S0-BWS-589

Countries of the World

and Their Leaders Yearbook 2014

ISSN 0196-2809

Countries of the World

and Their Leaders Yearbook 2014

A Compilation of U.S. Government Reports on Contemporary Political and Economic Conditions, Government Personnel and Policies, Political Parties, Religions, History, Education, Press, Radio and TV, Climate, and Other Characteristics of Selected Countries of the World; Together with Travel Alerts, Passport and Visa Information, World Health Information for Travelers, and Customs and Duty Tips for Returning Residents

Volume 1

Status of the World's Nations
Background Notes: Afghanistan — Mozambique

GALE
CENGAGE Learning®

Detroit • New York • San Francisco • New Haven, Conn • Waterville, Maine • London

Countries of the World and Their Leaders Yearbook 2014

Karen Ellicott, Editor

Product Management: Betz Des Chenes, Associate Publisher

Project Editor: Laurie J. Fundukian

Manufacturing: Rita Wimberley

Gale
27500 Drake Rd.
Farmington Hills, MI 48331-3535

ISBN-13: 978-1-56995-850-6 (set) ISBN-10: 1-56995-850-5 (set)
ISBN-13: 978-1-56995-851-3 (vol. 1) ISBN-10: 1-56995-851-3 (vol. 1)
ISBN-13: 978-1-56995-852-0 (vol. 2) ISBN-10: 1-56995-852-1 (vol. 2)

ISSN 0196-2809

This title is also available as an e-book.
ISBN-13: 978-1-56995-859-9
ISBN-10: 1-56995-859-9
Contact your Gale, Cengage Learning sales representative for ordering information.

Printed in Mexico
1 2 3 4 5 6 7 17 16 15 14 13

Contents

VOLUME 1

Status of the World's Nations and Background Notes: Afghanistan—Mozambique

VOLUME 2

Background Notes (continued): Namibia—Zimbabwe; International Treaty Organizations; Foreign Travel, including Country Reports on Terrorism

---

Background Notes on Countries of the World (Vol. 2)

International Treaty Organizations (Vol. 2)

Foreign Travel (Vol. 2)

INTRODUCTION AND ABBREVIATIONS

The majority of the information in these volumes was provided by the U.S. Department of State and is the most recent release of that information as of February 2013. However, changes in countries and governments occur rapidly. Therefore, the reader is advised to check directly with the consulate of the country he or she intends to visit before making final plans. The reader is also advised to visit www.state.gov for more detailed and current information on travel to the countries of the world.

Recent events in all parts of the world—Europe, Asia, the Americas, and Africa—have demonstrated dynamic changes that quickly affect the world's political and economic structures. This 2014 edition of *Countries of the World* continues the tradition of past editions in meeting the need for current information by monitoring and presenting a wealth of statistical and narrative data from pertinent U.S. government publications. Publications from the U.S. Department of State (State Department) and Central Intelligence Agency (CIA) have been used to present current basic information available on the countries of the world, their leaders, and U.S. embassies worldwide. Key government reports from these and other federal agencies have been gathered together in these volumes and presented in a format that is easily accessible to the reader.

For this 2014 edition, all 204 "Background Notes" from the previous publication of *Countries of the World* have been updated. In past editions, each "Background Note" contained information drawn primarily from the U.S. Department of State's own publications that were also known as "Background Notes." As of May 2012, these "Background Notes" are no longer being updated or produced by the government. Instead, they are being replaced by fact sheets that focus on U.S. relations with each country.

In this 2014 edition, historical information on each country is drawn from the State Department archives. Updated information on topics such as the political conditions and the economy has been compiled from other publications that were available as of January 2013 from the State Department, the U.S. Department of Commerce, and the CIA. Country specific information on travel, intercountry adoption, and international parental child abduction has been updated as well and can again be found within the "Background Notes" of those countries to which this information is pertinent.

In addition, the sections on International Treaty Organizations and Foreign Travel have been fully updated, revised, and reformatted as new information has been made available through the U.S. Department of State and other federal agencies.

ORGANIZATION

The two volumes in this set contain four sections:

- Status of the World's Nations
- Background Notes
- International Treaty Organizations
- Foreign Travel

A comprehensive index is included at the end of volume two.

Status of the World's Nations

This section begins the set by providing tables listing the independent nations of the world and the dependencies and areas of special sovereignty. Also included are alphabetical and chronological checklists of new nations since 1943.

Background Notes

This section provides basic information on the nation's history, government, economy, and diplomatic relations with the United States. Current and archived reports used to compile the information in this edition can be found on the State Department's web site at http://www.state.gov and on the CIA website at http://www.cia.gov. The "Background Notes" have been supplemented by the editors with the following additional information: Principal U.S. Embassy Officials, Principal Government Officials, Intercountry Adoption, International Parental Child Abduction, Consular Information Sheets, and Travel Warnings. This and other supplemental information has been compiled from a variety of reports available from the State Department. The maps appearing in the "Background Notes" were created by Maryland Cartographics, Inc. and were added by the editors to supplement the government information. They were not part of the original government publication.

Principal U.S. Embassy Officials

This section contains information from the State Department's report *Key Officers of Foreign Service Posts*. The address and telephone number of each embassy, consulate, or foreign service post are listed. Names and assignments are shown for principal U.S. embassy officials to aid in making direct inquiry.

A key to abbreviations related to foreign service assignments follows:

ACM Assistant Chief of Mission
ADB Asian Development Bank
ADV Adviser
AGR Agricultural Section (USDA/FAS)
AID Agency for International Development
AIT American Institute in Taiwan
ALT Alternate
AMB Ambassador
AMB OMS Ambassador's Office Management Specialist
APHIS Animal and Plant Health Inspection Service
APO Army Post Office
ARSO Assistant Regional Security Officer
ATF Alcohol, Tobacco, and Firearms
ATO Agricultural Trade Office (USDA/FAS)
B.P. Boite Postale
BBG Broadcasting Board of Governors
BCAO Branch Cultural Affairs Officer
BO Branch Office (of Embassy)
BUD Budget
BUREC Bureau of Reclamation
C.P. Caixa Postal
CA Consular Agent
CAO Cultural Affairs Officer
CDC Centers for Disease Control
Cdr Commander
CEO Cultural Exchange Officer
CG Consul General, Consulate General
CHG Charge d'Affaires
CINCAFSOUTH Commander-in-Chief Allied Forces Southern Europe
CINCEUR Commander-in-Chief U.S. European Command
CINCPAC Commander-in-Chief U.S. Pacific Command
CINCUSAFE Commander-in-Chief U.S. Air Forces Europe
CINCUSAREUR Commander-in-Chief, U.S. Army Europe
CM Chief of Mission
COM Commercial Section (FCS)
CON Consul, Consular Section
COUNS Counselor
CUS Customs Service (Treasury)
DAC Development Assistance Committee
DAO Office of the Defense Attache
DATT Defense Attache
DCM Deputy Chief of Mission
DEA Drug Enforcement Administration
DEF ADV Defense Adviser
DEL Delegation
DEP Deputy
DEP DIR Deputy Director
DEVEL Development
DIR Director
DOD Department of Defense
DOE Department of Energy
DOJ Department of Justice
DPAO Deputy Public Affairs Officer
DPO Deputy Principal Officer
DSA Defense Supply Adviser
E Embassy
EBRD Economic Board for Reconstruction and Development
ECO Economic Section
ECO/COM Economic/Commercial Section
ECOSOC Economic and Social Council
EDO Export Development Officer
ENV Environment
EPA Environmental Protection Agency
ERDA Energy Research and Development Administration
EST Environment, Science, and Technology
EX-IM Export-Import
EXEC Executive
FAA Federal Aviation Administration
FAA/CASLO Federal Aviation Administration Civil Aviation Security Liaison Officer
FAA/FSIDO Federal Aviation Administration Flight Standards International District Office
FAO Foreign Agricultural Office
FAS Foreign Agricultural Service
FBI Federal Bureau of Investigation
FBO Foreign Buildings Office
FCS Foreign Commercial Service
FIC/JSC Finance Committee and Joint Support Committee
FIN Financial Attache (Treasury)
FM Facilities Maintenance
FODAG Food and Agriculture Organizations
FPO Fleet Post Office
FSI Foreign Service Institute
GAO General Accounting Office
GSA General Services Administration
GSO General Services Officer
IAEA International Atomic Energy Agency
IAGS Inter-American Geodetic Survey
IBB International Broadcasting Bureau
ICAO International Civil Aviation Organization
IMO Information Management Officer
INS Immigration and Naturalization Service
IO Information Officer (USIS)
IPO Information Program Officer
IRM Information Resources Management
IRS Internal Revenue Service
ISM Information Systems Manager
ISO Information Systems Officer
ISSO Information Systems Security Officer
JCS Joint Chiefs of Staff
JUS/CIV Department of Justice, Civil Division
JUSMAG Joint U.S. Military Advisory Group
JUST Justice Department
LAB Labor Officer
LEGATT Legal Attache
LO Liaison Officer
M Mission
MAAG Military Assistance Advisory Group
Mg Major General
MGT Management Officer
MGT & RFM Management and Reform
MIL Military
MILGP Military Group
MIN Minister
MLO Military Liaison Office
MNL Minerals Officer
MSC Military Staff Committee
MSG Marine Security Guard
NARC Narcotics Officer
NAS Narcotics Affairs Section
NASA National Air and Space Administration
NATO North Atlantic Treaty Organization
NCIS Naval Criminal, U.S.
NIV Nonimmigrant Visas
NLO Naval Liaison Officer

OAS	Organization of American States
ODC	Office of Defense Cooperation
OIC	Officer in Charge
OMC	Office of Military Cooperation
OMS	Office Management Specialist
ORA	Office of Regional Affairs
PAA	Public Affairs Adviser
PAO	Public Affairs Officer
PC	Peace Corps
PER	Personnel
PERM REP	Permanent Representative
PO	Principal Officer
POL	Political Section
POL/ECO	Political/Economic Section
POL/LAB	Political and Labor Section
POLAD	Political Adviser
RCON	Regional Consular Affairs Officer
REDSO	Regional Economic Development Services Office
REF	Refugee Coordinator
RELO	Regional English Language Officer
REP	Representative
RES	Resources
RHUDO	Regional Housing and Urban Development Office
RMO	Regional Medical Officer
ROCAP	Regional Officer for Central American Programs
RPSO	Regional Procurement and Support Office
RSO	Regional Security Officer
SAO	Security Assistance Office
SCI	Scientific Attache
SCO	Senior Commercial Office
SEC	Secretary
SHAPE	Supreme Headquarters Allied Powers Europe
SLG	State and Local Government
SPA	Special Assistant
SPSH	Special Self Help
SR	Senior
STC	Security Trade Control
TAT	Tactical Analysis Team
TREAS	Treasury Department
UNEP	United Nations Environment Program
UNESCO	United Nations Educational, Scientific, and Cultural Organization
UNIDO	United Nations Industrial Development Organization
UNVIE	U.S. Mission to International Organizations in Vienna
USA	United States Army
USAF	United States Air Force
USCG	United States Coast Guard
USDA/APHIS	Animal and Plant Health Inspection Service
USDOC	U.S. Department of Commerce
USEO	United States Embassy Office
USEU	U.S. Mission to the European Union
USGS	U.S. Geological Survey
USINT	United States Interests Section
USLO	United States Liaison Office
USMC	United States Marine Corps
USMTM	U.S. Military Training Mission
USN	United States Navy
USNATO	U.S. Mission to the North Atlantic Treaty Organization
USOAS US	Mission to the Organization of American States
USOECD	U.S. Mission to the Organization for Economic Cooperation and Development
USOP US	Office Pristina
USTTA US	Travel and Tourism Agency
USUN US	Mission to the United Nations
VC	Vice Consul
VOA	Voice of America

Principal Government Officials

The information in this part of the "Background Note" is taken from the Central Intelligence Agency directory, *Chiefs of State and Cabinet Members of Foreign Governments,* which is updated monthly. The directory is intended to be used primarily as a reference aid and includes as many governments of the world as is considered practicable, some of them not officially recognized by the United States. In the directory, regimes with which the United States has no diplomatic exchanges are indicated by the initials NDE (no diplomatic exchange). The spelling of personal names follows transliteration systems generally agreed upon by government agencies, except in the case in which officials have stated a preference for alternate spellings of their names. Although the head of the central bank is listed for many countries, in most cases he or she is not a Cabinet member. Ambassadors to the United States and Permanent Representatives to the United Nations in New York have also been included. A key to the abbreviations related to members of foreign governments follows:

Adm.	Admiral
Admin.	Administrative/Administration
Asst.	Assistant
Brig.	Brigadier
Capt.	Captain
Cdr.	Commander
Cdte.	Comandante
Chmn.	Chairman
Col.	Colonel
Comdr.	Commodore
Ctte.	Committee
Del.	Delegate
Dep.	Deputy
Dept.	Department
Dir.	Director
Div.	Division
Dr.	Doctor
Eng.	Engineer
Fd. Mar.	Field Marshal
Fed.	Federal
Gen.	General
Govt.	Government
Intl.	International
Lt.	Lieutenant
Maj.	Major
Mar.	Marshal
Mbr.	Member
Min.	Minister, Ministry
NDE	No Diplomatic Exchange
Org.	Organization
Pres.	President
Prof.	Professor
RAdm.	Rear Admiral
Ret.	Retired
Sec.	Secretary
VAdm.	Vice Admiral
VMar.	Vice Marshal

Consular Information Sheets, Travel Warnings, and Travel Alerts

Consular Information Sheets (also referred to as Country Specific Information) are available for every country of the world. These pages include such information as location of the U.S. embassy or consulate in the subject country, unusual immigration practices, health conditions, minor political disturbances, unusual currency and entry regulations, crime and security information, and drug penalties. This country specific information provides only a general look at what are often very complex policies and procedures of a particular country. In some sections, readers may be directed to one of the following websites for more detailed information on safety and health issues affecting travelers.

Centers for Disease Control and Prevention: http://wwwnc.cdc.gov/travel/default.aspx

Federal Aviation Adminsitration, International Aviation Safety Assessments: http://www.faa.gov/about/initiatives/iasa/

Smart Traveler Enrollment Program: https://travelregistration.state.gov/ibrs/ui/

U.S. Department of State, International Travel Informaiton: http://travel.state.gov/travel/travel_1744.html

World Health Organization: http://www.who.int/countries/en/

Travel Warnings are issued to describe long-term, protracted conditions that make a country dangerous or unstable. A Travel Warning is also issued when the U.S. Government's ability to assist American citizens is constrained due to the closure of an embassy or consulate or because of a drawdown of its staff. Travel Alerts are issued to disseminate information about short-term conditions, generally within a particular country, that pose imminent risks to the security of U.S. citizens. Natural disasters, terrorist attacks, coups, anniversaries of terrorist events, election-related demonstrations or violence, and high-profile events such as international conferences or regional sports events are examples of conditions that might generate a Travel Alert.

International Treaty Organizations

This section provides information in "Background Note" format on important international organizations of which many of the world's nations are members. The information included in these articles is provided by the U.S. Department of State and additional government departments, agencies, or missions, which may be listed in the editor's note of the article.

Foreign Travel

This section provides useful information on travel to the countries of the world. Information is provided on customs, passports and visas, airport security measures, health concerns, specail needs travelers, international parental child abduction laws, intercountry adoption regulations, and numerous other travel related topics. A new section has been added containing an abridged version of the State Department's *Foreign Embassies and Consulates in the United States.* Travelers may wish to contact the offices of the country to which they wish to travel for specific information on entry requirements, customs, laws, and safety issues. Also included in this section is important U.S. government advice on global terrorism and its prevalence in countries and regions of the world.

Government Advice: Doing Business in International Markets

This section, primarily in question and answer format, provides explanations of the U.S. government services available to those engaged in business activities in other countries. Information on who to contact and how to make contacts by mail and telephone is outlined. In addition, contact information for the state and regional offices of the U.S. Department of Commerce devoted to international trade is provided.

Country Reports on Terrorism: 2011

This section presents a summary of the status of the U.S. government's efforts to combat international terrorism and summarizes the acts of terrorism recorded during 2010–11. It also provides descriptions of terrorist activities in the regions of the world and profiles active terrorist organizations.

FOR MORE INFORMATION

Government data presented in these volumes represents the most current release of such data as of Feburary 2013. However, some articles have been condensed and edited to be suitable for book format. Also, it must again be emphasized that because events and conditions in the world can change dramatically and quickly, readers should consult the web site of the State Department at http://www.state.gov for the latest information releases. The State Department has also established a toll-free number to assist individuals who need additional information or do not have access to the website. This toll-free number, 1-888-407-4747, is available from 8:00 a.m. to 8:00 p.m. Eastern Standard Time, Monday through Friday (except U.S. holidays). Callers who are unable to use toll-free numbers, such as those calling from overseas, may obtain information and assistance during these hours by calling 1-317-472-2328.

Status of the World's Nations

STATUS OF THE WORLD'S NATIONS

Listing of Nations, Dependencies, and Areas of Special Sovereignty

Editor's note: This section was adapted from *Geographic Notes*, issued by the Bureau of Intelligence and Research, U.S. State Department in April 1992 and updated by the editors of this volume in February 2013.

OVERVIEW

In this survey, the term "nation" refers to a people politically organized into a sovereign state with a definite, internationally recognized territory. The number of such nations has almost tripled since the end of World War II. On the eve of the war there were 70 nations; as of March 2011, there were 194.

In 1990 and 1991 several important changes took place in the status of the world's nations. Two nations, Yemen and Germany, were formed in 1990, each by unification of two formerly separate nations. In the case of Germany, the former German Democratic Republic was subsumed by the Federal Republic of Germany. The Republic of Yemen was formed by union of the former Yemen Arab Republic and the People's Democratic Republic of Yemen. Also in 1990, Namibia finally realized its Independence; the UN had terminated its status as a South African mandate in 1966.

The year 1990 also began a period of turmoil in the former Soviet Union. The independence of the three Baltic States—Estonia, Latvia, and Lithuania—was recognized by the central Soviet government in August 1991. The United States established diplomatic relations with the democratically elected governments of the Baltic States in September 1991. In December 1991 the 12 former Soviet republics became separate sovereign nations.

With the breakup of Yugoslavia, Bosnia and Herzegovina declared independence along with its neighbor Serbia and Montenegro in 1992. In 1993 Czechoslovakia dissolved into Slovakia and the Czech Republic. Also in 1993, Eritrea declared its independence from Ethiopia. In 2002, East Timor declared itself a nation after separating from Indonesia. Montenegro separated from Serbia to become an independent nation on June 3, 2006. On February 17, 2008, Kosovo declared its independence from Serbia. Following years of civil war, the nation of South Sudan gained independence on July 9, 2011.

The magnitude of these changes, though noteworthy, is not unprecedented in recent history. The unsettled international situations following each of the World Wars fostered the creation of new nations without an equal dissolution of existing ones. As a result of World War I, three nations in Europe ceased to exist—Austria, Hungary, Montenegro, and Serbia—but they were replaced by four new nations: Austria-Hungary, Czechoslovakia, and Yugoslavia. Poland reappeared on the map of Europe after an interval of almost a century and a quarter during which it had been partitioned among Austria-Hungary, Germany, and Russia.

In the early part of World War II, Estonia, Latvia, and Lithuania were forcibly incorporated into the USSR. Other nations disappeared temporarily from the world community during the period that led up to World War II. These include Ethiopia in 1936, Austria in 1938, and Czechoslovakia in 1939. In the aftermath of World War II, however, two new nations emerged through the partition of Germany and Israel was created within the United Kingdom's Palestine League of Nations Mandate.

Proliferation of Nations

The dramatic increase in the number of nations since World War II has occurred primarily through the breakup of larger territorial entities, particularly in Africa, along the southern periphery of Asia, in the Caribbean, and in the Pacific Ocean. The dissolution of the Soviet Union follows this proliferation pattern.

Several periods since 1945 were marked particularly by the emergence of new nations from colonial powers. In 1960 alone, 14 new nations appeared from French-controlled parts of Africa. Of the 69 nations formed worldwide between 1961 and 1992, 42 had been wholly or partly under British sovereignty at some time in their history, including seven of the 11 new Pacific island nations. Between September 1974 and November 1975, all five of Portugal's overseas provinces in Africa became nations.

Several exceptional situations since World War II have caused irregularities in the sovereignty structure. Syria in 1958 joined Egypt to form the United Arab Republic, a union that endured three years. In 1962 the West Indies Federation, just a few months before its scheduled independence, was dissolved in favor of sovereignty for Jamaica and Trinidad and Tobago. In another instance in which nations unsuccessfully attempted to merge, Kenya, Uganda, Tanganyika, and Zanzibar considered the creation of an East African federation with a single national government. These plans failed to materialize, but in April 1964 Tanganyika and Zanzibar merged to become one nation, Tanzania.

Geographical Attributes

The largest nation by size of territory is Russia, followed, in order by Canada, China, the United States, Brazil, and Australia, all with more than 5 million square kilometers of total area. The largest nation by population is China, followed, in order by India, the United States, and Indonesia, all with more than 190 million people. The Holy See (Vatican City) is the world's smallest nation, in both land area and population.

Of the 194 nations, 39 are islands that border no other country, 44 are landlocked, and the remaining 111 face one or more oceans or their embayments. As nations delimit their 200-nautical-mile exclusive economic zones (EEZs) under the provisions of the 1982 United Nations Convention on the Law of the Sea, including negotiating maritime boundaries with neighboring nations, some may face the possibility of being "zonelocked."

Dependent Areas

Government control over land areas varies widely, from full sovereignty to none. The term "dependent areas" encompasses a broad category of political entities that fall in some way within the jurisdiction of a nation. In this survey, dependent areas are "overseas" territories associated with a nation; they do not include offshore islands that belong to or make up civil divisions of a nation. Australia, Denmark, France, Netherlands, New Zealand, Norway, Portugal, Spain, the United Kingdom, and the United States maintain dependent areas. The level of political dependence ranges from self-governing in domestic affairs to administered directly from the national capital. The latter case often includes minor scattered islands with little or no permanent population.

Except for a sector of Antarctica, there are no significant land areas that are not either under the control of a nation or claimed by one. Antarctic claims have been made by seven of the 28 consultative nations to the 1959 Antarctic Treaty,* although the legal status of those claims remains in suspension under the provisions of the treaty. The unclaimed sector of Antarctica is between 90 and 150 degrees west longitude.

The United States has asserted no claim of sovereignty in Antarctica, although it reserves the right to make one; it recognizes none of the claims within the Antarctic Treaty area (south of 60 degrees south latitude) made by other nations.

*Argentina, Australia, Chile, France, New Zealand, Norway, and the United Kingdom are the seven signatories of the 1959 Antarctic Treaty which have claims in Antarctica. The remaining consultative nations are Belgium, Brazil, Bulgaria, China, Ecuador, Finland, Germany, India, Italy, Japan, Netherlands, Peru, Poland, Russia, South Africa, South Korea, Spain, Sweden, Ukraine, United States, and Uruguay.

NATIONS, DEPENDENCIES, AREAS OF SPECIAL SOVEREIGNTY

The following information is provided as reference material only. The data do not necessarily correspond to official statistics published by the various states. Status of the World's Nations should not be considered legally definitive.

Diplomatic Relations

The United States has established diplomatic relations with 189 of the listed nations. These are designated by an asterisk (*).

Name of Nation

The short-form name of the nation is commonly used; the long form is used for official documents and formal occasions. In a few instances no short form exists; the long form must serve for all usages. Conversely, a long form may not exist or may seldom be used.

Sovereignty

The sovereignty of dependencies and areas of special sovereignty is identified; where required, a note clarifies an entity's political status.

Capitals

For each state the conventionally accepted capital city name, recommended for use on maps, is listed. In the several instances where states have more than one capital, information on each is given. Some dependencies have no capital city and may be administered from another dependency of the same nation. In the case of small multi-island insular states or dependencies, the island on which the capital is located is given, unless it has the same name.

UN Membership

UN membership is indicated by a (+).

Independent States[1] in the World as of January 3, 2012

Short-form name	Long-form name	FIPS[2]	Capital
1. Afghanistan *+	Islamic Republic of Afghanistan	AF	*Kabul*
2. Albania *+	Republic of Albania	AL	*Tirana*
3. Algeria *+	People's Democratic Republic of Algeria	AG	*Algiers*
4. Andorra *+	Principality of Andorra	AN	*Andorra la Vella*
5. Angola *+	Republic of Angola	AO	*Luanda*
6. Antigua and Barbuda *+	(no long-form name)	AC	*Saint John's*
7. Argentina *+	Argentine Republic	AR	*Buenos Aires*
8. Armenia *+	Republic of Armenia	AM	*Yerevan*
9. Australia *+	Commonwealth of Australia	AS	*Canberra*
10. Austria *+	Republic of Austria	AU	*Vienna*
11. Azerbaijan *+	Republic of Azerbaijan	AJ	*Baku*
12. Bahamas, The *+	Commonwealth of The Bahamas	BF	*Nassau*
13. Bahrain *+	Kingdom of Bahrain	BA	*Manama*
14. Bangladesh *+	People's Republic of Bangladesh	BG	*Dhaka*
15. Barbados *+	(no long-form name)	BB	*Bridgetown*
16. Belarus *+	Republic of Belarus	BO	*Minsk*
17. Belgium *+	Kingdom of Belgium	BE	*Brussels*
18. Belize *+	(no long-form name)	BH	*Belmopan*
19. Benin *+	Republic of Benin	BN	*Porto-Novo*
20. Bhutan +	Kingdom of Bhutan	BT	*Thimphu*
21. Bolivia *+	Plurinational State of Bolivia	BL	*La Paz (administrative)* *Sucre (legislative/judiciary)*
22. Bosnia and Herzegovina *+	(no long-form name)	BK	*Sarajevo*
23. Botswana *+	Republic of Botswana	BC	*Gaborone*
24. Brazil *+	Federative Republic of Brazil	BR	*Brasília*
25. Brunei *+	Brunei Darussalam	BX	*Bandar Seri Begawan*
26. Bulgaria *+	Republic of Bulgaria	BU	*Sofia*
27. Burkina Faso *+	Burkina Faso	UV	*Ouagadougou*
28. Burma *+	Union of Burma	BM	*Rangoon* *Nay Pyi Taw (administrative)*
29. Burundi *+	Republic of Burundi	BY	*Bujumbura*
30. Cambodia *+	Kingdom of Cambodia	CB	*Phnom Penh*
31. Cameroon *+	Republic of Cameroon	CM	*Yaoundé*
32. Canada *+	(no long-form name)	CA	*Ottawa*
33. Cape Verde *+	Republic of Cape Verde	CV	*Praia*
34. Central African Republic *+	Central African Republic	CT	*Bangui*
35. Chad *+	Republic of Chad	CD	*N'Djamena*
36. Chile *+	Republic of Chile	CI	*Santiago*
37. China *+ (see note 3)	People's Republic of China	CH	*Beijing*
38. Colombia *+	Republic of Colombia	CO	*Bogotá*
39. Comoros *+	Union of Comoros	CN	*Moroni*
40. Congo (Brazzaville) *+ (4)	Republic of the Congo	CF	*Brazzaville*
41. Congo (Kinshasa) *+ (4)	Democratic Republic of the Congo	CG	*Kinshasa*
42. Costa Rica *+	Republic of Costa Rica	CS	*San José*
43. Côte d'Ivoire *+	Republic of Côte d'Ivoire	IV	*Yamoussoukro*
44. Croatia *+	Republic of Croatia	HR	*Zagreb*
45. Cuba +	Republic of Cuba	CU	*Havana*
46. Cyprus *+	Republic of Cyprus	CY	*Nicosia*
47. Czech Republic *+	Czech Republic	EZ	*Prague*
48. Denmark *+	Kingdom of Denmark	DA	*Copenhagen*
49. Djibouti *+	Republic of Djibouti	DJ	*Djibouti*
50. Dominica *+	Commonwealth of Dominica	DO	*Roseau*
51. Dominican Republic *+	Dominican Republic	DR	*Santo Domingo*
52. Ecuador *+	Republic of Ecuador	EC	*Quito*
53. Egypt *+	Arab Republic of Egypt	EG	*Cairo*

* Diplomatic relations with the United States; + Member of United Nations

Short-form name	Long-form name	FIPS[2]	Capital
54. El Salvador *+	Republic of El Salvador	ES	*San Salvador*
55. Equatorial Guinea *+	Republic of Equatorial Guinea	EK	*Malabo*
56. Eritrea *+	State of Eritrea	ER	*Asmara*
57. Estonia *+	Republic of Estonia	EN	*Tallinn*
58. Ethiopia *+	Federal Democratic Republic of Ethiopia	ET	*Addis Ababa*
59. Fiji *+	Republic of the Fiji Islands	FJ	*Suva*
60. Finland *+	Republic of Finland	FI	*Helsinki*
61. France *+	French Republic	FR	*Paris*
62. Gabon *+	Gabonese Republic	GB	*Libreville*
63. Gambia, The *+	Republic of The Gambia	GA	*Banjul*
64. Georgia *+	Georgia	GG	*T'bilisi*
65. Germany *+	Federal Republic of Germany	GM	*Berlin*
66. Ghana *+	Republic of Ghana	GH	*Accra*
67. Greece *+	Hellenic Republic	GR	*Athens*
68. Grenada *+	(no long-form name)	GJ	*Saint George's*
69. Guatemala *+	Republic of Guatemala	GT	*Guatemala*
70. Guinea *+	Republic of Guinea	GV	*Conakry*
71. Guinea-Bissau *+	Republic of Guinea-Bissau	PU	*Bissau*
72. Guyana *+	Co-operative Republic of Guyana	GY	*Georgetown*
73. Haiti *+	Republic of Haiti	HA	*Port-au-Prince*
74. Holy See *	Holy See	VT	*Vatican City*
75. Honduras *+	Republic of Honduras	HO	*Tegucigalpa*
76. Hungary *+	Hungary	HU	*Budapest*
77. Iceland *+	Republic of Iceland	IC	*Reykjavík*
78. India *+	Republic of India	IN	*New Delhi*
79. Indonesia *+	Republic of Indonesia	ID	*Jakarta*
80. Iran +	Islamic Republic of Iran	IR	*Tehran*
81. Iraq *+	Republic of Iraq	IZ	*Baghdad*
82. Ireland *+	(no long-form name)	EI	*Dublin*
83. Israel *+	State of Israel	IS	*Jerusalem (see note 5)*
84. Italy *+	Italian Republic	IT	*Rome*
85. Jamaica *+	(no long-form name)	JM	*Kingston*
86. Japan *+	(no long-form name)	JA	*Tokyo*
87. Jordan *+	Hashemite Kingdom of Jordan	JO	*Amman*
88. Kazakhstan *+	Republic of Kazakhstan	KZ	*Astana*
89. Kenya *+	Republic of Kenya	KE	*Nairobi*
90. Kiribati *+	Republic of Kiribati	KR	*Tarawa*
91. Korea, North +	Democratic People's Republic of Korea	KN	*P'yongyang*
92. Korea, South *+	Republic of Korea	KS	*Seoul*
93. Kosovo*	Republic of Kosovo	KV	*Pristina*
94. Kuwait *+	State of Kuwait	KU	*Kuwait*
95. Kyrgyzstan *+	Kyrgyz Republic	KG	*Bishkek*
96. Laos *+	Lao People's Democratic Republic	LA	*Vientiane*
97. Latvia *+	Republic of Latvia	LG	*Riga*
98. Lebanon *+	Lebanese Republic	LE	*Beirut*
99. Lesotho *+	Kingdom of Lesotho	LT	*Maseru*
100. Liberia *+	Republic of Liberia	LI	*Monrovia*
101. Libya *+	Great Socialist People's Libyan Arab Jamahiriya	LY	*Tripoli*
102. Liechtenstein *+	Principality of Liechtenstein	LS	*Vaduz*
103. Lithuania *+	Republic of Lithuania	LH	*Vilnius*
104. Luxembourg *+	Grand Duchy of Luxembourg	LU	*Luxembourg*
105. Macedonia*+	Republic of Macedonia	MK	*Skopje*
106. Madagascar *+	Republic of Madagascar	MA	*Antananarivo*
107. Malawi *+	Republic of Malawi	MI	*Lilongwe*
108. Malaysia *+	(no long-form name)	MY	*Kuala Lumpur*
109. Maldives *+	Republic of Maldives	MV	*Male*

* Diplomatic relations with the United States; + Member of United Nations

Short-form name	Long-form name	FIPS[2]	Capital
110. Mali *+	**Republic of Mali**	ML	*Bamako*
111. Malta *+	**Republic of Malta**	MT	*Valletta*
112. Marshall Islands *+	**Republic of the Marshall Islands**	RM	*Majuro*
113. Mauritania *+	**Islamic Republic of Mauritania**	MR	*Nouakchott*
114. Mauritius *+	**Republic of Mauritius**	MP	*Port Louis*
115. Mexico *+	**United Mexican States**	MX	*Mexico*
116. Micronesia, Federated States of *+	**Federated States of Micronesia**	FM	*Palikir*
117. Moldova *+	**Republic of Moldova**	MD	*Chisinau*
118. Monaco *+	**Principality of Monaco**	MN	*Monaco*
119. Mongolia *+	(no long-form name)	MG	*Ulaanbaatar*
120. Montenegro +	**Montenegro**	MJ	*Podgorica*
121. Morocco *+	**Kingdom of Morocco**	MO	*Rabat*
122. Mozambique *+	**Republic of Mozambique**	MZ	*Maputo*
123. Namibia *+	**Republic of Namibia**	WA	*Windhoek*
124. Nauru *+	**Republic of Nauru**	NR	*Yaren District (no capital city)*
125. Nepal *+	**Federal Democratic Republic of Nepal**	NP	*Kathmandu*
126. Netherlands *+	**Kingdom of the Netherlands**	NL	*Amsterdam* *The Hague (seat of gov't)*
127. New Zealand *+	(no long-form name)	NZ	*Wellington*
128. Nicaragua *+	**Republic of Nicaragua**	NU	*Managua*
129. Niger *+	**Republic of Niger**	NG	*Niamey*
130. Nigeria *+	**Federal Republic of Nigeria**	NI	*Abuja*
131. Norway *+	**Kingdom of Norway**	NO	*Oslo*
132. Oman *+	**Sultanate of Oman**	MU	*Muscat*
133. Pakistan *+	**Islamic Republic of Pakistan**	PK	*Islamabad*
134. Palau *+	**Republic of Palau**	PS	*Melekeok*
135. Panama *+	**Republic of Panama**	PM	*Panama*
136. Papua New Guinea *+	**Independent State of Papua New Guinea**	PP	*Port Moresby*
137. Paraguay *+	**Republic of Paraguay**	PA	*Asunción*
138. Peru *+	**Republic of Peru**	PE	*Lima*
139. Philippines *+	**Republic of the Philippines**	RP	*Manila*
140. Poland *+	**Republic of Poland**	PL	*Warsaw*
141. Portugal *+	**Portuguese Republic**	PO	*Lisbon*
142. Qatar *+	**State of Qatar**	QA	*Doha*
143. Romania *+	(no long-form name)	RO	*Bucharest*
144. Russia *+	**Russian Federation**	RS	*Moscow*
145. Rwanda *+	**Republic of Rwanda**	RW	*Kigali*
146. Saint Kitts and Nevis *+	**Federation of Saint Kitts and Nevis**	SC	*Basseterre*
147. Saint Lucia *+	(no long-form name)	ST	*Castries*
148. Saint Vincent and the Grenadines *+	(no long-form name)	VC	*Kingstown*
149. Samoa *+	**Independent State of Samoa**	WS	*Apia*
150. San Marino *+	**Republic of San Marino**	SM	*San Marino*
151. São Tomé and Príncipe *+	**Democratic Republic of São Tomé and Príncipe**	TP	*São Tomé*
152. Saudi Arabia *+	**Kingdom of Saudi Arabia**	SA	*Riyadh*
153. Senegal *+	**Republic of Senegal**	SG	*Dakar*
154. Serbia *+	**Republic of Serbia**	RB	*Belgrade*
155. Seychelles *+	**Republic of Seychelles**	SE	*Victoria*
156. Sierra Leone *+	**Republic of Sierra Leone**	SL	*Freetown*
157. Singapore *+	**Republic of Singapore**	SN	*Singapore*
158. Slovakia *+	**Slovak Republic**	LO	*Bratislava*
159. Slovenia *+	**Republic of Slovenia**	SI	*Ljubljana*
160. Solomon Islands *+	(no long-form name)	BP	*Honiara*
161. Somalia *+	(no long-form name)	SO	*Mogadishu*

* Diplomatic relations with the United States; + Member of United Nations

Short-form name	Long-form name	FIPS[2]	Capital
162. South Africa *+	Republic of South Africa	SF	*Pretoria (administrative)* *Cape Town (legislative)* *Bloemfontein (judiciary)*
163. South Sudan*+	Republic of South Sudan	OD	*Juba*
164. Spain *+	Kingdom of Spain	SP	*Madrid*
165. Sri Lanka *+	Democratic Socialist Republic of Sri Lanka	CE	*Colombo* *Sri Jayewardenepura Kotte (legislative)*
166. Sudan *+	Republic of the Sudan	SU	*Khartoum*
167. Suriname *+	Republic of Suriname	NS	*Paramaribo*
168. Swaziland *+	Kingdom of Swaziland	WZ	*Mbabane (administrative)* *Lobamba (legislative)*
169. Sweden *+	Kingdom of Sweden	SW	*Stockholm*
170. Switzerland *	Swiss Confederation	SZ	*Bern*
171. Syria *+	Syrian Arab Republic	SY	*Damascus*
172. Tajikistan *+	Republic of Tajikistan	TI	*Dushanbe*
173. Tanzania *+	United Republic of Tanzania	TZ	*Dar es Salaam* *Dodoma (legislative)*
174. Thailand *+	Kingdom of Thailand	TH	*Bangkok*
175. Timor-Leste*+	Democratic Republic of Timor-Leste	TT	*Dili*
176. Togo *+	Togolese Republic	TO	*Lomé*
177. Tonga *+	Kingdom of Tonga	TN	*Nuku'alofa*
178. Trinidad and Tobago *+	Republic of Trinidad and Tobago	TD	*Port-of-Spain*
179. Tunisia *+	Tunisian Republic	TS	*Tunis*
180. Turkey *+	Republic of Turkey	TU	*Ankara*
181. Turkmenistan *+	(no long-form name)	TX	*Ashgabat*
182. Tuvalu *+	(no long-form name)	TV	*Funafuti*
183. Uganda *+	Republic of Uganda	UG	*Kampala*
184. Ukraine *+	(no long-form name)	UP	*Kyiv*
185. United Arab Emirates *+	United Arab Emirates	AE	*Abu Dhabi*
186. United Kingdom *+	United Kingdom of Great Britain and Northern Ireland	UK	*London*
187. United States +	United States of America	US	*Washington, DC*
188. Uruguay *+	Oriental Republic of Uruguay	UY	*Montevideo*
189. Uzbekistan *+	Republic of Uzbekistan	UZ	*Tashkent*
190. Vanuatu *+	Republic of Vanuatu	NH	*Port-Vila*
191. Venezuela *+	Bolivarian Republic of Venezuela	VE	*Caracas*
192. Vietnam *+	Socialist Republic of Vietnam	VM	*Hanoi*
193. Yemen *+	Republic of Yemen	YM	*Sanaa*
194. Zambia *+	Republic of Zambia	ZA	*Lusaka*
195. Zimbabwe *+	Republic of Zimbabwe	ZI	*Harare*

* Diplomatic relations with the United States; + Member of United Nations

Other

Taiwan[6]	(no long-form name)	TW	*T'ai-pei*

Notes

Note 1: In this listing, the term "independent state" refers to a people politically organized into a sovereign state with a definite territory recognized as independent by the U.S.

Note 2: Federal Information Processing Standard (FIPS) 10-4 codes.

Note 3: With the establishment of diplomatic relations with China on January 1, 1979, the U.S. Government recognized the People's Republic of China as the sole legal government of China and acknowledged the Chinese position that there is only one China and that Taiwan is part of China.

Note 4: "Congo" is the official short-form name for both the Republic of the Congo and the Democratic Republic of the Congo. To distinguish one from the other, the U.S. Department of State adds the capital in parentheses. This practice is unofficial and provisional.

Note 5: Israel proclaimed Jerusalem as its capital in 1950. The U.S., like nearly all other countries maintains its embassy in Tel Aviv.

Note 6: Claimed by both the Government of the People's Republic of China and the authorities on Taiwan. Administered by the authorities on Taiwan (see note 3)

Dependencies and Areas of Special Sovereignty as of November 29, 2011*

Short-form name	Long-form name	Sovereignty	Code[1]	Capital
Akrotiri [15]	**Akrotiri**	United Kingdom	AX	*Episkopi*[16]
American Samoa	**Territory of American Samoa**	United States	AQ	*Pago Pago*
Anguilla	**Anguilla**	United Kingdom	AV	*The Valley*
Antarctica	(no long-form name)	None (see note 2)	AY	*None*
Aruba	(no long-form name)	Netherlands	AA	*Oranjestad*
Ashmore and Cartier Islands	**Territory of Ashmore and Cartier Islands**	Australia	AT	*Administered from Canberra*
Baker Island	(no long-form name)	United States	FQ	*Administered from Washington, D.C.*
Bermuda	**Bermuda**	United Kingdom	BD	*Hamilton*
Bouvet Island	(no long-form name)	Norway	BV	*Admin. from Oslo*
British Indian Ocean Territory[3]	**British Indian Ocean Territory**	United Kingdom	IO	*None*
Cayman Islands	**Cayman Islands**	United Kingdom	CJ	*George Town*
Christmas Island	**Territory of Christmas Island**	Australia	KT	*The Settlement (Flying Fish Cove)*
Clipperton Island	(no long-form name)	France	IP	*Administered from French Polynesia*
Cocos (Keeling) Islands	**Territory of Cocos (Keeling) Islands**	Australia	CK	*West Island*
Cook Islands	(no long-form name)	New Zealand	CW	*Avarua*
Coral Sea Islands	**Coral Sea Islands Territory**	Australia	CR	*Administered from Canberra*
Curaçao[11]	(no long-form name)	Netherlands	UC	*Willemstad*
Dhekelia[15]	**Dhekelia**	United Kingdom	DX	*Episkopi*[16]
Falkland Islands (Islas Malvinas)	**Falkland Islands (Islas Malvinas)**	United Kingdom[4]	FK	*Stanley*
Faroe Islands	(no long-form name)	Denmark	FO	*Tórshavn*
French Guiana[5]				
French Polynesia	(no long-form name)	France	FP	*Papeete*
French Southern & Antarctic Lands[6]	(no long-form name)	France	FS	*Administered from Paris*
Gibraltar	**Gibraltar**	United Kingdom	GI	*Gibraltar*
Greenland	(no long-form name)	Denmark	GL	*Nuuk (Godthåb)*
Guadeloupe[5]				
Guam	**Territory of Guam**	United States	GQ	*Hagatna*
Guernsey[7]	**Bailiwick of Guernsey**	British Crown Dependency	GK	*Saint Peter Port*
Heard Island & McDonald Islands	**Territory of Heard Island and McDonald Islands**	Australia	HM	*Administered from Canberra*
Hong Kong	**Hong Kong Special Administrative Region**	China[8]	HK	*None*
Howland Island	(no long-form name)	United States	HQ	*Administered from Washington, D.C.*
Isle of Man	(no long-form name)	British Crown Dependency	IM	*Douglas*
Jan Mayen	(no long-form name)	Norway	JN	*Administered from Oslo*[9]
Jarvis Island	(no long-form name)	United States	DQ	*Administered from Washington, D.C.*
Jersey	**Bailiwick of Jersey**	British Crown Dependency	JE	*Saint Helier*
Johnston Atoll	(no long-form name)	United States	JQ	*Administered from Washington, D.C.*
Kingman Reef	(no long-form name)	United States	KQ	*Administered from Washington, D.C.*

Short-form name	Long-form name	Sovereignty	Code[1]	Capital
Macau	**Macau Special Administrative Region**	China[10]	MC	*Macau*
Martinique[5]				
Mayotte	**Territorial Collectivity of Mayotte**	France	MF	*Mamoudzou*
Midway Islands	(no long-form name)	United States	MQ	*Administered from Washington, D.C.*
Montserrat	**Montserrat**	United Kingdom	MH	*Plymouth*
Navassa Island	(no long-form name)	United States	BQ	*Administered from Washington, D.C.*
Netherlands Antilles[11]	(no long-form name)	Netherlands	NT	*Willemstad*
New Caledonia	(no long-form name)	France	NC	*Nouméa*
Niue	(no long-form name)	New Zealand	NE	*Alofi*
Norfolk Island	**Territory of Norfolk Island**	Australia	NF	*Kingston*
Northern Mariana Islands	**Commonwealth of the Northern Mariana Islands**	United States	CQ	*Saipan*
Palmyra Atoll	(no long-form name)	United States	LQ	*Administered from Washington, D.C.*
Paracel Islands	(no long-form name)	undetermined[12]	PF	*None*
Pitcairn Islands	**Pitcairn, Henderson, Ducie, and Oeno Islands**	United Kingdom	PC	*Adamstown*
Puerto Rico	**Commonwealth of Puerto Rico**	United States	RQ	*San Juan*
Reunion[5]				
Saint Barthelemy	Saint Barthelemy	France	TB	*Gustavia*
Saint Helena[13]	**Saint Helena**	United Kingdom	SH	*Jamestown*
Saint Martin[17]	**Saint Martin**	France	RN	*Marigot*
Saint Pierre & Miquelon	**Territorial Collectivity of Saint Pierre and Miquelon**	France	SB	*Saint-Pierre*
Sint Maarten[11]	(no long-form name)	Netherlands	NN	*Philipsburg*
South Georgia & the South Sandwich Islands	**South Georgia and the South Sandwich Islands**	United Kingdom[4]	SX	*None*
Spratly Islands	(no long-form name)	undetermined[14]	PG	*None*
Svalbard	(no long-form name)	Norway	SV	*Longyearbyen*
Tokelau	(no long-form name)	New Zealand	TL	*None*
Turks & Caicos Islands	**Turks & Caicos Islands**	United Kingdom	TK	*Grand Turk*
Virgin Islands, U.S.	**United States Virgin Islands**	United States	VQ	*Charlotte Amalie*
Virgin Islands, British	**Virgin Islands, British**	United Kingdom	VI	*Road Town*
Wake Island	(no long-form name)	United States	WQ	*Administered from Washington, D.C.*
Wallis and Futuna	**Territory of the Wallis and Futuna Islands**	France	WF	*Matâ'utu*
Western Sahara	(no long-form name)	undetermined	WI	*None*

*accessed March 20, 2013

Notes

Note 1: Federal Information Processing Standard (FIPS) 10-4 codes. On September 2, 2008 the National Institute of Standards and Technology withdrew FIPS 10-4 as a United States Government standard. No successor standard for country codes has been identified.

Note 2: Antarctica consists of the territory south of 60 degrees south latitude. This area includes claims by Argentina, Australia, Chile, France, New Zealand, Norway, and the United Kingdom, the legal status of which remains in suspense under the terms of the Antarctic Treaty of 1959. The United States recognizes no claims to Antarctica.

Note 3: Chagos Archipelago (including Diego Garcia).

Note 4: U.K. Overseas Territory (also claimed by Argentina).

Note 5: French Guiana, Guadeloupe, Martinique and Reunion are departments (first-order administrative units) of France, and are therefore not dependencies or areas of special sovereignty. They are included in this list only for the convenience of the user. The Department of Guadeloupe includes the nearby islands of Marie-Galante, La Desirade, and Iles des Saintes, as well as Saint Barthelemy and the northern three-fifths of Saint Martin (the rest of which belongs to Netherlands Antilles). The islands of Bassas da India, Europa Island, Glorioso Islands, Juan de Nova Island, and Tromelin Island are administered from Reunion; all these islands are claimed by Madagascar, and Tromelin Island is claimed by Mauritius.

Note 6: "French Southern and Antarctic Lands" includes Île Amsterdam, Île Saint-Paul, Îles Crozet, and Îles Kerguelen in the southern Indian Ocean, along with the French-claimed sector of Antarctica, "Terre Adélie." The United States does not recognize the French claim to "Terre Adélie" (see note 2).

Note 7: The Bailiwick of Guernsey includes the islands of Alderney, Guernsey, Herm, Sark, and nearby smaller islands.

Note 8: Under a Sino-British declaration of September 1984, Hong Kong reverted to Chinese control on July 1, 1997. It is now a semi-autonomous entity that exists pursuant to international agreement and maintains its own government apart from the People's Republic of China.

Note 9: Administered from Oslo, Norway, through a governor resident in Longyearbyen, Svalbard.

Note 10: Under the Sino-Portuguese Joint Declaration on the Question of Macau signed in 1987, Macau reverted to Chinese control on December 20, 1999. It is now a semi-autonomous entity that exists pursuant to international agreement and maintains its own government apart from the People's Republic of China.

Note 11: The Netherlands Antilles dissolved on October 10, 2010. Curaçao and Sint Maarten (the Dutch two-fifths of the island of Saint Martin) became autonomous territories of the Kingdom of the Netherlands. Bonaire, Saba, and Sint Eustatius now fall under the direct administration of the Netherlands.

Note 12: South China Sea islands occupied by China but claimed by Vietnam.

Note 13: The territory of Saint Helena includes the Island group of Tristan da Cunha; Saint Helena also administers Ascension Island.

Note 14: South China Sea islands claimed in entirety by China and Vietnam and in part by the Philippines and Malaysia; each of these states occupies some part of the islands.

Note 15: U.K. military bases on the island of Cyprus.

Note 16: The joint force headquarters under the Commander of the British forces, Cyprus administers both sovereign base areas from Episkopi.

Note 17: The island of Saint Martin is divided: the northern three-fifths form the French collectivity of Saint-Martin, while the southern two-fifths (Sint Maarten) are part of the Netherlands Antilles.

Source: Office of the Geographer and Global Issues, Bureau of Intelligence and Research, U.S. Department of State, Washington, D.C.

Alphabetical Checklist of 128 New Nations Since 1943

Algeria....July 5, 1962
Angola....Nov. 11, 1976
Antigua and Barbuda....Nov. 1, 1981
Armenia....Sept. 23, 1991
Azerbaijan....Aug. 30, 1991
Bahamas, The....July 10, 1973
Bahrain....Aug. 14, 1971
Bangladesh....Apr. 4, 1972
Barbados....Nov. 30, 1966
Belarus....Aug. 25, 1991
Belize....Sept. 21, 1981
Benin....Aug. 1, 1960
Bosnia and Herzegovina....April 1, 1992
Botswana....Sept. 30, 1966
Brunei....Jan. 1, 1984
Burkina....Aug. 5, 1960
Burma....Jan. 4, 1948
Burundi....July 1, 1962
Cambodia....Nov. 8, 1949
Cameroon....Jan. 1, 1960
Cape Verde....July 5, 1975
Central African Republic....Aug. 13, 1960
Chad....Aug. 11, 1960
Comoros....Dec. 31, 1976
Congo, Dem. Rep. of (Zaire)....June 30, 1960
Congo, Rep. of....Aug. 15, 1960
Côte d'Ivoire (Ivory Coast)....Aug. 7, 1960
Croatia....June 25, 1991
Cyprus....Aug. 16, 1960
Czech Republic....Jan. 1, 1993
Djibouti....June 27, 1977
Dominica....Nov. 3, 1978
East Timor....May 20, 2002
Equatorial Guinea....Oct. 12, 1968
Eritrea....April 27, 1993
Estonia....Sept. 6, 1991
Fiji....Oct. 10, 1970
Gabon....Aug. 17, 1960
Gambia, The....Feb. 18, 1965
Georgia....April 9, 1991
Ghana....Mar. 6, 1957
Grenada....Feb. 7, 1974
Guinea....Oct. 2, 1958
Guinea-Bissau....Sept. 10, 1974
Guyana....May 26, 1966
Iceland....June 17, 1944
India....Aug. 15, 1947
Indonesia....Dec. 28, 1949
Israel....May 15, 1948
Jamaica....Aug. 6, 1962
Jordan....Mar. 22, 1946
Kazakhstan....Dec. 6, 1991
Kenya....Dec. 12, 1963
Kiribati....July 12, 1979
Korea, North....Sept. 9, 1948
Korea, South....Aug. 15, 1948
Kosovo....Feb. 17, 2008
Kuwait....June 19, 1961
Kyrgyzstan....Aug. 31, 1991
Laos....July 19, 1949
Latvia....Sept. 6, 1991
Lebanon....Nov. 22, 1943
Lesotho....Oct. 4, 1966
Libya....Dec. 24, 1951
Lithuania....Sept. 6, 1991
Macedonia....Nov. 20, 1991
Madagascar....June 27, 1960
Malawi....July 6, 1964
Malaysia....Aug. 31, 1957
Maldives....July 26, 1966
Mali....Sept. 22, 1960
Malta....Sept. 21, 1964
Marshall Islands....Oct. 21, 1986
Mauritania....Nov. 28, 1960
Mauritius....Mar. 12, 1968
Micronesia, Federated States of....Nov. 3, 1986
Moldova....Aug. 27, 1991
Montenegro....June 3, 2006
Morocco....Mar. 2, 1956
Mozambique....June 25, 1975
Namibia....March 21, 1990
Nauru....Jan. 31, 1968
Niger....Aug. 3, 1960
Nigeria....Oct. 1, 1960
Pakistan....Aug. 14, 1947
Palau....Jan. 1, 1981
Papua New Guinea....Sept. 16, 1976
Philippines....July 4, 1946
Qatar....Sept. 3, 1971
Russia....Aug. 24, 1991
Rwanda....July 1, 1962
Saint Kitts and Nevis....Sept. 19, 1983
Saint Lucia....Feb. 22, 1979
Saint Vincent and the Grenadines....Oct. 27, 1979
São Tomé and Príncipe....July 12, 1975
Senegal....Aug. 20, 1960
Serbia....April 11, 1992
Seychelles....June 28, 1976
Sierra Leone....Apr. 27, 1961
Singapore....Aug. 9, 1965
Slovakia....Jan. 1, 1993
Slovenia....June 25, 1991
Solomon Islands....July 7, 1978
Somalia....July 1, 1960
South Sudan....July 9, 2011
Sri Lanka....Feb. 4, 1948
Sudan....Jan. 1, 1956
Suriname....Nov. 25, 1975
Swaziland....Sept. 6, 1968
Syria....Jan. 1, 1944
Tajikistan....Sept. 9, 1991
Tanzania....Dec. 9, 1961
Togo....Apr. 27, 1960
Tonga....June 4, 1970
Trinidad and Tobago....Aug. 31, 1962
Tunisia....Mar. 20, 1956
Turkmenistan....Oct. 27, 1991
Tuvalu....Oct. 1, 1978
Uganda....Oct. 9, 1962
Ukraine....Dec. 1, 1991
Uzbekistan....Aug. 31, 1991
United Arab Emirates....Dec. 2, 1971
Vanuatu....July 30, 1980
Vietnam....Mar. 8, 1949
Western Samoa....Jan. 1, 1962
Yemen....May 22, 1990
Zambia....Oct. 24, 1964
Zimbabwe....Apr. 18, 1980

Chronological Checklist of 128 New Nations Since 1943

Year	Date	Nation
1943	Nov. 22	Lebanon
1944	Jan. 1	Syria
	June 17	Iceland
1946	Mar. 22	Jordan
	July 4	Philippines
1947	Aug. 14	Pakistan
	Aug. 15	India
1948	Jan. 4	Burma
	Feb. 4	Sri Lanka
	May 15	Israel
	Aug. 15	Korea, South
	Sept. 9	Korea, North
1949	Mar. 8	Vietnam
	July 19	Laos
	Nov. 8	Cambodia
	Dec. 28	Indonesia
1951	Dec. 24	Libya
1956	Jan. 1	Sudan
	Mar. 2	Morocco
	Mar. 20	Tunisia
1957	Mar. 6	Ghana
	Aug. 31	Malaysia
1958	Oct. 2	Guinea
1960	Jan. 1	Cameroon
	Apr. 27	Togo
	June 27	Madagascar
	June 30	Congo, Dem. Rep. of (Zaire)
	July 1	Somalia
	Aug. 1	Benin
	Aug. 3	Niger
	Aug. 5	Burkina
	Aug. 7	Côte d'Ivoire
	Aug. 11	Chad
	Aug. 13	Central African Republic
	Aug. 15	Congo, Rep of
	Aug. 16	Cyprus
	Aug. 17	Gabon
	Aug. 20	Senegal
	Sept. 22	Mali
	Oct. 1	Nigeria
	Nov. 28	Mauritania
1961	Apr. 27	Sierra Leone
	June 19	Kuwait
	Dec. 9	Tanzania
1962	Jan. 1	Western Samoa
	July 1	Burundi
	July 1	Rwanda
	July 5	Algeria
	Aug. 6	Jamaica
	Aug. 31	Trinidad and Tobago
	Oct. 9	Uganda
1963	Dec. 12	Kenya
1964	July 6	Malawi
	Sept. 21	Malta
	Oct. 24	Zambia
1965	Feb. 18	Gambia, The
	July 26	Maldives
	Aug. 9	Singapore
1966	May 26	Guyana
	Sept. 30	Botswana
	Oct. 4	Lesotho
	Nov. 30	Barbados
1968	Jan. 31	Nauru
1968	Mar. 12	Mauritius
	Sept. 6	Swaziland
	Oct. 12	Equatorial Guinea
1970	June 4	Tonga
	Oct. 10	Fiji
1971	Aug. 14	Bahrain
	Sept. 3	Qatar
	Dec. 2	United Arab Emirates
1972	Apr. 4	Bangladesh
1973	July 10	Bahamas, The
1974	Feb. 7	Grenada
	Sept. 10	Guinea-Bissau
1975	June 25	Mozambique
	July 6	Cape Verde
	July 12	São Tomé and Príncipe
	Sept. 16	Papua New Guinea
	Nov. 11	Angola
	Nov. 25	Suriname
	Dec. 31	Comoros
1976	June 28	Seychelles
1977	June 27	Djibouti
1978	July 7	Solomon Islands
	Oct. 1	Tuvalu
	Nov. 3	Dominica
1979	Feb. 22	Saint Lucia
	July 12	Kiribati
	Oct. 27	Saint Vincent and the Grenadines
1980	Apr. 18	Zimbabwe
	July 30	Vanuatu
1981	Jan. 1	Palau
	Sept. 21	Belize
	Nov. 1	Antigua and Barbuda
1983	Sept. 19	Saint Kitts and Nevis
1984	Jan. 1	Brunei
1986	Oct. 21	Marshall Islands
	Nov. 3	Micronesia, Federated States of
1990	Mar. 21	Namibia
	May 22	Yemen
1991	April 9	Georgia
	June 25	Croatia
	June 25	Slovenia
	Aug. 24	Russia
	Aug. 25	Belarus
	Aug. 27	Moldova
	Aug. 30	Azerbaijan
	Aug. 31	Uzbekistan
	Aug. 31	Kyrgyzstan
	Sept. 6	Latvia
	Sept. 6	Lithuania
	Sept. 6	Estonia
	Sept. 9	Tajikistan
	Sept. 23	Armenia
	Oct. 27	Turkmenistan
	Nov. 20	Macedonia
	Dec. 1	Ukraine
	Dec. 6	Kazakhstan
1992	April 1	Bosnia and Herzegovina
	April 11	Serbia
1993	Jan. 1	Czech Republic
	Jan. 1	Slovakia
	April 27	Eritrea
2002	May 20	East Timor
2006	June 3	Montenegro
2008	Feb. 17	Kosovo
2011	July 9	South Sudan

Background Notes on Countries of the World

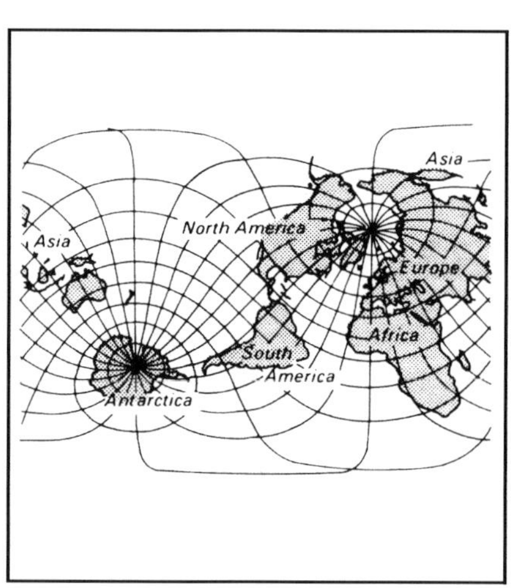

THE WORLD

February 2013

Editor's Note: This entry on The World is an abstract of current, key facts to provide a global context for the various national entries in this Yearbook. This information was provided by the U.S. Central Intelligence Agency; Background Notes on individual countries are from the U.S. Department of State.

PROFILE

Background: Globally, the 20th century was marked by: (a) two devastating world wars; (b) the Great Depression of the 1930s; (c) the end of vast colonial empires; (d) rapid advances in science and technology, from the first airplane flight at Kitty Hawk, North Carolina (US) to the landing on the moon; (e) the Cold War between the Western alliance and the Warsaw Pact nations; (f) a sharp rise in living standards in North America, Europe, and Japan; (g) increased concerns about the environment, including loss of forests, shortages of energy and water, the decline in biological diversity, and air pollution; (h) the onset of the AIDS epidemic; and (i) the ultimate emergence of the US as the only world superpower. The planet's population continues to explode: from 1 billion in 1820, to 2 billion in 1930, 3 billion in 1960, 4 billion in 1974, 5 billion in 1987, 6 billion in 1999, and 7 billion in 2012. For the 21st century, the continued exponential growth in science and technology raises both hopes (e.g., advances in medicine) and fears (e.g., development of even more lethal weapons of war).

GEOGRAPHY

The surface of the earth is approximately 70.9% water and 29.1% land. The former portion is divided into large water bodies termed oceans. The World Factbook recognizes and describes five oceans, which are in decreasing order of size: the Pacific Ocean, Atlantic Ocean, Indian Ocean, Southern Ocean, and Arctic Ocean.

The land portion is generally divided into several, large, discrete landmasses termed continents. Depending on the convention used, the number of continents can vary from five to seven. The most common classification recognizes seven, which are (from largest to smallest): Asia, Africa, North America, South America, Antarctica, Europe, and Australia. Asia and Europe are sometimes lumped together into a Eurasian continent resulting in six continents. Alternatively, North and South America are sometimes grouped as simply the Americas, resulting in a continent total of six (or five, if the Eurasia designation is used).

North America is commonly understood to include the island of Greenland, the isles of the Caribbean, and to extend south all the way to the Isthmus of Panama. The easternmost extent of Europe is generally defined as being the Ural Mountains and the Ural River; on the southeast the Caspian Sea; and on the south the Caucasus Mountains, the Black Sea, and the Mediterranean. Portions of Azerbaijan, Georgia, Kazakhstan, Russia, and Turkey fall within both Europe and Asia, but in every instance the larger section is in Asia. These countries are considered part of both continents. Armenia and Cyprus, which lie completely in Western Asia, are geopolitically European countries.

Asia usually incorporates all the islands of the Philippines, Malaysia, and Indonesia. The islands of the Pacific are often lumped with Australia into a "land mass" termed Oceania or Australasia. Africa's northeast extremity is frequently delimited at the Isthmus of Suez, but for geopolitical purposes, the Egyptian Sinai Peninsula is often included as part of Africa.

Although the above groupings are the most common, different continental dispositions are recognized or taught in certain parts of the world, with some arrangements more heavily based on cultural spheres rather than physical geographic considerations.

Map references: Political Map of the World, Physical Map of the World, Standard Time Zones of the World
Area: *total:* 510.072 million sq km; *land:* 148.94 million sq km; *water:*

361.132 million sq km; *note:* 70.9% of the world's surface is water, 29.1% is land

Area—comparative: land area about 16 times the size of the US; *Top fifteen World Factbook entities ranked by size:* Pacific Ocean 155.557 million sq km; Atlantic Ocean 76.762 million sq km; Indian Ocean 68.556 million sq km; Southern Ocean 20.327 million sq km; Russia 17,098,242 sq km; Arctic Ocean 14.056 million sq km; Antarctica 14 million sq km; Canada 9,984,670 sq km; United States 9,826,675 sq km; China 9,596,961 sq km; Brazil 8,514,877 sq km; Australia 7,741,220 sq km; European Union 4,324,782 sq km; India 3,287,263 sq km; Argentina 2,780,400 sq km

Top ten largest islands: Greenland 2,166,086 sq km; New Guinea (Indonesia, Papua New Guinea) 785,753 sq km; Borneo (Brunei, Indonesia, Malaysia) 751,929 sq km; Madagascar 587,713 sq km; Baffin Island (Canada) 507,451 sq km; Sumatra (Indonesia) 472,784 sq km; Honshu (Japan) 227,963 sq km; Victoria Island (Canada) 217,291 sq km; Great Britain (United Kingdom) 209,331 sq km; Ellesmere Island (Canada) 196,236 sq km

Land boundaries: the land boundaries in the world total 251,060 km (not counting shared boundaries twice); two nations, China and Russia, each border 14 other countries; *note:* 46 nations and other areas are landlocked, these include: Afghanistan, Andorra, Armenia, Austria, Azerbaijan, Belarus, Bhutan, Bolivia, Botswana, Burkina Faso, Burundi, Central African Republic, Chad, Czech Republic, Ethiopia, Holy See (Vatican City), Hungary, Kazakhstan, Kosovo, Kyrgyzstan, Laos, Lesotho, Liechtenstein, Luxembourg, Macedonia, Malawi, Mali, Moldova, Mongolia, Nepal, Niger, Paraguay, Rwanda, San Marino, Serbia, Slovakia, South Sudan, Swaziland, Switzerland, Tajikistan, Turkmenistan, Uganda, Uzbekistan, West Bank, Zambia, Zimbabwe; two of these, Liechtenstein and Uzbekistan, are doubly landlocked

Coastline: 356,000 km; *note:* 95 nations and other entities are islands that border no other countries, they include: American Samoa, Anguilla, Antigua and Barbuda, Aruba, Ashmore and Cartier Islands, The Bahamas, Bahrain, Baker Island, Barbados, Bermuda, Bouvet Island, British Indian Ocean Territory, British Virgin Islands, Cape Verde, Cayman Islands, Christmas Island, Clipperton Island, Cocos (Keeling) Islands, Comoros, Cook Islands, Coral Sea Islands, Cuba, Curacao, Cyprus, Dominica, Falkland Islands (Islas Malvinas), Faroe Islands, Fiji, French Polynesia, French Southern and Antarctic Lands, Greenland, Grenada, Guam, Guernsey, Heard Island and McDonald Islands, Howland Island, Iceland, Isle of Man, Jamaica, Jan Mayen, Japan, Jarvis Island, Jersey, Johnston Atoll, Kingman Reef, Kiribati, Madagascar, Maldives, Malta, Marshall Islands, Mauritius, Mayotte, Federated States of Micronesia, Midway Islands, Montserrat, Nauru, Navassa Island, New Caledonia, New Zealand, Niue, Norfolk Island, Northern Mariana Islands, Palau, Palmyra Atoll, Paracel Islands, Philippines, Pitcairn Islands, Puerto Rico, Saint Barthelemy, Saint Helena, Saint Kitts and Nevis, Saint Lucia, Saint Pierre and Miquelon, Saint Vincent and the Grenadines, Samoa, Sao Tome and Principe, Seychelles, Singapore, Sint Maarten, Solomon Islands, South Georgia and the South Sandwich Islands, Spratly Islands, Sri Lanka, Svalbard, Tokelau, Tonga, Trinidad and Tobago, Turks and Caicos Islands, Tuvalu, Vanuatu, Virgin Islands, Wake Island, Wallis and Futuna, Taiwan

Maritime claims: a variety of situations exist, but in general, most countries make the following claims measured from the mean low-tide baseline as described in the 1982 UN Convention on the Law of the Sea: territorial sea—12 nm, contiguous zone—24 nm, and exclusive economic zone—200 nm; additional zones provide for exploitation of continental shelf resources and an exclusive fishing zone; boundary situations with neighboring states prevent many countries from extending their fishing or economic zones to a full 200 nm

Climate: a wide equatorial band of hot and humid tropical climates—bordered north and south by subtropical temperate zones—that separate two large areas of cold and dry polar climates

Terrain: the greatest ocean depth is the Mariana Trench at 10,924 m in the Pacific Ocean

Elevation extremes: lowest point: Bentley Subglacial Trench (Antarctica) -2,555 m; *note:* in the oceanic realm, Challenger Deep in the Mariana Trench is the lowest point, lying -10,924 m below the surface of the Pacific Ocean; highest point: Mount Everest 8,850 m

Top ten highest mountains (measured from sea level): Mount Everest (China-Nepal) 8,850 m; K2 (Pakistan) 8,611 m; Kanchenjunga (India-Nepal) 8,598 m; Lhotse (Nepal) 8,516 m; Makalu (China-Nepal) 8,463 m; Cho Oyu (China-Nepal) 8,201 m; Dhaulagiri (Nepal) 8,167 m; Manaslu (Nepal) 8,163 m; Nanga Parbat (Pakistan) 8,125 m; Anapurna (Nepal) 8,091 m

Natural resources: the rapid depletion of nonrenewable mineral resources, the depletion of forest areas and wetlands, the extinction of animal and plant species, and the deterioration in air and water quality (especially in some countries of Eastern Europe, the former USSR, and China) pose serious long-term problems that governments and peoples are only beginning to address

Land use: arable land: 10.57%; *permanent crops:* 1.04%; *other:* 88.39% (2005); *Irrigated land:* 3,245,566 sq km (2003)

Natural hazards: large areas subject to severe weather (tropical cyclones); natural disasters (earthquakes, landslides, tsunamis, volcanic eruptions); *volcanism:* volcanism is a fundamental driver and consequence of plate tectonics, the physical process reshaping the Earth's lithosphere; the world is home to more than 1,500 potentially active volcanoes, with over 500 of these having erupted in historical times; an estimated 500 million people live near these volcanoes; associated dangers include lava flows, lahars (mudflows), pyroclastic flows, ash clouds, ash fall, ballistic projectiles, gas emissions, landslides, earthquakes, and tsunamis; in the 1990s, the International Association of Volcanology and Chemistry of the Earth's

Interior, created a list of 16 volcanoes worthy of special study because of their great potential for destruction: Avachinsky-Koryaksky (Russia), Colima (Mexico), Etna (Italy), Galeras (Colombia), Mauna Loa (United States), Merapi (Indonesia), Nyiragongo (Democratic Republic of the Congo), Rainier (United States), Sakurajima (Japan), Santa Maria (Guatemala), Santorini (Greece), Taal (Philippines), Teide (Spain), Ulawun (Papua New Guinea), Unzen (Japan), Vesuvius (Italy)

Environment—current issues: large areas subject to overpopulation, industrial disasters, pollution (air, water, acid rain, toxic substances), loss of vegetation (overgrazing, deforestation, desertification), loss of wildlife, soil degradation, soil depletion, erosion; global warming becoming a greater concern

Geography—*note:* the world is now thought to be about 4.55 billion years old, just about one-third of the 13.75-billion-year age estimated for the universe

PEOPLE

Languages: Mandarin Chinese 12.44%, Spanish 4.85%, English 4.83%, Arabic 3.25%, Hindi 2.68%, Bengali 2.66%, Portuguese 2.62%, Russian 2.12%, Japanese 1.8%, Standard German 1.33%, Javanese 1.25% (2009 est.); *note:* percents are for "first language" speakers only; the six UN languages—Arabic, Chinese (Mandarin), English, French, Russian, and Spanish (Castilian)—are the mother tongue or second language of about half of the world's population, and are the official languages in more than half the states in the world

Religions: Christian 33.35% (of which Roman Catholic 16.83%, Protestant 6.08%, Orthodox 4.03%, Anglican 1.26%), Muslim 22.43%, Hindu 13.78%, Buddhist 7.13%, Sikh 0.36%, Jewish 0.21%, Baha'i 0.11%, other religions 11.17%, non-religious 9.42%, atheists 2.04% (2009 est.)

Population: 7,021,836,029 (July 2012 est.)

Top ten most populous countries (in millions): China 1,343.24; India 1,205.07; United States 313.85; Indonesia 248.22; Brazil 205.72; Pakistan 190.29; Nigeria 170.12; Bangladesh 161.08; Russia 138.08; Japan 127.37 (July 2012 est.)

Age structure: *0-14 years:* 26.3% (male 944,987,919/female 884,268,378); *15-64 years:* 65.9% (male 2,234,860,865/female 2,187,838,153); *65 years and over:* 7.9% (male 227,164,176/female 289,048,221) (2012 est.)

Median age: *total:* 28.4 years; *male:* 27.7 years; *female:* 29 years (2009 est.)

Population growth rate: 1.096%; *note:* this rate results in about 145 net additions to the worldwide population every minute or 2.4 every second (2012 est.)

Birth rate: 19.14 births/1,000 population; *note:* this rate results in about 252 worldwide births per minute or 4.2 births every second (2012 est.)

Death rate: 7.99 deaths/1,000 population; *note:* this rate results in about 107 worldwide deaths per minute or 1.8 deaths every second (July 2012 est.)

Urbanization: urban population: 50.5% of total population (2010); *rate of urbanization:* 1.85% annual rate of change (2010–15 est.); *ten largest urban agglomerations:* Tokyo (Japan)—36,669,000; Delhi (India)—22,157,000; Sao Paulo (Brazil)—20,262,000; Mumbai (India)—20,041,000; Mexico City (Mexico)—19,460,000; New York-Newark (US)—19,425,000; Shanghai (China)—16,575,000; Kolkata (India)—15,552,000; Dhaka (Bangladesh)—14,648,000; Karachi (Pakistan)—13,125,000 (2009)

Sex ratio: *at birth:* 1.07 male(s)/female; *under 15 years:* 1.07 male(s)/female; *15-64 years:* 1.02 male(s)/female; *65 years and over:* 0.79 male(s)/female; *total population:* 1.01 male(s)/female (2011 est.)

Infant mortality rate: *total:* 39.48 deaths/1,000 live births; *male:* 41.42 deaths/1,000 live births; *female:* 37.4 deaths/1,000 live births (2012 est.)

Life expectancy at birth: total population: 67.59 years; *male:* 65.59 years; *female:* 69.73 years (2012 est.)

Total fertility rate: 2.47 children born/woman (2012 est.)

Hospital bed density: 2.94 beds/1,000 population (2005)

HIV/AIDS—adult prevalence rate: 0.8% (2009 est.)

HIV/AIDS—people living with HIV/AIDS: 33.3 million (2009 est.)

HIV/AIDS—deaths: 1.8 million (2009 est.)

Literacy: definition: age 15 and over can read and write; *total population:* 83.7%; *male:* 88.3%
female: 79.2%; *note:* over two-thirds of the world's 793 million illiterate adults are found in only eight countries (Bangladesh, China, Egypt, Ethiopia, India, Indonesia, Nigeria, and Pakistan); of all the illiterate adults in the world, two-thirds are women; extremely low literacy rates are concentrated in three regions, the Arab states, South and West Asia, and Sub-Saharan Africa, where around one-third of the men and half of all women are illiterate (2005 est.)

School life expectancy (primary to tertiary education): *total:* 11 years; *male:* 11 years; *female:* 11 years (2008)

GOVERNMENT

Administrative divisions: 195 countries, 72 dependent areas and other entities

Legal system: the legal systems of nearly all countries are generally modeled upon elements of five main types: civil law (including French law, the Napoleonic Code, Roman law, Roman-Dutch law, and Spanish law); common law (including United States law); customary law; mixed or pluralistic law; and religious law (including Islamic law); an additional type of legal system—international law—governs the conduct of independent nations in their relationships with one another

International law organization participation: all members of the UN are parties to the statute that established the International Court of Justice (ICJ) or World Court; 55 countries have accepted jurisdiction of the ICJ with reservations and 11 countries have accepted ICJ jurisdiction without reservations; states parties to the Rome Statute of the International Criminal Court (ICCt) are those countries that have ratified or acceded to the Rome Statute, the

Background Notes

treaty that established the Court; a total of 121 (effective 1 July 2012) countries have accepted jurisdiction of the ICCt (see Appendix B for a clarification on the differing mandates of the ICJ and ICCt)

ECONOMY

Overview

In 2011, world output—and per capita income—continued to recover from the 2008–09 recession, the first global downturn since 1946. Gross World Product (GWP) grew 3.7%, a slowdown from the 5.2% rate achieved in 2010. Growth was unevenly distributed: lower income countries—those with per capita incomes below $30,000 per year—averaged 4.1% growth, while higher income countries—with per capita incomes above $30,000—averaged 2.2% growth. Among large economies, China (+9.2%), Argentina (+8.9%), India (+7.2%), Nigeria (+7.2%), and Saudi Arabia (+6.8%) recorded the biggest GDP gains—although all were off the pace they set in 2010. Continuing uncertainties in financial markets slowed growth in Spain (+0.7%), Italy (+0.4%), and Greece (-6.9%), while the tsunami and Fukushima nuclear disaster hit Japan (-0.7%). Growth fell below 2% in both the US and the European Union, in part because of growing concern among consumers and investors about the size of government debt and its impact on the direction of fiscal policy. In 2011, global unemployment continued to creep upwards, reaching 9.0%—underemployment, especially in the developing world, remained much higher. Global gross fixed investment was a bright spot, jumping almost two percentage points to 24.8% of GWP, after a significant drop in 2009; direct investment across international borders climbed 7%. World trade grew 18% in 2011, but the pre-2009 pattern of surplus and deficit countries has returned. With the growth of international trade and investment, world external debt rose nearly 7%, reversing a 5% decline in 2010. Many, if not most, countries pursued expansionary monetary and fiscal policies, although at a reduced pace from 2010. The global money supply, narrowly defined, rose 7%, and broadly defined money increased roughly 8%, as central banks continued efforts to keep interest rates low. The global budget deficit was narrowed to roughly $3 trillion—4.2% of World GDP, as governments tried to rein in spending and slow the rise of public debt.

The international financial crisis of 2008–09 has presented the world economy with a major new challenge, together with several long-standing ones. The fiscal stimulus packages put in place in 2009–11 required most countries to run budget deficits. Treasuries issued new public debt—totaling $6.5 trillion since 2008—to pay for the additional expenditures. To keep interest rates low, many central banks monetized that debt, injecting large sums of money into the economies. When economic activity picks up, central banks will face the difficult task of containing inflation without raising interest rates so high they snuff out further growth. At the same time, governments will face the difficult task of spurring current growth and employment without saddling their economies with so much debt that they sacrifice long-term growth and financial stability.

Long-standing challenges the world faces are several. The addition of 80 million people each year to an already overcrowded globe is exacerbating the problems of underemployment, pollution, waste-disposal, epidemics, water-shortages, famine, over-fishing of oceans, deforestation, desertification, and depletion of non-renewable resources. The nation-state, as a bedrock economic-political institution, is steadily losing control over international flows of people, goods, funds, and technology. Internally, central governments often find their control over resources slipping as separatist regional movements—typically based on ethnicity—gain momentum, e.g., in many of the successor states of the former Soviet Union, in the former Yugoslavia, in India, in Iraq, in Indonesia, and in Canada. Externally, central governments are losing decisionmaking powers to international bodies, most notably the EU. The introduction of the euro as the common currency of much of Western Europe in January 1999, while paving the way for an integrated economic powerhouse, poses economic risks because the participating nations are culturally and politically diverse and have varying levels and rates of growth of income, and hence, differing needs for monetary and fiscal policies. In Western Europe, governments face the difficult political problem of channeling resources away from welfare programs in order to increase investment and strengthen incentives to seek employment. Because of their own internal problems and priorities, the industrialized countries devote insufficient resources to deal effectively with the poorer areas of the world, which, at least from an economic point of view, are becoming further marginalized. The terrorist attacks on the US on 11 September 2001 accentuated a growing risk to global prosperity, illustrated, for example, by the reallocation of resources away from investment to anti-terrorist programs. Wars in Iraq and Afghanistan added new uncertainties to global economic prospects. Despite these challenges, the world economy also shows great promise. Technology has made possible further advances in all fields, from agriculture, to medicine, alternative energy, metallurgy, and transportation. Improved global communications have greatly reduced the costs of international trade, helping the world gain from the international division of labor, raise living standards, and reduce income disparities among nations. Much of the resilience of the world economy in the aftermath of the financial crisis has resulted from government and central bank leaders around the globe working in concert to stem the financial onslaught, knowing well the lessons of past economic failures.

GDP (purchasing power parity): $80.33 trillion (2011 est.); $77.46 trillion (2010 est.); $73.65 trillion (2009 est.); *note:* data are in 2011 US dollars

GDP (official exchange rate): GWP (gross world product): $69.99 trillion (2011 est.)

GDP—real growth rate: 3.7% (2011); 5.2% (2010 est.); -0.8% (2009 est.)

GDP—per capita (PPP): $12,000 (2011 est.); $11,700 (2010 est.); $11,300 (2009 est.); *note:* data are in 2011 US dollars

GDP—composition by sector: *agriculture:* 6%; *industry:* 30.7%' *services:* 63.4% (2011 est.)

Labor force: 3.264 billion (2011 est.)

Labor force—by occupation: *agriculture:* 36.1%; *industry:* 21.5%; *services:* 42.4% (2007 est.)

Unemployment rate: 9.1% (2011 est.); 8.3% (2010 est.); *note:* 30% combined unemployment and underemployment in many non-industrialized countries; developed countries typically 4%-12% unemployment (2007 est.)

Household income or consumption by percentage share: *lowest 10%:* 2.7%; *highest 10%:* 27.8% (2007 est.)

Distribution of family income—Gini index: 39 (2007 est.); 37.2 (1998 est.)

Investment (gross fixed): 24.8% of GDP (2011 est.); 23% of GDP (2010 est.)

Budget: *revenues:* $20.23 trillion; *expenditures:* $23.05 trillion (2011 est.)

Taxes and other revenues: 28.9% of GDP (2011 est.)

Budget surplus (+) or deficit (-): -4% of GDP (2011 est.)

Public debt: 64.1% of GDP (2011 est.); 62.7% of GDP (2010 est.)

Inflation rate (consumer prices): world average 5% (2011 est.); developed countries 3% (2011 est.); developing countries 6.3% (2011 est.); *note:* the above estimates are weighted averages; inflation in developed countries is 0% to 4% typically, in developing countries, 5% to 10% typically; national inflation rates vary widely in individual cases; inflation rates have declined for most countries for the last several years, held in check by increasing international competition from several low wage countries, and by soft demand as a result of the world financial crisis (2010 est.)

Stock of narrow money: $25.64 trillion (31 December 2011 est.); $23.88 trillion (31 December 2010 est.)

Stock of broad money: $81.61 trillion (31 December 2011 est.); $75.57 trillion (31 December 2010 est.)

Stock of domestic credit: $110.3 trillion (31 December 2011); $100.4 trillion (31 December 2010)

Market value of publicly traded shares: $47.01 trillion (31 December 2011); $56.36 trillion (31 December 2010); $48.69 trillion (31 December 2009 est.)

Industries: dominated by the onrush of technology, especially in computers, robotics, telecommunications, and medicines and medical equipment; most of these advances take place in OECD nations; only a small portion of non-OECD countries have succeeded in rapidly adjusting to these technological forces; the accelerated development of new industrial (and agricultural) technology is complicating already grim environmental problems

Industrial production growth rate: 4.3% (2011 est.)

Exports: $17.97 trillion (2011 est.); $15.18 trillion (2010 est.)

Exports—commodities: the whole range of industrial and agricultural goods and services

Top ten—share of world trade: electrical machinery, including computers 14.8%; mineral fuels, including oil, coal, gas, and refined products 14.4%; nuclear reactors, boilers, and parts 14.2%; cars, trucks, and buses 8.9%; scientific and precision instruments 3.5%; plastics 3.4%; iron and steel 2.7%; organic chemicals 2.6%; pharmaceutical products 2.6%; diamonds, pearls, and precious stones 1.9%

Imports: $17.82 trillion (2011 est.); $14.96 trillion (2010 est.)

Imports—commodities: the whole range of industrial and agricultural goods and services

Top ten—share of world trade: see listing for exports

Debt—external: $69.08 trillion (31 December 2011 est.); $62.5 trillion (31 December 2010 est.); *note:* this figure is the sum total of all countries' external debt, both public and private

Stock of direct foreign investment—at home: $19.38 trillion (31 December 2011); $17.88 trillion (31 December 2010)

Stock of direct foreign investment—abroad: $20.63 trillion (31 December 2011); $19.32 trillion (31 December 2010)

ENERGY

Electricity—production: 20.68 trillion kWh (2009 est.)

Electricity—consumption: 19.01 trillion kWh (2009 est.)

Electricity—exports: 596.6 billion kWh (2010 est.)

Electricity—imports: 668.9 billion kWh (2010 est.)

Electricity—installed generating capacity: 4.821 billion kW (2009 est.)

Electricity—from fossil fuels: 66.6% of total installed capacity (2009 est.)

Electricity—from nuclear fuels: 7.9% of total installed capacity (2009 est.)

Electricity—from hydroelectric plants: 18.5% of total installed capacity (2009 est.)

Electricity—from other renewable sources: 4.9% of total installed capacity (2009 est.)

Crude oil—production: 84.82 million bbl/day (2011 est.)

Crude oil—exports: 40.22 million bbl/day (2009 est.)

Crude oil—imports: 41.79 million bbl/day (2009 est.)

Crude oil—proved reserves: 1.526 trillion bbl (1 January 2012 est.)

Refined petroleum products—production: 79.97 million bbl/day (2008 est.)

Refined petroleum products—consumption: 88.02 million bbl/day (2011 est.)

Refined petroleum products—exports: 22.67 million bbl/day (2008 est.)

Refined petroleum products—imports: 21.02 million bbl/day (2008 est.)

Natural gas—production: 3.359 trillion cu m (2010 est.)

Natural gas—consumption: 3.314 trillion cu m (2010 est.)

Natural gas—exports: 1.098 trillion cu m (2010 est.)
Natural gas—imports: 1.446 trillion cu m (2010 est.)
Natural gas—proved reserves: 191.3 trillion cu m (1 January 2011 est.)
Carbon dioxide emissions from consumption of energy: 31.78 billion Mt (2010 est.)

COMMUNICATIONS

Telephones—main lines in use: 1.2 billion (2008)
Telephones—mobile cellular: 5.4 billion (2010)
Telephone system: *general assessment:* NA; *domestic:* NA; *international:* NA
Internet users: 2.1 billion (2010)

TRANSPORTATION

Airports: total airports—43,794 (2012)
Top ten by passengers: Atlanta (ATL)—89,331,622; Beijing (PEK)—73,948,113; Chicago (ORD)—66,774,738; London (LHR)—65,884,143; Tokyo (HND)—64,211,074; Los Angeles (LAX)—59,070,127; Paris (CDG)—58,167,062; Dallas/Fort Worth (DFW)—56,906,610; Frankfurt (FRA)—53,009,221; Denver (DEN)—52,209,377 (2010)
Top ten by cargo (metric tons): Hong Kong (HKG)—4,165,852; Memphis (MEM)—3,916,811; Shanghai (PVG)—3,228,081; Incheon (ICN)—2,684,499; Anchorage (ANC)—2,646,695; Paris (CDG)—2,399,067; Frankfurt (FRA)—2,275,000; Dubai (DXB)—2,270,498; Tokyo (NRT)—2,167,853; Louisville (SDF)—2,166,656 (2010)
Heliports: 3,825 (2012)
Railways: *total:* 1,139,615 km (2008)
Roadways: *total:* 102,260,304 km (2008)
Waterways: 671,886 km
Top ten longest rivers: Nile (Africa) 6,693 km; Amazon (South America) 6,436 km; Mississippi-Missouri (North America) 6,238 km; Yenisey-Angara (Asia) 5,981 km; Ob-Irtysh (Asia) 5,569 km; Yangtze (Asia) 5,525 km; Yellow (Asia) 4,671 km; Amur (Asia) 4,352 km; Lena (Asia) 4,345 km; Congo (Africa) 4,344 km; *note:* if measured by volume, the Amazon is the largest river in the world
Ports and terminals: top ten container ports as measured by Twenty-Foot Equivalent Units (TEUs) throughput: Shanghai (China)—29,069,000; Singapore (Singapore)—28,431,100; Hong Kong (China)—23,669,242; Shenzhen (China)—22,509,700; Busan (South Korea)—14,194,334; Ningbo (China)—13,144,000; Guangzhou (China)—12,486,900; Qingdao (China)—12,012,000; Dubai (UAE)—11,575,775;—Rotterdam (Netherlands)- 11,145,804 (2010)
Transportation—*note:* the International Maritime Bureau (IMB) reports that 2011 saw a very slight (1%) decrease in global pirate activities with marginally fewer people taken hostage at sea; in 2011, pirates attacked a total of 439 ships worldwide including hijacking 45 ships, capturing 802 seafarers, and killing eight; while the Horn of Africa remains the most dangerous area for maritime shipping, accounting for more than 50% of all attacks in 2011, a number of attacks also occurred in the coastal waters of Indonesia, the South China Sea, Bangladesh, and West Africa; as of July 2012, there have been 189 attacks worldwide with 20 hijackings; the Horn of Africa remains the most dangerous region in 2012 with 70 attacks, 13 hijackings, 212 hostages seized; as of July 2012, Somali pirates hold 11 vessels and 174 hostages; the decrease in successful pirate attacks is due, in part, to more aggressive anti-piracy operations by international naval forces as well as the increased use of armed security teams aboard merchant ships

MILITARY

Military expenditures: roughly 2% of GDP of gross world product (2005 est.)

TRANSNATIONAL ISSUES

Disputes—international: stretching over 250,000 km, the world's 322 international land boundaries separate 195 independent states and 71 dependencies, areas of special sovereignty, and other miscellaneous entities; ethnicity, culture, race, religion, and language have divided states into separate political entities as much as history, physical terrain, political fiat, or conquest, resulting in sometimes arbitrary and imposed boundaries; most maritime states have claimed limits that include territorial seas and exclusive economic zones; overlapping limits due to adjacent or opposite coasts create the potential for 430 bilateral maritime boundaries of which 209 have agreements that include contiguous and non-contiguous segments; boundary, borderland/resource, and territorial disputes vary in intensity from managed or dormant to violent or militarized; undemarcated, indefinite, porous, and unmanaged boundaries tend to encourage illegal cross-border activities, uncontrolled migration, and confrontation; territorial disputes may evolve from historical and/or cultural claims, or they may be brought on by resource competition; ethnic and cultural clashes continue to be responsible for much of the territorial fragmentation and internal displacement of the estimated 6.6 million people and cross-border displacements of 8.6 million refugees around the world as of early 2006; just over one million refugees were repatriated in the same period; other sources of contention include access to water and mineral (especially hydrocarbon) resources, fisheries, and arable land; armed conflict prevails not so much between the uniformed armed forces of independent states as between stateless armed entities that detract from the sustenance and welfare of local populations, leaving the community of nations to cope with resultant refugees, hunger, disease, impoverishment, and environmental degradation

Refugees and internally displaced persons: the United Nations High Commissioner for Refugees (UNHCR) estimated in June 2011 that there were 43.7 million people forcibly displaced worldwide; this includes 15.1 million refugees and as many as 27.5 million IDPs in more than 40 countries (2011)
Trafficking in persons: current situation: approximately 800,000 people, mostly women and children, are trafficked annually across national borders, not including millions trafficked within their own countries; at least 80% of the victims are female and up to 50% are minors; 75% of all victims are trafficked into commercial sexual exploitation; almost two-thirds of the global victims are trafficked intra-regionally within East Asia and the Pacific (260,000 to 280,000 people) and Europe and Eurasia (170,000 to 210,000 people)
Tier 2 Watch List: (42 countries) Afghanistan, Angola, Azerbaijan, the Bahamas, Bahrain, Barbados, Belarus, Burma, Burundi, Chad, China, Comoros, Republic of the Congo, Cyprus, Djibouti, Ecuador, Federated States of Micronesia, The Gambia, Guinea-Bissau, Haiti, Iraq, Jamaica, Kenya, Lebanon, Liberia, Macau, Malawi, Malaysia, Maldives, Mauritania, Namibia, Niger, Russia, Senegal, Seychelles, Sierra Leone, South Sudan, Suriname, Thailand, Turkmenistan, Uzbekistan, Venezuela
Tier 3: (17 countries) Algeria, Central African Republic, Democratic Republic of Congo, Cuba, Equatorial Guinea, Eritrea, Iran, North Korea, Kuwait, Libya, Madagascar, Papua New Guinea, Saudi Arabia, Sudan, Syria, Yemen, Zimbabwe (2012)
Illicit drugs: *cocaine:* worldwide coca leaf cultivation in 2007 amounted to 232,500 hectares; Colombia produced slightly more than two-thirds of the worldwide crop, followed by Peru and Bolivia; potential pure cocaine production decreased 7% to 865 metric tons in 2007; Colombia conducts an aggressive coca eradication campaign, but both Peruvian and Bolivian Governments are hesitant to eradicate coca in key growing areas; 551 metric tons of export-quality cocaine (85% pure) is documented to have been seized or destroyed in 2005; US consumption of export quality cocaine is estimated to have been in excess of 380 metric tons

opiates: worldwide illicit opium poppy cultivation continued to increase in 2007, with a potential opium production of 8,400 metric tons, reaching the highest levels recorded since estimates began in mid-1980s; Afghanistan is world's primary opium producer, accounting for 95% of the global supply; Southeast Asia—responsible for 9% of global opium—saw marginal increases in production; Latin America produced 1% of global opium, but most was refined into heroin destined for the US market; if all potential opium was processed into pure heroin, the potential global production would be 1,000 metric tons of heroin in 2007

AFGHANISTAN

Compiled from publications that were available as of February 2013 from the U.S. Department of State, the U.S. Department of Commerce, and the Central Intelligence Agency (CIA). See the introduction to this set for explanatory notes.

Official Name:

Islamic Republic of Afghanistan

PROFILE

Geography

Area: total: 652,230 sq km; country comparison to the world: 41; land: 652,230 sq km; water: 0 sq km

Major cities: Kabul (capital) 3.573 million (2009)

Climate: arid to semiarid; cold winters and hot summers

Terrain: mostly rugged mountains; plains in north and southwest

People

Nationality: noun: Afghan(s); adjective: Afghan

Population: 30,419,928 (July 2012 est.)

Population growth rate: 2.22% (2012 est.)

Ethnic groups: Pashtun 42%, Tajik 27%, Hazara 9%, Uzbek 9%, Aimak 4%, Turkmen 3%, Baloch 2%, other 4%

Religions: Sunni Muslim 80%, Shia Muslim 19%, other 1%

Languages: Afghan Persian or Dari (official) 50%, Pashto (official) 35%, Turkic languages (primarily Uzbek and Turkmen) 11%, 30 minor languages (primarily Balochi and Pashai) 4%, much bilingualism, but Dari functions as the lingua franca

Literacy: definition: age 15 and over can read and write; total population: 28.1%; male: 43.1%; female: 12.6% (2000 est.)

Health: life expectancy at birth: total population: 49.72 years; male: 48.45 years; female: 51.05 years (2012 est.); Infant mortality rate: total: 121.63 deaths/1,000 live births; male: 129.51 deaths/1,000 live births; female: 113.36 deaths/1,000 live births (2012 est.)

Unemployment rate: 35% (2008 est.)

Work force: 15 million (2004 est.)

Government

Type: Islamic republic

Independence: 19 August 1919

Constitution: sixth constitution drafted 14 December 2003-4 January 2004; signed 16 January 2004; ratified 26 January 2004

Political subdivisions: 34 provinces (welayat, singular—welayat); Badakhshan, Badghis, Baghlan, Balkh, Bamyan, Daykundi, Farah, Faryab, Ghazni, Ghor, Helmand, Herat, Jowzjan, Kabul, Kandahar, Kapisa, Khost, Kunar, Kunduz, Lagh man, Logar, Nangarhar, Nimroz, Nuristan, Paktika, Paktiya, Panjshir, Parwan, Samangan, Sar-e Pul, Takhar, Uruzgan, Wardak, Zabul

Suffrage: 18 years of age; universal

Economy

GDP (purchasing power parity): $33.55 billion (2012 est.); $30.11 billion (2011 est.); $28.48 billion (2010 est.); $26.26 billion (2009 est.)

GDP real growth rate: 11% (2012 est.); 5.7% (2011 est.); 8.4% (2010 est.); 21% (2009 est.)

GDP per capita (PPP): $1,000 (2012 est.); $1,000 (2011 est.); $900 (2010 est.); $900 (2009 est.)

Natural resources: natural gas, petroleum, coal, copper, chromite, talc, barites, sulfur, lead, zinc, iron ore, salt, precious and semiprecious stones

Agriculture products: opium, wheat, fruits, nuts; wool, mutton, sheepskins, lambskins

Industries: small-scale production of textiles, soap, furniture, shoes, fertilizer, apparel, food-products, non-alcoholic beverages, mineral water, cement; handwoven carpets; natural gas, coal, copper

Exports: $376 million (2012 est.); $2.625 billion (2010 est.); $547 million (2009 est.)

Exports—commodities: opium, fruits and nuts, handwoven carpets, wool, cotton, hides and pelts, precious and semi-precious gems

Exports—partners: Pakistan 31.4%, India 28.8%, Tajikistan 8.3%, Russia 5.2%, Bangladesh 4.7% (2011)

Imports: $6.39 billion (2012 est.); $9.152 billion (2010 est.); $5.3 billion (2008 est.)

Imports—commodities: machinery and other capital goods, food, textiles, petroleum products

Imports—partners: US 31.4%, Pakistan 20.8%, Russia 8.4%, India 5.6%, Germany 4.1% (2011)

Debt—external: $1.28 billion (FY10/11); $2.7 billion (FY08/09)

Exchange rates: afghanis (AFA) per US dollar; 51 (2012 est.); 46.75 (2011); 46.45 (2010)

PEOPLE

Afghanistan's ethnically and linguistically mixed population reflects its location astride historic trade and invasion routes leading from Central Asia into South and Southwest Asia. While population data is somewhat unreliable for Afghanistan, Pashtuns make up the largest ethnic group at , followed by Tajiks, Hazaras, Uzbek, Aimaq, Turkmen, Baluch, and other small groups.

National/Racial/Ethnic Minorities

Ethnic tensions between Pashtun and non-Pashtun groups has resulted in conflict and occasional killings. Societal discrimination against Shia Hazaras continues along class, race, and religious lines in the form of extortion of money through illegal taxation, forced recruitment and forced labor, physical abuse, and detention.

Ethnic Hazaras have reported occasionally being asked to pay bribes at border crossings where Pashtuns were allowed to pass freely. Sikhs and Hindus reportedly continued to face discrimination, including unequal access to government jobs and harassment in their schools, as well as verbal and physical abuse in public places. The UNHCR has reported that Hindus, Sikhs, and Shia Muslims—particularly those from the Hazara ethnic group—have faced official obstacles and discrimination by the Sunni Muslim majority.

Religion

Reliable data on religious demography is not available because an official nationwide census has not been conducted in decades. Observers estimate that 80 percent of the population is Sunni Muslim, 19 percent Shia Muslim, and 1 percent other religious groups. According to self estimates by minority religious communities, there are approximately 2,000 Sikhs, more than 400 Baha'is, and approximately 100 Hindus. There is a small Christian community estimated between 500 and 8,000 persons. In addition, there are small numbers of adherents of other religious groups.

Different religious groups are concentrated in specific regions. Sunni Pashtuns dominate the south and east. The homeland of the Shia Hazaras is in the Hazarajat, the mountainous central highland provinces around Bamyan province. Ismaili populations are normally clustered in the northeast. Other areas, including Kabul, are more heterogeneous and include Sunni, Shia, Sikh, Hindu, and Baha'i populations.

The northern city of Mazar-e Sharif includes a mix of Sunnis (including ethnic Pashtuns, Turkmen, Uzbeks, and Tajiks) and Shia (Hazaras and Qizilbash), including Shia Ismailis. Nuristanis, a small but distinct ethno-linguistic group living in a mountainous eastern region, practiced an ancient polytheistic religion until they converted to Islam in the late 19th century. Some non-Muslim religious practices survive today as folk customs throughout remote areas.

In the 20th century, small communities of Baha'is, Buddhists, Christians, Hindus, Jews, and Sikhs lived in the country, although most members of these communities emigrated during the civil war and Taliban rule. By 2001, non-Muslim populations had been virtually eliminated except for a small population of native Hindus and Sikhs. Since the fall of the Taliban, some members of religious minorities have returned, but others have since left Kabul due to economic hardship and discrimination. Estimates from Hindu and Sikh religious leaders indicate that their population shrank in the past year as compared to the year before.

Followers of the Baha'i Faith have practiced in the country for approximately 150 years. The community is predominantly based in Kabul, where reportedly more than 300 Baha'i members live; another 100 live in other parts of the country.

Language

Dari (Afghan Farsi) and Pashto are official languages. Dari is spoken by more than one-third of the population as a first language and serves as a lingua franca for most Afghans, though Pashto is spoken throughout the Pashtun areas of eastern and southern Afghanistan. Tajik and Turkic languages are spoken widely in the north. Smaller groups throughout the country also speak more than 70 other languages and numerous dialects.

HISTORY

Afghanistan, often called the crossroads of Central Asia, has had a turbulent history. In 328 BC, Alexander the Great entered the territory of present-day Afghanistan, then part of the Persian Empire, and established a Hellenistic state in Bactria (present-day Balkh). Invasions by the Scythians, White Huns, and Turks followed in succeeding centuries. In AD 642, Arabs invaded the entire region and introduced Islam.

Arab rule gave way to the Persians, who controlled the area until conquered by the Turkic Ghaznavids in 998. Following Mahmud's short-lived dynasty, various princes attempted to rule sections of the country until the destructive Mongol invasion of 1219 led by Genghis Khan.

Following Genghis Khan's death in 1227, a succession of petty chiefs and princes struggled for supremacy until late in the 14th century, when one of his descendants, Tamerlane, incorporated Afghanistan into his own vast

Asian empire. In 1747, Ahmad Shah Durrani, the founder of what is known today as Afghanistan, established his rule. A Pashtun, Durrani was elected king by a tribal council after the assassination of the Persian ruler Nadir Shah at Khabushan in the same year. Throughout his reign, Durrani consolidated chieftainships, petty principalities, and fragmented provinces into one country. His rule extended from Mashad in the west to Kashmir and Delhi in the east, and from the Amu Darya (Oxus) River in the north to the Arabian Sea in the south.

European Influence

During the 19th century, collision between the expanding British Empire in the subcontinent and czarist Russia significantly influenced Afghanistan in what was termed "The Great Game." British concern over Russian advances in Central Asia and growing influence in Persia precipitated two Anglo-Afghan wars in 1839 and again in 1878.

The first resulted in the destruction of a British army. The latter conflict brought Amir Abdur Rahman to the Afghan throne. During his reign (1880–1901), the British and Russians officially established the boundaries of what would become modern Afghanistan through the demarcation of the Durand Line. The British retained effective control over Kabul's foreign affairs. Habibullah, Abdur Rahman's son and successor, was assassinated in 1919. His third son, Amanullah, regained control of Afghanistan's foreign policy after launching the third Anglo-Afghan war with an attack on India in the same year. During the ensuing conflict, the war-weary British relinquished their control over Afghan foreign affairs by signing the Treaty of Rawalpindi in August 1919. In commemoration of this event, Afghans celebrate August 19 as their Independence Day.

Reform and Reaction

King Amanullah (1919–29) moved to end his country's traditional isolation. He established diplomatic relations with most major countries and introduced several reforms intended to modernize Afghanistan. Some of these, such as the abolition of the traditional Muslim veil for women and the opening of a number of co-educational schools, quickly alienated many tribal and religious leaders.

Faced with overwhelming armed opposition, Amanullah was forced to abdicate in January 1929 after Kabul fell to forces led by Bacha-i-Saqao, a Tajik brigand. Prince Nadir Khan, a cousin of Amanullah's, in turn defeated Bacha-i-Saqao in October of the same year and, with considerable Pashtun tribal support, was declared King Nadir Shah. Four years later, however, he was assassinated in a revenge killing by a Kabul student.

Mohammad Zahir Shah, Nadir Khan's 19-year-old son, succeeded to the throne and reigned from 1933 to 1973. In 1964, King Zahir Shah promulgated a liberal constitution providing for a two-chamber legislature to which the king appointed one-third of the deputies. Although Zahir's "experiment in democracy" produced few lasting reforms, it permitted the growth of unofficial extremist parties on both the left and the right. These included the communist People's Democratic Party of Afghanistan (PDPA), which had close ideological ties to the Soviet Union.

In 1967, the PDPA split into two major rival factions: the Khalq (Masses) faction headed by Nur Muhammad Taraki and Hafizullah Amin and supported by elements within the military, and the Parcham (Banner) faction led by Babrak Karmal. The split reflected ethnic, class, and ideological divisions within Afghan society. Zahir's cousin, Sardar Mohammad Daoud, served as his Prime Minister from 1953 to 1963. During his tenure as Prime Minister, Daoud solicited military and economic assistance from both Washington and Moscow and introduced controversial social policies of a reformist nature. Daoud's alleged support for the creation of a Pashtun state in the Pakistan-Afghan border area heightened tensions with Pakistan and eventually resulted in Daoud's dismissal in March 1963.

Daoud's Republic (1973–78) and the April 1978 Coup

Amid charges of corruption and malfeasance against the royal family and poor economic conditions, former Prime Minister Daoud seized power in a military coup on July 17, 1973. Zahir Shah fled the country, eventually finding refuge in Italy. Daoud abolished the monarchy, abrogated the 1964 constitution, and declared Afghanistan a republic with himself as its first President and Prime Minister. His attempts to carry out badly needed economic and social reforms met with little success, and the new constitution promulgated in February 1977 failed to quell chronic political instability.

Seeking to exploit more effectively mounting popular disaffection, the PDPA reunified with Moscow's support. On April 27, 1978, the PDPA initiated a bloody coup, which resulted in the overthrow and murder of Daoud and most of his family. Nur Muhammad Taraki, Secretary General of the PDPA, became President of the Revolutionary Council and Prime Minister of the newly established Democratic Republic of Afghanistan. Opposition to the Marxist government emerged almost immediately. During its first 18 months of rule, the PDPA brutally imposed a Marxist-style "reform" program, which ran counter to deeply rooted Afghan traditions. In addition, thousands of members of the traditional elite, the religious establishment, and the intelligentsia were imprisoned, tortured, or murdered. Conflicts within the PDPA also surfaced early and resulted in exiles, purges, imprisonments, and executions. By the summer of 1978, a revolt began in the Nuristan region of eastern Afghanistan and quickly spread into a countrywide insurgency. In September 1979, Hafizullah Amin, who had earlier been Prime Minister and Minister of Defense, seized power from Taraki. Over the next 2 months, instability plagued Amin's regime as he moved against perceived enemies in the PDPA. By December, party morale was crumbling, and the insurgency was growing.

The Soviet Invasion

In December 1978, Moscow signed a new bilateral treaty of friendship and cooperation with Afghanistan, and the Soviet military assistance program increased significantly. The regime's survival increasingly was dependent upon Soviet assistance as the insurgency spread and the Afghan army began to collapse.

By October 1979, however, relations between Afghanistan and the Soviet Union were tense as Hafizullah Amin refused to take Soviet advice on how to stabilize and consolidate his government. Faced with a deteriorating security situation, on December 24, 1979, large numbers of Soviet airborne forces began to land in Kabul. They killed Hafizullah Amin and installed Babrak Karmal, exiled leader of the Parcham faction, as Prime Minister.

Following the invasion, the Karmal regime, although backed by 120,000 Soviet troops, was unable to establish authority outside Kabul. As much as 80% of the countryside, including parts of Herat and Kandahar, eluded effective government control. An overwhelming majority of Afghans opposed the communist regime, either actively or passively. Afghan fighters (mujahideen) made it almost impossible for the regime to maintain a system of local government outside major urban centers. Poorly armed at first, in 1984 the mujahideen began receiving substantial assistance in the form of weapons and training from the U.S. and other outside powers.

In May 1985, the seven principal Peshawar-based guerrilla organizations formed an alliance to coordinate their political and military operations against the Soviet occupation. Late in 1985, the mujahideen were active in and around Kabul. The failure of the Soviet Union to win over a significant number of Afghan collaborators or to rebuild a viable Afghan army forced it to bear an increasing responsibility for fighting the resistance and for civilian administration.

Soviet and popular displeasure with the Karmal regime led to its demise in May 1986. Karmal was replaced by Muhammad Najibullah, former chief of the Afghan secret police (KHAD). As Prime Minister, Najibullah was ineffective and highly dependent on Soviet support. Undercut by deep-seated divisions within the PDPA, regime efforts to broaden its base of support proved futile.

The Geneva Accords and Their Aftermath

By the mid-1980s, the tenacious Afghan resistance movement was exacting a high price from the Soviets, both militarily within Afghanistan and by souring the U.S.S.R.'s relations with much of the Western and Islamic world. Informal negotiations for a Soviet withdrawal from Afghanistan had been underway since 1982. In 1988 the Geneva accords were signed, which included a timetable that ensured full Soviet withdrawal from Afghanistan by February 15, 1989. About 14,500 Soviet and an estimated one million Afghan lives were lost between 1979 and the Soviet withdrawal in 1989.

Significantly, the mujahideen were party neither to the negotiations nor to the 1988 agreement and, consequently, refused to accept the terms of the accords. As a result, the civil war continued after the Soviet withdrawal, which was completed in February 1989. Najibullah's regime was able to remain in power until 1992 but collapsed after the defection of Gen. Abdul Rashid Dostam and his Uzbek militia in March. However, when the victorious mujahideen entered Kabul to assume control over the city and the central government, a new round of internecine fighting began between the various militias. With the demise of their common enemy, the militias' ethnic, clan, religious, and personality differences surfaced, and the civil war continued.

Seeking to resolve these differences, the leaders of the Peshawar-based mujahideen groups established an interim Islamic Jihad Council in mid-April 1992 to assume power in Kabul. Moderate leader Prof. Sibghatullah Mojaddedi was to chair the council for 2 months, after which a 10-member leadership council composed of mujahideen leaders and presided over by the head of the Jamiat-i-Islami, Prof. Burhanuddin Rabbani, was to be set up for 4 months. During this 6-month period, a Loya Jirga, or grand council of Afghan elders and notables, would convene and designate an interim administration which would hold power up to a year, pending elections.

But in May 1992, Rabbani prematurely formed the leadership council, undermining Mojaddedi's fragile authority. In June, Mojaddedi surrendered power to the Leadership Council, which then elected Rabbani as President. Nonetheless, heavy fighting broke out in August 1992 in Kabul between forces loyal to President Rabbani and rival factions, particularly those who supported Gulbuddin Hekmatyar's Hezb-i-Islami. After Rabbani extended his tenure in December 1992, fighting in the capital flared up in January and February 1993.

The Islamabad Accord, signed in March 1993, which appointed Hekmatyar as Prime Minister, failed to have a lasting effect. A follow-up agreement, the Jalalabad Accord, called for the militias to be disarmed but was never fully implemented. Through 1993, Hekmatyar's Hezb-i-Islami forces, allied with the Shi'a Hezb-i-Wahdat militia, clashed intermittently with Rabbani and Masood's Jamiat forces. Cooperating with Jamiat were militants of Sayyaf's Ittehad-i-Islami and, periodically, troops loyal to ethnic Uzbek strongman Abdul Rashid Dostam. On January 1, 1994, Dostam switched sides, precipitating large-scale fighting in Kabul and in northern provinces, which caused thousands of civilian casualties in Kabul and elsewhere and created a new wave of displaced persons and refugees. The country sank even further into anarchy, forces loyal to Rabbani and Masood, both ethnic Tajiks, controlled Kabul and much of the northeast, while local warlords exerted power over the rest of the country.

Rise and Fall of the Taliban

The Taliban had risen to power in the mid-1990s in reaction to the anarchy and warlordism that arose after the withdrawal of Soviet forces. Many Taliban had been educated in madrassas in Pakistan and were largely from rural southern Pashtun backgrounds. In 1994, the Taliban developed enough strength to capture the city of Kandahar from a local warlord and proceeded to expand its control throughout Afghanistan, occupying Kabul in September 1996. By the end of 1998, the Taliban occupied about 90% of the country, limiting the opposition largely to a small mostly Tajik corner in the northeast and the Panjshir valley.

The Taliban sought to impose an extreme interpretation of Islam—based upon the rural Pashtun tribal code—on the entire country and committed massive human rights violations, particularly directed against women and girls. The Taliban also committed serious atrocities against minority populations, particularly the Shi'a Hazara ethnic group, and killed noncombatants in several well-documented instances. In 2001, as part of a drive against relics of Afghanistan's pre-Islamic past, the Taliban destroyed two huge Buddha statues carved into a cliff face outside of the city of Bamiyan.

From the mid-1990s the Taliban provided sanctuary to Osama bin Laden, a Saudi national who had fought with the mujahideen resistance against the Soviets, and provided a base for his and other terrorist organizations. Bin Laden provided both financial and political support to the Taliban.

Bin Laden and his al-Qaeda group were charged with the bombing of the U.S. Embassies in Nairobi and Dar Es Salaam in 1998, and in August 1998 the United States launched a cruise missile attack against bin Laden's terrorist camp in southeastern Afghanistan. Bin Laden and al-Qaeda acknowledged their responsibility for the September 11, 2001 terrorist attacks against the United States.

Following the Taliban's repeated refusal to expel bin Laden and his group and end its support for international terrorism, the U.S. and its partners in an anti-terrorist coalition began a military campaign on October 7, 2001, targeting terrorist facilities and various Taliban military and political assets within Afghanistan. Under pressure from U.S. military and anti-Taliban forces, the Taliban disintegrated rapidly, and Kabul fell on November 13, 2001.

Afghan factions opposed to the Taliban met at a United Nations-sponsored conference in Bonn, Germany in December 2001 and agreed to restore stability and governance to Afghanistan—creating an interim government and establishing a process to move toward a permanent government. Under the "Bonn Agreement," an Afghan Interim Authority was formed and took office in Kabul on December 22, 2001 with Hamid Karzai as Chairman. The Interim Authority held power for approximately 6 months while preparing for a nationwide "Loya Jirga" (Grand Council) in mid-June 2002 that decided on the structure of a Transitional Authority.

The Transitional Authority, headed by President Hamid Karzai, renamed the government as the Transitional Islamic State of Afghanistan (TISA). One of the TISA's primary achievements was the drafting of a constitution that was ratified by a Constitutional Loya Jirga on January 4, 2004. On December 7, 2004, the country was renamed the Islamic Republic of Afghanistan.

On October 9, 2004, Afghanistan held its first national democratic presidential election. More than 8 million Afghans voted, 41% of whom were women. Hamid Karzai was announced as the official winner on November 3 and inaugurated on December 7 for a 5-year term as Afghanistan's first democratically elected president.

An election was held on September 18, 2005 for the "Wolesi Jirga" (lower house) of Afghanistan's new bicameral National Assembly and for the country's 34 provincial councils. Turnout for the election was about 53% of the 12.5 million registered voters. The Afghan constitution provides for indirect election of the National Assembly's "Meshrano Jirga" (upper house) by the provincial councils and by reserved presidential appointments. The first democratically elected National Assembly since 1969 was inaugurated on December 19, 2005. Younus Qanooni and Sigbatullah Mojadeddi were elected Speakers of the Wolesi Jirga and Meshrano Jirga, respectively.

The second national democratic presidential and provincial council elections were held in August 2009, and National Assembly elections were held September 2010. Hamid Karzai's main competitor, Abdullah Abdullah, forced a presidential runoff to be scheduled, but then withdrew. On November 2, 2009, officials of the Independent Election Commission (IEC) declared Hamid Karzai President of Afghanistan for another 5-year term. Unlike previous election cycles, the elections were coordinated by the IEC, with assistance from the UN. NATO officials announced in March 2009 that 15.6 million voters had registered to vote, roughly half of the country's population, and that 35% to 38% of registered voters were women.

Since the fall of the Taliban regime, destabilizing factors have included activities by the Taliban and other insurgents and by al-Qaeda. The government's authority is growing, although its ability to deliver necessary social services remains largely dependent on funds from the international donor community. U.S. assistance for Afghanistan's reconstruction from fiscal year 2001 to the present totals over $72 billion, including support for security services. Donors pledged continued assistance for the rebuilding of the country at the June 2008 international Afghanistan support conference in Paris. Overall, the international community has made multi-year reconstruction and security assistance pledges to Afghanistan totaling over $100 billion.

With international community support, including more than 49 countries participating in Operation Enduring Freedom and NATO-led International Security Assistance Force (ISAF), the government's capacity to secure Afghanistan's borders and maintain internal order is increasing.

As of October 2011, Afghan National Security Forces (ANSF) had reached approximately 170,700 Afghan National Army (ANA) soldiers, and over 136,800 police, including border and civil order police, had received training. Reform of the army and police, to include training, is an extensive and ongoing process, and the U.S. is working with NATO and international partners to further develop Afghanistan's National Security Forces.

As of October 2011, training and equipping programs for the ANSF remained at a steady pace to meet objectives of having 195,000 ANA and 157,000 Afghan National Police (ANP) by November 2012.

GOVERNMENT AND POLITICAL CONDITIONS

Afghanistan is an Islamic republic with a strong, directly elected presidency, a bicameral legislative branch, and a judicial branch. Widespread fraud and irregularities marred the September 2010 parliamentary elections, with observers concerned that the transparency of the electoral process would be undermined by President Hamid Karzai's 2010 appointment of a special tribunal, not envisioned in the constitution, to adjudicate the disputed election results. In 2009 citizens voted in their second presidential election. The constitutionally mandated Independent Elections Commission (IEC) declared Karzai president for a second term, after his challenger withdrew from a run-off election. Allegations of fraud also marred those elections. Civilian authorities generally maintained control over the security forces, although there were instances in which security forces acted independently.

Recent Elections

The September 2010 parliamentary elections were held amid significant security and logistical challenges. The elections themselves generally followed the constitutional process, although widespread fraud and corruption, particularly at the subnational level, hampered the election. International observers and civil society groups documented instances of ballot stuffing, ghost polling stations, and some interference by staff of electoral bodies; fraud was especially notable in areas with high levels of insecurity, limited observer and candidate agent coverage, and insufficient female electoral staff.

While security preparations improved relative to the 2009 presidential election, security was still inadequate in many locations, and numerous irregularities occurred, including pervasive intimidation of voters, polling staff, and candidates, especially women.

Due to newly implemented antifraud procedures, the IEC proactively threw out 1.3 million of the estimated total 5.6 million votes cast, based on evidence of fraud or other procedural irregularities. The IEC cited evidence of fraud at more than 2,500 polling stations and invalidated approximately 23 percent of the ballots cast.

The Electoral Complaints Commission (ECC) disqualified more than 300 polling stations and invalidated the votes for 24 preliminarily elected candidates due to evidence of fraud or noncompliance with IEC rules and regulations. Limited transparency on the part of both commissions during the tally and adjudication processes fueled the perception that political bias might have affected the invalidation process. The IEC certified the official election results on December 1, 2010.

In response to protests about the election results in December 2010, President Karzai appointed a special tribunal to investigate and recommend changes to the election results. The IEC, parliamentarians, and NGOs challenged the legality and constitutionality of the special tribunal, calling repeatedly for its dissolution. The parliamentarians viewed the special tribunal as an attempt by the executive to weaken parliament and interfere with its composition. Despite the special tribunal's ongoing review, parliament was inaugurated on January 26.

The special tribunal remained in place and the political impasse over the disputed races and the disposition of seats continued until June, virtually halting legislative action. In June the special tribunal recommended replacing 62 sitting members of parliament (MPs). On August 10, the president issued a decree that returned the review of the disputed cases from the special tribunal to the IEC for a final decision. On August 21, the IEC, which legally assumed the powers of the ECC, overturned nine of the ECC's disqualifications, and issued certificates to nine new MPs. After an internal boycott and heavy resistance to the IEC's decision, parliament had its first quorum after months in October and began voting on long-pending legislation.

In 2009 citizens voted in their second contested presidential election. The IEC declared Karzai president for a second term, after his challenger, Dr. Abdullah Abdullah, withdrew from a run-off election. The elections were similarly marred by serious allegations of widespread fraud.

Political Parties: Negative associations with warlords and the communists have led many citizens to view political parties with suspicion. The 2009 Party Law replaced the initial law of 2003, which granted parties the right to exist as formal institutions for the first time in the country's history. The new law required parties to have membership papers of 10,000 members (from a minimum of 22 provinces). The law was passed in September 2009 and allowed very little time for parties to complete the registration process in advance of the 2010 parliamentary elections.

The National Democratic Institute (NDI) reported that a number of parties complained about the process, citing fraud in the Ministry of Justice, which is responsible for registration of political parties, and the unequal treatment of parties by the registration department. As of November 2010, the MOJ had accredited 33 political parties under the law. By April 38 parties were registered, according to NDI. However, only five parties were accredited in time for the September 2010 elections, and very few parliamentary candidates were shown to be affiliated with a party during the campaign.

Political parties were not always able to conduct activities throughout the country, particularly in regions where antigovernment violence affected overall security. A total of 21 political parties had representation in the lower house.

Participation of Women and Minorities: The Pashtun ethnic group had more seats than any other ethnic group in both houses but did not have more than 50 percent of the seats. The Pashtuns lost seats in the September 2010 lower house elections. There was no evidence that there were societal groups that were specifically excluded. Traditional societal practices that limit women's participation in politics and activities outside the home community likely influenced the central government's composition.

For the Wolesi Jirga, the lower house of the national Assembly, 396 of the 2,510 candidates for the election were women, representing a significant increase in female candidate participation compared with the 2005 parliamentary elections. There were sufficient members to fill the two seats reserved for women in each province (68 of 249 total seats). Women active in public life continued to face disproportionate levels of threats and violence and were the targets of attacks by the Taliban and other insurgent groups. Most female MPs reportedly experienced some kind of threat or intimidation; many believed that the state could not or would not protect them.

There were reports that the female members of the High Peace Council established in September 2010 were marginalized by their male counterparts and that they were not permitted to take part in initial contacts with representatives from the Taliban or other insurgent groups. There were no laws preventing minorities from participating in political life; however, different ethnic groups complained that they did not have equal access to local government jobs in provinces where they were in the minority.

The constitution provides for seats for women and minorities in both houses of parliament. The constitution provides for at least 68 female delegates in the lower house of the national assembly, while 10 seats are provided for the Kuchi ethnic minority. According to the constitution, the president should appoint one-third of the members, including two members with physical disabilities and two Kuchis. Fifty percent of the president's appointees to the upper house must be women.

Principal Government Officials

Last Updated: 1/31/2013

Pres.: **Hamid KARZAI**
First Vice Pres.: **Mohammad FAHIM Khan**
Second Vice Pres.: **Abdul Karim KHALILI**
Min. of Agriculture, Irrigation, & Livestock: **Mohammad Asif RAHIMI**
Min. of Border & Tribal Affairs
Min. of Commerce & Industry: **Anwar Ul-Haq AHADY**
Min. of Communications: **Amirzai SANGIN**
Min. of Counternarcotics: **ZARAR Ahmad Moqbel Osmani**
Min. of Defense: **BISMULLAH Muhammadi Khan**
Min. of Economy: **Abdul Hadi ARGHANDIWAL**
Min. of Education: **Faruq WARDAK**
Min. of Energy & Water: **Ismail KHAN**
Min. of Finance: **Omar ZAKHILWAL**
Min. of Foreign Affairs: **Zalmay RASSOUL, Dr.**
Min. of Hajj & Islamic Affairs: **Mohammad Yusuf NIAZI**
Min. of Health: **Suraya DALIL, Dr.**
Min. of Higher Education: **Obaidullah OBAID**
Min. of Information & Culture: **Sayed Makhdum RAHIN**
Min. of Interior: **Ghulam Mujtaba PATANG, Lt. Gen.**
Min. of Justice: **Habibullah GHALEB**
Min. of Martyred, Disabled, Labor, & Social Affairs: **Amena AFZALI**
Min. of Mines: **Wahidullah SHAHRANI**
Min. of Public Works: **Najibullah AAZHANG**
Min. of Refugees & Repatriation: **Jamahir ANWARI**
Min. of Rural Rehabilitation & Development: **Wais BARMACK**
Min. of Transportation: **Daoud Ali NAJAFI, Dr.**
Min. of Urban Development: **Hassan ABDULHAI**
Min. of Women's Affairs: **Hasan Bano GHAZANFAR**
National Security Adviser: **Rangin Dadfar SPANTA**
Dir. Gen., National Directorate of Security: **Asadullah KHALID**
Governor, Da Afghanistan Bank: **Noorullah DELAWARI**
Ambassador to the US: **Eklil Ahmad HAKIMI**
Permanent Representative to the UN, New York: **Zahir TANIN**

ECONOMY

Afghanistan's economy is recovering from decades of conflict. The economy has improved significantly since the fall of the Taliban regime in 2001 largely because of the infusion of international assistance, the recovery of the agricultural sector, and service sector growth.

Despite the progress of the past few years, Afghanistan is extremely poor, landlocked, and highly dependent on foreign aid. Much of the population continues to suffer from shortages of housing, clean water, electricity, medical care, and jobs. Criminality, insecurity, weak governance, and the Afghan Government's difficulty in extending rule of law to all parts of the country pose challenges to future economic growth.

Afghanistan's living standards are among the lowest in the world. The international community remains committed to Afghanistan's development, pledging over $67 billion at nine donors' conferences between 2003-10. In July 2012, the donors at the Tokyo conference pledged an additional $16 billion in civilian aid through 2016. Despite this help, the Government of Afghanistan will need to overcome a number of challenges, including low revenue collection, anemic job creation, high levels of corruption, weak government capacity, and poor public infrastructure.

Labor Conditions

The labor law sets the minimum age for employment at 18 years but permits 14-year-olds to work as apprentices, allows children 15 years and older to do "light work," and permits children ages 16 to 18 to work up to 35 hours per week. Children younger than age 13 are prohibited from work under any circumstances. The labor law prohibits the employment of children in work likely to threaten their health or cause disability; however, there was no defined list of hazardous jobs.

Child labor remains a pervasive problem in practice. According to UNICEF estimates, at least 30 percent of primary school-age children undertook some form of work, and there were more than one million child laborers younger than the age of 14. A 2010 study by the AIHRC found that an even larger portion of the country's 15 million children—up to 40 percent—were likely to be engaged in some sort of paid work.

The minimum wage for government workers was 5,000 afghanis ($108) per month. No minimum wage was set for the private sector; however, the labor law states the minimum wage of the private sector may not be less than the minimum wage of the government sector. The labor law makes no mention of informal sector day workers, leaving them completely unprotected.

The law defines the standard workweek for both public-sector and private-sector employees as 40 hours: eight hours per day with one hour for lunch and noon prayers. Reduced standard workweeks were stipulated for youth, pregnant women, nursing mothers, miners, and others in other occupations that present health risks.

The law provides workers the right to receive wages, annual vacation time in addition to national holidays, compensation for injuries suffered in the line of work, overtime pay, health insurance for the employee and immediate family members, per diem for official trips, daily transportation, food allowances, night shift differentials, retirement rights, and compensation for funeral expenses in case of death while performing official duties. There were no officially adopted occupational health and safety standards and no regulations for occupational health and safety.

Labor violations against migrant workers were common in practice.

U.S.-AFGHAN RELATIONS

On May 2, 2012, the United States and Afghanistan signed the Enduring Strategic Partnership Agreement between the Islamic Republic of Afghanistan and the United States of America, a 10-year strategic partnership agreement (SPA) that demonstrates the United States' enduring commitment to strengthen Afghanistan's sovereignty, stability, and prosperity and continue cooperation to defeat al-Qaida and its affiliates. This agreement also signals the U.S. intent to designate Afghanistan as a Major Non-NATO Ally. The signing of the SPA marks the culmination of over 10 years of U.S. involvement in Afghanistan, supporting the elected government, providing development aid, and stabilizing the country. During that time, the core U.S. goal in Afghanistan has been to disrupt, dismantle, and defeat al-Qaida and its affiliates, and to prevent their return to Afghanistan.

At the December 2011 Bonn Conference, the U.S. and other international partners committed to assisting in Afghanistan's development through 2024. The U.S. continues to support a broad-based government in Afghanistan, representative of all Afghans. Afghan forces have begun taking the lead for security in many areas of the country, and the transition of full security responsibility for Afghanistan from the International Security Assistance Force (ISAF) to Afghan forces will be completed by the end of 2014.

U.S. Assistance to Afghanistan

The U.S. has made a long-term commitment to help Afghanistan rebuild itself after years of war. While the U.S. combat mission in Afghanistan is transitioning primary security responsibility to Afghan National Security Forces, the United States plans to remain politically, diplomatically, and economically engaged in Afghanistan for the long term. The U.S. and others in the international community currently provide resources and expertise to Afghanistan in a variety of areas, including humanitarian relief and assistance, capacity-building, security needs, counter-narcotic programs, and infrastructure projects.

The United States supports the Afghan Government's goals of focusing on reintegration and reconciliation, economic development, improving relations with Afghanistan's regional partners, and steadily increasing the security capability of Afghan security forces. The U.S. encourages the Afghan Government to take strong actions to combat corruption and improve governance, and to provide better services for the people of Afghanistan, while maintaining and expanding on the important democratic reforms and advances in women's rights that have been made since 2001.

Bilateral Economic Relations

Afghanistan has signed a Trade and Investment Framework Agreement with the United States, but a Bilateral Investment Treaty has not been negotiated. There is no Bilateral Taxation Treaty between Afghanistan and the United States. For 2011, U.S. goods imports from Afghanistan amounted to less than 1% of U.S. goods exports to the country. Efforts are underway to encourage improvements in the business climate to attract foreign trade and investment as well as to stimulate additional trade with the United States through trade capacity development, including through World Trade Organization (WTO) accession.

Afghanistan's Membership in International Organizations

Afghanistan and the United States belong to a number of the same international organizations, including the United Nations, International Monetary Fund, and World Bank. Afghanistan also is a Partner for Cooperation with the Organization for Security and Cooperation in Europe and is working toward accession to the WTO.

Bilateral Representation

Afghanistan maintains an embassy in the United States at 2341 Wyoming Avenue, NW, Washington, DC 20008 (tel: 202-483-6410).

Principal U.S. Embassy Officials

Last Updated: 1/14/2013

KABUL (E) Great Massoud Road, (VoIP, US-based) 301-490-1042,

INMARSAT Tel 011-873-761-837-725, Workweek: Saturday–Thursday 0800-1630, Website: kabul.usembassy.gov/

DCM OMS:	Sandra Slaughter
AMB OMS:	Rose S. Naputi
Co-CLO:	Christine E. McCarthy
DHS/CBP:	Jose S. Ramirez
DHS/ICE:	Richard M. Deasy
DHS/TSA:	Johannes Knudsen
ECON/COM:	Walter Koenig
FM:	Nathaniel (Jim) J. Pines
HHS:	Michael D. Lyman
HRO:	Constance M. Dierman
MGT:	Lawrence G. Richter
NAS/INL:	Thomas J. Hushek
PAO/ADV:	Jean E. Manes
POL/MIL:	James T. Heg
POSHO:	Dale A. Kerksiek
AMB:	James B. Cunningham
CON:	Valerie J. Chittenden
DCM:	Tina S. Kaidanow
PAO:	Masha Hamilton
GSO:	Wesley Green
RSO:	Fred Ketchem
AFSA:	Fougere D. Gordon
AGR:	Kaush Arha
AID:	S. Ken Yamashita
CLO:	Heidi L. Porter
DEA:	Michael T. Marsac
ECON:	Tara F. Erath
FAA:	Jan Brecht-Clark
FMO:	Ralph A. Hamilton
IMO:	Robert A. Hall
IPO:	A.J. Delucia
ISO:	Jesse T. Naputi
ISSO:	Lee Ackermann
LEGATT:	Stephen E. Vogt
POL:	Donald A. Blome

MAZAR-E-SHARIF (C)

CG OMS:	Sarah Cline
MGT:	William B. Connerley
CG:	Douglas P. Climan
IPO:	Daniel L. Reagan
POL:	Mark K Biedlingmaier

TRAVEL

Consular Information Sheet

January 28, 2013

Country Description: Afghanistan has made significant progress since the Taliban were deposed in 2001, but still faces daunting challenges, including fighting an insurgency, preventing the return or resurgence of al-Qaida, recovering from over three decades of civil strife, and rebuilding a shattered physical, economic, and political infrastructure. NATO and International Security Assistance (ISAF) forces work in partnership with Afghan security forces to combat violent extremist elements that terrorize the population and challenge the government. Violent extremists continue to pursue a strategy of terrorist attacks, relying largely on assassinations, suicide bombings, and improvised explosive devices (IEDs).

President Hamid Karzai won his second term as president of the Islamic Republic of Afghanistan on November 2, 2009, following elections marred by allegations of fraud. Internal problems following years of war have compromised efforts by the Afghan government to establish policies and procedures to improve governance and stability. The government faces challenges in trying to develop a more effective police force, a more effective and accessible legal system, and sub-national institutions that work in partnership with traditional and local leaders to meet the needs of the population. The United States works closely with the international community to increase security and bolster Afghan government capacity on national and sub-national levels, with the goal of transitioning responsibility for security to the Afghan government by the end of 2014.

Smart Traveler Enrollment Program (STEP)/Embassy Locations: If you are going to work, live, or travel in Afghanistan, please take the time to tell our Embassy about your trip. If you enroll, we can keep you up to date with important safety and security announcements. It will also help your friends and family get in touch with you in an emergency.

The U.S. Embassy in Kabul
Great Massoud (Airport) Road
Telephone: 0700–108-001
or 0700–108-002
Emergency after-hours telephone: 0700–201-908
Email: KabulACS@state.gov

Entry/Exit Requirements for U.S. Citizens: A passport and valid visa are required to enter and exit Afghanistan. Afghan entry visas are not available at Kabul International Airport. U.S. citizens who arrive without a visa are subject to confiscation of their passport and face heavy fines and difficulties in retrieving their passport and obtaining a visa, as well as possible deportation. U.S citizens who are also Afghan nationals do not require visas for entry into Afghanistan. Likewise, for U.S. passport holders born in Afghanistan (place of birth listed as Afghanistan on their passport), a visa is not required for entry. The Embassy of Afghanistan issues a letter confirming your nationality for entry into Afghanistan. However, you may wish to obtain a visa, as some Afghan-Americans have experienced difficulties at land border crossings because they do not have a visa in their passport. U.S. citizens arriving in the country via military air usually have considerable difficulties if they choose to depart Afghanistan on commercial air, because their passports are not stamped to show that they entered the country legally. Those arriving on military air should move quickly after arrival to legalizetheir status if there is any chance they will depart the country on anything other than military air. Travelers may be asked to register with a representative of the Ministry of Interior's Foreigners' Registration Office upon arrival at Kabul International Airport. Upon registration, the traveler will be issued a card that they should surrender upon departure. Immigration authorities in Afghanistan have also implemented a fingerprinting system for all foreign visitors upon entry to the country with the exception of diplomats and ISAF personnel traveling on official orders. Visit the Embassy of Afghanistan 's website for the most current visa information. The consular office of the Embassy of Afghanistan is located at 2233 Wisconsin Avenue, NW, Suite 216, Washington, DC 20007, telephone 202-298-9125.

The U.S. Department of State is unaware of any HIV/AIDS entry restrictions for visitors to or foreign residents of Afghanistan.

Threats to Safety and Security: The latest Travel Warning for Afghanistan warns U.S. citizens against travel to Afghanistan and states clearly that the security situation remains critical. No region in Afghanistan should be considered immune from violence, and the potential exists throughout the country for hostile acts, either targeted or random, against U.S. and other Western nationals at any time. There are remnants of the former Taliban regime and the terrorist al-Qaida network operating in various parts of Afghanistan, as well as narco-traffickers and other terrorist and insurgent groups that oppose the international community's presence and the strengthening of a democratic government. Those groups aim to weaken or bring down the Government of Afghanistan, and often, to drive Westerners out of the country. They do not hesitate to use violence to achieve their aims.

Terrorist actions may include, but are not limited to, suicide operations, bombings-including vehicle-borne explosives and improvised explosive devices-assassinations, carjackings, rocket attacks, assaults, or kidnappings. A number of such attacks were reported in Kabul city from January through October 2012, and many additional attacks were thwarted by Afghan and coalition forces.

Recent incidents include: a suicide attack against the Intercontinental Hotel in June 2011; a complex and sustained attack against multiple targets in Kabul on September 13, 2011 and again in April 2012, including the U.S. Embassy and ISAF Headquarters and the Afghan Parliament; a late October 2011 suicide bombing which killed 17 people including U.S. citizen contractors working with the military; and two significant improvised explosive device attacks in autumn 2012, including one attack which targeted a minivan near the airport carrying contractors working for the United States Agency for International Development (USAID), killing 10 non-US citizens and wounding another 11.

There is an ongoing risk of kidnapping and assassination of U.S. citizens and Non-Governmental Organization (NGO) employees throughout the country. In May 2012, a British and a Kenyan aid worker, along with two Afghan counterparts, were kidnapped in Badakhshan Province while riding on horseback to deliver medical supplies to a remote village; they were freed 11 days later in a NATO rescue operation. In December 2012, a U.S. citizen working with an NGO was kidnapped in Kabul province, and subsequently rescued by U.S. forces.

Riots-sometimes violent-have occurred in response to various political or other issues. U.S. citizens should avoid rallies and demonstrations; even demonstrations intended to be peaceful can turn confrontational and escalate into violence. Crime, including violent crime, remains a significant problem. The country faces a difficult period in the near term and U.S. citizens could be targeted or placed at risk by unpredictable local events. There is also a real danger from the presence of millions of unexploded land mines and other ordnance. Terrorists continue to use roadside or vehicle-borne improvised explosive devices. Private U.S. citizens should not come to Afghanistan unless they have made arrangements in advance to address security concerns.

The absence of records for ownership of property, differing laws from various regimes, and the chaos that comes from decades of civil strife have left property issues in great disorder. Afghan-Americans returning to Afghanistan to recover property, or U.S. citizens coming to the country to engage in business, have become involved in complicated real estate disputes and have faced threats of retaliatory action, including kidnapping for ransom and death.

Large parts of Afghanistan are extremely isolated, with few roads, mostly in poor condition, irregular cell phone signals, and none of the basic physical infrastructure found in Kabul or the larger cities. U.S. citizens traveling in these areas who find themselves in trouble may not even have a way to communicate their difficulties to the outside world.

Stay up to date by:

- Bookmarking our Bureau of Consular Affairs website, which contains the current Travel Warnings and Travel Alerts as well as the Worldwide Caution.
- Downloading our free Smart Traveler iPhone App for travel information at your fingertips.
- Following us on Twitter andFacebook.
- Calling 1-888-407-4747 toll-free within the United States and Canada, or 1-202-501-4444 from other countries.
- Taking some time before travel to consider your personal security.

Crime: A large portion of the Afghan population is unemployed, and many among the unemployed have moved to urban areas. These factors may directly contribute to crime and lawlessness. Diplomats and international relief workers have reported incidents of robberies and household burglaries as well as kidnappings and assault.

Any U.S. citizen who enters Afghanistan should remain vigilant for possible banditry, including violent attacks. Don't buy counterfeit and pirated goods, even if they are widely available. Not only are the bootlegs illegal in the United States, if you purchase them you may also be breaking local law.

Victims of Crime: If you or someone you know becomes the victim of a crime abroad, you should contact the local police and the nearest U.S. embassy or consulate. We can:

- Replace a stolen passport.

- Help you find appropriate medical care if you are the victim of violent crimes such as assault or rape.

- Put you in contact with the appropriate police authorities, and if you want us to, we can contact family members or friends.

- Help you understand the local criminal justice process and direct you to local attorneys, although it is important to remember that local authorities are responsible for investigating and prosecuting the crime.

The local equivalent to the "911" emergency line in Afghanistan is "199." Please note that local operators do not speak English. Most are limited to Dari or Pashto.

U.S. citizens in an emergency situation in Afghanistan can call the Embassy's 24-hour American Citizens Services line at 0700-201-908 or email us at KabulACS@state.gov.

Criminal Penalties: While you are traveling in Afghanistan, you are subject to its laws even if you are a U.S. citizen. Foreign laws and legal systems can be vastly different than our own and may not afford the protections available to you under U.S. law. Penalties for breaking the law can be more severe than in the United States for similar offenses. Engaging in sexual conduct with children or using or disseminating child pornography in a foreign country is a crime prosecutable in the United States. In some areas of Afghanistan you could be detained for questioning if you don't have your passport with you.

Taking pictures of military installations or personnel may result in questioning or detention. Driving under the influence could land you in jail for three to six months. If you break local laws in Afghanistan, your U.S. passport won't help you avoid arrest or prosecution. It's very important to know what's legal and what's not where you are going. Persons violating Afghan laws, even unknowingly, may be expelled, arrested, or imprisoned. Penalties for possessing, using, or trafficking in illegal drugs in Afghanistan are severe, and convicted offenders can expect long jail sentences and heavy fines.

During the last several years, there have been incidents involving the arrest and/or detention of U.S. citizens. Arrested U.S. citizens have faced periods of detention—sometimes in difficult conditions—while awaiting trial.

Although the Afghan constitution allows the free exercise of religion, proselytizing may be viewed as contrary to the beliefs of Islam and considered harmful to society. Authorities take these matters very seriously. Afghan law carries a maximum penalty of death for those charged with proselytizing, if convicted. Evidence may consist of possession of non-Islamic religious material, especially in local languages. Allegations of conversion of Afghan citizens are taken particularly seriously.

The testimony of three individuals or a group is enough to convict someone of proselytizing. The same penalty exists in law for Afghan citizens who convert to another religion. All Afghan citizens are considered Muslim from birth. Converts are subject to arrest regardless of where the conversion took place, and Afghan-U.S. dual nationals are also subject to this law. U.S. citizens have also been arrested by police in cases involving debt to Afghans. In Afghanistan, debts and business disputes are not exclusively civil matters as may be the case in the United States. Instead, the aggrieved party may successfully have a U.S. citizen arrested in cases where a debt is alleged to be owed to an Afghan. The Ministries of Commerce and Interior, Afghan Investment Support Agency, the Afghan National Police, and the courts have all played roles in recent disputes involving U.S. citizens. If involved in a commercial dispute, hiring an Afghan attorney early can be beneficial.

A list of English speaking attorneys in the consular district of the U.S. Embassy in Kabul can be found on the Embassy's website. The list comprises attorneys in Afghanistan officially registered with the Afghan Ministry of Justice who have expressed a willingness to carry out legal services for U.S. citizens. The Embassy does not endorse any particular attorney and the list is not comprehensive; we encourage those seeking legal advice in Afghanistan to utilize other means of finding an attorney.

While some countries will automatically notify the nearest U.S. embassy or consulate if a U.S. citizen is detained or arrested in a foreign country, that might not always be the case. To ensure that the United States is aware of your circumstances, request that the police and prison officials notify the nearest U.S. embassy or consulate as soon as you are arrested or detained.

Special Circumstances: Because of the poor infrastructure in Afghanistan, access to banking facilities is limited and unreliable. Afghanistan's economy operates on a "cash-only" basis for most transactions, but the use of credit cards is becoming more common. International bank transfers are limited. ATM machines exist at Standard Chartered Bank and Afghan International Bank (AIB) in the Wazir Akbar Khan neighborhood of Kabul, but some travelers have complained of difficulties using them.

International communications are difficult. Local telephone networks do not operate reliably. Most people rely on satellite or cellular telephone communications even to make local calls. Cellular phone service is available locally in many parts of the country, with service more reliable in Kabul and other large cities. Injured or distressed foreigners could face long delays before being able to communicate their needs to family or colleagues outside Afghanistan. Internet access through local service providers is limited.

In 2011, Afghanistan's Ministry of Interior ordered the organization of a committee for the purpose of bringing better security, traffic movements, and functionality to the streets of Kabul. This committee has implemented several restrictions, namely on tinted windows of vehicles operating in Kabul. Owners of vehicles with tinted windows can be arrested if they fail to eliminate tinting or replace their windshields and windows (several U.S. citizens have recently been detained on such charges).

U.S. citizens should be aware that an Afghan government-controlled security force, the Afghan Public Protection Force (APPF), will assume authority over the provision of most commercial security services in Afghanistan from private security companies this year. In August 2010, President Karzai issued Presidential Decree 62 ordering the disbandment of private security companies in Afghanistan. As a result, all security guard services being performed by private security companies, with the exception of diplomatic missions, will be transferred to the APPF.

By March 20, 2012, security guard services for all development site and convoys will transition to the APPF. By March 20, 2013, security for all ISAF bases and military construction sites will transition to the APPF. Only embassies and other accredited diplomatic missions will be permitted to continue using private security companies after March 2013.

In addition to being subject to all Afghan laws, U.S. citizens who are also citizens of Afghanistan may also be subject to other laws that impose special obligations on Afghan citizens. U.S. citizens who are also Afghan nationals do not require visas for entry into Afghanistan. The Embassy of Afghanistan issues a letter confirming your nationality for entry into Afghanistan.

However, you may wish to obtain a visa as some Afghan-Americans have experienced difficulties at land border crossings because they do not have a visa in their passport. We encourage U.S. citizens to carry a copy of their U.S. passport with them at all times, so that, if questioned by local officials, proof of identity and U.S. citizenship is readily available. Due to security conditions and travel difficulty, consular assistance for U.S. citizens in Afghanistan is limited, particularly for those persons outside the capital. Islam provides the foundation of Afghanistan's customs, laws, and practices. Foreign visitors—men and women—are expected to remain sensitive to the Islamic culture and not dress in a revealing or provocative manner, including the wearing of sleeveless shirts and blouses, halter-tops, and shorts. Women in particular, especially when traveling outside Kabul, may want to ensure that their tops have long sleeves and cover their collarbone and waistband, and that their pants/skirts cover their ankles. Almost all women in Afghanistan cover their hair in public; U.S. citizen women visitors should carry scarves for this purpose.

Afghan customs authorities may enforce strict regulations concerning temporary importation into or export from Afghanistan of items such as firearms, alcoholic beverages, religious materials, antiquities, medications, and printed materials. U.S. citizen travelers have faced fines and/or confiscation of items considered antiquities upon exiting Afghanistan. It is advisable to contact the Embassy of Afghanistan in Washington for specific information regarding customs requirements.

Travelers en route to Afghanistan may transit countries that have restrictions on firearms, including antique or display models. If you plan to take firearms or ammunition to another country, you should contact officials at that country's embassy and those that you will be transiting to learn about their regulations and fully comply with those regulations before traveling. Please consult the U.S. Customs and Border Protection website for information on importing firearms into the United States.

Accessibility: While in Afghanistan, individuals with disabilities may find accessibility and accommodation very different from what you would find in the United States. The Afghan constitution requires the state to assist and protect the rights of persons with disabilities, including the rights to health care and financial protection, but does not mandate access to buildings and transportation. Most buildings, public transportation, communication, and road crossings are inaccessible to persons with disabilities.

Medical Facilities and Health Information: Well-equipped medical facilities are few and far between throughout Afghanistan. European and American medicines are available in limited quantities and may be expensive or difficult to locate. There is a shortage of basic medical supplies.

Basic medicines manufactured in Iran, Pakistan, and India are available, but their reliability can be questionable. Several Western-style private clinics have opened in Kabul: the DK-German Medical Diagnostic Center (ph. 079-913-6210), French Children's Hospital, and CURE International Hospital (ph. 079-988-3830) offer a variety of basic and routine-type care but are not always open; if you are seeking treatment you should request American or Western health practitioners. Afghan public hospitals should be avoided. Individuals without government licenses or even medical degrees often operate private clinics; there is no public agency that monitors their operations. You will not be able to find Western-trained medical personnel in most parts of the country outside Kabul, although there are some international aid groups temporarily providing basic medical assistance in various cities and villages.

For any medical treatment, payment is required in advance. Commercial medical evacuation capability from Afghanistan is limited and could take days to arrange. Even medevac companies that claim to service the world may not agree to come to Afghanistan. If you have medevac insurance you should confirm with the insurance provider that it will be able to provide medevac assistance to this country and which clinics they recommend for evaluation.

You can find detailed information on vaccinations and other health precautions on the Centers for Disease Control's (CDC) website. For information about outbreaks of infectious diseases abroad, consult the World Health Organization (WHO) website. The WHO website also contains additional health information for travelers, including detailed country-specific health information.

Medical Insurance: You can't assume your insurance will go with you when you travel. It's very important to find out BEFORE you leave whether or not your medical insurance will cover you overseas. You need to ask your insurance company two questions:

- Does my policy apply when I'm out of the United States?
- Will it cover emergencies like a trip to a foreign hospital or a medical evacuation?

In many places, including Afghanistan, doctors and hospitals expect payment in cash at the time of service. Your regular U.S. health insurance may not cover doctors' and hospital visits in other countries. If your policy doesn't go with you when you travel, it's a very good idea to take out another one for your trip.

Traffic Safety and Road Conditions: While in Afghanistan, you may encounter road conditions that differ significantly from those in the United States. The information below concerning Afghanistan is provided for general reference only, and may not be totally accurate in a particular location or circumstance.

All drivers face the potential danger of encountering land mines that may have been planted on or near roadways. An estimated 5-7 million land mines and large quantities of unexploded ordnance exist throughout the countryside and alongside roads, posing a danger to travelers. Robbery and crime are also prevalent on highways outside Kabul.

The transportation system in Afghanistan is marginal, although the international community is constructing modern highways and provincial roads. Vehicles are poorly maintained, often overloaded, and traffic laws are not enforced. Roadside assistance is non-existent. Vehicular traffic is chaotic and must contend with numerous pedestrians, bicyclists, and animals.

Many urban streets have large potholes and are not well lit. Rural roads are not paved. With congested roads and abundant pedestrian traffic, vehicle accidents are a serious concern as they can escalate into violent confrontations. We strongly urge all drivers to drive defensively and pay close attention to their surroundings.

Aviation Safety Oversight: As there is no direct commercial air service to the United States by carriers registered in Afghanistan, the U.S. Federal Aviation Administration (FAA) has not assessed the government of Afghanistan's Civil Aviation Authority for compliance with International Civil Aviation Organization (ICAO) aviation safety standards. Further information may be found on the FAA's safety assessment page. U.S. government personnel are not permitted to travel on most Afghan airlines due to these ongoing safety concerns and the lack of Afghan government safety oversight capabilities.

U.S. government personnel may travel into and out of Afghanistan on international flights operated by airlines from countries whose civil aviation authorities meet the safety standards for the oversight of their air carrier operations under the FAA's International Aviation Safety Assessment (IASA) program. Such countries with airlines that operate to Afghanistan have included India, Pakistan, Bahrain, Germany, Turkey, and the United Arab Emirates.

Children's Issues: Please see the U.S. Dept. of State Office of Children's Issues web pages on intercountry adoption and international parental child abduction.

Travel Warning

January 29, 2013

The Department of State warns U.S. citizens against travel to Afghanistan. The security threat to all U.S. citizens in Afghanistan remains critical. This Travel Warning supersedes the Travel Warning for Afghanistan issued on June 27, 2012, and reminds U.S. citizens of ongoing security risks, including kidnapping and insurgent attacks.

No region in Afghanistan should be considered immune from violence, and the potential exists throughout the country for hostile acts, either targeted or random, against U.S. and other Western nationals at any time. Remnants of the former Taliban regime and the al-Qaida terrorist network, as well as other groups hostile to International Security Assistance Force (ISAF) military operations, remain active. Afghan authorities have a limited ability to maintain order and ensure the security of Afghan citizens and foreign visitors. Travel in all areas of Afghanistan is unsafe due to military combat operations, landmines, banditry, armed rivalry between political and tribal groups, and the possibility of insurgent attacks, including attacks using vehicle-borne or other improvised explosive devices (IEDs). The security situation remains volatile and unpredictable throughout the country.

There is an ongoing and significant risk of kidnapping and assassination of U.S. citizens and Non-Governmental Organization (NGO) employees throughout the country. In May 2012, a British and a Kenyan aid worker, along with two Afghan counterparts, were kidnapped in Badakhshan Province while riding on horseback to deliver medical supplies to a remote village; they were freed 11 days later in a NATO rescue operation. In December 2012, a U.S. citizen working with an NGO was kidnapped in Kabul Province, and subsequently rescued by U.S. forces.

Riots and incidents of civil disturbance can and do occur, often without warning. U.S. citizens should avoid rallies and demonstrations; even demonstrations intended to be peaceful can turn confrontational and escalate into violence. Following the unintentional mishandling of Korans by U.S. service members at Bagram Air Field base on February 21, 2012, violent demonstrations occurred in several locations throughout Afghanistan, resulting in the deaths of two U.S. service members during a protest outside of a military base in Nangarhar Province. Two additional U.S. service members were killed inside Kabul's Ministry of Interior during a shooting that was likely attributable to the mishandling of Korans. The release in mid-September 2012 of an anti-Islamic amateur film produced in the United States prompted demonstrations around Afghanistan, including in Kabul. Most of the protests were peaceful; however, on September 17, 2012, one rally in Kabul grew violent, leading to the destruction of two police vehicles. Kabul and its suburbs are also considered at high risk for militant attacks, including rocket attacks, vehicle-borne IEDs, direct-fire attacks and suicide bombings. A number of such attacks were reported in Kabul City from January to October 2012, and many additional attacks were thwarted by Afghan and coalition forces. In the last eighteen months, incidents involving Westerners have included a suicide attack against the Intercontinental Hotel in June 2011 in which U.S. citizens were critically injured, and an August 2011 attack against the British Council. Insurgents also carried out a complex sustained attack against multiple targets in Kabul on September 13, 2011, which included the U.S. Embassy and International Security Assistance Forces (ISAF) headquarters, and again on April 15, 2012, targeting the U.S. and neighbouring embassies as well as ISAF headquarters and the Afghan Parliament.

Insurgents have also targeted the offices, convoys, and individual implementing partners of the U.S. Agency for International Development (USAID). The Kabul-Jalalabad Road (commonly called Jalalabad Road) and the Kabul to Bagram road are highly restricted for Embassy employees. On May 2, 2012, insurgents with vehicle-borne explosives and suicide vests targeted Green Village, a compound on Jalalabad Road in Kabul that houses primarily international security contractors; several guards and local school children were killed at the gates of the compound as a result of explosions. On June 22, 2012, insurgents attacked Spozhmai Hotel west of Kabul City. This attack created a hostage situation which resulted in the deaths of a number of Afghan civilians.

Buildings or compounds that lack robust security measures in comparison to neighboring facilities may be viewed as targets of opportunity by insurgents.

Ambushes, robberies, and violent crime can add to the insecurity in many areas of the country. U.S. citizens involved in property or business disputes-a common legal problem in Afghanistan-have reported that their adversaries in the disputes have threatened their lives. U.S. citizens who find themselves in such situations should not assume that either local law enforcement or the U.S. Embassy will be able to assist them in resolving these disputes.

From time to time, depending on current security conditions, the U.S. Embassy places areas frequented by foreigners off limits to its personnel. Potential target areas include key national or international government establishments, international organizations and other locations with expatriate personnel, and public areas popular with the expatriate community such as restaurants and hotels. Private U.S. citizens are strongly urged to heed these restrictions as well. We encourage U.S. citizens to obtain the latest information by frequently consulting the Embassy's travel advisory website.

The U.S. Embassy's ability to provide emergency consular services to U.S. citizens in Afghanistan is limited, particularly for those persons outside the capital. U.S. citizens who choose to visit or remain in Afghanistan despite this Travel Warning are encouraged to enroll with the U.S. Embassy in Kabul through the State Department's Smart Traveler Enrollment Program (STEP) to obtain updated information on travel and security within Afghanistan. U.S. citizens without Internet access may enroll directly with the U.S. Embassy. Enrollment makes it easier for the Embassy to contact U.S. citizens in case of an emergency. The U.S. Embassy is located at Great Masood Road between Radio Afghanistan and the Ministry of Public Health (the road is also known as Bebe Mahro or Airport Road) in Kabul. The Embassy phone numbers are 93-(0)700-108-001 and 93-(0)700-108-002. For after-hours, life-or-limb emergencies involving U.S. citizens, the Consular Section can be reached at 93-(0)700-201-908; please direct routine consular correspondence to KabulACS@state.gov.

Current information on travel and security in Afghanistan may be obtained from the Department of State by calling 1-888-407-4747 toll free in the United States and Canada or, for callers outside the United States and Canada, a regular toll line at 1-202-501-4444. These numbers are available from 8:00 a.m. to 8:00 p.m. Eastern Time, Monday through Friday (except U.S. federal holidays).

For further information, please consult the Country Specific Information for Afghanistan and the current Worldwide Caution, which are available on the Bureau of Consular Affairs Internet website. You can also stay up to date by bookmarking our Bureau of Consular Affairs website, which also contains current Travel Warnings and Travel Alerts. Follow us on Twitter and the Bureau of Consular Affairs page on Facebook as well. You can also download our free Smart Traveler App, available through iTunes and the Android market, to have travel information at your fingertips.

Intercountry Adoption

October 2011

The information in this section has been edited from the latest report available as of February 2013 from the State Department Bureau of Consular Affairs, Office of Overseas Citizens Services. For more information, please read the *Intercountry Adoption* section of this book and review current reports online at http://adoption.state.gov.

Afghanistan is not party to the Hague Convention on Protection of Children and Co-operation in Respect of Intercountry Adoption (Hague Adoption Convention). Therefore, when the Hague Adoption Convention entered into force for the United States on April 1, 2008, intercountry adoption processing for Afghanistan did not change.

Afghan law does not allow for adoptions of Afghan children in Afghanistan. United States citizens considering adoption of Afghan children must obtain guardianship from an Afghan Family Court and then file an application for IR-4 status with USCIS, in order to facilitate adoption of the child in the courts of the United States. Prospective United States citizen guardians should refer to our flyer on Adoption of Children from Countries in which Islamic Shari'a Law is observed for more information on this issue.

The Afghan judicial system and Afghan family law are based on a strict interpretation of Islamic law. Islamic law does not allow for adoptions as generally understood in the United States. Guardianship is a limited proceeding and often does not terminate or grant full parental rights. U.S. immigrant visas can be issued in cases where the Afghan Family Court grants guardianship of an orphan (as defined under United States immigration law).

The court will require the petitioner to show that the child was clearly abandoned or otherwise orphaned. It must also be clear that the court understands and specifically rules that the child is permitted to leave the jurisdiction of Afghanistan and immigrate to the United States for the purpose of being adopted in the courts of the United States by the prospective parents. In Afghanistan, prospective parents who are non-Muslims may not adopt or be appointed as guardians of Muslim children. Strong cultural ties to Afghanistan (dual Afghan-American nationality, for example) may favorably influence the court's decision, but are not required.

Who Can Adopt? To bring an adopted child to the United States from Afghanistan, you must be found eligible to adopt by the U.S. Government. The U.S. Government agency responsible for making this determination is the Department of Homeland Security, U.S. Citizenship and Immigration Services (USCIS). Interested U.S. citizens are strongly encouraged to contact U.S. Consular officials in Kabul before formalizing any adoption agreement or making any adoption plans to ensure that appropriate procedures have been followed which will make it possible for the Embassy to issue a U.S. immigrant visa for the child. As Afghanistan has no statutory law on adoptions, there is no law setting forth age, residency, or marriage requirements. Prospective parents must comply with United States legal requirements in the I-600 process. Per Afghanistan's laws, prospective parents who are non-Muslims may not be appointed as guardians of Muslim children. According to officials at the Afghan Family Court, prospective guardians must be at least thirty (30) years old, demonstrate that they have sufficient resources to educate and raise the child, and may not have a criminal background.

Who Can Be Adopted? Afghanistan has no statutory law on adoptions or what constitutes an orphan. According to officials at the Afghan Family Court, a child may be declared an orphan if the birth parents are deceased or if they are no longer capable of raising the child, for instance due to poor health or physical infirmity. Under Islamic law, prospective parents may petition the family court for guardianship. Prospective parents should consult a lawyer in Afghanistan regarding guardianship requirements. If you have a particular child in mind for adoption, especially a relative, you should consult a lawyer or USCIS to assist you in determining whether this child meets the specific U.S. legal definition of orphan before proceeding.

Afghanistan's Adoption Authority: There is no central government adoption authority. Guardianship proceedings are filed in the family courts.

The Process: The first step in adopting a child from Afghanistan is usually to select a licensed agency in the United States that can help with your adoption. At a minimum you will need the services of someone licensed or authorized to perform a home study for your state of residence. Adoption service providers must be licensed by the U.S. state in which they operate.

If you are eligible to adopt, there is no central adoption authority in Afghanistan to provide you with a referral to a child. You will have to locate a child by contacting orphanages, charitable institutions or social welfare agencies. The child must be eligible to be adopted according to Afghanistan's requirements. The child must also meet the definition of an orphan under U.S. law.

Role of the Court: Prospective parents must petition the court for guardianship. The court will issue a "wasiqa" granting guardianship to the prospective parents.

Role of the Adoption Agencies: none

Time Frame: there is no specific time frame

Adoption Fees: n/a

Documents Required: Prospective parents must demonstrate that they intend to raise the child in accordance with Islamic tradition and norms.

Bringing Your Child Home: Once your adoption is complete (or you have obtained legal custody of the child), there are a few more steps to take before you can head home. Specifically, you need to apply for several documents for your child before he or she can travel to the United States, such as a birth certificate, a passport or travel document for your child from the country in which he or she was born, and a U.S. Immigration Visa.

For detailed and updated information on how to obtain these documents, review the *Intercountry Adoption* section in this publication and visit the U.S. Department of State Intercountry Adoption website at http://adoption.state.gov.

Child Citizenship Act: For adoptions finalized abroad, the Child Citizenship Act of 2000 allows your new child to acquire American citizenship automatically when he or she enters the United States as lawful permanent residents.

For adoptions finalized in the United States, the Child Citizenship Act of 2000 allows your new child to acquire American citizenship automatically when the court in the United States issues the final adoption decree. To learn more, review the *Intercountry Adoption* section in this publication and visit the U.S. Department of State Intercountry Adoption website at http://adoption.state.gov.

U.S. Embassy Kabul
Great Massoud Road, Kabul,
Afghanistan
Tel: 0700-108-499
Email: USConsulKabul@state.gov
Internet: http://kabul.usembassy.gov

Embassy of Afghanistan
2233 Wisconsin Ave., NW
Suite #216
Washington, DC 20007
Tel: 202-298-9125
Fax: 202-298-9127
Email:
consulate@embassyofafghanistan.org
Internet:
http://www.embassyofafghanistan.org/

Afghanistan also has consulates in New York and Los Angeles

Office of Children's Issues
U.S. Department of State
2201 C Street, NW
SA-29
Washington, DC 20520
Tel: 1-888-407-4747
E-mail: AskCI@state.gov
http://adoption.state.gov

For questions about immigration procedures, call the National Customer Service Center (NCSC) at 1-800-375-5283 (TTY 1-800-767-1833).

ALBANIA

Compiled from publications that were available as of February 2013 from the U.S. Department of State, the U.S. Department of Commerce, and the Central Intelligence Agency (CIA). See the introduction to this set for explanatory notes.

Official Name:

Republic of Albania

PROFILE

Geography

Area: total: 28,748 sq km; country comparison to the world: 145; land: 27,398 sq km; water: 1,350 sq km

Major cities: Tirana (capital) 433,000 (2009)

Climate: mild temperate; cool, cloudy, wet winters; hot, clear, dry summers; interior is cooler and wetter

Terrain: mostly mountains and hills; small plains along coast

People

Nationality: noun: Albanian(s); adjective: Albanian

Population: 3,002,859 (July 2012 est.)

Population growth rate: 0.28% (2012 est.)

Ethnic groups: Albanian 95%, Greek 3%, other 2% (Vlach, Roma (Gypsy), Serb, Macedonian, Bulgarian) (1989 est.)

Religions: Muslim 70%, Albanian Orthodox 20%, Roman Catholic 10%

Languages: Albanian (official—derived from Tosk dialect), Greek, Vlach, Romani, Slavic dialects

Literacy: definition: age 9 and over can read and write; total population: 98.7%; male: 99.2%; female: 98.3% (2001 census)

Health: life expectancy at birth: total population: 77.59 years; male: 74.99 years; female: 80.49 years (2012 est.); Infant mortality rate: total: 14.12 deaths/1,000 live births; male: 15.7 deaths/1,000 live births; female: 12.36 deaths/1,000 live births (2012 est.)

Unemployment rate: 13% (2012 est.)

Work force: 1.053 million (2010 est.)

Government

Type: parliamentary democracy

Independence: 28 November 1912

Constitution: approved by parliament 21 October 1998; adopted by popular referendum 22 November 1998; promulgated 28 November 1998

Political subdivisions: 37 municipalities (komunat/opstine, singular—komuna/opstina)

Suffrage: 18 years of age; universal

Economy

GDP (purchasing power parity): $25.86 billion (2012 est.); $25.23 billion (2011 est.); $24.74 billion (2010 est.); $23.9 billion (2009 est.)

GDP real growth rate: 0.5% (2012 est.); 2% (2011 est.); 3.5% (2010 est.); 3.3% (2009 est.)

GDP per capita (PPP): $8,000 (2012 est.); $7,800 (2011 est.); $7,700 (2010 est.); $7,500 (2009 est.)

Natural resources: petroleum, natural gas, coal, bauxite, chromite, copper, iron ore, nickel, salt, timber, hydropower

Agriculture products: wheat, corn, potatoes, vegetables, fruits, sugar beets, grapes; meat, dairy products

Industries: food processing, textiles and clothing; lumber, oil, cement, chemicals, mining, basic metals, hydropower

Exports: $2.121 billion (2012 est.); $1.954 billion (2011 est.); $1.548 billion (2010 est.)

Exports—commodities: textiles and footwear; asphalt, metals and metallic ores, crude oil; vegetables, fruits, tobacco

Exports—partners: Italy 48.8%, China 8.4%, Turkey 6.7%, Greece 5.6%, Spain 5.4%, India 4.9% (2010 est.)

Imports: $5.219 billion (2012 est.); $5.076 billion (2011 est.); $4.305 billion (2010 est.)

Imports—commodities: machinery and equipment, foodstuffs, textiles, chemicals

Imports—partners: Italy 34.8%, Greece 12.9%, China 6.2%, Turkey 6%, Germany 4.6% (2010 est.)

Debt—external: $5.281 billion (31 December 2012 est.); $5.7 billion (31 December 2011 est.)

Exchange rates: leke (ALL) per US dollar; 103.3 (2012 est.); 100.89 (2011 est.); 103.94 (2010 est.); 94.98 (2009); 79.546 (2008); 92.668 (2007)

GEOGRAPHY

Albania shares a border with Greece to the south/southeast, Macedonia to the east, Kosovo to the northeast, and Montenegro to the northwest. Western Albania lies along the Adriatic and Ionian Sea coastlines. Albania's primary seaport is Durres, which handles 90% of its maritime cargo.

PEOPLE

Scholars believe the Albanian people are descended from a non-Slavic, non-Turkic group of tribes known as Illyrians, who arrived in the Balkans around 2000 BC.

National/Racial/Ethnic Minorities

There were reports of significant societal discrimination against members of the Romani and Balkan-Egyptian communities.

The law permits official minority status for national groups and separately for ethnolinguistic groups. The government defined Greeks, Macedonians, and Montenegrins as national groups; Greeks constituted the largest of these. The law defined Aromanians (Vlachs) and Roma as ethnolinguistic minority groups.

Religion

No reliable data was available on religious participation or membership; the last official census including such data was conducted in 1939. The 2011 census concluded in November included an optional question for participants to acknowledge religious affiliation, but full survey results are not expected until mid-2012. The four traditional religious groups are Muslim (Sunni), Bektashi (a form of Shia Sufism), Orthodox Christian (the Autocephalous Orthodox Church of Albania), and Roman Catholic. In addition, there are numerous Protestant denominations and other religious groups, including the Baha'i Faith, Jehovah's Witnesses, and The Church of Jesus Christ of Latter-day Saints (Mormons). The State Committee on Cults reported more than 230 religious groups, organizations, foundations, and educational institutions operating in the country.

Languages

The national language of Albania is Albanian. Most educated people in Albania speak a foreign language. The most popular second languages are English, Italian, and Greek.

HISTORY

After falling under Roman authority in 165 BC, Albania was controlled nearly continuously by a succession of foreign powers until the mid-20th century, with only brief periods of self-rule.

Following the split of the Roman Empire in 395, the Byzantine Empire established control over present-day Albania. In the 11th century, Byzantine Emperor Alexius I Comnenus made the first recorded reference to a distinct area of land known as Albania and to its people.

The Ottoman Empire ruled Albania from 1385–1912. During this time, much of the population converted to the Islamic faith, and Albanians also emigrated to Italy, Greece, Egypt, and Turkey. Although its control was briefly disrupted during the 1443–78 revolt, led by Albania's national hero, Gjergj Kastrioti Skenderbeu, the Ottomans eventually reasserted their dominance.

The League of Prizren (1878) promoted the idea of an Albanian nation-state and established the modern Albanian alphabet, updating a language that survived the hundreds of years of Ottoman rule despite being outlawed. By the early 20th century, the weakened Ottoman Empire was no longer able to suppress Albanian nationalism. Following the conclusion of the First Balkan War, Albanians issued the Vlore Proclamation of November 28, 1912, declaring independence and the Great Powers established Albania's borders in 1913. Albania's territorial integrity was confirmed at the Paris Peace Conference in 1919, after U.S. President Woodrow Wilson dismissed a plan by the European powers to divide Albania among its neighbors.

During the Second World War, Albania was occupied first by Italy (1939–43) and then by Germany (1943–44). After the war, Communist Party leader Enver Hoxha, through a combination of ruthlessness and strategic alliances, managed to preserve Albania's territorial integrity during the next 40 years, but exacted a terrible price from the population, which was subjected to purges, shortages, repression of civil and political rights, a total ban on religious observance, and increased isolation. Albania adhered to a strict Stalinist philosophy, eventually withdrawing from the Warsaw Pact in 1968 and alienating its final remaining ally, China, in 1978.

Following Hoxha's death in 1985 and the subsequent fall of communism in 1991, Albanian society struggled to overcome its historical isolation and underdevelopment. During the initial transition period, the Albanian Government sought closer ties with the West in order to improve economic conditions and introduced basic democratic reforms, including a multi-party system.

In 1992, after the sweeping electoral victory of the Democratic Party, Sali Berisha became the first democratically elected President of Albania. Berisha began a more deliberate program of economic and democratic reform but progress on these issues stalled in the mid-1990s, due to political gridlock. At the same time, unscrupulous investment companies defrauded investors all over Albania using pyramid schemes. In early 1997, several of these pyramid schemes collapsed, leaving thousands of people bankrupt, disillusioned, and angry. Armed revolts broke out across the country, leading to the near-total collapse of government authority. During this time, Albania's already inadequate and antiquated infrastructure suffered tremendous damage, as people looted public works for building materials. Weapons depots all over the country were raided. The anarchy of early 1997 alarmed the world and prompted intensive international mediation.

A UN Multinational Protection Force restored order, and an interim national reconciliation government oversaw the general elections of June 1997, which returned the Socialists and their allies to power at the national level. President Berisha resigned, and the Socialists elected Rexhep Meidani as President of the Republic.

During the transitional period of 1997–2002, a series of short-lived Socialist-led governments succeeded one another as Albania's fragile democratic structures were strengthened. Additional political parties formed, media outlets expanded, non-governmental organizations (NGOs) and business associations developed. In 1998, Albanians ratified a new constitution via popular referendum, guaranteeing the rule of law and the protection of fundamental human rights and religious freedom. Fatos Nano, Chairman of the Socialist Party, emerged as Prime Minister in July 2002.

On July 24, 2002, Alfred Moisiu was sworn in as President of the Republic. The peaceful transfer of power from President Meidani to President Moisiu was the result of an agreement between the parties to engage each other within established parliamentary structures. This "truce" ushered in a new period of political stability in Albania, making possible significant progress in democratic and economic reforms, rule of law initiatives, and the development of Albania's relations with its neighbors and the United States.

The "truce" between party leaders began to fray in summer 2003 and progress on economic and political reforms suffered noticeably due to political infighting. The municipal elections of 2003 and national elections of 2005 were an improvement over past years, adding to the consolidation of democracy despite the continued presence of administrative errors and inaccuracies in voter lists.

In 2005, the Democratic Party and its allies returned to power, pledging to fight crime and corruption, decrease the size and scope of government, and promote economic growth. Their leader, Sali Berisha, was sworn in as Prime Minister on September 11, 2005. On July 20, 2007, President Bamir Topi was elected by Parliament for a 5-year mandate, succeeding Moisiu. On June 28, 2009, Albania held parliamentary elections. The Organization for Security and Cooperation in Europe (OSCE) Office for Democratic Institutions and Human Rights (ODIHR) described these elections as progress over past elections and found that the elections met most OSCE standards. However, ODIHR noted that they did not fully meet OSCE standards and observers noted problems, including misuse of national and municipal government resources by both sides for campaign purposes, shortcomings in electoral preparations for vote counting, and evidence of proxy voting, media bias, and pressure on public sector employees to participate in campaign events. The elections resulted in no single party gaining a majority of the 140 seats in Parliament, and the Movement for Socialist Integration (LSI) and the Democratic Party (DP) combined to form a coalition government, the first such in Albania's history.

The May 2011 local elections drew international attention, as Socialist Party (SP) reluctance to fulfill pre-election preparations gave rise to fears it would boycott the election in favor of unspecified protest action. The elections took place as scheduled; the campaign was spirited and vigorously contested, with voter participation high for local elections. In a majority of the districts, voting and counting occurred technically well. However, the Central Election Commission's (CEC) decision in the Tirana mayoral race to count contested ballots reversed preliminary results showing three-time mayor and Socialist Party leader Edi Rama ahead by 10 votes in favor of ruling Democrat Party candidate Luzim Basha. The process undermined public confidence in the independence and impartiality of the CEC as an institution.

GOVERNMENT AND POLITICAL CONDITIONS

The Republic of Albania is a parliamentary democracy. The constitution vests legislative authority in the unicameral Assembly (parliament), which elects both the prime minister and the president. The prime minister heads the government, while the president has limited executive power.

Recent Elections

On May 8, 2011 the country held nationwide elections for mayors and city councils that the OSCE/ODIHR election observation mission characterized as "competitive and transparent" but "highly polarized, with mistrust between political parties in government and opposition." The Central Election Commission's (CEC) decision to overturn initial results in the mayoral contest in Tirana was widely perceived to be partisan and undermined confidence in its independence and impartiality.

Participation of Women and Minorities: The law mandates that women fill 30 percent of appointed and elected positions, and the electoral code provides that 30 percent of candidates should be women. However, not all parties followed the electoral code. There were 23 women elected to the 140-seat parliament in 2009, an increase from nine in the previous parliament. These included the speaker and one woman in the Council of Ministers.

Civil registration requirements and lack of identification among the Roma population made it difficult for many of them to participate in the May 8 elections. Some Roma candidates were elected to local offices. International observers reported attempts to influence illiterate Roma voters. There were no Roma elected to parliament nor serving in ministerial or subministerial positions. Several members of the Greek minority served in parliament and in the executive branch in ministerial and subministerial positions, including as the minister of labor.

Principal Government Officials

Last Updated: 1/31/2013

Pres.: **Bujar NISHANI**
Prime Min.: **Sali BERISHA**
Dep. Prime Min.: **Edmond HAXHINASTO**
Min. of Agriculture, Food, & Consumer Protection: **Genc RULI**
Min. of Culture, Tourism, Youth, & Sports: **Aldo BUMCI**
Min. of Defense: **Arben IMAMI**
Min. of Economy, Trade, & Energy: **Edmond HAXHINASTO**
Min. of Education & Science: **Myqerem TAFAJ**
Min. of Environment, Forestry, & Water Management: **Fatmir MEDIU**
Min. of Finance: **Ridvan BODE**
Min. of Foreign Affairs: **Edmond PANARITI**
Min. of Health: **Vangjel TAVO**
Min. of Innovation, Technology, & Communications: **Genc POLLO**
Min. of Integration: **Majlinda BREGU**
Min. of Interior: **Flamur NOKA**
Min. of Justice: **Eduard HALIMI**
Min. of Labor, Social Issues, & Equal Opportunity: **Spiro KSERA**
Min. of Public Works,Transportation, & Telecommunications:**Sokol OLLDASHI**
Governor, Bank of Albania: **Ardian FULLANI**
Ambassador to the US: **Gilbert GALANXHI**
Permanent Representative to the UN, New York: **Ferit HOXHA**

ECONOMY

Albania, a formerly closed, centrally-planned state, is making the difficult transition to a more modern open-market economy. Macroeconomic growth averaged around 6% between 2004–08, but declined to about 3% in 2009–11, and 0.5% in 2012. Inflation is low and stable. The government has taken measures to curb violent crime, and recently adopted a fiscal reform package aimed at reducing the large gray economy and attracting foreign investment.

Remittances, a significant catalyst for economic growth declined from 12-15% of GDP before the 2008 financial crisis to 8% of GDP in 2010, mostly from Albanians residing in Greece and Italy. The agricultural sector, which accounts for almost half of employment but only about one-fifth of GDP, is limited primarily to small family operations and subsistence farming because of lack of modern equipment, unclear property rights, and the prevalence of small, inefficient plots of land.

Energy shortages because of a reliance on hydropower - 98% of the electrical power produced in Albania - and antiquated and inadequate infrastructure contribute to Albania's poor business environment and lack of success in attracting new foreign investment needed to expand the country's export base. FDI is among the lowest in the region, but the government has embarked on an ambitious program to improve the business climate through fiscal and legislative reforms.

The completion of a new thermal power plant near Vlore has helped diversify generation capacity, and plans to upgrade transmission lines between Albania and Montenegro and Kosovo would help relieve the energy shortages. Also, with help from EU funds, the government is taking steps to improve the poor national road and rail network, a long-standing barrier to sustained economic growth.

The country will continue to face challenges from increasing public debt, having slightly exceeded its former statutory limit of 60% of GDP in 2012. Strong trade, remittance, and banking sector ties with Greece and Italy make Albania vulnerable to spillover effects of the global financial crisis.

Labor Conditions

The law sets the minimum age of employment at 16 years and regulates the amount and type of labor that children under the age of 18 may perform. Children between the ages of 16 and 18 can work in certain specified jobs. While the law provides that the Ministry of Labor, Social Affairs, and Equal Opportunity is responsible for enforcing minimum age requirements through the courts, it lacked resources to adequately enforce the law.

The law criminalizes exploitation of children for labor or forced services, but the government did not enforce the law effectively. According to a CRCA estimate released in 2010, more than 50,000 children under the age of 18 worked at least part time. The CRCA reported that the majority of child laborers worked as street or shop vendors, beggars, farmers or shepherds, drug runners, vehicle washers, textile factory workers, miners, or shoeshine boys. Research suggested that begging started at a young age—as early as four or five years of age. While the criminal code prohibits the exploitation of children for begging, police generally did not enforce this law.

The national minimum wage was 20,000 leks ($183) per month ion 2011. According to INSTAT, the average wage for government workers in the second quarter of the year was 47,000 leks ($430) per month. In comparison, the national poverty threshold in 2010 was $61 per month.

The Albanian Institute of Statistics reported that average monthly wages in the public sector had increased 6.6 percent from 2010. The Ministry of Labor, Social Affairs, and Equal Opportunity is responsible for enforcing the minimum wage. The law establishes a 40-hour workweek; however, individual or collective agreements typically set the actual workweek.

The law establishes paid annual holidays, but in practice only employers in the formal labor market guaranteed the right to paid holidays. Many persons worked six days a week. The law requires payment of overtime and rest periods, but employers did not always observe these provisions in practice. The law limits the maximum hours of work per week to 50, and provides for premium pay for overtime.

The government had no standards for a minimum number of rest periods per week and rarely enforced laws related to maximum work hours, limits on overtime, or premium pay for overtime. In practice these laws did not often apply to workers in the informal sector such as domestic employees and migrant workers.

U.S.-ALBANIAN RELATIONS

The United States established diplomatic relations with Albania in 1922, following its 1912 independence from the Ottoman Empire. U.S.-Albanian diplomatic relations were ended in 1939 due to Albania's occupation by Italy (1939–43) and Germany (1943–44) during World War II. After the war, Albania saw 40 years of isolation and underdevelopment under its Stalinist leader, who died in 1985. With the 1991 fall of communism, the Albanian Government sought closer ties with the West in order to improve economic conditions and introduced basic democratic reforms. Diplomatic relations between the United States and Albania were reestablished in 1991.

The United States has been a strong partner and friend to Albania as it has made progress to consolidate democracy, to open up its economy, and to provide opportunity for all its people. Albania and the United States have signed and ratified a number of agreements, including a treaty on the prevention of proliferation of weapons of mass destruction and the promotion of defense and military relations; the Adriatic Charter on Euro-Atlantic integration; and an agreement regarding the non-surrender of persons to the International Criminal Court. The United States supports Albania's European Union membership goal, as it did Albania's pursuit of North Atlantic Treaty Organization (NATO) membership.

Albania has contributed to regional and global security. Albanians credit the 1999 NATO intervention against the then-Federal Republic of Yugoslavia with saving thousands of Kosovo Albanians, and supported United Nations mediation efforts in Kosovo. Albania has supported the U.S. policy of expanding the number of countries extending diplomatic recognition to Kosovo.

Within the Adriatic Charter, Albania has acted as a mentor to new NATO aspirants. It has provided military troops for U.S.-led actions in Afghanistan and Iraq, and has supported U.S. counterterrorism efforts by freezing terrorist assets, shutting down nongovernmental organizations with possible links to terrorist financing, and expelling extremists.

U.S. Assistance to Albania

U.S. Government assistance aims to help Albania strengthen democratic institutions and rule of law; promote sustainable, broad-based economic growth; and integrate the country into European and Euro-Atlantic structures. A fact sheet on U.S. assistance to Albania can be found here.

Bilateral Economic Relations

Trade with the United States accounts for an insignificant part of Albania's trade volume, focusing on a narrow range of goods and products. Major imports from the U.S. include food (mainly meat), transportation equipment (vehicles), machinery, and computer and electronic equipment, while the main exports to the United States are agricultural products, footwear, and textiles. Albania is eligible to export certain products duty-free to the United States under the Generalized System of Preferences program. The United States and Albania have signed a bilateral investment treaty.

Albania's Membership in International Organizations

Albania and the United States belong to a number of the same international organizations, including the United Nations, North Atlantic Treaty Organization, Euro-Atlantic Partnership Council, Organization for Security and Cooperation in Europe, International Monetary Fund, World Bank, and World Trade Organization. Albania also is an observer to the Organization of American States.

Bilateral Representation

Albania maintains an embassy in the United States at 1312 18th Street, NW, Floor 4, Washington, DC 20036 (tel. 202-223-4942).

Principal U.S. Embassy Officials

Last Updated: 1/14/2013

TIRANA (E) 103 Rruga Elbasanit, 355-4-224-7285, Fax (355) (4) 223-2222, Workweek: Monday-Friday, 8:00am-5:00pm, Website: 2222, Workweek: Monday-Friday, 8:00am-5:00pm, Website: http://tirana.usembassy.gov/

DCM OMS:	Vacant
AMB OMS:	Patricia Hart
FM:	Dennis Sprighetti
HRO:	Thomas Bevan
ICITAP:	Steve Bennett
MGT:	Christopher Volciak
OPDAT:	Cynthia Eldridge
POL/ECON:	Jenifer Moore
POSHO:	Dennis Sprighetti
SDO/DATT:	Glenn Brown
TREAS:	Robert Jelnick
AMB:	Alexander A. Arvizu
CON:	Lyra Carr
DCM:	Charge Henry Jardine
PAO:	Elisabeth Lewis
GSO:	Matthew Wright
RSO:	Barry Hale
AFSA:	Lyra Carr
AID:	Jim Barnhart
CLO:	Zosia Brown
ECON:	Nikhil Sudame
FMO:	Thomas Bevan
IMO:	Vacant
ISSO:	John Coyne
State ICASS:	Vacant

TRAVEL

Consular Information Sheet

August 27, 2012

Country Description: Albania is a parliamentary democracy with a market-oriented economic system. Albania's per capita income is among the lowest in Europe, but economic conditions in the country are steadily improving. Albania's economic integration into broader European markets is slowly underway and the Albanian economy continues to grow despite uncertainty in the region. Tourist facilities are not highly developed in much of the country, but are also steadily improving, and some goods and services taken for granted in Western European countries are not widely available. Hotel accommodations are plentiful in Tirana and in other major cities, but limited in smaller towns. Albanian is the official language; English is limited except for Tirana's main tourist areas.

Smart Traveler Enrollment Program (STEP)/Embassy Location: If you are going to live in or visit Albania, please take the time to tell our Embassy about your trip. If you enroll, we can keep you up to date with important safety and security announcements. It will also help your friends and family get in touch with you in an emergency.

U.S. Embassy Tirana
Rruga Elbasanit 103
Tirana, Albania
Telephone: (355)(4) 224 7285
Facsimile: (355) (04) 237 4957
Email: ACSTirana@state.gov

Entry/Exit Requirements for U.S. Citizens: To enter Albania, you will need a passport valid for at least six months. Immigration officers strictly enforce this law. You do not need a visa prior to entering Albania, but if you travel without a visa, you may be charged a fee for an entry stamp at the port of entry, which is valid for a stay of up to 90 days. Although at this time the fee has been waived, Albanian law allows for collection of an entry tax up to 10 Euros, or the equivalent in any easily convertible currency, including U.S. dollars, and it may be reinstated without notice.

If you are traveling without a visa, and you intend to stay in Albania for more than 90 days, please note that Albanian law allows you to remain in Albania for 90 days only within a specific 180-day period, starting from the date of first entry. For example, if you enter without a visa on January 1, you may remain in Albania for a total of 90 days during the period between January 1 and June 28. Departing

Albania during this period does not "restart the clock." If you attempt to re-enter Albania without a visa within 180 days of your previous entry, and after an aggregate stay of 90 days, you may be denied entry. If you intend to stay more than 90 days within a 180-day period, you must apply for a Residency Permit at the police station in the locality where you are residing in Albania. The U.S. Department of State is unaware of any HIV/AIDS entry restrictions for visitors to or foreign residents of Albania.

Threats to Safety and Security: Although the overall security situation in Albania has improved in recent years, organized criminal activity continues to operate in all regions. Corruption is pervasive. Large, public demonstrations occur frequently in Albania. Although the majority of demonstrations are peaceful, a demonstration in January 2011 turned violent and resulted in the death of four people and injuries to many others, including to Albania State Police Officers. Because of the possibility of violence, we urge U.S. citizens to avoid all demonstrations. U.S. citizens should stay up to date with media coverage of local events and be aware of their surroundings at all times. Police and news outlets often report small-scale, sporadic incidents of violence.

Although there is no direct prohibition for travel of U.S. Government employees throughout Albania, U.S. Government travelers to certain areas—such as the southern town of Lazarat and to the north in the Tropoje region—receive pre-travel security and safety briefings and, in some cases, security support. In most cases, police assistance and protection are limited. You should maintain a high level of security awareness at all times.

Stay up to date by:

- Bookmarking our Bureau of Consular Affairs website, which contains the current Travel Warnings and Travel Alerts as well as the Worldwide Caution.
- Following us on Twitter and the Bureau of Consular Affairs page on Facebook as well.
- Downloading our free Smart Traveler iPhone App to have travel information at your fingertips;
- Calling 1-888-407-4747 toll-free within the U.S. and Canada, or a regular toll line, 1-202-501-4444, from other countries.
- Taking some time before travel to consider your personal security.

Crime: When traveling in Albania, you should take the same precautions against becoming a victim of crime as you would in any U.S. city. Although violent crime does occur in Albania, violent crime aimed at U.S. citizens is rare and criminals do not seem to target U.S. citizens or other foreigners deliberately, but rather seek targets of opportunity, selecting those who appear to have anything of value. However, recent crime statistics indicate an increase in violent crimes throughout Albania since 2009.

Pick-pocketing, theft, and other petty street crimes are widespread, particularly in areas where tourists and foreigners congregate. Pickpockets use various diversionary tactics to distract victims, and panhandlers—particularly children—may become aggressive. U.S. citizens have reported the theft of their passports and portable electronic devices by pick-pockets. Exercise caution in bars and clubs in Tirana, where violent incidents, some involving the use of firearms, have occurred in the past.

Vehicle theft and theft from vehicles are not uncommon in Albania. You should avoid leaving valuables, including cell phones and electronic items, in plain view in unattended vehicles. You should lock the windows and doors of your residence securely when it is not occupied. In the event you are a victim of a carjacking, you should surrender your vehicle without resistance.

Organized crime is present in Albania; organized criminal activity occasionally results in violent confrontations between members of rival organizations. Armed crime continues to be more common in northern and northwestern Albania than in the rest of the country. Street crimes are more common at night. In 2011 there were 67 explosions in Albania, approximately 33 percent of which were in the district of Tirana. Since January 2012, approximately 39 explosions have occurred throughout Albania, the majority of which have occurred in the district of Tirana—most of which were either from remotely detonated car bombs or explosives placed at private residences. Although most of these cases are suspected to be the result of targeted violence against specific individuals, you should remain alert to avoid such situations.

Automated Teller Machine (ATM) use is generally safe in well-known locations; however, travelers should take standard safety precautions. Try to use ATMs located inside banks and check for any evidence of tampering with the machine before use. Be cautious when using publicly available Internet terminals, such as in Internet cafes, as sensitive personal information, account passwords, etc., may be subject to compromise.

Don't buy counterfeit and pirated goods, even if they are widely available. Not only are the bootlegs illegal in the United States, if you purchase them you may also be breaking local law.

Victims of Crime: If you or someone you know becomes the victim of a crime abroad, you should contact the local police and the nearest U.S. embassy or consulate. We can:

- Replace a stolen passport.
- Help you find appropriate medical care if you are the victim of violent crimes such as assault or rape.
- Put you in contact with the appropriate police authorities, and if you want us to, we can contact family members or friends.

- Help you understand the local criminal justice process and direct you to local attorneys, although it is important to remember that local authorities are responsible for investigating and prosecuting the crime.

The local equivalent to the "911" emergency line in Albania is 129; however, emergency response support is deemed unreliable.

Criminal Penalties: There are some things that might be legal in the country you visit, but still illegal in the United States. If you break local laws in Albania your U.S. passport won't help you avoid arrest or prosecution. It's very important to know what's legal and what's not wherever you go.

While you are traveling in Albania, you are subject to its laws even if you are a U.S. citizen. Foreign laws and legal systems can be vastly different from our own. For instance, it isillegal to take pictures of certain physical structures in Albania. Be alert for signage and guidance by security personnel.

In Albania, you may be taken in for questioning if you are not carrying your passport.

Engaging in sexual conduct with children or using or disseminating child pornography in a foreign country is a crime prosecutable in the United States. Engaging in sexual conduct with children is also a crime in Albania, as is the production and distribution of child pornography. Under Albanian law, police can detain any individual for up to 10 hours without filing formal charges. Although this is not a common occurance reported by U.S. citizens, the possibility remains. We encourage U.S. citizens to carry a copy of their U.S. passport with them at all times to show proof of identity and U.S. citizenship if questioned by local officials.

Persons violating Albanian laws, even unknowingly, may be expelled, arrested, or imprisoned. Penalties for possessing, using, or trafficking in illegal drugs in Albania are severe, and convicted offenders can expect long jail sentences and heavy fines. While some countries will automatically notify the nearest U.S. embassy or consulate if a U.S. citizen is detained or arrested in a foreign country, that might not always be the case. To ensure that the United States is aware of your circumstances, request that the police and prison officials notify the nearest U.S. embassy or consulate as soon as you are arrested or detained overseas.

Special Circumstances: Albania's customs authorities may enforce strict regulations concerning temporary importation into or export from Albania of some items. We suggest that you contact the Embassy of Albania in Washington, D.C. or one of Albania's Consulates in the United States for specific information regarding customs requirements.

The Albanian government considers any person in Albania who has at least one Albanian parent to be an Albanian citizen. In addition to being subject to all Albanian laws affecting U.S. citizens, dual nationals may be subject to Albanian laws that impose special obligations.

Albania is a cash economy. Credit cards are generally accepted only at major hotels in Tirana, large department/grocery stores, upscale restaurants, and some international airline offices. Travelers' checks are not widely used but can be changed at banks in larger towns or cities. ATMs are widely available in Tirana and in larger towns.

Accessibility: While in Albania, individuals with disabilities may find accessibility and accommodation very different from what you find in the United States. In December 2009, Albania signed the UN Convention on the Rights of Persons with Disabilities. However, very few of the convention's terms have been implemented, and it has not been ratified by Parliament. The national strategy on persons with disabilities adopted for the period 2004–2014 is aimed at improving living conditions through accessibility, support services, employment, and education; at present, it is only partly implemented. Only limited measures exist to support disabled persons. Most public buildings remain inaccessible and inconsistent inspection has resulted in construction of new facilities that are not always accessible for persons with disabilities. Public transportation for persons with disabilities is very limited.

Medical Facilities and Health Information: Medical care at private hospitals and clinics in Tirana has improved in recent years, but still remains below western standards, and medical facilities outside Tirana have very limited capabilities. Emergency and major medical care requiring surgery and hospital care outside Tirana is often inadequate because of a lack of medical specialists, diagnostic aids, medical supplies, and prescription drugs. If you have been previously diagnosed with (a) medical condition(s), you may wish to consult your personal health care provider before travel. As some prescription drugs may be unavailable locally, you may also wish to bring extra supplies of required medications.

Electricity shortages have resulted in sporadic blackouts throughout the country, which can affect food storage capabilities of restaurants and shops. While some restaurants and food stores have generators to store food properly, you should take care that food is cooked thoroughly to reduce the risk of food-borne illness. We do not recommend drinking the tap water in Albania. You should plan to purchase bottled water or drinks while in country.

You can find detailed information on vaccinations and other health precautions on the CDC website. For information about outbreaks of infectious diseases abroad, consult the World Health Organization (WHO) website. The WHO website also contains additional health information for travelers, including detailed country-specific health information.

Medical Insurance: You can't assume your insurance will go with you when you travel. It's very important to find out BEFORE you leave whether or not your medical insurance will cover you overseas. You need to ask your insurance company two questions:

- Does my policy apply when I'm out of the United States?
- Will it cover emergencies like a trip to a foreign hospital or a medical evacuation?

In Albania, doctors and hospitals still expect payment in cash at the time of service. Your regular U.S. health insurance may not cover doctor and hospital visits in other countries. If your policy doesn't go with you when you travel, it's a very good idea to take out another one for your trip.

Traffic Safety and Road Conditions: While in Albania you may encounter road conditions that differ significantly from those in the United States.

Although the government continues to make substantial investments in road improvements, many major roads in Albania are in poor condition. Disregard for traffic laws is widespread. Traffic accidents are frequent occurrences and can result in serious injury or death. If you choose to drive in Albania, please exercise caution and drive as defensively as possible. General outages of traffic signals and street lights are common, increasing the dangers of driving. You should avoid traveling at night outside the main urban areas as road conditions can be dangerous and road hazards are more difficult to see. During the winter months, roads throughout mountainous regions in northern Albania can be dangerously snowy and icy. Buses travel between most major cities almost exclusively during the day, but they do not always run according to schedule and can be uncomfortable relative to buses in the United States. Many travelers looking for public transport prefer to use privately owned vans, which function as an alternate system of bus routes and operate almost entirely without schedules or set fares. Please note that many of these privately owned vans may not have official permission to operate a bus service and may not adhere to accepted safety and maintenance standards; you should consider the condition of the van before you choose to travel in one. There are no commercial domestic flights and the rail conditions are poor, connections limited, and service unreliable.

You can only use an International driver's license for one year in Albania. If you wish to drive in Albania for a period of time in excess of one year, you must apply for an Albanian driver's license.

It is illegal to drive under the influence of alcohol and, if caught, the police may seize your driver's license and vehicle and impose additional penalties.

Using a cell phone while driving is only permitted when the driver utilizes a Bluetooth or other hands-free device and failure to use such a device can result in a fine.

Aviation Safety Oversight: As there is no direct commercial air service to the United States by carriers registered in Albania, the U.S. Federal Aviation Administration (FAA) has not assessed the government of Albania's Civil Aviation Authority for compliance with International Civil Aviation Organization (ICAO) aviation safety standards. Further information may be found on the FAA's safety assessment page.

Children's Issues: Please see the U.S. Dept. of State Office of Children's Issues web pages on intercountry adoption and international parental child abduction.

Intercountry Adoption
July 2010

The information in this section has been edited from the latest report available as of February 2013 from the State Department Bureau of Consular Affairs, Office of Overseas Citizens Services. For more information, please read the *Intercountry Adoption* section of this book and review current reports online at http://adoption.state.gov.

Albania is party to the Hague Convention on Protection of Children and Co-operation in Respect of Intercountry Adoption (Hague Adoption Convention). Therefore, all adoptions between Albania and the United States must meet the requirements of the Convention; the U.S. implementing legislation, the Intercountry Act of 2000 (IAA); and the IAA implementing regulations.

Who Can Adopt? Adoption between the United States and Albania is governed by the Hague Adoption Convention. Therefore to adopt from Albania, you must first be found eligible to adopt by the U.S. Government. The U.S. Government agency responsible for making this determination is the Department of Homeland Security, U.S. Citizenship and Immigration Services (USCIS).

In addition to these U.S. requirements for prospective adoptive parents, Albania also has the following requirements for prospective adoptive parents.

Residency Requirements: No known residency requirements.

Age Requirements: Under Albanian law, prospective adoptive parents must be a minimum of 18 years older than the adopted child.

Marriage Requirements: Both married and single prospective adoptive parents are permitted. When an adoptive parent is married, the consent of their spouse is required.

Income Requirements: Considered during the adoption process by the court as an indicator of the potential parents' ability to care for the child, but no guidelines are posted.

Other Requirements: Post has not discovered any additional restrictions on adoptive parents.

Who Can Be Adopted? Because Albania is party to The Hague Adoption Convention, children from Albania must meet the requirements of the Convention in order to be eligible for adoption. For example, the Convention requires that Albania attempt to place a child with a family in-country before determining that a child is eligible for intercountry adoption. In addition to Albania's requirements, a child must meet the definition of a Convention adoptee for you to bring him or her back to the United States.

Eligibility Requirements: Albanian Law number 9695, dated March 19, 2007, on the adoption procedures and Albanian Adoption Committee: Only children listed in the Albanian Adoption Committee are eligible to be adopted. In the lists of the Committee are registered those Albanian children, about whom:

- Abandonment has been declared by way of a final judgment (see article 250 of Albanian Family Code)
- Consent has been given by their biological parents; OR
- Consent has been given by the court for the children kept under care (see article 246 of Albanian Family Code).

Relinquishment Requirements: According to Article 246, the consent of both parents is required for the adoption of a minor. If one of the parents is deceased, is unable to express their will, or had their parental rights removed, the consent of the other parent is sufficient. When both parents of the child are deceased, or when their capacity to act has been removed or the parents are not known, the court decides if the child may be adopted. If the adoptee has reached the age of 10 years old, their opinion may be considered and if they are 12 years of age their consent is required.

Abandonment Requirements: The district court can declare as abandoned, a minor at a social care institution, public or private, or in the care of another person, when the parents, in an obvious manner, have not been involved with the child for a period of one year before the request for the declaration of the abandonment was submitted. If the minor has been housed in an institution since their birth, the timeframe of one year is reduced to three months.

Age Requirements: Child should be under 18 at the time of court decision granting adoption, but to be eligible for a U.S. visa through The Hague Adoption process the child must have been under the age of 16 when the court adoption decree was granted.

Sibling Requirements: No known restrictions

Requirements for Special Needs or Medical Conditions: No known restrictions

Waiting Period: An orphan must have been put up for local adoption for a period of six months before an international party may initiate adoption proceedings. This section of law covers all international adoptions, and requires confirmation that the child has had no chances to be adopted in Albania in the six months from the date of registration in Albanian Committee lists.

Revocation of Relinquishment of Rights: According to Article 248 consent for the adoption may be withdrawn by the biological parents within 3 months from the time it was given. This period serves as a probationary period for the relationships between the adoptive parents and the adoptee. The probationary period is needed to establish an adoptive relationship between a child and a family. The parents may withdraw their consent even after this three month period has elapsed, up until such time as the competent court enters its decision. The court, before it decides, must verify that the above-mentioned timeframes have been fulfilled, that all necessary efforts to return the child to the biological parents have been made and that the probationary period with the adoptive family has been successful. If the person, with whom the child was placed during the probationary period and after, refuses to return the child, the parents may petition the court for the return of the child, if this is in the child's best interest.

Family Adoptions: Under Albanian Family Code, there are two kinds of adoptions. The first type is legalized family adoption, whereby one relative transfers the parental rights of a child directly to another relative. Under this process, the child is never abandoned and the parents never relinquish parental rights. In these cases, the children are never available for adoption by any other party and never appear on the list of eligible children, which is where the Albanian Adoption Committee lists all children who are eligible to be adopted by any fit party. It is important to note that under Albanian law, any Albanian citizen who later acquires an additional citizenship is still considered an Albanian citizen. This means that naturalized Albanian-Americans are eligible to adopt under this procedure. Unfortunately, due to the process of transferring rights, this type of adoption will not qualify a child to receive a visa through Hague Adoption procedures.

Albania's Adoption Authority: The government office responsible for adoptions in Albania is the Albanian Adoption Committee. Individuals may not deal directly with the Albanian Adoption Committee or with individual orphanages or biological parents.

The Process: Because Albania is party to The Hague Adoption Convention, adopting from Albania must follow a specific process designed to meet the Convention's requirements. A brief summary of the Convention adoption process is given below. You must complete these steps in the following order so that your adoption meets all necessary legal requirements.

The first step in adopting a child from Albania is to select an adoption service provider in the United States that has been accredited. Only these agencies and attorneys can provide adoption services between the United States and Albania. All adoptions must be processed by an adoption agency accredited by the Albanian Adoption Committee. Currently, two U.S. adoption agencies have been accredited:

Bethany Christian Services
901 Eastern Avenue, NE
Grand Rapids, Michigan 49503–1295
Tel: (616) 459-6273
Fax: (616) 459-0343

International Children's Alliance
1101 17th Street, NW, Suite 1002
Washington, D.C. 20036
Tel: (202) 463-6874
Fax: (202) 463-6880
Email: adoptionop@aol.com

After you choose an accredited adoption service provider, you apply to be found eligible to adopt (Form I-800A) by the U.S. Government, Department of Homeland Security, U.S. Citizenship and Immigration Services (USCIS).

Once the U.S. government determines that you are "eligible" and "suitable" to adopt, you or your agency will forward your information to the adoption authority in Albania. Albania's adoption authority will review your application to determine whether you are also eligible to adopt under Albania's law.

If both the United States and Albania determine that you are eligible to adopt, and a child is available for intercountry adoption, the central adoption authority in Albania may provide you with a referral for a child. Each family must decide for itself whether or not it will be able to meet the needs of the particular child and provide a permanent family placement for the referred child.

The Albanian child must have a certificate from the Albanian Adoption Committee stating that s/he is adoptable. This means that the child has been in an orphanage for at least six months with no contact from his/her biological parents, and that the orphanage has been unsuccessful in placing the child with an Albanian family. The prospective adoptive parents may not go to an orphanage to select a child without authorization from the Albanian Adoption Committee. (Authorized local adoption agencies, i.e. International Children's Alliance, or Bethany Christian Services, can contact the Albanian Adoption Committee to obtain authorization for the prospective adoptive parents to visit an orphanage). In general the Committee will propose a child whom the prospective adoptive parents may accept if they wish.

After you accept a match with a child, you will apply to the U.S Government, Department of Homeland Security, U.S. Citizenship and Immigration Services (USCIS) for provisional approval to adopt that particular child (Form I-800). USCIS will determine whether the child is eligible under U.S. law to be adopted and enter the United States.

After this, your adoption service provider or you will submit a visa application for to a consular officer at the U.S. Embassy. The consular officer will review the child's information and evaluate the child for possible visa ineligibilities.

If the consular officer determines that the child appears eligible to immigrate to the United States, he or she will send a letter (an "Article 5 Letter") to the Albanian Central Authority. Do not adopt or obtain custody of a child in Albania before a U.S. consular officer issues the Article 5 Letter. The consular officer will make a final decision about the immigrant visa later in the adoption process.

Role of the Adoption Authority: Maintains the list of children eligible for adoption, suggests prospective children to prospective parents.

Role of the Court: Will review the case and determine if the adoption should be granted based on the welfare and best interest of the child.

Role of Adoption Agencies: Coordinate between the Adoption Committee and the prospective parents, prepare the paperwork and court documents for local adoption, schedule a court date, and assist parents to obtain the new birth certificate and passport.

Time Frame: Varies depending on court workload. Currently, the wait from the time the parents are matched with a child it will take approximately 2-3 months to have a finalized court decision. This process requires two court sessions, about two weeks apart.

Adoption Application: Handled by the accredited adoption agency.

Adoption Fees: In the adoption services contract that you sign at the beginning of the adoption process, your agency will itemize the fees and estimated expenses related to your adoption process.

Documents Required:

- A written request clearly stating the reasons why he/she/they want(s) to adopt a child;
- Birth certificate, marriage certificate of the adopting parent(s), divorce decree and former spouse's death certificate as applicable;
- Police records of the adopting parent(s);
- Personal, family, social and medical information on the adopting parent(s);
- Home Study (An evaluation study on the adopting family made by a social worker);

All the above-mentioned documents are submitted to one of the adoption agencies accredited by the Albanian Adoption Committee. Additional documents may be requested.

Bringing Your Child Home: Once your adoption is complete (or you have obtained legal custody of the child), there are a few more steps to take before you can head home. Specifically, you need to apply for several documents for your child before he or she can travel to the United States, such as a birth certificate, a passport or travel document for your child from the country in which he or she was born, and a U.S. Immigration Visa.

For detailed and updated information on how to obtain these documents, review the *Intercountry Adoption* section in this publication and visit the U.S. Department of State Intercountry Adoption website at http://adoption.state.gov.

Child Citizenship Act: For adoptions finalized abroad, the Child Citizenship Act of 2000 allows your new child to acquire American citizenship automatically when he or she enters the United States as lawful permanent residents. For adoptions finalized in the United States, the Child Citizenship Act of 2000 allows your new child to acquire American citizenship automatically when the court in the United States issues the final adoption decree. To learn more, review the *Intercountry Adoption* section in this publication and visit the U.S. Department of State Intercountry Adoption website at http://adoption.state.gov.

Obtaining Travel Documents: The final court decision and the child's travel documentation cannot be issued until 13 days after the court date. The child must remain in Albania during these 13 days, although s/he may reside with the adoptive parents during that time. Please remember: when traveling to the U.S. with your newly adopted child, since the child is an Albanian citizen, s/he will need to obtain a transit visa from the embassy of the country of transit in order to be permitted to travel through. The country of transit cannot issue this transit visa until the child is issued a passport. In many cases the transit visa application may take several days or more to process. (Note: this procedure is separate from the U.S. immigrant visa process.) Therefore, prospective adoptive parents should be prepared to arrive in Albania a day or two before the court date and to remain afterwards for approximately three weeks.

After Adoption: Post is unaware of any reporting or other requirements after the adoption is finalized. We strongly urge you to discuss any possible post-adoption requirements with the adoption agency you choose.

U.S. Embassy in Albania
Address: Elbasani Street, No.103, Tirana, Albania
Tel: ++355 (0)4 224 7285
Fax: +355 (0)4 223 2222
Email:TiranaUSConsulate@state.gov
http://Tirana.usembassy.gov

Albania's Adoption Authority
Address: Adresa: Rr: Mine Peza, Pallati 87/3, Shkalla 2, Tirana, Albania
Tel: +355 (0)42 227 487;:+355226465
Fax: +355 (0)42 227 487;
Email:
kshb@komitetibiresimeve. com.al
http://www.komitetibiresimeve.com.al/

Embassy of Albania
Address: 2100 S Street NW, Washington D.C. 20008
Tel: 202 223 4942; 202 2234942
Fax: 202 6287342
embassy.washington@mfa.gov.al

Office of Children's Issues
U.S. Department of State
2201 C Street, NW
SA-29
Washington, DC 20520
Tel: 1-888-407-4747
E-mail: AskCI@state.gov
http://adoption.state.gov

For questions about immigration procedures, call the National Customer Service Center (NCSC) at 1-800-375-5283 (TTY 1-800-767-1833).

ALGERIA

Compiled from publications that were available as of February 2013 from the U.S. Department of State, the U.S. Department of Commerce, and the Central Intelligence Agency (CIA). See the introduction to this set for explanatory notes.

Official Name:

People's Democratic Republic of Algeria

PROFILE

Geography

Area: total: 2,381,741 sq km; country comparison to the world: 10; land: 2,381,741 sq km; water: 0 sq km
Major cities: Algiers (capital) 2.74 million; Oran 770,000 (2009)
Climate: arid to semiarid; mild, wet winters with hot, dry summers along coast; drier with cold winters and hot summers on high plateau; sirocco is a hot, dust/sand-laden wind especially common in summer
Terrain: mostly high plateau and desert; some mountains; narrow, discontinuous coastal plain

People

Nationality: noun: Algerian(s); adjective: Algerian
Population: 37,367,226 (July 2012 est.)
Population growth rate: 1.165% (2012 est.)
Ethnic groups: Arab-Berber 99%, European less than 1%
Religions: Sunni Muslim (state religion) 99%, Christian and Jewish 1%
Languages: Arabic (official), French (lingua franca), Berber dialects: Kabylie Berber (Tamazight), Chaouia Berber (Tachawit), Mzab Berber, Tuareg Berber (Tamahaq)
Literacy: definition: age 15 and over can read and write; total population: 69.9%; male: 79.6%; female: 60.1% (2002 est.)
Health: life expectancy at birth: total population: 74.73 years; male: 72.99 years; female: 76.57 years (2012 est.); Infant mortality rate: total: 24.9 deaths/1,000 live births; male: 27.82 deaths/1,000 live births; female: 21.83 deaths/1,000 live births (2012 est.)
Unemployment rate: 10% (2012' est.)
Work force: 11.26 million (2012 est.)

Government

Type: republic
Independence: 5 July 1962
Constitution: 8 September 1963; revised 19 November 1976; effective 22 November 1976; revised several times
Political subdivisions: 48 provinces (wilayat, singular—wilaya)
Suffrage: 18 years of age; universal

Economy

GDP (purchasing power parity): $274.5 billion (2012 est.); $267 billion (2011 est.); $260.6 billion (2010 est.); $252.3 billion (2009 est.)
GDP real growth rate: 2.5% (2011 est.); 3.3% (2010 est.); 2.4% (2009 est.)
GDP per capita (PPP): $7,500 (2012 est.); $7,400 (2011 est.); $7,400 (2010 est.); $7,200 (2009 est.)
Natural resources: petroleum, natural gas, iron ore, phosphates, uranium, lead, zinc
Agriculture products: wheat, barley, oats, grapes, olives, citrus, fruits; sheep, cattle
Industries: petroleum, natural gas, light industries, mining, electrical, petrochemical, food processing
Exports: $76.84 billion (2012 est.); $72.66 billion (2011 est.); $57.09 billion (2010 est.)
Exports—commodities: petroleum, natural gas, and petroleum products 97%
Exports—partners: US 23.3%, Spain 12.2%, Canada 9.5%, France 9.5%, Brazil 5.4%, Netherlands 5.4%, Germany 4.3%, Italy 4.1% (2011)
Imports: $47.53 billion (2012 est.); $44.19 billion (2011 est.); $38.89 billion (2010 est.)
Imports—commodities: capital goods, foodstuffs, consumer goods
Imports—partners: France 18.5%, China 10.4%, Italy 9.5%, Spain 8%, Germany 4.5% (2011)
Debt—external: $4.344 billion (31 December 2012 est.); $4.699 billion (31 December 2011 est.)
Exchange rates: Algerian dinars (DZD) per US dollar; 77.84 (2012 est.); 72.938 (2011 est.); 74.386 (2010 est.); 72.65 (2009); 63.25 (2008)

GEOGRAPHY

Algeria, the second-largest state in Africa, has a Mediterranean coastline of about 998 kilometers (620 mi.). The Tellian and Saharan Atlas mountain ranges cross the country from east to west, dividing it into three zones. Between the northern zone, Tellian Atlas, and the Mediterranean is a narrow, fertile coastal plain—the Tel (hill)—with a moderate climate year round and rainfall adequate for agriculture. A high plateau region, averaging 914 meters (3,000 ft.) above sea level, with limited rainfall, great rocky plains, and desert, lies between the two mountain ranges. It is generally barren except for scattered clumps of trees and intermittent bush and pastureland.

The third and largest zone, south of the Saharan Atlas mountain range, is mostly desert. About 80% of the country is desert, steppes, wasteland, and mountains. Algeria's weather varies considerably from season to season and from one geographical location to another. In the north, the summers are usually hot with little rainfall. Winter rains begin in the north in October. Frost and snow are rare, except on the highest slopes of the Tellian Atlas Mountains.

Dust and sandstorms occur most frequently between February and May. Soil erosion—from overgrazing, other poor farming practices, and desertification—and the dumping of raw sewage, petroleum refining wastes, and other industrial effluents are leading to the pollution of rivers and coastal waters. The Mediterranean Sea, in particular, is becoming polluted from oil wastes, soil erosion, and fertilizer runoff. There are inadequate supplies of potable water.

PEOPLE

Nearly all Algerians are of Arab, Berber, or mixed Arab-Berber stock. More than 99 percent of the population is Sunni Muslim. A small community of Ibadi Muslims resides in the province of Ghardaia. Unofficial estimates of the number of Christian and Jewish citizens varied between 30,000 and 70,000, with Christians making up the overwhelming majority. This figure also includes expatriates living in the country. The vast majority of Christians and Jews fled the country following independence from France in 1962. In the 1990s, many of the remaining Christians and Jews emigrated due to acts of terrorism against them by violent extremists. Since 1994 the Jewish community has diminished to less than 2,000 members due to widespread violence in the 1990s that targeted all communities. Some religious leaders estimated that there were likely only a few hundred Jews remaining in the country. For security reasons, due mainly to the civil conflict, Christians concentrated in the cities of Algiers, Annaba, and Oran in the mid-1990s.

Languages

The national language of Albania is Albanian. Most educated people in Albania speak a foreign language. The most popular second languages are English, Italian, and Greek.

HISTORY

Since the 5th century B.C., the native peoples of northern Africa (first identified by the Greeks as "Berbers") were pushed back from the coast by successive waves of Phoenician, Roman, Vandal, Byzantine, Arab, Turkish, and, finally, French invaders. The greatest cultural impact came from the Arab invasions of the 8th and 11th centuries A.D., which brought Islam and the Arabic language. The effects of the most recent (French) occupation—French language and European-inspired socialism—are still pervasive.

North African boundaries have shifted during various stages of the conquests. Algeria's modern borders were created by the French, whose colonization began in 1830. To benefit French colonists, most of whom were farmers and businessmen, northern Algeria was eventually organized into overseas departments of France, with representatives in the French National Assembly. France controlled the entire country, but the traditional Muslim population in the rural areas remained separated from the modern economic infrastructure of the European community.

Algerians began their uprising on November 1, 1954 to gain rights denied them under French rule. The revolution, launched by a small group of nationalists who called themselves the National Liberation Front (FLN), was a guerrilla war in which both sides targeted civilians and used other brutal tactics. Eventually, protracted negotiations led to a cease-fire signed by France and the FLN on March 18, 1962, at Evian, France. The Evian Accords also provided for continuing economic, financial, technical, and cultural relations, along with interim administrative arrangements until a referendum on self-determination could be held. Over 1 million French citizens living in Algeria at the time, called the pieds-noirs (black feet), left Algeria for France.

The referendum was held in Algeria on July 1, 1962, and France declared Algeria independent on July 3. In September 1962 Ahmed Ben Bella was formally elected president. On September 8, 1963, a Constitution was adopted by referendum. On June 19, 1965, President Ben Bella was replaced in a non-violent coup by the Council of the Revolution headed by Minister of Defense Col. Houari Boumediene. Ben Bella was first imprisoned and then exiled. Boumediene, as President of the Council of the Revolution, led the country as Head of State until he was formally elected on December 10, 1976. Boumediene is credited with building "modern Algeria." He died on December 27, 1978.

Following nomination by an FLN Party Congress, Col. Chadli Bendjedid was elected president in 1979 and re-elected in 1984 and 1988. A new constitution was adopted in 1989 that allowed the formation of political parties other than the FLN. It also removed the armed forces, which had run the government since the days of Boumediene, from a designated role in the operation of the government.

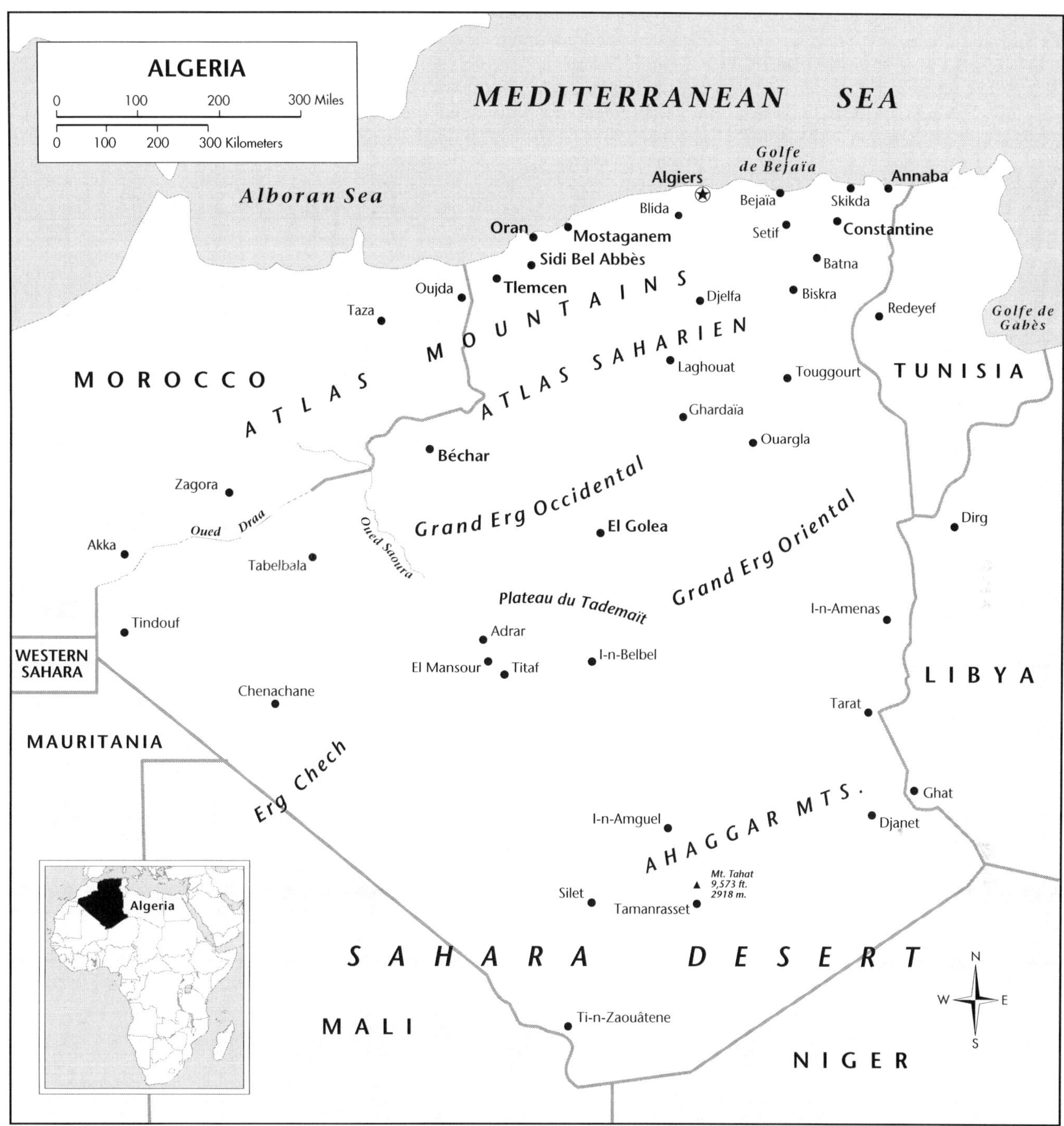

Among the scores of parties that sprang up under the new constitution, the militant Islamic Salvation Front (FIS) was the most successful, winning more than 50% of all votes cast in municipal elections in June 1990 as well as in the first stage of national legislative elections held in December 1991.

Faced with the real possibility of a sweeping FIS victory, the National People's Assembly was dissolved by presidential decree on January 4, 1992. On January 11, under pressure from the military leadership, President Chadli Bendjedid resigned. On January 14, a five-member High Council of State was appointed by the High Council of Security to act as a collegiate presidency and immediately canceled the second round of elections. This action, coupled with political uncertainty and economic turmoil, led to a violent reaction by Islamists. On January 16, Mohamed Boudiaf, a hero of the Liberation War, returned after 28 years of exile to serve as Algeria's fourth president. Facing sporadic outbreaks of violence and terrorism, the security forces took control of the FIS offices in early February, and the High Council of State declared a state of emergency. In March, following a court decision, the FIS Party was formally dissolved, and a series of arrests and trials of FIS members occurred resulting in more than 50,000 members being jailed. Algeria became caught in a cycle of violence, which became increasingly random and indiscriminate. On June 29, 1992, President Boudiaf was assassinated in Annaba in front of TV cameras by Army Lt. Lembarek Boumarafi, who allegedly confessed to carrying out the killing on behalf of the Islamists.

Despite efforts to restore the political process, violence and terrorism dominated the Algerian landscape during the 1990s. In 1994, Liamine Zeroual, former Minister of Defense, was appointed Head of State by the High Council of State for a 3-year term. During this period, the Armed Islamic Group (GIA) launched terrorist campaigns against government figures and institutions to protest the banning of the Islamist parties. A breakaway GIA group—the Salafist Group for Preaching and Combat (GSPC)—also undertook terrorist activity in the country. Government officials estimate that more than 150,000 Algerians died during this period.

Zeroual called for presidential elections in 1995, though some parties objected to holding elections that excluded the FIS. Zeroual was elected president with 75% of the vote. By 1997, in an attempt to bring political stability to the nation, the National Democratic Rally (RND) party was formed by a progressive group of FLN members. In September 1998, President Liamine Zeroual announced that he would step down in February 1999, 21 months before the end of his term, and that presidential elections would be held. Algerians went to the polls in April 1999, following a campaign in which seven candidates qualified for election. On the eve of the election, all candidates except Abdelaziz Bouteflika pulled out amid charges of widespread electoral fraud. Bouteflika, the candidate who appeared to enjoy the backing of the military, as well as the FLN and the RND party regulars, won with an official vote count of 70% of all votes cast. He was inaugurated on April 27, 1999 for a 5-year term.

President Bouteflika's agenda focused initially on restoring security and stability to the country. Following his inauguration, he proposed an official amnesty for those who fought against the government during the 1990s with the exception of those who had engaged in "blood crimes," such as rape or murder. This "Civil Concord" policy was widely approved in a nationwide referendum in September 2000. Government officials estimate that 80% of those fighting the regime during the 1990s have accepted the civil concord offer and have attempted to reintegrate into Algerian society. Bouteflika also launched national commissions to study education and judicial reform, as well as restructuring of the state bureaucracy.

In 2001, Berber activists in the Kabylie region of the country, reacting to the death of a youth in gendarme custody, unleashed a resistance campaign against what they saw as government repression. Strikes and demonstrations in the Kabylie region were commonplace as a result, and some spread to the capital. Chief among Berber demands was recognition of Tamazight (a general term for Berber languages) as an official language, official recognition and financial compensation for the deaths of Kabyles killed in demonstrations, an economic development plan for the area and greater control over their own regional affairs. In October 2001, the Tamazight language was recognized as a national language, but the issue remains contentious as Tamazight has not been elevated to an official language.

The April 8, 2004, presidential election was the first election since independence in which several candidates competed. Besides incumbent President Bouteflika, five other candidates, including one woman, competed in the election. Opposition candidates complained of some discrepancies in the voting list; irregularities on polling day, particularly in Kabylie; and of unfair media coverage during the campaign as Bouteflika, by virtue of his office, appeared on state-owned television daily. Bouteflika was re-elected in the first round of the election with 84.99% of the vote. Just over 58% of those Algerians eligible to vote participated in the election.

In November 2008, the parliament adopted a set of constitutional amendments that included a removal of presidential term limits. The parliament approved the proposed amendments by a wide margin with minimal debate. President Bouteflika won a third term in the April 9, 2009, elections with, officially, 90.2% of the vote. Opposition members again complained of unfair media coverage and irregularities during voting, and some parties boycotted the vote.

GOVERNMENT AND POLITICAL CONDITIONS

Algeria is a multiparty republic whose head of state and government (president) is elected by popular vote for a five-year term. The president has the constitutional authority to appoint and dismiss cabinet members and the prime minister. A 2008 constitutional amendment eliminated presidential term limits, and in April 2009 President Abdelaziz Bouteflika won reelection to his third term in office. Some opposition parties boycotted the election, arguing that restrictions on freedom of association skewed the election in favor of the incumbent.

Riots sparked by increases in staple food prices spread across 24 of the country's 48 provinces in January 2011. A fledgling political opposition coalition failed to garner widespread public support, and the government prevented the group from staging weekly marches in Algiers. In February the government lifted the state of emergency that had been in effect since 1992 but continued to prohibit marches in the capital and restrict freedom of association throughout the country. Beginning in March and extending through mid-April, dozens of groups staged protests and sit-ins in public spaces and in front of government ministries in Algiers, demanding higher wages, improved benefits, and better working conditions. Most protests remained peaceful and ended after the government agreed to meet most demands. In December both houses of parliament passed a series of reform laws on elections, political parties, female representation in elected bodies, associations, and media.

The constitution mandates presidential elections every five years. In 2008 President Abdelaziz Bouteflika announced his intention to seek parliamentary approval for a set of constitutional amendments that included removal of presidential term limits. One month later the parliament approved the proposed amendments by a wide margin with minimal debate.

Recent Elections

In 2009 the government held a contested, multiparty presidential election in which the incumbent was elected to a third term. Official election statistics indicated that President Bouteflika won the election with 90.2 percent of the votes and a voter turnout of 74.6 percent. Opposition parties and defeated candidates estimated voter turnout was actually in the range of 18 to 55 percent. Some international experts commented that observers monitored only election-day procedures and were not on the ground to evaluate preelection activities. Two opposition parties, the Rally for Culture and Democracy (RCD) and the Socialist Forces Front (FFS), boycotted the election. The LADDH pointed to a lack of critical debate in the media and favorable treatment of the incumbent by state-owned media.

Political Parties: The Ministry of Interior did not approve any political parties during 2011. In April Interior Minister Daho Ould Kablia indicated that the ministry had received 42 requests to authorize new political parties. In November Ould Kablia indicated that there were only five or six political parties that would meet the government's conditions for approval. Opposition candidates complained that the ministry regularly blocked registered parties from holding meetings and denied them access to larger and better-equipped government conference rooms while facilitating the activities of the pro-Bouteflika National Liberation Front (FLN).

A party must have received 4 percent of the vote, or at least 2,000 votes, in 25 wilayas (provinces) in one of the last three legislative elections to participate in national elections, making it very difficult in practice to create new political paties.

Membership in the Islamic Salvation Front (FIS), a political party banned in 1992, remained illegal due to the party's ties to the violence of the 1990s, which is estimated to have claimed 200,000 lives. The law also bans political party ties to nonpolitical associations and regulates party financing and reporting requirements. According to the law political parties cannot receive direct or indirect financial or material support from any foreign parties. The law also stipulates that resources are collected from contributions of the party's members, donations, and revenue from its activities, in addition to possible state funding.

Participation of Women and Minorities: In accordance with the law, the government promoted political rights for women by encouraging increased female representation within elected assemblies. In November both houses of parliament passed a law setting the terms for expanding women's representation in elected assemblies. In future elections, women must make up between 20 and 50 percent of candidates depending on the population and number of seats the wilaya holds in parliament's lower house.

There were three women in the cabinet. Women also held 30 of the 389 seats in the Popular Assembly of the Nation, the lower legislative chamber, and seven of the 144 seats in the Council of the Nation, the upper chamber. A woman led the Workers Party, and three major political parties—the FLN, National Rally for Democracy, and RCD—had women's divisions headed by women. The ethnic Amazigh (Berber) population of approximately 10 million participated freely and actively in the political process and represented one-third of the government.

Principal Government Officials

Last Updated: 1/31/2013

Pres.: **Abdelaziz BOUTEFLIKA**
Prime Min.: **Abdelmakek SELLAL**
Min. of Agriculture & Rural Development: **Rachid BENAISSA**
Min. of Commerce: **Mustapha BENBADA**
Min. of Communication: **Mohamed Oussaid BELAID**
Min. of Culture: **Khalida TOUMI**
Min. of Energy & Mining: **Youcef YOUSFI**
Min. of Finance: **Karim DJOUDI**
Min. of Fisheries & Fishing Resources: **Sid Ahmed FERROUKHI**
Min. of Foreign Affairs: **Mourad MEDELCI**
Min. of Health, Population, & Hospital Reform: **Abdelaziz ZIARI**
Min. of Higher Education & Scientific Research: **Rachid HARRAOUBIA**
Min. of Housing & Urban Development: **Abdelmadjid TEBBOUNE**
Min. of Industry, Small & Medium-Sized Enterprises, & Promotion of Investment: **Cherif RAHMANI**
Min. of Interior & Local Govts.: **Dahou OULD KABLIA**
Min. of Justice & Keeper of the Seals: **Mohamed CHARFI**
Min. of Labor, Employment, & Social Security: **Tayeb LOUH**
Min. of National Defense: **Abdelaziz BOUTEFLIKA**
Min. of National Education: **Abdelatif BABA AHMED**
Min. of National Solidarity & Family: **Souad BENDJABALLAH**
Min. of Postal Services & Information & Communication Technologies:**Moussa BENHAMADI**
Min. of Prospective Planning & Statistics: **Abdelhamid TEMMAR**
Min. of Public Works: **Amar GHOUL**
Min. of Relations With the Parliament: **Mahmoud KHEDRI**
Min. of Religious Affairs: **Bouabdellah GHLAMALLAH**
Min. of Territorial Management & the Environment: **Amara BENYOUNES**

Min. of Tourism & Handicrafts: **Mohamed BENMERADI**
Min. of Transport: **Amar TOU**
Min. of Vocational & Educational Training: **Mohamed MEBARKI**
Min. of War Veterans (Moudjahidine): **Mohamed Cherif ABBAS**
Min. of Water Resources: **Hocine NECIB**
Min. of Youth & Sports: **Mohamed TAHMI**
Min.-Del. to the Min. of Foreign Affairs in Charge of Maghreb & African Affairs: **Abdelkader MESSAHEL**
Min.-Del. to the Min. of National Defense: **Abdelmalek GUENAIZIA**
Sec. of State to the Prime Min. for Prospective & Statistics: **Bashir MASSAITFA**
Sec. of State to the Min. of Foreign Affairs for the National Community Abroad: **Belkacem SAHLI**
Sec. of State to the Min. of Territorial Management & the Environment: **Dalila BOUDJEMAA**
Sec. of State to the Min. of Tourism & Handicrafts for Tourism: **Mohamed Amine HADJ-SAID**
Sec. of State to the Min. of Youth & Sports for Youth: **Belkacem MELLAH**
Sec. Gen. to the Govt.: **Ahmed NOUI**
Governor, Bank of Algeria: **Mohamed LAKSACI**
Ambassador to the US: **Abdallah BAALI**
Permanent Representative to the UN, New York: **Mourad BENMEHIDI**

ECONOMY

Algeria's economy remains dominated by the state, a legacy of the country''s socialist post-independence development model. In recent years the Algerian Government has halted the privatization of state-owned industries and imposed restrictions on imports and foreign involvement in its economy.

Hydrocarbons have long been the backbone of the economy, accounting for roughly 60% of budget revenues, 30% of GDP, and over 95% of export earnings. Algeria has the 10th-largest reserves of natural gas in the world and is the sixth-largest gas exporter. It ranks 16th in oil reserves.

Thanks to strong hydrocarbon revenues, Algeria has a cushion of $173 billion in foreign currency reserves and a large hydrocarbon stabilization fund. In addition, Algeria''s external debt is extremely low at about 2% of GDP. Algeria has struggled to develop industries outside of hydrocarbons in part because of high costs and an inert state bureaucracy. The government''s efforts to diversify the economy by attracting foreign and domestic investment outside the energy sector have done little to reduce high youth unemployment rates or to address housing shortages.

A wave of economic protests in February and March 2011 prompted the Algerian Government to offer more than $23 billion in public grants and retroactive salary and benefit increases. Public spending has increased by 27% annually during the past five years. Long-term economic challenges include diversification from hydrocarbons, relaxing state control of the economy, and providing adequate jobs for younger Algerians.

Labor Conditions

The minimum legal age for employment is 16 years, but children that are younger may work as apprentices with permission from their parents or legal guardian. The law prohibits minors from working in dangerous or harmful work, but it does not establish a list of hazardous occupations prohibited to minors, nor does it cover work in the informal sector.

The national minimum wage of 15,000 dinars (approximately $203) per month was established in 2009 following a tripartite social pact between business, government and the official union. This did not provide a decent standard of living for a worker and family. In September the tripartite agreed to increase the monthly minimum wage to 18,000 dinars (approximately $244). Autonomous unions, which were not included in tripartite talks, reported the increase was inadequate and would not affect the majority of workers who already earn more than the minimum wage. Families making only 8,000 dinars (approximately $108) per month are considered to be living in poverty.

The standard workweek was 40 hours, including one hour for lunch per day. Employees who worked longer than the standard workweek received premium pay on a sliding scale from time-and-a-half to double-time, depending on whether the overtime was worked on a normal workday, a weekend, or a holiday.

The law contains occupational health and safety standards, which were not fully enforced. Economic migrants from sub-Saharan Africa and elsewhere working in the country without legal immigration status were not protected by the country's labor standards, making them vulnerable to exploitation. Labor law does not adequately cover migrant workers, who primarily are employed in the construction and domestic help sectors.

U.S.-ALGERIAN RELATIONS

The United States established diplomatic relations with Algeria in 1962 following its independence from France. Algeria severed relations with the United States in 1967, in the wake of the Arab-Israeli War. Relations were reestablished in 1974.

The United States and Algeria consult closely on key international and regional issues such as law enforcement cooperation, both in the field of counterterrorism and in countering more conventional transnational crimes. The two countries have finalized language for a customs mutual assistance agreement and have signed a mutual legal assistance treaty. The United States and Algeria have conducted bilateral military exercises. Exchanges between the Algerian and U.S. militaries are frequent, Algeria has hosted senior U.S. military officials and ship visits, and the United States hosted an Algerian port visit for the first time this year.

Algeria has remained relatively stable despite the turmoil that has engulfed the region beginning in 2011. While there have been sporadic demonstrations, they have remained primarily socio-economic in nature, with few calls for the government to step down. The United States viewed legislative elections held in 2012 as a welcome step in Algeria's progress toward democratic reform.

U.S. Assistance to Algeria

U.S. bilateral foreign assistance to Algeria is designed to strengthen Algeria's capacity to combat terrorism and crime, and support the building of stable institutions that contribute to the security and stability of the region. Foreign assistance supports Algeria's ongoing fight against al-Qaeda in the Islamic Maghreb and other hostile actors in the region.

Funding through the Middle East Partnership Initiative (MEPI) has been allocated to support the work of Algeria's developing civil society through programming that provides training to journalists, businesspeople, female entrepreneurs, legislators, legal professionals, and the heads of leading nongovernmental organizations. MEPI also has provided funding for economic development programs, and U.S. outreach programs support education in Algeria.

Bilateral Economic Relations

The United States is one of Algeria's top trading partners, and Algeria is one of the top U.S. trading partners in the Middle East/North African region. Most U.S. direct investment in Algeria has been in the hydrocarbon sector. The main U.S. import from Algeria is crude oil. The two countries have signed a trade and investment framework agreement, establishing common principles on which the economic relationship is founded and forming a platform for negotiating other bilateral agreements.

The U.S. Government encourages Algeria to make necessary changes to accede to the World Trade Organization, move toward transparent economic policies, and liberalize its investment climate. The United States has funded a program supporting Algerian efforts to develop a functioning, transparent banking and income tax system.

Algeria's Membership in International Organizations

Algeria and the United States belong to a number of the same international organizations, including the United Nations, International Monetary Fund, and World Bank. Algeria also is a Partner for Cooperation with the Organization for Security and Cooperation in Europe, an observer to the Organization of American States, and an observer to the World Trade Organization.

Bilateral Representation

Algeria maintains an embassy in the United States at 2118 Kalorama Road NW, Washington, DC 20008, tel: (202) 265-2800.

Principal U.S. Embassy Officials

Last Updated: 1/14/2013

ALGIERS (E) 5, Chemin Cheikh Bachir Ibrahimi, +213 (770) 08-2000, Fax +213 (21) 60-7335, Workweek: Sun–Thurs 08:00-17:00, Website: http://algiers.usembassy.gov

DCM OMS:	Jo Anne Jurkiewicz
AMB OMS:	Jeanne Kincaid
Co-CLO:	John Paul Mcpherson
DCM/CHG:	Elizabeth Moore Aubin
FCS:	No American Presence
FM:	Robert Bunge
HRO:	Dane C Ferguson
ICITAP:	Gary Bennett
MGT:	Darian Arky
MLO/ODC:	MAJ Maureen Paulk
POL/ECON:	Sahar Khoury-Kincannon
POL/MIL:	Emira Kasem
SDO/DATT:	COL Dean Vitale
AMB:	Henry S. Ensher
CON:	Julie Stinehart
PAO:	Tashawna Bethea
GSO:	Rhonda Wells
RSO:	Nicole Deal
AFSA:	Ronald Ward
AGR:	James R. Dever
EEO:	Manilka Wijesooriya
FMO:	Manilka Wijesooriya
ICASS Chair:	COL Dean Vitale
IMO:	Nancy Chaudhry
ISO:	Steve White
ISSO:	Steve White
LEGATT:	Lucas Beebe
State ICASS:	Fred Nelson

TRAVEL

Consular Information Sheet

June 14, 2011

Country Description: Algeria is the second-largest country in Africa, with over four-fifths of its territory covered by the Sahara desert. The country has a population of 35 million people mainly located near the northern coast. Algeria is a multi-party, constitutional republic. Facilities for travelers are available in populated areas but sometimes limited in quality and quantity.

Smart Traveler Enrollment Program (STEP)/Embassy Locations: If you are going to live in or visit Algeria, please take the time to tell our Embassy about your trip. If you enroll in the Smart Traveler Enrollment Program, we can keep you up to date with important safety and security announcements. It will also help your friends and family get in touch with you in an emergency.

U.S. Embassy, Algiers, Algeria
5 Chemin Cheikh Bachir Ibrahimi, El-Biar 16030 Alger Algerie
Telephone: [213] 770-08-20-00, which can also be reached after hours.
Email: ACSAlgiers@state.gov

Entry/Exit Requirements: Passports and visas are required for U.S. citizens traveling to Algeria. The Algerian visa application must be typed in all capital letters. The Algerian Embassy no longer accepts handwritten visa applications. Algerian-American dual nationals can enter Algeria with either an Algerian visa in their U.S. passport or using an Algerian passport. We recommend that such dual nationals travel to Algeria using an Algerian visa in their U.S. passport. For the most current information on entry/exit requirements, travelers may contact the Embassy of the People's Democratic Republic of Algeria at 2137 Wyoming Avenue NW, Washington, DC 20008, telephone (202) 265-2800.

The U.S. Department of State is unaware of any HIV/AIDS entry restrictions for visitors to or foreign residents of Algeria.

Threats to Safety and Security: Terrorism continues to pose a threat to the safety and security of U.S. citizens traveling to Algeria. Terrorist activities, including bombings, false roadblocks, kidnappings, ambushes, and assassinations occur regularly, particularly in the Kabylie region east of Algiers. Terrorists continue to use vehicle-borne explosive devices like the ones used in the 2007 bombings in Algiers of the Prime Ministry, the UN headquarters, and the Algerian Constitutional Council. Additionally, in 2010, terrorists began using homemade rockets as well as daisy-chain explosive attacks similar to those used in Iraq. Kidnapping by terrorist organizations is a real threat to U.S. citizens in Algeria, particularly outside major cities (see below). The same group that has claimed responsibility for these attacks, al-Qaida in the Islamic Maghreb (AQIM), operates throughout most of Algeria, including its southern region, and has kidnapped foreigners in neighboring countries.

The Department of State recommends that U.S. citizens avoid overland travel in Algeria. U.S. citizens who reside or travel in Algeria should take prudent security measures while in the country, including making provisions for reliable support in the event of an emergency. Additionally, sporadic episodes of civil unrest have been known to occur. U.S. citizens should avoid large crowds and maintain security awareness at all times. Visitors to Algeria are advised to stay only in hotels where adequate security is provided. All visitors to Algeria should remain alert and adhere to prudent security practices, such as avoiding predictable travel patterns and maintaining a low profile.

Currently, Embassy staffing is at full capacity but may not be able to provide full emergency consular services in certain areas of the country due to security restrictions. U.S. government employees traveling between cities must be accompanied by a security escort. Overland travel is not recommended. U.S. citizens should also carefully consider the security risks involved when using public transportation, such as buses and taxis.

Stay up to date by bookmarking our Bureau of Consular Affairs website, which contains the current Travel Warnings and Travel Alerts as well as the Worldwide Caution. Follow us on Twitter and become a fan of the Bureau of Consular Affairs page on Facebook as well.

You can also call 1-888-407-4747 toll-free within the United States and Canada, or by calling a regular toll line, 1-202-501-4444, from other countries. These numbers are available from 8:00 a.m. to 8:00 p.m. Eastern Time, Monday through Friday (except U.S. federal holidays).

Take some time before travel to improve your personal security—things are not the same everywhere as they are in the United States.

Crime: The crime rate in Algeria is moderate. Serious crimes have been reported in which armed men posing as police officers have entered homes and robbed the occupants at gunpoint. Petty theft and home burglary occur frequently, and muggings are on the rise, especially after dark in the cities. Theft of contents and parts from parked cars, pick-pocketing, theft on trains and buses, theft of items left in hotel rooms, and purse snatching are common. Alarms, grills, and/or guards help to protect most foreigners' residences.

Kidnappings, orchestrated by both criminals and terrorists, are a common occurrence in Algeria. Kidnappings for ransom occur intermittently in the Kabylie region. Kidnapping by terrorist organizations is an immediate threat in both the Kabylie region in northeastern Algeria and the trans-Sahara region in the south. An Italian tourist was kidnapped by AQIM in February 2011. In January 2011, two Frenchmen were kidnapped by AQIM in Niamey, Niger, and were killed during a rescue attempt on the Algeria-Mali border. In September 2010, AQIM kidnapped five French citizens along with a Togolese and a Malagasy national in Niger, and the four still in captivity are thought to be held in northeast Mali.

Don't buy counterfeit and pirated goods, even if they are widely available. Not only are the bootlegs illegal in the United States, you may be breaking local law, too.

Social unrest has become commonplace in Algeria. The frequency and intensity of localized, sporadic, and usually spontaneous civil disturbances rose dramatically in 2010 and 2011. These disturbances are overwhelmingly based in longstanding, deeply seated socio-economic grievances. Some people involved in these protests, demonstrations, and riots have ignited fireworks, thrown Molotov cocktails, brandished knives, looted businesses, damaged property, and robbed passersby. Most victims displayed obvious signs of wealth and were targets of opportunity. Travelers should avoid crowds, protests, demonstrations, and riots.

Victims of Crime: If you or someone you know becomes the victim of a crime abroad, you should contact the local police and the nearest U.S. embassy or consulate (see the Department of State's list of embassies and consulates). If your passport is stolen, we can help you replace it. For violent crimes such as assault and rape, we can, for example, help you find appropriate medical care, contact family members or friends, and help you receive money from them if you need it. Although the investigation and prosecution of any crime are solely the responsibility of local authorities, consular officers can help you to understand the local criminal justice process and to find an attorney, if needed.

The local equivalent to the "911" emergency line in Algeria is: 17 for the police and 14 in case of fire. These numbers may only be dialed from landline phones. From a mobile phone, dial 021-71-14-14 in case of fire; 021-23-63-81 for an ambulance; 021-73-53-50 for the police. Reliability and response time of emergency services vary but are not to U.S. standards. Emergency operators may or may not speak French and normally do not speak English.

Criminal Penalties: While you are traveling in another country, you are subject to its laws even if you are a U.S. citizen. Foreign laws and legal systems can be vastly different from our own. In some places, you may be taken in for questioning if you don't have your passport with you. In some places, it is illegal to take pictures of certain buildings. In some places, driving under the influence could land you immediately in jail. These criminal penalties will vary from country to country. There are also some things that might be legal in the country you visit but still illegal in the United States, and you can be prosecuted under U.S. law if you buy pirated goods. Engaging in sexual conduct with children or using or disseminating child pornography in a foreign country is a crime prosecutable in the United States. While you are overseas, U.S. laws don't apply. If you do something illegal in your host country, your U.S. passport won't help. It's very important to know what's legal and what's not where you are going. Persons violating Algerian laws, even unknowingly, may be expelled, arrested, or imprisoned. Penalties for possession, use, or trafficking in illegal drugs in Algeria are severe, and convicted offenders can expect long jail sentences and heavy fines. If you are arrested in Algeria authorities of Algeria are required to notify the nearest U.S. embassy or consulate of your arrest. If you are concerned the Department of State may not be aware of your situation, you should request the police or prison officials to notify the nearest U.S. embassy or consulate of your arrest.

Special Circumstances: ALL foreign currency being brought into Algeria should be disclosed when entering the country. While this requirement is not publicized when entering the country, upon arrival you should ask a customs official for a form to declare foreign currency. Each person leaving Algeria will be stopped and asked if he/she has any foreign money and will possibly be searched. If foreign currency was declared when entering the country, any disparity between the amount arrived with, and the amount held at departure, must be accounted for. If a traveler failed to declare any currency when entering Algeria, and is found to possess foreign currency while exiting the country, the penalties may be severe.

Foreign currency must be exchanged only at banks or authorized currency exchange locations, such as major hotels. Photography of military and government installations is prohibited. It is also illegal to import weapons, body armor, handcuffs, or binoculars.

Proselytizing: Islam is the state religion of Algeria. The Algerian government allows non-Muslim religious worship only in structures exclusively intended and approved for that purpose. Activities such as proselytizing, engaging in activities the Algerian authorities could view as encouraging conversion to another faith, and convening religious ceremonies in private residences are prohibited.

Accessibility: While in Algeria, individuals with disabilities, particularly physical ones limiting mobility, may find accessibility and accommodations lacking compared to the United States. The condition of sidewalks and streets is often poor, and there are almost no curb cuts or other modifications made for wheelchairs. Street curbs in Algeria stand much higher than those in the U.S., and a person in a wheelchair would require significant assistance in negotiating curbs. Hotels, restaurants, and most government buildings are not accessible to persons with physical disabilities. Restrooms and elevators rarely can accommodate wheelchairs. Very few vehicles, notably buses and taxis, are accessible for persons with serious physical disabilities.

Medical Facilities and Health Information: Hospitals and clinics in Algeria are available and improving in the large urban centers but are still not up to Western standards. Doctors and hospitals often expect immediate cash payment for services. Most medical practitioners speak French; English is not widely used.

Prescription medicines are not always readily available. Some pharmacies may at times be out-of-stock. In addition, the medicine may be sold under a different brand name and may contain a different dosage from in the United States. Please be aware that some newer medications may not yet be available in Algeria. It is usually easy to obtain over-the-counter products. Emergency services are satisfactory, but response time is often unpredictable. In all cases, response time is not as fast as in the United States.

Cases of tuberculosis are regularly reported but do not reach endemic levels. Every summer, public health authorities report limited occurrences of water-borne diseases, such as typhoid. In addition, HIV/AIDS is a concern in the remote southern part of the country, especially in border towns. You can find good information on vaccinations and other health precautions, on the CDC website. For information about outbreaks of infectious diseases abroad, consult the World Health Organization (WHO) website. The WHO website also contains additional health information for travelers, including detailed country-specific health information.

Medical Insurance: You can't assume your insurance will go with you when you travel. It's very important to find out BEFORE you leave.

You need to ask your insurance company two questions:

- Does my policy apply when I'm out of the U.S.?
- Will it cover emergencies like a trip to a foreign hospital or an evacuation?

In many places, doctors and hospitals still expect payment in cash at the time of service. Your regular U.S. health insurance may not cover doctors' and hospital visits in other countries. If your policy doesn't go with you when you travel, it's a very good idea to take out another one for your trip.

Traffic Safety and Road Conditions: While in a foreign country, U.S. citizens may encounter road conditions that differ significantly from those in the United States. The information below concerning Algeria is provided for general reference only, and may not be totally accurate in a particular location or circumstance. Algerian roads are overcrowded, and traffic-related accidents kill a large number of people every year. Drivers will encounter police and military checkpoints on major roads within and on the periphery of Algiers and other major cities. Security personnel at these checkpoints expect full cooperation. Motorists should be aware that terrorists employ false roadblocks as a tactic for ambushes and kidnappings, primarily in the central regions of Boumerdes and Tizi Ouzou and some parts of eastern Algeria. Travel overland, particularly in the southern regions, may require a permit issued by the Algerian government. For specific information concerning Algerian driver's permits, vehicle inspection, road tax, and mandatory insurance, contact the Algerian embassy.

Aviation Safety Oversight: As there is no direct commercial air service to the United States by carriers registered in Algeria, the U.S. Federal Aviation Administration (FAA) has not assessed the government of Algeria's Civil Aviation Authority for compliance with International Civil Aviation Organization (ICAO) aviation safety standards. Further information may be found on the FAA's safety assessment page.

Children's Issues: Please see the U.S. Dept. of State Office of Children's Issues web pages on intercountry adoption and international parental child abduction.

Travel Warning

January 19, 2013

The Department of State warns U.S. citizens of the risks of travel to Algeria. This replaces the Travel Warning for Algeria dated September 13, 2012, to update information on the current security situation in Algeria, the continuing threat posed by terrorism, and to reiterate information on security incidents and recommendations on security awareness.

On January 19, 2013, the Department of State authorized the departure from Algiers for eligible family members following the attack on the In Amenas BP Oil facility on January 16, 2013 and subsequent, credible threats of the kidnapping of western nationals. While the Consular Section is open for public services, the Embassy's ability to respond to emergencies involving U.S. citizens throughout Algeria is limited.

The Department of State urges U.S. citizens who travel to Algeria to evaluate carefully the risks posed to their personal safety. There is a high threat of terrorism and kidnappings in Algeria. This kidnapping threat was noted in the Department of State's Worldwide Caution dated July 18, 2012. Although the major cities are heavily policed, attacks could still potentially take place. The majority of terrorist attacks, including bombings, false roadblocks, kidnappings, and ambushes occur in areas of the country east and south of Algiers.

Al-Qaida in the Lands of the Islamic Maghreb (AQIM) is active and operates throughout Algeria. They claimed credit for the December 2007 United Nations bombings in Algeria, the last major attack in the capital, and have pledged to carry out more attacks. In February 2011, AQIM claimed responsibility for the kidnapping of an Italian citizen and her Algerian driver; and also the suicide bomb attack at the Algerian Military Academy in Cherchell, 48 miles west of Algiers in August 2011. The Movement for Unity and Jihad in West Africa (MUJAO) is also active in Algeria. In October 2011, they kidnapped two Spanish nationals and an Italian national from a refugee camp 1,088 miles southwest of Algiers in Tindouf. In March 2012, MUJAO claimed responsibility for the car bomb attack at an Algerian military base 1,196 miles south of Algiers in Tamanrasset and a similar car bomb attack at another base 478 miles south/southeast of Algiers in Ouargla.

The Department of State recommends that U.S. citizens avoid overland travel in Algeria. U.S. citizens who reside in or travel to Algeria should take personal security measures to include stocking adequate reserves of medicine, food, and water for use during an emergency. Additionally, sporadic episodes of civil unrest have been known to occur, such as the riots in Algiers and many other cities from January 2011 to the present. U.S. citizens should avoid large crowds and demonstrations because even demonstrations that are meant to be peaceful can become violent and unpredictable. U.S. citizens should be alert and aware of their surroundings and maintain security awareness at all times. U.S. citizens should regularly monitor the local news media for current news and information.

Visitors to Algeria are advised to stay only in hotels where adequate security is provided. All visitors to Algeria should remain alert, avoid predictable travel patterns and maintain a low profile. U.S. citizens should avoid political rallies of all kinds. Most political gatherings are peaceful but can turn violent without notice.

The U.S. government considers the potential threat to U.S. Embassy personnel assigned to Algiers sufficiently serious to require them to live and work under significant security restrictions. These practices limit, and may occasionally prevent, the movement of U.S. Embassy officials and the provision of consular services in certain areas of the country. The Government of Algeria requires U.S. Embassy personnel to seek permission to travel to the Casbah within Algiers or outside the province of Algiers and to have a security escort. Travel to the military zone established around the Hassi Messaoud oil center requires Government of Algeria authorization. Daily movement of Embassy personnel in parts of Algiers is limited, and prudent security practices ae required at all times. Travel by Embassy personnel within certain areas of the city requires coordination with the U.S. Embassy's Regional Security Office.

U.S. citizens living or traveling in Algeria are encouraged to enroll in the Department of State's Smart Traveler Enrollment Program (STEP) to receive the latest travel updates and to obtain updated information on security within Algeria. By enrolling, U.S. citizens make it easier for the Embassy to contact them in case of emergency.

For the latest security information, U.S. citizens living abroad should regularly monitor the Department of State's Bureau of Consular Affairs Internet website, where the current Worldwide Caution, Travel Alerts, Travel Warnings, and Country Specific Information can be found. Follow us on Twitter and the Bureau of Consular Affairs page on facebook as well. You can also download our free Smart Traveler App, available through iTunes and the Android market, to have travel information at your fingertips.

Up-to-date information on security can also be obtained by calling 1-888-407-4747 toll-free in the United States and Canada or, for callers outside the United States and Canada, on a regular toll line at 1-202-501-4444. These numbers are available from 8:00 a.m. to 8:00 p.m. Eastern Standard Time, Monday through Friday (except U.S. federal holidays).

The U.S. Embassy is located at 5 Chemin Cheikh Bachir El-Ibrahimi in the El Biar district of Algiers, and can be reached by telephone at (213) 770 08 20 00. The fax is {213} 21 98 22 99. The consular section email is ACSAlgiers@state.gov.

Intercountry Adoption

November 2011

The information in this section has been edited from the latest report available as of February 2013 from the State Department Bureau of Consular Affairs, Office of Overseas Citizens Services. For more information, please read the *Intercountry Adoption* section of this book and review current reports online at http://adoption.state.gov.

Algeria is not party to the Hague Convention on Protection of Children and Co-operation in Respect of Intercountry Adoption (Hague Adoption Convention). Therefore, when the Hague Adoption Convention entered into force for the United States on April 1, 2008, intercountry adoption processing for Algeria did not change.

Algerian family law is based on an interpretation of Islamic law. Algerian courts appoint a legal guardian ("Kafil"—see Algerian statute No. 84/11, articles 116 through 125) for a child. Such legal guardianship (called a "kafala") is treated as the functional equivalent of adoption. If a child has a known parent, the guardian can only be selected from blood relatives of the child (i.e., the child's next of kin). Obviously, if a child's parents are unknown, that does not apply. The prospective adoptive parent can request that the child's name be changed when the biological father of the child is unknown. However, if the identity of the child's biological mother is known and the biological mother is living, a formal consent deed for the name change must be executed by the biological mother. The executed consent deed is then attached to the name change request file, and decided upon by the president of the relevant Algerian court at the referral of the prosecutor. Algeria is the only Muslim country which will authorize a name change for an orphan. Any prospective adoptive parent of an Algerian child should start the application for a kafala at the Algerian Embassy in Washington, D.C.

Who Can Adopt? To bring an adopted child to United States from Algeria, you must be found eligible to adopt by the U.S. Government. The U.S. Government agency responsible for making this determination is the Department of Homeland Security, U.S. Citizenship and Immigration Services (USCIS).

Residency Requirements: An adoptive parent must be an Algerian citizen, and can be living either in Algeria or overseas. If the adoptive parent is living overseas, s/he must attach to the application form (i) a social investigation duly completed and signed by the Algerian consulate authorities in the country where that adoptive parent lives and (ii) a copy of the registration card given to Algerian citizens when they register with the Algerian consulate abroad.

Age Requirements: Men should not be over the age of 60, and women should not be over the age of 55. However, these criteria may be changed at the discretion of the commission reviewing the application file.

Marriage Requirements: The same rules apply to single, divorced or widowed individuals.

Income Requirements: A prospective adoptive parent must be able to prove sufficient income to support the child and provide decent accommodation. The prospective adoptive parent must have financial resources of at least the equivalent of 15,000 Algerian dinar per month. If the prospective adoptive parent is living overseas, the Algerian consulate may require a higher minimum income commensurate with income levels in that country.

Other Requirements: The prospective legal guardian must be of the Muslim faith and Algerian nationality, and supply medical certificates showing s/he is in good physical and mental health. In addition, s/he has to be a person of integrity, capable of protecting and entertaining the child, and capable of providing decent and salubrious accommodation for the child.

Who Can Be Adopted? Algeria has specific requirements that a child must meet in order to be eligible for adoption. You cannot adopt a child in Algeria unless he or she meets the requirements outlined below. In addition to these requirements, a child must meet the definition of an orphan under U.S. law for you to bring him or her back to the United States.

Relinquishment Requirements: A definitive agreement for the child's affiliation is given after the signature of the minute of abandonment by the mother.

Abandonment Requirements: The child's parents are unknown.

Age Requirements: Under nineteen (19) years old.

Sibling Requirements: not applicable

Waiting Period: Three months after the signing of the minute of abandonment by the biological mother and after the psychological interview of the prospective parents by the investigation team in the country of residence of the prospective adoptive parent.

The Process: There are no adoption agencies operating in Algeria. The first step in adopting a child from Algeria is to decide whether or not to use an Adoption Service Provider licensed agency in the United States that can help with your adoption. Adoption service providers must be licensed by the U.S. state in which they operate. To bring an adopted child from Algeria to the United States, you must apply to be found eligible to adopt (Form I-600A) by the U.S. Government, Department of Homeland Security, U.S. Citizenship and Immigration Services (USCIS). In addition to meeting the U.S. requirements for adoptive parents, you need to meet the requirements of Algeria If you are eligible to adopt, and a child is available for intercountry adoption, the Commission of the Ministry of National Solidarity in Algeria will provide you with a list of orphanages in Algeria that you can than consult with to determine if any eligible children are available. Each family must decide for itself whether or not it will be able to meet the needs of a particular child and provide a permanent family placement for that child. The child must be eligible to be adopted according to Algeria's requirements. The child must also meet the definition of an orphan under U.S. law.

Role of the Algerian Embassy: First, a prospective adoptive parent must submit a request for kafala to the Algerian Embassy in Washington, D.C. Once the Algerian Embassy receives this request and accompanying information, its social services division will begin an investigation of the prospective parents.

If the social services division provides a positive recommendation for adoption, the Algerian Embassy will forward the file to the Ministry of Foreign Affairs in Algeria, which will in turn forward the file to the Ministry of National Solidarity. The Commission of the Ministry of National Solidarity will ultimately make the decision of whether or not to grant kafala. The Commission of the Ministry of National Solidarity only meets every three months.

Role of the Court: Issues the name change document, if any.

Adoption Application: This consists of the request for kafala described elsewhere.

Time Frame: The U.S Embassy cannot predict how long the process will take. The process of obtaining kafala is generally a long one.

Adoption Fees: There are no fees for the process of obtaining kafala. The orphanages in Algiers (the "pouponnieres") do not require any payment.

Documents Required: When submitting a request for legal custody to the Algerian Embassy, the prospective parent should include: (1) a written request for kafala, including his or her reasons for desiring the kafala; (2) a birth certificate for each of the prospective adoptive parents; (3) the family form ('fiche familiale') for married prospective adoptive parents, (4) medical certificates; (5) a criminal records delivered by authorities of the country of residence; (6) work certificates; (7) pay stubs for the last three months, (8) a copy of the consular registration card(s); (9) citizenship certificate of the prospective adoptive parents, (10) recent photo ID of the prospective parents and (11) proof of title or the residential lease agreement for their home. See http://www.algeria-us.org/content/view/102/25/. All documents should be translated into French, and dollar amounts should be converted into Euros.

Bringing Your Child Home: Once your adoption is complete (or you have obtained legal custody of the child), there are a few more steps to take before you can head home. Specifically, you need to apply for several documents for your child before he or she can travel to the United States, such as a birth certificate, a passport or travel document for your child from the country in which he or she was born, and a U.S. Immigration Visa.

For detailed and updated information on how to obtain these documents, review the *Intercountry Adoption* section in this publication and visit the U.S. Department of State Intercountry Adoption website at http://adoption.state.gov.

Child Citizenship Act: For adoptions finalized abroad, the Child Citizenship Act of 2000 allows your new child to acquire American citizenship automatically when he or she enters the United States as lawful permanent residents. For adoptions finalized in the United States, the Child Citizenship Act of 2000 allows your new child to acquire American citizenship automatically when the court in the United States issues the final adoption decree. To learn more, review the *Intercountry Adoption* section in this publication and visit the U.S. Department of State Intercountry Adoption website at http://adoption.state.gov.

U.S. Embassy in Algeria
5 Chemin Cheikh Bachir
El-Ibrahimi, 16000, Alger, Algerie
Tel: +213 021 98 20 00
Fax: +213 021 60 73 35
Email:
Algiers_webmaster@state.gov
http://algiers.usembassy.gov

Algeria's Ministry of Social Action and National Solidarity
Route Nationale No. 1 les vergers BP No. 31 Bir khadem
Alger, Algerie
Tel: +213 021 44 99 46/47
Fax: +213 021 44 97 26

Algeria Adoption Authority
Ministry of National Solidarity
Route Nationale No. 1 les vergers BP No. 31 Bir khadem
Alger, Algerie
Tel.: +213 021 44 99 46, +213 021 44 99 47
Fax: +213 021 44 97 26

Embassy of Algeria
2118 Kalorama Road, NW
Tel: (202) 265-2800
Fax: (202) 667-2174
Email: mail@algeria-us.org
Internet: http://www.algeria-us.org

Office of Children's Issues
U.S. Department of State
2201 C Street, NW
SA-29
Washington, DC 20520
Tel: 1-888-407-4747
E-mail: AskCI@state.gov
http://adoption.state.gov

For questions about immigration procedures, call the National Customer Service Center (NCSC) at 1-800-375-5283 (TTY 1-800-767-1833).

ANDORRA

Compiled from publications that were available as of February 2013 from the U.S. Department of State, the U.S. Department of Commerce, and the Central Intelligence Agency (CIA). See the introduction to this set for explanatory notes.

Official Name:
Principality of Andorra

PROFILE

Geography

Area: total: 468 sq km; country comparison to the world: 196; land: 468 sq km; water: 0 sq km
Major cities: Andorra la Vella (capital) 25,000 (2009)
Climate: temperate; snowy, cold winters and warm, dry summers
Terrain: rugged mountains dissected by narrow valleys

People

Nationality: noun: Andorran(s); adjective: Andorran
Population: 85,082 (July 2012 est.)
Population growth rate: 0.274% (2012 est.)
Ethnic groups: Spanish 43%, Andorran 33%, Portuguese 11%, French 7%, other 6% (1998)
Religions: Roman Catholic (predominant)
Languages: Catalan (official), French, Castilian, Portuguese
Literacy: definition: age 15 and over can read and write; total population: 100%; male: 100%; female: 100%
Health: life expectancy at birth: total population: 82.5 years; male: 80.4 years; female: 84.74 years (2012 est.); Infant mortality rate: total: 3.76 deaths/1,000 live births; male: 3.74 deaths/1,000 live births; female: 3.79 deaths/1,000 live births
Unemployment rate: 1.9% (2011)
Work force: 38,220 (2011)

Government

Type: parliamentary democracy (since March 1993) that retains as its chiefs of state a coprincipality; the two princes are the president of France and bishop of Seu d'Urgell, Spain, who are represented in Andorra by the coprinces' representatives
Independence: 1278
Constitution: Andorra's first written constitution was drafted in 1991; approved by referendum 14 March 1993; effective 28 April 1993
Political subdivisions: 7 parishes (parroquies, singular—parroquia); Andorra la Vella, Canillo, Encamp, Escaldes-Engordany, La Massana, Ordino, Sant Julia de Loria
Suffrage: 18 years of age; universal

Economy

GDP (purchasing power parity): $3.119 billion (2012 est.); $3.169 billion (2011 est.); $3.227 billion (2010 est.); $3.3 billion (2009 est.)
GDP real growth rate: -1.6% (2012 est.); -1.8% (2011 est.); -2.2% (2010 est.); 3.8% (2009 est.)
GDP per capita (PPP): $37,200 (2011 est.); $37,200 (2011 est.); $37,700 (2010 est.)
Natural resources: hydropower, mineral water, timber, iron ore, lead
Agriculture products: small quantities of rye, wheat, barley, oats, vegetables; sheep
Industries: tourism (particularly skiing), cattle raising, timber, banking, tobacco, furniture
Exports: $70 million (2011); $89.5 million (2008)
Exports—commodities: tobacco products, furniture
Imports: $1.469 billion (2011); $1.801 billion (2008)
Imports—commodities: consumer goods, food, electricity
Debt—external: $NA
Exchange rates: euros (EUR) per US dollar; 0.7838 (2012 est.); 0.7194 (2011 est.); 0.755 (2010 est.); 0.7198 (2009 est.); 0.6827 (2008 est.)

PEOPLE

Andorrans live in seven valleys that form Andorra's political districts. Andorrans are a minority in their own country. Spanish, French, Portuguese, and other residents make up the more than 50% of the population.

Religion

No official government census exists based on religion; traditionally, approximately 90 percent of the population is Roman Catholic. The population consists largely of immigrants from Spain, Portugal, and France; citizens constitute only 37 percent of inhabitants. The country's immigrants are generally also Catholic.

There are nine other religious communities in the principality, which are well integrated into society. These include the following: the Muslim community, with an estimated 1,000 members; the Hindu community, with 500 members; the Anglican Church, with 500 members; and the Seventh-day Adventist Church, the Baha'i Faith, the Unification Church, and the New Apostolic Church, with approximately 100 members each.

There are also a small number of members of other Christian communities, including The Church of Jesus Christ of Latter-day Saints (Mormons) and Jehovah's Witnesses.

There are 51 Roman Catholic churches in the country. Additionally, there are 13 places of worship of other religious confessions. In most cases the cultural center serves as a place of worship.

Langauges

The national language is Catalan, a romance language related to the Provencal group. French and Spanish are also spoken.

Education

Education law requires school attendance for children up to age 16. A system of French, Spanish, and Andorran public schools provides education up to the secondary level. Schools are built and maintained by Andorran authorities, who pay also for Andorran teachers. French and Spanish schools pay for their own teachers. Andorran schools follow the Spanish curriculum, and their diplomas are recognized by the Spanish education system.

In 1997, the University of Andorra was established. The University of Andorra has two graduate schools; the Nursing School and the School of Computer Science. Students can obtain a degree in business administration, nursing, or education sciences as well as computer science. Students can also follow virtual studies with Spanish and French universities.

HISTORY

Andorra is the last independent survivor of the March states, a number of buffer states created by Charlemagne to keep the Muslim Moors from advancing into Christian France. Tradition holds that Charlemagne granted a charter to the Andorran people in return for their fighting the Moors. In the 800s, Charlemagne's grandson, Charles the Bald, made Count of Urgell overlord of Andorra. A descendant of the count later gave the lands to the diocese of Urgell, headed by Bishop of Seu d'Urgell. In the 11th century, fearing military action by neighboring lords, the bishop placed himself under the protection of the Lord of Caboet, a Spanish nobleman. Later, the Count of Foix, a French noble, became heir to Lord Caboet through marriage, and a dispute arose between the French Count and the Spanish bishop over Andorra.

In 1278, the conflict was resolved by the signing of a pareage, which provided that Andorra's sovereignty be shared between the Count of Foix and the Bishop of Seu d'Urgell of Spain. The pareage, a feudal institution recognizing the principle of equality of rights shared by two rulers, gave the small state its territory and political form. Over the years, the title was passed between French and Spanish rule until, in the reign of the French King Henry IV, an edict in 1607 established the head of the French state and the Bishop of Urgell as co-princes of Andorra.

Given its relative isolation, Andorra has existed outside the mainstream of European history, with few ties to countries other than France and Spain. In recent times, however, its thriving tourist industry and developments in transportation and communications have removed the country from its isolation.

GOVERNMENT AND POLITICAL CONDITIONS

The Principality of Andorra is a constitutional parliamentary democracy. Two co-princes—the president of France and the Spanish bishop of La Seu d'Urgell—serve with joint authority as heads of state, and a delegate represents each in the country.

The national police, the country's sole security force, reported to civilian authorities.

Recent Elections

On April 3, 2011, the country held free and fair multiparty elections for the 28 seats in the General Council of the Valleys (the parliament), which selects the head of government. Having won a majority in the parliament, the Democrats for Andorra (DA) elected Antoni Marti Petit as head of government. Observers considered the General Council elections on April 3 to be free and fair.

Participation of Women and Minorities: After the elections on April 3, there were 15 women in the 28-seat parliament, a majority for the first time. Two women sat in the nine-seat cabinet.

Citizens were ethnically and linguistically homogeneous but represented only 38 percent of the country's population. The majority of the population consists largely of immigrants from Spain, Portugal, and France. Because only citizens have the right to vote and hold official position, there were no members of minorities in government.

Principal Government Officials

Last Updated: 1/31/2013

Head of State (Co-Prince): **Francois HOLLANDE**
Head of State (Co-Prince): **Joan-Enric VIVES i SICILIA, Bishop**
Head of Govt.: **Antoni MARTI Petit**
Min. of Culture: **Albert Esteve GARCIA**
Min. of Economy & Territorial Planning: **Jordi ALCOBE**
Min. of Education, Youth, & Sports: **Roser SUNE**
Min. of Finance & Public Admin.: **Jordi CINCA Mateos**
Min. of Foreign Affairs: **Gilbert SABOYA Sunye**
Min. of Health: **Cristina RODRIGUEZ**
Min. of Justice & Interior: **Marc VILA**
Min. of Tourism & Environment: **Francesc CAMP**
Ambassador to the US: **Narcis CASAL de Fonsdeviela**
Permanent Representative to the UN, New York: **Narcis CASAL de Fonsdeviela**

ECONOMY

Tourism, retail sales, and finance are the mainstays of Andorra's tiny, well-to-do economy, accounting for more than three-quarters of GDP. About 9 million tourists visit annually, attracted by Andorra's duty-free status for some products and by its summer and winter resorts. The banking sector also contributes substantially to the economy. Andorra's comparative advantage as a tax haven eroded when the borders of neighboring France and Spain opened; its bank secrecy laws have been relaxed under pressure from the EU and OECD.

Agricultural production is limited—only 2% of the land is arable—and most food has to be imported, making the economy vulnerable to changes in fuel and food prices. The principal livestock activity is sheep raising. Manufacturing output and exports consist mainly of perfumes and cosmetic products, products of the printing industry, electrical machinery and equipment, clothing, tobacco products, and furniture.

Andorra is a member of the EU Customs Union and is treated as an EU member for trade in manufactured goods (no tariffs) and as a non-EU member for agricultural products. Andorra uses the euro and is effectively subject to the monetary policy of the European Central Bank. Slower growth in Spain and France has dimmed Andorra's prospects. In 2010 and 2011 a drop in tourism contributed to a contraction in GDP and a deterioration of public finances, prompting the government to implement several austerity measures.

Labor Conditions

Without exception, the law prohibits children younger than 14 from working. Children aged 14 and 15 may work up to two months per year during school holidays following strict regulations contained in the law. Laws limit work by children aged 14 and 15 to no more than six hours per day and by children aged 16 and 17 to eight hours per day, provide for safety restrictions, restrict the type of work children may perform, and outline other conditions. Laws protect children from exploitation in the workplace, and the government effectively enforced these laws. The labor inspection office in the Ministry of Social Welfare, Public Health, and Labor effectively enforced child labor regulations.

The national minimum wage is 5.36 euros ($ 6.97) per hour and 929.07 euros ($1,210) per month. The labor inspection office enforced the minimum wage effectively. The law limits the standard workweek to five eight-hour days for a total of 40 hours per week. Workers may work up to two overtime hours per day or 15 hours per week, 50 hours per month, and 426 hours per year.

The law provides for premium pay of time plus 25 percent the first four hours per week and time plus 50 percent the following four hours. There is a required rest period of 12 hours between working shifts. The labor inspection office sets occupational health and safety standards and has the authority to levy sanctions and fines against companies violating them. The law includes agricultural, domestic, and migrant workers.

U.S.-ANDORRAN RELATIONS

The United States established diplomatic relations with Andorra in 1995, following Andorra's 1993 adoption of a constitution establishing the country as a sovereign parliamentary democracy. It retains as its heads of state two co-princes — the Bishop of Urgell (Spain) and the French president. The United States and Andorra enjoy excellent relations based on common values including the promotion of democracy and human rights.

Since 2000, Andorra has participated in the Fulbright Exchange Program. The two countries have also signed a Bilateral Work Agreement for dependents of members of diplomatic missions and consular posts assigned to official duty in the respective countries and will soon conclude an agreement on the sharing of confiscated proceeds and instrumentalities of crimes. Andorra supports U.S. foreign policy positions and objectives, such as voting for U.S. candidates to international organizations.

The U.S. Ambassador to Spain is also accredited as Ambassador to Andorra. The U.S. Consul General based in Barcelona is responsible for the day-to-day management of relations with Andorra. She travels regularly to Andorra to carry out diplomatic demarches, represent U.S. interests, and administer consular services.

U.S. Assistance to Andorra

The United States provides no development assistance to Andorra.

Bilateral Economic Relations

The United States has no significant trade or investment with Andorra. The new investment law approved in mid- 2012 opens the country to foreign investment and this foreign investors will be able for the first time to gain full ownership of a business. The investment climate in the country has changed significantly with this new legislation liberalizing the Andorran economy.

Andorra participates in the Visa Waiver Program, which allows nationals of participating countries to travel to the United States for certain business or tourism purposes for stays of 90 days or less without obtaining a visa.

Andorra's Membership in International Organizations

Andorra and the United States belong to a number of the same international organizations, including the United Nations and Organization for Security and Cooperation in Europe; as well as the United Nations Educational, Scientific and Cultural Organization (UNESCO), and the World Health Organization (WHO). Andorra also is an observer to the World Trade Organization. A member of the Council of Europe, from November 2012 to May 2013, Andorra will chair its Committee of Ministers. Since 1991, Andorra has had a special agreement with the European Union.

Bilateral Representation

Andorra has no embassy in Washington, D.C., but maintains a permanent representative to the United Nations in New York who also is simultaneously accredited as ambassador to the United States.

Principal U.S. Embassy Officials

Last Updated: 1/14/2013

MADRID (E) C/ Serrano 75, (34) 91-587-2200, Fax (34) 91-587-2303, INMARSAT Tel 8816-763-10973, Workweek: 08:30 to 17:30, Website: http://madrid.usembassy.gov/

DCM OMS:	Marguerite Santos
AMB OMS:	Jennifer Garcia
CG OMS:	Maribel Gomez
Co-CLO:	Laura Smyth
DHS/ICE:	Alejandro Alonso
DHS/TSA:	Tere Franceschi
FCS:	Robert Jones
FM:	Matthew Jennings
GFS:	Frankfurt
HRO:	Matthew Johnson
MGT:	Kimberly Deblauw
MLO/ODC:	CAPT Gregory Molinari
POL/MIL:	Eric Mehler
POSHO:	Matthew Jennings
SDO/DATT:	CAPT Capt Scott Gage
AMB:	Alan D. Solomont
CG:	Kathleen Hennessey
DCM:	Luis G. Moreno
PAO:	Kate Byrnes
GSO:	Mary Lou Gonzales
RSO:	Lisa Grice
AFSA:	Klaudia Krueger
AGR:	Robert Hanson
CLO:	Julianne Price
DEA:	Richard Bendekovic
ECON:	Stephen Liston
EEO:	Christine Fagan
EST:	Ari Nathan
FMO:	Scarlet Feller
ICASS Chair:	Robert Hanson
IMO:	Marcellus Davis
IPO:	Jay Biddulph
ISO:	Clifton Reeves
ISSO:	Clifton Reeves
LEGATT:	Marc Varri
POL:	Amy Tachco
State ICASS:	Kathleen Hennessey

TRAVEL

Consular Information Sheet—Spain and Andorra

December 21, 2011

Country Description: Spain and Andorra are both advanced stable democracies and modern economies. Spain is a member of the North Atlantic Treaty Organization (NATO) and the European Union.

Smart Traveler Enrollment Program (Step)/Embassy Location: If you are going to live in or visit Spain or Andorra, please take the time to tell our Embassy (and/or Consulate) about your trip. If you enroll, we can keep you up to date with important safety and security announcements. It will also help your friends and family get in touch with you in an emergency.

U.S. Embassy Madrid
Calle Serrano, 75
28006 Madrid, Spain
Telephone: (34) 91 587 2240
Emergency after-hours telephone: (34) 91 587 2200
Facsimile: (34) 91 587 2303
Email: askacs@state.gov

U.S. Consulate General Barcelona
Paseo Reina Elisenda de Montcada, 23-25
08034 Barcelona, Spain
Telephone: (34) 93 280 2227
Emergency after-hours telephone: (34) 91 587 2200
Facsimile: (34) 93 280 6175 or (34) 93 205 5206
Email: consularbarcel@state.gov

You need to make an appointment for routine consular services. Additional information and appointments for routine services are available through the U.S. Citizen Services page on the embassy's website. To make an appointment, please visit the U.S. Embassy's online appointment system.

There are six consular agencies in Spain, which provide limited services to U.S. citizens, but are not authorized to issue passports. Anyone requesting service at one of the consular agencies should call ahead to verify that the service requested will be available on the day you expect to visit the agency. The agencies' contact information is below. Please note that the emergency after-hours telephone number for all of Spain is: (34) 91 587 2200. Ask to speak to the duty officer if you call this number for emergency assistance outside business hours. The U.S. Consulate General in Barcelona provides many services for U.S. citizens, including emergency passport services.

The U.S. Citizens Services Unit's assistance also includes, but is not limited to, routine passport services, notary services, and Consular Reports of Births Abroad. The Consulate General also assists in emergencies, including deaths, arrests and crisis situations. You need to make an appointment for routine consular services. For assistance regarding Andorra, please contact the U.S. Consulate General in Barcelona.

Entry/Exit Requirements for U.S. Citizens: Spain is a party to the Schengen Agreement. This means that U.S. citizens may enter Spain for up to 90 days for tourist or business purposes without a visa. Your passport should be valid for at least three months beyond the period of stay. You need sufficient funds and a return airline ticket. The Spanish Government scrutinizes visitors who overstay their visas or their visa-free entry per the Schengen Agreement. Immediate deportation after spending a number of days in jail is not uncommon.

You should leave Spain promptly at the end of the 90-day visa-free travel period or at the end of the time stated on your visa. U.S. citizens who wish to stay in Spain for longer than three months or who wish to apply for residency in Spain will also need to supply local authorities with an official criminal records check from their state of residence or from the Federal Bureau of Investigation's Criminal Justice Information Services office (CJIS).

Both types of documents must be apostilled by the state authority for state criminal records and by the Department of State for the FBI records. The embassy does not take fingerprints for the purpose of criminal records checks; rather, U.S. citizens can obtain a letter from the U.S. Embassy asking local police to take their fingerprints. Individuals need to make an appointment for notarial services to obtain the letter.

In an effort to prevent international child abduction, many governments have initiated procedures at entry/exit points. These often include requiring documentary evidence of relationship and permission for the child's travel from the parent(s) or legal guardian not present. Having such documentation on hand, even if not required, may facilitate entry/departure.

The U.S. Department of State is unaware of any HIV/AIDS entry restrictions for visitors to or foreign residents of Spain and Andorra. Visit the Embassy of Spain's website for the most current visa information.

For more information concerning entry requirements for Spain, travelers should contact the Embassy of Spain at 2375 Pennsylvania Avenue NW, Washington, DC 20037, telephone (202) 452-0100 or (202) 728-2340, or the nearest Spanish Consulate in Boston, Chicago, Houston, Los Angeles, Miami, New Orleans, New York, San Francisco, or San Juan. Information for the Spanish Embassy and consulates can be found at the Embassy of Spain's website.

Additional information can be found on the Spanish Ministry of Foreign Affairs website or obtained from the Tourist Office of Spain which has offices in several U.S. cities. Andorra does not have an airport, therefore all visitors to Andorra must enter via a land border with either Spain or France. There are no visa requirements for entry into Andorra for stays of up to three months; however, the relevant regulations for France or Spain should be followed, depending on which country is transited to reach Andorra. Andorra is not part of the Schengen area.

People entering Europe on a Schengen visa should therefore make sure that their visa entitles them to repeated visits to prevent them from being refused entry to Spain or France following a stay in Andorra.For more information on entry requirements to Andorra, travelers should contact the Andorran Mission to the UN, 2 U.N. Plaza, 25th floor, New York, NY 10018, telephone (212) 750-8064, email Andorra@un.int.

Threats to Safety and Security: Spain and Andorra share with the rest of the world an increased threat of international terrorist incidents.

Like other countries in the Schengen area, Spain's open borders with its Western European neighbors allow the possibility of terrorist groups entering and exiting the country with anonymity. Spain's proximity to North Africa makes it vulnerable to attack from al-Qa'ida terrorists in the Maghreb region. We remind U.S. citizens to remain vigilant with regard to their personal security and to exercise caution at all times.

In March 2004, Islamist extremists bombed four commuter trains entering Madrid, causing 191 deaths and over 1,400 injuries. Spanish authorities tried the suspected terrorists and their co-conspirators in February 2007 and they were convicted in October 2007. In October 2011, the Basque Fatherland and Liberty (ETA) terrorist organization publicly announced a "definitive cessation of armed activity" in the run-up to the November 20 Spanish general elections. While recent arrests have seriously weakened the organization and despite the October announcement, ETA remains a threat and has not disarmed or disbanded. ETA has historically avoided targeting foreigners, instead directing their attacks against the police, military, local politicians, and Spanish government targets as well as towards disrupting transportation and daily life. However, foreigners have been killed or injured collaterally in ETA attacks.

Two Ecuadorian nationals were killed in the Barajas Airport bombing in December 2006 , and 17 students were injured, including one American, in the bombing at the University of Navarre in October 2008. Though extortion threats have recently ceased in the Basque region, in the past, bombs have been used as part of criminal extortion of businesses.

The risk of being in the wrong place at the wrong time in event of an ETA action is a concern for foreign visitors and tourists. U.S. tourists traveling to Spain should remain vigilant, exercise caution, monitor local developments, and avoid demonstrations and other potentially violent situations. Bombings outside the Basque Country in Burgos and Palma de Mallorca in July 2009 underscore the importance of being vigilant.

Stay up to date by: Bookmarking our Bureau of Consular Affairs website, which contains the current Travel Warnings and Travel Alerts as well as the Worldwide Caution.; Following us on Twitter and the Bureau of Consular Affairs page on Facebook; Downloading our free Smart Traveler IPhone App to have travel information at your fingertips. Calling 1-888-407-4747 toll-free within the U.S. and Canada, or a regular toll line, 1-202-501-4444, from other countries; Taking some time before travel to consider your personal security.

Crime: Andorra has a low rate of crime. While most of Spain has a moderate rate of crime and most of the estimated one million U.S. citizen tourists have trouble-free visits to Spain each year, street crimes against tourists occur in the principal tourist areas. Madrid and Barcelona, in particular, report incidents of pickpocketing, mugging, and occasional violent attacks, some of which require the victim to seek medical attention. Although crimes occur at all times of day and night and to people of all ages, older tourists and Asian Americans seem to be particularly at risk.

Criminals tend to frequent tourist areas and major attractions such as museums, monuments, restaurants, outdoor cafes, Internet cafes, hotel lobbies, beach resorts, city buses, subways, trains, train stations, airports, and ATMs. In Madrid, incidents have been reported in all major tourist areas, including the area near the Prado Museum, near Atocha train station, in Retiro Park, in areas of old Madrid including near the Royal Palace, and in Plaza Mayor. There have been a number of passport and bag thefts reported at Madrid's Barajas Airport, local hotels, as well as in El Rastro (Madrid's flea market) and in the Metro.

In Barcelona, the largest number of incidents reported also occurred in major tourist areas--on Las Ramblas, Barcelona's El Prat Airport, Sants train station, Metro stations, in the Sagrada Familia Area, in the Gothic Quarter, in Park Güell, in Plaza Real, and along Barcelona's beaches. There have been a number of thefts reported at the Port Olimpic Area and nearby beaches.

Travelers should remain alert to their personal security and exercise caution. We suggest that travelers carry limited cash, only one credit card, and a copy of their passport; leaving extra cash, extra credit cards, passports and personal documents in a safe location. Be especially careful in crowds. Avoid placing passports, cash or other valuables in the outer pockets of backpacks or purses. Pickpockets often use the cover of a crowd to rob unsuspecting tourists and visitors. Do not leave belongings unattended in public areas. Do not put purses on the floor or on the backs of chairs at restaurants. Keep valuable belongings within sight and within easy reach at all times in public areas to reduce the risk of theft.

Thieves often work in teams of two or more people. In many cases, one person distracts a victim while the accomplices perform the robbery. For example, someone might wave a map in your face and ask for directions, "inadvertently" spill something on you, or help you clean up bird droppings thrown on you by a third unseen accomplice. While your attention is diverted, an accomplice makes off with your valuables. Thieves may drop coins or keys at your feet to distract you and try to take your belongings while you are trying to help. Physical assaults rarely happen. In the past, such attacks were initiated from behind, with the victim being grabbed around the neck and choked by one assailant while others rifle through or grab the belongings. A group of assailants may surround the victim in a crowded popular tourist area or on public transportation, and only after the group has departed does the person discover he/she has been robbed.

Purse snatchers may grab purses or wallets and run away, or immediately pass the stolen item to an accomplice. A passenger on a passing motorcycle sometimes robs pedestrians. There have been reports of thieves posing as plainclothes police officers, beckoning to pedestrians from cars and sometimes confronting them on the street asking for documents, or to inspect their cash for counterfeit bills, which they ultimately confiscate as "evidence." The U.S. Embassy in Madrid has received reports of cars on limited access motorways being pulled over by supposed unmarked police cars. The Spanish police do not operate in this fashion. We encourage U.S. citizens to ask for a uniformed law enforcement officer if approached.

Theft from vehicles is also common. "Good Samaritan" scams are unfortunately common, where a passing car or helpful stranger will attempt to divert the driver's attention by indicating there is a flat tire or mechanical problem. When the driver stops to check the vehicle, the "Good Samaritan" will appear to help the driver and passengers while the accomplice steals from the unlocked car. Drivers should be cautious about accepting help from anyone other than a uniformed Spanish police officer or Civil Guard. Items high in value like luggage, cameras, laptop computers, or briefcases are often stolen from cars. We recommend that travelers not leave baggage in open view inside parked cars, and keep doors locked, windows rolled up, and valuables out of sight when driving.

While the incidence of sexual assault is statistically very low, attacks do occur. We recommend that U.S. citizens remain aware of their surroundings at all times, and travel with a companion if possible, especially at night. Spanish authorities warn of the availability of so-called "date-rape" drugs and other drugs, including GBH and liquid ecstasy. U.S. citizens should not lower their personal security awareness because they are on vacation.

A number of U.S. citizens have been victims of various scams in Spain. One scheme involves a U.S. citizen receiving an email or telephone call requesting money to assist a relative or acquaintance who has been arrested, detained, robbed, or injured in Spain. If you receive such an email, we recommend that you not send money. Other scams include lottery or advance-fee scams in which a person is lured to Spain to finalize a financial transaction.

Often the victims are initially contacted via Internet or fax and informed they have won the Spanish Lottery (El Gordo), inherited money from a distant relative, or are needed to assist in a major financial transaction from one country to another. For more information, please see the Bureau of Consular Affairs' web page on International Financial Scams. Don't buy counterfeit and pirated goods, even if they are widely available. Not only are the bootlegs illegal in the United States, if you purchase them you are also breaking local law.

Victims of Crime: If you or someone you know becomes the victim of a crime abroad, you should contact the local police and the nearest U.S. embassy or consulate. We can:

- Replace a stolen passport.
- Help you find appropriate medical care if you are the victim of violent crimes such as assault or rape.
- Put you in contact with the appropriate police authorities, and if you want us to, we can contact family members or friends.
- Help you understand the local criminal justice process and direct you to local attorneys, although it is important to remember that local authorities are responsible for investigating and prosecuting the crime.

The local equivalent to the "911" emergency line in Europe, including in Spain and Andorra, is 112.

Criminal Penalties: While you are traveling in Spain and Andorra, you are subject to its laws even if you are a U.S. citizen. Foreign laws and legal systems can be vastly different from our own and criminal penalties will vary from country to country. In Spain, driving under the influence could land you immediately in jail. There are also some things that might be legal in the country you visit, but still illegal in the United States. You can be prosecuted under U.S. law if you buy pirated goods.

Engaging in sexual conduct with children or using or disseminating child pornography in a foreign country is a crime prosecutable in the United States. If you break local laws in Spain and Andorra, your U.S. passport or citizenship won't help you avoid arrest or prosecution. It's very important to know what's legal and what's not wherever you go.

Persons violating the laws of Spain and Andorra, even unknowingly, may be expelled, arrested, or imprisoned. Penalties for possessing, using, or trafficking in illegal drugs in Spain and Andorra are severe, and convicted offenders can expect long jail sentences and heavy fines. The cities of Madrid and Barcelona and the Balearic Islands regional government have banned the consumption of alcohol in the street, other than in registered street cafes and bars.

Visitors to Madrid, Barcelona, Mallorca, Ibiza, and Menorca should be aware that failure to respect this law might result in the imposition of fines. Throughout Spain and Andorra, driving under the influence could land you immediately in jail.

Spain takes illegal immigration seriously and police may stop people to ask for identification and proof of legal status. We recommend that you carry a copy of your U.S. passport at all times. While some countries will automatically notify the nearest U.S. embassy or consulate if a U.S. citizen is detained or arrested in a foreign country, that might not always be the case here. To ensure that the United States Government is aware of your circumstances, request that the police and prison officials notify the nearest U.S. embassy or consulate as soon as you are arrested or detained overseas.

Special Circumstances: Accessibility: While in Spain, individuals with disabilities may find accessibility and accommodation different from what you find in the United States. Spain has laws that prohibit discrimination against persons with physical, sensory, intellectual, and mental disabilities in employment, education, access to health care, access to information technology and communication, including social media, and the provision of other state services.

The law mandates access to buildings for persons with disabilities. While the government generally enforces these provisions, levels of assistance and accessibility differ between regions. Madrid, Barcelona and many of the other major cities have made great strides in making public transportation, museums and other public buildings accessible to those with physical disabilities. Most buses have ramps to accommodate wheelchairs and many metro stations have elevators for the same purpose.

Taxis are available which accommodate wheelchairs. However, in the downtown historic areas and in some other areas, sidewalks can be narrow and have uneven surfaces. Tourists should take this into account when planning their visit. Andorran law prohibits discrimination against persons with physical, sensory, intellectual and mental disabilities in employment, education, access to health care, and the provision of other state services. These nondiscrimination laws help to protect travelers with disabilities.

In practice, persons with disabilities have easy access to public buildings. The government continues to adapt infrastructure to the needs of disabled persons to ensure accessibility to public transportation, museums, commerce, restaurants, and other buildings in the country.

Medical Facilities and Health Information: Good medical care is available in both Spain and Andorra. Regulations regarding medications may vary from those in the United States. Spanish regulations do not permit the international shipment of medication, so please do not ship medication from the United States to Spain. U.S. citizens who plan a lengthy trip to Spain should bring their medication or obtain a prescription for that medication from a Spanish physician. For information about outbreaks of infectious diseases abroad, consult the World Health Organization (WHO) website.

Medical Insurance: You can't assume your insurance will go with you when you travel. It's very important to find out BEFORE you leave whether or not your medical insurance will cover you overseas. You need to ask your insurance company two questions:

- Does my policy apply when I'm out of the United States?
- Will it cover emergencies like a trip to a foreign hospital or a medical evacuation?

In many places, doctors and hospitals still expect payment in cash at the time of service. Your regular U.S. health insurance may not cover doctor' and hospital visits in other countries. If your policy doesn't go with you when you travel, it's a very good idea to take out another one for your trip.

Traffic Safety and Road Conditions: While in Spain and Andorra, you may encounter road conditions that differ significantly from those in the United States. Traffic in Madrid and Barcelona is faster paced than in U.S. cities and can be unnerving because of unfamiliar signs or motorbikes weaving between traffic lanes. Drivers should always obey the closest traffic light, as there are separate pedestrian lights in the cities.

Drivers should be alert when driving at night in urban areas because of the possibility of encountering drivers or pedestrians under the influence of alcohol.

Night driving in isolated rural areas can be dangerous because of farm animals and poorly marked roads. Rural traffic is generally heavier in July and August as well as during the Christmas and Easter seasons. Traffic regulations in effect in Spain include the prohibition on the use of a mobile phone without a hands-free device while driving a car. There is a fine of 300 euros for violation of this regulation and loss of driving privileges. In addition, all drivers and passengers are required to carry a reflective vest and put it on if they need to stop on the roadside.

A reflective triangle warning sign for a vehicle stopped on the side of the road is also mandatory. Those renting vehicles are encouraged to check with the rental company about traffic regulations and safety equipment. U.S. citizens must obtain International Driving Permits prior to their arrival if they plan to drive in Spain. You are not allowed to drive on your American license.

While rental car companies may rent a vehicle to you without the International Driving Permit, this is illegal and, if pulled over for a traffic violation, your rental car may be detained and towed to the nearest impound lot.

Pedestrians should use designated crossing areas when crossing streets and obey traffic lights. One of the facets of Spanish traffic laws that many U.S. citizens find troublesome is traffic stops by the Spanish National Police or the Guardia Civil. Unlike in the United States where drivers receive traffic tickets and then pay the court via mail or in person, Spanish police authorities may levy fines on the spot and issue a receipt for the payment. This is done to ensure the traffic fine is paid by foreigners who rarely come back to Spain to pay the fine. Public transportation in large Spanish cities is generally excellent.

All major cities have metered taxis, in which extra charges must be posted in the vehicle. We advise travelers to use only clearly identified cabs and to ensure that taxi drivers always switch on the meter. A green light on the roof indicates that the taxi is available. If you have a problem or suspect you are being over charged, ask for an official receipt. The license number for the taxi should be located in a metal plaque by the passenger window. This number identifies a specific taxi and can prove useful in the event of forgotten property or if you decide to file a complaint. Rail service is comfortable and reliable, but varies in quality and speed. Intercity buses are usually comfortable and inexpensive.

For specific information concerning Spanish driving permits, vehicle inspection, road tax and mandatory insurance, please contact the Spanish National Tourist Organization offices in New York. For information about driving in Andorra, refer to Andorra's Office of Tourism.

Aviation Safety Oversight: The U.S. Federal Aviation Administration (FAA) has assessed the government of Spain's Civil Aviation Authority as being in compliance with International Civil Aviation Organization (ICAO) aviation safety standards for oversight of Spain's air carrier operations. Further information may be found on the FAA's safety assessment page.

Children's Issues: Please see the U.S. Dept. of State Office of Children's Issues web pages on intercountry adoption and international parental child abduction.

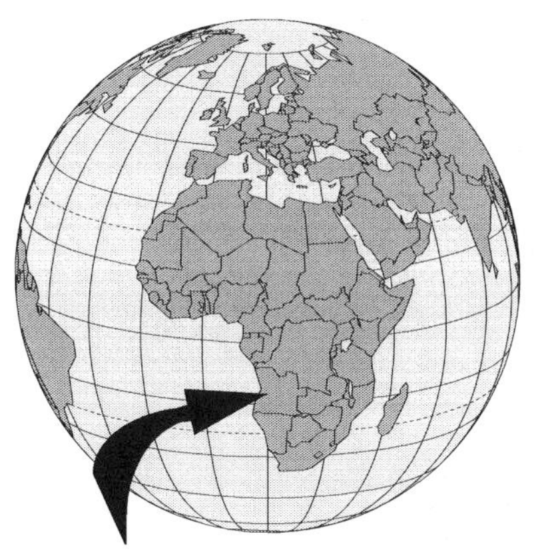

ANGOLA

Compiled from publications that were available as of February 2013 from the U.S. Department of State, the U.S. Department of Commerce, and the Central Intelligence Agency (CIA). See the introduction to this set for explanatory notes.

Official Name

Republic of Angola (Republica de Angola)

PROFILE

Geography

Area: total: 1,246,700 sq km; country comparison to the world: 23; land: 1,246,700 sq km; water: 0 sq km
Major cities: Luanda (capital) 4.511 million; Huambo 979,000 (2009)
Climate: semiarid in south and along coast to Luanda; north has cool, dry season (May to October) and hot, rainy season (November to April)
Terrain: narrow coastal plain rises abruptly to vast interior plateau

People

Nationality: noun: Angolan(s); adjective: Angolan
Population: 18,056,072 (July 2012 est.)
Population growth rate: 2.784% (2012 est.)
Ethnic groups: Ovimbundu 37%, Kimbundu 25%, Bakongo 13%, mestico (mixed European and native African) 2%, European 1%, other 22%
Religions: indigenous beliefs 47%, Roman Catholic 38%, Protestant 15% (1998 est.)
Languages: Portuguese (official), Bantu and other African languages
Literacy: definition: age 15 and over can read and write; total population: 70.1%; male: 82.7%; female: 58.1% (2010 est.)
Health: life expectancy at birth: total population: 54.59 years; male: 53.49 years; female: 55.73 years (2012 est.); Infant mortality rate: total: 83.53 deaths/1,000 live births; male: 87.39 deaths/1,000 live births; female: 79.47 deaths/1,000 live births (2012 est.)
Unemployment rate: NA
Work force: 8.468 million (2012 est.)

Government

Type: republic; multiparty presidential regime
Independence: 11 November 1975
Constitution: adopted by National Assembly 5 February 2010
Political subdivisions: 18 provinces (provincias, singular—provincia)
Suffrage: 18 years of age; universal

Economy

GDP (purchasing power parity): $126.2 billion (2012 est.); $117.2 billion (2011 est.); $113.3 billion (2010 est.); $109.6 billion (2009 est.)
GDP real growth rate: 6.8% (2012 est.); 3.4% (2011 est.); 3.4% (2010 est.); 2.4% (2009 est.)
GDP per capita (PPP): $6,200 (2012 est.); $6,000 (2011 est.); $5,900 (2010 est.); $5,900 (2009 est.)
Natural resources: petroleum, diamonds, iron ore, phosphates, copper, feldspar, gold, bauxite, uranium
Agriculture products: bananas, sugarcane, coffee, sisal, corn, cotton, cassava (manioc), tobacco, vegetables, plantains; livestock; forest products; fish

Industries: petroleum; diamonds, iron ore, phosphates, feldspar, bauxite, uranium, and gold; cement; basic metal products; fish processing; food processing, brewing, tobacco products, sugar; textiles; ship repair

Exports: $71.95 billion (2012 est.);; $65.69 billion (2011 est.); $50.59 billion (2010 est.)

Exports—commodities: crude oil, diamonds, refined petroleum products, coffee, sisal, fish and fish products, timber, cotton

Exports—partners: China 37.7%, US 21%, India 9.5%, Canada 4.1% (2011)

Imports: $22.32 billion (2012 est.); $21.74 billion (2011 est.); $16.67 billion (2010 est.)

Imports—commodities: machinery and electrical equipment, vehicles and spare parts; medicines, food, textiles, military goods

Imports—partners: Portugal 20.4%, China 17.7%, US 9.5%, Brazil 6.8%, South Africa 6.1%, France 5%, India 4.4% (2011)

Debt—external: $18.16 billion (31 December 2011 est.); $18.56 billion (31 December 2010 est.)

Exchange rates: kwanza (AOA) per US dollar; 95.54 (2012 est.); 93.741 (2011 est.); 91.906 (2010 est.); 79.33 (2009); 75.023 (2008); 76.6 (2007)

GEOGRAPHY

Angola is located on the South Atlantic coast of West Africa between Namibia on the south and, with the exception of the enclave of Cabinda, the Democratic Republic of the Congo (D.R.C.) on the north; the D.R.C. and Zambia form the eastern boundary. Cabinda is bounded by the Republic of the Congo (Brazzaville) on the north and east and by the D.R.C. on the south. The country is divided into an arid coastal strip stretching from Namibia to Luanda; a wet, interior highland; a dry savanna in the interior south and southeast; and rain forest in the north and in Cabinda. The upper reaches of the Zambezi River pass through Angola, and several tributaries of the Congo River have their sources in Angola. The coastal strip is tempered by the cool Benguela Current, resulting in a climate similar to coastal Baja California. The hot, humid rainy season lasts from November to April, followed by a moderate dry season from May to October. The interior highlands have a mild climate, with a rainy season from November through April, followed by a cool dry season from May to October, when overnight temperatures can fall to freezing. Elevations generally range from 3,000 to 6,000 feet. The far north and Cabinda enjoy rain throughout much of the year.

PEOPLE

Angola has three main ethnic groups, each speaking a Bantu language: Umbundu, Kimbundu, and Kikongo. Other groups include Chokwe, Lunda, Ganguela, Nhaneca-Humbe, Ambo, Herero, and Xindunga. In addition, mixed racial (European and African) people account for about 2%, with a small (1%) population of whites. Portuguese make up the largest non-Angolan population (though many native-born Angolans can claim Portuguese nationality under Portuguese law).

National/Racial/Ethnic Minorities

An estimated 3,500 San persons lived in small dispersed communities in Huila, Cunene, and Kuando Kubango provinces. The San are traditional hunter-gatherers who are linguistically and ethnically distinct from their Bantu fellow citizens. Their very limited participation in political life has increased, and Ocadec, a local NGO advocate for the San people, worked with provincial governments to increase services to San communities and to improve communication between these communities and the government.

Languages

Portuguese is the official language of Angola. Native languages include Kimbundu, Bakongo, Ovimbundu, and others. French is often spoken in the northern border regions and English is occasionally spoken near the Zambian and Namibian borders.

Religion

The majority of the population is Christian. The Roman Catholic Church estimates that 55 percent of the population is Catholic, while the government estimates 70 percent; neither figure could be verified independently. Data from the National Institute for Religious Affairs indicate that 25 percent of the population adheres to African Christian denominations (mixing Christian and traditional beliefs); 10 percent follows Protestant traditions, including Methodist, Baptist, Adventist, Congregationalist (United Church of Christ), and Assemblies of God; and 5 percent belongs to Brazilian evangelical churches.

A small portion of the rural population practices animism or indigenous religious beliefs. There is a small Muslim community, unofficially estimated at 80,000 to 90,000 adherents, the majority of whom are migrants from West Africa or of Lebanese origin. Some sources in the Muslim community put these figures much higher, although the accuracy of these estimates is questionable.

HISTORY

In 1482, when the Portuguese first landed in what is now northern Angola, they encountered the Kingdom of the Congo, which stretched from modern Gabon in the north to the Kwanza River in the south. Mbanza Congo, the capital, had a population of 50,000 people. South of this kingdom were various important states, of which the Kingdom of Ndongo, ruled by the ngola (king), was most significant. Modern Angola derives its name from the king of Ndongo. The Portuguese gradually took control of the coastal strip throughout the 16th century by a series of treaties and wars. The Dutch occupied Luanda from 1641 to 1648, during which the Ndongo Kingdom supported the Dutch in their attempt to drive away the Portuguese. In 1648, Brazilian-based Portuguese forces retook Luanda and initiated a process of military conquest of the Congo and Ndongo states that ended with Portuguese victory in 1671. Full Portuguese administrative control of the interior did not occur until the beginning of the 20th century.

Portugal's primary interest in Angola quickly turned to the slave trade. The slaving system began early in the 16th century with the purchase from African chiefs of people to work on sugar plantations in Sao Tome, Príncipe, and Brazil. Many scholars agree that by the beginning of the 19th century, Angola was the largest source of slaves not only for Brazil, but also for the Americas, including the United States. By the end of the 19th century, a forced labor system replaced formal slavery and continued until outlawed in 1961. This forced labor system provided the basis for the development of a plantation economy and, by the mid-20th century, a major mining sector. Forced labor combined with British financing allowed the construction of three railroads from the coast to the interior, the most important of which was the transcontinental Benguela railroad that linked the port of Lobito with the copper zones of the Belgian Congo and what is now Zambia, through which it connects to Dar es Salaam, Tanza-

nia. Colonial economic development did not translate into social development for native Angolans. The Portuguese regime encouraged white immigration, especially after 1950, which intensified racial antagonisms. As decolonization progressed elsewhere in Africa, Portugal, under the Salazar and Caetano dictatorships, rejected independence and treated its African colonies as overseas provinces. Consequently, three independence movements emerged: the Popular Movement for the Liberation of Angola (MPLA), led by Antonio Agostinho Neto, with a base among Kimbundu and the mixed-race intelligentsia of Luanda, and links to communist parties in Portugal and the Eastern Bloc; the National Front for the Liberation of Angola (FNLA), led by Holden Roberto, with an ethnic base in the Bakongo region of the north, and links to the United States and the Mobutu regime in Kinshasa; and the National Union for the Total Independence of Angola (UNITA), led by Jonas Malheiro Savimbi, with an ethnic and regional base in the Ovimbundu heartland in the center of the country, and links to the People's Republic of China (P.R.C.) and apartheid South Africa.

From the early 1960s, these movements fought against the Portuguese. A 1974 coup d'etat in Portugal established a military government that promptly ceased the war and agreed, in the Alvor Accords, to hand over power in Angola to a coalition of the three movements. The ideological differences among the three movements eventually led to armed conflict, with FNLA and UNITA forces attempting to wrest control of Luanda from the MPLA, and all parties backed by their respective international supporters. The intervention of troops from South Africa on behalf of UNITA, Zaire on behalf of the FNLA, and Cuba on behalf of the MPLA in 1975 effectively internationalized the conflict. After retaining control of Luanda, the coastal strip, and increasingly lucrative oil fields in Cabinda, the MPLA declared independence on November 11, 1975, the day the Portuguese abandoned the capital. UNITA and the FNLA formed a rival coalition government based in the interior city of Huambo. Agostinho Neto became the first president of the MPLA government that was recognized by the United Nations in 1976. Upon Neto's death from cancer in 1979, then-Planning Minister Jose Eduardo dos Santos ascended to the presidency.

The FNLA's military failures led to its increasing marginalization, internal divisions, and abandonment by international supporters. An internationalized conventional civil war between UNITA and the MPLA continued until 1989. For much of this time, UNITA controlled vast swaths of the interior and was backed by U.S. resources and South African troops. Similarly, tens of thousands of Cuban troops remained in support of the MPLA, often fighting South Africans on the front lines. A U.S.-brokered agreement resulted in withdrawal of foreign troops in 1989 and led to the Bicesse Accord in 1991, which spelled out an electoral process for a democratic Angola under the supervision of the United Nations. When UNITA's Jonas Savimbi failed to win the first round of the presidential election in 1992 (he won 40% to dos Santos's 49%, which required a runoff), he called the election fraudulent and returned to war. Another peace accord, known as the Lusaka Protocol, was brokered in Lusaka, Zambia, and signed in 1994. This agreement, too, collapsed into renewed conflict. The UN Security Council voted on August 28, 1997 to impose sanctions on UNITA. The Angolan military launched a massive offensive in 1999, which destroyed UNITA's conventional capacity and recaptured all major cities previously held by Savimbi's forces. Savimbi then declared a return to guerrilla tactics, which continued until his death in combat in February 2002.

On April 4, 2002, the Angolan Government and UNITA signed the Luena Memorandum of Understanding (MOU), which formalized the de facto cease-fire that prevailed following Savimbi's death. In accordance with the MOU, UNITA recommitted to the peace framework in the 1994 Lusaka Protocol, returned all remaining territory to Angolan Government control, quartered all military personnel in predetermined locations, and relinquished all arms. In August 2002, UNITA demobilized all military personnel, and the UN Security Council sanctions on UNITA were lifted on December 9, 2002. UNITA and the MPLA held their first post-war party congresses in 2003. The UNITA Congress saw the democratic transfer of power from interim leader General Paulo Lukumba "Gato" to former UNITA representative in Paris Isaias Henrique Samakuva, while the MPLA Congress reaffirmed President dos Santos' leadership of party structures. Samakuva was reelected to a second 4-year term as UNITA party president at a UNITA party congress in July 2007.

Founded in 1963, the Front for the Liberation of the Enclave of Cabinda (FLEC) fought for the enclave's independence from the Portuguese. Upon Angola's independence, MPLA forces gained control over Cabindan cities and oil resources, and the FLEC insurgency continued in predominately rural areas. The signing of the Memorandum of Understanding (MOU) for Peace and Reconciliation in Cabinda on August 1, 2006 was intended as a step toward ending conflict in Cabinda and in bringing about greater representation for the people of Cabinda. It followed a successful counterinsurgency campaign by the Angolan Armed Forces (FAA), which still maintain a strong troop presence there. The MOU rejected the notion of Cabindan independence, called for the demobilization and reintegration of former FLEC fighters into various government positions, and created a special political and economic status for the province of Cabinda. Many FLEC military combatants were integrated into the Angolan Armed Forces and National Police, including into some command positions. In addition, Cabindans were given a designated number of vice ministerial and other positions in the Angolan Government. Some FLEC members who did not sign onto the peace memorandum continue their independence efforts through public outreach, infrequent low-level attacks against FAA convoys and outposts, and occasional violent attacks on civilians.

GOVERNMENT AND POLITICAL CONDITIONS

Angola is a constitutional republic. The ruling Popular Movement for the Liberation of Angola (MPLA), led by President Jose Eduardo dos Santos, has been in power since independence in 1975 and exercised tight, centralized control over government planning, policymaking, and media outlets. In 2008 the government held the first legislative elections since 1992.

Domestic and international observers reported that polling throughout the country was peaceful and generally credible, despite a ruling party advantage due to state control of major media and other resources and serious logistical failures that marred polling in the capital, Luanda.

Recent Elections

After having postponed legislative elections for two years, the government held the first postwar elections in 2008. The ruling MPLA won 81.6 percent of the vote. Domestic and international observers reported that polling throughout the country was peaceful and generally credible, although the ruling party enjoyed advantages due to state control of major media and other resources. Serious logistical failures marred polling in the capital, Luanda. Opposition parties criticized many aspects of the electoral process, including state control of the major media, late disbursement of public campaign funds, the National Electoral Commission's (CNE) failure to accredit some opposition and civil society electoral observers, and the CNE's last-minute decision to discard the legal requirement that a voter registry be used at polling stations to verify a voter's identity and residence. Despite these and other irregularities, more than 87 percent of registered voters participated. Opposition parties generally accepted the electoral results.

Observers had expected a presidential election in 2009. However, elections did not occur due to a delay to accommodate constitutional reform. The new constitution called for elections within five years of the previous election. In August 2012 voters elected candidates from a party list, with the presidential candidate at the head of the list. Jose Eduardo Dos Santos of the MPLA was elected as president.

Political Parties: The ruling MPLA party dominated all political institutions. Political power was concentrated in the presidency and the Council of Ministers, through which the president exercised executive power. The council can enact laws, decrees, and resolutions, assuming most functions normally associated with the legislative branch. The National Assembly consists of 220 deputies elected under a party list proportional representation system. This body has the authority to draft, debate, and pass legislation, but in practice laws generally were drafted and proposed by the executive branch for the assembly's approval. After the 2008 legislative elections, opposition deputies held fewer than 20 percent of the parliamentary seats.

Opposition parties stated that their members were subject to harassment, intimidation, and assault by supporters of the MPLA. UNITA continued to argue that the MPLA had not lived up to the terms of the 2002 peace accord, and former combatants lacked the social services and assistance needed to reintegrate into society. Former combatants also reported difficulties obtaining pensions due to bureaucratic delays or discrimination. UNITA headquarters buildings in at least three provinces were denied access to public utilities, including electricity and water. During 2011 UNITA reported that its members suffered intimidation and harassment.

In February UNITA claimed that at least nine of its supporters were killed in Huambo Province for political reasons in the previous year. A parliamentary commission sent to investigate the claim found no political intolerance in Huambo Province. However, civil society criticized the report.

Opposition party members and civil society leaders cited examples of political intolerance during the 2008 election process.

Participation of Women and Minorities: Of the 220 deputies in the National Assembly, 79 were women (36 percent), exceeding the UN-recommended quota of 30 percent. Six women served as governors or vice governors, and 20 women were executive level officials (ministers, state secretaries, presidential appointees). The country has three dominant linguistic groups: the Ovimbundu, Mbundu, and Bakongo, which together constitute approximately 77 percent of the population. All were represented in government. Other groups also took part in governing at the national level. There were six members of smaller ethnic groups in the National Assembly and one minority member, a Chokwe, in the cabinet. Political parties must be represented in all 18 provinces; however, most political parties had limited national constituencies. By law no political party could limit party membership based on ethnicity, race, or gender.

Principal Government Officials

Last Updated: 1/31/2013

Pres.: **Jose Eduardo DOS SANTOS**
Vice Pres.: **Manuel Domingos VICENTE**
Min. of Agriculture: **Afonso Pedro CANGA**
Min. of Assistance & Social Reintegration: **Joao Baptista KUSSUMUA**
Min. of Commerce: **Rosa Escocio PACAVIRA DE MATOS**
Min. of Construction: **Fernando Alberto de Lemos Soares da FONSECA**
Min. of Culture: **Rosa Maria MARTINS DA CRUZ E SILVA**
Min. of Defense: **Candido Pereira dos Santos VAN DUNEM, Maj.Gen**
Min. of Economy: **Abraao Pio dos Santos GOURGEL**
Min. of Education: **Pinda SIMAO**
Min. of Energy & Water: **Joao Baptista BORGES**
Min. of Environment: **Maria de Fatima Monteiro JARDIM**
Min. of External Relations: **Georges Rebelo CHIKOTI**
Min. of Family & Women Promotion: **Maria Felomena de Fatima Lobao TELO DELGADO**
Min. of Finance: **Carlos Alberto LOPES**
Min. of Fisheries: **Victoria Francisco Lopes Cristovao DE BARROS NETO**
Min. of Former Combatants & Veterans of War: **Kundi PAIHAMA**
Min. of Geology & Mines: **Francisco Manuel Monteiro DE QUEIROZ**
Min. of Health: **Jose Vieira DIAS VAN-DUNEM**
Min. of Higher Education: **Adao Gaspar Ferreira DO NASCIMENTO**
Min. of Hotels & Tourism: **Pedro MUTINDE**
Min. of Industry: **Bernarda Goncalves Martins Henriques DA SILVA**
Min. of Interior: **Angelo de Barros Veiga TAVARES**

Min. of Justice & Human Rights: **Rui Jorge Carneiro MANGUEIRA**
Min. of Parliamentary Affairs: **Rosa Luis de Sousa MICOLO**
Min. of Petroleum: **Jose Maria Botelho de VASCONCELOS**
Min. of Planning & Territorial Development: **Job GRACA**
Min. of Public Admin., Employment, & Social Security:**Antonio Domingos da Costa Pitra NETO**
Min. of Science & Technology: **Maria Candida Pereira TEIXEIRA**
Min. of Social Communication: **Jose Luis DE MATOS**
Min. of Telecommunications & Information Technology: **Jose Carvalho DA ROCHA**
Min. of Territorial Admin.: **Bornito de Sousa Baltazar DIOGO**
Min. of Transport: **Augusto da Silva TOMAS**
Min. of Urban Affairs & Housing: **Jose Antonio DA CONCEICAO E SILVA**
Min. of Youth & Sports: **Goncalves Manuel MUANDUMBA**
Min. in the Office of the Presidency, Civil Affairs: **Edeltrudes Mauricio Fernandes GASPAR DA COSTA**
Min. in the Office of the Presidency, Military Affairs: **Manuel Helder "Kopelipa" VIEIRA DIAS**
Sec. of the Council of Ministers: **Frederico Manuel dos Santos e Silva CARDOSO**
Governor, National Bank of Angola: **Jose de Lima MASSANO**
Ambassador to the US: **Alberto do Carmo BENTO RIBEIRO**
Permanent Representative to the UN, New York: **Ismael Abraao GASPAR MARTINS**

ECONOMY

Angola's high growth rate in recent years was driven by high international prices for its oil. Angola became a member of OPEC in late 2006 and its current assigned a production quota of 1.65 million barrels a day (bbl/day). Oil production and its supporting activities contribute about 85% of GDP. Diamond exports contribute an additional 5%.

Subsistence agriculture provides the main livelihood for most of the people, but half of the country's food is still imported. Increased oil production supported growth averaging more than 17% per year from 2004 to 2008. A postwar reconstruction boom and resettlement of displaced persons has led to high rates of growth in construction and agriculture as well.

Much of the country's infrastructure is still damaged or undeveloped from the 27-year-long civil war. Land mines left from the war still mar the countryside, even though peace was established after the death of rebel leader Jonas SAVIMBI in February 2002. Since 2005, the government has used billions of dollars in credit lines from China, Brazil, Portugal, Germany, Spain, and the EU to rebuild Angola's public infrastructure.

The global recession that started in 2008 temporarily stalled economic growth. Lower prices for oil and diamonds during the global recession slowed GDP growth to 2.4% in 2009 and to 3.4% in 2010, and many construction projects stopped because Luanda accrued $9 billion in arrears to foreign construction companies when government revenue fell in 2008 and 2009.

Angola abandoned its currency peg in 2009, and in November 2009 signed onto an IMF Stand-By Arrangement loan of $1.4 billion to rebuild international reserves. Consumer inflation declined from 325% in 2000 to about 10% in 2012. Higher oil prices have helped Angola turn a budget deficit of 8.6% of GDP in 2009 into an surplus of 12% of GDP in 2012. Corruption, especially in the extractive sectors, also is a major challenge.

Labor Conditions

The law prohibits children under 14 from working. Although children could work from age 14 to 16 with parental permission, they could not do so if it interfered with schooling. The law was effectively enforced in the formal sector.

Child labor, especially in the informal sector, remains a problem. In October 2010 the newspaper Agora published a study conducted in Benguela that found more than 70,000 children worked in Benguela Province. A living standards survey published in 2010 reported that 20.4 percent of children between the ages of five and 14 worked; more children worked in rural than in urban areas. The study also reported that boys and girls were equally likely to work. Most work done by children was in the informal sector.

The minimum wage was 11,044 kwanza ($116) per month for all formal sectors. Workers in informal sectors, such as street vendors, subsistence agriculture, and domestic household, are not covered by the minimum wage law. The minimum wage law was effectively enforced in the formal sector.

By law the standard workweek is 40 hours with at least one unbroken period of 24 hours of rest per week. There is a limit on work of 54 hours per week. Required premium pay for overtime is time and a half for up to 30 hours of overtime and time and three-quarters from 30 to 40 hours. In the formal sector, there is a prohibition on excessive compulsory overtime, defined as more than two hours a day, 40 hours a month, or 200 hours a year. The government sets occupational health and safety standards. Workers have the right to remove themselves from situations that endanger health or safety without jeopardy to their employment.

Most wage earners held second jobs or depended on the agricultural or other informal sectors to augment their incomes. The majority of citizens derived their income from the informal sector or subsistence agriculture and therefore fell outside of government protection regarding working conditions.

In September 2010 the MPLA-linked labor union, Uniao Nacional dos Trabalhadores Angolana, published a report on working conditions that highlighted high unemployment, poor living conditions, and inequality as continuing problems despite various economic measures and new laws.

Workers found they did not have job stability, employers violated workers' rights, and workers unable to find employment in the formal sector had to seek work in the informal labor market.

U.S.-ANGOLAN RELATIONS

The United States established diplomatic relations in 1993 with Angola, which had become independent from Portugal in 1975. Post-independence, Angola saw 27 years of civil war among groups backed at various times by countries that included the United States, the Soviet Union, Cuba, China, and South Africa. Angola has had two presidents since independence.

The first president came to power in 1975; upon his 1979 death, the second president assumed power. Multiparty elections were held in 1992 under a process supervised by the United Nations, but the results were disputed and civil war continued until the 2002 death of one holdout guerilla leader.

Angola has a strong and capable military. Although the country is sub-Saharan Africa's second-largest oil producer and has great agricultural potential, two-thirds of the population live in poverty. U.S. foreign policy goals in Angola are to promote and strengthen Angola's democratic institutions, promote economic prosperity, improve health, and consolidate peace and security. The United States has worked with Angola to remove thousands of landmines and help war refugees and internally displaced people return to their homes. In 2009 Secretary Clinton declared Angola a "strategic partner" of the United States, one of three that the Obama Administration has identified on the African continent (the other two are Nigeria and South Africa). The U.S.—Angola Strategic Partnership Dialogue (SPD) was formalized with the signing of a Memorandum of Understanding in Washington in July 2010.

U.S. Assistance to Angola

U.S. assistance seeks to focus on preventing major infectious diseases, strengthening health systems, increasing access to family planning and reproductive health services, and building capacity within nongovernmental organizations working in health advocacy and health service delivery. U.S. assistance also promotes stabilization and security sector reform.

Bilateral Economic Relations

Angola is the second-largest trading partner of the United States in sub-Saharan Africa, mainly because of its petroleum exports. U.S. imports from Angola are dominated by petroleum, with some diamonds. U.S. exports to Angola include machinery, aircraft, poultry, and iron and steel products. Angola is eligible for preferential trade benefits under the African Growth and Opportunity Act. The United States and Angola have signed a trade and investment framework agreement, which seeks to promote greater trade and investment between the two countries.

Angola's Membership in International Organizations

Angola and the United States belong to a number of the same international organizations, including the United Nations, International Monetary Fund, World Bank, and World Trade Organization. Angola also is an observer to the Organization of American States.

Bilateral Representation

Angola maintains an embassy in the United States at 2100–2108 16th St., NW, Washington, DC 20009 (tel. 202-785-1156).

Principal U.S. Embassy Officials

Last Updated: 1/14/2013

LUANDA (E) Rua Houari Boumedienne #32, 011-244-222-641-000, Fax 011-244-222-641-232, INMARSAT Tel 011-871-683-133-246, Workweek: Monday thru Thursday, 8:00 am–6:00 pm; Fridays 8:00 am till 12 Noon, http://Luanda.usembassy.gov/

DCM OMS:	Jacqui Justin
AMB OMS:	Dionne Sims
CDC:	Dorotha Hall
FM:	William Keith
HRO:	John Kresge
MGT:	Ellen Tannor
POL/ECON:	Thomas Hastings
POL/MIL:	Guillermo De Las Heras
POSHO:	William Keith
SDO/DATT:	LTC Drew Henry
TREAS:	Patricia Bacchi
AMB:	Christopher McMullen
CON:	David Josar (Acting)
DCM:	Heather Merritt
GSO:	Roland Dixon
RSO:	Alston Richardson
AID:	Teresa McGhie
CLO:	Shawnon Hester
ECON:	Jonathan Magsaysay
FMO:	Mario Bedoya
IMO:	Mike Bostick (Acting)
ISO:	Mike Bostick
State ICASS:	Thomas Hastings

TRAVEL

Consular Information Sheet

March 20, 2012

Country Description: Angola is a large, developing country in southwest central Africa. The capital city is Luanda. Portuguese, the official language, is widely spoken throughout the country. Despite its extensive oil and mineral reserves and arable land suitable for large-scale production of numerous crops, Angola has some of the world's lowest social development indicators. Development was severely restricted by a 27-year long civil war that broke out upon independence in 1975 and destroyed most of the country's infrastructure.

Since the war ended in 2002, the economy grew at double digit annual growth until the global financial crisis undercut oil revenue. Although the government continues extensive infrastructure reconstruction and development projects, Angola still faces challenges with its infrastructure and with providing government services, especially in basic social services, aviation and travel safety, accommodations and communications. Tourism facilities, particularly outside the capital of Luanda, are often rudimentary.

Smart Traveler Enrollment Program (STEP)/Embassy Locations: If you are going to live in or visit Angola, please tell our Embassy about your trip. If you check in, we can keep you up to date with important safety and security announcements. Enrolling will also help your friends and family contact you in an emergency.

U.S. Embassy Luanda
Rua Houari Boumedienne #32
Miramar, Luanda
P.O. Box 6468
Telephone: (244) 222-641-000, (244) 222-447-028, (244) 222-445-481, (244) 222-446-224
Emergency after-hours telephone: (244) 222-641-000; (244) 923-640-154
Facsimile: (244) 222-641-259

Entry/Exit Requirements for U.S. Citizens: A passport and visa are required and must be obtained in advance of travel. An International Certificate of Vaccination is also required. If you are planning to live in or visit Angola, you should allow several weeks for the processing of your visa application. Angola does not issue airport visas, and persons arriving without visas are subject to arrest or exclusion. You may also encounter delays or exclusions if you do not have at least one blank visa page in your passport for entry stamps. Please note that Angolan embassies and consulates will not issue visas unless the passport has at least six month's validity remaining. Angola does not require travelers to have an exit visa.

If your international immunization card does not show inoculations against yellow fever within the past ten years, you may be subject to exclusion, on-the-spot vaccination, and/or heavy fines. If you remain in Angola beyond your authorized visa duration, you may be subject to fines and arrest. It is illegal to carry local currency out of Angola and anyone attempting to carry local currency out of Angola is subject to having this currency confiscated by customs officers. Current information on entry requirements may be obtained from the Embassy of Angola at 2100–2108 16th Street NW, Washington, DC, tel. (202) 785-1156, fax (202) 785-1258. Visit the Embassy of Angola's website for the most current visa information.

The U.S. Department of State is unaware of any HIV/AIDS entry restrictions for visitors or foreign residents of Angola.

Safety and Security: The overall security situation in Angola has improved markedly since the end of the civil war; however, you should still exercise caution when traveling in Angola. Ground travel in some parts of Angola can be problematic due to land mines and other remnants of war. Do not touch anything that resembles a mine or unexploded ordinance. Despite Angola's great progress in rebuilding highway and bridges, the infrastructure remains poor. Police and military officials are sometimes undisciplined, but their authority should not be challenged. Travel in most parts of Luanda is generally safe by day, but car doors should be locked, windows rolled up, and laptop, cell phones, packages stored out of sight. You should avoid travel after dark, and no travel should be undertaken on roads outside of cities after nightfall.

If you are living in, or planning to visit, the northern province of Cabinda, you should be aware of threats to your safety outside of Cabinda city. In 2007 and 2008, armed groups specifically targeted and attacked expatriates in Cabinda; these armed attacks resulted in the rape, robbery and murder of several expatriates working in Cabinda. During the African Nations Cup soccer tournament in January 2010, Front for the Liberation of the Enclave of Cabinda (FLEC) separatists attacked a vehicle carrying the visiting Togolese soccer team, killing three and injuring several others. Those responsible declared their intention to continue attacks against expatriates. Occasional attacks against police and Angolan Armed Forces (FAA) convoys and outposts continue to be reported. These incidents, while infrequent, have occurred with little or no warning. Exercise extreme caution when traveling outside of Cabinda city and limit travel.

You are advised to undertake only essential travel to Lunda North and South provinces. As the Government of Angola is sensitive to the travel of foreigners in the diamond-producing areas of the provinces, proper permission and documentation is required to frequent these areas.

You are advised not to take photographs of sites and installations of military or security interest, including government buildings, as this can result in fines and possibly arrest.

Stay up to date by:

- Bookmarking our Bureau of Consular Affairs website, which contains the current Travel Warnings and Travel Alerts as well as the Worldwide Caution.
- Following us on Twitter and the Bureau of Consular Affairs page on Facebook as well.
- Downloading our free Smart Traveler IPhone App to have travel information at your fingertips.
- Calling 1-888-407-4747 toll-free within the United States and Canada, or a regular toll line, 1-202-501-4444, from other countries.
- Taking some time before travel to consider your personal security.

Crime: Crime is a problem in Angola. While most violent crime occurs between Angolans, foreigners have been attacked as well. Street crime is a regular occurrence in Luanda. The most common crimes are pick-pocketing, purse-snatching, vehicle theft, and vehicle break-ins. Armed muggings, robberies, and carjacking involving foreigners also occur. U.S. citizens are advised to avoid Roque Santeiro and Rocha Pinto, and to only travel the "Serpentine Road" in front of the U.S. Embassy by car. In general, movement around Luanda is safer by day than by night. Touring after dark should be avoided.

Air travelers arriving in Luanda are strongly advised to arrange reliable and secure ground transportation in advance; there is no regular taxi service. U.S. citizens are advised to avoid the use of the public transportation known as "candongueiros" or "taxistas," because these multi-passenger vans are largely unregulated and often dangerous.

Motorists should stop at all police checkpoints if so directed. Police officers may solicit bribes or request immediate payment of "fines" for alleged minor infractions. U.S. citizens asked for bribes by the police should politely ask the traffic police to write them a ticket if the police allege a moving violation. If the police officer writes the ticket, then the motorist should pay the fine at the location indicated on the ticket. If no moving violation is alleged and the officer is asking for a bribe, the motorist should, without actually challenging the officer's authority, politely ask the officer for his/her name and badge number. Officers thus engaged will frequently let motorists go with no bribe paid if motorists follow this advice.

Motorists are reminded to have all proper documents in the vehicle at all times (i.e., vehicle registration, proof of insurance, and driver's license), as lack of documentation is also a traffic violation. Local law requires that every driver in Angola has the proper permission to drive. Police are not always responsive to reports of crime or requests for assistance. Most police are on foot and are assigned to designated stationary posts. The Rapid Intervention Police (PIR) unit is frequently seen patrolling various areas of the city. This well-trained and well-organized unit responds to major crimes.

There have been police operations against illegal aliens and private companies resulting in deportation of illegal resident foreign nationals and loss of personal and company property. Independent entrepreneurs in Angola should carry certified copies of relevant immigration and business documents at all times.

Travelers should be alert to fraud occasionally perpetrated by Luanda airport personnel. Immigration and customs officials sometimes detain foreigners without cause and then demand gratuities before allowing them to enter or depart Angola. Airport health officials sometimes demand that passengers arriving without proof of current yellow fever vaccination accept and pay for a vaccination at the airport.

Travelers are advised to carry their yellow fever vaccination card and ensure their yellow fever vaccine is up-to-date. If travelers forget to bring their yellow fever vaccination card and do not wish to receive the vaccine offered at the airport, they should be prepared to depart the country on the next available flight. Searches of travelers' checked baggage are common. Travelers should also be aware that criminals sometimes attempt to insert items into baggage at the airport, particularly for flights from Luanda to South Africa. It is important that travelers maintain control of their carry-on baggage at all times, and if they believe something has been inserted into their baggage, they should report the incident immediately to airport authorities.

In many countries around the world, counterfeit and pirated goods are widely available. Transactions involving such products may be illegal under local law. In addition, bringing them back to the United States may result in forfeitures and/or fines.

Don't buy counterfeit and pirated goods, even if they are widely available. Not only are the bootlegs illegal in the United States, you may be breaking local law too.

Victims of Crime: If you or someone you know becomes the victim of a crime abroad, you should contact the local police and the nearest U.S. embassy or consulate. We can:

- Replace a stolen passport.
- Help you find appropriate medical care if you are the victim of violent crimes such as assault or rape.
- Put you in contact with the appropriate police authorities, and if you want us to, we can contact family members or friend.
- Help you understand the local criminal justice process and direct you to local attorneys, although it is important to remember that local authorities are responsible for investigating and prosecuting the crime.

The local equivalent to the "911" emergency line in Angola for police is 113; for firefighters: 115, and for ambulance services: 112. Emergency numbers listed may not have an English speaking operator available.

Criminal Penalties: While you are traveling in another country, you are subject to its laws even if you are a U.S. citizen. Foreign laws and legal systems can be vastly different than our own. In some places driving under the influence could land you immediately in jail. These criminal penalties will vary from country to country. There are also some things that might be legal in the country you visit, but still illegal in the United States and you can be prosecuted under U.S. law if you buy pirated goods. Engaging in sexual conduct with children or using or disseminating child pornography in a foreign country is a crime prosecutable in the United States. If you do something illegal in your host country, your U.S. passport won't help. It's very important to know what's legal and what's not where you are going.

Persons violating Angola'slaws, even unknowingly, may be expelled, arrested or imprisoned. Penalties for possession, use, or trafficking in illegal drugs in Angola are severe, and convicted offenders can expect long jail sentences and heavy fines.

Customs Regulations: Angolan customs authorities may enforce strict regulations concerning temporary importation into or export from Angola of sensitive items including firearms, antiquities and currency. If you are planning on bringing in any of these items, you should contact the Embassy of Angola in Washington, DC or one of Angola's consulates in the United States for specific information regarding customs requirements.

Financial Transactions: Angola is generally a cash-only economy; neither traveler's checks nor credit cards are used outside the capital of Luanda. In Luanda, credit cards are accepted in extremely limited circumstances, namely large hotels. Despite a major campaign to expand credit card acceptance, this effort has yet to expand beyond the capital city. In general, Automated Teller Machine's (ATMs) are only accessible to those individuals who hold accounts with local banks.

Dollars are generally accepted for most commercial transactions in Luanda and in all provincial capitals; you should carry a sufficient supply of U.S. dollars with you during your travels. Only the newer series U.S. dollar bills are accepted. U.S. dollars can be converted to local currency at exchange businesses authorized by the Angolan government. Angolan currency (the Kwanza) may not be taken out of the country. Travelers who attempt to carry currency out of Angola are subject to having the currency confiscated, and being arrested and criminally prosecuted.

Personal Identification: You should carry a certified copy of your U.S. passport with you at all times so you can provide proof of identity and U.S. citizenship if questioned by local officials. To avoid the risk of theft or confiscation of original documentation, you should keep your passport in a secure place and carry only a certified copy. The Consular Section of the U.S. Embassy in Luanda can prepare copies of U.S. passports at no charge if you register with the Embassy.

Labor and Business Disputes: U.S. citizen performers, managers, booking agents and promoters traveling to Angola to perform and facilitate events should be aware that serious allegations have been made against Angolan talent agencies making arrangements for foreign performers. These allegations include, among other things, several charges of breach of contract and the forcible retention of passports and persons. In several cases, U.S. citizens have not been allowed to immediately leave the country until such disputes are settled. You should be sure of the reputation of any agency you choose to work with. It may be useful for you to contact performers who have previously worked in Angola and are familiar with agencies in Angola. Feel free to contact the U.S. Embassy directly for further information. If you experience any incidents of this nature in Angola you should report these to the local Angolan police and the U.S. Embassy.

Long Delays in Renewal of Visas: If you opt to renew your work or other visa while in Angola, you should expect delays of 10 weeks or more, during which time the Angolan immigration authorities will retain your passport and you will not be able to travel. You should plan your travel and visa renewals carefully to avoid complications.

If you must travel during this time, you can apply for a second U.S. passport PRIOR to turning over the primary passport to Angolan authorities for visa renewal. To apply for a second U.S. passport, you must write a letter explaining the need for the second passport, as well as meet all the requirements for a normal application for passport renewal, including being able to show a current valid passport. It can take up to 7-10 business days to receive a second passport. If you stay beyond your visa expiration date, you will be subject to a $150 per day fine.

Hotel Availability: Hotels are limited in Angola, and demand for the limited number of rooms is high. Hotels are often booked months in advance, especially in Luanda. Only a few large hotels in Luanda accept credit cards; hotels in the provinces generally do not accept credit cards. Adequate hotels are found in most provincial capitals, but some provide limited amenities.

Accessibility: While in Angola, individuals with disabilities may find accessibility and accommodations very different from what is found in the United States. There is no legislation that mandates any accommodations be made for persons with disabilities. While major hotels do have wheelchair-accessible ramps, most facilities make no such accommodations. If accessibility is a concern, please check with potential hotels and/or travel agencies before booking. The roads and sidewalks are poorly maintained and there are no wheelchair-access ramps for sidewalks.

Medical Facilities and Health Information: Medical facilities and services are available in Angola but are limited and often do not meet U.S. standards. Payment for services is generally required after delivery of services, and medical providers will accept U.S. dollars or local currency. A very small number of facilities accept credit cards. Adequate care for medical emergencies is limited to Luanda, where there are some good private clinics that usually have 24-hour service provided by a general practice physician and specialists on call. A list of such facilities can be found at our medical information web page.

Routine operations such as appendectomies can be performed. Local pharmacies provide a limited supply of prescriptions and over-the-counter medicines/drugs. You are urged to carry with you an adequate supply of properly-labeled medications that you may routinely require while you are living or visiting Angola. Please remember that malaria is endemic in most areas of Angola.

Angola and surrounding African countries have experienced outbreaks of viral hemorrhagic fevers. Most recent incidences are the 2005 Marburg hemorrhagic fever outbreak in Uige province, and the 2008 Ebola virus outbreak in the border region of neighboring Democratic Republic of Congo (DRC) that prompted the Government of Angola to close its border between Lunda Norte and the DRC.

Medical Insurance: You can't assume your insurance will go with you when you travel. It's very important to find out BEFORE you leave. You need to ask your insurance company two questions:

- Does my policy apply when I'm out of the United States.?
- Will it cover emergencies like a trip to a foreign hospital or a medical evacuation?

In many places, doctors and hospitals still expect payment in cash at the time of service. Your regular U.S. health insurance may not cover medical visits in other countries. If your policy doesn't cover you when you travel, it's a very good idea to take out another one for your trip.

Traffic Safety and Road Conditions: While in Angola, U.S. citizens may encounter road conditions that differ significantly from those in the United States. The information below concerning Angola is provided for general reference only, and may not be totally accurate in a particular location or circumstance.

Since the end of the civil war in 2002, overland access to the interior has improved considerably. Nonetheless, highways in some areas remain poor and at the infrastructure for travelers is poor or nonexistent.

Road travel can be dangerous, especially during the rainy season (October—March), which can cause large potholes and erosion. Landmines remain a problem on some secondary roads in more remote areas. Road conditions vary widely outside the capital from acceptable paved surfaces to virtually impassable dirt roads, particularly secondary routes. Many secondary roads, including secondary roads in urban areas, are impassable during the rainy season. Overloaded, poorly marked, and disabled vehicles, as well as pedestrians and livestock, pose hazards for motorists. Ground travel in rural areas should be undertaken during daylight hours only. Areas with suspected landmines are generally clearly marked and travelers should heed these warnings. Primary roads are considered to be landmine free in most provinces, but travelers should not venture far from the margins of the road. Extensive government, commercial, and NGO demining projects continue throughout the country.

Traffic in Luanda is heavy and often chaotic, and roads are often in poor condition. Few intersections have traffic lights or police to direct vehicles. Drivers often fail to obey traffic signals and signs, and there are frequent vehicle breakdowns, a problem exacerbated by missing manhole covers. Itinerant vendors, scooters, and pedestrians often weave in and out of traffic, posing a danger to themselves and to drivers.

Avoid most public transportation, including buses and van taxis, as the vehicles are generally crowded and may be unreliable. U.S. tourists to Angola can drive using a U.S. license for one month only, during which they should apply for an Angolan driving license.

Aviation Safety Oversight: As there is no direct commercial air service to the United States by carriers registered in Angola, the U.S. Federal Aviation Administration (FAA) has not assessed Angola's Civil Aviation Authority for compliance with International Civil Aviation Organization (ICAO) aviation safety standards. Further information may be found on the FAA's safety assessment page.

Children's Issues: Please see the U.S. Dept. of State Office of Children's Issues web pages on intercountry adoption and international parental child abduction.

Intercountry Adoption

January 2013

The information in this section has been edited from a report of the State Department Bureau of Consular Affairs, Office of Overseas Citizens Services. For more information, please read the *Intercountry Adoption* section of this book and review current reports online at http://adoption.state.gov.

Angola is not party to the Hague Convention on Protection of Children and Co-operation in Respect of Intercountry Adoption(the Hague Adoption Convention). Intercountry adoptions of children from non-Hague countries are processed in accordance with 8 Code of Federal Regulations, Section 204.3 as it relates to orphans as defined under the Immigration and Nationality Act, Section 101(b)(1)(F).

Adopting in Angola is a complex process. It can take years to identify a child for adoption and to complete all of the required steps and takes an Act of the National Assembly to approve each intercountry adoption. Prospective adoptive parents should note that Angolan adoption laws, which are currently being revised, are very strict. To ensure that the adoption process is completed successfully and in a timely manner, the U.S. Embassy in Angola strongly suggests that prospective adoptive parents consult an Angolan attorney.

Who Can Adopt? To bring an adopted child to United States from Angola, you must be found eligible to adopt by the U.S. Government. The U.S. Government agency responsible for making this determination is the Department of Homeland Security, U.S. Citizenship and Immigration Services (USCIS).

Residency: None.

Age of Adopting Parents: Prospective adoptive parents must be at least 25 years old and at least 16 years older than the prospective adoptive child.

Marriage: Prospective adoptive parents may be married, single, or in a common-law relationship.

Income: None.

Other: Prospective adoptive parent(s) must be in good physical and mental health, and financially capable of supporting and providing an education for the adopted child.

Who Can be Adopted? Angola has specific requirements that a child must meet in order to be eligible for adoption. You cannot adopt a child in Angola unless he or she meets the requirements outlined below. In addition to these requirements, a child must meet the definition of an orphan under U.S. law for you to bring him or her back to the United States.

Relinquishment: Adoption requires the consent of the prospective adoptive child's birth parent(s) or the legal guardian. Consent will be waived with regard to a child or adolescent whose parents are unknown or who have been stripped of their parental rights.

Abandonment: None.

Age of Adoptive Child: Less than 18 years old.

Sibling Adoptions: None.

Special Needs or Medical Conditions: None.

Waiting Period or Foster Care: Two years.

Prospective adoptive parents should be aware that not all children in orphanages or children's homes are adoptable. In many countries, birth parents place their child(ren) temporarily in an orphanage or children's home due to financial or other hardship, with the intention of returning for the child when they are able to do so. In such cases, the birth parent(s) have rarely relinquished their parental rights or consented to their child(ren)'s adoption.

Angola's Adoption Authority: National Office of Children and Adolescents of the Ministry of Social Assistance and Reintegration (MINARS); Ministry of Justice; and the National Parliament.

The Process: The recommended first step in adopting a child from Angola is to decide whether or not to use a licensed adoption service provider in the United States that can help you with your adoption. Adoption service providers must be licensed by the U.S. state in which they operate.

There are no specific adoption agencies in Angola. Prospective adoptive children can be selected from an orphanage or foster center. There are orphanages and foster children centers in all 18 provinces of Angola. After the selection of the child, prospective adoptive parents should inform MINARS and request assistance in completing the adoption process. A list of adoption attorneys in Angola may be found at the U.S. Embassy in Angola's website. The process for finalizing the adoption in Angola generally includes the following.

Role of Adoption Authority: There is no single adoption authority in Angola. The National Office of Children and Adolescents accepts adoption requests on behalf of MINARS. MINARS then processes and evaluates applications to be forwarded to the Family Court Room (a department of the Ministry of Justice).

Role of the Court: The Family Court Room reviews MINARS evaluations, provides permission for the prospective adoptive child be adopted, and forwards the file to the Assembleia Nacional (National Parliament) for final approval of the adoption.

Role of Adoption Agencies: There are no adoption service providers in Angola.

Adoption Application: Adoption by proxy is prohibited. Adoption requires the consent of the prospective adoptive child's birth parent(s) or the legal guardian. Consent will be waived with regard to a child or adolescent whose birth parents are unknown or who have forfeited their parental rights. A home study is required and will be evaluated by a Judge of the Family Court Room from the Provincial Court before the approval of the Parliament (National Assembly).

Prospective adoptive parent(s) should contact a local orphanage to identify a child for adoption through the National Office of Children and Adolescents. After a prospective adoptive child is identified, the orphanage contacts MINARS. If the prospective adoptive child is eligible for adoption, MINARS issues a document giving permission for the prospective adoptive child to be adopted. The process of identifying the child for adoption and receiving approval from MINARS can take 6-12 months. The prospective adoptive parent(s) then submit a request to the Family Court Room requesting approval from the National Assembly to adopt the child. Along with this request, the prospective adoptive parent attaches the following:

- A copy of the MINARS document giving permission for the child to be adopted;
- Birth certificates of the prospective adoptive parent(s);
- Marriage (and prior divorce) certificate of the prospective adoptive parents(s) (if applicable);
- Police clearance from home country and from Angola;
- Medical exam attesting good physical and mental health;
- Proof of financial support.

The process of approval from the Parliament can take between 12-18 months. Prospective adoptive parents should expect to submit certified copies of all documents. During the adoption process, the prospective adoptive parent(s) can submit a separate request to the Family Court Room requesting guardianship of the child. The request for guardianship can be submitted at the same time the request to the National Assembly is submitted. The request must be accompanied by the same documents listed above. A hearing will be scheduled at which the prospective adoptive parent(s) must be present. If the child is ten years of age or older, he/she will also be heard by the Trustee at the Family Court Room. This process may take three to six months to be completed. If the child is not an orphan, the prospective adoptive parent (s) will have to note that on their request and the Trustee of the Family Court Room will send a notification to the birth parents to appear in person and consent to the adoption of the child. Their consent will effectively permanently sever their parental rights. Once the National Assembly (Parliament) approves the adoption and the adoptive parent(s) receive the determination, that document must be submitted to the Family Court Room, and the Family Court Judge must issue the adoption decree.

Time Frame: An intercountry adoption in Angola can take anywhere from two to three years to complete from the time the child is identified.

Adoption Fees: The U.S. Embassy in Angola discourages the payment of any fees that are not properly receipted, "donations," or "expediting" fees, that may be requested from prospective adoptive parents. Such fees have the appearance of "buying" a baby and put all future adoptions in Angola at risk. Prospective adopting parents can expect to pay as much as $3,000.00 USD for government fees to complete the adoption. Attorney's fees are estimated to be an additional $10,000 USD.

Documents Required:

- Initial application can be made by a letter and should include the personal data of the prospective adoptive parents and the personal data of the prospective adoptive child. It does not need to be notarized;
- Criminal background check and clearance. The USCIS FBI background check is sufficient;
- Medical Evaluation can be conducted in the U.S. or Angola;
- Proof of income;
- Birth certificate of the prospective adoptive parent(s);
- Birth certificate (if available) for the prospective adoptive child or a statement from the institution where the child has been cared for;
- Marriage certificate and divorce decree(s) of prospective adoptive parent (s), if applicable;
- Consent from any living biological parent(s) of the child to adopt.

All documents must be translated into Portuguese. The translation needs to be done in Angola. The court will ask the translator to swear in court that the translation is correct.

Bringing Your Child Home: Once your adoption is complete (or you have obtained legal custody of the child), there are a few more steps to take before you can head home. Specifically, you need to apply for several documents for your child before he or she can travel to the United States, such as a birth certificate, a passport or travel document for your child from the country in which he or she was born, and a U.S. Immigration Visa. For detailed and updated information on how to obtain these documents, review the *Intercountry Adoption* section in this publication and visit the U.S. Department of State Intercountry Adoption website at http://adoption.state.gov.

Child Citizenship Act: For adoptions finalized abroad, the Child Citizenship Act of 2000 allows your new child to acquire American citizenship automatically when he or she enters the United States as lawful permanent residents. For adoptions finalized in the United States, the Child Citizenship Act of 2000 allows your new child to acquire American citizenship automatically when the court in the United States issues the final adoption decree.

U.S. Embassy in Angola
Rua Houari Boumedienne
#32 Miramar
Luanda, Angola
C.P. 6468
Consular Tel: (244)(222) 641-000
Fax: (244)(222) 641-259
Email: consularluanda@state.gov

Angola's Adoption Authorities:
Ministry of Justice, Family Court Room.
Sala da Familia, Tribunal Provincial de Luanda
Rua Amilcar Cabral No. 17, 5th and 7th Floor
Luanda, Angola

INAC—National Institute of the Child
Rua N'Gola M'Bambi
Luanda, Angola
Tel: 244-222 322 611; 222 323 683; 222 322 753

Embassy of Angola
2100-2108 16th Street, NW
Washington, DC 20009
Tel: 202-785-1156
Fax: 202-785-1258
Internet: http://www.angola.org

Office of Children's Issues
U.S. Department of State
2201 C Street, NW
SA-29
Washington, DC 20520
Tel: 1-888-407-4747
E-mail: AskCI@state.gov
http://adoption.state.gov

For questions about immigration procedures, call the National Customer Service Center (NCSC) at 1-800-375-5283 (TTY 1-800-767-1833).

ANTIGUA AND BARBUDA

Compiled from publications that were available as of February 2013 from the U.S. Department of State, the U.S. Department of Commerce, and the Central Intelligence Agency (CIA). See the introduction to this set for explanatory notes.

Official Name:
Antigua and Barbuda

PROFILE

Geography

Area: total: 442.6 sq km (Antigua 280 sq km; Barbuda 161 sq km); country comparison to the world: 201; land: 442.6 sq km; water: 0 sq km

Major cities: Saint John's (capital) 27,000 (2009)

Climate: tropical maritime; little seasonal temperature variation

Terrain: mostly low-lying limestone and coral islands, with some higher volcanic areas

People

Nationality: noun: Antiguan(s), Barbudan(s); adjective: Antiguan, Barbudan

Population: 89,018 (July 2012 est.)

Population growth rate: 1.276% (2012 est.)

Ethnic groups: black 91%, mixed 4.4%, white 1.7%, other 2.9% (2001 census)

Religions: Protestant 76.4% (Anglican 25.7%, Seventh-Day Adventist 12.3%, Pentecostal 10.6%, Moravian 10.5%, Methodist 7.9%, Baptist 4.9%, Church of God 4.5%), Roman Catholic 10.4%, other Christian 5.4%, other 2%, none or unspecified 5.8% (2001 census)

Languages: English (official), local dialects

Literacy: definition: age 15 and over has completed five or more years of schooling; total population: 85.8%; male: NA; female: NA (2003 est.)

Health: life expectancy at birth: total population: 75.69 years; male: 73.66 years; female: 77.83 years (2012 est.); Infant mortality rate: total: 14.17 deaths/1,000 live births; male: 16.32 deaths/1,000 live births; female: 11.91 deaths/1,000 live births (2012 est.)

Unemployment rate: 11% (2001 est.)

Work force: 30,000 (1991)

Government

Type: constitutional monarchy with a parliamentary system of government and a Commonwealth realm

Independence: 1 November 1981

Constitution: 1 November 1981

Political subdivisions: 6 parishes and 2 dependencies; Barbuda, Redonda, Saint George, Saint John, Saint Mary, Saint Paul, Saint Peter, Saint Philip

Suffrage: 18 years of age; universal

Economy

GDP (purchasing power parity): $1.535 billion (2012 est.); $1.595 billion (2011 est.); $1.603 billion (2010 est.); $1.76 billion (2009 est.)

GDP real growth rate: 1% (2012 est.); -0.5% (2011 est.); -8.9% (2010 est.); -10.3% (2009 est.)

GDP per capita (PPP): $17,500 (2012 est.); $18,200 (2011 est.); $18,300 (2010 est.); $20,100 (2009 est.)

Natural resources: NEGL; pleasant climate fosters tourism

Agriculture products: cotton, fruits, vegetables, bananas, coconuts, cucumbers, mangoes, sugarcane; livestock

Industries: tourism, construction, light manufacturing (clothing, alcohol, household appliances)

Exports: $37.9 million (2012 est.); $40.3 million (2011 est.); $45.33 million (2010 est.)

Exports—commodities: petroleum products, bedding, handicrafts, electronic components, transport equipment, food and live animals

Imports: $400 million (2012 est.); $437.4 million (2011 est.); $453.9 million (2010 est.)

Imports—commodities: food and live animals, machinery and transport equipment, manufactures, chemicals, oil

Debt—external: $359.8 million (June 2006)

Exchange rates: East Caribbean dollars (XCD) per US dollar; 2.7 (2012 est.); 2.7 (2011 est.)

PEOPLE

Antigua was first inhabited by the Siboney ("stone people"), whose settlements date at least to 2400 BC. The Arawaks—who originated in Venezuela and gradually migrated up the chain of islands now called the Lesser Antilles—succeeded the Siboney. The warlike Carib people drove the Arawaks from neighboring islands but apparently did not settle on either Antigua or Barbuda.

Religion

According to the 2001 census, 74 percent of the population is Christian. The Anglican Church is the largest religious group, accounting for an estimated 26 percent of the population. The Methodist, Moravian, and Roman Catholic churches account for less than 10 percent each. The United Evangelical Association, an organization that includes most independent evangelical churches, claims an estimated 25 percent of the population, and Jehovah's Witnesses number more than 1,000 members. Non-Christians include an estimated 1,000 to 1,500 Rastafarians, more than 200 Muslims, nearly 200 Hindus, and approximately 50 members of the Baha'i Faith.

HISTORY

Christopher Columbus landed on the islands in 1493, naming the larger one "Santa Maria de la Antigua." The English colonized the islands in 1632. Sir Christopher Codrington established the first large sugar estate in Antigua in 1674, and leased Barbuda to raise provisions for his plantations. Barbuda's only town is named after him. Codrington and others brought slaves from Africa's west coast to work the plantations.

Antiguan slaves were emancipated in 1834, but remained economically dependent on the plantation owners. Economic opportunities for the new freedmen were limited by a lack of surplus farming land, no access to credit, and an economy built on agriculture rather than manufacturing. Poor labor conditions persisted until 1939, which saw the birth of the trade union movement in Antigua and Barbuda. The Antigua Trades and Labour Union became the political vehicle for Vere Cornwall Bird, who was elected as the Labour Union's president in 1943. The Antigua Labour Party (ALP), formed by Bird and other trade unionists, first ran candidates in the 1946 elections and became the majority party in 1951, beginning a long history of electoral victories. Bird and the ALP were voted out of office in the 1971 general elections that swept the progressive labor movement into power, but returned to office in 1976, winning renewed mandates in every subsequent election under Vere Bird's leadership until 1994 and also under the leadership of his son, Lester Bird, until 2004. In March 2004 the ALP lost power in national elections that gave the United Progressive Party (UPP) 13 of the 17 seats in Parliament. In March 2009 elections, the ALP lost again to the Baldwin Spencer-led UPP, which won a slim majority, taking 9 of the 17 seats in Parliament; the ALP won 7 seats and the Barbuda People's Movement (BPM) won 1 seat.

GOVERNMENT AND POLITICAL CONDITIONS

Antigua and Barbuda is a multiparty, parliamentary democracy. In parliamentary elections in March 2009, which observers described as generally free and fair, the ruling United Progressive Party (UPP) defeated the Antigua Labour Party (ALP), and Baldwin Spencer was reelected as prime minister.

Recent Elections

In the March 2009 elections the ruling UPP won nine of 19 seats in the House of Representatives and 50 percent of the popular vote. Members of the Organization of American States observer group reported that the elections were generally free and fair. After the opposition ALP challenged the results of election, the Court of Appeal upheld the outcome, despite finding some technical problems in the election process.

Participation of Women and Minorities: There were two women in the House of Representatives and five women appointed to the 17-seat Senate. The governor general, the speaker of the House of Representatives, and the president of the Senate, all appointed positions, were women. There was one woman in the cabinet and one member of a minority in parliament.

Principal Government Officials

Last Updated: 1/31/2013

Governor Gen.: **Louise Agnetha LAKE-TACK**
Prime Min.: **Baldwin SPENCER**
Dep. Prime Min.: **Wilmoth DANIEL**
Min. of Agriculture, Lands, Housing, & the Environment:**Hilson BAPTISTE**
Min. of Education, Sports, Youth, & Gender Affairs: **Jacqui QUINN-LEANDRO**
Min. of Finance, the Economy, & Public Admin.: **Harold LOVELL**
Min. of Foreign Affairs: **Baldwin SPENCER**
Min. of Health, Social Transformation, & Consumer Affairs:**Wilmoth DANIEL**
Min. of National Security: **Errol CORT**
Min. of Tourism, Civil Aviation, & Culture: **John MAGINLEY**
Min. of Works & Transport: **Trevor WALKER**
Attorney Gen.: **Justin SIMON**
Ambassador to the US: **Deborah Mae LOVELL**
Permanent Representative to the UN, New York: **John W. ASHE**

ECONOMY

Tourism continues to dominate Antigua and Barbuda's economy, accounting for nearly 60% of GDP and 40% of investment. The dual-island nation's agricultural production is focused on the domestic market and constrained by a limited water supply and a labor shortage stemming from the lure of higher wages in tourism and con-

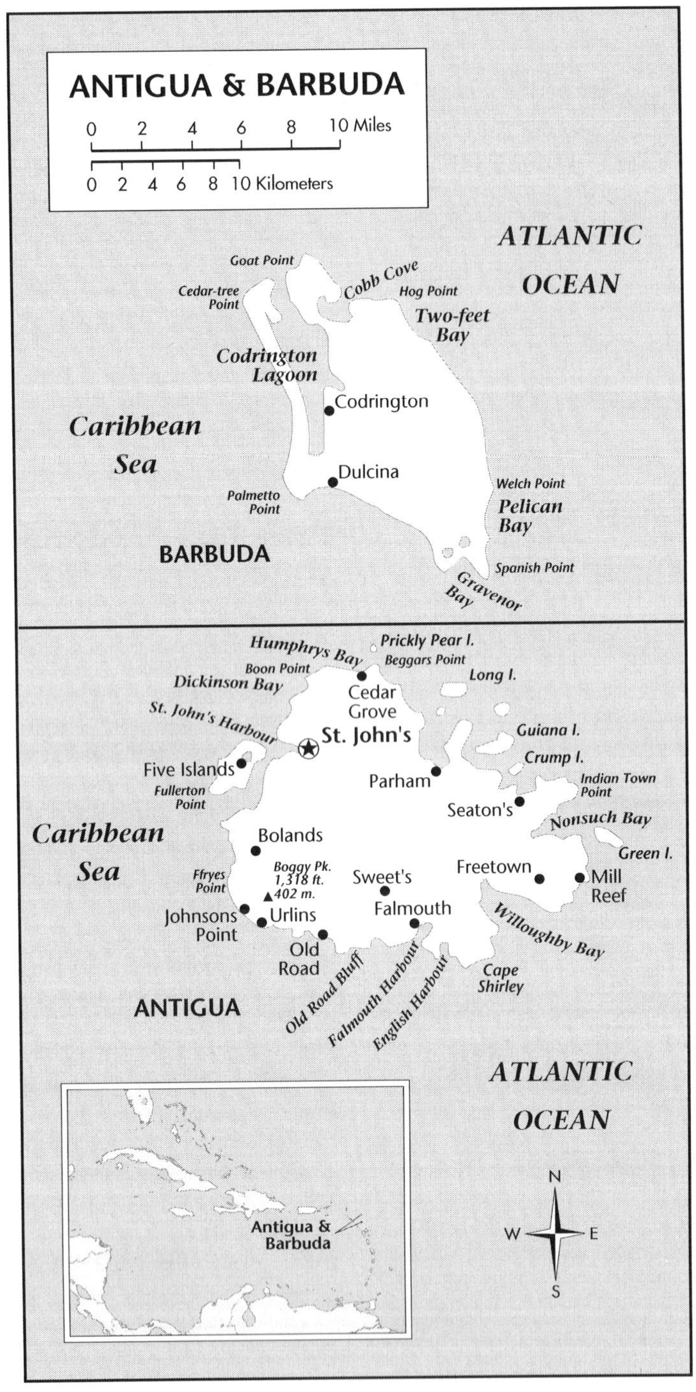

struction. Manufacturing comprises enclave-type assembly for export with major products being bedding, handicrafts, and electronic components. Prospects for economic growth in the medium term will continue to depend on tourist arrivals from the US, Canada, and Europe and potential damages from natural disasters. After taking office in 2004, the SPENCER government adopted an ambitious fiscal reform program and was successful in reducing its public debt-to-GDP ratio from 120% to about 90% in 2008. However, the global financial crisis that began in 2008, has led to a significant increase in the national debt, which topped 130% at the end of 2010.

The Antiguan economy experienced solid growth from 2003 to 2007, reaching over 12% in 2006 driven by a construction boom in hotels and housing associated with the Cricket World Cup, but growth dropped off in 2008 with the end of the boom. In 2009, Antigua's economy was severely hit by the global economic crisis and suffered from the collapse of its largest financial institution, a steep decline in tourism, a rise in debt, and a sharp economic contraction between 2009-11. Antigua has not yet returned to its pre-crisis growth levels.

Labor Conditions

The law stipulates a minimum working age of 16. In addition persons under age 18 must have a medical clearance to work and may not work later than 10 p.m. The Ministry of Labor, which is required by law to conduct periodic inspections of workplaces, effectively enforced this law. The Labor Commissioner's Office also had an inspectorate that investigated child labor. The government enforced these laws effectively, and child labor was not a problem.

The minimum wage was EC$7.50 ($2.78) an hour for all categories of labor. In practice the great majority of workers earned substantially more than the minimum wage.

The law provides that workers are not required to work more than a 48-hour, six-day workweek, but the standard workweek was 40 hours in five days. Laws provide for overtime work in excess of the standard workweek, requiring that employees be paid one and one half times the employees' basic wage per hour. Excessive or compulsory overtime is not specifically prohibited. There is a legal provision for paid annual holidays, which requires that no employee shall be obliged to work on a public holiday except in emergency situations. Employees receive their regular pay on holidays, unless an employee is required to work, in which case the employee would be paid an hourly rate of no less than 150 percent of the basic rate per hour worked.

The labor code includes provisions regarding occupational safety and health, but the government had not developed precise occupational health and safety laws or regulations apart from those regarding child labor.

U.S.-ANTIGUA AND BARBUDA RELATIONS

The United States established diplomatic relations with Antigua and Barbuda in 1981 following its independence from the United Kingdom. Relations between the United States and Antigua and Barbuda are friendly and cooperative. The United States has supported the Government of Antigua and Barbuda's efforts to encourage the country's economic development and to improve its citizens' security and standard of living.

Antigua and Barbuda's location close to the U.S. Virgin Islands and Puerto Rico makes it an attractive transshipment point for narcotics traffickers. To address these problems, the United States and Antigua and Barbuda have signed a series of counternarcotic and anticrime treaties and agreements, including a maritime law enforcement agreement, subsequently amended to include overflight and order-to-land provisions; a bilateral extradition treaty; and a mutual legal assistance treaty. The United States and Antigua and Barbuda also cooperate through partnerships including the Partnership Framework for HIV and AIDS, the Energy and Climate Partnership of the Americas, and the Caribbean Youth Empowerment Program.

Antigua and Barbuda is strategically situated in the Leeward Islands near maritime transport lanes of major importance to the United States. Antigua has long hosted a U.S. military presence. The U.S. Air Force operates a satellite tracking station under a lease agreement with the Government of Antigua and Barbuda.

The United States maintains no official diplomatic presence in Antigua. The Ambassador and Embassy officers are resident in Barbados and travel to Antigua frequently. A U.S. consular agent resident in Antigua assists U.S. citizens in Antigua and Barbuda.

U.S. Assistance to Antigua and Barbuda

U.S. assistance to Antigua and Barbuda is primarily channeled through multilateral agencies such as the World Bank and the Caribbean Development Bank, and through the U.S. Agency for International Development office in Bridgetown, Barbados. Antigua and Barbuda also receives U.S. counternarcotics assistance, and it benefits from U.S. military exercise-related and humanitarian civic assistance construction projects, including through the Caribbean Basin Security Initiative.

Bilateral Economic Relations

Antigua and Barbuda is a beneficiary of the U.S. Caribbean Basin Initiative (CBI), which grants duty-free entry into the United States for many goods. The CBI aims to facilitate the economic development and export diversification of the Caribbean Basin economies. Antigua and Barbuda is a member of the Caribbean Community and Common Market (CARICOM). At the 2012 meeting of the U.S.-CARICOM Trade and Investment Council, the parties approved an action agenda outlining priorities for strengthening and deepening the trading relationship.

Antigua and Barbuda's Membership in International Organizations

Antigua and Barbuda and the United States belong to a number of the same international organizations, including the United Nations, Organization of American States, International Monetary Fund, World Bank, and World Trade Organization.

Bilateral Representation

Antigua and Barbuda maintains an embassy in the United States at 3216 New Mexico Ave. NW, Washington, DC 20016 (tel. 202-362-5122).

Principal U.S. Embassy Officials

Last Updated: 1/14/2013

BRIDGETOWN (E) Wildey Business Park, Wildey, St. Michael BB 14006, 246-227-4000, Fax 246-227-4088, Workweek: Mon-Fri: 8.00–4.30, Website: http://bridgetown.usembassy.gov/

DCM OMS:	Frances Youmans
AMB OMS:	Ellen Benjamin-Leon
CDC:	Rachel Alabalak
Co-CLO:	Kathryn Mctigue Floyd
DHS/CBP:	Stephen Bows
FM:	Bruce Youmans
HRO:	Traci Cassilly
MGT:	Jeremey Neitzke
MLO/ODC:	CDR Michael Long
NAS/INL:	Kurt Van Der Walde
PAO/ADV:	Rachel Zaspel
POSHO:	Bruce Youmans
SDO/DATT:	CDR Michael Long
AMB:	Larry Palmer
CG:	Mark Bysfield
DCM:	Christopher Sandrolini
PAO:	Rebecca Ross
GSO:	M. Holly Peirce
RSO:	Thomas W.Baker
AFSA:	Vacant
AID:	Daniel Smolka
CLO:	Ylodia (Lisa) Robinson
DEA:	Charles Graham
ECON:	Brian Greaney
EEO:	Gregory Floyd
FAA:	Dawn Flanagan (Res. Washington)
FMO:	W. Lee Thompson
ICASS Chair:	Charles Graham
IMO:	Michael Cassilly
IRS:	Andrew Thornton
ISO:	Frederick Melton
ISSO:	Pic Jordan
LAB:	Gregory Floyd
LEGATT:	David Brooks
POL:	Brian Greaney
State ICASS:	Kurt Van Der Walde

TRAVEL

Consular Information Sheet

March 9, 2010

Country Description: Antigua and Barbuda is a dual island nation known for its beaches, and is a favorite destination for yachtsmen. Tourist facilities are widely available. English is the primary language. Banking facilities and ATMs are available throughout the island.

Smart Traveler Enrollment Program (STEP)/Embassy Location: If you are going to work, live, or travel abroad, please take the time to tell the local U.S. Embassy about your trip. If you enroll, the Embassy can keep you up to date with important safety and security announcements. It will also help your friends and family get in touch with you in an emergency. Antigua and Barbuda are covered by the U.S. Embassy in Bridgetown, Barbados, which is in located in the Wildey Business Park in suburban Wildey, southeast of downtown Bridgetown. The Consular Section can be reached by telephone at 246-227-4193, by fax at 246-431-0179, or by e-mail, ConsularBridge2 @state.gov. After hours the Embassy Duty Officer can be reached by calling (246) 227-4000. Hours of operation are 8:30 a.m.–4:00 p.m., Monday–Friday, except local and U.S. holidays. The U.S. Embassy maintains a Consular Agency in Antigua, located at Suite #2 Jasmine Court, Friars Hill Road, St. John's. The phone number is 268-463-6531, and the Consular Agent can also be reached via cell phone at 268-726-6531. The Agent can assist with routine American Citizens Services and with American citizen emergencies taking place in Antigua and Barbuda.

Entry Requirements: The Intelligence Reform and Terrorism Prevention Act of 2004 requires all travelers to and from the Caribbean, Bermuda, Panama, Mexico and Canada to have a valid passport to enter or re-enter the United States. U.S. citizens must have a valid U.S. passport if traveling by air, including to and from Mexico. If traveling by sea, U.S. citizens can use a passport or passport card. We strongly encourage all American citizen travelers to apply for a U.S. passport or passport card well in advance of anticipated travel. American citizens can visit http://travel.state.gov/ or call 1-877-4USA-PPT (1-877-487-2778) for information on how to apply for a passport. Immigration officials are strict about getting exact information about where visitors are staying and will often request to see a return ticket or ticket for onward travel, as well as proof of sufficient funds to cover the cost of the visitor's intended stay. There is a departure tax required upon departing the country.

For further information on entry requirements, travelers can contact the Embassy of Antigua and Barbuda, 3216 New Mexico Avenue, N.W., Washington, D.C. 20016, telephone 202-362-5122, or their consulate in Miami. Additional information may be found on the Internet on the home page of the Antigua and Barbuda Department of Tourism.

Safety and Security: For the latest security information, Americans traveling abroad should regularly monitor the Department's Internet web site at http://travel.state.gov where the current Worldwide Caution Travel Alert, Travel Warnings and Travel Alerts can be found. Up-to-date information on safety and security can also be obtained by calling 1-888-407-4747 toll free in the U.S., or for callers outside the U.S. and Canada, a regular toll line at 1-202-501-4444.

Crime: Violent crimes, including rape and murder, do occur, including at hotels and main tourist venues, and visitors should take precautions to ensure their safety. From 2008 to January 2010, four tourists were murdered in Antigua—a British couple on their honeymoon, an Australian yacht captain, and, most recently, an American citizen on a shore excursion from a cruise ship. Visitors should be especially vigilant on the beaches after dusk. Recently, tourists have been targeted on isolated beaches such as Pigeon Point, and visitors should always avoid visiting isolated beaches alone. Armed robbery and street crime also occur, and valuables left unattended on beaches, in rental cars or in hotel rooms are vulnerable to theft. Visitors to Antigua and Barbuda are advised to be alert and maintain the same level of personal security used when visiting major U.S. cities. Be especially vigilant when taking taxis in Antigua and Barbuda. Make certain that the taxi driver is licensed and is a member of the official taxi association. Unlicensed taxi operators have been known to extort money from passengers, despite having agreed to a fare beforehand. This can sometimes amount to double or triple the agreed-upon fare.

Information for Victims of Crime: If you or someone you know becomes the victim of a crime abroad, you should contact the local police and the nearest U.S. embassy or consulate. If your passport is stolen they can help you replace it. For violent crimes such as assault and rape, they can help you find appropriate medical care, contact family members or friends, and help them send you money if you need it. Although the investigation and prosecution of the crime are solely the responsibility of local authorities, consular officers can help you to understand the local criminal justice process and to find an attorney if you need one.

Medical Facilities and Health Information: There are many qualified doctors in Antigua and Barbuda, but medical facilities are limited to a public hospital and a private clinic and are not up to U.S. standards. The principal medical facility on Antigua is Holberton Hospital, on Hospital Road, St. John's (telephone (268) 462-0251). There is no hyperbaric chamber; divers requiring treatment for decompression illness must be evacuated from the island, to either Saba or Guadeloupe. Serious medical problems requiring hospitalization and/or medical evacuation to the United States can cost thousands of dollars. Doctors and hospitals often expect immediate cash payment for health services, and U.S. medical insurance is not always valid outside the United States.

HIV/AIDS entry restrictions may exist for visitors to and foreign residents of Antigua and Barbuda. Please verify the requirements with the Embassy of Antigua and Barbuda before you travel. Information on vaccinations and other health precautions, such as safe food and water and insect bite protection, may be obtained from the Centers for Disease Control and Prevention's hotline for international travelers at 1-877-FYI-TRIP (1-877-394-8747) or via the CDC's Internet site at http://www.cdc.gov/travel. For information about outbreaks of infectious diseases abroad, consult the World Health Organization's (WHO) website at http://www.who.int/en.

Medical Insurance: You can't assume your insurance will go with you when you travel. It's very important to find out BEFORE you leave. You need to ask your insurance company two questions: Does my policy apply when I'm out of the U.S.? Will it cover emergencies like a trip to a foreign hospital or an evacuation? In many places, doctors and hospitals still expect payment in cash at the time of service. Your regular U.S. health insurance may not cover doctors' and hospital visits in other countries. If your policy doesn't go with you when you travel, it's a very good idea to take out another one for your trip.

Traffic Safety and Road Conditions: While in a foreign country, U.S. citizens may encounter road conditions that differ significantly from those in the United States. The information below concerning Antigua and Barbuda is provided for general reference only, and may not be totally accurate in a particular location or circumstance. Traffic in Antigua and Barbuda moves on the left. Major roads are in average to poor condition, and drivers may encounter wandering animals and slow moving heavy equipment. Drivers often stop in the middle of the roadway without warning, so you should always maintain a safe distance from the vehicle in front of you and watch for signs of sudden braking. There is relatively little police enforcement of traffic regulations.

Aviation Safety Oversight: The U.S. Federal Aviation Administration (FAA) has assessed the Government of Antigua and Barbuda's Civil Aviation Authority as being in compliance with International Civil Aviation Organization (ICAO) aviation safety standards for the oversight of Antigua and Barbuda'sair carrier operations. For more information, travelers may visit the FAA's internet website at http://www.faa.gov.

Special Circumstances: Like all Caribbean countries, Antigua can be affected by hurricanes. The hurricane season normally runs from early June to the end of November, but there have also been hurricanes in December in recent years. General information about natural disaster preparedness is available via the Internet from the U.S. Federal Emergency Management Agency (FEMA) at www.fema.gov. Antiguan law prohibits same-sex marriage, and even the impression that a same-sex marriage is taking place can be construed as a violation of that law.

Visitors are warned against holding any type of ceremony or event that could appear to be a same-sex marriage. American citizens have been arrested by the Antiguan police for this type of activity in the recent past.

The justice system moves slowly in Antigua and Barbuda, and the police force is currently undergoing an overhaul due to corruption and ineffectiveness uncovered in a 2008 government-funded official inquiry. In mid-2008 a former Canadian police officer was appointed as police commissioner with the mandate of modernizing the 550-strong police force. At present, the police continue to be negligent in providing timely notification to the embassy of the arrest of an American citizen and access to American citizens post-arrest has on occasion been restricted. In 2009 and early 2010, some American visitors alleged that they were physically abused by arresting officers of the Antigua and Barbuda police force. These allegations are currently being investigated by the Government of Antigua and Barbuda.

Criminal Penalties: While in a foreign country, a U.S. citizen is subject to that country's laws and regulations, which sometimes differ significantly from those in the United States and may not afford the protections available to the individual under U.S. law. Penalties for breaking the law can be more severe than in the United States for similar offences. Persons violating Antigua and Barbuda's laws, even unknowingly, may be expelled, arrested or imprisoned. For instance, an American visitor was arrested recently for disorderly conduct and was imprisoned until sentencing, where she was fined a significant sum. She was found guilty of using foul language and resisting arrest. Penalties for possession, use, or trafficking in illegal drugs in Antigua and Barbuda are severe, and convicted offenders can expect long jail sentences and heavy fines. Engaging in sexual conduct with children or using or disseminating child pornography in a foreign country is a crime, prosecutable in the United States.

Children's Issues: For information on intercountry adoption of children and international parental child abduction, see the Office of Children's Issues website at http://travel.state.gov.

International Parental Child Abduction

January 2012

The information in this section has been edited from the last available report of the State Department Bureau of Consular Affairs, Office of Overseas Citizens Services (as of February 2013). For more information, please read the *International Parental Child Abduction* section of this book and check for potential updates online at www.travel.state.gov/abduction.

Disclaimer: The information in this flyer relating to the legal requirements of specific foreign countries is provided for general information only. Questions involving interpretation of specific foreign laws should be addressed to foreign legal counsel.

General Information: Antigua and Barbuda are not a party to the Hague Convention on the Civil Aspects of International Child Abduction, nor are there any international or bilateral treaties in force between Antigua and Barbuda and the United States dealing with international parental child abduction.

American citizens who travel to Antigua and Barbuda place themselves under the jurisdiction of local courts. American citizens planning a trip to Antigua and Barbuda with dual national children should bear this in mind.

Custody Disputes: In Antigua and Barbuda parents who are legally married share the custody of their children. If they are not married, by law the custody is granted to the mother unless there are known facts of inappropriate behavior, mental or social problems. Foreign court orders are not automatically recognized.

Enforcement of Foreign Judgments: Custody orders and judgments of foreign courts are not enforceable in Antigua and Barbuda if they potentially contradict or violate local laws and practices. For example, an order from a U.S. court granting custody to an American mother will not be honored in Antigua and Barbuda if the mother intends to take the child to live outside Antigua and Barbuda. Nor will Antigua and Barbuda courts enforce U.S. court decrees ordering a parent in Antigua and Barbuda to pay child support.

Visitation Rights: In cases where the father has custody of a child, the mother is guaranteed visitation rights. It has been the experience of the U.S. Embassy in Barbados that the father and the paternal grandparents of the child are generally open and accommodating in facilitating the right of the mother to visit and maintain contact with the child.

Dual Nationality: Dual nationality is recognized under Antiguan law. Children of Antigua and Barbuda parents and grandparents automatically acquire Antigua and Barbuda citizenship at birth, regardless of where the child was born. They are free to enter and leave the country on Antigua and Barbuda passports even if they are entitled to hold the passport of another country.

Passports for Minors and the Children's Passport Issuance Alert Program: For more information on these topics, see the International Parental Child Abduction section of this publication and review current reports from the U.S. Department of State at www.travel.state.gov/abduction.

Travel Restrictions: No exit visas are required to leave Antigua and Barbuda. However, a mother may face serious legal difficulties if she attempts to take her children out of Antigua and Barbuda without the permission of the father. Immigration officials at the airport or border may ask to see such permission in writing before allowing children to exit.

Criminal Remedies: For information on possible criminal remedies, please contact your local law enforcement authorities or the nearest office of the Federal Bureau of Investigation (FBI). Information is also available on the Internet at the web site of the U.S. Department of Justice, Office of Juvenile Justice and Delinquency Prevention (OJJDP) at http://www.ojjdp.ncjrs.org. Persons who wish to pursue a child custody claim in an Antiguan court should retain an attorney in Antigua and Barbuda. The U.S. Embassy in Barbados maintains a list of attorneys willing to represent American clients. A copy of this list may be obtained by requesting one from the Embassy at:

U.S. Embassy Bridgetown
Consular Section
ALICO Building, Cheapside
P O Box 302
Bridgetown
Barbados
Telephone: [246] 431-0225
Fax: [246] 431-0179
Web site: www.usembassy.state.gov/bridgetown

Questions involving Antiguan law should be addressed to an Antiguan attorney or to the Embassy of Antigua and Barbuda in the United States at:

Embassy of Antigua and Barbuda
3216 New Mexico Avenue, NW
Washington, DC 20016
Telephone: (202) 362-5122/5166/5211
AmbLHurst@aol.com

For further information on international parental child abduction, contact the Office of Children's Issues, U.S. Department of State at 1-888-407-4747 or visit its web site on the Internet at http://travel.state.gov.

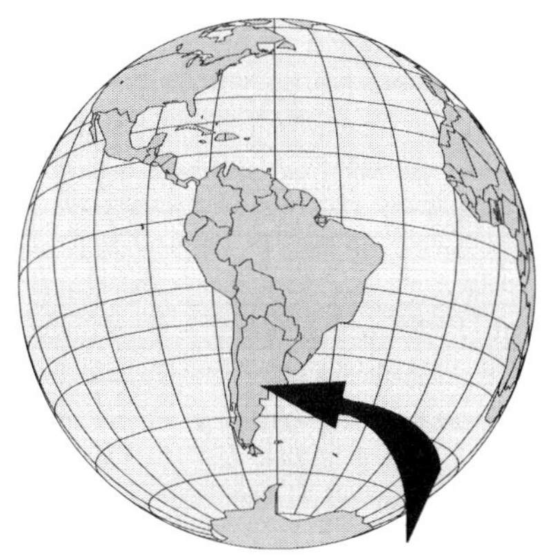

ARGENTINA

Compiled from publications that were available as of February 2013 from the U.S. Department of State, the U.S. Department of Commerce, and the Central Intelligence Agency (CIA). See the introduction to this set for explanatory notes.

Official Name:
The Argentine Republic

PROFILE

Geography

Area: total: 2,780,400 sq km; country comparison to the world: 8; land: 2,736,690 sq km; water: 43,710 sq km
Major cities: Buenos Aires (capital) 12.988 million; Cordoba 1.493 million; Rosario 1.231 million; Mendoza 917,000; San Miguel de Tucuman 831,000 (2009)
Climate: mostly temperate; arid in southeast; subantarctic in southwest
Terrain: rich plains of the Pampas in northern half, flat to rolling plateau of Patagonia in south, rugged Andes along western border

People

Nationality: noun: Argentine(s); adjective: Argentine
Population: 42,192,494 (July 2012 est.)
Population growth rate: 0.997% (2012 est.)
Ethnic groups: white (mostly Spanish and Italian) 97%, mestizo (mixed white and Amerindian ancestry), Amerindian, or other non-white groups 3%
Religions: nominally Roman Catholic 92% (less than 20% practicing), Protestant 2%, Jewish 2%, other 4%
Languages: Spanish (official), Italian, English, German, French, indigenous (Mapudungun, Quechua)
Literacy: definition: age 15 and over can read and write; total population: 97.2%; male: 97.2%; female: 97.2% (2001 census)
Health: life expectancy at birth: total population: 77.14 years; male: 73.9 years; female: 80.54 years (2012 est.); Infant mortality rate: total: 10.52 deaths/1,000 live births; male: 11.76 deaths/1,000 live births; female: 9.22 deaths/1,000 live births (2012 est.)
Unemployment rate: 7.2% (2012 est.)
Work force: 10.07 million (2012 est.)

Government

Type: republic
Independence: 9 July 1816
Constitution: 1 May 1853; amended many times starting in 1860
Political subdivisions: 23 provinces (provincias, singular—provincia) and 1 autonomous city
Suffrage: 18-70 years of age; universal and compulsory

Economy

GDP (purchasing power parity): $746.9 billion (2012 est.); $725.6 billion (2011 est.); $666.5 billion (2010 est.); $610.6 billion (2009 est.)
GDP real growth rate: 2.6% (2012 est.); 8.9% (2011 est.); 9.2% (2010 est.); 0.9% (2009 est.)
GDP per capita (PPP): $18,200 (2012 est.); $17,700 (2011 est.); $16,400 (2010 est.); $15,200 (2009 est.)
Natural resources: fertile plains of the pampas, lead, zinc, tin, copper, iron ore, manganese, petroleum, uranium
Agriculture products: sunflower seeds, lemons, soybeans, grapes, corn, tobacco, peanuts, tea, wheat; livestock
Industries: food processing, motor vehicles, consumer durables, textiles, chemicals and petrochemicals, printing, metallurgy, steel
Exports: $85.36 billion (2012 est.); $84.27 billion (2011 est.); $68.13 billion (2010 est.)
Exports—commodities: soybeans and derivatives, petroleum and gas, vehicles, corn, wheat
Exports—partners: Brazil 21.8%, China 7.4%, Chile 5.6%, US 5.5% (2011)
Imports: $67.33 billion (2012 est.); $70.73 billion (2011 est.); $53.87 billion (2010 est.)
Imports—commodities: machinery, motor vehicles, petroleum and natural gas, organic chemicals, plastics
Imports—partners: Brazil 33.2%, US 14.4%, China 12.4%, Germany 4.7% (2011)
Debt—external: $130.2 billion (31 December 2012 est.)
Exchange rates: Argentine pesos (ARS) per US dollar; 4.569 (2012 est.); 4.1101 (2011 est.); 3.8963 (2010 est.); 3.7101 (2009); 3.1636 (2008)

PEOPLE

Argentines are a mix of diverse national and ethnic groups, with descendants of Italian and Spanish immigrants predominant. Waves of immigrants from many European countries arrived in the late 19th and early 20th centuries. Syrian, Lebanese, and other Middle Eastern immigrants number about 500,000 to 600,000, mainly in urban areas.

Indigenous People

The constitution recognizes the ethnic and cultural identities of indigenous people and states that the congress shall protect their right to bilingual education, recognize their communities and the communal ownership of their ancestral lands, and allow for their participation in the management of their natural resources. In practice indigenous people did not fully participate in the management of their lands or natural resources, in part because responsibility for implementing the law is delegated to the 23 provinces, only 11 of which have constitutions recognizing indigenous rights. Although there is no formal process to recognize indigenous tribes or determine who is an indigenous person, indigenous communities can register with the provincial or federal government as civic associations.

Estimates of the indigenous population ranged from 700,000 to 1.5 million. Poverty rates were higher than average in areas with large indigenous populations. Indigenous people had greater than average rates of illiteracy, chronic disease, and unemployment. Indigenous women faced further discrimination based on gender and reduced economic status. The lack of trained teachers hampered government efforts to offer bilingual education opportunities to indigenous people.

Languages

Spanish is the national language of Argentina, although many businesspeople speak English as well as other European languages.

Religion

A study by the National Council of Scientific and Technical Research and the National Agency for the Promotion of Science and Technology, released in 2008, estimated that Roman Catholics constitute 76 percent of the population, and Baptists, Jews, Muslims, Jehovah's Witnesses, Lutherans, Methodists, and members of The Church of Jesus Christ of Latter-day Saints (Mormons) each total less than 5 percent of the population. Leaders of diverse religious groups noted the recent growth of evangelical Protestant communities. According to independent studies, the Jewish community consists of approximately 200,000-250,000 members.

HISTORY

Europeans arrived in the region with the 1502 voyage of Amerigo Vespucci. Spanish navigator Juan Diaz de Solias visited what is now Argentina in 1516. Spain established a permanent colony on the site of Buenos Aires in 1580, although initial settlement was primarily overland from Peru. The Spanish further integrated Argentina into their empire by establishing the Vice Royalty of Rio de la Plata in 1776, and Buenos Aires became a flourishing port. Argentina formally declared independence from Spain on July 9, 1816. Argentines revere Gen. Jose de San Martin—who campaigned in Argentina, Chile, and Peru—as the hero of their national independence. Following the defeat of the Spanish, centralist and federalist groups waged a lengthy conflict to determine the future of the nation. A modern constitution was promulgated in 1853, and a national unity government was established in 1861.

Two forces combined to create the modern Argentine nation in the late 19th century: the introduction of modern agricultural techniques and integration of Argentina into the world economy. Foreign investment and immigration from Europe aided this economic revolution. Investment, primarily from Britain, came in such fields as railroads and ports. As in the United States during this same period, the migrants who worked to develop Argentina's agricultural resources and early industrialization came principally from throughout Europe.

From 1880 to 1930, Argentina became one of the world's 10 wealthiest nations as a result of the rapid expansion of agriculture and foreign investment in infrastructure. The Great Depression brought a halt to this period of booming expansion, and combined with other social and political changes to usher in a period of less stable governance. The governments of the 1930s attempted to contain the currents of economic and political change that eventually led to a military coup and the subsequent emergence of Juan Domingo Peron (b. 1897). New social and political forces were seeking political power, including a modern military and labor movements that emerged from the growing urban working class.

The military ousted Argentina's constitutional government in 1943. Peron, then an army colonel, was one of the coup's leaders, and he soon became the government's dominant figure as Minister of Labor. Elections carried him to the presidency in 1946. He created the Partido Unico de la Revolucion, which became more commonly known as the Peronist or Justicialista party (PJ). He aggressively pursued policies aimed at empowering the working class and greatly expanded the number of unionized workers. In 1947, Peron announced the first 5-year plan based on the growth of industries he nationalized. He helped establish the powerful General Confederation of Labor (CGT). Peron's charismatic wife, Eva Duarte de Peron, known as Evita (1919–52), played a key role in developing support for her husband. Peron won re-election in 1952, but the military sent him into exile in 1955. In the 1950s and 1960s, military and civilian administrations traded power, trying, with limited success, to deal with diminished economic growth and continued social and labor demands. When military governments failed to revive the economy and suppress escalating domestic terrorism in the late 1960s and early 1970s, the way was open for Peron's return.

On March 11, 1973, Argentina held general elections for the first time in 10 years. Peron was prevented from running, but voters elected his stand-in, Dr. Hector Campora, as President. Peron's followers also commanded strong majorities in both houses of Congress. Campora resigned in July 1973, paving the way for new elections. Peron won a decisive victory and returned as President in October 1973 with his third wife, Maria Estela Isabel Martinez de Peron, as Vice President. During this period, extremists on the left and right carried out violent acts with a frequency that threatened public order. The government resorted to a number of emergency decrees, including the implementation of special executive authority to deal with violence. This allowed the government to imprison persons indefinitely without charge.

Peron died on July 1, 1974. His wife succeeded him in office, but a military coup removed her from office on March 24, 1976, and the armed forces formally exercised power through a junta composed of the three service commanders until December 10, 1983. The armed forces applied harsh measures against those they considered extremists and many others suspected of being their sympathizers. While they were able to gradually restore basic order, the human costs of what became known as "El Proceso," or the "Dirty War," were high. Official sources have identified approximately 9,000 persons who were "disappeared" during the 1976–83 military dictatorship, while some human rights groups put the figure as high as 30,000. Serious economic problems, mounting charges of corruption, public revulsion in the face of human rights abuses and, finally, the country's 1982 defeat by the United Kingdom in an unsuccessful attempt to seize the Falklands (Malvinas) Islands all combined to discredit the Argentine military regime. The junta lifted bans on political parties and gradually restored basic political liberties.

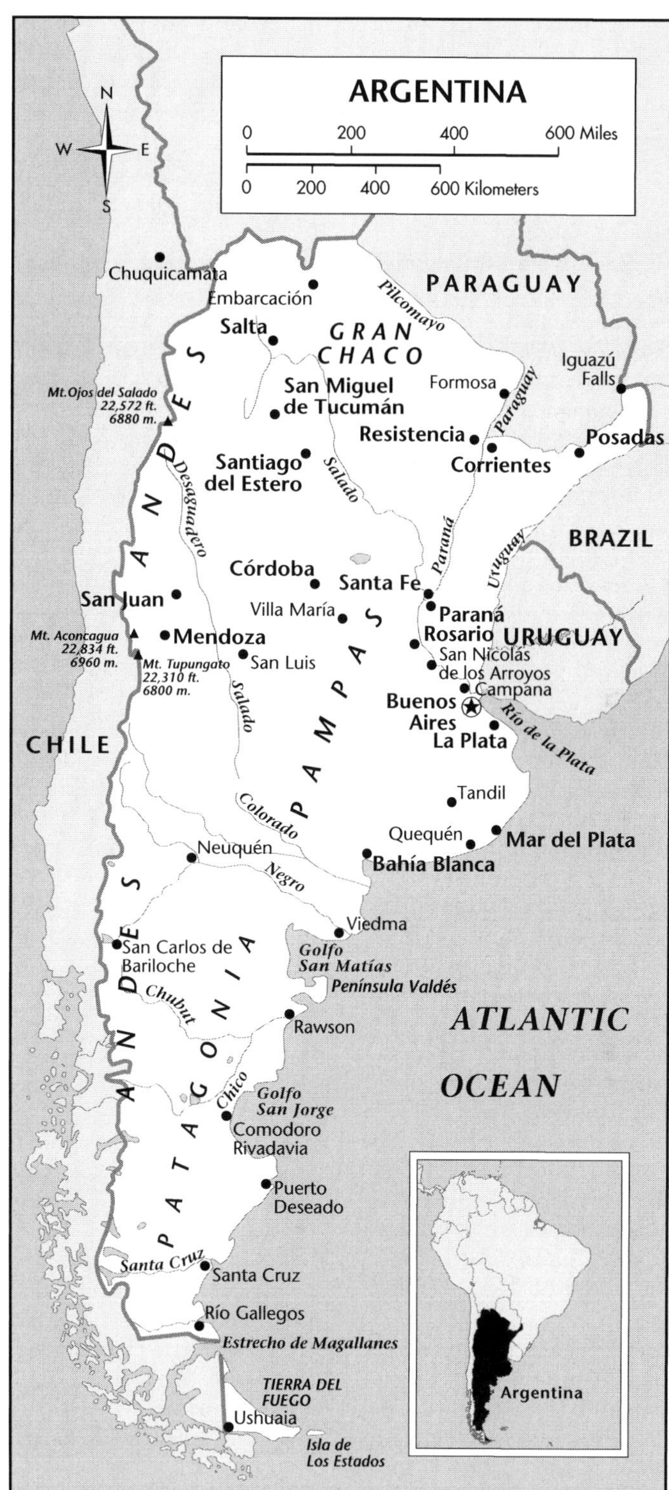

Democracy returned to Argentina in 1983, with Raul Alfonsin of the country's oldest political party, the Radical Civic Union (UCR), winning the presidency in elections that took place on October 30, 1983. He began a 6-year term of office on December 10, 1983. The UCR-led government took steps to resolve some of the nation's most pressing problems, including accounting for those who disappeared during military rule, establishing civilian control of the armed forces, and consolidating democratic institutions. However, inability to resolve endemic economic problems eventually undermined public confidence in Alfonsin, who left office 6 months early after Justicialista Party (PJ) candidate Carlos Saul Menem won the 1989 presidential elections.

President Menem imposed peso-dollar parity (convertibility) in 1992 to break the back of hyperinflation and adopted far-reaching market-based policies. Menem dismantled a web of protectionist trade and business regulations and reversed a half-century of statism by implementing an ambitious privatization program. These reforms contributed to significant increases in investment and growth with stable prices through most of the 1990s. Unfortunately, persistent allegations of corruption also accompanied many of the reforms, eventually undermining public confidence in the government and economy. Neither Menem nor his successor President Fernando De la Rua, who won election in 1999 at the head of a UCR-led coalition of center and center-left parties known as the "Alianza," were able to maintain public confidence and the recovery weakened. Also, while convertibility defeated inflation, its permanence undermined Argentina's export competitiveness and created chronic deficits in the current account of the balance of payments, which were financed by massive borrowing. The contagion effect of the Asian financial crisis of 1998 precipitated an outflow of capital that gradually mushroomed into a 4-year depression culminating in a financial panic in November 2001. In December 2001, amidst bloody riots, President De la Rua resigned.

After a period of political turmoil and several provisional presidents, a legislative assembly elected Eduardo Duhalde (PJ) President on January 1, 2002 to complete the term of former President De la Rua. Duhalde—differentiating himself from his three predecessors—quickly abandoned the peso's 10-year-old link with the dollar, a move that was followed by a sharp currency depreciation and rising inflation. In the face of increasing poverty and continued social unrest, Duhalde moved to bolster the government's social programs and to contain inflation. He stabilized the social situation and advanced presidential elections by 6 months in order to pave the way for a new president elected with a popular mandate.

In the first round of the presidential election on April 27, 2003, former President Carlos Menem (PJ) won 24.3% of the vote, Santa Cruz Governor Nestor Kirchner (PJ) won 22%, followed by smaller party/alliance candidates Ricardo Lopez Murphy with 16.4% and Elisa Carrio with 14.2%. Menem withdrew from the May 25 runoff election after polls showed overwhelming support for Kirchner in the second round of elections. After taking office, Kirchner focused on consolidating his political strength and alleviating social problems. He pushed for changes in the Supreme Court and military and undertook popular measures such as raising government salaries, pensions, and the minimum wage. On October 23, 2005, President Kirchner, bolstered by Argentina's rapid economic growth and recovery from its 2001–2002 crisis, won a major victory in the midterm legislative elections, giving him a strengthened mandate and control of a legislative majority in both the Senate and Chamber of Deputies.

Although Kirchner enjoyed approval ratings of over 60%, he announced in July 2007 that he would not seek re-election and backed his wife, then-Senator Cristina Fernandez de Kirchner, as the candidate to succeed him. Fernandez de Kirchner had a decades-long pedigree in politics, having served in the Chamber of Deputies and the Senate. She won 45% of the vote in the October 2007 presidential election and defeated her closest competitor, Elisa Carrio of the Civic Coalition, by 22.25 percentage points. Cristina Fernandez de Kirchner became the first Argentine woman elected to the presidency. "Cristina," as Argentines often refer to her, was sworn into office on December 10, 2007. Fernandez de Kirchner was overwhelmingly re-elected on October 23, 2011, winning 54% of the vote; Santa Fe Governor Hermes Binner (Socialist) received 17%, Ricardo Alfonsin (UCR) earned 11%, San Luis Governor Alberto Rodriguez Saa received 8%, and former president Eduardo Duhalde came in with 6%. Fernandez de Kirchner won the largest share of the vote and the widest margin of victory (37 percentage points) of any presidential candidate since the restoration of democracy in Argentina in 1983. She, Vice President Amado Boudou, and her cabinet were sworn into office on December 10, 2011.

GOVERNMENT AND POLITICAL CONDITIONS

Argentina is a federal constitutional republic. Cristina Fernandez de Kirchner was reelected to the presidency in October 2011 in multiparty elections that media and various nongovernmental organizations (NGOs) described as generally free and fair. Security forces report to civilian authorities but occasionally act independently of civilian control.

Recent Elections

On October 23, voters reelected President Cristina Fernandez de Kirchner of the Front for Victory Party in polling described by media and various NGOs as free and fair. In concurrent legislative elections, voters elected one-half of the members of the Chamber of Deputies representing all 24 provinces and one-third of those in the Senate representing eight provinces. Local observers considered these elections generally free and fair.

Participation of Women and Minorities: Decrees provide that one-third of the candidates on election slates for both houses of congress must be women. There were 28 women in the 72-seat Senate and 98 women in the 257-seat Chamber of Deputies. The president, two of the seven Supreme Court justices, and three cabinet ministers were women. There were no known ethnic or racial minorities in the national legislature. There were no known indigenous, ethnic, or racial minorities in the cabinet or on the Supreme Court.

Principal Government Officials

Last Updated: 1/31/2013

Pres.: **Cristina FERNANDEZ DE KIRCHNER**
Vice Pres.: **Amado BOUDOU**
Chief of Cabinet: **Juan Manuel ABAL MEDINA**
Min. of Agriculture: **Norberto YAUHAR**
Min. of Defense: **Arturo Antonio PURICELLI**
Min. of Economy & Public Finance: **Hernan Gaspar LORENZINO**
Min. of Education: **Alberto SILEONI**
Min. of Federal Planning, Public Investment, & Services:**Julio DE VIDO**
Min. of Foreign Relations & Worship: **Hector Marcos TIMERMAN**
Min. of Health: **Juan Luis MANZUR**
Min. of Industry: **Debora Adriana GIORGI de Ordonez**
Min. of Interior: **Anibal Florencio RANDAZZO**
Min. of Justice & Human Rights: **Julio Cesar ALAK**
Min. of Labor, Employment, & Social Security: **Carlos TOMADA**
Min. of Science, Technology, & Productive Innovation:**Lino BARANAO**
Min. of Security: **Nilda GARRE**
Min. of Social Development: **Alicia KIRCHNER**
Min. of Tourism: **Carlos Enrique MEYER**
Pres., Central Bank: **Mercedes MARCO DEL PONT**
Ambassador to the US: **Jorge Martin Arturo ARGUELLO**
Permanent Representative to the UN, New York:

ECONOMY

Argentina benefits from rich natural resources, a highly literate population, an export-oriented agricultural sector, and a diversified industrial base. Although one of the world's wealthiest countries 100 years ago, Argentina suffered during most of the 20th century from recurring economic crises, persistent fiscal and current account deficits, high inflation, mounting external debt, and capital flight. A severe depression, growing public and external indebtedness, and a bank run culminated in 2001 in the most serious economic, social, and political crisis in the country's turbulent history. Interim President Adolfo Rodriguez Saa declared a default—the largest in history—on the government's foreign debt in December of that year, and abruptly resigned only a few days after taking office. His successor, Eduardo Duhalde, announced an end to the peso's decade-long 1-to-1 peg to the US dollar in early 2002. The economy bottomed out that year, with real GDP 18% smaller than in 1998 and almost 60% of Argentines under the poverty line.

Real GDP rebounded to grow by an average 8.5% annually over the subsequent six years, taking advantage of previously idled industrial capacity and labor, an audacious debt restructuring and reduced debt burden, excellent international financial conditions, and expansionary monetary and fiscal policies. Inflation also increased, however, during the administration of President Nestor Kirchner, which responded with price restraints on businesses, as well as export taxes and restraints, and beginning in early 2007, with understating inflation data.

Cristina Fernandez De Kirchner succeeded her husband as President in late 2007, and the rapid economic growth of previous years began to slow sharply the following year as government policies held back exports and the world economy fell into recession. The economy in 2010 rebounded strongly from the 2009 recession, but has slowed since late 2011 even as the government continued to rely on expansionary fiscal and monetary policies, which have kept inflation in the double digits.

Labor Conditions

The minimum age for employment is 16 years old. In rare cases, the respective labor authority may authorize a younger child to work as part of a family unit. Children between the ages of 16 and 18 years may work in a limited number of job categories and for limited hours if they have completed compulsory schooling, which normally ends at age 18. Children under 18 cannot be hired to perform perilous, arduous, or unhealthy jobs. In December this prohibition expanded to include rural workers as well, and the congress passed a law to amend rural working conditions. The law requires employers to provide adequate care for workers' children during work hours to discourage child labor.

Child labor persists in practice. A 2004 government survey revealed that an estimated 450,000 children were working, or 7 percent of children between the ages of five and 13 years and 20 percent of children over the age of 14. In rural areas children worked in family and third-party farms producing such goods as blueberries, cotton, garlic, grapes, olives, strawberries, tobacco, tomatoes, and yerba mate.

In urban areas some children engaged in domestic service and worked on the street selling goods, shining shoes, and recycling trash. According to government sources, some children worked in the manufacturing sector producing such goods as bricks, matches, fireworks, and garments. Children were also found working in the mining, fishing, and construction sectors.The government increased the monthly minimum wage for most workers in September to 2,300 pesos ($550). This exceeded the amount of 1,386 pesos ($324) a month that the National Census and Statistics Institute estimated was needed by a family of four to remain above the poverty line.

Federal labor law sets standards in the areas of health, safety, and hours. The maximum workday is eight hours, and the maximum workweek is 48 hours. Overtime pay is required for hours worked in excess of these limits. The law sets minimums for periods of rest, requiring a minimum of 12 hours of rest to start a new workday. Sundays are holidays, and those required to work on Sundays are paid double. Paid vacations are mandatory for all workers for a minimum of 14 days and a maximum of 35 days, depending on the length of their service.

The law sets premium pay for overtime, adding an extra 50 percent of the hourly rate on ordinary days and 100 percent on Saturday afternoons, Sundays, and holidays. Employees cannot be forced to work overtime unless work stoppage would risk or cause injury, the need for overtime is caused by an act of God, or other exceptional reasons affecting the national economy or "unusual and unpredictable situations" affecting businesses occur. Workers have the right to remove themselves from dangerous or unhealthy work situations without jeopardy to continued employment. However, workers who leave the workplace before it has been proven unsafe risk being fired; in such cases, the worker has the right to judicial appeal, but the process was typically very lengthy.

The law requires employers to insure their employees against accidents at the workplace and when traveling to and from work. The law requires that employers either provide insurance through a labor risk insurance entity or provide its own insurance to employees to meet specified requirements set forth by the national insurance regulator.

Domestic employees, rural workers, free lance workers, and the volunteer firemen corps are excluded from the above provisions regarding minimum wages, hours of work, and occupational safety and health. The law includes separate minimum wage and hour regulations for domestic employees and rural workers.

Laws governing acceptable conditions of work were not enforced universally, particularly for workers in the informal sector. According to a 2007 ILO study, 60 percent of employed citizens ages 15 to 24 were engaged in informal labor. In practice, most workers in the formal sector earned significantly more than the minimum wage. Generally speaking, the minimum wage served to mark the minimum pay an informal worker should get, although formal workers' pay was usually higher.

U.S.-ARGENTINE RELATIONS

The United States established diplomatic relations with Argentina in 1823 following its independence from Spain. The bilateral relationship between the United States and Argentina is based on shared interests including regional peace and stability, non-proliferation, human rights, education, cultural exchanges, and commercial ties. The Government of Argentina has supported U.S. national and international security goals through participation in international peacekeeping operations and advocacy for the nonproliferation of weapons of mass destruction. U.S.-Argentine cooperation also includes science and technology initiatives in the fields of space, peaceful uses of nuclear energy, agricultural research and biotechnology, medicine, and the environment. The first bilateral joint science and technology working group meeting was held in 2010, and in 2011 the United States and Argentina signed an agreement on the peaceful uses of outer space. The United States and Argentina also have a binational energy working group.

U.S. Assistance to Argentina

U.S. assistance in Argentina promotes regional stability and democracy, and builds nonproliferation cooperation on export controls and border security.

Bilateral Economic Relations

The United States is one of Argentina's largest trading partners with a historic high of $22 million in trade in goods and services in the last year. U.S. exports to Argentina include machinery, oil, organic chemicals, and plastic. U.S. imports from Argentina include mineral fuel and oil, aluminum, wine, iron and steel products, and preserved foods. The two countries have signed a bilateral investment treaty, and the more than 500 U.S. companies are among the top investors in the country with nearly $15 billion invested in the country. U.S. direct investment in Argentina is mostly in mining, nonbank holding companies, and manufacturing. In 2007, the U.S. and Argentina modernized a bilateral civil aviation agreement to update safety and security and provide for more-frequent flights between the two countries, allowing for increased volumes of tourism and business travel.

Argentina's Membership in International Organizations

Argentina and the United States are active participants in many of the same international organizations and forums, including the United Nations, Organization of American States, International Atomic Energy Agency, the G-20, and the and World Trade Organization. Argentina will join the UN Security Council as a non-permanent member in January 2013.

Bilateral Representation

Argentina maintains an embassy in the United States at 1600 New Hampshire Ave. NW, Washington DC 20009; tel. (202) 238-6400.

Principal U.S. Embassy Officials

Last Updated: 1/14/2013

BUENOS AIRES (E) Avda. Colombia 4300, 54-11-5777-4533, Fax 54-11-5777-4240, Workweek: 0845 AM–0545 PM, Website: http://argentina.usembassy.gov/

DCM OMS:	Ginete, Malenereynee
AMB OMS:	Taylor, Wendy
Co-CLO:	Catan, Dena
DHS/ICE:	Aguilar, Raul
DHS/TSA:	Catan, Joseph
FCS:	Koloditch, James
FM:	Krueger, Steven
GFS:	Charleston Finance Center
HRO:	Patrick, Jane
MGT:	Dayringer, James
MLO/ODC:	COL Hall, Patrick
SDO/DATT:	COL Cook, Anthony
AMB:	Martinez, Vilma S.
CG:	Perrone, Daniel
CON:	Perrone, Daniel

DCM: Brown, Jefferson T.
PAO: Bosshardt, Marcia
GSO: Antolinez, Lori
RSO: Sivertson, Kristen
AFSA: Vacant
AGR: Sallyards, Melinda
APHIS: Perez-Marcano, Yvette
CLO: Murphey, Brooke
DEA: Gonzalez, Stephen
ECON: Stater, Timothy
EST: Cullinane, Mark
FMO: Wickersham, James
ICASS Chair: Gonzalez, Scott
IMO: Payton, Wayne
IPO: Schaffer, Craig
ISSO: Lee, John
LEGATT: Eckel, Michael
POL: Ludwig, Alexis
State ICASS: Ludwig, Alexis

Other Contact Information

American Chamber of Commerce in Argentina
Viamonte 1133, 8th floor
Buenos Aires, Argentina
Tel (54)(11) 4371-4500
Fax (54)(11) 4371-8400

U.S. Department of Commerce
Office of Latin America and the Caribbean
International Trade Administration
1401 Constitution Avenue, NW
Washington, DC 20230
Tel (202) 482-3872
Fax (202) 482-4157
Internet: http://trade.gov/

TRAVEL

Consular Information Sheet

November 2, 2011

Country Description: Argentina's cultural and culinary traditions, natural beauty and diversity, as well as its business opportunities attract nearly 500,000 U.S. citizen visitors each year. Buenos Aires, other large cities, as well as some rural destinations, have well-developed tourist facilities and services, including many four-and five-star hotels. The quality of tourist facilities in smaller towns outside the capital varies.

Smart Traveler Enrollment Program (STEP)/Embassy Locations: If you are going to live in or visit Argentina, please take the time to tell our Embassy about your trip. If you sign up, we can keep you up to date with important safety and security announcements. We can also help your friends and family get in touch with you in an emergency.

U.S. Embassy Buenos Aires, Argentina
Avenida Colombia 4300, Palermo
Telephone: (54) (11) 5777-4533
Emergency after-hours telephone: (54) (11) 5777-4873
Facsimile: (54) (11) 5777-4293

The Consular Section is open to the public from 8:30 a.m. to noon and from 2:30 p.m. to 4:00 p.m. Monday through Friday, except on U.S./Argentine holidays or administrative processing days. We are always available for emergencies. Additional information on Embassy services is available on the Internet at U.S. Embassy Buenos Aires, Argentina or by e-mail at American Citizen Services.

Entry/Exit Requirements for U.S. Citizens: A valid passport is required for U.S. citizens to enter Argentina. U.S. citizens do not need a visa for visits of up to 90 days for tourism or business. U.S. citizen tourist and business travelers arriving in Argentina at either Ezeiza or Jorge Newbery airports must pay an entry fee. It can be paid in dollars, by credit card, or with traveler's checks, and is valid for ten years and multiple entries. It applies only to bearers of tourist passports. Travelers bearing diplomatic or official passports are not charged, nor are travelers transiting and not entering Argentina. U.S. citizens who arrive in Argentina with expired or damaged passports may be refused entry and returned to the United States at their own expense. The U.S. Embassy cannot provide guarantees on behalf of travelers in such situations, and we encourage you to ensure that your travel documents are valid and in good condition prior to departure from the United States. Different rules apply to U.S. citizens who also have Argentine nationality, depending on their dates of U.S. naturalization. For more information, check the Argentine Ministry of the Interior website, which is currently only available in the Spanish language. Argentine-born naturalized U.S. citizens who enter Argentina as temporary visitors may depart using their U.S. passports as long as they remain for the period granted by the Argentine immigration officer at the time of entry (typically 60–180 days). Travelers in this category who overstay will be required to obtain an Argentine passport to depart. Children under 18 years of age who reside in Argentina, regardless of nationality, are required to present a notarized document that certifies both parents' permission for the child's departure from Argentina when the child is traveling alone, with only one parent, or in someone else's custody.

U.S. citizens wishing to enter Brazil or Paraguay from Argentina are required to obtain a visa in advance from the appropriate Embassy or consulate nearest to the traveler's place of residence. Travelers transiting between Brazil or Paraguay and Argentina should always make sure to present their passports to Argentine immigration officials to have their entry and exit from Argentina recorded. The U.S. Embassy in Buenos Aires cannot assist travelers with obtaining Brazilian or Paraguayan visas. For more information, see the Country Specific Information for Brazil and Paraguay.

HIV/AIDS Restrictions: The U.S. Department of State is unaware of any HIV/AIDS entry restrictions for visitors to or foreign residents of Argentina.

Threats to Safety and Security: Pedestrians and drivers should exercise caution, as drivers frequently ignore traffic laws and vehicles often travel at excessive speeds. The rate and toll of traffic accidents has been a topic of much local media attention. The U.S. government is supportive of coordinated efforts by Argentina, Brazil, and Paraguay to combat illegal activity in the tri-border region, where there is a long-standing pattern of trafficking of illicit goods. U.S.

citizens crossing from Argentina into Paraguay or Brazil may wish to consult the most recent Country Specific Information for Brazil and Paraguay.

Demonstrations are common in metropolitan Buenos Aires and occur in other major cities as well. Protesters on occasion block streets, highways, and major intersections, causing traffic jams and delaying travel. While demonstrations are usually nonviolent, some individuals break from larger groups and sometimes seek confrontation with the police and vandalize private property. Groups occasionally protest in front of the U.S. Embassy and U.S.-affiliated businesses. U.S. citizens should take common-sense precautions and avoid gatherings or any other event where crowds have congregated to protest. Information about the location of possible demonstrations is available from a variety of sources, including the local media.

Domestic flight schedules can be unreliable. Occasional work stoppages, over-scheduling of flights and other technical problems can result in flight delays, cancellations, or missed connections. Consult local media or the airline company for information about possible strikes or slow-downs before planning travel within Argentina.

Public transportation is generally reliable and safe. The preferred option for travel within Buenos Aires and other major cities is by radio taxi or "remise" (private car with driver). The best way to obtain safe taxis and remises is to call for one or go to an established stand, rather than hailing one on the street. Hotels, restaurants, and other businesses can order remises or radio taxis, or provide phone numbers for such services, upon request.

Passengers on buses, trains, and the subway should be alert for pickpockets and should also be aware that these forms of transport are sometimes interrupted by strikes or work stoppages. Argentina's mountains, forests, deserts, and glaciers make it a popular destination for outdoor and adventure sports enthusiasts. Despite the best efforts of local authorities, assisting visitors lost or injured in such remote areas can be difficult. U.S. citizens have died in recent years while mountain climbing, skiing, trekking, and hunting in Argentina. Travelers visiting isolated and wilderness areas should learn about local hazards and weather conditions and always inform park or police authorities of their itineraries. Reports of missing or injured persons should be made immediately to the police so that a search can be mounted or assistance rendered. Argentina boasts the highest peak outside of the Himalayas, Mount Aconcagua. Its guidebook billing as affordable and "requiring no climbing skills" attracts hundreds of U.S. citizens every year. However, inexperienced mountaineers should bear in mind that Aconcagua's 22,840-foot altitude, bitter cold, and savage storms make it, in fact, one of the world's most difficult climbs.

Stay up to date by:

- Bookmarking our Bureau of Consular Affairs website, which contains the current Travel Warnings and Travel Alerts as well as the Worldwide Caution.
- Following us on Twitter and the Bureau of Consular Affairs page on Facebook as well.
- Downloading our free Smart Traveler iPhone App to have travel information at your fingertips.
- Calling 1-888-407-4747 toll-free within the U.S. and Canada, or a regular toll line, 1-202-501-4444, from other countries.
- Taking some time before travel to consider your personal security.

Crime: Most U.S. citizens visit Argentina without incident. Nevertheless, street crime in the larger cities, especially greater Buenos Aires and Mendoza, is a problem for residents and visitors alike. As in any big city, visitors to Buenos Aires and popular tourist destinations should be alert to muggers, pickpockets, scam artists, and purse-snatchers on the street, in hotel lobbies, at bus and train stations, and in cruise ship ports. Be careful in San Telmo, an older traditional neighborhood specializing in antique stores and La Boca neighborhood (home to the famous "Caminito" street and "Boca Juniors" soccer stadium) in Buenos Aires, where violent robberies have been occurring with increasing frequency. Tourists who go to La Boca should limit their visit to the designated tourist areas during daylight hours. Criminals usually work in groups, and travelers should assume they are armed.

Criminals employ a variety of ruses to distract and victimize unsuspecting visitors. A common scam is to spray mustard or a similar substance on the tourist from a distance. A pickpocket will then approach the tourist offering to help clean the stain, and while doing so, he or an accomplice robs the victim. Another scam is to entice tourists into a bar known as a "wiskeria" with a flyer for a shopping discount or free show. Once inside, the victim is not allowed to leave until he or she pays an exorbitant amount for a drink.

Thieves regularly nab unattended purses, backpacks, laptops, and luggage, and criminals will often distract visitors for a few seconds to steal valuables. While most U.S. citizens are not physically injured when robbed, criminals are known to use force when they encounter resistance. Visitors are advised to immediately hand over all cash and valuables if confronted. Thieves may target visitors wearing expensive watches or jewelry, or carrying laptop computer cases.

Some travelers have received counterfeit currency in Argentina. Unscrupulous vendors and taxi drivers sometimes pretend to help tourists review their pesos, then trade bad bills for good ones. Characteristics of good currency can be reviewed at the Argentine Central Bank website. Along with conventional muggings, "express kidnappings" occur. Victims are grabbed off the street based on their appearance and vulnerability. They are made to withdraw as much money as possible from ATM machines, and then their family or co-workers are contacted and told to deliver all the cash that they have on hand or can gather in a couple of hours. Once the ransom is paid, the victim is usually quickly released unharmed. There have been some foreign victims. Visitors are particularly advised not to let children and adolescents travel alone.

Travelers worldwide are advised to avoid packing valuables in their checked baggage. In Argentina, officials have publicly acknowledged the systematic theft of valuables and money from checked baggage at Buenos Aires airports. Authorities are working to resolve the problem and have made a number of arrests, but travelers should exercise continued care and caution. Don't buy counterfeit and pirated goods, even if they are widely available. Not only are the bootlegs illegal in the United States, if you purchase them you may also be breaking local law. Your passport is a valuable document and should be guarded. Passports and other valuables should be locked in a hotel safe, and a photocopy of your passport should be carried for identification purposes. The U.S. Embassy has observed an increase in reports of stolen passports in the past years.

Victims of Crime: If you or someone you know becomes the victim of a crime abroad, you should contact the local police and the nearest U.S. embassy or consulate (see the Department of State's list of embassies and consulates). We can:

- Replace a stolen passport.
- Help you find appropriate medical care if you are the victim of violent crimes such as assault or rape.
- Put you in contact with the appropriate police authorities, and if you want us to, we can contact family members or friend.
- Help you understand the local criminal justice process and direct you to local attorneys, although it is important to remember that local authorities are responsible for investigating and prosecuting the crime.

The Argentine Federal Police have established a special Tourist Police Unit to receive complaints and investigate crimes against tourists. The unit, located at Corrientes 436 in Buenos Aires, responds to calls around the clock at 4346–5748 or toll-free 0800-999-5000 from anywhere in the country. The Mendoza Tourist Police Unit, open 7 a.m. to 10 p.m. daily, is located at San Martin 1143, telephone 0261-413-2135. After hours, the Mendoza unit may be reached by cell phone at 0261-15-6444-324. The local equivalent to the "911" emergency line in the city of Buenos Aires or in the surrounding Province of Buenos Aires is 911 for police assistance. In the city of Buenos Aires, dial 100 in case of fire and 107 for an ambulance. In the Province of Buenos Aires, fire and ambulance numbers vary by location.

Criminal Penalties: While you are traveling in Argentina, you are subject to its laws even if you are a U.S. citizen. Foreign laws and legal systems can be vastly different than our own. In some places you may be taken in for questioning if you don't have your passport with you. In some places, it is illegal to take pictures of certain buildings.

In some places driving under the influence could land you immediately in jail. There are also some things that might be legal in Argentina, but still illegal in the United States, and you can be prosecuted under U.S. law if you buy pirated goods. Engaging in sexual conduct with children or using or disseminating child pornography in a foreign country is a crime prosecutable in the United States. If you break local laws in Argentina, your U.S. passport won't help you avoid arrest or prosecution. It's very important to know what's legal and what's not wherever you go.Based on the Vienna Convention on Consular Relations, bilateral agreements with certain countries, and customary international law, if you are arrested in Argentina, you have the option to request that the police, prison officials, or other authorities alert the nearest U.S. embassy or consulate of your arrest, and to have communications from you forwarded to the nearest U.S. embassy or consulate.

Special Circumstances: In addition to being subject to all Argentine laws affecting U.S. citizens, dual nationals may also be subject to other laws that impose special obligations on Argentine citizens. In some instances, dual nationality may hamper U.S. Government efforts to provide protection abroad. Please see our information on Customs Regulations.

Accessibility: While in Argentina, individuals with disabilities may find accessibility and accommodation very different from what you find in the United States. It is important to note that a specific law mandates access to buildings for persons with disabilities; however, while the federal government has protective laws, many provinces have not adopted the laws and have no mechanisms to ensure enforcement.

Medical Facilities and Health Information: Information on vaccinations and other health precautions, such as safe food and water precautions and insect bite protection, may be obtained from the Centers for Disease Control and Prevention's (CDC) hotline for international travelers at 1-877-FYI-TRIP (1-877-394-8747) or via the CDC website. For information about outbreaks of infectious diseases abroad, consult the infectious diseases section of the World Health Organization (WHO) website. The WHO website also contains additional health information for travelers, including detailed country-specific health information.

Medical Insurance: You can't assume your insurance will go with you when you travel. It's very important to find out BEFORE you leave whether or not your medical insurance will cover you overseas. You need to ask your insurance company two questions:

- Does my policy apply when I'm out of the United States?

- Will it cover emergencies like a trip to a foreign hospital or a medical evacuation?

In many places, doctors and hospitals still expect payment in cash at the time of service. Your regular U.S. health insurance may not cover doctor and hospital visits in other countries. If your policy doesn't go with you when you travel, it's a very good idea to take out another one for your trip.

Traffic Safety and Road Conditions: While in Argentina, you may encounter road conditions that differ significantly from those in the United States. Driving in Argentina is generally more dangerous than driving in the United States. By comparison, drivers in Argentina tend to be aggressive, especially in Buenos Aires, and often ignore traffic regulations. U.S. driver's licenses are valid in the capital and the province of Buenos Aires, but Argentine or international licenses are required to drive in the rest of the country.

Aviation Safety Oversight: The U.S. Federal Aviation Administration (FAA) has assessed the government of Argentina's Civil Aviation Authority as being in compliance with International Civil Aviation Organization (ICAO) aviation safety standards for oversight of Argentina's air carrier operations. Further information may be found on the FAA's safety assessment page.

Children's Issues: Please see the U.S. Dept. of State Office of Children's Issues web pages on intercountry adoption and international parental child abduction.

Intercountry Adoption

November 2008

The information in this section has been edited from the latest report available as of February 2013 from the State Department Bureau of Consular Affairs, Office of Overseas Citizens Services. For more information, please read the *Intercountry Adoption* section of this book and review current reports online at http://adoption.state.gov. Argentina is not party to the Hague Convention on Protection of Children and Co-operation in Respect of Intercountry Adoption (Hague Adoption Convention). Therefore, when the Hague Adoption Convention entered into force for the United States on April 1, 2008, intercountry adoption processing for Argentina did not change. Argentina does not currently allow intercountry adoption. Adoption is restricted to Argentine citizens and permanent resident aliens residing in Argentina.

Who Can Adopt? To bring an adopted child to United States from Argentina, you must be found eligible to adopt by the U.S. Government. The U.S. Government agency responsible for making this determination is the Department of Homeland Security, U.S. Citizenship and Immigration Services (USCIS).

Residency Requirements: Applicants must be Argentine nationals or permanent resident aliens of Argentina for at least the five years immediately preceding the application for guardianship (first step in the adoption process).

Age Requirements: If single, the prospective adoptive parent must be at least 30 years of age. There is no minimum age requirement for married prospective adoptive parents. At least one member of the couple must be at least 18 years older than the adoptee.

Marriage Requirements: Married couples must be married at least three years and have no offspring. If the couple can prove they are physically unable to have a child, the court will consider marriages under 3 years. Married couples must adopt jointly except when there is a legal separation decree, the spouse is declared mentally incompetent by a court, or there is a judicial declaration of absence of spouse (presumption of death).

Income Requirements: Prospective adoptive parents must prove financial ability.

Who Can Be Adopted? Argentina has specific requirements that a child must meet in order to be eligible for adoption. You cannot adopt a child in Argentina unless he or she meets the requirements outlined below.

Eligibility Requirements: Biological parents may relinquish their children for adoption only through the courts. This release is irrevocable and can only be signed at the court by appointment set by a judge at least 60 days after the child's birth. It cannot be done immediately following the birth. The law provides for the 60-day window after the birth of the child to allow the birth mother time to think about her decision.

During this 60-day period, the court may review the personal conditions of the biological parents, their age, ability to take care of the child, reasons for the release for adoption and any other considerations and information pertinent to this act. A judge may request the opinion of, technical advice from, and/or the effective participation of a Defensor de Menores e Incapaces from the Minsterio Publico de la Defensa to determine the best interests of the child. A release by the biological parents will not be necessary in those instances when the child is a ward of the court, already an orphan on the streets, or has been housed in a government institution continuously for more than one year without any indication of interest from the birth parent(s).

Argentine Adoption Authority: While there is no official adoption authority, prospective adoptive parents must apply to Consejo Nacionalde Niñez, Adolescencia y Familia.

The Process: The first step in adopting a child is usually to select a licensed agency in the United States that can help with your adoption. Adoption service providers must be licensed by the U.S. state in which they operate. Because Argentina does not currently allow intercountry adoption, and adoption is restricted to Argentine citizens and permanent resident aliens residing in Argentina, the following information is meant to be a general overview of the process for those who are qualified to adopt. To bring an adopted child from Argentina to the United States, you must apply to be found eligible to adopt (Form I-600A) by the U.S. Government, Department of Homeland Security, U.S. Citizenship and Immigration Services (USCIS). Prospective adoptive parents must file an application with the court having jurisdiction over their domicile.

In that application, they may indicate their preference for the child's gender and age, and whether they consider themselves capable to adopt a child with health problems or other special needs. The prospective adoptive parents' names will be placed on a single nationwide list by filing date and be made public. The Consejo de la Ninez, Adolenscencia y Familia will inform them when their turn is reached. Adoptive parents may check their name status by contacting the Consejo at the address included in the Contact Information Section.

If you are eligible to adopt, and a child is available for intercountry adoption, the central adoption authority in Argentina will provide you with a referral to a child. Once matched with a child, the court will release a child in guardianship to the prospective adoptive parents. The child will remain under the jurisdiction of the court for the full period of guardianship. Application for adoption can only be filed after the guardianship period of no less than six months and not more than twelve months has elapsed. Birth parents will lose all rights and obligations after that time and these rights will be transferred to the prospective adoptive parents.

Role of the Court: The Argentine court releases a child in guardianship to the prospective adoptive parents when a suitable match has been determined.

Adoption Application: Adoption application can be filed after the guardianship period of 6-12 months has elapsed. After this guardianship period, birth parents lose all rights and obligations to the child.

Time Frame: Once guardianship has been awarded by the court, it takes between six months to a year to obtain the final adoption decree.

Adoption Fees: There are no fixed adoption fees to conclude an adoption in Argentina. Filing the petition for guardianship (to lead to adoption) is free. Prospective adoptive parents are responsible for attorney fees although some courts do provide free legal assistance. The judge may set fees for other services rendered.

Documents Required: The following documents are required for adoption in Argentina:

- Proof of Argentine citizenship or legal permanent residence in Argentine for the last five years
- Copy of the prospective adoptive parents' marriage certificate (if applicable)
- Evidence of good conduct
- Evidence of financial ability

The adopted child will be granted the father's surname or compound father and mother's surname is requested by the parents. The adoptive parents may request the issuance of a new birth certificate identifying the adoptive parents as the child's legal parents. After you finalize the adoption (or gain legal custody) in Argentina, the U.S Government, Department of Homeland Security, U.S. Citizenship and Immigration Services (USCIS) MUST determine whether the child is eligible under U.S. law to be adopted (Form I-600).

Bringing Your Child Home: Once your adoption is complete (or you have obtained legal custody of the child), there are a few more steps to take before you can head home. Specifically, you need to apply for several documents for your child before he or she can travel to the United States, such as a birth certificate, a passport or travel document for your child from the country in which he or she was born, and a U.S. Immigration Visa. For detailed and updated information on how to obtain these documents, review the *Intercountry Adoption* section on this publication and visit the USCIS Intercountry Adoption website at http://adoption.state.gov.

Child Citizenship Act: For adoptions finalized abroad, the Child Citizenship Act of 2000 allows your new child to acquire American citizenship automatically when he or she enters the United States as lawful permanent residents. To learn more, review the *Intercountry Adoption* section on this publication and visit the USCIS Intercountry Adoption website at http://adoption.state.gov.

After Adoption: By Argentine law, adoptive parents must inform the child of his/her adoption before the child turns 18 years of age. Parents must sign this commitment at the court at the time the adoption is granted. According to the laws in Argentina, adopted children have the right to know their true biological identity and will have access to their adoption file once they have reached the age of 18.

U.S. Embassy, Buenos Aires, Argentina
4300 Avenida Colombia
1425 Buenos Aires
Argentina
Main Telephone:
(011)(54)(11) 5777-4533
Consular Fax: (54)(11) 5777-4448
http://argentina.usembassy.gov

Argentine Adoption Authority
Secretaria National de la Ninez,
Adolescencia y Familia
Av. Peron 524 piso 1 (for adoptions)
Telephone: (54)(11) 4338-5800

Embassy of Argentina
1600 New Hampshire Ave., N.W.
Washington, D.C. 20009
Tel: (202) 939-6400

Office of Children's Issues
U.S. Department of State
2201 C Street, NW
SA-29
Washington, DC 20520
Tel: 1-888-407-4747
E-mail: AskCI@state.gov
http://adoption.state.gov

For questions about immigration procedures, call the National Customer Service Center (NCSC) 1-800-375-5283 (TTY 1-800-767-1833).

International Parental Child Abduction

January 2013

The information in this section has been edited from a report of the Bureau of Consular Affairs, Office of Overseas Citizens Services of the U.S. Department of State. For more information, please read the *International Parental Child Abduction* section of this book and review current reports online at www.travel.state.gov/abduction.

Disclaimer: The information in this flyer is provided for general information only, is not intended to be legal advice, and may change without notice. Questions involving interpretation of law should be addressed to an attorney licensed to practice in the relevant jurisdiction.

General Information: Argentina and the United States have been treaty partners under the 1980 Hague Convention on the Civil Aspects of International Child Abduction (Hague Abduction Convention) since June 1, 1991. In April 2012, the United States Department of State cited Argentina as demonstrating patterns of non-compliance with the Hague Abduction Convention in its annual "Report on Compliance with the Hague Convention on the Civil Aspects of International Child Abduction."

Hague Abduction Convention: The U.S. Department of State serves as the U.S. Central Authority (USCA) for the Hague Abduction Convention. Parents are strongly encouraged to contact the Department of State for assistance prior to initiating the Hague process directly with the foreign Central Authority.

United States Department of State
Office of Children's Issues
2201 C Street, N.W.
Washington, DC 20520
Telephone: 1-888-407-4747
Outside the United States or Canada: 1-202-501-4444
Fax: 202-736-9132

The Argentine Central Authority for the Hague Abduction Convention is the Ministry of Foreign Relations and Worship. The Ministry of Foreign Relations and Worship performs the duties given to central authorities under the Hague Abduction Convention, including processing Hague Abduction Convention applications for return of and access to children. They can be reached at:

Ministry of Foreign Relations and Worship
Legal Affairs Department
International Legal
Cooperation Department
Esmeralda 1212 - 4th floor
1007 Buenos Aires, Argentina
Telephone: +54 (11) 4819 7170; +54 (11) 4819 7172
Fax: +54 (11) 4819 7170; +54 (11) 4819 7172
Email: menores@mrecic.gov.ar
Website: http://www.menores.gov.ar/

To initiate a Hague case for return of, or access to, a child in Argentina, the left-behind parent must submit a Hague application to the Argentine Central Authority (the Ministry of Foreign Relations and Worship), either directly, or through the U.S. Central Authority (USCA).

Visitation/Access: A person may file an application under the Hague Abduction Convention for access to a child living in Argentina. The criteria for acceptance of a Hague access application vary from country to country. The U.S. Department of State can assist parents living in the United States to understand country-specific criteria and provide information on the process for submitting a Hague application.

Retaining an Attorney: In Argentina, Hague Abduction Convention cases cannot be filed in an Argentine court without legal representation. The Argentine Central Authority (Ministry of Foreign Relations and Worship) provides a list of lawyers licensed to practice in the appropriate jurisdiction. When parents cannot afford a private attorney and meet the Argentine Central Authority's financial requirements for assistance, the Argentine Central Authority will appoint a public defender or pro bono legal counsel. The U.S. Embassy in Buenos Aires, Argentina posts list of attorneys including those who specialize in family law. This list is provided as a courtesy service only and does not constitute an endorsement of any individual attorney. The Department of State assumes no responsibility or liability for the professional ability or reputation of, or the quality of services provided by, the persons or firms included in this list. Professional credentials and areas of expertise are provided directly by the lawyers.

Mediation: In Argentina, pre-trial mediation in Hague cases is not mandatory although the interested parties may request it. Mediation is performed by registered mediators, and the cost is established by law and varies depending on the outcome of mediation. The Argentine Central Authority does not provide or arrange mediation services. However, non-governmental organizations, such as the Legal Bar Association, and governmental organizations, including the Ministry of Justice and the Government of the City of Buenos Aires, offer mediation services free of charge to those who demonstrate financial need.

U.S. Embassy Argentina
Avenida Colombia 4300
Palermo neighborhood of Buenos Aires
Buenos Aires, Argentina
Telephone: (+54) (11) 5777–4533
Fax: (+54) (11) 5777– 4240
Email: BuenosAires-ACS@state.gov
Website: http://argentina.usembassy.gov

Embassy of Argentina
1600 New Hampshire Avenue, NW
Washington, DC, 20009–2512
Telephone: (202) 238-6400/6424
Fax: (202) 332-3171
http://www.embassyofargentina.us

ARMENIA

Compiled from publications that were available as of February 2013 from the U.S. Department of State, the U.S. Department of Commerce, and the Central Intelligence Agency (CIA). See the introduction to this set for explanatory notes.

Official Name:
Republic of Armenia

PROFILE

Geography

Area: total: 29,743 sq km; country comparison to the world: 143; land: 28,203 sq km; water: 1,540 sq km

Major cities: Yerevan (capital) 1.11 million (2009)

Climate: highland continental, hot summers, cold winters

Terrain: Armenian Highland with mountains; little forest land; fast flowing rivers; good soil in Aras River valley

People

Nationality: noun: Armenian(s); adjective: Armenian

Population: 2,970,495 (July 2012 est.)

Population growth rate: 0.107% (2012 est.)

Ethnic groups: Armenian 97.9%, Yezidi (Kurd) 1.3%, Russian 0.5%, other 0.3% (2001 census)

Religions: Armenian Apostolic 94.7%, other Christian 4%, Yezidi (monotheist with elements of nature worship) 1.3%

Languages: Armenian (official) 97.7%, Yezidi 1%, Russian 0.9%, other 0.4% (2001 census)

Literacy: definition: age 15 and over can read and write; total population: 99.6%; male: 99.7%; female: 99.4% (2010 est.)

Health: life expectancy at birth: total population: 73.49 years; male: 69.85 years; female: 77.56 years (2012 est.); Infant mortality rate: total: 18.21 deaths/1,000 live births; male: 22.63 deaths/1,000 live births; female: 13.28 deaths/1,000 live births (2012 est.)

Unemployment rate: 7% (2012 est.)

Work force: 1.194 million (2011 est.)

Government

Type: republic

Independence: 21 September 1991

Constitution: adopted by nationwide referendum 5 July 1995; amendments adopted through a nationwide referendum 27 November 2005

Political subdivisions: 11 provinces (marzer, singular—marz)

Suffrage: 20 years of age; universal

Economy

GDP (purchasing power parity): $18.95 billion (2012 est.); $18.17 billion (2011 est.); $17.41 billion (2010 est.); $17.05 billion (2009 est.)

GDP real growth rate: 3.8% (2012 est.); 4.4% (2011 est.); 2.1% (2010 est.); -14.2% (2009 est.)

GDP per capita (PPP): $5,600 (2012 est.); $5,500 (2011 est.); $5,300 (2010 est.); $5,200 (2009 est.)

Natural resources: small deposits of gold, copper, molybdenum, zinc, bauxite

Agriculture products: fruit (especially grapes), vegetables; livestock

Industries: diamond-processing, metal-cutting machine tools, forging-pressing machines, electric motors, tires, knitted wear, hosiery, shoes, silk fabric, chemicals, trucks, instruments, microelectronics, jewelry manufacturing, software development, food processing, brandy, mining

Exports: $1.495 billion (2012 est.); $1.305 billion (2011 est.); $1.113 billion (2010 est.)

Exports—commodities: pig iron, unwrought copper, nonferrous metals, diamonds, mineral products, foodstuffs, energy

Exports—partners: Russia 15.4%, Germany 13.9%, Iran 9.8%, Bulgaria 9.3%, Netherlands 7.8%, US 7.6%, Spain 7.6%, Canada 5.7%, Belgium 5.5%, Georgia 4.6% (2011)

Imports: $3.269 billion (2012 est.); $3.503 billion (2011 est.)

Imports—commodities: natural gas, petroleum, tobacco products, foodstuffs, diamonds

Imports—partners: Russia 20%, China 8.1%, Ukraine 6.8%, Iran 6.5%, Germany 5.9%, Italy 4.7% (2011)

Debt—external: $6.435 billion (31 December 2012 est.); $7.336 billion (30 September 2011)

Exchange rates: drams (AMD) per US dollar; 404.8 (2012 est.); 372.5 (2011 est.); 373.66 (2010 est.); 363.28 (2009); 303.93 (2008)

PEOPLE

Language

Armenian is the official language of the country and is used for all official documents. The majority of the population also speaks Russian, while English is a mandatory third language in many schools.

Religion

Approximately 90 percent of citizens belong to the Armenian Apostolic Church, one of six Oriental Orthodox churches. The Armenian Apostolic Church's spiritual center is the Etchmiadzin cathedral and monastery located near the capital of Yerevan.

There are small communities of other religious groups, each constituting less than 5 percent of the population: Roman Catholic, Armenian Uniate (Mekhitarist) Catholic, Orthodox Christian, Armenian Evangelical Christian, Molokan, Pentecostal, Seventh-day Adventist, Baptist, various groups of charismatic Christians, Jehovah's Witnesses, The Church of Jesus Christ of Latter-day Saints (Mormons), Yezidis (non-Muslim Kurds who practice Yezidism), Jews, Sunni Muslim Kurds, Shiite Muslims, pagans, and others.

Yezidis are concentrated primarily in agricultural areas around Mount Aragats, northwest of Yerevan. Armenian Catholics live primarily in the north, while most Jews, Mormons, and Orthodox Christians reside in Yerevan, along with a small community of Muslims, mostly Shiites, including Iranians and temporary residents from the Middle East.

HISTORICAL HIGHLIGHTS

Armenia first emerged around 800 BC as part of the Kingdom of Urartu or Van, which flourished in the Caucasus and eastern Asia Minor until 600 BC. After the destruction of the Seleucid Empire, the first Armenian state was founded in 190 BC. At its zenith, from 95 to 65 BC, Armenia extended its rule over the entire Caucasus and the area that is now eastern Turkey, Syria, and Lebanon. For a time, Armenia was the strongest state in the Roman East. It became part of the Roman Empire in 64 BC.

In 301 AD, Armenia became the first nation to adopt Christianity as a state religion, establishing a church that still exists independently of both the Roman Catholic and the Eastern Orthodox churches. Since then, the Armenian nation has depended on the church to preserve and protect its national identity. From around 1100 to 1350, the focus of the Armenian nation moved south, as the Armenian Kingdom of Cilicia, which had close ties to European Crusader states, flourished in southeastern Asia Minor until it was conquered by Muslim states. Between the 4th and 19th centuries, ethnic Armenians were conquered and ruled by, among others, Persians, Byzantines, Arabs, Mongols, and Ottoman Turks.

For a brief period from 1918 to 1920, Armenia re-emerged as an independent republic. In late 1920, local communists came to power following an invasion of Armenia by the Soviet Red Army, and in 1922, Armenia became part of the Trans-Caucasian Soviet Socialist Republic. In 1936, it became the Armenian Soviet Socialist Republic.

Independence

Armenians voted overwhelmingly for independence in a September 1991 referendum, followed by a presidential election in October 1991 that gave 83% of the vote to Levon Ter-Petrossian. Ter-Petrossian had been elected head of government in 1990, when the Armenian National Movement defeated the Communist Party. Ter-Petrossian was re-elected in 1996 in a disputed election. Following public demonstrations against Ter-Petrossian's policies on the predominantly ethnic Armenian enclave of Nagorno-Karabakh that is located within Azerbaijan, the President resigned under pressure in January 1998 and was replaced by Prime Minister Robert Kocharian, who was subsequently elected President in March 1998. Following the October 27, 1999 assassination in Parliament of Prime Minister Vazgen Sargsian, Parliament Speaker Karen Demirchian, and six other officials, a period of political instability ensued during which an opposition headed by elements of the former Armenian National Movement government attempted unsuccessfully to force Kocharian to resign. Riding out the unrest, Kocharian was later reelected in March 2003 in a contentious election that the Organization for Security and Cooperation in Europe (OSCE) and the U.S. Government deemed to have fallen short of international standards.

The Government of Armenia's stated aim is to build a Western-style parliamentary democracy as the basis of its form of government. However, international observers have been critical of the conduct of national elections in 1995, 1999, 2003, 2008, as well as the constitutional referendum of 2005.

The new constitution in 2005 increased the power of the legislative branch and allows for more independence of the judiciary; in practice, however, both branches remain subject to political pressure from the executive branch, which retains considerably greater power than its counterparts in most European countries.

GOVERNMENT AND POLITICAL CONDITIONS

Armenia's constitution provides for a republic with an elected head of state and a unicameral legislature, the National Assembly. In 2008 Serzh Sargsian became president after a significantly flawed election. The ruling coalition, led by Sargsian's Republican Party of Armenia, continued to dominate the political system.

Recent Elections

Observers criticized the 2008 presidential election as significantly flawed, with reports of favorable treatment of the government's candidate; ballot stuffing; vote buying; multiple voting; and intimidation of voters, candidates, and the media during the 2008 campaign. According to the OSCE, the vote count demonstrated deficiencies of accountability and transparency, and complaints and appeals procedures were not fully effective.

The Central Election Commission and the National Commission on Television and Radio did not ensure that media provided a level playing field for all candidates, and media bias was evident. There were continuing complaints that opposition parties had limited access to media.

On May 26, 2011 the National Assembly adopted a new electoral code that introduced many reforms that the Venice Commission and other international observers judged to be improvements. Nevertheless, these reforms did not dispel concerns about their implementation, the composition of the electoral commissions, or the continued possibility of fraud and abuse in connection with the estimated 500,000 to 800,000 registered voters who reside abroad.

Political Parties: There were no reports of undue legal restrictions on the registration or activity of political parties. Nevertheless, there were some complaints that the government used its administrative resources to discourage contributions to opposition parties, thereby limiting their activities. Additionally, there were allegations that the government discriminated against members of opposition political parties in hiring decisions.

Participation of Women and Minorities: Women's participation in political and public life, especially in decision-making bodies, remained low. As of the end of the year, there were 11 women in the 131-seat National Assembly, two in the cabinet, and no female governors. Only five of the elected 52 Yerevan City Council members were women, and no women headed any of Yerevan's 12 administrative districts.

The revised electoral code increased from 15 to 20 percent the required proportion of female candidates included on each party list of candidates for proportional voting. However, in the past a significant proportion of female candidates withdrew their candidacy after the election, with the result that the proportion of women in the National Assembly was well below that intended by the law. The new electoral code also introduced minimum gender balance requirements for the central and territorial election commissions.

Principal Government Officials

Last Updated: 1/31/2013

Pres.: **Serzh SARGSIAN**
Prime Min.: **Tigran SARGSIAN**
President's Chief of Staff: **Karen KARAPETIAN**
Min. of Agriculture: **Sergo KARAPETIAN**
Min. of Culture & Youth: **Hasmik POGHOSIAN**
Min. of Defense: **Seyran OHANIAN**
Min. of Diaspora: **Hranush HAKOBIAN**
Min. of Economy: **Tigran DAVTIAN**
Min. of Education & Science: **Armen ASHOTIAN**
Min. of Emergency Situations: **Armen YERITSIAN**
Min. of Energy & Natural Resources: **Armen MOVSISIAN**
Min. of Environmental Protection: **Aram HARUTYUNIAN**
Min. of Finance: **Vache GABRIELIAN**
Min. of Foreign Affairs: **Eduard NALBANDIAN**
Min. of Health: **Harutyun KUSHKIAN**
Min. of Justice: **Hrayr TOVMASIAN**
Min. of Labor & Social Affairs: **Artur GRIGORIAN**
Min. of Sport & Youth Affairs: **Artur PETROSIAN**
Min. of Territorial Admin.: **Armen GEVORGIAN**
Min. of Transport & Communication: **Manuk VARDANIAN**
Min. of Urban Development: **Vardan VARDANIAN**
Chmn., Central Bank of Armenia: **Artur JAVADIAN**
Ambassador to the US: **Tatoul MARKARIAN**
Permanent Representative to the UN, New York: **Garen NAZARIAN**

The U.S. Embassy in Yerevan, Armenia, is at 1 American Avenue; tel: 374-10-46-47-00; fax: 374-10-46-47-42.

ECONOMY

After several years of double-digit economic growth, Armenia faced a severe economic recession with GDP declining more than 14% in 2009, despite large loans from multilateral institutions. Sharp declines in the construction sector and workers' remittances, particularly from Russia, led the downturn.

The economy began to recover in 2010 with 2.1% growth, and picked up to 4.6% growth in 2011. Under the old Soviet central planning system, Armenia developed a modern industrial sector, supplying machine tools, textiles, and other manufactured goods to sister republics, in exchange for raw materials and energy. Armenia has since switched to small-scale agriculture and away from the large agroindustrial complexes of the Soviet era. Armenia has managed to reduce poverty, slash inflation, stabilize its currency, and privatize most small- and medium-sized enterprises. Armenia's geographic isolation, a narrow export base, and pervasive monopolies in important business sectors have made it particularly vulnerable to the sharp deterioration in the global economy and the economic downturn in Russia.

The conflict with Azerbaijan over the ethnic Armenian-dominated region of Nagorno-Karabakh contributed to a severe economic decline in the early 1990s and Armenia's borders with Turkey remain closed. Armenia is particularly dependent on Russian commercial and governmental support and most key Armenian infrastructure is Russian-owned and/or managed, especially in the energy

sector. The electricity distribution system was privatized in 2002 and bought by Russia's RAO-UES in 2005. Natural gas is primarily imported from Russia but construction of a pipeline to deliver natural gas from Iran to Armenia was completed in December 2008, and gas deliveries expanded after the April 2010 completion of the Yerevan Thermal Power Plant.

Armenia's severe trade imbalance has been offset somewhat by international aid, remittances from Armenians working abroad, and foreign direct investment. Armenia joined the WTO in January 2003. The government made some improvements in tax and customs administration in recent years, but anti-corruption measures have been ineffective and the economic downturn has led to a sharp drop in tax revenue and forced the government to accept large loan packages from Russia, the IMF, and other international financial institutions. Amendments to tax legislation, including the introduction of the first ever "luxury tax" in 2011, aim to increase the ratio of budget revenues to GDP, which still remains at low levels.

Armenia will need to pursue additional economic reforms and to strengthen the rule of law in order to regain economic growth and improve economic competitiveness and employment opportunities, especially given its economic isolation from two of its nearest neighbors, Turkey and Azerbaijan.

Labor Conditions

The minimum age for employment is 16, but children may work from the age of 14 with permission of a parent or a guardian. Persons under 18 are prohibited from working overtime; in harmful, strenuous, or dangerous conditions; at night; or on holidays. Authorities responsible for enforcing compliance with child labor law failed to implement the law in practice.

According to observers, many children, especially in rural regions, worked in family enterprises, mainly in agriculture. Observers also reported seeing children in Yerevan selling flowers and drawings and working in local markets after school hours. Children also worked in trade, construction, and car services, operated vehicles, and gathered waste metal and bottles. According to a 2008 UNICEF study on child labor, 4.7 percent of children between seven and 18 years of age had paying jobs. This percentage did not include children working on family farms or in family businesses. The survey also found almost one-third of working children were below the legal working age, almost all children worked without legal contracts, and some children were employed in heavy manual work as laborers and loaders.

The monthly minimum wage was 32,500 drams ($84.41), which was approximately equal to the poverty line.

The law provides for a 40-hour workweek, 28 days of mandatory annual leave, and compensation for overtime and nighttime work. The law provides that compulsory overtime cannot exceed four hours in two consecutive days and 180 hours within a year. In practice authorities did not effectively enforce these standards. Many private sector employees were unable to obtain paid leave and were required to work more than eight hours a day without compensation. According to representatives of some employment agencies, many employers also continued to hire employees for a "probationary" period of 10 to 30 days, during which they were not paid. Often these employees were subsequently dismissed and unable to claim payment for the time they worked because their initial employment was undocumented.

Occupational and health standards were established by government decree. Workers in the informal sector were excluded from any form of governmental protection. Work safety and health conditions remained substandard in numerous sectors.

U.S.-ARMENIAN RELATIONS

The dissolution of the Soviet Union in December 1991 brought an end to the Cold War and created the opportunity for bilateral relations with the New Independent States (NIS) as they began a political and economic transformation. The U.S. recognized the independence of Armenia on December 25, 1991, and opened an Embassy in Yerevan in February 1992.

In 1992 Armenia signed three agreements with the U.S. affecting trade between the two countries. They include an "Agreement on Trade Relations," (which entered into force in April 1992) an "Investment Incentive Agreement," (which also entered into force in April 1992) and a treaty on the "Reciprocal Encouragement and Protection of Investment" (generally referred to as the Bilateral Investment Treaty, or BIT, which entered into force in March 1996). The 1973 "Convention on matters of Taxation" concluded with the former USSR remains in force with Armenia. The 1994 Law on Foreign Investment governs all direct investments in Armenia, including those from the U.S.

In June 2011, the Department of State and the Ministry of Energy and Natural Resources of Armenia signed a Memorandum of Understanding on unconventional and conventional energy resources. The MOU aims to enhance cooperation between U.S. and Armenian experts to assess Armenia's potential energy resources, including shale gas.

Approximately 70 U.S.-owned firms currently do business in Armenia, including Dell, Microsoft, and IBM. Recent major U.S. investment projects include: the Hotel Armenia/Marriott; the Hotel Ani Plaza; Tufenkian Holdings (carpet and furniture production, hotels, and construction); several subsidiaries of U.S.-based information technology firms, including Viasphere Technopark, an IT incubator; Synopsys; a Greek-owned Coca-Cola bottling plant; jewelry and textile production facilities; several mining companies; and the Hovnanian International Construction Company.

U.S. Assistance to Armenia

The U.S. has made a concerted effort to help Armenia during its difficult transition from totalitarianism and a command economy to democracy and open markets. The cornerstone of this continuing partnership has been assistance provided through the Freedom for Russia and Emerging Eurasian Democracies and Open Markets (FREEDOM) Support Act, enacted in October 1992. In 2009, FREEDOM Support Act funds were merged with another account and was renamed Assistance to Europe, Eurasia and Central Asia (AEECA). Under this and other programs, the U.S. to date has provided Armenia with nearly $2 billion in development and humanitarian assistance. In addition, the U.S.-Armenia Joint Economic Task Force (USATF), established in 1999, is a bilateral commission that meets annually to deepen economic ties between Armenia and the U.S., advance market reforms in Armenia, and discuss opportunities for U.S. assistance to contribute to Armenia's long-term economic development. The most recent meeting was held in Washington, DC, in September 2011. The next meeting in 2012 will be held in Yerevan.

U.S. assistance supports Armenia's transition into a stable partner at peace with its neighbors, fully integrated into the regional economy, where principles of democracy are respected, the benefits of economic growth are shared by all segments of society, and Armenia's human capital potential is fully realized. The U.S. provides multifaceted assistance to Armenia through a variety of programs designed to promote economic growth, encourage democratic governance, improve health and social protection systems, and enhance Armenia's peace and security. The U.S. also provides humanitarian assistance to the poor, elderly, and other vulnerable groups. Assistance is provided through a "whole of government" approach that involves a number of U.S. government agencies, including the Departments of Agriculture, Commerce, Defense, Energy, Justice, and State, the Nuclear Regulatory Commission, the United States Agency for International Development (USAID), and the Peace Corps.

In 2006, Armenia signed a five-year, $236 million Millennium Challenge Corporation compact with the U.S. The MCA-Armenia program focused on reducing rural poverty through a sustainable increase in the economic performance of the agricultural sector. This included strategic investments in rural roads, irrigation infrastructure, and technical and financial assistance to water supply entities, farmers, and commercial agribusinesses. in 2009, MCC placed a hold on funding for a significant portion of the rural road rehabilitation project because of serious concerns about the 2008 presidential election. At the June 2009 MCC Board meeting, the decision was made not to resume funding for any further road construction and rehabilitation due to concerns about the status of democratic governance in Armenia. Funding for irrigation infrastructure and technical assistance, representing nearly $177 million of the compact's value, remained in effect and was implemented. The compact concluded in September 2011. Beneficiaries included 420,000 rural residents in about 350 communities across Armenia.

Promoting Economic Growth

U.S. assistance addresses Armenia's economic vulnerabilities, which have been exacerbated by the global economic crisis, while continuing to support economic competitiveness. The U.S. continues to work closely with international financial institutions like the International Monetary Fund and the World Bank to help Armenia continue its transition to a robust free-market economy. USAID and the U.S. Department of Agriculture (USDA) implement the largest portion of U.S. economic assistance activities. In addition to its broader assistance programs, USAID implements a range of economic assistance programs designed to enhance Armenia's macroeconomic foundation for growth, promote trade and investment, and focus on private sector competitiveness and workforce development in selected industries, including information technology and tourism, and development of the financial sector and fiscal authorities to achieve a business enabling environment.

The USDA Caucasus Agricultural Development Initiative provides targeted and sustained technical and marketing assistance to small and medium-sized agribusinesses, farmer-marketing associations, and the Government of Armenia. USDA's goal is to sustain the productivity of the agricultural sector by expanding access to markets and credit, increasing efficiency, and modernizing agriculture systems. USDA's priority assistance areas are: Farm Credit, Food Safety and Animal Health, support to the Armenian private sector through the NGO CARD, Agricultural Statistics and Agricultural Education. Also, as a training component of USDA projects in Armenia, the U.S. Department of Agriculture's Cochran Fellowship Program provides training in the U.S. to Armenian agriculturists.

Enhancing Democratic Governance

U.S. assistance programs enhance the Government of Armenia's capacity to govern justly and democratically. The programs strengthen democracy and the rule of law by improving legal education, promoting the capacity of both prosecutors and the defense bar, raising judicial ethics standards and human rights protections, fighting corruption and improving the transparency, accountability, and accessibility of government entities (particularly at the local level), increasing civic participation and government accountability by bolstering civil society, strengthening independent media and increasing access to information, and promoting free and fair elections and greater citizen participation in the political process.

U.S. assistance also encourages adoption of best practices within the criminal justice system by reforming procedures to promote greater police accountability, judicial independence, and fairness for those accused of crimes. Additionally, U.S. programs support international and domestic monitoring of Armenia's elections, thereby promoting transparency and democratic values.

Educational exchange programs also play an important role in supporting meaningful democratic and free-market reforms by instilling important core values in Armenia's youth.

Professional exchange programs serve as a vehicle to share U.S. experience with Armenian government officials, NGO activists, women leaders, bloggers, journalists, lawyers, political party members, business people, and other influential figures. These exchanges have focused on a range of topics, including U.S. elections, law enforcement, the American judiciary, women in business, conflict resolution, the media, human rights, and youth leadership.

Principal U.S. Embassy Officials

Last Updated: 1/14/2013

YEREVAN (E) 1 American Ave., (37410) 49-42-00, Fax (37410) 46-47-42, INMARSAT Tel Satellite 8821655530566; 8821655530392; 8821655530142, Workweek: Mon-Fri 9:00am-6:00pm, Website: http://yerevan.usembassy.gov/

DCM OMS:	Nicole Owens
AMB OMS:	Kimberly McKeown
FM:	Doug Barnes
HRO:	Christie Livingston
MGT:	Michael McKeown
NAS/INL:	Edward O'Brien
POL/ECON:	Brian Roraff
POSHO:	Doug Barnes
SDO/DATT:	Jeffrey Stimson
AMB:	John Heffern
CON:	George Lynn
DCM:	Bruce Donahue
PAO:	James Land
GSO:	Lisa Meyer
RSO:	Lance Leveque
AGR:	Lawrence Barbieri
AID:	Karen Hilliard
CLO:	Molly Rydzynski
FMO:	Christie Livingston
IMO:	Stephen Lavarn
ISO:	Sharmatie Baliram Singh
ISSO:	Sharmatie Baliram Singh
LEGATT:	John Lulejian
State ICASS:	James Land

TRAVEL

Consular Information Sheet

May 1, 2012

Country Description: Armenia is a constitutional republic with a developing economy. Tourist facilities, especially outside the capital city of Yerevan, are not very developed, and many of the goods and services taken for granted in other countries may be difficult to obtain.

Smart Traveler Enrollment Program (STEP)/Embassy Locations: If you are going to live in or visit Armenia, please take the time to tell our Embassy about your trip. If you enroll, we can keep you up to date with important safety and security announcements. It will also help your friends and family get in touch with you in an emergency.

Embassy Yerevan
1 American Avenue
Embassy switchboard:
374 10 46 47 00

Emergency after-hours telephone: 374 10 49 44 44
Facsimile: 374 46 47 37

Entry/Exit Requirements for U.S. Citizens: You need a passport and a visa to enter Armenia. You may purchase visas online in advance for a stay of up to 120 days at the Armenian Ministry of Foreign Affairs website. Several different visas are available at Armenian ports of entry, though the most commonly issued types are a single-entry visa valid for 21 days for a fee of 3,000 Armenian Drams (approx. $8), a single-entry visa valid for 120 days for a fee of 15,000 Armenian Drams (approx. $40), or a multiple-entry visa valid for 60 days for a fee of 20,000 Armenian Drams (approx. $54). All holders of official or diplomatic passports must have a valid visa upon arrival at the port of entry. Visas for up to 120 days may be obtained at the Armenian Embassy in Washington, D.C. or at the Armenian Consulate General in Los Angeles, for a fee of $40. For further information on entry requirements, contact the Armenian Embassy at 2225 R Street NW, Washington, DC 20008, tel. (202) 319-1976 and (202) 319-2982; or the Armenian Consulate General in Los Angeles at 50 N. La Cienega Blvd., Suite 210, Beverly Hills, CA 90211, tel. (310) 657-7320. Visit the Embassy of Armenia's website for the most current visa fee schedule.

The U.S. Department of State is unaware of any HIV/AIDS entry restrictions for visitors to or foreign residents of Armenia.

Threats to Safety and Security: A cease-fire has been in effect since 1994 around the self-proclaimed "Republic of Nagorno-Karabakh," an unrecognized ethnic-Armenian enclave within Azerbaijan. However, intermittent gunfire along the cease-fire line and along the border with Azerbaijan continues, often resulting in injuries and/or deaths. Because of the existing state of hostilities, consular services are not available to U.S. citizens in Nagorno-Karabakh. Be extremely cautious near the line of contact between Azerbaijani and Armenian positions in and around Nagorno-Karabakh and the surrounding areas and the Armenia-Azerbaijan border. Please consult the Country-Specific Information for Azerbaijan for more information. Armenia has land borders with Turkey, Iran, Georgia, and Azerbaijan (including the Nakhichevan Autonomous Republic of Azerbaijan). The borders with Turkey and Azerbaijan (including the Nakhichevan Autonomous Republic of Azerbaijan) remain closed and continue to be patrolled by armed troops and/or border guards who stop all people attempting to cross. Although de-mining operations have been largely completed, isolated land mines remain in some areas in and near the conflict zones with Azerbaijan and the Nagorno-Karabakh region.

Political rallies in the aftermath of the 2008 presidential elections turned violent, as clashes between government security forces and opposition demonstrators resulted in dozens of casualties, including 10 fatalities. While the opposition has continued to hold periodic protests, there have been no violent confrontations since 2008. Visitors should be mindful that even demonstrations intended to be peaceful could turn confrontational and possibly escalate into violence. U.S. citizens are urged to avoid the areas of demonstrations if possible, and to exercise caution if within the vicinity of any demonstrations. Information regarding demonstrations that have been brought to the attention of the U.S. Embassy can be found on the Messages for U.S. Citizens section of the Embassy website.

Armenia is an earthquake- and landslide-prone country. A Soviet-era Armenia Nuclear Power Plant is located in Metsamor, approximately 30 kilometers southwest of Yerevan; due to its age, the Armenian government plans to close the plant in coming years.

Stay up to date by:

- Bookmarking our Bureau of Consular Affairs website, which contains the current Travel Warnings and Travel Alerts as well as the Worldwide Caution;
- Following us on Twitter and the Bureau of Consular Affairs page on Facebook;
- Calling 1-888-407-4747 toll-free within the U.S. and Canada, or a regular toll line, 1-202-501-4444, from other countries; and
- Taking some time before travel to consider your personal security.

Crime: Crime against foreigners is relatively rare in Armenia. Break-ins—particularly of vehicles—and theft are the most common crimes, but there have been instances of violent crime. While the incidence of violent crime remains lower than in most U.S. cities, you should exercise caution and avoid traveling alone after dark in Yerevan. Several U.S. investors have also reported being involved in disputes over property ownership, and have had to seek legal recourse through long, and often unsuccessful, court proceedings.

Do not buy counterfeit and pirated goods, even if they are widely available. Not only are the bootlegs illegal to bring back into the United States, if you purchase them you may also be breaking local law.

Victims of Crime: If you or someone you know becomes the victim of a crime abroad, you should contact the local police and the nearest U.S. embassy or consulate. We can:

- Replace a stolen passport;
- Help you find appropriate medical care in instances of violent crimes such as assault or rape;
- Put you in contact with the appropriate police authorities and, if you want us to, we can contact family members or friends; and
- Help you understand the local criminal justice process and can direct you to local attorneys, though the local authorities are responsible for investigating and prosecuting the crime.

There is an emergency hot line in Armenia that can be reached by dialing 911. In addition, in case of emergency, one can dial 101 for fire, 102 for police, 103 for medical emergencies, and 104 for gas leaks.

Criminal Penalties: While you are traveling in Armenia, you are subject to its laws even if you are a U.S. citizen. Foreign laws and legal systems can be vastly different than our own, and criminal penalties vary from country to country. There are some things that might be legal in the country you visit, but still illegal in the United States; for instance you can be prosecuted under U.S. law if you buy pirated goods.

Engaging in sexual conduct with children or using or disseminating child pornography in a foreign country is a crime prosecutable in the United States. If you break local laws in Armenia, your U.S. passport won't help you avoid arrest or prosecution. It is very important to know what is legal and what is not where you are traveling.

Authorities of Armenia are required to notify the U.S. Embassy of your arrest. If you are concerned the Department of State may not be aware of your situation, you should request the police or prison officials to notify the U.S. Embassy.

Special Circumstances: Armenia remains largely a cash-only economy. Credit cards are accepted at some businesses, including major hotels and restaurants in Yerevan, but rarely outside of the capital. Limited facilities exist for cashing traveler's checks and wiring money into the country. There are a number of ATMs in the center of Yerevan. Beware that credit-card skimming is on the rise at ATMs throughout Armenia. Dollars are readily exchanged at market rates. You may experience problems with local officials seeking bribes to perform basic duties. Armenian customs authorities may enforce strict regulations concerning temporary importation into or export from Armenia of items such as firearms, pornographic materials, medication, and communications equipment. To export antiquities and other items that could have historical value, such as paintings, carpets, old books, or other artisan goods, you need to get special authorization in advance from the Armenian Ministry of Culture.

Dual nationals: Armenian legislation permits Armenian citizens to hold dual citizenship. U.S. citizens who emigrated from Armenia to the U.S. and subsequently acquired U.S. citizenship without explicitly giving up their Armenian citizenship are required by Armenian law to document their Armenian citizenship by obtaining an Armenian passport. Armenian citizens are entitled to certain rights, such as the right to vote in Armenian elections, though Armenian citizenship also entails specific legal obligations, including military service for certain males. U.S. citizens interested in obtaining Armenian citizenship must register their dual citizenship with the Passport and Visa Department of the Police of the Republic of Armenia (formerly OVIR) by simply presenting proof of their other citizenship (e.g. passport). For more information, please consult with the Passport and Visa Department of the Police (tel.: 374 53 69 42) and/or the Foreign Ministry's website.

Armenian law requires that all Armenian citizens enter and depart Armenian on their Armenian passports. If you are an Armenian citizen according the law of the Republic of Armenia, you will be required to obtain an Armenian passport prior to departing Armenia. The law applies to children considered Armenian citizens under Armenian law, including children born in the United States to two Armenian citizens, even if those children have never held an Armenian passport. Individuals who are dual citizens, or could be dual citizens, should inquire with the Armenian Embassy in Washington, D.C. prior to traveling to Armenia to determine if they will be required to obtain an Armenian passport to depart Armenia at the end of their visit. The full text of the Armenian Law on Citizenship is available online.

Compulsory military service: In addition to being subject to all Armenian laws affecting U.S. citizens, dual nationals are also subject to other laws that impose special obligations on Armenian citizens. Male U.S. citizens over the age of 18 who are also considered to be Armenian citizens are subject to conscription and compulsory military service upon arrival, and to other aspects of Armenian law while in Armenia. Armenian authorities have regularly detained U.S. citizens on these grounds upon their arrival in or attempted departure from Armenia. I n most cases, ethnic-Armenian travelers over the age of 18 accused of evading Armenian military service obligations are immediately detained and later found guilty of draft evasion. Penalties for those convicted are stiff and include jail time or a substantial fine. Those who may be affected are strongly advised to consult with Armenian officials at an Armenian embassy or consulate regarding their status before traveling.

Medical Facilities and Health Information: Though there are many competent physicians in Armenia, medical care facilities are limited, especially outside the major cities. The U.S. Embassy maintains a list of English-speaking physicians in the area. Most prescription medications are available, but the quality varies. Elderly travelers and those with existing health problems may be at risk due to inadequate medical facilities.

Good information on vaccinations and other health precautions can be found at the Centers for Disease Control and Prevention (CDC) website. For information about outbreaks of infectious diseases abroad, consult the infectious diseases section of the World Health Organization (WHO) website, which also contains additional health information for travelers, including detailed country-specific health information.

Accessibility: While in Armenia, individuals with disabilities may find accessibility and accommodation very different from what they find in the United States. Although Armenia has signed the Convention on the Rights of Persons with Disabilities as of

March 30, 2007, Armenian authorities have yet to enforce it. Therefore, assistance for handicapped individuals' needs, i.e., handicapped parking and/or wheelchair ramps, is nonexistent. This can make it difficult to frequent restaurants, stores and clubs.

Medical Insurance: You cannot assume your insurance will go with you when you travel. It is very important to find out BEFORE you leave. You need to ask your insurance company two questions:

- Does my policy apply when I am outside of the U.S?
- Will it cover emergencies like a trip to a foreign hospital or an evacuation?

In many places, doctors and hospitals still expect payment in cash at the time of service. Your regular U.S. health insurance may not cover visits to doctors and hospitals in other countries. If your policy doesn't go with you when you travel, it's a very good idea to take out another one for your trip.

Traffic Safety and Road Conditions: While in Armenia, U.S. citizens may encounter road conditions that differ significantly from those in the United States. Travel in Armenia requires caution. Public transportation, while very inexpensive, may be unreliable and uncomfortable. Minibuses are more dangerous than other forms of public transportation. These vehicles are often overcrowded and poorly maintained, commonly lack safety measures, including seatbelts, and are frequently involved in accidents.

Drivers in Armenia frequently ignore traffic laws, making roadways unsafe for unsuspecting travelers. Those driving in towns at night should be especially cautious. Pedestrians often fail to take safety precautions, and in cities at night it is common for pedestrians in dark clothing to cross unlighted streets in the middle of the block. "Road rage" is becoming a serious problem on Armenian streets and highways. To reduce your risk of being a victim of aggression, yield to aggressive drivers. Though crime along roadways is rare, the police sometimes seek bribes during traffic stops and sometimes harass drivers using U.S. or international driver's licenses.

We recommend you not travel at night. Winter travel can also be extremely hazardous, especially in mountain areas and higher elevations. Avoid the old highway between the towns of Ijevan and Noyemberyan in the Tavush region, as well as the main highway between the towns of Kirants and Baghanis/Voskevan; the U.S. Embassy has designated this portion of the road off-limits to all U.S. Government personnel because of its proximity to the cease-fire line between Armenian and Azerbaijani forces, which has experienced numerous cease-fire violations over the years.

On weekends, the number of intoxicated drivers on Armenian roads increases. Be extra careful on the main highway from Yerevan to the resort areas of Tsaghkadzor and Sevan. Traffic police will attempt to stop individuals driving erratically and dangerously, but the police presence outside of Yerevan is limited.

With the exception of a few major arteries, primary roads are frequently in poor repair, with sporadic stretches of missing pavement and large potholes. Some roads shown as primary roads on maps are unpaved and can narrow to one lane in width, while some newer road connections have not yet been marked on recently produced maps. Secondary roads are normally in poor condition and are often unpaved and washed out in certain areas. Signage is poor to nonexistent. Truck traffic is heavy on the main roads linking Yerevan to Iran and Georgia. Police and emergency medical services may take considerable time to reach remote regions.

The quality of gasoline in Armenia ranges from good at some of the more reliable stations in cities to very poor. The gasoline and other fuels sold out of jars, barrels, and trucks by independent roadside merchants should be considered very unreliable.

Aviation Safety Oversight: As there is no direct commercial air service to the United States by carriers registered in Armenia, the U.S. Federal Aviation Administration (FAA) has not assessed the government of Armenia's Civil Aviation Authority for compliance with International Civil Aviation Organization (ICAO) aviation safety standards. Further information may be found on the FAA safety assessment page.

Travelers on Armavia International Airways may experience prolonged delays and sudden cancellations of flights. Air travel to Armenia via European carriers is typically more reliable. Ticketed passengers on flights leaving Yerevan should reconfirm their reservations 24 hours prior to departure.

Children's Issues: Please see the U.S. Dept. of State Office of Children's Issues web pages on intercountry adoption and international parental child abduction.

Intercountry Adoption

November 2008

The information in this section has been edited from the latest report available as of February 2013 from the State Department Bureau of Consular Affairs, Office of Overseas Citizens Services. For more information, please read the *Intercountry Adoption* section of this book and review current reports online at http://adoption.state.gov.

Armenia is party to The Hague Convention on Protection of Children and Co-operation in Respect of Intercountry Adoption (Hague Adoption Convention). Therefore, all adoptions between Armenia and the United States must meet the requirements of the Convention and United States law implementing the Convention. For detailed and updated information on these requirements, please review the *Intercountry Adoption* section of this publication and visit the USCIS Intercountry Adoption website at http://adoption.state.gov.

Who Can Adopt? Adoption between the United States and Armenia is governed by The Hague Adoption Convention. Therefore to adopt from Armenia, you must first be found eligible to adopt by the United States Government. In addition to the United States requirements for prospective adoptive parents, Armenia also has the following requirements for prospective adoptive parents.

Residency Requirements: Prospective adoptive parents do not have to fulfill any residency requirements to adopt in Armenia.

Age Requirements: Single prospective adoptive parents must be at least 18 years older than the adopted child.

Marriage Requirements: Both single individuals and married couples are eligible to adopt.

Who Can Be Adopted? Because Armenia is party to The Hague Adoption Convention, children from Brazil must meet the requirements of the Convention in order to be eligible for adoption. In addition to Armenia's requirements, a child must meet the definition of a Convention adoptee for you to bring him or her back to the United States.

There are many children living in orphanages, however, ONLY those children whose parents have died, disappeared, or signed a statement of relinquishment of their parental rights, and whose families do not visit them, thus abandoning them, are available for adoption. In addition, consent for child adoption can only be given after the birth of the child.

Relinquishment Requirements: If biological parents are alive, the biological parents must sign a statement of relinquishment in order for a child to be eligible for adoption.

Age Requirements: A child's name must be listed on the national registry list for three months before he or she is declared available for intercountry adoption. For this reason, it is impossible to adopt a very young infant from Armenia.

Waiting Period: The names of children available for adoption are listed by the Ministry of Labor and Social Issues. A child's name must remain on the list for three months before he/she is declared available for intercountry adoption.

Armenia's Adoption Authority: National Adoption Committee of the Republic of Armenia

The Process: The first step in adopting a child from Armenia is to select an adoption service provider in the United States that has been accredited. After you choose an accredited adoption service provider, you apply to be found eligible to adopt (Form I-800A) by the USCIS. Once the United States Government determines that you are "eligible" and "suitable" to adopt, you or your agency will forward your information to the adoption authority in Armenia.

If both the United States and Armenia determine that you are eligible to adopt, and a child is available for intercountry adoption, the central adoption authority in Armenia may provide you with a referral for a child. In Armenia, the adoptive parents identify a child from the children eligible for inter-country adoption listed in the registry kept by the Ministry of Labor and Social Issues.

The prospective parents or their representative may go to the Ministry and view the list, or they may visit orphanages directly and identify a child. Once they identify a child, they must verify his/her status by reviewing the list.

Once the child has been identified, the prospective parents or their representative must submit their documents to the municipality in which the child resides. Once those documents are received, a court date is set.

After you accept a match with a child, you will apply to the USCIS for provisional approval to adopt that particular child (Form I-800). After this, your adoption service provider or you will submit a visa application to a Consular Officer at the United States Embassy. If the Consular office determines that the child appears eligible to immigrate to the United States, he/she will notify Armenia's adoption authority (Article 5 letter).

For Convention country adoptions, prospective adoptive parent(s) may not proceed with the adoption or obtain custody for the purpose of adoption until this takes place. Adoptive parents and the child, if over 14, must be present for court proceedings. The court may request the presence of biological parents, orphanage representatives, or the child if the child is over the age of 10. The court proceedings are closed to the public. Cases may be rejected on the basis of incomplete or fraudulent paperwork, among other issues addressed in Armenian law. Prospective adoptive parents may be disqualified based on mental disease, drug addiction, alcoholism, tuberculosis, HIV/AIDS, or other infectious diseases.

Role of the Adoption Authority: The National Adoption Committee reviews the prospective adoptive parents' registration documents and issues a conclusion on the ability to adopt.

Role of the Court: Once the child has been identified and the remaining documents are submitted, a court date is set. During the hearing, the judge makes decisions on any requests to change the child's name, birth date, etc. After the hearing, the court will issue a preliminary decision and 30 days later the Government registers the final court decision.

Role of Adoption Agencies: Armenian law does not recognize the involvement of professional facilitators, adoption agencies, or attorneys. It does allow prospective adoptive parents to grant power of attorney to an individual to handle most aspects of the adoption process on their behalf. Some United States adoption agencies have contacts with experienced local individuals who can be given power of attorney.

Time Frame: From start to finish, an adoption timeframe of one to two years is common. Once approval to adopt has been granted, it can take up to six months to identify a child and several more months to secure the proper paperwork from the different Government agencies to support an application to adopt that particular child.

Adoption Application: The prospective adoptive parents submit the adoption application to the National Adoption Committee.

Adoption Fee: The official fees necessary to procure the documents needed in support of the adoption are approximately $65 USD. The practice of charging official and unofficial expediting fees varies depending on the particular Government agency or local office. In addition, the attorneys or other individuals assisting the prospective adoptive parents with the adoption may charge fees for services rendered. In the adoption services contract that you sign at the beginning of the adoption process, your agency will itemize the fees and estimated expenses related to your adoption process.

Documents Required: Please note that fraud is pervasive in Armenia. Fabricated documents or real documents fraudulently obtained are readily available. As a result, the United States Embassy in Yerevan must carefully investigate all visa cases.

The following is a list of documents required to request registration as prospective adoptive parents.

- Copy of the prospective adoptive parents' United States passports
- USCIS approval (either of the Form I-600A in a transition case or the Form I-800A in a new case)
- Copy of certificate of home study, including a description of the family and the home where the adopted child will reside
- Work verification letters indicating position, salary, and three letters of reference
- Tax return for the most recent tax year
- Copy of marriage certificate, if applicable
- Copy of divorce decree, or spouse's death certificate, if applicable
- Spousal consent (if only one spouse is legally adopting the child)
- Medical evaluation report confirming that the prospective adoptive parent(s) do not suffer from any type of psychological condition, alcoholism or drug abuse, HIV AIDS or other STD, active tuberculosis or other infectious diseases
- Local police check for prospective adoptive parents
- Power of Attorney if documents will be submitted through an authorized representative

The following is a list of documents that must be submitted to the regional court presiding over the child's district:

- Full names of the prospective adoptive parent(s) and child
- Notification of prospective adoptive parents' plans to change the child's name, date or place of birth, or to list themselves as parents on new documents
- Prospective adoptive parents' passports or other identification
- Prospective adoptive parents' marriage certificate, if applicable
- Spousal consent (if married and only one spouse is legally adopting the child)
- Child's consent if the child is over 10 years of age
- Child's birth certificate and medical records
- Statement of child's centralized registration from the Ministry of Social Security
- Written consent of adoptive parents, birth parents, and the orphanage. If applicable, death certificates of birth parents and consent of biological grandparents if the biological parents are not legal adults.
- Government approval of prospective adoptive parents

For updates on document requirements and information on how to authenticate documents, visit the USCIS Intercountry Adoption website at http://adoption.state.gov.

Bringing Your Child Home: Once your adoption is complete (or you have obtained legal custody of the child), there are a few more steps to take before you can head home.

Specifically, you need to apply for several documents for your child before he or she can travel to the United States, such as a birth certificate, a passport or travel document for your child from the country in which he or she was born, and a U.S. Immigration Visa.

For detailed and updated information on how to obtain these documents, review the Intercountry Adoption section on this publication and visit the USCIS Intercountry Adoption website at http://adoption.state.gov.

Child Citizenship Act: For adoptions finalized abroad, the Child Citizenship Act of 2000 allows your new child to acquire American citizenship automatically when he or she enters the United States as lawful permanent residents. For adoptions finalized in the United States, the Child Citizenship Act of 2000 allows your new child to acquire American citizenship automatically when the court in the United States issues the final adoption decree. To learn more, review the *Intercountry Adoption* section on this publication and visit the USCIS Intercountry Adoption website at http://adoption. state.gov.

After Adoption: According to Armenian law, there are no post-adoption requirements for intercountry adoptions.

United States Embassy in Armenia
1 American Avenue
Yerevan, Republic of Armenia
Tel: (+374 10) 464-700, 494-686
Fax: (+374 10) 464-742, 464-737
Email: consular@usa.am

Armenian Adoption Authority
National Adoption Committee
of the Republic of Armenia
Ministry of Labor and Social Issues
Government Building
#1 Republic Square
Yerevan, Armenia
Tel: (374 10) 56-53-83 or 52-68-31

Embassy of the Republic of Armenia
2225 R Street, N.W.
Washington, D.C. 20008, USA
Tel: (202) 319-1976
Fax: (202) 319-2982
Email: armconsul@speakeasy.net
Internet: http://www.armeniaemb.org

Armenian Consulate General
50 North La Cienega Boulevard, Suite 210
Beverly Hills, CA 90211
Tel: (310) 657-7320
Email: armconla@aol.com

Office of Children's Issues
United States Department of State
2201 C Street, NW; SA-29
Washington, DC 20520
Tel: 1-888-407-4747
E-mail: AskCI@state.gov
http://adoption.state.gov.

ARUBA

Compiled from publications that were available as of February 2013 from the U.S. Department of State, the U.S. Department of Commerce, and the Central Intelligence Agency (CIA). See the introduction to this set for explanatory notes.

Official Name:
Aruba

PROFILE

Geography

Area: total: 180 sq km; country comparison to the world: 218; land: 180 sq km; water: 0 sq km
Major cities: Oranjestad (capital) 33,000 (2009)
Climate: tropical marine; little seasonal temperature variation
Terrain: flat with a few hills; scant vegetation

People

Nationality: noun: Aruban(s); adjective: Aruban; Dutch
Population: 107,635 (July 2012 est.)
Population growth rate: 1.413% (2012 est.)
Ethnic groups: mixed white/Caribbean Amerindian 80%, other 20%
Religions: Roman Catholic 80.8%, Protestant 7.8% (Evangelist 4.1%, Methodist 1.2%, other Protestant 2.5%), Jehovah's Witnesses 1.5%, Jewish 0.2%, other 5.1%, none or unspecified 4.6%
Languages: Papiamento (a Spanish-Portuguese-Dutch-English dialect) 66.3%, Spanish 12.6%, English (widely spoken) 7.7%, Dutch (official) 5.8%, other 2.2%, unspecified or unknown 5.3% (2000 census)
Literacy: definition: age 15 and over can read and write; total population: 97.3%; male: 97.5%; female: 97.1% (2000 census)
Health: life expectancy at birth: total population: 75.93 years; male: 72.89 years; female: 79.04 years (2012 est.); Infant mortality rate: total: 12.51 deaths/1,000 live births; male: 16.51 deaths/1,000 live births; female: 8.44 deaths/1,000 live births (2012 est.)
Unemployment rate: 6.9% (2005 est.)
Work force: 41,500 (2004 est.)

Government

Type: parliamentary democracy
Independence: none
Constitution: 1 January 1986
Political subdivisions: none (part of the Kingdom of the Netherlands)
Suffrage: 18 years of age; universal

Economy

GDP (purchasing power parity): $2.258 billion (2005 est.); $2.205 billion (2004 est.)
GDP real growth rate: 2.4% (2005 est.)
GDP per capita (PPP): $21,800 (2004 est.)
Natural resources: NEGL; white sandy beaches
Agriculture products: aloes; livestock; fish
Industries: tourism, transshipment facilities, banking
Exports: $1.276 billion (2011 est.); $265.8 million (2010 est.)
Exports—commodities: live animals and animal products, art and collectibles, machinery and electrical equipment, transport equipment
Exports—partners: US 83.6% (2011)
Imports: $2.016 billion (2011 est.); $1.343 billion (2010 est.)
Imports—commodities: machinery and electrical equipment, crude oil for refining and reexport, chemicals; foodstuffs
Imports—partners: US 50%, Netherlands 9.1%, Brazil 7%, UK 4.7% (2011)
Debt—external: $478.6 million (2005 est.)
Exchange rates: Aruban guilders/florins (AWG) per US dollar; 1.79 (2011 est.); 1.79 (2010 est.)

PEOPLE AND HISTORY

Aruba's first inhabitants were the Caquetios Indians from the Arawak tribe. Fragments of the earliest known Indian settlements date back to about 1000 A.D. Spanish explorer Alonso de Ojeda is regarded as the first European to arrive in about 1499. The Spanish garrison on Aruba dwindled following the Dutch capture of nearby Bonaire and Curacao in 1634. The Dutch occupied Aruba

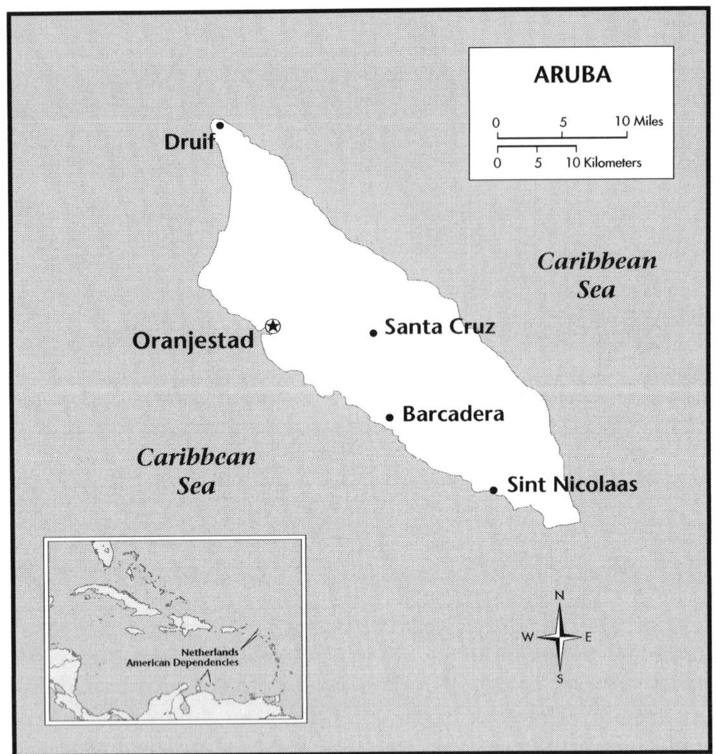

shortly thereafter, and retained control for nearly two centuries. In 1805, during the Napoleonic wars, the English briefly took control over the island, but it was returned to Dutch control in 1816. A 19th-century gold rush was followed by prosperity brought on by the opening in 1924 of an oil refinery. The last decades of the 20th century saw a boom in the tourism industry. In 1986 Aruba seceded from the Netherlands Antilles and became a separate, autonomous member of the Kingdom of the Netherlands. Movement toward full independence was halted at Aruba's prerogative in 1990. Aruba has a mixture of people from South America and Europe, the Far East, and other islands of the Caribbean.

GOVERNMENT

Part of the Kingdom of the Netherlands, Aruba has full autonomy on all internal affairs with the exception of defense, foreign affairs, and some judicial functions. The constitution was enacted in January 1986. Executive power rests with a governor, while a prime minister heads an eight-member Cabinet. The governor is appointed for a 6-year term by the monarch and the prime minister and deputy prime minister are elected by the legislature, or Staten, for 4-year terms. The Staten is made up of 21 members elected by direct, popular vote to serve 4-year terms. Aruba's judicial system, mainly derived from the Dutch system, operates independently of the legislature and the executive. Jurisdiction, including appeal, lies with the Common Court of Justice of Aruba and the Supreme Court of Justice in the Netherlands.

Principal Government Officials

Last Updated: 1/31/2013

Governor: **Fredis REFENJOL**
Prime Min.: **Michiel Godfried EMAN**
Min. of Education: **Fredis REFENJOL**
Min. of Finance & Economic Affairs: **Nilo SWAEN**
Min. of Gen. Affairs & Utilities: **Nelson ODUBER**
Min. of Justice: **Rudy CROES**
Min. of Public Health: **Booshi WEVER**
Min. of Public Works: **Marisol TROMP**
Min. of Sports, Culture, & Labor: **Ramon LEE**
Min. of Tourism & Transportation: **Eddy BRIESEN**
Attorney Gen.: **Ruud ROSINGH**
Pres., Central Bank: **A.R. CARAM**

POLITICAL CONDITIONS

The Aruba People's Party (AVP), led by Mike Eman, won the September 25, 2009 parliamentary elections, capturing 12 of the 21 seats; People's Electoral Movement (MEP) dropped from 11 to 8 seats, and Real Democracy Party (PDR) took the final seat. The Network of Eternal Democracy (RED) and Aruban Patriotic Movement (MPA) did not return to parliament.

ECONOMY

Tourism and offshore banking are the mainstays of the small open Aruban economy. Oil refining and storage ended in 2009. The rapid growth of the tourism sector over the last decade has resulted in a substantial expansion of other activities. Over 1.5 million tourists per year visit Aruba with 75% of those from the US. Construction continues to boom with hotel capacity five times the 1985 level. Tourist arrivals rebounded strongly following a dip after the 11 September 2001 attacks. The government has made cutting the budget and trade deficits a high priority.

U.S.-ARUBA RELATIONS

Aruba has semi-autonomy within the Kingdom of the Netherlands. It conducts foreign affairs, including with the United States, through the Netherlands, whose embassies and consulates issue visas for travel to the island. Tourism is the mainstay of Aruba's economy. Approximately 1.25 million tourists per year visit Aruba, with nearly 75% of those from the United States. In 2009, the U.S. accounted for more than 9% of

Aruba's exports and more than 49% of Aruba's imports by value. The U.S. Consulate General in Curacao is responsible for the day-to-day management of relations with the Dutch Caribbean, which includes Aruba, Bonaire, Curacao, Saba, Sint Eustatius, and Sint Maarten. Due to the strategic location of the Dutch Caribbean for the U.S., the consulate deals with issues such as securing U.S. borders, countering terrorism, and fighting international crime, especially narcotics trafficking and human trafficking.

The consulate provides a variety of services to U.S. citizens; it also can issue non-immigrant visas for certain travelers to the U.S. who wish to visit, work, or study for a temporary period. The consulate was opened in 1793. It was one of the earliest U.S. consulates, reflecting the importance of Caribbean trade to the new United States. The Consul General resides in the historic Roosevelt House, which was the local government's gift of property to the United States in 1950 as an expression of gratitude for U.S. protection during World War II.

Principal U.S. Embassy Officials

Last Updated: 1/14/2013

CURACAO (CG) J.B. Gorsiraweg #1, 599-9-461-3066, Fax 599-9-461-6489, INMARSAT Tel 00-874-383-133-190, Workweek: M-F 8AM–5 PM AST, http://curacao.usconsulate.gov

CM:	Valerie Belon
CON/POL/ECON:	Morgan Miles
DHS/CBP:	James Grimes
HRO:	Peggy Laurance
MGT:	Eric Kramp
CG:	Valerie Belon
RSO:	Robert Myers
DEA:	J. Gregory Garza
EEO:	Ricardo Cabrera
FMO:	Kevin Crews
IMO:	Jeffrey Yacobucci
State ICASS:	Morgan Miles

TRAVEL

Consular Information Sheet

November 16, 2009

Country Description: Aruba is an autonomous part of the Kingdom of the Netherlands. Tourist facilities are widely available.

Smart Traveler Enrollment Program (STEP)/Embassy Location: If you are going to work, live, or travel abroad, please take the time to tell the local U.S. Embassy about your trip. If you enroll, the Embassy can keep you up to date with important safety and security announcements. It will also help your friends and family get in touch with you in an emergency. The U.S. Consulate General is located at J.B. Gorsiraweg 1, Willemstad, Curaçao, telephone number (599-9) 461-3066; fax (599-9) 461-6489; e-mail address: acscuracao@state.gov.

Entry Requirements: All U.S. citizens must have a valid U.S. passport for all air travel, including to and from Aruba. All sea travelers must also now have a passport or passport card. We strongly encourage all American citizen travelers to apply for a U.S. passport or passport card well in advance of anticipated travel. American citizens can visit travel.state.gov or call 1-877-4USA-PPT (1-877-487-2778) for information on how to apply for their passports.

Visitors to Aruba may be asked to show onward/return tickets, proof of sufficient funds and proof of lodging accommodations for their stay. Length of stay for U.S. citizens is granted for thirty days and may be extended to 180 days by the office of immigration. For further information, travelers may contact the Royal Netherlands Embassy, 4200 Linnean Avenue NW, Washington, DC 20008, telephone (202) 244-5300, or the Dutch Consulate in Los Angeles, Chicago, New York, Houston or Miami. Visit the web site for the Embassy of the Netherlands and the Aruban Department of Immigration for the most current visa information. The U.S. Department of State is unaware of any HIV/AIDS entry restrictions for visitors to or foreign residents of Aruba.

Threats to Safety and Security: There are no known extremist groups, areas of instability or organized crime on Aruba, although drug trafficking rings do operate on the island. For the latest security information, Americans traveling abroad should regularly monitor the Department's Internet web site, where the current Worldwide Caution Travel Alert, Travel Warnings and Travel Alerts, can be found. Up-to-date information on safety and security can also be obtained by calling 1-888-407-4747 toll free in the U.S., or for callers outside the U.S. and Canada, a regular toll-line at 1-202-501-4444.

Crime: The crime threat in Aruba is generally considered low although travelers should always take normal precautions when in unfamiliar surroundings. There have been incidents of theft from hotel rooms and armed robberies have been known to occur. Valuables left unattended on beaches, in cars and in hotel lobbies are easy targets for theft. Car theft, especially of rental vehicles for joy riding and stripping, can occur. Vehicle leases or rentals may not be fully covered by local insurance when a vehicle is stolen or damaged. Be sure you are sufficiently insured when renting vehicles and jet skis. Parents of young travelers should be aware that the legal drinking age of 18 is not always rigorously enforced in Aruba, so extra parental supervision may be appropriate. Young travelers in particular are urged to take the same precautions they would when going out in the United States, e.g. to travel in pairs or in groups if they choose frequenting Aruba's nightclubs and bars, and if they opt to consume alcohol, to do so responsibly. Anyone who is a victim of a crime should make a report to Aruban police as well as report it immediately to the nearest U.S. consular office. Do not rely on hotel/restaurant/tour company management to make the report for you. In many countries around the world, counterfeit and pirated goods are widely available. Transactions involving such products may be illegal under local law. In addition, bringing them back to the United States may result in forfeitures and/or fines.

Victims of Crime: If you are the victim of a crime abroad, you should contact the local police and the nearest U.S. embassy or consulate (see end of this sheet or see the Department of State's list of embassies and consulates). This includes the loss or theft of a U.S. passport. The embassy/consulate staff can, for example, help you find appropriate medical care, contact family members or friends and explain how funds may be transferred. Although the investigation and prosecution of the crime are solely the responsibility of local authorities, consular officers can help you to understand the local criminal justice process and to find an attorney if needed. The emergency line in Aruba is 911.

Criminal Penalties: While in a foreign country, a U.S. citizen is subject to that country's laws and regulations, which sometimes differ significantly from those in the United States and may not afford the protections available to the individual under U.S. law. Penalties for breaking the law can be more severe than in the United States for similar offenses. Persons violating Aruba's laws, even unknowingly, may be expelled, arrested or imprisoned. Penalties for possession, use, or trafficking in illegal drugs in Aruba are severe, and convicted offenders can expect long jail sentences and heavy fines. Engaging in sexual conduct with children or using or disseminating child pornography in a foreign country is a crime, prosecutable in the United States.

Special Circumstances: Dutch law in principle does not permit dual nationality. However, there are several exceptions to the rule. For example, American citizens who are married to Dutch citizens are exempt from the requirement to abandon their American nationality when they apply to become a Dutch citizen by naturalization. For detailed information, contact the Embassy of the Netherlands in Washington, DC, or one of the Dutch consulates in the U.S.

Medical Facilities and Health Information: Medical care is good in Aruba. There is one hospital, Dr. H.E. Oduber Hospital, whose medical standards can be compared with an average small hospital in the U.S. The hospital has three classes of services and patients are accommodated according to the level of their insurance (i.e. first class: one patient to a room, TV, better food; second class: two to three patients to a room, shared bathroom, etc; third class: 15 to 20 people in one hall). There is a small medical center in San Nicolas. The many drug stores, or "boticas" provide prescription and over the counter medicine. Emergency services are usually quick to respond. There are no country-specific health concerns. Information on vaccinations and other health precautions, such as safe food and water precautions and insect bite protection, may be obtained from the Centers for Disease Control and Prevention's hotline for international travelers at 1-877-FYI-TRIP (1-877-394-8747) or via the CDC's Internet site at http://www.cdc.gov/travel. For information about outbreaks of infectious diseases abroad consult the World Health Organization's (WHO) website at http://www.who.int/en. Further health information for travelers is available at http://www.who.int/ith.

Medical Insurance: The Department of State strongly urges Americans to consult with their medical insurance company prior to traveling abroad to confirm whether their policy applies overseas and whether it will cover emergency expenses such as a medical evacuation.

Traffic Safety and Road Conditions: While in a foreign country, U.S. citizens may encounter road conditions that differ significantly from those in the United States. The information below concerning Aruba is provided for general reference only and may not be totally accurate for a particular location or circumstance. Driving in Aruba is on the right-hand side of the road. Local laws require drivers and passengers to wear seat belts and motorcyclists to wear helmets. Children under 5 years of age should be in a child safety seat; older children should ride in the back seat. Right turns on red are prohibited in Aruba.

Aruba's main thoroughfare, L.G. Smith Boulevard, is well lit and most hotels and tourist attractions can be easily located. There is a speed limit in Aruba and driving while intoxicated may result in the loss of a driver's license and/or a fine. However, these are not consistently enforced. Drivers should be alert at all times for speeding cars, which have caused fatal accidents. In the interior areas of the island, drivers should be alert for herds of goats or donkeys that may cross the roads unexpectedly. Buses provide convenient and inexpensive service to and from many hotels and downtown shopping areas. Taxis, while expensive, are safe and well regulated. As there are no meters, passengers should verify the price before entering the taxi. The emergency service telephone number is 911. Police and ambulance tend to respond fast to emergency situations. Also, travelers may wish to visit the website of the country's national tourist office and national authority responsible for road safety in Aruba for information: http://www. aruba.com/pages/traffic-tips.htm.

Aviation Safety Oversight: The U.S. Federal Aviation Administration (FAA) has assessed the Government of Aruba's Civil Aviation Authority as being in compliance with International Civil Aviation Organization (ICAO) aviation safety standards for oversight of Aruba's air carrier operations. For more information, travelers may visit the FAA's Internet web site at http://www.faa.gov.

Children's Issues: For information on intercountry adoption of children and international parental child abduction, see the Office of Children's Issues website at http://travel.state.gov.

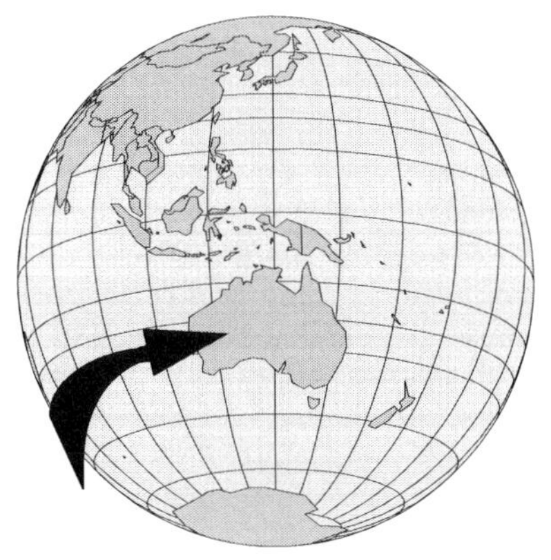

AUSTRALIA

Compiled from publications that were available as of February 2013 from the U.S. Department of State, the U.S. Department of Commerce, and the Central Intelligence Agency (CIA). See the introduction to this set for explanatory notes.

Official Name:
Commonwealth of Australia

PROFILE

Geography

Area: total: 7,741,220 sq km; country comparison to the world: 6; land: 7,682,300 sq km; water: 58,920 sq km

Major cities: Sydney 4.429 million; Melbourne 3.853 million; Brisbane 1.97 million; Perth 1.599 million; CANBERRA (capital) 384,000 (2009)

Climate: generally arid to semiarid; temperate in south and east; tropical in north

Terrain: mostly low plateau with deserts; fertile plain in southeast

People

Nationality: noun: Australian(s); adjective: Australian

Population: 22,015,576 (July 2012 est.)

Population growth rate: 1.126% (2012 est.)

Ethnic groups: white 92%, Asian 7%, aboriginal and other 1%

Religions: Protestant 27.4% (Anglican 18.7%, Uniting Church 5.7%, Presbyterian and Reformed 3%), Catholic 25.8%, Eastern Orthodox 2.7%, other Christian 7.9%, Buddhist 2.1%, Muslim 1.7%, other 2.4%, unspecified 11.3%, none 18.7% (2006 Census)

Languages: English 78.5%, Chinese 2.5%, Italian 1.6%, Greek 1.3%, Arabic 1.2%, Vietnamese 1%, other 8.2%, unspecified 5.7% (2006 Census)

Literacy: definition: age 15 and over can read and write; total population: 99%; male: 99%; female: 99% (2003 est.)

Health: life expectancy at birth: total population: 81.9 years; male: 79.48 years; female: 84.45 years (2012 est.); Infant mortality rate: total: 4.55 deaths/1,000 live births; male: 4.87 deaths/1,000 live births; female: 4.21 deaths/1,000 live births (2012 est.)

Unemployment rate: 5.2% (2012 est.)

Work force: 12.27 million (2012 est.)

Government

Type: federal parliamentary democracy and a Commonwealth realm

Independence: 1 January 1901

Constitution: 9 July 1900; effective 1 January 1901

Political subdivisions: 6 states and 2 territories; Australian Capital Territory, New South Wales, Northern Territory, Queensland, South Australia, Tasmania, Victoria, Western Australia

Suffrage: 18 years of age; universal and compulsory

Economy

GDP (purchasing power parity): $960.7 billion (2012 est.); $926.2 billion (2011 est.); $907.7 billion (2010 est.); $885.2 billion (2009 est.)

GDP real growth rate: 3.3% (2012 est.); 2% (2011 est.); 2.5% (2010 est.); 1.4% (2009 est.)

GDP per capita (PPP): $42,400 (2012 est.); $40,800 (2011 est.); $40,400 (2010 est.)

Natural resources: bauxite, coal, iron ore, copper, tin, gold, silver, uranium, nickel, tungsten, rare earth elements, mineral sands, lead, zinc, diamonds, natural gas, petroleum

Agriculture products: wheat, barley, sugarcane, fruits; cattle, sheep, poultry

Industries: mining, industrial and transportation equipment, food processing, chemicals, steel

Exports: $263.9 billion (2012 est.); $272.1 billion (2011 est.)

Exports—commodities: coal, iron ore, gold, meat, wool, alumina, wheat, machinery and transport equipment

Exports—partners: China 27.4%, Japan 19.2%, South Korea 8.9%, India 5.8% (2011)

Imports: $258.1 billion (2012 est.); $243.4 billion (2011 est.)

Imports—commodities: machinery and transport equipment, computers and office machines, telecommunication equipment and parts; crude oil and petroleum products

Imports—partners: China 18.5%, US 11.4%, Japan 7.9%, Singapore 6.3%, Germany 4.7% (2011)

Debt—external: $1.466 trillion (31 December 2012 est.); $1.376 trillion (31 December 2011 est.)

Exchange rates: Australian dollars (AUD) per US dollar; 0.963 (2012 est.); 0.9695 (2011 est.); 1.0902 (2010); 1.2822 (2009); 1.2059 (2008)

PEOPLE

Australia's indigenous inhabitants, a hunting-gathering people collectively referred to today as Aboriginals and Torres Straits Islanders, arrived more than 40,000 years ago. Although their technical culture remained static—depending on wood, bone, and stone tools and weapons—their spiritual and social life was highly complex. Most spoke several languages, and confederacies sometimes linked widely scattered tribal groups. When Captain James Cook claimed Australia for Great Britain in 1770, the native population may have numbered 300,000 in as many as 500 tribes speaking many different languages.

Immigration has been vital to Australia's development since the beginning of European settlement in 1788. For generations, most settlers came from the British Isles, and the people of Australia are still predominantly of British or Irish origin. Non-British/Irish immigration has increased significantly since World War II through an extensive, planned immigration program. Since 1945, over 7 million migrants have settled in Australia, including 700,000 refugee and humanitarian entrants. About 80% have remained; 24%—almost one in four—of Australians are foreign-born. Britain, Ireland, Italy, Greece, New Zealand, and the former Yugoslavia were the largest sources of post-war immigration. In 2010–2011, China was the largest source country for permanent migrants to Australia, with New Zealand, India, Britain, and the Philippines making up the rest of the top five. Although Australia has fewer than three people per square kilometer, it is one of the world's most urbanized countries. Less than 2.5% of the population lives in remote or very remote areas.

National/Racial/Ethnic Minorities

According to the 2006 census, Aboriginals and Torres Strait Islanders numbered approximately 517,200 persons, roughly 2.5 percent of the total population.

The government expressed a commitment to "closing the gap" on indigenous inequalities and since 2008 the prime minister has reported to Parliament the progress on this effort at the beginning of each year. In August 2011 the Productivity Commission released a report that noted improvements in 13 areas of indigenous well-being but worsening or no change in 17 areas. It found that infant and child mortality rates had "improved significantly" since the early 1990s; median household income had increased from 2002–2008; school retention to year 10 had increased from 83 to 96 percent from 1998–2010; and there were improvements in employment. However, "virtually all the indicators in this report" showed wide gaps between indigenous and other Australians.

According to the ABS, in 2010 indigenous adults were 14 times as likely as nonindigenous adults to be imprisoned and comprised 26 percent of the prison population. Life expectancy for indigenous men was estimated to be 67.2 years, compared with 78.7 years for nonindigenous men; life expectancy for indigenous women was estimated to be 72.9 years, compared with 82.6 years for nonindigenous women; and the indigenous unemployment rate was 18 percent, compared with 5 percent for the nonindigenous population.

The National Congress of Australia's First Peoples, established in May 2010, is the national representative body for Aboriginals and Torres Strait Islanders. It was designated to receive A$29.2 million ($29.7 million) over five years from the federal government.

Language

Australia is an English-speaking country.

Religion

According to the 2006 census, 64 percent of citizens consider themselves Christian, including 26 percent Roman Catholic, 19 percent Anglican, and 19 percent other Christian denominations. Buddhists constitute 2.1 percent of the population, Muslims 1.7 percent, Hindus 0.7 percent, Jews 0.4 percent, and all others professing a religion 0.5 percent.

According to the 2006 census, 5,206 persons, or less than 0.03 percent of respondents, reported practicing indigenous traditional religions. The 2006 census reported almost 64 percent of indigenous persons identify themselves as Christian, and 20 percent list no religion.

HISTORY

Australia was uninhabited until stone-culture peoples arrived, perhaps by boat across the waters separating the island from the Indonesia archipelago more than 40,000 years ago. Portuguese, Spanish, Dutch, and English explorers observed the island before 1770, when Captain Cook explored the east coast and claimed it for Great Britain. (Three American colonists were crew members aboard Cook's ship, the Endeavour.)

On January 26, 1788 (now celebrated as Australia Day), the First Fleet under Captain Arthur Phillip landed at Sydney, and formal proclamation of the establishment of the Colony of New South Wales followed on February 7. Many of the first settlers were convicts, some condemned for offenses that today would often be thought trivial. From the mid-19th century convict transportation to Australia significantly declined; the last ship to arrive was in 1868. The discovery of gold in 1851 led to increased population, wealth, and trade.

The six colonies that now constitute the states of the Australian Commonwealth were established in the following order: New South Wales, 1788; Tasmania, 1825; Western Australia, 1829; South Australia, 1836; Victoria,

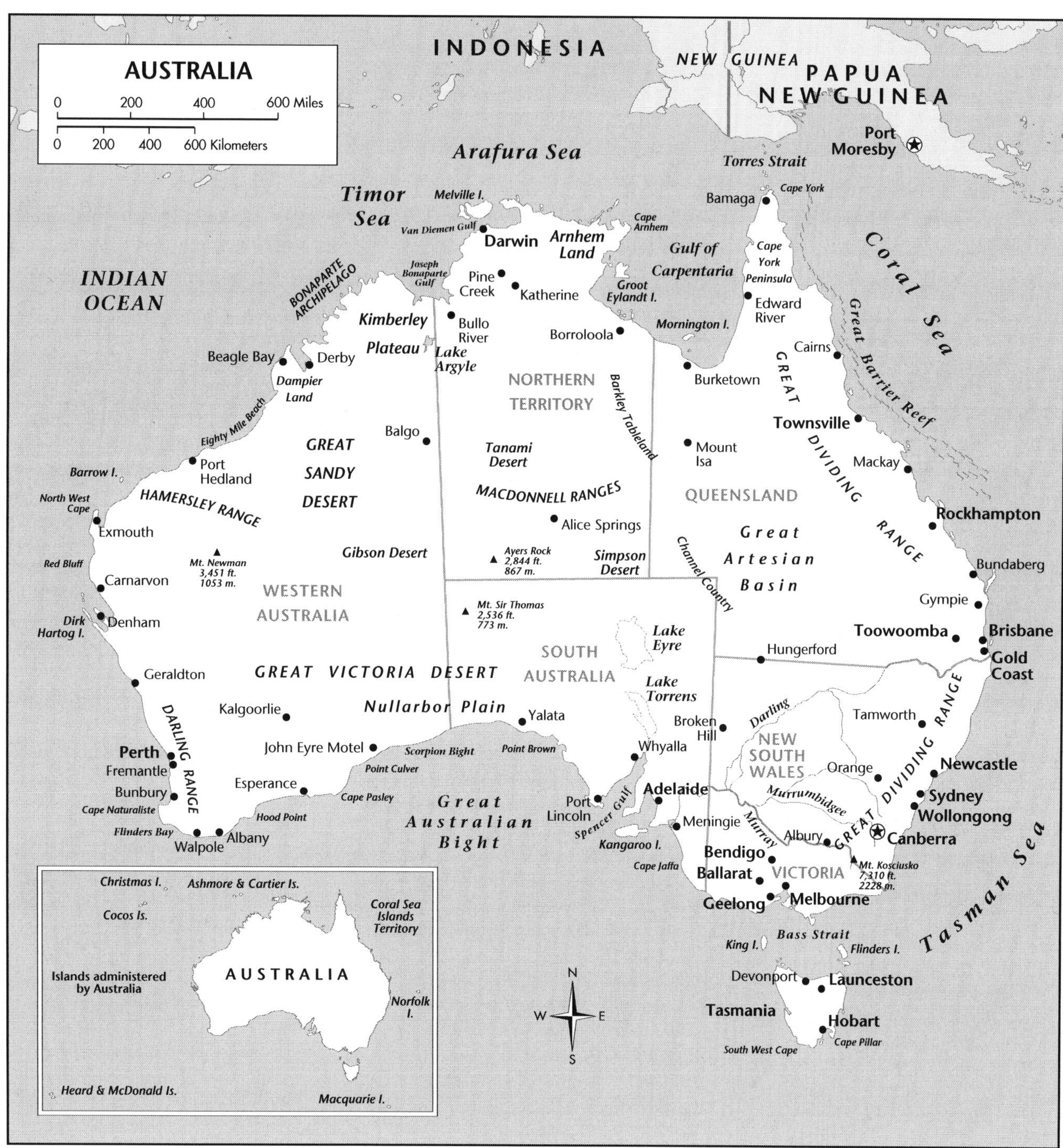

1851; and Queensland, 1859. Settlement preceded these dates in most cases. Discussions between Australian and British representatives led to adoption by the British Government of an act to constitute the Commonwealth of Australia in 1900, effective January 1, 1901. In 1911, control of the Northern Territory was transferred from South Australia to the Commonwealth. Also that year, the Australian Capital Territory (where the national capital, Canberra, is located), was established. The Northern Territory and Australian Capital Territory were granted self-government in 1978 and 1988, respectively.

The first federal Parliament was opened at Melbourne in May 1901 by the Duke of York (later King George V). In May 1927, the seat of government was transferred to Canberra, a city designed by American Walter Burley Griffin. The first session of Parliament in Canberra was opened by another Duke of York (later King George VI). Australia passed the Statute of Westminster Adoption Act on October 9, 1942 (with effect as of September 3, 1939), which officially established Australia's complete autonomy in both internal and external affairs and formalized a situation that had existed for years. The Australia Act (effective March 3, 1986) eliminated almost all remaining vestiges of British legal authority, including the ability to appeal to the British Privy Council. "Advance Australia Fair" was adopted as the national anthem in 1984.

GOVERNMENT AND POLITICAL CONDITIONS

Australia is a constitutional democracy with a freely elected federal parliamentary government. In free and fair federal parliamentary elections held in August 2010, neither the Australian Labor Party (ALP) nor the opposition Liberal Party and National Party coalition won enough seats to form a government. Subsequently, the ALP secured the support of the Greens Party member of Parliament (MP) and three independent MPs to gain a majority of 76 seats in the 150-seat House of Representatives and formed a government with Julia Gillard as prime minister.

Recent Elections

In federal elections held in August 2010, the incumbent ALP government won 72 seats in the 150-seat lower house of Parliament; the opposition Liberal-National Party coalition won 73; and others won five. The ALP formed a government with the support of one Greens Party and three independent MPs.

Participation of Women and Minorities: There are no legal impediments to public office for women or indigenous persons. Following the August 2010 elections, there were 64 women in the 226-seat federal Parliament (37 in the House of Representatives and 27 in the Senate). There were five female ministers in the 21-member federal cabinet, two women among the 10 ministers outside the cabinet, and four women among the 12 parliamentary secretaries. There were two women among the eight premiers and chief ministers of the six states and two territories. The prime minister and the governor-general were women, and there were three female judges on the seven-member High Court.

Indigenous persons generally were underrepresented among the political leadership. In August 2010 an indigenous person was elected to the federal House of Representatives for the first time. There was one indigenous citizen in the Tasmania State parliament, one in the New South Wales State parliament, two in the Western Australia State parliament, five in the Northern Territory legislative assembly, and one in the Australian Capital Territory legislative assembly. There was an Asian-Australian in the federal cabinet.

Principal Government Officials

Last Updated: 1/31/2013

Governor Gen.: **Quentin Alice Louise BRYCE**

Prime Min.: **Julia Eileen GILLARD**

Dep. Prime Min.: **Wayne Maxwell SWAN**

Min. for Agriculture, Fisheries, & Forestry: **Joseph William LUDWIG**

Min. for the Arts: **Simon Findlay CREAN**

Min. for Broadband, Communications, & the Digital Economy:**Stephen Michael CONROY**

Min. for Climate Change & Energy Efficiency: **Gregory Ivan COMBET**

Min. for Community Services: **Julie Maree COLLINS**

Min. for Defense: **Stephen Francis SMITH**

Min. for Defense Materiel: **Jason Dean CLARE**

Min. for Defense Science & Personnel: **Warren Edward SNOWDON**

Min. for Disability Reform: **Jennifer Louise MACKLIN**

Min. for Early Childhood & Childcare: **Katherine Margaret ELLIS**

Min. for Emergency Management: **Nicola Louise ROXON**

Min. for Employment & Workplace Relations: **William Richard SHORTEN**

Min. for Employment Participation: **Katherine Margaret ELLIS**

Min. for Families, Community Services, & Indigenous Affairs:**Jennifer Louise MACKLIN**

Min. for Finance & Deregulation: **Penelope "Penny" Yingyen WONG**

Min. for Financial Services & Superannuation: **William Richard SHORTEN**

Min. for Foreign Affairs: **Robert John CARR**

Min. for Foreign Trade & Competitiveness: **Craig Anthony EMERSON**

Min. for Health: **Tanya Joan PLIBERSEK**

Min. for Home Affairs: **Jason Dean CLARE**

Min. for Homelessness: **Brendan Patrick John O'CONNOR**

Min. for Housing: **Brendan Patrick John O'CONNOR**

Min. for Human Services: **Kim John CARR**

Min. for Immigration & Citizenship: **Christopher Eyles Guy BOWEN**

Min. for Indigenous Employment & Economic Development:**Julie Maree COLLINS**

Min. for Indigenous Health: **Warren Edward SNOWDON**

Min. for Infrastructure & Transport: **Anthony Norman ALBANESE**

Min. for Industry & Innovation: **Gregory Ivan COMBET**

Min. for Justice: **Jason Dean CLARE**

Min. for Manufacturing: **Kim John CARR**

Min. for Mental Health & Aging: **Mark Christopher BUTLER**

Min. for Multicultural Affairs: **Kate LUNDY**

Min. for the Public Service & Integrity: **Gary GRAY**

Min. for Regional Australia, Regional Development, & Local Govt.:**Simon Findlay CREAN**

Min. for Resources & Energy: **Martin John FERGUSON**

Min. for School Education, Early Childhood, & Youth: **Peter Robert GARRETT**

Min. for Small Business: **Brendan Patrick John O'CONNOR**

Min. for Social Inclusion: **Mark Christopher BUTLER**

Min. for Sport: **Kate LUNDY**

Min. for the Status of Women: **Julie Maree COLLINS**

Min. for Sustainability, Environment, Water, Population, & Communities: **Anthony Stephen BURKE**

Min. for Tertiary Education, Skills, Science, & Research:**Christopher Vaughan EVANS**
Min. for Tourism: **Martin John FERGUSON**
Min. for Veterans Affairs: **Warren Edward SNOWDON**
Treasurer: **Wayne Maxwell SWAN**
Asst. Treasurer: **David John BRADBURY**
Min. Assisting the Prime Min. on the Centenary of ANZAC:**Warren Edward SNOWDON**
Min. Assisting the Prime Min. for Deregulation: **David John BRADBURY**
Min. Assisting the Prime Min. on Digital Productivity: **Stephen Michael CONROY**
Min. Assisting the Prime Min. on Industry & Innovation:**Kate LUNDY**
Min. Assisting the Prime Min. on Mental Health Reform:**Mark Christopher BUTLER**
Min. Assisting on Queensland Floods Recovery: **Joseph William LUDWIG**
Min. Assisting for School Education: **Brendan Patrick John O'CONNOR**
Special Min. of State: **Gary GRAY**
Attorney Gen.: **Nicola Louise ROXON**
Governor, Reserve Bank of Australia: **Glenn STEVENS**
Ambassador to the US: **Kim Christian BEAZLEY**
Permanent Representative to the UN, New York: **Gary Francis QUINLAN**

POLITICAL CONDITIONS

Three political parties dominate the center of the Australian political spectrum. The Liberal Party (LP), nominally representing urban business interests, and its smaller coalition partner, the Nationals, nominally representing rural interests, are the center-right parties. The center-left Australian Labor Party, founded by labor unions, nominally represents workers and left-of-center groups. While traditionally moderately socialist in its policies, today it is best described as a social democratic party. There is strong bipartisan sentiment on many international issues, including Australia's commitment to its alliance with the United States.

Julia Gillard assumed the office of Prime Minister in June 2010, succeeding Kevin Rudd following her unopposed election as Labor leader in a caucus ballot.

The August 21, 2010, federal election produced a hung parliament, with neither the Labor Party, under the leadership of Gillard, nor the Liberal/National Coalition, led by Opposition Leader Tony Abbott, holding a majority of seats. The Coalition gained 8 seats while the Labor Party lost 11. Subsequently, the Labor Party secured the support of the Greens Party Member of Parliament (MP) and three independent MPs to gain a majority of 76 seats. The government was sworn in 14 September 2010. The composition of the new Senate, to take effect in July 2011, is 34 seats for the coalition, 31 for the ALP, nine for the Greens, one for the Democratic Labor Party, and one independent.

Gillard is pursuing her campaign promises to build a national broadband network and price carbon. The Australian Government's foreign policy shows strong continuity with that of its predecessors, including support for the U.S. alliance, engagement in the Asia-Pacific, and commitment to the mission in Afghanistan where it has deployed about 1,550 troops.

ECONOMY

Australia's abundant and diverse natural resources attract high levels of foreign investment and include extensive reserves of coal, iron ore, copper, gold, natural gas, uranium, and renewable energy sources. A series of major investments, such as the US$40 billion Gorgon Liquid Natural Gas project, will significantly expand the resources sector. Australia also has a large services sector and is a significant exporter of natural resources, energy, and food. Key tenets of Australia's trade policy include support for open trade and the successful culmination of the Doha Round of multilateral trade negotiations, particularly for agriculture and services.

The Australian economy grew for 17 consecutive years before the global financial crisis. Subsequently, the former RUDD government introduced a fiscal stimulus package worth over US$50 billion to offset the effect of the slowing world economy, while the Reserve Bank of Australia cut interest rates to historic lows. These policies—and continued demand for commodities, especially from China—helped the Australian economy rebound after just one quarter of negative growth. The economy grew by 1.4% during 2009 - the best performance in the OECD—by 2.5% in 2010, 2.1% in 2011, and 3.3% in 2012.

Unemployment, originally expected to reach 8-10%, peaked at 5.7% in late 2009 and fell to 5.2% in 2012. As a result of an improved economy, the budget deficit dropped to 0.8% of GDP in 2012 and the government could return to budget surpluses before 2015. Australia was one of the first advanced economies to raise interest rates, with seven rate hikes between October 2009 and November 2010. The Gillard government is focused on raising Australia's economic productivity to ensure the sustainability of growth, and continues to manage the symbiotic, but sometimes tense, economic relationship with China. Australia is engaged in the Trans-Pacific Partnership talks and ongoing free trade agreement negotiations with China, Japan, and Korea.

Labor Conditions

There is no federally mandated minimum age of employment, but state-imposed compulsory educational requirements, enforced by state educational authorities, effectively prevented most children from joining the work force full time until they were age 17. Federal, state, and territorial governments effectively monitored and enforced a network of laws, which varied among jurisdictions, governing the minimum age for leaving school, claiming unemployment benefits, and engaging in specified occupations. The ACTU also monitored adherence to these laws.

On June 5, 2011, Fair Work Australia increased the national minimum wage for adults working full time (38 hours per week) from A$569.90 ($580.20) toA$589.30 ($599.90) per week, based on a minimum hourly rate of A$15.51 ($15.80). There is no official poverty-level income figure, but the minimum wage, combined with welfare payments, is intended to provide a decent standard of living for a worker and family. Although a formal minimum wage exists, most workers received higher wages through enterprise agreements or individual contracts. Abovc minimum wage classifications apply to certain trades and professions.

A taxpayer-funded, paid parental leave benefit began January 1, 2011. The Paid Parental Leave Scheme pays the minimum wage rate for up to 18 weeks. To qualify, a worker must have worked for at least 10 of the 13 months prior to the birth or adoption of the child and worked for at least 330 hours during that 10-month period.

Under the Fair Work Act, maximum weekly hours are 38 plus "reasonable" additional hours (determined according to the act, taking into account factors such as an employee's health, family responsibilities, ability to claim overtime, pattern of hours in the industry, and amount of notice given). Industry standards or awards mandate rest periods and pay for overtime. Migrant worker visas require that employers respect these protections and provide bonds to cover health insurance, worker's compensation insurance, unemployment insurance, and other benefits.

Federal or state occupational health and safety laws apply to every workplace. Federal and state laws provide employees with the right to cease work without endangering their future employment if they believe that particular work activities pose an immediate threat to individual health or safety.

Over the past two decades, the percentage of the workforce regarded as temporary workers increased substantially. Temporary workers include both part-time and casual employees. Part-time employees have set hours and the same entitlements as full-time employees. The ABS reported that, as of June, approximately 3.43 million persons (30 percent of the workforce) were employed as part-time workers, of whom 70 percent were women. Casual employees are employed on a daily or hourly wage basis. They do not receive paid annual or sick leave, but the law mandates they receive additional pay to compensate for this.

U.S.-AUSTRALIAN RELATIONS

The United States established diplomatic relations with Australia in 1940, following the United Kingdom's recognition of Australia's domestic and external autonomy within the British Empire and the Government of Australia's formal adoption of the codification. U.S. relations with Australia are strong and close. The two share a traditional friendship, similarities in culture and historical background, democratic values, common interests, and similar views on most major international questions. Ties range from commercial, cultural, and environmental contacts to political and defense cooperation. Australian forces have fought beside the United States and other Allies in every significant conflict since World War I.

The United States and Australia attach high priority to controlling and eventually eliminating chemical weapons, other weapons of mass destruction, and anti-personnel landmines; and they work closely on global environmental issues such as slowing climate change and preserving coral reefs. The ANZUS Treaty with the United States enjoys broad bipartisan support in Australia as its pre-eminent formal security treaty alliance. Australia participates in bilateral AUSMIN consultations with the United States and in a trilateral security dialogue with the United States and Japan.

A number of U.S. institutions conduct cooperative scientific activities in Australia because of its geographical position, large land mass, and advanced technology. The two countries have signed a tax treaty and agreements on science and technology, emergency management cooperation, and social security. They also have concluded a mutual legal assistance treaty, enhancing bilateral cooperation on legal and counternarcotics issues.

U.S. Assistance to Australia

The United States provides no development assistance to Australia.

Bilateral Economic Relations

U.S. exports to Australia include machinery, vehicles, optic and medical instruments, aircraft, and agricultural products. U.S. imports from Australia include precious stones/metals, agricultural products, and optic and medical instruments. The United States is one of the largest foreign investors in Australia.

The bilateral Australia-U.S. Free Trade Agreement (AUSFTA) liberalized an already vibrant trade and investment relationship. The AUSFTA created ongoing working groups and committees to explore further bilateral trade reform. The two countries share a commitment to liberalizing global trade. They work together closely in the World Trade Organization, and both are active members of the Asia-Pacific Economic Cooperation forum. They also participate in the Trans-Pacific Partnership negotiations that seek to develop a regional trade agreement.

Australia's Membership in International Organizations

Australia and the United States belong to a number of the same international organizations, including the United Nations, ASEAN Regional Forum, Asia-Pacific Economic Cooperation forum, G-20, International

Monetary Fund, World Bank, Organization for Economic Cooperation and Development, and World Trade Organization. Australia also is a Partner for Cooperation with the Organization for Security and Cooperation in Europe.

Bilateral Representation

Australia maintains an embassy in the United States at 1601 Massachusetts Avenue NW, Washington, DC 20036 (tel. 202-797-3000).

Principal U.S. Embassy Officials

Last Updated: 1/14/2013

CANBERRA (E) American Embassy Canberra, Moonah Place, Yarralumla ACT 2600 AUSTRALIA, 61-2-6214-5600, Fax 61-2-6214-5970, INMARSAT Tel Reach Kit, Workweek: Mon–Fri / 8:00am to 5:00pm, Website: http://canberra.usembassy.gov/

DCM OMS:	Susan Christy
AMB OMS:	Susan Adams
Co-CLO:	Heidi Paul
FM:	Mark L. Moore
HRO:	Nancy Long
MGT:	Kathy Johnson
MLO/ODC:	COL Peter Tremblay
POSHO:	Mark L. Moore
SDO/DATT:	COL Chris Stockton
AMB:	Jeffrey L. Bleich
CON:	Walker Murray
DCM:	Jason P. Hyland
PAO:	Paul Houge
GSO:	Bernt Johnson
RSO:	Peter Gibbons
AGR:	Joseph Carroll
CLO:	Pamela Gilbert
DEA:	David Cali
ECON:	Jonathan Fritz
EEO:	Nancy Chen
EST:	Jonathan Habjan
FMO:	Calvin Watlington
ICASS Chair:	Jonathan Fritz
IMO:	Kevin Wagganer
IPO:	Philip Wilkin
ISO:	Mark Chalkley
ISSO:	Erik Connaway
LEGATT:	Henry Gittleman
POL:	Nan Fife
State ICASS:	Jonathan Fritz

MELBOURNE (CG) 553 St. Kilda Road, Melbourne, VIC, Australia, 3004, + 61 3 9526 5900, Fax + 61 3 9510-4646, INMARSAT Tel Iridium 014-716-9057, Workweek: M-F, 8:00–5:00, Website: http://melbourne.usconsulate.gov/

CG OMS:	Deborah Pines
MGT:	Joseph Marcus
POL/ECON:	Andrew Moore
POSHO:	Joseph Marcus
SDO/DATT:	John Dowling
CG:	Mary Warlick
CON:	Nathan Flook
PAO:	Suzan Shultz
IPO:	Maurio Lopez
ISSO:	Andrew Moore

SYDNEY (CG) MLC Centre–Level 59, 19-29 Martin Place, Sydney 2000, 61-2-9373-9200, Fax 61-2-9373-9125, Workweek: M-F, 08:00–17:00.

CG OMS:	Sue Heckman
FCS:	Joe Kaesshaefer
MGT:	Scott Simpson
POL/ECON:	Chris Meade
POSHO:	Caren Brown
CG:	Niels Marquardt
PO:	Niels Marquardt
CON:	Eric Fichte
PAO:	Karen Choe-Fichte
GSO:	Caren Brown
RSO:	Matt O'Brien
CLO:	Vacant
ECON:	Vacant
EEO:	Vacant
IPO:	Freddy Mendez
IRS:	Greg Monahan
ISO:	Steve Adams
LEGATT:	Renn Cannon

PERTH (C) Level 13, 16 St Georges Tce, 61-8-6144-5100, Fax 61-8-9231-9444, Workweek: M–F; 8:00 am–5:30 pm, http://perth.usconsulate.gov/perth/index.html.

CG OMS:	Mariane Primrose (Les)
MGT:	Seth Cornell
PAO/ADV:	Lisa Marino (Les)
CG:	Aleisha Woodward
CON:	Robert Reeves
GSO:	Anoutchka Payet (Les)
ECON:	Gina Soos (Les)
POL:	Claire Smith

TRAVEL

Consular Information Sheet

September 12, 2012

Country Description: Australia is a highly developed, stable democracy with a federal-state system. Tourist facilities are widely available.

Smart Traveler Enrollment Program (STEP)/Embassy Locations: If you are going to live in or visit Australia, please take the time to tell our Embassy and Consulates about your trip. If you enroll, we can keep you up to date with important safety and security announcements. It will also help your friends and family get in touch with you in an emergency.

Australian Capital Territory (ACT) or Queanbeyan:
U.S. Embassy in Canberra
Moonah Place
Yarralumla, ACT 2600
Telephone: (61) (2) 6214–5600
Emergency after-hours telephone: (61) (2) 411-424-608
Facsimile: (61) (2) 6214–5970

NOTE: The Embassy in Canberra only provides emergency assistance for U.S. citizens in the ACT. The U.S. Embassy does not issue U.S. passports or visas. Passports and other routine citizen services for Canberra and the rest of the ACT are provided by the U.S. Consulate General in Sydney.

New South Wales, Norfolk Island, Lord Howe Island, and Queensland:
U.S. Consulate General Sydney
Level 10, MLCCentre, 19-29 Martin Place, Sydney, NSW 2000
Telephone: (61) (2) 9373–9200
Emergency after-hours telephone: (61) (2) 4422–2201
Facsimile: (61) (2) 9373–9184

NOTE: The Consulate General offers an online appointment system for U.S. citizens seeking routine non-emergency services such as registration, passport, and other consular

Background Notes

services. To make an appointment, visit their web site. Hours open to the public: 8:00 a.m. to 11:30 a.m., Monday to Friday (except U.S. and Australian holidays and the first Wednesday of each month). For emergency services (e.g., the arrest, death, or serious injury of a U.S. citizen) after 5:00 p.m. weekdays, holidays and weekends, please call (61) (2) 4422–2201.

Victoria, Tasmania, South Australia, and the Northern Territory:
U.S. Consulate General Melbourne
553 St. Kilda Road, Melbourne
VIC 3004
Telephone: (61) (3) 9526–5900
Emergency after-hours telephone: (61) (3) 9389–3601
Facsimile: (61) (3) 9525–0769
Email: MelbourneACS@state.gov

NOTE: The Consulate General offers an online appointment system for U.S. citizens seeking routine non-emergency services such as registration, passport, and other consular services. To make an appointment, visit their web site. Hours open to the public: 8:00am—3:30pm Monday to Friday. All services other than emergencies require an appointment.

For emergency services (e.g., the arrest, death, or serious injury of a U.S. citizen) after 4:30 p.m. or on holidays and weekends, please call (61) (3) 9389–3601.

Western Australia:
U.S. Consulate General Perth
16 St. Georges Terrace
Perth WA 6000
Telephone: (61)(8) 9202–1224
Emergency after-hours telephone: (61) (8) 9476–0081
Facsimile: (61)(8) 9231–9444

NOTE: The Consulate General offers an online appointment system for U.S. citizens seeking routine non-emergency services such as registration, passport, and other consular services. To make an appointment, please visit the Consulate's web site. Hours open to the public for American Citizen Services: 8:30 to 11:30 a.m., Monday through Thursday. For emergency services (e.g., the arrest, death, or serious injury of a U.S. citizen) outside of business hours, please call (61) (8) 9476–0081.

Entry/Exit Requirements for U.S. Citizens: You must have a valid U.S. passport and a visa to enter Australia. Most U.S. passport holders traveling to Australia for tourism or business purposes for less than 90 days can obtain an Electronic Travel Authority (ETA). The ETA is an electronic label-free visa and can be obtained at the ETA website for a small service fee. Airlines and many travel agents in the United States are also able to apply for ETAs on behalf of travelers.

If you overstay your ETA or any other visa, even for short periods, you may be subject to exclusion, detention, and removal by the Australian Department of Immigration and Citizenship (DIAC). You can find more information about the ETA, other visas, and entry requirements from the Embassy of Australia at 1601 Massachusetts Avenue, NW, Washington, DC 20036, via the Australian Visa Information Service at 905-280-1437 (toll charges to Canada apply) or their website.

HIV/AIDS Entry Restrictions: Some HIV/AIDS entry restrictions exist for visitors to and foreigners seeking permanent residence in Australia. Depending on the type of visa you apply for, the length of your stay, and your intended activities in Australia, you may be required to undergo a medical examination before the Australian Department of Immigration and Citizenship (DIAC) will issue you a visa.

If during the course of the application process, you are found to be HIV positive, a decision on the application will be considered on the same grounds as any other pre-existing medical condition (such as tuberculosis or cancer), with the main focus being placed on the cost of the condition to Australia's health care and community services.

Threats to Safety and Security: Australia has an alert system for possible terrorist attacks. The threat levels range from "low" to "high." The Australian Attorney General's Office web site has up-to-date information regarding the current terrorism threat level. Depending on the alert, you should maintain a high level of vigilance and take appropriate steps to increase your security awareness. Travelers may also contact the Australian National Security Hotline at 61-1-800-123-400.

Stay up to date by:

- Bookmarking our Bureau of Consular Affairs website, which contains the current Travel Warnings and Travel Alerts as well as the Worldwide Caution.
- Following us on Twitter and the Bureau of Consular Affairs page on Facebook as well.
- Downloading our free Smart Traveler iPhone App to have travel information at your fingertips.
- Calling 1-888-407-4747 toll-free within the U.S. and Canada, or a regular toll line, 1-202-501-4444, from other countries.
- Taking some time before travel to consider your personal security.

Crime: Although Americans are not specifically targeted for crime, travelers should be aware that robberies, burglaries, assault, and auto theft are common in Australia's larger cities. Weapons are increasingly used in such crimes, which also may be associated with drug trafficking, gang activities, and drug or alcohol usage.

Foreign visitors in popular tourist areas are targets for pickpockets, purse-snatchers, and petty thieves. Be careful when consuming alcohol with unfamiliar people, as drink spiking can occur; appropriate security precautions should be taken, especially at night, to avoid becoming a target of opportunity. Do not buy counterfeit and pirated goods, even if they are widely available. Not only are the bootlegs illegal in the United States, if you purchase them you may also be breaking local law.

Victims of Crime: If you or someone you know becomes the victim of a crime abroad, you should contact the local police and the nearest U.S. embassy or consulate. We can:

- Replace a stolen passport.
- Help you find appropriate medical care if you are the victim of violent crimes such as assault or rape.
- Put you in contact with the appropriate police authorities, and if you want us to, we can contact family members or friends.
- Help you understand the local criminal justice process and direct you to local attorneys, although it is important to remember that local authorities are responsible for investigating and prosecuting the crime.

Every state in Australia has an assistance program for victims of crimes and these programs will be able to generally assist you, even if you are only visiting Australia. For more information on local programs in Australia, please visit Victim Assistance Online's website.

The local equivalent to the "911" emergency line in Australia is:000 (Triple 0). To call for fire/police/ambulance services throughout Australia, dial "000" for urgent assistance.

Criminal Penalties: While you are traveling in Australia, you are subject to its laws even if you are a U.S. citizen. While you are overseas, U.S. laws don't apply. Foreign laws and legal systems can be vastly different than our own. You may be taken in for questioning if you don't have your passport with you. In some places, it is illegal to take pictures of certain buildings, such as inside certain areas of Australian airports and near prisons. It is prohibited to take photographs at military bases.

If you break local laws, your U.S. passport won't help. It's very important to know what's legal and what's not where you are going. In Australia, driving under the influence could land you immediately in jail. If you violate Australian laws, even unknowingly, you may be expelled, arrested, or imprisoned. There are also some things that might be legal in the country you visit, but still illegal in the United States. You can be prosecuted under U.S. law if you buy pirated goods. Engaging in sexual conduct with children or using or disseminating child pornography in a foreign country is a crime prosecutable in the United States. If you break local laws in Australia, your U.S. passport won't help you avoid arrest or prosecution. Penalties for possessing, using, or trafficking in illegal drugs in Australia are severe, and convicted offenders can expect long jail sentences and heavy fines.

Please be aware that all objectionable material is subject to declaration and inspection and may be illegal in Australia. Objectionable material includes child pornography, bestiality, explicit sexual violence, and graphic degradation, as well as terrorism-related material and anything providing instruction in or encouraging drug use, crime, or violence. It's very important to know what's legal and what's not wherever you go.

While some countries will automatically notify the nearest U.S. embassy or consulate if a U.S. citizen is detained or arrested in a foreign country, that might not always be the case. To ensure that the United States is aware of your circumstances, request that the police and prison officials notify the nearest U.S. embassy or consulate as soon as you are arrested or detained overseas.

Potential Health Screening: The 1908 Quarantine Law gives Australian authorities broad powers to prevent the entry of diseases and other materials into Australia that might pose a threat to its welfare. In the event of a public health emergency involving a communicable disease, passengers arriving in Australia may be subject to strict health screening measures, including testing, monitoring, and assessment for possible quarantine.

For information about outbreaks of infectious diseases abroad, please consult the infectious diseases section of the World Health Organization (WHO) web site. The WHO website also contains additional health information for travelers, including detailed country-specific health information.

Customs: Australian customs authorities enforce very strict regulations concerning the importation from all countries of items such as agricultural and wood products, as well as very strict quarantine standards for other products, animals, and pets. These regulations also apply to items you bring with you, including small quantities of food such as fruit.

Safety Concerns: Be aware that Australian fauna can be dangerous. From jellyfish off the Great Barrier Reef to crocodiles, sharks, poisonous insects, and snakes, the continent and its waters host wildlife that merit awe and respect in equal doses. Visit the Wet Tropics Management Authority visitor info guide for information on Australian wildlife and marine life.

While swimming, take important safety precautions, such as swimming only between the flags where a lifeguard is present, and never swimming alone. SCUBA diving can be a treacherous sport. Over the past few years, there have been numerous deaths related to diving incidents. We urge divers to follow recommended precautions and never dive alone.

Accessibility: While in Australia, individuals with disabilities may find accessibility and accommodation very different from what you find in the United States. Australia has and enforces laws prohibiting discrimination for access of premises, facilities and accommodation; however, please keep in mind, that many of the downtown areas of Australian cities were built in the 1800s. These cities often have narrow sidewalks crowded with pedestrians and tourists. Also, many of the tourist spots at the beach or in the outback may have varying degrees of accessibility.

Generally, most public transit means, parking, streets, and buildings are accessible to disabled travelers. Modern accessibility improvements include ramps, tactile indicators, and audible street crossing indicators. Many websites offer information on accessible hotels, motels, and rental properties. Parks, gardens, stadiums and other public venues often share accessibility information on their websites.

Medical Facilities and Health Information: Excellent medical care is available in Australia. Serious medical problems requiring hospitalization and/or medical evacuation to the United States can cost tens of thousands of dollars. Most doctors and hospitals expect immediate cash/credit card payment for health services. We recommend travel insurance.

You can find detailed information on vaccinations and other health precautions on the CDC website. For information about outbreaks of infectious diseases abroad, consult the World Health Organization (WHO) website. The WHO website also contains additional health information for travelers, including detailed country-specific health information.

Medical Insurance: You can't assume your insurance will go with you when you travel. It's very important to find out BEFORE you leave whether or not your medical insurance will cover you overseas. You need to ask your insurance company two questions:

- Does my policy apply when I'm out of the United States?
- Will it cover emergencies like a trip to a foreign hospital or a medical evacuation?

In many places, doctors and hospitals still expect payment in cash at the time of service. Your regular U.S. health insurance may not cover doctor and hospital visits in other countries. If your policy doesn't go with you when you travel, it's a very good idea to take out another one for your trip.

Traffic Safety and Road Conditions: While in Australia, you may encounter road conditions that differ significantly from those in the United States. The information below concerning driving in Australia is provided for general reference only and may not be totally accurate in a particular location or circumstance.

Traffic operates on the left side of the road, and all vehicles use right-hand drive. Please use caution when crossing streets and when driving. When crossing roads on foot, make sure you look carefully in all directions. Wearing a seat belt is mandatory, and fines apply for not wearing them. Speed limits and laws regarding driving while intoxicated are rigorously enforced, and random breath testing of a driver's blood alcohol limit is a common occurrence.

Roads and streets are frequently narrower and less graded than U.S. highways. Outside major metropolitan areas, most highways are two-lane roads with significant distances between destinations. Speed limits vary throughout Australia and are measured in kilometers, not miles. Be aware that speed cameras are everywhere and you will be ticketed for driving over the speed limit.

When driving in Australia, exercise caution while passing or merging with adjacent traffic. If driving in rural areas, be cautious of free-roaming animals, such as kangaroos, and "road-trains" (several semi-truck trailers connected together). Passing road-trains is dangerous, and you should pull over to allow on-coming road-trains to pass to avoid being sideswiped. A number of fatalities have occurred in the Northern Territory where vehicles driven at high rates of speed have skidded and overturned after hitting loose gravel on the shoulder of the road. If you have no experience with a 4-wheel drive vehicle, you should exercise commonsense when driving in the Australian outback. Texting or holding your phone while driving is against the law, but you can use a hands-free system to communicate while driving. For specific information concerning Australian driving permits, vehicle inspection, road tax, mandatory insurance, and the rental and operation of motor vehicles in Australia, visit the Australian Tourist Commission web site.

Each state/territory has different rules about using a foreign driver's license and the conditions under which a visitor might have to get an international driver's license. In some cases, you can apply for a driver's license from the state in Australia where you intend to remain for the duration of your stay in Australia. More information about driving rules and regulations is available by state.

Aviation Safety Oversight: The U.S. Federal Aviation Administration (FAA) has assessed the government of Australia's Civil Aviation Authority as being in compliance with International Civil Aviation Organization (ICAO) aviation safety standards for oversight of Australia's air carrier operations. Further information may be found on the FAA's safety assessment page.

Children's Issues: Please see the U.S. Dept. of State Office of Children's Issues web pages on intercountry adoption and international parental child abduction.

Intercountry Adoption

December 2010

The information in this section has been edited from the latest report available as of February 2013 from the State Department Bureau of Consular Affairs, Office of Overseas Citizens Services. For more information, please read the *Intercountry Adoption* section of this book and review current reports online at http://adoption.state.gov.

Australia is party to the Hague Convention on Protection of Children and Co-operation in Respect of Intercountry Adoption (Hague Convention). Therefore all inter-country adoptions in Australia must meet the requirements of the Convention. Under the Hague Convention, Australia is a receiving country only and does not have an outgoing inter-country adoption program to place Australian children with families seeking to adopt from overseas. For domestic and intercountry adoptions by prospective adoptive parents residing in Australia, each State and Territory is responsible for assessing and approving adoption applications in accordance with its particular legislation. Depending on the applicable State legislation, prospective adoptive parents must generally be resident in that State and at least one applicant should be either an Australian citizen or a permanent resident of Australia to be eligible to adopt.

Who Can Adopt? Each State and Territory in Australia has its own legislation relating to domestic and intercountry adoption by residents of Australia. The legislation is generally referred to as the State's 'Adoption Act' and is supported by regulations which govern the process of adoption in that particular State or Territory. Prospective adoptive parents residing in Australia and seeking to adopt children domestically or from overseas must meet the legislative requirements of the relevant State or Territory in order to be eligible for adoption.

Residency Requirements: Australian residency requirements are dependent on the State or Territory in which the prospective adoptive parents reside. Generally, to be eligible to adopt, at least one of the prospective applicants must be an Australian citizen or a permanent resident of Australia. Information about residency in Australia may be obtained from the Australian Embassy in Washington, DC, from any Australian Embassy or Consulate, or from the website of the Department of Immigration and Citizenship at: http://www.immi.gov.au.

Age Requirements: Varies depending on the relevant State or Territory. Prospective adoptive parents must generally be at least 18 years of age.

Marriage Requirements: Varies depending on the relevant State or Territory. Generally married couples, de-facto couples, and single persons are able to adopt.

Income Requirements: Criteria used to assess suitability to adopt vary depending on the relevant State or Territory. Prospective adoptive parents' income may be relevant to determining their suitability to adopt in some States and Territories.

Who Can Be Adopted? Australia is party to the Hague Convention, but is a receiving country only and does not have an outgoing inter-country adoption program.

Eligibility Requirements: Requirements vary depending upon the relevant State or Territory. Generally the child must be under 18 years old and unmarried. Adoption should only occur if there are no other alternatives available for the child to remain with their family of origin. The welfare and the interests of the child are regarded as the paramount consideration at all times. Information about State-specific eligibility requirements is available from the website of the relevant State or Territory Central Authority (listed at the end of this flyer in the Contact Information section).

Australia's Adoption Authorities: The Australian Central Authority for Inter-country Adoption is the Australian Government Attorney-General's Department, Intercountry Adoption Branch. The Commonwealth Government, through the Attorney-General's Department, has responsibility for the establishment and overall management of Australia's inter-country adoption programs. State and Territory Central Authorities have responsibility for processing individual adoption applications and assessing prospective adoptive parents to determine their suitability to adopt.

The Process: All intercountry adoption processes by Australian citizens and/or permanent residents living in Australia are conducted in accordance with the Hague Convention. The intercountry adoption process used in each State and Territory is similar, but not identical. Generally, the adoption process in each State and Territory begins with a formal application and a detailed assessment of the applicant. If a prospective parent is deemed suitable by the State their application is forwarded overseas for approval.

If successful, the overseas authority then sends a placement proposal to the State or Territory Central Authority for approval. Finally, the parents are invited to travel to meet the child they have been matched with overseas.

Waiting times between approval and placement proposal may vary on depending on the country the child is being adopted from. Differences in process and requirements may also occur in each overseas country with which Australia has a program. State and Territory Central Authorities provide support and supervision following placement. The way in which an adoption is finalized depends upon the process used in the country of origin and the relevant State or Territory procedures.

Further general information on the adoption process can be obtained by visiting the Australian Government Attorney-General's Department website: http://www.ag.gov.au.

U.S. Mission in Australia U.S. Consulate General, Sydney

Level 59 MLC Centre
19-29 Martin Place
Sydney, NSW 2000
Australia
Tel: 61 2 9373 9200
Email: sydneyacs@state.gov.au
http://sydney.usconsulate.gov

The Embassy of Australia
1601 Massachusetts Avenue, NW
Washington, DC 20036
Tel: (202) 797-3000
Fax: (202) 797-3209
Email: http://www.austemb.org

Office of Children's Issues
U.S. Department of State
2201 C Street, NW
SA-29
Washington, DC 20520
Tel: 1-888-407-4747
E-mail: AskCI@state.gov
http://adoption.state.gov

For questions about immigration procedures, call the National Customer Service Center (NCSC) 1-800-375-5283 (TTY 1-800-767-1833).

International Parental Child Abduction

January 2012

The information in this section has been edited from the latest report available from the State Department Bureau of Consular Affairs, Office of Overseas Citizens Services as of February 2013. For more information, please read the *International Parental Child Abduction* section of this book and check for updated reports online at www.travel.state.gov/abduction.

Disclaimer: The information in this flyer relating to the legal requirements of specific foreign countries is provided for general information only. Questions involving interpretation of specific foreign laws should be addressed to foreign legal counsel.

General Information: Custody in Australia is referred to as "parental responsibility." Unless there is a court order to the contrary, the parents of a child are assumed to have "joint parental responsibility." A court-issued "residence" order specifies who will be the primary physical custodian of the child. A "contact" order is similar to a U.S. visitation or access order. Australian family courts adjudicate petitions on a case-by-case basis with the judge applying the "best interests of the child" standard.

The amount of access allowed a non-custodial parent is also decided on a case-by-case basis, and may be denied under certain egregious circumstances. Legitimacy of the child is not a factor in a judge's determination. If your child has a claim to Australian citizenship, you may be able to prevent the issuance of an Australian passport to your child. Please contact a consular officer at the Australian Embassy in Washington, D.C. (202-797-3000) for further information. There is also an Australian Consulate in California (310-229-4800).

Passports for Minors and the Children's Passport Issuance Alert Program: For more information on these topics, see the *International Parental Child Abduction* section of this publication and review current reports from the U.S. Department of State at www.travel.state.gov/abduction.

The Hague Convention: The United States is a party to the Hague Convention on the Civil Aspects of International Child Abduction. Its purpose is to discourage international parental child abduction and to ensure that children who are abducted or wrongfully retained, are returned to their country of habitual residence. The Convention does not deal with child custody itself, but determines the jurisdiction where those custody issues should be adjudicated. The Hague Convention entered into force between the United States and Australia on July 1, 1988. Therefore, Hague Convention provisions for return would apply to children abducted to or retained in Australia after July 1, 1988.

Under certain circumstances, parents and legal guardians of children taken to Australia prior to July 1, 1988, may still submit applications for access to the child under the Hague Convention. The designated Central Authority for all of Australia is the Commonwealth Attorney General's Department, International Family Law Section, which is part of the Family Law and Legal Assistance Division. Their address is Robert Garran Offices, National Circuit, Barton, ACT 2600, Australia. The international telephone number is 011-61-2-6250-6724 and the international telefax number is 011-61-2-6250-5917. The Section maintains a website, which is located at http://www.law.gov.au/childabduction.

For more information, please read the *International Parental Child Abduction* section of this book and review current reports online at www.travel.state.gov/ abduction.

Criminal Remedies: For information on possible criminal remedies, please contact your local law enforcement authorities, or the nearest office of the Federal Bureau of Investigation. Information is also available on the Internet at the web site of the U.S. Department of Justice, Office of Juvenile Justice and Delinquency Prevention at http://www.ojjdp.ncjrs.org.

You should be aware that filing criminal child abduction charges in the United States against a taking parent may jeopardize an Australian Hague Convention case.

Mirror Orders: A final U.S. court order can be registered in the Australian Family Court. The Family Court is a federal court, so orders are enforceable throughout Australia. The process for registration is set out in Regulation 23 of the Australian Family Law Regulations.

The parent who wishes to register a U.S. Court order in Australia should write a cover letter requesting registration. The letter should include the address in Australia where the child will be located. Attached to the letter must be three certified copies of the U.S. court order and documentation by a court officer that the copy is a true copy of the original order made by the Court. The court officer must also certify that the order is enforceable in that particular jurisdiction and that no subsequent orders have been made. The documents may be sent directly to the Australian Central Authority or to the Office of Children's Issues for forwarding to the Australian Central Authority. There is no fee for this service.

The registration of the order will be effective as soon as the Registrar of the Australian court files the order and notes the registration. However, a U.S. temporary or interim order for custody and visitation cannot be registered in Australia through the above process. The parent seeking Australian "consent orders" (orders agreed to by both parents) should apply to the Australian Family Court. Two documents must be filed. They are (1) a Form 12A signed by both parties and witnessed by a lawyer or Justice of the Peace and (2) the Consent Orders signed by both parties and witnessed by a person over the age of 18 years. Orders can duplicate the U.S. orders. A notation should be added that they are identical to orders made in the U.S. The notation should include the name and address of the Court where the orders were made and the date when they were made.

To expedite the process, a parent physically located in the United States can telefax a signed copy of the orders to the Australian Court in accordance with the Rule 7 Order 2. When filing by telefax, the document must be accompanied by a letter to the Court Registrar setting out (a) the nature and immediacy of the damage or harm which may result if the document is not lodged by telefax and (b) any other circumstances justifying lodging the document by facsimile.

The original signed copy should be sent to the Australian Court by an international courier service, such as Federal Express or DHL. There is no filing fee for an application for consent orders. Obviously, this process requires the cooperation of both parents. Should you have any questions, please contact the Office of Children's Issues.

If you are currently in Australia, you may contact the Central Authority of Australia directly. For further information on international parental child abduction, contact the Office of Children's Issues, U.S. Department of State at 1-888-407-4747 or visit its web site on the Internet at http://travel.state.gov.

AUSTRIA

Compiled from publications that were available as of February 2013 from the U.S. Department of State, the U.S. Department of Commerce, and the Central Intelligence Agency (CIA). See the introduction to this set for explanatory notes.

Official Name:
Republic of Austria

PROFILE

Geography

Area: total: 83,871 sq km; country comparison to the world: 114; land: 82,445 sq km; water: 1,426 sq km
Major cities: Vienna (capital) 1.693 million (2009)
Climate: temperate; continental, cloudy; cold winters with frequent rain and some snow in lowlands and snow in mountains; moderate summers with occasional showers
Terrain: in the west and south mostly mountains (Alps); along the eastern and northern margins mostly flat or gently sloping

People

Nationality: noun: Austrian(s); adjective: Austrian
Population: 8,219,743 (July 2012 est.)
Population growth rate: 0.026% (2012 est.)
Ethnic groups: Austrians 91.1%, former Yugoslavs 4% (includes Croatians, Slovenes, Serbs, and Bosniaks), Turks 1.6%, German 0.9%, other or unspecified 2.4% (2001 census)
Religions: Roman Catholic 73.6%, Protestant 4.7%, Muslim 4.2%, other 3.5%, unspecified 2%, none 12% (2001 census)
Languages: German (official nationwide) 88.6%, Turkish 2.3%, Serbian 2.2%, Croatian (official in Burgenland) 1.6%, other (includes Slovene, official in Carinthia, and Hungarian, official in Burgenland) 5.3% (2001 census)
Literacy: definition: age 15 and over can read and write; total population: 98%; male: NA; female: NA
Health: life expectancy at birth: total population: 79.91 years; male: 77 years; female: 82.97 years (2012 est.); Infant mortality rate: total: 4.26 deaths/1,000 live births; male: 5.16 deaths/1,000 live births; female: 3.33 deaths/1,000 live births (2012 est.)
Unemployment rate: 4.4% (2012 est.)
Work force: 3.665 million (2012 est.)

Government

Type: federal republic
Independence: 12 November 1918
Constitution: 1 October 1920; revised 1929; reinstated 1 May 1945; revised many times; note—during the period 1 May 1934-1 May 1945 there was a fascist (corporative) constitution in place
Political subdivisions: 9 states (Bundeslaender, singular—Bundesland); Burgenland, Karnten (Carinthia), Niederosterreich (Lower Austria), Oberosterreich (Upper Austria), Salzburg, Steiermark (Styria), Tirol (Tyrol), Vorarlberg, Wien (Vienna)
Suffrage: 16 years of age; universal; note—reduced from 18 years of age in 2007

Economy

GDP (purchasing power parity): $357.8 billion (2012 est.); $356.5 billion (2011 est.); $345.8 billion (2010 est.); $338 billion (2009 est.)
GDP real growth rate: $391.5 billion (2012 est.); 3.1% (2011 est.); 2.3% (2010 est.); -3.8% (2009 est.)
GDP per capita (PPP): $42,500 (2012 est.); $42,400 (2011 est.); $41,200 (2010 est.); $40,400 (2009 est.)
Natural resources: oil, coal, lignite, timber, iron ore, copper, zinc, antimony, magnesite, tungsten, graphite, salt, hydropower
Agriculture products: grains, potatoes, wine, fruit; dairy products, cattle, pigs, poultry; lumber
Industries: construction, machinery, vehicles and parts, food, metals, chemicals, lumber and wood processing, paper and paperboard, communications equipment, tourism
Exports: $164.1 billion (2012 est.); $173.6 billion (2011 est.)
Exports—commodities: machinery and equipment, motor vehicles and parts, paper and paperboard, metal goods, chemicals, iron and steel, textiles, foodstuffs
Exports—partners: Germany 32.2%, Italy 7.8%, Switzerland 4.4%, France 4.2% (2011)

Imports: $173.9 billion (2012 est.); $183.3 billion (2011 est.)
Imports—commodities: machinery and equipment, motor vehicles, chemicals, metal goods, oil and oil products; foodstuffs
Imports—partners: Germany 42.8%, Italy 6.8%, Switzerland 5.6%, Netherlands 4.1% (2011)
Debt—external: $883.5 billion (30 June 2011); $755 billion (30 June 2010)
Exchange rates: euros (EUR) per US dollar; 0.7838 (2012 est.); 0.7194 (2011 est.); 0.755 (2010 est.); 0.7198 (2009 est.); 0.6827 (2008 est.)

PEOPLE

Austrians are relatively homogeneous; about 90% speak German as their everyday language. However, there has been a significant amount of immigration, particularly from former Yugoslavia and Turkey, over the past 2 decades.

National/Racial/Ethnic Minorities

Interior Ministry statistics released in September 2011 cited 580 neo-Nazi, right-wing extremist, xenophobic, or anti-Semitic incidents in 2010. The government continued to express concern over the activities of extreme right-wing and neo-Nazi groups, many with links to organizations in other countries.

Human rights groups continued to report that Roma faced discrimination in employment and housing. The head of the Austrian Romani Cultural Association reported that the situation of the Romani community, estimated at more than 6,200 indigenous, and between 15,000 and 20,000 nonindigenous, individuals, continued to improve. Government programs, including financing for tutors, helped school-age Romani children move out of "special needs" and into mainstream classes.

NGOs reported that Africans living in the country experienced verbal harassment in public. In some cases black Africans were stigmatized for perceived involvement in the drug trade or other illegal activities. Federal law recognizes Croats, Czechs, Hungarians, Roma, Slovaks, and Slovenes as national minorities.

Language

Although most Austrians speak German, it is no problem for a traveler to get around the country with little or no knowledge of the language. Many Austrians speak English, which is mandatory in school, and are quite willing to help.

Religion

According to estimates from religious organizations and the Austrian Integration Fund, membership in major religious groups is as follows: Roman Catholic, 64 percent, and Muslim, 6 percent. Groups that constitute less than 5 percent of the population include Protestants, including the Lutheran and Swiss Reformed churches (Evangelical Church-Augsburg and Helvetic confessions); Eastern Orthodox (Russian, Greek, Serbian, Romanian, and Bulgarian); other Christian churches; Jehovah's Witnesses; other non-Christian religious groups; and the Jewish community.

According to a 2009 media survey of citizens who attend religious services, 2 percent attend services more than once a week, 10 percent attend weekly, 9 percent attend a minimum of once a month, 24 percent attend several times a year (on special occasions), and 55 percent rarely attend.

The provinces of Carinthia and Burgenland have higher percentages of Protestants than the national average at 10.3 percent and 13.3 percent, respectively. The numbers of Muslims in Vienna and in the province of Vorarlberg are higher than the national average, at 7.8 percent and 8.4 percent, respectively. Industry in these areas historically drew a disproportionately higher number of guest workers from Turkey and the former Yugoslavia.

HISTORY

Austrian history dates back to 976, when Leopold von Babenberg became the ruler of much of present-day Austria. In 1276 Rudolf I became the first Habsburg to ascend to the throne.

The Habsburg Empire

Although never unchallenged, the Habsburgs ruled Austria for nearly 750 years. Through political marriages, the Habsburgs were able to accumulate vast land wealth encompassing most of central Europe and stretching even as far as the Iberian Peninsula. After repulsing challenges from the Ottoman Empire in the 16th and 17th centuries, Austrian territory became increasingly consolidated in the central European part of the Danube basin.

In 1848 Franz Josef I ascended to the throne and remained in power until his death in 1916. Franz Josef saw many milestones in Austrian history. The Compromise of 1867 gave greater political rights to Hungary within the Empire, creating what became known as the Dual Monarchy. Political unity deteriorated further in the beginning of the 20th century, culminating, under the stress of World War I, in the collapse of the Empire and proclamation of an Austrian Republic on territory roughly identical to modern-day Austria. In 1919, the Treaty of St. Germain officially ended Habsburg rule and established the Republic of Austria.

Political Turmoil During the Inter-War Years and the Anschluss

From 1918 to 1934, Austria experienced sharpening political strife. In the late 1920s and early 1930s, paramilitary political organizations were engaged in strikes and violent conflicts. Unemployment rose to an estimated 25%. In 1934, a corporatist and authoritarian government came into power in Austria. Austrian National Socialists (NS) launched an unsuccessful coup d'etat in July 1934. In February 1938, under threats of military intervention from Germany,

Chancellor Kurt Schuschnigg was forced to accept Austrian National Socialists (Nazis) in his government. On March 12, Germany sent military forces into Austria and annexed the country ("Anschluss"), an action that received enthusiastic support from many Austrians.

The Holocaust in Austria

From March 1938 to April 1945, most of the Jewish population of the country was murdered or forced into exile. Other minorities, including the Sinti and Roma, homosexuals, and many political opponents of the Nazis also received similar treatment. Prior to 1938, Austria's Jewish population constituted 200,000 persons, or about 3% to 4% of the total population. Most Jews lived in Vienna, where they comprised about 9% of the population. Following Anschluss, Jews were forced out of many professions and lost access to their assets. In November 1938, the Nazis launched the Kristallnacht pogrom in Austria as well as in Germany. Jewish businesses were vandalized and ransacked. Thousands of Jews were arrested and deported to concentration camps. Jewish emigration increased dramatically.

Between 1938 and 1940, over half of Austria's Jewish population fled the country. Some 35,000 Jews were deported to the Ghettos in eastern Europe. Some 67,000 Austrian Jews (or one-third of the total 200,000 Jews residing in Austria) were sent to concentration camps. Those in such camps were murdered or forced into dangerous or severe hard labor that accelerated their death. Only 2,000 of those:in the death camps survived until the end of the war.

Austria Post-World War II

After April 1945, the victorious allies divided Austria into zones of occupation similar to those in Germany with a four-power administration of Vienna. Under the 1945 Potsdam agreements, the Soviets took control of German assets in their zone of occupation. These included 7% of Austria's manufacturing plants, 95% of its oil resources, and about 80% of its refinery capacity.

The properties were returned to Austria under the Austrian State Treaty. This treaty, signed in Vienna on May 15, 1955, came into effect on July 27. Under its provisions, all occupation forces departed by October 25, 1955. Austria became free and independent for the first time since 1938.

Austrian Compensation Programs and Acknowledgement of its Nazi Role

During the immediate postwar period, Austrian authorities introduced certain restitution and compensation measures for Nazi victims, but many of these initial measures were later seen as inadequate and/or unjust. There is no official estimate of the amount of compensation made under these programs. More disturbing for many was the continuation of the view that prevailed since 1943 that Austria was the "first free country to fall victim" to Nazi aggression. This "first victim" view had been fostered by the Allied Powers in the Moscow Declaration of 1943, in which the Allies declared as null and void the Anschluss and called for the restoration of the country's independence.

The Allied Powers did not ignore Austria's responsibility for the war, but nothing was said explicitly about Austria's responsibility for Nazi crimes on its territory. The controversial debate about the long-hidden wartime past of former UN Secretary General Kurt Waldheim, who was elected Austrian President in 1986, painfully forced Austrians to confront the country's role before and during World War II.

With the collapse of the Soviet Union in 1991, greater attention was given in many countries, including Austria, to unresolved issues from World War II. On November 15, 1994, Austrian President Thomas Klestil addressed the Israeli Knesset, noting that Austrian leaders.".. spoke far too rarely of the fact that some of the worst henchmen of the NS dictatorship were in fact Austrians..... In the name of the Republic of Austria, I bow my head before the victims of that time." Since 1994, Austria has committed to providing victims and heirs some $1 billion in restitution. Payments are made through the National Fund for Victims of National Socialism (established in 1995), which provides lump-sum payments to victims of Nazi persecution and their heirs, and the General Settlement Fund (established in 2001), which addresses gaps and deficiencies in postwar restitution programs. The Reconciliation Fund (established in 2000 and disbanded in 2005) provided one-time payments to Nazi-era forced and slave laborers. Its successor organization, the Future Fund (established 2006) supports projects with an emphasis on Holocaust and tolerance education.

GOVERNMENT AND POLITICAL CONDITIONS

The Republic of Austria is a parliamentary democracy with constitutional power shared between a popularly elected president and a bicameral parliament (Federal Assembly), in which the members of one house are directly elected and the other named by the constituent states. In practice the multiparty parliament and the coalition government it elects exercise most day-to-day governmental powers. National parliamentary elections in 2008 and presidential elections in 2009 were free and fair.

Recent Elections

The country held national parliamentary elections in 2008 and presidential elections in 2009; there were no reports of serious abuse or irregularities in either election.

Participation of Women and Minorities: The parliament consists of the National Council, which is popularly elected, and the Federal Council, whose members are named by the federal states. At the end of 2011, 50 women were in the 183-seat National Council and 19 women in the 62-member Federal Council. There were six women in the 14-member Council of Ministers (cabinet).

There appeared to be relatively little representation of ethnic minorities at the national level. The Federal Council includes one Muslim woman.

Principal Government Officials

Last Updated: 1/31/2013

Pres.: **Heinz FISCHER**
Chancellor: **Werner FAYMANN**
Vice Chancellor: **Michael SPINDELEGGER**
Min. for Agriculture, Forestry, Environment, & Water Management:**Nikolaus BERLAKOVICH**
Min. for Economics, Family, & Youth: **Reinhold MITTERLEHNER**
Min. for Education, Arts, & Culture: **Claudia SCHMIED**
Min. for European & International Affairs: **Michael SPINDELEGGER**
Min. for Finance: **Maria FEKTER**
Min. for Health: **Alois STOEGER**
Min. for Interior: **Johanna MIKL-LEITNER**
Min. for Justice: **Beatrix KARL**
Min. for Labor, Social Affairs, & Consumer Protection:**Rudolf HUNDSTORFER**
Min. for National Defense & Sports: **Norbert DARABOS**
Min. for Science & Research: **Karlheinz TOECHTERLE**
Min. for Transportation, Innovation, & Technology: **Doris BURES**
Min. for Women & Public Service: **Gabriele HEINISCH-HOSEK**
Governor, Austrian National Bank: **Ewald NOWOTNY**
Ambassador to the US: **Hans Peter MANZ**
Permanent Representative to the UN, New York: **Martin SAJDIK**

ECONOMY

Austria, with its well-developed market economy, skilled labor force, and high standard of living, is closely tied to other EU economies, especially Germany's. Its economy features a large service sector, a sound industrial sector, and a small, but highly developed agricultural sector.

Following several years of solid foreign demand for Austrian exports and record employment growth, the international financial crisis of 2008 and subsequent global economic downturn led to a sharp but brief recession. Austrian GDP contracted 3.9% in 2009 but saw positive growth of about 2% in 2010 and 3% in 2011. Unemployment did not rise as steeply in Austria as elsewhere in Europe, partly because the government subsidized reduced working hour schemes to allow companies to retain employees. Stabilization measures, stimulus spending, and an income tax reform pushed the budget deficit to 4.7% in 2010 and 3.6% in 2011, from only about 1.3% in 2008.

The international financial crisis of 2008 caused difficulties for Austria's largest banks whose extensive operations in central, eastern, and southeastern Europe faced large losses. The government provided bank support—including in some instances, nationalization—to support aggregate demand and stabilize the banking system. Austria's fiscal position compares favorably with other eurozone countries, but it faces considerable external risks, such as Austrian banks'' continued high exposure to central and eastern Europe as well as political and economic uncertainties caused by the European sovereign debt crisis. In 2011 the government attempted to pass a constitutional amendment limiting public debt to 60% of GDP by 2020, but it was unable to obtain sufficient support in parliament and instead passed the measure as a simple law. In March 2012, the Austrian parliament approved an austerity budget that will bring public finances into balance by 2016. In 2012, the budget deficit rose to 2.9% of GDP.

Labor Conditions

The minimum legal working age is 15, with the exception that children at least 12 years old may engage in certain forms of light work on family farms or businesses. Children age 15 and older are subject to the same regulations on hours, rest periods, overtime wages, and occupational health and safety restrictions as adults, except for additional limitations on hazardous forms of work or limitations for ethical reasons. Laws and policies protect children from exploitation in the workplace and prohibit forced or compulsory labor, and the government generally enforced these laws and policies effectively.

There is no legislated national minimum wage. Instead, nationwide collective bargaining agreements set minimum wages by job classification for each industry.

All collective bargaining agreements provide for a minimum wage of 1,000 euros ($1,300) per month—the official poverty level was 951 euros ($1,236) per month. Wages where no such collective agreements exist, such as for domestic workers, janitorial staff, and au pairs, are regulated in pertinent law and are generally lower than those covered by collective bargaining agreements.

The law provides for a maximum workweek of 40 hours, but collective bargaining agreements also give more than half of all employees 38- or 38.5-hour workweeks. Regulations to increase flexibility in work hours allow firms to increase the maximum regular time from 40 hours to 50 hours per week with overtime. In special cases work hours can be increased to a maximum of 60 hours per week, including overtime, for a maximum of 24 weeks annually. However, these 24 weeks can only be in eight-week segments, with at least a two-week break between each eight-week period.

Overtime is officially limited to five hours per week and 60 hours per year; however, authorities did not enforce these laws and regulations effectively, and some employers exceeded legal limits on compulsory overtime.

Collective bargaining agreements can specify higher limits. The law stipulates premium pay of 50 percent for overtime and requires time off on weekends and official holidays. An employee must have at least 11 hours off between workdays. Wage and hour standards were equitably enforced across all groups.

Foreign workers in both the formal and informal sectors make up approximately 13 percent of the country's workforce. Wage and hour regulations were not effectively enforced in the informal sector.

U.S.-AUSTRIAN RELATIONS

Austria is a free and stable democracy with a social market economy. As the inheritor of the Habsburg monarchy's historic links to eastern and southeastern Europe, Austria sees a role for itself in helping countries in these regions integrate successfully into an enlarged European Union. The United States and Austria share many common values and common perspectives, including a commitment to reducing the threats posed by climate change and nuclear proliferation, a support for human rights and the rule of law, and a shared vision of peace and freedom for all. The two countries are bound together through myriad people-to-people contacts in business, the arts, scholarship, recreation, and a host of other exchanges.

The Austro-Hungarian Empire recognized the United States in 1797, when we established consular relations with a Consul in Trieste, then part of the Austrian empire. Diplomatic relations were established with the naming of Henry A. Muhlenberg as first American Minister to Vienna in 1838. Relations were generally good until World War I (1914–18) and the United States' declaration of war on the Austro-Hungarian Empire in 1917. Friendly diplomatic relations with the new Republic of Austria were established in 1921 and lasted until Nazi Germany annexed Austria in 1938. After World War II (1939–45), the four allied powers (the United States, Great Britain, France, and the Soviet Union) divided Austria and Vienna into four occupation zones, with an Allied Council for Austria assuming authority over matters affecting the whole country. In 1955, these four powers and the Republic of Austria signed the Austrian State Treaty, which ended the occupation and declared Austria to be a free, independent, and neutral state. The U.S. played an essential role in the country's reconstruction and in the Austrian State Treaty. Since the post-World War II period, the United States and Austria have enjoyed strong relations. Austria and the United States are partners in promoting global security and prosperity. During the immediate postwar period, Austrian authorities introduced certain restitution and compensation measures for Nazi victims, but many of these initial measures were later seen as inadequate and/or unjust. Since 1994, Austria has committed to providing victims and heirs some $1 billion in restitution.

U.S. Assistance to Austria

The United States provides no foreign assistance to Austria.

Bilateral Economic Relations

Austria is a member country of the European Union and World Trade Organization, offering export opportunities for U.S. companies of all sizes, with no significant trade barriers. The country represents a desirable, affluent market for U.S.-made products in Europe. Recent Austrian governments have sought to encourage Austria's reputation as an attractive regional headquarters location through economic reforms and by highlighting Austria's historical and economic ties to the surrounding region.

Austria's Membership in International Organizations

Austrian leaders emphasize the country's role as both an East-West hub and a moderator between industrialized and developing countries. Austria hosts the International Atomic Energy Agency and several other UN bodies, the Organization of Petroleum Exporting Countries, and the Organization for Security and Cooperation in Europe (OSCE).

Austria and the United States belong to a number of the same international organizations, including the United Nations, OSCE, Organization for Economic Cooperation and Development, Euro-Atlantic Partnership Council, International Monetary Fund, World Bank, and World Trade Organization. Austria also is an observer to the Organization of American States. Austria currently serves in the UN Human Rights Council and is on the Executive Board of UNESCO.

Bilateral Representation

Austria maintains an embassy in the United States at 3524 International Court, NW, Washington, DC 20008 (tel. 202-895-6700). It also maintains Consulates General in Los Angeles and New York and additional trade promotion offices in Atlanta and Chicago.

Principal U.S. Embassy Officials

Last Updated: 1/14/2013

VIENNA (E) Boltzmanngasse 16, 1090 Wien, 011-43-1-31339-0, Fax 011-43-1-31339-2510, Workweek: M-F 0830–1700 local, Website: http://vienna.usembassy.gov/

DCM OMS: Kathy Alexander
AMB OMS: Malgorzata Lamot
DHS/CIS: Pamela Hutchings
DHS/ICE: James Plitt
FCS: Thomas Brennan
FM: Dennis Nice
HRO: Michael Greer
MGT: Charles J. Slater
MLO/ODC: LTC Chad Lemond
POL/ECON: Shawn Crowley
POSHO: Dennis Nice
SDO/DATT: LTC Scott Ogledzinski
AMB: William C. Eacho
CG: Timothy Eydelnant
DCM: Lee A. Brudvig
PAO: Jan Krc
GSO: Mira Piplani
RSO: Mary-Jo Swinimer
AFSA: James Zellinger
AGR: Paul Spencer
APHIS: Karen Sliter
CLO: Raghda Assad
DEA: Ira Israel
EEO: Cheryl Schaefle
FMO: Anne Wennerstrom
ICASS Chair: Jennifer Hall-Godfrey
IMO: Dave Mango
IPO: Barbara Debbage
IRS: Thomas E. Stevens
ISO: Leo Parpart
ISSO: Ryan Harvey
LEGATT: Steven Paulson
State ICASS: Jennifer Hall-Godfrey

UNVIE (VIENNA) (M) Wagramerstrasse 17-19, A-1220 Vienna, Austria, 43 1 31339 74 3501, Fax 43 1 367 07 64, Workweek: 0830-1700, Website: http://vienna.usmission.gov/

DCM OMS: Seifa Hauptmann
AMB OMS: Kathryn Martin
DEP DIR: John Godfrey
DIR: Sharon White
FM: Dennis Nice
HRO: Michael Greer
MGT: Charles J. Slater
POL/ECON: David Bame
POSHO: Dennis Nice
AMB: Charge Joseph E. Macmanus
DCM: Robert Wood
PAO: Jennifer Hall Godfrey
GSO: Mira Piplani
RSO: Michael Mclean
CLO: Raghda Assad
EEO: Cheryl Schaefle
FMO: Anne Wennerstrom
ICASS Chair: Jennifer Hall Godfrey
IMO: Dave Mango
IPO: Barbara Debbage
ISO: Leo Parpart
ISSO: Ryan Harvey

USOSCE (M) Obersteinergasse 11 1190 Vienna, Austria, 011-43-131339-3141, Fax 011-43-1-369-1585, Workweek: M-F 0830-1700 local, Website: http://osce.usmission.gov/

DCM OMS: Daniele Schoenauer
AMB OMS: Elizabeth Babroski
HRO: Michael Greer
MGT: Charles J. Slater
POSHO: Dennis Nice
SDO/DATT: JCS Col Jeffrey Fischer
AMB: Ian Kelly
DCM: Gary Robbins
PAO: Christopher Midura
GSO: Mira Piplani
RSO: John Pigman
AFSA: James Zellinger
CLO: Raghda Assad
EEO: Cheryl Schaefle
FMO: Anne Wennerstrom
ICASS Chair: Jennifer Hall Godfrey
IMO: Dave Mango
IPO: Barbara Debbage
IRS: Thomas E. Stevens
ISO: Leo Parpart
ISSO: Ryan Harvey
POL: Chris Robinson

TRAVEL

Consular Information Sheet

July 27, 2012

Country Description: Austria is a highly developed, stable democracy with a modern economy. Tourism is an important pillar of the Austrian economy and facilities are widely available.

Smart Traveler Enrollment Program (STEP): If you are going to live in or visit Austria, please take the time to tell our Embassy about your trip via the Department of State's Smart Traveler Enrollment Program (STEP). If you enroll, we can keep you up to date with important safety and security announcements. It will also help your friends and family get in touch with you in an emergency.

U.S. Embassy in Vienna
Consular Section
Parkring 12a
Telephone: 43- 1-31339–7535
After hours: 43-1-31339
Facsimile: 43-1-512 58 35
Email: ConsulateVienna@state.gov

Entry/Exit Requirements for U.S. Citizens: Austria is a party to the Schengen Agreement. As such, U.S. citizens may enter Austria for up to 90 days in any 180-day period for tourist or business purposes without a visa. The passport used should be valid at least for the period of the intended stay (usually the date of the return flight).

Anyone intending to stay longer than 90 days must obtain the appropriate visa issued by the Austrian Embassy in the United States. Specifically students attending a college/university in Austria should consult with the Austrian Embassy/Consulate before coming to Austria. Information for students is available from the Austrian agency for international mobility and cooperation in education, science and research (OeAD). For visa holders entering Austria, the passport should be valid for at least three months beyond the period of intended stay. Visit the Embassy of Austria website for the most current visa information. There are four Austrian Consulates General in the United States; please contact the appropriate office for assistance. If you reside outside the United States, please contact the Austrian Embassy or Consulate in your country of residence.

There are no vaccination requirements for international travelers. The U.S. Department of State is unaware of any HIV/AIDS entry restrictions for visitors to or foreign residents of Austria.

Threats to Safety and Security: Austria remains largely free of terrorist incidents; however, like other countries in the Schengen area, Austria's open borders with its Western European neighbors allow the possibility of terrorist groups entering and exiting the country with anonymity. U.S. citizens are reminded to remain vigilant with regard to their personal security and to exercise caution.

Austrian intelligence experts have registered increased radicalization of immigrant Muslim individuals and of small conspiratorial groups, as well as intensified use of the Internet as a propaganda and communications platform. Despite some terrorism-related incidents in 2007 directed against individual Austrian nationals or the Government of Austria, Austrian authorities believe the likelihood of terrorist attacks in Austria remains relatively low.

Every year, a number of avalanche deaths occur in Austria's alpine regions. Many occur when skiers/snowboarders stray from designated ski slopes. Leaving designated slopes to ski off-piste may pose serious risks and may delay rescue attempts in case of emergency. Skiers and snowboarders should monitor weather and terrain conditions, and use available avalanche rescue equipment. Avalanche beepers (transceivers) are the most common rescue devices and, when properly used, provide the fastest way of locating an avalanche victim, usually enabling authorities to begin rescue operations within minutes.

Stay up-to-date by:

- Bookmarking our Bureau of Consular Affairs website, which contains the current Travel Warnings and Travel Alerts as well as the Worldwide Caution;
- Following us on Twitter and the Bureau of Consular Affairs page on Facebook as well;
- Downloading our free Smart Traveler iPhone App to have travel information at your fingertips;
- Calling 1-888-407-4747 toll-free within the U.S. and Canada, or a regular toll line, 1-202-501-4444, from other countries; and
- Taking some time before travel to consider your personal security.

Crime: Austria has one of the lowest crime rates in Europe, and violent crime is rare. However, crimes involving theft of personal property do occur. As such, most crimes involving U.S. citizens are crimes of opportunity, involving theft of personal belongings. Travelers are also targets of pick-pockets who operate where tourists tend to gather. Some of the spots where such crimes are most frequently reported include Vienna's two largest train stations, the plaza around St. Stephen's Cathedral, and the nearby pedestrian shopping areas (in Vienna's First District).

The U.S. Embassy receives reports of theft and pick-pocketing on public transportation lines, especially on those lines coming into and out from the city center. Secure your personal belongings and always take precautions while on public transportation and in public places such as cafes and tourist areas. Don't buy counterfeit and pirated goods, even if they are widely available. Not only are the bootlegs illegal to bring back into the United States, by buying them, you may also be breaking local law.

Victims of Crime: If you or someone you know becomes the victim of a crime abroad, you should contact the local police. If you are the victim of a crime, you can contact the nearest U.S. embassy or consulate.

We can:

- Replace a stolen passport;
- Help you find appropriate medical care for violent crimes such as assault or rape;
- Put you in contact with the appropriate police authorities;
- Contact family members or friends, with your permission;
- Help you understand the local criminal justice process and can direct you to local attorneys, although it is important to remember that local authorities are responsible for investigating and prosecuting crime.

The local equivalent to the "911" emergency line in Austria is "133."

Criminal Penalties: While traveling in Austria, you are subject to its laws. While you are overseas, U.S. laws do not apply, and if you do something illegal in your host country, your U.S. passport won't help you avoid arrest or prosecution. It is very important to know what is legal and what is not, since foreign laws and legal systems can be vastly different from our own. Criminal penalties also vary from country to country. There are also some things that may be legal where you are traveling but illegal in the United States. If you engage in sexual conduct with children or use or disseminate child pornography in a foreign country, you can be prosecuted in the United States.

Persons violating Austrian laws, even unknowingly, may be expelled, arrested or imprisoned. Penalties for possessing, using, or trafficking illegal drugs in Austria are severe, and convicted offenders can expect long jail sentences and heavy fines.

Arrest Notifications: Based on the Vienna Convention on Consular Relations, bilateral agreements with certain countries, and customary international law, if you are arrested in Austria, you have the option to request that the police, prison officials, or other authorities alert the U.S. Embassy of your arrest, and to have communications from you forwarded to the Embassy.

Special Circumstances: You may have ATM problems with a U.S.-issued debit card. If your request for cash is rejected, check your accounts immediately to see whether the money was in fact debited. If this is the case, notify your banking institution immediately. Prompt action may result in a refund of the debited amount. Keep your receipts.

Accessibility: While in Austria, individuals with disabilities may find accessibility and accommodation very different from what you find in the United States. Austrian federal law mandates access to public buildings for persons with physical disabilities; as a result, accessibility has substantially improved in recent years.

While many stores and restaurants in Austria frequently lack ramp or elevator access, most tourist attractions are accessible. A comprehensive assessment of public buildings, including tourist sites, restaurants, cafes, and hotels in Vienna, is available at the Vienna Tourist Information website.

Streetcars: Vienna's streetcar fleet is phasing in newer trains that are easily accessible for those who use wheelchairs. Approximately one-third of the fleet has been upgraded, although older trains with stair-like entrances are still quite common.

Buses: Public buses in Vienna are equipped with a "kneeling" capability, to permit easier passenger boarding. The center of each bus has generous space and is equipped with tether lines.

Subway stations: All subway stations in Austria have elevator access, although not at every entrance. Stations are also equipped with a ridged/raised surface to help guide sight-impaired passengers from the entrance to the platform.

Crosswalks: Motorists in Vienna are quite observant of local law and usually yield to pedestrians waiting to cross in designated "zebra" crosswalks. Major intersections also offer an audible cue for the sight-impaired to cross.

Guide dogs: Austria is a very dog-friendly country and dogs are welcome in almost every venue, including taxis, public transportation, stores, and most restaurants. In addition, guide dogs are also permitted in normally restricted venues, such as major tourist attractions.

Medical Facilities and Health Information: There are an adequate number of hospitals available in Austria. Local hospitals will not settle their accounts directly with American insurance companies. You must pay the bill to the local hospital and later claim a refund from the insurance carrier in the United States. Medicare payments are not available outside the United States.

The Austrian Medicine Import Act generally prohibits the import of prescription drugs into Austria, with two exceptions:

- Travelers residing outside the European Union are allowed to carry with them (as part of their personal luggage) drugs and medicines, but only a quantity the individual requires during the course of the stay; and,
- Travelers, while staying in Austria, may receive drugs and medicines for their personal use by mail. The quantity is limited to the length of their stay in Austria and must never exceed three packages.

We recommend you have either a prescription or written statement from your personal physician that you are under a doctor's care and that the medicine is necessary for your physical well-being while traveling.

Public health in Austria is excellent. Community sanitation in Vienna meets or exceeds that of most U.S. cities. Disease incidence and type are similar to the rest of Europe and the United States. At the present time, air pollution is not a major health problem in Vienna.

You can find information on vaccinations and other health precautions on the Centers for Disease Control and Prevention (CDC) website. For information about outbreaks of infectious diseases abroad, consult the World Health Organization (WHO) website, which also contains additional health information for travelers, including detailed country-specific health information.

Medical Insurance: You can't assume your insurance will go with you when you travel. It's very important to find out BEFORE you leave whether or not your medical insurance will cover you overseas. You need to ask your insurance company two questions:

- Does my policy apply when I'm out of the United States?
- Will it cover emergencies like a trip to a foreign hospital or a medical evacuation?

In many places, doctors and hospitals still expect payment in cash at the time of service. Your regular U.S. health insurance may not cover doctor and hospital visits in other countries. If your policy doesn't go with you when you travel, it's a very good idea to take out another one for your trip.

Any person, regardless of citizenship, who wants to take up residence in Austria, must be covered by some health insurance plan that covers full medical treatment in Austria. U.S. citizens interested in joining the health insurance plan under the Austrian system should apply to the Health Insurance Agency (Gebietskrankenkasse) in the province (Bundesland) where they reside. Applicants for short-term visas require travel insurance; a list of insurance carriers is available here.

Traffic Safety and Road Conditions: While in Austria, you may encounter road conditions that differ significantly from those in the United States. Road conditions in Austria are generally excellent. During the winter, however, roads in alpine areas may become dangerous due to snowfall, ice, or avalanches. Some mountain roads may be closed for extended periods and tire chains are often required. Be extra careful during the heavily traveled vacation periods (i.e., December-February, Easter, and July-August). Be alert when you drive through autobahn construction zones, particularly on the A-1 East/West Autobahn. Reduced lanes and two-way traffic in these zones have resulted in several deadly accidents in recent years. Traffic information and road conditions are broadcast on the English-language channel, fm4, located between 91 and 105 FM depending on the locale.

A U.S. driver's license alone is not sufficient to drive in Austria. You must also get an international driver's permit (obtainable in the U.S. from the American Automobile Association and the American Automobile Touring Alliance) or by an official translation of the U.S. driver's license, which can be obtained at one of the Austrian automobile clubs (OEAMTC or ARBOE). This arrangement is only acceptable for the first six months of driving in Austria, after which all drivers must obtain an Austrian license.

Austria requires all vehicles using the autobahn to display an "Autobahn Vignette" highway-tax sticker on the inside of the vehicle's windshield. The sticker may be purchased at border crossings, gas stations in Austria, and small "Tabak" shops located in Austrian towns. Fines for failing to display a valid autobahn vignette on the windshield of your car are usually around $150. Austrian autobahns have a maximum speed limit of 130 km/hr, although drivers often drive much faster and pass aggressively. The use of hand-held cell phones while driving is prohibited. Turning right on red is also prohibited throughout Austria. The legal limit for blood alcohol content in Austria is.05 percent and penalties for driving under the influence tend to be stricter than in many U.S. states. It is mandatory for cars on Austrian motorways and highways to leave an emergency corridor, even when no emergency vehicle is approaching. When traffic stops, create an emergency corridor in between the far-left lane and all others to the right; vehicles should also be using the shoulder. Failure to comply carries a fine of about $2,700.

Between November 1 and April 15, the use of winter tires is mandated by law. All-season tires comply if they carry the "M S" mark and have at least 4 mm of tread. In addition, local police may require snow chains in heavy snow. Failure to comply with the law results in a substantial fine and the suspension of the cited vehicle's use. Insurance is deemed void if a vehicle which is involved in an accident between November 1 and April 15 is not fitted with winter tires. Tourists driving rented vehicles must ensure that the vehicle is equipped with the proper tires and pay close attention to the provisions of their rental contract. Many contracts prohibit drivers from taking rented vehicles into eastern European countries. Drivers attempting to enter countries listed as "prohibited" on the car rental contract may be arrested, fined, and/or charged with attempted auto theft. Austrian police are authorized to hold the rented vehicle for the car rental company.

Emergency roadside help and information may be reached by dialing 123 or 120 for vehicle assistance and towing services (Austrian automobile clubs), 122 for the fire department, 133 for police, and 144 for ambulance. The European emergency line is 112.

Austrian Federal Railroads (Österreichische Bundesbahnen) offer excellent railroad service to all major towns of the country and also direct connections with all major cities in Europe. Trains are well maintained and fares are reasonable. There is also an extensive network of bus lines operated by the Austrian Postal Service (Österreichische Post). All major cities also offer excellent public transportation services.

Aviation Safety Oversight: The U.S. Federal Aviation Administration (FAA) has assessed the government of Austria's Civil Aviation Authority as being in compliance with International Civil Aviation Organization (ICAO) aviation safety standards for oversight of Austria's air carrier operations. Further information may be found on the FAA safety assessment page.

Children's Issues: Please see the U.S. Dept. of State Office of Children's Issues web pages on intercountry adoption and international parental child abduction.

Intercountry Adoption

March 2009

The information in this section has been edited from the latest report available as of February 2013 from the State Department Bureau of Consular Affairs, Office of Overseas Citizens Services. For more information, please read the *Intercountry Adoption* section of this book and review current reports online at http://adoption.state.gov.

Austria is party to the Hague Convention on Protection of Children and Co-operation in Respect of Intercountry Adoption (Hague Adoption Convention). Therefore all adoptions between Austria and the United States must meet the requirements of the Convention and U.S. law implementing the Convention. Austria is not considered a country of origin in intercountry adoption.

The information provided is intended primarily to assist in extremely rare adoption cases from Austria, including adoptions of Austrian children by relatives in the United States, as well as adoptions from third countries by Americans living in Austria.

Who Can Adopt? Adoption between the United States and Austria is governed by the Hague Adoption Convention. Therefore to adopt from Austria, you must first be found eligible to adopt by the U.S. Government. The U.S. Government agency responsible for making this determination is the Department of Homeland Security, U.S. Citizenship and Immigration Services (USCIS).

Residency Requirements: The adoptive parents need to be legal residents of Austria.

Age Requirements: The adopting father must be at least 30 years old and the adopting mother 28 years old. The prospective adoptive parent must be 18 years older than the adoptee, with limited exceptions. There is no maximum age limit.

Marriage Requirements: The Austrian government prefers that the prospective adoptive parents be married, although the law does not officially specify this. If married, the couple must apply jointly. If not married, only one prospective adoptive parent may apply.

Other Requirements: If the adoptive parents already have children of their own (either biological or adopted), they may have less of a chance to adopt. The adoptive parents must also meet certain personal, social, health, and economic conditions determined by the local youth welfare authority,. If they are found to be suitable an extensive home study is prepared by their social workers. In some Austrian Provinces it is obligatory for prospective adoptive parents to attend a training seminar. Finally, the adoptive parents must have no criminal record.

Who Can be Adopted? Because Austria is party to the Hague Adoption Convention, children from Austria must meet the requirements of the Convention in order to be eligible for adoption. For example, the Convention requires that Austria attempt to place a child with a family in-country before determining that a child is eligible for intercountry adoption. In addition to Austria's requirements, a child must meet the definition of a Convention adoptee for you to bring him or her back to the United States. There are few Austrian children eligible for intercountry adoption.

Eligibility Requirements: If the child is legitimate, the prospective adoptive parent(s) must enter into a contract with the child's biological father (if contact can be made). This contract must contain certain legal requirements, including both of the birthparents' consents.

Abandonment Requirements: If the child is an orphan or illegitimate child, his/her legal guardian must sign the adoption contract. In addition, the child's mother (again, if contact is possible) must give her written consent to the adoption, unless she herself signed the adoption contract as legal guardian of the child. All signatures on the adoption contract as well as the biological mother's signature on her consent to the adoption must be notarized either by an Austrian notary public (within Austria) or by a notary public outside of Austria whose signature is authenticated via the "apostille" procedure. A fact sheet outlining this latter procedure may be accessed on the Internet at http://www.HCCH.net (Hague Legalization Convention.)

The Process: Because Austria is party to the Hague Adoption Convention, adopting from Austria must follow a specific process designed to meet the Convention's requirements. For detailed and updated information on these requirements, please review the *Intercountry Adoption* section of this publication and visit the U.S. Department of State Intercountry Adoption website at http://adoption.state.gov.

Role of the Adoption Authority: Investigations and inquiries to assess the eligibility and suitability of prospective parents are performed independently by the local youth welfare authorities acting under the authority and according to the instructions of the competent provincial governments.

Role of the Court: If the court is satisfied that the adoption would be in the best interest of the child, it issues a decree (Beschluss) certifying the adoption contract. This decree makes the adoption final and legally valid, and a new birth certificate for the child giving any new name(s) may be obtained from the appropriate Bureau of Vital Statistics (Standesamt). If the court does not approve the adoption, the contract is void.

Role of the Adoption Agencies: Youth welfare agencies, as well as non-governmental agencies in Oberosterreich, Salzburg, and Vienna, place children eligible for adoption with prospective adoptive parents.

Time Frame: Austrian adoptions take about 12 months to complete. This includes the 6 months during which the child lives with the adoptive parents while under the supervision of provincial adoption authorities and an additional 6 months needed to complete legal requirements.

Adoption Application: The district court granting the adoption is the competent authority per Art. 23 of the Convention

Adoption Fees: In the adoption services contract that you sign at the beginning of the adoption process, your agency will itemize the fees and estimated expenses related to your adoption process. With respect to adopting from Austria, prospective adoptive parents can expect to pay notary fees and that of any attorney selected.

There are court costs and an adoption contract fee to be paid in connection with an adoption. The U.S. Embassy in Austria discourages the payment of any fees that are not properly receipted, "donations," or "expediting" fees, that may be requested from prospective adoptive parents.

Documents Required: The adoption contract and the mother's release are submitted to the appropriate Austrian court with a petition for certification (Bestätigung).

The court may require evidence of the adopting parent's financial status. The court may also require a "home study" in the United States or at the place of residence abroad through an appropriate agency.

Bringing Your Child Home: Once your adoption is complete (or you have obtained legal custody of the child), there are a few more steps to take before you can head home. Specifically, you need to apply for several documents for your child before he or she can travel to the United States, such as a birth certificate, a passport or travel document for your child from the country in which he or she was born, and a U.S. Immigration Visa. For detailed and updated information on how to obtain these documents, review the *Intercountry Adoption* section in this publication and visit the U.S. Department of State Intercountry Adoption website at http://adoption.state.gov.

Child Citizenship Act: For adoptions finalized abroad, the Child Citizenship Act of 2000 allows your new child to acquire American citizenship automatically when he or she enters the United States as lawful permanent residents. For adoptions finalized in the United States, the Child Citizenship Act of 2000 allows your new child to acquire American citizenship automatically when the court in the United States issues the final adoption decree.

To learn more, review the *Intercountry Adoption* section in this publication and visit the U.S. Department of State Intercountry Adoption website at http://adoption.state.gov.

After Adoption: Post-adoption services are provided by the youth welfare authorities. If requested by states of origin post-adoption reports can be made a social worker or by a private organization entrusted to do so by the competent youth welfare authority.

U.S. Embassy in Austria
Address: Boltzmanngasse 16
A-1090 Vienna
Tel.: (+43-1) 31339-0
Fax: (+43-1) 310 06 82
E-mail: embassy@usembassy.at
Internet: http://www.usembassy.at/en

Austria's Adoption Authority
Bundesministerium für Justiz
(Federal Ministry of Justice)
Abteilung I 10
Postfach 63
1016 WIEN
Tel.: +43 (1) 52152 2731
telefax number: +43 (1) 52152 2829
E-mail: robert.fucik@bmj.gv.at

Embassy of Austria
Address: 3524 International Court, Washington D.C. 20008
Tel: 202-895-6711
Fax: 202-895-6773
Internet: http://www.austria.org

Office of Children's Issues
U.S. Department of State
2201 C Street, NW
SA-29
Washington, DC 20520
Tel: 1-888-407-4747
E-mail: AskCI@state.gov
http://adoption.state.gov

For questions about immigration procedures, call the National Customer Service Center (NCSC) at 1-800-375-5283 (TTY 1-800-767-1833).

International Parental Child Abduction

November 2012

The information in this section has been edited from a report of the State Department Bureau of Consular Affairs, Office of Overseas Citizens Services. For more information, please read the *International Child Abduction* section of this book and review current reports online at www.travel.state.gov/abduction.

Disclaimer: The information in this flyer is provided for general information only, is not intended to be legal advice, and may change without notice. Questions involving interpretation of law should be addressed to an attorney licensed to practice in the relevant jurisdiction.

General Information: Austria and the United States have been treaty partners under the 1980 Hague Convention on the Civil Aspects of International Child Abduction (Hague Abduction Convention) since October 1, 1988.

Hague Abduction Convention: The U.S. Department of State serves as the U.S. Central Authority (USCA) for the Hague Abduction Convention. In this capacity, the Department's Bureau of Consular Affairs, Directorate for Overseas Citizens Services, Office of Children's Issues facilitates the submission of applications under the Hague Abduction Convention for the return of, or access to, children located in countries that are U.S. treaty partners, including Austria. Parents are strongly encouraged to contact the Department of State for assistance prior to initiating the Hague process directly with the foreign Central Authority.

United States Department of State
Office of Children's Issues
2201 C Street, N.W.
Washington, DC 20520
Telephone: 1-888-407-4747
Outside the United States or Canada: 1-202-501-4444
Fax: 202-736-9132

The Austrian Central Authority (ACA) for the Hague Abduction Convention is the Bundesministerium fur Justiz, located in the Federal Ministry of Justice. The ACA has an administrative role in processing Hague applications. The Federal Ministry of Justice forwards completed Hague petitions to the appropriate Austrian court. A single judge in the local court (Bezirksgericht) holds a hearing and makes the initial Hague decision. The appeal of the first instance may be made to a panel of judges in the Regional court (Landesgericht). The second and final appeal maybe made to a panel of judges in the Supreme Court.

Austria Central Authority
Bundesministerium fur Justiz
Abteilung I 10
Museumstrasse
1016 Vienna
Austria
Telephone: +43 (1) 52152 2147
Fax: +43 (1) 525152 2829

To initiate a Hague case for return of, or access to, a child in Austria, the USCA encourages a parent or legal guardian to review the eligibility criteria and instructions for completing the Hague application form located at a the Department of State website and contact the Department of State for assistance prior to initiating the Hague process directly with the ACA. Austria took no reservations to the Convention under Article 24, translations of the documents are not required. The USCA is available to answer questions about the Hague application process, to forward a completed application to ACA, and to subsequently monitor its progress through the foreign administrative and legal processes.

There are no fees for filing Hague applications with either the United States or Austria central authorities. The Austrian courts will appoint an attorney to represent the applicant, and the Austrian government covers the legal expenses when filing a Hague petition in Austria. Additional costs may include airplane tickets for court appearances and for the return of the child, if so ordered.

Return: A parent or legal guardian may file an application under the Hague Abduction Convention for return to the United States of a child abducted to, or wrongfully retained in, Austria. The U.S. Department of State can assist parents living in the United States to understand whether the Convention is an available civil remedy and can provide information on the process for submitting a Hague application.

Visitation/Access: A person may file an application under the Hague Abduction Convention for access to a child living in Austria. The criteria for acceptance of a Hague access application vary from country to country. The U.S. Department of State can assist parents living in the United States to understand Austria-specific criteria and provide information on the process for submitting a Hague application.

Retaining an Attorney: The U.S. Embassy in Vienna, Austria, posts a list of attorneys, including those who specialize in family law at http://austria.usembassy.gov/attorney.html. A parent or guardian who hires private counsel should notify both the Austrian and the U.S. central authorities. This list is provided as a courtesy service only and does not constitute an endorsement of any individual attorney. The Department of State assumes no responsibility or liability for the professional ability or reputation of, or the quality of services provided by, the persons or firms included in this list. Professional credentials and areas of expertise are provided directly by the lawyers.

Mediation: The Austrian federal government is extremely supportive of mediation programs to resolve international parental child abduction cases. While courts cannot order cases into mediation, judges can and do strongly encourage mediated resolutions and can stay hearings to permit parties the time to mediate. The Austrian Federal Ministry of Justice offers a list of officially recognized mediation organizations, which can be found at in Austrian): http://www.mediatorenliste.justiz.gv.at/mediatoren/mediatorenliste.nsf/docs/home. Fees are normally based on hourly rates, but a sliding scale or negotiated rate is sometimes available. The process involves two mediators: one with training in a psychosocial field (such as a social worker or therapist) and the other with legal training (such as an attorney or a judge). All recognized mediators have completed specialized training in addition to their professional qualifications.

Embassy of the United States
Boltzmanngasse 16
1090 Vienna
Tel.: (+43-1) 31339–0
Fax: (+43-1) 310 06 82
Email: consulatevienna@state.gov
Website: U. S. Embassy in Vienna

Embassy of Austria
3524 International Court, NW
Washington, DC 20008
Telephone: 202-895-6700
Email: http://www.austria.org
Website: Embassy of Austria in the United States

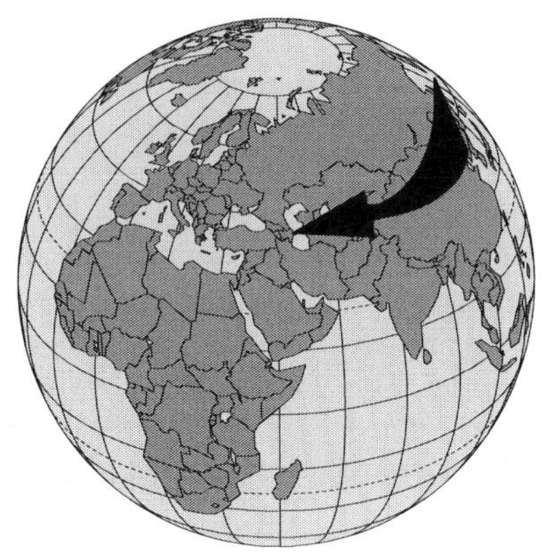

AZERBAIJAN

Compiled from publications that were available as of February 2013 from the U.S. Department of State, the U.S. Department of Commerce, and the Central Intelligence Agency (CIA). See the introduction to this set for explanatory notes.

Official Name:
Republic of Azerbaijan

PROFILE

Geography

Area: total: 86,600 sq km; country comparison to the world: 113; land: 82,629 sq km; water: 3,971 sq km

Major cities: Baku (capital) 1.95 million (2009)

Climate: dry, semiarid steppe

Terrain: large, flat Kur-Araz Ovaligi (Kura-Araks Lowland, much of it below sea level) with Great Caucasus Mountains to the north, Qarabag Yaylasi (Karabakh Upland) in west; Baku lies on Abseron Yasaqligi (Apsheron Peninsula) that juts into Caspian Sea

People

Nationality: noun: Azerbaijani(s); adjective: Azerbaijani

Population: 9,493,600 (July 2012 est.)

Population growth rate: 1.017% (2012 est.)

Ethnic groups: Azeri 90.6%, Dagestani 2.2%, Russian 1.8%, Armenian 1.5%, other 3.9% (1999 census)

Religions: Muslim 93.4%, Russian Orthodox 2.5%, Armenian Orthodox 2.3%, other 1.8% (1995 est.)

Languages: Azerbaijani (Azeri) (official) 90.3%, Lezgi 2.2%, Russian 1.8%, Armenian 1.5%, other 3.3%, unspecified 1% (1999 census)

Literacy: definition: age 15 and over can read and write; total population: 99.8%; male: 99.9%; female: 99.7% (2010 census)

Health: life expectancy at birth: total population: 71.32 years; male: 68.38 years; female: 74.68 years (2012 est.); Infant mortality rate: total: 28.76 deaths/1,000 live births; male: 29.48 deaths/1,000 live births; female: 27.93 deaths/1,000 live births (2012 est.)

Unemployment rate: 1% (2012 est.)

Work force: 6.2 million (2012 est.)

Government

Type: republic

Independence: 30 August 1991

Constitution: adopted 12 November 1995; modified by referendum 24 August 2002

Political subdivisions: 66 rayons (rayonlar; rayon—singular), 11 cities (saharlar; sahar—singular)

Suffrage: 18 years of age; universal

Economy

GDP (purchasing power parity): $98.16 billion (2012 est.); $94.25 billion (2011 est.); $94.16 billion (2010 est.); $89.71 billion (2009 est.)

GDP real growth rate: 3.8% (2012 est.); 0.1% (2011 est.); 5% (2010 est.); 9.3% (2009 est.)

GDP per capita (PPP): $10,700 (2012 est.); $10,300 (2011 est.); $10,400 (2010 est.)

Natural resources: petroleum, natural gas, iron ore, nonferrous metals, bauxite

Agriculture products: cotton, grain, rice, grapes, fruit, vegetables, tea, tobacco; cattle, pigs, sheep, goats

Industries: petroleum and natural gas, petroleum products, oilfield equipment; steel, iron ore; cement; chemicals and petrochemicals; textiles

Exports: $30.58 billion (2012 est.); $34.49 billion (2011 est.)

Exports—commodities: oil and gas 90%, machinery, cotton, foodstuffs

Exports—partners: Italy 32.4%, France 13.2%, US 7.5%, Germany 6.2%, Indonesia 5.4%, Czech Republic 5.3% (2011)

Imports: $10.78 billion (2012 est.); $10.17 billion (2011 est.)

Imports—commodities: machinery and equipment, oil products, foodstuffs, metals, chemicals

Imports—partners: Turkey 18.1%, Russia 15.5%, China 7.8%, Germany 7.2%, UK 6.1%, Ukraine 4.6%, Italy 4.2% (2011)

Debt—external: $4.074 billion (31 December 2011 est.); $4.033 billion (31 December 2010 est.)

Exchange rates: Azerbaijani manats (AZN) per US dollar; 0.7839 (2012 est.); 0.7897 (2011 est.); 0.8027 (2010 est.); 0.8038 (2009); 0.8219 (2008)

PEOPLE

National/Racial/Ethnic Minorities

Some of the approximately 20,000 to 30,000 citizens of Armenian descent living in the country historically complained of discrimination in employment, housing, and the provision of social services. Citizens who were ethnic Armenians often concealed their ethnicity by legally changing the ethnic designation in their passports.

Some groups reported sporadic incidents of discrimination, restrictions on their ability to teach in their native languages, and harassment by local authorities. These groups included Talysh in the south, Lezghi in the north, Meskhetian Turks, and Kurds displaced from the regions controlled by Armenia-supported Nagorno-Karabakh separatists.

Religion

Approximately 96 percent of the population is Muslim, with the remainder consisting mostly of Russian Orthodox, Armenian Apostolic, followers of other Christian groups, Jews, and nonbelievers. Approximately 65 percent are Shia and 35 percent are Sunni, according to the State Committee on Work with Religious Associations (SCWRA), the government body tasked with implementing policy on religious issues, enforcing relevant regulations, and interacting with religious organizations. Christians are mainly concentrated in Baku and other urban centers. The majority of Christians are Russian Orthodox whose identity, like that of Muslims, tends to be based more on culture and ethnicity than on religion. Approximately 20,000 Jews live in Baku, with smaller communities throughout the country.

Other small religious groups have existed in the country for more than 100 years, including Lutherans, Roman Catholics, Baptists, Molokans, Seventh-day Adventists, and Baha'is. Since independence in 1991, a number of religious groups considered by the government as foreign or "nontraditional" have established a presence, including Salafist Muslims, Pentecostal and other evangelical Christians, Jehovah's Witnesses, and Hare Krishnas. There are significant foreign resident Christian communities in Baku.

HISTORICAL HIGHLIGHTS

Azerbaijan combines the heritage of two venerable civilizations—the Seljuk Turks of the 11th century and the ancient Persians. Its name is thought to be derived from the Persian phrase "Land of Fire," referring both to its petroleum deposits, known since ancient times, and to its status as a former center of the Zoroastrian faith. The Azerbaijani Republic borders the Iranian provinces of East and West Azerbaijan, which are predominantly populated by ethnic Azeris.

Little is known about Azerbaijan's history until its conquest and conversion to Islam by the Arabs in 642 AD. Centuries of prosperity as a province of the Muslim caliphate followed. After the decline of the Arab Empire, Azerbaijan was ravaged during the Mongol invasions but regained prosperity in the 13th-15th centuries under the Mongol II-Khans, the native Shirvan Shahs, and under Persia's Safavid Dynasty.

Due to its location on the shore of the Caspian Sea and astride the trade routes connecting Europe to Central Asia and the Near East, Azerbaijan was fought over by Russia, Persia, and the Ottomans. Finally, the Russians split Azerbaijan's territory with Persia in 1828 by the Treaty of Turkmenchay, establishing the present frontiers and extinguishing the last native dynasties of local Azerbaijani khans. The beginning of modern exploitation of the oil fields in the 1870s led to a period of unprecedented prosperity and growth in the years before World War I.

Following the collapse of the Russian Empire in 1917, an independent republic was proclaimed in 1918 after an abortive attempt to establish a Transcaucasian Republic with Armenia and Georgia. The first democratic republic in the Muslim world, it gave women the right to vote in 1919. Azerbaijan received de facto recognition by the Allies as an independent nation in January 1920, an independence terminated by the arrival of the Red Army in April. Incorporated into the Transcaucasian Federated Soviet Socialist Republic in 1922, Azerbaijan became a union republic of the U.S.S.R. (Soviet Union) in 1936. The late 1980s were characterized by increasing unrest, eventually leading to a violent confrontation when Soviet troops killed 190 nationalist demonstrators in Baku on January 19-20, 1990. Azerbaijan declared its independence from the U.S.S.R. on August 30, 1991. Azerbaijan's first parliament was elected in 1995.

GOVERNMENT AND POLITICAL CONDITIONS

The Azerbaijan constitution provides for a republic with a presidential form of government. Legislative authority is vested in the Milli Mejlis (parliament). In practice the president dominated the executive, legislative, and judicial branches of government. November 2010 Milli Mejlis elections did not meet a number of key standards of the Organization for Security and Cooperation in Europe (OSCE) for democratic elections. Although there were more than 50 political parties, the president's party, the Yeni Azerbaijan Party, dominated the political system. Ethnic Armenian separatists, with Armenia's support, continued to control most of the Nagorno-Karabakh region of the country and seven surrounding Azerbaijani territories. The government did not exercise any control over developments in those territories.

Recent Elections

Although both progovernment and opposition political parties participated in the November 2010 parliamentary elections, these elections did not meet a number of international standards for democratic elections. According to domestic and international observers, shortcomings included a biased candidate registration process, constraints on freedom of assembly and expression, a restrictive political environment, unbalanced media coverage of candidates, and unequal treatment of candidates by authorities. The OSCE observation mission final report concluded that overall, the elections did not meet a number of key OSCE commitments for democratic elections or important elements of domestic legislation. There also were reports of pressure on domestic election observers, candidates, and family members. Such pressure included the firing of such individuals from their jobs and, in Nakhchivan, beatings.

President Ilham Aliyev, the son of former president Heydar Aliyev, was elected to a second term in 2008, also in a flawed election.

Political Parties: There were 50 registered political parties. However, the ruling Yeni Azerbaijan Party continued to dominate the political system. Domestic observers reported that membership in the ruling party conferred advantages, such as being given preference for public positions. For the first time since the country's independence, the Milli Mejlis after the 2010 election did not include representatives of the Musavat and Popular Front opposition parties.

Members of the opposition were more likely to experience official harassment and arbitrary arrest and detention than other citizens. Members of regional and central branches of opposition parties reported that local authorities often took actions to prevent routine party activities, for example, by pressuring restaurant owners not to allow opposition parties to use their facilities for meetings and events. During 2011 there were reports that these types of pressure occurred in Baku. Regional party members often had to conceal the purpose of their gatherings and hold them in remote locations. Opposition party members reported that police often dispersed small gatherings at tea houses and detained participants for questioning. Opposition parties continued to have difficulty renting office space, reportedly because landlords were afraid of official pressure; some parties operated out of their leaders' apartments

Participation of Women and Minorities: There were 19 women in the Milli Mejlis. The percentage of female members of parliament increased from 11 to 16 percent between 2005 and 2010. One woman held a ministerial-level position. Members of minority groups such as the Talysh, Avars, Russians, and Jews served in the Milli Mejlis and in government.

Principal Government Officials

Last Updated: 1/31/2013

Pres.: **Ilham ALIYEV**
Prime Min.: **Artur RASIZADE**
First Dep. Prime Min.: **Yaqub EYYUBOV**
Dep. Prime Min.: **Elchin EFENDIYEV**
Dep. Prime Min.: **Ali HASANOV**
Dep. Prime Min.: **Abid SHARIFOV**
Min. of Agriculture: **Ismat ABBASOV**

Min. of Communications & Information Technology: **Ali ABBASOV**
Min. of Culture & Tourism: **Abulfaz GARAYEV**
Min. of Defense: **Safar ABIYEV, Gen. Col.**
Min. of Defense Industry: **Yavar JAMALOV**
Min. of Ecology & Natural Resources: **Huseyngulu BAGIROV**
Min. of Economic Development: **Shahin MUSTAFAYEV**
Min. of Education: **Misir MARDANOV**
Min. of Emergency Situations: **Kamaladdin HEYDAROV**
Min. of Finance: **Samir SHARIFOV**
Min. of Foreign Affairs: **Elmar MAMMADYAROV**
Min. of Health: **Oqtay SHIRALIYEV**
Min. of Industry & Energy: **Natiq ALIYEV**
Min. of Internal Affairs: **Ramil USUBOV, Gen. Col.**
Min. of Justice: **Fikret MAMEDOV**
Min. of Labor & Social Security: **Fizuli ALEKPEROV**
Min. of National Security: **Eldar MAHMUDOV**
Min. of Sports & Youth: **Azad RAHIMOV**
Min. of Taxation: **Fazil MAMEDOV**
Min. of Transport: **Ziya MAMMADOV**
Chmn., National Bank: **Elman RUSTAMOV**
Ambassador to the US: **Elin SULEYMANOV**
Permanent Representative to the UN, New York: **Agshin MEHDIYEV**

ECONOMY

Azerbaijan's high economic growth during 2006–08 was attributable to large and growing oil exports, but some non-export sectors also featured double-digit growth, including construction, banking, and real estate, although most of this increase was tied to growth in the hydrocarbon sector. In 2011, economic growth slowed to 0.2%, largely because oil production reached a plateau.

The current global economic slowdown presents some challenges for the Azerbaijani economy as oil prices remain volatile, highlighting Azerbaijan's reliance on energy exports and lackluster attempts to diversify its economy. Oil exports through the Baku-Tbilisi-Ceyhan Pipeline remain the main economic driver while efforts to boost Azerbaijan's gas production are underway. However, Azerbaijan has made only limited progress on instituting market-based economic reforms. Pervasive public and private sector corruption and structural economic inefficiencies remain a drag on long-term growth, particularly in non-energy sectors. Several other obstacles impede Azerbaijan's economic progress, including the need for stepped up foreign investment in the non-energy sector and the continuing conflict with Armenia over the Nagorno-Karabakh region.

Trade with Russia and the other former Soviet republics is declining in importance, while trade is building with Turkey and the nations of Europe. Long-term prospects depend on world oil prices, the location of new oil and gas pipelines in the region, Azerbaijan's ability to negotiate export routes for its growing gas production, and its ability to manage its energy wealth to promote growth and spur employment in non-energy sectors of the economy.

Labor Conditions

The minimum age for employment depended on the type of work. In most instances the law permits children to work from age 15; children age 14 may work in family businesses or, with parental consent, in daytime after-school jobs that pose no hazard to their health. Children under 16 may not work more than 24 hours per week; children between the ages of 16 and 17 may not work more than 36 hours per week. The law prohibits employing children

under 18 in difficult and hazardous work conditions and identifies specific work and industries from which children are barred, including work with toxic substances and underground, at night, in mines, in night clubs, bars, casinos or other businesses that serve alcohol. The law provides for the protection of children from exploitation in the workplace and from work that is dangerous to their health.

The government raised the national minimum wage to 93.50 manat ($117) per month on December 1. The government defined the 2011 poverty line, on average, to be 95 manat per month ($119), adjusting the level for certain categories to 102 manat ($128) for able-bodied persons, 72 manat ($90) for pensioners, and 76 manat ($95) per child.

The law provides for a 40-hour workweek; the maximum daily work shift is 12 hours. Workers in hazardous occupations may not work more than 36 hours per week. The law requires lunch and rest periods, which are determined by labor contracts and collective agreements. It was not known whether local companies provided the legally required premium compensation for overtime, although international companies generally did. There was no prohibition on excessive compulsory overtime. However, most individuals worked part-time in the informal economy, where the government did not enforce contracts or labor laws.

The law provides equal rights to foreign and domestic workers. However, local human rights groups, including the Oil Workers Rights Defense Council, maintained that employers, particularly foreign oil companies, did not always treat foreign and domestic workers equally. Domestic employees of foreign oil companies often received lower pay and worked without contracts or health care.

U.S.-AZERBAIJAN RELATIONS

The United States established diplomatic relations with Azerbaijan in 1992, following its independence from the Soviet Union. The United States is committed to strengthening democracy and the formation of an open market economy in Azerbaijan. It stands to gain benefits from an Azerbaijan that is peaceful, democratic, prosperous, and strategically linked to the United States and U.S. allies in Europe. The United States seeks new ways to partner with Azerbaijan to promote regional security and stability, enhance energy security, and strengthen economic and political reforms. The United States supports efforts to peacefully resolve the Nagorno-Karabakh conflict and reopen the closed border with Armenia.

U.S. Assistance to Azerbaijan

U.S. Government assistance to Azerbaijan aims to encourage reforms that promote the development of democratic institutions and processes, sustainable economic growth, and regional security. A fact sheet on U.S. assistance to Azerbaijan can be found here.

Bilateral Economic Relations

The United States and Azerbaijan have a bilateral trade agreement and a bilateral investment treaty. U.S. companies are involved in offshore oil development projects with Azerbaijan and have been exploring emerging investment opportunities in Azerbaijan in telecommunications and other fields. Azerbaijan has been designated as a beneficiary country under the Generalized System of Preferences (GSP) program, under which a range of products that Azerbaijan might seek to export are eligible for duty-free entry to the United States. The GSP program provides an incentive for investors to produce in Azerbaijan and export selected products duty-free to the U.S. market.

Azerbaijan's Membership in International Organizations

Azerbaijan and the United States belong to a number of the same international organizations, including the United Nations, Euro-Atlantic Partnership Council, Organization for Security and Cooperation in Europe, International Monetary Fund, and World Bank. Azerbaijan also is an observer to the Organization of American States and the World Trade Organization and a participant in the North Atlantic Treaty Organization's (NATO) Partnership for Peace program.

Bilateral Representation

Azerbaijan maintains an embassy in the United States at 2741 34th Street NW, Washington, DC 20008; tel. (202) 337-3500.

Principal U.S. Embassy Officials

Last Updated: 1/14/2013

BAKU (E) 83 Azadlig Prospect, Azerbaijan, AZ 1007, +994-12-498-03-35; safe haven phone–dial like IVG–736-4161, Fax +994-12-465-66-71, INMARSAT Tel Iridium: 8816-2245-7891, Workweek: M-F, 9:00–17:30, Website: http://baku.usembassy.gov/

DCM OMS:	Rebecca Nassar
AMB OMS:	Grace Tift
Co-CLO:	Annalise Rivas
HRO:	Linda Fenton
MGT:	John C Dockery
POL/MIL:	Jonathan Giuliano
POSHO:	George Rivas
SDO/DATT:	COL Daniel Grillone
AMB:	Richard Morningstar
CON:	Eric Morin
DCM:	Adam Sterling
PAO:	Victoria Sloan
GSO:	Rhonda Slusher
RSO:	Rebecca Dockery
AID:	Michael J Greene
ATO:	Randy Ayers
CLO:	Evangeline Taylor
ECON:	Erin C. McConaha
FMO:	Linda Fenton
ICASS Chair:	Michael J Greene
IMO:	Lysa C Giuliano
ISSO:	Lysa Giuliano
LEGATT:	Eric Peterson
POL:	Anthony Baird
State ICASS:	Anthony Baird

TRAVEL

Consular Information Sheet

August 7, 2012

Country Description: Azerbaijan is a constitutional republic with a developing economy. Western-style amenities are found in the capital, Baku, but infrastructure and access to goods and services outside the city, while improving, are less well-developed.

Smart Traveler Enrollment Program (STEP)/Embassy Locations: If you are going to live in or visit Azerbaijan, please take the time to inform the U.S. Embassy about your trip. If you enroll, we can keep you up to date with important safety and security announcements. Enrolling will also help your friends and family get in touch with you in an emergency.

The U.S. Embassy is located at 83 Azadlig Prospekt; tel. (994-12) 498-03-35, 36, or 37; Emergency after-hours telephone: (994-12) 498-03-35, 36, or 37; Facsimile: (994-12) 465-66-71.

If you have registered with the embassy and are leaving Azerbaijan permanently, please check out by sending us an email.

Entry/Exit Requirements for U.S. Citizens: You need a passport and a visa to enter Azerbaijan. Get your visa before you travel and make sure the visa validity dates correspond with your travel. With limited exceptions (persons with invitations from high-ranking officials of the Government of Azerbaijan) you cannot get a visa at the airport, nor can you get a visa at the land borders with Georgia, Russia, Turkey, or Iran.

Currently, U.S. citizens may apply for a single or double-entry tourist or visitor visa valid for 90 days (cost: $160), or a one-year multiple-entry business visa (cost: $160). U.S. citizen tourists booking accommodations through a licensed Azerbaijani travel agency may receive a voucher that entitles them to receive a tourist visa for $20. The Embassy of Azerbaijan in Washington, D.C. recently started using a visa courier service that charges $21 for processing and service fees in addition to the basic cost of the visa. Visa applicants are required to use this service. Please see the website of the Azerbaijani Embassy in Washington, D.C. for more details. The Embassy of Azerbaijan states on its website that visas take 10 business days to process, but recently, U.S. citizens have been experiencing delays of up to 2 months between applying for a visa and the visa being issued.

According to Azerbaijani law, foreign nationals intending to remain in Azerbaijan for more than 30 days must register with local police within three days of their arrival. If this applies to you, go to the passport section of the local district police office and fill out an application form. The registration fee is AZN 9.90 (approximately $12 USD).

U.S. citizens of Armenian ancestry—or even those with Armenian last names—may have their visa applications denied by the Government of Azerbaijan on the grounds that their safety cannot be guaranteed.

A valid visa is required in order to depart Azerbaijan. If you are already in Azerbaijan, your visa applications, extensions, or renewals must be made at the State Migration Service of Azerbaijan, 202 Binagadi Highway, 3123 Block, Binagadi District, Baku; tel (994-12)562-56-23. If you are staying longer than 30 days, you should make sure your visa and local identification card are current and valid. We recommend you carry at least a photocopy of your current passport and valid visa with you at all times if you do not normally carry your passport.

The U.S. Department of State is unaware of any restriction on entry to Azerbaijan for travelers with HIV/AIDS. However, medical tests are required for those applying for temporary or permanent residence permits. The applications by people with health issues, including HIV/AIDS, are reviewed by the State Migration Service and approved on a case-by-case basis.

Azerbaijan does not recognize dual citizenship and dual U.S.–Azerbaijani citizens could encounter problems living and traveling in Azerbaijan. Azerbaijan has compulsory military service for males aged 18 to 35. Men who currently have U.S. citizenship and who previously held Azerbaijani citizenship and have not completed their military requirement could face fines or arrest unless they have officially renounced their Azerbaijani citizenship. Dual citizens may renounce their Azerbaijani citizenship at any Azerbaijan Embassy or Consulate.

Threats to Safety and Security: In light of ongoing global and regional threats against U.S. and foreign interests, the U.S. Embassy has recently released several Emergency Messages to U.S. citizens advising them to remain vigilant, particularly in public places associated with Western and Israeli communities. In January 2012, the Azerbaijani National Security Ministry disrupted a plot, reportedly backed by Iran, to attack prominent foreigners in Baku.You should avoid travel to the region of Nagorno-Karabakh and the surrounding occupied areas, as well as regions along the line of contact between Azerbaijani and Armenian positions. Because of the existing state of hostilities, we cannot offer consular services to U.S. citizens in Nagorno-Karabakh.

U.S. citizens of Armenian ancestry considering travel to Azerbaijan should remain particularly vigilant when visiting the country, as the Government of Azerbaijan has claimed it is unable to guarantee your safety.

Stay up to date by:

- Bookmarking our Bureau of Consular Affairs website, which contains the current Travel Warnings and Travel Alerts as well as the Worldwide Caution;
- Following us on Twitter and the Bureau of Consular Affairs page on Facebook;
- Calling 1-888-407-4747 toll-free within the United States and Canada, or a regular toll line, 1-202-501-4444, from other countries; and
- Taking some time before travel to consider your personal security. Here are some useful tips for traveling abroad safely.

Crime: Azerbaijan has seen a downward trend in the number of crimes committed against foreigners. Most of the crime in Baku affects local residents, with burglary and assault being the most common crimes.

Foreigners are at a greater risk in areas attracting large crowds or in very isolated areas. Although not common, petty theft and assault against foreign citizens do occur in Baku. Pick-pockets tend to frequent tourist sites, public transportation (especially minibuses), and pedestrian streets or large public squares where people congregate. Travelers should be mindful of their wallets, purses, and computer bags, as they make for tempting targets.

Avoid traveling alone at night. Late-night targeted attacks against lone males, while not common, are the most common crimes committed against foreigners; these usually involve victims who have been drinking.

There have been several reports from individuals who have been victims of crimes occurring late at night in bars frequented by Westerners. The crime occurs when a male patron is approached by a young woman who asks the individual to buy her a drink; after buying the drink and talking for a while, the customer is presented with an exorbitant bill. When the customer protests, he is approached by several men, detained, and forced to pay the full amount of the bill under threat of physical violence.

An American reported that a stranger, posing as a plumber, gained entry to his apartment and stole money and valuables. You should be very cautious about allowing unknown people to enter your hotel room or apartment.

A number of Western women have reported incidents of unwanted male attention, including groping and other offensive behavior while walking on the streets alone. Travelers should remain alert when visiting tourist areas in Baku, such as Fountain Square and the Maiden's Tower.

We recommend that you avoid traveling alone in these areas after nightfall.

There have been reports of vehicle break-ins at regional tourist sites outside Baku. Whenever possible, vehicles should be parked in guarded or controlled parking lots, and valuables should never be left in plain sight.

There have been two recently reported cases of U.S. citizens being asked by new Internet friends to help pay a "return guarantee fee" to the Azerbaijani Immigration Service before a short trip abroad. There is no such law requiring Azerbaijani citizens to post a deposit for foreign travel, and the Internet friends were later determined to have fraudulent Azerbaijani identification cards. Please see this website for information about avoiding Internet financial scams.

Don't buy counterfeit and pirated goods, even if they are widely available. Not only are the bootlegs illegal to bring back into the United States, but purchasing them may also be against local law.

Victims of Crime: If you or someone you know becomes the victim of a crime abroad, you should contact the local police and the nearest U.S. embassy or consulate. We can:

- Replace a stolen passport;
- Help you find appropriate medical care following violent crimes such as assault or rape;
- Put you in contact with the appropriate police authorities and, if you want us to, we can contact family members or friends; and
- Help you understand the local criminal justice process and can direct you to local attorneys, although local authorities are responsible for investigating and prosecuting the crime.

The Ministry of Internal Affairs established a special Office of Crimes By and Against Foreigners at which English-speaking officers are available until 8:00 PM at (994 12) 590-99-66. The Ministry of Internal Affairs also has a Duty Officer available after hours, at 590-93-31 or 590-94-31.

The local equivalents of the "911" emergency lines in Azerbaijan are: 101—Fire Brigade; 102—Police; 103—Ambulance; 104—Gas services; and 112—Ministry of Emergency Situations. English speaking operators are on duty 24 hrs at 102—Police.

Criminal Penalties: While you are traveling in Azerbaijan, you are subject to its laws even if you are a U.S. citizen. Foreign laws, legal systems, and criminal penalties can be vastly different from our own. In some places, you may be taken for questioning if you don't have your passport with you, it may be illegal to take pictures of certain buildings, and driving under the influence could land you immediately in jail.

There are also some things that might be legal in the country you visit, but still illegal in the United States; for instance, you can be prosecuted under U.S. law if you buy pirated goods. Engaging in sexual conduct with children or using or disseminating child pornography in a foreign country is a crime prosecutable in the United States. If you break local laws in Azerbaijan, your U.S. passport won't help you avoid arrest or prosecution. It's very important to know the local laws of your destination.

Azerbaijan's security apparatus is sensitive to photography, so both professional and tourist photographers have been stopped for taking photographs of facilities that may not appear to be sensitive, including oil fields, buildings, and public squares. If police stop you for taking photographs, you should cooperate. If your photographic equipment is confiscated, you should contact the Embassy Consular Section to report the incident.

Azerbaijan is a signatory to the Vienna Convention on Consular Relations. If you are arrested in Azerbaijan, the authorities are required to notify the Embassy of your arrest, and to have communications from you forwarded to the Embassy.

Special Circumstances: The Republic of Azerbaijan has a mostly cash economy. Traveler's checks and credit cards are accepted only in some hotels and a few restaurants and supermarkets.

Azerbaijani customs authorities may enforce strict regulations concerning temporary importation into or export from Azerbaijan of items such as firearms, religious materials, antiquities (including carpets), medications, and caviar, and any amount of currency over $1,000 USD. Visitors who purchase carpets will generally require an export permit issued by the State Museum of Azerbaijan Carpet and Applied Art; many carpet-selling shops will obtain that permit for the buyer for a fee. It is advisable to contact the Embassy of Azerbaijan in Washington for specific information regarding customs requirements.

Accessibility: While in Azerbaijan, individuals with disabilities may find accessibility and accommodation very different from what you find in the United States. Accessibility for those with disabilities, including stores, foot paths, road crossings, most tourists spots, and on public transportation is lacking throughout the country. There are no laws mandating access to public or other buildings, information, and communications for persons with disabilities.

Medical Facilities and Health Information: There is one Western-type medical clinic operating in Baku, run by International SOS, which provides 24-hour care of quality comparable to that in Western countries. It is adequate for urgent care and minor acute medical problems only. Surgeries, unless urgent for life-saving problems, are not advisable here. There is often a shortage of basic medical supplies, including disposable needles and vaccines. Bring adequate amounts of prescription medicines for the duration of your visit, as pharmacies often do not carry all brands or doses.

You can find good information on vaccinations and other health precautions on the Centers for Disease Control and Prevention (CDC) website. For information about outbreaks of infectious diseases abroad, consult the World Health Organization (WHO) website, which also contains additional health information for travelers, including detailed country-specific health information. Tuberculosis (TB), especially in multi drug-resistant forms, is an increasingly serious health concern in Azerbaijan. For further information, please consult the CDC's information on TB.

Medical Insurance: You can't assume your insurance will go with you when you travel. It's very important to find out BEFORE you leave. You need to ask your insurance company two questions:

- Does my policy apply when I'm outside of the United States?
- Will it cover emergencies like a trip to a foreign hospital or an evacuation?

Doctors and hospitals still expect payment in cash at the time of service. Your regular U.S. health insurance may reimburse you for medical expenses incurred overseas with the proper submission of claims once you return home, but you should not expect insurance to cover doctors' and hospital visits in other countries. Cash is almost always the only accepted form of payment.

If your policy does not provide international coverage, it's a very good idea to take out another one for your trip, for the sake of claiming reimbursement at a later date. It is advisable to purchase medical evacuation insurance, if not included in your medical insurance policy, in case urgent medical evacuation by air ambulance is needed.

Traffic Safety and Road Conditions: While in Azerbaijan, U.S. citizens may encounter road conditions that differ significantly from those in the United States. Fatalities from traffic accidents are high and continue to rise each year. The information below concerning Azerbaijan is provided for general reference only, and may not be totally accurate in a particular location or circumstance.

Azerbaijan is in the midst of a massive infrastructure re-building project, with virtually every major highway under construction at this time. The original roads are poorly constructed and poorly lighted. Although the newer sections of the road system are a marked improvement, the unfinished sections remain dangerous due to lack of proper construction and hazard signage.

Driving hazards such as open manholes, debris, sinkholes, and potholes are common in Baku. Many drivers do not pay attention to traffic regulations, signals, lane markings, pedestrians, or other drivers. Drivers often travel at extremely high speeds, and accidents are frequent and often serious. Pedestrians do not use crosswalks to cross the street and often stand in the median between lanes of traffic, even at night. Driving in Baku should be considered extremely hazardous. Outside the city, even where roads are present, conditions are similar. Roads are often in poor repair and unlighted, and lack lane markings, traffic signs, and warnings. Many rural roads are largely unpaved.

Throughout Azerbaijan, traffic police enforce traffic laws inconsistently and routine traffic stops are common. If stopped, drivers should have all required documents with them, including passport or local registration documents, driver's license, vehicle registration documents, and proof of insurance. Talking on the cell phone while driving carries a fine of AZN 50 (about $64 USD). Driving under the influence carries a fine of AZN 80-100 (about $102-$128 USD) and 5 points. If you get 10 points in one year, the fine is AZN 120-150 AZN (about $153-$191 USD) and 2 years suspension of license.

Most taxis in Baku are neither metered nor regulated. Older Russian-produced cars used as private taxis are widely regarded as unsafe. Visitors must negotiate the fare before entering a taxi. Recently, a fleet of new, London-style taxis have been deployed in Baku. They are metered and can be found near most places catering to tourists.

Although the city of Baku has invested in new buses and the quality of its underground metro system is very good, public transportation throughout remainder of the country remains overcrowded and poorly maintained.

Aviation Safety Oversight: As there is no direct commercial air service to the United States by carriers registered in Azerbaijan, the U.S. Federal Aviation Administration (FAA) has not assessed the Government of Azerbaijan's Civil Aviation Authority for compliance with International Civil Aviation Organization (ICAO) aviation safety standards. Further information may be found on the FAA's safety assessment page. Travelers on regional airlines in the Caucasus may experience delays and sudden cancellations of flights. Even basic safety features such as seat belts are sometimes missing. Air travel to Azerbaijan on international carriers via Europe is typically more reliable.

Children's Issues: Please see the U.S. Dept. of State Office of Children's Issues web pages on intercountry adoption and international parental child abduction.

Intercountry Adoption

August 2012

The information in this section has been edited from a report of the Bureau of Consular Affairs, Office of Overseas Citizens Services of the U.S. Department of State. For more information, please read the *Intercountry Adoption* section of this book and review current reports online at http://adoption.state.gov.

Azerbaijan is party to the Hague Convention on Protection of Children and Co-operation in Respect of Intercountry Adoption (Hague Adoption Convention). Intercountry adoption processing in Hague countries is done in accordance with the requirements of the Convention; the U.S. implementing legislation, the Intercountry Adoption Act of 2000 (IAA); and the IAA's implementing regulations, as well as the implementing legislation and regulations of Azerbaijan.

Below is the adoption information that the Department has obtained from the adoption authority of Azerbaijan. U.S. citizens interested in adopting children from Azerbaijan should contact the Central Authority of Azerbaijan to inquire about applicable laws and procedures. U.S. citizen prospective adoptive parents living in Azerbaijan who would like to adopt a child from the United States or from a third country should also contact Azerbaijan's Central Authority.

The U.S. Embassy in Tbilisi, Georgia, issues immigrant visas for Azerbaijan nationals. The consular officer will send a letter (referred to as an "Article 5 letter") to Azerbaijan's Central Authority for any intercountry adoption involving U.S. citizen parents and a child from Azerbaijan where all Convention requirements are met and the consular officer determines that the child appears eligible to immigrate to the United States.

This letter will inform Azerbaijan's Central Authority that the parents are eligible and suited to adopt, that all indications are that the child may enter and reside permanently in the United States, and that the U.S. Central Authority agrees that the adoption may proceed.

Do not attempt to adopt or obtain custody of a child in Azerbaijan before a U.S. consular officer issues the Article 5 letter in any adoption case.

The consular officer will make a final decision about a child's eligibility for an immigrant visa later in the adoption process.

Azerbaijan's Adoption Authority:
State Committee for Family, Women and Children Affairs
AZ 1000, Baku, Azerbaijan
40 U. Hajibeyov Str.
Government House, Gate IV
Tel: +994 (12) 493-70-39
Fax: +994 (12) 493 58 72
Email: office@scfwca.gov.az
Internet: scfwca.gov.az

BAHAMAS

Compiled from publications that were available as of February 2013 from the U.S. Department of State, the U.S. Department of Commerce, and the Central Intelligence Agency (CIA). See the introduction to this set for explanatory notes.

Official Name:
Commonwealth of The Bahamas

PROFILE

Geography

Area: total: 13,880 sq km; country comparison to the world: 161; land: 10,010 sq km; water: 3,870 sq km
Major cities: Nassau (capital) 248,000 (2009)
Climate: tropical marine; moderated by warm waters of Gulf Stream
Terrain: long, flat coral formations with some low rounded hills

People

Nationality: noun: Bahamian(s); adjective: Bahamian
Population: 316,182 (July 2012 est.)
Population growth rate: 0.904% (2012 est.)
Ethnic groups: black 85%, white 12%, Asian and Hispanic 3%
Religions: Protestant 67.6% (Baptist 35.4%, Anglican 15.1%, Pentecostal 8.1%, Church of God 4.8%, Methodist 4.2%), Roman Catholic 13.5%, other Christian 15.2%, none or unspecified 2.9%, other 0.8% (2000 census)
Languages: English (official), Creole (among Haitian immigrants)
Literacy: definition: age 15 and over can read and write; total population: 95.6%; male: 94.7%; female: 96.5% (2003 est.)
Health: life expectancy at birth: total population: 71.44 years; male: 69.04 years; female: 73.91 years (2012 est.); Infant mortality rate: total: 13.09 deaths/1,000 live births; male: 12.9 deaths/1,000 live births; female: 13.29 deaths/1,000 live births (2012 est.)
Unemployment rate: 14.2% (2009 est.)
Work force: 184,000 (2009)

Government

Type: constitutional parliamentary democracy and a Commonwealth realm
Independence: 10 July 1973
Constitution: 10 July 1973
Political subdivisions: 31 districts
Suffrage: 18 years of age; universal

Economy

GDP (purchasing power parity): $11.04 billion (2012 est.); $10.92 billion (2011 est.); $10.71 billion (2010 est.); $10.61 billion (2009 est.)
GDP real growth rate: 2.5% (2012 est.); 2% (2011 est.); 1% (2010 est.)
GDP per capita (PPP): $31,300 (2012 est.); $31,400 (2011 est.); $31,100 (2010 est.)
Natural resources: salt, aragonite, timber, arable land
Agriculture products: citrus, vegetables; poultry
Industries: tourism, banking, cement, oil transshipment, salt, rum, aragonite, pharmaceuticals, spiral-welded steel pipe
Exports: $709.7 million (2011 est.); $702.4 million (2010 est.)
Exports—commodities: mineral products and salt, animal products, rum, chemicals, fruit and vegetables
Exports—partners: Singapore 26.8%, US 25.6%, Dominican Republic 11.2%, Ecuador 8.1%, Mexico 4.9%, Switzerland 4.9% (2011)
Imports: $2.854 billion (2011 est.); $2.591 billion (2010 est.)
Imports—commodities: machinery and transport equipment, manufactures, chemicals, mineral fuels; food and live animals
Imports—partners: US 25.9%, India 18.8%, South Korea 14.4%, Venezuela 9.6%, Singapore 7.8%, China 4.2% (2011)
Debt—external: $342.6 million (2004 est.)
Exchange rates: Bahamian dollars (BSD) per US dollar; 1 (2012 est.); 1 (2011 est.); 1 (2010 est.); 1 (2008)

PEOPLE

More than 80% of the Bahamian population is of African heritage. About two-thirds of the population resides on New Providence Island (the location of Nassau). Many ancestors arrived in The Bahamas when the islands served as a staging area for the slave trade in the early 1800s. Others accompanied thousands of British loyalists who fled the Ameri-

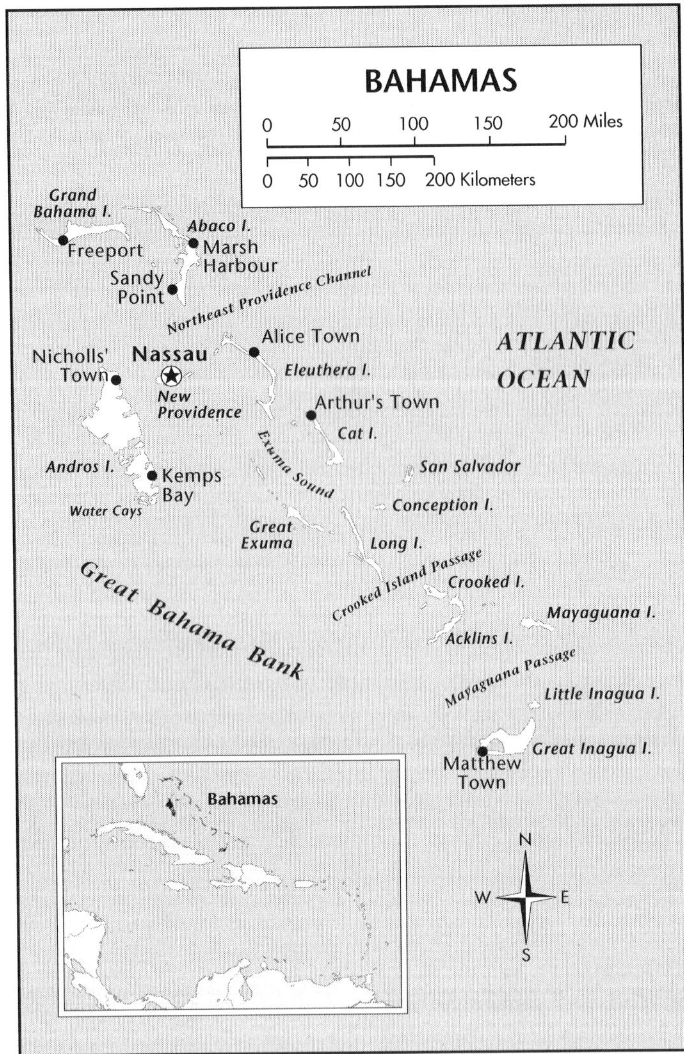

citizenship, residence, or work permits. Members of the Haitian community complained of discrimination in the job market, specifically that identity and work-permit documents were controlled by employers seeking leverage by threat of deportation. Some also complained of tactics used by immigration officials in raids of Haitian or suspected Haitian communities.

Language

The national language of The Bahamas is English, sometimes spoken with a distinctive local accent and the use of colorful local expressions.

Religion

More than 90 percent of the population professes a religion. Protestant Christian denominations including Baptists (35 percent), Anglicans (15 percent), Pentecostals (8 percent), Church of God (5 percent), Seventh-day Adventists (5 percent), and Methodists (4 percent) are in the majority; there are also significant Roman Catholic (14 percent) and Greek Orthodox populations. The local Greek Orthodox Church estimates that there are approximately 500 practicing Orthodox Christians on New Providence Island.

Smaller Jewish, Baha'i Faith, Jehovah's Witnesses, Rastafarian, and Muslim communities also are active. A small number of Bahamians and Haitians, particularly those living in the Family Islands, practice Obeah, a version of voodoo. Some members of the small resident Guyanese and Indian populations practice Hinduism and other South Asian religions. Although many unaffiliated Protestant congregations are almost exclusively black and Greek Orthodox and Jewish religious groups are almost exclusively white, most mainstream churches are integrated racially.

can colonies during the Revolutionary War. Haitians form the largest immigrant community in The Bahamas. 30,000-60,000 are estimated to be resident legally or illegally, concentrated on New Providence, Abaco, and Eleuthera islands.

School attendance is compulsory between the ages of 5 and 16. The College of The Bahamas, established in Nassau in 1974, provides programs leading to bachelors and associates degrees. Several non-Bahamian colleges also offer higher education programs in The Bahamas.

National/Racial/Ethnic Minorities

The country's racial and ethnic groups generally coexisted in a climate of peace. However, anti-Haitian prejudice and resentment regarding Haitian immigration was widespread. According to unofficial estimates, between 10 and 25 percent of the population were Haitians or persons of Haitian descent, making them the largest ethnic minority. Many persons of Haitian origin lived in shantytowns with limited sewage and garbage services, law enforcement, or other infrastructure.

Haitian children generally were granted access to education and social services, but interethnic tensions and inequities persisted. The Haitian community was characterized by high poverty, high unemployment, poor educational achievement, and poor health conditions. Haitians generally had difficulty in securing

HISTORY

In 1492, Christopher Columbus made his first landfall in the Western Hemisphere in The Bahamas. Spanish slave traders later captured native Lucayan Indians to work in gold mines in Hispaniola, and within 25 years, all Lucayans perished. In 1647, a group of English and Bermudan religious refugees, the Eleutheran Adventurers, founded the first permanent European settlement in The Bahamas and gave Eleuthera Island its name. Similar groups of settlers formed governments in The Bahamas until the islands became a British Crown Colony in 1717. The late 1600s to the early 1700s were the golden age for pirates and privateers.

Many famous pirates and privateers—including Sir Francis Drake and Blackbeard—used the islands of The Bahamas as a base. The numerous islands and islets with their complex shoals and channels provided excellent hiding places for the plundering ships near well-traveled shipping lanes. The first Royal Governor, Woodes Rogers, brought law and order to The Bahamas in 1718 when he expelled the buccaneers.

During the American Revolution, American colonists loyal to the British flag settled in The Bahamas. These Loyalists and new settlers from Britain brought Colonial building skills and agricultural expertise. Until 1834, when Britain abolished slavery, they also brought slaves, importing the ancestors of many modern Bahamians from Western Africa.

Proximity to the U.S. continued to provide opportunity for illegal shipping activity. In the course of the American Civil War, The Bahamas prospered as a center of Confederate blockade-running. During Prohibition, the islands served as a base for American rumrunners. Today, The Bahamas is a major transshipment point for narcotics on the way to the U.S.Bahamians achieved self-government through a series of constitutional and political steps, attaining internal self-government in 1964 and full independence within the Commonwealth on July 10, 1973. Since independence, The Bahamas has continued to develop into a major tourist and financial services center.

GOVERNMENT AND POLITICAL CONDITIONS

The Commonwealth of The Bahamas is a constitutional, parliamentary democracy. Prime Minister Hubert Ingraham's Free National Movement (FNM) regained control of the government in May 2007 elections that observers found to be generally free and fair.

Recent Elections

In 2007 national elections generally considered free and fair, the FNM won 23 of 41 seats in the House of Assembly and formed the new government under Hubert Ingraham. During 2011, a Boundary Commission redrew the lines for voting districts in preparation for the next elections. Members of the opposition Progressive Liberal Party and Democratic National Alliance (DNA) accused the FNM of gerrymandering and a biased process. Local civil society members criticized the government for lack of transparency in campaign finance, potentially exposing politicians to unethical influence by major contributors. There is no legislation in place to regulate election finance, which means that politicians are not required to declare campaign contributions and are not bound to utilize contributions for campaign purposes.

Participation of Women and Minorities: The House of Assembly had five elected female members; there were five appointed female senators, including its president, in the 14-seat Senate. There was one woman in the cabinet. Information on racial background was not collected, but there were several members of minorities in prominent positions in parliament and the cabinet.

Principal Government Officials

Last Updated: 1/31/2013

Governor Gen.: **Arthur FOULKES**
Prime Min.: **Perry CHRISTIE**
Dep. Prime Min.: **Philip DAVIS**
Min. of Agriculture, Marine Resources, & Local Govt.: **Alfred GRAY**
Min. of Education, Science, & Technology: **Jerome FITZGERALD**
Min. of the Environment & Housing: **Kendred DORSETT**
Min. of Finance: **Perry CHRISTIE**
Min. of Financial Services: **Ryan PINDER**
Min. of Foreign Affairs & Immigration: **Frederick MITCHELL**
Min. for Grand Bahama: **Michael DARVILLE**
Min. of Health: **Perry GOMEZ**
Min. of Labor & National Insurance: **Shane GIBSON**
Min. of Legal Affairs: **Allyson MAYNARD GIBSON**
Min. of National Security: **Bernard NOTTAGE**
Min. of Social Services: **Melanie GRIFFIN**
Min. of Tourism: **Obediah WILCHCOMBE**
Min. of Transport & Aviation: **Glenys Hanna MARTIN**
Min. of Works & Urban Development: **Philip DAVIS**
Min. of Youth, Sports, & Culture: **Daniel JOHNSON**
Attorney Gen.: **Allyson MAYNARD GIBSON**
Governor, Central Bank: **Wendy CRAIGG**
Ambassador to the US: **Cornelius SMITH**
Permanent Representative to the UN, New York: **Paulette A. BETHEL**

ECONOMY

The Bahamas is one of the wealthiest Caribbean countries with an economy heavily dependent on tourism and offshore banking. Tourism together with tourism-driven construction and manufacturing accounts for approximately 60% of GDP and directly or indirectly employs half of the archipelago's labor force.

Prior to 2006, a steady growth in tourism receipts and a boom in construction of new hotels, resorts, and residences led to solid GDP growth but since then tourism receipts have begun to drop off. The global recession in 2009 took a sizeable toll on The Bahamas, resulting in a contraction in GDP and a widening budget deficit. The decline was reversed in 2010–11 as tourism from the US and sector investment returned. Financial services constitute the second-most important sector of the Bahamian economy and, when combined with business services, account for about 36% of GDP. However, the financial sector currently is smaller than it has been in the past because of the enactment of new and stricter financial regulations in 2000 that caused many international businesses to relocate elsewhere.

Manufacturing and agriculture combined contribute approximately a 10th of GDP and show little growth, despite government incentives aimed at those sectors. Overall growth prospects in the short run rest heavily on the fortunes of the tourism sector and foreign investment in tourism related infrastructure projects. The government also completed the sale of 51% of the telecommunications company in 2011 after 14 years of trying to privatize the state-owned enterprise.

Labor Conditions

The law prohibits the employment of children under age 14 for industrial work or work during school hours. Children under age 16 may not work at night. There was no legal minimum age for employment in other sectors. Occupational health and safety restrictions apply to all younger workers. The Ministry of Labor and Social Development is responsible for enforcing laws regulating working hours for children, as well as occupational health and safety restrictions. Some children as young as 12 years old worked part time in service jobs in the evenings after school.

The minimum wage was B$4.45 ($4.45) per hour for hourly workers, B$35 ($35) per day for daily workers, and B$150 ($150) per week for weekly-paid workers. The law provides for a 40-hour workweek, a 24-hour rest period, and time-and-a-half payment for hours worked beyond the standard workweek. The law stipulates paid annual holidays and does not provide for compulsory overtime.

U.S.-BAHAMIAN RELATIONS

The United States established diplomatic relations with The Bahamas in 1973 following its independence from the United Kingdom. As a neighbor, The Bahamas and its political stability are especially important to the United States. The U.S. and the Bahamian Government have worked together on reducing crime and addressing illegal migration issues. With the closest island only 45 miles from the coast of Florida, The Bahamas often is used as a gateway for drugs, weapons and illegal aliens bound for the United States.

The United States and The Bahamas cooperate closely to address these threats. U.S. assistance and resources have been essential to Bahamian efforts to mitigate the persistent flow of illegal narcotics, guns, and migrants through the archipelago. The United States and The Bahamas also actively cooperate on law enforcement, civil aviation, marine research, meteorology, and agricultural issues. The U.S. Navy operates an underwater research facility on Andros Island.

U.S. Assistance to The Bahamas

U.S. foreign assistance to The Bahamas supports the key goals of bolstering law enforcement and counternarcotics efforts, including demand reduction, strengthening the criminal justice system, and improving interdiction capabilities. Regional security programs complement bilateral aid, providing further assistance for law enforcement, citizen safety, and rule-of-law programs. Additional support provided through the President's Emergency Plan for AIDS Relief (PEPFAR) funds programs in HIV prevention and awareness and stigma mitigation.

Bilateral Economic Relations

The Bahamian economy is driven by tourism and financial services. Most of the U.S.-affiliated businesses operating in The Bahamas are associated with tourism and banking. Historically, a majority of the 4-5 million tourists visiting The Bahamas each year have been from the United States. The Bahamas imports nearly all its food and manufactured goods from the United States, although it is beginning to diversify its supply chain to include Asian and Latin American suppliers. U.S. goods and services tend to be favored by Bahamians due to cultural similarities and exposure to U.S. advertising. Due to its dependence on U.S. tourism and trade, the Bahamian economy is affected by U.S. economic performance. The Bahamas is a beneficiary of the U.S.-Caribbean Basin Trade Partnership Act. The U.S. Department of Homeland Security's Bureau of Customs and Border Protection maintains "preclearance" facilities at the airports in Nassau and Freeport. Travelers to the U.S., including business people and tourists, are interviewed and inspected before departure, allowing faster connection times in the U.S.

The Bahamas' Membership in International Organizations

The Bahamas and the United States belong to a number of the same international organizations, including the United Nations, Organization of American States, International Monetary Fund, International Maritime Organization, and the World Bank. The Bahamas also is an observer to the World Trade Organization.

Bilateral Representation

The Bahamas maintains an embassy in the United States at 2220 Massachusetts Ave., NW, Washington, DC 20008 (tel: 202-319-2660).

Principal U.S. Embassy Officials

Last Updated: 1/14/2013

NASSAU (E) #42 Queen Street;PO: Box N-8197; Nassau, 242-322-1181,

Fax 242-328-7838 (GSO), Workweek: Mon-Thurs 8:00am-5:00pm; Fri 8:00am-3:30pm, Website: http://nassau.usembassy.gov/

DCM OMS:	Sandra Castillo
AMB OMS:	Mary Cross
DHS/CBP:	R. Allen Smith
DHS/ICE:	Elizabeth Conner
DHS/TSA:	Lawrence Mizell
FM:	Leonardo Moxey
HRO:	Kathryn Dare Morgan
MGT:	Cheryl Moore
MLO/ODC:	LCDR Samuel Wartell
NAS/INL:	David Jea
OMS:	Elizabeth Tucker
POL/ECON:	Alex Sokoloff
POSHO:	Nazima Razick
USCS OIC:	LCDR Louie C. Parks Jr..
AMB:	Vacant
CON:	Acting DCM John Armstrong
DCM:	Charge John Dinkelman
PAO:	Erica Thibault
GSO:	Nazima Razick
RSO:	Bradley Lynn
CLO:	Thomas Garcia
DEA:	James Connolly
EEO:	Sandra Castillo
FMO:	Anthony Bibbo
ICASS Chair:	David Jea
IMO:	Will Lanzet
ISO:	Sherri Hummel
ISSO:	Will Lanzet
LEGATT:	William Nicholson
State ICASS:	David Jea

Other Contact Information

U.S. Department of Commerce International Trade Administration Office of Latin America and the Caribbean
14th and Constitution, NW
Washington, DC 20230
Tel: 202-482-0704; 800-USA-TRADE
Fax: 202-482-0464

Caribbean/Latin American Action
1818 N Street, NW, Suite 310
Washington, DC 20036
Tel: 202-466-7464
Fax: 202-822-00:75

TRAVEL

Consular Information Sheet

November 30, 2010

Country Description: The Bahamas is a developed, English-speaking Caribbean nation composed of hundreds of islands covering a territory approximately the size of California. Tourism and financial services comprise the two largest sectors of the economy. Independent from the United Kingdom since 1973, the Bahamas is a Commonwealth nation with a century-old democratic tradition. The capital, Nassau, is located on New Providence Island.

Smart Traveler Enrollment Program (STEP)/Embassy Location: If you are going to work, live, or travel abroad, please take the time to tell the local U.S. Embassy about your trip. If you enroll, the Embassy can keep you up to date with important safety and security announcements. It will also help your friends and family get in touch with you in an emergency. The U.S. Embassy is located at Queen Street #19. Telephone: 242-322-1181. Emergency after-hours telephone: 242-357-7004. Facsimile: 242-356-7174

Entry Requirements: All U.S. citizens are required to present a valid U.S. passport in order to enter or re-enter the United States when travelling be air. U.S. citizens do not need visas for short trips to The Bahamas for tourist/business purposes. It is important to note that although the Bahamian government only requires proof of citizenship and identity in order to enter The Bahamas, the U.S. government requires that Americans have a valid passport in order to fly home. Most airlines will not permit a U.S. citizen to fly to The Bahamas without a valid U.S. passport and risk getting stranded.

Travel by Sea: Americans may enter the Unites States from The Bahamas by sea using a passport, passport card, or other Western Hemisphere Travel Initiative (WHTI) compliant document. Travelers arriving via private watercraft are charged docking fees.

We strongly encourage all American citizen travelers to apply for a U.S. passport or passport card well in advance of anticipated travel. American citizens can visit travel.state.gov or call 1-877-4USA-PPT (1-877-487-2778) for information on how to apply for their passports. U.S. citizens planning on an extended stay should be prepared to present proof or evidence of financial solvency upon entry to The Bahamas. Visit the Embassy of The Bahamas website for the most current visa information. The Bahamian Ministry of Health states there are no travel restrictions for persons with HIV entering The Bahamas.

Safety and Security: The water sports and scooter rental industries in The Bahamas are not carefully regulated. Every year people are killed or injured due to improper, careless, or reckless operation of scooters, jet-skis, and personal watercraft or scuba/snorkeling equipment. Visitors should rent equipment only from reputable operators, and should insist on sufficient training before using the equipment. There have been reports that some operators do not actually provide insurance coverage even when the renter opted (and paid) for insurance coverage. Visitors should insist on seeing proof that operators have sufficient medical and liability insurance.

Visitors should exercise caution and good judgment at all times. Engaging in high-risk behavior such as excessive consumption of alcohol can ultimately be dangerous as it greatly increases the vulnerability of an individual to accidents or opportunistic crime. Visitors should not accept rides from strangers or from unlicensed taxi drivers.

For the latest security information, Americans traveling abroad should regularly monitor the Department's web site, where the current Worldwide Caution Travel Alert, Travel Warnings and other Travel Alerts can be found. Up-to-date information on safety and security can also be obtained by calling 1-888-407-4747 toll-free in the U.S. and Canada, or for callers outside the U.S. and Canada, a regular toll line at 1-202-501-4444.

Crime: The Bahamas has a high crime rate. New Providence Island in particular has experienced a spike in crime that has adversely affected the traveling public. Pickpocketing and theft remain the most common crimes perpetrated against tourists. However, there has been a spate of more violent criminal activity in 2009. Three separate groups of tourists were held at gunpoint and robbed at popular tourist sites in and near Nassau; each of these incidents occurred during daylight hours and involved groups of more than eight persons. Several other groups of tourists allegedly were victims of armed robbery at more remote locations. The U.S. Embassy has received reports of assaults, including sexual assaults, in diverse areas such as in casinos, outside hotels, or on cruise ships. In several incidents the victim had reportedly been drugged. The Bahamas has the highest incidence of rape in the Caribbean according to a 2007 United Nations report on crime, violence, and development trends. Much of the violent crime occurs outside of areas frequented by tourists, such as the "over-the-hill" section of Nassau. Two American citizens were murdered in Nassau in 2009, both allegedly in residential areas. Home break-ins, theft, and robbery are not confined to any specific part of the island. The upsurge in criminal activity has also led to incidents which, while not directed at tourists, could place innocent bystanders at risk. An altercation at a major resort resulted in the shooting of two security officers, while several daytime robberies in Nassau led to exchanges of gunfire on busy streets.

Criminal activity in the outlying family islands does occur, but on a much lesser degree than on New Providence Island. The Embassy has received reports of burglaries and thefts, especially thefts of boats and/or outboard motors on Abaco and Bimini. The Embassy has not received reports of harassment or hate crimes motivated by race, religion, or citizenship. There have been reports of harassment of persons based on sexual orientation. In addition, women have reported incidents of verbal harassment and unwanted attention.

Counterfeit and pirated goods are available in The Bahamas. Transactions involving such products may be illegal under Bahamian law, even though those laws are not routinely enforced. In addition, bringing such products into the United States may result in forfeitures and/or fines. Some organized crime activity is believed to occur in The Bahamas, primarily related to the illegal importation and smuggling of illicit drugs or human trafficking. The Bahamas, due to its numerous uninhabited islands and cays, has historically been favored by smugglers and pirates. Most visitors to The Bahamas would not have noticeable interaction with organized crime elements; however, persons who operate their own water craft or air craft should be alert to the possibility of encountering similar vessels operated by smugglers engaged in illicit activities on the open seas or air space in or near The Bahamas.

Visitors are advised to report crime to the Royal Bahamas Police Force as quickly as possible. Early reports frequently improve the likelihood of identifying and apprehending suspected perpetrators In general, the Royal Bahamian Police Force is responsive to reports of crime and takes the threat of crime against tourists very seriously. However, the police response is sometimes slowed by a lack of resources or by the physical constraints imposed by geography and infrastructure.

Victims of Crime: If you or someone you know becomes the victim of a crime abroad, you should contact the local police and the nearest U.S. embassy or consulate. If your passport is stolen they can help you replace it. For violent crimes such as assault and rape, they can help you find appropriate medical care, contact family members or friends, and help them send you money if you need it. Although the investigation and prosecution of the crime are solely the responsibility of local authorities, consular officers can help you to understand the local criminal justice process and to find an attorney if you need one. The local equivalent to the "911" emergency line in the Bahamas is 919 or 911.

Criminal Penalties: While in a foreign country, a U.S. citizen is subject to that country's laws and regulations, which sometimes differ significantly from those in the United States and may not afford the protections available to the individual under U.S. law. Penalties for breaking the law can be more severe than in the United States for similar offenses. Engaging in sexual conduct with children or using or disseminating child pornography in a foreign country is a crime prosecutable in the United States. Persons violating Bahamian laws, even unknowingly, may be expelled, arrested, or imprisoned.

Customs Regulations: The Bahamas' customs authorities may enforce strict regulations concerning temporary importation or exportation of firearms. It is advisable to contact the Embassy of the Commonwealth of the Bahamas in Washington or one of the Bahamian consulates in the U.S. for specific information regarding customs requirements. Tourists who arrive by private boat are required to declare firearms to Bahamian Customs and leave firearms on the boat while in the Bahamas.

Boating/Fishing: Boaters should be aware that long-line fishing in Bahamian waters is illegal. All long-line fishing gear is required to be stowed below deck while transiting through Bahamian waters. Fishermen should note that stiff penalties are imposed for catching crawfish (lobster) or other marine life out of season or in protected areas.

Wildlife: Hunting of certain types of fowl in The Bahamas requires a special license and may only be done in season. All other hunting is prohibited in The Bahamas. A number of endangered and/or protected species reside in The Bahamas. U.S. citizens should not disturb, harass, or otherwise threaten wildlife, including species that may be huntable in the U.S. Americans have been arrested and prosecuted in The Bahamas for disturbing and/or hunting wild animals. Specific information is available from the Bahamian Ministry of Agriculture and Marine Resources.

Time-Shares: U.S. citizens should exercise caution when considering time-share investments and be aware of the aggressive tactics used by some time-share sales representatives. Bahamian law allows time-share purchasers five days to cancel the contract for full reimbursement. Disputes that arise after that period can be very time-consuming and expensive to resolve through the local legal system.

Hurricanes: The Bahamas, like all countries in the Caribbean basin, is vulnerable to hurricanes. Hurricane season officially runs from June 1 to November 30, although hurricanes have been known to occur outside that time period. Visitors to the Bahamas during hurricane season are advised to monitor weather reports in order to be prepared for any potential threats.

Be aware that airports and seaports invariably cease operations well before a predicted storm actually arrives, and that seats on most commercial transportation are sold out far in advance. General information about disaster preparedness is available via the Internet from the U.S. Federal Emergency Management Agency (FEMA) at http://www.fema.gov.

Medical Facilities and Health Information: Adequate medical care is available on New Providence and Grand Bahama islands. Medical care is more limited elsewhere. Serious health problems requiring hospitalization and/or medical evacuation to the United States can cost tens of thousands of dollars, and air ambulance companies generally require payment or an insurer's guarantee of payment up front. Bahamian physicians and hospitals do not usually accept U.S. medical insurance policies and typically expect immediate cash payment for professional services.

There is a chronic shortage of blood at Princess Margaret Hospital in Nassau, where most emergency surgery is performed. Travelers with rare blood types should know the names and locations of possible blood donors should the need arise. The Lyford Cay Hospital has a hyperbaric chamber for treatment of decompression illness. Ambulance service is available, but may not be able to respond quickly in the event of a major emergency or disaster. Information on vaccinations and other health precautions, such as safe food and water precautions and insect bite protection, may be obtained from the Centers for Disease Control and Prevention's hotline for international travelers at 1-877-FYI-TRIP (1-877-394-8747) or via the CDC's website at http://wwwn.cdc.gov/travel. For information about outbreaks of infectious diseases abroad, consult the World Health Organization's (WHO) web site at http://www.who.int/en. Further health information for travelers is available at http://www.who.int/ith/en.

Medical Insurance: You can't assume your insurance will go with you when you travel. It's very important to find out BEFORE you leave. You need to ask your insurance company two questions: Does my policy apply when I'm out of the U.S.? Will it cover emergencies like a trip to a foreign hospital or an evacuation? In many places, doctors and hospitals still expect payment in cash at the time of service. Your regular U.S. health insurance may not cover doctors' and hospital visits in other countries. If your policy doesn't go with you when you travel, it's a very good idea to take out another one for your trip.

Traffic Safety and Road Conditions: While in a foreign country, U.S. citizens may encounter road conditions that differ significantly from those in the United States. The information below concerning the Bahamas is provided for general reference only, and may not be totally accurate in a particular location or circumstance.

Traffic in The Bahamas moves on the left side of the roadway (i.e. opposite from that in the United States). Traffic congestion in Nassau is endemic, and drivers occasionally display aggressive tendencies. Round-abouts are a common feature. Some major streets do not have adequate shoulders or even passable sidewalks, compelling pedestrians to walk in the right-of-way. Motorcyclists frequently swerve through slow traffic and drive between lanes of moving vehicles. It is not uncommon to see poorly maintained or excessively loaded vehicles on roadways. Rural roads can be narrow, winding, and in poor condition.

Flooding frequently occurs on roads in many areas, including Nassau and Freeport, during and after storms. Drivers should be alert for unmarked or poorly marked construction zones. Travel by moped or bicycle can be quite hazardous, especially in the heavy traffic conditions prevalent in Nassau. Visitors should exercise appropriate caution when renting vehicles in The Bahamas. Those who choose to ride a moped or bicycle in particular should follow Bahamian helmet law and drive very defensively. Accidents involving U.S. tourists on motorbikes have resulted in severe injuries and fatalities.

Pedestrians need to remember that vehicular traffic comes from the right, as many tourists have been struck by cars after failing to check properly for oncoming traffic.

Emergency ambulance service is generally available and can be reached by dialing 911. Roadside assistance is also widely available through private towing services, listed in the phone book. For specific information concerning driver's permits, vehicle inspection, road tax, and mandatory insurance in the Bahamas, please contact the Bahamas Tourist Board in New York at http://bahamas.com, (tel.1-800-823-3136).

Aviation Safety Oversight: The U.S. Federal Aviation Administration

(FAA) has assessed the Government of the Bahamas' Civil Aviation Authority as being in compliance with International Civil Aviation Organization (ICAO) aviation safety standards for oversight of the Bahamas' air carrier operations. For more information, travelers may visit the FAA's web site at http://www.faa.gov.

Children's Issues: For information on intercountry adoption of children and international parental child abduction, see the Office of Children's Issues website at http://travel.state.gov.

Intercountry Adoption

December 2008

The information in this section has been edited from the latest report available as of February 2013 from the State Department Bureau of Consular Affairs, Office of Overseas Citizens Services. For more information, please read the *Intercountry Adoption* section of this book and review current reports online at http://adoption.state.gov.

The Bahamas is not party to the Hague Convention on Protection of Children and Co-operation in Respect of Intercountry Adoption (Hague Adoption Convention). Therefore, when the Hague Adoption Convention entered into force for the United States on April 1, 2008, intercountry adoption processing for The Bahamas did not change. Bahamian law allows adoption by any person with legal status in The Bahamas (even foreign tourists). However, the number of children available for adoption is very small and the waiting list for prospective adoptive parents is very long. Bahamian citizens or legal permanent residents are generally given preference in adopting children, especially if they have a blood relationship to the child.

Who Can Adopt? To bring an adopted child to United States from The Bahamas, you must be found eligible to adopt by the U.S. Government. The U.S. Government agency responsible for making this determination is the Department of Homeland Security, U.S. Citizenship and Immigration Services (USCIS).

Residency Requirements: There are no residency requirements for prospective adoptive parents.

Age Requirements: At least one prospective adoptive parent must be at minimum 25 years of age and more than 21 years older than the child except for cases of relative adoption. The Bahamas requires relatives who pursue adoption to be at least 18 years of age.

Marriage Requirements: Single people as well as married couples may adopt. According to the laws of The Bahamas it is extremely difficult for single men to adopt girls, though the courts may make exceptions based on special circumstances.

Who Can Be Adopted? The Bahamas has specific requirements that a child must meet in order to be eligible for adoption. You cannot adopt a child in The Bahamas unless he or she meets the requirements outlined below.

Eligibility Requirements: Children may be adopted by foreigners, if they are orphans (both or only known parent deceased), if they have been abandoned (the court must be satisfied that parents cannot be found), or released for adoption by their parents or legal guardian (if the child was born out-of-wedlock, only the mother needs to release the child for adoption).

Age Requirements: A child must be at least 6 weeks old to be eligible for release for adoption.

The Bahamas Adoption Authority: The Department of Social Services in the Ministry of Social Services and Community Development.

The Process: The first step in adopting a child from The Bahamas is usually to select a licensed agency in the United States that can help with your adoption. Adoption service providers must be licensed by the U.S. state in which they operate. To bring an adopted child from The Bahamas to the United States, you must apply to be found eligible to adopt (Form I-600A) by the U.S. Government, Department of Homeland Security, U.S. Citizenship and Immigration Services (USCIS). If you are eligible to adopt, and a child is available for intercountry adoption, the central adoption authority in The Bahamas will provide you with a referral to a child. The child must be eligible to be adopted according to The Bahamas requirements, as described in the Who Can be Adopted section. The child must also meet the definition of an orphan under U.S. law.

Role of the Adoption Authority: The Department of Social Services acts as the representative of the child's interests and a lawyer is required to guide the process through the Supreme Court.

Time Frame: The Bahamian adoption process typically takes a minimum of three months to complete, though can take longer.

Adoption Fees: The U.S. Embassy in The Bahamas discourages the payment of any fees that are not properly receipted, "donations," or "expediting" fees, that may be requested from prospective adoptive parents. Such fees have the appearance of "buying" a baby and put all future adoptions in The Bahamas. The Bahamian government does not charge fees for adoptions. Attorneys will charge fees ranging from $1,500 to $2,000 which covers the work involved and the filing fees. The prospective adoptive parent (s) will also have to pay the costs of the guardian ad litem.

Documents Required: Prospective adoptive parents must provide the following list of documents, through a Bahamian attorney, to the Supreme Court:

- Originating Summons
- Notice of Hearing of the Originating Summons

- Consent to Act as the Guardian Ad Litem
- Consent of the birth mother and/ or father or legal Guardian
- Affidavit of Applicants–the truth of the Statement in Support of the Application
- Annex to Statement in Support of Application
- Statement in Support of Application exhibits—birth certificate of applicant(s) Marriage certificate of the prospective adoptive parent(s)
- First 5 pages of passport applicant(s)
- Undertaking to pay costs of the Guardian Ad Litem
- Appearance Report that is prepared by the Guardian Ad Litem
- Letter of listing officer with Notice of Hearing for an Adoption Summons to go before the Judge on the Adoption. The documents number 1—8 are filed and within fourteen (14) days of the date of the Originating Summons

After you finalize the adoption (or gain legal custody) in The Bahamas, the U.S Government, Department of Homeland Security, U.S. Citizenship and Immigration Services (USCIS) MUST determine whether the child is eligible under U.S. law to be adopted (Form I-600).

For detailed and updated information on these requirements, please review the Intercountry Adoption section of this publication and visit the USCIS Intercountry Adoption website at http://adoption.state.gov.

Bringing Your Child Home: Once your adoption is complete (or you have obtained legal custody of the child), there are a few more steps to take before you can head home. Specifically, you need to apply for several documents for your child before he or she can travel to the United States, such as a birth certificate, a passport or travel document for your child from the country in which he or she was born, and a U.S. Immigration Visa. For detailed and updated information on how to obtain these documents, review the Intercountry Adoption section on this publication and visit the USCIS Intercountry Adoption website at http://adoption.state.gov.

Child Citizenship Act: For adoptions finalized abroad, the Child Citizenship Act of 2000 allows your new child to acquire American citizenship automatically when he or she enters the United States as lawful permanent residents.

For adoptions finalized in the United States, the Child Citizenship Act of 2000 allows your new child to acquire American citizenship automatically when the court in the United States issues the final adoption decree. To learn more, review the *Intercountry Adoption* section on this publication and visit the USCIS Intercountry Adoption website at http://adoption.state.gov.

U.S. Embassy Nassau
42 Queen Street
Nassau
Phone: (242) 322-1181
Fax: (242) 356-7174

The Bahamas' Adoption Authority
Tel: 242-356-0765
Fax: 242-323-3883

Embassy of The Bahamas
2220 Massachusetts Ave NW,
Washington, DC 20008
Phone: (202) 319-2660

Office of Children's Issues
U.S. Department of State
2201 C Street, NW
SA-29
Washington, DC 20520
Tel: 1-888-407-4747
E-mail: AskCI@state.gov
http://adoption.state.gov

For questions about immigration procedures, call the National Customer Service Center (NCSC) 1-800-375-5283 (TTY 1-800-767-1833).

International Parental Child Abduction

January 2012

The information in this section has been edited from the latest report available as of February 2013 from the State Department Bureau of Consular Affairs, Office of Overseas Citizens Services. For more information, please read the *International Parental Child Abduction* section of this book and check for updated reports online at www.travel.state.gov/abduction.

Disclaimer: The information in this flyer relating to the legal requirements of specific foreign countries is provided for general information only. Questions involving interpretation of specific foreign laws should be addressed to foreign legal counsel.

General Information: The Hague Convention on the Civil Aspects of International Child Abduction (the "Hague Convention") came into force between the United States and The Bahamas on January 1, 1994. Therefore, Hague Convention provisions for return would apply to children abducted or retained after January 1, 1994. Parents and legal guardians of children taken to The Bahamas prior to January 1, 1994, may still submit applications for access to the child under the Hague Convention in some cases.

The Bahamas is currently listed as a country of concern in the State Department's Compliance Report, which is submitted to Congress on a yearly basis, for their implementation of the Hague Convention for the return of children to the United States. Hague applications sent to The Bahamas for return of abducted children have not been acted on for years; Bahamian courts have then refused to order the return of abducted children on the grounds that they have become acclimated to life in The Bahamas.

Please Note: Submit your completed, signed application as soon as possible. Do not wait to get a custody order to begin the application process. A custody order issued after the taking or retention (a "chasing order") is not relevant to your Hague case and may, in fact, complicate it. For more information, please read the *International Parental Child Abduction* section of this book and review current reports online at www.travel.state.gov/abduction.

Central Authority
Ministry of Foreign Affairs
P O Box N-3746
East Hill Street
Nassau, New Providence
The Bahamas
Tel: (242) 322-7624/5; (242) 322-7590; (242) 328-1808
Fax: (242) 328-8212; (242) 326-2123

Legal Counsel: You will require an attorney to file the Hague application with the court and to represent your interests in hearings on your application. You will be required to give evidence as to the circumstances of your child's removal or retention, usually in the form of a sworn statement or affidavit. Under the Convention, The Bahamas is not obligated to pay for or in any way assume any costs resulting from court proceedings.

Legal assistance is available, however. Qualification for assistance is based on economic need. Information regarding availability for legal assistance may be obtained from the Central Authority office.

Criminal Remedies: For information on possible criminal remedies, please contact your local law enforcement authorities or the nearest office of the Federal Bureau of Investigation. Information is also available on the Internet at the web site of the U.S. Department of Justice, Office of Juvenile Justice and Delinquency Prevention at http://www.ojjdp.ncjrs.org. Please note that criminal charges may complicate a Hague Convention case. Contact the country officer in the Office of Children's Issues for specific information.

Passports for Minors and the Children's Passport Issuance Alert Program: For more information on these topics, see the *International Parental Child Abduction* section of this publication and review current reports from the U.S. Department of State at www.travel.state.gov/abduction. For further information on international parental child abduction, contact the Office of Children's Issues, U.S. Department of State at 1-888-407-4747 or visit its web site on the Internet at http://travel.state.gov.

You may also direct inquiries to: Office of Children's Issues, U.S. Department of State, Washington, DC 20520-4811; Phone: (202) 736-9090; Fax: (202) 312-9743.

BAHRAIN

Compiled from publications that were available as of February 2013 from the U.S. Department of State, the U.S. Department of Commerce, and the Central Intelligence Agency (CIA). See the introduction to this set for explanatory notes.

Official Name:
Kingdom of Bahrain

PROFILE

Geography

Area: total: 760 sq km; country comparison to the world: 188; land: 760 sq km; water: 0 sq km
Major cities: Manama (capital) 163,000 (2009)
Climate: arid; mild, pleasant winters; very hot, humid summers
Terrain: mostly low desert plain rising gently to low central escarpment

People

Nationality: noun: Bahraini(s); adjective: Bahraini
Population: 1,248,348
Population growth rate: 2.652% (2012 est.)
Ethnic groups: Bahraini 46%, non-Bahraini 54% (2010 census)
Religions: Muslim (Shia and Sunni) 81.2%, Christian 9%, other 9.8% (2001 census)
Languages: Arabic (official), English, Farsi, Urdu
Literacy: definition: age 15 and over can read and write; total population: 94.6%; male: 96.1%; female: 91.6% (2010 census)
Health: life expectancy at birth: total population: 78.29 years; male: 76.16 years; female: 80.48 years (2012 est.); Infant mortality rate: total: 10.2 deaths/1,000 live births; male: 11.43 deaths/1,000 live births; female: 8.92 deaths/1,000 live births (2012 est.)
Unemployment rate: 15% (2005 est.)
Work force: 705,900 (2012 est.)

Government

Type: constitutional monarchy
Independence: 15 August 1971
Constitution: adopted 14 February 2002
Political subdivisions: 5 governorates; Asamah, Janubiyah, Muharraq, Shamaliyah, Wasat
Suffrage: 20 years of age; universal; note—Bahraini Cabinet in May 2011 endorsed a draft law lowering eligibility to 18 years

Economy

GDP (purchasing power parity): $32.44 billion (2012 est.); $31.5 billion (2011 est.); $30.95 billion (2010 est.); $29.61 billion (2009 est.)
GDP real growth rate: 2% (2012 est.); 1.8% (2011 est.); 4.5% (2010 est.); 3.1% (2009 est.)
GDP per capita (PPP): $28,200 (2012 est.); $27,900 (2011 est.); $28,000 (2010 est.); $28,500 (2009 est.)
Natural resources: oil, associated and nonassociated natural gas, fish, pearls
Agriculture products: fruit, vegetables; poultry, dairy products; shrimp, fish
Industries: petroleum processing and refining, aluminum smelting, iron pelletization, fertilizers, Islamic and offshore banking, insurance, ship repairing, tourism
Exports: $20.95 billion (2012 est.); $19.91 billion (2011 est.)
Exports—commodities: petroleum and petroleum products, aluminum, textiles
Exports—partners: Saudi Arabia 3.3%, UAE 2.2%, Japan 2%, India 1.9% (2011)
Imports: $14.95 billion (2012 est.); $12.11 billion (2011 est.)
Imports—commodities: crude oil, machinery, chemicals
Imports—partners: Saudi Arabia 27.5%, US 10.2%, India 7.9%, China 7.4%, Brazil 5.8%, Germany 4.7% (2011)
Debt—external: $14.93 billion (31 December 2011 est.); $14.5 billion (31 December 2010 est.)
Exchange rates: Bahraini dinars (BHD) per US dollar; 0.376 (2012 est.) ; 0.376 (2011 est.); 0.376 (2010 est.); 0.376 (2009); 0.376 (2008)

PEOPLE

Bahrain is one of the most densely populated countries in the world; nearly 90% of the population lives in the two principal cities of Manama and Al Muharraq. Approximately 66% of the indigenous population is

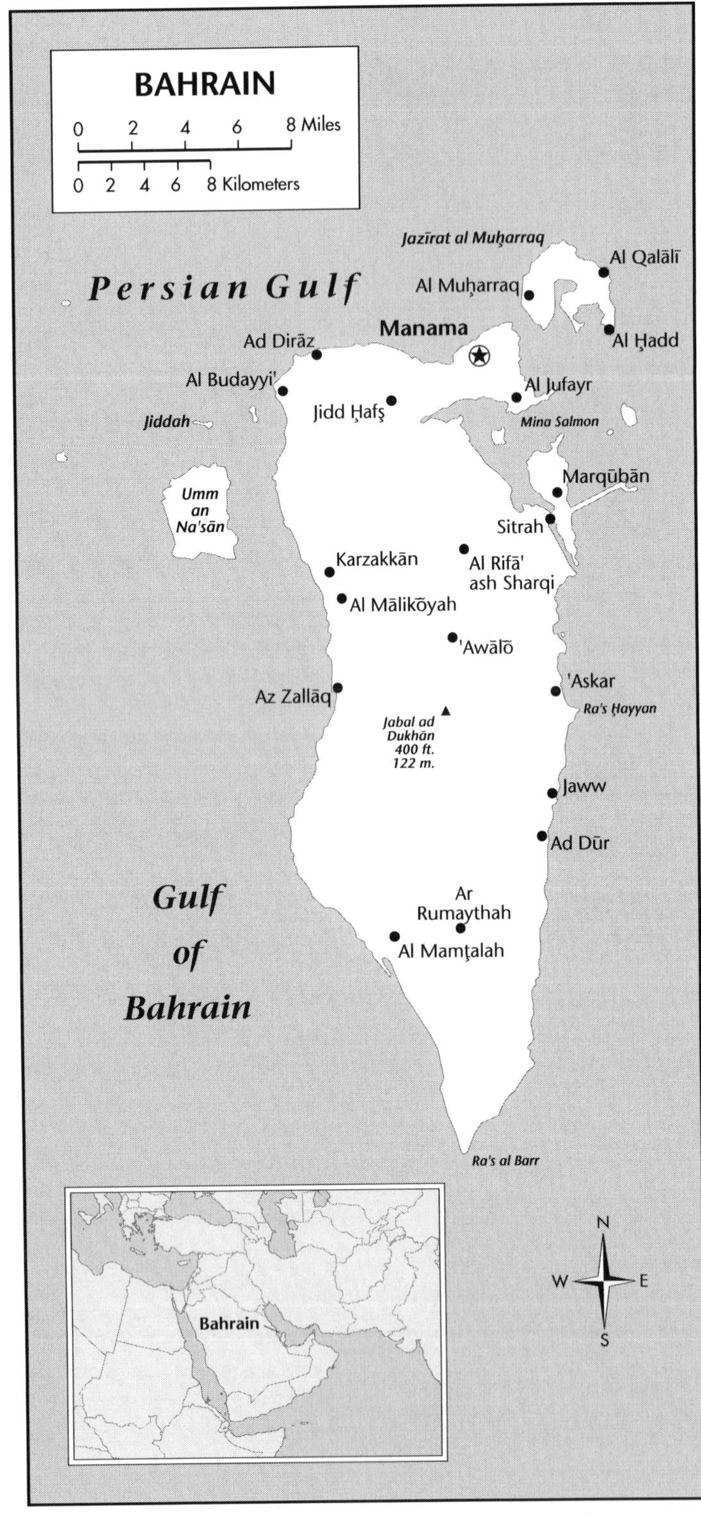

originally from the Arabian Peninsula and Iran. Bahrain has a sizeable foreign labor force. The government's policies on naturalization remain controversial. In June 2002, the King issued a decree allowing citizens of the Gulf Cooperation Council (GCC) to take up dual Bahraini nationality. Opposition political groups charge that the government is granting citizenship to foreign nationals who have served in the Bahraini armed forces and security services to alter the demographic balance of the country, which is primarily Shi'a. According to passport officials, about 40,000 individuals have been naturalized over the past 50 years.

Education

Bahrain has invested its oil revenues in developing an advanced educational system. The first public schools for girls and boys were opened in the 1920s. The government continues to pay for all schooling costs. Although school attendance is not compulsory, primary and secondary attendance rates are high, and literacy rates are currently among the highest in the region. Higher education is available for secondary school graduates at the Bahrain University, Arabian Gulf University and specialized institutes including the College of Health Sciences — operating under the direction of the Ministry of Health — which trains physicians, nurses, pharmacists, and paramedics. The government has identified providing educational services to the Gulf Cooperation Council as a potential economic growth area, and is actively working to establish Bahrain as a regional center for higher education.

Language

The official language of Bahrain is Arabic, but English is widely spoken as the standard language of business and higher education. Hindi, Farsi, Urdu, and various languages of South Asia are common.

Religion

The citizen population, which constitutes slightly less than half of the residents, is 99 percent Muslim. Jews, Christians, Hindus, and Baha'is constitute the remaining 1 percent. Muslims belong to the Shia and Sunni branches of Islam. The government does not publish statistics regarding the sectarian breakdown among Shia and Sunni citizens, although many international organizations and media outlets have stated that Shia represent a majority of the country's citizen population.

As of 2008, there were approximately 350 licensed Sunni mosques, while the number of licensed Shia places of worship included 863 mosques and 589 matams. In newer developments such as Hamad Town and Isa Town, which often have mixed Shia and Sunni populations, there tended to be a disproportionate number of Sunni mosques.

Foreigners, mostly from South Asia and from other Arab countries, constitute an estimated 54 percent of the population. Approximately half of resident foreigners are non-Muslim, including Hindus, Buddhists, Christians (primarily Roman Catholic, Protestant, Syrian Orthodox, and Mar Thoma from South India), Baha'is, and Sikhs.

HISTORY

The site of the ancient Bronze Age civilization of Dilmun, Bahrain was an important center linking trade routes between Mesopotamia and the Indus Valley as early as 5,000 years ago. The Dilmun civilization began to decline about 2,000 B.C. as trade from India was cut off. From 750 B.C. on, Assyrian kings repeatedly claimed sovereignty over the islands. Shortly after 600 B.C., Dilmun was formally incorporated into the new Babylonian empire. There are no historical references to Bahrain until Alexander the Great's arrival in the Gulf in the 4th century B.C. Although Bahrain was ruled variously by the Arab tribes of Bani Wa'el and Persian governors, Bahrain continued to be known by its Greek name Tylos until the 7th century, when many of its inhabitants converted to Islam. A regional pearling and trade center, Bahrain came under the control of the Ummayad Caliphs of Syria, the Abbasid Caliphs of Baghdad, Persian, Omani and Portuguese forces at various times from the 7th century until the Al Khalifa family, a branch of the Bani Utbah tribe that have ruled Bahrain since the 18th century, succeeded in capturing Bahrain from a Persian garrison controlling the islands in 1783.

In the 1830s the Al Khalifa family signed the first of many treaties establishing Bahrain as a British Protectorate. Similar to the binding treaties of protection entered into by other Persian Gulf principalities, the agreements entered into by the Al Khalifas prohibited them from disposing of territory and entering into relationships with any foreign government without British consent in exchange for British protection against the threat of military attack from Ottoman Turkey. The main British naval base in the region was moved to Bahrain in 1935 shortly after the start of large-scale oil production.

In 1968, when the British Government announced its decision (reaffirmed in March 1971) to end the treaty relationships with the Persian Gulf sheikdoms, Bahrain initially joined the other eight states (Qatar and the seven Trucial Sheikhdoms now the United Arab Emirates) under British protection in an effort to form a union of Arab emirates. The nine sheikhdoms still had not agreed on terms of union by 1971, however, prompting Bahrain to declare itself fully independent on August 15, 1971.

Bahrain promulgated a constitution and elected its first parliament in 1973, but just 2 years later, in August 1975, the Amir disbanded the National Assembly after it attempted to legislate the end of Al-Khalifa rule and the expulsion of the U.S. Navy from Bahrain. In the 1990s, Bahrain suffered from repeated incidents of political violence stemming from the disaffection of the Shi'a majority.

In response, the Amir instituted the first Bahraini cabinet change in 20 years in 1995 and also increased the membership of the Consultative Council, which he had created in 1993 to provide advice and opinion on legislation proposed by the cabinet and, in certain cases, suggest new laws on its own, from 30 to 40 the following year. These steps led to an initial decline in violent incidents, but in early 1996 a number of hotels and restaurants were bombed, resulting in several fatalities.

Over 1,000 people were arrested and held in detention without trial in connection with these disturbances. The government has since released these individuals.

GOVERNMENT AND POLITICAL CONDITIONS

Bahrain is a monarchy. Noncitizens make up slightly more than half of the population. King Hamad Bin Isa Al-Khalifa, the head of state, appoints the cabinet of ministers; approximately half are members of the Sunni Al-Khalifa ruling family. The parliament consists of an appointed upper house (the Shura Council) and the elected Council of Representatives. Approximately 17 percent of eligible voters participated in parliamentary by-elections on September 24. Independent human rights organizations did not consider these elections to be free and fair; a boycott by opposition political societies affected the outcome in the already extensively gerrymandered districts.

Beginning in February 2011 the country experienced a sustained period of unrest, including mass protests calling for political reform. Gulf Cooperation Council (GCC) Peninsula Shield Forces (PSF) troops were stationed in the country as a result of the unrest. Royal Decree Number 18 implemented an emergency State of National Safety (SNS) from March 15 to June 1 in accordance with the constitution. Military and civilian security forces carried out extensive security operations, including attacks on peaceful protesters at the former GCC Roundabout (commonly referred to as the Pearl Roundabout and subsequently renamed Al Farooq Junction) in Manama on February 17. Fifty-two confirmed deaths during the year may be linked to the unrest. There were 35 deaths between February 14 and April 15 alone, according to the Bahrain Independent Commission of Inquiry (BICI), and there were reports of an additional 17 related deaths throughout the rest of the year. Five of the 35 persons died as a result of torture inflicted by elements of security services during the SNS. During that year rioters attacked South Asian residents, killing at least two.

Recent Elections

The September 24, 2011 Council of Representatives by-elections were marred by irregularities. Several registered political societies declined to participate. The by-elections which were organized to replace 18 members from the largest Shia political society, Wifaq, who resigned in February to protest government actions against demonstrators. The opposition political societies asserted that the government gerrymandered electoral districts in 2002 to provide for a progovernment, mostly Sunni, majority in the Council of Representatives. Progovernment political societies declined to run candidates in the election, primarily because the 18 districts in contention were majority Shia districts and progovernment Sunni candidates faced likely defeat, although those societies encouraged their members to vote. Approximately 17 percent of eligible voters participated in the two rounds of voting on September 24 and October 1. The majority of the winning candidates were self-declared independents, with only two candidates claiming ties to official political societies.

Many alleged that the government engineered the victory of some female and Shia candidates by encouraging their competitors to withdraw from the race, and there were accusations that some opposition political societies attempted to intimidate voters. Despite instructions to their members by the main opposition groups to refrain from harassing those citizens who chose to vote, MOI officials reported that members of an unnamed opposition group attempted to disrupt voting at a predominantly Shia precinct in A'ali by throwing rocks to intimidate candidates and voters. Some candidates alleged there was a concerted effort by Shia election boycotters to force them to withdraw from the race. One newly elected candidate reported that a homemade explosive hit his house the evening that his victory was announced.

Political Parties: The government did not allow the formation of political parties, but more than a dozen "political societies" developed political platforms, held internal elections, and hosted political gatherings. Individuals active with these societies and other opposition political society groups faced repercussions during 2011. The government arrested and detained individual members of some political societies, including Wifaq and Wa'ad, for their political activities. They were charged with various crimes, including inciting hatred of the regime and attending an illegal gathering. Six members of the General Secretariat of the Amal political society were detained, tried, and convicted in as SNS court; the defendants remained imprisoned and their cases were under appeal at year's end.

During 2011 a number of elected municipal councils suspended several Wifaq political society municipal councilors because of their participation in antigovernment protests. In municipal councils where Wifaq members constituted a minority, Sunni members voted for their expulsion, sometimes in contradiction to the councils' bylaws. The minister of municipal affairs and urban planning petitioned the king's cabinet to dissolve municipal councils in which Wifaq members constituted the majority, but the cabinet did not address the petition during the year, and those councils continued to function without hindrance.

A new, predominantly Sunni, political society, the National Unity Gathering, received legal recognition in June. Political societies were highly critical of provisions in the law requiring them to notify the government before contacting political groups abroad.

Participation of Women and Minorities: The newly elected parliamentarians included three women, one of whom won by default when her opponents withdrew and two of whom won contested races, a first in the country's history. The elections brought the number of female members of the elected chamber to four. The Shura Council, the appointed 40-member upper house, included 11 women. Two women served as cabinet members, five women sat as judges on the criminal courts, and one was a judge on the Constitutional Court.

Although Shia and Sunni citizens have equal rights before the law, Sunnis dominated political life even though the majority of citizens were Shia. The Shura Council included 19 Shia members, including the speaker, as well as one Jewish member and one Christian member. Four of the 26 cabinet ministers were Shia, including one of the four deputy prime ministers.

Principal Government Officials

Last Updated: 1/31/2013

King: **HAMAD bin Isa Al Khalifa**
Prime Min.: **KHALIFA bin Salman Al Khalifa**
Dep. Prime Min.: **ALI bin Khalifa bin Salman Al Khalifa**
Dep. Prime Min.: **Jawad bin Salim al-ARAIDH**
Dep. Prime Min.: **KHALID bin Abdallah Al Khalifa**
Dep. Prime Min.: **MUHAMMAD bin Mubarak Al Khalifa**
Min. of Culture: **MAI bint Muhammad Al Khalifa**
Min. of Education: **Majid bin Ali Hasan al-NUAYMI**
Min. of Energy: **Abd al-Husayn MIRZA**
Min. of Finance: **AHMAD bin Muhammad bin Hamad bin Abdallah Al Khalifa**
Min. of Foreign Affairs: **KHALID bin Ahmad bin Muhammad Al Khalifa**
Min. of Health: **Sadiq bin Abd al-Karim al-SHIHABI**
Min. of Housing: **Basim bin Yacub al-HAMAR**
Min. of Human Rights & Social Development: **Fatima bint Ahmad al-BALUSHI**
Min. of Industry & Commerce: **HASAN bin Abdallah Fakhru**

Min. of Interior: **RASHID bin Abdallah bin Ahmad Al Khalifa**
Min. of Justice & Islamic Affairs: **KHALID bin Ali Al Khalifa**
Min. of Labor: **Jamil Muhammad Ali HUMAYDAN**
Min. of Municipal Affairs & Urban Planning: **JUMA bin Ahmad al-Ka'abi**
Min. of the Royal Court: **KHALID bin Ahmad bin Salman Al Khalifa**
Min. of the Royal Court for Follow-Up Affairs: **AHMAD BIN ATIYATALLAH Al Khalifa**
Min. of Royal Court Affairs: **ALI bin Isa bin Salman Al Khalifa**
Min. of Transportation: **KAMAL bin Ahmad Muhammad**
Min. of Works: **ISSAM bin Abdallah Khalaf**
Min. of State for Defense Affairs: **MUHAMMAD bin Abdallah Al Khalifa**
Min. of State for Follow-Up Affairs: **Muhammad bin Ibrahim al-MUTAWA**
Min. of State for Foreign Affairs: **Ghanim bin Fadhil al-BUAYNAYN**
Min. of State for Human Rights Affairs: **Salah ALI, Dr.**
Min. of State for Information Affairs: **Samira RAJAB**
Min. of State for Shura Council & Parliament Affairs: **Abd al-Aziz bin Muhammad al-FADHIL**
Attorney Gen.: **ALI bin Fadhil al-Buaynayn**
Governor, Central Bank of Bahrain: **Rashid bin Muhammad al-MARAJ**
Ambassador to the US: **Huda Azra Ibrahim NUNU**
Permanent Representative to the UN, New York: **Jamal Faris al-RUWAYI**

ECONOMY

Bahrain is one of the most diversified economies in the Persian Gulf. Highly developed communication and transport facilities make Bahrain home to numerous multinational firms with business in the Gulf. As part of its diversification plans, Bahrain implemented a Free Trade Agreement (FTA) with the US in August 2006, the first FTA between the US and a Gulf state. Bahrain's economy, however, continues to depend heavily on oil. Petroleum production and refining account for more than 60% of Bahrain's export receipts, 70% of government revenues, and 11% of GDP (exclusive of allied industries).

Other major economic activities are production of aluminum—Bahrain's second biggest export after oil—finance, and construction. Bahrain competes with Malaysia as a worldwide center for Islamic banking and continues to seek new natural gas supplies as feedstock to support its expanding petrochemical and aluminum industries.

In 2011 and into 2012, Bahrain experienced economic setbacks as a result of domestic unrest. Bahrain's reputation as a financial hub of the Gulf has been damaged, and the country now risks losing financial institutions to other regional centers such as Dubai or Doha. Economic policies aimed at restoring confidence in Bahrain's economy, such as the suspension of an expatriate labor tax, will make Bahrain's foremost long-term economic challenges—youth unemployment and the growth of government debt—more difficult to address.

Labor Conditions

The minimum age for employment is 16. The Ministry of Labor made rare exceptions on a case-by-case basis for juveniles between the ages of 14 and 16 who have an urgent need to assist in providing financial support for their families. Minors may not work in industries that the Ministry of Health deems hazardous or unhealthy, including construction, mining, and oil refining. Minors may work no more than six hours a day and may be present on the employment premises no more than seven hours a day. These regulations do not apply to family-operated businesses in which the only other employees are family members.

There is no national minimum wage. Public sector workers are covered by a standardized government pay scale, with a set minimum of 300 dinars ($798) pay per month. Citizens who earned less received a government stipend to offset the difference. There was no official poverty level.

The standard workweek is 48 hours. Workers are entitled to paid annual holidays and premium pay for overtime. Excessive compulsory overtime in excess of 60 hours per week requires permission from the Ministry of Labor.

The Ministry of Labor enforced the labor law and mandated acceptable conditions of work for all adult workers except domestic workers. According to NGOs, workplace safety standards were generally adequate, but inspection and compliance were substandard.

A ministerial decree prohibits outdoor work between noon and 4 p.m. during July and August. The ban is not strictly enforced and violations were common.

Unskilled foreign workers, mostly from South and Southeast Asia, made up approximately 60 percent of the workforce (76 percent of the private-sector workforce). They were particularly vulnerable to forced labor and in some cases were subject to withholding of passports, restrictions on movement, contract substitution, nonpayment of wages, threats, and physical and sexual abuse. A 2009 study by the country's Labor Market Regulatory Authority (LMRA) found that 65 percent of foreign workers had not seen their employment contract and that 89 percent were unaware of their terms of employment. Some foreign workers arrived in the country under the sponsorship of an employer and then switched jobs while continuing to pay a fee to their original sponsor, which made it difficult to monitor and control their employment. Some employers illegally charged workers exorbitant fees to remain in the country and work for other employers.

Estimates of the proportion of migrant workers in the country under illegal "free visa" arrangements—a practice that can contribute to debt bondage—ranged from 10 to 25 percent. In numerous cases employers withheld salaries from foreign workers for months or years and refused to grant them permission to leave the country. The fear of deportation or employer retaliation prevented many foreign workers from complaining to authorities. The labor law does not protect domestic workers, and this group was particularly vulnerable to exploitation. There were credible reports that many of the country's 70,000 domestic workers, most of them women, were forced to work 12- to 16-hour days, had to give their identity documents to employers, had little time off, were malnourished, and were subject to verbal and physical abuse, including sexual molestation and rape.

U.S.-BAHRAINI RELATIONS

The United States established diplomatic relations with Bahrain in 1971 following its independence from the United Kingdom. The U.S. embassy at Manama was opened September 21, 1971, and a resident ambassador was sent in 1974. The Bahraini Embassy in Washington, D.C., opened in 1977. The American Mission Hospital has operated continuously in Bahrain for more than a century.

Bahrain plays a key role in regional security architecture and is a vital U.S. partner in defense initiatives. Bahrain hosts the U.S. Navy's Fifth Fleet and participates in U.S.-led military coalitions. Bahraini forces have supported the International Security Assistance Force in Afghanistan, providing perimeter security at a military base. Bahrain was the first Arab state to lead a Coalition Task Force patrolling the Gulf and has supported the coalition counter-piracy mission with a deployment of its flagship. The U.S. designated Bahrain a Major Non-NATO Ally in 2002.

The U.S-Bahrain Free Trade Agreement entered into force in 2006, generating additional commercial opportunities for both countries. In 2011, bilateral trade exceeded $1.7 billion.

Recent political and social unrest has highlighted the need for reform and reconciliation. Following the release of the royally appointed Bahrain Independent Commission of Inquiry's (BICI) findings, which recommended a series of reforms, the Government of Bahrain has taken initial steps to redress past abuses and implement reforms. Despite these efforts, unrest and clashes have continued. The United States has urged the Government of Bahrain to implement the full range of BICI recommendations and take steps to implement additional reforms.

U.S. Assistance to Bahrain

U.S. assistance helps Bahrain, which lacks the oil wealth of its neighbors, obtain the equipment and training it needs to operate alongside U.S. air and naval forces. With the help of the U.S., Bahrain has made significant efforts to upgrade its defense systems and modernize its armed forces over the last 20 years. Since the 1991 Gulf War, the U.S. has provided military and defense technical assistance and training to Bahrain from Foreign Military Sales (FMS), commercial sources, and excess defense article sales (EDA), and under the International Military and Education Training (IMET) program. U.S. military sales to Bahrain since 2000 total $1.4 billion. Military exercises are conducted on a regular basis to increase the BDF's readiness and improve coordination with the U.S. and other GCC forces. The BDF also sends personnel to the United States for military training. This training includes courses from entry-level technical training to graduate-level professional military education.

To protect and advance U.S. interests, the United States uses all tools available, including foreign assistance, to encourage Bahrain's leadership to implement reforms and respect human rights standards; make Bahrain a stronger and more interoperable partner for regional peace, security and counter-terrorism cooperation; improve the ability to deny terrorist sponsorship, support, and sanctuary; and boost Bahrain's maritime defenses against smuggling and terrorism.

Bilateral Economic Relations

Due to its relatively limited energy reserves, Bahrain has been diversifying its economy away from oil and gas production and is seeking to attract foreign investment and businesses. The U.S.-Bahrain Free Trade Agreement took effect on August 1, 2006 and is generating increased U.S. commercial interest in Bahrain. Bilateral trade between the U.S. and Bahrain has increased each since the signing of the Free Trade Agreement, exceeding $1.7 billion USD in 2011. U.S. exports to Bahrain include machinery, aircraft, vehicles, and agricultural products. U.S. imports from Bahrain include fertilizers, aluminum, textiles, apparel, and organic chemicals.

Bahrain's Membership in International Organizations

Among other regional and global organizations, Bahrain is a member of the United Nations, International Monetary Fund, World Bank, and World Trade Organization.

Bilateral Representation

Bahrain maintains an embassy in the United States at 3502 International Drive NW, Washington, DC 20008; tel: (202) 342-1111.

Principal U.S. Embassy Officials:

Last Updated: 1/14/2013

MANAMA (E) Building 979, Road 3119, Block 331, Zinj District, 973-1724-2700/VoIP:202-448-5131, Fax 973-1727-2594, Workweek: Sun to Thurs, 0800-1700, Website: http://manama.usembassy.gov/

DCM OMS:	Vicki Byrd
AMB OMS:	Maria Huscilowitc
DHS/ICE:	Steve Igyarto (Res. In Riyadh)
FM:	Dennis Tabligan
HRO:	Virginia Smith
MGT:	Daniel Stoian
MLO/ODC:	COL John West
POL/ECON:	Kari Paetzold
POSHO:	Dennis Tabligan

SDO/DATT:	COL John West
AMB:	Thomas J. Krajeski
CG:	Daniela Dipierro
CON:	Daniela Dipierro
DCM:	Stephanie T. Williams
PAO:	Bradley Niemann
GSO:	Joy Yamamura
RSO:	R. Kevin Helm
ATO:	David Williams (Res. Dubai)
CLO:	Roxane Cooper
DEA:	Sa Mike Zivkovic (Res. In Dubai)
ECON:	Kelly Diiro
FAA:	Roy Barnett (Res. Abu Dabi)
FMO:	Alan Monetta
IMO:	Vacant
IRS:	Kathy J. Beck (Res. In Paris)
ISSO:	Brian Anderson
LEGATT:	Sa Scott Maccracken (Resident Doha)

TRAVEL

Consular Information Sheet

November 13, 2012

Country Description: The Kingdom of Bahrain is a constitutional hereditary monarchy governed by the Al-Khalifa family. In 2002, the country adopted a new constitution that reinstated a parliament, which consists of one elected and one appointed chamber. Islamic ideals and beliefs provide the conservative foundation of the country's customs, laws, and practices. Bahrain is a modern, developed country, and tourist facilities are widely available. The capital is Manama.

Smart Traveler Enrollment Program (STEP)/Embassy Locations: If you are going to live in or visit Bahrain, please take the time to tell our Embassy about your trip. If you enroll, we can keep you up to date with important safety and security announcements. It will also help your friends and family get in touch with you in an emergency.

The U.S. Embassy in Manama
Building No. 979
Road 3119, Block 331
Zinj District
Manama
Telephone: (973) 1724–2700
Emergency after-hours telephone: (973) 1727–5126
Facsimile: (973) 1725–6242
The workweek in Bahrain is Sunday through Thursday.

Entry/Exit Requirements for U.S. Citizens: You must have a passport valid for at least six months and a visa to enter Bahrain. U.S. passport holders outside Bahrain may apply and pay for a two-week tourist eVisa online through the Bahraini government website, or may obtain and pay for a visa upon arrival at any of the ports of entry. Bahraini authorities encourage U.S. citizens to apply for eVisas prior to arriving in Bahrain. U.S. diplomatic passport holders can get a no-fee two-week visa upon arrival. Prior to travel, visitors may also obtain a five-year multiple-entry visa valid for stays as long as one month from Bahraini embassies overseas.

All travelers to Bahrain face close scrutiny from Bahraini authorities, and should be prepared to answer questions regarding their purpose of travel to Bahrain. The Government of Bahrain has refused some U.S. citizens permission to enter Bahrain.

Exit permits are not required; however, visitors must be in legal status before they will be allowed to depart. You may be prevented from departing if you are involved in legal proceedings, have unpaid debt, or are a child subject to a custody dispute. Bahrain assesses heavy fines on visitors who fail to extend their legal status or depart the country at the end of their authorized stays. An exit tax is included in the ticket price for flights out of Bahrain, so no additional exit fees are required upon departure. Residents of Bahrain who intend to return should obtain a re-entry permit before departing.

For the most current information on entry and exit requirements, please contact the Embassy of the Kingdom of Bahrain at 3502 International Drive NW, Washington, DC 20008, telephone (202) 342-1111; or the Bahrain Permanent Mission to the UN at 2 United Nations Plaza, East 44th St., New York, NY 10017, telephone (212) 223-6200. U.S. citizens who need to extend their visas or residence permits in Bahrain should contact the General Directorate of Nationality and Passports.

Some HIV/AIDS restrictions exist for visitors to and foreign residents of Bahrain. While U.S. citizens do not have to declare their HIV status upon applying for entry into Bahrain, the government revokes the visas of non-Bahrainis who are discovered to be HIV positive. Please verify this information with the Embassy of the Kingdom of Bahrain before you travel.

Threats to Safety and Security: Spontaneous and at times violent anti-government demonstrations occur in some neighborhoods, particularly at night and on weekends. These demonstrations have included blockades of major highways, trash-can fires, and establishment of unofficial checkpoints. Participants have thrown rocks, Molotov cocktails and used various other homemade weapons, including crude improvised explosive devices. The Ministry of Interior maintains official checkpoints in some areas and routinely uses tear gas and stun grenades, along with birdshot and other crowd control measures against demonstrators. Violent clashes between security forces and demonstrators can make travel in and around Bahrain dangerous without advance warning.

There have been no direct attacks on U.S. citizens; however, Westerners and U.S. citizens have been caught in the middle of clashes anti-U.S. sentiment has been seen on the streets and U.S. flags have occasionally been burned during demonstrations. U.S. citizens are urged to remain alert to local security developments and to be vigilant regarding their personal safety by knowing the locations of police and fire stations, hospitals, and the U.S. Embassy. The Department of State strongly urges U.S. citizens to avoid all demonstrations, as even peaceful ones can quickly become unruly, and a foreigner could become a target of harassment or worse. If you are in immediate danger, call the police at 999.

The U.S. Embassy restricts its employees from traveling to specific areas and advises all U.S. citizens to do the same. Please check the Updated Travel Alert Map on the Embassy's website for the latest travel restrictions. We continue to urge U.S. citizens to stay current with media coverage of local events and be aware of their surroundings at all times. Please check our Demonstration Notices for information on demonstrations, security guidance, and a map outlining areas that are off-limits to Embassy U.S. citizen employees and their family members. The Department of State remains concerned about the possibility of terrorist attacks against U.S. citizens and U.S. interests throughout the world. U.S. citizens should maintain a low profile, vary routes and times for all required travel, and treat mail and packages from unfamiliar sources with caution. In addition, U.S. citizens are urged to avoid contact with any suspicious objects or people, and to report their presence to local authorities.

Stay up to date by:

- Bookmarking our Bureau of Consular Affairs website, which contains the current Travel Warnings and Travel Alerts as well as the Worldwide Caution.
- Following us on Twitter and the Bureau of Consular Affairs page on Facebook as well.
- Downloading our free Smart Traveler IPhone App to have travel information at your fingertips.
- Calling 1-888-407-4747 toll-free within the U.S. and Canada, or a regular toll line, 1-202-501-4444, from other countries.
- Taking some time before travel to consider your personal security.

Crime: The crime rate in Bahrain is low and violent crime is rare. However, burglary, petty theft, and robberies do occur. Take the same security precautions in Bahrain that you would practice in the United States. Hotel room doors should be locked when visitors are in their rooms, and travelers are encouraged to store valuables in hotel room safes when they are available.

Women are encouraged to keep their purses firmly under their arms, and men should avoid keeping their wallets in their hip pockets while in the old market area. Embassy Manama recommends that travelers using local taxis insist on the use of a meter to avoid being overcharged. Bahrain has a professional police force: contact the police if you encounter problems.

Do not buy counterfeit and pirated goods, even if they are widely available. Not only are the bootlegs illegal in the United States, if you purchase them you may be breaking local law.

Victims of Crime: If you or someone you know becomes the victim of a crime abroad, you should contact the local police and the nearest U.S. embassy or consulate. We can:

- Replace a stolen passport.
- Help you find appropriate medical care if you are the victim of violent crimes such as assault or rape.
- Put you in contact with the appropriate police authorities, and if you want us to, we can contact family members or friend.
- Help you understand the local criminal justice process and direct you to local attorneys, although it is important to remember that local authorities are responsible for investigating and prosecuting the crime.

The local equivalent to the "911" emergency line in Bahrain is: 999 for fire, ambulance, and police; 199 for traffic accidents (no injuries) or 999 (injuries).

Criminal Penalties: While you are traveling in Bahrain, you are subject to its laws even if you are a U.S. citizen. Foreign laws and legal systems can be vastly different from our own. In some places you may be taken in for questioning if you don't have your passport with you. In some places, it is illegal to take pictures of certain buildings. In some places driving under the influence could land you immediately in jail. These criminal penalties will vary from country to country. There are also some things that might be legal in the country you visit, but still illegal in the United States, and you can be prosecuted under U.S. law if you buy pirated goods. Engaging in sexual conduct with children or using or disseminating child pornography in a foreign country is a crime prosecutable in the United States. If you break local laws in Bahrain, your U.S. passport won't help you avoid arrest or prosecution. It's very important to know what's legal and what's not where you are going.

Persons violating Bahrain's laws, even unknowingly, may be expelled, arrested, or imprisoned. Penalties for possessing, using, or trafficking in illegal drugs in Bahrain are severe, and convicted offenders can expect long jail sentences and heavy fines. The use of vulgar language or hand gestures can result in heavy fines or criminal charges. Although alcohol is available, public drunkenness and disorderly behavior can result in arrest and one drink may be sufficient grounds for a drunken driving arrest.

While some countries will automatically notify the nearest U.S. embassy or consulate if a U.S. citizen is detained or arrested in a foreign country, that might not always be the case. To ensure that the United States is aware of your circumstances, request that the police and prison officials notify the nearest U.S. embassy or consulate as soon as you are arrested or detained overseas.

Special Circumstances: Individuals subject to Bahraini court orders or involved in court proceedings arising from indebtedness, labor disagreements, family disputes, or other legal disputes may be prevented from departing Bahrain until their cases are resolved. Instances have occurred in which departure was prohibited for several years, since the legal process can be both lengthy and complex. Embassy Manama's Consular Section maintains a list of local attorneys willing to represent U.S. citizens but cannot provide financial assistance for legal costs or living expenses while a person is prohibited from leaving Bahrain.

If you will be working in Bahrain, we urge you to have a valid work permit and signed employment contract prior to arriving in Bahrain. In particular, the contract should be clear in the provisions related to relocation expenses, type of housing and number of occupants, any visa fees to be paid by the employee, when salaries will be paid, any salary penalties, who will pay transportation costs if the contract is terminated by either the employee or the employer, and whether different provisions apply within the probation period. Under no circumstances should you take up employment while in Bahrain on a tourist visa. Bahraini authorities will hold you personally liable for remaining in legal immigration status, regardless of incorrect advice received from the employer or the employer's failure to obtain a valid work permit for the employee. It is illegal for Bahraini employers to confiscate or otherwise retain an employee's passport. Questions regarding employment in Bahrain can be directed to Bahrain's Ministry of Labour hotlines, or to a local attorney. While many U.S. citizens have a wonderful experience working in Bahrain, some individuals have complained of unfair employment practices. Specifically, the U.S. Embassy in Bahrain has received a number of complaints from U.S. citizens employed in the education sector.

Obtaining an employment permit may require providing properly authenticated documents. Failure to provide these documents may delay the issuance of the work permit or residence permits for the employee's family. Applicants may visit the website of Bahrain's Labour Market Regulatory Authority for complete requirements, and the Department of State's Office of Authentications and Authentication of American Academic Credentials for Use Abroad pages for authentication procedures.

The Kingdom of Bahrain generally does not permit dual nationality. U.S. citizens eligible for Bahraini citizenship will usually be required to relinquish their U.S. passport to Bahrain's General Directorate of Nationality, Passports, and Residence before they will be issued a Bahraini passport. However, the Kingdom of Bahrain has been known to make exceptions.

There are no treaties in force between Bahrain and the United States dealing with international parental child abduction and custody cases. Child custody decrees issued in a U.S. court may be ignored by Bahraini courts, and may be unenforceable in Bahrain. Bahraini family law is different from U.S. family law. U.S. citizens who are divorced from or in the process of getting a divorce from a Bahraini citizen should seek legal counsel and ascertain their rights in Bahrain before visiting Bahrain, especially with their children.

Accessibility: While in Bahrain, individuals with disabilities may find accessibility and accommodation very different from what you find in the United States. Outside of a few of the more expensive hotels in the capital, individuals with disabilities will find almost no accessible accommodations. Similarly there are very few accessible restaurants, shops, or historical sites. Transportation is not accessible, and sidewalks and crosswalks, even in the main cities, are not accessible. Handicap accessible toilets and bathrooms, even in major hospitals, are generally not available. New public buildings in the central municipality must include facilities for persons with disabilities. The law does not mandate access to nonresidential buildings for persons with disabilities.

Medical Facilities and Health Information: Basic modern medical care and medicines are available in several hospitals and health centers in Bahrain. Two government hospitals, several private hospitals, and numerous private clinics located throughout the country offer a wide range of medical services. Cardiac care, general surgery, internal medicine, obstetrics, gynecology, pediatrics, orthopedics, and dentistry services are readily available, as are x-rays, CT-scan, and MRI testing. The government hospitals house both trauma and ICU units. Pharmacies are common throughout Bahrain and carry a wide range of medications. Prescriptions are normally required. Payment at all medical facilities is due at the time of service. Some hospitals have limited direct billing capability for certain insurance carriers. Billing and insurance practices vary among the medical facilities. You can find good information on vaccinations and other health precautions on the CDC website. For information about outbreaks of infectious diseases abroad, consult the World Health Organization (WHO) website. The WHO website also contains additional health information for travelers, including detailed country-specific health information.

Medical Insurance: You can't assume your insurance will go with you when you travel. It's very important to find out BEFORE you leave whether or not your medical insurance will cover you overseas. You need to ask your insurance company two questions:

- Does my policy apply when I'm out of the U.S.?
- Will it cover emergencies like a trip to a foreign hospital or an evacuation?

In many places, doctors and hospitals still expect payment in cash at the time of service. Your regular U.S. health insurance may not cover doctors' and hospital visits in other countries. If your policy doesn't go with you when you travel, it's a very good idea to take out another one for your trip.

Traffic Safety and Road Conditions: While in a foreign country, U.S.

citizens may encounter road conditions that differ significantly from those in the United States. The information below concerning Bahrain is provided for general reference only, and may not be totally accurate in a particular location or circumstance.

Travel by road in Bahrain is generally safe although unsafe driving practices are common. Highways and major roads in the northern third of Bahrain are four to six lanes wide and well maintained; roads in villages and older parts of Manama and Muharraq are narrow and twisting. As in the United States, traffic in Bahrain moves on the right. Roundabouts (traffic circles) follow the British system, with those automobiles within the traffic circle having right of way over those attempting to enter.

Although the Bahraini penal code calls for fines of up to 100 Bahraini dinars ($270.00) or imprisonment of up to six months for driving above posted speed limits, drivers frequently drive well over the posted speed limits of 50-100 km per hour. The law allows the police to detain drivers for traffic violations until they can appear before a magistrate. It is illegal to use a cell phone while driving.

Under Bahraini law, any sign of having consumed alcohol may be taken as prima facie evidence of driving under the influence, which can lead to imprisonment and/or fines of up to 1,000 Bahraini dinars (about $2,700). Except for minor accidents, drivers may not move their vehicles after an accident until a report has been filed with the traffic police. This is true even in cases of single-car accidents. Insurance companies may not provide coverage if the cars are moved. However, drivers involved in minor, non-injury accidents no longer need to wait at the scene for the police. Individuals should get their vehicles off the road to avoid further accidents.

Drivers should call the accident hotline at 199 (if there are no injuries) or 999 (when someone is injured) where they will be directed to one of five centers to file the accident report. This report must be filed within 24 hours of the accident. Both drivers may be prohibited from leaving the country until the matter is resolved if an accident results in legal proceedings. The main switchboard at the traffic department is 1787–2222.

Aviation Safety Oversight: As there is no direct commercial air service to the United States by carriers registered in Bahrain, the U.S. Federal Aviation Administration (FAA) has not assessed the government of Bahrain's Civil Aviation Authority for compliance with International Civil Aviation Organization (ICAO) aviation safety standards. Further information may be found on the FAA's safety assessment page

Children's Issues: Please see the U.S. Dept. of State Office of Children's Issues web pages on intercountry adoption and international parental child abduction.

Intercountry Adoption

April 2011

The information in this section has been edited from the latest report available as of February 2013 from the State Department Bureau of Consular Affairs, Office of Overseas Citizens Services. For more information, please read the *Intercountry Adoption* section of this book and review current reports online at http://adoption.state.gov.

Bahrain is not party to the Hague Convention on Protection of Children and Co-operation in Respect of Intercountry Adoption (Hague Adoption Convention). Therefore, when the Hague Adoption Convention entered into force for the United States on April 1, 2008, intercountry adoption processing for Bahrain did not change.

The Department of State does not maintain files on the adoption process in Bahrain because adoptions from Bahrain are rare. Fewer than five adoptions by American citizen parents have taken place in over a decade.

International Parental Child Abduction

January 2012

The information in this section has been edited from the latest report available as of February 2013 from the State Department Bureau of Consular Affairs, Office of Overseas Citizens Services. For more information, please read the *International Parental Child Abduction* section of this book and check for updated reports online at www.travel.state.gov/abduction.

Disclaimer: The information in this flyer relating to the legal requirements of specific foreign countries is provided for general information only. Questions involving interpretation of specific foreign laws should be addressed to foreign legal counsel.

General Information: Bahrain is not a party to the Hague Convention on the Civil Aspects of International Child Abduction, nor are there any international or bilateral treaties in force between Bahrain and the United States dealing with international parental child abduction. American citizens who travel to Bahrain are subject to the jurisdiction of Bahraini courts, as well as to the country's laws and regulations. This holds true for all legal matters including child custody. Parents planning to travel with their children to Bahrain should bear this in mind.

Custody Disputes: There is no specific law in Bahrain governing child custody, with each dispute examined on a case-by-case basis. When child custody disputes arise between parents, one of whom is a citizen of Bahrain, custody decisions are based on Islamic (Sharia) law. Two separate Islamic courts, representing the jurisprudence of the Sunni and Shia Islamic sects, enforce divergent interpretations of Islamic law. In general, the marriage contract determines which court will exercise jurisdiction. If the contract is silent on this issue, the court representing the husband's sect will have jurisdiction. Non-Bahraini nationals, whether married to a Bahraini or other national, may file custody cases through a lawyer approved to practice in Bahrain in the court in which the marriage was legalized, whether Sunni, Shia or civil. Non-Muslims are permitted to file cases in the Bahrain civil court. In determining issues of custody, Bahraini courts consider the parents' religion, place of permanent residence, income, and the mother's subsequent marital status.

Priority is generally given to a Muslim father, irrespective of his nationality. Under Sharia law a Muslim mother is usually granted custody of girls under the age of nine and boys under the age of seven, at which time custody is transferred to the father. If the mother is unavailable, an infant may be given to the grandmother on the mother's side until s/he reaches the age of seven or nine. If the court finds the mother "incompetent," custody of the child, regardless of age, can be given to the father, or to the child's paternal grandmother.

A finding of incompetence is left to the discretion of the Sharia judge. Sharia courts have found parents incompetent if they are not Muslim or if they engage in behavior that is considered to be inconsistent with the Islamic faith. Remarriage to a non-Bahraini may be considered grounds for a finding of incompetence. Under Sharia law, if a mother removes a child from the father thus denying him access, the mother's custody rights can be severed. If both the mother and father are ruled incompetent, custody of the children is given to the women on the father's side of the family.

If a child has attained the "age of discretion," that child may be allowed to choose the parent with whom he or she wishes to live. Since the "age of discretion" has no clear definition, a Bahraini lawyer should be contacted to discuss any specific case.

Persons who wish to pursue a child custody claim in a Bahraini court should retain an attorney in Bahrain. The U.S. Embassy in Manama maintains a list of attorneys willing to represent American clients.

A copy of this list may be obtained by contacting the Embassy or the U.S. Department of State. U.S. government officials cannot recommend an attorney and make no claim as to the professional ability or integrity of the attorneys on this list. The U.S. government does not pay legal expenses. A copy of this list may be obtained by contacting the following offices.

American Embassy
Box 26431
Manama, Bahrain
Phone: 973-273-300
After hours: 973-275-126
Fax: 973-272-594

U.S. Department of State
Office of Children's Issues
SA-29
U.S. Department of State
2201 C Street, NW
Washington, DC 20520-2818
Phone: (202) 736-9090
Fax: (202) 312-9743

Embassy of the State of Bahrain
3502 International Drive, NW
Washington, DC 20008
Phone: (202) 342-0741
Fax: (202) 362-2192

Enforcement of Foreign Judgments: Custody orders and judgments of foreign courts are not enforceable in Bahrain if they potentially contradict or violate local laws and practices. For example, an order from a U.S. court granting custody to an American mother may not be honored in Bahrain if the mother intends to take the child to live outside Bahrain. Courts in Bahrain will not enforce U.S. court decrees ordering a parent in Bahrain to pay child support.

Visitation Rights: Non-custodial parents (both the mother and father) are entitled to visitation by prior arrangement of the competent court. Neither the court nor a custodial parent has the authority to stop a non-Bahraini parent from entering Bahrain to visit the child.

Dual Nationality: Dual nationality is not recognized under Bahraini law. Children of Bahraini fathers automatically acquire Bahraini citizenship at birth, regardless of where the child was born. Bahraini women can only transmit citizenship in rare instances when there is official intervention from the Bahraini government. Bahrainis must enter and leave the country on Bahraini passports even if they are entitled to hold the passport of another country.

Travel Restrictions: No exit visas are required to leave Bahrain. When a custody case is before the local court, children, regardless of their nationality, are generally subject to court-imposed travel restrictions. Either parent can request that a court issue an order restricting the travel of minor children, and immigration authorities will enforce that travel restriction. This travel restriction applies to children who are American citizens.

Criminal Remedies: For information on possible criminal remedies, please contact your local law enforcement authorities or the nearest office of the Federal Bureau of Investigation (FBI). Information is also available on the Internet at the web site of the U.S. Department of Justice, Office of Juvenile Justice and Delinquency Prevention (OJJDP) at http://www.ojjdp.ncjrs.org. For further information on international parental child abduction, contact the Office of Children's Issues, U.S. Department of State at (202) 736-9090 or visit its web site on the Internet at http://travel.state.gov/abduction.

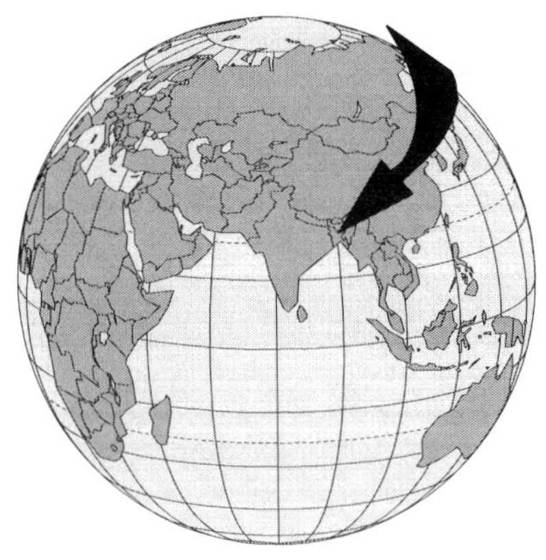

BANGLADESH

Compiled from publications that were available as of February 2013 from the U.S. Department of State, the U.S. Department of Commerce, and the Central Intelligence Agency (CIA). See the introduction to this set for explanatory notes.

Official Name:
People's Republic of Bangladesh

PROFILE

Geography

Area: total: 143,998 sq km; country comparison to the world: 95; land: 130,168 sq km; water: 13,830 sq km

Major cities: Dhaka (capital) 14.251 million; Chittagong 4.816 million; Khulna 1.636 million; Rajshahi 853,000 (2009)

Climate: tropical; mild winter (October to March); hot, humid summer (March to June); humid, warm rainy monsoon (June to October)

Terrain: mostly flat alluvial plain; hilly in southeast

People

Nationality: noun: Bangladeshi(s); adjective: Bangladeshi

Population: 161,083,804 (July 2012 est.)

Population growth rate: 1.579% (2012 est.)

Ethnic groups: Bengali 98%, other 2% (includes tribal groups, non-Bengali Muslims) (1998)

Religions: Muslim 89.5%, Hindu 9.6%, other 0.9% (2004)

Languages: Bangla (official, also known as Bengali), English

Literacy: definition: age 15 and over can read and write; total population: 56.8%; male: 61.3%; female: 52.2% (2010 est.)

Health: life expectancy at birth: total population: 70.06 years; male: 68.21 years; female: 71.98 years (2012 est.); Infant mortality rate: total: 48.99 deaths/1,000 live births; male: 51.48 deaths/1,000 live births; female: 46.39 deaths/1,000 live births (2012 est.)

Unemployment rate: 5% (2012 est.)

Work force: 77 million (2012 est.)

Government

Type: parliamentary democracy

Independence: 16 December 1971

Constitution: enacted 4 November 1972; effective 16 December 1972; suspended following coup of 24 March 1982; restored 10 November 1986; amended many times

Political subdivisions: 7 divisions; Barisal, Chittagong, Dhaka, Khulna, Rajshahi, Rangpur, Sylhet

Suffrage: 18 years of age; universal

Economy

GDP (purchasing power parity): $305.5 billion (2012 est.); $285.8 billion (2011 est.); $269.5 billion (2010 est.); $253.4 billion (2009 est.)

GDP real growth rate: 6.1% (2012 est.); 6.1% (2011 est.); 6.4% (2010 est.); 5.9% (2009 est.)

GDP per capita (PPP): $2,000 (2012 est.); $1,700 (2011 est.); $1,600 (2010 est.); $1,600 (2009 est.)

Natural resources: natural gas, arable land, timber, coal

Agriculture products: rice, jute, tea, wheat, sugarcane, potatoes, tobacco, pulses, oilseeds, spices, fruit; beef, milk, poultry

Industries: jute, cotton, garments, paper, leather, fertilizer, iron and steel, cement, petroleum products, tobacco, drugs and pharmaceuticals, ceramic, tea, salt, sugar, edible oil, soap and detergent, fabricated metal products, electricity and natural gas

Exports: $25.79 billion (2012 est.); $23.86 billion (2011 est.)

Exports—commodities: garments, knitwear, agricultural products, frozen food (fish and seafood), jute and jute goods, leather

Exports—partners: US 19.7%, Germany 16.1%, UK 9.5%, France 7.2%, Italy 4.3%, Netherlands 4.3%, Spain 4.3%, Canada 4% (2011)

Imports: $35.06 billion (2012 est.); $31.75 billion (2011 est.)

Imports—commodities: machinery and equipment, chemicals, iron and steel, textiles, foodstuffs, petroleum products, cement

Imports—partners: China 18.2%, India 13.5%, Malaysia 4.9% (2011)

Debt—external: $36.21 billion (31 December 2012 est.); $25.22 billion (31 December 2011 est.)

Exchange rates: taka (BDT) per US dollar; 82.17 (2012 est.) ; 74.152 (2011 est.); 69.649 (2010 est.); 69.04 (2009); 68.554 (2008)

GEOGRAPHY

Bangladesh is a low-lying, riparian country located in South Asia with a largely marshy jungle coastline of 710 kilometers (440 mi.) on the northern littoral of the Bay of Bengal. Formed by a deltaic plain at the confluence of the Ganges (Padma), Brahmaputra (Jamuna), and Meghna Rivers and their tributaries, Bangladesh's alluvial soil is highly fertile but vulnerable to flood and drought. Hills rise above the plain only in the Chittagong Hill Tracts in the far southeast and the Sylhet division in the northeast. Straddling the Tropic of Cancer, Bangladesh has a subtropical monsoonal climate characterized by heavy seasonal rainfall, moderately warm temperatures, and high humidity. Natural calamities, such as floods, tropical cyclones, tornadoes, and tidal bores affect the country almost every year. Bangladesh also is affected by major cyclones on average 16 times a decade.

Urbanization is proceeding rapidly, and it is estimated that only 30% of the population entering the labor force in the future will be absorbed into agriculture, although many will likely find other kinds of work in rural areas. The areas around Dhaka and Comilla are the most densely settled. The Sundarbans, an area of coastal tropical jungle in the southwest and last wild home of the Bengal tiger, and the Chittagong Hill Tracts on the southeastern border with Burma and India, are the least densely populated.

PEOPLE

The area that is now Bangladesh has a rich historical and cultural past, combining Dravidian, Indo-Aryan, Mongol/Mughul, Arab, Persian, Turkic, and west European cultures. Residents of Bangladesh, about 98% of whom are ethnic Bengali and speak Bangla, are called Bangladeshis. Urdu-speaking, non-Bengali Muslims of Indian origin, and various tribal groups, mostly in the Chittagong Hill Tracts, comprise the remainder.

Language

Although Bangla (Bengali) is the official language of Bangladesh, English is widely spoken and used in official and business circles. U.S. business people may greet their Bangladeshi counterparts with normal English salutations.

Religion

According to the 2001 census, Sunni Muslims constitute 90 percent of the population and Hindus make up 9 percent. The remaining 1 percent of the population is predominantly Christian (mostly Roman Catholic) and Theravada-Hinayana Buddhist. Ethnic and religious minority communities often overlap and are concentrated in the Chittagong Hill Tracts and northern districts. Buddhists are predominantly found among the indigenous (non-Bengali) populations of the Chittagong Hill Tracts. Bengali and ethnic minority Christians live in communities across the country, concentrating in Barisal City, Gournadi in Barisal District, Baniarchar in Gopalganj, Monipuripara in Dhaka, Christianpara in Mohakhal, Nagori in Gazipur, and Khulna City. There also are small populations of Shia Muslims, Sikhs, Baha'is, animists, and Ahmadi Muslims. Estimates of their numbers varied from a few thousand to 100,000 adherents per group. There is no indigenous Jewish community and no significant immigrant Jewish population.

Most foreign residents are of Bangladeshi descent and practice Islam. Separately, there are approximately 30,000 registered Rohingya refugees and 200,000 to 500,000 unregistered Rohingyas practicing Islam in the southeast around Coxs Bazar.

HISTORY

Bengal was absorbed into the Mughul Empire in the 16th century, and Dhaka, the seat of a nawab (the representative of the emperor), gained some importance as a provincial center. But it remained remote and thus a difficult to govern region—especially the section east of the Brahmaputra River—outside the mainstream of Mughul politics. Portuguese traders and missionaries were the first Europeans to reach Bengal in the latter part of the 15th century. They were followed by representatives of the Dutch, French, and British East India Companies. By the end of the 17th century, the British presence on the Indian subcontinent was centered in Calcutta. During the 18th and 19th centuries, the British gradually extended their commercial contacts and administrative control beyond Calcutta to Bengal. In 1859, the British Crown replaced the East India Company, extending British dominion from Bengal, which became a region of India, in the east to the Indus River in the west.

The rise of nationalism throughout British-controlled India in the late 19th century resulted in mounting animosity between the Hindu and Muslim communities. In 1885, the All-India National Congress was founded with Indian and British membership. Muslims seeking an organization of their own founded the All-India Muslim League in 1906. Although both the League and the Congress supported the goal of Indian self-government within the British Empire, the two parties were unable to agree on a way to ensure the protection of Muslim political, social, and economic rights. The subsequent history of the nationalist movement was characterized by periods of Hindu-Muslim cooperation, as well as by communal antagonism. The idea of a separate Muslim state gained increasing popularity among Indian Muslims after 1936, when the Muslim League suffered a decisive defeat in the first elections under India's 1935 constitution. In 1940, the Muslim League called for an independent state in regions where Muslims were in the majority. Campaigning on that platform in provincial elections in 1946, the League won the majority of the Muslim seats contested in Bengal. Widespread communal violence followed, especially in Calcutta.

When British India was partitioned and the independent dominions of

India and Pakistan were created in 1947, the region of Bengal was divided along religious lines. The predominantly Muslim eastern half was designated East Pakistan—and made part of the newly independent Pakistan—while the predominantly Hindu western part became the Indian state of West Bengal. Pakistan's history from 1947 to 1971 was marked by political instability and economic difficulties. Dominion status was rejected in 1956 in favor of an "Islamic republic within the Commonwealth." Attempts at civilian political rule failed, and the government imposed martial law between 1958 and 1962, and again between 1969 and 1971. Almost from the advent of independent Pakistan in 1947, frictions developed between East and West Pakistan, which were separated by more than 1,000 miles of Indian territory. East Pakistanis felt exploited by the West Pakistan-dominated central government. Linguistic, cultural, and ethnic differences also contributed to the estrangement of East from West Pakistan. Bengalis strongly resisted attempts to impose Urdu as the sole official language of Pakistan. Responding to these grievances, Sheikh Mujibur Rahman in 1948 formed a students' organization called the Chhatra League. In 1949, Maulana Abdul Hamid Khan Bhasani and some other Bengali leaders formed the East Pakistan Awami Muslim League (AL), a party designed mainly to promote Bengali interests. This party dropped the word Muslim from its name in 1955 and came to be known as Awami League. Mujib became president of the Awami League in 1966 and emerged as leader of the Bengali autonomy movement. In 1966, he was arrested for his political activities. After the Awami League won almost all the East Pakistan seats of the Pakistan national assembly in 1970–71 elections, West Pakistan opened talks with the East on constitutional questions about the division of power between the central government and the provinces, as well as the formation of a national government headed by the Awami League. The talks proved unsuccessful, however, and on March 1, 1971, Pakistani President Yahya Khan indefinitely postponed the pending national assembly session, precipitating massive civil disobedience in East Pakistan. Mujib was arrested again; his party was banned, and most of his aides fled to India and organized a provisional government. On March 26, 1971, following a bloody crackdown by the Pakistan Army, Bengali nationalists declared an independent People's Republic of Bangladesh. As fighting grew between the army and the Bengali mukti bahini ("freedom fighters"), an estimated 10 million Bengalis, mainly Hindus, sought refuge in the Indian states of Assam and West Bengal. On April 17, 1971, a provisional government was formed in Meherpur district in western Bangladesh bordering India with Sheikh Mujibur Rahman, who was in prison in Pakistan, as President, Syed Nazrul Islam as Acting President, and Tajuddin Ahmed as Prime Minister.

The crisis in East Pakistan produced new strains in Pakistan's troubled relations with India. The two nations had fought a war in 1965, mainly in the west, but the refugee pressure in India in the fall of 1971 produced new tensions in the east. Indian sympathies lay with East Pakistan, and in November, India intervened on the side of the Bangladeshis. On December 16, 1971, Pakistani forces surrendered, and Bangladesh—meaning "Bengal country"—was born; the new country became a parliamentary democracy under a 1972 constitution. The first government of the new nation of Bangladesh was formed in Dhaka with Justice Abu Sayeed Choudhury as President, and Sheikh Mujibur Rahman ("Mujib")—who was released from Pakistani prison in early 1972—as Prime Minister.

Sheikh Mujibur Rahman, 1972–75

Mujib came to office with immense personal popularity but had difficulty transforming this popular support into the political strength needed to function as head of government. The new constitution, which came into force in December 1972, created a strong executive prime minister, a largely ceremonial presidency, an independent judiciary, and a unicameral legislature on a modified Westminster model. The 1972 constitution adopted as state policy the Awami League's (AL) four basic principles of nationalism, secularism, socialism, and democracy.

The first parliamentary elections held under the 1972 constitution were in March 1973, with the Awami League winning a massive majority. No other political party in Bangladesh's early years was able to duplicate or challenge the League's broad-based appeal, membership, or organizational strength. Relying heavily on experienced civil servants and members of the Awami League, the new Bangladesh Government focused on relief, rehabilitation, and reconstruction of the economy and society. Economic conditions remained precarious, however. In December 1974, Mujib decided that continuing economic deterioration and mounting civil disorder required strong measures. After proclaiming a state of emergency, Mujib used his parliamentary majority to win a constitutional amendment limiting the powers of the legislative and judicial branches, establishing an executive presidency, and instituting a one-party system, the Bangladesh Krishak Sramik Awami League (BAKSAL), which all members of Parliament (and senior civil and military officials) were obliged to join.

Despite some improvement in the economic situation during the first half of 1975, implementation of promised political reforms was slow, and criticism of government policies became increasingly centered on Mujib. In August 1975, Mujib, and most of his family, were assassinated by mid-level army officers. His daughters, Sheikh Hasina and Sheikh Rehana, were out of the country. A new government, headed by former Mujib associate Khandakar Moshtaque, was formed.

Ziaur Rahman, 1975–81

Successive military coups resulted in the emergence of Army Chief of Staff Gen. Ziaur Rahman ("Zia") as strongman. He pledged the army's support to the civilian government headed by President Chief Justice Sayem. Acting at Zia's behest, Sayem dissolved Parliament, promising fresh elections in 1977, and instituted martial law.

Acting behind the scenes of the Martial Law Administration (MLA), Zia sought to invigorate government policy and administration. While continuing the ban on political parties, he sought to revitalize the demoralized bureaucracy, to begin new economic development programs, and to emphasize family planning. In November 1976, Zia became Chief Martial Law Administrator (CMLA) and assumed the presidency upon Sayem's retirement 5 months later, promising national elections in 1978.

As President, Zia announced a 19-point program of economic reform and began dismantling the MLA. Keeping his promise to hold elections, Zia won a 5-year term in June 1978 elections, with 76% of the vote. In November 1978, his government removed the remaining restrictions on political party activities in time for parliamentary elections in February 1979. These elections, which were contested by more than 30 parties, marked the culmination of Zia's transformation of Bangladesh's Government from the MLA to a democratically elected, constitutional one. The AL and the Bangladesh Nationalist Party (BNP), founded by Zia, emerged as the two major parties.

In May 1981, Zia was assassinated in Chittagong by dissident elements of the military. The attempted coup never spread beyond that city, and the major conspirators were either taken into custody or killed. In accordance with the constitution, Vice President Justice Abdus Sattar was sworn in as acting president. He declared a new national emergency and called for election of a new president within 6 months—an election Sattar won as the BNP's candidate. President Sattar sought to follow the policies of his predecessor and retained essentially the same cabinet, but the army stepped in once again.

Hussain Mohammed Ershad, 1982–90

Army Chief of Staff Lt. Gen. H.M. Ershad assumed power in a bloodless coup in March 1982. Like his predecessors, Ershad suspended the constitution and—citing pervasive corruption, ineffectual government, and economic mismanagement—declared martial law. The following year, Ershad assumed the presidency, retaining his positions as army chief and CMLA. During most of 1984, Ershad sought the opposition parties' participation in local elections under martial law. The opposition's refusal to participate, however, forced Ershad to abandon these plans. Ershad sought public support for his regime in a national referendum on his leadership in March 1985. He won overwhelmingly, although turnout was small. Two months later, Ershad held elections for local council chairmen. Pro-government candidates won a majority of the posts, setting in motion the President's ambitious decentralization program. Political life was further liberalized in early 1986, and additional political rights, including the right to hold large public rallies, were restored. At the same time, the Jatiya (National) Party, designed as Ershad's political vehicle for the transition from martial law, was established.

Despite a boycott by the BNP, led by President Zia's widow, Begum Khaleda Zia, parliamentary elections were held on schedule in May 1986. The Jatiya Party won a modest majority of the 300 elected seats in the National Assembly. The participation of the Awami League—led by the late President Mujib's daughter, Sheikh Hasina Wajed—lent the elections some credibility, despite widespread charges of voting irregularities.

Ershad resigned as Army Chief of Staff and retired from military service in preparation for the presidential elections, scheduled for October. Protesting that martial law was still in effect, both the BNP and the AL refused to put up opposing candidates. Ershad easily outdistanced the remaining candidates, taking 84% of the vote. Although Ershad's government claimed a turnout of more than 50%, opposition leaders, and much of the foreign press, estimated a far lower percentage and alleged voting irregularities.

Ershad continued his stated commitment to lift martial law. In November 1986, his government mustered the necessary two-thirds majority in the National Assembly to amend the constitution and confirm the previous actions of the martial law regime. The President then lifted martial law, and the opposition parties took their elected seats in the National Assembly.

In July 1987, however, after the government hastily pushed through a controversial legislative bill to include military representation on local administrative councils, the opposition walked out of Parliament. Passage of the bill helped spark an opposition movement that quickly gathered momentum, uniting Bangladesh's opposition parties for the first time. The government began to arrest scores of opposition activists under the country's Special Powers Act of 1974. Despite these arrests, opposition parties continued to organize protest marches and nationwide strikes. After declaring a state of emergency, Ershad dissolved Parliament and scheduled fresh elections for March 1988.

All major opposition parties refused government overtures to participate in these polls, maintaining that the government was incapable of holding free and fair elections. Despite the opposition boycott, the government proceeded. The ruling Jatiya Party won 251 of the 300 seats. The Parliament, while still regarded by the opposition as an illegitimate body, held its sessions as scheduled, and passed a large number of bills, including, in June 1988, a controversial constitutional amendment making Islam Bangladesh's state religion and provision for setting up High Court benches in major cities outside of Dhaka. While Islam remains the state religion, the provision for decentralizing the High Court division has been struck down by the Supreme Court.

By 1989, the domestic political situation in the country seemed to have quieted. The local council elections were generally considered by international observers to have been less violent and more free and fair than previous elections. However, opposition to Ershad's rule began to regain momentum, escalating by the end of 1990 in frequent general strikes, increased campus protests, public rallies, and a general disintegration of law and order.

On December 6, 1990, Ershad offered his resignation. On February 27, 1991, after 2 months of widespread civil unrest, an interim government headed by Acting President Chief Justice Shahabuddin Ahmed oversaw what most observers believed to be the nation's most free and fair elections to that date.

Khaleda Zia, 1991–96

The center-right BNP won a plurality of seats and formed a government with support from the Islamic fundamentalist party Jamaat-I-Islami, with Khaleda Zia, widow of Ziaur Rahman, obtaining the post of prime minister. Only four parties had more than 10 members elected to the 1991 Parliament: The BNP, led by Prime Minister Begum Khaleda Zia; the AL, led by Sheikh Hasina; the Jamaat-I-Islami (JI), led by Ghulam Azam; and the Jatiya Party (JP), led by acting chairman Mizanur Rahman Choudhury while its founder, former President Ershad, served out a prison sentence on corruption charges. The electorate approved still more changes to the constitution, formally re-creating a parliamentary system and returning governing power to the office of the prime minister, as in Bangladesh's original 1972 constitution. In October 1991, members of Parliament elected a new head of state, President Abdur Rahman Biswas.

In March 1994, controversy over a parliamentary by-election, which the opposition claimed the government had rigged, led to an indefinite boycott of Parliament by the entire opposition. The opposition also began a program of repeated general strikes to press its demand that Khaleda Zia's government resign and a caretaker government supervise a general election. Efforts to mediate the dispute, under the auspices of the Commonwealth Secretariat, failed. After another attempt at a negotiated settlement failed narrowly in late December 1994, the opposition resigned en masse from Parliament. The opposition then continued a campaign of marches, demonstrations, and strikes in an effort to force the government to resign. The opposition, including the Awami League's Sheikh Hasina, pledged to boycott national elections scheduled for February 15, 1996.

In February, Khaleda Zia was reelected by a landslide in voting boycotted and denounced as unfair by the three main opposition parties. In March 1996, following escalating political turmoil, the sitting Parliament enacted a constitutional amendment to allow a neutral caretaker government to assume power and conduct new parliamentary elections; former Chief Justice Mohammed Habibur Rahman was named Chief Adviser (a position equivalent to prime minister) in the interim government. New parliamentary elections were held in June 1996 and the Awami League won plurality and formed the government with support from the Jatiya Party led by deposed president Ershad; party leader Sheikh Hasina became Prime Minister.

Sheikh Hasina, 1996–2001

Sheikh Hasina formed what she called a "Government of National Consensus" in June 1996, which included one minister from the Jatiya Party and another from the Jatiyo Samajtantric Dal, a very small leftist party. The Jatiya Party never entered into a formal coalition arrangement, and party president H.M. Ershad withdrew his support from the government in September 1997. Only three parties had more than 10 members elected to the 1996 Parliament: The Awami League, BNP, and Jatiya Party. Jatiya Party president, Ershad, was released from prison on bail in January 1997.

International and domestic election observers found the June 1996 election free and fair, and ultimately, the BNP party decided to join the new Parliament. The BNP soon charged that police and Awami League activists were engaged in large-scale harassment and jailing of opposition activists. At the end of 1996, the BNP staged a parliamentary walkout over this and other grievances but returned in January 1997 under a four-point agreement with the ruling party. The BNP asserted that this agreement was never implemented and later staged another walkout in August 1997. The BNP returned to Parliament under another agreement in March 1998.

In June 1999, the BNP and other opposition parties again began to abstain from attending Parliament. Opposition parties staged an increasing number of nationwide general strikes, rising from 6 days of general strikes in 1997 to 27 days in 1999. A four-party opposition alliance formed at the beginning of 1999 announced that it would boycott parliamentary by-elections and local government elections unless the government took steps demanded by the opposition to ensure electoral fairness. The government did not take these steps, and the opposition subsequently boycotted all elections, including municipal council elections in February 1999, several parliamentary by-elections, and the Chittagong city corporation elections in January 2000.

In July 2001, the Awami League government stepped down to allow a caretaker government to preside over parliamentary elections. Political violence that had increased during the Awami League government's tenure continued to increase through the summer in the run up to the election. In August, Khaleda Zia and Sheikh Hasina agreed during a visit of former President Jimmy Carter to respect the results of the election, join Parliament win or lose, foreswear the use of hartals (violently enforced strikes) as political tools, and if successful in forming a government allow for a more meaningful role for the opposition in Parliament. The caretaker government was successful in containing the violence, which allowed a parliamentary general election to be successfully held on October 1, 2001.

Khaleda Zia, 2001–2006

The four-party alliance led by the BNP won over a two-thirds majority in Parliament. Begum Khaleda Zia was sworn in on October 10, 2001, as Prime Minister for the third time (first in 1991, second after the February 15, 1996 elections).

Despite her August 2001 pledge and all election monitoring groups declaring the election free and fair, Sheikh Hasina condemned the election, rejected the results, and boycotted Parliament. In 2002, however, she led her party legislators back to Parliament, but the Awami League again walked out in June 2003 to protest derogatory remarks about Hasina by a State Minister and the allegedly partisan role of the Parliamentary Speaker. In June 2004, the AL returned to Parliament without having any of their demands met. They then attended Parliament irregularly before announcing a boycott of the entire June 2005 budget session.

On August 17, 2005, near-synchronized blasts of improvised explosive devices in 63 out of 64 administrative districts targeted mainly government buildings and killed two persons. An extremist Islamist group named Jama'atul Mujahideen, Bangladesh (JMB) claimed responsibility for the blasts, which aimed to press home JMB's demand for a replacement of the secular legal system with Islamic sharia courts. Subsequent attacks on the courts in several districts killed 28 people, including judges, lawyers, and police personnel guarding the courts. A government campaign against the Islamic extremists led to the arrest of hundreds of senior and mid-level JMB leaders. Six top JMB leaders were tried and sentenced to death for their role in the murder of two judges; another leader was tried and sentenced to death in absentia in the same case.

In February 2006, the AL returned to Parliament, demanded early elections, and requested significant changes in the electoral and caretaker government systems to stop alleged moves by the ruling coalition to rig the next election. The AL blamed the BNP for several high-profile attacks on opposition leaders and asserted the BNP was bent on eliminating Sheikh Hasina and the Awami League as a viable force. The BNP and its allies accused the AL of maligning Bangladesh at home and abroad out of jealousy over the government's performance on development and economic issues. Dialogue between the Secretaries General of the main ruling and opposition parties failed to sort out the electoral reform issues.

Caretaker Government, October 2006–January 2009

The 13th Amendment to the constitution required the president to offer the position of the Chief Adviser to the immediate past Chief Justice of the Supreme Court, Justice K.M. Hasan, once the previous parliamentary session expired on October 28, 2006. The AL opposed Justice Hasan, alleging that he belonged to the ruling BNP in the past and that the BNP government in 2004 amended the constitution to extend the retirement age for the Supreme Court judges to ensure Justice Hasan became the Chief Adviser to help BNP win the elections. Justice Hasan declined the position, and after 2 days of violent protests, President Iajuddin Ahmed also assumed the role of Chief Adviser to the caretaker government.

On January 3, 2007, the Awami League announced it would boycott the January 22 parliamentary elections. The Awami League planned a series of country-wide general strikes and transportation blockades.

On January 11, 2007, President Iajuddin Ahmed declared a state of emergency, resigned as Chief Adviser, and indefinitely postponed parliamentary elections. On January 12, 2007, former Bangladesh Bank governor Fakhruddin Ahmed was sworn in as the new Chief Adviser, and ten new advisers (ministers) were appointed. Under emergency provisions, the government suspended certain fundamental rights guaranteed by the constitution and detained a large number of politicians and others on suspicion of involvement in corruption and other crimes. In January 2008, a reshuffle of the caretaker government took place, which included the appointment of special assistants to help oversee the functioning of the administration.

On July 16, 2007 the government arrested Awami League president and former Prime Minister Sheikh Hasina on charges of extortion during her tenure as Prime Minister. Hasina was released on parole in June 2008 and allowed to travel to the United States for medical treatment. The cases against her continue. On September 3, 2007, the government arrested BNP chairperson and former Prime Minister Khaleda Zia on charges of corruption. Sheikh Hasina returned from abroad and Khaleda Zia was released from prison to lead their respective parties in the parliamentary election campaign in the fall of 2008.

Municipal elections were held in 13 city corporations and municipalities on August 4, 2008. These elections were judged free and fair by international and domestic observers. The Election Commission registered over 80 million voters in preparation for parliamentary elections, which were held December 29, 2008. The Awami League swept to a landslide victory in what domestic and international observers declared a free, fair and credible election. The caretaker government ended on January 6, 2009 when Awami League President Sheikh Hasina became Prime Minister.

Sheikh Hasina, 2009–Present

Prime Minister Sheikh Hasina appointed a cabinet of relative newcomers upon taking office in January 2009. The BNP-led opposition attended the opening of the Parliament session, but has since mounted several boycotts in protest of perceived slights by the ruling party. Both sides struggle to break free from their shared history of confrontational politics, and key institutions necessary for strengthening democracy remain weak. As the new government was settling into office, it was rocked by a mutiny by border guards on February 25-26, 2009 in which more than 50 army officers were murdered.

Prime Minister Hasina has sought to increase Bangladesh's presence on the world stage. As leader of one of the countries most vulnerable to climate change, Hasina has been a vocal advocate for mitigation and adaptation by both developed and developing countries, aligning with the Copenhagen Accord in January 2010. In a sharp change from previous administrations, her government has actively confronted violent extremist groups to deny space to terrorist networks and activities within its borders. The simultaneous elections of the Awami League and the Congress Party in India set the stage for renewed bilateral talks between the countries, an atmosphere which has been improved by counterterrorism cooperation. In January 2010, Hasina traveled to New Delhi to meet with Indian Prime Minister Singh, where they signed three agreements on mutual legal assistance in criminal matters, transfer of sentenced persons, and countering terrorism, organized crime, and illegal drug trafficking; and two memoranda of understanding on energy sharing and cultural exchange programs.

GOVERNMENT AND POLITICAL CONDITIONS

Bangladesh is a parliamentary democracy. Prime Minister Sheikh Hasina Wazed led the Awami League (AL) alliance, a 14-party coalition with an overwhelming majority of parliamentary seats. International and domestic observers considered the 2008 elections to be free and fair, with isolated irregularities and sporadic violence. There were instances in which elements of the security forces acted independently of civilian control.

On June 30, 2011, the AL-led parliament passed the 15th amendment to the constitution over an opposition boycott, abolishing the provision mandating that elections be held under a neutral, caretaker government. The caretaker government system was established before the 1996 parliamentary general elections in response to the electoral system's perceived vulnerability to political manipulation. The amendment followed a May supreme court ruling that declared the caretaker system unconstitutional.

Under the 15th amendment, the 2013 parliamentary general elections and all subsequent elections are to be supervised by an independent electoral commission operating under the political government in power, which in 2013 would still be the current AL-led government. Many independent observers criticized the change because they believed that the electoral system's vulnerabilities to political manipulation that had necessitated the creation of the caretaker system had not been addressed and would resurface, leaving the electoral system vulnerable to political manipulation. This issue became a matter of enormous partisan concern and attention during 2011.

The parliament had 350 members, 300 of whom were directly elected. Selection for these seats was based on each political party's proportional representation within the 300-member group of directly elected legislators. An additional 50 seats are reserved for women, who are selected by political parties. Party leaders appointed candidates for elections, and there were allegations that wealthy candidates could purchase nominations from party leaders with campaign contributions or personal gifts.

Opposition parties continued to boycott parliament throughout the year but returned on certain days to fulfill the procedures necessary to retain their seats. They demanded fair treatment by the speaker and the ruling party legislators as preconditions for their return to the house. The parliament formed all 48 standing committees in the first session with participation from opposition parties. The opposition MPs continued to participate in standing committee meetings despite their absence from parliament.

Recent Elections

Sheikh Hasina, leader of the AL, became prime minister in 2009, following the parliamentary elections of 2008, which international and local observers deemed free and fair. The 14-party AL alliance held 229 of the 300 available seats. Hasina's cabinet included representatives from the other parties in her coalition. Hasina replaced Fakhruddin Ahmed, chief adviser to the caretaker government, as the head of government. BNP chairperson and former prime minister Khaleda Zia became leader of the opposition.

Participation of Women and Minorities: According to the law, women are eligible to contest any seat among the 345 MPs, but 45 additional seats were reserved for women. In June the 15th amendment raised this number to 50 out of 350 MPs. There was no provision to provide parliamentary seats for minorities.

The indigenous community experienced widespread discrimination and abuses, despite government quotas for indigenous participation in the civil service and higher education. The government also failed to protect indigenous persons from societal violence.

During 2011 the government released several statements announcing that the country's indigenous population was not "indigenous" and henceforth would be known as "small ethnic minorities" instead. The 15th amendment to the constitution codified this new category. Indigenous leaders disputed the new nomenclature, citing their long history in the Chittagong Hill Tracts and the plains land of Bengal. Indigenous leaders also objected to the term "small ethnic minorities" because its Bangla translation, upojati, is a pejorative term connoting "tribal."

Principal Government Officials

Last Updated: 1/31/2013

Pres.: **Zillur RAHMAN**
Prime Min.: **Sheikh HASINA Wajed**
Min. of Agriculture: **Matia CHOWDHURY**
Min. of Civil Aviation & Tourism: **Faruq KHAN, Lt. Col. (Ret.)**
Min. of Commerce: **Ghulam Muhammad QUADER**
Min. of Communications: **Obaidul QUADER**
Min. of Cultural Affairs: **Abdul Kalam AZAD**
Min. of Defense: **Sheikh HASINA Wajed**
Min. of Disaster Management & Relief: **A. H. Mahmood ALI**
Min. of Education: **Nurul Islam NAHID**
Min. of Environment & Forest: **Hasan MAHMUD**
Min. of Expatriates' Welfare & Overseas Employment: **Khandaker Mosharraf HOSSAIN**
Min. of Finance: **Abu Maal Abdul MUHITH**
Min. of Fisheries & Livestock: **Abdul Latif BISWAS**
Min. of Food: **Abdur RAZZAQUE**
Min. of Foreign Affairs: **Dipu MONI**
Min. of Health & Family Welfare: **A. F. M. Ruhul HAQUE**
Min. of Home Affairs: **Mohiuddin Khan ALAMGIR**
Min. of Industries: **Dilip BARUA**
Min. of Information: **Hasan Haq INU**
Min. of Information & Communication Technology: **Mostafa FARUQ Mohammad**
Min. of Labor & Employment: **Raziuddin Ahmed RAJU**
Min. of Land: **Rezaul Karim HIRA**
Min. of Law, Justice, & Parliamentary Affairs: **Shafique AHMED**
Min. of Local Govt., Rural Development, & Cooperatives:**Syed Ashraful ISLAM**
Min. of Planning: **A. K. KHANDEKAR, Air VMar. (Ret.)**
Min. of Posts & Telecommunications: **Sahara KHATUN**
Min. of Power, Energy, & Mineral Resources: **Sheikh HASINA Wajed**
Min. of Primary & Mass Education: **Afsarul AMEEN**
Min. of Public Admin.: **Sheikh HASINA Wajed**
Min. of Railways: **Mujibul HUQ**
Min. of Shipping: **Shahkahan KHAN**
Min. of Social Welfare: **Enamul Haq Mostafa SHAHID**
Min. of Textiles & Jute: **Abdul Latif SIDDIQUI**
Min. of Water Resources: **Ramesh Chandra SEN**
Min. Without Portfolio: **Suranjit Sen GUPTA**
Governor, Bangladesh Bank: **Atiur RAHMAN**
Ambassador to the US: **Akramul QADER**
Permanent Representative to the UN, New York: **Abdulkalam Abdul MOMEN**

Bangladesh maintains an Embassy in the United States at 3510 International Drive NW, Washington, DC 20008 (tel: 202-244-0183; fax: 202-244-5366). Bangladesh has Consulates General in New York and Los Angeles.

ECONOMY

The economy has grown 5-6% per year since 1996 despite political instability, poor infrastructure, corruption, insufficient power supplies, and slow implementation of economic reforms. Bangladesh remains a poor, overpopulated, and inefficiently-governed nation. Although more than half of GDP is generated through the service sector, 45% of Bangladeshis are employed in the agriculture sector with rice as the single-most-important product. Bangladesh's growth was resilient during the 2008–09 global financial crisis and recession. Garment exports, totaling $12.3 billion in FY09 and remittances from overseas Bangladeshis, totaling $11 billion in FY10, accounted for almost 12% of GDP.

Labor Conditions

By law every child must attend school through grade five or the age of 10 years, but there is no effective legal mechanism to enforce this provision, and child labor was widespread. The BLA regulates child employment depending on the type of work and the child's age. The law specifies penalties for child labor violations, typically nominal fines of less than 5,000 taka ($63).

According to a 2003 government survey of urban areas, street children, mostly boys, engaged in various forms of work, such as begging, working as porters, shining shoes, collecting paper, and selling flowers. Boys and girls, often those living on the streets, were exploited in illicit activities, including smuggling and trading arms and drugs. Children routinely performed domestic work. The government occasionally brought criminal charges against employers who abused domestic servants.

For the five-year period 2007–12, the National Minimum Wage Board (NMWB) established the minimum monthly wage at 1,500 taka ($19) for all economic sectors not covered by industry-specific wages. The NMWB may convene at any time, but it must meet every five years in a tripartite forum to set wage structures and benefits industry by industry. In the garment industry, the Ministry of Labor raised the minimum wage in June 2010 from 1,662 taka ($21) per month to 3,000 taka ($38) per month; however, wages were sometimes higher than the minimum wage. Wages in the EPZs were typically higher than general national wage levels. None of the set minimum wages provided a sufficient standard of living for urban dwellers. It was common practice for garment factories to force workers to work overtime, delay their pay for months, and deny full leave benefits. According to the Welfare Monitoring Survey published by the Bangladesh Bureau of Statistics, the poverty rate was 31.9 percent.

By law a standard workday is eight hours, but workers may work 10 hours a day in certain instances. Overtime is permitted, but the employer must pay double the basic wage and interim wages for the overtime work. A standard workweek is 48 hours but can be extended up to 60 hours, subject to the payment of overtime allowances. By law the average workweek should not exceed 56 hours. Workers must have one hour of rest if they work for more than six hours a day, a half-hour of rest for more than five hours a day, and one hour's rest at intervals for more than eight hours' work in a day. Factory workers receive one day off every week. Shop workers receive one-and-one-half days off per week.

In practice these legal limits were routinely violated and enforcement of the provisions was weak. In the ready-made garment sector, employers often required workers to work 12 hours a day or more to meet export deadlines, but they did not always properly compensate workers for their time.

The BLA established occupational health and safety standards. Workers groups stated that legally established standards were sufficient, but they were rarely implemented. Safety conditions at many workplaces were extremely poor. Because of high unemployment rates and inadequate enforcement of laws, workers who demanded redress of dangerous working conditions or who refused to work under hazardous conditions risked losing their jobs.

U.S.-BANGLADESH RELATIONS

Although the U.S. relationship with Bangladesh was initially troubled because of strong U.S. ties with Pakistan, U.S.-Bangladesh friendship and support developed quickly following Bangladesh's independence from Pakistan in 1971.

U.S.-Bangladesh relations are excellent. These relations were boosted in March 2000 when President Clinton visited Bangladesh, the first-ever visit by a sitting U.S. President, when Secretary of State Colin Powell visited in June 2003, as well as when Secretary of Defense Donald Rumsfeld visited in June 2004. A centerpiece of the bilateral relationship is a large U.S. aid program, totaling about $163 million for 2009. U.S. economic and food aid programs, which began as emergency relief following the 1971 war for independence, now concentrate on long-term development. U.S. assistance objectives include stabilizing population growth, protecting human health, encouraging broad-based economic growth, and building democracy. In total, the United States has provided more than $5.5 billion in food and development assistance to Bangladesh. Food aid under Titles I, II, and III of PL-480 (congressional "food-for-peace" legislation) has been designed to help Bangladesh meet minimum food requirements, promote food production, and moderate fluctuation in consumer prices. Other U.S. development assistance emphasizes family planning and health, agricultural development, and rural employment. The United States works with other donors and the Bangladesh Government to avoid duplication and ensure that resources are used to maximum benefit.

Since 1986, with the exception of 1988–89, when an aircraft purchase made the trade balance even, the U.S. trade balance with Bangladesh has been negative, due largely to growing imports of ready-made garments. Jute carpet backing is the other major U.S. import from Bangladesh. Total imports from Bangladesh were about $2.6 billion (excluding services) in FY 2005, up from $2.1 billion in 2002. In 2007 total imports reached $3.4 billion. U.S. exports to Bangladesh (some $333 million—excluding services—in 2005, and $456 million in 2007) include wheat, fertilizer, cotton, communications equipment, aircraft, and medical supplies, a portion of which is financed by the U.S. Agency for International Development (USAID). A bilateral investment treaty was signed in 1989.

Another trade related issue between the two countries involves the export processing zones (EPZs). The government provides several tax, foreign exchange, customs and labor incentives to investors in the EPZs. One such incentive provided in recent years was an exemption from certain labor laws, which had the practical effect of prohibiting trade unions from the zones. The U.S. Generalized System of Preferences (GSP) law requires the beneficiary country to satisfy certain conditions relating to labor rights. On July 13, 2004, the government passed a bill allowing limited trade unionism in the EPZs effective November 1, 2006. Implementation of the law has been slow, however, and a U.S. labor organization has filed a petition with the U.S. Government to suspend Bangladesh's GSP privileges in the absence of progress on labor rights issues.

Relations between Bangladesh and the United States were further strengthened by the participation of Bangladesh troops in the 1991 Gulf war coalition, and alongside U.S. forces in numerous UN peacekeeping operations, including Haiti in 1994, as well as by the assistance of a U.S. naval task force after a disastrous March 1991 cyclone in Bangladesh. The relief efforts of U.S. troops are credited with having saved as many as 200,000 lives. In response to Bangladesh's worst flooding of the century in 1998, the United States donated 700,000 metric tons of food grains, helping to mitigate shortages. In July 2006, the U.S. Navy's hospital ship Mercy visited Bangladesh and U.S. personnel worked with Bangladeshi medical personnel to provide medical treatment to Bangladeshi patients. Between 2005 and 2008, the United States obligated $2.2 million in grant aid funding (Foreign Military Financing) to purchase Defender class small boats for the Coast Guard of Bangladesh, and allocated $934,000 in IMET (International Military Education and Training) for 2007. In addition to heavy flooding at the end of summer 2007, Cyclone Sidr hit the country on November 15, causing widespread devastation and affecting the lives of millions of people. Following the cyclone, U.S. troops and two U.S. naval vessels assisted in the delivery of relief supplies to cyclone victims. USAID provided approximately $36.5 million in food and relief items to Cyclone Sidr-affected people and has continued its support through rebuilding houses for people in the cyclone-affected areas. An additional $80 million will be provided to rebuild livelihoods, strengthen local government, generate economic recovery through income-generation activities, and to plan and construct cyclone shelters in the disaster-prone areas.

Additionally, Bangladesh has become a valuable United States ally in global efforts to defeat terrorism. As part of these efforts, the Government of Bangladesh has begun to address problems of money laundering and weak border controls to ensure that Bangladesh does not become a terrorist safe-haven. Despite porous borders, ungoverned spaces, and poor service delivery, Bangladesh's strong national identity and moderate Islamic tradition help it serve as a key player in combating extremism.

U.S. Development Efforts in Bangladesh

USAID is the principal U.S. Government agency providing development assistance in Bangladesh. USAID has had a full-fledged cooperation program in Bangladesh since 1971. It works closely with the Government of Bangladesh, non-governmental organizations, the private sector, and other donors. USAID's yearly development budget for Bangladesh averages $100 million. In 2009, planned assistance amounted to roughly $163 million, including help for people living in the Cyclone Sidr-affected regions.

Since 1971, USAID has provided over $5.5 billion in development assistance, with half of that amount provided in food aid. With USAID assistance, Bangladesh has seen significant improvements in living conditions. Today, Bangladeshis have better access to health care and electricity, increased agricultural productivity and better nutrition. USAID works with communities in disaster preparedness and to improve their ability to manage emergency food supplies. USAID programs assist Bangladeshi organizations and communities in addressing their needs in the areas of health and family planning, income generation, agriculture and food security, disaster management, democracy and human rights, and education.

U.S. Foreign Assistance Program Areas

USAID supports the provision of low-cost, quality family planning services, maternal and child health care, and treatment for tuberculosis through a network of nongovernmental clinics and community health workers. USAID promotes the social marketing of contraceptives and selected maternal and child health products through private sector outlets. USAID-supported programs serve 38% of all couples using modern family planning methods. In 2008, USAID programs provided 1 million pregnancy-related checkups, vaccinations for 300,000 children, and essential care for 40,000 newborns. USAID targets the most at-risk populations with messages about the treatment of sexually transmitted infections. Although enrollment in primary school has improved in recent years, an estimated 40% of children still do not complete the second grade. USAID's pioneering work in early childhood education, including its support for 1,800 preschools and learning programs for older children, improves schools' ability to address poor attendance, low achievement, and high dropout rates in primary school. The USAID-funded Sesame Street television program "Sisimpur" is the most widely viewed children's television program in Bangladesh, reaching over 9 million viewers weekly.

Bangladesh is highly vulnerable to natural disasters, including cyclones, floods, landslides, droughts, and earthquakes. USAID's food security, disaster readiness, and humanitarian assistance programs target 3,500 of the most at-risk villages and help to provide a safety net of short-term emergency assistance during natural disasters, as well as long-term solutions that raise incomes, improve health, and enhance food security.

Since 2005, USAID has financed various asset protection activities, such as raising the ground of rural homes for 4,400 vulnerable farming households to protect assets such as vegetable gardens and farming animals. USAID has funded the construction of earthen embankments, which protect crops and allow more time to harvest, and walls to stop erosion in low-lying areas. In 11 southern coastal districts impacted by Cyclone Sidr, USAID plans to build 100 schools that will serve as shelters in the event of a disaster.

USAID's most significant contribution in Bangladesh has been to help bring electricity to rural areas. In 1971, only 3% of the population had electricity; today, 44% do. To protect natural resources and empower local people who depend on them for their livelihoods, USAID works with communities to establish management systems that encourage the wise use of aquatic and tropical forest resources and restore habitats and ecosystems. USAID also expands access to global markets by assisting key sectors, such as aquaculture and horticulture, to improve the quality of their products, increase sales, create jobs, and promote investment, particularly for the benefit of women, youth, and small and medium enterprise suppliers.

Elected officials and public institutions frequently fail to effectively address citizens' needs, and large- and small-scale corruption is pervasive. To fight these trends, USAID addresses the root causes of corruption by improving the quality of governance by elected leaders, developing fair and open election processes, improving the functioning of political parties, and increasing parliamentary and citizen oversight of the national budget. USAID also works with nongovernmental organizations, local governments, and municipal associations to improve government accountability and the delivery of social services. These efforts have led to direct budget allocations from the national government to local government associations for the first time ever. In addition, these programs have achieved a 50% increase in local revenues in targeted areas.

Trafficking in persons is a significant transnational crime in Bangladesh. With USAID's support, the Bangladesh Government made significant progress in dealing with human trafficking, removing the country from prospective U.S. sanctions. USAID has provided assistance to more than 500 trafficking survivors since 2006. The United States and Bangladesh have been friends and close allies for many years. Through its development assistance programs, the U.S. Government will continue to be a strong and close partner of the Bangladeshi people.

Principal U.S. Embassy Officials

Last Updated: 1/14/2013

DHAKA (E) Madani Avenue, Baridhara, Dhaka, Bangladesh, +880-2885-5500/22, Fax +880-2-882-3744 (Tel Operator) or 880 2 882 3159 (Mail Room), INMARSAT Tel +881-676-311-001–PCC, Workweek: 0800 to 1630 Sun–Thurs, Website: http://dhaka.usembassy.gov/

DCM OMS:	Cristina Moreau
AMB OMS:	Elizabeth Hamilton
CDC:	Dr. James Heffelfinger
FCS:	Lela Mulgaokr
FM:	Bill Hedges (Tdy)
HRO:	Tamara Comiskey
MGT:	Colette Marcellin
MLO/ODC:	MAJ Patrick Bunch
POL/MIL:	Andrei Cotton
POSHO:	Bill Hedges (Tdy)
SDO/DATT:	LTC Lance Jacobsen
AMB:	Dan Mozena
CON:	Jamie Fouss
DCM:	Jon Danilowicz
PAO:	Veraj Lebailly
GSO:	Bradley Page
RSO:	Bernard Nixon
AFSA:	Gshayman/Syoung
AGR:	David Leishman
AID:	Richard Greene
CLO:	Magdalena Dimitrowa
ECON:	Tobias Glucksman
EEO:	Catherine McFarland
FMO:	Priyadarshi Sen
ICASS Chair:	Karl Clark
IMO:	D. Charles Eckert
IPO:	Gabriel Cudal
ISO:	Craig Carter
ISSO:	Craig Carter
POL:	Pushpinder Dhillon
State ICASS:	Jamie Fouss

TRAVEL

Consular Information Sheet

January 6, 2012

Country Description: Bangladesh is located on the northern edge of the Bay of Bengal, bordered on three sides by India, and also shares a border with Burma. One hundred and fifty million people inhabit Bangladesh, which has a land area of 55,598 square miles, slightly smaller than the size of Iowa. This seventh most populous nation is one of the most crowded countries in the world. Bangladesh consists primarily of low-lying deltaic plains. The Ganges and Brahmaputra Rivers (known as the Padma and Jamuna in Bangladesh) and countless smaller tributaries crisscross the country. The capital, Dhaka, is fewer than 25 feet above sea level.

During the monsoon season from June to October between 30% and 70% of the country is under water due to flooding of rivers. Heavy rainfall is characteristic of Bangladesh, with most parts of the country receiving at least 200 centimeters of rainfall per year. Annual cyclones can cause extreme flooding and have led to great losses of life and property damage. Bangladesh is a democratic republic with a parliamentary form of government. Bangladesh remains a developing country with severe infrastructure shortcomings. Tourist facilities are minimal as are capacities to deal with emergency situations.

Smart Traveler Enrollment Program (STEP)/Embassy Locations: If you are going to live in or visit Bangladesh, please take the time to tell our Embassy about your trip. If you enroll, we can keep you up to date with important safety and security announcements. We can also help your friends and family get in touch with you in an emergency.

U.S. Embassy, Dhaka, Bangladesh
Madani Avenue, Baridhara,
Dhaka, 1212
Embassy telephone: (88-02) 885-5500
American Citizen Services telephone: (88-02) 882-3805
Emergency after-hours telephone: (88-02) 885-5500, press "0" and ask for the duty officer
American Citizen Services Email: DhakaACS@state.gov
Facsimile: (88-02) 882-4449

The Consular Section's American Citizens Services unit operates Sunday through Thursday from 8:00 a.m. to 4:30 p.m. All American Citizens Services are by appointment only, except in the event of an emergency.

Entry/Exit Requirements for U.S. Citizens: A passport valid for six months longer than your planned length of stay in Bangladesh and at least one blank visa page, visa, and onward or return ticket are required to enter Bangladesh. The United States is on a list of countries eligible for visitor (tourist) visas on arrival at Hazrat Shahjalal International Airport in Dhaka, Bangladesh. However, Bangladesh has not widely publicized their policies for visas on arrival. You may encounter delays in airport visa issuance or be refused entry to countries enroute to Bangladesh if you do not have a visa prior to arrival in Bangladesh. Therefore, we highly recommend that you obtain a visa prior to arrival.

While visas on arrival can be issued with validity up to a maximum of 30 days, most visas on arrival are issued only with the validity of the duration of the visitor's planned travel in Bangladesh. The visa on arrival fee is US $150 plus taxes, payable upon arrival in Dhaka in US dollars, cash only. All applicants must provide one passport-sized photograph; there are no facilities for obtaining passport-sized photos at Hazrat Shahjalal International Airport in Dhaka. Please note that visas on arrival are not available at Shah Amanat International Airport located in Chittagong or Osmani International Airport in Sylhet. A valid visa in an expired or canceled U.S. passport is not acceptable to Bangladeshi authorities. If you are issued a new U.S. passport for any reason, you will need a new visa. You may obtain a visa in your new passport at the Immigration Office at the Hazrat Shahjalal International Airport in Dhaka. The fee is USD $150.

Please carry photocopies of the biodata page of your U.S. passport and the pages containing the Bangladeshi visa and Bangladeshi immigration stamps. If your passport is lost or stolen, copies will help you apply for a replacement passport and an exit visa from the Bangladesh government. Replacing a lost visa, which is required in order to exit the country, may take three to four business days.

Bangladeshi-Americans and their immediate family members are eligible for a "No Visa Required for Travel to Bangladesh" seal, which can be issued by the nearest Bangladeshi Embassy or Consulate. This endorsement allows travelers multiple entries into Bangladesh with no restriction on duration of stay, for the validity of the bearer's passport. As with visas, "No Visa Required" seals are no longer valid in expired passports. If the passport bearing your original "No Visa Required" seal is lost or expires, you must obtain a new seal in a valid passport prior to entering or departing Bangladesh.

If you intend to use Dhaka as a hub to visit other countries in the region, ensure that you obtain a multiple-entry Bangladeshi visa before your arrival. If you intend to work for a non-governmental organization (NGO) in Bangladesh, you should ensure that your sponsor hasprovided you with up-to-date advice on the kind of visa you must obtain before your arrival. It is difficult and time-consuming to change your immigration status after you have arrived in Bangladesh.

Visas to Bangladesh that are expiring may be extended at the Directorate of Immigration and Passport, located at Sher-e-Bangla Nagar, Agargaon, and Dhaka. The phone numbers are (880-2) 913-1891 and 913-4011.

Visa rules introduced in October 2006 require foreign nationals who come to Bangladesh to work or for long-term visits to have the appropriate work permits and clearances on arrival. There are increased financial penalties for overstaying visas. Additionally, those who overstay for more than 90 days could be charged with violating the Foreigners Act of 1946. For further information on these rules, please check with the nearest Bangladeshi Embassy or Consulate (U.S. addresses listed below) before traveling, or visit the Bangladeshi Immigration Police website for further details on rules relating to foreigner registration.

When traveling by air, all foreigners except children under the age of two must pay a departure tax. This tax is often included when air tickets are purchased. Otherwise, it is collected at the airport at the time of departure. The amount of the departure tax varies depending on the destination (e.g., the departure tax for the

United States is the most expensive, at Bangladesh Taka (BDT) 2,500). There is no tax for transit passengers transiting Bangladesh without a visa and in country for 72 hours or fewer. These requirements are subject to change, and travelers are advised to check with the Embassy of Bangladesh before traveling.

If your visa or "No Visa Required" seal has expired or is in a passport that is no longer valid, you should expect delays upon departure. Travelers who have overstayed by 1 – 15 days will be fined 200 Bangladeshi Taka (Tk) per day, which can be paid at the Shah Jalal International Airport Immigration Office. Fines for overstays in excess of 15 days cannot be paid at the Shah Jalal International Airport. Travelers who have overstayed 15 – 90 days are subject to a fine of 500 Tk per day, which must be paid at the Immigration and Passport Office at 7th Sher-E-Bangla Nagar, Agargaon, Dhaka. Individuals who overstay in excess of 90 days face prosecution by the Bangladeshi Immigration and Passport Authority.

The Government of Bangladesh has announced that a new security surcharge will be levied on departing passengers, but no date of implementation has been set.

The Government of Bangladesh has no written policy regarding the entry of individuals with HIV/AIDS. However, according to anecdotal reports, some HIV/AIDS entry restrictions may exist for visitors to and foreign residents of Bangladesh. The Government of Bangladesh has informed the Embassy that a health officer or immigration officer at the airport who has concerns about an individual's possible HIV/AIDS status will make a case-specific determination regarding that individual's entry. For further information on entry requirements and possible exceptions to the exit requirements, please contact the Embassy of Bangladesh, 3510 International Drive NW, Washington, DC 20008, telephone 202-244-0183/7248/7216/3830/3571, fax 202-244-2771/7830, or the Bangladeshi Consulates in New York at 211 E. 43rd Street, Suite 502, New York, NY 10017, telephone 212-599-6767/6850/1874, fax 212-682-9211 or Los Angeles at 10850 Wilshire Boulevard, Suite 1250, Los Angeles, CA 90024, telephone 323-932-0100, fax 323-932-9703.

Threats to Safety and Security: The security situation in Bangladesh is fluid, and U.S. citizens are urged to exercise caution at all times and check with the U.S. Embassy for the latest information. U.S. citizens should always practice good personal security. Be aware of your surroundings and keep a low profile. Monitor local news reports, vary your routes and times in carrying out daily activities, and consider the level of security present when you visit public places, including religious sites, or choosing hotels, restaurants, and entertainment and recreation venues.

Spontaneous demonstrations take place in Bangladesh. U.S. citizens are reminded that even demonstrations intended to be peaceful can turn confrontational and escalate into violence quickly and unexpectedly. U.S. citizens are therefore urged to avoid the areas of demonstrations if possible, and to exercise caution if within the vicinity of any demonstrations. Many demonstrations occur on college and university campuses. For this reason, the U.S. Embassy recommends that U.S. citizens proceed with caution when visiting universities and colleges in Bangladesh.

The U.S. Embassy also recommends that U.S. citizens avoid Road 86 in the Gulshan-2 area of Dhaka. One of the major national political party's headquarters is located on this road. Large unscheduled events occur frequently and usually spill out on to the road, making it impassable. Baitul Mukarram Mosque (National Mosque), Muktangan (bordered by Baitul Mukarram Mosque to the east, the General Post Office or GPO to the south, the Secretariat to the West, and Topkhana Road to the North), and Topkhana-Motijheel Road should be avoided on Fridays from noon to 6:00 pm. Protests involving workers from the large garment-manufacturing industry are common. Visitors to Bangladesh should check U.S. Embassy Dhaka's website for updated information on the current political and security situation. A hartal or general strike is a mass protest, and can involve a total shutdown of the country. It is a recognized political method for articulating any political demand. Hartals can turn violent if the population, or political groups, enforce the shut down. Even demonstrations that are meant to be peaceful can become violent and unpredictable. You should avoid them if at all possible. Be alert and aware of your surroundings and pay attention to local news reports.

U.S. citizens are advised against traveling to the Khagrachari, Rangamati, and Bandarban Hill Tracts districts (collectively known as the Chittagong Hill Tracts) due to kidnappings and other security incidents. Foreigners traveling in the Chittagong Hill Tracts are required to register with local authorities.

Additionally, the U.S. Embassy has received reports of incidents of kidnapping, arms, and narcotics smuggling and clashes between local Bangladeshis and Rohingya refugees in areas near Rohingya refugee camps in the Teknaf, Kutupalong, Ukhia, and Ramu areas of the Cox's Bazaar district. The U.S. Embassy recommends against travel to these areas. Individuals who choose to visit these districts are urged to exercise extreme caution.

The fire department is accessible by dialing 199 if in Dhaka and (88) (02) 199 if outside of Dhaka. The fire department can also be reached by mobile phone from anywhere in Bangladesh by dialing (88) 01713-038181, (88) 01713-038182 or (88) 01730-336699. Improper storage of chemicalaccelerants,improperly installed electrical systems, lack of fire escapes, burglar bars on windows preventing escape, and hours-long fire department response make fires common in Bangladesh and extremely dangerous. One fire in June 2010 in Dhaka led to the deaths of over 120 individuals. In case of fire leave the area immediately.

Stay up to date by:

- Bookmarking our Bureau of Consular Affairs website, which contains the current Travel Warnings and Travel Alerts as well as the Worldwide Caution.
- Following us on Twitter and the Bureau of Consular Affairs page on Facebook as well.
- Downloading our free Smart Traveler IPhone App to have travel information at your fingertips.
- Calling 1-888-407-4747 toll-free within the U.S. and Canada, or a regular toll line, 1-202-501-4444, from other countries.
- Taking some time before travel to consider your personal security.

Crime: The Department of State rates Dhaka as having a high crime rate; the types of crime are comparable to any other world capital or large city. Always take precautions such as being alert and aware, locking home and vehicle doors, varying routes and schedules, traveling in groups, never walking alone at night, and parking near entrances or security lamps. Hiring a 24-hour guard is highly recommended due to the possibility of trespassing and break-ins. In general, crime dramatically increases in the hours of darkness; this includes dusk and dawn. Urban crime can be organized or opportunistic, conducted by individuals or groups, and commonly encompasses fraud, theft (larceny, pick-pocketing, and snatch-and-grab), robbery (armed and unarmed), carjacking, rape, assault, and burglary (home and auto). Incidents of crime and levels of violence are higher in low-income residential and congested commercial areas, but are seen in wealthier areas as well, including the Diplomatic Enclave in Dhaka. Many of the reported attacks occurred while the victims were riding in rickshaws; other incidents involved the targeting of small groups of foreigners on foot. To reduce your risk while riding in a rickshaw, keep your bags or valuables under your legs or behind you, away from passing vehicle traffic, and ensure that your bag's carrying straps are not visible. For security reasons, Embassy personnel are prohibited from riding in taxis, buses, rickshaws in Dhaka (outside of Dhaka's Diplomatic Enclave) and engine-powered rickshaws (also known as CNGs or auto rickshaws) and recommends that U.S. citizens exercise similar caution. Although U.S. embassy personnel may use trains in Bangladesh, travelers are warned to use extreme caution as trains in Bangladesh are known to be boarded by robbers at all hours of the day on all routes and larceny commonly occurs. In late August 2011, one man was killed and several injured during an attempted robbery of a train departing Dhaka. Avoid carrying or displaying large sums of money or wearing expensive jewelry and be aware of your surroundings when you use ATMs. Valuables should be stored in hotel safety deposit boxes and should not be left unattended in hotel rooms.

Taxis, if available at all, are unsafe and unreliable. Long-term visitors typically hire a car and driver; short-term visitors should hire a car through their hotel and arrange in advance with their hotel or other reliable party for pickup by hotel vehicle or similar transportation.

Women should observe stringent security precautions, including avoiding use of public transport after dark without the company of known and trustworthy companions, restricting evening entertainment to well-known venues, and avoiding isolated areas when alone at any time of day. Keep your hotel room number confidential and make sure hotel room doors have chains, deadlocks, and spy-holes. Hire only reliable cars and drivers and avoid traveling in vehicles hailed on the street.

Police are generally responsive to reports of crimes against U.S. citizens. However, crimes often go unsolved.

If you are assaulted, the Embassy recommends that you not fight with your attacker. Flee to a safe area and report the situation to the local authorities. We encourage all U.S. citizens to carry their mobile phones with them at all times.

Don't buy counterfeit and pirated goods, even if they are widely available. Not only is it illegal in the United States, you may be breaking local law too.

Victims of Crime: If you or someone you know becomes the victim of a crime abroad, you should contact the local police and the nearest U.S. embassy or consulate. We can:

- Replace a stolen passport.
- Help you find appropriate medical care if you are the victim of violent crimes such as assault or rape.
- Put you in contact with the appropriate police authorities, and if you want us to, we cancontact family members or friend.
- Help you understand the local criminal justice process and direct you to local attorneys, although it is important to remember that local authorities are responsible for investigating and prosecuting the crime.

The local equivalent to the "911" emergency line in Bangladesh is (88) (02) 999, which connects you to the Dhaka Metro Police Exchange. There is no guarantee that English will be spoken or understood at the Dhaka Metro Police Exchange. The Police Exchange can only transfer calls to the appropriate police station within the Dhaka metropolitan area, and the caller will have to speak with that police station in order to actually have any police services performed. There is similarly no guarantee that English will be spoken or understood at the local police station.

The Dhaka Metropolitan Police Department has established the following special phone number and e-mail address to assist non-Bangladeshi citizen victims of crime: mobile number (88) 01713-398355 and e-mail diplomathelpdesk@gmail.com. The Sylhet Metropolitan Police also have a Foreigners' Help Desk with the following phone number: (88) 01713-374364.

Outside Dhaka, the caller will need to directly contact the nearest police station. If you do not have the contact information for the nearest police station, call (88) (02) 999 to reach the Dhaka Metropolitan Police Switchboard, which should be able to provide the number of the appropriate police station within Bangladesh. However, they are unlikely to be able to transfer the call to a police station outside Dhaka. The caller should then hang up and dial the number provided by the Dhaka Metro Police Exchange. The ability to speak and/or understand English is even more unlikely at local police stations outside of Dhaka. The Police Exchange can also be reached by mobile phone from anywhere in Bangladesh at (88) (02) 712-4000.

Criminal Penalties: While you are traveling in another country, you are subject to its laws even if you are a U.S. citizen. Foreign laws and legal systems can be vastly different from our own. In some places, you may be taken in for questioning if you don't have your passport with you. In some places, it is illegal to take pictures of certain buildings. In some places, driving under the influence could land you immediately in jail. These criminal penalties will vary from country to country. There are also some things that might be legal in the country you visit, but still illegal in the United States, and you can be prosecuted under U.S. law if you buy pirated goods. Engaging in sexual conduct with children or using or disseminating child pornography in a foreign country is a crime prosecutable in the United States. If you break local laws in Bangladesh, your U.S. passport won't help you avoid arrest or prosecution. It's very important to know what's legal and what's not wherever you go. Persons violating Bangladeshi laws, even unknowingly, may be expelled, arrested, or imprisoned. The death penalty does exist in Bangladesh. Penalties for possession, use, or trafficking in illegal drugs in Bangladesh are severe, and convicted offenders can expect long jail sentences and heavy fines. While some countries will automatically notify the nearest U.S. embassy or consulate if a U.S. citizen is detained or arrested in a foreign country, that might not always be the case. To ensure that the United States is aware of your circumstances, request that the police and prison officials notify the nearest U.S. embassy or consulate as soon as you are arrested or detained overseas.

Special Circumstances: Air quality in Dhaka is extremely poor. Press reports indicate that Dhaka's Sulfur Dioxide and Nitrogen Dioxide concentrations far exceed World Health Organization permissible levels. Particulate matter, largely from diesel engine exhaust, is exceedingly high in Dhaka, far exceeding any permissible norms. Bangladesh's national encyclopedia calls the air pollution problem in Dhaka "acute" and further notes that lead levels, both suspended in air and blood levels in children and others far exceed allowable levels. The encyclopedia further notes that levels of Volatile Organic Compounds greatly exceed norms, that dust pollution causes many respiratory diseases, including asthma, in Bangladesh, and that 200 different organic compounds have been detected in Dhaka's atmosphere.

Traffic Congestion: Roads in Bangladesh, particularly in Dhaka, are extraordinarily crowded. In addition to inconvenience, congestion can delay arrival of emergency services including fire, ambulance, and police responses by multiple hours.

Ferry Safety: Bangladesh is a country criss-crossed with rivers, and thus uses a wide network of water-based public transportation. Ferries and other boats compete with the railroads as a major means of public transport. Typically overloaded and top-heavy, ferries do capsize, particularly during the monsoon season from June to October or during unexpected thunderstorms or windstorms. Dozens of people die in ferry accidents every year.

Maritime Piracy: The International Maritime Bureau, a specialized division of the International Chamber of Commerce, reports that Bangladesh is still listed as an area at high risk of maritime piracy with most attacks at Chittagong anchorages and moorages. Press reports indicate fishing vessels in Bangladeshi waters are frequently attacked and seized; crew members are sometimes lost. Mariners entering Bangladeshi waters should take appropriate precautionary measures.

Customs Restrictions: Bangladesh customs authorities may enforce strict regulations concerning temporary importation or export of items such as currency, household appliances, alcohol, cigarettes, and weapons. While there is no restriction on the amount of U.S. currencyvisitors may bring into Bangladesh, amounts in excess of USD $5000 must be declared to customs authorities at the time of arrival. The Government of Bangladesh does not allow the exchange of Taka for U.S. dollars, unless the customer has a ticket for travel outside of Bangladesh and an airplane ticket in hand. This is true for both cash and traveler's checks. Contact the Bangladeshi Embassy or Consulates for specific information regarding customs requirements.

Commercial and Land Disputes: If you are involved in commercial or property matters, be aware that the legal environment in Bangladesh is complex, and formal, regulated, transparent dispute mechanisms are not fully developed. Individuals and businesses cite corruption and an ineffective and painfully slow court system as serious problems. For more information, please contact the U.S. Trade Center at ustc-dhaka@state.gov.

Land disputes are common in Bangladesh and are extremely difficult to resolve through legal channels. Court cases can last for months, and sometimes years, without a final and accurate determination as to which party has legitimate claim to the title. The U.S. Embassy receives reports of numerous cases of U.S. citizens who claim to have been victimized in land-grabbing disputes. Rarely are these simple cases of a legitimate property owner versus an opportunistic land-grabber. More often, it is a case of disagreement between an owner who believes he or she has historical ownership of the property and a buyer who has just purchased the same property. One of them has been swindled, both of them have deeds, and it is next to impossible to determine whose deed is valid.

The dangers in becoming involved in a property dispute range from being threatened, injured, or murdered by hired thugs to being involved in a lengthy court dispute. Those involved in a court dispute run the risk of having cases filed against them, and may be arrested and jailed, sometimes for months. U.S. citizens wishing to purchase property in Bangladesh should be thoroughly aware of the risks involved and should only purchase property from a seller whose ownership is beyond doubt. Additionally, buyers should recognize the risks associated if they are not physically present to oversee their property. U.S. citizens should bear in mind that the U.S. Embassy cannot protect personal property and cannot take sides in a legal dispute.

Natural Disasters: Bangladesh is considered at extreme risk for natural disasters related to weather or other natural events. Flooding is the most common hazard, having killed untold hundreds of thousands of people even within the modern era. During the monsoon season, generally from June to October, between 30% and 70% of the country is under water due to flooding from the Ganges, Meghna, and the Brahmaputra Rivers. Cyclones, the local name for hurricanes, occur most frequently in May and October. Severe cyclones strike Bangladesh on average once every three years. Storm surges of up to 10 meters associated with these cyclones are relatively common. According to the World Bank, 60%of the worldwide deaths caused by cyclones in the last 20 years were in Bangladesh. Tornadoes are also common in Bangladesh, one of the most hard-hit countries in the world for these storms. Earthquakes are most common in the northern and eastern parts of Bangladesh, but as Bangladesh is close to the intersection of the Indian, Eurasian, and Australian tectonic plates, the potential for catastrophic earthquakes anywhere in the country is ever-present.

Forced Marriages: The U.S. Embassy occasionally receives reports of parents attempting to force their sons or daughters into an unwanted marriage. A marriage must be entered into with the full and free consent of both individuals. The parties involved should feel that they have a choice. If a U.S. citizen is being forced into a marriage against his or her will, help and advice from the Embassy are available. Please refer to the U.S. Embassy's information on forced marriage, contact the American Citizens Services unit by e-mail at DhakaACS@state.gov, or by phone at (88-02) 885-5500 from the United States, (02) 885-5500 from inside Bangladesh, or 885-5500 from within the city of Dhaka. All travelers to Bangladesh should maintain possession of their passports and return plane tickets to ensure independence to travel.

Visas to Other Countries: Visitors seeking to travel onward to India should obtain a visa to India in their home country. Appointments to apply for Indian visitor visas are extraordinarily difficult to obtain and visas issued to U.S. citizens in Bangladesh are limited to a single entry and are valid for only three months. Following the initial entry those who wish to re-enter India must wait two months to reapply for another visa. An Indian visitor visa issued in the United States is valid for multiple entries and for up to ten years. U.S. citizens seeking to obtain visas to Saudi Arabia in Bangladesh will encounter bureaucratic difficulties that render it effectively impossible to obtain that visa. We recommend all visa applications for Saudi Arabia be made in the United States.

Accessibility: While in Bangladesh individuals with disabilities may find accessibility and accommodation very different from what you find in the United States. Most roads in Bangladesh do not have proper footpaths and those that do are not easily accessible by persons with disabilities. Few roads have proper road crossings for pedestrians and those that do are large flyovers scaling the length of the road. These flyovers are accessible only by climbing stairs and walking across; there are no ramps or elevators to assist those with disabilities. The public transportation system is overcrowded and not easily accessible by those with disabilities. Most public places, including buildings, hotels, and restaurants, have little to no accommodation for persons with disabilities.

Disabled persons are legally afforded the same access to information rights as their non-disabled peers. The Ministry of Social Welfare, the Department of Social Services, and the National Foundation for the Development of the Disabled are the Bangladesh government agencies responsible for protecting the rights of persons with disabilities. Government facilities for treating persons with mental disabilities are largely inadequate. Several private initiatives existfor medical and vocational rehabilitation, as well as for employment of persons with disabilities. Several NGOs, including Handicap International, have programs focusing on helping and raising awareness of the challenges faced by the disabled.

Medical Facilities and Health Information: The general level of sanitation and health care in Bangladesh is far below U.S. standards. There is limited ambulance service in Bangladesh and attendants seldom are trained to provide the level of care seen in the United States. Traffic congestion and lack of a centralized emergency services system (911) makes patient transport slow and inefficient. Several hospitals in Dhaka (e.g., United, Apollo, and Square Hospitals) have emergency rooms that are equipped at the level of a community hospital, but most expatriates leave the country for all but the simplest medical procedures. Hospitals in the provinces are less well-equipped and supplied. Psychological and psychiatric services are limited throughout Bangladesh. There have been reports of counterfeit medications within the country, but medication from major pharmacies and hospitals is generally reliable. Medical evacuations to Bangkok or Singapore are often necessary for serious conditions or invasive procedures and can cost thousands of dollars. Despite government efforts, community sanitation and public health programs are inadequate in Bangladesh. Water supplies in Bangladesh are not potable. Typhoid fever, cholera, infectious hepatitis, giardia, cyclospora, and bacillary and amebic dysentery are only a few of the serious diseases transmitted by impure drinking water. Bottled drinking water, especially major brands, is generally safe for consumption. Fecal-oral contamination is common; improperly prepared meat and improperly cleaned vegetables can lead to food-borne illnesses such as cysticercosis, meurocysticercosis, and campylobacteriosis plus hepatitis A, B, C, and E.

Press reports indicate that fish and other raw foods are frequently treated with formalin to slow decomposition, that fruits, particularly bananas, are generally treated with chemicals to speed ripening, that milk products are adulterated with melamine, and vegetables tend to show elevated levels of arsenic due to contaminated groundwater. Washing, soaking, peeling, and /or thoroughly cooking food are mandatory procedures to minimize chemical, insecticide, bacterial, and parasitic contamination. Multiple strains of influenza continue to circulate in Bangladesh including H1N1 influenza A pandemic strain. H5N1 (Bird flu) was confirmed present in Dhaka in May of 2008 and sporadic outbreaks continue to occur. Any questions or concerns about influenza or other illnesses should be directed to a medical professional. Although the Embassy cannot provide medical advice or provide medical services to the public, a list of hospitals and doctors in Dhaka can be found on the Embassy website.

Bangladesh's Ministry of Health requires incoming travelers to complete a health questionnaire and if they report flu symptoms a sputum sample is collected. If the test result is positive for H1N1 influenza the traveler is contacted by the Ministry after 24 hours for further treatment.

Dengue fever, a mosquito-borne illness, is prevalent in Dhaka and surrounding areas, in particular from October through January. Prevention is key, as there is no vaccine or treatment once infected. Malaria is a problem in the surrounding areas outside Dhaka. If you are planning to travel outside Dhaka, consider starting prophylaxis medication prior to travel. Japanese B encephalitis, also a mosquito-borne disease, is a problem throughout Bangladesh, although less so in Dhaka. Chikungunya was found in Bangladesh in 2008 and this mosquito-borne illness is slowly making headway throughout the country, including in Dhaka. Use of mosquito repellent and bed nets is strongly recommended.

In 2009 and 2010, there were multiple outbreaks of anthrax in rural communities in Bangladesh among persons who slaughtered sick animals. Individuals who avoid this activity are not at risk. Human vaccination against anthrax is not recommended. Rabies is a more serious problem, with several thousand dying yearly in Bangladesh from this endemic disease, generally passed on via bites from infected dogs. Seek prophylactic advice from your healthcare practitioner before coming to Bangladesh and immediate medical attention if bitten by any animal. According to the World Health Organization, Bangladesh has also seen cases of polio, nipah virus, and Kala-Azar, (visceral leishmaniasis). Kala-Azar is a deadly disease caused by parasitic protozoa leishmaniadonovani, transmitted to humans by the bite of infected female sandflies, phlebotomusargentipes, which lowers immunity, causes persistent fever, anemia, liver and spleen enlargement, loss of body weight and if left untreated, kills. Tuberculosis (TB) is a major public health problem and endemic in Bangladesh. In 2008, the World Health Organization (WHO) ranked Bangladesh sixth among the world's 22 high-burden TB countries.

You can find good information on vaccinations and other health precautions on the CDC website. For information about outbreaks of infectious diseases abroad, consult the World Health Organization (WHO) website. The WHO website also contains additional health information for travelers including detailed country-specific health information.

Medical Insurance: You can't assume your insurance will go with you when you travel. It's very important to find out BEFORE you leave whether or not your medical insurance will cover you overseas. You need to ask your insurance company two questions:

- Does my policy apply when I'm out of the United States?
- Will it cover emergencies like a trip to a foreign hospital or a medical evacuation?

In many places, doctors and hospitals still expect payment in cash at the time of service. Your regular U.S. health insurance may not cover doctors' and hospital visits in other countries. If your policy doesn't go with you when you travel, it's a very good idea to take out another one for your trip.

Traffic Safety and Road Conditions: While in a foreign country, you may encounter road conditions that differ significantly from those in the United States. The information below concerning Bangladesh is provided for general reference only, and may not apply to every location or circumstance. Conditions differ around the country.

Traffic in Bangladesh moves on the left, the opposite of U.S. traffic. Roads are extremely crowded, particularly in the cities, with bicycle rickshaws, three-wheeled mini-taxis (CNGs), cars, overloaded buses, and trucks. Drivers are often aggressive and poorly trained, and many vehicles, particularly large trucks and buses, are badly maintained. Exercise extreme caution when crossing streets, even in marked pedestrian areas, and try to use only cars that have seatbelts. Seatbelts are not common in taxis. Helmets should always be worn on motorcycles and bicycles. Roads, including most major highways, are poorly maintained and often have numerous potholes, sharp drop-offs, and barriers that are not sign-posted. Drivers should exercise extreme caution when traveling at night by road, as many vehicles do not have proper illumination or dimmers and most roads are inadequately lighted or signed. Travel by road without an experienced local driver or guide is not recommended.

On Bangladeshi roads, the safest driving policy is to always assume that other drivers will not respond to a traffic situation in the same way you would in the United States. On Bangladeshi roads large vehicles generally take the right-of-way. Buses and trucks often run red lights and merge directly into traffic at yield points and traffic circles. Cars, autorickshaws, bicycles, and pedestrians behave only slightly more cautiously. Use your horn or flash your headlights frequently to announce your presence.

Road accidents, including fatal head-on collisions, are common in Bangladesh. If a serious accident occurs, or if a driver hits a pedestrian or a cow, crowds quickly gather and the vehicle and its occupants are at severe risk of being attacked. Such attacks pose significant risk of injury or death to the vehicle's occupants or at least of incineration of the vehicle. It is unsafe to remain at the scene of an accident of this nature, and drivers may instead wish to seek out the nearest police station. Travelers are strongly urged not to use public transportation, including buses, rickshaws, and CNGs due to their high accident rate and crime issues. An alternative to consider is a rental car and driver. Banditry and carjacking, particularly along inter-city highways, are a problem and those using these roads should exercise particular vigilance. Protestors often use road blockage as a means of publicizing their grievances, causing severe inconvenience to travelers. Visitors should monitor local news reports for any reports of road disturbances.

Aviation Safety Oversight: The U.S. Federal Aviation Administration (FAA) has assessed the Government of Bangladesh's Civil Aviation Authority as not being in compliance with International Civil Aviation Organization (ICAO) aviation safety standards for the oversight of Bangladesh's air carrier operations. Further information may be found on the FAA's website at FAA's safety assessment page.

Children's Issues: Please see the U.S. Dept. of State Office of Children's Issues web pages on intercountry adoption, international parental child abduction and the U.S. Embassy in Dhaka information on forced marriage.

Intercountry Adoption

August 2011

The information in this section has been edited from the latest report available as of February 2013 from the State Department Bureau of Consular Affairs, Office of Overseas Citizens Services. For more information, please read the *Intercountry Adoption* section of this book and review current reports online at http://adoption.state.gov.

Bangladesh is not party to the Hague Convention on Protection of Children and Co-operation in Respect of Intercountry Adoption (Hague Adoption Convention). Therefore, when the Hague Adoption Convention entered into force for the United States on April 1, 2008, intercountry adoption processing for Bangladesh did not change. Bangladeshi law does not allow for full adoptions of Bangladeshi children. Americans considering adoption of Bangladeshi children must obtain guardianship from a Bangladeshi court and subsequently adopt the child in the United States.

Only citizens of Bangladesh may be appointed/declared guardians of a Bangladeshi child. Since Bangladesh allows for dual citizenship, however, American citizens who are also Bangladeshi citizens may be appointed guardians of Bangladeshi children.

There have been a number of instances in which Americans have been poorly advised by legal practitioners and have entered into fostering/adoption arrangements which, even though endorsed by local Bangladeshi courts, do not meet the requirements of Bangladeshi adoption law. Adoptions that do not meet these requirements will not meet the requirements for the issuance of U.S. immigrant visas for the children. Americans intending to adopt a child in Bangladesh should not attempt to circumvent the proper processes. Interested U.S. citizens are strongly encouraged to contact the U.S. Citizenship and Immigration Services (USCIS) in New Delhi and the Consular Section in the U.S. Embassy in Dhaka before applying for guardianship of a child to ensure that appropriate procedures have been followed. Obtaining legal guardianship under Bangladesh law does not guarantee that the child will qualify for a U.S. immigrant visa.

Who Can Adopt? To bring an adopted child to United States from Bangladesh, you must be found eligible to adopt by the U.S. Government. The U.S. Government agency responsible for making this determination is the Department of Homeland Security, U.S. Citizenship and Immigration Services (USCIS). In addition to these U.S. requirements for prospective adoptive parents, Bangladesh also has the following requirements for prospective guardians.

Residency Requirements: There are no residency requirements; however, prospective parents must provide proof of Bangladeshi citizenship.

Age Requirements: Prospective guardians must be at least 18 years old.

Family Court Requirements: An application for legal guardianship must be made to the Family Court. In Bangladesh, the Family Court has sole jurisdiction over family matters.

Marriage Requirements: There is no legal requirement regarding marital status.

Income Requirements: While there is no specific income requirement, prospective adoptive parents must be able to provide food, shelter, and education for the proposed ward.

Other Requirements: While there is no specific income requirement, prospective adoptive parents must be able to provide food, shelter, and education for the proposed ward.

Who Can Be Adopted? Bangladesh has specific requirements that a child must meet in order to be eligible for adoption. You cannot adopt a child in Bangladesh unless he or she meets the requirements outlined below.

Relinquishment Requirements: The biological parent(s) must sign an irrevocable release of the child before a Notary Public or Magistrate in Bangladesh.

Abandonment Requirements: There is no specific requirement regarding abandonment, but if the legal guardians are alive, they will have to relinquish their rights of guardianship.

Age Requirements: The child must be under 18 years of age. Please note that U.S. immigration requirements state that children over the age of 16 are not eligible for entry into the United States unless being adopted as part of a sibling pair or group.

Sibling Requirements: There is no specific provision of the law relating to the guardianship of siblings. Guardianship proceedings for siblings can be completed together.

Waiting Period: There is no required waiting period.

Bangladesh's Guardianship Authority: Family Court

The Process: The first step in adopting a child from Bangladesh is usually to select a licensed agency in the United States that can help with your adoption. Adoption service providers must be licensed by the U.S. state in which they operate. There are no adoption agencies in Bangladesh; however, there at least 25,000 lawyers in Bangladesh who may initiate guardianship proceedings. Prospective guardians who choose to work with U.S. adoption service providers in the context of obtaining guardianship of Bangladeshi children are advised to fully research any adoption agency or facilitator they plan to use. For U.S.-based agencies, it is suggested that prospective adoptive parents contact the Better Business Bureau and/or the licensing office of the appropriate state government agency in the U.S. state where the agency is located or licensed. The Bangladesh government does not approve adoption agencies or attorneys. The U.S. Embassy can provide a list of Bangladeshi attorneys conversant with family law in Bangladesh. The Embassy can also assist in providing contact information for local established charitable orphanages.

To bring an adopted child from Bangladesh to the United States, you must apply to be found eligible to adopt (Form I-600A) by the U.S. Government, Department of Homeland Security, U.S. Citizenship and Immigration Services (USCIS). In addition to meeting the U.S. requirements for adoptive parents, you need to meet the requirements of Bangladesh. If you are eligible to adopt, and a child is available for intercountry adoption, the central adoption authority in Bangladesh will provide you with a referral to a child. In the case of Bangladesh, after the biological parents have signed a release of the child, an application for legal guardianship must be made to the Family Court. In Bangladesh, the Family Court has sole jurisdiction over family matters. The child must be eligible to be adopted according to Bangladesh's requirements. The child must also meet the definition of an orphan under U.S. law.

Role of the Adoption Authority: There is no formal adoption authority in Bangladesh.

Role of the Court: The Family Court is located in all districts of Bangladesh. If the applicant needs to contact the Family Court, he/she may contact the concerned Desk Officer or dealing section of the Family Court in person. The Family Court reviews the character and capacity of the proposed guardian in considering the welfare of the minor.

Role of the Adoption Agencies: There are no adoption agencies in Bangladesh.

Adoption Application: The application for legal guardianship must be made to the Family Court.

Time Frame: There is no set time frame for completing legal guardianship in Bangladesh. The following are some rough estimates on the processing times for specific stages of the Process:

- Processing time at an Orphanage—three days to one month
- Processing time at Family Court—one to three months
- Processing time at the Ministry of Home Affairs—15 days to two months

Guardianship Fees: There is a government court fee of Tk.60. There is no set lawyer's fee but it generally ranges from Tk.5000 to Tk.50,000, roughly $85 USD to $850 USD.

Documents Required:

- Birth certificate of the minor
- Guardianship Certificate
- Irrevocable release/undertaking of the biological parents (if any) of the child before a Notary Public, 1 st Class Magistrate, or before the relevant Family Court in Bangladesh
- No Objection certificate from the Ministry of Home Affairs

The Bangladeshi procedure for authenticating documents to be used in Bangladesh is as follows:

- Any foreign document should be attested by the Bangladeshi Mission abroad and then re-attested by the Foreign Ministry in Bangladesh. If the document is of a legal nature, then it should revalidated by the relevant treasury in Bangladesh.

- Any Bangladeshi (local) document can be treated as authenticated if it is attested by any First Class Government officer, any Magistrate or any Notary Public in Bangladesh.

Bringing Your Child Home: Once your adoption is complete (or you have obtained legal custody of the child), there are a few more steps to take before you can head home. Specifically, you need to apply for several documents for your child before he or she can travel to the United States, such as a birth certificate, a passport or travel document for your child from the country in which he or she was born, and a U.S. Immigration Visa. For detailed and updated information on how to obtain these documents, review the *Intercountry Adoption* section in this publication and visit the U.S. Department of State Intercountry Adoption website at http://adoption.state.gov.

Child Citizenship Act: For adoptions finalized abroad, the Child Citizenship Act of 2000 allows your new child to acquire American citizenship automatically when he or she enters the United States as lawful permanent residents. For adoptions finalized in the United States, the Child Citizenship Act of 2000 allows your new child to acquire American citizenship automatically when the court in the United States issues the final adoption decree. To learn more, review the *Intercountry Adoption* section in this publication and visit the U.S. Department of State Intercountry Adoption website at http://adoption.state.gov.

After Adoption: There are no requirements post-obtaining guardianship.

U.S. Embassy in Bangladesh
Madani Avenue, Baridhara,
Dhaka 1212, Bangladesh
Tel: (880) (2) 885–5500
Fax: (880) (2) 882–3744
http://dhaka.usembassy.gov

Embassy of Bangladesh
3510, International Drive NW
Washington, D.C. 20008
Tel: (202) 244–0183, (202) 244–7830
Fax: (202) 244–5366
http://www.bangladoot.org

Consulate General of the People's Republic of Bangladesh— New York
211 E. 43rd Street, Suite 502
New York, NY 10017
Tel: (212) 599–6767, (212) 599–6850
Fax: (212) 682–9211
E-mail: bdcgny@aol.com

Consulate General of the People's Republic of Bangladesh— Los Angeles
4201 Wilshire Blvd
Suite # 605
Los Angeles, CA 90010
Tel: (323) 932–0100
Fax: (323) 932–9703
E-mail: bcgla@earthlink.net
www.bangladeshconsulatela.com

Office of Children's Issues
U.S. Department of State
2201 C Street, NW
SA-29
Washington, DC 20520
Tel: 1–888–407–4747
E-mail: AskCI@state.gov
http://adoption.state.gov

For questions about immigration procedures, call the National Customer Service Center (NCSC) 1-800-375-5283 (TTY 1-800-767-1833).T

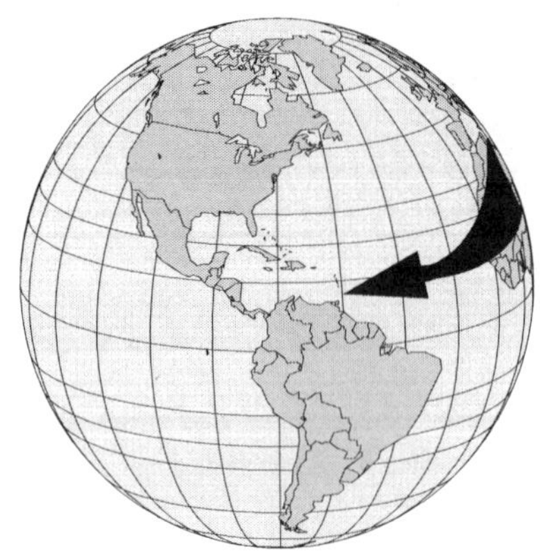

BARBADOS

Compiled from publications that were available as of February 2013 from the U.S. Department of State, the U.S. Department of Commerce, and the Central Intelligence Agency (CIA). See the introduction to this set for explanatory notes.

Official Name:
Barbados

PROFILE

Geography

Area: total: 430 sq km; country comparison to the world: 202; land: 430 sq km; water: 0 sq km
Major cities: Bridgetown (capital) 112,000 (2009)
Climate: tropical; rainy season (June to October)
Terrain: relatively flat; rises gently to central highland region

People

Nationality: noun: Barbadian(s) or Bajan (colloquial); adjective: Barbadian or Bajan (colloquial)
Population: 287,733 (July 2012 est.)
Population growth rate: 0.354% (2012 est.)
Ethnic groups: black 93%, white 3.2%, mixed 2.6%, East Indian 1%, other 0.2% (2000 census)
Religions: Protestant 63.4% (Anglican 28.3%, Pentecostal 18.7%, Methodist 5.1%, other 11.3%), Roman Catholic 4.2%, other Christian 7%, other 4.8%, none or unspecified 20.6% (2008 est.)
Languages: English
Literacy: definition: age 15 and over has ever attended school; total population: 99.7%; male: 99.7%; female: 99.7% (2002 est.)
Health: life expectancy at birth: total population: 74.52 years; male: 72.25 years; female: 76.82 years (2012 est.); Infant mortality rate: total: 11.63 deaths/1,000 live births; male: 12.98 deaths/1,000 live births; female: 10.27 deaths/1,000 live births (2012 est.)
Unemployment rate: 11.2% (2011 est.)
Work force: 145,000 (2011 est.)

Government

Type: parliamentary democracy and a Commonwealth realm
Independence: 30 November 1966
Constitution: 30 November 1966
Political subdivisions: 11 parishes and 1 city; Bridgetown, Christ Church, Saint Andrew, Saint George, Saint James, Saint John, Saint Joseph, Saint Lucy, Saint Michael, Saint Peter, Saint Philip, Saint Thomas
Suffrage: 18 years of age; universal

Economy

GDP (purchasing power parity): $7.091 billion (2012 est.); $6.576 billion (2011 est.); $6.544 billion (2010 est.); $6.53 billion (2009 est.)
GDP real growth rate: 0.7% (2012 est.); 0.5% (2011 est.); 0.2% (2010 est.); -4.2% (2009 est.)
GDP per capita (PPP): $25,500 (2012 est.); $23,700 (2011 est.); $23,700 (2010 est.)
Natural resources: petroleum, fish, natural gas
Agriculture products: sugarcane, vegetables, cotton
Industries: tourism, sugar, light manufacturing, component assembly for export
Exports: $491.1 million (2012 est.); $447.3 million (2011 est.)
Exports—commodities: manufactures, sugar and molasses, rum, other foods and beverages, chemicals, electrical components
Exports—partners: Trinidad and Tobago 18.7%, France 10.6%, US 9.6%, St. Lucia 8.7%, St. Vincent and the Grenadines 5.4%, Venezuela 4.8%, Antigua and Barbuda 4.4%, St. Kitts and Nevis 4.2% (2011)
Imports: $1.633 billion (2012 est.); $1.55 billion (2011 est.)
Imports—commodities: consumer goods, machinery, foodstuffs, construction materials, chemicals, fuel, electrical components
Imports—partners: Russia 26.6%, Trinidad and Tobago 24.8%, US 18.6%, China 6.1% (2011)
Debt—external: $4.49 billion (2010 est.)
Exchange rates: Barbadian dollars (BBD) per US dollar; 2 (2012 est.); 2 (2011 est.); 2 (2010 est.)

PEOPLE

The people of Barbados are primarily of African or mixed descent. English is the primary langauge.

According to the 2000 official census, more than 95 percent of the population is Christian. The 2000 census indicates that the Anglican (28 percent) and Pentecostal (18 percent) denominations are the two most represented religious denominations in Barbados followed by the Seventh-day Adventists (5 percent), Methodists (5 percent), and Roman Catholics (4 percent). There are small numbers of Baptists, Moravians, and members of The Church of Jesus Christ of Latter-day Saints (Mormons).

The number of non-Christians is small. There are 4,000 Muslims, most of whom trace their ancestry to the Indian state of Gujarat. A few immigrants from Guyana, Trinidad, South Asia, and the Middle East, as well as approximately 200 native-born persons, constitute the rest of the growing Muslim community. There are three mosques and an Islamic center. Other religious groups include Jews, Rastafarians, Hindus, Buddhists, and members of the Baha'i Faith.

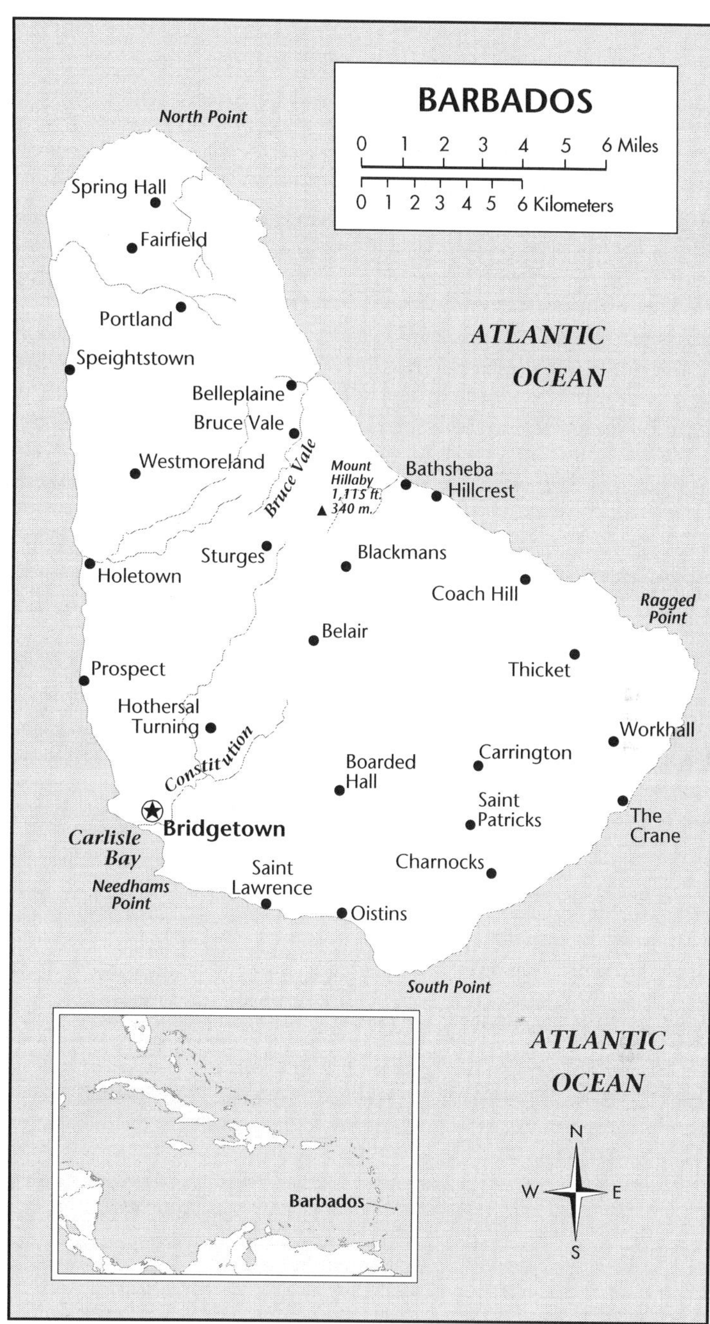

HISTORY

British sailors who landed on Barbados in the 1620s at the site of present-day Holetown on the Caribbean coast found the island uninhabited. As elsewhere in the eastern Caribbean, Arawak Indians may have been annihilated by invading Caribs, who are believed to have subsequently abandoned the island. From the arrival of the first British settlers in 1627-28 until independence in 1966, Barbados was a self-funding colony under uninterrupted British rule. Nevertheless, Barbados always enjoyed a large measure of local autonomy. Its House of Assembly, which began meeting in 1639, is the third-oldest legislative body in the Western Hemisphere, preceded only by Bermuda's legislature and the Virginia House of Burgesses.

As the sugar industry developed into the main commercial enterprise, Barbados was divided into large plantation estates, which replaced the small holdings of the early British settlers. Some of the displaced farmers relocated to British colonies in North America. To work the plantations, slaves were brought from Africa; the slave trade ceased a few years before the abolition of slavery throughout the British empire in 1834.

Plantation owners and merchants of British descent dominated local politics. It was not until the 1930s that the descendants of emancipated slaves began a movement for political rights. One of the leaders of this movement, Sir Grantley Adams, founded the Barbados Labour Party in 1938. Progress toward more democratic government for Barbados was made in 1951, when the first general election under universal adult suffrage occurred. This was followed by steps toward increased self-government, and in 1961, Barbados achieved the status of self-governing autonomy.

From 1958 to 1962, Barbados was one of 10 members of the West Indies Federation, and Sir Grantley Adams served as its first and only prime minister. When the federation was terminated, Barbados reverted to its former status as a self-governing colony. Following several attempts to form another federation composed of Barbados and the Leeward and Windward Islands, Barbados negotiated its own independence at a constitutional conference with the United Kingdom in June 1966. After years of peaceful and democratic progress, Barbados became an independent state within the British Commonwealth on November 30, 1966.

GOVERNMENT AND POLITICAL CONDITIONS

Barbados is a multiparty, parliamentary democracy. In 2008 national elections, voters elected Prime Minister David Thompson of the Democratic Labour Party (DLP). International observers assessed the vote as generally free and fair. Prime Minister Thompson died in office in October 2010 and was replaced by Deputy Prime Minister Freundel Stuart.

Recent Elections

In general elections held in 2008, the DLP, in opposition since 1994, defeated the Barbados Labour Party, led by then prime minister Owen Arthur. The DLP won 20 of the 30 seats in the parliament's House of Assembly, and DLP leader David Thompson became prime minister. Following Thompson's death in October 2010, the DLP parliamentary group selected Deputy Prime Minister Freundel Stuart to be prime minister.

Participation of Women and Minorities: Two cabinet members were female; there were three women in the House of Assembly. There were four women and three minorities in the 21-member appointed Senate.

Principal Government Officials

Last Updated: 1/31/2013

Governor Gen.: **Elliot BELGRAVE**
Prime Min.: **Freundel STUART**
Dep. Prime Min.
Min. of Agriculture, Food, Fisheries, & Water Resource Management:**David ESTWICK**
Min. of Civil Service: **Freundel STUART**
Min. of Commerce & Trade: **Haynesley BENN**
Min. of Education & Human Resource Development: **Ronald JONES**
Min. of Environment & Drainage: **Denis LOWE**
Min. of Family, Culture, Sports, & Youth: **Stephen LASHLEY**
Min. of Finance & Economic Affairs: **Christopher SINCKLER**
Min. of Foreign Affairs & Foreign Trade: **Maxine Pamela Ometa MCCLEAN**
Min. of Health: **Donville INNISS**
Min. of Home Affairs: **Adriel BRATHWAITE**
Min. of Housing & Lands: **Michael LASHLEY**
Min. of Industry, Small Business, & Rural Development: **Denis KELLMAN**
Min. of Intl. Transport & Intl. Business: **George HUTSON**
Min. of Labor & Social Security: **Esther BYER-SUCKOO**
Min. of National Security: **Freundel STUART**
Min. of Social Care, Constituency Empowerment, & Community Development: **Steve BLACKETT**
Min. of Tourism: **Richard SEALY**
Min. of Transport & Works: **John BOYCE**
Min. of Urban Development: **Freundel STUART**
Attorney Gen.: **Adriel BRATHWAITE**
Governor, Central Bank: **DeLisle WORRELL**
Ambassador to the US: **John E. BEALE**
Permanent Representative to the UN, New York: **Joseph GODDARD**

ECONOMY

Historically, the Barbadian economy was dependent on sugarcane cultivation and related activities. However, in recent years the economy has diversified into light industry and tourism with about four-fifths of GDP and of exports being attributed to services. Growth has rebounded since 2003, bolstered by increases in construction projects and tourism revenues, reflecting its success in the higher-end segment, but the sector faced declining revenues in 2009 with the global economic downturn.

The country enjoys one of the highest per capita incomes in the region. Offshore finance and information services are important foreign exchange earners and thrive from having the same time zone as eastern US financial centers and a relatively highly educated workforce. The government continues its efforts to reduce unemployment, to encourage direct foreign investment, and to privatize remaining state-owned enterprises. The public debt-to-GDP ratio rose to over 100% in 2009–11, largely because a sharp slowdown in tourism and financial services led to a wide budget deficit.

Labor Conditions

The law provides for a minimum working age of 16 for certain sectors but does not cover sectors such as agriculture. Compulsory primary and secondary education policies reinforced minimum age requirements. The law prohibits children under the age of 18 from engaging in work likely to harm their heath, safety, or morals but does not specifically note which occupations fall under this prohibition. The law prohibits the employment of children of compulsory school age (through age 16) during school hours. The law also prevents young people from night work (after 6:00 p.m.). These laws were effectively enforced. Child labor laws were generally observed in practice. According to the chief labor inspector, no underage employment cases were filed during the past few years.

The law provides for, and the authorities established, minimum wage rates for household domestics and shop assistants. The minimum wage for these employees was BDS$5 ($2.50) per hour. The Ministry of Labor recommended companies in all other sectors use this as the de facto minimum wage.

The standard legal workweek is 40 hours in five days, and the law provides employees with three weeks of paid holiday for the first four years of service and four weeks' holiday after five years of service. An employee's length of service is linked to the anniversary of the commencement date with current employer. The law requires overtime payment of time and one-half for hours worked in excess and prescribes that all overtime must be voluntary.

The Ministry of Labor did not identify any specific group of workers that were subject to hazardous or exploitive working conditions. According to the ministry, labor laws apply to all workers and are enforced across the board. However, foreign workers in high risk sectors such as domestic service, agriculture, or construction may not be aware of their rights and protections under the law. In practice the prevailing wage on the island was higher than the legal minimum wage. However, there were occasional press reports alleging that migrant workers received less than the minimum wage.

U.S.-BARBADIAN RELATIONS

The United States and Barbados have had friendly bilateral relations since Barbados' independence from the United Kingdom in 1966. Barbados and U.S. authorities cooperate closely in the fight against narcotics trafficking and other forms of transnational crime. The two countries have signed a mutual legal assistance treaty; an updated extradition treaty covering all common offenses, including conspiracy and organized crime; and a maritime law enforcement agreement.

U.S. Assistance to Barbados

The United States has supported the government's efforts to expand the country's economic base and to provide a higher standard of living for its citizens. U.S. assistance is channeled primarily through multilateral agencies such as the Inter-American Development Bank and the World Bank, as well as the U.S. Agency for International Development (USAID). USAID's Eastern Caribbean program, which includes Barbados, has focused on promoting economic growth through an improved business and investment climate, helping governments and the private sector compete in the global marketplace, combating HIV/AIDS, and protecting fragile ecosystems. Barbados receives counternarcotics and youth development assistance from the United States under the regional Caribbean Basin Security Initiative (CBSI) and is eligible to benefit from the U.S. military's exercise-related and humanitarian assistance construction program.

Bilateral Economic Relations

Barbados has an open economy with a marked dependence on imports, 40% of which come from the United States. Barbados is a beneficiary of the U.S. Caribbean Basin Initiative, which aims to facilitate the economic development and export diversification of the Caribbean Basin economies by providing countries with duty-free access to the U.S. market for most goods.

Barbados's Membership in International Organizations

As a small nation, the primary thrust of Barbados' diplomatic activity has been within international organizations. Barbados and the United States belong to a number of the same international organizations, including the United Nations, Organization of American States, Inter-American Development Bank, International Monetary Fund, World Bank, and World Trade Organization.

Bilateral Representation

Barbados maintains an embassy in the United States at 2144 Wyoming Avenue, NW, Washington, D.C. 20008 (tel. 202-939-9200).

Principal U.S. Embassy Officials

Last Updated: 1/14/2013

BRIDGETOWN (E) Wildey Business Park, Wildey, St. Michael BB 14006, 246-227-4000, Fax 246-227-4088, Workweek: Mon-Fri: 8.00–4.30, Website: http://bridgetown.usembassy.gov/

DCM OMS:	Frances Youmans
AMB OMS:	Ellen Benjamin-Leon
CDC:	Rachel Alabalak
Co-CLO:	Kathryn Mctigue Floyd
DHS/CBP:	Stephen Bows
FM:	Bruce Youmans
HRO:	Traci Cassilly
MGT:	Jeremey Neitzke
MLO/ODC:	CDR Michael Long
NAS/INL:	Kurt Van Der Walde
PAO/ADV:	Rachel Zaspel
POSHO:	Bruce Youmans
SDO/DATT:	CDR Michael Long
AMB:	Larry Palmer
CG:	Mark Bysfield
DCM:	Christopher Sandrolini
PAO:	Rebecca Ross
GSO:	M. Holly Peirce
RSO:	Thomas W.Baker
AFSA:	Vacant
AID:	Daniel Smolka
CLO:	Ylodia (Lisa) Robinson
DEA:	Charles Graham
ECON:	Brian Greaney
EEO:	Gregory Floyd
FAA:	Dawn Flanagan (Res. Washington)
FMO:	W. Lee Thompson
ICASS Chair:	Charles Graham
IMO:	Michael Cassilly
IRS:	Andrew Thornton
ISO:	Frederick Melton
ISSO:	Pic Jordan
LAB:	Gregory Floyd
LEGATT:	David Brooks
POL:	Brian Greaney
State ICASS:	Kurt Van Der Walde

Other Contact Information

U.S. Department of Commerce
International Trade Administration
Office of Latin America and the Caribbean
14th & Constitution Avenue, NW
Washington, DC 20230
Tel: 202-482-1658, 800-USA-Trade
Fax: 202-482-0464

Caribbean/Latin American Action
1818 N Street, NW
Suite 310
Washington, DC 20036
Tel: 202-466-7464
Fax: 202-822-00:75

TRAVEL

Consular Information Sheet

April 13, 2011

Country Description: Barbados is an independent Caribbean island nation with a developed economy. The capital is Bridgetown. Facilities for tourism are widely available. The U.S. Embassy in Barbados has consular responsibility for Antigua and Barbuda, Dominica, St. Kitts and Nevis, St. Lucia, St. Vincent and the Grenadines, as well as the British dependent territories of Anguilla, British Virgin Islands and Montserrat, and the French islands of Martinique, Guadeloupe, St. Barthélemy and St. Martin.

Smart Traveler Enrollment Program (STEP)/Embassy Locations: If you are going to live in or visit Barbados, please take the time to tell our Embassy about your trip. If you check in, we can keep you up to date with important safety and security announcements. It will also help your friends and family get in touch with you in an emergency.

U.S. Embassy in Bridgetown
Wildey Business park
Wildey
St. Michael, Barbados
Telephone: (246) 227-4399
Emergency after-hours telephone: (246) 227-4000
Facsimile: (246) 431-0179
Email: BridgetownACS@state.gov

Hours of operation are 8:30 a.m.–4:30 p.m. Monday through Friday, except Barbadian and U.S. holidays.

Entry/Exit Requirements for U.S. Citizens: U.S. citizens must have a valid U.S. passport to enter Barbados. No visa is needed to enter Barbados for stays up to 28 days. For further information, travelers may contact the Embassy of Barbados, 2144 Wyoming Avenue, N.W., Washington, D.C. 20008, telephone (202) 939-9200, fax (202) 332-7467, e-mail: washington@foreign.gov.bb; or the consulates of Barbados in Los Angeles, Miami or New York.

All U.S. citizens traveling outside of the United States are required to present a passport or other valid travel document to enter the United States. This extended to all sea travel (except closed-loop cruises), including ferry service on June 1, 2009. Travelers must now present a Western Hemisphere Travel Initiative (WHTI) compliant document such as a passport or a passport card for entry to the United States.

While passport cards and enhanced driver's licenses are sufficient for entry into the United States, they may not be accepted by the particular country you plan to visit; please be sure to check with your cruise line and countries of destination for any foreign entry requirements. We strongly encourage all U.S. citizen travelers to apply for a U.S. passport or passport card well in advance of anticipated travel. U.S. citizens can visit travel.state.gov or call 1-877-4USA-PPT (1-877-487-2778) for information on how to apply for their passports.

NOTE: Be aware that Caribbean cruises that begin and end in the U.S. (closed loop cruises) do not require that you travel with a valid passport. However, should you need to disembark due to an emergency and you do not have a valid passport, you may encounter difficulties entering or remaining in a foreign country. You may also have difficulty attempting to re-enter the United States by air because many airlines will require a valid passport before allowing you to board the aircraft. As such, it is strongly recommended that you always travel abroad with your valid passport.

HIV/AIDS entry restrictions may exist for visitors to and foreign residents of Barbados. Please contact the Embassy of Barbados before you travel at:

2144 Wyoming Avenue N.W.
Washington, DC 20008
(202) 939-9200 through 9202

Safety and Security: Stay up to date by bookmarking our Bureau of Consular Affairs' website, which contains the current Travel Warnings and Travel Alerts, as well as the Worldwide Caution.

You can also call 1-888-407-4747 toll-free in the U.S. and Canada, or by calling a regular toll-line at 1-202-501-4444, from other countries. These numbers are available from 8:00 a.m. to 8:00 p.m. Eastern Time, Monday through Friday (except U.S. federal holidays). Follow us on Twitter and become a fan of the Bureau of Consular Affairs page on facebook as well.

Take some time before travel to improve your personal security—things are not the same everywhere as they are in the United States.

Crime: Crime in Barbados is characterized primarily by petty theft and street crime. Incidents of violent crime, including rape, do occur. Visitors should be especially vigilant on the beaches at night. In October, 2010,two female tourists were reportedly sexually assaulted in separate attacks while walking alone during the day in the Holetown area on the West Coast of Barbados.

As always, visitors to and residents in Barbados should always be aware of their surroundings and exercise caution, especially when walking alone and even during the day. If walking alone, avoid secluded areas. Always secure valuables in a hotel safe, and always lock and secure hotel room and rental home doors and windows.

Don't buy counterfeit and pirated goods, even if they are widely available. Not only are the bootlegs illegal in the United States, if you purcahase them you may be breaking local law.

Victims of Crime: If you or someone you know becomes the victim of a crime abroad, you should contact the local police and the nearest U.S. embassy or consulate (see the Department of State's list of embassies and consulates). If your passport is stolen we can help you replace it. For violent crimes such as assault and rape, we can, for example, help you find appropriate medical care, contact family members or friends and help you get money from them if you need it. Although the investigation and prosecution of the crime are solely the responsibility of local authorities, consular officers can help you to understand the local criminal justice process and to find an attorney if needed.

The local equivalent to the "911" emergency line in Barbados are: Fire: 311, Police: 211, Ambulance: 511.

Criminal Penalties: While you are traveling in Barbados, you are subject to its laws even if you are a U.S. citizen. Foreign laws and legal systems can be vastly different than our own. In some places you may be taken in for questioning if you don't have your passport with you. In some places, it is illegal to take pictures of certain buildings. In some places, driving under the influence could land you immediately in jail. These criminal penalties will vary from country to country. There are also some things that might be legal in the country you visit, but still illegal in the United States and you can be prosecuted under U.S. law if you buy pirated goods.Engaging in sexual conduct with children or using or disseminating child pornography in a foreign country is a crime prosecutable in the United States. If you break local laws in Barbados, your U.S. passport won't help you avoid arrest or prosecution. It's very important to know what's legal and what's not where you are going. Persons violating Barbados laws, even unknowingly, may be expelled, arrested or imprisoned. Penalties for possession, use, or trafficking in illegal drugs in Barbados are severe, and convicted offenders can expect long jail sentences and heavy fines.

Special Circumstances: All Caribbean countries can be affected by hurricanes. The hurricane season normally runs from early June to the end of November, but there have been hurricanes in December in recent years. General information about natural disaster preparedness is available via the Internet from the U.S. Federal Emergency Management Agency (FEMA).

U.S. citizens are encouraged to carry a copy of their citizenship documents with them at all times so, if questioned by local officials, proof of identity and U.S. citizenship are readily available.

Accessibility: While in Barbados, individuals with disabilities may find accessibility and accommodation very different from what you find in the United States. There are no laws that specifically prohibit discrimination against persons with disabilities in employment, education, or the provision of other state services, other than constitutional provisions asserting equality for all. While no legislation mandates provision of accessibility to public thoroughfares or public or private buildings, the Town and Country Planning Department set provisions for all public buildings to include accessibility to persons with disabilities. As a result, many new buildings have ramps, reserved parking, and special sanitary facilities for such persons.

However, in general, access to buildings, pedestrian paths and transportation is extremely difficult for persons with disabilities. Sidewalks (if they exist) are very uneven and will only occasionally have ramps at intersections. Pedestrian crossings are also very infrequent. Many restaurants, hotels and residential buildings have stairs at the entrance without wheelchair ramps, except perhaps major hotels and retail areas. Buses and taxis do not have special accommodations for disabled persons.

Medical Facilities and Health Information: The main medical facility in Barbados is Queen Elizabeth Hospital. Medical care is generally good, but medical transport can take hours to respond and ambulance attendants are prohibited from applying lifesaving techniques during transport. Minor problems requiring a visit to the emergency room can involve a wait of several hours; private clinics and physicians offer speedier service. Serious medical problems requiring hospitalization and/or medical evacuation to the United States can cost thousands of dollars. Doctors and hospitals expect immediate cash payment for health services, and U.S. medical insurance is not always valid outside the United States. U.S. Medicare and Medicaid programs do not provide payment for medical services outside the United States.

You can find good information on vaccinations and other health precautions, on the CDC website. For information about outbreaks of infectious diseases abroad, consult the World Health Organization (WHO) website. The WHO website also contains additional health information for travelers, including detailed country-specific health information.

Medical Insurance: You can't assume your insurance will go with you when you travel. It's very important to find out BEFORE you leave. You need to ask your insurance company two questions:

- Does my policy apply when I'm out of the U.S.?
- Will it cover emergencies like a trip to a foreign hospital or an evacuation?

In many places, doctors and hospitals still expect payment in cash at the time of service. Your regular U.S. health insurance may not cover doctors' and hospital visits in other countries. If your policy doesn't go with you when you travel, it's a very good idea to take out another one for your trip.

Traffic Safety and Road Conditions: While in Barbados, you may encounter road conditions that differ significantly from those in the United States. Driving in Barbados is on the left-hand side of the road. Registered taxis and large public buses are generally safe. Private vans and small buses are often crowded and tend to travel at excessive speeds. Travelers are cautioned against riding in private mini-buses, known as "Z buses," as the owners frequently drive erratically. Night driving should be done with caution because of narrow roads with no shoulders and pedestrian/bicycle traffic. Visitors are warned to be extremely careful when driving, riding in a vehicle, or crossing roads on foot.

Aviation Safety Oversight: The U.S. Federal Aviation Administration (FAA) has assessed the government of Barbados' Civil Aviation Authority as not being in compliance with International Civil Aviation Organization (ICAO) aviation safety standards for oversight of Barbados' air carrier operations. Further information may be found on the FAA's safety assessment page.

Children's Issues: Please see the U.S. Dept. of State Office of Children's Issues web pages on intercountry adoption and international parental child abduction.

Intercountry Adoption

April 2009

The information in this section has been edited from the latest report available as of February 2013 from the State Department Bureau of Consular Affairs, Office of Overseas Citizens Services. For more information, please read the *Intercountry Adoption* section of this book and review current reports online at http://adoption.state.gov.

Barbados is not party to the Hague Convention on Protection of Children and Co-operation in Respect of Intercountry Adoption (Hague Adoption Convention). Therefore, when the Hague Adoption Convention entered into force for the United States on April 1, 2008, intercountry adoption processing for Barbados did not change.

Only citizens of countries with which Barbados has diplomatic or consular relations may adopt Barbadian children.

Who Can Adopt? To bring an adopted child to United States from Barbados, you must be found eligible to adopt by the U.S. Government. The U.S. Government agency responsible for making this determination is the Department of Homeland Security, U.S. Citizenship and Immigration Services (USCIS). For detailed and updated information on these requirements, please review the *Intercountry Adoption* section of this publication and visit the USCIS Intercountry Adoption website at http://adoption.state.gov.

Residency Requirements: The adoption of a Barbadian child can take place in Barbados or in the applicants' country of residence. Applicants wishing to adopt a child in Barbados will be required to reside on the island for a period of at least 18 months. If applicants wish the adoption to take place in their country of residence, the applicants are required to come to Barbados for at least a few weeks in order to receive the child into their care and must attend the High Court hearing for the license to take the child out of Barbados for the purpose of adoption.

Age Requirements: Prospective adoptive parents who are already related to the child they plan to adopt must be at least 18 years old. Otherwise, at least one prospective adoptive parent must be 25 years old and at least 18 years older than the child.

Marriage Requirements: Both married and single people may adopt.

Who Can Be Adopted? Barbados has specific requirements that a child must meet in order to be eligible for adoption. You cannot adopt a child in Barbados unless he or she meets the requirements outlined below.

Barbados Adoption Authority: The adoption agency for all of Barbados is the Child Care Board. There are no private adoption agencies operating in Barbados.

The Process: The first step in adopting a child from Barbados is usually to select a licensed agency in the United States that can help with your adoption. Adoption service providers must be licensed by the U.S. state in which they operate. To bring an adopted child from Barbados to the United States, you must apply to be found eligible to adopt (Form I-600A) by the U.S. Government, Department of Homeland Security, U.S. Citizenship and Immigration Services (USCIS). If you are eligible to adopt, and a child is available for intercountry adoption, the central adoption authority in Barbados will provide you with a referral to a child.

Role of the Adoption Authority: The laws that govern adoptions in Barbados are the Child Care Act and the Adoption Act. The Child Care Board administers these laws. Upon being notified of a prospective parent's intent to adopt, the Child Care Board will contract a social welfare agency abroad to do a home study. The home study conducted for U.S. immigration procedures (form I-600A) is acceptable. Upon completion of the home study, the adoptive parents should submit it to the Child Care Board for review. After the Child Care Board approves the home study, the Child Care Board will identify a child based on the adoptive parents' requests.

Role of the Court: The adoptive parents (using an attorney) will need to obtain an order from a Barbadian court authorizing the care and custody of the minor after they have been matched with a child by the Child Care Board. The adoptive parents are required to come to Barbados to attend the High Court hearing for the license and to receive the child into their care.

Time Frame: It will typically take non-Barbadians, including U.S. citizens, between six months and a year to adopt a Barbadian child, but it can take longer due to sometimes-lengthy Barbadian court procedures.

Adoption Fees: The U.S. Embassy in Barbados discourages the payment of any fees that are not properly receipted, "donations," or "expediting" fees, that may be requested from prospective adoptive parents. Such fees have the appearance of "buying" a baby and put all future adoptions in Barbados at risk. Average adoption attorney fees in Barbados are approximately U.S. $3000, which includes court fees. However, fees may vary depending on the attorney. It is necessary for the applicants to use an attorney in Barbados who will apply for the license on their behalf. There are no fees for filing adoption paperwork with the Child Care Board.

Documents Required:

- A completed home study and supporting documents:
- Birth certificate of each prospective adoptive parent;
- Marriage certificate and divorce documents (if applicable);
- Medical report of each prospective adoptive parent, to be conducted in the parent's country of residence;
- Police reference;
- Three (3) personal references known for a period of at least five (5) years and not family members;
- Statement of applicant(s) income.

After you finalize the adoption (or gain legal custody) in Barbados, the U.S Government, Department of Homeland Security, U.S. Citizenship and Immigration Services (USCIS) MUST determine whether the child is eligible under U.S. law to be adopted (Form I-600). For detailed and updated information on these requirements, please review the *Intercountry Adoption* section of this publication and visit the USCIS Intercountry Adoption website at http://adoption.state.gov.

Bringing Your Child Home: Once your adoption is complete (or you have obtained legal custody of the child), there are a few more steps to take before you can head home. Specifically, you need to apply for several documents for your child before he or she can travel to the United States, such as a birth certificate, a passport or travel document for your child from the country in which he or she was born, and a U.S. Immigration Visa. For detailed and updated information on how to obtain these documents, review the *Intercountry Adoption* section on this publication and visit the USCIS Intercountry Adoption website at http://adoption.state.gov.

Child Citizenship Act: For adoptions finalized abroad, the Child Citizenship Act of 2000 allows your new child to acquire American citizenship automatically when he or she enters the United States as lawful permanent residents. For adoptions finalized in the United States, the Child Citizenship Act of 2000 allows your new child to acquire American citizenship automatically when the court in the United States issues the final adoption decree. To learn more, review the *Intercountry Adoption* section on this publication and visit the USCIS *Intercountry Adoption* website at http://adoption.state.gov.

U.S. Embassy in Barbados
Consular Section
Wildey Business Park
Wildey
St. Michael, Barbados
Tel: (246) 227-4000
Fax: (246) 431-0179
Email: consularbridge2@state.gov
http://bridgetown.usembassy.gov

Barbadian Adoption Authority
Child Care Board
The Fred Edghill Building
Cheapside, Fontabelle, Barbados
Tel: 1 (246) 426-2577

Embassy of Barbados
2144 Wyoming Avenue, NW
Washington, DC 20008
Tel: (202) 939-9200
Fax: (202) 332-7467

Barbados also has consulates in: Los Angeles, Miami, and New York.

Office of Children's Issues
U.S. Department of State
2201 C Street, NW
SA-29
Washington, DC 20520
Tel: 1-888-407-4747
E-mail: AskCI@state.gov
http://adoption.state.gov

For questions about immigration procedures, call the National Customer Service Center (NCSC) 1-800-375-5283 (TTY 1-800-767-1833).

International Parental Child Abduction

January 2012

The information in this section has been edited from the latest report available as of February 2013 from the State Department Bureau of Consular Affairs, Office of Overseas Citizens Services. For more information, please read the *International Parental Child Abduction* section of this book and check for updated reports online at www.travel.state.gov/abduction.

Disclaimer: The information in this flyer relating to the legal requirements of specific foreign countries is provided for general information only. Questions involving interpretation of specific foreign laws should be addressed to foreign legal counsel.

General Information: Barbados is not a party to the Hague Convention on the Civil Aspects of International Child Abduction, nor are there any international or bilateral treaties in force between Barbados and the United States dealing with international parental child abduction. American citizens who travel to Barbados place themselves under the jurisdiction of local courts.

Custody Disputes: In Barbados, if parents are legally married they share the custody of their children. If they are not married, by law the custody is granted to the mother unless there are known facts of inappropriate behavior, mental or social problems. Foreign court orders are not automatically recognized.

Enforcement of Foreign Judgments: Custody orders and judgments of foreign courts are not enforceable in Barbados.

Visitation Rights: In cases where one parent has been granted custody of a child, the other parent is usually granted visitation rights.

The American Embassy in Bridgetown has reported few problems for non-custodial parents exercising their visitation rights.

If a custodial parent fails to allow visitation, the non-custodial parent may appeal to the court.

Dual Nationality: Dual nationality is recognized under Barbadian law.

Passports for Minors and the Children's Passport Issuance Alert Program: For more information on these topics, see the *International Parental Child Abduction* section of this publication and review current reports from the U.S. Department of State at www.travel.state.gov/abduction.

Travel Restrictions: No exit visas are required to leave Barbados.

Criminal Remedies: For information on possible criminal remedies, please contact your local law enforcement authorities or the nearest office of the Federal Bureau of Investigation (FBI). Information is also available on the Internet at the web site of the U.S. Department of Justice, Office of Juvenile Justice and Delinquency Prevention (OJJDP) at http://www.ojjdp.ncjrs.org.

Persons who wish to pursue a child custody claim in a Barbadian court should retain an attorney in Barbados. The U.S. Embassy in Barbados maintains a list of attorneys willing to represent American clients. A copy of this list may be obtained by requesting one from the Embassy at:

U.S. Embassy Bridgetown
Consular Section
ALICO Building
Cheapside
Barbados

Mailing Address:
P O Box 302
Bridgetown
Barbados
Telephone: [246] 431-0225
Fax: [246] 431-0179
Web site:
http://www.usembassy.state.gov

The workweek for the Embassy is Monday through Friday from 8:00am to 4:30pm.

Questions involving Barbadian law should be addressed to a Barbadian attorney or to the Embassy of Barbados in the United States at:

Embassy of Barbados
2144 Wyoming Avenue, NW
Washington, DC 20008
Telephone: (202) 939-9200

For further information on international parental child abduction, contact the Office of Children's Issues, U.S. Department of State at 1-888-407-4747 or visit its web site on the Internet at http://travel.state.gov/family.

BELARUS

Compiled from publications that were available as of February 2013 from the U.S. Department of State, the U.S. Department of Commerce, and the Central Intelligence Agency (CIA). See the introduction to this set for explanatory notes.

Official Name:
Republic of Belarus

PROFILE

Geography

Area: total: 207,600 sq km; country comparison to the world: 86; land: 202,900 sq km; water: 4,700 sq km

Major cities: Minsk (capital) 1.837 million (2009)

Climate: cold winters, cool and moist summers; transitional between continental and maritime

Terrain: generally flat and contains much marshland

People

Nationality: noun: Belarusian(s); adjective: Belarusian

Population: 9,643,566 (July 2012 est.)

Population growth rate: -0.362% (2012 est.)

Ethnic groups: Belarusian 83.7%, Russian 8.3%, Polish 3.1%, Ukrainian 1.7%, other 3.2% (2009 census)

Religions: Eastern Orthodox 80%, other (including Roman Catholic, Protestant, Jewish, and Muslim) 20% (1997 est.)

Languages: Belarusian (official) 23.4%, Russian (official) 70.2%, other 6.4% (includes small Polish- and Ukrainian-speaking minorities) (1999 census)

Literacy: definition: age 15 and over can read and write; total population: 99.6%; male: 99.8%; female: 99.5% (2009 census)

Health: life expectancy at birth: total population: 71.48 years; male: 65.88 years; female: 77.42 years (2012 est.); Infant mortality rate: total: 6.16 deaths/1,000 live births; male: 7.14 deaths/1,000 live births; female: 5.11 deaths/1,000 live births (2012 est.)

Unemployment rate: 1% (2009 est.)

Work force: 5 million (2009)

Government

Type: republic in name, although in fact a dictatorship

Independence: 25 August 1991

Constitution: 15 March 1994; revised by national referendum 24 November 1996 giving the presidency greatly expanded powers; became effective 27 November 1996; revised again 17 October 2004 removing presidential term limits

Political subdivisions: 6 provinces (voblastsi, singular—voblasts') and 1 municipality (horad); Brest, Homyel' (Gomel), Horad Minsk (Minsk City), Hrodna (Grodno), Mahilyow (Mogilev), Minsk, Vitsyebsk (Vitebsk)

Suffrage: 18 years of age; universal

Economy

GDP (purchasing power parity): $150.3 billion (2012 est.); $143.6 billion (2011 est.); $136.3 billion (2010 est.); $126.5 billion (2009 est.)

GDP real growth rate: 4.3% (2012 est.; 5.3% (2011 est.); 7.7% (2010 est.); 0.2% (2009 est.)

GDP per capita (PPP): $16,000 (2012 est.); $15,200 (2011 est.); $14,400 (2010 est.); $13,300 (2009 est.)

Natural resources: timber, peat deposits, small quantities of oil and natural gas, granite, dolomitic limestone, marl, chalk, sand, gravel, clay

Agriculture products: grain, potatoes, vegetables, sugar beets, flax; beef, milk

Industries: metal-cutting machine tools, tractors, trucks, earthmovers, motorcycles, televisions, synthetic fibers, fertilizer, textiles, radios, refrigerators

Exports: $46.6 billion (2012 est.); $39.62 billion (2011 est.)

Exports—commodities: machinery and equipment, mineral products, chemicals, metals, textiles, foodstuffs

Exports—partners: Russia 31%, Netherlands 12.6%, Ukraine 11.4%, Latvia 7.2%, Germany 4.7%, Brazil 4.3% (2011)

Imports: $48.18 billion (2012 est.); $42.18 billion (2011 est.)

Imports—commodities: mineral products, machinery and equipment, chemicals, foodstuffs, metals

Imports—partners: Russia 45.8%, Germany 6.5%, Ukraine 5.7%, China 4.5% (2011)

Debt—external: $33.73 billion (31 December 2011 est.); $23.5 billion (31 December 2010 est.)

Exchange rates: Belarusian rubles (BYB/BYR) per US dollar; 8,307.1 (2012 est.) ; 4,974.6 (2011 est.); 2,978.5 (2010 est.); 2,789.49 (2009); 2,130 (2008); 2,145 (2007)

PEOPLE

National/Racial/Ethnic Minorities

Governmental and societal discrimination against the ethnic Polish population and Roma persisted. There were also expressions of societal hostility toward proponents of Belarusian national culture, which the government often identified with actors of the democratic opposition.

Official and societal discrimination continued against the country's 10,000 to 20,000 Roma. The Romani community continued to experience high unemployment and low levels of education. Authorities estimated the unemployment rate among Roma to be as high as 80 percent, according to the latest available information. Roma often were denied access to higher education in state-run universities. In 2009, however, the Office of the Plenipotentiary Representative for Religious and Nationality Affairs stated that the country's Romani community had no problems that required the government's attention.

While the Russian and Belarusian languages have equal legal status, in practice Russian was the primary language used by the government. According to independent polling, the overwhelming majority of the population spoke Russian as its mother tongue. Because the government viewed proponents of the Belarusian language as political opponents of the regime, authorities continued to harass and intimidate academic and cultural groups that sought to promote use of the Belarusian language. Proposals to widen use of the language were rejected routinely.

Religion

According to a November 2011 survey by the state-controlled Information and Analytical Center, approximately 80 percent of citizens belong to the BOC, 10 percent to the Roman Catholic Church, and 2 percent to other religious groups, including Protestant, Muslim, Jewish, and other groups. There are also adherents of the Greek Catholic Church ("Uniate") and of Orthodox groups other than the BOC. Jewish groups stated that between 30,000 and 40,000 persons are Jewish. Other registered communities include the Old Believers, Lutherans, Jehovah's Witnesses, Greek Catholics, Apostolic Christians, Hare Krishnas, Baha'is, members of Christ's Church, members of The Church of Jesus Christ of Latter-day Saints (Mormons), members of the Messianic and Reform churches, Presbyterians, Armenian Apostolics, Latin Catholics, and members of St. Jogan Church.

HISTORICAL HIGHLIGHTS

While archeological evidence points to settlement in today's Belarus at least 10,000 years ago, recorded history begins with settlement by Baltic and Slavic tribes in the early centuries A.D. With distinctive features by the ninth century, the emerging Belarusian state was then absorbed by Kievan Rus' in the ninth century. Belarus was later an integral part of what was called Litva, which included today's Belarus as well as today's Lithuania. Belarus was the site of the Union of Brest in 1597, which created the Greek Catholic Church, for long the majority church in Belarus until suppressed by the Russian empire. Occupied by the Russian empire from the end of the 18th century until 1918, Belarus declared its short-lived National Republic on March 25, 1918, only to be forcibly absorbed by the Bolsheviks into what became the Soviet Union (U.S.S.R.). Suffering devastating population losses under Soviet leader Josef Stalin and the German Nazi occupation, including mass executions of 800,000 Jews, Belarus was retaken by the Soviets in 1944. It declared its sovereignty on July 27, 1990, and independence from the Soviet Union on August 25, 1991. It has been run by the authoritarian leader Alyaksandr Lukashenka since 1994.

GOVERNMENT AND POLITICAL CONDITIONS

Belarus is an authoritarian state. The country's constitution provides for a directly elected president, who is chief of state, and a bicameral parliament, the national assembly. A prime minister appointed by the president is the nominal head of government. In practice, however, power is concentrated in the presidency. Since his election as president in 1994, Alyaksandr Lukashenka has consolidated his power over all institutions and undermined the rule of law through authoritarian means, including manipulated elections and arbitrary decrees. Subsequent presidential elections, including the one held in December 2010, were neither free nor fair and fell well short of meeting international standards. The 2008 parliamentary elections also failed to meet international standards.

Since his election in 1994 to a five-year term as the country's first president, Lukashenka steadily consolidated power in the executive branch to dominate all branches of government, effectively ending any separation of powers among the branches of government. Flawed referenda in 1996 and 2004 amended the constitution to broaden his powers, extend his term in office, and remove presidential term limits. Subsequent presidential elections, including the one held in December 2010, continued to deny citizens the right to express their will to choose between opposing candidates in an honest and transparent process with fair access to media and resources.

Recent Elections

The December 2010 presidential election was marred by numerous violations of procedures and an absence of transparency and accountability that led the Organization for Security and Cooperation in Europe (OSCE) Office for Democratic Institutions and Human Rights (ODIHR) observer mission to report that the country still had "a considerable way to go in meeting its international commitments." OSCE/ODIHR observers assessed the vote count as "bad or very bad in almost half of all observed polling stations," with clear instances of ballot stuffing and tampering. Although opposition candidates enjoyed somewhat greater freedom to enter the race and promote their candidacies than in earlier elections, pre-election campaigning remained extremely limited, and government harassment of independent newspapers, opposition political parties, and independent NGOs throughout the year limited the opposition's ability to mount effective campaigns.

According to the OSCE/ODIHR mission, broadcasters nationwide devoted 90 percent of their political coverage to Lukashenka, and coverage of opposition candidates was overwhelmingly negative. Despite a nominal increase in opposition representation, authorities continued to exclude opposition representatives from election commissions at all levels. The majority of observers at local polling places appeared to be from government-sponsored NGOs; many of them received instructions in advance to report to foreign observers that the proceedings were "in order."

However, the most serious violations took place after the polls closed, when, as the OSCE/ODIHR mission observed, the situation "deteriorated significantly." In many instances international observers reported that counting was conducted silently and at a sufficient distance as to make evaluation of the count impossible. There were a number of reports that vote totals changed as the ballot boxes were transported between local precincts and the territorial election commission offices. No genuinely independent organizations were permitted to conduct exit polls, but in the opinion of the independent NGO "For Fair Elections," which monitored 250 polling stations across the country, the president failed to gain the 50 percent of the vote necessary to avoid a runoff. The official results gave Lukashenka 79.65 percent of the vote against nine other candidates.

The September 2008 parliamentary elections also fell significantly short of international standards for democratic elections, according to the final report by the OSCE/ODIHR observer mission.

Political Parties: Authorities routinely harassed and impeded the activities of independent political parties and activists. There were several instances of violence against prominent members of the political opposition during 2011. Some opposition parties lacked legal status, as authorities refused to register them, and the government routinely interfered with the right to organize, stand for election, seek votes, and publicize views. Approximately half a dozen largely inactive political parties loyal to the regime were allowed to operate freely, even though they appeared to be little more than fig leaves for a system that had de facto excluded party politics.

Political parties continued to receive formal "warnings" for minor offenses under a law that allows authorities to suspend parties for six months after one warning and close them after two. The law also prohibits political parties from receiving support from abroad and requires all political groups and coalitions to register with the Ministry of Justice.

Authorities continued to harass the unrecognized Union of Poles and its members.

Participation of Women and Minorities: While there were no laws that prevented women or minorities from voting or participating in political life on the same basis as men or minorities, statements by Lukashenka against female political leadership was cited as one of the obstacles to advancing women's political participation. Of the 24 ministries in the government, one was led by a woman.

Principal Government Officials

Last Updated: 1/31/2013

The spellings of names of Belarusian officials reflect widely recognized Russian spellings.

Pres.: **Aleksandr LUKASHENKO**
Prime Min.: **Mikhail MYASNIKOVICH**
First Dep. Prime Min.: **Vladimir SEMASHKO**
Dep. Prime Min.: **Anatoliy KALININ**
Dep. Prime Min.
Dep. Prime Min.: **Mikhail RUSYY**
Dep. Prime Min.: **Anatoliy TOZIK**
Min. of Agriculture & Food: **Leonid MARINICH**
Min. of Architecture & Construction: **Anatoliy NICHKASOV**
Min. of Communications & Information Technology: **Nikolay PANTELEY**
Min. of Culture: **Barys SVYATLOW**
Min. of Defense: **Yuriy ZHADOBIN**
Min. of Economics: **Nikolay SNOPKOV**
Min. of Education: **Sergey MASKEVICH**
Min. of Emergency Situations: **Vladimir VASHCHENKO**
Min. of Energy: **Aleksandr OZERETS**
Min. of Finance: **Andrey KHARKOVETS**
Min. of Foreign Affairs: **Vladimir MAKEY**
Min. of Forestry: **Mikhail AMELYANOVICH**
Min. of Health: **Vasiliy ZHARKO**
Min. of Housing & Municipal Services: **Andrey SHORETS**
Min. of Industry: **Dmitriy KATERINICH**
Min. of Information: **Oleg PROLESKOVSKIY**
Min. of Internal Affairs: **Anatoliy KULESHOV**
Min. of Justice: **Oleg SLIZHEVSKIY**
Min. of Labor & Social Security: **Marianna SHCHETKINA**
Min. of Natural Resources & Environmental Protection: **Vladimir TSALKO**
Min. of Sports & Tourism: **Aleksandr SHAMKO**
Min. of Taxes & Duties: **Vladimir POLUYAN**
Min. of Trade: **Valentin CHEKANOV**
Min. of Transport & Communication: **Anatol SIVAK**
Chief, Presidential Admin.: **Andrey KOBYAKOV**
Chmn., Ctte. for State Security (KGB): **Valery VAKULCHIK**
State Sec., Security Council: **Leonid MALTSEV**
Prosecutor Gen.: **Aleksandr KONYUK**
Chmn., National Bank: **Nadezhda YERMAKOVA**
Ambassador to the US:
Permanent Representative to the UN, New York: **Andrey DAPKYUNAS**

ECONOMY

As part of the former Soviet Union, Belarus had a relatively well-developed industrial base; it retained this industrial base—which is now outdated, energy inefficient, and dependent on subsidized Russian energy and preferential access to Russian markets—following the breakup of the USSR. The country also has a broad agricultural base which is inefficient and dependent on government subsidies. After an initial burst of capitalist reform from 1991–94, including privatization of state enterprises, creation of institutions of private property, and development of entrepreneurship, Belarus' economic development greatly slowed. About 80% of all industry remains in state hands, and foreign investment has been hindered by a climate hostile to business. A few banks, which had been privatized after independence, were renationalized. State banks account for 75% of the banking sector. Economic output, which had declined for several years following the collapse of the Soviet Union, revived in the mid-2000s thanks to the boom in oil prices. Belarus has only small reserves of crude oil, though it imports most of its crude oil and natural gas from Russia at prices substantially below the world market. Belarus exported refined oil products at market prices produced from Russian crude oil purchased at a steep discount.

In late 2006, Russia began a process of rolling back its subsidies on oil and gas to Belarus. Tensions over Russian energy reached a peak in 2010, when Russia stopped the export of all subsidized oil to Belarus save for domestic needs. In December 2010, Russia and Belarus reached a deal to restart the export of discounted oil to Belarus.

In November 2011, Belarus and Russia reached an agreement to drastically reduce the price of natural gas in exchange for selling to Russia the remaining share of Beltransgaz, the Belarusian natural gas pipeline operator. Little new foreign investment has occurred in recent years. In 2011, a financial crisis began, triggered by government directed salary hikes unsupported by commensurate productivity increases.

The crisis was compounded by an increased cost in Russian energy inputs and an overvalued Belarusian ruble, and eventually led to a near three-fold devaluation of the Belarusian ruble in 2011. In November 2011, Belarus agreed to sell to Russia its remaining shares in Beltransgaz, the Belarusian natural gas pipeline operator, in exchange for reduced prices for Russian natural gas. Receiving more than half of a $3 billion loan from the Russian-dominated Eurasian Economic Community Bail-out Fund, a $1 billion loan from the Russian state-owned bank Sberbank, and the $2.5 billion sale of Beltranzgas to Russian state-owned Gazprom helped stabilize the situation in 2012; nevertheless, the Belarusian currency lost more than 60% of its value.

Labor Conditions

The minimum age for employment is 16; however, a child as young as age 14 may conclude a labor contract with the written consent of one parent or a legal guardian. The Prosecutor General's Office reportedly enforced the law effectively. Minors under age 18 were allowed to work in nonhazardous jobs but were not allowed to work overtime, on weekends, or on government holidays. Work was not to be harmful to the minors' health or hinder their education.

The law forbids the exploitation of children in the workplace, including a prohibition on forced and compulsory labor, and specifies policies for acceptable working conditions. The government generally implemented these laws in practice. However, there were reports that some children were compelled into forced labor.

As of December 1, the national minimum monthly wage was 925,520 rubles ($112). As of December 31, the average monthly wage was 2,877,658 rubles ($348). As of November 1, the government set the poverty line at 574,790 rubles ($69) a month per capita. The first deputy minister of labor and social security reported on December 28 that 59 organizations paid their workers wages below the established national minimum monthly compensation.

The law establishes a standard workweek of 40 hours and provides for at least one 24-hour rest period per week. Because of the country's difficult economic situation, many workers worked considerably less than 40 hours per week, and factories often required workers to take unpaid furloughs due to lack of demand for the factories' products. In May amid deepening financial crisis and lack of foreign currency proceeds, the head of the National Statistics Committee stated that approximately 600,000 workers in industries were on furloughs due to their companies' failure to import raw materials.

Given higher wages in Russia, labor migration to Russia, where Belarusians have the legal right to work, increased noticeably. The law provides for mandatory overtime and holiday pay and restricts overtime to four hours every two days, with a maximum of 120 hours of overtime each year. The law establishes minimum conditions for workplace safety and worker health; however, employers often ignored these standards.

U.S.-BELARUS RELATIONS

The United States established diplomatic relations with Belarus in 1991, following its independence from the Soviet Union. Belarus has been led by the authoritarian Alyaksandr Lukashenka since 1994. Bilateral relations cooled following his election and have remained at a low level, despite U.S. efforts with the European Union to set benchmarks for improving Belarus' human rights and electoral practices.

The United States calls for new presidential and parliamentary elections that comply with Organization for Security and Cooperation in Europe standards, and for the release and rehabilitation of all political prisoners. The United States has imposed a variety of sanctions against Belarusian officials and entities.

U.S. Assistance to Belarus

U.S. Government assistance to Belarus focuses on supporting the Belarusian people in achieving a government that respects their democratic rights and fundamental freedoms. A fact sheet on U.S. assistance to Belarus can be found here.

Bilateral Economic Relations

The U.S. Government continues to support the development of the private sector in Belarus and its transition to a free-market economy. Under the Lukashenka regime, Belarusian authorities have pursued a generally hostile policy toward the private sector and have refused to initiate the basic economic reforms necessary to create a market-based economy. Most of the Belarusian economy remains under government control. The U.S. Government currently does not encourage U.S. companies to invest in Belarus. Belarus' opaque legal and regulatory systems do not create a business environment the U.S. Government recommends for investment.

Belarus's Membership in International Organizations

Belarus and the United States belong to a number of the same international organizations, including the United Nations, Euro-Atlantic Partnership Council, Organization for Security and Cooperation in Europe, International Monetary Fund, and World Bank. Belarus also is an observer to the World Trade Organization.

Bilateral Representation

Belarus maintains an embassy in the United States at 1619 New Hampshire Ave., NW, Washington, DC 20009 (tel. 202-986-1604).

Principal U.S. Embassy Officials

Last Updated: 1/14/2013

MINSK (E) 46, Starovilenskaya St., Minsk Belarus 220002, (375) (17) 210-1283, Fax (375) (17) 334-7853, INMARSAT Tel NONE, Workweek: M-F / 0830–1730, Website: http://belarus.usembassy.gov/

DCM OMS:	Vacant
AMB OMS:	Vacant
DCM/CHG:	Ethan A. Goldrich
FM:	Vacant
MGT:	Andrea Gastaldo
SDO/DATT:	Vacant
AMB:	Vacant
CON:	Carrie Lee
AGR:	(Res In Moscow)
AID:	John Riordon
DEA:	(Res In Vienna)
FAA:	(Res In Brussels)
IMO:	Nijay P. Saini
IRS:	Res. In Frankfurt
ISO:	Vacant
LEGATT:	(Res In Kiev)
POL:	Chris Panico
State ICASS:	Vacant

TRAVEL

Consular Information Sheet

December 19, 2012

Country Description: Belarus has been headed by President Alexander Lukashenka since 1994. Under Lukashenka's rule, economic and political reform has stalled and the government's human rights record has steadily deteriorated. Both Belarusian and Russian are official languages, and Russian is widely spoken throughout the country, particularly in the cities. Tourist facilities are not highly developed, but food and lodging in the capital and some regional centers are adequate.

Smart Traveler Enrollment Program (STEP)/Embassy Locations: If you are going to live in or visit Belarus, please take the time to tell our embassy about your trip. Enrolling in the Smart Traveler Enrollment Program will keep you up to date with important safety and security announcements, and help your friends and family get in touch with you in an emergency.

U.S. Embassy Minsk
46 Starovilenskaya St. Minsk 220002
Telephone: (375 17) 210-1283 or after hours (375 29) 676-0134
Fax (375 17) 334-7853 or (375 17) 17-217-7160 (consular section)

Entry/Exit Requirements for U.S. Citizens: You need a passport and a visa to enter Belarus. You must obtain a visa in advance to visit or transit through Belarus. All U.S. citizens visiting or residing in Belarus are required to register with the local office of the Citizenship and Migration Department of the Ministry of Interior (formerly OVIR) within 5 business days of arrival; if you plan to spend only 7 days (5 working days weekend) in Belarus, you are not required to register. The registration fee is currently approximately $12(the exact amount can be calculated by taking half of one National Minimum Tariff Unit) regardless of the duration of stay. Failure to register can result in fines and difficulties when departing. If you plan to stay at a hotel, you will be automatically registered at check-in. Registration performed by a hotel is free of charge.

Visas: Visa validity dates are strictly enforced; you should request a visa of sufficient length to allow for changes in arrival and departure plans, and should carefully review the beginning and ending dates of your visa before traveling.

The U.S. Department of State is unaware of any HIV/AIDS entry restrictions for visitors to Belarus on a 30-day visit. Long-term residents (more than 90 days a year) or students must obtain an HIV/AIDS test in Belarus and submit the results to the Department of Citizenship and Migration when applying for an extension of stay or residency in Belarus.

Exit Visa: A valid exit visa is necessary to depart Belarus. Generally, the visa issued by a Belarusian Embassy or Consulate is valid for both entry and exit. Photocopies of visas may be helpful in the event of loss, but note that a copy of a visa will not be sufficient for entry or departure, as Belarusian border officials always require original travel documents. If you overstay your visa's validity—even by one day—you will be prevented from leaving until you have been granted an extension by the Department of Citizenship and Migration. If you are not in a possession of a valid visa, you will face delays in leaving Belarus and may have trouble finding adequate accommodation. By Belarusian law, foreign travelers with an expired visa may not check in at any hotel or other lodging establishment.

If you plan to travel through Belarus to other countries, you are advised that there is a transit-visa requirement for entering and leaving Belarus. Transit visas are required even if you are transiting on a direct overnight train with no stops or transfers on Belarusian territory. Transit visas should be obtained prior to any journey that requires travel through Belarus. Transit visas are good only for transiting Belarus from one country into another. If you attempt to reenter the country from which you originally entered on your transit visa, you will not be let out of Belarus without paying a fine and obtaining an exit visa. Commonwealth of Independent States (CIS) and Russian visas are not a substitute for the transit visa. Many travel agencies, including those in Russia and CIS countries, as well as train ticket sales personnel, are often not aware of this visa requirement and may not seek a transit visa for a traveler unless instructed by the traveler to do so.

U.S. citizens attempting to transit Belarus without a valid Belarusian transit visa have been denied entry into the country and forcibly removed from trains. In some instances, local border and railway authorities have threatened passengers who did not possess a valid transit visa with jail or extorted "fines." It is our recommendation that you should not pay any border or railway officials for transit visas or "transit-visa fines," as these officials are not authorized to issue such visas. If you find yourself in Belarus without transit visas, if confronted by border or train personnel, you should request to be put in contact with consular officials at the U.S. Embassy in Minsk.

If your travel route to Belarus goes through Russia, you must possess a Russian transit visa in addition to your Belarusian visa. Russian embassies outside of the United States, including the Russian Embassy in Belarus, generally do not issue transit or tourist visas to U.S. citizens. Russian transit visas are not normally obtainable at Russian airports.

Limitations on Length of Stay: The Law on the Legal Status of Foreign Citizens and Stateless Persons in the Republic of Belarus states that all foreign citizens may be granted permission for a temporary stay (up to 90 days within a 365-day period), temporary residence (up to one year), or permanent residence. Belarusian Embassies and Consulates will issue visas for temporary stays. A temporary stay visa will allow you to be present physically in Belarus for a maximum of 90 days within the 365-day period for which the visa is issued. Once you have spent 90 days in Belarus, at one time or through a combination of visits, you will not be eligible to receive another visa until the original 365-day period has passed.

If you receive a visa for a temporary stay, but wish to remain in Belarus for longer than 90 days, you must apply for temporary or permanent residence with the Ministry of Interior. You must make the application in Belarus within the 90 days allotted for a temporary stay. Permission for temporary residence can be granted to students, spouses, or close relatives of Belarusian citizens, or for "work, business, or other activities." You may contact the Consular Section at the U.S. Embassy in Minsk for more information about application procedures for temporary or permanent residence. Every foreigner entering Belarus is required to fill out a migration card. You should retain this card for the whole period of stay and present it to the border authorities when exiting Belarus.

As a foreign citizen without a valid Belarusian visa, migration card, or proper registration with the Department of Citizenship and Migration as a temporary visitor or resident, you can be subject to sanctions up to and including deportation under the provisions of the Code of Administrative Violations. Depending on the circumstances, as a deportee, you also can be banned from returning to Belarus for a period from one to ten years.

Visiting and transiting Belarus, you also should be prepared to demonstrate sufficient financial means to support your stay. For individuals staying in Belarus for less than one month, this amount is equal to approximately $15/day/person. For those staying for longer than one month, the requirements call for $375/month/person. Belarusian officials may request this proof of funds at the time of visa application, at the border, or during registration. According to the Ministry of Interior, cash, credit cards, paid hotel reservations, or a letter from an inviting party pledging full financial support are sufficient means to demonstrate financial wherewithal.

Belarus also requires all foreign nationals (other than accredited diplomats) entering the country to purchase medical insurance at the port-of-entry, regardless of any other insurance they might have. For more information, see the "Medical Insurance" section below.

When entering Belarus, you may be charged 2 Euros per kilogram of luggage in excess of 50 Kg (121lbs). That fee must be paid in dollars or Euros. In accordance with current customs regulations, you may enter Belarus and exit the country with up to $3,000 in cash without submitting a written declaration.. For additional information on customs rules for Belarus, please see the Belarusian State Customs Committee official website.

Belarus enforces a requirement for special permits to travel in "protected border zones." The Government of Belarus has not provided information defining the parameters of those zones. You should be alert for warning signs, road barriers, and/or border guard posts, and are advised not to cross into such areas without permission.

Religious Group Travel: Foreign missionaries may not engage in religious activities outside the institutions that invited them unless they have a religious worker visa. One-year validity, multiple-entry, "spiritual-activities" visas, which are required of foreign missionaries, can be difficult to get, even for faiths that are registered with the government and have a long history in the country. Approval often involves a difficult bureaucratic process.

Belarusian law requires all religious groups and organizations to register with the Government; most organizations have done so. Unregistered religious groups may not legally gather for religious purposes. Many unregistered groups continue to meet, however, leaving themselves vulnerable to selective implementation of the law by authorities. The law also stipulates that only Belarusian citizens can head religious organizations in Belarus. In recent years, authorities have harassed, warned, fined, and briefly detained members of some unregistered and so-called "non-traditional" faiths for engaging in unsanctioned worship or proselytism. U.S. Embassy Minsk strongly recommends that should you choose to attend a religious service of an unregistered religious group, you do so only after consulting with members of the group about the risk of harassment or possible arrest by local law enforcement authorities. You are also urged to contact U.S. Embassy Minsk in the event you encounter any problems with authorities due to your participation in such services or events.

Dual Nationality: If you were a Belarusian citizen and obtained U.S. citizenship through naturalization, you may not have automatically lost your Belarusian citizenship. In the majority of cases, naturalized U.S. citizens retain their Belarusian citizenship unless they take specific steps to renounce it. The Belarusian authorities will allow naturalized U.S. citizens from Belarus to enter the country without a valid Belarusian passport on a "certificate of return" issued by Belarusian Embassies and Consulates. Please note that a valid Belarusian passport will be required to leave the country. It can take two to four weeks to receive a new Belarusian passport. For additional information please consult with the Embassy of Belarus in Washington, D.C.

Belarusian citizens, including dual nationals, are subject to Belarusian laws requiring service in Belarus's armed forces, as well as other laws pertaining to passports and nationality. If you are a U.S.-Belarusian dual national of military age who does not wish to serve in the Belarusian armed forces, you should contact the Embassy of Belarus in Washington, D.C. to learn more about an exemption or deferment from Belarusian military service before going to

Belarus. Without this exemption or deferment document, you may not be able to leave Belarus without completing military service, or may be subject to criminal penalties for failure to serve.

Children born to Belarusian parents or to one Belarusian parent and one foreign parent, even if born in the United States and in possession of a U.S. passport, may not be issued a Belarusian visa for travel to Belarus. The Belarusian government considers these children to be Belarusian citizens until age 16, when they may choose to accept or reject that claim to citizenship. Instead of a visa, a "certificate of return" is issued that will allow the child to enter Belarus. It is imperative that parents of such children understand that, in order to leave the country, the child will be required to have a Belarusian passport if he/she does not already have one. It can take anywhere from two to four weeks to complete the application procedures and receive a new Belarusian passport.

Visit the Embassy of Belarus website for the most current visa information, or contact the Embassy of Belarus at 1619 New Hampshire Avenue, NW, Washington, DC 20009, tel: 202-986-1604 fax: 202-986-1805.

Threats to Safety and Security: Both organized and spontaneous demonstrations occur in Belarus. Localized street disturbances relating to political events occur most frequently in Minsk or larger cities. In some instances, authorities may use force to disperse protesters. Bystanders, including foreign nationals, may face the possibility of arrest, beating, or detention. Even demonstrations intended to be peaceful can sometimes become confrontational and escalate into violence. For this reason, it is recommended that you, as a U.S. citizen, avoid all demonstrations and protest gatherings.

Security personnel may at times place you, as a foreigner, under surveillance; your hotel rooms, telephones, and fax machines may be monitored, and personal possessions in your hotel rooms may be searched. Taking photographs of anything that could be perceived as being of military or security interest may result in problems with authorities; these sites are not always clearly marked and application of these restrictions is subject to interpretation.

Stay up to date by:

- Bookmarking our Bureau of Consular Affairs website, which contains the current Travel Warnings and Travel Alerts as well as the Worldwide Caution;
- Following us on Twitter and the Bureau of Consular Affairs page on Facebook;
- Downloading our free Smart Traveler iPhone App or Smart Traveler Android App to have travel information at your fingertips;
- Calling 1-888-407-4747 toll-free within the U.S. and Canada, or a regular toll line, 1-202-501-4444, from other countries; and,
- Taking some time before travel to consider your personal security.

Crime: If you or someone you know becomes the victim of a crime abroad, you should contact the local police and the nearest U.S. embassy or consulate. We can:

- Replace a stolen passport;
- Help you find appropriate medical care if you are the victim of a violent crime such as assault or rape;
- Put you in contact with the appropriate police authorities, and if you want us to, we cancontact family members or friends; and
- Help you understand the local criminal justice process and direct you to local attorneys, although it is important to remember that local authorities are responsible for investigating and prosecuting the crime.

Belarus has a moderate rate of street crime. Criminal activity in Minsk is comparable to the level found in other large cities, while in the rural areas it is very limited. Though violent crime against foreigners is rare, criminals have been known to use force if met with resistance from victims. Common street crime, such as mugging and pocket picking, occurs most frequently near public transportation venues, near hotels frequented by foreigners, and/or at night in poorly-lighted areas. In Minsk, you should be especially alert in metro and bus stations.

Visiting night clubs, you should pay particular attention to your surroundings and drinks, because the drugging of drinks is not uncommon. Prostitutes at hotels may attempt to open hotel room doors in search of customers. Local and transnational organized criminal activity also exists in Belarus. Most casinos and adult clubs are operated by criminal elements, but street-level organized criminal violence is rare and does not generally affect foreigners. Carjacking is also rare, but theft of vehicles parts and car vandalism is not. Sport-utility and luxury vehicles tend to be the most sought-after. Parking in a secure area overnight is highly recommended.

Sexual assaults on women are as commonplace in Minsk as they are in most large urban areas in the United States. Women are advised to exercise the same caution as they would in any large city in the United States. Keep a copy of your passport in a separate location from your original passport.

Internet-Dating Schemes and Cyber-Crime: "Internet brides" are advertised on several websites and are not always legitimate. Often, potential suitors in the United States lose thousands of dollars when they send money to people they have never met and never hear from again. A growing variant on this theme is the suitor invited to Belarus to visit a "friend," who arranges lodging and transportation for him (at hugely inflated prices) and disappears when the money has changed hands.

Cyber-crime of all kinds is well developed in Belarus. Merchandise orders with fraudulent credit cards, ID theft, hacking/blackmail schemes, and advanced-fee fraud are gaining in popularity. If you are doing business with persons or firms in Belarus electronically, you should proceed with extreme caution. You should avoid using credit and debit cards, except at ATMs located inside major banks. Not only is electronic fraud common at ATMs and grocery stores, serious injuries have been inflicted during assaults at street-side ATMs. Please note that transferring funds from abroad, replacing stolen traveler's checks or airline tickets, or canceling credit cards can be difficult and time consuming, especially due to the lack of English-speaking tourist agencies and an undeveloped tourism industry in Belarus. In many countries around the world, counterfeit and pirated goods are widely available. Transactions involving such products may be illegal under local law. In addition, bringing them back to the United States may result in forfeitures and/or fines.

The local equivalents to the "911" emergency lines in Belarus are: 101 for Fire and Rescue Squad; 102 for Police; and 103 for Ambulance (Medical Emergency).

Belarus police organizations are well trained and professional, but severely restricted by an un-reformed Soviet-era legal system, corruption, and politicization of the police force and other government authorities. Due to low salaries, it is not uncommon for officers to collect bribes during traffic stops. Sophisticated criminal investigations are often inconclusive because of a lack of resources and/or political will. Some U.S. citizens have reported harassment at border crossings. Despite these problems, the Regional Security Officer recommends that you report any crimes immediately to the local police and the U.S. Embassy in Minsk.

Criminal Penalties: While you are traveling in Belarus, you are subject to its laws even if you are a U.S. citizen. Foreign laws and legal systems can be vastly different than our own. There are also some things that might be legal in the country you visit, but still illegal in the United States; for instance, you can be prosecuted under U.S. law if you buy pirated goods. Engaging in sexual conduct with children or using or disseminating child pornography in a foreign country is a crime prosecutable in the United States. If you do something illegal in Belarus, your U.S. passport won't help you avoid arrest or prosecution. It's very important to know what's legal and what's not where you are going.

While some countries will automatically notify the nearest U.S. embassy or consulate if a U.S. citizen is detained or arrested in a foreign country, that might not always be the case. To ensure that the United States is aware of your circumstances, you should immediately request that police and prison officials notify the embassy in the event you are arrested or detained.

Special Circumstances: Traveler's checks are normally not accepted in Belarus as a means of payment, but can be exchanged for cash at any bank. Most hotels, restaurants, and stores accept major credit cards. All Belarusian banks provide cash from major credit cards. All payments in Belarus are made in Belarusian rubles. Authorized currency exchange centers are widely available throughout major cities. Black-market currency exchange or payment in U.S. dollars to firms or individuals without a special license is a criminal offense in Belarus. Only a few large firms (such as state-owned gas stations and large travel agencies) are licensed to accept U.S. dollars. You may be offered "an unofficial" exchange rate at what seems a good rate, but the U.S. Embassy in Minsk advises to use widely available licensed exchange locations.

Credit Card and ATM Card Use: ATMs are also available for use, and it has become easier to use credit cards and debit cards in Belarus, especially in Minsk; however, this does not mean that it is safer to do so. There have been instances in which U.S. citizens have had their card numbers "skimmed" and the money in their accounts stolen, or their credit cards fraudulently charged. ("Skimming" is the theft of credit card information by an employee of a legitimate merchant or bank, manually copying down numbers or using a magnetic stripe reader.) In addition to skimming, the risk of physical theft of credit or debit cards also exists. To prevent such theft, the U.S. Embassy Minsk recommends that you keep close track of personal belongings and only carry what is needed when out. If you choose to use credit cards, you should regularly check your account status to ensure its integrity. You should avoid using credit and debit cards, except at ATMs located inside major banks.

Identification: As a foreigner, you are expected to carry your passport on you at all times. Failure to prove your identity with an internationally recognizable ID, if stopped by the police for a registration (visa) spot check, may result in detention by the police until your identity is established.

Accessibility: While in Belarus, individuals with disabilities may find accessibility and accommodation very different from what is found in the United States. Many existing buildings as well as public transportation systems are less adapted to individuals with disabilities. You should check ahead with your hotel/destination to learn more about options to accommodate disabled traveler needs before visiting Belarus.

Radiation: The 1986 release of nuclear material from the Chernobyl nuclear station in Ukraine affected Belarus. The city of Minsk was mostly spared, but other areas of Belarus were badly contaminated. Several years of monitoring have shown that radiation levels in Minsk have not exceeded internationally acceptable standards, and periodic testing of foodstuffs from various locations in Belarus has not revealed a level of radiation that would be considered harmful.

Marriage: If you plan to marry in Belarus, you should consult the information located on the U.S. Embassy Minsk website. Please note that only marriages performed at a registrar's office (ZAGS—Office for Matrimonial Acts Registration) are legally valid in Belarus.

Medical Facilities and Health Information: Medical care in Belarus is neither modern nor easily accessible, especially for those who do not speak Russian. There are no hospitals in Belarus that provide a level of medical care equal to that of Western hospitals, and none accept U.S. health insurance plans for payment. Despite the recent emergence of facilities which offer private "advanced" medical services, modern diagnostic equipment and even basic supplies are still lacking. Traumatic injuries are especially serious as the level of care and competence to deal with them are well below U.S. standards.

Ambulances are poorly equipped and unreliable; a wait time of 30 minutes or more is not unusual. The fastest way to secure Western-level care is medical evacuation to Western Europe. You should consider purchasing medical evacuation insurance prior to travel, or have access to substantial credit to cover evacuation costs. There are no air ambulance services in Belarus. Local health insurance for non-residents is required for all visitors by the government and may be purchased at points of entry. The medical emergency number for Belarus is 103 from any telephone.

Tuberculosis (TB) is an increasingly serious health concern in Belarus. For further information, please consult the Centers for Disease Control and Prevention's (CDC) information on TB. You can find good information on vaccinations and other health precautions, on the Centers for Disease Control and Prevention (CDC) website. For information about outbreaks of infectious diseases abroad, consult the World Health Organization (WHO) website, which also contains additional health information for travelers, including detailed country-specific health information.

Medical Insurance: You can't assume your insurance will go with you when you travel. It's very important to find out BEFORE you leave. You need to ask your insurance company two questions:

- Does my policy apply when I'm out of the United States?
- Will it cover emergencies like a trip to a foreign hospital or an evacuation?

In many places, doctors and hospitals still expect payment in cash at the time of service. Your regular U.S. health insurance may not cover doctors' and hospital visits in other countries. If your policy doesn't go with you when you travel, it's a very good idea to take out another one for your trip.

As a foreign national, you will be required to purchase local medical insurance at the port-of-entry, regardless of any other insurance you might have. Costs for this insurance will vary according to the length of stay. (Subject to change, current information puts costs at 2 euros for a one-to-three-day stay, 5 euros for a stay of 4-10 days, 15 euros for a stay of up to 31 days, and 85 euros for a stay of one year.)

Traffic Safety and Road Conditions: U.S. citizens on short-term visits to Belarus (up to 90 days) are permitted to drive with a valid U.S. state or international driver's license. Therefore, you should always carry your passport with you to prove date of entry into the country in the event that police stop you. If residing in Belarus for more than 90 days, you should apply for a Belarusian driver's license (regardless of the type of license you have, state or international), in which case you will be required to pass a two-part test in Russian. The first part of this test is a computer-based multiple-choice test on local driving rules, and the second part is a driving test. To receive a local driver's license, you will also need to complete a medical exam at a special medical clinic, which will include a general physical, approval form from a neuro-pathologist, a surgeon, and an EENT specialist, as well as an EKG, a chest x-ray, and an eye exam. Roads in Belarus are in generally good condition, but modern cars share the highways with tractors, horse-drawn carts, and pedestrians. Drunk driving is also common, even with a zero-tolerance law. Ice and snow in the winter months pose an added hazard. Should you get involved in an automobile accident, report it immediately to the road police, and remain at the scene until after the police arrive and complete the investigation. You may leave the scene of an accident only if you believe your personal safety is in danger.

Except for a stretch of the main east-west highway where the speed limit is 120 km/h (75 mph), the maximum speed limit on divided highways or main roads outside village, town, or city limits is 90 km/h (55 mph). Speed limits in cities are 60 km/h unless marked and will usually range between 40 km/h and 80 km/h, with frequent radar traps. Fines for speeding depend on the speed over the speed limit, and can vary from 2 to 10 minimum tariff units (from $26 to $130). Visible and hidden dangers exist, including potholes, unlighted or poorly lighted streets, inattentive and dark-clothed pedestrians walking on unlighted roads, drivers and pedestrians under the influence of alcohol, and disregard for traffic rules. Driving in winter is especially dangerous because of ice and snow. Driving with caution is urged at all times.

DUI fines vary from 15 to 35 minimum tariff units (from $200 to $500) for the first detected offense. Repeated offenders within 365 days may be subject to criminal persecution (up to 6 months in prison or up to two years of corrective labor). Drivers are expected to yield for pedestrians crossing at pedestrian crossings marked by respective road signs or road markings, and intersections not controlled by a traffic signal or a road policeman.

Use of hand-held mobile phones while driving is prohibited. Radio-dispatched taxi services are generally reliable, arrive promptly once called, and usually offer the lowest fare. Most radio-dispatched taxis are metered. Current fare is approximately $0.75 per mile. With the majority of taxi services, the rates are the same during the day and in the overnight hours. The use of informal, unregistered taxis is not recommended.

Minsk has a clean, safe, and efficient subway system that easily reaches most of the city center. Service is stopped from 1:00 a.m.to 5:30 a.m., but otherwise runs regularly throughout the day. Ticket prices are extremely low by western standards. Though their routes are extensive, buses and trolleys lack cooling capabilities in the summer and are usually crowded. When travelling on public transportation of any kind, you should be wary of pickpockets and other petty crime. If you are interested in car rentals, there are several western rental agencies currently operating in Minsk. In general, rental-car networks in Belarus are not well developed. You may experience significant delays (of several hours) in crossing the border by road into neighboring countries.

Aviation Safety Oversight: As there is no direct commercial air service to the United States by carriers registered in Belarus, the U.S. Federal Aviation Administration (FAA) has not assessed the Government of Belarus' Civil Aviation Authority for compliance with International Civil Aviation Organization (ICAO) aviation safety standards. Further information may be found on the FAA's safety assessment page.

Children's Issues: Please see the U.S. Dept. of State Office of Children's Issues web pages on intercountry adoption and international parental child abduction.

Intercountry adoption

February 2006

As of February 2013, the Department of State did not have country specific information pertaining to adoption from Belarus available on its Intercountry Adoption website. The information in this section was edited from previous reports. Prospective parents should read the *Intercountry Adoption* section of this book and check for current reports online at http://adoption.state.gov for the latest information.

The Government of Belarus has not completed any U.S. adoptions of Belarusian children since October 2004. Although the Government of Belarus changed its adoption procedures in 2005, intercountry adoptions involving U.S. families have yet to proceed. Thus, the information in this flyer relates to how the process should work, according to Belarusian law, if and when the Government of Belarus again begins allowing U.S. adoptions. The very small number of immigrant visas that the U.S. Government was able to issue to Belarusian orphans in Fiscal Year 2005 reflects adoptions approved in Belarus before the Belarusian government stopped processing adoptions. The Department of State encourages U.S. citizens contemplating adopting from Belarus to monitor closely the Important Notices page of the U.S. Department of State, Bureau of Consular Affairs web site for the most recent information on Belarusian adoptions. The government of Belarus stresses that American citizens interested in adopting a child in Belarus should not travel to that country until the stipulated adoption procedures have been completed. Belarus requires post placement reports on Belarusian orphans for the first five years after an adoption.

Belarusian National Adoption Center
Ms. Natalia Pospelova, Director
Platonova Str. 22, 11 th Floor
Minsk, BELARUS
Tel: 375—17-232-6701
Fax: 375—17-231-0617

Adoption Procedures: Interested American citizens should find and work with a licensed adoption agency or provider that employs representatives or facilitators in Belarus. Because prospective parents are advised that they should not travel to Belarus until a suitable child has been selected for them, a representative in Belarus is absolutely essential in order to work through the adoption process.

Belarusian Citizenship: Under Belarusian law, children adopted from Belarus remain citizens of Belarus at least until their 16th birthdays, notwithstanding the children's acquisition of a new citizenship in their new country. When the child turns 16, the adoptive parents may apply to the Belarusian embassy in Washington to have the child's Belarusian citizenship terminated. Parents with more detailed questions concerning this process should contact the Belarusian embassy.

Embassy of the Republic of Belarus
1619 New Hampshire Avenue, NW
Washington, D.C. 20009
Tel: (202) 986-1606
fax: (202) 986-1805
Email: consul@belarusembassy.org
http://www.belarusembassy.org

U.S. Immigration Requirements: Prospective adopting parents are strongly encouraged to consult USCIS publication M-249, *The Immigration of Adopted and Prospective Adoptive Children,* as well as the Department of State publication, *Intercountry Adoptions.*

U.S. Embassy Belarus
Consular Section, U.S. Embassy
46 Starovilenskaya St.
220002 Minsk, Belarus
Tel: 375-17-210-1283

Additional Information: Specific questions about adoption in Belarus may be addressed to the U.S. Embassy in Belarus. General questions regarding intercountry adoption may be addressed to the Office of Children's Issues, U.S. Department of State, CA/OCS/CI, SA-29, 4th Floor, 2201 C Street, NW, Washington, D.C. 20520-4818, toll-free Tel: 1-888-407-4747.

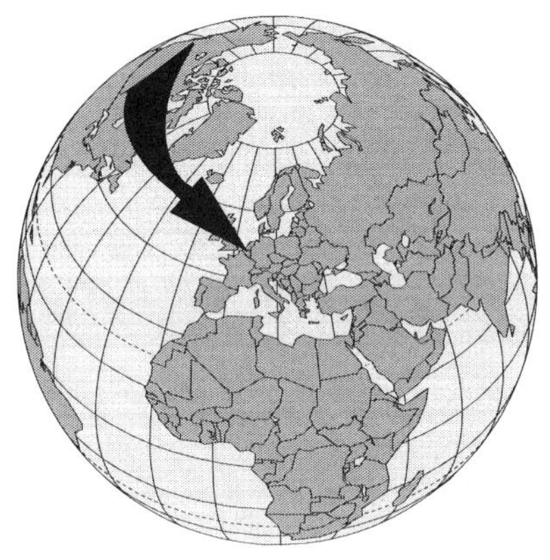

BELGIUM

Compiled from publications that were available as of February 2013 from the U.S. Department of State, the U.S. Department of Commerce, and the Central Intelligence Agency (CIA). See the introduction to this set for explanatory notes.

Official Name:
Kingdom of Belgium

PROFILE

Geography

Area: total: 30,528 sq km; country comparison to the world: 141; land: 30,278 sq km; water: 250 sq km

Major cities: Brussels (capital) 1.892 million; Antwerp 961,000 (2009)

Climate: temperate; mild winters, cool summers; rainy, humid, cloudy

Terrain: flat coastal plains in northwest, central rolling hills, rugged mountains of Ardennes Forest in southeast

People

Nationality: noun: Belgian(s); adjective: Belgian

Population: 10,438,353 (July 2012 est.)

Population growth rate: 0.061% (2012 est.)

Ethnic groups: Fleming 58%, Walloon 31%, mixed or other 11%

Religions: Roman Catholic 75%, other (includes Protestant) 25%

Languages: Dutch (official) 60%, French (official) 40%, German (official) less than 1%, legally bilingual (Dutch and French)

Literacy: definition: age 15 and over can read and write; total population: 99%; male: 99%; female: 99% (2003 est.)

Health: life expectancy at birth: total population: 79.65 years; male: 76.49 years; female: 82.95 years (2012 est.); Infant mortality rate: total: 4.28 deaths/1,000 live births; male: 4.79 deaths/1,000 live births; female: 3.74 deaths/1,000 live births (2012 est.)

Unemployment rate: 7.6% (2012 est.)

Work force: 5.055 million (2012 est.)

Government

Type: federal parliamentary democracy under a constitutional monarchy

Independence: 4 October 1830

Constitution: drafted 25 November 1830; approved by a Belgium National Congress 7 February 1831; entered into force 26 July 1831; amended many times; revised 14 July 1993 to create a federal state; in 1967 an official Dutch version of the constitution was adopted; in 1991 an official German version of the constitution was adopted; in 1993 an official consolidated version of the constitution was adopted

Political subdivisions: 3 regions (French: regions, singular—region; Dutch: gewesten, singular—gewest); Brussels-Capital Region, also known as Brussels Hoofdstedelijk Gewest (Dutch), Region de Bruxelles-Capitale (French long form), Bruxelles-Capitale (French short form); Flemish Region (Flanders), also known as Vlaams Gewest (Dutch long form), Vlaanderen (Dutch short form), Region Flamande (French long form), Flandre (French short form); Walloon Region (Wallonia), also known as Region Wallone (French long form), Wallonie (French short form), Waals Gewest (Dutch long form), Wallonie (Dutch short form)

Suffrage: 18 years of age; universal and compulsory

Economy

GDP (purchasing power parity): $420.6 billion (2012 est.); $418.6 billion (2011 est.); $410.8 billion (2010 est.); $401.7 billion (2009 est.)

GDP real growth rate: 0% (2012 est.); 1.9% (2011 est.); 2.3% (2010 est.); -2.8% (2009 est.)

GDP per capita (PPP): $38,100 (2012 est.); $38,200 (2011 est.); $37,900 (2010 est.)

Natural resources: construction materials, silica sand, carbonates

Agriculture products: sugar beets, fresh vegetables, fruits, grain, tobacco; beef, veal, pork, milk

Industries: engineering and metal products, motor vehicle assembly, transportation equipment, scientific instruments, processed food and beverages, chemicals, basic metals, textiles, glass, petroleum

Exports: $314.6 billion (2012 est.); $344.9 billion (2011 est.);

Exports—commodities: machinery and equipment, chemicals, finished diamonds, metals and metal products, foodstuffs
Exports—partners: Germany 18.7%, France 16.9%, Netherlands 12.5%, UK 7.2%, Italy 4.6%, US 4.5% (2011)
Imports: ; $355.1 billion (2011 est.); $284.4 billion (2010 est.)
Imports—commodities: raw materials, machinery and equipment, chemicals, raw diamonds, pharmaceuticals, foodstuffs, transportation equipment, oil products
Imports—partners: Netherlands 19.9%, Germany 14.8%, France 10.7%, UK 6%, US 5.3%, Ireland 4.5%, China 4.2% (2011)
Debt—external: $1.399 trillion (30 June 2011); $1.241 trillion (30 June 2010)
Exchange rates: euros (EUR) per US dollar; 0.7838 (2012 est.); 0.7194 (2011 est.); 0.755 (2010 est.); 0.7198 (2009 est.); 0.6827 (2008 est.)

GEOGRAPHY

Belgium is located in Western Europe, bordered by the Netherlands, Germany, Luxembourg, France, and the North Sea. Although generally flat, the terrain becomes increasingly hilly and forested in the southeast (Ardennes) region. Climate is cool, temperate, and rainy; summer temperatures average 77°F, winters average 45°F. Annual extremes (rarely attained) are 10°F and 100°F.

PEOPLE

Geographically and culturally, Belgium is at a crossroads of Europe, and during the past 2,000 years has witnessed a constant ebb and flow of different races and cultures. Consequently, Belgium is one of Europe's true melting pots with Celtic, Roman, Germanic, French, Dutch, Spanish, and Austrian cultures having made an imprint.

Belgium is divided ethnically into the Dutch-speaking Flemings and French-speaking Walloons, the 75,000 residents of the eastern German cantons, and the bilingual capital of Brussels. The population density is the second highest in Europe, after the Netherlands.

Language

Belgium has three national languages: Dutch (also referred to as Flemish), French, and German. English is spoken and understood throughout most of Belgium.

Religion

The government does not collect or publish statistics on religious affiliation. In a 2011 report, the King Baudouin Foundation said the religious affiliations of the population were as follows: 50 percent Roman Catholic, 32 percent no affiliation, 9.2 percent atheist, 5 percent Muslim, 2.5 percent other Christian, 0.4 percent Jewish, and 0.3 percent Buddhist.

According to a 2007 report, larger non-recognized religious groups who do not receive funds from the state include Jehovah's Witnesses with 23,701 baptized and 50,000 "churchgoers"; The Church of Jesus Christ of Latter-day Saints (Mormons) with 4,000 members; Seventh-day Adventists with 2,000; Hindus with 5,000; Sikhs with 3,000; Hare Krishnas with 1,500; and the Church of Scientology with 200 to 300 members. Experts consider these statistics to be accurate still.

HISTORY

Belgium derives its name from the Belgae, a Celtic tribe. The Belgae were forced to yield to Roman legions during the first century B.C. For some 300 years thereafter, what is now Belgium flourished as a province of Rome. But Rome's power gradually lessened. In about A.D. 300, Attila the Hun invaded what is now Germany and pushed Germanic tribes into northern Belgium. About 100 years later, the Germanic tribe of the Franks invaded and took possession of Belgium. The northern part of present-day Belgium became an overwhelmingly Germanized and Germanic-Frankish-speaking area, whereas in the southern part people continued to be Roman and spoke derivatives of Latin. After coming under the rule of the Dukes of Burgundy and, through marriage, passing into the possession of the Hapsburgs, Belgium was occupied by the Spanish (1519–1713) and the Austrians (1713–1794).

Under these various rulers, and especially during the 500 years from the 12th to the 17th century, the great cities of Ghent, Bruges, Brussels, and Antwerp took turns at being major European centers for commerce, industry (especially textiles), and art. Flemish painting—from Van Eyck and Breugel to Rubens and Van Dyck—became the most prized in Europe. Flemish tapestries hung on castle walls throughout Europe.

Following the French Revolution, Belgium was invaded and annexed by Napoleonic France in 1795. Following the defeat of Napoleon's army at the Battle of Waterloo, fought just a few miles south of Brussels, Belgium was separated from France and made part of the Netherlands by the Congress of Vienna in 1815.

In 1830, Belgium won its independence from the Dutch as a result of an uprising of the Belgian people. A constitutional monarchy was established in 1831, with a monarch invited in from the House of Saxe-Coburg Gotha in Germany.

Belgium was invaded by Germany in 1914 and again in 1940. Those invasions, plus disillusionment over postwar Soviet behavior, made Belgium one of the foremost advocates of collective security within the framework of European integration and the Atlantic partnership.

Since 1944, when British, Canadian, and American armies liberated Belgium, the country has lived in security and at a level of increased wellbeing.

Language, economic, and political differences between Dutch-speaking Flanders and Francophone Wallonia have led to increased divisions in Bel-

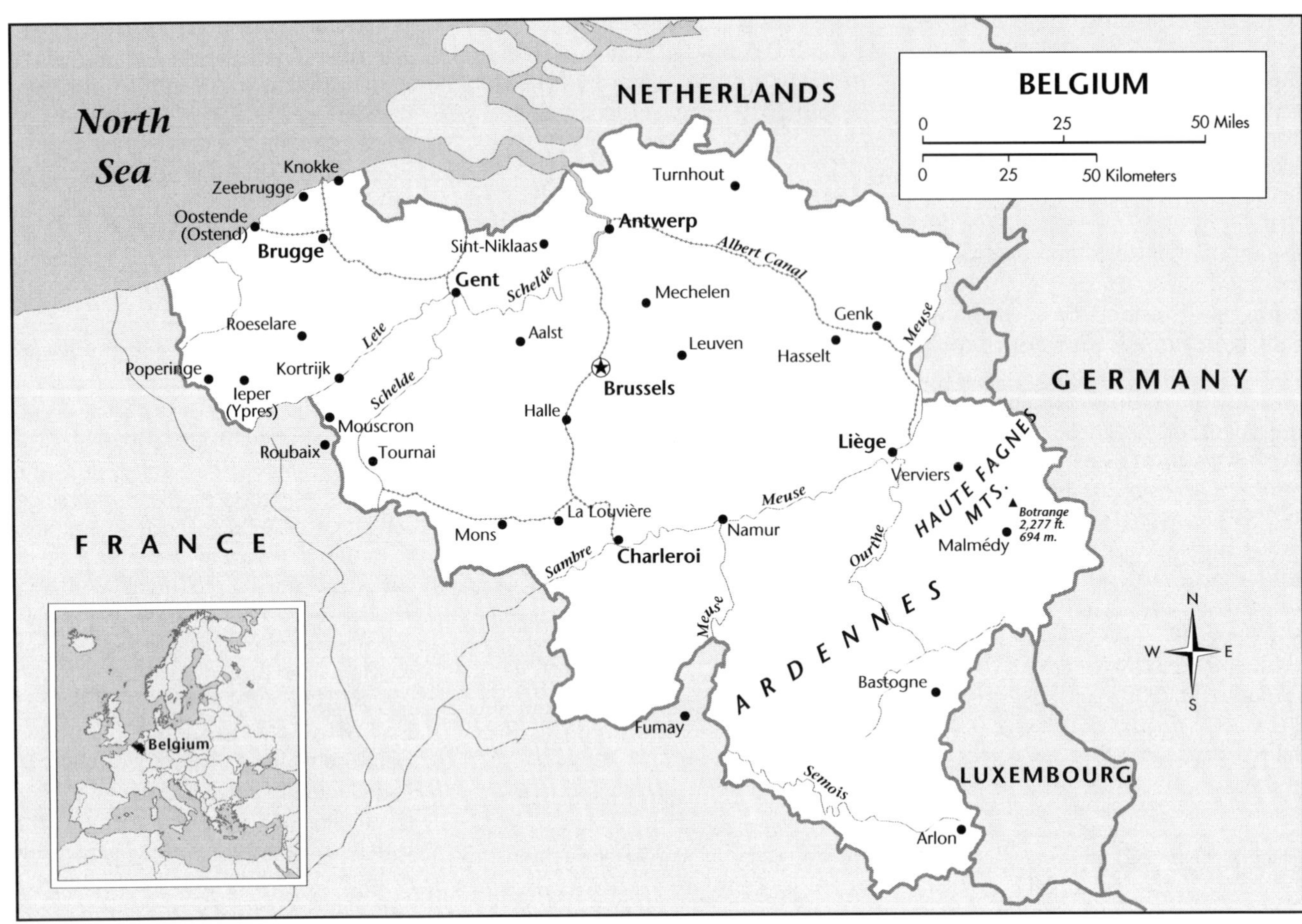

gian society. The Industrial Revolution of the late 18th and the 19th century accentuated the linguistic North-South division. Francophone Wallonia became an early industrial boom area, affluent and politically dominant. Dutch-speaking Flanders remained agricultural and was economically and politically outdistanced by Brussels and Wallonia. The last 50 years have marked the rapid economic development of Flanders while the coal and steel industries of Wallonia went into sharp decline, resulting in a corresponding shift of political and economic power to the Flemish, who now constitute an absolute majority (58%) of the population.

Demonstrations in the early 1960s led to the establishment of a formal linguistic border in 1962, and elaborate rules made to protect minorities in linguistically mixed border areas. In 1970, Flemish and Francophone cultural councils were established with authority in matters of language and culture for the two-language groups. Each of the three economic regions—Flanders, Wallonia, and Brussels—was granted a significant measure of political autonomy.

Since 1984, the German language community of Belgium (in the eastern part of Liege Province) has had its own legislative assembly and executive, which have authority in cultural, language, and subsequently educational affairs.

In 1988–89, the Constitution was again amended to give additional responsibilities to the regions and communities. The most sweeping change was the devolution of educational responsibilities to the community level. As a result, the regions and communities were provided additional revenue, and Brussels was given its own legislative assembly and executive.

Another important constitutional reform occurred in the summer of 1993, changing Belgium from a unitary to a federal state. It also reformed the bicameral parliamentary system and provided for the direct election of the members of community and regional legislative councils. The bilingual Brabant province, which contained the Brussels region, was split into separate Flemish and Walloon Brabant provinces. The revised Constitution came into force in 1994.

As a parliamentary democracy, Belgium has been governed by successive coalitions of two or more political parties. The centrist Christian Democratic Party often provided the Prime Minister. In the 1999 general election, Belgian voters rejected Jean Luc Dehaene's longstanding coalition government of Christian Democrats and Socialists and voted into power a coalition led by Flemish Liberal Leader Guy Verhofstadt. The first Verhofstadt government (1999–2003) was a six-party coalition between the Flemish and Francophone Liberals, Socialists, and Greens. It was the first

Liberal-led coalition in generations and the first six-party coalition in 20 years. It also was the first time the Greens had participated in Belgium's federal government. In the general election of 2003, the Greens suffered significant losses, while the Socialists posted strong gains and the Liberals also had modest growth in electoral support. Liberal Prime Minister Guy Verhofstadt reconstituted the coalition as a four-party government in July 2003, with only the Liberals and Socialists in power.

In the 2007 general elections, the Flemish Christian Democratic CD&V recouped the lost ground, becoming the country's largest party. The two Socialist parties and Prime Minister Guy Verhofstadt's Open VLD lost support. The Francophone Liberal MR became the largest party of Wallonia and Brussels. Following the election, the King tasked CD&V leader Yves Leterme with forming a new government. The ruling coalition was composed of Flemish Christian Democrats (CD&V), Francophone Christian Democrats (CDH), Flemish Liberals (Open VLD), Francophone Liberals (MR), and the Francophone Socialists (PS). However, it took over 9 months to form a government, which remained subject to intense strains. Leterme stepped down in December 2008 and was replaced as Prime Minister and head of the same coalition by the CD&V's Herman Van Rompuy.

Van Rompuy's appointment as President of the European Council under the Treaty of Lisbon paved the way for Leterme to regain his position as Prime Minister in November 2009. However, an electoral dispute between the Francophone and Flemish parties continually plagued his government coalition, which finally collapsed in April 2010.

The Francophone Socialist (PS) and Flemish nationalist (New Flemish Alliance—N-VA) parties won the largest proportion of seats during parliamentary elections in June 2010. The N-VA became the largest party in the House of Representatives, winning 27 seats compared to 4 in 2007, indicating growing support for regional autonomy in Flanders. Throughout 2011, no governing coalition was formed due to continued inability of the Francophone and Flemish parties to reach a compromise over state reforms. Prime Minister Leterme and his cabinet remained in office in a caretaker capacity. In September 2011, the six negotiating parties achieved a breakthrough agreement on local government of an electoral district with a Francophone majority comprising both Brussels and parts of the surrounding Flemish region.

The agreement was finalized in October 2011, with only the remaining hurdle of budget allocation among Belgium's local regions. After further austerity measures were agreed to in November 2011, a new government with francophone Socialist Elio Di Rupo as Prime Minister was formed on December 5, 2011.

GOVERNMENT AND POLITICAL CONDITIONS

The Kingdom of Belgium is a parliamentary democracy and a limited constitutional monarchy. The current monarch is King Albert II, who took the oath of office on August 9, 1993.

As titular head of state, the King plays a largely ceremonial and symbolic role in the nation. His primary political function is to designate a political leader to attempt to form a new cabinet following either an election, the resignation of a government, or a parliamentary vote of no confidence. The King is seen as playing a symbolic unifying role, representing a common national Belgian identity.

The country is a federal state with several levels of government: national, regional (Flanders, Wallonia, and Brussels), language community (Flemish, French, and German), provincial, and local. The Federal Council of Ministers, headed by the prime minister, remains in office as long as it retains the confidence of the lower house (Chamber of Representatives) of the bicameral parliament. Federal parliamentary elections held in 2010 were considered free and fair.

Recent Elections

Federal elections held in June 2010 were considered free and fair.

Participation of Women and Minorities: The constitution requires the presence of men and women in federal, regional, and local governments, and the law requires an equal number of male and female candidates on party tickets in European, federal, regional, provincial, and local elections. Failure to meet the requirement would nullify the elections and render any government thereby created illegal.

Following the 2010 federal elections, there were 59 women in the 150-seat federal Chamber of Representatives and 25 women in the 71-seat Senate (of the 40 directly elected senators, 17 were women). Five of the 23 federal cabinet ministers and state secretaries were women.

There are seven members of Moroccan and Turkish origin in the Chamber of Representatives and five in the Senate.

Principal Government Officials

Last Updated: 10/31/2012

King: **ALBERT II**
Prime Min.: **Elio DI RUPO**
Vice Prime Min.: **Joelle MILQUET**
Vice Prime Min.: **Laurette ONKELINX**
Vice Prime Min.: **Didier REYNDERS**
Vice Prime Min.: **Steven VANACKERE**
Vice Prime Min.: **Vincent VAN QUICKENBORNE**
Min. of Budget & Admin. Simplification: **Olivier CHASTEL**
Min. of Defense: **Pieter DE CREM**
Min. of Economy, Consumers, & the North Sea: **Johan VANDE LANOTTE**
Min. of Employment: **Monica DE CONINCK**
Min. of Finance & Sustainable Development: **Steven VANACKERE**
Min. of Foreign Affairs, Foreign Trade, & European Affairs: **Didier REYNDERS**
Min. of Interior: **Joelle MILQUET**

Min. of Justice: **Annemie TURTELBOOM**
Min. of the Middle Class, Small & Medium-Sized Enterprises, Self-Employed, & Agriculture: **Sabine LARUELLE**
Min. of Pensions: **Vincent VAN QUICKENBORNE**
Min. of Public Enterprise, Scientific Policy, & Development Cooperation: **Paul MAGNETTE**
Min. of Social Affairs & Public Health: **Laurette ONKELINX**
Governor, National Bank of Belgium: **Guy QUADEN**
Ambassador to the US: **Jan Jozef MATTHYSEN**
Permanent Representative to the UN, New York: **Jan GRAULS**

ECONOMY

This modern, open, and private-enterprise-based economy has capitalized on its central geographic location, highly developed transport network, and diversified industrial and commercial base. Industry is concentrated mainly in the more heavily-populated region of Flanders in the north.

With few natural resources, Belgium imports substantial quantities of raw materials and exports a large volume of manufactures, making its economy vulnerable to volatility in world markets. Roughly three-quarters of Belgium's trade is with other EU countries, and Belgium has benefited most from its proximity to Germany. In 2011 Belgian GDP grew by 2.0%, the unemployment rate decreased slightly to 7.7% from 8.3% the previous year, and the government reduced the budget deficit from a peak of 6% of GDP in 2009 to 4.2% in 2011 and 3.3% in 2012.

Despite the relative improvement in Belgium's budget deficit, public debt hovers near 100% of GDP, a factor that has contributed to investor perceptions that the country is increasingly vulnerable to spillover from the euro-zone crisis. Belgian banks were severely affected by the international financial crisis in 2008 with three major banks receiving capital injections from the government, and the nationalization of the Belgian arm of a Franco-Belgian bank. An ageing population and rising social expenditures are mid- to long-term challenges to public finances.

Labor Conditions

The minimum age of employment is 15. Persons between the ages of 15 and 18 may participate in part-time work and study programs and work full time during school vacations. The Ministry of Employment regulates industries that employ juvenile workers to ensure that labor laws are followed and occasionally grants waivers for children temporarily employed by modeling agencies and in the entertainment business.

The monthly national minimum wage was 1,443.54 euro (approximately $1,877) for workers 21 years of age, 1,481.86 euro ($1,927) for workers 21 1/2 years of age with six months of service, and 1,498.87 euro ($1,949) for workers 22 years of age with one year of service. The poverty income level in 2011 was 899 euros ($1,169) per month for a single adult.

The standard workweek is 38 hours, and workers are entitled to four weeks of annual leave. Departure from these norms can occur under a collective bargaining agreement, but work may not exceed 11 hours per day and 50 hours per week. An 11-hour rest period is required between two work periods. Overtime is paid at a time-and-a-half premium Monday through Saturday and at double time on Sundays. The Ministry of Labor and the labor courts effectively enforced these laws and regulations. The law forbids or limits excessive overtime. Without specific authorization, no employee can accumulate more than 65 hours of overtime during one quarter.

U.S.-BELGIAN RELATIONS

The United States established diplomatic relations with Belgium in 1832 following Belgium's declaration of independence from the Netherlands. The United States and Belgium are good friends and allies, with a cooperative relationship despite occasional disagreements on a limited number of foreign policy issues. Good will and affection for Americans is widely held as a result of the U.S. role during and after the two World Wars, including Belgium's liberation from Nazi Germany by British, Canadian, and U.S. forces in 1944.

As an outward-looking nation, Belgium works closely with the United States bilaterally and in international and regional organizations to encourage economic and political cooperation and assistance to developing countries. The United States appreciates Belgian activism in international affairs, including its participation in the International Security Assistance Force in Afghanistan; its humanitarian, reconstruction, and development assistance to Africa, Iraq, and Afghanistan; its peacekeeping missions in the Balkans and Lebanon; its frequent provision of airlift in international crises; and its hosting of transatlantic dialogues between European foreign ministers and the Secretary of State.

U.S. Assistance to Belgium

The United States provides no development assistance to Belgium.

Bilateral Economic Relations

Belgium is a member of the European Union (EU) and seeks to diversify and expand trade opportunities with non-EU countries. Bilaterally, there are few points of friction with the United States in the trade and economic area. The Belgian authorities are, as a rule, anti-protectionist and try to maintain a hospitable and open trade and investment climate. As a result, the U.S. Government focuses its market-opening efforts on the EU Commission and larger member states. Moreover, the Commission negotiates on trade issues for all member states, which in turn lessens bilateral trade disputes with Belgium. Belgium has welcomed hundreds of U.S. firms to its territory, many of which have their European headquarters there. U.S. companies are heavily represented in investments in the chemical sector, automotive assembly, petroleum refining, and pharmaceutical sectors. A number of U.S. service industries have followed in the wake of these investments—banks, law firms, public relations, accounting, and executive search firms. Belgium participates in the Visa Waiver Program, which allows nationals of participating countries to travel to the United States for certain business or tourism purposes for stays of 90 days or less without obtaining a visa.

Belgium's Membership in International Organizations

Belgium and the United States belong to a number of the same international organizations, including the United Nations, North Atlantic Treaty Organization, Euro-Atlantic Partnership Council, Organization for Security and Cooperation in Europe, Organization for Economic Cooperation and Development, International Monetary Fund, World Bank, and World Trade Organization. Belgium also is an observer to the Organization of American States.

Bilateral Representation

Belgium maintains an embassy in the United States at 3330 Garfield Street NW, Washington, DC 20008 (tel. 202-333-6900).

Principal U.S. Embassy Officials

Last Updated: 1/14/2013

BRUSSELS (E) 27 Blvd. du Regent, 1000 Brussels, (32-2) 811-4000, Fax (32-2) 811-4500, Workweek: E: 9-6 JAS 8-5, Website: http://Brussels.usembassy.gov/

DCM OMS: Beverly M Fenwick
AMB OMS: Augustine Peterson-Becker
Co-CLO: Dani Burke
DHS/CBP: Brian M. Demore
DHS/TSA: Russell Vieco
FCS: Laurie Farris
FM: Michael Jackson
HHS: Susanne Radtke
HRO: Christian Charette
MGT: Martin Hohe
MLO/ODC: COL Dean King
POL/ECON: Timothy Richardson
POSHO: Mike Dilks
SDO/DATT: COL Jeff Saunders
AMB: Howard W. Gutman
CON: David Seckler
DCM: Robert Faucher
PAO: Jason Davis
GSO: Rafael Rodriguez
RSO: Lon Fairchild
AGR: Resident In The Hague
AID: Sarah Gonzales
CLO: Philana Quick
DEA: Daniel Dodds
EEO: Jacqueline S. Deley
FAA: Steven Creamer
FMO: James Martin
IMO: Thomas Daley
IPO: Blanca Neve
IRS: Kathy Beck (Resident In Paris)
ISO: Bill Bonnett
ISSO: Thomas Gresham
LEGATT: Kevin McGee
State ICASS: David Seckler

USEU (M) Rue Zinner 13, B-1000 Brussels, (32) (2)811-4100, Fax (32-2) 811-4500, Workweek: 9:00 a.m.–6:00 p.m., Website: http://useu.usmission.gov/

DCM OMS: Noel Taylor
AMB OMS: Linda Loth
DHS/ICE: David Trissell
DHS/TSA: Richard Kolodner
FCS: Beryl Blecher
FM: Michael Jackson
HRO: Christian Charette
MGT: Martin Hohe
TREAS: Susan Baker
AMB: William E. Kennard
CON: Thomas Rogan
DCM: Thomas J White
PAO: John Sullivan
GSO: Rafael Rodriguez
RSO: Lon Fairchild
AGR: Maurice House
AID: Sarah Gonzales
APHIS: Marc Gilkey
CLO: Philana Quick
DEA: Carrie Thompson
ECON: Robert Pollard
IMO: Thomas Daley
IPO: Blanca Neve
IRS: Kathy J. Beck (Resident In Paris)
ISO: Bill Bonnett
ISSO: Richard Livingston
LEGATT: Kevin McGee
POL: Michelle Labonte

USNATO (M) Blvd Leopold III, 1110 Brussels, Belgium, (32-2) 724-3111, Fax +32 2 724 3404, Workweek: 08:30–18:00, Website: http://nato.usmission.gov/

DCM OMS: Chris Temen
AMB OMS: Karen Pennington
CA: Please See U.S. Embassy Brussels
MGT: Nancy Zmyslinski
AMB: Ivo H. Daalder
DCM: Joseph Manso
PAO: David Siefkin
GSO: Lori Mikesell
RSO: Joe Clark
ICASS Chair: Randy Hoag
IMO: Thomas Daley
IPO: Warren Talley
IRS: Please See U.S. Embassy Brussels
ISO: Andy Jordan
ISSO: Troy Williams
POL: Kurt Donnelly

TRAVEL

Consular Information Sheet

December 14, 2011

Country Description: Belgium is a highly developed and stable democracy with a modern economy. Tourist facilities are widely available.

Smart Traveler Enrollment Program (Step)/Embassy Location: If you are going to live in or visit Belgium, please take the time to tell our Embassy about your trip. By registering with the Smart Traveler Enrollment Program, we can keep you up to date with important safety and security announcements, and help your friends and family get in touch with you in an emergency.

U.S. Embassy Brussels, Belgium
27 Boulevard du Régent
(the Consular Section is at
25 Boulevard du Régent)
B-1000 Brussels
Telephone: 011-32-2-811-4000
(available 24/7)
Consular Section Fax:
011-32-2-811-4546

Entry/Exit Requirements for U.S. Citizens: Visit the Embassy of Belgium website for the most current visa information. If you need additional information about entry requirements, including visas for employment or study in Belgium, you can contact the Embassy of Belgium at 3330 Garfield Street NW, Washington, DC 20008, telephone (202) 333-6900, fax (202) 338-4960; or one of the Belgian Consulates General in Atlanta, Los Angeles, or New York. Belgium is a party to the Schengen Agreement. This means that U.S. citizens may enter Belgium for up to 90 days for tourist or business purposes without a visa. Your passport should be valid for at least three months beyond the period of stay. You need sufficient funds and a return airline ticket.

The U.S. Department of State is unaware of any HIV/AIDS entry restrictions for visitors to or foreign residents of Belgium.

Threats to Safety and Security: Belgium has been largely free of major terrorist incidents. As with other countries in the Schengen area, Belgium maintains open borders with its neighbors, allowing the possibility of terrorist operatives entering/exiting the country with anonymity. Belgian law enforcement and security officials, in close cooperation with neighboring countries, maintain an effective anti-terrorism effort and a welcoming environment for tourism and business.

Prior police approval is required for all public demonstrations in Belgium, and police are present to ensure adequate security for participants and passers-by. Nonetheless, spontaneous demonstrations do take place in Belgium from time to time in response to world events or local developments. Even demonstrations that are meant to be peaceful can become violent and unpredictable; you should avoid them if at all possible. Be alert and aware of your surroundings, and pay attention to what the local news media have to say. In general, larger public demonstrations are announced on the Demonstration Notices page within the U.S. Embassy Brussels website.

Stay up to date by:

- Bookmarking our Bureau of Consular Affairs website, which contains the current Travel Warnings and Travel Alerts as well as the Worldwide Caution;
- Following us on Twitter and the Bureau of Consular Affairs page on Facebook;
- Downloading our free Smart Traveler IPhone App to have travel information at your fingertips; and
- Calling 1-888-407-4747 toll-free within the U.S. and Canada, or a regular toll line, 1-202-501-4444, from other countries.

Take some time before travel to consider your personal security.

Crime: Belgium remains relatively free of violent crime, but low-level street crime is common. As in any major city in the United States, you should always be watchful and aware of your surroundings. Muggings, purse snatchings, and pocket picking occur frequently, particularly in the major cities. Thieves often loiter in transportation hubs like the Metro (subway) and train stations to take advantage of disoriented or distracted travelers. In Brussels, pocket picking, purse snatching, and theft of light luggage and laptops are common at the three major train stations: the North Station (Noordstation or Gare du Nord); the Central Station (Centraal Station or Gare Central); and especially the South Station (Zuidstation or Gare du Midi, the primary international train hub). We advise you to pay particularly close attention to your personal belongings when in Metro and train stations. One common trick is for the thief to ask you for directions while an accomplice steals your luggage. Thieves also watch for people who put their luggage down and are inattentive for even a moment. It is a good idea to hold onto your hand luggage at all times, and not to place carry-on luggage on overhead racks in trains.

Another growing problem, especially in Brussels, is theft from vehicles, both moving and parked. Do not leave your valuables in plain sight where a thief may spot them. Thieves will sometimes position themselves at traffic lights to scan for valuables in stopped cars. If they see a purse or other valuable item, they break the window and steal the item before you have time to react. Always drive with your windows up and doors locked. Whenever possible, park your car in secure areas or parking garages.

You should be aware that small groups of young men sometimes prey on unwary tourists, usually at night and often in metro stations in Brussels. These thieves typically seek small, high-value items such as mobile phones and MP3 players. You should carry only a minimum amount of cash, credit cards, and necessary personal identification (see Special Circumstances, below, for acceptable forms of identification).

We advise U.S. citizens to avoid wearing expensive jewelry and watches. Don't buy counterfeit and pirated goods, even if they are widely available. Not only are the bootlegs illegal to bring back into the United States, you may also be breaking local law.

Victims of Crime: If you or someone you know becomes the victim of a crime abroad, you should contact the local police and the nearest U.S. embassy or consulate. We can:

- Replace a stolen passport;
- Help you find appropriate medical care if you are the victim of a violent crime such as assault or rape;
- Put you in contact with the appropriate police authorities, and, if you want us to, we can contact family members or friends; and
- Help you understand the local criminal justice process and can direct you to local attorneys, although the local authorities are responsible for investigating and prosecuting the crime.

The local equivalent to the "911" emergency line in Belgium is 101 for emergencies requiring police assistance. For all other emergencies, please dial 112. The Belgian "Commission for financial assistance to victims of intentional acts of violence" provides financial compensation, under specific circumstances, for victims of crime and for those who have suffered injuries and consequent loss caused by such incidents. The Commission also provides for dependents or immediate family members of homicide victims. For more information, contact the Commission by phone at 32 2 542-7208; 32 2 542-7218; 32 2 542-7224; 32 2 542-7229, or 32 2 542-7244; by e-mail at commission.victimes@just.fgov.be or commissie.slachtoffers@just.fgov.be; or visit the Ministry website (French, Dutch, and German only).

Criminal Penalties: While you are traveling in Belgium, you are subject to its laws even if you are a U.S. citizen. Foreign laws and legal systems can be vastly different than our own, and criminal penalties will vary from country to country. There are also some things that might be legal in the country you visit, but still illegal in the United States; for instance, you can be prosecuted under U.S. law if you buy pirated goods.

Engaging in sexual conduct with children or using or disseminating child pornography in a foreign country is a crime prosecutable in the United States. If you break local laws in Belgium, your U.S. passport won't help you avoid arrest or prosecution. It's very important to know what's legal and what's not where you are going.

Persons violating Belgian laws, even unknowingly, may be expelled, arrested, or imprisoned. Penalties for possessing, using, or trafficking in illegal drugs in Belgium are severe, and convicted offenders can expect long jail sentences and heavy fines. Based on the Vienna Convention on Consular Relations, bilateral agreements, and customary international law, if you are arrested in Belgium, you have the right to request that the police, prison officials, or other authorities alert the U.S. Embassy of your arrest, and to have communications from you forwarded to the Embassy.

Arrest notifications in host country: While some countries will automatically notify the nearest U.S. embassy or consulate if a U.S. citizen is detained or arrested in a foreign country, that might not always be the case. To ensure that the United States is aware of your circumstances, request that the police and prison officials notify the nearest U.S. embassy or consulate as soon as you are arrested or detained overseas.

Special Circumstances: Belgian law requires that everyone carry official identification at all times. This ID must be displayed upon request to any Belgian police official. U.S. citizens who are not residents of Belgium will need to present a U.S. passport. While most monetary transactions are available (cash, credit cards), U.S. money orders cannot be negotiated in Belgium. Personal checks may only be cleared through a bank at which a person holds an account, and clearance can take two to four weeks. Banks and exchange facilities may refuse U.S. dollar denominations of $50 and $100 if they are not equipped with devices to identify counterfeit currency. Automated Teller Machines (ATMs) are widespread in Belgium and accept most U.S. ATM cards for fund withdrawals. If you want to purchase Euros, you are likely to find a more favorable exchange rate at banks than at money exchange facilities located at tourist locations, train stations, and airports.

Non-EU citizens visiting Belgium and staying in a private residence must register with local Commune authorities within three days of their arrival. You must request any change in visa or resident status through Commune authorities. You must complete any such request prior to the expiration of the current status. You should note that given the substantial requirements to change status, it is nearly impossible to do so within the 90 days permitted to remain in Belgium without a visa under the Visa Waiver Program.

Business visitor and employee registration requirement: Since April 1, 2007, non-Belgian employees and self-employed persons or their employees who carry out short-term assignments in Belgium must declare these activities in advance.

This mandatory "Limosa" declaration applies to: (1) Employees and apprentices who come to Belgium to execute certain temporary work and who, because of the nature of their short term assignment, are not subject to the Belgian social security system; (2) Self-employed individuals and self-employed apprentices who come to work in Belgium temporarily, irrespective of whether they are subject to the Belgian social security system. For more information, please see the Limosa website. For more information about working in Belgium, please visit the website of the Belgian Federal Public Service Employment, Labour and Social Dialogue.

Accessibility: While in Belgium, individuals with disabilities may find accessibility and accommodation very different from what you find in the United States. Although Belgian law requires that any new building with public or community space has to be accessible for persons with disabilities, many existing buildings as well as public transportation systems are less adapted to individuals with disabilities. General information on the accessibility of tourist accommodations, public transportation, museums, etc. can be found on the Belgian Tourist Office's website.

Medical Facilities and Health Information: High-quality medical facilities are widely available in Belgium. The large university hospitals can handle almost every medical problem. Hospitals may not necessarily have staff members who are fluent in English. The Embassy's Consular Section maintains a list of English-speaking doctors. You can find good information on vaccinations and other health precautions, on the Centers for Disease Control and Prevention (CDC) website. For information about outbreaks of infectious diseases abroad, consult the World Health Organization (WHO) website, which also contains additional health information for travelers, including detailed country-specific health information.

Medical Insurance: You can't assume your insurance will go with you when you travel. It's very important to find out BEFORE you leave. You need to ask your insurance company two questions:

- Does my policy apply when I'm out of the U.S.?
- Will it cover emergencies like a trip to a foreign hospital or an evacuation?

In many places, doctors and hospitals still expect payment in cash at the time of service. Your regular U.S. health insurance may not cover doctors' and hospital visits in other countries. If your policy doesn't go with you when you travel, it's a very good idea to take out another one for your trip.

Traffic Safety and Road Conditions: While in Belgium, you may encounter road conditions that differ significantly from those in the United States.

Belgium's road network is generally well built and maintained, but you may occasionally encounter potholes, even on principal roads. Sufficient lighting exists on major highways, but on rural roads it is often insufficient or nonexistent. Belgian rules for right-of-way differ from those in the U.S., and new drivers should thoroughly understand these rules before driving in Belgium. For instance, traffic coming from the right generally has priority at uncontrolled intersections and roundabouts, even if coming from a smaller street. The maximum speed limit on Belgian highways is 120 kilometers (72 miles) per hour, but is not always posted. The maximum speed in urban areas is normally 50 km (30 miles) per hour; however, in the Brussels city limits it is now only 30 km per hour. While Belgian authorities strictly enforce speed limits, many Belgians still drive significantly faster than the posted limit. Claiming ignorance may not prevent you getting a significant fine for speeding, and your vehicle may be impounded if you can't pay the fine on the spot. Belgian police also conduct breath analysis checks for alcohol use, particularly at night and during major holidays. The legal limit for operating a motor vehicle is.05 percent blood alcohol content.

Roadside assistance and information on road conditions are available in English from Touring Mobilis, tel: 02 286-3040. Belgian police will also provide information on road conditions, tel: 02-642-6666. Emergency services are efficient and responsive. For police emergencies, dial 101 by phone within Belgium. For all other emergencies, dial 112.

Aviation Safety Oversight: The U.S. Federal Aviation Administration (FAA) has assessed the government of Belgium's Civil Aviation Authority as being in compliance with International Civil Aviation Organization (ICAO) aviation safety standards for oversight of Belgium's air carrier operations. Further information may be found on the FAA's safety assessment page.

Children's Issues: Please see the U.S. Dept. of State Office of Children's Issues web pages on intercountry adoption and international parental child abduction.

Intercountry Adoption

March 2009

The information in this section has been edited from the latest report available as of February 2013 from the State Department Bureau of Consular Affairs, Office of Overseas Citizens Services. For more information, please read the *Intercountry Adoption* section of this book and review current reports online at http://adoption.state.gov. Belgium is party to the Hague Convention on Protection of Children and Co-operation in Respect of Intercountry Adoption (Hague Adoption Convention). Therefore all adoptions between Belgium and the United States must meet the requirements of the Convention and U.S. law implementing the Convention. Belgium is not considered a country of origin in intercountry adoption. While legally possible, intercountry adoption of a Belgian orphan by foreigners is unlikely. No Belgian orphans have received U.S. immigrant visas in the past five fiscal years.

The information provided is intended primarily to assist in extremely rare adoption cases from Belgium, including adoptions of Belgian children by relatives in the United States, as well as adoptions from third countries by Americans living in Belgium.

Who Can Adopt? Adoption between the United States and Belgium is governed by the Hague Adoption Convention. Therefore to adopt from Belgium, you must first be found eligible to adopt by the U.S. Government. The U.S. Government agency responsible for making this determination is the Department of Homeland Security, U.S. Citizenship and Immigration Services (USCIS).

Residency Requirements: Prospective adoptive parents must be resident in Belgium to adopt.

Age Requirements: Minimum age to adopt is 25, and the minimum age difference between the prospective adoptive parents and the adopted child is 15 years. For the adoption of a child of the spouse/cohabiting partner, the minimum age is 18 and the minimum age difference is 10 years.

Marriage Requirements: To adopt together prospective adoptive parents must be married, be legally registered as a cohabiting couple or have lived together on an ongoing basis and having an emotional commitment for at least three years.

Income Requirements: Income is discussed in the home study. There are no minimum requirements but the prospective adoptive parents must be able to take financial care of an adoption child.

Who Can Be Adopted? Because Belgium is party to the Hague Adoption Convention, children from Belgium must meet the requirements of the Convention in order to be eligible for adoption. For detailed and updated information on these requirements, please review the *Intercountry Adoption* section of this publication and visit the USCIS Intercountry Adoption website at http://adoption.state.gov.

Belgium's Adoption Authority: Residents of the Flemish-speaking part of Belgium should contact:

Kind en Gezin
Hallepoortlaan 27
1060 Brussels
E-mail: adoptie@kindengezin.be
tel.: (02) 533 14 76

Residents of the French-speaking part of Belgium should contact:
Autorité Communautaire pour l'Adoption Internationale (ACAI)
Boulevard Leopold II, 44
1080 Brussels
tel.: (02) 413 2726.

Ministerium der Deutschsprachigen Gemeinschaft
Zentrale Behörde der Deutschsprachigen Gemeinschaft für Adoptionen
Gospertstrasse 1
B-4700 Eupen
Tel.: + 32 (87) 59 63 46

The Process: Because Belgium is party to the Hague Adoption Convention, adopting from Belgium must follow a specific process designed to meet the Convention's requirements.

Role of the Adoption Authority: Apply to the central authority of your community (Flemish or French speaking). After submitting your application, you will be invited to take a preparation course required for all prospective adoptive parents.

Role of the Court: With the certificate of completion of the preparation course, a request is filed with the court to find you eligible to adopt. The court will order a home study. A service for the home study will invite you for four interviews. A social worker and psychologist will do the interview and make a report to advise the judge. The judge will then decide whether you are eligible to adopt. Note: The adoption of a Belgian child by citizens living in the United States (very exceptional, normally only for adoption of family-members) will be pronounced by a Belgian court.

Role of Adoption Agencies: Prospective adoptive parents should contact the adoption authority for the region of Belgium where they reside for information on Belgian adoption agencies. The adoption agency will send the file of the applicant(s) to the country of origin and wait for them to propose a child for adoption. The country of origin will send the file on an adoptable child to the adoption agency. After the approval of the match by the central authority, the prospective adoptive parents will be informed and the procedure in the country of origin may continue.

Time Frame: The time it takes to complete an adoption varies, depending on the child's country of origin.

Adoption Fees: Most fees will depend on the child's country of origin. Belgian fees, not including preapproved fees (including the home study), vary depending on which community (Flemish-speaking, French speaking) the prospective adoptive parents reside in.

Documents Required: Judgment of eligibility and home study are always necessary. Other documents depend on the country of origin of the child.

Bringing Your Child Home: Once your adoption is complete (or you have obtained legal custody of the child), there are a few more steps to take before you can head home. Specifically, you need to apply for several documents for your child before he or she can travel to the United States, such as a birth certificate, a passport or travel document for your child from the country in which he or she was born, and a U.S. Immigration Visa. For detailed and updated information on how to obtain these documents, review the *Intercountry Adoption* section on this publication and visit the USCIS Intercountry Adoption website at http://adoption state.gov.

Child Citizenship Act: For adoptions finalized abroad, the Child Citizenship Act of 2000 allows your new child to acquire American citizenship automatically when he or she enters the United States as lawful permanent residents. For adoptions to be finalized in the United States, the Child Citizenship Act of 2000 allows your child to typically acquire American citizenship when the U.S. state court issues the final adoption decree. To learn more, review the *Intercountry Adoption* section of this publication.

U.S. Embassy in Belgium
Boulevard du Regent 25
1000 Brussels
tel.: (02) 508-2537
Fax: (02) 513- 0409
E-mail: uscitizenbrussels@state.gov
Telephone: +358-9-616-25730

Embassy of Belgium
3330 Garfield Street N.W.
Washington, D.C. 20008
tel.: (202) 333-6900
Fax: (202) 333-5457
E-mail: washington@diplobel.org

Office of Children's Issues
U.S. Department of State
2201 C Street, NW
SA-29
Washington, DC 20520
Tel: 1-888-407-4747
E-mail: AskCI@state.gov
Internet: http://adoption.state.gov

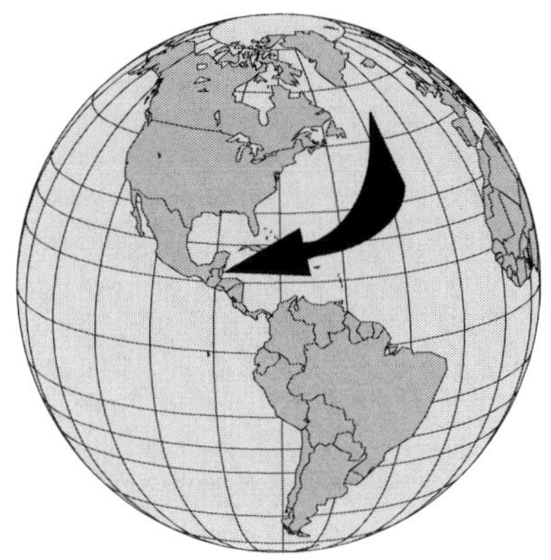

BELIZE

Compiled from publications that were available as of February 2013 from the U.S. Department of State, the U.S. Department of Commerce, and the Central Intelligence Agency (CIA). See the introduction to this set for explanatory notes.

Official Name:
Belize

PROFILE

Geography

Area: total: 22,966 sq km; country comparison to the world: 152; land: 22,806 sq km; water: 160 sq km
Major cities: Belmopan (capital) 20,000 (2009)
Climate: tropical; very hot and humid; rainy season (May to November); dry season (February to May)
Terrain: flat, swampy coastal plain; low mountains in south

People

Nationality: noun: Belizean(s); adjective: Belizean
Population: 327,719 (July 2012 est.)
Population growth rate: 2.011% (2012 est.)
Ethnic groups: mestizo 48.7%, Creole 24.9%, Maya 10.6%, Garifuna 6.1%, other 9.7% (2000 census)
Religions: Roman Catholic 39.3%, Pentacostal 8.3%, Seventh Day Adventist 5.3%, Anglican 4.5%, Mennonite 3.7%, Baptist 3.5%, Methodist 2.8%, Nazarene 2.8%, Jehovah's Witnesses 1.6%, other 9.9% (includes Bahai Faith, Buddhism, Hinduism, Islam, and Mormon), other (unknown) 3.1%, none 15.2% (2010 census)
Languages: Spanish 46%, Creole 32.9%, Mayan dialects 8.9%, English 3.9% (official), Garifuna 3.4% (Carib), German 3.3%, other 1.4%, unknown 0.2% (2000 census)
Literacy: definition: age 15 and over can read and write; total population: 76.9%; male: 76.7%; female: 77.1% (2000 census)
Health: life expectancy at birth: total population: 68.28 years; male: 66.61 years; female: 70.04 years (2012 est.); Infant mortality rate: total: 21.37 deaths/1,000 live births; male: 23.85 deaths/1,000 live births; female: 18.78 deaths/1,000 live births (2012 est.)
Unemployment rate: 13.1% (2009)
Work force: 120,500

Government

Type: parliamentary democracy and a Commonwealth realm
Independence: 21 September 1981
Constitution: 21 September 1981
Political subdivisions: 6 districts; Belize, Cayo, Corozal, Orange Walk, Stann Creek, Toledo
Suffrage: 18 years of age; universal

Economy

GDP (purchasing power parity): $2.896 billion (2012 est.); $2.836 billion (2011 est.); $2.767 billion (2010 est.); $2.693 billion (2009 est.)
GDP real growth rate: 2.3% (2012 est.); 2.5% (2011 est.); 2.7% (2010 est.); 0% (2009 est.)
GDP per capita (PPP): $8,400 (2012 est.); $8,400 (2011 est.); $8,300 (2010 est.); $8,200 (2009 est.)
Natural resources: arable land potential, timber, fish, hydropower
Agriculture products: bananas, cacao, citrus, sugar; fish, cultured shrimp; lumber
Industries: garment production, food processing, tourism, construction, oil
Exports: $555.8 million (2012 est.); $603.3 million (2011 est.); $475.7 million (2010 est.)
Exports—commodities: sugar, bananas, citrus, clothing, fish products, molasses, wood, crude oil
Exports—partners: US 37.7%, UK 16.4%, Costa Rica 9.9%, Nigeria 4.3% (2011)
Imports: $770.1 million (2012 est.); $773.9 million (2011 est.)
Imports—commodities: machinery and transport equipment, manufactured goods; fuels, chemicals, pharmaceuticals; food, beverages, tobacco
Imports—partners: US 38.5%, Mexico 10.5%, Cuba 9.2%, Guatemala 5.5%, China 5.1%, Trinidad and Tobago 4.1% (2011)
Debt—external: $1.457 billion (31 December 2012 est.); $1.079 billion (31 December 2011 est.)
Exchange rates: Belizean dollars (BZD) per US dollar; 2 (2012 est.); 2 (2011 est.); 2 (2010 est.); 2 (2009); 2 (2008); 2 (2007)

PEOPLE

Belize is the most sparsely populated nation in Central America. It is larger than El Salvador and compares in size to the State of Massachusetts. Slightly more than half of the population lives in rural areas. About one-fifth live in Belize City, the principal port, commercial center, and former capital. More than one-third of the population is comprised of persons younger than 14 years of age.

Most Belizeans are of multiracial descent. More than 40% of the population is of mixed Mayan and European descent (mestizo); over 20%% are of African and Afro-European (Creole) ancestry; about 11.0% are Mayan; and about 6% are Afro-Amerindian (Garifuna). The remainder, about 8%, includes European, East Indian, Chinese, Middle Eastern, and North American groups.

Language

English, the official language, is spoken by virtually all except the refugees who arrived during the past decades. Spanish is the native tongue of about 50% of the people and is spoken as a second language by another 20%. The various Mayan groups still speak their indigenous languages, and an English-Creole dialect similar to the Creole dialects of the English-speaking Caribbean Islands is spoken by most. The rate of functional literacy is 76%.

Religion

Roman Catholics are the largest religious group, accounting for 40 percent of the population in 2010 according to the government census. Pentecostals are 9 percent of the population, Seventh-day Adventists 6 percent, Anglicans 5 percent, Mennonites 4 percent, Baptists 4 percent, Methodists 3 percent, members of the Church of the Nazarene 3 percent, and Jehovah's Witnesses 2 percent. Smaller religious groups include The Church of Jesus Christ of Latter-day Saints (Mormons), Buddhists, Hindus, Muslims, Rastafarians, the Salvation Army, and the Baha'i Faith. Those stating they did not belong to any religious group constituted 15 percent of the population.

No religious group is a majority in any of the country's six districts. Catholics are found throughout the country. Mennonites and Pentecostals live mostly in the rural areas of the Cayo and Orange Walk districts, and members of other religious groups tend to be concentrated in Belize City.

HISTORY

The Mayan civilization spread into the area of Belize between 1500 BC and AD 300 and flourished until about AD 1200. Several major archeological sites—notably Caracol, Lamanai, Lubaantun, Altun Ha, and Xunantunich—reflect the advanced civilization and much denser population of that period. European contact began in 1502 when Christopher Columbus sailed along the coast. The first recorded European settlement was established by shipwrecked English seamen in 1638. Over the next 150 years, more English settlements were established. This period also was marked by piracy, indiscriminate logging, and sporadic attacks by Indians and neighboring Spanish settlers.

Great Britain first sent an official representative to the area in the late 18th century, but Belize was not formally termed the "Colony of British Honduras" until 1840. It became a crown colony in 1862. Subsequently, several constitutional changes were enacted to expand representative government. Full internal self-government under a ministerial system was granted in January 1964. The official name of the territory was changed from British Honduras to Belize in June 1973, and full independence was granted on September 21, 1981.

GOVERNMENT AND POLITICAL CONDITIONS

Belize is a constitutional parliamentary democracy. In February 2008 Prime Minister Dean Barrow's United Democratic Party (UDP) won 25 of the 31 seats in the House of Representatives following generally free and fair multiparty elections. There were instances in which elements of the security forces acted independently of civilian control.

Recent Elections

In February 2008 the UDP obtained a parliamentary majority in generally free and fair elections.

Participation of Women and Minorities: There were five women, among them the president, in the 12-member appointed Senate, but there were no women in the 31-seat elected House of Representatives. Mestizo, Creole, Maya, Garifuna, Mennonite, and other minority and immigrant groups participated in the National Assembly and at high levels of government.

There were no elected women in the national parliament and no female ministers, although there were several deputy ministers (known as chief executive officers). In March the National Women's Commission launched a collaborative initiative to explore ways to increase the participation of women at the highest level of decision making.

Principal Government Officials

Last Updated: 1/31/2013

Governor Gen.: **Colville YOUNG, Sir**
Prime Min.: **Dean Oliver BARROW**
Dep. Prime Min.: **Gaspar VEGA**
Min. of Communications: **Melvin HULSE**
Min. of Culture: **Jose Manuel HEREDIA, Jr.**
Min. of Economic Development, Commerce, Industry, & Consumer Protection: **Erwin CONTRERAS**

Background Notes

Min. of Education, Youth, & Sports: **Patrick FABER**
Min. of Energy, Science, Technology, & Public Utilities: **Joy GRANT**
Min. of Finance & Economic Development: **Dean Oliver BARROW**
Min. of Foreign Affairs: **Wilfred Peter ELRINGTON**
Min. of Forestry, Fisheries, Sustainable Development, & Indigenous Peoples: **Liselle ALAMILLA**
Min. of Health: **Pablo MARIN**
Min. of Housing: **Michael FINNEGAN**
Min. of Human Development, Social Transformation, & Poverty Alleviation: **Mark KING**
Min. of Information, Broadcasting, & Public Utilities: **Elvin PENNER**
Min. of Labor: **Godwin HULSE**
Min. of Local Govt.: **Gabriel MARTINEZ**
Min. of Natural Resources & Agriculture: **Gaspar VEGA**
Min. of National Security, Police, and Belize Defense Force: **John Birchman SALDIVAR**
Min. of Public Services & Elections & Boundaries: **Charles GIBSON**
Min. of Rural Development: **Gabriel MARTINEZ**
Min. of Tourism & Culture: **Jose Manuel HEREDIA, Jr.**
Min. of Transport: **Melvin HULSE**
Min. of Works: **Anthony MARTINEZ**
Attorney Gen.: **Wilfred Peter ELRINGTON**
Governor, Central Bank: **Glenford YSAGUIRRE**
Ambassador to the US: **Nestor MENDEZ**
Permanent Representative to the UN, New York: **Janine Elizabet COYE-FELSON**

ECONOMY

Tourism is the number one foreign exchange earner in this small economy, followed by exports of marine products, citrus, cane sugar, bananas, and garments. The government's expansionary monetary and fiscal policies, initiated in September 1998, led to GDP growth averaging nearly 4% in 1999–2007. Oil discoveries in 2006 bolstered this growth. Exploration efforts have continued and production has increased a small amount. In February 2007, the government restructured nearly all of its public external commercial debt, which helped reduce interest payments and relieved some of the country's liquidity concerns. Growth slipped to 0% in 2009, 2.7% in 2010, and 2.5% in 2011 as a result of the global slowdown, natural disasters, and a temporary drop in the price of oil. With weak economic growth and a large public debt burden, fiscal spending is likely to be tight.

A key government objective remains the reduction of poverty and inequality with the help of international donors. Although Belize has the second highest per capita income in Central America, the average income figure masks a huge income disparity between rich and poor. The 2010 Poverty Assessment shows that more than 4 out of 10 people live in poverty. The sizable trade deficit and heavy foreign debt burden continue to be major concerns.

Labor Conditions

The law prohibits the employment of children under age 14. Persons ages 14 to 18 may be employed only in an occupation that a labor officer has determined is "not injurious to the moral or physical development of nonadults." Children under age 16 are excluded from work in factories, and those under age 18 are excluded from working at night or in certain kinds of employment deemed dangerous. The National Child Labor Policy, enforced by the Department of Labor and the National Commission for Families and Children, contains a list of hazardous occupations for young workers.

The law permits children to work on family farms and in family-run businesses. National legislation does not address a situation in which child labor is contracted between a parent and the employer. The National Child Labor Policy distinguishes between children engaged in work that is beneficial to their development and those engaged in the worst forms of child labor. The policy identifies children involved in the worst forms of child labor as those engaged in hazardous work, trafficking and child slavery, commercial sexual activities, and illicit activities.

The national minimum wage was BZ$3.10 ($1.55) per hour. A full-time worker receiving the minimum wage earned between one and one-half and two times the poverty-limit income, depending on the district. The law sets the workweek at no more than six days or 45 hours and requires premium payment for overtime work. Workers are entitled to two working weeks' paid annual holiday. Additionally, there are 13 days designated as public and bank holidays. Employees who work on public and bank holidays are entitled to pay at time and a half except for Good Friday and Christmas, which are paid at twice the normal rate.

Several different health and safety regulations cover numerous industries. The law, which applies to all sectors, prescribes that the employer must take "reasonable care" for the safety of employees in the course of their employment. The law further states that every employer who provides or arranges accommodation for workers to reside at or in the vicinity of a place of employment shall provide and maintain sufficient and hygienic housing accommodations, a sufficient supply of wholesome water, and sufficient and proper sanitary arrangements. Workers have the legal right to leave a dangerous workplace situation without jeopardy to continued employment.

The minimum wage was generally respected in practice. Nevertheless, anecdotal evidence from NGOs and employers suggested that undocumented Central American workers, particularly young service workers and agricultural laborers, were regularly paid below the minimum wage.

U.S.-BELIZEAN RELATIONS

The United States and Belize traditionally have had close and cordial relations. The United States is home to the largest Belizean community outside Belize, estimated to be over 100,000. Belize's economic growth and accompanying democratic political stability are important U.S. objectives. The United States and Belize are working as partners to address the issues of citizen security and transnational crime. The two countries have mutual legal assistance treaties with each other covering stolen vehicles and extraditions. Both governments seek to control the flow of illegal migrants to the United States through Belize.

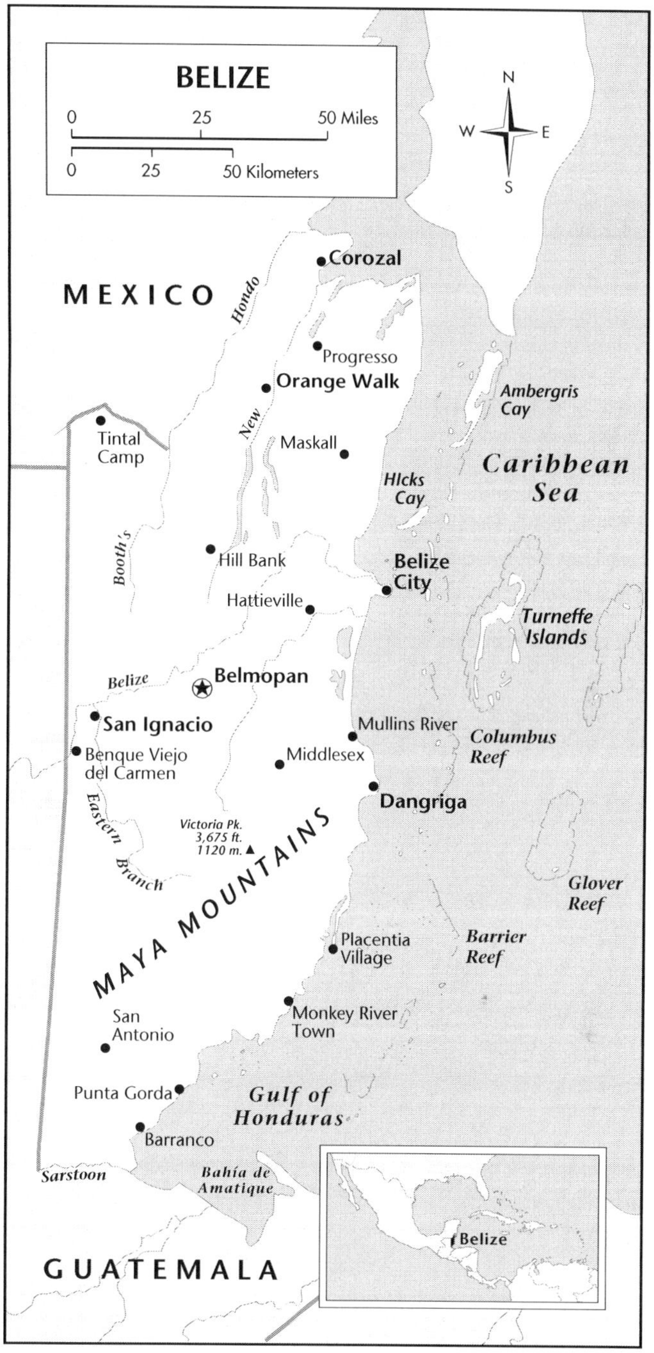

U.S. Assistance to Belize

The United States works closely with the Government of Belize to fight illicit narcotics trafficking, and Belize benefits from the Central America Regional Security Initiative (CARSI). Through CARSI, the U.S. Government seeks to strengthen citizen safety and improve the government's capacity to confront and disrupt criminal organizations. The Belize Defense Force receives military assistance from the United States. The U.S. military's assistance program in Belize has included the construction and renovation of several schools and youth hostels, medical assistance programs, and drug reduction programs. U.S. military assistance was also critical in establishing Belize's coast guard. Belize benefits from U.S. Agency for International Development regional programs, and there is a Peace Corps program in the country. Belize has signed a 5-year Central American regional framework agreement with the U.S. President's Emergency Plan for AIDS Relief.

Bilateral Economic Relations

The United States is Belize's principal trading partner and major source of investment funds. In 2010, the United States provided 47.9% of Belizean merchandise imports and accounted for 49.1% of Belize's merchandise exports. Some 185 U.S. companies have operations in Belize. Tourism attracts the most foreign direct investment, although U.S. investment also is found in the telecommunications, petroleum, and agricultural sectors. A Country Commercial Guide for Belize is available from the U.S. Embassy's Economic/ Commercial section.

Belize's Membership in International Organizations

Belize became a member of the United Nations following its 1981 independence from the United Kingdom. Belize and the United States belong to a number of the same international organizations, including the UN, Organization of American States, International Monetary Fund, World Bank, and World Trade Organization.

Bilateral Representation

Belize maintains an embassy in the United States at 2535 Massachusetts Avenue NW, Washington, DC 20008 (tel: 202-332-9636).

Principal U.S. Embassy Officials

Last Updated: 1/14/2013

BELMOPAN (E) Floral Park Road, 011-501-822-4011, Fax 011-501-822-4012, Workweek: 08:00–17:00, Mondays–Fridays, Website: http://belize.usembassy.gov

DCM OMS:	Joy Dellinger
AMB OMS:	Deb Mahoney
MGT:	Philip Wilson
MLO/ODC:	LTC Darren Lynn
POL/ECON:	Joe Boski
POSHO:	Henry Weiss
AMB:	Vinai Thummalapally
CON:	Christopher Derrick
DCM:	Margaret Hawthorne
PAO:	Eric Heyden
GSO:	Quinette Adams-Boston
RSO:	Lawrence Casselle
AFSA:	Alia Carter
APHIS:	John Hurley
CLO:	Yulia Lukasheva Melara
DEA:	Daktor Holguin
ICASS Chair:	Matthew Cain
IMO:	Krishnan Sridhar

Other Contact Information

Caribbean/Latin American Action
1818 N Street, NW
Washington, DC 20036
Tel: 202-466-7464
Fax: 202-822-0075

U.S. Department of Commerce International Trade Administration
Office of Latin American and the Caribbean
14th & Constitution, NW
Washington, DC 20230
Tel: 202-482-1658; 202-USA-TRADE-
Fax: 202-482-0464

TRAVEL

Consular Information Sheet

March 2, 2012

Country Description: Belize is a parliamentary democracy and British Commonwealth country. Belize has a developing economy based primarily upon agriculture and tourism. Tourist facilities vary in quality, from a limited number of business-class hotels in Belize City and luxury resorts in the offshore cayes (pronounced: "keys") to a range of luxury resorts, eco-tourism lodges and very basic accommodations in the countryside. Violent crime, especially in areas of Belize City, remains a serious concern.

Smart Traveler Enrollment Program (STEP)/Embassy Locations: If you are going to visit or live in Belize, please take the time to tell our Embassy about your trip. If you enroll, we can keep you up to date with important safety and security announcements. It will also help your friends or family get in touch with you in an emergency.

U.S. Embassy Belmopan
4 Floral Park Road
Belmopan, Cayo District
Belize, Central America
Telephone: 011-501-822-4011
Emergency after-hours telephone: 011-501-610-5030
Facsimile: 011-501-822-4050

Entry/Exit Requirements: All U.S. citizens must have a U.S. passport valid for at least six months from the date of arrival in Belize and proof of an onward or return ticket. No visas are required for citizens of the United States for tourist visits of up to 30 days, but they must have onward or return air tickets and proof of sufficient funds to maintain themselves in Belize.

All tourists and non-Belizean citizens are required to pay an exit fee of U.S. $39.25. As of October 2010, all U.S. airlines include this fee in the price of the ticket. Cruise ship passengers are charged U.S. $7 whether they leave the ship or remain onboard. This charge is included in the price of the cruise ticket. At the land borders, U.S. citizens are charged U.S. $15 if their stay was less than 24 hours and U.S. $18.75 if the stay was more than 24 hours.

Belize allows visitors a maximum of one month's stay in the country before they require an extension obtained through the Belize Ministry of Defense and Immigration. No specific immunizations are required for visitors to Belize. Visit the Embassy of Belize to the United States website (http://embassyofbelize.org/) for the most current visa information.

Cruise ship passengers: U.S. citizens on closed-loop cruises (i.e., cruises that begin and end at the same U.S. port) will be permitted to depart or enter the U.S. with a birth certificate and a government-issued photo ID, but a U.S. passport is preferable. Check with your cruise line to ensure you have the appropriate documentation. U.S. citizen passengers leaving their cruise ship and returning, for any reason, by air to the U.S. will be required to present their valid U.S. passports to airline officials before being permitted to board the aircraft.

Embassy of Belize
2535 Massachusetts Avenue, NW
Washington, DC 20008
Telephone: (202) 332-9636
Facsimile: (202) 332-6888
Website:
http://www.embassyofbelize.org

Consulate General of Belize
4801 Wilshire Boulevard, Suite 250
Los Angeles, CA 90010
Telephone: (323) 634-9900
Facsimile: (323) 634-9903
Email: belizeconsulate@sbcglobal.net

Permanent Mission of Belize to the United Nations
675 Third Avenue, Suite 1911
New York, NY 10017
Telephone: (212) 986-1240
Facsimile: (212) 593-0932
Email: blzun@belizemission.com

HIV/AIDS restrictions: The U.S. Department of State is unaware of any HIV/AIDS entry restrictions for visitors to or foreign residents of Belize.

Special Notice for Dual Nationals: A person who is a citizen of both the U.S. and Belize is able to enter Belize with only a Belizean passport.

However, a person who is a citizen of both the U.S. and Belize must enter the U.S. on the U.S. passport.

Terrorism and Security: The potential for domestic terrorist activity such as bombings, kidnappings, or hijackings is considered low in Belize. However, domestic gang members and other criminals have used fragmentation grenades and firearms to settle disputes. Neither U.S. citizens nor other foreign nationals are known to have been the victims or targets of terrorist activity in Belize. U.S. citizens are not believed to be specifically targeted for robbery or other crimes but are instead targets of opportunity. No areas are closed to travel but visitors should exercise caution, particularly in southern Belize City and remote areas along Belize's borders.

General Safety: Visitors should exercise situational awareness and good judgment while visiting Belize. Crime is a serious and growing problem throughout Belize. Road accidents are common (see Traffic Safety and Road Conditions) and traffic fatalities have included U.S. citizens. Public buses and taxis are frequently in poor condition and lack basic safety equipment.

Many unlicensed taxis are present in Belize and U.S. citizens are encouraged to avoid traveling in them; genuine taxis may be identified by their green-colored license plates. Medical care is limited in many areas, including the larger cities of Belize City and Belmopan, and emergency response services such as ambulances or paramedics may be either unavailable or limited in capability and equipment (see Medical Facilities and Health Information).

Water Safety: Boats serving the public, especially water taxis, often do not carry sufficient safety equipment. Many carry an excessive number of passengers and may sail in inclement weather. Rental diving equipment may not always be properly maintained or inspected, and some local dive masters fail to consider the skill levels of individual tourists when organizing dives to some of Belize's more challenging sites. Deaths and serious injuries have occurred as a result of the negligence of dive tour operators, the lack of strict enforcement of tour regulations, water taxis diverging from routes when tourists are in the water, and tourists' neglect of their physical limitations. The Embassy strongly recommends that anyone interested in scuba diving or snorkeling while in Belize check the references, licenses, and equipment of tour operators before agreeing to or paying for a tour.

The Embassy further recommends that U.S. citizens be forthcoming in reporting pre-existing medical conditions to their dive tour operators, and comply when a dive tour operator prohibits participation in such activities due to a U.S. citizen's health condition. Safety precautions and emergency response capabilities may not be up to U.S. standards. All tour guides and boat captains are now required to be licensed by the Government of Belize. The only hyperbaric recompression chamber in Belize is located in San Pedro Town, Ambergris Caye.

Cave Tubing: As a result of a fatal accident at the Cave's Branch Archeological Park in September 2008, the Belize Tourism Board (BTB) implemented new regulations, effective as of October 15, 2008. However, deaths from cave tubing accidents continue to occur. Cave tubing policies include an enhanced, mandatory guest-to-guide ratio of eight-to-one for all cave tubing tour companies operating in Belize. Signage is required at each cave tubing excursion site to inform participants of park rules, current water conditions, and/or warnings. Mandatory specialty training for each cave tubing guide continues and includes education on new regulations. Helmets are required for each cave tubing participant.

Additionally, the National Institute of Culture and History (NICH), which manages the Cave's Branch Archeological Park, has installed additional monitoring equipment for cave tubing excursions which measure currents and other factors. The Embassy encourages U.S. citizens participating in cave tubing to do so only with a guide and cave tubing tour companies that adhere to the above requirements and guidelines, and when water currents are deemed safe by those tour companies.

Border Areas: A long-standing border dispute between Belize and Guatemala has not been resolved and many areas of the border area are not adequately patrolled. Smugglers, narcotics traffickers and wildlife poachers enter Belize in the shared border region, and there have been incidents of clashes between some of these individuals and Belize military and law enforcement personnel, some of which included the exchangeof gunfire.

Visitors should avoid trekking or other activities near the Belize-Guatemala border to ensure that they do not inadvertently cross the border into Guatemala. The Embassy cautions U.S. citizens who choose to travel on cross-border public buses between Guatemala and Belize in response to a spike in armed bus attacks by bandits in January 2011. Illegal cross-border activities increase after nightfall. Visitors to the border areas should travel only during daylight.

During the month of January 2011, there were a total of four reported bus-related robberies occurring in the border area in Guatemala near Belize. Among these robberies, U.S. tourists were robbed in two separate incidents near Melchor, Guatemala, while traveling with the San Juan Bus Company from Flores, Guatemala into Belize.

Although no one was harmed in either incident, armed bandits boarded the buses and robbed passengers of cash and valuables. There is no current information available to suggest that the alleged perpetrators were attempting to target individuals or tourists of any specific nationality and the victims appear to have been targets of opportunity.

Take some time before travel to improve your personal security—things are not the same everywhere as they are in the United States.

Crime: Organized crime beyond street gangs is primarily connected to drug trafficking or trafficking in persons. Incidents of crime remain high, including violent crimes such as armed robbery, home invasions, shootings, stabbings, murders, and rapes. The Embassy has noted an increase in crimes against tourists at resorts and on the roads and river ways. U.S. citizens are primarily the victims of opportunistic crime.

There is no evidence suggesting criminals specifically target U.S. citizens, but nonetheless, foreigners have been targeted for crime due to their perceived wealth. Incidents of crime (such as theft, burglary, home invasion, purse-snatching, and pick-pocketing) increase during the winter holidays and during spring break. Several victims who resisted when confronted by criminals received serious injuries, including gunshot wounds and broken limbs. Although the majority of reported incidents occur in Belize City, particularly southern Belize City, crime may occur anywhere including tourist destinations such as San Pedro Town (Ambergris Caye), Caye Caulker, San Ignacio, Dangriga, Corozal, and Placencia.

Belize recorded 125 homicides in 2011, a decrease of five percent from 2010. Prior to 2011, homicide rates in Belize rose at least five percent every year since 2000, with the exception of 2009 when homicide rates again decreased slightly. With a population of only 312,698 according to the 2010 country census, Belize's per capita homicide rate of 39 homicides per 100,000 inhabitants in 2011 ranks it as the sixth highest in the world. While the country's per capita homicide rate is still lower than that of other Central American countries, such as Honduras, El Salvador, and Guatemala, its year-on-year increase is of concern.

The majority of homicides in 2011 occurred in the Belize district. The majority of these fatalities occurred in the southern portion of Belize City, an area that has become increasingly violent due to ongoing gang warfare between local groups for control of lucrative narcotics smuggling routes and sales rights. In late 2011, the Government of Belize brokered a truce among the major gangs which brought about a precarious peace resulting in the lower 2011 end-of-year homicide rate.

While increased police patrols, coordinated tours among resort security managers, and the arrest of perpetrators may reduce the frequency of crimes, these measures do not guarantee safety. Armed robberies of tourists remain a possibility at archeological sites, national parks, and other areas frequented by visitors. In July 2011, there was an increase in the number of robberies, home invasions, and daytime assaults in the Cayo District near the town of San Ignacio. There is no information suggesting the perpetrators were targeting tourists of any specific nationality; rather, the victims appear to have been targets of opportunity.

We encourage U.S. citizens to exercise caution and good situational awareness in all their travel activities. Visitors to tourist attractions should travel in groups and stick to the main plazas at Maya ruins and the central areas. Although there are armed guards stationed at many of the archeological sites, armed criminals have been known to prey on persons walking alone or in small groups from one site to another.

While many victims of theft are unharmed and only robbed of personal belongings and cash, victims who resist assailants have suffered injury. U.S. citizens who become victims of a robbery should report it immediately to the nearest police station as well as notifying the Embassy.

The Embassy recommends that visitors travel in groups and only during daylight hours. Avoid wearing jewelry, or carrying valuable or expensive items. As a general rule, valuables should not be left unattended, including in vehicles, hotel rooms or on the beach. Care should be taken when carrying high value items such as cameras. Women's handbags should be zipped and held close to the body. Men should carry wallets in their front pants pocket. Large amounts of cash should always be handled discreetly.

Specific groups such as the elderly, women, or homosexuals are not specifically singled out for victimization; however neither are they immune from being targeted for robbery or assault. Homosexuality is not widely accepted in Belize culture and homosexual behavior may be subject to prosecution as an "Unnatural crime" under Section 53 of the Belize Criminal Code.

Sexual harassment and/or assault of persons traveling alone or in small groups have occurred in recent years. From July to September 2011, there were a handful of sexual assaults on American citizen women after leaving night clubs, and even during daylight hours while walking with friends or while cycling alone on a deserted portion of the Hummingbird Highway.

A lack of resources and training impedes the ability of the police to effectively investigate crime and apprehend serious offenders. As a result, a number of crimes against U.S. citizens in Belize remain unresolved.

"Confidence scams" also occur in Belize, especially in resort areas. While there is no indication U.S. citizens are specifically singled out because of their nationality, tourists in general are particularly vulnerable to these crimes, resulting in visitors being pick-pocketed or robbed. More serious crimes have included armed robbery, physical assault, and being swindled out of large sums of money from fraudulent real estate and land sales, and other business deals.

With regard to business investments and contractual relationships, U.S. citizens should always conduct their own due diligence before entering into business ventures or other commercial arrangements. The Embassy cannot intervene to settle business disputes. Local business and trade associations, including the American Chamber of Commerce and Belize Chamber of Commerce, as well as government offices, may be able to provide information regarding Belize commercial requirements, validity of businesses, and reputable vendors and business agents. There have also been recent cases where investors have disputed commercial agreements with the Government of Belize through formal commercial dispute resolution procedures and the Government of Belize has failed to honor its agreements.

Drug use is common in some tourist areas. U.S. citizens should not buy, sell, hold, or take illegal drugs under any circumstances. Penalties for possession of drugs or drug paraphernalia are generally more severe than in the U.S. Visitors are cautioned that Belize classifies marijuana or ganja (i.e., cannabis) as an illegal drug for which a conviction of possession of even small amounts could result in heavy fines or imprisonment. Belize does not recognize the medical use of marijuana as permitted in some U.S. states, and U.S. citizens will be charged, fined or serve time in jail for possession of an illegal substance.

Possession of a firearm or ammunition requires a license from the Government of Belize. Residents and tourists found by Belize law enforcement to be in the possession of such items without a license may be sentenced to a prison term in Belize.

Don't buy counterfeit and pirated goods, even if they are widely available. Not only are the bootleg items illegal in the United States, if you purchase them you may also be breaking local law.

Victims of Crime: If you are the victim of a crime abroad, you should contact the local police first to obtain a Belize police report and then the nearest U.S. embassy or consulate (see the Department of State's list of embassies and consulates). This includes the loss or theft of a U.S. passport. The embassy's consular staff can, for example, help you find appropriate medical care, contact family members or friends, and explain how U.S. funds may be transferred to Belize. Although the investigation and prosecution of the crime are solely the responsibility of local Belize authorities, consular officers can help you to understand the local criminal justice process and to find a Belizean attorney if needed.

The local equivalent to the "911" emergency line in Belize is also 911. Please see the Department's information on victims of crime at www.travel.state.gov, including possible victim compensation programs in the United States.

Criminal Penalties: While you are traveling in Belize, you are subject to Belize's laws even if you are a U.S. citizen. Foreign laws and legal systems can be vastly different than our own. Penalties for breaking the law can be more severe than in the United States for similar offenses. Belize law enforcement reserves the right to hold any individual for up to 48 hours to verify identity and conduct other security checks prior to a formal arrest at which time the Embassy would be given consular access to that U.S. citizen. Persons violating Belize's laws may be expelled, arrested, or imprisoned.

Penalties for possessing, using, or trafficking in illegal drugs in Belize are severe, and convicted offenders can expect long jail sentences and heavy fines. Belize has strict laws making possession of a firearm, ammunition, or anti-ballistic body armor illegal unless a valid permit is obtained. Penalties for firearms violations are severe. U.S. gun licenses or permits have no validity in Belize. Engaging in sexual conduct with children, using or disseminating child pornography in a foreign country, including Belize, is a crime, prosecutable in the United States, under the Protect Act. U.S. law requires that all sex offenders notify U.S. law enforcement authorities of any travel outside of the U.S.

Consular access for U.S. citizens who are detained or arrested is uniformly good. If you are arrested in Belize, the Belize arresting officials are required to notify the U.S. embassy of your arrest. If you are concerned the Department of State may not be aware of your situation, you should request the police or prison officials to notify the U.S. embassy or consulate of your arrest.

Special Circumstances: Visitors entering Belize must make a customs declaration of any currency or financial instruments exceeding a total value of U.S. $10,000.

U.S. citizens visiting Belize for vacation, transit, or business purposes do not ordinarily require a Belize visa in advance of their arrival. Belize's Department of Defense and Immigration routinely issues visitor's permits at border crossings and at the Philip S.W. Goldson International Airport for stays of up to 30 days. Visitor's permits may be renewed or extended by application to any of the Department of Defense and Immigration's field offices while in Belize.

According to the Embassy of Belize in Washington, D.C., all visitors to Belize must be in a possession of a valid passport, an onward or return ticket and sufficient funds (a minimum of U.S. $60 per day) to cover the cost of the length of stay. U.S. citizens wishing to obtain visas in advance of their arrival may apply at the Embassy of Belize or one of its constituent consulates.

Cruise ship passengers disembarking and rejoining their cruise ship the same day may do so while in possession of valid, U.S. government-issued identification and an original copy of their U.S. birth certificate.

U.S. citizens traveling with their children may be asked by immigration officials to show U.S. birth certificates for each child. When children are not traveling with both parents, immigration officials often request signed documentation to establish the children are traveling with the permission of both parents.

Such documentation may include notarized letters from the parent(s), custody or adoption papers, and even death certificates in situations where one or both parents are deceased.

Persons who are citizens of both the U.S. and Belize are able to enter Belize with only a Belizean passport. Such dual nationals should be aware, however, that a valid U.S. passport will be required in order to board a U.S.-bound flight from Belize. The average processing time to obtain a full-validity U.S. passport at the Embassy is approximately 10 working days.

Persons illegally present in Belize may face a sentence of imprisonment of up to six months if they are unable to pay the fine imposed by a court. Persons violating Belize's laws, even unknowingly, may be expelled, arrested, or imprisoned. Illegal presence in Belize remains a civil matter, and one in which the U.S. Embassy does not have the jurisdiction to resolve on behalf of U.S. citizens.

Accessibility: While in Belize, individuals with disabilities may find accessibility and accommodation very different from what one would find in the United States. While some government buildings, schools, businesses and restaurants are accessible for individuals with disabilities, many places remain inaccessible. Accessibility may be especially difficult in the rural and non-tourist areas. Paved roads and sidewalks are rare outside tourist areas. Public buses and taxis are not accessible. Please check with hotels, restaurants, and tour operators in advance for information about accessibility.

Medical Facilities and Health Information: Medical care for minor ailments is generally available in urban areas. Trauma care or advanced medical treatment is limited, even in Belize City or Belmopan, and may be extremely limited or unavailable in rural and remote areas. Pharmacy services are generally good in larger towns; many medications such as antibiotics which are available only by prescription in the U.S. can be obtained over-the-counter from licensed pharmacists. More specialized prescription medications may be completely unavailable. U.S. citizens bringing their own prescription medications with them must ensure they carry a current doctor's prescription for each medication.

In much of the country, emergency services will be either unavailable or delayed. Serious injuries or illnesses often require evacuation to another country. The Embassy strongly suggests visitors obtain traveler's insurance and medical evacuation coverage in advance of their travel to cover unexpected medical emergencies.

The Government of Belize last reported an outbreak of Dengue fever in July 2011, and of H1N1 influenza in May and September 2009.

Information on vaccinations and other health precautions, such as safe food and water precautions and insect bite protection, may be obtained from the Centers for Disease Control and Prevention's (CDC) hotline for international travelers at 1-877-FYI-TRIP (1-877-394-8747) or via the CDC website. For information about outbreaks of infectious diseases abroad, consult the infectious diseases section of the World Health Organization (WHO) website. The WHO website also contains additional health information for travelers, including detailed country-specific health information.

Belize does not recognize the medical use of marijuana as permitted in some U.S. states, and U.S. citizens will be charged, fined or serve time in jail for possession of an illegal substance.

Medical Insurance: U.S. citizens must not assume that their medical insurance automatically provides overseas coverage. It's very important to find out BEFORE you leave the United States whether or not your medical insurance will cover you overseas. Questions to ask your insurance company are the following:

- Does my medical insurance policy apply when I'm outside of the United States?
- Will my medical insurance policy cover emergencies such as a trip to a foreign hospital or a medical evacuation?

In many places in Belize, doctors and hospitals still expect payment in cash at the time of service. Regular U.S. medical insurance may not cover doctors' and hospital visits in other countries. U.S. Medicare does not cover treatment received outside of the U.S. Purchasing medical coverage specific to a trip is always encouraged.

Traffic Safety and Road Conditions: While in a foreign country, U.S. citizens may encounter road conditions that differ significantly from those in the United States.

Valid U.S. or international driver's permits are accepted in Belize only for a period of three months after initial entry.

Public buses and private vehicles are the main mode of transportation in Belize; no railways currently operate in the country. Like in the United States, drivers operate vehicles on the right side of the road and road signs are in English with distances indicated in miles. Driving norms do not always follow U.S. practice, and due caution must be exercised at all times.

Roadside assistance can be difficult to summon as there are very few public telephones along the road and emergency telephone numbers do not always function properly. While cell phone service is fairly reliable, reception in remote areas such as on Hummingbird Highway is spotty or nonexistent. The Belize Department of Transportation is responsible for road safety.

Roads in Belize vary from two-lane paved roads to dirt or gravel tracks. The few paved roads are high-crowned, meaning that the roads are built to a slight point in the middle and slope down on the sides. There are usually no shoulders on the sides of the roads such that when vehicles get too close to the edge, the vehicle may lose traction on the loosely packed gravel, which contributes to cars overturning. There are few markings or reflectors. Even in urban areas, most streets lack lane markings, leading many motorists to create as many lanes as possible in any given stretch of street or road. Bridges on the major highways are often only a single lane. The Manatee Road (Coastal Road), leading from the Western Highway east of Belmopan to Dangriga, is mostly unpaved, easily flooded after storms and without services. The Southern Highway from Dangriga to Punta Gorda is now completely paved and in good condition. Service stations are available along the major roads although there are some significant gaps in the rural areas.

Belize's official hurricane season from May to November annually creates hazardous road conditions. During Tropical Storm Alma/Arthur in late May 2008, the Southern Highway Bridge over the Sittee River, north of Kendal (Stann Creek District), was destroyed. In the interim, the temporary causeway constructed pending permanent replacement of the Kendall Bridge is at times impassable due to high water on the Sittee River. The causeway itself has had to be replaced several times following major rainfall and flooding. Motorists should not attempt to cross any low bridge with water flowing over the surface of the bridge as both the strength and depth of the current may be stronger than is apparent.

Poor road and/or vehicle maintenance cause many fatal accidents on Belize's roads. Speed limits are a maximum of 55 miles per hour on highways and 25 miles per hour on most other roads, but they are seldom obeyed or even posted. Drivers should particularly watch for speed bumps and rumble strips as they pass through villages on the major highways. These usually denote pedestrian crossings and are not always marked by clear signage or reflective yellow paint.

Many vehicles on the road do not have functioning safety equipment such as turn signals, flashers, or brake lights. Seatbelts for drivers and front-seat passengers are mandatory, but children's car seats are not required and are not widely available for purchase. Maintaining a safe driving distance will avoid accidents. Driving while intoxicated is punishable by a fine; however, if an alcohol-related road accident results in a fatality, the driver may face manslaughter charges. U.S. citizens can and have been imprisoned in Belize as a result of road accidents, even where alcohol is not a factor.

Unusual local traffic customs include: pulling to the right before making a left turn; passing on the right of someone who is signaling a right-hand turn; stopping in the middle of the road to talk to someone while blocking traffic, carrying passengers, including small children, in the open beds of trucks; and tailgating at high speeds.

Bicycles are numerous and constitute a traffic hazard at all times. Bicyclists often ride against traffic and do not obey even basic traffic laws such as stopping at red lights or stop signs. Although commonly encountered after nightfall, few bicycles have lights or wear reflective clothing. It is common to see bicyclists carrying heavy loads or passengers, including small children balanced in their laps or across the handlebars.

During daylight hours, particularly during weekends, highway drivers may encounter cross-country racing bicyclists, engaged in either training or in organized competitions. These may be accompanied by slow-moving vehicles such as pickup trucks or even motor cycles. Exercise caution when passing such persons as their attention may be on each other rather than passing motorists. The driver of a vehicle that strikes a bicyclist or pedestrian is almost always considered to be at fault, regardless of circumstances. U.S. citizens who have struck bicyclists in Belize have faced significant financial penalties or even prison sentences. Driving at night is not recommended even in populated areas. Major driving hazards include poor signage and road markings, a tendency by drivers to not dim their lights when approaching other vehicles, drunk driving, and poor or unfamiliar road conditions. Pedestrians and motorcyclists without reflective clothing; and bicyclists without lights or reflectors also constitute very serious after-dark hazards exacerbated by the lack of street lighting at night. Local wildlife, dogs and cattle in the road are also hazards even outside of rural areas. For safety reasons, travelers should not stop to offer assistance to others whose vehicles appear to have broken down as it may be a robbery scheme.

Aviation Safety Oversight: The U.S. Federal Aviation Administration (FAA) has assessed the Government of Belize's Civil Aviation Authority as not being in compliance with International Civil Aviation Organization (ICAO) aviation safety standards for oversight of Belize's air carrier operations. Further information may be found on the FAA's safety assessment page. All direct commercial air service to the United States is by U.S. air carriers registered in Belize.

Children's Issues: Please see the U.S. Dept. of State Office of Children's Issues web pages on intercountry adoption and international parental child abduction.

Intercountry Adoption

January 2012

The information in this section has been edited from the latest report available as of February 2013 from the State Department Bureau of Consular Affairs, Office of Overseas Citizens Services. For more information, please read the *Intercountry Adoption* section of this book and review current reports online at http://adoption.state.gov.

Belize is party to the Hague Convention on Protection of Children and Co-operation in Respect of Intercountry Adoption (Hague Adoption Convention). Therefore all adoptions between Belize and the United States must meet the requirements of the Convention; the U.S. implementing legislation, the Intercountry Adoption Act of 2000 (IAA); and the IAA implementing regulations.

Who Can Adopt? Adoption between the United States and Belize is governed by the Hague Adoption Convention. Therefore to adopt from Belize, you must first be found eligible to adopt by the U.S. Government. The U.S. Government agency responsible for making this determination is the Department of Homeland Security, U.S. Citizenship and Immigration Services (USCIS).

Residency Requirements: Belizean law prohibits the issuance of a final adoption order unless the non-Belizean prospective adoptive parent resides in Belize with the Belizean child for 12 months. A social worker will visit periodically to assess the parent-child relationship.

Age Requirements: At least one of the prospective adoptive parents must be a minimum of 25 years old and no fewer than 12 years older than the child.

Marriage Requirements: Both married and single individuals can adopt in Belize. Single men cannot adopt female children. These restrictions can be waived if the court finds that special circumstances warrant it.

Income Requirements: While there are no specific income requirements, prospective adoptive parents' financial status will be included as part of the home study.

Other Requirements: A person who is not a citizen of Belize may adopt a Belizean child if he or she does not have a criminal record and has a current recommendation concerning his suitability to adopt a child from his country's probation and welfare office or other competent authority. A social services practitioner must verify this recommendation in writing as well as submit a report of the findings of the inquiry to the court. (Please note that U.S. immigration law requires that in Hague Convention countries like Belize the determination of suitability (home study) must be completed, supervised, or approved by a U.S. based Hague accredited or approved adoption service provider.) In addition, the court may request a report/recommendation from an additional person or authority A person must also satisfy the court that his country of origin will respect and recognize the adoption order.

Who Can Be Adopted? Because Belize is party to the Hague Adoption Convention, children from Belize must meet the requirements of the Convention in order to be eligible for adoption. For example, the Convention requires that Belize attempt to place a child with a family in-country (i.e. in Belize) before determining that a child is eligible for intercountry adoption. In addition to Belize's requirements, a child must meet the definition of a Convention adoptee for you to bring him or her back to the United States. Belizean law only provides for the adoption of children who are citizens of Belize. A child who is not a Belizean citizen cannot be the subject of an adoption in a Belizean court, although Belizean courts can issue custody orders for any child residing in Belize.

Eligibility Requirements: Children in Belize may only be adopted through the judicial process. There are no private adoptions or adoptions through extra-judicial processes. Intercountry adoption placements are made on a case-by-case basis. Belizean law requires that prospective adoptive parents complete a one year probationary period of custody of the child before a final adoption decree for purposes of immigration can be issued.

Relinquishment Requirements: Under Belizean law, consents provided by birth parents or legal guardians of the child become irrevocable upon issuance of a provisional adoption order. However, once entered with the court, the consents by the parent or legal custodian are not revocable by the parent or guardian themselves, but are only revocable by court action.

Abandonment Requirements: Determined on a case-by-case basis.

Age Requirements: Determined on a case-by-case basis.

Sibling Requirements: Determined on a case-by-case basis.

Requirements for Special Needs or Medical Conditions: Determined on a case-by-case basis.

Waiting Period: Belizean law requires that prospective adoptive parents complete a one year probationary period of custody of the child before a final adoption decree for purposes of immigration can be issued. Prospective adoptive parents may fulfill this one year period in Belize, or may be authorized by the Supreme Court of Belize to fulfill the probationary period in their country of residence. "Provisional," "Interim" or "Preliminary" adoption decrees issued by the Supreme Court of Belize before the one year probationary period of custody is fulfilled can be considered permission for the prospective adoptive parents to take the child out of Belize during the probationary period, and to pursue an adoption process in accordance with the laws of their country of residence after fulfillment of the one year probationary period of custody.

Belize's Adoption Authority: Belize Department of Human Services, within the Belize Ministry of Human Development

The Process: The first step in adopting a child from Belize is to select an accredited or approved adoption service provider in the United States. Only these agencies and attorneys can provide adoption services between the United States and Belize. Intercountry adoptions must be decided by a Supreme Court Judge and require the services of a local attorney authorized to present cases to the Supreme Court of Belize. Contact the Belize Central Authority or a Belizean attorney for forms and procedures for intercountry adoption. A list of local attorneys can be found at http://belize.usembassy.gov/legal_information.html.

Prospective adoptive parents should fully research any adoption agency or facilitator they plan to use for adoption services. For U.S.-based agencies, prospective adoptive parents may wish to contact the Better Business Bureau and/or the licensing authority in the U.S. state where the agency is located or licensed. After you choose an accredited or approved adoption service provider, you apply to be found eligible to adopt (Form I-800A) by the U.S. Government, Department of Homeland Security, U.S. Citizenship and Immigration Services (USCIS). Once the U.S. government determines that you are "eligible" and "suited" to adopt, you or your agency will forward your information to the adoption authority in Belize.

Belize's adoption authority will review your application to determine whether you are also eligible to adopt under Belize's adoption law. Sections 137 and 141 of Belizean Adoption Law specify the requirements for Non-Belizean citizens who would like to adopt a Belizean child. If both the United States and Belize determine that you are eligible to adopt, and a child is available for intercountry adoption, the central adoption authority in Belize may provide you with a referral for a child. Each family must decide for itself whether or not it will be able to meet the needs of the particular child and provide a permanent family placement for the referred child.

A child who is not a Belizean citizen cannot be the subject of an adoption in a Belizean court, although Belizean courts can issue custody for any child residing in Belize. After you accept a match with a child, you will apply to the U.S. Government, Department of Homeland Security, U.S. Citizenship and Immigration Services (USCIS) for provisional approval of a petition to immigrate a child through adoption (Form I-800). Form I-800, like Form I-800A, must be submitted in the United States. USCIS will determine whether the child is eligible under U.S. law to be adopted and enter the United States. After the I-800 is provisionally approved by USCIS, the entire case file is transferred to the U.S. Department of State's National Visa Center, which immediately forwards the case file to the U.S. Embassy.

Upon receipt of the file the Embassy makes contact with your adoption service provider to arrange for submission of a visa application. The Embassy will ask for an immigrant visa application form known as the DS 230 Parts I and II, an original or certified birth certificate for the child, photos of the child and, if practicable, a medical exam conducted by a panel physician. Once the Consular officer receives the visa application, the officer reviews the child's information and evaluates the case and the application for compliance with the Hague Convention and for possible visa ineligibilities. If the Consular officer determines that the child appears eligible to immigrate to the United States, he or she will notify the Belize Central Authority of this initial determination in a letter known as the Article 5 letter. When the Belize Central Authority receives the Article 5 letter from the Embassy, it will issue a letter known as the Article 17 letter to the prospective adoptive parent(s) and the Adoption Service Provider. The Article 17 letter notifies the prospective adoptive parents that they may proceed with the adoption.

For Convention country adoptions, prospective adoptive parent(s) may not proceed with the adoption or obtain custody for the purpose of adoption until both the Article 5 and Article 17 letters have been issued. You cannot initiate the adoption process prior to issuance of the Article 5 and Article 17 letters. The Consular officer will make a final decision about the immigrant visa later in the adoption process.

Role of the Court: Upon any application for an adoption order, the court may postpone the determination of the application and may make an interim order giving the custody of the child to the applicant for a probationary period not exceeding two years with terms regarding provision for the maintenance, education, supervision of the welfare of the child specified as the court may think fit.

All consents required for a full and final adoption order are also required for an interim adoption order. Under Belizean law, consents provided by birth parents or legal guardians of the child become irrevocable upon issuance of a provisional adoption order. However, once entered with the court, the consents by the parent or legal custodian are not revocable by the parent or guardian themselves, but are only revocable by court action. As mentioned above, according to sections 137 and 141 of Belizean adoption law, the Supreme Court of Belize may (and usually does) postpone the granting of a final adoption decree and instead issues an interim or provisional adoption order. Under this circumstance, the prospective adoptive parent(s) will have custody of the child for a probationary period of one year during which there must be quarterly reports regarding the child's care and progress.

Prospective parents who receive an interim order from the Supreme Court of Belize and would like to carry it out in the U.S. may seek an IH-4 visa for the child. This visa is granted to the prospective parents only with the understanding and agreement that they will also seek a final adoption decree from their state of legal residence. Even though the child will be living in the U.S., the Supreme Court of Belize may request home study reports from U.S. Social Services agencies during the interim.

Prospective adoptive parents may fulfill the interim one year probationary period in Belize. In this case prospective adoptive parents would obtain a final adoption decree from the Supreme Court of Belize after fulfilling the one year period and would then apply to the U.S. Embassy for an IH-3 immigrant visa for the child.

Role of Adoption Agencies: International adoptions occur before a Supreme Court Judge and require the services of a local attorney authorized to present cases to the Supreme Court of Belize. Those persons desirous of information regarding the forms and procedures to follow for adoptions should contact a Belizean attorney see list of attorneys in Belize.

Time Frame: The processing time for adoptions can vary, depending on the circumstances of the case. The Belize Department of Human Services reports that "ward adoptions" (children in the custody of the Department of Human Services) can take up to one year or more to process because of the need for home study reports, matching, placement and legal proceedings. For children not in the custody of the Belize Department of Human Services, the processing time can be shorter. If the prospective adoptive parents request a specific child, the matching and placement determination can take less time. These adoption proceedings take from 3 months to one year.

Adoption Application: The prospective adoptive parents will file the adoption application to the Belize Human Services Department.

Adoption Fees: In the adoption services contract that you sign at the beginning of the adoption process, your agency will itemize the fees and estimated expenses related to your adoption process.

Prospective adoptive parents can expect to pay attorney's fees for adoption services in Belize ranging from $1,500 USD to $5,000 USD. The cost can vary based on the attorney selected, the type of adoption (local vs. international) and the number of children being adopted. Attorneys' fees include all costs related to the adoption process, such as court costs and filing fees.

The U.S. Embassy in Belize discourages the payment of any fees that are not properly receipted. In addition, "donations," or "expediting" fees, which may be requested from prospective adoptive parents, have the appearance of "buying" a baby and put all future adoptions in Belize at risk. U.S. citizens adopting a child in Belize should report any exorbitant fees to the U.S. Embassy in Belize or to the U.S. Department of State.

Documents Required: The following documents are required by the Belize Human Services Department:

- A valid police certificate;
- An approved home study;
- Proof of home government approval to adopt (for U.S. citizens, this is an approved I-800 or I-800A).

Additional documents may be requested. If you are asked to provide proof that a document from the United States is authentic, we can help. Read more on Traveling Abroad to learn about Authenticating U.S. Documents.

Bringing Your Child Home: Once your adoption is complete (or you have obtained legal custody of the child), there are a few more steps to take before you can head home. Specifically, you need to apply for several documents for your child before he or she can travel to the United States, such as a birth certificate, a passport or travel document for your child from the country in which he or she was born, and a U.S. Immigration Visa. For detailed and updated information on how to obtain these documents, review the *Intercountry Adoption* section in this publication and visit the U.S. Department of State Intercountry Adoption website at http://adoption.state.gov.

Child Citizenship Act: For adoptions finalized abroad, the Child Citizenship Act of 2000 allows your new child to acquire American citizenship automatically when he or she enters the United States as lawful permanent residents. For adoptions finalized in the United States, the Child Citizenship Act of 2000 allows your new child to acquire American citizenship automatically when the court in the United States issues the final adoption decree. To learn more, review the *Intercountry Adoption* section in this publication and visit the U.S. Department of State Intercountry Adoption website at http://adoption.state.gov.

After Adoption: Under Belizean law, adoption orders made under section 141 remain provisional for 12 months during which time quarterly reports regarding the progress of the child must be submitted to the court by a competent authority in the country where the adopted child lives. After the 12 month period has expired, an application can be made to a designated court for the adoption to be made final. We strongly urge you to comply with Belizean reporting requirements and complete all post-adoption requirements in a timely manner. Your adoption agency may be able to help you with this process. Your cooperation will contribute to Belize's history of positive experiences with American parents.

U.S. Embassy in Belize
4 Floral Park Road
Belmopan, Belize
Tel: ++501-822-4011

Belizean Adoption Authority:
Department of Human Services
40 Regent Street
P.O. Box 41
Belize City, Belize
Tel: ++501-227-7451, 501-227-2057
Fax: ++501-227-1276

Belize Immigration and Nationality Department
Dry Creek Street
Belmopan
Tel: ++501-822-3860, 501-822-0739

Belize Vital Statistics Unit
Gabourel Lane
Belize City, Belize
Tel: ++501-223-7405
Fax: ++501-223-5635

Embassy of Belize
2535 Massachusetts Ave. NW
Washington, DC 20008
Tel: 202-332-9636

Office of Children's Issues
U.S. Department of State
2201 C Street, NW
SA-29
Washington, DC 20520
Tel: 1-888-407-4747
E-mail: AskCI@state.gov
http://adoption.state.gov

For questions about immigration procedures, call the National Customer Service Center (NCSC) at 1-800-375-5283 (TTY 1-800-767-1833).

International Parental Child Abduction

January 2013

The information in this section has been edited from a report of the State Department Bureau of Consular Affairs, Office of Overseas Citizens Services. For more information, please read the *International Child Abduction* section of this book and review current reports online at www.travel.state.gov/abduction.

Disclaimer: The information in this flyer is provided for general information only, is not intended to be legal advice, and may change without notice. Questions involving interpretation of law should be addressed to an attorney licensed to practice in the relevant jurisdiction.

General Information: Belize and the United States have been treaty partners under the 1980 Hague Convention on the Civil Aspects of International Child Abduction (Hague Abduction Convention) since November 1, 1989.

Hague Abduction Convention: The U.S. Department of State serves as the U.S. Central Authority (USCA) for the Hague Abduction Convention. In this capacity, the Department's Bureau of Consular Affairs, Directorate for Overseas Citizens Services, Office of Children's Issues facilitates the submission of applications under the Hague Abduction Convention for the return of, or access to, children located in countries that are U.S. treaty partners, including Belize. Parents are strongly encouraged to contact the Department of State for assistance prior to initiating the Hague process directly with the foreign central authority.

United States Department of State
Office of Children's Issues
2201 C Street, N.W.
Washington, DC 20520
Telephone: 1-888-407-4747
Outside the United States or Canada: 1-202-501-4444
Fax: 202-736-9132

The Belize Central Authority for the Hague Abduction Convention is the Ministry of Human Development and Social Transformation. The role of the Ministry of Human Development and Social Transformation is to perform the duties given to central authorities under the Hague Abduction Convention, including processing Hague Abduction Convention applications for return of and access to children. They can be reached at:

Ministry of Human Development and Social Transformation
West Block, Independence Hill
Belmopan
Telephone: 501-822-2161
or 501-822-2684
Email: secretary@humandev.gov.bz

To initiate a Hague case for return of, or access to, a child in Belize, the left-behind parent must submit a Hague application to the Ministry of Human Development and Social Transformation. The USCA is available to answer questions about the Hague application process, to forward a completed application to the Ministry of Human Development and Social Transformation and to subsequently monitor its progress through the foreign administrative and legal processes. There are no fees for filing Hague applications with either the United States or Belize central authorities. Attorney fees, if necessary, are the sole responsibility of the person hiring the attorney. Additional costs may include airplane tickets for court appearances and for the return of the child, if so ordered.

Return: A parent or legal guardian may file an application under the Hague Abduction Convention for return to the United States of a child abducted to, or wrongfully retained in Belize. The U.S. Department of State can assist parents living in the United States to understand whether the Convention is an available civil remedy and can provide information on the process for submitting a Hague application.

Visitation/Access: A person may file an application under the Hague Abduction Convention for access to a child living in Belize. The criteria for acceptance of a Hague access application vary from country to country. The U.S. Department of State can assist parents living in the United States to understand country-specific criteria and provide information on the process for submitting a Hague application.

Retaining an Attorney: Retaining a local private attorney is required in Belize Hague Abduction Convention return cases if the LBP is not present in Belize. The case will not be filed in court if a LBP lives outside of Belize and does not hire an attorney. LBPs living in Belize may file a case in court without legal representation. Local attorneys are not provided by the Belize Central Authority, and the litigant in a Hague Abduction Convention case in Belize is responsible for all legal fees. U.S. Embassy Belmopan maintains a list of attorneys who specialize in family law on their website. This list is provided as a courtesy service only and does not constitute an endorsement of any individual attorney. The Department of State assumes no responsibility or liability for the professional ability or reputation of, or the quality of services provided by, the persons or firms included in this list. Professional credentials and areas of expertise are provided directly by the lawyers.

Mediation: Mediation may be offered by the Family Court in Belize free of charge, but this service is limited to individuals with cases already being handled by the court. Parents interested in mediation outside of a court case should consult a local attorney.

U.S. Embassy Belmopan
4 Floral Park Road
Belmopan, Cayo
Belize
Telephone: + (501) 822-4011
Fax: + (501) 822-4050
Email: ACSBelize@state.gov

Embassy of Belize
2535 Massachusetts Avenue, NW
Washington D.C., DC 20008
Telephone: (202) 332-9636

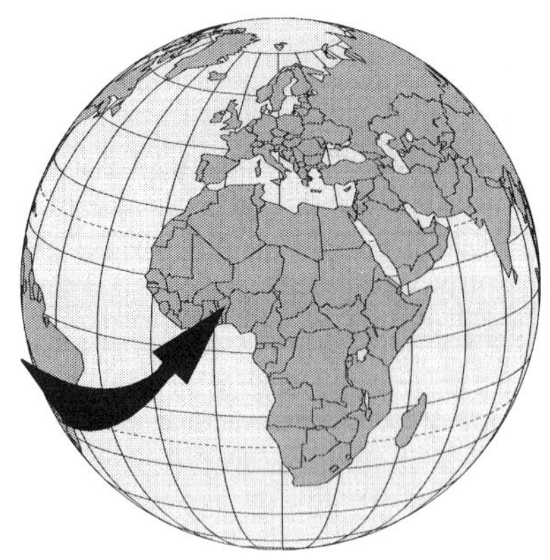

BENIN

Compiled from publications that were available as of February 2013 from the U.S. Department of State, the U.S. Department of Commerce, and the Central Intelligence Agency (CIA). See the introduction to this set for explanatory notes.

Official Name:
Republic of Benin

PROFILE

Geography

Area: total: 112,622 sq km; country comparison to the world: 102; land: 110,622 sq km; water: 2,000 sq km

Major cities: Cotonou (seat of government) 815,000; Porto-Novo (capital) 276,000 (2009)

Climate: tropical; hot, humid in south; semiarid in north

Terrain: mostly flat to undulating plain; some hills and low mountains

People

Nationality: noun: Beninese (singular and plural); adjective: Beninese

Population: 9,598,787 (July 2012 est.)

Population growth rate: 2.877% (2012 est.)

Ethnic groups: Fon and related 39.2%, Adja and related 15.2%, Yoruba and related 12.3%, Bariba and related 9.2%, Peulh and related 7%, Ottamari and related 6.1%, Yoa-Lokpa and related 4%, Dendi and related 2.5%, other 1.6% (includes Europeans), unspecified 2.9% (2002 census)

Religions: Catholic 27.1%, Muslim 24.4%, Vodoun 17.3%, Protestant 10.4% (Celestial 5%, Methodist 3.2%, other Protestant 2.2%), other Christian 5.3%, other 15.5% (2002 census)

Languages: French (official), Fon and Yoruba (most common vernaculars in south), tribal languages (at least six major ones in north)

Literacy: definition: age 15 and over can read and write; total population: 42.4%; male: 55.2%; female: 30.3% (2010 census)

Health: life expectancy at birth: total population: 60.26 years; male: 59 years; female: 61.59 years (2012 est.); Infant mortality rate: total: 60.03 deaths/1,000 live births; male: 63.3 deaths/1,000 live births; female: 56.59 deaths/1,000 live births (2012 est.)

Unemployment rate: NA%

Work force: 3.662 million (2007 est.)

Government

Type: republic

Independence: 1 August 1960

Constitution: adopted by referendum 2 December 1990

Political subdivisions: 12 departments; Alibori, Atakora, Atlantique, Borgou, Collines, Kouffo, Donga, Littoral, Mono, Oueme, Plateau, Zou

Suffrage: 18 years of age; universal

Economy

GDP (purchasing power parity): $15.51 billion (2012 est.); $14.87 billion (2011 est.); $14.43 billion (2010 est.); $14.07 billion (2009 est.)

GDP real growth rate: 3.5% (2012 est.); 3.1% (2011 est.); 2.6% (2010 est.); 2.7% (2009 est.)

GDP per capita (PPP): $1,700 (2012 est.); $1,500 (2011 est.); $1,500 (2010 est.); $1,500 (2009 est.)

Natural resources: small offshore oil deposits, limestone, marble, timber

Agriculture products: cotton, corn, cassava (manioc), yams, beans, palm oil, peanuts, cashews; livestock

Industries: textiles, food processing, construction materials, cement

Exports: $1.578 billion (2012 est.); $1.849 billion (2011 est.)

Exports—commodities: cotton, cashews, shea butter, textiles, palm products, seafood

Exports—partners: India 30.8%, China 20.2%, Indonesia 6.9%, Niger 4.9%, Singapore 4.5%, Nigeria 4.3% (2011)

Imports: ; $1.802 billion (2010 est.); $2.213 billion (2011 est.)

Imports—commodities: foodstuffs, capital goods, petroleum products

Imports—partners: China 31.3%, France 12.3%, UK 7.6%, US 6.8%, India 5.8%, Netherlands 4.6%, Belgium 4.3% (2011)

Debt—external: $953.5 million (31 December 2012 est.)

Exchange rates: Communaute Financiere Africaine francs (XOF) per US dollar; 514.1 (2012 est.); 471.87 (2011 est.); 495.28 (2010 est.); 472.19 (2009); 447.81 (2008)

GEOGRAPHY

Benin, a narrow, north-south strip of land in West Africa, lies between the Equator and the Tropic of Cancer. Benin's latitude ranges from 6o30N to 12o30N and its longitude from 1oE to 3o40E. Benin is bounded by Togo to the west, Burkina Faso and Niger to the north, Nigeria to the east, and the Bight of Benin to the south. With an area of 112,622 square kilometers, roughly the size of Pennsylvania, Benin extends from the Niger River in the north to the Atlantic Ocean in the south, a distance of 700 kilometers (about 500 mi.).

Although the coastline measures 121 kilometers (about 80 mi.), the country measures about 325 kilometers (about 215 mi.) at its widest point. It is one of the smaller countries in West Africa: eight times smaller than Nigeria, its neighbor to the east. It is, however, twice as large as Togo, its neighbor to the west. A relief map of Benin shows that it has little variation in elevation (average elevation 200 meters).

The country can be divided into four main areas from the south to the north. The low-lying, sandy, coastal plain (highest elevation 10 meters) is, at most, 10 kilometers wide. It is marshy and dotted with lakes and lagoons communicating with the ocean. The plateaus of southern Benin (altitude between 20 meters and 200 meters) are split by valleys running north to south along the Couffo, Zou, and Oueme Rivers. An area of flat lands dotted with rocky hills whose altitude seldom reaches 400 meters extends around Nikki and Save. Finally, a range of mountains extends along the northwest border and into Togo; this is the Atacora, with the highest point, Mont Sokbaro, at 658 meters. Two types of landscape predominate in the south. Benin has fields of lying fallow, mangroves, and remnants of large sacred forests. In the rest of the country, the savanna is covered with thorny scrubs and dotted with huge baobab trees. Some forests line the banks of rivers. In the north and the northwest of Benin the Reserve du W du Niger and Pendjari National Park attract tourists eager to see elephants, lions, antelopes, hippos, and monkeys.

Benin's climate is hot and humid. Annual rainfall in the coastal area averages 36 cm. (14 in.), not particularly high for coastal West Africa. Benin has two rainy and two dry seasons. The principal rainy season is from April to late July, with a shorter less intense rainy period from late September to November. The main dry season is from December to April, with a short cooler dry season from late July to early September. Temperatures and humidity are high along the tropical coast. In Cotonou, the average maximum temperature is 31°C (89°F); the minimum is 24°C (75°F).

Variations in temperature increase when moving north through a savanna and plateau toward the Sahel. A dry wind from the Sahara called the Harmattan blows from December to March. Grass dries up, the vegetation turns reddish brown, and a veil of fine dust hangs over the country, causing the skies to be overcast. It also is the season when farmers burn brush in the fields.

PEOPLE

The majority of Benin's people live in the south. About 42 African ethnic groups live in this country; these various groups settled in Benin at different times and also migrated within the country. Ethnic groups include the Yoruba in the southeast (migrated from Nigeria in the 12th century); the Dendi in the north-central area (they came from Mali in the 16th century); the Bariba and the Fulbe (Peul) in the northeast; the Betammaribe and the Somba in the Atacora Range; the Fon in the area around Abomey in the South Central and the Mina, Xueda, and Aja (who came from Togo) on the coast.

Recent migrations have brought other African nationals to Benin that include Nigerians, Togolese, and Malians. The foreign community also includes many Lebanese and Indians involved in trade and commerce. The personnel of the many European embassies and foreign aid missions and of nongovernmental organizations and various missionary groups account for a large number of the European population.

Language

French is the lingua franca of Benin, which has multiple ethnicities with distinct languages. English is not commonly used.

Religion

According to the 2002 census (the most recent official population survey), the population is 27 percent Roman Catholic, 24 percent Muslim, 17 percent Voudon (Voodoo), 6 percent other indigenous religious groups, and 5 percent Celestial Christian. Groups that constitute less than 5 percent each include Methodists, the Church of Jesus Christ of Latter-day Saints (Mormons), Jehovah's Witnesses, Rosicrucians, Baha'is, Baptists, Pentecostals, and those who follow the Unification Church and Eckankar. Seven percent claim no religious affiliation.

Many individuals who identify themselves as Christian or Muslim also practice Voodoo or other traditional religions.

Nearly all Muslims are Sunni. The few Shia Muslims are primarily foreign residents and reside in Benin for commercial reasons.

HISTORY

Benin was the seat of one of the great medieval African kingdoms called Dahomey. Europeans began arriving in the area in the 18th century, as the kingdom of Dahomey was expanding its territory. The Portuguese, the French, and the Dutch established trading posts along the coast (Porto-Novo, Ouidah, Cotonou), and traded weapons for slaves. Slave trade ended in 1848. Then, the French signed treaties with Kings of Abomey

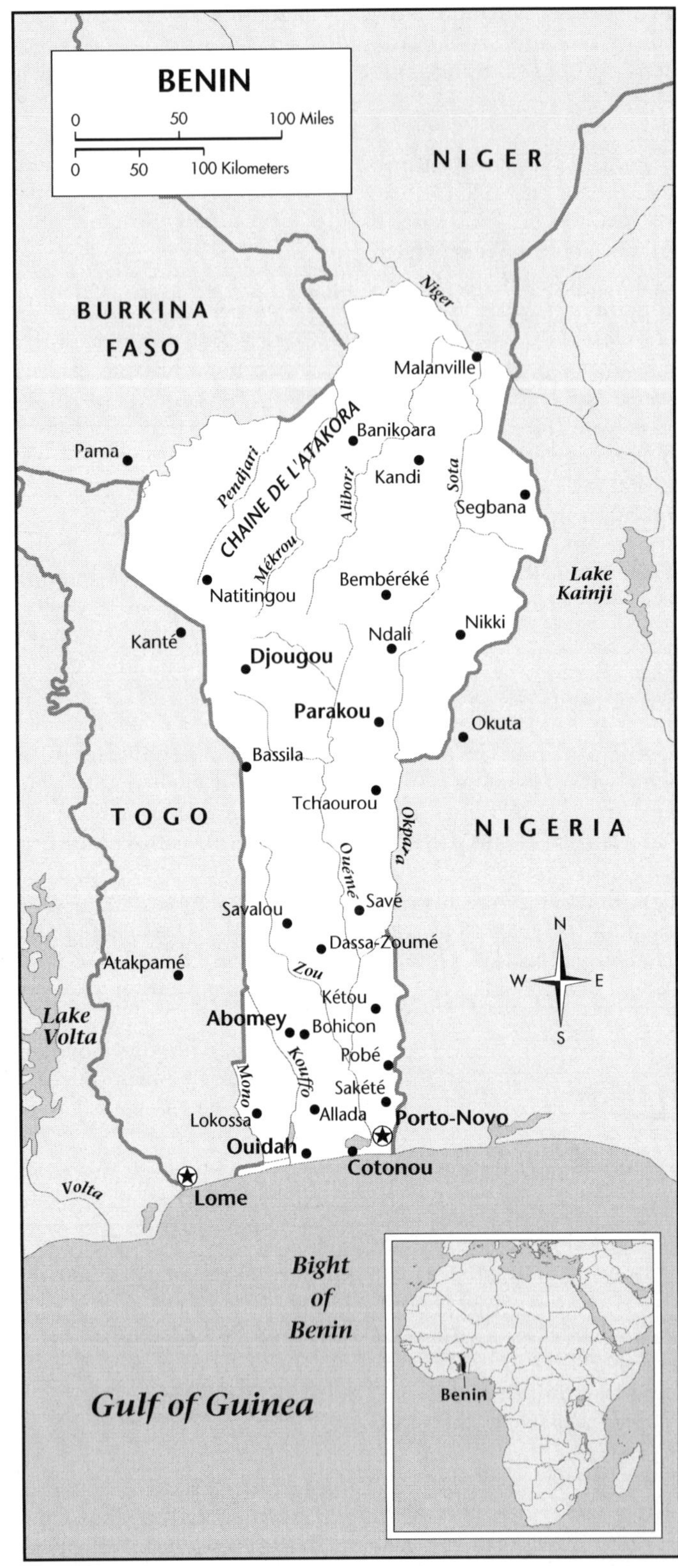

(Guezo, Glele) and Hogbonou (Toffa) to establish French protectorates in the main cities and ports. However, King Behanzin fought the French influence, which cost him deportation to Martinique. As of 1900, the territory became a French colony ruled by a French Governor. Expansion continued to the North (kingdoms of Parakou, Nikki, Kandi), up to the border with former Upper Volta. On December 4, 1958, it became the Republique du Dahomey, self-governing within the French community, and on August 1, 1960, the Republic of Benin gained full independence from France.

Post-Independence Politics

Between 1960 and 1972, a succession of military coups brought about many changes of government. The last of these brought to power Major Mathieu Kerekou as the head of a regime professing strict Marxist-Leninist principles. The Revolutionary Party of the People of Benin (PRPB) remained in complete power until the beginning of the 1990s.

Kerekou, encouraged by France and other democratic powers, convened a national conference that introduced a new democratic constitution and held presidential and legislative elections. Kerekou's principal opponent at the 1991 presidential poll, and the ultimate victor, was Prime Minister Nicephore Soglo. Supporters of Soglo also secured a majority in the National Assembly. In the 1996 presidential poll Kerekou defeated Soglo, and was reelected in 2001. At the end of his second term in 2006, Kerekou successfully handed power over to Boni Yayi, elected with 75% of the votes cast.

In December 2002, Benin held its first municipal elections since before the institution of Marxism-Leninism. The process was smooth with the significant exception of the 12th district council for Cotonou, the contest that would ultimately determine who would be selected for the mayoralty of the capital city. That vote was marred by irregularities, and the electoral commission was forced to repeat that single election. Nicephore Soglo's Renaisance du Benin (RB) party won the new vote, paving the way for the former president to be elected Mayor of Cotonou by the new city council in February 2002.

On April 20 and May 1, 2008, Benin held its second local and municipal elections, which were marred by fraud allegations and irregularities. Voters filed appeals with the

Supreme Court, which nullified results in a number of communes and ordered new elections and recounting of votes in constituencies where results were contested.

Former West African Development Bank Director Boni Yayi won the March 2006 election for the presidency in a field of 26 candidates. International observers including the United Nations, the Economic Community of West African States (ECOWAS), and others called the election free, fair, and transparent. President Kerekou was barred from running under the 1990 constitution due to term and age limits. President Yayi was inaugurated on April 6, 2006.

Benin held legislative elections on March 31, 2007 for the 83 seats in the National Assembly. The "Force Cowrie for an Emerging Benin" (FCBE), a coalition of parties closely linked to President Yayi, won a plurality of the seats in the National Assembly, providing the president with considerable influence over the legislative agenda.

The "G-13" deputies from minor political parties who had joined the FCBE to help President Yayi obtain a majority in the National Assembly subsequently left this coalition and joined undeclared opposition parties, including G4 and Force Cle, forming an unstable though blocking majority.

Seeking to improve the electoral system, the Government of Benin, with the support of international donors, developed a permanent digital voter's list in 2010. In the first election since the list was created, incumbent President Yayi won a second term with 53% of the vote in March 2011.

The United Nations, ECOWAS, the African Union, and the international community praised Benin for once again holding fair and transparent elections. Legislative elections were held on April 30, 2011. The FCBE won 41 out of the 83 seats in the National Assembly.

GOVERNMENT AND POLITICAL CONDITIONS

Benin is a constitutional democracy. On March 13, President Boni Yayi won a second, and final, five-year term in multiparty elections. In the April 30 legislative elections, President Yayi's supporting coalition, Cowry Force for an Emerging Benin, won 41 of 83 seats in the National Assembly and formed a majority coalition with the Renaissance of Benin Party and other minor supporting parties for a total of 61 seats. As a result the coalition controlled the Bureau of the National Assembly with six of the seven seats. International observers viewed both the presidential and legislative elections as free, fair, and transparent.

Recent Elections

The country held presidential elections on March 13, 2011 and legislative elections on April 30. International observers viewed both the presidential and legislative elections as generally free and fair. Both elections were hampered by delays on the days of the vote, usually in receiving voting materials or due to polling staff arriving late. Even with delays, all polling stations remained open the full nine hours required by law. There were no reports of eligible voters unable to cast ballots.

Political Parties: Parties could freely run candidates for election. There were no government restrictions on the political opposition. No single party or group has recently dominated politics. For legislative elections, all candidates must be associated with a political party; there were no independent candidates.

Participation of Women and Minorities: There were eight women out of 83 members in the National Assembly and eight female ministers in the 26-member cabinet. The Constitutional Court had two women among its seven justices. The country has no majority ethnic group. Various ethnic groups were well represented in government agencies, including the civil service, and the armed forces. Nine cabinet ministers were from the Bariba, Somba, and Dendi ethnic groups; eleven were from the Fon, Goun, and Adja ethnic groups; and six were from the Yoruba and Nago ethnic groups.

Principal Government Officials

Last Updated: 1/31/2013

Pres.: **Thomas YAYI Boni**

Prime Min.: **Pascal KOUPAKI**

Min. of State of National Defense: **Issifou Kgui N'DOURO**

Min. of Admin. & Institutional Reform: **Martial SOUNTON**

Min. of Agriculture, Livestock, & Fisheries: **Kate SADAI**

Min. of Air Transport & Public Works: **Nicaise Kotchami FAGNON**

Min. of Communications & Information & Information Technology:**Max AWEK**

Min. for Coordination of Govt. Action, Evaluation of Public Policy, Privatization, & Social Dialogue: **Pascal KOUPAKI**

Min. of Culture, Literacy, & Tourism: **Valentin DJENONTIN**

Min. of Decentralization, Local Government, Administration, & Territorial Management: **Raphael EDOU**

Min. of Economy & Finance: **Adidjatou MATHYS**

Min. of Energy, Water, & Mines: **Jonas Aliou GBIAN**

Min. of Environment, Housing, & Urban Development:**Blaise Ahanhanzo GLELE**

Min. of Family, Social Affairs, National Solidarity, Disabled Persons, & the Elderly: **Fatouma Amadou DJIBRIL**

Min. of Foreign Affairs, African Integration, Francophonie, & Beninese Diaspora: **Nassirou Arifari BAKO**

Min. of Health: **Akoko Kinde GAZARD**

Min. of Higher Education & Scientific Research: **Francois ABIOLA**

Min. of Industry, Commerce, Small & Medium Enterprises:**Madina SEPHOU**

Min. of Interior & Public Security: **Benoit Assounan DEGLA**

Min. of Justice, Legislation, & Human Rights, & Keeper of the Seals:**Marie Elise GBEDO**

Min. of Labor & Public Service: **Kora Madina MEMOUNA**

Min. of Maritime Economy & Govt. Spokesman: **Jean-Michel ABIMBOLA**

Min. of Microfinance: **Reckya MADOUGOU**

Min. of Planning: **Marcel de SOUZA**

Min. of Primary Education: **Eric N'DAH**

Min. of Public Works & Transportation: **Lambert KOTY**

Min. of Relations With Institutions & Religions: **Safiatu BASSABI**

Min. of Secondary Education, Technical & Professional Training, & Integration of Youth:**Ake NATONDE**

Min. of Urban Development, Housing, Land Reform, & Erosion Prevention:**Francois Gbendoukpo NOUDEGBESSI**

Min. of Youth, Sports, & Leisure: **Didier APLOGAN**

Min.-Del. to the Pres. in Charge of Communications & Information Technologies: **Desire ADADJA**

Min.-Del. to the Pres. in Charge of Maritime Economy: **Issa BADAROU SOULE**

Governor, Central Bank: **Charles Konan BANNY**

Ambassador to the US: **Cyrille Segbe OGUIN**

Permanent Representative to the UN, New York: **Jean-Francis Regis ZINSOU**

ECONOMY

The economy of Benin remains underdeveloped and dependent on subsistence agriculture, cotton production, and regional trade. Growth in real output had averaged almost 4% before the global recession but fell to 2.7% in 2009 and 2.6% in 2010. Inflation has subsided over the past several years.

In order to raise growth, Benin plans to attract more foreign investment, place more emphasis on tourism, facilitate the development of new food processing systems and agricultural products, and encourage new information and communication technology. Specific projects to improve the business climate by reforms to the land tenure system, the commercial justice system, and the financial sector were included in Benin's $307 million Millennium Challenge Account grant signed in February 2006. The 2001 privatization policy continues in telecommunications, water, electricity, and agriculture.

The Paris Club and bilateral creditors have eased the external debt situation with Benin benefiting from a G-8 debt reduction announced in July 2005, while pressing for more rapid structural reforms. An insufficient electrical supply continues to adversely affect Benin's economic growth though the government recently has taken steps to increase domestic power production. Private foreign direct investment is small, and foreign aid accounts for the majority of investment in infrastructure projects.

Cotton, a key export, suffered from flooding in 2010–11, but high prices supported export earnings. The government agreed to 25% increase in civil servant salaries in 2011, following a series of strikes, has increased pressure on the national budget. Benin has appealed for international assistance to mitigate piracy against commercial shipping in its territory.

Labor Conditions

The labor code prohibits the employment or apprenticeship of children under 14 years of age in any enterprise; however, children between 12 and 14 years may perform domestic work and temporary or seasonal light work if it does not interfere with their compulsory schooling. Child labor remained a problem due in part to limited government enforcement of the law. To help support their families, children of both sexes—including those as young as seven—continued to work on family farms, in small businesses, on construction sites in urban areas, in public markets as street vendors, and as domestic servants under the practice of vidomegon.

A majority of children working as apprentices were under the legal age for apprenticeship of 14, including children working in construction, car and motorcycle repair, hairdressing, and dressmaking. Children worked as laborers with adults in quarries in many areas. Forced child labor, including street children engaged in prostitution, street hawking, and begging, was a problem.

Children under age 14 worked in either the formal or informal sectors in the following activities: agriculture, hunting and fishing, industry, construction and public works, trade/vending and food/beverage, transportation, and communication and other services, including employment as household staff. Some parents indentured their children to "agents" recruiting farm hands or domestic workers, often on the understanding that the children's wages would be sent to the parents. In some cases these agents took the children to neighboring countries, including Nigeria, Cote d'Ivoire, Togo, and Ghana, for labor. Many rural parents sent their children to cities to live with relatives or family friends to perform domestic chores in return for receiving an education. Host families did not always honor their part of the arrangement, and abuse of child domestic servants was a problem.

The government set minimum wage scales for a number of occupations. The minimum wage was 30,000 CFA ($66) per month. Many workers had to supplement their wages by subsistence farming or informal sector trade. Most workers in the wage sector earned more than the minimum wage; many domestics and other laborers in the informal sector earned less. The Office of Labor enforced the minimum wage; however, its efforts were impeded by the small number of labor inspectors. Significant parts of the work force and foreign workers were not covered by minimum wage scales.

The labor code establishes a workweek of between 40 and 46 hours, depending on the type of work, and provides for at least one 24-hour rest period per week. Domestic and agricultural workers frequently worked 70 hours or more per week, above the maximum provided for under the labor code of 12 hours per day or 60 hours per week. The labor code also mandates premium pay for overtime and prohibits excessive compulsory overtime. The authorities generally enforced legal limits on workweeks in the formal sector. The government did not effectively monitor or control foreign or migrant workers' conditions of work.

U.S.-BENINESE RELATIONS

The United States established diplomatic relations with Benin (then called Dahomey) in 1960, following its independence from France. Between 1960 and 1972, a succession of military coups brought about many changes of government, followed by one-party, Marxist-Leninist rule until the early 1990s, when the country transitioned to a democratic government. In the years since then, the history of bilateral relations has been excellent. The United States supports the consolidation of democracy and economic liberalization in Benin. Presidential and legislative elections in 2011 were peaceful and benefited from strong citizen participation and robust press freedom. However, poor health care, low quality of public education, and insufficiently transparent governance persist as obstacles to national development.

U.S. Assistance to Benin

The United States supports efforts to improve the health of Beninese families by reducing the malaria disease burden, improving the health of mothers and young children, and strengthening the health system. U.S. assistance also provides support to Benin's defense and military capacity enhancement, enabling the country to maintain domestic peace and security while contributing to regional stability.

Bilateral Economic Relations

Benin is eligible for preferential trade benefits under the African Growth and Opportunity Act. Trade between Benin and the United States is small, but interest in U.S. products is growing. U.S. exports to Benin include vehicles, oil, machinery, low-value shipments, and perfumery/cosmetics. U.S. imports from Benin include Shea butter and cashews. The United States aims to promote increased trade with Benin and thereby with Benin's neighbors, particularly Nigeria, Niger, and Burkina Faso, whose imports pass through Benin. The United States also works to stimulate U.S. investment in key sectors such as energy, telecommunications, and transportation. Benin and the United States have a bilateral investment agreement. The United States also has a trade and investment framework agreement with the West African Economic and Monetary Union, of which Benin is a member.

Benin's Membership in International Organizations

Benin and the United States belong to a number of the same international organizations, including the United Nations, International Monetary Fund, World Bank, and World Trade Organization. Benin also is an observer to the Organization of American States.

Bilateral Representation

Benin maintains an embassy in the United States at 2124 Kalorama Road, Washington, DC 20008, tel. 202-232-6656.

Principal U.S. Embassy Officials

Last Updated: 1/14/2013

COTONOU (E) Rue Caporal Bernard Anani, (229) 21 30 06 50, Fax (229) 21 30 19 74, INMARSAT Tel 762768573, 763682952, 763682956, Workweek: Mon-Thurs 8:00-5:30, Fri 7:30-1:30, Website: http://cotonou.usembassy.gov/

AMB OMS:	Tammy Lubulu
CDC:	Peter Thomas
MGT:	Greg Keller
PAO/ADV:	Alexis Wolff
POL/ECON:	Marilyn Gayton
POL/MIL:	Mackenzie Rowe
AMB:	Michael A Raynor
CON:	William Astillero
DCM:	Susan Tuller
PAO:	Doug Johnston
GSO:	Wesley Shelton
RSO:	Billy Alfano
AFSA:	Shirpaul Mclaughlin
AID:	Kevin Armstrong
CLO:	Jennie Orloff
EEO:	Tbd
FMO:	David Hamiel
ICASS Chair:	Kevin Armstrong
IMO:	Bill Bridgeland
ISSO:	Bill Bridgeland
State ICASS:	Tbd

TRAVEL

Consular Information Sheet

January 20, 2012

Country Description: Benin is a developing country in West Africa. Its political capital is Porto Novo; however, its administrative capital, Cotonou, is Benin's largest city and the site of most government, commercial, and tourist activity.

Smart Traveler Enrollment Program (STEP)/Embassy Locations: If you are going to live in or visit Benin, please take the time to tell our Embassy about your trip. If you enroll, we can keep you up to date with important safety and security announcements. It will also help your friends and family get in touch with you in an emergency. The Embassy is located at Rue Caporal Bernard Anani in Cotonou. The Embassy's mailing address is: B.P. 2012, Cotonou, Benin; Telephone: The 24-hour telephone numbers are (229) 21-30-06-50, 21-30-05-13, and 21-30-17-92. Facsimile: (229) 21-30-66-82.

Entry/Exit Requirements for U.S. Citizens: A passport and visa are required. Visas are not routinely available at the airport. Visitors to Benin should also carry the WHO Yellow Card ("Carte Jaune") indicating that they have been vaccinated for yellow fever. Visit the Embassy of Benin website for the most current visa information. The Embassy is located at: 2124 Kalorama Road, NW, Washington, DC 20008; tel.: 202-232-6656.

The U.S. Department of State is unaware of any HIV/AIDS entry restrictions for visitors to or foreign residents of Benin.

Threats to Safety and Security: U.S. citizens should avoid crowds, political rallies, and street demonstrations and maintain security awareness at all times.

U.S. citizens should not walk on the beach, at any time of day, alone. It is also highly recommended not to carry a passport or valuables when walking in any part of the city. Travelers should carry a notarized photocopy of the photo page of their passport (see Crime section). They should not walk around the city after dark, and should take particular care to avoid the beach and isolated areas near the beach after dark.

The ocean currents along the coast are extremely strong and treacherous, with rough surf and a strong undertow, and several people drown each year.

Stay up to date by:

- Bookmarking our Bureau of Consular Affairs website, which contains the current Travel Warnings and Travel Alerts as well as the Worldwide Caution.
- Following us on Twitter and the Bureau of Consular Affairs page on Facebook as well.
- Downloading our free Smart Traveler IPhone App to have travel information at your fingertips.
- Calling 1-888-407-4747 toll-free within the United States and Canada, or a regular toll line, 1-202-501-4444, from other countries.
- Taking some time before travel to consider your personal security.

Crime: Street crime is a significant problem in Cotonou. Robbery and muggings occur along the Boulevard de France (the beach road by the Marina and Novotel Hotels) and on the beaches near hotels frequented by international visitors. Most of the reported incidents involve the use of force, often by armed persons, with occasional minor injury to the victim. Travelers should avoid isolated and poorly lit areas and should not walk around the city or the beaches between dusk and dawn. U.S. diplomatic personnel are prohibited from visiting the Dantokpa market between the hours of dusk and dawn. Even during daylight hours, foreigners on the beach near Cotonou are frequently victims of robberies. When visiting the beach, travelers should not carry valuables, and should carry only a photocopy of their passport. If you are a victim of crime, you should contact the U.S. Embassy immediately.

There has been a continued increase in the number of robberies after dark, both within metropolitan Cotonou and on highways and rural roads outside of major metropolitan areas. Motorists are urged to be wary of the risk of carjacking in both urban and rural areas. Keep the windows of your vehicle rolled up and the doors locked, and stay alert for signs of suspicious behavior by other motorists or pedestrians that may lead to carjacking, such as attempts to stop a moving vehicle for no obvious reason. Travelers should avoid driving outside the city of Cotonou after dark and should exercise extreme caution when driving inside of Cotonou after dark (see Traffic Safety and Road Conditions below). Overland travel to Nigeria is dangerous near the Benin/Nigeria border due to unofficial checkpoints and highway banditry.

Travelers should exercise extreme caution when using credit cards and automated teller machines (ATMs) in Benin due to a high rate of fraud. Perpetrators of business and other kinds of fraud often target foreigners, including U.S. citizens. While such fraud schemes in the past have been largely associated with Nigeria, they are now prevalent throughout West Africa, including Benin, and are more frequently perpetrated by Beninese criminals. Business scams are not always easy to recognize, and any unsolicited business proposal should be carefully scrutinized. There are, nevertheless, some indicators that are warnings of a probable scam. Look out for:

- Any offer of a substantial percentage of a very large sum of money to be transferred into your account, in return for your "discretion" or "confidentiality;"
- Any deal that seems too good to be true;
- Requests for signed and stamped, blank letterhead or invoices, or for bank account or credit card information;
- Requests for urgent air shipment, accompanied by an instrument of payment whose genuineness cannot immediately be established;
- Solicitations claiming the soliciting party has personal ties to high government officials;
- Requests for payment, in advance, of transfer taxes or incorporation fees;
- Statements that your name was provided to the soliciting party either by someone you do not know or by "a reliable contact;"
- Promises of advance payment for services to the Beninese government; and
- Any offer of a charitable donation.

These scams, which may appear to be legitimate business deals requiring advance payments on contracts, pose a danger of both financial loss and physical harm. Recently, more U.S. citizens have been targeted. The perpetrators of such scams sometimes pose as attorneys. One common ploy is to request fees for "registration" with fictitious government offices or regulatory authorities. The best way to avoid becoming a victim of advance-fee fraud is common sense—

if something looks too good to be true, it probably is. Travelers should carefully check out any unsolicited business proposal originating in Benin before committing funds, providing goods or services, or undertaking travel. For additional information, please see the Department of State's webpage on International Financial Scams. Scams may also involve persons posing as singles on Internet dating sites or as online acquaintances who then get into trouble and require money to be "rescued." If someone you met online asks you to send them money, please contact the U.S. Embassy before doing so.

Don't buy counterfeit and pirated goods, even if they are widely available. Not only are the bootlegs illegal in the United States, if you purchase them you may also be breaking local law.

Over the last six months of 2011, there has been an increase of reports of pirate attacks off the coast of Benin. The attacks have been focused on chemical tanker ships, not container or other types of boats. It is unlikely that any tourist would become a victim of piracy, but caution should be used if approached by an unknown vessel while at sea. If you see any suspected pirates, do not approach them but contact port officials, local police, and the U.S. Embassy.

Victims of Crime: If you are the victim of a crime abroad, you should contact the local police and the nearest U.S. embassy or consulate. We can:

- Replace a stolen passport.
- Help you find appropriate medical care if you are the victim of violent crimes such as assault or rape.
- Put you in contact with the appropriate police authorities, and if you want us to, we can contact family members or friend.
- Help you understand the local criminal justice process and direct you to local attorneys, although it is important to remember that local authorities are responsible for investigating and prosecuting the crime.

The local equivalent to the "911" emergency line in Benin is 117 for Police and 118 for Fire.

Criminal Penalties: While you are traveling in Benin, you are subject to its laws and regulations even if you are a U.S. citizen. Foreign laws and legal systems can be vastly different from those in the United States and may not afford the protections available to the individual under U.S. law. Penalties for breaking the law can be more severe than in the United States for similar offenses. Engaging in sexual conduct with children or using or disseminating child pornography in a foreign country is a crime prosecutable in the United States.

While some countries will automatically notify the nearest U.S. embassy or consulate if a U.S. citizen is detained or arrested in a foreign country, that might not always be the case. To ensure that the United States is aware of your circumstances, request that the police and prison officials notify the nearest U.S. embassy or consulate as soon as you are arrested or detained overseas.

Special Circumstances: U.S. citizens are advised to keep a notarized photocopy of the photo page of their passport with them at all times when traveling in Benin.

The Embassy has had a few reports of officials requesting a "gift" to facilitate official administrative matters (e.g., customs entry). Such requests should be politely but firmly declined.

It is prohibited to photograph government buildings and other official sites, such as military installations, without the formal consent of the Government of Benin. In general, it is always best to be courteous and ask permission before taking pictures of people. Beninese citizens may react angrily if photographed without their prior approval.

Obtaining customs clearance at the port of Cotonou for donated items shipped to Benin from the United States may be a lengthy process. In addition, to obtain a waiver of customs duties on donated items, the donating organization must secure prior written approval from the Government of Benin. Please contact the U.S. Embassy in Cotonou for more detailed information.

Accessibility: While in Benin, individuals with disabilities may find accessibility and accommodation very different from what you find in the United States. The condition of the sidewalks, where they exist, is often poor. It is unusual to find curb cuts or other modifications for wheelchairs. Cars and motorcycles often park on sidewalks, making navigation difficult. Only major roads are paved. The unpaved roads may be full of holes, rocks, and other debris. There are few marked pedestrian crossings. Some hotels, restaurants, and other stores are accessible via wheelchair, but many are not. The primary method of public transportation is the zemidjan (moped taxi). The passenger rides in the back and there are no special accommodations for people with disabilities.

Discrimination against persons with physical and mental disabilities is not prohibited by law, and there are no legal requirements for the construction or alteration of buildings to permit access for persons with disabilities. The labor code includes provisions to protect the rights of workers with disabilities, but they are enforced with limited effectiveness.

Medical Facilities and Health Information: Medical facilities in Benin are limited and not all medicines are available. Travelers should carry their own supplies of prescription drugs and preventive medicines. Not all medicines and prescription drugs available in Benin are USFDA-approved. U.S. citizens should be prepared to pay for medical services, including consulations and tests, before medical advice or treatment is received. Credit cards are not accepted.

Information on vaccinations and other health precautions, such as safe food and water precautions and insect bite protection, may be obtained from the Centers for Disease Control and Prevention's (CDC) hotline for international travelers at 1-877-FYI-TRIP (1-877-394-8747) or via the CDC website. For information about outbreaks of infectious diseases abroad, consult the infectious diseases section of the World Health Organization (WHO) website. The WHO website also contains additional health information for travelers, including detailed country-specific health information.

Malaria is a serious risk to travelers to Benin. For information on malaria, its prevention, protection from insect bites, and anti-malarial drugs, please visit the CDC's malaria webpages.

Medical Insurance: You can't assume your insurance will go with you when you travel. It's very important to find out BEFORE you leave whether or not your medical insurance will cover you overseas. You need to ask your insurance company two questions:

- Does my policy apply when I'm out of the United States?
- Will it cover emergencies like a trip to a foreign hospital or a medical evacuation?

In many places, doctors and hospitals still expect payment in cash at the time of service. Your regular U.S. health insurance may not cover doctor and hospital visits in other countries. If your policy doesn't go with you when you travel, it's a very good idea to take out another one for your trip.

Traffic Safety and Road Conditions: While in Benin, you may encounter road conditions that differ significantly from those in the United States. The information below concerning Benin is provided for general reference only, and may not be totally accurate in a particular location or circumstance.

With the exception of the road linking Cotonou in the south to Malanville on the border with Niger in the north, and from Parakou in central Benin to Natitingou in the northwestern part of the country, roads in Benin are generally in poor condition and are often impassable during the rainy season. Benin's unpaved roads vary widely in quality; deep sand and potholes are common. During the rainy season from mid-June to mid-September, dirt roads often become impassable. Four-wheel drive vehicles with full spare tires and emergency equipment are recommended.

Most of the main streets in Cotonou are paved, but side streets are often made of dirt and have deep potholes. Traffic moves on the right, as in the United States. Cotonou has no public transportation system; many Beninese people rely on bicycles, mopeds, motorbikes, and zemidjans. U.S. Embassy personnel are required to wear safety helmets when on a motorcycle and are strongly discouraged from using zemidjans. Travelers using zemidjans, particularly at night, are much more vulnerable to being mugged, assaulted or robbed. Buses and bush taxis offer service in the interior.

Gasoline smuggled from Nigeria is widely available in glass bottles and jugs at informal roadside stands throughout Cotonou and much of the country. This gasoline is of unreliable quality, often containing water or other contaminants that can damage or disable your vehicle. Drivers should purchase fuel only from official service stations. There are periodic gas shortages, which can be particularly acute in the north of the country where there are few service stations.

U.S. citizens traveling by road should exercise extreme caution. Poorly maintained and overloaded transport and cargo vehicles frequently break down and cause accidents. Drivers often place branches or leaves in the road to indicate a broken down vehicle is in the roadway. Undisciplined drivers move unpredictably through traffic. Construction work is often poorly indicated. Speed bumps, commonly used on paved roads in and near villages, are seldom indicated. Drivers must be on guard against people and livestock wandering into or across the roads. Nighttime driving is particularly hazardous as vehicles frequently lack headlights and/or taillights, and brake lights are often burned out.

With few exceptions, Cotonou and other cities lack street lighting, and lighting on roads between population centers is non-existent. The U.S. Embassy in Cotonou prohibits non-essential travel outside of metropolitan areas after dusk by diplomatic personnel and strongly urges all U.S. citizens to avoid night driving as well. There have been numerous carjackings and robberies on roads in Benin after dark, several of which resulted in murder when the driver refused to comply with the assailants' demands. The national police periodically conduct vehicle checks at provisional roadblocks in an effort to improve road safety and reduce the increasing number of carjackings. When stopped at such a roadblock, you must have all of the vehicle's documentation available to present to the authorities.

Aviation Safety Oversight: As there is no non-stop commercial air service to the United States by carriers of Benin, the U.S. Federal Aviation Administration (FAA) has not assessed the government of Benin's Civil Aviation Authority for compliance with International Civil Aviation Organization (ICAO) aviation safety standards. Further information may be found on the FAA's safety assessment page.

Children's Issues: Please see the U.S. Dept. of State Office of Children's Issues web pages on intercountry adoption and international parental child abduction.

Intercountry Adoption

April 2012

The information in this section has been edited from the latest report available as of February 2013 from the State Department Bureau of Con-

sular Affairs, Office of Overseas Citizens Services. For more information, please read the *Intercountry Adoption* section of this book and review current reports online at http://adoption.state.gov.

Benin is not party to the Hague Convention on Protection of Children and Co-operation in Respect of Intercountry Adoption (the Hague Adoption Convention). Intercountry adoptions of children from non-Hague countries are processed in accordance with 8 Code of Federal Regulations, Section 204.3 as it relates to orphans as defined under the Immigration and Nationality Act, Section 101(b)(1)(F).

Below is the limited adoption information that the Department has obtained from the adoption authority of Benin. U.S. citizens adopting children from Benin, as well as U.S. citizen prospective adoptive parents living in Benin who would like to adopt from the United States or from a third country, should contact the adoption authority of Benin to inquire about applicable laws and procedures. See contact information below.

The type of adoption in Benin that resembles U.S. adoption practice most closely is adoption plenière ("Plenary Adoption"). Adoption pleniere provides the same rights and privileges to an adopted child as biological children of the adopting parent(s). Benin may have particular requirements on the age, marital status and family size for prospective adoptive parents, as well as requirements for which children can be adopted. Prospective adoptive parents should verify these requirements directly with the adoption authority of Benin.

Caution: Prospective adoptive parents should be aware that not all children in orphanages or children's homes are adoptable. In many countries, birth parents place their child(ren) temporarily in an orphanage or children's home due to financial or other hardship, with the intention of returning for the child when they are able to do so. In such cases, the birth parent(s) rarely would have relinquished their parental rights or consented to their child(ren)'s adoption.

Benin's Adoption Authority:
Ministère de la Famille et de la Solidarité Nationale
Direction de la Famille de l'Enfance et de l'Adolescence (D.F.E.A.)
Address: 01 B.P. 2802 Cotonou, Bénin
Tel: (229) 21 31 67 07/21 31 67 08/21 30 03 33
Fax: (229) 21 31 64 62
Email: mfpss2003@yahoo.fr/mfpss@intnet.bj
Internet: http://www.gouv.bj/spip.php?rubrique170

BERMUDA

Compiled from publications that were available as of February 2013 from the U.S. Department of State, the U.S. Department of Commerce, and the Central Intelligence Agency (CIA). See the introduction to this set for explanatory notes.

Official Name:
Bermuda

PROFILE

Geography

Area: total: 54 sq km; country comparison to the world: 232; land: 54 sq km; water: 0 sq km

Major cities: Hamilton (capital) 12,000 (2009)

Climate: subtropical; mild, humid; gales, strong winds common in winter

Terrain: low hills separated by fertile depressions

People

Nationality: noun: Bermudian(s); adjective: Bermudian

Population: 69,080 (July 2012 est.)

Population growth rate: 0.572% (2012 est.)

Ethnic groups: black 54.8%, white 34.1%, mixed 6.4%, other races 4.3%, unspecified 0.4% (2000 census)

Religions: Protestant 52% (Anglican 23%, African Methodist Episcopal 11%, other Protestant 18%), Roman Catholic 15%, other 12%, unaffiliated 6%, unspecified 1%, none 14% (2000 census)

Languages: English (official), Portuguese

Literacy: definition: age 15 and over can read and write; total population: 98%; male: 98%; female: 99% (2005 est.)

Health: life expectancy at birth: total population: 80.82 years; male: 77.6 years; female: 84.1 years (2012 est.); Infant mortality rate: total: 2.47 deaths/1,000 live births; male: 2.58 deaths/1,000 live births; female: 2.36 deaths/1,000 live births (2012 est.)

Unemployment rate: 2.1% (2004 est.)

Work force: 38,360 (2004)

Government

Type: parliamentary; self-governing territory

Independence: none

Constitution: 8 June 1968; amended 1989 and 2003

Political subdivisions: 9 parishes and 2 municipalities; Devonshire, Hamilton, Hamilton, Paget, Pembroke, Saint George, Saint George's, Sandys, Smith's, Southampton, Warwick

Suffrage: 18 years of age; universal

Economy

GDP (purchasing power parity): $4.5 billion (2004 est.)

GDP real growth rate: 4.6% (2004 est.)

GDP per capita (PPP): $69,900 (2004 est.)

Natural resources: limestone, pleasant climate fostering tourism

Agriculture products: bananas, vegetables, citrus, flowers; dairy products, honey

Industries: international business, tourism, light manufacturing

Exports: $16 million (2011 est.); $15 million (2010 est.)

Exports—commodities: reexports of pharmaceuticals

Imports: $940 million (2011 est.); $988 million (2010 est.)

Imports—commodities: clothing, fuels, machinery and transport equipment, construction materials, chemicals, food and live animals

Debt—external: $160 million (FY99/00)

Exchange rates: Bermudian dollars (BMD) per US dollar—1 (2011); 1 2010

HISTORICAL HIGHLIGHTS

Bermuda is an archipelago consisting of seven main islands and many smaller islands and islets lying about 1,050 kilometers (650 mi.) east of North Carolina. The main islands—with hilly terrain and subtropical climate—are clustered together, connected by bridges, and are considered to be a geographic unit, referred to as the Island of Bermuda.

Bermuda was discovered in 1503 by a Spanish explorer, Juan de Bermudez, who made no attempt to land because of the treacherous reef surrounding the uninhabited islands.

In 1609, a group of British colonists led by George Somers was shipwrecked and stranded on the islands for 10 months. Their reports aroused great interest about the islands in England, and in 1612 King James extended the Charter of the Virginia Company to include them. Later that year, about 60 British colonists arrived and founded the town of St. George, the oldest continuously inhabited English-speaking settlement in the Western Hemisphere. When representative government was introduced to Bermuda in 1620, it became a self-governing colony.

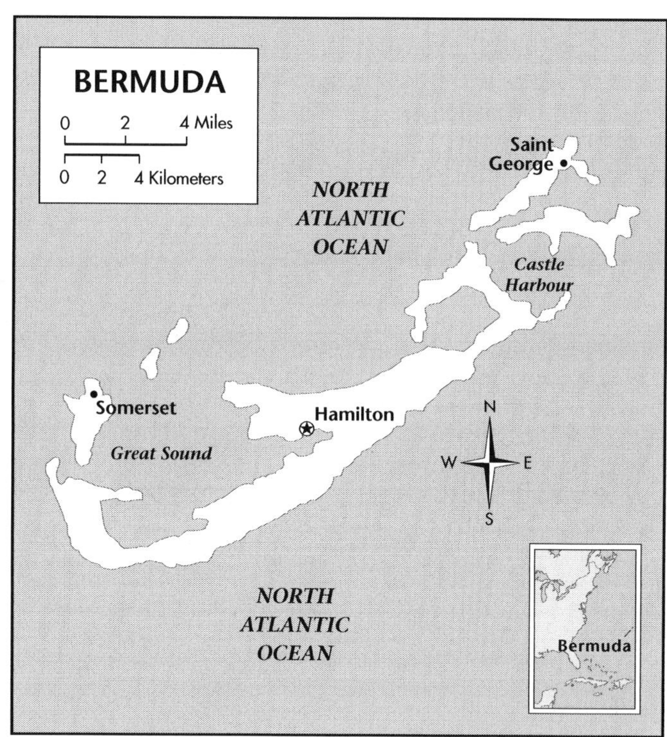

Due to the islands' isolation, for many years Bermuda remained an outpost of 17th-century British civilization, with an economy based on the use of the islands' endemic cedar trees for shipbuilding and the salt trade. Hamilton, a centrally located port founded in 1790, became the seat of government in 1815.

Slaves from Africa were brought to Bermuda soon after the colony was established. The slave trade was outlawed in Bermuda in 1807, and all slaves were freed in 1834. Today, about 60% of Bermudians are of African descent. The establishment of a formal constitution in 1968 bolstered internal self-government; debate about independence ensued, although a 1995 independence referendum was defeated. The government re-opened the independence debate in 2004.

GOVERNMENT AND POLITICAL CONDITIONS

Bermuda is the oldest self-governing overseas territory in the British Commonwealth. Its 1968 constitution provides the island with formal responsibility for internal self-government, while the British Government retains responsibility for external affairs, defense, and security. The Bermudian Government is consulted on any international negotiations affecting the territory. Bermuda participates, through British delegations, in the UN and some of its specialized and related agencies.

Unsatisfied aspirations, particularly among young blacks, led to a brief civil disturbance in December 1977, following the execution of two men found guilty of the 1972-73 assassinations of Governor Richard Sharples and four others. In the 1980s, the increasing prosperity of Bermudians, combined with limited land area, caused a housing shortage. Despite a general strike in 1981 and economic downturn in the early 1980s, Bermuda's social, political, and economic institutions remained stable.

Government Structure

Queen Elizabeth II is head of state and is represented in Bermuda by a governor, whom she appoints. Internally, Bermuda has a parliamentary system of government. The premier is head of government and leader of the majority party in the House of Assembly. The cabinet is composed of ministers selected by the premier from among members of the House of Assembly and the Senate. The 36-member House is elected from 36 electoral districts (one representative from each district) for a term not to exceed 5 years. The Senate, or reviewing house, serves concurrently with the House and has 11 members—five appointed by the governor in consultation with the premier, three by the opposition leader, and three at the governor's discretion.

The judiciary is composed of a chief justice and associate judges appointed by the governor.

For administrative purposes, Bermuda is divided into nine parishes, with Hamilton and St. George considered autonomous corporations.

Political Parties

Bermuda's first political party, the Progressive Labor Party (PLP), was formed in May 1963 with predominantly black adherents. In 1965, the two-party system was launched following the formation of the United Bermuda Party (UBP), which had the support of the majority of white voters and of some black voters. A third party, the Bermuda Democratic Party (BDP), was formed in the summer of 1967 with a splinter group from the PLP as a nucleus. The BDP disbanded in 1970 and was later replaced by the National Liberal Party (NLP), which has since also disbanded.

In the fall of 2009 several UBP parliamentarians broke away from the party and in November formed a third party, the Bermuda Democratic Alliance (BDA). In May 2011, the UBP voted overwhelmingly to disband after 47 years. The majority of its members united with the breakaway BDA and together formed a new opposition party, the One Bermuda Alliance (OBA).

Bermuda's first election held on the basis of universal adult suffrage and equal voting took place on May 22, 1968; previously, the franchise had been limited to property owners. In the 1968 election, the UBP won 30 House of Assembly seats, while the PLP won 10 seats and the BDP lost the 3 seats it had previously held. The UBP continued to maintain control of the government, although by decreasing margins in the Assembly, until 1998 when the PLP won the general election for the first time.

Following a bitter and divisive general election on December 18, 2007—which many predicted would be very close—the PLP under Premier Ewart Brown was returned to power with the same number of seats as it had going into the election. The opposition UBP lost its third successive election, leading to calls for major change that resulted in the demise of the party and the formation of the new opposition OBA in 2011.

Independence

The PLP and UBP both discussed the possibility of complete independence. An independence referendum called by a sharply divided UBP in the summer of 1995 was resoundingly defeated and resulted in the resignation of the premier and UBP leader, John Swan. Just over 58% of the electorate voted in the independence referendum, with over 73% voting against independence and only 25% in favor. Eventual independence from the United Kingdom (U.K.) has been a goal of the PLP since the party's inception in 1963. In February 2004 then-Premier (and PLP party leader) Alex Scott announced his decision to commence an open and objective debate on the subject of independence. The government-appointed Bermuda Independence Commission held hearings island-wide where there was considerable focus on the mechanics of deciding independence, whether through an independence referendum, a general election, or some combination of the two. However, several recent polls indicated little support for independence.

Currently citizens of Britain's overseas territories, including Bermuda, are entitled to British citizenship. The British Overseas Territories Bill, passed in February 2002, provides automatic acquisition of British citizenship, including automatic transmission of citizenship to their children; the right of abode, including the right to live and work in the U.K. and the European Union (EU); the right not to exercise or to formally renounce British citizenship; and the right to use the European Union/ European Economic Area (EU/EEA) channel at the airport. The U.K. has indicated that citizens of an independent Bermuda would no longer be automatically entitled to British citizenship and the EU benefits that accrue to it by this method.

There are no conditions attached to the grant of British citizenship to the overseas territories, a fact of particular importance to Bermuda where the issue of independence is being debated. A 1999 U.K. government White Paper states: "The new grant of British citizenship will not be a barrier, therefore, to those Overseas Territories choosing to become independent of Britain. Our Overseas Territories are British for as long as they wish to remain British. Britain has willingly granted independence where it has been requested; and we will continue to do so where this is an option."

Principal Government Officials

Last Updated: 1/31/2013

Governor: **Richard GOZNEY, Sir**
Premier: **Alex SCOTT**
Dep. Premier: **Ewart BROWN**
Min. of Education: **Terry LISTER**
Min. of Environment: **Neletha BUTTERFIELD**
Min. of Finance: **Paula COX**
Min. of Health & Family Services: **Patrice PARRIS**
Min. of Housing, Works, & Engineering: **Ashfield DEVENT**
Min. of Justice: **Larry MUSSENDEN**
Min. of Labor & Home Affairs: **Randy NORTON**
Min. of Legislative Affairs: **Michael SCOTT**
Min. of Sports & Community Affairs: **Dale BULTER**
Min. of Tourism, Telecommunications, and e-Commerce: **Renee WEBB**
Min. of Transport: **Ewart BROWN**
Min. of Works, Engineering, Parks, & Housing: **Alex SCOTT**
Attorney Gen.: **Larry MUSSENDEN**
Cabinet Sec.:
Chmn., Bermuda Monetary Authority:

ECONOMY

Bermuda enjoys the fourth highest per capita income in the world, more than 50% higher than that of the US; the average cost of a house by the mid-2000s exceeded $1,000,000. Its economy is primarily based on providing financial services for international business and luxury facilities for tourists. A number of reinsurance companies relocated to the island following the 11 September 2001 attacks on the US and again after Hurricane Katrina in August 2005 contributing to the expansion of an already robust international business sector. Bermuda's tourism industry—which derives over 80% of its visitors from the US—continues to struggle but remains the island's number two industry. Most capital equipment and food must be imported. Bermuda's industrial sector is largely focused on construction and agriculture is limited, with only 20% of the land being arable.

FOREIGN RELATIONS AND U.S.-BERMUDIAN RELATIONS

Bermuda is a British Overseas Territory with significant autonomy. U.S. policy toward the United Kingdom is the basis of U.S.-Bermuda relations. Bermuda has executed a Tax Information Exchange Agreement in a treaty between the United States, the United Kingdom, and Bermuda. The United States and the Government of Bermuda have signed a Mutual Legal Assistance Treaty, authorizing authorities in the U.S. and Bermuda to request and obtain assistance from each other in criminal investigations and prosecutions and related administrative and other proceedings. The treaty provides for cooperation between the U.S. and Bermuda in combating a wide variety of crimes, including economic crimes and money laundering, by facilitating the collection of evidence needed by authorities in one country but located within the other country. The U.S. Coast Guard provides search and rescue assistance to Bermuda as needed.

U.S. Assistance to Bermuda

The United States provides no foreign assistance to Bermuda.

Bilateral Economic Relations

The United States is Bermuda's principal trading partner. The economy is based primarily on international business and tourism. Bermuda is an important regional and global offshore financial center. It has large insurance and reinsurance sectors, with firms based in the jurisdiction writing significant volumes of business in the United States and United Kingdom. The government cooperates with the United States to prevent money laundering and terrorist financing. An estimated 8,000 registered U.S. citizens live in Bermuda, many of them employed in the international business community. There also are a large number of American businesses incorporated in Bermuda. Areas of opportunity for U.S. investment are principally in the reinsurance and financial services industries. U.S. visitors are critical to the island's tourism industry.

Bermuda's Membership in International Organizations

The United Kingdom is formally responsible for Bermuda's foreign and defense policy.

Bilateral Representation

The United Kingdom's embassy in the United States is at 3100 Massachusetts Avenue, NW, Washington, DC 20008; tel: 202-588-6500.

Principal U.S. Embassy Officials

Last Updated: 1/14/2013

HAMILTON (CG) 16 Middle Road, Devonshire DV 03 Bermuda, 1-441-295-1342 x0, Fax 1-441-296-9233 or 1-441-295-1592, Workweek: 8:00 AM–4:30 PM, M-F

CG OMS:	Gemma V. Newton
DHS/CBP:	Robert J. Scarberry
DPO:	Adam R. Vogelzang
ECON/COM:	Eleesha M. Lewis
FM:	Andre Krol (Wash DC)
HRO:	Peggy Laurance (Frc–Fort Lauderdale)
MGT:	Eleesha M. Lewis
POSHO:	Eleesha M. Lewis
SDO/DATT:	Dao London
CG:	Robert W. Settje
CON:	Adam R. Vogelzang
GSO:	Eleesha M. Lewis
RSO:	Paul P. Avallone (Usun-Ny); Arso Ed Swoyer
AFSA:	Adam R. Vogelzang
APHIS:	Robert J. Scarberry
CLO:	Jodi Szabo
DEA:	Frank Carine (Not At Post)
EEO:	Under S/Ocr Regional Support
FMO:	Eleesha M. Lewis
ICASS Chair:	Robert J. Scarberry
IMO:	Jeffrey A. Yacobucci (At Frc)
IPO:	Jeffrey A. Yacobucci (At Frc)
IRS:	Raul Pertierra (Not At Post)
ISO:	Jeffrey A. Yacobucci (At Frc)
ISSO:	Adam R. Vogelzang/Alt: Jeffrey A. Yacobucci
LEGATT:	Bill Nicholson (Embassy Nassau)
POL:	Eleesha M. Lewis
State ICASS:	Adam R. Vogelzang

TRAVEL

Consular Information Sheet

March 7, 2011

Country Description: Bermuda is a British overseas territory with a stable democracy and developed economy. Tourist facilities are widely available.

Smart Traveler Enrollment Program (Step)/Embassy Location: If you are going to live in or visit Bermuda please take the time to tell our Embassy or Consulate about your trip. If you enroll, we can keep you up to date with important safety and security announcements. It will also help your friends and family get in touch with you in an emergency.

American Consulate General
Hamilton
16 Middle Road
Devonshire DV 03
Telephone: 441 295-1342
Emergency after-hours telephone: 441 335-3828
Facsimile: 441 295-1592

Entry/Exit Requirements for U.S. Citizens: All persons travelling between the United States and Bermuda are required to present a passport to enter Bermuda or re-enter the United States. Travelers with questions concerning travel to Bermuda may contact the British Embassy in Washington DC or any one of the British Consulate Generals across the U.S. Visit the British Embassy website for the most current visa information. The U.S. Department of State is unaware of any HIV/AIDS entry restrictions for visitors to or foreign residents of Bermuda.

Safety and Security: Stay up to date by bookmarking our Bureau of Consular Affairs website, which contains the current Travel Warnings and Travel Alerts as well as the Worldwide Caution. Follow us on Twitter and Facebook as well.

You can also call 1-888-407-4747 toll-free within the U.S. and Canada, or by calling a regular toll line, 1-202-501-4444, from other countries. These numbers are available from 8:00 a.m. to 8:00 p.m. Eastern Time, Monday through Friday (except U.S. federal holidays). Take some time before travel to improve your personal security—things are not the same everywhere as they are in the United States.

Crime: Bermuda has a moderate but growing crime rate. Recent crime statistics can be viewed at the official website of the Bermuda Police Service. Examples of common crimes include theft of unattended baggage and items from rental motorbikes, purse snatching (often perpetrated by thieves riding motorbikes), mugging, and theft from unsecured hotel rooms. Valuables left in hotel rooms or left unattended in public areas are vulnerable to theft. Criminals often target visitors on rental motorbikes and at popular tourist attractions.

The back streets of the city of Hamilton are often the setting for nighttime assaults, particularly late at night after the bars close. Travelers should exercise caution when walking after dark or visiting out-of-the-way places on the island as they can be vulnerable to theft and assault, and because narrow and dark roadways can contribute to accidents. In the past, there have been reports of sexual assault and acquaintance rape and occasional use of "date rape" drugs.

Travelers should note an increase in gang presence and illegal drug activity in Bermuda. There have been no reports of gang violence targeted towards visitors to Bermuda, although gunfire between gang members has occurred throughout the island

Don't buy counterfeit and pirated goods, even if they are widely available. Not only are the bootlegs illegal in the United States, you may be breaking local law too.

Victims of Crime: If you or someone you know becomes the victim of a crime abroad, you should contact the local police and the nearest U.S. embassy or consulate (see the Department of State's list of embassies and consulates). If your passport is stolen we can help you replace it. For violent crimes such as assault and rape, we can, for example, help you find appropriate medical care, contact family members or friends and help you get money from them if you need it.

Although the investigation and prosecution of the crime are solely the responsibility of local authorities, consular officers can help you to understand the local criminal justice process and to find an attorney if needed. Although Bermuda does not have a formalized Victims of Crime program, there is a Criminal Injuries Compensation Board c/o The Supreme Court, 113 Front Street, Hamilton HM 12, Bermuda. Tel; (441) 292-1350 Fax: (441)292-2268.

The local equivalent to the "911" emergency line in Bermuda is 911.

Criminal Penalties: While you are traveling in Bermuda, you are subject to its laws even if you are a U.S. citizen. Foreign laws and legal systems can be vastly different than our own. In some places you may be taken in for questioning if you don't have your passport with you. In some places, it is illegal to take pictures of certain buildings. In some places driving under the influence could land you immediately in jail. These criminal penalties will vary from country to country.

There are also some things that might be legal in the country you visit, but still illegal in the United States, For example, you can be prosecuted under U.S. law if you buy pirated goods.Engaging in sexual conduct with children or using or disseminating child pornography in a foreign country is a crime, prosecutable in the United States. If you break local laws in Bermuda, your U.S. passport won't help you avoid arrest or prosecution. It's very important to know what's legal and what's not where you are going. Bermuda has zero tolerance for possession or importation of controlled substances, and possession or importation of dangerous weapons including stun guns and pepper spray. Violations have resulted in fines and prison sentences. Cruise ships and cruise ship passengers visiting Bermuda are searched by Bermuda Customs officials and persons with controlled substances are fined, imprisoned and/or not allowed to re-board the ship.

Recent changes to Bermuda's laws allow police to require DNA testing for certain criminal offenses.

If you are arrested in Bermuda, authorities of Bermuda are required to alert the U.S. Consulate in Hamilton of your arrest. If you are concerned that the Department of State may not be aware of your situation, you should request the police to notify the U.S. Consulate General in Hamilton of your arrest.

Special Circumstances: The Department of State warns U.S. citizens against taking any type of firearm, ammunition or component of a firearm into Bermuda. Entering Bermuda with a firearm, some bladed instruments or even a single round of ammunition or ammunition magazine is illegal, even if the weapon or ammunition is taken into the country unintentionally.

Pepper sprays and stun guns are considered dangerous weapons in Bermuda and are illegal. The Bermudian Government strictly enforces its laws restricting the entry of weapons and ammunition. Permission to import or own a gun in Bermuda must be sought in advance from the Bermuda Police Service. Any privately owned firearms must be secured at Bermuda Police Headquarters. Violations may result in arrests, convictions and potentially long prison sentences.

Medical Facilities and Health Information: Adequate medical care is available for routine procedures, though extremely expensive. The hospital performs general surgery and has an intensive care unit. Serious or complex medical problems will likely require medical evacuation to the United States. Most Bermudian health care providers including the local hospital do not accept overseas insurance and will expect payment at the time of service. You can find good information on vaccinations and other health precautions on the CDC website.

For information about outbreaks of infectious diseases abroad, consult the World Health Organization (WHO) website. The WHO website also contains additional health information for travelers, including detailed country-specific health information.

Medical Insurance: You can't assume your insurance will go with you when you travel. It's very important to find out BEFORE you leave. You need to ask your insurance company two questions:

- Does my policy apply when I'm outside the United States?
- Will it cover emergencies like a trip to a foreign hospital or an evacuation?

In Bermuda, places, doctors and hospitals expect payment in cash at the time of service. Your regular U.S. health insurance may not cover doctors' and hospital visits in other countries. If your policy doesn't go with you when you travel, it's a very good idea to take out another one for your trip.

Traffic Safety and Road Conditions: While in Bermuda you may encounter road conditions that differ significantly from those in the United States. Traffic in Bermuda moves on the left side and the roads are very narrow, often with no defined shoulder. The maximum speed in the city of Hamilton is 25 kph (15mph) and 35 kph (21 mph) on the rest of the island. Under Bermudian law, non residents are not allowed to own, rent or drive four-wheeled vehicles. Non residents must rely on taxis, the local bus system or rented motorbikes. Traffic is moderately heavy. Road accidents—particularly involving motorbikes—are common and can result in serious injuries or death. Rental motorbikes are readily available, and the required helmet is provided. However, visitors should carefully consider whether or not it is worth the risk to ride a motorbike. Motorbikes provide the greatest road peril in Bermuda; local operators tend to abuse the speed limit and they will often pass on the left or right side with no warning. Those unfamiliar with driving on the left side are likely to find the roundabouts and regulations for yielding at junctions confusing and dangerous. In addition, vehicles often stop on the side of the road, blocking one lane of traffic.

Main roads, while generally in good condition, are extremely narrow and tend to be bordered by heavy vegetation or stone walls. Taxis are readily available. The local bus system, serves the length of the island and stops close to most beaches, hotels, the downtown shopping area and other points of interest. In addition, water ferry service to a variety of stops around the island is available seven days a week and is a very safe and enjoyable mode of transportation. For specific information concerning Bermuda's drivers permits, vehicle inspection, road tax and mandatory insurance, please contact the Bermuda Department of Tourism offices at 310 Madison Avenue, Suite 201, New York, NY Tel: (212) 818-9800.

Aviation Safety Oversight: The U.S. Federal Aviation Administration (FAA) has assessed the government of Bermuda's Civil Aviation Authority as being in compliance with International Civil Aviation Organization (ICAO) aviation safety standards for oversight of Bermuda's air carrier operations. Further information may be found on the FAA's safety assessment page.

Children's Issues: Please see the U.S. Dept. of State Office of Children's Issues web pages on intercountry adoption and international parental child abduction.

International Parental Child Abduction

January 2012

The information in this section has been edited from the latest report available from the State Department Bureau of Consular Affairs, Office of Overseas Citizens Services as of February 2013. For more information, please read the *International Parental Child Abduction* section of this book and check for updated reports online at www.travel.state.gov/abduction.

Disclaimer: The information in this flyer relating to the legal requirements of specific foreign countries is provided for general information only. Questions involving interpretation of specific foreign laws should be addressed to foreign legal counsel.

General Information: Bermuda is a British overseas territory. The United Kingdom of Great Britain and Northern Ireland has extended the Hague Convention on the Civil Aspects of International Child Abduction 1980 to cover Bermuda, Cayman Islands, Falkland Islands, Isle of Man, and Montserrat.

For further information on the filing of a Hague application for one of these territories, please contact the appropriate case officer in the Office of Children's Issues at 202-736-9090. American citizens who travel to the British overseas territories place themselves under the jurisdiction of their local courts. American citizens planning a trip to the British overseas territories with dual national children should bear this in mind.

Custody Disputes: In the British overseas territories, if parents are legally married they share the custody of their children. If they are not married, by law the custody is granted to the mother unless there are known facts of inappropriate behavior, mental or social problems. Foreign court orders are not automatically recognized.

Enforcement of Foreign Judgments: Custody orders and judgments of foreign courts are not enforceable in the British overseas territories.

Visitation Rights: In cases where one parent has been granted custody of a child, the other parent is usually granted visitation rights. If a custodial parent fails to allow visitation, the non-custodial parent may appeal to the court.

Dual Nationality: Dual nationality is recognized under the British overseas territories' laws.

Passports for Minors and the Children's Passport Issuance Alert Program: For more information on these topics, see the *International Parental Child Abduction* section of this publication and review current reports from the U.S. Department of State at www.travel.state.gov/abduction.

Travel Restrictions: No exit visas are required to leave any of the British overseas territories.

Criminal Remedies: For information on possible criminal remedies, please contact your local law enforcement authorities or the nearest office of the Federal Bureau of Investigation (FBI). Information is also available on the Internet at the web site of the U.S. Department of Justice, Office of Juvenile Justice and Delinquency Prevention (OJJDP) at http://www.ojjdp.ncjrs.org. Persons who wish to pursue a child custody claim in any British overseas territory court should retain an attorney in the British overseas territory that they are pursuing the child custody claim. The U.S. embassies in Barbados, Jamaica, and The Bahamas maintain lists of attorneys who are willing to represent American clients.

For further information on international parental child abduction, contact the Office of Children's Issues, U.S. Department of State at 1-888-407-4747 or visit its web site on the Internet at http://travel.state.gov/abduction.

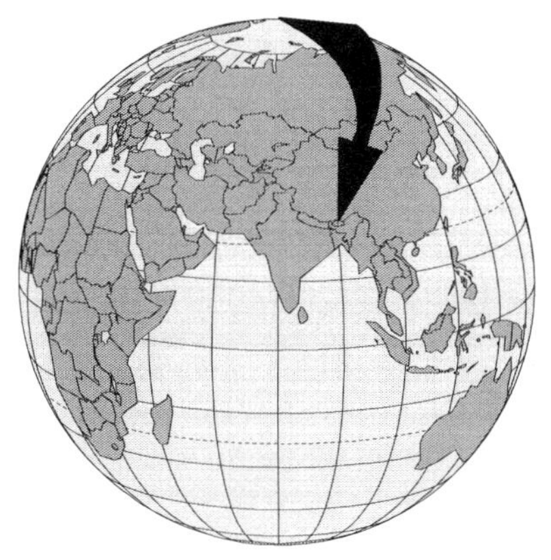

BHUTAN

Compiled from publications that were available as of February 2013 from the U.S. Department of State, the U.S. Department of Commerce, and the Central Intelligence Agency (CIA). See the introduction to this set for explanatory notes.

Official Name:
Kingdom of Bhutan

PROFILE

Geography

Area: total: 38,394 sq km; country comparison to the world: 137; land: 38,394 sq km; water: 0 sq km

Major cities: Thimphu (capital) 89,000 (2009)

Climate: varies; tropical in southern plains; cool winters and hot summers in central valleys; severe winters and cool summers in Himalayas

Terrain: mostly mountainous with some fertile valleys and savanna

People

Nationality: noun: Bhutanese (singular and plural); adjective: Bhutanese

Population: 716,896 (July 2012 est.)

Population growth rate: 1.175% (2012 est.)

Ethnic groups: Bhote 50%, ethnic Nepalese 35% (includes Lhotsampas—one of several Nepalese ethnic groups), indigenous or migrant tribes 15%

Religions: Lamaistic Buddhist 75%, Indian- and Nepalese-influenced Hinduism 25%

Languages: Sharchhopka 28%, Dzongkha (official) 24%, Lhotshamkha 22%, other 26%

Literacy: definition: age 15 and over can read and write; total population: 47%; male: 60%; female: 34% (2003 est.)

Health: life expectancy at birth: total population: 67.88 years; male: 67.01 years; female: 68.79 years (2012 est.); Infant mortality rate: total: 42.17 deaths/1,000 live births; male: 42.82 deaths/1,000 live births; female: 41.49 deaths/1,000 live births (2012 est.)

Unemployment rate: 4% (2009)

Work force: 299,900

Government

Type: constitutional monarchy

Independence: 1907

Constitution: ratified 18 July 2008

Political subdivisions: 20 districts (dzongkhag, singular and plural)

Suffrage: 18 years of age; universal

Economy

GDP (purchasing power parity): $4.813 billion (2012 est.); $4.342 billion (2011 est.); $4.101 billion (2010 est.); $3.708 billion (2009 est.)

GDP real growth rate: 9.9% (2012) 5.9% (2011 est.); 10.6% (2010 est.); 6.7% (2009 est.)

GDP per capita (PPP): $6,500 (2012 est.); $6,200 (2011 est.); $5,900 (2010 est.); $5,300 (2009 est.)

Natural resources: timber, hydropower, gypsum, calcium carbonate

Agriculture products: rice, corn, root crops, citrus; dairy products, eggs

Industries: cement, wood products, processed fruits, alcoholic beverages, calcium carbide, tourism

Exports: $725.2 million (2012 est.); $665.3 million (2011 est.)

Exports—commodities: electricity (to India), ferrosilicon, cement, calcium carbide, copper wire, manganese, vegetable oil

Imports: $1.28 billion (2012 est.); $1.185 billion (2011 est.)

Imports—commodities: fuel and lubricants, passenger cars, machinery and parts, fabrics, rice

Debt—external: $1.275 billion (2011); $836 million (2009)

Exchange rates: ngultrum (BTN) per US dollar; 46.67 (2011 est.); 45.73 (2010 est.); 41.487 (2007)

PEOPLE

The people of Bhutan can be divided into three broad ethnic categories—Ngalops, Sharchops, and Lhotsampas. The Ngalops make up the majority of the population, living mostly in the western and central areas. The Ngalops are thought to be of Tibetan origin, arriving in Bhutan during the 8th and 9th centuries A.D. and bringing Buddhism with them. Most Ngalops follow the Drukpa Kagyupa

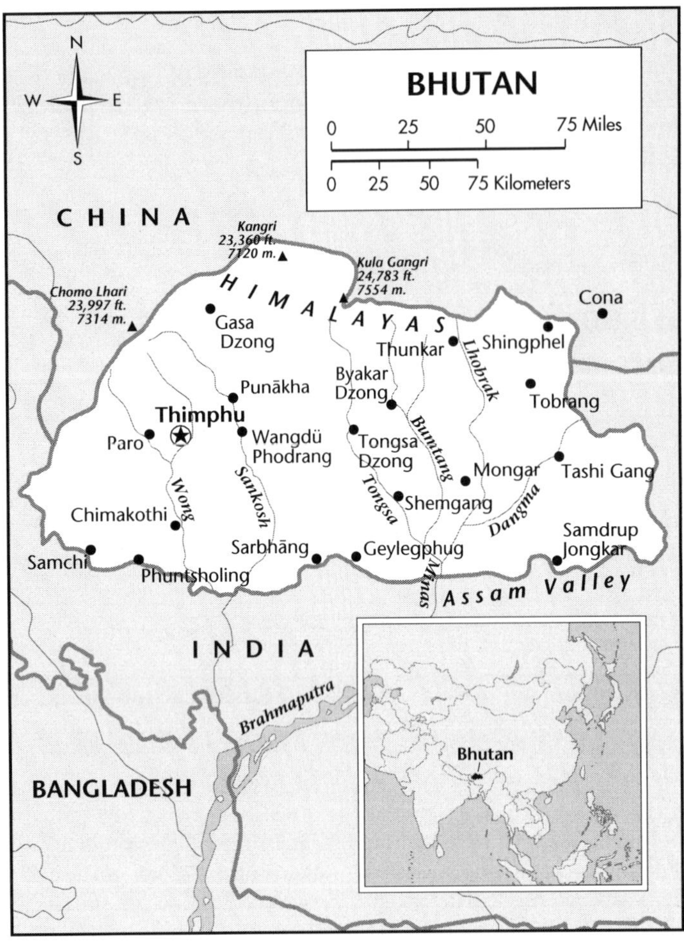

discipline of Mahayana Buddhism. In a country that is deeply rooted within the Buddhist religion, many people's sect of religion, as opposed to their ethnic group, characterizes them. The Ngalops predominate in the government, and the civil service and their cultural norms have been declared by the monarchy to be the standard for all citizens. The Sharchops, who live in the eastern section of Bhutan, are considered to be descendants of the earliest major group to inhabit Bhutan. Most follow the Ningmapa discipline of Mahayana Buddhism. Sharchop is translated as "people of the east."

The Ngalops, Sharchops, and the indigenous tribal people are collectively known as Drukpas and account for about 65% of the population.

The Lhotsampas are people of Nepali descent, currently making up 35% of the population. They came to Bhutan in the 19th and 20th centuries, mostly settling in the southern foothills to work as farmers. They speak a variety of Nepali dialects and are predominantly Hindu.

National/Racial/Ethnic Minorities

Organizations representing exiled Nepali-speaking Bhutanese claimed that Nepali-speaking Bhutanese were subjected to discrimination and prejudice in employment, but the government stated they were proportionally represented in civil service and government jobs. English and Dzongkha languages are the mediums of instruction taught in all schools. The Committee on the Rights of the Child expressed concern about the rights of minority children, specifically the Nepali-speaking minority, to take part in their culture, practice their religion, or use their language.

Religion

A majority of the population practices Drukpa Kagyu or Nyingmapa Buddhism, both of which are disciplines of Mahayana Buddhism. The Nepali-speaking minority population practices Hinduism, Christianity, and Buddhism. Hindu temples exist in southern areas, and in October, the government approved the construction of a Hindu temple in the capital, Thimphu. Christianity is said to be concentrated in towns and in the south.

According to unconfirmed estimates, there are between 6,000 and 21,000 Christians in the country. There are also reports of a few Muslims in the country. Although priests of the Bon tradition (animism) often officiate and include Bon rituals in Buddhist festivals, very few citizens adhere exclusively to this religious group. Some citizens from the eastern part of the country, known as Sharchops, reportedly practice Buddhism combined with elements of the Bon tradition and Hinduism.

HISTORY

Bhutan's early history is steeped in mythology and remains obscure. It may have been inhabited as early as 2000 B.C., but not much was known until the introduction of Tibetan Buddhism in the 9th century A.D. when turmoil in Tibet forced many monks to flee to Bhutan. In the 12th century A.D., the Drukpa Kagyupa school was established and remains the dominant form of Buddhism in Bhutan today. The country's political history is intimately tied to its religious history and the relations among the various monastic schools and monasteries. The consolidation of Bhutan occurred in 1616 when Ngawana Namgyal, a lama from Tibet, defeated three Tibetan invasions, subjugated rival religious schools, codified an intricate and comprehensive system of law, and established himself as ruler (shabdrung) over a system of ecclesiastical and civil administrators. After his death, infighting and civil war eroded the power of the shabdrung for the next

200 years when in 1885, Ugyen Wangchuck was able to consolidate power and cultivated closer ties with the British in India. In 1907, Ugyen Wangchuck was elected as the hereditary ruler of Bhutan, crowned on December 17, 1907, and installed as the head of state Druk Gyalpo (Dragon King). In 1910, King Ugyen and the British signed the Treaty of Punakha which provided that British India would not interfere in the internal affairs of Bhutan if the country accepted external advice in its external relations.

When Ugyen Wangchuck died in 1926, his son Jigme Wangchuck became the next ruler, and when India gained independence in 1947, the new Indian Government recognized Bhutan as an independent country. In 1949, India and Bhutan signed the Treaty of Peace and Friendship, which provided that India would not interfere in Bhutan's internal affairs but would be guided by India in its foreign policy. Succeeded in 1952 by his son Jigme Dorji Wangchuck, Bhutan began to slowly emerge from its isolation and began a program of planned development. Bhutan became a member of the United Nations in 1971, and during his tenure the National Assembly was established and a new code of law, as well as the Royal Bhutanese Army and the High Court.

In 1972, Jigme Singye Wangchuck ascended the throne at age 16. He emphasized modern education, decentralization of governance, the development of hydroelectricity and tourism and improvements in rural developments. He was perhaps best known internationally for his overarching development philosophy of "Gross National Happiness." It recognizes that there are many dimensions to development and that economic goals alone are not sufficient. Satisfied with Bhutan's transitioning democratization process, he abdicated in December 2006 rather than wait until the promulgation of the new constitution in 2008. His son, Jigme Khesar Namgyel Wangchuck, became King upon his abdication.

GOVERNMENT AND POLITICAL CONDITIONS

Bhutan is a democratic, constitutional monarchy whose king, Jigme Khesar Namgyel Wangchuck, is the head of state, with executive power vested in the cabinet, headed by Prime Minister Jigme Thinley. The country held its first general election for the National Assembly in 2008, and an EU election-monitoring team declared that it met international standards and was free and fair. During 2011 local nonpartisan elections were held, with Danish election observers reporting no significant irregularities.

In 2008 the country completed a successful transition from an absolute hereditary monarchy to a constitutional monarchy with a bicameral elected parliament, marking the final step in the transition to a parliamentary democracy. The law provides limited rights for changing the government, and it provides for a separation of powers.

Recent Elections

From January through July 2011, the government held nonpartisan local elections at the district and subdistrict levels, with 1,128 candidates elected. A woman was elected to head one of 205 subdistricts in the country. A new round of local elections took place in December to fill one-quarter of the unfilled local positions (371 out of 1,499), and 304 candidates were elected.

In 2008 voters elected the country's first National Assembly, the lower house of the parliament. The ruling Druk Phensum Tshogpa (DPT) party won 45 of 47 seats. Human Rights Watch reported that the government excluded 13 percent of the Nepali-speaking population from voting because they were considered "non-nationals" in the 2005 census. International monitors reported that the elections were generally free and fair with no reports of irregularities during the election process.

Political Parties: The constitution states that political parties shall promote national unity and shall not resort to regionalism, ethnicity, and religion to incite voters for electoral gain. Political parties are required to be broad based with cross-national membership and are not permitted to receive money or any assistance from foreign sources. During 2011 political parties experienced debt challenges, as they could not sustain their operations solely on membership dues. The government provides funding only for general elections.

In 2007 the government began allowing political parties to register under the terms of a draft constitution. Three parties registered with the Election Commission, which disqualified the Bhutan People's United Party (BPUP) for "failing to prove its credibility" as a national political party. The Election Commission indicated that BPUP candidates did not meet the commission's education requirements. The Election Act specifies that candidates for parliament must have earned at least a bachelor's degree to run for office. The government took no action in response to the party's appeal of the decision.

The Druk National Congress, established in 1994 by Bhutanese refugees in exile, continued to claim that the government denied independent parties the ability to operate effectively. The government regarded political parties organized by Nepali-speaking individuals living in exile in refugee camps as illegal, terrorist, and antinational in nature. These parties, which sought repatriation of refugees and democratic reforms, were unable to conduct activities inside the country.

Participation of Women and Minorities: Women comprised 31.6 percent of civil servants. Ten members of parliament were women, including six in the National Council and four in the National Assembly. There was one woman on the High Court, and one female judge at the district court. Female parliamentarians increased from 9 percent in 2005 to 14 percent during 2011.

The Election Commission reported there were 20 Nepali-speaking minorities in parliament, 15 in the National Assembly and five in the National Council. One Hindu and one Christian also served in the National Council.

Principal Government Officials

Last Updated: 1/31/2013

King: **Jigme Khesar Namgyel WANGCHUCK**
Prime Minister: **Jigme THINLEY**
Min. of Agriculture: **Pema GYAMTSHO**
Min. of Economic Affairs: **Khandu WANGCHUK**
Min. of Education: **Thakur Singh POWDYEL**
Min. of Finance: **Wangdi NORBU**
Min. of Foreign Affairs: **Ugyen TSHERING**
Min. of Health: **Zangley DUKPA**
Min. of Home & Cultural Affairs: **Minjur DORJI**
Min. of Information & Communication: **Nandalal RAI**
Min. of Labor & Human Resources: **Dorji WANGDI**
Min. of Works & Human Settlements: **Yeshey ZIMBA**
Chmn., Royal Advisory Council: **Rinzin GYALTSHEN**
Governor, Royal Monetary Authority: **Daw TENZIN**
Permanent Representative to the UN, New York: **Lhatu WANGCHUK**

ECONOMY

The economy, one of the world's smallest and least developed, is based on agriculture and forestry, which provide the main livelihood for more than 40% of the population. Agriculture consists largely of subsistence farming and animal husbandry. Rugged mountains dominate the terrain and make the building of roads and other infrastructure difficult and expensive.

The economy is closely aligned with India's through strong trade and monetary links and dependence on India's financial assistance. The industrial sector is technologically backward with most production of the cottage industry type. Most development projects, such as road construction, rely on Indian migrant labor. Model education, social, and environment programs are underway with support from multilateral development organizations.

Each economic program takes into account the government's desire to protect the country's environment and cultural traditions. For example, the government, in its cautious expansion of the tourist sector, encourages visits by upscale, environmentally conscientious tourists. Complicated controls and uncertain policies in areas such as industrial licensing, trade, labor, and finance continue to hamper foreign investment.

Hydropower exports to India have boosted Bhutan's overall growth. New hydropower projects will be the driving force behind Bhutan's ability to create employment and sustain growth in the coming years. GDP has rebounded strongly since the global recession began in 2008.

Labor Conditions

According to the law, the minimum age of employment is 18. However, the law allows for employment of children between the ages of 13 and 17 in environments that will not be harmful to their health or safety. Children younger than 18 often performed agricultural and construction work, completed chores on family farms, or worked in shops and restaurants after school and during holidays. Girls were employed primarily as domestic workers, where they were vulnerable to abuse and exploitation. UNICEF estimated that 19 percent of children between ages five and 14 were child laborers. Labor inspectors operating under the Ministry of Labor and Human Resources enforce child labor laws.

The law addresses issues such as minimum wage, sexual harassment, workers' associations, acceptable forms of child labor, and labor inspection regulations. According to civil society, the national minimum wage rate was Nu 3,000 ($67) per month, and the labor minister stated that half the country's workers earned more than the minimum wage. The workday is defined as eight hours with a one-hour lunch break, and employers must grant regular days of rest. Work in excess of this must be paid at 1.5 times the normal rate.

All citizens are entitled to free medical care. The government transported persons who could not receive adequate care in the country to other countries (usually India) for treatment. Workers are eligible for compensation in the case of partial or total disability, and in the event of death, their families were entitled to compensation. Labor regulations grant workers the right to leave work situations that endanger their health and safety.

U.S.-BHUTAN RELATIONS

Bhutan became a member of the United Nations in 1971. Bhutan does not have diplomatic relations with any of the permanent members of the UN Security Council, including the United States. The U.S. has no significant trade relations with the country. Informal contact is maintained through the Bhutanese Embassy in India and the Bhutanese Mission to the United Nations in New York.

Bhutan participates in a regional program for South Asia sponsored by the U.S. Agency for International Development (USAID) that helps countries develop their power infrastructure (SARI-E). A few Bhutanese military officers have attended courses at the Asia-Pacific Center for Security Studies. The U.S. Government annually brings several Bhutanese participants to the United States through its International Visitors and Fulbright Programs.

Bilateral Representation

The U.S. Embassy in New Delhi, India, has consular responsibilities for Bhutan, but U.S. citizens also may request assistance from U.S. Embassies in Kathmandu, Nepal, or Dhaka, Bangladesh.

Principal U.S. Embassy Officials

Last Updated: 1/14/2013

NEW DELHI (E) Shanti Path, Chanakya Puri New Delhi–110021, India, 91-11-24198000, Fax 91-11-24190017, Workweek: Monday thru Friday; 0830 hrs to 1700 hrs, Website: http://newdelhi.usembassy.gov/

DCM OMS:	Lisa Cantonwine
AMB OMS:	Suzonne M. Woytovech
CDC:	Kenneth Earhart
Co-CLO:	Cassandra Davis
DHS/CBP:	Steven King
DHS/CIS:	Bobbie Johnson
DHS/ICE:	Vacant
FCS:	Judy Reinke
FDA:	Bruce Ross
FM:	James Horner
HHS:	Steven T. Smith
HRO:	Thomas Steyer
MGT:	Michael Mullins
MLO/ODC:	CAPT Kenneth Spurlock
POSHO:	James Horner
SDO/DATT:	CAPT Timothy J. Maricle
AMB:	Nancy J. Powell
CON:	Julia R. Stanley
DCM:	Donald Lu
PAO:	Walter T. Douglas
GSO:	William McClure
RSO:	Tim Haley
AFSA:	Isabelle Chan
AGR:	Allan Mustard
AID:	William Hammink
CLO:	Alicia May
DEA:	Michael Brown
ECON:	Blair P. Hall
EEO:	Lisa Cantonwine
EST:	Blair P. Hall
FAA:	Aaron Wilkins
FMO:	Mary Jo Rasing
ICASS Chair:	Judy Reinke
IMO:	Aziz Ahmed
IPO:	Wesley M. Tompkins
IRS:	Elizabeth Kinney
ISO:	Joseph Conners
ISSO:	Michael Meaux
LEGATT:	Daniel Clegg
POL:	Herro Mustafa
State ICASS:	Julia R. Stanley

TRAVEL

Consular Information Sheet

July 19, 2012

Country Description: Bhutan is a small, land-locked Himalayan country which completed its transition from an absolute monarchy to a constitutional monarchy in 2008. The United States does not have diplomatic relations with Bhutan and there is no U.S. diplomatic presence there. Consular issues relating to Bhutan, including assistance to U.S. citizens, are handled by the U.S. Embassy in New Delhi.

Smart Traveler Enrollment Program (STEP)/Embassy Locations: If you are going to live in or visit Bhutan, please take the time to tell our Embassy in New Delhi about your trip. If you enroll, we can keep you up to date with important safety and security announcements. It will also help your friends and family get in touch with you in an emergency.

There is no U.S. Embassy or Consulate in Bhutan. Although no formal diplomatic relations exist between the United States and Bhutan, informal contact is maintained through the U.S. Embassy in New Delhi, India. Updated information on travel and security in Bhutan may be obtained at the U.S. Embassy in New Delhi, at any other U.S. Consulate in India, the U.S. Embassy in Kathmandu, Nepal, the U.S. Embassy in Dhaka, Bangladesh and the U.S. Embassy in Bangkok, Thailand. The U.S. Embassy in New Delhi is located on Shanti Path, Chanakya Puri, New Delhi 110 021, India, telephone (91)(11) 2419–8000, fax (91)(11) 2419–8407. In the case of an emergency involving a U.S. citizen, please call the 24-hour operator at (91)(11) 2419–8000 and ask for American Citizen Services.

A consular officer from the U.S. Embassy in New Delhi periodically visits Bhutan to renew passports, provide notarial services, and take applications for Consular Reports of Birth Abroad. The U.S. Embassy in New Delhi informs U.S. citizens enrolled in the Smart Traveler Enrollment Program in advance regarding dates for these visits.

As entry by air is available only via India, Bangladesh, Nepal, and Thailand, U.S. citizens traveling to Bhutan may also consider enrolling with consular sections in these locations:

The U.S. Consulate General in Chennai (Madras) is at 220 Anna Salai, Gemini Circle, 600006; telephone (91)(44) 2857–4000; fax (91)(44) 2857–4443. In case of emergency involving a U.S. citizen, please call the 24-hour operator at (91)(44) 2857–4000 and ask for American Citizen Services.

The U.S. Consulate General in Hyderabad is at Paigah Palace, 1-8-323 Chiran Fort Lane, Begumpet, Secunderabad, Andhra Pradesh, 500003; telephone (91)(40) 4033–8300; fax (91)(40) 4033–8301. In case of emergency involving a U.S. citizen, please call the 24-hour operator at (91)(40) 4033–8300 and ask for American Citizens Services.

The U.S. Consulate in Kolkata is located at 5/1 Ho Chi Minh Sarani, Kolkata 700 071, India, telephone (91)(33) 3984–2400, fax (91)(33) 2282–2335. If you are a U.S. citizen with an after-hours emergency, please call our primary hotline at (91) 99030. If unable to reach someone on the hotline, please call (91)(33)3984–2400, press "0" and ask for the duty officer.

The U.S. Consulate General in Mumbai (Bombay) is located at C-49, G-Block, Bandra Kurla Complex, Bandra East, Mumbai 400 051. In case of an emergency involving a U.S. citizen, please call the 24-hour operator at (91)(22) 2672–4000 and ask for American Citizens Services.

The U.S. Embassy in Kathmandu is located at Maharajgunj in Kathmandu, Nepal. The Consular Section can be reached through the Embassy switchboard at (977) (1) 400-7200 or directly by fax at (977) (1) 400-7281 or contacted by email. If you are a U.S. citizen with an after-hours emergency, please call the hotline at: (977)(1) 400-7266 and (977)(1) 400-7269.

The U.S. Embassy in Bangkok is located at 120/22 Wireless Road, Bangkok, Thailand, telephone 66-2-205-4000, fax 66-2-205-4103. If you are a U.S. citizen with an after-hours emergency, please call the Embassy switchboard at 66-2-205-4000 (from outside of Thailand), or 02-205-4000 (within Thailand), and request to speak with the duty officer.

The U.S. Embassy in Dhaka is located at Madani Avenue Baridhara, Dhaka 1212, Bangladesh, telephone (880) (2) 8855500, fax (880) (2) 8823744. If you are a U.S. citizen with an after-hours emergency, please call (880) (2) 885-5500. Press "0" and ask to speak to the duty officer.

Entry/Exit Requirements for U.S. Citizens: You will need a passport valid for at least six months following the date of your arrival to Bhutanand a visa to enter and exit Bhutan. All visas are approved from Thimphu and are only issued to tourists booked with a local licensed tour operator, directly or through a foreign travel agent. Applications for tourist visas are submitted by the tour operator (See the Association of Bhutanese Tour Operators website for further information). All visitors, including those on official U.S. government business, must obtain visa clearance from Thimphu before coming to Bhutan.

Visa clearance takes at least 10 days to process and air tickets to Bhutan cannot be purchased without visa clearance. At your point of entry into Bhutan, immigration authorities will stamp a visa into your passport upon payment of USD 20. You will also need to provide two passport photos. Tourist visas are usually granted for the scheduled travel period. More information, including a list of authorized tour operators in Bhutan, may be obtained from the Tourism Council of Bhutan, PO Box 126, Thimphu, Bhutan, telephone 975-2-323251, 2-323252, fax 975-2-323695.

The Tourism Council of Bhutan sets a non-negotiable minimum daily tariff for all visitors to Bhutan. The rate includes all accommodations, all meals, transportation, services of licensed guides and porters, and cultural programs where and when available.

The rate is the same for both cultural tours and treks. Travelers should contact the Tourism Council for the latest daily tariff.

At this time only Drukair, the Bhutanese government airline, services Bhutan. Entry by air is available only via India, Bangladesh, Nepal, and Thailand. The border with China is closed. Drukair will board only travelers with visa clearance from the Tourism Authority of Bhutan.

Some HIV/AIDS entry restrictions exist for visitors to and foreign residents of Bhutan. There are no disclosure regulations or restrictions for HIV/AIDS patients who enter Bhutan on a tourist visa for a maximum two-week visit. For longer stays, however, applicants must present the results of an HIV/AIDS test completed within the six months prior to their visit.

The test can also be administered by Bhutanese officials upon arrival. Travelers should verify this information with the Bhutan Mission to the United Nations before they travel.

For the most current information on entry and exit requirements, please contact the Bhutan Mission to the United Nations (Consulate General), 763 First Avenue, New York, NY 10017, telephone (212) 682-2268, fax (212) 661-0551. Outside the United States, inquiries should be made at the nearest Bhutan embassy or consulate.

Threats to Safety and Security: In May and October 2011 small improvised explosive devices were detonated in the southern border towns of Phuentsholing and Gelephu. These were the first such reported incidents since a series of small bombs exploded in Bhutan between October 2006 and December 2008. Except for one bombing that took place in the capital, Thimphu, most of the other incidents occurred in areas near the border, far from tourist destinations and resulted in little damage. The government has blamed various groups for these bombings. Groups demanding the repatriation of Nepali-speaking Bhutanese refugees currently living in camps in Nepal have in the past resorted to protests and small-scale violence.

Stay up to date by:

- Bookmarking our Bureau of Consular Affairs website, which contains the current Travel Warnings and Travel Alerts as well as the Worldwide Caution.
- Following us on Twitter and the Bureau of Consular Affairs page on Facebook as well.
- Downloading our free Smart Traveler IPhone App to have travel information at your fingertips.
- Calling 1-888-407-4747 toll-free within the U.S. and Canada, or a regular toll line, 1-202-501-4444, from other countries.
- Taking some time before travel to consider your personal security.

Crime: There is relatively little crime in Bhutan. Petty crime, such as pick-pocketing and purse snatching, is occasionally reported. While generally safe, the capital Thimphu has begun to see burglaries, street fights and an increasing, although still small, number of drug abusers. Reasonable precautions should be taken when visiting the town and, in particular, when going out at night. Do not buy counterfeit and pirated goods, even if they are widely available. Not only are the bootlegs illegal in the United States, you may also be breaking local law.

Victims of Crime: If you or someone you know becomes the victim of a crime abroad, you should contact the local police and the U.S. Embassy in New Delhi. We can:

- Help you find appropriate medical care if you are the victim of violent crimes such as assault or rape.
- Put you in contact with the appropriate police authorities, and if you want us to, we can contact family members or friend.
- Help you understand the local criminal justice process and direct you to local attorneys, although it is important to remember that local authorities are responsible for investigating and prosecuting the crime.

Because there is no U.S. Embassy presence in Bhutan, getting your lost or stolen U.S. passport replaced can be complicated and costly. If you are without a passport you will be required to seek permission to exit Bhutan from Bhutanese immigration authorities, and also obtain advance permission to enter the receiving country from that country's immigration authorities.

The receiving country's immigration officials may or may not grant such permission. If permission is not granted, a consular officer from the U.S. Embassy or Consulate in the receiving country must meet you at the receiving country airport prior to immigration checks to bring you a new passport. The State Department charges fees for this call-out service, which can total several hundred dollars per hour, in addition to the passport fees.

The local equivalent to the "911" emergency line for Bhutan police in Bhutan is 113. The emergency number for ambulance service is 112.

Criminal Penalties: While you are traveling in Bhutan, you are subject to its laws even if you are a U.S. citizen. Foreign laws and legal systems can be vastly different from our own. In some places you may be taken in for questioning if you don't have your passport with you. In some places, it is illegal to take pictures of certain buildings. In some places driving under the influence could land you immediately in jail. These criminal penalties will vary from country to country. There are also some things that might be legal in the country you visit, but still illegal in the United States, and you can be prosecuted under U.S. law if you buy pirated goods. Engaging in sexual conduct with children or using or disseminating child pornography in a foreign country is a crime, prosecutable in the United States. If you break local laws in Bhutan, your U.S. passport won't help you avoid arrest or prosecution. It's very important to know what's legal and what's not where you are going.

While some countries will automatically notify the nearest U.S. embassy or consulate if a U.S. citizen is detained or arrested in a foreign country, that might not always be the case. To ensure that the United States is aware of your circumstances, request that the police and prison officials notify the nearest U.S. embassy or consulate as soon as you are arrested or detained overseas. Although no formal diplomatic relations exist between the United States and Bhutan, informal contact is maintained through the U.S. Embassy in New Delhi, India.

Special Circumstances: Visitors are advised to carry cash or travelers checks, since credit cards are not widely accepted in Bhutan, particularly outside the cities. Indian rupees up to the 100 rupee denomination are accepted for purchases in Bhutan. The Bhutan Royal Monetary Authority has instructed shopkeepers and businesses not to accept Indian rupees in denominations above 100. Such money can be confiscated if found. International ATMs are not available in Bhutan.

Flights into and out of Paro Airport are restricted to daylight hours and are dependent on weather conditions. Flights can be delayed or cancelled due to weather conditions, particularly during the monsoon season between May and September. Passengers are advised to allow at least 24 hours' transit time for connecting flights to and from Paro Airport and to travel on non-restricted air tickets so that they can be rebooked on the first available air carrier if a connecting flight is missed. Passengers transiting through India will need a transit visa if they intend to leave the airport or spend a night in India.

Drukair has rigid restrictions on the amount and size of luggage passengers may carry into the country. Passengers are advised to send bulky items ahead as unaccompanied baggage, since the aircraft servicing Bhutan have limited space available for large bags, and airline employees may not load large pieces of luggage.

Bhutanese customs authorities enforce strict regulations concerning temporary importation into or export from Bhutan of items such as firearms, ammunition, explosives and military stores; narcotics and drugs (except medically prescribed drugs); tobacco products; wildlife products, especially those of endangered species; and antiques. It is advisable to contact the Bhutan Mission to the United Nations (Consulate General), 763 First Avenue, New York, NY 10017, telephone (212) 682-2268, fax (212) 661-0551, for specific information regarding customs requirements.

Accessibility: While in Bhutan, individuals with disabilities may find accessibility and accommodation very different from what you find in the United States. Persons with physical disabilities living in or traveling to the country may find that Bhutan lacks the necessary infrastructure to accommodate their disability.

Medical Facilities and Health Information: Medical facilities in the populated areas in Bhutan such as Thimphu and Paro are available but may be limited or unavailable in rural areas. U.S. citizens in need of urgent medical care should try to get to the Jigme Dorji Wangchuck National Referral Hospital in the capital city, Thimphu. For emergency services in Thimphu, dial 113 for police or 112 for ambulance.

Medical services may not meet Western standards, and some medicines are in short supply. Certain emergency medical services are provided free of charge to all tourists. Visitors planning to trek in Bhutan should pay special attention to the risk of altitude illness. Altitude sickness is a risk above 8,000 feet and travelers to that altitude should consult an appropriate health care provider 4 to 6 weeks before their trip. Treks in Bhutan can take visitors days or weeks away from the nearest medical facility. Helicopter evacuation from remote areas in Bhutan is available through the registered tour operators at the U.S. citizen's expense. The U.S. Embassy in New Delhi can also help arrange evacuations through private companies at the U.S. citizen's expense. We strongly urge you to ensure that your medical insurance covers such evacuations, which can be extremely expensive.

The Government of Bhutan recommends that visitors obtain tetanus, typhoid, and hepatitis A inoculations before traveling to Bhutan. Hepatitis B, Japanese Encephalitis, and rabies vaccines are recommended for prolonged stays for people at risk. The influenza vaccine is also recommended.

Tuberculosis is an increasingly serious health concern in Bhutan. For further information, please consult the CDC's information on TB.

According to the Centers for Disease Control and Prevention (CDC), the risk of malaria exists in rural areas below 1,700m (5,577ft) in the southern belt districts of Bhutan (Chirang, Geylegphug, Samchi, Samdrup Jongkhar, and Shemgang) along the border with India. Dengue is also a risk; you should take measures to prevent insect/mosquito bites in the higher risk areas in the south from July to December.

Although yellow fever is not a disease risk in Bhutan, the government requires travelers arriving from countries where yellow fever is present to present proof of yellow fever vaccination.

You can find detailed information on vaccinations and other health precautions on the CDC website. For information about outbreaks of infectious diseases abroad, consult the World Health Organization (WHO) website. The WHO website also contains additional health information for travelers, including detailed country-specific health information.

Medical Insurance: You can't assume your insurance will go with you when you travel. It's very important to find out BEFORE you leave. You need to ask your insurance company two questions:

- Does my policy apply when I'm out of the United States?
- Will it cover emergencies like a trip to a foreign hospital or an evacuation?

In many places, doctors and hospitals still expect payment in cash at the time of service. Your regular U.S. health insurance may not cover doctors' and hospital visits in other countries. If your policy doesn't go with you when you travel, it's a very good idea to take out another one for your trip.

The Royal Insurance Corporation of Bhutan has initiated a travel and medical plan solely for visitors to Bhutan. When booking your trip, you should get detailed information about the insurance plan from your travel agents in Bhutan. You may also visit their web site at www.ricb.com.bt.

Traffic Safety and Road Conditions: While in Bhutan, you may encounter road conditions that differ significantly from those in the United States. The information below concerning Bhutan is provided for general reference only and may not be totally accurate in a particular location or circumstance.

General road conditions outside urban areas are poor, and emergency services generally are not available. Because of the mountainous terrain, roads tend to have steep drop-offs and blind curves. During heavy rains there is a risk of falling rocks and landslides which can block roads. However, because Bhutan requires tourists to arrange their trips through registered tour operators and travel in groups with experienced drivers, most tourists will not drive themselves.

Aviation Safety Oversight: As there is no direct commercial air service to the United States by carriers registered in Bhutan, the U.S. Federal Aviation Administration (FAA) has not assessed the government of Bhutan's Civil Aviation Authority for compliance with International Civil Aviation Organization (ICAO) aviation safety standards. Further information may be found on the FAA's safety assessment page.

Children's Issues: Please see the U.S. Dept. of State Office of Children's Issues web pages on intercountry adoption and international parental child abduction.

Intercountry Adoption

Notice on Suspension of all Intercountry Adoptions in Bhutan
March 2012

Effective January 1, 2012, the Government of Bhutan temporarily suspended all intercountry adoptions pending approval of a new adoption law by the King. The adoption bill was drafted to clarify Bhutan's adoption procedures. The National Commission for Women and Children (NCWC), the Bhutanese government agency responsible for overseeing intercountry adoptions, is unable to estimate how long it will take for the adoption bill to be approved, but indicated it is not aware of any pending cases involving the adoption of a Bhutanese child by U.S. citizens.

Prospective adoptive parents who believe the suspension affects their adoption of a child from Bhutan may contact the NCWC by email at admin@ncwc.org.bt to inquire about the status of their case. The NCWC indicated it will review each case on an individual basis.

U.S. Embassy in New Delhi
Shantipath, Chanakya Puri
New Delhi—110 021 India
Telephone number:
091–011–24198000 or 24198062

(this number is answered from 10AM to 12 Noon IST)
Fax number: 091–011–24198407
Email ACSnd@state.gov
For American Citizens Services
IVnd@state.gov
For Immigrant Visa Unit
http://newdelhi.usembassy.gov/visa_services.html

Bhutan's Adoption Authority
The National Commission for Women and Children (NCWC)
Post Box 556
Thimpu, Bhutan
Tel: 00975–2-334549/334550
Contact: Rinchen Chopel, Executive Director
E-mail: Rinchophel@gmail.com
Contact: Pema Galmo, Assistant Program Officer
E-mail: Pgalmo@gmail.com

Bhutan Consulate General
2 U.N. Plaza, 27th Floor
New York, NY 10017
Telephone: (212) 826–1919
Fax: (212) 826–2998

Office of Children's Issues
U.S. Department of State
2201 C Street, NW
SA-29
Washington, DC 20520
Tel: 1–888–407–4747
E-mail: AskCI@state.gov
http://adoption.state.gov

For questions about immigration procedures, call the National Customer Service Center (NCSC) 1-800-375-5283 (TTY 1-800-767-1833).

BOLIVIA

Compiled from publications that were available as of February 2013 from the U.S. Department of State, the U.S. Department of Commerce, and the Central Intelligence Agency (CIA). See the introduction to this set for explanatory notes.

Official Name:
Plurinational State of Bolivia

PROFILE

Geography

Area: total: 1,098,581 sq km; country comparison to the world: 28; land: 1,083,301 sq km; water: 15,280 sq km

Major cities: La Paz (capital) 1.642 million; Santa Cruz 1.584 million; Sucre 281,000 (2009)

Climate: varies with altitude; humid and tropical to cold and semiarid

Terrain: rugged Andes Mountains with a highland plateau (Altiplano), hills, lowland plains of the Amazon Basin

People

Nationality: noun: Bolivian(s); adjective: Bolivian

Population: 10,290,003 (July 2012 est.)

Population growth rate: 1.664% (2012 est.)

Ethnic groups: Quechua 30%, mestizo (mixed white and Amerindian ancestry) 30%, Aymara 25%, white 15%

Religions: Roman Catholic 95%, Protestant (Evangelical Methodist) 5%

Languages: Spanish (official) 60.7%, Quechua (official) 21.2%, Aymara (official) 14.6%, foreign languages 2.4%, other 1.2% (2001 census)

Literacy: definition: age 15 and over can read and write; total population: 86.7%; male: 93.1%; female: 80.7% (2001 census)

Health: life expectancy at birth: total population: 67.9 years; male: 65.16 years; female: 70.77 years (2012 est.); Infant mortality rate: total: 40.94 deaths/1,000 live births; male: 44.68 deaths/1,000 live births; female: 37.02 deaths/1,000 live births (2012 est.)

Unemployment rate: 5.5% (2011 est.)

Work force: 4.718 million (2012 est.)

Government

Type: republic; note—the new constitution defines Bolivia as a "Social Unitarian State"

Independence: 6 August 1825

Constitution: 7 February 2009

Political subdivisions: 9 departments (departamentos, singular—departamento); Beni, Chuquisaca, Cochabamba, La Paz, Oruro, Pando, Potosi, Santa Cruz, Tarija

Suffrage: 18 years of age, universal and compulsory

Economy

GDP (purchasing power parity): $54.36 billion (2012 est.); $51.56 billion (2011 est.); $49.06 billion (2010 est.); $47.11 billion (2009 est.)

GDP real growth rate: 5% (2012 est.); 5.1% (2011 est.); 4.1% (2010 est.); 3.4% (2009 est.)

GDP per capita (PPP): $5,000 (2012 est.); $4,900 (2011 est.); $4,700 (2010 est.); $4,600 (2009 est.)

Natural resources: tin, natural gas, petroleum, zinc, tungsten, antimony, silver, iron, lead, gold, timber, hydropower

Agriculture products: soybeans, coffee, coca, cotton, corn, sugarcane, rice, potatoes; Brazil nuts; timber

Industries: mining, smelting, petroleum, food and beverages, tobacco, handicrafts, clothing, jewelry

Exports: $10.97 billion (2012 est.); $8.397 billion (2011 est.); $6.291 billion (2010 est.)

Exports—commodities: natural gas, soybeans and soy products, crude petroleum, zinc ore, tin

Exports—partners: Brazil 41.8%, US 12.2%, South Korea 6.4%, Peru 5.7%, Argentina 5.2%, Japan 4.6% (2011)

Imports: $8.14 billion (2012 est.); $7.613 billion (2011 est.); $5.007 billion (2010 est.)

Imports—commodities: petroleum products, plastics, paper, aircraft and aircraft parts, prepared foods, automobiles, insecticides

Imports—partners: Chile 23.6%, Brazil 23%, Argentina 10.4%, US 10.1%, Peru 6.9%, China 5.9% (2011)

Debt—external: $5.491 billion (31 December 2011 est.); $5.267 billion (31 December 2010 est.)

Exchange rates: bolivianos (BOB) per US dollar; 6.96 (2012 est.); 6.937 (2011 est.); 7.0167 (2010 est.); 7.07 (2009); 7.253 (2008); 7.8616 (2007)

PEOPLE AND CULTURE

More than 60% of the population is indigenous. The largest of the approximately three dozen indigenous groups are the Quechua, Aymara, Chiquitano, and Guarani. No other indigenous groups represent more than 0.5% of the population. German, Croatian, Serbian, Asian, Middle Eastern, Canadian and other minorities also live in Bolivia. Many of these minorities descend from families that have lived in Bolivia for several generations.

Bolivia is one of the least developed countries in South America. Almost two-thirds of its people, many of whom are subsistence farmers, live in poverty.

The socio-political development of Bolivia can be divided into three distinct periods: pre-Columbian, colonial, and republican. Important archaeological ruins, gold and silver ornaments, stone monuments, ceramics, and weavings remain from several important pre-Columbian cultures. Major ruins include Tiwanaku, Samaipata, Incallajta, and Iskanwaya. The country abounds in other sites that are difficult to reach and have seen little archaeological exploration.

The Spanish brought a tradition of religious art which, in the hands of local indigenous and mestizo builders and artisans, developed into a rich and distinctive style of architecture, painting, and sculpture known as "Mestizo Baroque." The colonial period produced the paintings of Perez de Holguin, Flores, Bitti, and others as well as the skilled work of unknown stonecutters, woodcarvers, goldsmiths, and silversmiths. An important body of native baroque religious music from the colonial period was recovered and has been performed internationally to wide acclaim since 1994.

Important 20th-century Bolivian artists include, among others, Guzman de Rojas, Arturo Borda, Maria Luisa Pacheco, and Marina Nunez del Prado. Bolivia has rich folklore. Its regional folk music is distinctive and varied. The "devil dances" at the annual Oruro carnival are among the great South American folkloric events, as are the lesser-known carnival at Tarabuco and the "Gran Poder" festival in La Paz.

National/Racial/Ethnic Minorities

In the 2001 census, approximately 62 percent of the population over the age of 15 identified themselves as indigenous, primarily from the Quechua and Aymara groups. The Inter-American Commission on Human Rights reported that 70 percent of indigenous persons lived in poverty or extreme poverty with little access to education or minimal services to support human health, such as clean drinking water and sanitation systems. The government carried out some programs to increase access to potable water and sanitation in rural areas where indigenous people predominated. The governmental Indigenous Fund initiated support in 2010 for development projects designed to primarily benefit indigenous communities. The fund had a budget of more than 900 million bolivianos ($129 million) but allotted only 70 million bolivianos ($10 million) for 82 projects in the year.

Indigenous lands were not fully demarcated, and land reform remained a central political issue. Historically, some indigenous persons shared lands collectively under the "ayllu" system, which was not legally recognized during the transition to private property laws. Despite laws mandating reallocation and titling of lands, recognition and demarcation of indigenous lands were not fully accomplished.

The law states that indigenous peoples have the right to control natural resources in their territories, but indigenous people protested outside exploitation of their resources and sometimes complained that authorities did not properly consult them.

Indigenous persons were well represented in government and politics, but they bore a disproportionate share of poverty and unemployment. Government educational and health services remained unavailable to many indigenous groups living in remote areas. The government continued to try to improve individual and family situations through the delivery of cash conditional transfers and retirement payments to low-income persons and the elderly. For example, under the cash conditional transfer program, pregnant women and children under the age of two receive money if they undergo medical checkups.

Language

Bolivia has 37 official languages including Spanish and 36 indigenous languages. The most prevalent of the indigenous languages are Aymara and Quechua. Many business officials who work with international partners speak English.

Religion

According to the 2001 census by the National Statistical Institute, 78 percent of the population identified themselves as Roman Catholic and 16 percent as Protestant or evangelical. Approximately 3 percent were members of smaller Christian groups, and less than 1 percent were non-Christians, including Muslims and Jews. The government's official registry of religious organizations includes 23 religious groups.

Many indigenous communities, concentrated in rural areas, practice a mix of Catholic and spiritual traditions. Some indigenous communities have incorporated traditional beliefs into Catholic ceremonies.

HISTORY

The Andean region has probably been inhabited for some 20,000 years. Around 2000 B.C., the Tiwanakan culture developed at the southern end of Lake Titicaca. The Tiwanakan culture centered around and was named after the great city Tiwanaku. The people developed advanced architectural and agricultural techniques before disappearing about 1200 A.D., probably because of extended drought.

Roughly contemporaneous with the Tiwanakan culture, the Moxos in the eastern lowlands and the Mollos north of present-day La Paz also developed advanced agricultural societies that had dissipated by the 13th century. Around 1450, the Quechua-speaking Incas entered the area of modern highland Bolivia and added it to their empire. They controlled the area until the Spanish conquest in 1525.

During most of the Spanish colonial period, this territory was called "Upper Peru" or "Charcas" and was under the authority of the Viceroy of Lima. Local government came from the Audiencia de Charcas located in Chuquisaca (La Plata—modern-day Sucre). Bolivian silver mines produced much of the Spanish empire's wealth. Potosi, site of the famed Cerro Rico—"Rich Mountain"—was, for many years, the largest city in the Western Hemisphere. As Spanish royal authority weakened during the Napoleonic wars, sentiment against colonial rule grew. Independence was proclaimed in 1809. Sixteen years of struggle followed before the establishment of the republic, named after Simon Bolivar, on August 6, 1825.

Independence did not bring stability. For nearly 60 years, short-lived, weak institutions and frequent coups characterized Bolivian politics. The War of the Pacific (1879–83) demonstrated Bolivia's weakness when it was defeated by Chile. Chile took lands that contained rich nitrate fields and removed Bolivia's access to the sea. An increase in world silver prices brought Bolivia prosperity and political stability in the late 1800s. Tin eventually replaced silver as the country's most important source of wealth during the early part of the 20th century. Successive governments controlled by economic and social elites followed laissez-faire capitalist policies through the first third of the century.

Indigenous living conditions remained deplorable. Forced to work under primitive conditions in the mines and in nearly feudal status on large estates, indigenous people were denied access to education, economic opportunity, or political participation. Bolivia's defeat by Paraguay in the Chaco War (1932–35) marked a turning point. Great loss of life and territory discredited the traditional ruling classes, while service in the army produced stirrings of political awareness among the indigenous people and more of a shared national identity. From the end of the Chaco War until the 1952 revolution, the emergence of contending ideologies and the demands of new groups convulsed Bolivian politics.

Revolution and Turmoil

Bolivia's first modern and broad-based political party was the Nationalist Revolutionary Movement (MNR). Denied victory in the 1951 presidential elections, the MNR led a successful revolution in 1952. Under President Victor Paz Estenssoro, the MNR introduced universal adult suffrage, carried out a sweeping land reform, promoted rural education, and nationalized the country's largest tin mines.

Twelve years of tumultuous rule left the MNR divided. In 1964, a military junta overthrew President Paz Estenssoro at the outset of his third term. The 1969 death of President Rene Barrientos, a former junta member elected president in 1966, led to a succession of weak governments. The military, the MNR, and others installed Col. (later General) Hugo Banzer Suarez as president in 1971. Banzer ruled with MNR support from 1971 to 1974. Then, impatient with schisms in the coalition, he replaced civilians with members of the armed forces and suspended political activities.

The economy grew impressively during most of Banzer's presidency, but human rights violations and fiscal crises undercut his support. He was forced to call elections in 1978, and Bolivia again entered a period of political turmoil. Elections in 1978, 1979, and 1980 were inconclusive and marked by fraud. There were coups, counter-coups, and caretaker governments.

In 1980, Gen. Luis Garcia Meza carried out a ruthless and violent coup. His government was notorious for human rights abuses, narcotics trafficking, and economic mismanagement. Later convicted in absentia for crimes, including murder, Garcia Meza was extradited from Brazil and began serving a 30-year sentence in 1995 in a La Paz prison.

After a military coup forced Garcia Meza out of power in 1981, three separate military governments in 14 months struggled unsuccessfully to address Bolivia's growing problems. Unrest forced the military to convoke the Congress elected in 1980 and allow it to choose a new chief executive. In October 1982–22 years after the end of his first term of office (1956–60)—Hernan Siles Zuazo again became president. Severe social tension, exacerbated by hyperinflation and weak leadership, forced him to call early elections and relinquish power a year before the end of his constitutional term.

Return to Democracy

In the 1985 elections, Gen. Banzer's Nationalist Democratic Action Party (ADN) won a plurality of the popular vote (33%), followed by former President Paz Estenssoro's MNR (30%) and former Vice President Jaime Paz Zamora's Movement of the Revolutionary Left (MIR, at 10%). With no majority, the Congress had constitutional authority to determine who would be president. In the congressional run-off, the MIR sided with MNR, and Paz Estenssoro was

selected to serve a fourth term as president. When he took office in 1985, he faced a staggering economic crisis. Economic output and exports had been declining for several years. Hyperinflation meant prices grew at an annual rate of 24,000%. Social unrest, chronic strikes, and drug trafficking were widespread.

In 4 years, Paz Estenssoro's administration achieved a measure of economic and social stability. The military stayed out of politics; all major political parties publicly and institutionally committed themselves to democracy. Human rights violations, which tainted some governments earlier in the decade, decreased significantly. However, Paz Estenssoro's accomplishments came with sacrifice. Tin prices collapsed in October 1985. The collapse came as the government moved to reassert control of the mismanaged state mining enterprise and forced the government to lay off over 20,000 miners. Although this economic "shock treatment" was highly successful from a financial point of view and tamed devastatingly high rates of hyperinflation, the resulting social dislocation caused significant unrest.

MNR candidate Gonzalo Sanchez de Lozada finished first in the 1989 elections (23%), but no candidate received a majority of popular votes. Again, Congress would determine the president. The Patriotic Accord (AP) between Gen. Banzer's ADN and Jaime Paz Zamora's MIR, the second- and third-place finishers (at 22.7% and 19.6%, respectively), led to Paz Zamora's assuming the presidency.

Even though Paz Zamora had been a Marxist in his youth, he governed as a moderate, center-left president, and marked his time in office with political pragmatism. He continued the economic reforms begun by Paz Estenssoro. Paz Zamora also took a fairly hard line against domestic terrorism, authorizing a 1990 attack on terrorists of the Nestor Paz Zamora Committee and the 1992 crackdown on the Tupac Katari Guerrilla Army (EGTK).

The 1993 elections continued the growing tradition of open, honest elections and peaceful democratic transitions of power. The MNR defeated the ruling coalition, and Gonzalo "Goni" Sanchez de Lozada was named president by a coalition in Congress.

Sanchez de Lozada pursued an aggressive economic and social reform agenda, relying heavily on successful entrepreneurs-turned-politicians like him. The most dramatic program—"capitalization," a form of privatization under which investors acquired 50% ownership and management control of the state oil corporation, telecommunications system, airlines, railroads, and electric utilities—was used to generate funds for a new pension and healthcare system called BonoSol. BonoSol funding was popular in the country but the concept of capitalization was strongly opposed by certain segments of society, with frequent and sometimes violent protests from 1994 through 1996. During his term, Sanchez de Lozada also created the "Popular Participation Law," which devolved much of the central government's authority to newly-created municipalities, and the INRA law, which significantly furthered land redistribution efforts begun under the MNR after the 1952 revolution.

In the 1997 elections, Gen. Hugo Banzer, leader of the ADN, returned to power democratically after defeating the MNR candidate. The Banzer government continued the free market and privatization policies of its predecessor. The relatively robust economic growth of the mid-1990s continued until regional, global, and domestic factors contributed to a decline in economic growth. Job creation remained limited throughout this period, and public perception of corruption was high. Both factors contributed to an increase in social protests during the second half of Banzer's term.

Rising international demand for cocaine in the 1980s and 1990s led to a boom in coca production and to significant peasant migration to the Chapare region. To reverse this, Banzer instructed special police units to physically eradicate the illegal coca in the Chapare. The policy produced a sudden and dramatic 4-year decline in Bolivia's illegal coca crop, to the point that Bolivia became a relatively small supplier of coca for cocaine. In 2001, Banzer resigned from office after being diagnosed with cancer. He died less than a year later. Banzer's U.S.-educated vice president, Jorge Quiroga, completed the final year of the term.

In the 2002 national elections, former President Sanchez de Lozada (MNR) again placed first with 22.5% of the vote, followed by coca union leader Evo Morales (Movement Toward Socialism, MAS) with 20.9%. The MNR platform featured three overarching objectives: economic reactivation (and job creation), anti-corruption, and social inclusion.

A 4-year economic recession, difficult fiscal situation, and longstanding tensions between the military and police led to the February 12-13, 2003, violence that left more than 30 people dead and nearly toppled Sanchez de Lozada's government. The government stayed in power, but was unpopular.

Trouble began again in the so-called "Gas Wars" of September/October 2003, which sparked over a proposed project to export liquefied natural gas, most likely through Chile. A hunger strike by Aymara leader and congressional deputy Felipe "Mallku" Quispe led his followers to begin blocking roads near Lake Titicaca. About 800 tourists, including some foreigners, were trapped in the town of Sorata. After days of unsuccessful negotiations, Bolivian security forces launched a rescue operation, but on the way out, were ambushed by armed peasants and a number of people were killed on both sides. The incident ignited passions throughout the highlands and united a loose coalition of protestors to pressure the government. Anti-Chile sentiment and memories of three major cycles of non-renewable commodity exports (silver through the 19th century, guano and rubber late in the 19th century, and tin in the 20th century) touched a nerve with many citizens. Tensions grew and La Paz was subjected to protesters' blockades. Violent confrontations ensued, and approximately 60 people died when security forces tried to bring supplies into the besieged city.

On October 17, large demonstrations under the leadership of Evo Morales forced Sanchez de Lozada to resign. Vice President Carlos Mesa Gisbert assumed office and restored order. Mesa appointed a non-political cabinet and promised to revise the constitution through a constituent assembly, revise the hydrocarbons law, and hold a binding referendum on whether to develop the country's natural gas deposits, including for export. The referendum took place on July 18, 2004, and Bolivians voted overwhelmingly in favor of development of the nation's hydrocarbons resources. But the referendum did not end social unrest. In May 2005, large-scale protests led to the congressional approval of a law establishing a 32% direct tax on hydrocarbons production, which the government used to fund new social programs. After a brief pause, demonstrations resumed, particularly in La Paz and El Alto. President Mesa offered his resignation on June 6, and Eduardo Rodriguez, the president of the Supreme Court, assumed office in a constitutional transfer of power. Rodriguez announced that he was a transitional president, and called for elections within 6 months.

Evo Morales Elected

On December 18, 2005, the Movement Toward Socialism (MAS) candidate Juan Evo Morales Ayma was elected to the presidency by 54% of the voters. Bolivia's first president to represent the indigenous majority, Morales continued to serve as leader of the country's coca unions. During his campaign, Morales vowed to nationalize hydrocarbons and to empower the indigenous population. Morales was highly critical of what he termed "neo-liberal" economic policies. On January 22, 2006, Morales and Vice President Alvaro Garcia Linera were inaugurated.

On May 1, 2006, the government issued a decree nationalizing the hydrocarbons sector and calling for the renegotiation of contracts with hydrocarbons companies. Morales promoted greater state control of natural resource industries, particularly hydrocarbons and mining, and of the telecommunications sector (see Economy section). These policies pleased Morales' supporters but complicated Bolivia's relations with some of its neighboring countries, foreign investors, and members of the international community.

Fulfilling another campaign promise, Morales convoked a constituent assembly to draft a new constitution. The assembly convened on August 6, 2006, and planned to complete its work by August 2007; however, the Congress extended its mandate to December 2007 after the assembly faced political deadlock over its voting rules. The MAS approved a constitution without the opposition vote in November 2007, in a controversial assembly session in which opposition delegates were blocked from voting by demonstrators and the armed forces. On December 14, 2007, Morales presented the constitutional text to the National Congress to request a referendum for its approval in 2008. The opposition-controlled Senate prevented the referendum legislation from moving forward.

Political tensions between the government and the opposition over the new constitution, autonomy statutes passed by some departmental legislatures, and disputes over the division of tax proceeds from the hydrocarbon industry led to civil unrest, which culminated in violent discord in August and September 2008 in eastern departments.

On October 21, 2008, with a crowd of at least 50,000 pro-government supporters surrounding the National Congress, the government and congressional opposition agreed on final draft text for the new constitution. Voters approved the new constitution on January 25, 2009, and it entered into force on February 7, 2009. The new constitution called for national elections, which were held in December.

Current Administration

President Morales was re-elected on December 6, 2009, with 64% of the vote, followed by former Cochabamba Prefect Manfred Reyes Villa (27%) and business leader Samuel Doria Medina (6%). The ruling MAS party won 88 out of 130 deputy races and 26 out of 36 Senate seats, gaining a two-thirds majority of the Plurinational Assembly.

After re-election, President Morales prioritized implementation of the new constitution. Morales and Vice President Garcia Linera pledged to move the country toward "communitarian socialism," with an "integrated" economic system featuring a strong state presence. The Morales administration promised greater investment in infrastructure, education, health, and a "great leap forward" in industrialization (including development of lithium reserves and the country's first satellite).

The 2009 constitution included mandates for implementing legislation, including five major pieces of legislation by July 2010. Required legislation included bills to codify and coordinate interactions between the co-equal "ordinary" and indigenous justice systems; reform and restructure the country's Supreme Court, Constitutional Tribunal, and National Electoral Court (considered the fourth branch of government); and define the roles and responsibilities of the central government and four autonomy levels: departmental, regional, municipal, and indigenous. On December 26, 2010, the Morales administration removed subsidies for gasoline overnight. Gas prices rose 73% and, following nationwide protests over the "gasolinazo," Morales reintroduced the subsidies. Morales' popularity also was affected by police intervention in a march by lowland indigenous persons on September 25, 2011 protesting the development of a road through their protected territory. On October 16, 2011, the government held popular elections for the four highest judicial courts in the country. A majority of votes were returned null or blank due to frustrations over campaign restrictions, the recent police intervention, and complicated ballots.

President Morales held a national summit in late 2011 and early 2012 to formulate a new set of laws to address foreign investment, the hydrocarbon industry, and other issues. On January 23, 2012 Morales announced a round of cabinet changes, removing seven ministers and replacing two others in his 20-person cabinet.

GOVERNMENT AND POLITICAL CONDITIONS

Bolivia is a constitutional, multiparty republic. In December 2009, in a process deemed free and fair by international observers, citizens reelected Evo Morales Ayma, leader of the Movement toward Socialism (MAS) party, as president.

Recent Elections

Monitoring groups from the Organization of American States, the EU, and the Carter center considered the 2009 national presidential and legislative elections peaceful, free, and fair.

The nation's first judicial elections, held on October 16, 2011, were deemed free and fair by observers from the Organization of American States and the Union of South American States. However, electoral laws prohibited media access to the candidates prior to the elections (see section 2.a.), and opposition leaders claimed the preselection of candidates by congress rendered the vote "legal but not legitimate."

Participation of Women and Minorities: Half the candidates on municipal election ballots must be women, a requirement that increased female representation to approximately 30 percent of municipal council positions. However, credible NGOs reported that women participating in politics sometimes faced challenges to running for municipal offices in the form of violence. There were 52 women among the 166 congressional deputies and senators and 10 women in the 21-member cabinet. In the October 16 judicial elections, the candidates for Supreme Court were categorized by gender to encourage equal representation in the court.

The constitution and electoral law set aside seven special indigenous districts to increase indigenous political participation in congress.

Principal Government Officials

Last Updated: 1/31/2013

Pres.: **Juan Evo MORALES Ayma**
Vice Pres.: **Alvaro GARCIA Linera**
Min. of Autonomy: **Claudia Stacy PENA Claros**
Min. of Communication: **Amanda DAVILA Torrez**
Min. of Culture: **Pablo Cesar GROUX Canedo**
Min. of Defense: **Ruben Aldo SAAVEDRA Soto**
Min. of the Economy & Public Finances: **Luis Alberto ARCE Catacora**
Min. of Education: **Roberto Ivan AGUILAR Gomez**
Min. of the Environment & Water: **Felipe QUISPE Quenta**
Min. of Foreign Relations & Worship: **David CHOQUEHUANCA Cespedes**
Min. of Govt.: **Carlos ROMERO Bonifaz**
Min. of Health & Sports: **Juan Carlos CALVIMONTES Camargo**
Min. of Hydrocarbons & Energy: **Juan Jose Hernando SOSA Soruco**
Min. of Institutional Transparency & Fighting Corruption: **Nardi SUXO Iturri**
Min. of Labor, Employment, & Social Security: **Daniel SANTALLA Torrez**
Min. of Legal Defense of the State: **Hugo MONTERO Lara**
Min. of Mining & Metals: **Mario VIRREYRA Iporre**
Min. of Planning & Development: **Elba Viviana CARO Hinojosa**
Min. of the Presidency: **Juan Ramon QUINTANA Taborga**
Min. of Productive Development & Pluralist Economics: **Ana Teresa MORALES Olivera**
Min. of Public Works, Services, & Housing: **Arturo Vladimir SANCHEZ Escobar**
Min. of Rural Development & Lands: **Nemecia ACHACOLLO Tola**
Min. Without Portfolio for Justice: **Cecilia Luisa AYLLON Quinteros**
Presidential Del. for Political Affairs:
Presidential Del. for Public Transparency & Integrity:
Pres., Central Bank: **Marcelo ZABALAGA**
Charge d'Affaires, Embassy, Washington: **Freddy BERSATTI**
Permanent Representative to the UN, New York: **Sacha Sergio LLORENTI Soliz**

ECONOMY

Bolivia is one of the poorest and least developed countries in Latin America. Following a disastrous economic crisis during the early 1980s, reforms spurred private investment, stimulated economic growth, and cut poverty rates in the 1990s. The period 2003–05 was characterized by political instability, racial tensions, and violent protests against plans - subsequently abandoned—to export Bolivia's newly discovered natural gas reserves to large Northern Hemisphere markets.

In 2005, the government passed a controversial hydrocarbons law that imposed significantly higher royalties and required foreign firms then operating under risk-sharing contracts to surrender all production to the state energy company in exchange for a predetermined service fee. The global recession slowed growth, but Bolivia recorded the highest growth rate in South America during 2009.

During 2010–12 high world commodity prices sustained rapid growth and large trade surpluses. However, a lack of foreign investment in the key sectors of mining and hydrocarbons, along with growing conflict among social groups pose challenges for the Bolivian economy.

Labor Conditions

The law prohibits all paid work by children under the age of 14. The law prohibits a range of dangerous, immoral, and unhealthy types of work for minors under 18. Labor law permits apprenticeship for 12- to 14-year-old children with various formal but poorly enforced restrictions that were criticized by the International Labor Organization (ILO). Children under 14 worked in a variety of industries, including historically dangerous sectors such as mining.

The Ministry of Labor is responsible for enforcing child labor laws but in general did not do so effectively, including laws pertaining to the minimum age and maximum hours for child workers, school completion requirements, and health and safety conditions for children in the workplace.

According to the ILO, in 2008 an estimated 848,000 children between the ages of five to 17 worked at least one hour a week. Approximately 800,000 children were under the age of 14 and working in risky labor conditions—354,000 in urban areas and 446,000 in rural areas. There were reports of Bolivian children subjected to forced labor in neighboring countries.

During 2011 the government raised the minimum monthly wage to 815 bolivianos ($117) for the public and private sectors. The official estimate of the poverty income level in 2005 was 336 bolivianos ($48) per month. Labor laws establish a maximum workweek of 48 hours and limit the workday to eight hours for men. The laws also set a 40-hour workweek for women, prohibit women from working at night, mandate rest periods, and require premium pay for work above a standard workweek. The law provides for a minimum of 15 days' annual leave and grants workers the right to remove themselves from dangerous situations without fear of losing their jobs. In practice the government did not effectively enforce these laws.

An estimated two-thirds of workers were part of the informal economy. There was no significant government effort to formalize or enforce labor laws in this portion of the economy. Working conditions in cooperative-operated mines remained poor. Miners were self-employed and continued to work with no scheduled rest for long periods in dangerous, unhealthy conditions.

U.S.-BOLIVIAN RELATIONS

The United States established diplomatic relations with Bolivia in 1849 following its independence from Spain. Bolivia is one of the poorest countries in the Western Hemisphere, with much of the population living in poverty, and it faces serious economic and social challenges. The United States and Bolivia have traditionally had cordial and cooperative relations.

Bolivia is a major producer of coca and cocaine, and its international obligation to control illegal narcotics is a primary issue in the bilateral relationship. For centuries, a limited quantity of Bolivian coca leaf has been chewed and used in traditional rituals, but in the 1970s and 1980s the emergence of the drug trade led to a rapid increase in coca cultivated to make cocaine. In 2006, Bolivia inaugurated as president Evo Morales, a coca union leader who was critical of what he termed "neo-liberal" economic policies.

Relations with the United States deteriorated as the Bolivian Government began to dismantle vital elements of the relationship. In 2008, the government expelled the U.S. Ambassador and the U.S. Drug Enforcement Administration from the country. It also expelled the U.S. Agency for International Development from Bolivia's largest coca-growing region.

The U.S. and Bolivia began a dialogue in 2009 to improve relations, which culminated in the 2011 signing of a bilateral framework agreement to normalize relations. The United States provides assistance to advance common goals in Bolivia through programs to promote health and welfare, advance economic development, and fight narcotics production and trafficking.

U.S. Assistance to Bolivia

U.S. assistance aims to support Bolivian Government counterparts, non-governmental organizations, and the private sector to address key social, economic, and law enforcement needs. U.S. assistance provides support for the Bolivian Government's health sector program that seeks to improve health conditions among vulnerable segments of the population, especially women and children under 5 years of age. U.S. assistance will provide limited administrative and logistical support for Bolivian counternarcotics efforts and seek to encourage greater Bolivian cooperation in this area. It will also help agricultural producers improve the volume, quality, and marketability of select crops grown as an alternative to coca.

Bilateral Economic Relations

The United States is one of Bolivia's top trade partners. U.S. exports to Bolivia include machinery, vehicles, aircraft, optical and medical instruments, and agricultural products. U.S. imports from Bolivia include silver and jewelry, crude oil, tin, and Brazil nuts and other agricultural products. Bolivia is generally open to foreign direct investment, but legal uncertainties include regulatory changes called for in the 2009 Bolivian constitution. The government has begun to nationalize companies that were privatized in the 1990s. The U.S.-Bolivia bilateral investment treaty that entered into force in 2001 was terminated by the Bolivian Government as of June 2012, although it will continue to apply for another 10 years to covered investments existing at the time of termination.

Bolivia's Membership in International Organizations

Bolivia and the United States belong to a number of the same international organizations, including the United Nations, Organization of American States, International Monetary Fund, World Bank, and World Trade Organization.

Bilateral Representation

Bolivia maintains an embassy in the United States at 3014 Massachusetts Ave., NW, Washington, DC 20008 (tel. 202-483-4410); consulates in Washington, DC (tel. 202-232-4827), Los Angeles, San Francisco, Miami, New Orleans, and New York; and honorary consulates in Atlanta, Chicago, Cincinnati, Houston, Mobile, Seattle, St. Louis, and San Juan.

Principal U.S. Embassy Officials

Last Updated: 1/14/2013

LA PAZ (E) Av. Arce # 2780, (591) (2) 216-8000, Fax (591) (2) 216-8111, Workweek: Mon-Fri, 08:30–17:30, http://bolivia.usembassy.gov/

DCM OMS:	Karin Gembus
AMB OMS:	Vacant
CM Charge:	Larry Memmott
CM OMS:	Megan E. Gallardo
Co-CLO:	Bonnie Stroup
FM:	Vacant
HRO:	Cristina Meaney
MGT:	Robert A. Frazier
MLO/ODC:	COL Dennis Fiemeyer
NAS/INL:	Donald Frerichs
POL/ECON:	A/Geoffresy Schadrack
SDO/DATT:	COL Dennis Fiemeyer
AMB:	Vacant
CON:	Victoria Coffineau

DCM:	Acting DCM Mitchell Ferguson
PAO:	Aruna Amirthanayagan
GSO:	Park F. Wollam
RSO:	Thomas Scanlon
AFSA:	Richmond Blake
AID:	Wayne R. Nilsestuen
CLO:	Vacant
EEO:	Megan Gallardo
FMO:	Mathew Miller
ICASS Chair:	Ginger Longworth
IMO:	Bradley Gabler
IPO:	Armando Asencio
ISO:	Deborah A. Gaymer
ISSO:	Jimmey Aucoin
State ICASS:	Geoffrey Schadrack

TRAVEL

Consular Information Sheet

July 27, 2012

Country Description: Bolivia is a constitutional democracy and one of the least-developed countries in South America. Tourist facilities are generally adequate, but vary greatly in quality. La Paz is the administrative capital of Bolivia, while Sucre is the constitutional capital and the seat of the Supreme Court. La Paz is accessible by the international airport in El Alto.

Smart Traveler Enrollment Program (STEP)/Embassy Locations: If you are going to live in or visit Bolivia, please take the time to tell our Embassy about your trip. If you enroll, we can keep you up-to-date with important safety and security announcements. It will also help your friends and family get in touch with you in an emergency.

United States Embassy, La Paz, Bolivia
Avenida Arce 2780, La Paz, Bolivia
Telephone: 591-2-216-8246
Emergency after-hours telephone: 591-715-33713
Facsimile: 591-2-216-8808

There are two consular agencies in Bolivia, which provide limited services to U.S. citizens, including receiving passport applications which are then processed in La Paz. If you request service at one of the consular agencies, please schedule an appointment through the Embassy's web page at http://bolivia.usembassy.gov.

United States Consular Agency, Santa Cruz, Bolivia
Avenida Roque Aguilera #146 (3er Anillo), Santa Cruz, Bolivia
Telephone: 591-3-351-3477/351-3479
Emergency after-hours telephone: 591-715-33713
Facsimile: 591-3-351-3478

United States Consular Agency, Cochabamba, Bolivia
Edificio "SAAL," Avenida Pando No. 1122, Piso 1, Suites B and C, Cochabamba, Bolivia
Telephone: 591-4-411-6313
Emergency after-hours telephone: 591-715-33713
Facsimile: 591-4- 448-9119

Entry/Exit Requirements for U.S. Citizens: To enter and depart Bolivia, you are required to have a U.S. passport valid for at least six months from the date of your proposed entry into Bolivia.

If you are a U.S. citizen seeking to enter Bolivia as a tourist, you must have an entry visa. You can apply for a Bolivian tourist visa by mail or in person at Bolivian consulates in the U.S., as well as at Bolivian ports of entry, such as at Bolivia's international airports and at land border crossings. Bolivian tourist visas are valid for five years from the date of issuance and allow the bearer to enter the country three times in a year for a cumulative stay of not more than ninety days. The tourist visa costs $135.00. You can pay the $135.00 fee in cash, by deposit to the Bolivian Consulate's bank account, or by money order. If you choose to apply for your visa upon your arrival to Bolivia, you must pay this fee in cash to immigration authorities. In addition to the $135.00 visa fee, you must present a visa application form with a 4cm x 4cm color photograph, a passport with a validity of not less than 6 months, evidence of a hotel reservation or a letter of invitation in Spanish, proof of economic solvency (credit card, cash, or a current bank statement), and an International Vaccination Certificate for yellow fever.

Please visit the Embassy of Bolivia web site for the most current visa information. Bolivian consulates in the United States are located in Houston, Los Angeles, Miami, Minneapolis, Oklahoma City, New York, and Washington, DC.

If you are a U.S. citizen whose passport has been lost or stolen in Bolivia, you must obtain a replacement passport and present it, together with reports of the loss or theft from the Tourist Police and/or Interpol, to a Bolivian government immigration office in order to obtain a replacement visa at a cost of $80.00. For more information on replacement passport procedures, please consult the U.S. Embassy's web site.

The Bolivian government charges an exit tax for air departures from the country. If you have Bolivian citizenship or residency, the Bolivian government requires an additional fee upon departure. While the Bolivian government does not currently require travelers to purchase round-trip air tickets in order to enter the country, some airlines have required travelers to purchase round-trip tickets prior to boarding aircraft bound for Bolivia. Some tourists arriving by land report that immigration officials did not place entry stamps in their passports, causing problems at checkpoints and upon departure. Travelers should ensure that they receive entry and exit stamps from the Bolivian authorities every time they leave or enter Bolivia.

The U.S. Department of State is unaware of any HIV/AIDS entry restrictions for visitors to or foreign residents of Bolivia.

Additional requirements for minors: In an effort to prevent international child abduction, the Bolivian government has initiated procedures at entry/exit points. Minors (under 18) who are citizens or residents of Bolivia and who are traveling alone, with one parent, or with a third party must obtain a travel permit from the Juzgado del Menor. In order to obtain this permit, the parent or guardian must present a copy of the minor's birth certificate, parents' identification, and written authorization from the absent parent(s) or legal guardian, specifically granting permission to travel alone, with one parent, or with a third party. When a parent is deceased, Bolivian authorities require a notarized copy of the death certificate in lieu of the written authorization. If documents are prepared in the United States, you must have the documents translated into Spanish, notarized, and authenticated by the Bolivian Embassy or a Bolivian consulate within the United States. If documents are prepared in Bolivia, only notarization by a Bolivian notary is required. This requirement does not apply to children who enter the country with a U.S. passport as tourists, unless they hold dual U.S./Bolivian citizenship or have been in Bolivia for more than 90 consecutive days. Upon departure, U.S./Bolivian citizen minors traveling alone, with one parent, or with a third party, who have been in Bolivia for ninety (90) days or longer, will be required to present a travel authorization issued by the Juzgado del Menor, a copy of the minor's birth certificate and a copy of parents' identifications to immigration at the airport or land border. These travel are only valid for 90 days after they are issued and notarized, and a child may be prevented from leaving the country with an expired authorization.

The new visa requirement states that unaccompanied minors to Bolivia must present an official Parental Authorization and Consent Certificate duly provided by the appropriate authorities. Until the Bolivian government provides further specifics on this document, the embassy recommends that all unaccompanied minors to Bolivia carry a letter of permission from their parents or legal guardians authorizing travel.

Threats to Safety and Security: Protests, strikes, and other civic actions are common and disrupt transportation on a local and national level. While protest actions generally begin peacefully, they have the potential to become violent. The police have used tear gas to break up protests. In addition to rallies and street demonstrations, protesters sometimes block roads and have reacted with force when travelers attempt to pass through or go around roadblocks. You should avoid roadblocks and demonstrations. Demonstrations protesting government or private company policies occur frequently, even in otherwise peaceful times. If you plan to travel to or from Bolivia, you should take into consideration the possibility of disruptions to air service in and out of La Paz and other airports due to protests. You should monitor Bolivian media reports and the U.S. Embassy website for updates. The embassy strongly recommends that U.S. citizens avoid areas where roadblocks or public demonstrations are occurring or planned. Political rallies should similarly be avoided in light of press reports of violence at some rallies in various parts of Bolivia.

If you find yourself in a roadblock, you should not attempt to run through it, as this may aggravate the situation and lead to physical harm. Instead, you should consider taking alternative, safe routes, or returning to where the travel started. If you plan to embark on a road trip, you should monitor news reports and contact the American Citizen Services Unit of the U.S. Embassy in La Paz at (591-2) 216-8246 or the U.S. Consular Agencies in Cochabamba at (591- 4) 411-6313 and/or Santa Cruz at (591-3) 351-3477 for updates. Given that roadblocks may occur without warning and have stranded travelers for several days, you should take extra food, water, and warm clothing. The U.S. Embassy also advises American citizens maintain at least two weeks' supply of drinking water and canned food in case roadblocks affect supplies. For more information on emergency preparedness, please consult the Federal Emergency Management Authority (FEMA) web site. That website includes a Spanish language version.

Visitors should be careful when choosing a tour operator and should not accept any type of medication or drugs from unreliable sources.

The countrywide emergency number for the police, including highway patrol, is 110. The corresponding number for the fire department is 119. The National Tourism Police has offices in La Paz and Cochabamba, providing free assistance to tourists. In the city of Santa Cruz, Interpol will provide these same services to tourists. These services include English-speaking officials who may assist tourists in filing police reports of lost/stolen documents or other valuables. The La Paz office is open 24 hours a day and is located at Plaza del Stadium, Edificio Olympia, Planta Baja, Miraflores, telephone number 222-5016. The Cochabamba office is located at Plaza 14 de Septiembre, Edificio Prefectura, tel. (4) 451-0023; it is open from 7:30 a.m. until 8:00 p.m. seven days a week. In the Chapare region between Santa Cruz and Cochabamba and the Yungas region northeast of La Paz, violence and civil unrest, primarily associated with anti-narcotics activities, periodically create a risk for travelers to those regions. Another risk in this region is the dangerous flooding of roads due to heavy rains from December to February.

Confrontations between area residents and government authorities over coca eradication have resulted in the use of tear gas and stronger force by government authorities to quell disturbances. Pro-coca groups have expressed anti-U.S. sentiments and may attempt to target U.S. government or private interests. If you plan to travel to the Chapare or Yungas regions, we encourage you to check with the Embassy's Consular Section prior to travel. Violence has also erupted between squatters unlawfully invading private land and security forces attempting to remove them.

Stay up-to-date by bookmarking our Bureau of Consular Affairs' website, which contains current Travel Warnings and Travel Alerts as well as the Worldwide Caution.

You can also call 1-888-407-4747 toll-free within the U.S. and Canada, or by calling a regular toll line, 1-202-501-4444, from other countries.

These numbers are available from 8:00 a.m. to 8:00 p.m. Eastern Time, Monday through Friday (except U.S. federal holidays).

There is nobody better at protecting you than yourself. Take some time before travel to improve your personal security—things are not the same everywhere as they are in the United States.

Crime: The U.S. Department of State currently classifies Bolivia as a medium to high crime threat country. Street crime, such as pick pocketing, assaults following ATM withdrawals, and theft from parked vehicles, occurs with some frequency in Bolivia. You should secure your belongings in a hotel safe and refrain from wearing expensive jewelry. U.S. citizens have also had backpacks, passports, and other property stolen at bus terminals or while traveling on buses, as well as at Internet cafes and in other situations where the U.S. citizen is distracted or leaves property unattended. Theft of cars and car parts, particularly late-model four-wheel-drive vehicles, is common. Hijacking of vehicles has occurred, and you should take appropriate precautions to avoid being victimized.

Express kidnappings are common in La Paz. The areas where these crimes are most known to occur include Plaza Humbolt (Zona Sur), Plaza Abaroa, Plaza del Estudiante, Plaza Isabel La Católica, Plaza San Francisco and through several places in the downtown section of the city. These incidents typically occur when the victim boards a taxi in which the driver is an accomplice. Once the victim is inside, an additional person or two (the kidnappers) board the vehicle. At this point, the victim is robbed of his/her belongings and/or driven to an ATM where he/she is forced to provide PINs for debit and credit card withdrawals. Recommended tips to avoid becoming a victim include using only radio taxis which one calls in advance and not traveling alone, particularly if under the influence of alcohol or out late at night.

We recommend that you avoid the Coronilla Hill, a Cochabamba landmark adjacent to the main bus terminal and near several markets, hostels, and restaurants. The Coronilla Hill has become an increasingly dangerous place for tourists and local citizens alike. The local police, tourist authorities, and press have declared the area off limits and cautioned people to enter the area at their own peril. U.S. citizens have been assaulted in the area. The police have made several sweeps of the area in an attempt to control the population of street people, most of whom are reportedly drug addicts and alcohol abusers. Nonetheless, incidents of crime continue. Police reports indicate that thieves in that area have gone from purse snatching and burglary to increasingly violent assaults on passerbys.

The U.S. Embassy in La Paz continues to receive reports of U.S. citizens traveling by bus from Copacabana to La Paz being kidnapped and robbed of their ATM cards and other valuables. This crime reportedly involves U.S. citizens taking an evening bus from Copacabana. While the bus is scheduled to stop at the La Paz bus terminal, the driver will stop short of that location, typically near the General Cemetery late at night. Disembarking and disoriented passengers then have little option but to hail a waiting taxi. Thieves in cooperation with the taxi driver enter the taxi to blindfold and coerce the U.S. citizen(s) into surrendering cash, cameras, ATM cards, and other valuables. U.S. citizen victims have reported that once the thieves withdrew funds using the ATM cards, the U.S. citizens were released without further harm. If you plan to travel from Copacabana, you should try to arrive during daylight hours, verify the final destination, and buy tickets directly at the Copacabana bus terminal rather than from third parties.

Bolivian police report that there are eight organized criminal groups operating in the La Paz area. The techniques employed by these groups vary, but there are a few major patterns that can be identified:

There have been reports of "false police"—persons using police uniforms, identification, and even buildings modified to resemble police stations—intercepting and robbing foreign tourists, including U.S. citizens. Under Bolivian law, police need a warrant from the "fiscal" (prosecutor) to detain a suspect. Any searches or seizures must occur at a bona fide police station in the presence of the prosecutor. The warrant requirement also applies to suspected drug trafficking cases, although such searches and seizures may occur without a prosecutor present. If detained, you should request to see the warrant and demand immediate contact with the nearest U.S. consular office (in La Paz, Cochabamba or Santa Cruz).

According to press reports, criminals using the "false police" method focus on foreigners in areas frequented by tourists, including bus terminals and tourist markets such as Sagarnaga Street in La Paz. The perpetrators will identify a potential victim and have an accomplice, typically driving a white taxi, offer taxi services to the potential victim. They focus on European and U.S. tourists who are not wearing a traditional "trekker" backpack and are traveling without a large number of bags. A few blocks after the potential victim boards the taxi, another accomplice, pretending to be a recently arrived tourist, boards the taxi with the potential victim. With all the accomplices then in place, the "false police" stop the taxi, "search" the passengers, and rob the victim. As part of this scam, the false police may take the victim to a false police station.

A similar variation also introduces a "tourist" to the victims. This introduction can take place on a bus, taxi, train, or just walking down the street. The "tourist" will befriend the victims and might seek assistance in some manner. After a period of time, the "police" intercept the victims and the "tourist." At this point, the "police" discover some sort of contraband (usually drugs) on the "tourist."

The entire group is then taken to the "police station." At this point, the "police" seize the documents, credit cards, and ATM cards of the victims. The perpetrators obtain personal identification numbers, sometimes by threat of violence, and the scam is complete.

Another technique introduces a "tourist" to the victims. This "tourist" can be any race or gender and will probably be able to speak the language of the victims. This meeting can happen anywhere, and the goal of the "tourist" is to build the trust of the victims. Once a certain level of trust is obtained, the "tourist" suggests a particular mode of transportation to a location (usually a taxi). The "taxi" picks up the victims and the "tourist" and delivers the group to a safe house in the area. At this point the victims are informed that they are now kidnapped and are forced to give up their credit cards and ATM cards with personal identification numbers. In most instances, the victims are released, but violence is always a possibility. The techniques and the perpetrators are convincing. Authentic uniforms, badges, and props help persuade the victims that the situation is real and valid.

You should exercise great caution if visiting Bolivia. If you have doubts about a situation, you should immediately remove yourself from the scene. Thefts of bags, wallets, and backpacks are a problem throughout Bolivia, but especially in the tourist areas of downtown La Paz and the Altiplano. Most thefts involve two or three people who spot a potential victim and wait until the bag or backpack is placed on the ground, often at a restaurant, bus terminal, Internet café, etc. In other cases, the thief places a disagreeable substance on the clothes or backpack of the intended victim and then offers to assist the victim with the removal of the substance. While the person is distracted, the thief or an accomplice grabs the bag or backpack and flees. If you find yourself in such a situation, you should decline assistance, secure the bag/backpack, and walk briskly from the area.

To steal wallets and bags, thieves may spray water on the victim's neck, and while the person is distracted, an accomplice takes the wallet or bag. At times, the thief poses as a policeman and requests that the person accompany him to the police station, using a nearby taxi. If this happens to you, you should indicate a desire to contact the U.S. Embassy and not enter the taxi. Under no circumstances should you surrender ATM or credit cards, or release a personal identification number. While most thefts do not involve violence, in some instances the victim has been physically harmed and forcibly searched for hidden valuables. This is particularly true in "choke and rob" assaults where the victims, including U.S. citizens, reported being choked from behind until they lost consciousness and later awoke to find all of their possessions gone. These assaults have happened during both day and night. You should avoid being alone on the streets, especially at night and in isolated areas.

Don't buy counterfeit and pirated goods, even if they are widely available. Not only are the bootlegs illegal in the United States, you may be breaking local law, too.

Victims of Crime: If you or someone you know becomes the victim of a crime abroad, you should contact the local police and the nearest U.S. Embassy or Consulate (see the Department of State's list of embassies and consulates). If your passport is stolen, we can help you replace it. For violent crimes such as assault and rape, we can, for example, help you find appropriate medical care, contact family members or friends and help you get money from them if you need it. Although the investigation and prosecution of the crime are solely the responsibility of local authorities, consular officers can help you to understand the local criminal justice process and to find an attorney if needed.

The local equivalent to the "911" emergency line in Bolivia is 110, but you are unlikely to find an English speaker answering your call.

Criminal Penalties: While you are traveling in another country, you are subject to the local laws even if you are a U.S. citizen. Foreign laws and legal systems can be vastly different from our own. In some places, you may be taken in for questioning if you do not have your passport with you. In some places, it is illegal to take pictures of certain buildings and driving under the influence could land you immediately in jail. There are also some things that might be legal in Bolivia, but still illegal in the United States, and you can be prosecuted under U.S. law if you buy pirated goods or engage in child pornography. While you are overseas, U. S. laws don't apply. If you do something illegal in your host country, your U.S. passport won't help. It is very important to know what is legal and what is not legal where you are going. If you violate Bolivian laws, even unknowingly, Bolivian authorities may expel, arrest, or imprison you. Penalties for possessing, using, or trafficking in illegal drugs in Bolivia are severe, and convicted offenders can expect long jail sentences and heavy fines.

Special Circumstances: In the run-up to the July 2006 Constituent Assembly elections, President Morales accused the U.S. military of infiltrating Bolivia with operatives disguised as "students and tourists." As an apparent result of these comments, some U.S. citizens have reported harassment by Bolivian officials and been subjected to unwanted media attention. If you plan to travel to Bolivia, be aware of the political atmosphere and the possibility of unwanted attention from pro-governmental groups and Bolivian officials.

For information on in-country visa procedures and requirements, please consult the Bolivian Immigration Service at fax/telephone (591-2) 211-0960, street address Avenida Camacho entre Calles Loayza y Bueno, La Paz, Bolivia. In emergency cases, the Immigration Service may permit temporary residency applicants to retrieve their passports from those applications. However, under current regulations in such cases, the applicant would need to commence the application anew, including paying the corresponding fees. Any U.S. documents, such as birth, marriage, divorce, or death certificates, to be presented in Bolivia must first be authenticated in the U.S. at the nearest Bolivian Embassy or consulate. For information on those procedures, please consult the Department of State Office of Authentications web site and the nearest Bolivian Embassy or consulate.

Mountain Trekking and Climbing Safety: The Embassy urges you to exercise extreme care when trekking or climbing in Bolivia. Since June 2002, four U.S. citizens have died in falls while mountain climbing in Bolivia. Three of the deaths occurred on Illimani, a 21,033-foot peak located southeast of La Paz. Many popular trekking routes in the Bolivian Andes cross passes as high as 16,000 feet. Trekkers must have adequate clothing and equipment, not always available locally, and should be experienced mountain travelers.

It is not prudent to trek alone. Solo trekking is the most significant factor contributing to injuries and robberies. The safest option is to join an organized group and/or use a reputable firm to provide an experienced guide and porter who can communicate in both Spanish and English. If you develop any of the following symptoms while climbing at altitude—severe headache, weakness, vomiting, shortness of breath at rest, cough, chest tightness, unsteadiness—descend to a lower altitude immediately. The Embassy strongly encourages trekkers and climbers to purchase adequate insurance to cover expenses in case of injury or death.

Medical Facilities and Health Information: Throughout the country, both personal hygiene and sanitary practices in food handling are far below U.S. standards. Food and beverage precautions are essential. Medical care in large cities is adequate for most purposes but of varying quality. Ambulance services are limited to non-existent. Medical facilities are generally not adequate to handle serious medical conditions. Pharmacies are located throughout Bolivia and prescription and over-the-counter medications are widely available. Western Bolivia, dominated by the Andes and high plains (Altiplano), is largely insect-free. However, altitude sickness (see below) is a major problem. Eastern Bolivia is tropical, and visitors to that area are subject to related illnesses. Insect precautions are recommended. Dengue is endemic throughout eastern Bolivia, including in Santa Cruz city. Since January 2007, there have been several thousand cases, representing a significantly increased incidence, and part of a region-wide trend.

Bolivia is a high risk area for rabies. Dog and bat bites and scratches should be taken seriously and post exposure prophylaxis sought. Yellow fever is present in subtropical Bolivia. Yellow fever vaccination certification is required for visa application and may be required by airlines flying into Bolivia and at entry into Bolivia.

High Altitude Health Risks: The altitude of La Paz ranges from 10,600 feet to over 13,000 feet (3,400 to 4,000 meters) above sea level. Much of Western Bolivia is at the same altitude or higher, including Lake Titicaca, the Salar de Uyuni, and the cities of Oruro and Potosi. The altitude alone poses a serious risk of illness, hospitalization, and even death, even for those in excellent health.

Prior to departing the U.S. for high-altitude locations (over 10,000 feet above sea level), you should discuss the trip with your healthcare provider and request information on specific recommendations concerning medication and lifestyle tips at high altitudes. Coca-leaf tea is a popular beverage and folk remedy for altitude sickness in Bolivia. However, possession of this tea, which is sold in bags in most Bolivian grocery stores, is illegal in the United States. "Sorojchi pills" sold locally at pharmacies contain high amounts of caffeine and are not usually recommended.

The State Department cautions travelers planning to visit La Paz to consider the following risks and advice:

- Sickle cell anemia or sickle cell trait:ersons with sickle cell trait may have a crisis at elevations of more than 8,000 feet. U.S. citizens with this condition have required urgent medical evacuation from La Paz to the United States.
- Heart disease: Any person who has heart disease, or known risk factors for heart disease, should consult their doctor about their risks of ascending to altitude, and whether any testing of their heart would be in order. Even U.S. citizens who adjust well initially to the altitude in La Paz have subsequently suffered heart attacks and been hospitalized.
- Lung Disease: Anyone with emphysema should consult closely with their doctor and seriously reconsider coming to La Paz or surrounding, high altitude areas. Anyone with asthma should consult their doctor; mild asthma may be manageable at high altitude, but it is important to remember that emergency care and intensive respiratory care are very limited even in the city of La Paz and are absent outside the city. U.S. citizens with respiratory ailments have previously been medically evacuated from La Paz to other countries to receive medical treatment.
- Given potential complications from altitude sickness, pregnant women should consult their doctor before travel to La Paz and other high-altitude areas of Bolivia. A higher number of miscarriages and other pregnancy-related complications have been noted at altitude.

All people, even healthy and fit persons, will feel symptoms of hypoxia (lack of oxygen) upon arrival at high altitude. Most people will have increased respiration and increased heart rate. Many people will have headaches, difficulty sleeping, lack of appetite, minor gastric and intestinal upsets, and mood changes. Many travelers limit physical activity for the first 36 to 48 hours after arrival and avoid alcohol and smoking for at least one week after arrival.

Good information on vaccinations and other health precautions can be found on the CDC website. For information about outbreaks of infectious diseases abroad, consult the World Health Organization (WHO) website. The WHO website also contains additional health information for travelers, including detailed country-specific health information.

Medical Insurance: You can't assume your insurance will go with you when you travel. It is very important to find out BEFORE you leave. You need to ask your insurance company two questions:

- Does my policy apply when I'm out of the U.S.?
- Will it cover emergencies like a trip to a foreign hospital or a medical evacuation?

In many places, doctors and hospitals still expect payment in cash at the time of service. Your regular U.S. health insurance may not cover doctors' and hospital visits in Bolivia. If your policy doesn't go with you when you travel, it's a very good idea to take out another one for your trip.

Traffic Safety and Road Conditions: While in a foreign country, U.S. citizens may encounter road conditions that differ significantly from those in the United States. The information below concerning Bolivia is provided for general reference only and may not be totally accurate in a particular location or circumstance. If you plan on driving in Bolivia, despite the hazards described below, you should obtain an international driver's license through your local automobile club before coming to Bolivia.

Road conditions in Bolivia are hazardous. A lthough La Paz, Santa Cruz, and Cochabamba are connected by improved highways, the vast majority of roads in Bolivia are unpaved. Few highways have shoulders, fencing or barriers, and highway markings are minimal. Yielding for pedestrians in the cities is not the norm. For trips outside the major cities, especially in mountainous areas, a four-wheel-drive vehicle is highly recommended. Travel during the rainy season (November through March) is difficult, as most routes are potholed, and some roads and bridges are washed out. Added dangers are the absence of formal training for most drivers, poor maintenance and overloaded vehicles, lack of lights on some vehicles at night, and intoxicated or overly tired drivers, including commercial bus and truck drivers.

The majority of intercity travel in Bolivia is by bus, with varying levels of safety and service. Bus accidents, at times attributed to drunk drivers or mechanical failures, have caused scores of deaths and severe injuries. In recent years, there have been major bus crashes on the highway between La Paz and Oruro, Cochabamba and Santa Cruz, Oruro and Cochabamba and on the Yungas road. The old Yungas road is considered one of the most dangerous routes in the world.

Taxis, vans, and buses dominate intracity transportation. From a crime perspective, public transportation is relatively safe, and violent assaults are rare. However, petty theft of unattended backpacks and other personal items does occur. For safety purposes, the Embassy advises you to use radio taxis whenever possible. U.S. citizens taking unlicensed taxis have reported being robbed and assaulted.

Drivers of vehicles involved in traffic accidents are expected to remain at the scene until the arrival of local police authorities. Any attempt to leave the scene is in violation of Bolivian law. The Embassy believes any attempt to flee the scene of an accident would place the driver and passengers at greater risk of harm than remaining at the scene until the arrival of local police.

Aviation Safety Oversight: The U.S. Federal Aviation Administration (FAA) has assessed the Government of Bolivia's Civil Aviation Authority as being in compliance with International Civil Aviation Organization (ICAO) aviation safety standards for oversight of Bolivia's air carrier operations. For more information, visit the FAA's safety assessment page.

There are limited flights within Bolivia and to neighboring countries. Flight delays and cancellations are common. You should keep this information in mind when making your travel plans.

Children's Issues: Please see the U.S. Dept. of State Office of Children's Issues web pages on intercountry adoption and international parental child abduction.

Intercountry Adoption

October 2009

The information in this section has been edited from the latest report available as of February 2013 from the State Department Bureau of Consular Affairs, Office of Overseas Citizens Services. For more information, please read the *Intercountry Adoption* section of this book and review current reports online at http://adoption.state.gov.

Bolivia is party to the Hague Convention on Protection of Children and Co-operation in Respect of Intercountry Adoption (Hague Adoption Convention). Therefore all adoptions between Bolivia and the United States must meet the requirements of the Convention and U.S. law implementing the Convention.

Who Can Adopt? Adoption between the United States and Bolivia is governed by the Hague Adoption Convention. Therefore to adopt from Bolivia, you must first be found eligible to adopt by the U.S. Government. The U.S. Government agency responsible for making this determination is the Department of Homeland Security, U.S. Citizenship and Immigration Services (USCIS).

Residency Requirements: U.S. citizens must be legal residents of Bolivia in order to adopt in Bolivia.

Age Requirements: Prospective adoptive parents must be between 25 to 50 years of age or 15 years older than the adopted child to adopt a child in Bolivia.

Marriage Requirements: Bolivia allows both married and single people to adopt.

Who Can be Adopted? Because Bolivia is party to the Hague Adoption Convention, children from Bolivia must meet the requirements of the Convention in order to be eligible for adoption. For example, the Convention requires that Bolivia attempt to place a child with a family in-country before determining that a child is eligible for intercountry adoption. In addition to Bolivia's requirements, a child must meet the definition of a Convention adoptee for you to bring him or her back to the United States.

Abandonment Requirements: In order to be eligible for adoption, a Bolivian child must be "abandoned." Abandonment is a legal finding made by the Bolivian court, and must occur before the child is assigned to prospective adoptive parents. In effect, this prohibits so-called "direct" adoptions, in which the birth parent gives a child directly (or via an intermediary) to specific prospective adoptive parents for adoption. In addition, this effectively bars adoptive parents from searching for and locating a child on their own. Prospective adoptive parents must work with the Vice-Ministry of Gender and Generational Affairs to locate a child that is eligible for adoption.

Waiting Period: Adoption proceedings can, by law, take from 25 to 45 working days from the date of the first hearing, although it is not uncommon for the procedures to take even longer. The length of the process often depends on which court has jurisdiction over the case.

The Process: Because Bolivia is party to the Hague Adoption Convention, adopting from Bolivia must follow a specific process designed to meet the Convention's requirements. For detailed and updated information on these requirements, please review the *Intercountry Adoption* section of this publication and visit the U.S. Department of State Intercountry Adoption website at http://adoption.state.gov.

Role of the Adoption Authority: Once the final adoption decree has been issued, the adoption is recorded in a national registry maintained by the Vice-Ministry of Gender and Generational Affairs. At this point, at least one of the adoptive parents will need to the I-800A and I-800 in the United States with the Department of Homeland Security.

If approved, the 800 petition will be returned to the Consular Section's Immigrant Visa (IV) Unit in La Paz for visa processing. The Immigrant Visa Unit will then coordinate with the adoptive parents to arrange an immigrant visa interview on behalf of the child.

Time Frame: Bolivian adoptions can be time-consuming. Recent experience suggests that the total time required will be several months to over one year. When a married couple is adopting, it is sufficient for one spouse to remain in Bolivia for the duration of the adoption process; it is not necessary that both do so. However, both adoptive parents must be present for the preliminary hearing on provisional placement, the evaluation, and the ratification of the adoption by the court.

At least one prospective adoptive parent should plan to stay in Bolivia for approximately four to six weeks. Adoptive parents are advised NOT to make travel plans for an adoptive child until they have the child's U.S. visa. The Immigrant Visa Unit at the U.S. Embassy in La Paz will do its best to process adoption visa paperwork quickly; however, unexpected delays in the adoption process are possible. The U.S. Citizenship and Immigration Service and consular officials have no authority to intervene in any Bolivian legal process.

Adoption Fees: In the adoption services contract that you sign at the beginning of the adoption process, your agency will itemize the fees and estimated expenses related to your adoption process. The U.S. Embassy in Bolivia discourages the payment of any fees that are not properly receipted, "donations," or "expediting" fees, that may be requested from prospective adoptive parents. Such fees have the appearance of "buying" a baby and put all future adoptions in Bolivia at risk.

Documents Required: The following is a general list of documents that are required for adoption in Bolivia. Prospective adoptive parents should be aware that other documents may be required. Prospective adoptive parents are advised to have several extra copies of each document on hand when traveling to Bolivia. Documents to be submitted by the prospective adoptive parents include (but are not limited to) the following:

- The adoptive parents' birth certificates;
- The adoptive parents' marriage certificate(s), if applicable;
- Home study conducted by an approved adoption service provider;
- Physical and psychological health certificates;
- Financial and employment certifications;
- 2-3 Personal references and police clearances;
- Evidence that prospective parent(s) has participated in and completed a parenting workshop (this may be undertaken in the United States).

Bringing Your Child Home: Once your adoption is complete (or you have obtained legal custody of the child), there are a few more steps to take before you can head home. Specifically, you need to apply for several documents for your child before he or she can travel to the United States, such as a birth certificate, a passport or travel document for your child from the country in which he or she was born, and a U.S. Immigration Visa.

For detailed and updated information on how to obtain these documents, review the *Intercountry Adoption* section in this publication and visit the U.S. Department of State Intercountry Adoption website at http://adoption.state.gov.

Child Citizenship Act: For adoptions finalized abroad, the Child Citizenship Act of 2000 allows your new child to acquire American citizenship automatically when he or she enters the United States as lawful permanent residents.

For adoptions finalized in the United States, the Child Citizenship Act of 2000 allows your new child to acquire American citizenship automatically when the court in the United States issues the final adoption decree. To learn more, review the *Intercountry Adoption* section in this publication and visit the U.S. Department of State Intercountry Adoption website at http://adoption.state.gov.

U.S. Embassy in Bolivia
Avenida Arce 2780, between calles Cordero and Campos
La Paz, Bolivia

Bolivia's Adoption Authority
Av. 16 de Julio #1219
La Paz, Bolivia
Telephone: 591-2-212 4725
591-2-212 4727
Email: vicejunite@alamo.entelnet.bo

Embassy of Bolivia in U.S.
3014 Massachusetts Ave., N.W.
Washington, D.C. 20008
Tel: (202) 483-4410

Office of Children's Issues
U.S. Department of State
2201 C Street, NW
SA-29
Washington, DC 20520
Tel: 1-888-407-4747
E-mail: AskCI@state.gov
http://adoption.state.gov

BOSNIA AND HERZEGOVINA

Compiled from publications that were available as of February 2013 from the U.S. Department of State, the U.S. Department of Commerce, and the Central Intelligence Agency (CIA). See the introduction to this set for explanatory notes.

Official Name:
Bosnia and Herzegovina

PROFILE

Geography

Area: total: 51,197 sq km; country comparison to the world: 129; land: 51,187 sq km; water: 10 sq km
Major cities: Sarajevo (capital) 392,000 (2009)
Climate: hot summers and cold winters; areas of high elevation have short, cool summers and long, severe winters; mild, rainy winters along coast
Terrain: mountains and valleys

People

Nationality: noun: Bosnian(s), Herzegovinian(s); adjective: Bosnian, Herzegovinian
Population: 3,879,296 (July 2012 est.)
Population growth rate: -0.003% (2012 est.)
Ethnic groups: Bosniak 48%, Serb 37.1%, Croat 14.3%, other 0.6% (2000)
Religions: Muslim 40%, Orthodox 31%, Roman Catholic 15%, other 14%
Languages: Bosnian (official), Croatian (official), Serbian
Literacy: definition: age 15 and over can read and write; total population: 97.9%; male: 99.4%; female: 96.5% (2010 est.)
Health: life expectancy at birth: total population: 78.96 years; male: 75.42 years; female: 82.77 years (2012 est.); Infant mortality rate: total: 8.47 deaths/1,000 live births; male: 9.72 deaths/1,000 live births; female: 7.13 deaths/1,000 live births (2012 est.)

Unemployment rate: 43.3% (2011 est.)

Work force: 2.6 million (2010 est.)

Government

Type: emerging federal democratic republic

Independence: 1 March 1992

Constitution: the Dayton Peace Accords, signed 14 December 1995 in Paris, included a constitution; note—each of the entities also has its own constitution

Political subdivisions: 2 first-order administrative divisions and 1 internationally supervised district—Brcko district (Brcko Distrikt), the Bosniak/Croat Federation of Bosnia and Herzegovina (Federacija Bosna i Hercegovina) and the Bosnian Serb-led Republika Srpska; note—Brcko district is in northeastern Bosnia and is a self-governing administrative unit under the sovereignty of Bosnia and Herzegovina and formally held in condominium between the two entities; the District remains under international supervision

Suffrage: 18 years of age, 16 if employed; universal

Economy

GDP (purchasing power parity): $32.08 billion (2012 est.); $32.04 billion (2011 est.); $31.51 billion (2010 est.); $31.29 billion (2009 est.)
GDP real growth rate: 0% (2012 est.); 1.7% (2011 est.); 0.7% (2010 est.); -2.9% (2009 est.)
GDP per capita (PPP): $8,300 (2012 est.); $8,200 (2011 est.); $8,100 (2010 est.); $8,000 (2009 est.)
Natural resources: coal, iron ore, bauxite, copper, lead, zinc, chromite, cobalt, manganese, nickel, clay, gypsum, salt, sand, timber, hydropower
Agriculture products: wheat, corn, fruits, vegetables; livestock
Industries: steel, coal, iron ore, lead, zinc, manganese, bauxite, aluminum, vehicle assembly, textiles, tobacco products, wooden furniture, ammunition, domestic appliances, oil refining
Exports: $5.427 billion (2012 est.); $6.03 billion (2011 est.); $4.937 billion (2010 est.)
Exports—commodities: metals, clothing, wood products
Exports—partners: Slovenia 18.3%, Croatia 15.1%, Italy 14.8%, Germany 13.9%, Austria 12.4% (2011)
Imports: $10.18 billion (2012 est.); $11.06 billion (2011 est.); $9.23 billion (2010 est.)
Imports—commodities: machinery and equipment, chemicals, fuels, foodstuffs
Imports—partners: Croatia 20%, Germany 13.3%, Slovenia 13.1%,

Italy 9.7%, Russia 7.7%, Austria 6.2%, Hungary 4.8% (2011)
Debt—external: $10.54 billion (31 December 2011 est.); $8.457 billion (31 December 2010 est.)
Exchange rates: konvertibilna markas (BAM) per US dollar; 1.533 (2012 est.) ; 1.4069 (2011 est.); 1.4767 (2010 est.); 1.4079 (2009); 1.3083 (2008); 1.4419 (2007)

PEOPLE

The three constituent peoples of Bosnia and Herzegovina are Bosniaks, Serbs, and Croats, and languages are Bosnian, Serbian, and Croatian. Religions include Islam, Serbian Orthodoxy, Roman Catholicism, Judaism, some Protestant sects, and some others.

National/Racial/Ethnic Minorities

Ethnic differences remained a powerful destructive force in society, although mixed communities existed peacefully in some areas. Ethnic discrimination in employment and education remained key problems.

An estimated 80,000 to 100,000 Roma were in the country. Some Romani leaders reported an increase in Romani emigration from the country and asylum-seeking abroad during the year due to discrimination in access to social benefits. Roma experienced serious difficulties in enjoying the full range of fundamental human rights provided to them under the law. The Roma Information Council estimated that only 1 percent of the working-age Romani population were employed and indicated that employers usually downsized Roma first during a reduction in force. Many Roma lacked birth certificates, identification cards, or a registered residence, preventing them from accessing health care and public education services or registering to vote.

In April 2011, "Kali Sari," a Roma Decade watchdog NGO, released a report that noted substantial progress in improving the status of the country's Roma population. The report noted the government's programs for improving Romani employment, housing, and health care, as well as for completing a census of Roma, creating a database documenting the needs of Roma, and adopting a new Romani education action plan. However, the report criticized the government for excluding Roma from the decision-making process for allocating assistance to the Romani population. Romani human-rights leaders complained about the lack of transparency in awarding government contracts and allegations of corruption in implementing Roma Decade programs.

Religion

The country's territory is divided into two entities, the Federation of Bosnia and Herzegovina (BiH) and the Republika Srpska (RS), with a separate administrative district for Brcko (Brcko District). According to unofficial estimates from the State Statistics Agency, Muslims constitute 45 percent of the country's population, Serb Orthodox Christians 36 percent, Roman Catholics 15 percent, Protestants 1 percent, and other groups, including Jews, 3 percent. Bosniaks are generally associated with Islam, Bosnian Croats with the Roman Catholic Church, and Bosnian Serbs with the Serb Orthodox Church. The Jewish community, with approximately 1,000 members, maintains a historic place in society by virtue of centuries of coexistence with other religious communities and its active role in the Inter-Religious Council, which mediates among the communities.

The degree of religious observance varies among the traditional religious groups; however, some areas of significantly greater observance exist, particularly in more rural areas. For many persons religion often serves as a community or ethnic identifier, and they might confine their religious practice to significant rites of passage such as birth, marriage, and death.

The majority of Serb Orthodox adherents lives in the RS, and the majority of Muslims and Catholics resides in the Federation. Within the Federation distinct Muslim and Catholic majority areas remain, with most Catholics living in Herzegovina and areas of central Bosnia and most Muslims living elsewhere in central Bosnia and Sarajevo. The Jewish community, like Protestants and most other small religious groups in the country, has its largest membership in Sarajevo.

HISTORY

For the first centuries of the Christian era, present-day Bosnia was part of the Roman Empire. After the fall of Rome, it was contested by Byzantium and Rome's successors in the west. Slavs settled the region in the 7th century. The medieval kingdom of Bosnia emerged in the 12th century and ended in 1463, when Ottoman Turks conquered the region.

During Ottoman rule, many Bosnians converted from Christianity to Islam. Bosnia was under Ottoman rule until 1878, when the Congress of Berlin transferred administrative control to Austria-Hungary. Austria-Hungary annexed Bosnia in 1908. While those living in Bosnia came under the rule of the Austro-Hungarian Empire, South Slavs in Serbia and elsewhere were calling for a South Slav state. World War I began when Serb nationalist Gavrilo Princip assassinated the Archduke Franz Ferdinand in Sarajevo. Following the Great War, Bosnia became part of the South Slav state of Yugoslavia, only to be given to the Nazi-puppet state, the Independent State of Croatia (NDH) during World War II. Many atrocities were committed against Jews, Serbs, and others who resisted the occupation from 1941–45. The end of the war saw the establishment of a Communist, federal Yugoslavia under wartime leader Josip Broz Tito, with Bosnia and Herzegovina as one of six republics in the Yugoslav federation.

After Tito died in 1980, Yugoslavia's unraveling was hastened by Slobodan Milosevic's rise to power in 1986. Milosevic's embrace of Serb national-

ism led to intrastate ethnic strife. Slovenia and Croatia both declared independence from Yugoslavia in June 1991. By late September 1991, Bosnian Serb Radovan Karadzic's Serbian Democratic Party (SDS) had declared four self-proclaimed "Serb Autonomous Regions (SAO)" in Bosnia. In October 1991, the Bosnian Serbs announced the formation within Bosnia of a "Serbian Republic of Bosnia-Herzegovina" that would have its own constitution and parliamentary assembly. In January 1992, Radovan Karadzic publicly proclaimed a fully independent "Republic of the Serbian People in Bosnia-Herzegovina." On March 1, 1992, the Bosnian Government held a referendum on independence. Bosnia's parliament declared the republic's independence on April 5, 1992. However, this move was opposed by Serb representatives, who had voted in their own referendum in November 1991 in favor of remaining in Yugoslavia. Bosnian Serbs, supported by neighboring Serbia, responded with armed force in an effort to partition the republic along ethnic lines. Recognition of Bosnia and Herzegovina's independence by the United States and the European Community occurred on April 6-7, and Bosnia and Herzegovina was admitted to the United Nations on May 22, 1992.

In March 1994, Muslims and Croats in Bosnia signed an agreement creating the Federation of Bosnia and Herzegovina, ending a period of Muslim-Croat conflict. The conflict with the Bosnian Serbs continued through most of 1995. Many atrocities were committed, including acts of genocide committed by members of the Army of Republika Srpska in and around Srebrenica in July 1995, where approximately 8,000 Bosnian Muslim men and boys were killed. The conflict ended with the November 21, 1995 Dayton Peace Agreement, which was formally signed on December 14, 1995 in Paris.

Radovan Karadzic and Ratko Mladic, the political and military leaders of the Bosnian Serbs, were indicted by the International Criminal Tribunal for the Former Yugoslavia (http://www.icty.org/) in The Hague in July 1995 on charges of genocide and crimes against humanity stemming from their role in crimes against civilians throughout Bosnia and Herzegovina culminating in the Srebrenica massacre. Karadzic was apprehended and transferred to the ICTY in The Hague by Serbian authorities on July 21, 2008. Mladic was apprehended in Serbia on May 26, 2011 and transferred to The Hague on June 1, 2011.

Bosnia and Herzegovina today consists of two Entities—the Federation of Bosnia and Herzegovina (FBiH), which is largely Bosniak and Croat, and the Republika Srpska (RS), which is primarily Serb. In July 2000, the Constitutional Court of Bosnia and Herzegovina rendered a decision whereby Bosniaks, Croats, and Serbs are recognized as constituent peoples throughout the territory of Bosnia and Herzegovina. In March 2002, this decision was formally recognized and agreed on by the major political parties in both Entities.

The most recent national elections took place in October 2010, electing new state presidency members; state, Entity, and cantonal parliaments; and the RS presidency. The BiH presidency was sworn in on November 10, 2010. The RS government was formed in December 2010, and the Federation government was formed in March 2011. The BiH Council of Ministers was formed in February 2012. The next municipal elections are scheduled to occur in 2012, and the next general elections will take place in 2014. In October 2008, Bosnia and Herzegovina held municipal elections, where mayors and members of municipal assemblies were directly elected (in all municipalities except Mostar and Brcko District).

The international community retains an extraordinary civilian and military presence in Bosnia and Herzegovina (BiH) stemming from the Dayton Peace Accords. The Dayton Accords created the position of High Representative, an international official charged with overseeing implementation of the civilian aspects of the agreement. The current High Representative (since March 2009) is Austria's Valentin Inzko (www.ohr.int).

In December 1995, NATO deployed a 60,000-troop Implementation Force (IFOR) to oversee implementation of the military aspects of the peace agreement. IFOR transitioned into a smaller Stabilization Force (SFOR) in 1996. With the end of the SFOR mission in December 2004, the European Union (EU) assumed primary responsibility for military stabilization operations. Approximately 600 EU troops remain deployed in Bosnia (www.euforbih.org). NATO maintains a small headquarters operation with responsibility to assist with defense reform.

GOVERNMENT AND POLITICAL CONDITIONS

Bosnia and Herzegovina consists of two entities within the state, the Federation of Bosnia and Herzegovina (the Federation) and the Republika Srpska (RS). The 1995 General Framework Agreement for Peace (the Dayton Accords) provides for a democratic republic with a bicameral parliament but assigns many governmental functions to the two entities. The Dayton Accords also provide for a high representative who has the authority to impose legislation and remove officials. In October 2010 the country held general elections that international observers deemed free and fair. As of year's end the country had not formed a government, although leaders reached an agreement to do so early in 2012.

Deep-seated ethnic divisions continued to foster widespread discrimination in most aspects of daily life, undermined the rule of law, distorted public discourse in the media, and obstructed the return of persons who were displaced during the 1992–95 conflict.

Recent Elections

Observers from the OSCE concluded that the October 2010 general election largely was conducted in line with international standards but noted problems, including deficiencies in the registration process, group voting, and irregularities in the counting process. The OSCE observation mission noted that private media, particularly print, tended to favor certain candidates. Smaller parties complained about systematic underexposure in the media. On December 28, political leaders reached a deal to form a new Council of Ministers, but work on implementing that decision would continue into 2012. At the end of 2011, political leaders failed to form a new government in one canton, leaving officials whose party had lost representation in office on a "technical mandate."

Nationalist rhetoric from leaders of all ethnic groups dominated political exchanges. In particular Serb politicians regularly called into question the validity and existence of the state of Bosnia and Herzegovina and threatened to call a referendum in the RS to secede from the state.

Participation of Women and Minorities: The law requires that at least 30 percent of political party candidates be women. Eight of 42 members of the state-level House of Representatives were women. There were no women in the nine-member Council of Ministers, although there were two female deputy ministers.

At the entity level, women held three of 23 leadership positions in the Federation, including one ministerial position, one speaker position, and one deputy speaker position in parliament. Following the 2010 elections, 19 women were elected to the Federation House of Representatives and 14 to the Federation House of Peoples. In the RS two of 16 ministers and one deputy speaker in parliament were women. As of August 2011 women comprised 31 percent of the delegates in the RS National Assembly, 30 percent of RS government ministers, and 5 percent of RS mayors.

The law provides that Serbs, Croats, Bosniaks, and "others" must be adequately represented in entity, cantonal, and municipal government institutions, based on the 1991 census, until the returns process detailed by the Dayton Accords is completed. However, the government did not respect this law in practice. In addition to the three constituent peoples, there were 16 recognized national minority groups.

Minorities not regarded as "constituent peoples" under the country's constitution remained severely underrepresented in government. There were no members of a minority group in the parliament and only one member in the Council of Ministers.

Principal Government Officials

Last Updated: 1/31/2013

Bosnia's central government is headed by a tripartite presidency, with one representative of each of the three major ethnic constituencies. The chairmanship of the presidency rotates among the three presidency members every eight months.

National Govt.

Presidency Chmn. (Serb): **Nebojsa RADMANOVIC**
Presidency Member (Bosniak): **Bakir IZETBEGOVIC**
Presidency Member (Croat): **Zeljko KOMSIC**
Chmn., Council of Ministers: **Vjekoslav BEVANDA**
Dep. Chmn., Council of Ministers: **Zlatko LAGUMDZIJA**
Min. of Civil Affairs: **Sredoje NOVIC**
Min. of Defense: **Muhamed IBRAHIMOVIC**
Min. of Finance: **Nikola SPIRIC**
Min. of Foreign Affairs: **Zlatko LAGUMDZIJA**
Min. of Foreign Trade: **Mirko SAROVIC**
Min. of Human Rights & Refugees: **Damir LJUBIC**
Min. of Justice: **Barisa COLAK**
Min. of Security: **Sadik AHMETOVIC**
Min. of Transport & Communication: **Damir HADZIC**
Governor, Central Bank: **Kemal KOZARIC**
Ambassador to the US: **Jadranka NEGODIC**
Permanent Representative to the UN, New York: **Mirsada COLAKOVIC**

Federation Govt.

Pres.: **Zivko BUDIMIR**
Vice Pres.: **Mirsad KEBO**
Vice Pres.: **Svetozar PUDARIC**
Prime Min.: **Nermin NIKSIC**
Dep. Prime Min.: **Jerko LIJANOVIC**
Dep. Prime Min.: **Desnica RADIVOJEVIC**
Min. of Agriculture, Water Industry, & Forestry: **Jerko LIJANOVIC**
Min. of Culture & Sports: **Salmir KAPLAN**
Min. of Development, Entrepreneurship, & Crafts: **Sanjin HALIMOVIC**
Min. of Education & Science: **Damir MASIC**
Min. of Energy, Mining, & Industry: **Erdal TRHULJ**
Min. of Environment & Tourism: **Branka DJURIC**
Min. of Finance: **Ante KRAJINA**
Min. of Health: **Rusmir MESIHOVIC**
Min. of Interior: **Predrag KURTES**
Min. of Justice: **Zoran MIKULIC**
Min. of Labor & Social Welfare: **Vjekoslav CAMBER**
Min. of the Liberation War Veterans & Disabled Veterans Issues:**Zukan HELEZ**
Min. of Refugees & Displaced Persons: **Adil OSMANOVIC**
Min. of Trade: **Milorad BAHILJ**
Min. of Traffic & Communications: **Enver BIJEDIC**
Min. of Urban Planning: **Desnica RADIVOJEVIC**

Republika Srpska Govt.

Pres.: **Milorad DODIK**
Vice Pres.: **Enes SULJKANOVIC**
Vice Pres.: **Emil VLAJKI**
Prime Min.: **Aleksandar DZOMBIC**
Min. of Agriculture: **Miroslav MILOVANOVIC**
Min. of Economic Relations & Coordination: **Zeljka CVIJANOVIC**
Min. of Education & Culture: **Anton KASIPOVIC**
Min. of Finance: **Zoran TEGELTIJA**
Min. of Health & Social Protection: **Ranko SKRBIC**
Min. of Industry, Energy, & Mining: **Zeljko KOVACEVIC**
Min. of Interior: **Stanislav CADJO**
Min. of Justice: **Dzerard SELMAN**
Min. of Labor & Veterans Affairs: **Petar DJOKIC**
Min. of Public Admin. & Local Self-Govt.: **Lejla RESIC**
Min. of Refugees & Displaced Persons: **Davor CORDAS**
Min. of Science & Technology: **Jasmin KOMIC**
Min. of Trade & Tourism: **Gorana ZLATKOVIC**
Min. of Transport & Communications: **Nedeljko CUBRILOVIC**
Min. of Urban Planning & Ecology: **Srebrenka GOLIC**
Min. of Youth, Families, & Sport: **Nada TESANOVIC**

ECONOMY

Bosnia has a transitional economy with limited market reforms. The economy relies heavily on the export of metals as well as on remittances and foreign aid. A highly decentralized government hampers economic policy coordination and reform, while excessive bureaucracy and a segmented market discourage foreign investment.

The interethnic warfare in Bosnia and Herzegovina caused production to plummet by 80% from 1992 to 1995 and unemployment to soar. With an uneasy peace in place, output recovered in 1996–99 but slowed in 2000–02 and picked up again during 2003–08, when GDP growth exceeded 5% per year. However, the country experienced a decline in GDP of nearly 3% in 2009 reflecting local effects of the global economic crisis. GDP has stagnated since then. Foreign banks, primarily from Austria and Italy, now control most of the banking sector. The konvertibilna marka (convertible mark or BAM) - the national currency introduced in 1998 - is pegged to the euro, and confidence in the currency and the banking sector has increased. Bosnia's private sector is growing, but foreign investment has dropped off sharply since 2007.

Government spending, at roughly 50% of GDP, remains high because of redundant government offices at the state, entity and municipal level. Privatization of state enterprises has been slow, particularly in the Federation, where political division between ethnically-based political parties makes agreement on economic policy more difficult. High unemployment remains the most serious macroeconomic problem. Successful implementation of a value-added tax in 2006 provided a predictable source of revenue for the government and helped rein in gray-market activity. National-level statistics have also improved over time but a large share of economic activity remains unofficial and unrecorded. Bosnia and Herzegovina became a full member of the Central European Free Trade Agreement in September 2007.

Bosnia and Herzegovina's top economic priorities are: acceleration of integration into the EU; strengthening the fiscal system; public administration reform; World Trade Organization (WTO) membership; and securing economic growth by fostering a dynamic, competitive private sector. In 2009, Bosnia and Herzegovina was granted an International Monetary Fund (IMF) stand-by arrangement, necessitated by sharply increased social spending and a fiscal crisis exacerbated by the global economic downturn. Disbursement of IMF aid was suspended in 2011 after a parliamentary deadlock left Bosnia without a state-level government for over a year. The IMF concluded a new stand-by arrangement with Bosnia in October 2012, with the first tranches paid in November and December 2012.

Labor Conditions

The minimum age for employment of children in the Federation and the RS is 15; minors between the ages of 15 and 18 must provide a valid health certificate to work. The law prohibits children from performing hazardous labor. In the Federation, the law prohibits minors from night work except in exceptional circumstances.

The monthly minimum wage in the Federation was 343 convertible marks ($227). In the RS, the monthly minimum wage was 370 convertible marks ($245) except in the textiles and footwear sectors where it was 320 convertible marks ($212). The Brcko District did not have a separate minimum wage or an independent pension fund, and employers typically used the minimum wage rate of whichever entity to which its workers decided to direct their pension funds.

The legal workweek in both entities and the Brcko District is 40 hours; however, seasonal workers may work up to 60 hours per week. The law limits overtime to 10 hours per week in both entities; the Federation has no provision for premium pay, while the RS requires a 30 percent premium. A 2010 study found that employers routinely denied workers overtime and sick leave in the private commercial sector in both entities and the Brcko District, particularly those employed in large shopping malls. An employee in the RS may volunteer for an additional 10 hours in exceptional circumstances. Federation and RS laws require a minimum rest period of 30 minutes during the workday. The entities and the Brcko District did little to enforce regulations on working hours, daily and weekly rest, or annual leave, and these protections were generally believed to be lacking. Entity labor laws prescribe a maximum overtime of 10 hours per week and prohibit excessive compulsory overtime. The law also sets mandatory occupational health and safety standards, especially for those industry sectors where there are hazardous working conditions for workers. Employers in each entity and the Brcko District must provide a minimum of nine paid annual holidays. People can choose which holidays to observe depending on ethnic or religious affiliation.

Workers' rights extended to all official, that is, registered, workers including migrant and temporary workers. According to informal estimates, approximately 40 percent of the total work force was unregistered. Workers in certain industries often worked in hazardous conditions, particularly those in metal- and steel-processing plants and coalmines.

U.S.-BOSNIAN RELATIONS

The United States established diplomatic relations with Bosnia and Herzegovina in 1992 following its independence from Yugoslavia. A period of conflict followed among Bosnia's Muslims, Croats, and Serbs, some of whom wished to remain part of Yugoslavia. The 1992–95 war in Bosnia and Herzegovina was ended with the crucial participation of the United States in brokering the 1995 Dayton Peace Agreement. After leading the diplomatic and military effort to secure the Dayton accords, the United States has continued to lead the effort to ensure its implementation. The United States maintains command of the North Atlantic Treaty Organization (NATO) headquarters in Sarajevo. It also has donated hundreds of millions of dollars to help with reconstruction, humanitarian assistance, economic development, and military reconstruction in Bosnia and Herzegovina.

The United States supports Bosnia and Herzegovina on its path toward full integration into Euro-Atlantic institutions. The country's progress toward Euro-Atlantic structures—and the democratic, economic, and security commitments that this entails—are essential to the broader stability of the western Balkans. Bosnia and Herzegovina is working toward activation of its Membership Action Plan with NATO and has signed a Stabilization and Association Agreement with the European Union.

U.S. Assistance to Bosnia and Herzegovina

U.S. Government assistance to Bosnia and Herzegovina aims to fully anchor the country in European and Euro-Atlantic institutions, strengthen multi-ethnic democratic institutions and civil society, support strong State-level judiciary and law enforcement sectors, and increase prosperity and attractiveness to foreign investors. A fact sheet on U.S. assistance to Bosnia and Herzegovina can be found here.

Bilateral Economic Relations

Bosnia and Herzegovina is a transitional economy that is pursuing membership in the European Union and the World Trade Organization. More than 40 U.S. and U.S.-affiliated companies have established a full-time presence in the country. Bosnia and Herzegovina has been designated as a beneficiary country under the Generalized System of Preferences (GSP) program, under which a range of products that Bosnia and Herzegovina might seek to export are eligible for duty-free entry to the United States. The GSP program provides an incentive for investors to produce in Bosnia and Herzegovina and export selected products duty-free to the U.S. market.

Bosnia and Herzegovina's Membership in International Organizations

Bosnia and Herzegovina and the United States belong to a number of the same international organizations, including the United Nations, Euro-Atlantic Partnership Council, Organization for Security and Cooperation in Europe, International Monetary Fund, and World Bank. Bosnia and Herzegovina also is an observer to the World Trade Organization and the Organization of American States and a participant in the North Atlantic Treaty Organization's (NATO) Partnership for Peace program.

Bilateral Representation

Bosnia and Herzegovina maintains an embassy in the United States at 2109 E Street NW, Washington, DC 20037 (tel. 202-337-1500).

Principal U.S. Embassy Officials

Last Updated: 1/14/2013

SARAJEVO (E) Roberta C. Frasurea 1, 71000 Sarajevo, +387 33 704 000, Fax +387 33 659 722, Workweek: Monday–Friday 8:00AM to 5:00PM, Website: http://sarajevo.usembassy.gov/

DCM OMS: Mary Beth Laclair
AMB OMS: Teresa Coddington
FM: Allan Mitchell
HRO: Kimberly Murphy
ICITAP: James J. Tillman
MGT: Adam Lamoreaux
MLO/ODC: Karin Wagner
POSHO: Allan Mitchell
SDO/DATT: COL Scott Miller
AMB: Patrick Moon
CON: Cynthia Ebeid
DCM: Nicholas Hill
PAO: Thomas Mesa
GSO: Gerald W. Blackburn
RSO: Christine Putz
AFSA: Matt Blevins
AGR: James R.Dever (Resident In Rome)
AID: David Barth
CLO: Lori A. Long
ECON: Lian Von Wantoch
EEO: James Bayer
FMO: Kimberly Murphy
ICASS Chair: Thomas Mesa
IMO: James W. Bayer
IPO: Chad O'Brien
ISSO: Jim Bayer
LEGATT: Frank J. Teixeira
POL: Tamir Waser
State ICASS: Thomas Mesa

BANJA LUKA (BO) Jovana Ducica 5, Banja Luka, +387-51-211-500, Fax +387-51-218-291, Workweek: Monday–Friday, Website: http://sarajevo.usembassy.gov/

DCM OMS: Mary Beth Laclair
AMB OMS: Teresa A. Coddington
FM: Allan Mitchell
HRO: Kimberly Murphy
ICITAP: James J. Tillman
MGT: Adam Lamoreaux
SDO/DATT: COL Scott Miller
AMB: Patrick S. Moon
CON: Cynthia Ebeid
DCM: Nicholas Hill
PAO: Thomas Mesa
GSO: Gerald Blackburn
RSO: Wade Boston
AID: Alan E. Reed
CLO: Lori A. Long
ECON: Eric W. Luftman
EST: Karyn Posner (Resident In Budapest)
FAA: Gregory Joyner (Resident In Rome)
FMO: Kimberly Murphy
IMO: James Bayer
ISSO: James Bayer
LEGATT: Milton Chalkley
POL: Aaron Schwoebel

MOSTAR (BO) Husnije Repca 3, Mostar, +387 36 580 580, Fax +387 36 580 581, Workweek: Monday–Friday 8:00 a.m.–5:00 p.m., Website: http://sarajevo.usembassy.gov/

DCM OMS: Mary Beth Laclair
AMB OMS: Teresa Coddington
HRO: Judy Marcouiller
ICITAP: James J. Tillman
MGT: Adam D. Lamoreaux
SDO/DATT: Michael V. Schleicher
AMB: Patrick S. Moon
CON: Ann-Marie Casella
DCM: Jonathan M. Moore
PAO: Janet W. Miller
GSO: Gerald Blackburn
AGR: James Dever (Resident In Vienna)
AID: Alan E. Reed
EEO: James Bayer
EST: Karyn Posner (Resident In Budapest)
FAA: (Resident In Rome)
FMO: Judy Marcouiller
IRS: Kathy J. Beck (Resident In Paris)
ISSO: James Bayer
LEGATT: Frank J. Teixeira
POL: Elise H. Kleinwaks

TRAVEL

Consular Information Sheet

July 27, 2012

Country Description: Bosnia and Herzegovina has experienced significant progress in restoring peace and stability since the 1992–95 war; nonetheless, political tensions among its ethnic groups persist. Progress has been made to reconstruct the physical infrastructure that was devastated during the war, but roads, railroads, and other infrastructural improvements lag behind other countries in the region. Hotels and travel amenities are available in the capital, Sarajevo, and other major towns. In more remote areas of the country, public facilities vary in quality.

Smart Traveler Enrollment Program (STEP)/Embassy Locations: If you are going to live in or visit Bosnia and Herzegovina, please take the time to tell our Embassy about your trip. If you enroll, we can keep you up to date with important safety and security announcements. It will also help your friends and family get in touch with you in an emergency.

U.S. Embassy Sarajevo
1 Robert C. Frasure Street
71000 Sarajevo
Telephone: (387) 33 704 000
Emergency after-hours telephone: (387) 33 704 000. If after dialing you receive a recorded message, press "0" and ask for the embassy duty officer.
Facsimile: (387) 33 221 837
Email: rws@state.gov

Entry/Exit Requirements for U.S. Citizens: You need a passport to travel to Bosnia and Herzegovina. U.S. citizens do not need a visa for stays up to three months. The Government of Bosnia and Herzegovina does not issue visas to U.S. travelers prior to travel for any length of stay and purpose of travel, including diplomatic assignments. If you are not staying at a hotel but in a private residence, you must register with the local police within 24 hours of arrival. If you are planning to remain in Bosnia and Herzegovina for more than three months, you must apply for a temporary residence permit from the local field office of the Foreigners' Affairs Department of the Ministry of Security that has jurisdiction over your place of residence. You should submit your application for a temporary residence permit at least 15 days prior to the expiration of the initial three-month visa-free period of stay. The maximum duration of a temporary residence permit is 12 months, with the possibility of extension. The fee is 100 convertible marks (KM), or approximately 70 USD. To apply for this permit, you must first obtain a police certificate from your U.S. state of residence indicating that you have no criminal record. For additional information, please contact the Embassy of Bosnia and Herzegovina at 2109 E Street, NW, Washington, DC 20037, telephone 202-337-1500. Visit the Embassy of Bosnia and Herzegovina website (www.bhembassy.org) for the most current visa information.

Bosnia and Herzegovina immigration authorities strictly enforce a law requiring any unaccompanied minor (under 18) to have written permission from both parents in order to enter and leave the country. If traveling with only one parent, the minor is required to have written permission for the trip from the non-traveling parent.

The U.S. Department of State is unaware of any HIV/AIDS entry restrictions for visitors to or foreign residents of Bosnia and Herzegovina.

Threats to Safety and Security: Landmines remain a problem in Bosnia and Herzegovina. As of 2010, there were still an estimated 11,000 minefields and an estimated 220,000 active land mines throughout the country. The area of suspected landmine contamination is estimated at over 1460 square kilometers— more than 2.85% of the country's territory. A new Bosnia and Herzegovina Mine Action Center (BHMAC) study of the mine problem in Bosnia and Herzegovina has identified a total of 1631 local communities affected by mines. BHMAC estimates that mines directly affect the safety of 921,513 people. Since 1996, 1,669 people were injured due to mine accidents, of which 588 people died. While most urban areas have been largely cleared, you should still take special care when near the former lines of conflict, including the suburbs of Sarajevo. The de-mining community recommends staying on hard surfaced areas and out of abandoned buildings. Families traveling with children in Bosnia and Herzegovina should be especially aware of the danger posed by mines and unexploded ordnance. For more information about landmines and unexploded ordinance please visit the website of the Bosnia and Herzegovina Mine Action Center.

Localized political difficulties continue and random violence may occur with little or no warning, but politically-related violence in recent years has been rare.

Bosnian criminals may use firearms and explosives to settle personal, business, and political disputes. In June 2010, local religious extremists were responsible for a bomb exploding outside a police station in Bugojno; one officer was killed. Local media outlets reported 38 incidents involving the use of hand-grenades in Bosnia and Herzegovina since the beginning of 2011. The foreign community is rarely the target of such violence, but there is always the danger of being in the wrong place at the wrong time.

There was a terrorist shooting attack targeting the U.S. Embassy in Sarajevo on October 28, 2011, in which one local police officer was wounded. While most Bosnian citizens appreciate the assistance of the international community, you might occasionally encounter anti-foreign sentiment.

Stay up to date by:

- Bookmarking our Bureau of Consular Affairs website, which contains the current Travel Warnings and Travel Alerts as well as the Worldwide Caution.

- Following us on Twitter and the Bureau of Consular Affairs page on Facebook as well.
- Downloading our free Smart Traveler IPhone App to have travel information at your fingertips.
- Calling 1-888-407-4747 toll-free within the U.S. and Canada, or a regular toll line, 1-202-501-4444, from other countries.
- Taking some time before travel to consider your personal security.

Crime: The overall crime rate throughout the country remains moderate, although Sarajevo has a consistently high rate of property crimes. The Embassy has noted a recent sharp increase in criminal activity throughout Sarajevo in the form of armed robberies, residential break-ins, thefts from motor vehicles, and pick-pocketing. In many of these incidents, members of the international community were victims. On average, four motor vehicles are stolen in Bosnia and Herzegovina each day. The persistent difficult economic situation, including an officially reported unemployment rate over 40 percent, may be fueling an increase in criminal aggressiveness. Be alert to your surroundings at all times, but in particular, after dark and in locations visited by foreigners such as cafés and restaurants.

Take normal precautions to protect your property from theft and exercise common sense personal security measures, such as traveling in groups and staying in well-lighted areas after dark. Try to avoid confrontations with local citizens resulting from traffic incidents or public disagreements. Avoid carrying large sums of money on your person and avoid keeping money in one place. Be careful of beggars or others who may be attempting to distract you or directly pick your pocket. There are also documented cases of pick-pocketing and other scams to obtain money from foreign passengers aboard public transportation (especially aboard the trams). Most local citizens in Bosnia and Herzegovina do not use backpacks. People wearing backpacks tend to attract the attention of pickpockets who quite easily gain access to backpacks without the owners' knowledge. Keep purses and bags closed and avoid placing valuables in purses and bags. Items placed on the chair next to you, hung on the coat rack, or placed on the back of a chair are more easily stolen or pilfered.

Don't buy counterfeit and pirated goods, even if they are widely available. Not only are the bootlegs illegal in the United States, if you purchase them you may also be breaking local law.

Victims of Crime: If you or someone you know becomes the victim of a crime abroad, you should contact the local police and the nearest U.S. embassy or consulate. We can:

- Replace a stolen passport.
- Help you find appropriate medical care if you are the victim of violent crimes such as assault or rape.
- Put you in contact with the appropriate police authorities, and if you want us to, we can contact family members or friends.
- Help you understand the local criminal justice process and direct you to local attorneys, although it is important to remember that local authorities are responsible for investigating and prosecuting the crime.

The local equivalents to the "911" emergency line in Bosnia and Herzegovina are: Police—122; Ambulance—124; and Fire—123.

Criminal Penalties: While you are traveling in Bosnia and Herzegovina, you are subject to its laws even if you are a U.S. citizen. Foreign laws and legal systems can be vastly different from our own. In Bosnia and Herzegovina, photographing military or secure installations including airports, equipment, bridges, government checkpoints, troops and the U.S. Embassy, is forbidden. If in doubt, please ask permission before taking photographs. Remember that there are some things that might be legal in the country you visit, but still illegal in the United States. Engaging in sexual conduct with children or using or disseminating child pornography in a foreign country is a crime prosecutable in the United States. If you break local laws in Bosnia and Herzegovina, your U.S. passport won't help you avoid arrest or prosecution. It is very important to know what is legal and what is not wherever you go.

Persons violating Bosnia and Herzegovina's laws, even unknowingly, may be expelled, arrested, or imprisoned. Penalties for possessing, using, or trafficking in illegal drugs in Bosnia and Herzegovina are severe, and convicted offenders can expect long jail sentences and heavy fines. While some countries will automatically notify the nearest U.S. embassy or consulate if a U.S. citizen is detained or arrested in a foreign country, that might not always be the case. To ensure that the United States is aware of your circumstances, request that the police and prison officials notify the nearest U.S. embassy or consulate as soon as you are arrested or detained overseas.

Special Circumstances: Bosnia and Herzegovina is still predominantly a cash economy. Although the use of credit cards has become widespread in recent years, travelers still should not expect to use them to cover all expenses. Automated Teller Machines (ATMs) are available in sufficient numbers at international banks in Sarajevo and other major cities and towns. Traveler's checks can be cashed in every bank immediately, without delays; bank fees for these transactions are usually 2%. Cash transfers from abroad may involve delays, but Western Union transfers are available in many banks and post offices throughout the country.

The convertible mark (KM), the national currency, is pegged to the euro under a currency-board regime, which guarantees its stability. All official payments must be made in convertible marks. Any bank in Bosnia and Herzegovina should be able to exchange U.S. dollars into convertible marks with the usual bank commission (between one and two percent).

During the winter months, flights into and out of Sarajevo are frequently delayed or canceled due to heavy fog. Travelers should be prepared for last-minute schedule changes, lengthy delays, alternate routings, or time-consuming overland transportation.

Accessibility: While in Bosnia and Herzegovina, individuals with disabilities may find accessibility and accommodation very different from what you find in the United States. The law prohibits discrimination against persons with physical, sensory, intellectual, and mental disabilities; however, there is discrimination against persons with disabilities in employment, education, and access to health care and other state services. The law mandates that all public buildings be retrofitted to provide access to persons with disabilities. Changes in new buildings are expected by the end of the year. However, in practice, buildings are rarely accessible to persons with disabilities.

Medical Facilities and Health Information: The lack of adequate medical facilities, especially outside Sarajevo, may cause problems for visitors. Because many medicines are not obtainable, travelers should bring their own supply of prescription drugs and preventive medicines. Private practitioners and dentists are becoming more common; however, quality of care varies and rarely meets U.S. or Western European standards. All major surgery is performed in public hospitals.

Individuals with asthma or other chronic respiratory conditions may react negatively to the air quality and allergens in Bosnia and Herzegovina, especially in Sarajevo. Additionally, persons with mental health conditions may not be able to locate English-speaking mental health providers or support groups.

You can find detailed information on vaccinations and other health precautions on the CDC website. For information about outbreaks of infectious diseases abroad, consult the World Health Organization (WHO) website. The WHO website also contains additional health information for travelers, including detailed country-specific health information.

Tuberculosis is an increasingly serious health concern in Bosnia and Herzegovina. For further information, please consult the CDC's information on TB.

Medical Insurance: You can't assume your insurance will go with you when you travel. It's very important to find out BEFORE you leave whether or not your medical insurance will cover you overseas. You need to ask your insurance company two questions:

- Does my policy apply when I'm out of the United States?
- Will it cover emergencies like a trip to a foreign hospital or a medical evacuation?

In many places, doctors and hospitals still expect payment in cash at the time of service. Your regular U.S. health insurance may not cover doctor and hospital visits in other countries. If your policy doesn't go with you when you travel, it's a very good idea to take out another one for your trip.

Traffic Safety and Road Conditions: While in Bosnia and Herzegovina, you may encounter road conditions that differ significantly from those in the United States.

Road travel is possible throughout most of the country, but many roads are poorly maintained and are sometimes blocked because of landslides, de-mining activity, and traffic accidents. Bosnia and Herzegovina has fewer than forty kilometers of four-lane highways. The existing two-lane roads between major cities are quite narrow in places, lack guardrails, and are full of curves. Travel by road can be risky because of poorly maintained roads and morning and evening fog in the mountains. Driving in winter is hazardous because of fog, snow and ice.

Local driving habits can be challenging given the road conditions, and many vehicles are in bad condition; approximately 100 motor vehicle accidents are reported daily throughout Bosnia and Herzegovina. Many accidents occur when drivers exceed safe speeds along winding mountain roads. Accidents involving drunk driving are an increasing problem. Driving after dark is especially dangerous, and street lighting is not common outside major towns. Road construction may be poorly marked, and automobiles share the road with heavy vehicles and agricultural equipment. Travelers should try to convoy with other vehicles, if possible, and plan their trip to ensure they travel only during daylight hours.

Although the number of service stations outside major cities has increased in recent years, many do not offer mechanical services. The emergency number for vehicle assistance and towing service is 1282. Speed limit signs are not always obvious or clear. The speed limit on the majority of roads is 60 km/h (37 mph); on straight stretches of road it is generally 80 km/h (50 mph). The use of seat belts is mandatory. Talking on a cell phone while driving is prohibited. The tolerated blood alcohol level is.03 percent. Bosnian law requires having a safety vest, spare tire, jack, first aid kit, safety triangle, towing rope, and spare light bulbs in the car at all times.

In order to drive legally in Bosnia and Herzegovina, you must have an international driving permit in addition to your U.S. license.

Aviation Safety Oversight: As there is no direct commercial air service to the United States by carriers registered in Bosnia and Herzegovina, the U.S. Federal Aviation Administration (FAA) has not assessed the government of Bosnia and Herzegovina's Civil Aviation Authority for compliance with International Civil Aviation Organization (ICAO) aviation safety standards. Further information may be found on the FAA'ssafety assessment page.

Children's Issues: Please see the U.S. Dept. of State Office of Children's Issues web pages on intercountry adoption and international parental child abduction.

Intercountry Adoption

July 2010

The information in this section has been edited from the latest report available as of February 2013 from the State Department Bureau of Consular Affairs, Office of Overseas Citizens Services. For more information, please read the *Intercountry Adoption* section of this book and review current reports online at http://adoption.state.gov.

Bosnia-Herzegovina is not party to the Hague Convention on Protection of Children and Co-operation in Respect of Intercountry Adoption (Hague Adoption Convention). Therefore, when the Hague Adoption Convention entered into force for the United States on April 1, 2008, intercountry adoption processing for Bosnia-Herzegovina did not change.

Who Can Adopt? To bring an adopted child to the United States from Bosnia-Herzegovina, you must be found eligible to adopt by the U.S. Government. The U.S. Government agency responsible for making this determination is the Department of Homeland Security, U.S. Citizenship and Immigration Services (USCIS).

Residency Requirements: Foreign citizens can adopt in BiH only exceptionally. While there is nothing in Bosnian law that specifically prohibits foreigners from applying to adopt a Bosnian child, the law stresses that there must be overwhelming justification and exceptionally compelling reasons for a foreigner to be permitted to do so.

The definition of "overwhelming justification" is judged on a case-by-case basis. The law says specifically that a foreign citizen may appear as an adoptive parent "if the adoption is in the best interest of the child and if the child cannot be adopted in Bosnia and Herzegovina."

Age Requirements: Adoptive parents must be between 25 and 45 and must be older than the child at least 18 years. If there are justified reasons, the adoptive parent may be older than 45, but the age difference between the parent and child must not be greater than 45.

Marriage Requirements: In addition to married couples, common-law marriage partners who have lived together for at least 5 years or single people may adopt; however the latter cases are the exception.

Income Requirements: Not specified in the Family Law; is considered by Social Services Centers when they conduct the home study.

Other Requirements: The BiH Family Law does not provide any information on adoption by same-sex couples.

Who Can be Adopted? Bosnia-Herzegovina has specific requirements that a child must meet in order to be eligible for adoption. You cannot adopt a child in Bosnia-Herzegovina unless he or she meets the requirements outlined below.

Eligibility Requirements: For adoption, the approval of both parents or sole parent is required. The parent has to state specifically whether he/she agrees to full or partial adoption. (Only a child up to the age of 10 can be adopted fully. Full adoption implies an irreversible relationship equal to a blood relationship. Partial adoption implies all the rights and duties that exist between parents and children under the law, but partial adoption does not affect the rights and duties of the adopted child towards his/her biological parents and other relatives.)

Abandonment Requirements: A child whose parents are unknown may be adopted only after 3 months have passed since his/her abandonment.

Age Requirements: A child less than 3 months old cannot be adopted. A child of parents who are minors cannot be adopted. Exceptionally, such child may be adopted after he/she is one year old if there are no family prospects. A child up to the age of 18 can be adopted partially. Children older than age 10 must give their approval for the adoption.

Waiting Period: The municipal Center for Social Work publishes its decision regarding its recommendation on an adoption within two months of receiving the adoption application. However, in practice it usually takes longer for the Center to make a decision. Once the Center reaches a decision they then forward the application package to the Ministry of Social Policy with their recommendation. The Ministry is supposed to reach a decision about a request for adoption in two months. Once the Ministry makes a decision, it is sent back to the Center that accepted the application. If the decision is favorable, the prospective adoptive parents must be personally present at the official ceremony (act) of adoption.

The Process: The U.S. Embassy in Sarajevo maintains a list of attorneys that may be useful. Prospective adoptive parents may contact the Embassy directly for a copy of that list. Prospective parents are normally expected to contact the Social Services Center in the area where they plan to adopt directly. Persons falling into any of the following groups are prohibited from adopting Bosnian children:

- persons whose parental rights have been taken away;
- persons with a limited or no ability to work;
- persons who provide insufficient guarantees that they will raise the child correctly;
- persons who are mentally ill, retarded, or suffering from any illness that could endanger the health and life of the adopted child.

A home study conducted by the Center for Social Work is required in all cases. If you are eligible to adopt, and a child is available for intercountry adoption, the central adoption authority in Bosnia-Herzegovina will provide you with a referral to a child. Persons who wish to apply to adopt a particular child can do so by contacting the Center for Social Work of the municipality/district in which the child is resident and submitting the documents listed below. [The Center for Social Work is the Bosnian equivalent of the county or municipal social services department in the United States.] Prospective adoptive parents who do not have a particular child in mind can contact the Center for Social Work for a designated area to inquire if there are any children eligible for adoption.

If the Center affirms that a child is eligible for adoption, the Center will request the documents listed below to determine the eligibility of the prospective adoptive parent(s). It should be noted that it is entirely possible that a Center will not respond at all to an inquiry from a foreign national, since under Bosnian law, inter-country adoption is permitted only in exceptional circumstances (typically when there is a compelling medical need, or one of the adopting parents is of Bosnian origin). The Center then forwards the application package, along with its recommendation, to the Ministry of Social Policy.

The Ministry makes a final decision and sends the package back to the Center. The Center then notifies the prospective adoptive parents. If the decision is favorable, the prospective adoptive parents must be personally present at the official ceremony (act) of adoption. This is an official act signed by the adoptive parents in person and representatives of the government. It takes place at the Center for Social Work. The court then issues an official decision or decree ratifying the proceedings conducted by the Center for Social Work. The court does not have the authority to overrule the Ministry's decision.

Role of the Adoption Authority: The Ministry of Social Policy will make the final decision, upon the referral (proposal) of the Center for Social Work.

Role of the Court: The court will issue an official decree ratifying the proceedings conducted by the Center for Social Work.

Role of the Adoption Agencies: None.

Adoption Application: There is no specific application form. The prospective adoptive parent(s) must write a signed letter to the relevant Center for Social Work providing basic information about them. It can be submitted by mail or through an authorized representative.

Time Frame: See above

Adoption Fees: None

Documents Required: The application must be accompanied by the following documents about each of the adoptive parents;

- Certified Birth certificate.
- Certified Marriage certificates (if applicable). Medical certificate of good health, preferably provided by a hospital or general practice clinic, rather than a private physician.
- Proof of citizenship (certified copy of a birth certificate, naturalization certificate or passport).
- Police certificate (i.e., certificate that no criminal record exists) issued by local law enforcement authorities from every place of residence where the applicant has lived for more than a year since the age of 18.
- Court certificate (i.e., certificate proving that the prospective adoptive parent is not under any court investigation at the present time).
- Certificate about capacity for gainful employment. This should take the form of a resume of previous employment records, and an original letter (on official stationery) signed by the current employer, stating the job title, if the position is full-or part-time, how long the person has been employed and the salary.
- Certificate proving that the prospective adoptive parent has never been charged with child neglect or abuse. This may take the form of an official letter from the local department of child welfare.
- Documents testifying to the prospective adoptive parent's income and property.
- Home study (social worker's analysis) about the prospective adoptive family, including its ability to care for a child. For non-Bosnian applicants, including Americans, the social services department of the applicant's country must conduct the study.

All original documents and the application letter must be in English and each must be accompanied by a translation into Bosnian/Serbian/Croatian done by an official court translator. It is easier and less expensive to have the translations done in Bosnia. The U.S. Embassy in Sarajevo can provide a list of court translators. The Embassy itself cannot, however, do the translations.

Bringing Your Child Home: Once your adoption is complete (or you have obtained legal custody of the child), there are a few more steps to take before you can head home. Specifically, you need to apply for several documents for your child before he or she can travel to the United States, such as a birth certificate, a passport or travel document for your child from the country in which he or she was born, and a U.S. Immigration Visa. For detailed and updated information on how to obtain these documents, review the *Intercountry Adoption* section in this publication and visit the U.S. Department of State Intercountry Adoption website at http://adoption.state.gov.

Child Citizenship Act: For adoptions finalized abroad, the Child Citizenship Act of 2000 allows your new child to acquire American citizenship automatically when he or she enters the United States as lawful permanent residents.

For adoptions finalized in the United States, the Child Citizenship Act of 2000 allows your new child to acquire American citizenship automatically when the court in the United States issues the final adoption decree.

To learn more, review the *Intercountry Adoption* section in this publication and visit the U.S. Department of State Intercountry Adoption website at http://adoption.state.gov.

U.S. Embassy in Bosnia-Herzegovina
Alipasina 43, 71000 Sarajevo
Bosnia and Herzegovina
Tel: +387 33 445 700
Fax: +387 33 221 837
Email: rws@state.gov
http://sarajevo.usembassy.gov

Bosnia-Herzegovina's Adoption Authority
Ministry of Labor and Social Policy of the Federation of Bosnia and Herzegovina
Vilsonovo setaliste 10, 71000 Sarajevo, Bosnia and Herzegovina
Tel: +387 33 661 782
Fax: +387 33 661 783
Email: info@fmrsp.gov.ba
Internet: www.fmrsp.gov.ba

Embassy of Bosnia-Herzegovina
2109 E Street NW
Washington, DC 20037
Tel: (202) 337 1500
Fax: (202) 337 2909
consularaffairs@bhembassy.org
http://www.bhembassy.org/consular_information.html

Office of Children's Issues
U.S. Department of State
2201 C Street, NW
SA-29
Washington, DC 20520
Tel: 1-888-407-4747
E-mail: AskCI@state.gov
http://adoption.state.gov

For questions about immigration procedures, call the National Customer Service Center (NCSC) at 1-800-375-5283 (TTY 1-800-767-1833).

BOTSWANA

Compiled from publications that were available as of February 2013 from the U.S. Department of State, the U.S. Department of Commerce, and the Central Intelligence Agency (CIA). See the introduction to this set for explanatory notes.

Official Name:
Republic of Botswana

PROFILE

Geography

Area: total: 581,730 sq km; country comparison to the world: 48; land: 566,730 sq km; water: 15,000 sq km

Major cities: Gaborone (capital) 196,000 (2009)

Climate: semiarid; warm winters and hot summers

Terrain: predominantly flat to gently rolling tableland; Kalahari Desert in southwest

People

Nationality: noun: Motswana (singular), Batswana (plural); adjective: Motswana (singular), Batswana (plural)

Population: 2,098,018 (July 2012 est.)

Population growth rate: 1.477% (2012 est.)

Ethnic groups: Tswana (or Setswana) 79%, Kalanga 11%, Basarwa 3%, other, including Kgalagadi and white 7%

Religions: Christian 71.6%, Badimo 6%, other 1.4%, unspecified 0.4%, none 20.6% (2001 census)

Languages: Setswana 78.2%, Kalanga 7.9%, Sekgalagadi 2.8%, English (official) 2.1%, other 8.6%, unspecified 0.4% (2001 census)

Literacy: definition: age 15 and over can read and write; total population: 84.5%; male: 84%; female: 84.9% (2010 est.)

Health: life expectancy at birth: total population: 55.74 years; male: 56.93 years; female: 54.51 years (2012 est.); Infant mortality rate: total: 10.49 deaths/1,000 live births; male: 11.03 deaths/1,000 live births; female: 9.94 deaths/1,000 live births (2012 est.)

Unemployment rate: 7.5% (2007 est.)

Work force: 1.269 million

Government

Type: parliamentary republic

Independence: 30 September 1966

Constitution: March 1965; effective 30 September 1966

Political subdivisions: 9 districts and 5 town councils; Central, Francistown, Gaborone, Ghanzi, Jwaneng, Kgalagadi, Kgatleng, Kweneng, Lobatse, North East, North West, Selebi-Pikwe, South East, Southern

Suffrage: 18 years of age; universal

Economy

GDP (purchasing power parity): $31.49 billion (2012 est.); $30.09 billion (2011 est.); $28.76 billion (2010 est.); $26.83 billion (2009 est.)

GDP real growth rate: 3.8% (2012 est.); 4.6% (2011 est.); 7.2% (2010 est.); -4.9% (2009 est.)

GDP per capita (PPP): $16,800 (2012 est.); $16,200 (2011 est.); $15,700 (2010 est.); $14,800 (2009 est.)

Natural resources: diamonds, copper, nickel, salt, soda ash, potash, coal, iron ore, silver

Agriculture products: livestock, sorghum, maize, millet, beans, sunflowers, groundnuts

Industries: diamonds, copper, nickel, salt, soda ash, potash, coal, iron ore, silver; livestock processing; textiles

Exports: $5.887 billion (2012 est.); $6.031 billion (2011 est.)

Exports—commodities: diamonds, copper, nickel, soda ash, meat, textiles

Imports: $5.883 billion (2012 est.); $6.211 billion (2011 est.); $4.767 billion (2010 est.)

Imports—commodities: foodstuffs, machinery, electrical goods, transport equipment, textiles, fuel and petroleum products, wood and paper products, metal and metal products

Debt—external: $1.968 billion (31 December 2012 est.); $1.973 billion (31 December 2011 est.); $1.709 billion (31 December 2010 est.)

Exchange rates: pulas (BWP) per US dollar; 7.65 (2012 est.); 6.8382 (2011 est.); 6.7936 (2010 est.); 7.1551 (2009); 6.7907 (2008); 6.2035 (2007)

PEOPLE

Batswana, a term also used to denote all citizens of Botswana, refers to the country's major ethnic group (the "Tswana" in South Africa), which came into the area from South Africa during the Zulu wars of the early 1800s. Prior to European contact, the Batswana lived as herders and farmers under tribal rule.

National/Racial/Ethnic Minorities

An estimated 50,000-60,000 people belong to one of the many scattered, diverse tribal groups known as San or Basarwa. The San represented approximately 3 percent of the population and are culturally and linguistically distinct from most other residents. The law prohibits discrimination against the San with respect to employment, housing, health services, and cultural practices; however, the San remained economically and politically marginalized and generally did not have access to their traditional land. The San continued to be geographically isolated, had limited access to education, lacked adequate political representation, and were not fully aware of their civil rights.

Language

English is the official language of government and business in Botswana. Setswana is the predominant indigenous language and the first language of most Batswana.

Religion

Approximately 70 percent of citizens identify themselves as Christians. Anglicans, Methodists, and members of the United Congregational Church of Southern Africa make up the majority of Christians. There are also congregations of Lutherans, Roman Catholics, The Church of Jesus Christ of Latter-day Saints (Mormons), Seventh-day Adventists, Jehovah's Witnesses, Baptists, the Dutch Reformed Church, Mennonites, and other Christian denominations. The Muslim community, primarily of South Asian origin, numbers slightly more than 5,000. There are small numbers of Hindus and Baha'is. Approximately 20 percent of citizens espouse no religion.

HISTORY

In the 19th century, hostilities broke out between the Batswana and Boer settlers from the Transvaal. After appeals by the Batswana for assistance, the British Government in 1885 put "Bechuanaland" under its protection. The northern territory remained under direct administration and is today's Botswana, while the southern territory became part of the Cape Colony and is now part of the northwest province of South Africa; the majority of Setswana-speaking people today live in South Africa.

Despite South African pressure, inhabitants of the Bechuanaland Protectorate, Basutoland (now Lesotho), and Swaziland in 1909 asked for and received British assurances that they would not be included in the proposed Union of South Africa. An expansion of British central authority and the evolution of tribal government resulted in the 1920 establishment of two advisory councils representing Africans and Europeans. Proclamations in 1934 regularized tribal rule and powers. A European-African advisory council was formed in 1951, and the 1961 constitution established a consultative legislative council.

In June 1964, Britain accepted proposals for democratic self-government in Botswana. The seat of government was moved from Mafikeng, in South Africa, to newly-established Gaborone in 1965. The 1965 constitution led to the first general elections and to independence in September 1966. General elections serve to elect members of parliament, and the presidential candidate from the party that wins the most seats in the general election becomes the president. Seretse Khama, a leader in the independence movement and the legitimate claimant to traditional rule of the Bamangwato, became the country's first president, was re-elected twice, and died in office in 1980. The presidency passed to the sitting vice president, Ketumile Masire, who was elected in his own right in 1984 and re-elected in 1989 and 1994. Masire retired from office in 1998. The presidency passed to the sitting vice president, Festus Mogae, who was elected in his own right in 1999. Mogae won a second term in elections held October 30, 2004 and stepped down in accordance with national term limits on March 31, 2008. On April 1, 2008 former Vice President Ian Khama assumed the presidency. Khama was elected as President in his own right during the general election held on October 16, 2009.

GOVERNMENT AND POLITICAL CONDITIONS

Botswana has been a multiparty democracy since independence in 1966. Its constitution provides for indirect election of a president and popular election of a National Assembly. In 2009 the ruling Botswana Democratic Party (BDP) won the majority of parliamentary seats in an election deemed generally free and fair. President Ian Khama, who has held the presidency since the resignation of President Festus Mogae in 2008, retained his position. The BDP has held the presidency and a majority of National Assembly seats since independence.

Recent Elections

In 2009 the ruling BDP won the majority of National Assembly seats in a general election deemed by international and domestic observers to be generally free and fair. President Ian Khama retained the presidency, which he has held since 2008.

Political Parties: At the end of 2011, the BDP held 39 seats in parliament, the new Botswana Movement for Democracy (BMD) party led the opposition with six seats, the BNF controlled six seats, the BCP had five

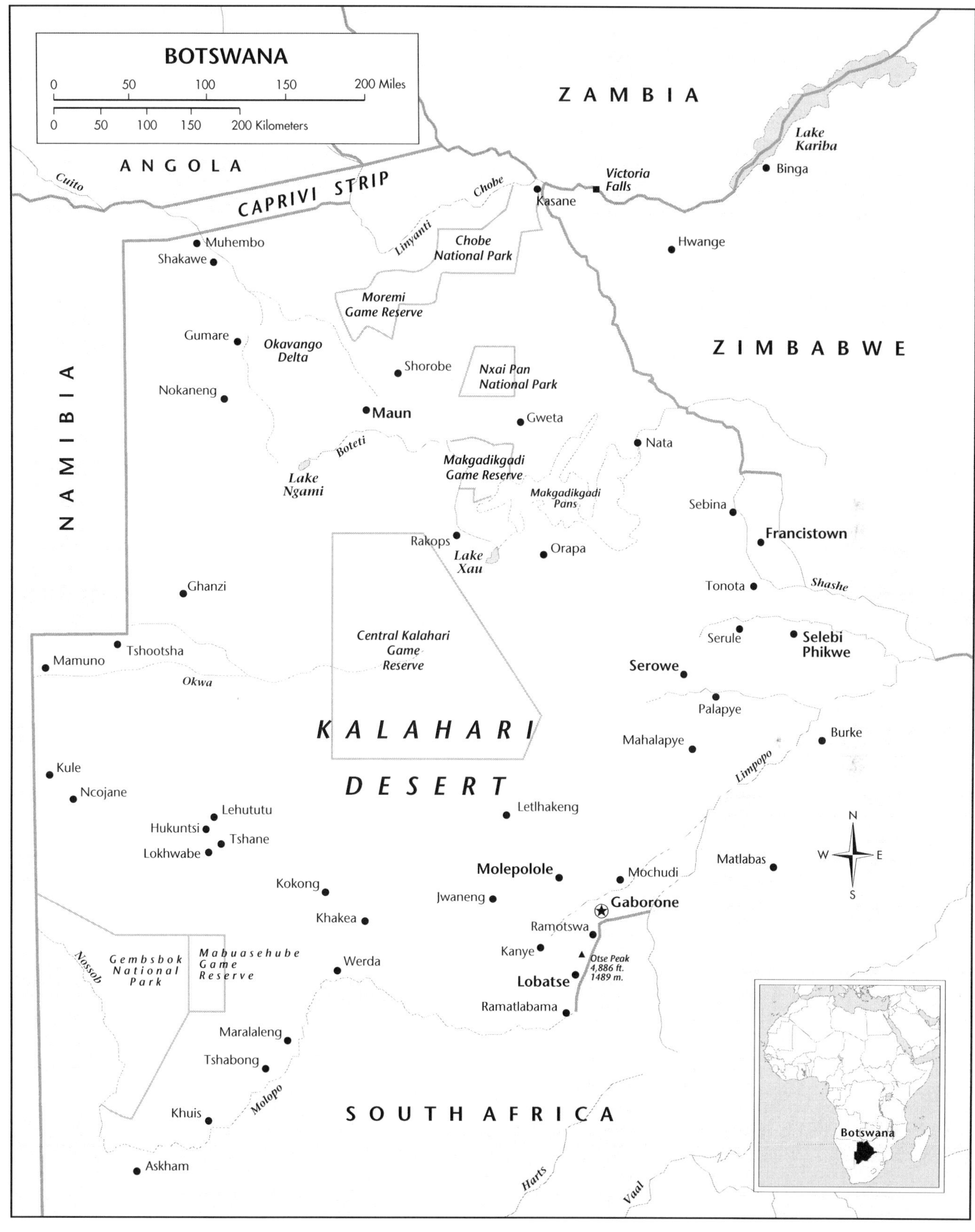
BOTSWANA
0 50 100 150 200 Miles
0 50 100 150 200 Kilometers
ZAMBIA
ANGOLA
CAPRIVI STRIP
ZIMBABWE
NAMIBIA
SOUTH AFRICA
KALAHARI
DESERT
Lake Kariba
Binga
Victoria Falls
Kasane
Chobe
Linyanti
Cuito
Chobe National Park
Muhembo
Shakawe
Hwange
Moremi Game Reserve
Gumare
Okavango Delta
Shorobe
Nxai Pan National Park
Nokaneng
Maun
Gweta
Nata
Boteti
Makgadikgadi Game Reserve
Makgadikgadi Pans
Lake Ngami
Sebina
Francistown
Rakops
Lake Xau
Orapa
Ghanzi
Tonota
Shashe
Central Kalahari Game Reserve
Serule
Selebi Phikwe
Tshootsha
Mamuno
Okwa
Serowe
Palapye
Mahalapye
Burke
Limpopo
Kule
Ncojane
Lehututu
Hukuntsi
Tshane
Lokhwabe
Letlhakeng
Molepolole
Mochudi
Matlabas
Kokong
Jwaneng
Gaborone
Khakea
Ramotswa
Kanye
Otse Peak 4,886 ft. 1489 m.
Lobatse
Ramatlabama
Werda
Nossob
Gembsbok National Park
Mabuasehube Game Reserve
Maralaleng
Tshabong
Molopo
Khuis
Askham
Harts
Vaal
N
W
E
S
Botswana

seats, and there was one independent. The BMD, which split from the BDP in 2010, had two of its eight MPs return to the BDP in 2011.

The House of Chiefs consists of eight paramount chiefs, five chiefs chosen by the president, and 22 elected chiefs from designated regions. It acts as an advisory upper chamber to the National Assembly on any legislation affecting tribal organization and property, customary law, and administration of the customary courts. The paramount chiefs are members of the House of Chiefs for life, while the chosen and elected chiefs serve five-year terms since 2009. The first election, based on amendments made to the constitution in 2006, was held the same year. In order to hold concurrent elections with Parliament, another election was held in 2009.

Political parties operated without restriction or outside interference.

Participation of Women and Minorities: There were five women in the 61-seat National Assembly, one of whom was the speaker; four in the 24-member cabinet; and four in the expanded 35-seat House of Chiefs.

While the constitution formally recognizes eight principal ethnic groups of the Tswana nation, amendments to the constitution also allow minority tribes to be represented in the expanded House of Chiefs. Under the law members from all groups enjoy equal rights, and minority tribes have representation that is at least equal to that of the eight principal tribes. There were members of minority tribes in the assembly, the cabinet, and on the High Court.

Principal Government Officials

Last Updated: 1/31/2013

Pres.: **Seretse Khama Ian KHAMA**
Vice Pres.: **Ponatshego KEDIKILWE**
Min. of Agriculture: **Christian DE GRAF**
Min. of Defense, Justice, & Security: **Dikgakgamatso Ndelu SERETSE**
Min. of Environment, Wildlife, & Tourism: **Tshekedi KHAMA**
Min. of Education & Skills Development: **Pelonomi VENSON-MOITI**
Min. of Finance & Development Planning: **Ontefetse Kenneth MATAMBO**
Min. of Foreign Affairs & Intl. Cooperation: **Phandu Tombola Chaka SKELEMANI**
Min. of Health: **John SEAKGOSING**
Min. of Infrastructure, Science, & Technology: **Johnnie K. SWARTZ**
Min. of Labor & Home Affairs: **Edwin BATSHU**
Min. of Lands & Housing: **Nonofo MOLEFHI**
Min. of Local Govt.: **Peter SEELE**
Min. of Minerals, Energy, & Water Resources: **Kitso MOKAILA**
Min. of Presidential Affairs & Public Admin.: **Mokgweetsi MASISI**
Min. of Trade & Industry: **Baledzi GAOLATHE**
Min. of Transport & Communication: **Lebonaamang MOKALAKE**
Min. of Youth, Sports, & Culture: **Shaw KHATHI**
Min. in the Office of the Pres. Responsible for Public Service:**Margaret NASHA**
Attorney Gen.: **Athalia MOLOKOMME**
Governor, Bank of Botswana: **Linah MOHOHLO**
Ambassador to the US: **Tebelelo Mazile SERETSE**
Permanent Representative to the UN, New York: **Charles Thembani NTWAAGAE**

ECONOMY

Botswana has maintained one of the world's highest economic growth rates since independence in 1966. However, economic growth was negative in 2009, with the industrial sector shrinking by 30%, after the global crisis reduced demand for Botswana's diamonds.

The economy has since recovered, with GDP growth in 2010 at 7.2% and estimated GDP growth in 2011 of 6.2%. Through fiscal discipline and sound management, Botswana transformed itself from one of the poorest countries in the world to a middle-income country with a per capita GDP of $16,300 in 2011.

Two major investment services rank Botswana as the best credit risk in Africa. Diamond mining has fueled much of the expansion and currently accounts for more than one-third of GDP, 70-80% of export earnings, and about half of the government's revenues. Botswana's heavy reliance on a single luxury export was a critical factor in the sharp economic contraction of 2009.

Tourism, financial services, subsistence farming, and cattle raising are other key sectors. Although unemployment was 7.5% in 2007 according to official reports, unofficial estimates place it closer to 40%. The prevalence of HIV/AIDS is second highest in the world and threatens Botswana's impressive economic gains. An expected leveling off in diamond mining production within the next two decades overshadows long-term prospects.

Labor Conditions

Children 14 years or older may be employed in light work that is "not harmful to [their] health and development" and is approved by a parent or guardian. The law provides that work shall not exceed six hours per day when a child is not in school, and five hours when a child is in school. The law provides that adopted children may not be exploited for labor and prohibits the exploitation or coercion into prostitution.

The Ministry of Labor and Home Affairs is responsible for enforcing child labor laws and policies in all sectors; however, resources were too limited for effective oversight in remote areas. Despite the laws and policies designed to protect children from exploitation in the workplace, there were reports of child labor, mostly on subsistence-level cattle posts or farms.

Of the children employed, approximately half were below the legal working age of 14. Two-thirds of employed children were working in rural villages, and more than 60 percent worked in the agricultural sector. According to the 2005–06 labor survey, slightly fewer than 38,000 children between the ages of seven and 17 were employed in 2006.

Approximately half of those were under 14. More than 60 percent of employed children worked in agriculture, 20 percent in retail trade, and 4 percent in private homes. Children also worked as domestic laborers and in informal bars. Outside of supermarkets they sometimes assisted truck drivers with unloading goods and carried bags for customers. Many orphans also left school to work as caregivers for sick relatives. Most employed children worked up to 28 hours per week.

The minimum hourly wage for most full-time labor in the private sector was 3.80 pula ($0.58). Formal sector jobs generally paid well above minimum wage levels. Informal sector employment, particularly in the agricultural and domestic service sectors, where housing and food were provided, frequently paid below the minimum wage. The minimum wage for domestic workers was two pula ($0.30) per hour, or approximately 16 pula ($2.40) a day. The minimum for workers in the agricultural sector was 408 pula ($62) per month; however, the cost of feeding a worker who lived on the employer's premises could be deducted from the wages. A 2003 government household income survey found that 23 percent of people lived on less than a dollar a day. The government defines poverty as a lack of food, shelter, clothing, etc. rather than an absolute income level; the same survey estimated that 30 percent of people lived in poverty. A smaller survey in 2009 estimated that 23 percent were impoverished.

The cabinet determined wage policy based on recommendations from the National Economic, Manpower, and Incomes Committee, which consists of representatives of the government, private sector, and Botswana Federation of Trade Unions. The Ministry of Labor and Home Affairs is responsible for enforcing the minimum wage, and each of the country's districts had at least one labor inspector.

The law permits a maximum 48-hour workweek, exclusive of overtime, which is payable at time-and-a-half. The law does not specifically outline rest periods or prohibit excessive compulsory overtime. The law prescribes 40-hour workweek for most modern private sector jobs, and a 48-hour workweek for the public sector. The labor law also applies to farm and migrant workers.

The government generally enforced wage, hour, health, and safety requirements, but the number of labor inspectors was insufficient to inspect all workplaces. Foreign migrant workers were vulnerable to exploitative working conditions, mainly in domestic labor. Employers in the formal sector generally provided for worker safety.

U.S.-BOTSWANA RELATIONS

The United States considers Botswana an excellent partner and an advocate of and model for stability in Africa. Botswana has consistently maintained a democratic government, responsibly managed its natural resources, and invested in its people and infrastructure. The bilateral relationship is strong, grounded in a shared commitment to democracy, good governance, and human rights. The United States and Botswana also share an interest in ensuring the sustainability of Botswana's success by deepening economic diversification and promoting regional economic growth and development.

U.S. Assistance to Botswana

The United States has been a major partner in Botswana's development since its independence from the United Kingdom in 1966. The U.S. Agency for International Development (USAID) phased out its bilateral partnership with Botswana in the mid-1990s, after successful programs emphasizing education, training, entrepreneurship, environmental management, and reproductive health. Botswana benefits along with its neighbors in the region from USAID's Initiative for Southern Africa, based in Pretoria, and USAID's Southern Africa Trade Hub, headquartered in Gaborone. The U.S. International Board of Broadcasters operates a major Voice of America relay station in Botswana serving most of the African continent.

Botswana is one of the focus countries for PEPFAR, the President's Emergency Plan for Aids Relief. PEPFAR assistance to Botswana supports sustainable, high-quality, cost-effective HIV/AIDS prevention, treatment, and care interventions. The Centers for Disease Control and Prevention has undertaken many projects and has assisted many organizations in the fight against the HIV/AIDS epidemic in Botswana. HIV/AIDS-related programs also are a focus of the Peace Corps.

The International Law Enforcement Academy (ILEA), which is jointly financed, managed, and staffed by the Governments of Botswana and the United States, provides training to police and government officials from across the sub-Saharan region. Over 4,300 law enforcement professionals from 26 countries in sub-Saharan Africa have received training from ILEA since it began offering classes in 2001.

Bilateral Economic Relations

Botswana is eligible for preferential trade benefits under the African Growth and Opportunity Act. The country belongs to the Southern African Customs Union, which has signed a Trade, Investment, and Development Cooperative Agreement (TIDCA) with the United States. The TIDCA establishes a forum for consultative discussions, cooperative work, and possible agreements on a wide range of trade issues, with a special focus on customs and trade facilitation, technical barriers to trade, sanitary and phytosanitary measures, and trade and investment promotion.

Botswana's Membership in International Organizations

Botswana puts a premium on economic and political integration in Southern Africa. Botswana and the United States belong to a number of the same international organizations, including the United Nations, International Monetary Fund, World Bank, and World Trade Organization.

Bilateral Representation

Botswana maintains an embassy at 1531-1533 New Hampshire Avenue NW, Washington DC 20036 (tel. 202-244-4990; fax 202-244-4164). Its mission to the United Nations is at 103 E. 37th Street, New York NY 10017 (tel. 212-889-2277; fax 212-725-5061).

Principal U.S. Embassy Officials

Last Updated: 1/14/2013

GABORONE (E) P.O. Box 90, Gaborone, Botswana, (267) 395-3982, Fax (267) 395-6947, Workweek: M-Th 7:30 AM to 5:00 PM, Fri 7:30 AM to 1:30 PM, Website: http://botswana.usembassy.gov/

DCM OMS:	Lisa G Knight
AMB OMS:	Megan Walton
CDC:	Kathleen Toomey
Co-CLO:	Shonnie Franta
ECON/COM:	Domingo Villaronga
HRO:	Charlie Franta
IBB:	Charles Shepard
MGT:	Arlen J. Holt
MLO/ODC:	LTC Joshua Reitz
POL/ECON:	Katherine Dueholm
SDO/DATT:	LTC Joshua Reitz
TREAS:	James Day
AMB:	Michelle Gavin
CON:	Stephen Wilger
DCM:	Michael Murphy
PAO:	John Warner
COM:	Janet Kennedy
GSO:	Andrew Prater
RSO:	William McCarthy
AFSA:	Stephen Wilger
AID:	Joan Larosa
CLO:	Sue McCarthy
EEO:	Megan Walton
FMO:	Carol Vargas
ICASS Chair:	Seana Lammers
IMO:	Mehari Tesfamicael
ISSO:	Mehari Tesfamicael
State ICASS:	Katherine Dueholm

TRAVEL

Consular Information Sheet

August 2, 2012

Country Description: Botswana, a country in southern Africa roughly the size of Texas with a population of approximately 1.8 million, has a stable democratic, parliamentary government and a stable economy. Diamond and mineral mining are key components of the economy, while facilities for tourism are also widely available.

Smart Traveler Enrollment Program (STEP): If you are going to live in or visit Botswana, please take the time to tell our Embassy about your trip. If you enroll, we can keep you up to date with important safety and security announcements. It will also help your friends and family get in touch with you in an emergency. If you do not have internet access, you can stop by the Embassy and complete your registration.

The U.S. Embassy Gaborone is located on Embassy Drive in the Government Enclave.

Mailing address:
P.O. Box 90, Gaborone, Botswana
Telephone: 267 395-3982
After-hours Emergency Telephone: 267 395-7111
Fax 267 318-0232

Entry/Exit Requirements for U.S. Citizens: A passport with at least six months of validity remaining is required. U.S. citizens are permitted stays up to 90 days total within a 12-month periodwithout a visa. Travelers who attempt to enter Botswana with a temporary travel document (12-page emergency photo-digitized passport (EPDP)) must have a visa to enter. It is not possible to obtain a visa upon arrival in Botswana, and U.S. citizens without a visa in a temporary passport will face possible fines and long administrative delays.

For additional information on entry requirements, travelers may contact the Embassy of the Republic of Botswana, 1531–1533 New Hampshire Avenue NW, Washington, DC 20036, telephone (202) 244-4990/1, fax (202) 244-4164 or the Permanent Mission of the Republic of Botswana to the United Nations, 103 E. 37th St., New York, NY, 10016, telephone (212) 889-2277, fax (212) 725-5061. There are also honorary consuls in Los Angeles, San Francisco and Houston. Visit the Embassy of Botswana's web site for the most current visa information. As a general precaution, all travelers are advised to carry a photocopy of the photo/bio information page of their passport and keep it in a location separate from the passport. Visitors to Botswana who also intend to visit South Africa should be advised that the passports of all travelers to South Africa must contain at least two blank (unstamped) visa pages each time entry to South Africa is sought; these pages are in addition to the endorsement/amendment pages at the back of the passport. Otherwise, the traveler, even when in possession of a valid South African visa, may be refused entry into South Africa, fined, and returned to their point of origin at the traveler's expense.

The U.S. Department of State is unaware of any HIV/AIDS entry restrictions for visitors to or foreign residents of Botswana.

Threats to Safety and Security: Civil unrest and disorder are rare, but in the event of a protest, U.S. citizens should avoid crowds, political rallies, and street demonstrations and maintain security awareness at all times.

Stay up to date by:

- Bookmarking our Bureau of Consular Affairs website, which contains the current Travel Warnings and Travel Alerts as well as the Worldwide Caution.

- Following us on Twitter and the Bureau of Consular Affairs page on Facebook as well.
- Downloading our free Smart Traveler iPhone App to have travel information at your fingertips.
- Calling 1-888-407-4747 toll free within the U.S. and Canada, or a regular toll line, 1-202-501-4444 from other countries.
- Taking some time before travel to consider your personal safety.

Crime: Crime is a serious concern in Botswana. Visitors must be vigilant and take common-sense security precautions. Petty street crime and crimes of opportunity, primarily the theft of money and personal property, are not uncommon. Home invasions, "smash and grabs" from vehicles, and cell phone thefts, often at knife point, are routinely reported to the police. Hotels and lodges are not immune from criminal activity, and visitors should remain alert and take reasonable precautions in safeguarding personal property (particularly money and electronic equipment). Visitors are urged to exercise extreme caution near the Gaborone Dam and Kgale Hill in Gaborone due to the high number of reported criminal incidents. Travelers arriving in Botswana via South Africa should be aware that there is a serious continuing baggage pilferage problem at OR Tambo (Johannesburg) and Cape Town International Airports. Travelers are encouraged to use an airport plastic wrapping service and to avoid placing electronics, jewelry, cameras, designer athletic gear, or other valuables in checked luggage. Also, make an inventory of items in checked baggage to aid in claims processing if theft does occur.

In many countries around the world, counterfeit and pirated goods are widely available. Transactions involving such products may be illegal under local law. In addition, bringing them back to the United States may result in forfeitures and/or fines.

Victims of Crime: If you are the victim of a crime abroad, you should contact the local police and the nearest U.S. embassy or consulate. We can:

- Replace a stolen passport.
- Help you find appropriate medical care if you are the victim of violent crimes such as assault or rape.
- Put you in contact with the appropriate police authorities and we can, if you want us to, contact family members or friends.
- Help you understand the local criminal justice process and direct you to local attorneys, although it is important to remember that local authorities are responsible for investigating and prosecuting the crime.

Botswana has three numbers equivalent to the "911" emergency line. For police assistance, dial "999." For an ambulance, dial "997." In the event of a fire, dial "998."

Criminal Penalties: While you are traveling in Botswana, you are subject to its laws even if you are a U.S. citizen. Foreign laws and legal systems can be vastly different than our own and may not afford the protections available to the individual under U.S. law. Penalties for breaking the law can be more severe than in the United States for similar offenses. Persons violating Botswana's laws, even unknowingly, may be expelled, arrested or imprisoned. Penalties for possession, use, or trafficking in illegal drugs in Botswana are severe, and convicted offenders can expect long jail sentences and heavy fines.

Engaging in sexual conduct with children or using or disseminating child pornography in a foreign country is a crime, prosecutable in the United States. Motorists should note that it is illegal to use a cell phone while driving; failure to comply could result in fines and/or confiscation of the cell phone. If you break local laws in Botswana, your U.S. passport won't help you avoid arrest or prosecution. It's very important to know what's legal and what's not where you are going.

Based on the Vienna Convention on Consular Relations, bilateral agreements with certain countries, and customary international law, if you are arrested in Botswana, you have the option to request that the police, prison officials, or other authorities alert the nearest U.S. embassy or consulate of your arrest, and to have communications from you forwarded to the nearest U.S. embassy or consulate.

Special Circumstances: Botswana experiences occasional periods of rolling electric power outages that can leave areas without power for several hours. Visitors are urged to carry flashlights. American citizens are also urged to be aware of how power outages might affect home security systems, garage doors and gates, and kitchen equipment, such as stoves and refrigerators. The power fluctuations could cause power surges that might harm computers, televisions, or other electrical appliances.

Botswana strictly enforces its laws controlling the trade in animal products. The hunting of lions is explicitly prohibited and leopards and elephants are covered under a strict quota regime. Botswana's Wildlife Conservation and National Parks Act makes it illegal to possess or remove from Botswana without a government permit any living or dead animal or animal trophy. A trophy is any horn, ivory, tooth, tusk, bone, claw, hoof, hide, skin, hair, feather, egg, or other durable portion of an animal, whether the item has been processed or not. Curio shops and vendors throughout the country sell items such as animal skins, plain and decorated ostrich eggs and eggshells, and carved bones or teeth of animals protected by this law. All of the souvenirs, although widely sold, are subject to this act. Travelers departing the country with a trophy must have a receipt from a store licensed to sell such items. Ivory and endangered rhinoceros horn products obtained in Botswana may not be removed from the country under any circumstances;

elephant hair jewelry may be removed only with the appropriate license from the Department of Wildlife and National Parks. Trophies may not be taken from the wild without a permit. Violators are subject to arrest and may face a penalty of up to five years imprisonment and a substantial fine. Wild animals may pose a danger to tourists. Tourists should bear in mind that, even in the most serene settings, the animals are wild and can pose a threat to life and safety. Tourists should use common sense when approaching wildlife, observe all local or park regulations, and heed all instructions given by tour guides. In addition, tourists are advised that potentially dangerous areas sometimes lack fences and warning signs. Exercise appropriate caution in all unfamiliar surroundings.

Accessibility: While in Botswana, individuals with disabilities may find accessibility and accommodation very different from what you find in the United States. Botswana law prohibits discrimination against persons with physical and mental disabilities in education, employment, access to health care, or the provision of other state services. While the government mandates access to public buildings or transportation for persons with disabilities, most privately owned buildings and business, and older government buildings remain inaccessible.

Medical Facilities and Health Information: Medical facilities in Gaborone are adequate for simple medical problems, but facilities outside of Gaborone are limited. Adequately equipped emergency rooms and trained physicians are available in the capital but services are rudimentary elsewhere. Professional private emergency rescue services operate air and ground ambulances throughout the country, but care is rendered only after a patient's ability to pay is established.

Response times are often slow in less populated areas. Outside of Gaborone, most airports are either not equipped or may have malfunctioning night lighting capability, so airborne medical evacuations can often only be conducted during daylight hours. Malaria is prevalent only in the north of the country, particularly around the Chobe and Okavango National Parks. Malaria prophylaxis is not required in Gaborone but is suggested for travel to the north. For advanced care Americans often choose to travel to South Africa. Many South African manufactured prescription drugs are available in Gaborone.

Travelers through South Africa from countries where yellow fever is endemic are required to present their yellow World Health Organization (WHO) vaccination record or other proof of inoculation. This requirement may be imposed on travelers flying to South Africa via yellow fever countries, even when transiting passengers are required to stay on board the plane (e.g., South African Airways flights stopping in Dakar, Senegal).

Please note that yellow fever inoculations are no longer administered at South African ports of entry. If a yellow fever inoculation is not obtained in accordance to these new guidelines, passengers may be turned around at the South African port of entry.

The Embassy recommends that you carry your certificate of vaccination with you whenever traveling through South Africa as we have received reports that authorities will inspect them even from passengers who did not arrive from or transit through yellow fever countries.

Approximately one-quarter of the population of Botswana is infected with HIV, the virus that causes AIDS. Travelers are advised to exercise appropriate precautions if engaging in sexual activity, or if exposed to blood products through injuries or rendering assistance to accident victims. Tuberculosis is also endemic to Botswana. Several hundred cases of extensively drug resistant tuberculosis (XDR-TB) have been identified in Botswana since January 2008 when Botswana first obtained the ability to test for this form of TB. Individuals who plan to reside or stay in Botswana for extended periods are advised to obtain a tuberculosis skin test (PPD test) prior to arrival and again upon departure from Botswana. There are occasional diarrhea outbreaks in areas affected by heavy rains. Travelers in those regions are encouraged to take necessary precautions when handling food and drinking water.

Information on vaccinations and other health precautions, such as safe food and water precautions and insect bite protection, may be obtained from the Centers for Disease Control and Prevention's (CDC) hotline for international travelers at 1-877-FYI-TRIP (1-877-394-8747) or via the CDC web site. For information about outbreaks of infectious diseases abroad, consult the infectious diseases section of the World Health Organization (WHO) web site. The WHO web site also contains additional health information for travelers, including detailed country-specific health information.

Medical Insurance: You can't assume your insurance will go with you when you travel. It's very important to find out BEFORE you leave whether your medical insurance will cover you overseas. You need to ask your insurance company two questions:

- Does my policy apply when I am out of the United States?
- Will it cover emergencies like a trip to a foreign hospital or a medical evacuation?

In many places, doctors and hospitals still expect payment in cash at the time of service. Your regular U.S. health insurance may not cover doctors' and hospital visits in other countries. If your policy doesn't go with you when you travel, it's a very good idea to take out another one for your trip.

Traffic Safety and Road Conditions: While in a foreign country, U.S. citizens may encounter road conditions that differ significantly from those in the United States. The information below concerning Botswana is provided for general reference only, and may not be totally accurate in a particular location or circumstance.

Driving in Botswana is challenging and motorists must drive defensively. As elsewhere in the region, traffic circulates on the left in Botswana. While the roads in major population centers are generally good, rural roads can be in poor condition and treacherous. Rolling power outages mean that many traffic lights and street lamps do not work properly. The combination of long, tedious stretches of two-lane highways without shoulders, high speed limits, free-range domestic animals (even in urban centers), and large numbers of pedestrians and hitchhikers in the roadways make fatal accidents a frequent occurrence. Smash and grab robberies from vehicles are not uncommon in Botswana, particularly in urban areas at traffic lights. Motorists should avoid carrying anything of value (hand bags, briefcases, purses, cell phones, etc.) in the passenger compartment that could attract potential assailants.

Aviation Safety Oversight: As there is no direct commercial air service to the United States by carriers registered in Botswana, the U.S. Federal Aviation Administration (FAA) has not assessed the government of Botswana's Civil Aviation Authority for compliance with International Civil Aviation Organization (ICAO) aviation safety standards. Further information may be found on the FAA's safety assessment page.

On October 14, 2011, a Cessna Caravan C208B 12-seater aircraft operated by Moremi Air Services crashed shortly after takeoff at Xakanaka airstrip in the Okavango Delta, northwest Botswana, killing seven passengers and the pilot. Tourists flying on small aircraft are advised to be aware of and comply with safety regulations limiting the weight of the baggage they may bring on board, to listen carefully to the pre-flight safety briefing given by pilots (and demand such a briefing if one is not given), and during the briefing ask any safety-related questions they deem appropriate.

Children's Issues: Please see the U.S. Dept. of State Office of Children's Issues web pages on intercountry adoption and international parental child abduction.

Intercountry Adoption

June 2012

The information in this section has been edited from a report of the Bureau of Consular Affairs, Office of Overseas Citizens Services of the U.S. Department of State. For more information, please read the *Intercountry Adoption* section of this book and review current reports online at http://adoption.state.gov.

Botswana is not party to the Hague Convention on Protection of Children and Co-operation in Respect of Intercountry Adoption(the Hague Adoption Convention). Intercountry adoptions of children from non-Hague countries are processed in accordance with 8 Code of Federal Regulations, Section 204.3 as it relates to orphans as defined under the Immigration and Nationality Act, Section 101(b)(1)(F).

The Ministry of Local Government maintains a list of families (currently over 200 families, both citizens and foreigners) who wish to adopt children. Currently, this list is much longer than the number of available children and families can wait many months or years before being matched.

In traditional Setswana culture, adoption is neither common nor a preferred option for orphans or abandoned children. Extended families usually assume the role left to the state in many other countries. The Government of Botswana does not prefer these unofficial arrangements, and is currently re-writing the Adoption Act of 1952 in order to implement clear and compulsory legal procedures for custody, guardianship, and adoption of minors.

Who Can Adopt? To bring an adopted child to the United States from Botswana, you must meet eligibility and suitability requirements. The U.S. Department of Homeland Security, U.S. Citizenship and Immigration Services (USCIS) determines Who Can Adopt under U.S. immigration law. Additionally, a child must meet the definition of orphan under U.S. law in order to be eligible to immigrate to the United States on an IR-3 or IR-4 immigrant visa.

Residency: While prospective adoptive parents are not required to be permanent residents of Botswana in order to adopt, officials of the Department of Social Work within the Ministry of Local Government will verify work and residency documents before placing a prospective adoptive parent's name on the adoption "wait list."

Age of Adopting Parents: No person under the age of 25 may adopt a child, either either individually or jointly with their spouse.

Marriage: A married couple, widower, widow, unmarried, separated, or divorced person may adopt a child in Botswana.

Income: Even though there are no set income requirements, social workers will verify that prospective parents have adequate financial resources to care for a child.

Other: While Botswana society is broadly tolerant, the penal code contains provisions that are widely understood to penalize same sex relations and there are no laws that protect the LGBT community from discrimination.

The U.S. Embassy is unaware of any successful adoptions of children from Botswana by same sex couples from the United States. Same sex couples contemplating adopting a child from Botswana should seek legal advice in Botswana.

Who Can Be Adopted? In addition to U.S. immigration requirements, Botswana has specific requirements that a child must meet in order to be eligible for adoption.

Relinquishment or Abandonment: Consent to the adoption must be given by:

- Both parents of the child or, if the child is born out of wedlock, by the mother of the child;
- The guardian of the child if both parents are dead, or in the case of a child born out of wedlock, if the mother is dead;
- By the surviving parent if one parent is dead and by any guardian of the child who may have been appointed by the deceased parent;
- If one parent has deserted the child, by the other parent;
- A guardian of the child appointed by the Minister of Local Government when both parents are dead, have deserted the child, or are incapable by reason of mental disorder or defect of consenting to the adoption.

Age of Adoptive Child: There is no specific age requirement. However, in order to be eligible to adopt a child over the age of 16, the prospective adoptive parents must be at least 25 years older than the child.

Sibling Adoptions: Reasonable efforts will be made to prevent the separation of siblings during the adoption process.

Special Needs or Medical Conditions: Children with special needs can be adopted in Botswana, but special consideration or expedited processing is not possible.

Waiting Period or Foster Care: Prospective adoptive parents must foster a prospective adoptive child for a period of six months in Botswana before they may conclude a full and final adoption. Once a child is legally adopted in Botswana, the adoptive parents must remain in Botswana with the child for a period of 12 months before they can legally remove the child to a different country. The Ministry of Local Government will grant exceptions where there is a compelling need (such as employment or schooling) for the adoptive family to depart Botswana. This legal requirement makes intercountry adoption from Botswana extremely difficult for anyone other than long term residents.

If prospective adoptive parents wish to leave Botswana for a vacation or due to employment or school requirements during the six months in which they are fostering a prospective adoptive child, the Magistrate (Children's) court must provide written permission prior to departure. The same permission is required should the adoptive parents wish to temporarily depart Botswana during the 12 month period in which they are required to remain in Botswana after the adoption is finalized.

The U.S. Embassy will require both the court order granting custody and notice that the child is free to travel outside of Botswana before issuing a non-immigrant visa to the adoptive or prospective adoptive child. In addition, it must be demonstrated to the satisfaction of the consular officer that the child has sufficient ties to Botswana to compel his/her return after a short visit to the United States.

Prospective adoptive parents should be aware that not all children in orphanages or children's homes are adoptable. In many countries, birth parents place their child(ren) temporarily in an orphanage or children's home due to financial or other hardship, with the intention of returning for the child when they are able to do so. In such cases, the birth parent(s) rarely would have relinquished their parental rights or consented to their child(ren)'s adoption.

Botswana's Adoption Authority: Ministry of Local Government. While the Ministry of Local Government has oversight of the entire process, the Magistrate Court is the only body which issues binding legal decisions regarding children's issues. The Magistrate Court is referred to as the Children's Court when it hears cases involving children.

The Magistrate Court gives priority to children's cases, therefore custody and adoption cases do not queue with other matters before the court. While the court is under no legal obligation to involve social workers in children's issues, they typically do. However, social workers have described rare cases in which custody has been granted solely at the judge's discretion.

The Process: The recommended first step in adopting a child from Botswana is to decide whether or not to use a licensed adoption service provider in the United States that can help you with your adoption. Adoption service providers must be licensed by the U.S. state in which they operate.

Private adoptions outside of government regulations are not recognized in Botswana. The system is designed in such a way that legal representation or utilization of an adoption agency or broker is not required. While there is no specific law prohibiting their existence, there are currently no adoption service providers recognized in Botswana. Some families retain an attorney believing that to do so may help them navigate the bureaucracy more quickly, but often end up being frustrated that they have spent considerable sums of money for no apparent advantage.

In order to adopt a child from Botswana, you will need to meet the requirements of the Government of Botswana and U.S. immigration law. You must submit an application to be found eligible to adopt with the Ministry of Local Government of Botswana. (Insert instructions and/or link for filing application with host government here.)

To meet U.S. immigration requirements, you may also file an I-600A, Application for Advance Processing of an Orphan Petition with U.S. Department of Homeland Security's U.S. Citizenship and Immigration Services to be found eligible and suitable to adopt.

If you are eligible to adopt, and a child is available for intercountry adoption, the central adoption authority or other authorized entity in Botswana will provide you with a referral. Each family must decide for itself whether or not it will be able to meet the needs of and provide a permanent home for a particular child.

The child must be eligible to be adopted according to Botswana requirements, as described in the Who Can Be Adopted section. The child must also meet the definition of an orphan under U.S. immigration law.

The Ministry of Local Government maintains a list of families (currently over 200 families, both citizens and foreigners) who wish to adopt children. Currently, this list is much longer than the number of available children and families can wait many months or years before being matched. If you are eligible to adopt, and a child is available for intercountry adoption, the central adoption authority in Botswana will match you with a child. Each family must decide whether or not it will be able to meet the needs and provide a permanent home for the child with whom they are matched.

Once a child is matched with a family, and the family agrees to the match, the family must submit an application to the Magistrate (Children's) Court to obtain legal custody and foster the child.

Once a child is matched with a family, the family must submit an application to the Magistrate (Children's) Court to obtain legal custody and become the child's foster parents. This is not a long term arrangement, and after six months the family must either terminate custody or begin proceedings to legally adopt the child. During this period, a social worker monitors the family by conducting visits to the home to interview family members and to observe family life and living conditions.

Role of Adoption Authority: While the Adoption Act of 1952 provides that the Minister of Local Government acts as the child's guardian ad litem, in practice the courts assign social workers to act in this capacity. Once the adoption is complete, social workers attempt to make follow-up visits with families.

Role of the Court: During the actual adoption hearing, the social worker can submit any information to the Children's (Magistrate) Court that was obtained during the course of their home visits or interviews. Only children over ten years of age are interviewed by social workers regarding custody and adoption issues.

The court will not grant the application unless it is satisfied that:

- The applicant(s) are qualified to adopt the child;
- The applicant(s) are of good repute and are fit and proper to be entrusted with the custody of the child;
- The applicant(s) have adequate means to maintain and educate the child;
- The proposed adoption will serve the best interests and be conducive to the welfare of the child;
- That consent to the adoption has been given (see relinquishment and abandonment requirements).

Role of Adoption Agencies: None.

Adoption Application: Current applications will be provided and explained by the social worker assigned to the case.

Time Frame: After six months, during which the prospective adoptive parents foster the prospective adoptive child, they may apply to the Magistrate (Children's) Court for adoption.

Adoption Fees: An unspecified sum of money sufficient to cover all expenses incurred. Fees are paid directly to the Government of Botswana, through the Ministry of Local Government and/or the Magistrate's Court.

Documents Required: Documentary requirements will be provided and explained by the social worker assigned to the case. Additional documents may be requested. You may be asked to provide proof that a document from the United States is authentic.

Bringing Your Child Home: Once your adoption is complete (or you have obtained legal custody of the child), there are a few more steps to take before you can head home. Specifically, you need to apply for several documents for your child before he or she can travel to the United States, such as a birth certificate, a passport or travel document for your child from the country in which he or she was born, and a U.S. Immigration Visa. For detailed and updated information on how to obtain these documents, review the *Intercountry Adoption* section in this publication and visit the U.S. Department of State Intercountry Adoption website at http://adoption.state.gov.

Child Citizenship Act: For adoptions finalized abroad, the Child Citizenship Act of 2000 allows your new child to acquire American citizenship automatically when he or she enters the United States as lawful permanent residents. For adoptions finalized in the United States, the Child Citizenship Act of 2000 allows your new child to acquire American citizenship automatically when the court in the United States issues the final adoption decree. To learn more, review the *Intercountry Adoption* section in this publication and visit the U.S. Department of State Intercountry Adoption website at http://adoption.state.gov.

After Adoption: The Department of State is not aware of any post-adoption reporting requirements at this time governing adoptions from Botswana.

U.S. Embassy in Botswana
Address: Embassy Drive, Government Enclave
Gaborone, Botswana
Tel: 267-395-3982
Fax: 267-318-0232
Email: consulargaborone@state.gov
Internet: botswana.usembassy.gov

Botswana's Adoption Authority:
Ministry of Local Government
Address:
Bag 0097, Gaborone, Botswana
Tel: 267-397-1916

Embassy of Botswana
Address:
1531 New Hampshire Ave. N.W.,
Washington, DC 20036
Tel: 202-244-4990
Fax: 202-244-4164
Internet: botswanaembassy.org

U.S. Consulate General in Johannesburg, South Africa
Mailing Address:
P.O. Box 787197, Sandton, 2146
Johannesburg, South AfricaPhysical
Address: 1 Sandton Drive, Sandhurst
(opposite Sandton City Mall)
Johannesburg, South Africa
Tel: (27 11) 290-3000
Fax: (27 11) (011) 884-0396
Email:
consularjohannesburg@state.gov

Office of Children's Issues
U.S. Department of State
2201 C Street, NW
SA-29
Washington, DC 20520
Tel: 1-888-407-4747
E-mail: AskCI@state.gov
http://adoption.state.gov

BRAZIL

Compiled from publications that were available as of February 2013 from the U.S. Department of State, the U.S. Department of Commerce, and the Central Intelligence Agency (CIA). See the introduction to this set for explanatory notes.

Official Name:
Federative Republic of Brazil

PROFILE

Geography

Area: total: 8,514,877 sq km; country comparison to the world: 5; land: 8,459,417 sq km; water: 55,460 sq km

Major cities: Sao Paulo 19.96 million; Rio de Janeiro 11.836 million; Belo Horizonte 5.736 million; Porto Alegre 4.034 million; BRASILIA (capital) 3.789 million (2009)

Climate: mostly tropical, but temperate in south

Terrain: mostly flat to rolling lowlands in north; some plains, hills, mountains, and narrow coastal belt

People

Nationality: noun: Brazilian(s); adjective: Brazilian

Population: 199,321,413 (July 2012 est.)

Population growth rate: 1.102% (2012 est.)

Ethnic groups: white 53.7%, mulatto (mixed white and black) 38.5%, black 6.2%, other (includes Japanese, Arab, Amerindian) 0.9%, unspecified 0.7% (2000 census)

Religions: Roman Catholic (nominal) 73.6%, Protestant 15.4%, Spiritualist 1.3%, Bantu/voodoo 0.3%, other 1.8%, unspecified 0.2%, none 7.4% (2000 census)

Languages: Portuguese (official and most widely spoken language)

Literacy: definition: age 15 and over can read and write; total population: 88.6%; male: 88.4%; female: 88.8% (2004 est.)

Health: life expectancy at birth: total population: 72.79 years; male: 69.24 years; female: 76.53 years (2012 est.); Infant mortality rate: total: 20.5 deaths/1,000 live births; male: 23.9 deaths/1,000 live births; female: 16.93 deaths/1,000 live births (2012 est.)

Unemployment rate: 6.2% (2012 est.)

Work force: 107.1 million (2012 est.)

Government

Type: federal republic

Independence: 7 September 1822

Constitution: 5 October 1988

Political subdivisions: 26 states (estados, singular—estado) and 1 federal district (distrito federal)

Suffrage: voluntary between 16 to under 18 years of age and over 70; compulsory 18 to 70 years of age; note—military conscripts do not vote by law

Economy

GDP (purchasing power parity): $2.362 trillion (2012 est.); $2.324 trillion (2011 est.); $2.262 trillion (2010 est.); $2.103 trillion (2009 est.)

GDP real growth rate: 1.3% (2012 est.); 2.7% (2011 est.); 7.5% (2010 est.); -0.3% (2009 est.)

GDP per capita (PPP): $12,000 (2012 est.); $11,900 (2011 est.); $11,700 (2010 est.); $11,000 (2009 est.)

Natural resources: bauxite, gold, iron ore, manganese, nickel, phosphates, platinum, tin, rare earth elements, uranium, petroleum, hydropower, timber

Agriculture products: coffee, soybeans, wheat, rice, corn, sugarcane, cocoa, citrus; beef

Industries: textiles, shoes, chemicals, cement, lumber, iron ore, tin, steel, aircraft, motor vehicles and parts, other machinery and equipment

Exports: $256 billion (2012 est.); $256 billion (2011 est.); $201.9 billion (2010 est.)

Exports—commodities: transport equipment, iron ore, soybeans, footwear, coffee, autos

Exports—partners: China 17.3%, US 10.1%, Argentina 8.9%, Netherlands 5.3% (2011)

Imports: $238.8 billion (2012 est.); $219.6 billion (2011 est.); $181.8 billion (2010 est.)

Imports—commodities: machinery, electrical and transport equipment, chemical products, oil, automotive parts, electronics

Imports—partners: US 15.1%, China 14.5%, Argentina 7.5%, Germany 6.7%, South Korea 4.5% (2011)

Debt—external: $405.3 billion (31 December 2012 est.); $397.5 billion (31 December 2011 est.); $347 billion (31 December 2010 est.)

Exchange rates: reals (BRL) per US dollar; 2.1 (2012 est.); 1.6728 (2011 est.); 1.7592 (2010 est.); 2 (2009); 1.8644 (2008); 1.85 (2007)

PEOPLE

With its 190 million inhabitants, Brazil has the largest population in Latin America and ranks fifth in the world. The majority of people live in the south-central area, which includes the industrial cities of Sao Paulo, Rio de Janeiro, and Belo Horizonte. Brazil underwent rapid urban growth; by 2005, 81% of the total population was living in urban areas. This growth aids economic development but also creates serious social, security, environmental, and political problems for major cities.

Six major groups make up the Brazilian population: the Portuguese, who colonized Brazil in the 16th century; Africans brought to Brazil as slaves; various other European, Middle Eastern, and Japanese and other Asian immigrant groups who settled in Brazil since the mid-19th century; and indigenous peoples of Tupi and Guarani language stock. Intermarriage between the Portuguese and indigenous people or slaves was common. Although the major European ethnic stock of Brazil was originally Portuguese, subsequent waves of immigration contributed to a diverse ethnic and cultural heritage.

From 1875 until 1960, about 5 million Europeans immigrated to Brazil, settling mainly in the four southern states of Sao Paulo, Parana, Santa Catarina, and Rio Grande do Sul. Immigrants came mainly from Italy, Germany, Spain, Japan, Poland, and the Middle East. The largest Japanese community outside Japan is in Sao Paulo. Despite class distinctions, national identity is strong. Brazil prides itself on being open to all races. It recently began a national conversation on racial equality and entered into a memorandum of understanding with the United States on addressing racial inequality. Indigenous people, located mainly in the northern and western border regions and in the upper Amazon Basin, make up less than 1% of the population. Their numbers are declining as contact with the outside world and commercial expansion into the interior increase. Brazilian Government programs to establish indigenous reservations and to provide other forms of assistance for these groups have existed for years but are controversial.

Language

Brazil is the only Portuguese-speaking nation in the Americas. English proficiency varies among Brazilian business persons.

Religion

The 2000 census indicated that approximately 74 percent of the population identified themselves as Roman Catholic (about 125 million persons). Fifteen percent were Protestant, of which an estimated 74 percent were from evangelical churches. There were 1,104,886 Jehovah's Witnesses and 199,645 members of The Church of Jesus Christ of Latter-day Saints (Mormons).

Members of African and syncretic religious groups totaled 127,582 adherents of Candomble and 397,431 followers of Umbanda. There were also 214,873 Buddhists, 86,825 Jews, 27,239 Muslims, 2,905 Hindus, 151,080 adherents of other eastern religions, and 17,088 adherents of indigenous religious beliefs.

While the 2000 census reported 27,239 Muslims, the Federation of Muslim Associations of Brazil estimated in 2010 that there were 1.5 million Muslims in the country. There are significant Muslim communities in the cities of Sao Paulo, Rio de Janeiro, Curitiba, and Foz do Iguazu, as well as in smaller cities in the states of Parana, Rio Grande do Sul, Sao Paulo, and Rio de Janeiro.

According to the Jewish Confederation of Brazil, there are more than 125,000 Jews, 65,000 of whom reside in Sao Paulo State and 40,000 in Rio de Janeiro State. Many other cities have smaller Jewish communities.

HISTORY

Pedro Alvares Cabral claimed Brazil for Portugal in 1500. The colony was ruled from Lisbon until 1808, when Dom Joao VI and the rest of the Portuguese royal family fled from Napoleon's army, and established its seat of government in Rio de Janeiro. Dom Joao VI returned to Portugal in 1821. His son declared Brazil's independence on September 7, 1822, and became emperor with the title of Dom Pedro I. His son, Dom Pedro II, ruled from 1831 to 1889, when a federal republic was established in a coup led by Deodoro da Fonseca, Marshal of the Army. Slavery had been abolished a year earlier by the Princess Regent Isabel while Dom Pedro II was in Europe.

From 1889 to 1930, the government was a constitutional republic, with the presidency alternating between the dominant states of Sao Paulo and Minas Gerais. This period ended with a military coup that placed Getulio Vargas, a civilian, in the presidency; Vargas remained as dictator until 1945. Between 1945 and 1961, Brazil had six presidents: Jose Linhares, Gaspar Dutra, Vargas himself, Cafe Filho, Carlos Luz, Nereu Ramos, Juscelino Kubitschek, and Janio Quadros. When Quadros resigned in 1961, Vice President Joao Goulart succeeded him.

Goulart's years in office were marked by high inflation, economic stagnation, and the increasing influence of radical political elements. The armed forces, alarmed by these developments, staged a coup on March 31, 1964. The coup leaders chose Humberto Castello Branco as president, followed by Arthur da Costa e Silva (1967-69), Emilio Garrastazu Medici (1969-74), and Ernesto Geisel (1974-79), all of whom were senior army officers. Geisel began a democratic opening that was continued by his successor, Gen. Joao Baptista de Oliveira Figueiredo (1979-85). Figueiredo permitted the return of politicians exiled or banned from political activity during the 1960s and 1970s and allowed them to run for state and federal offices in 1982.

Concurrently, an electoral college consisting of all members of Congress and six delegates chosen from each state continued to choose the president. In January 1985, the electoral college voted Tancredo Neves from the opposition Brazilian Democratic Movement Party (PMDB) into office as President. Neves died 39 days later, before his presidential inauguration, from abdominal complications. Vice President Jose Sarney became President upon Neves' death. Brazil completed its transition to a popularly elected government in 1989, when Fernando Collor de Mello won 53% of the vote in the first direct presidential election in 29 years. In 1992, a major corruption scandal led to his impeachment and, ultimately, resignation. Vice President Itamar Franco took his place and governed for the remainder of Collor's term.

To date, all democratically elected presidents that followed Itamar Franco started and finished their mandate with no interruptions in the constitutional order. On October 3, 1994 Fernando Henrique Cardoso was elected President with 54% of the vote. Cardoso took office January 1, 1995, and pursued a program of ambitious economic reform. He was re-elected in 1998 for a second 4-year term. Luiz Inacio Lula da Silva, commonly known as Lula, was elected president in 2002, after his fourth campaign for the office. He was re-elected in 2006 for a second 4-year term.

President Lula, a former union leader, was Brazil's first working-class president. In office, he took a prudent fiscal path, warning that social reforms would take years and that Brazil had no alternative but to maintain tight fiscal austerity policies. At the same time, he made fighting poverty through conditional transfer payments an important element of his policies. In October 2010, Brazil held its sixth consecutive presidential and general elections since the reinstatement of democracy in 1985. About 130 million Brazilians, two-thirds of the country's population, were eligible to vote, a mandatory civic duty. Up for election were the President, the governors of all 26 states and of the federal district of Brasília; all 513 federal deputies; 54 senators (two-thirds of the total); and 1,057 delegates to the 27 state assemblies.

Dilma Vana Rousseff, the Workers' Party (PT) candidate, won a runoff election against the Brazilian Social Democratic Party candidate, becoming the first woman president of Brazil. President Rousseff had previously served as the Minister of Mines and Energy and as the Chief of Cabinet in President Lula's administration. Rousseff took office on January 1, 2011 and has prioritized growth with equity policies to eradicate poverty and fiscal austerity. She has been a vocal defender of human rights and promoter of social inclusion, most notably gender equality, and is generally seen as a strong advocate for transparency in government. Within the first year of her government, several cabinet ministers resigned at Rousseff's urging due to accusations of graft.

GOVERNMENT AND POLITICAL CONDITIONS

Brazil is a constitutional, multiparty republic. In October 2010 voters chose Dilma Rousseff as president in elections considered free and fair.

Recent Elections

In the October 2010 national elections, considered free and fair, Workers' Party candidate Dilma Rousseff won a four-year term as president.

Participation of Women and Minorities: Women have full political rights. The law requires that 30 percent of the candidates registered by each political party be women. According to the Electoral Supreme Court, there were 3,968 female candidates in the October 2010 elections, compared with 15,504 male candidates. Thirteen women were elected to the 81-member Senate and 44 women to the 513-member Chamber of Deputies. Of the 27 governors elected, two were women. There were 25 Afro-Brazilians in Congress (three senators and 22 deputies). There was one Afro-Brazilian in the cabinet and one each on the Federal Supreme Court and Superior Court of Justice.

Principal Government Officials

Last Updated: 1/31/2013

Pres.: **Dilma ROUSSEFF**
Vice Pres.: **Michel TEMER**
Chief of the Civilian Household of the Presidency: **Gleisi Helena HOFFMANN**
Sec. Gen. of the Presidency: **Gilberto CARVALHO**
Min. of Agrarian Development: **Pepe VARGAS**
Min. of Agriculture, Livestock, & Supply: **Mendes RIBEIRO Filho**
Min. of Cities: **Aguinaldo RIBEIRO**
Min. of Communications: **Paulo BERNARDO**
Min. of Culture: **Marta SUPLICY**
Min. of Defense: **Celso Luiz Nunes AMORIM**
Min. of Development, Industry, & Trade: **Fernando Damata PIMENTEL**
Min. of Education: **Aloizio MERCADANTE Oliva**
Min. of the Environment: **Izabella TEIXEIRA**
Min. of Finance: **Guido MANTEGA**
Min. of Fishing & Aquaculture: **Marcello CRIVELLA**
Min. of Foreign Relations: **Antonio de Aguiar PATRIOTA**
Min. of Health: **Alexandre PADILHA**
Min. of Justice: **Jose Eduardo Martins CARDOZO**
Min. of Labor & Employment: **Carlos Daudt BRIZOLA**
Min. of Mines & Energy: **Edison LOBAO**
Min. of National Integration: **Fernando BEZERRA COELHO**
Min. of Planning, Budget, & Management: **Miriam Aparecida BELCHIOR**
Min. of Science & Technology: **Marco Antonio RAUPP**
Min. of Social Development & Hunger Alleviation: **Tereza CAMPELO**
Min. of Social Security: **Garibaldi ALVES FILHO**
Min. of Sports: **Aldo REBELO**
Min. of Tourism: **Gastao VIEIRA**
Min. of Transportation: **Paulo Sergio PASSOS**
Head, Office of the Inspectorate Gen.: **Jorge HAGE**
Head, Office of Institutional Security: **Jose ELITO Carvalho Siqueira**
Head, Office of the Solicitor Gen.: **Luis Inacio Lucena ADAMS**
Head, Secretariat of Civil Aviation: **Wagner BITTENCOURT**
Head, Secretariat of Institutional Relations: **Ideli SALVATTI**
Head, Secretariat for Social Communication: **Helena CHAGAS**
Head, Secretariat of Strategic Affairs: **Moreira FRANCO**
Head, Special Secretariat for Human Rights: **Maria do ROSARIO**
Head, Special Secretariat for Promotion of Racial Equality:**Luiza BAIRROS**
Head, Special Secretariat for Women's Rights: **Eleonora MENICUCCI de Oliveira**
Head, Special Secretariat of Ports: **Leonidas CRISTINO**
Pres., Central Bank: **Alexandre Antonio TOMBINI**
Ambassador to the US: **Mauro Luiz Iecker VIEIRA**
Permanent Representative to the UN, New York: **Maria Luiza Ribeiro VIOTTI**

ECONOMY

Characterized by large and well-developed agricultural, mining, manufacturing, and service sectors, Brazil's economy outweighs that of all other South American countries, and Brazil is expanding its presence in world markets. Since 2003, Brazil has steadily improved its macroeconomic stability, building up foreign reserves, and reducing its debt profile by shifting its debt burden toward real denominated and domestically held instruments.

In 2008, Brazil became a net external creditor and two ratings agencies awarded investment grade status to its debt. After strong growth in 2007 and 2008, the onset of the global financial crisis hit Brazil in 2008. Brazil experienced two quarters of recession, as global demand for Brazil's commodity-based exports dwindled and external credit dried up. However, Brazil was one of the first emerging markets to begin a recovery. In 2010, consumer and investor confidence revived and GDP growth reached 7.5%, the highest growth rate in the past 25 years.

Rising inflation led the authorities to take measures to cool the economy; these actions and the deteriorating international economic situation slowed growth to 2.7% in 2011, and 1.5% in 2012. Despite slower growth, in 2011 Brazil overtook the United Kingdom as the world's seventh largest economy in terms of GDP. Unemployment is at historic lows and Brazil's traditionally high level of income inequality has declined for each of the last 14 years. Brazil's historically high interest rates have made it an attractive destination for foreign investors.

Large capital inflows over the past several years have contributed to the appreciation of the currency, hurting the competitiveness of Brazilian manufacturing and leading the government to intervene in foreign exchanges markets and raise taxes on some foreign capital inflows. President Dilma ROUSSEFF has retained the previous administration's commitment to inflation targeting by the central bank, a floating exchange rate, and fiscal restraint. In an effort to boost growth, in 2012 the administration implemented a series of more expansionary monetary and fiscal policies that have failed to stimulate much growth.

Labor Conditions

The minimum working age is 16 years, and apprenticeships may begin at age 14. The law bars all minors under age 18 from work that constitutes a physical strain or occurs in unhealthy, dangerous, or morally harmful conditions. In 2008 domestic service was added to the list of hazardous work prohibited for minors under 18. The law requires parental permission for minors to work as apprentices.

Child labor continues to be a problem. The 2009 IBGE National Household Survey (PNAD), reflecting the most recent data available, showed that 4.25 million of an estimated 44 million children between the ages of five and 17 were engaged in some form of child labor. According to 2010 data from the MTE, the majority of those were employed in street vending (42 percent), followed by automobile washing (10 percent), manufacturing (8 percent), and agriculture (3 percent).

The 2010 census reported that 132,000 children between the ages 10 and 14 were the sole providers for their families. Approximately half of child laborers received no income, and 90 percent worked in the unregistered informal sector. Slightly more than half of child laborers worked in rural areas.

In January the minimum wage increased to 545 reais ($292) per month. According to 2010 IBGE data released on June 2, 56 percent of households had per capita incomes of less than the minimum wage. Between 2001 and 2009, the income growth rate of the poorest 10 percent of the population was 7 percent per year, while that of the richest 10 percent was 1.7 percent, decreasing income inequality. Nevertheless, a 2010 IGBE study revealed 8.5 percent of the population (16.2 million) was considered "extremely poor" or earning less than 70 reais per month ($38).

The law limits the workweek to 44 hours and specifies a weekly rest period of 24 consecutive hours, preferably on Sundays. The law also provides for paid annual vacation, prohibits excessive compulsory overtime, and stipulates that hours worked above the weekly limit must be compensated at time-and-a-half pay; these provisions generally were enforced in the formal sector.

The MTE sets occupational, health, and safety standards that are consistent with internationally recognized norms, although unsafe working conditions were prevalent throughout the country.

According to the Institute for Applied Economic Research, the informal sector shrank by 1.6 percent in the first six months of 2011, compared with the same period in 2010, to an average of 35.6 percent, the lowest level since 2003. Most unregistered workers were in the agricultural sector. Not all foreign migrant workers, informal sector workers, and unregistered workers were subject to hazardous working conditions, but these groups were at a higher risk of being subjected to such conditions and/or to working conditions analogous to slave labor.

U.S.-BRAZILIAN RELATIONS

The United States and Brazil have traditionally enjoyed cooperative, active relations encompassing a broad political and economic agenda. The United States was the first country to recognize Brazil's independence from Portugal in 1822, and as the two largest democracies and economies in the Western Hemisphere, the United States and Brazil are currently consolidating a foundation for a new partnership for the 21st century with a focus on global issues that affect both countries. Ten bilateral agreements signed during President Obama's visit to Brazil in March 2011 and five more signed during President Rousseff's visit to the United States in April 2012 testify to an intensification of bilateral engagement in a broad range of areas of mutual interest. Since 2011, a series of high-level dialogues have been created or upgraded, including four Presidential Dialogues: the Global Partnership Dialogue, Economic and Financial Dialogue, Strategic Energy Dialogue, and Defense Cooperation Dialogue. Formal intergovernmental dialogues engage multiple U.S. and Brazilian agencies on issues including bilateral and multilateral issues, economics, trade, finance, agriculture, energy, aviation, technology, innovation, the environment, education, culture, defense, and nonproliferation. These dialogues are the primary vehicles for policy coordination and for defining partnership priorities.

Bilateral relations are complemented by people-to-people initiatives and trilateral and multilateral cooperation. The United States and Brazil's long history of exchange in education is one example; the bi-national Fulbright Commission was established in 1957, and thousands of scholars have traveled between the two countries. Education cooperation continues to thrive as President Obama's "100,000 Strong in the Americas" goal and Brazilian President Rousseff's "Science without Borders" initiative create opportunities for new academic and research partnerships. EducationUSA centers around helping Brazil advise students on study in the United States and host events to assist U.S. higher education institutions recruit Brazilian students. The United States is also working closely with Brazilian counterparts to expand opportunities for English language learning and professional development for Brazilian teachers. These exchanges strengthen U.S. and Brazilian institutional partnerships, develop a workforce prepared for 21st century opportunities, and contribute to long-term economic growth for both countries.

The United States and Brazil also share a commitment to combat discrimination based on race, gender, ethnicity, or lesbian, gay, bisexual, and transgender (LGBT) status; to advance gender equality; to fight exploitative child and forced labor; and to promote human rights. The U.S.-Brazil Joint Action Plan to Eliminate Racial and Ethnic Discrimination and Promote Equality, the first bilateral instrument that targets racism, and the U.S.-Brazil Memorandum of Understanding on the Advancement of Women provide platforms for cooperation to combat racial discrimination and women's empowerment broadly, and to share best practices in tackling discrimination in STEM education, law enforcement, labor, health, gender-based violence, economic empowerment, and many other areas. Multilateral cooperation and collaboration at the United Nations and Organization of American States has also proven effective in the promotion of LGBT human rights.

The United States and Brazil also partner on trilateral cooperation in third countries, particularly in support of biofuels and agricultural development, food security, health, and women's rights. Successful programs include joint technical cooperation and training in support of trilateral development programs in Mozambique in agricultural research and technology and food security, with plans to extend this cooperation to additional countries in Africa, Central America, and the Caribbean. Multilaterally, the power of U.S.-Brazil collaboration is evidenced by the success of the Open Government Partnership, a multi-country initiative to foster transparency launched and co-chaired in its inaugural year by the United States and Brazil.

U.S. Assistance to Brazil

The United States, through the U.S. Agency for International Development (USAID), and Brazil are committed to forging a strong partnership that promotes development in other countries, principally in Africa and the Western Hemisphere. Innovative trilateral collaboration will prioritize transnational challenges that are of mutual interest, including food security, health, the environment, agriculture, and economic development. USAID is concluding its bilateral support to prevent and control tuberculosis, support HIV/AIDS prevention, promote clean energy technologies in Brazil, and mitigate climate change. Ongoing programs continue to preserve natural ecosystems, and foster sustainable forest management. Through public-private partnerships, USAID is helping develop basic workplace skills and expand access to English language training for disadvantaged youth, and foster corporate social responsibility goals and projects conducted by U.S. companies operating in Brazil.

Bilateral Economic Relations

In 2007, the United States and Brazil launched the Economic Partnership Dialogue, a multi-agency technical consultative mechanism that addresses bilateral, trilateral, and hemispheric initiatives. The two countries also signed an agreement in 2011 to enhance cooperation on trade and investment. The agreement aims to expand the direct trade and investment relationship by providing a framework to deepen cooperation on innovation, trade facilitation, and technical barriers to trade. The Economic Partnership Dialogue promotes economic cooperation across a range of issues.

In 2011, the United States accounted for 10% of Brazil's exports and 15% of Brazil's imports. The flow of investment between the United States and Brazil is increasingly important, as the United States is one of Brazil's top foreign investor. Brazil has been designated a priority market under both the President's National Export Initiative (NEI) and for FY 2012 via SelectUSA to promote exports and two-way investment. As the world's largest biofuels producers, the two countries have worked together to help make sustainable biofuels a global commodity.

In March 2011 the U.S. Ambassador and Brazilian Foreign Minister signed the U.S.-Brazil Air Transport Agreement that, once in force, will establish an Open Skies air transportation relationship between our two countries. In April 2012 the Secretary and the Brazilian Foreign Minister signed the bilateral Aviation Partnership Memorandum of Understanding (MOU), which will provide a coordinated venue for both countries to address aviation sector priorities, including technical cooperation on aviation infrastructure, air transportation, and air traffic management technologies. The U.S. Trade and Development Agency (USTDA) also held an Airports Modernization Technologies Reverse Trade Mission for Brazilian officials in June 2012. This was the inaugural activity of the U.S. Brazil Aviation Partnership.

Some 150,000 U.S. citizens visit Brazil annually. In 2011, more than 1.5 million Brazilians visited the United States, spending more than $6.8 billion, extending the arrivals expansion streak to eight years and setting a second consecutive record. Travel and tourism exports now account for 34% of all U.S. services exports to Brazil. In 2012, the U.S. government embarked on a national strategy to make the United States the world's top travel and tourism destination, to generate jobs and revitalize the U.S. economy. Goals include increasing visitor visa processing capacity at U.S. missions in Brazil and China by 40% in 2012.

Brazil's Membership in International Organizations

Brazil and the United States belong to a number of the same international organizations, including the United Nations, Organization of American States, Inter-American Development Bank, G-20, International Monetary Fund, World Bank, and World Trade Organization. Brazil has also traditionally been a leader in the inter-American community, and is a member of the sub-regional Mercosur and UNASUR groups.

Bilateral Representation

Brazil maintains an embassy in the United States at 3006 Massachusetts Avenue NW, Washington, DC 20008 (tel. 202-238-2700). Brazil has consulates general in New York, Chicago, Los Angeles, Miami, Houston, Boston, Atlanta, San Francisco, Hartford, and Washington, DC.

Principal U.S. Embassy Officials

Last Updated: 1/14/2013

BRASILIA (E) SES Av. das Naces Qd. 801–Lt. 03–70403-900–Brasilia, DF–Brasil, 5561-3312-7000, Fax 55-61-3312-7676, Workweek: M-F/8:00-5:00, Website: http://brasilia.usembassy.gov/

DCM OMS:	Liliana Carlson
AMB OMS:	Teresa Bascue
Co-CLO:	Liz Hilliard
DHS/CBP:	Jaime Ramsay
DHS/ICE:	Gabriel Gonzalez
FCS:	Devin Rambo
FM:	John Beauchamp
HRO:	Jay Williams
MGT:	Charles Grover
MLO/ODC:	Eric Snadecki
NAS/INL:	Matthew Sandelands
SDO/DATT:	Samuel H. Prugh
AMB:	Thomas A. Shannon
CON:	Donald Jacobson
DCM:	Todd Chapman
PAO:	John Matel
GSO:	Elias Parra
RSO:	Paul Kennedy
AFSA:	Kevin O'Connor
AGR:	Robert Hoff
AID:	Lawrence Hardy
APHIS:	Mark Prescott
CLO:	Heidi Inder
DEA:	Alex Toth
ECON:	James Dudley
EEO:	Dale R Rice
EST:	Kirsten Schulz
FMO:	James Inder
ICASS Chair:	Brian Brisson
IMO:	Dale R Rice
IPO:	Hector Torres
ISO:	Aaron Bascue
ISSO:	Alex Peterson
LEGATT:	Richard E. Cavalieros
POL:	Stefanie Amadeo
State ICASS:	James Dudley

RIO DE JANEIRO (CG) Avenida Presidente Wilson, 147. Rio de Janeiro. RJ 20030-020, 55-21-3823-2000, Fax 55-21-3823-2003, INMARSAT Tel 683-142-238, Workweek: Mon–Fri/08:00–17:00 hrs.

FCS:	Alan Long
FM:	James Hill
MGT:	Patti Hoffman
MLO/ODC:	Anne Restrepo
POL/ECON:	Alfred Boll
SDO/DATT:	John Morris
CG:	John S. Creamer
CON:	Phillip Min
PAO:	Mark Pannell
GSO:	Matthew Myers
RSO:	Michael Brown
IPO:	David Aliprandi

SAO PAULO (CG) Rua Henri Dunant, 700, Chacara Santo Antonio, Sao Paulo/SP, 04709-110, (55-11) 5186-7000, Fax (55-11) 5186-7099; (55-11) 5186-7350 (Mgmt), Workweek: Mon-Fri, 7:30 AM to 4:30 PM, Website: http://saopaulo.usconsulate.gov/

CA:	Michael Jacobsen
CG OMS:	Michelle Ethridge
Co-CLO:	Vacant
DHS/CBP:	Arnaldo Perez
FCS:	Rick De Lambert
FM:	Paul R. Bottse
HRO:	Glenn Jake Fairhurst
MGT:	Raymond H. Murphy
POL/ECON:	Samantha Carl-Yoder
POSHO:	Paul Bottse
TREAS:	Vacant
CG:	Dennis Hankins
CON:	Michael Jacobsen
PAO:	Laura Gould
GSO:	Jeffery Bournes
RSO:	Delvis Jimenez
AFSA:	Vacant
ATO:	Frederick Giles
CLO:	Beth Konvalinka
DEA:	William Matthews
EEO:	Laura Chamberlin
FMO:	Raymond H. Murphy
IPO:	Andrew Hoff
POL:	Kathryn Hoffman

RECIFE (C) Rua Goncalves Maia, 163, Boa Vista, Recife,PE, 55-81-3416-3050, Fax 55-81-3231-1906, Workweek: M-F 7:30 am–4:30 pm.

FCS:	Adierson Azevedo
MGT:	James Bredeck
POL/ECON:	Douglas Flitter

PO:	Usha Pitts
CON:	Lesley Hayden
PAO:	Heidi R. Arola
GSO:	Greg E Holliday
RSO:	Roberto I Quiroga
CLO:	Claudia Bredeck
ISSO:	James Bredeck

TRAVEL

Consular Information Sheet

August 23, 2012

Country Description: The fifth largest country in the world, Brazil is a Portuguese-speaking country with a robust economy. It consists of 26 states. Tourist facilities are excellent in major cities, but vary in quality in remote areas.

Smart Traveler Enrollment Program (STEP)/Embassy Locations: We encourage U.S. citizens living or traveling in Brazil to sign up for the Smart Traveler Enrollment Program with the nearest U.S. embassy or consulate to obtain updated information on local travel and security. U.S. citizens without internet access may sign up directly with the nearest U.S. embassy or consulate. Enrolling is important; it allows us to keep you up to date with important safety and security announcements. It will also help your friends and family get in touch with you in an emergency.

U.S. Embassy, Brasilia
SES 801—Avenida das Nacoes,
Lote 3
Telephone: 011-55-61-3312–7000
Emergency after-hours telephone: 011-55-61-3312–7400
Facsimile: 011-55-61-3312–7676

U.S. Consular Agency Belem
Avenida Conselheiro Furtado 2865,
Edificio Sintese 21, Rooms 1104/1106
Telephone: 011-55-91-3259–4566

U.S. Consular Agency Manaus
Rua Franco de Sa, 230,
Sao Francisco,
Edificio Atrium, Room 306
Telephone: 011-55-92-3611–3333

U.S. Consulate General Recife
Rua Goncalves Maia, 163, Boa Vista
Telephone: 011-55-81-3416–3050
Emergency after-hours telephone: 011-55-81-3416–3060 or 011-55-81-9916–9470
Facsimile: 011-55-81-3231–1906

U.S. Consular Agency Fortaleza
Avenida Santos Dumont 2828
Aldeota, Suite 708
Telephone 011-55-85-3021–5200
Fascimile: 011-55-85-3021–3888

U.S. Consulate General
Rio de Janeiro
Avenida Presidente Wilson, 147, Castelo
Telephone: 011-55-21-3823–2000
Emergency after-hours telephone: 011-55-21-3823–2000
Facsimile: 011-55-21-3823–2093

U.S. Consular Agency Salvador da Bahia
Avenida Tancredo Neves, 1632,
Caminho das Arvores,
Salvador Trade Center—Torre Sul, Room 1401
Telephone:
011-55-71-3113–2090/2091/2092

U.S. Consulate General Sao Paulo
Rua Henri Dunant, 500,
Chacara Santo Antonio
Telephone: 011-55-11-5186–7000
Emergency after-hours telephone: 011-55-11-5186–7373
Facsimile: 011-55-11-5186–7099

U.S. Consular Agency Porto Alegre
Assis Brasil 4320 Store 84 (Boulevard Strip Mall)
Parque Sao Sebastiao 91110–000
Porto Alegre, RS
Telephone 011-55-51-3226–3344

Entry/Exit Requirements for U.S. Citizens: Brazil requires U.S. citizens to carry a valid U.S. passport and visa when traveling to Brazil for any purpose. You must obtain your Brazilian visa in advance from the Brazilian Embassy or Consulate nearest to your place of residence in the United States.

There are no "airport visas" and immigration authorities will refuse entry into Brazil to anyone not possessing a valid visa. The U.S. government cannot assist you if you arrive in Brazil without proper documentation. Travelers under 18 years of age and their parents should carefully review the visa application requirements. The adjudicating official at the Brazilian Embassy or Consulate may require a birth certificate and notarized travel authorization to issue a visa to a minor.

U.S. citizens and other foreign travelers must fill out a small immigration form on arrival that will be stamped and handed back by immigration officials at the airport. It is important to retain this form to hand back to immigration officials upon exit from the country. According to the Brazilian Embassy's website, visitors who lose this form will have to get clearance from the Brazilian Federal Police to leave the country and may have to pay a fine.

Remember that while in Brazil, you are subject to local law. Showing contempt to a Brazilian government official at the port of entry, or elsewhere, is a serious offense. Additionally, if you have recently visited certain countries, including most other Latin American countries, you may be required to present an inoculation card indicating you had a yellow fever inoculation or you may not be allowed to board the plane or enter the country. Check with the Brazilian Embassy for more information.

The U.S. Department of State is unaware of any HIV/AIDS entry restrictions for visitors to or foreign residents of Brazil.

For current entry and customs requirements for Brazil, travelers may contact the Brazilian Embassy, which is temporarily located at 1025 Thomas Jefferson St., NW, Suite 300 W (3rd floor), Washington, D.C. 20007–5250, Phone: (202) 238-2805. Travelers may also contact the Brazilian Consulates in Atlanta, Boston, Chicago, Hartford, Houston, Los Angeles, Miami, New York, and San Francisco. Addresses, phone numbers, web and e-mail addresses, and jurisdictions of these consulates may be found at the Brazilian Embassy website.

Special Entry/Exit Requirements for Dual Nationals: U.S. citizens who also have Brazilian nationality cannot be issued Brazilian visas and must obtain a Brazilian passport from the Brazilian Embassy or Consulate nearest to their place of residence to enter and depart Brazil. In addition to being subject to all Brazilian laws affecting U.S. citizens, dual nationals may also be subject to other laws that impose special obligations on Brazilian citizens. Information about dual nationality can be found on our website.

Special Entry/Exit Requirements for Minors: Brazilian minors age 17 years and under, including minors who have both Brazilian and U.S. citizenship, are subject to strict exit requirements. Brazilian minors departing Brazil, if not accompanied by both parents, must prove that both parents authorized the departure. If accompanied by only one parent, the minor must have a notarized letter from the other parent indicating permission to depart the country, a court order proving that the accompanying parent has sole custody, or a Brazilian court order authorizing the child's departure.

If accompanied by neither parent, the minor must have a notarized letter from both parents authorizing departure, or a Brazilian court order authorizing the same. There are no exceptions, even if the child remained in Brazil only a short time. The authorization must be notarized by a Brazilian notary to be considered valid by the Brazilian authorities. If prepared in the United States, the authorization must be in Portuguese or accompanied by an official translation into Portuguese, and must be notarized by either the Brazilian Embassy or a Brazilian Consulate, or notarized by a U.S. notary public and then authenticated at the Brazilian Embassy or Consulate. Prior to departing the United States, parents traveling to Brazil with children who are Brazilian nationals may wish to obtain an authorization for each parent to return with the children to the United States without the other parent, just in case. Note that children adopted from Brazil are still considered Brazilian citizens and must be documented as such should they return to Brazil.

Minors age 17 years and under who are not Brazilian nationals are not technically subject to the same strict travel requirements as Brazilian minors. However, there have been cases where the travel of non-Brazilian minors has been delayed or prevented when accompanied by only one parent or a third party. To avoid potential difficulties, parents of non-Brazilian minors may want to follow the procedures above if their children will be traveling to Brazil accompanied by only one parent or by a third party.

Parents contemplating separation or divorce should resolve custody matters before leaving the country. Pursuant to the Hague Convention on the Civil Aspects of International Child Abduction, to which both Brazil and the United States are party, custody will ultimately be decided by a court in the country where the child is a habitual resident. Information about the prevention of international child abduction can be found on our website. The State Department hotline for Child Abduction Prevention during regular business hours is: (202) 663-3330 and after hours: (888) 407-4747.

Threats to Safety and Security: Demonstrations and political or labor strikes can occur in urban areas and may cause temporary disruption to public and private transportation. Protests anywhere in the world have the potential to become violent. U.S. citizens traveling or residing in Brazil are advised to take common-sense precautions, avoid large gatherings or other events where crowds have congregated to demonstrate or protest, and comply with the instructions of local authorities.

Individuals with ties to criminal entities and traffickers operate along all the Brazilian borders. These organizations are involved in the trafficking of illicit goods and drugs. U.S. citizens crossing into bordering countries should consult the Country Specific Information for those locations.

Colombian terrorist groups have been known to operate in the border areas of neighboring countries. Although there have been reports of isolated small-scale armed incursions from Colombia into Brazil in the past, we know of no specific threat directed against U.S. citizens across the border in Brazil at this time.

Colombian groups have kidnapped residents and tourists along the Colombian border. If you are traveling or residing in these areas we urge you to exercise caution when visiting remote parts of the Amazon basin, and respect local laws and customs. You should ensure that your outfitter/guide is familiar with the Amazon region.

Brazil's beaches can pose a threat to the safety of travelers. Many beaches have very strong and dangerous riptides, including those in Rio de Janeiro and Fortaleza. Make sure to observe posted flags and signs for strong swells and currents, and never swim while under the influence of alcohol. Even if the water looks safe there may be strong riptides. Ocean currents and waves are unpredictable, even in well-populated beaches frequented by tourists. In 2011, one U.S. citizen suffered serious injuries and two died while swimming in Copacabana beach. Travelers are advised to adhere to local authorities' guidance and refrain from swimming alone in areas marked with red warning signs or at beaches where there are no municipal lifeguards and first responder services. There is a possibility of shark attacks in the waters of many of the beaches in northeastern Brazil, including those in Recife, Natal, and Maceio. We advise visitors to heed signs posted on any beach they visit.

Blackouts in the large cities have struck areas with high concentrations of hotels and resident U.S. citizens. During these blackouts, local authorities responded quickly to increase police presence and maintain public security. In addition, most tourist hotels are equipped with generators, minimizing the impact of a blackout on visitors. Nonetheless, you should use caution in the event of a blackout during your visit to Brazil. Residents should keep flashlights and sufficient supplies of food and potable water in their residences to prepare for blackouts.

Flooding and mudslides can occur throughout the country, and can be fatal. Monitor news and weather reports and adhere to municipal advisories before traveling to areas prone to flooding or landslides. Many of Brazil's larger cities have frequent heavy rainstorms that may cause flash flooding and cripple traffic for hours.

The U.S. Embassy restricts travel of U.S. government employees in areas where narcotics traffickers and other criminals have recently engaged in violence. The violence is usually directed against rival groups, local security forces, local government authorities, and occasionally civilians.

The travel of U.S. government employees is restricted in all shanty towns, or "favelas," in the following areas: Recife, Rio de Janeiro, Sao Paulo, any area within 150 km of the borders with Venezuela, Colombia, Peru, Bolivia, Guyana, Suriname, French Guiana, Paraguay and, between the hours of 6:00 p.m. and 6:00 a.m., in Brasilia's "satellite cities" of Ceilandia, Santa Maria, Sao Sebastiao and Paranoa. This restriction does not include commonly used transit routes that often pass near or through favelas.

Strikes by police and other emergency service providers are not uncommon. Police strikes in Fortaleza, Ceará, in December 2011 and Salvador, Bahia, in January 2012 undermined public security and caused a worrisome increase in crime and lawlessness.

Stay up to date on safety and security information by:

- Bookmarking our Bureau of Consular Affairs website which contains the current Travel Warnings and Travel Alerts as well as the Worldwide Caution.
- Following us on Twitter and the Bureau of Consular Affairs page on Facebook.
- Downloading our free Smart Traveler iPhone App for travel information at your fingertips.
- Calling 1-888-407-4747 toll-free within the U.S. and Canada, or a regular toll line, 1-202-501-4444, from other countries. These numbers are available from 8:00 a.m. to 8:00 p.m. Eastern Time, Monday through Friday (except U.S. federal holidays).
- Taking some time before travel to consider your personal security.

Crime: Brazilian police and media report that the crime rate remains high in most urban centers, including the cities of Rio de Janeiro and Sao Paulo, and is also growing in rural areas within those states. Brazil's murder rate is more than four times higher than that of the United States, and rates for other crimes are similarly high. Criminal convictions for crimes are rare.

Street crime remains a problem for visitors and local residents alike. Foreign tourists, including U.S. citizens, are often targets, especially in Sao Paulo, Rio de Janeiro, Salvador, and Recife. While the risk is greater during the evening and at night, street crime also occurs during the day, and safer areas of cities are not immune. Incidents of theft on city buses are frequent. You should keep a copy of your passport with you while in public and keep your passport in a hotel safe or other secure place. You should also carry proof of your health insurance with you.

In May/June 2012, armed groups in Sao Paulo targeted restaurants, robbing patrons during busiest parts of the day. These criminal events are not isolated to one area of the city and target both rich and poor neighborhoods.

The incidence of crime against tourists is greater in areas surrounding beaches, hotels, discotheques, bars, nightclubs, and other tourist destinations and is especially prevalent prior to and during Carnival (Brazilian Mardi Gras), but also occurs throughout the year. Several Brazilian cities have established specialized tourist police units to patrol areas frequented by tourists.

Use caution with regard to evening and night travel through rural areas and satellite cities due to reported incidents of roadside robberies that randomly target passing vehicles. Robberies and "quick-nappings" outside of banks and ATMs occur regularly. In a "quick-napping," criminals abduct victims for a short time in order to receive a quick payoff from the family, business, or the victim's ATM card. Some victims have been beaten and/or raped. You should also take precautions to avoid being carjacked, especially in Sao Paulo, Rio de Janeiro, Recife, and other cities.

In airports, hotel lobbies, bus stations, and other public places, pick pocketing and the theft of hand-carried luggage and laptop computers are common. You should "dress down" when in public and avoid carrying valuables or wearing jewelry or expensive watches. "Good Samaritan" scams are common. If a tourist looks lost or seems to be having trouble communicating, a seemingly innocent bystander offering help may actually be a participant in a scam. Take care at and around banks and ATMs that take U.S. credit or debit cards. Travelers using personal ATM or credit cards sometimes receive billing statements with unauthorized charges after returning from a visit to Brazil or have had their cards cloned or duplicated without their knowledge. If you use such payment methods, carefully monitor your banking for the duration of your visit.

While the ability of Brazilian police to help recover stolen property is limited, we strongly advise you to obtain a "boletim de ocorrencia" (police report) at a "delegacia" (police station) if any of your possessions are lost or stolen. This will facilitate your exit from Brazil and assist with insurance claims. Be aware, however, that the police in tourist areas are on the lookout for false reports of theft for purposes of insurance fraud. Do not buy counterfeit and pirated goods, even if they are widely available. These goods are illegal in the United States, and if you purchase them you may also be breaking local law.

Brasilia: Brasilia has significant crime problems. Reports of residential burglaries continue to occur in the generally affluent residential sections of the city. Public transportation, hotel sectors, and tourist areas report the highest crime rates, but statistics show that these incidents can happen anywhere and at anytime. The "satellite cities" that surround Brasilia have per-capita crime rates comparable to much larger cities. Police reports indicate that rates of all types of crime, including "quick-nappings," have risen dramatically in Brasilia in the last two years. Brasilia's Central Bus Station or "Rodoviaria" is a particularly dangerous area, especially at night. This location is known to have a large concentration of drug dealers and users. Illegal drugs such as crack cocaine and "oxi" (a derivative of cocaine base produced with cheaper chemicals) have become very common in the "Plano Piloto" area and satellite cities.

Rio de Janeiro: The city continues to experience high incidences of crime. Tourists are particularly vulnerable to street thefts and robberies in the evening and at night especially in areas adjacent to major tourist attractions.There have been attacks, including shootings, along trails leading to the famous Corcovado Mountain and in other parts of the Tijuca Forest. If robbed, do not attempt to resist or fight back, but rather relinquish your personal belongings. At all times, pay close attention to your surroundings and the behavior of those nearby. There have been reports of thieves and rapists slipping incapacitating drugs into drinks at bars, hotel rooms, and street parties. While crime occurs throughout the year, it is more frequent during Carnival and the weeks prior.

Choose lodging carefully, considering location, security, and the availability of a safe to store valuables. Do not answer your hotel room door until you positively confirm who is on the other side. Look out the peephole, or call the front desk to confirm the visitor. There have been several recent incidents where mass holdups of guests have occurred at hotels and hostels in the city.

Rio de Janeiro's favelas are a subject of curiosity for many U.S. citizen travelers. A favela pacification program, instituted in 2008, has installed police stations in some favelas, primarily in the Zona Sul area. However, most favelas exist outside the control of city officials and police. Travelers are urged to exercise caution when entering any "pacified" favelas and should not go into favelas that are not "pacified" by the state government. Even in some "pacified" favelas, the ability of police to provide assistance, especially at night, may be limited. Several local companies offer "favela jeep tours" targeted at foreign tourists. Be aware that neither the tour company nor the city police can guarantee your safety when entering favelas.

Be vigilant while on the roads, especially at night. There have been shootings and carjackings on the Linha Vermelha, which links the airport to the Southern Zone of the city. In Rio de Janeiro, motorists should be especially vigilant at stoplights and when stuck in traffic. Carjackings and holdups can occur at intersections, especially at night.

Visitors should also remain alert to the possibility of manhole cover explosions. There have been multiple manhole cover explosions in Rio de Janeiro in the past few years, with a higher incidence in the Centro and Copacabana neighborhoods.

Report all incidents to Rio's tourist police (DEAT) at (21) 2332–2924. The tourist police have been very responsive to victims and cooperative with the U.S. Consulate General.

Sao Paulo: All areas of Greater Sao Paulo have a high rate of armed robbery of pedestrians and drivers at stoplights and during rush hour traffic. The "red light district" of Sao Paulo located on Rua Augusta north of Avenida Paulista and the Estacao de Luz metro areas are especially dangerous. There are regular reports of young women slipping various drugs into men's drinks and robbing them of all their belongings while they are unconscious. Armed holdups of pedestrians and motorists by young men on motorcycles ("motoboys") are a common occurrence in Sao Paulo. Criminals have also begun targeting restaurants throughout the city including, but not limited to, establishments in the upscale neighborhoods of Jardins, Itaim Bibi, Campo Belo, Morumbi and Moema. Victims who resist run the risk of violent attack. Laptop computers, other electronics, and luxury watches are the targets of choice for criminals in Sao Paulo.

Efforts of incarcerated drug lords to exert their power outside of their jail cells have resulted in sporadic disruptions in the city, violence directed at the authorities, bus burnings and vandalism at ATM machines, including the use of explosives. Be aware of your surroundings and exercise caution at all times. Respect police roadblocks and be aware that some municipal services may be disrupted.

As in Rio de Janeiro, favela tours have recently become popular among foreign tourists in Sao Paulo. We advise you to avoid Sao Paulo's favelas, as neither the tour company nor the city police can guarantee your safety when entering favelas.

Recife: Recife has one of the highest per capita murder rates in all of Brazil. As in Rio de Janeiro, tourists in Recife should take special care while on the beaches, as robberies may occur in broad daylight. In the upscale Boa Viagem neighborhood, carjackings can occur at any time of the day or night.

Victims of Crime: If you or someone you know becomes the victim of a crime abroad, you should contact the local police and the nearest U.S. Embassy or Consulate (see the Department of State's list of embassies and consulates). We can:

- Replace a stolen passport;
- Help you find appropriate medical care if you are the victim of a violent crime such as assault or rape;
- Put you in contact with the appropriate police authorities and contact family members or friends;
- Help you understand the local criminal justice process and direct you to local attorneys, although the investigation and prosecution of the crime are solely the responsibility of local authorities.

The local equivalent to the "911" emergency line in Brazil is: 190—Policia/Police 192—Ambulancia/Ambulance 193—Bombeiros/Fire Department.

Criminal Penalties: While in Brazil, you are subject to its laws even though you are a U.S. citizen. Foreign laws and legal systems can be vastly different from our own. Penalties for breaking the law can be more severe than in the United States for similar offenses. Persons violating Brazilian laws, even unknowingly, may be expelled, arrested, or imprisoned. Penalties for possession, use, or trafficking of illegal drugs in Brazil are severe, and convicted offenders can expect long jail sentences and heavy fines. There are also some things that might be legal in Brazil, but still illegal in the United States.

For instance, you can be prosecuted under U.S. law if you buy pirated goods. In addition, engaging in sexual conduct with children or using or disseminating child pornography in a foreign country is a crime, prosecutable in the U.S. In November 2008, Brazil passed a series of laws designed to strengthen protection of children against sexual exploitation. Brazilian police in tourist areas such as Rio de Janeiro are on the lookout for foreigners inappropriately touching or photographing minors. If you break local laws in Brazil, your U.S. passport will not help you avoid arrest or prosecution. It is very important to know what is legal and what is not where you are going. Based on the Vienna Convention on Consular Relations, and customary international law, if you are arrested in Brazil, you have the option to request that the authorities alert the nearest U.S. Embassy or Consulate. We recommend that you carry with you the contact information for the nearest U.S. Embassy or Consulate.

Special Circumstances: Brazilian customs authorities may enforce strict regulations concerning temporary importation into or export from Brazil of items such as firearms, antiquities, mineral samples, tropical plants, medications, and business equipment. In the Amazon region, there is a special concern for the export of biological material, which could have genetic value. People propagating or exporting biological material without proper permits run the risk of being accused of "biopiracy," a serious offense in Brazil. Contact the Brazilian Embassy in Washington, D.C. or one of Brazil's Consulates in the United States for specific information regarding customs requirements.

Accessibility: While in Brazil, individuals with disabilities may find accessibility and accommodation very different from what you find in the United States. Brazilian law prohibits discrimination against persons with physical and mental disabilities in employment, education, and access to health care, and the federal government effectively enforces these provisions. While federal and state laws have provisions ensuring access to buildings for persons with disabilities, states do not have programs to enforce them effectively. Accessibility to public transportation and the ability to accommodate the needs of physically disabled persons are limited in many areas.

Medical Facilities and Health Information: Medical care is generally good but it varies in quality, particularly in remote areas, and it may not meet U.S. standards outside the major cities. Expatriates regularly use the Albert Einstein Hospital in Sao Paulo. It is inspected and certified by the Joint Commission International and offers international service assistance. The hospital phone is 011-55-11-3747–1233.

In Rio, many expatriates go to Hospital Samaritano (Rua Bambina 98, Botafogo; tel. 2537–9722) or Pro-Cardiaco, which specializes in cardiac care but offers other specialty services (Rua Dona Mariana 219, Botafogo; tel. 2537–4242, ambulance tel. 2527–6060; http://www.procardiaco.com.br/

Prescription and over-the-counter medicines are widely available. Emergency services are responsive. Travelers may call a private ambulance company or call 192 and request an ambulance for a public hospital. Callers must stay on the line to provide the location as there is no automatic tracking of phone calls. Other important phone numbers include, Emergency 199, Police 190, and Fire Department 193.

All travelers should visit either their personal physician or a travel health clinic 4-8 weeks before departure, as some vaccines and malaria prophylaxis must be given a few weeks before travel. The following vaccines or vaccine boosters are recommended for all travelers, regardless of country of destination: Hepatitis A, typhoid, hepatitis B, MMR (measles, mumps, rubella), and Td (tetanus-diphtheria). Yellow fever vaccine is only recommended if traveling outside the coastal areas between Fortaleza and Uruguay border, and then only given to children older than 9 months of age. Note that yellow fever vaccination is recommended if traveling to Iguaçu Falls. Cholera, polio and rabies vaccines are not recommended except under specific circumstances. Consult the CDC Yellow Book for more information.

Travelers' diarrhea (TD) is the most common travel-related ailment. The cornerstone of prevention is food and water precautions: (1) Do not drink tap water unless it has been boiled, filtered or chemically disinfected. (2) Do not drink un-bottled beverages or drinks with ice. Do not eat raw or undercooked meat or fish, including ceviche. The most important measure for TD is rehydration, best performed with oral rehydration solution available almost universally in pharmacies in Brazil.

Insect-borne illnesses are common in Brazil. In addition to yellow fever, malaria, leishmaniasis, and dengue, for which there are no vaccines, are the principal ones. Dengue usually presents with fever, rash and body aches, or without symptoms, and clears relatively quickly; however, it can be rapidly fatal in a minority of cases, if severe. Consult CDC Yellow Book for the signs and symptoms of severe dengue. Malaria is present throughout the year in forested areas of the Amazon region, but tends to be seasonal (southern summer) elsewhere in the country; mostly on the periphery of cities and towns in the Amazon region. There is little to no risk of malaria in other areas of Brazil.

The first-line protection against all insect bites is the use of insect repellents (less than or equal to 30% DEET content—above 2 months of age), but mosquito nets, mosquito coils, aerosol sprays, protective clothing, use of screens or staying in air-conditioned environment, when available are also alternatives. Medications to prevent malaria infection (prophylaxis) are available, and travelers should consult with their health care provider or travel health clinic. Chagas disease (American trypanosomiasis) transmission has been eliminated in every state except Bahia and Tocantins through an aggressive program of insecticide spraying.

Brazil is an endemic area for schistosomiasis, a water-borne parasite, and travelers should avoid wading, swimming or other contact with fresh water.

Brazil is a high-burden country for tuberculosis, but short-term travelers are not considered at high risk for infection unless visiting crowded environments, hospitals, prisons or homeless shelters. Consult with your health care provider or travel health clinic for possible use of tuberculin skin testing before and after return from travel.

Plastic and other elective/cosmetic surgery is a major medical industry in Brazil. While Brazil has many plastic surgery facilities that are on par with those found in the United States, the quality of care varies widely. If arranging plastic surgery, make sure that emergency medical facilities are available. Some "boutique" plastic surgery operations offer luxurious facilities but are not hospitals and are therefore unable to deal with unforeseen emergencies.

Several U.S. citizens have died while visiting non-traditional healers outside of urban areas. While this is not surprising given that this type of treatment often attracts the terminally ill, U.S. citizens are advised to ensure they have access to proper medical care when visiting such sites. In the unfortunate event of a death, relatives or friends of any deceased U.S. citizen are advised to immediately contact the U.S. Embassy in Brasilia or the U.S. Consulate in Sao Paulo, Rio de Janeiro, or Recife, and not to contract local mortuary services before seeking embassy assistance.

Information on vaccinations and other health precautions, such as safe food and water precautions and insect bite protection, may be obtained from the Centers for Disease Control and Prevention's hotline for international travelers at 1-877-FYI-TRIP (1-877-394-8747) or via the CDC's web site, http://wwwnc.cdc.gov/travel/, and the Yellow Book. For information about outbreaks of infectious diseases abroad and for general health information for travelers, consult the World Health Organization (WHO) website, http://www.who.int/ith/en/.

Medical Insurance: You should not assume that your medical insurance will go with you when you travel. The Department of State strongly urges you to consult with your medical insurance company PRIOR to traveling abroad to determine whether the policy applies overseas and whether it covers emergency expenses such as a medical evacuation. It is very important to find out BEFORE you leave whether your medical insurance will cover you overseas. You need to ask your insurance company two questions:

- Does my policy apply when I'm out of the United States?
- Will it cover emergencies like a trip to a foreign hospital or a medical evacuation?

In many places, doctors and hospitals still expect payment in cash at the time of service. Your regular U.S. health insurance may not cover doctors' and hospital visits in other countries. If your policy does not go with you when you travel, it's a very good idea to take out another policy for your trip.

Traffic Safety and Road Conditions: While in Brazil, U.S. citizens may encounter road conditions that differ significantly from those in the United States. The information below concerning Brazil is provided for general reference only, and may not be totally accurate in a particular location or circumstance.

Travelers should consider obtaining an Inter-American Driving Permit to carry along with their valid U.S. license if they plan to drive while in Brazil. Such permits can be obtained through AAA or other sources.

Road conditions in Brazil vary widely throughout the country. State roads (especially in the south) are often excellent, while federal, interstate roads (designated "BR") are often very poor due to lack of maintenance. There are occasional stretches of modern divided highway that rival European or U.S. roads. In municipal areas, however, signs, shoulders, exits, and merge lanes tend to be haphazard. There are many potholes and surfaces are frequently uneven and bumpy. Some stretches of federal roads and rural state roads are so potholed that high-clearance vehicles are needed to traverse them. Pedestrians, bicyclists, and horse-drawn vehicles all pose hazards and can be encountered even on major routes. Travel after dark outside city centers is not recommended because of animals and disabled vehicles. Dirt roads are the rule in remote areas. These vary widely in quality and may quickly become more dangerous, even impassable, in rainy weather. Passenger car travel can be reasonably safe in most areas if you take into account the prevailing conditions described above and exercise due prudence and caution. Passenger-bus hijacking, usually non-violent, occurs at random in some areas of the country.

Driving on Brazil's inter-city roads can pose significant risks. As is the case elsewhere in the region, poor driving skills, bad roads, and a high density of trucks combine to make travel via roads considerably more hazardous than in the U.S. There are no laws requiring truckers to take mandatory rest stops and they often drive for excessive periods of time. All major inter-city routes are saturated with heavy truck traffic and for the most part have only two lanes. Road maintenance is inadequate and some long-distance roads through the Amazon forest are impassable much of the year.

There are few railroads and passenger train travel is almost nonexistent. Private cars and public buses are the main modes of inter-city road travel. Buses can range (depending on the route and the price) from luxurious and well-maintained to basic and mechanically unsound.

The Brazilian Federal Government maintains a (Portuguese language) website with up-to-date information on road conditions throughout Brazil; the site also has downloadable state roadmaps. A private Brazilian company, Quatro Rodas, publishes road maps that contain local phone numbers to ascertain the current conditions of roads on the map. Apart from toll roads, which generally have their own services, roadside assistance is available only very sporadically and informally through local private mechanics.

The fastest way to summon assistance in an emergency anywhere in the country is to dial 193, a universal number staffed by local fire departments. This service is in Portuguese only. Many motorists in major urban areas and more developed parts of the country carry cellular phones, and can be asked to assist in calling for help.

Brazilian traffic laws impose severe penalties for a number of traffic offenses. Enforcement ranges from sporadic to non-existent, so motorists should not assume that others will necessarily follow even the most fundamental and widely accepted rules of the road. Some important local rules and customs include the following.

Seatbelts/Child Car Seats: Brazil requires the use of seatbelts for everyone in the car. Brazilian federal law requires car seats for all children under the age of 7 ½. From age 7 ½ years to 10, children cannot ride in the front seat of the car, and must be in the back seat wearing a seatbelt.

Speed Limits: The maximum speed limit on major, divided highways is 120 kmph (74 mph). Lower limits (usually 60 kmph/40 mph) are often posted in urban areas, depending on the road and the nature of the neighborhood. Speed limits are widely ignored and rarely enforced. However, an increasing number of towns and cities have electronic/photographic devices (marked "Fiscalisacao Electronica"), which verify speed and take photos of violators' cars and license plates as a basis for issuing speeding tickets. Brazilian drivers tend to brake suddenly when encountering these devices. Many cities and towns have erected speed bumps, which are sometimes severe and may be unpainted and unmarked.

Yielding the Right of Way: Drivers must yield the right of way to cars on their right. Compliance with stop signs is rarely enforced; so many motorists treat them as yield signs.

Driving Under the Influence: Drivers with any measurable content of alcohol in their blood are in violation of the law. Checkpoints are often set up in urban areas where randomly chosen drivers are required to exit their vehicles and perform a breathalyzer test.

Turns at Red Lights:Not permitted, except for right turns where there is a sign with an arrow pointing to the right and the words "Livre a Direita."

Penaltiesfor Drivers Involved in an Accident Resulting in Injury or Death: In addition to possible criminal charges and penalties, compensatory and punitive damages may also apply.

Local Driving Customs: Drivers often use flashes or wave a hand out of the window to signal other drivers to slow down. In addition, pedestrian "zebra" crossings are strictly observed in some places (especially in Brasilia) and ignored most everywhere else.

Aviation Safety Oversight: The U.S. Federal Aviation Administration (FAA) has assessed the government of Brazil's Civil Aviation Authority as being in compliance with International Civil Aviation Organization (ICAO) aviation safety standards for oversight of Brazil's air carrier operations. Further information may be found on the FAA's safety assessment page.

Children's Issues: For information see the U.S. Dept. of State Office of Children's Issues web pages on intercountry adoption and international parental child abduction. If you have an emergency call the U.S. State Department's emergency after hours phone number: (888) 407-4747, or the American Citizen Services officer at the closest U.S. Embassy or Consulate.

Intercountry Adoption

March 2010

The information in this section has been edited from the latest report available as of February 2013 from the State Department Bureau of Consular Affairs, Office of Overseas Citizens Services. For more information, please read the *Intercountry Adoption* section of this book and review current reports online at http://adoption.state.gov.

Brazil is party to the Hague Convention on Protection of Children and Co-operation in Respect of Intercountry Adoption (Hague Adoption Convention). Therefore, all adoptions between Brazil and the United States must meet the requirements of the Convention and U.S. law implementing the Convention.

Who Can Adopt? Adoption between the United States and Brazil is governed by the Hague Adoption Convention. Therefore to adopt from Brazil, you must first be found eligible to adopt by the U.S. Government. The U.S. Government agency responsible for making this determination is the Department of Homeland Security, U.S. Citizenship and Immigration Services (USCIS).

Adoption in Brazil can be a complicated process, sometimes involving long waits. Brazilian adoption law gives preference to Brazilian citizens and citizens of countries that have implemented the Hague Adoption Convention. Please be aware that without Brazilian citizenship, it is unlikely that a U.S. citizen will be able to adopt a healthy, single child under the age of 5 years. The following types of children are most commonly available to U.S. citizens without Brazilian citizenship:

- Generally older children between the ages of 9 to 12
- Sibling groups of any number and of all ages
- Special needs children of all ages

Intercountry adoption will only be considered after all possibilities of finding a national adoption match are exhausted. Brazilian citizens living abroad will have priority to adopt over foreign citizens from other countries.

Residency Requirements: Brazilian law requires foreign prospective adoptive parents to live in Brazil with the prospective adoptive child for 30 days prior to the adoption.

Age Requirements: Persons over the age of 18 may adopt, regardless of marital status. The adopting party must be at least 16 years older than the potential adoptee.

Marriage Requirements: Adults over the age of 18 may adopt, regardless of marital status. Joint adoption is granted if parents are legally married or have a stable union contract. Divorced or legally separated couples may adopt together if they agree on the guardianship, schedule of visits, and have proof of relationship with the child.

The Process: Because Brazil is party to the Hague Adoption Convention, adopting from Brazil must follow a specific process designed to meet the Convention's requirements. For detailed and updated information on these requirements, please review the *Intercountry Adoption* section of this publication and visit the U.S. Department of State Intercountry Adoption website at http://adoption.state.gov.

Role of the Central Authority: The State Judiciary Commission of Adoption (CEJA) is the division of government responsible for *Intercountry Adoption* in Brazil. Each Brazilian state maintains a CEJA that acts as the Central Authority and is the sole organization authorized to approve foreign adoption parents.

Role of the Court: In October 1990, Brazil promulgated a new Federal Statute for the protection of children and adolescents. In accordance with this law, priority in adoptions is given to Brazilian citizens. Adoption by Proxy is prohibited. A child will only be allowed to depart Brazilian territory when the adoption has been finalized

Role of the Adoption Agencies: Prospective adoptive parents are required to use the services of an accredited or approved adoption service provider in the United States, and are advised to fully research any adoption agency or facilitator they plan to use for adoption services in Brazil. Because Brazil is a Convention country, adoption services must be provided by an approved service provider.

Time Frame: The average time to complete an intercountry adoption in Brazil varies from three months to three years.

Adoption Application: To begin the adoption process, prospective adoptive parents must apply for permission to adopt from the CEJA. CEJA will process the application; a lawyer is not required for this service. CEJA provides the prospective adoptive parents with a "Habilitation Approval Certificate" and eventually identifies the child(ren) eligible for adoption from a database of prospective children.

The U.S. Consulate in Rio de Janeiro provides a letter addressed to the CEJA stating that the United States will comply with the Hague Adoption Convention (i.e. that the adopted child will be a United States citizen and have all rights as any United States citizen). This letter is provided only after the USCIS has provisionally approved the I-800A application and a copy of the approval is received by the United States Consulate in Rio de Janeiro.

The U.S. Consulate in Rio de Janeiro provides the Article 5 letter. The letter is addressed to the CEJA stating that the child(ren) appear(s) to be eligible to receive a visa, and that the United States agrees that the adoption process may continue. Once the adoptive parents satisfy Brazilian adoption requirements, a judge may grant a final adoption. The Brazilian government will then allow the child to leave Brazil.

Adoption Fees: There are no government fees to open a dossier with the CEJA. Unfortunately it is difficult to determine an average cost for attorneys in Brazil since prices vary from state to state, and on the qualifications of the attorney.

The U.S. Embassy in Brazil discourages and the Brazilian National Adoption Law prohibits payment of any fees that are not properly receipted. "Donations," or "expediting" fees, which may be requested from prospective adoptive parents, have the appearance of "buying" a baby and put all future adoptions in Brazil at risk. Any expected expenses should have been itemized in the fees and estimated expenses section of your adoption services contract.

Documents Required: According to CEJA statutes, petitioners must provide at a minimum the following:

- A home study including a psychological evaluation and medical report(s) of prospective adoptive parent(s) stating they are in good health and capable to adopt;
- Certificate of Residence—proof of home ownership or an affidavit from landlord regarding the apartment lease;
- Photos of the prospective adoptive parent's(s') residence (inside and outside);
- Pictures of prospective adoptive family and grandparents, if possible;
- Notice of Approval of I-800A petition;
- Copy of Petitioner's U.S. passport(s), photo and signature page;
- Police records, requested within one year;
- Last filed Federal Income Tax return;
- Marriage certificate (if applicable);
- Birth certificate(s) of prospective adoptive parent(s);
- Divorce Decree (if applicable);
- Copy of applicant's current state of residence law on adoptions, including statement that the law is still in effect (generally obtained at a state Court House, from a Senator's office, or lawyer);
- Handwritten signed statement from prospective adoptive parent(s) saying they are aware that adoption in Brazil is free and irrevocable; and
- Statement that prospective adoptive parent(s) is(are) aware that they must not establish any contact in Brazil with prospective child's birth parent(s) or guardian (if applicable) before the authorization from CEJA is issued.

Bringing Your Child Home: Once your adoption is complete (or you have obtained legal custody of the child), there are a few more steps to take before you can head home. Specifically, you need to apply for several documents for your child before he or she can travel to the United States, such as a birth certificate, a passport or travel document for your child from the country in which he or she was born, and a U.S. Immigration Visa. For detailed and updated information on how to obtain these documents, review the *Intercountry Adoption* section in this publication and visit the U.S. Department of State Intercountry Adoption website at http://adoption.state.gov.

Child Citizenship Act: For adoptions finalized abroad, the Child Citizenship Act of 2000 allows your new child to acquire American citizenship automatically when he or she enters the United States as lawful permanent residents. For adoptions finalized in the United States, the Child Citizenship Act of 2000 allows your new child to acquire American citizenship automatically when the court in the United States issues the final adoption decree. To learn more, review the *Intercountry Adoption* section in this publication and visit the U.S. Department of State Intercountry Adoption website at http://adoption.state.gov.

After Adoption: According to Brazilian law, there are post-adoption requirements of adoptive parents. Adoptees may have access to their background records after the age of 18; before the age of 18 access to background records is only granted with judicial approval. Brazilian legislation requires ASPs to send post-adoption follow-up reports to CEJA and ACAF on the adopted children every six months for up to two years after the adoption is granted and/or until the child gets the naturalization certificate; they suggest that PAPs sign a document releasing their privacy act so that Brazilian authorities could be informed about the child's progress and adjustment to the new family; ACAF may also request ASPs information about an adopted child at any moment and ASPs need to send a copy of the child's naturalization certificate as soon as it is issued to ACAF.

U.S. Consulate in Rio de Janeiro
Avenida Presidente Wilson, 147, Castelo
Rio de Janeiro RJ 20030-020
Tel: (55) (21) 3823-2000
Fax: (55) (21) 3823-2083
Email: adoptionrio@state.gov

Brazil's Central Authority: The State Judiciary Commission of Adoption (CEJA) is the division of government responsible for intercountry adoption in Brazil. Each Brazilian state maintains a CEJA that acts as the Central Authority and is the sole organization authorized to approve foreign adopting parents. For a list of contacts, visit the U.S. Department of State Intercountry Adoption website at http://adoption.state.gov.

Brazilian Embassy
3006 Massachusetts Avenue, NW
Washington, DC 20008
Tel: (202) 238-2700
Fax: (202) 238-2827
www.brasilemb.org

Office of Children's Issues
U.S. Department of State
2201 C Street, NW
SA-29
Washington, DC 20520
Tel: 1-888-407-4747
E-mail: AskCI@state.gov
http://adoption.state.gov

For questions about immigration procedures, contact the National Customer Service Center (NCSC) at 1-800-375-5283 (TTY 1-800-767-1833).

International Parental Child Abduction

January 2013

The information in this section has been edited from a report of the

Bureau of Consular Affairs, Office of Overseas Citizens Services of the U.S. Department of State. For more information, please read the *International Parental Child Abduction* section of this book and review current reports online at www.travel.state.gov/abduction.

Disclaimer: The information in this flyer is provided for general information only, is not intended to be legal advice, and may change without notice. Questions involving interpretation of law should be addressed to an attorney licensed to practice in the relevant jurisdiction.

General Information: Brazil and the United States have been treaty partners under the 1980 Hague Convention on the Civil Aspects of International Child Abduction (Hague Abduction Convention) since December 1, 2003.

In April 2012, the U.S. Department of State cited Brazil as demonstrating patterns of non-compliance with the Hague Abduction Convention in its annual "Report on Compliance with the Hague Convention on the Civil Aspects of International Child Abduction." The report is located here.

Hague Abduction Convention: The U.S. Department of State serves as the U.S. Central Authority (USCA) for the Hague Abduction Convention. In this capacity, the Department's Bureau of Consular Affairs, Directorate for Overseas Citizen Services, Office of Children's Issues facilitates the submission of applications under the Hague Abduction Convention for the return of, or access to, children located in countries that are U.S. treaty partners, including Brazil. Parents are strongly encouraged to contact the Department of State for assistance prior to initiating the Hague process directly with the foreign Central Authority.

The Brazilian Central Authority for the Hague Abduction Convention is the Secretaria de Estado dos Direitos Humanos (SEDH). SEDH's role is to perform the duties given to central authorities under the Hague Abduction Convention, including processing Hague Abduction Convention applications for return of and access to children. They can be reached at:

Secretaria de Estado dos Direitos Humanos
Setor Comercial Sul—B, Quadra 9, Lote C
Edifício Parque Cidade Corporate
Torre "A," 10º andar
70308–200, BRASILIA-DF
Telephone/Fax:
+55-61-2025–3481
and +55-61-2025–3975
Website:
http://www.direitoshumanos.gov.br/

To initiate a Hague case for return of, or access to, a child in Brazil, the left-behind parent may submit a Hague application to the BCA. The USCA is available to answer questions about the Hague application process, to forward a completed application to the BCA, and to subsequently monitor its progress through the foreign administrative and legal processes.

Petitioning parents may also initiate a Hague case for return of, or access to a child in Brazil by retaining a private Brazilian attorney and directly filing a Hague case before a federal court. However, if a Hague case is directly filed before a federal court, the BCA will not monitor the progress of the case and will have no authority to assist in any manner.

There are no fees for filing Hague applications with either the United States or Brazil. Attorney fees, if necessary, are the sole responsibility of the person hiring the attorney. Additional costs may include airplane tickets for court appearances and for the return of the child, if so ordered.

Return: A parent or legal guardian may file an application under the Hague Abduction Convention for return to the United States of a child abducted to, or wrongfully retained in Brazil. The U.S. Department of State can assist parents living in the United States to understand whether the Convention is an available civil remedy and can provide information on the process for submitting a Hague application.

Visitation/Access: A person may file an application under the Hague Abduction Convention for access to a child living in Brazil. The criteria for acceptance of a Hague access application vary from country to country. The U.S. Department of State can assist parents living in the United States to understand country-specific criteria and provide information on the process for submitting a Hague application.

Retaining an Attorney: Retaining a private attorney is not required in order to file Hague Abduction Convention applications with courts in Brazil. However, parents should consider hiring a private attorney to follow up on cases, directly provide information to courts, and generally advise courses of action appropriate for their individual circumstances.

A privately-hired attorney should contact the BCA as soon as possible after the Hague Abduction Convention application has been filed. If a parent does not hire a private attorney, the Office of the Attorney General (OAG) will act as the legal representative of the state of Brazil on behalf of Hague applications, because Brazilian law considers Hague abduction cases to be public cases. Therefore, it is important to note that the OAG does not represent the interests of either party. The OAG will file cases with a federal court.

The Brazilian Bar Association and the Brazil's Defensoria Publica Da Uniao (Public Defender's Office) offer free legal assistance for any type of legal proceeding to those who demonstrate financial need. For additional information, please contact the Brazilian Bar Association, Sao Paulo Section, Legal Assistance Committee at: assistencia.judiciaria@oabsp.org.br.

The U.S. Embassy in Brasilia, Brazil posts a list of attorneys including those who specialize in family law. This list is provided as a courtesy service only and does not constitute an endorsement of any individual attorney. The Department of State assumes no responsibility or liability for the professional ability or reputation of, or the quality of services provided by, the following persons or firms. Professional credentials and areas of expertise are provided directly by the lawyers..

Mediation: In Hague Abduction Convention cases, the BCA always promotes mediation between parents before sending the case to the courts. Voluntary agreements are also strongly encouraged by the courts. Upon receiving a case, judges schedule a formal conciliation hearing to determine if parties can reach an a agreement which would then be formalized by the court. If a voluntary agreement is not reached, the court will then conduct further hearings and rule on the merits of the application. There are no NGOs or non-profit organizations that mediate between parents in abduction cases in Brazil.

U.S. Embassy Brasilia
SES—Av. das Nações, Quadra 801, Lote 03
70403–900 - Brasília, DF
Telephone: + (61) 3312–7000
Fax: +(61) 3312–7651
Email: BrasiliaACS@state.gov
Website: http://brazil.usembassy.gov

Embassy of Brazil
Consular Services
1030 15th Street, NW
Washington D.C., DC 20005
Telephone: (202) 461-3000
Email: consular@consbrasdc.org
Website: http://www.brasilemb.org/

BRUNEI

Compiled from publications that were available as of February 2013 from the U.S. Department of State, the U.S. Department of Commerce, and the Central Intelligence Agency (CIA). See the introduction to this set for explanatory notes.

Official Name:
Negara Brunei Darussalam

PROFILE

Geography

Area: total: 5,765 sq km; country comparison to the world: 173; land: 5,265 sq km; water: 500 sq km
Major cities: Bandar Seri Begawan (capital) 22,000 (2009)
Climate: tropical; hot, humid, rainy
Terrain: flat coastal plain rises to mountains in east; hilly lowland in west

People

Nationality: noun: Bruneian(s); adjective: Bruneian
Population: 408,786 (July 2012 est.)
Population growth rate: 1.691% (2012 est.)
Ethnic groups: Malay 66.3%, Chinese 11.2%, indigenous 3.4%, other 19.1% (2004 est.)
Religions: Muslim (official) 67%, Buddhist 13%, Christian 10%, other (includes indigenous beliefs) 10%
Languages: Malay (official), English, Chinese
Literacy: definition: age 15 and over can read and write; total population: 92.7%; male: 95.2%; female: 90.2% (2001 census)
Health: life expectancy at birth: total population: 76.37 years; male: 74.09 years; female: 78.75 years (2012 est.); Infant mortality rate: total: 11.15 deaths/1,000 live births; male: 13.31 deaths/1,000 live births; female: 8.9 deaths/1,000 live births (2012 est.)
Unemployment rate: 2.7% (2010)
Work force: 198,800 (2010 est.)

Government

Type: constitutional sultanate (locally known as Malay Islamic Monarchy)
Independence: 1 January 1984
Constitution: 29 September 1959 (some provisions suspended under a State of Emergency since December 1962, others since independence on 1 January 1984)
Political subdivisions: 4 districts (daerah-daerah, singular—daerah); Belait, Brunei-Muara, Temburong, Tutong
Suffrage: 18 years of age for village elections; universal

Economy

GDP (purchasing power parity): $21.94 billion (2012 est.); $21.24 billion (2011 est.); $20.84 billion (2010 est.); $20.31 billion (2009 est.)
GDP real growth rate: 2.7% (2012 est.); 1.9% (2011 est.); 2.6% (2010 est.); -1.8% (2009 est.)
GDP per capita (PPP): $50,500 (2012 est.); $50,000 (2011 est.); $50,300 (2010 est.); $50,000 (2009 est.)
Natural resources: petroleum, natural gas, timber
Agriculture products: rice, vegetables, fruits; chickens, water buffalo, cattle, goats, eggs
Industries: petroleum, petroleum refining, liquefied natural gas, construction
Exports: $10.67 billion (2008); $8.25 billion (2007)
Exports—commodities: crude oil, natural gas, garments
Exports—partners: Japan 45.6%, South Korea 16.5%, Australia 11.8%, Indonesia 8.4%, India 4.8%, China 4.6% (2011)
Imports: $2.61 billion (2008 est.); $2.055 billion (2007 est.)
Imports—commodities: machinery and transport equipment, manufactured goods, food, chemicals
Imports—partners: Singapore 33.2%, China 15.5%, South Korea 12.2%, Malaysia 10.7%, Germany 9.6% (2011)
Debt—external: $0 (2005)
Exchange rates: Bruneian dollars (BND) per US dollar; 1.25 (2012 est.); 1.2579 (2011); 1.3635 (2010 est.); 1.45 (2009)

PEOPLE

Many cultural and linguistic differences make Brunei Malays distinct from the larger Malay populations in nearby Malaysia and Indonesia, even

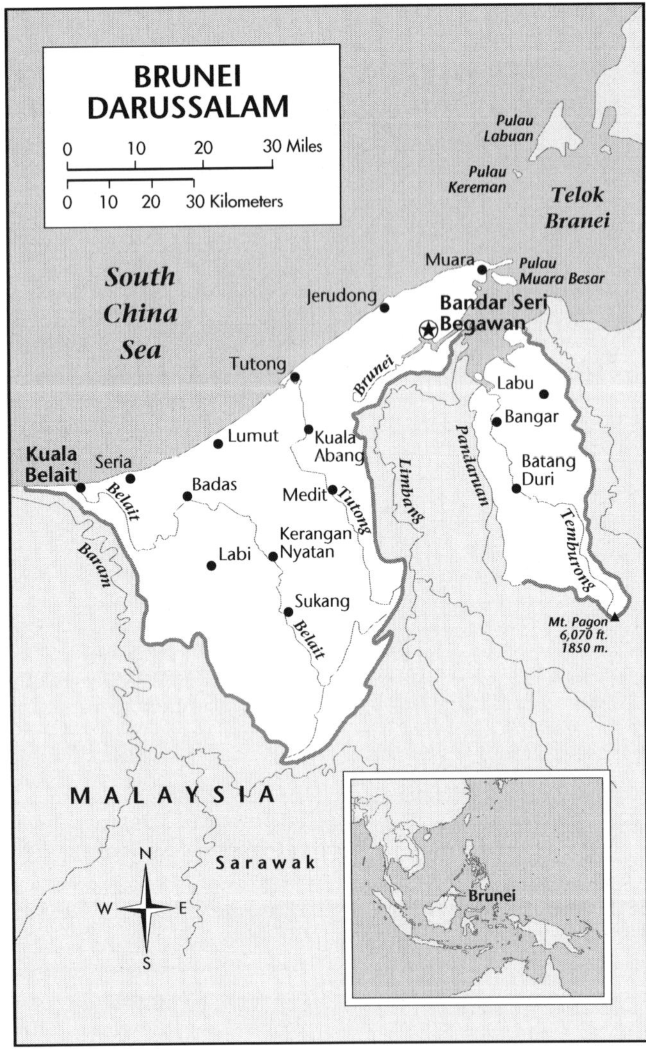

though they are ethnically related and share the Muslim religion. Brunei has hereditary nobility, carrying the title Pengiran. The Sultan can award to commoners the title Pehin, the equivalent of a life peerage awarded in the United Kingdom. The Sultan also can award his subjects the title Dato, the equivalent of a knighthood in the United Kingdom, and Datin, the equivalent of damehood.

Bruneians adhere to the practice of using complete full names with all titles, including the title Haji (for men) or Hajah (for women) for those who have made the Haj pilgrimage to Mecca. Many Brunei Malay women wear the tudong, a traditional head covering. Men wear the songkok, a traditional Malay cap. Men who have completed the Haj can wear a white songkok. The requirements to attain Brunei citizenship include passing tests in Malay culture, customs, and language as well as the national Malay Islamic Monarchy (MIB) philosophy. Stateless permanent residents of Brunei are given International Certificates of Identity, which allow them to travel overseas. The majority of ethnic Chinese in Brunei are permanent residents, and many are stateless. An amendment to the National Registration and Immigration Act of 2002 allowed female Bruneian citizens to transfer their nationality to their children.

In May 2006, the law changed to allow citizenship to permanent residents who have contributed to the country's economic growth, to women married to a citizen for 2 years, to women married to permanent residents for 5 years, and to children of permanent resident fathers after the age of 2 years and 6 months. According to unofficial sources there are approximately 20,000 "stateless" persons in the country, including persons born and raised in the country who were not automatically accorded citizenship and its attendant rights but were granted permanent resident status. In July 2009, the Land Code Strata Act, which allows permanent residents to own units of multistory property for a maximum of 99 years, came into force.

Oil wealth allows the Brunei Government to provide the population with one of Asia's finest health care systems. Malaria has been eradicated, and cholera is virtually nonexistent. There are five general hospitals—in Bandar Seri Begawan, Tutong, Kuala Belait, Bangar, and Seria—and there are numerous health clinics throughout the country.

Education

Education starts with preschool, followed by 6 years of primary education and up to 7 years of secondary education. Nine years of education are mandatory. Most of Brunei's college students attend universities and other institutions abroad, but approximately 4,880 (2009) study at the University of Brunei Darussalam. Opened in 1985, the university has a faculty of more than 300 instructors and is located on a sprawling campus overlooking the South China Sea.

A second university, Sultan Sharif Ali Islamic University, was established in 2007 and offers programs such as Islamic finance and law. As of December 2009, the university had about 300 students. Upgraded to university status as of October 2008, Institut Teknologi Brunei (ITB) began offering degree programs in addition to its "Higher National Diploma" programs and had about 700 students.

Language

The official language is Malay. The bulk of the population speaks Malay but many speak English well. English is normally the language of business. Menus and signs in English are common. The Chinese community that makes up 10% of the total population generally speaks Mandarin and the Hokkien dialect.

Religion

According to official statistics, the population is 82 percent Muslim, 7 percent Buddhist, 3 percent Christian, and less than 1 percent a combination of other faiths (including Hindu, Baha'i, Taoist, Sikh, Nasrani, atheists, and others); 7 percent did not state their religious affiliation. The government categorizes Catholics as distinct from other Christians. There is also an indigenous population that adheres to traditional animistic beliefs, although many have converted either to Islam or Christianity. According to the latest information available, there are 110 mosques and Islamic prayer halls, six Christian churches (three Roman Catholic, two Anglican and one Baptist), three Chinese Buddhist temples, and one Hindu temple, all officially registered in the country. Several Christian congregations operate without registration.

HISTORY

Historians believe there was a forerunner to the present Brunei Sultanate, which the Chinese called Po-ni. Chinese and Arabic records indicate that this ancient trading kingdom existed at the mouth of the Brunei River as early as the seventh or eighth century A.D. This early kingdom was apparently conquered by the Sumatran Hindu Empire of Srivijaya in the early ninth century, which later controlled northern Borneo and the Philippines. It was subjugated briefly by the Java-based Majapahit Empire but soon regained its independence and once again rose to prominence.

The Brunei Empire had its golden age from the 15th to the 17th centuries, when its control extended over the entire island of Borneo and north into the Philippines. Brunei was particularly powerful under the fifth sultan, Bolkiah (1473-1521), who was famed for his sea exploits and even briefly captured Manila; and under the ninth sultan, Hassan (1605-19), who fully developed an elaborate Royal Court structure, elements of which remain today.

After Sultan Hassan, Brunei entered a period of decline due to internal battles over royal succession as well as the rising influences of European colonial powers in the region that, among other things, disrupted traditional trading patterns, destroying the economic base of Brunei and many other Southeast Asian sultanates. In 1839, the English adventurer James Brooke arrived in Borneo and helped the Sultan put down a rebellion. As a reward, he became governor and later "Rajah" of Sarawak in northwest Borneo and gradually expanded the territory under his control.

Meanwhile, the British North Borneo Company was expanding its control over territory in northeast Borneo. In 1888, Brunei became a protectorate of the British Government, retaining internal independence but with British control over external affairs. In 1906, Brunei accepted a further measure of British control when executive power was transferred to a British resident, who advised the ruler on all matters except those concerning local custom and religion.

In 1959, a new constitution was written declaring Brunei a self-governing state, while its foreign affairs, security, and defense remained the responsibility of the United Kingdom. An attempt in 1962 to introduce a partially elected legislative body with limited powers was abandoned after the opposition political party, Parti Rakyat Brunei, launched an armed uprising, which the government put down with the help of British forces. In the late 1950s and early 1960s, the government also resisted pressures to join neighboring Sabah and Sarawak in the newly formed Malaysia. The Sultan eventually decided that Brunei would remain an independent state.

In 1967, Sultan Omar abdicated in favor of his eldest son, Hassanal Bolkiah, who became the 29th ruler. The former Sultan remained as Defense Minister and assumed the royal title Seri Begawan. In 1970, the national capital, Brunei Town, was renamed Bandar Seri Begawan in his honor. The Seri Begawan died in 1986. On January 4, 1979, Brunei and the United Kingdom signed a new treaty of friendship and cooperation. On January 1, 1984, Brunei Darussalam became a fully independent state.

GOVERNMENT AND POLITICAL CONDITIONS

Brunei Darussalam is a sultanate that has been ruled by the same family for more than 600 years. Sultan Haji Hassanal Bolkiah governed under longstanding emergency powers that placed few limits on his power. The Legislative Council, made up of appointed, indirectly elected, and ex officio members, met during the year and exercised a limited role in recommending and approving legislation.

Recent Elections

Political authority and control rested entirely with the sultan. A 33-person legislative council (LegCo) of primarily appointed members and little independent power provides a forum for public discussion of proposed government programs, as well as administrative deficiencies. It convenes once a year for approximately two weeks, after which it is dissolved. The Seventh LegCo session met in March 2011. Council members may be disqualified from service on the basis of various offenses, including disloyalty to the sultan.

Persons age 18 years and above may vote by secret ballot in village consultative council elections, which are based on a traditional system of village chiefs. Candidates must be Muslim, approved by the government, and citizens or permanent residents for more than 15 years. The councils communicate constituent wishes through a variety of channels, including periodic meetings chaired by the minister of home affairs. The government also meets with mukim (collections of villages) representatives to allow for airing of local grievances and concerns.

Political Parties: The Brunei National Development Party was the country's only registered political party. The party pledged to support the sultan and the government. Although the party criticized administrative deficiencies, its few activities received limited publicity, and it was hindered by membership restrictions.

Participation of Women and Minorities: In 2009 the sultan appointed the first female cabinet member, Datin Hayati, as attorney general. Two other women held ministerial rank—the sultan's sister, Princess Masna, ambassador-at-large in the Ministry of Foreign Affairs and Trade; and Deputy Minister for Culture Youth and Sports Datin Adina, appointed in 2010. There were four female permanent secretaries—in the Ministries of Defense, Foreign Affairs and Trade, and Industry and Primary Resources. There were two women appointed to the LegCo. Ethnic Chinese held one Cabinet-level post and two LegCo positions.

Principal Government Officials

Last Updated: 1/31/2013

Sultan: **HASSANAL Bolkiah, Sir**

Prime Min.: **HASSANAL Bolkiah, Sir**

Min. of Communications: **ABDULLAH bin Bakar**

Min. of Culture, Youth, & Sports: **HAZAIR bin Abdullah**

Min. of Defense: **HASSANAL Bolkiah, Sir**

Min. of Development: **SUYOI bin Osman**

Min. of Education: **Awang ABU BAKAR bin Apong**

Min. of Energy: **Mohammad YASMIN bin Umar**

Min. of Finance: **HASSANAL Bolkiah, Sir**

Min. of Finance II: **ABDUL RAHMAN bin Ibrahim**

Min. of Foreign Affairs & Trade: **MOHAMED Bolkiah, Prince**

Min. of Foreign Affairs & Trade II: **LIM Jock Seng**

Min. of Health: **ADANAN bin Mohd Yusof**

Min. of Home Affairs: **BADARUDDIN bin Othman**

Min. of Industry & Primary Resources: **YAHYA bin Bakar**

Min. of Religious Affairs: **MOHAMMAD bin Abd Rahman**

Senior Min. in the Prime Min.'s Office: **Al-Muhtadee BILLAH, Crown Prince**

Ambassador to the US: **YUSOFF bin Abdul Hamid**

Permanent Representative to the UN, New York: **LATIF bin Tuah**

ECONOMY

Brunei has a small well-to-do economy that encompasses a mixture of foreign and domestic entrepreneurship, government regulation, welfare measures, and village tradition. Crude oil and natural gas production account for just over half of GDP and more than 90% of exports. Per capita GDP is among the highest in Asia, and substantial income from overseas investment supplements income from domestic production.

The government provides for all medical services and free education through the university level and subsidizes rice and housing. A new monetary authority was established in January 2011 with responsibilities that include monetary policy, monitoring of financial institutions, and currency trading activities.

Labor Conditions

Various domestic laws prohibit the employment of children under age 16. Parental consent and approval by the Labor Commission is required for those under 18. Female workers under 18 may not work at night or on offshore oil platforms. The Department of Labor, which is part of the Ministry of Home Affairs, effectively enforced laws related to the employment of children. There were no reports of violations of child labor laws. The law does not set a minimum wage, but most employed citizens command good salaries; per capita income stands at BN$40,700 (US$31,300). Some foreign embassies set minimum wage requirements for their nationals working in Brunei. The standard workweek is Monday through Thursday, then Saturday, with Friday and Sunday off, allowing for two rest periods of 24 hours each week. The law provides for paid annual holidays, overtime for work in excess of 48 hours per week, and double time for work performed on legal holidays, but laws regarding hours were frequently not observed in practice.

Occupational health and safety standards were established by government regulations. The government generally enforced labor, health and safety regulations effectively, but enforcement in the unskilled labor sector was lax. This was true especially for foreign laborers at construction sites, where pay arrearage and inadequate safety and living conditions were reported. The government may close a workplace where health, safety, or working conditions are unsatisfactory. Foreign migrant workers often signed contracts with employment agents or other sponsors in their home countries that reduced their promised salaries through payments to the agencies or sponsors.

The government forbade wage deductions to agencies or sponsors and mandated that employees receive their full salaries; nevertheless, foreign workers continued to pay high fees to manpower agents to obtain work in the country. The government now requires recruiting agencies to be registered.

U.S.-BRUNEI RELATIONS

In 1850, the United States and Brunei concluded a Treaty of Peace, Friendship, Commerce and Navigation, which remains in force. In 1984, Brunei became a fully independent state following a century of partial autonomy under the United Kingdom. The United States opened an embassy in Brunei upon the country's independence. A memorandum of understanding on defense cooperation was signed in 1994. Brunei's armed forces engage in joint exercises, training programs, and other military cooperation with the United States.

Bruneian military personnel have attended U.S. military academies. The two countries work closely together on a bilateral and regional agenda to tackle some of the most pressing issues. They also have cooperated to increase English language instruction in Association of Southeast Asian Nations (ASEAN) countries, promote commercial interests, and expand educational opportunities and people-to-people connections.

The United States shares Brunei's commitment to the environment and supports the Heart of Borneo rainforest conservation initiative.

U.S. Assistance to Brunei

The United States provides no foreign assistance to Brunei.

Bilateral Economic Relations

Brunei encourages foreign investment in the domestic economy through various incentives, marketing opportunities for investors in new industries and economic activities, although oil and gas and government spending still account for most economic activity.

Brunei's non-petroleum industries include agriculture, forestry, fishing, aquaculture, and banking. U.S. firms are consulting on aquaculture projects. Bilateral trade is expanding and the United States was the third-largest supplier of imports to Brunei in 2009.

Brunei's garment-for-export industry has been shrinking since the United States eliminated its garment quota system at the end of 2004. However, with 75% of total garment exports valued at $66 million, the United States remains the largest export market for garments.

Brunei's Membership in International Organizations

Brunei gives its ASEAN membership the highest priority in its foreign relations. The United States and Brunei participate in many of the same international organizations, including the United Nations, the East Asia Summit, the ASEAN Regional Forum, the Asia-Pacific Economic Cooperation (APEC) forum, the International Monetary Fund, the World Bank, and the World Trade Organization.

Bilateral Representation

Brunei maintains an embassy in the United States at 3520 International Court, NW, Washington, DC 20008; tel. 202-237-1838.

Principal U.S. Embassy Officials

Last Updated: 1/14/2013

BANDAR SERI BEGAWAN (E) Simpang 336-52-16-9, Jalan Kebangsaan, (673)238-4616, Fax (673)238-4603, 238-4604, Workweek: 7:45am-4:30pm M-F, Website: http://bandar.usembassy.gov/

AMB OMS:	Supin Horton
CON/POL/ECON:	Christin Ho
DHS/CIS:	(Singapore)
FM:	(Singapore)
MGT:	Paul E. Brand
POSHO:	Paul E. Brand
SDO/DATT:	(Singapore)
AMB:	Daniel L. Shields
DCM:	Melinda M. Pavek
PAO:	Deidra D. Avendasora
RSO:	Andrew J. Loftus
EEO:	(Singapore)
FMO:	(Singapore)
IMO:	Ronald F. Dugger
IRS:	(Singapore)

TRAVEL

Consular Information Sheet

January 30, 2012

Country Description: Brunei Darussalam is a small Islamic Sultanate on the northwest coast of the Island of Borneo. It is divided into four districts: Brunei/Muara, Tutong, Belait and Temburong. The capital, Bandar Seri Begawan, is its major city. Brunei's official language is Malay, but English is widely understood and used in business. Tourist facilities and services are generally available throughout the country.

Smart Traveler Enrollment Program (STEP)/Embassy Locations: If you are going to live in or visit Brunei, please take the time to tell our Embassy about your trip. If you enroll, we can keep you up to date with important safety and security announcements. It will also help your friends and family get in touch with you in an emergency.

U.S. Embassy Bandar Seri Begawan
Simpang 336-52-16-9
Jalan Kebangsaan
Bandar Seri Begawan BC4115, Brunei Darussalam.

Mail from the United States can be sent to the Embassy's address:
U.S. Embassy, P.O. Box 2991, Bandar Seri Begawan BS8675, Negara Brunei Darussalam.
Telephone: 673-238-4616
After hour emergency telephone: (673) 873-0691
Fax number: (673) 238-4606

Entry/Exit Requirements for U.S. Citizens: U.S. passport-holders must have at least six months' validity remaining on their passport before entering Brunei for business or pleasure and are required to obtain a visa prior to arrival in Brunei for visits of 90 days or longer. Diplomatic and official passport-holders are also required to apply for a visa to enter Brunei Darussalam for assignments to Brunei of more than 90 days There

Background Notes

is an airport departure tax. For further information about entry or exit requirements, travelers may consult the Consular Section of the Embassy of Brunei, 3520 International Court NW, Washington, DC 20008, tel. (202) 237-1838, or visit the Embassy of Brunei website for the most current visa information.

Immigration offenses are punishable by caning. Workers who overstay their visas can face jail sentences, fines, and caning. Persons associated with violators, such as contractors or employers, are subject to the same penalties if the violator is found guilty.

Brunei has imposed HIV/AIDS travel restrictions as part of a ban on communicable diseases. The Ministry of Health (MOH) of Brunei Darussalam requires all travelers entering Brunei to fill out a Health Declaration Card and submit it to the Officer-In-Charge (MOH) upon disembarkation. Under Section 7, Infectious Diseases Order 2003 of MOH, travelers may be subjected to a medical examination upon arrival in Brunei Darussalam. Travelers also may be quarantined if infected or suspected to be infected with an infectious disease or if travelers have had contact with such a person, under Section 15 of the same order of MOH. Please verify this information with the Embassy of Brunei before you travel.

Threats to Safety and Security: Noting several past terrorist bombings in Indonesia, the Department of State continues to be concerned that terrorist groups such as Jemaah Islamiyah (JI) have the capability to carry out terrorist attacks throughout the region. U.S. citizens in Brunei should be vigilant with regard to their personal security, maintain a low profile, vary times and routes during their daily routines, and report any suspicious activity to the local police or to the U.S. Embassy.

Brunei adheres to conservative Islamic social values, and Americans are advised to learn and respect local customs and traditions. Typically non-Muslims are not expected to follow the same customs enforced on practicing Muslims. Persons violating Brunei's laws, even unknowingly, may be deported, arrested, or imprisoned. Any public criticism of His Majesty the Sultan or other members of the Royal Family is strongly discouraged. Alcohol cannot be purchased legally in Brunei; however, two liters of spirits/wine and 12 cans of beer may be imported per border entry by adult non-Muslims for personal consumption in privacy. Importing more than the prescribed amount of alcohol per border entry will result in arrest. The Royal Brunei Police Force is generally professional and courteous. Most officers speak English but some, especially from the reserve units, have limited to no English speaking capability. Travelers are strongly urged to carry a copy of their passport on their person as police will most always ask for identification for all parties involved in any type of incident. In the event of police detention, Americans should request to contact the US Embassy. The Embassy local guard force operates 24 hours a day, seven days a week, and all guards speak English. The 24-hour number of the Embassy is 673-238-4616 and the Duty Officer is 673-873-0691. The emergency number for the police is 993.

In terms of natural disasters, earthquakes and typhoons are not major concerns in Brunei. Brunei has not been affected by industrial accidents and kidnappings are not common.

Stay up to date by:

- Bookmarking our Bureau of Consular Affairs website, which contains the current Travel Warnings and Travel Alerts as well as the Worldwide Caution.
- Follow us on Twitter and the Bureau of Consular Affairs page on Facebook as well.
- Calling 1-888-407-4747 toll-free within the U.S. and Canada, or a regular toll line, 1-202-501-4444, from other countries.
- Taking some time before travel to consider your personal security.

Crime: Most crimes that occur in Brunei are non-violent and crimes of opportunity, including residential burglaries and vehicle break-ins. While traveling or residing in Brunei, you can easily avoid being victim to a crime of opportunity by simply practicing good security awareness. For example, securing valuables (remove from plain view), avoid secluded locations, properly secure your residence and vehicle, and not traveling alone late at night.

Crime in Brunei peaks in July and December, due to the holidays and schools being out of session. Overall, many crimes carry severe penalties, and punishments such as jail, fines, caning, or deportation (for foreigners).

Victims of Crime: If you or someone you know becomes the victim of a crime abroad, you should contact the local police and the nearest U.S. embassy or consulate. We can:

- Replace a stolen passport.
- For violent crimes such as assault or rape,help you find appropriate medical care,
- Put you in contact with the appropriate police authorities, and contact family members or friends.
- Although the local authorities are responsible for investigating and prosecuting the crime, consular officers can help you understand the local criminal justice process and can direct you to local attorneys.

In Brunei, the local equivalents to the "911" emergency line are: 993 for Brunei Police, 995 for Fire & Rescue, and 998 for Search & Rescue.

Criminal Penalties: While you are traveling in Brunei, you are subject to its laws even if you are a U.S. citizen. Foreign laws and legal systems can be vastly different than our own. In some places you may be taken in for questioning if you don't have your passport with you. In some places, it is illegal to take pictures of certain buildings. In some places driving under the influence could land you immediately in jail. These criminal penalties will vary from country to country. There are also some things that might be legal in the country you visit, but still illegal in the United States, and you can be prosecuted under U.S. law if you buy pirated goods, which are prevalent in Brunei. Engaging in sexual conduct with children or using or disseminating child pornography in a foreign country is a crime prosecutable in the United States. If you break local laws in Brunei, your U.S. passport won't help you avoid arrest or prosecution. It's very important to know what's legal and what's not where you are going.

If you violate Brunei laws, even unknowingly, you may be expelled, arrested, or imprisoned. Penalties for possession, use of, or trafficking in illegal drugs in Brunei are severe, and convicted offenders can expect long jail sentences, heavy fines, and, possibly, death. Brunei has a mandatory death penalty for many narcotics offenses. Under the current law, possession of heroin, ecstasy, and morphine derivatives of more than 15 grams, Cocaine of more than 30 grams, Cannabis of more than 500 grams, Syabu (Methamphetamine) of more than 50 grams, or Opium of more than 1.2 kg., carries the death penalty. Possession of lesser amounts can result in a minimum twenty-year jail term and caning. Importation of firearms is prohibited; the illegal possession of firearms or explosives and drug use/possession carry severe penalties, including the possibility of the death penalty. Any attempts to circumvent alcohol controls can result in arrest and criminal prosecution. Gambling in Brunei is illegal.

Prostitution is illegal and harsh penalties can result from engaging in the solicitation of prostitution. In addition, due to the conservative Muslim culture, any extramarital relations between a Muslim and non-Muslim, from simple acts such as holding hands or public displays of affection to sexual activity may be considered a crime in Brunei.

If you are arrested in Brunei, authorities of Brunei are required to alert the U.S. Embassy of your arrest. If you are concerned the Department of State may not be aware of your situation, you should request the police to notify the closest U.S. embassy of your arrest.

Immigration Violations: U.S. citizens in Brunei are subject to the laws of the country and may be arrested for violation of immigration regulations or any other law. In such cases, the U.S. Embassy will provide consular services to U.S. citizens arrested in Brunei, in accordance with international law and U.S. regulations. However, the Embassy may not intervene in local judicial matters.

Dual Nationality: Brunei does not recognize or permit dual nationality. Brunei nationals are expected to enter and exit the country on their Brunei passports. Should Brunei authorities learn that a person is a dual national, they may require immediate renunciation of the citizenship of either the other nation or Brunei.

Customs Regulations: Brunei customs authorities may enforce strict regulations concerning temporary importation or export of items such as firearms, religious materials, antiquities, medications, business equipment, currency, ivory, and alcohol. For non-Muslims, limited amounts of alcohol for personal consumption are permitted. It is advisable to contact the Embassy of Brunei in Washington, D.C., for specific information regarding customs requirements.

Accessibility: While in Brunei, individuals with disabilities may find accessibility and accommodation very different from what you find in the United States

Medical Facilities and Health Information: There is adequate care for basic medical conditions in Brunei; however, for certain elective surgery or complicated care, the best medical care in the region is obtained in Singapore. Brunei has a number of public hospitals and clinics. The biggest ones are RIPAS Hospital in Bandar Seri Begawan and Tutong Hospital in the district of the same name. The largest private hospital is Jerudong Park Medical Center about 20 minutes by car outside of Bandar Seri Begawan, which is a facility comparable to those in the U.S. Brunei also hosts a number of private clinics, many of which are staffed by expatriates. More information can be found at the U.S. Embassy Website at Medication and prescriptions are readily available, but may not be the same brands as those found in the U.S. There are no major health concerns in Brunei..

You can find good information on vaccinations and other health precautions, on the CDC website. For information about outbreaks of infectious diseases abroad, consult the World Health Organization (WHO) website. The WHO website also contains additional health information for travelers, including detailed country-specific health information.

Medical Insurance: You can't assume your insurance will go with you when you travel. It's very important to find out BEFORE you leave whether or not your medical insurance will cover you overseas. You need to ask your insurance company two questions:

- Does my policy apply when I'm out of the United States?
- Will it cover emergencies like a trip to a foreign hospital or a medical evacuation?

In many places, doctors and hospitals still expect payment in cash at the time of service. Your regular U.S. health insurance may not cover doctors' and hospital visits in other countries. If your policy doesn't go with you when you travel, it's a very good idea to take out another one for your trip.

Traffic Safety and Road Conditions: While in a foreign country, you may encounter road conditions that differ significantly from those in the United States.

Brunei has an extensive network of roads comparable to most western countries' and they are well maintained. Traffic moves on the left side of the road. Holders of a foreign driver's license are permitted to drive in Brunei Darussalam for 90 days only. For longer stays, a foreign driver's license must be endorsed to a Brunei driver's license, available at any Land Transport Department office.

Drivers must obey traffic rules at all times and should take extra caution when approaching traffic signals. In urban areas, several deadly accidents have occurred in recent years when local drivers drove through red lights.

The Royal Brunei Police Force routinely sets up checkpoints and traffic stops, particularly at night. These checkpoints are normally set up for one of two reasons: 1) for routine license and registration checks and 2) DWI/search for contraband (drugs and alcohol). In case you are stopped, be prepared to show identification card and vehicle registration. In addition to registration, you should always have your insurance policy in the car. In case of an accident you will need all three.

Aviation Safety Oversight: The U.S. Federal Aviation Administration (FAA) has assessed the government of Brunei's Civil Aviation Authority as being in compliance with International Civil Aviation Organization (ICAO) aviation safety standards for oversight of Brunei's air carrier operations. Further information may be found on the FAA's safety assessment page.

Children's Issues: Please see the U.S. Dept. of State Office of Children's Issues web pages on intercountry adoption and international parental child abduction.

Intercountry Adoption

April 2011

Brunei is not party to the Hague Convention on Protection of Children and Co-operation in Respect of Intercountry Adoption (Hague Adoption Convention). Therefore, when the Hague Adoption Convention entered into force for the United States on April 1, 2008, intercountry adoption processing for Brunei did not change. The Department of State does not maintain files on the adoption process in Brunei because adoptions from Brunei are rare; fewer than five adoptions by American citizen parents have not taken place in over a decade.

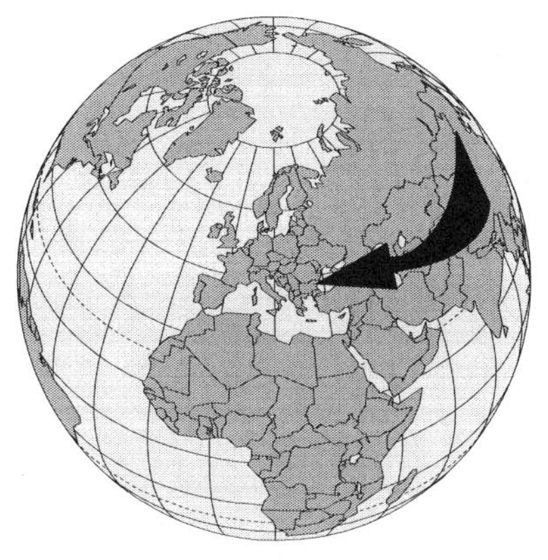

BULGARIA

Compiled from publications that were available as of February 2013 from the U.S. Department of State, the U.S. Department of Commerce, and the Central Intelligence Agency (CIA). See the introduction to this set for explanatory notes.

Official Name:
Republic of Bulgaria

PROFILE

Geography

Area: total: 110,879 sq km; country comparison to the world: 105; land: 108,489 sq km; water: 2,390 sq km
Major cities: Sofia (capital) 1.192 million (2009)
Climate: temperate; cold, damp winters; hot, dry summers
Terrain: mostly mountains with lowlands in north and southeast

People

Nationality: noun: Bulgarian(s); adjective: Bulgarian
Population: 7,037,935 (July 2012 est.)
Population growth rate: -0.796% (2012 est.)
Ethnic groups: Bulgarian 76.9%, Turk 8%, Roma 4.4%, other 0.7% (including Macedonian, Armenian, Tatar, Circassian), other (unknown) 10% (2011 census)
Religions: Eastern Orthodox 59.4%, Muslim (Sunni) 7.4%, Muslim (Shia) 0.4%, other (including Catholic, Protestant, Armenian Apostolic Orthodox, and Judaism) 1.7%, other (unknown) 27.4%, none 3.7% (2011 census)
Languages: Bulgarian (official) 76.8%, Turkish 8.2%, Roma 3.8%, other 0.7%, other (unknown) 10.5% (2011 census)
Literacy: definition: age 15 and over can read and write; total population: 98.4%; male: 98.7%; female: 98% (2011)
Health: life expectancy at birth: total population: 73.84 years; male: 70.24 years; female: 77.65 years (2012 est.); Infant mortality rate: total: 16.13 deaths/1,000 live births; male: 19.29 deaths/1,000 live births; female: 12.79 deaths/1,000 live births (2012 est.)
Unemployment rate: 9.9% (2012 est.)
Work force: 2.451 million (2012 est.)

Government

Type: parliamentary democracy
Independence: 3 March 1878
Constitution: adopted 12 July 1991
Political subdivisions: 28 provinces (oblasti, singular—oblast)
Suffrage: 18 years of age; universal

Economy

GDP (purchasing power parity): $$103.7 billion (2012 est.); 102.3 billion (2011 est.); $100.7 billion (2010 est.); $100.3 billion (2009 est.)
GDP real growth rate: 1% (2012 est.); 1.7% (2011 est.); 0.4% (2010 est.); -5.5% (2009 est.)
GDP per capita (PPP): $14,200 (2012 est.); $13,800 (2011 est.); $13,400 (2010 est.); $13,300 (2009 est.)
Natural resources: bauxite, copper, lead, zinc, coal, timber, arable land
Agriculture products: vegetables, fruits, tobacco, wine, wheat, barley, sunflowers, sugar beets; livestock
Industries: electricity, gas, water; food, beverages, tobacco; machinery and equipment, base metals, chemical products, coke, refined petroleum, nuclear fuel
Exports: $27.67 billion (2012 est.); $28.12 billion (2011 est.); $20.6 billion (2010 est.)
Exports—commodities: clothing, footwear, iron and steel, machinery and equipment, fuels
Exports—partners: Germany 12.2%, Romania 9.8%, Italy 8.5%, Turkey 8.2%, Greece 7%, Belgium 5.1%, France 4.3% (2011)
Imports: $30.32 billion (2012 est.); $30.86 billion (2011 est.); $24.29 billion (2010 est.)
Imports—commodities: machinery and equipment; metals and ores; chemicals and plastics; fuels, minerals, and raw materials
Imports—partners: Russia 18%, Germany 11%, Italy 7.3%, Romania 7%, Greece 5.7%, Turkey 4.6%, Spain 4.3%, Ukraine 4% (2011)
Debt—external: $43.24 billion (31 December 2012 est.); $46.84 billion (31 December 2011 est.)
Exchange rates: leva (BGN) per US dollar; 1.533 (2012 est.); 1.4065 (2011 est.); 1.4774 (2010 est.); 1.404 (2009); 1.3171 (2008); 1.4366 (2007)

GEOGRAPHY

Bulgaria shares a border with Turkey and Greece to the south, Macedonia and Serbia to the west, Romania to the north, and the Black Sea to the east. The capital, Sofia, lies in the western region of the country.

PEOPLE

National/Racial/Ethnic Minorities

Ethnic groups include Bulgarian, Turkish, Roma, and others.

According to the 2011 census, there were 325,345 Roma in the country, i.e., less than 5 percent of the population. Ethnic Turks numbered 588,318, or less than 9 percent of the population. Observers asserted that these figures were inaccurate, because more than 600,000 persons did not answer the census question about their ethnic origin, and officials did not conduct a proper count in most Romani communities but rather either made assumptions or failed to include them altogether.

Societal discrimination and popular prejudice against Roma and other minority groups remained a problem, and there were incidents of violence between members of different ethnic groups.

Langauge

Bulgarian is a Slavic language that uses the Cyrillic alphabet. In business, the usage of English is increasing rapidly. Many Bulgarians have some comprehension of the Russian language. German and French are also widely spoken.

Religion

According to the 2011 census, 76 percent of the population identifies itself as Orthodox Christian. Orthodox Christianity, Hanafi Sunni Islam, Judaism, and Roman Catholicism are generally understood as collectively holding a historic place in the country's culture. Muslims comprise the largest minority, estimated at 10 percent of the population. Groups that in total constitute about 2 percent of the population include Catholics, Armenian Christians, Jews, evangelical Protestants, and others. There are 114 registered religious groups in addition to the Bulgarian Orthodox Church (BOC).

Some religious minorities are concentrated geographically. The Rhodope Mountains (along the country's southern border with Greece) are home to many Muslims, including ethnic Turks, Roma, and "Pomaks" (descendants of Slavic Bulgarians who converted to Islam under Ottoman rule). Ethnic Turkish and Roma Muslims also live in large numbers in the northeast and along the Black Sea coast. Nearly 40 percent of the country's Catholics are located in and around Plovdiv. The majority of the small Jewish community lives in Sofia and along the Black Sea coast. Protestants are more widely dispersed throughout the country but are more numerous in areas with large Roma populations.

HISTORY

Ancient Thrace was partially located on the territory of modern Bulgaria, and Thracian culture provides a wealth of archeological sites within Bulgaria. In the second century A.D., the Bulgars came to Europe from their old homeland, the Kingdom of Balhara situated in the Mount Imeon area (present Hindu Kush in northern Afghanistan).

The first Bulgarian state was established in 635 A.D., located along the north coast of the Black Sea. In 681 A.D. the first Bulgarian state on the territory of modern Bulgaria was founded. This state consisted of a mixture of Slav and Bulgar peoples. In 864, Bulgaria adopted Orthodox Christianity. The First Bulgarian Kingdom, considered to be Bulgaria's "Golden Age," emerged under Tsar Simeon I in 893-927. During this time, Bulgarian art and literature flourished. Followers of Saints Cyril and Methodius are believed to have developed the Cyrillic alphabet in Bulgaria in the early 10th century.

In 1018, the Byzantine Empire conquered Bulgaria. In 1185 the Bulgarians broke free of Byzantine rule and established the Second Bulgarian Kingdom. A number of Bulgaria's famous monasteries were founded during this period. Following the 1242 Mongol invasion, this kingdom began losing territory to its neighbors. Ottoman expansion into the Balkan Peninsula eventually reached Bulgaria, and in 1396 Bulgaria became part of the Ottoman Empire. During the 5 centuries of Ottoman rule, most of Bulgaria's indigenous cultural centers were destroyed. Several Bulgarian uprisings were brutally suppressed and a great many people fled abroad. The April uprising of 1876, the Russo-Turkish War (1877–78), and the Treaty of San Stefano (March 3, 1878, the date of Bulgaria's national holiday), began Bulgaria's liberation from the Ottoman Empire, but complete independence was not recognized until 1908.

During the first half of the 20th century, Bulgaria was marred by social and political unrest. Bulgaria participated in the First and Second Balkan Wars (1912 and 1913) and sided with the Central Powers, and later the Axis Powers, during the two World Wars. Although allied with Germany during World War II, Bulgaria never declared war on the Soviet Union and never sent troops abroad to fight under Nazi command. Near the end of World War II, Bulgaria changed sides to fight the German army all the way to Austria; 30,000 Bulgarian troops were killed.

Bulgaria had a mixed record during World War II, when it was allied with Nazi Germany under a March 1941 agreement. The Law for the Protection of the Nation, enacted in January 1941, divested Jews of property, livelihood, civil rights, and personal security. Despite a February 1943 agreement requiring Bulgaria to transfer Bulgaria's Jews to Nazi extermination camps in Poland, Bulgaria did not actually deport any Bulgarian Jews or Roma to Nazi

concentration camps. Under that agreement, however, Bulgarian forces transferred approximately 11,000 Jews from Bulgarian-occupied territory (Thrace and Macedonia) to Nazi concentration camps.

In June 1943 the government "re-settled" Sofia's 25,000 Jews to rural areas. Tsar Boris—supported by the parliament (especially its prominent Deputy Speaker, Dimitar Peshev), the Orthodox Church, and the general public—aided the Jewish community and helped its 50,000 members survive the war, despite harsh conditions. The Bulgarian Jews remained safe, and when they were permitted to emigrate to Israel after the war, most of them did.

King Simeon II assumed control of the throne in 1943 at the age of six following the death of his father Boris III. With the entry of Soviet troops into Bulgaria in September 1944 and the defeat of the Axis Powers in World War II, communism emerged as the dominant political force within Bulgaria. Simeon, who later returned and served as Prime Minister, was forced into exile in 1946 and resided primarily in Madrid, Spain. By 1946, Bulgaria had become a satellite of the Soviet Union, remaining so throughout the Cold War period. Todor Zhivkov, the head of the Bulgarian Communist Party, ruled the country for much of this period. During his 27 years as leader of Bulgaria, democratic opposition was crushed; agriculture was collectivized and industry was nationalized; and the Bulgarian Orthodox Church fell under the control of the state.

In 1989, Zhivkov was removed from power, and democratic change began. The first multi-party elections since World War II were held in 1990. The ruling communist party changed its name to the Bulgarian Socialist Party and won the June 1990 elections. Following a period of social unrest and passage of a new constitution, the first fully democratic parliamentary elections were held in 1991 in which the Union of Democratic Forces won. The first direct presidential elections were held the next year.

As Bulgaria emerged from the throes of communism, it experienced a period of social and economic turmoil that culminated in a severe economic and financial crisis in late 1996–early 1997. With the help of the international community, former Prime Minister Ivan Kostov initiated a series of reforms in 1997 that helped stabilize the country's economy and put Bulgaria on the Euro-Atlantic path. Elections in 2001 ushered in a new government and president. In July 2001, Bulgaria's ex-king Simeon Saxe-Coburg-Gotha became the first former monarch in post-communist Eastern Europe to become Prime Minister. His government continued to pursue Euro-Atlantic integration, democratic reform, and development of a market economy. Bulgaria became a member of the North Atlantic Treaty Organization on March 29, 2004, and a member of the European Union (EU) on January 1, 2007.

Following June 2005 general elections, Sergei Stanishev of the Bulgarian Socialist Party became the new Prime Minister of a coalition government on August 16, 2005. In October 2006, Georgi Parvanov, the former leader of the Bulgarian Socialist Party, became the first Bulgarian president to win re-election. Despite his limited constitutional powers, President Parvanov played an important role in helping to ensure a consistent, pro-Western foreign policy. The Stanishev government continued Bulgaria's integration with the Euro-Atlantic world and its close partnership with the United States. Bulgaria has attracted large amounts of American and European investment, and is an active partner in coalition operations in Afghanistan as well as in UN-led peacekeeping operations in the Balkans.

In the July 2009 general elections, Bulgarian voters punished the Socialist-led government for corruption scandals and frozen EU funds. Citizens for the European Development of Bulgaria (GERB) took 116 of 240 seats in parliament, and its leader (and former Sofia mayor) Boyko Borissov became the Prime Minister. Borissov formed a minority government supported by the Blue Coalition, ATAKA, and Order, Law, Justice (RZS), but in the course of its second year in office, these parties gradually withdrew their support for GERB. The government's priorities include: promoting economic stability, unblocking the frozen EU funds, and fighting corruption.

GOVERNMENT AND POLITICAL CONDITIONS

The Republic of Bulgaria is a parliamentary democracy. The constitution vests legislative authority in the unicameral National Assembly (Narodno Sabranie). A minority government headed by a prime minister led the country. Observers characterized the 2011 presidential elections as reflecting "a respect for fundamental rights and freedoms," but they also noted reports of vote buying and organizational weaknesses.

Recent Elections

Despite a new electoral code, concerns about the effectiveness of law enforcement and the judiciary, and allegations of vote-buying which negatively affected the election environment, observers widely regarded the results of the 2011 local and presidential elections free and fair. The final report of the Limited Election Observation Mission of OSCE's Office for Democratic Institutions and Human Rights (ODIHR) found the election generally was conducted in accordance with OSCE commitments and Council of Europe standards.

The law prohibits campaigning in languages other than Bulgarian. In its report on the 2009 elections, ODIHR noted that this requirement, as well as the absence of official voter information in minority languages, limited the ability of some members of the Romani and Turkish minority groups to understand the election rules and to participate effectively in the election process.

Political Parties: The law requires a political party to have 2,500 members to register officially. Voters of Romani or Turkish origin were legally limited in that the constitution does not allow for the establishment of political parties along ethnic lines. In practice this prohibition did not appear to weaken the role of some ethnic minorities in the political process, and a number of parties represented various ethnic minority groups.

Participation of Women and Minorities: There were 57 women in the 240-seat National Assembly. There were three female ministers out of 16 ministers in total. Women held key positions in the National Assembly, including those of speaker of the assembly, one deputy speaker, and chairmen of seven of the 20 standing committees.

There were 28 members of minority groups (27 ethnic Turks and one Rom) in the National Assembly. There was one ethnic Turkish minister in the cabinet. While the ethnic Turkish minority was well represented, Roma were underrepresented, particularly in appointed leadership positions. Pomaks (ethnic Bulgarians who are Muslims) held elected positions at the local level.

Principal Government Officials

Last Updated: 1/31/2013

Pres.: **Rosen PLEVNELIEV**
Vice Pres.: **Margarita POPOVA**
Prime Min.: **Boyko BORISOV**
Dep. Prime Min.: **Simeon DJANKOV**
Dep. Prime Min.: **Tsvetan TSVETANOV**
Min. of Agriculture & Forestry: **Miroslav NAYDENOV**
Min. of Culture: **Vezhdi RASHIDOV**
Min. of Defense: **Anyu ANGELOV**

Min. of Economy, Energy, & Tourism: **Delyan DOBREV**
Min. of Education & Science: **Sergey IGNATOV**
Min. of Environment & Waters: **Nona KARADZHOVA**
Min. of EU Funds: **Tomislav DONCHEV**
Min. of Finance: **Simeon DJANKOV**
Min. of Foreign Affairs: **Nikolay MLADENOV**
Min. of Health: **Desislava ATANASOVA**
Min. of Interior: **Tsvetan TSVETANOV**
Min. of Justice: **Diana KOVACHEVA**
Min. of Labor & Social Policy: **Totyu MLADENOV**
Min. of Physical Education & Sports: **Svilen NEIKOV**
Min. of Regional Development & Public Works: **Lilyana PAVLOVA**
Min. of Transport, Information Technology, & Communications: **Ivaylo MOSKOVSKI**
Chmn., Bulgarian National Bank: **Ivan ISKROV**
Ambassador to the US: **Elena POPTODOROVA**
Permanent Representative to the UN, New York: **Stephan TAFROV**

ECONOMY

Bulgaria, a former Communist country that entered the EU on 1 January 2007, averaged more than 6% annual growth from 2004 to 2008, driven by significant amounts of bank lending, consumption, and foreign direct investment. Successive governments have demonstrated a commitment to economic reforms and responsible fiscal planning, but the global downturn sharply reduced domestic demand, exports, capital inflows, and industrial production. GDP contracted by 5.5% in 2009, stagnated in 2010, despite a significant recovery in exports, and grew approximately 2.2% in 2011.

Despite having a favorable investment regime, including low, flat corporate income taxes, significant challenges remain. Corruption in public administration, a weak judiciary, and the presence of organized crime continue to hamper the country's investment climate and economic prospects.

Labor Conditions

The law sets the minimum age for employment at 16 and the minimum age for dangerous work at 18. To employ children under the age of 18, employers must obtain a work permit from the General Labor Inspectorate of the Ministry of Labor and Social Policy. Employers can hire children under the age of 16 with special permits for light work that is not risky or harmful to the child's development and that does not interfere with the child's education or training.

Employment of children without a work permit is a criminal offense and entails a punishment of up to six months in prison. Child labor laws generally were enforced well in the formal sector, but NGOs reported that children were exploited in certain industries (particularly small family-owned shops, textile production, restaurants, construction businesses, and periodical sales) and by organized crime (notably for prostitution, pickpocketing, and the distribution of narcotics). Besides child sex trafficking, the worst forms of child labor included heavy physical labor and labor on family tobacco farms, a significant health hazard.

The national minimum wage was 270 levs ($180) per month. The poverty income level as of October, according to the trade unions, was 198.48 levs ($132.67), up 7.2 percent compared with June 2010. In November the government set the poverty line at 236 levs ($158).

The law provides for a standard workweek of 40 hours with at least one 24-hour rest period per week; the law prohibits excessive compulsory overtime. The law prohibits overtime work for children under age 18, pregnant women, and women with children up to age six. The law stipulates that the pay premium for overtime cannot be less than 150 percent during workdays, 175 percent during weekends, and 200 percent during 12 official holidays. With a significant grey market economy, many informal workers are not covered by legal protections or government inspections.

U.S.-BULGARIAN RELATIONS

The United States established diplomatic relations with Bulgaria in 1903. A Consular Agency was established in Sofia on January 12, 1912. It reported to the Consulate General in Bucharest. The first American Consular Agent in Bulgaria was actually a Bulgarian national, Asen Kermekchiev (later Ace Kermek), a businessman, physician, and journalist. Kermekchiev served the United States Government even while working as a field doctor for Bulgaria in the First Balkan War, and was praised for protecting American lives and property while at the front. He also founded the first American Chamber of Commerce in Sofia. Bulgaria was allied with Germany in World War II, and became a satellite of the Soviet Union at the war's end. As Bulgaria emerged from communism in the 1990s, the United States moved to encourage development of multi-party democracy and a market economy.

Bulgaria is a reliable ally in an area of strategic importance to the United States. The U.S.-Bulgarian Defense Cooperation Agreement gives the United States military access to and shared use of several Bulgarian military facilities. The access facilitates joint training between the U.S. military and the Bulgarian and Romanian militaries. Bulgaria has participated in North Atlantic Treaty Organization (NATO), European Union (EU), and coalition operations, including in Libya, Iraq, Afghanistan, Kosovo, and Bosnia. We work closely with the government of Bulgaria in strengthening the rule of law and have strong cooperation in law enforcement.

On any given day, there are approximately 7,000 Americans in Bulgaria. In 2011, approximately 5,900 Bulgarians visited the United States. The American University of Bulgaria in Blagoevgrad draws students from throughout southeast Europe and beyond, and is the only U.S.-accredited university in the region.

U.S. Assistance to Bulgaria

U.S. Government investment in modernization and NATO interoperability for Bulgaria's military helps create stronger, more effective Bulgarian military units that can deploy alongside U.S. forces when needed.

Bilateral Economic Relations

Bulgaria is a member of the European Union. Upon its accession to the EU, the country adopted regulations and standards that conform to EU norms. U.S. companies conduct business across the major industry sectors, and the business climate is generally positive.

The top foreign investor in Bulgaria is a U.S. company. The United States and Bulgaria have a treaty on avoidance of double taxation and a bilateral investment treaty. U.S. citizens traveling on a U.S. passport for business or tourism purposes can enter and stay in Bulgaria for up to 90 days in a 6-month period without requiring issuance of a visa.

Bulgaria's Membership in International Organizations

Bulgaria and the United States belong to a number of the same international organizations, including the United Nations, North Atlantic Treaty Organization, Euro-Atlantic Partnership Council, Organization for Security and Cooperation in Europe, International Monetary Fund, World Bank, and World Trade Organization. Bulgaria also is an observer to the Organization of American States.

Bilateral Representation

Bulgaria maintains an embassy in the United States at 1621 22nd Street, NW, Washington DC 20008 (tel. 202-387-0174).

Principal U.S. Embassy Officials

Last Updated: 1/14/2013

SOFIA (E) 16 Kozyak Street, 1408 Sofia, Bulgaria, (359) (2) 937-5100, Fax 939-5790/GSO; 937-5231/HR, INMARSAT Tel 683-13-1345;683-13-1346, Workweek: M-F 07:00–19:00, http://bulgaria.usembassy.gov/

DCM OMS:	Sarah Madrid
AMB OMS:	Nicole Mock
DHS/CIS:	Marla Belvedere (Resident Vienna)
DHS/ICE:	James Plitt (Vienna)
FCS:	Barbara Lapini
FM:	Walter O'Banion
HRO:	Margaret Genco
MGT:	Andrew Siegel
MLO/ODC:	CDR Mark Imblum
POL/ECON:	Rebecca Dunham
POL/MIL:	Joseph J. Fitzgerald
POSHO:	Walter O'Banion
SDO/DATT:	COL Ray Schultz
AMB:	Marcie B. Ries
CG:	Deborah Campbell
DCM:	Bryan Dalton
PAO:	Elizabeth Fitzsimmons
GSO:	Glenn Tosten, Karlene Frelich
RSO:	Seth Green
AGR:	Michael Henney (Based In Warsaw, Poland)
CLO:	Catherine Siegel, Greg Dix
DEA:	Sheila Lyons
EEO:	Kristen Stolt
FMO:	Margaret Genco
IMO:	James Keller
IRS:	Kathy Beck (Resident Paris)
ISO:	John Miller
ISSO:	James Keller
LEGATT:	Timothy Langan Jr..
State ICASS:	Deborah Campbell

TRAVEL

Consular Information Sheet

November 7, 2011

Country Description: After joining the European Union in 2007, Bulgaria experienced rapid economic development, especially in urban and resort areas. However, since a recession during the 2008 financial crisis, growth continues at a slower pace. Tourist facilities are widely available, although conditions vary and some facilities, infrastructure, and services may not be up to Western standards.

Smart Traveler Enrollment Program (STEP)/Embassy Locations: If you are going to live or visit Bulgaria, please take the time to tell our Embassy about your trip. If you enroll in the Smart Traveler Enrollment Program, we can keep you up to date with important safety and security announcements, and help your friends and family get in touch with you in an emergency.

U.S. Embassy Sofia
16, Kozyak St., Sofia1408;
tel.: (359 2) 937-5100;
fax: (359 2) 937-5209;
Non-immigrant Visa Matters: NIV_Sofia@state.gov
Immigrant Visa Matters: IV_Sofia@gov
American Citizen Services Matters: ACS_Sofia@state.gov

Entry/Exit Requirements for U.S. Citizens: A U.S. passport is required for U.S. citizens who are not Bulgarian nationals. As a U.S. citizen, you are authorized to stay for a total of 90 days within a six-month period without a Bulgarian visa. This law is strictly enforced. You can file an application to extend your stay beyond the original 90 days for urgent or humanitarian reasons, but the application must be submitted to regional police authorities no later than five days prior to the end of the original 90-day period. Travelers who have been in the country for 90 days and then leave will not be able to re-enter Bulgaria before the six-month period expires. Travelers using official or diplomatic passports must secure visas prior to arrival. Please plan and apply for your visa early. Upon entering the country, Bulgarian immigration authorities request that all foreigners declare the purpose of their visit and provide their intended address. For further information on entry and exit requirements, contact the Embassy of the Republic of Bulgaria at 1621 22nd Street NW, Washington, DC 20008; tel. (202) 387-7969 (main switchboard (202) 387-0174), or the Bulgarian Consulate in New York City at 121 East 62nd Street,

New York, NY 10021; tel. (212) 935-4646. If you intend to live or work in Bulgaria for more than 90 days within six months (or more than six months within a year), you must obtain a "D" visa prior to arrival. As of July 2008, U.S. citizens must apply for a "D" visa at a Bulgarian Embassy/Consulate in the country where they are legally resident. If you wish to obtain a "D" visa while already present in Bulgaria — having entered as a tourist, for example — you will have to leave Bulgaria and apply at a Bulgarian embassy or consulate in the United States. U.S. citizens residing in the United States should apply at the Bulgarian representative office (either the Embassy or a Consulate) nearest their home. Visit the Bulgarian Ministry of Foreign Affairs or Bulgarian Embassies/Consulates websites for more information on visas. The U.S. Embassy in Sofia also has entry requirements and the "D" visa application online. Bulgarian authorities do not consider presentation of a copy of the passport sufficient for identification purposes. Visitors should carry their original passports with them at all times; however, this is not a requirement for U.S. citizens who hold residence permits in Bulgaria. A U.S. passport card is also recognized as a proof of citizenship and identity, but is not accepted for use for international air travel to and from Bulgaria.

Traveling with Bulgarian Citizen Minors: Bulgarian authorities are particularly strict in matters involving the travel of Bulgarian children. If a dual or multi-national Bulgarian child is traveling out of Bulgaria with only one parent or another adult, the absent parent(s) must sign a certified/legalized declaration authorizing custody for travel purposes. This declaration must be presented to authorities upon departure. If the declaration is signed in Bulgaria, certification by a Bulgarian notary public is required. If signed in the United States, the declaration must be certified by a notary public and the court in the jurisdiction where the notary is licensed. The declaration must then be legalized with an apostille issued by the individual state's Secretary of State or Governor's office, and a Bulgarian translation by a licensed translation company to be certified by the Bulgarian Ministry of Foreign Affairs. Please note Bulgarian authorities do not require such documentation for minors who are not Bulgarian. However, in cases of minor children who do not have Bulgarian citizenship but, one or both parents are Bulgarian citizens, migration officials may request a certified/legalized declaration authorizing custody for travel purposes. We are unaware of any HIV/AIDS entry restrictions for visitors to or foreign residents of Bulgaria.

Threats to Safety and Security: While Bulgaria's accession to the European Union has enhanced the overall security environment for tourist and business travelers, violence related to criminal groups occurs sporadically in public locations. Recent incidents include bombings and shootings, likely the result of turf wars between rival organized crime syndicates, which remain highly prevalent in Bulgaria's largely cash economy. In January 2010, a journalist who had published a book containing details on Bulgarian organized crime was assassinated in Sofia in daylight hours. Public protests, demonstrations, and strikes in response to world or local events can occur sporadically.

Traffic disruptions in Bulgaria, particularly in the central city, have occurred as a result of demonstrations. While these demonstrations are normally peaceful, confrontational demonstrations have occurred, and even demonstrations intended to be peaceful can turn confrontational and possibly escalate into violence. Nationwide demonstrations in October 2011 resulted in some violence and destruction of property. You are urged to avoid demonstration areas if possible, and to exercise caution if traveling within the vicinity of any demonstrations. You should monitor media coverage to stay abreast of local events and should be aware of your surroundings at all times. Information regarding demonstrations in Bulgaria can be found on the Embassy website.

Stay up to date by:

- Bookmarking our Bureau of Consular Affairs website, which contains the current Travel Warnings and Travel Alerts as well as the Worldwide Caution;
- Following us on Twitter and the Bureau of Consular Affairs page on Facebook; Downloading our free Smart Traveler iPhone App to have travel information at your fingertips;
- Calling 1-888-407-4747 toll-free within the U.S. and Canada, or a regular toll line, 1-202-501-4444, from other countries; and
- Taking some time before travel to consider your personal security.

Crime: Pick-pocketing and purse snatching are frequent occurrences, especially in crowded markets, on shopping streets, and aboard the busiest tram and bus lines. Con artists operate on public transportation and in bus and train stations. Credit cards and ATMs should be used with caution. Be wary of people who approach you at an ATM and offer assistance. Do not give your PIN to anyone under any circumstances.Travelers should be suspicious of "instant friends" and should also require persons claiming to be government officials to show identification. We recommend that you report crimes immediately to the police, as they have helped recover money and valuables on more than one occasion. To avoid becoming a victim of more serious crimes, use the same personal safety precautions that you would use in large urban areas of the United States. You should pay special attention to the drink prices at high-end bars and nightclubs. There have been instances of travelers being charged exorbitant prices, especially for champagne and hard alcohol. Bills have been as high as several thousand dollars for drinks, and in some establishments the management may use force to secure payment.

Taxi drivers occasionally overcharge unwary travelers, particularly at

Sofia Airport and the Central Train Station. We recommend that you use taxis with meters and clearly marked rates displayed on a sticker on the passenger side of the windshield. The standard rates normally range between BGL 0.59 and 0.70 (about 40 U.S. cents) per kilometer. Some taxis charged BGL 6.59 or 6.70 (about $5) per kilometer. However, because these exorbitant prices were clearly displayed on the taxi, there was no current law being violated. A recent law established the maximum amount a taxi can charge per kilometer; however, it is a new law, and enforcement is still sporadic. At the airport, there is a clearly marked booth within the arrival terminal, which arranges for metered taxis at a fair rate; finding reputable taxis at the Central Train Station is more difficult. We recommend inquiring about the fare first, to avoid excessive payment if a metered taxi cannot be found. Always ensure that you account for all luggage, packages, and hand-carried items before you pay and release a taxi. The likelihood of retrieving articles left behind in a taxi is remote.

Automobile theft is a concern, with four-wheel-drive vehicles and late-model European sedans being the most popular targets. Very few vehicles are recovered. Automobile break-ins are common in residential areas or near parks, especially when valuables are left in plain sight. Residential burglaries are also a frequent occurrence as in any major city. If you plan to reside in Bulgaria on a long-term basis, you should take measures to protect your dwelling and should consider installation of window grills, steel doors with well-functioning locks, and an alarm system. You should also be cautious about making credit card charges over the Internet to unfamiliar websites. Recent experience has shown that offers for merchandise and services may be scam artists posing as legitimate businesses. A recent example involves Internet credit card payments to alleged tour operators via Bulgaria-based websites. In several cases, the corresponding businesses did not actually exist. Don't buy counterfeit and pirated goods, even if they are widely available. Not only are the bootlegs illegal to bring back into the United States, if you purchase them you may also be breaking local law.

Victims of Crime: If you or someone you know becomes the victim of a crime abroad, you should contact the local police and the Embassy. We can:

- Replace a stolen passport;
- Help you find appropriate medical care if you are the victim of violent crimes such as assault or rape;
- Put you in contact with the appropriate police authorities, and if you want us to, we can contact family members or friend; and
- Help you understand the local criminal justice process and direct you to local attorneys, although it is important to remember that local authorities are responsible for investigating and prosecuting the crime.

You must also report a lost/stolen passport to the Bulgarian migration authorities located at 48, Maria Luisa in Sofia or the local police station if you are in the countryside. Emergency services, including police, fire or ambulance services, are reached by dialing 112, the local equivalent to 911 in the U.S.

Criminal Penalties: While in Bulgaria, you are subject to its laws and regulations, which sometimes differ significantly from those in the United States and may not afford the protections available to an individual under U.S. law. Penalties for breaking the law can be more severe than in the United States for similar offenses. Engaging in sexual conduct with children or using or disseminating child pornography in a foreign country is a crime prosecutable in the United States. You may be taken in for questioning if you don't have your passport, U.S. passport card, or long-term residence card with you.

Penalties for possessing, using, or trafficking in illegal drugs in Bulgaria are severe, and convicted offenders can expect long jail sentences and heavy fines. While some countries will automatically notify the nearest U.S. embassy or consulate if a U.S. citizen is detained or arrested in a foreign country, that might not always be the case. To ensure that the United States is aware of your circumstances, request that the police and prison officials notify the nearest U.S. embassy or consulate as soon as you are arrested or detained overseas.

Special Circumstances: Bulgaria is still largely a cash economy. Due to the potential for fraud and other criminal activity, credit cards should be used sparingly and with extreme caution. Skimming devices, surreptitiously attached to ATMs by criminals, are used to capture cards and PINs for later criminal use, including unauthorized charges or withdrawals, and are common in Bulgaria. If you choose to use credit cards, we recommend you use ATMs located in banks or malls as opposed to the more vulnerable locations on the street. You should check your account status regularly to ensure its integrity. In connection with such scams, be extremely wary of friendly bystanders near ATMs who offer assistance. Any time a card is not returned, you should immediately report the card as lost/stolen to the card-issuing company. You may exchange cash at banks or Exchange Bureaus, but should know that Exchange Bureaus sometimes post misleading rate quotations that confuse travelers. People on the street who offer high rates of exchange are usually con artists intent on swindling unwary travelers. Damaged or very worn U.S. dollar bank notes are often not accepted at banks or Exchange Bureaus. Major branches of the following Bulgarian banks will cash travelers' checks on the spot for Leva, the Bulgarian currency, or another desired currency: Unicredit Bulbank, Bulgarian Postbank, First Investment Bank, and United Bulgarian Bank (UBB). UBB also serves as a Western Union agent and provides direct transfer of money. There are also many Western Union branches in major towns and cities. Most shops, hotels, and restaurants, with the exception of the major hotels, do not accept travelers' checks or credit cards. Only some local banks can cash U.S. Treasury checks and the payee may need to wait up to a month to receive funds. Corruption remains an important concern of the Bulgarian government. The Commission for Coordinating of the Activity for Combating Corruption manages the efforts of each government agency's internal inspectorate in fighting public corruption and engages in public awareness campaigns. Complaints of public corruption can be made by mail to the Ministry of Finance, 2A Knyaz Dondukov Blvd., 1055 Sofia, Bulgaria and 1 Slavyanska St., 1000 Sofia, 359 2 987 06 97; or to the Ministry of Finance by phone at 080018018. For more information, visit Ministry of Justice web site or by email form. If you are planning to import an automobile to Bulgaria, be aware that customs duties on personal automobiles can be high.

Accessibility: While in Bulgaria, individuals with disabilities may find accessibility and accommodation very different from what is found in the United States. The law requires improved access to buildings for persons with disabilities, and new public works projects take this requirement into account; however, enforcement of this law lags in existing, unrenovated buildings. Bulgarian law prohibits discrimination against persons with physical and mental disabilities in employment, education, access to health care, and the provision of other state services; however, the government does not effectively enforce these provisions in practice. Societal discrimination against persons with disabilities persists. Public transportation and general commuting in Sofia or around Bulgaria is nearly impossible for disabled individuals. Buses, trams, and trolleys are generally old and extremely crowded, and lack facilities for disabled travelers. Some newer vehicles claim to have access for disabled individuals, but in reality, access is extremely limited and disabled travelers must rely on fellow passengers to help them on and off the vehicles. The Sofia metro is the most accessible system for disabled individuals, but its reach is limited in the city until a planned extension is completed. Disabled travelers should consider traveling with a friend or family member who can assist them in navigating the transportation systems in Bulgaria.

Medical Facilities and Health Information: While Bulgarian physicians are trained to a very high standard, most hospitals and clinics, especially in village areas, are generally not equipped and maintained to meet U.S. or Western European standards. Basic medical supplies and over-the-counter and prescription medications are widely available, but highly specialized treatment may not be obtainable. Pediatric facilities are in need of funding and lack equipment. Serious medical problems requiring hospitalization and/or medical evacuation to the United States may cost thousands of dollars. Doctors and hospitals often expect immediate cash payment for health services. A list of hospitals and physicians in Bulgaria can be found on the U.S. Embassy's website. You can find good information on vaccinations and other health precautions on the Centers for Disease Control and Prevention's (CDC) website. For information about outbreaks of infectious diseases abroad, consult the World Health Organization (WHO) website, which also contains additional health information for travelers, including detailed country-specific health information.

Medical Insurance: If you are traveling to Bulgaria, be prepared to present valid evidence of health insurance to the Bulgarian border authorities in order to be admitted into the country. The insurance should be valid for the duration of the traveler's stay in Bulgaria. It's very important to find out BEFORE you leave. You need to ask your insurance company two questions:

- Does my policy apply when I'm out of the U.S.?
- Will it cover emergencies like a trip to a foreign hospital or an evacuation?

In many places, doctors and hospitals still expect payment in cash at the time of service. Your regular U.S. health insurance may not cover doctor and hospital visits in other countries. If your policy doesn't go with you when you travel, it's a very good idea to take out another one for your trip.

Traffic Safety and Road Conditions: While in a foreign country, U.S. citizens may encounter road conditions that differ significantly from those in the United States. The Bulgarian road system is largely underdeveloped. There are few sections of limited-access divided highway. Some roads are in poor repair and full of potholes. Rockslides and landslides may be encountered on roads in mountainous areas. Livestock and animal-drawn carts present road hazards throughout the country, especially during the agricultural season. Travel conditions deteriorate during the winter as roads become icy and potholes proliferate. The U.S. Embassy in Sofia advises against driving at night because such road conditions are more dangerous in the dark. Some roads lack pavement markings and lights, and motorists often drive with dim or missing headlights.

Driving in Bulgaria is extremely dangerous. Aggressive driving habits, the lack of safe infrastructure, and a mixture of late model and old model cars on the country's highways contribute to a high fatality rate for road accidents. Motorists should avoid confrontations with aggressive drivers in Bulgaria. In particular, drivers of late-model sedans are known to speed and drive dangerously. Motorists should exercise caution and avoid altercations with the drivers of such vehicles, which may be driven by armed organized crime figures. In some cities, traffic lights late at night blink yellow in all directions, leaving right-of-way unclear and contributing to frequent accidents. A form of "Russian road roulette" has taken hold in Sofia wherein drivers make bets about speeding through red lights at speeds that exceed 120mph in the late hours of the evening; bets are also taken challenging drivers to go the wrong way around roundabouts at high speeds. Heavy truck traffic along the two-lane routes from the Greek border at Kulata to Sofia, and from the Turkish border at Kapitan Andre to Plovdiv, creates numerous hazards. Motorists should expect long delays at border crossings. A U.S. state driver's license is valid in Bulgaria only when used in conjunction with an International Driving Permit. For information on how to obtain a permit, http://www.bulgariatravel.org/eng/index.php please see our Road Safety Overseas information. If pulled over by a police officer, you should be aware that under a recently changed Bulgarian law police officers may collect fines on the spot, and may confiscate your driver's license depending upon the offense.

The use of seat belts is mandatory in Bulgaria for all passengers, except pregnant women. Children under 12 years of age may ride in the front seat only if seated in a child car seat. In practice, these rules are often not followed. Speed limits are 50 km/h (31 mph) in the cities/towns, 90 km/h (56 mph) out of town, and 130 km/h (80 mph) on the highways. For motorcycles, speed limits are 50 km/h in the cities/towns, 80 km/h out of town, and 100 km/h on the highways. Motorcyclists must drive with helmets and with lights on at all times. At crossings that are not regulated, the driver who is on the right has the right-of-way, but this rule is frequently ignored. Drivers may be charged with driving under the influence of alcohol with a blood level as low as 0.05 percent. Right turns on red lights are not permitted unless specifically authorized. The penalties for drivers involved in an accident resulting in injury or death range from a US $25 fine up to imprisonment for life. A new law requires the use of headlights day and night from November 1st through March 31st. In case of emergency, drivers should call 112 (equivalent to 911 in the U.S.). For specific information concerning Bulgarian driving permits, vehicle inspection, road tax, and mandatory insurance, please visit the Bulgarian Embassy website.

Aviation Safety Oversight: The U.S. Federal Aviation Administration (FAA) has assessed the government of Bulgaria's Civil Aviation Authority as being in compliance with International Civil Aviation Organization (ICAO) aviation safety standards for oversight of Bulgaria's air carrier operations. Further information may be found on the FAA's safety assessment page.

Children's Issues: Please see the U.S. Dept. of State Office of Children's Issues web pages on intercountry adoption and international parental child abduction.

Intercountry Adoption

November 2008

The information in this section has been edited from the latest report available as of February 2013 from the State Department Bureau of Consular Affairs, Office of Overseas Citizens Services. For more information, please read the *Intercountry Adoption* section of this book and review current reports online at http://adoption.state.gov.

Bulgaria is party to The Hague Convention on Protection of Children and Co-operation in Respect of Intercountry Adoption (Hague Adoption Convention). Therefore all adoptions between Bulgaria and the United States must meet the requirements of the Convention and United States law implementing the Convention. For more detailed and updated information on these requirements, please review the *Intercountry Adoption* section of this publication and visit the USCIS Intercountry Adoption website at http://adoption.state.gov.

Who Can Adopt? Adoption between the United States and Bulgaria is governed by The Hague Adoption Convention. Therefore to adopt from Bulgaria, you must first be found eligible to adopt by the United States Government. In addition to the United States requirements for prospective adoptive parents, Bulgaria also has the following requirements for prospective adoptive parents.

Residency Requirements: There are no residency requirements to complete an intercountry adoption in Bulgaria. However, prospective adoptive parents are expected to spend five days with their adoptive child before the orphanage director will release the child.

Age Requirements: Prospective adoptive parents must be at least 15 years older than their adoptive children, but no more than forty-five years older.

Marriage Requirements: Prospective adoptive parents may be married or single.

Who Can Be Adopted? Because Bulgaria is party to The Hague Adoption Convention, children from Bulgaria must meet the requirements of the Convention in order to be eligible for adoption. In addition to Bulgaria's requirements, a child must meet the definition of a Convention adoptee for you to bring him or her back to the United States.

Bulgarian Adoption Authority: Ministry of Justice

The Process: The first step in adopting a child from Bulgaria is to select an adoption service provider in the United States that has been accredited. Prospective adoptive parents also must use a Bulgarian-licensed United States adoption agency or a Bulgarian adoption agency accredited by the Bulgarian Ministry of Justice. The Ministry of Justice is currently reviewing license applications for several United States-based adoption agencies.

For a complete list of adoption agencies visit the web site of the U.S. Embassy in Sofiaat http://bulgaria.usembassy.gov. After you choose an accredited adoption service provider, you apply to be found eligible to adopt (Form I-800A) by the USCIS. Once the United States Government determines that you are "eligible" and "suitable" to adopt, you or your agency will forward your information to the adoption authority in Bulgaria.

Bulgaria's adoption authority will review your application to determine whether you are also eligible to adopt under Bulgarian law. After completing the United States pre-adoption requirements through USCIS, United States citizens specifically interested in pursuing an adoption from Bulgaria must also contact a Bulgarian or United States adoption agency which has been licensed by the Bulgarian Ministry of Justice. All required documents must be deposited at the Ministry of Justice by the accredited agency. If the prospective parent(s) application is accepted, their names are placed on a registry. Separately, the Bulgarian Ministry of Justice (MOJ) also maintains a registry of Bulgarian children eligible for intercountry adoption. Under Bulgarian law, a child may appear on this registry only if three Bulgarian families have declined to adopt him/her. If both the United States and Bulgaria determine that you are eligible to adopt, and a child is available for intercountry adoption, the central adoption authority in Bulgaria may provide you with a referral for a child.

The Bulgarian Government does not process prospective adoptive parents' applications in chronological order. Priority is given to persons willing to adopt a handicapped child. Furthermore, the Adoption Council abides very strictly by the principle that its goal is to find appropriate parents for a child in need, and not to find a child for prospective parents who want one. The Adoption Council within the Ministry of Justice reviews the registries of prospective parents and available children, including all relevant documentation, and proposes a match. The MOJ provides the adoptive parents through their accredited agency photographs of the child and information about his/her medical condition.

If the family declines to adopt a specific child, the Council should be informed within two months and a match with a different child will be offered. There is no limitation as to the number of times prospective adoptive parents may decline to adopt a Bulgarian orphan. The decision to decline is passed by prospective adoptive parents to the MOJ through the accredited adoption agency. It is important to note that if prospective adoptive parents decline to adopt a specific child, they must notify the MOJ within two months of the referral. Once the prospective adoptive parent(s) select a child and the Council approves the application, the case is forwarded to the Minister of Justice for final approval. When the Minister signs the parents' application, the paperwork is transferred directly to Sofia City Court, which sets a date for a court hearing.

The judges take into consideration the MOJ's referral and review the documentation related to the adoption process. If they require additional documents, the court sets a date for a new hearing. After all requirements have been met, the court grants custody of the child to the adoptive parents.

Time Frame: If there is a child available for intercountry adoption, it normally takes several months to complete the adoption process in Bulgaria; however, there are very few children on the waiting list, which means that the adoptive parents may wait many months and even years until the Ministry of Justice offers them a Bulgarian orphan for adoption.

Adoption Fees: The United States Embassy in Sofia is aware of the following Bulgarian fees for adoption. These fees are subject to change. All fees are given in Euros as the Bulgarian currency is linked to the Euro.

- Application fee at the MOJ: 100.00 EUR
- Court fee: 750 EUR
- Transcript of the Court Decree: 25 EUR
- Passport fee for child under 14: 7.00 EUR
- Passport fee for child over 14: 14.00 EUR
- Birth Certificate fee: 3.00 EUR

In the adoption services contract that you sign at the beginning of the adoption process, your agency will itemize the fees and estimated expenses related to your adoption process.

Documents Required:

- Application, including personal data, family history, financial information. The application is a letter prepared by the accredited adoption agency.
- Document certifying that the adoptive parent(s) has/have not been deprived of custody rights. An FBI fingerprint clearance shows whether there were prior arrests or criminal convictions which would render them ineligible to adopt a child in Bulgaria.
- Home Study.
- Medical Certificate (signed by a general practitioner).
- Police Certificate.
- Marriage Certificate (if applicable).
- Approval by the USCIS (I-171H).

All documents should be submitted should be originals. They must be translated and apostilled.

Bringing Your Child Home: Once your adoption is complete (or you have obtained legal custody of the child), there are a few more steps to take before you can head home. Specifically, you need to apply for several documents for your child before he or she can travel to the United States, such as a birth certificate, a passport or travel document for your child from the country in which he or she was born, and a U.S. Immigration Visa. For detailed and updated information on how to obtain these documents, visit the USCIS Intercountry Adoption website at http://adoption.state.gov.

Child Citizenship Act: For adoptions finalized abroad, the Child Citizenship Act of 2000 allows your new child to acquire American citizenship automatically when he or she enters the United States as lawful permanent residents. For adoptions finalized in the United States: The Child Citizenship Act of 2000 allows your new child to acquire American citizenship automatically when the court in the United States issues the final adoption decree.

To learn more, review the *Intercountry Adoption* section on this publication and visit the USCIS Intercountry Adoption website at http://adoption.state.gov.

After Adoption: Bulgaria requires adoptive parents to submit post adoption reports. We strongly urge you to comply with the wish of Bulgaria and complete all post-adoption requirements in a timely manner. Your adoption agency may be able to help you with this process. Your cooperation will contribute to Bulgaria's history of positive experiences with American parents.

United States Embassy in Bulgaria
16 Kozyak Street
Sofia 1407
Bulgaria
Tel: (359 2) 937-5100
e-mail: iv_sofia@state.gov
Internet:
http://bulgaria.usembassy.gov

Bulgarian Adoption Authority
Ministry of Justice
Slavyanska Street # 1, Sofia 1000
Tel: (359 2) 923-7303 (Bulgarian only)
http://www.mjeli.Government.bg/ (Bulgarian only)

Embassy of Bulgaria
1621 22nd Street, N.W.
Washington, D.C. 20008
Tel: 202-387-0174 (main)
Email: office@Bulgaria-Embassy.org,
http://www.bulgaria-embassy.org.

Office of Children's Issues
United States Department of State
2201 C Street, NW; SA-29
Washington, DC 20520
Tel: 1-888-407-4747
E-mail: AskCI@state.gov.
http://adoption.state.gov.

BURKINA FASO

Compiled from publications that were available as of February 2013 from the U.S. Department of State, the U.S. Department of Commerce, and the Central Intelligence Agency (CIA). See the introduction to this set for explanatory notes.

Official Name:
Burkina Faso

PROFILE

Geography

Area: total: 274,200 sq km; country comparison to the world: 75; land: 273,800 sq km; water: 400 sq km

Major cities: Ouagadougou (capital) 1.777 million (2009)

Climate: tropical; warm, dry winters; hot, wet summers

Terrain: mostly flat to dissected, undulating plains; hills in west and southeast

People

Nationality: noun: Burkinabe (singular and plural); adjective: Burkinabe

Population: 17,275,115 (July 2012 est.)

Population growth rate: 3.073% (2012 est.)

Ethnic groups: Mossi over 40%, other approximately 60% (includes Gurunsi, Senufo, Lobi, Bobo, Mande, and Fulani)

Religions: Muslim 60.5%, Catholic 19%, animist 15.3%, Protestant 4.2%, other 0.6%, none 0.4%

Languages: French (official), native African languages belonging to Sudanic family spoken by 90% of the population

Literacy: definition: age 15 and over can read and write; total population: 21.8%; male: 29.4%; female: 15.2% (2003 est.)

Health: life expectancy at birth: total population: 54.07 years; male: 52.09 years; female: 56.1 years (2012 est.); Infant mortality rate: total: 79.84 deaths/1,000 live births; male: 87.26 deaths/1,000 live births; female: 72.19 deaths/1,000 live births (2012 est.)

Unemployment rate: 77% (2004)

Work force: 6.668 million

Government

Type: parliamentary republic

Independence: 5 August 1960

Constitution: approved by referendum 2 June 1991; formally adopted 11 June 1991; last amended January 2002

Political subdivisions: 13 regions; Boucle du Mouhoun, Cascades, Centre, Centre-Est, Centre-Nord, Centre-Ouest, Centre-Sud, Est, Hauts-Bassins, Nord, Plateau-Central, Sahel, Sud-Ouest

Suffrage: 18 years of age; universal

Economy

GDP (purchasing power parity): $24.03 billion (2012 est.); $22.32 billion (2011 est.); $21.14 billion (2010 est.); $19.59 billion (2009 est.)

GDP real growth rate: 7% (2012 est.); 5.6% (2011 est.); 7.9% (2010 est.); 3.2% (2009 est.)

GDP per capita (PPP): $1,400 (2012 est.); $1,500 (2011 est.); $1,400 (2010 est.); $1,400 (2009 est.)

Natural resources: manganese, limestone, marble; small deposits of gold, phosphates, pumice, salt

Agriculture products: cotton, peanuts, shea nuts, sesame, sorghum, millet, corn, rice; livestock

Industries: cotton lint, beverages, agricultural processing, soap, cigarettes, textiles, gold

Exports: $2.734 billion (2012 est.); $2.173 billion (2011 est.); $1.417 billion (2010 est.)

Exports—commodities: gold, cotton, livestock

Exports—partners: China 22%, Turkey 17.7%, Singapore 8.8%, Indonesia 7%, Thailand 5.2% (2011)

Imports: $2.868 billion (2012 est.); $2.327 billion (2011 est.); $1.708 billion (2010 est.)

Imports—commodities: capital goods, foodstuffs, petroleum

Imports—partners: Cote dIvoire 16.4%, France 14.9%, Ghana 4.9%, Togo 4.6%, Belgium 4.1% (2011)

Debt—external: $2.442 billion (31 December 2012 est.); $2.335 billion (31 December 2011 est.); $2.053 billion (31 December 2010 est.)

Exchange rates: Communaute Financiere Africaine francs (XOF) per US dollar; 514.1 (2012 est.); 471.87 (2011 est.); 495.28 (2010 est.)

GEOGRAPHY

Burkina Faso is a landlocked country located in the middle of West Africa's "hump." It is geographically in the Sahel—the agricultural region between the Sahara Desert and the coastal rain forests. Most of central Burkina Faso lies on a savanna plateau, 200 meters-300 meters (650 ft.-1,000 ft.) above sea level, with fields, brush, and scattered trees. The largest river is the Mouhoun (Black Volta), which is partially navigable by small craft. Burkina Faso has West Africa's largest elephant population. Game preserves also are home to lions, hippos, monkeys, warthogs, and antelope.

Infrastructure and tourism are, however, not well developed. Annual average rainfall varies from about 100 centimeters (40 in.) in the south to less than 25 centimeters (10 in.) in the north and northeast, where hot desert winds accentuate the dryness of the region. The cooler season, November to February, is pleasantly warm and dry (but dusty), with cool evenings. March-June can be very hot. In July-September, the rains bring a 3-month cooler and greener humid season.

PEOPLE

Burkina Faso is an ethnically integrated, secular state. Burkina Faso's people belong to two major West African cultural groups—the Voltaic and the Mande (whose common language is Dioula).

The dominant ethnic group is the Mossi, with the Voltaic Mossi making up about one-half of the population. The Mossi claim descent from warriors who migrated to present-day Burkina Faso from Ghana and established an empire that lasted more than 800 years. The group is mainly farmers and is led by the Mogho Naba (emperor of the Mossi kingdom), whose court is in Ouagadougou. The Mogho Naba is a revered figure who speaks with greater moral authority than any other Burkinabe and plays an important, informal role in fostering national harmony and dialogue. Few Burkinabe have had formal education. Schooling is in theory free and compulsory until the age of 16. The University of Ouagadougou, founded in 1974, was the country's first institution of higher education. The Polytechnical University in Bobo-Dioulasso was opened in 1995. The University of Koudougou was founded in 2005 to substitute for the former teachers' training school, Ecole Normale Superieure de Koudougou.

Religion

Approximately 61 percent of the population practices Islam, with the majority being Sunni. The government estimates that 19 percent of the population is Roman Catholic, 15 percent maintain exclusively indigenous beliefs, and 4 percent are members of various Protestant denominations. Statistics on religious affiliation are approximate because Islam and Christianity are consistently practiced in tandem with indigenous religious beliefs.

Muslims reside largely in the northern, eastern, and western border regions, and Christians live in the center of the country. Persons practice indigenous religious beliefs throughout the country, especially in rural communities. Ouagadougou, the capital, has a mixed Muslim and Christian population.

HISTORY

Until the end of the 19th century, the history of Burkina Faso was dominated by the empire-building Mossi. The French arrived and claimed the area in 1896, but Mossi resistance ended only with the capture of their capital Ouagadougou in 1901. The colony of Upper Volta was established in 1919, but it was dismembered and reconstituted several times until the present borders were recognized in 1947.

The French administered the area indirectly through Mossi authorities until independence was achieved on August 5, 1960. The first President, Maurice Yameogo, resigned in 1966 following continuous worker strikes and handed power over to Lt. Col. Sangoule Lamizana, who was head of a government of senior army officers. Lamizana remained in power throughout the 1970s, as President of military and then elected governments.

Following more worker strikes, Col. Saye Zerbo overthrew President Lamizana in 1980. Colonel Zerbo also encountered resistance from workers' unions and was overthrown 2 years later by Maj. Dr. Jean-Baptiste Ouedraogo and the Council of Popular Salvation (CSP). Factional infighting developed between moderates in the CSP and radicals led by Capt. Thomas Sankara, who was appointed Prime Minister in January 1983, but was subsequently arrested. Efforts to bring about his release, directed by Capt. Blaise Compaore, resulted in yet another military coup d'etat, led by Sankara and Compaore on August 4, 1983.

Sankara and Compaore established the National Revolutionary Committee with Sankara as President, and he vowed to "mobilize the masses." But the committee's membership remained secret and was dominated by Marxist-Leninist military officers. In 1984, Upper Volta changed its name to Burkina Faso, meaning "the country of honorable people." But many of the strict security and austerity measures taken by Sankara provoked resistance. Despite his initial popularity and personal charisma, Sankara was killed in a coup which brought Capt. Blaise Compaore to power in October 1987.

Compaore pledged to pursue the goals of the revolution but to "rectify" Sankara's "deviations" from the original aims. In fact, Compaore reversed most of Sankara's policies and combined the leftist party he headed with more centrist parties after the 1989 arrest and execution of two military officers, Major Jean-Baptiste Boukary Lingini and Captain Henri Zongo, who had supported Compaore and governed with him up to that point.

GOVERNMENT AND POLITICAL CONDITIONS

Burkina Faso is a presidential republic. In November 2010 President Blaise Compaore was reelected to a fourth term with more than 80 percent of the vote. Despite some irregularities and the resource advantage held by the president, international observers considered the election to have been free and transparent. The president, assisted by members of his party, the Congress for Democracy and Progress (CDP), continued to dominate the government. The CDP won a majority in the 2007 legislative elections, which observers declared generally free and orderly despite irregularities, including fraud involving voter identification cards. There were instances in which elements of the security forces acted independently of civilian control.

Recent Elections

In November 2010 President Blaise Compaore won reelection with more than 80 percent of the vote. Opposition candidate Hama Arba Diallo, the runner-up, received 7.96 percent. Despite some irregularities, international observers considered the election to have been free and transparent despite the resource advantage held by the president.

Political Parties: Political parties operated freely. Individuals and parties may declare their candidacies and stand for election in presidential elections provided the Constitutional Council validates their candidacy; however, individuals must be members of a registered political party to run in legislative or municipal elections.

In the 2007 legislative elections, the ruling CDP won 73 seats in the 111-seat National Assembly. Of the 38 non-CDP members of parliament, 25 belonged to parties allied with the government. Election observers declared the elections free and orderly, except in four cities where they noted irregularities, including several cases of fraud involving voter identification cards. Opposition leaders denounced the elections.

CDP membership conferred advantages, particularly for businessmen and traders seeking ostensibly open government contracts. There were no cabinet members from the political opposition

Participation of Women and Minorities: There were 16 women in the 111-seats National Assembly and three women in the 30-member presidential cabinet. One of the four higher courts was led by a woman, the national ombudsman was a woman, 22 elected mayors were women, and an estimated 40 to 45 percent of new communal councilors were women. There are more than 60 ethnic groups in the country. Major ethnic groups include Mossi (50 percent of the population), Fulanis (12 percent), and Dioula (10 percent). Ethnicity is not a factor in cabinet appointments.

Principal Government Officials

Last Updated: 1/31/2013

Pres.: **Blaise COMPAORE**

Prime Min.: **Luc-Adolphe TIAO**

Min. of Agriculture, Water, & Fisheries: **Laurent SEDOGO**

Min. of Animal Resources: **Jeremie OUEDRAOGO**

Min. of Basic Education & Literacy: **Koumba BOLY-BARRY**

Min. of Civil Service, Labor, & Social Security: **Soungalo Appolinaire OUATTARA**

Min. of Communication & Spokesperson of the Govt.: **Alain Edouard TRAORE**

Min. of Culture & Tourism: **Baba HAMA**

Min. of Defense: **Blaise COMPAORE**

Min. of Economy & Finance: **Lucien Marie Noel BEMBAMBA**

Min. of Employment, Professional Development, & Youth:**Achille Marie Joseph TAPSOBA**

Min. of Environment & Sustainable Development: **Jean COULDIATY**

Min. of Foreign Affairs & Regional Cooperation: **Djibril BASSOLE**

Min. of Health: **Adama TRAORE**

Min. of Housing & Urbanization: **Yacouba BARRY**

Min. of Industry, Commerce, & Artisans: **Patiende Arthur KAFANDO**

Min. of Infrastructure & Improvement of Landlocked Situation:**Jean Bertin OUEDRAOGO**

Min. of Justice, Human Rights Promotion, & Keeper of the Seal:**Jerome TRAORE**

Min. of Mines & Energy: **Lamoussa Salif KABORE**

Min. of Parliamentary Relations & Political Reforms: **Boungnessan Arsene YE**

Min. of Scientific Research & Innovation: **Gnissa Isaie KONATE**

Min. of Secondary & Higher Education: **Albert OUEDRAOGO**

Min. of Social Action & National Solidarity: **Clemence TRAORE-SOME**

Min. of Sports & Leisure: **Yacouba OUEDRAOGO**

Min. of Territorial Admin., Security, & Decentralization:**Jerome BOUGOUMA**

Min. of Transportation, Posts, & Telecommunications: **Gilbert Noel OUEDRAOGO**

Min. of Women's Affairs: **Nestorine SANGARE-COMPAORE**

Min.-Del. in Charge of Agriculture: **Abdoulaye COMBARY**

Min.-Del. in Charge of Budget: **Francois Marie Didie ZOUNDI**

Min.-Del. in Charge of Literacy: **Zakaria TIEMTORE**

Min.-Del. in Charge of Local Collectives: **Toussaint Abel COULIBALY**

Min.-Del. in Charge of Regional Cooperation: **Vincent ZAKANE**

Ambassador to the US: **Seydou BOUDA**

Permanent Representative to the UN, New York: **Der KOGDA**

ECONOMY

Burkina Faso is a poor, landlocked country that relies heavily on cotton and gold exports for revenue. The country has few natural resources and a weak industrial base. About 90% of the population is engaged in subsistence agriculture, which is vulnerable to periodic drought. Cotton is the main cash crop.

Since 1998, Burkina Faso has embarked upon a gradual privatization of state-owned enterprises and in 2004 revised its investment code to attract foreign investment. As a result of this new code and other legislation favoring the mining sector, the country has seen an upswing in gold exploration and production. By 2010, gold had become the main source of export revenue. Gold mining production doubled between 2009 and 2010. Two new mining projects were launched the third quarter of 2011. Local community conflict persists in the mining and cotton sectors, but the Prime Minister has made efforts to defuse some of the economic cause of public discontent, including announcing income tax reductions, reparations for looting victims, and subsidies for basic food items and fertilizer. An IMF mission to Burkina Faso in October 2011 expressed general satisfaction with the measures. The risk of a mass exodus of the 3 to 4 million Burinabe who live and work in Cote D'Ivoire has dissipated and trade, power, and transport links are being restored.

Labor Conditions

The law sets the minimum age for employment at 16 and prohibits children less than 18 years of age from working at night except in times of emergency. The minimum age for employment was consistent with the age for completing educational requirements, which was 16 years. In the domestic and agricultural sectors, the law permits children under the age of 15 to perform limited activities for up to four and one-half hours per day. There were no explicit restrictions regarding occupational health and safety in the law.

The law prohibits the worst forms of child labor, including the commercial sexual exploitation of children, child pornography, and jobs that harm their health. The 2008 antitrafficking legislation provides for penalties of up to 10 years for violators and increases maximum prison terms from five to 10 years. The law also allows terms as high as 20 years to life imprisonment under certain conditions. However, the government did not effectively enforce the law.

Child labor was a problem. According to the National Institute of Statistics and Demography 41.1 percent of the children between five and 17 years were engaged in some form of economic activity. Children mostly worked in the following areas: agriculture (69.2 percent), mining (2.2 percent), trade (5 percent) and sometimes as domestic servants in the informal sector (19 percent). Some children, particularly those working as cattle herders and street hawkers did not attend school. A 2010 UNICEF study found that of 50,000 gold miners, 19,881 were children. The main reason for this phenomenon was poverty and insufficient access to education.

The law mandates a minimum monthly wage of 30,684 CFA francs ($61) in the formal sector; the minimum wage does not apply to subsistence agriculture or other informal occupations.

The law mandates a standard workweek of 40 hours for non-domestic workers and a 60-hour workweek for household employees, and it provides for overtime pay. There are also regulations pertaining to rest periods, limits on hours worked, and prohibition of excessive compulsory overtime, but these standards were not effectively enforced.

The government sets occupational health and safety standards. Government inspectors under the Ministry of Civil Service, Labor, and Social Security and the labor tribunals are responsible for overseeing occupational health and safety standards in the small industrial and commercial sectors, but these standards do not apply in subsistence agriculture and other informal sectors. These standards were generally not effectively enforced. Employers often paid less than the minimum wage. Wage-earners usually supplemented their income through reliance on the extended family, subsistence agriculture, or trading in the informal sector.

U.S.-BURKINA RELATIONS

The United States established diplomatic relations with Burkina Faso (then called Upper Volta) in 1960, following its independence from France. U.S. relations with Burkina Faso are excellent. In addition to regional peace and stability, U.S. interests in Burkina Faso are to promote continued democratization and greater respect for human rights and to encourage sustainable economic development. Countering terrorism and strengthening border security are of growing importance in Burkina Faso.

The United States and Burkina Faso engage in a number of military training and exchange programs, including in counterterrorism and humanitarian assistance. The country is contributing to the support of U.S. efforts in the Sahel. Burkina Faso is a partner in the Africa Contingency Operations Training and Assistance program for peacekeeping and is a member of the Trans-Sahara Counterterrorism Partnership.

U.S. Assistance to Burkina Faso

U.S. assistance to Burkina Faso focuses on increasing food security for mothers and children in food deficit areas, improving the education of girls, strengthening malaria control and reproductive health services, addressing threats of meningitis and influenza, increasing production of high-potential agricultural zones, enhancing access to markets, and increasing investment in land and rural productivity.

Bilateral Economic Relations

Burkina Faso is eligible for preferential trade benefits under the African Growth and Opportunity Act. U.S. exports to Burkina Faso include machinery, vehicles, aircraft, and rice. The top U.S. import from Burkina Faso is gold. Investment possibilities include Burkina Faso's mining and communications sectors. The United States has signed a trade and investment framework agreement with the West African Economic and Monetary Union, of which Burkina Faso is a member.

Burkina Faso's Membership in International Organizations

Burkina Faso and the United States belong to a number of the same international organizations, including the United Nations, International Monetary Fund, World Bank, and World Trade Organization.

Bilateral Representation

Burkina Faso maintains an embassy in the United States at 2340 Massachusetts Ave. NW, Washington, DC 20008 (tel. 202-332-5577).

Principal U.S. Embassy Officials

Last Updated: 1/14/2013

OUAGADOUGOU (E) Secteur 15, Ouaga 2000, Avenue Sembene Ousmane, Rue 15.873, (226) 5049-5300, Fax (226) 50-49-53-32, Workweek: M-F 08:00-17:00, Website: http://ouagadougou.usembassy.gov/

DCM OMS:	Pamela Lee-Pow Ayoung
AMB OMS:	Patti Hagopian
CDC:	Diomande Fabien
ECON/COM:	Timothy Swett
FM:	James Sisson
HRO:	Clare Ann Fagan
MGT:	Susan N'Garnim
MLO/ODC:	Michael Lee
POSHO:	James Sisson
SDO/DATT:	Andrew Brosnan
AMB:	Thomas Dougherty
CON:	Kelly McCaleb
DCM:	Christopher Davis
PAO:	Meg Riggs
GSO:	Tdy Frank Skinner Acting
RSO:	Jeffrey Hicks
AID:	Janet Trucker
CLO:	Ima Essien Jones
EEO:	Meg Riggs
ICASS Chair:	Meg Riggs
IMO:	Dale Jones
IPO:	Katina Caldwell
IRS:	Brenda.J.Morgan
POL:	Chris Farlow
State ICASS:	Meg Riggs

TRAVEL

Consular Information Sheet

February 21, 2012

Country Description: Burkina Faso, previously known as Upper Volta, is a landlocked, developing country in the Sahel region of West Africa. Its capital is Ouagadougou. Burkina Faso is a former French colony; the official language is French. With a population of nearly 17 million, it is one of the world's least-developed countries, and infrastructure for tourism is limited.

Smart Traveler Enrollment Program (STEP)/Embassy Locations: If you are going to live in or visit Burkina Faso, please take the time to tell our Embassy about your trip by enrolling in the Smart Traveler Enrollment Program (STEP). If you enroll, we can keep you up to date with important safety and security announcements via email and SMS. It will also help your friends and family get in touch with you in an emergency.

U.S. Embassy Ouagadougou
Avenue Sembene Ousmane, Secteur 15, Ouaga 2000
Ouagadougou, Burkina Faso
Telephone: 226 50 49 53 00
Facsimile: 226 50 49 56 23

Entry/Exit Requirements: U.S. citizens are strongly urged to acquire visas for Burkina Faso before traveling to the country.

U.S. citizens traveling to Burkina Faso should apply for a visa at the Embassy of Burkina Faso in Washington, D.C., where they will benefit from visa reciprocity, receiving a five-year multiple entry visa for USD $100. If a visa is obtained at the port of entry, it will cost 94,000 francs CFA (approximately USD $190) because visa reciprocity is not yet recognized by the local issuing authority. The U.S. Embassy in Ouagadougou is working with the Government of Burkina Faso (GOBF) to implement the visa reciprocity agreement when visas are issued at the port of entry. Travelers entering Burkina Faso are required to present their current and valid "International Certificate of Vaccination as approved by the World Health Organization (WHO)" (commonly called a "yellow card") showing that their Yellow Fever vaccination is up-to-date.

The Embassy of Burkina Faso in Washington is located at 2340 Massachusetts Avenue, NW, Washington, DC 20008, telephone (202) 332-5577. Visas are also available from Burkina Faso's Mission to the United Nations in New York City. Overseas, inquiries should be made at the nearest Burkinabe embassy or consulate. Visit the Embassy of Burkina Faso website for the most current visa information, or contact their offices directly. Several companies that offer visa-services but have no affiliation with the Government of Burkina Faso have set up sites to resemble that of the Embassy of Burkina Faso. The correct web address for the Embassy of Burkina Faso in Washington DC is www.burkina-usa.org; the site for Burkina Faso's Permanent Mission is www.burkina-onu.org.

The U.S. Department of State is unaware of any HIV/AIDS entry restrictions for visitors to or foreign residents of Burkina Faso.

Threats to Safety and Security: U.S. citizens traveling to, and residing in, Burkina Faso are urged to exercise caution and maintain a high level of security awareness at all times. Kidnapping remains a threat in the northern areas of the country bordering Mali and Niger. Due to ongoing security concerns in the these areas, the U.S. Embassy deems the area north of the road stretching from Djibo to Dori off-limits to official government travelers unless prior authorization for such travel is expressly given. There have been no known terrorist incidents (bombings, hijackings, or kidnappings) directed against foreigners in Burkina Faso; however, the al-Qaida in the Islamic Maghreb (AQIM) terrorist organization and their affiliates could target westerners in the porous border regions of the north, near Mali and Niger. The Sahel region of Burkina Faso is extremely remote, and the Government of Burkina Faso as well as the Embassy's ability to render assistance in the event of an emergency there is limited. Ouagadougou occasionally experiences demonstrations and civil unrest. Although most demonstrations are generally peaceful, there have been incidents of violence, looting, and destruction within recent years. Instances may arise where the best course of action may be to shelter temporarily in place if it is otherwise generally safe to do so. U.S. citizens should remain informed of current developments; avoid crowds, political gatherings, and street demonstrations, even if they appear to be peaceful.

Stay up to date by:

- Bookmarking our Bureau of Consular Affairs website which contains the current Travel Warnings and Travel Alerts as well as the Worldwide Caution.
- Following us on Twitter and the Bureau of Consular Affairs page on Facebook as well.
- Downloading our free Smart Traveler IPhone App to have travel information at your fingertips.
- Calling 1-888-407-4747 toll-free within the U.S. and Canada, or a regular toll line, 1-202-501-4444, from other countries.
- Taking some time before travel to consider your personal security.

Crime: Street crime in Burkina Faso poses risks for visitors. Most reported incidents involve purse-snatchers, pickpockets, and street scam artists who target wallets, jewelry, cell phones, and other valuables. Thieves are especially active during international meetings or events which draw large crowds to the capital. The areas near and around the U.N. Circle, Avenue Kwame N'Krumah, and the Central Market in Ouagadougou experience the highest incidence of street crime. Travelers should stay alert, remain in groups, and avoid poorly lit areas. Be especially cautious at night when most reported incidents have taken place.

Incidents of highway banditry continue to occur countrywide. Although the bandits typically operate at night, there have been daytime attacks. They have injured or killed individuals who refused their demands or attempted to drive through their roadblocks. In 2010 a police officer, escorting a bus, was shot and killed while attempting to stop a roadside robbery. Several attacks have been directed at intercity public buses. U.S. citizen travelers should avoid all intercity and highway travel at night. Check with the Embassy for the latest security information before setting out on your journey.

Perpetrators of business fraud often target foreigners, including Americans. Recent scams that have victimized U.S. citizens have taken many forms, including fraudulent transactions for gold and antiquities. Such fraud schemes are now prevalent throughout West Africa, including Burkina Faso. The scams pose a danger of both financial loss and physical harm. A typical sign of a business scam is the demand for advance payments on contracts. Persons contemplating business deals in Burkina Faso should contact the commercial section of the U.S. Embassy in Ouagadougou if they have any doubts about the legitimacy of a potential business client or partner.

Normally, fraud schemes begin with an unsolicited communication (usually by e-mail) from an unknown individual who describes a situation that promises quick financial gain, often by assisting in the transfer of a large sum of money or gold dust out of the country. A series of "advance fees" must then be paid in order to conclude the transaction. In fact, the final payoff does not exist; the purpose of the scam is simply to collect the advance fees. Common variations of this scheme involve individuals claiming to be refugees, victims of various African conflicts, or former political leaders in need of help in transferring large sums of money. Sometimes perpetrators manage to induce victims to provide bank account and credit card information, and financial authorizations that allow them to incur large debts against the victim's credit. In some instances, victims have lost their life savings.

The best way to avoid becoming a victim of advance-fee fraud is common sense. If a proposition looks too good to be true, it probably is. Research thoroughly any unsolicited business proposal originating from Burkina Faso or any other source before committing funds, providing goods or services, or undertaking travel.

Don't buy counterfeit and pirated goods, even if they are widely available. Not only are the bootlegs illegal in the United States, but if purchased, you may also be breaking local law.

Victims of Crime: If you or someone you know becomes the victim of a crime abroad, you should contact the local police and the nearest U.S. embassy or consulate. We can:

- Replace a stolen passport.
- Help you find appropriate medical care if you are the victim of violent crimes such as assault or rape.
- Put you in contact with the appropriate police authorities, and if you want us to, we can contact family members or friend.
- Help you understand the local criminal justice process and direct you to local attorneys, although it is important to remember that local authorities are responsible for investigating and prosecuting the crime.

There is no local equivalent to the all-purpose "911" emergency line in Burkina Faso; there are separate numbers for different types of services and also for different cities. Within Ouagadougou, emergency numbers are as follows: fire department, 50-30-69-47, 50-30-69-48, or simply dial 18; ambulance service, 50-30-66-44 or 50-30-66-45; police, 50-30-63-83, 50-30-71-00, or simply dial 17; Gendarmerie, 50-31-33-39 or 50-31-33-40. You can also dial 10-10 which will connect to the Ministry of Security who will then dispatch the appropriate law enforcement entity.

Criminal Penalties: While you are traveling in Burkina Faso, you are subject to its laws even if you are a U.S. citizen. Foreign laws and legal systems can be vastly different than our own. In some places you may be taken in for questioning if you don't have your passport with you. In some places, it is illegal to take pictures of certain buildings. In some places driving under the influence could land you immediately in jail. These criminal penalties will vary from country to country. There are also some things that might be legal in the country you visit, but still illegal in the United States, and you can be prosecuted under U.S. law if you buy pirated goods. Engaging in sexual conduct with children or using or disseminating child pornography in a foreign country is prosecutable in the United States. If you break the law in Burkina Faso, your U.S. passport won't help you avoid arrest or prosecution. It's very important to know what's legal and what's not wherever you go.

Persons violating Burkina Faso's laws, even unknowingly, may be expelled, arrested, or imprisoned. Penalties for possessing, using, or trafficking in illegal drugs in Burkina Faso can be severe, and convicted offenders can expect long jail sentences and heavy fines. Burkina Faso is not a party to a bilateral agreement that requires mandatory notification.

Based on the Vienna Convention on Consular Relations, bilateral agreements with certain countries and customary international law, if you are arrested in Burkina Faso you have the option to request that the police, prison officials, or other authorities alert the nearest U.S. embassy or consulate of your arrest, and to have communications from you forwarded to the nearest U.S. embassy or consulate.

Special Circumstances: Burkina Faso's customs authorities may enforce strict regulations concerning export from Burkina Faso of items such as masks, religious materials, and antiquities. The Director of the National Museum has stated that all exportation of objects of art (old or traditional artists' works, and all old material of the national cultural patrimony) is subject to the prior approval of the Ministry of Culture. Contact the Embassy of Burkina Faso in Washington (see contact information in the Entry Requirements section) for specific information regarding customs requirements.

Foreigners should carry photocopies of the biographic page of their passport and their visa with them at all times. If a passport is lost and a valid visa cannot be presented by the traveler upon departure, a police report documenting the loss of the visa may be required.

Credit cards are accepted at only a few high-end establishments in Ouagadougou. Travelers' checks may be cashed at local banks, but euro-denominated traveler's checks are much more widely accepted than dollar-denominated ones. There are a few ATMs in Ouagadougou and Bobo-Dioulasso, but they do not always accept cards from foreign banks. ATMs generally accept Visa and MasterCard credit cards with a personal identification number.

Burkina Faso's laws concerning photography have recently changed. Photo permits from the Tourist Office are no longer required for tourists. Film crews still do require permits. Note that the Tourist Office publishes a list of buildings, installations, and areas that may not be photographed at all.

Local telephone service is adequate but expensive. Cell phone networks are available in most urban areas, although service can be unreliable. Telephone coverage in rural areas is limited, though increasing. International calls cannot always be made from hotels; it may be necessary to make international calls from a Post and Telecommunications Office, where only local currency is accepted. Collect calls are not possible. Cybercafes for Internet access are common in both Ouagadougou and Bobo-Dioulasso.

Accessibility: While in Burkina Faso, individuals with disabilities may find accessibility and accommodation very different from what you find in the United States.

Medical Facilities and Health Information: Medical facilities and emergency hospital care are very limited and of poor quality, particularly in areas outside of Ouagadougou. Emergency response services, such as ambulances, are in very short supply, poorly equipped, and in many regions simply nonexistent.

Some medicines are available through local pharmacies, though supplies can be limited and quality is inconsistent. Travelers requiring specific medicines should bring an adequate supply for the duration of their stay in Burkina Faso. Malaria is a serious risk to travelers in Burkina Faso and can be fatal. Travelers who become ill with a fever or flu-like illness while traveling in a malaria-risk area and up to one year after returning home should seek prompt medical attention and tell the physician their travel history and what anti-malarial drugs they have been taking. There are vaccines not routinely given in the United States that are strongly advised before traveling to Burkina Faso. Meningitis is endemic in Burkina Faso, and cases are most frequent during the drier, dustier months of January through June. Travelers should confirm that their meningitis inoculation is up to date. Tuberculosis remains to be a health concern in Burkina Faso.

You can find good information on vaccinations and other health precautions, on the CDC website. For information about outbreaks of infectious diseases abroad, consult the World Health Organization (WHO) website. The WHO website also contains additional health information for travelers, including detailed country-specific health information.

Medical Insurance: You can't assume your insurance will go with you when you travel. It's very important to find out BEFORE you leave. You need to ask your insurance company two questions:

- Does my policy apply when I'm out of the United States?
- Will it cover emergencies like a trip to a foreign hospital or an evacuation?

In many places, doctors and hospitals still expect payment in cash at the time of service. Your regular U.S. health insurance may not cover doctors' and hospital visits in other countries. If your policy doesn't go with you when you travel, it's a very good idea to take out another one for your trip. It is strongly advised you have medical evacuation insurance before you travel to Burkina Faso.

Traffic Safety and Road Conditions: While in Burkina Faso, you may encounter road conditions that differ significantly from those in the United States. The information which follows is for general reference only, and may not be applicable in a particular location or circumstance within Burkina Faso.

Travelers should exercise great caution when traveling by road in Burkina Faso. While several major urban and intercity roads are paved, they can be narrow and full of potholes. Dirt roads are common, even in large cities. Vehicles will often enter oncoming traffic to pass or maneuver around obstacles. Broken-down vehicles may be abandoned on the road. Rural roads outside of major arteries are often in poor condition and roadside assistance is not available. Some rural roads are impassible in the rainy season. Livestock and children may dart onto the road without warning. Road travel at night is especially dangerous and, if at all possible, should be avoided. At night, there is a high volume of truck traffic passing through the country and pedestrians, bicycles, and donkey carts pose a major hazard on unlit, unmarked roads. Vehicles are often dangerously overloaded and poorly maintained.

Drivers, including motorcyclists and bicyclists, are at times careless. The police rarely enforce traffic laws and are virtually absent from rural roads. Emergency services in case of accidents are scarce, underequipped, and practically nonexistent in most rural areas. Caution is urged while using any form of public transportation to travel by road, and travelers should remain aware of their personal belongings at all times.

Aviation Safety Oversight: As there is no direct commercial air service to the United States by carriers registered in Burkina Faso, the U.S. Federal Aviation Administration (FAA) has not assessed the government of Burkina Faso's Civil Aviation Authority for compliance with International Civil Aviation Organization (ICAO) aviation safety standards. Further information may be found on the FAA's safety assessment page.

Children's Issues: Please see the U.S. Dept. of State Office of Children's Issues web pages on intercountry adoption and international parental child abduction.

Intercountry Adoption

November 2010

The information in this section has been edited from the latest report available as of February 2013 from the State Department Bureau of Consular Affairs, Office of Overseas Citizens Services. For more information, please read the *Intercountry Adoption* section of this book and review current reports online at http://adoption.state.gov.

Burkina Faso is party to the Hague Convention on Protection of Children and Co-operation in Respect of Intercountry Adoption (Hague Adoption Convention). Therefore all adoptions between Burkina Faso and the United States must meet the requirements of the Convention and U.S. law implementing the Convention.

Who Can Adopt? Adoption between the United States and Burkina Faso is governed by the Hague Adoption Convention. Therefore to adopt from Burkina Faso, you must first be found eligible to adopt by the U.S. Government. The U.S. Government agency responsible for making this determination is the Department of Homeland Security, U.S. Citizenship and Immigration Services (USCIS).

Residency Requirements: With the Hague Convention now implemented, American citizens residing in the United States can apply to adopt a child from Burkina Faso.

Age Requirements: Each prospective adoptive parent must be at least 15 years older than the prospective adoptee, unless the prospective adoptee is the biological child of one of the spouses, in which case the age difference between the child and the other spouse must be at least 10 years. Prospective parents must generally be under the age of 60, though certain exceptions may be made based upon the specifics of the case.

Marriage Requirements: Married, cohabiting, heterosexual couples who have been married for at least five years may adopt a child. Single applicants are almost never permitted to adopt children in Burkina Faso. Married prospective adoptive parents without children of their own are given priority. In some cases, couples that already have two or more children may have greater difficulty with the adoption process.

Other Requirements: The authorities must be convinced that an adoption will not generate a material profit for anyone involved in the adoption (except service providers such as lawyers).

Who Can be Adopted? Because Burkina Faso is party to the Hague Adoption Convention, children from Burkina Faso must meet the requirements of the Convention in order to be eligible for adoption. For example, the Convention requires that Burkina Faso attempt to place a child with a family in Burkina Faso before determining that a child is eligible for intercountry adoption. In Burkina Faso, children identified for adoption are mostly from one of the following categories: orphans whose parents are unknown or have died, children with mentally ill mothers, abandoned children, and children who were born of incestuous or adulterous relationships.

Eligibility Requirements: If the child's biological parents are known, there must be a consent act, a family council report or a declaration of abandonment.

Age Requirements: Under local law, children can be adopted at any time up to age 18. If the adoptive child is aged 15 or above, however, he/she must give his/her personal consent before the adoption can take place. U.S. citizens considering adopting a Burkinabe child aged 16 or older should contact the U.S. Embassy in Ouagadougou prior to initiating the adoption process, as U.S. law requires a child to be under the age of sixteen to qualify for a U.S. immigrant visa.

The Process: Because Burkina Faso is party to the Hague Adoption Convention, adopting from Burkina Faso must follow a specific process designed to meet the Convention's requirements. For detailed and updated information on these requirements, please review the *Intercountry Adoption* section of this publication and visit the U.S. Department of State Intercountry Adoption website at http://adoption.state.gov.

Role of the Adoption Authority: The office of Placements and Adoptions at the Ministry of Social Affairs and National Solidarity (La Direction de la Protection de l'Enfant et de L'Adolescent, Ministère de l'Action Sociale et de la Solidarité Nationale) receives and examines all adoption applications and identifies adoptable children. When the prospective parents agree to adopt the child that is proposed to them, the Office of Placements and Adoptions then drafts an agreement to pursue the procedure together with the child's birth certificate and home study. If the child's biological parents are known, there must be a consent act, a family council report or a declaration of abandonment. The agreement to pursue the adoption procedure is given to the local representative of the accredited agency. This exchange of agreement to pursue the procedure must be completed before the adoption court hearing. Unless this condition is respected, the adoption cannot be recognized by the authorities of Burkina Faso. At the end of the procedure, the adoptive family must travel to Burkina Faso to get the child. The adoptive parents must remain in the country for at least 10 to 15 business days to finalize the adoption process.

Role of the Court: After committing themselves to adopt the child, the prospective parents hire a lawyer in Burkina Faso to follow the procedure in court. The Office of Placements and Adoptions forwards the completed adoption file to the tribunal where the child resides or to the main tribunal in Ouagadougou.When the file is received by the tribunal, they contact a notary to establish an act of adoption.

This act of adoption is first sent to the institution that is responsible for the welfare of the child to initial and sign the act before it is forwarded to the Office of Placement and adoption for a final signature. There is a three month waiting period after the signature of the act before the court announces the final adoption. The lawyer then gets a copy of the judgment to request the issuance of a new birth certificate and a new passport for the child. In Burkina Faso, birth certificates are issued by the local mayor's office (the "Mairie"). Passports are issued by the Ministry of Security's "Division du Contrôle des Migrations" upon presentation of the child's birth certificate with name changes and the adoption decree. The passport costs about 50,000 (110 USD). Copies of the judgment and the certificate of non appeal are sent to the Office of Placement and Adoptions for the issuance of the certificate of conformity and the authorization to leave the country. The certificate of non appeal is delivered 1 month after the final court decision. Unless all the conditions are met, the office of placement and adoptions is unable to issue the certificate of conformity and the authorization to leave the country. These documents can only be given to the adoptive parents when they get to Burkina Faso.

Role of Adoption Agencies: Accredited Adoption Agencies may have fully accredited representatives in Burkina Faso who act on behalf of prospective adoptive parents.

Time Frame: It takes about twelve months from the time the prospective parents submit their initial application until the child is identified and custody is given to the adoptive family. It takes six months or more for the case to be finalized in court. Finalization includes the final adoption decree, the issuance of child's new birth certificate, the issuance of the "Certificat de Conformité" and the authorization for the child to leave the country. Generally, the child is placed in the adoptive parents' care as soon as s/he is identified, and lives with them until the final court hearing. In the absence of those parents (for Americans who reside in the U.S. and are adopting in Burkina Faso) the child is placed in a host family or in an orphanage.

The court hearing is usually just a formality, as the government Social Service Agency has already vetted the parents. Adoption cases may take longer when not properly followed up with the court. The Placements and Adoptions Office suggests that adoptive parents hire a lawyer, especially when cases fall under the jurisdiction of the civil court in Ouagadougou. The Placements and Adoptions office maintains a list of local lawyers who can be consulted. In small cities, prospective adoptive parents might not need to hire a lawyer.

Adoption Application: Prospective adoptive parents should understand that there are two kinds of adoption available in Burkina Faso, and for U.S. immigration purposes, the "full" adoption option is the only one that can confer immigrant status to an adopted child. An "open" adoption—one which gives a biological parent the right to revoke the adoption at any time—does not meet the requirements established by U.S. immigration law for issuing visas to adopted orphans. There are two ways to submit adoption applications in Burkina Faso:

- Through accredited Adoption Agencies who have a fully accredited representative in Burkina Faso to act on their behalf.
- Apply to the Ministry of Social Affairs, Infant and Adolescent Welfare office through the Central Authority in the prospective adoptive parents' home country for transmission to the Burkina Faso Central Authority.

Applications are evaluated with respect to the following factors:

- The family's ability to financially support the child/
- The family's way of life.
- The findings of a social and psychological report on the prospective adoptive parents.
- The family's motivations and their attitude towards adoption.
- The marital status, age and state of health of the adoptive parents.
- The point of view and welfare of children already members of the adoptive family.
- The size of the family (applications from families with more than two children may not be given priority).

Adoption Fees: In the adoption services contract that you sign at the beginning of the adoption process, your agency will itemize the fees and estimated expenses related to your adoption process. The U.S. Embassy in Burkina Faso discourages the payment of any fees that are not properly receipted, "donations," or "expediting" fees, that may be requested from prospective adoptive parents. Such fees have the appearance of "buying" a baby and put all future adoptions in Burkina Faso at risk.

The following adoption fees are covered by the adoptive parents:

- Fees for home study conducted on the child: 150,000 (approximately 320 USD).
- Initial filing fee: 26,500 CFA (65 USD) per file. The payment receipt must be included when first applying for consideration as an adoptive parent.
- Case processing by the Central Authority once the child is identified: 100,000 CFA (210 USD).
- Stamps: 5000 CFA (12 USD) for each application.
- Medical exam (Tests that are compulsory include hepatitis A and B, HIV, blood and sickle cells detection) All expenses related to the medical exams are born by the adoptive parents..
- Food allowance: 100,000 CFA (about 210 USD) per month and per child. This amount is payable from the time the adoptive family commits themselves to adopting the child.

In the event of a serious illness, the adoptive parents may be asked to bear the cost of hospitalization and or the transportation of the child. Adoptive parents must also cover the expenses of lawyers' and notary services. Fees are collected by a finance agent appointed to work at the Ministry of Social Action.

Documents Required: Only certified copies of these documents are acceptable to the Burkinabe authorities.

- Two motivation letters stamped with 5,000 FCFA revenue stamps (available at the local mayor's office), one addressed to the Chief Judge of the court in Ouagadougou and the other to the Ministry of Social Affairs, explaining in detail the motivation for adopting, and specifying the profile of the child they would like to adopt.
- A marriage certificate for the couple showing that they have been married for more than 5 years.
- A copy of the family book (official record of spouse, children) when/if available.
- Proof of residence.
- Proof of income.
- Birth certificate for each prospective parent.
- An authorization to adopt (agreement) issued by the authorities of the receiving country.
- Medical documents certifying that both prospective adoptive parents are physically and psychologically health.
- A home study report done by a Social Services agency of the adoptive parents habitual residence.
- A certificate of nationality (when it applies).
- A certificate stating that the parents have received training as potential adoptive parents.
- A commitment to send a report twice a year during the two first years of adoption and then once a year until the child reaches the age of 18.
- Police certificates for both prospective parents.
- A copy of the first two pages of both prospective parents' passports.

Bringing Your Child Home: Once your adoption is complete (or you have obtained legal custody of the child), there are a few more steps to take before you can head home. Specifically, you need to apply for several documents for your child before he or she can travel to the United States, such as a birth certificate, a passport or travel document for your child from the country in which he or she was born, and a U.S. Immigration Visa. For detailed and updated information on how to obtain these documents, review the *Intercountry Adoption* section in this publication and visit the U.S. Department of State Intercountry Adoption website at http://adoption.state.gov.

Child Citizenship Act: For adoptions finalized abroad, the Child Citizenship Act of 2000 allows your new child to acquire American citizenship automatically when he or she enters the United States as lawful permanent residents. For adoptions finalized in the United States, the Child Citizenship Act of 2000 allows your new child to acquire American citizenship automatically when the court in the United States issues the final adoption decree. To learn more, review the *Intercountry Adoption* section in this publication and visit the U.S. Department of State Intercountry Adoption website at http://adoption.state.gov.

After Adoption: When the adoption procedure is completed and the child joins the adoptive family, a periodic follow-up on the integration of the child in the family must be done by the competent social services of the child place of residence. The office of placements and adoptions at the Ministry of Social Affairs and National Solidarity must hear about the child twice a year during the first 2 years of the child's life with the adoptive family and once a year up to the child's 18th birthday.

U.S. Embassy in Burkina Faso
Avenue Sembene Ousmane
Secteur 15, Ouaga 2000
01 BP 35, Ouagadougou 01
Tel: (226) 50-49-53-00
Fax: (226) 50-49-56-23
Email: consularouaga@state.gov
http://ouagadougou.usembassy.gov

Burkina Faso's Adoption Authority
Ministère de l'Action Sociale et de la Solidarité Nationale
Immeuble Baoghin, Secteur 10
01 BP 515, Ouagadougou 01
Burkina Faso
Tel: (226) 50 30 68 80 (Switchboard)
Fax: (226) 50 31 67 37

Embassy of Burkina Faso
2340 Massachusetts Avenue, N.W.
Washington, D.C. 20008
Tel: (202) 332-5577/6895

Fax: (202) 667-1882
Email: ambawdc@verizon.net
http://www.burkina-usa.org

Office of Children's Issues
U.S. Department of State
2201 C Street, NW
SA-29
Washington, DC 20520
Tel: 1-888-407-4747
E-mail: AskCI@state.gov
http://adoption.state.gov

For questions about immigration procedures, call the National Customer Service Center (NCSC) at 1-800-375-5283 (TTY 1-800-767-1833).

International Parental Child Abduction

November 2012

The information in this section has been edited from a report from the State Department Bureau of Consular Affairs, Office of Overseas Citizens Services. For more information, please read the *International Parental Child Abduction* section of this book and check for updated reports online at www.travel.state.gov/abduction.

Disclaimer: The information in this flyer is provided for general information only, is not intended to be legal advice, and may change without notice. Questions involving interpretation of law should be addressed to an attorney licensed to practice in the relevant jurisdiction.

General Information: Burkina Faso and the United States have been treaty partners under the 1980 Hague Convention on the Civil Aspects of International Child Abduction (Hague Abduction Convention) since November 1, 1992.

Hague Abduction Convention: The U.S. Department of State serves as the U.S. Central Authority (USCA) for the Hague Abduction Convention. In this capacity, the Department's Bureau of Consular Affairs, Directorate for Overseas Citizens Services, Office of Children's Issues facilitates the submission of applications under the Hague Abduction Convention for the return of, or access to, children located in countries that are U.S. treaty partners, including Burkina Faso. Parents are strongly encouraged to contact the Department of State for assistance prior to initiating the Hague process directly with the foreign Central Authority.

United States Department of State
Office of Children's Issues
2201 C Street, N.W.
Washington, DC 20520
Telephone: 1-888-407-4747
Outside the United States or Canada: 1-202-501-4444
Fax: 202-736-9132

The Burkina Faso Central Authority (BFCA) for the Hague Abduction Convention is the Ministry of Social Action and National Solidarity. The BFCA plays the role of facilitator in Hague Abduction Convention cases, taking measures to locate the child and taking parent, to visit the home and interview the taking parent, and to seek a voluntary return. If the taking parent does not agree to a voluntary return, the BFCA will forward the Hague application to the public prosecutor and act as the formal applicant in return proceedings before the court. Contact the BFCA at:

Ministère de l'Action Sociale et de la Solidarité Nationale
01 BP 515
OUAGADOUGOU 01
Burkina Faso
Telephone numbers: +226 5030–6880 /5031–0055
Fax: +226 5031–8530

Return: A parent or legal guardian may file an application under the Hague Abduction Convention for return to the United States of a child abducted to, or wrongfully retained in, Burkina Faso. The U.S. Department of State can assist parents living in the United States to understand whether the Convention is an available civil remedy and can provide information on the process for submitting a Hague application.

For more information, please read the *International Parental Child Abduction* section of this book and review current reports online at www.travel.state.gov/abduction.

Visitation/Access: A person may file an application under the Hague Abduction Convention for access to a child living in Burkina Faso. The criteria for acceptance of a Hague access application vary from country to country. The U.S. Department of State can assist parents living in the United States to understand country-specific criteria and provide information on the process for submitting a Hague application

Retaining an Attorney: The BFCA does not provide an attorney to left-behind parents, but it provides a list of attorneys. Parents or legal guardians have the option to hire a private attorney to represent them, but all attorney fees will be the applicant's responsibility.

The U.S. Embassy in Ouagadougou, Burkina Faso, posts a list of attorneys including those who specialize in family law at: http://ouagadougou.usembassy.gov/medical_information.html. This list is provided as a courtesy service only and does not constitute an endorsement of any individual attorney.

Mediation: Mediation may be available for abduction and access cases. The BFCA will contact Burkina Faso Social Services officials and attempt to initiate mediation services in all Hague Abduction Convention cases. Mediation is voluntary.

U.S. Embassy Ouagadougou
Avenue Sembene Ousmane, Secteur 15, Ouaga 2000
Ouagadougou, Burkina Faso
Telephone: 226 50 49 53 00
Fax: +226 50 49 56 23
Email: consularouaga@state.gov
Website:
http://ouagadougou.usembassy.gov/

Embassy of Burkina Faso
2340 Massachusetts Avenue, NW
Washington, DC 20008
Telephone (202) 332-5577
Fax: (202) 667-1882
Email: contact@burkina-usa.org
Website: http://burkina-usa.org/

BURMA

Compiled from publications that were available as of February 2013 from the U.S. Department of State, the U.S. Department of Commerce, and the Central Intelligence Agency (CIA). See the introduction to this set for explanatory notes.

Official Name:
Union of Burma

Editor's Note: Since 1989 the military authorities in Burma have promoted the name Myanmar as a conventional name for their state; the US Government did not adopt the name, which is a derivative of the Burmese short-form name Myanma Naingngandaw

PROFILE

Geography

Area: total: 676,578 sq km; country comparison to the world: 40; land: 653,508 sq km; water: 23,070 sq km
Major cities: Rangoon (capital) 4.259 million; Mandalay 1.009 million; Nay Pyi Taw 992,000 (2009)
Climate: tropical monsoon; cloudy, rainy, hot, humid summers (southwest monsoon, June to September); less cloudy, scant rainfall, mild temperatures, lower humidity during winter (northeast monsoon, December to April)
Terrain: central lowlands ringed by steep, rugged highlands

People

Nationality: noun: Burmese (singular and plural); adjective: Burmese
Population: 54,584,650 (July 2012 est.)
Population growth rate: 1.07% (2012 est.)
Ethnic groups: Burman 68%, Shan 9%, Karen 7%, Rakhine 4%, Chinese 3%, Indian 2%, Mon 2%, other 5%
Religions: Buddhist 89%, Christian 4% (Baptist 3%, Roman Catholic 1%), Muslim 4%, animist 1%, other 2%
Languages: Burmese (official)
Literacy: definition: age 15 and over can read and write; total population: 89.9%; male: 93.9%; female: 86.4% (2006 est.)
Health: life expectancy at birth: total population: 65.24 years; male: 62.91 years; female: 67.71 years (2012 est.); Infant mortality rate: total: 47.74 deaths/1,000 live births; male: 54.51 deaths/1,000 live births; female: 40.57 deaths/1,000 live births (2012 est.)
Unemployment rate: 5.4% (2012 est.)
Work force: 33.41 million (2012 est.)

Government

Type: nominally civilian parliamentary government took power in March 2011
Independence: 4 January 1948
Constitution: approved by referendum 29 May 2008; reformed by a series of acts in 2011
Political subdivisions: 7 regions (taing-myar, singular—taing) and 7 states (pyi ne-myar, singular—pyi ne)
Suffrage: 18 years of age; universal

Economy

GDP (purchasing power parity): $89.23 billion (2012 est.); $83.74 billion (2011 est.); $79.4 billion (2010 est.); $75.38 billion (2009 est.)
GDP real growth rate: 6.2% (2012 est.); 5.5% (2011 est.); 5.3% (2010 est.); 5.1% (2009 est.)
GDP per capita (PPP): $1,400 (2012 est.); $1,300 (2011 est.); $1,300 (2010 est.); $1,300 (2009 est.)
Natural resources: petroleum, timber, tin, antimony, zinc, copper, tungsten, lead, coal, marble, limestone, precious stones, natural gas, hydropower
Agriculture products: rice, pulses, beans, sesame, groundnuts, sugarcane; fish and fish products; hardwood
Industries: agricultural processing; wood and wood products; copper, tin, tungsten, iron; cement, construction materials; pharmaceuticals; fertilizer; oil and natural gas; garments, jade and gems
Exports: $8.529 billion (2012 est.); $8.206 billion (2011 est.); $7.831 billion (2010 est.)
Exports—commodities: natural gas, wood products, pulses, beans, fish, rice, clothing, jade and gems
Exports—partners: Thailand 37.1%, China 19%, India 12.3%, Japan 6.7% (2011)
Imports: $7.137 billion (2012 est.); $5.982 billion (2011 est.); $4.376 billion (2010 est.)
Imports—commodities: fabric, petroleum products, fertilizer, plastics, machinery, transport equip-

ment; cement, construction materials, crude oil; food products, edible oil

Imports—partners: China 39.2%, Thailand 22.9%, Singapore 9.8%, South Korea 5.4%, $5.448 billion (31 December 2012 est.); Japan 4.1% (2011)

Debt—external: $5.811 billion (31 December 2011 est.); $6.352 billion (31 December 2010 est.)

Exchange rates: kyats (MMK) per US dollar; 867.6 (2012 est.); 5.39 (2011 est.); 5.58 (2010 est.); 1,055 (2009); 1,205 (2008); 1,296 (2007)

PEOPLE

The majority of Burma's people are ethnic Burman. Shan, Karen, Rohingya, Arakanese (Rakhine), Kachin, Chin, and Mon, together with other smaller indigenous ethnic groups, represent about 30% of the population. Indians and Chinese are the largest non-indigenous groups.

According to Burmese Government budget data, public health expenditure has accounted for less than 1% of total government spending. High infant mortality rates and short life expectancies further highlight poor health and living conditions. Tuberculosis, diarrheal disease, malaria, and HIV/AIDS pose serious threats to the Burmese population. The Global Fund to Fight AIDS, Tuberculosis and Malaria re-entered Burma in early 2011. In 2009, the UNDP's Human Development Index, which measures achievements in terms of life expectancy, educational attainment, and adjusted real income, ranked Burma 138 out of 182 countries.

Burmese authorities have perpetrated numerous documented human rights violations, including extrajudicial killings, disappearances, rape, torture, and incommunicado detentions. Internal displacement and refugee outflows of ethnic minorities are prevalent. Over two million Burmese, many of them ethnic minorities, have fled for economic and political reasons to Thailand, Bangladesh, India, China, Indonesia, Malaysia, and elsewhere. In Burma, there are approximately 750,000 stateless Rohingya in Northern Rakhine State. Elsewhere, there are roughly 150,000 Burmese living in nine refugee camps in Thailand along the border with Burma. Approximately 28,000 Burmese Rohingya are registered as living in two official refugee camps in Bangladesh, and more than 200,000 unregistered Rohingya live in surrounding towns and villages outside of the two camps.

Malaysia hosts more than 90,000 refugees and asylum seekers, primarily in urban areas, 91% of whom are from Burma. Chin and Rohingya comprise the largest groups of this population. Up to 100,000 unregistered Burmese Chin are living in India's Mizoram State, with another 7,500 Burmese refugees and asylum seekers (primarily Chin) in Delhi, India, of which up to 4,000 are UN High Commissioner for Refugees (UNHCR)-registered refugees.

Language

Burmese is the most widely spoken language (approx. 32 million native speakers). Ethnic groups have retained their own identities and languages. Some of the most prominent are Shan; various Karen, Karenni and Chin languages; Arakanese; Kachin; Mon; Palaung; Parauk; Wa; and Yangbye. English is spoken in many areas frequented by tourists. Indian and Chinese residents speak various languages and dialects of their homelands: Hindi, Urdu, Tamil, Bengali, Mandarin, Fujian, and Cantonese.

Religion

Theravada Buddhism is the dominant religion. It coexists with astrology, numerology, fortune telling, and veneration of indigenous pre-Buddhist era deities called "nats." The principal minority religious groups include Christians (primarily Baptists, Roman Catholics, and Anglicans, along with several other small Protestant denominations), Muslims (mostly Sunni), Hindus, and practitioners of traditional Chinese and indigenous religions. According to official statistics, approximately 90 percent of the population practices Buddhism, 4 percent practices Christianity, and 4 percent practices Islam. These statistics almost certainly underestimated the non-Buddhist proportion of the population. There has not been a census since 1983. Independent researchers place the Muslim population as being between 6 and 10 percent. A very small Jewish community in Rangoon has a synagogue but no resident rabbi.

The country is ethnically diverse, with some correlation between ethnicity and religion. Theravada Buddhism is the dominant religion among the majority Burman ethnic group and also among the Shan, Arakanese, and Mon ethnic minorities. Christianity is dominant among the Kachin, Chin, and Naga ethnic groups. Protestant Christian groups reported recent rapid growth among animist communities in Chin State. Christianity also is practiced widely among the Karen and Karenni ethnic groups; although many Karen and Karenni are Buddhist and some Karen are Muslim. Citizens of Indian origin, who are concentrated in major cities and in the south central region, predominantly practice Hinduism or Islam, although some are Christian. Islam is practiced widely in Rakhine State and in Rangoon, Irrawaddy, Magwe, and Mandalay Divisions, where some Burmese, Indians, and ethnic Bengalis practice the religion. Chinese ethnic minorities generally practice traditional Chinese religions. Traditional indigenous beliefs are practiced widely among smaller ethnic groups in the highland regions.

HISTORY

Burma was unified by Burman dynasties three times during the past millennium. The first such unification came with the rise of the Bagan (Pagan) Dynasty in 1044 AD, which is considered the "Golden Age" in Burmese history. During this period, Theravada Buddhism first made its appearance in Burma, and the Bagan kings built a massive city with thousands of pagodas and monasteries along the Irrawaddy River. The Bagan Dynasty lasted until 1287 when Mongol invaders destroyed the city. Ethnic Shan rulers, who established a political center at Ava (near Mandalay), filled the ensuing political vacuum for a short time.

In the 15th century, the Taungoo Dynasty succeeded again in unifying under Burman rule a large, multiethnic kingdom. This dynasty, which lasted from 1486 until 1752, left little cultural legacy, but expanded the kingdom through conquest of the Shans. Internal power struggles and the cost of protracted warfare led to the eventual decline of the Taungoo Dynasty.

The final Burman royal dynasty, the Konbaung, was established in 1752 under the rule of King Alaungpaya and lasted until the fall of King Thibaw to Britain in 1885. Like the Taungoo Kings, the Konbaung rulers focused on warfare and conquest. Wars were fought with the ethnic Mons and Arakanese, and with the Siamese.

The Burmese sacked the Siamese capital of Ayuthaya in 1767. This period also saw four invasions by the Chinese and three devastating wars with the British. The British began their conquest of Burma in 1824, expanding their holdings after each of the three wars. At the end of the third war in 1885, the British gained complete control of Burma, annexing it to British India. A group of Burmese nationalists known as the "30 Comrades," led by General Aung San, joined the Japanese forces in driving out the British at the outbreak of World War II. However, the Burmese Army switched sides in mid-1945 and aided U.S. and British forces in their drive to Rangoon against the Japanese.

After the war, the Burmese, with General Aung San at the helm, demanded complete political and economic independence from Britain. The British Government acceded to these demands. A constitution was completed in 1947 and independence granted in January 1948. General Aung San was assassinated with most of his cabinet before the constitution went into effect. During the constitutional period from 1948 to 1962, Burma had a democratic, parliamentary government. However, the country suffered widespread conflict and internal struggle. Constitutional disputes and persistent division among political and ethnic groups contributed to the democratic government's weak hold on power. In

1958, Prime Minister U Nu accepted military rule temporarily to restore political order. The military stepped down after 18 months.

In 1962 General Ne Win led a military coup, abolishing the constitution and establishing a xenophobic military government. Under his "Burmese Way to Socialism," he established socialist economic policies that had devastating effects on the country's economy and business climate. In 1974 Ne Win established the Burma Socialist Program Party (BSPP), the sole political party allowed in the country.

On November 25, 1974, former UN Secretary General U Thant died in New York. His body was flown back to Rangoon, where Ne Win had ordered that he be buried without any official honors. On the day of his funeral, December 5, tens of thousands of Burmese came out to pay their respects. Student demonstrators took U Thant's coffin and paraded through the streets before the demonstrators buried him on the site of the former Rangoon University Students Union. Demonstrations and anti-government speeches continued until December 11, when government troops stormed the campus, killing several students and taking away U Thant's coffin to bury it near the Shwedagon Pagoda. Riots broke out in Rangoon and the government declared martial law in order to crush the student demonstrations. Student protests that broke out in subsequent years were also similarly suppressed.

In March 1988, student-led demonstrations broke out in Rangoon in response to the worsening economic situation and evolved into a call for regime change. Despite repeated violent crackdowns by the military and police, the demonstrations increased in size and many in the general public joined the students. During mass demonstrations on August 8, 1988, military forces killed more than 1,000 demonstrators. At a rally following this massacre, Aung San Suu Kyi, the daughter of General Aung San, made her first political speech and assumed the role of opposition leader.

In September 1988, a group of generals deposed Ne Win's Burmese Socialist Program Party, suspended the constitution, and established a new ruling junta called the State Law and Order Restoration Council (SLORC). In an effort to "restore order," the SLORC sent the army into the streets to suppress the ongoing public demonstrations. An estimated additional 3,000 were killed, and more than 10,000 students fled into the hills and border areas. Many left the country.

The SLORC ruled by martial law until national parliamentary elections were held in May 1990. These elections were judged generally to be free and fair. The military made little effort to intimidate voters, erroneously assuming their preferred candidates would win. The results were an overwhelming victory for Aung San Suu Kyi's National League for Democracy party, which won nearly 60% of the vote and 392 of the 485 seats, even though she was under house arrest at the time of the elections. The SLORC refused to honor the results or call the parliament into session, instead imprisoning many political activists and maintaining its grip on power.

The ruling junta changed its name to the State Peace and Development Council (SPDC) in 1997, but did not change its policy of autocratic control and repression of the democratic opposition. It continued to subject Aung San Suu Kyi to varying forms of detention and other restrictions on her movement, which it periodically lifted only to reinstate later. In May 2002, Aung San Suu Kyi was allowed to leave her home, and she subsequently traveled widely throughout the country, where she was greeted by large crowds. On May 30, 2003, Aung San Suu Kyi and a convoy of her supporters were attacked by a group of regime-affiliated thugs. Many members of the convoy were killed or injured, and others disappeared. Aung San Suu Kyi and other members of her party were detained.

In October 2004, hard-line members of the senior leadership consolidated their power by ousting Prime Minister General Khin Nyunt and removing him and his allies from control of the government and military intelligence apparatus. Following a sharp increase in fuel prices on August 15, 2007, pro-democracy groups began a series of peaceful marches and demonstrations to protest the deteriorating economic situation in Burma. The regime responded by arbitrarily detaining over 150 pro-democracy activists in August and September 2007, including Min Ko Naing and Ko Ko Gyi, both previously-imprisoned key figures in the 1988 demonstrations. On August 28, 2007, as popular dissatisfaction spread, Buddhist monks began leading peaceful marches. On September 5, 2007, security forces in the town of Pakkoku violently broke up demonstrations by monks, resulting in injuries and triggering calls for a nationwide response and a government apology for the incident.

Beginning on September 18, 2007, monks resumed their peaceful protests in several cities throughout the country. These marches grew quickly to include ordinary citizens, culminating in a large gathering of protestors in Rangoon on September 24. On September 26 and 27, the regime renewed its violent crackdown, shooting, beating, and arbitrarily detaining thousands of monks, pro-democracy activists, and onlookers. The regime confirmed the deaths of only 10 protestors. However, some non-governmental organizations (NGOs) estimated the number of casualties to be much higher, and in his December 7, 2007, report to the UN General Assembly, Special Rapporteur on the Situation of Human Rights in Myanmar Paulo Sergio Pinheiro stated that there were over 30 fatalities in Rangoon associated with the September 2007 protests. In retribution for leading protest marches, monks were beaten and arrested, many monks were disrobed, and several monasteries were raided, ransacked, and closed. In addition to the more than 1,100 political prisoners whose arrests predate the crackdown, another thousand or more were detained due to their participation in the September 2007 protests.

Following the regime's 1993 proclamation of a seven-step roadmap to democracy and a subsequent national convention which convened intermittently, the regime in September 2007 concluded the process of "drafting" principles for the new constitution. Delegates to the convention were not allowed to debate freely, discuss, or attempt to amend the principles. In October 2007, the SPDC appointed 54 pro-regime persons to sit on a constitution drafting committee. The government declared the completion of the constitution drafting committee's work in February 2008, and announced that it would hold a national referendum on the constitution in May 2008, with multi-party elections planned for 2010. While the referendum law provided for a secret ballot, free debate was not permitted and activities considered "interfering with the referendum" carried a 3-year prison sentence. The government carried out the referendum in May 2008 amidst the aftermath of the humanitarian disaster caused by Cyclone Nargis. Although the referendum was rife with irregularities, the government announced that 92.48% of voters approved the constitution, with a 98% voter turnout. Independent observers do not consider those figures to be credible.

Cyclone Nargis hit Irrawaddy and Rangoon Divisions May 2-3, 2008. The storm devastated a huge swath of the Irrawaddy Delta region, wiping out entire villages, leaving an estimated 138,000 Burmese dead or missing, and affecting approximately 2.4 million people, according to the UN Office for the Coordination of Humanitarian Affairs (OCHA). Burmese authorities were criticized for their initial reluctance to grant access to the affected region by international donors, though such access was granted in the ensuing months.

Starting in November 2008, the government imposed harsh sentences on large numbers of political prisoners it had arrested over the course of the previous year, including Min Ko Naing and Ko Ko Gyi. The trials were closed and did not appear to meet minimum standards of due process. The imprisoned activists were convicted, mainly in closed-door hearings, of unlawful association, illegally distributing print and video media, or generally destabilizing public security and the security of the state and were given lengthy sentences, some as long as 68 years.

On May 14, 2009, security forces took Aung San Suu Kyi from house arrest to Insein prison and charged her and her two assistants with baseless crimes related to an uninvited U.S. citizen who swam to her home. Following a trial that was widely viewed as unfair, on August 11, 2009, Aung San Suu Kyi and her two assistants were convicted of violating the terms of her house arrest. The international community criticized her conviction and subsequent sentence to an additional 18 months of house arrest. The SPDC government released Aung San Suu Kyi on November 13, 2010, after more than 7 years' continuous detention. However, the government continues to hold an estimated 2,100 other political prisoners.

In March 2010, the government published widely criticized election and party registration laws to govern the conduct of elections planned for 2010. The laws annulled the results of the 1990 elections, barred political prisoners from party membership and parliamentary candidacy, and granted broad authority to the regime-appointed Union Election Commission to oversee and regulate political party activities. In April 2010, all active-duty cabinet ministers resigned their military commissions, reportedly to prepare for candidacy in the 2010 elections. Prime Minister Thein Sein was appointed head of the pro-government Union Solidarity and Development Party.

The country held its first elections in 20 years on November 7, 2010. The United States condemned the planning and the execution of the elections as neither free nor fair. The regime proxy Union Solidarity and Development Party won over three-quarters of elective parliamentary seats, although observers around the country reported widespread electoral malfeasance, including abuse of advance voting procedures. Per Burma's 2008 constitution, military appointees fill one-quarter of all parliamentary seats. The new, nominally civilian government took office on April 1, 2011, and the SPDC was dissolved. Insiders from the SPDC era fill almost all key positions at the national level and most at the state/region level. The current roles of the former top two SPDC leaders, Senior General Than Shwe and Vice Senior General Maung Aye, remain unclear.

GOVERNMENT AND POLITICAL CONDITIONS

Burma's government is headed by President Thein Sein; the military-run State Peace and Development Council was officially dissolved in 2011, although former and active military officers continued to wield authority at each level of government. In November 2010 the then-military regime held the country's first parliamentary elections since 1990, which were neither free nor fair. The government's main party, the ruling Union Solidarity and Development Party (USDP), claimed an overwhelming majority of seats in the national parliament and state/regional assemblies. Military security forces report to military channels, and civilian security forces, such as the police, report to a nominally civilian ministry headed by an active-duty military general.

Significant developments during 2011 included the emergence of a legislature that allowed opposition parties to contribute substantively to debates; democratic reforms such as the amendment of laws allowing opposition parties to register and Aung San Suu Kyi to announce her bid for Parliament; the release of hundreds of political prisoners; the relaxation of a number of censorship controls, the opening of some space in society for the expression of dissent; and an easing of restrictions on some internal and foreign travel for citizens.

Recent Elections

In November 2010 the country held its first election in 20 years, which the international community assessed as neither free nor fair due to an array of flaws including political party registration restrictions, detention of political activists, restrictions on free reporting and freedom of assembly, inadequate time to develop candidate lists and to prepare campaigners, lack of media access, the lack of independence of the electoral commission, allegations of fraud via advance voting irregularities, the cancellation of elections in certain ethnic areas, and widespread reports of official intimidation.

Political Parties: The ruling USDP dominated the electoral field. Membership in the USDP conferred advantages in many areas. According to human rights activists and legal sources, citizens could present USDP cards in place of national identification cards for travel and to purchase express bus, train, boat, or plane tickets. USDP members reportedly were given priority enrollment in foreign language universities in Rangoon and Mandalay and were exempt from the visitor registration process—required for everyone else—for overnight stays in townships other than the member's own.

In November 2011, however, the president signed into law an amended Political Parties Registration Law that opened registration to opposition parties. The amended party registration law, among other improvements, deleted a clause that previously prevented former convicts from becoming a party member, implying that freed political prisoners have the right to join a political party and run for office. Following the law's passage, the NLD submitted its application for registration on November 25, and on December 23, Aung San Suu Kyi traveled to Naypyitaw to officially register the party. In total 11 parties applied for registration, and five were registered at year's end.

Participation of Women and Minorities: Following the 2010 elections, in some instances in the newly convened Parliament, opposition and ethnic parties contributed substantively to debates of current issues and the nation's future. Lawmakers adopted important legislation, such as a labor law that granted workers the right to organize and strike and a law providing the right to peaceful assembly. Participation of women and minorities in political life also increased. Prior to 2010 there were no women in the upper ranks of political leadership, and members of certain minority groups were denied a role in politics. During 2011 two women were deputy ministers, and five ethnic states elected persons of their own ethnicity as chief minister. There were 12 women in the 440-seat Pyithu Hluttaw (House of Representatives, or lower house), or 2.7 percent of members; six in the 224-seat Amyotha Hluttaw (House of Nationalities, or upper house), or 2.7 percent; and 24 among the 882 total seats in the seven state and seven regional Hluttaws, or 2.7 percent. The representation of women at both the national and the state/regional level was approximately 3 percent. There were 44 ethnic representatives from ethnic parties (non-USDP) in the Pyithu Hluttaw, or 10 percent, 29 in the Amyotha Hluttaw, or 12.9 percent, five among the 544 seats in the seven regional Hluttaws, or 0.9 percent, and 98 among the 338 seats in the seven state Hluttaws, or 29 percent. The representation of ethnic parliamentarians from ethnic parties at both the national and state/regional level was thus approximately 11 percent.

Principal Government Officials

Last Updated: 1/31/2013

Pres.: **THEIN SEIN**
Vice Pres.: **NYAN TUN**
Vice Pres.: **SAI MAUK KHAM, Dr.**
Min. for Agriculture & Irrigation: **MYINT HLAING**
Min. for Border Affairs: **THEIN HTAY, Maj. Gen.**
Min. of Commerce: **WIN MYINT**
Min. of Communications, Post, & Telegraph: **THEIN TUN**
Min. of Construction: **KYAW LWIN**
Min. for Cooperatives: **KYAW HSAN**
Min. of Culture: **AYE MYINT KYU**
Min. of Defense: **WAI LWIN, Lt. Gen.**
Min. of Education: **MYA AYE**
Min. of Electric Power: **KHIN MAUNG SOE**
Min. of Energy: **THAN HTAY**
Min. of Environmental Conservation & Forestry: **WIN TUN**
Min. of Finance & Revenue: **WIN SHEIN**
Min. of Foreign Affairs: **WUNNA MAUNG LWIN**
Min. of Health: **PE THET KHIN, Dr.**
Min. of Home Affairs: **KO KO, Lt. Gen.**
Min. of Hotels & Tourism: **HTAY AUNG**
Min. of Immigration & Population: **KHIN YI**
Min. of Industry: **AYE MYINT**
Min. of Information: **AUNG KYI**
Min. of Labor: **MAUNG MYINT**
Min. of Livestock & Fisheries: **OHN MYINT**
Min. of Mines: **MYINT AUNG**
Min. of National Planning & Economic Development: **KAN ZAW**
Min. of Rail Transport: **ZEYAR AUNG**
Min. of Religious Affairs: **MYINT MAUNG**
Min. of Science & Technology: **KO KO OO**
Min. of Social Welfare, Relief, & Resettlement: **MYAT MYAT OHN KHIN**
Min. of Sports: **TINT HSAN**
Min. for Transport: **NYAN TUN AUNG**
Min. in the Office of the Pres.: **AUNG MIN**
Min. in the Office of the Pres.: **HLA TUN**
Min. in the Office of the Pres.: **SOE MAUNG**
Min. in the Office of the Pres.: **SOE THEIN**
Min. in the Office of the Pres.: **THEIN NYUNT**
Min. in the Office of the Pres.: **TIN NAING THEIN**
Governor, Central Bank of Burma: **THAN NYEIN**
Ambassador to the US: **THAN SWE**
Permanent Representative to the UN, New York: **TIN KYAW**

ECONOMY

Burma, a resource-rich country, suffers from pervasive government controls, inefficient economic policies, corruption, and rural poverty. Despite Burma's emergence as a natural gas exporter, socio-economic conditions have deteriorated under the mismanagement of the previous regime. Approximately 32% of the population lives in poverty and Burma is the poorest country in Southeast Asia. The business climate is widely perceived as opaque, corrupt, and highly inefficient. Wealth from country's ample natural resources is concentrated in the hands of an elite group of military leaders and business associates.

In 2010–11, the transfer of state assets—especially real estate—to military families under the guise of a privatization policy further widened the gap between the economic elite and the public. The economy suffers from serious macroeconomic imbalances—including multiple official exchange rates that overvalue the Burmese kyat, fiscal deficits, lack of commercial credit further distorted by a non-market interest rate regime, unpredictable inflation, unreliable economic data, and an inability to reconcile national accounts.

Burma's poor investment climate—including weak rule of law—hampers the inflow of foreign investment; in recent years, foreign investors have shied away from nearly every sector except for natural gas, power generation, timber, and mining. The exploitation of natural resources does not benefit the population at large. The most productive sectors will continue to be in extractive industries—especially oil and gas, mining, and timber—with the latter two causing significant environmental degradation. Other areas, such as manufacturing, tourism, and services, struggle in the face of poor infrastructure, unpredictable trade policies, undeveloped human resources (the result of neglected health and education systems), endemic corruption, and inadequate access to capital for investment.

Private banks still operate under tight domestic and international restrictions, limiting the private sector's access to credit. The United States, the European Union, and Canada have imposed financial and economic sanctions on Burma. US sanctions, prohibiting most financial transactions with Burmese entities, impose travel bans on senior Burmese military and civilian leaders and others connected to the ruling regime, and ban imports of Burmese products.

These sanctions affect the country's fledgling garment industry, isolate the struggling banking sector, and raise the costs of doing business with Burmese companies, particularly firms tied to Burmese regime leaders. Remittances from overseas Burmese workers—who had provided significant financial support for their families—have driven the Ministry of Finance to license domestic banks to carry out overseas operations.

In 2011 the government took initial steps toward reforming and opening up the economy by lowering export taxes, easing restrictions on its financial sector, and reaching out to international organizations for assistance. Although the Burmese government has good economic relations with its neighbors, significant improvements in economic governance, the business climate, and the political situation are needed to promote serious foreign investment.

Labor Conditions

The law sets a minimum age of 13 for the employment of children. The 1993 Child Law provides for the protection of children in the workplace by classifying children ages 14 to 17 as youths and allowing them to engage in light duties. The legislation does not define what constitutes "light duties." Forced child labor is illegal under Order 1/99, which also prohibits recruitment of children into the military. The military law also prohibits recruitment of children into the military.

In practice the Child Law was not enforced. Child labor remained prevalent and highly visible. In cities children work mostly in the food-processing and light-manufacturing industries, as street vendors or refuse collectors, and as restaurant and teashop attendants. In rural areas children routinely worked in family agricultural activities, often as the result of poverty.

Despite legal provisions outlining criminal penalties for those guilty of recruiting child soldiers, the government army continued to recruit and use children in military-related activities. Ethnic armed groups and some cease-fire groups also allegedly recruited child soldiers.

Only government employees and employees of a few traditional industries were covered by minimum wage provisions. The Ministry of Finance and Revenue sets the minimum wage. It was not clear what methodology or process it uses.

The minimum monthly wage for salaried public employees remained on par with the market monthly wage of 50,000 kyat ($110) for what was in effect an eight-hour workday. The rate for day laborers was 2,000 kyat ($4.44) per day. Various subsidies and allowances supplemented this sum. The national poverty income level was estimated at less than 1,000 kyat ($2.22) per day.

Low real wages in the public sector fostered widespread corruption and absenteeism. In the private sector, urban laborers performing unskilled work earned 2,000 to 2,500 kyat ($4.44 to $5.56) per day, while rural agricultural workers generally earned less. Skilled workers in the private sector tended to earn somewhat more than rural agricultural workers and urban laborers; for example, a skilled factory worker earned 50,000 to 100,000 kyat ($110 to $220) per month, according to private sector employers.

The law prescribes a five-day, 35-hour workweek for employees in the public sector and a six-day, 44-hour workweek for private sector employees, with overtime paid for additional work. Factory workers at state-owned enterprises must work 44 to 48 hours per week, depending on the type of factory.

The law also allows for one 24-hour rest period per week, and workers are permitted 21 paid holidays per year; however, in practice provisions related to wages and hours benefited only a small portion of the labor force, since they were rarely enforced and most workers were engaged in rural agriculture or the informal sector.

U.S.-BURMA RELATIONS

The United States supports a peaceful, prosperous, and democratic Burma that respects the human rights of all its peoples. After the military coup government's 1988 crackdown on Burma's democratic opposition and its failure to honor the results of the country's 1990 parliamentary election, bilateral relations between the United States and Burma became strained. The United States and other members of the international community began to impose a range of economic, financial, and travel sanctions against Burma and support resolutions at the United Nations to mobilize international attention on the deplorable human rights situation. In 1990, the United States downgraded its level of diplomatic representation from Ambassador to Charge d'Affaires.

In 2009, the United States launched a new policy principled engagement including direct, senior-level dialogue with Burmese authorities. Relations between the United States and Burma began to improve, following the formation in March 2011 of a more civilian government under President Thein Sein. The new Burmese Government has implemented a series of reform efforts including releasing hundreds of political prisoners, signing preliminary ceasefire agreements with several ethnic armed groups, and holding credible parliamentary by-elections in which pro-democracy leader Aung San Suu Kyi and her opposition party won a landslide victory.

Secretary Clinton traveled to Burma in December 2011, marking the first visit by a U.S. Secretary of State in 56 years and an important turning point in U.S-Burma ties. The Burmese Government has continued on the path of reform since Secretary Clinton's visit and the United States has demonstrated its commitment to supporting Burma's reform agenda through principled engagement and an "action-for-action" strategy to respond to the reforms and incentivize further progress.

The U.S. seeks to deepen cooperation on a wide range of issues that promote democratization and national reconciliation. In recent months, the United States has fully restored diplomatic relations, taken steps to re-establish a USAID Mission in country, provided support for assessment missions and technical assistance by international financial institutions, and eased financial and investment sanctions against Burma.

The Barack Obama administration regularly consults with the U.S. Congress as well as U.S. allies and friends in Europe and Asia in appropriate ways to respond to developments in the country.

The military government changed the country name to "Myanmar" in 1989. It remains U.S. policy to refer to the country as Burma.

U.S. Assistance to Burma

As part of its response to Burma's steps toward reform, the U.S. is re-establishing an in-country U.S. Agency for International Development (USAID) mission. The United States has also decided to support a normal country program for the United Nations Development Program, and to enable private organizations in the U.S. to pursue a broad range of nonprofit activities from democracy building to health and education

Bilateral Economic Relations

The United States had imposed an array of economic sanctions on Burma, including bans on the importation of Burmese products into the U.S. and the export of financial services from the U.S. to Burma. Although U.S. exports to Burma (other than financial services) have been permitted, very little trade has flowed in that direction. As a result of Burma's political and economic reform progress, the United States eased the bans on the export of U.S. financial services and new investment in July. This sanctions easing is part of a broader effort to help accelerate broad based economic growth and recognize and encourage political reform. The United States continues to maintain a ban on all imports from Burma including rubies and jadeite substantially transformed in a third country.

Burma's Membership in International Organizations

Burma became a member of the United Nations in 1948 following independence from the United Kingdom. Burma and the United States belong to a number of the same international organizations, including the UN, International Monetary Fund, World Bank, and World Trade Organization.

Bilateral Representation

Burma maintains an embassy to the United States at 2300 S Street NW, Washington, DC 20008, tel.: (202) 332-3344; fax: (202) 332-4351.

Principal U.S. Embassy Officials

Last Updated: 1/14/2013

RANGOON (E) Rangoon, 110 University Avenue (GPO:521), (95) (1)536509, Fax 95-1-511069, INMARSAT Tel 383131573 or 383131574, Workweek: M-F 0800–1630, Website: http://burma.usembassy.gov/

DCM OMS:	Chin Hui Han-Quinlan
AMB OMS:	Leza Olson
Co-CLO:	Melissa Finkenbiner
FM:	Jim Libruk
MGT:	L. Eric Lindberg
POSHO:	Jim Libruk
SDO/DATT:	COL William Dickey
AMB:	Derek Mitchell
CON:	Andrew Webster-Main
DCM:	Virginia Murray
PAO:	Adrienne Nutzman
GSO:	Alla Kamins
RSO:	Justin J. Otto
AGR:	Dr. Tun Winn
CLO:	Stacie M. Kennedy

DEA: John M. Whalen
ECON: Machut Shishak
EEO: Craig A. Halbmaier
FMO: Patricia Pettet
IMO: Marco McGill
IPO: Marco McGill
ISO: Eric C. Finkenbiner
ISSO: Eric C. Finkenbiner
POL: Douglas E. Sonnek
State ICASS: Vacant

TRAVEL

Consular Information Sheet

June 29, 2011

Country Description: Burma (Myanmar) is an underdeveloped agrarian country ruled by an authoritarian military regime. The country's government suppresses all expression of opposition to its rule. The Government of Burma held nationwide elections on November 7, 2010, the first such elections in Burma in two decades. President Obama stated that Burma's elections were neither free nor fair and failed to meet any of the internationally accepted standards associated with legitimate elections.

After a long period of isolation, Burma has started to encourage tourism. As a foreigner, you can expect to pay more than locals do for accommodations, domestic airfares, and entry to tourist sites. Tourist facilities in Rangoon, Bagan, Ngapali Beach, Inle Lake, and Mandalay are superior to tourist facilities in other parts of the country, where they are limited or nonexistent. Please note that you should travel with sufficient cash to cover your expenses for the duration of your visit. Traveler's checks and credit cards are not accepted anywhere, and ATM machines are nonexistent in Burma.

Smart Traveler Enrollment Program (STEP)/Embassy Locations: If you are going to live in or visit Burma, please take the time to tell our Embassy about your trip. If you enroll, we can keep you up to date with important safety and security announcements. By enrolling, you will also help your friends and family get in touch with you in an emergency.

The U.S. Embassy is located at 110 University Ave., Kamayut Township, Rangoon. The Consular Section telephone number is (95-1) 536-509, ext. 4240; email consular-rangoon@state.gov. Travelers may visit the U.S. Embassy website at http://burma.usembassy.gov. The after-hours emergency number is 09-512-4330, or (95-1) 536-509, ext. 4014. The Consular Section is open from 8:00 am to 4:30 p.m., with non-emergency American Citizens Services from 2:00 to 3:30 pm, Monday through Friday except on U.S. and Burmese holidays.

Entry/Exit Requirements for U.S. Citizens: The Government of Burma strictly controls travel to, from, and within Burma. Since October 1, 2006, Burmese authorities have often prohibited entry or exit at most land border crossings, unless the traveler is part of a package-tour group that has received prior permission from the Burmese authorities. You must have a valid passport with at least six months remaining validity and visa to enter Burma. You should apply for your Burmese visa at a Burmese embassy or consulate abroad before you arrive in Burma. On September 1, 2010, the Government of Burma suspended its "Visa on Arrival" program, which had been in effect since May 2010. In Burma, you will be required to show your passport with a valid visa at all airports, train stations, and hotels. Security checkpoints are common outside of tourist areas.

Burmese authorities rarely issue visas to persons with occupations they deem "sensitive," including journalists. Many journalists and writers traveling to Burma on tourist visas have been denied entry. Journalists — and tourists mistaken for journalists — have been harassed. Some journalists have had film and notes confiscated upon leaving the country.

In an effort to prevent international child abduction, many governments have initiated procedures at entry/exit points. These often include requiring documentary evidence of relationship and permission from the absent parent(s) or legal guardian for the child's travel. Having such documentation on hand, even if not required, may help you with entry/departure.

You can get information about entry requirements as well as other information from the Burmese Embassy's (Embassy of the Union of Myanmar) website, 2300 S Street NW, Washington, DC 20008, telephone 202-332-4350 or the Permanent Burma Mission (Mission of Myanmar) to the UN, 10 East 77th St., New York, NY 10021, (212-535-1311) 212-744-1271, fax 212-744-1290.

The U.S. Department of State is unaware of any HIV/AIDS entry restrictions for visitors to or foreign residents of Burma.

Threats to Safety and Security: Over a period of years, Burma has experienced sporadic bombing attacks. In April 2010, a series of explosions among a crowd of revelers at a Water Festival celebration in Rangoon killed at least ten people and wounded as many as 170. In June 2011, bombings targeted a variety of local facilities, including government offices, public restrooms, a public phone booth, markets, and in one instance a train traveling from Mandalay to Rangoon. There is no indication that these attacks targeted U.S. citizens or U.S. interests.

In September 2007, the Government of Burma brutally cracked down on peaceful demonstrators, using gunfire, rubber bullets, batons, and tear gas against them and nearby observers. The authorities killed at least 30 people during the crackdown and arrested more than 3,000. On September 27, 2007, security forces shot and killed a Japanese journalist in the Sule Pagoda downtown area during a demonstration. The Government of Burma has a standing law, which is selectively enforced, that bans all gatherings of more than five people.

Burma experienced major political unrest in 1988 when the military regime jailed or killed thousands of Burmese democracy activists. In 1990, the military government refused to recognize the results of an election that the opposition won overwhelmingly. Major demonstrations by opposition activists occurred in 1996 and 1998.

In May 2003, individuals affiliated with the Burmese regime attacked a convoy carrying opposition leader Aung San Suu Kyi in Sagaing Division; dozens were killed or injured. Conflicts between the government and various ethnic minority groups continue in a number of border regions in Burma, and anti-personnel landmines in some border areas pose an additional danger. Occasional fighting between government forces and various rebel groups has occurred in Chin State and Sagaing Division near India and along Burma's Kachin, Shan, Mon, Kayah (Karenni), and Karen State's borders with China and Thailand.

Most recently, in June 2011, Burmese government troops clashed with Kachin militias, prompting a number of civilians to flee from Burma into China. Several recent skirmishes have also reportedly taken place between Burmese government troops and armed groups in Karen and Shan State. From time to time, the governments of Burma and Thailand have closed the border between the two nations on short notice.

In light of these incidents, you should exercise caution in public places at all times. Be alert to your surroundings and the presence of unattended packages or bags or suspicious objects/ activity in public areas.

Furthermore, avoid crowded public places, such as large public gatherings, demonstrations, and any areas cordoned off by security forces; problems can develop quickly. While in Burma, you should closely follow media reports and public information about the security situation in Burma. Given the Government of Burma's restrictions on travel by U.S. diplomats, U.S. Government assistance to U.S. citizens affected by incidents in remote areas of Burma may be difficult.

Stay up to date by:

- Bookmarking our Bureau of Consular Affairs website, which contains the current Travel Warnings and Travel Alerts as well as the Worldwide Caution.
- Downloading our free Smart Traveler iPhone App for travel information at your fingertips.
- Following us on Twitter and Facebook.
- Calling 1-888-407-4747 toll-free within the United States and Canada, or 1-202-501-4444 from other countries.

Crime: Crime rates in Burma, especially toward foreigners, are lower than those of many other countries in the region. Nevertheless, the crime rate has been increasing. Violent crime against foreigners is rare.

Don't buy counterfeit and pirated goods, even if they are widely available. Not only are the bootlegs illegal in the United States, but if you purchase them, you may also be breaking local law.

Victims of Crime: If you or someone you know becomes the victim of a crime abroad, you should contact the local police and the U.S. Embassy.. We can:

- Replace a stolen passport.
- For violent crimes such as assault or rape, help you find appropriate medical care.
- Put you in contact with the appropriate police authorities, and contact family members or friends.
- Although the local authorities are responsible for investigating and prosecuting the crime, consular officers can help you understand the local criminal justice process and can direct you to local attorneys.

There is no equivalent number to the "911" emergency line in Burma.

Criminal Penalties: While you are traveling in Burma, you are subject to its laws, even if you are a U.S. citizen. Foreign laws and legal systems can be vastly different than our own. In Burma, you may be taken in for questioning if you don't have your passport with you. It is illegal to take pictures of Burmese officials and of certain buildings, such as military installations and government buildings. There are also some things that might be legal in Burma, but still illegal in the United States.

You can be prosecuted under U.S. law if you buy pirated goods.Engaging in sexual conduct with children or using or disseminating child pornography in a foreign country is a crime prosecutable in the United States. If you break local laws in Burma, your U.S. passport won't help you avoid arrest or prosecution. It's very important to know what's legal and what's not in Burma.

While in Burma, you should carry your U.S. passport or a photocopy of passport data and visa pages at all times so that if you are questioned by Burmese officials, you will have proof of your U.S. citizenship readily available

Some foreigners have been denied even minimal rights in criminal proceedings in Burma, especially when suspected of engaging in political activity of any type. This includes, but is not limited to, denial of access to an attorney, denial of access to court records, and denial of family and consular visits. The criminal justice system is controlled by the military junta, which orders maximum sentences for most offenses.

In the past, the Government of Burma has deported a number of U.S. citizens engaged in teaching and training programs in Mandalay and other locations in Upper Burma. In some cases, the individuals were sponsored by the U.S. Embassy. Although their activities were apolitical, their deportations demonstrate the Government of Burma's sensitivity to activities by foreigners. Burmese authorities often did not inform the Embassy of these deportations and did not give the individuals an explanation for their deportations. However, in subsequent discussions with the Embassy, Burmese authorities stated that some of the deportations were due to the visitors' violation of the terms of their Burmese visas. The authorities told us that in one case, a U.S. citizen was detained, questioned, and "asked to leave Burma" because of her boyfriend's political activities in the United States.

If you travel to Burma, and especially to Mandalay and remote regions of the country, you should be aware of these potential risks and make informed choices about your travel and activities in Burma. Based on the Vienna Convention on Consular Relations and customary international law, if you are arrested in Burma, you have the option to request that the police, prison officials, or other authorities alert the U.S. Embassy of your arrest, and to have communications from you forwarded to the U.S. Embassy.

Accessibility: While in Burma, individuals with disabilities may find accessibility and accommodation very different from what they find in the United States. Roads and sidewalks are often extremely difficult to cross even in the best of circumstances.

Ramps or handicapped-accessible facilities do not exist even in Rangoon and other areas popular with tourists. Individuals confined to wheelchairs or those with other physical ailments should be prepared to face difficulties throughout Burma.

Photography: Do not photograph or videotape the military or police, or anything that could be perceived as being of military or security interest— such as bridges, airfields, government buildings or government vehicles. Burmese authorities might interpret these actions as being provocative and may question and/or arrest you. U.S. citizens have been detained, arrested, tried, and deported for, among other activities, distributing pro-democracy literature and visiting the homes and offices of Burmese pro-democracy leaders. Burmese authorities have warned U.S. Embassy officials that those who engage in similar activities in the future will be jailed rather than deported, although this has not yet occurred.

Foreigner Travel within Burma: Burmese authorities require that hotels and guesthouses furnish information about the identities and activities of their foreign guests. Burmese who interact with foreigners may be compelled to report on those interactions to Burmese authorities.

Security personnel may at times place foreign visitors under surveillance, and you should assume your actions, such as meeting with Burmese citizens, particularly in public spaces like hotel lobbies, rooms, and restaurants, are being monitored.

You should assume that telephones (including cell phones) and fax machines are monitored and that your personal possessions in hotel rooms may be searched. You will not generally be required to obtain advance permission to travel to the main tourist areas of Mandalay and the surrounding area, Bagan, Inle Lake, Ngapali, and other beach resorts. However, some tourists traveling to places where permission is not expressly required have reported delays due to questioning by local security personnel.

Additionally, the military regime restricts access to some areas of the country on an ad-hoc basis, and in 2005, the regime stated it could not guarantee the safety of foreigners traveling in eastern Shan State, specifically in Wa territory, also known as Special Region 2. If you plan to travel in Burma, you should check with Burmese tourism authorities to see whether travel to specific destinations is permitted.

Even if the Burmese authorities allow travel to specific destinations in Burma, you may not be safe traveling in those areas. Wherever you travel in Burma, you should be careful to respect the differences between the United States and the Burmese culture and customs.

Dual Nationals: According to Burmese officials at the Burmese Embassy in Washington D.C., Burmese citizens will automatically lose their Burmese citizenship when they obtain another country's citizenship. Burmese authorities reportedly require former Burmese citizens to inform the Burmese government about their acquisition of U.S. citizenship and the change of address associated with their move to the United States, and to surrender their Burmese nationality. They also demand surrender of any National Registration Card or National Scrutiny Card, which is evidence of Burmese citizenship.

On occasion, Burmese authorities have detained and pursued criminal proceedings against Burmese-Americans who have returned to Burma on U.S. passports and who have had in their possession evidence of Burmese citizenship, such as a National Registration Card. If you have U.S. citizenship and have not surrendered your Burmese citizenship, you should check with the nearest Burmese embassy prior to your travel to Burma to be sure you are not at risk of arrest if you travel to Burma.

Irrawaddy Delta Region: On May 2, 2008, Cyclone Nargis devastated Burma's Irrawaddy Delta region and surrounding areas, killing over 130,000 people. Like other areas of Burma, the Delta region is still without many basic necessities.

The United Nations, ASEAN, and other members of the international community, including the United States, continue to provide international relief assistance to assist communities recovering from the storm. Rangoon, Burma's most populous city and other areas outside of the Irrawaddy Delta are recovering. Electrical power and water supply have been restored in most areas, and markets are now operating normally.

Customs Regulations: Customs regulations in Burma are restrictive and strictly enforced. Customs authorities closely search travelers' luggage upon their arrival and departure from Burma. It is illegal to enter or exit Burma with items such as firearms, religious materials, antiquities, medications, business equipment, currency, gems, ivory, and other restricted items. On several occasions in the past two decades, foreigners have been detained, searched, and imprisoned for attempting to take restricted items out of the country.

Customs officials also strictly limit the items that can be brought into the country. Among other items, they ban pornography and political material or literature critical of the regime or supportive of the opposition. Travelers have also reported problems bringing in high-tech electronic devices and equipment, ranging from toys to computers. The military regime has never provided a complete list of prohibited import items.

For information on restricted items for import into Burma and specific customs' requirements, please contact the nearest Burmese embassy (Embassy of the Union of Myanmar) or the Burmese Embassy in Washington, D.C., or Burma's Mission in New York.

Computers, Internet, and Email: The military regime carefully controls and monitors all Internet use in Burma and restricts Internet access through software-based censorship that limits the materials individuals can access online. The government has allowed cyber cafes to open, but access to the Internet is very expensive, and access to most "free" international e-mail services such as Hotmail and Yahoo is prohibited. Currently, Gmail (Google mail) accounts can be accessed in Burma, and many locals and resident expatriates use it.

It is illegal to own an unregistered modem in Burma. You may bring one laptop computer into Burma, but you must declare it upon arrival. Limited email service is available at some large hotels. All emails are subject to monitoring by Burmese security services. It is very expensive to send photographs via email. One foreign visitor was presented a bill for $2,000 after transmitting one photograph via a major hotel's e-mail system. During September and October 2007, the military government disconnected all Internet access across the country for extended periods of time.

Telephone Services: Telephone service is poor in Rangoon and other major cities and non-existent in many areas. Calling the United States from Burma is difficult and extremely expensive.

Consular Notification and Access: U.S. consular officers do not always receive timely notification of the detention, arrest, or deportation of U.S. citizens. In addition, Burmese authorities have on occasion refused to give Embassy consular officers access to arrested or detained U.S. citizens. If you are arrested or detained, you should request immediate contact with the U.S. Embassy.

Please carry your U.S. passport with you at all times, so that if questioned by local officials, you have proof of identity and U.S. citizenship readily available. Should an emergency arise involving the detention of a U.S. citizen, especially outside of Rangoon, U.S. Embassy personnel may not be able to assist quickly, because travel inside Burma can be slow and difficult.

The Burmese authorities do not routinely notify the U.S. Embassy of the arrest of U.S. citizens and have obstructed regular access by U.S. consular officers to U.S. citizen detainees.

Currency: Traveler's checks, credit cards, and ATM cards can rarely, if ever, be used. Although moneychangers sometimes approach travelers with an offer to change dollars into Burmese kyat at the market rate, it is illegal to exchange currency except at authorized locations such as the airport, banks and government stores. It is also illegal for Burmese to possess foreign currency without a permit. Foreigners are required to use U.S. dollars, other hard currency, or Foreign Exchange Certificates (FEC) for the payment of plane tickets, train tickets, and most hotels bills. Please be sure to bring pristine bills, as most establishments will not accept torn or old U.S. currency.

Burmese kyats are accepted for nearly all other transactions. Executive Order 13310, signed by President Bush on July 28, 2003, imposed a ban on the exportation of financial services to Burma In recent months, U.S. financial institutions have increased scrutiny of on-line financial transactions taking place on Burmese Internet providers.

As a result, the bank accounts of some U.S. citizens working or traveling in Burma have been frozen. To avoid this potential problem, customers of U.S. banks should avoid on-line banking while using a Burmese Internet Service Provider (ISP). Those who believe their accounts have been subject to similar restrictions in error are asked to contact the Consular Section of the U.S. Embassy in Rangoon.

U.S. Treasury Sanctions: As of August 27, 2003, U.S. Treasury sanctions ban the import of almost all goods from Burma into the United States. This ban includes Burmese-origin products such as gifts, souvenirs, and items for personal use, even if carried in personal luggage.

These sanctions are part of a much larger U.S. sanctions regime for Burma, which includes a ban on new U.S. investment among other measures. For specific information, contact the U.S. Department of the Treasury, Office of Foreign Assets Control (OFAC) home page or via OFAC's Info-by-Fax service at 202-622-0077, or by phone toll-free at 1-800-540-6322.

Medical Facilities and Health Information: Medical facilities in Burma are inadequate for even routine medical care. There are few adequately trained medical personnel. We recommend that you have medevac insurance in case you need to be transported to a regional medical center outside of Burma for emergency care. Most foreign drugs on sale in Burma have been smuggled into the country, and many are counterfeit or adulterated and thus unsafe to use. Travelers should bring adequate supplies of their medications for the duration of their stay in Burma. HIV/AIDS is widespread among high-risk populations, such as prostitutes and illegal drug users. Malaria, tuberculosis, hepatitis, and other infectious diseases are endemic in many parts of the country.

In early 2006 throughout 2007, and again in early 2010, brief avian influenza outbreaks resulted in the death of domestic poultry and some wild birds. In December 2007, the World Health Organization and Burmese Ministry of Health confirmed Burma's first case of human infection with the H5N1 avian influenza virus.

If you travel to Burma and other South Asian countries affected by avian influenza, we caution you to avoid poultry farms, contact with animals in live food markets, and any other surfaces that appear to be contaminated with feces from poultry or other animals. There were no reported human cases on H5N1 in Burma during the 2010 outbreaks.

You can find good information on vaccinations and other health precautions, on the CDC website. The WHO website also contains additional health information for travelers, including detailed country-specific health information. For information about avian influenza (H5N1), please see the U.S. Department of State's Avian Influenza Fact Sheet. Tuberculosis is an increasingly serioushealth concern in Burma. For further information, please consultthe CDC's information on TB.

Medical Insurance: You can't assume your insurance will go with you when you travel. It's very important to find out BEFORE you leave whether or not your medical insurance will cover you overseas. You need to ask your insurance company two questions:

- Does my policy apply when I'm out of the United States?
- Will it cover emergencies like a trip to a foreign hospital or a medical evacuation?

In many places, doctors and hospitals still expect payment in cash at the time of service. Your regular U.S. health insurance may not cover doctors' and hospital visits in other countries. If your policy doesn't go with you when you travel, it's a very good idea to take out another one for your trip.

Traffic Safety and Road Conditions: While in a foreign country, you may encounter road conditions that differ significantly from those in the United States. The information below concerning Burma is provided for your general reference only, and may not be accurate in a particular location or circumstance. Rangoon's main roads are generally in poor condition.

Traffic in the capital is increasing rapidly, but heavy congestion is still uncommon. Some roads are in serious disrepair. Slow-moving vehicles, bicycles, animals, and heavy pedestrian traffic create numerous hazards for drivers on Rangoon's streets. If you drive in Burma, you must remain extremely alert to avoid hitting pedestrians. Most roads outside of Rangoon consist of one to two lanes and are potholed, often unpaved, and unlit at night. Many of the truck drivers traveling from China to Rangoon are believed to drive under the influence of methamphetamines and other stimulants.

Drunken and/or drugged drivers are also common on the roads during the four-day Buddhist water festival in mid-April. Driving at night is particularly dangerous. Few, if any, streets are adequately lit. Most Burmese drivers do not turn on their headlights until the sky is completely dark; many do not use headlights at all. Many bicyclists use no lights or reflectors. Vehicular traffic moves on the right side, as in the United States; however, a majority of vehicles have the steering wheel positioned on the right.

The "right of way" concept is generally respected, but military convoys and motorcades always have precedence. Most vehicle accidents are settled between the parties on site, with the party at fault paying the damages. In the event of an accident with a pedestrian, the driver is always considered to be at fault and subject to fines or arrest, regardless of the circumstances.

Accidents that require an investigation are concluded quickly and rarely result in criminal prosecution. There is no roadside assistance and ambulances are not available. Vehicles generally do not have seat belts. Child car seats are also not available.

Aviation Safety Oversight: As there is no direct commercial air service to the United States by carriers registered in Burma, the U.S. Federal Aviation Administration (FAA) has not assessed Burma's Civil Aviation Authority for compliance with International Civil Aviation Organization (ICAO) aviation safety standards.

The safety records of Burma's domestic airlines are not open to the public, nor is public information available concerning the Burma government's oversight of domestic airlines. These factors raise concerns about aviation safety for all Burmese domestic air carriers.

Children's Issues: Please see the U.S. Dept. of State Office of Children's Issues web pages on intercountry adoption and international parental child abduction.

Intercountry Adoption

November 2011

Burma is not party to the Hague Convention on Protection of Children and Co-operation in Respect of Intercountry Adoption (Hague Adoption Convention). Therefore, when the Hague Adoption Convention entered into force for the United States on April 1, 2008, intercountry adoption processing for Burma did not change. Burmese law does not allow for the adoption of Burmese children by non-Burmese nationals.

The Government of Burma does not recognize dual citizenship and only those prospective adoptive parents that are Burmese citizens and Buddhist are able to complete an adoption under Burmese law.

U.S. Embassy in Burma
110 University Ave
Kamayut Township
Rangoon, Burma
Phone: (95)-(1)-536–509 (and then press 1 to get to the Consular section)
Fax: (95)-(1)-650–480
Email: ConsularRangoon@state.gov
http://burma.usembassy.gov

Embassy of Burma
2300 S Street, NW
Washington, D.C. 20008
Phone: 202–332–3344, 202–332–4350, or 202–332–4352
Fax: 202–332–4351
Email: info@mewashingtondc.com
Internet: www.mewashingtondc.com

Office of Children's Issues
U.S. Department of State
2201 C Street, NW
SA-29
Washington, DC 20520
Tel: 1–888–407–4747
E-mail: AskCI@state.gov
http://adoption.state.gov

For questions about immigration procedures, call the National Customer Service Center (NCSC) at 1-800-375-5283 (TTY 1-800-767-1833).

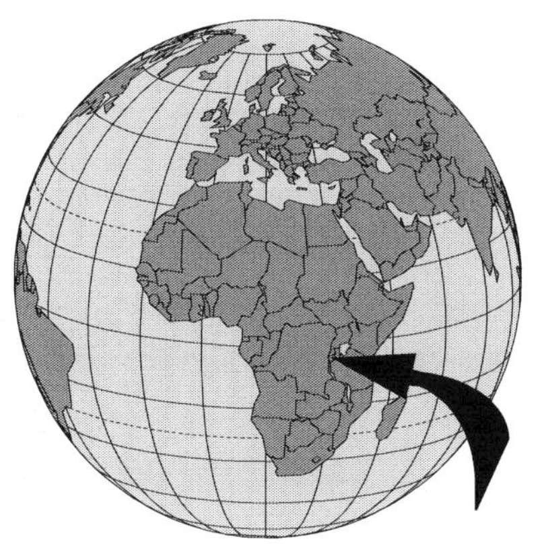

BURUNDI

Compiled from publications that were available as of February 2013 from the U.S. Department of State, the U.S. Department of Commerce, and the Central Intelligence Agency (CIA). See the introduction to this set for explanatory notes.

Official Name:
Republic of Burundi

PROFILE

Geography

Area: total: 27,830 sq km; country comparison to the world: 147; land: 25,680 sq km; water: 2,150 sq km

Major cities: Bujumbura (capital) 455,000 (2009)

Climate: equatorial; high plateau with considerable altitude variation (772 m to 2,670 m above sea level); average annual temperature varies with altitude from 23 to 17 degrees centigrade but is generally moderate as the average altitude is about 1,700 m; average annual rainfall is about 150 cm; two wet seasons (February to May and September to November), and two dry seasons (June to August and December to January)

Terrain: hilly and mountainous, dropping to a plateau in east, some plains

People

Nationality: noun: Burundian(s); adjective: Burundian

Population: 10,557,259 (July 2012 est.)

Population growth rate: 3.104% (2012 est.)

Ethnic groups: Hutu (Bantu) 85%, Tutsi (Hamitic) 14%, Twa (Pygmy) 1%, Europeans 3,000, South Asians 2,000

Religions: Christian 67% (Roman Catholic 62%, Protestant 5%), indigenous beliefs 23%, Muslim 10%

Languages: Kirundi (official), French (official), Swahili (along Lake Tanganyika and in the Bujumbura area)

Literacy: definition: age 15 and over can read and write; total population: 67.2%; male: 72.9%; female: 61.8% (2010 est.)

Health: life expectancy at birth: total population: 59.24 years; male: 57.52 years; female: 61.02 years (2012 est.); Infant mortality rate: total: 60.32 deaths/1,000 live births; male: 64.85 deaths/1,000 live births; female: 55.67 deaths/1,000 live births (2012 est.)

Unemployment rate: NA%

Work force: 4.245 million (2007)

Government

Type: republic

Independence: 1 July 1962

Constitution: ratified by popular referendum 28 February 2005

Political subdivisions: 17 provinces; Bubanza, Bujumbura Mairie, Bujumbura Rural, Bururi, Cankuzo, Cibitoke, Gitega, Karuzi, Kayanza, Kirundo, Makamba, Muramvya, Muyinga, Mwaro, Ngozi, Rutana, Ruyigi

Suffrage: 18 years of age; universal

Economy

GDP (purchasing power parity): $5.489 billion (2012 est.); $5.25 billion (2011 est.); $5.04 billion (2010 est.); $4.855 billion (2009 est.)

GDP real growth rate: 4.2% (2012 est.); 4.2% (2011 est.); 3.8% (2010 est.); 3.5% (2009 est.)

GDP per capita (PPP): $600 (2012 est.); $600 (2011 est.); $600 (2010 est.); $600 (2009 est.)

Natural resources: nickel, uranium, rare earth oxides, peat, cobalt, copper, platinum, vanadium, arable land, hydropower, niobium, tantalum, gold, tin, tungsten, kaolin, limestone

Agriculture products: coffee, cotton, tea, corn, sorghum, sweet potatoes, bananas, cassava (manioc); beef, milk, hides

Industries: light consumer goods such as blankets, shoes, soap; assembly of imported components; public works construction; food processing

Exports: $107.4 million (2012 est.); $99.5 million (2011 est.); $101.9 million (2010 est.)

Exports—commodities: coffee, tea, sugar, cotton, hides

Exports—partners: Germany 15.7%, China 10.5%, Sweden 9.5%, Belgium 9%, Pakistan 7.4%, US 7.4%, France 4.3% (2011)

Imports: $569.7 million (2012 est.); $533.3 million (2011 est.); $440.3 million (2010 est.)

Imports—commodities: capital goods, petroleum products, foodstuffs

Imports—partners: Saudi Arabia 16.8%, Belgium 8.2%, China 7.5%, Uganda 7.4%, Kenya 6.5%, Zambia 6.4%, US 6.2%, France 5% (2011)
Debt—external: $231.7 million (31 December 2012 est.); $573.4 million (31 December 2011 est.); $533.8 million
Exchange rates: Burundi francs (BIF) per US dollar; 1,439.5 (2012 est.); 1,261.1 (2011 est.); 1,230.8 (2010 est.); 1,230.18 (2009); 1,198 (2008); 1,065 (2007)

PEOPLE

Most people live on subsistence farms near areas of fertile volcanic soil. The population is made up of three major ethnic groups--Hutu, Tutsi, and Twa. Intermarriage takes place frequently between the Hutus and Tutsis. Although Hutus encompass the majority of the population, historically Tutsis have been politically and economically dominant.

National/Racial/Ethnic Minorities

The Batwa, the original hunter-gatherer inhabitants who number approximately 80,000 persons, less than 1 percent of the population, generally remained economically, politically, and socially marginalized. Lack of education, employment, and access to land were cited as the major problems. Local administrations must provide free schoolbooks and health care for all Batwa children and two acres of land per family (comparable with the nationwide average size of a farmstead). Local administrations largely fulfilled these requirements. The constitution provides three appointed seats for Batwa in each of the houses of parliament. Following the 2010 election, however, one of these three Senate seats was awarded to a non-Batwa.

Langauge

The indigenous language is Kirundi, which is spoken throughout the country. French is the administrative and official language. Kiswahili is widely spoken in the capital and in the eastern region of the country near the border with Tanzania. In response to Burundi's 2007 entry into the East African Community, the government added English and Swahili instruction, beginning in first grade, to public school curricula. While a number of government officials and business people are making an effort to speak English, it is absolutely essential for foreigners to speak French or have access to a reliable interpreter.

Religion

Although reliable statistics on the size of various religious groups are not available, sources estimate approximately 60 percent of the population is Roman Catholic, 20 percent includes members of indigenous religious groups, and 15 percent is Protestant. The Muslim population is estimated to be between 2 and 5 percent, the majority of whom live in urban areas. Sunnis make up the majority of Muslims; the remainder is Shia.

HISTORY

In the 16th century, Burundi was a kingdom characterized by a hierarchical political authority and tributary economic exchange. A king (mwani) headed a princely aristocracy (ganwa) that owned most of the land and required a tribute, or tax, from local farmers and herders. In the mid-18th century, this predominantly-Tutsi royalty consolidated authority over land, production, and distribution with the development of the ubugabire—a patron-client relationship in which the populace received royal protection in exchange for tribute and land tenure.

Although European explorers and missionaries made brief visits to the area as early as 1856, it was not until 1899 that Burundi came under German East African administration. In 1916 Belgian troops occupied the area. In 1923, the League of Nations mandated to Belgium the territory of Ruanda-Urundi, encompassing modern-day Rwanda and Burundi. The Belgians administered the territory through indirect rule, building on the Tutsi-dominated aristocratic hierarchy. Following World War II, Ruanda-Urundi became a United Nations Trust Territory under Belgian administrative authority. After 1948, Belgium permitted the emergence of competing political parties. Two political parties emerged: the Union for National Progress (UPRONA), a multi-ethnic party led by Tutsi Prince Louis Rwagasore and the Christian Democratic Party (PDC) supported by Belgium. In 1961, Prince Rwagasore was assassinated following an UPRONA victory in legislative elections.

Full independence was achieved on July 1, 1962. In the context of weak democratic institutions at independence, Ganwa King Mwambutsa IV established a constitutional monarchy comprising equal numbers of Hutus and Tutsis. The 1965 assassination of the Hutu prime minister set in motion a series of destabilizing Hutu revolts and subsequent governmental repression. In 1966, King Mwambutsa was deposed by his son, Prince Ntare IV, who himself was deposed the same year by a military coup led by Capt. Michel Micombero. Micombero abolished the monarchy and declared a republic, although a de facto military regime emerged. In 1972, an aborted Hutu rebellion triggered the flight of hundreds of thousands of Burundians. Civil unrest continued throughout the late 1960s and early 1970s.

In 1976, Col. Jean-Baptiste Bagaza took power in a bloodless coup. Although Bagaza led a Tutsi-dominated military regime, he encouraged land reform, electoral reform, and national reconciliation. In 1981, a new constitution was promulgated. In 1984, Bagaza was elected head of state, as the sole candidate. After his election, Bagaza's human rights record deteriorated as he suppressed religious activities and detained political opposition members.

In 1987, Maj. Pierre Buyoya overthrew Colonel Bagaza. He dissolved opposition parties, suspended the 1981 constitution, and instituted his ruling Military Committee for

National Salvation (CSMN). During 1988, increasing tensions between the ruling Tutsis and the majority Hutus resulted in violent confrontations between the Tutsi-dominated army, the Hutu opposition, and Tutsi hardliners. During this period, an estimated 150,000 people were killed, with tens of thousands of refugees flowing to neighboring countries. Buyoya formed a commission to investigate the causes of the 1988 unrest and to develop a charter for democratic reform.

In 1991, Buyoya approved a constitution that provided for a president, multi-ethnic government, and a parliament. Burundi's first Hutu president, Melchior Ndadaye, of the Hutu-dominated FRODEBU Party, was elected in 1993. He was assassinated by factions of the Tutsi-dominated armed forces in October 1993.

The country was then plunged into civil war, in which tens of thousands of people were killed and hundreds of thousands were displaced by the time the FRODEBU government regained control and elected Cyprien Ntaryamira president in January 1994. Nonetheless, the security situation continued to deteriorate.

In April 1994, President Ntaryamira and Rwandan President Juvenal Habyarimana died in a plane crash. This act marked the beginning of the Rwandan genocide, while in Burundi the death of Ntaryamira exacerbated the violence and unrest. Sylvestre Ntibantunganya was installed as president for a 4-year term on April 8, but the security situation further deteriorated. The influx of hundreds of thousands of Rwandan refugees and the activities of armed Hutu and Tutsi groups further destabilized the regime.

Burundi's civil war officially ended in 2006 under a South Africa-brokered cease-fire agreement with the last of Burundi's rebel groups. In 2009, the PALIPEHUTU-FNL, the last rebel group, disarmed, demobilized and registered as a political party (the FNL), in accordance with the terms of the agreement. Today the government is focused on rebuilding its infrastructure and reestablishing external relations with its regional neighbors.

GOVERNMENT AND POLITICAL CONDITIONS

The Republic of Burundi is a democratic, multiparty republic. The 2005 constitution provides for an executive branch that reports to the president, a bicameral parliament, and an independent judiciary. In June 2010 voters reelected President Pierre Nkurunziza, and in July 2010 they selected a new National Assembly (lower house) in elections that international observers found largely free, fair, peaceful, and consistent with international standards. The armed forces and other.

While observers considered the military generally professional and apolitical, the intelligence service and the police tended to be influenced directly by and responsive to the ruling National Council for the Defense of Democracy-Forces for the Defense of Democracy party (CNDD-FDD).

Recent Elections

Between May and September 2010 the government held five separate elections: communal councils (in May), presidential (in June), National Assembly (in July), Senate (in July), and village councils (in September). Voter turnout in the communal elections was more than 90 percent. Following the communal elections, a coalition of 12 parties withdrew and boycotted the remaining four elections. Following the withdrawal of the opposition coalition, the CNDD-FDD's presidential candidate, Pierre Nkurunziza, ran unopposed, and the ruling CNDD-FDD party won absolute majorities in the National Assembly and Senate.

The EU's Election Observation Mission, which monitored the five elections, noted that the June 28 presidential and July 23 National Assembly elections were largely peaceful and generally well managed by the Independent Electoral Commission, but that the political and electoral environment was characterized by unfair use by the ruling CNDD-FDD of government facilities and financial resources during the campaigns, the absence of pluralistic competition, and restrictions by the government and ruling party on the freedoms of political party expression and assembly of its competitors. Members of the youth wings of the CNDD-FDD and of several rival political parties engaged in intimidation and violence before, during, and after the elections.

Political Parties: There were 43 registered political parties, the vast majority based on family, clan, or region and representing localized interests. Only six parties fielded candidates in all 17 provinces and 129 communes in the May 2010 communal elections. In July the National Assembly mandated that all parties reregister by the end of the year. According to the new law, in order to qualify for public campaign funding and to compete in the 2015 legislative and presidential elections, parties must be "nationally" based (i.e., be ethnically and regionally diverse) and demonstrate in writing that they have party membership and organizations in all of the provinces.

A provision that all party presidents must reside in Burundi was rejected by the coalition of political parties that boycotted the 2010 elections, given that the presidents of three of the parties in the coalition remain in self-imposed exile abroad.

Participation of Women and Minorities: The constitution reserves 30 percent of the seats in the National Assembly, the Senate, and the communal councils for women. There were 32 women in the 106-seat National Assembly and 19 women in the 41-seat Senate. The constitution also mandates that 30 percent of appointed government positions be set aside for women. After a cabinet reshuffle in December, women held eight of 21 ministerial positions; there were seven women on the 17-seat Supreme Court, and three

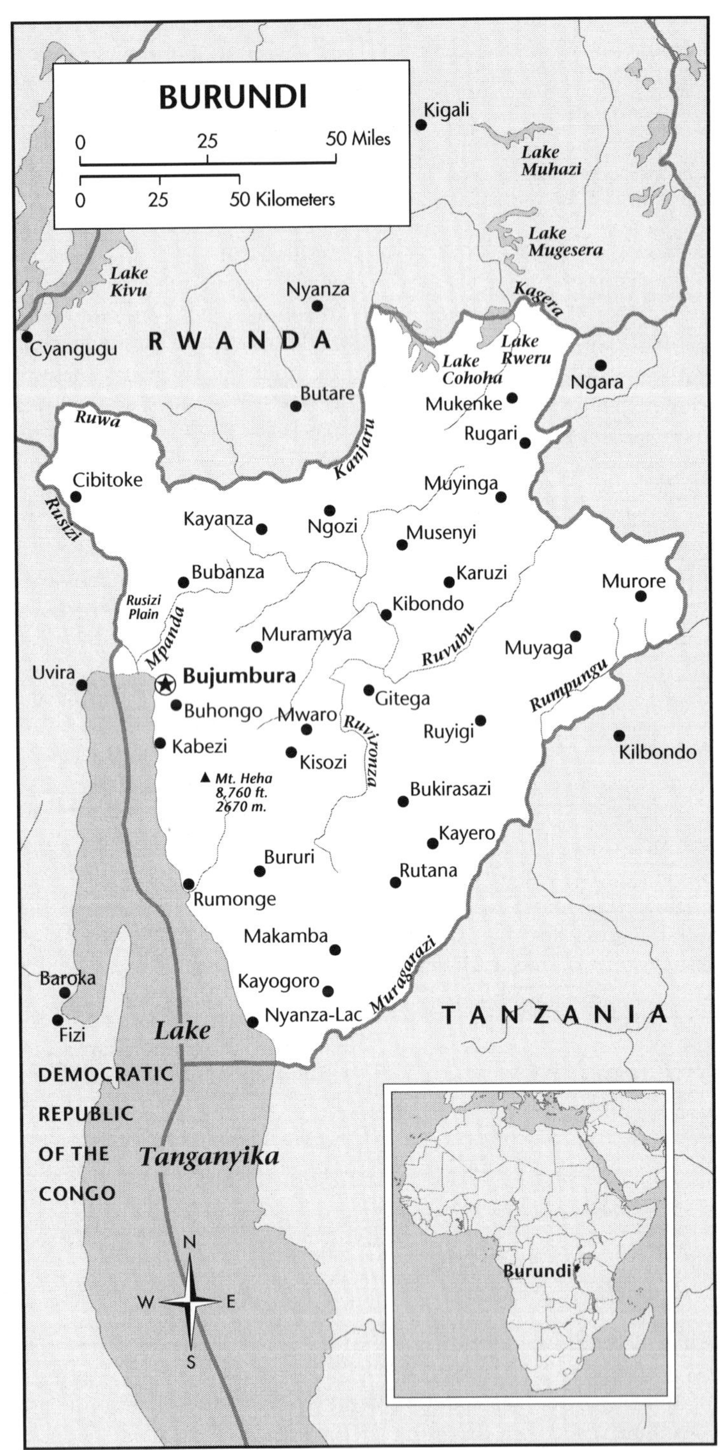

women on the seven-seat Constitutional Court. The constitution provides for representation in all elected and appointed government positions for the two main ethnic groups: the Hutu majority is entitled to no more than 60 percent and the Tutsi minority to no less than 40 percent. In addition, the Batwa ethnic group, which makes up less than 1 percent of the population, is allotted three seats in each chamber of parliament. However, in 2010 the government named a non-Batwa to one of three Senate seats reserved for Batwas, a decision challenged by the Batwa community but upheld by the Constitutional Court in 2010.

Principal Government Officials

Last Updated: 1/31/2013

Pres.: **Pierre NKURUNZIZA**

First Vice Pres.: **Therence SINUNGURUZA**

Second Vice Pres.: **Gervais RUFYIKIRI**

Min. of Agriculture & Livestock: **Odette KAYITESI**

Min. of of Basic Education, Secondary Education, Handicrafts, Training,& Literacy: **Severin BUZINGO**

Min. of Civil Service, Labor, & Social Security: **Annonciate SENDAZIRASA**

Min. of Commerce, Trade, Industry, Posts, & Tourism: **Victoire NDIKUMANA**

Min. of Communal Development: **Martin NIVIYABANDI**

Min. of East African Community Affairs: **Hafsa MOSSI**

Min. of Energy & Mines: **Come MANIRAKIZA**

Min. of External Relations & Intl. Cooperation: **Laurent KAVAKURE**

Min. of Finance, Plans, & Development: **Tabu Abdallah MANIRAKIZA**

Min. of Good Governance & Privatization: **Issa NGENDAKUMANA**

Min. of Higher Education & Scientific Research: **Julien NIMUBONA**

Min. of Interior: **Edouard NDUWIMANA**

Min. of Justice & Keeper of the Seals: **Pascal BARANDAGIYE**

Min. of National Defense & War Veterans: **Pontien GACIYUBWENGE, Maj. Gen.**

Min. of National Solidarity, Human Rights, & Gender: **Clotilde NIRAGIRA**

Min. of Public Health & Fight Against AIDS: **Sabine NTAKARUTIMANA, Dr.**

Min. of Public Security: **Gabriel NIZIGAMA**

Min. of Telecommunications, Information, Communication, & Relations With Parliament: **Concile NIBIGIRA**

Min. of Transport, Public Works, & Equipment: **Moise BUCUMI**

Min. of Water, Environment, Territorial Admin., & Urban Planning: **Jean-Marie NIBIRANTIJE**

Min. of Youth, Sports, & Culture: **Jean-Jacques NYENIMIGABO**

Attorney Gen.: **Pascal BARANDAGIYE**

Governor, Central Bank: **Gaspard SINDAYIGAYA**

Ambassador to the US: **Angele NIUHIRE**
Permanent Representative to the UN, New York: **Hermenegilde NIYONZIMA**

ECONOMY

Burundi is a landlocked, resource-poor country with an underdeveloped manufacturing sector. The economy is predominantly agricultural. It accounts for just over 30% of GDP and employs more than 90% of the population. Burundi's primary exports are coffee and tea, which account for 90% of foreign exchange earnings, though exports are a relatively small share of GDP.

Burundi's export earnings—and its ability to pay for imports—rests primarily on weather conditions and international coffee and tea prices. The Tutsi minority, 14% of the population, dominates the coffee trade. An ethnic-based war that lasted for over a decade resulted in more than 200,000 deaths, forced more than 48,000 refugees into Tanzania, and displaced 140,000 others internally. Only one in two children go to school, and approximately one in 15 adults has HIV/AIDS.

Food, medicine, and electricity remain in short supply. Less than 2% of the population has electricity in its homes. Burundi's GDP grew around 4% annually in 2006–11. Political stability and the end of the civil war have improved aid flows and economic activity has increased, but underlying weaknesses—a high poverty rate, poor education rates, a weak legal system, a poor transportation network, overburdened utilities, and low administrative capacity—risk undermining planned economic reforms. The purchasing power of most Burundians has decreased as wage increases have not kept up with inflation.

Burundi will remain heavily dependent on aid from bilateral and multilateral donors—foreign aid represents 42% of Burundi's national income, the second highest rate in Sub-Saharan Africa; the delay of funds after a corruption scandal cut off bilateral aid in 2007 reduced government's revenues and its ability to pay salaries. Burundi joined the East African Community, which should boost Burundi's regional trade ties, and received $700 million in debt relief in 2009. Government corruption is also hindering the development of a healthy private sector as companies seek to navigate an environment with ever changing rules.

Labor Conditions

The law states that enterprises may not employ children under the age of 16, barring exceptions permitted by the labor ministry. These exceptions include light work or apprenticeships that do not damage children's health, interfere with their normal development, or prejudice their schooling. In accordance with the law, the minister of labor may permit children aged 12 and up to be employed in "light labor," such as selling newspapers, herding cattle, or preparing food. Under the law the legal age for most types of "nondangerous" labor varies from 16 to 18. Children are legally prohibited from working at night and are legally limited to 40 hours per week. The law makes no distinction between the formal and informal sector. The labor ministry is responsible for enforcing child labor laws and had multiple enforcement tools, including criminal penalties, civil fines, and court orders.

The government did not effectively enforce these laws. Because of extreme poverty, child labor was an economic necessity for many families and remained a problem. Children younger than 16 in rural areas regularly performed heavy manual labor in the daytime during the school year, primarily in the agricultural sector. Children working in agriculture could be subject to using potentially dangerous machinery and tools, carrying heavy loads, and applying harmful pesticides. They also herded cattle and goats, which could expose them to the elements and force them to work with large or dangerous animals. Many children worked in the informal sectors. Children were obliged by custom and economic necessity to participate in subsistence farming, family businesses, and other informal sector activity such as street vending. Children also worked in small, local brick-making enterprises. In urban areas children worked as domestic servants.

The informal daily minimum wage in Bujumbura for unskilled laborers was 2,500 Burundian francs ($2.00). In the past the minimum wage was set by the government, but the government has stopped setting it, and during the year the minimum wage was set by market forces. In the interior of the country, the daily minimum wage was 1,000 Burundian francs ($0.80), with a lunch provided. The government estimated that 60 percent of the population lived below the poverty line which the World Bank defined for Burundi as being the equivalent of $0.50 in urban areas and $0.38 in rural areas. More than 90 percent of the population participated in the informal economy. The wages in the informal sector average between 2,500 and 3,000 Burundian francs ($2.00 to $2.40) in Bujumbura and 1,500 Burundian francs ($1.20) in the interior of the country. There were no reports of enforcement of minimum wage laws in recent years.

The labor code stipulates an eight-hour workday and a 40-hour workweek, except for workers involved in national security activities. Supplements must be paid for overtime work: 35 percent for the first two hours and 60 percent thereafter. The weekends and holiday premium pay is 200 percent. There is no statute concerning compulsory overtime. Rest periods include 30 minutes for lunch. There is no differentiation made between foreign or migrant workers and citizen workers.

The labor code establishes occupational safety and health (OSH) standards that require safe workplaces. The Department of Inspection within the Labor Ministry is charged with enforcing the law regarding minimum wage and work hours and the OSH standards. The government did not effectively enforce these laws.

U.S.-BURUNDI RELATIONS

The United States established diplomatic relations with Burundi in 1962, following its independence from a Belgian-administered trusteeship. From 1993 to 2006, the country saw civil war driven by ethnic tensions. The 2000 Arusha Peace and Reconciliation Accords provided a negotiated settlement to the conflict. National elections in 2010 were judged by domestic and international observers to be free and fair. Democratic consolidation remains critical, as does the need to demonstrate peace dividends to the population. Burundi is one of the poorest countries in the world.

U.S. Government goals in Burundi are to help the people of Burundi realize a just and lasting peace based on democratic principles and sustainable economic development. The United States encourages political stability, ongoing democratic reforms, political openness, respect for human rights, and economic development. In the long term, the United States seeks to strengthen the process of internal reconciliation and democratization within all the states of the region to promote a stable, democratic community of nations that will work toward mutual social, economic, and security interests on the African continent. As the situation in Burundi normalizes, the United States seeks to facilitate its integration into regional and international markets, as a means to promote sustainable economic development.

U.S. Assistance to Burundi

U.S. foreign assistance aims to promote private sector-led economic growth, emphasizing agricultural production and trade (particularly within the East African Community Common Market); improve health care delivery; combat HIV/AIDS; reduce malnutrition in children under the age of 2 years; strengthen good governance and government effectiveness; and build the capacity of Burundi to maintain peace and security both at home and elsewhere in Africa. All development assistance programs seek to prioritize women and youth.

Bilateral Economic Relations

Burundi is eligible for preferential trade benefits under the African Growth and Opportunity Act. The United States has signed trade and investment framework agreements with the East African Community and with the Common Market for Eastern and Southern Africa. Burundi is a member of both regional organizations. U.S. exports to Burundi include iron and steel products, baking-related products, pharmaceutical products, wheat, and furniture and bedding. The primary import from Burundi to the United States is coffee.

Burundi's Membership in International Organizations

Burundi and the United States belong to a number of the same international organizations, including the United Nations, International Monetary Fund, World Bank, and World Trade Organization.

Bilateral Representation

Burundi maintains an embassy in the United States at Suite 212, 2233 Wisconsin Ave. NW, Washington, DC 20007 (tel. 202-342-2574).

Principal U.S. Embassy Officials

Last Updated: 1/14/2013

BUJUMBURA (E) Avenue des Etats-Unis, 257-22-207-000, Fax 257-22-222-926, INMARSAT Tel Iridium: 8816-3145-8703/8704/8705, Workweek: 5 days–Mon–Thu 7:30-5:30–Fri–7:30–12:30, Website: http://bujumbura.usembassy.gov/

AMB OMS:	Marsha Thomas
Co-CLO:	Vacant
FM:	Doyle Daniels
HRO:	Hannah Eagleton
MGT:	Irvin Hicks Jr..
POSHO:	Doyle Daniels
SDO/DATT:	MAJ Dan Ebert
AMB:	Dawn Liberi
CON:	Stacey Maupin
DCM:	Samuel R. Watson
PAO:	Anita Doll
GSO:	Lynn Marshall
RSO:	Yvon Guillaume
AID:	Douglas Sheldon
CLO:	Victoria Hill
ECON:	Patrick Gan
FMO:	Hannah Eagleton
ICASS Chair:	Kim Jordan
IMO:	Todd Lowder
IPO:	Bruce Macewen
ISSO:	Todd Lowder
POL:	Kim Jordan
State ICASS:	Vacant

TRAVEL

Consular Information Sheet

September 24, 2012

Country Description: One of the poorest countries in the world, Burundi is a small, francophone, densely populated central African nation bordering Lake Tanganyika, Rwanda, Tanzania, and the Democratic Republic of Congo. Burundi was plagued by a civil war from 1993 to 2006 that often involved non-governmental and non-combatant targets. In December 2008, the last rebel group agreed to demobilize and register as a political party. Between May and September 2010, Burundi held a series of five elections covering elected offices at all levels of government which domestic and international observers considered to be credible. Years of fighting have devastated a historically fragile economy that depends largely on subsistence agriculture.

Poor public health and education, weather disasters such as drought and floods, crop diseases, soaring food and fuel prices, and lack of infrastructure exacerbate the effects of conflict and delay recovery. Limited facilities for tourism are slowly becoming available around Bujumbura. Outside the capital, particularly towards the southern town of Rumonge, tourist facilities are developing along the lakeshore. However, road and safety guidelines should be considered when traveling outside of Bujumbura.

Smart Traveler Enrollment Program (STEP)/Embassy Locations: If you are going to live in or visit Burundi, please take the time to tell our Embassy about your trip. If you enroll, we can keep you up to date with important safety and security announcements. It will also help your friends and family get in touch with you in an emergency.

U.S. Embassy Bujumbura
Avenue des Etats-Unis
Telephone: 257 22 20 7000
Emergency after-hours telephone: 257 79 938 841
Facsimile: 257 22 24 3467

Entry/Exit Requirements for U.S. Citizens: A passport valid for six months and evidence of immunization against yellow fever are required for entry into Burundi. In January 2010, the Government of Burundi issued a diplomatic note stating that travelers would no longer be able to obtain entry visas upon arrival at ports of entry and should apply for visas from their nearest Burundian Embassy or consulate. To date, however, all ports of entry continue to issue three-day and one-month tourism visas upon entry. Travelers to Burundi should inquire about visa procedures with their nearest Burundian Embassy or Immigration Office before planning a trip. Travelers with an expired visa are not permitted to leave the country without acquiring an exit visa prior to departure.

The latest information about visas may be obtained from the Embassy of the Republic of Burundi, Suite 212, 2233 Wisconsin Avenue, NW, Washington, DC 20007, telephone (202) 342-2574, or from the Permanent Mission of Burundi to the United Nations in New York at telephone (212) 499-0001 thru 0006. Visit the Embassy of Burundi website for the most current visa information.

The U.S. Department of State is unaware of any HIV/AIDS entry restrictions for visitors to or foreign residents of Burundi.

Threats to Safety and Security: See the Department of State's Travel Warning for Burundi. In October 2009, al-Shabaab publically threatened to attack Burundi to retaliate for its participation in the African Union Mission in Somalia (AMISOM). The U.S. Embassy takes this threat seriously and regularly reviews the current security posture for U.S. government personnel and travel warnings for U.S. citizens in the region. Remain vigilant while performing your daily activities or while traveling outside of major cities to decrease the likelihood of becoming a victim of crime or other violent acts.

Public demonstrations are generally nonviolent and well controlled by the police. However, any demonstration or spontaneous gathering has the potential to become violent. Avoid them.

Stay up to date by:

- Bookmarking our Bureau of Consular Affairs website, which contains the current Travel Warnings and Travel Alerts as well as the Worldwide Caution.
- Following us on Twitter and the Bureau of Consular Affairs page on Facebook as well.
- Downloading our freeSmart Traveler App, available through iTunes and the Android marketplace, to have travel information at your fingertips.
- Calling 1-888-407-4747 toll-free within the United States and Canada, or a regular toll line, 1-202-501-4444, from other countries.
- Taking some time before travel to consider your personal security.

Crime: Crime poses a high risk for foreign visitors to Bujumbura and Burundi in general. Due to insufficient resources, local authorities in any part of Burundi are often unable to provide timely assistance in cases of emergency. U.S. government personnel are prohibited from walking on the streets after dusk or using local public transportation. Foreigners, whether in vehicles or at home, are always potential crime targets. Common crimes, often committed by groups of armed bandits, include mugging, purse-snatching, pick-pocketing, burglary, automobile break-ins and carjacking. Don't leave valuable items unattended in a hotel room. Many criminal incidents involve armed attackers. Criminals in Bujumbura often operate in pairs or in small groups involving six or more individuals.

The Department of State advises you to use caution when traveling, paying particular attention when traveling to and from frequent destinations including work, home, and popular shops or restaurants. You should also avoid establishing routines and vary routes between regularly-traveled destinations in order to reduce vulnerability to targeted criminal or terrorist acts. In general, you should pay close attention to your personal security at locations where foreigners are commonly known to congregate and avoid demonstrations and large gatherings. U.S. citizens living and working in Bujumbura should take this opportunity to ensure your security and emergency action plans are up-to-date.

Likewise, outside of Bujumbura, vulnerability to criminal attacks on the roads continues to be a serious concern. The U.S. Embassy strongly cautions against traveling outside of towns after nightfall. When traveling upcountry, the best practice is to use convoys of multiple vehicles to prevent becoming a victim of crime in the event of mechanical failure or emergency while traveling. Furthermore, the U.S. Embassy recommends travelers be equipped with satellite telephones, maps and navigation equipment, medical gear to include trauma supplies, and vehicle maintenance and recovery equipment, especially when traveling off main routes.

Don't buy counterfeit and pirated goods, even if they are widely available. Not only are the bootlegs illegal in the United States, if you purchase them you may also be breaking local law.

Victims of Crime: If you or someone you know becomes the victim of a crime abroad, you should contact the local police and the nearest U.S. embassy or consulate.

We can:

- Replace a stolen passport.
- Help you find appropriate medical care if you are the victim of violent crimes such as assault or rape.
- Put you in contact with the appropriate police authorities, and if you want us to, we can contact family members or friends.
- Help you understand the local criminal justice process and direct you to local attorneys, although it is important to remember that local authorities are responsible for investigating and prosecuting the crime.

In the city of Bujumbura, the number for emergency assistance is 112. In practice the number often goes unanswered and you may wish to seek police assistance in person; there is no comparable number outside the capital.

Criminal Penalties: While you are traveling in Burundi, you are subject to its laws even if you are a U.S. citizen. Foreign laws and legal systems can be vastly different than those of the United States. There are also some things that might be legal in the country you visit, but still illegal in the United States. For example, you can be prosecuted under U.S. law if you buy pirated goods. Engaging in sexual conduct with children or using or disseminating child pornography in a foreign country is also a crime prosecutable in the United States.

Burundian law requires that you carry some form of identification at all times. You can be held for questioning if you do not have an identification document when one is requested by a member of the Burundian Police. It is illegal to take pictures of certain sensitive buildings/installations in Burundi. If you see Burundian Police near an installation, it's safer to seek permission before taking photographs. Driving under the influence can land you immediately in jail. Penalties for possessing, using, or trafficking in illegal drugs in Burundi are severe, and convicted offenders can expect long jail sentences and heavy fines.

If you break local laws in Burundi, your U.S. passport won't help you avoid arrest or prosecution. It's very important to know what's legal and what's not where you are going.

Based on the Vienna Convention on Consular Relations, bilateral agreements with certain countries, and customary international law, if you are arrested in Burundi, you have the option to request that the police, prison officials, or other authorities alert the U.S. embassyof your arrest, and to have communications from you forwarded to the U.S. embassy.

Accessibility: While in Burundi, individuals with disabilities may find accessibility and accommodation very different from what you find in the United States. Although local law prohibits discrimination against people with handicaps, this law is not enforced. Furthermore, there are no laws requiring access to transportation, communication, or public buildings for persons with disabilities. There are few sidewalks and no curb-cuts. Most buildings do not have functioning elevators. People living in Burundi with disabilities must rely on their families for support.

Currency: There are a few international ATMs in Burundi. However, frequent power outages and connectivity issues prevent them from being a reliable source for currency. Additionally, most Burundian hotels and businesses do not accept credit cards. Many hotels in Bujumbura accept payment in U.S. dollars or Euros from non-Burundians. Travelers should be aware that Burundian banking practices prohibit acceptance of U.S. currency printed before the year 2006.

Same Gender Sexual Relations: The Government of Burundi adopted a penal code in April 2009 that, while stipulating increased penalties for forced labor and human trafficking, also contains language criminalizing same gender sexual relations. To date, however, there are no reports that anyone has been arrested or prosecuted for such activities.

Photography: The U.S. Embassy recommends that you not photograph airports, military installations, or other government buildings, and obtain permission from individuals before taking their photographs.

Power Shortages: At times, the power supply in Bujumbura can be a serious problem, particularly during the dry season and after nightfall.

Medical Facilities and Health Information: Medical facilities in Burundi do not meet United States standards. You should carry an ample supply of properly-labeled prescription drugs and other medications with you, as certain medications and prescription drugs are unavailable or in short supply. Sterility of equipment is questionable, and treatment is unreliable. Ambulance assistance is non-existent and emergency services are all but unavailable. Hospital care in Burundi should be considered in only the most serious cases and when no reasonable alternatives are available. Malaria prophylaxis is strongly recommended for travel to all parts of Burundi.

You can find good information on vaccinations and other health precautions, on the CDC website. For information about outbreaks of infectious diseases abroad, consult the World Health Organization (WHO) website. The WHO website also contains additional health information for travelers, including detailed country-specific health information.

Tuberculosis is an increasingly serious health concern in Burundi. For further information, please consult the CDC's information on TB.

Medical Insurance: You can't assume your insurance will go with you when you travel. It's very important to find out before you leave whether or not your medical insurance will cover you overseas. You need to ask your insurance company two questions:

- Does my policy apply when I'm out of the United States?
- Will it cover emergencies like a trip to a foreign hospital or a medical evacuation?

Medical evacuation is very expensive and having your own medical evacuation insurance is highly recommended. In many places, doctors and hospitals still expect payment in cash at the time of service. Your regular U.S. healthinsurance may not cover doctors' and hospital visits in other countries. If your policy doesn't go with you when you travel, it's a very good idea to take out another one for your trip.

Traffic Safety and Road Conditions: While in Burundi, you may encounter road conditions that differ significantly from those in the United States.

The information below concerning Burundi is provided for general reference only, and may not be totally accurate in a particular location or circumstance.

While travel on most roads is generally safe during the day, travelers must maintain constant vigilance. There have been reports of violent attacks on vehicles traveling the roads throughout the country outside of Bujumbura. U.S. government personnel are required to travel upcountry via two-vehicle convoy to certain areas, have their trips pre-approved by the Embassy's Regional Security Officer, and carry a satellite phone with them. The U.S. Embassy recommends that U.S. citizens not travel on the national highways from dusk to dawn. Drivers without valid permits, and the ease with which a driver's license can be acquired without training, make Burundian drivers less careful, predictable, or mindful of driving rules than U.S. drivers may expect.

There are no functioning traffic signals in Bujumbura, and virtually nothing of the kind elsewhere in the country. Roadways are not marked, and the lack of streetlights or shoulders makes driving in the countryside at night especially dangerous.

Additionally, drivers may encounter cyclists, pedestrians, and livestock in the roadway, including in and around the capital. Mini-vans used as buses for 18 persons should be given a wide berth as they start and stop abruptly, often without pulling to the side of the road.

Large holes or damaged portions of roadway may be encountered anywhere in the country, including in Bujumbura; when driving in the countryside off main roads, travelers should carry multiple spare tires. During the rainy season, many side roads are passable only with four-wheel drive vehicles. Burundi's supplies of gasoline and diesel fuel are imported predominantly from Kenya and Tanzania, and are relatively expensive due to high transportation costs. Service stations are rare outside of the major cities.

Third-party insurance is required, and it will cover any damages in the event of an accident (property, injury, or death). If you are found to have caused an accident, you automatically will be fined 10,000 Burundian francs (approximately $7.00 U.S.) and your driver's license will be confiscated until the police investigation is completed. Although the law provides for the arrest of drunk drivers, in practice, the police do not act on this law.

In the city of Bujumbura, the number for police assistance is 112, although frequently calls to this number are unanswered; there is no comparable number outside the capital. If you are involved in an accident causing death, it is advised that you leave the scene of the accident and proceed to the nearest police station.

Aviation Safety Oversight: As there is no direct commercial air service to the United States by carriers registered in Burundi, the U.S. Federal Aviation Administration (FAA) has not assessed the government of Burundi's Civil Aviation Authority for compliance with International Civil Aviation Organization (ICAO) aviation safety standards. Further information may be found on the FAA's safety assessment page.

Children's Issues: Please see the U.S. Dept. of State Office of Children's Issues web pages on intercountry adoption and international parental child abduction.

Travel Warning

November 8, 2012

The Department of State warns U.S. citizens of the risks of traveling to Burundi. This Travel Warning replaces the Travel Warning for Burundi dated April 18, 2012, to reiterate existing security concerns and to note that security restrictions on travel for Embassy personnel remain in place.

Because Burundi participates in peacekeeping operations in Somalia, the terrorist organization al-Shabaab, based in Somalia, has threatened to conduct terror attacks in Burundi. It may also target U.S. interests in Burundi.

The Burundian civil war that lasted from 1993 to 2006 often involved non-governmental and non-combatant targets. In December 2008, the government and the last rebel group signed their final cease-fire agreement in which the rebel group agreed to demobilize and register as a political party. Burundi held general elections in 2010 which were generally considered credible. However, political tensions ran high and there were incidents of violence during the campaign period. Low-level political violence persists; the areas of Bujumbura Rural, Makamba, Rumonge, and the area neighboring the Kibira forest are of particular concern.

There are no known armed militia groups operating in Burundi; however, weapons are easy to obtain and some ex-combatants have turned to crime or political violence. Crime, often committed by groups of armed bandits or street children, poses the highest risk for foreign visitors to both Bujumbura and Burundi in general. Exchanges of gunfire and grenade attacks are common even in densely populated urban areas. You should stay indoors, in a ground floor interior room, if gunfire or explosions occur nearby. Common crimes include muggings, burglaries, and robberies. Visitors should keep vehicle doors locked and windows up, and be careful when stopped in heavy traffic, due to the threat of robbery and theft. The U.S. Embassy has received reports of armed criminals ambushing vehicles, particularly on the roads leading out of Bujumbura. The U.S. Embassy prohibits U.S. government personnel from walking on the streets after dark and from using local public transportation at any time. Due to a lack of resources, local authorities in any part of Burundi are often unable to provide timely assistance during an emergency. U.S. citizens should be aware that even gatherings and demonstrations intended to be peaceful can turn violent. U.S. citizens residing in or traveling to Burundi are reminded to maintain a high level of security awareness at all times and avoid political rallies, demonstrations, and crowds of any kind. Even seemingly peaceful sporting events can become politicized and turn violent. U.S. citizens should routinely monitor local media sources and the internet for reports of demonstrations and unrest.

The U.S. Embassy continues to caution U.S. citizens that travel outside the capital, Bujumbura, presents significant risks, especially after nightfall. The U.S. Embassy restricts the travel of its personnel in Burundi. Within 30 km/18 miles of the city, Embassy employees may travel in single vehicles, but are advised to check in and out with the Embassy. The Embassy's Regional Security Officer (RSO) must pre-approve all Embassy personnel travel outside this approximately 30-km radius of Bujumbura, and employees must travel via an approved itinerary in two-vehicle convoys equipped with satellite phones, GPS, and emergency equipment. All employee movement outside the city after dark is forbidden; the Embassy recommends that U.S. citizens not travel on national highways from dusk to dawn. U.S. citizens are also encouraged to avoid traveling within the city of Bujumbura after midnight.

Corruption is endemic in Burundi and contributes to an environment where the rule of law is not respected. Government officials may ask for bribes for providing routine services. Travelers are frequently stopped, questioned, and asked for bribes by security forces at numerous official and unofficial road blocks throughout the country. Likewise, criminals who have paid off local officials may operate without fear of prosecution. U.S. citizens who travel to or remain in Burundi despite this Travel Warning are urged to contact the U.S. Embassy in Bujumbura for information on the latest Embassy security guidance, and to enroll in the Smart Traveler Enrollment Program(STEP) so they can receive the most up-to-date security information. Please keep all of your information in STEP current. It is important when enrolling or updating information to include multiple phone numbers and email addresses to facilitate communication in the event of an emergency.

U.S. citizens without Internet access may register directly with the U.S. Embassy in Bujumbura at Avenue des Etats-Unis. The hours for non-emergency American Citizens Services are 9:00 a.m. to 12:00 p.m. and 1:30 p.m. to 3:00 p.m. on Mondays and Tuesdays, and 9:00 a.m. to 12:00 p.m. on Fridays. The Embassy Consular section can be reached by telephone, including for after-hours emergencies, at +257-22-20-7000, or by fax at +257-22-22-2926. Security information for U.S. citizens in Burundi is posted at Embassy Bujumbura's website.

For further information, consult the Department of State's Country Specific Information for Burundi and the current Worldwide Caution, available on the Bureau of Consular Affairs Internet website. Current information on safety and security can also be obtained by calling 1-888-407-4747 toll-free in the United States and Canada or, a regular toll line at-1-202-501-4444 for callers from other countries. These numbers are available from 8:00 a.m. to 8:00 p.m. Eastern Time, Monday through Friday (except U.S. federal holidays). Stay up to date by bookmarking our Bureau of Consular Affairs website, which contains the current Travel Warnings and Travel Alerts as well as the Worldwide Caution. Follow us on Twitter and the Bureau of Consular Affairs page on Facebook as well. You can also download our free Smart Traveler App, available through iTunes and the Android market to have travel information at your fingertips.

Intercountry Adoption

July 2008

The information in this section has been edited from the latest report available as of February 2013 from the State Department Bureau of Consular Affairs, Office of Overseas Citizens Services. For more information, please read the *Intercountry Adoption* section of this book and review current reports online at http://adoption.state.gov.

Burundi is party to the Hague Convention on Protection of Children and Co-operation in Respect of Intercountry Adoption (Hague Adoption Convention). Therefore all adoptions between Burundi and the United States must meet the requirements of the Convention and U.S. law implementing the Convention.

Who Can Adopt? Adoption between the United States and Burundi is governed by the Hague Adoption Convention. Therefore to adopt from Burundi, you must first be found eligible to adopt by the U.S. Government. The U.S. Government agency responsible for making this determination is the Department of Homeland Security, U.S. Citizenship and Immigration Services (USCIS).

Residency Requirements: There are no residency requirements for prospective adoptive parents of Burundian children.

Age Requirements: An adopting parent should be at least thirty years of age. A waiver of this requirement can be requested from the County Court. (There is no age requirement if adopting the child of a spouse). An adopting parent must be a minimum of fifteen years older than the child to be adopted. However, a waiver can be obtained from the County Court.

Marriage Requirements: If married, adopting parents must have been married and living together for at least the past five years, and consent of the spouse is required. Adoption by more than one person is not possible except when the couple is legally married.

Other Requirements: Adopting parents must have moral qualities and material resources necessary to support the child. Adopting parents must be found eligible to adopt through examination of a psycho-medical report and a home study.

Who Can be Adopted? Because Burundi is party to the Hague Adoption Convention, children from Burundi must meet the requirements of the Convention in order to be eligible for adoption.

For detailed and updated information on these requirements, please review the *Intercountry Adoption* section of this publication and visit the U.S. Department of State Intercountry Adoption website at http://adoption.state.gov.

Role of the Adoption Authority: All adoption cases are submitted to the Central Authority in the Ministry of Social Action. Once a case has been approved by the Ministry, it must then be approved by the County Court.

Role of the Court: Once approval is received from Central Authority, the case will be passed to the County Court for ruling.

Role of Adoption Agencies: There are no recognized adoption service organizations in Burundi, only associations who care for children. Adoption cases are prepared and processed by private lawyers. Cases are submitted to the Ministry of Social Action and the County Court for approval.

Time Frame: The local adoption process can take between three and six months.

Adoption Application:

- Select and contact a lawyer in Burundi who will process the case;
- Submit all required documentation for prospective parents;
- Submit all required documentation for adoptive child / children;
- Lawyer will prepare case for adjudication by the Central Authority in the Ministry of Social Action.

The following elements will be reviewed:

- The home study report presented and performed by the adoption authority in the country of the adopting parents. Usually the home study completed when applying for the I-600A.
- The child/children's eligibility to be adopted: identification, status, social background, personal and family development, medical history, education and socio-cultural issued and any other special needs;
- The best interest of the child/children;
- The adoption consent must be given freely, and legally in a notarized attestation by persons authorized to agree to the adoption and with the understanding of the consequences of intercountry adoption; the biological mother must give consent to relinquish the child/children after birth, if applicable;
- With respect to age and maturity, the adoptive child/children must be fully informed of the consequences of intercountry adoption;
- The child's/children's views must be taken into consideration. If over 13 years of age, the consent of the adoptive child/children must be given freely, and legally in a notarized attestation;
- Evidence of the prospective adoptive parents' eligibility to adopt.

Adoption Fees: In the adoption services contract that you sign at the beginning of the adoption process, your agency will itemize the fees and estimated expenses related to your adoption process.

The U.S. Embassy in Burundi discourages the payment of any fees that are not properly receipted, "donations," or "expediting" fees, that may be requested from prospective adoptive parents. Such fees have the appearance of "buying" a baby and put all future adoptions in Burundi at risk.

Fees can vary and it is advisable to contact an attorney to obtain accurate fee information.

Documents Required: The following documents will be required and must be attached to an intercountry adoption request:

For the Child/Children:

- Attestations of the adoptive child/children's family situation and status;
- An attestation of acceptance from the prospective family guaranteeing their material support of the adoptive child/children;
- Travel document (i.e. Burundian passport) for the adoptive child/children.

For the Prospective Adoptive Parents:

- Marriage, Birth and Judicial/Police Certificates;
- Attestations of good behavior and of family composition;
- Financial/income declaration;

- Family psychological and medical report.

Civil documents, such as "attestations," can be obtained at the Mayor Office or through the civil offices.

Bringing Your Child Home: Once your adoption is complete (or you have obtained legal custody of the child), there are a few more steps to take before you can head home.

Specifically, you need to apply for several documents for your child before he or she can travel to the United States, such as a birth certificate, a passport or travel document for your child from the country in which he or she was born, and a U.S. Immigration Visa.

For detailed and updated information on how to obtain these documents, review the *Intercountry Adoption* section in this publication and visit the U.S. Department of State Intercountry Adoption website at http://adoption.state.gov.

Child Citizenship Act: For adoptions finalized abroad, the Child Citizenship Act of 2000 allows your new child to acquire American citizenship automatically when he or she enters the United States as lawful permanent residents. For adoptions finalized in the United States, the Child Citizenship Act of 2000 allows your new child to acquire American citizenship automatically when the court in the United States issues the final adoption decree. To learn more, review the *Intercountry Adoption* section in this publication and visit the U.S. Department of State Intercountry Adoption website at http://adoption.state.gov.

U.S. Embassy in Burundi
B.P. 1720
Avenue Des Etats-Unis
Bujumbura, Burundi
Tel: (257) 22-34-54
Tel (after hours): (257) 21-48-53
Fax: (257) 22-29-26
http://bujumbura.usembassy.gov

Embassy of Burundi
2233 Wisconsin Ave., NW, Suite 212
Washington, DC 20007
Tel: 202-342-2574; 202-749-0885
Fax: 202-342-2578

Office of Children's Issues
U.S. Department of State
2201 C Street, NW
SA-29
Washington, DC 20520
Tel: 1-888-407-4747
E-mail: AskCI@state.gov
http://adoption.state.gov

For questions about immigration procedures, call the National Customer Service Center (NCSC) at 1-800-375-5283 (TTY 1-800-767-1833).

CAMBODIA

Compiled from publications that were available as of February 2013 from the U.S. Department of State, the U.S. Department of Commerce, and the Central Intelligence Agency (CIA). See the introduction to this set for explanatory notes.

Official Name:
Kingdom of Cambodia

PROFILE

Geography

Area: total: 181,035 sq km; country comparison to the world: 90; land: 176,515 sq km; water: 4,520 sq km
Major cities: Phnom Penh (capital) 1.519 million (2009)
Climate: tropical; rainy, monsoon season (May to November); dry season (December to April); little seasonal temperature variation
Terrain: mostly low, flat plains; mountains in southwest and north

People

Nationality: noun: Cambodian(s); adjective: Cambodian
Population: 14,952,665 (July 2012 est.)
Population growth rate: 1.687% (2012 est.)
Ethnic groups: Khmer 90%, Vietnamese 5%, Chinese 1%, other 4%
Religions: Buddhist (official) 96.4%, Muslim 2.1%, other 1.3%, unspecified 0.2% (1998 census)
Languages: Khmer (official) 95%, French, English
Literacy: definition: age 15 and over can read and write; total population: 73.6%; male: 84.7%; female: 64.1% (2004 est.)
Health: life expectancy at birth: total population: 63.04 years; male: 60.66 years; female: 65.53 years (2012 est.); Infant mortality rate: total: 54.08 deaths/1,000 live births; male: 61.02 deaths/1,000 live births; female: 46.82 deaths/1,000 live births (2012 est.)
Unemployment rate: 3.5% (2007 est.)
Work force: 8.8 million (2010 est.)

Government

Type: multiparty democracy under a constitutional monarchy
Independence: 9 November 1953
Constitution: promulgated 21 September 1993
Political subdivisions: 23 provinces (khett, singular and plural) and 1 municipality (krong, singular and plural)
Suffrage: 18 years of age; universal

Economy

GDP (purchasing power parity): $36.59 billion (2012 est.); $33.89 billion (2011 est.); $31.95 billion (2010 est.); $30.15 billion (2009 est.)
GDP real growth rate: 6.5% (2012 est.); 6.1% (2011 est.); 6% (2010 est.); 0.1% (2009 est.)
GDP per capita (PPP): $2,400 (2012 est.); $2,200 (2011 est.); $2,100 (2010 est.); $2,000 (2009 est.)
Natural resources: oil and gas, timber, gemstones, iron ore, manganese, phosphates, hydropower potential
Agriculture products: rice, rubber, corn, vegetables, cashews, cassava (manioc), silk
Industries: tourism, garments, construction, rice milling, fishing, wood and wood products, rubber, cement, gem mining, textiles
Exports: $6.148 billion (2012 est.); $5.35 billion (2011 est.); $5.068 billion (2010 est.)
Exports—commodities: clothing, timber, rubber, rice, fish, tobacco, footwear
Exports—partners: US 41.5%, Canada 8.6%, Germany 8.2%, UK 7.9%, Japan 4.6% (2011)
Imports: $8.84 billion (2012 est.); $6.963 billion (2011 est.); $6.791 billion (2010 est.)
Imports—commodities: petroleum products, cigarettes, gold, construction materials, machinery, motor vehicles, pharmaceutical products
Imports—partners: Thailand 29.6%, China 23.9%, Singapore 9.4%, Hong Kong 7.2%, Vietnam 5.1%, South Korea 4.6% (2011)
Debt—external: $5.071 billion (31 December 2012 est.); $5.028 billion (31 December 2011 est.); $4.676 billion (31 December 2010 est.)
Exchange rates: riels (KHR) per US dollar; 4,075.4 (2012 est.); 4,058.5 (2011 est.); 4,184.9 (2010 est.); 4,139 (2009); 4,070.94 (2008); 4,006 (2007)

GEOGRAPHY

Cambodia is located on mainland Southeast Asia between Thailand to the west and north and Vietnam to the east and southeast. It shares a land border with Laos in the northeast. Cambodia has a sea coast on the Gulf of Thailand. The Dangrek mountain range in the north and Cardamom Mountains in the southwest form natural boundaries. Principal physical features include the Tonle Sap lake and the Mekong and Bassac Rivers. Cambodia remains one of the most heavily forested countries in the region, although deforestation continues at an alarming rate.

PEOPLE AND CULTURE

Ninety percent of Cambodia's population is ethnically Cambodian. Other ethnic groups include Chinese, Vietnamese, hill tribes, Cham, and Lao.

National/Racial/Ethnic Minorities

The rights of minorities under the nationality law are not explicit; constitutional protections are extended only to "Khmer people." Citizens of Chinese and Vietnamese ethnicity constituted the largest ethnic minorities. Ethnic Chinese citizens were accepted in society, but animosity continued toward ethnic Vietnamese, who were seen as a threat to the country and culture. Some groups, including political groups, continued to make strong anti-Vietnamese statements. They complained of political control of the CPP by the Vietnamese government, border encroachment, and other problems for which they held ethnic Vietnamese at least partially responsible.

Language

Khmer is the official language. Even with the increasing use of English, most business and official meetings are conducted in Khmer. Chinese, French, Thai, and Vietnamese are also widely spoken.

Religion

An estimated 96 percent of the population is Theravada Buddhist. The vast majority of ethnic-Khmer Cambodians is Buddhist, and there is a close association between Buddhism, Khmer cultural traditions and identity, and daily life. According to the Ministry of Cults and Religion, the Mahayana school of Buddhism claims approximately 19,550 followers and has 167 temples throughout the country.

Approximately 2.4 percent of the population, predominantly ethnic Cham, is Muslim and typically live in towns and rural fishing villages on the banks of the Tonle Sap Lake and the Mekong River, as well as in Kampot Province. There are four branches of Islam represented in the country: the Malay-influenced Shafi branch, practiced by as much as 90 percent of Muslims; the Saudi-Kuwaiti-influenced Salafi (Wahhabi) branch; the indigenous Iman-San branch; and the Kadiani branch. The remaining 1.6 percent of the population is Baha'i, Jewish, ethnic Vietnamese Cao Dai, or members of various Christian denominations.

Angkor Wat

Over a period of 300 years, between 900 and 1200 AD, the Khmer Kingdom of Angkor produced some of the world's most magnificent architectural masterpieces on the northern shore of the Tonle Sap, near the present town of Siem Reap. The Angkor area stretches 15 miles east to west and 5 miles north to south. Some 72 major temples or other buildings dot the area. Suryavarman II built the principal temple, Angkor Wat, between 1112 and 1150. With walls nearly one-half mile on each side, Angkor Wat portrays the Hindu cosmology with the central towers representing Mount Meru, home of the gods; the outer walls, the mountains enclosing the world; and the moat, the oceans beyond. Angkor Thom, the capital city built after the Cham sack of 1177, is surrounded by a 300-foot wide moat. Construction of Angkor Thom coincided with a change from Hinduism to Buddhism. Temples were altered to display images of the Buddha, and Angkor Wat became a major Buddhist shrine. During the 15th century, nearly all of Angkor was abandoned after Siamese attacks. The exception was Angkor Wat, which remained a shrine for Buddhist pilgrims. The great city and temples remained largely cloaked by the forest until the late 19th century when French archaeologists began a long restoration process.

Concerned about further destruction and dilapidation of the Angkor complex and cultural heritage, the Cambodian Government in 1995 established the Authority for the Protection and Management of Angkor and the Region of Siem Reap (APSARA) to protect, maintain, conserve, and improve the value of the archaeological park. In December 1995 the World Heritage Committee confirmed Angkor's permanent inscription on the World Heritage List. Tourism is now the second-largest foreign currency earner in Cambodia's economy.

MODERN HISTORY

Although Cambodia had a rich and powerful past under the Hindu state of Funan and the Kingdom of Angkor, by the mid-19th century the country was on the verge of dissolution. After repeated requests for French assistance, a protectorate was established in 1863. By 1884, Cambodia was a virtual colony; soon after it was made part of the Indochina Union with Annam, Tonkin, Cochin-China, and Laos. France continued to control the country even after the start of World War II through its Vichy government. In 1945, the Japanese dissolved the colonial administration, and King Norodom Sihanouk declared an independent, anti-colonial government under Prime Minister Son Ngoc Thanh in March 1945. The Allies deposed this government in October. In January 1953, Sihanouk named his father as regent and went into self-imposed exile, refusing to return until Cambodia gained genuine independence.

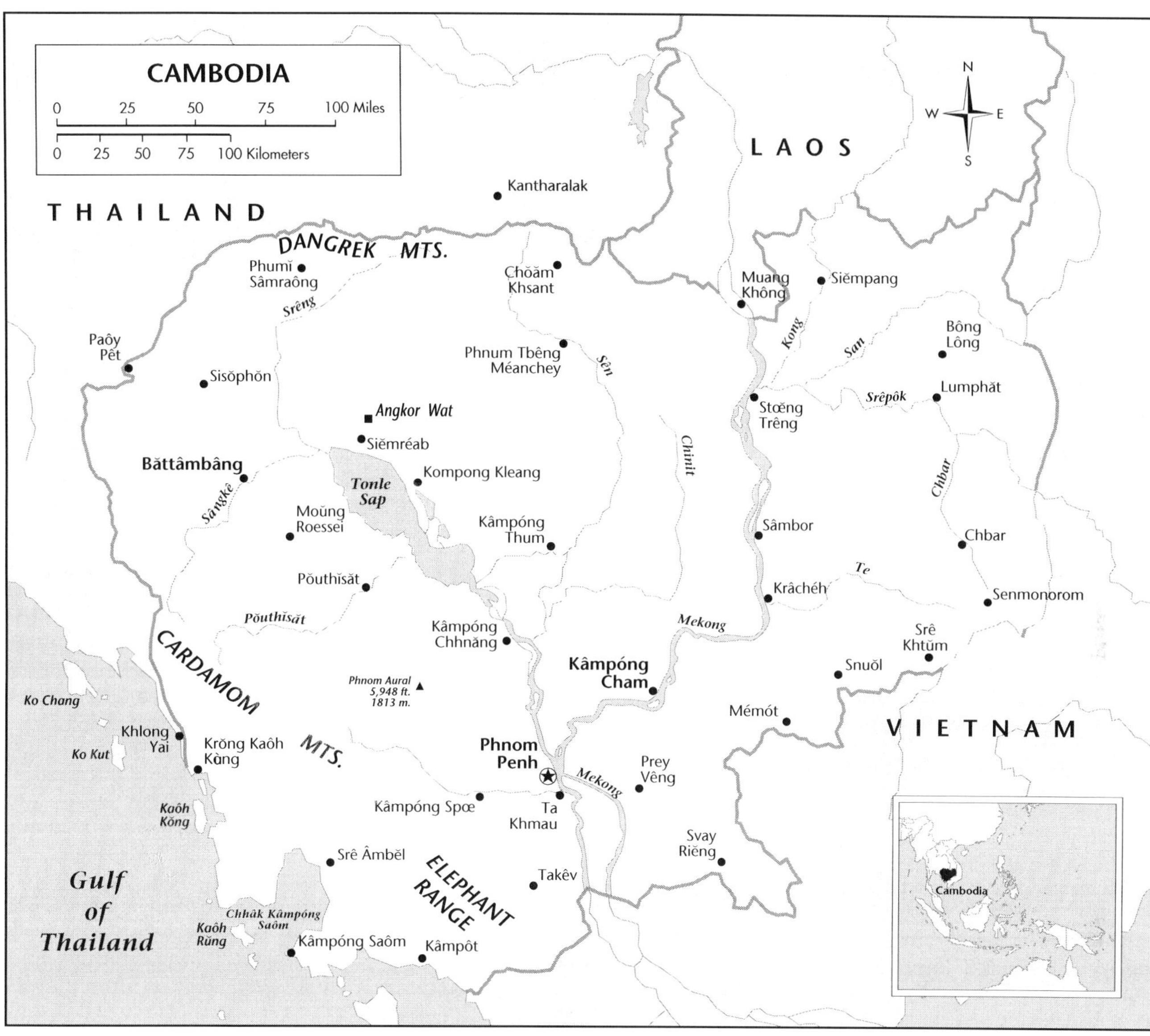

Full Independence

Sihanouk's actions hastened the French Government's July 4, 1953 announcement of its readiness to grant independence, which came on November 9, 1953. The situation remained uncertain until a 1954 conference was held in Geneva to settle the French-Indochina war. All participants, except the United States and the State of Vietnam, associated themselves (by voice) with the final declaration.

The Cambodian delegation agreed to the neutrality of the three Indochinese states but insisted on a provision in the cease-fire agreement that left the Cambodian Government free to call for outside military assistance should the Viet Minh or others threaten its territory.

Neutral Cambodia

Neutrality was the central element of Cambodian foreign policy during the 1950s and 1960s. By the mid-1960s, parts of Cambodia's eastern provinces were serving as bases for North Vietnamese Army and Viet Cong (NVA/VC) forces operating against South Vietnam, and the port of Sihanoukville was being used to supply them. As NVA/VC activity grew, the United States and South Vietnam became concerned, and in 1969, the United States began a series of air raids against NVA/VC base areas inside Cambodia. Throughout the 1960s, domestic politics polarized. Opposition grew within the middle class and among leftists, including Paris-educated leaders such as Son Sen, Ieng Sary, and Saloth Sar (later known as Pol Pot), who led an insurgency under the clandestine Communist Party of Kampuchea (CPK).

The Khmer Republic and the War

In March 1970, Gen. Lon Nol deposed Prince Sihanouk and assumed power. On October 9, the Cambodian monarchy was abolished, and the country was renamed the Khmer Republic.

Hanoi rejected the new republic's request for the withdrawal of NVA/VC troops and began to re-infiltrate some of the 2,000-4,000 Cambodians who had gone to North Vietnam in 1954. They became a cadre in the insurgency. The United States moved to provide material assistance to the new government's armed forces, which were engaged against both the Khmer Rouge insurgents and NVA/VC forces. In April 1970, U.S. and South Vietnamese forces entered Cambodia in a campaign aimed at destroying NVA/VC base areas. Although a considerable quantity of equipment was seized or destroyed, NVA/VC forces proved elusive and moved deeper into Cambodia. NVA/VC units overran many Cambodian Army positions while the Khmer Rouge expanded their small scale attacks on lines of communication.

The Khmer Republic's leadership was plagued by disunity among its members, the problems of transforming a 30,000-man army into a national combat force of more than 200,000 men, and spreading corruption. The insurgency continued to grow, with supplies and military support provided by North Vietnam. But inside Cambodia, Pol Pot and Ieng Sary asserted their dominance over the Vietnamese-trained communists, many of whom were purged. At the same time, the Khmer Rouge forces became stronger and more independent of their Vietnamese patrons. By 1974, Lon Nol's control was reduced to small enclaves around the cities and main transportation routes. More than 2 million refugees from the war lived in Phnom Penh and other cities. On New Year's Day 1975, communist troops launched an offensive that, in 117 days of the hardest fighting of the war, destroyed the Khmer Republic. Simultaneous attacks around the perimeter of Phnom Penh pinned down Republican forces, while other Khmer Rouge units overran fire bases controlling the vital lower Mekong resupply route. A U.S.-funded airlift of ammunition and rice ended when Congress refused additional aid for Cambodia. Phnom Penh surrendered on April 17, 1975—5 days after the U.S. mission evacuated Cambodia.

Democratic Kampuchea

Many Cambodians welcomed the arrival of peace, but the Khmer Rouge soon turned Cambodia—which it called Democratic Kampuchea (DK)—into a land of horror. Immediately after its victory, the new regime ordered the evacuation of all cities and towns, sending the entire urban population out into the countryside to till the land. Thousands starved or died of disease during the evacuation. Many of those forced to evacuate the cities were resettled in new villages, which lacked food, agricultural implements, and medical care. Many starved before the first harvest, and hunger and malnutrition—bordering on starvation—were constant during those years.

Those who resisted or who questioned orders were immediately executed, as were most military and civilian leaders of the former regime who failed to disguise their pasts. Within the CPK, the Paris-educated leadership—Pol Pot, Ieng Sary, Nuon Chea, and Son Sen—was in control, and Pol Pot was made Prime Minister. Prince Sihanouk was put under virtual house arrest. The new government sought to restructure Cambodian society completely. Remnants of the old society were abolished, and Buddhism suppressed.

Agriculture was collectivized, and the surviving part of the industrial base was abandoned or placed under state control. Cambodia had neither a currency nor a banking system. The regime controlled every aspect of life and reduced everyone to the level of abject obedience through terror. Torture centers were established, and detailed records were kept of the thousands murdered there. Public executions of those considered unreliable or with links to the previous government were common. Few succeeded in escaping the military patrols and fleeing the country. Solid estimates of the numbers who died between 1975 and 1979 are not available, but it is likely that hundreds of thousands were brutally executed by the regime. Hundreds of thousands more died from forced labor, starvation, and disease—both under the Khmer Rouge and during the Vietnamese invasion in 1978. Estimates of the dead range from 1.7 million to 3 million, out of a 1975 population estimated at 7.3 million.

Democratic Kampuchea's relations with Vietnam and Thailand worsened rapidly as a result of border clashes and ideological differences. While communist, the CPK was fiercely anti-Vietnamese, and most of its members who had lived in Vietnam were purged. Democratic Kampuchea established close ties with China, and the Cambodian-Vietnamese conflict became part of the Sino-Soviet rivalry, with Moscow backing Vietnam. Border clashes worsened when Democratic Kampuchea's military attacked villages in Vietnam.

In mid-1978, Vietnamese forces invaded Cambodia, advancing about 30 miles before the arrival of the rainy season. In December 1978, Vietnam announced formation of the Kampuchean United Front for National Salvation (KUFNS) under Heng Samrin, a former DK division commander. It was composed of Khmer communists who had remained in Vietnam after 1975 and officials from the eastern sector—like Heng Samrin and Hun Sen—who had fled to Vietnam from Cambodia in 1978. In late December 1978, Vietnamese forces launched a full invasion of Cambodia, capturing Phnom Penh on January 7, 1979 and driving the remnants of Democratic Kampuchea's army westward toward Thailand.

The Vietnamese Occupation

On January 10, 1979, the Vietnamese installed Heng Samrin as head of state in the new People's Republic of Kampuchea (PRK). The Vietnamese Army continued to pursue Khmer Rouge forces. An estimated 600,000 Cambodians were displaced during the Pol Pot era and the Vietnamese invasion streamed to the Thai border in search of refuge between 1979 and 1981. The international community responded with a massive relief effort coordinated by the United States through the UN Children's Fund (UNICEF) and the World Food Program. More than $400 million was provided between 1979 and 1982, of which the United States contributed nearly $100 million. Vietnam's occupation army of an estimated 180,000 troops was posted throughout the country from 1979 to September 1989.

The Heng Samrin regime's 30,000 troops were plagued by poor morale and widespread desertion. Resistance to Vietnam's occupation was extensive. A remainder of the Khmer Rouge's military forces eluded Vietnamese troops and established themselves in remote regions. A noncommunist resistance movement consisting of groups that had been fighting the Khmer Rouge after 1975—including Lon Nol-era soldiers—coalesced in 1979-80 to form the Khmer People's National Liberation Armed Forces (KPNLAF), which pledged loyalty to former Prime Minister Son Sann, and Moulinaka (Movement pour la Liberation Nationale de Kampuchea), loyal to Prince Sihanouk.

In 1979, Son Sann formed the Khmer People's National Liberation Front (KPNLF) to lead a political struggle for Cambodia's independence. Prince Sihanouk formed his own organization, National United Front for an Independent, Neutral, Peaceful, and Cooperative Cambodia (FUNCINPEC), and its military arm, the Armee Nationale Sihanoukienne (ANS) in 1981.

Within Cambodia, Vietnam had only limited success in establishing its client Heng Samrin regime, which was dependent on Vietnamese advisers at all levels. Security in some rural areas was tenuous, and major transportation routes were subject to interdiction by resistance forces. The presence of Vietnamese throughout the country and their intrusion into nearly all aspects of Cambodian life alienated much of the populace. The settlement of Vietnamese nationals, both former residents and new immigrants, further exacerbated anti-Vietnamese sentiment. Reports of the numbers involved vary widely, with some estimates as high as 1 million. By the end of the decade, Khmer nationalism began to reassert itself against the traditional Vietnamese enemy. In 1986, Hanoi claimed to have begun withdrawing part of its occupation forces. At the same time, Vietnam continued efforts to strengthen its client regime, the PRK, and its military arm, the Kampuchean People's Revolutionary Armed Forces (KPRAF). These withdrawals continued over the next 2 years, and the last Vietnamese troops left Cambodia in September 1989.

Peace Efforts

From July 30 to August 30, 1989, representatives of 18 countries, the four Cambodian parties, and the UN Secretary General met in Paris in an effort to negotiate a comprehensive settlement. They hoped to achieve those objectives seen as crucial to the future of post-occupation Cambodia—a verified withdrawal of the remaining Vietnamese occupation troops, the prevention of the return to power of the Khmer Rouge, and genuine self-determination for the Cambodian people. A comprehensive settlement was agreed upon on August 28, 1990.

Cambodia's Renewal

On October 23, 1991, the Paris Conference reconvened to sign a comprehensive settlement giving the UN full authority to supervise a cease-fire, repatriate the displaced Khmer along the border with Thailand, disarm and demobilize the factional armies, and prepare the country for free and fair elections. Prince Sihanouk, President of the Supreme National Council of Cambodia (SNC), and other members of the SNC returned to Phnom Penh in November 1991, to begin the resettlement process in Cambodia. The UN Advance Mission for Cambodia (UNAMIC) was deployed at the same time to maintain liaison among the factions and begin demining operations to expedite the repatriation of approximately 370,000 Cambodians from Thailand.

On March 16, 1992, the UN Transitional Authority in Cambodia (UNTAC) arrived in Cambodia to begin implementation of the UN Settlement Plan. The UN High Commissioner for Refugees began full scale repatriation in March 1992. UNTAC grew into a 22,000-strong civilian and military peacekeeping force to conduct free and fair elections for a constituent assembly.

Over 4 million Cambodians (about 90% of eligible voters) participated in the May 1993 elections, although the Khmer Rouge or Party of Democratic Kampuchea (PDK), whose forces were never actually disarmed or demobilized, barred some people from participating. Prince Ranariddh's FUNCINPEC Party was the top vote recipient with a 45.5% vote, followed by Hun Sen's Cambodian People's Party and the Buddhist Liberal Democratic Party, respectively. FUNCINPEC then entered into a coalition with the other parties that had participated in the election.

The parties represented in the 120-member assembly proceeded to draft and approve a new constitution, which was promulgated September 24, 1993. It established a multiparty liberal democracy in the framework of a constitutional monarchy, with the former Prince Sihanouk elevated to King. Prince Ranariddh and Hun Sen became First and Second Prime Ministers, respectively, in the Royal Cambodian Government (RGC). The constitution provides for a wide range of internationally recognized human rights.

In 1997, most of the remaining Khmer Rouge fighters accepted a government amnesty and laid down their arms, putting an end to nearly 3 decades of war. On October 4, 2004, the Cambodian National Assembly ratified an agreement with the United Nations on the establishment of a tribunal to try senior leaders responsible for the atrocities committed by the Khmer Rouge. The tribunal held its first trial, against former S-21 prison chief Kaing Guek Eav (aka Duch), in 2009, resulting in a guilty verdict and a 35 year sentence in July 2010. Duch will serve 19 years after his sentence was reduced by five years for being illegally detained by a Cambodian Military court, and by 11 years for time served since his 1999 arrest. Four more former Khmer

Rouge leaders are currently being tried, and two additional investigations are in progress that may result in additional indictmentrs. Donor countries have provided over $100 million to date in support of the tribunal, including $6.8 million from the United States.

GOVERNMENT AND POLITICAL CONDITIONS

Cambodia is a constitutional monarchy with an elected parliamentary form of government. In the most recent national elections, held in 2008, the Cambodian People's Party (CPP) won 90 of 123 National Assembly seats. Most observers assessed that the election process improved over previous elections but did not fully meet international standards. The CPP consolidated control of the three branches of government and other national institutions, with most power concentrated in the hands of Prime Minister Hun Sen.

Recent Elections

The most recent national elections, held in 2008 for the National Assembly, were peaceful overall, with a process that was generally considered an improvement over past elections. However, observers noted that the elections did not fully meet international standards. Although some election day irregularities persisted, they were low in number and did not appear to affect the outcome or distort the will of the electorate.

Parties could register, and individuals were free to declare their candidacy without restrictions.

Political Parties: Some NGOs and political parties alleged that membership in the dominant CPP party provided advantages, such as gifts, access to government emergency aid, and economic land concessions. There were no reports of members of the opposition parties receiving similar economic land concessions.

Participation of Women and Minorities: Traditional culture limited the role of women in government; however, women took part in the May 2009 indirect provincial and district council elections. There were 26 women in the 123-seat National Assembly and nine women in the 61-seat Senate.

There was a female deputy prime minister and 62 female ministers, secretaries of state, undersecretaries of state, and National Election Commission officials. Women also served as advisers, and there were 51 female judges and prosecutors in the municipal and provincial courts, appeals court, and Supreme Court. Although there were no female governors, the government appointed women as deputy governors in all of the 23 provinces and the Phnom Penh Municipality (there are a number of deputy governors in each province). The National Election Committee reported that women held 15 percent of commune council seats and 13 percent of district and provincial council seats.

There were five members of minorities—four Cham and one Tampuan—in the National Assembly. There also were three members of minorities in the Senate. At least eight officials in senior positions in the government were from minority groups.

Principal Government Officials

Last Updated: 1/31/2013

King: **Norodom SIHAMONI**
Prime Min.: **HUN SEN**
Permanent Dep. Prime Min.: **MEN SAM AN**
Dep. Prime Min.: **BIN CHHIN**
Dep. Prime Min.: **HOR NAMHONG**
Dep. Prime Min.: **KE KIMYAN**
Dep. Prime Min.: **KEAT CHHON**
Dep. Prime Min.: **NHEK BUNCHHAY**
Dep. Prime Min.: **SAR KHENG**
Dep. Prime Min.: **SOK AN**
Dep. Prime Min.: **TEA BANH, Gen.**
Dep. Prime Min.: **YIM CHHAI LY**
Min. of the Office of the Council of Ministers: **SOK AN**
Min. of Agriculture, Forestry, & Fisheries: **CHAN SARUN**
Min. of Commerce: **CHAM PRASITH**
Min. of Cults & Religious Affairs: **MIN KHIN**
Min. of Culture & Fine Arts: **HIM CHHEM**
Min. of Economy & Finance: **KEAT CHHON**
Min. of Education, Youth, & Sport: **IM SITTHI**
Min. of Environment: **MOK MARET**
Min. of Foreign Affairs & Intl. Cooperation: **HOR NAMHONG**
Min. of Health: **MAM BUN HENG**
Min. of Industry, Mines, & Energy: **SUY SEM**
Min. of Information: **KHIEU KANHARITH**
Min. of Interior: **SAR KHENG**
Min. of Justice: **ANG VONG VATTANA**
Min. of Labor & Vocational Training: **VONG SOTH**
Min. of Land Management, Urbanization, & Construction:**IM CHHUN LIM**
Min. of National Defense: **TEA BANH, Gen.**
Min. of Planning: **CHHAY THAN**
Min. of Posts & Telecommunications: **SO KHUN**
Min. of Public Works & Transportation: **TRAM IV TOEK**
Min. of Relations With the National Assembly, Senate, & Inspection:**SAOM KIM SUO**
Min. of Rural Development: **CHEA SOPHARA**
Min. of Social Affairs, War Veterans, & Youth Rehabilitation:**IT SAM-HENG**
Min. of Tourism: **THONG KHON**
Min. of Water Resources & Meteorology: **LIM KEAN-HAO**
Min. of Women's Affairs: **UNG KUNTHA PHAVY**
Governor, State Bank: **CHEA CHANTO**
Ambassador to the US: **HEM HENG**
Permanent Representative to the UN, New York: **SEA KOSAL**

ECONOMY

Since 2004, garments, construction, agriculture, and tourism have driven Cambodia's growth. GDP climbed more than 6% per year between 2010 and 2012. The garment industry currently employs more than 335,000 people and accounts for more than 75% of Cambodia's total exports. In 2005, exploitable oil deposits were found beneath Cambodia's territorial waters, representing a potential revenue stream for the government, if commercial extraction becomes feasible. Mining also is attracting some investor interest and the government has touted opportunities for mining bauxite, gold, iron and gems. The tourism industry has continued to grow rapidly with foreign arrivals exceeding 2 million per year since 2007. Cambodia, nevertheless, remains one of the poorest countries in Asia and long-term economic development remains a daunting challenge, inhibited by endemic corruption, limited educational opportunities, high income inequality, and poor job prospects.

Approximately 4 million people live on less than $1.25 per day and 37% of Cambodian children under the age of 5 suffer from chronic malnutrition. More than 50% of the population is less than 25 years old. The population lacks education and productive skills, particularly in the impoverished countryside, which also lacks basic infrastructure. The Cambodian government is working with bilateral and multilateral donors, including the World Bank and IMF, to address the country's many pressing needs; more than 50% of the government budget comes from donor assistance. The major economic challenge for Cambodia over the next decade will be fashioning an economic environment in which the private sector can create enough jobs to handle Cambodia's demographic imbalance.

Labor Conditions

The law establishes 15 years as the minimum age for employment and 18 years as the minimum age for hazardous work. The law permits children between 12 and 15 to engage in "light work" that is not hazardous to their health and does not affect school attendance. The law limits the working hours of children ages 12 to 15 to no more than four hours on school days and seven hours on nonschool days, and prohibits work between 8:00 p.m. and 6:00 a.m. The government also bans employment of children in sectors that pose major safety or health risks to minors.

Child labor was widespread in agriculture, brick making, salt production, shrimp processing, fishing, domestic service, and rubber production. Child labor was also reported in the garment, footwear, and hospitality sectors but to a much lesser extent. According to a 2006 study conducted by the World Bank and other sources, more than 750,000 economically active children were below the absolute minimum working age of 12.

An additional 500,000 children (12 to 14 years old) conducting nonlight economic activity were below the minimum age for this type of work. According to the report, more than 250,000 children ages 15 to 17 worked more than 43 hours per week or in hazardous sectors. Three-quarters of economically active children were in the agriculture sector, 15 percent in commerce, 5 percent in small-scale manufacturing, and 2 percent in services. A 2007 study of child domestic workers found that they typically did not attend school, worked long hours with no medical benefits, and received little or no pay.

The law requires the MOLVT to establish a garment-sector minimum wage based on recommendations from the Labor Advisory Committee. At the end of 2011, the minimum monthly wage was KHR244,000 (approximately $59). The law does not mandate a minimum wage for any other sector. The World Bank defines the poverty level as KHR5,000 ($1.22) per day.

The law provides for a standard legal workweek of 48 hours, not to exceed eight hours per day. The law establishes a rate of 130 percent of daytime wages for nightshift work and 150 percent for overtime, which increases to 200 percent if overtime occurs at night, on Sunday, or on a holiday. Employees are allowed to work up to two hours of overtime each day. The law prohibits excessive overtime, states that all overtime must be voluntary, and also provides for paid annual holidays. The law states that the workplace should have health and safety standards adequate to provide for workers' well-being.

The government did not effectively enforce standards regarding hours worked and overtime compensation. Workers reported that overtime was often excessive and sometimes mandatory. Outside the garment industry, regulations on working hours were rarely enforced. Involuntary overtime remained a problem, although the practice decreased during 2011. Employers used coercion to force employees to work. Workers often faced fines, dismissal, or loss of premium pay if they refused to work overtime.

Although workers had the right to remove themselves from dangerous situations, those who did so sometimes risked loss of employment. In practice work-related injuries and health problems were common. Most large garment factories producing for markets in developed countries met relatively high health and safety standards as conditions of their contracts with buyers. Working conditions in some small-scale factories and cottage industries were poor and often did not meet international standards.

On December 5, 2011, the government launched the National Social Protection Strategy (NSPS) for the Poor and Vulnerable, scheduled to remain in effect until 2015. The NSPS envisions a "sustainable, affordable, and effective national social protection system" with programs designed to end chronic poverty, hunger, and unemployment. The government committed to reducing the poverty rate from 25.8 percent in 2010 to 19.5 percent in 2015.

U.S.-CAMBODIAN RELATIONS

Over the last several decades of the 20th century, the United States and Cambodia established, broke off, and reestablished relations as a result of armed conflict and government changes in Cambodia. Full diplomatic relations were established after the freely elected Royal Government of Cambodia was formed in

1993. In recent years, bilateral relations between the U.S. and Cambodia have deepened and broadened. The two countries have worked together to increase trade and address challenges from promoting regional security and democracy to expanding global health and development.

The U.S. supports efforts in Cambodia to combat terrorism, reduce the prevalence of HIV/AIDS, build democratic institutions, promote human rights, foster economic development, eliminate corruption and trafficking in persons, achieve the fullest possible accounting for Americans missing from the Indochina conflict in the 1960s and 1970s, and to bring to justice those most responsible for serious violations of international humanitarian law committed under the 1975–79 Khmer Rouge regime.

U.S. Assistance to Cambodia

Cambodia is at peace after decades of conflict, although important challenges remain. Cambodia relies heavily on foreign assistance—about half of the central government budget depends on donor aid. U.S. assistance makes significant contributions to the country's development.

In 2010, U.S. Agency for International Development (USAID)-administered assistance was approximately $70 million for programs in health, education, governance, and economic growth.

Bilateral Economic Relations

Cambodia's economy suffers from the legacy of decades of war and internal strife. The economy is heavily dollarized; the dollar and riel can be used interchangeably. The U.S. normalized economic relations with the country in 1992 and is one of Cambodia's major trading partners. Manufacturing output is concentrated in the garment sector, and garments dominate Cambodia's exports, especially to the U.S. and the European Union.

Cambodia's Membership in International Organizations

Cambodia became a member of the United Nations in 1955 following independence from France in 1953. Cambodia and the United States belong to a number of the same international organizations, including the UN, International Monetary Fund, World Bank, and World Trade Organization.

Bilateral Representation

Cambodia's embassy in the United States is located at 4530 16th Street NW, Washington DC 20011; tel: (202) 726-7742; fax: (202) 726-8381.

Principal U.S. Embassy Officials

Last Updated: 1/14/2013

PHNOM PENH (E) #01, St. 96, (855) 23 728 000, Fax (855) 23 728 600, Workweek: 8AM–5PM, Website: http://cambodia.usembassy.gov/ >http://cambodia.usembassy.gov/

DCM OMS:	Koji Kanazawa
AMB OMS:	Niceta Redd
Co-CLO:	Ingrid Gillette
FM:	Philip C. Steinhauser
HRO:	Paula A. Mendez
MGT:	Terry L. Murphree
POL/ECON:	David Myers
SDO/DATT:	COL Mark Gillette
AMB:	William E. Todd
CON:	Eric Meyer
DCM:	Jeff Daigle
PAO:	Sean J. McIntosh
GSO:	Dianne Syrvalin
RSO:	Luis Matus
AID:	Laurie De Freese
CLO:	Alandra Ellington
FMO:	Geoge Meray
ICASS Chair:	Mark Gillette
IMO:	Arthur J. Mendez
LEGATT:	Sharon Kuo
POL:	Darren Hultman

TRAVEL

Consular Information Sheet

January 27, 2012

Country Description: Cambodia is a developing country with a constitutional monarchy and an elected government. King Norodom Sihamoni is the constitutional monarch and head of state. Elections for Members of the National Assembly were held in July 2008 and are scheduled to take place again in July 2013. The July 2008 elections sent representatives from five different parties to the National Assembly, with the Cambodian People's Party holding a majority of seats. The country has a market economy, with approximately 80 percent of the population of 13.4 million engaged in subsistence farming. The quality of tourist facilities varies widely in Cambodia, with the highest standards found in Phnom Penh, Siem Reap, and Sihanoukville.

Smart Traveler Enrollment Program (STEP)/Embassy Locations: If you are going to live in or visit Cambodia, please take the time to tell our Embassy about your trip. If you enroll, we can keep you up to date with important safety and security announcements. It will also help your friends and family get in touch with you in an emergency.

US Embassy Phnom Penh
No. 1, Street 96 (near Wat Phnom), Phnom Penh, Cambodia
Telephone: (855-23) 728-000
Fax: (855-23) 728-700

Entry/Exit Requirements for U.S. Citizens: You will need a valid passport and a Cambodian visa to travel to Cambodia. Tourist and business visas are valid for one month beginning with the date of entry into Cambodia. Cambodia offers on-line visa processing. You may also apply in person at the Cambodian Embassy located at 4530 16th Street NW, Washington, DC 20011, tel. 202-726-7742, fax 202-726-8381. Tourists and business travelers may also obtain a

Cambodian visa at the airports in Phnom Penh, Siem Reap, and at all major border crossings. Cambodian airports now collect fingerprints upon entry using an inkless, electronic process. You will need two passport-sized (4cm by 6cm) photographs and a passport valid for a minimum of six months beyond the date of entry into Cambodia. Cambodia regularly imposes fines for overstay of an expired visa. If the overstay is 30 days or less, the charge is USD $5.00 per day; for overstays of more than 30 days, the charge is USD $6.00 per day. You should contact the nearest embassy or consulate of Cambodia or visitthe Embassy of the Kingdom of Cambodia web site for the most current visa information.

The U.S. Department of State is unaware of any HIV/AIDS entry restrictions for visitors to or foreign residents of Cambodia.

Threats to Safety and Security: The State Department is concerned that individuals and groups may be planning terrorist actions against U.S. citizens and interests, as well as at sites frequented by Westerners in Southeast Asia, including in Cambodia. Extremist groups in Southeast Asia have transnational capabilities to carry out attacks against locations where Westerners congregate.

U.S. citizens residing in, or traveling to, Cambodia should therefore exercise caution in clubs, discos, bars, restaurants, hotels, places of worship, schools, outdoor recreation venues, tourist areas, beach resorts, and other places frequented by foreigners. U.S. citizens should remain vigilant with regard to their personal security and avoid crowds and demonstrations. From time to time, the U.S. Embassy places local establishments off limits to Embassy personnel due to safety and security incidents. You can contact the Embassy for notification on the current restrictions in place for Embassy personnel, or register with the Embassy through STEP for security updates and alerts.

Although the political situation is relatively stable, Cambodian political activities have turned violent in the past, and the possibility for politically-motivated violence remains. On January 2, 2009, three explosive devices were found near the Ministry of National Defense in downtown Phnom Penh. While there is no indication these incidents were directed at U.S. or other Western interests, the possibility remains that further attacks could be carried out, potentially harming innocent bystanders.

The U.S. Embassy frequently receives reports of random gunfire in the vicinity of bars, nightclubs, and other entertainment venues. While U.S. citizens have not been injured and do not appear to have been targeted, the potential exists for serious injury. U.S. citizens should be vigilant in these areas.

The U.S. Embassy recommends that U.S. citizens avoid travel along the Cambodian-Thai border in the provinces of Preah Vihear, Oddar Meanchey, and the Banteay Ampil district of Banteay Meanchey province because of a continuing border dispute between the two countries. Thai and Cambodian soldiers have been stationed along the border in this area since July 2008 and have exchanged gunfire on several occasions.

Land mines and unexploded ordnance are found in rural areas throughout Cambodia, and especially in Battambang, Banteay Meanchey, Pursat, Siem Reap, and Kampong Thom provinces. Travelers in these regions should never walk in forested areas or even in dry rice paddies without a local guide. Areas around small bridges on secondary roads are particularly dangerous. Travelers should not touch anything that resembles a mine or unexploded ordnance; they should notify the Cambodia Mine Action Center at 023-368-841/981-083 or 084.

You should exercise extreme caution when traveling on boat tours and excursions in the coastal areas of the country. In April 2011, a boat containing 90 tourists capsized off the coast of Sihanoukville. While no one was seriously injured, such incidents could recur anytime as boat tour operators do not take into account basic safety concerns and rarely provide life jackets for all passengers.

Stay up to date:

- Bookmark our Bureau of Consular Affairs website, which contains the current Travel Warnings and Travel Alerts as well as the Worldwide Caution.
- Follow us on Twitter and the Bureau of Consular Affairs page on Facebook.
- Download our free Smart Traveler IPhone App to have travel information at your fingertips.
- Call 1-888-407-4747 toll-free within the U.S. and Canada, or a regular toll line, 1-202-501-4444, from other countries.
- Taking some time before travel to consider your personal security.

Crime: Cambodia has a high crime rate, including street crime. Military weapons and explosives are readily available to criminals despite authorities' efforts to collect and destroy such weapons. Armed robberies occur frequently, and foreign residents and visitors are among the victims. Armed burglaries are also a concern. In April 2010, a U.S. citizen reported that he and his female companion were bound with wire, assaulted, and robbed in his home in Siem Reap. In July 2010, another U.S. citizen sustained injuries during a burglary of his home in Phnom Penh. The Embassy also received reports that hotel rooms of U.S. citizen visitors in Phnom Penh have been burglarized while the occupants were asleep. The most common type of theft is "snatch and grab" robbery, and anything that can be quickly grabbed is at risk: cameras, jewelry, purses, backpacks, mobile phones, etc. Exercise caution and keep belongings out of sight if you travel via "tuk-tuk," as passengers in these open-air vehicles have been targeted by thieves. If walking along the street, make yourself less of a target by carrying bags or items in the hand or on the shoulder away from the street.

If you encounter these circumstances, you should surrender your valuables immediately, since any perceived resistance may be met with physical violence, including lethal force. To avoid the risk of theft or confiscation of original documents, the U.S. Embassy advises its personnel and all U.S. citizens traveling to, or residing in, Cambodia to carry photocopies of their U.S. passport, driver's license, and other important documents and leave the originals in a hotel safe or other secure place. Local police rarely investigate reports of crime against tourists, and travelers should not expect to recover stolen items.

In July 2010, the U.S. Embassy received several reports that U.S. citizens and other foreigners had been attacked by rocks or pieces of brick that were thrown from moving vehicles in the vicinity of the riverfront in Phnom Penh. Several of the victims reportedly suffered facial lacerations and concussions. All of the attacks took place at night, and the victims included both foreign men and women. You should exercise caution, especially at night, and report any attacks to both the Embassy and to the local tourist police.

In 2011, the U.S. Embassy received several reports of presumed ATM/ debit card fraud. ATM fraud can take place in many different ways, but the most common is by "skimming" card data as a transaction is made, while simultaneously recording the Personal Identification Number (PIN) that corresponds with the card. Several people have reported that unauthorized transactions have occurred after using their ATM cards in Cambodia. In light of these events, you should exercise caution by planning ahead and making copies of your ATM card, front and back, so that if you lose it, you still have the card number and contact information.

Use ATMs located in secured areas, such as bank or hotel lobbies. Consider only using a few ATMs, and be aware of their appearance. If something looks unfamiliar about a machine, don't use it until you have verified that any modification is legitimate. You should also be aware of your surroundings when using an ATM. Robberies are more likely as you depart an ATM, so please stay alert to your surroundings and depart an ATM quickly. The U.S. Embassy advises its personnel who travel to the provinces to exercise extreme caution outside the provincial towns at all times.

Many rural parts of the country remain without effective policing. Avoid walking alone after dusk anywhere in Sihanoukville, especially along the waterfront. Some of the beaches are secluded, and the Embassy has received reports that women have been attacked along the Sihanoukville waterfront during the evening.

Take security precautions when visiting the Siem Reap(Angkor Wat) area. You should be particularly vigilant during annual festivals and at tourist sites in Phnom Penh, Siem Reap, and Sihanoukville, where there have been marked increases in motorcycle "snatch and grab" thefts of bags and purses. Pickpockets, some of whom are beggars, are present in the markets and at the tourist sites. Sometimes they may act overly friendly, placing their hand on your shoulder or back to distract you. As mentioned above, tourists are often victims of purse snatching and other snatch-and-grab assaults. These crimes are typically not violent unless the victim resists; if such a crime is attempted, do not fight back.

If you are visiting Cambodia, you should practice sound personal security awareness by varying your routes and routines, maintaining a low profile, not carrying or displaying large amounts of cash, not wearing flashy or expensive jewelry, and not walking alone after dark. In addition, you should travel by automobile and not use local moto-taxis or cyclos (passenger-carrying bicycles). These vehicles are more vulnerable to armed robberies and offer no protection against injury when involved in traffic accidents. Don't buy counterfeit and pirated goods, even if they are widely available. Not only are the 'bootlegs' illegal in the United States, if you purchase them or try to bring them back into the United States you may also be breaking local or federal laws.

Victims of Crime: If you or someone you know becomes the victim of a crime abroad, you should contact the local police and the nearest U.S. embassy or consulate.

We can:

- Replace a stolen passport.
- For violent crimes such as assault or rape, help you find appropriate medical care.
- Put you in contact with the appropriate police authorities and, if you want us to, we can contact your family members or friends.
- Although the local authorities are responsible for investigating and prosecuting the crime, consular officers can help you understand the local criminal justice process and can direct you to local attorneys.

The American Citizen Services (ACS) unit is located in the Consular Section of the U.S. Embassy at #1, St. 96 (entrance on St. 51 between St. 96 and 102), Phnom Penh. The Consular Section telephone number is 855-23-728-801 Monday thru Friday 8:00 a.m. to 5:00 p.m. and 855-23-728-000 after business hours and weekends.

The local equivalent to the "911" emergency line in Cambodia is 117 for police, 118 for fire, and 119 for ambulance.

Criminal Penalties: While you are traveling in Cambodia, you are subject to its laws even if you are a U.S. citizen. Foreign laws, legal systems, and criminal penalties can be vastly different than our own. In some places, it is illegal to take pictures of certain buildings. Criminal penalties will vary from country to country. There are also acts that might be legal in the country you visit, but still illegal in the United States.

You can be prosecuted under U.S. law if you buy pirated goods. Engaging in sexual conduct with children or using or disseminating child pornography in a foreign country is a crime prosecutable in the United States. If you break local laws in Cambodia, your U.S. passport won't help you avoid arrest or prosecution. It is very important to know what's legal and what's not where you are going. Based on the Vienna Convention on Consular Relations, bilateral agreements with certain countries, and customary international law, if you are arrested in Cambodia, you have the option to request that the police, prison officials, or other authorities alert the nearest U.S. embassy or consulate of your arrest, and to have communications from you forwarded to the nearest U.S. embassy or consulate.

Accessibility: While in Cambodia, individuals with disabilities may find accessibility and accommodation very different from what you find in the United States. Currently, except for buildings and hotels that have been built under international standards, most public places and public transportation are not accessible.

Persons with disabilities will face difficulties with Cambodia's sidewalks, rest rooms, road crossings, and tourist areas.

Water Festival: During this annual festival which takes place in Phnom Penh in November, the population of the city nearly quadruples as millions of Cambodians from every town and province flock to the capital for three days. In November 2010, this festival was marred by a tragic stampede killing more than 300 people. Please avoid crowded areas near the riverfront during the Water Festival holiday.

Customs: Cambodian customs authorities may enforce strict regulations concerning temporary importation into or export from Cambodia of items such as drugs, firearms, antiquities, or ivory. It is advisable to contact the Embassy of Cambodia in Washington for specific information regarding customs requirements.

Dual Nationality: Dual nationality is allowed under Cambodia's 1996 nationality law. In addition to being subject to all Cambodian laws affecting U.S. citizens, individuals who possess Cambodian nationality may also be subject to laws that impose special obligations on Cambodian citizens.

Business Transactions: Some U.S. citizens have reported threats of personal injury, extortion, detention, or kidnapping related to personal business disputes, in particular those involving real estate. If you are planning to engage in real estate deals or other significant financial transactions, please proceed with caution and retain the appropriate legal counsel. If you do not have confidence in the ability of the local police to protect you, you may wish to consider departing the country expeditiously.

Financial Transactions: The U.S. dollar is widely used, especially for larger transactions, and most prices are quoted in dollars. Ripped or torn U.S. bills are not accepted. The Cambodian riel can also be used, but it is less favored and is mostly given to tourists as change for dollar purchases. The riel is commonly used in smaller towns and rural areas. Credit cards are increasingly accepted within Cambodia, and a number of banks in Phnom Penh accept Visa cards for cash advances.

Credit cards are often subject to a service charge. Banks and major hotels accept travelers' checks but usually charge a service fee. Several international banks operate ATM machines that allow travelers to obtain U.S. dollar currency in Phnom Penh, Siem Reap, and other urban centers. Please see the section on crime for information on ATM and credit card fraud. Personal checks are not generally accepted. Several banks serve as Western Union agents to which funds can be wired, including in Phnom Penh, Siem Reap, Sihanoukville, and other provincial cities. Information on Western Union can be found at http://www.westernunion.com

Photography: Taking photographs of anything that could be perceived as being of military or security interest—including government buildings, military installations, airfields, and bridges—may result in problems with the authorities and confiscation of the camera.

Medical Facilities and Health Information: Medical facilities and services in Cambodia do not meet international standards. Both Phnom Penh and Siem Reap have a limited number of internationally-run clinics and hospitals that can provide basic medical care and stabilization. Medical care outside these two cities is almost non-existent. Local pharmacies provide a limited supply of prescription and over-the-counter medications, but because the quality of locally obtained medications can vary greatly, make sure to bring an adequate supply of your medications for the duration of your stay in Cambodia. You should be wary of purchasing local medication. Counterfeit medication is readily available, often indiscernible from authentic medication, and potentially lethal. You can find good information on vaccinations and other health precautions, on the CDC website. For information about outbreaks of infectious diseases abroad, consult the World Health Organization (WHO) website.

Medical Insurance: You can't assume your insurance will go with you when you travel. It's very important to find out BEFORE you leave whether or not your medical insurance will cover you overseas. You need to ask your insurance company two questions:

- Does my policy apply when I'm out of the United States?
- Will it cover emergencies like a trip to a foreign hospital or a medical evacuation?

In many places, doctors and hospitals still expect payment in cash at the time of service. Your regular U.S. health insurance may not cover doctors' and hospital visits in other countries. If your policy doesn't go with you when you travel, it's a very good idea to take out another one for your trip.

Traffic Safety and Road Conditions: While in Cambodia, you may encounter road conditions that differ significantly from those in the United States. The information below concerning Cambodia is provided forgeneral reference only and may not be totally accurate in a particular location or circumstance. You should not drive at night in Cambodia outside of city limits. Road maintenance is sporadic in both urban and rural areas. Roads between major areas are adequate; however, roads leading to areas that are more rural are poor. During the rainy season, both urban and rural road conditions deteriorate considerably. Roadside assistance is non-existent. The safety of road travel outside urban areas varies greatly. Cambodian drivers routinely ignore traffic laws, and vehicles are poorly maintained. Intoxicated drivers are commonplace, particularly during the evening hours, and penalties for DUI offenses vary greatly.

Banditry occurs even on heavily traveled roads, so all travel should be done in daylight between the hours of 7:00 a.m. and 5.00 p.m. Serious flooding occurs in both Phnom Penh and the rest of Cambodia starting at the end of July or early August and continuing into November. The unimproved highways to Prey Veng, Pailin, Stung Treng, and Poipet become more difficult and dangerous during this time of the year, and travel on unpaved or dirt roads is virtually impossible. The National Route highways are the only roads that can be traveled with caution during this time of the year. The U.S. Embassy advises its personnel not to travel by train because of low safety standards and the high risk of banditry. Although speed boats operate between Phnom Penh and Siem Reap, travel by boat should be avoided because boats are often overcrowded and lack adequate safety equipment, including life jackets. Boat owners accept no liability for accidents. Travelers also should exercise caution when using inter-city buses, including those to popular tourist destinations such as Siem Reap and Sihanoukville. Moto-taxis and cyclos are widely available; however, you should not use them due to safety concerns and because personal belongings can be easily stolen. Organized emergency services for victims of traffic accidents are non-existent outside of major urban areas, and those available in major urban areas are inadequate.

Aviation Safety Oversight: As there is no direct commercial air service to the United States by carriers registered in Cambodia, the U.S. Federal Aviation Administration (FAA) has not assessed the government of Cambodia's Civil Aviation Authority for compliance with International Civil Aviation Organization (ICAO) aviation safety standards. Furtherinformation may be found on the FAA safety assessment page.

Children's Issues: Please see the U.S. Dept. of State Office of Children's Issues web pages on intercountry adoption and international parental child abduction.

Intercountry Adoption

Update on Status of Intercountry Adoptions between the United States and Cambodia
January 2, 2013

The United States has determined that it will not be able to process intercountry adoptions in Cambodia at this time, under the Hague Convention on Protection of Children and Co-Operation in Respect of Intercountry Adoption (the Convention). Despite Cambodia's initiatives to strengthen its child welfare system and improve the integrity of its domestic and intercountry adoption processes, it does not yet have a fully functional Convention process in place.

We caution adoption service providers and prospective adoptive parents that important steps, consistent with the requirements of the Convention, must take place before intercountry adoptions between the United States and Cambodia may resume. Adoption service providers should neither initiate nor claim to initiate adoption services in Cambodia for prospective adoptive parents in the United States until they receive notification from the Department of State.

The Department of State will provide updated information on adoption.state.gov as it becomes available. If you have any questions about this notice, please contact the Office of Children's Issues at 1-888-407-4747 within the United States, or 202-501-4444 from outside the United States. Email inquiries may be directed to AdoptionUSCA@state.gov.

The Embassy of the United States of America, Phnom Penh

Consular Section
#1, Street 96
Phnom Penh, Cambodia
Tel: (855-23) 728-000
Fax: (855-23) 728-600
Email: adoptionscambodia@state.gov
http://cambodia.usembassy.gov

CAMEROON

Compiled from publications that were available as of February 2013 from the U.S. Department of State, the U.S. Department of Commerce, and the Central Intelligence Agency (CIA). See the introduction to this set for explanatory notes.

Official Name:
Republic of Cameroon

PROFILE

Geography

Area: total: 475,440 sq km; country comparison to the world: 54; land: 472,710 sq km; water: 2,730 sq km

Major cities: Douala 2.053 million; Yaounde (capital) 1.739 million (2009)

Climate: varies with terrain, from tropical along coast to semiarid and hot in north

Terrain: diverse, with coastal plain in southwest, dissected plateau in center, mountains in west, plains in north

People

Nationality: noun: Cameroonian(s); adjective: Cameroonian

Population: 20,129,878 (July 2012 est.)

Population growth rate: 2.082% (2012 est.)

Ethnic groups: Cameroon Highlanders 31%, Equatorial Bantu 19%, Kirdi 11%, Fulani 10%, Northwestern Bantu 8%, Eastern Nigritic 7%, other African 13%, non-African less than 1%

Religions: indigenous beliefs 40%, Christian 40%, Muslim 20%

Languages: 24 major African language groups, English (official), French (official)

Literacy: definition: age 15 and over can read and write; total population: 75.9%; male: 84%; female: 67.8% (2001 est.)

Health: life expectancy at birth: total population: 54.71 years; male: 53.82 years; female: 55.63 years (2012 est.); Infant mortality rate: total: 59.7 deaths/1,000 live births; male: 64.19 deaths/1,000 live births; female: 55.07 deaths/1,000 live births (2012 est.)

Unemployment rate: 30% (2001 est.)

Work force: 8.264 million (2012 est.)

Government

Type: republic; multiparty presidential regime

Independence: 1 January 1960

Constitution: approved by referendum 20 May 1972; adopted 2 June 1972; revised January 1996; amended April 2008

Political subdivisions: 10 regions (regions, singular—region); Adamaoua, Centre, Est, Extreme-Nord, Littoral, Nord, North-West (Nord-Ouest), Ouest, Sud, South-West (Sud-Ouest)

Suffrage: 20 years of age; universal

Economy

GDP (purchasing power parity): $50.32 billion (2012 est.); $47.86 billion (2011 est.); $45.97 billion (2010 est.); $44.67 billion (2009 est.)

GDP real growth rate: 4.7% (2012 est.); 4.1% (2011 est.); 2.9% (2010 est.); 2% (2009 est.)

GDP per capita (PPP): $2,300 (2012 est.); $2,300 (2011 est.); $2,300 (2010 est.); $2,200 (2009 est.)

Natural resources: petroleum, bauxite, iron ore, timber, hydropower

Agriculture products: coffee, cocoa, cotton, rubber, bananas, oilseed, grains, cassava (manioc); livestock; timber

Industries: petroleum production and refining, aluminum production, food processing, light consumer goods, textiles, lumber, ship repair

Exports: $6.538 billion (2012 est.); $5.549 billion (2011 est.); $4.485 billion (2010 est.)

Exports—commodities: crude oil and petroleum products, lumber, cocoa beans, aluminum, coffee, cotton

Exports—partners: Spain 13.3%, China 11.4%, Netherlands 9.7%, Italy 8.8%, India 6.6%, France 6.4%, US 5.9%, Germany 4.8%, Belgium 4% (2011)

Imports: $6.597 billion (2012 est.); $6.108 billion (2011 est.); $4.663 billion (2010 est.)

Imports—commodities: machinery, electrical equipment, transport equipment, fuel, food

Imports—partners: China 16.9%, France 16.8%, Nigeria 12.4%, Belgium 5.3%, Italy 4.3%, US 4.3% (2011)

Debt—external: $3.343 billion (31 December 2012 est.); $3.147 billion (31 December 2011 est.); $2.964 billion (31 December 2010 est.)

Exchange rates: Cooperation Financiere en Afrique Centrale francs (XAF) per dollar; 514.1 (2012 est.); 471.87 (2011 est.); 495.28 (2010 est.); 472.19 (2009); 447.81 (2008); 493.51 (2007)

PEOPLE

Cameroon's estimated 250 ethnic groups form five large regional-cultural groups: western highlanders (or grassfielders), including the Bamileke, Bamoun, and many smaller entities in the northwest; coastal tropical forest peoples, including the Bassa, Douala, and many smaller entities in the Southwest; southern tropical forest peoples, including the Ewondo, Bulu, and Fang (all Beti subgroups), Maka and Pygmies (officially called Bakas); predominantly Islamic peoples of the northern semi-arid regions (the Sahel) and central highlands, including the Fulani, also known as Peuhl in French; and the "Kirdi," non-Islamic or recently Islamic peoples of the northern desert and central highlands.

Although Yaounde is Cameroon's capital, Douala is the largest city, main seaport, and main industrial and commercial center.

The western highlands are among the most fertile regions in Cameroon and have a relatively healthy environment in higher altitudes. This region is densely populated and has intensive agriculture, commerce, cohesive communities, and historical emigration pressures. From here, Bantu migrations into eastern, southern, and central Africa are believed to have originated about 2,000 years ago. Bamileke people from this area have in recent years migrated to towns elsewhere in Cameroon, such as the coastal regions, where they form much of the business community. About 20,000 non-Africans, including more than 6,000 French and 2,400 U.S. citizens, reside in Cameroon.

National/Racial/Ethnic Minorities

The population consists of more than 250 ethnic groups, among which there were frequent and credible allegations of discrimination. Ethnic groups commonly gave preferential treatment to fellow ethnic group members in business and social practices. Members of the president's Beti/Bulu ethnic group from southern areas held key positions and were disproportionately represented in the government, state-owned businesses, security forces, and the ruling CPDM party.

Northern areas continued to suffer from ethnic tensions between the Fulani (or Peuhl) and the Kirdi, who remained socially, educationally, and economically disadvantaged relative to the Fulani in the three northern regions.

Traditional Fulani rulers, called lamibe, continued to wield great power over their subjects, who often included Kirdi, and sometimes subjected them to tithing and forced labor. Isolated cases of hereditary servitude were alleged, largely Fulani enslavement of Kirdi. Many Fulani hired Kirdi at exploitive wage levels to perform tasks that the Fulani considered menial and beneath them.

Vigilante violence against persons suspected of theft resulted in at least two deaths during 2011. Public frustration over police ineffectiveness and the release without charge of many individuals arrested for serious crimes contributed to vigilante violence.

An estimated 50,000 to 100,000 Baka, including Bakola and Bagyeli (Pygmies), resided primarily (and were the earliest known inhabitants) in the forested areas of the South and East regions. While no legal discrimination exists, other groups often treated the Baka as inferior and sometimes subjected them to unfair and exploitative labor practices. The government did not effectively protect their civil and political rights. Some observers believed that sustained logging was destroying the Baka's unique, forest-oriented belief system, forcing them to adapt their traditional social and economic systems to a more rigid modern society similar to their Bantu neighbors.

The Ministry of Social Affairs continued efforts begun in 2005 to provide birth certificates and national identity cards to Baka; however, 95 percent of Baka did not have identity cards at year's end. Ministry teams reported that efforts to reach Baka were impeded by the difficulty in accessing their homes deep in the forest, but that slow progress was being made. During 2011 ministry teams located dozens of Baka to assist them with registration and voting.

Language

Although both French and English are official languages in Cameroon, at least two-thirds of the population speaks French, which is the dominant business language. A majority of working-class Cameroonians understand, even though they may not speak, both languages. Pidgin English is a local lingua franca in the two English-speaking regions (the South West and North West Regions) of Cameroon and is widely used in several parts of Cameroon. The staff at most hotels and restaurants are usually bilingual-English and French.

Religion

According to the 2005 census, 69 percent of the population is Christian, 21 percent Muslim, and 6 percent animist. Groups that constitute less than 5 percent of the population include Jews and Baha'is. As defined by the census, the Christian population is divided among Roman Catholics (38.4 percent of the total population), Protestants (26.3 percent), and other Christian denominations (4 percent), including Jehovah's Witnesses.

Muslims and Christians are found in every region, although Christians are concentrated primarily in the southern and western regions. Large cities have significant populations of both groups. The two Anglophone regions of the country are largely Protestant, and the eight Francophone regions are mostly Catholic. In the northern regions, the dominant Fulani (or Peuhl) ethnic group is mainly Muslim, but the overall population in those regions is fairly evenly divided among Muslims, Christians, and followers of indigenous religions, who are mostly located in rural areas. The Bamoun ethnic group of the West Region is predominately Muslim.

HISTORY

The earliest inhabitants of Cameroon were probably the Bakas (Pygmies). They still inhabit the forests of the South and East regions. During the late 1770s and early 1800s, the Fulani, a pastoral Islamic people of the western Sahel, conquered most of what is now northern Cameroon, subjugating or displacing its largely non-Muslim inhabitants.

Although the Portuguese arrived on Cameroon's coast in the 1500s, malaria prevented significant European settlement and conquest of the interior until the late 1870s, when large supplies of the malaria suppressant, quinine, became available. The early European presence in Cameroon was primarily devoted to coastal trade and the acquisition of slaves. The northern part of Cameroon was an important part of the Muslim slave trade network. The slave trade was largely suppressed by the mid-19th century. Christian missions established a presence in the late 19th century and continue to play a role in Cameroonian life. Beginning in 1884, all of present-day Cameroon and parts of several of its neighbors became the German colony of Kamerun, with a capital first at Duala (Douala) and later Buea and then Jaunde (present day Yaounde). After World War I, this colony was partitioned between Britain and France under a June 28, 1919 League of Nations mandate. France gained the larger geographical share, transferred outlying regions to neighboring French colonies, and administered the rest from Yaounde. Britain's territory—a strip bordering Nigeria from the sea to Lake Chad, with an equal population—was governed from Lagos.

In 1955, the outlawed Union of the Peoples of Cameroon (UPC), based largely among the Bamileke and Bassa ethnic groups, began an armed struggle for independence in French Cameroon. This rebellion continued, with diminishing intensity, even after independence. Estimates of deaths from this conflict vary from tens of thousands to hundreds of thousands.

French Cameroon achieved independence in 1960 as the Republic of Cameroon. The following year the largely Muslim northern two-thirds of British Cameroon voted to join Nigeria; the largely Christian southern third voted to join with the Republic of Cameroon to form the Federal Republic of Cameroon. The formerly French and British regions each maintained substantial autonomy. Ahmadou Ahidjo, a French-educated Fulani, became President of the federation in 1961. Ahidjo, relying on a pervasive internal security apparatus, outlawed all political parties but his own (the Cameroon National Union, CNU) in 1966. He successfully suppressed the UPC rebellion, capturing the last high-ranking rebel leader in 1970. In 1972, Ahidjo introduced a new constitution, which replaced the federation with a unitary state.

Ahidjo resigned as President in 1982 and was constitutionally succeeded by his Prime Minister, Paul Biya, a career official from the Bulu-Beti ethnic group. Ahidjo later regretted his choice of successors, but his supporters failed to overthrow Biya in a 1984 coup attempt. Biya won single-candidate elections in 1984 and 1988 and flawed multiparty elections in 1992, 1997, 2004, and 2011. His Cameroon People's Democratic Movement (CPDM) party, formerly the CNU, holds a sizeable majority in the legislature following 2007 elections—153 deputies out of a total of 180. The next parliamentary elections will take place in mid-2012.

GOVERNMENT AND POLITICAL CONDITIONS

Cameroon is a republic dominated by a strong presidency. The country has a multiparty system of government, but the Cameroon People's Democratic Movement (CPDM) has remained in power since it was created in 1985. It has unfettered control of all government branches. The president retains the power to control legislation and rule by decree.

On October 9, 2011, CPDM leader Paul Biya won reelection as president, a position he has held since 1982. The election was flawed by irregularities, including the failure to properly distribute all voter cards, late opening of polling stations, multiple voting, ballot-box stuffing, the absence of indelible ink, and intimidation of voters. There were instances in which elements of the security forces acted independently of civilian control.

Recent Elections

On October 9, 2011, CPDM leader Paul Biya, who garnered more than 77 percent of the vote, won reelection as president, a position he has held since 1982. The election was peaceful but marred by irregularities, including polls that opened late, a voter list that contained numerous duplicate entries, insufficient time to distribute registration cards, inadequate training of polling officials, and the absence of indelible ink. These shortcomings effectively disfranchised an unknown number of voters and created opportunities for multiple voting and ballot box stuffing. Domestic and international observers concluded that the irregularities did not significantly affect the election outcome. Citizens residing overseas registered and voted.

The opposition's failure to unite behind a single candidate divided the opposition vote 22 ways and contributed to voter apathy and cynicism. According to the Centre for Human Rights and Peace Advocacy

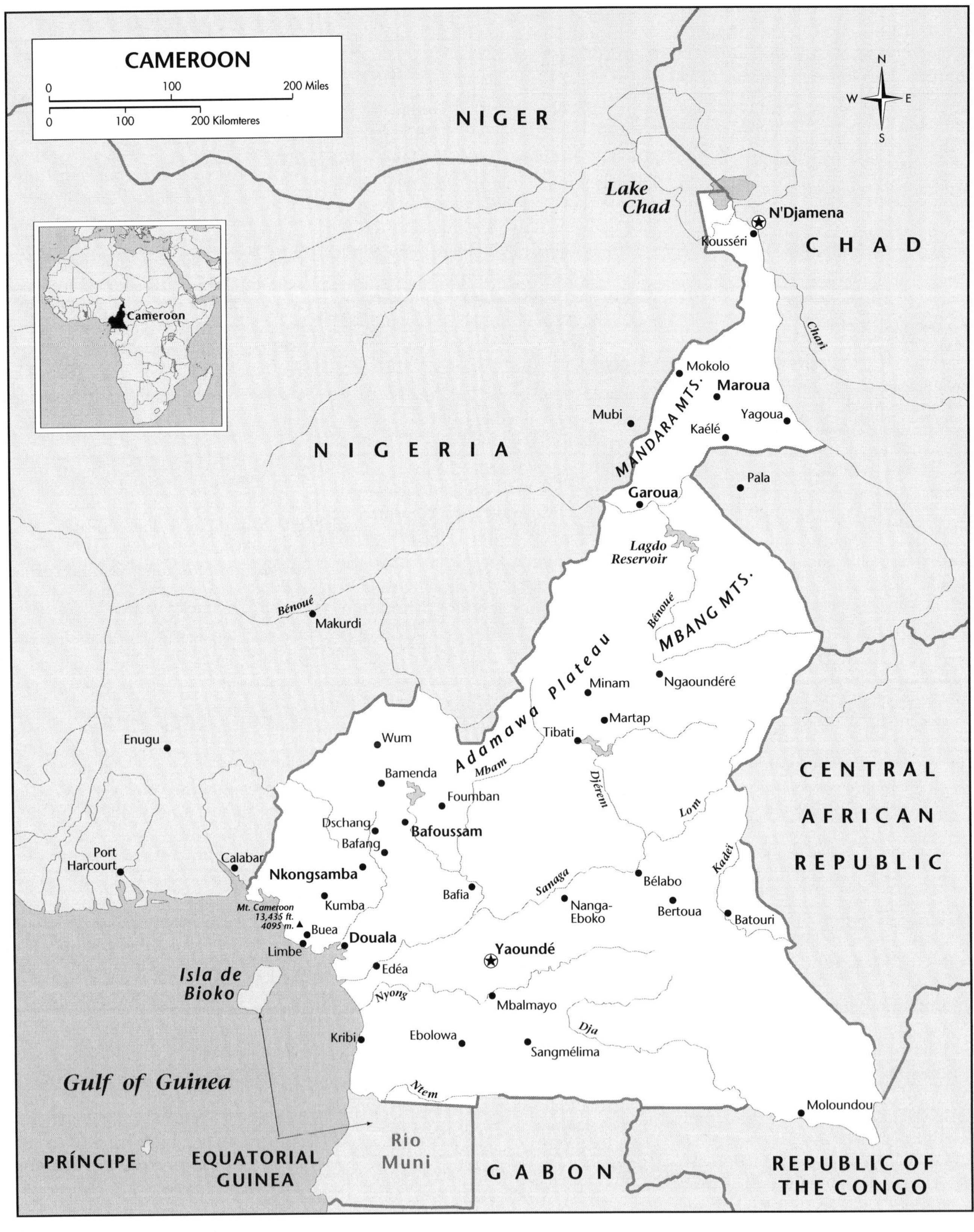
CAMEROON
0 100 200 Miles
0 100 200 Kilomteres
N
W E
S
NIGER
Lake Chad
N'Djamena
Kousséri
CHAD
Cameroon
Chari
Mokolo
Maroua
Mubi
Yagoua
Kaélé
MANDARA MTS.
NIGERIA
Pala
Garoua
Lagdo Reservoir
MBANG MTS.
Bénoué
Makurdi
Adamawa Plateau
Minam
Ngaoundéré
Martap
Tibati
Enugu
Wum
Bamenda
Mbam
Foumban
Djérem
Lom
CENTRAL AFRICAN REPUBLIC
Dschang
Bafoussam
Bafang
Port Harcourt
Calabar
Nkongsamba
Kadeï
Bafia
Sanaga
Bélabo
Kumba
Nanga-Eboko
Bertoua
Batouri
Mt. Cameroon 13,435 ft. 4095 m.
Buea
Douala
Limbe
Yaoundé
Isla de Bioko
Edéa
Nyong
Mbalmayo
Dja
Kribi
Ebolowa
Sangmélima
Gulf of Guinea
Ntem
Moloundou
Rio Muni
PRÍNCIPE
EQUATORIAL GUINEA
GABON
REPUBLIC OF THE CONGO

(CHRAPA), an organization with special consultative status at the UN, less than 30 percent of the population voted. The government claimed that 66 percent of the population cast ballots.

The election was administered by Elections Cameroon (ELECAM), which was established in 2006 and whose members were appointed by the president. ELECAM's original 12 Electoral Council members were formerly active CPDM members, resulting in public skepticism of ELECAM's credibility and objectivity. In May the government amended electoral legislation to increase the number of council members from 12 to 18. In July the president appointed six new members, who included prominent figures from civil society. On October 7, one of the new appointees was dismissed for allegedly receiving money from the CPDM to manage part of its public relations campaign.

After the election the Supreme Court received 20 complaints from political parties, 10 of which demanded either the partial or complete annulment of results as a result of irregularities. On October 19, the court dismissed all the cases for lack of evidence or late submission.

According to CHRAPA, coverage of campaign activities by the state media was biased, providing extensive coverage of the campaign activities of the incumbent but not of opposition parties.

The government greatly increased the number of municipalities run by presidentially appointed delegates, who have authority over elected mayors, effectively disenfranchising the residents of those localities. Delegate-run cities included most of the provincial capitals and some division capitals in pro-opposition regions; however, this practice was almost nonexistent in the southern regions, which tended to support the ruling CPDM party. In municipalities with elected mayors, local autonomy was limited, since elected local governments relied on the central government for most of their revenue and administrative personnel.

Political Parties: There were more than 253 registered political parties. Fewer than 10, however, had significant levels of support, and only five had seats in the National Assembly. The CPDM held an absolute majority in the National Assembly. Opposition parties included the Social Democratic Front (SDF), based in the Anglophone regions and some major cities, the National Union for Democracy and Progress, the Cameroon Democratic Union, and the Union of the Peoples of Cameroon.

Membership in the ruling political party conferred significant advantages, including in the allocation of key jobs in parastatals and the civil service. The president appoints all ministers, including the prime minister, and also directly appoints the governors of each of the 10 regions who also serve as CPDM officials. The president has the power to appoint important lower level members of the 58 regional administrative structures as well. Onerous requirements for registration of parties and candidates restricted political activity.

In 2008 the National Assembly passed a constitutional amendment that removed presidential term limits and added provisions for presidential immunity. Although considerable national discussion of the proposal ensued, the National Assembly ultimately passed the revisions in a manner that allowed no debate and underscored the CPDM's unfettered control of all government branches. Neither the electorate nor its elected representatives had an opportunity to affect the outcome of the constitutional exercise.

Authorities sometimes refused to grant opposition parties permission to hold rallies and meetings and arrested SCNC activists for participating in SCNC activities. The government considered the SCNC illegal because it advocates secession and has never registered as a political party or organization.

Participation of Women and Minorities: Women held 23 of 180 seats in the National Assembly, six of 61 cabinet posts, and a few of the higher offices within the major political parties, including the CPDM. Pygmies were not represented in the National Assembly or in the higher offices of government.

Principal Government Officials

Last Updated: 1/31/2013

Pres.: **Paul BIYA**
Prime Min.: **Philemon YANG**
Dep. Prime Min.: **Amadou ALI**
Dep. Prime Min.: **Jean NKUETE**
Sec. Gen. of the Presidency: **Laurent ESSO**
Min.-Delegate at the Presidency in Charge of Defense: **Alain Mebe NGO'O**
Min. in Charge of Special Duties at the Presidency: **Paul ATANGA NJI**
Min. in Charge of Special Duties at the Presidency: **Victor MENGOT**
Min. in Charge of Special Duties at the Presidency: **Hamadou MUSTAPHA**
Min. in Charge of Special Duties at the Presidency: **Rene Emmanuel SADI**
Min. of Agriculture & Rural Development: **Jean NKUTE**
Min. of Basic Education: **Alim YOUDDOUF**
Min. of Commerce: **Luc Magloire MBARGA ATANGANA**
Min. of Communication: **Issa Tchiroma BAKARY**
Min. of Culture: **Ama Tutu MUNA**
Min. of Economy, Planning, & Regional Development: **Louis Paul MOTAZE**
Min. of Employment & Professional & Technical Training:**Zacharie PEREVET**
Min. of Energy & Water Resources: **Michael Ngako TOMDIO**
Min. of Environment & Nature Protection: **Pierre HELE**
Min. of External Relations: **Pierre Moukoko MBONJO**
Min. of Finance: **Lazare Essimi MENYE**
Min. of Forestry & Wildlife: **Elvis NGOLLE NGOLLE**
Min. of Higher Education: **Jacques Fame NDONGO**
Min. of Industry, Mines, & Technological Development:**Badel Ndanga NDINGA**
Min. of Justice: **Amadou ALI**
Min. of Labor & Social Security: **Robert NKILI**
Min. of Lands & Titles: **Jean-Baptiste BELEOKEN**
Min. of Livestock & Fisheries: **Aboubakary SARKI**

Min. of Post & Telecommunications: **Jean-Pierre Biyiti Bi ESSAM**
Min. of Public Health: **Andre Mama FOUDA**
Min. of Public Service & Admin. Reform: **Emmanuel BONDE**
Min. of Public Works: **Bernard Messengue AVOM**
Min. of Scientific Research & Innovation: **Madeleine TCHUENTE**
Min. of Secondary Education: **Louis BAPES BAPES**
Min. of Social Affairs: **Catherine Bakang MBOCK**
Min. of Sports & Physical Education: **Michel ZOA**
Min. of Territorial Admin. & Decentralization: **Hamidou Yaya MARAFA**
Min. of Tourism: **Baba HAMADOU**
Min. of Transport: **Bello Bouba MAIGARI**
Min. of Urban Development & Housing: **Colbert TCHATAT**
Min. of Women & Family Protection: **Marie Theresa Abena ONDOA**
Min. of Youth: **Adoum GAROUA**
Governor, Central Bank: **Philibert ANDZEMBE**
Ambassador to the US: **Joseph FOE-ATANGANA**
Permanent Representative to the UN, New York: **Michel Tommo MONTHE**

ECONOMY

Because of its modest oil resources and favorable agricultural conditions, Cameroon has one of the best-endowed primary commodity economies in sub-Saharan Africa. Still, it faces many of the serious problems confronting other underdeveloped countries, such as stagnant per capita income, a relatively inequitable distribution of income, a top-heavy civil service, endemic corruption, and a generally unfavorable climate for business enterprise.

Since 1990, the government has embarked on various IMF and World Bank programs designed to spur business investment, increase efficiency in agriculture, improve trade, and recapitalize the nation's banks.

The IMF is pressing for more reforms, including increased budget transparency, privatization, and poverty reduction programs. Subsidies for electricity, food, and fuel have strained the budget. New mining projects—in diamonds, for example—have attracted foreign investment, but large ventures will take time to develop. Cameroon's business environment—one of the world's worst—is a deterrent to foreign investment.

Labor Conditions

The law generally protects children from exploitation in the workplace and specifies penalties ranging from fines to imprisonment for infringement. The law sets a minimum age of 14 for child employment, prohibits children from working at night or longer than eight hours a day, and enumerates tasks that children under the age of 18 cannot legally perform, including moving heavy objects, dangerous and unhealthy tasks, working in confined areas, and prostitution. Employers were required to train children between the ages of 14 and 18, and work contracts must contain a training provision for minors. These provisions of the law were not adequately enforced.

The use of child labor, particularly in informal sectors, remained rampant. According to ILO's 2008 survey, 51 percent of children between the ages of 10 and14 years were engaged in work; 41 percent of children between five and 17 years old also worked.

According to 2008 government statistics on child labor, 85.2 percent of working children were employed in the agriculture sector, either on family subsistence plots or on cocoa, tea, banana, and palm oil plantations, and fisheries. In the urban informal sector, children worked as street vendors, car washers, and domestic workers. Some children also worked in mines and quarries. Many urban street vendors were less than 14 years of age. Children worked as household help, and some children were involved in prostitution. In the North there were credible reports that children from needy homes were placed with other families to do household work for pay, which normally went to the child's family. Parents viewed child labor as both a tradition and a rite of passage. Relatives often employed rural youth, especially girls, as domestic helpers, and these jobs seldom allowed time for the children to attend school. In rural areas, many children began work at an early age on family farms. The cocoa industry also employed child laborers. These children originated, for the most part, from the three northern and the Northwest regions.

The minimum wage in all sectors was 28,246 CFA francs ($56) per month. MINLESI was responsible for enforcing the minimum wage nationally.

The law establishes a standard workweek of 40 hours in public and private nonagricultural firms and 48 hours in agricultural and related activities. There are exceptions for guards and firemen (56 hours a week), service sector staff (45 hours), and household and restaurant staff (54 hours). The law mandates at least 24 consecutive hours of weekly rest. Premium pay for overtime ranges from 120 to 150 percent of the hourly pay depending on amount and whether it is for weekend or late-night overtime. There is a prohibition on excessive compulsory service. MINLESI inspectors were responsible for monitoring these standards.

Despite the minimum wage law, employers often negotiated with workers for lower salaries, in part due to the high rate of unemployment in the country. Salaries lower than the minimum wage were prevalent in the public works sector, where many positions required unskilled labor.

U.S.-CAMEROONIAN RELATIONS

The United States established diplomatic relations with Cameroon in 1960, following its independence from a French-administered trusteeship. Cameroon has had two presidents since independence. U.S. relations with Cameroon are positive, although from time to time they have been affected by concerns over human rights abuses and the pace of political and economic liberalization. The two countries are partners in addressing issues of democracy, good governance, and economic development. The United States hopes to continue to work with Cameroon to consolidate democratic gains and economic growth, particularly as Cameroon embarks upon municipal and legislative elections planned for 2013. The United States supports Cameroon's efforts to strengthen electoral institutions, enhance transparency, and allow for contestation of results.

U.S. Assistance to Cameroon

The U.S. Agency for International Development (USAID) runs a number of programs in Cameroon, mainly through its regional office in Ghana, and primarily in the health sector. The Centers for Disease Control (CDC) also has activities in Cameroon, mainly in HIV/AIDS prevention. Peace Corps volunteers work in five program sectors: agroforestry, community health, education and information technology, small business development, and youth development (focused primarily on girls and young women). The Public Affairs section of the U.S. Embassy in Cameroon organizes and funds diverse cultural, educational, and informational exchanges.

It maintains a library and helps foster the development of Cameroon's independent press by providing information in a number of areas, including U.S. human rights and democratization policies. The Embassy administers both the Ambassador's Special Self-Help and Democracy and Human Rights Fund programs and the Ambassador's Fund for Cultural Preservation. Through several State Department and USAID regional funds, the Embassy also provides funds for biodiversity protection, refugees, HIV/AIDS, democratization, and girl's scholarships.

Bilateral Economic Relations

Cameroon is eligible for preferential trade benefits under the African Growth and Opportunity Act. Cameroon's exports to the United States include mineral fuel and oil, cocoa, rubber, wood, and coffee while imports from the United States include machinery, articles for donation, aircraft, vehicles, and plastics.

The United States is a leading investor in Cameroon, largely through the Chad-Cameroon petroleum pipeline project and energy provider AES Sonel. The United States and Cameroon have a bilateral investment treaty.

Cameroon's Membership in International Organizations

Cameroon supports the principle of noninterference in the affairs of third countries and increased assistance to underdeveloped countries. Cameroon and the United States belong to a number of the same international organizations, including the United Nations, International Monetary Fund, World Bank, and World Trade Organization.

Bilateral Representation

Cameroon maintains an embassy in the United States at 1700 Wisconsin Avenue NW, Washington, DC 20007 (tel.: 202-265-8790).

Principal U.S. Embassy Officials

Last Updated: 1/14/2013

YAOUNDE (E) 6.050 Avenue Rosa Parks , BP 817, (237) 2220-1500, Fax (237) 2220-1500 Ext. 4531, Workweek: Monday–Thursday: 0730–1700; Friday: 0730–1230, Website: http://yaounde.usembassy.gov/

DCM OMS:	Patricia McCarty
AMB OMS:	Nelda Villines
CDC:	Dr. Omotayo Bolu
FM:	Gid Bullock
HRO:	Amanda Arriga
MGT:	Chanh Nguyen
POL/ECON:	Cleverley, Mikael
AMB:	Robert P. Jackson
CON:	Phillips Doni
DCM:	Gregory D. Thome
PAO:	Matthew McKeever
GSO:	Femi Akinyemi
RSO:	Jeffrey Rusinek
CLO:	Dawn McKeever
EEO:	Dianne Brisson
FMO:	Gia Parker
ICASS Chair:	Vacant
IMO:	William Johnson
ISO:	Elton Sankoh
ISSO:	Elton Sankoh
State ICASS:	Matt McKeever

DOUALA (BO), (237) 3342-5331, Workweek: Monday-Thursday 0730-1700/Friday 0730-1230, Website: http://yaounde.usembassy.gov/

AMB OMS:	See Yaounde
DIR:	Michael Margolies
FM:	See Yaounde
HRO:	See Yaounde
POL/ECON:	See Yaounde
SDO/DATT:	See Yaounde
AMB:	See Yaounde
CG:	See Yaounde
CON:	See Yaounde
DCM:	See Yaounde
PAO:	See Yaounde
GSO:	See Yaounde
RSO:	See Yaounde
FMO:	See Yaounde

TRAVEL

Consular Information Sheet

April 18, 2012

Country Description: Cameroon is a developing country in central Africa that offers many natural and cultural attractions, but lacks modern tourism facilities. The busy port and commercial center of Douala, its largest city, contrasts with the relative calm of inland Yaounde, the capital. Cameroon is officially bilingual. French dominates as the language of education and government in all regions except the Southwest and Northwest, where English is widely spoken. Most educated people and staff at major hotels speak both languages.

In February 2008, social and political discord led to civil unrest; however, since that time the country has experienced relative stability and peace. Crime continues to be a significant concern throughout Cameroon.

Smart Traveler Enrollment Program (STEP)/Embassy Locations: If you are going to live in or travel to Cameroon, please take the time to tell Embassy Yaounde about your trip by enrolling in the Smart Traveler Enrollment Program (STEP). If you enroll, we can keep you up to date with important safety and security announcements. It will also help your friends and family get in touch with you in an emergency. You should remember to keep all of your information in STEP up to date. It is important during enrollment or updating of information to include your current phone number and current email address where you can be reached in case of an emergency.

U.S. Embassy Yaounde
Avenue Rosa Parks in the Mbankolo Quartier, adjacent to the Mount Febe Golf Club
Mailing address: P.O. Box 817, Yaounde, Cameroon
Telephone: +237 2220–1500
Emergency after-hours telephone: +237 2220–1500
Facsimile: +237 2220–157

Embassy Branch Office, Douala, Cameroon
Corner of Rue Ivy and Rue French in the Ecobank Building in Bonanjo
Telephone: +237 3342–5331
Facsimile: +237 3342–7790.

Entry/Exit Requirements: A valid passport, visa, evidence of yellow-fever vaccination, and current immunization records are required for entry into Cameroon. You may be denied entry if you lack the proper documentation before entering the country. Obtaining a visa at the airport is not an option. You must obtain your visa before traveling to Cameroon.

Cameroon does not recognize dual nationality and considers U.S. citizens of Cameroonian descent to have lost their Cameroonian citizenship. Naturalized U.S. citizens of Cameroonian descent should enter Cameroon using their U.S. passports, and should be sensitive to possible hostility on the part of Cameroonian officials regarding their changed citizenship.

Visit the website of the Embassy of Cameroon for the most current visa information. You should obtain the latest information on entry requirements from this website or directly from the Embassy of the Republic of Cameroon, 1700 Wisconsin Ave. NW, Washington, D.C. 20007, tel.: (202) 265-8790, fax: (202) 387-3826.

The U.S. Department of State is unaware of any HIV/AIDS entry restrictions for visitors to or foreign residents of Cameroon.

Safety and Security: Cameroon experienced significant civil unrest in half of its ten regions in February 2008. Although a rapid resumption of violence is considered unlikely, if you are living in or visiting Cameroon, you are encouraged to stay abreast of local political and social developments that could signal additional instability for the country. Legislative and municipal elections are expected in 2013, although a date has not yet been set. You should remain alert as these elections approach.

Embassy employees have been instructed to refrain from travel outside of city limits after dark, and to be cautious in their movements in centrally located areas within cities and towns. You should follow the same guidelines and not travel by night on Cameroon's dangerous highways. Armed highway bandits (most notably in border areas); poorly lit and maintained roads; hazardous, poorly maintained vehicles; and unskilled, aggressive, and intoxicated drivers all pose threats to motorists. Attacks and accidents are most common outside major towns, especially in the regions bordering Chad and the Central African Republic, but occur in all areas of the country.

The U.S. Department of State continues to warn U.S. citizens against travel to neighboring Central African Republic (CAR). On occasion, conflict between insurgents and government security forces in CAR has spilled across the border into Cameroon, affecting outposts in the Adamaoua and East regions. Humanitarian and religious workers in eastern Cameroon are strongly encouraged to coordinate their efforts with the Embassy and the Office of the United Nations High Commission for Refugees (UNHCR) in Yaoundé.

In February 2008, an attack by rebel insurgents on Ndjamena, the capital of Chad, forced the evacuation of the U.S. Embassy in Chad and sent up to 50,000 refugees across the border into the town of Kousseri in Cameroon. If you are in Cameroon and considering crossing into Chad, you should review the U.S. Department of State's Travel Warning for Chad and Travel Warning for the Central African Republic.

Cameroon assumed control of the Bakassi peninsula in August 2008. Over the last few years, there have been attacks on Cameroonian military forces and clashes between armed groups and Cameroonian security forces in the Bakassi area. Cameroon military authorities restrict access to the Bakassi Peninsula. U.S. official travelers must receive prior approval through the U.S. Defense Attaché Office at the U.S. Embassy in Yaoundé. U.S. employees are not permitted to make personal travel to the region.

Piracy in coastal areas remains a problem. While mostly occurring at sea, criminal groups have also conducted armed raids against lucrative coastal targets including banks. Heightened security measures begun in 2009 have reduced the number of attacks. If you are visiting any coastal areas in Cameroon, you should be alert to the threat of piracy and move inland if you detect a potential threat.

Stay up to date by:

- Bookmarking our Bureau of Consular Affairs website, which contains the current Travel Warnings and Travel Alerts as well as the Worldwide Caution.

- Following us on Twitter and the Bureau of Consular Affairs page on Facebook as well.
- Downloading our free Smart Traveler iPhone App to have travel information at your fingertips.
- Calling 1-888-407-4747 toll-free within the United States and Canada, or a regular toll line, 1-202-501-4444, from other countries.
- Taking some time before travel to consider your personal security.

Crime: Crime is a serious problem throughout Cameroon that increased in some areas of the country in 2011. U.S. citizens should exercise caution when traveling in Cameroon. Internet-based crime based in Cameroon is escalating rapidly, and everyone, including businesses and other institutions, should be extremely skeptical of any financial transactions that involve sending money for goods, services, or adoptions. Crimes against property, such as carjacking and burglaries, have often been accompanied by violent acts and resulted in fatalities. All foreigners are potential targets for theft with possible attendant violence. Armed banditry has been a problem throughout all ten regions in Cameroon. In January 2011, more than 20 Peace Corps volunteers were robbed at gunpoint in Kribi. In December 2010, a U.S citizen who was residing in Douala was murdered, and in Yaounde, a U.S. citizen and a British citizen were sexually assaulted in separate incidents in March 2011.

In the past, armed bandits have erected road barricades to steal vehicles. While there have been no major incidents of banditry involving westerners since 2010, travelers may encounter random security checkpoints intended to curb the practice. Cameroonian law requires that you must carry identification at all times, and security personnel may request that travelers show their passport, residence card, driver's license, and/or vehicle registration at these roadblocks. You should keep certified copies of these important documents in a secure location separate from the originals. Security personnel have been known to ask for bribes, but in many instances allow expatriate travelers who refuse to pay, to continue with their travels after a short delay. The U.S. government does not condone bribery or corruption of any kind.

There have been many crimes involving public transportation. Taxis can be dangerous and U.S. Embassy personnel are not permitted to use taxi cabs in Cameroon. Taxis in Cameroon function more like a U.S. bus system, with drivers stopping along the road to pick up additional passengers as long as there is space left in the vehicle. Taxi drivers and accomplices posing as passengers often conspire to commit serious crimes including rape, robbery, and assault. If you must use a taxi, consider hiring a driver you know and his/her private taxi for your exclusive use for that particular trip. Taxi passengers should be particularly vigilant at night.

The risk of street and residential crime is high. Incidents often involve gangs and relate to home invasion and kidnapping. Periodic efforts by authorities in Yaoundé to clear streets and public spaces of illegally constructed homes and market stalls can become confrontational, and may contribute to surges in criminality as these very modest homes and businesses are destroyed.

Many crimes involve an "inside man" and target individuals or locations involved with payrolls or other activities involving large sums of cash. Carjackings and robberies have also been reported on rural highways, especially in the northern region near Cameroon's border with the Central African Republic and Chad.

The Embassy has identified a wide range of internet scams based in Cameroon. These schemes cover a broad spectrum of bogus activities, including adoptions, insurance claims, dating, real estate, the provision of domestic services (such as nannies and household help), agricultural products, antiques, and exotic and domesticated animals. Often, these are advance-fee scams where "the victim pays money to someone in anticipation of receiving something of greater value, such as a loan, contract, investment, or gift, and then receives little or nothing in return." U.S. citizens should never send money or travel to Cameroon to meet someone contacted via the Internet without first checking with the Embassy's Commercial Section. Commercial scams targeting foreigners, many including U.S. citizens, continue to be a problem. The scams generally involve phony offers of lucrative sales and repeated requests for additional funds to pay for unforeseen airport and/or customs fees. Do not share your personal financial or account information.

Additionally, the U.S. Embassy is aware of complaints by U.S. citizens shipping vehicles or other merchandise to Cameroon who are unable to complete the transaction as they had expected, and who have ended up being detained based on these commercial disputes. The ability of U.S. Embassy officers to extricate U.S. citizens from the legal consequences of unlawful business deals is limited. U.S. citizens are urged to complete financial transactions in writing with trusted partners only, and to avoid informal agreements.

For more information on international financial scams, including those involving internet dating, a promise of an inheritance windfall, a promise of a work contract overseas, overpayment for goods purchased online, or money-laundering, see the Department of State's publication International Financial Scams. If you have concerns about the legitimacy of a transaction in Cameroon, contact the U.S. Embassy in Cameroon. The Embassy's commercial section regularly assists U.S. citizens seeking to determine the legitimacy of commercial transactions.

In many countries around the world, counterfeit and pirated goods are widely available. Transactions involving such products may be illegal under local law. In addition, bringing them back to the United States may result in forfeitures and/or fines.

Victims of Crime: If you or someone you know becomes the victim of a crime abroad, you should contact the local police and the nearest U.S. embassy or consulate. We can:

- Replace a stolen passport.
- Help you find appropriate medical care if you are the victim of violent crimes such as assault or rape.
- Put you in contact with the appropriate police authorities, and if you want us to, we can contact family members or friend.
- Help you understand the local criminal justice process and direct you to local attorneys, although it is important to remember that local authorities are responsible for investigating and prosecuting the crime.

Cameroon has no local equivalent to the "911" emergency line; dial 112 in major cities to contact ambulance services.

Criminal Penalties: While you are in a foreign country, you are subject to that country's laws and regulations, even if you are a U.S. citizen. Foreign laws and legal systems can be vastly different than our own. Cameroonian law does not afford many of the protections to which you may be accustomed in the United States. Legal proceedings tend to be complex, lengthy, and subject to inappropriate influence. If you violate the law in Cameroon, even unknowingly, you may be expelled, arrested, or imprisoned. Penalties for breaking the law can be more severe than in the United States for similar offenses, and the condition of detention centers, while improving, is poor. During the February 2008 civil unrest, there were reports of arbitrary arrests by law enforcement officials. Although no expatriates were known to have been arrested, the Department of State cautions you against venturing out during such periods of unrest. Penalties for possession, use, or trafficking in illegal drugs in Cameroon are severe, and convicted offenders can expect long jail sentences and heavy fines. There are also some things that might be legal in Cameroon, but still illegal in the United States. You can be prosecuted under U.S. law if you buy pirated goods. Engaging in sexual conduct with children or using or disseminating child pornography in a foreign country is a crime prosecutable in the United States. If you break local laws in your host country, your U.S. passport won't help you avoid arrest or prosecution. It's very important to know what's legal and what's not where you are going.

Based on the Vienna Convention on Consular Relations, bilateral agreements with certain countries, and customary international law, if you are arrested in Cameroon, you have the option to request that the police, prison officials, or other authorities alert nearest U.S. Embassy or the Embassy Branch Office in Douala of your arrest, and to have communications from you forwarded to the Embassy or Branch Office. In Cameroon, the U.S. Embassy contact number is 22 20 15 00, and is staffed 24 hours a day, 7 days a week.

U.S. citizens of Cameroonian descent: Cameroon does not recognize dual nationality and considers U.S. citizens of Cameroonian descent to have lost their Cameroonian citizenship. Naturalized U.S. citizens should enter Cameroon using their U.S. passports, and should be alert to possible hostility on the part of Cameroonian officials regarding their changed citizenship. Cameroonian law enforcement, customs, and other officials wield significant authority, and disputes with Cameroonian authorities can result in detention, confiscation of documents, and considerable expense and delays to the traveler. You should show the same deference and respect to Cameroonian officials as you would give to similarly ranked individuals in the United States.

Currency: Cash in local currency, the Central African franc (FCFA), is the most common (and almost only) form of payment accepted throughout the country. A few large hotels in Yaoundé and Douala will change U.S. dollars at a poor exchange rate. Larger banks in Yaoundé, Douala, and other cities often have ATMs. Credit card cash advances are not available, and most banks do not cash personal checks for non-clients. U.S-dollar-denominated traveler's checks are not accepted in Cameroon, and while credit cards are accepted at some larger hotels and shops in Yaoundé and Douala, you should be cautious, as identity theft is endemic in the region. Western Union and other money transfer services have extensive networks in many parts of Cameroon. The U.S. Embassy does not provide currency exchange, check cashing, or other financial services. In recent years, business travelers have experienced difficulty in obtaining adequate services from Cameroon's banking sector. Business travelers find it useful to employ the services of a local agent in the Cameroon market. Counterfeit currency appears to be a growing problem.

Customs: Cameroonian customs authorities may enforce strict import and export regulations, particularly with regard to pharmaceuticals and wood products. Customs regulations restrict trade in ivory and items protected under the Convention on International Trade in Endangered Species. Some wood products available in Cameroon may be made from endangered tropical hardwood. Trading in such banned woods is a federal offense, punishable by civil and criminal penalties in the United States.

Game Parks: While visiting game parks and reserves, tourists should bear in mind that they are ultimately responsible for maintaining their own safety. Tourists should use common sense when approaching wildlife, maintain a safe distance from animals, and heed all instructions given by guides or trackers. Even in the most serene settings, the animals in Cameroon's game parks are wild and can pose a lethal threat.

Most game parks require that a professional guide accompany visitors.

You should not pressure or pay those persons to be more flexible in their duties.

Same Gender Sexual Relations: Same gender sexual relations are illegal in Cameroon, and the Government of Cameroon has prosecuted and convicted people under these laws, as recently as 2012. Allegations concerning a person's sexual orientation may be raised in business and personal disputes, sometimes resulting in criminal charges.

Corruption: The Government of the Republic of Cameroon has sporadically enforced laws against corruption. Charges of corruption are also made and enforced indiscriminately in the course of business or personal disputes.

Photography: While photography is not officially forbidden, security officials are sensitive about photographs taken of government buildings, military installations, and other public facilities, many of which are unmarked. Photography of these subjects may result in seizure of photographic equipment by Cameroonian authorities. Due to the threat of harassment and the lack of signs designating sites prohibited for photography, and the fact that some Cameroonians object to having their picture taken, you should ask permission before taking photographs.

Medical Facilities and Health Information: Medical facilities in Cameroon are extremely limited. Even in large cities, emergency care and hospitalization for major illnesses and surgery are hampered by the lack of trained specialists, outdated diagnostic equipment, and poor sanitation. Medical services in outlying areas may be completely nonexistent. Doctors and hospitals often require immediate payment for health services in cash, and require family members or friends to locate and purchase any medical supplies they will need. Pharmacies in larger towns are well stocked, but in other areas many medicines are unavailable. You should carry your own properly-labeled supply of prescription and over-the-counter medicines.

The Centers for Disease Control has a comprehensive review of infectious disease issues and overall health recommendations for traveling to Cameroon.

Malaria is a serious and sometimes fatal disease. If you will be visiting Cameroon, you will need to discuss with your doctor the best ways for you to avoid getting sick with malaria. Ways to prevent malaria include the following:

- Taking a prescription antimalarial drug,
- Using insect repellent and wearing long pants and sleeves to prevent mosquito bites, and
- Sleeping in air-conditioned or well-screened rooms and/or using bednets.

All of the following antimalarial drugs are equal options for preventing malaria in Cameroon: Atovaquone-proguanil, doxycycline, or mefloquine. For information that can help you and your doctor decide which of these drugs would be best for you, please see Choosing a Drug to Prevent Malaria. Chloroquine is NOT an effective antimalarial drug in Cameroon and should not be taken to prevent malaria in this region.

If you become ill with a fever or flu-like illness while traveling in Cameroon, or up to one year after returning home, you should seek prompt medical attention and tell the physician your travel history and what antimalarials you have been taking.

Schistosomiasis is endemic in Cameroon. Avoid wading, swimming, bathing, or washing in, or drinking from bodies of fresh water such as canals, lakes, rivers, streams, or springs.

There are periodic outbreaks of cholera in Cameroon. People in high-risk areas can protect themselves by following a few simple rules of good hygiene and safe food preparation. These include scrupulous washing of hands under running water, especially before food preparation and eating, thorough cooking of food and consumption while hot, boiling or treatment of drinking water, and use of sanitary facilities. Above all, be very careful with food and water, including ice.

Yellow fever can cause serious medical problems and the vaccine, required for entry into Cameroon, is very effective. Measles and meningitis are also present in northern Cameroon. You should be sure your vaccinations are current. Polio remains a threat in northern Nigeria and Chad, which share porous borders with Cameroon.

Tuberculosis is an increasingly serious health concern in Cameroon.

You can find more information on vaccinations and other health precautions on the CDC website. For information about outbreaks of infectious diseases abroad, consult the World Health Organization (WHO) website. The WHO website also contains additional health information for travelers, including detailed country-specific health information.

Medical Insurance: You can't assume your insurance will go with you when you travel. It's very important to find out BEFORE you leave whether or not your medical insurance will cover you overseas. You need to ask your insurance company two questions:

- Does my policy apply when I'm out of the United States?
- Will it cover emergencies like a trip to a foreign hospital or a medical evacuation?

In many places, doctors and hospitals still expect payment in cash at the time of service. Your regular U.S. health insurance may not cover doctors' and hospital visits in other countries. If your policy doesn't cover you when you travel, it is a good idea to take out another policy for your trip.

Traffic Safety and Road Conditions: While in a foreign country, U.S. citizens may encounter road conditions that differ significantly from those in the United States. Cameroon's road networks, both paved and unpaved, are poorly maintained and unsafe at all times of the year. Drivers frequently ignore road safety rules. There are few road and traffic signs, and speed limits are neither posted nor enforced. Vehicles are poorly maintained and there is no mechanism or requirement to inspect them for roadworthiness. Livestock and pedestrians create constant road hazards (especially at night). Buses and logging trucks travel at excessive speed and are a constant threat to other road traffic. During the rainy season, many roads are barely passable even with four-wheel-drive vehicles. Travelers on roads near the borders with the Central African Republic and Chad should ensure that they have adequate vehicle fuel, cooking fuel, food, and or radio. There are no national or local ordinances governing the use of mobile telephones, text messaging, and other electronic communications while operating a motor vehicle.

Visitors who do not have a valid passport and a visa may experience difficulties at police roadblocks or other security checkpoints. It is not uncommon for a uniformed member of the security forces to stop motorists on the pretext of a minor or non-existent violation of local motor vehicle regulations in order to extort small bribes. The Embassy advises you not to pay bribes, and to request that police officers provide a citation to be paid at the local court.

Local law states that vehicles involved in an accident should not be moved until the police arrive and a police report can be made. However, if an accident results in injury, be aware that a "village justice" mentality may develop. If an angry crowd forms, drive directly to the U.S. Embassy or another location where you can receive assistance. Contact the local police once you are safely away from danger. Cameroon has no roadside emergency telephone numbers, but you can dial 112 in major cities to contact ambulance services. U.S. citizens should contact the U.S. Embassy +237 2220–1500 if emergency assistance is needed.

Aviation Safety Oversight: As there is no direct commercial air service to the United States by carriers registered in Cameroon, the U.S. Federal Aviation Administration (FAA) has not assessed Cameroon's Civil Aviation Authority for compliance with International Civil Aviation Organization (ICAO) aviation safety standards. Further information may be found on the FAA's safety assessment page.

Limited domestic air service is available from the recently re-started Cameroonian national airline and from small operators that are not firmly established. Service is routinely suspended or cancelled.

Children's Issues: Please see the U.S. Dept. of State Office of Children's Issues web pages on intercountry adoption and international parental child abduction.

Intercountry Adoption

February 2009

The information in this section has been edited from the latest report available as of February 2013 from the State Department Bureau of Consular Affairs, Office of Overseas Citizens Services. For more information, please read the *Intercountry Adoption* section of this book and review current reports online at http://adoption.state.gov. Cameroon is not party to the Hague Convention on Protection of Children and Co-operation in Respect of Intercountry Adoption (Hague Adoption Convention). Therefore, when the Hague Adoption Convention entered into force for the United States on April 1, 2008, intercountry adoption processing for Cameroon did not change.

Fraud Warning: Recently many Americans have become victims of Cameroonian scam artists offering adoption services through the Internet. Americans should be very cautious about sending money or traveling to Cameroon to adopt a child from an orphanage they have only heard about through e-mails. Prospective adoptive parents MUST travel to Cameroon and participate in person in the legal procedures that govern Cameroonian adoptions. In order to protect themselves and the children from the possibility of fraud or other serious problems, prospective adoptive parents are advised to consider first the list of accredited orphanages available at the Ministry of Social Affairs. Should prospective adoptive parents wish to hire a Cameroonian attorney to assist with the adoption, they can obtain a list of attorneys from the U.S. Embassy in Yaounde.

Who Can Adopt? To bring an adopted child to United States from Cameroon, you must be found eligible to adopt by the U.S. government. The U.S. government agency responsible for making this determination is the Department of Homeland Security, U.S. Citizenship and Immigration Services (USCIS).

Residency Requirements: The prospective adoptive parents must have the child in their care and custody for at least three consecutive months before the High Court will consider issuing an adoption decree.

Age Requirements: At least one adoptive parent in the couple must be older than 40 years of age. If neither parent meets the age requirement, at least one must be at least 35 years old and they must have been married for a minimum of 10 years. If neither of these requirements can be met, the couple can submit a medical certificate confirming their infertility in order to have the age requirement waived. The couple should bring a medical certificate from a U.S. or local doctor.

Marriage Requirements: Adoptive parents must be married. Single people can adopt–with certain restrictions on age. As homosexuality is illegal in Cameroon, gay or lesbian marriages are not recognized.

Income Requirements: The couple must provide evidence of financial capacity to support the adopted child. This evidence can be proven with a report of a home study from the U.S. along with bank statements, evidence of assets, pay slips, etc.

Other Requirements:

- Both parties in a couple must be in agreement over the adoption. One spouse may not adopt without the other's consent.
- PAPs must submit a medical certificate from either a U.S. or local doctor showing that they are medically fit.
- Evidence of consent of the birth parent(s) (if they are alive). The consent must be witnessed either in court, by a diplomatic consulate or by a public notary.
- Evidence of the consent of the adoptee if s/he is 16 or older. The consent must be witnessed either in court, by a diplomatic consulate or by a public notary.
- Prospective adoptive parents must come to Cameroon for an extended period of time and participate (in person) in the elaborate legal procedures.

Who Can Be Adopted? Cameroon has specific requirements that a child must meet in order to be eligible for adoption. You cannot adopt a child in Cameroon unless he or she meets the requirements outlined below. In addition to these requirements, a child must meet the definition of an orphan under U.S. law for you to bring him or her immediately to the United States.

Eligibility Requirements: Adopted individuals cannot have children of their own at the time of the adoption, nor have any legal descendants. Adopted individuals may not marry their adoptive parents or siblings.

Cameroon's Adoption Authority: Ministry of Social Affairs and the High Court (Tribunal de Grande Instance) having jurisdiction over the place of residence of the child to be adopted.

The Process: The first step in adopting a child is usually to select a licensed agency in the United States that can help with your adoption. Adoption service providers must be licensed by the U.S. state in which they operate. Cameroon does not have adoption agencies. In general, any orphanage may release an orphan for adoption. However, in order to help protect themselves and the children from the possibility of fraud or other serious problems, prospective adoptive parents are advised to consider the list of accredited orphanages available at the Ministry of Social Affairs.

Parents wishing to hire a Cameroonian attorney to assist with the adoption can obtain a list of attorneys from the U.S. Embassy in Yaounde. Due to repeated scams involving the impersonation of legitimate lawyers or law offices, the Embassy has removed this information from its website.

This information can be obtained by e-mailing the American Citizen Services Unit at YaoundeACS@state.gov. If you are eligible to adopt, and a child is available for intercountry adoption, the central adoption authority in Cameroon will provide you with a referral to a child.

A social worker will be assigned to follow up the case and assist the prospective adoptive parents with identifying a child for adoption and monitoring the family during the foster care period. The local lawyer, if hired by the prospective adoptive parents, must also be involved in the process. The social worker's final report determines whether prospective adoptive parents can proceed with the case to the High Court.

The adoptive parents may choose either to be present or to be represented by a lawyer during the hearing at the High Court. Under Cameroonian law, the High Court must determine that the following four criteria have been met before it can issue an adoption decree.

- That every person whose consent is necessary has consented to and understands the nature and effect of the adoption. Such consent is irrevocable and permanently servers all legal ties between the biological parents and the child.
- That the child's welfare will be improved by the adoption. Parents must provide proof of what they can provide for the child in a way that other cannot.
- That no payment or reward has been the reason for the adoption.
- That the prospective adoptive parent is healthy.

Role of the Court: The High Court will consent to the adoption and issue a final adoption decree.

Time Frame: Prospective adoptive parents should expect that a minimum of three months will pass between the date they submit their adoption application to the Ministry of Social Affairs and the date the High Court's Public Prosecutor completes his/her review of the file. Only when the review is completed will a hearing date be scheduled.

In addition, a Cameroonian adoption is likely to be affected by administrative and judicial delays, insufficient or misplace paperwork, and other factors. Most parents have found that hiring a local attorney to monitor the case and keep pressure on the High Court has been crucial in expediting its processing. Once all of the Cameroonian procedures have been completed and an adoption decree has been issued, the U.S. Embassy requires a minimum of two weeks to complete the immigrant visa process and may need longer depending on the specific circumstances. This includes the mandatory I-604 orphan investigation to verify a child qualifies as an orphan.

Adoption Fees: There are moderate court fees involved in the adoption, but legal fees for correct and complete adoptions typically run to several thousand USD.

Documents Required: The following documents are required for adoption in Cameroon:

- Application bearing a 1000 FCFA (approximately $2 USD) fiscal stamp, addressed to the President of the High Court

- Certified copy of the child's Cameroonian birth certificate
- Biographical information of the biological parents of the child to be adopted
- Biographical information of the adoptive parents
- If applicable, a notarized deed of agreement from surviving biological parents, or the orphanage director having custody over the child and prospective adoptive parents; This deed expressly states that the child is released irrevocable for adoption
- Report of the home study (U.S. Home Study is acceptable)
- Evidence of finances and income
- Legal authorization from the biological parents, if applicable
- Notarized affidavit of support of the child from the adoptive parents
- Deposit of 3,000 CFA Francs (approximately $6 USD) made at the court registry
- A separate, non-refundable deposit of 78,000 CFA Francs (approximately $160 USD) made at the court registry
- Written application
- Certified copy of the child's birth certificate
- Certified copy of the adoptive parents' identification
- Prison/court record clearance
- Adoptive parents' proof of residency; For married parents who do not meet the age requirements, they must bring a medical certificate attesting their infertility
- Medical certificate for the adoptive parents, attesting that they are medically fit
- Report of the social home study

Bringing Your Child Home: Once your adoption is complete (or you have obtained legal custody of the child), there are a few more steps to take before you can head home. Specifically, you need to apply for several documents for your child before he or she can travel to the United States, such as a birth certificate, a passport or travel document for your child from the country in which he or she was born, and a U.S. Immigration Visa.

For detailed and updated information on how to obtain these documents, review the *Intercountry Adoption* section on this publication and visit the USCIS Intercountry Adoption website at http://adoption. state.gov. Regarding the adoption procedure in Cameroon, please note that the U.S. Consulate will only accept final FULL/FULL adoption court judgment issued by the competent High Court having jurisdiction over the place of residence of the adoptee.

Under no circumstance should a simple adoption be submitted during the processing of the immigrant visa. Therefore, the adoptive parent(s) should note the distinction between a simple adoption and a full adoption when applying to the High Court. Simple Adoption (same as in French) does not confer a full custody to the adoptive parents over the adoptee.

In other words, the adopted child maintains the link with his/her natural parents, who could revoke their consent at any time, and demand the child back. Whereas a full adoption (adoption plénière in French) gives legal custody to adoptive parent(s), cuts the link with the natural family, and is irrevocable.

For this reason, and because the U.S. Immigration law requires a full adoption for immigration purposes, ONLY a FULL adoption (adoption plénière) decree granted by the Cameroonian High Court of the adoptee's place of residence is accepted at the Consular section of the US Embassy in Yaounde, during immigrant visa processing.

This document must be accompanied a notarized letter of irrevocable release of the child issued and signed by the surviving parent(s), before a local Commissioner of Oaths.

Child Citizenship Act: For adoptions finalized abroad, the Child Citizenship Act of 2000 allows your new child to acquire American citizenship automatically when he or she enters the United States as lawful permanent residents.

For adoptions finalized in the United States, the Child Citizenship Act of 2000 allows your new child to acquire American citizenship automatically when the court in the United States issues the final adoption decree.

To learn more, review the *Intercountry Adoption* section on this publication and visit the USCIS Intercountry Adoption website at http://adoption.state.gov.

After Adoption: Cameroon does not require post-adoption reporting at this time.

U.S. Embassy in Cameroon
Avenue Rosa Parks
P.O. Box 817
Yaoundé, Cameroon
Tel: (237) 2220-15-00
YaoundeACS@state.gov

Embassy of the Republic of Cameroon
2349 Massachusetts Avenue, N.W
Washington, D.C. 20036
Tel: (202) 265-8790
Fax: (202) 387-3826
http://www.ambacam-usa.org

Office of Children's Issues
U.S. Department of State
2201 C Street, NW
SA-29
Washington, DC 20520
Tel: 1-888-407-4747
E-mail: AskCI@state.gov
http://adoption.state.gov

For questions about immigration procedures, call the National Customer Service Center (NCSC) 1-800-375-5283 (TTY 1-800-767-1833).

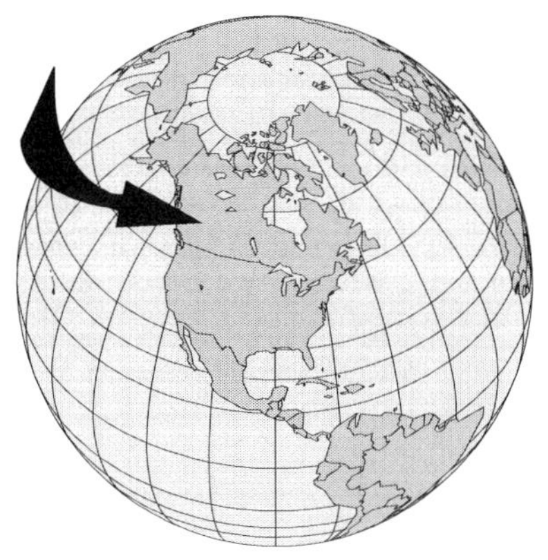

CANADA

Compiled from publications that were available as of February 2013 from the U.S. Department of State, the U.S. Department of Commerce, and the Central Intelligence Agency (CIA). See the introduction to this set for explanatory notes.

Official Name:

Canada

PROFILE

Geography

Area: total: 9,984,670 sq km; country comparison to the world: 2; land: 9,093,507 sq km; water: 891,163 sq km

Major cities: Toronto 5.377 million; Montreal 3.75 million; Vancouver 2.197 million; Ottawa (capital) 1.17 million; Calgary 1.16 million (2009)

Climate: varies from temperate in south to subarctic and arctic in north

Terrain: mostly plains with mountains in west and lowlands in southeast

People

Nationality: noun: Canadian(s); adjective: Canadian

Population: 34,300,083 (July 2012 est.)

Population growth rate: 0.784% (2012 est.)

Ethnic groups: British Isles origin 28%, French origin 23%, other European 15%, Amerindian 2%, other, mostly Asian, African, Arab 6%, mixed background 26%

Religions: Roman Catholic 42.6%, Protestant 23.3% (United Church 9.5%, Anglican 6.8%, Baptist 2.4%, Lutheran 2%), other Christian 4.4%, Muslim 1.9%, other and unspecified 11.8%, none 16% (2001 census)

Languages: English (official) 58.8%, French (official) 21.6%, other 19.6% (2006 Census)

Literacy: definition: age 15 and over can read and write; total population: 99%; male: 99%; female: 99% (2003 est.)

Health: life expectancy at birth: total population: 81.48 years; male: 78.89 years; female: 84.21 years (2012 est.); Infant mortality rate: total: 4.85 deaths/1,000 live births; male: 5.19 deaths/1,000 live births; female: 4.5 deaths/1,000 live births (2012 est.)

Unemployment rate: 7.3% (2012 est.)

Work force: 18.85 million (2012 est.)

Government

Type: a parliamentary democracy, a federation, and a constitutional monarchy

Independence: 1 July 1867

Constitution: made up of unwritten and written acts, customs, judicial decisions, and traditions; the written part of the constitution consists of the Constitution Act of 29 March 1867, which created a federation of four provinces, and the Constitution Act of 17 April 1982, which transferred formal control over the constitution from Britain to Canada, and added a Canadian Charter of Rights and Freedoms as well as procedures for constitutional amendments

Political subdivisions: 10 provinces and 3 territories; Alberta, British Columbia, Manitoba, New Brunswick, Newfoundland and Labrador, Northwest Territories, Nova Scotia, Nunavut, Ontario, Prince Edward Island, Quebec, Saskatchewan, Yukon

Suffrage: 18 years of age; universal

Economy

GDP (purchasing power parity): $1.446 trillion (2012 est.); $1.414 trillion (2011 est.); $1.38 trillion (2010 est.); $1.337 trillion (2009 est.)

GDP real growth rate: 1.9% (2012 est.); 2.5% (2011 est.); 3.2% (2010 est.); -2.8% (2009 est.)

GDP per capita (PPP): $41,500 (2012 est.); $41,100 (2011 est.); $40,500 (2010 est.); $39,700 (2009 est.)

Natural resources: iron ore, nickel, zinc, copper, gold, lead, rare earth elements, molybdenum, potash, diamonds, silver, fish, timber, wildlife, coal, petroleum, natural gas, hydropower

Agriculture products: wheat, barley, oilseed, tobacco, fruits, vegetables; dairy products; fish; forest products

Industries: transportation equipment, chemicals, processed and unprocessed minerals, food products, wood and paper products, fish products, petroleum and natural gas

Exports: $481.7 billion (2012 est.); $462.4 billion (2011 est.); $393 billion (2010 est.)
Exports—commodities: motor vehicles and parts, industrial machinery, aircraft, telecommunications equipment; chemicals, plastics, fertilizers; wood pulp, timber, crude petroleum, natural gas, electricity, aluminum
Exports—partners: US 73.7%, UK 4.2% (2011)
Imports: $480.9 billion (2012 est.); $461 billion (2011 est.); $401.7 billion (2010 est.)
Imports—commodities: machinery and equipment, motor vehicles and parts, crude oil, chemicals, electricity, durable consumer goods
Imports—partners: US 49.5%, China 10.8%, Mexico 5.5% (2011)
Debt—external: $1.181 trillion (30 June 2011); $1.181 trillion (30 June 2011); $1.009 trillion (30 June 2010)
Exchange rates: Canadian dollars (CAD) per US dollar; 1.001 (2012 est.); 0.9895 (2011 est.); 1.0302 (2010 est.); 1.1431 (2009); 1.0364 (2008); 1.0724 (2007)

PEOPLE

Language

Canada, as a country, has two official languages: English and French. All Government of Canada services and documents are available in these two languages. English, however, is the official and most commonly spoken language of most provinces, except Quebec. In Quebec, French is the official work and most commonly spoken language. New Brunswick, home to many French-speaking people, is the only officially bilingual province in Canada. Canada has attracted a huge influx of immigrants in recent years, many of whom speak Spanish, Mandarin, Cantonese, and a variety of Arabic dialects.

Religion

According to the most recent census that included questions about religious affiliation (2001), approximately 77.1 percent of the population is Christian. Roman Catholics (44 percent of the population) constitute the largest group followed by Protestant denominations (29 percent). The United Church and the Anglican, Presbyterian, Lutheran, Baptist, and Pentecostal churches are the largest Protestant groups. The Muslim population stands at 2 percent while approximately 1.1 percent of the population is Jewish. Groups that constitute 1 percent or less of the population include Buddhists, Hindus, Sikhs, Scientologists, Baha'is , and adherents of Shintoism and Taoism.

According to the 2001 census, 0.1 percent of the population identifies itself as followers of "aboriginal spirituality." Approximately 16 percent of the population claims no religious affiliation.

Most recent immigrants were born in Asia and generally practice religious beliefs different from the majority of native-born citizens. According to the 2006 census, "visible minorities" constitute 16.2 percent of the overall population, with 96 percent in urban areas, mostly in metropolitan Toronto, Montreal, and Vancouver.

GOVERNMENT AND POLITICAL CONDITIONS

Canada is a constitutional monarchy with a federal parliamentary government. In a free and fair multiparty federal election held on May 2, 2011, the Conservative Party, led by Stephen Harper, won a majority of seats in the federal Parliament and formed a government.

Recent Elections

On May 2, 2011, the Conservative Party won a majority of seats in the federal Parliament and formed a national majority government.

Participation of Women and Minorities: There were 76 women and seven indigenous individuals in the 308-member federal House of Commons; 38 members were born outside the country. There were 36 women and six indigenous persons in the 105-seat Senate (whose members are appointed by the governor general on the advice of the prime minister); 12 members were born outside the country. Women held 10 seats in the 39-member cabinet. Four of the nine members of the Supreme Court, including the chief justice, were women.

Principal Government Officials

Last Updated: 1/31/2013

Governor Gen.: **David JOHNSTON**
Prime Min.: **Stephen Joseph HARPER**
Min. of Aboriginal Affairs & Northern Development: **John DUNCAN**
Min. of Agriculture & Agri-Food & the Canadian Wheat Board: **Gerry RITZ**
Min. for the Asia-Pacific Gateway: **Edward FAST**
Min. for the Atlantic Gateway: **Keith ASHFIELD**
Min. of Canadian Heritage & Official Languages: **James MOORE**
Min. of the Canadian Northern Economic Development Agency: **Leona AGLUKKAQ**
Min. of Citizenship, Immigration, & Multiculturalism: **Jason KENNEY**
Min. of the Economic Development Agency of Canada for the Regions of Quebec: **Denis LEBEL**
Min. of the Environment: **Peter KENT**
Min. for the Federal Economic Development Initiative for Northern Ontario: **Anthony Peter CLEMENT**
Min. of Finance: **James Michael FLAHERTY**
Min. of Fisheries & Oceans: **Keith ASHFIELD**
Min. of Foreign Affairs: **John Russell BAIRD**
Min. of Health: **Leona AGLUKKAQ**
Min. of Human Resources & Skills Development: **Diane FINLEY**
Min. of Industry: **Christian PARADIS**
Min. of Intergovernmental Affairs: **Peter PENASHUE**
Min. of Intl. Cooperation: **Julian FANTINO**
Min. of Intl. Trade: **Edward FAST**
Min. of Justice & Attorney Gen.: **Robert Douglas NICHOLSON**
Min. of Labor: **Lisa RAITT**
Min. of National Defense: **Peter Gordon MACKAY**

Min. of National Revenue: **Gail SHEA**
Min. of Natural Resources: **Joe OLIVER**
Min. of Public Safety: **Victor TOEWS**
Min. of Public Works & Govt. Services: **Rona AMBROSE**
Min. for Status of Women: **Rona AMBROSE**
Min. of Transport, Infrastructure, & Communities: **Denis LEBEL**
Min. of Veterans Affairs: **Steven BLANEY**
Associate Min. of National Defense: **Bernard VALCOURT**
Min. of State (Agriculture): **Christian PARADIS**
Min. of State (Atlantic Canada Opportunities Agency): **Bernard VALCOURT**
Min. of State (Democratic Reform): **Tim UPPAL**
Min. of State (Federal Economic Development Agency for Southern Ontario): **Gary GOODYEAR**
Min. of State (Finance): **Ted MENZIES**
Min. of State (La Francophonie): **Bernard VALCOURT**
Min. of State (Science & Technology): **Gary GOODYEAR**
Min. of State (Seniors): **Alice WONG**
Min. of State (Small Business & Tourism): **Maxime BERNIER**
Min. of State (Sport): **Bal GOSAL**
Min. of State (Transport): **Steven John FLETCHER**
Min. of State (Western Economic Diversification): **Lynne YELICH**
Min. of State of Foreign Affairs (Americas and Consular Affairs): **Diane ABLONCZY**
Min. of State & Chief Govt. Whip: **Gordon O'CONNOR**
Pres., Queen's Privy Council: **Peter PENASHUE**
Pres., Treasury Board: **Anthony Peter CLEMENT**
Leader of the Govt. in the House of Commons: **Peter VAN LOAN**
Leader of the Govt. in the Senate: **Marjory LEBRETON**
Governor, Bank of Canada: **Mark CARNEY**
Ambassador to the US: **Gary DOER**
Permanent Representative to the UN, New York: **Guillermo RISHCHYNSKI**

ECONOMY

As an affluent, high-tech industrial society in the trillion-dollar class, Canada resembles the US in its market-oriented economic system, pattern of production, and affluent living standards. Since World War II, the impressive growth of the manufacturing, mining, and service sectors has transformed the nation from a largely rural economy into one primarily industrial and urban.

The 1989 US-Canada Free Trade Agreement (FTA) and the 1994 North American Free Trade Agreement (NAFTA) (which includes Mexico) touched off a dramatic increase in trade and economic integration with the US its principal trading partner. Canada enjoys a substantial trade surplus with the US, which absorbs about three-fourths of Canadian exports each year. Canada is the US's largest foreign supplier of energy, including oil, gas, uranium, and electric power.

Given its great natural resources, highly skilled labor force, and modern capital plant, Canada enjoyed solid economic growth from 1993 through 2007. Buffeted by the global economiccrisis, the economy dropped into a sharp recession in the final months of 2008, and Ottawa posted its first fiscal deficit in 2009 after 12 years of surplus.

Canada's major banks, however, emerged from the financial crisis of 2008–09 among the strongest in the world, owing to the financial sector's tradition of conservative lending practices and strong capitalization. Canada achieved marginal growth in 2010 and 2011 and plans to balance the budget by 2015. In addition, the country's petroleum sector is rapidly becoming an even larger economic driver with Alberta's oil sands significantly boosting Canada's proven oil reserves, ranking the country third in the world behind Saudi Arabia and Venezuela.

Labor Conditions

Child labor legislation varies by province, and there are sufficient laws to protect children from exploitation in the workplace. Most provinces restrict the number of hours of work to two or three hours on a school day and eight hours on a nonschool day and prohibit children under age 15 or 16 from working without parental consent, after 10 or 11 p.m., or in any hazardous employment. During official school or academic breaks, the federal government employed youths between ages 15 and 17 for work that is unlikely to endanger their health or safety.

Child labor laws and policies were enforced effectively, and the child labor inspections were carried out by federal and provincial labor ministries. Child labor was not a problem in the country.

Minimum wage rates ranged from C$8.80 to C$11.00 ($8.62 to $10.78). Some provinces exempt agricultural, hospitality, and other specific categories of workers from minimum-wage rates, and Ontario has a minimum-wage rate for youths under age 18 who work less than 28 hours per week when school is in session that is lower than the respective minimum for adult workers.

Standard work hours vary by province, but in each the limit is 40 or 48 hours per week, with at least 24 hours of rest. The law requires payment of a premium for work above the standard workweek. Entitlement to paid annual leave varies by province, but the law requires a minimum of 10 days paid annual leave per year (or payment of 4 percent of wages in lieu) after one year of continuous employment. Some provinces mandate an additional week of paid leave to employees who have completed a specified length of service. There is no specific prohibition on excessive compulsory overtime, which is regulated by means of the required rest periods in the labor code that differ by industry. Some categories of workers have specific employment rights that differ from the standard, including commercial fishermen, oil field workers, loggers, home caregivers, professionals, managers, and some sales staff.

Some NGOs reported that migrants, new immigrants, young workers, and the unskilled were vulnerable to violations of the law on minimum wage, overtime pay, unpaid wages, and

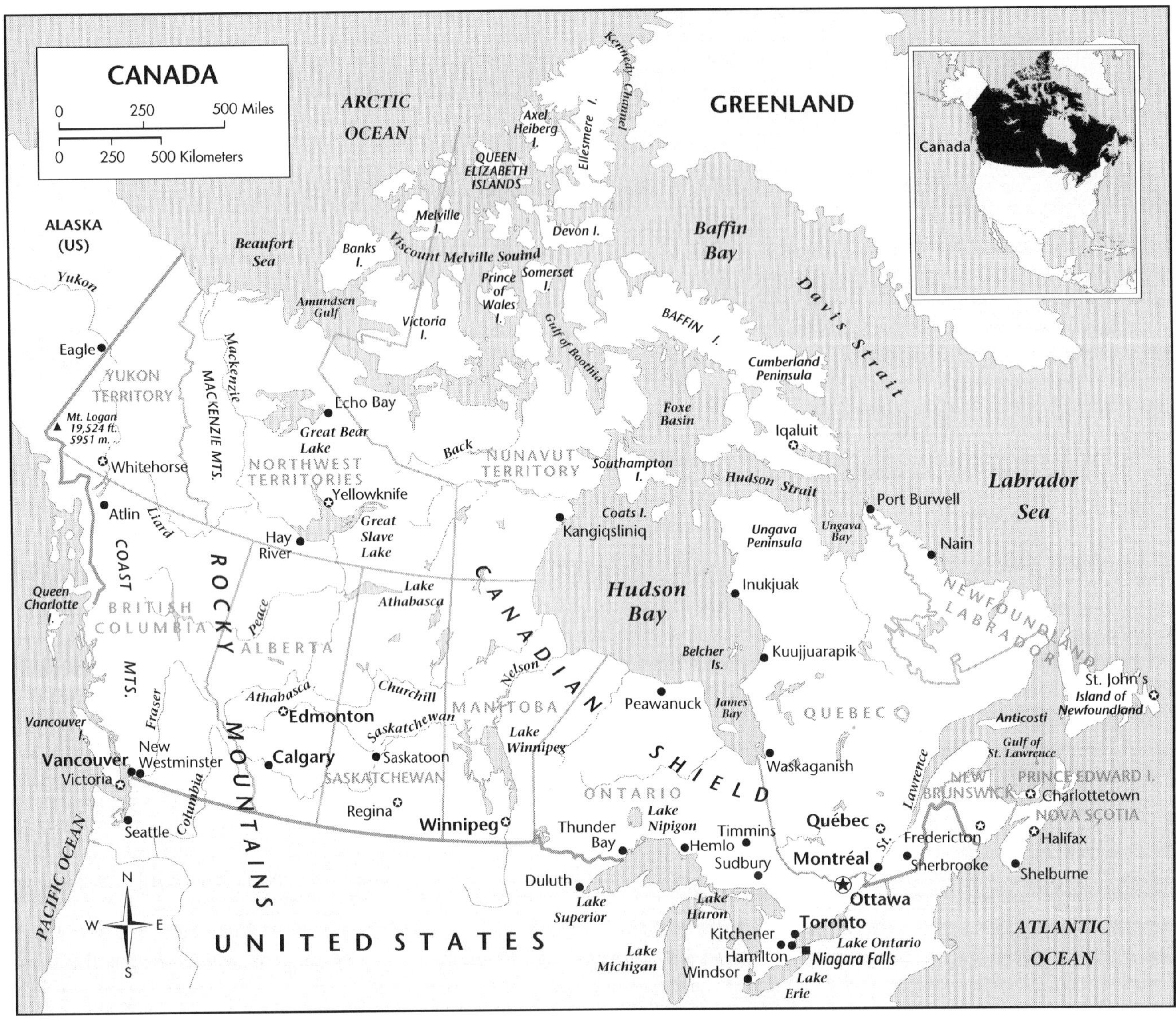

excessive hours of work, and they alleged that restrictions on the type of labor complaints accepted for investigation and delays in processing cases discouraged the filing of complaints in practice.

UNITED STATES-CANADA RELATIONS

The United States and Canada share two borders and their bilateral relationship is among the closest and most extensive in the world. It is reflected in the high volume of bilateral trade—the equivalent of $1.6 billion a day in goods—as well as in people-to-people contact. About 300,000 people cross between the countries every day by all modes of transport. In fields ranging from security and law enforcement to environmental protection to free trade, the two countries work closely on multiple levels from federal to local.

U.S. defense arrangements with Canada are more extensive than with any other country. The Permanent Joint Board on Defense provides policy-level consultation on bilateral defense matters and the United States and Canada share North Atlantic Treaty Organization (NATO) mutual security commitments. U.S. and Canadian military forces cooperate on continental defense within the framework of the binational North American Aerospace Defense Command (NORAD).

The Beyond the Border initiative outlines a vision for perimeter security and economic competitiveness whereby the United States and Canada work in partnerships within, at, and away from our borders to achieve enhanced security and accelerate the legitimate flow of people, goods, and services between our two countries. The United States has several successful joint law enforcement programs with Canada such as the Integrated Border Enforcement Teams (IBET), Border Enforcement Security Taskforces (BEST), and the ShipRider Integrated Cross Border

Maritime Law Enforcement program. Senior leadership engages in these efforts through fora such as the Cross Border Crime Forum (CBCF), which is chaired by the U.S. Attorney General and the Secretary of Homeland Security with their Canadian counterparts. As part of the Beyond the Border Action Plan, U.S. and Canadian officials are enhancing cross-border law enforcement radio interoperability and building on the successes of programs such as IBET, BEST, and ShipRider to develop the next generation of integrated cross-border law enforcement.

U.S. Customs and Border Protection (CBP) conducts preclearance operations at eight Canadian airports, allowing air travelers to arrive at domestic terminals in the United States by screening and making admissibility decisions about U.S.-bound travelers and their accompanying goods or baggage prior to departure. The United States and Canada intend to enhance preclearance operations and expand them to also cover land, rail, and ferry/cruise travel as part of the Beyond the Border Action Plan.

The United States and Canada work together to resolve and manage transboundary environmental and water issues. A principal instrument of this cooperation is the International Joint Commission established under the 1909 Boundary Waters Treaty. Under the Columbia River Treaty, Canada and the United States jointly regulate and manage the Columbia River as it flows from British Columbia into the United States. The two countries cooperate on a range of bilateral fisheries issues and international high seas governance initiatives, and are both founding members of the Arctic Council.

The bilateral Clean Energy Dialogue is charged with expanding clean energy research and development; developing and deploying clean energy technology; and building a more efficient electricity grid based on clean and renewable energy in order to reduce greenhouse gases and combat climate change in both countries. Canada is an ally of the United States in international climate change negotiations. Canada participates in the U.S.-led Major Economies Forum on Energy and Climate; the Asia Pacific Partnership on Clean Development and Climate, which aims to accelerate the development and deployment of clean energy technologies in major industrial sectors; and the International Carbon Sequestration Leadership Forum, which researches effective ways to capture and store carbon dioxide.

U.S. Assistance to Canada

The United States provides no foreign assistance to Canada.

Bilateral Economic Relations

The United States and Canada share the world's largest and most comprehensive trading relationship, which supports millions of jobs in each country. Canada is the single largest foreign supplier of energy to the United States. Recognition of the commercial viability of Canada's oil sands has made it the world's third largest holder of oil reserves after Saudi Arabia and Venezuela and is the only non-OPEC member in the top five. Canada and the United States operate an integrated electricity grid that meets jointly developed reliability standards, and they provide all of each other's electricity imports. Canadian uranium helps fuel U.S. nuclear power plants.

The North American Free Trade Agreement (NAFTA) among the United States, Canada, and Mexico aims to reduce trade barriers and establish agreed upon trade rules. It has resolved long-standing bilateral irritants and liberalized rules in several areas, including agriculture, services, energy, financial services, investment, and government procurement. The Regulatory Cooperation Council seeks to further stimulate trade by increasing regulatory transparency and cooperation between the United States and Canada and eliminating unnecessary regulatory differences and duplicative actions that hinder cross-border trade and investment. Canada and the United States have one of the world's largest investment relationships. The United States is Canada's largest foreign investor, and Canada is the fifth-largest foreign investor in the United States. U.S. investment is primarily in Canada's mining and smelting industries, petroleum, chemicals, the manufacture of machinery and transportation equipment, and finance. Canadian investment in the United States is concentrated in finance and insurance, manufacturing, banking, information and retail trade, and other services.

Bilateral trade disputes are managed through bilateral consultative forums or referral to NAFTA or World Trade Organization (WTO) dispute resolution procedures. Canada has challenged U.S. trade remedy law in NAFTA and WTO dispute settlement mechanisms. The two countries negotiated the application to Canadian goods of "Buy American" provisions for state and local procurement under the American Recovery and Reinvestment Act. The United States has encouraged Canada to strengthen its intellectual property laws and enforcement. Canada passed an important copyright law on June 28, 2012.

Canada's Membership in International Organizations

In addition to their close bilateral ties, Canada and the United States cooperate in multilateral fora, including international efforts to combat terrorist financing and money laundering. The two countries belong to a number of the same international organizations, including the United Nations, NATO, WTO, G8, G20, Organization for Security and Cooperation in Europe, Organization for Economic Cooperation and Development, Organization of American States, and Asia-Pacific Economic Cooperation forum. Canada accepted an invitation to join the Trans-Pacific Partnership regional trade agreement being negotiated among the United States and other countries.

Bilateral Representation

Canada maintains an embassy in the United States at 501 Pennsylvania Avenue, NW, Washington DC 20001.

Principal U.S. Embassy Officials

Last Updated: 1/14/2013

OTTAWA (E) 490 Sussex Drive, (613) 688-5335, Fax (613) 688-3080, Workweek: M-F 08:30-17:00, Website: http://canada.usembassy.gov/

DCM OMS:	Margaret W. Baker
AMB OMS:	Louise J. Ramsay
Co-CLO:	Vera Fitch
DCM/CHG:	James D. Nealon
DHS/CBP:	Alan L. Langford
DHS/ICE:	Matthew Stentz
DHS/TSA:	James Libovicz
FCS:	Richard Steffens
FM:	John Harvey
HHS:	Brad Austin
HRO:	Scott Learmonth
MGT:	Chris Riche
POSHO:	John Harvey
SDO/DATT:	COL Creg Paulk
AMB:	David Jacobson
CG:	Sylvia D. Johnson
CON:	Bryan Harrison
PAO:	Susan Crystal
GSO:	Paul D. Yeskoo
RSO:	David Brackins
AGR:	Scott Reynolds
APHIS:	Vacant
ATF:	William A. Temple
CLO:	Cindy Cooper
DEA:	Daniel Mylius
ECON:	Sue Saarnio
EPA:	Nikki Brajevich
EST:	Lucy K. Abbott
FMO:	Susan Astley-Cass
ICASS Chair:	Rick Ortiz
IMO:	Vacant
IPO:	James Fieser
IRS:	Jeff Cooper
ISO:	Ricky Kay Brown
ISSO:	Hector Matienzo
LEGATT:	Alan Bradstock (Acting)
POL:	Samuel Brock

CALGARY (CG) 1000–615 Macleod Trail SE / Calgary, AB / T2G 4T8, (403) 266-8962, Fax (403) 264-6630, Workweek: (Mon-Fri) 0800-1630, Website: http://calgary.usconsulate.gov/

CG OMS:	John Andrews
FCS:	Cindy Biggs
MGT:	Stephen Macleod
POL/ECON:	Brett D. Mattei
CG:	Peter Kujawinski
CON:	Richard Hanrahan
AFSA:	Cassy Allen

HALIFAX (CG) 1969 Upper Water St., Ste 904, Halifax, NS B3J 3R7, (902) 429-2480, Fax (902) 423-6861, Workweek: Mon-Fri, 8:30 a.m.-5:00 p.m., Public Hours-8:30 a.m.-11:30 a.m./2:00 p.m.-4:30 p.m., Website: http://halifax.usconsulate.gov/

CG:	Richard H. Riley
CON:	Scott L. Whitmore

MONTREAL (CG) 1155 St. Alexandre, Montreal, Qc, Canada, H3B 3Z1, 514-398-9695, Fax 514-398-0973, Workweek: 8:15AM to 5:00PM, Mon-Fri, Website: http://montreal.usconsulate.gov/

CG OMS:	Daniel J Pellegrino
DHS/ICE:	Scott Bocksel
HRO:	Scott Learmonth
MGT:	Michelle N. Ward
POL/ECON:	Jamie S. White
Port DIR:	Gregory D. Starr
CG:	Andrew C. Parker
CON:	Scott D. Boswell
PAO:	Caitlin Bergin
COM:	No Com Officer At This Post
RSO:	Michael Jordan
CLO:	Tricia Saucier
FAA:	David Behrens
IPO:	William Manuel

QUEBEC (CG) 2, rue de la Terrasse Dufferin, C.P. 939, Quebec (Quebec) Canada G1R 4T9, 1-418-692-2106, Fax 1-418-692-4640 / 1-418-692-4068, Workweek: Monday thru Friday, 0830 to 1700, Website: http://quebec.usconsulate.gov/

PO:	Peter A. O'Donohue
CON:	Stuart R. Wilson

TORONTO (CG) 360 University Avenue, Toronto M5G 1S4, 416-595-1700, Fax 416-595-1090, Workweek: M-F, 8:15-5:00, Website: http://toronto.usconsulate.gov/

CG OMS:	Tracey A De Rosa
DHS/CIS:	Donald Anderson
DHS/ICE:	John A. Ward
FCS:	Frank Carrico
HRO:	J.David Kay
MGT:	J.David Kay
POSHO:	J. David Kay
CG:	James Dickmeyer
CON:	Patricia L.Fietz
PAO:	Scott Walker
RSO:	Christian J. Rodgers
AFSA:	Nancy Brant
ATF:	Peter Forcelli
CLO:	Chloe Jl Walker
IPO:	Ali Nikooazm
ISSO:	Ali Nikooazm
LEGATT:	Daniel A. Bodony
POL:	Jeffery R. Izzo

VANCOUVER (CG) 1095 W. Pender St., 19th Fl, Vancouver, B.C., V6E 2M6, (604) 685-4311, Fax (604) 685-5285/685-7304, Workweek: Mon-Fri, 8:00 a.m.–4:30 p.m., Website: http://vancouver.usconsulatc.gov/

CG OMS:	Susan McDermott
Co-CLO:	Catherine Sarreal
DHS/ICE:	Brian Patrick Mize
DPO:	Joseph E. Salazar
MGT:	Michael J. Kelly
POL/ECON:	Marisa Ferguson
Port DIR:	Richard Roberts
POSHO:	Michael J. Kelly
CG:	Anne Callaghan
CON:	Camille D. Hill
PAO:	Jeanne M. Briganti
RSO:	Anthony A. McGinley
AFSA:	Bryan Giblin
ATF:	James S. Higgins
CLO:	Lauren Salazar
DEA:	David F. Lenartowicz
EEO:	Janie M. Carpenter
IPO:	David R. Krough
ISSO:	David R. Krough
LEGATT:	Jeffrey Harris

US ICAO (MONTREAL) (M) 999 University Street, Suite 1410 Montreal, Quebec, H3C-5J9, Canada, 514-954-8304, Fax 514-954-8021, Workweek: 9:00 a.m.–6:00 p.m. M-F.

AMB OMS:	Cynthia J. Loyet
AMB:	Duane E. Woerth
DCM:	Joseph L. Novak
FAA:	(Anc) David Behrens
FAA/CASLO:	(Anc Asst.) Belinde Riedler

WINNIPEG (BO) 201 Portage Ave., Suite 860 Winnipeg, MB R3B 3K6, (204) 940-1801, Fax (204) 940-1809, Workweek: M-F, 8 AM–5 PM, Website: http://winnipeg.usconsulate.gov/

PO:	Timothy L. Cipullo

TRAVEL

Consular Information Sheet

November 3, 2011

Country Description: Canada, where English and French are the official languages, is the world's second largest country in land area with urban cities, small towns, large mountain ranges and vast coastlines. It is a highly developed, stable democracy with a vibrant economy. Tourist facilities are widely available in much of the country, but the northern and wilderness areas are less developed and facilities there can be vast distances apart.

Smart Traveler Enrollment Program (STEP)/Embassy Locations: If you are going to live in or visit Canada, please take the time to register with the U.S. Embassy or nearest U.S. Consulate. If you enroll, we can keep you up to date with important safety and security announcements. It will also help your friends and family get in touch with you in an emergency.

U.S. Embassy
490 Sussex Drive, K1N 1G8
Ottawa, Ontario, Canada
Telephone: (613) 238-5335
Emergency after-hours telephone: (613) 238-5335
Facsimile: (613) 688-3082

The Embassy's consular district includes Ottawa, Eastern Ontario (Kingston, Lanark, Leeds, Prescott, Refrew, Russell, and Stormont) as well as those parts of Quebec (Outaouais and Abitibi-Témiscamingues) near Ottawa.

U.S. Consulates General are located in:
Calgary, Alberta
615 Macleod Trail SE, 10th Floor
Telephone: (403) 266-8962
Emergency after-hours telephone: (403) 266-8962 then press '0'
Facsimile: (403) 263-2241

The consular district includes Alberta, Manitoba, Saskatchewan, and the Northwest Territories, excluding Nunavut.

Halifax, Nova Scotia
Upper Water Street, Suite 904, Purdy's Wharf Tower II
Telephone: (902) 429-2480
Emergency after-hours telephone: (902) 429-2485
Facsimile: (902) 423-6861

The consular district includes New Brunswick, Newfoundland, Nova Scotia, Prince Edward Island, and the French islands of Saint Pierre and Miquelon.

Montreal, Quebec
1155 rue St. Alexandre
Telephone: (514) 398-9695
Emergency after-hours telephone: (514) 981-5059
Facsimile: (514) 398-9748

The consular district includes Greater Montreal and the regions of Southern Quebec Province (Laurentides, Lanaudiere, Laval, Montreal, Montregie, Estrie, and the southern parts of Centre-du-Quebec), including Joliete, Drummondville, and Sherbrooke.

Quebec City, Quebec
2 rue de la Terrasse Dufferin
Telephone: (418) 692-2095
Emergency after-hours telephone: (418) 692-2096
Facsimile: (418) 692-4640.

The consular district includes Quebec City and those regions of Quebec Province to the North and East of the Montreal and Ottawa Districts (indicated above), plus the Territory of Nunavut.

Toronto, Ontario
360 University Avenue (please note that consular clients must enter the Consulate at 225 Simcoe Street)
Telephone: (416) 595-1700
Emergency after hours telephone: (416) 201-4100
Facsimile: (416) 595-5466

The consular district includes the province of Ontario except for the counties of Kingston, Lanark, Leeds, Prescott, Refrew, Russell, and Stormont, which are served by the U.S. Embassy in Ottawa.

Vancouver, British Columbia
1095 West Pender Street (please note that consular clients must enter the Consulate at 1075 West Pender Street)
Telephone: (604) 685-4311
Facsimile: (604) 685-7175

The consular district includes British Columbia and the Yukon Territory.

Winnipeg, Manitoba
201 Portage Street, Suite 860
Telephone: (204) 940-1800
Facsimile: (204) 940-1809

The consulate provides only emergency services for U.S. citizens in distress; it does not provide consular services. Manitoba-related consular matters such as visas, passports and notarials are handled at other U.S. Consulates General, primarily Calgary. Applicants for U.S. visas require interview appointments. Information on visa appointments is available at the CSC Visa Information Service website. For information on consular and U.S. passport services for U.S. citizens who live in Canada please see website. No visa or consular/passport information is available by calling the embassy or consulate switchboards.

Entry/Exit Requirements for U.S. Citizens: For temporary visits to Canada for less than 180 days, a visa is not required for U.S. citizens in most cases. For information on entering Canada for any purpose other than a visit (e.g. to work, study or immigrate), contact the Canadian Embassy or nearest consulate and consult the Canadian immigration website.

Entry into Canada is solely determined by Canadian Border Services Agency (CBSA) officials in accordance with Canadian law. Please see the CBSA's website for details. Canadian law requires that all persons entering Canada carry both proof of citizenship and proof of identity. A valid U.S. passport, passport card, or NEXUS card (see below) satisfies these requirements for U.S. citizens.

Please Note: Anyone with a criminal record (including misdemeanors or alcohol-related driving offenses) may not be able to enter Canada without first obtaining a special waiver well in advance of any planned travel. To determine whether you may be inadmissible and how to overcome this finding, please refer to the Canadian citizenship and immigration website.

For further information on entry requirements, travelers may contact the Canadian Embassy at 501 Pennsylvania Avenue NW, Washington DC 20001, tel. (202) 682-1740; or the Canadian consulates in Atlanta, Boston, Buffalo, Chicago, Dallas, Detroit, Los Angeles, Miami, Minneapolis, New York, San Juan or Seattle.

Travel Documents: Both the U.S. and Canadian governments urge frequent travelers to join the NEXUS trusted traveler program. NEXUS members receive a special travel card that allows expedited border crossings for both private and commercial travelers through both U.S. and Canadian border controls.

If a U.S. citizen traveling to Canada does not have a passport, passport card, or approved alternate document such as a NEXUS card, they must show a government-issued photo ID (e.g. Driver's License) and proof of U.S. citizenship such as a U.S. birth certificate, naturalization certificate, or expired U.S. passport. Children under 16 need only present proof of U.S. citizenship. (Please see below for important information concerning re-entry into the United States.)

U.S. citizens entering Canada from a third country must have a valid U.S. passport.

When returning to the United States from Canada, it is very important to note that all U.S. citizens are required to present a valid U.S. passport to enter or re-enter the United States via air. For entry into the United States via land and sea borders, U.S. citizens must present either a U.S. passport, passport card, NEXUS card, Enhanced Drivers License, or other Western Hemisphere Travel Initiative (WHTI)-compliant document. The only exception to this requirement is for U.S. citizens under the age of 16 (or under 19, if traveling with a school, religious, or other youth group) who need only present a birth certificate (original, photocopy or certified copy), Consular Report of Birth Abroad, or naturalization certificate.

WHTI: U.S. citizen travelers are urged to obtain WHTI-compliant documents well in advance of their planned travel to Canada. For the most recent information on WHTI and WHTI-compliant documents, please see the U.S. Department of State's WHTI website. One of the WHTI-compliant documents for crossing the land border is the U.S. Passport Card. The card may not be used to travel by air and is available only to U.S. citizens. U.S. citizens can visit the U.S. Department of State's website or call 1-877-4USA-PPT (1-877-487-2778) for information on how to apply for their passports.

Travel for Private Boaters and Recreational Vessels: Canadian law requires all foreign private boaters, including recreational vessels, to present themselves upon their arrival in Canada to the CBSA. Private boaters who depart Canada, enter foreign waters, and subsequently return to Canada also must present themselves to the CBSA when they return. The reporting obligation exists regardless of the boater's activities while outside of Canada or planned activities while in Canada. Arrival in Canada occurs when the pleasure craft crosses the international boundary into Canadian waters. This provision applies regardless of whether or not boaters drop anchor, land, enter an inland tributary or moor alongside another vessel while in foreign waters. Failure to report entry may result in detention, seizure or forfeiture of the vessel and/or monetary penalties. The minimum fine for failing to report to the CBSA upon entry to Canada is C$1,000. Upon entering Canadian waters, private boaters who qualify can present themselves to the CBSA by calling the Telephone Reporting Centre (TRC) at 1-888-226-7277. All other private boaters, including vessels carrying foreign nationals (other than U.S. citizens or permanent residents), must proceed directly to a designated marine telephone reporting site and place a call to the TRC in order to obtain CBSA clearance.

For procedures to report arrivals in the United States through the Small Vessels Reporting System, please refer to the Small Vessel Reporting System and Pleasure Boat Reporting Requirements web pages of the U.S. Customs and Border Protection.

Travel with Minors: If you plan to travel to Canada with a minor who is not your own child or for whom you do not have full legal custody, CBSA may require you to present a notarized affidavit of consent from the minor's parents. There is no specific form for this document, but it should include dates of travel, parents' names and photocopies of their state-issued IDs.

The U.S. Department of State is unaware of any HIV/AIDS entry restrictions for visitors to or foreign residents of Canada.

Threats to Safety and Security: Stay up to date by:

- Bookmarking our Bureau of Consular Affairs website, which contains the current Travel Warnings and Travel Alerts as well as the Worldwide Caution.
- Following us on Twitter and the Bureau of Consular Affairs page on Facebook as well.
- Downloading our free Smart Traveler iPhone App to have travel information at your fingertips.
- Calling 1-888-407-4747 toll-free within the U.S. and Canada, or a regular toll line, 1-202-501-4444, from other countries.
- Taking some time before travel to consider your personal security—

Crime: Although Canada generally has a lower crime rate than the U.S., violent crimes do occur throughout the country, especially in urban areas. Visitors to large cities should be aware that parked cars are regularly targeted for opportunistic smash-and-grab thefts, and they are cautioned to avoid leaving any possessions unattended in a vehicle, even in the trunk. Due to the high incidence of such crimes, motorists in Montreal, Vancouver and some other jurisdictions can be fined for leaving their car doors unlocked or for leaving valuables in view. Auto theft in Montreal and Vancouver, including theft of motor homes and recreational vehicles, may even occur in patrolled and apparently secure parking lots and decks. SUVs appear to be particular targets of organized theft. While Canadian gun control laws are much stricter than those in the United States, such laws have not prevented gun-related violence in certain areas.

In many countries around the world, counterfeit and pirated goods are widely available. Do not buy counterfeit and pirated goods, even if they are widely available. Not only are the bootlegs illegal in the United States, if you purchase them you may also be breaking local law.

Victims of Crime: If you or someone you know becomes the victim of a crime abroad, you should contact the local police and the nearest U.S. embassy or consulate. We can:

- Replace a stolen passport.
- Help you find appropriate medical care if you are the victim of violent crimes, such as assault or rape.
- Put you in contact with the appropriate police authorities, and if you want us to, we cancontact family members or friends.
- Help you understand the local criminal justice process and direct you to local attorneys, although it is important to remember that local authorities are responsible for investigating and prosecuting the crime.

Each of Canada's provinces has a Crime Victim Compensation Board from which U.S. citizen victims of crime in Canada may seek redress.

As in the United States, emergency assistance can be reached by dialing 911.

Criminal Penalties: While in a foreign country, a U.S. citizen is subject to that country's laws and regulations, which sometimes differ significantly from those in the United States and may not afford the protections available to the individual under U.S. law. Penalties for breaking the law can be more severe than in the United States for similar offenses. Persons violating Canada's laws, even unknowingly, may be expelled, arrested or imprisoned. Penalties for possession, use, or trafficking in illegal drugs in Canada are severe, and convicted offenders can expect long jail sentences and heavy fines. Engaging in sexual conduct with children or using or disseminating child pornography in a foreign country is a crime, prosecutable in the United States.

Canadian law prohibits the unlawful importation or trafficking of controlled substances and narcotics. A number of travelers, including U.S. citizens, have been arrested for attempting to smuggle khat, a narcotic from East Africa, into Canada. Smugglers risk substantial fines, a permanent bar from Canada, and imprisonment.

Based on the Vienna Convention on Consular Relations, bilateral agreements with certain countries, and customary international law, if you are arrested in Canada, you have the option to request that the police, prison officials, or other authorities alert the nearest U.S. embassy or consulate of your arrest, and to have communications from you forwarded to the nearest U.S. embassy or consulate.

Tax Issues: For information on U.S. Federal tax issues please refer to the IRS Website for International Taxpayers.

Importation of Firearms: Firearms are much more strictly controlled in Canada than in the United States. Violation of firearms restrictions may result in prosecution and imprisonment. Visitors bringing any firearms into Canada, or planning to borrow and use firearms while in Canada, must declare the firearms in writing using a Non-Resident Firearm Declaration form. Visitors planning to borrow a firearm in Canada must obtain a Temporary Firearms Borrowing License in advance. These forms must be signed before a CBSA officer at the border and no photocopies are available at the border. Full details and downloadable forms are available at the Canadian Firearms Centre website, under the heading "Visitors to Canada." Canadian law requires that officials confiscate firearms and weapons from persons crossing the border who deny having the items in their possession. Confiscated firearms and weapons are never returned. Possession of an undeclared firearm may result in arrest and imprisonment.

Canada has three classes of firearms: non-restricted, restricted, and prohibited. Non-restricted firearms include most ordinary hunting rifles and shotguns. These may be brought temporarily into Canada for sporting or hunting use during hunting season, use in competitions, in-transit movement through Canada, or personal protection against wildlife in remote areas of Canada. Anyone wishing to bring hunting rifles into Canada must be at least 18 years old, must properly store the firearm for transport, and must follow the declaration requirements described above. Restricted firearms are primarily handguns; however, pepper spray, mace, and some knives also are included in this category. A restricted firearm may be brought into Canada, but an Authorization to Transport permit must be obtained in advance from a Provincial or Territorial Chief Firearms Officer. Prohibited firearms include fully automatic, converted automatics and assault-type weapons. Prohibited firearms are not allowed into Canada.

Pornography: Canada has strict laws concerning child pornography, and in recent years there has been an increase in random checks of electronic media of travelers entering Canada. Computers are subject to searches without a warrant at the border and illegal content can result in the seizure of the computer as well as detention, arrest, and prosecution of the bearer.

Accessibility: Although Canada has effectively implemented laws mandating access to buildings for persons with disabilities, individuals with disabilities may find accessibility and accommodation very different from what you find in the United States.

Medical Facilities and Health Information: The level of public health and sanitation in Canada is high. Canada's medical care is of a high standard but is government-controlled and rationed. Quick and easy access to ongoing medical care is difficult for temporary visitors who are not members of each province's government-run health care plans.

Many physicians will not take new patients. Access to a specialist is only by referral and may take months to obtain. Emergency room waits can be very long. Some health care professionals in the province of Quebec may speak only French. No Canadian health care provider accepts U.S. domestic health insurance, and Medicare coverage does not extend outside the United States. Visitors who seek any medical attention in Canada should be prepared to pay cash in full at the time the service is rendered. Traveler's medical insurance is highly recommended even for brief visits.

You can find good information on vaccinations and other health precautions on the CDC website. For information about outbreaks of infectious diseases abroad, consult the World Health Organization (WHO) website. The WHO website also contains additional health information for travelers, including detailed country-specific health information.

Medical Insurance: You can't assume your insurance will go with you when you travel. It's very important to find out BEFORE you leave whether or not your medical insurance will cover you overseas. You need to ask your insurance company two questions:

- Does my policy apply when I'm out of the United States?
- Will it cover emergencies like a trip to a foreign hospital or a medical evacuation?

In many places, doctors and hospitals still expect payment in cash at the time of service. Your regular U.S. health insurance may not cover doctors' and hospital visits in other countries. If your policy doesn't go with you when you travel, it's a very good idea to take out another one for your trip.

Traffic Safety and Road Conditions: While in Canada, you may encounter road conditions that differ significantly from those in the United States. The information below concerning Canada is provided for general reference only, and may not be totally accurate in a particular location or circumstance. As in the United States, all emergency assistance in Canada can be reached by dialing 911.

Transport Canada is the Canadian federal government agency responsible for road safety, although each province or territory has the authority to establish its own traffic and safety laws and issue driving licenses. For detailed information on road conditions throughout Canada, as well as links to provincial government web sites, please see the Transport Canada website or the Canadian Automobile Association (CAA) website. The CAA honors American Automobile Association membership. Some automobile warranties of vehicles purchased in the United States may be invalid in Canada; please check the warranty of your vehicle.

Driving in Canada is similar to driving in many parts of the United States. Distances and speeds, however, are posted in kilometers per hour and some signs, particularly in Quebec, may only be in French. U.S. driver's licenses are valid in Canada. Proof of auto insurance is required. U.S. auto insurance is accepted as long as an individual is a tourist in Canada. U.S. insurance firms will issue a Canadian insurance card, which should be obtained and carried prior to driving into Canada. For specific information concerning Canadian driving permits, mandatory insurance and entry regulations, please contact the Canadian National Tourist Organization.

Unless otherwise posted, the maximum speed limit in Canada is 50km/hr in cities and 80km/hr on highways. On rural highways, the posted speed limit may be 100km/hr (approximately 60 miles/hr). Seat belt use is mandatory for all passengers, and child car seats must be used by children under 40 pounds. Some provinces require drivers to keep their vehicles' headlights on during the day and some have banned driving while using a hand-held cell phone.

Motorcycles cannot share a lane, and safety helmets for motorcycle riders and passengers are mandatory. Many highways do not have merge lanes for entering traffic. Tailgating and rapid lane-changes without signaling are common. Emergency vehicles frequently enter the oncoming traffic lane to avoid congestion. Drivers should be aware that running a red light is a serious concern throughout Canada and motorists are advised to pause before proceeding when a light turns green.

Alcohol-related driving offenses, such as driving while intoxicated (DWI), driving while ability-impaired, and driving under the influence (DUI) of alcohol, are criminal offenses in Canada. Penalties are heavy, and any prior conviction (no matter how old or how minor the infraction) is grounds for exclusion from Canada. Americans with a DWI record must seek a waiver of exclusion from Canadian authorities before traveling to Canada, which requires several weeks or months to process.

It is illegal to take automobile radar detectors into Quebec, Ontario, Manitoba, the Yukon or the Northwest Territories, regardless of whether they are used or not. Police there may confiscate radar detectors, operational or not, and impose substantial fines.

Winter travel can be dangerous due to heavy snowfalls and hazardous icy conditions. Some roads and bridges are subject to periodic winter closures. Snow tires are required in some provinces. The CAA has tips for winter driving in Canada. Travelers also should be cautious of deer, elk, and moose while driving at night in rural areas.

Highway 401, from Detroit to Montreal, is one of the busiest highways in North America. It has been the scene of numerous, deadly traffic accidents due to sudden, severe, and unpredictable weather changes, high rates of speed, and heavy truck traffic. There have been numerous incidents involving road racing and dangerous truck driving. Drivers tend to be aggressive, often exceeding speed limits and passing on both sides, and police enforcement is spotty.

In addition, approaches to border crossings into the United States may experience unexpected traffic backups. Drivers should be alert, as lane restrictions at border approaches exist for drivers in NEXUS and FAST expedited inspection programs.

Aviation Safety Oversight: The U.S. Federal Aviation Administration (FAA) has assessed the government of Canada's Civil Aviation Authority as being in compliance with International Civil Aviation Organization (ICAO) aviation safety standards for oversight of Canada's air carrier operations. Further information may be found on the FAA's safety assessment page.

Children's Issues: Please see the U.S. Dept. of State Office of Children's Issues web pages on intercountry adoption and international parental child abduction.

Intercountry Adoption

June 2009

The information in this section has been edited from the latest report available as of February 2013 from the State Department Bureau of Consular Affairs, Office of Overseas Citizens Services. For more information, please read the *Intercountry Adoption* section of this book and review current reports online at http://adoption.state.gov.

Canada is party to the Hague Convention on Protection of Children and Co-operation in Respect of Intercountry Adoption (Hague Adoption Convention). Therefore all adoptions between Canada and the United States must meet the requirements of the Convention and U.S. law implementing the Convention. Canada is not considered a country of origin in intercountry adoption. Only 14 Canadian orphans have received U.S. immigrant visas in the past five fiscal years. The information provided is intended primarily to assist in extremely rare adoption cases from Canada, including adoptions of Canada children by relatives in the United States, as well as adoptions from third countries by Americans living in Canada.

Who Can Adopt? Adoption between the United States and Canada is governed by the Hague Adoption Convention. Therefore to adopt from Canada, you must first be found eligible to adopt by the U.S. Government. The U.S. Government agency responsible for making this determination is the Department of Homeland Security, U.S. Citizenship and Immigration Services (USCIS).

Residency Requirements: Eligibility and residence requirements vary by province. In general, non-residents of Canada cannot adopt children for emigration from Canada. There are some very limited exceptions, usually involving relatives of the children. Contact the provincial adoption authorities for specific information on additional eligibility requirements to adopt, including any age, marriage, and income requirements.

Who Can Be Adopted? Because Canada is party to the Hague Adoption Convention, children from Canada must meet the requirements of the Convention in order to be eligible for adoption. For example, the Convention requires that Canada attempt to place a child with a family in-country before determining that a child is eligible for intercountry adoption. In addition to Canada's requirements, a child must meet the definition of a Convention adoptee for you to bring him or her back to the United States. For detailed and updated information on these requirements, please review the *Intercountry Adoption* section of this publication and visit the USCIS Intercountry Adoption website at http://adoption.state.gov.

Canada's Adoption Authority: In Canada, the various provinces are responsible for setting and administering adoption policies and procedures.

The Process: Because Canada is party to the Hague Adoption Convention, adopting from Canada must follow a specific process designed to meet the Convention's requirements. For detailed and updated information on these requirements, please review the *Intercountry Adoption* section of this publication and visit the USCIS Intercountry Adoption website at http://adoption.state.gov.

The process for finalizing the adoption (or gaining legal custody) in Canada varies according to the province. Contact the provincial adoption authorities for specific information on the process for adoption, including application instructions and fees, and documents required.

Bringing Your Child Home: Once your adoption is complete (or you have obtained legal custody of the child), there are a few more steps to take before you can head home. Specifically, you need to apply for several documents for your child before he or she can travel to the United States, such as a birth certificate, a passport or travel document for your child from the country in which he or she was born, and a U.S. Immigration

Visa. For detailed and updated information on how to obtain these documents, review the *Intercountry Adoption* section on this publication and visit the USCIS Intercountry Adoption website at http://adoption.state.gov.

Child Citizenship Act: For adoptions finalized abroad, the Child Citizenship Act of 2000 allows your new child to acquire American citizenship automatically when he or she enters the United States as lawful permanent residents.

For adoptions finalized in the United States, the Child Citizenship Act of 2000 allows your new child to acquire American citizenship automatically when the court in the United States issues the final adoption decree. To learn more, review the *Intercountry Adoption* section on this publication and visit the USCIS Intercountry Adoption website at http://adoption.state.gov.

After Adoption: Information on post-adoption procedures and requirements for each province and territory can be found on the Social Development Canada website at: www.hrsdc.gc.ca.

United States Consulate General Montreal
1155 rue Saint-Alexandre
Montreal, Quebec H3B 3Z1
Canada
Tel: (514) 398-9695
Fax: (514) 398-0973
Telephone: +358-9-616-2

Canada's Adoption Authority
Intercountry Adoption Services (IAS)
Human Resources and Social Development Canada
333 North River Road/
Place Vanier, Tower A/2nd floor
OTTAWA, Ontario
Canada
K1A 0L1
Tel.: (613)-954-0880
Fax: (613)-948-7537
http://www.cic.gc.ca/english/immigrate/adoption/authorities.asp

Canadian Embassy
501 Pennsylvania Ave., NW
Washington, DC 20001
202-682-1740; Fax: 202-682-7701
http://www.canadainternational.gc.ca/washington

Canada also has consulates in: Atlanta, Boston, Buffalo, Chicago, Dallas, Denver, Detroit, Houston, Los Angeles, Miami, Minneapolis, New York, Raleigh, San Diego, San Francisco, and Seattle.

Office of Children's Issues
U.S. Department of State
2201 C Street, NW
SA-29
Washington, DC 20520
Tel: 1-888-407-4747
E-mail: AskCI@state.gov
Internet: http://adoption.state.gov

For questions about immigration procedures, call the National Customer Service Center (NCSC) 1-800-375-5283 (TTY 1-800-767-1833).

International Parental Child Abduction

January 2012

The information in this section has been edited from the latest report available as of February 2013 from the State Department Bureau of Consular Affairs, Office of Overseas Citizens Services. For more information, please read the *International Parental Child Abduction* section of this book and check for updated reports online at www.travel.state.gov/abduction.

Disclaimer: The information in this flyer relating to the legal requirements of specific foreign countries is provided for general information only. Questions involving interpretation of specific foreign laws should be addressed to foreign legal counsel.

General Information: Canada is a federal state comprising ten provinces and three territories. With the exception of Quebec, all provinces or territories are based on a Common Law jurisdiction. Quebec is a civil law province or territory and its laws are codified. Each province or territory administers its own court system.

The Hague Convention: The United States is a party to the Hague Convention on the Civil Aspects of International Child Abduction (the "Hague Convention"). The Convention is an international treaty. Its purpose is to discourage international parental child abduction and to ensure that children who are abducted or wrongfully retained, are returned to their country of habitual residence.

The Convention does not address child custody, but determines the jurisdiction in which custody should be adjudicated.

The Hague Convention came into force between the United States and Canada on July 1, 1988. Therefore, Hague Convention provisions for return would apply to children abducted or retained on or after July 1, 1988. Parents and legal guardians of children taken to Canada prior to July 1, 1988 may still submit applications for access to the child under the Hague Convention.

For more information on The Hague Convention, see the *International Parental Child Abduction* section of this publication and review current reports from the U.S. Department of State at www.travel.state.gov/abduction. Each province and territory in Canada has its own Central Authority. If the whereabouts of the child is known or there is reason to believe the child is located in a specific province or territory, applications under the Hague Convention are forwarded to the Provincial Central Authority. If the child's whereabouts are not known, the applications are forwarded to the Federal Central Authority in Ottawa, Ontario. For a list of contact names and addresses for Central Authorities, review current reports online at www.travel. state.gov/abduction.

Criminal Remedies: For information on possible criminal remedies, please contact your local law enforcement authorities or the nearest office of the Federal Bureau of Investigation. Information is also available on the Internet at the web site of the U.S. Department of Justice, Office of

Juvenile Justice and Delinquency Prevention, at http://www.ojjdp.ncjrs.org.

PLEASE NOTE THAT CRIMINAL CHARGES MAY COMPLICATE A HAGUE CONVENTION CASE IN CANADA.

Canadian Federal Central Authority
Ms. Sandra Zed Finless
Justice Legal Services
Foreign Affairs
and International Trade
125 Sussex Drive, Tower C, 7th Floor
Ottawa, Ontario K1A 0G2
Tel: (613) 996-1300 or 992-6300
Fax: (613) 992-6485

Passports for Minors and the Children's Passport Issuance Alert Program: For more information on these topics, see the *International Parental Child Abduction* section of this publication and review current reports from the U.S. Department of State at www.travel.state.gov/abduction.

More Information: For further information and/or assistance in either preventing or responding to an international parental child abduction, contact the Office of Children's Issues, U.S. Department of State at (202) 736-9090 or visit its web site at www.travel.state.gov/abduction.

CAPE VERDE

Compiled from publications that were available as of February 2013 from the U.S. Department of State, the U.S. Department of Commerce, and the Central Intelligence Agency (CIA). See the introduction to this set for explanatory notes.

Official Name:
Republic of Cape Verde

PROFILE

Geography

Area: total: 4,033 sq km; country comparison to the world: 176; land: 4,033 sq km; water: 0 sq km
Major cities: Praia (capital) 125,000 (2009)
Climate: temperate; warm, dry summer; precipitation meager and erratic
Terrain: steep, rugged, rocky, volcanic

People

Nationality: noun: Cape Verdean(s); adjective: Cape Verdean
Population: 523,568 (July 2012 est.)
Population growth rate: 1.428% (2012 est.)
Ethnic groups: Creole (mulatto) 71%, African 28%, European 1%
Religions: Roman Catholic (infused with indigenous beliefs), Protestant (mostly Church of the Nazarene)
Languages: Portuguese (official), Crioulo (a blend of Portuguese and West African words)
Literacy: definition: age 15 and over can read and write; total population: 84.3%; male: 89.3%; female: 79.4% (2010 est.)
Health: life expectancy at birth: total population: 71 years; male: 68.78 years; female: 73.27 years (2012 est.); Infant mortality rate: total: 26.02 deaths/1,000 live births; male: 29.77 deaths/1,000 live births; female: 22.16 deaths/1,000 live births (2012 est.)
Unemployment rate: 21% (2000 est.)
Work force: 196,100 (2007)

Government

Type: republic
Independence: 5 July 1975
Constitution: 25 September 1992; a major revision on 23 November 1995 substantially increased the powers of the president; a 1999 revision created the position of national ombudsman (Provedor de Justica)
Political subdivisions: 17 municipalities (concelhos, singular—concelho); Boa Vista, Brava, Maio, Mosteiros, Paul, Porto Novo, Praia, Ribeira Brava, Ribeira Grande, Ribeira Grande de Santiago, Sal, Santa Catarina, Santa Catarina do Fogo, Santa Cruz, Sao Domingos, Sao Filipe, Sao Lourenco dos Orgaos, Sao Miguel, Sao Salvador do Mundo, Sao Vicente, Tarrafal, Tarrafal de Sao Nicolau
Suffrage: 18 years of age; universal

Economy

GDP (purchasing power parity): $2.188 billion (2012 est.); $2.078 billion (2011 est.); $1.978 billion (2010 est.); $1.88 billion (2009 est.)
GDP real growth rate: 4.8% (2012 est.); 5% (2011 est.); 5.2% (2010 est.); 3.7% (2009 est.)
GDP per capita (PPP): $4,100 (2012 est.); $4,000 (2011 est.); $3,900 (2010 est.); $3,700 (2009 est.)
Natural resources: salt, basalt rock, limestone, kaolin, fish, clay, gypsum
Agriculture products: bananas, corn, beans, sweet potatoes, sugarcane, coffee, peanuts; fish
Industries: food and beverages, fish processing, shoes and garments, salt mining, ship repair
Exports: $205.1 million (2012 est.); $191.4 million (2011 est.); $135.3 million (2010 est.)
Exports—commodities: fuel, shoes, garments, fish, hides
Exports—partners: Spain 65.9%, Portugal 18.9% (2011)
Imports: $1.038 billion (2012 est.); $980.5 million (2011 est.); $814.2 million (2010 est.)
Imports—commodities: foodstuffs, industrial products, transport equipment, fuels
Imports—partners: Portugal 37%, Netherlands 25.4%, Spain 7%, Italy 5.2%, China 5.2% (2011)
Debt—external: $741.3 million (31 December 2012 est.); $657.7 million (31 December 2011 est.); $652.5 million
Exchange rates: Cape Verdean escudos (CVE) per US dollar; 86.42 (2012 est.); 79.323 (2011 est.); 83.259 (2010 est.); 79.38 (2009)

GEOGRAPHY

The Cape Verde Islands are located in the mid-Atlantic Ocean some 450 kilometers (about 300 mi.) off the west coast of Africa. The archipelago includes 10 islands and 5 islets, divided into the windward (Barlavento) and leeward (Sotavento) groups. The main islands in the Barlavento group are Santo Antao, Sao Vicente, Santa Luzia, Sao Nicolau, Sal, and Boa Vista; those of the Sotavento group include Maio, Santiago, Fogo, and Brava. All islands but Santa Luzia are inhabited.

Three islands—Sal, Boa Vista, and Maio—generally are level and very dry. Mountains higher than 1,280 meters (4,200 ft.) are found on Santiago, Fogo, Santo Antao, and Sao Nicolau.

Sand carried by high winds has created spectacular rock formations on all islands, especially the windward ones. Sheer, jagged cliffs rise from the sea on several of the mountainous islands. Natural vegetation is sparse in the uplands and coast, but interior valleys support denser growth. Rainfall is irregular, and the archipelago suffers periodic droughts and consequent food shortages. The average precipitation per year in Praia is 24 centimeters (9.5 in.). During the winter, storms blowing from the Sahara sometimes cloud the sky, but sunny days are the norm year round.

PEOPLE

The Cape Verde archipelago was uninhabited until the Portuguese discovered the islands in 1456. Enslaved Africans were brought to the islands to work on Portuguese plantations. They were joined by entrepreneurs and refugees fleeing religious persecution in Europe, leading to a rich cultural and ethnic mix. The influence of African culture is most pronounced on the island of Santiago, where nearly half of the population resides. Sparse rain and few natural resources historically have induced Cape Verdeans to emigrate. It is believed that of the more than 1 million individuals of Cape Verdean ancestry, fewer than half actually live on the islands. Some 500,000 people of Cape Verdean ancestry live in the United States, mainly in New England. Portugal, Netherlands, Italy, France, Senegal, and Sao Tome and Principe also have large Cape Verdean communities.

Language

The official language is Portuguese, but Cape Verdeans also speak Cape Verdean Creole, which is based on archaic Portuguese and influenced by African and European languages.

Religion

According to the 2010 Census, the country's population is 77 percent Roman Catholic; however, an informal poll taken by local churches places this figure at more than 85 percent. The second largest religious group is the Church of the Nazarene. Other groups include Seventh-day Adventists, The Church of Jesus Christ of Latter-day Saints (Mormons), Assemblies of God, Universal Church of the Kingdom of God, and other Pentecostal and evangelical groups. There are small Baha'i communities and a small but growing Muslim community that has 6,008 members, according to government statistics.

HISTORY

In 1462, Portuguese settlers arrived at Santiago and founded Ribeira Grande (now Cidade Velha), the first permanent European settlement city in the tropics. In the 16th century, the archipelago prospered from the transatlantic slave trade. Pirates occasionally attacked the Portuguese settlements. Sir Francis Drake sacked Ribeira Grande in 1585. After a French attack in 1712, the city declined in importance relative to Praia, which became the capital in 1770.

With the decline in the slave trade, Cape Verde's early prosperity slowly vanished. However, the islands' position astride mid-Atlantic shipping lanes made Cape Verde an ideal location for re-supplying ships. Because of its excellent harbor, Mindelo (on the island of Sao Vicente) became an important commercial center during the 19th century.

Portugal changed Cape Verde's status from a colony to an overseas province in 1951 in an attempt to blunt growing nationalism. Nevertheless, in 1956, Amilcar Cabral, a Cape Verdean, and a group of Cape Verdeans and Guinea-Bissauans organized (in Guinea-Bissau) the clandestine African Party for the Independence of Guinea-Bissau and Cape Verde (PAIGC), which demanded improvement in economic, social, and political conditions in Cape Verde and Portuguese Guinea and formed the basis of the two nations' independence movement. Moving its headquarters to Conakry, Guinea in 1960, the PAIGC began an armed rebellion against Portugal in 1961. Acts of sabotage eventually grew into a war in Portuguese Guinea that pitted 10,000 Soviet bloc-supported PAIGC soldiers against 35,000 Portuguese and African troops.

By 1972, the PAIGC controlled much of Portuguese Guinea despite the presence of the Portuguese troops, but the organization did not attempt to disrupt Portuguese control in Cape Verde. Portuguese Guinea declared independence in 1973 and was granted de jure independence in 1974. Following the April 1974 revolution in Portugal, the PAIGC became an active political movement in Cape Verde. In December 1974, the PAIGC and Portugal signed an agreement providing for a transitional government composed of Portuguese and Cape Verdeans. On June 30, 1975, Cape Verdeans elected a National Assembly, which received the instruments of independence from Portugal on July 5, 1975.

Immediately following the November 1980 coup in Guinea-Bissau, relations between Cape Verde and Guinea-Bissau became strained. Cape Verde abandoned its hope for unity with Guinea-Bissau and formed the African Party for Indepen-

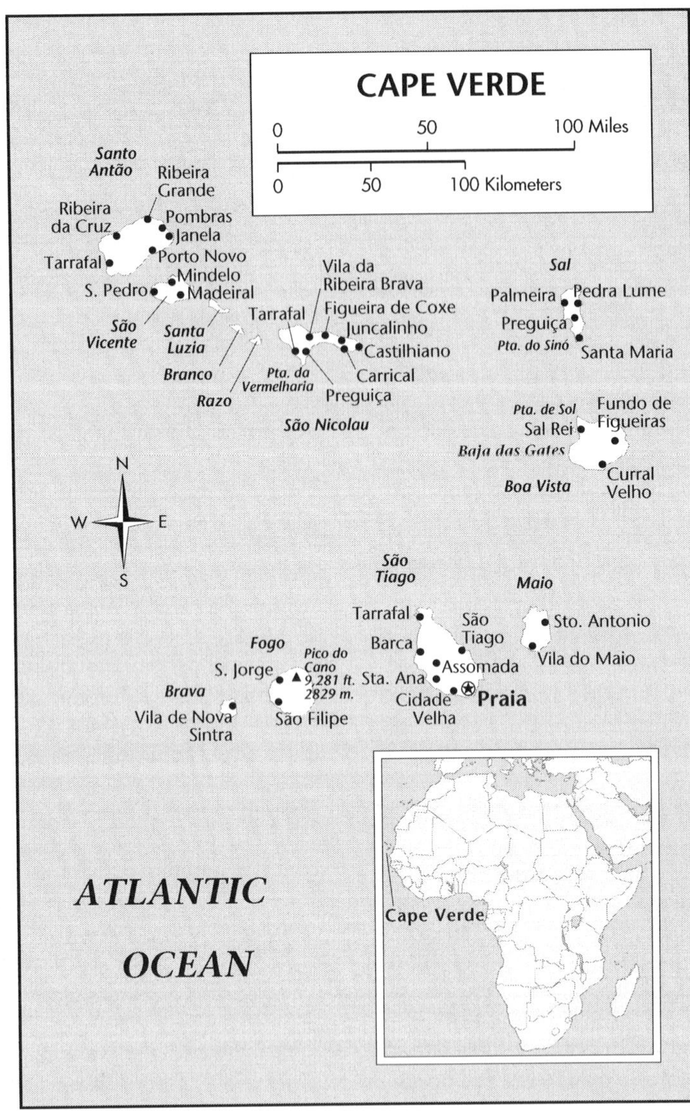

dence of Cape Verde (PAICV). The PAICV and its predecessor established a one-party system and ruled Cape Verde from independence until 1990.

Responding to growing pressure for pluralistic democracy, the PAICV called an emergency congress in February 1990 to discuss proposed constitutional changes to end one-party rule. Opposition groups came together to form the Movement for Democracy (MPD) in Praia in April 1990. Together, they campaigned for the right to contest the presidential election scheduled for December 1990. The one-party state was abolished September 28, 1990, and the first multi-party elections were held in January 1991. The MPD won a majority of the seats in the National Assembly, and MPD presidential candidate Mascarenhas Monteiro defeated the PAICV's candidate with 73.5% of the votes. Legislative elections in December 1995 increased the MPD majority in the National Assembly. The party won 50 of the National Assembly's 72 seats. A February 1996 presidential election returned President Mascarenhas Monteiro to office.

Legislative elections in January 2001 returned power to the PAICV, with the PAICV holding 40 of the National Assembly seats, MPD 30, and Party for Democratic Convergence (PCD) and Party for Labor and Solidarity (PTS) 1 each. In February 2001, the PAICV-supported presidential candidate, Pedro Pires, defeated former MPD leader Carlos Veiga. In 2006, the PAICV won legislative elections again, and Pires was re-elected as President.

GOVERNMENT AND POLITICAL CONDITIONS

Cape Verde is a multiparty parliamentary democracy in which constitutional powers are shared between the newly elected (in August) head of state, President Jorge Carlos Fonseca, and Prime Minister Jose Maria Neves, who is serving a third term after his party won the parliamentary elections in February. President Fonseca was elected to a five-year term in generally free and fair elections. The Supreme Court and the National Electoral Commission also declared the 2011 nationwide legislative elections generally free and fair. There continue to be isolated instances in which elements of the security forces acted independently of civilian control.

Recent Elections

In the 2011 legislative elections, individuals and parties were free to declare their candidates. The ruling African Party for the Independence of Cape Verde (PAICV) won 38 seats in the National Assembly with approximately 52 percent of the vote; the main opposition party, Movement for Democracy (MpD), won 32 seats with 42 percent; and the Union for a Democratic and Independent Cape Verde won the remaining two seats with 4 percent. International observers characterized these elections as generally free and fair. The presidential election also was held in 2011.

Economic Community of West African States and African Union election observers characterized these elections as free, transparent, and credible. However, they noted some irregularities, including cases of pressuring voters near polling stations and also of vote buying.

Jorge Carlos Fonseca, the candidate supported by the opposition MpD, won the election with approximately 54 percent of the vote, while Manuel Inocencio Sousa, the candidate supported by the PAICV, received 46 percent of votes.

Political Parties: Political parties acted without restriction or external interference. Individuals could declare their candidacies and parties could select their candidates without interference.

Participation of Women and Minorities: Of the 72 National Assembly seats, women held 19, and there were eight women working in cabinet-level positions in government ministries out of 21 such positions. Women filled three of eight seats on the SCJ.

Principal Government Officials

Last Updated: 1/31/2013

Pres.: **Jorge Carlos de Almeida FONSECA**
Prime Min.: **Jose Maria Pereira NEVES**
Min. of Communication: **Maria Fernanda TAVARES Fernandes**
Min. of Culture: **Mario Lucio Matias de SOUSA Mendes**
Min. of Defense: **Jorge TOLENTINO**
Min. of Education & Sports: **Fernanda Maria de BRITO Marques**
Min. of Environment, Housing, & Territorial Admin.: **Sara Maria Duarte LOPES**
Min. of Finance & Planning: **Cristina Isabel Lopes da Silva Monteiro DUARTE**
Min. of Fisheries: **Adalberto Filomeno Carvalho Santos VIEIRA**
Min. of External Relations: **Victor BORGES**
Min. of Health: **Maria Cristina Lopes Almeida FONTES Lima**
Min. of Infrastructure & Maritime Economy: **Jose Maria Fernandes da VEIGA**
Min. of Internal Admin.: **Marisa Helena do Nascimento MORAIS**
Min. of Justice: **Jose Carlos Lopes CORREIA**
Min. of Labor, Youth, & Human Services: **Janira Isabel Fonseca Hopffer ALMADA**
Min. of National Defense: **Jorge Homero TOLENTINO**
Min. of Parliamentary Business: **Rui Mendes SEMEDO**
Min. of Public Admin.: **Romeu Fonseca MODESTO**
Min. of Rural Affairs: **Eva Verona Teixeira ORTET**
Min. of Secondary Schools, Science, & Innovation: **Antonio Leao de Aguair CORREIA E SILVA**
Min. of Social Development & Family: **Felisberto Alves VIEIRA**
Min. of Tourism, Industry, & Energy: **Humberto Santos de BRITO**
Sec. of State for Foreign Affairs: **Jorge Alberto da Silva BORGES**
Governor, Central Bank: **Carlos BURGO**
Ambassador to the US: **Fatima Lima VEIGA**
Permanent Representative to the UN, New York: **Antonio Pedro Monteiro LIMA**

ECONOMY

The economy is service oriented with commerce, transport, tourism, and public services accounting for about three-fourths of GDP. This island economy suffers from a poor natural resource base, including serious water shortages exacerbated by cycles of long-term drought and poor soil for agriculture on several of the islands.

Although about 40% of the population lives in rural areas, the share of food production in GDP is low. About 82% of food must be imported. The fishing potential, mostly lobster and tuna, is not fully exploited. Cape Verde annually runs a high trade deficit financed by foreign aid and remittances from its large pool of emigrants; remittances supplement GDP by more than 20%. Despite the lack of resources, sound economic management has produced steadily improving incomes.

Continued economic reforms are aimed at developing the private sector and attracting foreign investment to diversify the economy and mitigate high unemployment. Future prospects depend heavily on the maintenance of aid flows, the encouragement of tourism, remittances, and the momentum of the government's development program. Cape Verde became a member of the WTO in July 2008.

Labor Conditions

The legal minimum age for work is 15 years, and the minimum age for hazardous work is 18. According to the labor code, children ages 15 to 18 are not allowed to work more than 38 hours a week or more than seven hours a day. Children under 15, according to the constitution, can work only in agriculture; as part of an apprenticeship or training program; or to help support the family. Children 16 to 18 are allowed to work overtime in an emergency. However, in these cases the children cannot work more than two hours a day, and these extra hours cannot exceed 30 hours a year. Several laws prohibit child labor, but enforcement was not consistent. Barriers, mostly cultural, remained to the effective implementation of these laws. For example, not all citizens see children working to help support their families as a negative thing, especially in small, remote communities. There is no official data on child labor. Child labor occurred mainly in the informal sector.

The law does not stipulate a minimum wage. The government defines the poverty income level as 105 escudos ($1.25) a day. The law stipulates a maximum of eight hours per day and 44 hours work per week. The law requires rest periods, the length depending on sector, and that the minimum rest period be 12 hours between workdays. The law also provides for daily and annual overtime hours granted in exceptional circumstances. The law states that a worker is entitled to 22 days of paid vacation.

Overtime must be compensated with at least time and a half. Work done on holidays must be compensated with double pay.

In general, it is the responsibility of the employer to ensure the workplace is healthy and hygienic. Although companies tended to respect laws on working hours, many employees such as domestic workers, health professionals, farmers, fishermen, and commercial workers commonly worked for longer periods of time than the law allows. Some sources stated it was "likely" foreign migrant workers were more often exploited than others.

U.S.-CAPE VERDEAN RELATIONS

The United States and Cape Verde have strong historical roots. As early as the 1740's, U.S. whaling ships began recruiting crews from the islands of Brava and Fogo, and other ships from the American colonies routinely anchored in Cape Verdean ports to trade. The tradition of emigration to the United States began at that time and continues today. Some 4,000 American citizens now reside in the country, while Cape Verde's Diaspora in the United States (primarily Massachusetts and Rhode Island) almost rivals the islands' current population of over 500,000.

The first U.S. consulate in sub-Saharan Africa was established in Cape Verde in 1818. The United States established diplomatic relations with Cape Verde in 1975, following its independence from Portugal. Cape Verde was under one-party rule from independence until 1990; the first multiparty elections were held in 1991. A model of democratic governance, the country enjoys relatively high literacy rates, high per capita income, and positive health indicators. Cape Verde has few natural resources, although fish and shellfish are plentiful. The economy is service-oriented, notably tourism.

Relations between the United States and Cape Verde are cordial. Cape Verde is one of Africa's success stories and an important U.S. partner in West Africa. Its strategic location means that Cape Verde is increasingly at the crossroads of the transatlantic narcotics trade. The country has cooperated with U.S. law enforcement officials to fight drug trafficking. Top U.S. priorities in Cape Verde are maritime security, domain awareness, and border control, as well as the crosscutting areas of bilateral engagement and development.

U.S. Assistance to Cape Verde

Given that Cape Verde has the best development indicators of any country in the region and has become a lower middle-income country, U.S. assistance is more focused and limited. There is no bilateral USAID program.

In October 2010, Cape Verde became the first African state—and the second worldwide—to complete its first Millennium Challenge Corporation (MCC) Compact (for $110 million, signed in July 2005), which strengthened the investment climate, reformed the financial sector and public policy, increased agricultural productivity, built or rebuilt roads, bridges, and ports; and improved public access to markets, jobs, and social services. On February 10, 2012, Cape Verde signed a second MCC Compact for $66.2 million, which is focused on water, sanitation, and land management reforms. Limited U.S. security, counternarcotics, and law enforcement assistance seeks to build the capacity of Cape Verde's military and police to respond more effectively to various maritime security challenges.

Bilateral Economic Relations

Cape Verde is eligible for preferential trade benefits under the African Growth and Opportunity Act. U.S. exports to Cape Verde include poultry, low-value shipments, vehicles, machinery, and perfumery and cosmetics. U.S. imports from Cape Verde include machinery, rum and tafia, prepared meats and fish, toys and sports equipment, and baking-related goods. Cape Verde and the United States have signed an Open Skies agreement to facilitate air travel safety and expansion, which have led to the establishment of direct flights to and from Boston. Lacking natural resources and fresh water, Cape Verde has become a global leader in solar and wind energy and has sought expanded ties with American companies to develop these renewable resources.

Cape Verde's Membership in International Organizations

Cape Verde and the United States belong to a number of the same international organizations, including the United Nations, International Monetary Fund, World Bank, and World Trade Organization.

Bilateral Representation

Cape Verde maintains an embassy in the United States at 3415 Massachusetts Avenue, NW, Washington DC 20007 (tel. 202-965-6820).

Principal U.S. Embassy Officials

Last Updated: 1/14/2013

PRAIA (E) Rua Abilio Macedo, No. 6, Plateau, (238) 260-8900, Fax (238) 261-1355, INMARSAT Tel 683-135898/9, Workweek: Mon-Fri 8:00 a.m.-12:30p.m./1:30–5:00 p.m., Website: http://capeverde.usembassy.gov/

AMB OMS:	Ronald S. Collins
HRO:	Alvin C. Thomas
MGT:	Alvin C. Thomas
POL/ECON:	Jason Hughes
POSHO:	Thomas Marotta
SDO/DATT:	LTC Matthew Sousa
AMB:	Adrienne S. O'Neal
CON:	Robert Dahlke
DCM:	Pedro G. Erviti
PAO:	Rebecca Marquez
GSO:	Thomas Marotta
RSO:	Thad Osterhout
CLO:	Marco Marquez
FMO:	Alvin C. Thomas
ICASS Chair:	Larry Blake
IMO:	Neil Brans
IRS:	Kathy Beck
LEGATT:	Ralph Hope

TRAVEL

Consular Information Sheet

August 9, 2012

Country Description: The Republic of Cape Verde is a developing country that consists of nine inhabited and several uninhabited volcanic islands off the western coast of Africa. Most islands (Santiago, Sao Vicente, Santo Antao, Sao Nicolau, Fogo and Brava) are rugged and mountainous; three (Sal, Maio, and Boa Vista) are flat, desert islands with vast white sand beaches. Praia, the capital and largest city (with a population of 140,000), is on the island of Santiago. Cape Verde's major shipping port and second-largest city, Mindelo (population 75,000), is on the island of São Vicente. Two languages are spoken widely in Cape Verde: Portuguese (the official language, spoken by many but not all Cape Verdeans) and Cape Verdean Crioulo (a mixture of Portuguese and African languages). While the tourist industry brings ever-growing numbers of visitors, tourist facilities on most of the islands remain limited. Sal and Boa Vista islands, however, each have a well- developed tourism infrastructure and extensive nonstop flight connections via charter to various European airports.

Cape Verde enjoys a stable, democratic parliamentary government, with a popularly elected president and a unicameral national assembly (of 72 members), as well as a prime minister who leads the majority party in parliament and heads the government. At present, the presidency and parliament are controlled by rival political parties. The judicial system consists of the national supreme court in Praia and municipal courts throughout the islands.

Smart Traveler Enrollment Program (STEP)/Embassy Locations: If you plan either to visit or reside in Cape Verde, please take the time to inform the Embassy of your plans. If you enroll in the Smart Traveler Enrollment Program (STEP), we can keep you up to date with important safety and security announcements. Enrolling in STEP will also help your friends and family get in touch with you in an emergency.

Embassy Praia
Address: Rua Abilio Macedo 6, Praia, Santiago, Cape Verde
Telephone: 238-260-8900 (general switchboard)
238-260-8948 (American Citizen Services)
Emergency after-hours telephone: 238-991-3325
Facsimile: 238-261-1355

Entry/Exit Requirements for U.S. Citizens: A U.S. passport and a Cape Verdean visa are required. Two types of visas are available: a single-entry visa valid for up to 90 days or a multiple-entry visa valid for five years. You can apply for a visa at the Cape Verdean Embassy in Washington, DC (3415 Massachusetts Avenue NW, Washington DC 20007, tel. 202-965-6820) or the Cape Verdean Consulate General in Boston, MA (607 Boylston Street, 4th Floor, Boston, MA 02116, tel. 617-353-0014). Visit the website of the U.S. Embassy to Cape Verde for the most current visa information.

Alternatively, if you are unable to travel to the Cape Verdean Embassy or Consulate, you may apply for a visa upon arrival at one of the country's four international airports (Nelson Mandela/Praia, Cesaria Evora / Mindelo, Amilcar Cabral/Sal and Aristides Pereira/Boa Vista). The current fee for such a visa is 2500 CVE (also payable in U.S. dollars) but is subject to change.

In theory, Visa credit cards (no Mastercard or American Express) are accepted, but intermittent power cuts in airport terminals often make electronic processing of credit card transactions impossible. We therefore strongly advise being prepared to pay in U.S. currency.

World Health Organization (WHO) vaccination cards are not required upon entry via flights from the U.S. However, the Cape Verdean Health Ministry intermittently imposes such a requirement on persons, including U.S. citizens, arriving on flights from Senegal or other West African countries. Outbreaks of malaria and dengue fever in recent years have prompted such measures. If you plan any such West African travel en route to to Cape Verde, you should ensure that you have your WHO card up to date.

The U.S. Department of State is unaware of any HIV/AIDS entry restrictions for visitors to or foreign residents of Cape Verde.

Threats to Safety and Security: Visitors traveling to Cape Verde who wish to participate in water sports, swimming, boating, and fishing should exercise extreme caution since the tides and currents around the islands are very strong. Several small fishing boats have been lost at sea in recent years, an inter-island ferry sank in 2009, and drownings occur each year even on the beaches in Praia.

Cape Verde, similar to Hawaii, is an archipelago of volcanic islands. Although volcanoes on most of the islands are now inactive, seismologists still consider the entire island of Fogo to be an active volcano; its last eruption occurred in 1995. Future eruptions remain a threat, as do earth tremors throughout the islands, especially on Fogo, Brava, and Santo Antão, and beneath the ocean channels that separate them. General information about natural disaster preparedness is available via the Internet from the U.S. Federal Emergency Management Agency.

National parliamentary and presidential elections in 2011, including campaign rallies and demonstrations, were peaceful. However, the Embassy advises you to avoid crowds at local festivals, cultural events, etc. to minimize exposure to pick-pockets or involvement in disturbances caused by the widespread availability of alcohol.

Stay up to date by:

- Bookmarking our Bureau of Consular Affairs website, which contains the current Travel Warnings and Travel Alerts as well as the Worldwide Caution.

- Following us on Twitter and the Bureau of Consular Affairs page on Facebook as well.
- Downloading our free Smart Traveler IPhone App to have travel information at your fingertips.
- Calling 1-888-407-4747 toll-free within the U.S. and Canada, or a regular toll line, 1-202-501-4444, from other countries.
- Taking some time before travel to consider your personal security.

Crime: Petty thievery and burglary are common in Cape Verde, especially in marketplaces, and at festivals, street fairs and public gatherings. Criminals do not necessarily target U.S. citizens, but rather anyone perceived to be affluent, regardless of nationality. Often the perpetrators of petty theft and pickpocketing are gangs of street children, so visitors should avoid groups of children who appear to have no adult supervision. Muggings occur often, particularly at night and in more isolated areas, and increasingly involve violence. The perpetrators are predominantly males between the ages of 14 and 25 operating in groups of two or three to attack their victims. Due to inadequate lighting in many public areas, often caused by rolling power cuts in urban neighborhoods, you should be especially vigilant after dark, carry a small flashlight to illuminate your path, never go out alone, keep vehicle doors and windows locked, and avoid isolated places.

National police statistics showing a decrease in crime in general in Cape Verde conflict with a public perception that crime is actually growing, particularly in the cities of Praia and Mindelo. This perception has been fueled by intense media coverage, a marked uptick in violent(often drug-related) robberies, physical assaults and murders. Over the past two years, there have been several murders and attempted murders, including some on the tourist islands of Sal and Boa Vista, although none have targeted U.S. citizens.

The Embassy emphasizes the particular dangers of using hillside stairways connecting neighborhoods in Praia and many other Cape Verdean cities and towns. These stairways, although offering convenient shortcuts through hilly terrain, have been scenes of some of the most notorious assaults in recent months, even in broad daylight with many people present. The Embassy strongly advises against using these any time of day.

As reported in the Department of State's Country Reports on Human Rights Practices, domestic abuse against women is widespread in Cape Verde. Although the Cape Verdean national assembly adopted a law criminalizing it in July 2010, implementing legislation remains a work in progress. Counterfeit and pirated goods, although widely available in street markets in Praia, Mindelo and elsewere, are nevertheless illegal in both Cape Verde and the U.S. U.S. citizens who buy them risk legal penalties under Cape Verdean law.

Victims of Crime: If you or someone you know becomes the victim of a crime in Cape Verde or elsewhere outside the U.S., you should contact the local police and the nearest U.S. embassy or consulate. We can:

- Replace a stolen passport.
- Help you find appropriate medical care if you are the victim of violent crimes such as assault or rape.
- Put you in contact with the appropriate police authorities, and if you want us to, we can contact family members or a friend.
- Help you understand the local criminal justice process and direct you to local attorneys, although it is important to remember that local authorities are responsible for investigating and prosecuting the crime.

The local equivalent to the "911" emergency line in Cape Verde is: 132 (police) and 131 (fire).

Criminal Penalties: While you are traveling in Cape Verde, you are subject to its laws even if you are a U.S. citizen. Foreign laws and legal systems can be vastly different than our own. In some places,you may be taken in for questioning if you don't have your passport with you. In some places, driving under the influence could land you immediately in jail. These criminal penalties will vary from country to country. There are also some things that might be legal in the country you visit, but still illegal in the United States, and you can be prosecuted under U.S. law if you buy pirated goods. Engaging in sexual conduct with children or using or disseminating child pornography in a foreign country is a crime prosecutable in the United States. If you break local laws in Cape Verde, your U.S. passport won't help you avoid arrest or prosecution. It's very important to know what's legal and what's not wherever you go.

Persons violating Cape Verdean laws, even unknowingly, may be expelled, arrested, or imprisoned. Penalties for possessing, using, or trafficking in illegal drugs in Cape Verde are severe, and convicted offenders can expect long jail sentences and heavy fines.

Arrest notifications in host country: Based on the Vienna Convention on Consular Relations, if you are arrested in Cape Verde, you have the option to request that the police, prison officials, or other authorities alert the nearest U.S. embassy or consulate of your arrest, and to have communications from you forwarded to the nearest U.S. embassy or consulate. To ensure that the United States is aware of you circumstances in the event of an arrest, request that the police and prison officials notify the nearest U.S. embassy or consulate as soon as you are arrested or detained overseas.

Special Circumstances: Inter-island travel is generally via ferry or 45-seat propeller planes. The islands of Brava and Santo Antao, however, are only accessible by boat. Not all flights between islands are direct, even if originally scheduled as such, and airline services may be delayed, re-routed or cancelled due to poor visibility from dust or rain and related safety concerns. During peak travel seasons (summer and Christmas holidays), air travelers arriving from abroad into Praia and other major airports for connecting flights to other islands may experience luggage delays at their final destination because of the limited carrying capacity of inter-island aircraft. Prudence dictates having a change of clothing and all vital materials (including medications) in your carry-on luggage to tide you over for the first 24-48 hours in country.

There is regular daily inter-island ferry service between Santo Antão and São Vicente. Ferry services are also available between Santiago, Brava, and Fogo but do do not operate daily and the service schedules frequently change. Those planning to travel by ferry should plan well in advance, and confirm a few days before departure that the ferry service is still operating. Regardless of whether your inter-island travel is by air or sea, be aware that poor weather and sea conditions often cause last minute delays or cancellations.

CV Telecom is currently the only provider for fixed-line voice, data service, and Internet service (dial-up, ISDN, and ADSL). Mobile phone service is on the GSM standard and is available from both CV Telecom and a competitor called T Mais. Only major cities and towns have Internet cafes, and international telecommunications services in Cape Verde are dependent on transatlantic fiber-optic cables. Visitors who need reliable communication to other countries may want to consider bringing satellite-based voice and/or data equipment. The international country code for Cape Verde is 238. Fixed and mobile line numbers all have seven digits. Land lines all begin with the number "2," and mobile numbers, which all began with the number "9" until the end of 2009, may now begin with either "5" or "9." Telephone connections are good, but calls made to numbers outside the archipelago are very expensive.

Accessibility: While in Cape Verde, individuals with disabilities may find accessibility and accommodation considerably more limited than in the United States. The country's rugged terrain, the widespread use of cobblestone streets and pathways, and the frequency of power outages that shut down elevators in large urban buildings all constitute significant hardships for persons with limited mobility. Although the Cape Verdean constitution guarantees that persons with disabilities will receive priority in the provision of government services and stipulates that public buildings must be accessible to the disabled, in reality few such accommodations have been made. However, the country does have national advocacy organizations for the visually and hearing impaired that actively seek to expand such accommodations.

Medical Facilities and Health Information: Medical facilities in Cape Verde are limited, and despite an extensive network of local pharmacies some medications are in short supply or otherwise unavailable. The country's largest hospitals (all public) are in Praia and Mindelo, but smaller public health centers and private medical clinics, of variable quality in both personnel and equipment, are located throughout the country. The islands of Brava and Santo Antão do not have airports, so air evacuation from them in the event of a medical emergency is impossible.

Malaria exists in Cape Verde, but is mainly limited to the island of Santiago. Nationwide, malaria is far less prevalent than in mainland African countries with approximately 20-40 cases occurring annually, almost always among recent West African migrants who contracted the illness before arriving in the islands. Although many expatriates do not believe there is a need for malaria prophylaxis, it is important to be aware that there is an elevated risk of contracting the disease from July to December, especially during the rainiest months (August-October).

In 2009, Cape Verde experienced its first-ever epidemic of dengue fever, another mosquito-borne illness, the spread of which was facilitated by an unusually heavy rainy season. Unlike malaria, no prophylaxis exists against dengue fever. Ultimately, 21,000 cases were reported, affecting all nine inhabited islands, with six fatalities nationwide. Since then, the number of dengue cases has dropped drastically. In 2010, the Cape Verdean government received notification of 405 cases, 16 of which were confirmed by a laboratory. No deaths were reported. No final data has been received for 2011. At least two cases were reported in 2011, with no confirmed deaths.

Even with reduced risk of dengue as a public health threat in Cape Verde, travelers are advised to minimize exposure to both dengue and malaria by taking precautions against mosquito bites, which are most common at dawn and dusk, particularly from July to December. Like malaria, no vaccine exists for dengue, so travelers in Cape Verde who exhibit symptoms as described on the CDC's dengue fact sheet should immediately seek medical attention. Depending on how long you are in Cape Verde, symptoms may not present themselves until after you return to the United States. Since medical professionals in the United States often do not test patients for either illness, make sure you tell the doctor evaluating your symptoms that you have recently been in a country where both malaria and dengue fever exist.

If you need a doctor in Cape Verde, a list of medical providers and hospitals is available on the website of the U.S. Embassy in Praia.

You can find detailed information on vaccinations and other health precautions on the CDC website. For information about outbreaks of infectious diseases abroad, consult the World Health Organization (WHO) website. The WHO website also contains additional health information for travelers, including detailed country-specific health information.

Medical Insurance: You can't assume your insurance will go with you when you travel. It's very important to find out BEFORE you leave whether or not your medical insurance will cover you overseas. You need to ask your insurance company two questions:

- Does my policy apply when I'm out of the United States?
- Will it cover emergencies like a trip to a foreign hospital or a medical evacuation?

In many places, doctors and hospitals still expect payment in cash at the time of service. Your regular U.S. health insurance may not cover doctor and hospital visits in other countries. If your policy doesn't go with you when you travel, it's a very good idea to take out another one for your trip.

Traffic Safety and Road Conditions: While in Cape Verde, or any foreign country, U.S. citizens may encounter road conditions that differ significantly from those in the United States. The information below concerning Cape Verde is provided for general reference only, and may not apply in a particular location or circumstance.

Cape Verde has an extensive road system. Asphalt roads used to be relatively uncommon, except for airport connector roads. However, on the islands of Santiago, Sal, and São Vicente, many urban and rural roads are now asphalt. On the other islands (Fogo, Brava, Maio, São Nicolau, and Boa Vista), the roads are still narrow, winding, and mostly cobblestone, though there are ongoing projects to convert them to asphalt. Although a clear improvement in terms of the country's overall transportation infrastructure, the new asphalt roads often lack speed bumps and as a result enable a degree of reckless, high-speed driving previously unseen in Cape Verde. During the rainy season, cobblestone roads are especially slippery, and mud and rockslides are common on roads that cut through mountains. Houses are often located adjacent to roadways, and drivers must be on the lookout for pedestrians, especially children, as well as herds of livestock. Roads and streets are often unlit, so driving at night is hazardous. Most accidents result from aggressive driving, excessive speed, passing in blind curves, and/or on inclines or declines in the rain.. Driving while under the influence of alcohol is a problem in Cape Verde. The peak time for drunk drivers is on Sundays, but one can encounter them at any time. Also, extreme caution toward both pedestrians and other drivers should be exercised after celebrations, festivals and open-air concerts as well as during holiday periods, such as Christmas, New Year's Eve and Mardi Gras ("Carnaval").

Full-service gas stations (no self-service) are available and quite modern, often with their own convenience stores. Taxis and buses generally offer clean, dependable service on all islands. Bus service in Praia is reliable and inexpensive, and most buses are fairly new. Intra-island service usually consists of minivans (typically a Toyota Hiace) or converted pickup trucks that have benches along the edges of the pickup bed. However, intra-island service can be dangerous because some drivers overload their vehicles, exceed the speed limit, or drive after drinking alcohol. Before entering any vehicle, riders should pay close attention to the appearance and behavior of the driver.

In Cape Verde, traffic moves on the right side of the road, as in the United States. At intersections, the vehicle on the right has the right-of-way, but at roundabouts (traffic circles), cars inside the circle have the right-of-way. Under Cape Verdean law, seat belts must be worn at all times by the driver as well as the person in the front passenger seat. Children under 12 must sit in the back seat. Motorcyclists must wear crash helmets and use headlights at all times. Bicycling is common in Praia and in some other areas. The use of helmets, gloves, and /or other protective gear while bicycling is more widespread than in mainland African countries but not governed by local laws/regulations and not at all universal. Pedestrian striped crosswalks are common in Praia, Mindelo, and other large cities/towns, and are widely used and heeded by motorists.

Aviation Safety Oversight: The U.S. Federal Aviation Administration (FAA) has assessed the government of Cape Verde's Civil Aviation Authority as being in compliance with International Civil Aviation Organization (ICAO) aviation safety standards for oversight of Cape Verde's air carrier operations. Further information may be found on the FAA's safety assessment page.

Children's Issues: Please see the U.S. Dept. of State Office of Children's Issues web pages on intercountry adoption and international parental child abduction.

Intercountry Adoption

Interim Notice on Adopting in Cape Verde
September 2011

The Hague Adoption Convention entered into force in Cape Verde on January 1, 2010. Any adoptions finalized in Cape Verde since that date by U.S. citizens seeking to obtain U.S. immigrant visas for the adopted children are subject to the U.S. Hague Adoption Convention process. However, Cape Verde has not yet implemented procedures for the processing of Hague Adoption cases and as such is not processing Convention intercountry adoption cases at this time.

In general, it is no longer possible for a U.S. family to complete an intercountry adoption from Cape Verde by filing a Form I-600A, Application for Advance Processing of an Orphan Petition and/or a Form I-600, Petition to Classify Orphan as an Immediate Relative, because intercountry adoption between the United States and Cape Verde are now subject to the Hague Adoption Convention. One limited exception would be for cases involving full and final adoption decrees issued in Cape Verde before the Hague Adoption Convention entered into force in Cape Verde on

January 1, 2010. Such cases could be processed for U.S. immigration purposes as non-Hague cases.

U.S. citizen families interested in adopting in Cape Verde may initiate a Hague adoption case on behalf of a child in Cape Verde by filing a Form I-800A, Application for Determination of Suitability to Adopt a Child from a Convention Country. However, U.S. citizen families should be mindful of the limited validity of the I-800A approval in choosing when to file the application. The U.S. Department of State cannot predict when Cape Verde will have procedures in place and be ready to process Convention adoption cases. In the event that the Form I-800A approval expires before Cape Verde starts processing Convention adoptions, U.S. citizen families will need to file a new Form I-800A with a new filing fee.

In addition, once implemented, the Hague procedures may include specific requirements for Cape Verde that must be addressed in the family's home study, which families filing now would not be able to anticipate or address. Families filing now could thus find themselves incurring costs for cases that will not be able to proceed before their Form I-800A approval expires or that will not completely comply with whatever requirements Cape Verde ultimately puts in place. For information on expiration of I-800A approval, see the Instructions for Form I-800A, page 10, under the heading Processing Information, in the paragraph entitled Decision.

The U.S. Embassy in Praia will continue to monitor developments and will provide information about Cape Verde's progress toward developing and implementing Hague Convention adoption procedures. As information becomes available, the Department will post it on the website, http://adoption.state.gov.

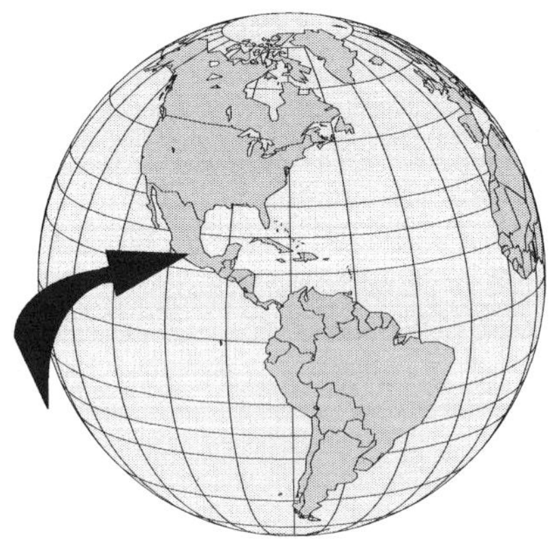

CAYMAN ISLANDS

Compiled from publications that were available as of February 2013 from the U.S. Department of State, the U.S. Department of Commerce, and the Central Intelligence Agency (CIA). See the introduction to this set for explanatory notes.

Official Name:
Cayman Islands

PROFILE

Geography

Area: total: 264 sq km; country comparison to the world: 211; land: 264 sq km; water: 0 sq km
Major cities: George Town (capital) 32,000 (2009)
Climate: tropical marine; warm, rainy summers (May to October) and cool, relatively dry winters (November to April)
Terrain: low-lying limestone base surrounded by coral reefs

People

Nationality: noun: Caymanian(s); adjective: Caymanian
Population: 52,560 (July 2012 est.)
Population growth rate: 2.239% (2012 est.)
Ethnic groups: mixed 40%, white 20%, black 20%, expatriates of various ethnic groups 20%
Religions: Protestant 67.7% (Church of God 25.5%, Presbyterian/United Church 9.2%, Seventh-Day Adventist 8.4%, Baptist 8.3%, Pentecostal 6.7%, Anglican 3.9%, non-denominational 5.7%), Roman Catholic 12.6%, other religions 4%, other 6.5%, none 6.1%, unspecified 3.2% (2007)
Languages: English (official) 95%, Spanish 3.2%, other 1.8% (1999 census)
Literacy: definition: age 15 and over has ever attended school; total population: 98%; male: 98%; female: 98% (1970 est.)
Health: life expectancy at birth: total population: 80.8 years; male: 78.12 years; female: 83.51 years (2012 est.); Infant mortality rate: total: 6.49 deaths/1,000 live births; male: 7.43 deaths/1,000 live births; female: 5.53 deaths/1,000 live births (2012 est.)
Unemployment rate: 4% (2008)
Work force: 39,000

Government

Type: parliamentary democracy
Independence: none
Constitution: The Cayman Islands Constitution Order 2009, 6 November 2009
Political subdivisions: 8 districts; Creek, Eastern, Midland, South Town, Spot Bay, Stake Bay, West End, Western
Suffrage: 18 years of age; universal

Economy

GDP (purchasing power parity): $2.25 billion (2008 est.); $2.23 billion (2003 est.)
GDP real growth rate: 1.1% (2008 est.); 0.9% (2004 est.)
GDP per capita (PPP): $43,800 (2004 est.)
Natural resources: fish, climate and beaches that foster tourism
Agriculture products: vegetables, fruit; livestock; turtle farming
Industries: tourism, banking, insurance and finance, construction, construction materials, furniture
Exports: $42.6 million (2012 est.); $40.5 million (2011 est.); $40.72 million (2010 est.)
Exports—commodities: turtle products, manufactured consumer goods
Imports: $796.8 million (2012 est.); $851.7 million (2011 est.); $745.3 million (2010 est.)
Imports—commodities: foodstuffs, manufactured goods, fuels
Debt—external: $70 million (1996)
Exchange rates: Caymanian dollars (KYD) per US dollar; 0.83 (2012 est.); 0.83 (2011 est.); 0.83 (2010 est.)

PEOPLE

The Cayman Islands remained largely uninhabited until the 17th century. A variety of people settled on the islands, including pirates, refugees from the Spanish Inquisition, shipwrecked sailors, deserters from Oliver Cromwell's army in Jamaica, and slaves. The majority of Caymanians are of African and British descent, with considerable interracial mixing.

HISTORICAL HIGHLIGHTS

Great Britain took formal control of the Cayman Islands, along with Jamaica, under the Treaty of Madrid in 1670. Following several unsuccessful attempts, permanent settlement of the islands began in the 1730s. The Cayman Islands historically have been popular as a tax-exempt destination. Legend has it that Caymanians in 1788 rescued the crews of a Jamaican merchant ship convoy which had struck a reef at Gun Bay and that the Caymanians were rewarded with King George III's promise to never again impose any tax.

The Cayman Islands, initially administered as a dependency of Jamaica, became an independent colony in 1959; they now are a largely self-governing British Overseas Territory.

GOVERNMENT AND POLITICAL CONDITIONS

The Cayman Islands' physical isolation under early British colonial rule allowed the development of an indigenous set of administrative and legal traditions, which were codified into a Constitution in 1959. Although still a British Overseas Territory, the islands today are self-governed in nearly all respects. The Constitution, or the Cayman Islands Constitution Order 2009, that governs the islands came into effect on November 6, 2009.

The Cayman Islands' political system is very stable, bolstered by a tradition of restrained civil governance, sustained economic prosperity, and its relative isolation from foreign policy concerns by virtue of its colonial relationship with the United Kingdom. Public discussion revolves around public sector expenditure and social services, the pace of additional economic development, and the status of the large foreign national community on the islands.

Government Structure

The Cayman Islands form a British Overseas Territory with a large measure of self-government. Under the 2009 Constitution, the islands are administered by a government that is headed by a Governor, a Legislative Assembly, and a Cabinet. The Governor is recruited from the U.K. Government Service, serves as the British government administrator, and retains responsibility for the civil service, defense, external affairs, and internal security.

The Governor also chairs the Cabinet and appoints to the Cabinet the Chief Secretary, the Attorney General, and the Financial Secretary, while the Legislative Assembly elects the Cabinet's other five members. Unlike other Caribbean Overseas Territories there is no Chief Minister but a Premier (formerly called the Leader of Government Business). The Premier is an elected politician, while the Chief Secretary is the most senior civil servant. Currently, the Premier is also the Minister of Financial Services, Tourism, and Development. Responsibility for defense and external affairs resides with the United Kingdom; however, the Chief Secretary has responsibility for the Portfolio of Internal and External affairs, and the Cayman Government may negotiate certain bilateral matters directly with foreign governments. The elected members of the Cabinet divide the remaining administrative portfolios.The 18-seat unicameral Legislative Assembly is presided over by an independent speaker. Elections are held at the discretion of the Governor at least every 4 years. Members of the Assembly may introduce bills, which, if passed, are then approved, returned, or disallowed by the Governor. The U.K. Government also reserves the right to disallow bills approved by the Governor. The four-tiered judicial system is based on English common law and colonial and local statutes. The Cayman Islands Court of Appeal is the highest court on the islands, but Her Majesty's Privy Council sitting in London may hear a final appeal.

Political Coalitions

Since 2000, there have been two official political parties: The United Democratic Party (UDP) and the People's Progressive Movement (PPM). While there has been a shift to political parties, many contending for an office still run as independents.

In May 2009 elections, the United Democratic Party (UDP) defeated the incumbent People's Progressive Movement, receiving nine of the 15 seats.

Principal Government Officials

Last Updated: 10/31/2012

Head of State: **Queen Elizabeth II**
Governor: **Duncan Taylor**
Head of Government Business: **W McKeeva Bush**

ECONOMY

With no direct taxation, the islands are a thriving offshore financial center. More than 93,000 companies were registered in the Cayman Islands as of 2008, including almost 300 banks, 800 insurers, and 10,000 mutual funds. A stock exchange was opened in 1997. Tourism is also a mainstay, accounting for about 70% of GDP and 75% of foreign currency earnings. The tourist industry is aimed at the luxury market and caters mainly to visitors from North America. Total tourist arrivals exceeded 1.9 million in 2008, with about half from the US. Nearly 90% of the islands' food and consumer goods must be imported. The Caymanians enjoy a standard of living comparable to that of Switzerland.

FOREIGN RELATIONS AND U.S.-CAYMANIAN RELATIONS

The Cayman Islands is a largely self-governing British Overseas Territory

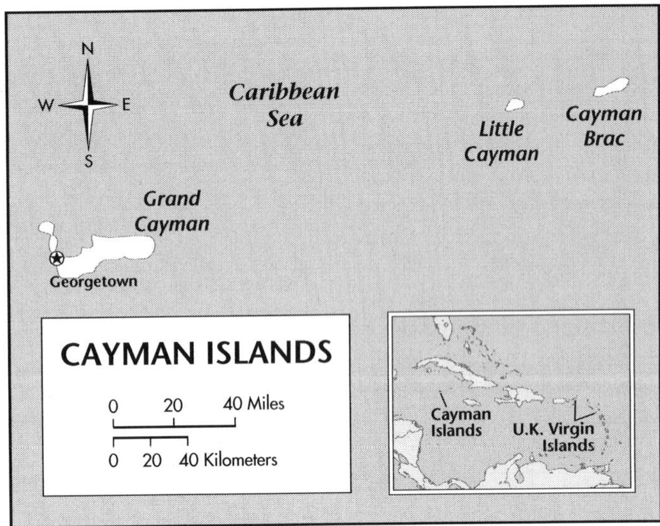

with close historic and political links to the United Kingdom and Jamaica. U.S. policy toward the United Kingdom is the basis of U.S.-Cayman Islands relations. Responsibility for defense and external affairs resides with the United Kingdom, although the Cayman Government may negotiate certain bilateral matters directly with foreign governments. With the rise in international narcotics trafficking, the Cayman Government has entered into a narcotics agreement and a mutual legal assistance treaty with the United States in order to reduce the use of its facilities for money laundering operations.

U.S. Assistance to the Cayman Islands

The United States provides no development assistance to the Cayman Islands.

Bilateral Economic Relations

The role of tourism and international finance in the Cayman Islands's economy has made the United States one of its most important trade and economic partners. The United States is a major source country for tourists visiting the Cayman Islands.

For U.S. and other foreign investors and businesses, the Cayman Islands's main appeal as a financial center is the absence of all major direct taxes, free capital movement, a minimum of government regulations, and a well-developed financial infrastructure.

The Cayman Islands's Membership in International Organizations

The United Kingdom is formally responsible for the Cayman Islands's foreign and defense policy.

Bilateral Representation

The United States does not maintain diplomatic offices in the Cayman Islands. Diplomatic relations are conducted through the U.S. Embassy in London and the British Embassy in Washington, DC. The Cayman Islands are part of the consular district administered by the U.S. Embassy in Jamaica. There also is a U.S. consular agency in the Cayman Islands to assist in providing services for U.S. citizens. The United Kingdom's embassy in the United States is at 3100 Massachusetts Avenue, NW, Washington, DC 20008; tel: 202-588-6500.

Principal U.S. Embassy Officials

Last Updated: 1/14/2013

KINGSTON (E) 142 Old Hope Road, Kingston 6, 876-702-6000, Fax 876-702-6001, Workweek: M-F; 07:15 to 16:00; most offices allow flex time; all offices staffed core hours, some staff take Friday afternoons off, working longer on other days, Website: http://kingston.usembassy.gov/

DCM OMS:	Janelle Walker
AMB OMS:	Jacqueline Lawrence
CDC:	Rachel Albalak
CG OMS:	Cheri Champ
DHS/CIS:	Adijatu Abiose
DHS/ICE:	James Stitzel
FM:	Wall, David
HRO:	Judith Glen
MGT:	Leslie Degraffenried
NAS/INL:	Gary Rex
POL/ECON:	Alexander Martschenko
POSHO:	Wall, David
SDO/DATT:	LTC Thomas Newman
AMB:	Pamela Bridgewater
CG:	David Stone
DCM:	Brown, Raymond
PAO:	Yolonda Kerney
GSO:	Lloyd Champ
RSO:	Vincent Cooper
AGR:	Margaret Bauer
AID:	Denise Herbol
APHIS:	Steve Crook
CLO:	Newman, Jade
DEA:	Gavin Kersellius
EEO:	Alexander Martschenko
FAA:	Allan B. Hurr
FMO:	Melissa Huth
ICASS Chair:	Gavin Kersellius
IMO:	Anbess Keffelew
ISO:	Cynthia Atnip
ISSO:	Anbess Keffelew
LEGATT:	Donitta Clark
State ICASS:	David Stone

TRAVEL

Consular Information Sheet

November 17, 2011

Country Description: The Cayman Islands are a British overseas territory consisting of three main islands with a total area of approximately 100 square miles and located about 500 miles west of Jamaica. There is an international airport located in Grand Cayman, and facilities for tourists are widely available. The U.S. Embassy in Kingston, Jamaica, has consular responsibility for the Cayman Islands.

Smart Traveler Enrollment Program(STEP)/Embassy Location: If you are going to live or visit the Cayman Islands, please take the time to tell our Embassy about your trip. If you enroll, we can keep you up to date with important safety and security announcements. It will also help your friends and family get in touch with you in an emergency.

U.S. Embassy Kingston
142 Old Hope Road
Kingston, Jamaica
Telephone: (876) 702-6000
Email: KingstonACS@state.gov

U.S. Consular Agency
Cayman Islands
Cayman Centre Unit B-1, 118 Dorcy Drive
George Town, Grand Cayman
Public Hours are M-F, from 8:00 a.m.-2:00 p.m.
Telephone: (345) 945-8173
E-Mail: CaymansACS@state.gov

Entry/Exit Requirements for U.S. Citizens: Visas are not required for U.S. citizens traveling to the Cayman Islands for short-term visits. U.S. citizens traveling to the Cayman Islands for work must obtain a work permit from the Department of Immigration of the Cayman Islands, telephone (345) 949-8344. There is a departure tax for travelers age twelve and older, which is regularly included in airfare. For further information, travelers may contact Cayman Islands Department of Tourism offices in Miami at (305) 599-9033, New York (212) 889-9009, Houston (713) 461-1317 and Chicago (630) 705-0650.

Although there are no express HIV/AIDS entry restrictions for visitors to the Cayman Islands, persons suffering from HIV/AIDS can be denied permission to land if a Health Officer certifies that their entry to the Islands would be dangerous to the community pursuant to Section 82 (c) of the Cayman Immigration Law (2007 Revision), which states:

The following persons, not being Caymanian or permanent residents, are prohibited immigrants—a person certified by a Health Officer to be suffering from a communicable disease that makes his entry into the Islands dangerous to the community.

Threats to Safety and Security: Following a period of more than seven months in which no homicides were reported, the Cayman Islands recently experienced a surge in gang-related criminal activity. Several murders, believed to be gang-related executions, occurred on Grand Cayman in September 2011. Local law enforcement authorities are aggressively addressing these challenges, which mostly affect the West Bay area, although at least one of the murders occurred in East Bay.

Stay up to date by bookmarking our Bureau of Consular Affairs website, which contains the current Travel Warnings and Travel Alerts as well as the Worldwide Caution. Follow us on Twitter and the Bureau of Consular Affairs page on facebook as well.

You can also call 1-888-407-4747 toll-free within the United States and Canada, or by calling a regular toll line, 1-202-501-4444, from other countries. These numbers are available from 8:00 a.m. to 8:00 p.m. Eastern Time, Monday through Friday (except U.S. federal holidays).

Take some time before travel to improve your personal security—things are not the same everywhere as they are in the United States.

Crime: The crime threat in Cayman Islands is generally considered low, although travelers should always take normal precautions when in unfamiliar surroundings. Petty theft, pick-pocketing and purse snatchings occur. A few cases involving sexual assault have been reported to the Embassy. Police in the Cayman Islands rigorously enforce laws against illegal drugs. U.S. citizens should avoid buying, selling, holding or taking illegal drugs under any circumstances. Don't buy counterfeit and pirated goods, even if they are widely available. Not only are the bootlegs illegal in the United States, if you purchase them you may also be breaking local law.

Victims of Crime: If you or someone you know becomes the victim of a crime abroad, you should contact the local police and the nearest U.S. embassy or consulate (see the Department of State's list of embassies and consulates). If your passport is stolen we can help you replace it. For violent crimes such as assault and rape, we can help you find appropriate medical care, contact family members or friends, and help them send you money if you need it. Although the investigation and prosecution of the crime are solely the responsibility of local authorities, consular officers can help you to understand the local criminal justice process and to find an attorney if you need.

The local equivalent to the "911" emergency line in the Cayman Islands is "911."

Criminal Penalties: While you are traveling in the Cayman Islands, you are subject to its laws even if you are a U.S. citizen. Foreign laws and legal systems can be vastly different than our own. In some places you may be taken in for questioning if you don't have your passport with you. In some places, it is illegal to take pictures of certain buildings. In some places driving under the influence could land you immediately in jail. These criminal penalties will vary from country to country. There are also some things that might be legal in the country you visit, but still illegal in the United States, and you can be prosecuted under U.S. law if you buy pirated goods. Engaging in sexual conduct with children or using or disseminating child pornography in a foreign country is a crime prosecutable in the United States. If you break local laws in the Cayman Islands, your U.S. passport won't help you avoid arrest or prosecution. It's very important to know what's legal and what's not where you are going.

Persons violating Caymanian laws, even unknowingly, may be expelled, arrested, or imprisoned. Penalties for possessing, using, or trafficking in illegal drugs in the Cayman Islands are severe, and convicted offenders can expect long jail sentences and heavy fines. If you are arrested in the Cayman Islands, authorities of the Cayman Islands are required to notify the nearest U.S. embassy or consulate of your arrest. If you are concerned the Department of State may not be aware of your situation, you should request the police or prison officials to notify the nearest U.S. embassy or consulate of your arrest.

Special Circumstances: Cayman Islands customs authorities may enforce strict regulations concerning temporary importation into or export from the Cayman Islands of items such as firearms of any kind, ammunition, spear guns (or pole spears or Hawaiian slings), live plants and plant cuttings. Raw fruits and vegetables are also restricted. Visitors from the United States should be aware that products made from farmed green sea turtles at the Cayman Turtle Farm Ltd. are offered for local consumption; however, the importation of genuine sea turtle products is strictly prohibited by the United States, as well as other countries that have signed the Convention on International Trade in Endangered Species. In addition, U.S. Customs prohibits the transshipment of turtle products through the United States and any products discovered will be confiscated. It is advisable to contact the Cayman Government Collector of Customs (345) 949-2473 for specific information regarding customs requirements.

The Cayman Islands, like all Caribbean countries, can be affected by hurricanes. Hurricane season runs from June 1 to November 30 each year. Hazard Management Cayman Islands is responsible for disaster preparedness and response on the islands. General information on the subject of hurricane preparedness is also available via the Internet from the U.S. Federal Emergency Management Agency (FEMA)

Accessibility: While in the Cayman Islands, individuals with disabilities may find accessibility and accommodation very different from what they find in the United States. The Cayman Islands lack comprehensive disability legislation and while many hotels and resorts well-equipped for disabled guests, other tourist facilities, such as the airport and dock, are much less so. The Cayman Islands lack a suitable dock for large passenger ships, for instance, so passengers aboard cruise vessels who wish to visit the Cayman Islands are transported to shore in smaller vessels. You may wish to consult websites and blogs that focus on accessible travel for practical information and first-hand accounts of traveling in the Cayman Islands.

Medical Facilities and Health Information: The quality of medical care in the Cayman Islands is generally comparable to that available in the United States; however, some procedures and cases requiring critical care may require medical evacuation to the United States. Several American citizens each year drown or suffer cardiac arrest while snorkeling or SCUBA diving in the Cayman Islands. These deaths may be attributed in part to tourists attempting to do more than they are trained to do or to poor physical conditioning or pre-existing medical conditions that are exacerbated when snorkeling or diving. A hyperbaric chamber is available for treatment of decompression illness. Doctors and hospitals often expect immediate payment for health services. Emergency response services in the Cayman Islands are on par with those generally available in the United States.

You can find good information on vaccinations and other health precautions, on the CDC website. For information about outbreaks of infectious diseases abroad, consult the World Health Organization (WHO) website. The WHO website also contains additional health information for travelers, including detailed country-specific health information.

Medical Insurance: You can't assume your insurance will go with you when you travel. It's very important to find out BEFORE you leave whether or not your medical insurance will cover you overseas. You need to ask your insurance company two questions:

- Does my policy apply when I'm out of the United States?
- Will it cover emergencies like a trip to a foreign hospital or a medical evacuation?

In many places, doctors and hospitals still expect payment in cash at the time of service. Your regular U.S. health insurance may not cover doctors' and hospital visits in other countries. If your policy doesn't go with you when you travel, it's a very good idea to take out another one for your trip.

Traffic Safety and Road Conditions: While in the Cayman Islands, you may encounter road conditions that differ significantly from those in the United States. The information below concerning the Cayman Islands is provided for general reference only, and may not be totally accurate in a particular location or circumstance.

As in Great Britain and its other territories, vehicles in the Cayman Islands travel on the left-hand side of the road (the opposite side compared with driving in the United States). Due to their size, the Caymans have little highway infrastructure to maintain.

Local driving standards, the risk of accidents, the availability of emergency roadside service, quality and frequency of signage, and enforcement of traffic laws, generally meet the standards of the United States. Visitors must obtain a temporary driver's license, easily granted upon presentation of a valid state driver's license and payment of a small fee, at a car rental agency or a police station. Laws against driving while intoxicated are strictly enforced, with a legal maximum blood alcohol level set at 100 milligrams per 100 milliliters of blood (equivalent to a.10 blood/alcohol level in the United States). Seatbelt laws are also enforced and require the driver and all passengers to wear seatbelts while in motion.

Aviation Safety Oversight: The U.S. Federal Aviation Administration (FAA) has assessed the government of Cayman Islands' Civil Aviation Authority as being in compliance with International Civil Aviation Organization (ICAO) aviation safety standards for oversight of Cayman Islands' air carrier operations. Further information may be found on the FAA's safety assessment page.

Children's Issues: Please see the U.S. Dept. of State Office of Children's Issues web pages on intercountry adoption and international parental child abduction.

Intercountry Adoption

February 2007

As of February 2013, the Department of State did not have country specific information pertaining to adoption from the Cayman Islands available on its Intercountry Adoption website. The information in this section was edited from previous reports. Prospective parents should read the *Intercountry Adoption* section of this book and check for current reports online at http://adoption.state.gov for the latest information.

Adoption Authority:
Department of Children and Family Services
Ground Floor, Brit Cay Building
George Town
P.O. Box 10653
Grand Cayman KY1-1006
Cayman Islands
Tel. 345-949-0290
Fax. 345-949-4167

Adoption Agencies and Attorneys: Prospective adoptive parents are advised to fully research any adoption agency or facilitator they plan to use for adoption services. For U.S.-based agencies, it is suggested that prospective adoptive parents contact the Better Business Bureau and/or the licensing office of the appropriate state government agency in the U.S. state where the agency is located or licensed.

Adoption Procedures: Prospective adoptive parents should contact the Adoption Coordinator, who works within the Department of Children and Family Services, to arrange for an initial interview. The adoption process will be explained and if everything is in order, prospective adoptive parents will be given the application packet to take away and complete.

The Cayman Islands are represented in the United States by the Embassy of the United Kingdom:

United Kingdom Embassy
3100 Massachusetts Avenue
Washington DC 20008
Telephone: 202-462-1340
Fax: 202-898-4255.

U.S. Immigration Requirements: Prospective adoptive parents are strongly encouraged to consult USCIS publication M-249, *The Immigration of Adopted and Prospective Adoptive Children*, as well as the Department of State publication, *Intercountry Adoptions.*

U.S. Embassy
142 Old Hope Rd.
Kingston 6
Jamaica, West Indies
Phone: 876-702-6000
Fax: 876-702-6018

Additional Information: Specific questions about adoption in the Cayman Islands may be addressed to the U.S. Embassy in Kingston, Jamaica. General questions regarding intercountry adoption may be addressed to the Office of Children's Issues, U.S. Department of State, CA/OCS/CI, SA-29, 4th Floor, 2201 C Street, NW, Washington, D.C. 20520-4818, toll-free Tel: 1-888-407-4747.

International Parental Child Abduction

January 2012

The information in this section has been edited from the latest report available as of February 2013 from the State Department Bureau of Consular Affairs, Office of Overseas Citizens Services. For more information, please read the *International Parental Child Abduction* section of this book and check for updated reports online at www.travel.state.gov/abduction.

General Information: Cayman Islands is a British overseas territory. The United Kingdom of Great Britain and Northern Ireland has extended the Hague Convention on the Civil Aspects of International Child Abduction 1980 to cover Bermuda, Cayman Islands, Falkland Islands, Isle of Man, and Montserrat.

For further information on the filing of a Hague application for one of these territories, please contact the appropriate case officer in the Office of Children's Issues at 202-736-9090. American citizens who travel to the British overseas territories place themselves under the jurisdiction of their local courts. American citizens planning a trip to the British overseas territories with dual national children should bear this in mind.

Custody Disputes: In the British overseas territories, if parents are legally married they share the custody of their children. If they are not married, by law the custody is granted to the mother unless there are known facts of inappropriate behavior, mental or social problems. Foreign court orders are not automatically recognized.

Enforcement of Foreign Judgments: Custody orders and judgments of foreign courts are not enforceable in the British overseas territories.

Visitation Rights: In cases where one parent has been granted custody of a child, the other parent is usually granted visitation rights. If a custodial parent fails to allow visitation, the non-custodial parent may appeal to the court.

Dual Nationality: Dual nationality is recognized under the British overseas territories' laws.

Passports for Minors and the Children's Passport Issuance Alert Program: For more information on these topics, see the *International Parental Child Abduction* section of this publication and review current reports from the U.S. Department of State at www.travel.state.gov/abduction.

Criminal Remedies: For information on possible criminal remedies, please contact your local law enforcement authorities or the nearest office of the Federal Bureau of Investigation (FBI).

Information is also available on the Internet at the web site of the U.S. Department of Justice, Office of Juvenile Justice and Delinquency Prevention (OJJDP) at http://www.ojjdp.ncjrs.org.

Persons who wish to pursue a child custody claim in any British overseas territory court should retain an attorney in the British overseas territory that they are pursuing the child custody claim. The U.S. embassies in Barbados, Jamaica, and The Bahamas maintain lists of attorneys who are willing to represent American clients. For further information on international parental child abduction, contact the Office of Children's Issues, U.S. Department of State at 1-888-407-4747 or visit its web site on the Internet at http://travel.state.gov/abduction.

CENTRAL AFRICAN REPUBLIC

Compiled from publications that were available as of February 2013 from the U.S. Department of State, the U.S. Department of Commerce, and the Central Intelligence Agency (CIA). See the introduction to this set for explanatory notes.

Official Name:
Central African Republic

PROFILE

Geography

Area: total: 622,984 sq km; country comparison to the world: 45; land: 622,984 sq km; water: 0 sq km
Major cities: Bangui (capital) 702,000 (2009)
Climate: tropical; hot, dry winters; mild to hot, wet summers
Terrain: vast, flat to rolling, monotonous plateau; scattered hills in northeast and southwest

People

Nationality: noun: Central African(s); adjective: Central African
Population: 5,057,208 (July 2012 est.)
Population growth rate: 2.142% (2012 est.)
Ethnic groups: Baya 33%, Banda 27%, Mandjia 13%, Sara 10%, Mboum 7%, M'Baka 4%, Yakoma 4%, other 2%
Religions: indigenous beliefs 35%, Protestant 25%, Roman Catholic 25%, Muslim 15%
Languages: French (official), Sangho (lingua franca and national language), tribal languages
Literacy: definition: age 15 and over can read and write; total population: 56%; male: 69.3%; female: 43.2% (2010 est.)
Health: life expectancy at birth: total population: 50.48 years; male: 49.23 years; female: 51.76 years (2012 est.); Infant mortality rate: total: 97.17 deaths/1,000 live births; male: 105.04 deaths/1,000 live births; female: 89.06 deaths/1,000 live births (2012 est.)
Unemployment rate: 8% (2001 est.)
Work force: 1.926 million (2007)

Government

Type: republic
Independence: 13 August 1960
Constitution: ratified by popular referendum 5 December 2004; effective 27 December 2004
Political subdivisions: 14 prefectures (prefectures, singular—prefecture), 2 economic prefectures (prefectures economiques, singular—prefecture economique), and 1 commune
Suffrage: 18 years of age; universal

Economy

GDP (purchasing power parity): $3.847 billion (2012 est.); $3.688 billion (2011 est.); $3.576 billion (2010 est.); $3.461 billion (2009 est.)
GDP real growth rate: 4.1% (2012 est.); 3.1% (2011 est.); 3.3% (2010 est.); 1.7% (2009 est.)
GDP per capita (PPP): $800 (2012 est.); $800 (2011 est.); $800 (2010 est.); $800 (2009 est.)
Natural resources: diamonds, uranium, timber, gold, oil, hydropower
Agriculture products: cotton, coffee, tobacco, manioc (tapioca), yams, millet, corn, bananas; timber
Industries: gold and diamond mining, logging, brewing, textiles, footwear, assembly of bicycles and motorcycles
Exports: $198.5 million (2012 est.); $169.2 million (2011 est.); $152.8 million (2010 est.)
Exports—commodities: diamonds, timber, cotton, coffee, tobacco
Exports—partners: Belgium 29.1%, China 16.4%, Morocco 7.6%, Democratic Republic of the Congo 7.6%, France 6.8%, Indonesia 6% (2011)
Imports: $341.2 million (2012 est.); $380.1 million (2011 est.); $313 million (2010 est.)
Imports—commodities: food, textiles, petroleum products, machinery, electrical equipment, motor vehicles, chemicals, pharmaceuticals
Imports—partners: South Korea 45.6%, Netherlands 8.8%, France 7.1%, Cameroon 5.1% (2011)
Debt—external: $469.5 million (31 December 2012 est.); $483.9 million (31 December 2011 est.); $404 million (31 December 2010 est.)
Exchange rates: Cooperation Financiere en Afrique Centrale francs (XAF) per US dollar; 514.1 (2012 est.); 471.87 (2011); 495.28 (2010); 472.19 (2009); 447.81 (2008); 493.51 (2007)

PEOPLE

There are more than 80 ethnic groups in the Central African Republic (C.A.R.), each with its own language. Sango, the language of a small group along the Oubangui River, is the national language spoken by the majority of Central Africans. Only a small part of the population has more than an elementary knowledge of French, the official language.

Approximately 61% of the population of the C.A.R. lives in rural areas. The chief agricultural areas are around Bossangoa, Bouar, and Bambari. Bangui, Berberati, Bangassou, and Bossangoa are the most densely populated urban centers.

National/Racial/Ethnic Minorities

Violence by unidentified persons, bandits, and other nonstate armed entities against the Mbororo was a problem, as they continued to suffer disproportionately from the civil disorder in the north. Their cattle wealth made them attractive targets to the bandits and other nonstate armed entities. Additionally, since many citizens viewed the Mbororo as inherently foreign due to their transnational migratory patterns, they faced occasional discrimination with regard to government services and protections.

Despite constitutional protections and the ratification of the International Labor Organization (ILO's) Convention on Indigenous and Tribal Peoples, there was societal discrimination against Ba'aka (Pygmies), the earliest known inhabitants of the rain forest in the south. Ba'aka constitute approximately 1 to 2 percent of the population. They continued to have little say in decisions affecting their lands, culture, traditions, and the exploitation of natural resources. Forest-dwelling Ba'aka in particular were subject to social and economic discrimination and exploitation, which the government has done little to prevent. Despite repeated promises the government took no steps to issue and deliver identity cards to Ba'aka, lack of which, according to many human rights groups, effectively denied them access to greater civil rights.

The Ba'aka, including children, were often coerced into agricultural, domestic, and other types of labor. They were considered to be the slaves of members of other local ethnic groups, and even when they were remunerated for labor, their wages were far below those prescribed by the labor code and lower than wages paid to members of other groups.

Refugees International reported that Ba'aka were effectively "second-class citizens," and the popular prejudice that they were barbaric and subhuman further caused them to be excluded from mainstream society.

Religion

According to the 2003 census, Protestants constitute 51 percent of the population, Roman Catholics 29 percent, and Muslims 15 percent. Others practice indigenous beliefs (animism), which are often incorporated into Christian and Islamic practice throughout the country.

HISTORY

The C.A.R. appears to have been settled from at least the 7th century on by overlapping empires, including the Kanem-Bornou, Ouaddai, Baguirmi, and Dafour groups based in Lake Chad and the Upper Nile. Later, various sultanates claimed present-day C.A.R., using the entire Oubangui region as a slave reservoir, from which slaves were traded north across the Sahara and to West Africa for export by European traders. Population migration in the 18th and 19th centuries brought new migrants into the area, including the Zande, Banda, and M'Baka-Mandjia.

In 1875 the Egyptian sultan Rabah governed Upper-Oubangui, which included present-day C.A.R. Europeans, primarily the French, German, and Belgians, arrived in the area in 1885. The French consolidated their legal claim to the area through an 1887 convention with Congo Free State, which granted France possession of the right bank of the Oubangui River. Two years later, the French established an outpost at Bangui, and in 1894, Oubangui-Chari became a French territory. However, the French did not consolidate their control over the area until 1903 after having defeated the forces of the Egyptian sultan Rabah and established colonial administration throughout the territory. In 1906, the Oubangui-Chari territory was united with the Chad colony; in 1910, it became one of the four territories of the Federation of French Equatorial Africa (A.E.F.), along with Chad, Congo (Brazzaville), and Gabon. The next 30 years were marked by small-scale revolts against French rule and the development of a plantation-style economy.

In August 1940, the territory responded, with the rest of the A.E.F., to the call from Gen. Charles de Gaulle to fight for Free France. After World War II, the French Constitution of 1946 inaugurated the first of a series of reforms that led eventually to complete independence for all French territories in western and equatorial Africa. In 1946, all A.E.F. inhabitants were granted French citizenship and allowed to establish local assemblies. The assembly in C.A.R. was led by Barthelemy Boganda, a Catholic priest who also was known for his forthright statements in the French Assembly on the need for African emancipation. In 1956 French legislation eliminated certain voting inequalities and provided for the creation of some organs of self-government in each territory. The French constitutional referendum of September 1958 dissolved the A.E.F., and on December 1 of the same year the Assembly declared the birth of the Central African Republic with Boganda as head of government. Boganda ruled until his death in a March 1959 plane crash. His cousin, David Dacko, replaced him, governing the country until 1965 and overseeing the country's declaration of independence on August 13, 1960.

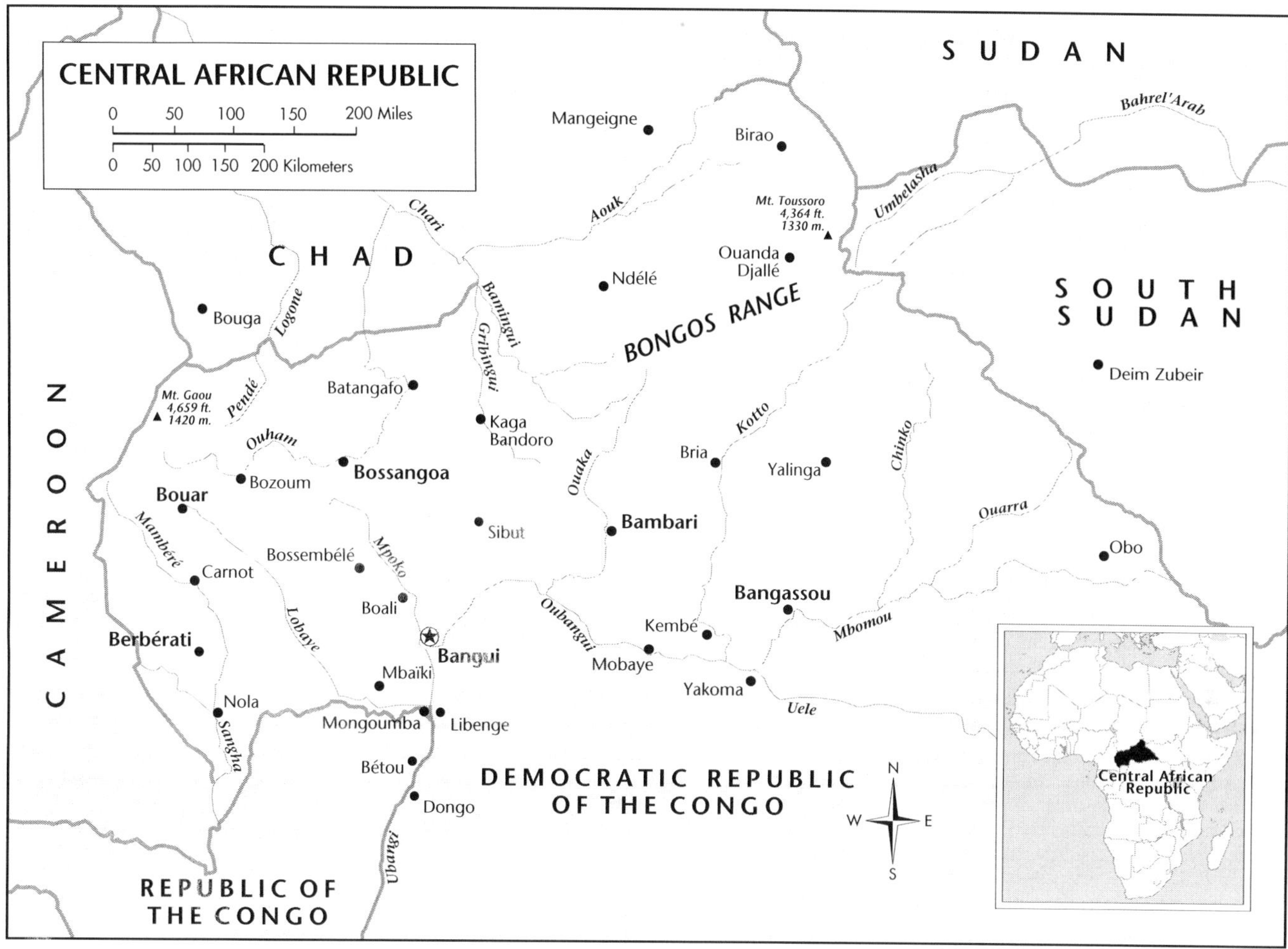

On January 1, 1966, following a swift and almost bloodless coup, Col. Jean-Bedel Bokassa assumed power as President of the Republic. Bokassa abolished the constitution of 1959, dissolved the National Assembly, and issued a decree that placed all legislative and executive powers in the hands of the president. On December 4, 1976, the republic became a monarchy with the promulgation of the imperial constitution and the proclamation of the president as Emperor Bokassa I. His regime was characterized by numerous human rights atrocities.

Following riots in Bangui and the murder of between 50 and 200 schoolchildren, former President Dacko led a successful French-backed coup against Bokassa on September 20, 1979. Dacko's efforts to promote economic and political reforms proved ineffectual, and on September 1, 1981, he in turn was overthrown in a bloodless coup by Gen. Andre Kolingba. For 4 years, Kolingba led the country as head of the Military Committee for National Recovery (CRMN). In 1985 the CRMN was dissolved, and Kolingba named a new cabinet with increased civilian participation, signaling the start of a return to civilian rule. The process of democratization quickened in 1986 with the creation of a new political party, the Rassemblement Democratique Centrafricain (RDC), and the drafting of a new constitution that subsequently was ratified in a national referendum. General Kolingba was sworn in as constitutional President on November 29, 1986. The constitution established a National Assembly made up of 52 elected deputies, elected in July 1987. Due to mounting political pressure, in 1991 President Kolingba announced the creation of a national commission to rewrite the constitution to provide for a multi-party system. Multi-party presidential elections were conducted in 1992 but were later cancelled due to serious logistical and other irregularities. Ange Felix Patasse won a second-round victory in rescheduled elections held in October 1993, and was re-elected for another 6-year term in September 1999.

Salary arrears, labor unrest, and unequal treatment of military officers from different ethnic groups led to three mutinies against the Patasse government in 1996 and 1997. The French succeeded in quelling the disturbances, and an African peacekeeping force (MISAB) occupied Bangui until 1998 when they were relieved by a UN peacekeeping mission (MINURCA). Economic difficulties caused by the looting and destruction during the 1996 and 1997 mutinies, energy crises, and government mismanagement continued to trouble Patasse's government through 2000. In March 2000 the last of the

MINURCA forces departed Bangui. In May 2001 rebel forces within the C.A.R. military, led by former President and Army General Andre Kolingba, attempted a military coup. After several days of heavy fighting, forces loyal to the government, aided by a small number of troops from Libya and the Congolese rebel Movement for the Liberation of the Congo (MLC), were able to put down the coup attempt. In November 2001, there were several days of sporadic gunfire between members of the Presidential Security Unit and soldiers defending sacked Chief of Staff of the Armed Forces Francois Bozize, who fled to Chad. In mid-2002 there were skirmishes on the C.A.R.-Chad border. In October 2002, former Army Chief of Staff Francois Bozize launched a coup attempt that culminated in the March 15, 2003 overthrow of President Patasse and the takeover of the capital. General Bozize declared himself President, suspended the constitution, and dissolved the National Assembly.

Since seizing power, President Francois Bozize has made significant progress in restoring order to Bangui and parts of the country, and professed a desire to promote national reconciliation, strengthen the economy, and improve the human rights situation. A new constitution was passed by referendum in December 2004. In spring 2005, the country held its first elections since the March 2003 coup. The first round of presidential and legislative elections were held in March 2005, and in May, President Bozize defeated former Prime Minister Martin Ziguele in a second-round runoff. On June 13, Bozize named Elie Dote, an agricultural engineer who had worked at the African Development Bank, his new Prime Minister. Following a countrywide strike, Elie Dote resigned on January 18, 2008.

In September 2006, rebel activity in the northwestern and northeastern part of the country intensified, resulting in the government losing control over parts of its territory. The subsequent fighting between government troops and rebels displaced nearly 300,000 citizens. In January 2007, the Libyan Government brokered a peace agreement between the government and the Democratic Front of the Central African People (FPDC), a rebel group operating in the northeastern part of the country headed by Abdoulaye Miskine. Other rebels disavowed the peace agreement, but by May 2008, most rebel groups had either entered into a peace agreement with the government—the peace agreement with the Popular Army for the Restoration of Democracy (APRD) being the most significant—or declared a cease-fire.

In June 2008, the government signed the Libreville Comprehensive Peace Agreement with the APRD and the Union of Democratic Forces for Unity (UFDR), led by Zakaria Damane, in Libreville, Gabon. One rebel group, the Convention of Patriots for Justice and Peace (CPJP) remained outside of the comprehensive peace process. The CPJP attacked the Central African Army on numerous occasions, including in November 2010 when they briefly captured the town of Birao.

In June 2011, the government signed a cease-fire agreement with CPJP. Since that time, the government and CPJP have not fought; however, the CPJP engaged in skirmishes with UFDR in the northeastern region of C.A.R. in September 2011. CPJP and UFDR signed a cease-fire agreement in October 2011.

Implementation of the Comprehensive Peace Agreement, particularly its provisions granting amnesty to former fighters, furthered an Inclusive Political Dialogue (IPD) intended to help end instability in the C.A.R. In December 2008, the Inclusive Political Dialogue formally convened and issued its recommendations, which included, among other items, the establishment of a government of national unity and of an independent electoral commission in advance of planned 2010 elections. As of December 2011, the implementation of the results of the IPD remained incomplete.

In January 2009, a new coalition government was appointed. While there was little change in the government's composition, with key ministers allied with the President remaining in place, some members of the political opposition and rebel groups obtained ministerial portfolios.

In early 2010, President Bozize twice delayed constitutionally mandated elections scheduled for April and May due to a poorly functioning Independent Electoral Commission (IEC) and bickering between C.A.R.'s political parties. The first round of presidential and parliamentary elections took place in January 2011.

The elections, though not without flaws, were held peacefully and without major incident during polling. The IEC declared President Bozize the winner of the presidential election in the first round and determined that a third of the 105 parliamentary races were also decided in this round. Nine members of President Bozize's family, also members of his KNK party, won victory in the first round.

Members of the opposition, citing irregularities in the counting process, filed 88 challenges with the Constitutional Court and called unsuccessfully for a boycott of the second round of elections, which took place in March 2011. In April 2011, the Constitutional Court invalidated the results of 13 races run in January and ordered a special election to rerun those races.

In May 2011, the Constitutional Court again intervened to reverse the results of nine races in the second round March elections. A special election, also protested by the opposition, was held in September 2011. In the end, the KNK party won at least 64 of 105 parliamentary seats.

While international observers cited some irregularities in the election, the fragmented nature of the opposition likely meant that it could not pose a credible challenge to the KNK or President Bozize.

GOVERNMENT AND POLITICAL CONDITIONS

Central African Republic (CAR) is a constitutional republic governed by a strong executive branch and weak legislative and judicial branches. Armed forces Chief of Staff General Francois Bozize seized power in a military coup in 2003. In January 2011 citizens reelected Bozize president in what was considered by national and international observers to be a flawed election.

Recent Elections

During 2011 the country held three rounds of multiparty presidential and legislative elections that resulted in the reelection of Francois Bozize as president. Bozize had seized power in a 2003 military coup, declared himself president, and headed a transitional government until winning election in 2005. Domestic and international election observers judged the 2011 elections to be flawed, citing fraud, intimidation, and lack of ballot secrecy, among other problems. Observers also reported irregularities, including an unexplained increase of 40 percent in registered voters between 2005 and 2010, and high levels of "par derogation" votes indicating voters casting ballots outside their home districts.

Political Parties: Political parties were not prevented from participating in the elections, and 861 candidates from 41 parties competed for 105 legislative seats. Membership within the president's Kwa Na Kwa party generally conferred special advantages, including access to government resources to conduct political campaigns.

Political parties continued to be subject to close scrutiny and restrictions by the government. Members of political parties were not always able to move about the country without restriction; many had to obtain authorization from the government before traveling.

Participation of Women and Minorities: Women and minority citizens are not prevented by law from voting or participating in political life on the same basis as men or nonminority citizens. The new government, chosen in April, included a number of female ministers, including the minister of commerce, minister for primary and secondary education, minister of international cooperation, minister of tourism, and minister of social affairs. During 2011 there were eight female deputies in the 105-member legislature.

Principal Government Officials

Last Updated: 1/31/2013

Pres.: **Francois BOZIZE**

Prime Min.: **Faustin-Archange TOUADERA**

Min. of Agriculture: **Parfait MBAYE**

Min. of Civil Service: **Jacques BOTI**

Min. of Defense: **Jean-Francois BOZIZE**

Min. of Economy: **Sylvain MALIKO**

Min. of Education:

Min. of Equipment, Transport, & Civil Action: **Jean-Prospere WODOBODE**

Min. of Finance & Budget: **Sylvain NDOUTINGAI**

Min. of Foreign Affairs, Regional Integration, & Francophonie Affairs: **Antoine GAMBI**

Min. of Interior & Security: **Raymond Paul NDOUGOU, Brig. Gen.**

Min. of Justice: **Paul OTTO**

Min. of Mining & Energy: **Sylvain NDOUTINGAI**

Min. of Public Health: **Bernard Lala KONAMNA**

Min. of Social Affairs: **Solange Pagonendji N'DACKALA**

Min. of Tourism, Development, & Crafts: **Yvonne MBOISSONA**

Min. of Trade, Industry, & Small & Medium-Size Enterprises: **Rosalie KOUDOUNGERE**

Min. of Transport & Equipment: **Charles MASSI**

Min. of Youth, Sports, and Culture: **Desire KOLINGBA**

Min. of State for Communications, National Reconciliation, Democratic Culture, & Human Rights: **Jabdoul Karim MECKASSOUA**

Min. of State for Rural Development: **Charles MASSI**

Min., Office of the Prime Min., & Govt. Spokesman: **Aurelian Simplice ZINGAS**

Governor, Regional Central Bank: **Alphonse KOYAMBA**

Ambassador to the US: **Emmanuel TOUABOY**

Permanent Representative to the UN, New York: **Charles-Armel DOUBANE**

ECONOMY

Subsistence agriculture, together with forestry, remains the backbone of the economy of the Central African Republic (CAR), with about 60% of the population living in outlying areas. The agricultural sector generates more than half of GDP. Timber and diamonds account for most export earnings, followed by cotton. Important constraints to economic development include the CAR's landlocked position, a poor transportation system, a largely unskilled work force, and a legacy of misdirected macroeconomic policies. Factional fighting between the government and its opponents remains a drag on economic revitalization.

Since 2009 the IMF has worked closely with the government to institute reforms that have resulted in some improvement in budget transparency, but other problems remain. The government's additional spending in the run-up to the election in 2011 worsened CAR's fiscal situation. Distribution of income is extraordinarily unequal. Grants from France and the international community can only partially meet humanitarian needs.

In 2012 the World Bank approved $125 million in funding for transport infrastructure and regional trade, focused on the route between CAR's capital and the port of Douala in Cameroon. After a two year lag in donor support, the IMF's first review of CAR's extended credit facility for 2012–2015 praised improvements in revenue collection but warned of weak management of spending.

Labor Conditions

The labor code forbids the employment of children younger than 14 years of age without specific authorization from the Ministry of Labor and Civil Service, but the law also provides that the minimum age for employment could be as young as 12 years of age for some types of light work in traditional agricultural activities or home services. The law prohibits children younger than 18 years old from performing hazardous work or working at night. Although the law defines hazardous work as any employment that endangers children's physical and mental health, it does not define the worst forms of child labor. The mining code specifically prohibits child or underage labor.

The government did not enforce these provisions. Child labor was common in many sectors of the economy, especially in rural areas. Throughout the country children as young as seven years old frequently performed agricultural work. Children often worked as domestic workers, fishermen, and in mines, often in dangerous conditions. Children also worked in the diamond fields alongside adult relatives, transporting and washing gravel, as well as mining gold, digging holes, and carrying heavy loads. Despite the law prohibiting child labor in mining, many children were seen working in and around diamond mining fields.

The labor code states that the minister of labor must set minimum wages in the public sector by decree. The minimum wages in the private sector are established on the basis of sector-specific collective conventions resulting from negotiations between the employer and workers' representatives in each sector.

The minimum wage in the private sphere varies by sector and kind of work. For example, the monthly minimum wage was 8,500 CFA francs ($17) for agricultural workers and 26,000 CFA francs ($51) for government workers.

The minimum wage applies only to the formal sector, leaving most of the economy unregulated in terms of wages. The monthly minimum wage increased 12 percent during the year from 25,000 CFA ($50) to 28,000 CFA ($55). The law applies to foreign and migrant workers as well. Most labor was performed outside the wage and social security system (in the extensive informal sector), especially by farmers in the large subsistence agricultural sector.

The law sets a standard workweek of 40 hours for government employees and most private sector employees. Household employees may work up to 52 hours per week. The law also requires a minimum rest period of 48 hours per week for both citizens and foreign and migrant workers. Overtime policy varied according to the workplace; violations of overtime policy were taken to the Ministry of Labor, although it was unknown whether this occurred in practice during 2011. The government did not enforce labor standards, and violations were common through all sectors of the economy.

U.S.-C.A.R. RELATIONS

The United States established diplomatic relations with the Central African Republic (C.A.R.) in 1960, following its independence from France. The United States and C.A.R. enjoy generally good relations, although the U.S. continues to have concerns about the pace of political and economic liberalization, social development, and respect for human rights.

C.A.R. is one of the world's least developed nations, and has experienced several periods of political instability since independence. The two countries share a vision of a more stable Central African Republic that enjoys greater economic growth, contributes to regional stability, and is a reliable partner on issues of mutual importance. The United States continues to work with C.A.R. and through the United Nations and other international bodies to support the country as it combats the Lord's Resistance Army (LRA). The United States also encourages C.A.R. to develop institutions that will improve transparency, strengthen the rule of law, and promote unity among Central Africans.

The U.S. Embassy in C.A.R. was briefly closed as a result of 1996–97 military mutinies. It reopened in 1998 with limited staff, but U.S. Agency for International Development and Peace Corps missions previously operating there did not return. The Embassy again temporarily suspended operations in November 2002 in response to security concerns raised by the October 2002 launch of a rebellion that resulted in a coup in 2003. The Embassy reopened in 2005. A resident U.S. Ambassador was appointed to C.A.R. in 2007. Currently, there is limited U.S. diplomatic/consular representation in the country, and the Embassy's ability to provide services to U.S. citizens is extremely limited. Due to unrest, the U.S. Department of State warns U.S. citizens against travel to C.A.R.

U.S. Assistance to Central African Republic

Central African Republic is located in a volatile and poor region and has a long history of development, governance, and human rights problems. U.S. assistance in Central African Republic is largely humanitarian in nature, with substantial contributions to multilateral organizations. Other smaller assistance programs target military professionalization, human rights, and strengthening the rule of law. Restrictions on U.S. aid that were imposed after the 2003 military coup were lifted in 2005.

C.A.R. ranks 179 out of 187 on the United Nations' Human Development Index. Significant portions of the country's territory remain uncontrolled and ungoverned, with the presence of multiple armed actors creating insecurity in much of the north and northeast. The Lord's Resistance Army continues to terrorize civilians in the southeastern part of the country. While the 2008 Inclusive Political Dialogue and subsequent peace and cease-fire agreements brought an end to much of the internal fighting, true stability has not been cemented because of the government's lack of capacity to fully secure its territory. Insecurity continues throughout the country, particularly outside of Bangui, and the government recognizes the urgent need to protect its citizens against threats from internal and external actors. In October 2011, President Barack Obama announced that the United States would deploy a small number of U.S. forces to act as advisors to the national militaries in the region that are pursuing the LRA, including the Ugandan People's Defense Force and the Central African Armed Forces. Forces were deployed to C.A.R. in December 2011.

Bilateral Economic Relations

The United States and C.A.R. have a small amount of bilateral trade. In 2004, the United States removed C.A.R. from the list of countries eligible for preferential trade benefits under the African Growth and Opportunity Act. The two countries have a bilateral investment agreement and investment treaty.

Central African Republic's Membership in International Organizations

The Central African Republic is an active member in several Central African organizations. A major foreign policy objective of the C.A.R. Government is standardization of tax, customs, and security arrangements among Central African countries. The Central African Republic and the United States belong to a number of the same international organizations, including the United Nations, International Monetary Fund, World Bank, and World Trade Organization. C.A.R. generally joins other African and developing countries in consensus positions on major policy issues.

Bilateral Representation

The Central African Republic maintains an embassy in the United States at 2704 Ontario Road, NW, Washington, DC, 20009 (tel: 202-483-7800/01, fax: 202-332-9893).

Principal U.S. Embassy Officials

Last Updated: 1/14/2013

BANGUI (E) Avenue David Dacko, Bangui, (236) 21-61-02-00, Fax (236) 21-61-44-94, INMARSAT Tel 870-77-233-7490, Workweek: Mon-Thurs 7:30-17:00 Fri 7:30-13:30, Website: http://Bangui.usembassy.gov

AMB OMS:	Gloria Mangum
CON/POL/ECON:	Robert J. Cavese
FM:	Gustavo Mejia
HRO:	Gustavo Mejia
MGT:	Gustavo Mejia
POSHO:	Vacant
AMB:	Laurence D. Wohlers
DCM:	Brennan M. Gilmore
PAO:	Vacant
GSO:	Vacant
CLO:	Vacant
FMO:	Gustavo Mejia
State ICASS:	Rob Cavese

TRAVEL

Consular Information Sheet

April 9, 2012

Country Description: The Central African Republic (CAR) is one of the world's least developed nations, and has experienced several periods of political instability since independence from France in 1960. Despite an on-going peace process and the presence of a democratically-elected government in the capital, Bangui, rebels still control large portions of the country's northern and eastern provinces. In the Dzanga-Sangha National Park in the southwest, facilities for tourists are being developed but remain limited.

The U.S. Embassy in Bangui resumed operations in January 2005, following the evacuation of all U.S. staff in 2002. The Embassy continues to operate with limited staffing, and can provide only basic services to U.S. citizens in the CAR.

Smart Traveler Enrollment Program (STEP)/Embassy Locations: If you are going to live in or visit the Central African Republic, please take the time to tell our Embassy about your trip. If you enroll, we can keep you up to date with important safety and security announcements. It will also help your friends and family get in touch with you in an emergency.

The United States Embassy, Bangui
Avenue David Dacko
B.P. 924
Bangui
Telephone: 236 2161–0200
Facsimile: 236 2161–4494
Emergency after-hours telephone: 236 7554–2276 and 236 7550–1293

Entry/Exit Requirements for U.S. Citizens: A valid passport, visa, and evidence of yellow fever vaccination are required for entry. Travelers should obtain the latest information and details from the Embassy of the Central African Republic, 2704 Ontario Road, NW

Washington, DC 20009, telephone: (202) 483–7800/7801, fax: (202) 332–9893. Overseas, inquiries should be made to the nearest Central African Republic Embassy or Consulate. NOTE: In any country where there is no Central African Republic diplomatic mission, the French Embassy has authorization to issue a visa for entry into the Central African Republic. The Embassy of the Central African Republic does not have a website.

The U.S. Department of State is unaware of any HIV/AIDS entry restrictions for visitors to or foreign residents of the Central African Republic.

There are several restrictions on foreigners who wish to travel within the CAR. Both residents and tourists must ensure that they have proper paperwork for any travel outside of Bangui. Travel to the southwest in particular requires a permit for all foreign travelers due to the presence of sensitive mining areas. Travelers are encouraged to check with the authorities in Bangui, such as the Gendarmerie National, and/or the U.S. Embassy about possible restrictions in the areas where they wish to travel.

Threats to Safety and Security: Spontaneous demonstrations take place in CAR from time-to-time in response to world events or local developments. We remind you that even demonstrations intended to be peaceful can turn confrontational and possibly escalate into violence. You are therefore urged to avoid the areas of demonstrations if possible, and to exercise caution if within the vicinity of any demonstrations.

You should stay current with media coverage of local events and be aware of your surroundings at all times. Armed rebel groups, bandits, and poachers present real dangers, and the Central African government is unable to guarantee the safety of visitors in most parts of the country. Northwestern and eastern CAR, especially the areas bordering Chad and Sudan, are particularly dangerous due to clashes between government and rebel forces.

There have been repeated attacks on Central African and expatriate travelers throughout CAR over the last 10 years. The continued presence of the Lord's Resistance Army in eastern CAR poses a particular safety and security threat. Bandits, militias, and cross-border rebel activity in the north and northeast also threaten the security of residents and travelers. Limited infrastructure and the great distance from Bangui mean that the U.S. Embassy can provide few services to U.S. citizens in these areas. Travel to these regions is therefore strongly discouraged.

Bangui itself, though safer, suffers from elevated crime rates, as well as severely limited transport and medical options. CAR military and civilian security forces (and people posing as such) staff checkpoints throughout the city, frequently harassing local and expatriate travelers for bribes. The U.S. Department of State advises against travel outside of the capital. Please see the Department of State's Travel Warning for the CAR for more information.

Stay up to date by:

- Bookmarking our Bureau of Consular Affairs website, which contains the current Travel Warnings and Travel Alerts as well as the Worldwide Caution.
- Following us on Twitter and the Bureau of Consular Affairs page on Facebook as well.
- Downloading our free Smart Traveler iPhone App to have travel information at your fingertips.
- Calling 1-888-407-4747 toll-free within the United States and Canada, or a regular toll line, 1-202-501-4444, from other countries.
- Taking some time before travel to consider your personal security.

Crime: Crime remains a concern in the capital although it has decreased in recent years. You should exercise caution while traveling around the city and its immediate environs. Petty theft remains a problem in large market areas, particularly in the crowded markets near KM 5 on the outskirts of the city. Armed gangs may operate in outlying residential areas.

During previous periods of civil unrest and civil conflict, including most recently in 2002 and 2003, foreign mercenaries and citizens engaged in widespread looting and damaged much of the city's infrastructure. In the northern and western parts of the country, there are frequent reports of armed robbery and kidnapping by highway bandits (called "coupeurs de routes" or "zaraguinas"), especially during the December to May dry season. When a crime does occur in Bangui, the victim may have to pay to send a vehicle to pick up police officers due to the shortage of police vehicles and fuel.

In many countries around the world, counterfeit and pirated goods are widely available. Transactions involving such products may be illegal under local law. In addition, bringing them back to the United States may result in forfeitures and/or fines. The Computer Crime and Intellectual Property Division in the U.S. Department of Justice has more information on this serious problem.

Victims of Crime: If you or someone you know becomes the victim of a crime abroad, you should contact the local police and the nearest U.S. embassy or consulate. We can:

- Replace a stolen passport.
- Help you find appropriate medical care if you are the victim of violent crimes such as assault or rape.
- Put you in contact with the appropriate police authorities, and if you want us to, we can contact family members or friend.
- Help you understand the local criminal justice process and direct you to local attorneys, although it is important to remember that local authorities are responsible for investigating and prosecuting the crime.

The local equivalent to the "911" emergency line in the Central African Republic is 117, and you can call the Gendarmerie at 2161–2200.

Criminal Penalties: While you are traveling in the CAR, you are subject to its laws even if you are a U.S. citizen. Foreign laws and legal systems can be vastly different than our own. Penalties for breaking the law can be more severe than in the United States for similar offenses. Persons violating Central African laws, even unknowingly, may be expelled, arrested, or imprisoned.

Penalties for possession, use, or trafficking in illegal drugs in the CAR are severe, and convicted offenders can expect long jail sentences and heavy fines. Engaging in sexual conduct with children or using or disseminating child pornography in a foreign country is a crime prosecutable in the United States. If you break local laws in the CAR your U.S. passport won't help you avoid arrest or prosecution. It's very important to know what's legal and what's not where you are going. Based on the Vienna Convention on Consular Relations, bilateral agreements with certain countries, and customary international law, if you are arrested in CAR, you have the option to request that the police, prison officials, or other authorities alert the nearest U.S. embassy or consulate of your arrest, and to have communications from you forwarded to the nearest U.S. embassy or consulate.

Photography: Taking photographs of police or military installations, or any other government buildings, is prohibited. Unauthorized photography may result in the seizure of photographic equipment by CAR authorities. Police or other government authorities can provide information and grant permission for photographing a particular subject or location.

Corruption: Corruption remains a serious problem among CAR security forces, some members of which have harassed travelers for bribes. At night, the roads in the capital are often manned with impromptu checkpoints, at which police or other military members ask motorists and travelers for money.

Banking: Banking infrastructure remains limited in the CAR, and facilities for monetary exchange exist only in the capital. There are no ATMs in the CAR. Exchange bureaus and banks normally accept dollars and euros, but not West African Francs (CFA). Credit cards are not used in the CAR, and purchases of goods and services are made in cash, including hotel rooms and airline tickets.

Accessibility: While in the CAR, individuals with disabilities may find accessibility and accommodation very different from what you find in the United States. Public infrastructure is generally in poor condition and sidewalks, buildings, and public transportation do not cater to special accessibility needs.

Medical Facilities and Health Information: Medical facilities are extremely limited in the CAR, and the quality of care is unreliable. Sanitation levels are low. Many medicines are not available; you should carry properly labeled prescription drugs and other medications with you that will suffice for your entire visit.

Routine immunizations and protection from vaccine-preventable diseases such as yellow fever, rabies, polio, meningitis, typhoid, and hepatitis A and B are recommended. Malaria (predominantly P. falciparum) exists throughout the year and chemoprophylaxis is strongly recommended. Information on vaccinations and other health precautions, such as safe food and water precautions and insect bite protection, may be obtained from the CDC website. For information about outbreaks of infectious diseases abroad, consult the World Health Organization (WHO) website. The WHO website also contains additional health information for travelers, including detailed country-specific health information. Tuberculosis is an increasingly serious health concern in the CAR. For further information, please consult the CDC's information on TB. Insect-borne illnesses are of concern as is Schistosomiasis, an illness related to contact with fresh water. Insect precautions and avoiding freshwater are recommended.

Medical Insurance: You can't assume your insurance will go with you when you travel. It's very important to find out BEFORE you leave whether or not your medical insurance will cover you overseas. You need to ask your insurance company two questions:

- Does my policy apply when I'm out of the United States?
- Will it cover emergencies like a trip to a foreign hospital or a medical evacuation?

In many places, doctors and hospitals still expect payment in cash at the time of service. Your regular U.S. health insurance may not cover doctors' and hospital visits in other countries. If your policy doesn't go with you when you travel, it's a very good idea to take out another one for your trip.

Traffic Safety and Road Conditions: While in a foreign country, U.S. citizens may encounter road conditions that differ significantly from those in the United States. The information below concerning the CAR is provided for general reference only, and may not be totally accurate in a particular location or circumstance.

In Bangui, road conditions vary, and many roads have large holes and degraded areas that prevent the normal flow of traffic. Only a small portion of the roads in the country, including in the capital, are paved, and many of the compacted dirt roads have been degraded. Drivers tend to prefer to drive on the smoothest portion of the road and ignore basic traffic laws, thus slowing the flow of traffic and increasing the risk of collision. The city of Bangui does have a public transportation system consisting of green buses and yellow taxis, though these vehicles are often dangerously overcrowded and very badly maintained.

Due to the risk of armed attacks on motorists in the northern and western regions of the country, overland travel in these areas should be avoided. Any driving outside the capital should be only during daylight hours. Most remote areas in the CAR that are frequented by tourists are accessible only by four-wheel drive vehicles, although some roads are not passable at all during the rainy season, from May to October. There are currently no distracted driving laws in effect in the Central African Republic, but police may pull over drivers who talk or text while driving for not following unspecific safe driving procedures.

Aviation Safety Oversight: As there is no direct commercial air service to the United States by carriers registered in the CAR, the U.S. Federal Aviation Administration (FAA) has not assessed the government of the CAR's Civil Aviation Authority for compliance with International Civil Aviation Organization (ICAO) aviation safety standards. Further information may be found on the FAA's safety assessment page.

Children's Issues: For information see the U.S. Dept. of State Office of Children's Issues web pages on intercountry adoption and international parental child abduction.

Travel Warning

December 28, 2012

The Department of State warns U.S. citizens against all travel to the Central African Republic at this time. As a result of the deteriorating security situation, the U.S. Embassy in Bangui suspended its operations on December 28, 2012, and therefore cannot provide protection or routine consular services to U.S. citizens in the Central African Republic. U.S. citizens who have decided to stay in CAR should review their personal security situation and seriously consider departing, taking advantage of commercial flights. This replaces the Travel Warning of December 23, 2012, to reflect the deterioration of the security situation.

The U.S. Embassy staff in Bangui cannot provide services to U.S. citizens at this time. U.S. citizens in CAR who seek consular assistance should contact the Office of Overseas Citizens Services at CARemergency-USC@state.gov.

If you are going to live in or travel to the Central African Republic despite this Travel Warning, please take the time to tell us about your trip by enrolling in the Smart Traveler Enrollment Program (STEP). By enrolling in STEP, we can keep you up to date with important safety and security announcements. Enrolling in STEP will also make it easier for us to contact you in the event of an emergency. You should remember to keep all of your information in STEP up to date; it is particularly important when you enroll or update your information to include a current phone number and e-mail address in order to receive emergency messages.

For information on general crime and security issues, you should also consult the Department of State's Country Specific Information of Central African Republic as well as The Worldwide Caution located on the Bureau of Consular Affairs website. Follow us on Twitter and the Bureau of Consular Affairs page on Facebook, and download our free Smart Traveler app, available through iTunes and the Android market, to have travel information at your fingertips. Travelers may obtain up-to-date information on security conditions by calling 1-888-407-4747 toll free in the United States and Canada, or from other countries on a regular toll-line at 1-202-501-4444.

Intercountry Adoption

June 2012

The information in this section has been edited from the latest report available as of February 2013 from the State Department Bureau of Consular Affairs, Office of Overseas Citizens Services. For more information, please read the *Intercountry Adoption* section of this book and review current reports online at http://adoption.state.gov.

The Central African Republic is not party to the Hague Convention on Protection of Children and Co-operation in Respect of Intercountry Adoption (the Hague Adoption Convention). Intercountry adoptions of children from non-Hague countries are processed in accordance with 8 Code of Federal Regulations, Section 204.3 as it relates to orphans as defined under the Immigration and Nationality Act, Section 101(b)(1)(F).

Below is the limited adoption information that the Department has obtained from the adoption authority of the Central African Republic. U.S. citizens adopting children in rare adoption cases from the Central African Republic, as well as U.S. citizen prospective adoptive parents living in the Central African Republic, who would like to adopt from the United States or from a third country, should contact the adoption authority of the Central African Republic to inquire about applicable laws and procedures. See contact information below.

There are two types of adoptions in the Central African Republic: simple adoption and plenary adoption (adoption plénière). Plenary adoption severs the familial relationship between the child and the birth parents. This adoption gives the adopted child the same rights as a child born to the adoptive parent.

In a simple adoption, the biological parents (if living) retain inheritance rights and other privileges over the child, and must be consulted if the adoptive parents want to change the child's name or make significant changes in the life of the child. A simple adoption does not meet the requirements of U.S. immigration law and therefore cannot be the basis for granting an immigrant visa to an adopted child. Prospective adoptive parents should be aware that not all children in orphanages or children's homes are adoptable. In many countries, birth parents place their child(ren) temporarily in an orphanage or children's home due to financial or other hardship, with the intention of returning for the child when they are able to do so. In such cases, the birth parent(s) rarely would have relinquished their parental rights or consented to their child(ren)'s adoption.

Central African Republic's Adoption Authority:
Ministère de la Famille et des Affaires Sociales
Comité d'Adoption
B.P. 917
Bangui, République Centrafricaine
Chef de Service des Actions Sociales
Jules Gueret 90 07 93
Assistant aux Services des Actions Sociales
Bernard Azoumi 03 96 90

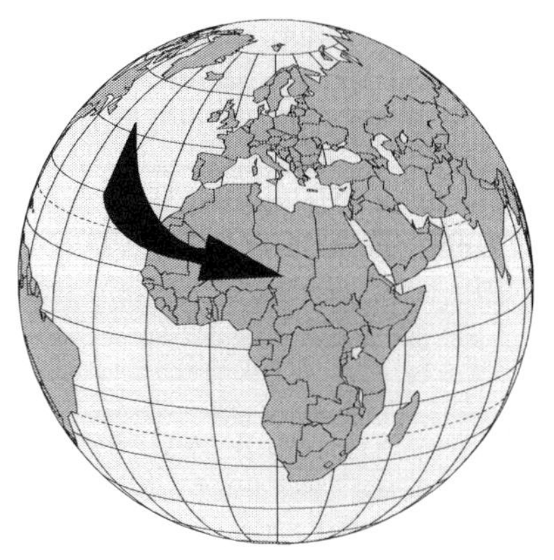

CHAD

Compiled from publications that were available as of February 2013 from the U.S. Department of State, the U.S. Department of Commerce, and the Central Intelligence Agency (CIA). See the introduction to this set for explanatory notes.

Official Name:
Republic of Chad

PROFILE

Geography

Area: total: 1.284 million sq km; country comparison to the world: 21; land: 1,259,200 sq km; water: 24,800 sq km
Major cities: N'djamena (capital) 808,000 (2009)
Climate: tropical in south, desert in north
Terrain: broad, arid plains in center, desert in north, mountains in northwest, lowlands in south

People

Nationality: noun: Chadian(s); adjective: Chadian
Population: 10,975,648 (July 2012 est.)
Population growth rate: 1.98% (2012 est.)
Ethnic groups: Sara 27.7%, Arab 12.3%, Mayo-Kebbi 11.5%, Kanem-Bornou 9%, Ouaddai 8.7%, Hadjarai 6.7%, Tandjile 6.5%, Gorane 6.3%, Fitri-Batha 4.7%, other 6.4%, unknown 0.3% (1993 census)
Religions: Muslim 53.1%, Catholic 20.1%, Protestant 14.2%, animist 7.3%, other 0.5%, unknown 1.7%, atheist 3.1% (1993 census)
Languages: French (official), Arabic (official), Sara (in south), more than 120 different languages and dialects
Literacy: definition: age 15 and over can read and write French or Arabic; total population: 34.5%; male: 45%; female: 24.2% (2010 est.)
Health: life expectancy at birth: total population: 48.69 years; male: 47.61 years; female: 49.82 years (2012 est.); Infant mortality rate: total: 93.61 deaths/1,000 live births; male: 99.39 deaths/1,000 live births; female: 87.6 deaths/1,000 live births (2012 est.)
Unemployment rate: NA%
Work force: 4.293 million (2007)

Government

Type: republic
Independence: 11 August 1960
Constitution: passed by referendum 31 March 1996; a June 2005 referendum removed constitutional term limits
Political subdivisions: 22 regions (regions, singular—region)
Suffrage: 18 years of age; universal

Economy

GDP (purchasing power parity): $21.34 billion (2012 est.); $19.79 billion (2011 est.); $19.48 billion (2010 est.); $17.23 billion (2009 est.)
GDP real growth rate: 7.3% (2012 est.); 1.6% (2011 est.); 13% (2010 est.); -1.2% (2009 est.)
GDP per capita (PPP): $2,000 (2012 est.); $1,900 (2011 est.); $1,900 (2010 est.); $1,700 (2009 est.)
Natural resources: petroleum, uranium, natron, kaolin, fish (Lake Chad), gold, limestone, sand and gravel, salt
Agriculture products: cotton, sorghum, millet, peanuts, rice, potatoes, manioc (tapioca); cattle, sheep, goats, camels
Industries: oil, cotton textiles, meatpacking, brewing, natron (sodium carbonate), soap, cigarettes, construction materials
Exports: $4.951 billion (2012 est.); $4.114 billion (2011 est.); $3.16 billion (2010 est.)
Exports—commodities: oil, cattle, cotton, gum arabic
Exports—partners: US 83.2%, China 6.8%, France 5.6% (2011)
Imports: $3.936 billion (2012 est.); $3.512 billion (2011 est.); $2.94 billion (2010 est.)
Imports—commodities: machinery and transportation equipment, industrial goods, foodstuffs, textiles
Imports—partners: Cameroon 16.9%, France 15.7%, China 10.7%, Finland 6.5%, Sweden 6%, Saudi Arabia 5%, Belgium 4.4% (2011)
Debt—external: $1.749 billion (31 December 2012 est.); $1.769 billion (31 December 2011 est.); $1.725 billion (31 December 2010 est.)
Exchange rates: Cooperation Financiere en Afrique Centrale francs (XAF) per US dollar; 514.1 (2012 est.); 471.87 (2011 est.); 495.28 (2010 est.); 472.19 (2009); 447.81 (2008); 480.1 (2007)

GEOGRAPHY

Chad is a landlocked country in north central Africa, with a territory twice the size of Texas. Population densities range from 54 persons per square kilometer in southern zones to 0.1 persons in the vast northern desert region, itself larger than France. The population of the capital city of N'Djamena, situated at the confluence of the Chari and Logone Rivers, is representative of Chad's ethnic and cultural diversity.

Chad has four bioclimatic zones. The northernmost Saharan Desert zone averages less than 200 mm (8") of rainfall annually. The central Sahelian zone receives between 200 and 600 mm (24") of rainfall and has vegetation ranging from grass/shrub steppe to thorny, open savanna. The southern zone, often referred to as the Sudanian zone, receives between 600 and 1,000 mm (39"), with woodland savanna and deciduous forests for vegetation. Rainfall in the small Guinea zone, limited to Chad's southwestern tip, ranges between 1,000 and 1,200 mm (47").

The country's topography is generally flat, with the elevation gradually rising as one moves north and east away from Lake Chad. The highest point in Chad is Emi Koussi, a mountain that rises 3,100 meters (10,200 ft.) in the northern Tibesti Mountains. The Ennedi Plateau and the Ouaddai highlands in the east complete the image of a gradually sloping basin, which descends toward Lake Chad. There also are central highlands in the Guera region rising to 1,500 meters (4,900 ft.).

Lake Chad, one of the most important wetlands on the continent and home to hundreds of species of fish and birds, shrank dramatically over 4 decades due to increased water use and inadequate rainfall. The lake, the second-largest in West Africa, covered 25,000 square kilometers in 1963 but had decreased to 1,350 square kilometers as of 2002.

The Chari and Logone Rivers, both of which originate in the Central African Republic and flow northward, provide most of the water entering Lake Chad.

PEOPLE

About 80% of the Chadian population is rural. There are over 250,000 refugees near the eastern border from the Sudanese conflict in Darfur; more than 60,000 Central African Republic refugees in the south; and approximately 130,000 internally displaced persons in eastern Chad.

National/Racial/Ethnic Minorities

There are approximately 200 ethnic groups, many of which were concentrated regionally. They speak 128 distinct primary languages. Although most ethnic groups were affiliated with one of two regional and cultural traditions—Arabs and Muslims in the North, Center, and East; and Christian or animist groups in the South—internal migrations in response to urbanization and desertification resulted in the integration of these groups in some areas.

Language

French and Arabic are the official languages of Chad. Chadian Arabic varies considerably from Classical Arabic, and while Chadians may be able to understand the latter, speakers of Classical Arabic may have difficulty understanding Chadian Arabic. English speakers in the government and business communities are rare.

Religion

More than half of the population is Muslim, approximately one-third is Christian, and the remainder follows indigenous religious beliefs or has no religion. Most northerners practice Islam, and most southerners practice Christianity or indigenous religions. Population patterns are becoming more complex, especially in urban areas, and there has been a proliferation of mosques in the traditionally Christian south.

The majority of Muslims adhere to the Sufi Tijaniyah tradition. A minority of Muslims (5 to 10 percent) hold beliefs in some cases associated with Wahhabism or Salafism. There has been a slow though steady movement towards membership in these groups.

Catholics represent the largest Christian group. Most Protestants affiliate with various evangelical Christian groups. Small Baha'i and Jehovah's Witnesses communities are also present.

HISTORY

The region has been known to traders and geographers since the late Middle Ages. Since then, Chad has served as a crossroads for the Muslim peoples of the desert and sahelian regions, and the animist African tribes of the savanna regions to the south. While the former developed coherent political entities that became the powerful kingdoms of Kanem-Bornu, Baguirmi, and Ouaddai, controlling much of northern and central Chad as well as parts of Nigeria and Sudan, the southern regions were much less politically developed and remained splintered into small, local, tribal chiefdoms. Contact between the two regions was dominated by regular raids conducted by Muslims into the non-Muslim south to secure slaves for their own use and for trade into North Africa and the Middle East.

The French first entered Chad in 1891, establishing their authority through military expeditions that reduced the politically backward south and by defeating the armies of the northern and central Muslim kingdoms, culminating in decisive victory over the powerful kingdom of Baguirmi in the battle of Kousseri (today in Cameroon). The French did not consider the territory pacified until 1911; armed clashes between French forces and local resistance fighters continued for years thereafter.

France ruled southern Chad ("le Tchad Utile," or Useful Chad) as a

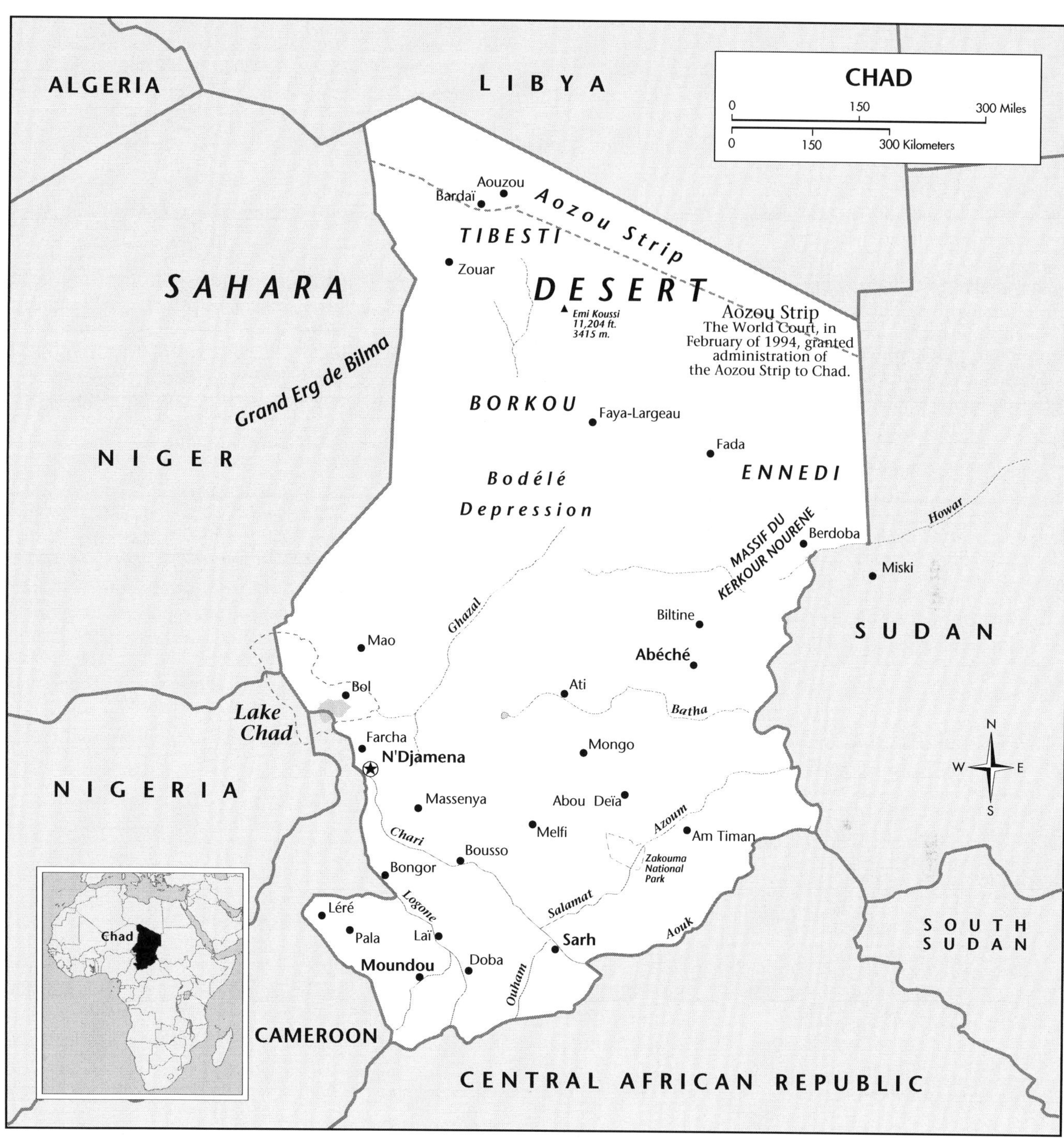

typical colony with civil administration, basic education, urbanization of major centers, and missionary activity, while exploiting the region's agricultural potential.

The French ruled northern and central Chad ("le Tchad des Sultans," or Chad of the Sultans) differently, confining the colonial footprint to a few military garrisons and relying on traditional tribal and religious leaders to administer the local populations in time-tried ways. The French made Chad, along with what are today Gabon, the Central African Republic, and the Republic of the Congo, part of a colonial federation called French Equatorial Africa, under a governor-general resident at Brazzaville in what is now the Republic of the Congo.

In 1959, the territory of French Equatorial Africa was dissolved, and its four constituent states—Gabon, the Central African Republic, the Republic of the Congo, and Chad—became autonomous members of the French Community. In August 1960 Chad became an independent nation under its first president, Francois Tombalbaye, a southerner.

Tombalbaye's authoritarianism and distrust of democracy led him in 1962 to ban all political parties except his own Chadian Progressive Party (PPT) and to attempt to concentrate all power in his own hands. His treatment of opponents, real or imagined, was extremely harsh, filling the prisons with thousands of political prisoners. His discrimination against the mostly Muslim central and northern regions and his attempt to impose his own ethnic group's customs on other tribes in Chad resulted in a tax revolt in 1965 that precipitated civil war with northern and central militants taking up arms to oust Tombalbaye and end the South's political dominance.

Despite the help of French combat forces, the Tombalbaye government was never able to quell the insurgency. Tombalbaye's rule became more irrational and brutal, leading the military to carry out a coup in 1975, assassinating Tombalbaye and installing General Felix Malloum, another southerner, as head of state. In 1978, Malloum's government was broadened to include more northerners. Internal dissent within the government led the northern prime minister, Hissein Habre, to send his fighters against the national army in the capital in 1979, reigniting the civil war. Nigeria and the Organization of African Unity (OAU) attempted to bring the Chadian factions together. In August 1979, the Lagos accord established a transitional government pending national elections planned within 18 months. Goukouni Oueddei, a northerner, was named President; Colonel Kamougue, a southerner, Vice President; and Habre, Minister of Defense. Early in 1980, however, the accord broke down and fighting broke out again between Goukouni's and Habre's partisans. With assistance from Libya (which asserted a claim to the northern Chadian territory called the Aouzou Strip), Goukouni regained control of the capital and other urban centers and Habre retreated into Sudan. Goukouni's policy of political union of Chad and Libya, however, was unpopular and generated support for Habre, whose forces took N'Djamena in June 1981. He proclaimed himself President. French troops and an OAU peacekeeping force of 3,500 Nigerian, Senegalese, and Zairian troops remained neutral during the conflict.

Habre continued to face armed opposition on various fronts and brutally repressed opposition to his rule. In 1983, Goukouni's forces launched an offensive against the Habre government's positions in northern and eastern Chad with Libyan military support. This provoked French and Zairian forces to intervene to support Habre, pushing Goukouni's and Libyan forces northward. In 1984, the French and Libyan Governments announced the mutual withdrawal of their forces from Chad. The French and Zairian troops withdrew, but Libyan forces backing Goukouni continued to occupy northern Chad.

Habre defeated southern rebel groups and began a process of national reconciliation with former armed enemies and regime opponents. In 1986, Habre's forces, with French and U.S. financial and logistical support, attacked and decisively defeated the Libyans and Goukouni's forces in northern Chad in what was known as the Toyota War, from Habre's desert warriors' preference for using light trucks and desert-warfare tactics in overcoming the more numerous and better-armed and -equipped enemy. With Libyan forces expelled from nearly all of Chadian territory, a cease-fire was declared in 1987 and Chad and Libya restored normal relations in 1989. In 1994 the International Court of Justice confirmed Chadian sovereignty over the Aouzou Strip, effectively ending residual Libyan occupation of parts of Chad.

Habre's increasingly authoritarian rule and perceived favoritism of his own Gorane ethnic group weakened the coalition of northern and central groups on which he depended for support. In 1989, Idriss Deby, one of Habre's leading generals and a Zaghawa, defected and fled to Darfur in Sudan, from which he mounted a Zaghawa-supported series of attacks on the Habre regime. In December 1990, with Libyan and Sudanese assistance, Deby's forces successfully marched on N'Djamena, causing Habre to flee the country. Deby's Patriotic Salvation Movement (MPS) approved a national charter on February 28, 1991, with Deby as president.

During the 1990s and into the new century, Deby ruled in an authoritarian fashion, although proclaiming a desire for a democratic transition while surviving frequent coup and assassination attempts. He promulgated a new constitution in 1996, legalized political parties in 1992, and held an inclusive "National Conference" in 1993 aimed at political and electoral reform leading to a pluralist democratic regime.

In 1996, Deby won the country's first multi-party presidential election, defeating General Kamougue. In 1997, Deby's MPS party won 63 of 125 seats in legislative elections. International observers noted numerous serious irregularities in both electoral events. In 2001, Deby won reelection in a flawed contest, gaining 63% of the votes. In 2002, the MPS was successful in similarly flawed legislative elections.

In 2004, the National Assembly voted to amend the constitution to abolish presidential term limits; the amendment was approved in a 2005 national referendum. In 2006, Deby was elected to his third 5-year presidential term with 78% of the vote.

As a result, opposition parties boycotted the 2006 National Assembly elections, precipitating a political crisis. The government responded by signing an agreement with the opposition coalition for a program of political and electoral reforms aimed at credible national legislative, municipal, and presidential elections, codified in an August 13, 2007 accord. The accord also extended the mandate of the 2002 Assembly until such time as the reforms were achieved and the elections held.

Dissatisfaction with Deby's long rule among many ethnic groups, including subsets of Deby's own Zaghawa ethnic group, and tensions between Chad and Sudan caused by the Darfur crisis led in 2004 to the creation of a renewed and serious rebel threat: several newly-formed Chadian rebel groups found refuge in Sudan and support from the Sudanese Government, enabling them to mount frequent armed attacks into Chad, with the intention of violently toppling the Deby regime. Deby's situation was complicated by the influx of 300,000 Darfuri refugees into Chad and the displacement of 200,000 Chadians in eastern Chad. The Governments of Chad and Sudan soon became involved in a deadly proxy war, with the Government of Chad supporting Sudanese rebels committed to regime change in Khartoum and the Government of Sudan supporting Chadian rebels with the same goal vis-a-vis Chad. Sudanese rebels reached the Chadian capital twice, in 2006 and 2008, nearly overrunning the city in the latter instance, before being repulsed by government forces.

In 2008-2009, after the Chadian Army had defeated three major rebel attacks, and the Sudanese Army repulsed a rebel attack that reached the suburbs of Khartoum, international pressure for the normalization of Chad-Sudan relations intensified. Several Chad-Sudan agreements brokered by third parties had failed from 2006 to 2008, following which N'Djamena and Khartoum moved to resolve their differences bilaterally. This resulted in January 2010 in a Chad-Sudan peace accord, according to which the sides agreed to end the proxy war by breaking with rebel clients, normalize relations, and secure their border through joint military cooperation. President Deby publicly renounced past support for Sudanese rebels, a key Sudanese and international demand, and committed Chad to assist international efforts to resolve the Darfur crisis through peaceful negotiation.

The humanitarian effort to assist refugees and displaced persons in eastern Chad led to the deployment of two international peacekeeping operations, a European one from 2007-2008, and a UN one called MINURCAT, beginning in 2008. In 2010, the Government of Chad declined to agree to a renewal of MINURCAT's mandate, claiming that the project had been ineffective and proposing to provide better security with its own resources. MINURCAT ceased operations in December 2010. Chad provides security in and around refugee camps and to humanitarian personnel providing assistance through the Detachement Integre de Securite (DIS), a Chadian national police force created by the Chadian Government expressly for this purpose.

The August 13, 2007 accord on political and electoral reforms continues to be implemented. The accord has been facilitated through technical and political support from the European Union (EU), the U.S., France, Germany, the African Union (AU), and Switzerland, and they and the UN actively support the electoral process. In February 2011, Chad held legislative elections. Approximately 56% of the electorate voted, and the election was conducted without major incidents or any violence. On February 27, Chad's electoral commission announced that the ruling MPS and its allies had won 133 of 188 National Assembly seats. Opposition leaders alleged that fraud and irregularities invalidated the elections, but Chad's Constitutional Court did not nullify the results. International observers noted the lack of election preparation and some irregularities, but did not consider the government to have engaged in fraud.

Chad held presidential elections in April 2011. President Deby won easily, with approximately 88% of the vote, although turnout appeared low to international observers. Leading opposition figures boycotted the presidential elections due to concerns that deficiencies in the legislative elections had not been corrected. Municipal elections took place in January 2012.

GOVERNMENT AND POLITICAL CONDITIONS

Chad is a centralized republic in which the executive branch dominates the legislature and judiciary. Legislative and presidential elections were held during 2011. In April President Idriss Deby Itno, leader of the Patriotic Salvation Movement (MPS), was elected to a fourth term with 83.6 percent of valid votes. However, major opposition figures chose to boycott the presidential election, which was marked by low voter turnout. Deby has ruled the country since taking power in a 1990 coup. In February's legislative elections, the ruling MPS won 118 of the National Assembly's 188 seats. International observers deemed these elections to be legitimate and credible. Despite logistical issues, both the legislative and presidential elections occurred without violence.

Recent Elections

Although fraught with operational problems, international observers including the EU, African Union, and the Organisation Internationale de la Francophonie, the pan-African civil society group Coordination des Experts Electoraux Africains, and government and opposition-affiliated Chadian civil society actors deemed the February 2011 legislative elections to be legitimate and credible. No violence was associated with the elections, and there was no evidence of a systematic effort to deny voters their right to freely choose. Opposition candidates were given equal access to and treatment by national television, and security and government officials generally maintained a neutral posture during the campaigns.

The presidential vote in April occurred without violence or incident, and the election was organized in a manner sufficiently consistent with international standards and local laws that the electorate was in general permitted free expression of choice. However, local groups criticized the lack of participation by the three opposition candidates and low voter turnout.

Political Parties: There were approximately 120 registered political parties. The main opposition coalition was well-treated, in part to provide proof that the country had a multiparty system; however, smaller opposition parties were subjected to government interference. Northerners, particularly members of the Zaghawa ethnic group, including the Bideyat subclan to which the president belongs, were overrepresented in key institutions of state power, including the military officer corps, elite military units, and the presidential staff.

Opposition leaders accused the government of denying funds and equal broadcast time on state-run media.

Participation of Women and Minorities: There were 10 women in the 188-seat National Assembly. Five of the 40 cabinet ministers were women. Both the cabinet and the National Assembly had diverse ethnic representation.

Principal Government Officials

Last Updated: 1/31/2013

Pres.: **Idriss DEBY Itno**
Prime Min.: **Emmanuel NADINGAR**
Min. of Agriculture: **Albert Pahimi PADACKE**
Min. of Civil Service, Labor, & Employment: **Abdoulaye ABAKAR**
Min. of Commerce & Industry: **Youssouf ABASSALLAH**
Min. of Communications & Spokesperson for the Govt.: **Kedallah YOUNOUS**
Min. of Culture, Youth, & Sports: **Djibert YOUNOUS**
Min. of Defense: **BICHARA Issa Djadallah**
Min. of Economy & Urban Planning: **Mahamat Ali HASSAN**
Min. of Environment & Fisheries: **Terap Kabak HASSAN**
Min. of Finance & Budget: **Gata NGOULOU**
Min. of Foreign Affairs, African Integration, & Intl. Cooperation: **Moussa FAKI Mahamat**
Min. of Good Governance & Public Stabilization: **Ahmadaye Al-HASSAN**
Min. of Higher Learning, Scientific Research, & Professional Training: **Ahmat TABOYE**
Min. of Infrastructure: **Adoum YOUNOUSMI**
Min. of Interior & Public Security: **Ahmat Mahamat BACHIR**
Min. of Justice: **M'Bailou Naimbaye LOSSIMIAN**
Min. of Livestock & Animal Husbandry: **Ahmat Rakhis MANANI**
Min. of Mines & Energy: **Hassan SALINE**
Min. of National Education: **Abderahim Younous ALI**
Min. of Petroleum: **Mahamat Nasser HASSANE**
Min. of Postal Service, New Technology, & Communications: **Jean Bawoyeu ALINGUE**
Min. of Public Health: **Toufta BOGUENA**
Min. of Social Action, Solidarity, & Family: **Ngarmbatina Carmel SOU IV**
Min. of Territorial Development:
Min. of Tourism Development: **Mahamat Allahou TAHER**
Min. of Urban Planning & Housing: **Djimrangar DADNADJI**
Min. of Water: **Ahmat Mahamat KARAMBAL**
Min. in Charge of Auditing Govt. Depts.: **Mahamat Bechir OKORMI**
Min. in Charge of Decentralization: **Hamid Mahamat DAHALOB**
Min. in Charge of Human Rights: **Abderaman DJASNABAILLE**
Min. in Charge of Microfinance & Poverty Reduction: **Fatime TCHOMBI**
Min. & Sec. Gen. of the Govt., in Charge of Relations With the National Assembly: **Assia ABBO**
Dep. Sec. Gen. of the Govt., in Charge of Relations With the National Assembly: **Ousmane Moussa MAHAMAT**
Sec. of State for Agriculture: **Mariam ATTAHIR**
Sec. of State for the Economy & Urban Planning, in Charge of Microfinance & Poverty: **Azziza BAROUD**
Sec. of State for Environment, in Charge of Rural Hydraulics & Livestock: **Tahar SOUGOUDI**
Sec. of State for Finance, in Charge of the Budget: **Habiba SAHOULBA**
Sec. of State for Foreign Relations, Intl. Cooperation, & African Integration: **Mahamat BECHIR Okormi**
Sec. of State for Higher Education: **Yaya DJABAYE**
Sec. of State for Infrastructure, in Charge of Transport: **Mahamat Mahamadou ADDY**
Sec. of State for the Interior: **Bichara Issa DJADALLAH**
Sec. of State for National Defense, in Charge of War Veterans & Victims: **Hassan Saleh Al Gadam AL-DJINNEDI**
Sec. of State for National Education, in Charge of Basic Education: **Khadidja HASSABALLAH**
Sec. of State for Public Health: **Mahadie Outhman ISSA**
Sec. of State for Social Action: **Naima ABDELMOUTI**
Sec. of State for Urban Development and Housing: **Raoul Laouna GONG**
Ambassador to the US: **Maitine DJOUMBE**
Permanent Representative to the UN, New York: **Ahmad ALLAM-MI**

ECONOMY

Chad's primarily agricultural economy will continue to be boosted by major foreign direct investment projects in the oil sector that began in 2000. At least 80% of Chad's population relies on subsistence farming and livestock raising for its livelihood. Chad's economy has long been handicapped by its landlocked position, high energy costs, and a history of instability. Chad relies on foreign assistance and foreign capital for most public and private sector investment projects. Remittances are also an important source of income. The Libyan conflict disrupted inflows of remittances to Chad's impoverished western region that relies on income from Chadians living in Libya.

A consortium led by two US companies has been investing $3.7 billion to develop oil reserves—estimated at 1.5 billion barrels—in southern Chad. Chinese companies are also expanding exploration efforts and have completed a 311-km pipeline and the country's first refinery. The nation's total oil reserves are estimated at 1.5 billion barrels. Oil production came on stream in late 2003. Chad began to export oil in 2004. Cotton, cattle, and gum arabic provide the bulk of Chad's non-oil export earnings.

Labor Conditions

The labor code stipulates that the minimum age for employment is 14, except that children may work as apprentices beginning at age 13. The Office of Labor Inspection is responsible for enforcement of child labor laws and policies; however, the laws were not effectively enforced. Child labor was a serious problem. The low legal minimum age for employment, lack of any schooling opportunities in some areas, and tribal initiation rites rendering children informally adults by the age of 14 contributed to a general perception that child labor did not constitute exploitation unless the victims were less than age 13 or 14.

An estimated 20 percent of children between the ages of six and 18 worked in exploitive labor in the urban informal sector, according to a 2005 study published by Human Rights Without Borders. Children were regularly employed as herders, domestics, crop-pickers, and in panning for gold. They also were employed in the commercial sector, particularly in the capital, as street vendors, manual laborers, and helpers in small shops. Contracts were typically entered into informally between parents and herders and generally included compensation (including a small monthly salary and generally one animal at the end of six months). Local NGOs reported that compensation was often not paid.

Children worked as domestic servants, mainly in the capital. According to a 2005 UNICEF-government survey of child domestics in N'Djamena (the most recent data source available), 62 percent of child domestics were boys, 24 percent were between eight and 14 years of age, 68 percent were between 15 and 17, and 86 percent were illiterate. Local human rights organizations reported an increase in the number of child domestic workers during the year.

The labor code requires the government to set minimum wages. The monthly minimum wage was raised during the year from 28,000 CFA ($56) to 60,000 CFA ($120); however, the minimum wage was not effectively enforced. The law limits most employment to 39 hours per week, with overtime paid for supplementary hours. Agricultural work was limited to 2,400 hours per year, an average of 46 hours per week. All workers were entitled to unbroken rest periods of between 24 and 48 hours. The labor code mandates occupational health and safety standards and gives inspectors the authority to enforce them. Workers had the right to remove themselves from dangerous working conditions. The labor code explicitly covers all workers, including foreign and illegal workers.

Nearly all private sector and state-owned firms paid at least the minimum wage, but it was largely ignored in the vast informal sector. Salary arrears remained a problem, although less so than in previous years.

Workers did not always avail themselves of their rights concerning work hour limits, largely because they preferred the additional pay. Workers had the right to remove themselves from dangerous working conditions, however, in practice, with so few jobs in the formal sector, doing so for any reason often meant jeopardizing their employment. The protections legally provided for foreign and illegal workers were not always respected in practice.

U.S.-CHAD RELATIONS

The United States established diplomatic relations with Chad in 1960, following its independence from France. Relations between the United States and Chad are good. Chad is emerging from half a century of regionalized conflict and internal turmoil, and it has the potential to lay foundations for better governance and development. A 2010 peace agreement with Sudan continues to hold, and Chad currently enjoys relative stability; however, the risk of spillover of tensions from Libya, the Central African Republic, and Nigeria remains. Chad ranked 183rd out of 187 countries in the 2011 United Nations Development Program Human Development Index and is one of the most food-insecure countries in the world.

The Chadian Government is taking steps to improve infrastructure and foster stability. The United States continues to encourage Chad to advance good governance.

U.S. Assistance to Chad

U.S. interests in Chad include continued provision of humanitarian assistance to Sudanese and Central African Republic refugees and internally displaced persons in eastern Chad; continued Chadian commitment to efforts to reinforce regional stability and security; continued Chadian progress toward deepening democratization, including promotion of human rights and the rule of law; more responsible public-revenue management to promote sustainable socio-economic development; and continued U.S.-Chadian cooperation on regional and international counterterrorism efforts. The U.S. Government utilizes a combination of global, multilateral, regional, and bilateral programs, along with diplomacy, to achieve its goals in Chad. U.S. bilateral foreign assistance priorities for Chad focus on professionalizing the Chadian military and improving food security and maternal health. There is no U.S. Agency for International Development mission or Peace Corps program in Chad.

Bilateral Economic Relations

Chad is eligible for preferential trade benefits under the African Growth and Opportunity Act. Chad's exports to the United States are dominated by oil, while imports from the United States include machinery, plastics, and cereals. The United States is a leading investor in Chad, largely through the Chad-Cameroon petroleum pipeline project. The United States does not have an investment treaty or a bilateral tax agreement with Chad.

Chad's Membership in International Organizations

Chad and the United States belong to a number of the same international organizations, including the United

Nations, International Monetary Fund, World Bank, and World Trade Organization.

Bilateral Representation

The Republic of Chad maintains an embassy in the United States at 2401 Massachusetts Ave., NW, Washington, DC 20008 (tel: 202-652-1312; fax 202-758-0341).

Principal U.S. Embassy Officials

Last Updated: 1/14/2013

NDJAMENA (E) Ave. Felix Eboue, (235) (2) 251-6211, Fax (235) (2) 251-5654, INMARSAT Tel 76-364-4730, Workweek: Mon-Thu 0730-1700; Fri. 0730-1230, Website: http://ndjamena.usembassy.gov/

AMB OMS:	Debra Clark-Ware
ECON/COM:	Paul Colombini
FM:	Andy Deubel
HRO:	Lora West
MGT:	Luis Chirichigno
POL/ECON:	Beth Lampron
POL/MIL:	Brian Kennedy
POSHO:	Andy Deubel
SDO/DATT:	Vacant
AMB:	Mark Boulware
CON:	Elliot Repko
DCM:	Todd C. Holmstrom
PAO:	Lisbeth Keefe
GSO:	Francis Mbenna
RSO:	Nick Pietrowicz
AFSA:	Elliot Repko
AID:	Les Mcbride
CLO:	Cristina Pietrowicz
FMO:	Vacant
IMO:	Kasey Snyder
IPO:	Ricky Dabbs
State ICASS:	Shannon Brady

TRAVEL

Consular Information Sheet

June 27, 2012

Country Description: Chad is a developing country in north central Africa with one of the lowest per capita incomes in the world. Chad faces challenges in the areas of political stability and economic development. Years of war, drought, and lack of economic growth have severely damaged the country's institutions and its infrastructure. Facilities for tourism are limited. The capital is N'Djamena. French and Arabic are the primary languages.

Smart Traveler Enrollment Program (STEP)/Embassy Locations: If you are going to live in or visit Chad, please take the time to tell our Embassy about your trip. If you enroll, we can keep you up-to-date with important safety and security announcements. It will also help your friends and family get in touch with you in an emergency.

U.S. Embassy in Chad
Avenue Felix Eboue
N'Djamena
Mailing Address: BP 413 N'djamena Chad
Telephone: 235 2251–62-11, 2251–70-09, 2251–77-59, 2251–90-52, 2251–92-18 and 2251–92-33,
Emergency after-hours telephone: 235 6662–2100
Facsimile: 235 2251–56-54

Entry/Exit Requirements for U.S. Citizens: A valid passport and visa are required to enter Chad, but if you are entering from a high-risk country for yellow fever, you will need to show proof of vaccination. Visitors must check in with the National Police and obtain a registration stamp within 72 hours of arrival. You may obtain further entry information from the Embassy of the Republic of Chad at 2401 Massachusetts Avenue, N.W., Washington D.C. 20008, telephone (202) 652-1312. If you are overseas, you should inquire at the nearest Chadian embassy or consulate. The Government of Chad recently announced that it would not grant airport visas for tourists or business visitors. Anyone traveling on either a tourist, diplomatic, or official passport must obtain a Chadian visa prior to arrival.

The U.S. Department of State is unaware of any HIV/AIDS entry restrictions for visitors to or foreign residents of Chad.

Threats to Safety and Security: U.S. citizens planning travel to Chad should read the current Worldwide Caution Travel Alert and the Travel Warning for Chad, which warns U.S. citizens of the risks of traveling to Chad.

Due to the insecurity caused by high levels of violent crime, the continuing risk of clashes between Chadian government and rebel forces, and the constant risk of sudden outbreak of conflict among the populations living in these areas, we recommend that you avoid all travel to eastern Chad, the Chad/Sudan border area, and the Chad/Central African Republic border area. Kidnapping for ransom or as part of factional conflict continues to be a concern. The U.S. Embassy in Chad prohibits official government travel to eastern Chad without express authorization. If you are affiliated with humanitarian relief efforts, you should review security precautions and consider measures to mitigate your exposure to violent crime. If you are residing in Chad, you should exercise extreme caution throughout the country.

Stay up to date by:

- Bookmarking our Bureau of Consular Affairs website, which contains the current Travel Warnings and Travel Alerts as well as the Worldwide Caution.
- Following us on Twitter and the Bureau of Consular Affairs page on Facebook as well.
- Downloading our free Smart Traveler iPhone App to have travel information at your fingertips.
- Calling 1-888-407-4747 toll-free within the U.S. and Canada, or a regular toll line, 1-202-501-4444, from other countries.
- Taking some time before travel to consider your personal security.

Crime: U.S. citizens and Europeans are perceived to be wealthy, and should take precautions to avoid becoming crime victims. Travelers are advised not to leave cash or valuables unsecured in their hotel rooms, and not to wear expensive jewelry or show large amounts of cash. Travelers are also advised to dress modestly, not to walk outside after dark, and to lock their car doors. Petty crimes such as purse snatching, pickpocketing, and theft from vehicles do occur, particularly in areas frequented by expatriates. Violent crime against expatriates is a growing concern, especially in the eastern parts of the country. Carjacking, burglary, and vehicle thefts increase during times of political instability. Expatriate residences have been targeted for armed robbery, and some foreigners have been assaulted in the process. Travelers to northern Cameroon should contact the U.S. Embassy's Regional Security Officer in N'Djamena prior to crossing the Chad/Cameroon border because of the high incidence of road attacks there.

Victims of Crime: If you or someone you know becomes the victim of a crime abroad, you should contact the local police and the nearest U.S. embassy or consulate. We can:

- Replace a stolen passport.
- Help you find appropriate medical care if you are the victim of violent crimes such as assault or rape.
- Put you in contact with the appropriate police authorities, and contact family members or friends.
- Help you understand the local criminal justice process and direct you to local attorneys, although it is important to remember that local authorities are responsible for investigating and prosecuting the crime.

There is no local equivalent to the "911" emergency line in Chad.

Criminal Penalties: While you are traveling in Chad, you are subject to its laws even if you are a U.S. citizen. Foreign laws and legal systems can be vastly different than our own. In some places you may be taken in for questioning if you don't have your passport with you. In some places, it is illegal to take pictures of certain buildings. In some places driving under the influence could land you immediately in jail. These criminal penalties will vary from country to country. There are also some things that might be legal in the country you visit, but still illegal in the United States, and you can be prosecuted under U.S. law if you buy pirated goods. Engaging in sexual conduct with children or using or disseminating child pornography in a foreign country is a crime prosecutable in the United States. If you break local laws in Chad, your U.S. passport won't help you avoid arrest or prosecution. It's very important to know what's legal and what's not where you are going.

Based on the Vienna Convention on Consular Relations, bilateral agreements with certain countries, and customary international law, if you are arrested in Chad, you have the option to request that the police, prison officials, or other authorities alert the nearest U.S. embassy or consulate of your arrest, and to have communications from you forwarded to the nearest U.S. embassy or consulate.

Photography: All photography requires a government permit. Taking photos of military sites, official buildings, and airports is strictly prohibited, even with a permit. Such sites are not always clearly marked. Film and cameras may be confiscated, often by undercover police.

Accessibility: While in Chad, individuals with disabilities may find accessibility and accommodation very different from what you find in the United States.

Medical Facilities and Health Information: Medical facilities in Chad are extremely limited. Medicines are in short supply or unavailable, including many over-the-counter preparations sold in the United States. Travelers should carry any needed, properly labeled, medicines with them. In the event of major injury or illness, visitors generally will require medical evacuation.

There are two medical clinics in the capital of N'Djamena which offer "international standard" medical care; International SOS and Europ-Assistance. These are not walk-in clinics and advance membership is required to access services.

Malaria is a serious and sometimes fatal disease. Plasmodium falciparum malaria, the type that predominates in Chad, is resistant to the antimalarial drug chloroquine. Because travelers to Chad are at high risk for contracting malaria, the Centers for Disease Control and Prevention (CDC) advise that travelers should take one of the following antimalarial drugs: mefloquine (Lariam), doxycycline, or atovaquone/proguanil (Malarone). Travelers who become ill with a fever or flu-like illness while traveling in a malaria-risk area, and up to one year after returning home, should seek prompt medical attention and tell the physician their travel history and what antimalarials they have been taking. For additional information on malaria, including protective measures, visit the CDC Travelers' Health web site.

Other widespread illnesses in Chad include diarrhea and upper respiratory infections. HIV/AIDS is becoming an increasingly serious problem as infection rates are at alarming levels (up to 25 percent in high-risk groups). Meningitis outbreaks usually occur annually and several other diseases (cholera, diphtheria, chicken pox, typhoid) periodically appear.

You can find more information on vaccinations and other health precautions, on the CDC website. For information about outbreaks of infectious diseases abroad, consult the World Health Organization (WHO) website. The WHO website also contains additional health information for travelers, including detailed country-specific health information.

Medical Insurance: You can't assume your insurance will go with you when you travel. It's very important to find out BEFORE you leave whether or not your medical insurance will cover you overseas.

You need to ask your insurance company two questions:

- Does my policy apply when I'm out of the United States?
- Will it cover emergencies like a trip to a foreign hospital or a medical evacuation?

In many places, doctors and hospitals still expect payment in cash at the time of service. Your regular U.S. health insurance may not cover doctors' and hospital visits in other countries. If your policy doesn't go with you when you travel, it's a very good idea to take out another one for your trip. Medical evacuation out of Chad is difficult and expensive. There are only two companies that have agents and medical clinics in Chad capable of handling emergencies including medical evacuation; International SOS (ISOS) and Europ Assistance.

Traffic Safety and Road Conditions: While in a foreign country, you may encounter road conditions that differ significantly from those in the United States. The information below concerning Chad is provided for general reference only, and may not be totally accurate in a particular location or circumstance.

Roads are in poor condition and dangerous. In the capital city of N'Djamena, only the main roads are paved; the rest of the roads are either hard-packed dirt or looser dirt and sand. During the rainy season (mid-June to mid-September) many roads become impassable or are restricted by rain barriers, while during the drier season, clouds of dust rising from the roads reduce visibility.

Visitors should take great care while driving. Both paved and unpaved roads are poorly maintained, and often have large ruts and potholes. All drivers should adjust their speed accordingly. At night, streets are not lit; it is imperative to watch for pedestrians, bicyclists, motorcyclists, and livestock, as they may not be visible until they are in very close proximity.

Driving in Chad tends to be erratic both in cities and in rural areas. In cities, particularly N'Djamena, motorists share the roads with bicycles, motor scooters, pedestrians, and non-motorized wheelchairs. Lanes are not marked, and it is not uncommon for a normally two-lane thoroughfare to become a four-lane road during rush hours (generally 7:00 a.m.—9:00 a.m. and 3:00 p.m.—6:00 p.m. Monday—Thursday; 7:00 a.m.—9:00 a.m. and 11:00 a.m.—12:30 p.m. on Friday). Drivers are urged to be particularly observant at these times because motorists often attempt to overtake slower traffic by moving into oncoming lanes, usually at high speeds. There are only a few traffic lights in N'Djamena, and these are often out of service. Drivers yield to traffic on their right, particularly when entering the many traffic circles.

In rural areas, drivers should watch for livestock crossing the roads, and for large hawks that rest on the roads. These birds can be fearless, and cause damage by smashing into drivers' windshields; drivers may avoid this by slowing down when approaching the hawks, and allowing them sufficient time to fly away. Finally, drivers should be alert to older transport trucks traveling between cities, which do not always have functioning headlights.

No emergency services exist, so drivers should exercise extreme caution. Travelers should always wear seat belts. When traveling by car, be sure to carry a spare tire. Roadside service is limited to good Samaritans and children who will help push cars to the side or out of holes. When traveling outside the capital, it is imperative to carry sufficient quantities of drinking water. Drivers should ensure that their gas tanks are at least half-full at all times, as gas stations are not widely available. Gas may be purchased in an emergency in bottles from roadside stands, but it is generally of poor quality.

Travelers on roads in all areas of the country are subject to attack by armed bandits.

Aviation Safety Oversight: As there is no direct commercial air service between the United States and Chad, the U.S. Federal Aviation Administration (FAA) has not assessed Chad's Civil Aviation Authority for compliance with International Civil Aviation Organization (ICAO) aviation safety standards. Further information may be found on the FAA's safety assessment page.

Children's Issues: The government of Chad has prohibited international adoptions. Please see the U.S. Dept. of State Office of Children's Issues web pages on intercountry adoption and international parental child abduction.

Travel Warning

November 21, 2012

The Department of State warns U.S. citizens of the risks of travel to Chad and recommends citizens avoid all travel to eastern Chad and border regions. Because of security concerns the U.S. Embassy in Chad reviews all proposed travel by official U.S. government personnel to areas outside the capital, N'Djamena, and its immediate surroundings before approving such arrangements. U.S. citizens affiliated with humanitarian relief efforts similarly should review security precautions and consider measures to mitigate exposure to violent crime and other threats. U.S. citizens residing in Chad should exercise caution throughout the country. This Travel Warning replaces the Travel Warning for Chad dated March 29, 2012, to update U.S. citizens on the current security situation in Chad.

The U.S. Embassy in Chad operates as a fully accompanied post, meaning minor dependents of U.S. government employees are permitted to travel to or accompany family members to N'Djamena. The security situation in Chad has slowly but steadily improved since the conclusion of an effective peace agreement between Sudan and Chad in early 2010. You should note, however, that despite recent stability, the security environment has been historically volatile and could still deteriorate unexpectedly. The Embassy, therefore, strongly recommends that all U.S. citizens in Chad exercise caution and be prepared to implement their personal evacuation or safe haven plans on short notice should the situation warrant. U.S. citizens in Chad should closely monitor news media and register with the U.S. Embassy N'Djamena as well as monitor its website.

The frequency of violent crime in rural Chad is highly variable. Incidents of robbery, carjacking at gunpoint, and murder have been reported throughout the country. While there have been no kidnapping for ransom incidents in Chad since 2010, regional trends suggest this still could be a potential threat in the future. Violence is occasionally associated with car accidents and other events causing injury to Chadian nationals. Robbery victims have been beaten and killed, surgeons conducting unsuccessful medical interventions have been threatened with bodily harm, and law enforcement/military officials have been implicated in violent crime. In addition, although the last active rebel group was recently disarmed, armed groups might reemerge with little warning. The Government of Chad has few resources to guarantee the safety of visitors in rural Chad.

U.S. citizens affiliated with humanitarian relief efforts in rural Chad are strongly urged to adhere closely to the policies and procedures of their host organizations to mitigate risks from violent crime. The Government of Chad requires all individuals traveling to or residing in areas hosting refugee populations in Chad to obtain movement permits issued by the Ministry of Territorial Administration in N'Djamena, and to register in Abéché upon arrival in eastern Chad. U.S. citizens intending to enter Cameroon, Central African Republic, Libya, Niger, Nigeria, or Sudan from Chad should consult the Department's Travel Warnings for those countries and obtain any requisite visas or travel permits prior to traveling.

The U.S. Embassy communicates with U.S. citizens residing in Chad through its warden system; however in the case of an emergency, including an evacuation, the support that can be offered to those in remote and rural areas is limited. All U.S. citizens affiliated with humanitarian relief efforts in eastern Chad must have an evacuation plan developed with the United Nations agency coordinating their work on the ground.

Medical services in Chad are extremely limited. All U.S. citizens entering Chad are strongly encouraged to verify their coverage extends to traveling within Chad—including medical evacuation—prior to arrival. SOS International and Europ Assistance are the only two clinics in Chad that offer an international standard of care and provide medical evacuation services. The preceding information is provided for informational purposes only and in no way constitutes an endorsement, expressed or implied, by the United States Department of State.

Embassy updates are available at the U.S. Embassy N'Djamena web site. The current Worldwide Caution, Travel Warnings, Travel Alerts, and Country Specific Information as well as global updates are available at the U.S. Department of State's Bureau of Consular Affairs. Travelers may obtain up-to-date information on security conditions by calling 1-888-407-4747 toll free in the United States and Canada, or from other countries on a regular toll-line at 1-202-501-4444. Follow us on Twitter and the Bureau of Consular Affairs page on Facebook as well. You can also download our free Smart Traveler App, available through iTunes and the Android market, to have travel information at your fingertips.

U.S. citizens residing in or traveling to Chad are encouraged to inform the Department prior to traveling and enroll in the Smart Traveler Enrollment Program (STEP). By enrolling in STEP, the Department can keep travelers apprised of important safety and security announcements. Enrolling in STEP will also make for easier communication in the event of an emergency. Travelers should remember to keep all of their information in STEP up to date; it is particularly important to include a current phone number and e-mail address in order to receive the Embassy's emergency messages.

The U.S. Embassy in N'Djamena is located on Avenue Felix Eboue in N'Djamena and the mailing address is BP 413 N'Djamena Chad. The Embassy telephone numbers are 235 2251–62-11, 2251–70-09, 2251–77-59, 2251–90-52, 2251–92-18, and 2251–92-33. The Embassy fax number is 235 2251–56-54.

For after-hours emergencies, U.S. citizens in N'Djamena should call 235 6662–2100 and ask to speak with the duty officer.

Intercountry Adoption

July 2012

The information in this section has been edited from the latest report available as of February 2013 from the State Department Bureau of Consular Affairs, Office of Overseas Citizens Services. For more information, please read the *Intercountry Adoption* section of this book and review current reports online at http://adoption.state.gov.

Chad is not party to the Hague Convention on Protection of Children and Co-operation in Respect of Intercountry Adoption (the Hague Adoption Convention). Intercountry adoptions of children from non-Hague countries are processed in accordance with 8 Code of Federal Regulations, Section 204.3 as it relates to orphans as defined under the Immigration and Nationality Act, Section 101(b)(1)(F).

Below is the limited adoption information that the Department has obtained from the adoption authority of Chad. U.S. citizens adopting children in rare adoption cases from Chad, as well as U.S. citizen prospective adoptive parents living in Chad who would like to adopt from the United States or from a third country, should contact the Ministry of Justice to inquire about applicable laws and procedures.

The Government of Chad does allow intercountry adoptions, however, prospective adoptive parents should be aware that the lack of clear legal procedures for adopting in Chad can, and often does, result in protracted, difficult, and expensive adoption proceedings. Presently two sorts of adoptions are available in Chad; adoption simple and adoption pleinière. The adoption simple appears to be a form of traditional adoption whereby parents who are not able to provide for their child(ren) allow them to live with locally-based adoptive parents who can provide for the child(ren). The adoption simple does not allow the adoptive parents to change the adoptive child's legal name. An adoption pleinière appears to be a fuller and more finalized form of adoption in Chad. The adoption pleinière does permit adoptive parents to change their adoptive child's legal name. Prospective adoptive parents should not consider an adoption simple as final or irrevocable for custody and immigration purposes.

Chad's Tribunal de la Première Instance appears to have final jurisdiction when determining adoption cases for immigration and custody purposes. All questions should be directed to the Secretary General of the Ministry of Justice at +235.22.52.36.67

Caution: Prospective adoptive parents should be aware that not all children in orphanages or children's homes are adoptable. In many countries, birth parents place their child(ren) temporarily in an orphanage or children's home due to financial or other hardship, with the intention of returning for the child when they are able to do so. In such cases, the birth parent(s) rarely would have relinquished their parental rights or consented to their child(ren)'s adoption.

Chad's Adoption Authority: Ministry of Justice; +235.22.52.36.67.

CHILE

Compiled from publications that were available as of February 2013 from the U.S. Department of State, the U.S. Department of Commerce, and the Central Intelligence Agency (CIA). See the introduction to this set for explanatory notes.

Official Name:
Republic of Chile

PROFILE

Geography

Area: total: 756,102 sq km; country comparison to the world: 38; land: 743,812 sq km; water: 12,290 sq km

Major cities: Santiago (capital) 5.883 million; Valparaiso 865,000 (2009)

Climate: temperate; desert in north; Mediterranean in central region; cool and damp in south

Terrain: low coastal mountains; fertile central valley; rugged Andes in east

People

Nationality: noun: Chilean(s); adjective: Chilean

Population: 17,067,369 (July 2012 est.)

Population growth rate: 0.884% (2012 est.)

Ethnic groups: white and white-Amerindian 95.4%, Mapuche 4%, other indigenous groups 0.6% (2002 census)

Religions: Roman Catholic 70%, Evangelical 15.1%, Jehovah's Witnesses 1.1%, other Christian 1%, other 4.6%, none 8.3% (2002 census)

Languages: Spanish (official), Mapudungun, German, English

Literacy: definition: age 15 and over can read and write; total population: 95.7%; male: 95.8%; female: 95.6% (2002 census)

Health: life expectancy at birth: total population: 78.1 years; male: 75.08 years; female: 81.25 years (2012 est.); Infant mortality rate: total: 7.36 deaths/1,000 live births; male: 7.84 deaths/1,000 live births; female: 6.85 deaths/1,000 live births (2012 est.)

Unemployment rate: 6.4% (2012 est.)

Work force: 8.231 million (2012 est.)

Government

Type: republic

Independence: 18 September 1810

Constitution: 11 September 1980, effective 11 March 1981; amended several times

Political subdivisions: 15 regions (regiones, singular—region); Aisen del General Carlos Ibanez del Campo, Antofagasta, Araucania, Arica y Parinacota, Atacama, Biobio, Coquimbo, Libertador General Bernardo O'Higgins, Los Lagos, Los Rios, Magallanes y de la Antartica Chilena, Maule, Region Metropolitana (Santiago), Tarapaca, Valparaiso

Suffrage: 18 years of age; universal and compulsory

Economy

GDP (purchasing power parity): $319.4 billion (2012 est.); $303.5 billion (2011 est.); $286.5 billion (2010 est.); $269.9 billion (2009 est.)

GDP real growth rate: 5% (2012 est.); 5.9% (2011 est.); 6.1% (2010 est.); -0.9% (2009 est.)

GDP per capita (PPP): $18,400 (2012 est.); $17,400 (2011 est.); $16,700 (2010 est.); $15,900 (2009 est.)

Natural resources: copper, timber, iron ore, nitrates, precious metals, molybdenum, hydropower

Agriculture products: grapes, apples, pears, onions, wheat, corn, oats, peaches, garlic, asparagus, beans; beef, poultry, wool; fish; timber

Industries: copper, lithium, other minerals, foodstuffs, fish processing, iron and steel, wood and wood products, transport equipment, cement, textiles

Exports: $83.66 billion (2012 est.); $81.71 billion (2011 est.); $71.03 billion (2010 est.)

Exports—commodities: copper, fruit, fish products, paper and pulp, chemicals, wine

Exports—partners: China 22.4%, US 11.3%, Japan 11%, Brazil 5.5%, South Korea 5.4%, Netherlands 4.7% (2011)

Imports: $70.2 billion (2012 est.); $70.92 billion (2011 est.); $55.17 billion (2010 est.)

Imports—commodities: petroleum and petroleum products, chemicals, electrical and telecommunications equipment, industrial machinery, vehicles, natural gas
Imports—partners: US 20.9%, China 17.9%, Brazil 8.8%, Argentina 6.7%, Japan 4.2% (2011)
Debt—external: $102.1 billion (31 December 2012 est.); $99.4 billion (31 December 2011 est.); $86.35 billion (31 December 2010 est.)
Exchange rates: Chilean pesos (CLP) per US dollar; 488.9 (2012 est.); 483.67 (2011 est.); 510.25 (2010 est.); 560.86 (2009); 509.02 (2008); 526.25 (2007)

GEOGRAPHY

The northern Chilean desert contains great mineral wealth, principally copper, but also gold, potash, and lithium salts. The central area dominates the country in terms of population and agricultural resources. This area also is the cultural and political center from which Chile expanded in the late 19th century, when it incorporated its northern and southern regions. Southern Chile is rich in forests and grazing lands and features a string of volcanoes and lakes. The southern coast is a labyrinth of fjords, inlets, canals, twisting peninsulas, and islands. The Andes Mountains are located on the eastern border.

PEOPLE

About 85% of Chile's population lives in urban areas; greater Santiago is home to more than six million people and dominates Chile's political and economic institutions. Chile is a multiethnic society, and a majority of the population can claim some European ancestry, mainly Spanish (Castilian, Andalusian, and Basque), but also German, Italian, Irish, French, British, Swiss, and Croatian, in various combinations.

A small yet influential number of Irish and English immigrants came to Chile during the colonial period. German immigration began in the mid-1800s and continued into the 20th century; the southern provinces of Valdivia, Llanquihue, and Osorno show a strong German influence. In addition, there are a significant number of Middle Eastern, mainly Palestinian, immigrants and their descendants. About 800,000 Native Americans, mostly Mapuche, reside in the south-central area. The Aymara, Atacameno, and Diaguita groups can be found mainly in Chile's northern desert valleys and oases. Easter Island (Rapa Nui) is home to the Rapa Nui, an indigenous population.

Indigenous People

Indigenous people (approximately 5 percent of the total population) have the right to participate in decisions affecting their lands, cultures, and traditions, including the exploitation of energy, minerals, timber, or other natural resources on indigenous lands. However, the INDH noted in its 2011 annual report that government policies and judicial decisions regarding consultation with indigenous peoples limited their participation and restricted the measures and subjects of discussion. Indigenous people also experienced societal discrimination, and there were reported incidents in which they were attacked and harassed. Indigenous women faced triple discrimination on the basis of their gender, indigenous background, and reduced economic status, and they were especially vulnerable to violence, poverty, and illness.

Language

Spanish is the language of Chile. Among the business community, there is a fair level of English language capability.

Religion

According to the most recent census in 2002, 70 percent of the population over the age of 14 identified themselves as Roman Catholic and 15 percent as evangelical. In the census, the term "evangelical" referred to all non-Catholic Christian churches with the exception of The Church of Jesus Christ of Latter-day Saints (Mormons), Jehovah's Witnesses, Orthodox churches (Armenian, Greek, Persian, Serbian, and Ukrainian), and Seventh-day Adventists. Approximately 90 percent of those identified as evangelicals are Pentecostal. Anglican, Baptist, Episcopalian, Lutheran, Methodist, Presbyterian, Reformed Evangelical, and Wesleyan church members constitute the remaining 10 percent. Baha'is, Buddhists, Jews, Muslims, and members of the Unification Church collectively constitute less than 5 percent of the population.

Indigenous persons make up 5 percent of the population. Sixty-five percent of indigenous persons identify themselves as Catholic, 29 percent as Protestant, and 6 percent as "other." Mapuche communities, constituting 87 percent of indigenous citizens, continue to respect traditional religious leaders (Longkos and Machis), and anecdotal information indicates a high degree of syncretism in worship and traditional healing practices.

HISTORY

About 10,000 years ago, migrating indigenous peoples settled in fertile valleys and along the coast of what is now Chile. The Incas briefly extended their empire into what is now central Chile, but the northern area's barrenness prevented extensive settlement. The first Europeans to arrive in Chile were Diego de Almagro and his band of Spanish conquistadors, who came from Peru seeking gold in 1536.

The Spanish encountered hundreds of thousands of Indians from various cultures in the area that modern Chile now occupies. These cultures supported themselves principally through slash-and-burn agriculture, hunting, and fishing. The conquest of Chile began in earnest in 1540 and was carried out by Pedro de Valdivia, one of Francisco Pizarro's lieutenants, who founded the city of Santiago on February 12, 1541. Although the Spanish did not find the extensive gold and silver they sought, they recognized the agricultural potential of Chile's central valley, and Chile became part of the Viceroyalty of Peru. The drive for independence from Spain was precipitated by usurpation of the Spanish throne by Napoleon's brother Joseph in 1808. A national junta in the name of Ferdinand—heir to the deposed king—was formed on September 18, 1810. The junta proclaimed Chile an autonomous republic within the Spanish monarchy. A movement for total independence soon won a wide following. Spanish attempts to reimpose rule during what was called the "Reconquista" led to a prolonged struggle.

Intermittent warfare continued until 1817, when an army led by Bernardo O'Higgins, Chile's most renowned patriot, and Jose de San Martin, hero of Argentine independence, crossed the Andes into Chile and defeated the royalists. On February 12, 1818, Chile was proclaimed an independent republic under O'Higgins' leadership. The political revolt brought little social change, however, and 19th century Chilean society preserved the essence of the stratified colonial social structure, which was greatly influenced by family politics and the Roman Catholic Church.

A strong presidency eventually emerged, but wealthy landowners remained extremely powerful. Toward the end of the 19th century, the government in Santiago consolidated its position in the south by suppressing the indigenous Mapuche. In 1881, it signed a treaty with Argentina confirming Chilean sovereignty over the Strait of Magellan. As a result of the War of the Pacific with Peru and Bolivia (1879-83), Chile expanded its territory northward by almost one-third and acquired valuable nitrate deposits, the exploitation of which led to an era of national affluence.

Chile established a parliamentary democracy in the late 19th century, but this degenerated into a system protecting the interests of the ruling oligarchy. By the 1920s, the emerging middle and working classes were powerful enough to elect a reformist president, whose program was frustrated by a conservative congress. A new constitution that gave heightened power to the executive and formally separated church and state went into effect 1925. In the 1920s, Marxist groups with strong popular support arose. Continuing political and economic instability resulted with the rule of the quasi-dictatorial General Carlos Ibanez (1927-32). When constitutional rule was restored in 1932, a strong middle-class party, the Radicals, emerged. It became the key force in coalition governments for the next 20 years. During the period of Radical Party dominance (1932-52), the state increased its role in the economy. The 1964 presidential election of Christian Democrat Eduardo Frei Montalva by an absolute majority initiated a period of major reform. Under the slogan "Revolution in Liberty," the Frei administration embarked on far-reaching social and economic programs, particularly in education, housing, and agrarian reform, including rural unionization of agricultural workers.

By 1967, however, Frei encountered increasing opposition from leftists, who charged that his reforms were inadequate, and from conservatives, who found them excessive. At the end of his term, Frei had accomplished many noteworthy objectives, but he had not fully achieved his party's ambitious goals. In 1970, Senator Salvador Allende, a Marxist and member of Chile's Socialist Party, who headed the "Popular Unity" (UP) coalition of socialists, communists, radicals, and dissident Christian Democrats, won a plurality of votes in a three-way contest and was named President by the Chilean Congress. His program included the nationalization of private industries and banks, acceleration of agrarian reform and land expropriation, and collectivization. Allende's program also included the nationalization of U.S. interests in Chile's major copper mines.

Elected with only 36% of the vote and by a plurality of only 36,000 votes, Allende never enjoyed majority support in the Chilean Congress. Not all of his coalition's members agreed on his "Chilean Road to Socialism," and some pushed for more radical measures. Domestic production declined; severe shortages of consumer goods, food, and manufactured products were widespread; and inflation reached 1,000% per annum. Mass demonstrations, recurring strikes, violence by both government supporters and opponents, and widespread rural unrest ensued in response to the general deterioration of the economy. By 1973, Chilean society had split into two hostile camps. A military coup overthrew Allende on September 11, 1973. As the armed forces bombarded the presidential palace, Allende reportedly committed suicide. A military government, led by General Augusto Pinochet, took over control of the country. The regime was marked by serious human rights violations and the stifling of civil liberties and political expression.

Through a new authoritarian constitution, approved by a plebiscite on September 11, 1980, General Pinochet became President of the Republic for an 8-year term. In its later years, the regime gradually permitted greater freedom of assembly, speech, and association, to include trade union activity. In contrast to its authoritarian political rule, the military government pursued decidedly laissez-faire economic policies.

During its 16 years in power, Chile moved away from economic statism toward a largely free market economy that fostered an increase in domestic and foreign private investment. In a plebiscite on October 5, 1988, Chileans voted for elections to choose a new president and the majority of members of a two-chamber congress, denying General Pinochet a second 8-year term as president.

On December 14, 1989, Christian Democrat Patricio Aylwin, the candidate of a coalition of 17 political parties called the Concertacion, was elected president. Pinochet remained as commander-in-chief of the Army until 1998, when he became senator for life. Aylwin served from 1990 to 1994 and was succeeded by another Christian Democrat, Eduardo Frei Ruiz-Tagle (son of Frei Montalva), leading the same coalition, for a 6-year term. Ricardo Lagos Escobar of the Socialist Party and the Party for Democracy led the Concertacion to a narrower victory in the 2000 presidential elections. His term ended on March 11, 2006, when President Michelle Bachelet Jeria, of the Socialist Party, took office for a 4-year term.

In 2010, center-right Alianza coalition candidate Sebastian Pinera's inauguration marked the first time the Concertacion had not held the presidency since the return to democracy in 1990. President Pinera's inauguration came less than 2 weeks after a devastating magnitude 8.8 earthquake (at that time, the fifth-largest ever recorded) that struck Chile on February 27, 2010.

The earthquake and its aftershocks were felt throughout the central part of Chile, home to 75% of the population. The earthquake and subsequent tsunamis caused considerable damage in the two regions nearest the epicenter about 70 miles from Concepcion (200 miles southwest of Santiago); over 500 people were killed, hundreds of thousands of homes were destroyed or damaged, and nearly two million people were affected. By 2011, the economy had recovered from the effects of the earthquake, and most of the damaged infrastructure was restored. In certain areas heavily affected by the earthquake, some groups expressed concern about the availability of permanent housing.

Chile achieved global recognition for the successful rescue of 33 trapped miners in 2010. On August 5, 2010 the access tunnel collapsed at the San Jose copper and gold mine in the Atacama Desert near Copiapo in northern Chile, trapping 33 men 700 meters (2,300 ft.) below ground. A rescue effort organized by the Chilean Government located the miners 17 days later. All 33 men were brought to the surface on October 13, 2010, over a period of almost 24 hours, an effort that was carried on live television around the world.

GOVERNMENT AND POLITICAL CONDITIONS

Chile is a constitutional multiparty democracy. In January 2010 voters chose Sebastian Pinera Echenique of the center-right Coalition for Change as president in elections that were generally considered free and fair.

Recent Elections

In January 2010 voters chose Sebastian Pinera Echenique of the center-right Coalition for Change as president in free and fair run-off elections. In December 2009 voters also elected 18 of the 38 senators and all members of the Chamber of Deputies in elections generally considered free and fair.

Participation of Women and Minorities: There were 17 women in the 120-seat Chamber of Deputies and five women in the 38-seat Senate. There were four women in the 22-member cabinet. Indigenous people have the legal right to participate freely in the political process, but relatively few were active apart from those elected at the municipal level.

Principal Government Officials

Last Updated: 1/31/2013

Pres.: **Sebastian PINERA Echenique**
Min. of Agriculture: **Luis MAYOL**
Min. of Communications & the Press: **Andres CHADWICK**
Min. for the Economy, Development, & Reconstruction: **Juan Pablo LONGUEIRA**
Min. of Education: **Harald BEYER**
Min. of Energy: **Jorge BUNSTER**
Min. for the Environment: **Maria Ignacia BENITEZ Pereira**
Min. of Finance: **Felipe LARRAIN Bascunan**
Min. of Foreign Affairs: **Alfredo MORENO Charme**
Min. of Health: **Jaime MANALICH Muxi**
Min. of Housing & Urban Development: **Rodrigo PEREZ Mackenna**
Min. of Interior & Public Security
Min. of Justice: **Patricia PEREZ**
Min. of Labor & Social Security: **Evelyn MATTHEI Fornet**
Min. of Mining: **Hernan DE SOLMINIHAC Tampier**
Min. of the National Council for Culture & the Arts: **Luciano CRUZ-COKE Carvallo**
Min. of National Defense: **Rodrigo HINZPETER Kirberg**
Min. of National Patrimony: **Catalina PAROT Donoso**
Min. of the National Service for Women: **Carolina SCHMIDT Zaldivar**
Min. of Planning & Cooperation: **Joaquin LAVIN Infante**
Min. of Policy Coordination: **Cristian LARROULET Vignau**
Min. of Public Works: **Laurence GOLBORNE Riveros**
Min. of Transport & Telecommunications: **Pedro Pablo ERRAZURIZ Dominguez**
Pres., Central Bank: **Rodrigo VERGARA Montes**
Ambassador to the US: **Felipe BULNES**
Permanent Representative to the UN, New York: **Octavio ERRAZURIZ Guilisasti**

ECONOMY

Chile has a market-oriented economy characterized by a high level of foreign trade and a reputation for strong financial institutions and sound policy that have given it the strongest sovereign bond rating in South America. Exports account for more than one-third of GDP, with commodities making up some three-quarters of total exports. Copper alone provides one-third of government revenue. During the early 1990s, Chile's reputation as a role model for economic reform was strengthened when the democratic government of Patricio AYLWIN—which took over from the military in 1990—deepened the economic reform initiated by the military government.

Since 1999, growth has averaged 4% per year. Chile deepened its long-standing commitment to trade liberalization with the signing of a free trade agreement with the US, which took effect on 1 January 2004. Chile claims to have more bilateral or regional trade agreements than any other country. It has 59 such agreements (not all of them full free trade agreements), including with the European Union, Mercosur, China, India, South Korea, and Mexico. Over the past seven years, foreign direct investment inflows have quadrupled to some $15 billion in 2010, but foreign direct investment had dropped to about $7 billion in 2009 in the face of diminished investment throughout the world.

The Chilean government conducts a rule-based countercyclical fiscal policy, accumulating surpluses in sovereign wealth funds during periods of high copper prices and economic growth, and allowing deficit spending only during periods of low copper prices and growth.

As of November 2011, those sovereign wealth funds - kept mostly outside the country and separate from Central Bank reserves - amounted to more than $18 billion. Chile used this fund to finance fiscal stimulus packages during the 2009 economic downturn. In December 2009, the OECD invited Chile to become a full member, after a two year period of compliance with organization mandates, and in May 2010 Chile signed the OECD Convention, becoming the first South American country to join the OECD.

The economy started to show signs of a rebound in the fourth quarter of 2009, and GDP has grown more than 5% per year in the three years since. Chile achieved this growth despite the 8.8 magnitude earthquake that struck in February 2010, which was one of the top 10 strongest earthquakes on record. The earthquake and subsequent tsunamis it generated caused considerable damage near the epicenter, located about 70 miles from Concepcion - and about 200 miles southwest of Santiago.

Labor Conditions

The law sets the minimum age for employment at 18, although it provides that children between the ages of 15 and 18 may work with the express permission of their parents or guardians as long as they attend school. They may perform only light work that does not require hard physical labor or constitute a threat to health or child development. When attending school, children may not work more than 30 hours a week and in no case more than eight hours a day or between the hours of 10 p.m. and 7 a.m. Employers must register their work contracts at the local Ministry of Labor inspector's office.

Child labor was a problem in the informal economy and in agriculture. The use of children in the production, sale, and transport of drugs in the border area with Peru and Bolivia continued to be a problem. Children worked in the production of ceramics and books and in the repair of shoes and garments. In urban areas it was common to find boys carrying loads in agricultural loading docks and assisting in construction activities, while girls sold goods on the streets and worked as domestic servants. Children in rural areas were involved in caring for farm animals, as well as harvesting, collecting, and selling crops, such as wheat, potatoes, oats, and quinoa.

On July 1, the minimum wage increased 5.5 percent to 182,000 pesos (approximately $376) a month. As of March 1, the minimum wage for domestic servants was raised from 92 to 100 percent of that for other occupations. The minimum wage for workers over age 65 and under 18 was 135,494 pesos ($280). The 2009 official poverty level, the latest government figure available, was 64,134 pesos ($133) a month.

The law sets the legal workweek at six days or 45 hours. The maximum workday length is 10 hours (including two hours of overtime pay), but some categories of workers, such as caretakers and domestic servants, are exempt. The law mandates at least one 24-hour rest period during the workweek, except for workers at high altitudes, who may exchange a work-free day each week for several consecutive work-free days every two weeks.

The law establishes fines for employers who compel workers to work in excess of 10 hours a day or do not provide adequate rest days. Annual leave for full-time workers is 15 work days, and workers with more than 10 years of service are eligible for an additional day of annual leave for every three years worked. Overtime is considered to be any time worked beyond the 45-hour work week. Workers receive time and a half pay for any overtime performed.

U.S.-CHILEAN RELATIONS

From 1973 to 1990, Chile was ruled by a military government that came to power in a coup. The U.S. Government applauded the rebirth of democratic practices in Chile in the late 1980s and early 1990s and sees the maintenance of a vibrant democracy and a healthy and sustainable economy as among the most important U.S. interests in Chile. The two countries consult frequently on issues of mutual concern, including in the areas of trade, multilateral diplomacy, security, culture, and science. The U.S. Government and the Government of Chile have frequent high-level interaction.

U.S.-Chile collaboration on the environment includes sustainable development, climate change, energy efficiency, conservation and wildlife management, marine protected areas, environmental law enforcement, glacier monitoring, and agricultural best practices. Many U.S. technical agencies are actively engaged in Chile, including the U.S. Environmental Protection Agency, the Department of Interior, the U.S. Geological Survey, the National Park Service, and the National Oceanographic and Atmospheric Administration. The two countries have three sister park agreements.

The U.S.-Chile Equal Opportunities Scholarship Program was established to sponsor English and academic studies for Chilean PhD students who come from disadvantaged and rural areas that have not traditionally had access to English language schools or study abroad opportunities. The program has become a model for other international scholarships programs with Chile.

Under the U.S.-Chile Trilateral Development Cooperation initiative, the two countries have worked together on development projects in several countries. These projects have focused on issues such as citizen security, social inclusion, improving agricultural standards, and export promotion. At the U.S. state level, the Chile-California Partnership for the 21st Century fosters collaboration between individuals, government, and the private sector in areas such as agriculture, energy efficiency, environmental resource management, and education. Chile and Massachusetts have entered into a similar agreement.

U.S. Assistance to Chile

The United States provides no foreign development assistance to Chile.

Bilateral Economic Relations

The United States has a bilateral free trade agreement with Chile. The agreement eliminates tariffs and opens markets, reduces barriers for trade in services, provides protection for intellectual property, ensures regulatory transparency, guarantees nondiscrimination in the trade of digital products, commits the parties to maintain competition laws that prohibit anticompetitive business conduct, and requires effective labor and environmental enforcement. The United States and Chile participate in the Trans-Pacific Partnership trade negotiations that seek to develop a regional trade agreement.

Chile's Membership in International Organizations

Since its return to democracy in 1990, Chile has been an active participant in the international arena. Chile and the United States belong to a number of the same international organizations, including the United Nations, Organization of American States, Community of Democracies, Asia-Pacific Economic Cooperation forum, Organization for Economic Cooperation and Development, International Monetary Fund, World Bank, and World Trade Organization. Chile is also a member of the Pacific Alliance, Union of South American Nations (UNASUR), and Community of Latin American and Caribbean States (CELAC).

Bilateral Relations

Chile maintains an embassy in the United States at 1732 Massachusetts Avenue, NW, Washington, DC 20036; tel: 202-785-1746.

Principal U.S. Embassy Officials

Last Updated: 1/14/2013

SANTIAGO (E) 2800 Av. Andres Bello, +56-2-2330-3000, Fax +56-2-2330-3710, Workweek: Mon-Fri 8:30-17:00, Website: http://santiago.usembassy.gov/

DCM OMS:	Anastasia Ioda
AMB OMS:	Jackie Valenzuela
Co-CLO:	Mindee Davis
FCS:	Ellen Lenny-Pesagno
FDA:	Edmundo Garcia
FM:	Stephen Tuntland
HRO:	Karen Conole
MGT:	Jennifer Johnson
MLO/ODC:	COL James Quinn
NAS/INL:	Brian Manning
POL/ECON:	Brian Doherty
POSHO:	Steve Tuntland
SDO/DATT:	CAPT Ronald P. Townsend
AMB:	Alejandro D. Wolff
CG:	Mark Leoni
CON:	Tristan Spiceland
DCM:	James L. Williams
PAO:	Lawrence Corwin
GSO:	Paul Salarano
RSO:	Liseli Pennings
AGR:	Rachael Bickford
APHIS:	Judith Hall
CLO:	Shanna Ridenour
DEA:	Jorge Marrero
EEO:	Tristan Spiceland
FMO:	Donna Edmonds
ICASS Chair:	Rachel Bickford
IMO:	John Adams
ISO:	Heidi Dignan
ISSO:	Steven Stockdale
LAB:	Pablo Valdez
LEGATT:	Eric Metz

TRAVEL

Consular Information Sheet

August 26, 2011

Country Description: In addition to its stunning natural beauty, the Republic of Chile has a large, educated middle class and a robust free-market economy. Santiago and other large cities have well-developed tourist facilities and services, although the quality of tourist facilities may vary outside major populated areas.

Smart Traveler Enrollment Program (STEP)/Embassy Locations: If you are going to live in or visit Chile, please take the time to tell our Embassy about your trip. If you check in, we can keep you up to date with important safety and security announcements.

It will also help your friends and family get in touch with you in an emergency.

U.S. Embassy Santiago
Address: Avenida Andres Bello 2800, Las Condes, Santiago
Telephone switchboard: 56-2-330-3000
Telephone from the United States: 011-56-2-330-3000
U.S. Department of State Emergency Assistance: 1-888-407-4747
Consular Section fax number: 56-2-330-3017
E-mail address for U.S. citizens: santiagoamcit@state.gov
Internet address for hours and general information: http://chile.usembassy.gov

Entry/Exit Requirements for U.S. Citizens: U.S. citizens entering Chile must have a valid passport. U.S. citizens traveling to Chile for recreation, tourism, business, or academic conferences do not need to obtain a visa prior to their arrival to Chile. A Tourist Card will be issued for a stay of up to 90 days upon payment of a reciprocity fee, currently US $140. Currently, the fee is only charged at the Santiago International Airport. Payment can be made in U.S. currency or by credit card.

An extension of stay for another 90 days is possible upon payment of an extension fee at the Chilean Immigration Office located at San Antonio 580, Santiago; telephone 56-2-550-2469. The Tourist Card must be surrendered upon departure. Failure to submit this card upon departure may result in delays until a replacement is obtained. If lost or stolen, the tourist card must be replaced by the International Police branch of the PDI at their nearest headquarters or at the international airport prior to departure.

Ensure that you have appropriate documentation to enter Chile. U.S. passports must be in good condition and valid for the period of stay. The U.S. Embassy cannot secure entry on your behalf if you arrive without a valid U.S. passport, with a passport that is damaged or mutilated, or if you arrive without a visa when one is required.

For up-to-date information on visa requirements, visit the website of the Embassy of Chile in Washington D.C. U.S. Citizens who intend to work, live, or study in Chile must apply in advance for a Chilean visa. Chile imposes severe restrictions on the importation of agricultural products. Visit the Ministry of Agriculture website for current guidelines.

The U.S. Department of State is unaware of any HIV/AIDS entry restrictions for visitors to or foreign residents of Chile.

Entry/Exit Requirements for Dual Nationals: Dual U.S./Chile nationals must enter and exit Chile using their Chilean passport, and they must enter and exit the United States using their U.S. passport. A naturalization certificate is not a valid travel document. Information about dual nationality can be found on our website.

Entry/Exit Requirements for Minors: In an effort to prevent international child abduction, Chile has put in place strict requirements for the entry/exit of minors under the age of 18. Even when the minor is traveling with both parents, the parents will be required to show evidence of their relationship to the child when departing the country. Please carry an original birth certificate or a certified copy of the original.

Minors who enter Chile on a visa category other than tourist will always be required to submit a written notarized authorization from any non-traveling parent(s) and a birth certificate at the time of departure. In Chile, the authorization can be executed before a local notary public. If the non-traveling parent(s) is in the United States, the written authorization can be notarized and executed directly at the Chilean Embassy or Consulate. If the non-traveling parent is in the United States and is unable to visit the Chilean Embassy or a Chilean Consulate, the authorization can be executed by a U.S. notary.

However, an authorization executed by a U.S. notary must be authenticated to be valid in Chile. This means that the after the document is notarized it must be authenticated through a chain of steps involving submission to local, state and national authorities before it can be submitted to the Chilean Embassy or Consulate.

Note that the final step in the process is to submit the document to the Chilean Ministry of Foreign Affairs in Chile to authenticate the signature of the Chilean official in the United States. This is a lengthy process and should be commenced well in advance of travel. A minor entering Chile as a tourist will generally not be required to present a written notarized authorization from the non-traveling parent(s) at the time of departure if the minor leaves with the same adult companion with whom the minor entered Chile. The minor's immigration record will be annotated to include the relevant information. If the minor will depart alone or in the company of another party, the minor will be required to submit a written notarized authorization from the non-traveling parent(s) and birth certificate.

The written notarized authorization should include the following: 1) the full name of the custodial and/or non-custodial parents(s) or legal guardians; 2) the parents' full address; 3) the full name of the child; 4) the child's date of birth, place of birth, passport number and date of issuance; 5) full name and passport details of the person accompanying the minor; 6) dates of travel, including arrival and departure information; 7) address where the minor will reside; and 8) explicit authorization that a minor can travel alone or in the company of another person. Find additional information at Travel.State.Gov regarding the prevention of international child abduction.

Threats to Safety and Security: The Republic of Chile is politically stable, and the potential for terrorist activity is low. Demonstrations are common on March 29, the Day of the Young Combatant, and September 11, the anniversary of the coup against the government of President Salvador Allende. Even demonstrations that are meant to be peaceful can become violent and unpredictable. Avoid them if possible.

Be alert and aware of your surroundings and pay attention to the local news media. Protest and anarchist groups are known to place small explosive devices at ATMs and other Chilean government/business locations, which have thus far resulted in few or no injuries. However, improvised explosive devices (IEDs) are increasingly being placed in high-traffic pedestrian areas. A larger explosive device detonated in a major international hotel in Santiago in November, 2009 resulting in broken glass and several injuries. U.S. citizens have not been targeted in these attacks. Visitors to Easter Island may encounter rare, non-violent demonstrations.

Such demonstrations have caused minor disruption at the airport and closure of some government facilities. Demonstrations may result in minor inconveniences and occasional delays.

Stay up to date by:

- Bookmarking our Bureau of Consular Affairs website, which contains the current Travel Warnings and Travel Alerts as well as the Worldwide Caution.
- Follow us on Twitter and the Bureau of Consular Affairs page on Facebook as well.
- Download our free Smart Traveler iPhone App to have travel information at your fingertips.
- Calling 1-888-407-4747 toll-free within the U.S. and Canada, or by calling a regular toll line, 1-202-501-4444, from other countries.

Take some time before travel to consider your personal security. Things are not the same everywhere as they are in the United States.

Crime: Most foreigners visit Chile without incident. Nevertheless, street crime is a problem, especially in Santiago and Valparaiso. As in any large city, be cautious and aware of your surroundings. Be alert for pick-pocketing, purse and camera snatching, and thefts from backpacks and rental cars. Crimes are common in major tourist destinations, in hotel lobbies and restaurants, internet cafes, at bus and subway stations, and in cruise ship ports. Criminals usually work in groups and employ a variety of ruses to distract and victimize unsuspecting visitors. A few taxi drivers engage in currency switching and overcharge with altered taxi meters.

Drivers should keep car doors locked at all times and valuables out of sight as there have been reports of thieves entering cars or breaking windows of cars stopped at traffic lights in different areas in Santiago. Your passport is a valuable document. Report the loss or theft of a U.S. passport to the police and the U.S. Embassy immediately. Secure your passport and other valuables in a hotel safe, and carry a photocopy of your passport for identification purposes. Leave copies of your passport and important documents with family members in case of emergency.

Counterfeit and pirated goods may sometimes be available in Chile, and transactions involving such products may be illegal under local law. In addition, bringing such goods back to the United States may result in forfeitures and/or fines.

Victims of Crime: If you or someone you know becomes the victim of a crime abroad, you should contact the local police and the nearest U.S. embassy or consulate. We can:

- Replace a stolen passport.
- For violent crimes such as assault or rape, help you find appropriate medical care.
- Put you in contact with the local police authorities, and contact family members or friends.

Although the local authorities are responsible for investigating and prosecuting the crime, consular officers can help you understand the local criminal justice process and can direct you to local attorneys. The local equivalents to the "911" emergency lines in Chile follow an ABC-123 plan:

131—Ambulancia/Ambulance
132—Bomberos/Fire Department
133—Carabineros/Police Department

Criminal Penalties: While in a Chile, you are subject to Chile's laws and regulations. Chilean laws may differ significantly from those in the United States. You may not have the same protections available to you as under U.S. law, and penalties for breaking the law can also be more severe than in the United States for similar offenses. Persons violating Chile's laws, even unknowingly, may be expelled, arrested, or imprisoned. Penalties for possession, use, or trafficking in illegal drugs in Chile are strict, and convicted offenders can expect lengthy jail sentences and fines.

Persons engaging in sexual conduct with children and using or disseminating child pornography in a foreign country may be prosecuted in the United States. Based on the Vienna Convention on Consular Relations, bilateral agreements with certain countries, and customary international law, if you are arrested in Chile, you have the option to request that the police, prison officials, or other authorities alert the nearest U.S. embassy or consulate of your arrest, and to have communications from you forwarded to the nearest U.S. embassy or consulate.

Special Circumstances: Chile lies in an active seismic zone and is prone to major earthquakes, landslides, tsunamis, and volcanic eruptions. Several of the strongest earthquakes in history have occurred in Chile. Prepare yourself for a natural disaster by consulting the U.S. Federal Emergency Management Agency (FEMA) and Chile's Oficina Nacional de Emergencia (ONEMI).

Minefields are found in Chile's northern border region with Peru and Bolivia and around the southern border with Argentina in Patagonia. Minefields are generally marked, but markers may have shifted or may not be visible. Follow clearly identified roads and trails when traveling in minefield areas. Border crossings should only be made at authorized locations. Consult with park or other local officials concerning minefields and other hazards.

Chile is a popular destination for outdoor and adventure sports. Despite the best efforts of local authorities, assisting persons lost or injured in isolated and wilderness areas can be problematic. Before you go, learn about local hazards and weather conditions. Obtain information about parks and wilderness areas from the Chilean Forestry Service and mountain climbing from the Federacion de Andinismo de Chile and weather forecasts from the Chilean Meteorological Service. Report missing or injured persons immediately to the police. Inform park rangers, police, or other local authorities of your itinerary.

Chile's mountains and ski resorts are the recreational destination for hundreds of skiers and snowboarders each year. The main ski centres in Chile have good safety standards with will groomed pistes, ski and snowboard lessons with certified instructors, and clear signals for closure and opening of pistes. Skiing and snowboarding, however, are inherently dangerous sports and a number of people die at Chile's ski resorts each year. Skiers and snowboarders should respect the rules of each ski resort and be aware that skiing or boarding out of the bounds is extremely dangerous.

Accessibility: While in Chile, individuals with disabilities may find accessibility and accommodation very different from what you did in the United States. While steps are being taken to improve conditions for persons with disabilities, many public places are not adapted to accommodate these needs. For information on handicap accessible locations in Santiago and other locations in Chile, you can visit www.mapcity.com/ciudadaccesible.

Medical Facilities and Health Information: Santiago has two main private hospitals that are accredited by The American Hospital Association and meet U.S. standards: Clinica Alemana and Clinica Las Condes. Both have international patient departments and experience with some international insurance. Medical care in Chile is generally good, though it may not meet U.S. standards in remote areas. Major hospitals accept credit cards, but many doctors and hospitals in Chile expect immediate payment in cash. Prescriptions written by local doctors and over-the-counter medicines are widely available.

Air pollution is a major source of health concern in Santiago, resulting in severe bronchial ailments affecting infants, small children and the elderly. The most severe air pollution occurs during the winter (May through August). The ozone layer is especially thin over parts of Chile. Take precautions to protect yourself from ultraviolet radiation. Information on vaccinations and other health precautions can be found on the Centers for Disease Control (CDC) website. For information about outbreaks of infectious diseases abroad, consult the World Health Organization (WHO) website.

Medical Insurance: You can't assume your insurance will go with you when you travel. It's very important to find out BEFORE you leave.

You need to ask your insurance company two questions: Does my policy apply when I'm out of the U.S.? Will it cover emergencies like a trip to a foreign hospital or an evacuation?

In many places, doctors and hospitals still expect payment in cash at the time of service. Your regular U.S. health insurance may not cover doctors' and hospital visits in other countries. If your policy doesn't go with you when you travel, it's a very good idea to take out another one for your trip.

Traffic Safety and Road Conditions: While in Chile, U.S. citizens may encounter road conditions that differ significantly from those in the United States:

- Right-hand turns are prohibited at red lights unless otherwise posted;
- Major highways in and around Santiago collect tolls through use of an electronic transmitter (available at www.concesiones.cl);
- Secondary and mountain roads may be poorly maintained, poorly lit, and may lack guardrails;
- Many drivers do not signal lane changes and rarely yield to merging traffic,
- Many drivers exceed posted speed limits, do not maintain safe distances, and do not observe posted road signs;
- Major arteries in Santiago may switch directions during morning and evening rush hours;
- Drivers must carry sufficient Chilean pesos to pay frequent highway tolls.

Chile has modern infrastructure. Taxis and public transportation are plentiful and relatively inexpensive. Agree to a taxi fare before embarking. To use the public bus system in Santiago you need to obtain the prepaid "Bip" card. This card can also be used when traveling on the Santiago subway. Driving under the influence of alcohol in Chile is severely punished, and can result in incarceration. Visitors must have an international driver's permit and their U.S. driver's license to legally drive in Chile. The international driver's license must be obtained in the United States before traveling to Chile. Although car rental firms may rent to customers with only a U.S. driver's license, the police may fine foreigners for driving without a valid international permit.

Aviation Safety Oversight: The U.S. Federal Aviation Administration (FAA) has assessed the Government of Chile's Civil Aviation Authority as being in compliance with International Civil Aviation Organization (ICAO) aviation safety standards for oversight of Chile's air carrier operations.

Children's Issues: Please see the U.S. Dept. of State Office of Children's Issues web pages on intercountry adoption and international parental child abduction.

Intercountry Adoption

April 2010

The information in this section has been edited from the latest report available as of February 2013 from the State Department Bureau of Consular Affairs, Office of Overseas Citizens Services. For more information, please read the *Intercountry Adoption* section of this book and review current reports online at http://adoption.state.gov.

Chile is party to the Hague Convention on Protection of Children and Co-operation in Respect of Intercountry Adoption (Hague Adoption Convention). Therefore all adoptions between Chile and the United States must meet the requirements of the Convention and U.S. law implementing the Convention.Chilean adoption law gives priority to Chile an families over non-Chilean families. Most Chilean children available for intercountry adoption are at least four years old. Not all children eligible for adoption in Chile meet U.S. immigration requirements to receive an orphan visa, so it is important that adopting families consult with the U.S. Embassy in Santiago before beginning any adoption procedures to ensure that the adoption complies with U.S. law.

Who Can Adopt? Adoption between the United States and Chile is governed by the Hague Adoption Convention. Therefore to adopt from Chile, you must first be found eligible to adopt by the U.S. Government. The U.S. Government agency responsible for making this determination is the Department of Homeland Security, U.S. Citizenship and Immigration Services (USCIS).

Residency Requirements: There are no residency requirements to adopt in Chile.

Age Requirements: The adoptive parents must both be at least 20 years older than the child being adopted.

Marriage Requirements: Only married couples between the ages of 25 and 60 can adopt in Chile.

Who Can be Adopted? Because Chile is party to the Hague Adoption Convention, children from Chile must meet the requirements of the Convention in order to be eligible for adoption. For example, the Convention requires that Chile attempt to place a child with a family in-country before determining that a child is eligible for intercountry adoption.

In addition to Chile's requirements, a child must meet the definition of a Convention adoptee for you to bring him or her back to the United States. Families interested in adopting in Chile must apply and be approved by SENAME, which keeps the national registry of children eligible for adoption.

The first stage of the application process is to send SENAME, at the address above, a letter or email that includes both prospective adoptive parents' names, dates of birth, contact information and any preferences, including the reasons for these preferences, for a child or children. The children on the national registry have been declared eligible for adoption (susceptible de ser adoptado) by a judge and all parental rights have been terminated. SENAME matches available children with prospective adoptive parents.

Blood relatives are always given priority, followed by unrelated Chilean families, then non-Chilean families. Prospective adoptive parents do have the right to decline a specific match, which they would do by simply notifying SENAME. Prospective adoptive parents should consider carefully declining a specific match as they will be required to begin the process again and will have to explain, in detail, the reason for their declination.

Waiting Period: After a child is successfully matched with a family, there is a wait to obtain a hearing with a judge. The normal wait time is between 6 to 12 months.

Chile's Adoption Authority: SENAME (Servicio Nacional de Menores) is the clearinghouse for adoptions and approves parents who wish to adopt. Prospective adopting families must contact SENAME first before beginning any adoption proceedings.

The Process: Because Chile is party to the Hague Adoption Convention, adopting from Chile must follow a specific process designed to meet the Convention's requirements.

Time Frame: Intercountry adoptions from Chile normally take about two (2) years from start to finish. This time is measured from the time the prospective adoptive parents contact SENAME expressing their intention to adopt until the time the adoption is finalized.

Adoption Fees: In the adoption services contract that you sign at the beginning of the adoption process, your agency will itemize the fees and estimated expenses related to your adoption process.

The U.S. Embassy in Chile discourages the payment of any fees that are not properly receipted, "donations," or "expediting" fees, that may be requested from prospective adoptive parents. Such fees have the appearance of "buying" a baby and put all future adoptions in Chile at risk. Fees vary, but prospective adoptive parents should expect to spend no more than $300. Prospective adoptive parents should report exorbitant fees to the U.S. Embassy or SENAME.

Documents Required: The following documents are required by SENAME after the initial letter or email from the prospective adoptive parents is received. They will not accept these documents with the initial letter or email.

Prospective parents will receive a letter from SENAME acknowledging receipt and asking for the following documents below. Once the package of documents is received, SENAME will begin the process of matching a child;

- Birth certificates and marriage certificate of the prospective adoptive parents;
- Certificate issued by a Chilean Consul in the U.S. that states that the parents have met all U.S. adoption requirements;
- Favorable home study conducted by an accredited agency in the U.S.;
- Physical and psychological exams demonstrating the well-being of the parents;
- Proof of parents' financial situation, i.e., ability to successfully support the child;
- Recent photographs of each of the prospective adoptive parent(s);
- Three notarized letters of recommendation from U.S. community, religious or other governmental authorities;
- Since all Immigrant Visas issued in Chile will be IH-3 visas, the U.S. Embassy will issue a certificate stating that the child is eligible for U.S. citizenship automatically after he/she legally enters the U.S. with an immigrant visa. In order to obtain this certificate, adopting parents and/or their agent must come to the Embassy Monday, Wednesday or Friday morning between 8:30-11:00am.

Bringing Your Child Home: Once your adoption is complete (or you have obtained legal custody of the child), there are a few more steps to take before you can head home. Specifically, you need to apply for several documents for your child before he or she can travel to the United States, such as a birth certificate, a passport or travel document for your child from the country in which he or she was born, and a U.S. Immigration Visa.

For detailed and updated information on how to obtain these documents, review the *Intercountry Adoption* section in this publication and visit the U.S. Department of State Intercountry Adoption website at http://adoption.state.gov.

Child Citizenship Act: For adoptions finalized abroad, the Child Citizenship Act of 2000 allows your new child to acquire American citizenship automatically when he or she enters the United States as lawful permanent residents. For adoptions finalized in the United States, the Child Citizenship Act of 2000 allows your new child to acquire American citizenship automatically when the court in the United States issues the final adoption decree. To learn more, review the *Intercountry Adoption* section in this publication and visit the U.S. Department of State Intercountry Adoption website at http://adoption.state.gov. For questions about immigration procedures, call the National Customer Service Center (NCSC) at 1-800-375-5283 (TTY 1-800-767-1833).

U.S. Embassy in Chile
Consular Section—Immigrant Visas
Avenida Andrés Bello 2800
Santiago, Chile
Tel: (56)(2) 335-6550
Fax: (56)(2) 330-3005
Santiagoimmigration@state.gov
http://chile.usembassy.gov

Chile's Adoption Authority
Servicio Nacional de Menores de Chile (SENAME)
Unidad de Adopción
Huerfanos 587
Santiago, Chile
Telephone: (56)(2) 398-4447
http://www.sename.cl

Embassy of Chile in the United States
1732 Massachusetts Avenue, N.W.
Washington, DC 20036
Tel: (202) 785-1746
Fax: (202) 887-5579
http://www.chile-usa.org

Office of Children's Issues
U.S. Department of State
2201 C Street, NW
SA-29
Washington, DC 20520
Tel: 1-888-407-4747
AskCI@state.gov
http://adoption.state.gov

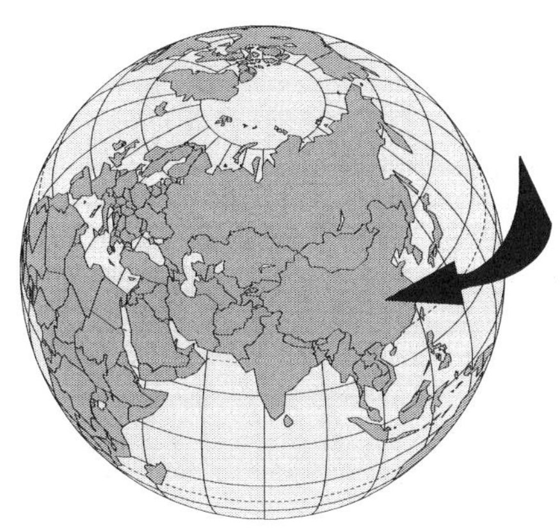

CHINA

Compiled from publications that were available as of February 2013 from the U.S. Department of State, the U.S. Department of Commerce, and the Central Intelligence Agency (CIA). See the introduction to this set for explanatory notes.

Official Name:
People's Republic of China

PROFILE

Geography

Area: total: 9,596,961 sq km; country comparison to the world: 4; land: 9,569,901 sq km; water: 27,060 sq km

Major cities: Shanghai 16.575 million; Beijing (capital) 12.214 million; Chongqing 9.401 million; Shenzhen 9.005 million; Guangzhou 8.884 million (2009)

Climate: extremely diverse; tropical in south to subarctic in north

Terrain: mostly mountains, high plateaus, deserts in west; plains, deltas, and hills in east

People

Nationality: noun: Chinese (singular and plural); adjective: Chinese

Population: 1,343,239,923 (July 2012 est.)

Population growth rate: 0.481% (2012 est.)

Ethnic groups: Han Chinese 91.5%, Zhuang, Manchu, Hui, Miao, Uighur, Tujia, Yi, Mongol, Tibetan, Buyi, Dong, Yao, Korean, and other nationalities 8.5% (2000 census)

Religions: Daoist (Taoist), Buddhist, Christian 3%-4%, Muslim 1%-2%

Languages: Standard Chinese or Mandarin (Putonghua, based on the Beijing dialect), Yue (Cantonese), Wu (Shanghainese), Minbei (Fuzhou), Minnan (Hokkien-Taiwanese), Xiang, Gan, Hakka dialects, minority languages (see Ethnic groups entry)

Literacy: definition: age 15 and over can read and write; total population: 92.2%; male: 96%; female: 88.5% (2007)

Health: life expectancy at birth: total population: 74.84 years; male: 72.82 years; female: 77.11 years (2012 est.); Infant mortality rate: total: 15.62 deaths/1,000 live births; male: 15.38 deaths/1,000 live births; female: 15.9 deaths/1,000 live births (2012 est.)

Unemployment rate: 6.4% (2012 est.)

Work force: 795.4 million

Government

Type: Communist state

Independence: 1 October 1949

Constitution: most recent promulgation 4 December 1982; amended several times

Political subdivisions: 23 provinces (sheng, singular and plural), 5 autonomous regions (zizhiqu, singular and plural), and 4 municipalities (shi, singular and plural)

Suffrage: 18 years of age; universal

Economy

GDP (purchasing power parity): $12.38 trillion (2012 est.); $11.44 trillion (2011 est.); $10.48 trillion (2010 est.); $9.486 trillion (2009 est.)

GDP real growth rate: 7.8% (2012 est.); 9.2% (2011 est.); 10.4% (2010 est.); 9.2% (2009 est.)

GDP per capita (PPP): $9,100 (2012 est.); $8,500 (2011 est.); $7,800 (2010 est.); $7,100 (2009 est.)

Natural resources: coal, iron ore, petroleum, natural gas, mercury, tin, tungsten, antimony, manganese, molybdenum, vanadium, magnetite, aluminum, lead, zinc, rare earth elements, uranium, hydropower potential (world's largest)

Agriculture products: world leader in gross value of agricultural output; rice, wheat, potatoes, corn, peanuts, tea, millet, barley, apples, cotton, oilseed; pork; fish

Industries: world leader in gross value of industrial output; mining and ore processing, iron, steel, aluminum, and other metals, coal; machine building; armaments; textiles and apparel; petroleum; cement; chemicals; fertilizers; consumer products, including footwear, toys, and electronics; food processing; transportation equipment, including automobiles, rail cars and locomotives, ships, and aircraft; telecommunications equipment, commercial space launch vehicles, satellites

Exports: $2.021 trillion (2012 est.); $1.904 trillion (2011 est.); $1.581 trillion (2010 est.)

Exports—commodities: electrical and other machinery, including data processing equipment, apparel, textiles, iron and steel, optical and medical equipment

Exports—partners: US 17.1%, Hong Kong 14.1%, Japan 7.8%, South Korea 4.4%, Germany 4% (2011)

Imports: $1.78 trillion (2012 est.); $1.743 trillion (2011 est.); $1.327 trillion (2010 est.)

Imports—commodities: electrical and other machinery, oil and mineral fuels, optical and medical equipment, metal ores, plastics, organic chemicals

Imports—partners: Japan 11.2%, South Korea 9.3%, US 6.8%, Germany 5.3%, Australia 4.6% (2011)

Debt—external: $710.7 billion (31 December 2012 est.); $697.2 billion (30 September 2011 est.); $548.6 billion (31 December 2010 est.)

Exchange rates: Renminbi yuan (RMB) per US dollar; 6.311 (2012 est.); 6.4615 (2011 est.); 6.7703 (2010 est.); 6.8314 (2009); 6.9385 (2008); 7.61 (2007)

PEOPLE

Ethnic Groups

The largest ethnic group is the Han Chinese. The remaining are Zhuang, Manchu, Hui, Miao, Uighur, Yi , Mongol, Tibetan, Buyi, Korean, and other ethnic minorities.

Language

There are seven major Chinese dialects and many subdialects. Mandarin (or Putonghua), the predominant dialect, is spoken by over 70% of the population. It is taught in all schools and is the medium of government. About two-thirds of the Han ethnic group are native speakers of Mandarin; the rest, concentrated in southwest and southeast China, speak one of the six other major Chinese dialects. Non-Chinese languages spoken widely by ethnic minorities include Mongolian, Tibetan, Uighur and other Turkic languages (in Xinjiang), and Korean (in the northeast). Some autonomous regions and special administrative regions have their own official languages. For example, Mongolian has official status within the Inner Mongolian Autonomous Region of China.

The Pinyin System of Romanization

On January 1, 1979, the Chinese Government officially adopted the pinyin system for spelling Chinese names and places in Roman letters. A system of Romanization invented by the Chinese, pinyin has long been widely used in China on street and commercial signs as well as in elementary Chinese textbooks as an aid in learning Chinese characters. Variations of pinyin also are used as the written forms of several minority languages.

Pinyin has now replaced other conventional spellings in China's English-language publications. The U.S. Government also has adopted the pinyin system for all names and places in China. For example, the capital of China is now spelled "Beijing" rather than "Peking."

Religion

A February 2007 survey conducted by East China Normal University and reported in state-run media concluded that 31.4% of Chinese citizens ages 16 and over are religious believers. While the Chinese constitution affirms "freedom of religious belief," the Chinese Government places restrictions on religious practice, particularly on religious practice outside officially recognized organizations. The five state-sanctioned "patriotic religious associations" are Buddhism, Taoism, Islam, Catholicism, and Protestantism. Buddhism is most widely practiced; the state-approved Xinhua news agency estimates there are 100 million Buddhists in China. According to the State Administration for Religious Affairs (SARA), there are more than 21 million Muslims in the country. Christians on the mainland number nearly 23 million, accounting for 1.8% of the population, according to The Blue Book of Religions (compiled by the Chinese Academy of Social Sciences' Institute of World Religions and released in August 2010). Other official figures indicate there are 5.3 million Catholics, though unofficial estimates are much higher. The Pew Research Center estimated in 2007 that 50 million to 70 million Christians practice in unregistered religious gatherings or "house" churches. There are no official statistics confirming the number of Taoists in China.

Although officially restricted from 1949 until the 1980s, Buddhism has regained popularity in China and has become the largest organized religion in the country. There continue to be strict government restrictions on Tibetan Buddhism.

Of China's 55 officially recognized minorities, 10 groups are predominately Muslim. According to government figures, there are 36,000 Islamic places of worship and more than 45,000 imams.

Only two Christian organizations—a "patriotic" Catholic association without official ties to Rome and the "Three-Self-Patriotic" Protestant church—are sanctioned by the Chinese Government. Unregistered "house" churches exist in many parts of the country. The extent to which local authorities have tried to control the activities of unregistered churches varies from region to region. However, the government suppresses the religious activities of "underground" Roman Catholic clergy who are not affiliated with the official patriotic Catholic association and have avowed loyalty to the Vatican, which the government accuses of interfering in the country's internal affairs. The government also severely restricts the activities of groups it designates as "evil cults," including several Christian groups and the Falun Gong spiritual movement.

Population Policy

With a population officially over 1.3 billion and an estimated population growth rate of 0.593% (2011 est.), China is very concerned about its population growth and has attempted with mixed results to implement a strict birth limitation policy. China's 2002 Population and Family Plan-

ning Law and policy permits one child per family, with allowance for a second child under certain circumstances, especially in rural areas, and with guidelines looser for ethnic minorities with small populations. Enforcement varies and relies largely on "social compensation fees" to discourage extra births. Official government policy prohibits the use of physical coercion to compel persons to submit to abortion or sterilization, but in some localities there are instances of local birth-planning officials using physical coercion to meet birth limitation targets. The government's goal is to stabilize the population in the first half of the 21st century, and 2009 projections from the U.S. Census Bureau were that the Chinese population would peak at around 1.4 billion by 2026.

HISTORY

Dynastic Period

China is the oldest continuous major world civilization, with records dating back about 3,500 years. Successive dynasties developed a system of bureaucratic control that gave the agrarian-based Chinese an advantage over neighboring nomadic and hill cultures. Chinese civilization was further strengthened by the development of a Confucian state ideology and a common written language that bridged the gaps among the country's many local languages and dialects. Whenever China was conquered by nomadic tribes, as it was by the Mongols in the 13th century, the conquerors sooner or later adopted the ways of the "higher" Chinese civilization and staffed the bureaucracy with Chinese.

The last dynasty was established in 1644, when the Manchus overthrew the native Ming dynasty and established the Qing (Ch'ing) dynasty with Beijing as its capital. At great expense in blood and treasure, the Manchus over the next half-century gained control of many border areas, including Xinjiang, Yunnan, Tibet, Mongolia, and Taiwan. The success of the early Qing period was based on the combination of Manchu martial prowess and traditional Chinese bureaucratic skills.

During the 19th century, Qing control weakened, and prosperity diminished. China suffered massive social strife, economic stagnation, explosive population growth, and Western penetration and influence. The Taiping and Nian rebellions, along with a Russian-supported Muslim separatist movement in Xinjiang, drained Chinese resources and almost toppled the dynasty. Britain's desire to continue its opium trade with China collided with imperial edicts prohibiting the addictive drug, and the First Opium War erupted in 1840. China lost the war; subsequently, Britain and other Western powers, including the United States, forcibly occupied "concessions" and gained special commercial privileges. Hong Kong was ceded to Britain in 1842 under the Treaty of Nanking, and in 1898, when the Opium Wars finally ended, Britain executed a 99-year lease of the New Territories, significantly expanding the size of the Hong Kong colony.

As time went on, the Western powers, wielding superior military technology, gained more economic and political privileges. Reformist Chinese officials argued for the adoption of Western technology to strengthen the dynasty and counter Western advances, but the Qing court played down both the Western threat and the benefits of Western technology.

Early 20th Century China

Frustrated by the Qing court's resistance to reform, young officials, military officers, and students—inspired by the revolutionary ideas of Sun Yat-sen—began to advocate the overthrow of the Qing dynasty and creation of a republic. A revolutionary military uprising on October 10, 1911, led to the abdication of the last Qing monarch. As part of a compromise to overthrow the dynasty without a civil war, the revolutionaries and reformers allowed high Qing officials to retain prominent positions in the new republic. One of these figures, Gen. Yuan Shikai, was chosen as the republic's first president. Before his death in 1916, Yuan unsuccessfully attempted to name himself emperor. His death left the republican government all but shattered, ushering in the era of the "warlords" during which China was ruled and ravaged by shifting coalitions of competing provincial military leaders.

In the 1920s, Sun Yat-sen established a revolutionary base in south China and set out to unite the fragmented nation. With Soviet assistance, he organized the Kuomintang (KMT or "Chinese Nationalist People's Party"), and entered into an alliance with the fledgling Chinese Communist Party (CCP). After Sun's death in 1925, one of his proteges, Chiang Kai-shek, seized control of the KMT and succeeded in bringing most of south and central China under its rule. In 1927, Chiang turned on the CCP and executed many of its leaders. The remnants fled into the mountains of eastern China. In 1934, driven out of their mountain bases, the CCP's forces embarked on a "Long March" across some of China's most desolate terrain to the northwestern province of Shaanxi, where they established a guerrilla base at Yan'an.

During the "Long March," the communists reorganized under a new leader, Mao Zedong (Mao Tse-tung). The bitter struggle between the KMT and the CCP continued openly or clandestinely through the 14-year-long Japanese invasion (1931-45), even though the two parties nominally formed a united front to oppose the Japanese invaders in 1937. The war between the two parties resumed after the Japanese defeat in 1945. By 1949, the CCP occupied most of the country.

Chiang Kai-shek fled with the remnants of his KMT government and military forces to Taiwan, where he proclaimed Taipei to be China's "provisional capital" and vowed to re-conquer the Chinese mainland. Taiwan still calls itself the "Republic of China."

The People's Republic of China

In Beijing, on October 1, 1949, Mao Zedong proclaimed the founding of the People's Republic of China (P.R.C.). The new government assumed control of a people exhausted by two generations of war and social conflict, and an economy ravaged by high inflation and disrupted transportation links. A new political and economic order modeled on the Soviet example was quickly installed.

In the early 1950s, China undertook a massive economic and social reconstruction program. The new leaders gained popular support by curbing inflation, restoring the economy, and rebuilding many war-damaged industrial plants. The CCP's authority reached into almost every aspect of Chinese life. Party control was assured by large, politically loyal security and military forces; a government apparatus responsive to party direction; and the placement of party members in leadership positions in labor, women's, and other mass organizations.

The "Great Leap Forward" and the Sino-Soviet Split

In 1958, Mao broke with the Soviet model and announced a new economic program, the "Great Leap Forward," aimed at rapidly raising industrial and agricultural production. Giant cooperatives (communes) were formed, and "backyard factories" dotted the Chinese landscape. The results were disastrous. Normal market mechanisms were disrupted, agricultural production fell behind, and China's people exhausted themselves producing what turned out to be shoddy, un-salable goods. Within a year, starvation appeared even in fertile agricultural areas. From 1960 to 1961, the combination of poor planning during the Great Leap Forward and bad weather resulted in one of the deadliest famines in human history.

The already-strained Sino-Soviet relationship deteriorated sharply in 1959, when the Soviets started to restrict the flow of scientific and technological information to China. The dispute escalated, and the Soviets withdrew all of their personnel from China in August 1960. In 1960, the Soviets and the Chinese began to have disputes openly in international forums.

The Cultural Revolution

In the early 1960s, State President Liu Shaoqi and his protege, Party General Secretary Deng Xiaoping, took over direction of the party and adopted pragmatic economic policies at odds with Mao's revolutionary vision. Dissatisfied with China's new direction and his own reduced authority, Party Chairman Mao launched a massive political attack on Liu, Deng, and other pragmatists in the spring of 1966. The new movement, the "Great Proletarian Cultural Revolution," was unprecedented in communist China's history. For the first time, a section of the Chinese communist leadership sought to rally popular opposition against another leadership group. China was set on a course of political and social anarchy that lasted the better part of a decade.

In the early stages of the Cultural Revolution, Mao and his "closest comrade in arms," National Defense Minister Lin Biao, charged Liu, Deng, and other top party leaders with dragging China back toward capitalism. Radical youth organizations, called Red Guards, attacked party and state organizations at all levels, seeking out leaders who would not bend to the radical wind. In reaction to this turmoil, some local People's Liberation Army (PLA) commanders and other officials maneuvered to outwardly back Mao and the radicals while actually taking steps to rein in local radical activity.

Gradually, Red Guard and other radical activity subsided, and the Chinese political situation stabilized along complex factional lines. The leadership conflict came to a head in September 1971, when Party Vice Chairman and Defense Minister Lin Biao reportedly tried to stage a coup against Mao; Lin Biao allegedly later died in a plane crash in Mongolia. In the aftermath of the Lin Biao incident, many officials criticized and dismissed during 1966-69 were reinstated. Chief among these was Deng Xiaoping, who reemerged in 1973 and was confirmed in 1975 in the concurrent posts of Party Vice Chairman, Politburo Standing Committee member, PLA Chief of Staff, and Vice Premier.

The ideological struggle between more pragmatic, veteran party officials and the radicals re-emerged with a vengeance in late 1975. Mao's wife, Jiang Qing, and three close Cultural Revolution associates (later dubbed the "Gang of Four") launched a media campaign against Deng. In January 1976, Premier Zhou Enlai, a popular political figure, died of cancer. On April 5, Beijing citizens staged a spontaneous demonstration in Tiananmen Square in Zhou's memory, with strong political overtones of support for Deng. The authorities forcibly suppressed the demonstration. Deng was blamed for the disorder and stripped of all official positions, although he retained his party membership.

The Post-Mao Era

Mao's death in September 1976 removed a towering figure from Chinese politics and set off a scramble for succession. Former Minister of Public Security Hua Guofeng was quickly confirmed as Party Chairman and Premier. A month after Mao's death, Hua, backed by the PLA, arrested Jiang Qing and other members of the "Gang of Four." After extensive deliberations, the Chinese Communist Party leadership reinstated Deng Xiaoping to all of his previous posts at the 11th Party Congress in August 1977. Deng then led the effort to place government control in the hands of veteran party officials opposed to the radical excesses of the previous 2 decades. The new, pragmatic leadership emphasized economic development and renounced mass political movements. At the pivotal December 1978 Third Plenum (of the 11th Party Congress Central Committee), the leadership adopted economic reform policies aimed at expanding rural income and incentives, encouraging experiments in enterprise autonomy, reducing central planning, and attracting foreign direct investment to China. The plenum also decided to accelerate the pace of legal reform, culminating in the passage of several new legal codes by the National People's Congress in June 1979.

After 1979, the Chinese leadership moved toward more pragmatic positions in almost all fields. The party encouraged artists, writers, and journalists to adopt more critical approaches, although open attacks on party authority were not permitted. In late 1980, Mao's Cultural Revolution was officially proclaimed a catastrophe. Hua Guofeng, a protege of Mao, was replaced as premier in 1980 by reformist Sichuan party chief Zhao Ziyang and as party General Secretary in 1981 by the even more reformist Communist Youth League chairman Hu Yaobang.

Reform policies brought great improvements in the standard of living, especially for urban workers and for farmers who took advantage of opportunities to diversify crops and establish village industries. Controls on literature and the arts were relaxed, and Chinese intellectuals established extensive links with scholars in other countries.

At the same time, however, political dissent as well as social problems such as inflation, urban migration, and prostitution emerged. Although students and intellectuals urged greater reforms, some party elders increasingly questioned the pace and the ultimate goals of the reform program. In December 1986, student demonstrators, taking advantage of the loosening political atmosphere, staged protests against the slow pace of reform, confirming party elders' fear that the current reform program was leading to social instability. Hu Yaobang, a protege of Deng and a leading advocate of reform, was blamed for the protests and forced to resign as CCP General Secretary in January 1987. Premier Zhao Ziyang was made General Secretary and Li Peng, former Vice Premier and Minister of Electric Power and Water Conservancy, was made Premier.

1989 Student Movement and Tiananmen Square

After Zhao became the party General Secretary, the economic and political reforms he had championed, especially far-reaching political reforms enacted at the 13th Party Congress in the fall of 1987 and subsequent price reforms, came under increasing attack. His proposal in May 1988 to accelerate price reform led to widespread popular complaints about rampant inflation and gave opponents of rapid reform the opening to call for greater centralization of economic controls and stricter prohibitions against Western influence. This precipitated a political debate, which grew more heated through the winter of 1988-89.

The death of Hu Yaobang on April 15, 1989, coupled with growing economic hardship caused by high inflation, provided the backdrop for a large-scale protest movement by students, intellectuals, and other parts of a disaffected urban population. University students and other citizens camped out in Beijing's Tiananmen Square to mourn Hu's death and to protest against those who would slow reform. Their protests, which grew despite government efforts to contain them, called for an end to official corruption, a greater degree of democracy, and for defense of freedoms guaranteed by the Chinese constitution. Protests also spread to many other cities, including Shanghai, Chengdu, and Guangzhou.

Martial law was declared on May 20, 1989. Late on June 3 and early on the morning of June 4, military units were brought into Beijing. They used armed force to clear demonstrators from the streets. There are no official estimates of deaths in Beijing, but most observers believe that casualties numbered in the hundreds. After June 4, while foreign governments expressed horror at the brutal suppression of the demonstrators, the central government eliminated remaining sources of organized opposition, detained large numbers of protesters, and required political reeducation not only for students but also for large numbers of party cadre and government officials.

Zhao was purged at the Fourth Plenum of the 13th Central Committee in June and replaced as Party General Secretary by Jiang Zemin. Deng's power was curtailed as more orthodox party leaders, led by Chen Yun, became the dominant group in the leadership.

Following this resurgence of conservatives in the aftermath of June 4, economic reform slowed until given new impetus by Deng Xiaoping's return to political dominance 2 years later, including a dramatic visit to southern China in early 1992. Deng's renewed push for a market-oriented economy received official sanction at the 14th Party Congress later in the year as a number of younger, reform-minded leaders began their rise to top positions.

Hu Jintao was elevated to the Politburo Standing Committee at the Congress. Deng and his supporters argued that managing the economy in a way that increased living standards should be China's primary policy objective, even if "capitalist" measures were adopted. Subsequent to the visit, the Communist Party Politburo publicly issued an endorsement of Deng's policies of economic openness. Though continuing to espouse political reform, China has consistently placed overwhelming priority on the opening of its economy.

Post-Deng Leadership

Deng's health deteriorated in the years prior to his death in 1997. During that time, Party General Secretary and P.R.C. President Jiang Zemin and other members of his generation gradually assumed control of the day-to-day functions of government. This "third generation" leadership governed collectively with Jiang at the center. In the fall of 1987, Jiang was re-elected Party General Secretary at the 15th Party Congress, and in March 1998 he was re-elected President during the 9th National People's Congress. Premier Li Peng was constitutionally required to step down from that post. He was elected to the chairmanship of the National People's Congress. The reform-minded pragmatist Zhu Rongji was selected to replace Li as Premier.

In November 2002, the 16th Communist Party Congress elected Hu Jintao as the new General Secretary. In 1992 Deng Xiaoping had informally designated Hu Jintao as the leading figure among the "fourth generation" leaders. A new Politburo and Politburo Standing Committee was also elected in November.

In March 2003, General Secretary Hu Jintao was elected President at the 10th National People's Congress. Jiang Zemin retained the chairmanship of the Central Military Commission. At the Fourth Party Plenum in September 2004, Jiang Zemin retired from the Central Military Commission, passing the Chairmanship and control of the People's Liberation Army to President Hu Jintao.

The Chinese Communist Party's 17th Party Congress, held in October 2007, saw the elevation of key "fifth generation" leaders to the Politburo and Standing Committee, including Xi Jinping, Li Keqiang, Li Yuanchao, and Wang Yang. At the National People's Congress plenary held in March 2008, Xi was elected Vice President of the government, and Li Keqiang was elected Vice Premier.

The 18th Party Congress was held in the fall of 2012. President Hu Jintao stepped down as the party's General Secretary in favor of Xi Jinping. The Congress elected the 18th Central Committee of the Communist Party of China.

GOVERNMENT AND POLITICAL CONDITIONS

The People's Republic of China (PRC) is an authoritarian state in which the Chinese Communist Party (CCP) constitutionally is the paramount authority. CCP members hold almost all top government, police, and military positions. Ultimate authority rests with the 25-member Political Bureau (Politburo) of the CCP and its nine-member Standing Committee. Hu Jintao holds the three most powerful positions as CCP general secretary, president, and chairman of the Central Military Commission. Civilian authorities generally maintained effective control of the security forces.

Recent Elections

The NPC, composed of 2,987 deputies, elects the president and vice president, the premier and vice premiers, and the chairman of the State Central Military Commission. In practice the NPC Standing Committee, which consists of 175 members, oversaw these elections and determined the agenda and procedure for the NPC.

The NPC Standing Committee remained under the direct authority of the CCP, and most legislative decisions require the concurrence of the CCP's nine-member Politburo Standing Committee. Despite its broad authority under the state constitution, the NPC does not set policy independently or remove political leaders without the CCP's approval.

According MCA statistics, almost all of the country's more than 600,000 villages had implemented direct elections for members of local subgovernment organizations known as village committees. The direct election of officials by ordinary citizens remained narrow in scope and strictly confined to the local level. The government estimated that one-third of all elections were marred by serious procedural flaws. Corruption, vote buying, and interference by township-level and CCP officials continued to be problems. The law permits each voter to cast proxy votes for up to three other voters.

The election law governs legislative bodies at all levels, although compliance and enforcement of the election law were uneven across the country. Under this law citizens have the opportunity to vote for local people's congress representatives at the county level and below every five years, although in most cases the nomination of candidates in those elections was controlled by higher-level government officials or CCP cadres. At higher levels legislators selected people's congress delegates from among their ranks. For example, provincial-level people's congresses selected delegates to the NPC. Local CCP secretaries generally served concurrently as the head of the local people's congress, thus strengthening CCP control over legislatures.

In local people's congress elections during 2011, more than 100 candidates declared via microblogs their intent to seek election without the approval of the CCP. By the end of 2011,most of the declared independent candidates had been kept off the ballots by the local governments despite meeting nomination criteria. None of the declared independent candidates had won election by year's end. Election officials pressured independent candidates to renounce their candidacies, manipulated the ballot to exclude independent candidates, refused to disclose electorate information to independent candidates, and sometimes adjusted electoral districts to dilute voter support for independent candidates. During the November 9, 2011, local people's congress elections in Beijing, authorities deployed a heavy security presence at many polling stations in districts where independent candidates sought office. Beijing Foreign Studies University, where high-profile independent candidates Wu Qing and Qiao Mu both stood for election, closed off the campus on election day to keep out journalists and independent observers. Extra security personnel guarded both entrances to the university and checked the identities of anyone seeking entry.

Political Parties: Official statements asserted that "the political party system [that] China has adopted is multiparty cooperation and political consultation under" CCP leadership. However, the CCP retained a monopoly on political power, and the government forbade the creation of new political parties. The government officially recognized nine parties founded prior to 1949, and 30 percent of NPC seats were held by parties other than the CCP. The establishment of new parties is functionally prohibited, and activists attempting to support unofficial parties have been arrested, detained, or confined. During 2011 the authorities took measures to restrict the participation of independent candidates.

Participation of Women and Minorities: The government placed no special restrictions on the participation of women or minority groups in the political process. However, women held few positions of significant influence in the CCP or government structure. Among the 2,987 delegates of the 11th NPC (term 2008–13), 637 were women (21.3 percent of the total). There was one female member of the CCP's 25-member Politburo, who also concurrently served as one of five state councilors. There were three women ministers within the 28 organs of the State Council: Minister of Supervision Ma Wen, Minister of Justice Wu Aiying, and Head of the National Population and Family Planning Commission Li Bin. According to government-provided information, there were more than 230 female provincial and ministerial officials, more than 670 female mayors—twice the number in 1995—and more than 15 million female CCP cadres (approximately one-fifth of the CCP membership).

The government encouraged women to exercise their right to vote in village committee elections and to run in those elections, although only a small fraction of elected members were women. In many locations a seat on the village committee was reserved for a woman, usually given responsibility for family planning. The election Law provides a general mandate for quotas for female and ethnic minority representatives; however, achieving these quotas often required election authorities to violate the election procedures specified in the election law. During the 2011–12 local people's congresses elections, many electoral districts in which independent candidates campaigned used these quotas as justification to thwart the candidacies of these independent candidates. A total of 411 delegates from 55 ethnic minorities were members of 11th NPC, accounting for 13.8 percent of the total number of delegates. All of the country's officially recognized minority groups were represented. The 17th Communist Party Congress elected 40 members of ethnic minority groups as members or alternates on the Central Committee. The only ministerial-level post held by an ethnic minority member was in the State Ethnic Affairs Commission, headed by Yang Jing, an ethnic Mongol from Inner Mongolia. In addition, there was one ethnic minority member, Vice Premier Hui Liangyu, of the Hui ethnic group, on the Politburo. Minorities held few senior CCP or government positions of significant influence.

Principal Government Officials

Last Updated: 1/31/2013

At the time of publication, the full list of confirmed cabinet members for 2013 was not available.

Pres.: **XI Jinping (as of March 2013)**
Vice Pres.: **LI Yuanchao (as of March 2013)**
Premier, State Council: **LI Keqiang (as of March 2013)**
Executive Vice Premier, State Council:
Vice Premier, State Council: **HUI Liangyu**
Vice Premier, State Council: **ZHANG Dejiang**
Vice Premier, State Council: **WANG Qishan**
State Councilor, State Council: **LIU Yandong**
State Councilor, State Council: **LIANG Guanglie, Gen.**
State Councilor, State Council: **MA Kai**
State Councilor, State Council: **MENG Jianzhu**
State Councilor, State Council: **DAI Bingguo**
Sec. Gen., State Council: **MA Kai**
Chmn., Central Military Commission: **HU Jintao**
Chmn., National Development & Reform Commission: **ZHANG Ping**
Min. in Charge of the State Population & Family Planning Commission: **LI Bin**
Min. in Charge of the State Ethnic Affairs Commission: **YANG Jing**
Min. of Agriculture: **HAN Changfu**
Min. of Civil Affairs: **LI Liguo**
Min. of Commerce: **CHEN Deming**
Min. of Culture: **CAI Wu**
Min. of Education: **YUAN Guiren**
Min. of Environmental Protection: **ZHOU Shengxian**
Min. of Finance: **XIE Xuren**
Min. of Foreign Affairs: **YANG Jiechi**
Min. of Health: **CHEN Zhu**
Min. of Housing & Urban-Rural Development: **JIANG Weixin**
Min. of Human Resources & Social Security: **YIN Weimin**
Min. of Industry & Information Technology: **MIAO Wei**
Min. of Justice: **WU Aiying**
Min. of Land & Resources: **XU Shaoshi**
Min. of National Defense: **LIANG Guanglie, Gen.**
Min. of Public Security: **MENG Jianzhu**
Min. of Railways: **SHENG Guangzu**
Min. of Science & Technology: **WAN Gang**
Min. of State Security: **GENG Huichang**
Min. of Supervision: **MA Wen**
Min. of Transportation: **YANG Chuantang**
Min. of Water Resources: **CHEN Lei**
Auditor Gen., National Audit Office: **LIU Jiayi**
Governor, People's Bank of China: **ZHOU Xiaochuan**
Ambassador to the US: **ZHANG Yesui**
Permanent Representative to the UN, New York: **LI Baodong**

ECONOMY

Since the late 1970s China has moved from a closed, centrally planned system to a more market-oriented one that plays a major global role - in 2010 China became the world's largest exporter. Reforms began with the phasing out of collectivized agriculture, and expanded to include the gradual liberalization of prices, fiscal decentralization, increased autonomy for state enterprises, creation of a diversified banking system, development of stock markets, rapid growth of the private sector, and opening to foreign trade and investment. China has implemented reforms in a gradualist fashion. In recent years, China has renewed its support for state-owned enterprises in sectors it considers important to "economic security," explicitly looking to foster globally competitive national champions.

After keeping its currency tightly linked to the US dollar for years, in July 2005 China revalued its currency by 2.1% against the US dollar and moved to an exchange rate system that references a basket of currencies. From mid 2005 to late 2008 cumulative appreciation of the renminbi against the US dollar was more than 20%, but the exchange rate remained virtually pegged to the dollar from the onset of the global financial crisis until June 2010, when Beijing allowed resumption of a gradual appreciation. The restructuring of the economy and resulting efficiency gains have contributed to a more than tenfold increase in GDP since 1978.

Measured on a purchasing power parity (PPP) basis that adjusts for price differences, China in 2012 stood as the second-largest economy in the world after the US, having surpassed Japan in 2001. The dollar values of China's agricultural and industrial output each exceed those of the US; China is second to the US in the value of services it produces. Still, per capita income is below the world average. The Chinese government faces numerous economic challenges, including: (a) reducing its high domestic savings rate and correspondingly low domestic demand; (b) sustaining adequate job growth for tens of millions of migrants and new entrants to the work force; (c) reducing corruption and other economic crimes; and (d) containing environmental damage and social strife related to the economy's rapid transformation. Economic development has progressed further in coastal provinces than in the interior, and by 2011 more than 250 million migrant workers and their dependents had relocated to urban areas to find work. One consequence of population control policy is that China is now one of the most rapidly aging countries in the world. Deterioration in the environment - notably air pollution, soil erosion, and the steady fall of the water table, especially in the North - is another long-term problem. China continues to lose arable land because of erosion and economic development.

The Chinese government is seeking to add energy production capacity from sources other than coal and oil, focusing on nuclear and alternative energy development. In 2010–11, China faced high inflation resulting largely from its credit-fueled stimulus program. Some tightening measures appear to have controlled inflation, but GDP growth consequently slowed to under 8% for 2012. An economic slowdown in Europe contributed to China's, and is expected to further drag Chinese growth in 2013. Debt overhang from the stimulus program, particularly among local governments, and a property price bubble challenge policy makers currently.

The government's 12th Five-Year Plan, adopted in March 2011, emphasizes continued economic reforms and the need to increase domestic consumption in order to make the economy less dependent on exports in the future. However, China has made only marginal progress toward these rebalancing goals.

Labor Conditions

The law prohibits the employment of children under the age of 16, but child labor remained a problem. The government does not publish statistics on the extent of child labor. However, based on print media and online reports, manufacturing in the electronics industry appeared to have the most prevalent use of child labor, although many reports indicated it occurred in a number of sectors.

NGOs continued to report some use of child labor in factories producing for export. There continued to be some reports that schools supplied factories with illegal child labor under the pretext of vocational training. There were reports that spot labor shortages, rising wage levels, and more demands made by adult workers, compounded by continued fierce competition, induced some small enterprises to run the risk of hiring child labor and some local authorities to ignore this practice to protect against employers moving to other areas.

There was no national minimum wage, but the labor law requires local and provincial governments to set their own minimum wage according to standards promulgated by the MOHRSS. Monthly minimum wages varied greatly with Shenzhen, Guangdong Province, the highest at 1,320 RMB ($207) and towns in remote Ningxia Province the lowest at 750 RMB ($118). During 2011 the country increased its "rural poverty level" to 192 RMB per month ($30). These laws apply to all workers. The regulation states that labor and social security bureaus at or above the county level are responsible for enforcement of the law. It provides that where the ACFTU finds an employer in violation of the regulation, it shall have the power to demand that the relevant labor bureaus deal with the case.

The labor law mandates a 40-hour standard workweek, excluding overtime, and a 24-hour weekly rest period. It also prohibits overtime work in excess of three hours per day or 36 hours per month and mandates premium pay for overtime work. However, in practice compliance with the law was weak, and standards were regularly violated. While excessive overtime still occurred, in many cases migrant workers encouraged noncompliance by requesting greater amounts of overtime to increase their overall wages.

The State Administration for Work Safety (SAWS) sets and enforces occupational health and safety regulations. While many labor laws and regulations on worker safety are fully compatible with international standards, implementation and enforcement were generally poor due to a lack of adequate resources. Inadequately enforced labor laws and occupational health and safety laws and regulations continued to put workers' livelihoods, health, and safety at risk. In practice almost all local and provincial governments raised minimum wage levels significantly during the year, as a result of changing economic and demographic conditions. Additionally, increased economic activity, spot shortages of skilled labor, increased inland investment, and successful strikes led to generally increased wage levels for workers in all parts of the country. A decrease in the migration of workers into Guangdong contributed to a changing factory workforce that was older and more likely to be married and have children. As the tenure of the PRD's workers continued to increase, their skills improved, adding additional upward pressure on wages.

U.S.-CHINA RELATIONS

The United States seeks to build a positive, cooperative, and comprehensive relationship with China by expanding areas of cooperation and addressing areas of disagreement, such as human rights. The United States welcomes a strong, peaceful, and prosperous China playing a greater role in world affairs and seeks to advance practical cooperation with China in order to build a partnership based on mutual benefit and mutual respect. The annual Strategic and Economic Dialogue (S&ED) has served as a unique platform to promote bilateral understanding, expand consensus, discuss differences, improve mutual trust, and increase cooperation.

The strategic track of the S&ED has produced benefits for both countries through a wide range of joint projects and initiatives and expanded avenues for addressing common regional and global challenges such as proliferation concerns in Iran and North Korea, the conflict between Sudan and South Sudan, and climate change. The United States has emphasized the need to enhance bilateral trust through increased high-level exchanges, formal dialogues, and expanded people-to-people ties. The U.S. approach to China is an integral part of reinvigorated U.S. engagement with the Asia-Pacific.

U.S. Assistance to China

U.S. Agency for International Development (USAID) and State's assistance programs in China focus on four principal areas: assisting Tibetan communities; addressing the threat of HIV/AIDS and other pandemic diseases; advancing the rule of law and human rights; and supporting environmental protection and climate change mitigation efforts. U.S. assistance programs are targeted, scalable with Chinese resources, and directly address U.S. interests such as limiting the transmission of infectious diseases such as tuberculosis, malaria, HIV/AIDS, and avian influenza that pose threats throughout the region and globally. Programs in Tibetan areas of China support activities that preserve the distinct Tibetan culture and promote sustainable development and environmental conservation in Tibetan communities through grants to U.S. organizations.

Bilateral Economic Relations

The U.S. approach to its economic relations with China has two main elements: the United States seeks to fully integrate China into the global, rules-based economic and trading system and seeks to expand U.S. exporters' and investors' access to the Chinese market. Total two-way trade between China and the United States grew from $33 billion in 1992 to over $503 billion in goods in 2011. The United States is China's second-largest trading partner (after the European Union—EU), and China is the fourth-largest trading partner for the United States (after the EU, Canada, and Mexico). During the economic track of the May 2012 S&ED, the two countries announced measures to enhance macroeconomic cooperation, promote open trade and investment, enhance international rules and global economic governance, and foster financial market stability and reform. For information on the economic track, see http://www.treasury.gov/initiatives/Pages/china.aspx.

China's Membership in International Organizations

The People's Republic of China assumed the China seat at the United Nations in 1971, replacing Taiwan, and is a permanent member of the UN Security Council. Over the years, China has become increasingly active in multilateral organizations in particular through the United Nations. China and the United States work closely with the international community to address threats to global security, including North Korea and Iran's nuclear programs.

Bilateral Relations

China maintains an embassy in the United States at 3505 International Place, NW, Washington, DC 20008; Tel.: (202) 495-2266.

Principal U.S. Embassy Officials

Last Updated: 1/14/2013

CHENGDU (CG) No. 4 Lingshiguan Lu, Chengdu, Sichuan 610041, PRC, 86-28-8558-3992, Fax 86-28-8558-3520, Workweek: 08:00–17:00, Website: http://chengdu.usconsulate.gov/

CG OMS:	Kathleen Ebert
FCS:	William Marshak
FM:	Sam Kelly
MGT:	Carol-Anne Chang
OMS:	Martha Hood
POL/ECON:	Michael Toyryla
CG:	Peter Haymond
PO:	Peter Haymond
CON:	Vlad Lipschutz
PAO:	Mary-Sue Fields
GSO:	Mark Reedy
RSO:	William W. Chang
ATO:	Chanda Beckman
CLO:	Claudia Benner
EEO:	Mary-Sue Fields
IPO:	Eric Peterson

GUANGZHOU (CG) #1 Shamian South St., Guangzhou 510133, (86) (20) 8121-8000, Fax (86) (20) 8121-6296, Workweek: 8:30 AM–5:30 PM, http://guangzhou.usconsulate.gov/

CG OMS:	Anh Zvinakis
Co-CLO:	Carol Chapman
DHS/CIS:	Brian Spalter
DHS/ICE:	Man Tse
FCS:	Greg Wong
FDA:	Irene Chan
MGT:	Michael Cragun
POL/ECON:	Robert Lee
POSHO:	Thomas Chapman
CG:	Jennifer Zimdahl Galt
CON:	James Levy
PAO:	Roxanne Cabral
GSO:	Guy Margalith
RSO:	James Reynolds
AFSA:	Thomas Weber
ATO:	Jorge Sanchez
CLO:	Jennifer O'Connor
EEO:	Daniel Cederberg
IPO:	Timothy Harrison

SHANGHAI (CG) 1469 Huai Hai Zhong Lu, Shanghai 200031 PRC, 86-21-6433-6880, Fax 86-21-6433-4122, INMARSAT Tel 86-21-6433-6880, Fax 86-21-6433-4122, INMARSAT Tel 881676310550, Workweek: 8:00 am–5:00 pm, http://shanghai.usembassy-china.org.cn/

CG OMS:	Jennifer Yahn
DHS/CIS:	Hien Vu
DPO:	Vacant
FCS:	William Brekke
FDA:	Frank Eng
FM:	Tom Nave
MGT:	Eliza Al-Laham
POL/ECON:	James Mullinax
POSHO:	Tom Nave
CG:	Robert Griffiths
CON:	Kristin Hagerstrom
PAO:	Dale Largent
GSO:	Kelia Cummins
RSO:	Vacant
ATO:	Keith Schneller
CLO:	Vacant
FAA:	Thomas Miller
IPO:	Harry Clark
ISO:	Leslie Hope
ISSO:	Eric Dunivant

SHENYANG (CG) 86-24-2322-1198, Fax 86-24-2322-1942, Workweek: 0830-1730, Website: http://shenyang.usconsulate.gov/

CG OMS:	Kim Cardascia
FM:	Ralph Delarue
MGT:	Lisa Povolni
POL/ECON:	Jeff Loree
CG:	Sean Stein
CON:	Tyler Allen
PAO:	Seth Bailey
GSO:	Kevin Fisher

RSO: Scott Kim
AGR: Philip Jarrell
EEO: Justin Walls
IPO: Ron Dick
ISO: Hugh Thompson
ISSO: Ron Dick

BEIJING (M) No. 55 An Jia Lou Road, Beijing 100600, 8610-8531-3000, Fax 8610-6532-6929, Workweek: 0800-1700, Website: http://beijing.usembassy.gov/

DCM OMS: Krause, Meredith
AMB OMS: Dennis Clark
CDC: Jeffrey McFarland
Co-CLO: Kerry Scott
DHS/CIS: Michael Hickman
DHS/ICE: James Nagle
DHS/TSA: Cindy Eickhoff
FCS: William Zarit
FDA: Christopher Hickey
FM: Paul Davenport
HRO: Julia Harlan
MGT: Jennifer Bonner
POSHO: Paul Davenport
SDO/DATT: BG David R. Stilwell
AMB: Ambassador Gary Locke
CON: Charles Bennett
DCM: Charge Robert Wang
PAO: Tom Hodges
GSO: Henry Kaminski
RSO: Jim Lemarie
AFSA: Holly A. Kirking
AGR: Scott Sindelar
AID: Maria Rendon-Labadan
APHIS: Lou Vanechanos
ATO: Michael Woolsey
CLO: Denise Shepherd
DEA: Daniel Baldwin
ECON: William Weinstein
EEO: Carmen Castro
EST: Erica Thomas
FAA: Pat Power
FMO: Carmen Castro
ICASS Chair: Christopher Quinlivan
IMO: Thomas Proctor
IPO: Brad Summers
IRS: Chinchie Killfoil
ISO: Elaine S. Tiang-Chu
ISSO: Doug Huyett
LAB: Roy Perrin
LEGATT: Russell L. Hunt
POL: Dan Kritenbrink

WUHAN 47F New World Intl Trade Tower I, No.568 Jianshe Ave, Hankou, Wuhan 430022, 86-27-8555-7791, Fax 86-27-8555-7761.

CG: Lipschutz, Vlad

TRAVEL

Consular Information Sheet

January 28, 2013

Country Description: The People's Republic of China was established on October 1, 1949, with Beijing as its capital city. With well over 1.3 billion citizens, China is the world's most populous country and the world's fourth-largest country in terms of territory. Although political power remains centralized in the Chinese Communist Party, China is undergoing profound economic and social changes. Modern tourist facilities are available in major cities, but many facilities in smaller provincial cities and rural areas may be below international standards.

Smart Traveler Enrollment Program (STEP)/Embassy Locations: If you are going to live in or visit China, please take the time to tell our Embassy and Consulates about your trip. If you enroll, we can keep you up to date with important safety and security announcements. It will also help your friends and family get in touch with you in an emergency.

The U.S. Embassy in Beijing China
No. 55 An Jia Lou Road
Chaoyang District, Beijing 100600
Telephone: (86) (10) 8531–4000
Emergency after-hours telephone: (86) (10) 8531–4000

The Embassy consular district includes the municipalities of Beijing and Tianjin and the provinces/autonomous regions of Gansu, Hebei, Henan, Hubei, Hunan, Inner Mongolia, Jiangxi, Ningxia, Qinghai, Shaanxi, Shandong, Shanxi, and Xinjiang.

The U.S. Consulate General
in Chengdu
Number 4, Lingshiguan Road,
Section 4, Renmin Nanlu,
Chengdu 610041.
Telephone: (86)(28) 8558–3992
Emergency after-hours telephone: (86) (10) 8531–4000

This consular district includes the provinces/autonomous region of Guizhou, Sichuan, Xizang (Tibet) and Yunnan, as well as the municipality of Chongqing.

The U.S. Consulate General
in Guangzhou
Number 1 South Shamian Street,
Shamian Island
Guangzhou 510133.
Telephone: (86)(20) 8518–7605
Emergency after-hours telephone: (86) (10) 8531–4000

This consular district includes: the provinces/autonomous region of Guangdong, Guangxi, Hainan, and Fujian.

The U.S. Consulate General
in Shanghai
Westgate Mall, 8th Floor,
1038 Nanjing Xi Lu,
Shanghai 200031
Telephone: (86)(21) 3217–4650
Emergency after-hours telephone: (86) (21) 3217–4650

This consular district includes Shanghai municipality and the provinces of Anhui, Jiangsu and Zhejiang.

The U.S. Consulate General
in Shenyang
No. 52, 14th Wei Road
Heping District,
Shenyang 110003
Telephone: (86)(24) 2322–1198
Emergency after-hours telephone: ((86) (10) 8531–4000

This consular district includes: the provinces of Heilongjiang, Jilin, and Liaoning.

The U.S. Consulate General
in Wuhan
New World International Trade Tower I
No. 568, Jianshe Avenue
Hankou, Wuhan 430022
Telephone: (86) (027) 8555–7791
Emergency after-hours telephone: (86) (10) 8531–4000

Entry/Exit Requirements for U.S. Citizens: To enter China, you need a visa as well as six months' validity remaining on your passport. If you do not have a valid passport and the appropriate Chinese visa, you will not be allowed to enter China, you will be fined, and you will be subject to immediate deportation. U.S. citizens traveling to China may apply for up to a one-year multiple-entry visa. Check your U.S. passport before applying for a visa to make sure that it has one year or more validity remaining; otherwise, you may be issued a visa for less than the time you request. The Chinese Embassy and consulates general in the United States do not always issue maximum validity visas even if requested to do so. A multiple-entry visa is essential if you plan to re-enter China, especially if you plan to visit either Hong Kong or Macau and return to China. China has recently instituted new supporting document requirements for tourist (L) visas. Visit the website of the Embassy of the People's Republic of China for the most current visa information.

Many regions, such as the Tibet Autonomous Region (TAR) and other remote areas, require special permits for tourist travel. Permits are not always granted, as during certain times the PRC may not allow foreigners to enter an area it deems restricted. The easiest way to apply for the appropriate permit is through a local Chinese travel agent. Permits usually cost approximately RMB 200, are single-entry, and are valid for a maximum of three months. The TAR remains a sensitive area for travel, and even when travel to Tibet is allowed, usually only Lhasa and part of Shan Nan are open to foreigners. If you do enter a restricted area without the requisite permit, you could be fined, taken into custody, and deported for illegal entry. A Border Travel Permit (bianfangzheng) is required for travel in and around the TAR and the Nepal border area. Applications for the permit are made at the Public Security Bureau's office in Lhasa. To learn more about specific entry requirements for restricted areas, check with the Visa Office of the Embassy of the People's Republic of China in the United States by telephone (202) 338-6688 between 9:30 a.m. and 3:30 p.m. Eastern Standard Time, Monday through Friday, fax (202) 588-9760, or e-mail chnvisa@bellatlantic.net.China no longer restricts tourists with HIV from visiting, but will not issue them residence permits. Please verify the restrictions with the Embassy of the People's Republic of Chinabefore you travel.

Upon Arrival: Once you are in China, the PRC expects you to comply with the requirements of your visa. For example, if you are on a tourist visa, you are not allowed to work; if you are on a work visa, you typically cannot become a full-time student. It is difficult to change or renew your visa within China. Visitors cannot change tourist (L) and exchange (F) visas to other visa types. Entry and exit requirements are strictly enforced.

Police, school administrators, airline and train officials, and hotel staff may check your visa to make sure you have not overstayed. You will typically not be allowed to check into a hotel or travel by plane or on some trains if your visa has expired, and you may be taken into custody. If you intentionally or inadvertently violate the terms of your Chinese visa, including staying after your visa has expired, you may be charged a RMB 500 fine per day up to a maximum of RMB 5,000, experience departure delays, and face possible detention.

Whether you are traveling to or living in China, you must register with the police within 24 hours of your arrival in the country. Even foreigners with residence permits are required to register after each re-entry. If you are staying in a hotel, the staff will automatically register you. However, if you are staying in a private home with family or friends, you should take your passport to the local police station to register. Failure to do so could result in fines and detention. Chinese law requires that you carry a valid U.S. passport and Chinese visa or residence permit at all times. If you are visiting China, you should carry your passport with you, out of reach of pickpockets. If you live in China and have a residence permit, you should carry that document and leave your passport in a secure location, except when traveling.

Some parts of China are off limits or accessible only if you travel with an organized tour. You should always use common sense and avoid unlawful entry to sensitive areas, including military zones or bases and places where there is current civil unrest. If problems arise, the U.S. Embassy has limited ability to provide assistance. The Chinese government will not usually authorize the travel of U.S. government personnel to Tibet or areas where there is civil unrest, even to provide consular assistance to U.S. citizens.

Leaving China: You must have a valid visa not only to enter China, but also to leave China. If your visa has expired or if you lose your passport while you are in China, immigration authorities will not permit you to exit the country until you receive a new visa. The time it takes to get a visa replaced varies depending on where you are in China; however, in Beijing, it can take at least one week from the date of application, regardless of your previously-scheduled departure date. You should not expect the Chinese visa renewal or replacement process to be expedited to meet your travel schedule.

When you overstay in China, you may be detained for various amounts of time, as well as fined up to RMB 5000. You must apply for a visa extension from the Entry/Exit Bureau before attempting to leave the country.

If your passport is lost or stolen in China, you will need to replace both the U.S. passport and the Chinese visa. The first step in this process is to immediately report the loss or theft of your passport to the Chinese authorities and obtain a report.. Reporting regulations vary from place to place in China. For instance, if you lose your passport in Beijing, the local authorities will require you to file a police report at the local police station before they will issue a replacement visa in your new passport, while in Shanghai you must report the loss to the Entry/Exit Bureau. In Chengdu and Chongqing, the local authorities will require you to file a report first with your local police station and then with your local Entry/Exit Bureau. Once you report the loss and are given a copy of the report, you will need to come into the U.S. Embassy or a consulate general to apply for a new U.S. passport. Once you have the passport, you will need to take it to the local Entry and Exit Bureau to obtain a replacement Chinese visa.

U.S. citizens named (or whose businesses are named) as respondents in civil suits are often barred from leaving China pending resolution of the case.

Transiting China: In general, if you are travelling through China en route to another country, you do not need a visa, as long as you stay in China less than 24 hours and do not leave the airport. If, however, you are a transit passenger and have more than one stopover in China, you must exit the transit lounge at the first stop to apply for an endorsement in your passport that permits multiple stops in China. As long as you have a ticket that continues on to an international destination, the endorsement should be routine.

If Shanghai Pudong airport is your international transit point, you may stay in Shanghai for 48 hours if you have a valid passport, a visa for your destination, and an onward plane ticket. Make sure you get an endorsement stamp at the immigration desk before you leave the airport.

Dual Nationality: China does not recognize dual nationality. Chinese authorities recognize the U.S. citizenship only of persons who enter China using a Chinese visa in a U.S. passport. If you use any other type of travel document to enter China, the Chinese government will likely not permit the U.S. Embassy or consulates general in China to provide you with consular assistance. For example, when U.S. citizens who have entered China using non-U.S. passports are arrested, the Government of China will neither notify the U.S. mission of their detention, nor allow U.S. consular officers to visit them while they are detained. If you are a dual national with valid U.S. and Chinese passports, you should take care in determining which passport to use to enter and exit China.

Chinese authorities generally consider a child born in China to be a Chinese citizen if one parent is a Chinese national, even if the child is issued a U.S. passport while in China. In such cases, prior to departing China with your child, you should contact the local Public Security Bureau and/or Entry-Exit Bureau for information on obtaining a travel document.

Threats to Safety and Security: For most visitors, China remains a very safe country. Petty street crime is the most common safety concern for U.S. citizens in China. However, business disputes between U.S. citizens and Chinese business partners can result in a physical confrontation or kidnapping.

Some parts of the country are restricted or you may need a special permit to travel there. Please keep in mind that you are a guest in a foreign country where U.S. laws do not apply. You are subject to Chinese law and legal procedures.

Violent crime is not common in China, but violent demonstrations can erupt without warning, and in past years there have been some fatal bombings and explosions which could pose a random threat to foreign visitors in the area. The vast majority of these local incidents are related to disputes over land seizures, social issues, employment disputes, environmental problems, or conflicts involving ethnic minorities. Some incidents have become large-scale and involved criminal activity, including hostage taking and vandalism.

Stay up to date:

- By bookmarking our Bureau of Consular Affairs website, which contains the current Travel Warnings and Travel Alertsas well as the Worldwide Caution.
- Follow us on Twitterand the Bureau of Consular Affairs page on Facebook as well.
- Downloading our free Smart Traveler IPhone Appor Android Appto have travel information at your fingertips.
- You can also call 1-888-407-4747 toll-free within the United States and Canada, or call a regular toll line, 1-202-501-4444, from other countries. These numbers are available from 8:00 a.m. to 8:00 p.m. Eastern Time, Monday through Friday (except U.S. federal holidays).

Take some time before traveling to improve your personal security—things are not the same everywhere else as they are in the United States.

Crime: When visiting China, you should always take routine safety precautions and pay attention to your surroundings. Petty theft remains the most prevalent type of crime encountered. Pickpockets target tourists at sightseeing destinations, airports, crowded subways, markets, and stores. Make sure you guard your passport and wallet, as most incidents tend to involve items kept in back pockets, backpacks, or bags/purses swung over a shoulder or set down in a taxi, another vehicle, a restaurant, or a shop.

Narcotics-related crimes and use are also on the rise in China. Chinese law enforcement authorities have little tolerance for illegal drugs, and they periodically conduct widespread sweeps of bar and nightclub districts, targeting narcotics distributors and drug users. Expatriates from various countries have been detained in such police actions. Con artists targeting visitors are also common in popular tourist sites. A common scam involves younger Chinese "English students," often women or a couple, offering a local tour and an invitation to tea at a nearby restaurant. When the bill comes, the restaurant owners force victims to pay an exorbitant bill before they can leave the premises.

Taxi drivers, especially at airports, sometimes target arriving travelers, refusing to use the meter or claiming they are a limousine and can charge higher fares. Always have the name of your destination written in Chinese to show the driver, and get a receipt when you arrive at your destination. It is a good practice to keep valuables such as purses, camera bags, and computer cases next to you or in your lap rather than in a less-accessible area of the taxi. Ask the driver to remove the bags from the trunk before you get out of the taxi and before you pay, so he cannot drive away with your luggage.

Do not buy counterfeit or pirated goods, even if they are widely available. Not only are the bootlegs illegal in the United States; if you purchase them, you may also be breaking local law. Some U.S. citizens report that items purchased, even at state-owned or museum stores, believed to be antiques or genuine gems are later determined to be reproductions.

Counterfeit currency is a significant concern in China. Cab drivers and businesses have given many people, not just tourists, counterfeit currency. Carrying small bills or using exact change, particularly in taxis, can help protect you. Some merchants will switch a large bill with a counterfeit bill and return it to you, claiming that you passed them the counterfeit bill. If you must pay with RMB 100 bills, it may be useful to note the last few serial numbers before paying in case they get switched. There have been cases of people receiving counterfeit bills from free-standing ATMs. Use only ATMs at financial institutions or those recommended by your hotel.

Political protest is not legal or permitted in China and is rarely encountered by foreigners. Travelers who have attempted to engage in political protest activities in public places have been deported quickly, in some cases at their own expense, usually before the U.S. Embassy is aware of the situation.

Participating in unauthorized political activities or protests against Chinese policy in China may result in lengthy detentions and may impact your eligibility for future visas to visit China. Foreigners engaging in pro-Falun Gong or pro-Tibetan activities have been detained or immediately deported from China, usually at their own expense, after being questioned. Several reported they were subject to interrogations and were physically abused during detention. In addition, some alleged that personal property, including clothing, cameras, and computers, was not returned.

U.S. citizens have been detained and expelled for distributing religious literature. Chinese customs authorities have enforced strict regulations concerning the importation of religious literature, including Bibles. If you bring religious literature with you, it should be a "reasonable amount" for your personal use only. If you attempt to bring larger quantities, the literature will likely be confiscated and you may be fined, detained, or deported.

Victims of Crime: If you or someone you know becomes the victim of a crime abroad, you should contact the local police and the nearest U.S. embassy or consulate (see the Department of State's list of embassies and consulates). We can:

- Replace a stolen passport.
- Help you find appropriate medical care if you are the victim of violent crimes such as assault or rape.
- Put you in contact with the appropriate police authorities, and if you want us to, we can contact family members or friend on your behalf.
- Help you understand the local criminal justice process and direct you to local attorneys, although it is important to remember that local authorities are responsible for investigating and prosecuting the crime.

The local equivalent to the "911" emergency line in China is "110"; however, very few English speakers staff this hotline. Please note that the local police can be reached only by calling "110" from the location where the crime occurred. Remember that if your passport is stolen, you must not only apply for a new passport at the U.S. Embassy or consulate but must also apply for a new visa. To receive the new visa, Chinese visa officials may require that you file a police report about your stolen passport at the police station nearest to where the theft occurred. You may also be directed to file a report at the local Entry/Exit Bureau as well. If someone steals your passport, save yourself possible inconvenience by filing the police report right away.

Criminal Penalties: While you are traveling in China, you are subject to its laws even if you are a U.S. citizen. Foreign laws and legal systems can be vastly different than our own. There are also some things that might be legal in the country you visit, but still illegal in the United States. For example, you can be prosecuted under U.S. law if you buy pirated goods. Engaging in sexual conduct with children or using or disseminating child pornography in a foreign country is a crime prosecutable in the United States. If you break local laws in China, your U.S. passport will not help you avoid arrest or prosecution. It is very important to know what is legal and what is not wherever you go.

China gives the police the authority to detain and deport foreigners for a wide variety of reasons, including engaging in prohibited religious activities and soliciting prostitutes. If you do not have your passport with you, you may be taken in for questioning. China has strict laws against driving under the influence of alcohol that can lead to immediate detention on a criminal charge.

If you are arrested in China, the U.S.-China Consular Convention requires Chinese authorities to notify the U.S. Embassy or nearest consulate general of your arrest within four days. Typically, the police will not allow anyone other than a consular officer to visit you during your initial detention period, including your family or even an attorney.

Bail is rarely granted in China, and you can be subject to detention for many months before being granted a trial.

Special Circumstances: North Korea—China shares a lengthy border with the Democratic People's Republic of Korea (North Korea or DPRK), a country with which the United States does not maintain diplomatic or consular relations. If you cross into North Korea, even inadvertently, you will become subject to North Korean law. For further information about travel to North Korea, consult the North Korea Country Specific Information webpage and the Travel Warning for North Korea.

Commercial Disputes: If you or your company becomes involved in a civil business dispute in China, the Chinese government may prohibit you from leaving China, without advance notice, and until the matter is resolved under Chinese law. There are cases of U.S. citizens being prevented from leaving China for months and even years while civil cases are pending. In some cases, defendants have even been put into police custody pending resolution of their civil cases.

Some local businesspeople who feel that they have been wronged by a foreign business partner may hire "debt collectors" to harass and intimidate the foreigner or his/her family in hopes of collecting the debt. Foreign managers or company owners have in some cases been physically detained as leverage during dispute negotiations. The Embassy and consulates general can provide a list of local attorneys who can be hired to provide counsel. For information on commercial contracts and disputes and for general assistance, please consult the U.S. Commercial Service website for China.

Surveillance and Monitoring: Security personnel carefully watch foreign visitors and may place you under surveillance. Hotel rooms (including meeting rooms), offices, cars, taxis, telephones, Internet usage, and fax machines may be monitored onsite or remotely, and personal possessions in hotel rooms, including computers, may be searched without your consent or knowledge. Business travelers should be particularly mindful that trade secrets, negotiating positions, and other business-sensitive information may be taken and shared with local interests.

Natural gas: U.S. citizens who rent apartments with gas appliances should be aware that, in some areas, natural gas is not scented to warn occupants of gas leaks or concentrations. In addition, heaters may not always be well vented, allowing excess carbon monoxide to build up in living spaces. Fatal accidents involving U.S. citizens have occurred. If you plan to live in China, you should ensure all gas appliances are properly vented or install gas and carbon monoxide detectors in your residence. These devices are not widely available in China, and if possible, you should purchase them prior to your arrival.

Cell phones: In China, most people use cell phones for calls and SMS messaging. Telephones and SIM cards are widely available, and minutes can be purchased at many convenience stores. Vendors require identification from anyone purchasing a SIM card, and the purchaser's identity is registered with the government.

Internet access: The Internet is used widely throughout China. Most hotels, even in remote areas, offer Internet access, often for a fee. Low-cost cyber cafes or Internet bars are widely available and are often open 24 hours a day. You may have to show your passport and have your photo taken before you can log on. Many websites are blocked, including social networking sites such as Facebook, and you can expect that your Internet activity may be monitored.

Contracts: Anyone entering into a commercial or employment contract in China should first have it reviewed by legal counsel, both in the United States and in China. The U.S. Foreign Commercial Servicecan assist you in identifying and vetting business contacts and opportunities. Many U.S. citizens have reported difficulty getting their contracts enforced by Chinese courts, and others have reported being forced out of profitable joint ventures and being unable to secure legal recourse in China. If you or your company are the subject of a court order requiring you to pay a settlement in a legal case, failure to make this payment may result in an exit ban which will prohibit your departure from China until payment is made.

English/Secondary School Teachers: English teachers in China frequently report being recruited through misrepresentations or having contract disputes which can result in termination, lost wages, having school authorities confiscate their passports, forced eviction from housing, and even threats of violence. It is important to research the school at which you will be teaching and also to make sure that you have the proper visa to legally teach English in China. Do not accept a one-way airline ticket from a school to teach English in China, as some U.S. citizens have reported that the school never provided their airfare home. If you do have a dispute with your school, you may wish to consult with or hire a local attorney; seek assistance from the police if your safety is threatened. Prospective teachers are encouraged to read the Teaching in China Guide on the U.S. Embassy's American Citizen Services website.

Social Insurance: China has a social insurance system to which foreigners who work in China must contribute. When you sign an employment contract, you must apply for a social insurance number, and it is important that your employer work with you to comply with the regulations. Please check the official website for updated information.

Air Quality in China: Air pollution is a significant problem in many cities and regions in China. Pollutants such as particle pollution and ozone are linked to a number of significant health effects, and those effects are likely to be more severe for sensitive populations, including people with heart or lung disease, children, and older adults. While the quality of air can differ greatly between cities or between urban and rural areas, U.S. citizens living in or traveling to

China may wish to consult their doctor when living in or prior to traveling to areas with significant air pollution.

The Chinese Ministry of Environmental Protection provides its own air quality data for cities throughout China. You can view the information at http://english.mep.gov.cn. The U.S. Embassy in Beijing and the U.S. Consulates in Chengdu, Guangzhou, and Shanghai make air quality data available to the U.S. citizen community. View these data from the following links:

U.S. Embassy Beijing air quality data:
http://beijing.usembassy-china.org.cn/070109air.html

U.S. Consulate in Chengdu air quality data:
http://chengdu.usembassy-china.org.cn/air-quality-monitor4.html

U.S. Consulate in Guangzhou air quality data:
http://guangzhou.usembassy-china.org.cn/guangzhou-air-quality-monitor.html

U.S. Consulate in Shanghai air quality data:
http://shanghai.usembassy-china.org.cn/airmonitor.html

Typhoons: The southeast coast of China is subject to strong typhoons and tropical storms, usually from July through September. For current information about typhoons and tropical storms, please consult the Joint Typhoon Warning Center in Honolulu and the National Weather Service's Central Pacific Hurricane Center.

Earthquakes: China is a seismically active country, and earthquakes occur throughout the country. Notable earthquakes include one in Qinghai in 2010 in which 3,000 people were killed and a major quake in Sichuan in 2008 when more than 87,000 people perished. U.S. citizens should make contingency plans and leave emergency contact information with family members outside of China. Check here for information about earthquake preparedness, and general information about natural disaster preparedness is available from the U.S. Federal Emergency Management Agency.

Accessibility: While in China, individuals with disabilities may find accessibility and accommodation very different from what they find in the United States. Standards adopted for making roads and buildings accessible to persons with disabilities are subject to the Law on the Handicapped, which calls for their "gradual" implementation; however, compliance with the law is lax. Even in newer areas of large cities, sidewalks often do not have curb cuts, making wheelchair or stroller use difficult. Many large streets can be crossed only via overhead pedestrian bridges not accessible except by staircase. Although some sidewalks have special raised "buttons" or strips to help those who are blind or have restricted sight to follow the pavement, they are unreliable. While most public buildings have elevators, they are often locked, and the responsible official with the key must be located before they can be used.

In major cities, public restrooms in places visited by tourists usually have a least one handicap-accessible toilet. International signage is used to identify handicap-accessible facilities. Free or reduced-entry fares on public transportation are sometimes provided for a handicapped person and a companion, although this is usually stated only in Chinese and is often restricted to residents with special identification cards.

Medical Facilities and Health Information: The standards of medical care in China are not equivalent to those in the United States. If you plan to travel outside of major Chinese cities, you should consider making special preparations.

Travelers have reported difficulty passing through customs inspection when arriving with large quantities of prescription medications. If you regularly take over-the-counter or prescription medication, bring your own supply in the original container, including each drug's generic name, and carry the doctor's prescription with you. Many commonly-used U.S. drugs and medications are not available in China, and some that bear names that are the same as or similar to prescription medications from the United States may not contain the same ingredients or may be counterfeit. If you try to have medications sent to you from outside China, you may have problems getting them released by Chinese Customs and/or you may have to pay high customs duties.

Reuse of medical supplies such as syringes and needles or poor sterilization practices are problems in China, contributing to transmission of diseases such as hepatitis, which is endemic in China. To avoid contamination, travelers should always ask doctors and dentists to use sterilized equipment and be prepared to pay for new syringe needles in hospitals or clinics.

In emergencies, Chinese ambulances are often slow to arrive, and most do not have sophisticated medical equipment or trained responders. In most parts of China, helicopter evacuations are not commercially available. Many travelers choose to take taxis or other vehicles to the nearest major hospital rather than wait for ambulances to arrive. Most hospitals demand cash payment or a deposit in advance for admission, procedures, or emergencies, although a few hospitals in major cities may accept credit cards.

Beijing, Shanghai, Guangzhou, and a few other large cities have medical facilities with some international staff. Many hospitals in major Chinese cities have so-called VIP wards (gaogan bingfang). Most VIP wards provide medical services to foreigners and have some English-speaking staff. However, even in the VIP/foreigner wards of major hospitals, you may have difficulty due to cultural, language, and regulatory differences. In China, it is customary for patients' families to help care for them in the hospital and to supply their toiletries, paper supplies, and meals. Hospitals often refuse to perform surgery or administer treatment without the written consent of the patient's family, even if they are not in China, and doctors frequently will only tell the family members the patient's diagnosis and prognosis, but will not discuss it with the patient. Physicians and hospitals sometimes refuse to give U.S. patients copies of their Chinese hospital medical records, including laboratory test results, scans, and x-rays.

Mental health facilities or medications are not widely available in China. If you are traveling to or studying abroad in China, before you go, put a plan in place for managing your mental health.

In most rural areas, only rudimentary medical facilities are available, often with poorly trained personnel who have little medical equipment and medications. Rural clinics are often reluctant to accept responsibility for treating foreigners, even in emergency situations.

If you elect to have surgery or other medical services performed in China, be aware that there is little legal recourse to protect you in case of medical malpractice. The U.S. Embassy and consulates general in China maintain lists of local English-speaking doctors and hospitals, which are published on their respective American Citizens Services web pages.

Most roads and towns in Tibet, Qinghai, parts of Xinjiang, and western Sichuan are situated at altitudes over 10,000 feet. If you plan to travel in these areas, you should seek medical advice in advance of travel, allow time for acclimatization to the high altitude, and remain alert to signs of altitude sickness. Air pollution is also a significant problem throughout China, and you should consult your doctor prior to travel and consider the impact seasonal smog and heavy particulate pollution may have on you.

You can find detailed information on vaccinations and other health precautions on the CDC website. Please note that the CDC recommends that travelers to China ensure that their polio vaccinations are up to date. For information about outbreaks of infectious diseases abroad, consult the World Health Organization (WHO) website. Tuberculosis is also an increasingly serious health concern in China. For further information, please consult the CDC's information on TB.

HIV is a significant concern in China. An estimated quarter of a million people in China are living with HIV, most of whom are not aware of their status. The WHO website also contains additional health information for travelers, including detailed country-specific health information.

Medical Insurance: You cannot assume your insurance will go with you when you travel. It is very important to find out BEFORE you leave whether or not your medical insurance will cover you overseas. You need to ask your insurance company two questions:

- Does my policy apply when I'm out of the United States?
- Will it cover emergencies like a trip to a foreign hospital or a medical evacuation?

In many places, doctors and hospitals expect payment in cash at the time of service and may not begin treatment without payment or may discontinue treatment if you become unable to pay.

Your regular U.S. health insurance may not cover doctors' and hospital visits in other countries. If your policy does not cover you when you are abroad, it might be a good idea to take out another one that covers you for the duration of your trip.

Traffic Safety and Road Conditions: While in China, you will encounter road conditions that differ significantly from those in the United States. Rules, regulations, and conditions vary greatly throughout China, but a general rule of thumb is that traffic safety is poor and driving in China can be dangerous.

Traffic is chaotic and largely unregulated, and right-of-way and other courtesies are usually ignored. The average Chinese driver has fewer than five years' experience behind the wheel and the rate of traffic accidents in China, including fatal accidents, is among the highest in the world. Cars, bicycles, motorbikes, trucks, and buses often treat road signs and signals as advisory rather than mandatory. Pedestrians never have the right of way, and you should always be careful while travelling in, or even walking near, traffic. Child safety seats are not widely available in China, and most taxis and other cars do not have seat belts in the back seats. Motorcycle and bicycle accidents are frequent and often serious. If you decide to ride a bike or motorcycle, wear a helmet.

You may not drive in China using your U.S. driver's license or an international license. If you have a resident permit, you can apply for a PRC driver's license, although regulations for obtaining a license vary from province to province. Liability issues and the difficulty of passing the driver's test may make it preferable to employ a local driver.

If you are involved in a traffic accident, stay calm; road altercations sometimes turn violent quickly. The safest course is tocall the policeand wait for them. Even minor traffic accidents can becomemajor public dramas. In some instances bystanders have surrounded accident scenes and nominated themselves to be an ad hoc jury. The parties involved in an accident may offer money to the crowd in exchange for favorable consideration. If there are no injuries and damage is minimal, the parties often come to agreement on the spot. If no agreement is reached and the police are called, the police may mediate or conduct an on-site investigation requiring those involved to come to the police station to sign statements.

Unresolved disputes are handled by the courts. In cases where there are injuries, the driver whose vehicle is determined to have inflicted the injury will often be held at least partially liable for the injured person's medical costs regardless of actual responsibility for the accident. Many foreigners have been involved in incidents where the victims appear to have purposely caused accidents and claimed to have been injured in order to get payment for their supposed damages and medical care. When foreigners are involved in an accident, the police will sometimes hold their passports until the other parties are satisfied with the compensation they receive.

Aviation Safcty Oversight: The U.S. Federal Aviation Administration (FAA) has assessed the government of China's Civil Aviation Authority as being in compliance with International Civil Aviation Organization (ICAO) aviation safety standards for oversight of China's air carrier operations. Further information may be found on the FAA's safety assessment page.

Children's Issues: Please see the U.S. Dept. of State Office of Children's Issues webpages on intercountry adoption and international parental child abduction.

Intercountry Adoption

June 2011

The information in this section has been edited from the latest report available as of February 2013 from the State Department Bureau of Consular Affairs, Office of Overseas Citizens Services. For more information, please read the *Intercountry Adoption* section of this book and review current reports online at http://adoption.state.gov. China is party to the Hague Convention on Protection of Children and Co-operation in Respect of Intercountry Adoption (Hague Adoption Convention). Therefore all adoptions between China and the United States must meet the requirements of the Convention and U.S. law implementing the Convention.

Who Can Adopt? Adoption between the United States and China is governed by the Hague Adoption Convention. Therefore to adopt from China, you must first be found eligible to adopt by the U.S. Government. The U.S. Government agency responsible for making this determination is the Department of Homeland Security, U.S. Citizenship and Immigration Services (USCIS).

Residency Requirements: China does not require that prospective adoptive parents reside in China for a specified period prior to completing an adoption. However, in order to finalize an adoption, at least one adopting parent must travel to China to execute the required documents in person before the appropriate Chinese authorities. If only one member of an adopting married couple travels to China, that person must have in his/her possession a power of attorney from the other spouse, notarized and authenticated by the Chinese Embassy in Washington or one of the Chinese Consulates General elsewhere in the United States.

Age Requirements: Both parents must be between the ages of 30 and 50. Those couples who apply to adopt a special needs child must be between the ages of 30 and 55.

Marriage Requirements: Chinese law only permits intercountry adoption by married couples, defined as one man and one woman. They must adopt the child jointly. In addition, they must have been married at least two years; if either person has previously divorced, the couple must have been married at least five years. No more than two divorces are allowed. Single Females may now adopt special needs children from China.

Income Requirements: At least one member of the couple must have stable employment and the family's annual income must equal at least $10,000 for each family member in the household (including the child to be adopted). Annual income excludes welfare, pensions, unemployment insurance, and government subsidies. The total value of the family's assets must be at least $80,000. Both prospective parents must be high school graduates or have vocational training equivalent to a high school education.

Health Requirements: Both partners must be physically and mentally fit, with none of the following conditions:

- AIDS;
- Mental disability;
- Infectious disease that is actively contagious;
- Blind in either eye;
- Hearing loss in both ears or loss of language function (those adopting children with hearing or language function loss are exempted from this requirement);
- Non-function or dysfunction of limbs or trunk caused by impairment, incomplete limbs, paralysis or deformation;
- Severe facial deformation;
- Severe diseases that require long-term treatment and that may affect life expectancy, including malignant tumors, lupus, nephrosis, epilepsy, etc;
- Major organ transplant within ten years;
- Schizophrenia;
- Severe mental disorders requiring medication for more than two years, including depression, mania, or anxiety neurosis; and
- Body Mass Index (BMI) of 40 or more.

Other Requirements: The family must have fewer than five children under the age of 18, and the youngest is at least one year old (those adopting special needs children are exempted from this requirement). Neither partner may have a significant criminal record, and both must have a history of honorable behavior and good moral character with no evidence of:

- Domestic violence, sexual abuse, abandonment or abuse of children;

- Use of narcotics or any potentially addictive medication prescribed for mental illness;
- Alcohol abuse, unless the individual can show she/he has been sober for at least ten years

Applications from persons with past criminal records will be considered on a case-by-case basis if the individual has fewer than three minor criminal convictions (none in the last ten years) and fewer than five minor traffic violations.

The prospective parents must demonstrate the ability to provide a safe family environment capable of meeting the needs of an orphaned child and providing for her/his development, and an understanding of the special risks (including potential diseases, developmental delays, and post-placement maladjustment) that could come with inter-country adoption.

Prospective adoptive parents must provide an adoption application letter that makes clear the willingness to allow post-placement follow-ups and provide post-placement reports as required. (Compliance with post-placement and post-adoption reports is extremely important for continued close cooperation on adoption between the United States and China.)

Who Can Be Adopted? Because China is party to the Hague Adoption Convention, children from China must meet the requirements of the Convention in order to be eligible for adoption. For example, the Convention requires that China attempt to place a child with a family in-country before determining that a child is eligible for intercountry adoption. In addition to China's requirements, a child must meet the definition of a Convention adoptee for you to bring him or her back to the United States.

Age Requirements: Chinese law allows for the adoption of children up to and including age 13; children ages 14 and up may not be adopted.

Waiting Period: It is hard to predict with certainty how much time is required to complete an adoption in China. The time frames provided in this flyer are intended as guidelines only, and the specific circumstances of each case could affect significantly how long the process takes.

Recent experience indicates that waiting periods are approximately 54 months from the time a U.S. adoption agency submits the paperwork of the prospective adopter to CCCWA until the CCCWA gives the prospective adoptive parent(s) their initial referral. Cases involving children with special needs are generally shorter.

After the referral is sent and the prospective parent(s) accept the referral (see the step-by-step description of the Chinese adoption process, below), at least four to eight more weeks may elapse before the prospective adoptive parents receive the CCCWA's final approval to travel to China.

Families should allow at least two weeks in China to finalize their child's adoption and immigration procedures. The CCCWA has advised local officials to try to complete the process within 15 days after the prospective parents arrive in China.

The child's Chinese passport, exit permits, and U.S. immigrant visa process will take another 7–10 days after the adoption is finalized.

Chinese Adoption Authority: The China Centre of Adoption Affairs (CCCWA)

The Process: Because China is party to the Hague Adoption Convention, adopting from China must follow a specific process designed to meet the Convention's requirements.

The first step in adopting a child from China is to select an adoption service provider in the United States that has been accredited. Only these agencies and attorneys can provide adoption services between the United States and China.

Prospective adoptive families must use an agency that is both U.S. Hague accredited and a CCCWA-licensed agency for all steps in the intercountry adoption process in both transition cases and Convention cases. After you choose an accredited adoption service provider, you apply to be found eligible to adopt (Form I-800A) by the U.S. Government, Department of Homeland Security, U.S. Citizenship and Immigration Services (USCIS). Once USCIS determines that you are "eligible" and "suitable" to adopt, your adoption service provider will submit your adoption application to the CCCWA, including any preferences you may have about the child's age, sex, physical/medical condition, or region of origin within China. This application package should also include a cover letter.

The CCCWA will review your application to determine whether you are eligible to adopt under Chinese law. It will also advise prospective adoptive parent(s), either directly or through their adoption agency, if additional documents or authentications are required.

If both the United States and China determine that you are eligible to adopt, and a child is available for intercountry adoption, the central adoption authority in China may provide you with a referral for a child.

Prospective adoptive parents either accept or refuse a referral and send the document to their agency, which forwards it to CCCWA. CCCWA requires a response on a referral within 45 days of sending a referral to a family. After you accept a match with a child, you will apply to the U.S Government, Department of Homeland Security, U.S. Citizenship and Immigration Services (USCIS) for provisional approval to adopt that particular child (Form I-800). USCIS will determine whether the child is eligible under U.S. law to be adopted and enter the United States.

The adoption service provider then submits the child's visa application (DS-230) to the U.S. Consulate General Guangzhou's Adopted Children's Immigrant Visa Unit (ACIVU). The ACIVU officer will review the child's information and evaluate the case for possible visa ineligibilities. If the officer determines that the child appears eligible to immigrate to the United States, he/she will notify China's adoption authority via the "Article 5" letter, which the adoption agency will forward to the CCCWA. After the ACIVU has issues an Article 5 letter and the adoption service provider submits the letter to the CCCWA, the CCCWA will then issue a "Travel Approval" CCCWA ("Notice of Coming to China for Adoption") to the agency, who will forward this information on to the family. This document will bear the "chops," or red-inked seals of the CCCWA. Prospective adoptive parents must have this approval notice in hand before departing for China to finalize the adoption.

Only at this point the adoption agency may submit an immigrant visa appointment request to the ACIVU. Once prospective adoptive parents have received confirmation of their ACIVU immigrant visa appointment, they may travel to China. Once in China they may proceed directly to the city in China where the Civil Affairs Bureau with jurisdiction over the appropriate Children's Welfare Institute is located. Although the CCCWA is headquartered in Beijing, prospective adoptive parents will not be required to travel to Beijing during this process. The CCCWA will have already forwarded a copy of the adoption approval notice to the locality where the child resides. Local Child Welfare Institutes, provincial Civil Affairs officials and Chinese notarial offices will not process adoptions unless they have seen this notice allowing the prospective adoptive parents take legal custody of the child.

Requirements for Adopting Children with Special Needs or Medical Conditions: Once prospective adoptive parents decide to accept a special needs referral, they have 72 hours to fill out the necessary forms to complete their dossier. Prospective adoptive parents can review the case, including the medical and growth records and a photo of the child. The reason the child is designated special needs is documented and the prospective adoptive parents can decide if they can meet the child's needs; for example, whether their insurance would cover the child's medical needs, and whether they themselves are able to provide any educational or rehabilitative needs, etc. If the prospective adoptive parents decide they are able to meet this child's needs, they indicate such to the CCCWA and from that point onward they have 72 hours to fill out the necessary forms to complete the dossier. The reason this short time limit is set is so that the child is not taken off the list until a family is truly committed to adopt that child. If the prospective adoptive parents have not completed the forms and submitted them within 72 hours, the child's name goes back on the list and other prospective adoptive parents can review that child's file. For detailed information about special needs programs, please consult your adoption service provider.

Role of the Adoption Authority: The provincial Departments of Civil Affairs, which are administered by the Ministry of Civil Affairs, issue the final adoption certificate.

Adoption Fees: Fees charged by Chinese authorities in connection with foreign adoptions may vary depending on the province where the child is adopted. However, for each adoption, there are standard fees that adoptive parents must pay.

The authentication/legalization of documents by the Chinese Embassy or Consulate in the United States costs $10 USD per document, whether the document is one or multiple pages. The fee is for authentication of the seal. The initial CCCWA fee is $750 USD, plus $300 USD for translation of the documents submitted in the dossier. The translations can be done in the United States or China, however, the CCCWA advises that the translations must be "correct" and that CCCWA will "rectify," and charge for correcting any errors.

Fees for issuance of the Chinese-notarized certificate approving the adoption, birth certificate and abandonment certificate may vary based on province. These documents normally come together in a packet notarized by the provincial notary office. The Guangzhou Consulate no longer requests the notarized adoption certificate but still requires the birth certificate and abandonment certificate to be notarized. Many provincial notary offices still issue these three notaries as a package. Additional documents such as death certificates, for the orphan's parents, or additional investigation is not included in this fee. Chinese passports cost $25 USD for the normal 15-working-day issuance. Charges for expedited service differ by province.

Individual Children's Welfare Institutes (where the child lived prior to adoption) may charge from $5000 USD to $5000 USD as a combined donation to the institution and a fee for caring for the child. U.S. adoptive parent(s) who believe that they were compelled at any point during the adoption process to pay exorbitant fees out of keeping with the general outline provided in this flyer should notify the U.S. Consulate General in Guangzhou. In the adoption services contract that you sign at the beginning of the adoption process, your agency will itemize the fees and estimated expenses related to your adoption process.

Documents Required: The following documents should be submitted in the original dossier:

- Adoption application letter
- Birth certificate(s) of the prospective adoptive parent(s)
- Marital status statement—Either a marriage certificate, divorce or death certificate (if applicable) or statement of single status is required.
- Certificates of profession, income and property including; verification of employment and salary notarized and authenticated; a certified and authenticated copy of your property trust deeds, if applicable(not notarized?); Bank statements notarized/certified and authenticated

- Health examination certificate(s) of the prospective adoptive parent(s)

- Certificate(s) of criminal or no-criminal record—A certificate of good conduct for the adoptive parent(s) from a local police department notarized or bearing the police department seal and authenticated. An FBI report is acceptable in lieu of a local police record. This is separate from the FBI check conducted by USCIS as part of the petition process. You can request an FBI record check by sending two sets of fingerprints, an $18 money order, your full name, date and place of birth, social security number and letter of request explaining purpose for clearance to: FBI ID Division, Room 10104, Washington, DC 20537–9700. The FBI certificate should also be authenticated.

- Home study report

- Certificate of child adoption approval by the competent department of the adopter's country of residence, also known as the Department of Homeland Security Bureau of Citizenship and Immigration Services I-171H Notice of Approval of an I-600A petition) along with copies of the U.S. passport(s) of the prospective adoptive parent(s)

- Each applicant parent should also submit two front-view photos and several other photos reflecting the family's life in the United States.

- Power of attorney notarized and authenticated (if only one spouse will travel to China). In case of married couples, if only one adopting parent comes to China, Chinese law requires that the spouse traveling bring a power of attorney from his/her spouse, notarized and properly authenticated by Chinese Embassy or one of the Chinese Consulates General in the United States.

Bringing Your Child Home: Once your adoption is complete (or you have obtained legal custody of the child), there are a few more steps to take before you can head home. Specifically, you need to apply for several documents for your child before he or she can travel to the United States, such as a birth certificate, a passport or travel document for your child from the country in which he or she was born, and a U.S. Immigration Visa. For detailed and updated information on how to obtain these documents, review the *Intercountry Adoption* section in this publication and visit the U.S. Department of State Intercountry Adoption website at http://adoption.state.gov.

Child Citizenship Act: For adoptions finalized abroad, the Child Citizenship Act of 2000 allows your new child to acquire American citizenship automatically when he or she enters the United States as lawful permanent residents. For adoptions finalized in the United States, the Child Citizenship Act of 2000 allows your new child to acquire American citizenship automatically when the court in the United States issues the final adoption decree. To learn more, review the *Intercountry Adoption* section in this publication and visit the U.S. Department of State Intercountry Adoption website at http://adoption.state.gov.

After Adoption: Prospective Adoptive Parents must provide an adoption application letter that makes clear the applicants' willingness to allow post-placement follow-ups and provide post-placement reports as required.

U.S. Embassy in China
No. 55 An Jia Lou road
Beijing, China 100600
Tel: (86–10) 8531–4000
Fax: (86–10) 8531–3300
Email: AmCitBeijing@state.gov

Consulate General of the United States in Guangzhou
Adopted Children Immigrant Visa Unit
Mailing #1 Shamian South Street
Guangzhou, P. R. C. 51033
Tel: 011–86–20–8121 8000;
011–86–20–8518 7653 (Direct Line)
Fax: 011–86–20–3884 4420
Email: GuangzhouA@state.gov

China's Adoption Authority
The China Centre of Adoption Affairs (CCCWA)
103 Beiheyan St.
Dongcheng District
Beijing 100006
Tel: 86–10–6522–3102;
86–10–6513–0607
Email: mail@ccaa.cn
Internet: www.china-ccaa.org

Ministry of Civil Affairs
No. 147 Beiheyan St.
Beijing, 100032

Embassy of the People's Republic of China
Consular Section
2300 Connecticut Ave., N.W.
Washington, D.C. 20008
Tel: 202–328–2500

China also has Consulates in Los Angeles, CA; San Francisco, CA; Chicago, IL; New York, NY, and Houston, TX.

Office of Children's Issues
U.S. Department of State
2201 C Street, NW
SA-29
Washington, DC 20520
Tel: 1–888–407–4747
E-mail: AskCI@state.gov
http://adoption.state.gov

For questions about immigration procedures, call the National Customer Service Center (NCSC) at 1-800-375-5283 (TTY 1-800-767-1833).

Concerns About Information on the Background of Children Adopted from China
August 15, 2011

The press has reported allegations that in 2005 local family planning officials in China, in the name of enforcing the "One Child Policy," seized children from their birth families and sold them to orphanages. Embassy Beijing has been in touch with China's Centre for Children's Welfare and Adoption (CCCWA) about the allegations mentioned in the articles and CCCWA has promised updates on their investigations when they have further information. We are not aware of any intercountry adoption by a U.S. family that has been confirmed to be linked to these alleged actions. In response to these concerns, we would like to remind adopting parents that verification of a child's eligibility for intercountry adoption is an integral part of the intercountry adoption process. If there is evidence that documents may have been falsified or are not accurate, then officials at a U.S. Embassy or Consulate conduct an investigation before the visa is approved. If you wish to get more information on your child's background, we suggest that you contact the adoption service provider that assisted you with the adoption. If you have any further questions about this notice please contact the Office of Children's Issues at: 1–888–407–4747 within the United States or 202–501–4444 from outside the United States.

China Single Female Adoption Notice
March 11, 2011

Government departments and adoption agencies in receiving countries, In order to promote special needs child adoption and guarantee the basic interests of the orphaned and disabled children, CCAA decides to accept the adoption applications from female single applicants to adopt according to the requirements listed in this notice, starting from March 15, 2011. Female single applicants are allowed to adopt special focus children listed on the Special Needs System of CCAA. One applicant can only adopt one special focus child at a time, with an interval of at least one year between two adoptions.

The applicant shall have reached the age of 30 years and are under 50. For applicants over 50, the age difference between the child to be adopted and the applicant shall be no more than 45 years.

The applicant shall provide her civil status certificate. Unmarried applicants shall provide certification for being single and non-homosexual; divorced applicants shall provide the divorce certificate of the last marriage; and widowed applicants shall provide the death certificate of their ex-spouse.

Applicants shall be healthy both physically and mentally according to the requirements by CCAA for prospective adoptive couples. Applicants shall be law abiding with no criminal records, and have good moral quality and conduct.

The family annual income shall reach $10,000 per family member, including the prospective adoptee and the family net assets value should reach $100,000. The applicant shall have good medical insurance which can cover the medical expense of the adopted child. Applicants shall be experienced in child caring or be occupied in child-related fields, such as doctor, nurse, teacher, child psychological counselor, etc. It's best that the applicants have already had successful experience in caring for special needs children. The number of children in the applicant's family under the age of 18 years shall be no more than two, and the youngest one should have reached the age of 6 years old. Applicants shall be fully prepared for adopting a special focus child. Social workers shall provide the following information fully and truly in the home study reports besides family visit interviews:

- Adoption motive. The decision to adopt a special focus child shall be well-considered. Applicants shall be capable of caring for a special need child and be responsible for the well-being of the child.
- The reason of being single and attitude towards marriage. Applicants shall have clear indication of willingness to appoint male figures as role models for the adopted child, and welcome male friends to join family gatherings.
- Applicants shall have received inter-country adoption training and training specifically for special needs child adoption so as to understand fully the physical and psychological needs of special needs children.
- Detailed nurturing and rehabilitation plan. Applicants shall be qualified personally and socially for caring special needs children and have wide social and family supporting network which can provide assistance any time.
- Other advantages for caring special needs children.

Guardians appointed by the applicants shall provide written statement as consent to act as the guardian of the adopted child.

If the applicant has a stable relationship and lives with a male partner, the requirements of couple applicants shall be applied. The Department will seek clarification on the details of the new policy and will make updates to our website as soon as we have additional details. If you have any further questions about this notice please contact the Office of Children's Issues at 1–888–407–4747 within the United States or 202–501–4444 from outside the United States.

International Parental Child Abduction

January 2012

The information in this section has been edited from the latest report available as of February 2013 from the State Department Bureau of Consular Affairs, Office of Overseas Citizens Services. For more information, please read the *International Parental Child Abduction* section of this book and check for updated reports online at www.travel.state.gov/abduction.

Disclaimer: The information in this flyer relating to the legal requirements of specific foreign countries is provided for general information only. Questions involving interpretation of specific foreign laws should be addressed to foreign legal counsel.

General Information: The Peoples Republic of China (PRC) is not a party to the Hague Convention on the Civil Aspects of International Child Abduction, nor are there any international or bilateral treaties in force between China and the United States dealing with international parental child abduction. American citizens who travel to China place themselves under the jurisdiction of local courts. American citizens planning a trip to China with dual national children should bear this in mind.

Custody Disputes: In China, parents who are legally married share the custody of their children. If they are not married and the parents cannot reach an agreement, custody is granted by the courts in the best interests of the child.

Enforcement of Foreign Judgments: Custody orders and judgments of foreign courts are not enforceable in China. Such judgments must be presented to a Chinese court for that courts consideration and decision. In China, there is a limited process to appeal a lower court's decision.

Visitation Rights: In cases where legal custody has been granted and the judgment has been rendered, the non-custodial parent's visitation rights are normally incorporated within the court ordered decision.

Dual Nationality: Dual nationality is not recognized under Chinese law. Some U.S. citizens who are also Chinese nationals (mostly U.S.-born children of Chinese nationals or Legal permanent Permanent Residents) have experienced difficulty entering and departing China on U.S. passports. In some cases, such dual nationals are required to use Chinese travel documents to depart China. Normally this causes inconvenience but no significant problems for affected persons; however, in child custody disputes, the ability of dual national children to depart from China could be affected. Generally, children who are Chinese nationals according to Chinese law are not permitted to depart China if one parent refuses to allow the travel requested by one parent, even if that parent is considered an abducting parent by United States courts. In those cases, children abducted to China are only permitted to return to the United States if both parents agree to their return, or if a Chinese court upholds a United States Court's decision to allow the left-behind parent sole custody. For more information, please read the *International Parental Child Abduction* section of this book and review current reports online at www.travel. state.gov/abduction.

Passports for Minors and the Children's Passport Issuance Alert Program: For more information on these topics, see the *International Parental Child Abduction* section of this publication and review current reports from the U.S. Department of State at www.travel.state.gov/abduction.

Travel Restrictions: While no exit visas are required to leave China, persons who replace passports are required to get an exit permit from the entry and exit police. The U.S. Embassy and Consulates will assist a traveler with a new passport in obtaining this document.

Criminal Remedies: For information on possible criminal remedies, please contact your local law enforcement authorities or the nearest office of the Federal Bureau of Investigation (FBI). Information is also available on the Internet at the web site of the U.S. Department of Justice, Office of Juvenile Justice and Delinquency Prevention (OJJDP) at http://www.ojjdp. ncjrs.org. Persons who wish to pursue a child custody claim in a Chinese court should retain an attorney in China.

The American Embassy and U.S. Consulates in China maintain lists of attorneys willing to represent American clients. A copy of this list may be obtained by requesting one from the Embassy or Consulate at:

U.S. Embassy in Beijing
Consular Section
3 Xiu Shui Bei Jie
Beijing 100600
People's Republic of China
Telephone: 011-86-10-6532-3431
Fax: 011-86-10-6532-4153
Web site: http://www.usembassy-china.org.cn
E-mail: amcitbeijing@state.gov

Questions involving Chinese law should be addressed to a Chinese attorney or to the Embassy of China in the United States at:

Embassy of the People's Republic of China
2201 Wisconsin Avenue, NW
Washington, DC 20007
Telephone: (202) 338-6688

For further information on international parental child abduction, contact the Office of Children's Issues, U.S. Department of State at 1-888-407-4747 or visit its web site on the Internet at www.travel.state.gov/abduction.

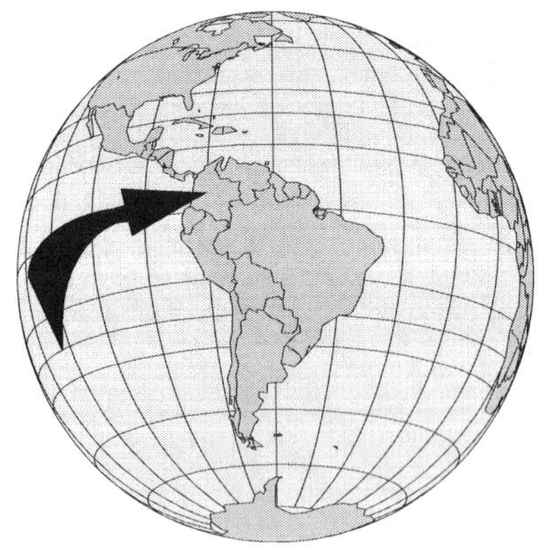

COLOMBIA

Compiled from publications that were available as of February 2013 from the U.S. Department of State, the U.S. Department of Commerce, and the Central Intelligence Agency (CIA). See the introduction to this set for explanatory notes.

Official Name:
Republic of Colombia

PROFILE

Geography

Area: total: 1,138,910 sq km; country comparison to the world: 26; land: 1,038,700 sq km; water: 100,210 sq km

Major cities: Bogota (capital) 8.262 million; Medellin 3.497 million; Cali 2.352 million; Barranquilla 1.836 million; Bucaramanga 1.065 million (2009)

Climate: tropical along coast and eastern plains; cooler in highlands

Terrain: flat coastal lowlands, central highlands, high Andes Mountains, eastern lowland plains

People

Nationality: noun: Colombian(s); adjective: Colombian

Population: 45,239,079 (July 2012 est.)

Population growth rate: 1.128% (2012 est.)

Ethnic groups: mestizo 58%, white 20%, mulatto 14%, black 4%, mixed black-Amerindian 3%, Amerindian 1%

Religions: Roman Catholic 90%, other 10%

Languages: Spanish (official)

Literacy: definition: age 15 and over can read and write; total population: 90.4%; male: 90.1%; female: 90.7% (2005 census)

Health: life expectancy at birth: total population: 74.79 years; male: 71.55 years; female: 78.23 years (2012 est.); Infant mortality rate: total: 15.92 deaths/1,000 live births; male: 19.34 deaths/1,000 live births; female: 12.3 deaths/1,000 live births (2012 est.)

Unemployment rate: 10.3% (2012 est.)

Work force: 23.08 million (2012 est.)

Government

Type: republic; executive branch dominates government structure

Independence: 20 July 1810

Constitution: 5 July 1991; amended many times

Political subdivisions: 32 departments (departamentos, singular—departamento) and 1 capital district (distrito capital)

Suffrage: 18 years of age; universal

Economy

GDP (purchasing power parity): $500 billion (2012 est.); $478 billion (2011 est.); $451.3 billion (2010 est.); $433.9 billion (2009 est.)

GDP real growth rate: 4.3% (2012 est.); 5.9% (2011 est.); 4% (2010 est.); 1.7% (2009 est.)

GDP per capita (PPP): $10,700 (2012 est.); $10,400 (2011 est.); $9,900 (2010 est.); $9,600 (2009 est.)

Natural resources: petroleum, natural gas, coal, iron ore, nickel, gold, copper, emeralds, hydropower

Agriculture products: coffee, cut flowers, bananas, rice, tobacco, corn, sugarcane, cocoa beans, oilseed, vegetables; shrimp; forest products

Industries: textiles, food processing, oil, clothing and footwear, beverages, chemicals, cement; gold, coal, emeralds

Exports: $59.96 billion (2012 est.); $56.22 billion (2011 est.); $39.55 billion (2010 est.)

Exports—commodities: petroleum, coal, emeralds, coffee, nickel, cut flowers, bananas, apparel

Exports—partners: US 38%, EU 15%, China 3.5%, Ecuador 3.4% (2011 est.)

Imports: $55.49 billion (2012 est.); $54.7 billion (2011 est.); $37.51 billion (2010 est.)

Imports—commodities: industrial equipment, transportation equipment, consumer goods, chemicals, paper products, fuels, electricity

Imports—partners: US 25%, China 15%, Mexico 11%, Brazil 5%, Germany 4.1% (2011 est.)

Debt—external: $73.41 billion (31 December 2012 est.); $68.76 billion (31 December 2011 est.); $63.06 billion (31 December 2010 est.)

Exchange rates: Colombian pesos (COP) per US dollar; 1,800.4 (2012 est.); 1,848.1 (2011 est.); 1,898.6 (2010 est.); 2,157.6 (2009); 2,243.6 (2008); 2,013.8 (2007)

PEOPLE

Colombia is the third-most populous country in Latin America, after Brazil and Mexico. Most of Colombia's population is concentrated around the northern and western departments. The nine eastern lowlands departments, constituting about 54% of Colombia's area, are sparsely populated (less than 3% of the population; density of less than one person per square kilometer).

Ethnic and cultural diversity in Colombia reflects the indigenous, European (mainly Spanish), and African heritages of its inhabitants. Afro-Colombians and indigenous groups have faced challenges related to integration into mainstream Colombian society.

Many Colombians live below the poverty line, and the country continues to face large income disparities and inadequate social services. The history of the country, including decades of violence involving outlawed armed groups and drug cartels coupled with human rights violations, has complicated the advancement of government social programs to address these problems. Colombia continues to make progress in improving citizen security, which is an essential building block for stability and democracy.

National/Racial/Ethnic Minorities

According to the 2005 national census, approximately 4.5 million persons, or 10 percent of the country's population, described themselves as of African descent. A November UN report estimated that Afro-Colombians composed 15 to 20 percent of the population, while human rights groups and Afro-Colombian organizations estimated the proportion to be 20 to 25 percent. Afro-Colombians are entitled to all constitutional rights and protections, but they faced significant economic and social discrimination. According to the UN report, 45.5 percent of the country's population lived below the poverty rate, but in Choco, the department with the highest percentage of Afro-Colombian residents, 70.5 percent of residents lived below the poverty line (41 percent in extreme poverty).

Choco continued to experience the lowest per capita level of social investment and ranked last in terms of infrastructure, education, and health. Maternal mortality in Choco was four times higher than the national average. It also continued to experience some of the country's worst political violence, as organized criminal gangs and FARC and ELN guerrillas struggled for control of the department's drug- and weapons-smuggling corridor (see section 1.g.). The UN report further explained that illiteracy rates were six times the national average in Narino, another department with a high percentage of Afro-Colombians.

In 2010 the government approved a policy to promote equal opportunity for black, Afro-Colombian, Palenquera, and Raizal populations. (Palenquera populations along some parts of the Caribbean coast, Raizal populations in the San Andres archipelago, and blacks and Afro-Colombians are all Afro-descendents who self-identify slightly differently based on their unique linguistic and cultural heritages.)

The constitution and laws give special recognition to the fundamental rights of indigenous people, who compose approximately 3.4 percent of the population, and require that the government consult beforehand with indigenous groups regarding governmental actions that could affect them. The law accords indigenous groups perpetual rights to their ancestral lands. However, many indigenous communities had no legal title to lands they claimed, and illegal armed groups often violently contested indigenous land ownership.

Through its land restitution and formalization "shock plan," as of July 2011 the government had restored 269,800 acres of land to indigenous communities.

Langauge

Spanish is the official language and spoken throughout the country. Many senior executives and government officials speak English.

Religion

The government does not keep statistics on religious affiliation, and estimates from religious leaders varied. A majority of the population is Roman Catholic. According to the Colombian Evangelical Council (CEDECOL), approximately 15 percent of the population is Protestant, whereas the Catholic Bishops' Conference estimates that 90 percent of the population is Catholic.

A 2007 article in the daily newspaper El Tiempo stated that 80 percent of the population is Catholic, 14 percent non-Catholic Christian, 2 percent agnostic, and the remaining 4 percent belongs to other religious groups, including Islam and Judaism.

Another estimate had the following figures for the non-Catholic population: 261,000 Seventh-Day Adventists, five million other Protestants and evangelicals, 150,000 The Church of Jesus Christ of Latter-Day Saints (Mormons), 10,000 Muslims, and 5,000 Jews. Practitioners of animism and various syncretic beliefs are also present in the country.

Some religious groups are concentrated in certain geographical regions. Most practitioners of syncretic beliefs that blend Catholicism with elements of African animism are Afro-Colombians and reside on the Pacific coast. Most Jews reside in major cities, Muslims on the Caribbean coast, and adherents of indigenous animistic religions in remote rural areas. A small Taoist commune is located in a mountainous region of Santander Department.

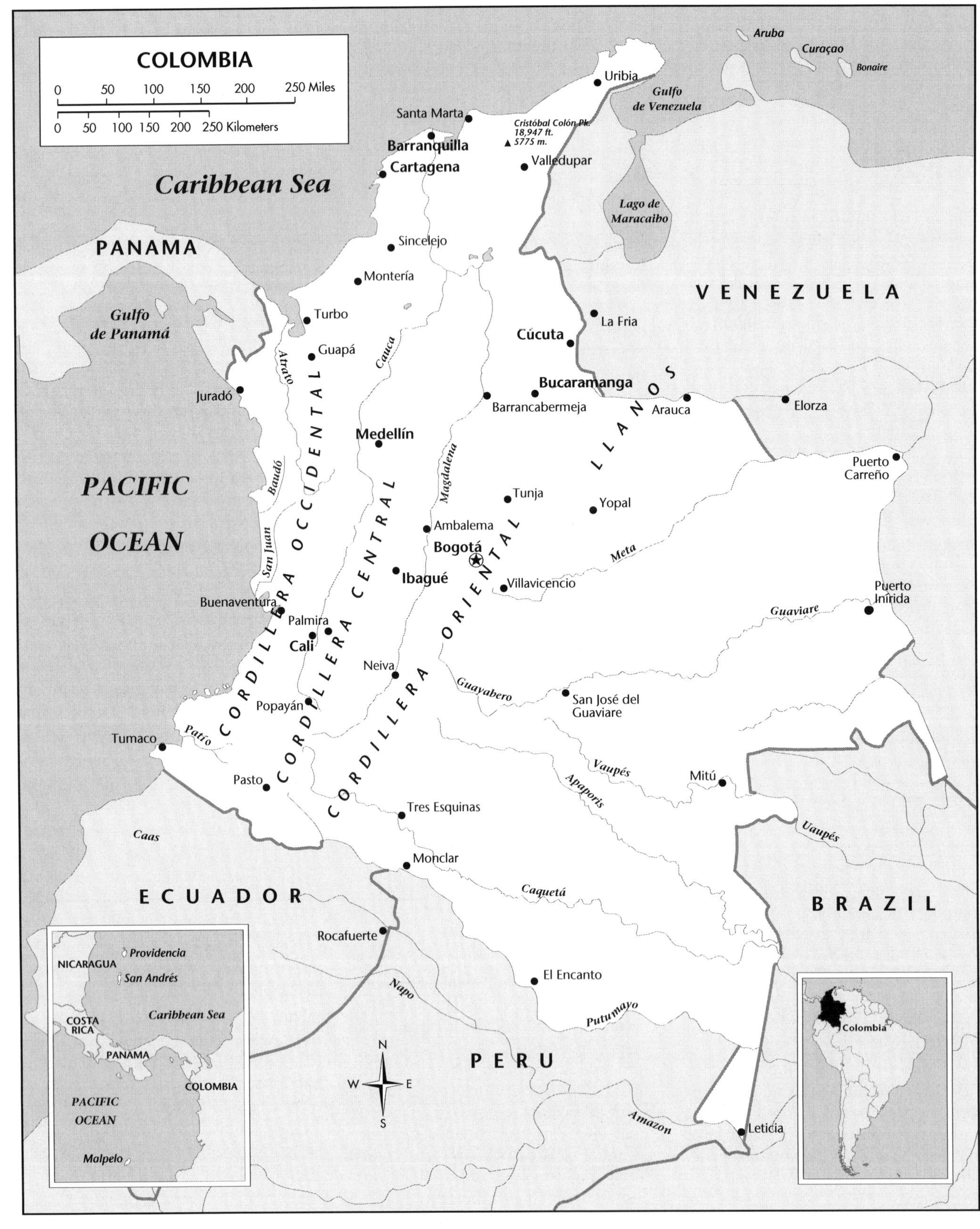
COLOMBIA
0 50 100 150 200 250 Miles
0 50 100 150 200 250 Kilometers
Aruba
Curaçao
Bonaire
Uribia
Gulfo de Venezuela
Santa Marta
Cristóbal Colón Pk. 18,947 ft. 5775 m.
Barranquilla
Cartagena
Valledupar
Caribbean Sea
Lago de Maracaibo
PANAMA
Sincelejo
Montería
VENEZUELA
Gulfo de Panamá
Turbo
La Fria
Cúcuta
Guapá
Atrato
Cauca
Juradó
Bucaramanga
Barrancabermeja
Arauca
Elorza
LLANOS
Medellín
CORDILLERA OCCIDENTAL
CORDILLERA CENTRAL
CORDILLERA ORIENTAL
Magdalena
Baudó
PACIFIC OCEAN
Puerto Carreño
Tunja
Yopal
Ambalema
Bogotá
San Juan
Meta
Ibagué
Villavicencio
Puerto Inírida
Buenaventura
Guaviare
Palmira
Cali
Neiva
Guayabero
San José del Guaviare
Popayán
Tumaco
Patía
Vaupés
Mitú
Pasto
Apaporis
Tres Esquinas
Caas
Uaupés
Monclar
Caquetá
ECUADOR
BRAZIL
Rocafuerte
Providencia
NICARAGUA
San Andrés
El Encanto
Napo
COSTA RICA
Caribbean Sea
Colombia
Putumayo
N
W
E
S
PANAMA
PERU
COLOMBIA
PACIFIC OCEAN
Amazon
Leticia
Malpelo

HISTORY

During the pre-Columbian period, the area now known as Colombia was inhabited by indigenous societies ranging from hunters and nomadic farmers to the highly structured economy of the Chibchas, who are considered to have been one of the most developed indigenous groups in South America.

Santa Marta, the first permanent Spanish settlement, was founded in 1525. The city of Santa Fe de Bogota was founded in 1538 and, in 1717, became the capital of the Viceroyalty of New Granada, which included what are now Colombia, Venezuela, Ecuador, and Panama. Bogota was one of three principal administrative centers of the Spanish possessions in the New World.

On July 20, 1810, the citizens of Bogota created the first representative council to defy Spanish authority. Full independence was proclaimed in 1813, and in 1819 the Republic of Greater Colombia was formed to include all the territory of the former Viceroyalty of New Granada. Simon Bolivar was elected its first president with Francisco de Paula Santander as vice president. Conflicts between followers of Bolivar and Santander led to the formation of two main political parties, Liberal and Conservative. Bolivar's supporters, who formed the nucleus of the Conservative Party, sought strong centralized government, alliance with the Roman Catholic Church, and a limited suffrage. Santander's followers, forerunners of the Liberals, wanted a decentralized government, state control over education and other civil matters, and broader voting rights.

Throughout the 19th and early 20th centuries, each party held the presidency for roughly equal periods of time. Colombia maintained a tradition of civilian government and regular, free elections. Notwithstanding the country's commitment to democratic institutions, Colombia's history has been characterized by widespread and violent conflict. Two civil wars resulted from bitter rivalry between the Conservative and Liberal parties: The War of a Thousand Days (1899–1903), which claimed an estimated 100,000 lives, and La Violencia (the Violence) (1946–1957), which resulted in about 300,000 deaths.

La Violencia (The Violence) and the National Front

The assassination of Liberal leader Jorge Eliecer Gaitan in 1948 sparked the bloody conflict known as La Violencia. Conservative Party leader Laureano Gomez came to power in 1950, but was ousted by a military coup led by General Gustavo Rojas Pinilla in 1953. In 1957, Rojas was overthrown by the military with the support of the Liberal and Conservative Parties after he failed to restore democratic rule and was implicated in corrupt schemes.

In July 1957, an alliance between former Conservative President Laureano Gomez (1950–53) and former Liberal President Alberto Lleras Camargo (1945–46) led to the creation of the National Front. This established a power-sharing agreement between the two parties ending the partisan violence. Under the agreement, the presidency would be determined by regular rotating elections every 4 years, and the two parties would have parity in all other elected and appointed offices. This arrangement was phased out in 1978.

Post-National Front Years

During the post-National Front years, successive Colombian governments made efforts to negotiate peace with the guerrilla organizations that were flourishing in Colombia's remote and undeveloped rural areas. These organizations were rooted in Marxist ideologies and mobilized by student leaders in the 1960s. The groups persisted at low levels of organization until the 1980s, when they gained power. In 1984, President Belisario Betancur, a Conservative, negotiated a cease-fire with the Revolutionary Armed Forces of Colombia (FARC) and the Democratic Alliance (M-19) that included the release of many imprisoned guerrillas. However, the National Liberation Army (ELN) rejected the government's cease-fire proposal. The M-19 pulled out of the cease-fire and resumed fighting in 1985. The army suppressed an M-19 and drug cartel-coordinated attack on the Palace of Justice in Bogota in November 1985, during which 115 people were killed, including 11 Supreme Court justices. The government and the M-19 renewed their truce in March 1989, which led to a peace agreement and the M-19's demobilization and reintegration into society and political life. The M-19 was one of the parties that participated in the process to enact a new constitution (see below), which took effect in 1991. The FARC ended its truce in 1990 after 2,000-3,000 demobilized members were murdered. Many of those killed were members of the FARC political party Union Patriotica (UP), sanctioned by Bentacur during the peace negotiations. Those killed included the UP 1985 presidential candidate and elected congressmen. The identities of the assassins were not entirely clear, but a combination of government, paramilitary, and private entities was suspected.

The 1991 constitution brought major reforms to Colombia's political institutions. While the new constitution preserved a presidential, three-branch system of government, it created institutions such as the Inspector General, a Human Rights Ombudsman, a Constitutional Court, and a Superior Judicial Council. It also re-established the position of Vice President. Other significant reforms in the 1991 constitution provided for civil divorce, dual nationality, and the establishment of a legal mechanism ("Tutela") that allows individuals to appeal government decisions affecting their constitutional rights and defined the state as pluri-ethnic, creating special seats for indigenous and Afro-Colombian representation in the Congress. The 1991 constitution also authorized the introduction of an accusatory system of criminal justice to be instituted gradually throughout the country, replacing the previous written inquisitorial system. A 2005 constitutional amendment allows the president to hold office for two consecutive 4-year terms.

Since the early 1980s, successive Colombian governments have had to contend with the terrorist and drug-trafficking activities of left-wing guerrillas, the rise of paramilitary self-defense forces in the 1990s, and the violence of drug cartels. Three presidential candidates were assassinated during the election campaign of 1990. After Colombian security forces killed Medellin cartel leader Pablo Escobar in December 1993, indiscriminate acts of violence associated with his organization abated as the cartels fragmented into multiple, smaller trafficking organizations that competed against one another in the drug trade. Guerrillas and paramilitary groups also entered into drug trafficking as a way to finance their military operations.

Pastrana Administration

The administration of Andres Pastrana (1998–2002), a Conservative, faced the challenges of increased countrywide attacks by the FARC and ELN, widespread drug production and associated crime, and the expansion of paramilitary groups. The Pastrana administration unveiled its "Plan Colombia" in 1999 as a 6-year strategy to deal with these longstanding problems and sought support from the international community. Plan Colombia was a comprehensive program to combat the narcotics trade, spur economic recovery, strengthen democratic institutions and respect for human rights, and provide humanitarian assistance to internally displaced persons.

In November 1998, Pastrana ceded a sparsely populated area the size of Switzerland in south-central Colombia to the FARC's control to serve as a neutral zone where peace negotiations could take place. The FARC negotiated with the government sporadically, while continuing to mount attacks against the military, communities, local authorities, and individuals and to expand coca production, which undermined the government's efforts to reach an agreement. Negotiations with the rebels in 2000 and 2001 were marred by rebel attacks, kidnappings, and fighting between rebels and paramilitaries for control of coca-growing areas in Colombia. In February 2002, after the FARC hijacked a commercial aircraft and kidnapped a senator, Pastrana ordered the military to attack rebel positions and reassert control over the neutral zone. The FARC withdrew into the jungle and increased attacks against Colombia's infrastructure but avoided large-scale direct conflicts with the military.

Uribe Administration

Alvaro Uribe, an independent, was elected president in May 2002 on a platform to restore security to the country. Among his promises was pursuing the broad goals of Plan Colombia within the framework of a long-term strategy. In the fall of 2002, Uribe released a democratic security strategy that employed political, economic, and military means to weaken all illegal armed groups. The Uribe government offered to negotiate a peace agreement with these groups if they would agree to a unilateral cease-fire and to end drug trafficking and kidnapping.

In December 2003, the Colombian United Self-Defense Forces (AUC) paramilitary group entered into a peace agreement with the government that led to the collective demobilization of over 31,000 AUC members. In addition, more than 20,000 members of the FARC, AUC, ELN, and other illegal armed groups have individually surrendered their arms. In July 2005, President Uribe signed the Justice and Peace Law, which provides reduced punishments for the demobilized if they renounce violence and return illegal assets, which are used by the government to provide reparations to victims.

In January 2007, Colombian leaders presented a new strategy to consolidate gains under Plan Colombia and its follow-on programs. This strategy eventually became known as the National Consolidation Plan (Plan Nacional de Consolidacion, or PNC). The PNC is a civilian-led, whole-of-government approach that builds upon successful Plan Colombia programs to establish state presence in traditionally ungoverned spaces. By improving access to social services, including justice, education, housing, and health; strengthening democracy; and supporting economic development through sustainable growth and trade, the Colombian Government seeks to permanently recover governance in Colombia's historically marginalized rural areas and break the cycle of guerilla violence.

In 2008, senior FARC commander Luis Edgar Devia-Silva, aka "Raul Reyes," was killed during a Colombian Government operation; FARC Commander Manuel Munoz-Ortiz, aka "Ivan Rios," was killed at the hands of his own chief of security; and FARC founding member Manuel Marulanda-Velez, aka "Tirofijo," died from a reported heart attack. Since 2000, the FARC has not carried out large-scale multi-front attacks, although it has mounted some operations that indicate it has not yet been broken. Government efforts on peace negotiations with the FARC stalled in 2010.

Santos Administration

On August 7, 2010, Juan Manuel Santos was inaugurated as President of Colombia. He previously served as Minister of National Defense for Uribe's second presidential term, as Minister of Finance under President Andres Pastrana, and as Minister of Trade under President Cesar Gaviria.

The Santos administration laid out an ambitious National Development Plan and has used a legislative majority to pass significant legislation, including a historic victims' law that will benefit approximately 4 million Colombians over the next 10 years with reparations and land restitution. Santos reorganized the executive branch, including new ministries of justice, labor, and the environment and abolished the discredited Administrative Department of Security (DAS) and replaced it with a new civilian intelligence agency. Executive branch reform was mandated, including the redistribution of royalties from mineral/natural resources, fiscal reforms, and the implementation of more tools to improve citizen safety. To improve national policies going forward, Santos also created new presidential programs for Afro-Colombian and indigenous issues. Vice President Angelino Garzon, a respected former labor leader, coordinates human rights and labor right issues. He has promptly condemned human rights abuses and threats against unions.

The Santos administration has also maintained positive trends in security consolidation. Security forces captured, killed, or demobilized over 4,200 guerrillas and members of criminal gangs in 2010 and over 3,000 more in 2011. The number of FARC fighters has decreased from 16,000 in 2001 to approximately 8,000 in 2011. The Colombian police and military successfully coordinated operations that resulted in the death of top FARC military commander "Mono Jojoy," ER-PAC (neo-paramilitary group) leader "Cuchillo," and FARC Supreme Commander "Alfonso Cano." Timoleon Jimenez, aka "Timochenko" was named Cano's successor in 2011. The successful operation against Cano was the continuation of a government strategy of pursuing high-value targets (HVTs) to weaken guerilla groups. In August 2011, Santos announced a revised counterinsurgency plan focused on degrading the FARC and its networks through coordinated intelligence, smaller operations, consolidation, and better protection for law enforcement officials. President Santos has also clearly defined his government's position on the possibility of peace negotiations—the FARC must release hostages, stop violence and lawlessness, and renounce the use of force to achieve political ends. Santos reemphasized, in December 2011, that the unilateral release of hostages was a non-negotiable first step. In February 2012, the FARC announced it would return hostages and cease its policy of kidnapping hostages for ransom, but it remains to be seen whether it follows through. Since 2002, more than 54,000 paramilitaries and guerrillas have demobilized, while kidnappings have fallen 91%, homicides 45%, terrorist attacks 91%, and attacks against oil pipelines 71%. Colombian law enforcement interdicted over 125 metric tons (MT) of cocaine and cocaine base in 2011. As a result of nationwide efforts to improve security, travel on Colombia's roads has doubled since 2000, and tourism has doubled since 2004.

The Victims and Land Restitution Law, signed into law by Santos in June 2011, focuses on making reparations available to 4 million victims affected by the country's ongoing civil conflict. This landmark law, the implementation of which began in January 2012, offers monetary compensation to the victims of human rights violations such as forced disappearance or homicide. It also offers monetary compensation or land restitution to people who lost their land as a result of the conflict. If the land is now uninhabitable because it is not secure or is now a natural park or other protected place, compensation will be made in the form of equivalent land in another part of the country. If land restitution does not fully compensate for the loss of land, a monetary award will be made. Victims (and the families of these victims) who were guerillas or paramilitaries will not be eligible for compensation, and it is unclear whether victims of criminal bands or state violence will be eligible for compensation. The law will continue to aid past and current victims through 2021.

Building on the "democratic security" agenda of the previous administration, President Santos campaigned on "democratic prosperity," focusing on economic development (jobs), security, and poverty reduction. The Santos administration passed an employment and formalization law, which seeks to create 2.5 million jobs, formalize 500,000 informal jobs, and reduce annual unemployment to single digits, all by 2014. His legislation to reduce the deficit through fiscal discipline measures was passed in late 2011.

In 2008, Colombia established an accusatorial judicial system, which should help critical human rights cases progress, but the country still needs to implement judicial reform legislation, provide more resources to the Prosecutor General, and show movement on emblematic human rights cases.

In December 2011, 64% of Colombians held a favorable opinion of the United States; 63% approved of President Barack Obama; and 72% favored the U.S.-Colombia Trade Promotion Agreement (CTPA). While security and counternarcotics continue to be key issues, the United States and Colombia are broadening their relationship. President Obama met with President Santos at the UN General Assembly in September 2010 and in Washington, DC in April 2011. The U.S. Congress ratified the CTPA on October 12, 2011, and President Obama signed it on October 24. The agreement will enter into force when Colombia demonstrates compliance with the obligations of the accord. In October 2010, more than 40 U.S. officials met with their counterparts in Bogota for the first High-Level Partnership Dialogue to discuss cooperation on issues like energy, human rights, and scientific exchange. A second round was held in Washington, DC in May 2011 and was expanded to include issues such as culture and education, and social and economic reform.

Colombia has taken an active, prominent role in global and regional institutions like the United Nations Security Council (UNSC) and the Union of South American Nations (UNASUR). Colombia chairs the Iran and Sudan Sanctions Committees in the UNSC, has contributed to three UN peacekeeping missions (Haiti, the Sinai, and Sierra Leone), and used its April 2011 UNSC presidency to focus attention on the reconstruction of Haiti. A Colombian is Secretary General of UNASUR until April 2012. Colombia will host the Summit of the Americas in April 2012 and the Pathways to Prosperity Ministerial Conference in October 2012. Additionally, Colombia has been sharing its unique security expertise throughout the region and globally through military and counternarcotics training exchanges with over 20 countries in Latin America, West Africa, and Afghanistan, and has committed to help the Central American Integration System (SICA) members. President Santos also successfully reestablished relations with Venezuela and Ecuador, allowing for greater collaboration on counternarcotics, border security, and trade.

GOVERNMENT AND POLITICAL CONDITIONS

Colombia is a constitutional, multiparty republic. In June 2010 Juan Manuel Santos was chosen president in elections that were considered generally free and fair. The internal armed conflict continued between the government and terrorist organizations, particularly the Revolutionary Armed Forces of Colombia (FARC) and the National Liberation Army (ELN).

Recent Elections

On October 30, 2011, the government held elections for local positions including governors, departmental representatives, mayors, and municipal councilors. The Electoral Observation Mission (MOE), an independent election-monitoring NGO, reported that between February and election day, of the approximately 102,000 candidates for local office, 41 were killed, 23 were attacked, seven were kidnapped, and 88 were threatened, for a total of 159 incidents of "political violence," compared with 149 during the previous local elections in 2007.

According to the NGO New Rainbow Foundation, electoral fraud remained a serious concern. The NGO reported that parties supported candidates with questionable financial ties paid voters to register and vote in municipalities in which they were not resident. According to New Rainbow Foundation, all parties' rosters included candidates with questionable ties. The MOE estimated that 600,000 people registered to vote in precincts where they were not legally resident. The government took steps to reduce fraud, introducing a new finance tool to ensure transparency of campaign funds, disqualifying candidates with pending criminal investigations, and canceling the national identification cards of voters who could not demonstrate residence or employment in the municipality where they registered to vote.

In June 2010 Juan Manuel Santos won a four-year term as president in elections that the OAS electoral observation mission considered generally free and fair. The OAS mission also noted that the 2010 elections involved the lowest levels of violence in 30 years.

Political Parties: Political parties could operate without restrictions or outside interference. The Liberal and Conservative parties previously dominated politics. The 2010 election of President Santos and the second-place showing of Antanas Mockus of the newly established Green Party reflected a continued widening of the political arena. More than a dozen political parties from across the political spectrum were represented in Congress.

Organized criminal gangs and the FARC threatened and killed government officials (see section 1.g.). According to the Presidential Program for Human Rights, seven municipal council members were killed through September, compared with eight in the same period in 2010.

Some local officials resigned because of threats from the FARC. A Ministry of Interior and Justice program provided protection to 199 mayors, 103 members of departmental congresses, and 2,448 council members as of July.

Participation of Women and Minorities: The law requires that women be placed in at least 30 percent of appointed government posts and that the government report to Congress each year the percentage of women in high-level government positions. There were 15 women in the 102-member Senate and 19 in the 165-member House of Representatives. There were four women in the 16-member cabinet and three on the 23-member Supreme Court. In January the country's first female prosecutor general was sworn in; however, the validity of her election was challenged on several grounds.

Two indigenous senators and two indigenous members of the House of Representatives occupied seats reserved for indigenous persons. There were no indigenous persons in the cabinet or on any of the high courts.

Eleven Afro-Colombians served in Congress. There were eight self-identified Afro-Colombian members of the House of Representatives—six were elected, and two occupied seats reserved for Afro-Colombians. Although there were no seats reserved for Afro-Colombians in the Senate, there were three Afro-Colombian senators. Two Afro-Colombians served as deputy magistrates on the Constitutional Court. There were no Afro-Colombian cabinet ministers.

Principal Government Officials

Last Updated: 1/31/2013

Pres.: **Juan Manuel SANTOS Calderon**
Vice Pres.: **Angelino GARZON**
Min. of Agriculture & Rural Development: **Juan Camilo RESTREPO**
Min. of Commerce, Industry, & Tourism: **Sergio DIAZ-GRANADOS**
Min. of Communication: **Diego MOLANO Vega**
Min. of Culture: **Mariana GARCES Cordoba**
Min. of Defense: **Juan Carlos PINZON Bueno**
Min. of Education: **Maria Fernanda CAMPO Saavedra**
Min. of Energy & Mines:
Min. of the Environment & Sustainable Development: **Frank PEARL Gonzalez**
Min. of Housing & Territorial Development: **Beatriz URIBE Botero**
Min. of Finance & Public Credit: **Mauricio CARDENAS Santa Maria**
Min. of Foreign Relations: **Maria Angela HOLGUIN Cuellar**

Min. of Interior: **German VARGAS LLERAS**
Min. of Justice: **Ruth Stella CORREA**
Min. of Labor: **Rafael PARDO Rueda**
Min. of Social Protection: **Mauricio SANTAMARIA Salamanca**
Min. of Transportation: **Cecilia ALVAREZ-CORREA**
Dir., National Planning: **Hernando Jose GOMEZ Restrepo**
Prosecutor Gen.:
Pres., Bank of the Republic: **Jose Dario URIBE Escobar**
Ambassador to the US: **Gabriel SILVA Lujan**
Permanent Representative to the UN, New York: **Nestor OSORIO Londono**

ECONOMY

Colombia's consistently sound economic policies and aggressive promotion of free trade agreements in recent years have bolstered its ability to face external shocks. Real GDP has grown more than 4% per year for the past three years, continuing almost a decade of strong economic performance. All three major ratings agencies have upgraded Colombia's government debt to investment grade. Nevertheless, Colombia depends heavily on oil exports, making it vulnerable to a drop in oil prices.

Economic development is stymied by inadequate infrastructure, weakened further by recent flooding. Moreover, the unemployment rate of 10.3% in 2012 is still one of Latin America's highest. The SANTOS Administration's foreign policy has focused on bolstering Colombia's commercial ties and boosting investment at home. The US-Colombia Free Trade Agreement (FTA) was ratified by the US Congress in October 2011 and implemented in 2012. Columbia has signed or is negotiating FTAs with a number of other countries, including Canada, Chile, Mexico, Switzerland, the EU, Venezuela, South Korea, Turkey, Japan, and Israel. Foreign direct investment—notably in the oil sector—reached a record $10 billion in 2008 but dropped to $7.2 billion in 2009, before beginning to recover in 2010, and reached a record high of nearly $16 billion in 2012. Colombia is the third largest Latin American exporter of oil to the US. Inequality, underemployment, and narcotrafficking remain significant challenges, and Colombia's infrastructure requires major improvements to sustain economic expansion.

Labor Conditions

The law sets the minimum age for employment at 15, and 18 for hazardous work. Children ages 15 and 16 may work no more than 30 hours per week, and children age 17 may work no more than 40 hours per week. Children under the age of 15 may work in arts, sports, or recreational or cultural activities for a maximum of 14 hours per week. In all of these cases, working children and adolescents must have signed documentation filed by their parents and approved by a labor inspector or other local authority.

Hazardous work includes an extensive list of activities within 11 occupational categories and subcategories identified as the "worst forms of child labor," including agriculture, hunting and forestry, fishing, mining and quarrying, manufacturing, construction, transport and storage, health services, and defense. The government, however, approved some agricultural apprenticeship programs for children from 14 to 17 through the National Service Learning Agency. For 14-year-old children, this program is education-only, and children are not permitted to work. Child workers are prohibited from working at night or where there is a risk of bodily harm or exposure to excessive heat, cold, or noise.

Child labor remained a problem in the informal and illicit sectors. According to a National Administrative Department of Statistics (DANE) study conducted in 2009 and published in 2011, of the 11.4 million children between the ages of five and 17, approximately one million worked. NGOs reported that 37.6 percent of children who worked did not receive payment. According to the DANE study, most child laborers were engaged in agriculture, commerce, retail, and manufacturing. Significant incidences of child labor occurred in the production of clay bricks, coal, emeralds, gold, coca, and pornography. There were instances of forced child labor in mines, quarries, and private homes. According to government officials and international organizations, children also worked, sometimes forcibly, in the illegal drug trade and other illicit activities.

The monthly minimum wage was approximately 535,600 pesos ($277), a 4 percent increase from 2010. In a study on poverty released in 2010, DANE estimated the poverty income level at 281,384 pesos ($146) monthly. In December, for the first time since 2006, the tripartite commission of employers, workers, and government representatives charged with negotiating the minimum wage came to an agreement on the 2012 wage, which was to increase by 5.8 percent to 566,700 pesos ($293).

The labor code provides for a regular workweek of 48 hours and a minimum rest period of eight hours within the week. The law provides for paid annual civil and religious holidays for all workers. Employees who work at least one full year are entitled to at least 15 days of paid vacation. The code stipulates that workers are entitled to receive premium compensation for additional hours worked over the regular workweek of 48 hours and for work performed on Sundays. Compulsory overtime is permitted only in exceptional cases where the work is considered essential for the company's functioning.

The government remained unable to enforce the minimum wage in the informal sector, which, according to the Office of the Inspector General, constituted approximately 60 percent of the workforce.

U.S.-COLOMBIAN RELATIONS

The United States established diplomatic relations with Colombia in

1822, following its independence from Spain. Colombia is a middle-income country and one of the oldest democracies in Latin America. It has seen nearly half a century of intense armed conflict with insurgent and paramilitary groups perpetuated by their involvement in widespread illegal drug production and trafficking, along with criminal and narcotics trafficking organizations. Peace talks between the Government of Colombia and the Revolutionary Armed Forces of Colombia (FARC) began in Oslo, Norway on October 18, 2012 and negotiations will move to Havana, Cuba in November 2012. Long-term U.S. interests in the region include promoting security, stability, and prosperity in Colombia, and Colombia has made progress in addressing its security, development, and governance challenges.

The country's National Consolidation Plan seeks to re-establish state control and legitimacy in strategically important areas previously dominated by illegal armed groups through a phased approach that combines security, counternarcotics, and economic and social development initiatives. U.S. policy toward Colombia supports the government's efforts to strengthen its democratic institutions, promote respect for human rights and the rule of law, foster socioeconomic development, address immediate humanitarian needs, and end the threats to democracy posed by narcotics trafficking and terrorism.

The United States and Colombia have signed agreements on trade, environmental protection, asset sharing, chemical control, ship-boarding, renewable and clean energy, science and technology, and civil aviation.

U.S. Assistance to Colombia

The U.S. Government supports the Colombian Government's National Consolidation Plan by selectively working in key "consolidation zones," where drug trafficking, violence, and the lack of government presence have historically converged. The U.S. Government coordinates its efforts in these areas through the Colombia Strategic Development Initiative, an inter-agency, whole-of-government approach to providing U.S. assistance in eradication and interdiction; capacity building of the military, national police, and prosecutor units; creation of viable options for citizens in the licit economy, particularly in the agricultural sector. Our programs also provide more general support for the implementation of Colombian Government reforms in land restitution; reparations for victims and vulnerable populations; demobilization and reintegration of ex-combatants; promoting respect for human rights and the rule of law and protection of vulnerable citizens (such as human rights and labor activists); and addressing global climate change and environmental issues in one of the most ecologically diverse countries in the world.

Bilateral Economic Relations

The United States is Colombia's largest trading partner, and the two countries' free trade agreement entered into force in May 2012. The U.S.-Colombia Trade Promotion Agreement aims to improve the investment environment, eliminate tariffs and other barriers to U.S. exports, expand trade, and promote economic growth in both countries.

U.S. exports to Colombia include machinery, oil, agricultural products, organic chemicals, and plastic. U.S. imports from Colombia include crude oil, gold, coffee, cut flowers, textiles, and bananas. Approximately 250 U.S. businesses conduct at least some operations in Colombia. U.S. direct investment in Colombia is primarily concentrated in the mining and manufacturing sectors.

Colombia's Membership in International Organizations

Colombia and the United States belong to a number of the same international organizations, including the United Nations, Organization of American States, International Monetary Fund, World Bank, and World Trade Organization.

Bilateral Representation

Colombia maintains an embassy in the United States at 2118 Leroy Place NW, Washington, DC 20008 (tel. 202-387-8338).

Principal U.S. Embassy Officials

Last Updated: 1/14/2013

BOGOTA (E) Cra. 45 No. 22D-45, (57-1) 275-2000, Fax (57-1) 275-2197, INMARSAT Tel 683131545/46, Workweek: 8:00am–5:00pm, Monday-Friday, Website: http://bogota.usembassy.gov/

DCM OMS:	Dominique Emery
AMB OMS:	Irene Willig
DHS/ICE:	Stephen Kleppe
FCS:	Cameron Werker
FM:	Nat Marchiano
HRO:	Deborah Pedroso
ICITAP:	Michael Yasofsky
MGT:	John Olson
MLO/ODC:	LTC Chris Buckley
NAS/INL:	James Story
OMS:	Karen Peterson
OPDAT:	Evelio J. Yera
POSHO:	Nat Marchiano
SDO/DATT:	COL Philip Abbott
TREAS:	Manny J Muriel
AMB:	P. Michael McKinley
CG:	Roberto Powers
CON:	Angela Kerwin
DCM:	Perry Holloway
PAO:	Linda Gonzalez
GSO:	Tom Palmer
RSO:	Stephen Brunette
AGR:	Joe Lopez
AID:	Peter Natiello
APHIS:	Peter Fernandez
ATF:	Raymond Fragoso
CLO:	Jennifer M. Cwiak-Alamo
DEA:	Jay Bergman
ECON:	Laura Lochman
FMO:	Jill Thompson
ICASS Chair:	Matt Donahue
IMO:	Ivan Watson
IPO:	Dave Odette
IRS:	Manny Muriel
ISO:	Vacant
ISSO:	David Kent
LEGATT:	Keith Byers
POL:	Drew Blakeney
State ICASS:	Brian Murphy

Other Contact Information

U.S. Department of State
2201 C Street, NW
Washington, DC 20520
Main Switchboard: 202-647-4000
Internet: http://www.state.gov

U.S. Department of Commerce Trade Information Center International Trade Administration
1401 Constitution Avenue NW
Washington, DC 20230
tel: 800-USA-TRADE
Internet: http://www.trade.gov

Colombian-American Chamber of Commerce
Calle 98, # 22-64, Oficina 1209
Apartado Aereo 8008
Bogota, Colombia
tel: (571) 587-7278
fax: (571) 587-7278-2

TRAVEL

Consular Information Sheet

August 23, 2011

Country Description: Colombia is a medium-income nation of some 46 million inhabitants. Its geography is very diverse, ranging from tropical coastal areas and rainforests to rugged mountainous terrain. Tourist facilities in Colombia vary in quality and safety, according to price and location. Security is a significant concern for travelers.

Smart Traveler Enrollment Program (STEP)/Embassy Locations: If you are going to live in or visit Colombia, please take the time to tell our Embassy about your trip. If you enroll, we can keep you up to date with important safety and security announcements. It will also help your friends and family get in touch with you in an emergency.

The United States Embassy Bogota
Calle 24 Bis No. 48-50 Bogotá, D.C. Colombia.
Mailing address: Carrera 45 No. 24B-27 Bogotá, D.C. Colombia.
Telephone: (571) 315-1566.
Emergency after-hours telephone: (571) 315-0811;
Facsimile: (571) 315-2197.

The United States Consular Agency Barranquilla
Calle 77B, No. 57-141, Piso 5, Centro Empresarial Las Americas, Barranquilla, Atlantico
Telephone: (575) 353-2001
Facsimile: (575) 353-5216

Entry/Exit Requirements for U.S. Citizens: All U.S. citizens who are not also Colombian citizens must present a valid U.S. passport to enter and depart Colombia, and to return to the United States. Dual U.S-Colombian citizens must present a Colombian passport to enter and exit Colombia, and a U.S. passport to return to the United States. Be aware that any person born in Colombia may be considered a Colombian citizen, even if never documented as such. U.S. citizens born in Colombia or who otherwise have Colombian citizenship will need both a Colombian passport and a U.S. passport for the trip. U.S. citizens traveling to Colombia do not need a Colombian visa for a tourist stay of 60 days or less. Travelers entering Colombia are sometimes asked to present evidence of return or onward travel, usually in the form of a round-trip plane ticket. Americans traveling overland must enter Colombia at an official border crossing. Travelers arriving by bus should ensure, prior to boarding, that their bus will cross the border at an official entry point. Entering Colombia at unauthorized crossings may result in fines or incarceration.

The length of stay granted to travelers is determined by the Colombian immigration officer at the point of entry and will be stamped in your passport. Extensions may be requested by visiting an office of the Colombian immigration authority, known as the Departamento Administrativo de Seguridad, or DAS, after arrival in Colombia. Fines are levied if a traveler remains in Colombia longer than authorized, and the traveler cannot leave Colombia until the fine is paid. Any traveler possessing a Colombian visa with more than three months' validity must register the visa at a DAS immigration office within 15 days of arrival in Colombia or face fines. The DAS immigration office in Bogota is located at Calle 100 and Carrera 11B 29, telephone (571) 408-8000. This office is open from Monday to Thursday from 7:00 a.m. to 4:00 p.m. and Fridays from 07:00 a.m. to 3:00 p.m.

No arrival tax is collected upon entry into Colombia, but travelers leaving by plane must pay an exit tax at the airport, in cash. According to "Aeronautica Civil" authorities in charge of the airport tax, the exit tax is divided in two categories: the Tasa Aeroportuaria of US$35.00 and Timbre Aeroportuario of $US37.00 (both of these fees are updated once a year.) There can be an additional exit tax, the Colombian Administrative fee, of US$15.00 (Normally the Colombian Administrative fee is not included in the tickets purchased in the U.S.) Some airlines include all or a portion of this tax in the cost of your airline ticket; check with your airline to find out how much you will have to pay at the airport. In some cases where foreign travelers have been in the country for less than 30 days, they have been able to obtain an exemption from this tax by taking their documents immediately to the Aeronautica Civil desk (usually booth no. 19 in the El Dorado international terminal) and requesting the exemption.

U.S. citizens whose U.S. passports are lost or stolen in Colombia must obtain a new U.S. passport before departing. They must then present the new passport, along with a police report describing the loss or theft, to a DAS office. Information about obtaining a replacement U.S. passport in Colombia is available on the U.S. Embassy web site under the heading "If your last passport was lost or stolen." Contact information for DAS is available in Spanish from the DAS web site. The Embassy in Bogota or the U.S. Consular Agency in Barranquilla can provide guidance on contacting DAS when you apply for your replacement passport. For further, specific guidance on Colombian entry requirements, including information about Colombian visas, travelers should contact the Colombian Embassy at 2118 Leroy Place NW, Washington, DC 20008; telephone (202) 387-8338; or the nearest Colombian consulate. Consulates are located in Atlanta, Boston, Chicago, Houston, Los Angeles, Miami, New Orleans, New York, San Francisco, Tampa, and San Juan, Puerto Rico.

Colombia has imposed HIV/AIDS travel restrictions on all travelers with HIV/AIDS except those with PLHIV. A waiver may be requested from the Colombian embassy (Source: NAM April 2006, USSD December 06). Please verify this information with the Embassy of Colombia before you travel

Additional Exit Requirements for Minors: To prevent international child abduction, Colombia has implemented special exit procedures for Colombian children under 18 who are departing the country without both their mother and their father or a legal guardian. These procedures apply to U.S. citizen children if they are also Colombian citizens or if they are legal residents of Colombia. The procedures do not apply to U.S. citizen children present in Colombia as tourists using a U.S. passport. Complying with the procedures can be complex and time-consuming, especially if an absent parent is outside Colombia at the time. Advance planning is essential as this can take some time.

The procedures are as follows: Upon exiting the country, the person traveling with the child (or the child him/herself) must present a certified copy of the child's birth certificate, along with written, signed authorization from the absent parent(s) or legal guardian. The authorization must explicitly grant permission for the child to travel alone, with one parent, or with a third party, by name.

When a parent is deceased, a notarized copy of a death certificate is required instead of written authorization. When one parent has sole custody of the child, that parent may present a custody decree instead of the other parent's written authorization. In cases where a Colombian citizen or dual national child has been adopted in a U.S. Court, the adoption decree will need to be legalized (Exequatur) by the Colombian Supreme Court. If the documents to be presented originated in the United States, they must first be translated into Spanish and then signed in front of a Colombian consul at a Colombian consulate. Then, upon arrival in Colombia, the documents must be presented to the Colombian Ministry of Foreign Affairs for certification of the consul's signature.

Alternatively, the documents can be translated into Spanish, then notarized by a notary public in the United States, and authenticated by requesting an apostille from the competent authority in the state where the documents were prepared. The document, translation, and apostille can then be presented to immigration officers at the airport when the child travels. If the documents originated in Colombia and are written in Spanish, only notarization by a Colombian notary is required. For documents originating in countries other than the United States or Colombia, please inquire with the Colombian embassy serving that country.

In cases where the absent parent refuses or is unable to provide consent, the other parent can request assistance from the Colombian child protective service, Instituto Colombiano de Bienestar Familiar (ICBF). In appropriate cases, ICBF will investigate and may issue a document that will allow the child to travel without both parents' consent. This process may take a significant amount of time and is not within the control of the U.S. government.

Threats to Safety and Security: The Department of State warns U.S. citizens of the dangers of travel to Colombia. Security in Colombia has improved significantly in recent years, including in tourist and business travel destinations like Cartagena and Bogota, but violence by narco-terrorist groups continues to affect some rural areas and large cities.

Terrorist activity remains a threat throughout the country. On August 12, 2010, a car bomb exploded outside the Caracol radio station in Bogota, injuring seven people. On October 21, 2010, Colombian authorities foiled another car bomb attack directed at the National Administrative Center in Bogota. On June 16, 2011, a satchel bomb exploded at a local monument in uptown Bogota, resulting in some damage to adjoining buildings, but no fatalities or injuries. Small towns and rural areas of Colombia can still be extremely dangerous due to the presence of narco-terrorists. While the Embassy possesses no information concerning specific and credible threats against U.S. citizens in Colombia, we strongly encourage you to exercise caution and remain vigilant.Emerging criminal gangs (BACRIM) began to develop after the demobilization of the paramilitary fighters from the Autodefensas Unidas de Colombia (AU.C). BACRIM competes and sometimes cooperates with the FARC in the drug trade. The violence associated to BACRIMs occurs throughout Colombia and is a major law enforcement challenge which has led to an increase in the murder rate within some urban areas.

The incidence of kidnapping in Colombia has diminished significantly from its peak at the beginning of this decade. Nevertheless, terrorist groups such as the Revolutionary Armed Forces of Colombia (FARC), the National Liberation Army (ELN), and other criminal organizations continue to kidnap and hold civilians for ransom or as political bargaining chips. No one is immune from kidnapping on the basis of occupation, nationality, or other factors. Kidnapping remains a serious threat, with two kidnapping cases of U.S. citizens reported since August 2010. One kidnapped citizen was rescued within 4 days and the other case resulted in the murder of the victim. Kidnapping in rural areas is of particular concern. On July 2, 2008, the Government of Colombia rescued 15 hostages, including three U.S. citizens, who had been held for more than five years. Although the U.S. government places the highest priority on the safe recovery of kidnapped U.S. citizens, it is U.S. policy not to make concessions to or strike deals with kidnappers. Consequently, the U.S. government's ability to assist kidnapping victims is limited.

U.S. government officials and their families in Colombia are permitted to travel to major cities in the country, but normally only by air. They may not use inter- or intra-city bus transportation, or travel by road outside urban areas at night. U.S. government officials and their families in Colombia must file a request to travel to any area in Colombia that is outside of two general vicinities. The first vicinity is outlined by the cities of Bogota, Anolaima, Cogua, and Sesquile. The second vicinity is on the Highway 90 corridor that connects Cartagena, Barranquilla, and Santa Marta. All U.S. citizens in Colombia are urged to follow these precautions and exercise extra caution outside of the aforementioned areas.

Stay up to date by:

- Bookmarking our Bureau of Consular Affairs website, which contains the current Travel Warnings and Travel Alerts as well as the Worldwide Caution.
- Follow us on Twitter and the Bureau of Consular Affairs page on Facebook as well.
- Download our free Smart Traveler iPhone App to have travel information at your fingertips.
- Calling 1-888-407-4747 toll-free within the U.S. and Canada, or a regular toll line, 1-202-501-4444, from other countries.
- Taking some time before travel to consider your personal security.

Crime: While both violent and petty crime remain significant concerns in Colombia, rates currently remain consistent with 2009 levels. Robbery and other violent crimes, as well as scams against unsuspecting tourists, are common in urban areas. Generally speaking, if you are the victim of a robbery, you should not resist. Firearms are prevalent in Colombia and altercations can often turn violent. Small towns and rural areas of Colombia can still be extremely dangerous due to the presence of narco-terrorists.

Theft also remains a significant problem in many urban and rural areas. () There has been an increase in petty crime, including a significant increase in pick pocketing of passports in the El Dorado Airport in Bogota, Colombia, and at luxury hotels, especially around the predominant Colombian holidays, Christmas, Easter Week, and summer holidays (July and August). Due to criminal activities the U.S. Embassy defines two areas in Bogota that are always off limits for all U.S. government officials and family members. These areas are:

- "Galerias" District (between Calles 53 and 54 with Carrera 24 through 27)
- "Plaza de las Americas" District (Avenida Primera de Mayo between Carrera 68 and Avenida Boyaca)

Some of the most common methods used by criminals in Colombia are noted below:

Robberies of ATM customers: Tourists and others have been robbed after using automatic teller machines (ATMs) on the street. In some cases, robbers have used motorcycles to approach their victims and later flee the scene. Americans are urged to use ATMs only inside shopping malls or other protected locations. Driving to and from the location—rather than walking—provides added protection. When using an ATM, you should be on the lookout for anyone watching or following you.

Robberies of taxi passengers: Robbery of taxi passengers is a serious problem in Bogota, as well as in Cali and Medellin. Typically, the driver—who is one of the conspirators—will pick up the passenger and then stop to pick up two or more armed cohorts, who enter the cab, overpower the passenger, and take his/her belongings. If the passenger has an ATM card, the perpetrators may force the passenger to withdraw money from various ATM locations. Such ordeals can last for hours. In almost every case of taxi-related crime, the victims have been riding alone and have hailed taxis off the street. Rather than hailing a taxi, you should use the telephone dispatch service that most taxi companies offer. Many hotels, restaurants, and stores will call a taxi for you, and the taxi usually arrives within minutes. When a taxi is dispatched by telephone, the dispatcher creates a record of the call and the responding taxi. When taking a taxi, it's important that the passenger take note of the license plate, company and other ID of the taxi.

Robberies of tourists departing airports: U.S. citizens arriving at major Colombian airports have occasionally been victimized by armed robbers and rogue taxi drivers while en route from the airport to their hotel or home. There are taxi booths both in El Dorado (international) and Puente Aereo (domestic) airports. Travelers may go to the booth, request a taxi, and provide the address of the service.

The taxi booth in the international terminal is located to the right, once you exit the baggage/customs area. The taxi booth in the domestic terminal is located to the left, once you exit the baggage area. The person in the booth will give you a ticket indicating the amount of money you will pay for the service. Dispatchers are right outside the exit to organize the waiting line. Authorized taxis are located in the designated area, close to the booth. The passenger should give one part of the ticket to the driver and retain one for their records. Non authorized taxis usually are located in front of the exit areas but not in the authorized areas. Criminals also sometimes scout out victims at the airport and then follow their vehicles before robbing the occupants at a stoplight. Travelers should remain vigilant at airports and report to local airport police if they suspect they may be under surveillance.

Robberies on hiking trails: Several U.S. citizens were robbed in 2010 while hiking on nature trails in and around Bogota. Because hiking trips generally take place in isolated settings, participants are especially vulnerable. Hikers in Colombia are more protected if they travel in large groups.

Attacks on Hostels: In the past twelve months (since April 2010), there have been reports of eight attacks on tourists in local hostels in the Candelaria area of Bogota, including one that involved the sexual assault of a U.S. citizen. Be careful when selecting a hotel, looking not just at price but at the general safety of the area.

Use of disabling drugs: The Embassy continues to receive reports of criminals in Colombia using disabling drugs to temporarily incapacitate tourists and others. At bars, restaurants, and other public areas, perpetrators may offer tainted drinks, cigarettes, or gum. Typically, victims become disoriented or unconscious, and are thus vulnerable to robbery, sexual assault, and other crimes. Avoid leaving food or drinks unattended at a bar or restaurant, and be suspicious if a stranger offers you something to eat or drink. Certain areas of Bogota are off-limits to U.S. Embassy personnel due to the prevalence of the use of disabling drugs. See map below for specific areas that U.S. citizens are encouraged to avoid.

Counterfeit money scams: U.S. citizens in Colombia routinely fall victim to a scam in which purported undercover police officers approach them on the street and request to examine their money, supposedly to determine if it is counterfeit. The "officers," who are in fact criminals, then flee with the money. In a variation of this scam, the thieves may ask to see jewelry. Legitimate Colombian police officers do not make such requests. Don't buy counterfeit and pirated goods, even if they are widely available. Not only are the bootlegs illegal in the United States, if you purchase them you may also be breaking local law.

Victims of Crime: If you or someone you know becomes the victim of a crime abroad, you should contact the local police and the U.S. embassy in Bogota or the Consular Agency in Baranquilla. We can:

- Replace a stolen passport.
- For violent crimes such as assault or rape, help you find appropriate medical care.
- Put you in contact with the appropriate police authorities, and contact family members or friends.
- Although the local authorities are responsible for investigating and prosecuting the crime, consular officers can help you understand the local criminal justice process and can direct you to local attorneys.

The local equivalent to the "911" emergency line in Colombia is 123 for police, ambulance, and fire. There will not be an English speaker answering the telephone. The Government of Colombia does not provide monetary compensation to foreign victims of crime. However, a U.S. citizen residing in Colombia who is a victim of violence by illegal armed groups may apply for compensation. More information is available at the Agencia Presidencial Para La Accion Social y Cooperacion Internacional.

Criminal Penalties: While you are traveling in Colombia, you are subject to its laws even if you are a U.S. citizen. Foreign laws and legal systems can be vastly different than our own. In some places driving under the influence could land you immediately in jail. These criminal penalties will vary from country to country. There are also some things that might be legal in the country you visit, but still illegal in the United States, and you can be prosecuted under U.S. law if you buy pirated goods. Engaging in sexual conduct with children or using or disseminating child pornography in a foreign country is a crime prosecutable in the United States. If you break local laws in Colombia, your U.S. passport won't help you avoid arrest or prosecution. It's very important to know what's legal and what's not where you are going. If you are arrested, the U.S. government cannot request your release. Colombia and the United States do not have a prisoner transfer agreement, and so any sentence for a crime committed in Colombia is ordinarily served in a Colombian prison.

Penalties for possession, use, or trafficking of illegal drugs in Colombia are severe, and convicted offenders can expect long prison sentences under harsh conditions, with significant expense and great hardship for themselves and their families. Colombian police make multiple arrests daily for drug trafficking at major airports, and have sophisticated means for detecting illegal drugs in baggage or on your person. Travelers are sometimes requested to undergo an x-ray to ensure that they are not smuggling narcotics within their own bodies. There are more than 40 Americans incarcerated in Colombia for attempting to smuggle drugs out of the country. The hardships resulting from imprisonment do not end even after release from prison. Colombian law requires that serious offenders remain in the country to serve a lengthy period of parole, during which the offender is given no housing and may lack permission to work. As a result, family members must often support the offender, sometimes for more than a year, until the parole period expires.

Arrest notifications in host country: Based on the Vienna Convention on Consular Relations, bilateral agreements with certain countries, and customary international law, if you are arrested in Colombia, you have the option to request that the police, prison officials, or other authorities alert the nearest U.S. embassy or consulate of your arrest, and to have communications from you forwarded to the nearest U.S. embassy or consulate.

Special Circumstances: Colombia employs strict screening procedures for detecting narcotics smuggling at its international airports. Americans and other travelers are occasionally questioned, searched, fingerprinted, and/or asked to submit to an abdominal x-ray upon arrival or departure. Most airport inspectors do not speak English, and travelers who do not speak Spanish may have difficulty understanding what is asked of them. Please refer to the section on Criminal Penalties for further information on the strict enforcement of Colombia's drug laws.

Customs Regulations: Travelers generally must not enter or exit Colombia while carrying cash or other financial instruments worth more than 10,000 U.S. dollars. If you do, you must declare it and be able to prove the legal source of the financial instruments. Even so, Colombian authorities may confiscate any amount over $10,000, and may initiate a criminal investigation into the source of the money and the traveler's reasons for carrying it. Recovery of the confiscated amount requires a lengthy, expensive legal process and may not always be possible. Americans wishing to send large sums of money to or from Colombia should contact their nearest Colombian consulate, or speak with Colombian customs officials, and should also consider seeking advice from an attorney or financial professional. Colombian law prohibits tourists and business travelers from bringing firearms into Colombia. Illegal importation or possession of firearms may result in incarceration. Colombian law forbids the export of pre-Columbian objects and other artifacts protected by cultural patrimony statutes. Under an agreement between the United States and Colombia, U.S. customs officials are obligated to seize pre-Columbian objects and certain colonial religious artwork when they are brought into the United States. In many countries around the world, counterfeit and pirated goods are widely available. Buying or selling them is illegal in Colombia, and bringing them back to the United States may result in forfeitures and fines.

Accessibility: While in Colombia, individuals with disabilities may find accessibility and accommodation very different from what you find in the United States. Colombian law prohibits discrimination against persons with physical and mental disabilities in employment, education, access to health care, or the provision of other state services, and the government seeks to enforce these prohibitions. No law mandates access to public buildings for persons with disabilities, thus limiting the power of the government to penalize those schools or offices without access, but both national and local governments address this with programs aimed at improving access. The law provides persons with physical disabilities access to voting stations. The Presidential Program for Human Rights is responsible for protecting the rights of persons with disabilities. Access to buildings, pedestrian paths and transportation is extremely difficult for persons with disabilities. A few major shopping centers and residential buildings in the wealthier neighborhoods of Bogotá have access ramps and elevators. One mall in Bogotá exclusively hires security guards who are disabled. Most hospitals in major cities are also wheelchair accessible. However, sidewalks (if they exist) are very uneven and rarely have ramps at intersections. Pedestrian crossings are also very infrequent and traffic almost never gives pedestrians (disabled or otherwise) the right of way. Most, but not all cafés, restaurants, hotels and residential buildings have stairs at the entrance without wheelchair ramps. Buses and taxis do not have special accommodations for disabled persons.

Medical Facilities and Health Information: Medical care is adequate in major cities but varies greatly in quality elsewhere. Emergency rooms in Colombia, even at top-quality facilities, are frequently overcrowded and ambulance service can be slow. Many private health care providers in Colombia require that patients pay for care before treatment, even in an emergency. Some providers in major cities may accept credit cards, but those who do not may request advance payment in cash. Uninsured travelers without financial resources may be unable to obtain care, or relegated to seeking treatment in public hospitals where care is far below U.S. standards.

The Embassy regularly receives reports of U.S. citizens in Colombia who have died or suffered complications from liposuction and other elective surgeries intended to treat obesity. Before undergoing such a procedure in Colombia, the Department of State recommends that you consult with your personal physician, research the credentials of the provider in Colombia, and carefully consider your ability to access emergency medical care if complications arise. It is important to confirm that your medical insurance provides coverage in Colombia, including treatment of complications from elective procedures or medical evacuation if necessary. Should you suffer complications as a result of medical malpractice, collecting damages from your surgeon may be difficult. Colombia has seen a recent increase in the use of unregulated drugs that purport to enhance sexual performance. Several American tourists recently died after using these substances, which come in liquid, powder, or tablet form. You are urged to seek guidance from a physician before ingesting any such substances in Colombia.

Travelers to the capital city of Bogota may need time to adjust to the altitude of 8,600 feet, which can affect blood pressure, digestion, and energy level, and cause mild dyspnea with exercise, headaches, sleeplessness, and other discomfort. Travelers should drink liberal fluids to maintain hydration, and should avoid strenuous exercise until they have acclimated to the altitude. Travelers with circulatory or respiratory problems should consult a physician before traveling to Bogota or other high-altitude locations. You can find good information on vaccinations and other health precautions such as malaria prevention, on the CDC website. For information about outbreaks of infectious diseases abroad, consult the World Health Organization (WHO) website. The WHO website also contains additional health information for travelers, including detailed country-specific health information.

Medical Insurance: You can't assume your insurance will go with you when you travel, Medicare for instance does not cover expenses incurred outside of the USA or its territories. It's very important to find out BEFORE you leave whether or not your medical insurance will cover you overseas. You need to ask your insurance company two questions:

- Does my policy apply when I'm out of the United States?
- Will it cover emergencies like a trip to a foreign hospital or a medical evacuation?

In many places, doctors and hospitals still expect payment in cash at the time of service. Your regular U.S. health insurance may not cover doctors' and hospital visits in other countries. If your policy doesn't go with you when you travel, it's a very good idea to take out another one for your trip.

Traffic Safety and Road Conditions: While in Colombia, you may encounter road conditions that differ significantly from those in the United States. Due to the security environment in Colombia, U.S. government officials and their families are not permitted to travel by road between most major cities. They also cannot use inter- or intra-city bus transportation, or travel by road outside urban areas at night. All Americans in Colombia are encouraged to follow these same precautions.

Traffic laws in Colombia, including speed limits, are often ignored and rarely enforced, creating dangerous conditions for drivers and pedestrians in major cities. Under Colombian law, seat belts are mandatory for front-seat passengers in a private vehicle. Car seats are mandatory for children, and a child under ten is not permitted to ride in a front seat. It is against the law to talk on a cellular phone while driving in Colombia, and violators may be fined. While driving outside major cities, it is mandatory to drive with your lights on. If an accident occurs, the involved parties must remain at the scene and not move their vehicles until the authorities arrive; this rule is strictly enforced, and moving a vehicle or leaving the scene of an accident may constitute an admission of guilt under Colombian law.

Americans seeking to import their own vehicles into Colombia should consult with their nearest Colombian consulate for information on Colombian taxes and licensing rules, which can be complicated and bureaucratic.

Aviation Safety Oversight: The U.S. Federal Aviation Administration (FAA) has assessed the government of Colombia's Civil Aviation Authority as being in compliance with International Civil Aviation Organization (ICAO) aviation safety standards for oversight of Colombia's air carrier operations. Further information may be found on the FAA's safety assessment page.

Children's Issues: Please see the U.S. Dept. of State Office of Children's Issues web pages on intercountry adoption and international parental child abduction.

Travel Warning

October 3, 2012

The Department of State reminds U.S. citizens of the dangers of travel to Colombia. Security in Colombia has improved significantly in recent years, including in tourist and business travel destinations such as Cartagena and Bogota, but violence linked to narco-trafficking continues to affect some rural areas and parts of large cities. This replaces the Travel Warning for Colombia issued February 21, 2012, to update information on recent security incidents and terrorist activity.

While the Embassy possesses no information concerning specific and credible threats against U.S. citizens in Colombia, we strongly encourage you to exercise caution and remain vigilant as terrorist and criminal activities remain a threat throughout the country. Two people were killed and approximately 60 injured by a car bomb during an assassination attempt on the life of a former Interior Minister on May 15, 2012. Explosions occur throughout Colombia on a regular basis, including some in Bogota itself. Small towns and rural areas of Colombia can still be extremely dangerous due to the presence of terrorists and narco-traffickers, including armed criminal gangs (referred to as "BACRIMs" in Spanish), that are active throughout much of the country. Violence associated with the BACRIM has spilled over into many of Colombia's major cities. These groups are heavily involved in the drug trade.

Although the incidence of kidnapping in Colombia has diminished significantly from its peak in 2000, it remains a threat, and is of particular concern in rural areas. Terrorist groups and other criminal organizations continue to kidnap and hold civilians for ransom or as political bargaining chips. No one is immune from kidnapping on the basis of occupation, nationality, or other factors. One U.S. citizen was kidnapped and killed in March 2011, and another was kidnapped and freed in May 2011. The U.S. government places the highest priority on the safe recovery of kidnapped U.S. citizens, but it is U.S. policy not to make concessions to or strike deals with kidnappers. Consequently, the U.S. government's ability to assist kidnapping victims is limited.

U.S. government officials and their families in Colombia are permitted to travel to major cities in the country, but normally only by air. They may not use inter- or intra-city bus transportation, or travel by road outside urban areas at night. U.S. government officials and their families in Colombia must file a request to travel to any area in Colombia outside of two general areas. The first area is outlined by the cities of Bogota, Anolaima, Cogua, and Sesquile. The second area is on the Highway 90 corridor that connects Cartagena, Barranquilla, and Santa Marta. All U.S. citizens in Colombia are urged to follow these precautions and exercise extra caution outside of the aforementioned areas. For more detailed information on staying safe in Colombia, please see the State Department's Country Specific Information for Colombia. For the latest security information, U.S. citizens traveling abroad should regularly monitor the Bureau of Consular Affairs' internet web site, where the current Worldwide Caution, Travel Warnings, and Travel Alerts can be found. Follow us on Twitter and the Bureau of Consular Affairs pageon Facebook as well. You can also download our free Smart Traveler App, available through iTunes and the Android market, to have travel information at your fingertips.

Up-to-date information on security can also be obtained by calling 1-888-407-4747 toll free in the United States and Canada or, for callers outside the United States and Canada, a regular toll line at 001-202-501-4444. These numbers are available from 8:00 a.m. to 8:00 p.m. Eastern Time, Monday through Friday (except U.S. federal holidays). U.S. citizens living or traveling in Colombia are encouraged to enroll with the State Department's Smart Traveler Enrollment Program to obtain updated information on travel and security within Colombia. For any emergencies involving U.S. citizens in Colombia, please contact the U.S. Embassy or the closest U.S. Consulate as listed below.

The U.S. Embassy is located at Calle 24 Bis No. 48-50 Bogota, D.C., Colombia. Mailing address: Carrera 45 No. 24B-27 Bogota, D.C., Colombia. In case of a serious emergency that jeopardizes the health or safety of a U.S. citizen in Colombia, please call the Embassy at (571) 275-2000; Embassy fax: (571) 275-4501; Consular Section phone: (571) 275-4900. The Embassy's American Citizens Services office provides routine information at http://bogota.usembassy.gov. For questions not answered there, inquiries may be sent by email to ACSBogota@state.gov.

The U.S. Consular Agency in Barranquilla, which accepts passport applications and performs notarial services, is located at Calle 77B, No. 57-141, Piso 5, Centro Empresarial Las Américas, Barranquilla, Atlántico, Colombia; telephone (575) 369-0419; fax (57-5) 353-5216.

Intercountry Adoption

Colombia's revised procedures for determining children's eligibility for intercountry adoption October 22, 2012

Colombia's Institute for Family Welfare (ICBF) recently announced revised procedures for determining a child's eligibility for intercountry adoption, which may affect some adoptions involving U.S. families. This process is known in Colombia as the "re-establishment of rights." ICBF implemented these new procedures as a result of a November 2011 Constitutional Court ruling that ICBF was not fully considering the rights of, and opportunities for placement with, biological and extended families before placing a child for domestic or intercountry adoption.

To comply with the Constitutional Court decision, ICBF has been reviewing approximately 1,300 declarations of adoptability to ensure they meet the revised procedures. ICBF has identified a number of cases in which the adoption eligibility determination for a child does not meet the new standards. ICBF has placed an administrative hold on these cases until it is satisfied that the adoptability determination is evaluated as to whether there might be an extended family member who could care for the child. ICBF will notify prospective adoptive families that have been matched with children whose cases require evaluation. For privacy reasons, ICBF cannot inform the prospective adoptive families of the specific reasons for the review, and ICBF cannot offer any guarantee of the final outcome of the review. As of September 2012, the U.S. Embassy in Bogota is aware of six instances involving U.S. families whose adoption proceedings required review; one adoption has since been finalized. These reviews represent a small percentage of the total number of intercountry adoptions between Colombia and the United States, and the Embassy continues to work with ICBF to encourage timely resolution. Families who learn that their adoption has been placed on hold should inform the U.S. Embassy in Bogota by contacting IVBogota@state.gov.

In addition to these formal reviews, both ICBF and the Colombian family court system appear to be scrutinizing proposed adoptions more carefully. Prospective adoptive families may experience delays while ICBF evaluates a family's suitability before finalizing the match with an available child. The issuance of the adoption decree by a family court judge may also take longer than in the past. Families should anticipate spending six to eight weeks in Colombia to obtain the final adoption decree. Given these delays, the Embassy strongly advises all families with less than three months' validity left on USCIS fingerprint results to make arrangements with USCIS (NBC.Hague@dhs.gov) to update these before traveling to Colombia to complete the adoption. The Department of State will provide updated information on adoption.state.gov as it becomes available. If you have any questions about this notice, please contact the Office of Children's Issues at 1-888-407-4747 within the United States, or 202-501-4444 from outside the United States. E-mail inquiries may be directed to Adoption-USCA@state.gov.

Adoption Process Overview June 2011

The information in this section has been edited from the latest report of the State Department Bureau of Consular Affairs, Office of Overseas Citizens Services that was available as of February 2013. For more information, please read the *Intercountry Adoption* section of this book and review current reports online at http://adoption.state.gov.

Colombia is party to the Hague Convention on Protection of Children and Co-operation in Respect of Intercountry Adoption (Hague Adoption Convention). Therefore, all adoptions between Colombia and the United States must meet the requirements of the Convention and U.S. law and regulations implementing the Convention.Colombia's Central Authority for adoptions, the Colombian Family Welfare Institute (ICBF), is the only means of adopting a Colombian child; Colombian law prohibits private adoptions. Please note ICBF does not allow for a Colombian child to travel to the United States to be adopted. Therefore, prospective adoptive parents must obtain a full and final adoption under Colombian law before the child can immigrate to the United States. Adopting parents are required to be physically present before a "family judge" at the time of adoption. No exceptions are made to this requirement.

Who Can Adopt? Adoption between the United States and Colombia is governed by the Hague Adoption Convention. Therefore to adopt from Colombia, you must first be found eligible to adopt by the U.S. Government. The U.S. Government agency responsible for making this determination is the Department of Homeland Security, U.S. Citizenship and Immigration Services (USCIS).

Residency Requirements: There are no residency requirements for intercountry adoptions from Colombia.

Age Requirements: Both parents are required to be 25 years old. In practice, newborns are assigned to younger couples and older children to older couples.

Marriage Requirements: Colombian law allows adoptions by a married man and woman and common law spouses of more than three years. Single men and women are only allowed to adopt children over the age of seven on a case-by-case basis.

Income Requirements: Prospective adoptive parents are required to submit documentation confirming their ability to provide for the adopted child. This requirement may be met by only one parent.

Other Requirements: Gay or Lesbian individual or couple prospective adoptive parents are advised that they should consult with the ICBF regarding Colombia's legal requirements prior to pursuing an adoption there. In addition, according to Colombian law, both parents must be found "physically and emotionally capable" to adopt.

Who Can Be Adopted? Because Colombia is a member of the Hague Adoption Convention, children from Colombia must meet the requirements of the Convention in order to be eligible for adoption. For example, the Convention requires that Colombia attempt to place a child with a family in Colombia before determining that a child is eligible for intercountry adoption. In addition to Colombia's requirements, a child must meet the definition of a Convention adoptee for you to bring him or her back to the United States.

Colombian Central Authority: Bienestar Familiar (ICBF)

The Process: Because Colombia is a member of the Hague Adoption Convention, adopting from Colombia must follow a specific process designed to meet the Convention's requirements.

The first step in adopting a child from Colombia is to select an accredited or approved adoption service provider in the United States. Only these agencies and attorneys can provide adoption services between the United States and Colombia. Once prospective adoptive parents decide that Colombia is the nation from which they wish to adopt, they must first contact the ICBF, or an accredited adoption service provider in Colombia, in order to obtain a list of adoption service provider in the United States, nearest to the couple's place of residence, that are accredited by both the Colombian and U.S. Governments. An accredited adoption service provider will conduct the home study and assist the prospective adoptive parents in preparing the paperwork necessary for Homeland Security, Citizenship and Immigration Services (USCIS). After you choose an accredited adoption agency, you apply to be found eligible to adopt (Form I-800A) by the U.S. government, Department of Homeland Security, U.S. Citizenship and Immigration Services (USCIS). Once the U.S. Government determines you "eligible" and "suitable" to be an adoptive parent, you or your adoption service provider will forward your information to ICBF in Colombia.

The Central Authority will review your application to determine whether you are also eligible to adopt under Colombian law.

Required Documents: Once USCIS has approved the documentation, parents must compile the following list of documents for submission to the ICBF:

- Application Form for adoption (this can be provided by the ICBF or found on the ICBF Website);
- Birth certificate(s)of the prospective adoptive parent(s);
- Marriage certificate or proof of common law relationship of prospective adoptive parents;
- Medical examination(s) by Board-certified physicians clearly stating that prospective adoptive parent(s) is (are) mentally and physically capable of caring for a child (or children);
- National law enforcement clearance issued by a competent police authority. For U.S. citizens, this consists of a set of fingerprints, and their results, issued by the Federal Bureau of Investigation (FBI). These cards may be requested from the Department of Homeland Security. When completed, the cards for the U.S. records check as well as the USD $85.00 fee and a letter of intent (for adoption purposes) should be sent to the National Visa Center, Fingerprint Unit, 32 Rochester Avenue, Portsmouth, New Hampshire 03801. The FBI may take as long as two to three months to return the completed results. The set of fingerprints submitted previously with the Form I-800A cannot be submitted to the ICBF;
- Birth certificates of any children previously adopted by the prospective adoptive parent(s);
- Certificate of financial ability and employment letters explaining time of service and monthly salary received in U.S. dollars;

- If self-employed, a certified document regarding the parent's(s') financial resources or last income tax return with supporting documents;

- Social and psychological study of the prospective adoptive family that establishes physical, mental, moral and social capacity. The home study required by USCIS can fulfill both the U.S. and the Colombian requirements;

- If there were previous marriages or partners of the prospective adoptive parent(s), proof of divorce and reasons for such dissolutions should be presented; and

- Notarized statement clarifying any changes in name or indicating, "also known as." Generally, Colombian women do not change their names to that of their husbands. As a result, Colombian courts are accustomed to birth certificates, marriage certificates, and passports with no variation in name. If you have documents in both maiden and marriage names, you must submit a notarized statement indicating the reasons for the discrepancies in your documents.

Once the ICBF approves the package of documents, it will be in a position to inform prospective adoptive parents, through their adoption service providers, about the availability of children in need of a family placement and the amount of time it is likely to take to complete an adoption. If both the United States and Colombia determine that you are eligible to adopt, and a child is available for intercountry adoption, the Central Authority in Colombia may provide you with a referral for a child.

ICBF will inform the parents, through the adoption service provider, once a child has officially been assigned to them. Medical, social, psychological, and nutritional assessments are provided to the prospective adoptive parents, as well as photographs of the child. Prospective adoptive parents are given two months to make a decision as to whether to adopt that particular child. After you accept a match with a child, you will apply to the USCIS for permission to adopt that child (Form I-800, Petition to Classify a Convention adoptee as an Immediate Relative). USCIS will determine whether the child is eligible under U.S. immigration law to be adopted and enter the United States. After this, your adoption service provider or you will submit a visa application for to a Consular Officer at the U.S. Embassy in Bogota. The Consular Officer will review the child's information and evaluate the child for possible visa ineligibilities. If the Consular Office determines that the child appears eligible to immigrate to the United States, he or she will notify the ICBF (Article 5 letter). For Convention country adoptions, prospective adoptive parent(s) may not proceed with the adoption until this takes place. At this point, you may travel to Colombia to begin the legal process with Colombian authorities. The ICBF or the Colombian adoption agency will assist with obtaining the documents needed to complete Colombian legal procedures. Remember: The Consular Officer will make a final decision about the immigrant visa later in the adoption process.

Role of the Central Authority: Colombian law does not allow for private adoptions. Children may be adopted only through the Colombian Family Welfare Institute (ICBF) and approved adoption agencies. The ICBF will match the child with the prospective adoptive parent(s) and help with obtaining paperwork before the case moves to the Colombian courts.

Role of the Court: The Colombian courts require a letter from the U.S. Embassy in Bogota stating that they will issue an immigrant visa to the child if all adoption and U.S. immigrant requirements are met. When all documentation is completed, the courts will provide the adoption decree, a new Colombian birth certificate, and a new Colombian passport. Colombian law requires that both adopting parents be physically present when the adoption is presented to a "family judge." No exceptions are made to this requirement. Role of Adoption Service Providers: Because Colombia is a Convention country, adoption services must be provided by an accredited agency, temporarily accredited agency, approved person, supervised provider, or exempted provider. It is essential that prospective adoptive parent(s) seeking to adopt from a Convention country use an accredited adoption service provider. The Department of State maintains a current list of accredited adoption service providers. The list of accredited adoption service providers is also provided on the website of the Hague Permanent Bureau at www.hcch.net.

Time Frame: There is no set time frame for completing an intercountry adoption from Colombia. There are many factors that determine how long the adoption and visa process takes, including paperwork approval times, desired sex and age of the child, and the age of the prospective adoptive parent(s). Adoptive parents have reported the entire process taking 18 to 30 months.

Adoption Application: Prospective adoptive parents must first contact the ICBF or an accredited adoption agency in Colombia in order to obtain a list of adoption service providers in the United States that are accredited by both the Colombian and U.S. Governments.

Adoption Fees: It is difficult to predict how much the entire adoption process will cost as each case has unique circumstances. Adoptive parents have reported spending between $12,000 USD and $20,000 USD. The Colombian passport fee is approximately $30 USD. These expenses should have been itemized in the fees and estimated expenses section of your adoption services contract.

Bringing Your Child Home: Once your adoption is complete (or you have obtained legal custody of the child), there are a few more steps to take before you can head home. Specifically, you need to apply for several documents for your child before he or she can travel to the United States, such as a birth certificate, a passport or travel document for your child from the country in which he or she was born, and a U.S. Immigration Visa.

For detailed and updated information on how to obtain these documents, review the *Intercountry Adoption* section in this publication and visit the U.S. Department of State Intercountry Adoption website at http://adoption.state.gov.

Child Citizenship Act: For adoptions finalized abroad, the Child Citizenship Act of 2000 allows your new child to acquire American citizenship automatically when he or she enters the United States as lawful permanent residents. For adoptions finalized in the United States, the Child Citizenship Act of 2000 allows your new child to acquire American citizenship automatically when the court in the United States issues the final adoption decree. To learn more, review the *Intercountry Adoption* section in this publication and visit the U.S. Department of State Intercountry Adoption website at http://adoption.state.gov.

After Adoption: Colombian law does not currently have any post-adoption requirements.

U.S. Embassy in Colombia
Carrera 45, No. 24B-27
Bogotá, Colombia
Tel: 011–571–383–2795, 2 p.m.—3:30 p.m. (EST)
Email: IVBogota@state.gov

Colombia's Central Authority
Bienestar Familiar (ICBF)
Grupo Nacional de Adopciones
Avenida 68 # 64–01
Bogotá, Colombia
Tel: 011–57–1-437 7630—Ext. 3158—3157
Website: www.icbf.gov.co (Spanish)

Embassy of Colombia
2118 Leroy Place, NW
Washington, DC 20008
Tel: (202) 387–8338
Fax: (202) 232–8643
Email: embassyofcolombia@olombiaemb.org
Website: http://www.colombiaemb.org

Office of Children's Issues
U.S. Department of State
2201 C Street, NW
SA-29
Washington, DC 20520
Tel: 1–888–407–4747
Email: AskCI@state.gov
Website:http://adoption.state.gov

For questions about immigration procedures, contact the National Customer Service Center (NCSC) at 1-800-375-5283 (TTY 1-800-767-1833).

International Parental Child Abduction

September 2012

The information in this section has been edited from a report of the Bureau of Consular Affairs, Office of Overseas Citizens Services of the U.S. Department of State. For more information, please read the *International Child Abduction* section of this book and review current reports online at www.travel.state.gov/abduction.

Disclaimer: The information below relating to the legal requirements of Colombia is provided for general information only. Questions involving interpretation of specific foreign laws should be addressed to foreign legal counsel.

General Information: Colombia is in the process of transforming its criminal justice system into an accusatorial one, with oral trials, in a way that resembles the U.S. justice system. For non-criminal matters, however, including divorce and custody cases, Colombia remains a civil law country.

Judicial proceedings in a civil law country generally differ from those in the United States, a common law country, in several significant ways. For example, juries are not used. Legal cases are heard and decided by a judge or panel of judges. Evidence can be presented and arguments can be made in oral hearings, but such hearings tend to play a secondary role, supplementing extensive written submissions to the judge. The judge normally can play a more active role in proceedings than is common in U.S. courts. A judge in a civil law country is free to seek evidence independently of what either side presents.

In Colombia, family court judges handle divorce and custody cases. In cases involving the Hague Convention on the Civil Aspects of International Child Abduction, recent legislation by the Colombian Congress has placed jurisdiction with family courts as well. In more remote areas of the country where there are no family courts, Hague cases are to be heard by civil court circuit judges. While Colombian courts can recognize or enforce U.S. custody orders, they generally refuse to do so. In a Colombian court, Colombian law takes precedence over U.S. law. A Colombian court order granting custody to one parent will prevail over an order issued by a U.S. court.

Custody/Rights of Visitation: In Colombia, married parents share equal rights of custody to their minor children. Under Colombian law, if a father acknowledges on a child's birth certificate that he is the father, then he shares equal custody rights with the mother, even if the child was born out of wedlock. A father who has acknowledged paternity may seek assistance from administrative or judicial authorities for a remedy if the mother interferes with his rights to custody or visitation. Custody cases are first assigned to family protection officers within the Colombian Institute of Family Welfare and then custody and/or visitation are determined before a family court judge. Family courts have heavy caseloads and cases involving a U.S. parent disputing custody with a Colombian parent take a long time to resolve. The U.S. Embassy in Bogota notes that Colombian courts favor parents of Colombian nationality and that it is very rare for a court in Colombia to grant custody to a parent residing in the U.S. when there is a parent residing in Colombia.

Criminal Aspects: The crime of international parental abduction is covered in the Colombian Penal Code as simple kidnapping, with circumstances that can increase or reduce the punishment. Colombia does not consider international parental kidnapping as an extraditable offense.

Colombian Citizenship: The Colombian Constitution provides that a child born abroad to a Colombian mother or father acquires Colombian citizenship once the birth is registered in a consular office or the child later becomes domiciled in Colombia. If a child is born in Colombia, he/she will obtain Colombian citizenship automatically as long as one parent is a Colombian national or one of the child's parents has legal resident status in Colombia.

Colombian Passports: In contrast to U.S. requirements, a Colombian passport for a minor child can be obtained with only one parent's consent. However, Colombian authorities have rules that restrict the departure of Colombian children from the country when they are not in the company of both parents.

Preventing Issuance of a Colombian Passport: If a parent wishes to prevent the issuance of a passport to their minor child, he or she must submit a request to the Ministerio de la Proteccion Social, Instituto Colombiano de Bienstar Familiar (ICBF). If ICBF concurs with the parent's request, it will notify the Colombian passport office to place a hold on issuance of a passport to the minor child. The Colombian passport agency will then notify Colombian Embassies and Consulates of the hold. Parents may only submit a request through ICBF, not through a Colombian Embassy or Consulate. Further information can be found at www.icbf.gov.co/icbf/directorio/portel/libreria/php/decide.php?patron=03.

The Hague Convention: The United States is a party to the Hague Convention on the Civil Aspects of International Child Abduction. The Hague Convention is an international treaty. Its purpose is to discourage international parental abduction and to ensure that children who are abducted or wrongfully retained are returned to their country of habitual residence. The Hague Convention does not govern who should get custody of a child, but only the jurisdiction where custody should be adjudicated.

The Hague Convention took effect between the United States and Colombia on June 1, 1996. Therefore, Hague Convention provisions for return apply only to children abducted or retained after that date. Parents and legal guardians of children taken to Colombia prior to June 1, 1996 may still submit applications for access to the child under the Hague Convention. All countries party to the Hague Convention have a Central Authority that is responsible for processing Hague applications.

The Colombian Central Authority performs an administrative role in processing Hague applications. The Central Authority is the Instituto Colombiano de Bienstar Familiar (ICBF), which is located within the Ministry of Social Protection. The address is Sede Nacional Avenida 68 No 64-01, PBX 4377630, Bogota, DC, Colombia. The international telephone number is 011-57-1-437-7630. The Central Authority's email address is churtado1@icbf.gov.co.

For more information on the Hague Convention, please read the *International Parental Child Abduction* section of this book and review current reports online at www.travel.state.gov/abduction.

Passports for Minors and the Children's Passport Issuance Alert Program: For more information on these topics, see the *International Parental Child Abduction* section of this publication and review current reports from the U.S. Department of State at www.travel.state.gov/abduction.

More Information: The State Department has general information about hiring a foreign attorney, service of process, and enforcement of child support and the international enforcement of judgments, which supplement the country-specific information provided in this flyer. In addition, the State Department publishes Country Specific Information (CSI) for every country in the world, providing information such as location of the U.S. Embassy, health conditions, political situations, and crime reports. When situations in a country are sufficiently serious, the State Department issues Travel Alerts or Travel Warnings that may recommend U.S. citizens defer travel to that country. These documents are available on www.travel.state.gov.

COMOROS

Compiled from publications that were available as of February 2013 from the U.S. Department of State, the U.S. Department of Commerce, and the Central Intelligence Agency (CIA). See the introduction to this set for explanatory notes.

Official Name:
Union of the Comoros

PROFILE

Geography

Area: total: 2,235 sq km; country comparison to the world: 180; land: 2,235 sq km; water: 0 sq km

Major cities: Moroni (capital) 49,000 (2009)

Climate: tropical marine; rainy season (November to May)

Terrain: volcanic islands, interiors vary from steep mountains to low hills

People

Nationality: noun: Comoran(s); adjective: Comoran

Population: 737,284 (July 2012 est.)

Population growth rate: 2.063% (2012 est.)

Ethnic groups: Antalote, Cafre, Makoa, Oimatsaha, Sakalava

Religions: Sunni Muslim 98%, Roman Catholic 2%

Languages: Arabic (official), French (official), Shikomoro (a blend of Swahili and Arabic)

Literacy: definition: age 15 and over can read and write; total population: 74.9%; male: 80.2%; female: 69.7% (2010 est.)

Health: life expectancy at birth: total population: 62.74 years; male: 60.54 years; female: 65.01 years (2012 est.); Infant mortality rate: total: 68.97 deaths/1,000 live births; male: 80.12 deaths/1,000 live births; female: 57.5 deaths/1,000 live births (2012 est.)

Unemployment rate: 20% (1996 est.)

Work force: 268,500 (2007 est.)

Government

Type: republic

Independence: 6 July 1975

Constitution: 23 December 2001

Political subdivisions: 3 islands and 4 municipalities; Grande Comore (N'gazidja), Anjouan (Ndzuwani), Domoni, Fomboni, Moheli (Mwali), Moroni, Moutsamoudou

Suffrage: 18 years of age; universal

Economy

GDP (purchasing power parity): $872 million (2012 est.); $847.7 million (2011 est.); $829.6 million (2010 est.); $813 million (2009 est.)

GDP real growth rate: 2.5% (2012 est.); 2.2% (2011 est.); 2.1% (2010 est.); 1.8% (2009 est.)

GDP per capita (PPP): $1,300 (2012 est.); $1,200 (2011 est.); $1,200 (2010 est.); $1,200 (2009 est.)

Agriculture products: vanilla, cloves, ylang-ylang (perfume essence), copra, coconuts, bananas, cassava (manioc)

Industries: fishing, tourism, perfume distillation

Exports: $27.5 million (2012 est.); $18.5 million (2011 est.); $13.2 million (2010 est.)

Exports—commodities: vanilla, ylang-ylang (perfume essence), cloves, copra

Exports—partners: Singapore 36%, Turkey 23.7%, France 10.5%, Netherlands 7.9% (2011)

Imports: $211.2 million (2012 est.); $219.9 million (2011 est.); $194 million (2010 est.)

Imports—commodities: rice and other foodstuffs, consumer goods, petroleum products, cement, transport equipment

Imports—partners: Pakistan 16.2%, France 15.8%, UAE 11.3%, Turkey 7.3%, Kenya 5.5%, India 4.6%, South Africa 4.2% (2011)

Debt—external: $279.3 million (31 December 2009 est.); $279.3 million (31 December 2009 est.); $485.4 million (31 December 2010 est.)

Exchange rates: Comoran francs (KMF) per US dollar; 386.4 (2012 est.); 353.9 (2011 est.); 371.46 (2010 est.)

PEOPLE

The Comorans, inhabiting the islands of Grande Comore (also known as Ngazidja), Anjouan, and Moheli, share African-Arab origins.

Language

The most common language is Shikomoro, a Swahili dialect. French and Arabic also are spoken.

Religion

The population is estimated at roughly 800,000 and is 99 percent Sunni Muslim. There are several hundred non-Sunni residents on the islands, including Shia Muslims, Sikhs, Hindus, Jehovah's Witnesses, Roman Catholics, and Protestants.

A few foreign faith-based nongovernmental organizations (NGOs), including two U.S.-based Protestant groups--the very small Bahari Foundation and the "Groupe de Service Volontaire"--have operated humanitarian and development programs for nearly 20 years with strong community ties and no government interference.

HISTORY

Over the centuries, the islands were chanced upon or invaded by a succession of diverse groups from the coast of Africa, the Persian Gulf, Indonesia, and Madagascar. Portuguese explorers visited the archipelago in 1505. "Shirazi" Arab migrants introduced Islam at about the same time. Between 1841 and 1912, France established colonial rule over Grande Comore, Anjouan, Mayotte, and Moheli and placed the islands under the administration of the governor general of Madagascar. Later, French settlers, French-owned companies, and wealthy Arab merchants established a plantation-based economy that used about one-third of the land for export crops.

After World War II, the islands became a French overseas territory and were represented in France's National Assembly. Internal political autonomy was granted in 1961. Agreement was reached with France in 1973 for Comoros to become independent in 1978. On July 6, 1975, however, the Comoran parliament passed a resolution declaring unilateral independence. The deputies of Mayotte abstained, preferring to maintain strong ties to France. As a result, the Comoran Government has control only over Grande Comore, Anjouan, and Moheli. Mayotte remains under French administration.

Until recently, Comoran politics were plagued by political instability and civil strife, with numerous coups and secession attempts since independence from France in 1975. The most recent secession attempt was on the island of Anjouan in 1997–1999, wherein rival factions on the island of Anjouan both wanted to secede but could not agree on whether to declare independence or to join France.

This disagreement erupted into violence, which eventually spread to the other islands as well. It was partially in response to this that then-Colonel Assoumani Azali took over the national government in 1999 in a bloodless coup d'etat. In May 1999, Azali decreed a constitution that gave him both executive and legislative powers. When Azali took power, he had pledged to step down in 2000 and relinquish control to a democratically elected president. Instead, in 2001, Azali resigned from the military and ran as a civilian candidate for the national presidency. He was elected in 2002 in flawed but fair elections.

In June 2007, individual island elections on Grande Comore and Moheli were held on schedule, but on Anjouan, island governor Mohamed Bacar refused to step down, held a sham election, and declared himself Island Governor for another term. In March 2008, Comoran and African Union (AU) forces restored constitutional rule on Anjouan. A new election for island governor was held peacefully in June 2008.

GOVERNMENT AND POLITICAL CONDITIONS

The Union of the Comoros is a constitutional, multiparty republic. The country consists of three islands—Grande Comore (also called Ngazidja), Anjouan, and Moheli—and claims a fourth, Mayotte, which France governs. In November and December 2010 elections were held to choose a new union president as well as governors for each of the three islands. Serious electoral irregularities on the island of Anjouan noted by some observers were not sufficient to change the outcome of the national contests, and the constitutional court upheld the results of the elections. On May 26, 2011, former vice president Ikililou Dhoinine became president of the Comoros.

The constitution provides for a rotating union government presidency in which every four years each island takes a turn at holding a primary for three presidential candidates. The constitution thus restricts, by island, those eligible to run for the presidency. However, aside from the rotation principle, anyone is free to run for election.

Recent Elections

In November and December 2010, elections were held to choose a new union government president, as well as governors for each of the three islands. The turn passed to Moheli. From the original 10 candidates (all natives of Moheli), Mohelian voters selected three to run in the national election. Although some observers noted serious irregularities on the island of Anjouan in the national election, these were not sufficient to change the outcome, and the constitutional court upheld the final election results. Former vice president Ikililou Dhoinine became the union president in May 2011.

In December 2009 legislative elections were held for both the union national assembly (parliament) and the three island assemblies. These elections were also considered generally free and fair.

Participation of Women and Minorities: There was one woman in the 33-member National Assembly and three women in the 10-member cabinet. No minorities held National Assembly seats or ministerial posts in the union or island governments.

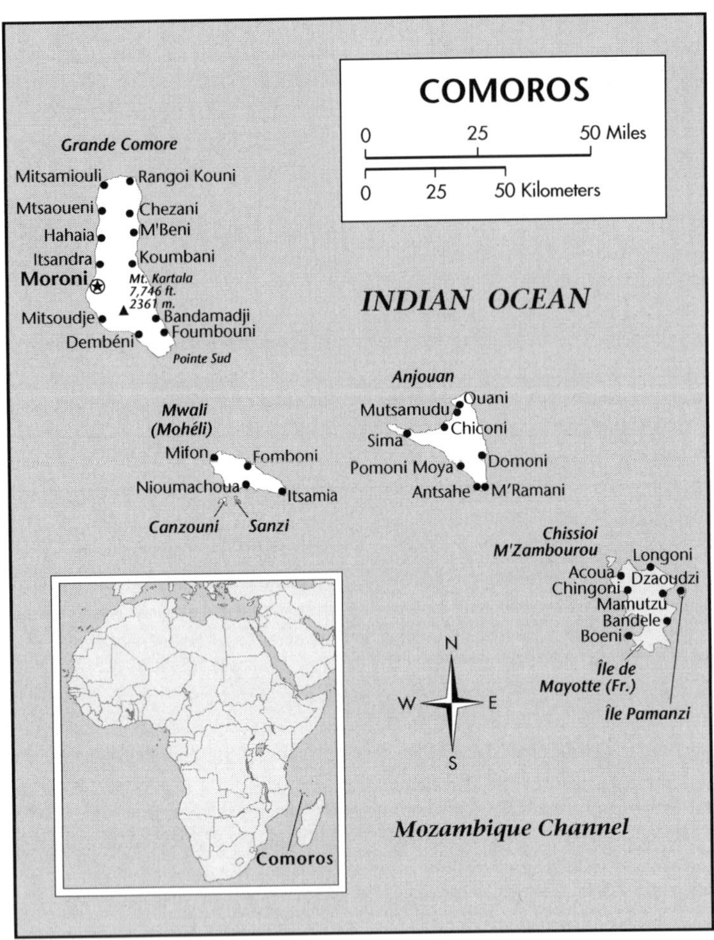

Principal Government Officials

Last Updated: 1/31/2013

Three main islands have been unified into the Union of Comoros, and the presidency of the Union will rotate between the different islands every four years.

Pres. of the Union: **Ikililou DHOININE**

Vice Pres. in Charge of the Min. of Finance, Economy, Budget, Investment, & External Trade Charged With Privatization: **Mohamed Ali SOILIHI**

Vice Pres. in Charge of the Min. of Land Planning, Urbanism, & Housing: **Nourdine BOURHANE**

Vice Pres. in Charge of the Min. of Production, Environment, Energy, Industry, & Craft: **Fouad MOHADJI**

Min. of Defense: **Hamadi MADI**

Min. of Employment, Labor, Vocational Training, & Women, Entrepreneurship & Govt. Spokesperson: **Sitti KASSIM**

Min. of External Relations & Cooperation in Charge of the Diaspora, Francophonie, & the Arab World: **Mohamed BAKRI Ben Abdoulfatah Sharif**

Min. of Health, Solidarity, Social Cohesion, & Gender Promotion: **Moinafouraha AHMED**

Min. of the Interior, Information, & Decentralization Charged With Relations With the Institutions: **HAMADA Abdallah**

Min. of Justice, Civil Service, Admin. Reform, Human Rights, & Islamic Affairs & Keeper of the Seals: **ANLIANE Ahmed**

Min. of National Education, Research, Culture, & Arts Charged With Youth & Sports: **Mohamed ISSIMAILA**

Min. of Posts & Telecommunications & the Promotion of New Information & Communication Technologies: **RASTAMI Mouhidine**

Governor, Central Bank: **Abdou Mohamed CHANFIOU**

Ambassador to the US: **Roubani KAAMBI**

Permanent Representative to the UN, New York: **Roubani KAAMBI**

ECONOMY

One of the world's poorest countries, Comoros is made up of three islands that have inadequate transportation links, a young and rapidly increasing population, and few natural resources. The low educational level of the labor force contributes to a subsistence level of economic activity, high unemployment, and a heavy dependence on foreign grants and technical assistance.

Agriculture, including fishing, hunting, and forestry, contributes 40% to GDP, employs 80% of the labor force, and provides most of the exports. Export income is heavily reliant on the three main crops of vanilla, cloves, and ylang-ylang and Comoros" export earnings are easily disrupted by disasters such as fires. The country is not self-sufficient in food production; rice, the main staple, accounts for the bulk of imports.

The government—which is hampered by internal political disputes—lacks a comprehensive strategy to attract foreign investment and is struggling to upgrade education and technical training, privatize commercial and industrial enterprises, improve health services, diversify exports, promote tourism, and reduce the high population growth rate. Political problems have inhibited growth, which averaged only about 1% in 2006–09 but more than 2% per year in 2010–11. Remittances from 150,000 Comorans abroad help supplement GDP. In September 2009 the IMF approved Comoros for a three-year $21 million loan, but the government has struggled to meet program targets, such as restricting spending on wages, strengthening domestic revenue collection, and moving forward on structural reforms.

Labor Conditions

Laws exist to protect children from exploitation in the workplace. The law establishes 15 as the minimum age for employment. The government did not enforce such laws. Children worked in subsistence farming, fishing, in the informal sector selling goods along roadsides, and extracting and selling marine sand. Children worked on food crops such as manioc and beans, and also on cash crops such as vanilla, cloves, and ylang-ylang (a flower used to make perfume). Some children worked under forced labor conditions, particularly in domestic service, roadside and market selling, and agriculture. In addition, some Qur'anic schools arranged for indigent students to receive lessons in exchange for labor, which sometimes was forced. Some families placed their children in the homes of wealthier families where they worked in exchange for food, shelter, or educational opportunities. Many children were not paid for their work.

The official estimate for the poverty income level is 250,000 Comoran francs ($700) per year. Although the union government and local governments did not enforce the minimum wage law and workweek standards, unions had adequate influence to negotiate de facto minimum wage rates for different skill levels for unionized jobs. These provisions applied to all workers, regardless of sector or country of origin. In practice unions promoted this dc facto minimum wage via their ability to strike against employers.

Some employers, particularly the government, were consistently remiss in paying salaries. Despite some strikes and other protests, the union government was unable regularly to pay government employees—including low-level officials, teachers, and medical workers—with arrears building up over years; most public sector employees did not receive more than one third of their expected pay in any given year. No safety or health standards exist for worksites.

U.S.-COMOROS RELATIONS

The United States established diplomatic relations with Comoros in 1977, following its 1975 independence from France. The United States and Comoros enjoy friendly relations. The United States seeks to help counter piracy and terrorism in the Indian Ocean region through maintaining a strong bilateral relationship with Comoros and enhancing its maritime security. The U.S. Ambassador to Comoros is also accredited to Madagascar and is resident there. The United States does not maintain an embassy in Comoros.

U.S. Assistance to Comoros

U.S. security assistance to Comoros focuses on training its military and security forces and developing a maritime defense force.

Bilateral Economic Relations

Comoros is eligible for preferential trade benefits under the African Growth and Opportunity Act. The United States receives a growing percentage of Comoros exports but supplies only a negligible fraction of its imports. The United States has signed a trade and investment framework agreement with the Common Market for Eastern and Southern Africa, of which Comoros is a member.

Comoros Membership in International Organizations

Comoros and the United States belong to a number of the same international organizations, including the United Nations, International Monetary Fund, and World Bank. Comoros also is an observer to the World Trade Organization.

Bilateral Representation

The U.S. Ambassador to Madagascar also is accredited to Comoros. Comoros has no embassy in Washington, DC, but has a permanent representative to the United Nations in New York who also is accredited as ambassador to the United States.

Principal U.S. Embassy Officials

Last Updated: 1/14/2013

ANTANANARIVO (E) Point Liberty, Andranoro, Antehiroka 105, Antsahavola B.P. 620 Antananarivo, Madagascar, (261) (20) 23-480 00 or 261-33-443-2000, Fax (261) (20) 23-480 35 or 261-33-443-2817, INMARSAT Tel 38-31-32673, Workweek: M-T 7:30AM–5:00PM/ F–7:30 AM–1:30 PM, http://www.antananarivo.usembassy.gov/

DCM OMS:	Tiffany Sims
AMB OMS:	Vacant
CDC:	Alyssa M. Finlay-Vickers
CG OMS:	Vacant
Co-CLO:	Bao Holy Andriamasinoro
DCM/CHG:	Charge Eric Wong
FCS:	Larry Farris
FM:	Ricardo Cruz
HRO:	Vonzett George
MGT:	Kevin Weishar
OMS:	Tiffany Sims
POL/ECON:	Jeremy Edwards
POSHO:	Ricardo Cruz
SDO/DATT:	CDR Michael Baker
AMB:	Vacant
CG:	Vacant
CON:	Jeffrey Osweiler
PAO:	Brett Bruen
GSO:	Kumi Ikeda
RSO:	Aaron Tambrini
AFSA:	Cathy Bowes
AGR:	Scott Reynolds (Pretoria)
AID:	Rudolph Thomas
CLO:	David Grist
DEA:	Jeffrey P. Breeden (Pretoria)
EEO:	Patty Baxer
FAA:	Edward Jones (Dakar)
FMO:	Tyrone Campbell
ICASS Chair:	John Reddy
IMO:	Joseph Farina
IPO:	Roger L. Smith
IRS:	Aziz Benbrahim (Paris)
ISSO:	Sonia Grigorian
LEGATT:	Wilford Rattigan
POL:	Nicolle Otallah
State ICASS:	Eric Atkins

TRAVEL

Consular Information Sheet

April 30, 2012

Country Description: The Union of the Comoros is a developing nation located in the Indian Ocean off the east coast of Africa. Comoros consists of three islands—Ngazidja (also known as Grand Comore), Moheli, and Anjouan—that cover about 900 square miles. A fourth island, Mayotte, officially changed status from a French "collectivity" to a French Département in March 2011. Mayotte is within the consular jurisdiction of Embassy Antananarivo. Ngazidja is home to the capital city, Moroni, and is the most developed of the three islands. Facilities for tourism are limited and telecommunication links are unreliable. French, Arabic, Swahili, and Comoran are spoken.

Smart Traveler Enrollment Program (STEP)/Embassy Location: If you are going to live in or visit the Comoros or Mayotte, please take the time to tell our embassy about your trip. If you enroll in our Smart Traveler Enrollment Program, we can keep you up to date with important safety and security announcements. Your enrollment will also help your friends and family get in touch with you in an emergency.

U.S. citizens without Internet access may enroll in person at the U.S. Embassy in Antananarivo. The U.S. Embassy in Antananarivo is located at Lot 207A, Point Liberty, Andranoro-Antehiroka, Antananarivo (105), Madagascar. The mailing address is B.P. 5253, Antananarivo (105) Madagascar. The telephone number is [261] (20) 23-480-00; the fax number is [261] (20) 23-480-35.

Entry/Exit Requirements for U.S. Citizens: A passport and onward/return ticket are required. Visas are available from the Comoran Mission to the United Nations in New York; U.S. citizens visiting Comoros can obtain a visa upon entry for a fee of sixty Euros. Travelers should obtain the latest details from the Mission of the Union of Comoros, 420 East 50th Street, New York, NY 10022; telephone number (212) 972-8010, fax (212) 983-4712.

The U.S. Department of State is unaware of any HIV/AIDS entry restrictions for visitors to or foreign residents of Comoros.

Threats to Safety and Security: Comoros has experienced occasional strikes and civil unrest, resulting in violent clashes between police and demonstrators, and has a history of coups since becoming independent. You should avoid political rallies and street demonstrations; even demonstrations intended to be peaceful can turn confrontational and possibly escalate into violence.

Conditions change rapidly on the islands of the Comoros due to weak political institutions and a lack of economic development. Religious intolerance and religious-based violence are very unusual in Comoros. Although foreign residents and visitors have not been targeted for violence, the potential for further outbreaks of civil disorder remains, and you should exercise caution and good judgment, keep a low profile, and remain vigilant. Running water and electric power are unreliable, even at the most upscale hotels on the islands, and nonexistent for the most part outside the few urban areas. Care should be taken to ensure that water is potable and the food is cleaned and properly cooked.

Stay up to date by:

- Bookmarking our Bureau of Consular Affairs website, which contains the current Travel Warnings and Travel Alerts as well as the Worldwide Caution.
- Following us on Twitter and the Bureau of Consular Affairs page on Facebook as well.
- Downloading our free Smart Traveler IPhone App to have travel information at your fingertips.
- Calling 1-888-407-4747 toll-free within the U.S. and Canada, or a regular toll line, 1-202-501-4444, from other countries.
- Taking some time before travel to consider your personal security.

Crime: You should be vigilant against pickpocketing and other forms of petty crime when visiting crowded market areas, parks, and at the beaches. Violent crime is uncommon; Moheli, for example, has not reported a homicide in decades. The most commonly reported crime is home break-ins. Most reported crimes are crimes of opportunity.

Don't buy counterfeit and pirated goods, even if they are widely available. Not only are the bootlegs illegal in the United States, if you purchase them you may also be breaking local law.

Victims of Crime: If you or someone you know becomes the victim of a crime abroad, you should contact the local police and the nearest U.S. embassy or consulate. We can:

- Replace a stolen passport.
- Help you find appropriate medical care if you are the victim of violent crimes such as assault or rape.
- Put you in contact with the appropriate police authorities, and if you want us to, we can contact family members or friends.
- Help you understand the local criminal justice process and direct you to local attorneys, although it is important to remember that local authorities are responsible for investigating and prosecuting the crime.

The local equivalent to the "911" emergency line in Comoros is: 17 for local police; 18 for the Gendarmerie.

Criminal Penalties: While you are traveling in another country, you are subject to its laws even if you are a U.S. citizen. Foreign laws and legal systems can be vastly different than our own. In some places you may be taken in for questioning if you don't have your passport with you. In some places driving under the influence could land you immediately in jail. These criminal penalties will vary from country to country. There are also some things that might be legal in the country you visit, but still illegal in the United States, and you can be prosecuted under U.S. law if you buy pirated goods. Engaging in sexual conduct with children or using or disseminating child pornography in a foreign country is a crime prosecutable in the United States. If you break local laws in in your host country, your U.S. passport won't help you avoid arrest or prosecution. It's very important to know what's legal and what's not where you are going.

Persons violating the laws of Comoros, even unknowingly, may be expelled, arrested, or imprisoned. Penalties for possession, use or trafficking in illegal drugs in Comoros are strict, with convicted offenders receiving a mandatory minimum five-year jail sentence and heavy fines.

Arrest notifications in host country: While some countries will automatically notify the nearest U.S. embassy or consulate if a U.S. citizen is detained or arrested in a foreign country, that might not always be the case. To ensure that the United States is aware of your circumstances, request that the police and prison officials notify the nearest U.S. embassy or consulate as soon as you are arrested or detained overseas. Please note that there is no official permanent U.S. presence in Comoros—such official notification to U.S authorities must be made to the U.S. Embassy in Madagascar, and may therefore be extremely slow.

Special Circumstances: While religions other than Islam are permitted in Comoros, evangelization is illegal. Violators of this law can be fined or imprisoned. Few establishments accept credit cards in the Comoros; cash transactions are preferred, in Comoran Francs or Euros. Dollars are not accepted.

Accessibility: While in Comoros individuals with disabilities will find virtually no accommodation for accessibility.

Medical Facilities and Health Information: Medical care is substandard throughout the country including Grande Comore. Adequate evacuation insurance coverage for all travelers is a high priority. Travelers should bring their own supplies of prescription drugs and preventive medicines. Malaria is prevalent in Comoros. The Center for Disease Control and Prevention (CDC) advises that travelers to Comoros should take one of the following anti-malarial drugs: mefloquine (Lariam), doxycycline, or atovaquone/proguanil (Malarone).

Other protective measures, such as the use of bed nets and insect repellants, help to reduce malaria risk. Travelers who become ill with a fever or flu-like illness while traveling in a malaria-risk area and up to one year after returning home should seek prompt medical attention and tell the physician their travel history and what antimalarials they have been taking.

For additional information on malaria, protection from insect bites, and anitmalarial drugs, please visit the CDC Travelers' Health web pages.The East African Indian Ocean islands have seen some cases of chikungunya, a viral dengue-like ailment, and dengue itself. As with malaria, chikungunya and dengue are transmitted by mosquitoes. Every effort should be made to use bed nets, repellants, proper clothing and other barriers that discourage/prevent mosquito bites.

The CDC has further information on chikungunya and dengue on their website. Rabies vaccines should be considered for shorter stays for adventure travelers, hikers, backpackers, or rural travelers who are staying more than 24 hours away from a reliable source of human rabies immune globulin and rabies vaccine for post-exposure treatment. All bat, carnivore, and other mammal bites or scratches while in this country should be taken seriously and post-exposure prophylaxis sought even in those already immunized.

There is a high risk of marine hazards (jellyfish, coral and sea urchins) as well as traveler's diarrhea throughout the country. Food and beverage precautions are essential in order to reduce chance of illness. Travelers should carry loperamide (Imodium) and/or a quinolone (Ciprofloxacin) antibiotic for presumptive self-treatment, if diarrhea occurs. More information on vaccinations and other health precautions is available from the CDC website. For information about outbreaks of infectious diseases abroad, consult the World Health Organization (WHO) website. The WHO website also contains additional health information for travelers, including detailed country-specific health information.

Medical Insurance: You can't assume your insurance will go with you when you travel. It's very important to find out BEFORE you leave whether or not your medical insurance will cover you overseas. You need to ask your insurance company two questions:

- Does my policy apply when I'm out of the United States?
- Will it cover emergencies like a trip to a foreign hospital or a medical evacuation?

In many places, doctors and hospitals still expect payment in cash at the time of service. Your regular U.S. health insurance may not cover doctors' and hospital visits in other countries. If your policy doesn't go with you when you travel, it's a very good idea to take out another one for your trip.

Traffic Safety and Road Conditions: While in Comoros, you will encounter road conditions that differ significantly from those in the United States. In Comoros, one drives on the right side of the street. Roads are ill-maintained, congested, very narrow and poorly lit at night. Travelers should exercise extreme caution when driving after dark, or walking along trafficked roads. Some urban roads are paved, but many rural roads are not. Most roads are full of potholes and dangerous curves. Roads have no posted speed limits, but road conditions limit speeds to well below 30 miles an hour. Drivers and front seat passengers are required to wear seat belts. There are no laws regarding child safety seats.

There are no organizations in Comoros that provide emergency or roadside assistance. Individuals involved in accidents rely on passersby for assistance. Taxis or a rental car with driver are preferable to public transportation.

Aviation Safety Oversight:: As there is no direct commercial air service to the United States by carriers registered in Comoros, the U.S. Federal Aviation Administration (FAA) has not assessed the government of Comoros' Civil Aviation Authority for compliance with International Civil Aviation Organization (ICAO) aviation safety standards. Further information may be found on the FAA's safety assessment page.

Children's Issues:: Please see the U.S. Dept. of State Office of Children's Issues web pages on intercountry adoption and international parental child abduction.

Intercountry Adoption

July 2011

Comoros is not party to the Hague Convention on Protection of Children and Co-operation in Respect of Intercountry Adoption (Hague Adoption Convention). Therefore, when the Hague Adoption Convention entered into force for the United States on April 1, 2008, intercountry adoption processing for Comoros did not change. Adoption is illegal under the laws and Constitution of Comoros. Comoran law recognizes a "Delegation de l'autorite parental", which delegates parental authority to someone other than the child's parent, but this is only available to Comoran citizens. While Comoran citizens can use this process to emigrate a child from Comoros, Comoran law forbids them to adopt the child after leaving Comoros. The Embassy is not aware of any mechanism in Comoran law that would allow non-Comoran citizens to assume guardianship of a child for the purpose of taking him/ her to the another country to conclude a full and final adoption.

Thus, there appears to be no legal mechanism for a Comoran child to qualify for an immigrant visa as an adopted child or a child to be adopted internationally.

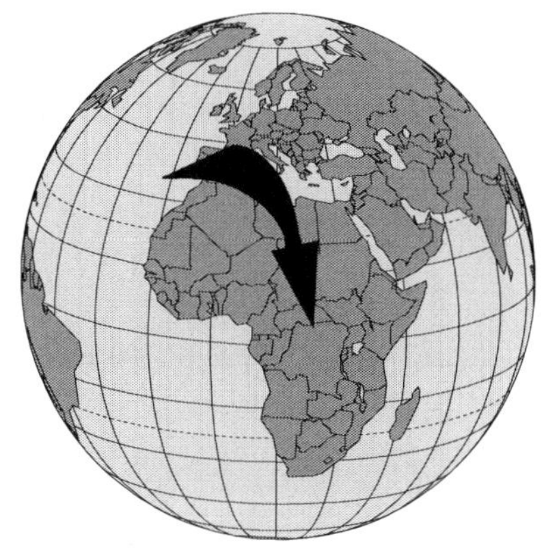

CONGO

Compiled from publications that were available as of February 2013 from the U.S. Department of State, the U.S. Department of Commerce, and the Central Intelligence Agency (CIA). See the introduction to this set for explanatory notes.

Official Name:
Democratic Republic of the Congo

PROFILE

Geography

Area: total: 2,344,858 sq km; country comparison to the world: 11; land: 2,267,048 sq km; water: 77,810 sq km

Major cities: Kinshasa (capital) 8.401 million; Lubumbashi 1.543 million; Mbuji-Mayi 1.488 million; Kananga 878,000; Kisangani 812,000 (2009)

Climate: tropical; hot and humid in equatorial river basin; cooler and drier in southern highlands; cooler and wetter in eastern highlands; north of Equator—wet season (April to October), dry season (December to February); south of Equator—wet season (November to March), dry season (April to October)

Terrain: vast central basin is a low-lying plateau; mountains in east

People

Nationality: noun: Congolese (singular and plural); adjective: Congolese or Congo

Population: 73,599,190 (July 2012 est.)

Population growth rate: 2.579% (2012 est.)

Ethnic groups: over 200 African ethnic groups of which the majority are Bantu; the four largest tribes—Mongo, Luba, Kongo (all Bantu), and the Mangbetu-Azande (Hamitic) make up about 45% of the population

Religions: Roman Catholic 50%, Protestant 20%, Kimbanguist 10%, Muslim 10%, other (includes syncretic sects and indigenous beliefs) 10%

Languages: French (official), Lingala (a lingua franca trade language), Kingwana (a dialect of Kiswahili or Swahili), Kikongo, Tshiluba

Literacy: definition: age 15 and over can read and write French, Lingala, Kingwana, or Tshiluba; total population: 66.8%; male: 76.9%; female: 57% (2010 est.)

Health: life expectancy at birth: total population: 55.74 years; male: 54.28 years; female: 57.23 years (2012 est.); Infant mortality rate: total: 76.63 deaths/1,000 live births; male: 80.36 deaths/1,000 live births; female: 72.79 deaths/1,000 live births (2012 est.)

Unemployment rate: NA%

Work force: 35.92 million (2012 est.)

Government

Type: republic

Independence: 30 June 1960

Constitution: 18 February 2006

Political subdivisions: 10 provinces (provinces, singular—province) and 1 city (ville); Bandundu, Bas-Congo (Lower Congo), Equateur, Kasai-Occidental (West Kasai), Kasai-Oriental (East Kasai), Katanga, Kinshasa, Maniema, Nord-Kivu (North Kivu), Orientale, Sud-Kivu (South Kivu)

Suffrage: 18 years of age; universal and compulsory

Economy

GDP (purchasing power parity): $27.53 billion (2012 est.); $25.59 billion (2011 est.); $23.93 billion (2010 est.); $22.36 billion (2009 est.)

GDP real growth rate: 7.1% (2012 est.); 6.9% (2011 est.); 7% (2010 est.); 2.8% (2009 est.)

GDP per capita (PPP): $400 (2012 est.); $400 (2011 est.); $300 (2010 est.); $300 (2009 est.)

Natural resources: cobalt, copper, niobium, tantalum, petroleum, industrial and gem diamonds, gold, silver, zinc, manganese, tin, uranium, coal, hydropower, timber

Agriculture products: coffee, sugar, palm oil, rubber, tea, cotton, cocoa, quinine, cassava (manioc), bananas, plantains, peanuts, root crops, corn, fruits; wood products

Industries: mining (diamonds, gold, copper, cobalt, coltan, zinc, tin), mineral processing, consumer products (textiles, plastics, footwear, cigarettes), metal products, processed foods and beverages, timber, cement, commercial ship repair

Exports: $11.28 billion (2012 est.); $10.93 billion (2011 est.); $8.35 billion (2010 est.)

Exports—commodities: diamonds, gold, copper, cobalt, wood products, crude oil, coffee
Exports—partners: China 48%, Zambia 21.2%, US 9.4%, Belgium 5.4% (2011)
Imports: $9.237 billion (2012 est.); $9.021 billion (2011 est.); $7.829 billion (2010 est.)
Imports—commodities: foodstuffs, mining and other machinery, transport equipment, fuels
Imports—partners: China 17.1%, South Africa 17%, Belgium 9%, Zambia 7.5%, Zimbabwe 6.1%, Kenya 5.1%, France 5% (2011)
Debt—external: $7.644 billion (31 December 2012 est.); $14.82 billion (31 December 2011 est.); $13.14 billion (31 December 2010 est.)
Exchange rates: Congolese francs (CDF) per US dollar; 920 (2012 est.); 919.49 (2011 est.); 905.91 (2010 est.); 472.19 (2009); 559 (2008); 516 (2007)

GEOGRAPHY

The Democratic Republic of the Congo (D.R.C.) includes the greater part of the Congo River basin, which covers an area of almost one million square kilometers (400,000 sq. mi.). The country's only outlet to the Atlantic Ocean is a narrow strip of land on the north bank of the Congo River.

The vast, low-lying central area is a basin-shaped plateau sloping toward the west and covered by tropical rainforest. This area is surrounded by mountainous terraces in the west, plateaus merging into savannas in the south and southwest, and dense grasslands extending beyond the Congo River in the north. High mountains are found in the extreme eastern region.

The D.R.C. lies on the Equator, with one-third of the country to the north and two-thirds to the south. The climate is hot and humid in the river basin and cool and dry in the southern highlands. South of the Equator, the rainy season lasts from October to May and north of the Equator, from April to November. Along the Equator, rainfall is fairly regular throughout the year. During the wet season, thunderstorms often are violent but seldom last more than a few hours. The average annual rainfall for the entire country is about 107 centimeters (42 in.).

PEOPLE

As many as 250 Sudanese, Nilotic, and Bantu ethnic groups have been distinguished and named; small groups of aboriginal Pygmies are found throughout the central Congo Basin. Some of the larger groups are the Kongo, Luba, Tetela, and Anamongo.

National/Racial/Ethnic Minorities

The country had a population of between 200,000 and 500,000 Pygmies (Twa, Mbuti, Aka, and others), believed to be the country's original inhabitants. The government did not effectively protect their civil and political rights, and societal discrimination against them was widespread. Most Pygmies took no part in the political process and lived in remote areas.

Fighting in the East between RMG and SSF caused displacement of some Pygmy populations. Since 2003, many Pygmies who had lived in IDP camps in the East were forced out of the camps by other IDPs, removing their access to humanitarian relief provided to camp residents.

In some areas, traditional leaders (mwami) and wealthy persons captured Pygmies and forced them into slavery. For 2009–10, the World Peasants/Indigenous Organization (WPIO) reported 644 new cases of enslavement of Pygmies.

Language

Four regional languages have official status: Kikongo (Bas-Congo and Bandundu), Kiswahili (Katanga, Kivus and Orientale), Lingala (Kinshasa and within the Congo River Valley), and Tshiluba (Kasais). French is the business language. Many expatriates and some Congolese businesspersons have some knowledge of English.

Religion

The population is approximately 50 percent Roman Catholic, 35 percent Protestant (including evangelicals), 5 percent Kimbanguist (a Christian-inspired Congolese church), and 5 percent Muslim. Other religious groups are represented in much smaller numbers and include Jehovah's Witnesses, The Church of Jesus Christ of Latter-day Saints (Mormons), Greek Orthodox Christians, and Jews. The remainder generally practices animist indigenous religious beliefs. Best estimates indicate that approximately 70 percent of the population attends religious services each week, but the last population census providing specific proportions was conducted in 1984.

Most religious groups are scattered throughout the country and are widely represented in cities and large towns. Muslims are concentrated mainly in the provinces of Maniema, Orientale, and Kinshasa. Although present throughout the country, Kimbanguists are primarily concentrated in Kinshasa and Bas-Congo.

HISTORY

The area known as the Democratic Republic of the Congo was populated as early as 10,000 years ago and settled in the 7th and 8th centuries A.D. by Bantus from present-day Nigeria. Portuguese navigator Diego Cao was the first European known to have visited the area (in 1482), and English journalist Henry Morton Stanley later explored much of the region in the mid to late 19th century. The area was officially colonized in 1885 as a personal possession of Belgian King Leopold II as the Congo Free State. In 1907, administration shifted to the Belgian Government, which renamed the country the Belgian Congo. Following a series of riots and unrest, the Belgian Congo gained its independence on June 30, 1960. Parliamentary elections in 1960 produced

Patrice Lumumba as prime minister and Joseph Kasavubu as president of the renamed Democratic Republic of the Congo.

The Mobutu Era

Within the first year of independence, several events destabilized the country: the army mutinied; the governor of Katanga Province attempted secession; a UN peacekeeping force was called in to restore order; Prime Minister Lumumba died under mysterious circumstances; and Col. Joseph Desire Mobutu (later Mobutu Sese Seko) took over the government and ceded it again to President Kasavubu.

Unrest and rebellion plagued the government until 1965, when Mobutu, by then a lieutenant general and commander-in-chief of the national army, again seized control of the country and declared himself president for 5 years. Mobutu quickly centralized power through the domination of his Popular Revolution Movement (MPR) party and was elected unopposed as president in 1970.

Embarking on a campaign of cultural awareness, in 1971, Mobutu renamed the country the Republic of Zaire and required citizens to adopt African names. Relative peace and stability prevailed until 1977 and 1978 when Katangese rebels, staged in Angola, launched a series of invasions into the Katanga region. The rebels were driven out with the aid of Belgian, Moroccan, and French paratroopers.

During the 1980s, Mobutu continued to enforce his one-party system of rule. Although Mobutu successfully maintained control during this period, opposition parties, most notably the Democracy and Social Progress Union (UDPS), were active. Mobutu's attempts to quell these groups drew significant international criticism.

As the Cold War came to a close, internal and external pressures on Mobutu increased. In late 1989 and early 1990, Mobutu was weakened by a series of domestic protests, heightened international criticism of his regime's human rights practices, and a faltering economy. In April 1990, Mobutu agreed to the principle of a multi-party system with elections and a constitution. As details of a reform package were delayed, soldiers in September 1991 began looting Kinshasa to protest their unpaid wages. Two thousand French and Belgian troops, some of whom were flown in on U.S. Air Force planes, arrived to evacuate the 20,000 endangered foreign nationals in Kinshasa. Soldiers went on a similar rampage in January 1993.

In 1992, after previous similar attempts, the long-promised Sovereign National Conference was staged, encompassing more than 2,000 representatives from various political parties. The conference gave itself a legislative mandate and elected Archbishop Laurent Monsengwo as its chairman, along with Etienne Tshisekedi, leader of the UDPS, as prime minister. Mobutu's opposition to the Sovereign National Conference led to the Limete Catholic Massacre on February 16, 1992, in which Mobutu's personal guards gunned down as many as 250 parishioners on their way to church. By the end of the year Mobutu had created a rival government with its own prime minister. The ensuing stalemate produced a compromise merger of the two governments into the High Council of the Republic-Parliament of Transition (HCR-PT) in 1994, with Mobutu as head of state and Leon Kengo Wa Dondo as prime minister. Although presidential and legislative elections were scheduled repeatedly over the next 2 years, they never took place.

Beginning in late 1994, the war and genocide in neighboring Rwanda spilled over to Zaire. Rwandan Hutu militia forces (Interahamwe), who fled Rwanda following the ascension of a Tutsi-led government, used Hutu refugee camps in eastern Zaire as bases for incursions against Rwanda.

In October 1996, Rwandan troops (RPA) entered Zaire, simultaneously with the formation of an armed coalition led by Laurent-Desire Kabila known as the Alliance of Democratic Forces for the Liberation of Congo-Zaire (AFDL). With the goal of forcibly ousting Mobutu, the AFDL, supported by Rwanda and Uganda, began a military campaign toward Kinshasa. Following failed peace talks between Mobutu and Kabila in May 1997, Mobutu left the country.

From Dictatorship to Disintegration

Laurent-Desire Kabila marched into Kinshasa on May 17, 1997, and declared himself president. He consolidated power around himself and the AFDL and renamed the country the Democratic Republic of the Congo (D.R.C.). Kabila's Army Chief and the Secretary General of the AFDL were Rwandan, and RPA units continued to operate tangentially with the D.R.C.'s military, which was renamed the Congolese Armed Forces (FAC).

Over the next year, relations between Kabila and his foreign backers deteriorated. In July 1998, Kabila ordered all foreign troops to leave the D.R.C. Most refused to leave. On August 2, nationwide fighting erupted as Rwandan troops in the D.R.C. "mutinied," and fresh Rwandan and Ugandan troops entered the country. Two days later, Rwandan troops flew to Bas-Congo, with the intention of marching on Kinshasa, ousting Kabila, and replacing him with the newly formed Rwandan-backed rebel group called the Congolese Rally for Democracy (RCD). The Rwandan campaign was thwarted at the last minute when Angolan, Zimbabwean, and Namibian troops intervened on behalf of the D.R.C. Government. The Rwandans and the RCD withdrew to eastern D.R.C., where they established de facto control over portions of eastern D.R.C. and continued to fight the Congolese army and its foreign allies.

In February 1999, Uganda backed the formation of a rebel group called the Congo Liberation Movement (MLC), which drew support from among ex-Mobutuists and ex-Zairian soldiers in Equateur Province (Mobutu's home province). Together, Uganda and the MLC established control over the northern third of the

D.R.C.At this stage, the D.R.C. was divided de facto into three segments—one controlled by Laurent Kabila, one controlled by Rwanda, and one controlled by Uganda—and the parties had reached military deadlock. In July 1999, a cease-fire was proposed in Lusaka, Zambia, which all parties signed by the end of August. The Lusaka Accord called for a cease-fire, the deployment of a UN peacekeeping operation, the withdrawal of foreign troops, and the launching of an "Inter-Congolese Dialogue" to form a transitional government leading to elections. The parties to the Lusaka Accord failed to fully implement its provisions in 1999 and 2000. Laurent Kabila drew increasing international criticism for blocking full deployment of UN troops, hindering progress toward an Inter-Congolese Dialogue, and suppressing internal political activity.

On January 16, 2001, Laurent Kabila was assassinated, allegedly by a member of his personal bodyguard corps who was in turn killed by an aide-de-camp. Kabila was succeeded by his son Joseph, who reversed many of his father's negative policies. Over the next year, the UN peacekeeping mission in the D.R.C. (United Nations Organization Mission in the Democratic Republic of the Congo, known by its French acronym

MONUC) deployed throughout the country, and the Inter-Congolese Dialogue proceeded. By the end of 2002, all Angolan, Namibian, and Zimbabwean troops had withdrawn from the D.R.C. Following D.R.C.-Rwanda talks in South Africa that culminated in the Pretoria Accord in July 2002, Rwandan troops officially withdrew from the D.R.C. in October 2002. However, there were continued, unconfirmed reports that Rwandan soldiers and military advisers remained integrated with the forces of an RCD splinter group (RCD/G) in eastern D.R.C. Ugandan troops officially withdrew from the D.R.C. in May 2003.

National Dialogue, Transitional Government, and Nascent Democracy

In October 2001, the Inter-Congolese Dialogue began in Addis Ababa under the auspices of a facilitator, former Botswana president Ketumile Masire. The initial meetings made little progress and were adjourned. On February 25, 2002, the dialogue was reconvened in South Africa. It included representatives from the government, rebel groups, political opposition, civil society, and Mai-Mai groups (Congolese local defense militias). The talks ended inconclusively on April 19, 2002, when the government and the MLC brokered an agreement that was signed by the majority of delegates at the dialogue but left out the RCD/G and opposition UDPS party, among others.

This partial agreement was never implemented, and negotiations resumed in South Africa in October 2002. This time, the talks led to an all-inclusive agreement, which was signed by delegates in Pretoria on December 17, 2002, and formally ratified by all parties on April 2, 2003. That same day, a transitional constitution was adopted.

Following nominations by each of the various signatory groups, President Joseph Kabila on June 30, 2003, issued a decree that formally announced the transitional government lineup. Four vice presidents (each representing a specific party, faction, or region) took their oaths of office on July 17, 2003, and most incoming ministers assumed their new functions within days thereafter.

During the transitional government period, President Joseph Kabila made significant progress in liberalizing domestic political activity and undertaking economic reforms in cooperation with the World Bank and International Monetary Fund (IMF). However, serious human rights problems remained in the security services and justice system.

GOVERNMENT AND POLITICAL CONDITIONS

The Democratic Republic of the Congo (DRC) is a nominally centralized, constitutional republic. The president and the lower house of parliament (National Assembly) are popularly elected. Provincial assemblies choose the members of the upper house (Senate). On November 28, the country held multiparty presidential and National Assembly elections, which many local and international observers judged lacked credibility and were seriously flawed. State security forces (SSF) acted independently of civilian control and of military command in many instances.

Recent Elections

Presidential and parliamentary elections were held on November 28, 2011 and on December 9, the CENI announced that President Joseph Kabila received approximately 49 percent of the vote, Etienne Tshisekedi received 32 percent, and Vital Kamerhe 8 percent. Several international observer missions, including the Carter Center and the EU Observer Mission, judged that the results of the elections "lacked credibility," due largely to irregularities and a lack of transparency in the vote tabulation process.

Election day was generally peaceful but chaotic and disorganized at a number of polling stations throughout the country. For example, many individuals could not find their names on the voting lists and therefore could not vote. Midway through election day, the CENI publicly announced that these "omitted" individuals could vote in the stations in which they registered, regardless of whether their names appeared on the rolls. In addition to the confusion, an RMG attacked a polling station in Lubumbashi on election day, and there were numerous incidents of violence in Kasai Occidental and parts of Kinshasa.

On December 12, Vital Kamerhe, on behalf of the opposition, filed a claim with the Supreme Court seeking to annul the presidential elections. On December 16, the Supreme Court upheld the CENI's provisional results declaring that President Kabila won the election. The opposition quickly denounced the Supreme Court's ruling, and some international stakeholders criticized the procedure employed by the court. President Kabila was sworn into office on December 20.

Meanwhile second place winner and Kabila's primary opponent Etienne Tshisekedi declared he had won the election and held his own "inauguration" at his home on December 23. SSF had prevented the inauguration from taking place at the Martyr's Stadium, as planned by Tshisekedi and his UDPS party. Up to five people died in small-scale clashes on that day. At the end of 2011, Tshisekedi remained in detention in his residence.

By the end of 2011, parliamentary election results had not been announced.

During 2011, a number of legal codes were changed concerning the elections process. Perhaps most significantly, on January 25, the Senate and the National Assembly adopted an amendment to the constitution that changed the presidential election from a two-round voting system to a single-round system whereby a simple majority determines the winner. In June and July, officials completed the voter registration process, registering approximately 32 million voters nationwide. In October the CENI began publishing voter lists on its Web site. Many observers, including the Carter Center, claimed that the voter registration process was flawed.

The registration of presidential and legislative candidates was accompanied by demonstrations, especially by opposition party UDPS and Alliance pour la Majorite Presidentielle (AMP) member PPRD.

Political Parties: The 2007 law on the status and rights of the political opposition recognizes opposition parties represented in parliament as well as those not in parliament. The law also details the various "sacred" rights and obligations of opposition parties. During 2011 political parties were able to operate most of the time without restriction or outside interference, but there were notable exceptions, particularly during the election period. Opposition members were sometimes harassed (see section 2.a.).

Participation of Women and Minorities: At the end of 2011, women held 10 percent of seats in the National Assembly (50 of 500) and approximately 6 percent in the provincial assemblies (43 of 690). This was a decrease from the 12 percent of seats held prior to the 2006 elections. In addition, four of the 108 senators were women. Among the 45 government ministers and vice ministers, four were women.

Many ethnic groups, including Pygmies, were not represented in the Senate, the National Assembly, or provincial assemblies. The lack of political participation of some ethnic groups may have been a result of continuing societal discrimination. The enslavement of and discrimination against Pygmies continued in some areas and undoubtedly contributed to their lack of political participation (see section 5).

Principal Government Officials

Last Updated: 1/31/2013

Pres.: **Joseph KABILA**

Prime Min.: **Augustin Matata PONYO Mapon**

Dep. Prime Min.: **Alexandre LUBA Ntambo**

Dep. Prime Min.: **Daniel MUKOKO Samba**

Min. of Agriculture & Rural Development: **Jean-Chrysistine VAHAMWITI**

Min. of Budget: **Daniel MUKOKO Samba**

Min. of Communications, Media, & Relations With Parliament: **Lambert MENDE Omalanga**

Min. of Defense & Veterans Affairs: **Alexandre LUBA Ntambo**

Min. of Economy & Trade: **Jean-Paul NEMOYATO**

Min. of Employment, Labor, & Social Welfare: **Modeste BAHATI Lukwebo**

Min. of Energy & Hydraulic Resources: **Bruno KAPANJI Kalala**

Min. of the Environment, Conservation, & Tourism: **Bavon BAVON N'sa Mputu Elima**

Min. of Finance: **Augustin Matata PONYO Mapon**

Min. of Foreign Affairs, Intl. Cooperation, & Francophone Affairs: **Raymond TSHIBANDA**

Min. of Gender, Family, & Children's Affairs: **Genevieve INAGOSI**

Min. of Health: **Felix KABANGE Numbi**

Min. of Hydrocarbons: **Crispin ATAMA Tabe**

Min. of Industry & Small & Medium-Sized Enterprises: **Remy MUSUNGAYI Bampale**

Min. of Infrastructure, Public Works, Town & Country Planning, Urban Planning, & Housing: **Fridolin KASWESHI Musoka**

Min. of Interior, Security, Decentralization, & Customary Affairs: **Richard MUYEJ**

Min. of Justice & Human Rights: **Wivine MUMBA Matipa**

Min. of Lands: **Robert MBUINGA**

Min. of Mines: **Martin KABWELULU Labilo**

Min. of Planning & Monitoring the Implementation of Modernity: **Celestin VUNABANDI**

Min. of Post, Telecommunications, & New Information Technologies: **Tryphon KIN-KIEYI Mulumba**

Min. of Primary, Secondary, & Vocational Education: **Maker MWANGU Famba**

Min. of Public Service: **Jean Claude KIBALA**

Min. of Social & Humanitarian Affairs & National Solidarity: **Charles NAWEJ Mundele**

Min. of Transportation & Commerce: **Justin KALUMBA Mwana Ngongo**

Min. of University & Higher Education: **Chelo LOTSIMA**

Min. of Youth, Sports, Leisure, Culture, & Arts: **Banza MUKALAYI Sungu**

Governor, Central Bank: **Jean-Claude MASANGU Mulongo**

Ambassador to the US: **Faida Maramuke MITIFU**

Permanent Representative to the UN, New York: **Ignace GATA MAVITA wa Lufuta**

ECONOMY

The economy of the Democratic Republic of the Congo—a nation endowed with vast potential wealth— is slowly recovering from decades of decline. Systemic corruption since independence in 1960, combined with country-wide instability and conflict that began in the mid-90s has dramatically reduced national output and government revenue, increased external debt, and resulted in the deaths of more than 5 million people from violence, famine, and disease.

With the installation of a transitional government in 2003 after peace accords, economic conditions slowly began to improve as the transitional government reopened relations with international financial institutions and international donors, and President Kabila began implementing reforms. Progress has been slow. An uncertain legal framework, corruption, and a lack of transparency in government policy are long-term problems for the mining sector and for the economy as a whole. Much economic activity still occurs in the informal sector and is not reflected in GDP data. Renewed activity in the mining sector, the source of most export income, boosted Kinshasa's fiscal position and GDP growth in recent years

The global recession cut economic growth in 2009 to less than half its 2008 level, but growth returned to around 7% per year in 2010–12. The DRC signed a Poverty Reduction and Growth Facility with the IMF in 2009 and received $12 billion in multilateral and bilateral debt relief in 2010, but the IMF at the end of 2012 suspended the last three payments under the loan facility - worth $240 million - because of concerns about the lack of transparency in mining contracts.

Labor Conditions

The minimum age for full-time employment without parental consent is 18 years. Employers may legally hire minors between the ages of 15 and 18 with the consent of a parent or guardian. Those under the age of 16 may work a maximum of four hours per day, and all minors are restricted from transporting heavy items.

Child labor, including forced child labor, was a problem throughout the country. Child labor was most common in the informal sector, particularly in mining and subsistence agriculture. For economic survival, families often encouraged children to work. According to data collected by a September 2010 UNICEF survey, approximately 42 percent of children between the ages of five and 14 were involved in child labor. The same survey indicated that children in rural areas are more likely to be involved in child labor than children in urban areas (46 percent compared to 34 percent). UNICEF considered children to be involved in labor if, during the week preceding the survey, a child five to 11 years old performed at least one hour of economic activity or at least 28 hours of domestic work, or a child 12 to 14 years old performed at least 14 hours of economic activity or at least 28 hours of domestic work.

Children were also exploited in the worst forms of child labor, many of them in exploitative work in agriculture, street vending, water selling, and domestic service. Children made up as much as 30 percent of the work force in the artisanal mining sector. In mining regions of the provinces of Katanga, Kasai Occidental, Orientale, North Kivu, and South Kivu, children performed dangerous mine work, often underground. In many areas of the country, children who were five to 12 years old broke rocks to make gravel for a small wage. The government sets regional minimum wages for all workers in private enterprise, with the highest pay scales applied to the cities of Kinshasa and Lubumbashi. In January 2009 the government established a minimum wage of 1,680 Congolese francs (approximately $3 at that time) per day. Given the continued devaluation of the currency, the minimum wage, which has never been adjusted, stood at $1.87 at year's end. While most foreign employers paid higher wages than the official minimum wage, the average worker has had to cope with falling real wages for over a decade.

The law defines different standard workweeks, ranging from 45 to 72 hours, for various jobs and prescribes rest periods and premium pay for overtime. However, the law establishes no monitoring or enforcement mechanism, and employers often did not respect these provisions. The law specifies health and safety standards. The law does not provide workers the right to remove themselves from dangerous work situations without jeopardizing their employment. Health and safety standards were not effectively enforced in either the formal and informal sectors.

Employers in the informal sector often did not respect the legally required minimum wage. The average monthly wage did not provide a decent standard of living for a worker and family. Government salaries remained low, ranging from 45,000 to 75,000 Congolese francs (approximately $50 to $83) per month, and salary arrears were common in both the civil service and public enterprises (parastatals). More than 90 percent of laborers worked in subsistence agriculture, informal commerce or mining, or other informal pursuits.

According to the World Bank, between 500,000 and two million miners worked in the informal sector nationwide and up to 16 percent of the population indirectly relied on artisanal mining. Overall estimates were notoriously challenging to verify, and determining the number of miners working specifically in the conflict areas was difficult. In 2010 the international NGO Pact estimated that between 200,000 and 250,000 miners worked in North Kivu and South Kivu. Many suffered violence from guards and SSF for illegally entering mining concession areas. Informal sector workers, who make up approximately 90 percent of the workforce, are subject to hazardous and/or exploitive working conditions.

U.S. CONGOLESE RELATIONS

The United States established diplomatic relations with the Democratic Republic of the Congo (D.R.C.) in 1960, following its independence from Belgium. Post-independence, the country saw a mix of unrest and rebellion, dictatorships, armed conflict with neighboring countries, and control of parts of the D.R.C.'s territory by neighboring countries. Following the 2001 assassination of the country's leader, a United Nations peacekeeping mission deployed throughout the country, and a transitional government took office in 2003. The D.R.C. held multiparty elections in 2006 and 2011.

Regional stability and security is dependent on durable peace in the D.R.C., due to the country's size and its location bordering nine nations. The D.R.C. faces challenges that include the destabilizing presence of armed groups in eastern D.R.C., rampant corruption, inadequate infrastructure and human resources, and a limited capacity to raise and manage revenues. U.S. relations with the D.R.C. are strong. The United States played a role in the D.R.C. peace process and has supported internal reconciliation and democratization in the country. U.S. foreign policy in the D.R.C. is focused on developing a nation that is stable and democratic, at peace with its neighbors, extends state authority across its territory, and provides for the basic needs of its citizens. The United States is the largest donor to the United Nations stabilization mission in the D.R.C.

U.S. Assistance to the Democratic Republic of the Congo

U.S. foreign assistance to the D.R.C. aims to support the security conditions and governance structures necessary for improvement of Congolese social and economic sectors and to permit extension of state authority across the country.

U.S. assistance in the D.R.C. seeks to bolster peace and stability, particularly in eastern D.R.C.; protect civilians; strengthen governance institutions and the rule of law; increase food security, agricultural productivity, and access to credit; and support economic recovery, growth, and the provision of basic social services, including access to quality health care and education.

Bilateral Economic Relations

U.S. exports to the D.R.C. include pharmaceutical products, poultry, machinery, and wheat. The top U.S. import from the D.R.C. is oil, accounting for more than 90% of all U.S. imports. The two countries have signed a bilateral investment treaty. The United States also has signed a trade and investment framework agreement with the Common Market for Eastern and Southern Africa, of which the D.R.C. is a member.

The Democratic Republic of the Congo's Membership in International Organizations

The D.R.C. and the United States belong to a number of the same international organizations, including the United Nations, International Monetary Fund, World Bank, and World Trade Organization.

Bilateral Representation

The Democratic Republic of the Congo maintains an embassy in the United States at 1726 M Street, NW, Suite 601, Washington, DC, 20036; tel. (202) 234-7690.

Principal U.S. Embassy Officials

Last Updated: 1/14/2013

KINSHASA (E) 310 AVENUE DES AVIATEURS, KINSHASAGOMBE, 011-243-81-556-0151, Fax 011-243-81-556-0169, INMARSAT Tel 881-6414-55177 (POST 1), Workweek: M-Th, 7:30–17:15 and Fri 07:30-12:30, http://kinshasa.usembassy.gov/

DCM OMS:	Adela Renna
AMB OMS:	Sheila Romine
CDC:	Kassim Sidibe
FM:	Greg Patterson
HRO:	Theresa Everett
MGT:	R. Chance Sullivan
SDO/DATT:	LTC Lee Whiteside
AMB:	James F. Entwistle
CON:	Brooke Knobel
DCM:	Eric Madison
PAO:	Ellen Masi Bienstock
GSO:	Elizabeth Harris
RSO:	Kenneth Greenblatt
AFSA:	Vincent Wing
AID:	Diana Putman
CLO:	Jacly Brock
ECON:	Kevan Higgins
EEO:	Daniel Renna
FMO:	Vincent Wing
IMO:	Papayoro, Diop
IPO:	Papayoro Diop
ISSO:	Papayoro Diop
POL:	David Alarid
State ICASS:	Fertik Elliot

TRAVEL

Consular Information Sheet

July 25, 2012

Country Description: The Democratic Republic of the Congo (Congo-Kinshasa) (DRC), located in central Africa, is the second largest country on the continent. The capital is Kinshasa. French is the official language. The country endured more than a decade of civil war that ended in 2003, but still faces continuing political and economic instability.

Smart Traveler Enrollment Program (STEP)/Embassy Locations: If you are going to live in or visit the DRC, please take the time to tell our Embassy about your trip by enrolling in the Smart Traveler Enrollment Program (STEP). If you enroll, we can keep you up-to-date with important safety and security announcements. It will also help your friends and family get in touch with you in an emergency. You should remember to keep all of your information in STEP up to date. It is important during enrollment or when you update your information to include your current phone number and email address where you can be reached in case of an emergency.

U.S. Embassy in the Democratic Republic of the Congo
310 Avenue de Aviateurs
Kinshasa
Telephone: 243-081-225-0151 (do not dial the zero when calling from abroad)

Consular Section
Avenue Dumi, opposite the Ste. Anne Residence
Kinshasa
Emergency after-hours telephone: 243-81-556-0151
Facsimile: 243-81-556-0173

Entry/Exit Requirements for U.S. Citizens: A passport, visa, and proof of yellow fever vaccination are required for entry. It is your responsibility to obtain a visa from a DRC embassy and arrange onward travel before arriving. U.S. citizens entering the country without visas have been detained and deported. Likewise, travelers arriving in the DRC without proper proof of yellow fever vaccination have been temporarily detained, fined, or had their passports confiscated. For inquiries and further information on entry/exit formalities, please visit the Congolese Immigration website (in French).

All journalists working in the DRC must obtain permission from the

Congolese Ministry of Information in Kinshasa. The U.S. Embassy recommends that journalists enter the DRC via Kinshasa. Visitors who wish to travel to any mining areas must first obtain government approval from the appropriate government agencies or ministries, a cumbersome and often time-consuming process.

On occasion, travelers to the DRC experience difficulties at the airport and other ports of entry, such as temporary detention, passport confiscation, and demands by immigration and security personnel for unofficial "fees." If confronted with harassment, please ask to contact the U.S. Embassy's Consular Section at 081-556-0151. All resident foreigners, including U.S. citizens, are required to register at the office of the Direction General of Migration (DGM) in the commune of their place of residence.

For departure from the DRC, airlines require a valid visa for all destination countries before they will issue a ticket or allow a passenger to board. All departing travelers, including U.S. officials, must pay a $50 airport exit fee, in cash. Airlines and the DGM also require that passengers have the correct entry stamp in the passport they wish to use to exit the country. Dual nationals arriving in the DRC should carefully consider which passport they use to enter the DRC. Passengers who are unable to leave the country on the passport they used to enter the DRC may not be able to continue on their travel itinerary. You may obtain additional information about visas from the Embassy of the Democratic Republic of the Congo, 1726 M Street NW, Washington, DC 20036, tel.: (202)234-7690, fax: (202) 234-2609 or the DRC's Permanent Mission to the UN, 866 United Nations Plaza, Room 511, New York, NY 10017, tel.: (212)319-8061, fax: (212)319-8232. Overseas, inquiries should be made at the nearest Congolese embassy or consulate.

The United States Department of State is unaware of any HIV/AIDS entry restrictions for visitors to or foreign residents of the DRC.

Threats to Safety and Security: Although the DRC is now more stable than it has been in the past decade, the security situation remains fluid and problematic. The Department of State's Security Environmental Threat List Report has designated the DRC as a Critical Crime and High Political Violence Post.

Visitors are encouraged to review the current Department of State Travel Warning for the DRC for additional details. Poor economic conditions, high unemployment, and the government's inability to pay its civil servants, military, and police on time often contribute to criminal activity in Kinshasa and throughout the country. Visitors are urged to remain vigilant at all times.

The country held presidential and national assembly elections on November 28, 2011, and the Congolese Supreme Court certified the provisional results of the presidential election on December 16, declaring the incumbent President Joseph Kabila the winner. The elections and their results were marred by political violence in Kinshasa and other parts of the DRC.

Both inside and outside Kinshasa, security forces are known to set up occasional roadblocks, especially after dark. Vehicles are often searched for weapons and valuables, and travelers are checked for identity papers. Security forces regularly seek bribes. If confronted with such a situation, it is best to remain courteous and calm. If detained, report the incident to the U.S. Embassy in Kinshasa as soon as possible.

The United Nations' largest peacekeeping operation in the world operates in the DRC. Known by its French acronym of MONUSCO, it has nearly 18,000 peacekeepers deployed in the country, primarily in the east. Violence, nevertheless, persists in the eastern DRC due to the presence of numerous militias and armed groups, with sporadic outbreaks occurring in North Kivu, South Kivu, and northern Katanga provinces, as well as in the Ituri, Bas-Uele and Haut-Uele Districts of Orientale province, and less frequently in Bas-Congo and Equateur provinces. A military offensive against the Lord's Resistance Army (LRA) in Haut Uele District commenced in mid-December 2008 and continues today. The LRA is still active in this area and especially areas on the border with the Central African Republic and South Sudan. The DRC military has conducted a series of operations against the Democratic Forces for the Liberation of Rwanda since January 2009.

In April 2012, members of a former rebel group that had previously been integrated into the Congolese military mutinied and heavy fighting has been reported in Masisi and Rutshuru territories as well as in Virunga National Park. As a result, over 200 people have been killed and the number of internally displaced persons has risen to 1.7 million. Moreover, renewed violence amongst foreign and Congolese rebel groups present in the northern part of North Kivu and former Rwandan militants in the southern part of the province and throughout South Kivu pose a serious and significant risk to travelers in the region. This fighting underscores the persistent insecurity arising from the activities of rebel and other armed groups operating in the Kivus, which contribute to the overall high risks and dangers associated with travel to eastern Congo.

The security situation in the DRC remains unstable and difficult to predict. All travel by Embassy personnel must be vetted for approval. Criteria used to consider approving or denying travel requests include, but are not limited to, political and violent activity, use of multiple-vehicle caravans, and armed protection by local police or MONUSCO. Travelers should take into consideration the above factors when making travel arrangements for the DRC.

Stay up to date by:

- Bookmarking our Bureau of Consular Affairs website, which contains the current Travel Warnings and Travel Alerts as well as the Worldwide Caution.

- Following us on Twitter and the Bureau of Consular Affairs page on Facebook as well.
- Downloading our free Smart Traveler iPhone App to have travel information at your fingertips.
- Calling 1-888-407-4747 toll-free within the U.S. and Canada, or a regular toll line, 1-202-501-4444, from other countries.
- Taking some time before travel to consider your personal security.

Crime: In the DRC, deteriorating economic conditions continue to foster crime, especially in urban areas. Most reported criminal incidents in Kinshasa involve crimes of opportunity, which include pick-pocketing and petty theft. The majority of the crimes are committed by "sheggehs," who are generally homeless street children. Travel in certain areas of Kinshasa, Kisangani, Lubumbashi and most other major cities is generally safe during daylight hours, but travelers are urged to be vigilant against criminal activity that targets non-Congolese, particularly in traffic jams and areas surrounding hotels, supermarkets, and restaurants. Outlying, remote areas are less secure because of high levels of criminal activity and the lack of adequate training, supervision, and salary for security forces. Individuals purporting to be security officials have detained and robbed U.S. citizens and other foreigners in Kinshasa. This type of crime occurs more frequently during the holiday season, including the Christmas and New Year's holidays and prior to the beginning of the school year.

Vehicle thefts, burglaries, and armed robberies occur throughout the country with reports of some carjackings in the North Kivu area resulting in deaths. The Embassy recommends that motorists drive with doors locked and windows closed at all times. Do not permit soldiers or police officers to enter your vehicle, and avoid getting into the vehicle of anyone purporting to be a security official. If confronted, remain courteous and calm and, if threatened, do not resist. Please report any incident to the U.S. Embassy in Kinshasa.

Laws and regulations are not administered consistently in the DRC. Legal recourse in cases of theft and robbery is limited. Valuable items should be kept at home or in a secure location.

If you use public transportation or visit busy areas, be on guard against robbery and pick-pocketing, which is a problem in all major cities in the DRC. The "sheggehs," particularly in Kinshasa, can be aggressive and persistent and many of them are involved in some type of criminal activity.

In many countries around the world, counterfeit and pirated goods are widely available. Transactions involving such products may be illegal under local law. In addition, bringing these items to the United States may result in forfeitures and/or fines.

Victims of Crime: If you are the victim of a crime abroad, you should contact the local police and the nearest U.S. embassy or consulate (see the Department of State's list of embassies and consulates). This includes the loss or theft of a U.S. passport. The embassy's consular staff may be able to help you find appropriate medical care, contact family members or friends, and explain how funds may be transferred. Although the investigation and prosecution of the crime are solely the responsibility of local authorities, consular officers can help you to understand the local criminal justice process and to find an attorney if needed.

There is no local equivalent to the "911" emergency line in the Congo.

Criminal Penalties: While in a foreign country, U.S. citizens are subject to that country's laws and regulations, which sometimes differ significantly from those in the United States and may not afford the protections available to the individual under U.S. law. Penalties for breaking the law can be more severe than in the United States for similar offenses. Engaging in sexual conduct with children or using or disseminating child pornography in a foreign country is a crime prosecutable in the United States.

While some countries will automatically notify the nearest U.S. embassy or consulate if a U.S. citizen is detained or arrested in a foreign country, that might not always be the case. To ensure that the United States is aware of your circumstances, request that the police and prison officials notify the nearest U.S. embassy or consulate as soon as you are arrested or detained overseas.

Photography: Travelers should note that photography is strictly forbidden in many public places in Kinshasa and around any public or government building in the DRC. Persons caught photographing such sites will likely be fined, have their photographic equipment confiscated and will risk detention and possible arrest.

Travel to and from Congo-Brazzaville (Republic of Congo): Passenger and VIP ferry service, known locally as "Carnot Rapide," is available to and from Kinshasa and Brazzaville. The ferries operate daily and make multiple stops throughout the day, with the last boat departing at 3PM. Prices for the ferries are: US $15 for the passenger and US $25 for the VIP ferry (Carnot Rapide). If ferry service is functioning, U.S. citizens are required to have a special exit permit from the DRC's Immigration Service and a visa from the Republic of the Congo (Congo-Brazzaville) to cross the Congo River from Kinshasa to Brazzaville.

Phone Service: In the DRC, cellular phones are the norm, as other telephone service is unreliable. Depending on the type of phone, it may be possible to purchase a SIM card locally to use a U.S.-compatible cell phone in the DRC.

Currency: U.S. currency is widely accepted in urban areas, but most vendors and banking institutions will accept only bills printed in 2006 and forward, with the large, off-center portraits that provide stronger protection against counterfeiting. In addition, bills must be in near perfect condition; even those with minor stains or small tears will be rejected. One-dollar bills are rarely accepted. You should examine U.S. bills before accepting them to ensure that they are legitimate: counterfeit currency is widely circulated. Currency exchange should be conducted only at reputable banks and not on the street.

Medical Facilities and Health Information: Medical facilities are severely limited, and medical materials are in short supply. It is wise to carry properly labeled prescription drugs and other medications; an adequate supply of prescription or over-the-counter drugs in local stores or pharmacies is generally not available. Payment for any medical services is expected in cash, in advance of treatment.

Malaria is common throughout the DRC and it is strongly advisable to consult your primary care provider concerning proper prophylaxis; outbreaks of polio, cholera, typhoid, yellow fever, the Ebola virus, measles, and hemorrhagic fever also occur. Tuberculosis is an increasingly serious health concern in the DRC. Travelers are encouraged to obtain tuberculosis testing pre-travel and repeat 8-12 weeks after return. Travelers should take appropriate precautions to prevent the spread of HIV/AIDS.

Many insect-borne illnesses are present. Follow insect precautions at all times, including using insect repellant and mosquito nets when possible. A yellow fever vaccine is required for entry into the country. Travelers are encouraged to avoid contact with non-chlorinated fresh water to prevent schistosomiasis.

There is a high risk of traveler's diarrhea and cholera throughout the country. This can be mitigated by using good judgment when choosing what food to eat and water to drink. When in restaurants, it is best to ask for bottled water and avoid ice.

Information on vaccinations and other health precautions, such as safe food and water precautions and insect bite protection, may be obtained from the Centers for Disease Control and Prevention's (CDC) hotline for international travelers at 1-877-FYI-TRIP (1-877-394-8747) or via the CDC's web site. For information about outbreaks of infectious diseases abroad, consult the World Health Organization's (WHO) web site. Further health information for travelers is available from the WHO.

Medical Insurance: The Department of State strongly urges you to consult with your medical insurance company prior to traveling abroad to confirm whether your policy applies overseas and whether it will cover emergency expenses such as a medical evacuation.

Traffic Safety and Road Conditions: While in a foreign country, you may encounter road conditions that differ significantly from those in the United States. The information below concerning the DRC is provided for general reference only, and may not be totally accurate in a particular location or circumstance.

Roads throughout the DRC are generally in poor condition, and often impassable in the rainy season. When driving in cities, keep windows up and doors locked. At roadblocks or checkpoints, documents should be shown through closed windows. In the event of an automobile accident involving bodily injury to a third party or pedestrian, do not stop to offer assistance under any circumstances. Attempts to provide assistance may further aggravate the incident, resulting in a hostile mob reaction such as stoning or beating. Proceed directly to the nearest police station or gendarmerie to report the incident.

Official motorcades pose serious risks to drivers and pedestrians in Kinshasa. If you hear sirens or see security forces announcing the approach of a motorcade, pull off the road as far as possible and extinguish your headlights. Do not attempt to move until the entire motorcade has passed; security forces will indicate when this has occurred. Failure to comply may result in arrest or vehicle damage with possible personal injury.

Use of cell phones while driving is prohibited in the DRC. As with other traffic regulations, enforcement of this law is inconsistent. Distracted drivers pose a threat in large cities, especially Kinshasa.

Any form of public transportation is unregulated, generally unsafe, and unreliable. Taxis, mini-buses, and trains are in poor mechanical condition and are often filled beyond capacity.

Drivers should stop their cars and pedestrians should stand still when passing a government installation during the raising and lowering of the Congolese flag. This ceremony occurs at roughly 7:30 a.m. and 6:00 p.m.

Aviation Safety Oversight: The U.S. Federal Aviation Administration (FAA) has assessed the government of the Democratic Republic of the Congo's Civil Aviation Authority as not being in compliance with International Civil Aviation Organization (ICAO) aviation safety standards for oversight of the DRC's air carrier operations. Further information may be found on the FAA's safety assessment page.

Civil aviation in the DRC experiences frequent air incidents and accidents; more than a dozen crashes and in-flight accidents resulted in more than 300 fatalities between 2000 and 2008. Incidents included hard landings, engine failures, collapsed landing gear, and planes veering off runways. In-country air travel schedules are unreliable and planes are frequently overloaded with passengers and/or cargo.

There have been several recent incidents causing deaths and injuries, including one on August 25, 2010 that killed all but one passenger. In April 2011, a flight crashed while landing in Kinshasa killing 32 passengers and crew. In July 2011, a flight crashed in Kisangani killing more than 70 passengers. The U.S.

Embassy prohibits official travel by U.S. government employees and certain contractors on most airlines flying domestic routes in the DRC due to safety and maintenance concerns. International flights on foreign-owned-and-operated carriers are not affected by this prohibition.

Children's Issues: The Congolese government has recently changed adoption procedures and now requires the Director General of Immigration to sign all exit visas for orphans. As a result, adoptive families may have to wait an additional two weeks or more before obtaining permission to leave with the child. For additional information, see the U.S. Dept. of State Office of Children's Issues web pages on intercountry adoption and international parental child abduction.

Travel Warning

November 21, 2012

The Department of State warns U.S. citizens of the risks of traveling to the Democratic Republic of the Congo (Congo-Kinshasa) (DRC). The Department strongly recommends you avoid all travel to the city of Goma and the province of North Kivu and all but essential travel to the province of South Kivu and the Ituri region in the province of Oriental. Because of ongoing instability and violence, the Department's ability to provide consular services to U.S. citizens in these regions of the DRC is extremely limited. This replaces the Travel Warning dated August 2, 2012, to update information on security in the Democratic Republic of the Congo. Armed groups, bandits, and elements of the Congolese military remain security concerns in eastern and northeastern DRC. These armed groups, primarily located in the North Kivu, South Kivu, and Orientale provinces, as well as the northern part of Katanga province, and the eastern part of Maniema province, are known to pillage, steal vehicles, kidnap, rape, kill, and carry out military or paramilitary operations in which civilians are indiscriminately targeted. The Lord's Resistance Army (LRA) is present near the border with Uganda, Central African Republic, and the Republic of South Sudan. The UN Organization Stabilization Mission in the DRC (MONUSCO) continues to assist the Congolese government with the protection of civilians and efforts to combat armed groups.

The region has been the scene of violent clashes that have resulted in the displacement of more than 1.9 million civilians since the start of the Rwandan conflict in 1994. In April 2012, members of a rebel group that previously had been integrated into the Congolese military mutinied and heavy fighting has been reported in Massisi and Ruthshuru territories as well as in Virunga National Park. In November 2012, members of this group captured several towns north of Goma and Goma itself, the provincial capital of North Kivu province. As a result, hundreds of people have been killed and the number of internally displaced persons has risen to 1.7 million. Moreover, violence amongst foreign and Congolese rebel groups present in the northern part of North Kivu and former Rwandan militants in the southern part of the province and throughout South Kivu pose a serious and significant risk to travelers in the region. This fighting underscores the persistent insecurity arising from activities of rebel and other armed groups operating in the Kivus, which contribute to the overall high risks and dangers associated with travel to eastern Congo. The U.S. Embassy in Kinshasa currently does not allow travel by official personnel to North Kivu. Travel to South Kivu and the Ituri region of Oriental province by Embassy personnel is permitted only under exceptional circumstances.

Travelers are frequently detained and questioned by poorly disciplined security forces at numerous official and unofficial roadblocks and border crossings throughout the country. Requests for bribes in such instances are extremely common, and security forces have occasionally injured or killed people who refuse to pay. In the past year, several U.S. citizens were illegally detained by government forces. Very poor infrastructure (road and air) makes the provision of consular services difficult outside of Kinshasa.

Kinshasa has a critical crime threat level, and U.S. citizens continue to be the victims of serious crimes, including armed robbery by groups posing as law enforcement officials in both urban and rural areas, especially after nightfall. Avoid walking alone and displaying cash and other personal property of value. Avoid taking photos in public, especially of government buildings and the airport (which are viewed as places of national security), police stations, the presidential palace, border crossings, and along the river, since doing so may lead to arrest.

Lock vehicle doors and keep windows closed when driving. You should not stop at the scene of an accident or at intersections where people have gathered, as mobs can develop quickly. In areas where the roads are in poor condition and the speed limit is minimal, be wary of gangs of street children who may approach your car, open your door, and steal your belongings. Roadblocks are often found throughout the country, especially near government buildings and installations in Kinshasa, and should be avoided when possible. If stopped at a roadblock, keep doors locked and crack the window in order to communicate.

Official Congolese motorcades pose hazards to motorists and pedestrians. Drivers should pull over to the far side of the road when sirens or security forces announce their presence. You should not take photographs of motorcades. Proceed only when security forces permit you to do so.

There is no reliable public transportation system in the DRC. Overcrowded vans and taxis, which often do not meet western safety standards, serve as public transportation in Kinshasa. Few independent taxis are available, operating largely out of the big hotels, and most do not meet safety standards. You should avoid all travel by public transportation, and hire private transport from a reliable source.

The DRC has few viable roads or railways, but does have several major waterways. Boat transport is widely used; however, the vessels are often overloaded or badly maintained, and accidents are commonplace. There were multiple accidents in 2011 on both rivers and lakes resulting in hundreds of fatalities.

Public health concerns pose a hazard to U.S. citizen travelers due to outbreaks of deadly viruses and other diseases, which can occur without warning and often without swift reporting by local health authorities. Information on personal protection for international travelers, including children, can be found on the Centers for Disease Control (CDC) website. Travelers are required to carry evidence of yellow fever vaccination in order to enter the DRC. Health officials at entry points, such as the airport in Kinshasa, will check for proof of vaccination. If you do not have evidence of a yellow fever vaccination, you may be denied entry or required to pay a fine. Malaria is common throughout the DRC and prophylaxis is recommended.

Due to the recent outbreak of Wild Polio Virus and measles in the DRC, you should update your polio and measles vaccinations, if necessary, and refer to the CDC for additional guidance. Due to the high levels of air borne irritants (i.e., dust, burning trash, debris, etc.) individuals with respiratory illnesses should carry all their necessary medications and equipment with adaptors.

There is a high risk of traveler's diarrhea and cholera throughout the country. This can be prevented by using good judgment when choosing what food to eat and water to drink. When in restaurants, it is best to ask for bottled water and avoid ice.

Due to the immense size of the country, the density of the Congo River rainforest, the terrible state of the roads, and the poor security situation, the only way to get around the country quickly is by plane. Domestic air travel on Congolese or other local airlines in the DRC is not recommended. The U.S. Federal Aviation Administration has assessed the government of the DRC as not being compliant with international standards for aviation safety oversight.

There have been several recent incidents causing deaths and injuries, including one on August 25, 2010, that killed all but one passenger. In April 2011, a United Nations operated flight crashed while landing in Kinshasa, killing 32 passengers and crew. In July 2011, a Boeing 737 crashed in Kisangani, killing more than 70 passengers. Crashes of private aircraft are even more common. The U.S. Embassy has prohibited official travel by U.S. government employees and certain contractors on most airlines flying domestic routes in the DRC due to safety and maintenance concerns. International flights on foreign-owned-and-operated carriers are not affected by this prohibition.

You should avoid all public demonstrations and areas where crowds have gathered because even peaceful events can become violent, and even deadly. You should exercise caution at all times, and closely monitor local and international news from reliable sources. Radio Okapi broadcasts in French on 103.5 FM at 0700, 0800, 1200, and 1800, and provides updates throughout the day. English-language news can be found on BBC at 92.6 FM. In emergencies, the Belgian Embassy operates a French-language radio broadcast system at FM 98.8. Changes in security conditions may occasionally restrict the travel of U.S. Mission personnel.

The U.S. Embassy in Kinshasa strongly encourages U.S. citizens who travel to or remain in the DRC despite this Travel Warning to enroll in the Smart Traveler Enrollment Program (STEP) so you can receive the most up-to-date security information.

You should remember to keep all of your information in STEP current. It is important to include your current phone number and email address where you can be reached in case of an emergency.

The U.S. Embassy is located at 310 Avenue des Aviateurs; the Consular Section entrance is located on Avenue Dumi, opposite Saint Anne's church. The Embassy's telephone number, including for after-hours emergencies, is 243-81-556-0151; callers within the DRC should dial 081-556-0151. All telephone lines in the DRC, cellular as well as landlines, are unreliable. Click here to visit the Embassy website.

For further information, consult the Department of State's Country Specific Information for Democratic Republic of the Congo and the current Worldwide Caution, available on the Bureau of Consular Affairs Internet website. Current information on safety and security can also be obtained by calling 1-888-407-4747 toll-free in the United States and Canada or, a regular toll line at-1-202-501-4444 for callers from other countries. These numbers are available from 8:00 a.m. to 8:00 p.m. Eastern Time, Monday through Friday (except U.S. federal holidays). Stay up to date by bookmarking our Bureau of Consular Affairs website, which contains the current Travel Warnings and Travel Alerts as well as the Worldwide Caution. Follow us on Twitter and the Bureau of Consular Affairs page on Facebook as well. You can also download our free Smart Traveler App, available through iTunes and the Android market to have travel information at your fingertips.

Intercountry Adoption

May 2012

The information in this section has been edited from the latest report available as of February 2013 from the State Department Bureau of Consular Affairs, Office of Overseas Citizens Services. For more information, please read the *Intercountry Adoption* section of this book and review current reports online at http://adoption.state.gov.

The Democratic Republic of the Congo is not party to the Hague Convention on Protection of Children and Co-operation in Respect of Intercountry Adoption (Hague Adoption Convention). Intercountry adoptions of children from non-Hague countries are processed in accordance with 8 Code of Federal Regulations, Section 204.3 as it relates to orphans as defined under the Immigration and Nationality Act, Section 101(b)(1)(F).

Who Can Adopt? To bring an adopted child to the United States from the Democratic Republic of the Congo, you must meet eligibility and suitability requirements. The U.S. Department of Homeland Security, U.S. Citizenship and Immigration Services (USCIS) determines Who Can Adopt under U.S. immigration law. Additionally, a child must meet the definition of orphan under U.S. law in order to be eligible to immigrate to the United States on an IR-3 or IR-4 immigrant visa.

Residency: No requirements.

Age of Adopting Parents: Prospective adoptive parents must be at least 15 years older than the intended adoptee. This "15-year rule" may be waived if the adoptee is a biological child of one of the parents. There is no age limit for adopting parents.

Marriage: Adopting parents may be married, single, widowed or divorced. Persons in the last three groups may not adopt a child of the opposite sex unless the court grants an exemption. Couples should have been married for at least five years.

Income: No requirements.

Other: Gays and lesbians or same-sex couples are not permitted to adopt by the Democratic Republic of the Congo. Any person who has a prior history of child abuse is also not permitted to adopt. No couple may adopt more than three children unless a subsequent prospective adoptee is the biological child of one of the parents. Parents may not already have more than two children when they adopt unless the child they are adopting is a sibling of one of their children. No adoptive parent may marry the adopted child. There is no medical ineligibility for adoptive parents.

Who Can Be Adopted? In addition to U.S. immigration requirements, the Democratic Republic of the Congo has specific requirements that a child must meet in order to be eligible for adoption.

Relinquishment: Parents must give written consent ("autorisation parentale").

Abandonment: Social Services must provide a PV Tutelage Report ("Proces-Verbal de Constat d'Abandon d'un Enfant") in all cases of abandonment, including an absence of parents due to loss, separation, death, desertion, or disappearance of the biological parents.

Age of Adoptive Child: There is no age limit for prospective adoptees. Adoptees fifteen years and older must give consent to the adoption. Please note, however, that in order for a child to meet the definition of orphan under U.S. immigration law, a Form I-600 petition must be filed while the child is under the age of 16 (or under the age of 18 if adopted, or to be adopted, together with a sibling under the age of 16).

Sibling Adoptions: No known requirements.

Special Needs or Medical Conditions: No known requirements.

Waiting Period or Foster Care: None

Democratic Republic of Congo's Adoption Authority: Ministry of Justice. While the Ministry of Justice has jurisdiction over adoption, several ministries in the Congolese government participate in enforcing adoption law and policies. Individual cases are handled by the Tribunal pour Enfants in the region where a prospective adoptive child resides. Attorneys have current contacts at appropriate courts. The local "commune" or township and its trustee council create the Abandonment document, designate the abandoned child as a Ward of the State, and consign the child to foster care or an orphanage. The Ministry of Social Affairs is charged with the role of protection of "vulnerable children," which can impact adoption policies. The Direction Generale d'Immigration (DGM) controls the departure of children from the Democratic Republic of the Congo.

The Process: The recommended first step in adopting a child from the Democratic Republic of the Congo is to decide whether or not to use a licensed adoption service provider in the United States that can help you with your adoption. Adoption service providers must be licensed by the U.S. state in which they operate.

There are no adoption agencies in Democratic Republic of the Congo, however, orphanages must be licensed or accredited by the Congolese government. It is customary and accepted practice to engage Congolese lawyers to carry out adoption proceedings. Lawyers are automatically accredited by the government by virtue of their professional training. The U.S. Embassy in Kinshasa maintains a list of attorneys on its website who have expressed a willingness to work with U.S. citizens. This list does not imply an endorsement of specific attorneys by the Embassy.

In order to adopt a child from the Democratic Republic of the Congo; you will need to meet the requirements of the government of the Democratic Republic of the Congo and U.S. immigration law. You must submit an application to be found eligible to adopt with the Ministry of Justice.

Prospective adoptive parents need to seek adoption through a lawyer directly with the court. There are no application forms to fill out. Prospective Adoptive Parents should know that, in the case of children who are Wards of the State, the "Guardianship Council" of the local government must first release the child for adoption.

You may also file an I-600A, Application for Advance Processing of an Orphan Petition with U.S. Department of Homeland Security's U.S. Citizenship and Immigration Services to be found eligible and suitable to adopt.

If you are eligible to adopt, and a child is available for intercountry adoption, the central adoption authority or other authorized entity in the Democratic Republic of the Congo will provide you with a referral. Each family must decide for itself whether or not it will be able to meet the needs of and provide a permanent home for a particular child. If prospective adoptive parents choose the adoptive child at an orphanage, they do so according to their own criteria (age, gender, etc.).

Role of the Adoption Authority: Although the Ministry of Justice has jurisdiction over adoptions, individual cases are handled by the Tribunal pour Enfants in the region where a prospective adoptive child resides. Mailing addresses do not exist as there is no mail service. Attorneys have current contacts at appropriate courts.

Role of the Court: The court requires consent to the adoption before granting a judgment. Biological parents, or appointed guardians, must give their consent, if applicable. If no family members or guardians are identified, the court will determine consent. Any child over the age of 15 must give his or her own consent.

After obtaining the proper consent, the prospective adoptive parents request a hearing in open court at the Tribunal pour Enfants in the area where the child resides. Parents must submit copies of their birth certificates and the birth certificate of the prospective adoptee. The court will require proof that any and all interested family members of the child have been informed of the adoption and have received notice of the court hearing. After the initial hearing, the court conducts an investigation to determine that all conditions for placement or final adoption have been met and that all documents are legitimate.

Once the investigation is completed and all requirements have been satisfied, the court will issue a judgment of adoption. The date of the adoption will be retroactive to the date of the first court appearance. The adopted child's name on the judgment will incorporate his/her original name along with the newly adopted family name, but adoptive parents must ensure that the names on the local and U.S. documents match. At the time of adoption, choices concerning Congolese citizenship will be made by the adoptive parent (in the case of minors) or by the adoptee (if 18 years or older). The adoptive parents must register the judgment at the local city hall or magistrate within one month or the adoption is null and void. This is done either where the adoptive parents live (if they live in the Democratic Republic of the Congo) or where the child resides (if the adoptive parents do not live in the Democratic Republic of the Congo).

Role of Adoption Agencies: There are no local adoption agencies in Democratic Republic of the Congo, however, many orphanages are licensed or accredited by the Congolese government. It is customary and accepted practice to engage Congolese lawyers to carry out adoption proceedings. Lawyers are automatically accredited by the government by virtue of their professional training. The U.S. Embassy in Kinshasa maintains a list of attorneys on its web site who have expressed a willingness to work with U.S. citizens. This list does not imply an endorsement of specific attorneys by the Embassy.

Adoption Application: Prospective parents apply for permission to adopt by sending a letter to the Tribunal pour Enfants in the region where the child resides. Postal delivery is not available, so a letter should be sent by messenger or delivered by hand. There is no application form. The Judge from the Tribunal pour Enfants approves foreign adoptive parents for adoption.

Time Frame: It can take from a minimum of three months to approximately one year to complete the adoption process from child placement to visa issuance, although some cases can take considerably longer.

Adoption Fees: Court fees for an adoption case range up to approximately $300. Lawyer fees can range from $5,000-6,000. Fees can be kept to a minimum if, prior to the first consultation, adopting parents secure any required documents such as birth, death, marriage and relevant court records on their own. In addition to these fees, prospective adoptive parents may be expected to pay for the care and feeding of the child after the adoption has concluded and before the U.S. immigrant visa is issued, as well as all fees for passport issuance and exit permits.

Documents Required: The adopting parents must submit copies of their own birth certificates, the birth certificate of the prospective adoptive child, police certificates from the adoptive parents' place of birth, and attestations of good conduct from their city hall or local embassy or consulate. Additional documents may be requested.

Bringing Your Child Home: Once your adoption is complete (or you have obtained legal custody of the child), there are a few more steps to take before you can head home. Specifically, you need to apply for several documents for your child before he or she can travel to the United States, such as a birth certificate, a passport or travel document for your child from the country in which he or she was born, and a U.S. Immigration Visa. For detailed and updated information on how to obtain these documents, review the *Intercountry Adoption* section in this publication and visit the U.S. Department of State Intercountry Adoption website at http://adoption.state.gov.

Child Citizenship Act: For adoptions finalized abroad, the Child Citizenship Act of 2000 allows your new child to acquire American citizenship automatically when he or she enters the United States as lawful permanent residents. For adoptions finalized in the United States, the Child Citizenship Act of 2000 allows your new child to acquire American citizenship automatically when the court in the United States issues the final adoption decree. To learn more, review the *Intercountry Adoption* section in this publication and visit the U.S. Department of State Intercountry Adoption website at http://adoption.state.gov.

After Adoption: The Democratic Republic of the Congo does not have any post-adoption requirements.

U.S. Embassy in the Democratic Republic of the Congo
310, Avenue des Aviateurs
Kinshasa, Gombe
République Démocratique du Congo
Tel: (243) 81 884-6623 or (243) 81 556-0151
Email: KinshasaAdoptions@state.gov
Website: Kinshasa.usembassy.gov

Democratic Republic of the Congo's Adoption Authority: The Ministry of Justice has jurisdiction over adoption; however, individual cases are handled by the Tribunal pour Enfants in the region where a prospective adoptive child resides. Attorneys have current contacts at appropriate courts.

The local "commune" or township and its trustee council generally create the Abandonment document and often designate an abandoned child as a Ward of the State, and consign the child to foster care or an orphanage. The Ministry of Social Affairs has a more centralized role in the protection of "vulnerable children." The Direction Generale d'Immigration (DGM) controls the departure of children from the Democratic Republic of the Congo.

Direction Generale de Migration
65, Boulevard du 30 Juin
Commune de la Gombe
Ville de Kinshasa, R.D.Congo
Tel: +243 81 030 07 55
Email: dgm@dgm.cd or dgmetatmajor@yahoo.fr
Internet: www.dgm.cd

Division of Urbaine des Affaires Sociale
33 Avenue Busudjano
Quartier Ancien Combattant
Commune de Kasavubu
Ville de Kinshasa, R.D. Congo
Tel: +243 82 209 7748

Tribunal Pour Enfants
Terrain Saint Therese
Quartier 5 Commune de N'Djili
Ville de Kinshasa, R.D. Congo

Embassy of the Democratic Republic of the Congo
1726 M Street, N.W.
Washington, D.C. 20036
Tel: (202) 234-7690

Office of Children's Issues
U.S. Department of State
2201 C Street, NW
SA-29
Washington, DC 20520
Tel: 1-888-407-4747
E-mail: AskCI@state.gov
http://adoption.state.gov

For questions about immigration procedures, call the National Customer Service Center (NCSC) at 1-800-375-5283 (TTY 1-800-767-1833).

Release of Adopted Children from Orphanages
March 5, 2012

Prospective adoptive parents considering adopting in the Democratic Republic of the Congo (DRC) should be aware that the U.S. Embassy has received reports that a number of legally adopted children, including those with valid immigration visas to the United States, have not been promptly released by the orphanages to their new adoptive U.S. citizen parents or their legal representatives. In most cases, the orphanages have eventually released the children into the care of their adoptive parents or legal representatives. Police intervention has been reported in some cases at the request of both orphanages and adoptive parents. The U.S. Embassy has limited authority to intervene in these situations, but encourages adoptive parents in such a situation to notify the Consular Section.

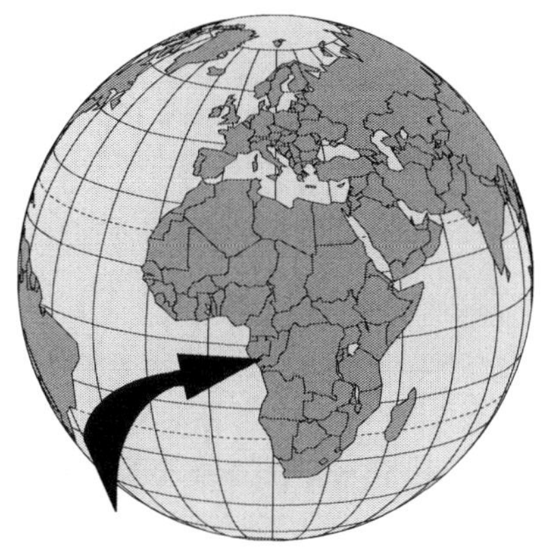

CONGO

Compiled from publications that were available as of February 2013 from the U.S. Department of State, the U.S. Department of Commerce, and the Central Intelligence Agency (CIA). See the introduction to this set for explanatory notes.

Official Name:
Republic of the Congo

PROFILE

Geography

Area: total: 342,000 sq km; country comparison to the world: 64; land: 341,500 sq km; water: 500 sq km

Major cities: Brazzaville (capital) 1.292 million (2009)

Climate: tropical; rainy season (March to June); dry season (June to October); persistent high temperatures and humidity; particularly enervating climate astride the Equator

Terrain: coastal plain, southern basin, central plateau, northern basin

People

Nationality: noun: Congolese (singular and plural); adjective: Congolese or Congo

Population: 4,366,266 (July 2012 est.)

Population growth rate: 2.849% (2012 est.)

Ethnic groups: Kongo 48%, Sangha 20%, M'Bochi 12%, Teke 17%, Europeans and other 3%

Religions: Christian 50%, animist 48%, Muslim 2%

Languages: French (official), Lingala and Monokutuba (lingua franca trade languages), many local languages and dialects (of which Kikongo is the most widespread)

Literacy: definition: age 15 and over can read and write; total population: 83.8%; male: 89.6%; female: 78.4% (2003 est.)

Health: life expectancy at birth: total population: 55.27 years; male: 53.95 years; female: 56.62 years (2012 est.); Infant mortality rate: total: 74.22 deaths/1,000 live births; male: 79.58 deaths/1,000 live births; female: 68.7 deaths/1,000 live births (2012 est.)

Unemployment rate: NA%

Work force: 1.514 million (2007)

Government

Type: republic

Independence: 15 August 1960

Constitution: approved by referendum 20 January 2002

Political subdivisions: 10 regions (regions, singular—region) and 1 commune; Bouenza, Brazzaville, Cuvette, Cuvette-Ouest, Kouilou, Lekoumou, Likouala, Niari, Plateaux, Pool, Sangha

Suffrage: 18 years of age; universal

Economy

GDP (purchasing power parity): $19.27 billion (2012 est.); $18.48 billion (2011 est.); $17.69 billion (2010 est.); $16.27 billion (2009 est.)

GDP real growth rate: 4.9% (2012 est.); 4.5% (2011 est.); 8.8% (2010 est.); 7.5% (2009 est.)

GDP per capita (PPP): $4,700 (2012 est.); $4,600 (2011 est.); $4,600 (2010 est.); $4,300 (2009 est.)

Natural resources: petroleum, timber, potash, lead, zinc, uranium, copper, phosphates, gold, magnesium, natural gas, hydropower

Agriculture products: cassava (tapioca), sugar, rice, corn, peanuts, vegetables, coffee, cocoa; forest products

Industries: petroleum extraction, cement, lumber, brewing, sugar, palm oil, soap, flour, cigarettes

Exports: $12.35 billion (2012 est.); $12.38 billion (2011 est.); $9.621 billion (2010 est.)

Exports—commodities: petroleum, lumber, plywood, sugar, cocoa, coffee, diamonds

Exports—partners: China 37.9%, US 20%, Australia 6.2%, France 6%, Spain 4.8%, Italy 4.3%, Netherlands 4.3% (2011)

Imports: $4.751 billion (2012 est.); $4.917 billion (2011 est.); $3.186 billion (2010 est.)

Imports—commodities: capital equipment, construction materials, foodstuffs

Imports—partners: France 17.3%, China 12.6%, India 9.5%, Italy 7.5%, Brazil 7.3%, US 5.8% (2011)

Debt—external: $4.225 billion (31 December 2012 est.); $4.955 billion (31 December 2011 est.)

Exchange rates: Cooperation Financiere en Afrique Centrale francs (XAF) per US dollar; 511.4 (2012 est.); 471.87 (2011 est.); 495.28 (2010 est.); 472.19 (2009); 447.81 (2008); 483.6 (2007)

PEOPLE

Congo's sparse population is concentrated in the southwestern portion of the country, leaving the vast areas of tropical jungle in the north virtually uninhabited. Thus, Congo is one of the most urbanized countries in Africa, with at least 70% of its total population living in Brazzaville, Pointe-Noire, or along the 332-mile railway that connects them.

Before the 1997 war, about 9,000 Europeans and other non-Africans lived in Congo, most of whom were French. Only a fraction of this number remains. The number of American citizens residing in Congo typically hovers around 300.

National/Racial/Ethnic Minorities

According to local NGOs, Pygmies were severely marginalized in regard to employment, health services, and education, in part due to their isolation in remote areas and their different cultural norms. Pygmies were often considered socially inferior and had little political voice; however, in recent years several Pygmy rights groups have developed programs to overcome this. Many Pygmies were not aware of the concept of voting and had minimal ability to influence government decisions affecting their interests.

The 2007 national census estimated the indigenous population to be 2 percent of the general population, equivalent to an estimated 74,000 persons.

Religion

According to the Government Information Bureau, nearly 80 percent of the population practices Buddhism. There are approximately 30,000 Roman Catholics (of whom over half are foreign domestic workers and expatriates residing in Macau) and more than 5,000 Protestants. Smaller religious groups include Baha'is (estimated at 2,500 persons); Muslims (estimated at 400 persons); and a small number of Falun Gong practitioners.

There are approximately 40 Buddhist temples, as well as dozens of village temples and houses dedicated to Buddhist deities; 30 Taoist temples; three Catholic cathedrals, 18 Catholic churches and 56 Catholic chapels within diocesan buildings; approximately 76 Protestant churches; four Baha'i centers; and one mosque.

Many Protestant denominations are represented, including Baptist, Anglican, Lutheran, Presbyterian, Methodist, and Pentecostal churches. There are also evangelical denominations and independent local churches.

An estimated 76 Protestant churches with 4,000 members conduct services in Chinese; approximately 5,000 worshippers attend every Sunday. An estimated 500 Protestants attend services conducted in foreign languages.

HISTORY

First inhabited by indigenous people, Congo was later settled by Bantu groups that also occupied parts of present-day Angola, Gabon, and Democratic Republic of the Congo (formerly Zaire), forming the basis for ethnic affinities and rivalries among those states. Several Bantu kingdoms--notably those of the Kongo, the Loango, and the Teke--built trade links leading into the Congo River basin. The first European contacts came in the late 15th century, and commercial relationships were quickly established with the kingdoms--trading for slaves captured in the interior. The coastal area was a major source for the transatlantic slave trade, and when that commerce ended in the early 19th century, the power of the Bantu kingdoms eroded. The area came under French sovereignty in the 1880s. Pierre Savorgnon de Brazza, a French empire builder, competed with agents of Belgian King Leopold's International Congo Association (later Zaire) for control of the Congo River basin. Between 1882 and 1891, treaties were secured with all the main local rulers on the river's right bank, placing their lands under French protection. In 1908, France organized French Equatorial Africa (AEF), comprising its colonies of Middle Congo (modern Congo), Gabon, Chad, and Oubangui-Chari (modern Central African Republic). Brazzaville was selected as the federal capital.

Economic development during the first 50 years of colonial rule in Congo centered on natural resource extraction by private companies. In 1924-34, the Congo-Ocean Railway (CFCO) was built at a considerable human and financial cost, opening the way for growth of the ocean port of Pointe-Noire and towns along its route.

During World War II, the AEF administration sided with Charles DeGaulle, and Brazzaville became the symbolic capital of Free France during 1940-43. The Brazzaville Conference of 1944 heralded a period of major reform in French colonial policy, including the abolition of forced labor, granting of French citizenship to colonial subjects, decentralization of certain powers, and election of local advisory assemblies. Congo benefited from the postwar expansion of colonial administrative and infrastructure spending as a result of its central geographic location within AEF and the federal capital at Brazzaville.

The Loi Cadre (framework law) of 1956 ended dual voting roles and provided for partial self-government for the individual overseas territories. Ethnic rivalries then produced sharp struggles among the emerging Congolese political parties and sparked severe riots in Brazzaville in 1959. After the September 1958 referendum approving the new French Constitution, AEF was dissolved. Its four territories became autonomous members of the French Community, and Middle Congo was renamed the

Congo Republic. Formal independence was granted in August 1960. Congo's first President was Fulbert Youlou, a former Catholic priest from the Pool region in the southeast. He rose to political prominence after 1956, and was narrowly elected President by the National Assembly at independence. Youlou's 3 years in power were marked by ethnic tensions and political rivalry. In August 1963, Youlou was overthrown in a 3-day popular uprising (Les Trois Glorieuses) led by labor elements and joined by rival political parties. All members of the Youlou government were arrested or removed from office.

The Congolese military took charge of the country briefly and installed a civilian provisional government headed by Alphonse Massamba-Debat. Under the 1963 constitution, Massamba-Debat was elected President for a 5-year term and named Pascal Lissouba to serve as Prime Minister. President Massamba-Debat's term ended abruptly in August 1968, when Capt. Marien Ngouabi and other army officers toppled the government in a coup. After a period of consolidation under the newly formed National Revolutionary Council, Major Ngouabi assumed the presidency on December 31, 1968. One year later, President Ngouabi proclaimed Congo to be Africa's first "people's republic" and announced the decision of the National Revolutionary Movement to change its name to the Congolese Labor Party (PCT).

On March 18, 1977, President Ngouabi was assassinated. Although the persons accused of shooting Ngouabi were tried and some of them executed, the motivation behind the assassination remains unclear. An 11-member Military Committee of the Party (CMP) was named to head an interim government with Colonel (later General) Joachim Yhomby-Opango to serve as President of the Republic. Accused of corruption and deviation from party directives, Yhomby-Opango was removed from office on February 5, 1979, by the Central Committee of the PCT, which then simultaneously designated Vice President and Defense Minister Col. Denis Sassou-Nguesso as interim President. The Central Committee directed Sassou-Nguesso to take charge of preparations for the Third Extraordinary Congress of the PCT, which proceeded to elect him President of the Central Committee and President of the Republic. Under a congressional resolution, Yhomby-Opango was stripped of all powers, rank, and possessions and placed under arrest to await trial for high treason. He was released from house arrest in late 1984 and ordered back to his native village of Owando.

After 2 decades of turbulent politics bolstered by Marxist-Leninist rhetoric, and with the collapse of the Soviet Union, the Congolese gradually moderated their economic and political views to the point that, in 1992, Congo completed a transition to multi-party democracy. Ending a long history of one-party Marxist rule, a specific agenda for this transition was laid out during Congo's national conference of 1991 and culminated in August 1992 with multi-party presidential elections. Sassou-Nguesso conceded defeat and Congo's new President, Prof. Pascal Lissouba, was inaugurated on August 31, 1992.

Congolese democracy experienced severe trials in 1993 and early 1994. President Lissouba dissolved the National Assembly in November 1992, calling for new elections in May 1993. The results of those elections were disputed, touching off violent civil unrest in June and again in November. In February 1994, all parties accepted the decisions of an international board of arbiters, and the risk of large-scale insurrection subsided.

Congo's democratic progress was derailed in 1997. As presidential elections scheduled for July 1997 approached, tensions between the Lissouba and Sassou-Nguesso camps mounted. When President Lissouba's government forces surrounded Sassou-Nguesso's compound in Brazzaville with armored vehicles on June 5, Sassou-Nguesso ordered his militia to resist. Thus began a 4-month conflict that destroyed or damaged much of Brazzaville. In early October, Angolan troops invaded Congo on the side of Sassou-Nguesso and, in mid-October, the Lissouba government fell. Soon thereafter, Sassou-Nguesso declared himself President and named a 33-member government.

In January 1998, the Sassou-Nguesso regime held a National Forum for Reconciliation to determine the nature and duration of the transition period. The forum, tightly controlled by the government, decided elections should be held in about 3 years, elected a transition advisory legislature, and announced that a constitutional convention would finalize a draft constitution. However, the eruption in late 1998 of fighting between Sassou-Nguesso's government forces and a pro-Lissouba and pro-Kolelas armed opposition disrupted the transition to democracy. This new violence also closed the economically vital Brazzaville-Pointe Noire railroad, caused great destruction and loss of life in southern Brazzaville and in the Pool, Bouenza, and Niari regions, and displaced hundreds of thousands of persons. In November and December 1999, the government signed agreements with representatives of many, though not all, of the rebel groups.

The December accord, mediated by President Omar Bongo of Gabon, called for follow-on, inclusive political negotiations between the government and the opposition. During the years 2000-2001, Sassou-Nguesso's government conducted a national dialogue (Dialogue Sans Exclusif), in which the opposition parties and the government agreed to continue on the path to peace. Ex-President Lissouba and ex-Prime Minister Kolelas refused to agree and were exiled. They were tried in absentia and convicted in Brazzaville of charges ranging from treason to misappropriation of government funds. Ex-militiamen were granted amnesty, and many were provided micro-loans to aid their reintegration into civil society. Not all opposition members participated. One group, referred to as "Ninjas," actively opposed the government in a low-level guerrilla war in the Pool region of the country. Other members of opposition parties have returned and have opted to participate to some degree in political life.

A new constitution was drafted in 2001, approved by the provisional legislature (National Transition Council), and approved by the people of Congo in a national referendum in January 2002. Presidential elections were held in March 2002, and Sassou-Nguesso was declared the winner. Legislative elections were held in May and June 2002. In March 2003, the government signed a peace accord with the Ninjas, and the country has remained stable and calm since the signing. President Sassou-Nguesso allowed Kolelas to return to Congo for his wife's funeral in October 2005 and subsequently asked that parliament grant Kolelas amnesty. Parliament complied with Sassou-Nguesso's request in December 2005.

In 2007, Sassou-Nguesso announced he would allow the return of former president Pascal Lissouba, along with a pardon for the 2001 in absentia conviction for "economic crimes" for which Lissouba had been sentenced to 30 years. Although a general amnesty has been granted to Lissouba since December 2009, he has not yet returned to the country. Now a health condition requiring regular treatment not available in Brazzaville seems to be the only real obstacle to his return. Former Prime Minister Joachim Yhombi-Opango returned to the country in August 2007, after the Council of Ministers granted him amnesty in May for a 2001 conviction in absentia for allegedly improperly selling the country's oil while in office. Legislative elections were held in June and August 2007 and were widely viewed as disorganized and marred by irregularities, with low voter turnout. Presidential elections were held in July 2009, and Sassou-Nguesso was declared the winner. Legislative elections are slated for 2012.

GOVERNMENT AND POLITICAL CONDITIONS

The Republic of the Congo is a parliamentary republic in which most of the decision-making authority and political power is vested in the president and his administration, although the method by which internal decision-making occurs is unclear. Denis Sassou-Nguesso was reelected president in 2009 with 78 percent of the vote, but the validity of these figures is questioned. The 2009 election was peaceful, and the African Union declared the elections to have been free and fair; however, opposition candidates and nongovernmental organizations (NGOs) cited irregularities. While the country has a multiparty political system, members of the president's Congolese Labor Party (PCT) occupy most senior government positions.

Recent Elections

Denis Sassou-Nguesso was reelected president in the 2009 election with a claimed 78 percent of the vote. Officially, 66 percent of eligible voters participated in the election, although the opposition estimated the turnout to be much lower. While the election was peaceful, opposition candidates and NGOs criticized the election for irregularities, such as gross manipulation of voter lists and discrepancies between the officially reported rates of voter participation and those observed by independent election observers. The African Union declared the elections free and fair.

On October 9, 2011, the country held a midterm senatorial election for one half of the senate's 72 seats. The president's ruling party—Parti Congolais du Travail (PCT)—and its allies won 28 seats, the opposition won three seats, and five independents were elected. Unlike the National Assembly and presidential elections, the senatorial elections are conducted through indirect suffrage.

Political Parties: Major political parties included the ruling PCT, the Pan-African Union for Social Development, the Congolese Movement for Democracy and Integrated Development, the Union for Democracy and the Republic, the Rally for Democracy and Social Progress, and the Union for Progress. Opposition parties encountered government restrictions, particularly with regard to the right to organize. Opposition parties were restricted from organizing before, during, and after the 2009 presidential election.

Following that election and the August 17, 2011 selection of three new ministers, the government included high-ranking politicians from northern ethnic tribes as well as representatives from other regions and ethnicities.

Participation of Women and Minorities: After the October Senate elections, there were nine women in the 72-seat Senate and nine women in the 137-seat National Assembly. There were five women in the 37-member cabinet.

Many indigenous persons—largely Pygmies—were excluded from the political process due to their isolation in remote areas, lack of registration, cultural barriers, and stigmatization by the majority Bantu population (see section 6).

However, indigenous rights were strengthened by the parliament's passage of an indigenous persons rights protection bill in December 2010, which became law on February 25 upon President Sassou-Nguesso's signature of the legislation.

Principal Government Officials

Last Updated: 1/31/2013

Pres.: **Denis SASSOU-Nguesso**

Min. of State, Min. of Transport, Civil Aviation, & Maritime Shipping: **Isidore MVOUBA**

Min. of State, Min. of Industrial Development & Private Sector Promotion: **Rodolphe ADADA**

Min. of State, Min. of Justice & Human Rights & Keeper of the Seals: **Aime Emmanuel YOKA**

Min. of State, Min. of Labor & Social Security: **Florent TSIBA**

Min. of State, Min. of Planning, Economy, Land Reform, & Integration: **Pierre MOUSSA**

Min. at the Presidency in Charge of National Defense, Veterans, & Disabled War Veterans: **Charles Zacharie BOWAO**

Min. at the Presidency in Charge of Special Economic Zones: **Alain Akouala ATIPAULT**

Min. of Agriculture & Livestock: **Rigobert MABOUNDOU**

Min. of Civic Education & Youth: **Anatole Collinet MAKOSSO**

Min. of Civil Service & State Reformation: **Guy Brice Parfait KOLELAS**

Min. of Commerce, Consumption, & Supplies: **Claudine MOUNARI**

Min. of Communications in Charge of Relations With Parliament: **Bienvenu OKIEMY**

Min. of Construction, Town Planning, & Housing: **Claude Alphonse NSILOU**

Min. of Culture & Arts: **Jean-Claude GAKOSSO**

Min. of Energy & Water: **Henri OSSEBI**

Min. of Equipment & Public Works: **Emile OUOSSO**

Min. of Finance, Budget, & Public Portfolio: **Gilbert ONDONGO**

Min. of Foreign Affairs & Intl. Cooperation: **Basile IKOUEBE**

Min. of Health & Population: **Georges MOYEN**

Min. of Higher Education: **Ange Antoine ABENA**

Min. of Hydrocarbons: **Andri Raphakl LOEMBA**

Min. of Interior & Decentrialization: **Raymond Ziphyrin MBOULOU**

Min. of Land Affairs & Public Domain: **Pierre MABIALA**

Min. of Maritime & Inland Fisheries, in Charge of Aquaculture: **Hellot Mampouya MATSON**

Min. of Mines, Mineral Industries, & Geology: **Pierre OBA**

Min. of Posts & Technology, in Charge of New Technologies: **Thierry MOUNGALA**

Min. of Primary & Secondary Education, in Charge of Literacy: **Rosalie KAMA NIAMAYOUA**

Min. for the Promotion of Women & the Integration of Women in Development: **Madeleine Yila BOUMPOTO**

Min. of Scientific Research & Technical Innovation: **Henri OSSEBI**

Min. of Small & Medium-Size Enterprises, in Charge of Cottage Industry: **Adelaide MOUGANY**

Min. of Social Affairs, Humanitarian Action, & Solidarity: **Emilienne RAOUL**

Min. of Sports & Sport Education: **Leon Alfred OPIMBAT**

Min. of Sustainable Development, Forestry Economy, & Environment: **Henri DJOMBO**

Min. of Technical Education & Professional Training: **Andri Okombi SALISSA**

Min. of Tourism Industries & Leisure: **Mathieu Martial KANI**

Min.-Del. for Land Reform & Integration, attached to the Min. of State for Planning, Economy, Land Reform, & Integration: **Josui Rodrigue NGOUONIMBA**

Min.-Del. for Maritime Commerce, attached to the Min. of Transport, Civil Aviation, & Maritime Shipping: **Martin Parfait Aimi COUSSOUD MAVOUNGOU**

Ambassador to the US: **Serge MOMBOULI**

Permanent Representative to the UN, New York: **Raymond Serge BALE**

ECONOMY

The economy is a mixture of subsistence agriculture, an industrial sector based largely on oil and support services, and government spending. Oil has supplanted forestry as the mainstay of the economy, providing a major share of government revenues and exports. In the early 1980s, rapidly rising oil revenues enabled the government to finance large-scale development projects with GDP growth averaging 5% annually, one of the highest rates in Africa.

Characterized by budget problems and overstaffing, the government has mortgaged a substantial portion of its oil earnings through oil-backed loans that have contributed to a growing debt burden and chronic revenue shortfalls. Economic reform efforts have been undertaken with the support of international organizations, notably the World Bank and the IMF. However, the reform program came to a halt in June 1997 when civil war erupted.

Denis Sassou-Nguesso, who returned to power when the war ended in October 1997, publicly expressed interest in moving forward on economic reforms and privatization and in renewing cooperation with international financial institutions. Economic progress was badly hurt by slumping oil prices and the resumption of armed conflict in December 1998, which worsened the republic's budget deficit.

The current administration presides over an uneasy internal peace and faces difficult economic challenges of stimulating recovery and reducing poverty. The drop in oil prices during the global crisis reduced oil revenue by about 30%, but the subsequent recovery of oil prices has boosted the economy's GDP and near-term prospects. In March 2006, the World Bank and the International Monetary Fund (IMF) approved Heavily Indebted Poor Countries (HIPC) treatment for Congo, which received $1.9 billion in debt relief under the program in 2010.

Labor Conditions

Although there are laws and policies designed to protect children from exploitation in the workplace, child labor was a problem. The minimum age for employment or internships was 16 years; however, this law generally was not enforced, particularly in rural areas and in the informal sector. The most common forms of child labor were in markets, commercial fishing, or in domestic servitude, where children were subject to harsh conditions, long hours, and little or no pay. Children worked with their families on farms or in small businesses in the informal sector without government monitoring. Children are engaged in the worst forms of child labor in agriculture and domestic service. There were no official government statistics on general child labor. However, a 2005 International Labor Organization survey showed that 85 percent of the sample of 47,000 working children resided in rural areas, and just over half (53 percent) were girls who performed household chores or worked in exchange for pay.

The national minimum wage was 54,000 CFA ($109) per month in the formal sector. There was no official minimum wage for the agricultural and other informal sectors. High urban prices and dependent extended families obliged many workers, including teachers and health workers, to seek secondary employment, mainly in the informal sector.

The law provides for a standard workweek of seven hours per day, five days a week, with a one-hour lunch break. There was no legal limit on the number of hours worked per week. The law stipulates that overtime must be paid for all work in excess of 42 hours per week; however, there is no legal prohibition against excessive compulsory overtime. Overtime was subject to agreement between employer and employee. These standards were generally observed, and workers were usually paid in cash for overtime work beyond 42 hours per week.

U.S.-CONGOLESE RELATIONS

The United States established diplomatic relations with the Republic of Congo in 1960, following the country's independence from France. Diplomatic relations were suspended in 1965, then resumed in 1977. In 1992, the Republic of Congo completed a transition to multi-party democracy; the country saw several years of civil conflict during 1997-2003. Due to this, the U.S. Embassy operated out of Kinshasa, DRC from 1997 to 2006. In 2009, a new Embassy compound was built and opened, restoring a full American diplomatic presence in the country.

U.S.- Republic of Congo relations are positive and cooperative. The two countries have worked together on issues such as strengthening regional security, improving the health of Congolese citizens, promoting English language learning, and safeguarding the environment. The United States has supported Congolese democratization efforts, contributing aid to the country's electoral processes and working alongside Congolese civil society and private sector leaders as well as government officials to improve human rights and help build a more stable, secure, democratic, and prosperous Congo.

U.S. Assistance to the Republic of Congo

U.S. foreign assistance to Republic of the Congo is focused on maintaining peace and security, professionalizing the armed forces, and helping prepare those forces to participate in regional peacekeeping missions. Increasing the country's capability in the area of maritime security (including port management) and training are vital to supporting its ability to prevent conflict and preserve the security it has developed.

Bilateral Economic Relations

The Republic of Congo's economy is based primarily on its petroleum sector, with U.S. companies playing a role in the petroleum production and services sectors. The country's top export to the United States is oil, while imports from the United States include machinery, poultry, optic and medical instruments, and vehicles. The Republic of Congo is eligible for preferential trade benefits under the African Growth and Opportunity Act. The deep-water port in the economic capital of Pointe Noire is International Ship and Port Facility Security certified, making it eligible to receive and send shipments directly with the United States. The two countries have a bilateral investment treaty designed to facilitate and protect foreign investment.

Republic of the Congo's Membership in International Organizations

The Republic of Congo and the United States belong to a number of the same international organizations, including the United Nations, International Monetary Fund, World Bank, and World Trade Organization.

Bilateral Representation

The Congo maintains an embassy in the United States at 4891 Colorado Avenue, NW, Washington, DC 20011 (tel: 202-726-5500).

Principal U.S. Embassy Officials

Last Updated: 1/14/2013

BRAZZAVILLE (E) Boulevard Denis Sassou Nguesso, No. 70-83, Section D, Centre Ville, Brazzaville, +242-6-612-2000, Workweek: M-Thurs–7:30 a.m. to 5:00 p.m./Fridays 7:30 a.m.–12:30 p.m., Website: http://brazzaville.usembassy.gov/

AMB OMS:	Pamela Roxanne Aulton
FM:	Gerald Toomey
HRO:	Theresa Everett (Resident In Kinshasa)
MGT:	Vallera Gibson
SDO/DATT:	COL Lee Whiteside (Resident In Kinshasa)
AMB:	Christopher W. Murray
CON:	Morgan O'Brien
DCM:	Margaret B. Diop
PAO:	James Jeffers
GSO:	Christopher Green
RSO:	William Ferrari
CLO:	Caroline Ferrari
ECON:	Demark Schulze
EEO:	Pamela Aulton
IMO:	Dennis Graves
POL:	Barry Junker

TRAVEL

Consular Information Sheet

July 27, 2012

Country Description: The Republic of the Congo (Congo-Brazzaville) is a developing nation in Central Africa. The official language is French, and Lingala, Kikongo, and Kituba are also widely spoken. The largest cities are the capital, Brazzaville, located on the Congo River, and Pointe Noire on the Atlantic coast. Parts of the capital and large areas in the south of the country were damaged during civil conflict in 1997 and 1998–1999. The last rebel group signed a cease-fire accord with the government in March 2003. Facilities for tourism are very limited.

Smart Traveler Enrollment Program (STEP)/ Embassy Locations:: If you are going to live in or travel to the Republic of the Congo, please take the time to tell Embassy Brazzaville about your trip by enrolling in the Smart Traveler Enrollment Program (STEP). If you enroll, we can keep you up to date with important safety and security announcements. It will also help your friends and family get in touch with you in an emergency. You should remember to keep all of your information in STEP up to date. It is important during enrollment or updating of information to include your current phone number and current email address where you can be reached in case of an emergency.

U.S. Embassy Brazzaville
Boulevard Denis Sassou Nguesso (across from Blanche Gomez Maternity Hospital)
Brazzaville
Republic of the Congo
Telephone: 242 06 612-2000
Emergency after-hours telephone: 242 04 444-0013
Email: BrazzavilleACS@state.gov

Entry/Exit Requirements for U.S. Citizens: A passport, visa, and evidence of yellow fever vaccination are required for entry. Visitors to the Republic of the Congo should also have a letter of invitation and/or written proof of a hotel reservation for presentation to immigration officials upon arrival. In some cases, invitation letters must be endorsed by local immigration authorities prior to the bearer's arrival in the country.

Possession of a valid visa is often not sufficient for admission to the Congo as immigration requirements are unclear and arbitrarily enforced. Additionally, local law prohibits exiting the country with the local currency, known as the Central African Franc or CFA. Travelers are advised to limit the amount of CFA they travel with to avoid any unnecessary forfeitures upon departure. See Currency under Special Circumstances below for more information.

Until January 2010, Congolese Embassies and Consulates issued unique visas for entry to the Republic of Congo. Visas should be identical regardless of where they are issued, however, some Embassies and Consulates, including the Congolese Consulate in New York, have not started issuing the new universal visas. The new Congolese visas are a passport-page-sized sticker with a map outline of the Republic of the Congo in the background. If you attempt to enter Congo with one of the old visas, you may be denied entry.

Additional information on entry requirements may be obtained from the Embassy of the Republic of the Congo, 4891 Colorado Ave., N.W., Washington, D.C. 20011, telephone (202) 726-5500, or from the Permanent Mission of the Republic of the Congo to the United Nations, 14 E. 65th St., New York, NY, 10021, telephone (212) 744-7840. Overseas inquiries should be made at the nearest Congolese embassy or consulate.

The U.S. Department of State is unaware of any HIV/AIDS entry restrictions for visitors to or foreign residents of the Republic of the Congo.

Threats to Safety and Security: Although the Republic of the Congo is still recovering from its civil war, there have been no serious episodes of unrest or violence since the March 2003 peace accord. Continued security awareness, however, remains a key consideration for all visitors.

You should avoid travel in the Pool region south of Brazzaville. Although terrorism has not been a recent problem in the ROC, the Ninjas (a former rebel group) reside in the Pool Region, especially in and around the village of Kinkala. Although they do not specifically target U.S. citizens, they do routinely establish roadblocks and conduct highway robberies. The passenger train connecting Brazzaville and Point Noire passes through this region and train passengers have been robbed. For this reason, the Embassy advises against travel by road or rail between Brazzaville and Pointe Noire.

You should also pay close attention to events in the Democratic Republic of the Congo as unrest in Kinshasa can also affect Brazzaville. In 2007, stray small arms fire originating in Kinshasa landed in Brazzaville.

Stay up to date by:

- Bookmarking our Bureau of Consular Affairs website, which contains the current Travel Warnings and Travel Alerts as well as the Worldwide Caution.
- Following us on Twitter and the Bureau of Consular Affairs page on Facebook as well.
- Downloading our free Smart Traveler iPhone App to have travel information at your fingertips.
- Calling 1-888-407-4747 toll-free within the United States and Canada, or a regular toll line, 1-202-501-4444, from other countries.
- Taking some time before travel to consider your personal security.

Crime: Several incidents of petty street crime against U.S. citizens have occurred recentlyand reports of violent crime in Brazzaville, although not specifically targeting U.S. citizens, are not uncommon. Incidents of armed robberies, vehicle break-ins, mugging, and pick-pocketing have been reported near the ports, outside popular restaurants, as well as in the Congolese neighborhoods surrounding the city center in both Pointe Noire and Brazzaville.

U.S. citizens are not typically singled out by criminal elements, but may become targets of opportunity depending on your dress, actions, behavior, and level of perceived vigilance. In late 2011, criminal elements targeted a few middle-class and affluent residences for burglary.

You should note that in cases of theft and robbery, legal recourse is limited; leave valuable items at home.

There are no areas that the Embassy considers "off-limits" in Brazzaville; however, in the neighborhoods of Poto-Poto, Bacongo and Makelekele, you can expect to be verbally harassed. Vendors often physically grab potential clients or say, "Mondele" (white/western person) to garner attention, and women traveling alone may experience greater verbal harassment.

Pointe Noire shares similar concerns to Brazzaville with one exception, petty crime is often committed near Pointe Noire's beaches. The Embassy recommends that you stay on main beaches, secure valuables and avoid all beaches completely at night, when crimes typically occur. You should also use caution when swimming because of riptides.

The main areas of concern in Pointe Noire are the coastline (currents), beachside after hours, and market areas (another popular area for petty crime, which should also be avoided after dark).

Victims of Crime: If you or someone you know becomes the victim of a crime abroad, you should contact the local police and the nearest U.S. embassy or consulate. We can:

- Replace a stolen passport.

- Help you find appropriate medical care if you are the victim of a violent crime such as assault or rape.
- Put you in contact with the appropriate police authorities, and if you want us to, we can contact family members or friend
- Help you understand the local criminal justice process and direct you to local attorneys, although it is important to remember that local authorities are responsible for investigating and prosecuting the crime.

The local equivalent to the "911" emergency line in the Republic of the Congo is 242 06 665-4804. Please note that police resources are limited and response to emergency calls is often slow (45 minutes or longer). In general, response or recourse for victims of crime is extremely limited, if not non-existent in the Republic of the Congo.

Criminal Penalties: While you are traveling in the Republic of the Congo, you are subject to its laws even if you are a U.S. citizen. Foreign laws and legal systems can be vastly different from our own. It is important to carry some form of identification at all times in the ROC. Wallets should contain only a small amount of cash and be free of all credit cards. In the Republic of the Congo you may be taken in for questioning if you are stopped by the police and are unable to produce an acceptable form of identification. A common practice among policemen in the ROC is to stop foreigners and accuse them of minor infractions (which may or may not be valid). When this occurs, the police do not want to write a ticket, but rather request the person to pay a fine on the spot. The U.S. Embassy does not encourage anyone to pay fines. The Embassy recommends that all travelers carry a copy of their U.S. passport and Congolese visa to prevent them from being taken by police or armed assailants during an attempted bribe.

If you travel within the Republic of the Congo, you should carry your passport, as you may be asked to register with immigration upon arrival in a new location. It is illegal to take pictures of government buildings, military installations, and other key parts of infrastructure such as ports, train stations, and airports. In general, it is best to keep your camera out of sight and ask permission prior to taking photos. If permission is refused, don't take the photo.

There are also some things that might be legal in the Republic of the Congo, but still illegal in the United States. You can be prosecuted under U.S. law if you buy pirated goods. Engaging in sexual conduct with children and using or disseminating child pornography in a foreign country is a crime prosecutable in the United States. If you break local laws in the Republic of the Congo, your U.S. passport will not help you avoid arrest or prosecution. If you are arrested in the Republic of the Congo, you have the option to request that the police, prison officials, or other authorities alert the U.S. embassy of your arrest, and to have communications from you forwarded to the U.S. embassy.

Currency: The Republic of the Congo is primarily a cash economy and uses the Central African Franc (CFA), a common currency used in Gabon, Chad, Cameroon, the Central African Republic, and Equatorial Guinea. U.S. dollars may be exchanged for local currency, but traveler's checks are generally not accepted and cannot be cashed at local banks. Some hotels in Brazzaville and in Pointe Noire now accept major credit cards, but cash remains the preferred method of payment. Most businesses accept cash only. Personal checks drawn on foreign accounts are not accepted. Western Union has offices in Brazzaville and Pointe Noire. There is one ATM at the Credit du Congo Bank in Brazzaville which accepts foreign debit cards. ATMs at several of Credit du Congo's branches in Pointe Noire also accept foreign debit cards. CFA are not available outside the CFA zone and there are tight restrictions on travelling with CFA. If you are caught attempting to leave the country in possession of CFA, airport authorities may confiscate all of your local currency. For this reason, the U.S. embassy recommends that you not travel via air with CFA, even if you are travelling directly to another country in the CFA zone.

Customs: Airport police and customs officials routinely inspect incoming and outgoing luggage, even for in-country travel. For a complete list of prohibited items, please contact the nearest Congolese embassy or consulate. Visitors who seek to export arts and crafts at the airports are frequently subject to an export tax and/ or solicitations for bribes from customs agents. There have also been repeated instances of travelers being questioned about how much currency they are carrying and expats have been asked to show customs officials how much money they have in their wallets.

Detention: Local security forces, especially traffic police, routinely detain foreigners to solicit bribes. Detention of U.S. citizens, particularly in remote areas, may not always be promptly reported to the U.S. embassy by Congolese authorities. You are encouraged to carry a copy of your passport and valid visa for the Congo with you at all times so that, if questioned by local officials, proof of identity and U.S. citizenship is readily available. If detained or arrested, U.S. citizens should always ask to be allowed to contact the U.S. embassy.

Ferry Service to Kinshasa: Commercial ferry service between Brazzaville and Kinshasa normally operates from 8 a.m. to 4 p.m. Monday through Saturday and 8 a.m. to 12 p.m. on Sunday, but the ports may close completely with minimal notice. A special exit permit from the Republic of the Congo's Immigration Service and a visa for the Democratic Republic of the Congo are required to cross the Congo River from Brazzaville to Kinshasa. Likewise, an ROC visa is required when arriving by boat in Brazzaville.

Accessibility: While in the Republic of the Congo, individuals with disabilities may find accessibility and accommodation very different from what they find in the United States. Although local law prohibits discrimination against people with handicaps, this law is not enforced. Furthermore, there are no laws requiring access to transportation, communication, or public buildings for persons with disabilities. There are few sidewalks and no curb-cuts. Most buildings do not have functioning elevators. People living in the Republic of the Congo with disabilities must rely on their families for support.

Medical Facilities and Health Information: Medical facilities are extremely limited. Some medicines are in short supply, particularly in rural areas. Travelers should carry their own supply of properly-labeled medications. The Consular Section maintains a list of clinics in Brazzaville and Pointe Noire. This list is provided as a service for U.S. citizens residing in or visiting the Republic of the Congo and in no way constitutes an endorsement or recommendation of any particular facility. The list is available on the Embassy Brazzaville web site and in person in the Consular Section.

An outbreak of acute poliomyelitis (polio) virus began in October 2010 with cases in Pointe Noire, Brazzaville, and most other parts of the Republic of the Congo. In response to the outbreak, the Government of Congo, in cooperation with the World Health Organization, has launched a nationwide emergency vaccination program. As of January 2011, the vaccination campaign appears to have halted the spread of the virus. However, it remains extremely important to make sure your polio vaccination is up-to-date prior to travel to the Republic of the Congo. Outbreaks of Measles and Chikunguny were declared in June 2011; travelers should carry and use mosquito repellents and sleep under mosquito nets if possible.

You can find more information on vaccinations and other health precautions on the CDC website. For information about outbreaks of infectious diseases abroad, consult the World Health Organization (WHO) website. The WHO website also contains additional health information for travelers, including detailed country-specific health information.

Malaria is a serious and sometimes fatal disease. Plasmodium falciparum malaria, the type that predominates in the Congo, is resistant to the anti-malarial drug chloroquine. Because travelers to the Republic of the Congo are at high risk for contracting malaria, the Centers for Disease Control and Prevention (CDC) advises that travelers should take one of the following anti-malarial drugs: mefloquine (Lariam), doxycycline, or atovaquone/proguanil (Malarone). Travelers who become ill with a fever or flu-like illness while traveling in a malaria-risk area and up to one year after returning home should seek prompt medical attention and tell the physician their travel history and what anti-malarials they have been taking. The CDC provides additional information on malaria protective measures.

Schistosomiasis, transmitted by waterborne larvae that penetrate intact skin, presents significant risk. Travelers should avoid freshwater exposure.

Tuberculosis is an increasingly serious health concern in the Republic of the Congo. For further information, please consult the CDC's information on TB.

Medical Insurance: You can't assume your insurance will go with you when you travel. It's very important to find out BEFORE you leave. You need to ask your insurance company two questions:

- Does my policy apply when I'm out of the U.S.?
- Will it cover emergencies like a trip to a foreign hospital or an evacuation?

In many places, doctors and hospitals still expect payment in cash at the time of service. Your regular U.S. health insurance may not cover doctors' and hospital visits in other countries. If your policy doesn't go with you when you travel, it's a very good idea to take out a specific policy for your trip.

Traffic Safety and Road Conditions: While in the Republic of the Congo, you may encounter road conditions that differ significantly from those in the United States. Traffic safety in general is hazardous due to high speeds, aggressive driving, poorly maintained vehicles, and general indifference toward the safety of pedestrians and cyclists. The information below concerning the Republic of the Congo is provided for general reference only, and may not be totally accurate in a particular location or circumstance.

Road conditions are generally poor and deteriorate significantly during the rainy season from November to May. The National Highway 2 which links Brazzaville to Pointe Noire is largely unpaved and often impassable in the rainy season. Unleaded gasoline and diesel fuel are frequently unavailable in the major cities and especially in the more isolated regions of the country. Maintenance of the few paved roads is limited. Overland travel off the main roads requires a four-wheel drive vehicle. Poorly marked checkpoints, sometimes manned by undisciplined soldiers, exist in many areas of the countryside.

Bus travel is strongly discouraged. While there are no officially registered taxi companies in Brazzaville or Pointe-Noire, taxis are required to have an operator permit. Many taxis drivers are owner-operators. In the past several years, there have not been any reported criminal incidents involving taxis in Brazzaville or Pointe Noire. The Embassy suggests a few guidelines for local taxi usage:

Hire only taxis painted in the government-authorized green and white color scheme in Brazzaville and blue and white color scheme in Pointe Noire. Taxis are not metered. Fares should be negotiated before passengers embark. Carry small bills: taxis are notorious for not having change and will always tend to round-up fares or not return change. The standard/typical day-time fare is CFA 1,000 within the city or municipalities within the city limits of Brazzaville. Night-time fares vary from CFA 1,500-2,000 in Brazzaville. Taxi fares are usually a little more in Pointe Noire at all times.

As a common-sense security precaution, passengers should take a note of vehicle registration in case of any incidents or issues with taxi-operators.

Taxis vary greatly in terms of operating state and are generally not air-conditioned. Taxis are not regularly inspected and in some case will not have functioning seat belts, windows, or doors. Therefore, personal safety, security, and liability issues should be evaluated when choosing local taxis.

While taxis are a convenient and relatively safe alternative for transportation in Brazzaville and Pointe Noire, the Embassy does not endorse the use of any local taxi operators in either city. It is your responsibility to determine whether the basic concerns and risks are commensurate with your transportation needs. Emergency services are limited within Brazzaville and Pointe Noire and virtually non-existent elsewhere in the Republic of the Congo. There are currently no Distracted Driving Laws in effect in the Republic of the Congo, but police may pull over drivers who talk or text while driving for not following safe driving procedures.

Aviation Safety Oversight: As there is no direct commercial air service to the United States by carriers registered in the Republic of the Congo, the U.S. Federal Aviation Administration (FAA) has not assessed the government of the Republic of the Congo's Civil Aviation Authority for compliance with International Civil Aviation Organization (ICAO) aviation safety standards. Further information may be found on the FAA's safety assessment page.

Children's Issues: Please see the U.S. Dept. of State Office of Children's Issues web pages on intercountry adoption and international parental child abduction.

Intercountry Adoption

December 2010

The Republic of the Congo (Congo-Brazzaville) is not party to the Hague Convention on Protection of Children and Co-operation in Respect of Intercountry Adoption (Hague Adoption Convention). Therefore, when the Hague Adoption Convention entered into force for the United States on April 1, 2008, intercountry adoption processing for Congo-Brazzaville did not change.

The Department of State does not maintain files on the adoption process in Congo-Brazzaville because adoptions from Congo-Brazzaville are rare; fewer than five adoptions by American citizen parents have taken place since 2005. Please visit the Department's Country Specific Information sheets for more information on travelling to Congo-Brazzaville and the U.S. Embassy Brazzaville's website for information on consular services.

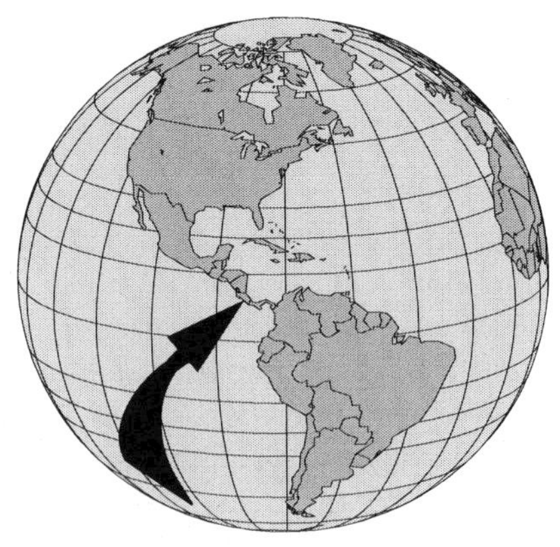

COSTA RICA

Compiled from publications that were available as of February 2013 from the U.S. Department of State, the U.S. Department of Commerce, and the Central Intelligence Agency (CIA). See the introduction to this set for explanatory notes.

Official Name:
Republic of Costa Rica

PROFILE

Geography

Area: total: 51,100 sq km; country comparison to the world: 130; land: 51,060 sq km; water: 40 sq km

Major cities: San Jose (capital) 1.416 million (2009)

Climate: tropical and subtropical; dry season (December to April); rainy season (May to November); cooler in highlands

Terrain: coastal plains separated by rugged mountains including over 100 volcanic cones, of which several are major volcanoes

People

Nationality: noun: Costa Rican(s); adjective: Costa Rican

Population: 4,636,348 (July 2012 est.)

Population growth rate: 1.288% (2012 est.)

Ethnic groups: white (including mestizo) 94%, black 3%, Amerindian 1%, Chinese 1%, other 1%

Religions: Roman Catholic 76.3%, Evangelical 13.7%, Jehovah's Witnesses 1.3%, other Protestant 0.7%, other 4.8%, none 3.2%

Languages: Spanish (official), English

Literacy: definition: age 15 and over can read and write; total population: 94.9%; male: 94.7%; female: 95.1% (2000 census)

Health: life expectancy at birth: total population: 77.89 years; male: 75.26 years; female: 80.65 years (2012 est.); Infant mortality rate: total: 9.2 deaths/1,000 live births; male: 10.03 deaths/1,000 live births; female: 8.32 deaths/1,000 live births (2012 est.)

Unemployment rate: 7.9% (2012 est.)

Work force: 2.196 million (2012 est.)

Government

Type: democratic republic

Independence: 15 September 1821

Constitution: 7 November 1949

Political subdivisions: 7 provinces (provincias, singular—provincia); Alajuela, Cartago, Guanacaste, Heredia, Limon, Puntarenas, San Jose

Suffrage: 18 years of age; universal and compulsory

Economy

GDP (purchasing power parity): $58.6 billion (2012 est.); $55.73 billion (2011 est.); $53.5 billion (2010 est.); $51.11 billion (2009 est.)

GDP real growth rate: 4.8% (2012 est.); 4.2% (2011 est.); 4.7% (2010 est.); -1% (2009 est.)

GDP per capita (PPP): $12,600 (2012 est.); $12,100 (2011 est.); $11,700 (2010 est.); $11,300 (2009 est.)

Natural resources: hydropower

Agriculture products: bananas, pineapples, coffee, melons, ornamental plants, sugar, corn, rice, beans, potatoes; beef, poultry, dairy; timber

Industries: microprocessors, food processing, medical equipment, textiles and clothing, construction materials, fertilizer, plastic products

Exports: $11.47 billion (2012 est.); $10.38 billion (2011 est.); $9.516 billion (2010 est.)

Exports—commodities: bananas, pineapples, coffee, melons, ornamental plants, sugar; beef; seafood; electronic components, medical equipment

Exports—partners: US 33.9%, China 12.6%, Netherlands 12.1%, UK 10.7% (2011)

Imports: $16.79 billion (2012 est.); $15.53 billion (2011 est.); $12.96 billion (2010 est.)

Imports—commodities: raw materials, consumer goods, capital equipment, petroleum, construction materials

Imports—partners: US 43.3%, Mexico 6.4%, China 6.2%, Japan 6% (2011)

Debt—external: $12.04 billion (31 December 2012 est.); $10.05 billion (31 December 2011 est.); $8.849 billion (31 December 2010 est.)

Exchange rates: Costa Rican colones (CRC) per US dollar; 504.5 (2012 est.); 505.66 (2011 est.); 525.83 (2010 est.); 573.29 (2009); 530.41 (2008); 519.53 (2007)

PEOPLE

Unlike many of their Central American neighbors, present-day Costa Ricans are largely of European rather than mestizo descent; Spain was the primary country of origin. However, an estimated 10% to 15% of the population is Nicaraguan, of fairly recent arrival and primarily of mestizo origin. Descendants of 19th-century Jamaican immigrant workers constitute an English-speaking minority, about 3% of the population. Few of the native Indians survived European contact; the indigenous population today is less than 1% of the population.

Language

Costa Rica is a Spanish-speaking country, although English is often taught in schools and used widely in business circles. Other native languages still spoken by indigenous people are; Bribrí, Maleku, Ngäbe (Guaymí) and Cabecar. Creole-English language (or Mekatelyu) is spoken on the Caribbean Coast.

Religion

According to a survey provided during the year by the University of Costa Rica, approximately 47 percent of the population identified itself as practicing Roman Catholic, 23 percent as non-practicing Catholic, 16 percent as evangelical Protestant, 6 percent as belonging to other religions, and 8 percent as having no religious affiliation.

Among Protestants approximately 92 percent of the population is Pentecostal and 8 percent is Baptist. The Church of Jesus Christ of Latter-day Saints estimates membership at 35,000 and the Lutheran Church estimates 5,500 members. The Jewish Zionist Center estimates that there are 2,800 Jews in the country. An estimated 1,000 Quakers live in the cloud forest reserve of Monteverde, Puntarenas, and an additional 1,000 persons attend Quaker meetings as nonmembers throughout the country. Although they represent less than 1 percent of the population, Jehovah's Witnesses have a strong presence on the Caribbean coast. Seventh-day Adventists operate a university that attracts students from throughout the Caribbean Basin. The Unification Church has its headquarters for Latin America in San Jose. Other religious groups include followers of Islam, Taoism, Krishna Consciousness, Scientology, Tenrikyo, and the Baha'i Faith. Indigenous peoples are more likely than nonindigenous peoples to practice animism.

HISTORY

In 1502, on his fourth and last voyage to the New World, Christopher Columbus made the first European landfall in the area. Settlement of Costa Rica began in 1522. For nearly 3 centuries, Spain administered the region as part of the Captaincy General of Guatemala under a military governor. The Spanish optimistically called the country "Rich Coast." Finding little gold or other valuable minerals in Costa Rica, however, the Spanish turned to agriculture.

The small landowners' relative poverty, the lack of a large indigenous labor force, the population's ethnic and linguistic homogeneity, and Costa Rica's isolation from the Spanish colonial centers in Mexico and the Andes all contributed to the development of an autonomous and individualistic agrarian society. An egalitarian tradition also arose. This tradition survived the widened class distinctions brought on by the 19th-century introduction of banana and coffee cultivation and consequent accumulations of local wealth.

Costa Rica joined other Central American provinces in 1821 in a joint declaration of independence from Spain. Although the newly independent provinces formed a Federation, border disputes broke out among them, adding to the region's turbulent history and conditions. Costa Rica's northern Guanacaste Province was annexed from Nicaragua in one such regional dispute. In 1838, long after the Central American Federation ceased to function in practice, Costa Rica formally withdrew and proclaimed itself sovereign.

An era of peaceful democracy in Costa Rica began in 1899 with elections considered the first truly free and honest ones in the country's history. This began a trend that continued until today with only two lapses: in 1917–19, Federico Tinoco ruled as a dictator, and, in 1948, Jose Figueres led an armed uprising in the wake of a disputed presidential election.

With more than 2,000 dead, the 44-day civil war resulting from this uprising was the bloodiest event in 20th-century Costa Rican history, but the victorious junta drafted a constitution guaranteeing free elections with universal suffrage and the abolition of the military. In 1949, Costa Rica dissolved its armed forces and Figueres became a national hero. He won the first election under the new constitution in 1953. Since then, Costa Rica has held 15 presidential elections, the latest in 2010.

GOVERNMENT AND POLITICAL CONDITIONS

Costa Rica is a constitutional, multiparty republic governed by a president and a unicameral legislative assembly that are directly elected in multiparty elections every four years. In 2010 voters chose Laura Chinchilla Miranda of the National Liberation Party (PLN), the country's first female president in elections that were generally considered free and fair.

Recent Elections

In national elections held in February 2010, Laura Chinchilla Miranda of the PLN won the presidency and became the country's first female

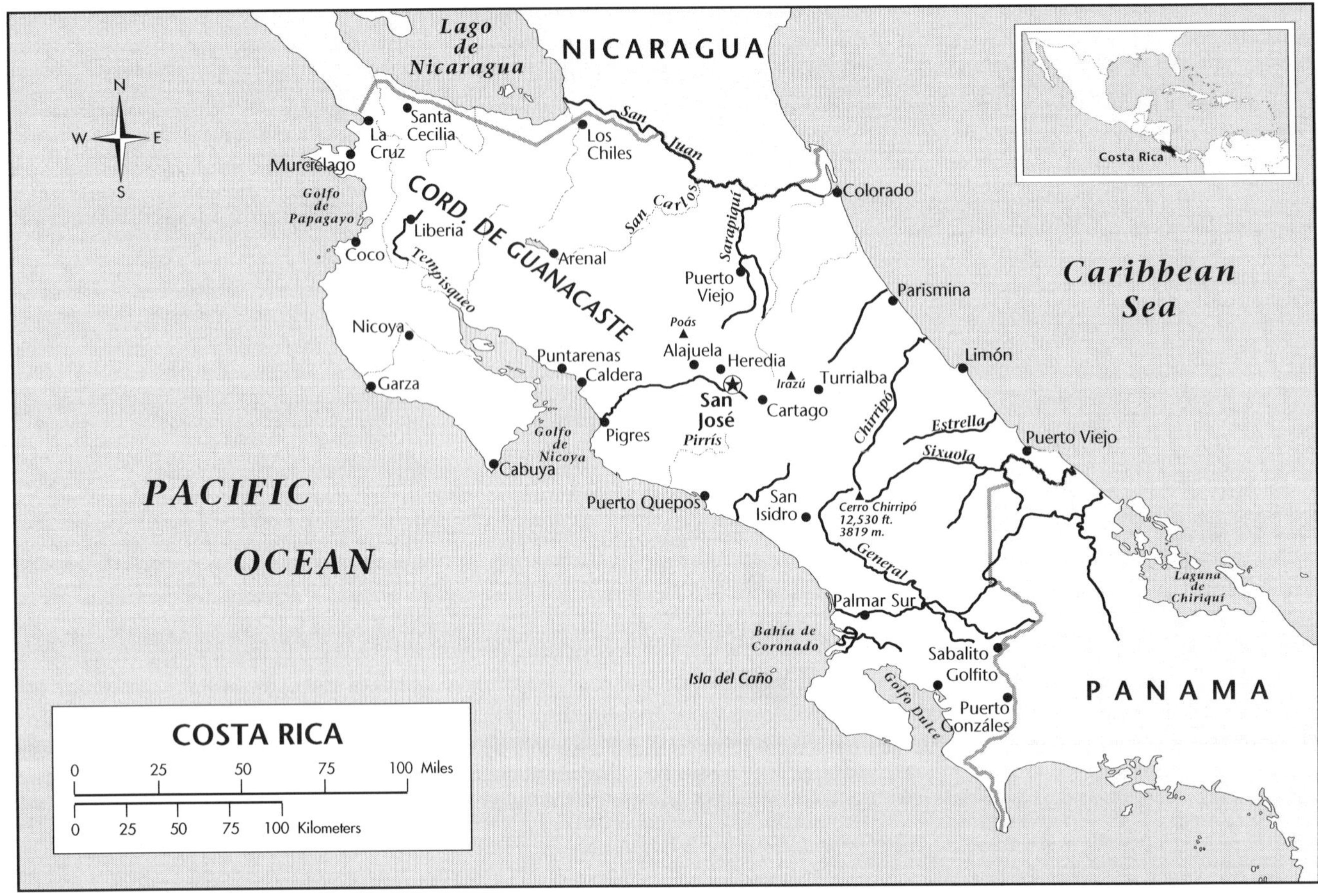

president in elections that generally were considered free and fair. The Organization of American States team that monitored the election praised the peaceful and democratic way in which the process unfolded.

Participation of Women and Minorities: Women were represented with a degree of visibility in government; indigenous people and people of African descent, representing approximately 4 percent of the population (2000 census), were not. The electoral code requires that a minimum of 50 percent of candidates for elective office be female and that women's names be placed alternately with men on the ballots by party slate. There were seven women among the 22 cabinet ministers. There were 22 women in the 57-seat Legislative Assembly, including the vice president of the assembly and nine legislative committee chairwomen. The deputy chief justice of the Supreme Court, president of the High Court of Civil Appeals, and president of the Constitutional Chamber were women. Indigenous persons did not play a significant role in politics or government. There were no indigenous or black members in the Legislative Assembly or the cabinet. A black person headed one government agency.

Principal Government Officials

Last Updated: 1/31/2013

Pres.: **Laura CHINCHILLA Miranda**

First Vice Pres.: **Alfio PIVA Mesen**

Second Vice Pres.: **Luis LIBERMAN Ginsburg**

Min. of Agriculture & Livestock: **Gloria ABRAHAM Peralta**

Min. of Communications: **Francisco CHACON Gonzalez**

Min. of Culture & Youth: **Manuel OBREGON Lopez**

Min. of Decentralization & Local Governments: **Juan MARIN Quiros**

Min. of Economy, Industry, & Trade: **Mayi ANTILLON Guerrero**

Min. of Education: **Leonardo GARNIER Rimolo**

Min. of Environment & Energy: **Rene CASTRO Salazar**

Min. of Finance: **Edgar AYALES Esna**

Min. of Foreign Relations: **Jose Enrique CASTILLO Barrantes**

Min. of Foreign Trade: **Anabel GONZALEZ Campabadal**

Min. of Health: **Daisy Maria CORRALES Diaz, Dr.**

Min. of Housing: **Guido MONGE**

Min. of Justice: **Fernando FERRARO**

Min. of Labor & Social Security: **Olman SEGURA**

Min. of Planning & Economic Policy: **Roberto Javier GALLARDO Nunez**

Min. of the Presidency: **Carlos Ricardo BENAVIDES Jimenez**

Min. of Public Security, Govt., & Police: **Mario ZAMORA Cordero**

Min. of Public Works & Transportation: **Pedro CASTRO**

Min. of Science & Technology: **Alejandro CRUZ Molina**

Min. of Social Welfare: **Fernando MARIN Rojas**

Min. of Sports: **William CORRALES Araya**
Min. of Tourism: **Allan FLORES Moya**
Attorney Gen.: **Jorge CHAVARRIA Guzman**
Pres., Central Bank: **Rodrigo BOLANOS Zamora**
Ambassador to the US: **Shanon Muni FIGUERES Boggs**
Permanent Representative to the UN, New York: **Eduardo ULIBARRI Bilbao**

POLITICAL CONDITIONS

Costa Rica has long emphasized the development of democracy and respect for human rights. The country's political system has steadily developed, maintaining democratic institutions and an orderly, constitutional scheme for government succession.

Several factors have contributed to this trend, including enlightened leadership, comparative prosperity, flexible class lines, educational opportunities that have created a stable middle class, and high social indicators. Also, because Costa Rica has no armed forces, it has avoided military involvement in political affairs, unlike other countries in the region.

On May 8, 2010 Laura Chinchilla, of the National Liberation Party (PLN), was sworn in as President of the Republic of Costa Rica. Chinchilla's top priority is strengthening security, and she is likely to push for fiscal reform to support her policies, seeking to boost revenue, possibly through revised tax legislation, to fund an increase in security services and education. Chinchilla is also focused on improving the country's infrastructure, reforming taxes, expanding jobs through a "green jobs" initiative, creating better living conditions for children and senior citizens, and supporting women's issues.

Following the 2010 elections, the 57-member unicameral Legislative Assembly fragmented into several parties, with no faction having a plurality—the PLN won 23 seats, the PAC 12 seats, PML 9 seats, and the PUSC 6 seats, with the remaining seats split among lesser known parties.

ECONOMY

Prior to the global economic crisis, Costa Rica enjoyed stable economic growth. The economy contracted 1.3% in 2009 but resumed growth at about 4.5% per year in 2010–12. While the traditional agricultural exports of bananas, coffee, sugar, and beef are still the backbone of commodity export trade, a variety of industrial and specialized agricultural products have broadened export trade in recent years.

High value added goods and services, including microchips, have further bolstered exports. Tourism continues to bring in foreign exchange, as Costa Rica's impressive biodiversity makes it a key destination for ecotourism. Foreign investors remain attracted by the country's political stability and relatively high education levels, as well as the incentives offered in the free-trade zones; and Costa Rica has attracted one of the highest levels of foreign direct investment per capita in Latin America. However, many business impediments remain such as high levels of bureaucracy, legal uncertainty due to overlapping and at times conflicting responsibilities between agencies, difficulty of enforcing contracts, and weak investor protection. Poverty has remained around 15-20% for nearly 20 years, and the strong social safety net that had been put into place by the government has eroded due to increased financial constraints on government expenditures. Unlike the rest of Central America, Costa Rica is not highly dependent on remittances as they only represent about 2% of GDP. Immigration from Nicaragua has increasingly become a concern for the government. The estimated 300,000-500,000 Nicaraguans in Costa Rica legally and illegally are an important source of mostly unskilled labor but also place heavy demands on the social welfare system.

The US-Central American-Dominican Republic Free Trade Agreement (CAFTA-DR) entered into force on 1 January 2009 after significant delays within the Costa Rican legislature. CAFTA-DR has increased foreign direct investment in key sectors of the economy, including the insurance and telecommunications sectors recently opened to private investors. President Chinchilla was not able to gain legislative approval for fiscal reform, her top priority, though she continued to pursue fiscal reform in 2012. President Chinchilla and the PLN were successful in passing a tax on corporations to fund an increase for security services.

Labor Conditions

The child and adolescence code prohibits labor of all children under age 15 without any exceptions; it supersedes the minimum working age of 12 established in the labor code, which had not been amended to reflect this change. Adolescents between the ages of 15 and 18 may work a maximum of six hours daily and 36 hours weekly. The law prohibits night work and overtime for minors. The law prohibits those under age 18 from engaging in hazardous or unhealthy activities.

The government generally enforced laws against child labor effectively in the formal sector. Child labor was a problem mainly in the informal economy, especially in agricultural, construction, sales, and small food-product manufacturing.

Monthly minimum wages for the private sector ranged from 135,000 colones (approximately $270) for household workers to 498,000 colones ($993) for university graduates. According to a 2011 INEC survey, the poverty line was 92,122 colones ($184) in urban areas and 70,970 colones in rural areas ($141). The constitution sets workday hours, overtime remuneration, days of rest, and annual vacation rights. Workers generally may work a maximum of eight hours a day or 48 hours weekly. Overtime work is paid at a rate of 50 percent above the stipulated wages or salaries. All workers are entitled to one day of rest after six consecutive days of work and annual paid vacations. Although there is no statutory prohibition against compulsory overtime, the labor code stipulates that the workday may not exceed 12 hours. The Labor Ministry generally enforced minimum wages effectively in the San Jose area but was not effective in enforcing the minimum wage law in rural areas, particularly where large numbers of migrants were employed. The national minimum wage also applied for migrant workers. The Labor Ministry publicly recognized that many workers, including in the formal sector, received less than the minimum wage. The government continued to implement the campaign for minimum wage compliance launched in 2010.

Unions also reported systematic violations of labor rights and provisions concerning working conditions, overtime, and wages in the EPZs. Labor unions reported that overtime pay violations, such as nonpayment, and mandatory overtime were common in the private sector and particularly in EPZ industries. There were reports that agricultural workers, particularly migrant laborers in the pineapple industry, worked in unsafe conditions, including exposure to chemicals without proper training.

U.S.-COSTA RICAN RELATIONS

The United States established diplomatic relations with Costa Rica in 1851, following its independence from Spain and the later dissolution of a federation of Central American states. The United States and Costa Rica have a history of close and friendly relations based on mutual respect for democratic government, human freedoms, free trade, and other shared values. Costa Rica's record on the environment, human rights, and advocacy for the peaceful settlement of disputes give it a weight in world affairs far beyond its size. This record also means that Costa Rica and the United States often share similar positions (votes) in international fora. The United States and Costa Rica enjoy robust bilateral law enforcement cooperation. The two countries have signed a maritime cooperation agreement that facilitates narcotics seizures, illegal migrant rescues, illegal fishing seizures, and search-and-rescue missions.

The United States and Costa Rica share a strong commitment to combating climate change, preventing environmental degradation, as well as preserving Costa Rica's important and rich biological diversity. The U.S. and Costa Rican Governments, the Central Bank of Costa Rica, and The Nature Conservancy have concluded agreements that provide funding for the conservation, restoration, and protection of tropical forests.

It is estimated that approximately 120,000 private American citizens, including many retirees, reside in the country and more than 1.2 million American citizens visit Costa Rica annually.

U.S. Assistance to Costa Rica

U.S. foreign assistance seeks to assist the Costa Rican Government improve public security, the primary concern of both Costa Rican citizens and political leaders. Providing a safe and secure domestic environment will contribute to greater economic growth and prosperity, and will help keep local and transnational crime from eroding the effectiveness of Costa Rica's democratic institutions. U.S. Peace Corps volunteers work in economic development, education, and youth empowerment programs.

Bilateral Economic Relations

The United States and Costa Rica are parties to the U.S.-Central America-Dominican Republic Free Trade Agreement (CAFTA-DR), which aims to facilitate trade and investment and further regional integration by eliminating tariffs, opening markets, reducing barriers to services, and promoting transparency. CAFTA-DR contains a chapter on investment similar to a bilateral investment treaty with the United States.

The United States is Costa Rica's most important trading partner accounting for almost half of Costa Rica's exports, imports, and tourism, and over half of its foreign direct investment. U.S. exports to Costa Rica include machinery, oil, agricultural products, plastic, and semiconductors. U.S. imports from Costa Rica include computer accessories, semiconductors, medical instruments, pineapples and bananas, and coffee.

Costa Rica's Membership in International Organizations

Costa Rica and the United States belong to a number of the same international organizations, including the United Nations, Organization of American States, International Monetary Fund, World Bank, and World Trade Organization.

Bilateral Representation

Costa Rica maintains an embassy in the United States at 2114 S Street NW, Washington, DC 20008 (tel. 202-480-2200).

Principal U.S. Embassy Officials

Last Updated: 1/14/2013

SAN JOSE (E) Pavas, San Jose, (506) 2519-2000 NetBox: 301-985-8648, Fax (506) 2519-2305, INMARSAT Tel 011-8816-2248-1250, 8648, Fax (506) 2519-2305, INMARSAT Tel 011-8816-2248-1250, Workweek: Monday-Friday, 8:00a.m.-4:30 p.m., Website: http://sanjose.usembassy.gov/

DCM OMS:	Allyson Cornish
AMB OMS:	Jean Smith
FCS:	Ireas Cook
FDA:	Michael C. Rogers
FM:	Jesus Vidal
HRO:	Anita A. Brown
MGT:	Leo F. Voytko
POSHO:	Jesus Vidal
AMB:	Anne Slaughter Andrew

CG:	Robin L. Haase
DCM:	Eric Nelson
PAO:	Mary Daschbach
GSO:	Nathan Boyack
RSO:	Patrick A. Mitchell
AGR:	Kelly Stange
AID:	Tim Callaghan
APHIS:	Eric Hoffman
CLO:	Eridania De Maria
DEA:	James Kenney
ECON:	Jason McInerney
EEO:	Jason McInerney
EST:	Alain G. Norman
FMO:	Christopher Scheffman
ICASS Chair:	Jane McEntee
IMO:	Kevin Rubesh
ISO:	Patricia Rainey
ISSO:	Patricia Rainey
POL:	Roy Perrin
State ICASS:	Eric Turner

Other Contact Information

U.S. Department of Commerce Trade Information Center International Trade Administration
14th and Constitution Avenue, NW
Washington, DC 20320
Tel: 800-USA-TRADE
www.trade.gov

Costa Rican American Chamber of Commerce
c/o Aerocasillas
P.O. Box 025216, Dept 1576
Miami, Florida 33102-5216
Tel: 506-22-0-22-00
Fax: 506-22-0-23-00
Email: Amchamcr@sol.racsa.co.cr

TRAVEL

Consular Information Sheet

May 29, 2012

Country Description: Costa Rica is a middle-income, developing country with a strong democratic tradition. Tourist facilities are generally extensive and adequate. While English is a second language for many Costa Ricans in tourist areas, knowledge of Spanish is necessary for legal matters and in non-tourist areas.

Smart Traveler Enrollment Program (STEP)/ :Embassy Locations: If you are going to live in or visit Costa Rica, please take the time to tell the Embassy about your trip by enrolling in STEP. If you enroll, we can keep you up to date with important safety and security announcements. It will also help your friends and family get in touch with you in an emergency.

We strongly encourage those seeking information to visit the Embassy website. For emergencies such as deaths and major accidents, arising outside of normal business hours, U.S. citizens may call (506) 2519–2000 and ask for the duty officer.

Embassy San Jose
Calle 120 Avenida 0,
Pavas, San José, Costa Rica
Telephone: [506] 2519–2000
Emergency after-hours telephone: [506] 2519–2000
Facsimile: [506] 2200–2455

Entry/Exit Requirements for U.S. Citizens: Visit the Embassy San Jose website for the most current visa information. For entry into Costa Rica, you must present both a valid passport and a roundtrip/outbound ticket. Your passport must be valid for at least 90 days after your arrival. Because of possible fines levied by Costa Rican Immigration, many airlines will not permit passengers without a roundtrip ticket to board flights to Costa Rica unless they have Costa Rican citizenship, residency or a visa. Immigration now also requires that travelers be able to demonstrate financial capacity of at least $100 per month while they are in Costa Rica as tourists. When you leave Costa Rica, you will have to pay a departure tax of $28 USD.

Passports should be in good condition; Costa Rican Immigration may deny entry if a passport is damaged in any way. Costa Rican authorities generally permit U.S. citizen tourists to stay up to ninety (90) days. To extend that period, you must submit an application for an extension to the Office of Temporary Permits in the Costa Rican Department of Immigration. Extension requests are evaluated on a case-by-case basis. Tourists who stay more than 90 days without receiving an extension may experience a delay at the airport when departing, may be fined $100, and/or may be denied entry to Costa Rica on future visits.

Individuals planning to study in Costa Rica can only apply for a student visa from Costa Rican Immigration after arriving in the country. Neither the Costa Rican Embassy in Washington, D.C. nor its Consulates in the United States have the authority to issue student visas. This has led to some confusion by airline employees who mistakenly believe that individuals traveling to Costa Rica as part of a legitimate exchange program must have a return travel date that is less than 90 days from their initial date of travel.

All persons—including American citizens—traveling to Costa Rica from certain countries in South America and Sub-Saharan Africa must provide evidence of a valid yellow fever vaccination prior to entry. The countries considered at risk are: Angola, Benin, Burkina Faso, Cameroon, Democratic Republic of Congo, Gabon, Gambia, Ghana, Guinea, Liberia, Nigeria, Sierra Leone, Sudan, Bolivia, Brazil, Colombia, Ecuador, Peru, Guyana and Venezuela. You can travel to Costa Rica no sooner than 10 days after receiving the vaccination.

The most authoritative and up-to-date information on Costa Rican entry and exit requirements may be obtained from the Consular Section of the Embassy of Costa Rica at 2114 "S" Street NW, Washington, D.C. 20008, telephone (202) 480-2200, fax (202) 265-4795. You may visit the Embassy of Costa Rica's website or contact the Embassy via email. You may also obtain information from the Costa Rican consulates in Atlanta, Houston, Los Angeles, Miami, New York, or the honorary consulates in Minnesota and Arizona..Please also see the Costa Rican Immigration Agency website. It is advisable to contact the Embassy of Costa Rica in Washington or one of Costa Rica's Consulates in the United States for specific information regarding customs requirements before shipping any items.

The U.S. Department of State is unaware of any HIV/AIDS entry restrictions for visitors to or foreign residents of Costa Rica.

Threats to Safety and Security: The incidence of crime in Costa Rica is higher than in many parts of the United States and has adversely affected the traveling public. Pickpocketing and theft remain the most common crimes perpetrated against tourists. U.S. citizens also have been the victims of violent crime including sexual assaults, robberies, car-jackings and murders. American tourists and residents can, however, take steps to protect themselves. You should exercise at least the same level of caution here that you would in major cities or tourist areas in the United States. Engaging in high-risk behavior, such as excessive consumption of alcohol or drugs, can increase the vulnerability of an individual to accidents or opportunistic crime.

Demonstrations in Costa Rica generally are peaceful and rarely affect tourists. However, demonstrators in Costa Rica have been known to block traffic on roads or disrupt travel. Visitors to Costa Rica may also be inconvenienced by infrequent work stoppages and strikes. The Costa Rica Constitution prohibits political activity by foreigners; such actions may result in detention and/or deportation. Travelers should avoid political demonstrations and other activities that might be deemed political by the Costa Rican authorities.. U.S. citizens are urged to exercise caution if in the vicinity of any protests.

There have been no recent acts of terrorism in Costa Rica.

On both the Caribbean and Pacific coasts currents are swift and dangerous, and there are few lifeguards or warning signs on dangerous beaches. A number of U.S. citizens drown every year in Costa Rica due to riptides or sudden drop-offs. There are many scenic areas in Costa Rica where a small incident may become life-threatening due to the rugged terrain or remote location. Foreign visitors have disappeared while hiking or traveling in Costa Rica.

Extreme caution, whether swimming, hiking, or driving, is advised. Adventure tourism is popular in Costa Rica, and many companies offer whitewater rafting, bungee jumping, jungle canopy tours, SCUBA diving, and other outdoor activities. U.S. citizens are urged to use caution in selecting adventure tourism companies. Although the Costa Rican government regulates most of these companies and local regulations require they meet certain safety standards and have insurance coverage, there is not uniform and effective enforcement of these regulations.

Even where strictly enforced, safety measures may not be as stringent nor as comprehensive as what you may be familiar with in the United States. Visitors have been injured or even killed due to improper, careless, or reckless operation of scooters, jet-skis, quads, and other recreational equipment. You should rent equipment only from reputable operators, and insist on sufficient training before using the equipment. Travelers to remote or isolated scenic venues should be aware that they may be some distance from ATMs, appropriate medical services, and law enforcement or consular assistance in an emergency. The Costa Rican Tourism Institute (ICT) web site has contact information for licensed tour operators and travel agencies.

Stay up to date by:

- Bookmarking our Bureau of Consular Affairs website, which contains the current Travel Warnings and Travel Alerts as well as the Worldwide Caution.
- Follow us on Twitter and the Bureau of Consular Affairs page on Facebook as well.
- Download our free Smart Traveler iPhone App to have travel information at your fingertips.
- Calling 1-888-407-4747 toll-free within the U.S. and Canada, or a regular toll line, 1-202-501-4444, from other countries.
- Taking some time before travel to consider your personal security.

Crime: Crime is a significant concern for Costa Ricans and visitors alike. Almost two million foreign tourists, about half of them U.S. citizens, visit Costa Rica annually. While the vast majority do not become victims of crime, all are potential targets for criminals. Criminals often operate in small groups, but may also operate alone. The most common crime perpetrated against tourists is theft, with thieves primarily looking for cash, jewelry, credit cards, electronic items and passports. Serious crimes, although less frequent, do occur. At least 14 U.S. citizens have been murdered in Costa Rica since January 2007. Daytime robberies in public places occur, and thieves have been known to brandish weapons or use violence if victims resist. Eleven U.S. citizens have been sexually assaulted in the past year in tourist areas.

While crimes occur throughout Costa Rica, they are more prevalent at certain times and in certain areas. The downtown area of San Jose for example, is a prime tourist destination during daylight hours. You are strongly encouraged, however, not to go there after dark. U.S. government officials, in fact, are not permitted to stay in hotels in that area due to safety concerns. If you plan to visit an unfamiliar area, you should consult with a trustworthy local (a concierge, a tour guide, etc.) regarding precautions or concerns.

Thieves often work in groups to set up a victim. A prevalent scam involves the surreptitious puncturing of tires of rental cars, often near restaurants, tourist attractions, airports, or close to the car rental agencies themselves. When the travelers pull over, "good Samaritans" quickly appear to help change the tire—and just as quickly remove valuables from the car, sometimes brandishing weapons. Drivers with flat tires are advised to drive, if at all possible, to the nearest service station or other public area and change the tire themselves, watching valuables at all times. Another common scam involves one person dropping change in a crowded area, such as on a bus. When the victim tries to assist, a wallet or other item is taken.

Take proactive steps to avoid becoming a crime victim. Do not walk, hike or exercise alone, and bear in mind that crowded tourist attractions and resort areas popular with foreign tourists are common venues for criminal activity. Ignore any verbal harassment, and avoid carrying your passport, large amounts of cash, jewelry or expensive photographic equipment. You should be particularly cautious of walking alone at night and should not leave bars or restaurants with strangers. Additionally, do not seekentertainment in groups of people you do not know. Do not consume food or drinks you have left unattended or accept food or drinks from "friendly" people.

Tourists should carry photocopies of their passport data page and Costa Rican entry stamp, and leave the original passport in a hotel safe or other secure place when doing day trips or touring the vicinity of where the hotel is located. Costa Rican immigration authorities conduct routine immigration checks at locations, such as bars in downtown San Jose and beach communities. U.S. citizens questioned during these checks who have only a copy of the passport may be asked to provide the original passport with appropriate stamps. Be sure you are certain of the location of your passport and will have ready access to it.

Travelers renting vehicles should purchase an adequate level of locally valid theft insurance, park in secure lots whenever possible, and never leave valuables in their vehicles. Please note that there are unlicensed "parking attendants" that will occasionally assist you in parking; however, parking where they indicate does not always guarantee that it is a legal parking spot. Drivers should be cautious of where they park their cars. The U.S. Embassy receives several reports daily of valuables, identity documents, and other items stolen from locked vehicles, primarily rental cars. Thefts from parked cars can occur nearly anywhere, although cities, at beaches, at the airport, in front of restaurants and hotels, and at national parks and other tourist attractions are common locations.

U.S. government personnel are not permitted to travel on city buses due to safety concerns, and must use caution when traveling on any other buses. If you choose to travel by bus, you are encouraged to keep your bag with valuables and identification on your lap. Personal items are frequently stolen from buses. Do not store your bags or other personal belongings in the storage bins, as theft from overhead bins is common. You should keep your belongings in your line of sight at all times and your valuables in your possession. If you choose to help another passenger stow his belongings, you should be especially cautious that your own belongings are not removed while you are doing so.

Travelers should use only licensed taxis, which are typically red with medallions (yellow triangles containing numbers) painted on the side. Licensed taxis at the airport are painted orange. All licensed taxis should have working door handles, locks, seatbelts and meters (called "marias"); passengers are encouraged to use seatbelts.

Don't buy counterfeit and pirated goods, even if they are widely available. Not only are the bootlegs illegal in the United States, if you purchase them you may also be breaking local law.

Victims of Crime: Local law enforcement agencies have limited capabilities and different standards than U.S. law enforcement. If you or someone you know becomes the victim of a crime abroad, you should contact the local police.

Report any crime to the OIJ police (800.800.3000) who are able to take your report, and also to the Consular Section of the U.S. Embassy at 2519–2000,from the U.S.: 011-506-2519–2000, or by email to: acssanjose@state.gov.

The loss or theft abroad of a U.S. passport should be reported immediately to the U.S. Embassy. This allows the Embassy to make the necessary notifications that may help catch criminals, including terrorists, who try to buy or use the passport.

The local equivalent to the "911" emergency line in Costa Rica is also "911"

In Costa Rica, there are various types of police. Those in uniform are La Fuerza Pública. Their role is crime prevention. OIJ, plain clothes police, are in charge of investigations. In general, only OIJ police can accept reports of crime. There are also tourist and traffic police.

The U.S. embassy can:

- Replace a stolen passport.
- For violent crimes such as assault or rape, help you find appropriate medical care.
- Put you in contact with the appropriate police authorities and, if you want us to, we can contact family members or friends.

Although the local authorities are responsible for investigating and prosecuting the crime, consular officers can help you understand the local criminal justice process and can provide you with the names of local attorneys.

Criminal Penalties: While you are traveling in Costa Rica, you are subject to its laws and regulations even if you are a U.S. citizen. Some laws in Costa Rica differ significantly from those in the United States and may not afford the protections available to the individual under U.S. law. Penalties for breaking the law can be more severe than in the United States for similar offenses. Persons violating Costa Rica's laws, even unknowingly, may be expelled, arrested or imprisoned. The law permits pre-trial detention of persons accused of serious crimes. Penalties for possession, use, or trafficking in illegal drugs in Costa Rica are severe, and convicted offenders can expect long jail sentences and heavy fines. Engaging in sexual conduct with minors or using or disseminating child pornography in a foreign country is a crime, prosecutable in the United States. It is also a crime in Costa Rica. Foreign laws and legal systems can be vastly different than our own. Driving under the influence of alcohol or drugs could land you immediately in jail. You can be prosecuted under U.S. law if you buy pirated goods. If you break local laws in Costa Rica, your U.S. passport will not help you avoid arrest or prosecution. It is very important to know what is legal and what is not where you are going.

If you are arrested in Costa Rica, authorities are required to notify the U.S. Embassy of your arrest. If you are concerned the Department of State may not be aware of your situation, you should request the police or prison officials to notify the U.S. embassy of your arrest.

Land Ownership and Shoreline Property: U.S. citizens are urged to use extreme caution when making real estate purchases or investments, to consult with reputable legal counsel, and to investigate thoroughly all aspects before entering into a contract. Check the San Jose Embassy website for a list of possible lawyers. You also are encouraged to review the Investment Climate Statement for Costa Rica on the State Department's website. Coastal land within 50 meters of the high tide line is open to the public and therefore closed to development, and construction on the next 150 meters inland is possible only with the approval of the local municipality.

Squatters: Organized squatter groups have invaded properties in various parts of the country. These squatter groups take advantage of legal provisions that allow people without land to gain title to unused property. Local courts may show considerable sympathy for the squatters. Victims of squatters have reported threats, harassment, and violence. There is very little that the U.S. Embassy can do to assist U.S. citizens who enter into land or business disputes in Costa Rica; you must be prepared to take your case to the local courts, which is often a very long and expensive process.

Documentation Requirements: Visitors are required to carry appropriate documentation at all times. However, due to the high incidence of passport theft, tourists are permitted and encouraged to carry photocopies of the data page and entry stamp from the passport, leaving the passport in a hotel safe or other secure place. As noted under the CRIME section of this report, Costa Rican immigration authorities conduct routine checks for illegal immigrants, especially in bars located in downtown San Jose and in beach communities. A U.S. citizen questioned during one of these checks and carrying only the copy of the passport will be required to produce the original passport. Therefore, tourists should carry their actual passports when taking domestic air flights, when traveling overnight, and when traveling a considerable distance from their hotel.

Local authorities have the right to detain U.S. citizens until their identity and immigration status have been verified. Tourists who carry passports are urged to place them securely in an inside pocket.

Exit Procedures for Costa Rican citizens and legal residents: All children born in Costa Rica acquire Costa Rican citizenship at birth, and may only depart the country upon presentation of an exit permit issued by immigration authorities. Unless the child is traveling with both parents, legal documentation is required to demonstrate that both parents grant permission for the child to leave the country. This policy, designed to prevent international child abduction, applies to dual national U.S./Costa Rican citizens as well as U.S. citizens who are legal residents in Costa Rica. Parents of minors who obtained Costa Rican citizenship through a parent or through birth in Costa Rica are advised to consult with appropriate Costa Rican authorities prior to travel to Costa Rica, especially if one (or both) parent(s) is not accompanying the child.

Disaster Preparedness: Costa Rica is located in an active earthquake and volcanic zone. When planning travel to the area, you should consider that such a disaster may strike without warning. Serious flooding occurs annually in the Caribbean Province of Limon and the Pacific Province of Puntarenas, and flash floods and severe landslides occur in other parts of Costa Rica as well, depending on the time of year and rainfall. General information about natural disaster preparedness is available from the U.S. Federal Emergency Management Agency (FEMA) and from the Center for Disease Control and Prevention.

Accessibility: While in Costa Rica, individuals with disabilities may find accessibility and accommodation limited. Costa Rica has legislation that mandates access to transportation, communication and public buildings for persons with disabilities, but the government does not effectively enforce these laws.

Medical Facilities and Health Information: Costa Rica actively promotes medical tourism. While there are advantages like affordable costs, quality health care, and a chance to recuperate and have a vacation at the same time, there are also risks.

Medical tourists should confirm that the facilities they intend to use are accredited and have an acceptable level of care. They should also purchase medical evacuation insurance before travelling, and should confirm that the cost and payment for their treatment is clearly understood by both parties. Persons with unpaid or disputed debts in Costa Rica may be legally prevented from leaving the country.

In the event of unforeseen medical complications or malpractice, medical tourists may not be covered by their personal insurance or may not be able to seek damages through malpractice lawsuits. Although many hospitals and clinics abroad have medical malpractice insurance, seeking compensation can prove to be difficult because insurance laws and legal options may not exist. Be aware that if you should need or wish to be transferred to a hospital in the United States and do not have medical evacuation issurance, an air ambulance flight can cost upwards of US$20,000 and will often take place only after you (or your loved ones) have paid for it.

Medical care in San Jose is adequate, but is limited in areas outside of San Jose. Most prescription and over-the-counter medications are available throughout Costa Rica. Doctors and hospitals often expect immediate cash payment for health services, and U.S. medical insurance is not always valid outside the United States. A list of local doctors and medical facilities can be obtained from the U.S. Embassy in San Jose 's website.. An ambulance may be summoned by calling 911. Most ambulances provide transportation but little or no medical assistance.

You can find good information on vaccinations and other health precautions on the CDC website. For information about outbreaks of infectious diseases abroad, consult the World Health Organization (WHO) website. The WHO website also contains additional health information for travelers, including detailed country-specific health information.

Medical Insurance: You cannot assume your insurance will go with you when you travel. It's very important to find out BEFORE you leave whether or not your medical insurance will cover you overseas. You need to ask your insurance company two questions:

- Does my policy apply when I'm out of the United States?
- Will it cover emergencies like a trip to a foreign hospital or a medical evacuation?

In many places, doctors and hospitals still expect payment in cash at the time of service. Your regular U.S. health insurance may not cover doctors' and hospital visits in other countries. If your policy doesn't go with you when you travel, it's a very good idea to take out another one for your trip. U.S. retirees living in Costa Rica without adequate insurance coverage can find themselves at the mercy of public hospitals with limited resources in providing care. Many retirees have also been the victims of unscrupulous home care providers. Some elderly retirees have been dumped on the street by unscrupulous "care takers" once their funds were exhausted.

Traffic Safety and Road Conditions: While in Costa Rica, you may encounter road conditions that differ significantly from those in the United States. The information below concerning Costa Rica is provided for general reference only, and may not apply to a particular location or circumstance.

Roads are often in poor condition. Large potholes with the potential to cause significant damage to vehicles are common. Traffic signs, even on major highways, are inadequate and few roads have clearly marked lanes. Except for the principal highways, few roads have names, making it difficult to find addresses. Shoulders are narrow or consist of drainage ditches. Visibility at intersections is often limited by hedges or other obstacles. Bridges, even on heavily traveled roads, may be only a single lane requiring vehicles traveling in one direction to cede the right of way to oncoming vehicles. Pedestrians, cyclists, and farm animals are common sights along or on main roads, creating additional potential driving hazards. Buses and cars frequently stop in travel lanes, even on expressways. Traffic laws and speed limits are often ignored, turn signals are rarely used, passing on dangerous stretches of highway is common, and pedestrians are not given the right of way. The abundant motorcyclists in particular, drive without respect to rules of the road, often passing on the right, weaving in and out without warning, and creating lanes where none officially exist. As a result, the fatality rate for pedestrians and those riding bicycles and motorcycles is disproportionately high. All of the above, in addition to poor visibility due to heavy fog or rain, can make driving treacherous. Landslides are common in the rainy season. Main highways and principal roads in the major cities are paved, but some roads to beaches and other rural locations are not. Additionally, rural roads sometimes lack bridges and motorists are compelled to ford waterways; you should exercise extreme caution in driving across moving water, as a small trickle in the dry season may become a strong torrent after a heavy rain upstream. Even a few inches of moving water may be sufficient to float your vehicle, and the river bed may not be stable.

In order to drive in Costa Rica, drivers need to show a valid U.S. driver's license or an international driving permit. Drunk driving is illegal in Costa Rica. There are individuals who drive while using their cell phone but anything that impedes one's ability to drive is discouraged.

Many destinations are accessible only with high clearance, four-wheel drive vehicles. When staying outside of urban areas, travelers should call ahead to their hotels to ask about the current status of access roads. Travelers should also minimize driving at night, especially outside of urban areas.

Costa Rica has a 911 system for reporting emergencies. In the event of a traffic accident, vehicles must be left where they are and should not be moved from where the accident occurred. Both the traffic police and an insurance investigator must make accident reports before the vehicles are moved.

Aviation Safety Oversight: The U.S. Federal Aviation Administration (FAA) has assessed the Government of Costa Rica's Civil Aviation Authority as being in compliance with International Civil Aviation Organization (ICAO) aviation safety standards for oversight of Costa Rica's air carrier operations. For more information, travelers may visit the FAA web site.

Children's Issues: Please see the U.S. Dept. of State Office of Children's Issues web pages on intercountry adoption and international parental child abduction.

Intercountry Adoption

February 2011

The information in this section has been edited from the latest report available as of February 2013 from the State Department Bureau of Consular Affairs, Office of Overseas Citizens Services. For more information, please read the *Intercountry Adoption* section of this book and review current reports online at http://adoption.state.gov.

The Hague Convention on Intercountry adoption, which entered into force for the United States on April 1, 2008, requires that all adoptions between the United States and Hague Partner countries have certain safeguards that ensure the adoption is in the best interest of the child. Every step of the Hague Adoption process was developed to address past abuses. The Costa Rican Central Authority for the Hague Convention in respect to Intercountry adoption is the Patronato Nacional de la Infancia (PANI). PANI is the Costa Rican child welfare authority. PANI will not accept private-direct-adoptions. There are no exceptions to this rule. Private adoptions are those that are not handled by the Costa Rican Council on Adoptions (PANI), but are arranged by an attorney and approved by a judge. There have been allegations of fraud in connection with private adoptions, and the Costa Rican National Council on adoptions strongly discourages them.

All international adoptions in Costa Rica should go through PANI. PANI prohibits adoption of children less than five years of age, except in cases in which the child is part of a family group, or in cases where the child may have disabilities that will cause difficulties in placing the child. Another important requirement is the post-adoption reporting that the adoptive parents need to send to the country of origin of the children. PANI is very strict with this requirement and they require a post-adoption report for a period of two years, every six months. U.S. adoption providers and adoptive parents must comply with this requisite Costa Rica is party to the Hague Convention on Protection of Children and Co-operation in Respect of Intercountry Adoption (Hague Adoption Convention). Therefore all adoptions between Costa Rica and the United States must meet the requirements of the Convention and U.S. law implementing the Convention.

Who Can Adopt? Adoption between the United States and Costa Rica is governed by the Hague Adoption Convention. Therefore to adopt from Costa Rica, you must first be found eligible to adopt by the U.S. Government. The U.S. Government agency responsible for making this determination is the Department of Homeland Security, U.S. Citizenship and Immigration Services (USCIS).

Residency Requirements: Costa Rican law requires that, at the initial stage of the adoption process, both prospective adoptive parents must be in Costa Rica to sign the official consent documents before the Costa Rican court. In the case of adoption by a single prospective adoptive parent, that individual must be present to sign the documents. At least 30 days should be allowed for this initial trip. At the end of the process, one of the adoptive parents, or the sole parent if it is a single-parent adoption, must be in Costa Rica to finish the paperwork for the adoption, obtain a travel document for the child, and complete immigration procedures at the U.S. Embassy. Since the length of time for the entire adoption process may vary (from eight months to a year), many prospective adoptive parents make two trips to Costa Rica; others prefer to remain in Costa Rica for the entire process. While in Costa Rica, the adopting parents need to take the following steps to satisfy local adoption requirements:

- Meet the child;
- Give formal consent for the adoption at the court;
- Obtain a decree of abandonment;
- Obtain a certified copy of the final adoption decree from the court;
- Register the adoption at the local Civil Registry;
- Obtain a birth certificate from the Civil Registry with the new name of the child;
- Obtain PANI authorization for the child to leave the country;
- Obtain a Costa Rican passport for the child.

Age Requirements: Prospective adoptive parents must be at least 25 years of age and under 60 years of age.

Marriage Requirements: Costa Rican law permits adoption by married and single persons. A foreign couple must have been married for at least five years.

Who Can Be Adopted? Because Costa Rica is party to the Hague Adoption Convention, children from Costa Rica must meet the requirements of the Convention in order to be eligible for adoption. For example, the Convention requires that Costa Rica attempt to place a child with a family in Costa Rica before determining that a child is eligible for intercountry adoption. In addition to Costa Rican requirements, a child must meet the definition of a Convention adoptee for you to bring him or her back to the United States.

Abandonment/Relinquishment Requirements: Under Costa Rican law, adopted children do not need to be orphans (both birth parents deceased). They must, however, be abandoned or irrevocably surrendered for adoption. Abandoned children may be living in a government facility, in a private orphanage or foster home or in the custody of a relative or friend. Children may also remain in the custody of a biological parent prior to formal relinquishment of custody before a judge.

Age Requirements: In foreign adoptions overseen by PANI, current Costa Rican law prohibits adoption of children less than four years of age, except in cases in which the child is part of a family group, or is difficult to place.

Costa Rican Adoption Authority: The Patronato Nacional de la Infancia (PANI), the Costa Rican child welfare authority, oversees adoptions of abandoned orphans who are in public institution.

The Process: Because Costa Rica is party to the Hague Adoption Convention, adopting from Costa Rica must follow a specific process designed to meet the Convention's requirements.

The first step in adopting a child from Costa Rica is to select an adoption service provider in the United States that has been accredited not only in the United States but also in Costa Rica. The accreditation of agencies in Costa Rica is done by the Costa Rican Central Authority, PANI. Prospective adoptive parent(s) seeking to adopt in Costa Rica need(s) to check with the Costa Rican Central Authority to find a current list of these agencies, You can find PANI's contact information at the end of this document. Only these agencies and attorneys can provide adoption services between the United States and Costa Rica.

After you choose an accredited adoption service provider, you apply to be found eligible to adopt (Form I-800A) by the U.S. Government, Department of Homeland Security, U.S. Citizenship and Immigration Services (USCIS). Once the U.S. Government determines that you are "eligible" and "suitable" to adopt, you or your agency will forward your information to the adoption authority in Costa Rica. Costa Rica's adoption authority will review your application to determine whether you are also eligible to adopt under Costa Rican law.

If both the United States and Costa Rica determine that you are eligible to adopt, and a child is available for intercountry adoption, the central adoption authority in Costa Rica may provide you with a referral for a child.

After you accept a match with a child, you will apply to the U.S Government, Department of Homeland Security, U.S. Citizenship and Immigration Services (USCIS) for provisional approval to adopt that particular child (Form I-800). USCIS will determine whether the child is eligible under U.S. law to be adopted and enter the United States.

After this, your adoption service provider or you will submit a visa application to a Consular Officer at the U.S. Embassy. The Consular Officer will review the child's information and evaluate the child for possible visa ineligibilities. If the Consular Office determines that the child appears eligible to immigrate to the United States, he/she will notify the Costa Rican adoption authority (Article 5 letter). For Convention country adoptions, prospective adoptive parent(s) may not proceed with the adoption or obtain custody for the purpose of adoption until this takes place.

Role of the Adoption Authority: PANI contacts a prospective adoptive family when PANI identifies a child for adoption, even calling collect if authorized by the family or through the adoption facilitator that is handling the case. Pictures and related information about the child will be sent by airmail. (Note that there is a backlog in pending cases.)

PANI must also authorize the child to leave the country. Foreigners, including U.S. citizens, must complete the adoption process in Costa Rica and the adoption must be formally registered in the civil registry before the Costa Rican authorities will grant permission for the child to leave the country. Because of Costa Rican government concerns about child smuggling and the need for follow-up in the adoption process, permission is rarely granted for a child to leave Costa Rica in the custody of a prospective adoptive parent for the purpose of being finally adopted in another country.

Role of the Court: The court reviews the qualifications of the prospective adoptive parents, with PANI playing a consultative role.

Time Frame: An adoption in Costa Rica generally takes from eight to twelve months from the time a decree of abandonment has been issued or an official request for adoption of a specific child is placed before the court.

Adoption Fees: The U.S. Embassy in Costa Rica discourages the payment of any fees that are not properly receipted, "donations," or "expediting" fees, that may be requested from prospective adoptive parents. Such fees have the appearance of "buying" a baby and put all future adoptions in Costa Rica at risk. In the adoption services contract that you sign at the beginning of the adoption process, your agency will itemize the fees and estimated expenses related to your adoption process.

Some of the fees specifically associated with adopting from Costa Rica include official fees for an adoption which are set at a minimum of $250, and represent the total court costs when an adoption is processed through PANI. Payments to parents or guardians are illegal under Costa Rican law and prospective adoptive parents who make such payments could be subject to investigation and possible prosecution. American adoptive parents may want to notify the Embassy and the Department of State if they feel they are being charged excessive fees.

Documents Required: The following documentation is normally required:

- Certified and authenticated copies of the adoptive parent(s)' birth certificate(s);
- Certified and authenticated copy of the adoptive parent(s)' marriage certificate (if applicable) and proof of termination of any previous marriages (certified copy of spouse's death certificate or divorce decree);
- Medical certificate(s) for adoptive parent(s) notarized. The certificate must be authenticated by the Costa Rican Embassy in the U.S. and translated into Spanish.

- A certificate of good conduct/no criminal record for each adoptive parent from a local police department, notarized or bearing police department seal and authenticated. An FBI report is acceptable in lieu of local police record. This is separate from the FBI check conducted by USCIS as part of the petition process;
- Verification of employment and salary, notarized and authenticated;
- Two letters of reference notarized and authenticated;
- A certified and authenticated copy of property trusts deeds, if applicable;
- A home study prepared by an authorized and licensed social agency, certified and authenticated, may be required in some cases by the Costa Rican authorities if necessary information was not included on the USCIS (I-800A).
- Bank statements, notarized/certified and authenticated;
- Family letter of intent to adopt, which states any general preferences requested by the family, i.e. a certain age, sex, etc. notarized and authenticated.

Bringing Your Child Home: Once your adoption is complete (or you have obtained legal custody of the child), there are a few more steps to take before you can head home. Specifically, you need to apply for several documents for your child before he or she can travel to the United States, such as a birth certificate, a passport or travel document for your child from the country in which he or she was born, and a U.S. Immigration Visa. For detailed and updated information on how to obtain these documents, review the *Intercountry Adoption* section in this publication and visit the U.S. Department of State Intercountry Adoption website at http://adoption.state.gov.

Child Citizenship Act: For adoptions finalized abroad, the Child Citizenship Act of 2000 allows your new child to acquire American citizenship automatically when he or she enters the United States as lawful permanent residents. For adoptions finalized in the United States, the Child Citizenship Act of 2000 allows your new child to acquire American citizenship automatically when the court in the United States issues the final adoption decree. To learn more, review the *Intercountry Adoption* section in this publication and visit the U.S. Department of State Intercountry Adoption website at http://adoption.state.gov.

U.S. Embassy in Costa Rica
APO AA 34020
Tel: (506) 2519- 2466
Fax: (506) 2220–2455
http://sanjose.usembassy.gov

Costa Rican Adoption Authority
Patronato Nacional de La Infancia
P.O. Box 5000–1000
San Jose, Costa Rica
Tel: (506) 25230794
Fax: (506) 25230895
Email: paniadop@racsa.co.cr

Embassy of Costa Rica
2112- S Street, N.W.
Washington, D.C. 20008
Tel: (202) 234–2945/46
Fax: (202) 265–4795
http://www.costarica-embassy. org

Costa Rica also has consulates in: Atlanta, Chicago, Houston, Los Angeles, Miami, New York, San Juan, San Francisco, and Tampa

Office of Children's Issues
U.S. Department of State2201 C Street, NW
SA-29
Washington, DC 20520
Tel: 1–888–407–4747
E-mail: AskCI@state.gov
http://adoption.state.gov

For questions about immigration procedures, call the National Customer Service Center (NCSC) 1-800-375-5283 (TTY 1-800-767-1833).

CÔTE D'IVOIRE

Compiled from publications that were available as of February 2013 from the U.S. Department of State, the U.S. Department of Commerce, and the Central Intelligence Agency (CIA). See the introduction to this set for explanatory notes.

Official Name:
Republic of Côte d'Ivoire

PROFILE

Geography

Area: total: 322,463 sq km; country comparison to the world: 69; land: 318,003 sq km; water: 4,460 sq km
Major cities: Abidjan (seat of government) 4.009 million; Yamoussoukro (capital) 808,000 (2009)
Climate: tropical along coast, semiarid in far north; three seasons—warm and dry (November to March), hot and dry (March to May), hot and wet (June to October)
Terrain: mostly flat to undulating plains; mountains in northwest

People

Nationality: noun: Ivoirian(s); adjective: Ivoirian
Population: 21,952,093 (July 2012 est.)
Population growth rate: 2.044% (2012 est.)
Ethnic groups: Akan 42.1%, Voltaiques or Gur 17.6%, Northern Mandes 16.5%, Krous 11%, Southern Mandes 10%, other 2.8% (includes 130,000 Lebanese and 14,000 French) (1998)
Religions: Muslim 38.6%, Christian 32.8%, indigenous 11.9%, none 16.7% (2008 est.)
Languages: French (official), 60 native dialects of which Dioula is the most widely spoken
Literacy: definition: age 15 and over can read and write; total population: 56.2%; male: 65.2%; female: 46.6% (2010 est.)
Health: life expectancy at birth: total population: 57.25 years; male: 56.21 years; female: 58.33 years (2012 est.); Infant mortality rate: total: 63.2 deaths/1,000 live births; male: 69.77 deaths/1,000 live births; female: 56.42 deaths/1,000 live births (2012 est.)
Unemployment rate: NA%
Work force: 8.97 million (2012 est.)

Government

Type: republic; multiparty presidential regime established 1960
Independence: 7 August 1960
Constitution: approved by referendum 23 July 2000
Political subdivisions: 19 regions
Suffrage: 18 years of age; universal

Economy

GDP (purchasing power parity): $39.64 billion (2012 est.); $36.53 billion (2011 est.); $38.34 billion (2010 est.); $37.45 billion (2009 est.)
GDP real growth rate: 8.1% (2012 est.); -4.7% (2011 est.); 2.4% (2010 est.); 3.8% (2009 est.)
GDP per capita (PPP): $1,700 (2012 est.); $1,600 (2011 est.); $1,700 (2010 est.); $1,800 (2009 est.)
Natural resources: petroleum, natural gas, diamonds, manganese, iron ore, cobalt, bauxite, copper, gold, nickel, tantalum, silica sand, clay, cocoa beans, coffee, palm oil, hydropower
Agriculture products: coffee, cocoa beans, bananas, palm kernels, corn, rice, cassava (manioc), sweet potatoes, sugar, cotton, rubber; timber
Industries: foodstuffs, beverages; wood products, oil refining, gold mining, truck and bus assembly, textiles, fertilizer, building materials, electricity
Exports: $10.99 billion (2012 est.); $11.41 billion (2011 est.); $10.47 billion (2010 est.)
Exports—commodities: cocoa, coffee, timber, petroleum, cotton, bananas, pineapples, palm oil, fish
Exports—partners: Netherlands 11.6%, US 11.5%, Germany 7.3%, Nigeria 6%, Canada 6%, France 5.9%, South Africa 5.4% (2011)
Imports: $8.406 billion (2012 est.); $7.92 billion (2011 est.); $7.014 billion (2010 est.)
Imports—commodities: fuel, capital equipment, foodstuffs
Imports—partners: Nigeria 35.6%, France 9.9%, China 5.6%, Colombia 5.4% (2011)
Debt—external: $4.742 billion (31 December 2012 est.)$11.44 billion (31 December 2011 est.)
Exchange rates: Communaute Financiere Africaine francs (XOF) per US dollar; 513.1 (2012 est.); 471.87 (2011 est.); 495.28 (2010 est.); 472.19 (2009); 447.81 (2008)

PEOPLE

Côte d'Ivoire has more than 60 ethnic groups, usually classified into five principal divisions: Akan (east and center, including Lagoon peoples of the southeast), Krou (southwest), Southern Mande (west), Northern Mande (northwest), Senoufo/Lobi (north center and northeast). The Baoules, in the Akan division, probably comprise the single largest subgroup. They are based in the central region around Bouake and Yamoussoukro. The Betes in the Krou division, the Senoufos in the north, and the Malinkes in the northwest and the cities are the next largest groups. Most of the principal divisions have a significant presence in neighboring countries.

Of the more than 5 million non-Ivoirian Africans living in Côte d'Ivoire, one-third to one-half are from Burkina Faso; the rest are from Ghana, Guinea, Mali, Nigeria, Benin, Senegal, Liberia, and Mauritania. The non-African expatriate community includes roughly 10,000 French and possibly 60,000 Lebanese.

National/Racial/Ethnic Minorities

The country has an ethnically diverse population, with more than 60 ethnic groups. Groups sometimes practiced societal discrimination against others on the basis of ethnicity. Approximately 25 percent of the population was considered foreign, although many within this category were second- or third-generation residents. Outdated or inadequate land ownership laws reportedly resulted in conflicts with ethnic and xenophobic overtones, often between the native populations and other groups.

Religion

Approximately 35 to 40 percent of the population is Christian, an equal percentage is Muslim, and an estimated 25 percent practice indigenous religious beliefs. Many persons who are nominally Christian or Muslim also practice some aspects of indigenous religious beliefs. Traditionally, the north is associated with Islam and the south with Christianity, although practitioners of both religions live throughout the country. In general, political and religious affiliations tend to follow ethnic and socioeconomic lines.

Christian groups include Roman Catholics, Jehovah's Witnesses, Seventh-day Adventists, Methodists, Assemblies of God, Southern Baptists, Copts, and The Church of Jesus Christ of Latter-day Saints (Mormons).

Other religious groups include Buddhists, Baha'is, followers of the International Society for Krishna Consciousness, and Bossonists, who follow a traditional practice of the Akan ethnic group.

HISTORY

The early history of Côte d'Ivoire is virtually unknown, although it is thought that a Neolithic culture existed. France made its initial contact with Côte d'Ivoire in 1637, when missionaries landed at Assinie near the Gold Coast (now Ghana) border. Early contacts were limited to a few missionaries because of the inhospitable coastline and settlers' fear of the inhabitants.

In the 18th century, the country was invaded from present-day Ghana by two related Akan groups—the Agni, who occupied the southeast, and the Baoule, who settled in the central section. In 1843–44, Admiral Bouet-Willaumez signed treaties with the kings of the Grand Bassam and Assinie regions, placing their territories under a French protectorate. French explorers, missionaries, trading companies, and soldiers gradually extended the area under French control inland from the lagoon region. However, complete pacification was not accomplished until 1915.

French Period

Côte d'Ivoire officially became a French colony in 1893. Captain Binger, who had explored the Gold Coast frontier, was named the first governor. He negotiated boundary treaties with Liberia and the United Kingdom (for the Gold Coast) and later started the campaign against Almany Samory, a Malinke chief, who fought against the French until 1898.

From 1904 to 1958, Côte d'Ivoire was a constituent unit of the Federation of French West Africa. It was a colony and an overseas territory under the French Third Republic. Until the period following World War II, governmental affairs in French West Africa were administered from Paris. France's policy in West Africa was reflected mainly in its philosophy of "association," meaning that all Africans in Côte d'Ivoire were officially French "subjects" without rights to citizenship or representation in Africa or France.

During World War II, France's Vichy regime remained in control until 1943, when members of Gen. Charles de Gaulle's provisional government assumed control of all French West Africa. The Brazzaville Conference in 1944, the first Constituent Assembly of the French Fourth Republic in 1946, and France's gratitude for African loyalty during World War II led to far-reaching governmental reforms in 1946. French citizenship was granted to all African "subjects," the right to organize politically was recognized, and various forms of forced labor were abolished.

A turning point in relations with France was reached with the 1956 Overseas Reform Act (Loi Cadre), which transferred a number of powers from Paris to elected territorial governments in French West Africa and also removed remaining voting inequalities.

Independence

In December 1958, Côte d'Ivoire became an autonomous republic within the French community as a result of a referendum that brought community status to all members of the old Federation of French West Africa (except Guinea, which had voted against association). Côte d'Ivoire became independent on August 7,

1960 and Felix Houphouet-Boigny assumed the presidency. Côte d'Ivoire's contemporary political history is closely associated with Houphouet-Boigny's 33-year presidency. He was the leader of the main political party until the 1990s, the Parti Democratique de la Côte d'Ivoire (PDCI), and one of the founders of the Rassemblement Democratique Africain (RDA), the leading pre-independence inter-territorial political party in French West African territories (except Mauritania). Houphouet-Boigny first came to political prominence in 1944 when he founded the Syndicat Agricole Africain, an organization that won improved conditions for African farmers and formed a nucleus for the PDCI. After World War II, he was elected by a narrow margin to the first Constituent Assembly, representing Côte d'Ivoire in the French National Assembly from 1946 to 1959. He devoted much of his effort to inter-territorial political organization and further improvement of labor conditions. In May 1959, he reinforced his position as a dominant figure in West Africa by leading Côte d'Ivoire, Niger, Upper Volta (Burkina), and Dahomey (Benin) into the Council of the Entente, a regional organization promoting economic development. He maintained that the road to African solidarity was through step-by-step economic and political cooperation, and his key principle was non-intervention in internal affairs of other African states.

After serving 13 years in the French National Assembly, including almost 3 years as a minister in the French Government, he became Côte d'Ivoire's first Prime Minister in April 1959. He was elected the first President of Côte d'Ivoire in 1960 and served for 33 years.

1999—Coup and Aftermath

In a region where many political systems are unstable, Côte d'Ivoire showed remarkable political stability from its independence from France in 1960 until late 1999. Under Felix Houphouet-Boigny, President from independence until his death on December 7, 1993, Côte d'Ivoire maintained a close political allegiance to the West while many countries in the region were undergoing repeated military coups, experimenting with Marxism, and developing ties with the Soviet Union and China. His successor, President Henri Konan Bedie, served from 1993 to 1999 and was familiar with the U.S., having served as Côte d'Ivoire's first ambassador to the U.S. Falling world market prices for Côte d'Ivoire's primary exports of cocoa and coffee put pressure on the economy and the Bedie presidency. Government corruption and mismanagement led to steep reductions in foreign aid in 1998 and 1999, and eventually to the country's first coup on December 24, 1999.

Following the bloodless coup, General Robert Guei formed a government of national unity and promised open elections. A new constitution was drafted and ratified by the population in the summer of 2000. It retained clauses that underscored national divisions between north and south and Christians and Muslims, and established stricter eligibility requirements for contesting political office, including that both parents of anyone wishing to run for president must be born in Côte d'Ivoire. Elections were scheduled for fall 2000, but when the general's hand-picked Supreme Court disqualified all of the candidates from the two major parties—the PDCI and Rassemblement des Republicaines (RDR)—Western election support and monitors were withdrawn. The RDR called for a boycott, setting the stage for low election turnout in a race between Guei and Front Populaire Ivoirien (FPI) candidate Laurent Gbagbo. When early polling results showed Gbagbo in the lead, Guei stopped the process—claiming polling fraud—disbanded the election commission, and declared himself the winner. Within hours Gbagbo supporters took to the streets of Abidjan. A bloody fight followed as crowds attacked the guards protecting the presidential palace. Many gendarmes and soldiers joined the fight against the junta government, forcing Guei to flee. Having gained the most votes, Gbagbo was declared President. The RDR then took to the streets, calling for new elections because the Supreme Court had declared their presidential candidate and all the candidates of the PDCI ineligible. More violence erupted as forces loyal to the new government joined the FPI youth to attack RDR demonstrators. Hundreds were killed in the few days that followed before RDR party leader Alassane Ouattara called for peace and recognized the Gbagbo presidency.

2001—Attempted Coup

Although there was another coup attempt on January 7, 2001, local municipal elections were conducted in the spring without violence and with the full participation of all political parties. The RDR, which had boycotted the presidential and legislative elections, won the most local seats, followed by the PDCI and FPI. Some economic aid from the European Union began to return by the summer of 2001, and the International Monetary Fund (IMF) re-engaged the government. Questions surrounding severe human rights abuses by the government during the 2000 presidential and legislative elections remained unresolved (e.g., a mass grave at Yopougon), but day-to-day life began to return to normal. In August 2002, President Gbagbo formed a de facto government of national unity that included the RDR party.

2002—The Country Divides

On September 19, 2002, exiled military personnel and co-conspirators in Abidjan simultaneously attacked government ministers and government and military/security facilities in Abidjan, Bouake, and Korhogo. In Abidjan, government forces managed to stop the coup attempt within hours, but the attacks resulted in the deaths of Minister of Interior Emile Boga Doudou and several high-ranking military officers. General Guei was killed under still-unclear circumstances. Almost immediately after the coup attempt, the government launched an aggressive security operation, in which shantytowns—occupied by thousands of immigrants and Ivoirians—were searched for weapons and rebels. Government security forces burned down or demolished a number of these shantytowns, which displaced over 12,000 people.

The failed coup attempt quickly evolved into a rebellion, split the country in two, and escalated into the country's worst crisis since independence in 1960. The rebel group, calling itself the "Patriotic Movement of Côte d'Ivoire" (MPCI), retained control in Bouake and Korhogo, and within 2 weeks moved to take the remainder of the northern half of the country. In mid-October 2002, government and MPCI representatives signed a ceasefire and French military forces already present in the country agreed to monitor the ceasefire line. In late November 2002, the western part of the country became a new military front with the emergence of two new rebel groups—the Ivoirian Popular Movement for the Great West (MPIGO) and the Movement for Justice and Peace (MJP). MPIGO and MJP were allied with the MPCI, and the three groups subsequently called themselves the "New Forces." In January 2003, the Economic Community of West African States (ECOWAS) placed approximately 1,500 peacekeeping troops from five countries—Senegal (commander), Ghana, Benin, Togo, and Niger—on the ground beside the 4,000 French peacekeepers. The troops maintained the east-west ceasefire line, known as the Zone of Confidence, dividing the country.

2003–2006—Reunification Attempts

In late January 2003, the country's major political parties and the New Forces signed the French-brokered Linas-Marcoussis Accord (LMA), agreeing to a power-sharing national reconciliation government to include rebel New Forces representatives. The parties agreed to work together on modifying national identity, eligibility for citizenship, and land tenure laws that many observers considered among the root causes of the conflict. The LMA also stipulated a UN Monitoring Committee to report on implementation of the accord. The same month, President Gbagbo appointed Seydou Diarra as the consensus Prime Minister. In March 2003, Prime Minister Diarra formed a government of national reconciliation of 41 ministers. On July 4, 2003, the government and New Forces militaries signed an "End of the War" declaration that recognized President Gbagbo's authority and vowed to work for the implementation of the LMA and a program of demobilization, disarmament, and reintegration (DDR). On September 13, 2003, 6 months after the formation of the reconciliation government, President Gbagbo named politically neutral Defense and Security Ministers, after consulting with the political parties and New Forces.

2004 saw serious challenges to the Linas-Marcoussis Accord. Violent flare-ups and political deadlock in the spring and summer led to the Accra III talks in Ghana. Signed on July 30, 2004, the Accra III Agreement reaffirmed the goals of the LMA with specific deadlines and benchmarks for progress. Unfortunately, those deadlines—late September for legislative reform and October 15 for rebel disarmament—were not met by the parties. The ensuing political and military deadlock was not broken until November 4, when government forces initiated a bombing campaign of rebel targets in the north. On November 6, a government aircraft bombed a French military installation in Bouake, killing nine French soldiers and one American civilian. Claiming that the attack was deliberate (the Ivoirian Government claimed it was a mistake), French forces retaliated by destroying most of the small Ivoirian air force. Mayhem ensued for several days as anti-French mobs rioted in Abidjan and violence flared elsewhere. On November 15, 2004 the United Nations Security Council issued an immediate arms embargo on Côte d'Ivoire and gave leaders 1 month to get the peace process back on track or face a travel ban and an asset freeze. In April 2005, South African President Thabo Mbeki invited the leaders to South Africa for an African Union-sponsored mediation effort. The result was the Pretoria Agreement, signed April 6, 2005. The Pretoria Agreement formally ended the country's state of war, and addressed issues such as disarmament, demobilization, and reintegration, the return of New Forces Ministers to government, and the reorganization of the Independent Electoral Commission. A follow-up agreement in June 2005 laid out another framework for disarmament, elections, and the adoption of legislation required under the Linas-Marcoussis Accord.

In September 2005, the government postponed presidential elections scheduled for October 30, 2005. In October 2005, the UN Security Council, via UN Security Council Resolution (UNSCR) 1633, endorsed an African Union decision to extend the Linas-Marcoussis peace process for an additional 12 months. As called for under 1633, a new Prime Minister, Charles Konan Banny, was selected by the international community and given broad powers designed to reunify the country. Banny selected a new cabinet in December 2005 in collaboration with the opposition, the President, and the New Forces. In January 2006, militias loyal to President Gbagbo mounted violent protests against statements by the UN Operation in Côte d'Ivoire (UNOCI) regarding the role of the National Assembly during the ongoing transition period. These protests threatened the independence of the Banny government and the ability of UNOCI and the International Working Group (created by the UN Security Council to oversee the peace process) to help the country achieve a stable, lasting reconciliation.

Initial steps toward disarmament and elections began in May 2006. The government began a pilot identification program for citizens and foreign residents lacking birth and nationality certificates. Government and rebel New Forces military formations began pre-groupment activities as a prelude to actual disarmament. Neither initiative was completed, and elections did not take place on October 31, 2006, as mandated by UN Security Council Resolution 1633. In November 2006, the UN Security Council issued a new resolution, 1721, which extended Prime Minister Banny's mandate for an additional 12 months. Prime Minister Banny was effectively blocked, however, from exercising control over the government as envisioned by the international community. President Gbagbo closed out 2006 with a speech to the nation in which he called for direct talks with the New Forces and the elimination of the Zone of Confidence.

Ouagadougou Political Agreement

On March 4, 2007, after weeks of closed-door negotiations led by Burkinabe President Compaore in Ouagadougou, Burkina Faso, President Gbagbo and New Forces leader Guillaume Soro announced they had agreed to a peace agreement aimed at reunifying the country and holding new elections. The Ouagadougou Agreement foresaw a new transitional government and the re-launch of the stalled voter registration and identification process to enable elections to be held within 10 months. It also called for the near-immediate elimination of the Zone of Confidence; the disarmament, demobilization, and reintegration of former combatants; and for rebel and government forces to form a joint integrated Command Center that would implement the measures for the restructuring of the Defense and Security Forces.

At the end of March, Soro was named Prime Minister, and several days later, a new cabinet—consisting of most of the ministers from the previous cabinet—was named. Subsequently, UNOCI withdrew from within the Zone of Confidence, although it was still positioned on both sides, and six mixed brigades of New Forces, national Gendarmerie soldiers, and impartial forces were established. The Zone of Confidence was dismantled in September 2007, but both the mixed brigades and impartial forces continued to carry out patrols throughout the ex-Zone of Confidence.

On June 29, 2007, an attack against Prime Minister Soro's aircraft occurred at the Bouake Airport, killing several persons in his entourage, but he escaped unharmed. Government ministries (particularly Health, Education, Finance, and Interior) and officials returned to their posts in the northern part of the country and the disarmament, demobilizaton, and reintegration (DDR) of former combatants began on a limited scale. As part of the DDR process, in January 2008, the Defense and Security Forces completed regroupment. In late 2009, cantonment of some New Forces had begun in Bouake, with preparations continuing in other areas of the north.

In September 2007, the first step in the identification of voters commenced when a series of mobile courts began issuing birth certificates to those who never had them. In April 2008, the government announced elections would be held on November 30, 2008. In early November 2008, those elections were postponed; a new date of November 29, 2009 was later set. In late December 2008, the parties to the Ouagadougou Political Agreement (OPA) signed the fourth supplementary agreement to the OPA. Under the terms of this agreement, disarmament, demobilization, and reintegration was to be completed 2 months before presidential elections. Citizen identification and voter registration continued to pose operational challenges. Identification and registration was launched nationwide in early December 2008 and proceeded fairly smoothly, although with some delays. On November 11, 2009, the Independent Electoral Commission (CEI) announced that the elections scheduled for November 29 would again be postponed to allow for the completion of the registration process. No new election date was set at the time of postponement. A provisional electoral list was completed on November 10, 2009, to be posted at all election sites throughout the country. A 30-day dispute period was to begin when the lists had been physically posted, allowing anyone to challenge the names on the provisional list.

On February 12, 2010, President Gbagbo announced the dissolution of the government and the CEI, amid claims of fraud during the voter registration process. The decision, as well as frustration regarding several localized cases of mismanagement of the voter list, sparked riots in several cities outside of Abidjan that resulted in at least 12 deaths. Following several weeks of negotiations, a new government was announced and a new head of the CEI was appointed.

2010 Presidential Elections

After several years of delays, the first round of presidential elections was held on October 31, 2010. The election was hailed by all candidates and observers as peaceful and fair, with nearly 80% voter turnout and no significant irregularities reported. The November 28 runoff between Alassane Ouattara and incumbent President Gbagbo was again characterized by high voter turnout and largely peaceful participation by the Ivoirian people, and Ouattara was declared the winner by the CEI. Credible and accredited observers assessed both rounds as fair and free of irregularities that would have affected the results. Gbagbo refused to cede power, and a period of fighting ensued. Ouattara was formally inaugurated in May 2011.

GOVERNMENT AND POLITICAL CONDITIONS

Côte d'Ivoire is a democratic republic. On May 21, Alassane Ouattara, leader and candidate of the opposition party Rally for Republicans (RDR), was officially inaugurated president. The inauguration followed the April 11 capture of Laurent Gbagbo, the former president who refused to accept the results of the October and November 2010 presidential election. The UN and international and domestic observer missions declared the vote fair and democratic and recognized Ouattara as the country's duly elected president; however, President Ouattara and former president Gbagbo took separate oaths of office in December 2010 and remained in a standoff over the presidency until Gbagbo's capture. Post-electoral violence perpetrated by both sides, but attributable primarily to pro-Gbagbo forces, resulted in approximately 3,000 deaths, significant population displacement, torture, sexual violence, and widespread property destruction.

On March 17, 2011, President Ouattara combined the former rebel Forces Nouvelles (FN) with cooperating elements of the Defense and Security Forces (FDS), the former government's security forces, into the Republic Forces of Côte d'Ivoire (FRCI), the country's new official military. Until President Ouattara's official inauguration in May, security forces, who largely supported former president Gbagbo, did not report to civilian authorities. Following the inauguration, violence significantly decreased, but there still were instances in which elements of the security forces acted independently of civilian control—particularly FRCI members ineligible for the unified military, armed pro-Gbagbo groups supported under the former regime, and endemic militia groups in the West.

Recent Elections

In October 2010 the country held its first presidential election in 10 years. Incumbent President Laurent Gbagbo, candidate of the Ivoirian People's Front (FPI), and opposition RDR party leader Alassane Ouattara advanced to the November 2010 presidential runoff. In December 2010 the Independent Electoral Commission (CEI) declared Ouattara the winner of the runoff with 54.1 percent of the vote; Gbagbo received 45.9 percent. Voter turnout was recorded at 81 percent. The UN Special Representative of the Secretary General independently certified the results of the election, determining Ouattara the winner by a margin similar to that announced by the CEI. As a result the African Union, ECOWAS, the UN, and multiple international and domestic observer teams also recognized Ouattara as the new president. Gbagbo, however, refused to accept the results, and the Constitutional Council, which was made up entirely of Gbagbo appointees, overturned the CEI ruling, citing voter "irregularities." More than 500,000 votes for Ouattara were annulled, and Gbagbo was declared the winner. Ouattara and Gbagbo remained in a standoff over the presidency and took separate oaths of office in December 2010. Gbagbo retained control of state resources including the national television station, the security forces, and the treasury.

The political stalemate plunged the country into crisis. Violence perpetrated by both sides resulted in approximately 3,000 deaths, significant population displacement, torture, sexual violence, and widespread property destruction. On March 17, 2011, President Ouattara signed a decree to unify former rebel forces, the FN and former government security forces, and the FDS into the FRCI, the country's new official army. On April 11, the FRCI—with limited assistance from UN peacekeepers and French military forces—captured Gbagbo. On May 21, President Ouattara was inaugurated.

On December 11, the country held elections for representatives to the National Assembly. The elections were peaceful and generally free and fair, despite minor administrative problems. Voter turnout was 37 percent, which was higher than the 32 percent recorded for the 2000 legislative elections.

Preliminary results indicated that President Ouattara's RDR party won a majority with 127 seats. The PDCI, a pro-Ouattara party, won 77 seats. Independents, some reported to be pro-FPI, won 35 seats. At the end of 2011, the political opposition was poised to have limited representation in the National Assembly.

Participation of Women and Minorities: Initial results indicate there were 29 women elected to the National Assembly.

Principal Government Officials

Last Updated: 1/31/2013

Pres.: **Alassane Dramane OUATTARA**

Min. to the Pres. of the Republic & Chief of Staff of the Presidency:

Min. to the Pres. of the Republic in Charge of Defense: **Paul Kofi KOFI**

Min. to the Pres. of the Republic in Charge of Relations With Republican Institutions:

Min. in Charge of Presidential Affairs:

Senior Min. & Sec. Gen. of the Presidency of the Republic:

Prime Min.: **Daniel Kablan DUNCAN**

Min. to the Prime Min. in Charge of Economy & Finance: **Niale KABA**

Min. of African Integration & Ivoirians Abroad: **Ally COULIBALY**

Min. of Agriculture: **Mamadou Sangafoa COULIBALY**

Min. of Civil Service & Admin. Reform: **Gnamien KONAN**

Min. of Commerce: **Jean-Louis BILLON**

Min. of Communication: **Affoussiata Bamba LAMINE**

Min. of Construction & Housing: **Mamadou SANOGO**

Min. of Culture & Francophone Affairs: **Maurice Kouakou BANDAMA**

Min. of Defense: **Alassane Dramane OUATTARA**

Min. of Economic Infrastructure: **Patrick ACHI**

Min. of Economy & Finance: **Daniel Kablan DUNCAN**

Min. of Employment, Social Affairs, & Professional Training: **Moussa DOSSO**

Min. of Environment & Sustainable Development: **Remi Alla KOUADIO**

Min. of Foreign Affairs: **Charles Koffi DIBY**

Min. of Handicrafts & Promotion of Small & Medium-Sized Enterprises .

Min. of Health & HIV/AIDS Control: **Raymonde Goudou COFFIE**

Min. of Higher Education & Scientific Research: **Ibrahima Cisse BACONGO**

Min. of Industry: **Jean-Claude BROU**

Min. of Interior & Security: **Hamed BAKAYOKO**

Min. of Justice, Human Rights, & Civil Liberties: **Gnenema Mamadou COULIBALY**

Min. of Livestock & Fisheries: **Kobena Kouassi ADJOUMANI**

Min. of Mines, Oil, & Energy: **Adama TOUNGARA**

Min. of National Education & Technical Training: **Kandia Kamissoko CAMARA**

Min. of Planning & Development: **Albert Mabri TOIKEUSSE**

Min. of Post, Information, & Communication Technologies & Govt.Spokesperson: **Bruno Nabagne KONE**

Min. of Solidarity & the Family: **Anne Desiree OULOTO**

Min. of Tourism: **Roger KAKOU**

Min. of Transports: **Gaoussou TOURE**

Min. of Veteran Affairs & War Victims

Min. of Water & Forestry: **Babaud DARRET**

Min. of Youth, Sports, & Leisure: **Alain Michel LOBOGNON**

Ambassador to the US: **Daouda DIABATE**

Permanent Representative to the UN, New York: **Youssoufou BAMBA**

ECONOMY

Côte d'Ivoire is heavily dependent on agriculture and related activities, which engage roughly 68% of the population. Côte d'Ivoire is the world's largest producer and exporter of cocoa beans and a significant producer and exporter of coffee and palm oil. Consequently, the economy is highly sensitive to fluctuations in international prices for these products, and, to a lesser extent, in climatic conditions.

Cocoa, oil, and coffee are the country's top export revenue earners, but the country is also producing gold. Since the end of the civil war in 2003, political turmoil has continued to damage the economy, resulting in the loss of foreign investment and slow economic growth. In late 2011, Côte d'Ivoire's economy began to recover from a severe downturn of the first quarter of the year that was caused by widespread post-election fighting. In June 2012 the IMF and the World Bank announced $4.4 billion in debt relief for Côte d'Ivoire under the Highly Indebted Poor Countries Initiative. Côte d'Ivoire's long term challenges include political instability and degrading infrastructure.

Labor Conditions

There were laws against forced labor and the exploitation of children in the workplace; however, child labor reportedly remained a widespread problem, particularly in cocoa and coffee plantations, and gold mines.

In most instances the legal minimum working age is 14; however, the Ministry of Civil Service and Administrative Reform and the Ministry of Labor, Social Affairs, and Solidarity enforced this provision effectively only in the civil service and in large multinational companies. Children were not allowed to work between 7 p.m. and 6 a.m. They reportedly routinely worked on family farms or as vendors, shoe shiners, errand boys, domestic helpers, street restaurant vendors, and car watchers and washers in the informal sector in cities. Some girls as young as nine reportedly worked as domestic servants, often within their extended family networks.

Children reportedly continued to work under hazardous conditions on cocoa farms. A Tulane University survey published in 2009 found that 24.1 percent of children between the ages of five and 17 in the cocoa-growing regions had worked on a cocoa farm in the previous 12 months. The survey showed that a number of these children were involved in or exposed to hazardous conditions, including operating tools (93.9 percent) and carrying heavy loads (79.8 percent). Similar hazardous conditions reportedly existed during the year. A small percentage of the children working on cocoa farms had no family ties to the farmers, but most worked on family farms or with their parents.

Minimum wages varied according to occupation, with the lowest set at FCFA 36,607 ($73) per month for the industrial sector; a slightly higher minimum wage rate applied for construction work. The official estimate for the poverty income level is between FCFA 500 ($1) and FCFA 700 ($1.40) a day. The government enforced the minimum wage rates only for salaried workers employed by the government or registered with the social security office. Labor federations attempted to fight for just treatment under the law for workers when companies failed to meet minimum salary requirements or discriminated among classes of workers, such as local and foreign workers.

Under Gbagbo and Ouattara, no government action was reportedly taken to rectify the large salary discrepancies between expatriate non-African employees and their African colleagues who were employed by the same company.

The standard workweek was 40 hours. The law requires overtime compensation for additional hours and provides for at least 24-hour rest period per week. The law does not prohibit compulsory overtime. The law also provides for regulations on occupational, safety, and health standards in the workplaces. The government did not enforce occupational, safety and health standards effectively in the informal sector. Several million foreign workers, mostly from neighboring countries, typically worked in the informal labor sector, where labor laws were not enforced.

U.S.-IVOIRIAN RELATIONS

The United States established diplomatic relations with Côte d'Ivoire (then called Ivory Coast) in 1960 following its independence from France. A coup in 1999 ushered in several years of coup attempts, disputed elections, rebellions, and attempts at reunification. In 2011, a new president was formally inaugurated after a period of fighting brought on by the incumbent's refusal to cede power following 2010 elections.

U.S.-Ivoirian relations have traditionally been friendly and close. The United States participates in the international effort to assist Côte d'Ivoire in moving beyond its decade-long crisis, providing more than a quarter of the funding for the UN Operation in Côte d'Ivoire. The U.S. Government's overriding interests in Côte d'Ivoire have long been to help restore peace, encourage disarmament and reunification of the country, and support a democratic government whose legitimacy can be accepted by all the citizens of Côte d'Ivoire.

U.S. Assistance to Côte d'Ivoire

U.S. assistance aims to support multi-ethnic participation in the democratic process in lieu of violence and separation; enhance capacity of national, provincial, and local governmental institutions, the media, and civil society leading to better governance and increased public confidence in the democratic process; support electoral and follow-on activities; increase respect for the rule of law and human rights; and address the HIV/AIDS epidemic through expanded access to prevention, care, and treatment services.

Bilateral Economic Relations

Côte d'Ivoire is eligible for preferential trade benefits under the African Growth and Opportunity Act. U.S. exports to Côte d'Ivoire include plastics, machinery, oil, agricultural products, vehicles, and iron and steel products. U.S. imports from Côte d'Ivoire include cocoa, oil, rubber, wood, and cashew nuts. U.S. firms have made investments in oil and gas, banking, cocoa, and international courier services. The United States has a trade and investment framework agreement with the West African Economic and Monetary Union, of which Côte d'Ivoire is a member.

Côte d'Ivoire's Membership in International Organizations

Côte d'Ivoire and the United States belong to a number of the same international organizations, including the United Nations, International Monetary Fund, World Bank, and World Trade Organization.

Bilateral Representation

Côte d'Ivoire maintains an embassy at 2424 Massachusetts Avenue, NW, Washington, DC 20007; tel: 202-797-0300.

Principal U.S. Embassy Officials

Last Updated: 1/14/2013

ABIDJAN (E) Riviera Golf, 01 B.P. 1712, Abidjan 01, Côte d'Ivoire, (225) 22.49.40.00, Fax (225) 22.49.43.23, INMARSAT Tel 8816-414-45393 (Iridium), Workweek: M–F 8:00–17:00, Website: http://abidjan.usembassy.gov/

DCM OMS:	Soto, Liz
AMB OMS:	Markley, Tim
CDC:	Wingate, Therese
FM:	Dr. Ike Khan
HHS:	Jefferson, Melissa
HRO:	Harby, Issa
MGT:	Lyman, Thomas
SDO/DATT:	LTC Ginther, Christopher
AMB:	Carter,Phillip III
CON:	Bongiovanni, Kristin
DCM:	Sim, Cheryl
PAO:	Cebra, Jonathan
GSO:	Vogel, Kevin
RSO:	(Acting) Richard Fisher
AID:	Slocum, Glenn
CLO:	Everson, Monique R
ECON:	Cely, Sean
EEO:	Arcieri, Kate
FMO:	Tracey, Debra C
IMO:	Vega, Edna
IPO:	Clark, Michael
POL:	Schiebel, Russ

TRAVEL

Consular Information Sheet

August 17, 2012

Country Description: Côte d'Ivoire (Ivory Coast) is a developing country on the western coast of Africa. The official capital is Yamoussoukro, but Abidjan is the largest city, the main commercial center, and the location of the Ivorian government and the U.S. Embassy. The official language is French; English is not widely used. Côte d'Ivoire is a republic whose constitution provides for separate branches of government under a strong president.

Since 1999, Côte d'Ivoire has experienced several episodes of political unrest and violence—most recently, the post-electoral crisis following presidential elections in late 2010. After President Alassane Ouattara's inauguration in May 2011, violence and instability subsided significantly. As of March 26, 2012, the U.S. Embassy in Côte d'Ivoire returned to operating as a fully accompanied post, allowing minor dependents of U.S. government employees to travel or accompany family members to Abidjan. Since the post-electoral crisis ended, schools and businesses have reopened and government services such as police and gendarme activity have nearly returned to pre-crisis levels. The airport and ports have also fully resumed operations. The Embassy continues to monitor the host country's capacity for providing basic services to its population, particularly related to safety and security issues. Police and gendarmes are not always able to fulfill their public security mandate due to antiquated training and an acute lack of resources, such as weapons, transportation, and communications equipment. The potential for civil unrest, however, remains. The government faces significant challenges in terms of security, the economy, national reconciliation, and humanitarian needs.

Tourist facilities in and near Abidjan, the commercial capital, are good; accommodations in many other locations are limited in quality and availability.

Smart Traveler Enrollment Program (STEP)/Embassy Locations: If you are going to live in or visit Côte d'Ivoire, please take the time to tell our Embassy about your trip. If you enroll, we can keep you up to date with important safety and security announcements. It will also help your friends and family get in touch with you in an emergency.

Embassy Abidjan
Address: 01 B.P. 1712
Abidjan 01 Côte d'Ivoire.
Telephone: 225-22-49-40-00
Emergency after-hours telephone: 225-22-49-44-50
Facsimile: 225-22-49-42-02
Email: AbjAmcit@state.gov

Entry/Exit Requirements for U.S. Citizens: The Ivorian government requires U.S. citizens to have a valid visa for entry into Côte d'Ivoire, as well as a passport with more than six months of remaining validity. U.S. citizens traveling to Côte d'Ivoire should check with the nearest Ivorian embassy or consulate for details regarding the latest visa procedures and fees. Please note that visas are not available at the airport upon arrival, and that airport immigration control officials in Abidjan have both detained and denied entry to U.S. citizens arriving in Côte d'Ivoire without a visa. In addition to visa and passport requirements, an international health certificate showing current yellow fever immunization is required for entry into Côte d'Ivoire. Without it, the traveler may be required to submit to vaccination at entry before clearing immigration, at a cost of 5,000 CFA (a little over $10).

An exit permit is required for all art objects being removed from Côte d'Ivoire. The export permit costs 2000

CFA plus 500 CFA per object(approximately one to four U.S. dollars). Only the National Museum has the authority to issue the permits.

Foreign travelers are sometimes approached at ports of entry by individuals with offers to expedite passport control and customs, and are then asked to pay an exorbitant fee, both for the service and for the passport and customs officers. Travelers to Côte d'Ivoire are advised that there is no need to pay a police officer or customs officer for any service rendered during an arrival or departure, and that they should not surrender their passports or other important documents to anyone except easily identifiable government officials in uniform.

U.S. citizens intending to establish a residence in Côte d'Ivoire must apply for a residency permit "carte de séjour" at the Office d'Identification Nationale. (Note: "Cartes de séjour" are not issued to children under the age of 16 who are documented on their parents' visas.)

Travelers may obtain the latest information and details on entry requirements from the Embassy of the Republic of Côte d'Ivoire, 2424 Massachusetts Avenue NW, Washington, DC 20007, tel. (202) 797-0300. Côte d'Ivoire has a Consulate in Los Angeles located at 3550 Wilshire Blvd, Ste 1728, Los Angeles, CA 90010, tel. (310) 358-3339. There are honorary consulates for Côte d'Ivoire in San Francisco, Stamford, Orlando, Houston, and Detroit. If you are currently overseas, you should inquire at the nearest Ivorian embassy or consulate.

The U.S. Department of State is unaware of any HIV/AIDS entry restrictions for visitors to or foreign residents of Côte d'Ivoire.

Threats to Safety and Security: Since President Ouattara fully assumed office in May 2011, the country is no longer divided, although some political tensions persist and sometimes lead to localized violent incidents. The normal security infrastructure of police and gendarmerie is in a state of transition and reestablishment. The military often performs traditional civilian law enforcement functions for which is it not properly trained, and the military and police themselves have also recently been the subject of targeted attacks in which several soldiers and policemen were killed.

The banking system is open and money-wire services are operational in Côte d'Ivoire.

The Embassy's ability to provide consular services outside of the Abidjan area, including emergency assistance, is severely limited. Many areas of Côte d'Ivoire are difficult to access, and travel in these areas is hazardous. Outside the major cities, infrastructure is poor, medical care is limited, and there are few facilities for tourists.

The U.S. Embassy in Abidjan and the Department of State continue to monitor the securitysituation in Côte d'Ivoire closely. U.S. citizens are reminded that even demonstrations and/or political events intended to be peaceful can turn confrontational and possibly escalate into violence. U.S. citizens are therefore urged to avoid the areas of demonstrations, and to exercise caution if within the vicinity of any demonstrations or political events. U.S. citizens in Côte d'Ivoire are advised to stay current on media coverage of local events and to remain aware of their surroundings at all times. U.S. citizens should avoid crowds and demonstrations, be aware of their surroundings, and use common sense to avoid situations and locations that could be dangerous. Swimming in coastal waters is dangerous and strongly discouraged, even for excellent swimmers. The ocean currents along the coast are powerful and treacherous, and several people drown each year.

Stay up to date by:

- Bookmarking our Bureau of Consular Affairs website, which contains the current Travel Warnings and Travel Alerts, as well as the Worldwide Caution.
- Following us on Foursquare, Twitter, and the Bureau of Consular Affairs page on Facebook as well.
- Downloading our free Smart Traveler iPhone App to have travel information at your fingertips.
- Calling 1-888-407-4747 toll-free within the United States and Canada, or a regular toll line, 1-202-501-4444, from other countries.
- Taking some time before travel to consider your personal security.

Crime: Crime continues to be a major public security concern in Côte d'Ivoire. Armed carjackings, robberies of businesses, and home invasions have occurred and targeted residents, including expatriates, who are perceived as wealthy. U.S. citizens, either visiting or residing in Côte d'Ivoire, are strongly encouraged to remain alert and aware of their surroundings to prevent becoming a victim of crime. The general guidance for travel to Côte d'Ivoire is to exercise the same prudence and caution you that you would in any metropolitan area in the United States. Common sense steps include refraining from displaying jewelry and other valuables and carrying limited amounts of cash and only photocopies of key documents. In addition, home and car doors should be locked at all times.

When moving about the city, stay in well-lit areas and walk confidently at a steady pace on the side of the street facing traffic close to the curb. Avoid crowds, mass transit, alleys, and sparsely populated areas. Take caution when walking past concealed areas such as doorways and bushes. Whenever possible, travel in pairs or small groups. If you go out at night and need transportation, orange taxis are metered, although no safer than any other taxis. There have been reports of muggings and robbery scams even in metered taxis. Always carry identification and be discreet about your transactions, especially on the street. Normal spending habits of Westerners may appear extravagant to Ivoirians. Be particularly alert when visiting Abidjan's Koumassi, Yopougon, and Abobo districts. When traveling outside of Abidjan, you should avoid traveling after dark and should be aware that police and security forces often use vehicular checkpoints to extort money from drivers and passengers. If you must travel after dark, use extreme caution.

U.S. citizens who are stopped by police/security forces are urged to be polite and cooperate. If you are ticketed, you should ask the officer for a receipt for any items confiscated by the police, such as a driver's license or other identification. Drivers issued a ticket should note, however, that it is legal to pay the police officer money by the side of the road, but the amount paid should not exceed the amount printed on the ticket itself. The fees generally range from 500 CFA to 2,000 CFA (approximately one to four U.S. dollars).

U.S. citizens detained by the police should ask that the U.S. Embassy be notified immediately at 225 2249–4000/4050.

Contact information for local authorities includes:
Abidjan Prefecture of Police:
225 2021–0022
Police Headquarters:
225 2022–0822
Ministry of Security:
225 2022–1950/1941
Police Emergency Number: 225 3163–3536/4503

While there have been relatively few reported cases of sexual assault against foreigners, the actual rate of assault may be higher. U.S. citizens have been economic targets. Travelers should avoid large gatherings and political demonstrations, as they can quickly turn violent.

Credit card use in Côte d'Ivoire is limited, particularly outside Abidjan, and credit card fraud is an increasing problem. Business fraud is common and the perpetrators often target foreigners. Schemes previously associated with Nigeria are now prevalent throughout West Africa, including Côte d'Ivoire, and pose a risk of grave financial loss. Typically these scams begin with unsolicited communication (usually by e-mail) from strangers who promise quick financial gain, often by transferring large sums of money or valuables out of the country, but then require a series of "advance fees" to be paid, such as fees for legal documents or taxes. Of course, the final payoff does not exist; the purpose of the scam is simply to collect the advance fees.

A common variation is the scammer's claim to be a refugee or émigré of a prominent West African family, who needs assistance transferring large sums of cash. Another common scam involves alleged victims of a serious accident or injury in need of money for life-saving medical care. Still other variations appear to be legitimate business deals that require advance payments on contracts or large purchases of merchandise using fraudulent credit cards. Sometimes victims are convinced to provide bank account and credit card information, and authorize financial transactions that drain their accounts, causing them to incur large debts.

The best way to avoid becoming a victim of advance-fee fraud is common sense, if a proposition looks too good to be true it is probably a scam, particularly if you have never met the correspondent. You should carefully check and research any unsolicited business proposal before committing funds, providing goods or services, or undertaking travel. A good clue to a scam is the phone number given to the victim; legitimate businesses and offices provide fixed line numbers, while scams typically use only cellular (cell) phones. In Côte d'Ivoire, most cell phone numbers start with 44, 45, 46, 48, 60, 66, or 67. It is virtually impossible to recover money lost through these scams. For additional information, please consult the Department of State's brochure on international financial scams.

Don't buy counterfeit and pirated goods, even if they are widely available. Not only are the bootlegs illegal in the United States, if you purchase them, you may also be breaking local law.

Victims of Crime: If you or someone you know becomes the victim of a crime abroad, you should contact the local police and the nearest U.S. embassy or consulate (see the Department of State's list of embassies and consulates).

- Replace a stolen passport.
- Help you find appropriate medical care if you are the victim of violent crimes such as assault or rape.
- Put you in contact with the appropriate police authorities, and if you want us to, we can contact family members or friend.
- Help you understand the local criminal justice process and direct you to local attorneys, although it is important to remember that local authorities are responsible for investigating and prosecuting the crime.

The local equivalent to the "911" emergency line in Côte d'Ivoire is 111.

Criminal Penalties: While you are traveling in Côte d'Ivoire, you are subject to its laws even if you are a U.S. citizen. Foreign laws and legal systems can be vastly different than our own. In some places you may be taken in for questioning if you don't have your passport with you. In some places, it is illegal to take pictures of certain buildings. In some places driving under the influence could land you immediately in jail. These criminal penalties will vary from country to country. There are also some things that might be legal in the country you visit, but still illegal in the United States, and you can be prosecuted under U.S. law if you buy pirated goods, for example. Engaging in sexual conduct with children or using or disseminating child pornography in a foreign country is a crime prosecutable in the United States. If you break local laws in Côte d'Ivoire, your U.S. passport won't help you avoid arrest or prosecution. It's very important to know what's legal and what's not where you are going. Persons violating Ivorian laws, even unknowingly, may be expelled, arrested, or imprisoned. Penalties for possessing, using, or trafficking in illegal drugs in Côte d'Ivoire are severe, and convicted offenders can expect long jail sentences and heavy fines.

Under the Vienna Convention on Consular Relations, bilateral agreements with certain countries, and customary international law, if you are arrested in Côte d'Ivoire, you may request that police, prison officials, and other authorities alert the nearest U.S. embassy or consulate of your arrest. You may also ask that they forward communications to the U.S. embassy or consulate on your behalf.

Special Circumstances: Ivorian customs authorities encourage the use of an ATA (Admission Temporaire/Temporary Admission) Carnet for the temporary admission of professional equipment, commercial samples, and/or goods for exhibitions and fair purposes. ATA Carnet Headquarters, at the U.S. Council for International Business, 1212 Avenue of the Americas, New York, NY 10036, issues and guarantees the ATA Carnet in the United States. For additional information, call (212) 354-4480 or e-mail ATA Carnet Headquarters.

If traveling to another West African Economic and Monetary Union (WAEMU) country, expatriate residents leaving Côte d'Ivoire must declare the amount of currency being taken out of the country. Residents traveling to countries that use the CFA franc currency, but are not WAEMU members, are prohibited from taking CFA francs out of Côte d'Ivoire and are authorized to carry up to the equivalent of 2,000,000 CFA francs (approximately $4,000) in any other currency. You can take funds in excess of that amount out of the country in the form of travelers or bank checks. If going to any other country, tourists are prohibited from taking more than 500,000 CFA francs (approximately $1,000) and business operators are prohibited from taking more than 2,000,000 CFA francs (approximately $4,000) without government approval.

Carry a photocopy of your U.S. passport, visa, and entry stamps. You should also carry your international driver's license, especially if you plan to drive anywhere in Côte d'Ivoire. U.S. driver's licenses are not valid in Côte d'Ivoire. Government corruption remains a serious problem in Côte d'Ivoire, and has an impact on judicial proceedings, contract awards, customs, and tax issues. Uniformed security forces (police, military, gendarmes) routinely stop vehicles for traffic violations and security checks. If you are stopped, politely present your identification. Police and security officials rarely speak English. If you are stopped at one of these checkpoints and asked to pay a bribe, politely refuse and present your photocopy of your U.S. passport, visa, and entry stamp.

Taking pictures is prohibited near sensitive installations, including military sites, government buildings such as radio and television stations, the Presidency building, the airport, and the DeGaulle and Houphouet-Boigny bridges in Abidjan.

Accessibility: Individuals with disabilities should be aware that there are almost no accommodations made for individuals with disabilities in Côte d'Ivoire.

Medical Facilities and Health Information: Abidjan has privately-run medical and dental facilities that are adequate, but do not fully meet U.S. standards. Good physician specialists can be found, though few speak English. While pharmacies are well-stocked with medications produced in Europe, newer drugs may not be available. If you plan a lengthy trip to Côte d'Ivoire, you should bring enough medication to last the entire stay, not just a prescription, in your carry-on luggage. Medical care outside of Abidjan is extremely limited.

Malaria is a serious health problem in Côte d'Ivoire. For more information on malaria, including protective measures, visit the U.S. Centers for Disease Control and Prevention (CDC) web site.

The avian influenza or "bird flu" virus (H5N1) was confirmed in animals in Côte d'Ivoire as of June 2006 and could recur. For more information regarding avian influenza, please visit the CDC's avian influenza web page, and read the State Department's "2009–H1N1, Pandemic Influenza, and H5N1" influenza Fact Sheet.

In January 2011, the Ministry of Health of Côte d'Ivoire and the World Health Organization (WHO) announced a yellow fever outbreak in the central and northern districts of Beoumi, Katiola, Seguela, and Mankono. Based on the ongoing nationwide risk of yellow fever, the CDC has a long-standing recommendation for all travelers to Côte d'Ivoire to obtain the yellow fever vaccine, and the government of Côte d'Ivoire requires it for entry into the country. In response to the current outbreak, at the end of January 2011, the Ministry of Health of Côte d'Ivoire conducted a mass vaccination campaign in the affected districts.

There are yearly cholera outbreaks. The risk of contracting acute watery diarrhea, including cholera, can be significantly reduced by drinking purified water, bleaching produce, and eating meat and seafood that are thoroughly cooked and hot.

You can find good information on vaccinations and other health precautions on the CDC website. For information about outbreaks of infectious diseases abroad, consult the World Health Organization (WHO) website. The WHO website also contains additional health information for travelers, including detailed country-specific health information. Tuberculosis is an increasingly serious health concern in Côte d'Ivoire. For further information, please consult the CDC's information on TB.

Medical Insurance: You can't assume your insurance will go with you when you travel. It's very important to find out BEFORE you leave whether or not your medical insurance will cover you overseas. You need to ask your insurance company two questions:

- Does my policy apply when I'm out of the United States?
- Will it cover emergencies like a trip to a foreign hospital or a medical evacuation?

In Côte d'Ivoire, doctors and hospitals still expect payment in cash at the time of service. Your regular U.S. health insurance may not cover doctors' and hospital visits in other countries. If your policy doesn't go with you when you travel, it's a very good idea to take out another one for your trip. Medevac insurance is usually separate from medical insurance, and is recommended for visits to Côte d'Ivoire.

Traffic Safety and Road Conditions: While in Côte d'Ivoire, you may encounter road conditions that differ significantly from those in the United States. The information below concerning Côte d'Ivoire is provided for general reference only, and may not be totally accurate in a particular location or circumstance. Serious traffic accidents, one of the greatest threats to U.S. citizens in Côte d'Ivoire, occur regularly in Abidjan. Unsafe road conditions, unskilled drivers, and poorly maintained and overloaded vehicles create very poor driving conditions. Speed limits, lane markings, and signals are not respected, and drivers do not yield for pedestrians or bicyclists. Drive defensively, watch out for public transportation vehicles that stop and start without warning, and be especially cautious at intersections because traffic lights often malfunction. If you drive at night, beware of vehicles without headlights or taillights and pedestrians and bicycles along the roadside. In case of an accident, do not move your vehicle until a police officer tells you to do so. However, if there is no other vehicle to take the injured to a hospital, or if you believe your life is in danger from others at the site of the accident, go to the nearest hospital or police station.

Abidjan has a poor public transportation system; if you choose to travel by bus despite the risks, the "Express" line is believed to be the safest and most reliable. In Abidjan, taxis are readily available, inexpensive (metered), but poorly maintained and notorious for not respecting the rules of the road. There have been reports of robberies in metered or Orange taxis, widely thought to be the most secure form of public transportation. Communal taxis ("woro-woros"), used only within the limits of each commune, are not metered and are dangerous. Don't use local vans ("Gbaka") because they are frequently involved in accidents.

While carjacking incidents are not as frequent as in other high-crime cities, they do occur, including vehicles with diplomatic plates. The Embassy recommends that motorists drive with doors locked and windows closed at all times. While stopped in traffic, allow enough room between your car and the one in front to maneuver out if needed. Before getting into your car, look around to see if there is anyone paying unusual attention and, if someone appears to be watching, don't go to your vehicle, get assistance instead. If confronted, remain courteous and calm and, if threatened, do not resist. Please report any incident to the U.S. Embassy in Abidjan.
Emergency services such as ambulance service (SAMU) exist in Abidjan and larger towns, but such service is unreliable. Call 185 or 2244–5553. In smaller towns there is usually no ambulance service available, but ambulances may be dispatched from larger towns.

Aviation Safety Oversight: The U.S. Federal Aviation Administration (FAA) has assessed the government of Côte d'Ivoire's Civil Aviation Authority as not being in compliance with International Civil Aviation Organization (ICAO) aviation safety standards for oversight of Côte d'Ivoire's air carrier operations. You can find further information on the FAA's safety assessment page.

Children's Issues: Please see the U.S. Dept. of State Office of Children's Issues web pages on intercountry adoption and international parental child abduction.

Travel Warning

November 16, 2012

The Department of State warns U.S. citizens of the risks of travel to Côte d'Ivoire. U.S. citizens who reside in or travel to Côte d'Ivoire should monitor conditions carefully, maintain situational awareness, and pay very close attention to their personal security. While the security situation has improved since the post-electoral crisis that ended May 2011, the potential for civil unrest remains. Security conditions could change quickly and without warning. This Travel Warning updates U.S. citizens on the current security situation in Côte d'Ivoire, replacing the Travel Warning of April 23, 2012.

This year there have been several serious security incidents in the southwestern and southeastern regions of Côte d'Ivoire. For example, in June, UN peacekeepers were attacked in the Tai region; in August, there were attacks on a local police station in Yopougon and a military camp in Akouedou; and in October, there was an attack on a powerplant in Abidjan as well as a military checkpoint and police office in the town of Bonoua. While neither U.S. citizens nor U.S. interests were targets in these incidents, the U.S. Embassy in Côte d'Ivoire recommends that all U.S. citizens take appropriate steps to maintain a high level of vigilance and security awareness.

If you are planning travel to Côte d'Ivoire, particularly to destinations outside of Abidjan, you should consult the U.S. Embassy or your host organization for the most recent security assessments of the areas to which you plan to travel. Official U.S. Embassy personnel must obtain approval for travel within the neighborhoods of Abobo and Yopougon and outside of Abidjan, including travel to western Côte d'Ivoire. The Embassy's ability to assist you in an emergency outside of Abidjan may be limited.

Crimes, such as muggings, robbery, burglary, and carjacking, pose risks for foreign visitors in Abidjan and around the country. You should take precautions when stopped in heavy traffic or at road blocks due to the threat of assault and/or robbery, and avoid travel outside Abidjan after dark to minimize risk. Additionally, the generally poor road conditions are also a factor in driving after sunset. Local law enforcement authorities have limited capacity to respond to emergencies.

The U.S. Embassy instructs its staff to avoid large gatherings, crowds, demonstrations, and political events. You are reminded that even demonstrations and/or political events intended to be peaceful can turn confrontational and possibly escalate into violence. You are therefore urged to avoid the areas of demonstrations, and to exercise caution if within the vicinity of any demonstrations or political events.

U.S. citizens traveling and residing in Côte d'Ivoire are urged to enroll in the State Department's Smart Traveler Enrollment Program (STEP) to receive the most up-to-date security information. By enrolling, you make it easier for the Embassy to contact you in case of emergency.

For further information, consult the Department of State's Country Specific Information for Côte d'Ivoire and the Worldwide Caution, both located on the Department of State's Bureau of Consular Affairs website. Current information on safety and security can also be obtained by calling 1-888-407-4747 toll-free in the United States and Canada, or a regular toll line at 1-202-501-4444 from other countries. These numbers are available from 8:00 a.m. to 8:00 p.m. Eastern Time, Monday through Friday (except U.S. federal holidays).

Stay up to date by bookmarking our Bureau of Consular Affairs website, which contains the current Travel Warnings and Travel Alerts as well as the Worldwide Caution. Follow us on Twitter and the Bureau of Consular Affairs page on Facebook as well. You can also download our free Smart Traveler App, available through iTunes and the Android market to have travel information at your fingertips.

The Embassy is located at 01 B.P. 1712 Abidjan 01 Côte d'Ivoire. If you have questions or concerns about safety or related issues, you are encouraged to contact the consular section at the Embassy by sending an email message to AbjAmcit@state.gov. The Embassy Consular's section can be reached by telephone at 225-22-49-45-94 and emergency after-hours telephone at 225-22-49-44-50.

Intercountry Adoption

July 2012

The information in this section has been edited from a report of the Bureau of Consular Affairs, Office of Overseas Citizens Services of the U.S. Department of State. For more information, please read the *Intercountry Adoption* section of this book and review current reports online at http://adoption.state.gov.

Côte d'Ivoire is not party to the Hague Convention on Protection of Children and Co-operation in Respect of Intercountry Adoption (Hague Adoption Convention). Intercountry adoptions of children from non-Hague countries are processed in accordance with 8 Code of Federal Regulations, Section 204.3 as it relates to orphans as defined under the Immigration and Nationality Act, Section 101(b)(1)(F).

Who Can Adopt? To bring an adopted child to the United States from Côte d'Ivoire, you must meet eligibility and suitability requirements. The U.S. Department of Homeland Security, U.S. Citizenship and Immigration Services (USCIS) determines who can adopt under U.S. immigration law. Additionally, a child must meet the definition of orphan under U.S. immigration law in order to be eligible to immigrate to the United States on an IR-3 or IR-4 immigrant visa. In addition to U.S. immigration requirements, you must also meet the following requirements in order to adopt a child from Côte d'Ivoire.

Residency: The adoption law requires a mandatory home study and a six-month integration period. Prospective adoptive parents may wish to inquire with counsel about whether the court of justice may modify this requirement for foreign prospective adoptive parent(s) residing abroad by waiving the requirement and/or reducing the length of integration time if the adoptive parent(s) can prove that they have seen the adoptive child and that they have been contributing to her or his upkeep.

Age of Adopting Parents: The prospective adoptive parent(s) must be more than 30 years old and must be at least 15 years older than the adoptive child.

Marriage: A prospective adoptive couple must be married for at least five years, and both individuals must consent to the adoption.

Income: The income requirement is not specifically addressed in the adoption law. The law states that "the adoption is not possible unless there are clear and convincing reasons and if it will confer advantages to the adopted child." That is, the adoption should be beneficial for the child at all levels. The judge will, therefore, verify whether the adoptive parent(s) are financially capable of providing good care for the child. In addition, in order to be eligible to adopt, adoptive parent(s) must include in their application, addressed to the Direction de la Protection Sociale (Department of Social Welfare), any proof of income whether they are employed or self-employed.

Other: In Côte d'Ivoire, gay and lesbian individuals and couples are not legally recognized as eligible to adopt.

Who Can Be Adopted? In addition to U.S. immigration requirements, Côte d'Ivoire has specific requirements that a child must meet in order to be eligible for adoption.

Relinquishment: Children placed in an orphanage by the biological parent(s) for financial inability or other personal reasons are not available for adoption unless the parent(s) officially relinquish their parental rights over the child and irrevocably consent to the child's adoption.

Abandonment: Foundlings, directly placed in public orphanages, are considered abandoned if after three months of police investigation, the biological parents cannot be located.

Age of Adoptive Child: With regard to the full adoption, the law states that the child must be under 15 years old. However, the maximum age for an orphan to be placed in a public orphanage is five years old.

Sibling Adoptions: Sibling adoptions are accepted.

Special Needs or Medical Conditions: A medical examination is required for the orphan before the child can be released from the orphanage. The medical examination is the responsibility of the prospective adoptive parent(s).

Waiting Period or Foster Care: The law requires a mandatory six months period for foster care.

Prospective adoptive parents should be aware that not all children in orphanages or children's homes are adoptable. In many countries, birth parents place their child(ren) temporarily in an orphanage or children's home due to financial or other hardship, intending that the child return home when this becomes possible. In such cases, the birth parent(s) have rarely relinquished their parental rights or consented to their child(ren)'s adoption.

Côte d'Ivoire's Adoption Authority: The government offices responsible for adoption in Côte d'Ivoire are the Ministère de l'Emploi, des Affaires Sociales et de la Solidarité (Ministry of Employment, Social Welfare and Solidarity) and the Ministère de la Justice (Ministry of Justice). More specifically, the Direction de la Protection Sociale (Department of Social Welfare) has jurisdiction over the child's identification process, the home study, and the issuance of a certificate authorizing the orphanage to release the child to the adoptive parent(s). The Tribunal de Première Instance (Court of First Instance) has sole authority to grant or deny legal adoption.

The Process: The recommended first step in adopting a child from Côte d'Ivoire is to decide whether or not to use a licensed adoption service provider in the United States that can help you with your adoption. Adoption service providers must be licensed by the U.S. state in which they operate.

There are no private adoption agencies in Côte d'Ivoire. All adoption matters are processed through the Department of Social Welfare and/or the Court of First Instance. The Department of Social Welfare requires that foreign prospective adoptive parent(s) living abroad submit an official authorization for adoption issued by authorized U.S. adoption agencies from their state of residence. This can be a formal U.S. home study.

In order to adopt a child from Côte d'Ivoire you will need to meet the requirements of the Government of Côte d'Ivoire and U.S. immigration law. If the adoptive parent already identified the child, the request for adoption is directly processed through the Court of First Instance. When a child is not yet identified, the first step must be followed with the Department of Social Welfare of Côte d'Ivoire.

Prospective adoptive parent(s) must submit an application to be found eligible to adopt with the Department of Social Welfare of Côte d'Ivoire. The application includes a written request from the prospective parent(s) addressed to the Head of Social Welfare Department along with specific supporting documents. The request should mention the motives for adoption and must indicate the preferred age range and the gender of the adoptive child.

Documents Required:

- Birth certificates of the adoptive parent(s);
- Police Clearance;
- Copy of passport or National ID card;
- One ID photograph;
- Certified copy of the Marriage certificate for legally married couples;
- Proof of income (pay slips or other proof);
- Medical certificate confirming sterility if this is the reason the prospective adoptive parents are pursuing adoption;
- The foreign state authorization for adoption.

The complete file should be sent to or dropped off at the following address in order to receive a registration number: Direction de la Protection Sociale, BP V 200 Immeuble le Général, 5e étage, Plateau, Abidjan 01, Côte d'Ivoire. You may also call (+225) 22 32 42 33 for directions.

The registration is subject to the payment of fees which are separate from the court fees. The fee for foreign citizens residing in or outside Côte d'Ivoire is currently USD 123. This fee is non-refundable.

The committee in charge of placing children in foster-homes will review the applications for adoption, conduct the home study, and will start looking for a child matching the criteria indicated by the prospective adoptive parents. This committee meets four times per year, on a quarterly basis, in March, June, September and December.

The application remains open for two years from the date of registration and will be reviewed during each quarterly session if no decision has yet been made. The prospective adoptive parent(s) will be notified in writing of the final decision.

To meet U.S. immigration requirements, you may also file an I-600A, Application for Advance Processing of an Orphan Petition with U.S. Department of Homeland Security's U.S. Citizenship and Immigration Services to be found eligible and suitable to adopt.

If you are eligible to adopt, and a child is available for intercountry adoption, the central adoption authority or other authorized entity in Côte d'Ivoire will provide you with a referral. Each family must decide for itself whether or not it will be able to meet the needs of and provide a permanent home for a particular child. The child must also meet the definition of orphan under U.S. immigration law.

Once the application is approved and a child is identified for adoption, the committee issues to the prospective adoptive parent(s) an authorization to take the child from the orphanage for a mandatory medical examination. The prospective adoptive parents are responsible for paying the medical fees which are currently USD 400. Upon the completion of the medical examination, the adoptive parent(s) are required to confirm in writing their intent to adopt. Once their confirmation is received, the committee will issue an authorization to the orphanage to release the child for foster care to the adoptive parent(s). However, the release is also subject to the payment of a compulsory financial contribution to the orphanage for the upkeep of the other abandoned children. The amount set for foreign adoptive parents whether living in country or abroad is currently USD 616.

Once the child is officially placed in foster care, the adoptive parent(s) may submit a request for legal adoption to the court. Although the law states that it is only upon the completion of a six-month period that the judge may receive a request for and grant a full adoption, in practice, the court is more lenient with international adoptions and considers various factors when making the decision.

There are two types of adoptions in Côte d'Ivoire: the simple adoption (Adoption Simple) and the full adoption (Adoption Plénière). The simple adoption is roughly equivalent of a guardianship order. The full adoption is a permanent, irrevocable severing of parental rights with the biological parents and the creation of a legal parent-child relationship with the adoptive parent(s) with the same rights as a biological child. However, please note that only a full adoption is considered a valid adoption for U.S. immigration purposes.

Upon receipt of the request for legal adoption, the court will review the facts surrounding the adoption and the documents supporting the request. The court may verify the biological parents' consent, if applicable. When satisfied, the court schedules a date for the hearing to render the official adoption judgment. At the same time, the judge can order a name change for the adopted child and authorize the birth certificate to be amended to reflect the name of the adoptive parent(s) as the new legal surname of the child.

Please note that if the child is not an orphan, the biological parents are required by law to consent in writing to the adoption. The written consent must be attached to the application for adoption along with the other supporting documents.

Adoption Application: The documentary requirements for processing adoptions before the court are the following:

- A written request for legal full adoption from the adoptive parent(s);
- Birth certificates of the adoptive parent(s);
- Marriage certificate for legally married couples;
- Proof of income (pay slips or other proof);
- Medical certificate confirming sterility, if this is the reason the prospective adoptive parents are pursuing adoption;
- The official certificate issued by the local Department of Social Welfare authorizing foster care.
- A U.S. home study may be useful, if translated into French;
- Consent for adoption, in writing, with the signature(s) of the biological parent(s), if known, duly attested by a Notary Public.

Time Frame: The legal process may be finalized within a year.

Adoption Fees: The adoption process involves administrative fees associated with the medical examination, as well as for court procedures. The administrative and medical fees are described in section 2 (c) and section 3. The court fees consist of USD 59.00 to register the case at court. Additional fees involve the purchase of a revenue stamp of USD 1.60 for issuance of the birth certificate, and the payment of a USD 75.00 application fee for an Ivoirian passport.

Additional documents may be requested. If you are asked to provide proof that a document from the United States is authentic, we can help.

Authentication of Documents: You may be asked to provide proof that a document from the United States is authentic.

Bringing Your Child Home: Once your adoption is complete (or you have obtained legal custody of the child), there are a few more steps to take before you can head home. Specifically, you need to apply for several documents for your child before he or she can travel to the United States, such as a birth certificate, a passport or travel document for your child from the country in which he or she was born, and a U.S. Immigration Visa. For detailed and updated information on how to obtain these documents, review the *Intercountry Adoption* section in this publication and visit the U.S. Department of State Intercountry Adoption website at http://adoption.state.gov.

Child Citizenship Act: For adoptions finalized abroad, the Child Citizenship Act of 2000 allows your new child to acquire American citizenship automatically when he or she enters the United States as lawful permanent residents. For adoptions finalized in the United States, the Child

Citizenship Act of 2000 allows your new child to acquire American citizenship automatically when the court in the United States issues the final adoption decree. To learn more, review the *Intercountry Adoption* section in this publication and visit the U.S. Department of State Intercountry Adoption website at http://adoption.state.gov.

After Adoption: We strongly urge you to comply with Côte d'Ivoire's post-adoption requirements in a timely manner. Your adoption agency may be able to help you with this process. Your cooperation will contribute to that country's positive experiences with American parents.

U.S. Embassy in Côte d'Ivoire
01 B.P. 1712, Abidjan 01
Côte d'Ivoire
Tel: (225) 22-49-40-00
Fax: (225) 22-49-42-02
Email: abjamcit@state.gov
Internet: abidjan.usembassy.gov

Côte dIvoire Adoption Authority:
Mr. le Directeur
Direction de la Protection Sociale
Direction Générale des Affaires Sociales
Ministère d'Etat, Ministère de l'Emploi, des Affaires Sociales et de la Solidarité
BP V 200 Abidjan 01
Tel: (225) 20 322 683 or 20 324 233

Monsieur le Président
Tribunal de Première Instance d'Abidjan
BP V 33 Abidjan, Côte d'Ivoire
Tel: (225) 20 223 586

Embassy of Côte dIvoire
2424 Massachusetts Avenue, NW
Washington, D.C. 20007
Telephone: (202) 797-0300.

Côte d'Ivoire also has consulates in: San Francisco, Stamford (CT), Orlando, Houston, and Detroit.

Office of Children's Issues
U.S. Department of State
2201 C Street, NW
SA-29
Washington, DC 20520
Tel: 1-888-407-4747
E-mail: AskCI@state.gov
http://adoption.state.gov

For questions about immigration procedures, call the National Customer Service Center (NCSC) at 1-800-375-5283 (TTY 1-800-767-1833).

CROATIA

Compiled from publications that were available as of February 2013 from the U.S. Department of State, the U.S. Department of Commerce, and the Central Intelligence Agency (CIA). See the introduction to this set for explanatory notes.

Official Name

Republic of Croatia

PROFILE

Geography

Area: total: 56,594 sq km; country comparison to the world: 127; land: 55,974 sq km; water: 620 sq km

Major cities: Zagreb (capital) 685,000 (2009)

Climate: Mediterranean and continental; continental climate predominant with hot summers and cold winters; mild winters, dry summers along coast

Terrain: geographically diverse; flat plains along Hungarian border, low mountains and highlands near Adriatic coastline and islands

People

Nationality: noun: Croat(s), Croatian(s); adjective: Croatian

Population: 4,480,043 (July 2012 est.)

Population growth rate: -0.092% (2012 est.)

Ethnic groups: Croat 89.6%, Serb 4.5%, other 5.9% (including Bosniak, Hungarian, Slovene, Czech, and Roma) (2001 census)

Religions: Roman Catholic 87.8%, Orthodox 4.4%, other Christian 0.4%, Muslim 1.3%, other and unspecified 0.9%, none 5.2% (2001 census)

Languages: Croatian (official) 96.1%, Serbian 1%, other and undesignated (including Italian, Hungarian, Czech, Slovak, and German) 2.9% (2001 census)

Literacy: definition: age 15 and over can read and write; total population: 98.8%; male: 99.5%; female: 98.2% (2010 est.)

Health: life expectancy at birth: total population: 75.99 years; male: 72.38 years; female: 79.8 years (2012 est.); Infant mortality rate: total: 6.06 deaths/1,000 live births; male: 6.16 deaths/1,000 live births; female: 5.96 deaths/1,000 live births (2012 est.)

Unemployment rate: 19% (2012 est.)

Work force: 1.745 million (2012 est.)

Government

Type: presidential/parliamentary democracy

Independence: 25 June 1991

Constitution: adopted 22 December 1990; revised 2000, 2001

Political subdivisions: 20 counties (zupanije, zupanija—singular) and 1 city (grad—singular

Suffrage: 18 years of age; universal

Economy

GDP (purchasing power parity): $79.67 billion (2012 est.); $81.36 billion (2011 est.); $81.4 billion (2010 est.); $82.38 billion (2009 est.)

GDP real growth rate: -1.1% (2012 est.); 0% (2011 est.); -1.2% (2010 est.); -6% (2009 est.)

GDP per capita (PPP): $18,100 (2012 est.); $18,400 (2011 est.); $18,400 (2010 est.); $18,600 (2009 est.)

Natural resources: oil, some coal, bauxite, low-grade iron ore, calcium, gypsum, natural asphalt, silica, mica, clays, salt, hydropower

Agriculture products: arable crops (wheat, corn, barley, sugar beet, sunflower, rapeseed, alfalfa, clover); vegetables (potatoes, cabbage, onion, tomato, pepper); fruits (apples, plum, mandarins, olives), grapes for wine; livestock (cattle, cows, pigs); dairy products

Industries: chemicals and plastics, machine tools, fabricated metal, electronics, pig iron and rolled steel products, aluminum, paper, wood products, construction materials, textiles, shipbuilding, petroleum and petroleum refining, food and beverages, tourism

Exports: $13.04 billion (2012 est.); $12.28 billion (2011 est.); $12.07 billion (2010 est.)

Exports—commodities: transport equipment, machinery, textiles, chemicals, foodstuffs, fuels

Exports—partners: Italy 16.6%, Bosnia and Herzegovina 12.7%, Germany 10.4%, Slovenia 8.2%, Austria 5.8%, Luxembourg 4.5% (2011)

Imports: $21.13 billion (2012 est.); $20.4 billion (2011 est.); $19.96 billion (2010 est.)

Imports—commodities: machinery, transport and electrical equipment; chemicals, fuels and lubricants; foodstuffs

Imports—partners: Italy 16.2%, Germany 12.8%, China 7.2%, Russia 7.2%, Slovenia 6.4%, Austria 4.4% (2011)

Debt—external: $64.25 billion (31 December 2012 est.); $66.3 billion (31 December 2011 est.); $61.62 billion (31 December 2010 est.)

Exchange rates: kuna (HRK) per US dollar; 5.891 (2012 est.); 5.3439 (2011 est.); 5.498 (2010 est.); 5.2692 (2009); 4.98 (2008)

GEOGRAPHY

Croatia serves as a gateway to eastern Europe. It lies along the east coast of the Adriatic Sea and shares a border with Serbia, Montenegro, Bosnia and Herzegovina, Hungary, and Slovenia. The republic has a distinct boomerang shape, arching from the Pannonian Plains of Slavonia between the Sava, Drava, and Danube Rivers, across hilly, central Croatia to the Istrian Peninsula, then south through Dalmatia along the rugged Adriatic coast. Croatia is made up of 20 counties plus the city of Zagreb and controls 1,185 islands in the Adriatic Sea, 67 of which are inhabited.

PEOPLE

The Croats are believed to be a Slavic people who migrated from Ukraine and settled in present-day Croatia during the 6th century.

Language

While Croatian is the official language, many business people in Croatia speak foreign languages, mostly English, German, and Italian (along the coast).

Religion

Approximately 85 percent of the population is Roman Catholic, and 6 percent is Serbian Orthodox Christian (SPC). Groups that constitute less than 5 percent of the population include Muslims, Jews, and followers of other religions. Religious affiliation correlates closely with the country's ethnic makeup. SPC followers, predominantly ethnic Serbs, live primarily in cities and areas bordering Bosnia and Herzegovina (BiH), Serbia, and Montenegro. Most members of other minority religious groups reside in urban areas. Most immigrants are Roman Catholic ethnic Croats from Bosnia and Herzegovina.

HISTORY

After a period of self-rule and the establishment of an independent kingdom, Croatians agreed to the Pacta Conventa in 1091, submitting themselves to Hungarian authority. By the mid-1400s, concerns over Ottoman expansion led the Croatian Assembly to invite the Habsburgs, under Archduke Ferdinand, to assume control over Croatia. Habsburg rule proved successful in thwarting the Ottomans, and by the 18th century, much of Croatia was free of Turkish control. The Austrian monarchy also acquired control over Dalmatia at the close of the Napoleonic wars following centuries of rule by the Venetian Republic.

In 1868, Croatia gained domestic autonomy under Hungarian authority. Following World War I and the demise of the Austro-Hungarian Empire, Croatia joined the Kingdom of Serbs, Croats, and Slovenes (the Kingdom of Serbs, Croats, and Slovenes became Yugoslavia in 1929). During World War II, German and Italian troops invaded and occupied Yugoslavia and set up a puppet, Fascist regime to rule a nominally-independent Croatian state. This regime, under the hard-line nationalist Croatian Ustasha party, was responsible for the deaths of large numbers of ethnic Serbs, Jews, Roma, and other civilians in a network of concentration camps. It was eventually defeated by the Partisans, led by Josip Broz Tito, in what was essentially a civil war as well as a struggle against the Axis occupiers. The pro-Yugoslav Partisans included many ethnic groups, including a large number of Croatians, and were supplied in large part by the United States and the United Kingdom. Yugoslavia changed its name once again after World War II. The new state became the Federal Socialist Republic of Yugoslavia and united Croatia and several other republics together under the communist leadership of Marshal Tito.

After the death of Tito and with the fall of communism throughout Eastern Europe, the Yugoslav federation began to unravel. Croatia held its first multi-party elections since World War II in 1990. Long-time Croatian nationalist Franjo Tudjman was elected President, and 1 year later, Croatia declared independence from Yugoslavia. Conflict between Serbs and Croats in Croatia escalated, and 1 month after Croatia declared independence, the Yugoslav Army intervened and war erupted.

The United Nations mediated a cease-fire in January 1992, but hostilities resumed the next year when Croatia fought to regain one-third of the territory lost the previous year. A second cease-fire was enacted in May 1993, followed by a joint declaration the next January between Croatia and Yugoslavia. However, in September 1993, the Croatian Army led an offensive against the Serb-held self-styled "Republic of Krajina." A third cease-fire was called in March 1994, but it, too, was broken in May and August 1995, after which Croatian forces regained large portions of the Krajina, prompting an exodus of Serbs from this area. In November 1995, Croatia agreed to peacefully reintegrate Eastern Slavonia, Baranja, and Western Sirmium under terms of the Erdut Agreement, and the Croatian government re-established political and legal authority over those territories in January 1998. In December 1995, Croatia signed the Dayton peace agreement, committing itself to a permanent cease-fire and the return of

all refugees. The death of President Tudjman in December 1999, followed by the election of a coalition government and President Stjepan Mesic in early 2000, brought significant changes to Croatia. The government, under the leadership of Prime Minister Ivica Racan, progressed in implementation of the Dayton Peace Accords, regional cooperation, refugee returns, national reconciliation, and democratization. National parliamentary elections held in November 2003 brought back into power the Croatian Democratic Union party (HDZ), which had governed Croatia from independence until 2000.

The HDZ government, headed by Prime Minister Ivo Sanader, was narrowly re-elected in a November 2007 ballot. The Sanader government's priorities included membership for Croatia in the European Union (EU) and the North Atlantic Treaty Organization (NATO); Croatia joined NATO in April 2009. In July 2009, Prime Minister Sanader unexpectedly resigned, and Deputy Prime Minister Jadranka Kosor took over as Croatia's first female Prime Minister. While in office, Prime Minister Kosor focused on tackling corruption at home, while pushing to overcome the last remaining hurdles to Croatia's EU accession.

In January 2010, Ivo Josipovic won the final round of presidential elections to replace two-term President Mesic. In December 2010, former Prime Minister Sanader fled the country in the face of a corruption investigation and was arrested in Austria. In July 2011, Sanader was extradited to Croatia, where he remained in custody until December 2011. Sanader's trial on multiple corruption-related charges continued as of March 2012. President Josipovic and Prime Minister Kosor signed the EU Accession Treaty in Brussels in December 2011.

The center-left "Kukuriku Coalition," made up of the Social Democratic Party (SDP), Croatian People's Party (HNS), Croatian Peasant Party (HSS), and Istrian Democratic Assembly (IDS), gained a majority of seats in parliamentary elections held December 4, 2011. Prime Minister Zoran Milanovic and his new government took office on December 23, 2011.

In a national referendum held January 22, 2012, Croatia took an important step on its path to EU accession with a two-thirds vote in favor of becoming the EU's 28th member. The referendum saw a relatively low turnout, with only 43.51% of the electorate voting. A tentative date of July 2013 has been established for full EU membership.

GOVERNMENT AND POLITICAL CONDITIONS

The Republic of Croatia is a constitutional parliamentary democracy. Legislative authority is vested in the unicameral parliament (Sabor). The president serves as head of state and nominates the prime minister, who leads the government. Domestic and international observers stated that parliamentary elections held in December were in accordance with international standards.

Recent Elections

Parliamentary elections held on December 4, 2011, took place in a pluralistic environment and were administered in a professional and transparent manner, according to the limited election observation mission of the OSCE Office for Democratic Institutions and Human Rights. The group noted, however, that further steps should be taken to improve the legal framework, particularly in reference to the voter list and relative constituency size.

Participation of Women and Minorities: There were 33 women in the 151-seat parliament and four women in the 22-seat cabinet, including a deputy prime minister and the foreign minister. There were five women among the 13 Constitutional Court justices, including the president of the court and 20 women among the 40 Supreme Court justices, including the vice president.

The law governing gender equality requires that political parties balance the representation of genders on their candidate lists for local and national elections as well as in elections for seats in the European Parliament. By the next round of local elections due in May 2013, the share of either gender on candidate lists should be no lower than 40 percent. The law stipulates fines for the violation of this provision. Local NGOs criticized the law on the grounds that the fines were too small to be a deterrent and that the government rarely enforced previous laws for quotas. Female candidates made up 30 percent of the "Kukuriku" coalition candidate list that won parliamentary elections in December, while female candidates made up 22 percent of the HDZ list.

The law reserves three parliamentary seats for ethnic Serb representatives; five additional seats are set aside for the 21 other recognized national minority groups. All national minority voters may choose between voting in the general parliamentary elections and voting for candidates on their declared national minority list. Ethnic Serbs and other ethnic minorities in principle can win additional seats under this system if candidates of their minority group obtain sufficient votes in one or more of the regular voting districts. Mainstream, nonethnically-based political parties placed ethnic Serbs in some leading positions on their candidate lists. As a result, the new government has a number of ethnic Serb ministers including deputy prime ministers. According to records published by political parties at year's end, the parties remained within campaign spending limits; i.e. 15 million kunas ($2.6 million) total per party or coalition across Croatia's 10 districts.

Principal Government Officials

Last Updated: 1/31/2013

Pres.: **Ivo JOSIPOVIC**
Prime Min.: **Zoran MILANOVIC**
First Dep. Prime Min.: **Vesna PUSIC**
Dep. Prime Min.: **Branko GRCIC**
Dep. Prime Min.: **Neven MIMICA**
Dep. Prime Min.: **Milanka OPACIC**
Min. of Administration: **Arsen BAUK**
Min. of Agriculture: **Tihomir JAKOVINA**
Min. of Construction & Physical Planning: **Anka MRAK-TARITAS**
Min. of Culture: **Andrea ZLATAR VIOLIC**
Min. of Defense: **Ante KOTROMANOVIC**
Min. of Economy: **Ivan VRDOLJAK**
Min. of Entrepreneurship & Trade: **Gordan MARAS**
Min. of Environmental & Nature Protection: **Mihael ZMAJLOVIC**
Min. of Finance: **Slavko LINIC**
Min. of Foreign & European Affairs: **Vesna PUSIC**
Min. of Health: **Rajko OSTOJIC**
Min. of Home, Foreign, & European Affairs: **Neven MIMICA**
Min. of Interior: **Ranko OSTOJIC**
Min. of Justice: **Orsat MILJENIC**
Min. of Labor & Pension System: **Mirando MRSIC**
Min. of Maritime Affairs, Transport, & Infrastructure: **Sinisa Hajdas DONCIC**
Min. of Regional Development & European Funds: **Branko GRCIC**
Min. of Science, Education, & Sports: **Zeljko JOVANOVIC**
Min. of Social Welfare & Youth Policy: **Milanka OPACIC**
Min. of Tourism: **Veljko OSTOJIC**
Min. of War Veterans: **Predrag MATIC**
Governor, Croatian National Bank: **Boris VUJCIC**
Ambassador to the US: **Josko PARO**
Permanent Representative to the UN, New York: **Ranko VILOVIC**

ECONOMY

Though still one of the wealthiest of the former Yugoslav republics, Croatia's economy suffered badly during the 1991–95 war. The country's output during that time collapsed and Croatia missed the early waves of investment in Central and Eastern Europe that followed the fall of the Berlin Wall. Between 2000 and 2007, however, Croatia's economic fortunes began to improve slowly with moderate but steady GDP growth between 4% and 6% led by a rebound in tourism and credit-driven consumer spending.

Inflation over the same period remained tame and the currency, the kuna, stable. Croatia experienced an abrupt slowdown in the economy in 2008 and has yet to recover. Difficult problems still remain, including a stubbornly high unemployment rate, a growing trade deficit, uneven regional development, and a challenging investment climate. The new government has announced a more flexible approach to privatization, including the sale in the coming years of state-owned businesses that are not of strategic importance.

While macroeconomic stabilization has largely been achieved, structural reforms lag. Croatia will face significant pressure as a result of the global financial crisis, due to reduced exports and capital inflows. Croatia reentered a recession in 2012 and Zagreb cut spending, particularly on social programs. Croatia's high foreign debt, anemic export sector, strained state budget, and over-reliance on tourism revenue will hinder economic progress over the medium term.

Labor Conditions

The minimum age for the employment of children is 15 years. Minors under the age of 15 may work if they receive prior approval from the state labor inspectorate and if it is determined that the child is not expected to suffer physically or mentally from the work. The law prohibits workers under the age of 18 from working overtime, at night, or under dangerous conditions. Labor law amendments that went into effect on January 1 further impose strict regulations on the employment of minors, forbidding their employment in work environments that could pose health threats. The Ministry of Economy, Labor, and Entrepreneurship, in conjunction with the ombudsman for children and the State Labor Inspectorate, is responsible for enforcing this regulation.

The minimum wage as determined by the government is 2,814 kunas ($482) per month; the net minimum monthly wage is between 2,000 and 2,200 kunas ($342 and $377), depending on exemptions. The government's official monthly income poverty line is 2,100 kunas ($360) for single households and 4,410 kunas ($755) for a four-person household. The government enforced the minimum wage.

The law provides for a standard workweek of 40 hours. Workers are entitled to a 30-minute break daily, one day off out of seven, and a minimum of four weeks of paid vacation annually. The law entitles workers to time-and-a-half pay for overtime and limits overtime to eight hours per week. The labor inspectorate must be notified if overtime work by an employee continues for more than four consecutive weeks or for more than 12 weeks during a calendar year or if the combined overtime of employees of an employer exceeds 10 percent of the total working hours in a particular month. Pregnant women, mothers with children less than three years of age, and single parents of children under six years of age may work overtime only if they freely give written consent to perform such work. An amendment to the labor law that went into effect on January 1, 2011, further requires pregnant women to obtain a note from a doctor indicating their fitness to work overtime and that such work would not adversely affect their health or that of the fetus. The government set health and safety standards, which the Health Ministry enforced; its inspectorate has jurisdiction over enforcement of health and safety laws in the workplace. In practice many industries often did not meet worker protection standards.

U.S.-CROATIAN RELATIONS

The United States established diplomatic relations with Croatia in 1992 following its independence from Yugoslavia. Following Croatia's independence, U.S. engagement aimed to support Croatia's development as a democratic, secure, and market-oriented society and as a strong partner in Euro-Atlantic institutions, and the United States welcomed Croatia's desire to play a positive and stabilizing role in the region. U.S. assistance has been important in enabling Croatia to become a leading partner in Southeast Europe and a model for its neighbors. Bilateral relations between the United States and Croatia are very strong.

Croatia has joined forces with the United States to address regional and global challenges. Croatia has participated in North Atlantic Treaty Organization (NATO) operations including the International Security Assistance Force in Afghanistan, the Kosovo Force, and Operation Unified Protector in Libya, and United Nations peacekeeping missions in Lebanon, Cyprus, India and Pakistan, the Western Sahara, and the Golan Heights. Croatia's mentoring of neighbors in NATO's Partnership for Peace, and especially the Adriatic Charter, has helped those NATO candidates advance their membership aspirations by initiating defense reforms and contributing to Alliance operations.

U.S. Assistance to Croatia

Croatia actively supports its international commitments to prevent the proliferation of weapons of mass destruction. The United States will continue its work to strengthen Croatia's strategic trade control system, border controls, and law enforcement mechanisms. The U.S. Department of Defense has a robust military-to-military relationship with Croatia. The U.S. provides military assistance to Croatia in the form of training, equipment, equipment loans, and education in U.S. military schools. Croatia also has a state partnership with the Minnesota National Guard.

Bilateral Economic Relations

Croatia is a strong democracy with a market economy, but retains significant state control or involvement in a number of industries. The Croatian Government has said it wants to strengthen economic reforms, consolidate public spending, improve the business climate, and foster economic growth. The United States and Croatia have a bilateral investment treaty and investment protection agreement. Croatia is slated to formally enter the European Union (EU) in July 2013 if its accession treaty is ratified by all EU member states. With Croatia's EU accession, U.S. companies exporting to the EU will have an additional market opportunity.

Croatia's Membership in International Organizations

Croatia and the United States belong to a number of the same international organizations, including the United Nations, North Atlantic Treaty Organization, Euro-Atlantic Partnership Council, Organization for Security and Cooperation in Europe, International Monetary Fund, World Bank, and World Trade Organization. Croatia also is an observer to the Organization of American States.

Bilateral Representation

Croatia maintains an embassy in the United States at 2343 Massachusetts Avenue NW, Washington DC, 20008–2853, tel. (202) 588-5899.

Principal U.S. Embassy Officials

Last Updated: 1/14/2013

ZAGREB (E) Thomasa Jeffersona 2, Zagreb 10010, 385-1-661-2200, Fax 385-1-661-2373, Workweek: Mon–Fri 8:00am–16:30pm, Website: http://zagreb.usembassy.gov/

DCM OMS:	Christina L. Gerhardson
AMB OMS:	Terri Gilbert
Co-CLO:	Lika Johnston
DHS/CIS:	James Plitt (Vienna)
FCS:	Robert Peaslee
FM:	Kevin Tregaskis
HRO:	Brian A. Randall
MGT:	John K. Madden
MLO/ODC:	LTC Troy Eggum
POSHO:	Kevin Tregaskis
SDO/DATT:	COL Calvin T. Carlsen
AMB:	Kenneth H. Merten
CON:	Robert Neus
DCM:	Hoyt B. Yee
PAO:	Timothy E. Gerhradson
GSO:	Linda L. Rosalik
RSO:	Orlando Velasquez
CLO:	Nichole Snethen
ECON:	Thomas L. Johnston
FMO:	Brian A. Randall
IMO:	Aaron Luffman
IRS:	Kathy J. Beck
ISO:	Jerel Eastham
LEGATT:	Cary Gleicher (Vienna)
POL:	David Allen
State ICASS:	Ward Kempker

TRAVEL

Consular Information Sheet

January 10, 2013

Country Description: Croatia is a well-developed nation under a parliamentary democracy and is in the process of accession to the European Union (EU). Facilities for tourism are available throughout the country, and the Adriatic coast is a popular tourist destination.

Smart Traveler Enrollment Program (STEP)/Embassy Locations: If you are going to live in or visit Croatia, please take the time to tell our embassy about your trip. If you enroll, we can keep you up to date with important safety and security announcements. Your enrollment will also help your friends and family get in touch with you in an emergency.

U.S. Embassy Zagreb
2 Thomas Jefferson Street
10010 Zagreb
Telephone: 385 (1) 661-2200
Emergency After-Hours Telephone: 385 (1) 661-2400
Facsimile: 385 (1) 665-8933
Email: ZagrebACS@state.gov

The U.S. Embassy Zagreb is located in the southern outskirts of Zagreb near the airport.

Entry/Exit Requirements for U.S. Citizens: You need a passport to visit Croatia. You don't need a visa if you are a U.S. passport holder coming for tourist or business trips of fewer than 90 days within a six-month period. Visit the Embassy of Croatia website for the most current visa information.

All foreign citizens must register with the local police within 24 hours of arrival and inform them of any change in their address. If you are staying in a hotel or in accommodations rented through an accommodation company, the hotelier or accommodation company will register you automatically. Failure to register is a misdemeanor offense; some U.S. citizens have been fined for failing to register. U.S. citizens already in Croatia who wish to remain in Croatia for more than 90 days must obtain a temporary residence permit. Please note that the first temporary stay permit must be obtained from the Croatian Embassy or Consulate in the United States.

In support of a residency application, applicants will need to provide a copy of their birth and, if applicable, marriage and divorce certificates, obtained no more than 90 days before application, as well as an FBI Identification Record Request authenticated for use abroad. All documents should be translated into Croatian and have an "apostille" stamp certifying their authenticity. Information on apostilles and authentication of documents is available from the Bureau of Consular Affairs website.

U.S. citizens who need extensions of approved temporary stays should submit requests to the local police having jurisdiction over their place of residence in Croatia. You should submit requests no later than 30 days in advance of the last day of authorized stay. Please also see the embassy's website for the latest information on procedures for obtaining residence or work permits.

The U.S. Department of State is unaware of any HIV/AIDS entry restrictions for visitors to or foreign residents of Croatia.

Threats to Safety and Security: Although hostilities in all parts of the country ended in 1995, de-mining of areas along former confrontation lines is not complete. We estimate that de-mining operations will continue until at least 2018. Mine-affected areas are well-marked with Croatian-language warning signs using the international symbol for mines—a skull and crossbones inside a red, upside-down triangle.

Be cautious in former conflict areas, including Eastern Slavonia, Brodsko-Posavska County, Karlovac County, areas around Zadar, and in more remote areas of the Plitvice Lakes National Park, and stay on known safe roads and areas. Mine-clearance work may lead to the closure of roads in former conflict areas. For more information about mine-affected areas and de-mining operations in Croatia, please visit the Croatian Mine Action Center's website.

Stay up to date by:

- Bookmarking our Bureau of Consular Affairs website, which contains the current Travel Warnings and Travel Alerts as well as the Worldwide Caution;
- Following us on Twitter and the Bureau of Consular Affairs page on Facebook as well;
- Downloading our free Smart Traveler iPhone App to have travel information at your fingertips;
- Calling 1-888-407-4747 toll-free within the United States and Canada, or call a regular toll line, 1-202-501-4444, from other countries; and
- Taking some time before travel to improve your personal security.

Crime: While violent crime is rare, there have been isolated attacks targeting specific persons or property, which may have been racially motivated or prompted by lingering ethnic tensions from Croatia's war for independence. Foreigners do not appear to be singled out by criminals. We advise you to safeguard your belongings in public areas, especially in bus or railroad stations, airports, and gas stations, and on public transportation. As in many countries, outward displays of wealth may increase your chances of being targeted by thieves.

We urge U.S. citizens to avoid going to so-called "gentlemen's clubs;" a few such establishments have presented foreign customers with grossly inflated bar bills, sometimes in the thousands of dollars, and threatened those customers who refuse to pay.

Don't buy counterfeit and pirated goods, even if they are widely available. Not only are the bootlegs illegal to bring back into the United States, if you purchase them you may also be breaking local law.

Victims of Crime: If you or someone you know becomes the victim of a crime abroad, you should contact the local police and the U.S. Embassy. We can:

- Replace a stolen passport;
- Help you find appropriate medical care if you are the victim of violent crimes such as assault or rape;
- Put you in contact with appropriate police authorities, and if you sign a privacy act waiver, we can contact family members or friends; and
- Help you understand the local criminal justice process and direct you to local attorneys, although it is important to remember that local authorities are responsible for investigating and prosecuting the crime.

The local equivalent to the "911" emergency line in Croatia is 112.

Criminal Penalties: While you are traveling in Croatia, you are subject to its laws even if you are a U.S. citizen. Foreign laws and legal systems can be vastly different from our own, and criminal penalties vary from country to country. There are also some things that might be legal in the country you visit, but still illegal in the United States, and you can be prosecuted under U.S. law if you buy pirated goods. Engaging in sexual conduct with children or using or disseminating child pornography in a foreign country is a crime prosecutable in the United States. If you break local laws in Croatia, your U.S. passport won't help you avoid arrest or prosecution. It's very important to know what's legal and what's not where you are going.

While some countries will automatically notify the nearest U.S. embassy or consulate if a U.S. citizen is detained or arrested in a foreign country, that might not always be the case. To ensure that the United States is aware of your circumstances, request that the police and prison officials notify the nearest U.S. embassy or consulate as soon as you are arrested or detained overseas.

Special Circumstances: With numerous automated teller machines (ATMs) and ever-wider acceptance of credit cards in Croatia, traveler's checks are accepted less frequently or exchanged at an unfavorable rate. Facilities are available for the wiring or transferring of funds.

Recreational Boating: The Croatian Government requires all recreational skippers chartering Croatian flagged vessels to have a certificate of competence. Under Croatian law, the Ministry of Maritime Affairs, Transport, and Infrastructure recognizes licenses issued by the national authorities of other countries.

Although no such national licensing regime exists in the United States, Croatia does recognize certain certificates issued by the US Sailing Association. Regulations are complex and vary by class of license. Details on class of license recognized by country can be found at the Ministry's website. Tourists in Croatia can also be certified at harbormasters' offices in Pula, Rijeka, Senj, Zadar, Sibenik, Split, Ploce, and Dubrovnik, as well as at the Ministry in Zagreb by passing a test.

Accessibility: While in Croatia, individuals with disabilities may find accessibility and accommodation very different from what is found in the United States. Croatian law mandates access to transportation, communication and public buildings for persons with disabilities. However, the law does not demand that facilities be retrofitted. Persons with disabilities will find marked differences in new construction compared to old construction, where access can still be limited. Croatia's geography is hilly and often steep, including along the coast, presents challenges to some persons with disabilities, as well as fitting facilities and transport for universal access. Outside of urban areas, accessibility generally worsens significantly.

Climbing and Hiking: If you intend to hike in the Croatian mountains or climb in the numerous rock climbing areas, always seek local guides' expert advice. The weather in the Croatian mountains can change quickly, even in the summer months, and temperatures can get very low overnight. There have been reports of hikers getting lost in the mountains when they have gone out alone, without expert guides, and left marked paths. Hikers have also been lost in stormy weather, and there have been fatal accidents as well. If in trouble, call the emergency number 112 and the Croatian Mountain Rescue Service will help you as best they can. Rock climbers in the famous Paklenica National Park should consult a local guide or contact the National Park for more information.

Medical Facilities and Health Information: Health-care facilities in Croatia, although generally of Western caliber, are under severe budgetary strains. Some medicines are in short supply in public hospitals and clinics. The number of private medical and dental practitioners is substantial, and private pharmacies stock a variety of medicines not readily available through public health facilities. Tick-borne encephalitis, a disease preventable with a three-shot vaccination series, is found throughout inland Croatia but is not prevalent along the coast.

You can find detailed information on vaccinations and other health precautions on the Centers for Disease Control and Prevention (CDC) website. For information about outbreaks of infectious diseases abroad, consult the World Health Organization (WHO) website, which also contains additional health information for travelers, including detailed country-specific health information.

Medical Insurance: You can't assume your insurance will go with you when you travel. It's very important to find out BEFORE you leave whether or not your medical insurance will cover you overseas. You need to ask your insurance company two questions:

- Does my policy apply when I'm out of the United States?
- Will it cover emergencies like a trip to a foreign hospital or a medical evacuation?

In many places, doctors and hospitals still expect payment in cash at the time of service, and generally will not accept credit cards. Your regular U.S. health insurance may not cover doctor and hospital visits in other countries. If your policy doesn't go with you when you travel, it's a very good idea to take out another one for your trip.

U.S. citizens who plan to stay in Croatia for more than 90 days may be required by Croatian authorities to pay into the Croatian health insurance system for the period of their stay in Croatia, regardless of whether they hold private insurance from the United States.

Traffic Safety and Road Conditions: While in Croatia, you may encounter road conditions that differ significantly from those in the United States.

Road conditions and maintenance in Croatia vary widely. Modern highways linking Zagreb with Rijeka and Split opened in 2004. Construction work is still ongoing between Split and Dubrovnik, causing delays and road closures. Highway tolls are higher than those in the United States and can be paid by cash or credit card. Information on tolls and fees is also available from the Croatian Automobile Association website. Primary roads, including roads along the coast, are generally adequate, but most have only one lane in each direction. Coastal roads are narrow and congested, and tend to be slippery when wet. Rock slides are also possible on roads along the coast, as well as through the mountain regions of Lika and Gorski Kotar. There is heavy congestion on major routes on weekends (towards the coast, for example) and in major cities during rush hours. Congestion on coastal routes, at border crossings, and at tunnels is especially heavy in the summer months. Drivers should be prepared for sudden slowdowns when approaching tunnels at any time of year.

Drivers tend to be aggressive in Croatia. Passing on curves or in oncoming lanes is common on highways and poses a higher risk of accidents. Accidents, when they do happen, very often involve fatalities. Drivers traveling though former conflict areas should stay on paved roads to reduce the risk of encountering unmarked mines and unexploded ordnance left over from the 1991–1995 war. In Zagreb, motorists and pedestrians alike should also pay special attention to trams (streetcars), which in downtown areas may travel at a high rate of speed through the narrow, congested streets. Additionally, drivers in towns and cities should be aware that pedestrians crossing streets in designated white striped crosswalks have the right of way. Drivers must stop to allow these pedestrians to cross.

Right turns on red lights are strictly forbidden in Croatia unless an additional green light (in the shape of an arrow) allows it. At unmarked intersections, right of way is always given to the vehicle entering from the right. The use of front seat belts is obligatory, and passengers in vehicles equipped with rear seat belts are required to use them. Special seats are required for infants, and children under age 12 may not sit in the front seat of an automobile. The use of cellular phones while operating a motor vehicle is prohibited unless the driver is using a hands-free device. By law, headlights of vehicles must be used all winter, as well as during fog and other inclement weather.

According to Croatian law, a driver may drive with a blood alcohol level of up to 0.05 percent; however it is illegal for a professional driver and those younger than 24 years of age to drive with a blood alcohol level greater than 0.00 percent. A driver with an alcohol level greater than 0.00 may be found guilty if involved in an accident. Police routinely spot-check motorists for drinking and driving and administer breath-analyzer tests at the scene of even the most minor accident. Drivers who refuse to submit to a breath-analyzer test are automatically presumed to have admitted to driving while intoxicated. In case of accidents resulting in death or serious injury, Croatian law requires police to take blood samples to test blood alcohol levels. Punishment for traffic violations can be severe, including fines up to 2,000 euros and even prison sentences.

Within Croatia, emergency road help and information may be reached 24 hours a day by dialing 1987, a service of the Croatian Automobile Association (HAK), staffed by English-speaking operators. The police can be reached by dialing 112 or 192,and the ambulance service by dialing 194.Additional road condition and safety information may be obtained from HAK at tel. (385 1) 464-0800 (English-speaking operators available 24 hours), or (385 1) 661-1999. Croatian Radio broadcasts programs in foreign languages designed for tourists in Croatia on several frequencies. A daily program is broadcast in English at 8:05 pm on channel one, lasting approximately 10 minutes.

During the summer season, approximately mid-June through mid-September, channel two of the Croatian Radio (98.5 Mhz in northwestern Croatia and the Dubrovnik area, 105.3 Mhz in Istria, 96.1 Mhz in Split, 98.9 Mhz in Makarska, 93.3 Mhz in Gorski kotar) broadcasts foreign news, traffic information, and other important information in English, German, and Italian, in addition to their normal reporting.

According to Croatian law, U.S. citizens visiting Croatia for tourism or business may use a U.S. driver's license for up to three months, but should also have an International Driver's Permit.U.S. citizens with an approved extended tourist visa or a permit for permanent residence may continue to use a U.S. driver's license for up to twelve months; however, a Croatian driver's license is required for stays longer than twelve months.

A driver must be at least 23 years old and have a valid driver's license in order to rent a car. Foreigners who have been granted temporary residence in Croatia and who are in possession of a vehicle registered abroad (with valid registration documents and insurance) may use their car a maximum of three months following the day of entry into Croatia, after which period the vehicle must be re-registered in Croatia. For specific information concerning Croatian driver's permits, vehicle inspection, road tax, and mandatory insurance, please contact the Croatian National Tourist Office, P.O. Box 2651,NY 10108. In cases of traffic accidents involving a foreign-registered vehicle, the investigating police officer on the scene is required to issue a vehicle damage certificate to the owner of the foreign-registered vehicle. This certificate is necessary to cross the border. Upon written request, the police station in the area where the accident occurred will issue a Traffic Accident Investigation Record.

Aviation Safety Oversight: The U.S. Federal Aviation Administration (FAA) has assessed the government of Croatia's Civil Aviation Authority as being in compliance with International Civil Aviation Organization (ICAO) aviation safety standards for oversight of Croatia's air carrier operations. Further information may be found on the FAA's safety assessment page.

Children's Issues: Please see the U.S. Dept. of State Office of Children's Issues web pages on intercountry adoption and international parental child abduction.

Intercountry Adoption

April 2011

Croatia is not party to the Hague Convention on Protection of Children and Co-operation in Respect of Intercountry Adoption (Hague Adoption Convention). Therefore, when the Hague Adoption Convention entered into force for the United States on April 1, 2008, intercountry adoption processing for Croatia did not change. The Department of State does not maintain files on the adoption process in Croatia because adoptions from Croatia are rare. Fewer than five adoptions by American citizen parents have taken place since 2003.

CUBA

Compiled from publications that were available as of February 2013 from the U.S. Department of State, the U.S. Department of Commerce, and the Central Intelligence Agency (CIA). See the introduction to this set for explanatory notes.

Official Name:
Republic of Cuba

PROFILE

Geography

Area: total: 110,860 sq km; country comparison to the world: 106; land: 109,820 sq km; water: 1,040 sq km

Major cities: Havana (capital) 2.14 million (2009)

Climate: tropical; moderated by trade winds; dry season (November to April); rainy season (May to October)

Terrain: mostly flat to rolling plains, with rugged hills and mountains in the southeast

People

Nationality: noun: Cuban(s); adjective: Cuban

Population: 11,075,244 (July 2012 est.)

Population growth rate: -0.115% (2012 est.)

Ethnic groups: white 65.1%, mulatto and mestizo 24.8%, black 10.1% (2002 census)

Religions: nominally Roman Catholic 85%, Protestant, Jehovah's Witnesses, Jewish, Santeria

Languages: Spanish (official)

Literacy: definition: age 15 and over can read and write; total population: 99.8%; male: 99.8%; female: 99.8% (2002 census)

Health: life expectancy at birth: total population: 77.87 years; male: 75.61 years; female: 80.27 years (2012 est.); Infant mortality rate: total: 4.83 deaths/1,000 live births; male: 5.19 deaths/1,000 live births; female: 4.45 deaths/1,000 live births (2012 est.)

Unemployment rate: 3.6% (2012 est.)

Work force: 5.18 million (2012 est.)

Government

Type: Communist state

Independence: 20 May 1902

Constitution: 24 February 1976; amended July 1992 and June 2002

Political subdivisions: 15 provinces (provincias, singular—provincia) and 1 special municipality (municipio especial); Artemisa, Camaguey, Ciego de Avila, Cienfuegos, Granma, Guantanamo, Holguin, Isla de la Juventud, La Habana, Las Tunas, Matanzas, Mayabeque, Pinar del Rio, Sancti Spiritus, Santiago de Cuba, Villa Clara

Suffrage: 16 years of age; universal

Economy

GDP (purchasing power parity): $114.1 billion (2010 est.); $112.4 billion (2009 est.); $110.8 billion (2008 est.)

GDP real growth rate: 1.5% (2010 est.); 1.4% (2009 est.); 4.1% (2008 est.)

GDP per capita (PPP): $9,900 (2010 est.); $9,800 (2009 est.); $9,700 (2008 est.)

Natural resources: cobalt, nickel, iron ore, chromium, copper, salt, timber, silica, petroleum, arable land

Agriculture products: sugar, tobacco, citrus, coffee, rice, potatoes, beans; livestock

Industries: sugar, petroleum, tobacco, construction, nickel, steel, cement, agricultural machinery, pharmaceuticals

Exports: $6.35 billion (2012 est.); $6.347 billion (2011 est.); $4.598 billion (2010 est.)

Exports—commodities: sugar, nickel, tobacco, fish, medical products, citrus, coffee

Exports—partners: China 24.9%, Canada 21.6%, Venezuela 7.2%, Netherlands 7.1%, Spain 6.5% (2011)

Imports: $14.12 billion (2012 est.); $13.26 billion (2011 est.); $10.65 billion (2010 est.)

Imports—commodities: petroleum, food, machinery and equipment, chemicals

Imports—partners: Venezuela 37.6%, China 9.9%, Spain 8.5%, Brazil 5.2%, Canada 4.4% (2011)

Debt—external: $22.36 billion (31 December 2012 est.); $21.52 billion (31 December 2011 est.)

Exchange rates: Cuban pesos (CUP) per US dollar; 1 (2012 est.) ; 0.9847 (2011 est.); 0.9259 (2010 est.); 0.9259 (2009); 0.9259 (2008); 0.9259 (2007)

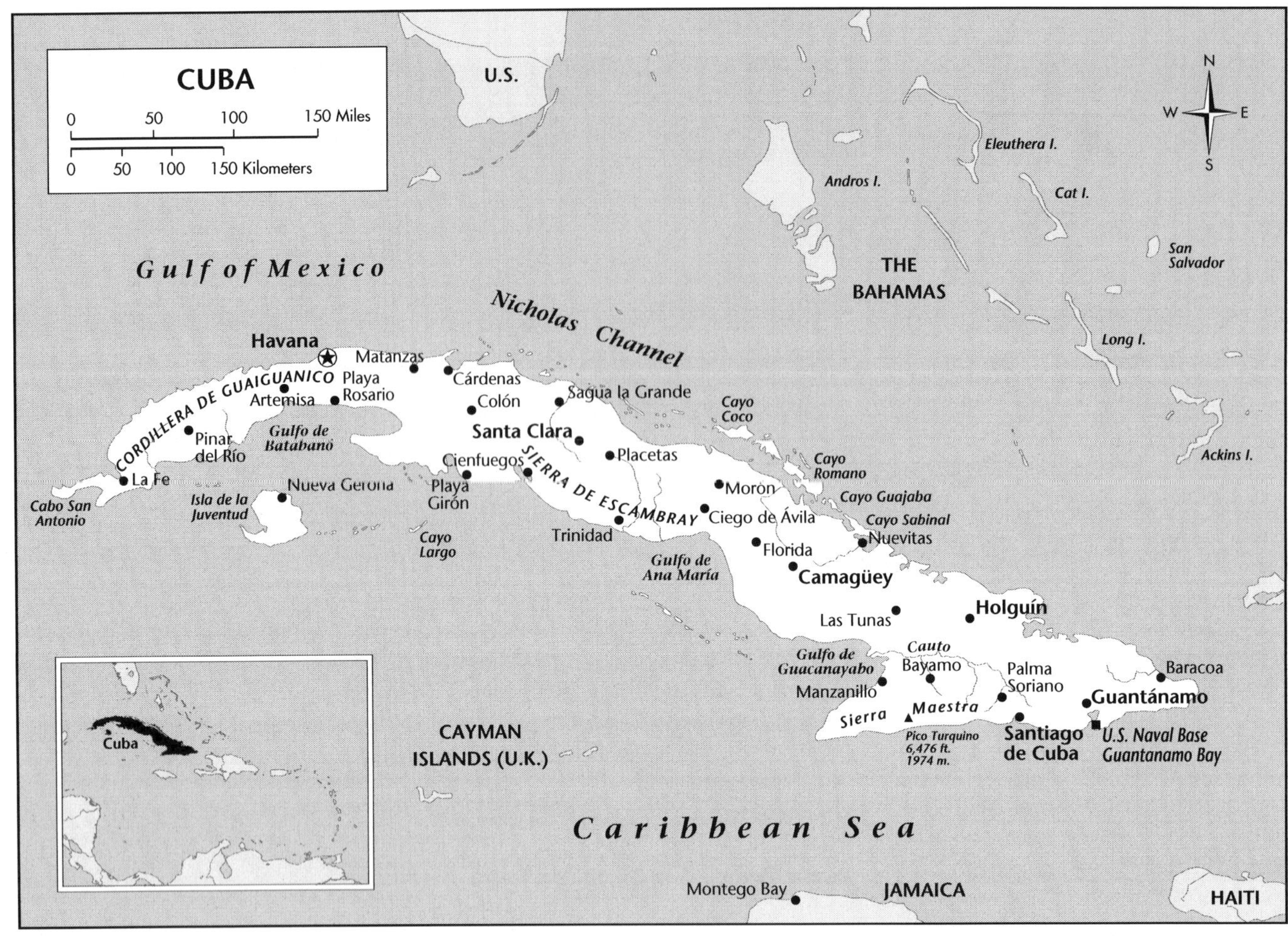

PEOPLE

Cuba is a multiracial society with a population of mainly Spanish and African origins. Spanish is the official language.

Religion

There is no independent authoritative source on the size or composition of religious institutions and their membership. The Roman Catholic Church estimates that 60 to 70 percent of the population is Catholic but that only 4 to 5 percent regularly attend mass. Membership in Protestant churches is estimated at 5 percent of the population.

Baptists and Pentecostals are likely the largest Protestant denominations. Jehovah's Witnesses reported approximately 94,000 members; Seventh-day Adventists and Methodists each estimated 30,000; Anglicans, 22,000; Presbyterians, 15,000; Quakers, 300; and The Church of Jesus Christ of Latter-day Saints (Mormons), 50. The Jewish community estimated 1,500 members of whom 1,200 reside in Havana. According to the Islamic League, there are approximately 6,000 to 8,000 Muslims, although only an estimated 1,000 are Cubans. Other religious groups include the Greek and Russian Orthodox churches, Buddhists and Baha'is.

Many persons consult with practitioners of religions with roots in West Africa and the Congo River basin, known as Santeria. These religious practices are commonly intermingled with Catholicism, and some even require Catholic baptism for full initiation, making it difficult to estimate accurately the total membership of these syncretistic groups.

HISTORY

Spanish settlers established the raising of cattle, sugarcane, and tobacco as Cuba's primary economic pursuits. As the native Indian population died out, African slaves were imported to work the ranches and plantations. Slavery was abolished in 1886.

Cuba was the last major Spanish colony to gain independence, following a lengthy struggle begun in 1868. Jose Marti, Cuba's national hero, helped initiate the final push for independence in 1895. In 1898, the United States entered the conflict after the USS Maine sank in Havana Harbor on February 15 due to an explosion of undetermined origin. In December of that year, Spain relinquished control of Cuba to the United States with the Treaty of Paris.

On May 20, 1902, the United States granted Cuba its independence but retained the right to intervene to preserve Cuban independence and stability in accordance with the Platt Amendment. In 1934, the Platt Amendment was repealed. The United States and Cuba concluded a Treaty of Relations in 1934 which, among other things, continued the 1903 agreements that leased the Guantanamo Bay naval base to the United States.

Independent Cuba was often ruled by authoritarian political and military figures who either obtained or remained in power by force. Fulgencio Batista, an army sergeant, organized a non-commissioned officer revolt in September 1933 and wielded significant power behind the scenes until he was elected president in 1940. Batista was voted out of office in 1944 and did not run in 1948. Both those elections were won by civilian political figures with the support of party organizations.

Running for president again in 1952, Batista seized power in a bloodless coup 3 months before the election was to take place, suspended the balloting, and began ruling by decree. Many political figures and movements that wanted a return to the government according to the constitution of 1940 disputed Batista's undemocratic rule.

On July 26, 1953, Fidel Castro, who had been involved in increasingly violent political activity before Batista's coup, led a failed attack on the Moncada army barracks in Santiago de Cuba in which more than 100 died. After defending himself in a trial open to national and international media, he was convicted and jailed, and subsequently was freed in an act of clemency, before going into exile in Mexico. There he organized the "26th of July Movement" with the goal of overthrowing Batista, and the group sailed to Cuba on board the yacht Granma, landing in the eastern part of the island in December 1956. Batista's dictatorial rule fueled increasing popular discontent and the rise of many active urban and rural resistance groups, a fertile political environment for Castro's 26th of July Movement. Faced with a corrupt and ineffective military—itself dispirited by a U.S. Government embargo on weapons sales to Cuba—and public indignation and revulsion at his brutality toward opponents, Batista fled on January 1, 1959. Although he had promised a return to constitutional rule and democratic elections along with social reforms, Castro used his control of the military to consolidate his power by repressing all dissent from his decisions, marginalizing other resistance figures, and imprisoning or executing thousands of opponents.

An estimated 3,200 people were executed by the Cuban Government between 1959 and 1962 alone. As the revolution became more radical, hundreds of thousands of Cubans fled the island.

Castro declared Cuba a socialist state on April 16, 1961. For the next 30 years, Castro pursued close relations with the Soviet Union and worked to advance the geopolitical goals of the Soviet Union, funding and fomenting violent subversive and insurrectional activities and participating in foreign interventions until the demise of the U.S.S.R. in 1991.

Relations between the United States and Cuba deteriorated rapidly as the Cuban Government expropriated U.S. properties and moved toward adoption of a one-party communist system. In response, the United States imposed an embargo on Cuba in October 1960, and, in response to Castro's provocations, broke diplomatic relations on January 3, 1961. Tensions between the two governments peaked during the October 1962 missile crisis.

GOVERNMENT AND POLITICAL CONDITIONS

Cuba is a totalitarian state led by Raul Castro, who is the chief of state, president of the council of state and council of ministers, and commander in chief of the armed forces. At the Sixth Communist Party Congress held in April, delegates also elected Castro as party first secretary. The constitution recognizes the Communist Party (CP) as the only legal party and "the superior leading force of society and of the state." The 2008 legislative elections were neither free nor fair. A CP candidacy commission preapproved all candidates, and all 614 members ran unopposed.

Recent Elections

All 614 candidates for the National Assembly at the 2008 national elections were prevetted by government-run bodies and ran unopposed. They in turn elected Raul Castro to succeed his brother as chief of state and president by unanimous vote.

Political Parties: All candidates for office were preapproved by government-run commissions, which rejected independent candidacies without explanation or the right of appeal. All but seven of the 614 candidates were CP members. In the 2010 municipal elections, scores of candidates were summarily refused the opportunity to run. Some independent candidates managed to run, although they were all defeated in open, nonsecret voting.

Participation of Women and Minorities: There are no official restrictions on women or minorities, and the government actively promotes participation of both in government. President (and CP First Secretary) Castro highlighted that the composition of the newly elected Central Committee included 48 women (42 percent) and 36 Afro-Cubans (31 percent). Following the selection of the National Assembly in 2008, the government reported the composition as approximately 63 percent white, 20 percent black, and 17 percent mixed race.

Principal Government Officials

Last Updated: 1/31/2013

Pres., Council of State: **Raul Modesto CASTRO Ruz, Gen.**

First Vice Pres., Council of State: **Jose Ramon MACHADO Ventura**
Vice Pres., Council of State: **Gladys BEJERANO Portela**
Vice Pres., Council of State: **Abelardo COLOME Ibarra, Corps Gen.**
Vice Pres., Council of State: **Esteban LAZO Hernandez**
Vice Pres., Council of State: **Ramiro VALDES Menendez**
Min. Sec., Council of State: **Homero ACOSTA Alvarez**
Pres., Council of Ministers: **Raul CASTRO Ruz, Gen.**
First Vice Pres., Council of Ministers: **Jose Ramon MACHADO Ventura**
Vice Pres., Council of Ministers: **Ricardo CABRISAS Ruiz**
Vice Pres., Council of Ministers: **Miguel DIAZ-CANEL Bermudez**
Vice Pres., Council of Ministers: **Adel IZQUIERDO Rodriguez**
Vice Pres., Council of Ministers: **Antonio Enrique LUSSON Batlle, Div. Gen.**
Vice Pres., Council of Ministers: **Marino MURILLO Jorge**
Vice Pres., Council of Ministers: **Ulises ROSALES del Toro**
Vice Pres., Council of Ministers: **Ramiro VALDES Menendez**
Sec., Executive Ctte., Council of Ministers: **Jose Amado RICARDO Guerra, Brig. Gen.**
Min. of Agriculture: **Gustavo RODRIGUEZ Rollero**
Min. of Construction: **Rene MESA Villafana**
Min. of Culture: **Rafael BERNAL Alemany**
Min. of Domestic Trade: **Mary Blanca ORTEGA Barredo**
Min. of Economy & Planning: **Adel IZQUIERDO Rodriguez**
Min. of Education: **Ena Elsa VELAZQUEZ Cobiella**
Min. of Energy & Mines: **Alfredo LOPEZ Valdes**
Min. of Finance & Prices: **Lina PEDRAZA Rodriguez**
Min. of the Food Industry: **Maria del Carmen CONCEPCION Gonzalez**
Min. of Foreign Trade & Investment: **Rodrigo MALMIERCA Diaz**
Min. of Foreign Relations: **Bruno RODRIGUEZ Parrilla**
Min. of Higher Education: **Rodolfo ALARCON Ortiz**
Min. of Industry: **Salvador PARDO Cruz**
Min. of Information Science & Communication: **Maimir MESA Ramos**
Min. of Interior: **Abelardo COLOME Ibarra, Corps Gen.**
Min. of Justice: **Maria Esther REUS Gonzalez**
Min. of Labor & Social Security: **Margarita Marlene GONZALEZ Fernandez**
Min. of Public Health: **Roberto MORALES Ojeda**
Min. of the Revolutionary Armed Forces: **Leopoldo CINTRA FRIAS, Corps Gen.**
Min. of Science, Technology, & Environment: **Elba Rose PEREZ Montoya**
Min. of Tourism: **Manuel MARRERO Cruz**
Min. of Transportation: **Cesar Ignacio AROCHA Masid**
Attorney Gen.: **Dario DELGADO Cura**
Pres., Central Bank of Cuba: **Ernesto MEDINA Villaveiran**
Permanent Representative to the UN, New York: **Pedro NUNEZ Mosquera**

ECONOMY

The government continues to balance the need for loosening its socialist economic system against a desire for firm political control. The government in April 2011 held the first Cuban Communist Party Congress in almost 13 years, during which leaders approved a plan for wide-ranging economic changes. President Raul CASTRO said such changes were needed to update the economic model to ensure the survival of socialism.

The government has expanded opportunities for self employment and has introduced limited reforms, some initially implemented in the 1990s, to increase enterprise efficiency and alleviate serious shortages of food, consumer goods, services, and housing. The average Cuban's standard of living remains at a lower level than before the downturn of the 1990s, which was caused by the loss of Soviet aid and domestic inefficiencies.

Since late 2000, Venezuela has been providing oil on preferential terms, and it currently supplies over 100,000 barrels per day of petroleum products. Cuba has been paying for the oil, in part, with the services of Cuban personnel in Venezuela including some 30,000 medical professionals.

Labor Conditions

The legal minimum working age is 17, although the labor code permits the employment of 15-and 16-year-old children to obtain training or fill labor shortages. The labor code does not permit 15- and 16-year-olds to work more than seven hours per day or 40 hours per week, or on holidays. Children ages 13 to 18 cannot work in specified hazardous occupations, such as mining, or at night. There were no known government programs to prevent child labor or remove children from such labor. Antitruancy programs, however, helped ensure that children were in school and not in the labor market. Inspections and penalties were adequate to enforce the law, and in practice it was rare that children under 17 worked.

The monthly minimum wage was fixed at 225 pesos (approximately $9). The minimum wage requirement does not apply to the small nonstate sector. The government supplemented the minimum wage with free education, subsidized medical care (daily pay is reduced by 40 percent after the third day of a hospital stay), housing, and some food. Even with subsidies the government acknowledged that the average wage of 448 pesos per month (approximately $19) did not provide a reasonable standard of living.

The standard workweek is 44 hours, with shorter workweeks in hazardous occupations, such as mining. The law provides workers with a weekly 24-hour rest period, and 24 days of paid annual holidays. These standards applied to state workers as well as to the small nonstate sector (but not to the self-employed). The law does not provide for premium pay for overtime or prohibit obligatory overtime but generally caps the number of overtime hours at 12 per week or 160 per year. However, the law provides little grounds for a worker to refuse to work overtime. Refusal to work overtime could result in a notation in the employee's official work history that could imperil subsequent requests for vacation time. The Ministry of Labor has the authority to establish different overtime caps as needed. Compensation for overtime is paid in cash at the regular hourly rate or in additional rest time, particularly for workers directly linked to production or services, and does not apply to management.

The Ministry of Labor effectively enforced minimum wage and hours of work standards through offices at the national, provincial, and municipal levels, but the government lacked mechanisms to enforce occupational safety and health standards.

Workers frequently complained that overtime compensation was either not paid or not paid in a timely manner. The government continued to expand the number of trades that could be plied privately, to 181, and for the first time allowed the self-employed to hire labor. Foreign companies operated in a limited number of sectors, such as hotels, tourism, and mining.

Such companies operated on the basis of a joint venture policy, in which the government contracted and paid company workers in pesos, an amount that was a small fraction of what the company remitted to the state for labor costs. Employers are prohibited from contracting or paying the workers directly, although many reportedly made supplemental payments under the table.

The independent and illegal Confederation of Independent Workers of Cuba reported numerous violations of health and safety laws at worksites throughout the country, including inadequate and poorly maintained equipment and protective gear.

U.S.-CUBAN RELATIONS

Cuba's authoritarian regime assumed power by force in 1959 and has severely restricted fundamental freedoms, repressed political opponents, and violated human rights. The United States imposed an embargo on Cuba in 1960 and broke diplomatic relations in 1961, following the Cuban Government's expropriation of U.S. properties and its move toward adoption of a one-party communist system.

U.S. policy toward Cuba is focused on encouraging democratic and economic reforms and increased respect for human rights on the part of the Cuban Government. The U.S. Government has taken steps to reach out to the Cuban people in support of their desire to freely determine their country's future.

Although Cuba is subject to U.S. trade sanctions, the United States remains Cuba's second largest supplier of food. The United States is committed to supporting safe, orderly, and legal migration from Cuba through the effective implementation of the 1994–95 U.S.-Cuba Migration Accords.

U.S. Assistance to Cuba

U.S. programs in Cuba include humanitarian support to political prisoners and their families, human rights and democracy promotion, and facilitating the free flow of information to, from and within the island.

Bilateral Economic Relations

Remittances play an important role in Cuba's state-controlled economy, with much of that funding coming from families in the United States. In 2009, the United States announced the lifting of restrictions on family travel and remittances to Cuba, expanded the list of items eligible for humanitarian export to Cuba, and announced new regulations for U.S. telecommunications companies to expand the flow of information to Cuba.

In 2011, the United States announced regulatory changes that increase purposeful travel including religious, cultural, educational, and people-to-people travel; expand the individuals and groups eligible to send and receive remittances; and allow all U.S. international airports to apply to provide charter services to Cuba (previously only three airports were authorized).

Travel to Cuba is restricted by U.S. regulations to licensed travelers engaged in a set of specified activities. All U.S. travel to Cuba must be licensed by the Department of Treasury's Office of Foreign Assets Control (OFAC), and must fall into one of 12 categories. Further information on the licensing process can be obtained from OFAC or at its website. Those contemplating a visit to Cuba should consult the consular information page about the country.

All exports to Cuba must be licensed by the Commerce Department's Bureau of Industry and Security (BIS). Further information on exports to Cuba can be found at the BIS website.

Cuba's Membership in International Organizations

Cuba has an activist foreign policy and aims to find new sources of trade, aid, foreign investment, and political support, as well as to promote opposition to U.S. policy toward Cuba, in particular U.S. trade sanctions. Cuba and the United States belong to a number of the same international organizations, including the United Nations and the World Trade Organization. Cuba was readmitted to the Organization of American States in 2009 after having been expelled in 1962, but the country has refused to rejoin.

Bilateral Representation

Cuba is represented in the United States by the Cuban Interests Section in Washington, D.C.

Principal U.S. Embassy Officials

Last Updated: 1/14/2013

HAVANA (USINT) Calzada between L & M Streets, 011-537-839-4100,

Fax 011-537-833-2095, INMARSAT Tel ., Workweek: Monday–Friday, 8:00 am–4:30 pm, Website: http://havana.usinterestsection.gov/

DCM OMS:	Enid Anglero
CM:	John Caulfield
CM OMS:	Kellie Reifstenzel
DHS/CIS:	Jorge Medina
FM:	Paul Davis
HRO:	Peggy Guttierrez
MGT:	Acting Peggy Guttierrez
POL/ECON:	Thomas Palaia
POSHO:	Paul Davis
CG:	Timothy Roche
DCM:	Conrad Tribble
PAO:	Lynn Roche
GSO:	Hunter Crowder
RSO:	Brent Brown
AFSA:	Derek Kolb
CLO:	Steven Quartell
FMO:	Peggy Guttierrez
ICASS Chair:	Jorge Medina
IMO:	Michael Cifarelli
IPO:	Mohammad Chaudhry
ISO:	Scott Cullum
ISSO:	Scott Cullum
State ICASS:	Kellie Reifstenzel

TRAVEL

Consular Information Sheet

April 30, 2012

Country Description: Cuba is an authoritarian state which controls most aspects of Cuban life through the Communist Party, its affiliated mass organizations, and the state security apparatus. The Communist Party is constitutionally recognized as Cuba's only legal political party and the Ministry of Interior is the principal organ of state security and control. The Cuban government routinely employs repressive methods against internal dissent and monitors and responds to perceived threats to its authority. These methods include intense physical and electronic surveillance, and in some cases may involve detention and interrogation of both Cuban citizens and foreign visitors. Travel to Cuba by U.S. citizens and permanent residents is restricted by U.S. law and regulations, and travelers generally must obtain a license or qualify for an existing license from the Department of Treasury. Such licenses restrict the activities and transactions in which U.S. citizens and residents may engage while in Cuba. Licensed U.S. travelers visiting Cuba should be aware that any on-island activities could be subject to surveillance, and their contacts with Cuban citizens monitored closely. The United States Government, which does not maintain full diplomatic relations with Cuba, is represented by the U.S. Interests Section (USINT) in Havana, which provides a range of consular and other services. U.S. diplomats, however, are not allowed to travel freely outside the capital and may be prevented from providing assistance to U.S. citizens outside Havana.

Smart Traveler Enrollment Program (STEP)/Embassy Locations: The United States does not maintain full diplomatic relations with Cuba. Consular and other services are provided to the extent possible by the U.S. Interests Section (USINT). USINT is limited in its capacity to provide protection or routine consular services to U.S. citizens in Cuba because the Cuban government restricts U.S. diplomatic travel to the city of Havana. Additionally, the Cuban government in most instances does not recognize the U.S. citizenship of Cuban-American nationals for consular purposes and denies U.S. officials consular access to such individuals. U.S. citizens who travel to Cuba are encouraged to contact and enroll with USINT's American Citizen Services section.

U.S. citizens who enroll through the Smart Traveler Enrollment Program at the U.S. Interests Section in Havana may obtain updated information on travel and security within the country. There is no access to the U.S. Naval Base at Guantanamo Bay from within Cuba. The U.S. Embassy in Kingston, Jamaica handles consular issues for Guantanamo Bay. For further information on Guantanamo Bay, please contact the U.S. Embassy in Kingston by telephone at (876) 929-5374.

Switzerland serves as the protecting power for U.S. interests in Cuba; however, the U.S. Interests Section is not co-located with the Swiss Embassy. The U.S. Interests Section is located in Havana at Calzada between L and M Streets, Vedado; telephone numbers (537) 833-3551 through 833-3559. Hours are Monday through Thursday, 8:00 a.m. to 4:30 p.m., and Friday, 8:00 a.m. to 3:30 p.m. For emergency assistance after hours and on weekends, individuals should call (537) 833-2302 or (535) 280-5791 and request to speak with the duty officer. Routine information is available through the American Citizen Services office of the U.S. Interests Section.

USINT staff members provide briefings on U.S.-Cuba policy to U.S. citizen individuals and groups visiting Cuba. These briefings or meetings can be arranged through USINT's Public Diplomacy Office.

Cuban Requirements for Authorized Travelers: The Cuban government requires a valid passport and visa for entry into Cuba. Although Cuba may issue visas upon arrival to U.S. citizens, the U.S. government strongly recommends that all travelers to Cuba, including religious workers, obtain the appropriate type of visa ahead of time and, if required, specific authorization from Cuban authorities in order to avoid any potential problems with documentation upon arrival in Cuba. Attempts to enter or exit Cuba illegally, or to aid the irregular exit of Cuban nationals or other persons, are contrary to Cuban law and may be punishable by stiff jail terms. Entering Cuban territory, territorial waters or airspace (within 12 nautical miles of the Cuban coast) without prior authorization from the Cuban government may result in arrest or other enforcement action by Cuban authorities. Immigration violators are subject to prison terms ranging from four years for illegal entry or exit to as many as 30 years for aggravated cases of alien smuggling.

The Cuban government requires individuals visiting Cuba to engage only in activities authorized under the category for which the Cuban visa is issued (e.g. religious, educational, etc.). Participating in activities that go beyond the reason for which a visa is granted may result in arrest or other enforcement action by Cuban authorities. Visa violations are subject to lengthy prison terms ranging up to 25 years or more. In recent years, the Cuban government has detained U.S. citizens suspected of visa violations for engaging in activities it perceives as counterrevolutionary or subversive to state security. In 2009, the Cuban government arrested a U.S. citizen who was in Cuba facilitating access to the internet. In 2011, he was convicted of crimes against the security of the state and sentenced to 15 years in prison.

Entry/Exit Requirements, Travel Transaction Limitations: The U.S. Department of the Treasury enforces the Cuban Assets Control Regulations, which apply to all U.S. citizens and permanent residents wherever they are located, all people and organizations physically located in the United States, and branches and subsidiaries of U.S. organizations throughout the world.

The regulations require that persons subject to U.S. jurisdiction be licensed in order to engage in any travel-related transactions pursuant to travel to, from, and within Cuba. Transactions related to travel for tourist activities are not licensable.

This restriction also prohibits tourist travel to Cuba from or through a third country such as Mexico or Canada. U.S. law enforcement authorities enforce these regulations at U.S. airports and pre-clearance facilities in third countries. Travelers who fail to comply with Department of the Treasury regulations could face civil penalties and criminal prosecution upon return to the United States.

Cuba requires visitors to have non-U.S. medical insurance and sells a temporary policy to those who do not have it. Questions about this insurance requirement should be directed to the Cuban Interests Section. Some HIV/AIDS entry restrictions exist for visitors to and foreign residents of Cuba. Cuban authorities do not demand HIV tests of travelers to Cuba, with the exception of foreign students on scholarships.

The Cuban authorities currently accept the results of HIV tests conducted by labs in the United States. Please verify this information with the Cuban Interests Section in Washington before traveling.

For the latest information on U.S. regulations governing travel to Cuba and to view the most accurate and updated travel restrictions information, please see the Department of Treasury's OFAC website at http://www.treasury.gov/resource-center/sanctions/Programs/Pages/cuba.aspx

General licenses for Travel: General licenses are granted to the following categories of travelers, who are permitted to spend money to travel to Cuba and to engage in other transactions directly incident to the purpose of their travel, without the need to obtain a specific license from the U.S. Department of the Treasury's Office of Foreign Assets Control (OFAC):

- Persons visiting a close relative (any individual related to a person by blood, marriage, or adoption who is no more than three generations removed from that person or from a common ancestor with that person) who is a national of Cuba, and persons traveling with them who share a common dwelling as a family with them. There is no limit on the duration or frequency of such travel. (According to the Cuban Assets Control Regulations, third country nationals who reside in Cuba are considered Cuban nationals.)

- Journalists and supporting broadcasting or technical personnel (regularly employed in that capacity by a news reporting organization and traveling for journalistic activities).

- Official government travelers on official business.

- Members of international organizations of which the United States is also a member (traveling on official business).

- Religious organizations, including members and staff, traveling for the purpose of participating and engaging in religious activities. Organizations may open accounts at Cuban financial institutions for the purpose of accessing funds in Cuba for transactions related to such activities.

- Students and all members of faculty and staff of accredited U.S. graduate and undergraduate degree granting institutions can participate in academic activities in Cuba through any sponsoring U.S. academic institution, not only through the accredited U.S. academic institution at which the student is pursuing a degree, if the traveler's study in Cuba will be accepted for credit toward the student's degree.

- Persons teaching at a Cuban academic institution if regularly employed in a teaching capacity at the sponsoring U.S. academic institution and provided the teaching activities are related to an academic program at the Cuban institution and the duration of the teaching will be no shorter than 10 weeks.

- Full-time professionals, whose travel transactions are directly related to research in their professional areas, provided that their research: 1) is of a noncommercial, academic nature; 2) comprises a full work schedule in Cuba; and 3) has a substantial likelihood of public dissemination.

- Full-time professionals whose travel transactions are directly related to attendance at professional meetings or conferences in Cuba that are organized by an international professional organization, institution, or association that regularly sponsors such meetings or conferences in other countries. An organization, institution, or association headquartered in the United States may not sponsor such a meeting or conference unless it has been specifically licensed to sponsor it. The purpose of the meeting or conference cannot be the promotion of tourism in Cuba or other commercial activities involving Cuba, or to foster production of any bio-technological products.

- Employees of a U.S. telecommunications services provider or an entity duly appointed to represent such a provider traveling incident to: 1) the commercial marketing, sales negotiation, accompanied delivery, or servicing of authorized telecommunications-related items; or 2) participation in certain telecommunications-related professional meetings for the commercial marketing of, sales negotiation for, or performance under contracts for the provision of telecommunications services, or the establishment of facilities to provide telecommunications services.

- Individuals regularly employed by a producer or distributer of agricultural commodities, medicine, or medical devices or an entity duly appointed to represent such a producer or distributer traveling incident to the commercial marketing, sales negotiation, accompanied delivery, or servicing in Cuba of such items.

Specific Licenses to Visit Close Relatives in Cuba who are non-Cuban nationals: Travelers wishing to visit a close relative in Cuba who is authorized to be in Cuba, but is not a national of Cuba or a third country national residing in Cuba, may apply for a specific license from OFAC.

Specific Licenses for People to People Transactions: Specific licenses may be issued by OFAC to travelers involved in educational activities under the auspices of an organization that sponsors and organizes such programs to promote people-to-people contact but are not involved in academic study pursuant to a degree program.

Specific Licenses for Educational Institutions: Specific licenses may be issued by OFAC to authorize travel transactions incident to an individual's educational activities of certain types. Once an academic institution has applied for and received such a specific license, travelers affiliated with that academic institution are authorized to engage in the following activities without seeking further authorization from OFAC.

- Academic institutions may sponsor or co-sponsor academic seminars, conferences, and workshops related to Cuba or global issues involving Cuba and faculty, staff, and students may attend these events.

- U.S. academic institutions may open accounts at Cuban financial institutions for the purpose of accessing funds in Cuba for transactions related to such events.

Specific Licenses for Religious Organizations: Specific licenses may be issued by OFAC to religious organizations for travel related transactions incident to religious activities that are not authorized by the new general license.Licenses authorizing transactions for multiple trips over an extended period of time are available to applicants with plans to engage in a full-time program of religious activities in Cuba. Religious travelers to Cuba should be aware that Cuban officials require specific authorization to travel to Cuba for religious purposes. Religious travelers to Cuba should contact the Cuban Interests Section regarding proper authorization to travel to Cuba for religious purposes and should wait for their response before traveling.

Other Specific Licenses: Specific licenses may be issued by OFAC, on a case-by-case basis, authorizing travel transactions by the following categories of persons in connection with the following activities:

- Humanitarian Projects and Support for the Cuban People—1) Persons traveling in connection with activities that are intended to provide support for the Cuban people, such as activities of recognized human rights organizations; and 2) persons whose travel transactions are directly related to certain humanitarian projects in or related to Cuba that are designed to directly benefit the Cuban people. Licenses authorizing transactions for multiple trips over an extended period of time are available.

- Free-Lance Journalism—Persons with a suitable record of publication who are traveling to Cuba to do research for free-lance journalistic projects. Licenses authorizing transactions for multiple trips over an extended period of time are available for applicants demonstrating a significant record of journalism.

- Professional Research and Professional Meetings—Persons traveling to Cuba to do professional research or to attend a professional meeting that does not meet the requirements of the relevant general license (described above). Licenses authorizing transactions for multiple trips over an extended period of time are available.

- Public Performances, Athletic or Other Competitions, and Exhibitions—Persons traveling to participate in a public performance, athletic or other competition or exhibition. The event must be open for attendance, and in relevant situations, participation by the Cuban public, and all profits from the event after costs must be donated to an independent non-governmental organization in Cuba or a U.S.-based charity with the objective, to the extent possible, of benefiting the Cuban people.

- Amateur or semi-professional athletes or teams traveling to participate in an athletic competition. The athletes must have been selected for the competition by the relevant U.S. sports federation, and the competition must be one that is open for attendance, and in relevant situations, participation by the Cuban people.

- Clinic or Workshop Participants—Persons traveling to Cuba for the purpose of participating in a clinic or workshop that is being organized and run, at least in part, by the licensee.
- Activities of Private Foundations or Research or Educational Institutions—Persons traveling to Cuba on behalf of private foundations or research or educational institutes that have an established interest in international relations to collect information related to Cuba for noncommercial purposes. Licenses authorizing transactions for multiple trips over an extended period of time are available.
- Exportation, Importation, or Transmission of Information or Informational Materials—Persons traveling to engage in activities directly related to the exportation, importation, or transmission of information or informational materials.
- Licensed Exportation—Persons traveling to Cuba incident to marketing, sales negotiation, accompanied delivery, or servicing in Cuba of exports that appear consistent with the export or re-export policy of the Department of Commerce and are not authorized by the general licenses described above.

Applying for a Specific License: Persons wishing to travel to Cuba under a specific license should send a letter specifying the details of the proposed travel, including any accompanying documentation, to the Licensing Division, Office of Foreign Assets Control, U.S. Department of the Treasury, 1500 Pennsylvania Ave, NW, Washington, DC 20220. Academic institutions wishing to obtain one of the two-year specific licenses described above should send a letter to the same address requesting such a license and establishing that the institution is accredited by an appropriate national or regional accrediting association. Religious organizations wishing to obtain one of the specific licenses described above should send a letter to the same address requesting such a license and setting forth examples of religious activities to be undertaken in Cuba.

The United States maintains a broad embargo against trading with Cuba, and most commercial imports from Cuba are prohibited by law. Sales of items in certain sectors, including medicine, medical devices and supplies, and agricultural commodities, have been approved for export by specific legislation. The Department of the Treasury may issue licenses on a case-by-case basis authorizing Cuba travel-related transactions directly incident to marketing, sales negotiation, accompanied delivery, and servicing of exports and re-exports that appear consistent with the licensing policy of the Department of Commerce.

Additional information may be obtained by contacting:

Licensing Division
Office of Foreign Assets Control
U.S. Department of the Treasury
1500 Pennsylvania Avenue NW
Treasury Annex
Washington, DC 20220
Telephone (202) 622-2480;
1-800-540-6322
Fax (202) 622-1657

Internet users can also log onto the Department of Treasury's OFAC website.

Civilian Aircraft Travel: The Cuban Air Force shot down two U.S.-registered civilian aircraft in international airspace in 1996. As a result of this action, the President of the United States and the Federal Aviation Administration (FAA) issued an "Emergency Cease and Desist Order and Statement of Policy," which allows for vigorous enforcement action against U.S.-registered aircraft that violate Cuban airspace. For additional information on restrictions on aircraft flying between the United States and Cuba, see the FAA's web site.

For current information on Cuban entry and customs requirements, travelers should contact:

Cuban Interests Section (an office of the Cuban government)
2630 16th Street NW
Washington, DC 20009
Telephone (202) 797-8518/8520
Fax (202) 797-8521

Consular Section (part of the Cuban Interests Section)
2639 16th Street NW
Washington, DC 20009
Telephone (202) 797-8609/8610/8615
Fax (202) 986-7283

Temporary Sojourn License: Exports of aircraft or vessels on temporary sojourn to Cuba will be considered on a case-by-case basis by the U.S. Department of Commerce. Temporary sojourn licenses are not available for pleasure boaters. Additional information is available at the Bureau of Industry and Security website. Vessels of the United States, as defined in 33 CFR §107.200, may not enter Cuban territorial waters without advance permission from the U.S. Coast Guard. The U.S. Coast Guard provides permission information at (305) 415-6920.

Threats to Safety and Security: The security environment in Cuba is relatively stable and characterized by a strong military and police presence throughout the country. Demonstrations against the United States are more infrequent and smaller than in past years, are usually approved and monitored by the Cuban Government, and are generally peaceful in nature. The same cannot be said about state-organized demonstrations against domestic opposition groups, which can be violent. U.S. citizens should avoid all demonstrations. Cuba tightly restricts the departure of its citizens, although illegal departures are not uncommon. Hijackings of vessels to depart Cuba are much less common. The United States Government has publicly and repeatedly announced that any person who hijacks (or attempts to hijack) an aircraft or vessel (whether common carrier or other) will face the maximum penalties pursuant to U.S. law, regardless of that person's nationality.

In recent years, the Cuban government has detained U.S. citizens it suspects of engaging in activities perceived to undermine state security. In 2011, it convicted a U.S. citizen of crimes against the security of the state and sentenced the individual to 15 years in prison after being detained for 14 months without charge. U.S. citizens traveling to Cuba should be aware that the Cuban Government can detain anyone at anytime for any purpose and should not expect that justice will be carried out according to international norms and practice.

Cuban territorial waters are extremely dangerous and difficult to navigate, even for experienced mariners. The potential for running aground is very high and the bottom type is unforgiving. Search and rescue capability in Cuba is limited and running aground will often lead to the complete destruction and loss of the vessel. U.S. boaters who enter Cuban waters (legitimately or illegitimately) have encountered problems that required repairs and/or salvage; costs for both are significantly higher than comparable services in the United States or elsewhere in the Caribbean.

In addition, the Government of Cuba does not allow the use of the U.S. dollar for transactions and U.S. credit cards are not accepted in Cuba. Cuban authorities typically hold boats as collateral payment. U.S.-registered/flagged vessels belonging to U.S. citizens have been permanently seized by Cuban authorities. Due to the lack of resources, the quality of repairs in Cuba is inconsistent. Repairs take significantly longer in Cuba than they would in the United States due to lack of the most basic materials and to bureaucratic impediments. Boaters are often confined to their boats while repairs are made. Boaters can be detained while Cuban authorities investigate the circumstances of their entry to Cuba, especially if their travel documents are not in order or they are suspected of illegal activities. Mariners and their passengers should not navigate close to Cuban territorial waters without possessing a valid passport, unless seeking a safe port due to emergencies.

The ability of the U.S. Interests Section to assist mariners in distress is extremely limited due to current limitations on travel by U.S. personnel outside of Havana. Notifying the U.S. Interests Section, regardless of legitimately or illegitimately entering Cuban territorial seas is the most reliable way to obtain assistance.

The transfer of funds from the United States to Cuba to pay for boat repair and salvage is subject to restrictions codified in U.S. law relating to commercial transactions with the Government of Cuba. A Department of the Treasury license is required for such payments and applicants should be prepared to provide documentary evidence demonstrating the emergency nature of the repairs. U.S. credit or debit cards, personal checks, and travelers' checks cannot be used in Cuba so boaters should be prepared to pay for all transactions in cash. It is difficult to transfer money to Cuba and travelers have frequently been required to spend several hundred dollars for transportation to Havana to receive transferred funds.

For the latest security information, U.S. citizens traveling abroad should regularly monitor the Department of State Bureau of Consular Affairs' website, which posts current Travel Warnings and Travel Alerts, and lists Worldwide Cautions.

Up-to-date information on safety and security can also be obtained by calling 1-888-407-4747 toll-free in the U.S. and Canada, or for other callers, a regular toll line at 1-202-501-4444. These numbers are available from 8:00 a.m. to 8:00 p.m. Eastern Time, Monday through Friday (except U.S. federal holidays).

The Department of State urges U.S. citizens to take responsibility for their own personal security while traveling overseas.

Crime: Official crime statistics are not published by the Cuban government, but reporting by U.S. citizens and other foreign travelers indicates that the majority of incidents are non-violent and theft-related—i.e., pick-pocketing, purse snatching, or the taking of unattended/valuable items. Sources claim, however, that violent crime has increased in Cuba and is generally associated with assaults committed during a burglary or robbery. The U.S. Government cannot confirm this information, but rates the threat of crime in Cuba as medium. In the event of a confrontation, travelers should not resist as perpetrators may be armed. Thefts generally occur in crowded areas such as markets, beaches, and other gathering points, including Old Town Havana and the Prado neighborhood. Travelers should exercise basic situational awareness at all times and are advised not to leave belongings unattended, nor to carry purses and bags loosely over one shoulder.

Visitors should avoid wearing flashy jewelry or displaying large amounts of cash. When possible, visitors should carry a copy of their passport with them and leave the original at a secure location. U.S. visitors should also beware of Cuban "jineteros" (hustlers) who specialize in swindling tourists. While most jineteros speak English and go out of their way to appear friendly, e.g., by offering to serve as tour guides or to facilitate the purchase of cheap cigars, many are in fact professional criminals who may resort to violence in their efforts to acquire tourists' money and other valuables. When exchanging currency, use state-run offices to convert dollars and avoid independent/street vendors as we have seen a slight increase in the number of persons trying to pass counterfeit bills at the Interests Section.

All travelers should ensure that valuables remain under their personal control at all times and are never put into checked baggage.

Victims of Crime: The loss or theft abroad of a U.S. passport should be reported immediately to the local police and the U.S. Interests Section in Havana. If you are the victim of a crime while in Cuba, in addition to reporting to local police, please contact the U.S. Interests Section for assistance. The Interests Section staff can, for example, assist you to find appropriate medical care, contact family members or friends and explain how funds may be transferred. However, U.S. diplomats' travel is restricted to inside Havana and may be prevented from providing some assistance to U.S. citizens outside the capital. Although the investigation and prosecution of the crime is solely the responsibility of local authorities, consular officers can help you to understand the local criminal justice process and to find an attorney if needed.

The local equivalent to the "911" emergency line in Cuba is: 106 for police and 105 for Fire.

Criminal Penalties: While in a foreign country, a U.S. citizen is subject to that country's laws and regulations, which sometimes differ significantly from those in the United States and may not afford the protections available to the individual under U.S. law. Penalties for breaking the law can be more severe than in the United States for similar offenses. Persons violating Cuba's laws, even unknowingly, may be expelled, arrested, or imprisoned. Penalties for possession, use, or trafficking in illegal drugs in Cuba are severe, and convicted offenders can expect long jail sentences and heavy fines. Those accused of drug-related and other crimes face long legal proceedings and delayed due process. In one 2009 drug conviction, a U.S. citizen was sentenced to 18 years in prison. Another U.S. citizen was arrested for drugs in 2011 but because he is a dual national, the Cuban Government has refused to grant USINT access to visit.

Criminal penalties are also harsh for foreigners or dual nationals suspected of assisting Cuban migrants who attempt to leave Cuba illegally. Average jail sentences for individuals charged with migrant smuggling range from 10 to 20 years. In a 2007 case, a U.S. citizen was arrested for attempting to facilitate the illegal departure of his Cuban family members via raft. He was charged with migrant smuggling and received a jail sentence of 16 years. A U.S.-Cuba dual national arrested in 2010 was sentenced to 7 years in prison for alien smuggling. The Cuban government considers him Cuban and has denied USINT access to visit him due to his Cuban citizenship.

For more information, please contact the U.S. Interests Section's American Citizens Services Unit at:

U.S. Interests Section
American Citizen Services Unit
Calzada, entre L y M
Vedado, Havana, Cuba
Phone: 53-7-833-3551 (through 3559)
Fax: 53-7-833-1653

Engaging in sexual conduct with children or using or disseminating child pornography in a foreign country is a crime, prosecutable in the United States.

Medical Facilities and Health Information: Medical care in Cuba does not meet U.S. standards. While medical professionals are generally competent, many health facilities face shortages of medical supplies and bed space. Many medications are unavailable, so travelers to Cuba should bring with them any prescribed medicine in its original container and in amounts commensurate with personal use. Travelers may also wish to consider bringing additional amounts of prescribed medicines and over-the-counter remedies in the event that a return to the United States is delayed for unforeseen reasons. A copy of the prescription and a letter from the prescribing physician explaining the need for prescription drugs may facilitate their entry into the country.

Travelers to the Havana area should be aware that U.S. and other foreign visitors are generally limited to using only the "tourist" Cira Garcia Hospital located in the Miramar neighborhood of Havana. Treatment at Cira Garcia and any other medical consultation requires payment in cash (see section on Medical Insurance below).

Information on vaccinations and other health precautions, such as safe food and water precautions and insect bite protection, may be obtained from the Centers for Disease Control and Prevention's hotline at 1-800-CDC-INFO (1-800-232-4636) or via the CDC's website. For information about outbreaks of infectious diseases abroad, consult the World Health Organization's (WHO) website. Further health information for travelers is available at the WHO's international travel and health web page.

Medical Insurance: As of May 1, 2010, tourists, foreigners with temporary residence in Cuba, and Cubans living abroad who visit Cuba have to purchase medical insurance. The insurance is sold by foreign companies approved by the Cuban government or by Cuban firms at the ports of entry in Cuba according to Cuba's Official Gazette. Diplomats and representatives of accredited international organizations do not have to be insured.

Questions about this requirement should be directed to the Cuban Interests Section. For more information, travelers may also wish to visit the website for Cuba's Travel Insurance Agency, Asistur S.A.

No medical facility in Cuba will accept U.S. issued insurance cards, credit cards, or checks and medical services must be paid for in cash. The Department of State strongly urges U.S. citizens to consult with their medical insurance company prior to traveling abroad to confirm whether their policy applies overseas and whether it will cover emergency expenses such as a medical evacuation.

Traffic Safety and Road Conditions: While in a foreign country, U.S. citizens may encounter road conditions that differ significantly from those in the United States. The information below concerning Cuba is provided for general reference only, and may not be totally accurate in a particular location or circumstance.

Driving is on the right-hand side of the road; speed limits are sometimes posted and generally respected in urban areas. Passengers in automobiles are generally required to wear seatbelts, and all motorcyclists are required to wear helmets.

Unconfirmed reports suggest that accidents involving motor vehicles are now the leading cause of accidental death in Cuba. Many accidents involve motorists striking pedestrians or bicyclists. Drivers found responsible for accidents resulting in serious injury or death are subject to prison terms of up to 10 years, and Cuban authorities may prohibit drivers of rental cars who are involved in accidents from leaving the country until all claims associated with an accident are settled. Witnesses to vehicular accidents may not be permitted to leave Cuba until an investigation into the accident has been completed.

Taxis are available in busy commercial and tourist areas; radio-dispatched taxis are generally clean and reliable. Travelers should be cautious in sharing information with taxi drivers or other strangers. In addition, travelers should not accept rides in unlicensed taxis as they may be used by thieves to rob passengers. Buses designated for tourist travel, both between and within cities, generally meet international standards for both cleanliness and safety. Public buses used by Cubans, known as "guaguas," are crowded and unreliable and are havens for pickpockets. These public buses usually will not offer rides to foreign visitors.

Although popular with tourists, the three-wheeled, yellow-hooded "Co-Co" taxis are highly unsafe and should be avoided. "Co-Co" taxis are modified motorcycles that reach speeds of up to 40 mph, but have no seat belts or other safety features.

Drivers should exercise extreme care. Although the main arteries of Havana are generally well-maintained, secondary streets often are not. Many roads and city streets are unlit, making night driving dangerous, especially as some cars and most bicycles lack running lights or reflectors. Street signage tends to be insufficient and confusing. Many Cuban cars are old, in poor condition and lack turn signals and other standard safety equipment.

The principal Cuban east-west highway is in good condition, but it lacks lights and extends only two-thirds of the way from Havana to the eastern tip of the island. The principal highway to the east is in poor condition in many areas, with washed out sections and deep potholes. Road signage on highways is minimal. Night driving should be strictly avoided outside urban areas. Secondary rural roads are narrow, and some are in such bad condition as to be impassable by cars. Due to the rarity of cars on rural roads, pedestrians, bicycles, horse-drawn carts, and farm equipment operators wander onto the roads without any regard to possible automobile traffic. Unfenced livestock constitute another serious road hazard.

Rental car agencies provide roadside assistance to their clients as a condition of the rental contract. Cuban authorities may prohibit drivers of rental cars who are involved in accidents from leaving the country, even if they are injured and require medical evacuation, until all claims associated with an accident are settled.

Travelers should not permit unauthorized persons to drive the rental vehicle. Automobile renters are provided telephone numbers to call in Havana or in other places where they might be motoring; agencies generally respond as needed with tow trucks and/or mechanics. A similar service is available to foreign residents of Cuba who insure cars with the National Insurance Company.

Aviation Safety Oversight: As there is no direct commercial air service to the United States by carriers registered in Cuba, the U.S. Federal Aviation Administration (FAA) has not assessed Cuba's Civil Aviation Authority for compliance with International Civil Aviation Organization (ICAO) aviation safety standards. For more information, travelers may visit the FAA's website.

The U.S. Interests Section has instructed its employees and official visitors to avoid domestic or international travel on Cuban air carriers, including the Cuban flag carrier Cubana de Aviación, whenever possible due to serious concerns regarding Cuba's ability to meet international safety oversight standards. U.S. citizens considering travel on any Cuban airline may wish to defer their travel or pursue an alternative means of transportation.

Special Circumstances: Photographing military or police installations or personnel, or harbor, rail, and airport facilities is forbidden.

Dual Nationality: The Government of Cuba does not recognize the U.S. nationality of U.S. citizens who are born in Cuba and may not recognize the U.S. nationality of those born in the U.S. to Cuban parents.

These individuals are treated as Cuban citizens and may be subject to a range of restrictions and obligations, including military service. The Cuban government may require U.S.-Cuban dual citizens ("dual nationals") to enter and depart Cuba using a Cuban passport. Using a Cuban passport for this purpose does not jeopardize one's U.S. citizenship; however, such persons must use their U.S. passport to enter and depart the United States. In some instances, dual nationals may be required to obtain exit permission from the Cuban government in order to return to the United States. There have been cases of dual nationals being forced by the Cuban government to surrender their U.S. passports. Despite these restrictions, dual nationals who fall ill may only be treated at hospitals for foreigners (except in emergencies). See the Consular Access paragraph below for information on Cuba's denial of consular services to dual nationals who have been arrested, as well as the Children's Issues paragraph below for information on how dual nationality may affect welfare inquiries and custody disputes.

Dual nationals should be especially wary of any attempt by Cuban authorities to compel them to sign "repatriation" documents. The Government of Cuba views a declaration of repatriation as a legal statement on the part of the dual national that she/he intends to resettle permanently in Cuba.

In several instances, the Government of Cuba has seized the U.S. passports of dual nationals signing declarations of repatriation and has denied these individuals permission to return to the United States.

Consular Access: U.S. citizens are encouraged to carry a copy of their U.S. passport with them at all times so that, if questioned by local officials, proof of identity and U.S. citizenship is readily available. The original should be kept in a secure location, preferably in a safe or locked suitcase.

Cuba does not recognize the right of the U.S. Government to protect Cuban-born U.S. citizens, whom the Cuban government views as Cuban citizens only. Cuban authorities consistently fail to notify the U.S. Interests Section of the arrest of dual nationals and may deny U.S. consular officers access to them. They also withhold information concerning the welfare and treatment of dual nationals.

Currency Regulations: Since November 2004, the U.S. dollar has not been accepted for commercial transactions. U.S. issued debit and credit cards also are not accepted in Cuba. The Cuban government requires the use of convertible Cuban pesos or non-convertible Cuban pesos ("moneda nacional") for all transactions. The official exchange rate for convertible Cuban pesos (CUC) is 1 USD = 1 CUC, however the Cuban government charges a 10 percent fee for exchanging U.S. dollars and assesses other transaction fees (approximately 3 percent), making the effective exchange rate at hotels, the airport, and currency exchange houses 1 USD = 0.87 CUC. The current exchange rate for CUC to non-convertible Cuban pesos (CUP) is 1 CUC = 24 CUP.

Cuba-Related Travel Transactions: Only persons whose travel falls into the categories mentioned above (under "Entry Requirements/ Travel Transaction Limitations") may be authorized by the U.S. Department of the Treasury to spend money related to travel to, from, or within Cuba. Persons licensed to engage in travel-related transactions in Cuba may spend up to the State Department Travel Per Diem Allowance for Havana, Cuba, for purchases directly related to travel in Cuba, such as hotel accommodations, meals, local transportation, and goods personally used by the traveler in Cuba. Most licensed travelers may also spend additional money for transactions directly related to the activities for which they received their license. For example, journalists traveling in Cuba under the journalism general license (described above) may spend money over and above the current per diem for extensive local transportation and other costs that are directly related to covering a story in Cuba. Purchases of services unrelated to travel or a licensed activity, such as non-emergency medical services, are prohibited. The purchase of publications and other information materials is not restricted.

General licenses for Remittances: U.S. persons aged 18 or older may send remittances to a close relative in Cuba or to a Cuban national in a third country, provided that no member of the household is a prohibited official of the Government of Cuba or a prohibited member of the Cuban Communist Party. (The term "prohibited official of the Government of Cuba" means: Ministers and Vice-Ministers, members of the Council of State, and the Council of Ministers; members and employees of the National Assembly of People's Power; members of any provincial assembly; local sector chiefs of the Committees for the Defense of the Revolution; sub-Directors General, Directors General and higher officials of all Cuban ministries and state agencies; employees of the Ministry of the Interior (MININT); employees of the Ministry of Defense (MINFAR); secretaries and first secretaries of the Confederation of Labor of Cuba (CTC) and its component unions; chief editors, editors, and deputy editors of Cuban state-run media organizations and programs, including newspapers, television, and radio; and members and employees of the Supreme Court (Tribuno Supremo Nacional). The term "prohibited members of the Cuban Communist Party" means: members of the Politburo, the Central Committee, Department Heads of the Central Committee; employees of the Central Committee; and secretaries and first secretaries of the provincial Party central committees.) There is no limit on the amount of such remittances or the frequency with which they may be sent. Authorized family travelers may carry up to $3000 of their own family remittances to Cuba. Carrying remittances on behalf of others is prohibited.

U.S. persons are also authorized to send two one-time $1,000 emigration related remittances per payee to enable the payee to emigrate from Cuba to the United States. The U.S. person can send a maximum of $1,000 prior to payee receiving a valid visa issued by the State Department or other approved U.S. immigration documents and a maximum of $1,000 after payee has received a valid visa issued by the State Department or other approved U.S. immigration documents. A remitter must be able to provide the visa recipient's full name, date of birth, visa number, and visa date of issuance at the time this remittance is sent.

U.S. persons can remit up to $500 in any consecutive three-month period to any Cuban national, except prohibited officials of the Government of Cuba or prohibited members of the Cuban Communist Party, to support the development of private businesses, among other purposes.

U.S. persons can send unlimited remittances to religious organizations in Cuba in support of religious activities. A U.S. person sending remittances to close relatives who are students in Cuba, pursuant to an educational license, for the purpose of funding transactions is authorized to do so per the license under which the student is traveling.

Specific licenses for RemittancesSpecific licenses may be issued by OFAC, on a case-by-case basis, authorizing the following activities:

A U.S. person sending remittances to a person in Cuba, directly or indirectly, for transactions to facilitate non-immigrant travel by an individual in Cuba to the United States under circumstances where humanitarian need is demonstrated, including but not limited to illness or other medical emergency.

A U.S. person sendingremittances to independent nongovernmental entities in Cuba including but not limited to prodemocracy groups and civil society groups, and to members of such groups or organizations, or to individuals or independent non-governmental entities to support the development of private businesses, including small farms.

Remittances may be made from a depository institution or licensed Remittance Forwarder. They may not be couriered by third parties.

U.S. citizens and permanent resident aliens are prohibited from using credit cards in Cuba. U.S. credit card companies do not accept vouchers from Cuba, and Cuban shops, hotels and other places of business do not accept U.S. credit cards. Neither personal checks nor travelers' checks drawn on U.S. banks are accepted in Cuba.

Exportation of Accompanied Baggage: As of September 3, 2009, there is no longer a weight limit on the accompanied baggage per traveler.

What Can Be Brought Back: If U.S. travelers return from Cuba with goods of Cuban origin, such goods, with the exception of informational materials, may be seized at Customs' discretion [Section 515.204 of the Regulations]. Cuban cigars and rum are routinely confiscated at U.S. ports of entry. Purchasing Cuban cigars and rum in a "duty-free" shop at the Havana Airport does not exempt them from seizure by U.S. Customs. There are no limits on the import or export of informational materials [Section 515.206 of the Regulations]. Information and informational materials such as books, films, artworks, posters, photographs, tapes, CDs and certain artwork are statutorily exempt from regulation under the embargo and may be transported freely; however, blank tapes and CDs are not considered informational materials and may be seized. To be considered informational material, artworks must be classified under Chapter subheading 9701, 9702, or 9703 of the Harmonized Tariff Schedule of the United States (for example, original paintings, drawings, pastels, engravings, prints, and sculptures are all exempt.)

Fair Business Practices: Anyone authorized by the U.S. Department of the Treasury to provide Cuban travel services or services in connection with sending money to Cuba is prohibited from participating in the discriminatory practices of the Cuban government against individuals or particular classes of travelers.

The assessment of consular fees by the Cuban government, which are applicable worldwide, is not considered to be a discriminatory practice; however, requiring the purchase of services not desired by the traveler is prohibited. Information provided to the U.S. Department of the Treasury regarding arbitrary fees, payments for unauthorized purposes, or other possible violations will be handled confidentially.

Children's Issues: Cuba does not allow adoption of children by U.S. citizens. Additionally, the Government of Cuba does not recognize dual citizenship. It considers children who maintain both Cuban and American citizenship to be Cuban citizens. Consequently, it is often difficult for U.S. consular officers to ascertain the welfare and whereabouts of U.S.-Cuba dual citizen children living with their Cuban parents or relatives. In the event of a custody dispute, the U.S. citizen parent may need to pursue a legal hearing in Cuba with the assistance of a Cuban attorney. The U.S. Interests Section can provide to interested parties a list of attorneys practicing in the Havana area.

For more information, see the U.S. Dept. of State Office of Children's Issues web pages on intercountry adoption and international parental child abduction. In an effort to prevent international child abduction, many governments have initiated procedures at entry/exit points. These often include requiring documentary evidence of relationship and permission for the child's travel from the parent(s) or legal guardian not present. Having such documentation on hand, even if not required, may facilitate entry/departure.

Intercountry Adoption

May 2011

Cuba is party to the Hague Convention on Protection of Children and Co-operation in Respect of Intercountry Adoption (Hague Adoption Convention). Therefore, adoptions between Cuba and the United States are governed by the requirements of the Convention and the laws and regulations implementing the Convention in both the United States and Cuba. The Department of State does not maintain files on the adoption process in Cuba because adoptions from Cuba are rare. Fewer than five adoptions by American citizen parents have taken place in the last five years.

International Parental Child Abduction

January 2012

The information in this section has been edited from the latest report available as of February 2013 from the State Department Bureau of Consular Affairs, Office of Overseas Citizens Services. For more information, please read the *International Parental Child Abduction* section of this book and check for updated reports online at www.travel.state.gov/abduction.

Disclaimer: The information in this flyer relating to the legal requirements of specific foreign countries is provided for general information only. Questions involving interpretation of specific foreign laws should be addressed to foreign legal counsel.

General Information: Cuba is not a party to the Hague Convention on the Civil Aspects of International Child Abduction, nor are there any international or bilateral treaties in force between Cuba and the United States dealing with international parental child abduction. American citizens who travel to Cuba place themselves under the jurisdiction of local courts. American citizens planning a trip to Cuba with dual national children should bear this in mind.

Custody Disputes: In Cuba, if parents are legally married they share the custody of their children. If they are not married and the parents cannot reach an agreement, custody is granted by the courts in the best interests of the child. Foreign court orders are not automatically recognized.

Enforcement of Foreign Judgments: Custody orders and judgments of foreign courts are not enforceable in Cuba.

Visitation Rights: In cases where one parent has been granted custody of a child, the other parent is usually granted visitation rights. If a custodial parent fails to allow visitation, the non-custodial parent may appeal to the court.

Dual Nationality: Dual nationality is not recognized under Cuban law.

Passports for Minors and the Children's Passport Issuance Alert Program: For more information on these topics, see the International Parental Child Abduction section of this publication and review current reports from the U.S. Department of State at www.travel.state.gov/abduction.

Travel Restrictions: Cuban citizen children (including dual nationals) are required to have exit visas to depart Cuba.

Criminal Remedies: For information on possible criminal remedies, please contact your local law enforcement authorities or the nearest office of the Federal Bureau of Investigation (FBI). Information is also available on the Internet at the web site of the U.S. Department of Justice, Office of Juvenile Justice and Delinquency Prevention (OJJDP) at http://www.ojjdp.ncjrs.org.

Persons who wish to pursue a child custody claim in a Cuban court should retain an attorney in Cuba. The U.S. Interests Section at the Embassy of Switzerland in Cuba maintains a list of attorneys willing to represent American clients. A copy of this list may be obtained by requesting one from the U.S. Interests Section of the Embassy at:

Embassy of Switzerland

U.S. Interests Section

Calzada between L & M Streets
Vedado, Havana, Cuba
Telephone: 011-53-7-33-3551/59
Fax: 011-53-7-33-3700
Web site: www.usembassy. state.gov

Questions involving Cuban law should be addressed to a Cuban attorney or to the Cuban Interests Section of the Embassy of Switzerland in the United States at:

Embassy of Switzerland
Cuban Interests Section

2630 16th Street, NW
Washington, DC 20009
Telephone: (202) 797-8518

For further information on international parental child abduction, contact the Office of Children's Issues, U.S. Department of State at 1-888-407-4747 or visit its web site on the Internet at www.travel.state.gov/abduction.

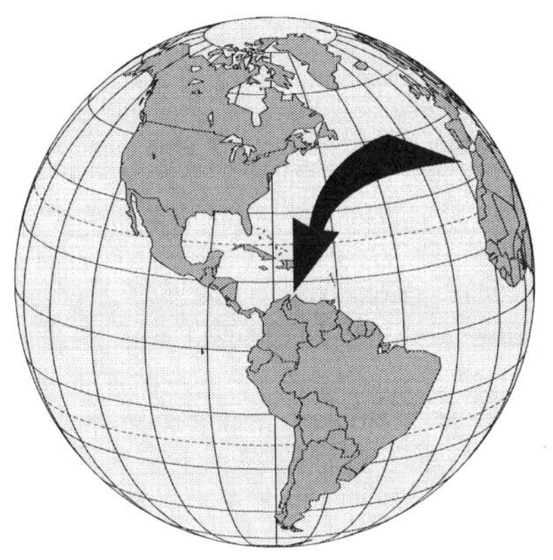

CURAÇAO

Compiled from publications that were available as of February 2013 from the U.S. Department of State, the U.S. Department of Commerce, and the Central Intelligence Agency (CIA). See the introduction to this set for explanatory notes.

Official Name:
Curaçao

PROFILE

Geography

Area: total: 444 sq km; country comparison to the world: 200; land: 444 sq km; water: 0 sq km
Climate: tropical marine climate, ameliorated by northeast trade winds, results in mild temperatures; semi-arid with average rainfall of 600 mm/year
Terrain: generally low, hilly terrain

People

Population: 145,834 (est. January 2010)
Religions: Roman Catholic 80.1%, Protestant 11.2% (Pentecostal 3.5%, Seventh-Day Adventist 2.2%, other Protestant 5.5%), none 4.6%, Jehovah's Witnesses 1.7%, Jewish 0.8%, other 1.3%, not reported 0.3% (2001 census)
Languages: Papiamentu (a Spanish-Portuguese-Dutch-English dialect) 81.2%, Dutch (official) 8%, Spanish 4%, English 2.9%, other 3.9% (2001 census)
Health: life expectancy at birth: total: NA; males: 72.4 years; females: 80.1 years (2009);
Unemployment rate: 10.3% (2008 est.)
Work force: 63,000 (2008 est.) (2008)

Government

Type: parliamentary
Independence: none
Constitution: Staatsregeling adopted by island council 5 September 2010; entered into force 10 October 2010; revised Kingdom Charter pending
Political subdivisions: none (part of the Kingdom of the Netherlands)
Suffrage: 18 years of age; universal

Economy

GDP (purchasing power parity): $2.838 billion (2008 est.); $2.606 billion (2007 est.); $2.452 billion (2006 est.)
GDP real growth rate: 3.5% (2008); 2.2% (2007)
GDP per capita (PPP): $15,000 (2004 est.)
Natural resources: calcium phosphates, aloes, sorghum, peanuts, vegetables, tropical fruit
Agriculture products: aloe, sorghum, peanuts, vegetables, tropical fruit
Industries: tourism, petroleum refining, petroleum transshipment facilities, light manufacturing
Exports: $1.5 billion (2011 est.); $1.4 billion (2010 est.)
Exports—commodities: petroleum products
Imports: $2.5 billion (2011 est.); $2.8 billion (2010 est.)
Imports—commodities: crude petroleum, food, manufactures
Exchange rates: Netherlands Antillean guilders (ANG) per US dollar; 1.79 (2011 est.); 1.79 (2010 est.); 1.79 (2009); 1.79 (2008); 1.79 (2007)

PEOPLE AND HISTORY

The Arawaks are recognized as the first human civilization to inhabit the island of Curaçao.

A Spanish expedition led by Alonso de Ojeda claimed Curaçao for Spain in 1499, and it remained under Spanish rule until the Dutch took control in 1634. Curaçao was a strategically important point for Dutch military advances against the Spanish and as the center of the Dutch Caribbean slave trade. In 1845 the Dutch Windward islands united with Curaçao, Bonaire, and Aruba in a political unit. The islands' economy remained weak until the early part of the 20th century when oil was discovered in Venezuela's Lake Maracaibo and a refinery was established on Curaçao. During the same period, an offshore financial sector was created to serve Dutch business interests. Curaçao became the seat of the Netherlands Antilles Government in 1954. The federation of the Netherlands Antilles (Aruba, Curaçao, Sint Maarten, Bonaire, St. Eustatius, and Saba) was a constituent part of the Kingdom of the Netherlands and was semi-autonomous in most internal affairs. The Kingdom retained authority over foreign affairs, defense, final judicial review, and "Kingdom matters," including human rights and good governance. Aruba was part of this federation until January 1, 1986, when it gained a separate status within the Kingdom of the Netherlands.

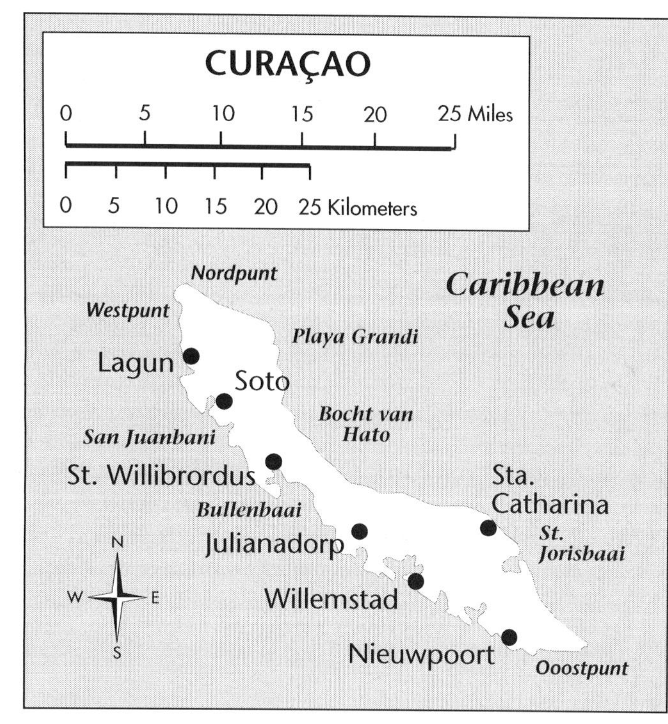

The Netherlands Antilles ceased to exist on October 10, 2010. The islands that formed the Netherlands Antilles assumed new positions within the Kingdom of the Netherlands. Curaçao and Sint Maarten gained semi-autonomous status similar to Aruba, and the remaining BES islands (Bonaire, St. Eustatius, and Saba) became special overseas public entities, much like municipalities, within the Netherlands. About 85% of Curaçao's population is of African derivation.

The remaining 15% is made up of various races and nationalities, including Dutch, Portuguese, North Americans, natives from other Caribbean islands, Latin Americans, Sephardic Jews, Lebanese, and Asians. Roman Catholicism predominates, but several other religions are represented, including Anglican, Jewish, Protestant, Mormon, Baptist, Muslim, and Hindu. The Jewish community is the oldest in the Western Hemisphere, dating back to 1634.

GOVERNMENT AND POLITICAL CONDITIONS

Current political relations among the Netherlands, Aruba, Curaçao, Sint Maarten, Bonaire, St. Eustatius, and Saba stem from 1954. They are based on the Charter for the Kingdom of the Netherlands, a voluntary arrangement among the Netherlands, Suriname, and the Netherlands Antilles. At the time, the Charter represented an end to colonial relations and the acceptance of a new legal system in which each of the three would look after its own interests independently, as well as provide mutual assistance and promote common interests on the basis of equality. Suriname left the Kingdom's political alliance and became independent in 1975. Aruba has had a separate status within the Kingdom since 1986 when it left the Netherlands Antilles.

The Netherlands Antilles dissolved on October 10, 2010, and its successor political entities remain part of the Kingdom of the Netherlands. Curaçao and Sint Maarten now have a status similar to Aruba, and the remaining BES islands (Bonaire, St. Eustatius, and Saba) are special overseas municipalities within the Netherlands. Aruba, Curaçao, and Sint Maarten enjoy autonomy on most internal matters and defer to the Kingdom of the Netherlands in matters of defense, foreign policy, final judicial review, human rights, and good governance.

Curaçao is governed by a popularly elected unicameral "Staten" (parliament) of 21 members. It chooses a Prime Minister and a Council of Ministers, consisting of six to eight other ministers. A governor, who serves a 6-year term, represents the monarch of the Kingdom of the Netherlands. Following August 27, 2010 elections, an 11-seat coalition government was formed consisting of the Movement for the Future of Curaçao (MFK), the Sovereign Party (PS), and the MAN party. The MFK, led by Gerrit Schotte, and the PS, led by Helmin Wiels, won 5 and 4 seats respectively, and the MAN party won 2 seats.

The Real Alternative Party (PAR) won 8 seats, and the Workers' Liberation Front (FOL) and People's National Party (PNP) won 1 seat each. Drug smuggling and trafficking in persons continue to be issues for Curaçao. Drug smuggling has been significantly reduced through intensive cooperation among U.S., Dutch, Curaçao, and international law enforcement authorities.

Principal Government Officials

Last Updated: 10/31/2012

Chief of State: **Queen Beatrix**
Governor: **Frits GOEDGEDRAG**
Prime Minister and General Affairs: **Gerrit SCHOTTE** (MFK)

ECONOMY

Tourism, petroleum refining, and offshore finance are the mainstays of this small economy, which is closely tied to the outside world. Although GDP grew slightly during the past decade, the island enjoys a high per capita income and a well-developed infrastructure compared with other countries in the region. Curaçao has an excellent natural harbor that can accommodate large oil tankers.

The Venezuelan state oil company leases the single refinery on the island from the government; most of the oil for the refinery is imported from Venezuela; most of the refined products are exported to the US. Almost all consumer and capital goods are imported, with the US, Brazil, Italy, and Mexico being the major suppliers. The government is attempting to diversify its industry and trade and has signed an Association Agreement with the EU to expand business there. Poor soils and inadequate water supplies hamper the development of agriculture. Budgetary problems complicate reform of the health and pension systems for an aging population.

U.S.-CURAÇAO RELATIONS

Curaçao has semi-autonomy within the Kingdom of the Netherlands. It conducts foreign affairs, including with the United States, through the Netherlands, whose embassies and consulates issue visas for travel to the island.

Tourism and financial services are mainstays of Curaçao's economy. Approximately 800,000 tourists per year visit Curaçao, with almost 25% of those from the United States. Oil refining is a key part of the economy; most of the refined products are exported to the U.S. The U.S. is a major supplier of consumer and capital goods imported by Curaçao. In 2010, the U.S. accounted for 40% of Curaçao's exports and 37% of Curaçao's imports. The U.S. Consulate General in Curaçao is responsible for the day-to-day management of relations with the Dutch Caribbean, which includes Aruba, Bonaire, Curaçao, Saba, Sint Eustatius, and Sint Maarten.

Due to the strategic location of the Dutch Caribbean for the U.S., the consulate deals with issues such as securing U.S. borders, countering terrorism, and fighting international crime, especially narcotics trafficking and human trafficking.

The consulate provides a variety of services to U.S. citizens; it also can issue non-immigrant visas for certain travelers to the U.S. who wish to visit, work, or study for a temporary period.

The consulate was opened in 1793. It was one of the earliest U.S. consulates, reflecting the importance of Caribbean trade to the new United States. The Consul General resides in the historic Roosevelt House, which was the local government's gift of property to the United States in 1950 as an expression of gratitude for U.S. protection during World War II.

Principal U.S. Embassy Officials

Last Updated: 1/14/2013

CURACAO (CG) J.B. Gorsiraweg #1, 599-9-461-3066, Fax 599-9-461-6489, INMARSAT Tel 00-874-383-133-190, Workweek: M-F 8AM–5 PM AST, http://curacao.usconsulate.gov

CM:	Valerie Belon
CON/POL/ECON:	Morgan Miles
DHS/CBP:	James Grimes
HRO:	Peggy Laurance
MGT:	Eric Kramp
CG:	Valerie Belon
RSO:	Robert Myers
DEA:	J. Gregory Garza
EEO:	Ricardo Cabrera
FMO:	Kevin Crews
IMO:	Jeffrey Yacobucci
State ICASS:	Morgan Miles

Other Contact Information

U.S. Department of Commerce
International Trade Administration
Trade Information Center
14th and Constitution, NW
Washington, DC 20230
Tel: 1-800-USA-TRADE

TRAVEL

Consular Information Sheet

April 13, 2011

Country Description: Curaçao is a semi-autonomous part of the Kingdom of the Netherlands. The economy is well-developed and tourist facilities are widely available. Tourism and the financial services sector have been the mainstays of the Curaçao economy since the 1970s.

Smart Traveler Enrollment Program (STEP)/Embassy Locations: U.S. citizens living or traveling in Curaçao are encouraged to sign up for the Smart Traveler Enrollment Program in order to obtain updated information on local travel and security. U.S. citizens without Internet access may sign up directly with the nearest U.S. embassy or consulate. Enrolling is important; it allows the State Department to assist U.S. citizens in an emergency.

United States Consulate
General Curaçao
J.B. Gorsiraweg 1
Willemstad, Curaçao
Telephone: (599-9) 461-3066
Emergency after-hours telephone: (599-9) 510-6870
Facsimile: (599-9) 461-6489

Entry/Exit Requirements: All U.S. citizens must have a valid U.S. passport for all air travel, including to and from Curaçao. All sea travelers must also now have a passport or passport card. We strongly encourage all American citizen travelers to apply for a U.S. passport or passport card well in advance of anticipated travel.

American citizens can visit travel.state.gov or call 1-877-4USA-PPT (1-877-487-2778) for information on how to apply for their passports. Visitors to Curaçao may be asked to show onward/return tickets, proof of sufficient funds and proof of lodging accommodations for their stay. Length of stay for U.S. citizens is granted for thirty days and may be extended to 180 days by the office of immigration. For further information, travelers may contact the Royal Netherlands Embassy, 4200 Linnean Avenue NW, Washington, DC 20008, telephone (202) 244-5300, or the Dutch Consulates in Los Angeles, Chicago, New York, Houston or Miami. Visit the web site for the Embassy of the Netherlands and the island of Curaçao website for the most current visa information. The U.S. Department of State is unaware of any HIV/AIDS entry restrictions for visitors to or foreign residents of Curaçao.

Safety and Security: There are no known terrorist or extremist groups, areas of instability or organized crime on Curaçao, although drug trafficking rings do operate on the island. Stay up to date by bookmarking our Bureau of Consular Affairs website, which contains the current Travel Warnings and Travel Alerts as well as the Worldwide Caution. Follow us on Twitter and the Bureau of Consular Affairs page on Facebook as well. You can also call 1-888-407-4747 toll-free within the United States and Canada, or by calling a regular toll line, 1-202-501-4444, from other countries. These numbers are available from 8:00 a.m. to 8:00 p.m. Eastern Time, Monday through Friday (except U.S. federal holidays). Take some time before travel to improve your personal security—things are not the same everywhere as they are in the United States.

Crime: The crime threat in Curaçao is generally considered low although travelers should always take normal precautions when in unfamiliar surroundings. Drug smuggling and trafficking in persons continue to be issues in Curaçao. Drug smuggling, in particular, has been significantly reduced through intensive cooperation among U.S., Dutch, Curaçao and international law enforcement authorities. Valuables left unattended on beaches, in cars and in hotel lobbies are easy targets for theft. Car theft, especially of rental vehicles for joy riding and stripping, can occur. Vehicle leases or rentals may not be fully covered by local insurance when a vehicle is stolen or damaged. Be sure you are sufficiently insured when renting vehicles, jet skis, and other items. Parents of young travelers should be aware that the legal drinking age of 18 is not always rigorously enforced in Curaçao, so extra parental supervision may be appropriate. Young travelers in particular are urged to take the same precautions they would when going out in the United States, e.g. to travel in pairs or in groups if they choose to frequent Curaçao's nightclubs and bars, and if they opt to consume alcohol, to do so responsibly. Anyone who is a victim of a crime should make a report to Curaçao police as well as report it immediately to the nearest U.S. consular office. Do not rely on hotel/restaurant/tour company management to make the report for you.

Don't buy counterfeit and pirated goods, even if they are widely available. Not only are the bootlegs illegal in the United States, if you purchase them you may also be breaking local law.

Victims of Crime: If you or someone you know becomes the victim of a crime abroad, you should contact the local police and the nearest U.S. embassy or consulate (see the Department of State's list of embassies and consulates). If your passport is stolen we can help you replace it. For violent crimes such as assault and rape, we can help you find appropriate medical care, contact family members or friends, and help them send you money if you need it. Although the investigation and prosecution of the crime are solely the responsibility of local authorities, consular officers can help you to understand the local criminal justice process and to find an attorney if you need. The emergency line in Curaçao is 911.

Criminal Penalties: While you are traveling in Curaçao, you are subject to its laws even if you are a U.S. citizen. Foreign laws and legal systems can be vastly different than our own. In some places you may be taken in for questioning if you don't have your passport with you. In some places, it is illegal to take pictures of certain buildings. In some places driving under the influence could land you immediately in jail. These criminal penalties will vary from country to country. There are also some things that might be legal in the country you visit, but still illegal in the United States, and you can be prosecuted under U.S. law if you buy pirated goods. Engaging in sexual conduct with children or using or disseminating child pornography in a foreign country is a crime prosecutable in the United States. If you break local laws in Curaçao, your U.S. passport won't help you avoid arrest or prosecution. It's very important to know what's legal and what's not where you are going.

Special Circumstances: Dutch law in principle does not permit dual nationality. However, there are several exceptions to the rule. For example, American citizens who are married to Dutch citizens are exempt from the requirement to abandon their American nationality when they apply to become a Dutch citizen by naturalization. For detailed information, contact the Embassy of the Netherlands in Washington, DC, or one of the Dutch consulates in the U.S.

Medical Facilities and Health Information: Medical care is good in Curaçao. There is one general hospital, St. Elisabeth Hospital, whose medical standards can be compared with to a small hospital in the U.S. St. Elizabeth's hospital has a decompression chamber and qualified staff to assist scuba divers suffering from decompression sickness. The hospital has three classes of services and patients are accommodated according to the level of their insurance: First Class: one patient to a room, air conditioning, etc.; Second Class: two to six patients to a room; Third Class: 15 to 30 people in one hall. Several private clinics such as Dr. Taams Clinic and Advent Clinic, provide good to excellent medical service. The many drug stores or "boticas" provide prescription and over the counter medicine. Emergency services are usually quick to respond. There have been cases of dengue fever in recent months. You can find good information on vaccinations and other health precautions, on the CDC website. For information about outbreaks of infectious diseases abroad, consult the World Health Organization (WHO) website. The WHO website also contains additional health information for travelers, including detailed country-specific health information.

Medical Insurance: You can't assume your insurance will go with you when you travel. It's very important to find out BEFORE you leave whether or not your medical insurance will cover you overseas. You need to ask your insurance company two questions:

- Does my policy apply when I'm out of the United States?
- Will it cover emergencies like a trip to a foreign hospital or a medical evacuation?

In many places, doctors and hospitals still expect payment in cash at the time of service. Your regular U.S. health insurance may not cover doctors' and hospital visits in other countries. If your policy doesn't go with you when you travel, it's a very good idea to take out another one for your trip.

Traffic Safety and Road Conditions: While in Curaçao, U.S. citizens may encounter road conditions that differ significantly from those in the United States. Driving in Curaçao is on the right-hand side of the road. Local laws require drivers and passengers to wear seat belts and motorcyclists to wear helmets. Children under 5 years of age should be in a child safety seat; older children should ride in the back seat. Right turns on red are prohibited in Curaçao.

Curaçao's main roads are fairly well lit and most hotels and tourist attractions can be easily located. Nonexistent or hidden and poorly maintained street signs are the major road hazard in Curaçao. Therefore, drivers should proceed through intersections with caution. Roads in Curaçao are extremely slippery during rainfall. Night driving is reasonably safe as long as drivers are familiar with the route and road conditions. There are speed limits in Curaçao and driving while intoxicated may result in the loss of a driver's license and/or a fine. However, these are not consistently enforced. Drivers should be alert at all times for speeding cars, which have caused fatal accidents. In the rural areas of the island, drivers should be alert for herds of goats that may cross the roads unexpectedly. Minibuses are inexpensive and run non-stop during the daytime with no fixed schedule. Each minibus has a specific route displayed in the front windshield. Buses, which run on the hour, have limited routes. Taxis, while relatively expensive, are safe and well regulated. As there are no meters, passengers should verify the price before entering the taxi. The emergency service telephone number is 911. Police and ambulances tend to respond quickly to emergency situations.

Aviation Safety Oversight: Prior to October 10, 2010, Curaçao was a part of the Netherlands Antilles. On that date, Curaçao acquired a new independent status within the Kingdom of the Netherlands. The U.S. Federal Aviation Administration (FAA) assessed the government of the Netherlands Antilles as being in compliance with International Civil Aviation Organization (ICAO) aviation safety standards for oversight of Netherlands Antilles air carrier operations. However, under its new status, Curaçao has not been assessed by the FAA for compliance with ICAO aviation standards.

Children's Issues: Please see the U.S. Dept. of State Office of Children's Issues web pages on intercountry adoption and international parental child abduction.

CYPRUS

Compiled from publications that were available as of February 2013 from the U.S. Department of State, the U.S. Department of Commerce, and the Central Intelligence Agency (CIA). See the introduction to this set for explanatory notes.

Official Name:
Republic of Cyprus

PROFILE

Geography

Area: total: 9,251 sq km (of which 3,355 sq km are in north Cyprus); country comparison to the world: 171; land: 9,241 sq km; water: 10 sq km

Major cities: Nicosia (capital) 240,000 (2009)

Climate: temperate; Mediterranean with hot, dry summers and cool winters

Terrain: central plain with mountains to north and south; scattered but significant plains along southern coast

People

Nationality: noun: Cypriot(s); adjective: Cypriot

Population: 1,138,071 (July 2012 est.)

Population growth rate: 1.571% (2012 est.)

Ethnic groups: Greek 77%, Turkish 18%, other 5% (2001)

Religions: Greek Orthodox 78%, Muslim 18%, other (includes Maronite and Armenian Apostolic) 4%

Languages: Greek (official), Turkish (official), English

Literacy: definition: age 15 and over can read and write; total population: 97.6%; male: 98.9%; female: 96.3% (2001 census)

Health: life expectancy at birth: total population: 78 years; male: 75.21 years; female: 80.92 years (2012 est.); Infant mortality rate: total: 9.05 deaths/1,000 live births; male: 10.72 deaths/1,000 live births; female: 7.3 deaths/1,000 live births (2012 est.)

Unemployment rate: 8% (2012 est.)

Work force: 416,900 (2012 est.)

Government

Type: republic
Independence: 16 August 1960
Constitution: 16 August 1960
Political subdivisions: 6 districts; Famagusta, Kyrenia, Larnaca, Limassol, Nicosia, Paphos; note—Turkish Cypriot area's administrative divisions include Kyrenia, all but a small part of Famagusta, and small parts of Nicosia (Lefkosia) and Larnaca
Suffrage: 18 years of age; universal

Economy

GDP (purchasing power parity): $23.57 billion (2012 est.); $24.03 billion (2011 est.); $23.91 billion (2010 est.); $23.64 billion (2009 est.)
GDP real growth rate: -2.3% (2012 est.); 0.5% (2011 est.); 1.1% (2010 est.); -1.9% (2009 est.)

GDP per capita (PPP): $26,900 (2012 est.); $29,400 (2011 est.); $29,800 (2010 est.); $29,700 (2009 est.)

Natural resources: copper, pyrites, asbestos, gypsum, timber, salt, marble, clay earth pigment

Agriculture products: citrus, vegetables, barley, grapes, olives, vegetables; poultry, pork, lamb; dairy, cheese

Industries: tourism, food and beverage processing, cement and gypsum production, ship repair and refurbishment, textiles, light chemicals, metal products, wood, paper, stone and clay products

Exports: $1.889 billion (2012 est.); $2.165 billion (2011 est.); $1.518 billion (2010 est.)

Exports—commodities: citrus, potatoes, pharmaceuticals, cement, clothing

Exports—partners: Greece 26.2%, UK 10.2%, Germany 5.6% (2011)

Imports: $7.716 billion (2012 est.); $8.034 billion (2011 est.); $8.032 billion (2010 est.)

Imports—commodities: consumer goods, petroleum and lubricants, machinery, transport equipment

Imports—partners: Greece 21.5%, Israel 10.4%, UK 9.2%, Italy 8.3%, Germany 8.1%, France 5.7%, China 4.8%, Netherlands 4.6% (2011)

Debt—external: $NA $35.87 billion (31 December 2011 est.); $30.77 billion (31 December 2010 est.)

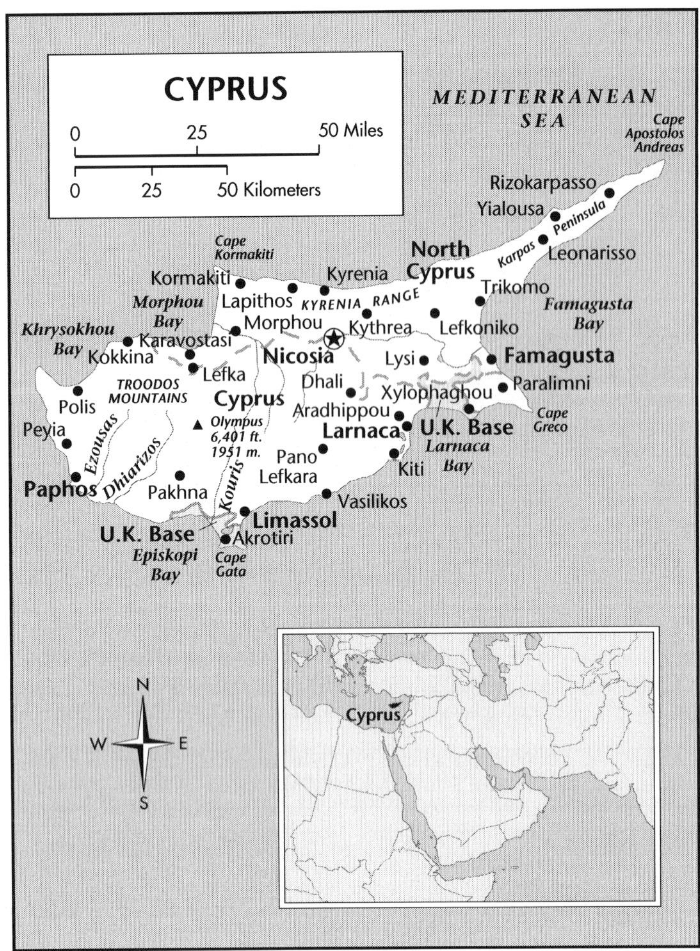

Exchange rates: euros (EUR) per US dollar; 0.7838 (2012 est.) ; 0.7194 (2011 est.); 0.755 (2010 est.); 0.7198 (2009 est.); 0.6827 (2008 est.); 0.7345 (2007 est.)

PEOPLE

Since 1974, Cyprus has been divided de facto into the government-controlled two-thirds of the island and the remaining one-third of the island, which is administered by Turkish Cypriots. Greek and Turkish Cypriots share many customs but maintain distinct identities based on religion, language, and close ties with their respective "motherlands."

Language

The official languages in Cyprus are Greek, Turkish, and English. Greek and English are widely spoken in the government-controlled area of the island. Press is available in many languages. English is usually preferred in business dealings. Turkish is widely spoken in the area administered by Turkish Cypriots.

Religion

Prior to 1974, the country experienced a long period of strife between its Greek Cypriot and Turkish Cypriot communities. In response the UN Force in Cyprus (UNFICYP) began peacekeeping operations in 1964. The island has been divided since Turkish military intervention in 1974. The southern part of the island is under the control of the government of the Republic of Cyprus (ROC), while the northern part is administered by Turkish Cypriots. In 1983 their administration proclaimed itself the "Turkish Republic of Northern Cyprus" ("TRNC"). The United States does not recognize the "TRNC," nor does any other country except Turkey. A buffer zone, or "green line," patrolled by the UNFICYP, separates the two parts. The area administered by Turkish Cypriots is discussed in a separate section in this report.

According to the most recent census information available (2001), 95 percent of the permanent population in the government-controlled area belongs to the Autocephalous Greek Orthodox Church of Cyprus. All other religious groups combined constitute less than 5 percent of the population and include Roman Catholic, Protestant, Muslim, Maronite Catholic, Armenian Orthodox, Jewish, Jehovah's Witnesses, Baha'i, Buddhist, and other groups.

Recent immigrants and migrant workers generally practice religions different from those of native-born citizens, who are predominantly Greek Orthodox. There is a Buddhist meditation center in Nicosia and a synagogue in Larnaca; both are used primarily by foreign residents. The Jewish community, numbering approximately 2,150, includes a very small number of native Jewish Cypriots and a greater number of Jews who are part of the foreign resident community.

In the area administered by the Turkish Cypriots, nominally 98 percent of population is Sunni Muslim. An estimated 10,000 mostly immigrant workers from Turkey of Turkish, Kurdish, or Arab origin, are Alevis. There are also followers of other schools of Islam. There is a Turkish Cypriot Baha'i community of approximately 200 persons, a small Jewish community of foreign expatriates, a Russian Orthodox Church of approximately 200 persons, and a Jehovah's Witness community of approximately 40 members. Most non-Muslims residing in the area are foreigners from Western Europe who are generally members of the Roman Catholic or Anglican churches.

The large majority of the secular Turkish Cypriot community observes Islamic holidays through cultural events and family gatherings, rather than attending service or through specifically religious ceremonies. This is in contrast to students, residents, immigrants, and workers of Turkish, Kurdish, or Arab origin who celebrate and practice most of the spiritual and traditional aspects of their religions through mosque services.

HISTORY

Human settlement on Cyprus stretches back nearly eight millennia and by 3700 BC, the island was a crossroads between East and West. The island fell successively under Assyrian, Egyptian, Persian, Greek, and Roman domination. For 800 years, beginning in 364 AD, Cyprus was ruled by Byzantium. After brief possession by King Richard I (the Lion-Hearted) of England during the Crusades, the island came under Frankish control in the late 12th century. It was ceded to the Venetian Republic in 1489 and conquered by the Ottoman Turks in 1571. The Ottomans applied the millet system to Cyprus, which allowed religious authorities to govern their own non-Muslim minorities.

This system reinforced the position of the Orthodox Church and the cohesion of the ethnic Greek population. Most of the Turks who settled on the island during the 3 centuries of Ottoman rule remained when control of Cyprus—although not sovereignty—was ceded to Great Britain in 1878. Many, however, left for Turkey during the 1920s. The island was annexed formally by the United Kingdom in 1914 at the outbreak of World War I and became a crown colony in 1925.

Cyprus gained its independence from the United Kingdom and established a constitutional republic in 1960, after an anti-British campaign by the Greek Cypriot EOKA (National Organization of Cypriot Fighters), a guerrilla group that desired political union, or enosis, with Greece. Archbishop Makarios, a charismatic religious and political leader, was elected president.

Shortly after the founding of the republic, serious differences arose between the two communities about the implementation and interpretation of the constitution. The Greek Cypriots argued that the complex mechanisms introduced to protect Turkish Cypriot interests were obstacles to efficient government. In November 1963, President Makarios advanced a series of constitutional amendments designed to eliminate some of these special provisions.

The Turkish Cypriots opposed such changes. The confrontation prompted widespread intercommunal fighting in December 1963, after which Turkish Cypriots ceased to participate in the government. Following the outbreak of intercommunal violence, many Turkish Cypriots (and some Greek Cypriots) living in mixed villages began to move into enclaved villages or elsewhere. UN peacekeepers were deployed on the island in 1964. Following another outbreak of intercommunal violence in 1967–68, a Turkish Cypriot provisional administration was formed.

In July 1974, the military junta in Athens sponsored a coup led by extremist Greek Cypriots against the government of President Makarios, citing his alleged pro-communist leanings and his perceived abandonment of enosis.

Turkey, citing the 1960 Treaty of Guarantee, intervened militarily to protect Turkish Cypriots. In a two-stage offensive, Turkish troops took control of 38% of the island. Almost all Greek Cypriots subsequently fled south while almost all Turkish Cypriots moved to the north. Since the events of 1974, UN peacekeeping forces have maintained a buffer zone between the two sides.

Except for occasional demonstrations or infrequent incidents between soldiers in the buffer zone, the island was free of violent conflict from 1974 until August 1996, when violent clashes led to the death of two demonstrators and escalated tension. The situation has been quiet since 1996.

GOVERNMENT AND POLITICAL CONDITIONS

The Republic of Cyprus is a constitutional republic and multiparty presidential democracy. On May 22, 2011, 56 representatives were elected to the 80-seat Vouli Antiprosopon (House of Representatives) in free and fair elections, and in 2008 President Demetris Christofias was elected in free and fair elections. He was replaced by Nikos Anastasiadis in February 2013.

Recent Elections

On May 22, 2011, free and fair elections were held for the 56 seats assigned to Greek Cypriots in the 80-seat House of Representatives.

Participation of Women and Minorities: Women held six of the 56 seats filled in the House of Representatives and three of 11 ministerial posts. They also held senior positions in the judicial branch. There were no members of minorities in the House of Representatives. The small Armenian Orthodox, Maronite Christian, and Roman Catholic communities elected special nonvoting observer representatives from their respective communities to the House of Representatives. Twenty-four seats assigned to Turkish Cypriots were unfilled.

Principal Government Officials

Last Updated: 2/31/2013

Pres.: **Nikos ANASTASIADIS**
Min. of Agriculture, Natural Resources, & Environment: **Nikos KOUGIALIS**
Min. of Commerce, Industry, & Tourism: **Georgios LAKKOTRYPIS**
Min. of Communications & Works: **Tasos MITSOPOULOS**
Min. of Defense: **Fotis FOTIOU**
Min. of Education & Culture: **Kyriakos KENEVEZOS**
Min. of Finance: **Michalis SARRIS**
Min. of Foreign Affairs: **Ioannis KASOULIDIS**
Min. of Health: **Petros PETRIDIS**
Min. of Interior: **Sokratis CHASIKOS**

Min. of Justice & Public Order: **Ionas NIKOLAOU**
Min. of Labor & Social Insurance: **Charis GEORGIADIS**
Governor, Central Bank: **Panikos DIMITRIADIS**
Ambassador to the US:
Permanent Representative to the UN, New York: **Nikolaos EMILIOU**

ECONOMY

The area of the Republic of Cyprus under government control has a market economy dominated by the service sector, which accounts for four-fifths of GDP. Tourism, financial services, and real estate are the most important sectors. Erratic growth rates over the past decade reflect the economy's reliance on tourism, the profitability of which can fluctuate with political instability in the region and economic conditions in Western Europe. Nevertheless, the economy in the area under government control has grown at a rate well above the EU average since 2000.

Cyprus joined the European Exchange Rate Mechanism (ERM2) in May 2005 and adopted the euro as its national currency on 1 January 2008. An aggressive austerity program in the preceding years, aimed at paving the way for the euro, helped turn a soaring fiscal deficit (6.3% in 2003) into a surplus of 1.2% in 2008, and reduced inflation to 4.7%.

This prosperity came under pressure in 2009, as construction and tourism slowed in the face of reduced foreign demand triggered by the ongoing global financial crisis. Although Cyprus lagged behind its EU peers in showing signs of stress from the global crisis, the economy tipped into recession in 2009, contracting by 1.7%, and has been slow to bounce back since, posting anemic growth in 2010–11 before contracting again by 2.3% in 2012.

Serious problems surfaced in the Cypriot financial sector in early 2011 as the Greek fiscal crisis and euro zone debt crisis deepened. Cyprus's borrowing costs have risen steadily because of its exposure to Greek debt. Two of Cyprus's biggest banks are among the largest holders of Greek bonds in Europe and have a substantial presence in Greece through bank branches and subsidiaries. Cyprus experienced numerous downgrades of its credit rating in 2012 and has been cut off from international money markets.

The Cypriot economy contracted in 2012 following the writedown of Greek bonds. A liquidity squeeze is choking the financial sector and the real economy as many global investors are uncertain the Cypriot economy can weather the EU crisis. The budget deficit rose to 7.4% of GDP in 2011, a violation of the EU's budget deficit criteria - no more than 3% of GDP. In response to the country's deteriorating finances and serious risk of contagion from the Greek debt crisis, Nicosia implemented measures to cut the cost of the state payroll, curb tax evasion, and revamp social benefits, and trimmed the deficit to 4.2% of GDP in 2012. In July, Nicosia became the fifth euro zone government to request an economic bailout program from the European Commission, the European Central Bank, and the International Monetary Fund - known collectively as the "Troika." Negotiations over the final details of the plan are ongoing.

Labor Conditions

The law prohibits the employment of children, defined as persons under 15, except in specified circumstances, such as combined work-training programs for children who have attained the age of 14 or employment in cultural, artistic, sports, or advertising activities, subject to certain rules limiting work hours. Nighttime work and engagement of children in street trading is prohibited. The law also permits the employment of adolescents, defined as persons between the ages of 15 and 18, provided it is not harmful, damaging, or dangerous, and also subject to rules limiting hours of employment. Employment of adolescents between midnight and 4:00 a.m. is not permitted. The minimum age for employment in an "industrial undertaking" is 16.

Although there is no national minimum wage, there is a minimum wage for certain groups that are deemed vulnerable to exploitation. The official poverty line is set at 2,062 euros ($2,680) a month for a family of four; the rate was established in 2009. The minimum wage for shop assistants, nurses' assistants, clerks, hairdressers, and nursery assistants was 855 euros ($1,110) per month for the first six months and 909 euros ($1,180) per month thereafter. For asylum seekers working in the agricultural sector, the minimum monthly wage was either 425 euros ($553) with accommodation and food provided or 767 euros ($997) without accommodation and food.

The minimum starting salary for foreign nationals working as live-in housekeepers was 456 euros ($593) per month. Medical insurance, visa fees, travel, and repatriation expenses were covered by the employers. Cabaret performers' contracts typically stipulated that they receive at least 205 euros ($267) per week for 36 hours of work. Workers in almost all other occupations, including unskilled labor, were covered under collective bargaining agreements. The wages set in these agreements were significantly higher than the minimum wage.

Foreign workers were allowed to claim pensions, and in some cases bilateral agreements existed that allowed workers to claim credit in their home countries. Unions and labor confederations were generally effective in enforcing negotiated wage rates (collectively bargained rates), which were generally much higher than the minimum wage. The Migration Service was responsible for enforcing the minimum wage for foreign workers but did not actively do so.

The legal maximum workweek was 48 hours, including overtime. Unions and employers within the same economic sector collectively determined the actual working hours. In the private sector, white-collar employees typically worked 39 hours a week, and blue-collar employees worked 38 hours a week. In the public sector, the workweek was 38 hours in the winter and 35 hours in the summer. The law does not require premium pay for overtime or mandatory rest periods; however, these benefits were sometimes stipulated in contracts and collective agreements. The law provides that foreign and local workers receive equal treatment. Labor ministry inspectors are responsible for enforcing these laws. Labor unions, however, reported enforcement problems in sectors not covered by collective agreements. They also reported that certain employers, mainly in the building industry, exploited illegal foreign workers by paying them very low wages.

There were reports that foreign domestic workers, primarily from East or South Asia, were mistreated by their employers or fired without cause in violation of their contracts. Some domestic workers, particularly live-in maids, reported working excess hours for employer families at all times, night and day, without additional compensation or time off. Although the law protects domestic workers who file a complaint with the Ministry of Labor and Social Insurance from being deported until their cases have been adjudicated, NGOs reported that many domestic workers did not complain to authorities about mistreatment due to fear of deportation.

U.S.-CYPRUS RELATIONS

The United States established diplomatic relations with Cyprus in 1960 following its independence from the United Kingdom. Shortly after the founding of the republic, serious differences arose between the Greek Cypriot and Turkish Cypriot communities about the implementation and interpretation of the constitution. The 1960s and early 1970s saw intercommunal violence and foreign intervention by Greece and Turkey. Since 1974, Cyprus has been divided de facto into the Republic of Cyprus controlled two-thirds of the island and the remaining one-third of the island, which is administered by Turkish Cypriots. In 1983, the Turkish Cypriots declared an independent "Turkish Republic of Northern Cyprus" ("TRNC"). The United States does not recognize the "TRNC," nor does any country other than Turkey. United Nations peacekeeping forces have maintained a buffer zone between the two sides.

The United States regards the status quo on Cyprus as unacceptable and supports efforts to reach a comprehensive settlement to reunify the island as a bizonal, bicommunal federation. Successive U.S. administrations have viewed intercommunal negotiations under UN auspices as the best means to achieve a fair and permanent settlement. The United States has urged all parties to intensify their work on behalf of peace and progress.

The United States works closely with Cyprus to advance our shared transatlantic priorities both bilaterally and in the context of our strategic partnership with the European Union, which Cyprus joined in 2004. Our bilateral partnership continues to grow in areas of common interest, such as promoting peace and security in the region, fostering opportunities for greater trade and investment, and protecting cultural heritage. A mutual legal assistance treaty and a Proliferation Security Initiative agreement on ship boarding facilitate bilateral cooperation.

U.S. Assistance to Cyprus

The U.S. goal in Cyprus is to build regional stability through a comprehensive settlement of the Cyprus dispute. U.S. assistance focuses on creating conditions conducive to the resolution of the dispute by promoting mutual understanding between the Greek Cypriot and Turkish Cypriot communities through support for activities that bring them together to design Cypriot solutions to common problems. U.S. assistance also seeks to address economic disparities between the two communities and promote expanded business and economic relationships between them.

Bilateral Economic Relations

The Republic of Cyprus is a member of the European Union. The EU's body of common rights and obligations (acquis communautaire) is suspended in the area administered by Turkish Cypriots pending a Cyprus settlement. U.S. exports and projects involving U.S. investment are primarily in the energy, financial services, tourism, logistics, and consumer goods sectors. There may be additional opportunities for investment in Cyprus' growing energy sector. U.S. imports from Cyprus include agricultural products, salt, and minerals. Bilateral business ties also encompass a healthy exchange in services.

Cyprus's Membership in International Organizations

Cyprus and the United States belong to a number of the same international organizations, including the United Nations, Organization for Security and Cooperation in Europe, International Monetary Fund, World Bank, and World Trade Organization. Cyprus also is an observer to the Organization of American States.

Bilateral Representation

Cyprus maintains an embassy in the United States at 2211 R Street NW, Washington, DC 20008 (tel. 202-462-5772).

Principal U.S. Embassy Officials

Last Updated: 1/14/2013

NICOSIA (E) Metochiou & Ploutarchou, Engomi 2407, Nicosia, Cyprus, 357-22-39-3939, Fax 357-22-780-944, Workweek: M-F, 08:00–17:00, Website: http://nicosia.usembassy.gov/

DCM OMS:	Cheryl L. Payne
AMB OMS:	Daphney T. Auguste
ECON/COM:	Susan M. Delja
FM:	Laura M. Alexander
HRO:	Raoul A. Russell
MGT:	Tracy H. Harding
POSHO:	Laura M. Alexander
SDO/DATT:	COL William H. Woods
AMB:	John M. Koenig

CON:	Steven B. Royster
DCM:	Andrew J. Schofer
PAO:	Keith Peterson
GSO:	Rita W. Bopp
RSO:	Jorge A. Espinoza
AID:	Jed Barton (Resident In Kiev)
CLO:	Meital May
DEA:	Jack M. Sparks
EEO:	Juliette A. Dickstein
FMO:	Raoul A. Russell
ICASS Chair:	Christopher W. Smith
IMO:	James H. May
IRS:	Aziz Benbrahim (Resident In Paris)
ISSO:	James H. May
LEGATT:	Vacant (Resident In Athens)
POL:	Kristen L. Pisani
State ICASS:	Christopher W. Smith

TRAVEL

Consular Information Sheet

March 14, 2012

Country Description: Since 1974, Cyprus, a Mediterranean island nation, has been divided de facto into a government-controlled area comprising the southern two-thirds of the island, and a northern third (the self-declared "Turkish Republic of Northern Cyprus"), administered by Turkish Cypriots. The United States does not recognize the "Turkish Republic of Northern Cyprus," nor does any country other than Turkey. Facilities for tourism in Cyprus are highly developed. Cyprus joined the European Union in 2004.

Smart Traveler Enrollment Program (STEP)/Embassy Locations: If you are going to live in or visit Cyprus, please take the time to tell our embassy about your trip. If you enroll, we can keep you up to date with important safety and security announcements. It will also help your friends and family get in touch with you in an emergency.

U.S. Embassy Nicosia
Metochiou & Ploutarchou Street
2407, Engomi
Nicosia, Cyprus
Tel: 357-22-393939
Fax: 357-22-780944
Emergency after-hours telephone: 357-22-393939; wait for the recorded message and press 0.

Entry/Exit Requirements for U.S. Citizens: You need a passport to travel to Cyprus. You don't need a visa if you are staying for less than 90 days. For longer stays, you need a visa or residence permit. Be mindful that the Government of Cyprus does not recognize the residence permits issued by Turkish Cypriot authorities for the portions of the island under Turkish Cypriot administration. The Government of Cyprus does not issue residency permits to individuals who live in the areas outside government control. On occasion, U.S. citizens who resided in the areas which are not under the effective control of the Republic of Cyprus for more than 90 days have been detained by officials at Larnaca airport and denied entry into Government-controlled areas.

Read the "Special Circumstances" section of this fact sheet for important additional information about entry requirements into the Turkish Cypriot-administered areas. For further information on entry requirements for the Republic of Cyprus, contact the Embassy of Cyprus at 2211 R Street NW, Washington, DC 20008–4082, tel. (202) 462-5772, or the Cypriot Consulate in New York at 13 East 40th St., 5th Floor, New York, NY 10016, tel. (212) 686-6016/17.

Some HIV/AIDS entry restrictions exist for visitors to and foreign residents of Cyprus. Legislation mandates that aliens known to have certain communicable diseases and HIV be denied entry into the country. If you think you may be included in this restriction, check with the Embassy of Cyprus before you travel.

Threats to Safety and Security: Do not, under any circumstances, attempt to enter the U.N. buffer zone at any place other than a designated crossing point. This area is mined and militarized. Never photograph military installations or anything that could be perceived as being of security interest (especially in the areas not under the effective control of the Government of the Republic of Cyprus). Pay particular attention to areas marked with "no photography" signs. Police on both sides strictly enforce these restrictions.

The Embassy has reports of instances of discrimination and sexual harassment against U.S. citizens of Eastern European or non-European descent, particularly against U.S. citizens of Asian descent.

Stay up to date by:

- Bookmarking our Bureau of Consular Affairs website, which contains the current Travel Warnings and Travel Alerts as well as the Worldwide Caution.
- Following us on Twitter and the Bureau of Consular Affairs page on Facebook as well.
- Downloading our free Smart Traveler iPhone App to have travel information at your fingertips.
- Calling 1-888-407-4747 toll-free within the U.S. and Canada, or a regular toll line, 1-202-501-4444, from other countries.
- Taking some time before travel to consider your personal security.

Crime: The crime rate in Cyprus is low. Visitors in urban areas should take the normal precautions they would take in any large city. Avoid so-called "cabarets," bars which sometimes employ women brought to Cyprus for sexual exploitation. These establishments can also present foreign patrons with grossly inflated bar tabs, and customers who refuse to pay may be threatened.

Don't buy counterfeit and pirated goods, even if they are widely available. Not only are these counterfeit, bootleg goods illegal to bring back into the United States, f you purchase them you may also be breaking local law.

There is a reported increase in the rate of home break-ins particularly in the Nicosia area of Cyprus. Although most home break-ins take place overnight, these types of crimes can take place at any time of day and night as perpetrators seek the best targets of opportunity whenever available. As in any major metropolitan area, all travelers and residents should exercise care by locking all doors and windows of their homes and offices and not leaving any valuables out in public view.

Victims of Crime: If you or someone you know becomes the victim of a crime abroad, you should contact the local police and the nearest U.S. embassy or consulate. We can:

- Replace a stolen passport.
- Help you find appropriate medical care if you are the victim of violent crimes such as assault or rape.
- Put you in contact with the appropriate police authorities, and if you want us to, we can contact family members or friend.
- Help you understand the local criminal justice process and direct you to local attorneys, although it is important to remember that local authorities are responsible for investigating and prosecuting the crime.

The local equivalents to the "911" emergency line in the Republic of Cyprus are 199 and 112. Emergency assistance is available in the area administered by Turkish Cypriots by calling 155.

Criminal Penalties: While you are traveling in Cyprus, you are subject to its laws even if you are a U.S. citizen. Foreign laws and legal systems can be vastly different than our own, and criminal penalties vary from country to country. There are also some things that might be legal in the country you visit, but still illegal in the United States; for instance, you can be prosecuted under U.S. law if you buy pirated goods. Engaging in sexual conduct with children or using or disseminating child pornography in a foreign country is a crime prosecutable in the United States. If you break local laws in Cyprus, your U.S. passport won't help you avoid arrest or prosecution. It's very important to know what's legal and what's not wherever you go.

If you are arrested in Cyprus, authorities of Cyprus are required to notify the U.S. Embassy of your arrest. If you are concerned the Department of State may not be aware of your situation, you should request the police or prison officials to notify the U.S. Embassy of your arrest. You also have the option to request to have communications from you forwarded to the U.S. Embassy.

Special Circumstances: Since 1974, the Republic of Cyprus has designated Larnaca and Paphos international airports, and the seaports of Limassol, Larnaca, and Paphos, as the only legal points of entry into and exit from Cyprus; these ports are all in the government-controlled southern part of the island. Entry or exit via any other air or seaport is considered an illegal act by the Republic of Cyprus. Formerly, visitors choosing to arrive at non-designated airports and seaports in the area administered by Turkish Cypriots were not allowed to cross the U.N.-patrolled buffer zone to the government-controlled area in the south. Since 2004, when the Republic of Cyprus implemented new EU-related crossing regulations, U.S. citizens (and citizens of other non-EU countries not requiring visas) have been able to cross regardless of their port of entry into Cyprus.

Most U.S. citizen visitors to Cyprus are able to cross the buffer zone without hindrance, although on occasion difficulties are encountered at both the government and Turkish Cypriot checkpoints. Cypriot officials at the buffer zone checkpoints or at airports and seaports in the government-controlled areas may detain and prosecute U.S. citizens who have been present for more than 90 days in the areas which are not under the effective control of the Government of the Republic of Cyprus if they do not possess a residency permit issued by the relevant authorities of the Republic of Cyprus.

For visits of less than 90 days, U.S. citizens may enter the Turkish Cypriot-administered area by displaying a valid U.S. passport. Stays for 90 days or longer require a "temporary residency visa" issued by Turkish Cypriot authorities. Turkish Cypriot authorities have deported foreigners who violate this law. Turkish Cypriot authorities emphasize that the requirement to obtain a temporary residency visa within 90 days of arriving in the Turkish Cypriot-administered area cannot be avoided by periodically visiting the southern part of the island controlled by the Republic of Cyprus.

Policy and procedures regarding travel across the buffer zone are subject to change. More information on current procedures may be obtained at the U.N. buffer zone Ledra Palace checkpoint in Nicosia.

Cyprus customs authorities enforce strict regulations concerning temporary importation into or export from Cyprus of items such as firearms. There are no restrictions on contemporary religious materials and medication for personal use; however, Cyprus restricts the export of Byzantine period ecclesiastical material and all archaeological material, including ancient coins. The U.S. Customs Service may impose corresponding import restrictions in accordance with the Convention on Cultural Property Implementation Act. You should contact the Embassy of the Republic of Cyprus in Washington, DC for specific information regarding customs requirements or visit their online Customs information.

Dual nationals may be subject to laws that impose special obligations on citizens of Cyprus. For example, U.S. citizens whom the Republic of Cyprus considers to be Cypriot citizens may be subject to compulsory military service and other aspects of Cypriot law while in Cyprus. U.S. citizen males between the ages of 16 and 26 years who reside in the United States and whose parents or grandfather were Greek Cypriots or have Greek Cypriot names should get written confirmation that they reside permanently outside of Cyprus from the Cypriot

Embassy in Washington, D.C. before they travel to Cyprus. After their arrival in Cyprus, they should present their foreign residency confirmation statement to the Cypriot National Guard Registration office to obtain an exit permit. Those who believe they may be affected should inquire at the Embassy of Cyprus regarding their status. U.S. citizens whom the Turkish Cypriot authorities consider to be "citizens" may also be subject to compulsory military service in the area administered by Turkish Cypriots. The U.S. Embassy Nicosia is unable to exempt dual nationals from such service.

U.S. Citizens who buy or lease property, particularly in the area administered by Turkish Cypriots, may find their ownership challenged by people displaced as a result of the 1974 conflict. Prospective property buyers should always seek legal advice before buying.

On October 20, 2006, the Government of the Republic of Cyprus passed Article 303A of the Criminal Code which makes it a felony to buy, rent or sell property in Cyprus without the consent of the registered owner. Cypriot courts have used the law to prosecute people involved in the sale or purchase of property in the area administered by the Turkish Cypriots.

The Government of Cyprus has also attempted to enforce Cypriot legal judgments in property matters in other EU countries. Cypriot customs authorities routinely detain anyone arriving in Cyprus or crossing the buffer zone found to be in possession of documents relating to property purchases in the area administered by Turkish Cypriots.

Since 2006, the Immovable Property Commission (IPC) in the north has accepted claims for compensation or restitution from Greek Cypriots for property in the north. The Government of the Republic of Cyprus does not recognize the legitimacy of the IPC. However, in 2010, the European Court of Human Rights (ECHR) ruled that the IPC is an effective, domestic remedy; thus, persons claiming rights to properties in the north who want to file a property claim at the ECHR must first apply to the IPC.

Accessibility: While in Cyprus, individuals with disabilities may find accessibility and accommodation to be very different from what you find in the United States. Cypriot law prohibits discrimination against persons with disabilities in employment, education, access to health care, or in the provision of other state services, and in practice the government generally enforces the provisions.

The People with Disabilities Law also mandates that public buildings and tourist facilities built after 1999 be accessible to all, however, older buildings frequently lack access for persons with disabilities. Narrow or nonexistent sidewalks and lack of transport, parking spaces, accessible toilets and elevators all pose problems for persons with disabilities.

Medical Facilities and Health Information: Medical care is available both at government hospitals and private clinics. Emergency rooms offer adequate care to stabilize patients, most of who are then transferred to private hospitals. Many of the private-sector doctors have been trained in the United Kingdom or the United States. While fees are generally lower than those in the United States, medical supplies are often more expensive. Paramedics do not staff ambulances. The standard of medical care in the area administered by Turkish Cypriots is improving, but still falls below that found in the government-controlled area. The World Health Organization considers Cyprus to be one of the healthiest areas of the Mediterranean. Water supplies are potable, and the refuse collection/sewage disposal system is adequate. Communicable diseases such as typhoid are rare. Respiratory ailments and allergies are sometimes exacerbated by the dry and dusty climate.

You can find good information on vaccinations and other health precautions, on the Centers for Disease Control and Prevention (CDC) website. For information about outbreaks of infectious diseases abroad, consult the World Health Organization (WHO) website, which also contains additional health information for travelers, including detailed country-specific health information.

Medical Insurance: You can't assume your insurance will go with you when you travel. It's very important to find out BEFORE you leave. You need to ask your insurance company two questions:

- Does my policy apply when I'm out of the U.S.?
- Will it cover emergencies like a trip to a foreign hospital or an evacuation?

In many places, doctors and hospitals still expect payment in cash at the time of service. Your regular U.S. health insurance may not cover doctors' and hospital visits in other countries. If your policy doesn't go with you when you travel, it's a very good idea to take out another one for your trip.

Traffic Safety and Road Conditions: While in Cyprus, U.S. citizens may encounter road conditions that differ significantly from those in the United States.

In recent years, Cyprus ranked among the top three countries in Europe, on a per capita basis, in traffic fatalities. Speeding, tailgating, overtaking, and the running of caution lights are commonplace and major causes of accidents. Emergency assistance is available in the Republic of Cyprus by calling 112 or 199. Emergency assistance is available in the area administered by Turkish Cypriots by calling 155.

There are few public buses and no rail lines in Cyprus. Taxis are widely available. Traffic moves on the left side of the road, British style, and modern motorways link the major cities. Secondary roads, especially in mountainous areas, tend to be narrow and winding, and not as well maintained as major highways. Traffic laws, signs, and speed limits are consistent with the standards used throughout Europe. Traffic circles (roundabouts) are often utilized at major intersections.

The use of seat belts (in front seats) and child car seats is required. Motorcyclists are required to wear helmets and the use of cellular phones while driving is prohibited unless used with some form of hands-free kit. Liability insurance is mandatory. Road safety conditions in the area administered by Turkish Cypriots are similar to conditions in the south, except that the road network is less developed. Insurance purchased in the government-controlled area is not valid in the area administered by Turkish Cypriots, but insurance for that area may be purchased near the U.N. buffer zone checkpoints.

Aviation Safety Oversight: As there is no direct commercial air service to the United States by carriers registered in Cyprus, the U.S. Federal Aviation Administration (FAA) has not assessed the government of Cyprus's Civil Aviation Authority for compliance with International Civil Aviation Organization (ICAO) aviation safety standards. Further information may be found on the FAA's safety assessment page.

Children's Issues: In an effort to prevent international child abduction, many governments have initiated strict identification procedures at entry/exit points. These often include requiring documentary evidence of relationship and permission for the child's travel from the parent(s) or legal guardian, if not present. Having such documentation on hand, even if not required, may facilitate entry and departure. Although Cyprus is party to The Hague Convention on the Civil Aspects of International Child Abduction, the Convention cannot be used effectively to recover a child abducted to the area administered by Turkish Cypriots.

Please see the U.S. Dept. of State Office of Children's Issues web pages on intercountry adoption and international parental child abduction.

Intercountry Adoption

March 2009

The information in this section has been edited from the latest report available as of February 2013 from the State Department Bureau of Consular Affairs, Office of Overseas Citizens Services. For more information, please read the *Intercountry Adoption* section of this book and review current reports online at http://adoption.state.gov.

Cyprus is party to the Hague Convention on Protection of Children and Co-operation in Respect of Intercountry Adoption (Hague Adoption Convention). Therefore all adoptions between Cyprus and the United States must meet the requirements of the Convention and U.S. law implementing the Convention. Cyprus is not considered a country of origin in intercountry adoption. There are virtually no children available for adoption in Cyprus.

Cypriot couples who wish to adopt usually look to other countries for adoption possibilities. No Cypriot orphans have received U.S. immigrant visas in the past five years. The information provided is intended primarily to assist in rare adoption cases from Cyprus, including adoptions of Cypriot children by relatives in the United States, as well as adoptions from third countries by Americans living in Cyprus.

Who Can Adopt? Adoption between the United States and Cyprus is governed by the Hague Adoption Convention. Therefore to adopt from Cyprus, you must first be found eligible to adopt by the U.S. Government.

The U.S. Government agency responsible for making this determination is the Department of Homeland Security, U.S. Citizenship and Immigration Services (USCIS). For detailed and updated information on these requirements, please review the *Intercountry Adoption* section of this publication and visit the USCIS Intercountry Adoption website at http://adoption.state.gov.

Residency Requirements: Prospective adoptive parents must be permanent residents of Cyprus or have resided in Cyprus for at least two years prior to the submission of the application.

Age Requirements: At least one parent must be 25 years old. If the adopting parents are relatives of the child, one of them must be at least 21 years old.

Marriage Requirements: Married couples must adopt jointly unless one spouse is incapable of giving consent or cannot be located. Unmarried couples may not adopt jointly. The court may approve adoptions by single adoptive parents if that person has applied alone and if the court determines that special reasons exist. "Special reasons" are not listed or defined in the Cypriot adoption code, but the prevailing view in Cyprus is that a family with two parents is in children's best interests.

Who Can Be Adopted? Because Cyprus is party to the Hague Adoption Convention, children from Cyprus must meet the requirements of the Convention in order to be eligible for adoption.

Cypriot Adoption Authority: Social Welfare Services of the Ministry of Labor & Social Insurance

The Process: Because Cyprus is party to the Hague Adoption Convention, adopting from Cyprus must follow a specific process designed to meet the Convention's requirements. For detailed and updated information on these requirements, please review the *Intercountry Adoption* section of this publication and visit the USCIS Intercountry Adoption website at http://adoption.state.gov. There are no adoption agencies in Cyprus. The Consular Section at the U.S. Embassy in Nicosia maintains a list of English-speaking lawyers who are licensed to practice in Cyprus.

Role of the Adoption Authority: The Social Welfare Services´ main responsibilities during the adoption process are:

- To investigate whether an individual or a family are eligible to become adoptive parents.
- To safeguard the best interests of children as soon as the application for adoption is submitted to the Court.
- To submit to the Court a report indicating whether the adoption is in the best interests of a child.
- To act as a temporary guardian to a child and to submit to the Court the report in order to issue the adoption order.
- Post adoption counseling.

Role of the Court: The court with jurisdiction over the case reviews the application for adoption and issues the adoption order provided that the adoption is in the best interests of the child.

Role of Adoption Agencies: There are no adoption agencies in Cyprus. The Consular Section at the U.S. Embassy in Nicosia maintains a list of English-speaking lawyers who are licensed to practice in Cyprus. The U.S. Embassy cannot recommend the services of any specific attorney.

Adoption Application: Prospective adopting parents need only to submit a written application signed by both spouses to the District Welfare officer of the district of their habitual residence. During the eligibility study they will be requested to undergo full medical tests.

Documents Required: Contact Social Welfare Services directly for list.

Adoption Fees: In the adoption services contract that you sign at the beginning of the adoption process, your agency will itemize the fees and estimated expenses related to your adoption process. Attorneys in Cyprus provide legal services only when Cypriot families adopt children from abroad. Fees vary from case to case.

Bringing Your Child Home: Once your adoption is complete (or you have obtained legal custody of the child), there are a few more steps to take before you can head home. Specifically, you need to apply for several documents for your child before he or she can travel to the United States, such as a birth certificate, a passport or travel document for your child from the country in which he or she was born, and a U.S. Immigration Visa. For detailed and updated information on how to obtain these documents, review the *Intercountry Adoption* section on this publication and visit the USCIS Intercountry Adoption website at http://adoption.state.gov.

Child Citizenship Act: For adoptions finalized abroad, the Child Citizenship Act of 2000 allows your new child to acquire American citizenship automatically when he or she enters the United States as lawful permanent residents. For adoptions to be finalized in the United States, the Child Citizenship Act of 2000 allows your child to typically acquire American citizenship when the U.S. state court issues the final adoption decree. To learn more, review the *Intercountry Adoption* section on this publication and visit the USCIS Intercountry Adoption website at http://adoption.state.gov.

After Adoption: There are no post-adoption reporting requirements.

U.S. Embassy in Cyprus
Embassy of the United States of America, Nicosia
Metohiou & Ploutarchou Street
P.O.Box 24536
1385 Nicosia—Cyprus
Telephone number: 357-22-393939
Fax: 357-22-776841
Email: consularnicosia@state.gov
http://cyprus.usembassy.gov

Cypriot Adoption Authority
Social Welfare Services
Ministry of Labor & Social Insurance
63 Prodromou Street
1468 Nicosia
Cyprus
Tel: 357-22-406650/406655
Fax: 357-22-667907
E-mail: central.sws@sws.mlsi.gov.cy
http://www.mlsi.gov.cy/sws

Embassy of Cyprus
2224 Wyoming Ave N.W.
Washington, D.C. 20008
Tel. 202/232-4517 or -4528
http://www.Cyprusembassy.org.

Cyprus also has consulates in Chicago, Los Angeles, and New York.

Office of Children's Issues
U.S. Department of State
2201 C Street, NW
SA-29
Washington, DC 20520
Tel: 1-888-407-4747
E-mail: AskCI@state.gov
http://adoption.state.gov

For questions about immigration procedures, call the National Customer Service Center (NCSC) 1-800-375-5283 (TTY 1-800-767-1833).

CZECH REPUBLIC

Compiled from publications that were available as of February 2013 from the U.S. Department of State, the U.S. Department of Commerce, and the Central Intelligence Agency (CIA). See the introduction to this set for explanatory notes.

Official Name:
Czech Republic

PROFILE

Geography

Area: total: 78,867 sq km; country comparison to the world: 116; land: 77,247 sq km; water: 1,620 sq km
Major cities: Prague (capital) 1.162 million (2009)
Climate: temperate; cool summers; cold, cloudy, humid winters
Terrain: Bohemia in the west consists of rolling plains, hills, and plateaus surrounded by low mountains; Moravia in the east consists of very hilly country

People

Nationality: noun: Czech(s); adjective: Czech
Population: 10,177,300 (July 2012 est.)
Population growth rate: -0.134% (2012 est.)
Ethnic groups: Czech 90.4%, Moravian 3.7%, Slovak 1.9%, other 4% (2001 census)
Religions: Roman Catholic 26.8%, Protestant 2.1%, other 3.3%, unspecified 8.8%, unaffiliated 59% (2001 census)
Languages: Czech 94.9%, Slovak 2%, other 2.3%, unidentified 0.8% (2001 census)
Literacy: definition: NA; total population: 99%; male: 99%; female: 99% (2003 est.)
Health: life expectancy at birth: total population: 77.38 years; male: 74.11 years; female: 80.83 years (2012 est.); Infant mortality rate: total: 3.7 deaths/1,000 live births; male: 4.03 deaths/1,000 live births; female: 3.35 deaths/1,000 live births (2012 est.)
Unemployment rate: 8.6% (2012 est.)
Work force: 5.545 million (2012 est.)

Government

Type: parliamentary democracy
Independence: 1 January 1993
Constitution: ratified 16 December 1992, effective 1 January 1993; amended several times
Political subdivisions: 13 regions (kraje, singular—kraj) and 1 capital city (hlavni mesto); Jihocesky (South Bohemia), Jihomoravsky (South Moravia), Karlovarsky, Kralovehradecky, Liberecky, Moravskoslezsky (Moravia-Silesia), Olomoucky, Pardubicky, Plzensky (Pilsen), Praha (Prague), Stredocesky (Central Bohemia), Ustecky, Vysocina, Zlinsky
Suffrage: 18 years of age; universal

Economy

GDP (purchasing power parity): $286.7 billion (2012 est.); $288.6 billion (2011 est.); $283.9 billion (2010 est.); $276.3 billion (2009 est.)
GDP real growth rate: -1% (2012 est.); 1.7% (2011 est.); 2.7% (2010 est.); -4.7% (2009 est.)
GDP per capita (PPP): $27,200 (2012 est.); $27,400 (2011 est.); $27,000 (2010 est.); $26,400 (2009 est.)
Natural resources: hard coal, soft coal, kaolin, clay, graphite, timber
Agriculture products: wheat, potatoes, sugar beets, hops, fruit; pigs, poultry
Industries: motor vehicles, metallurgy, machinery and equipment, glass, armaments
Exports: $134.1 billion (2012 est.); $138.5 billion (2011 est.); $116.7 billion (2010 est.)
Exports—commodities: machinery and transport equipment, raw materials and fuel, chemicals
Exports—partners: Germany 32.4%, Slovakia 9%, Poland 6.3%, France 5.5%, Austria 4.6%, UK 4.6%, Italy 4.2% (2010 est.)
Imports: $129 billion (2012 est.); $133.2 billion (2011 est.); $113.9 billion (2010 est.)
Imports—commodities: machinery and transport equipment, raw materials and fuels, chemicals
Imports—partners: Germany 29.7%, China 7.6%, Poland 7.1%, Slovakia 7%, Netherlands 5.7%, Russia 4.8%, Austria 4.4% (2010 est.)
Debt—external: $90.18 billion (2012 est.); $101.6 billion (31 December 2011 est.); $95.4 billion (31 December 2010 est.)

Exchange rates: koruny (CZK) per US dollar; 19.59 (2012 est.); 17.696 (2011 est.); 19.098 (2010 est.); 19.063 (2009); 17.064 (2008); 20.53 (2007)

PEOPLE

The majority of the 10.5 million inhabitants of the Czech Republic are ethnically and linguistically Czech. Other ethnic groups include Germans, Roma, Vietnamese, and Poles.

National/Racial/Ethnic Minorities

Minority groups in the country included Roma, Ukrainians, Slovaks, Vietnamese, Poles, Russians, and Germans. Roma, who numbered approximately 200,000 experienced high levels of poverty, unemployment, and illiteracy and faced varying levels of discrimination in education, employment, and housing. Societal prejudice against the country's Romani population at times resulted in violence.

Members and sympathizers of neo-Nazi organizations were the most frequent perpetrators of acts of interethnic violence, particularly against Roma. The Workers' Party (DS), which was conspicuous for its hostility to Roma and other minorities, was banned in February 2010, but it was replaced by the Workers' Party for Social Justice (DSSS) soon afterward. DSSS and DS membership and leadership were virtually the same.

Language

The official language of the Czech Republic is Czech, part of the Slavic family of languages. Czechs have very strong linguistic abilities. Many older Czechs speak Russian, German, or English as second and third languages. Younger Czechs are more likely to speak English. Czech is an extremely difficult language to learn.

Religion

The population of 10.6 million is largely homogeneous with a dominant Christian tradition. In a 2011 opinion poll, 32 percent of respondents claimed to believe in God, while 42 percent stated they did not personally believe in God.

According to the 2011 census, there are 2.2 million religious believers in the country. Eleven percent of the population is Roman Catholic; 1.5 percent belongs to Protestant churches; 1.3 percent professes adherence to other religious faiths, including Judaism, Islam, and Buddhism; and 6.7 percent lists no specific religion. Eight percent of the population attends religious services regularly. Leaders of the local Muslim community estimate there are 15,000 Muslims in the country. There are approximately 3,100 persons officially registered as members of the Jewish community, although the overall Jewish population may be larger.

HISTORY

The Czech Republic was the western part of the Czech and Slovak Federal Republic. Formed into a common state after World War I (October 28, 1918), the Czechs, Moravians, and Slovaks remained united for almost 75 years. On January 1, 1993, the two republics split to form two separate states.

The Czechs lost their national independence to the Hapsburg Empire in 1620 at the Battle of White Mountain and for the next 300 years were ruled by the Austrian Monarchy. With the collapse of the monarchy at the end of World War I, the independent country of Czechoslovakia was formed, encouraged by, among others, U.S. President Woodrow Wilson.

Despite cultural differences, the Slovaks shared with the Czechs similar aspirations for independence from the Hapsburg state and voluntarily united with the Czechs. For historical reasons, Slovaks were not at the same level of economic and technological development as the Czechs, but the freedom and opportunity found in Czechoslovakia enabled them to make strides toward overcoming these inequalities. However, the gap never was fully bridged, and the discrepancy played a continuing role throughout the 75 years of the union.

Although Czechoslovakia was the only east European country to remain a parliamentary democracy from 1918 to 1938, it was plagued with minority problems, the most important of which concerned the country's large German population. Constituting more than 22% of the interwar state's population and largely concentrated in the Bohemian and Moravian border regions (the Sudetenland), members of this minority, including some who were sympathetic to Nazi Germany, undermined the new Czechoslovak state. Internal and external pressures culminated in September 1938, when France and the United Kingdom yielded to Nazi pressures at Munich and agreed to force Czechoslovakia to cede the Sudetenland to Germany.

Fulfilling Hitler's aggressive designs on all of Czechoslovakia, Germany invaded what remained of Bohemia and Moravia in March 1939, establishing a German "protectorate." By this time, Slovakia had already declared independence and had become a puppet state of the Germans. Hitler's occupation of the Czech lands was a clear betrayal of the Munich Pact and still stirs passions in modern-day Czech society, but at the time it was met by muted resistance; the brunt of Nazi aggression was felt by Czech Jews and other minorities who were rounded up and deported to concentration camps in systematic waves. Over 100,000 Jews lived in the Czech lands in 1939. Only several thousand remained or returned after the Holocaust in 1945.

At the close of World War II, Soviet troops overran all of Slovakia, Moravia, and much of Bohemia, including Prague. In May 1945, U.S. forces liberated the city of Plzen and most of western Bohemia. A civilian uprising against the German garrison took place in Prague in May 1945. Following Germany's surrender, some 2.9 million ethnic Germans were expelled from Czechoslovakia with Allied approval under the Benes

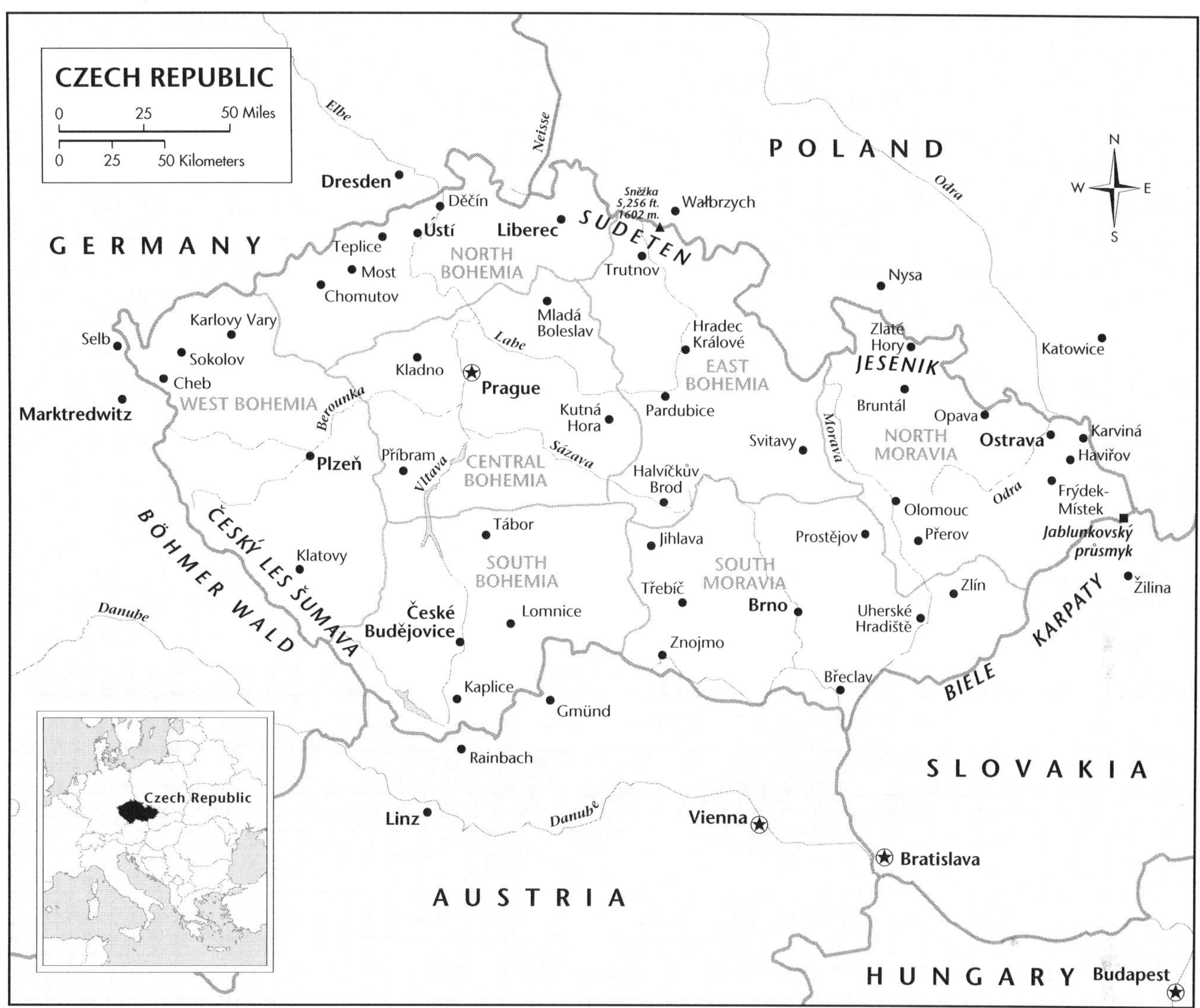

Decrees. Reunited after the war, the Czechs and Slovaks set national elections for the spring of 1946. The democratic elements, led by President Eduard Benes, hoped the Soviet Union would allow Czechoslovakia the freedom to choose its own form of government and aspired to a Czechoslovakia that would act as a bridge between East and West.

The Czechoslovak Communist Party, which won 38% of the vote, held most of the key positions in the government and gradually managed to neutralize or silence the anti-communist forces. Although the communist-led government initially intended to participate in the Marshall Plan, it was forced by Moscow to back out. Under the cover of superficial legality, the Communist Party seized power in February 1948. After extensive purges modeled on the Stalinist pattern in other east European states, the Communist Party tried 14 of its former leaders in November 1952 and sentenced 11 to death. For more than a decade thereafter, the Czechoslovak communist political structure was characterized by the orthodoxy of the leadership of party chief Antonin Novotny.

The 1968 Soviet Invasion

The communist leadership allowed token reforms in the early 1960s, but discontent arose within the ranks of the Communist Party central committee, stemming from dissatisfaction with the slow pace of the economic reforms, resistance to cultural liberalization, and the desire of the Slovaks within the leadership for greater autonomy for their republic. This discontent expressed itself with the removal of Novotny from party leadership in January 1968 and from the presidency in March. He was replaced as party leader by a Slovak, Alexander Dubcek.

After January 1968, the Dubcek leadership took practical steps toward political, social, and economic reforms. In addition, it called for politico-military changes in the Soviet-dominated Warsaw Pact and Council for Mutual Economic Assistance. The leadership affirmed its loyalty to socialism and the Warsaw Pact but also expressed the desire to improve relations with all countries of the world regardless of their social systems.

A program adopted in April 1968 set guidelines for a modern, humanistic socialist democracy that would guarantee, among other things, freedom of religion, press, assembly, speech, and travel; a program that, in Dubcek's words, would give socialism "a human face." After 20 years of little public participation, the population gradually started to take interest in the government, and Dubcek became a truly popular national figure.

The internal reforms and foreign policy statements of the Dubcek leadership created great concern among some other Warsaw Pact governments. On the night of August 20, 1968, Soviet, Hungarian, Bulgarian, East German, and Polish troops invaded and occupied Czechoslovakia. The Czechoslovak Government immediately declared that the troops had not been invited into the country and that their invasion was a violation of socialist principles, international law, and the UN Charter.

The principal Czechoslovak reformers were forcibly and secretly taken to the Soviet Union. Under obvious Soviet duress, they were compelled to sign a treaty that provided for the "temporary stationing" of an unspecified number of Soviet troops in Czechoslovakia. Dubcek was removed as party First Secretary on April 17, 1969, and replaced by another Slovak, Gustav Husak. Later, Dubcek and many of his allies within the party were stripped of their party positions in a purge that lasted until 1971 and reduced party membership by almost one-third.

The 1970s and 1980s became known as the period of "normalization," in which the apologists for the 1968 Soviet invasion prevented, as best they could, any opposition to their conservative regime. Political, social, and economic life stagnated. The population, cowed by the "normalization," was quiet.

The Velvet Revolution

The roots of the 1989 Civic Forum movement that came to power during the "Velvet Revolution" lie in human rights activism. On January 1, 1977, more than 250 human rights activists signed a manifesto called the Charter 77, which criticized the government for failing to implement human rights provisions of documents it had signed, including the state's own constitution; international covenants on political, civil, economic, social, and cultural rights; and the Final Act of the Conference for Security and Cooperation in Europe. Although not organized in any real sense, the signatories of Charter 77 constituted a citizens' initiative aimed at inducing the Czechoslovak Government to observe formal obligations to respect the human rights of its citizens.

On November 17, 1989, the communist police violently broke up a peaceful pro-democracy demonstration and brutally beat many student participants. In the days that followed, Charter 77 and other groups united to become the Civic Forum, an umbrella group championing bureaucratic reform and civil liberties. Its leader was the dissident playwright Vaclav Havel. Intentionally eschewing the label "party," a word given a negative connotation during the previous regime, Civic Forum quickly gained the support of millions of Czechs, as did its Slovak counterpart, Public Against Violence.

Faced with an overwhelming popular repudiation, the Communist Party all but collapsed. Its leaders, Husak and party chief Milos Jakes, resigned in December 1989, and Havel was elected President of Czechoslovakia on December 29. The astonishing quickness of these events was in part due to the unpopularity of the communist regime and changes in the policies of its Soviet guarantor as well as to the rapid, effective organization of these public initiatives into a viable opposition.

A coalition government, in which the Communist Party had a minority of ministerial positions, was formed in December 1989. The first free elections in Czechoslovakia since 1946 took place in June 1990 without incident and with more than 95% of the population voting. As anticipated, Civic Forum and Public Against Violence won landslide victories in their respective republics and gained a comfortable majority in the federal parliament. The parliament undertook substantial steps toward securing the democratic evolution of Czechoslovakia. It successfully moved toward fair local elections in November 1990, ensuring fundamental change at the county and town level.

Civic Forum found, however, that although it had successfully completed its primary objective—the overthrow of the communist regime—it was ineffectual as a governing party. The demise of Civic Forum was viewed by most as necessary and inevitable.

By the end of 1990, unofficial parliamentary "clubs" had evolved with distinct political agendas. Most influential was the Civic Democratic Party, headed by Vaclav Klaus, who later became Prime Minister. Other notable parties that came to the fore after the split were the Czech Social Democratic Party, Civic Movement, and Civic Democratic Alliance.

By 1992, Slovak calls for greater autonomy effectively blocked the daily functioning of the federal government. In the election of June 1992, Klaus's Civic Democratic Party won handily in the Czech lands on a platform of economic reform. Vladimir Meciar's Movement for a Democratic Slovakia emerged as the leading party in Slovakia, basing its appeal on fairness to Slovak demands for autonomy. Federalists, like Havel, were unable to contain the trend toward the split. In July 1992, President Havel resigned. In the latter half of 1992, Klaus and Meciar hammered out an agreement that the two republics would go their separate ways by the end of the year.

Members of the federal parliament, divided along national lines, barely cooperated enough to pass the law officially separating the two nations. The law was passed on December 27,

1992. On January 1, 1993, the Czech Republic and the Republic of Slovakia were simultaneously and peacefully founded.

Relationships between the two states, despite occasional disputes about the division of federal property and governing of the border, have been peaceful. Both states attained immediate recognition from the U.S. and their European neighbors.

GOVERNMENT AND POLITICAL CONDITIONS

The Czech Republic is a multiparty parliamentary democracy. Legislative authority is vested in the bicameral parliament, consisting of a Chamber of Deputies (Poslanecka snemovna) and Senate (Senat). The president, elected every five years by parliament, is head of state and appoints a prime minister from the majority party or coalition. In 2008 the bicameral parliament elected Vaclav Klaus as president for a second term. The elections for the Chamber of Deputies in May 2010 were considered free and fair, as were October 2010 elections for one-third of the seats in the Senate.

Recent Elections

In May 2010 the country held elections for seats in the Chamber of Deputies, the lower chamber of parliament. In October 2010 elections were held for one-third of the seats in the Senate and for municipal governments. Both elections were considered free and fair.

Participation of Women and Minorities: There were 45 women in the 200-seat Chamber of Deputies, including the speaker and two of three deputy speakers, and 15 women in the 81-seat Senate. There were two women in the 15-member cabinet. Fifteen percent of judges were women, including five women on the 15-member Constitutional Court. One of the country's 13 regional governors was a woman. One justice of the constitutional court was an ethnic Slovak. Few of the country's estimated 200,000 Roma were integrated into political life. No Roma were members of parliament, had cabinet portfolios, or sat on the Supreme Court. Some Roma were appointed to national and regional advisory councils dealing with Romani affairs.

Representatives from the 12 national minority groups were included in the 31-member Government Council for National Minorities, an advisory group that includes government officials. Each minority group may nominate up to three representatives to the council.

Principal Government Officials

Last Updated: 1/31/2013

Pres.: **Vaclav KLAUS**

Prime Min.: **Petr NECAS**

First Dep. Prime Min.: **Karel SCHWARZENBERG**

Dep. Prime Min.: **Karolina PEAKE**

Min. of Agriculture: **Petr BENDL**

Min. of Culture: **Alena HANAKOVA**

Min. of Defense

Min. of Education, Youth, & Sports: **Petr FIALA**

Min. of Environment: **Tomas CHALUPA**

Min. of Finance: **Miroslav KALOUSEK**

Min. of Foreign Affairs: **Karel SCHWARZENBERG**

Min. of Health: **Leos HEGER**

Min. of Industry & Trade: **Martin KUBA**

Min. of the Interior: **Jan KUBICE**

Min. of Justice: **Pavel BLAZEK**

Min. of Labor & Social Affairs: **Ludmila MULLEROVA**

Min. for Regional Development: **Kamil JANKOVSKY**

Min. of Transportation: **Zbynek STANJURA**

Min. Without Portfolio: **Petr MLSNA**

Governor, Czech National Bank: **Miroslav SINGER**

Ambassador to the US: **Petr GANDALOVIC**

Permanent Representative to the UN, New York: **Edita HRDA**

ECONOMY

The Czech Republic is a stable and prosperous market economy, which harmonized its laws and regulations with those of the EU prior to its EU accession in 2004. While the conservative, inward-looking Czech financial system has remained relatively healthy, the small, open, export-driven Czech economy remains sensitive to changes in the economic performance of its main export markets, especially Germany.

When Western Europe and Germany fell into recession in late 2008, demand for Czech goods plunged, leading to double digit drops in industrial production and exports. As a result, real GDP fell 4.7% in 2009, with most of the decline occurring during the first quarter. Real GDP, however, has slowly recovered with positive quarter-on-quarter growth starting in the second half of 2009 and continuing throughout 2011.

The auto industry remains the largest single industry, and, together with its upstream suppliers, accounts for nearly 24% of Czech manufacturing. The Czech Republic produced more than a million cars for the first time in 2010, over 80% of which were exported. Foreign and domestic businesses alike voice concerns about corruption especially in public procurement.

Other long term challenges include dealing with a rapidly aging population, funding an unsustainable pension and health care system, and diversifying away from manufacturing and toward a more high-tech, services-based, knowledge economy.

Labor Conditions

The minimum legal working age is 15. Employment conditions for children ages 15 to 18 were subject to strict standards of safety, permitted hours, and noninterference with education. Infringement of child labor rules is subject to fines of up to two million korunas ($103,000). The State Bureau for Labor Inspections (SBLI) effectively enforced these regulations. During the year the SBLI did not report any cases of child labor law violations.

The Ministry of Labor and Social Affairs establishes and enforces minimum wage standards. During 2011 the national minimum wage was 8,000 korunas ($410) per month. By comparison, the "Existence Minimum Cost," described as the minimum amount needed to satisfy the basic needs of a working-age adult for a month, was 2,200 korunas ($115). Enforcement of the minimum wage was one of the primary objectives of SBLI inspections.

The law provides for a 40-hour workweek, two days of rest per week, and a break of at least 30 minutes during the standard eight-hour workday. Employees are entitled to 20 days of paid annual leave. Employers may require up to eight hours per week of overtime to meet increased demand, but not more than 150 hours of overtime in a calendar year. Additional overtime is subject to the consent of the employee. Premium pay for overtime, equal to at least 125 percent of the average earnings, is governed by the provisions of the labor code.

According to the International Organization for Migration, the standard conditions of work were not always observed in situations involving migrant workers. Relatively unskilled foreign workers from less developed countries were sometimes dependent upon temporary employment agencies to find and retain work. According to trade unions and NGOs, migrants sometimes worked under substandard conditions and were subject to inhumane treatment by these agencies. Most commonly, salaries were paid to the agencies, which then garnished wages, resulting in workers receiving subminimum wages, working overtime without proper compensation, or working without any compensation at all. Since migrant workers seldom filed formal complaints of such abuses, authorities had fewer opportunities to intervene.

U.S.-CZECH RELATIONS

Czechoslovakia's communist regime fell in 1989, and the country split into two republics in 1993 — the Czech Republic and the Slovak Republic. Although the U.S. Government encouraged political and economic transformation in Czechoslovakia, it was initially opposed to the idea of the country forming two separate states, due to concerns that a split might aggravate existing regional political tensions.

The United States established diplomatic relations with the Czech Republic in 1993, and the Czech Republic made integration into Western institutions its chief foreign policy objective. Relations between the United States and the Czech Republic are excellent and reflect their common approach to the many challenges facing the world.

The Czech Republic is a member of the North Atlantic Treaty Organization (NATO) and the European Union (EU), and is an important and reliable ally in promoting U.S. interests. The two countries have worked together to strengthen security, promote economic development and democratic values, and defend basic human rights. The United States looks to the Czech Republic as a partner in issues ranging from Afghanistan to the Balkans, and seeks opportunities to continue to deepen the relationship.

U.S. Assistance to the Czech Republic

U.S. security assistance programs for the Czech Republic help secure the benefits of peace and stability for the Afghanistan region, and help support further participation by the Czech Republic in coalition operations alongside the United States in pursuit of mutual security interests and goals.

Bilateral Economic Relations

The Czech Republic is a member of the European Union. The U.S. economic relationship with the EU is the largest and most complex in the world, and the United States and the EU continue to pursue initiatives to create new opportunities for transatlantic commerce.

The United States and the Czech Republic have a bilateral investment treaty. Successive Czech governments have welcomed U.S. investment, and the United States has been one of the Czech Republic's top investors. Leading sectors for U.S. exports to and investment in the Czech Republic include automotive parts and equipment, education, energy, franchising, information technology, medical equipment, scientific equipment, EU-funded projects, and the agricultural sector. The Czech Republic participates in the Visa Waiver Program, which allows nationals of participating countries to travel to the United States for certain business or tourism purposes for stays of 90 days or less without obtaining a visa.

The Czech Republic's Membership in International Organizations

The Czech Republic and the United States belong to a number of the same international organizations, including the United Nations, North Atlantic Treaty Organization, Euro-Atlantic Partnership Council, Organization for Security and Cooperation in Europe, Organization for Economic Cooperation and Development, International Monetary Fund, World Bank, and World Trade Organization. The Czech Republic also is an observer to the Organization of American States.

Bilateral Representation

The Czech Republic maintains an embassy in the United States at 3900 Spring of Freedom Street, NW, Washington, DC 20008; tel. (202) 274-9101.

Principal U.S. Embassy Officials

Last Updated: 1/14/2013

PRAGUE (E) Trziste 15, 118 01 Praha 1, CR, (420) 257 022 000, Fax (420) 257 022 806, Workweek: 8:00–4:30 Monday-Friday, Website: http://prague.usembassy.gov/

DCM OMS:	Janice Green
AMB OMS:	Nelia Hill
Co-CLO:	Leslie Silkworth
DHS/ICE:	James Plitt (Vienna)
FCS:	Stuart Schaag
FM:	Robert Warner
HRO:	Jenny Traille
IBB:	Adam Gartner
MGT:	Erica Renew
POL/ECON:	William Silkworth
POSHO:	Robert Warner
SDO/DATT:	COL Patrick Sullivan
AMB:	Norman Eisen
CG:	Charles Jess
DCM:	Joseph Pennington
PAO:	Robert Zimmerman
GSO:	Jonathan Earle
RSO:	Teji Thiara
AGR:	Michael Henney (Resident In Warsaw)
CLO:	Cale McCausland
ECON:	Steven Butler
EST:	Smith, Alan
FMO:	Jenny Traille
ICASS Chair:	William Silkworth
IMO:	Eric Rose
IRS:	Barbara Franklin (Resident In Frankfurt)
LEGATT:	Paul Haertel
State ICASS:	William Silkworth

TRAVEL

Consular Information Sheet

January 30, 2012

Country Description: The Czech Republic is centrally located in the heart of Europe. It has a democratic parliamentary system of government and a well-developed economy. The Czech Republic is a member of NATO and the European Union. Tourist facilities in the capital city of Prague are at the level of those found in most European capitals, although travelers can expect varying standards outside of Prague.

Smart Traveler Enrollment Program (STEP)/Embassy Locations: If you are going to live in or visit the Czech Republic, please take the time to tell our Embassy about your trip. If you enroll, we can keep you up to date with important safety and security announcements. It will also help your friends and family get in touch with you in an emergency.

Local embassy information is available below:

The U.S. Embassy in Prague
Telephone: (420) 257 022 000
Emergency after-hours telephone: (420) 257 022 000
Fax: (420) 257 022 809

Entry/Exit Requirements: You need a valid passport to enter the Czech Republic. The Czech Republic is a party to the Schengen Agreement. This means that U.S. citizens may enter the Czech Republic and other Schengen member states for a total of up to 90 days for tourism or business purposes without a visa. Your passport should be valid for at least three months beyond your period of stay. For further details about travel to and within Schengen countries, please see our Schengen Fact Sheet.

Note: Although European Union regulations require that non-European Union visitors obtain a stamp in their passports upon initial entry to a Schengen country, many borders are not staffed with officers carrying out this function. If you wish to ensure that your entry is properly documented, you may need to request a stamp at an official point of entry. Under local law, travelers without a stamp in their passports may be questioned and asked to document the length of their stay in Schengen countries at the time of departure or at any other point during their visit, and could face possible fines or other repercussions if unable to do so.

You will need a visa for longer stays or to work or study in the Czech Republic. When a visa is required, it is important that you submit your application to the Embassy of the Czech Republic or the nearest Czech Consulate at least 3-4 months in advance of traveling to the Czech Republic. The Embassy of the Czech Republic's website provides the most current information on applying for a Czech visa. When a visa is required, we do not recommend departing for the Czech Republic without a valid visa. Please be aware that the U.S. Embassy is not able to expedite or help with the issuance of Czech visas in any way.The Czech Government requires travelers to the Czech Republic to have proof of finances to pay for their stay. All foreigners seeking entry into the Czech Republic must also carry proof of a medical insurance policy contracted for payment of all costs for hospitalization and medical treatment while in the Czech Republic. According to the Czech Government, if you have a health insurance card or an internationally recognized credit card with health insurance included, it will generally be accepted as proof of insurance to enter the country.

The U.S. Department of State is unaware of any HIV/AIDS entry restrictions for U.S. citizen visitors or U.S. citizen foreign residents in the Czech Republic.

Threats to Safety and Security: The Czech Republic remains largely free of terrorist incidents. However, like other countries in the Schengen Zone, the Czech Republic's open borders with its neighbors allow for the possibility of terrorist groups entering/exiting the country undetected. Civil disorder is rare in the Czech Republic, although strikes and demonstrations may occur. You should be vigilant in protecting your security, bearing in mind that even demonstrations intended to be peaceful may turn violent. Avoid street demonstrations whenever possible.

Stay up-to-date by:

- Bookmarking our Bureau of Consular Affairs website, which contains the current Travel Warnings and Travel Alerts as well as the Worldwide Caution;
- Following us on Twitter and Facebook;

- Downloading our free Smart Traveler iPhone App to have travel information at your fingertips; and
- Calling1-888-407-4747 toll-free within the U.S. and Canada, or a regular toll line, 1-202-501-4444, from other countries.

Take some time before you travel to improve your personal security—things often work differently outside the United States.

Crime: The Czech Republic generally has a low crime rate. However, pick-pocketing is a problem, especially in major tourist areas in Prague. Travelers are at a particularly high risk when:

- On public transportation (trains, trams or the Prague metro);
- In the city center;
- In crowded areas; and
- Eating at outdoor cafes.

As the individuals may operate in groups, and could conceivably be armed with simple weapons, victims should avoid direct confrontation with potential criminals. Pick-pocketing rings in the Czech Republic tend to be professional and highly organized.

Keep a copy of your passport biodata page (and any pages with valid visas) in a safe place separate from the passport itself; this can help you to apply for a new passport if yours is lost or stolen. Under Czech law, you must verify your identity by presenting a travel document, a residence permit card, or an identity card issued by the Ministry of Foreign Affairs, if asked by Czech police. If you are a tourist, this means that you are expected to carry your passport with you. Please ensure the security of your passport while traveling to prevent incidents of pick-pocketing or theft. Incidents of violent crime, while still relatively infrequent, are possible. U.S. citizens have reported incidents of sexual assault in recent years. You should be aware of the reported use of rohypnol and other "date rape" drugs in the Czech Republic. Use caution when accepting open drinks at bars or clubs, and don't leave your drinks unattended.

You should only change money at banks or legitimate money kiosks. An offer to change money by an unknown person on the street is most likely a scam. Automated Teller Machines (ATMs) are widely available throughout major cities in the Czech Republic. Most Czech ATMs offer instructions in multiple languages and allow access to U.S. bank accounts. The press has reported that criminal organizations are illegally obtaining users' ATM card numbers and PIN codes by electronically "skimming" the information from victims' cards at ATMs. This activity has reportedly occurred at ATMs in public areas— even bank lobbies covered by security cameras. Visitors requiring ATM services should attempt to use machines at more secure or heavily traveled and monitored locations, such as commercial banks, large hotels, and the airport.

American citizens have reported being overcharged by merchants on credit card transactions. Visitors to the Czech Republic should carefully verify that charges are correct before signing for purchases, keep all receipts, and check your credit card accounts online to ensure that you are billed properly for credit card payments.

Auto thefts and break-ins are common in the Czech Republic, especially in major cities. To avoid vehicle-related crimes, you should use parking garages and anti-theft devices. You should also not leave valuables in plain sight inside vehicles, as this increases the possibility of theft.

Czech bars and dance clubs are generally safe. However, as with many cities, you may be approached to purchase illicit drugs; this is against the law in the Czech Republic. Be mindful that security at nightclubs could respond more forcefully than at similar venues in the United States. Be aware that casinos and gaming establishments are government-regulated, but some have been affiliated with, or attracted the interest of, organized crime.

Taxis: You should be alert to the potential for substantial overcharging by taxis, particularly in areas frequented by tourists. Some taxi drivers charge unsuspecting foreigners two or three times the standard rate. To minimize the possibility of being overcharged, you should obtain a price estimate in advance and ensure that the driver is using the meter.

The Embassy has also received limited reports of passengers being assaulted or robbed by taxi drivers after hailing a random cab on the street. We strongly recommend that you call for a taxi, rather than hail one on the street. If calling is not possible, visitors should obtain a taxi at one of the clearly marked "Fair Place" taxi stands, which are regulated by the Prague city government. All taxis should be clearly marked.

Victims of Crime: If you or someone you know becomes the victim of a crime abroad, you should contact the local police and the U.S. Embassy. We can:

- Replace a stolen passport during regular business hours;
- Help you find appropriate medical care for violent crimes such as assault or rape;
- Put you in contact with the appropriate police authorities;
- Contact family members or friends; and
- Although local authorities are responsible for investigating and prosecuting the crime, Consular officers can help you understand the local criminal justice process and can provide you with a list of local attorneys.

The local equivalent to the "911" emergency line in the Czech Republic is 112. English-speaking assistance is not always available from the local police, but the police station located next to the Embassy at Vlašská # 3 usually has an English-speaker available.

Criminal Penalties: While you are traveling in the Czech Republic, you are subject to its laws even if you are a U.S. citizen. Foreign laws and legal systems can be vastly different from our own. The Czech Republic has a zero-tolerance policy for drinking and driving, and this is strictly enforced. Criminal penalties vary from country to country. There are also some things that might be legal in the country you visit, but still illegal in the United States; for instance, you can be prosecuted under U.S. law if you buy pirated goods. Don't buy counterfeit and pirated goods, even if they are widely available. Not only are the bootlegs illegal to bring back into the United States, by purchasing them you may also be breaking local law. Engaging in sexual conduct with children or using or disseminating child pornography in a foreign country is a crime prosecutable in the United States. If you break local laws in the Czech Republic, your U.S. passport won't help you avoid arrest or prosecution. It's very important to know what's legal and what's not where you are traveling.

If you are arrested in the Czech Republic, authorities are required to notify the U.S. Embassy in Prague of your arrest. If you are concerned the Embassy may not be aware of your situation, you should request the police or prison officials to notify the U.S. Embassy.

Special Circumstances: Czech customs authorities enforce strict regulations concerning temporary import or export of items such as firearms, antiquities, medications, business equipment, etc. You should contact the Embassy of the Czech Republic in Washington, D.C. or the Consulates General of the Czech Republic in New York or Los Angeles for specific information regarding customs requirements. For more information, please also see our Customs Information page. The Embassy is not able to assist with clearing goods through Czech Customs that have been mailed to private American citizens.

Accessibility: While in the Czech Republic, individuals may find accessibility and accommodation very different from what you find in the United States. The law prohibits discrimination against persons with disabilities in employment, education, access to health care, and the provision of other state services; the government generally enforces these provisions. Most buses and new tram cars are configured for special needs access, but only 60 percent of Prague's metro stations are accessible to persons with disabilities. Of 15 major metro stations in the city center, only five were barrier-free in 2011. Accessibility outside of Prague is generally less available.

Public Transportation: Passengers on public transportation should buy a ticket prior to boarding to avoid being fined. The ticket must be validated at the outset of the trip by inserting it into the yellow box found on trams and buses and in the entry halls of Metro stations. In Prague, ticket offices are located in many Metro stations. Tickets can also be purchased at tabak shops, newspaper stands, post offices, and from vending machines at all metro stations and at major tram stops. Those travelers who do not validate their tickets face the possibility of encountering an inspector at any time. The transportation inspectors operate in plainclothes, but should display a small metal badge (emblazoned with the words "P%u0159epravníKontrola") when inspecting travelers' tickets. Fines range from 50 to 950 CZK, but the standard on-the-spot payment for traveling without a valid ticket is 700 CZK. Inspectors should provide a receipt upon payment. Information on the types of tickets and pricing can be found here.

Medical Facilities and Health Information: Prague has adequate Western-style medical clinics with English-speaking doctors and dentists. However, the Czech medical system is organized differently from the medical system in the United States. Even though central emergency rooms exist in most hospitals, patients are often sent to the facility which treats the specific medical condition (i.e., broken noses are sent to the Ear, Nose, and Throat specialist rather than to the General Practitioner). There are family practices in the Czech Republic that function like those in the United States, but they are located mostly in larger cities.

All major hospitals accept credit cards or cash as a method of payment. Private specialists usually expect cash payment for health services, though some private facilities accept credit cards as well. Administrative staff at the majority of Czech medical facilities may not speak English. Hospitalization in the Czech Republic is much more liberal than in the United States; conditions that would be treated on an outpatient basis in the United States are often treated on an inpatient basis in the Czech Republic. Ambulance services are on par with U.S. standards. Response time is generally less than 15 minutes. Ambulance companies generally expect payment at the time of service. Serious medical problems requiring hospitalization and/or medical evacuation to the United States can cost thousands of dollars or more. Please note that because euthanasia is not permitted under Czech law, U.S. living wills stipulating no exceptional interventions to prolong life cannot be honored in the Czech Republic.

Tick-Borne Illness: If you plan to camp or hike in long grass or woodlands from March -October, you run the risk of both tick-borne encephalitis and Lyme disease. You should take precautions to prevent tick bites. While there is no vaccine for Lyme disease, you may obtain a vaccine for tick-borne encephalitis in a three-shot series. The first two shots are given 2-4 weeks apart, and the last shot 6 -12 months after the second. You can find good Information on vaccinations and other health precautions on the Centers for Disease Control (CDC) website. For information about outbreaks of infectious diseases abroad, consult the World Health Organization (WHO) website, which also contains additional health information for travelers, including detailed country-specific health information.

Medical Insurance: You can't assume your insurance will go with you when you travel. It's very important to find out BEFORE you leave whether or not your medical insurance will cover you overseas. You need to ask your insurance company two questions:

- Does my policy apply when I'm out of the United States?
- Will it cover emergencies like a trip to a foreign hospital or a medical evacuation?

In many places, doctors and hospitals still expect payment in cash at the time of service. Your regular U.S. health insurance may not cover doctor and hospital visits in other countries. If your policy doesn't cover you when you travel, you are strongly advised to take out another one for your trip. Please note that Medicaid/ Medicare does not apply outside the United States.For more information, please see our medical insurance overseas page.

Traffic Safety and Road Conditions: While in the Czech Republic, U.S. citizens may encounter road conditions that differ significantly from those in the United States. The information below concerning the Czech Republic is provided for general reference only, and may not be totally accurate in a particular location or circumstance.

Road fatalities in the Czech Republic in 2011 were at their lowest level since 1947, according to Czech safety experts, but caution should be exercised while driving. Driving speeds on European highways are higher than in the U.S., and drivers are expected to stay in the right lane except when passing. Highways in the Czech Republic generally meet European standards, however, on two-lane roads, drivers should be prepared to encounter uneven surfaces, irregular lane markings, and sign placements that are not clear. Streets in towns are not always in good condition. You should pay special attention to driving on cobblestone and among streetcars in historic city centers, especially in wet or icy conditions. Traffic lights are placed before the intersection, so be aware of where you stop at signaled intersections. Speed limits are 50 km/h in towns, 90 km/h outside of towns, and 130 km/h on highways, but drivers routinely flout the limits. An International Driving Permit (IDP), available from AAA (in the United States only), must accompany a U.S. driver's license; failure to have the IDP with a valid license may result in denial of an insurance claim after an accident. Persons driving into the Czech Republic should be aware that a toll sticker is required to drive legally on major highways. Signs stating this requirement are posted near the border, but are easy to miss. The stickers are available at most gas stations. The fine for failing to display a toll sticker is assessed on the spot. Czech law requires that drivers have their headlights on at all times when driving in the Czech Republic.

The law also requires that all private cars, including those of foreign visitors, carry each of the following items: fluorescent green high visibility safety jacket, first aid kit, spare pair of prescription glasses kept in the glove compartment (if necessary), warning triangle, and complete set of spare bulbs.

Czech law allows for breathalyzer testing of drivers stopped by local law enforcement officials for any reason. There is a zero-tolerance policy for alcohol and driving; driving with any trace of detected alcohol, however slight, is illegal and those caught usually face immediate fines and possible criminal proceedings. U.S. citizens have reported instances of motorists stopped on the shoulders of highways waving at drivers as if they needed assistance.

Some drivers have reported being pressured into giving money to the person who has purportedly broken down, and it was unclear in those situations if the motorist was truly in need or trying to scam those who stopped to offer assistance. For specific information concerning Czech requirements for driver's permits, vehicle inspection, road tax and mandatory insurance, please contact the Czech Tourist Authority offices in New York by telephone at (212) 288-0830 or by email. Also, we suggest that you visit the website of the Czech Republic's national tourist office and the Ministry of Transport.

Aviation Safety Oversight: The U.S. Federal Aviation Administration (FAA) has assessed the government of the Czech Republic's Civil Aviation Authority as being in compliance with International Civil Aviation Organization (ICAO) aviation safety standards for oversight of the Czech Republic's air carrier operations. Further information may be found on the FAA's safety assessment page.

Children's Issues: Please see the U.S. Dept. of State Office of Children's Issues web pages on intercountry adoption and international parental child abduction.

Intercountry Adoption

May 2011

The information in this section has been edited from the latest report available as of February 2013 from the State Department Bureau of Consular Affairs, Office of Overseas Citizens Services. For more information, please read the *Intercountry Adoption* section of this book and review current reports online at http://adoption.state.gov.

The Department of State does not maintain files on the intercountry adoption process from the Czech Republic because adoptions from the Czech Republic are rare; fewer than five adoptions by U.S. citizen parents have taken place since 2006. U.S. citizens adopting children in rare adoption cases from the Czech Republic, as well as U.S. citizen prospective adoptive parents living in the Czech Republic who plan to adopt from the United States or from a third country, should contact the Central Authority of the Czech Republic below to inquire about applicable laws and procedures.

Czech Republic's Central Authority for Adoption:
Úrad pro mezinárodne

právní ochranu detí
(Office for International Legal Protection of Children)
Silingrovo namestí ¾
60200 BRNO
Czech Republic
tel. & fax: +420 (5) 4221 2836
Internet: www.umpod.cz

International Parental Child Abduction

October 2012

The information in this section has been edited from a report from the State Department Bureau of Consular Affairs, Office of Overseas Citizens Services. For more information, please read the *International Parental Child Abduction* section of this book and check for updated reports online at www.travel.state.gov/abduction.

Disclaimer: The information in this flyer is provided for general information only, is not intended to be legal advice, and may change without notice. Questions involving interpretation of law should be addressed to an attorney licensed to practice in the relevant jurisdiction.

General Information: Czech Republic and the United States have been treaty partners under the 1980 Hague Convention on the Civil Aspects of International Child Abduction (Hague Abduction Convention) since March 1, 1998.

Hague Abduction Convention: The U.S. Department of State serves as the U.S. Central Authority (USCA) for the Hague Abduction Convention. Parents are strongly encouraged to contact the Department of State for assistance prior to initiating the Hague process directly with the foreign Central Authority.

United States Department of State
Office of Children's Issues
2201 C Street, N.W.
Washington, DC 20520
Telephone: 1-888-407-4747
Outside the United States or Canada: 1-202-501-4444
Fax: 202-736-9132

The Office for International Legal Protection of Children discharges the obligations of a central authority under the Hague Abduction Convention, including reviewing Hague applications for completeness, initiating location efforts for missing children, and approaching taking parties about whether or not abduction situations may be resolved voluntarily. The Czech Republic Central Authority (CCA) can be reached at:

Office for International Legal Protection of Children
Silingrovo namestí ¾
60200 BRNO
Czech Republic
Telephone: +420 (5) 4221 5522
Fax: +420 (5) 4221 2836
Internet: www.umpod.cz

To initiate a Hague case for return of, or access to, a child in Czech Republic, the USCA encourages a parent or legal guardian to review the eligibility criteria and instructions for completing the Hague application form.

Return: A parent or legal guardian may file an application under the Hague Abduction Convention for return to the United States of a child abducted to, or wrongfully retained in, Czech Republic. The U.S. Department of State can assist parents living in the United States to understand whether the Convention is an available civil remedy and can provide information on the process for submitting a Hague application.

Visitation/Access: A person may file an application under the Hague Abduction Convention for access to a child living in Czech Republic. The criteria for acceptance of a Hague access application vary from country to country. The U.S. Department of State can assist parents living in the United States to understand country-specific criteria and provide information on the process for submitting a Hague application.

Retaining an Attorney: The Czech system does not require parents to retain a private attorney in order to file a Hague Abduction Convention application with a court; however, the CCA recommends that parents have legal representation. Parents may hire a private attorney to assist them with their case and to advise them as to the best course of action for their individual circumstances. A privately hired attorney should contact the CCA and the USCA as soon as possible after the CCA receives the Hague Abduction Convention application. The CCA can provide referrals to assist applicants to find a private attorney or the applicants may represent themselves. The CCA's role is not to assign attorneys to cases but to facilitate the Hague process until such time as an attorney submits the Hague petition to the Czech court. The U.S. Embassy in Prague, Czech Republic, posts a list of attorneys including those who specialize in family law at: http://prague.usembassy.gov/acs_legal.html. This list is provided as a courtesy service only and does not constitute an endorsement of any individual attorney.

Mediation: Mediation may be available for both abduction and access cases. The CCA offers mediation services directly, in English, at no cost to parents. The CCA also provides referrals to private and non-governmental organizations that offer mediation services. Mediation in Czech Republic is voluntary and can occur at any stage of the Hague process.

U.S. Embassy Prague
Tržište 15
118 01 Praha 1 - Malá Strana
Czech Republic
Telephone: (+420) 257 022 000
Website:
http://prague.usembassy.gov/

Embassy of Czech Republic
3900 Spring of Freedom Street NW
Washington, D.C. 20008
Telephone: 202-274-9100
Email: Washington@embassy.mzv.cz
Website:
http://www.mzv.cz/washington/

DENMARK

Compiled from publications that were available as of February 2013 from the U.S. Department of State, the U.S. Department of Commerce, and the Central Intelligence Agency (CIA). See the introduction to this set for explanatory notes.

Official Name:
Kingdom of Denmark

PROFILE

Geography

Area: total: 43,094 sq km; country comparison to the world: 134; land: 42,434 sq km; water: 660 sq km

Major cities: Copenhagen (capital) 1.174 million (2009)

Climate: temperate; humid and overcast; mild, windy winters and cool summers

Terrain: low and flat to gently rolling plains

People

Nationality: noun: Dane(s); adjective: Danish

Population: 5,543,453 (July 2012 est.)

Population growth rate: 0.239% (2012 est.)

Ethnic groups: Scandinavian, Inuit, Faroese, German, Turkish, Iranian, Somali

Religions: Evangelical Lutheran (official) 95%, other Christian (includes Protestant and Roman Catholic) 3%, Muslim 2%

Languages: Danish, Faroese, Greenlandic (an Inuit dialect), German (small minority)

Literacy: definition: age 15 and over can read and write; total population: 99%; male: 99%; female: 99% (2003 est.)

Health: life expectancy at birth: total population: 78.78 years; male: 76.39 years; female: 81.31 years (2012 est.); Infant mortality rate: total: 4.19 deaths/1,000 live births; male: 4.25 deaths/1,000 live births; female: 4.12 deaths/1,000 live births (2012 est.)

Unemployment rate: 6.4% (2012 est.)

Work force: 2.848 million (2012 est.)

Government

Type: constitutional monarchy

Independence: ca. 965

Constitution: 5 June 1953; note—constitution allowed for a unicameral legislature and a female chief of state

Political subdivisions: metropolitan Denmark—5 regions (regioner, singular—region); Hovedstaden, Midtjylland, Nordjylland, Sjaelland, Syddanmark

Suffrage: 18 years of age; universal

Economy

GDP (purchasing power parity): $208.5 billion (2012 est.); $209.2 billion (2011 est.); $207.1 billion (2010 est.); $204.4 billion (2009 est.)

GDP real growth rate: -0.4% (2012 est.); 1.1% (2011 est.); 1.3% (2010 est.); -5.8% (2009 est.)

GDP per capita (PPP): $37,700 (2012 est.); $37,600 (2011 est.); $37,400 (2010 est.); $37,100 (2009 est.)

Natural resources: petroleum, natural gas, fish, salt, limestone, chalk, stone, gravel and sand

Agriculture products: barley, wheat, potatoes, sugar beets; pork, dairy products; fish

Industries: iron, steel, nonferrous metals, chemicals, food processing, machinery and transportation equipment, textiles and clothing, electronics, construction, furniture and other wood products, shipbuilding and refurbishment, windmills, pharmaceuticals, medical equipment

Exports: $110.8 billion (2012 est.); $111.7 billion (2011 est.); $95.77 billion (2010 est.)

Exports—commodities: machinery and instruments, meat and meat products, dairy products, fish, pharmaceuticals, furniture, windmills

Exports—partners: Germany 16.9%, Sweden 13.2%, UK 9.9%, Norway 5.7%, US 5.5%, Netherlands 4.9%, France 4.4% (2011)

Imports: $97.91 billion (2012 est.); $102.1 billion (2011 est.); $87.13 billion (2010 est.)

Imports—commodities: machinery and equipment, raw materials and semimanufactures for industry, chemicals, grain and foodstuffs, consumer goods

Imports—partners: Germany 20.8%, Sweden 13.6%, Netherlands 7.1%, UK 6.3%, China 6.3%, Norway 5.8% (2011)

Debt—external: $626.9 billion (30 June 2011); $559.5 billion (30 June 2010)

Exchange rates: Danish kroner (DKK) per US dollar; 5.847 (2012 est.); 5.3687 (2011 est.); 5.6241 (2010 est.); 5.361 (2009); 5.0236 (2008); 5.4797 (2007)

PEOPLE

The Danes, a homogeneous Gothic-Germanic people, have inhabited Denmark since prehistoric times. Danish is the principal language. English is a required school subject, and fluency is high. A small German-speaking minority lives in southern Jutland; a mostly Inuit population inhabits Greenland; and the Faroe Islands have a Nordic population with its own language. Education is compulsory from ages seven to 16 and is free through the university level.

Religion

Based on 2011 official statistics, approximately 80 percent of the population belongs to the ELC. Although only 2 to 3 percent of citizens attend services regularly, approximately 50 percent of them utilize the church at least once annually for baptisms, confirmations, weddings, funerals, and religious holidays.

As a result of immigration trends, the second largest religion is Islam, constituting approximately 4 percent of the population (approximately 230,000 individuals). Muslim communities tend to concentrate in the largest cities, particularly in Copenhagen, Odense, and Aarhus. Groups that constitute less than 1 percent of the population include (from largest to smallest): Catholics, Jehovah's Witnesses, Serbian Orthodox Christians, Jews, Baptists, Buddhists, members of The Church of Jesus Christ of Latter-day Saints (Mormons), and Pentecostals.

HISTORY

During the Viking period (9th-11th centuries), Denmark was a great power based on the Jutland Peninsula, the Island of Zealand, and the southern part of what is now Sweden. In the early 11th century, King Canute united Denmark and England for almost 30 years.

Viking raids brought Denmark into contact with Christianity, and in the 12th century, crown and church influence increased. By the late 13th century, royal power had waned, and the nobility forced the king to grant a charter, considered Denmark's first constitution. Although the struggle between crown and nobility continued into the 14th century, Queen Margrethe I succeeded in uniting Denmark, Norway, Sweden, Finland, the Faroe Islands, Iceland, and Greenland under the Danish crown. Sweden and Finland left the union in 1520; however, Norway remained until 1814. Iceland, in a "personal union" under the king of Denmark after 1918, became independent in 1944.

The Reformation was introduced in Denmark in 1536. Denmark's provinces in today's southwestern Sweden were lost in 1658, and Norway was transferred from the Danish to the Swedish crown in 1814, following the defeat of Napoleon, with whom Denmark was allied.

The Danish liberal movement gained momentum in the 1830s, and in 1849 Denmark became a constitutional monarchy. After the war with Prussia and Austria in 1864, Denmark was forced to cede Schleswig-Holstein to Prussia and adopt a policy of neutrality. Toward the end of the 19th century, Denmark inaugurated important social and labor market reforms, laying the basis for the present welfare state.

Denmark remained neutral during World War I. Despite its declaration of neutrality at the beginning of World War II, it was invaded by the Germans in 1940 and occupied until liberated by the Allied forces in May 1945. Resistance against the Germans was sporadic until late 1943. By then better organized, the resistance movement and other volunteers undertook a successful rescue mission in which nearly the entire Jewish population of Denmark was shipped to Sweden (whose neutrality was honored by Germany). However, extensive studies are still being undertaken for the purpose of establishing a clearer picture of the degree of Danish cooperation—official and corporate—with the occupying power. Denmark became a charter member of the United Nations and was one of the original signers of the North Atlantic Treaty.

Cultural Achievements

Denmark's rich intellectual heritage has made multifaceted contributions to modern culture. The discoveries of astronomer Tycho Brahe (1546-1601), the work of geologist, anatomist, and bishop Blessed Niels Steensen (1639-86—beatified in 1988 by Pope John Paul II), and the contributions of Nobel laureates Niels Bohr (1885-1962) to atomic physics and Niels Finsen (1860-1904) to medical research indicate the range of Danish scientific achievement.

The fairy tales of Hans Christian Andersen (1805-75), the philosophical essays of Soeren Kierkegaard (1813-55), and the short stories of Karen Blixen (pseudonym Isak Dinesen; 1885-1962) have earned international recognition, as have the symphonies of Carl Nielsen (1865-1931). Danish applied art and industrial design have won many awards for excellence, with the term "Danish Design" becoming synonymous with high quality, craftsmanship, and functionalism.

Among the leaders in architecture and design was Arne Jacobsen (1902-1971), the "father of modern Danish design." Georg Jensen (1866-1935) was known for outstanding modern design in silver, and "Royal Copenhagen" is among the finest porcelains.

Entertainer and pianist Victor Borge (1909-2000), who emigrated to the

United States under Nazi threat in 1940 and became a naturalized U.S. citizen, had a worldwide following.The Danish Film Institute, one of the oldest in Scandinavia, holds daily public screenings of Danish and international movies in their original language and works to maintain and restore important archival prints. Movie directors who have won international acclaim include Gabriel Axel (Babette's Feast, 1987 Oscar for Best Foreign Film), Bille August (Buster's World, 1984; Pelle the Conqueror, 1988 Oscar for Best Foreign Film; The House of the Spirits, 1993), Lars von Trier (Breaking the Waves, 1996; Dancer in the Dark, 2000 Cannes Golden Palm; and Antichrist 2009, Nordic Council's Film Prize 2009), and Susanne Bier (In a Better World, 2011 Golden Globe for Best Foreign Language Film). Danes became involved early on in the "Dogma film" genre's development, in which small, hand-held digital cameras permitted greater rapport between director and actor and gave a documentary film feel to increasingly realistic works. Examples of the Dogma concept include von Trier's The Idiots (1998) and Dogville (2003, starring Nicole Kidman), Thomas Vinterberg's The

Celebration (1998 Cannes Special Jury prize), Soeren Kragh-Jacobsen's Mifune's Last Song (1999 Berlin Silver Bear award), and Lone Scherfig's Italian for Beginners (2000 Berlin Silver Bear award). Mads Mikkelsen is one of Denmark's best-known actors internationally, with film roles in King Arthur (2004), Casino Royale (2006), After the Wedding (2006, which was nominated for an Oscar), and Clash of The Titans (2010).

The Louisiana Museum north of Copenhagen, "Arken" south of Copenhagen, and the North Jutland Art Museum in Aalborg showcase international collections of modern art. The State Museum of Art and the Glyptotek, both in Copenhagen, contain masterpieces of Danish and international art.

Denmark's National Museum building in central Copenhagen holds most of the state's anthropological and archeological treasures, with notable prehistoric and Viking Age collections; two of its best satellite collections are the Viking Ship Museum in Roskilde west of the metropolis and the Open Air Museum in a nearby northern suburb, where buildings have been transported from their original locations around the country and reassembled on plots specially landscaped to evoke the original site.

The Museum of Applied Art and Industrial Design in Copenhagen exhibits the best in Danish design. The internationally-known Royal Copenhagen Porcelain Factory exports worldwide. Danish ceramic designers have included Bjoern Wiinblad, whose whimsical creations first appeared in the 1950s, Gertrude Vasegaard, and Michael Geertsen. Denmark has a number of impressive castles, many of which have been converted to museums.

Frederiksborg Castle, on a manmade island in a lake north of Copenhagen, was restored after a catastrophic fire in the 1800s and features important collections and manicured gardens. Kronborg (or Hamlet's) Castle in Helsingoer (Elsinore), which once exacted tribute from passing ships, holds furniture and art collections of the period and hosts touring summer productions of Shakespearean works. Copenhagen's Rosenborg Castle, with public gardens in the heart of the city, houses the kingdom's crown jewels.

For American readers, probably the best-known contemporary Danish writer is Peter Hoeg (Smilla's Sense of Snow; Borderliners). Poems by poet, novelist, playwright, and screenwriter Klaus Rifbjerg and by poet, short-story writer, and composer Benny Andersen have been translated into English by Curbstone Press.

Suzanne Broegger's works focus on the changing roles of women in society. Kirsten Thorup's "Baby" won the 1980 Pegasus Prize and was printed in English by the University of Louisiana Press. The psychological thrillers of Anders Bodelsen and political thrillers by Leif Davidsen also appear in English. In music, Hans Abrahamsen and Per Noergaard are two well-known composers, and Abrahamsen's works have been performed by the National Symphony Orchestra in Washington, DC.

Other international names are Poul Ruders, Bo Holten, and Karl Aage Rasmussen. Danes such as bass player Niels Henning Oersted Petersen have won broad international recognition, and the Copenhagen Jazz Festival held each year in July attracts international jazz enthusiasts. Rock and roll band Metallica's drummer, Lars Ulrich, is Danish.

The Royal Danish Ballet specializes in the work of Danish choreographer August Bournonville (1805-79). Danish dancers also feature regularly on the U.S. ballet scene, notably Peter Martins as head of New York City Ballet.

Cultural Policy

The Ministry of Cultural Affairs was created in 1961. Cultural life and meaningful leisure time were then and remain now subjects of debate by politicians and parliament as well as the general public.

The democratization of cultural life promoted by the government's 1960s cultural policy has come to terms with the older "genteel culture;" broader concepts of culture now generally accepted include amateur and professional cultural, media, sports, and leisure-time activities.

Denmark's cultural policy is characterized by decentralized funding, program responsibility, and institutions. Danish cultural direction differs from that of other countries with a Ministry of Culture and a stated policy in that special laws govern each cultural field—e.g., the Theater Act of 1990 (as amended) and the Music Law of 1976 (as amended).

The Ministry of Cultural Affairs includes among its responsibilities international cultural relations; training of librarians and architects; copyright legislation; and subsidies to archives, libraries, museums, literature, music, arts and crafts, theater, and film production. During 1970-82, the Ministry also recognized protest movements and street manifestations as cultural events, because social change was viewed as an important goal of Danish cultural policy. Danish governments exercise caution in moderating this policy and practice. Radio and TV broadcasting also fall under the Ministry of Culture.

Government expenditures for culture totaled just over 1.0% of the public budget in 2008 and government expenditures for culture totaled 0.33% of gross domestic product (GDP). Viewed against the government's firm objective to limit public expenditures, contributions are unlikely to increase in the future and have remained about $1.2 billion for the last couple of years.

Municipal and county governments assume a relatively large share of the costs for cultural activities in their respective districts, 57% to the government's 43%. Most support goes to libraries and archives, theater, museums, arts and crafts training, and films.

Foundations

Large, private foundations play an important part in supporting the spectrum of cultural activities from supporting struggling young artists to paying for large-scale restoration work, operating museums, and supporting scientific research.

Private organizations such as the New Carlsberg Foundation, the Velux Foundation, and the Augustinus Foundation enjoy an almost semi-public stature due to their long records of working for the public good. U.S.-style corporate sponsorship of the arts is very limited in Denmark.

GOVERNMENT AND POLITICAL CONDITIONS

The Kingdom of Denmark is a constitutional monarchy with democratic parliamentary rule. Queen Margrethe II is head of state. A prime minister, usually the leader of the majority party or coalition, is head of government and presides over the cabinet, which is accountable to a unicameral parliament (Folketing). Elections on September 15, 2011, which observers deemed free and fair, gave a plurality to a left-of-center coalition led by the Social Democratic Party.

The territories of Greenland and the Faroe Islands have democratically elected home rule governments whose powers may encompass all matters except foreign and national security affairs, police services, and monetary matters. Greenlanders and Faroese have the same rights throughout the kingdom as other citizens. Each territory elects two representatives to the Danish parliament.

Recent Elections

Free and fair parliamentary elections took place on September 15, 2011. They gave a plurality to a left-of-center coalition led by the Social Democratic Party.

Participation of Women and Minorities: Following the September 15 elections, there were 70 women in the 179-seat parliament, and nine in the 23-seat cabinet. Following municipal and regional elections in November 2009, 32 percent of the members of municipal councils and 35 percent of the members of regional councils were women.

Four citizens of other than Danish, Greenlandic, or Faroese origin were elected to the parliament in the 2011 elections. There was one member of an ethnic minority in the 23-seat cabinet. In the November 2009 municipal elections, 65 persons of non-Danish ethnic origin were elected to municipal councils.

Principal Government Officials

Last Updated: 1/31/2013

Queen: **MARGRETHE II**
Prime Min.: **Helle THORNING-SCHMIDT**
Dep. Prime Min.: **Margrethe VESTAGER**
Min. of Agriculture, Food, & Fisheries: **Mette GJERSKOV**
Min. of Business Affairs & Growth: **Annette VILHELMSEN**
Min. of Children & Education: **Christine ANTORINI**
Min. of Climate, Energy, & Construction: **Martin LIDEGAARD**
Min. of Cultural Affairs: **Marianne JELVED**
Min. of Defense: **Nick HAEKKERUP**
Min. for Development Cooperation: **Christian Friis BACH**
Min. of Ecclesiastical Affairs: **Manu SAREEN**
Min. of Economic Affairs: **Margrethe VESTAGER**
Min. of Employment: **Mette FREDERIKSEN**
Min. of Environment: **Ida AUKEN**
Min. of Equality: **Manu SAREEN**
Min. of European Cooperation: **Nicolai WAMMEN**
Min. of Finance: **Bjarne CORYDON**
Min. of Foreign Affairs: **Villy SOVNDAL**
Min. of Health & Prevention: **Astrid KRAG**
Min. of Interior Affairs: **Margrethe VESTAGER**
Min. of Justice: **Morten BODSKOV**
Min. of Nordic Cooperation: **Manu SAREEN**
Min. of Research, Innovation, & Continuing Education: **Morten OSTERGAARD**
Min. of Social Affairs & Integration: **Karen HAEKKERUP**
Min. of Taxation: **Holger NIELSEN**
Min. of Towns, Housing, & Rural Affairs: **Carsten HANSEN**
Min. of Trade & Investment: **Pia Olsen DYHR**
Min. of Transport: **Henrik Dam KRISTENSEN**
Chmn., Board of Governors, Danish National Bank: **Nils BERNSTEIN**
Ambassador to the US: **Peter TAKSOE-JENSEN**
Permanent Representative to the UN, New York: **Carsten STAUR**

ECONOMY

This thoroughly modern market economy features a high-tech agricultural sector, state-of-the-art industry with world-leading firms in pharmaceuticals, maritime shipping and renewable energy, and a high dependence on foreign trade.

Denmark is a member of the European Union (EU); Danish legislation and regulations conform to EU standards on almost all issues. Danes enjoy a high standard of living and the Danish economy is characterized by extensive government welfare measures and an equitable distribution of income.

Denmark is a net exporter of food and energy and enjoys a comfortable balance of payments surplus but depends on imports of raw materials for the manufacturing sector. Within the EU, Denmark is among the strongest supporters of trade liberalization. After a long consumption-driven upswing, Denmark's economy began slowing in 2007 with the end of a housing boom. Housing prices dropped markedly in 2008–09 and, following a short respite in 2010, has since continued to decline.

The global financial crisis has exacerbated this cyclical slowdown through increased borrowing costs and lower export demand, consumer confidence, and investment. The global financial crises cut Danish real GDP in 2008–09. Denmark made a modest recovery in 2010 with real GDP growth of 1.3%, in part because of increased government spending; however, the country experienced a technical recession in late 2010–early 2011.

Historically low levels of unemployment rose sharply with the recession and have remained at about 6% in 2010–12, based on the national measure, about two-thirds average EU unemployment. An impending decline in the ratio of workers to retirees will be a major long-term issue. Denmark maintained a healthy budget surplus for many years up to 2008, but the budget balance swung into deficit in 2009.

In spite of the deficits, the new coalition government delivered a modest stimulus to the economy in 2012. Nonetheless, Denmark's fiscal position remains among the strongest in the EU with public debt at about 45% of GDP in 2012. Despite previously meeting the criteria to join the European Economic and Monetary Union (EMU), so far Denmark has decided not to join, although the Danish krone remains pegged to the euro.

Denmark held the EU presidency during the first half of 2012; priorities included promoting a responsible, dynamic, green, and safe Europe, while working to steer Europe out of its euro zone economic crisis.

Labor Conditions

The law prohibits the exploitation of children in the workplace, and the government effectively enforced this prohibition in practice. There were no reported instances of unlawful child labor.

The minimum legal age for full-time employment is 15 years. The law sets a minimum age for part-time employment of 13 years and limits school-age children to less strenuous tasks. The law limits work hours and sets occupational health and safety restrictions for children, and the government effectively enforced these laws in practice. The law does not mandate a national minimum wage; unions and employer associations negotiate minimum wages. The average minimum wage for all private and public sector collective bargaining agreements was 109 kroner (approximately $19) per hour, exclusive of pension benefits. Migrant workers are entitled to the same minimum wages and working conditions, and must adhere to the same employment regulations, as Danes.

Workers generally worked a 37.5-hour week, established by contract rather than by law. Workers received premium pay for overtime, and there was no compulsory overtime. Working hours were determined by collective bargaining agreements that adhered to the EU directive that an average workweek not exceed 48 hours. These agreements also guarantee workers at least five weeks' paid vacation per year.

The law prescribes conditions of work, including safety and health standards; authorities ensured compliance with labor legislation in practice. The same laws protect legal migrants and foreign workers.

U.S.-DANISH RELATIONS

Denmark and the United States have long enjoyed a close and mutually beneficial relationship. The two countries consult closely on European and other regional political and security matters and cooperate extensively to promote peace and stability well beyond Europe's borders. Denmark largely shares U.S. views on the positive ramifications of North Atlantic Treaty Organization (NATO) enlargement. Danish troops support International Security Assistance Force-led stabilization efforts in Afghanistan.

The U.S. Air Force base and early warning radar facility at Thule, in northwest Greenland, serves as a vital link in Western and NATO defenses. In 2004, the Danish and Greenland Home Rule governments signed agreements allowing for an upgrade of the Thule early warning radar in connection with a role in the U.S. ballistic missile defense system. The same agreements also created new opportunities for both sides to enhance economic, technical, and environmental cooperation between the United States and Greenland.

American culture—and particularly popular culture, from jazz, rock, and rap to television shows and literature—is very popular in Denmark. More than 300,000 U.S. tourists visit Denmark annually.

Bilateral Economic Relations

Denmark's active liberal trade policy in the European Union (EU), Organization for Economic Cooperation and Development, and World Trade Organization largely coincides with U.S. interests. There have been differences of opinion between the U.S. and the EU on how to manage and resolve recent global and regional financial crises, but not on the importance of action.

Denmark's role in European environmental and agricultural issues and its strategic location at the entrance to the Baltic Sea have made Copenhagen a center for U.S. agencies and the private sector dealing with the Nordic/Baltic region.

The U.S. is Denmark's largest non-European trade partner. Among major Danish exports to the United States are industrial machinery, chemical products, furniture, pharmaceuticals, canned ham and pork, windmills, and plastic toy blocks (Lego).

In addition, Denmark has a significant services trade with the U.S., a major share of it stemming from Danish-controlled ships engaged in container traffic to and from the United States (notably by Maersk-Line). Over 400 U.S. companies have subsidiaries in Denmark.

Denmark's Membership in International Organizations

Danish foreign policy is founded upon four cornerstones: the United Nations, NATO, the EU, and Nordic cooperation. Denmark and the United States belong to a number of the same international organizations, including the UN, NATO, the Organization for Security and Cooperation in Europe, Organization for Economic Cooperation and Development, International Monetary Fund, World Bank, and World Trade Organization.

Bilateral Representation

Denmark maintains an embassy at 3200 Whitehaven Street NW, Washington, DC 20008-3683 (tel. 202-234-4300). Danish consulates general are located in Chicago and New York.

Principal U.S. Embassy Officials

Last Updated: 1/14/2013

COPENHAGEN (E) Dag Hammerskjolds Alle 24, 2100 Copenhagen, Denmark, +45 3341 7100, Fax +45 3543 0223, INMARSAT Tel +1 8816-314-39096, Workweek: 8:30 am until 5:00 pm, Website: http://denmark.usembassy.gov/

DCM OMS:	Michelle Stokes
AMB OMS:	Christine Kucera
DHS/ICE:	Vacant
MGT:	Jonathan Bayat
POL/ECON:	Diana Brown
POSHO:	Daniel McManus
SDO/DATT:	CAPT Alistair Borchert
AMB:	Laurie S. Fulton
CON:	Jonathan Webster
DCM:	Stephen Cristina
PAO:	Robert Kerr
GSO:	Daniel McManus
RSO:	Dimas Jaen
AGR:	Steve Heute (Res. The Hague) X 482
CLO:	Ewa Dickson
DEA:	Christopher Urban
EEO:	Michelle Stokes
EST:	Edward Canuel
ICASS Chair:	Bjarke Frederiksen
IMO:	Anup Shah
IPO:	Anup Shah
ISSO:	Will Dickson
LEGATT:	Johannes Vandenhoogen
State ICASS:	Robert Kerr

TRAVEL

Consular Information Sheet

April 16, 2012

Country Description: The Kingdom of Denmark is a highly developed, stable democracy with a modern economy. Greenland is a self-governing part of the Kingdom of Denmark, and the Faroe Islands have home rule within the Kingdom of Denmark.

Smart Traveler Enrollment Program (STEP)/Embassy Locations: If you are going to live in or visit Denmark, please take the time to tell us about your trip. If you enroll, we can keep you up to date with important safety and security announcements. It will also help us get in touch with your friends and family in an emergency.

United States Embassy in Denmark
Dag Hammarskjölds Allé 24
2100 Copenhagen
Telephone: 45 3341 7100
Emergency after-hours telephone: 45 3341 7400
Fax: 45 3538 9616

Entry/Exit Requirements for U.S. Citizens: Denmark is a party to the Schengen Agreement. You may enter the country for up to 90 days on your U.S. passport for tourist or business purposes without a visa. Your passport should be valid for at least three months beyond your period of stay. More information about travel into and within Schengen countries can be found on our Schengen Fact Sheet. Visit the Danish Embassy in Washington's website for the most current visa information. Another source of useful information, available in both English and Danish, is the Danish Immigration Service website.

If you are coming to Denmark to study, your student visa will allow you to enter Denmark 14 days prior to the start of your study program and remain for 14 days after the end of your program. These days are non-transferrable, meaning if you enter the Schengen zone only ten days before the start of your student visa's validity, you may not add four extra days to the 14 days that you may stay after your visa has expired. Your Danish student visa is a Schengen visa which will allow you to travel in the Schengen zone for the period of validity. It does not allow you to travel to other Schengen countries after the end of the 14 days of lawful travel, and you cannot immediately benefit from the 90 day visa-free tourist travel at the end of your study period.

Greenland and the Faroe Islands are not party to the Schengen Agreement. However, you may travel to those places for 90 days for business or tourism without a visa. Residence and work permits issued exclusively for Greenland or the Faroe Islands are not valid for travel to Schengen countries.

The U.S. Department of State is unaware of any HIV/AIDS entry restrictions for visitors to or foreign residents of Denmark.

Threats to Safety and Security: Denmark remains largely free of terrorist incidents; however, like other Western European nations, Denmark faces an increased threat of terrorism. In the past year, the police arrested individuals accused of planning terrorist attacks in Denmark. In particular, the 2005 publishing of cartoons of the Prophet Muhammad continues to impact Danish relations with the Muslim world and draw the attention of extremists. The Department of State recently re-issued the Worldwide Caution which includes information about the potential for terrorists attacks in Europe.

As with other countries in the Schengen area, Denmark's open borders allow for the possibility of terrorist groups entering and exiting the country with anonymity. You are reminded to remain vigilant with regard to your personal security and to exercise caution. In general, Copenhagen is a safe city. However, certain areas pose more of a threat than others, and you should avoid downtown Vesterbro and Nørrebro late at night. Public demonstrations occasionally occur in Copenhagen and other cities, and are generally peaceful events. Prior police approval is required for public demonstrations, and police oversight is routinely provided to ensure adequate security for participants and passers-by. Nonetheless, as with any large crowd composed of diverse groups, situations may develop which could pose a threat to public safety. You should avoid areas where public demonstrations are taking place. Be aware that participation in illegal demonstrations or street riots may result in immediate imprisonment and long-term bans on re-entering Denmark.

Stay up to date by:

- Bookmarking our Bureau of Consular Affairs website, which contains the current Travel Warnings and Travel Alerts as well as the Worldwide Caution;
- Following us on Twitter and the Bureau of Consular Affairs page on Facebook;.
- Downloading our free Smart Traveler iPhone App to have travel information at your fingertips;
- Calling 1-888-407-4747 toll-free within the U.S. and Canada, or a regular toll line, 1-202-501-4444, from other countries; and,
- Taking some time before travel to consider your personal security.

Crime: Denmark, Greenland, and the Faroes all have relatively low violent-crime rates. Muggings, sexual assault, and racially motivated violence are rare. Violent confrontations occasionally take place between the various immigrant gangs and outlaw motorcycle gangs operating in Denmark. The confrontations do not typically affect tourists and law-abiding Danish citizens, but there is always a possibility that travelers could be caught in the wrong place at the wrong time. Travellers should be aware of their surroundings and immediately leave the area if they feel threatened. Be particularly vigilant in the Nørrebro and Vesterbro areas of Copenhagen. Pickpockets and purse-snatchers operate mainly at train stations—the Copenhagen Central Station in particular—and on crowded trains or buses. Sophisticated thieves target the Copenhagen Airport and cruise ship quays. The best precaution is to keep an eye on your belongings at all times. Do not put any bags containing valuables, such as your passport, credit cards, and airline tickets, down on the ground or on the back of a chair. Watch your computer bag, which is particularly desirable. Popular tourist attractions, like shopping streets and restaurants, also attract pickpockets and thieves. Hotel lobbies and breakfast rooms attract professional, well-dressed criminals who blend in with guests and target purses and briefcases left unguarded by unsuspecting tourists and business travelers.

Pickpockets and purse-snatchers often work in pairs or groups with one person distracting the victim while another grabs the valuables. Since car and home break-ins have become more prevalent in recent years, we strongly recommend that you not leave any valuables in parked vehicles.

Don't buy counterfeit and pirated goods, even if they are widely available. Not only are the bootlegs illegal in the United States, if you purchase them, you may also be breaking local law.

Victims of Crime: If you or someone you know becomes the victim of a crime abroad, you should contact the local police and the nearest U.S. embassy or consulate. We can:

- Replace a stolen passport.
- Help you find appropriate medical care if you are the victim of violent crimes such as assault or rape.
- Put you in contact with the appropriate police authorities, and if you want us to, we can contact family members or a friend.
- Help you understand the local criminal justice process and direct you to local attorneys, although it is important to remember that local authorities are responsible for investigating and prosecuting the crime.

Denmark has a program to provide financial compensation to victims who suffer serious injuries due to crime. The victim must report the incident to the police within 24 hours. Danish police routinely inform victims of serious crime of their right to seek compensation.

The relevant forms are available from the police or from the Danish Criminal Injuries Compensation Board, Gyldenløvesgade 11, 1600 Copenhagen V. TEL: 45-3392 3334; FAX: 45-3920 4505. Claim processing time is a minimum of three months. While there is no maximum award limit, victim compensation payments are generally far lower than equivalent payments in the United States, given Denmark's social welfare coverage. More information about compensation payments to victims of serious crime is available at the Compensation Board's website.

The local equivalent to the "911" emergency line in Denmark is 112.

Criminal Penalties: While you are traveling in Denmark, you are subject to Danish laws. Foreign laws and legal systems can be vastly different from our own. In Denmark, the police may take you in for questioning if you violate the law and don't have proper identification with you. However, most forms of identification, such as student ID or driver's license, are acceptable, and there is no legal requirement for foreigners to carry their passports.

Under Danish law, the police are permitted to detain someone for up to eight hours without charge. In addition, possessing knives with a locking blade longer than seven centimeters in a public place carries an immediate jail sentence. Some activities may be legal in Denmark, but are illegal in the United States. For instance, you can be prosecuted under U.S. law if you buy pirated goods.

Engaging in sexual conduct with minors under U.S. law and using or disseminating child pornography is a crime prosecutable in the United States. If you break local laws in Denmark, your U.S. passport won't help you avoid arrest or prosecution. It's very important to know what is legal at your travel destination.

Greenland has very strict laws on the removal of natural resources, including precious and semi-precious metals, stones, and gemstones found there. Before attempting to extract or export any of these materials, make certain that it is not against the law.

Persons violating Denmark's laws, even unknowingly, may be expelled, arrested, or imprisoned. Penalties for possessing, using, or trafficking in illegal drugs in Denmark are severe, and convicted offenders can expect long jail sentences and heavy fines, depending on the drug type. The possession of heroin, speed, ecstacy, cocaine, etc. will, in most cases, result in a jail sentence. A tourist's possession of smaller amounts of marijuana or hashish for personal use will in most cases result in a warning or deportation. For larger quantities and trafficking, jail sentences are likely.

Based on the Vienna Convention on Consular Relations, bilateral agreements with certain countries, and customary international law, if you are arrested in Denmark, you have the option to request that the police, prison officials, or other authorities alert the U.S. Embassy of your arrest. You also have the right to have your communications forwarded to the Embassy.

Greenland: If you are contemplating travel on cruise ships near Greenland, you should be aware that search and rescue capabilities are limited due to long distances between populated areas. Currently, the combined search and rescue ship capacity is less than would be needed to cope with even one of the large cruise ships that frequent the area. Search and rescue ships offer basic transport and basic medical care, but are not capable of advanced life-support.

There are uncharted waters in some fjords, and water temperatures can be frigid even during summer months. Emergency medical facilities outside of Nuuk are limited in number and types of services offered. Eastern Greenland is even more remote, and services are even more limited. If you are thinking of such a trip, please carefully consider these factors and check the operational records and the experience of captains and crews operating vessels in Arctic waters when selecting cruises off the shores of Greenland.

If you wish to explore Greenland by land, we strongly encourage you to hire experienced guides. Trekking in the coastal areas generally requires no official permission, but any travel into the huge National Park in northeastern Greenland and any treks across the central ice fields do require official permission. Please check with your tour operator to make sure that the company has received the necessary permission for such trips.

Given the similarity of landscape, long periods of darkness, and the potential for fast-changing weather, persons unfamiliar with the area can become disoriented easily and risk long-term exposure to the elements. While the mountains in Greenland are of moderate altitude, they are technically difficult; familiarity with ascent and descent routes is a must. While the authorities will rescue individuals in difficulty, land search and rescue capabilities are limited and subject to weather restrictions. In some circumstances, you may be billed for the cost of rescue services.

Given the remoteness of Greenland, you should strongly consider obtaining travel insurance which could pay any expenses relating to illness, injury, or death. Although emergency medical assistance is mainly free of charge, even to tourists, all additional services will have an extremely high cost. Queen Ingrid's Hospital, the main hospital in Nuuk, offers a full range of medical services, but medical facilities in outlying towns and settlements are very basic.

In most cases, evacuation to Nuuk would be required. Most medicines are available in Greenland, and medical staff will suggest appropriate alternatives if necessary. Expect emergency medical evacuations from Nuuk to Denmark or Iceland to be very costly. Evacuations from remote interior regions will cost significantly more. The cost of funeral services in Greenland is significantly higher than in Denmark.

Other Topics: If you wish to bring your pet to Denmark, please visit the website of the Danish Veterinary & Food Administration.

Accessibility: While in Denmark, individuals with disabilities may find accessibility and accommodation very different from what they find in the United States. However, the law prohibits discrimination against persons with physical and mental disabilities in employment, education, access to health care or other state services, and other areas.

In addition, the law mandates access to buildings, education, information, and communications for persons with disabilities. The Danish government generally enforces these provisions. All forms of public transportation have accommodations for persons with disabilities, though many buildings are not easily accessible for the disabled.

Accessibility information is available on the Danish tourist organization's web site, VisitDenmark. A parliamentary ombudsman monitors the equal treatment of disabled persons and receives a significant number of complaints related to discrimination against disabled persons each year.

Medical Facilities and Health Information: Excellent medical facilities are widely available in Denmark. In Greenland and the Faroe Islands, medical facilities are limited, and evacuation is required for serious illness or injury. Although emergency medical treatment is free of charge, the patient is charged for follow-up care. There are modern, fully equipped hospitals throughout Denmark; the largest—also called University Hospitals—are located in Copenhagen, Odense, and Aarhus.

Information on vaccinations and other health precautions can be found via the Centers for Disease Control and Prevention (CDC) website. For information about outbreaks of infectious diseases abroad, consult the the World Health Organization (WHO) website. The WHO website also contains additional health information for travelers, including detailed country-specific health information.

Medical Insurance: You can't assume your insurance will go with you when you travel. It's very important to find out BEFORE you leave. You need to ask your insurance company two questions:

- Does my policy apply when I'm out of the United States?
- Will it cover emergencies like a trip to a foreign hospital or an evacuation?

In many places, doctors and hospitals still expect payment in cash at the time of service. Your regular U.S. health insurance may not cover doctor and hospital visits in other countries. If your policy doesn't go with you when you travel, it is advisable to take out another one for your trip.

Traffic Safety and Road Conditions: While in Denmark, you may encounter road conditions that differ significantly from those in the United States. You must be 18 years of age to drive a car in Denmark. U.S tourists may use their state driver's license in Denmark for up to 90 days. Long-term residents must obtain a valid Danish driver's license.

Driving in Denmark is on the right side of the road. Road signs use standard international symbols. Many urban streets have traffic lanes reserved for public transport only, and bicycle lanes are common. Unless otherwise noted on traffic signs, the speed limit is 50km/h in urban areas, 80 km/h on open roads, and 110 km/h on expressways.

Use of seat belts is mandatory for drivers and all passengers. Children under three years of age must be secured with approved safety equipment appropriate to the child's age, size, and weight. Children from three to six years of age may use approved child or booster seats instead of seat belts.

Driving any vehicle, including bicycles, under the influence of alcohol or drugs is considered a very serious offense. The rules are stringently enforced and violations can result in stiff fines and jail sentences. It is against to law to drive while using a hand-held cell phone.

Denmark has an extensive and efficient public transportation system. Trains, buses, and ferries connect Copenhagen with other major cities in Denmark and with Norway, Sweden, and Germany. Bicycles are also widely used in Denmark. Passengers exiting public or tourist buses, as well as tourists driving rental cars, are especially reminded to watch for bicycles in designated lanes and paths, which are usually located between the pedestrian sidewalk and the motor-vehicle lane. Danish expressways, highways, and secondary roads are of high quality and connect all areas of the country. It is possible to drive from the northern tip of Denmark to the German border in the south in just four hours. Greenland has no established road system, and domestic travel is by foot, boat, or air.

The majority of the Faroe Islands are interconnected by roads and tunnels as well as by boat, and on the large islands, even small hamlets are accessible by road. On the smaller islands, travel is mostly done on foot. There is excellent mobile telephone coverage throughout the islands.

Aviation Safety Oversight: The U.S. Federal Aviation Administration (FAA) has assessed the government of Denmark's Civil Aviation Authority as being in compliance with International Civil Aviation Organization (ICAO) aviation safety standards for oversight of Denmark's air carrier operations. Further information may be found on the FAA's safety assessment page.

Children's Issues: Please see the U.S. Dept. of State Office of Children's Issues web pages on intercountry adoption and international parental child abduction.

Intercountry Adoption

January 2012

The information in this section has been edited from the latest report available as of February 2013 from the State Department Bureau of Consular Affairs, Office of Overseas Citizens Services. For more information, please read the *Intercountry Adoption* section of this book and review current reports online at http://adoption.state.gov.

Denmark is party to the Hague Convention on Protection of Children and Co-operation in Respect of Intercountry Adoption (Hague Adoption Convention). Therefore all adoptions between Denmark and the United States must meet the requirements of the Convention and U.S. law implementing the Convention.

There are few children eligible for intercountry adoption from Denmark, with a long waiting list of Danish prospective adoptive parents. While legally possible, intercountry adoption of a Danish orphan by foreigners is unlikely. No Danish orphans have received U.S. immigrant visas in the past five fiscal years. The information provided is intended primarily to assist in rare adoption cases from Denmark, including adoptions of Danish children by relatives in the United States, as well as adoptions from third countries by Americans living in Denmark.

Who Can Adopt? Adoption between the United States and Denmark is governed by the Hague Adoption Convention. Therefore to adopt from

Denmark, you must first be found eligible to adopt by the U.S. Government. The U.S. Government agency responsible for making this determination is the Department of Homeland Security, U.S. Citizenship and Immigration Services (USCIS). In addition to these U.S. requirements for prospective adoptive parents, Denmark also has the following requirements for prospective adoptive parents.

Residency Requirements: Adoptive parents must be legally admitted residents of Denmark to adopt domestically or intercountry. Temporary visitors without an established home in Denmark cannot apply.

Age Requirements: The age difference between the applicant and the prospective child should not be more than 40 years, and the adoptive parents must be at least 25 years old.

Marriage Requirements: Married couples and same sex couples who have entered into a registered partnership must adopt as a couple. In addition, couples must be married and have lived in the same household for at least 2½ years. Single people can also adopt.

Health Requirements: The physical and psychological health of the applicants must meet certain criteria.

Income and Property Requirements: The prospective adoptive parents must be of proper financial standing and their home must be suitable to house a child.

Criminal Background Check: The applicants cannot have a criminal record that would make them unfit to become adoptive parents.

Who Can Be Adopted? Because Denmark is party to the Hague Adoption Convention, children from Denmark must meet the requirements of the Convention in order to be eligible for adoption. For example, the Convention requires that Denmark attempt to place a child with a family in-country before determining that a child is eligible for intercountry adoption. In addition to Denmark's requirements, a child must meet the definition of a Convention adoptee for you to bring him or her back to the United States.

Denmark's Adoption Authority:
Danish Ministry of Justice
Department of Family Law
Kristineberg 6
2100 Copenhagen

The Danish Ministry of Justice is the adoption law-making branch of the Danish government and is also the Central Authority for the Hague Intercountry Adoption Convention. The local Joint Council of the Regional State Administration serves as the regional adoption authority. Joint Councils are established at the five Regional State Administrations (Statsforvaltning) in Denmark. The Regional State Administration mainly concentrates on family issues: divorce, child custody, maintenance, etc.

The Process: Because Denmark is party to the Hague Adoption Convention, adopting from Denmark must follow a specific process designed to meet the Convention's requirements. The first step in adopting a child from Denmark is to select an adoption service provider that has been accredited.

Private adoption agencies are accredited by the Danish Ministry of Justice, Department of Family Affairs to provide adoption services. The Department certifies adoption agencies and monitors their work to ensure that they comply with the law. In special circumstances such as relative adoptions, the Danish Central authority can allow the adoption to take place without the assistance of an adoption agency.

After you choose an accredited adoption service provider, you apply to be found eligible to adopt (Form I-800A) by the U.S. Government, Department of Homeland Security, U.S. Citizenship and Immigration Services (USCIS). Once the U.S. government determines that you are "eligible" and "suitable" to adopt, you or your agency will forward your information to the adoption authority in Denmark. Denmark's adoption authority will review your application to determine whether you are also eligible to adopt under Danish law.

If both the United States and Denmark determine that you are eligible to adopt, and if a child is available for intercountry adoption, the central adoption authority in Denmark may provide you with a referral for a child. Each family must decide for itself whether or not it will be able to meet the needs of the particular child and provide a permanent family placement for the referred child.

After you accept a match with a child, you will apply to the U.S. Government, Department of Homeland Security, U.S. Citizenship and Immigration Services (USCIS) for provisional approval to adopt that particular child (Form I-800). USCIS will determine whether the child is eligible under U.S. law to be adopted and enter the United States.

After this, your adoption service provider or you will submit a visa application for to a Consular officer at the U.S. Embassy. The Consular officer will review the child's information and evaluate the child for possible visa ineligibilities.

If the Consular officer determines that the child appears eligible to immigrate to the United States he or she will send a letter (an "Article 5 Letter") to Denmark Central Authority. Do not adopt or obtain custody of a child in Denmark before a U.S. consular officer issues the Article 5 Letter.

Role of the Regional State Administration: Prospective adoptive parents file their initial application with the local Joint Council of the Regional State Administration in the jurisdiction where they reside. A Joint Council consists of three members - a social worker, a lawyer, and a medical officer. The Joint Council determines whether the initial application for adoption may be approved for further processing. A complete list of Joint Councils can be found at http://www.statsforvaltning.dk.

The Danish National Board of Adoption supervises the Joint Councils, observes national and international developments in adoption matters, collects information concerning adoption, negotiates with authorities and organizations in other countries, and supplies general information. Decisions reached by the Joint Councils may be appealed to the Danish National Board of Adoption at:

Danish National Board of Adoption
Kristineberg 6
1470 Copenhagen
Tel: +45-3392 3302
Fax: +45-3927 1889
Email: an@adoptionsnaevnet.dk
Web site: http://www.adoptionsnaevnet.dk

Domestic adoptions in Denmark are processed via the five Regional State Administrations in the jurisdiction where the prospective parents reside. Prospective adoptive parents file an application with the Joint Council of their Regional State Administration. The application is processed in three phases. For more detailed information, please visit the web site for the Danish National Board of Adoption, http://www.adopt.dk, and click on "English Language Version."

The first phase determines whether the applicants meet the general eligibility requirements for adoptive parents. Applicants cannot proceed to phase two without approval by the Joint Council.

The second phase is a pre-adoption counseling training program, mandatory for all applicants who have not previously adopted a child. The purpose of the training is to supply applicants with information concerning different aspects of adoption, and to provide a basis for the applicants themselves to determine whether or not they possess the necessary resources (financial as well as parenting abilities) to adopt a child.

The training course runs over a weekend and a half (one weekend session, followed by one Saturday or Sunday session). Participation in a pre-adoption training program costs Danish Kroner 2,500 (approximately USD 450). The third phase includes one or more interviews with the secretariat of the Joint Council. At the end of the third phase, a home study report is presented to the Joint Council for final decision and approval. The prospective parents proceed by submitting their approval to one of the Danish government-authorized adoption agencies.

Role of the Court: The Regional State Administration is responsible for issuing the Adoption Certificate, and finalizing the adoption. According to Danish law, the adopted child has the same rights as a biological child.

Role of Adoption Agencies: Adoption agencies are accredited by the Danish government to provide adoption services.

Time Frame: From the initial contact with the Joint Council at the Regional State Administration until the adoptive parents can be united with the child, the time frame is on average 35 months.

Adoption Fees: In the adoption services contract that you sign at the beginning of the adoption process, your agency will itemize the fees and estimated expenses related to your adoption process.

Domestic adoptions of Danish children are free of charge. The cost of an intercountry adoption (adopting a child in a third country and then taking him or her to Denmark to reside) can be high, often ranging between USD 20,000—30,000 depending on the country of the child's origin. Travel expenses must be added to this amount. Once the adoption has been finalized, the adoptive parents are entitled to a Danish Government lump-sum relief benefit to help reduce their overall expenses.

Documents Required: The initial application form, which can be obtained from the Regional State Administration (Statsforvaltning), must be accompanied by the following documents: birth certificate, marriage certificate, latest tax return, and certificate of health.

An application to participate in the pre-adoption counseling program must be filed with the Department of Family Affairs, office of Training Programs. If the applicants wish to continue the process after they complete the counseling program, a third application must be filed to start phase three.

In the case of an adoption from a third country, when the child arrives in Denmark from his or her country of origin (after that country's adoption procedures have been completed), the adoptive parents must apply to the Regional State Administration for an Adoption Certificate. With the Adoption Certificate, the adoption is finalized, and pursuant to Danish law, the adopted child has the same rights as a biological child.

Additional documents may be requested. You may be asked to provide proof that a document from the United States is authentic, read more on Traveling Abroad to learn about authenticating U.S. Documents.

U.S. Embassy in Denmark
Dag Hammarskjolds Alle 24
2100 Copenhagen
Tel: +45-3341 7100
Fax: +45-3538 9616
Email: CopenhagenACS@state.gov
Web site:
http://www.denmark.usembassy.gov

Denmark's Adoption Authority
Danish Ministry of Justice
Department of Family Law
Kristineberg 6
2100 Copenhagen
Tel: +45-7268 8000
Fax: +45-7268 8001
Email: familiestyrelsen@famstyr.dk
Web site:
http://www.families tyrelsen.dk

Danish Accredited Adoption Agencies
AC Boernehjaelp
Elkjaervej 31
8230 Aabyhoj
Tel: +45-8612 6522
Fax: +45-8619 7853
Email: adoption@a-c.dk
Web site: www.a-c.dk

DanAdopt
Hovedgaden 24
3460 Birkerod
Tel: +45-4581 6333
Fax: +45-4581 7482
Email: mail@danadopt.dk
Web site: www.danadopt.dk

Royal Danish Embassy
3200 Whitehaven Street NW
Washington, DC 20008–3683
Tel: (202) 234-4300
Fax: (202) 328-1470
Email: wasamb@.um.dk
Web site:
http://www.denmarkemb.org

Denmark also has Consulates General in Chicago and New York City.

Office of Children's Issues
U.S. Department of State
2201 C Street, NW
SA-29
Washington, DC 20520
Tel: 1-888-407-4747
E-mail: AskCI@state.gov
http://adoption.state.gov

For questions about immigration procedures, call the National Customer Service Center (NCSC) at 1-800-375-5283 (TTY 1-800-767-1833).

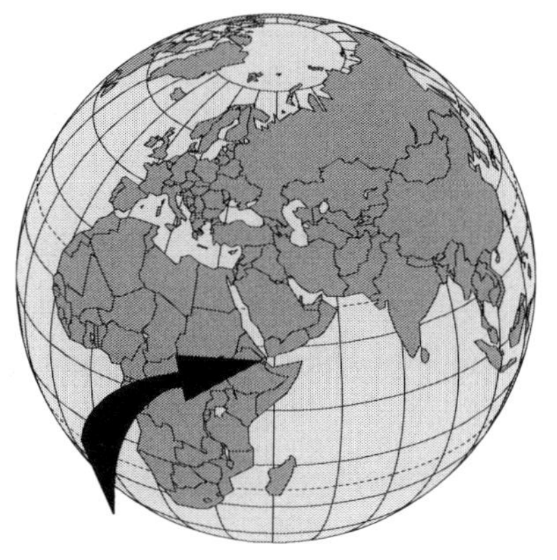

DJIBOUTI

Compiled from publications that were available as of February 2013 from the U.S. Department of State, the U.S. Department of Commerce, and the Central Intelligence Agency (CIA). See the introduction to this set for explanatory notes.

Official Name:
Republic of Djibouti

PROFILE

Geography

Area: total: 23,200 sq km; country comparison to the world: 151; land: 23,180 sq km; water: 20 sq km
Major cities: Djibouti (capital) 567,000 (2009)
Climate: desert; torrid, dry
Terrain: coastal plain and plateau separated by central mountains

People

Nationality: noun: Djiboutian(s); adjective: Djiboutian
Population: 774,389 (July 2012 est.)
Population growth rate: 2.285% (2012 est.)
Ethnic groups: Somali 60%, Afar 35%, other 5% (includes French, Arab, Ethiopian, and Italian)
Religions: Muslim 94%, Christian 6%
Languages: French (official), Arabic (official), Somali, Afar
Literacy: definition: age 15 and over can read and write; total population: 67.9%; male: 78%; female: 58.4% (2003 est.)
Health: life expectancy at birth: total population: 61.57 years; male: 59.15 years; female: 64.07 years (2012 est.); Infant mortality rate: total: 53.31 deaths/1,000 live births; male: 60.88 deaths/1,000 live births; female: 45.5 deaths/1,000 live births (2012 est.)
Unemployment rate: 59% (2007 est.)
Work force: 351,700 (2007)

Government

Type: republic
Independence: 27 June 1977
Constitution: approved by referendum 4 September 1992; note—constitution allows for multiparties
Political subdivisions: 6 districts (cercles, singular—cercle); Ali Sabieh, Arta, Dikhil, Djibouti, Obock, Tadjourah
Suffrage: 18 years of age; universal

Economy

GDP (purchasing power parity): $2.377 billion (2012 est.); $2.26 billion (2011 est.); $2.163 billion (2010 est.); $2.09 billion (2009 est.)
GDP real growth rate: 4.8% (2012 est.); 4.5% (2011 est.); 3.5% (2010 est.); 5% (2009 est.)
GDP per capita (PPP): $2,700 (2012 est.); $2,700 (2011 est.); $2,600 (2010 est.); $2,600 (2009 est.)
Natural resources: potential geothermal power, gold, clay, granite, limestone, marble, salt, diatomite, gypsum, pumice, petroleum
Agriculture products: fruits, vegetables; goats, sheep, camels, animal hides
Industries: construction, agricultural processing
Exports: $$101.7 million (2012 est.); 96.3 million (2011 est.); $85.1 million (2010 est.)
Exports—commodities: reexports, hides and skins, coffee (in transit)
Exports—partners: Somalia 77.2%, Egypt 8.6% (2011)
Imports: $465.1 million (2012 est.); $413.7 million (2011 est.); $363.8 million (2010 est.)
Imports—commodities: foods, beverages, transport equipment, chemicals, petroleum products
Imports—partners: Saudi Arabia 18.1%, China 16.6%, India 14%, Indonesia 6.1%, Malaysia 5.3%, US 4.3%, Pakistan 4.2% (2011)
Debt—external: $802.9 million (31 December 2012 est.); $812.5 million (31 December 2011 est.); $754 million
Exchange rates: Djiboutian francs (DJF) per US dollar; 177.7 (2012 est.); 177.72 (2011 est.); 177.72 (2010 est.)

PEOPLE

About two-thirds of the Republic of Djibouti's inhabitants live in the capital city. The indigenous population is divided between the majority Somalis (predominantly of the Issa tribe, with minority Issaq and Gadabursi representation) and the Afars (Danakils). All are Cushitic-speaking peoples. Among the 15,000 foreigners residing in Djibouti, the French are the most numerous. Among the French are approximately 3,000 troops.

Religion

More than 99 percent of the population is Sunni Muslim. There are a small number of Roman Catholics, Protestants, Copts, Ethiopian Orthodox, Greek Orthodox, Jehovah's Witnesses, Hindus, and Baha'is. Foreign-born citizens, as well as many expatriate residents, are often members of these religious groups. Citizens are officially considered Muslims if they do not specifically identify with another religious group.

HISTORY

The Republic of Djibouti gained its independence on June 27, 1977. It is the successor to French Somaliland (later called the French Territory of the Afars and Issas), which was created in the first half of the 19th century as a result of French interest in the Horn of Africa. However, the history of Djibouti, recorded in poetry and songs of its nomadic peoples, goes back thousands of years to a time when Djiboutians traded hides and skins for the perfumes and spices of ancient Egypt, India, and China. Through close contacts with the Arabian Peninsula for more than 1,000 years, the Somali and Afar tribes in this region became the first on the African continent to adopt Islam.

It was Rochet d'Hericourt's exploration into Shoa (1839–42) that marked the beginning of French interest in the African shores of the Red Sea. Further exploration by Henri Lambert, French Consular Agent at Aden, and Captain Fleuriot de Langle led to a treaty of friendship and assistance between France and the sultans of Raheita, Tadjourah, and Gobaad, from whom the French purchased the anchorage of Obock (1862).

Growing French interest in the area took place against a backdrop of British activity in Egypt and the opening of the Suez Canal in 1869. In 1884–85, France expanded its protectorate to include the shores of the Gulf of Tadjourah and Somaliland. Boundaries of the protectorate, marked out in 1897 by France and Emperor Menelik II of Ethiopia, were affirmed further by agreements with Ethiopian Emperor Haile Selassie I in 1945 and 1954.

The administrative capital was moved from Obock to Djibouti in 1892. In 1896, Djibouti was named French Somaliland. Djibouti, which has a good natural harbor and ready access to the Ethiopian highlands, attracted trade caravans crossing East Africa as well as Somali settlers from the south. The Franco-Ethiopian railway, linking Djibouti to the heart of Ethiopia, was begun in 1897 and reached Addis Ababa in June 1917, further facilitating the increase of trade.

During the Italian invasion and occupation of Ethiopia in the 1930s and during World War II, constant border skirmishes occurred between French and Italian forces. The area was ruled by the Vichy (French) government from the fall of France until December 1942, and fell under British blockade during that period. Free French and the Allied forces recaptured Djibouti at the end of 1942. A local battalion from Djibouti participated in the liberation of France in 1944.

On July 22, 1957, the colony was reorganized to give the people considerable self-government. On the same day, a decree applying the Overseas Reform Act (Loi Cadre) of June 23, 1956, established a territorial assembly that elected eight of its members to an executive council. Members of the executive council were responsible for one or more of the territorial services and carried the title of minister. The council advised the French-appointed governor general.

In a September 1958 constitutional referendum, French Somaliland opted to join the French community as an overseas territory. This act entitled the region to representation by one deputy and one senator in the French Parliament, and one counselor in the French Union Assembly.

The first elections to the territorial assembly were held on November 23, 1958, under a system of proportional representation. In the next assembly elections (1963), a new electoral law was enacted. Representation was abolished in exchange for a system of straight plurality vote based on lists submitted by political parties in seven designated districts. Ali Aref Bourhan, allegedly of Turkish origin, was selected to be the president of the executive council.

French President Charles de Gaulle's August 1966 visit to Djibouti was marked by 2 days of public demonstrations by Somalis demanding independence. On September 21, 1966, Louis Saget, appointed governor general of the territory after the demonstrations, announced the French Government's decision to hold a referendum to determine whether the people would remain within the French Republic or become independent. In March 1967, 60% chose to continue the territory's association with France.

In July of that year, a directive from Paris formally changed the name of the region to the French Territory of Afars and Issas. The directive also reorganized the governmental structure of the territory, making the senior French representative (formerly the governor general) a high commissioner. In addition, the executive council was redesignated as the council of government, with nine members.

In 1975, the French Government began to accommodate increasingly insistent demands for independence. In June 1976, the territory's citizenship law, which favored the Afar minority, was revised to reflect more closely the weight of the Issa Somali.

The electorate voted for independence in a May 1977 referendum. The Republic of Djibouti was established on June 27, 1977, and Hassan Gouled

Aptidon became the country's first president. In 1981, he was again elected president of Djibouti. He was re-elected, unopposed, to a second 6-year term in April 1987 and to a third 6-year term in May 1993 multiparty elections. In early 1992, the constitution permitted the legalization of four political parties for a period of 10 years, after which a complete multiparty system would be installed. By the time of the December 1992 national assembly elections, only three had qualified. They were the Rassemblement Populaire Pour le Progres (People's Rally for Progress—RPP), which was the only legal party from 1981 until 1992; the Parti du Renouveau Democratique (The Party for Democratic Renewal—PRD); and the Parti National Democratique (National Democratic Party—PND).

Only the RPP and the PRD contested the national assembly elections, and the PND withdrew, claiming that there were too many unanswered questions on the conduct of the elections and too many opportunities for government fraud. The RPP won all 65 seats in the national assembly, with a turnout of less than 50% of the electorate. In early November 1991, civil war erupted in Djibouti between the government and a predominantly Afar rebel group, the Front for the Restoration of Unity and Democracy (FRUD). The FRUD signed a peace accord with the government in December 1994, ending the conflict. Two FRUD members were made cabinet members, and in the presidential elections of 1999 the FRUD campaigned in support of the RPP.

In 1999, Ismail Omar Guelleh—President Hassan Gouled Aptidon's chief of staff, head of security, and key adviser for over 20 years—was elected to the presidency as the RPP candidate. He received 74% of the vote, with the other 26% going to opposition candidate Moussa Ahmed Idriss of the Unified Djiboutian Opposition (ODU). For the first time since independence, no group boycotted the election. Moussa Ahmed Idriss and the ODU later challenged the results based on election "irregularities" and the assertion that "foreigners" had voted in various districts of the capital; however, international and locally based observers considered the election to be generally fair, and cited only minor technical difficulties. Guelleh took the oath of office as the second President of the Republic of Djibouti on May 8, 1999, with the support of an alliance between the RPP and the government-recognized section of the Afar-led FRUD.

In February 2000, another branch of FRUD signed a peace accord with the government. On May 12, 2001, President Guelleh presided over the signing of what was termed the final peace accord officially ending the decade-long civil war between the government and the armed faction of the FRUD. The peace accord successfully completed the peace process begun on February 7, 2000 in Paris. Ahmed Dini Ahmed represented the FRUD.

GOVERNMENT AND POLITICAL CONDITIONS

Djibouti is a republic with a strong elected president and a weak legislature. In April 2010 parliament amended the constitution to remove term limits, facilitating the April 8, 2011, reelection of President Ismail Omar Guelleh for a third term. The president won with 80 percent of the vote against one independent candidate, who was supported by one of two opposition coalitions that had boycotted the election until April 3; the other coalition did not participate in the election. International observers characterized the election as free and fair, although they criticized pre-election planning and the presence of security forces at polling stations.

The 2010 constitutional amendment removing presidential term limits, general dissatisfaction with the government, student unrest, and high levels of unemployment contributed to popular protests in February 2011. On February 18, security forces used tear gas and rubber bullets to disperse violent young protestors who remained following a peaceful demonstration.

One civilian and one police officer were killed, and numerous demonstrators were injured. The subsequent security crackdown resulted in numerous arrests, detentions, and criminal proceedings against demonstrators. Between March 25 and April 8, 2011, the official campaign period, the government banned opposition rallies.

Recent Elections

In April 2010 parliament amended the constitution to remove term limits, facilitating the April 8, 2011 reelection of President Ismail Omar Guelleh for a third term. The president won with 80 percent of the vote against independent candidate Mohamed Warsama Ragueh. Political opposition parties, claiming that the Guelleh administration had made it impossible to conduct a fair election, initially chose not to nominate candidates for the presidential election, effectively boycotting it. However, one week prior to election day, the Union of Democratic Movements, the most active opposition coalition, asked its supporters to vote for Ragueh, the former head of the Constitutional Council. The Union for a Democratic Change, the other coalition, did not participate in the election. International observers from the African Union, La Francophonie, the Arab League, and the Inter-Governmental Authority on Development declared the elections to be free, fair, and transparent. However, observers criticized pre-election planning and the number of security personnel at polling stations.

The government banned opposition rallies between March 25 and April 8 and harassed opposition leaders (see section 2.b.).

For example, on March 11, security forces detained four opposition leaders for approximately four hours while they were on their way to a planned demonstration. The detained leaders were PND president Aden Robleh Awaleh, PDD president Mohamed Daoud Chehem, UDJ president Guedi Hared, and MRD president Souleiman Farah Lodon. The four leaders were loaded into a truck and driven around the outskirts of Djibouti, after which they were returned to the residence of UDJ president Guedi. The leaders said they were not mistreated but considered the government's action a clear effort to prevent them from organizing the demonstration. The demonstration planned for the day did not take place.

In March the government expelled Democracy International (DI) from the country after accusing it of being an "illegal organization" that supported the opposition's "seditious activities," according to Human Rights Watch and Freedom House. The international election monitoring organization had been working to assist the government in preparations for the election and training of both ruling and opposition parties in campaign methods. The expulsion followed campaign monitoring activities by DI during the February 18 unrest that the government perceived as a violation of unbiased participation in the process.

Political Parties: The government arrested, harassed, and threatened opposition leaders, restricted the operations of opposition parties, and denied opposition groups permits to organize protests (see sections 1.a., 1.c., and 2.b.). According to Freedom House, opposition parties were also "disadvantaged by electoral rules and the government's abuse of the administrative apparatus."

Participation of Women and Minorities: The 2008 legislative elections brought two more women into the National Assembly, raising to nine the number of female parliamentarians in the 65-seat body. There was one woman in the 21-member cabinet, and the president of the Supreme Court, who by law acts in the president's stead in case of death or incapacitation, was a woman.

The legislature included members of all clans. Membership was approximately 41 percent Issa, 43 percent Afar, and 16 percent representatives of smaller minority groups. Elected from a single list (opposition parties did not contest the legislative elections in 2008 after the government declined to accept their conditions), the legislature's members reflected the governing coalition's intent to ensure balance.

The cabinet was similarly balanced: there were six Afars, including the prime minister and the foreign minister. However, some Afars continued to claim they were not as well represented at lower governmental levels. There were three representatives from Somali clans other than the Issa in the cabinet, and one of Yemeni origin.

Principal Government Officials

Last Updated: 1/31/2013

Pres.: **Ismail Omar GUELLEH**

Prime Min.: **Mohamed Dileita DILEITA**

Min. of Agriculture, Livestock, & Fisheries: **Mohamed Ahmed AWALEH**

Min. of Communication & Culture: **Abdi Houssein AHMED**

Min. of Defense: **Mohamed Kamil ADBOULKADER**

Min. of Economy, Finance, & Planning: **Ilyas Moussa DAWALEH**

Min. of Energy & Water: **Fouad Ahmed AYE**

Min. of Foreign Affairs & Intl. Cooperation: **Mahamoud Ali YOUSSOUF**

Min. of Health: **Ali Yacoub MAHAMOUD**

Min. of Higher Education & Research: **Nabil Mohamed AHMED**

Min. of Housing, Urban Planning, & Environment: **Hassan Omar Mohamed BOURHAN**

Min. of Infrastructure & Transport: **Mohamed Moussa Ibrahim BALALA**

Min. of Interior: **Hassan Darar HOUFFANEH**

Min. of Justice, Penal, & Muslim Affairs: **Ali Farah ASSOWEH**

Min. of Labor: **Ali Hassan BAHDON**

Min. for Mosque Properties & Muslim Affairs: **Hamoud Abdi SULTAN**

Min. of National Education & Professional Training: **Moussa Ahmed HASSAN**

Min. for the Promotion of Women & Family Planning: **Hasna Barkat DAOUD**

Governor, Central Bank: **Mahamoud Haid DJAMA**

Ambassador to the US: **Roble OLHAYE Oudine**

Permanent Representative to the UN, New York: **Roble OLHAYE Oudine**

ECONOMY

Djibouti's economy is based on service activities connected with the country's strategic location and status as a free trade zone in the Horn of Africa. Three-fourths of Djibouti's inhabitants live in the capital city; the remainder are mostly nomadic herders. Scanty rainfall limits crop production to fruits and vegetables, and most food must be imported.

Djibouti provides services as both a transit port for the region and an international transshipment and refueling center. Imports and exports from landlocked neighbor Ethiopia represent 70% of port activity at Djibouti's container terminal. Djibouti has few natural resources and little industry. The nation is, therefore, heavily dependent on foreign assistance to help support its balance of payments and to finance development projects. An unemployment rate of nearly 60% in urban areas continues to be a major problem.

While inflation is not a concern, due to the fixed tie of the Djiboutian franc to the US dollar, the artificially high value of the Djiboutian franc adversely affects Djibouti's balance of payments. Djibouti holds foreign reserves amounting to less than six months of import coverage. Per capita consumption dropped an estimated 35% between 1999 and 2006 because of recession, civil war, and a high population growth rate (including immigrants and refugees).

Djibouti has experienced relatively minimal impact from the global economic downturn, but its reliance on diesel-generated electricity and imported food leave average consumers vulnerable to global price shocks. Djibouti in 2012 began construction of a third port to secure its position as a critical transshipment hub in the Horn of Africa and the principal conduit for Ethiopia's trade.

Djibouti also received funding in late 2012 for a desalination plant to begin address the severe freshwater shortage affecting Djibouti City, and particularly its poorest residents.

Labor Conditions

The law prohibits all labor by, and employment of, children under age 16.

Government enforcement of child labor legislation was ineffective. Child labor existed throughout the country, including the worst forms of child labor. Children engaged in the sale of the mild narcotic khat, legal under local law. Family-owned businesses such as restaurants and small shops employed children at all hours. Children were involved in a range of activities such as shining shoes, washing and guarding cars, selling items, working as domestic servants, working in subsistence farming and with livestock, and other activities in the informal sector. Children of both sexes worked as domestic servants. The 2006 labor code canceled minimum wage rates for occupational categories and provides that wages be set after common agreement between employers and employees. T

he legal workweek is 48 hours, normally spread over six days. This limit applies to workers regardless of gender or nationality. The law mandates a weekly rest period of 24 consecutive hours and the provision of overtime pay, and limits compulsory overtime to a maximum of five hours per week. The law provided for paid holidays. The government sets occupational safety and health standards.

There were no laws or regulations permitting workers to refuse to carry out dangerous work assignments without jeopardizing their continued employment. Although more flexible hiring regulations applied in the Djibouti Free Zone, a commercial export processing zone near the Djibouti City port, other labor code provisions applied to all workers, including foreign workers and workers in the Free Zone.

U.S.-DJIBOUTIAN RELATIONS

The United States established diplomatic relations with the Republic of Djibouti in 1977, following its independence from France, and had consular representation in the former colony of French Somaliland since 1929. Since independence, Djibouti has had two presidents — Hassan Gouled Aptidon, was first elected in 1977 and ruled for 22 years until the current president, Ismail Omar Guelleh, was elected in 1999.

The country had a single legal party from 1981 to 1992. Additional political parties became legal and formed beginning in 1992. The country's nearly decade-long internal conflict between the government and a rebel group officially ended in 2001.

Djibouti is located at a strategic point in the Horn of Africa and is a strong U.S. partner on security, regional stability, and humanitarian efforts in the greater Horn. The Djiboutian Government has been supportive of U.S. and interests and takes a proactive position against terrorism.

Djibouti hosts a U.S. military presence at Camp Lemonnier, a former French Foreign Legion base in the capital. Djibouti has also allowed the U.S. military, as well as other militaries with presences in Djibouti, access to its port facilities and airport.

The U.S. Agency for International Development's (USAID) Food for Peace program maintains a warehouse for pre-positioned emergency food relief in Djibouti — the only one of its kind outside the continental United States — allowing expedient delivery of humanitarian assistance to famine-stricken countries from Africa to Asia. International Broadcasting Bureau facilities in Djibouti transmit Arabic-language Radio Sawa programming, and Voice of America Somali Service broadcasts to neighboring Somalia and the Arabian Peninsula.

U.S. Assistance to Djibouti

Djibouti's prosperity is hindered by serious unemployment, poor health, food insecurity, and less than effective governance. U.S. assistance aims to help improve health and education and to promote stability, which is critical to improving Djibouti's capacity to provide basic services to its people in the long term.

Bilateral Economic Relations

Djibouti is eligible for preferential trade benefits under the African Growth and Opportunity Act. The government has spearheaded the creation of a deep-sea port, which has increased private sector investment. U.S. exports to Djibouti include vegetable oil, wheat, machinery, and foodstuffs. U.S. imports almost always transit Djibouti from origin countries farther inland, like Ethiopia. These imports include coffee, vegetables, and perfumery and cosmetics. The United States has signed a trade and investment framework agreement with the Common Market for Eastern and Southern Africa, of which Djibouti is a member.

Djibouti's Membership in International Organizations

Djibouti and the United States belong to a number of the same international organizations, including the United Nations, International Monetary Fund, World Bank, and World Trade Organization.

Bilateral Representation

Djibouti's embassy in Washington is located at Suite 515, 1156 15th Street, NW, Washington, DC 20005 (tel. 202-331-0270; fax 202-331-0302).

Principal U.S. Embassy Officials

Last Updated: 1/14/2013

DJIBOUTI (E) American Embassy–B.P. 185–Lot number 350-B,Lotissement Haramous-Republic of Djibouti, (253) 21-453-000, Fax (253) 21–453-020, Workweek: Sunday-Thursday, 08:00-16:30, Website: http://djibouti.usembassy.gov/

DCM OMS: Linda Adams
AMB OMS: Jennifer Sparks
DHS/CIS: Dennis Becker
ECON/COM: Fausto Degusman
FM: Felipe Cayabyab
HRO: Thomas Zeitler
MGT: Todd Katschke
POSHO: Felipe Cayabyab
SDO/DATT: Edward William
AMB: Geeta Pasi
CON: Chad Wesen
DCM: Julie Stufft
PAO: Stuart Denyar
GSO: Philip Kern
RSO: William Inman
AID: Mark Mitchell (Acting)
CLO: Arlene Degusman
EEO: Phil Kern
FMO: Melanie Parris
ICASS Chair: Stuart Denyar
IMO: Edgar Ruiz
IPO: William Kasey
IRS: Kathy Beck (Resident In Paris)
ISO: Edgar Ruiz
POL: Chansonetta Cummings
State ICASS: Chad Wesen

TRAVEL

Consular Information Sheet

September 20, 2012

Country Description: Djibouti is a developing country located at the juncture of the Red Sea and the Indian Ocean. It is a multi-party democracy with a legal system based on French civil law (Djibouti was a French colony until 1977), though modified by traditional practices and Islamic (Sharia) law.

Although exact numbers are unavailable, unemployment is estimated to be in excess of 50% of the working-age population. Over two-thirds of the country's estimated 850,000 residents live in the capital, also called Djibouti. Modern tourist facilities and communications links exist in the city of Djibouti but are limited outside the capital

Smart Traveler Enrollment Program (STEP)/Embassy Locations: If you are going to live in, or visit Djibouti, please take the time to tell our Embassy about your trip. If you enroll, we can keep you up to date with important safety and security announcements. It will also help your friends and family get in touch with you in an emergency.

U.S. Embassy Djibouti
Lotissement Haramous Lot # 350B
Djibouti City, Republic of Djibouti
Phone: 253-21-453-000
Email: ConsularDjibouti@State.gov

Entry/Exit Requirements for U.S. Citizens: A passport, visa, and evidence of yellow fever vaccination are required for entry. Those travelling by air can obtain 30-day visas at Ambouli International Airport for 10,000 Djiboutian francs ($60); however, it is advisable to obtain visas prior to travel to Djibouti whenever possible. If visas are obtained prior to travel, one year, multiple entry visas are issued.

Travelers may obtain the latest information on entry requirements from the Embassy of the Republic of Djibouti, 1156 15th Street, NW, Washington, DC 20005, telephone (202) 331-0270, or at the Djibouti Mission to the United Nations, 866 United Nations Plaza, Suite 4011, New York, NY 10017, telephone (212) 753-3163. Overseas, inquiries may be made at the nearest Djiboutian embassy or consulate. In countries where there is no Djiboutian diplomatic representation, travelers may sometimes obtain visas at the French Embassy. The validity of the Djiboutian visa is also the amount of time one may stay in the country without a residency permit. If one overstays his/her visa validity, an exit tax of 10,000 Djiboutian francs ($60) must be paid.

U.S. citizen journalists or any U.S. citizen connected with the media must contact the U.S. Embassy's Public Affairs section prior to travel to facilitate entry into Djibouti. If you are unclear whether this applies to you, please contact the U.S. Embassy for more information.

HIV/AIDS Restrictions: The U.S. Department of State is unaware of any HIV/AIDS entry restrictions for visitors to or foreign residents of Djibouti.

Threats to Safety and Security: Djibouti enjoys a stable political climate. Its international borders are porous. Terrorism poses a threat in East Africa. In particular, al-Shabaab poses a threat to U.S. citizens in Djibouti. After Djibouti announced it would join the AMISOM peacekeeping mission to Somalia, al Shabaab threatened to retaliate by launching attacks inside Djibouti. al-announced that it had formally merged with al-Qa'ida in February 2012.

On October 29, 2008, terrorists launched several coordinated and near-simultaneous attacks involving multiple car bombs against local and international targets in the regions of Somaliland and Puntland. On July 11, 2010, Al-Shabaab launched simultaneous suicide attacks at two popular venues in Kampala, Uganda where people had gathered to watch the World Cup. One American was killed and several wounded. Many Ugandans lost their lives and many more were injured. This is significant as it was the first such attack coordinated outside of Somalia and demonstrated this terrorist organization's regional capabilities.

U.S. citizens traveling in East Africa should be aware of the potential for indiscriminate attacks on civilian targets in public places, including hotels, and tourist sites where Westerners are known to congregate. Read our Worldwide Caution for the most current travel warning on East Africa. Kidnapping of westerners for ransom is a growing concern in the region.

Tensions exist between neighboring Ethiopia and Eritrea due to their long-running border dispute. Since April, 2008, there has been increased tension on Djibouti's border with Eritrea after an incursion by Eritreans in that area. In January 2012, ethnic Afar gunmen attacked a western tourist convoy travelling in Ethiopia's north-western region which borders Djibouti. The attackers were most likely criminally motivated. Since the Afar people live in an area spanning the Ethiopia-Eritrea-Djibouti border area, the attack significantly worsened Ethiopia-Eritrea relations. In March and May, Ethiopia staged raids across the Eritrean border—bringing tensions to near their highest point since the 1998–2000 war between the two countries.

Pirates and other criminals have specifically targeted and kidnapped foreigners working in Somalia. In October 2011, a U.S. citizen aid worker living in Somalia was kidnapped, and in January 2012, another U.S. citizen was kidnapped while on work-related travel in Somalia. In both cases, as well as in recent kidnappings of other westerners, the victims took precautionary measures by hiring local security personnel, but those hired to protect them appear to have played a key role in the abductions.

A strong familiarity with Somalia and/or extensive prior travel to the region does not reduce travel risk. Any U.S. citizens travelling to Somalia, including Somaliland and Puntland, are advised to obtain Kidnap and Recovery Insurance, as well as Medical Evacuation Insurance, prior to travel.

Civil unrest or armed conflict in neighboring countries could disrupt air travel to and from Djibouti or otherwise negatively affect its security. Travelers should exercise caution when traveling to any remote area of Djibouti, especially near the borders with Eritrea, Ethiopia, and Somalia.

Seaborne travel is extremely dangerous. There have been hundreds of incidents of armed attacks and robberies at sea by pirate groups on ships transiting around the Horn of Africa. On February 21, 2011, pirates hijacked a yacht carrying four Americans in the Gulf of Aden, who were subsequently killed. Additionally, after the April 2009 hijacking of a U.S. cargo vessel and subsequent rescue of the vessel's captain by U.S. forces, Somali pirates threatened to retaliate against U.S. citizens transiting the region.

In the event that seaborne travel is unavoidable, vessels should convoy in groups and maintain good communications contact at all times. Marine channels 12, 13 and 16 VHF-FM are international call-up and emergency channels and are commonly monitored by ships at sea. 2182 MHz is the HF international call-up and emergency channel. In the Gulf of Aden, use of transit routes farther offshore appears to reduce, but does not eliminate, the risk of contact with assailants.

Wherever possible, travel in trafficked sea-lanes. Avoid loitering in or transiting isolated or remote areas. In the event of an attack, consider activating the Emergency Position Indicating Radio Beacon. Due to distances involved, there may be a considerable delay before assistance arrives. Vessels may also contact the Yemeni Coast Guard 24-hour Operations Center at 967-1-562-402. Operations Center staff members speak English.

The United States Maritime Administration (MARAD) has advised that elevated regional tensions have increased the risk of maritime attacks being conducted by extremist to vessels operating in the Gulf of Oman, North Arabian Sea, Gulf of Aden, and the Bab el Mandeb regions.

MARAD recommends vessels at anchor, operating in restricted maneuvering environments, or at slow speeds should be especially vigilant, and report suspicious activity. U.S. flag vessels that observe suspicious activity in the area are advised to report such suspicious activity or any hostile or potentially hostile action to Commander, U.S. Naval Forces Central Command (COMUSNAVCENT) battlewatch captain at phone number 011-973-1785–3879.

All suspicious activities and events are also to be reported to the U.S. Coast Guard National Response Center at the following toll free telephone: 1-800-424-8802, direct telephone 202-267-2675, or TDD 202-267-4477. The complete advisory is available on the MARAD website at www.MARAD.DOT.gov.

U.S. citizens are encouraged to carry a photocopy of their U.S. passports with them at all times for ready proof of identity and U.S. citizenship if questioned by local officials. Police occasionally stop travelers on the main roads leading out of the capital to check identity documents.

Stay up to date by:

- Bookmarking our Bureau of Consular Affairs website, which contains the current Travel Warnings and Travel Alerts as well as the Worldwide Caution.
- Following us on Twitter and the Bureau of Consular Affairs page on Facebook as well.
- Downloading our free Smart Traveler IPhone App to have travel information at your fingertips.
- Calling 1-888-407-4747 toll-free within the U.S. and Canada, or a regular toll line, 1-202-501-4444, from other countries.
- Taking some time before travel to consider your personal security.

Crime: Accurate crime statistics are not available, but the majority of crimes are petty thefts and crimes of opportunity. There has been anecdotal evidence of an increasing trend in the frequency of violent crimes against Djiboutian citizens and burglaries of residences in established neighborhoods. Violent crimes against foreigners are a rarity in Djibouti. However, foreigners are frequent victims of snatch and grab type robberies and price gouging by unscrupulous taxi drivers.

Do not buy counterfeit and pirated goods, even if they are widely available. Not only are the bootlegs illegal in the United States, if you purchase them you may also be breaking local law.

Victims of Crime: If you or someone you know becomes the victim of a crime abroad, you should contact the local police and the nearest U.S. embassy or consulate. We can:

- Replace a stolen passport.
- Help you find appropriate medical care if you are the victim of violent crimes such as assault or rape.
- Put you in contact with the appropriate police authorities, and if you want us to, we can contact family members or friend.
- Help you understand the local criminal justice process and direct you to local attorneys, although it is important to remember that local authorities are responsible for investigating and prosecuting the crime.

The local equivalent to the "911" emergency line in Djibouti is 18.

Criminal Penalties: While you are traveling in Djibouti, you are subject to its laws even if you are a U.S. citizen. Foreign laws and legal systems can be vastly different than our own. In some places you may be taken in for questioning if you don't have your passport with you. In some places, it is illegal to take pictures of certain buildings.

In some places, driving under the influence of drugs or alcohol could land you immediately in jail. These criminal penalties will vary from country to country. There are also some things that might be legal in the country you visit, but still illegal in the United States.

For example, you can be prosecuted under U.S. law if you buy pirated goods. Engaging in sexual conduct with children or using or disseminating child pornography in a foreign country is a crime prosecutable in the United States. If you break local laws in Djibouti, your U.S. passport won't help you avoid arrest or prosecution. It's very important to know what is legal and what is not wherever you go.

If you are arrested in Djibouti, you have the right to request authorities alert the U.S. Embassy of your arrest. The U.S. does not have an agreement with Djibouti requiring notification of the U.S. Embassy upon your arrest. If you are arrested in Djibouti you should use whatever means of communication available to alert the U.S. Embassy of your situation.

Special Circumstances: Although the narcotic khat is legal and widely chewed in Djibouti, it is illegal in many countries, including the United States. Driving under the influence of drugs and alcohol could result in legal penalties.

Djiboutians are generally conservative in dress and manner, especially in rural areas. Photography of public infrastructure (including, but not limited to, public buildings, seaports, the airport, bridges, military facilities or personnel) is not allowed in Djibouti. Use extreme caution when photographing anyone or anything near prohibited areas. Photographic equipment will be confiscated, and the photographer may be arrested.

Djibouti is a cash-based economy and credit cards are not widely accepted. Automated teller machines (ATMs) are limited. Changing money on the street is legal, but be aware of possible scams as well as personal safety considerations if people observe you carrying large amounts of cash. The exchange rate on the street will be similar to that at a bank or hotel. It is important that the U.S. banknotes that you carry have a date of 2003 or newer because many currency exchanges will not accept U.S. paper money older than 2003.

Djiboutian customs authorities may enforce strict regulations concerning temporary importation and exportation of firearms. It is advisable to contact the Embassy of Djibouti in Washington, DC, for specific information regarding customs requirements.

Accessibility: While in Djibouti individuals with disabilities may find accessibility and accommodations very different from what you find in the United States.The government does not mandate accessibility to buildings or government services for persons with disabilities, thus accessibility is limited. The constitution does not prohibit discrimination against persons with disabilities; however, the labor code prohibits discrimination in employment against such persons. Such persons have access to education and public health services.

Medical Facilities and Health Information: Adequate medical facilities in the capital of Djibouti are limited, and medicines are often unavailable. Medicines that are available are extremely expensive. Medical services in some outlying areas may be completely nonexistent. Motorists should be especially aware that, in case of an accident outside the capital, emergency medical treatment would depend almost exclusively on passersby. In addition, cell phone coverage in outlying areas is often unavailable, making it impossible to summon help.

Malaria and dengue fever are prevalent in Djibouti. Travelers who become ill with a fever or flu-like illness while traveling in a malaria-risk area and even up to one year after returning home should seek prompt medical attention, tell the physician their travel history, and let health care providers know what anti-malarial drugs they have been taking.

In 2005, polio was found in all of Djibouti's neighbors (Somalia, Ethiopia, Eritrea and Yemen), and health professionals strongly suspect it is present in Djibouti.

The Advisory Committee on Immunization Practices (ACIP) recommends that all infants and children in the United States should receive four doses of inactivated poliovirus vaccine (IPV) at 2, 4, 6–18 months and 4–6 years of age. Adults traveling to polio-endemic and epidemic areas and who have received a primary series with either IPV or oral polio vaccine should receive another dose of IPV. For adults, available data does not indicate the need for more than a single lifetime booster dose with IPV.

Tuberculosis is a serious health concern in Djibouti, including multi-drug resistant strains. For further information, please consult the CDC's information on TB.

In May 2006, avian influenza was confirmed in three chickens and one human in Djibouti. For more information about this illness, see the Department of State's Avian Flu Fact Sheet.

In an effort to combat H1N1, immigration authorities at Ambouli International Airport take travelers' temperature before admittance to the country. If a visitor is found to have a fever or otherwise appears to be sick, she or he may be detained or denied entrance.

You can find detailed information on vaccinations and other health precautions on the CDC website. For information about outbreaks of infectious diseases abroad, consult the World Health Organization (WHO) website. The WHO website also contains additional health information for travelers, including detailed country-specific health information.

Medical Insurance: You cannot assume your insurance will go with you when you travel. It is very important to find out BEFORE you leave whether or not your medical insurance will cover you overseas. You need to ask your insurance company two questions:

- Does my policy apply when I'm outside of the United States?
- Will it cover emergencies like a trip to a foreign hospital or a medical evacuation?

In many places, doctors and hospitals still expect payment in cash at the time of service. Your regular U.S. health insurance may not cover doctor and hospital visits in other countries. If your policy does not cover you when you travel, it is a very good idea to take out another one for your trip.

Traffic Safety and Road Conditions: While in a foreign country, U.S. citizens may encounter road conditions that differ significantly from those in the United States. The information below concerning Djibouti is provided for general reference only, and may not be totally accurate in a particular location or circumstance.

Driving on Djiboutian roads can be hazardous. Since most roads do not have shoulders or sidewalks, pedestrians and livestock use the roadways both day and night. Driving at night is extremely dangerous and strongly discouraged on all roads outside Djibouti City. While some main roads in Djibouti are well maintained, roads are often narrow, poorly lit, or rutted. Many secondary roads are in poor repair or are rutted dirt roads.

Drivers and pedestrians should exercise extreme caution. Minibuses and cars often break down; when breakdowns occur, local drivers usually place branches or rocks behind the vehicle to indicate trouble, but these warning signals are barely visible and hazardous in and of themselves. Excessive speed, unpredictable local driving habits, pedestrians and livestock in the roadway, and the lack of basic safety equipment on many vehicles are daily hazards. Speed limits are posted occasionally but are not enforced.

The leafy narcotic—khat, is widely used, particularly in the afternoons, creating other traffic hazards. The Djiboutian Gendarmerie and the National Police Force share responsibility for road safety in Djibouti. In March 2012 a "Road Police" was created, though its role has yet to be clearly defined. Djiboutian authorities recently erected traffic lights to help regulate the flow of traffic.

Be very cautious approaching these lights, as many other drivers continue to disregard them. Travelers should be aware that police use large obstacles as roadblocks on some of the major roads, and these may be difficult to see at night.

Drivers who do not have a four-wheel drive vehicle will encounter problems driving on rural roads. There are no emergency services for stranded drivers, and it is always advisable to carry a cell phone or satellite phone when undertaking a trip outside of the capital. Many parts of the country, however, do not have cell phone coverage.

While Djibouti has been declared a "mine-safe" country, this indicates landmines have been identified and marked, not that they have been removed. Landmines are known to be present in northern Tadjourah and Obock districts. In addition, there may be mines in the Ali Sabieh area of the south.

In March 2012, a 12-year-old boy was seriously injured by a land mine in the vicinity of Lac Assal and Ghoubet, two popular tourist destinations. The incident occurred in the area known as Dabaleh Gahar, east of where National Route 10 splits off from National Route 9. This location is approximately 20 km southeast of where most people visit Lac Assal; about one kilometer from the paved road. This area was home to a Djiboutian military encampment during the civil war (1991–1994) and the mine likely remained in place after that conflict.Travelers should stay on paved roads and should check with local authorities before using unpaved roads.

There are two main international highways to the capital city, via Dire Dawa, Ethiopia, and Obock, Djibouti, and both demand that drivers remain vigilant. The route towards Dire Dawa is in very poor condition. Both have a high volume of Ethiopian trucks transporting large cargo. Railroad crossings are not clearly marked.

The only means of public inter-city travel is by bus. Buses are poorly maintained and their operators often drive erratically with little regard for passenger safety. Taxis should be avoided at all costs.

Aviation Safety Oversight: As there is no direct commercial air service to the United States by carriers registered in Djibouti, the U.S. Federal Aviation Administration (FAA) has not assessed the government of Djibouti's Civil Aviation Authority for compliance with International Civil Aviation Organization (ICAO) aviation safety standards. Further information may be found on the FAA's safety assessment page.

Children's Issues: Please see the U.S. Dept. of State Office of Children's Issues web pages on intercountry adoption and international parental child abduction.

Intercountry Adoption

May 2012

The information in this section has been edited from the latest report available as of February 2013 from the State Department Bureau of Consular Affairs, Office of Overseas Citizens Services. For more information, please read the *Intercountry Adoption* section of this book and review current reports online at http://adoption.state.gov. Djibouti is not party to the Hague Convention on Protection of Children and Co-operation in Respect of Intercountry Adoption (the Hague Adoption Convention). Intercountry adoptions of children from non-Hague countries are processed in accordance with 8 Code of Federal Regulations, Section 204.3 as it relates to orphans as defined under the Immigration and Nationality Act, Section 101(b)(1)(F).

Adoption in Djibouti is a complicated, time consuming process with many legal hurdles. There is no clear, uniform adoption procedure. Generally, only non-Djiboutian children considered to be abandoned in Djibouti are available for adoption.

Djiboutian children can be adopted only in very exceptional cases (mostly by other family members) and at the discretion of the Djiboutian government. Adoption in Djibouti is divided into two types: simple and plénier. Simple adoption is when someone cares for the child as his/her own, but the child's name is not changed and the biological parents retain parental rights.

A plénier adoption is when the biological parents irrevocably relinquish parental rights and the child's last name is changed to match the adoptive parents. For the purposes of U.S. immigration law, a plénier adoption is required.

Who Can Adopt? To bring an adopted child to the United States from Djibouti, you must meet eligibility and suitability requirements. The U.S. Department of Homeland Security, U.S. Citizenship and Immigration Services (USCIS) determine Who Can Adopt under U.S. immigration law. Additionally, a child must meet the definition of orphan under U.S. immigration law in order to be eligible to immigrate to the United States on an IR-3 or IR-4 immigrant visa.

In addition to U.S. immigration requirements, you must also meet the following requirements in order to adopt a child from Djibouti.

Residency Requirements: Prospective adoptive parents must be physically present in Djibouti at the time of the proposed adoption, but need not be residents. The child must be both physically present and a resident of Djibouti.

Age of Adopting Parents: Prospective adoptive parents must be at least 25 years of age and must be at least 15 years older than the child. If the prospective adoptive parent is a relative, he/she need only be 21 years old. The prospective adoptive parent(s) must also be morally and physically sound, as determined by the Government of Djibouti.

Marriage: Prospective adoptive parents do not need to be married in order to complete the adoption process.

Income: Djiboutian law does not stipulate any specific income requirements; only that prospective adoptive parents should demonstrate that they have a steady, monthly income.

Other: Gays and lesbians adopting as individuals and same-sex couples are not eligible to adopt in Djibouti. It is unclear whether the Government of Djibouti would allow non-Muslim prospective parents to adopt a child that was born to Muslim biological parents.

Who Can Be Adopted? In addition to U.S. immigration requirements, Djibouti has specific requirements that a child must meet in order to be eligible for adoption.

Relinquishment: Only children considered to be abandoned or children whose parents are willing to irrevocably relinquish their parental rights are eligible for adoption.

Abandonment: Djibouti does not have a clear definition of what is legally considered to be abandonment; each case is individually examined by a local court.

Age of Adoptive Child: Children must be 17 years of age or younger. Please note, however, that in order for a child to meet the definition of orphan under U.S. immigration law, a Form I-600 petition must be filed while the child is under the age of 16 (or under the age of 18 if adopted, or to be adopted, together with a sibling under the age of 16).

Sibling Adoptions: There are no known sibling requirements; however this may vary on a case by case basis.

Special Needs or Medical Conditions: There are no known requirements.

Waiting Period or Foster Care: There is no defined waiting period; however, the process may take a year or more.

Prospective adoptive parents should be aware that not all children in orphanages or children's homes are adoptable. In many countries, biological parents place their child(ren) temporarily in an orphanage or children's home due to financial or other hardship, intending that the child return home when this becomes possible. In such cases, the birth parent(s) rarely would have relinquished their parental rights or consented to their child(ren)'s adoption.

Djibouti's Adoption Authority: Tribunal de Première Instance de Djibouti

The Process: The recommended first step in adopting a child from Djibouti is to decide whether or not to use a licensed adoption service provider in the United States that can help you with your adoption. Adoption service providers must be licensed by the U.S. state in which they operate.

There are no adoption service providers in Djibouti to assist with the Djiboutian portion of the adoption process. A U.S. adoption service provider can assist in the U.S. immigration portion of an adoption from Djibouti. According to court officials, adoptions do not require the participation of a lawyer, but may be beneficial to engage someone familiar with Djiboutian family law.

In order to adopt a child from Djibouti; you will need to meet the requirements of the Government of Djibouti and U.S. immigration law. You must submit an application to be found eligible to adopt with the Tribunal de Première Instance de Djibouti. Please see instructions below under Adoption Application.

You may also file an I-600A, Application for Advance Processing of an Orphan Petition with U.S. Department of Homeland Security's U.S. Citizenship and Immigration Services to be found eligible and suitable to adopt under U.S. Immigration Law.

There is no official process for matching you with a Djiboutian child, and there are no agencies available to assist you in Djibouti. Most matches are done through family connections. Each family must decide for itself whether or not it will be able to meet the needs of and provide a permanent home for a particular child.

Role of Adoption Authority: All adoptions are facilitated through the Tribunal de Première Instance de Djibouti, which serves as Djibouti's adoption authority.

Role of the Court: The court will issue final paperwork stating that the child has been adopted and that legal custody has been transferred to the prospective adoptive parents.

Role of Adoption Agencies: There are no adoption service providers in Djibouti to assist with an adoption.

Adoption Application: Once a child has been identified, adoption procedures must be initiated with a written request from the prospective adoptive parent(s) to the President of Tribunal de Première Instance to open an adoption case on their behalf.

The court has two responsibilities: it must verify whether the necessary legal conditions have been met, and that the adoption is in the best interest of the child. To that effect, it is mandatory that adoptive parent(s) attach the U.S. documents listed in the section below to their application. The court can order an additional social investigation report to complement the one already attached to the initial request (see below), and one or more types of specific medical examinations. The clerk of the District Court will then forward the request to the police for a background check to be performed (if the prospective adoptive parents are resident in Djibouti).

Procedures for a child with identified biological parent(s): The biological parents must agree to irrevocably relinquish their parental rights (i.e. a plénier adoption).

The biological parents must appear before the court with their identification and the child's birth certificate and sign a consent document. A three-month appeal period follows, during which time the biological parents may reclaim their parental rights or the prospective adoptive parents may decide to cancel the adoption.

At the end of that period, if no appeal is made, the prospective adoptive parents must submit a request to the court to continue the process, at which time the court will fix a hearing date. At the hearing, the judge will rule whether to grant a delegation of parental authority, which technically shifts parental authority from the biological to the adoptive parents. If the adoptive parents are residents of Djibouti, or if they plan to stay for some time, they may be granted temporary custody of the child, to allow the child to physically live with them.

The biological parents then have an additional two-month window within which they may reclaim the child. If they do not, the adoptive parents have to submit to the court a request for finalizing the adoption. At the hearing, the court will make a final ruling to grant the adoption.

However, for an additional two months the Public Ministry (office of the District Attorney) or any other concerned individual (family member), excluding the natural parents, may appeal for reversal if they can provide "serious evidence" that the adoption will adversely affect the child. The court can refuse to grant an adoption and may order the adoptive parents not to break the child's bonds with its biological family.

The judgment is always given in a public hearing. Whether the adoption is approved or rejected, the decision can be appealed, and the ensuing appeal may also be subject to a final appeal at the Supreme Court.

Procedure for an abandoned child with unknown parents: The process is similar to that of a child with identified biological parents, excluding steps pertaining to the biological parents. Instead, after the prospective adoptive parents have submitted a written request to the court, the court will order a police investigation to try and find the biological parents and establish their identity (this may take up to a month). If biological parents cannot be found and no one claims the child, the police will deliver a certificate of abandonment to the court, after which the court will proceed with the case.

Time Frame: It may take a year or more from the time the adoption application is submitted to the Tribunal de Première Instance until the prospective adoptive parents receive the final documents. Factors bearing on the length of time may include court-ordered investigations, parents' citizenship, court calendar, appeals, and individual case anomalies.

Adoption Fees: The Government of Djibouti processes all adoptions. All procedures undertaken by the court (Adoption Authority) are free of charge. Prospective adoptive parents should expect to pay for any/all required medical examinations for the child, as well as for their own travel expenses.

Adoption Fees: The Government of Djibouti processes all adoptions. All procedures undertaken by the court (Adoption Authority) are free of charge. Prospective adoptive parents should expect to pay for any/all required medical examinations for the child, as well as for their own travel expenses.

- **Documents Required:**
  Police clearance (indicating no arrest record);
- Home study report;
- Proof of adequate financial means and stability (last three pay slips, tax return, etc.)

Additional documents may be requested. You may be asked to provide proof that a document from the United States is authentic. If so, the Department of State, Authentications office may be able to assist.

Bringing Your Child Home: Once your adoption is complete (or you have obtained legal custody of the child), there are a few more steps to take before you can head home. Specifically, you need to apply for several documents for your child before he or she can travel to the United States, such as a birth certificate, a passport or travel document for your child from the country in which he or she was born, and a U.S. Immigration Visa.

For detailed and updated information on how to obtain these documents, review the *Intercountry Adoption* section in this publication and visit the U.S. Department of State Intercountry Adoption website at http://adoption.state.gov.

Child Citizenship Act: For adoptions finalized abroad, the Child Citizenship Act of 2000 allows your new child to acquire American citizenship automatically when he or she enters the United States as lawful permanent residents.

For adoptions finalized in the United States, the Child Citizenship Act of 2000 allows your new child to acquire American citizenship automatically when the court in the United States issues the final adoption decree. To learn more, review the *Intercountry Adoption* section in this publication and visit the U.S. Department of State Intercountry Adoption website at http://adoption.state.gov.

After Adoption: The government of Djibouti does not have any post-adoption requirements.

U.S. Embassy in Djbouti
Lot Number 350-B
Lotissement Haramous
Djibouti City
Tel: (253) 21-453-000
Fax: (253) 21-453-340
Email: ConsularDjibouti@state.gov
Internet: djibouti.usembassy.gov/

Djibouti's Adoption Authority
Office of the Secretary
Tribunal de Première Instance
Ministère de la Justice
B.P. 12
Djibouti
République de Djibouti
Tel: (253) 21-353-389

Embassy of Djibouti
1156 15th St., NW, Suite 515
Washington, DC 20005
Tel: 202-331-0270

Office of Children's Issues
U.S. Department of State
2201 C Street, NW
SA-29
Washington, DC 20520
Tel: 1-888-407-4747
E-mail: AskCI@state.gov
http://adoption.state.gov

For questions about immigration procedures, call the National Customer Service Center (NCSC) at 1-800-375-5283 (TTY 1-800-767-1833).

DOMINICA

Compiled from publications that were available as of February 2013 from the U.S. Department of State, the U.S. Department of Commerce, and the Central Intelligence Agency (CIA). See the introduction to this set for explanatory notes.

Official Name:
Commonwealth of Dominica

PROFILE

Geography

Area: total: 751 sq km; country comparison to the world: 189; land: 751 sq km; water: 0 sq km
Major cities: Roseau (capital) 14,000 (2009)
Climate: tropical; moderated by northeast trade winds; heavy rainfall
Terrain: rugged mountains of volcanic origin

People

Nationality: noun: Dominican(s); adjective: Dominican
Population: 73,126 (July 2012 est.)
Population growth rate: 0.216% (2012 est.)
Ethnic groups: black 86.8%, mixed 8.9%, Carib Amerindian 2.9%, white 0.8%, other 0.7% (2001 census)
Religions: Roman Catholic 61.4%, Protestant 20.6% (Seventh-Day Adventist 6%, Pentecostal 5.6%, Baptist 4.1%, Methodist 3.7%, Church of God 1.2%), Jehovah's Witnesses 1.2%, other Christian 7.7%, Rastafarian 1.3%, other or unspecified 1.6%, none 6.1% (2001 census)
Languages: English (official), French patois
Literacy: definition: age 15 and over has ever attended school; total population: 94%; male: 94%; female: 94% (2003 est.)
Health: life expectancy at birth: total population: 76.18 years; male: 73.23 years; female: 79.29 years (2012 est.); Infant mortality rate: total: 12.38 deaths/1,000 live births; male: 16.54 deaths/1,000 live births; female: 8.01 deaths/1,000 live births (2012 est.)
Unemployment rate: 23% (2000 est.)
Work force: 25,000 (2000 est.)

Government

Type: parliamentary democracy
Independence: 3 November 1978
Constitution: 3 November 1978
Political subdivisions: 10 parishes; Saint Andrew, Saint David, Saint George, Saint John, Saint Joseph, Saint Luke, Saint Mark, Saint Patrick, Saint Paul, Saint Peter
Suffrage: 18 years of age; universal

Economy

GDP (purchasing power parity): $1.035 billion (2012 est.); $989.5 million (2011 est.); $984.8 million (2010 est.); $981.5 million (2009 est.)
GDP real growth rate: 0.4% (2012 est.); 0.5% (2011 est.); 0.3% (2010 est.); -0.7% (2009 est.)
GDP per capita (PPP): $14,600 (2012 est.; $14,000 (2011 est.); $13,900 (2010 est.); $13,900 (2009 est.)
Natural resources: timber, hydropower, arable land
Agriculture products: bananas, citrus, mangos, root crops, coconuts, cocoa
Industries: soap, coconut oil, tourism, copra, furniture, cement blocks, shoes
Exports: $41 million (2012 est.); $40.4 million (2011 est.); $36.21 million (2010 est.)
Exports—commodities: bananas, soap, bay oil, vegetables, grapefruit, oranges
Exports—partners: Japan 45.8%, Antigua and Barbuda 8.2%, Jamaica 7.3%, Guyana 7%, Trinidad and Tobago 4.5% (2011)
Imports: $218.6 million (2012 est.); $207.1 million (2011 est.); $197.7 million (2010 est.)
Imports—commodities: manufactured goods, machinery and equipment, food, chemicals
Imports—partners: Japan 34.3%, US 15.7%, Trinidad and Tobago 14%, China 5.7%, Singapore 5.5% (2011)
Debt—external: $253.8 million (31 December 2012 est.); $303 million (2008); $213 million (2004)
Exchange rates: East Caribbean dollars (XCD) per US dollar; 2.7 (2012 est.); 2.7 (2011 est.); 2.7 (2010 est.); 2.7 (2009)

PEOPLE

Almost all Dominicans are descendants of enslaved Africans brought in by colonial planters in the 18th century. Dominica is the only island in the eastern Caribbean to retain some of its pre-Columbian population—the Carib Indians—about 3,000 of whom live on the island's east coast. The population growth rate is very low, due primarily to emigration to more prosperous Caribbean Islands, the United Kingdom, the United States, and Canada.

National/Racial/Ethnic Minorities

There is a Kalinago, or Carib, population estimated at about 3,000 persons, most of whom lived in the 3,782-acre Carib Territory, an area not clearly delineated by law. The Carib Act states that any child of a Kalinago is also Kalinago. Non-Kalinagos may become Kalinagos if they are invited to live in the Carib Territory and do so continuously for 12 years.

The Kalinago people continued to suffer from low levels of unofficial and societal discrimination. Kalinago women in particular suffered from these types of discrimination. Unemployment in the territory generally was higher than in the rest of the country, and mean income was below the national mean. There were few jobs in the territory, because of the decline of the agricultural sector and the inability to obtain bank financing due to the lack of collateral in terms of privately owned land. Many Kalinagos who moved to the capital city of Roseau did not report any significant discrimination. The vast majority of Kalinagos have intermarried, and it was not always easy to identify someone as Kalinago.

Language

English is the official language; however, because of historic French domination, the most widely spoken dialect is a French-based Creole.

Religion

According to the 2001 population and housing census, approximately 61 percent of the population is Roman Catholic. Seventh-day Adventists and Pentecostals represent 6 percent each, and Baptists and Methodists 4 percent each. There are also Anglicans, members of the Baha'i Faith, Christian Brethren, members of the Church of Christ, Jehovah's Witnesses, Muslims, Nazarenes, and Rastafarians. Six percent of the population claims no religious affiliation.

HISTORY

The island's indigenous Arawak people were expelled or exterminated by Caribs in the 14th century. Columbus landed there in November 1493. Spanish ships frequently landed on Dominica during the 16th century, but fierce resistance by the Caribs discouraged Spain's efforts at settlement.

In 1635, France claimed Dominica. Shortly thereafter, French missionaries became the first European inhabitants of the island. Carib incursions continued, though, and in 1660, the French and British agreed that both Dominica and St. Vincent should be abandoned. Dominica was officially neutral for the next century, but the attraction of its resources remained; rival expeditions of British and French foresters were harvesting timber by the start of the 18th century.

Largely due to Dominica's position between Martinique and Guadeloupe, France eventually became predominant, and a French settlement was established and grew. As part of the 1763 Treaty of Paris that ended the Seven Years' War, the island became a British possession. In 1778, during the American Revolutionary War, the French mounted a successful invasion with the active cooperation of the population. The 1783 Treaty of Paris, which ended the war, returned the island to Britain. French invasions in 1795 and 1805 ended in failure.

In 1763, the British established a legislative assembly, representing only the white population. In 1831, reflecting a liberalization of official British racial attitudes, the Brown Privilege Bill conferred political and social rights on free nonwhites. Three Blacks were elected to the legislative assembly the following year. Following the abolition of slavery, in 1838 Dominica became the first and only British Caribbean colony to have a Black-controlled legislature in the 19th century. Most Black legislators were smallholders or merchants who held economic and social views diametrically opposed to the interests of the small, wealthy English planter class. Reacting to a perceived threat, the planters lobbied for more direct British rule.

In 1865, after much agitation and tension, the colonial office replaced the elective assembly with one comprised of one-half elected members and one-half appointed. Planters allied with colonial administrators outmaneuvered the elected legislators on numerous occasions. In 1871, Dominica became part of the Leeward Island Federation. The power of the Black population progressively eroded. Crown Colony government was re-established in 1896. All political rights for the vast majority of the population were effectively curtailed. Development aid, offered as compensation for disenfranchisement, proved to have a negligible effect.

Following World War I, an upsurge of political consciousness throughout the Caribbean led to the formation of the Representative Government Association. Marshaling public frustration with the lack of a voice in the governing of Dominica, this group won one-third of the popularly elected seats of the legislative assembly in 1924 and one-half in 1936. Shortly thereafter, Dominica was transferred from the Leeward Island Administration and was governed as part of the Windwards until 1958, when it joined the short-lived West Indies Federation.

After the federation dissolved, Dominica became an associated state of the United Kingdom in 1967 and formally took responsibility for its internal affairs. On November 3, 1978, the Commonwealth of Dominica was granted independence by the United Kingdom.

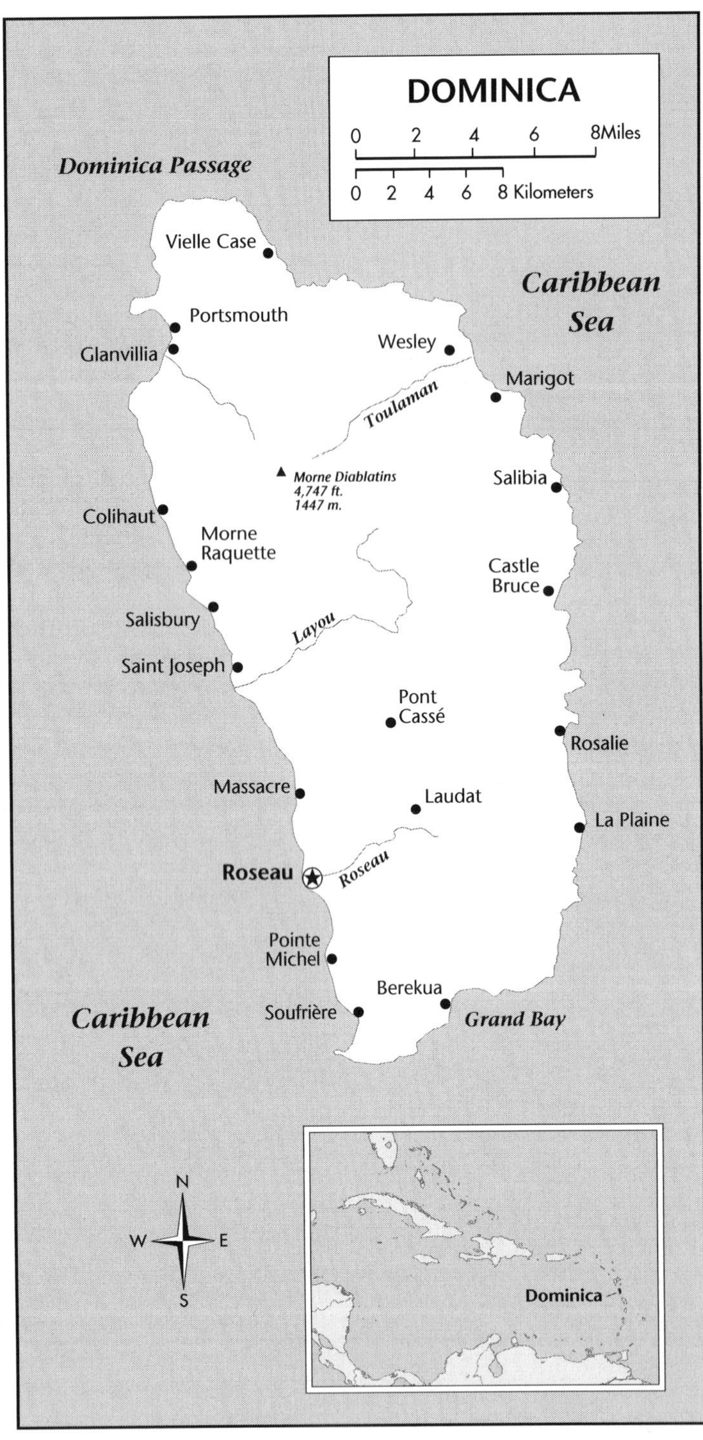

Independence did little to solve problems stemming from centuries of economic underdevelopment, and in mid-1979, political discontent led to the formation of an interim government. It was replaced after the 1980 elections by a government led by the Dominica Freedom Party under Prime Minister Eugenia Charles, the Caribbean's first female prime minister. Chronic economic problems were compounded by the severe impact of hurricanes in 1979 and in 1980. By the end of the 1980s, the economy recovered, but weakened again in the 1990s due to a decrease in banana prices. In the 2000s, the economy was hit by a spate of disasters, including the removal of the European preferential trade for bananas, the impact of Hurricane Dean, and the global financial meltdown. Dominica has managed quite well during the current global recession as a smaller percentage of its economy is based on tourism and foreign investment.

In the January 2000 elections, the Edison James United Workers Party (UWP) was defeated by the Dominican Labour Party (DLP), led by Roosevelt P. "Rosie" Douglas. Douglas died after only a few months in office and was replaced by Pierre Charles, who died in office in January 2004. Roosevelt Skerrit, also of the DLP, replaced Charles as Prime Minister. Under Prime Minister Skerrit's leadership, the DLP won elections in May 2005 and in December 2009. In 2009, the DLP won 18 of the 21 constituencies, with the UWP collecting 3 seats. Currently the opposition has decided to boycott parliament over allegations of campaign improprieties. Due to the absence in parliament of 2 UWP members, the government held by-elections on July 9, 2010 with both seats won by the UWP.

GOVERNMENT AND POLITICAL CONDITIONS

Dominica is a multiparty, parliamentary democracy. In 2009 elections Prime Minister Roosevelt Skerrit's Dominica Labour Party (DLP) prevailed over the opposition United Workers Party (UWP) by a margin of 18 seats to three seats. Although outside observers found the elections generally free and fair, the opposition continued to boycott Parliament over alleged electoral abuses.

Recent Elections

In parliamentary elections held in December 2009, the ruling DLP won 18 seats in the House of Assembly, defeating the UWP, which won three seats. Two of the three opposition members boycotted Parliament to pressure the government to call new elections. As a result of the boycott, after six months the government declared the two seats vacant by operation of law and called by-elections in those two constituencies, both won again by the opposition. The newly elected opposition members continued to boycott full participation in Parliament; they appear for each sitting, sign in, and then walk out.

The Caribbean Community and the Organization of American States sent teams of election observers, who declared the election to be fair and transparent. After the election, the opposition filed court complaints of election irregularities regarding a number of complaints, but the court rejected the claims except for one of ineligibility to hold office against two ministers over dual-nationality issues. After a full evidentiary trial, the court ruled against the opposition and determined the two ministers were eligible under the law.

Participation of Women and Minorities: Voters elected two women to the House of Assembly, and these women held two cabinet positions: the minister for social services, community development, and gender affairs; and the minister for culture, youth, and sports. The appointed Speaker of the House of Assembly was a woman, and the ruling DLP appointed one woman to serve in the 10-person appointed Senate.

The parliamentary representative for the constituency that includes the Carib Territory was a Carib.

Principal Government Officials

Last Updated: 1/31/2013

Pres.: **Eliud WILLIAMS**

Prime Min.: **Roosevelt SKERRIT**

Min. of Agriculture & Forestry: **Matthew WALTER**

Min. of Carib Affairs: **Ashton GRANEAU**

Min. of Culture, Youth, & Sports: **Justina CHARLES**

Min. of Education & Human Resource Development: **Peter ST. JEAN**

Min. of Employment, Trade, Industry, & Diaspora Affairs: **John Collin MCINTYRE**

Min. of Environment, Natural Resources, Physical Planning, & Fisheries: **Kenneth DARROUX**

Min. of Finance: **Roosevelt SKERRIT**

Min. of Foreign Affairs: **Roosevelt SKERRIT**

Min. of Health: **Julius TIMOTHY**

Min. of Information, Telecommunication, & Constituency Empowerment: **Ambrose GEORGE**

Min. of Lands, Housing, Settlements, & Water Resource Management: **Reginald AUSTRIE**

Min. of National Security, Labor, & Immigration: **Charles SAVARIN**

Min. of Public Works, Energy, & Ports: **Rayburn BLACKMOORE**

Min. of Social Services, Community Development, & Gender Affairs: **Gloria SHILLINGFORD**

Min. of Tourism & Legal Affairs: **Ian DOUGLAS**

Attorney Gen.: **Levi PETER**

Permanent Representative to the UN, New York: **Vince HENDERSON**

ECONOMY

The Dominican economy has been dependent on agriculture - primarily bananas - in years past, but increasingly has been driven by tourism as the government seeks to promote Dominica as an "ecotourism" destination. In order to diversify the island's production base, the government also is attempting to develop an offshore financial sector and has signed an agreement with the EU to develop geothermal energy resources.

In 2003, the government began a comprehensive restructuring of the economy - including elimination of price controls, privatization of the state banana company, and tax increases - to address an economic and financial crisis and to meet IMF requirements.

This restructuring paved the way for an economic recovery and helped to reduce the debt burden, which remains at about 80% of GDP. Hurricane Dean struck the island in August 2007 causing damages equivalent to 20% of GDP.

In 2009, the economy contracted as a result of the global recession and growth remains anemic.

Labor Conditions

Although two laws prohibit employment of children, one law defines a "child" as under age 12 and the other as under age 14 for hazardous work. Nonetheless, the government set a policy that defines 15 years as the minimum age for employment and enforced this standard. Children between the ages of 12 and 14 were allowed to work only in certain family enterprises such as farming.

Safety standards limit the type of work, conditions, and hours of work for children over the age of 14. The government effectively enforced these standards, and there were no abuses reported. Although resources were insufficient to engage in inspections on a comprehensive basis, the laws and penalties were generally adequate to remove children from illegal child labor.

The minimum wage law establishes a base wage of EC$5.00 (approximately $1.87) per hour for all public and private workers. The minimum wage varies according to category of worker, with the lowest minimum wage set at EC$4.00 ($1.50), and the maximum at EC$5.50 ($2.06) per hour. Most workers (including domestic employees) earned more than the legislated minimum wage as prevailing wages were much higher than statutory minimum wages. Enforcement is the responsibility of the labor commissioner. Labor laws provide that the labor commissioner may authorize the employment of a person with disabilities at a wage lower than the minimum rate to enable that person to be employed gainfully. The labor commissioner has not authorized subminimum wages for the last few years.

The standard legal workweek is 40 hours in five days. The law provides overtime pay for work above the standard workweek; moreover, excessive overtime is not prohibited. The law stipulates paid holidays.

The government effectively enforced all labor standards, including in the informal sector, which accounted for close to 50 percent of total employment, and in which workers were not unionized.

U.S.-DOMINICAN RELATIONS

The United States established diplomatic relations with Dominica in 1979 following its independence from the United Kingdom. Relations between the United States and Dominica are friendly. The United States supports the Dominican Government's efforts to expand its economic base and to provide a higher standard of living for its citizens. The two countries work together in the battle against illegal drugs. Dominica cooperates with U.S. agencies and participates in counternarcotics programs in an effort to curb narco-trafficking and marijuana cultivation. The two governments have signed a maritime law enforcement agreement to strengthen counternarcotics coordination as well as mutual legal assistance and extradition treaties to enhance joint efforts in combating international crime. The United States maintains no official presence in Dominica. The Ambassador and Embassy officers are resident in Barbados and travel frequently to Dominica.

U.S. Assistance to Dominica

U.S. assistance to Dominica is primarily channeled through multilateral agencies such as the World Bank and the Caribbean Development Bank, and through the U.S. Agency for International Development office in Bridgetown, Barbados. The Peace Corps provides technical assistance to Dominica, and has volunteers on the island working mostly in education, youth development, and health. The United States provides training, equipment, and material to Dominican security and defense forces, including through the Caribbean Basin Security Initiative

Bilateral Economic Relations

Dominica is a beneficiary of the U.S. Caribbean Basin Initiative (CBI), which grants duty-free entry into the United States for many goods. The CBI aims to facilitate the economic development and export diversification of the Caribbean Basin economies. Dominica is a member of the Caribbean Community and Common Market (CARICOM). At the 2012 meeting of the U.S.-CARICOM Trade and Investment Council, the parties approved an action agenda outlining priorities for strengthening and deepening the trading relationship.

Dominica's Membership in International Organizations

Dominica and the United States belong to a number of the same international organizations, including the United Nations, Organization of American States, International Monetary Fund, World Bank, and World Trade Organization.

Bilateral Representation

Dominica maintains an embassy in the United States at 3216 New Mexico Ave., NW, Washington, DC 20016 (tel. 202-364-6781).

Principal U.S. Embassy Officials

Last Updated: 1/14/2013

BRIDGETOWN (E) Wildey Business Park, Wildey, St. Michael BB 14006, 246-227-4000, Fax 246-227-4088, Workweek: Mon-Fri: 8.00–4.30, Website: http://bridgetown.usembassy.gov/

DCM OMS:	Frances Youmans
AMB OMS:	Ellen Benjamin-Leon
CDC:	Rachel Alabalak
Co-CLO:	Kathryn Mctigue Floyd
DHS/CBP:	Stephen Bows
FM:	Bruce Youmans
HRO:	Traci Cassilly
MGT:	Jeremey Neitzke
MLO/ODC:	CDR Michael Long
NAS/INL:	Kurt Van Der Walde
PAO/ADV:	Rachel Zaspel
POSHO:	Bruce Youmans
SDO/DATT:	CDR Michael Long
AMB:	Larry Palmer
CG:	Mark Bysfield
DCM:	Christopher Sandrolini
PAO:	Rebecca Ross
GSO:	M. Holly Peirce
RSO:	Thomas W.Baker
AFSA:	Vacant
AID:	Daniel Smolka
CLO:	Ylodia (Lisa) Robinson
DEA:	Charles Graham
ECON:	Brian Greaney
EEO:	Gregory Floyd
FAA:	Dawn Flanagan (Res. Washington)
FMO:	W. Lee Thompson
ICASS Chair:	Charles Graham
IMO:	Michael Cassilly
IRS:	Andrew Thornton
ISO:	Frederick Melton
ISSO:	Pic Jordan
LAB:	Gregory Floyd
LEGATT:	David Brooks
POL:	Brian Greaney
State ICASS:	Kurt Van Der Walde

Other Contact Information

International Trade Administration
U.S. Department of Commerce
1401 Constitution Ave NW
Washington, DC 20230
Tel: 1-800-USA-TRADE
http://trade.gov/

Caribbean/Latin American Action
1818 N Street, NW, Suite 310
Washington, DC 20036
Tel: (202) 466-7464
Fax: (202) 822-0075

TRAVEL

Consular Information Sheet

April 13, 2011

Country Description: Dominica is an English-speaking developing Caribbean island nation. The tourism industry is in the early stages of development; first-class tourist facilities are limited, but medium-range facilities are widely available.

Smart Traveler Enrollment Program (STEP)/Embassy Locations: If you are going to live in or visit Dominica, please take the time to tell our Embassy in Bridgetown, Barbados about your trip. If you check in, we can keep you up to date with important safety and security announcements. It will also help your friends and family get in touch with you in an emergency.

U.S. Embassy in Bridgetown
Wildey Business Park
St. Michael, Barbados
Telephone: (246) 227-4399
Emergency after-hours telephone: (246) 227-4000
Facsimile: (246) 431-0179
Email: BridgetownACS@state.gov
Hours of operation are 8:30 a.m.—4:30 p.m. Monday through Friday, except Barbadian and U.S. holidays.

Entry/Exit Requirements For U.S. Citizens: In addition to a valid passport, U.S. citizens may be asked to present a return or onward ticket. U.S. citizens should take special care to secure their passports while traveling as it can be time-consuming and difficult to acquire new proof of citizenship to facilitate return travel should the passport be lost or stolen. There is a departure tax of US$22 assessed when leaving Dominica.

Children under twelve years of age are exempt from the departure tax. For further information concerning entry requirements, travelers can contact the Embassy of the Commonwealth of Dominica, 3216 New Mexico Avenue, N.W., Washington, D.C. 20016, telephone (202) 364-6781, e-mail: embdomdc@aol.com, or the Consulate General of Dominica in New York at (212) 768-2480. Visit the Dominica Division of Tourism offical website for more information.

All U.S. citizens traveling outside of the United States are required to present a passport or other valid travel document to enter the United States. This extended to all sea travel (except closed-loop cruises), including ferry service on June 1, 2009. Travelers must now present a Western Hemisphere Travel Initiative (WHTI) compliant document such as a passport or a passport card for entry to the United States. While passport cards and enhanced driver's licenses are sufficient for entry into the United States, they may not be accepted by the particular country you plan to visit; please be sure to check with your cruise line and countries of destination for any foreign entry requirements. We strongly encourage all U.S. citizen travelers to apply for a U.S. passport or passport card well in advance of anticipated travel. U.S. citizens can visit travel.state.gov or call 1-877-4USA-PPT (1-877-487-2778) for information on how to apply for their passports.

Be aware that Caribbean cruises that begin and end in the U.S. (closed loop cruises) do not require that you travel with a valid passport. However, should you need to disembark due to an emergency and you do not have a valid passport, you may encounter difficulties entering or remaining in a foreign country. You may also have difficulty attempting to re-enter the United States by air because many airlines will require a valid passport before allowing you to board the aircraft. As such, it is strongly recommended that you always travel abroad with your valid passport.

The U.S. Department of State is unaware of any HIV/AIDS entry restrictions for visitors to or foreign residents of Dominica. Please contact the Embassy of Dominicabefore you travel.

Threats to Safety and Security: Stay up to date by bookmarking our Bureau of Consular Affairs' website, which contains the current Travel Warnings and Travel Alerts, as well as the Worldwide Caution. Follow us on Twitter and become a fan of the Bureau of Consular Affairs page on facebook as well. You can also call 1-888-407-4747 toll-free in the U.S. and Canada, or by calling a regular toll-line at 1-202-501-4444, from other countries.

These numbers are available from 8:00 a.m. to 8:00 p.m. Eastern Time, Monday through Friday (except U.S. federal holidays). Take some time before travel to improve your personal security—things are not the same everywhere as they are in the United States.

Crime: Petty street crime occurs in Dominica. Valuables left unattended, especially on beaches, are vulnerable to theft. If renting a private property on Dominica, be certain to request proof of insurance from the property owner. Rented villas are sometimes robbed, especially those in the Calibishie area, and if the owner has no insurance for theft you will be unable to recoup your losses. Don't buy counterfeit and pirated goods, even if they are widely available. Not only are the bootlegs illegal in the United States, if you purchase them you may be breaking local law.

Victims of Crime: If you or someone you know becomes the victim of a crime abroad, you should contact the local police and the nearest U.S. embassy or consulate (see the Department of State's list of embassies and consulates). If your passport is stolen we can help you replace it. For violent crimes such as assault and rape, we can, for example, help you find appropriate medical care, contact family members or friends and help you get money from them if you need it. Although the investigation and prosecution of the crime are solely the responsibility of local authorities, consular officers can help you to understand the local criminal justice process and to find an attorney if needed.

The local equivalent to the "911" emergency line in Dominica is 911 or 999. The Roseau police can be reached at 767-448-2222.

Criminal Penalties: While you are traveling in Dominica, you are subject to its laws even if you are a U.S. citizen. Foreign laws and legal systems can be vastly different than our own. In some places you may be taken in for questioning if you don't have your passport with you. In some places, it is illegal to take pictures of certain buildings. In some places driving under the influence could land you immediately in jail. These criminal penalties will vary from country to country. There are also some things that might be legal in the country you visit, but still illegal in the United States, and you can be prosecuted under U.S. law if you buy pirated goods.Engaging in sexual conduct with children or using or disseminating child pornography in a foreign country is a crime prosecutable in the United States. If you break local laws in Dominica, your U.S. passport won't help you avoid arrest or prosecution. It's very important to know what's legal and what's not where you are going. Persons violating Dominica's laws, even unknowingly, may be expelled, arrested or imprisoned. Penalties for possession, use, or trafficking in illegal drugs in Dominicaare severe, and convicted offenders can expect long jail sentences and heavy fines.

Special Circumstances: All Caribbean countries can be affected by hurricanes. The hurricane season normally runs from early June to the end of November, but there have been hurricanes in December in recent years. General information about natural disaster preparedness is available via the Internet from the U.S. Federal Emergency Management Agency (FEMA).

There is no U.S. Embassy or Consulate in Dominica. The U.S. Embassy in Bridgetown, Barbados is responsible for American Citizens Services on the island of Dominica. U.S. citizens are encouraged to carry a copy of their citizenship documents with them at all times so, if questioned by local officials, proof of identity and U.S. citizenship are readily available.

Accessibility: While in Dominica, individuals with disabilities may find accessibility and accommodation very different from what you find in the United States. There is no legal requirement in Dominica mandating access to buildings for persons with disabilities. Access to buildings, pedestrian paths and transportation is extremely difficult for persons with disabilities. Sidewalks (if they exist) are very uneven and will only occasionally have ramps at intersections. Pedestrian crossings are also very infrequent. In general, restaurants, hotels and residential buildings have stairs at the entrance without wheelchair ramps, except perhaps major hotels and retail areas. Buses and taxis do not have special accommodations for disabled persons.

Medical Facilities and Health Information: Medical care is limited. The major hospital is Princess Margaret Hospital (telephone (767) 448-2231/5720). In addition, there is one other hospital in Dominica and several clinics. There is an operational hyperbaric chamber at the main hospital. The private hospital and clinics will take emergency cases. There is limited ambulance service on most of the island, and a sea rescue service is now available at the North end of the island. Serious medical problems requiring hospitalization and/or medical evacuation to the United States can cost thousands of dollars.

Doctors and hospitals often expect immediate cash payment for health services. You can find good information on vaccinations and other health precautions, on the CDC website. For information about outbreaks of infectious diseases abroad, consult the World Health Organization (WHO) website. The WHO website also contains additional health information for travelers, including detailed country-specific health information.

Medical Insurance: You can't assume your insurance will go with you when you travel. It's very important to find out BEFORE you leave. You need to ask your insurance company two questions:

- Does my policy apply when I'm out of the U.S.?
- Will it cover emergencies like a trip to a foreign hospital or an evacuation?

In many places, doctors and hospitals still expect payment in cash at the time of service. Your regular U.S. health insurance may not cover doctors' and hospital visits in other countries. If your policy doesn't go with you when you travel, it's a very good idea to take out another one for your trip.

Traffic Safety and Road Conditions: While in Dominica, you may encounter road conditions that differ significantly from those in the United States. Vehicles are driven on the left in Dominica. Seatbelt laws are not strictly enforced. Roads are narrow with steep inclines throughout the island. There are few guardrails in areas that have precipitous drop-offs from the road.

Be especially careful on the two hour trip from the airport to the capital, Roseau, that winds through the mountainous interior. Serious accidents involving tourist vehicles occur periodically. Road signs are limited outside of the major towns. Drivers should be alert for minibus (taxi) drivers, who often make sudden stops or pull out into traffic without warning or signaling. A local temporary driver's license is required. These can be purchased at all car rental offices and from the Traffic Department in Roseau.

Aviation Safety Oversight: The U.S. Federal Aviation Administration (FAA) has assessed the Government ofDominica's Civil Aviation Authority as being in compliance with International Civil Aviation Organization (ICAO) aviation safety standards for oversight of Dominica's air carrier operations. Further information may be found on the FAA's safety assessment page.

Children's Issues: Please see the U.S. Dept. of State Office of Children's Issues web pages on intercountry adoption and international parental child abduction.

Intercountry Adoption

December 2008

The information in this section has been edited from the latest report available as of February 2013 from the State Department Bureau of Consular Affairs, Office of Overseas Citizens Services. For more information, please read the *Intercountry Adoption* section of this book and review current reports online at http://adoption.state.gov.

Dominica is not party to the Hague Convention on Protection of Children and Co-operation in Respect of Intercountry Adoption (Hague Adoption Convention). Therefore, when the Hague Adoption Convention entered into force for the United States on April 1, 2008, intercountry adoption processing for Dominica did not change.

Who Can Adopt? To bring an adopted child to United States from Dominica, you must be found eligible to adopt by the U.S. Government. The U.S. Government agency responsible for making this determination is the Department of Homeland Security, U.S. Citizenship and Immigration Services (USCIS).

Residency Requirements: The Dominica government has no specific residency requirements for prospective adoptive parents.

Age Requirements: Adoptive parents should not be under the age of twenty-five (25) years old.

Income Requirements: The adopting parent(s) should be employed or have means of supporting the child. There is no specific income requirement.

Who Can be Adopted? Dominica has no specific requirements that a child must meet in order to be eligible for adoption. In addition to these requirements, a child must meet the definition of an orphan under U.S. law for you to bring him or her back to the United States.

The Process: The first step in adopting a child from Dominica is usually to select a licensed agency in the United States that can help with your adoption. Adoption service providers must be licensed by the U.S. state in which they operate. If you are eligible to adopt, and a child is available for intercountry adoption, the central adoption authority in Dominica will provide you with a referral to a child. Each family must decide for itself whether or not it will be able to meet the needs of a particular child and provide a permanent family placement for the referred child.

Role of the Adoption Authority: Parents are not matched to children. An adoption process begins when a child has been identified for adoption. Prospective adoptive parents must submit to the Welfare Division a copy of their home study report and W2 tax form.

Time Frame: There is no specified period. A short hearing is required after all requirements are met and all documents are in order.

Adoption Fees: Adoption fees vary from lawyer to lawyer but an adoptive parent can expect to pay at least US $700 to $1000 for an adoption, including stamp duty.

Documents Required:

- Petition for Adoption (from country of adoptive parents)
- Affidavit of support (from country of adoptive parents)
- Consent of biological parents
- Birth certificate of child
- Application to appoint Guardian Ad Litem
- Guardian Ad Litem Report
- Home study report from prospective adoptive parents' country if not a citizen of Dominica and W2 tax forms to be submitted to the Welfare Division
- If married a marriage certificate and if one spouse is adopting the consent of the other spouse
- Application for Adoption and Draft Adoption Order

Bringing Your Child Home: Once your adoption is complete (or you have obtained legal custody of the child), there are a few more steps to take before you can head home. Specifically, you need to apply for several documents for your child before he or she can travel to the United States, such as a birth certificate, a passport or travel document for your child from the country in which he or she was born, and a U.S. Immigration Visa. For detailed and updated information on how to obtain these documents, review the *Intercountry Adoption* section in this publication and visit the U.S. Department of State Intercountry Adoption website at http://adoption.state.gov.

Child Citizenship Act: For adoptions finalized abroad, the Child Citizenship Act of 2000 allows your new child to acquire American citizenship automatically when he or she enters the United States as lawful permanent residents. For adoptions finalized in the United States, the Child Citizenship Act of 2000 allows your new child to acquire American citizenship automatically when the court in the United States issues the final adoption decree. To learn more, review the *Intercountry Adoption* section in this publication and visit the U.S. Department of State Intercountry Adoption website at http://adoption.state.gov.

U.S. Embassy in Barbados
Wildey Business Park
St. Michael, BB 14006
Barbados, W.I.
Phone: 246-431-0225
Mailing Address:
P.O. Box 302
Bridgetown BB 11000
Bridgetown, Barbados
Phone: 246-431-0225
Fax: 246-431-0179

Dominica's Adoption Authority
Welfare Division
Government Head Quarters
Roseau, Dominica.
Telephone: 767-448-2401, extensions 3019, 3020, 3334 or 3254

Embassy of Dominica
3216 New Mexico Avenue, NW
Washington, DC 20016
Telephone: (202) 364-6781
Fax: (202) 364-6791

Office of Children's Issues
U.S. Department of State
2201 C Street, NW
SA-29
Washington, DC 20520
Tel: 1-888-407-4747
E-mail: AskCI@state.gov
http://adoption.state.gov

For questions about immigration procedures, call the National Customer Service Center (NCSC) at 1-800-375-5283 (TTY 1-800-767-1833).

International Parental Child Abduction

January 2012

The information in this section has been edited from the latest report available as of February 2013 from the State Department Bureau of Consular Affairs, Office of Overseas Citizens Services. For more information, please read the *International Parental Child Abduction* section of this book and check for updated reports online at www.travel.state.gov/abduction.

Disclaimer: The information in this flyer relating to the legal requirements of specific foreign countries is provided for general information only. Questions involving interpretation of specific foreign laws should be addressed to foreign legal counsel.

General Information: The Government of the Commonwealth of Dominica is not a party to the Hague Convention on the Civil Aspects of International Child Abduction, nor are there any international or bilateral treaties in force between Dominica and the United States dealing with international parental child abduction. Recommendations to be a signatory to the Hague Convention on Civil Aspects of International Child Abduction have been submitted to the Government for consideration. American citizens who travel to Dominica place themselves under the jurisdiction of local courts. American citizens planning a trip to Dominica with dual national children should bear this in mind.

Custody Disputes: In Dominica if parents are legally married they share the custody of their children, in the sense that the children live with them and are taken care of by them in the matrimonial home. However, legal custody lies with the father. When parents are not married the custody of the child usually lies with the mother. Due to the death of the mother, mental problems, or a declaration made by the Court that the mother is unfit based on an application by the father, a father may apply to the court for custody of the child. Foreign court orders are not automatically recognized.

Enforcement of Foreign Judgments: Custody orders and judgments of foreign courts may be enforced in Dominica once there has been compliance with The Commonwealth Judgments Reciprocal Enforcements Act, which provides for reciprocal enforcement in the state of judgments in Courts of the United Kingdom and other Commonwealth Countries; or The Foreign Judgments Reciprocal Enforcement Act, which provides for judgments given in foreign countries that accord reciprocal treatment to judgments given in Dominica.

Visitation Rights: In cases where one parent has been granted custody of a child, the other parent is usually granted visitation rights. Under the Maintenance Act 15 of 2001, when a parent has been made to maintain a child under a Maintenance Order, a parent can apply to the court for access to the child at the time when the order is made or thereafter once the order is in force. If a custodial parent fails to allow visitation, the non-custodial parent may appeal to the court.

Dual Nationality: Dual nationality is recognized under Dominican law.

Passports for Minors and the Children's Passport Issuance Alert Program: For more information on these topics, see the *International Parental Child Abduction* section of this publication and review current reports from the U.S. Department of State at www.travel.state.gov/abduction.

Travel Restrictions: No exit visas are required to leave Dominica.

Criminal Remedies: For information on possible criminal remedies, please contact your local law enforcement authorities or the nearest office of the Federal Bureau of Investigation (FBI). Information is also available on the Internet at the web site of the U.S. Department of Justice, Office of Juvenile Justice and Delinquency Prevention (OJJDP) at http://www.ojjdp.ncjrs.org.

Persons who wish to pursue a child custody claim in a Dominican court should retain an attorney in Dominica. The U.S. Embassy in Barbados maintains a list of attorneys willing to represent American clients. A copy of this list may be obtained by requesting one from the Embassy at:

U.S. Embassy Bridgetown
Consular Section
ALICO Building, Cheapside
P O Box 302
Bridgetown
Barbados
Telephone: [246] 431-0225
Fax: [246] 431-0179
http://www.usembassy.state.gov/bridgetown

Questions involving Dominican law should be addressed to a Dominican attorney or to the Embassy of Dominica in the United States at:

Embassy of the Commonwealth of Dominica
3216 New Mexico Avenue, NW
Washington, DC 20016
Telephone: (202) 364-6791

More Information: For further information and/or assistance in either preventing or responding to an international parental child abduction, contact the Office of Children's Issues, U.S. Department of State at (202) 736-9090 or visit its web site at www.travel.state.gov/abduction.

DOMINICAN REPUBLIC

Compiled from publications that were available as of February 2013 from the U.S. Department of State, the U.S. Department of Commerce, and the Central Intelligence Agency (CIA). See the introduction to this set for explanatory notes.

Official Name:
Dominican Republic

PROFILE

Geography

Area: total: 48,670 sq km; country comparison to the world: 132; land: 48,320 sq km; water: 350 sq km
Major cities: Santo Domingo (capital) 2.138 million (2009)
Climate: tropical maritime; little seasonal temperature variation; seasonal variation in rainfall
Terrain: rugged highlands and mountains with fertile valleys interspersed

People

Nationality: noun: Dominican(s); adjective: Dominican
Population: 10,088,598 (July 2012 est.)
Population growth rate: 1.305% (2012 est.)
Ethnic groups: mixed 73%, white 16%, black 11%
Religions: Roman Catholic 95%, other 5%
Languages: Spanish (official)
Literacy: definition: age 15 and over can read and write; total population: 87%; male: 86.8%; female: 87.2% (2002 census)
Health: life expectancy at birth: total population: 77.44 years; male: 75.28 years; female: 79.69 years (2012 est.); Infant mortality rate: total: 21.3 deaths/1,000 live births; male: 23.27 deaths/1,000 live births; female: 19.25 deaths/1,000 live births (2012 est.)
Unemployment rate: 14.7% (2012 est.)
Work force: 4.806 million (2012 est.)

Government

Type: democratic republic
Independence: 27 February 1844
Constitution: 28 November 1966; amended 25 July 2002 and January 2010
Political subdivisions: 31 provinces (provincias, singular—provincia) and 1 district (distrito)
Suffrage: 18 years of age, universal and compulsory; married persons regardless of age can vote; note—members of the armed forces and national police cannot vote by law

Economy

GDP (purchasing power parity): $98.74 billion (2012 est.); $94.58 billion (2011 est.); $90.52 billion (2010 est.); $84.01 billion (2009 est.)
GDP real growth rate: 4% (2012 est.); 4.5% (2011 est.); 7.8% (2010 est.); 3.5% (2009 est.)
GDP per capita (PPP): $9,600 (2012 est.); $9,400 (2011 est.); $9,200 (2010 est.); $8,700 (2009 est.)
Natural resources: nickel, bauxite, gold, silver
Agriculture products: sugarcane, coffee, cotton, cocoa, tobacco, rice, beans, potatoes, corn, bananas; cattle, pigs, dairy products, beef, eggs
Industries: tourism, sugar processing, ferronickel and gold mining, textiles, cement, tobacco
Exports: $9.467 billion (2012 est.); $8.536 billion (2011 est.); $6.598 billion (2010 est.)
Exports—commodities: ferronickel, sugar, gold, silver, coffee, cocoa, tobacco, meats, consumer goods
Exports—partners: US 49.3%, Haiti 16.9% (2011)
Imports: $18.2 billion (2012 est.); $17.42 billion (2011 est.); $15.3 billion (2010 est.)
Imports—commodities: foodstuffs, petroleum, cotton and fabrics, chemicals and pharmaceuticals
Imports—partners: US 43.4%, Venezuela 7.1%, Mexico 6%, China 5.7% (2011)
Debt—external: $16.58 billion (31 December 2012 est.); $14.42 billion (31 December 2011 est.); $12.86 billion (31 December 2010 est.)
Exchange rates: Dominican pesos (DOP) per US dollar; 39.42 (2012 est.); 38.232 (2011 est.); 37.307 (2010 est.); 36.03 (2009); 34.775 (2008); 33.113 (2007)

PEOPLE

Slightly fewer than half of Dominicans live in rural areas; many are small landholders. Haitians form the largest foreign minority group. Spanish is the primary language.

National/Racial/Ethnic Minorities

Haitians continued to immigrate to the country in search of economic opportunity and relief, especially following the January 2010 earthquake. However, the Migration Directorate continued to carry out "devoluciones" or "returns" of undocumented Haitians to Haiti.

Some Haitian immigrants and others lived in shantytowns or sugarcane work camps known as bateyes. As in many poor areas in other parts of the country, these were harsh environments with limited or no electricity, running water, sanitary facilities, or adequate schooling. In many bateyes medical assistance either was rudimentary or not readily available, and clean water was rarely available. Many batey residents, lacking documentation, felt they had little choice but to remain in their communities, where they felt relatively safe from the risks of deportation and harassment that existed elsewhere in the country.

Religion

The largest religious group is the Roman Catholic Church. Traditional Protestants, evangelical Christian groups (particularly Assemblies of God, Church of God, Baptists, and Pentecostals), Seventh-day Adventists, Jehovah's Witnesses, and The Church of Jesus Christ of Latter-day Saints (Mormons) have a smaller but growing presence. According to a 2006 population survey by the Gallup Organization, the population was approximately 40 percent Catholic (practicing), 29 percent Catholic (nonpracticing), and 18 percent evangelical Protestant. In the same study, approximately 11 percent stated they had no religion.

The Dominican Confederation of Evangelical Unity claimed evangelicals represented 16 to 20 percent of the population. There are approximately 350 Jews. Most live in Santo Domingo, which has two synagogues and one rabbi. There is a synagogue for the small Jewish community in Sosua, which is led by a community leader, but there is no ordained rabbi.

There are approximately 800 Muslims, including foreign students. There are a small number of Buddhists and Hindus. Some Catholics practice a combination of Catholicism and Afro-Caribbean beliefs (santeria), witchcraft (brujeria), or voodoo (vodou), but because these practices are usually concealed the number of adherents is unknown.

HISTORY

The island of Hispaniola, of which the Dominican Republic forms the eastern two-thirds and Haiti the remainder, was originally occupied by Tainos, an Arawak-speaking people. The Tainos welcomed Columbus in his first voyage in 1492, but subsequent colonizers were brutal, reducing the Taino population from about 1 million to about 500 in 50 years. To ensure adequate labor for plantations, the Spanish brought African slaves to the island beginning in 1503.

In the next century, French settlers occupied the western end of the island, which Spain ceded to France in 1697, and which, in 1804, became the Republic of Haiti. The Haitians conquered the whole island in 1822 and held it until 1844, when forces led by Juan Pablo Duarte, the hero of Dominican independence, drove them out and established the Dominican Republic as an independent state.

In 1861, the Dominicans voluntarily returned to the Spanish Empire; in 1865, independence was restored. Economic difficulties, the threat of European intervention, and ongoing internal disorders led to a U.S. occupation in 1916 and the establishment of a military government in the Dominican Republic. The occupation ended in 1924, with a democratically elected Dominican Government.

In 1930, Rafael L. Trujillo, a prominent army commander, established absolute political control. Trujillo promoted economic development—from which he and his supporters benefited—and severe repression of domestic human rights. Mismanagement and corruption resulted in major economic problems. In August 1960, the Organization of American States (OAS) imposed diplomatic sanctions against the Dominican Republic as a result of Trujillo's complicity in an attempt to assassinate President Romulo Betancourt of Venezuela. These sanctions remained in force after Trujillo's death by assassination in May 1961. In November 1961, the Trujillo family was forced into exile.

In January 1962, a council of state that included moderate opposition elements with legislative and executive powers was formed. OAS sanctions were lifted January 4, and, after the resignation of President Joaquin Balaguer on January 16, the council under President Rafael E. Bonnelly headed the Dominican Government.

In 1963, Juan Bosch was inaugurated president. Bosch was overthrown in a military coup in September 1963. Another military coup, on April 24, 1965, led to violence between military elements favoring the return to government by Bosch and those who proposed a military junta committed to early general elections. On April 28, U.S. military forces landed to protect U.S. citizens and to evacuate U.S. and other foreign nationals.

Additional U.S. forces subsequently established order. In June 1966, President Balaguer, leader of the Reformist Party (now called the Social Christian Reformist Party—PRSC), was elected and then re-elected to office in May 1970 and May 1974, both times after the major opposition parties withdrew late in the campaign. In the May 1978 election, Balaguer was defeated in his bid for a fourth successive term by Antonio Guzman of the Dominican Revolu-

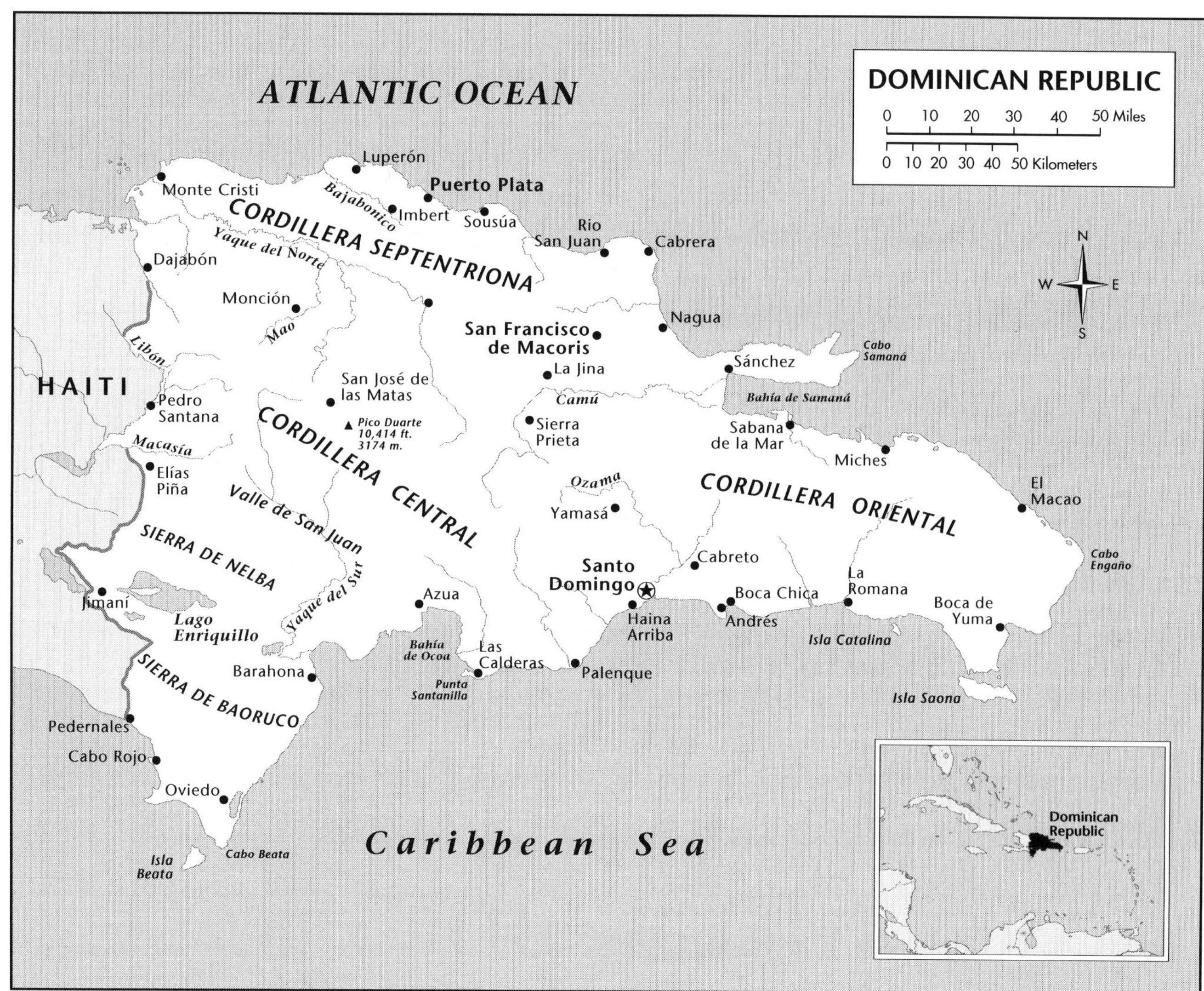

tionary Party (PRD). Guzman's inauguration on August 16 marked the country's first peaceful transfer of power from one freely elected president to another.

The PRD's presidential candidate, Salvador Jorge Blanco, won the 1982 elections, and the PRD gained a majority in both houses of Congress. In an attempt to cure the ailing economy, the Jorge administration began to implement economic adjustment and recovery policies, including an austerity program in cooperation with the International Monetary Fund (IMF). In April 1984, rising prices of basic foodstuffs and uncertainty about austerity measures led to riots.

Balaguer was returned to the presidency with electoral victories in 1986 and 1990. Upon taking office in 1986, Balaguer tried to reactivate the economy through a public works construction program.

Nonetheless, by 1988 the country had slid into a 2-year economic depression, characterized by high inflation and currency devaluation. Economic difficulties, coupled with problems in the delivery of basic services—e.g., electricity, water, transportation—generated popular discontent that resulted in frequent protests, occasionally violent, including a paralyzing nationwide strike in June 1989.

In 1990, Balaguer instituted a second set of economic reforms. After concluding an IMF agreement, balancing the budget, and curtailing inflation, the Dominican Republic experienced a period of economic growth marked by moderate inflation, a balance in external accounts, and a steadily increasing GDP that lasted through 2000.

The voting process in 1986 and 1990 was generally seen as fair, but allegations of electoral board fraud tainted both victories. The elections of 1994 were again marred by charges of fraud. Following a compromise calling for constitutional and electoral reform, President Balaguer assumed office for an abbreviated term and Congress amended the constitution to bar presidential succession.

Since 1996, the Dominican electoral process has been seen as generally free and fair. In June 1996, Leonel Fernandez Reyna of the Dominican Liberation Party (PLD) was elected to a 4-year term as president. Fernandez's political agenda was one of economic and judicial reform. He helped enhance Dominican participation in hemispheric affairs, such as the OAS and the followup to the Miami Summit. On May 16, 2000, Hipolito Mejia, the PRD candidate, was elected president in another free and fair election, defeating PLD candidate Danilo Medina and former president Balaguer. Mejia championed the cause of free trade and Central American and Caribbean economic integration.

The Dominican Republic signed a free trade agreement (CAFTA-DR) with the United States and five Central American countries in August 2004, in the last weeks of the Mejia administration. During the Mejia administration, the government sponsored and obtained anti-trafficking and anti-money-laundering legislation, sent troops to Iraq for Operation Iraqi Freedom, and ratified the Article 98 agreement it had signed in 2002. Mejia faced mounting domestic problems as a deteriorating economy—caused in large part by the government's measures to deal with massive bank fraud—and constant power shortages plagued the latter part of his administration.

During the Mejia administration, the constitution was amended to permit an incumbent president to seek a second successive term, and Mejia ran for re-election. On May 16, 2004, Leonel Fernandez was elected president, defeating Mejia 57.11% to 33.65%. Eduardo Estrella of the PRSC received 8.65% of the vote. Fernandez took office on August 16, 2004, promising in his inaugural speech to promote fiscal austerity, to fight corruption and to support social concerns. Fernandez said the Dominican Republic would support policies favoring international peace and security through multilateral mechanisms in conformity with the United Nations and the OAS.

On May 16, 2008, President Fernandez was re-elected president with 53.8% of the vote. The Fernandez administration works closely with the United States on law enforcement, immigration, and counterterrorism matters.

Congressional and municipal elections were held in May 2010, with Fernandez's PLD winning a slim majority of seats in the House of Representatives and 31 of 32 Senate seats, as well as a plurality of mayoral seats. President Fernandez's role in the victorious congressional campaign led his supporters to promote his candidacy for re-election in 2012. The new constitution promulgated in January 2010 would seem to prohibit this, and ultimately Fernandez announced that he would not run in the 2012 elections. Following primary contests, the 2012 presidential race is divided between the ruling PLD's candidate, Danilo Medina, and the opposition PRD's candidate, former President Hipolito Mejia.

GOVERNMENT AND POLITICAL CONDITIONS

The Dominican Republic is a representative constitutional democracy. In 2008 voters elected President Leonel Fernandez of the Dominican Liberation Party (PLD) for a third term, and in 2010 elections the PLD and its allies won majorities in both chambers of Congress. Impartial outside observers assessed these elections as generally free and fair. There were instances in which elements of the security forces acted independently of civilian control.

Recent Elections

Observers also described the May 2010 congressional and municipal elections as generally free and fair. On December 21 the National Judicial Council named three new members to the five-person Supreme Electoral Tribunal, which has final authority to adjudicate questions over election issues. In May 2012, Danilo Medina Sanchez won the presidency in an election described as generally free and fair by the Organization of American States, other independent observers, and the government electoral board.

Participation of Women and Minorities: By law parties must reserve for women 33 percent of positions on their lists of candidates for the House of Representatives and city councils. There were four women in the 32-member Senate, 37 women in the 183-member House of Representatives, two women in the cabinet, and four women on the 17-seat Supreme Court. The law requires each party's candidates for mayor and deputy mayor to be of different genders, and there were 12 female mayors and 145 female deputy mayors.

Principal Government Officials

Last Updated: 1/31/2013

Pres.: **Danilo MEDINA Sanchez**

Vice Pres.: **Margarita CEDENO DE FERNANDEZ**

Min. of Agriculture: **Luis Ramon RODRIGUEZ**

Min. of the Armed Forces: **Sigfrido Aramis PARED Perez**

Min. of Culture: **Jose Antonio RODRIGUEZ**

Min. of Economy, Planning, & Development: **Juan Temistocles MONTAS Dominguez**

Min. of Education: **Josefina PIMENTEL**

Min. of the Environment & Natural Resources: **Bautista ROJAS Gomez**

Min. of Finance: **Simon LIZARDO Mezquita**

Min. of Foreign Relations: **Carlos MORALES Troncoso**

Min. of Higher Education, Science, & Technology: **Ligia AMADA MELO Viuda Cardona**

Min. of Industry & Commerce: **Jose DEL CASTILLO Savinon**

Min. of Interior & Police: **Jose Ramon FADUL**

Min. of Labor: **Maritza HERNANDEZ**

Min. of the Presidency: **Gustavo MONTALVO**

Min. of Public Admin.: **Ramon VENTURA Camejo**

Min. of Public Health & Social Welfare: **Freddy HIDALGO**
Min. of Public Works & Communications: **Gonzalo CASTILLO**
Min. of Sports: **Jaime David FERNANDEZ Mirabal**
Min. of Tourism: **Francisco Javier GARCIA Fernandez**
Min. of Women: **Alejandrina GERMAN**
Min. of Youth: **Jorge MINAYA**
Min. Without Portfolio for Citizen Security: **Franklin ALMEYDA**
Min. Without Portfolio for Economic Development: **Antonio Isa CONDE**
Min. Without Portfolio for Regional Integration Policy: **Miguel MEJIA, Dr.**
Admin. Sec. of the Presidency: **Jose Ramon PERALTA**
Attorney Gen.: **Francisco DOMINGUEZ Brito**
Governor, Central Bank: **Hector VALDEZ Albizu**
Ambassador to the US: **Anibal de Jesus DE CASTRO Rodriguez**
Permanent Representative to the UN, New York: **Hector Virgilio ALCANTARA MEJIA**

ECONOMY

The Dominican Republic has long been viewed primarily as an exporter of sugar, coffee, and tobacco, but in recent years the service sector has overtaken agriculture as the economy's largest employer, due to growth in telecommunications, tourism, and free trade zones. The economy is highly dependent upon the US, the destination for more than half of exports. Remittances from the US amount to about a 10th of GDP, equivalent to almost half of exports and three-quarters of tourism receipts.

The country suffers from marked income inequality; the poorest half of the population receives less than one-fifth of GDP, while the richest 10% enjoys nearly 40% of GDP. High unemployment and underemployment remains an important long-term challenge. The Central America-Dominican Republic Free Trade Agreement (CAFTA-DR) came into force in March 2007, boosting investment and exports and reducing losses to the Asian garment industry. The growth of the Dominican Republic's economy rebounded from the global recession in 2010–12 and remains one of the fastest growing in the region although its fiscal situation is weak; the fiscal deficit climbed from 2.6% in 2011 to approximately 8% in 2012.

Labor Conditions

The law prohibits employment of children younger than 14 years of age and places restrictions on the employment of children under the age of 16, limiting their working hours to six hours per day. For those under age 18, the law limits night work and prohibited employment in dangerous work, such as work involving hazardous substances, heavy or dangerous machinery, and heavy loads. Minors are also prohibited from selling alcohol, certain work at hotels, handling cadavers, and various tasks involved in the production of sugarcane. Fines and legal sanctions may be applied to firms employing underage children.

The Ministry of Labor in coordination with the National Council for Children and Adolescents (CONANI) is responsible for enforcing child labor laws. While the ministry and CONANI effectively enforced regulations in the formal sector, child labor in the informal sector was a problem largely beyond regulatory reach. In 2010 one NGO estimated that 364,000 minors between five and 17 years of age worked illegally.

Child labor took place primarily in the informal economy, small businesses, private households, and agriculture. In particular, there were reports that children worked in the production of garlic, potatoes, coffee, sugarcane, tomatoes, and rice.

Children also worked as domestic servants, and many were victims of forced labor. There were credible reports that poor Haitian families arranged for Dominican families to "adopt" and employ their children. In some cases adoptive parents reportedly did not treat the children as full family members, expecting them to work in the households or family businesses rather than to attend school, which resulted in a kind of indentured servitude for children and adolescents.

There were 14 different minimum wages, depending on the industry. The minimum wage for workers in free trade zones was 6,376 pesos ($1,674). The minimum wage for workers outside the zones ranged from 6,035 pesos ($158) to 9,400 pesos ($247). The minimum wage for the public sector was 5,117 pesos ($134) per month. The daily minimum wage for farm workers covered by minimum wage regulations, which included all agricultural products except sugarcane, was 175 pesos ($4.60) based on a 10-hour day. Sugarcane workers were subject to a special, lower minimum wage for the sugar industry of 110 pesos ($2.88) per 8-hour workday, an increase from 2009. Although no official estimate of the poverty income level was available, one estimate put the cost of the cheapest common basket of goods at over 10,000 pesos ($262) per month. All workers, including migrants, are covered by minimum wage provisions.

The law establishes a standard work period of 44 hours per week and stipulates that all workers are entitled to 36 hours of uninterrupted rest each week. The law includes paid annual holidays and requires premium pay for overtime, although enforcement was ineffective. The law prohibits excessive or compulsory overtime. While the law requires that employers provide a safe working environment, in practice workers could not remove themselves from hazardous working situations without losing their jobs, and employers may terminate an employment contract at will.

The labor code covers domestic workers, but does not provide for them the payment of notice, severance, or bonus, and they are only guaranteed the payment of two weeks' vacation after one year of continuous work and the Christmas bonus. Workers in the free trade zones are also covered by the labor code, but are not entitled to the payment of bonuses.

In practice the Ministry of Labor did not always enforce the minimum wage. The Dominican Social Security Institute (IDSS) sets workplace safety and health conditions.

According to the 2007 National Urban Labor Force study completed by the Central Bank, the most recent national estimate available, about 54 percent of the workforce is in the informal sector, often outside the reach of government enforcement efforts.

Mandatory overtime continued to be a common practice in factories and was sometimes enforced through loss of pay or employment for those who refused. Some companies also started a practice to pay every eight days instead of every seven days, which resulted in a loss of wages for workers.

On sugar plantations cane cutters usually were paid by the weight of cane cut rather than the hours worked. Cane cutters continued to suspect fraud by weigh station operators, although company officials denied it. The amount of cane a worker could cut varied, but most young able-bodied workers were able to cut two to three tons of cane in a workday, yielding a daily wage of 160-240 pesos (approximately $4.19-$6.29). Less able-bodied workers, who were often older, were paid only for the amount of the cane they actually cut, even if the amount was less than the minimum wage. During the six-month off-season, some workers in sugar plantations remained in their communities and worked part-time jobs clearing land or cleaning sugarcane. Such workers generally were not paid the legally mandated minimum wage.

Conditions for agricultural workers were poor, with many workers working long hours and exposed to hazardous working conditions including the exposure to pesticides, excessive exposure to the sun, and use of sharp and heavy tools. Sugarcane workers often did not receive medical services or pensions due to the lack of documentation even though deductions were taken from their pay.

U.S.-DOMINICAN REPUBLIC RELATIONS

The United States established diplomatic relations with the Dominican Republic in 1884 following its independence from Spain. Post-independence, the country saw a mix of coups, U.S. military intervention and occupations, military government, and democratic government. The Dominican Republic's first peaceful transfer of power from one freely elected president to another was in 1978.

U.S. relations with the Dominican Republic are excellent. The country is an important partner in hemispheric affairs due to its standing in the Caribbean as the largest economy and second-largest country in terms of population and land mass, its large bilateral trade with the United States, and its proximity to the United States and other smaller Caribbean nations. The Dominican Government has been supportive of many U.S. initiatives in the United Nations and related agencies. The two governments cooperate in the fight against trafficking in illegal substances. The Dominican Republic has worked closely with U.S. law enforcement officials on issues such as the extradition of fugitives and measures to hinder illegal migration.

The United States has a strong interest in a democratic, stable, and economically healthy Dominican Republic and supports its democratic and economic development. Obstacles to sustainable development include the poor quality of the country's education system, the inability of the health system to adequately respond to the population's needs, weak economic competitiveness, and severe inefficiencies in the energy sector. Violence has increased in the Dominican Republic in recent years. While there have been coordinated efforts to address corruption, improving transparency is a priority in order to consolidate the country's democratic gains. The U.S. Government collaborates with Dominican authorities to address these issues while working with local and international partners to strengthen institutional and technical capacity.

U.S. Assistance to the Dominican Republic

U.S. assistance helps build accountable and transparent institutions that can better serve the needs of the Dominican people and strengthen democratic governance. In addition, U.S. assistance stimulates income generation opportunities for small businesses and rural communities, improves the protection of the environment, enables local organizations to promote ecological and cultural tourism, and furthers the equitable provision of quality health and education services. The Caribbean Basin Security Initiative complements bilateral programs in the Dominican Republic and provides additional assistance for law enforcement, citizen safety, and rule of law programs.

Bilateral Economic Relations

The Dominican Republic's most important trading partner is the United States. The two countries are parties to the Dominican Republic-Central America-United States Free Trade Agreement (CAFTA-DR), along with five Central American countries. This agreement creates new economic opportunities by eliminating tariffs, opening markets, reducing barriers to services, and promoting transparency. It facilitates trade and investment among the seven countries and furthers regional integration.

U.S. exports to the Dominican Republic include oil, agricultural products, machinery, vehicles, and cotton, yarn, and fabric. U.S. imports from the Dominican Republic include optical and medical instruments, jewelry and gold, agricultural products, machinery, tobacco, and knit apparel. U.S. firms, mostly manufacturers of apparel, footwear, and light electronics, as well as U.S. energy companies, account for much of the foreign private investment in the Dominican Republic.

The Dominican Republic's Membership in International Organizations

The Dominican Republic and the United States belong to a number of the same international organizations, including the United Nations, Organization of American States, International Monetary Fund, World Bank, and World Trade Organization.

Bilateral Representation

The Dominican Republic maintains an embassy in the United States at 1715 22nd Street NW, Washington, DC 20008 (tel. 202-332-6280).

Principal U.S. Embassy Officials

Last Updated: 1/14/2013

SANTO DOMINGO (E) Cesar Nicolas Penson esq. Leopoldo Navarro, 809 221-2171, Fax 809 686-7437, INMARSAT Tel 683 142-873, Workweek: Mon-Fri/0800-1645.

DCM OMS:	Katherine Ramirez
AMB OMS:	Rachel Griego
CDC:	Samuel Martinez Alberto
CG OMS:	Cristina Guzman
DHS/CIS:	Crispina Castillo
DHS/ICE:	Donald Bruckschen
FCS:	Isabella Cascarano
HRO:	Anita A. Brown
MGT:	Jennifer Haskell
MLO/ODC:	LTC Terry A. Bayliss
NAS/INL:	Mario A. Fernandez
PO/CON:	Sharon Ann Weber
POL/ECON:	Francisco Fernandez
TREAS:	Jennifer Fox
AMB:	Raul H. Yzaguirre
CG:	William J. Weissman
CON:	William Weissman
DCM:	Dan Foote
PAO:	Todd Haskell
GSO:	Kristin Rockwood
RSO:	John Aybar
AFSA:	Hart Nelson
AGR:	Margie Bauer
AID:	Alexandra Panehal
APHIS:	Eric Hoffman
CLO:	Esther Rodriguez
DEA:	John Niedzialek
ECON:	Kristina Dunne
EEO:	Silje Grimstad
IMO:	Richard T. Bowen III
IPO:	Jose A. Rivera
ISO:	Mark Wecker
ISSO:	Joseph Brooks
LEGATT:	Lazaro Andino
POL:	Alex Henegar
State ICASS:	Todd Haskell

Other Contact Information

U.S. Department of Commerce International Trade Administration
Trade Information Center
14th and Constitution Avenue, NW
Washington, DC 20230
Tel: 1-800-USA-TRADE
Internet: http://trade.gov

Caribbean/Latin American Action
1818 N. Street, NW, Suite 310
Washington, DC 20036
Tel: (202) 466-7464
Fax: (202) 822-0075

American Chamber of Commerce in the Dominican Republic
Torre Empresarial, 6to.
Piso, Ave. Sarasota No. 25,
Santo Domingo, Dominican Republic
Tel: (809) 381-0777
Fax: (809) 381-0303
E-mail: amcham@codetel.net.do

TRAVEL

Consular Information Sheet

June 22, 2012

Country Description: The Dominican Republic covers the eastern two-thirds of the Caribbean island of Hispaniola. The capital city is Santo Domingo, located on the south coast of the island. Tourist facilities vary according to price and location. Spanish is the official language. Though English is widely spoken in major cities and tourist areas, it is much less common outside these areas.

Smart Traveler Enrollment Program (STEP)/Embassy Locations: If you are going to live in or travel to the Dominican Republic, please take the time to tell us about your trip. If you sign up for the Smart Traveler Enrollment Program with the U.S. Embassy in Santo Domingo, we will be able to keep you up to date with the latest safety and security announcements. Your enrollment can also help us reach your family and friends in case of emergency. If you don't have Internet access, you may sign up directly with the nearest U.S. Embassy or Consulate.

The Consular Section of the U.S. Embassy is located at the corner of Calle César Nicolás Penson and Avenida Máximo Gómez. The American Citizens Services (ACS) Unit can be reached by telephone at 809-731-4294, or via email at acssantodom@state.gov. ACS Unit office hours are 7:30 a.m. to 4:30 p.m., Monday through Thursday, Friday 7:30 a.m. to 12:15 p.m., except on U.S. and Dominican holidays. The Chancery of the U.S. Embassy is located a quater-mile away from the Consular Section, at the corner of Calle César Nicolás Penson and Calle Leopoldo Navarro. The telephone number is 809-221-2171.

There is a consular agency in the north coast city of Puerto Plata at Calle Villanueva esq. Avenida John F. Kennedy, Edificio Abraxa Libraria, 2nd floor, telephone 809-586-4204, 809-586-8017, 809-586-8023; office hours are 9:00 a.m. to 12:00 p.m., and 2:30 p.m. to 5:00 p.m., Monday through Friday, except holidays.

Entry/Exit Requirements for U.S. Citizens: If you are traveling by air outside of the United States, you are required to present a passport or other valid travel document to enter or re-enter the United States. This requirement was extended to sea travel (except closed loop cruises), including ferry service, during the summer of 2009. U.S. citizens traveling by sea must now have either a U.S. passport, passport card, or other WHTI- compliant document. Be aware that the "enhanced driver's licenses" or "enhanced ID cards" offered by many states are not accepted by Dominican authorities for ferry travel from Puerto Rico. We strongly recommend that all U.S. citizens have a valid U.S. passport in their possession prior to their arrival in the Dominican Republic. Attempting to enter on expired or invalid documents can result in direct return to the United States. Sea travelers should also check with their cruise line and countries of destination for any foreign entry requirements.

Applications for the U.S. passport card are now being accepted and have been in full production since July 2008. The card may not be used to travel by air and is available only to U.S. citizens. Further information on the passport card and upcoming changes to U.S. passport policy can be found on our web site. We strongly encourage you to apply for a U.S. passport well in advance of anticipated travel. Visit the Bureau of Consular Affairs website or call 1-877-4USA-PPT (1-877-487-2778) for information on how to apply for your passport.

For information concerning entry and exit requirements, travelers may contact the Embassy of the Dominican Republic at 1715 22nd Street NW, Washington, DC 20008, tel. (202) 332-6280. There are also Dominican consulates in Boston, Chicago (Northfield, IL), Mayaguez, Miami, New Orleans, New York, and San Juan. Visit the Embassy of the Dominican Republic web site for the most current visa information.

Visas: Visitors who do not obtain a Dominican visa prior to entry must purchase a tourist card upon arrival to enter the country. Tourist cards cost ten U.S. dollars, which must be paid in U.S. currency. Tourist cards may be purchased at the Dominican Embassy in Washington or Dominican consulates prior to arrival, as well as at Dominican airports at the time of entry. Tourist cards normally permit a legal stay of up to 60 days. Visitors who would like to extend their time in the Dominican Republic should visit the Migration Department in Santo Domingo and request an extension. Failure to request an extension will subject the visitor to a surcharge at the airport upon departure. The surcharge, assessed on a sliding scale, ranges from $30 for one month to as high as $500 for five years.

Travel of children and exit requirements: Strict exit requirements apply to minors under 18 years of age (of any nationality) who are residents in the Dominican Republic. Such children traveling alone, without one parent, or with anyone other than the parent(s), must present written authorization from a parent or legal guardian.

This authorization must be in Spanish, and it must be notarized at a Dominican consulate in the United States, or notarized and then certified at the Dominican Attorney General's office (Procuraduria de la Republica) if done in the Dominican Republic. The fee for this service is 1000 Dominican pesos, payable at Dominican immigration in Santo Domingo. More information can be found at the immigration office's website. Though not a requirement for non-resident minors (in the Dominican Republic), we recommendthat any minor traveling to the Dominican Republic without one or both parents have a notarized document from the absent parent(s). In addition to clarifying the reason for travel, this will facilitate departure from the Dominican Republic.

Dominican regulations governing the travel of children in the Dominican Republic can be found in Spanish on the Dirección General de Migración web site.

The U.S. Department of State is unaware of any HIV/AIDS entry restrictions for visitors to or foreign residents of the Dominican Republic.

Safety and Security: Foreign tourists are often considered attractive targets for criminal activity and you should maintain a low profile to avoid becoming a victim of violence or crime. In dealing with local police, you should be aware that the standard of professionalism might vary. Police attempts to solicit bribes have been reported, as have incidents of police using excessive force.

Protests, demonstrations, and general strikes occur periodically. Previous political demonstrations have sometimes turned violent, with participants rioting and erecting roadblocks, and police sometimes using deadly force in response. Political demonstrations do not generally occur in areas frequented by tourists and are generally not targeted at foreigners. However, it is advisable to exercise caution when traveling throughout the country. Street crowds should be avoided. In urban areas, travel should be conducted on main routes whenever possible. Power outages occur frequently throughout the Dominican Republic, and travelers should remain alert during blackout periods, as crime rates often increase during these outages.

If you are considering overland travel between the Dominican Republic and Haiti, you should first consult the Country Specific Information Sheet and the Travel Warning for Haiti as well as the Warden Information website of the U.S. Embassy in Port-au-Prince for information about travel conditions in Haiti. While Santo Domingo and the majority of the tourist destinations within the Dominican Republic are located several hours from the Haitian border, the January 12, 2010 earthquake in Haiti has contributed to increased congestion in the area between Barahona, Dominican Republic, and the Haitian border along route 44.

There were two incidents involving attacks against U.S. citizen relief workers as they traveled from Haiti to Santo Domingo. In both cases, the U.S. citizens observed common safety practices such as traveling in a large group and in conjunction with other vehicles. Despite the extra precautions, the groups were attacked. In one incident, armed men blocked the highway with burning tires and opened fire on a passing bus. The armed men also shattered a bus window with a rock and the bus driver was forced to ram the burning blockade in order to escape to safety. In another incident, armed gunmen and men with machetes detained a group of U.S. citizen relief workers for several hours.

The U.S. Embassy cautions its staff to use extreme caution while in Haiti.

Other than official business, travel to Haiti for U.S. Embassy personnel is discouraged. The Department of State has issued a Travel Warning for Haiti. U.S. citizens who travel to Haiti despite this Warning, especially in the area along route 44 near the border of Haiti, should travel in groups during daylight hours and use caution. Drivers who encounter illegal roadblocks should stop a significant distance away, drive in reverse or turn around, and drive to the nearest town to report the blockade to local authorities. Drivers should do their best to leave the danger zone and get to safety.

Stay up to date by bookmarking our, Bureau of Consular Affairs' website, which contains the current Travel Warnings and Travel Alerts, as well as the Worldwide Caution. Follow us on Twitter and the Bureau of Consular Affairs page on Facebook as well.

For additional information on U.S. Embassy safety and security recommendations, please review the embassy's Warden and Security Notices. You can also call 1-888-407-4747 toll-free in the U.S. and Canada or, for callers outside the U.S. and Canada, a regular toll line at 1-202-501-4444. These numbers are available from 8:00 a.m. to 8:00 p.m. Eastern Standard Time, Monday through Friday (except U.S. federal holidays).

Take some time before travel to improve your personal security—things are not the same everywhere as they are in the United States. Here are some useful tips for a safe trip abroad.

Crime: Crime continues to be a problem throughout the Dominican Republic. Street crime and petty theft involving U.S. tourists does occur, and you should take precautions to avoid becoming a target. While pick pocketing and mugging are the most common crimes against tourists, reports of violence against both foreigners and locals are growing. Valuables left unattended in parked automobiles, on beaches, and in other public places are vulnerable to theft, and car theft remains a problem.

Travelers to the Dominican Republic should strongly consider leaving valuable property at home. We recommend bringing no item on your trip that cannot be easily replaced, and to make contingency plans in case of theft. These precautions include: making photocopies of all credit cards and licenses which include the numbers to call in order to report theft; photocopies of passports and birth certificates; and leaving emergency funds with someone at home in case it is necessary for money to be sent on short notice.

Carry cellular telephones in a pocket rather than on a belt or in a purse. Avoid wearing headphones, which make the bearer more vulnerable and readily advertise the presence of a valuable item. Limit or avoid display of jewelry; it attracts attention and could prompt a robbery attempt. Limit cash and credit cards carried on your person. Be sure to store valuables, wallet items, and passports in a safe place.

There are continuing reports of thefts that target tourists en route from the airport to their hotel or home. Some U.S. citizens have been victimized in taxis. In a typical case, a taxi with rolled-down windows stops at a traffic light, and a motorcyclist reaches in and steals a purse or other valuables.. You are advised to utilize the taxi service authorized by the airport if you didn't make arrangements before arrival. Even when using such an authorized taxi service, you should always be aware of the potential for a criminal to stalk travelers leaving the airport parking area. U.S. citizens in privately owned vehicles have also been targeted, and you should always keep doors and windows locked at all times to deter criminals. Some travelers returning to local residences in privately owned vehicles have been followed, assaulted, and robbed upon arrival at their home.

Several U.S. citizens have also been targeted and robbed at bus stations, possibly as a result of gang activity. Take measures to safeguard your personal security at all times.

The dangers present in the Dominican Republic are similar to those of many major U.S. cities. Criminals can be dangerous—many have weapons and are likely to use them if they meet resistance. Visitors walking the streets should always be aware of their surroundings. Be wary of strangers, especially those who seek you out at celebrations or nightspots. Travel with a partner or in a group if possible.

Many public transportation vehicles are unsafe, especially the route taxis or "carros publicos" in urban areas. These are privately owned cars that run along certain routes, can take up to six or more passengers, and are inexpensive. Passengers in "carros publicos" are frequently the victims of pick pocketing, and passengers have on occasion been robbed by "carro publico" drivers. Urban buses ("guaguas") are only marginally better. We are also aware of at least one incident in which the driver of a "motoconcho" (motorcycle taxi) robbed a U.S. citizen passenger. The U.S. Embassy cautions its staff not to use these modes of transportation. As an alternative, some scheduled interurban bus services use modern buses and run on reliable timetables. These are generally the safest means of intercity travel.

With respect to taxis, visitors to the Dominican Republic are strongly advised to take only hotel taxis or taxis operated by services whose cabs are arranged in advance by phone and can subsequently be identified and tracked. Drivers should exercise extreme caution when driving at night and use major highways when possible. In 2009, a U.S. citizen riding her moped was stopped and robbed on a rural road near Samana.

Although kidnappings are not common in the Dominican Republic, in 2007, two U.S. citizens were kidnapped and held for ransom, in separate instances.

The U.S. Embassy calls attention to certain criminal techniques that have surprised U.S. citizens and other victims in recent years. Several individuals reported robberies perpetrated by criminals on mopeds (often coasting with the engine turned off so as not to draw attention). The driver approaches a pedestrian, grabs his or her cell phone, purse or backpack, and then speeds away. This type of robbery is particularly dangerous because the motorcyclist reaches the intended victim at 15–20 miles per hour and often knocks the victim to the ground. There were several such crimes against U.S. citizens in 2009, some in upscale neighborhoods of Santo Domingo.

The embassy has received reports of crime involving apparent police collaboration. A seemingly-friendly stranger shakes hands with a tourist, who then finds that the stranger has placed a small baggie of cocaine or other substance into the tourist's hand. The tourist is then immediately apprehended by a police officer, and pays a "fine" to the police to be set free.

U.S. citizens have been victimized at the airports in Santo Domingo and Punta Cana as they checked in their luggage and prepared to leave the country. Smugglers obtained an authentic airline baggage tag in a U.S. citizen's name and placed it on baggage that contained drugs, presumably to be retrieved by a confederate at the other end of the flight.

Criminals may also misrepresent themselves in an effort to gain access to your residence or hotel room. In one case, Dominican police arrested a building's maintenance man and an accomplice for a violent crime against a U.S. citizen. There have been instances when U.S. citizens were robbed of large amounts of cash immediately prior to a scheduled financial transaction by thieves with apparent inside knowledge of the transaction. In one case, a U.S. citizen was robbed just outside his attorney's office, and in another case a U.S. citizen reported he was victimized by two police officers.

U.S. citizens residing in private homes have been the victims of robberies, sometimes resulting in fatal violence. In one case, an elderly couple in San Pedro de Macoris was violently assaulted in their home and the husband murdered. In another case, a home in Puerto Plata was broken into and the visiting U.S. citizen occupants assaulted, tied up, and robbed. In still another case, two elderly U.S. citizens in Santiago were robbed and attacked in their home with a machete. One died and the other was hospitalized with critical injuries.

The U.S. Embassy continues to receive reports from U.S. citizens who have been stopped while driving and asked for "donations" by someone who may appear to be a police officer before they are allowed to continue on their way. Usually, the person(s) stopping the U.S. citizen drivers had approached from behind on a motorcycle; several of these motorcyclists pulled up alongside the driver's window and indicated that they were carrying a firearm. In some cases, the perpetrators were dressed in the light green uniform of "AMET," the Dominican traffic police; however, they often seemed too young to be police officers or wore ill-fitting uniforms that might have been stolen.

In another incident, individuals dressed in military fatigues told the victim they were police and requested the victim to follow them to the police station prior to robbing him. Such incidents should be reported to the police and to the consular section. If Dominican police stop you for a traffic violation, you should request a traffic ticket rather than paying an on-the-spot fine. You also have the right to ask police for identification. Regulations require police to wear a nametag with their last name. While everyone driving in the Dominican Republic should abide by traffic laws and the instructions of legitimate authorities, U.S. citizens finding themselves in the aforementioned scenarios should exercise caution. In general, you should keep your doors locked and windows closed at all times and leave yourself an escape route when stopping in traffic in the event of an accident or other threat. Incidents involving police may be reported to the Internal Affairs Department of the National Police at 809-688-1777 or 809-688-0777.

You should use credit cards judiciously while in the Dominican Republic. Credit card fraud is common, and recent reports indicate that its incidence has increased significantly, in Santo Domingo as well as in the resort areas of the country.

If you elect to use your credit or debit cards, you should never let the cards leave your sight. You should also pay close attention to credit card bills following time spent in the Dominican Republic. There have been reports of fraudulent charges appearing months after card usage in thc Dominican Republic. Victims of credit card fraud should contact the bank that issued the credit card immediately.

Minimize the use of automated teller machines (ATMs), which are present throughout Santo Domingo and other major cities. One local ATM fraud scheme involves sticking photographic film or pieces of paper in the card feeder of the ATM so that an inserted card becomes jammed. Once the card owner has concluded the card is irretrievable, the thieves extract both the jamming material and the card, which they then use. There are other more sophisticated ATM scams as well, including operations that involve "insiders" who can access and manipulate electronic data entered by legitimate card holders at properly functioning ATMs. Exercise caution and be aware of your surroundings when using an ATM card.

The overall level of crime tends to rise during the Christmas season, and you should take extra precautions when visiting the Dominican Republic between November and January.

Beaches and Resorts: The embassy regularly receives reports of individuals and families who have become victims of crime while within the boundaries of their resort hotel. A growing number of these crimes involve the burglary of the room and even the removal of the room safe. In general, the criminals do not commit their crime in the presence of the guest, but it is not unheard of for guests to be victimized in their own room, caught off guard in their sleep. We strongly recommend vigilance. Hotels generally will not assume responsibility for valuables left in a room.

The embassy occasionally receives reports of instances of sexual assault at the resorts, particularly while at the beach. Some hotel employees have ingratiated themselves with guests as a ruse to ultimately isolate and force the victim into compromising circumstances. Many hotels have policies that discourage employee fraternization with guests. Please report any unwanted attention you receive to hotel management. Be aware of cultural differences and stay in the company of your traveling companions. It has also been reported that some predators will use date rape drugs, or take advantage of alcohol consumption, to render their victims unaware. Be cautious of accepting any drink or food from a stranger, as it may have been tampered with. Again, the embassy strongly encourages vigilance. "All-inclusive" resorts are well known for serving abundant quantities of alcohol and there are no laws in the Dominican Republic against serving alcohol to intoxicated persons. Drink responsibly. Remember that excessive alcohol consumption may decrease your awareness of your surroundings, making you an easy target for crime.

If you become a victim of sexual assault and other violent crimes, we urge you to report the incident immediately to the American Citizen Services unit during working hours, or to the U.S. Embassy's duty officer after hours. You should also report the incident to local authorities for a police report. It is essential that sexual assault victims insist on an immediate examination by an authorized police medical examiner (medica legista) to ensure that a documented report is available for any future prosecution of the case. Please be aware that crime can happen anywhere and that everyone must take personal responsibility to stay alert of their surroundings at all times.

The embassy also receives reports of individuals who have suffered accidents or medical crisis at resorts. Check your insurance coverage prior to going overseas or consider travelers' insurance. Hospitalization in the Dominican Republic can be extremely expensive and patients are expected to pay for services immediately. For additional information, see the section below on medical insurance.

Don't buy counterfeit and pirated goods, even if they are widely available. Not only are the bootlegs illegal in the United States, if you purchase them you may also be breaking local law.

Tourist Police: The Dominican Republic has police that are specially trained to assist tourists who require assistance. This public institution is called Politur and represents a cooperative effort between the National Police, Secretary of the Armed Forces, and the Secretary of Tourism. Politur typically has personnel in tourist areas to provide first responder type assistance to tourists. If you are the victim of a crime, Politur can help you get to a police station so that you may file a police report and seek further assistance. Politur is located at the corner of 30 de Marzo and Mexico, Bloque D, Governmental Building, Santo Domingo. The general phone number is 809-686-8639.

Victims of Crime: If you or someone you know becomes the victim of a crime abroad, you should contact the local police and the nearest U.S. embassy or consulate (see the Department of State's list of embassies and consulates). If your passport is stolen we can help you replace it. For violent crimes such as assault and rape, we can help you find appropriate medical care, contact family members or friends, and help them send you money if you need it. Although the investigation and prosecution of the crime are solely the responsibility of local authorities, consular officers can help you to understand the local criminal justice process and to find an attorney if you need.

The emergency telephone number in the Dominican Republic is 911.

Criminal Penalties: While you are traveling in The Dominican Republic, you are subject to its laws. Foreign laws and legal systems can be vastly different than our own. In some places you may be taken in for questioning if you don't have your passport with you. In some places, it is illegal to take pictures of certain buildings. In some places driving under the influence could land you immediately in jail. These criminal penalties will vary from country to country. There are also some things that might be legal in the country you visit, but still illegal in the United States, and you can be prosecuted under U.S. law if you buy pirated goods. Engaging in sexual conduct with children or using or disseminating child pornography in a foreign country is a crime prosecutable in the United States as well as the Dominican Republic, If you break local laws in The Dominican Republic, your U.S. passport won't help you avoid arrest or prosecution. It's very important to know what's legal and what's not where you are going.

Persons violating laws of the Dominican Republic, even unknowingly, may be expelled, arrested, or imprisoned. Penalties for possessing, using, or trafficking in illegal drugs in the Dominican Republic are severe, and convicted offenders can expect long jail sentences and heavy fines.

Arrest notifications in host country: Based on the Vienna Convention on Consular Relations, bilateral agreements with certain countries, and customary international law, if you are arrested in the Dominican Republic, you have the option to request that the police, prison officials, or other authorities alert the nearest U.S. Embassy of your arrest, and to have communications from you forwarded to the U.S. Embassy.

Currency Regulations: It is legal to exchange currency at commercial banks, exchange booths in hotels and exchange houses. The exchange rate is set by the Central Bank, based on prevailing market conditions. The market determines the exchange rate. No more than USD $10,000 or its equivalent in another currency, including Dominican pesos, may be taken out of the Dominican Republic at the time of departure without declaring it.

Real Estate: Real estate investments in the Dominican Republic require a high level of caution, as property rights are irregularly enforced and investors often encounter problems in receiving clear title to land. Title searches in the Dominican Republic may not undergo the same rigorous examination as in the United States. We recommend consultation with a reputable attorney before signing documents or closing on any real estate transactions. Real estate investments by U.S. citizens have been the subject of both legal and physical takeover attempts. Absentee landlords and absentee owners of undeveloped land are particularly vulnerable. Investors should seek solid property title and not just a "carta de constancia," which is often confused by foreigners with a title. An official land registry measurement (also known as 'deslinde' or 'mensura catastral') is also desirable for the cautious overseas investor. Investors should also consider purchasing title insurance. Squatters, sometimes supported by governmental or non-governmental organizations, have invaded properties belonging to U.S. citizens, threatening violence and blocking the owners from entering their property. In at least one instance, a U.S. citizen landowner was physically assaulted by squatters. Several U.S. citizens with long-standing expropriation disputes with the Dominican government are still without compensation. On several occasions, U.S. citizens have faced lawsuits founded on false documentation that result in costly, protracted court proceedings. Litigation can last for years, preventing any productive use of the property. Eviction of squatters can also take years. The U.S. Embassy does not generally attend property dispute hearings on behalf of U.S. citizens and encourages you to take the necessary steps to safeguard your investment by researching the situation thoroughly beforehand. The embassy maintains a list of attorneys on its website that can be consulted should legal representation be necessary.

Gambling: Many U.S. citizens have reported losing large amounts of money at Dominican casinos by playing a game (or variations thereof) known as "Super Keno," "Caribbean Keno," "Progressive Keno," or "Progressive Roulette." Players have complained that the game's rules are unclear and/or misleading. Casinos have also been associated with cases involving credit card fraud. Any complaints arising from a casino should be directed to the Office of Casinos at the Secretary of Finance. To register a complaint with this office, call 809-687-5131, ext. 2120.

Divorce: In recent years, there have been a number of businesses, primarily on the Internet, which advertise "Quickie Dominican Divorces." The services of these businesses should be used with caution, as they may misrepresent the process of obtaining a divorce in the Dominican Republic. While it is relatively simple for foreigners to obtain a divorce in the Dominican Republic, such divorces are only valid if specific steps are taken. Those seeking information regarding divorce should first consult with an attorney in their home state. Additional information is available in U.S. Embassy's flyer on Divorce in the Dominican Republic.

Alien Smuggling: Dominican authorities may prosecute anyone arrested for organizing the smuggling of aliens into or out of the Dominican Republic. This is in addition to any charges individuals may face in the other country involved, including the United States.

Hurricanes: The Dominican Republic is situated in an area of the Caribbean prone to hurricanes. In the event of a hurricane alert, a notice will be posted on the U.S. Embassy in Santo Domingo's web page. Further information can be obtained from the National Weather Service National Hurricane Center. General information about natural disaster preparedness is available from the U.S. Federal Emergency Management Agency. Travelers are encouraged to register with the U.S. Embassy.

Carnival Celebrations: Visitors attending Carnival celebrations throughout the Dominican Republic should be aware that participants will frequently use sticks, whips, or rubber bags filled with bits of tire and rocks to physically strike spectators on their backside. Such attacks can produce serious injuries and catch spectators off guard. Spectators are encouraged to safeguard their person against such attacks by taking appropriate precautions. Visitors are also advised that Carnival celebrations tend to attract pickpockets and other violent criminals who will prey on spectators.

Water Sports: Visitors to the Dominican Republic, including to local resort areas, should carefully assess the potential risk of recreational activities. Some of the swimming areas at popular beaches around the Dominican Republic are subject to dangerous undertows. Many beaches lack life guards and/or warnings of unsafe conditions. Resort managers usually offer current information on local swimming & surf conditions. You should not swim alone, particularly at isolated beaches. You are further cautioned to weigh carefully the risks inherent in white water sports such as rafting or activities involving jumping from or swimming near waterfalls, particularly following heavy rains when swollen rivers and streams increase the potential for dangerous flash floods. In flash flood conditions, helmets and life vests may not provide adequate protection. U.S. citizens have perished during flash floods that followed rains, even though they were wearing helmets and life jackets. Participants in ecotourism adventures should carefully assess the risks of any activity as safety standards and first response assistance are often not comparable to those found in the United States. Exercise caution while visiting isolated beaches with severe conditions. Areas of dangerous surf and undertow are often unmarked.

Scams: be alert to a relatively recent scam which targets elderly citizens in the United States. The perpetrator contacts a grandparent on the telephone pretending to be a law enforcement official or attorney and informs them that a loved one has been arrested overseas. The caller instructs the victim to wire cash through a money transfer service to pay fines or secure bail. In some instances, impersonators are used to portray the role of the scared grandchild, effectively perpetuating the fraud. Local law enforcement in the Dominican Republic follows a protocol to allow U.S. citizens that have been arrested to contact the nearest U.S. Consulate or Embassy. When in doubt, please contact the American Citizens Services Unit of the U.S. Embassy to confirm the welfare of a family member in the Dominican Republic.

Agricultural Products: Visitors to the Dominican Republic are reminded to review the information provided by the U.S. Department of Agriculture before attempting to import or export food or agricultural products. Severe penalties apply for violations.

Accessibility: While in the Dominican Republic, individuals with disabilities may find accessibility and accommodation very different from what you find in the United States. The law provides for physical access for persons with disabilities to all new public and private buildings, but the authorities do not enforce this provision. While public sidewalks can often accommodate persons with disabilities, many parts of sidewalks are in disrepair and pose a hazard to all pedestrians.Public transportation, lodging and restaurants generally do not have the same accommodations for persons with disabilities as found in the United States.

Medical Facilities and Health Information: While adequate medical facilities can be found in large cities, particularly in private hospitals, the quality of care can vary greatly outside major population centers. There is an emergency 911 service within Santo Domingo, but its reliability is questionable. Outside the capital, emergency services range from extremely limited to nonexistent. Blood supplies at both public and private hospitals are often limited, and not all facilities have blood on hand even for emergencies. Many medical facilities throughout the country do not have staff members who speak or understand English. A private nationwide ambulance service, ProMed, operates in Santo Domingo, Santiago, Puerto Plata and La Romana; the telephone number is 809-412-5555. ProMed expects full payment at the time of transport.

Consult closely with your medical practitioner in the United States regarding any locally available treatments or therapies before traveling to the Dominican Republic for procedures which are not licensed and approved in the United States. Experimental procedures carry certain risks as the quality of treatment varies from U.S. standards.

The U.S. Embassy maintains a non-comprehensive list of providers of medical care in the Dominican Republic. The availability of prescription drugs varies depending upon location. Also, specific brand name drugs may not be available in the Dominican Republic. There have been some instances of counterfeit drugs infiltrating the Dominican market. You are advised to make sure you are traveling with an adequate supply of prescription drugs to meet their needs while in the Dominican Republic.

Tap water is unsafe to drink and should be avoided. Bottled water and beverages are safe.

Dengue: Dengue is endemic to the Dominican Republic. To reduce the risk of contracting dengue, the U.S. Center for Disease Control (CDC) recommends wearing clothing that exposes as little skin as possible and applying a repellent containing the insecticide DEET (concentration 30 to 35 percent) or Picaridin (concentration 20 percent or greater for tropical travelers). Because of the increased risk of dengue fever and the ongoing risk of malaria in the Dominican Republic (see below), practicing preventative measures is recommended by the CDC. For further information on dengue fever, please visit the Centers for Disease Control and Prevention's (CDC) web site.

Malaria: There are occasional reports of cases of malaria in areas frequented by U.S. and European tourists including La Altagracia Province, the easternmost province in which many beach resorts are located. Malaria risk is significantly higher for travelers who go on some of the excursions to the countryside offered by many resorts. Prior to visiting the Dominican Republic, travelers should consult the CDC web site for more information and recommendations on malarial prophylaxis.

Sexually Transmitted Diseases: Be aware that sexually transmitted diseases are common in the Dominican Republic. Please take appropriate precautions to help stop the spread of sexually transmitted diseases.

Cosmetic Surgery: The U.S. Embassy in Santo Domingo and the CDC are aware of several cases in which U.S. citizens experienced serious complications or died following elective cosmetic surgery in the Dominican Republic. The CDC's Website contains a report on patients who suffered postoperative infections following cosmetic surgery in the Dominican Republic. Patients considering travel to the Dominican Republic for cosmetic surgery may also wish to contact the Dominican Society of Plastic Surgeons (tel. 809-688-8451) to verify the training, qualifications, and reputation of specific doctors.

You can find good information on vaccinations and other health precautions, on the CDC website. For information about outbreaks of infectious diseases abroad, consult the World Health Organization (WHO) website. The WHO website also contains additional health information for travelers, including detailed country-specific health information.

Information on vaccinations and other health precautions, such as safe food and water precautions and insect bite protection, may be obtained from the Centers for Disease Control and Prevention's hotline for international travelers at 1-877-FYI-TRIP (1-877-394-8747) or via the CDC's website.

Medical Insurance: You can't assume your insurance will go with you when you travel. It's very important to find out BEFORE you leave whether or not your medical insurance will cover you overseas. You need to ask your insurance company two questions:

- Does my policy apply when I'm out of the United States?
- Will it cover emergencies like a trip to a foreign hospital or a medical evacuation?

In many places, doctors and hospitals still expect payment in cash at the time of service. Your regular U.S. health insurance may not cover doctors' and hospital visits in other countries. If your policy doesn't go with you when you travel, it's a very good idea to take out another one for your trip.

Traffic Safety and Road Conditions: While in the Dominican Republic, you may encounter road conditions that differ significantly from those in the United States. The information below concerning the Dominican Republic is provided for general reference only.

Traffic in the Dominican Republic moves on the right side of the road. Speed limits vary from 25 mph in the city to 60 mph on rural roads, but they are generally not enforced. Drivers are required to carry liability insurance.

If you do drive in the Dominican Republic, you should be aware that the utmost caution and defensive driving are necessary. Traffic laws are similar to those in the United States, but undisciplined driving is common, due to a lack of adequate traffic controls. Many drivers will not use turn indicators. It is common for a vehicle operator to stick his hand out the window to signal a turn. Drivers can also be aggressive and erratic, often failing to yield the right-of-way even when road signs or signals indicate that they should. Turning right on red lights is permitted, but should be done with caution.

Travel at night on intercity highways and in rural areas should be avoided, due to animals on the road, poor road conditions, poor lane markers, missing manhole covers, large potholes, unmarked speed bumps, and other vehicles being driven at excessive speeds, often with malfunctioning headlights or taillights. Drivers should be aware that road hazards and closures are often indicated by piles of debris littered across the roadway, without any lettered signs or reflective surfaces to help call attention to the road condition. Often times, there is no indication of the road hazard whatsoever. Blackouts also increase the danger of night travel. Mudslides and bridge washouts can be a problem during and after heavy rains. The distances between reliable roadside services or major population centers can be considerable, which also increases the risk involved in driving after dark.

Traffic accidents often result in serious injury or death. This is often the case when heavy vehicles, such as buses or trucks, are involved. Traditionally, vehicles involved in accidents in the Dominican Republic are not moved (even to clear traffic), until authorized by a police officer. Drivers who violate this norm may be held legally liable for the accident.

Dominican law requires that a driver be taken into custody for driving under the influence or being involved in an accident that causes serious injury or death, even if the driver is insured and appears not to have been at fault. The minimum detention period is 48 hours; however, detentions frequently last until a judicial decision is reached (often weeks or months), or until a waiver is signed by the injured party (usually as the result of a cash settlement).

Visitors to the Dominican Republic might want to consider hiring a professional driver during their stay in lieu of driving themselves. Licensed drivers who are familiar with local roads can be hired through local car rental agencies. In case of accidents, only the driver will be taken into custody.

Pedestrians tend to step out into traffic without regard to corners, crosswalks, or traffic signals. Many pedestrians die every year crossing the street (including major, multi-lane highways) at seemingly random locations. Pedestrians do not have the right-of-way, and walking along or crossing busy streets—even at intersections with traffic lights or traffic police present—can be very dangerous.

Seat belts are required by law, and those caught not wearing them will be fined. There are no child car seat laws. The law also requires the use of hands-free cellular devices while driving. Police stop drivers using cell phones without the benefit of these devices. Penalties for those driving under the influence and those involved in accidents resulting in injury or death can be severe.

Motorcycles and motor scooters are common in the Dominican Republic, and they are often driven erratically. Dominican law requires that motorcyclists wear helmets, but local authorities rarely enforce this law. Motor vehicle authorities report that less than one percent of motorcyclists in the country are actually licensed. As noted previously, public transportation vehicles such as the route taxis ("carros publicos") and urban buses ("guaguas") are unsafe.

Aviation Safety Oversight: The U.S. Federal Aviation Administration (FAA) has assessed the Government of the Dominican Republic's Civil Aviation Authority as being in compliance with International Civil Aviation Organization (ICAO) aviation safety standards for oversight of the Dominican Republic's air carrier operations. For more information, travelers may visit the FAA website.

Children's Issues: Please see the U.S. Dept. of State Office of Children's Issues web pages on intercountry adoption and international parental child abduction.

Intercountry Adoption

September 2010

The information in this section has been edited from the latest report available as of February 2013 from the State Department Bureau of Consular Affairs, Office of Overseas Citizens Services. For more information, please read the *Intercountry Adoption* section of this book and review current reports online at http://adoption.state.gov. The Dominican Republic is party to the Hague Convention on Protection of Children and Co-operation in Respect of Intercountry Adoption (Hague Adoption Convention). Therefore all adoptions between the Dominican Republic and the United States must meet the requirements of the Hague Adoption Convention and U.S. law implementing the Convention.

Who Can Adopt? Adoption between the United States and the Dominican Republic is governed by the Hague Adoption Convention. Therefore to adopt from the Dominican Republic, the adopting family must first be found eligible to adopt by the U.S. Government. The U.S. Government agency responsible for making this determination is the Department of Homeland Security, U.S. Citizenship and Immigration Services (USCIS).

Residency Requirements: Both prospective adoptive parents must comply simultaneously with the period of cohabitation required by Law. If adopting a child under 12 years old, cohabitation shall be for at least 60 days. If adopting a child over 12 years of age, cohabitation shall be for at least 30 days.

Age Requirements: The prospective adoptive parents must be between 30 and 60 years of age and at least 15 years older than the child they wish to adopt.

Marriage Requirements: Only heterosexual couples who have been married for five years or more are allowed to adopt from the Dominican Republic. Single individuals and unmarried couples are not permitted to adopt.

Who Can be Adopted? Because the Dominican Republic is party to the Hague Adoption Convention, children from the Dominican Republic must meet the requirements of the Hague Adoption Convention in order to be eligible for adoption. For example, the Hague Adoption Convention requires that the Dominican Republic attempt to place a child with a family in-country before determining that a child is eligible for intercountry adoption. In addition to the Dominican Republic's requirements, a child must meet the definition of a Convention adoptee for the adopting family to bring him or her back to the United States.

The Process: Because the Dominican Republic is party to the Hague Adoption Convention, adopting from the Dominican Republic must follow a specific process designed to meet the Convention's requirements. For detailed and updated information on these requirements, please review the *Intercountry Adoption* section of this publication and visit the U.S. Department of State Intercountry Adoption website at http://adoption.state.gov.

Documentary Requirements: Prospective adoptive parents must meet the documentary requirements of Dominican law (see below). Once all the required documents are complete, the PAP(s) must submit the original along with two set of copies to the Department of Adoptions of CONANI.

- Adoption application letter signed by the PAPs.
- Special Power of Representation of the lawyer for the PAPs, if applicable.
- Photograph of the future adoptive family.
- Photocopies of the passports of the PAPs.
- Psychological evaluation report made to the PAPs.
- Social assessment report made to the PAPs.
- Birth certificates of the PAPs.
- Marriage certificate of the PAPs.
- Certificates of no criminal record of the PAPs.
- Medical certificates of the PAPs.
- Proof of economic solvency of each of the PAPs.
- Certification from an entity of a civic, community, or religious group on the social and moral suitability of the PAPs.
- Certificate of no objection from the PAPs children over 12 years of age (if applicable).
- Certification of suitability of the PAPs, issued by the USCIS (Approval of I-800A).
- Certification issued by the officially authorized agency (Adoption Service Provider) or authority of commitment for post-adoption monitoring.

Role of the Central Authority: After the prospective adoptive parents receive and accept the referral of a child, CONANI reviews the prospective adoptive parents' file for required documents and, if satisfied, issues a Certificate of Suitability.

Role of the Dominican Court of Minors (the Court): Dominican adoption law is governed by the Dominican Code of Fundamental Protection and Rights for Children and Adolescents, Law 136-03, Articles 111-167. The Dominican Court of Minors receives the formal, legal application for adoption. If the application is approved, the Court issues a Final Order of Adoption.

Role of Adoption Service Providers: The adoption service provider (ASP) forwards the prospective adoptive parents' application to CONANI. The ASP also is responsible for obtaining further permissions from the U.S. and Dominican authorities as well as ensuring that the PAPs are fully versed in the remaining procedures to be completed.

Time Frame: An adoption can be completed within nine to ten months of U.S. and Dominican requirements being met. It should be noted that many variables can affect the total time it takes to complete the *Intercountry Adoption* of a Dominican child.

Adoption Application: The prospective adoptive parents initiate contact with CONANI (via their attorney) and begin the process of locating a child who meets the definition of "Convention adoptee" under both Dominican and U.S. law.

Adoption Fees: Attorney fees for the adoption of a Dominican child range from $5,000 to $8,000 USD. All adoption-related expenses, including court costs and document fees, are included in this estimate. These expenses should have been itemized in the fees and estimated expenses section of the adoption services contract. Learn more about adoption service provider responsibilities.

Socialization: If the PAPs accept the child placement, then the socialization period begins. This is the first contact between the child and prospective adoptive parents. CONANI issues a certificate of completion of the administrative phase of the adoption process and refers the case to the Court of Children and Adolescents territorial jurisdiction. This begins the judicial phase of the adoption process.

the Judicial Process: Requests from future adoptive parents are treated in strict chronological order, starting from the date of entry of the file to the Adoption Department. All documents coming from abroad should be legalized or authenticated by the competent authority, and they should be translated into Spanish by a certified court interpreter. Currently, the waiting time for records that are complete and on the waiting list for adoption is between two years to two and half years until being assigned to prospective adoptive parents.

Bringing Your Child Home: Once your adoption is complete (or you have obtained legal custody of the child), there are a few more steps to take before you can head home. Specifically, you need to apply for several documents for your child before he or she can travel to the United States, such as a birth certificate, a passport or travel document for your child from the country in which he or she was born, and a U.S. Immigration Visa. For detailed and updated information on how to obtain these documents, review the *Intercountry Adoption* section in this publication and visit the U.S. Department of State Intercountry Adoption website at http://adoption.state.gov.

Child Citizenship Act: For adoptions finalized abroad, the Child Citizenship Act of 2000 allows your new child to acquire American citizenship automatically when he or she enters the United States as lawful permanent residents. For adoptions finalized in the United States, the Child Citizenship Act of 2000 allows your new child to acquire American citizenship automatically when the court in the United States issues the final adoption decree. To learn more, review the *Intercountry Adoption* section in this publication and visit the U.S. Department of State Intercountry Adoption website at http://adoption.state.gov.

After Adoption: CONANI requires post adoption reports to be submitted by the ASP for 5 years after the child has entered the United States; the first report must be submitted 6 months after the child entered the US, the second report after the first year, then once a year for the next 5 years. The reports are to be submitted to the closest Embassy or Consulate of the Dominican Republic to the residence of the child in the United States. Adoptive parent are reminded that they are required by law and international treaty to complete all post-adoption reporting requirements in a timely manner. The ASP is required to assist families as well.

U.S. Embassy in the Dominican Republic
IV Unit (Adoptions)
Unit 3470, Box 531
APO AA 34041-0531

Dominican Republic's Central Authority
Consejo Nacional para la Niñez y la Adolescencia (CONANI)
Av. Máximo Gómez esq. República de Paraguay # 154
Ensanche La Fe
(Frente a la Bomba Esso)
Santo Domingo
República Dominicana
Tel: 809-567-2233
(Office of Adoptions, ext. 1157)
Email: adopciones@conani.gov.do
Website: www.conani.gov.do

Embassy of the Dominican Republic
1715 22nd Street, N.W.
Washington, D.C. 20008
Tel: (202) 332-6280
Fax: (202) 265-8057

Office of Children's Issues
U.S. Department of State
2201 C Street, NW
SA-29
Washington, DC 20520
Tel: 1-888-407-4747
E-mail: AskCI@state.gov
http://adoption.state.gov

For questions about general immigration procedures, call the National Customer Service Center (NCSC) at 1-800-375-5283 (TTY 1-800-767-1833).

ECUADOR

Compiled from publications that were available as of February 2013 from the U.S. Department of State, the U.S. Department of Commerce, and the Central Intelligence Agency (CIA). See the introduction to this set for explanatory notes.

Official Name:
Republic of Ecuador

PROFILE

Geography

Area: total: 283,561 sq km; country comparison to the world: 74; land: 276,841 sq km; water: 6,720 sq km

Major cities: Guayaquil 2.634 million; Quito (capital) 1.801 million (2009)

Climate: tropical along coast, becoming cooler inland at higher elevations; tropical in Amazonian jungle lowlands

Terrain: coastal plain (costa), inter-Andean central highlands (sierra), and flat to rolling eastern jungle (oriente)

People

Nationality: noun: Ecuadorian(s); adjective: Ecuadorian

Population: 15,223,680 (July 2012 est.)

Population growth rate: 1.419% (2012 est.)

Ethnic groups: mestizo (mixed Amerindian and white) 65%, Amerindian 25%, Spanish and others 7%, black 3%

Religions: Roman Catholic 95%, other 5%

Languages: Spanish (official), indigenous (Quechua, Shuar)

Literacy: definition: age 15 and over can read and write; total population: 91%; male: 92.3%; female: 89.7% (2001 census)

Health: life expectancy at birth: total population: 75.94 years; male: 73 years; female: 79.04 years (2012 est.); Infant mortality rate: total: 19.06 deaths/1,000 live births; male: 22.37 deaths/1,000 live births; female: 15.59 deaths/1,000 live births (2012 est.)

Unemployment rate: 5.9% (2012 est.)

Work force: 4.769 million (2012 est.)

Government

Type: republic

Independence: 24 May 1822

Constitution: 20 October 2008; this is Ecuador's 20th constitution

Political subdivisions: 24 provinces (provincias, singular—provincia)

Suffrage: 18-65 years of age, universal and compulsory; 16 and other eligible voters, optional

Economy

GDP (purchasing power parity): $134.7 billion (2012 est.); $129.1 billion (2011 est.); $119.7 billion (2010 est.); $115.6 billion (2009 est.)

GDP real growth rate: 4% (2012 est.); 7.8% (2011 est.); 3.6% (2010 est.); 0.4% (2009 est.)

GDP per capita (PPP): $8,800 (2012 est.; $8,600 (2011 est.); $8,100 (2010 est.); $7,900 (2009 est.)

Natural resources: petroleum, fish, timber, hydropower

Agriculture products: bananas, coffee, cocoa, rice, potatoes, manioc (tapioca), plantains, sugarcane; cattle, sheep, pigs, beef, pork, dairy products; fish, shrimp; balsa wood

Industries: petroleum, food processing, textiles, wood products, chemicals

Exports: $23.77 billion (2012 est.); $22.29 billion (2011); $18.06 billion (2010 est.)

Exports—commodities: petroleum, bananas, cut flowers, shrimp, cacao, coffee, wood, fish

Exports—partners: US 38.3%, Panama 10.1%, Peru 6.3%, Venezuela 5.3%, Chile 5%, Russia 4.6% (2009 est.)

Imports: $24.67 billion (2012 est.); $23.23 billion (2011 est.); $19.64 billion (2010 est.)

Imports—commodities: industrial materials, fuels and lubricants, nondurable consumer goods

Imports—partners: US 27.9%, China 10.3%, Colombia 9.2%, Panama 4.6%, Peru 4.6%, Brazil 4.3%, South Korea 4.1% (2009 est.)

Debt—external: $20.03 billion (31 December 2012 est.); $10.05 billion (31 December 2011 est.); $14.81 billion (31 December 2010 est.)

PEOPLE

Ecuador's population is ethnically mixed. A large majority of the population is mestizo (mixed Amerindian-Caucasian), followed by smaller percentages of indigenous, Afro-Ecuadorian, and European-descendent criollos. Although Ecuadorians were heavily concentrated in the mountainous central highland region a few decades ago, today's population is divided about equally between that area and the coastal lowlands. Migration toward cities—particularly larger cities—in all regions has increased the urban population to over 60% of the total. The tropical forest region (or Amazon region) to the east of the mountains remains sparsely populated and contains only about 3% of the population.

National/Racial/Ethnic Minorities

Afro-Ecuadorian citizens, who account for approximately 7 percent of the population according to the 2010 census, suffered pervasive discrimination, particularly with regard to educational and economic opportunity. The constitution declares the state to be plurinational and affirms the principle of nondiscrimination by recognizing the rights of indigenous, Afro-Ecuadorian, and Montubio (a rural, farming population recognized as an independent ethnic group) communities.

According to the 2010 census, 7 percent of the population self-identified as indigenous. Indigenous organizations estimated that up to 30 percent of the population maintained their indigenous cultural identity and lived in indigenous communities. The vast majority of indigenous citizens resided in rural areas, including the highlands and Amazonian provinces. Indigenous persons continued to suffer discrimination at many levels of society and, with few exceptions, were at the bottom of the socioeconomic scale.

The law recognizes the rights of indigenous communities to hold property communally. Land in many cases is titled to the indigenous community. In other cases indigenous groups managed a reserve that the government set aside for biodiversity protection. The government worked with indigenous communities to help them gain titles to their lands. The constitution allows indigenous persons to participate in the benefits that natural resource extraction projects may bring and to receive compensation for any damages that result.

Language

Ecuador's official language is Spanish, but Quechua, the lingua franca of the Inca Empire, is spoken by many of the indigenous peoples. Nine additional indigenous languages are also spoken in Ecuador. English is spoken in major visitor centers.

Religion

According to PROLADES (the Latin American Socio-Religious Studies Program which categorizes religious groups in Latin American and the Caribbean), 85 percent of citizens are Roman Catholic, 12 percent are Protestant, 1 percent are other religions, and the remaining 2 percent include atheists, agnostics, and those who did not respond. Some groups follow a syncretic form of Catholicism that combines indigenous beliefs with orthodox Catholic doctrine.

Included in the 12 percent of citizens who are Protestants are Southern Baptists, members of the Church of Jesus Christ of Latter-day Saints (Mormons), Jehovah's Witnesses, and Pentecostals. Pentecostals particularly draw their membership from indigenous people in the highland provinces. Hundreds of evangelical churches exist, many of which are not affiliated with a particular denomination. These groups include the Gospel Missionary Union, now called Avant Ministries, the Christian and Missionary Alliance, and Hoy Cristo Jesus Bendice (Today Jesus Christ Blesses).

Other registered religious groups, including Anglicans, Baha'is, Buddhists, Episcopalians, Jews, Lutherans, Muslims, members of the Eastern Orthodox Church, Presbyterians, members of the Unification Church, and followers of Inti (the traditional Inca sun god), have small numbers of members.

HISTORY

The Inca Empire and Spanish Conquest

Advanced indigenous cultures flourished in Ecuador long before the area was conquered by the Inca Empire in the 15th century. In 1534, the Spanish arrived and defeated the Inca armies, and Spanish colonists became the new elite. The indigenous population was decimated by disease in the first decades of Spanish rule—a time when the natives also were forced into the "encomienda" labor system for Spanish landlords. In 1563, Quito became the seat of a royal "audiencia" (administrative district) of Spain.

Independence and Historical Developments

After independence forces defeated the royalist army in 1822, Ecuador joined Simon Bolivar's Republic of Gran Colombia, only to become a separate republic in 1830. The 19th century was marked by instability, with a rapid succession of rulers. The conservative Gabriel Garcia Moreno unified the country in the 1860s with the support of the Catholic Church. In the late 1800s, world demand for cocoa tied the economy to commodity exports and led to migrations from the highlands to the agricultural frontier on the coast.

A coastal-based liberal revolution in 1895 under President Eloy Alfaro reduced the power of the clergy and opened the way for capitalist development. The end of the cocoa boom produced renewed political instability and a military coup in 1925. The 1930s and 1940s were marked by populist politicians, such as five-time President Jose Velasco Ibarra. In January 1942, Ecuador signed the Rio Protocol to end a brief war with

Peru the year before. Ecuador agreed to a border that conceded to Peru much of the territory Ecuador had previously claimed in the Amazon region. After World War II, a recovery in the market for agricultural commodities and the growth of the banana industry helped restore prosperity and political peace. From 1948–60, three presidents—beginning with Galo Plaza—were freely elected and completed their terms. Political turbulence returned in the 1960s, followed by a period of military dictatorship between 1972 and 1979. The 1980s and beginning of the 1990s saw a return to democracy, but instability returned by the middle of the decade.

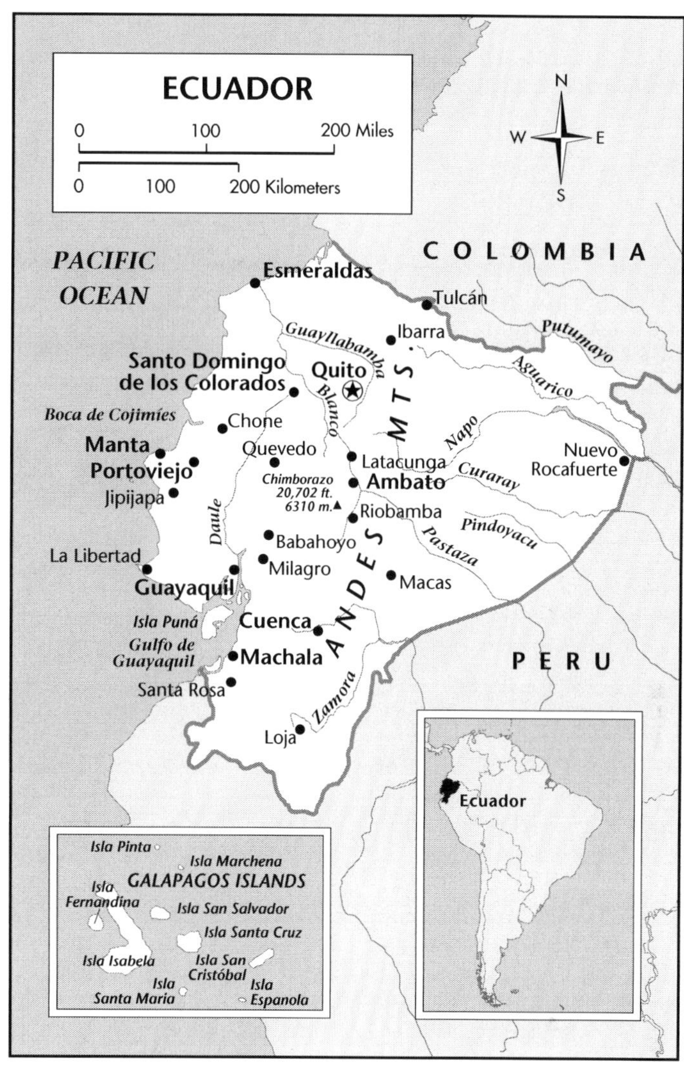

Political Instability (1997–2006)

Abdala Bucaram, from the Guayaquil-based Ecuadorian Roldosista Party (PRE), won the presidency in 1996 on a platform that promised populist economic and social policies, and challenged what Bucaram termed as the power of the nation's oligarchy. During his short term of office, Bucaram's administration was severely criticized for corruption. Bucaram was deposed by the Congress in February 1997 on grounds of alleged mental incompetence. In his place, Congress named Fabian Alarcon interim president. Alarcon's presidency was endorsed by a May 1997 popular referendum.

Quito mayor Jamil Mahuad of the Popular Democracy party was elected president by a narrow margin in July 1998. Mahuad concluded a historic peace agreement with Peru on October 26, 1998, but increasing economic, fiscal, and financial difficulties drove his popularity steadily lower. On January 21, 2000, during demonstrations in Quito by indigenous groups, the military and police refused to enforce public order. Demonstrators entered the congressional building and declared a three-person "junta" in charge of the country. Field-grade military officers declared their support for the concept. During a night of confusion and negotiations, President Mahuad fled the presidential palace. Vice President Gustavo Noboa took charge and Mahuad went on national television to endorse Noboa as his successor. Congress met in emergency session in Guayaquil the same day, January 22, and ratified Noboa as President of the Republic.

Completing Mahuad's term, Noboa restored some stability to Ecuador. He implemented the dollarization of the economy that Mahuad had announced and obtained congressional authorization for the construction of Ecuador's second major oil pipeline, this one financed by a private consortium. Noboa turned over the government on January 15, 2003, to his successor, Lucio Gutierrez, a former army colonel who first came to public attention as a member of the short-lived "junta" of January 21, 2000. Gutierrez' campaign featured an anti-corruption and leftist, populist platform. After taking office, however, Gutierrez adopted relatively conservative fiscal policies and defensive tactics, including replacing the Supreme Court and declaring a state of emergency in the capital to combat mounting opposition.

The situation came to a head on April 20, 2005, when political opponents and popular uprisings in Quito prompted Congress to strip Gutierrez of the presidency for allegedly "abandoning his post." When the military withdrew its support, Gutierrez went into temporary exile. Congress declared Vice President Alfredo Palacio the new president. A semblance of stability returned, but the Palacio administration failed to achieve congressional support for major reforms.

The Correa Administration (2007–present)

In October 2006 presidential elections, third-time candidate Alvaro Noboa won the first round. Rafael Correa bested Noboa in the second-round presidential runoff in November 2006. Correa was Palacio's former finance minister; he ran on an anti-establishment reform platform and successfully presented himself as the "change" candidate. Election observers characterized the elections as generally free, fair, and transparent. Noboa's National Institutional Renovation and Action Party won the largest bloc in Congress in 2006 elections, followed by Gutierrez's Patriotic Society Party; Correa's Proud and Sovereign Fatherland (PAIS) movement did not field any congressional candidates. Traditional parties saw their congressional representation cut in half.

The new Congress took office on January 5, 2007, and Correa was sworn in as President on January 15, 2007. In March 2007, the Supreme Electoral Tribunal dismissed 57 members of Congress on the grounds that they violated campaign laws. Following that, the Congress was largely deadlocked and later effectively replaced by a constituent assembly that was voted into power on September 30, 2007. The assembly, which was inaugurated on November 29, 2007, drafted a new constitution that voters approved in a referendum and that went into effect in October 2008. The new constitution was Ecuador's 20th since independence.

As required under the new constitution, elections for the president, vice president, members of the National Assembly, and provincial and local offices were held in April 2009, 2 years into Correa's first term. President Correa was re-elected in the first round, taking 52% of the vote, compared to 28% for former president Lucio Gutierrez, his nearest rival. Correa's PAIS movement also won the largest legislative bloc in the new National Assembly, although not a majority.

Correa has asserted that his political project, which he calls the "Citizens' Revolution," intends to search for social justice and reassert the supremacy of human labor over capital. His government has increased spending on housing, health care, and other popular social programs.

GOVERNMENT AND POLITICAL CONDITIONS

Ecuador is a constitutional multiparty republic with an elected president and unicameral legislature. In April 2009 voters reelected President Rafael Correa and chose members of the National Assembly in elections that were considered generally free and fair. In May voters approved amendments to the constitution in a process also considered free and fair.

Recent Elections

On May 7, 2011, citizens voted in a national referendum on constitutional changes including reform of the judiciary and ownership and regulation of financial and media institutions, as well as regulatory changes on gambling, animal cruelty, and social security. The referendum was considered free and fair by a small team of observers from the Organization of American States (OAS), but there were delays and irregularities in the vote-counting process. Local observers expressed concern over violations of campaign spending rules.

Elections for offices at all levels of government, including the presidency and the multiparty National Assembly, were held in 2009. OAS and EU observers concluded that the elections were generally free and fair, with local irregularities. Domestic observers also observed elections throughout the country. Although the international and domestic observation teams reported no major fraud, there were some reports of missing or marked ballots, counting and vote-calculation irregularities, and incidents of violence.

Participation of Women and Minorities: The constitution provides for state-promoted, gender-balanced representation in the public sector, including in the lists of political parties' candidates for the National Assembly and other representative institutions. The law mandates that electoral lists be gender-balanced and structured in an alternating male-female (or vice versa) pattern, both for primary and stand-in candidates.

There were 42 women in the 124-seat National Assembly, 11 women in the 28-member cabinet, and two female secretaries of state with the rank of minister. There were seven Afro-Ecuadorians and indigenous persons in the National Assembly but no Asian-Ecuadorians. There were no Afro-Ecuadorians, Asian-Ecuadorians, or indigenous persons in the cabinet.

Principal Government Officials

Last Updated: 1/31/2013

Pres.: **Rafael CORREA Delgado**
Vice Pres.: **Lenin MORENO Garces**
Min. of Agriculture, Livestock, Fisheries, & Aquaculture: **Javier PONCE Cevallos**
Min. of the Coast: **Nicolas ISSA Wagner**
Min. of Culture: **Erika SILVA**
Min. of Economic & Social Inclusion: **Doris SOLIZ Carrion**
Min. of Education: **Gloria VIDAL**
Min. of Electricity & Renewable Energy: **Esteban ALBORNOZ**
Min. of Environment: **Lorena TAPIA Nunez**
Min. of Finance: **Patricio RIVERA**
Min. of Foreign Relations, Foreign Trade, & Integration: **Ricardo PATINO Aroca**
Min. of Industry & Competitiveness: **Veronica SION de Josse**
Min. of Interior: **Jose SERRANO**
Min. of Justice & Human Rights: **Johanna PESANTEZ**
Min. of Labor Relations: **Jose FRANCISCO Vacas**

Min. of Nonrenewable Natural Resources: **Wilson PASTOR**
Min. of National Defense: **Maria Fernanda ESPINOSA Garces**
Min. of Public Health: **Karina VANCE**
Min. of Sports: **Sandra VELA Davila**
Min. of Telecommunication & Information: **Jaime GUERRERO**
Min. of Tourism: **Freddy EHLERS**
Min. of Transportation & Public Works: **Maria de los ANGELES Duarte**
Min. of Urban Development & Housing: **Pedro JARAMILLO**
Min. Coordinator of Economic Policy: **Jeannette SANCHEZ Zurita**
Min. Coordinator of Internal & External Security Policy: **Homero ARELLANO, Adm. (Ret.)**
Min. Coordinator of Natural & Cultural Heritage: **Maria BELEN Moncayo**
Min. Coordinator of Policy: **Betty TOLA**
Min. Coordinator of Production: **Santiago LEON**
Min. Coordinator of Social Development: **Richard ESPINOSA**
Min. Coordinator of Strategic Sectors: **Rafael PROVEDA Bonilla**
National Sec. of Planning & Development: **Fander FALCONI**
Sec. Gen. of Public Admin.: **Vinicio ALVARADO Espinel**
Pres., Central Bank: **Pedro DELGADO**
Ambassador to the US: **Nathalie CELY Suarez**
Permanent Representative to the UN, New York:

ECONOMY

Ecuador is substantially dependent on its petroleum resources, which have accounted for more than half of the country's export earnings and approximately two-fifths of public sector revenues in recent years. In 1999/2000, Ecuador's economy suffered from a banking crisis, with GDP contracting by 5.3% and poverty increasing significantly.

In March 2000, the Congress approved a series of structural reforms that also provided for the adoption of the US dollar as legal tender. Dollarization stabilized the economy, and positive growth returned in the years that followed, helped by high oil prices, remittances, and increased non-traditional exports. From 2002–06 the economy grew an average of 5.2% per year, the highest five-year average in 25 years. After moderate growth in 2007, the economy reached a growth rate of 7.2% in 2008, buoyed by high global petroleum prices and increased public sector investment. President Rafael Correa, who took office in January 2007, defaulted in December 2008 on Ecuador's sovereign debt, which, with a total face value of approximately US$3.2 billion, represented about 30% of Ecuador's public external debt.

In May 2009, Ecuador bought back 91% of its "defaulted" bonds via an international reverse auction. Economic policies under the Correa administration - for example, an announcement in late 2009 of its intention to terminate 13 bilateral investment treaties, including one with the United States - have generated economic uncertainty and discouraged private investment.

The Ecuadorian economy slowed to 0.4% growth in 2009 due to the global financial crisis and to the sharp decline in world oil prices and remittance flows. Growth picked up to a 3.6% rate in 2010 and 7.8% in 2011, before falling to 4% in 2012. China has become Ecuador's largest foreign bilateral lender since Quito defaulted in 2008, allowing the government to maintain a high rate of social spending; Quito owes the Chinese government more than $9 billion in oil for cash loans as of December 2012.

Labor Conditions

The law sets the minimum working age for minors at 15 for all types of labor and the maximum hours a minor may work at six hours per day, five days per week. The law lists jobs that are not suitable for children and prohibits minors from working in hazardous conditions, including in agriculture, mines, domestic work, garbage dumps, slaughterhouses, or in jobs requiring exposure to toxic or dangerous substances or loud noises. The law requires employers to pay minors the same wages received by adults for the same type of employment. Penalties for violations of the child labor laws include fines of $50 to $300 for parents or guardians and fines of $200 to $1,000 for employers hiring children younger than 15. An employer's business is subject to closure for repeated infractions.

The Ministries of Labor and of Economic and Social Inclusion and the Minors' Tribunal enforce child labor laws, but enforcement, while improving, remained inadequate. Child labor remained a severe problem in the informal sector. Children were most likely to be found working on banana plantations or as street vendors. Children also worked in the production of broccoli, sugarcane, and strawberries and were involved in brick making and small-scale gold mining. Forced child labor took the form of involuntary domestic work, forced begging, and forced labor in mines. Some children were forced to engage in criminal activity, such as drug trafficking, and were recruited by Colombian terrorist groups along the northern border.

In urban areas many children under the age of 15 worked in family-owned businesses in the informal sector, shining shoes, or as street peddlers. Other children were employed in messenger services, domestic services, and begging. Children as young as five or six often sold newspapers or candy on the street to support themselves or augment family income.

The National Institute of Statistics and Census found that in 2009, 374,000 children were engaged in labor not permitted by law, primarily working in rural areas or in the informal sector. In 2010 UNICEF estimated the number of child laborers at approximately 340,000.

The minimum monthly wage was $264. The official estimate of the poverty level was $72.87 per month. The law limits the standard work period to 40 hours a week, eight hours a day, with two consecutive days of rest per week. Underground workers, such as miners, are limited to six hours a day and may only work one additional hour a day with premium pay. Premium pay is 1.5 times the basic salary for work done from 6:00 a.m. to

12:00 a.m. Work done from 12:00 a.m. to 6:00 a.m. receives twice the basic salary, although workers whose standard shift is at night receive a premium of 25 percent instead. Premium pay also applies to work done on weekends and holidays. Overtime is limited to no more than four hours a day and a total of 12 hours a week. Mandatory overtime is prohibited. Workers are entitled to a continuous 15-day annual vacation, including weekends, plus one extra day per year after five years of service. Different regulations regarding schedule and vacations apply to live-in domestic workers.

The law provides for the health and safety of workers. Health and safety standards are outlined in the labor code. Workers do not have the right to remove themselves from situations that endanger health or safety without jeopardy to their employment. Foreign and migrant workers are subject to the same labor standards.

A law passed by national referendum in May 2011 made it mandatory for employers to register their employees with Social Security and established criminal penalties for noncompliance. The government ran an active campaign to register workers and labor inspectors focused on ensuring that workers had contracts and were registered with Social Security.

Most workers worked in the large informal sector and in rural areas and were not subject to the minimum wage laws or legally mandated benefits. There were no specific regulations governing health and safety standards in the small-scale agricultural sector.

U.S.-ECUADORIAN RELATIONS

The United States established diplomatic relations with Ecuador in 1848 following its withdrawal from its federation with Colombia. The United States and Ecuador share a history of partnership and cooperation, and have mutual interests in combating narco-trafficking, reducing poverty, fostering Ecuador's economic development, increasing trade, protecting U.S. citizens and interests, and promoting a commitment to representative democracy.

The United States and Ecuador are making efforts to improve diplomatic relations. The two countries launched a bilateral dialogue in 2008, which was suspended in April 2011, after the Government of Ecuador declared the then-U.S. Ambassador persona non grata, citing alleged confidential cables released to the public by the WikiLeaks organization. The Ecuadorian Ambassador to the United States was expelled shortly after. In September 2011, both countries announced that they would resume Ambassadorial-level relations. Ecuadorian Ambassador to the United States Nathalie Cely arrived in Washington in December 2011; U.S. Ambassador to Ecuador Adam Namm arrived in Quito in May 2012.

Ecuador shares U.S. concern over narco-trafficking and the activities of illegal armed groups. The government has maintained Ecuador virtually free of coca production since the mid-1980s, and is working to combat money laundering and the transshipment of drugs and chemicals essential to the processing of cocaine (with U.S. support). Ecuador also gives priority to combating child labor and trafficking in persons.

U.S. Assistance to Ecuador

U.S. assistance in Ecuador is designed to strengthen democratic participation and the rule of law, improve citizen security, counter illicit trafficking, conserve biodiversity, address climate change, and develop economic alternatives for marginalized Ecuadorians. The United States will work with the Government of Ecuador and broader civil society to advance the long-term objectives of stability, strengthened democratic institutions, including the press, and environmental protection. Working with the Government of Ecuador to increase their capability to counter illicit trafficking and improve citizen security is vital to U.S. national security interests, because these efforts support U.S. security efforts in the region.

Bilateral Economic Relations

The United States is Ecuador's principal trading partner. Major U.S. exports to Ecuador include machinery, chemicals and fertilizers, computers and electronic equipment, petroleum products, transportation equipment, cereals and grains, and paper. Ecuador benefits from duty-free entry into the United States for many of its products under the Andean Trade Promotion and Drug Eradication Act and under the Generalized System of Preferences. U.S. imports from Ecuador include crude oil, shrimp and prawns, bananas and plantains, cocoa, and cut flowers (roses). The two countries have signed a bilateral investment treaty. U.S. direct investment in Ecuador is led by the manufacturing and wholesale/retail sectors.

Ecuador's Membership in International Organizations

Ecuador and the United States belong to a number of the same international organizations, including the United Nations, Organization of American States, International Monetary Fund, World Bank, and World Trade Organization. Ecuador is also a member of the Bolivarian Alternative for the Americas (ALBA) and of the United Nations of the South (UNASUR).

Bilateral Representation

Ecuador maintains an embassy in the United States at 2535 15th Street NW, Washington, DC 20009 (tel. 202-234-7200).

Principal U.S. Embassy Officials

Last Updated: 1/14/2013

QUITO (E) Avigiras E12-170 y Eloy Alfaro, 011-593-2-398-5000, Fax 011-

593-2-398-1000, Workweek: Monday through Friday: 8:00–17:00, Website: http://spanish.ecuador.usembassy.gov/

DCM OMS:	Maggie Johnson
AMB OMS:	Rusell Potter
Co-CLO:	Jennifer Lemos
DHS/ICE:	Marshall Heeger
FM:	George Robb
HRO:	Carol Fajardo
MGT:	Kemp L. Long
MLO/ODC:	COL Alfred Brooks
NAS/INL:	Kevin O'Connor
POSHO:	George Robb
AMB:	Adam E. Namm
CG:	David Lindwall
DCM:	Timothy Zuniga-Brown
PAO:	Heide Bronke Fulton
GSO:	Ramon Best
RSO:	Daniel Hernandez
AGR:	Emiko Purdy
AID:	Andrew Herscowitz
APHIS:	Darya Chehrezad
CLO:	Erzsebet Best
DEA:	A.J. Collazo
ECON:	Nicole Weber
FMO:	Christopher Bergaust
ICASS Chair:	Joe Relk
IMO:	Michelle Zentis
LEGATT:	Gabriel Ramirez
POL:	William Mozdzierz
State ICASS:	Heide Bronke Fulton

GUAYAQUIL (CG) 9 de Octubre y Garcia Moreno, 593-4-232-3570, Fax 593-4-232-5286, Workweek: M-F 8:00-5:00, Website: Guayaquil.USConsulate.gov/

CA:	Jack Nelson (Galapagos)
CG OMS:	Alexandra Vasconez
DHS/ICE:	Paul Salomon
FM:	Roger Riojas
MGT:	David Liboff
NAS/INL:	Daniel Ramboer
POL/ECON:	Christine Buzzard
CG:	David Lindwall
CON:	Ronald Packowitz
PAO:	Mark Kendrick
GSO:	Rosalind Zavras
RSO:	Jeremy Sims
CLO:	Alexander Zavras
DEA:	Stephen Briggs
EEO:	Christine Buzzard
IPO:	Arthur Saunders
ISSO:	Arthur Saunders

TRAVEL

Consular Information Sheet

December 12, 2011

Country Description: Ecuador is a Spanish-speaking country approximately the size of Colorado. It has a democratically elected government. In general, tourist facilities are adequate but vary in quality. Crime is a significant concern. Ecuador uses the U.S. dollar as its official currency, and U.S. bills and both U.S. and locally minted coins are accepted everywhere.

Smart Traveler Enrollment Program (STEP): If you are going to live in or visit Ecuador, please take the time to let our Embassy in Quito or Consulate General in Guayaquil know when you'll be here. If you enroll, we can keep you up to date with important safety and security announcements. It will also help your friends and family get in touch with you in an emergency.

The U.S. Embassy in Quito
For visitors: Ave. Avigiras E12-170 y Ave. Eloy Alfaro; Quito, Ecuador
For local mail and package delivery: Ave. Guayacanes N52-205 y Ave. Avigiras
Quito, Ecuador
Telephone during business hours (8:00 a.m. to 5:00 p.m.):
(011) 593-2-398-5000
Emergency after-hours telephone:
(011) 593-2-398-5000
Facsimile: (011) 593-2-398-5100

The American Citizen Services unit in Quito uses an online appointment system for passport services, notary services, and reports of birth abroad. For detailed information or to make an appointment, visit the Embassy's American Citizen Services website. Walk-in service for emergencies, passport pick-up, or reports of death are available from 1:00 p.m. to 3:00 p.m., Monday through Thursday.

The U.S. Consulate General in Guayaquil
For visitors, local mail, and packages:
9 de Octubre y Garcia Moreno; Guayaquil, Ecuador
Telephone during business hours (8:00 a.m. to 5:00 p.m.):
(011) 593-4-232-3570
Emergency after-hours telephone:
(011) 593-4-232-1152
Facsimile: (011) 593-4-232-0904

The American Citizen Services unit in Guayaquil uses an online appointment system for passport services, notary services, and reports of birth abroad. For detailed information about services or to make an appointment, visit the Consulate's American Citizen Services website. Walk-in service for those with questions regarding Social Security is available from 8:00 a.m. to 11:00 a.m., Monday through Thursday. All other walk-in service is available for emergencies only. Both the Embassy and the Consulate are closed on U.S. and local holidays.

The Galápagos Islands fall within the consular district of the U.S. Consulate General in Guayaquil, Ecuador. The U.S. government also maintains a Consular Agent within the Galápagos Islands to provide support in case of U.S. citizen emergencies.

U.S. Consular Agent to the Galápagos Islands: Mr. Jack Nelson
Location: Av. Charles Darwin
Puerto Ayora, Santa Cruz Island
(at the former Hotel Galápagos)
Telephone: (05)252-6330
(From the United States, dial 011-593-5-252-6330)
Cell phone: 091-33-4815
(From the United States, dial 011-593-9-133-4815)

Visa Requirements to Enter Ecuador: If you are a U.S. citizen wishing to enter Ecuador, you must present a U.S. passport with at least six months remaining validity. Ecuadorian immigration officials also sometimes request evidence of return or onward travel, such as an airline ticket.

Under Ecuadorian law, U.S. citizens traveling for business or tourism on a tourist passport can enter Ecuador for up to 90 days per calendar year without a visa. Extensions for up to another 90 days can be requested through the provincial migration offices. If you are planning a visit longer than 90 days, you must obtain a visa in advance of your arrival.

More detailed information and requirements for visas in Ecuador can be found at the website of Ecuador's Ministry of Foreign Affairs. You can also visit the website for the Embassy of Ecuador in the United States for the most current visa information, or for further information regarding entry, exit or customs requirements. If you stay in Ecuador beyond the terms of your visa, you may be deported or barred from re-entering Ecuador in the future. A substantial fine may be imposed by Ecuadorian Immigration prior to your departure.

The U.S. Department of State is unaware of any HIV/AIDS entry restrictions for visitors to or foreign residents of Ecuador.

Proof of Legal Status While In Ecuador: Once you have entered Ecuador, Ecuadorian authorities require you to carry identification, including proof of U.S. citizenship, at all times. Because of the frequency of passport theft in Ecuador, you should carry a photocopy of your passport (including the personal data page and the entry stamp and/or visa) rather than your actual passport.

Departing Ecuador: To depart Ecuador, you must again present a U.S. passport with at least six months validity remaining.

Special Entry/Exit Instructions for U.S. Citizens Born in Ecuador: The Government of Ecuador considers any person born in Ecuador to be an Ecuadorian citizen. U.S. citizens born in Ecuador will be required to show an Ecuadorian passport or national ID card ("cedula") to Ecuadorian Immigration authorities upon entering and exiting the country. Dual citizens who do not comply with this requirement may not be allowed to enter or exit the country. Be aware that all U.S. citizens, regardless of dual citizenship, must present a valid U.S. passport upon returning to the United States. For additional information, visit the Ecuadorian Ministry of Foreign Affairs' Travel Documents website. Information about dual nationality can be found on our website.

Special Exit Requirements for Minors: Ecuador has implemented specific procedures to prevent international child abduction. Under Ecuadorian law, children under the age of 18 who are citizens or residents of Ecuador and who are traveling alone, with one parent, or with a third party, must present a copy of a birth certificate and written authorization from the absent parent(s) or legal guardian. When a parent is deceased, a notarized copy of the death certificate is required in lieu of written authorization.

Lost/Stolen Passports: If your U.S. passport is lost or stolen in Ecuador, you must obtain a police report in order to replace your passport at the U.S. Embassy or Consulate, and then obtain a "Movimiento Migratorio" from an Ecuadorian immigration office in order to leave the country.

Natural Disasters: Ecuador has many active and potentially active volcanoes, including around the capital of Quito and other popular tourist destinations. Other potential environmental threats include flooding, earthquakes, and tsunamis. In the event of a natural disaster, transportation, water, communications, and power systems may fail due to damaged infrastructure or heavy ash fall. Roads may close and flights in or out of Ecuadorian airports might be cancelled due to adverse conditions.

Three active volcanoes within 100 kilometers of Quito threaten the city primarily with ash fall. Baños, a popular tourist destination, is located at the base of the Tungurahua volcano. Tungurahua has erupted explosively several times in the last decade, including several eruptions throughout 2010 and 2011 that produced significant ash fall. Travelers to Baños, especially on the western side of town, should be aware that mud or lava flows could pose a significant and immediate threat. If you are in Baños when a volcanic eruption occurs, stay alert to the sirens and instructions from local authorities, and follow the arrows on the street to reach the evacuation shelters in the Santa Ana neighborhood on the main road on the east side of town, towards Puyo.

Earthquakes sometimes trigger deadly tsunamis, which could strike coastal areas of Ecuador or the Galápagos Islands. Ecuadorian national authorities put out warnings of potential tsunamis, but the response on the local level is uneven, and on one recent occasion in the Galapagos Islands, there was no coordinated evacuation when a tsunami struck. Ecuador's National Risk Management Secretariat and the Ecuadorian Geophysical Institute monitor Ecuadorian volcanoes, earthquakes, and tsunamis in Ecuador, issuing regular reports on their activity. In the event of a natural disaster, pay close attention to the news media for updates.

Civil Unrest: Political demonstrations occur frequently throughout Ecuador. During demonstrations, protesters often block city streets and rural highways, including major arteries such as the Pan American Highway, disrupting public and private transportation. Protesters sometimes burn tires, throw rocks, damage cars and other personal property, and on occasion detonate small improvised explosive devices. Police response to demonstrations varies, but may include water cannons and tear gas. U.S. citizens and U.S.-affiliated interests are not usually targeted, but you should avoid areas where demonstrations are in progress and be prepared with back-up transportation plans. Peaceful demonstrations can turn violent with little or no warning, and you could become a target.

Northern Border Region: Due to the spread of organized crime, drug and small-arms trafficking, and incursions by terrorist organizations near Ecuador's border with Colombia, the U.S. Embassy in Quito advises caution when traveling to northern Ecuador, including the provinces of Sucumbios, northern Orellana, Carchi, and northern Esmeraldas. U.S. government personnel are prohibited from traveling alone or staying overnight in these areas. At least 11 U.S. citizens are known to have been victims of kidnapping in this region in the past 11 years.

Safety in the Galapagos Islands: The Galápagos archipelago is located more than 600 miles to the west of continental Ecuador. Geographic isolation and the lack of local resources may present challenges to travelers there. Dangers posed by lax enforcement of marine safety laws and rudimentary medical facilities are exacerbated by the difficulty of performing evacuations from the islands. A significant number of Ecuadorian tour vessels operating in the Galápagos do not meet international safety standards. The Government of Ecuador requires that vessels carrying more than 16 passengers comply with the International Safety Management Code established by the International Maritime Organization. However, the quality of oversight, crewmember proficiency, and other requisites for safe vessel operation may vary substantially. Travelers should inquire about safety features when boarding vessels. Be sure to look for life boats, flotation devices and, if possible, take a moment to inspect the life vest you would be using if there were an accident. Medical resources in the Galápagos Islands are severely limited. Acute surgical, cardiac, and other types of specialty medicine are not available. There are two hospitals, located on the Santa Cruz and San Cristobal Islands. These facilities have limited personnel and resources, and often do not have basic medical supplies. Some cruise ships have on-board physicians available, who charge a fee for their services. Scuba divers in the Galápagos Islands should be aware of limited facilities for decompression. Serious injury or illness in the Galápagos typically requires costly medical evacuation to the Ecuadorian mainland or the United States for treatment. Medical evacuations by air ambulance can run upwards of $50,000 and take significant time to arrange. For that reason, the purchase of traveler's health insurance that includes air evacuation is strongly recommended.

Stay up to date by:

- Bookmarking our Bureau of Consular Affairs website, which contains the current Travel Warnings and Travel Alerts as well as the Worldwide Caution;
- Following us on Twitter and the Bureau of Consular Affairs page on Facebook;
- Downloading our free Smart Traveler iPhone App to have travel information at your fingertips;
- Calling 1-888-407-4747 toll-free within the U.S. and Canada, or a regular toll line, 1-202-501-4444, from other countries; and,
- Taking some time before travel to consider your personal security.

Crime: Crime is a severe problem in Ecuador. Crimes against U.S. citizens in the past year have ranged from petty theft to violent offenses, including armed robbery, home invasion, sexual assault, and several instances of murder and attempted murder. Very low rates of apprehension and conviction of criminals—due to limited police and judicial resources—contribute to Ecuador's high crime rate.

"Secuestro Express" Taxi Assaults: Robberies and assaults against taxi passengers, known locally as "secuestro express" continue to present a significant safety concern, especially in Guayaquil and Manta, but also with increasing regularity in Quito. Shortly after the passenger enters a taxi, the vehicle is typically intercepted by armed accomplices of the driver, who threaten passengers with weapons, rob passengers of their personal belongings, and force victims to withdraw money from ATMs. Increasingly, victims have been beaten or raped during these incidents. In the Guayaquil area, you should call to order a taxi by phone or use a service affiliated with major hotels. If you must hail a taxi on the street, seek out those that are officially registered and in good condition.

Registered taxis in Ecuador are usually yellow, display matching unit numbers on their windshields and doors, feature a taxi cooperative name on the door, and are identified with an orange license plate. Still, be aware that passengers have been victimized even in taxis that meet these criteria. U.S. officials associated with the U.S. Consulate in Guayaquil are forbidden from hailing street taxis.

If you become a victim of express kidnapping and/or robbery, cooperation with the assailant usually results in the best outcome, as nothing material is as valuable as your life. Following a criminal incident, U.S. citizens are encouraged to immediately file a police report with the local authorities and to inform the American Citizens Services Unit at the U.S. Embassy in Quito or the U.S. Consulate General in Guayaquil.

Violent Robberies: Armed or violent robberies can occur in all parts of Ecuador, not just the major cities. Many travelers have been robbed after using ATMs or when exiting banks. Travelers should avoid withdrawing large amounts of cash at one time from banks and ATMs, and should use ATMs in protected indoor areas like well-guarded shopping malls. In some cases, robbers have used motorcycles to approach their victims and flee the scene. Tourists have also been robbed at gunpoint on beaches and along hiking trails.

Non-Violent Robberies: Pick-pocketing, purse-snatching, robbery, bag-slashing, and hotel room theft are the most common types of crimes committed against U.S. citizens in Ecuador. They occur throughout Ecuador and incidents have increased significantly in recent years. Pickpockets and other petty thieves are particularly active in airports, restaurants, on public transportation, in crowded streets, bus terminals, public markets, and grocery stores. Backpackers are frequently targeted for robbery, as are travelers carrying laptop computer bags. On buses, luggage stowed below the bus or at a traveler's feet is sometimes stolen. Thieves in Ecuador often distract the victim, sometimes by purposefully spilling liquid on the victim and pretending to help the victim clean it up, while accomplices snatch the victim's bag or pick the victim's pocket. To lower your risk of these or other non-violent crimes, leave valuables in a safe place, or don't travel with them. Make use of hotel safes when available, avoid wearing obviously expensive jewelry or designer clothing, and carry only the cash or credit cards that you will need on each outing. Stay alert to pickpockets when in crowds and when taking public transportation, and be conscious that distractions can be created to target you.

Carjacking and Thefts from Vehicles: To avoid carjacking or theft from your vehicle while you are stopped at intersections, drive with your doors locked and windows rolled up. "Smash and grabs" occur when thieves break into parked vehicles, but have also been known to occur in slow-moving or stopped traffic, particularly when cars are driven by females in the car alone. Do not leave anything of value in plain view in a car, including sunglasses, sports equipment, purses, briefcases or valuables. Always be aware of your surroundings, and try to travel in groups.

Sexual Assault: Incidents of sexual assault and rape have increased, including in well-traveled tourist areas. Criminals generally target women who are alone, and use alcohol or incapacitating drugs on unsuspecting tourists to rob and/or sexually assault them. These so-called date-rape drugs disorient the victim and can cause prolonged unconsciousness and serious medical problems. To lower your risk, travel in groups, don't leave food or drinks unattended in public places, and never allow a stranger to give you a drink.

Murder: Since September 2009, at least four U.S. citizens in Ecuador have been victims of murder. In most cases, the victims and alleged perpetrators personally knew each other. Investigation and prosecution of the perpetrators is the responsibility of the Ecuadorian government, and do not proceed with the speed and thoroughness we are accustomed to in the United States. Although the U.S. Embassy and U.S. Consulate General monitor and encourage these investigations, our ability to intervene is extremely limited. The Ecuadorian government has established an emergency hotline that callers can use to inform police about murders or contract killings. The number is 1-800-DELITO (1800 335486).

Credit Card Fraud: Increasing numbers of U.S. citizens in Ecuador have fallen victim to fraud related to their credit or debit cards. "Skimming," the theft of credit card informationduring an otherwise legitimate transaction, is most likely to occur in restaurants or bars, where the skimmer takes the victim's card out of the owner's view. To avoid skimming, take the credit/debit card to the register yourself and never let the card out of your sight. Also, be sure to monitor your bank account or credit card statement frequently.

Staying Alert in Quito: Stay particularly alert for crime on the crowded streets of south Quito, at the Panecillo, the Historic District, and in the areas of El Tejar, Parroquia San Sebastian, Avenida Cristobal Colon, and Gonzalez Suarez. Quito's Mariscal Sucre district, a popular tourist area with restaurants, bars, hotels, hostels, and shopping, is increasingly a site of crimes; reported incidents in recent years range from petty theft and sexual assault to shootings. In Mariscal Sucre, travel in groups when possible, avoid hailing taxis off the street or using unofficial taxis, and exercise caution in the early morning hours. Outside the city, stay alert if hiking to the summit of Pichincha, as violent crime has been known to occur there.

Staying Alert in Guayaquil and Elsewhere on the Coast: In Guayaquil, visitors should exercise extreme caution in the downtown area and the southern part of the city. Tourist sites such as the Christ statue (Sagrado Corazon de Jesus) on Cerro del Carmen, the Malecon 2000, and Las Peñas, though well-patrolled by police, are still targeted by criminals hoping to prey on unsuspecting tourists. There have also been reports of armed robberies at restaurants in the fashionable areas of Urdesa and Samborondon.At the airport in both Quito and Guayaquil, arriving passengers have been targeted by armed robbers who follow them from the airport to rob them. Cases have been reported involving multiple vehicles that cut off and intercept the victim as well as just a single motorcycle rider who robs the victim while they are getting out of their car. The perpetrators appear to focus on travelers who are returning from overseas trips laden with gifts and large amounts of cash.

Victims of Crime: If you or someone you know becomes the victim of a crime, you should immediately contact the local police to file a crime report (known as a "denuncia") and inform the U.S. Embassy or Consulate General.

The Ecuadorian Tourist Security Service has opened a number of service centers throughout Quito, which provide general information and a location to file police reports. If you are a victim of crime, the U.S. Embassy or Consulate General can:

- Help you find appropriate medical care for violent crimes such as assault or rape.
- Put you in contact with the appropriate police authorities and contact family members or friends on your behalf.
- Replace your stolen passport.
- Help you understand the local criminal justice process and direct you to Ecuadorian attorneys or law enforcement officials.

If you are a victim of domestic violence, regardless of your gender, you may receive assistance from a local branch of the Commissioner's Office for Women and Family Issues, which has a listing of their branches available on their Spanish-language website. Emergency phone numbers in Ecuador vary by region. In Quito and Ibarra, dial 911 for all emergencies. In Guayaquil, Cuenca and Loja, the number is 112. Elsewhere, dial 101 for police,102 for firefighters or ambulance, or 131 for the local Red Cross. Operators typically speak Spanish only.

Criminal Penalties: While you are traveling in Ecuador, you are subject to Ecuadorian laws even though you are a U.S. citizen. Foreign laws and legal systems can be vastly different from our own. Criminal penalties will vary from country to country. There are also some things that might be legal in the country you visit, but still illegal in the United States. For example, you can be prosecuted under U.S. law if you buy pirated goods. Engaging in sexual conduct with children or using or disseminating child pornography in a foreign country is also a crime prosecutable in the United States. If you break local laws in Ecuador, your U.S. passport won't help you avoid arrest or prosecution. It's very important to know what's legal and what's not where you are going.

If you are arrested in Ecuador, under the Vienna Convention on Consular Relations and customary international law, you have the option to request that the police, prison officials, or other authorities alert the nearest U.S. Embassy or Consulate. Outside of Quito and Guayaquil, awareness of international protocols is uneven. If you are arrested in Ecuador, request that the Ecuadorian authorities do this on your behalf. Please note, however, that the U.S. government has no authority to intervene in Ecuadorian legal matters. Don't buy counterfeit and pirated goods, even if they are widely available. Not only are the bootlegs illegal to bring back into the United States, if you purchase them, you may also be breaking local law.

Drug Trafficking: Each year, approximately 20 to 25 U.S. citizens are arrested by Ecuadorian authorities for attempting to traffic drugs between Ecuador and the United States, or between mainland Ecuador and the Galápagos Islands. Many of those arrested claim not to have known they were transporting drugs. Under no circumstances should you ever accept gifts, packages, or suitcases from anyone you do not trust and know well. If you are arrested for drug trafficking, you can expect to serve a lengthy period in pre-trial detention, and if convicted you will likely be sentenced to a long prison term and fined heavily. In nearly all cases, U.S. citizens convicted of drug trafficking in Ecuador must serve their sentences in Ecuador, where conditions of confinement are harsh and far below U.S. standards.

Retiring In Ecuador: In recent years, Ecuador has become a top overseas destination for retiring U.S. citizens. Bear in mind that organizations promoting Ecuador or any other place as a retirement destination may have a financial incentive to attract retirees, and may not always present a balanced picture. Consider multiple sources before choosing a destination. Remain vigilant when contracting professional services for assistance with Ecuadorian visas, real estate transactions, or customs brokering for imported household effects. U.S. citizen retirees regularly complain about unethical practices by lawyers, real estate agents, and others who have taken advantage of their lack of knowledge about local language, laws, and culture, resulting in costly losses and little hope for a remedy through the local judicial system.

As in any country, Ecuadorian rules governing visas and customs are subject to change with little notice. The Ministry of Foreign Relations and other Ecuadorian government agencies publish little information in English, increasing foreigners' reliance on lawyers or other facilitators, some of whom have distorted the true cost or requirements for obtaining Ecuadorian visas. Staff members at the U.S. Embassy and U.S. Consulate General are not in a position to give detailed advice about Ecuadorian immigration law.

Accessibility for Disabled Persons: While in Ecuador, individuals with disabilities may find accessibility and accommodation very different from U.S. standards. Although Ecuador's constitution prohibits discrimination against the disabled, travelers with disabilities may have great difficulty traversing public walkways and accessing buildings.

Medical Facilities and Health Information: Adequate medical and dental care is available in the major cities of Ecuador. In smaller communities and in the Galápagos Islands, services are limited, and the quality is generally well below U.S. standards. Ambulances, with or without trained emergency staff, are in short supply in cities, but even more so in rural areas.

Pharmacies are readily available in any city; however, you might find that the availability of some medications is sporadic, and formulations and brand names will differ from products available in the United States. Narcotics and tranquilizers are extremely limited in availability. Pharmacists sometimes dispense medications without requesting a prescription. These individuals may have little training and often prescribe broad-spectrum antibiotics. Consider any advice from them accordingly. Folk healers and traditional markets in some parts of the country offer herbal and folk remedies. You should exercise caution when exploring these remedies, as the formulations can be questionable and some components may interact with other prescription medications.

Many tropical diseases are present in Ecuador, including malaria, dengue and yellow fever (which are transmitted by mosquitoes at lower altitudes), leishmaniaisis (transmitted by sand flies), chagas disease (transmitted by triatomine bugs) and tuberculosis (transmitted from person to person via respiratory droplets). To protect yourself from insect-borne diseases while at lower altitudes, use insect repellants, clothing treated with permethrin, and bed nets.

In Ecuador, yellow fever is found only in the Amazon basin. Ecuadorian authorities might require you to show a certificate of yellow fever vaccination when entering or leaving this area, or when continuing travel to other areas of South America. If possible, you should obtain a yellow fever vaccine prior to departure from the United States. You can also obtain the vaccination in Guayaquil from the Jefatura Provincial de Salud, Panama y Padre Aguirre, (tel): 04-230-3160, Monday through Friday from 8:30 a.m. to 12:00 p.m. The vaccine is free if you do not need an international certification; otherwise it costs $10.40. Antimalarial medication significantly reduces the risk of contracting malaria. There are no vaccines or prophylactic medications for dengue, leishmaniaisis or chagas. If you become ill with fever or flu-like symptoms during or after travel in a high-risk area, you should promptly seek medical attention. Note that the onset of these diseases may be delayed by up to a year.

You can find good information on vaccinations and other health precautions, on the Centers for Disease Control and Prevention website. For information about outbreaks of infectious diseases abroad, consult the World Health Organization (WHO) website. The WHO website also contains additional health information for travelers, including detailed country-specific health information.

Your Health and High Altitudes: If you travel to Quito (elevation: 9,400 feet) or other highland areas, you will typically require some time to adjust to the altitude, which can adversely affect your blood pressure, digestion, and energy level. Mountain climbers in particular should be cautioned not to underestimate the time required to adjust before beginning a challenging climb at altitude. Consult with your personal health care providers before undertaking high-altitude travel, as there are medications available to help combat the effects. If you have heart or lung problems or the sickle cell trait, you may develop serious health complications at high altitudes.

Medical Insurance: Do not assume your insurance will go with you when you travel. It's very important to find out BEFORE you travel whether your medical insurance will cover you overseas. Ask your insurance company two questions:

- Does my policy apply when I'm outside the United States?
- Will it cover emergencies like a trip to a foreign hospital or a medical evacuation?

In Ecuador, doctors and hospitals expect payment in cash at the time of service. If your policy does not offer overseas coverage, you should take out another one for your trip. Even if you have insurance, you may have to pay in advance and seek reimbursement from your insurer. If you are unable to pay for medical care, you may be relegated to Ecuador's public hospitals, where care is far below U.S. standards. If you are staying in Ecuador long-term, consider taking out a local insurance plan.

Medical evacuations, particularly from the Galapagos Islands, can cost tens of thousands of dollars and are typically not covered by U.S. insurance policies. For this reason, travelers are advised to purchase traveler's insurance that includes evacuation insurance. The Social Security Medicare Program does not provide coverage for hospital or medical costs outside of the United States.

Driving in Ecuador: Although some of Ecuador's roads and highways have greatly improved in recent years,road travel throughout Ecuador can still be dangerous, especially at night. Some roads are poorly maintained, or affected by heavy rains and mudslides. Mountain roads may lack safety features such as crash barriers or guard rails, and conditions are frequently made more treacherous by heavy fog. Highways are often unmarked and unlit, and do not have signs indicating destinations. In addition, slow-moving buses and trucks frequently stop in the middle of the road unexpectedly. In the countryside, livestock is often herded along roads or grazes on roadsides. Lacking sidewalks, many roads are also used by pedestrians. Driving practices differ from U.S. standards, and drivers often disobey traffic laws and signals. In all areas, buses stop without warning to pick up or drop off passengers. Drivers often turn right and left from any lane and rarely yield to pedestrians and cyclists. You might encounter intoxicated drivers at any time, though the chances of a drunk-driving accident are higher on weekends and Ecuadorian holidays. On the coast in particular, many vehicles are poorly maintained and breakdowns are common.

If you are the driver of a vehicle involved in an automobile accident, even if you are not at fault, you may be taken into police custody, especially if injuries are involved or if you do not have insurance. If injuries or damages are serious, you may face criminal charges.

Driver's Licenses: You may drive in Ecuador using your state-issued driver's license for up to 90 days. If you are staying in Ecuador for a prolonged period, you should contact the Comision de Transito del Ecuador to obtain a valid driver's license.

Importing a Vehicle: You should investigate local regulations before attempting to import any vehicle into Ecuador on a temporary or permanent basis. If you are able to register a vehicle in Ecuador, you will be required to buy local liability insurance, called SOAT.

Bus Travelers: Intra- and inter-city bus passengers are often targets of crime, including robbery and sexual assault. Numerous bus accidents occur every year in Ecuador, and many buses are overcrowded, poorly maintained, and lack seat belts or other safety features. In Guayaquil, security on public transportation is a major concern. Armed criminals have been known to board local city buses and rob passengers of jewelry, money, and other valuables. There have been instances in which routes between cities are blocked by criminals, who force the bus to stop and then board the bus to rob passengers.

Aviation Safety Oversight: The U.S. Federal Aviation Administration (FAA) has assessed the Government of Ecuador's Civil Aviation Authority as being in compliance with International Civil Aviation Organization (ICAO) aviation safety standards for oversight of Ecuador's air carrier operations. Further information may be found on the FAA's safety assessment page.

Children's Issues: Please see the U.S. Dept. of State Office of Children's Issues web pages on intercountry adoption and international parental child abduction.

Intercountry Adoption

December 2012

The information in this section has been edited from a report of the State Department Bureau of Consular Affairs, Office of Overseas Citizens Services. For more information, please read the *Intercountry Adoption* section of this book and review current reports online at http://adoption.state.gov.

Ecuador is party to the Hague Convention on Protection of Children and Co-operation in Respect of Intercountry Adoption (Hague Adoption Convention). Therefore, all adoptions between Ecuador and the United States must meet the requirements of the Convention and U.S. law implementing the Convention.

Ecuadorian law does not allow for an Ecuadorian child to travel to the United States to be adopted. Therefore, prospective adoptive parents must obtain a full and final adoption under Ecuadorian law before the child can immigrate to the United States. Adoption in Ecuador can be a complicated process. Ecuadorian adoption law gives preference to adoptions made by Ecuadorian nationals within Ecuador. Intercountry adoptions are permitted only in exceptional cases, normally when there are no relatives or other Ecuadorians able to adopt orphans or become their guardians.

Who Can Adopt? Adoption between the United States and Ecuador is governed by the Hague Adoption Convention. Therefore to adopt from Ecuador, you must first be found eligible to adopt by the U.S. Government. The U.S. Government agency responsible for making this determination is the Department of Homeland Security, U.S. Citizenship and Immigration Services (USCIS).

Residency Requirements: Prospective adoptive parent(s) must travel to Ecuador and expect to remain there for three to four weeks to finalize the adoption. Once an adoption decree is issued, only one parent needs to remain in Ecuador with the child, usually for an additional week.

Age Requirements: If married, both parents must be over 25 years of age and have been married for more than three years. There must be an age difference of at least 14 years between the younger parent and the child and no more than 45 years between either parent and the child.

Marriage Requirements: Both single and married individuals may adopt a child in Ecuador. Married couples must be heterosexual. An unmarried (single, widowed, or divorced) adoptive parent may only adopt a child of the same sex, unless the National Adoption Direction issues a favorable report for adoption of a child of the opposite sex. Priority is given to heterosexual married couples.

Other Requirements: The Childhood and Adolescence Court (Juzgado de la Niñez y Adolescencia) or a Notary Public must grant permission for the child to depart the country if only one member of the couple is present in Ecuador to travel with the child. This permission is only valid for one year. Additionally, prospective adoptive parents residing outside Ecuador may not adopt more than two children at a time, except in the case of sibling adoptions.

Who Can Be Adopted? Because Ecuador is a member of the Hague Adoption Convention, children from Ecuador must meet the requirements of the Convention in order to be eligible for adoption. For example, the Convention requires that Ecuador attempt to place a child with a family in-country before determining that a child is eligible for intercountry adoption. In addition to Ecuador's requirements, a child must meet the definition of a Convention adoptee for you to bring him or her back to the United States. Learn more about the Convention's requirements for adoptable children.

Ecuador's Central Authority: National Council of Childhood and Adolescence, (Consejo Nacional de la Niñez y Adolescencia, CNNA).

Ecuadorian Adoption Authorities: The National Adoption Direction, the Family Assignment Committee (Comité de Asignación Familiar) and The Technical Adoptions Unit (Unidad Técnica Adopciones)

The Process:. Because Ecuador is party to the Hague Adoption Convention, adopting from Ecuador must follow a specific process designed to meet the Convention's requirements. For detailed and updated information on these requirements, please review the *Intercountry Adoption* section of this publication and visit the U.S. Department of State Intercountry Adoption website at http://adoption.state.gov.

The first step in adopting a child from Ecuador is to select an accredited or approved adoption service provider in the United States that has signed an Agreement with the Government of Ecuador. Only these agencies and attorneys can provide adoption services between the United States and Ecuador. A list of U.S. accredited and approved adoption service providers may be obtained in person from the Consular Section of the U.S. Embassy in Quito or Consulate General in Guayaquil or online from the Department of State. After you choose an accredited or approved adoption service provider, you apply to be found eligible to adopt (Form I-800A) by the Department of Homeland Security, U.S. Citizenship and Immigration

Services (USCIS). Once the U.S. Government determines that you are "eligible" and "suitable" to be an adoptive parent, your information will be forwarded to the Central Authority in Ecuador. The Technical Adoptions Unit will review your application to determine whether you are also eligible to adopt under Ecuadorian law.

If both the United States and Ecuador determine that you are eligible to adopt, and a child is available for intercountry adoption, The Family Assignment Committee (Comites de Asignacion Familiar), will provide a referral for a child and assign a child to the prospective adoptive parent(s) and forward this information regarding the assigned child to the parent's(s') adoption service provider. You cannot identify a specific child that you would like to adopt prior to the referral.

Prospective adoptive parent(s) must express acceptance of the referral in writing, after which, they must travel to Ecuador to complete the judicial part of the process. If married, both spouses are required to travel to Ecuador for an adaptation period. The length of the adaptation period with the child depends on each orphanage's policy and program, but it usually takes three or four days.

After this, based on the prospective adoptive parents' relationship with the child, the orphanage will send a report to the Technical Adoption Unit. That office will then give the report along with other adoption documents to the adoption service provider's representative. The documents will be filed at the Minor's Court along with the adoption petition, which must be signed (jointly by the petitioners if a married couple). The judge will then schedule an appointment (usually one or two days later) with the prospective adoptive parent(s) to acknowledge the signature(s) on the adoption request. The prospective adoptive parent(s) must go personally to that appointment and bring their passport(s).

After you accept a match with a child, you will apply to the USCIS for provisional approval to adopt that specific child (Form I-800, Petition to Classify a Convention adoptee as an Immediate Relative). USCIS will determine whether the child is eligible under U.S. immigration law to be adopted and enter the United States. If the Consular Officer determines that the child appears eligible to immigrate to the United States, he or she will notify the Central Authority (Consejo Nacional de la Niñez y Adolescencia, CNNA) and the Adoption Service Provider (Article 5 letter).

Role of the Court: The courts in Ecuador issue adoption decrees. The Childhood and Adolescence Court, Juzgado de la Niñez y Adolescencia, must grant permission for the child to depart the country if only one member of the couple is present in Ecuador to travel with the child.

Role of Adoption Service Providers: The Government of Ecuador requires that prospective adoptive parents work through an accredited or approved U.S. adoption service provider that has signed an Agreement with the Government of Ecuador. The agency can give you an estimate of the cost of an adoption in Ecuador. A list of these agencies may be obtained in person from the Consular Section of the U.S. Embassy in Quito or Consulate General in Guayaquil.

Time Frame: The adoption process in Ecuador generally takes between nine and sixteen months to complete. Adopting families must first contact an Ecuadorian-approved U.S. adoption service provider that will provide general instructions about intercountry adoption procedures, and will assist prospective adoptive parents with the preparation and filing of preliminary U.S. immigration documentation.

This process generally takes approximately three months (USCIS Form I-800A). An additional six months to one year is needed for further adjudication once these documents are forwarded to an agency or lawyer in Ecuador.

Adoption Fees: The cost of adoptions varies with different adoption service providers. In the adoption services contract that you sign at the beginning of the adoption process, your agency will itemize the fees and estimated expenses related to your adoption process.

Documents Required: Certifications, notarizations and apostilles must be completed in the United States before the prospective adoptive parents travel to Ecuador or the application for adoption is submitted. Translations can be completed in Ecuador. Documents must be apostilled in the United States.

The prospective adoptive parent(s) must present the following documents to the American adoption service provider which will represent them in Ecuador:

- Certified copies of birth certificates of prospective adoptive parent(s);
- Certified copy of marriage certificate and proof of termination of prior marriages (death certificates/divorce decrees), if applicable;
- Certified copy of the state law that regulates the adoption of minors (especially foreign minors) in the adoptive parent's(s') state of U.S. residence;
- Home study report on the adoptive parent(s) and institutional criteria on the suitability of the adoptive parent(s) from the entity performing the home study (all these documents are part of the I-800A);
- Certificate of no criminal record for each adoptive parent from a local police department (an FBI report is acceptable in lieu of local police record);
- Verification of employment and salary;
- Notarized adoption authorization letter from the adoption service provider to the family certifying that the family is duly prepared to adopt an Ecuadorian child;

- Certificate of physical and mental health of prospective adoptive parent(s); and
- Photocopies of the passports of the prospective adoptive parent(s).

The adoption hearing will take place three or four days after the judge schedules the meeting to verify signature(s). The judge will review the parent's(s') qualifications, including psychological and financial situations. After the hearing, prospective adoptive parent(s) and the judge sign the minutes. The judge will issue the final adoption decree unless the judge identifies false statements or documents. The adoption decree becomes final three days after issuance. At this point, the adoptive parent(s) can obtain a new birth certificate for their child from the Civil Registry Office.

The new birth certificate will include the name(s) of parent(s) and any change of name for the child. With the new birth certificate, the parent(s) (or the adoption service provider on their behalf) can obtain an Ecuadorian identity card and Ecuadorian passport for the child.

Bringing Your Child Home: Once your adoption is complete (or you have obtained legal custody of the child), there are a few more steps to take before you can head home. Specifically, you need to apply for several documents for your child before he or she can travel to the United States, such as a birth certificate, a passport or travel document for your child from the country in which he or she was born, and a U.S. Immigration Visa. For detailed and updated information on how to obtain these documents, review the *Intercountry Adoption* section in this publication and visit the U.S. Department of State Intercountry Adoption website at http://adoption.state.gov.

Child Citizenship Act: For adoptions finalized abroad, the Child Citizenship Act of 2000 allows your new child to acquire American citizenship automatically when he or she enters the United States as lawful permanent residents. For adoptions finalized in the United States, the Child Citizenship Act of 2000 allows your new child to acquire American citizenship automatically when the court in the United States issues the final adoption decree. To learn more, review the *Intercountry Adoption* section in this publication and visit the U.S. Department of State Intercountry Adoption website at http://adoption.state.gov.

After Adoption: In accordance with the International Adoption agreement, the Central Authority has the responsibility to periodically follow up on the residence and living conditions of the adopted children. The Central Authority will request annual reports from the international adoption agencies in accordance with international agreements. Ecuadorian adoption law stipulates that the follow-up report must be completed quarterly during the first year and every six months during the second year. Adoption follow-ups cease two years after the adoption date.

United States Embassy
Avigirias E12–170 y Eloy Alfaro
Quito—Ecuador
P.O. Box: 17–17–1538
Telephone: 011–593–2- 398–5000
Fax: 011–593–2- 398–5100

U.S. Consulate in Guayaquil
9 de Octubre y Garcia Moreno
Guayaquil, Ecuador
Tel: 011–593–4-2323–570 ext. 224, 222
Fax: 011–593–4-320–904, 011–593–4-2325–286

Ecuador's Central Authority
National Council of Childhood and Adolescence, (Consejo Nacional de la Niñez y Adolescencia, CNNA).
Mariscal Foch E4–38 entre Colon y Cordero. Quito, Ecuador

Embassy of Ecuador
2535 15th Street, N.W.
Washington, DC 20009
Tel: (202) 234–7200
Fax: (202) 667–3482
Email: consuladodc@ecuador.org
Website: http://ecuador.org/main.htm

Ecuador also has consulates in Chicago, Houston, Miami, Jersey City, New York, New Orleans, San Francisco, and Los Angeles.

Office of Children's Issues
U.S. Department of State
2201 C Street, NW
SA-29
Washington, DC 20520
Tel: 1–888–407–4747
Email: AskCI@state.gov
Website:http://adoption.state.gov

For questions about immigration procedures, contact the National Customer Service Center (NCSC) at 1-800-375-5283 (TTY 1-800-767-1833).

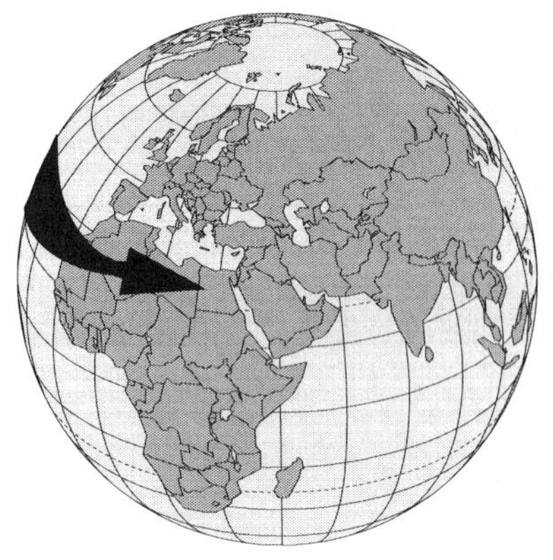

EGYPT

Compiled from publications that were available as of February 2013 from the U.S. Department of State, the U.S. Department of Commerce, and the Central Intelligence Agency (CIA). See the introduction to this set for explanatory notes.

Official Name:
Arab Republic of Egypt

PROFILE

Geography

Area: total: 1,001,450 sq km; country comparison to the world: 30; land: 995,450 sq km; water: 6,000 sq km

Major cities: Cairo (capital) 10.902 million; Alexandria 4.387 million (2009)

Climate: desert; hot, dry summers with moderate winters

Terrain: vast desert plateau interrupted by Nile valley and delta

People

Nationality: noun: Egyptian(s); adjective: Egyptian

Population: 83,688,164 (July 2012 est.)

Population growth rate: 1.922% (2012 est.)

Ethnic groups: Egyptian 99.6%, other 0.4% (2006 census)

Religions: Muslim (mostly Sunni) 90%, Coptic 9%, other Christian 1%

Languages: Arabic (official), English and French widely understood by educated classes

Literacy: definition: age 10 and over can read and write; total population: 72%; male: 80.3%; female: 63.5% (2010 est.)

Health: life expectancy at birth: total population: 72.93 years; male: 70.33 years; female: 75.66 years (2012 est.); Infant mortality rate: total: 24.23 deaths/1,000 live births; male: 25.8 deaths/1,000 live births; female: 22.59 deaths/1,000 live births (2012 est.)

Unemployment rate: 12.5% (2012 est.)

Work force: 27.54 million (2012 est.)

Government

Type: republic

Independence: 28 February 1922

Constitution: provisional constitution passed by referendum 19 March 2011; adopted 30 March 2011

Political subdivisions: 27 governorates (muhafazat, singular—muhafazat)

Suffrage: 18 years of age; universal and compulsory

Economy

GDP (purchasing power parity): $537.8 billion (2012 est.); $525.6 billion (2011 est.); $516.5 billion (2010 est.); $491.2 billion (2009 est.)

GDP real growth rate: 2% (2012 est.); 1.8% (2011 est.); 5.1% (2010 est.); 4.7% (2009 est.)

GDP per capita (PPP): $6,600 (2012 est.); $6,600 (2011 est.); $6,600 (2010 est.); $6,400 (2009 est.)

Natural resources: petroleum, natural gas, iron ore, phosphates, manganese, limestone, gypsum, talc, asbestos, lead, rare earth elements, zinc

Agriculture products: cotton, rice, corn, wheat, beans, fruits, vegetables; cattle, water buffalo, sheep, goats

Industries: textiles, food processing, tourism, chemicals, pharmaceuticals, hydrocarbons, construction, cement, metals, light manufactures

Exports: $28.37 billion (2012 est.); $27.91 billion (2011 est.); $25.02 billion (2010 est.)

Exports—commodities: crude oil and petroleum products, cotton, textiles, metal products, chemicals, processed food

Exports—partners: Italy 8.8%, Germany 5.5%, US 5.5%, India 5.2%, Saudi Arabia 5.1%, Spain 4.7%, France 4.5% (2011)

Imports: $58.76 billion (2012 est.); $53.97 billion (2011 est.); $52.7 billion (2010 est.)

Imports—commodities: machinery and equipment, foodstuffs, chemicals, wood products, fuels

Imports—partners: China 11.5%, US 9.8%, Italy 5.6%, Germany 4.9%, Turkey 4.4%, Brazil 4.1% (2011)

Debt—external: $34.88 billion (31 December 2012 est.); $33.74 billion (31 December 2011 est.); $34.84 billion (31 December 2010 est.)

Exchange rates: Egyptian pounds (EGP) per US dollar; 6.05 (2012 est.); 5.9328 (2011 est.); 5.6219 (2010 est.); 5.545 (2009); 5.4 (2008); 5.67 (2007)

PEOPLE

Egypt is the most populous country in the Arab world and the second-most populous on the African continent. Nearly all of the country's 80 million people live in the following locations: Cairo and Alexandria; elsewhere on the banks of the Nile; in the Nile delta, which fans out north of Cairo; and along the Suez Canal. These regions are among the world's most densely populated, containing an average of over 3,820 persons per square mile (1,540 per sq. km.), as compared to about 200 persons per sq. mi. for the country as a whole.

Small communities spread throughout the desert regions of Egypt are clustered around oases and historic trade and transportation routes. The government has tried with mixed success to encourage migration to newly irrigated land reclaimed from the desert. However, the proportion of the population living in rural areas has continued to decrease as people move to the cities in search of employment and a higher standard of living.

The Egyptians are a fairly homogeneous people of Hamitic origin. Mediterranean and Arab influences appear in the north, and there is some mixing in the south with the Nubians of northern Sudan. Ethnic minorities include a small number of Bedouin Arab nomads in the eastern and western deserts and in the Sinai, as well as some 50,000-100,000 Nubians clustered along the Nile in Upper (southern) Egypt.

Education is free through university and compulsory from ages 6 through 15. Major universities include Cairo University (100,000 students), Alexandria University, and the 1,000-year-old Al-Azhar University, one of the world's major centers of Islamic learning.

Language

Arabic is the spoken language of Egypt. Colloquial Cairene Arabic is expressive and rich in words of Coptic, European, and Turkish origins. The written language differs from the spoken. Modern standard Arabic, based on the language of the Koran, is heard on radio, television, and in formal speeches. English, and to a lesser extent French, is widely spoken amongst the business community and at hotel and tourist destinations.

Egypt's vast and rich literature constitutes an important cultural element in the life of the country and in the Arab world as a whole. Egyptian novelists and poets were among the first to experiment with modern styles of Arabic literature, and the forms they developed have been widely imitated. Egyptian novelist Naguib Mahfouz was the first Arab to win the Nobel prize for literature. Egyptian books and films are available throughout the Middle East.

Religion

Approximately 90 percent of the population is Sunni Muslim. Shia Muslims constitute significantly less than 1 percent of the population. Estimates of the percentage of Christians range from 8 to 12 percent (6 to 10 million), the majority of whom belong to the Coptic Orthodox Church. The country's Jewish community numbers about 100 persons, mostly senior citizens.

Other Christian communities together constitute less than 2 percent of the population and include the Armenian Apostolic, Catholic (Armenian, Chaldean, Greek, Melkite, Roman, and Syrian), Maronite, and Orthodox (Greek and Syrian) churches, which range in size from several thousand to hundreds of thousands. A Protestant community, established in the mid-19th century, includes 16 Protestant denominations: Presbyterian, Anglican, Baptist, Brethren, Open Brethren, Revival of Holiness (Nahdat al-Qadaasa), Faith (Al-Eyman), Church of God, Christian Model Church (Al-Mithaal Al-Masihi), Apostolic, Grace (An-Ni'ma), Pentecostal, Apostolic Grace, Church of Christ, Gospel Missionary (Al-Kiraaza bil Ingil), and the Message Church of Holland (Ar-Risaala). There are also followers of the Seventh-day Adventist Church, which was granted legal status in the 1960s. There are 1,000 to 1,500 Jehovah's Witnesses, less than 1,500 Baha'is, and a small number of foreign members of The Church of Jesus Christ of Latter-day Saints (Mormons), but the government does not recognize these faiths. Estimates of the number of Shia Muslims vary widely, but the community most likely numbers in the low tens of thousands. There are also small groups of Qur'anists and Ahmadiya Muslims.

Christians reside throughout the country, although the percentage of Christians is higher in Upper Egypt (the southern part of the country) and in some sections of Cairo and Alexandria.

There are many foreign religious groups, especially Roman Catholics and Protestants, which have had a presence in the country for more than a century. These groups are engaged in education, social, and development work.

HISTORY

Egypt has endured as a unified state for more than 5,000 years, and archeological evidence indicates that a developed Egyptian society has existed for much longer. Egyptians take pride in their "pharaonic heritage" and in their descent from what they consider mankind's earliest civilization. The Arabic word for Egypt is Misr, which originally connoted "civilization" or "metropolis."

Archeological findings show that primitive tribes lived along the Nile long before the dynastic history of the pharaohs began. By 6000 B.C., organized agriculture had appeared.

In about 3100 B.C., Egypt was united under a ruler known as Mena, or Menes, who inaugurated the 30 pharaonic dynasties into which Egypt's ancient history is divided—the Old and the Middle Kingdoms and the New Empire. The pyramids at Giza (near Cairo), which were built in the fourth dynasty, testify to the power of the pharaonic religion and state. The

Great Pyramid, the tomb of Pharaoh Khufu (also known as Cheops), is the only surviving monument of the Seven Wonders of the Ancient World. Ancient Egypt reached the peak of its power, wealth, and territorial extent in the period called the New Empire (1567–1085 B.C.).

Persian, Greek, Roman, and Arab Conquerors

In 525 B.C., Cambyses, the son of Cyrus the Great, led a Persian invasion force that dethroned the last pharaoh of the 26th dynasty. The country remained a Persian province until conquered by Alexander the Great in 322 B.C., ushering in Ptolemaic rule in Egypt that lasted for nearly 300 years.

Following a brief Persian reconquest, Egypt was invaded and conquered by Arab forces in 642 A.D. A process of Arabization and Islamization ensued. Although a Coptic Christian minority remained—and constitutes about 10% of the population today—the Arab language inexorably supplanted the indigenous Coptic tongue. For the next 1,300 years, a succession of Arab, Mameluke, and Ottoman caliphs, beys, and sultans ruled the country.

European Influence

The Ottoman Turks controlled Egypt from 1517 until 1882, except for a brief period of French rule under Napoleon Bonaparte. In 1805, Mohammed Ali, commander of an Albanian contingent of Ottoman troops, won autonomy from the Ottoman Empire and founded the dynasty that ruled Egypt until his great-great grandson, Farouk, was overthrown in 1952. Mohammed Ali ruled Egypt until 1848, ushering in the modern history of Egypt. The rapid growth of Cairo as an urban center began in the reign of Ismail (1863–79). Eager to modernize the capital, he ordered the construction of a European-style city to the west of the medieval core. The Suez Canal was completed in Ismail's reign in 1869, and its completion was celebrated by many events, including the commissioning of Verdi's "Aida" for a new opera house and the building of great palaces, such as the Omar Khayyam (originally constructed to entertain the French Empress Eugenie, and now the central section of the Cairo Marriott Hotel).

In 1882, British expeditionary forces crushed an Egyptian revolt led by Ahmed Orabi Pasha, marking the beginning of British occupation and the virtual inclusion of Egypt within the British Empire. Egypt became independent from the British Empire in 1922. British influence, however, continued to dominate Egypt's political life.

Between 1922 and 1952, three main political forces competed with one another: the Wafd, a broadly-based nationalist political organization strongly opposed to British influence; King Fuad, whom the British had installed during World War I; and the British themselves, who were determined to maintain control over the Suez Canal. Other political forces emerging in this period included the Communist Party (1925) and the Muslim Brotherhood (1928), which eventually became a potent political and religious force.

During World War II, British troops used Egypt as a base for Allied operations throughout the region. British troops were withdrawn to the Suez Canal area in 1947, but nationalist, anti-British feelings continued to grow after the war. On July 22-23, 1952, a group of disaffected army officers (the "Free Officers") led by Lt. Col. Gamal Abdel Nasser overthrew King Farouk, whom the military blamed for Egypt's poor performance in the 1948 war with Israel. Following a brief experiment with civilian rule, they abrogated the 1923 constitution and declared Egypt a republic on June 19, 1953. Nasser evolved into a charismatic leader, not only of Egypt, but of the Arab world, promoting and implementing "Arab socialism." He nationalized much of Egypt's economy.

Nasser helped establish the Non-Aligned Movement of developing countries in September 1961, and continued to be a leading force in the movement until his death in 1970. When the United States held up military sales in reaction to Egyptian neutrality toward Moscow, Nasser concluded a seminal arms deal with Czechoslovakia in September 1955.

When the U.S. and the World Bank withdrew their offer to help finance the Aswan High Dam in mid-1956, Nasser nationalized the privately owned Suez Canal Company. The crisis that followed, exacerbated by growing tensions with Israel over guerrilla attacks from Gaza and Israeli reprisals, resulted in the invasion of Egypt that October by France, Britain, and Israel; U.S. political intervention helped reverse the invasion, and the Canal remained nationalized.

Nasser's domestic policies were frequently oppressive, yet generally popular. All opposition was stamped out, and opponents of the regime frequently were imprisoned without trial. Nasser's foreign and military policies helped provoke the Israeli attack of June 1967 that virtually destroyed Egypt's armed forces along with those of Jordan and Syria. Israel also occupied the Sinai Peninsula, the Gaza Strip, the West Bank, and the Golan Heights. Nasser, however, was revered by the masses in Egypt and elsewhere in the Arab world until his death in 1970.

After Nasser's death, another of the original "Free Officers," Vice President Anwar el-Sadat, was elected President. In 1971, Sadat concluded a treaty of friendship with the Soviet Union, but a year later, ordered Soviet advisers to leave. In 1973, he launched the October war with Israel, in which Egypt's armed forces achieved initial successes but were driven back by Israeli counterattacks.

Camp David and the Peace Process

In a momentous change from the Nasser era, President Sadat shifted Egypt from a policy of confrontation with Israel to one of peaceful accommodation through negotiations. Following the Sinai Disengagement Agreements of 1974 and 1975, Sadat

created a fresh opening for progress by his dramatic visit to Jerusalem in November 1977. This led to President Jimmy Carter's invitation to President Sadat and Prime Minister Begin to join him in trilateral negotiations at Camp David. The historic Camp David accords were signed by Egypt and Israel and witnessed by the United States on September 17, 1978. The accords led to the March 26, 1979 signing of the Egypt-Israel Treaty of Peace, by which Egypt regained control of the Sinai in May 1982. Throughout this period, U.S.-Egyptian relations steadily improved, but Sadat's willingness to break ranks by making peace with Israel antagonized most other Arab states.

Domestic Politics after Camp David

Sadat introduced greater political freedom and a new economic policy, the most important aspect of which was the "infitah" or "open door." This relaxed government controls over the economy and encouraged private, including foreign, investment. Sadat dismantled much of the existing political machine and brought to trial a number of former government officials accused of criminal excesses during the Nasser era.

On October 6, 1981, Islamic extremists assassinated President Sadat. Hosni Mubarak, Vice President since

1975 and an air force commander during the October 1973 war, was elected President later that month. He was subsequently confirmed by popular referendum for four more 6-year terms; the most recent referendum took place in September 2005. Egypt was readmitted to the Arab League in 1989 after being expelled for reaching a peace agreement with Israel.

Between 1991 and 2011, Egypt undertook a domestic economic reform program to reduce the size of the public sector and expand the role of the private sector. Political reform stalled, however. The government repressed civil society and opposition groups and maintained Egypt's long-standing state of emergency. The first competitive presidential elections, held in 2005, were marked by low voter turnout and charges of fraud. Parliamentary elections in 2005 saw significant opposition gains but also violence, low turnout, fraud, and vote rigging.

In one notable case, Ayman Nour, member of parliament and popular leader of the opposition Al-Ghad (Tomorrow) Party, was arrested in 2005 and ultimately sentenced to five years' imprisonment. He was released in 2009. Following parliamentary elections in 2010 that saw significant irregularities and pre-election restrictions, the ruling National Democratic Party (NDP) continued to dominate national politics by maintaining an overriding majority in the People's Assembly and Shura Council.

The Arab Spring in Egypt: Revolution at Tahrir Square

After an 18-day massive, popular revolution centered on Cairo's Tahrir (Liberation) Square, Hosni Mubarak was forced to resign as the President of Egypt on February 11, 2011. He relinquished the administration of power first to his Vice President and then to a transitional government led by the Egyptian military's Supreme Council of the Armed Forces (SCAF), which then appointed a civilian prime minister and cabinet to run the Egyptian government. In a March 19, 2011 referendum, Egyptians voted overwhelmingly to amend Egypt's constitution, thus setting the legal groundwork for democratic parliamentary and presidential elections. The referendum included amendments that set term limits for the president, affirmed judicial oversight of elections, and prevented the state of emergency from remaining in effect for longer than six months unless approved by a public referendum. It also provided for the establishment of a 100-member constituent assembly to draft a new constitution.

GOVERNMENT AND POLITICAL CONDITIONS

Egypt is a republic governed at year's end by the Supreme Council of the Armed Forces (SCAF), a transitional authority of senior military officers that rules by decree. The appointed civilian Cabinet of Ministers carries out the SCAF's executive responsibilities. Legislative elections began on November 28 and extended into in February 2012. Nongovernmental (NGO) observers reported the first two rounds of elections that took place during the calendar year to be generally free from state interference. There were instances in which elements of the security forces acted independently of civilian control.

On February 11, 2011, then president Muhammad Hosni Mubarak transferred executive authority to the SCAF following antigovernment demonstrations that began on January 25. On February 13, the SCAF suspended the 1971 constitution and dissolved the popularly elected People's Assembly and the partially elected Shura (Consultative) Council. On March 19, voters approved a constitutional referendum that mandated new legislative elections and the drafting of a new constitution. The referendum balloting was considered free and fair. On March 30, the SCAF issued a provisional constitution.

Recent Elections

On March 19, 2011, voters participated in a constitutional referendum to approve or reject eight amendments to the 1971 constitution. The process generally was considered fair, but there were scattered reports of voter intimidation.

On October 1, the SCAF announced that it would permit local and international NGOs to "witness" the elections under guidelines determined by the Higher Elections Commission. The SCAF's previous position as articulated on July 20 was that it would not allow international organizations to observe the elections, terming it an affront to national sovereignty. The segment of the electoral process completed by year's end generally was considered free from state interference, but local and international NGOs monitoring the elections noted administrative issues including delays in opening polling stations and inadequate supplies of indelible ink, ballot boxes, and ballots.

There were also reports that some parties violated electoral regulations stipulating that no campaigning could occur within 48 hours of the elections or in close proximity to polling stations. In addition, during the electoral period (although not targeting election participants or locations), security forces used excessive force to disperse demonstrations, the government censored and harassed media outlets, and Ministry of Justice investigators raided the offices of NGOs involved in electoral monitoring and administration activities.

On January 23, 2012, Egypt's newly elected lower house of parliament, the People's Assembly, convened for the first time; the SCAF transferred legislative authority to the parliament on the same day. The new members of Egypt's upper house of parliament, the Shura Council, met on February 28, 2012. Presidential elections took place on May 23-24, 2012, with a run-off on June 16-17. Muhammad Mursi was elected to the presidency.

Political Parties: The freedom to form, legally register, and operate political parties improved significantly during 2011. Before the revolution the law stipulated that party "principles, targets, programs, policies, or means of practicing activities" had to conform to national security and other requirements (as interpreted by the government). On March 28, the SCAF passed a new law that eased most restrictions on the legal establishment of new political parties. However, the law prohibits parties formed on the basis of religion, class, sect, profession, geography, language, or gender, and new parties are required to have a minimum of 5,000 members from at least 10 provinces. Previously, new parties were required to have 1,000 members.

Authorities rejected one party application during the year, from the reportedly Shia-oriented Tahrir Party, on the grounds that the party was based on religious principles. The committee asked several parties to provide further documentation to ensure they were in compliance with the law. Some parties, such as Al-Wasat, had unsuccessfully sought to register for more than a decade under the previous government. Approximately 40 new parties successfully registered after the revolution.

On April 16, an administrative court dissolved the former ruling National Democratic Party and transferred its assets to the state.

Participation of Women and Minorities: Religious and cultural barriers strongly inhibited women's political participation and leadership. The SCAF and political parties, among other groups, excluded women from the political process during 2011. On July 21, the SCAF announced that it abolished the quota established in 2009 that reserved 64 People's Assembly seats for women. In late September the SCAF amended the election law to require at least one female candidate on each party list competing in the legislative elections.

Media and NGO observer groups reported high voter turnout among women and Coptic Christians for the first two rounds of parliamentary elections that took place in November and December. Since the elections continued at year's end, it was unclear how many women or minorities would serve in parliament. At the end of 2011, the cabinet included one woman and two Coptic Christians. There were no women or members of religious minorities serving on the SCAF; women were excluded from military service, and non-Muslims were generally selected for retirement before reaching senior active-duty ranks. No women or members of religious minorities were among the appointed governors of the country's 27 governorates.

Principal Government Officials

Last Updated: 1/31/2013

Pres.: **Muhammad MURSI**
Vice Pres.: **Mahmoud MEKKY**
Prime Min.: **Hisham QANDIL**
Min. of Agriculture & Land Reclamation: **Mohamed Salah Abdel MO'MEN**
Min. of Antiquities: **Mohamed Ibrahim ALI**
Min. of Awqaf (Religious Affairs): **Talaat AFIFI**
Min. of Civil Aviation: **Samir IMBABY**
Min. of Communication & Information Technology: **Hany MAHMOUD**
Min. of Culture: **Mohamed Saber ARAB**
Min. of Defense: **Abdelfattah Said ELSISI, Lt. Gen.**
Min. of Education: **Ibrahim Ahmed Ghoneim DEIF**
Min. of Electricity & Energy: **Mahmoud BALBA'**
Min. of Finance: **Momtaz SAEED**
Min. of Foreign Affairs: **Mohamed Kamel AMR**
Min. of Foreign Trade & Industry: **Hatem SALEH**
Min. of Health & Population: **Mohamed Hamed MUSTAFA**
Min. of Higher Education: **Moustafa MOSAD**
Min. of Housing, Utilities, & Urban Communities: **Tarek WAFIQ**
Min. of Information: **Salah Abdel MAQSOOD**
Min. of Interior: **Ahmed Gamal AL-DIN**
Min. of Intl. Cooperation & Planning: **Ashraf AL ARABY**
Min. of Irrigation & Water Resources: **Mohamed Baha AL DIN AHMED**
Min. of Justice: **Ahmed MEKKY**
Min. of Legal Affairs & Parliamentary Councils: **Mohamed MAHSOUB**
Min. of Manpower & Immigration: **Khaled Mahmoud AL AZHARY**
Min. of Military Production: **Abdelfattah Said ELSISI, Lt. Gen.**
Min. of Petroleum & Metallurgical Wealth: **Osama KAMAL**
Min. of Science, Technology, & Scientific Research: **Nadia ZAKHARY**
Min. of Social Affairs & Insurance: **Nagwa KHALIL**
Min. of Sport: **El Amry FAROUK**
Min. of Supply & Internal Trade: **Abou Zeid Mohamed ABOU ZEID**
Min. of Tourism: **Hisham ZAAZOU**
Min. of Transport: **Mohamed RASHAD**
Min. of Youth: **Osama YASSIN**
Min. of State for Environmental Affairs: **Khaled ABDEL AZIZ**
Min. of State for Local Development: **Ahmed Zaki ABDEEN**
Min. of State for Military Production: **Reda Hafiz AL-MAJID, Air Mar.**
Governor, Central Bank of Egypt: **Farouk Abdel Baky El OKDAH**
Ambassador to the US: **Mohamed TAWFIK**
Permanent Representative to the UN, New York: **Mootaz Ahmadein KHALIL**

ECONOMY

Occupying the northeast corner of the African continent, Egypt is bisected by the highly fertile Nile valley, where most economic activity takes place. Egypt's economy was highly centralized during the rule of former President Gamal Abdel Nasser but opened up considerably under former Presidents Anwar El-Sadat and Mohamed Hosni Mubarak. Cairo from 2004 to 2008 aggressively pursued economic reforms to attract foreign investment and facilitate GDP growth. Despite the relatively high levels of economic growth in recent years, living conditions for the average Egyptian remained poor and contributed to public discontent.

After unrest erupted in January 2011, the Egyptian Government backtracked on economic reforms, drastically increasing social spending to address public dissatisfaction, but political uncertainty at the same time caused economic growth to slow significantly, reducing the government's revenues. Tourism, manufacturing, and construction were among the hardest hit sectors of the Egyptian economy, and economic growth is likely to remain slow during the next several years.

The government drew down foreign exchange reserves by more than 50% in 2011 and 2012 to support the Egyptian pound and the dearth of foreign financial assistance - as a result of unsuccessful negotiations with the International Monetary Fund over a multi-billion dollar loan agreement which have dragged on more than 20 months - could precipitate fiscal and balance of payments crises in 2013.

Labor Conditions

The Child Law sets the minimum age for regular employment at 15, and at age 12 for seasonal employment. The labor code bars children under age 18 from 44 specific hazardous occupations, while the Child Law prohibits employment of children (all under 18) from any work that "puts the health, safety, or morals of the child into danger." Provincial governors, with the approval of the minister of education, may authorize seasonal work (often agricultural) for children who are 12 or older, provided that duties are not hazardous and do not interfere with schooling. The labor code and Child Law limit working children's hours and mandate breaks. However, the labor code explicitly excludes domestic work, work in family businesses, and children working in agriculture from minimum age and other restrictions.

The government did not effectively enforce child labor laws in the informal sector, and child labor in the informal sector remained prevalent. In July 2011 the government estimated that 1.6 million children, just under 10 percent of the total population of children, were engaged in labor. The majority of child labor occurred in agriculture and domestic work, although children also worked in light industry, on construction sites, and in service businesses such as auto repair shops. The National Council of Wages established an LE 700 ($120) monthly minimum wage for public sector workers. At least initially, the minimum wage applied only to direct government employees and used existing benefits and bonuses to calculate the total salary. Most government workers, therefore, already earned a total above the minimum wage. The government initiated a 15 percent wage hike designed to lift those below the threshold above the LE 700 level. According to Central Agency for Public Mobilization and Statistics figures, from July 2010 to June 2011, the poverty line was LE 256 ($41) per person, per month. The agency defined "extreme poverty" as less than LE 171.50 ($28) per month.

Although the wage council determined working hours for government and public sector employees, there were no standards for the private sector. The law stipulates that the maximum workweek is 48 hours. The law provides for premium pay for overtime and work on rest days and national holidays. Most private sector employees worked five days per week, usually Sunday through Thursday. The law prohibits excessive compulsory overtime, but the government enforced these prohibitions only in the public sector, and it did so selectively.

Many private and informal sector workers throughout the country, including in special economic zones, faced poor working conditions. Domestic workers were not covered by labor laws, making them vulnerable to abuse and forced labor. There were reports of employer abuse of citizen and undocumented foreign workers, especially domestic workers.

U.S.-EGYPTIAN RELATIONS

The United States established diplomatic relations with Egypt in 1922, following its independence from protectorate status under the United Kingdom. The United States and Egypt share a relationship based on mutual interest in Middle East peace and stability, revitalizing the Egyptian economy and strengthening trade relations, and promoting regional security. Egypt has been a key U.S. partner in ensuring regional stability and on a wide range of common security issues, including Middle East peace and countering terrorism.

Egypt's historic transition to democracy, launched in early 2011, will have a profound impact on the political future, not only of Egypt, but also the Middle East and North Africa (MENA) region at large. Supporting a successful transition to democracy and economic stability in Egypt, one that protects the basic rights of its citizens and fulfills the aspirations of the Egyptian people, will continue to be a core objective of U.S. policy toward Egypt. A prosperous and democratic Egypt, buoyed by economic growth and a strong private sector, can be an anchor of stability for the MENA region.

U.S. Assistance to Egypt

U.S. assistance to Egypt has long played a central role in Egypt's economic and military development, and in furthering the strategic partnership. With Egypt embarking on a transition to democracy, U.S. support can bolster Egypt's nascent democratic system and achieve inclusive economic growth. U.S. assistance supports Egyptian efforts to protect civil liberties and human rights, introduce transparency and accountability in government, foster economic growth and democratic institutions, and develop a robust, independent civil society.

Bilateral Economic Relations

Egypt has one of the most diversified economies in the Middle East. U.S. exports to Egypt include wheat and corn, mineral fuel and oil, machinery, aircraft, and iron and steel products. U.S. imports from Egypt include apparel, natural gas and oil, fertilizers, textile coverings, and agricultural products. Under the Qualifying Industrial Zone agreement, the

United States waives duties on imports from Egypt if the value includes 10.5% Israeli content; this program is meant to promote stronger ties between the region's peace partners. Egypt and the United States have signed a trade and investment framework agreement, a step toward creating freer trade and increasing investment flows. The two also have a bilateral investment treaty that provides for fair, equitable, and nondiscriminatory treatment for investors of both nations.

Egypt's Membership in International Organizations

Egypt and the United States belong to a number of the same international organizations, including the United Nations, International Monetary Fund, World Bank, and World Trade Organization. Egypt also is a Partner for Cooperation with the Organization for Security and Cooperation in Europe, an observer to the Organization of American States, and a nonparty state to the International Criminal Court.

Bilateral Representation

Egypt maintains an embassy in the United States at 3521 International Court NW, Washington, DC, 20008 (tel. 202-895-5400).

Principal U.S. Embassy Officials

Last Updated: 1/14/2013

CAIRO (E) 8 Kamal El Din Salah St., Garden City, Cairo., (20) (2) 2797-3300, Fax (20) (2) 2797-3200, Workweek: SUN-THU—0800-1630, Website: http://cairo.usembassy.gov/

DCM OMS:	Stephen Rogerson
AMB OMS:	Cecile Sakla
DHS/CBP:	Carl Jaigobind
DHS/ICE:	Timothy Hicks
FCS:	Ann Bacher
FM:	Craig Flanagan
HRO:	Gong Li
MGT:	Amy Hyatt
MLO/ODC:	MG Richard Clark
POL/MIL:	Eva Shinagel
POSHO:	Craig Flanagan
SDO/DATT:	MG Richard Clark
AMB:	Anne Patterson
CG:	J Richard Walsh
CON:	John Coe
DCM:	Marc Sievers
PAO:	Patricia Kabra
GSO:	John Griffith
RSO:	Todd Brown
AFSA:	Andrew Mitchell
AGR:	Jonathan Gressel
AID:	John Beed (Acting)
APHIS:	Sharon Williams
CLO:	Tricia Canton
DEA:	Thomas Riddles
ECON:	Ian Campbell
FMO:	Vivian Lesh
ICASS Chair:	David Witty
IMO:	Alma Pabst
IPO:	Gwen Sell
IRS:	Aziz Benbrahim (Resident In Paris)
ISO:	Gwen Sell
ISSO:	Monique C Theriot
LEGATT:	Tom Sobocinski
POL:	David Ranz

ALEXANDRIA (CG) 3 Pharaana Street, (20) (3) 486-1009, Fax (20) (3) 487-3811, Workweek: SUN-THU, 8:00am-4:30pm.

DPO:	Jennifer Dewitt Walsh
MGT:	Jennifer Dewitt Walsh
POSHO:	Craig Flanagan
PO:	Candace Putnam
PAO:	Naima Green
ISSO:	Monique C Theriot

TRAVEL

Consular Information Sheet

July 27, 2012

Country Description: Egypt is a republic with a developing economy. It has extensive facilities for tourists.

Smart Traveler Enrollment Program (STEP)/Embassy Locations: If you are going to live in or visit Egypt, please take the time to tell our Embassy about your trip. If you enroll, we can keep you up to date with important safety and security announcements. It will also help your friends and family get in touch with you in an emergency. U.S. citizens without Internet access may enroll directly with the Embassy.

U.S. Embassy Cairo
Consular Section
5 Tawfik Diab Street
Garden City, Cairo
Telephone: (20) 2-2797–2301
fax: (20) 2-2797–2472
Email: consularcairoacs@state.gov

For after-hours emergencies involving U.S. citizens, call (20) 2-2797–3300.

The American Citizens Services unit uses an online appointment system for those coming to receive routine consular services from Sunday through Thursday, except for official holidays (U.S. and Egyptian) and the last Tuesday of each month. Phone-inquiry hours are between 1:00 p.m. and 3:00 p.m. The latest Embassy Emergency or Security Message for U.S. Citizens can be heard on (20) 2-2797–3000.

The mailing address from the United States is: Consular Section, Unit 64900, Box 15, APO AE 09839–4900. Within Egypt or from a third country, it is 8 Kamal el-Din Salah Street, Garden City, Cairo. Consular information is available on the U.S. Embassy Cairo web site. Visa-related inquiries should be sent by e-mail.

Once a month, American Citizens Services are available at the American Center, 3 Pharana Street, Azarita, Alexandria. Every five to 10 weeks, American Citizens Services are available at the Cairo American College in Maadi. Please check the Embassy website for dates and times of available services.

Entry/Exit Requirements for U.S. Citizens: A passport and visa are required. Tourists can obtain a renewable 30-day tourist visa on arrival at an Egyptian airport for a $15 fee, payable in U.S. dollars. Tourists arriving overland and/or those who previously experienced difficulty with their visa status in Egypt should obtain a visa prior to arrival. Travelers arriving from Israel at the Taba border crossing are advised to obtain a visa prior to their arrival, otherwise they are granted either a no-fee, 14-day visa valid for travel within Sinai only, or they may buy a 30-day tourist visa for $15 upon submission of a travel agency support letter. The letters are obtainable from travel agents at the border; however, their fees for providing this service vary.

Diplomatic and official passport holders are required without exception to have a visa before arrival in Egypt. Please note that holders of official or diplomatic passports who arrive without diplomatic visas will not be granted admission to Egypt. The Embassy in Cairo is unable to intercede with Egyptian officials to obtain entry permission for diplomatic and official passport holders who do not have visas in their passports. Such travelers will be required to remain in transit at Cairo Airport until their departure from Egypt at their expense can be arranged. Military personnel arriving on commercial flights are not exempt from passport and visa requirements. The Egyptian Embassy in Washington is currently requiring at least 7-10 working days, and sometimes much longer, to process official visa requests, an expedite letter from the Department of State notwithstanding, so it is incumbent upon all official travelers to submit their visa requests and passports to the Egyptian Embassy well in advance of travel.

Foreigners who wish to come to Egypt for work must obtain a work permit and work/business visa before arrival. Foreigners can acquire a work permit from the Ministry of Manpower and Immigration offices in the district of the employer, and accordingly are authorized residency in the country. Work permits must be obtained through the employer. Foreigners who arrive as tourists but want to change their status after arrival in country are allowed a three-month tourist/non-working residency visa to change their status from tourist to work. Foreigners in Egypt on tourist visas are not permitted to work.

Proof of yellow fever immunization is required if arriving from an infected area.

Foreign residents and their dependents aged 15 or older who are in Egypt applying for work, study, or training permits and staying longer than 30 days require HIV testing. A test performed in the United States may be accepted under certain conditions. Please verify this information with the Egyptian Embassy before you travel.

Threats to Safety and Security: Political protests and demonstrations have turned violent multiple times in the past year. In early May 2012, clashes between protesters, military and police in the Abbasiya neighborhood of Cairo left eleven dead and hundreds injured. Demonstrations in downtown Cairo near Tahrir Square in the October to December 2011 period often turned violent and resulted in deaths and injuries as well as extensive property damage. Politically-motivated rallies and demonstrations are likely to continue to occur with little or no warning.. U.S. citizens are urged to remain alert to local security developments and to be vigilant regarding their personal security. The U.S. Department of State strongly urges U.S. citizens to avoid all demonstrations, as even peaceful ones can quickly become unruly and lead to clashes with security forces or even rival groups. There have been instances of instability and public disorder in some other areas of Egypt, most notably in the Nile Valley governorates of Assiut and Sohag, located between Cairo and Luxor. These governorates, along with the adjacent governorates of Minya and Qena, have been areas of extremist activity in the past. U.S. Embassy personnel traveling to these areas (apart from Luxor and adjacent tourist destinations) require advance approval. Egyptian authorities also restrict the travel of foreigners to these governorates. U.S. citizens planning to travel in these areas should contact the Embassy prior to travel.

Sporting events in Egypt, especially soccer matches, can cause heavy traffic disruptions and even violent demonstrations. On February 1, 2012, violence erupted at a soccer match in Port Said which left more than 70 people dead and hundreds injured. Reaction to the tragedy in Port Said led to multiple demonstrations in Cairo and other cities by supporters of the soccer clubs involved; some of these demonstrations also turned violent. From 2009–2012, demonstrations have occurred at soccer stadiums and in front of foreign embassies in Cairo when Egypt's teams have played in international matches. U.S. citizens should exercise extreme caution if attending soccer matches in Egypt and should be aware of the potential for an increase in traffic and crowds after sporting events and should avoid areas where large numbers of people are gathering to watch the events. As always, we strongly urge you to avoid areas where you see heavy police presence or crowds assembling, to exercise caution if within the vicinity of any large public gatherings, and to stay away from demonstrations.

Egypt has also experienced several terrorist incidents over the past several years. On January 1, 2011, a bombing attack occurred in Alexandria at a Coptic church. More than 20 deaths were reported and almost 100 were injured, from both the Christian and the Muslim communities. In February 2009, a small bomb exploded in the main square in front of the Khan al Khalili bazaar in Cairo, causing numerous casualties among foreign visitors, including the death of a young French tourist. A second explosive device was discovered and detonated by police.

U.S. citizens who plan to visit the Sinai in spite of the persistent threat of terrorist attacks should exercise great caution. Travelers should remain alert to their surroundings and are reminded that crowded tourist areas have been the target of terrorist activities. Travelers should use caution when visiting destination resorts and hotels without significant physical setback and security procedures. U.S. citizens are encouraged to visit the U.S. Embassy in Cairo website for the most up-to-date security information.

The Egyptian government screens travelers before allowing entry/exit through the Rafah border crossing with Gaza. U.S. travel groups and/or humanitarian aid convoys that need to cross this border should contact the Egyptian Embassy in Washington and arrange for permission for their trip before travel. Travelers to Gaza from Egypt should read the Travel Warning for Israel, the West Bank, and Gaza.. If the travel is urgent, U.S. citizens should consult the U.S. Embassy Consular Section in Cairo upon arrival as Egyptian authorities may require that they execute an affidavit that they have read the Travel Warning for Israel, the West Bank, and Gaza. The affidavit is an Egyptian requirement but is not a guarantee for crossing the border. The fee for the affidavit is $50. Official U. S. government travel to the areas of Rafah and Al Arish in the North Sinai is restricted.

In the past, Egypt has suffered deadly terrorist attacks in or near tourist sites often coinciding with major local holidays. U.S. citizens should be especially vigilant in crowded tourist areas, practice good personal security measures, and be alert to their surroundings. A heavy security presence is apparent to travelers throughout the country. U.S. citizens do not appear to have been targeted in any of these incidents.

Restricted Areas: Travelers to Egypt's frontiers, including the borders with Libya, Sudan, and Israel and parts of the Sinai off the main, paved roads, must obtain permission from the Travel Permits Department of the Ministry of the Interior, located at the corner of Sheikh Rihan and Nubar Streets in downtown Cairo. Reports indicate that the security situation in the northern Sinai area, which is generally defined as the area north of the Cairo-Nekhl-Taba road, remains difficult due to the continuing potential for violence.

Travelers should be aware of the possible dangers of overland travel. There have been multiple kidnappings in the Sinai of U.S. citizens over the past four years. Kidnappings of foreign tourists in the Sinai have increased since January 2012. Kidnappers hold foreign tourists for several days in an attempt to seek concessions from Egyptian officials for detained family members. While thus far all known foreign kidnap victims have been released unharmed in 2012, the danger of overland travel in the Sinai is significant. In May 2012, two U.S. citizens were kidnapped and released a day later; in July 2012, two U.S. citizens were kidnapped and released a few days later. Overland travel from Israel to the Sinai is strongly discouraged.

U.S. Embassy personnel in Egypt are currently prohibited from traveling to the Sinai, except by air to Sharm El Sheikh. Overland travel by U.S. government (USG) employees anywhere in the Sinai outside of Sharm El Sheikh is prohibited. In addition, travel by road by USG employees west of Marsa Matruh on the north coast is prohibited. Travel between Fayoum, Asyut, Sohag, and Qena; and Fayoum is only approved on a case by case basis.

In addition, travelers should be aware that landmines have caused many casualties, including deaths of U.S. citizens, in Egypt. All travelers should check with local authorities before embarking on off-road travel. Known minefields are not reliably marked by signs, but are sometimes enclosed by barbed wire. After heavy rains, which can cause flooding and the consequent shifting of landmines, travelers should be careful when driving through build-ups of sand on roadways. Though mines are found in other parts of Egypt, the highest concentrations are in World War II battlefields along the Mediterranean coast west of Alexandria, the Eastern Desert between Cairo, and the Suez Canal, and much of the Sinai Peninsula. Travelers are urged to be especially prudent in these areas.

Stay up to date by:

- Bookmarking our Bureau of Consular Affairs website, which contains the current Travel Warnings and Travel Alerts as well as the Worldwide Caution.
- Following us on Twitter and the Bureau of Consular Affairs page on Facebook as well.
- Downloading our free Smart Traveler IPhone App to have travel information at your fingertips.
- Calling 1-888-407-4747 toll-free within the U.S. and Canada, or a regular toll line, 1-202-501-4444, from other countries.
- Taking some time before travel to consider your personal security.

Crime: Since the January 25, 2011 revolution, there have been increased reports of crime. While the majority of incidents reported are crimes of opportunity, such as purse snatching and theft, there is growing concern of more serious incidents that involve weapons, including carjackings. There have been multiple reports of a motorcyclist or vehicle driving by a pedestrian and grabbing a purse or other valuables. U.S. citizens are advised to carry cellular telephones in a pocket rather than on a belt or in a purse. Avoid wearing headphones, which make the bearer more vulnerable and readily advertise the presence of a valuable item. Limit or avoid display of jewelry; it attracts attention and could prompt a robbery attempt. Limit cash and credit cards carried on your person.

Be sure to store valuables, wallet items, and passports in a safe place.Travelers are strongly cautioned not to leave valuables such as cash, jewelry, and electronic items unsecured in hotel rooms or unattended in public places. Unescorted women are vulnerable to sexual harassment and verbal abuse. The Embassy has received increasing reports over the last several months of foreigners being sexually groped in taxis and in public places. Travelers are cautioned to be aware of their surroundings and to be cautious going anywhere with a stranger alone.

Many marriages between Egyptians and U.S. citizens are successful. However, the Embassy warns against marriage fraud on the part of the U.S. citizen or the Egyptian. Entering into a marriage contract for the principal purpose of facilitating immigration to the United States for an alien is against U.S. law and can result in serious penalties, including fines and imprisonment for the U.S. citizen and the Egyptian. At the same time, it is not uncommon for Egyptians to enter into marriages with U.S. citizens solely for immigration purposes. Relationships developed via correspondence, particularly those begun on the Internet, are particularly susceptible to manipulation.

The U.S. government urges U.S. citizens who meet Egyptians on the Internet or while touring the country to take the time necessary to get to know them before considering marriage. Unfortunately, the Embassy sees many cases of abuse against U.S. citizen spouses and often those marriages end in divorce when the Egyptian acquires permanent residency (a "green card") or citizenship in the United States. These cases invariably occur when the relationship is based mostly on Internet communication and very little face-to-face interaction. Don't buy counterfeit and pirated goods, even if they are widely available. Not only are the bootlegs illegal in the United States, if you purchase them you may also be breaking local law.

Victims of Crime: If you or someone you know becomes the victim of a crime abroad, you should contact the local police and the nearest U.S. embassy or consulate. We can:

- Replace a stolen passport.
- Help you find appropriate medical care if you are the victim of violent crimes such as assault or rape.
- Put you in contact with the appropriate police authorities, and if you want us to, we can contact family members or friends.
- Help you understand the local criminal justice process and direct you to local attorneys, although it is important to remember that local authorities are responsible for investigating and prosecuting the crime.

The local equivalent to the "911" emergency line in Egypt is 122.

U.S. citizen tourists can forward their complaints for investigation by the-Tourist Police Headquarters. For crimes involving children, you may call the child emergency help line at 16000. For issues involving violence against women and/or general complaints, dial 138.

The Embassy has received increasing reports of U.S. citizen women subject to domestic violence, sexual harassment, verbal abuse, and rape in Egypt. Women have been groped in taxis and public places. The Consular Section strongly encourages women who seek our assistance to take legal action against perpetrators in order to bring them to justice. Some Egyptian NGOs provide assistance to victimized women within the Egyptian community. Women victimized overseas may be entitled to receive compensation for counseling and/or other services such as relocating back to the U.S.

Criminal Penalties: While you are traveling in Egypt, you are subject to its laws even if you are a U.S. citizen. Foreign laws and legal systems can be vastly different from our own. In some places you may be taken in for questioning if you don't have your passport with you. In some places, it is illegal to take pictures of certain buildings. In some places driving under the influence could land you immediately in jail. These criminal penalties will vary from country to country. There are also some things that might be legal in the country you visit, but still illegal in the United States, and you can be prosecuted under U.S. law if you buy pirated goods. Engaging in sexual conduct with children or using or disseminating child pornography in a foreign country is a crime prosecutable in the United States. If you break local laws in Egypt, your U.S. passport won't help you avoid arrest or prosecution. It's very important to know what's legal and what's not where you are going.

While some countries will automatically notify the nearest U.S. embassy or consulate if a U.S. citizen is detained or arrested in a foreign country, that might not always be the case. To ensure that the United States is aware of your circumstances, request that the police and prison officials notify the nearest U.S. embassy or consulate as soon as you are arrested or detained in Egypt.

Special Circumstances: There are restrictions on photographing military personnel and sites, bridges, and canals, including the Suez Canal. Egyptian authorities may broadly interpret these restrictions to include other potentially sensitive structures, such as embassies, other public buildings with international associations, and some religious edifices. Visitors should also refrain from taking photographs of any uniformed personnel.

In addition to being subject to all Egyptian laws, U.S. citizens of Egyptian origin may also be subject to other laws that impose special obligations on Egyptian citizens. The Government of Egypt considers all children born to Egyptian fathers to be Egyptian citizens even if they were not issued an Egyptian birth certificate or a passport. U.S. citizen women married to Egyptians do not need their spouse's permission to depart Egypt as long as they have a valid Egyptian visa. Dual nationals residing in Egypt for more than six months from the date of arrival or whose entry visa has an annotation "original Egyptian" require proof of Egyptian citizenship, such as a family I.D. card or Egyptian birth certificate. In some cases where U.S. citizens fail to renew their residency visas or lose their U.S. passports, dual nationals are required to present their parents' Egyptian birth certificates and be documented as Egyptian citizens in order to obtain a temporary /replacement entry stamp to facilitate their travel out of Egypt. Male dual nationals staying in Egypt for more than six months from the date of arrival and who have not completed military service are not generally required to enlist in the armed forces. However, they must obtain an exemption certificate through the Ministry of Defense Draft Office before they can leave Egypt.

Individuals who may be affected can inquire at an Egyptian consulate abroad before traveling to Egypt. Dual Egyptian-American nationals may enter and leave Egypt on their U.S. passports. Persons with dual nationality who travel to Egypt on their Egyptian passports are normally treated as Egyptian citizens by the local government. The ability to provide U.S. consular assistance to those traveling on Egyptian passports is extremely limited.

The Government of Egypt is very firm in dealing with anyone attempting to illegally adopt a child in Egypt. Islamic Shari'a law does not allow for full adoption of a child, as generally understood in the United States. Laws in Egypt regarding adoption are unclear and may vary according to a prospective adoptive parent's religious background. There have been cases of U.S. citizen couples sentenced to two years' imprisonment for attempting to circumvent Egyptian laws on birth registrations and adoption.

Services for U.S. Companies: The U.S. Department of Commerce's Officers and Commercial Specialists are available for counseling U.S. business representatives on market-entry opportunities and techniques. They actively support U.S. companies who are bidding on projects, advocate on their behalf, and assist in removing trade barriers. For specific questions, visit the U.S. Commercial Service website, or contact them by email.

Marriage in Egypt: The Egyptian government allows U.S. citizens to marry in Egypt. For further information, please refer to the website of the U.S. Embassy in Cairo.

Accessibility: While in Egypt, individuals with disabilities will find accessibility and accommodation very different from what you find in the United States. Businesses and institutions in Egypt generally do not make special accommodation for persons with disabilities. Additionally, Egyptian authorities do not effectively enforce laws mandating access to transportation, communication, and public buildings by persons with disabilities. Pedestrian sidewalks and walkways are limited, and when present, often end abruptly, causing accidents. Accommodations on public transportation are not offered for elderly individuals or persons with disabilities. Pedestrian crosswalks are rarely established and not adhered to, creating risk for pedestrians traversing roads in both business and residential areas.

Medical Facilities and Health Information: Medical care in Egypt falls short of U.S. standards. The U.S. Embassy in Cairo can provide a list of local hospitals and English-speaking physicians. Emergency and intensive care facilities are limited. Most Nile cruise boats do not have a ship's doctor, but some employ a medical practitioner of uncertain qualification. Hospital facilities in Luxor and Aswan are inadequate, and they are nonexistent at most other ports-of-call. The Egyptian ambulance service hotline is 123, but Egyptian ambulance service is not reliable.

Beaches on the Mediterranean and Red Sea coasts are generally unpolluted. Persons who swim in the Nile or its canals, walk barefoot in stagnant water, or drink untreated water are at risk of exposure to bacterial and other infections and the parasitic disease schistosomiasis (bilharzia).

It is generally safe to eat properly prepared, thoroughly cooked meat and vegetables in tourist hotels, on Nile cruise boats, and in tourist restaurants. Eating uncooked vegetables should be avoided. Tap water in many locations is not potable. It is best to drink bottled water or water that has been boiled and filtered. Well-known brands of bottled beverages are generally considered to be safe.

Influenza: As of February 2010, the Egyptian Ministry of Health has confirmed 102 human cases of the H5NI strain of avian influenza in Egypt since March 2006. Commonly known as "bird flu," the disease has resulted in 30 deaths. Travelers to Egypt and other countries where the virus is being isolated or identified are cautioned to avoid poultry farms, contact with animals in live food markets, and any surfaces that appear to be contaminated with feces from poultry or other animals. In addition, the CDC and WHO recommend eating only fully cooked poultry and eggs.

You can find detailed information on vaccinations and other health precautions on the CDC website. For information about outbreaks of infectious diseases abroad, consult the World Health Organization (WHO) website. The WHO website also contains additional health information for travelers, including detailed country-specific health information.

Medical Insurance: You can't assume your insurance will go with you when you travel. It's very important to find out BEFORE you leave. You need to ask your insurance company two questions:

- Does my policy apply when I'm out of the U.S.?
- Will it cover emergencies like a trip to a foreign hospital or an evacuation?

In many places, doctors and hospitals still expect payment in cash at the time of service. Your regular U.S. health insurance may not cover doctors' and hospital visits in other countries. If your policy doesn't go with you when you travel, it's a very good idea to take out another one for your trip.

Traffic Safety and Road Conditions: While in Egypt, you may encounter road conditions that differ significantly from those in the United States. The information below concerning Egypt is provided for general reference only, and may not be totally accurate in a particular location or circumstance.

Driving in Egypt, a country with one of the world's highest rates of road fatalities per mile driven, is a challenge. Even seasoned residents of Cairo must use extraordinary care and situational awareness to navigate the hectic streets of the capital. Traffic rules appear to be routinely ignored by impatient drivers. Any visiting U.S. citizens thinking about driving in Cairo should carefully consider their options, take the utmost precautions, and drive defensively. Drivers should be prepared for unlit vehicles at night; few, if any, road markings; vehicles traveling at high rates of speed; vehicles traveling the wrong way on one-way streets; divided highways and connecting ramps; pedestrians constantly dodging in and out of traffic; and a variety of animals on the roads.

Most traffic lights in Cairo appear not to function, but rather intersections are staffed by policemen who use subtle finger movements to indicate which cars may move. Pedestrians should also exercise extreme caution when traversing roadways, especially in high-volume/high-velocity streets such as Cairo's Corniche, which follows the east bank of the Nile River. Motorists in Egypt should be especially cautious during the rare winter rains, which can cause extremely slippery road surfaces or localized flooding.

Public mini- and microbuses are not safe; the Embassy strongly recommends that its personnel not use them. In the early morning of December 26, 2010, a bus carrying 34 U.S. tourists hit a dump truck on the highway just outside Aswan on the road to Abu Simbel. Eight U.S. tourists were killed and 21 were injured. In 2009, there was a serious accident involving international tourist buses on highways outside Cairo in which a number of foreign tourists were killed. Intercity roads are generally in good condition, but unmarked surfaces, stray animals, and disabled vehicles without lights or reflectors are among the many hazards that can be encountered on highways, especially after dark. Embassy personnel in Egypt are prohibited from traveling by road outside Cairo after sunset. In addition, some roads, especially in the Sinai and southeastern part of the country, are off-limits to foreigners. Traffic warning signs should be respected.

Trains are usually a safe means of transportation in Egypt. However, in 2009, there were several collisions involving third-class passenger and cargo trains in the greater Cairo and Upper Egypt areas in which a number of Egyptian nationals were killed or injured. Visit the website of Egypt's national tourist office and national authority for road safety.

Aviation Safety Oversight: The U.S. Federal Aviation Administration (FAA) has assessed the government of Egypt's Civil Aviation Authority as being in compliance with International Civil Aviation Organization (ICAO) aviation safety standards for oversight of Egypt's air carrier operations. Further information may be found on the FAA's safety assessment page.

Children's Issues: Please see the U.S. Dept. of State Office of Children's Issues web pages on intercountry adoption and international parental child abduction.

Intercountry Adoption
August 2009

The information in this section has been edited from the latest report available as of February 2013 from the State Department Bureau of Consular Affairs, Office of Overseas Citizens Services. For more information, please read the *Intercountry Adoption* section of this book and review current reports online at http://adoption.state.gov.

Egypt is not party to the Hague Convention on Protection of Children and Co-operation in Respect of Intercountry Adoption (Hague Adoption Convention). Therefore, when the Hague Adoption Convention entered into force for the United States on April 1, 2008, intercountry adoption processing for Egypt did not change. Laws in Egypt regarding adoption are unclear and may vary according to a prospective adoptive parent's religious background.

Islamic Shari'a law does not allow for full adoption of a child, as generally understood in the United States. U.S. citizens wishing to adopt a non-Muslim child may wish to seek legal advice from a local Egyptian attorney. Fostering, which assumes no blood relationship, is sometimes permitted in Egypt through the Ministry of Social Affairs. Most commonly, a foster parent will agree to partially or fully support a child who remains in an orphanage.

On occasion, however, a foster parent will enter into a contract with the orphanage, and will be permitted to raise the child at home. To begin this process, the foster family submits a request to the Ministry of Social Services. If the Ministry of Social Affairs approves the request, it will grant permission to allow an orphanage to release a child to be fostered at the home of the foster family. Egypt has both Muslim and Christian orphanages, though not all orphanages release orphans to be fostered at one's home. Prospective guardians may only foster children of their same religion. The Egyptian government assigns names to all orphans of unknown parentage. In some circumstances, an orphan may be issued a birth certificate that also contains fictitious names for the mother and father. Christians may request that the child's name be changed during the fostering process.

Who Can Adopt? To bring an adopted child to United Stated from Egypt, you must be found eligible to adopt by the U.S. Government. The U.S. Government agency responsible for making this determination is the Department of Homeland Security, U.S. Citizenship and Immigration Services (USCIS).

Residency Requirements: There are no residency requirements provided that the prospective parents have satisfied the Egyptian legal requirements and are awarded legal custody with the right to remove the child from Egypt for immigration. For guardianship, a lawyer can move the prospective parent's case through the court system without the guardians being present. However, at least one of the prospective parents applying for guardianship or fostering needs to be able to show proof of Egyptian citizenship (e.g. an Egyptian passport or national ID card).

Age Requirements: Prospective adoptive parents must be at least 25 years old and not more than 55 years old.

Marriage Requirements: Only married couples can foster or obtain guardianship of an orphan in Egypt.

Income Requirements: While there are no specific income requirements, the prospective adoptive family's income should be enough to cover the basic needs of the family including the child.

Other requirements:

- At least one of the prospective parents should be of Egyptian nationality.
- The number of children in the family should not exceed two unless they are old enough to depend on themselves.
- The family is not allowed to provide care for more than one child until they obtain an approval from the Ministry of Social Affairs.
- The foster mother should have enough time to take care of the child as well as the other family members.
- Egyptian law does not allow for same-sex couples to apply for adoption.

Who Can Be Adopted? Egypt has specific requirements that a child must meet in order to be eligible for fostering and or guardian. You cannot adopt a child in Egypt unless he or she meets the requirements outlined below. In addition to these requirements, a child must meet the definition of an orphan under U.S. law for you to bring him or her back to the United States.

Eligibility Requirements: A relinquished child is determined by the Ministry of Social Affairs to be a child whose parents are incapable of taking care of them and who do not have any relatives to take the parents' place. In this case the foster parent will enter into a contract with the orphanage and agree to fully support the child. To begin this process, the foster family is asked to submit a fostering request to the Ministry of Social Affairs with all documentation proving that they are capable of supporting the child.

Abandoned children include: children born out-of-wedlock who were abandoned by their parents, lost children, and children who were abandoned by their divorced parents. There are two ways to foster these children. The most common way is that a person would benevolently agree to partially or fully support the child who remains in an orphanage. It is also possible to foster a child in one's home, in which case the foster parent will enter into a contract with the orphanage and agree to fully support the child. To begin this process, the foster family is asked to submit a fostering request to the Ministry of Social Affairs with all documentation and with proof that they are able to support the child.

Age Requirements: There are no age requirements.

Sibling Requirements: The number of children in a prospective family should not exceed two unless they are old enough to depend on themselves. Prospective parents are not allowed to foster more than one child except after obtaining permission from the Ministry of Social Affairs.

Waiting Period: Impossible to predict. To satisfy the requirements of the Egyptian family law and be awarded legal custody or permission to foster an orphan at home with an approval to remove the child for immigration is a long and difficult process. However, once a child has been identified, an I-600A application for advance processing of orphan petition has been approved by the USCIS office having jurisdiction over the prospective parents' place of residence, and prospective parents have satisfied Egyptian law and been awarded legal custody, the immigration process takes between 1-2 weeks.

Egypt's Adoption Authority: Obtaining permission to foster an Egyptian child is a difficult process. Prospective foster parents are required to undergo a pre-qualification process through the Ministry of Social Affairs. This is similar to the U.S. screening process for foster parents and includes, among other things, regular visits by a social worker to determine whether prospective parents are able to care for the child properly. The number of visits is determined by the social worker.

The Process: The first step in fostering a child from Egypt is usually to select a licensed agency in the United States that can help with your adoption. Adoption service providers must be licensed by the U.S. state in which they operate. Not all orphanages release orphans to be fostered at one's home. Adoptive parents are encouraged to seek the advice of the Ministry of Social Affairs about orphanages which release orphans to be fostered in the foster family's home. To bring a fostered child from Egypt to the United States, you must apply to be found eligible to adopt (Form I-600A) by the U.S. Government, Department of Homeland Security, U.S. Citizenship and Immigration Services (USCIS). If you are eligible to adopt (foster), and a child is available for intercountry adoption, the central fostering authority in Egypt will provide you with a referral to a child.

Role of the Adoption Authority: All prospective parents are required to apply to the Ministry of Social Affairs to qualify to become foster parents. To begin the process, foster parents need to submit the following documents:

- A copy of the marriage decree.
- Employment status and proof that they will be able to financially support a child (proof of income).
- Proof that one of the parents is infertile.
- Proof that one of the foster parents is an Egyptian citizen.

A social worker from the Ministry of Social Affairs will visit the parents to make sure that the foster family will be able to provide all types of support to the child. Once all documents are complete, they will be sent to the Ministry of Social Affairs Committee for adjudication. If all conditions are met, the Ministry of Social Affairs will issue an approval or denial. Foster parents are notified and then are free to visit an orphanage and choose a child.

The foster family will sign a contract with the orphanage showing that the orphanage is officially releasing the child to the foster family and that the foster family will allow a social worker from the Ministry of Social Affairs to visit the child on a regular basis to determine whether the foster parents are able to care for the child properly. (If the parents are planning to move the child permanently to the U.S., they should discuss this in detail with the Ministry of Social Affairs in advance.)

Role of the Court: Christians wishing to adopt in Egypt should seek legal counsel from an Egyptian attorney in order to receive the most updated information regarding the proper procedures and documentation for adopting or acquiring custody of an Egyptian orphan.

Role of Adoption Agencies: There are no adoption agencies in Egypt. Attorneys and/or prospective adoptive parents handle the cases themselves.

Adoption Application: All prospective parents are required to apply to the Ministry of Social Affairs to qualify to become foster parents. A social worker from the Ministry of Social Affairs will visit the parents to make sure that the foster family will be capable to provide all types of support to an infant. Once all documents are complete, they will be sent to the Ministry of Social Affairs Committee for adjudication. If all conditions are met, Ministry of Social Affairs will issue an approval or denial. Foster parents are notified and then are free to visit an orphanage to choose a child.

The foster family will sign a contract with the orphanage showing that the orphanage is officially releasing the child to the foster family and that the foster family will allow a social worker from the Ministry of Social Affairs to visit the infant on a regular basis to determine whether the foster parents are able to care for the child properly. (This issue should be discussed in detail with the Ministry of Social Affairs in advance, if the parents are planning to move the child permanently to the U.S.).

Christians wishing to foster in Egypt should seek legal counsel from an Egyptian attorney in order to receive the most updated information regarding the proper procedures and documentation for fostering or acquiring custody of an Egyptian orphan.

Time Frame: The time frame is typically impossible to predict. To satisfy the requirements of the Egyptian family law and be awarded legal custody or permission to foster an orphan at home with an approval to remove the child for immigration is a long and difficult process.

However, once a child has been identified, an I-600A application for advance processing of orphan petition has been approved by the U.S Citizenship of Immigration Services (CIS) office having jurisdiction over the prospective parents' place of residence, and prospective parents have satisfied Egyptian law and been awarded legal custody, the immigration process takes between 1-2 weeks.

Adoption Fees: The U.S. Embassy in Egypt discourages the payment of any fees that are not properly receipted, "donations," or "expediting" fees, that may be requested from prospective fostering parents. Such fees have the appearance of "buying" a baby, this is criminalized by the 2008 Child Law, and may put all future fostering in Egypt at risk.

Documents Required: To begin the process, foster parents need to submit the following documents:

- A copy of the marriage decree.
- Employment status and proof that they will be able financially to support a child (proof of income).
- Proof that one of the parents is infertile (can not give birth).
- Proof that one of the foster parents is an Egyptian citizen.

After you finalize the fostering process (or gain legal custody) in Egypt, the U.S Government, Department of Homeland Security, U.S. Citizenship and Immigration Services (USCIS) MUST determine whether the child is eligible under U.S. law to be adopted (Form I-600).

Bringing Your Child Home: Once your fostering is complete (or you have obtained legal custody of the child), there are a few more steps to take before you can head home. Specifically, you need to apply for several documents for your child before he or she can travel to the United States, such as a birth certificate, a passport or travel document for your child from the country in which he or she was born, and a U.S. Immigration Visa. For detailed and updated information on how to obtain these documents, visit the USCIS Intercountry Adoption website at http://adoption.state.gov.

Child Citizenship Act: For adoptions finalized abroad, the Child Citizenship Act of 2000 allows your new child to acquire American citizenship automatically when he or she enters the United States as lawful permanent residents. For adoptions finalized in the United States, the Child Citizenship Act of 2000 allows your new child to acquire American citizenship automatically when the court in the United States issues the final adoption decree. To learn more, review the *Intercountry Adoption* section on this publication and visit the USCIS Intercountry Adoption website at http://adoption.state.gov.

After Adoption: The Ministry of Social Affairs conducts regularly scheduled visits after the fostering of the child to determine whether the foster parents are able to care for the child properly. However, if parents are planning to travel to the United States, they should discuss the possibility of waiving the visit requirements.

U.S. Embassy in Egypt
Address: Consular Section, IV Unit
Embassy of the United States of America
5 Tawfik Diab Street
Garden City, Cairo
Egypt
Tel: +(202) 2797-2200 or +(202) 2797-2201
Internet: http://cairo.usembassy.gov

Egypt's Adoption Authority
Address: Ministry of Social Affairs
Main office: 19, AlMarghani Street, Agouza
Cairo, Egypt
Tel: +202-3761-8183/+202-3337-5404

Embassy of Egypt
Address: 3521 International Ct. N.W.
Washington DC 20008
Tel: 202.895.5400
Fax: 202.244.4319/202.244.5131
Email:Embassy@egyptembassy.net
http://www.egyptembassy.net

Office of Children's Issues
U.S. Department of State
2201 C Street, NW
SA-29
Washington, DC 20520
Tel: 1-888-407-4747
E-mail: AskCI@state.gov
http://adoption.state.gov

International Parental Child Abduction

January 2012

The information in this section has been edited from the latest report available as of February 2013 from the State Department Bureau of Consular Affairs, Office of Overseas Citizens Services. For more information, please read the *International Parental Child Abduction* section of this book and check for updated reports online at www.travel.state.gov/abduction.

Disclaimer: The information in this circular relating to the legal requirements of specific foreign countries is provided for general information only. Questions involving interpretation of specific foreign laws should be addressed to foreign counsel. Currently there are no international or bilateral treaties in force between Egypt and the United States dealing with international parental child abduction. The Hague Convention on the Civil Aspects of International Child Abduction cannot be invoked if a child is taken from the United States to Egypt, or vice versa, by one parent against the wishes of the other parent or in violation of a U.S. custody order.

Parental Kidnapping: The removal of a child by the non-custodial parent to or within Egypt is not a crime in Egypt unless the child is subject to Egyptian court-ordered travel restrictions. Additionally, parents should be aware that they must work within the Egyptian court system in order to obtain legal custody of the child in Egypt. Once the custody order is obtained, the parent must go to the district family court for its implementation. The president of the court has the authority to request that the police enforce the custody order and/or impose a penalty on the noncustodial parent for noncompliance with the custody order.

Dual Nationality: Egypt recognizes the concept of dual nationality. Under Egyptian law, children born to an Egyptian father are automatically considered citizens of Egypt. Egyptian mothers of children born to a non-Egyptian father, however, should submit requests to the Egyptian Passports, Immigration and Nationality Authority, Egyptian Embassies or Consulates overseas, and/or the Civil Registration Office to register their children as Egyptian citizens.

Enforcement of Foreign Court Orders: A parent can request that a foreign custody order be recognized in Egypt, but enforcement will result only if the order does not contravene Sharia law and "paternal rights." Therefore, as a practical matter, foreign custody orders are not generally automatically recognized in Egypt, and the parent must seek legal representation in Egypt.

Jurisdiction: Egyptian Family Courts within the jurisdiction of each summary court have legal jurisdiction to hear child custody petitions.

Presumptive Custody: Under Egyptian law, the courts generally favor the mother. Mothers are most commonly considered to be the appropriate custodians of children up to age 15. Normally, if custody disputes arise between parents, Egyptian courts uphold presumptive custody.

Conditions for "Presumptive Custody:" Courts in Egypt generally uphold presumptive custody for the mother if she is a "person of the book" (i.e., Muslim, Christian or Jewish) and if she is deemed to be a "fit" mother. If the father is Muslim, the court generally requires that the mother commit herself to raise the child as a Muslim in Egypt. If a non-Egyptian mother's custody is upheld in court, she generally must still request the permission of the court to take the children out of Egypt. Also, under Egyptian law, if the mother (Muslim or non-Muslim) remarries she may lose her claim to custody of her children, depending on the court's determination based on the best interests of the child. This law, however, does not apply to the father; he would normally retain custody rights if he remarries.

Order of Preference for Non-Parental Custody: The mother may lose presumptive custody due to remarriage or inability to counter court findings that she is an "unfit mother." In such cases, the courts recognize an order of preference of alternate adult custodians with priority given to the mother's family in the following order: maternal grandmother or great-grandmother; paternal grandmother or great-grandmother; maternal aunt; paternal aunt; maternal niece; paternal niece.

If these relatives do not exist, the right of custody shifts to a male in the following order of priority: maternal grandfather; maternal brother; maternal nephew; paternal brother.

Right of Visitation: By law, visitation depends on the willingness of the custodial parent. If a father has custody and does not voluntarily agree to visitation, the local authorities will generally not force the issue without a court order. The parent will have to seek a court order to enforce visitation.

Egyptian/American MOU on Parental Access: In October 2003, the U.S. and Egypt signed a Memorandum of Understanding (MOU) that confirms both countries' commitment to facilitating parental access to children in the other country. Both the U.S. and Egypt agree that a left-behind parent should have meaningful access to his or her child or children. However, the MOU recognizes that facilitating parental access may occur in tandem with efforts to return children to their custodial parents. Currently, however, there are no international or bilateral treaties in force between Egypt and the United States dealing with international parental child abduction.

Egypt is not a signatory to the Hague Convention on the Civil Aspects of International Child Abduction. Thus, this treaty cannot be invoked if a child is taken from the U.S. to Egypt by one parent against the wishes of the other parent or in violation of a U.S. custody order.

Travel: Currently, the father's permission is not required for children to depart Egypt unless there is a custody order that explicitly grants custody to the father. Egyptian fathers no longer have absolute control over their children's right to travel abroad. They can still prevent their children from traveling, but must do so by means of a court order.

Travel Restrictions (Wife): Due to a Supreme Court decision in March 2000, an Egyptian wife no longer requires the permission of her Egyptian husband to obtain a passport and depart the country. In the case of a child custody dispute, however, either spouse may obtain a court order preventing the other spouse from traveling until the dispute has been resolved.

Visa Stamps—Departure: Immigration officials will prevent the departure of any foreign national whose passport lacks a valid entry stamp and visa. Egyptian procedures to obtain valid entry stamps and residencies must be followed by the bearer when the U.S. Embassy issues a parent or a child a new U.S. passport. In some recent cases, pending a review of law, children of Egyptian-citizen fathers who have been in Egypt for more than six months, but less than one year, have been considered dual nationals by the Egyptian authorities and have been issued temporary residency stamps which permitted departure with a U.S. passport.

In such cases, the Immigration officials required full names, dates, and places of birth of the fathers. Dual national children who have resided in Egypt for more than one year may be required to obtain Egyptian birth certificates in order to depart Egypt.

Visas: Should a parent declare a child's passport stolen or lost, the new passport plus a police report of loss or theft is generally sufficient for the re-issuance of a tourist visa. If the Immigration Authority's records indicate the bearer has a prolonged stay in Egypt, however, issuance of the visa may halt pending issuance of an Egyptian birth certificate.

Issuance of Egyptian Passports: Under Egyptian law, either parent may apply for an Egyptian passport for his/her child, provided there have been no court-ordered restrictions placed on the child's departure. In some recent cases, minors have been able to obtain Egyptian passports on their own behalf.

U.S. Embassy in Cairo
5 Latin America Street
Garden City
Cairo, Egypt
Telephone: 20-2-797-3000
Consular Section Telephone:
20-2-797-2301
Fax: 20-2-797-2472
Web Site: http://egypt.usembassy.gov

Embassy of the Arab Republic of Egypt
3521 International Court, NW
Washington, D.C. 20008
Telephone: (202) 895-5400
Fax: (202) 244-4319/5131
Consular Section: (202) 966-6342

For further information on international parental child abduction, contact the Office of Children's Issues, U.S. Department of State at 1-888-407-4747 or visit its web site on the Internet at http://travel.state.gov/abduction.

EL SALVADOR

Compiled from publications that were available as of February 2013 from the U.S. Department of State, the U.S. Department of Commerce, and the Central Intelligence Agency (CIA). See the introduction to this set for explanatory notes.

Official Name:
Republic of El Salvador

PROFILE

Geography

Area: total: 21,041 sq km; country comparison to the world: 153; land: 20,721 sq km; water: 320 sq km
Major cities: San Salvador (capital) 1.534 million (2009)
Climate: tropical; rainy season (May to October); dry season (November to April); tropical on coast; temperate in uplands
Terrain: mostly mountains with narrow coastal belt and central plateau

People

Nationality: noun: Salvadoran(s); adjective: Salvadoran
Population: 6,090,646 (July 2012 est.)
Population growth rate: 0.303% (2012 est.)
Ethnic groups: mestizo 90%, white 9%, Amerindian 1%
Religions: Roman Catholic 57.1%, Protestant 21.2%, Jehovah's Witnesses 1.9%, Mormon 0.7%, other religions 2.3%, none 16.8% (2003 est.)
Languages: Spanish (official), Nahua (among some Amerindians)
Literacy: definition: age 15 and over can read and write; total population: 81.1%; male: 82.8%; female: 79.6% (2007 census)
Health: life expectancy at birth: total population: 73.69 years; male: 70.41 years; female: 77.12 years (2012 est.); Infant mortality rate: total: 19.66 deaths/1,000 live births; male: 21.73 deaths/1,000 live births; female: 17.5 deaths/1,000 live births (2012 est.)
Unemployment rate: 6.9% (2012 est.)
Work force: 2.593 million (2012 est.)

Government

Type: republic
Independence: 15 September 1821
Constitution: 20 December 1983
Political subdivisions: 14 departments (departamentos, singular—departamento); Ahuachapan, Cabanas, Chalatenango, Cuscatlan, La Libertad, La Paz, La Union, Morazan, San Miguel, San Salvador, San Vicente, Santa Ana, Sonsonate, Usulutan
Suffrage: 18 years of age; universal

Economy

GDP (purchasing power parity): $45.98 billion (2012 est.); $45.15 billion (2011 est.); $44.52 billion (2010 est.); $43.9 billion (2009 est.)
GDP real growth rate: 1.5% (2012 est.); 1.4% (2011 est.); 1.4% (2010 est.); -3.1% (2009 est.)
GDP per capita (PPP): $7,700 (2012 est.); $7,600 (2011 est.); $7,600 (2010 est.); $7,500 (2009 est.)
Natural resources: hydropower, geothermal power, petroleum, arable land
Agriculture products: coffee, sugar, corn, rice, beans, oilseed, cotton, sorghum; beef, dairy products
Industries: food processing, beverages, petroleum, chemicals, fertilizer, textiles, furniture, light metals
Exports: $5.804 billion (2012 est.); $5.309 billion (2011 est.); $4.577 billion (2010 est.)
Exports—commodities: offshore assembly exports, coffee, sugar, textiles and apparel, gold, ethanol, chemicals, electricity, iron and steel manufactures
Exports—partners: US 44.6%, Guatemala 13.2%, Honduras 9.8%, Nicaragua 5.1%, Germany 4.1% (2011)
Imports: $10.44 billion (2012 est.); $9.75 billion (2011 est.); $8.189 billion (2010 est.)
Imports—commodities: raw materials, consumer goods, capital goods, fuels, foodstuffs, petroleum, electricity
Imports—partners: US 39.4%, Guatemala 9.9%, Mexico 9%, China 5.2% (2011)
Debt—external: $12.84 billion (31 December 2012 est.); $12.95 billion (31 December 2011 est.); $11.77 billion (31 December 2010 est.)
Exchange rates: the US dollar is used as a medium of exchange and circulates freely in the economy

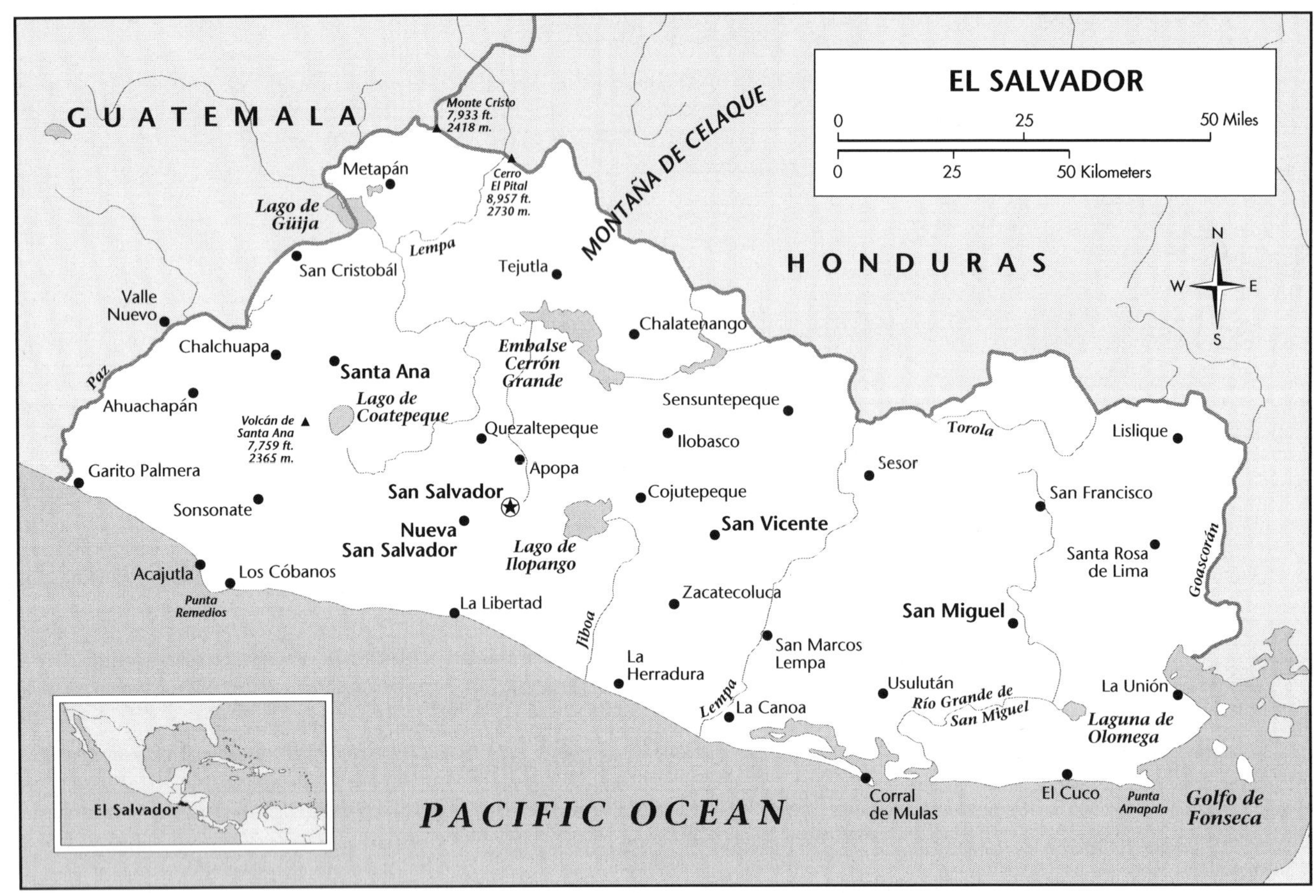

PEOPLE

Almost 90% of the population is of mixed Indian and Spanish extraction. About 1% is indigenous; very few Indians have retained their customs and traditions.

National/Racial/Ethnic Minorities

While the constitution states that native languages are part of the national heritage and should be preserved and respected, the law does not recognize indigenous communities and accords no special rights to indigenous people. Births of indigenous persons were reportedly more likely not to be registered officially, reducing educational opportunities, since school registration requires a birth certificate.

Although few individuals publicly identified themselves as indigenous, members of a few small indigenous communities continued to maintain traditional customs without repression or interference by the government or nonindigenous groups. Government estimates in 2004, the most recent available, indicated that approximately 99 percent of indigenous persons lived below the poverty level.

Language

Spanish is the official language. English is spoken in business circles and by educated Salvadorans.

Religion

According to a November 2011 survey by the Institute of Public Opinion of the University of Central America, 46 percent of the population identifies itself as Roman Catholic; 33 percent as evangelical; 2 percent as Jehovah's Witnesses; 1 percent as traditional Protestant; and 1 percent as "other." Among the evangelicals, 59 percent identified themselves as Pentecostals, 22 percent as Baptists, and 19 percent as "other." The survey reported 17 percent as having "no religion." There are small communities of The Church of Jesus Christ of Latter-day Saints (Mormons), Jehovah's Witnesses, Hare Krishnas, Muslims, Jews, and Buddhists. A small segment of the population observes indigenous religious practices.

HISTORY

The Pipil Indians, descendants of the Aztecs, and the Pocomames and Lencas were the original inhabitants of El Salvador.

The first Salvadoran territory visited by Spaniards was Meanguera Island, located in the Gulf of Fonseca, where Spanish Admiral Andres Nino led an expedition to Central America and disembarked on May 31, 1522. In June 1524, the Spanish Captain

Pedro de Alvarado started a war to conquer Cuscatlan. His cousin Diego de Alvarado established the village of San Salvador in April 1525. In 1546, Charles I of Spain granted San Salvador the title of city.

During the subsequent years, the country evolved under Spanish rule; however, toward the end of 1810 many people began to express discontent. On November 5, 1811, when Priest Jose Matias Delgado rang the bells of La Merced Church in San Salvador calling for insurrection, the people began to band together for freedom.

In 1821, El Salvador and the other Central American provinces declared their independence from Spain. When these provinces were joined with Mexico in early 1822, El Salvador resisted, insisting on autonomy for the Central American countries. In 1823, the United Provinces of Central America was formed of the five Central American states under Gen. Manuel Jose Arce. When this federation was dissolved in 1838, El Salvador became an independent republic. El Salvador's early history as an independent state—as with others in Central America—was marked by frequent revolutions; not until the period 1900–30 was relative stability achieved. Following a deterioration in the country's democratic institutions in the 1970s a period of civil war followed from 1980–1992. More than 75,000 people are estimated to have died in the conflict. In January 1992, after prolonged negotiations, the opposing sides signed peace accords which ended the war, brought the military under civilian control, and allowed the former guerillas to form a legitimate political party and participate in elections.

GOVERNMENT AND POLITICAL CONDITIONS

El Salvador is a constitutional multiparty republic. In March 2009 voters elected Carlos Mauricio Funes Cartagena of the Farabundo Marti National Liberation Front (FMLN) as president for a five-year term in generally free and fair elections.

Recent Elections

In March 2009 FMLN candidate Carlos Mauricio Funes Cartagena won the presidential election, which the Organization of American States and other international observers reported was generally free and fair with few irregularities. During the 2009 elections, as in prior elections, the main opposition political party, ARENA, and the FMLN accused each other of registering voters from other countries under the registration law, which allows a person to register with two witnesses who swear to his/her identity; however, no parties filed any formal complaints after the election.

In the January 2009 legislative elections, described as free and fair by international observers, no party won an outright majority.

Political Parties: Political parties could operate without restrictions or outside interference. On June 16, the Legislative Assembly passed a law to allow Salvadorans for the first time to vote for individual candidates instead of voting only for parties. On April 29, the Constitutional Chamber canceled El Salvador's oldest political parties, the National Conciliation Party and the Christian Democratic Party. Both parties registered as new political parties with similar logos and colors. The Supreme Electoral Tribunal (TSE) registered nine political parties plus five independent candidates to compete in the 2012 elections. Some independent candidates asserted that the TSE improperly denied their registration, and several reported receiving threats, which caused some of them to drop their candidacies.

Participation of Women and Minorities: There were 16 women in the 84-member Legislative Assembly, five women on the 15-member Supreme Court, and two women in the 13-member cabinet. No persons on the Supreme Court or in the legislature or other government entities identified themselves as members of an ethnic minority or indigenous community, and there were no political party positions or parliamentary seats designated for ethnic minorities.

Principal Government Officials

Last Updated: 1/31/2013

Pres.: **Carlos Mauricio FUNES Cartagena**
Vice Pres.: **Salvador SANCHEZ CEREN**
Min. of Agriculture & Livestock: **Pablo Alcides OCHOA**
Min. of Defense: **Jose Atilio BENITEZ Parada**
Min. of Economy: **Armando FLORES**
Min. of Education: **Hato HASBUN**
Min. of Environment & Natural Resources: **Herman ROSA Chavez**
Min. of Finance: **Juan Carlos CACERES Chavez**
Min. of Foreign Relations: **Hugo Roger MARTINEZ Bonilla**
Min. of Govt.: **Ernesto ZELAYANDIA**
Min. of Health: **Maria Isabel RODRIGUEZ, Dr.**
Min. of Justice & Public Security: **David Victoriano MUNGUIA Payes**
Min. of Labor & Social Welfare: **Humberto CENTENO**
Min. of Public Works: **Gerson MARTINEZ**
Min. of Tourism: **Jose Napoleon DUARTE Duran**
Attorney Gen.: **Romeo Benjamin BARAHONA Melendez**
Pres., Central Reserve Bank: **Carlos Gerardo ACEVEDO**
Ambassador to the US: **Francisco Robert ALTSCHUL Fuentes**
Permanent Representative to the UN, New York: **Joaquin Alexander Maza MARTELLI**

ECONOMY

The smallest country in Central America geographically, El Salvador has the third largest economy in the region. With the global recession in 2009, real GDP contracted by 3.1%. The economy slowed even further during 2010–12. Remittances accounted for 17% of GDP in 2011 and were received by about a third of all households.

In 2006, El Salvador was the first country to ratify the Dominican Republic-Central American Free Trade Agreement (CAFTA-DR), which has bolstered the export of processed foods, sugar, and ethanol, and supported investment in the apparel sector amid increased Asian competition. El Salvador has promoted an open trade and investment environment and has embarked on a wave of privatizations extending to telecom, electricity distribution, banking, and pension funds.

The Salvadoran Government maintained fiscal discipline during post-war reconstruction and reconstruction following earthquakes in 2001 and hurricanes in 1998 and 2005. Taxes levied by the government include a value added tax (VAT) of 13%, income tax of 30%, excise taxes on alcohol and cigarettes, and import duties. The VAT accounted for about 51.7% of total tax revenues in 2011. El Salvador's external debt amounts to about one-fourth of GDP.

In 2012, El Salvador successfully completed a $461 million compact with the Millennium Challenge Corporation (MCC)—a United States Government agency aimed at stimulating economic growth and reducing poverty in the country's northern region, the primary conflict zone during the civil war, through investments in education, public services, enterprise development, and transportation infrastructure. In December 2011, the MCC approved El Salvador's eligibility to develop a proposal for a program for consideration.

Labor Conditions

The law prohibits the employment of children under age 14, except that children age 12 and older are allowed to engage in light work on coffee and sugar plantations and in the fishing industry, so long as it does not harm their health or interfere with their education. Children under age 16 are prohibited from working more than six hours per day and 34 hours per week; those under age 18 are prohibited from working at night or in occupations considered hazardous. In August 2011 the Ministry of Labor published a list of the types of work considered hazardous and prohibited for children, which includes repairing heavy machinery; using chainsaws; mining; handling weapons, including knives and machetes, handling munitions and inflammable or radioactive substances; fishing and harvesting mollusks; working as stevedores; and working at heights above five feet while doing construction, erecting antennas, and working on billboards.

The Ministry of Labor was responsible for enforcing child labor laws but did so with limited effectiveness. The ministry attributed its limited enforcement to traditional cultural attitudes that support the use of child labor.

Child labor remained a serious and widespread problem. According to the 2010 School Registration Census, the most recent available, there were approximately 91,300 child workers, with the largest number engaged in agricultural work. The worst forms of child labor occurred in coffee and sugarcane cultivation, fishing, mollusk shucking, and fireworks production. There were reports of children engaged in garbage scavenging. Orphans and children from poor families frequently worked for survival as street vendors and general laborers in small businesses. Children also worked as domestic servants, and faced long work hours and abuse by employers. Children were subjected to commercial sexual exploitation. Children were recruited into illegal gangs to perform illicit activities related to the arms and drug trades, including homicide.

There is no national minimum wage; the minimum wage is determined by sector. The minimum monthly wage was $224.29 for retail and service employees, $219.40 for industrial laborers, and $187.68 for apparel assembly workers. The agricultural minimum wage was $104.97 per month, although some agricultural workers, including coffee workers, were paid by the amount harvested rather than a daily wage. The government reported that the poverty income level was $183.41 for urban areas and $145 for rural areas.

The law sets a maximum normal workweek of 44 hours, limited to no more than six days, and to no more than eight hours per day, but allows overtime if a bonus is paid. The law mandates that full-time employees be paid for an eight-hour day of rest in addition to the 44-hour normal workweek. The law provides that employers must pay double time for work on designated annual holidays, as well as a Christmas bonus based on the time of service of the employee, and 15 days of paid annual leave. The law prohibits compulsory overtime.

The ministry received complaints regarding failure to pay overtime, minimum wage violations, unpaid overtime and unpaid salaries, as well as cases of employers illegally withholding benefits (including social security and pension funds) from workers. According to the Ministry of Labor, immigrant workers have the same rights as Salvadorans, but, in practice, the ministry does not enforce these rights. In practice there were reports of overtime and wage violations in several sectors.

In some cases, the country's high crime rate negatively impacted acceptable conditions of work, as well as workers' psychological and physical health. Some workers, such as bus drivers, bill collectors, messengers, and teachers in high risk areas reported being subject to extortion and death threats.

U.S.-SALVADORAN RELATIONS

The United States established diplomatic relations with El Salvador in 1863 following its independence from Spain and the later dissolution of a federation of Central American states. Post-independence, the country saw a mix of revolutions, democracy, and a 1980–1992 civil war. The United States and El Salvador share a strong commitment to democracy, rule of law, and inclusive economic development. Ties are further enriched by 1.6 million Salvadorans who call the United States home.

El Salvador is a key partner in efforts to dampen the threats posed by transnational criminal organizations and gangs. The country has been a strong, durable partner on security and defense issues. However, endemic crime and impunity threaten El Salvador's progress by undermining the legitimacy of state institutions and impeding economic growth. U.S. policy toward El Salvador promotes the strengthening of El Salvador's democratic institutions, rule of law, judicial reform, national reconciliation and reconstruction, and economic opportunity and growth. Through the Partnership for Growth, the two countries are committed to working closely to boost economic prosperity and create a safer, more prosperous, and more democratic future for all their citizens.

U.S. Assistance to El Salvador

El Salvador is one of four countries worldwide selected to participate in the Partnership for Growth initiative. A joint U.S.-El Salvador multidisciplinary team identified the two most critical constraints to economic growth: crime and insecurity; and low productivity in tradables. The governments of El Salvador and the United States subsequently identified 20 goals in a 5-year Joint Country Action Plan to work in partnership with local organizations, the private sector, and other donors. As part of this effort, the majority of U.S. assistance for El Salvador will be aligned to support of the Joint Country Action Plan.

Bilateral Economic Relations

The United States and El Salvador are parties to the U.S.-Central America-Dominican Republic Free Trade Agreement (CAFTA-DR), which aims to facilitate trade and investment and further regional integration by eliminating tariffs, opening markets, reducing barriers to services, and promoting transparency. CAFTA-DR contains a chapter on investment similar to a bilateral investment treaty with the United States. More than 300 U.S. companies have established either a permanent commercial presence in El Salvador or work through representative offices in the country. U.S. exports to El Salvador include agricultural products, oil, machinery, knit crocheted fabrics, and low-value and donated relief articles. U.S. imports from El Salvador include apparel, agricultural products, and gold. Remittances from Salvadorans working in the United States are an important source of income for many families in El Salvador.

El Salvador's Membership in International Organizations

El Salvador and the United States belong to a number of the same international organizations, including the United Nations, Organization of American States, International Monetary Fund, World Bank, Inter-American Development Bank, and World Trade Organization.

Bilateral Representation

El Salvador maintains an Embassy in the United States at 1400 16th Street NW, Washington, DC, 20036 (tel: 202-595-7500).

Principal U.S. Embassy Officials

Last Updated: 1/14/2013

SAN SALVADOR (E) Blvd. Santa Elena, Antiguo Cuscatlan, (503) 2501-2999, Fax (503)2501-2150, INMARSAT Tel 683-130-825, Workweek: Mon-Fri, 8:00 a.m. to 4:30 p.m., Website: http://sansalvador.usembassy.gov/

DCM OMS:	Leilani Boyle
AMB OMS:	Harriet Noonan
DHS/CIS:	Paul Mitchell
DHS/ICE:	Thomas Almond
FCS:	Ireas Cook
FM:	Mark Schroeppel
HRO:	Karen Klaver
MGT:	Michael A. Barrow
MLO/ODC:	COL Carlos Figueroa
NAS/INL:	Michael Rittley
POSHO:	Steven Morse
SDO/DATT:	COL Carlos Figueroa
AMB:	Mari Carmen Aponte
CG:	Kathryn A. Cabral
DCM:	Sean Murphy
PAO:	Mari Tolliver
GSO:	Douglas Demaggio
RSO:	Mike Wilkins
AFSA:	Tbd
AGR:	Henry Schmick
AID:	William Elderbaum
ATF:	Harry Penate
CLO:	Christine Rose
DEA:	Michael A. Smith
ECON:	John Barrett
EEO:	Doug Demaggio
FAA:	Ruben Qui?Onez
FAA/CASLO:	Victor Guardia (Miami)
FMO:	Carl C. Scott
IMO:	Allen Gandy
IPO:	David Jefferson
LEGATT:	Joseph Deters
POL:	Maeve Dwyer
State ICASS:	Mark Seibel

TRAVEL

Consular Information Sheet

December 2, 2011

Country Description: El Salvador is a democratic country with a developing economy. Tourism facilities are not fully developed. The capital is San Salvador, accessible by El Salvador's International Airport at Comalapa. The U.S. Dollar is the primary currency in El Salvador and the economy is fully dollarized. Americans traveling with U.S. Dollars should not exchange them for Colones.

Smart Traveler Enrollment Program (STEP)/Embassy Locations: If you are going to live or visit El Salvador, please take the time to tell our Embassy about your trip. If you enroll, we can keep you up to date with important safety and security announcements. It will also help your friends and family get in touch with you in an emergency.

U.S. Embassy San Salvador
Final Boulevard Santa Elena Sur
Urbanizacion Santa Elena, Antiguo Cuscatlan
La Libertad
Telephone 011-503-2501-2999
Fax 011-503-2278-5522
Email: CongenSansal@state.gov

The Consular Section is open for U.S. citizens' services from 8:15 a.m. to 11:30 a.m. weekdays, excluding U.S. and Salvadoran holidays. After business hours, the Embassy can be contacted by telephone at 011-503-2501-2316 or 011-503-2501-2253.

Entry/Exit Requirements: To enter the country by air or sea, U.S. citizens must present a current U.S. passport and either a Salvadoran visa or a one-entry tourist card. The tourist card may be obtained from immigration officials for a ten-dollar fee upon arrival in country at an airport or seaport. U.S. travelers who plan to remain in El Salvador for more than thirty days can apply in advance for a multiple-entry visa, issued free of charge, from the Embassy of El Salvador in Washington, DC or from a Salvadoran consulate in Boston, Chicago, Dallas, Houston, Las Vegas, Long Island, Los Angeles, Miami, New York City, or San Francisco. Travelers may contact the Embassy of El Salvador at 1400 16th Street NW, Washington, DC 20036, tel. (202) 595 7500; fax (202) 232-3763; or visit the Embassy of El Salvador web site (Spanish language only). When applying for a visa, travelers may be asked to present evidence of U.S. employment and adequate finances for their visit at the time of visa application or upon arrival in El Salvador. For passengers departing by air or sea, El Salvador has an exit tax, which is usually included in the price of the airline ticket.

Travelers should be aware that El Salvador's entry requirements vary in accordance with agreements the country has with foreign governments. Citizens of several countries in addition to the United States may enter El Salvador by air or sea with a current passport and either a visa or tourist card. Citizens of many other countries, including many Latin American and western European nations, may enter with only a current passport. However, citizens of most nations are required to present both a current passport and a visa to enter El Salvador by air or sea. Non-U.S. citizen travelers are advised to contact a Salvadoran embassy or consulate to determine the entry requirements applicable to them. In June 2006, El Salvador entered into the "Central America-4 (CA-4) Border Control Agreement" with Guatemala, Honduras, and Nicaragua. Under the terms of the agreement, citizens of the four countries may travel freely across land borders from one of the countries to any of the others without completing entry and exit formalities at immigration checkpoints. U.S. citizens and other eligible foreign nationals, who legally enter any of the four countries, may similarly travel among the four without obtaining additional visas or tourist entry permits for the other three countries. Immigration officials at the first port of entry determine the length of stay, up to a maximum period of 90 days. Foreign tourists who wish to remain in the four-country region beyond the period initially granted for their visit must request a one-time extension of stay from local immigration authorities in the country where the traveler is physically present, or they must leave the CA-4 countries and reapply for admission to the region. Foreigners "expelled" from any of the four countries are excluded from the entire CA-4 region. In isolated cases, the lack of clarity in the implementing details of the CA-4 Border Control Agreement has caused temporary inconvenience to some travelers and has resulted in others being fined more than one hundred dollars or detained in custody for 72 hours or longer.

Airlines operating out of El Salvador International Airport require all U.S. citizen passengers boarding flights for the United States (including U.S.-Salvadoran dual nationals) to have a current U.S. passport. U.S. citizens applying for passports at the U.S. Embassy in San Salvador are reminded that proof of citizenship and identity are required before a passport can be issued. Photographic proof of identity is especially important for young children because of the high incidence of fraud involving children. Since non-emergency passports are printed in the United States, and not at the U.S. Embassy in El Salvador, citizens submitting applications in El Salvador should be prepared to wait approximately 10 business days for receipt of their new passports. The U.S. Embassy in El Salvador reminds U.S. citizen travelers that their activities in El Salvador are governed by Salvadoran law and the type of visa they are issued. Under Salvadoran law, all foreigners who participate directly or indirectly in the internal political affairs of the country (i.e. political rallies, protests) lose the right to remain in El Salvador, regardless of visa status or residency in El Salvador.

HIV Info: The U.S. Department of State is unaware of any HIV/AIDS restrictions for temporary visitors. Salvadoran Immigration Law does not specifically refer to HIV/AIDS but persons wishing to apply for residency must undergo a medical exam and be certified free of communicable diseases.

In an effort to prevent international child abduction, many governments have initiated procedures at entry/exit points. These often include requiring documentary evidence of relationship and permission for the child's travel from the parent(s) or legal guardian if not present. Having such documentation on hand, even if not required, may facilitate entry/departure. Minors traveling on Salvadoran passports and who are traveling alone, with one parent or with a third party must have the written permission of the absent parent(s) or legal guardian to depart El Salvador. A Salvadoran notary must notarize this document. If the absent parent(s) or legal guardian is (are) outside of El Salvador, the document must be notarized by a Salvadoran consul. If a court decree gives custody of the child traveling on a Salvadoran passport to one parent, the decree and a passport will allow the custodial parent to depart El Salvador with the child. Although Salvadoran officials generally do not require written permission for non-Salvadoran minors traveling on U.S. or other non-Salvadoran passports, it would be prudent for the parents of minor children traveling on U.S. passports to provide similar documentation if both parents are not traveling with their children.

For any questions concerning U.S. visas for either temporary travel to or permanent residence in the U.S., please contact our regional U.S. Visa Information Center. From El Salvador, the Visa Information Center may be reached by calling 900-6011 from any landline operated by Telecomm, or by purchasing a VISAS-USA calling card from any location that sells Telefonica phone cards. Calling instructions are on the back of the card. Calls using the 900 number will be charged to the caller's telephone bill. The Telefonica phone card permits a seven-minute call. From the U.S., the Visa Information Center can be contacted by dialing 866-730-2089 and charging the call to a Visa or MasterCard credit card.

Volunteers, Mission Groups, and Non-Profits: Groups bringing donated supplies, equipment, and medicine may experience difficulties with customs. To avoid potential problems, all donated material should be cleared with the appropriate office well before traveling to El Salvador. For medicines, please contact the Consejo Superior De Salud Publica (Superior Council for Public Health) at Superior Council for Public Health. For all other donated goods, please contact the Secretaria de Inclusion Social (Secretariat of Social Inclusion) via email at Secretariat of Social Inclusion.

Threats to Safety and Security: Most travelers to El Salvador experience no safety or security problems, but the criminal threat in El Salvador is critical. Random and organized violent crime is endemic throughout El Salvador. U.S. citizens have not been singled out by reason of their nationality, but are subject to the same threat as all other persons in El Salvador. See the section below on Crime for additional related information.

Political or economic issues in the country may give rise to demonstrations, sit-ins, or protests at any time or place, but these activities occur most frequently in the capital or on its main access roads. U.S. citizens are cautioned to avoid areas where demonstrations are being held and to follow local news media reports or call the U.S. Embassy for up-to-date information. Strong undertows and currents can make swimming at El Salvador's Pacific Coastal beaches and the country's lakes extremely dangerous for even strong and experienced swimmers. Since 2008, eight Americans have drowned while swimming in Salvadoran waters. Stay up to date by bookmarking our Bureau of Consular Affairs website, which contains the current Travel Warnings and Travel Alerts as well as the Worldwide Caution. Follow us on Twitter and the Bureau of Consular Affairs page on Facebook as well.

You can also call 1-888-407-4747 toll free within the United States and Canada, or by calling a regular toll line, 202-501-4444, from other countries. These numbers are available from 8 a.m. to 8 p.m. Eastern Time, Monday through Friday (except U.S. federal holidays). Take some time before travel to consider your personal security—things are not the same everywhere as they are in the United States.

Crime: The State Department considers El Salvador a critical-crime-threat country. El Salvador has one of the highest homicide rates in the world; violent crimes, as well as petty crimes are prevalent throughout El Salvador, and U.S. citizens have been among the victims. Central America has been identified as the most violent region in the world, with El Salvador reporting the highest death rate due to armed violence. According to a recent study, El Salvadorhas the highest rate of violent fatalities, with over 70 deaths recorded for every 100,000 inhabitants.

The Embassy is aware of at least thirteen U.S. citizens who were murdered in El Salvador since 2010.

Extortion is on the rise and U.S. citizens and their family members have been victims in various incidents. Violent, organized gangs are a major factor in the crime situation and are often behind extortion attempts. Some areas of El Salvador are effectively controlled by gangs. Many gangs have access to military-style hardware, including automatic weapons and hand grenades. Extortion tactics have included indiscriminate grenade attacks on buses, businesses, and restaurants, resulting in the death or injury of dozens of people, including children. These types of attacks are unpredictable and the U.S. Embassy advises its personnel to remain alert to their surroundings and to minimize risk to themselves. Criminals have ready access to firearms and shootouts are not uncommon. Foreigners, however, may not carry guns even for their own protection without first obtaining firearms licenses from the Salvadoran government. Failure to do so will result in the detention of the bearer and confiscation of the firearm, even if it is licensed in the United States. Armed holdups of vehicles traveling on El Salvador's roads are common, and we encourageU.S. citizens to remain aware of their surroundings and to drive with their doors locked and windows up. If confronted, do not resist the armed assailant(s).

Travelers should remain in groups and avoid remote or isolated locations in order to minimize their vulnerability. Travelers should also avoid displaying or carrying valuables in public places. Passports and other important documents should not be left in private vehicles. Armed assaults and carjackings take place both in San Salvador and in the interior of the country, but are especially frequent on roads outside the capital where police patrols are scarce. Criminals have been known to follow travelers from the international airport to private residences or secluded stretches of road where they carry out assaults and robberies. Armed robbers are known to shoot if the vehicle does not come to a stop. Criminals often become violent quickly, especially when victims fail to cooperate immediately in surrendering valuables. Frequently, victims who argue with assailants or refuse to give up their valuables are shot. Kidnapping for ransom continues to occur, but has decreased in frequency since 2001. U.S. citizens in El Salvador should exercise caution at all times and practice good personal security procedures throughout their stay.

The U.S. Embassy warns its personnel to drive with their doors locked and windows raised, to avoid travel outside of major metropolitan areas after dark, and to avoid travel on unpaved roads at all times because of criminal assaults and lack of police and road service facilities. Travelers with conspicuous amounts of luggage, late-model cars, or foreign license plates are particularly vulnerable to crime, even in the capital.

Travel on public transportation, especially buses, both within and outside the capital, is risky and not recommended. The Embassy advises official visitors and personnel to avoid using mini-buses and buses and to use only radio-dispatched taxis or those stationed in front of major hotels. U.S. citizens using banking services should be vigilant while conducting their financial exchanges either inside local banks or at automated teller machines. There have been several reports of armed robberies in which victims appear to have been followed from the bank after completing their transactions. Credit-card skimming is also a problem.

Visitors to El Salvador should use caution when climbing volcanoes or hiking in other remote locations. Armed robberies of climbers and hikers are common. Mine-removal efforts ceased several years ago, but land mines and unexploded ordnance in backcountry regions still pose a threat to off-road tourists, backpackers, and campers. The Embassy strongly recommends engaging the services of a local guide certified by the national or local tourist authority when hiking in backcountry areas, even when within the national parks.

Don't buy counterfeit and pirated goods, even if they are widely available. Not only are the bootlegs illegal in the United States, if you purchase them, you may also be breaking the local law.

Victims of Crime: If you, or someone you know, becomes the victim of a crime abroad, you should contact the local police and the nearest U.S. Embassy or Consulate (see the Department of State's list of embassies and consulates). If your passport is stolen, we can help you replace it. For violent crimes such as assault and rape, we can help you to find appropriate medical care, contact family members or friends, and help them send you money if you need it. We can also put you in contact with the appropriate police authorities, and, if you want us to, contact family members or friends. Although the investigation and prosecution of the crime are solely the responsibility of local authorities, consular officers can help you to understand the local criminal justice process and to find an attorney if needed. Victims of crime should bear in mind that law enforcement resources are limited and judicial processes are uneven in El Salvador. Most crimes in the country (including murder) go unsolved and the likelihood for redress through the judicial system is limited. As a result, only a small percentage of cases result in conviction.

The local equivalent to the "911" emergency line in El Salvador is also 911.

Criminal Penalties: While you are traveling in another country, you are subject to its laws even if you are a U.S. citizen. Foreign laws and legal systems can be vastly different than our own. In some places, you may be taken in for questioning for not having your passport with you. In some places, it is illegal to take pictures of certain buildings. In some places, driving under the influence could land you immediately in jail. These criminal penalties will vary from country to country. There are also some things that might be legal in the country you visit, but are still illegal in the United States, and you can be prosecuted under U.S. law. For example, buying pirated goods, engaging in sexual conduct with children, or using or disseminating child pornography in a foreign country is a crime prosecutable in the United States. If you break local laws in your host country, your U.S. passport won't help you avoid arrest or prosecution. It's very important to know what's legal and what's not where you are going.

Penalties for breaking the law can be more severe than in the United States for similar offences. Persons violating El Salvador's laws, even unknowingly, may be expelled, arrested, or imprisoned. Penalties for possession, use, or trafficking in illegal drugs in El Salvador are severe, and convicted offenders can expect long jail sentences and heavy fines. If you are arrested in El Salvador, you have the right to request authorities to alert the U.S. Embassy of your arrest.

Guns: El Salvador has strict laws requiring a locally obtained license to possess or carry a firearm in the country. The Embassy strongly advises persons without a Salvadoran firearms license not to bring guns into the country or use a firearm while in El Salvador. The Embassy cannot intervene in the judicial process when a U.S. citizen is charged with a firearms violation. Conviction for possessing an unlicensed firearm can carry a prison sentence of three to five years.

Disaster Preparedness: El Salvador is an earthquake-prone country. Flooding and landslides during the rainy season (June to November) also pose a risk. In November of 2009, heavy and constant rain over a four-day period caused severe flooding and triggered landslides that severely damaged roads, bridges, and houses. Almost 200 people died and 14,000 more were left homeless. In October 2011, ten days of heavy rains destroyed crops and towns in Central America, hitting El Salvador particularly hard with mudslides and flooding that killed 34 persons and forced 50,000 to seek temporary shelter. General information about natural disaster preparedness is available from the U.S. Federal Emergency Management Agency (FEMA). Additional information in Spanish about earthquakes (sismos) in El Salvador can be found on the Government of El Salvador's web page.

Medical Facilities and Health Information: There are a few private hospitals with an environment that would be acceptable to visiting U.S. citizens. The Embassy recommends that these hospitals be used only for emergency care, to stabilize a condition prior to returning to the U.S. for definitive evaluation and treatment. Private hospitals and physicians expect up-front payment (cash or, for hospitals, credit card) for all bills.

Priority Ambulance (503-2264-7911) is the only private ambulance service with a fleet of vehicles in San Salvador that has trained personnel and medical equipment to manage emergencies. The response time is often less than ideal because of the heavy traffic in San Salvador. Therefore, whenever possible, people should transport themselves directly to the hospital by private vehicle.

Pharmacies are plentiful but not all medicines found in the U.S. are available in El Salvador. Medicines often have a different brand name and are frequently more expensive than in the U.S. We recommend that U.S. citizens traveling to El Salvador carry an adequate supply of any medication they require in its original container, which should be clearly labeled. A copy of the prescription from your doctor will be helpful in the event that it is requested by immigration or customs authorities.

No specific vaccinations are required for entry into El Salvador from the United States. Travelers coming from countries where yellow fever is endemic must have had a yellow fever vaccination in order to enter the country. For more information, visit El Salvador's Immigration web site.

You can find good information on vaccinations and other health precautions, on the Centers for Disease Control (CDC) website. For information about outbreaks of infectious diseases abroad, consult the infectious diseases section of the World Health Organization (WHO) website. The WHO website also contains additional health information for travelers, including detailed country-specific health information.

Medical Insurance: You can't assume your insurance will go with you when you travel. It's very important to find out BEFORE you leave whether or not your medical insurance will cover you overseas. You need to ask your insurance company two questions:

- Does my policy apply when I'm out of the United States?
- Will it cover emergencies like a trip to a foreign hospital or a medical evacuation?

In many places, doctors and hospitals still expect payment in cash at the time of service. Your regular U.S. health insurance may not cover doctors' and hospital visits in other countries. If your policy doesn't go with you when you travel, it's a very good idea to take out another one for your trip. For more information, please see our medical insurance overseas page.

Traffic Safety and Road Conditions: While in a foreign country, you may encounter road conditions that differ significantly from those in the United States. The information below concerning El Salvador is provided for general reference only, and may not be totally accurate in a particular location or circumstance.

Major highways and thoroughfares are among the best in Central America, but road conditions throughout El Salvador are not up to U.S. standards. Road travel at night is particularly dangerous outside the capital as there are few road lights and many vehicles lack adequate safety lighting or reflectors. The Embassy advises against driving outside the capital during night time or periods of low visibility. Mini-buses, buses, and taxis are often poorly maintained. Drivers are often not trained, and generally do not adhere to traffic rules and regulations. Because of inconsistent enforcement of traffic laws in El Salvador, drivers must make an extraordinary effort to drive defensively. Passing on blind corners or across several lanes of traffic is commonplace. Salvadoran law requires that the driver of a vehicle that injures or kills another person must be arrested and detained until a judge can determine responsibility for the accident. This law is uniformly enforced. Visitors to El Salvador may drive on their U.S. license for up to thirty days. After that time, a visitor is required to obtain a Salvadoran license. Further information on traffic and road conditions is available in Spanish from Automovil Club de El Salvador, at telephone number 011-503-2221-0557.

Aviation Safety Oversight: The U.S. Federal Aviation Administration (FAA) has assessed the government of El Salvador's Civil Aviation Authority as being in compliance with International Civil Aviation Organization (ICAO) aviation safety standards for oversight of El Salvador's air carrier operations. Further information may be found on the FAA's safety assessment page.

Children's Issues: Please see the U.S. Dept. of State Office of Children's Issues web pages on intercountry adoption and international parental child abduction.

Travel Warning

January 23, 2013

The Department of State has issued this Travel Warning to inform U.S. citizens about the security situation in El Salvador. Tens of thousands of U.S. citizens safely visit El Salvador each year for study, tourism, business, and volunteer work. However, crime and violence are serious problems throughout the country. In 2011, El Salvador had the second highest murder rate in the world: 71 per 100,000 people (by comparison, the murder rate in Massachusetts, with a similar geographical area and population, was 2.6 per 100,000). In 2012, a truce between El Salvador's two principal street gangs contributed to a decline in the homicide rate. However, the sustainability of the decline is unclear, and the truce had little impact on robbery, assaults, and other violent crimes. Most of these crimes go unsolved. In March 2012, as a result of an administrative review of the security situation, Peace Corps El Salvador substantially reduced the number of its volunteers in country.

U.S. citizens do not appear to be targeted based on their nationality. However, 22 U.S. citizens have been murdered in El Salvador since January 2010. During the same time period, 230 U.S. citizens reported having their passports stolen. Armed robberies of climbers and hikers in El Salvador's national parks are common, and the Embassy strongly recommends engaging the services of a local guide certified by the national or local tourist authority when hiking in back country areas, even within the national parks. In 2000, the National Civilian Police (PNC) established a special tourist police force (POLITUR) to provide security and assistance to tourists, as well as protection for the cultural heritage of El Salvador. It has officers located in 19 tourist destinations.

A majority of serious crimes are never solved; only five of the 22 murders committed against U.S. citizens since January 2010 have resulted in convictions. The Government of El Salvador lacks sufficient resources to properly investigate and prosecute cases and to deter violent crime. The PNC is still developing into a modern and effective police force that can protect the public. While several of the PNC's investigative units have shown great promise, routine street level patrol techniques, anti-gang, and crime suppression efforts are limited.

Transnational criminal organizations conduct narcotics, arms trafficking, and other unlawful activities throughout the country and use violence to control drug trafficking routes and carry out other criminal activity. Other criminals, acting both individually and in gangs, commit crimes such as murder-for-hire, carjacking, extortion, armed robbery, rapes, and other aggravated assaults. El Salvador, a country of roughly six million people, has hundreds of known street gangs totaling more than 20,000 members. Gangs and other criminal elements roam freely day and night, targeting affluent areas for burglaries, and gang members are quick to engage in violence if resisted.

Extortion is a particularly serious and common crime in El Salvador. Many extortion attempts are no more than random cold calls that originate from imprisoned gang members using cellular telephones, and the subsequent threats against the victim are made through social engineering and/or through information obtained about the victim's family. U.S. citizens who are visiting El Salvador for extended periods may be at higher risk for extortion demands. Hitting its peak a few years ago, extortion has dropped in the last two years; however, recent reports show that there is an increase in the level of violence associated with extortion cases, including media reports of extortion victims and witnesses being killed. Extortion attempts can be transnational in nature and can include kidnapping of victims. For example, in 2011, a 2 year old U.S. citizen was kidnapped from the home of his grandparents in El Salvador by 8 to 10 armed men. Ransom demands made to family members in both El Salvador and the United States were traced back to a local prison used exclusively to incarcerate gang members.

U.S. citizens should be vigilant of their surroundings at all times, especially when entering or exiting their homes or hotels, cars, garages, schools, and workplaces. Whenever possible, travel in groups of two or more persons. Avoid wearing jewelry, and do not carry large sums of money or display cash, ATM/credit cards, or other valuables. Avoid walking at night in most areas of El Salvador, and do not walk alone near beaches, historic ruins, or trails. Incidents of crime along roads, including carjacking, are common in El Salvador. Motorists should avoid traveling at night and always drive with their doors locked to deter potential robberies at traffic lights and on congested downtown streets. Travel on public transportation, especially buses, both within and outside the capital, is risky and not recommended. The Embassy advises official visitors and personnel to avoid using mini-buses and regular buses and to use only radio-dispatched taxis or those stationed in front of major hotels. The location and timing of criminal activity is unpredictable. We recommend that all travelers exercise caution when traveling anywhere in El Salvador. However, certain areas of the country demonstrate higher levels of criminal activity than others. Salvadoran "departments" (a geographic designation similar to U.S. states) with homicide rates higher than the national average include:

- La Paz
- La Union
- Santa Ana
- San Miguel
- San Salvador
- San Vicente
- Sonsonate

In addition, the following municipalities are experiencing chronic high levels of reported criminal activity:

- Acajutla/Metalio
- Apopa
- Ilopango
- La Libertad
- La Union/Tamarindo Beaches
- Lourdes-Colon
- Mejicanos
- San Francisco Gotera
- San Miguel
- Santa Rosa de Lima
- Soyopango

For more detailed information regarding personal security, please see the State Department's Country Specific Information for El Salvador. For the latest security information, U.S. citizens traveling abroad should regularly monitor the Bureau of Consular Affairs' Web site, where the

Worldwide Caution, Travel Warnings, and Travel Alerts can be found. U.S. citizens living or traveling in El Salvador are strongly encouraged to sign up for the State Department's Smart Traveler Enrollment Program (STEP) to obtain updated information on travel and security within El Salvador. The Embassy is located on Final Boulevard Santa Elena Sur, Urbanización Santa Elena, Antiguo Cuscatlán, La Libertad, and can be reached by telephone at 011-503-2501–2999 or by fax at 011-503-2278–5522. For after-hours emergencies, please call 011-503-2501–2253. The Embassy's American Citizen Services (ACS) Unit can be reached directly by fax at 011-503-2501–6020 or by e-mail at ACSSanSal@state.gov. Travelers may register with the Consular Section of the U.S. Embassy in San Salvador through the Smart Traveler Enrollment Program (STEP). Travelers may obtain up-to-date information on security conditions by calling 1-888-407-4747 toll-free in the United States or outside the U.S. and Canada on a regular toll line at 1-202-501-4444.

For information on general crime and security issues, U.S. citizens should also consult the U.S. Embassy in El Salvador. Stay up to date by bookmarking our Bureau of Consular Affairs Web site, which contains Travel Warnings and Travel Alerts as well as the Worldwide Caution. Follow us on Twitter and the Bureau of Consular Affairs page on Facebook as well. You can also download our free Smart Traveler App, available through iTunes and the Android market, to have travel information at your fingertips.

Intercountry Adoption

January 2013

The information in this section has been edited from a report of the State Department Bureau of Consular Affairs, Office of Overseas Citizens Services. For more information, please read the *Intercountry Adoption* section of this book and review current reports online at http://adoption.state.gov.

El Salvador is party to the Hague Convention on Protection of Children and Co-operation in Respect of Intercountry Adoption(Hague Adoption Convention). Intercountry adoption processing in Hague countries is done in accordance with the requirements of the Convention; the U.S. implementing legislation, the Intercountry Act of 2000 (IAA); and the IAA's implementing regulations, as well as the implementing legislation and regulations of the government of El Salvador.

In order for an adoption application for an adopted child to meet the Convention requirements, a U.S. consular officer must review the case file and issue an "Article 5 Letter" to the Salvadoran Central Authority before an adoption is completed. The process for international adoptions in El Salvador can be lengthy and complicated for prospective adoptive parents. The Salvadoran authorities responsible for administering adoptions are still working on effectively transitioning to the Hague process and significant delays in the process are common and should be expected.

It is important to note that U.S. citizens temporarily resident in El Salvador who are considering petitioning for their adoptive child as an immediate relative may be expected to reside in El Salvador for a minimum of three years. This includes the one year of residency mandated by Salvadoran law to adopt domestically, plus the required two years of physical and legal custody of the child in order to file an I-130 petition.

If you plan to pursue a local adoption and then file the I-130, please contact the U.S. Embassy in San Salvador as soon as possible for more information. Please note that although the competent authority responsible for placing children in foster care may grant you permission to reside with and care for your prospective adoptive child, this may not constitute legal custody; taking the child outside of El Salvador during the adoption process is generally not permitted.

Who Can Adopt? To bring an adopted child to the United States from El Salvador, you must meet eligibility and suitability requirements. The U.S. Department of Homeland Security, U.S. Citizenship and Immigration Services (USCIS) determines who can adopt under U.S. immigration law. Additionally, a child must meet the definition of Convention adoptee under U.S. law in order to immigrate to the United States on an IH-3 or IH-4 immigrant visa.

Residency Requirements: Under Article 176 of the Salvadoran Family Code, adoptive parents who reside in El Salvador and who wish to adopt a child who is not related to them must be prepared to reside with the child in El Salvador for at least one year prior to the finalization of the adoption. To satisfy this requirement, the adoptive parent(s) must be appointed the foster parent(s) or guardian of the child, subject to approval by the Salvadoran Institute for the Development of Children and Adolescents (ISNA), prior to the beginning of the one year co-residency period. Prospective adoptive parents who claim a residence other than El Salvador are exempt from the one year cohabitation requirement.]

Age of Adopting Parents: Prospective adoptive parents must be at least 15 years older than the child.

Marriage: Single individuals may adopt in El Salvador if they are at least 25 years old and at least 15 years older than the child to be adopted. Married couples must both be over the age of 25, unless the marriage is at least five years old, in which case the requirement applies only to one spouse. The Salvadoran family code provides that only legally married couples may adopt as a couple in El Salvador; same-sex marriages are not recognized under Salvadoran law.

Income: Prospective adoptive parents must demonstrate that they are financially, morally, mentally, and physically able to provide for the adopted child.

Who Can Be Adopted? Because El Salvador is party to the Hague Adoption Convention, children from El Salvador must meet the requirements of the Convention in order to be eligible for adoption. For example, the Convention requires that El Salvador attempt to place a child with a family in-country before determining that a child is eligible for intercountry adoption. In addition to El Salvador's requirements, a child must meet the definition of a Convention adoptee for you to bring him or her back to the United States.

Relinquishment: Salvadoran law states that a child less than 18 years of age may be eligible for international adoption if the child is abandoned or orphaned and a family court determines that the adoption is in the best interest of the child. Salvadoran law also permits the adoption of a child more than 18 who is under the care of a parent or relative if a court determines the adoption is in the child's best interest.

Abandonment: According to Salvadoran family code, a child is abandoned if the biological parents are no longer providing care for their child. This definition is very broad and can include parents that are incarcerated or who left their children in the care of other family members. In most cases, however, the parental rights are still intact and the legal relinquishment or revocation of parental rights does not occur until after the child has been matched with a family for adoption. This is one of the lengthiest and most complex steps in the Salvadoran adoption process. Prospective adoptive parents should not assume that the legal relinquishment of parental rights has occurred prior to being matched with a child.

Age of Adoptive Child: Although Salvadoran law permits adoptions of children over the age of 18 in certain cases, prospective adoptive parents should bear in mind that foreign adoptions of children over 16 years of age are not valid for immigration purposes for the United States, except for specific cases of sibling adoptions.

Sibling Adoptions: The Salvadoran Central Authority makes an effort to keep biological siblings together whenever possible. If the children are abandoned in different municipalities, however, biological siblings may be adopted by different families without the Central Authority's knowledge.

Special Needs or Medical Conditions: The adoption of children with special needs is a top priority for the Salvadoran Central Authority. Prospective adoptive parents must pass a suitability review to ensure they are able to care for a child with special needs.

Waiting Period or Foster Care: Foreign adoptive parents must formally adopt Salvadoran children in El Salvador, in accordance with Salvadoran laws and procedures, before taking the children out of the country to live. Prospective adoptive parents who reside in El Salvador and who wish to adopt a child who is not related to them must first be appointed the foster parent or guardian of the child, and be prepared to reside with the child in El Salvador for at least one year prior to the finalization of the adoption.

The Process: The recommended first step in adopting a child from El Salvador is to select an adoption service provider in the United States that has been accredited or approved to provide services to U.S. citizens in Convention cases. The primary adoption service provider is responsible for ensuring that all adoption services in the case are done in accordance with the Hague Adoption Convention and U.S. laws and regulations. In addition, the adoption service provider must also be authorized by El Salvador's designated Central Authority for Adoptions, OPA. Prospective adoptive parents interested in adopting from El Salvador should contact OPA for up-to-date information prior to initiating a new adoption process. The following U.S. Hague-accredited adoption service providers have been authorized to provide services in El Salvador: New Hope Child and Family Agency, New Hope Adoption international (Adopciones Nueva Esperanza Internacional),The Open Door Adoption Agency, Hope Cottage, Inc., America World Adoptions, All Blessings/Kentucky Adoption Services, Villa Hope, Inc., Christian Adoption Services, Inc., Adoption Hope International, Inc., Madison Adoption Associates. Prospective adoptive parents are advised to fully research any adoption agency or facilitator they plan to use for adoption services.

After you choose an accredited or approved adoption service provider, you must apply to be found eligible to adopt by the responsible U.S. government agency, the Department of Homeland Security, U.S. Citizenship and Immigration Services (USCIS). For more information, please read the *Intercountry Adoption* section of this book and review current reports online at http://adoption.state.gov.

If both the United States and El Salvador determine that you are eligible to adopt, and the central authority for Convention adoptions has determined that a child is available for adoption and that intercountry adoption is in that child's best interests, the central authority for Convention adoptions in El Salvador may provide you with a referral for a child. If you accept the referral, the adoption service provider communicates that to the adoption authority in El Salvador.

The Supreme Court of El Salvador prohibits granting of guardianships to prospective adoptive parents for the purpose of allowing children to leave El Salvador for subsequent adoption abroad. ISNA investigates the circumstances of an orphaned or neglected child's family and seeks to find a close relative who may be willing to care for the child. Once satisfied that intercountry adoption is in the child's best interest, ISNA determines which prospective adoptive parents are suitable matches for the child. OPA is responsible for coordinating with ISNA when a child is matched with prospective adoptive parents.

After you accept a match with a child, you will apply to the U.S. Department of Homeland Security, U.S. Citizenship and Immigration Services (USCIS) for provisional approval for the child to immigrate to the United

States (Form I-800). For more information, please read the *Intercountry Adoption* section of this book and review current reports online at http://adoption.state.gov.

The process for finalizing the adoption (or gaining legal custody) in El Salvador generally includes the following:

Role of Adoption Authority: OPA will review the adoption documents to ensure they are complete. Due to the complexity of the Salvadoran adoption process, the authority may not inform prospective adoptive parents in a timely manner that their case has missing, incomplete, or incorrect documentation. This can cause additional delays. The U.S. Embassy recommends calling, emailing or visiting OPA on a regular basis during the process.

Role of the Court: The Salvadoran family court will issue a final adoption decree that adoptive parents will need to obtain the child's new birth certificate and passport with the child's new surname. The time to obtain new civil documents varies in different parts of the country and can take anywhere from 24 hours to two weeks depending on the judge. The court is also responsible for the legal relinquishment or revocation of parental rights; and in some cases, this does not occur until after the child has been matched with a family for adoption. This is one of the lengthiest and most complex steps in the Salvadoran adoption process.

Role of the Adoption Agencies: The adoption service provider is responsible for ensuring that home studies are completed and for assisting prospective adoptive parents with providing required documentation to the Salvadoran government, including the family court judges. The adoption service provider should also regularly communicate with the U.S. Embassy's Consular Section to ensure consistency with the Hague process.

Time Frame: Salvadoran adoption procedures can take 18 to 36 months to complete, but have often taken much longer. This does not include the time necessary for the U.S. Embassy to complete its own investigation, as required by immigration regulations. Because adoption fraud in El Salvador has taken a variety of forms, an investigation of each adoption is necessary to ensure that the child is an orphan, as defined by U.S. immigration law, and that the birth mother is aware that the child is being adopted irrevocably and will be taken from the country. Investigation times vary depending on the complexity of each case.

Adoption Application: Filing an adoption application can be done by visiting OPA in San Salvador or by sending a legal representative to submit your documentation. The prospective adoptive parents should be prepared to travel to El Salvador regularly as personal appearances will be required throughout the adoption process.

Adoption Fees: The Salvadoran Central Authority currently does not charge any fees for their administrative services. Prospective adoptive parents may choose to retain a Salvadoran attorney to assist with an adoption and will be charged for those services by the attorney. We advise prospective adoptive parents to discuss options with their adoption service provider. In the adoption services contract that you sign at the beginning of the adoption process, your agency will itemize the fees and estimated expenses related to your adoption process. Some of the fees specifically associated with adopting from El Salvador include:

- Salvadoran Attorney's Fee-Typically $3,000-$10,000
- Medical Exam for the Child-Costs generally may run between $250-$600 (includes vaccinations for all children; includes x-rays for children between 14-16)
- U.S. Immigrant Visa - $230
- Salvadoran passport fee - $25
- Photos for U.S. Immigrant Visa - $5 (for two photos)
- Hotel stay for one night, two adults at the Hilton Princess, Sheraton Presidente, or Marriott Courtyard Hotel (please confirm prices if you book a room) - $130-170

The State Department discourages the payment of any fees that are not properly receipted. "Donations" or "expediting" fees, which may be requested from prospective adoptive parents, have the appearance of "buying" a child and put all future adoptions in El Salvador at risk.

Documents Required: Each of the U.S. documents listed here must be either authenticated at a Salvadoran Embassy, or a Salvadoran Consulate, or apostilled by the competent authority of the adopting parents' country (see below). U.S. documents listed below must also be translated into Spanish by an individual appointed for that purpose by a Salvadoran notary public.

- Certified birth certificate for the adopting parents
- Certified marriage certificate, if applicable
- Police clearance from the adopting parents' municipality
- Financial statements
- Home study certification
- Health certificate for the adopting parents
- Certification stating that the adopting parents meet the legal requirements of their home State to adopt and that the State will monitor the welfare of the child after adoption
- Statement regarding who will care for the adopted child in the absence of the adoptive parents due to illness, disability or death
- Certified copies of the adopting parents' passports

Background Notes

- Certified copies of birth and health certificates for any other biological or adopted children in the family
- Photographs of the exterior and interior of the adopting parents' home
- Photocopy of the identity card and certified birth certificate of the Salvadoran attorney
- Health certificate for the child to be adopted
- Photographs of the adopting parents, adopted child, and attorney
- Power of attorney for a specified Salvadoran attorney to represent the adopting parents, which must be executed before a Salvadoran notary public or by Salvadoran Consul at a Salvadoran Embassy or Consulate.
- The designated Salvadoran lawyer must present two files of all the documentation (one with originals, and the other with certified copies). If the files exceed two hundred pages, both files must be divided in halves with a closing and opening statement from the notary attached to the divided files. The Salvadoran attorney must comply with the requirements stipulated in Article 42 of the Salvadoran Family Code of Proceedings.

Bringing Your Child Home: Once your adoption is complete (or you have obtained legal custody of the child), there are a few more steps to take before you can head home. Specifically, you need to apply for several documents for your child before he or she can travel to the United States, such as a birth certificate, a passport or travel document for your child from the country in which he or she was born, and a U.S. Immigration Visa. For detailed and updated information on how to obtain these documents, review the *Intercountry Adoption* section in this publication and visit the U.S. Department of State Intercountry Adoption website at http://adoption.state.gov.

Child Citizenship Act: For adoptions finalized abroad, the Child Citizenship Act of 2000 allows your new child to acquire American citizenship automatically when he or she enters the United States as lawful permanent residents.

For adoptions finalized in the United States, the Child Citizenship Act of 2000 allows your new child to acquire American citizenship automatically when the court in the United States issues the final adoption decree. To learn more, review the *Intercountry Adoption* section in this publication and visit the U.S. Department of State Intercountry Adoption website at http://adoption.state.gov.

After Adoption: El Salvador requires post-adoption reports, from six months and to two years after the adoption is finalized.

U.S. Embassy in El Salvador
Final Boulevard y Urb. Santa Elena
Antiguo Cuscatlán, La Libertad
Tel. (outside the El Salvador): 011+503–2501–2999 within El Salvador: 2501–2999
Fax: (503) 2278–6020
E-mail: AdoptSanSal@state.gov

Salvadoran Adoption Authority
Oficina Para Adopciones
Coordinador OPA
Procuraduría General de la República
9ª. Calle Poniente y 13 Ave. Norte, Torre PGR,
Centro de Gobierno
San Salvador, El Salvador
Phone (503) 2231–9418—2231–9424 or 2231–9412
http://www.pgr.gob.sv/ado.html

Embassy of El Salvador
Consular Section
1400 16th Street, Suite 100, N.W.
Washington, D.C, 20036
Tel: (202) 595–7500
Fax: (202) 232 3763
Email: correo@elsalvador.org

El Salvador also has consulates in Atlanta, Boston, Chicago, Dallas, Elizabeth (NJ), Houston, Las Vegas, Los Angeles, Santa Ana (CA), Woodbridge (VA), Duluth (GA), Miami, New York, Long Island (NY), Nogales (AZ), San Francisco, and Washington, DC. Contact information for these consulates can be found at the web site listed above.

Office of Children's Issues
U.S. Department of State
2201 C Street, NW
SA-29
Washington, DC 20520
Tel: 1–888–407–4747
E-mail: AskCI@state.gov
http://adoption.state.gov

For questions about immigration procedures, call the National Customer Service Center (NCSC) 1-800-375-5283 (TTY 1-800-767-1833).

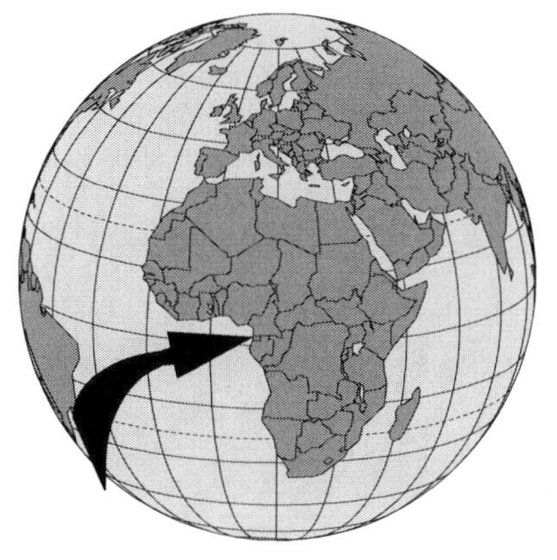

EQUATORIAL GUINEA

Compiled from publications that were available as of February 2013 from the U.S. Department of State, the U.S. Department of Commerce, and the Central Intelligence Agency (CIA). See the introduction to this set for explanatory notes.

Official Name:
Republic of Equatorial Guinea

PROFILE

Geography

Area: total: 28,051 sq km; country comparison to the world: 146; land: 28,051 sq km; water: 0 sq km
Major cities: Malabo (capital) 128,000 (2009)
Climate: tropical; always hot, humid
Terrain: coastal plains rise to interior hills; islands are volcanic

People

Nationality: noun: Equatorial Guinean(s) or Equatoguinean(s); adjective: Equatorial Guinean or Equatoguinean
Population: 685,991 (July 2012 est.)
Population growth rate: 2.607% (2012 est.)
Ethnic groups: Fang 85.7%, Bubi 6.5%, Mdowe 3.6%, Annobon 1.6%, Bujeba 1.1%, other 1.4% (1994 census)
Religions: nominally Christian and predominantly Roman Catholic, pagan practices
Languages: Spanish (official) 67.6%, other (includes French (official), Fang, Bubi) 32.4% (1994 census)
Literacy: definition: age 15 and over can read and write; total population: 93.9%; male: 97.1%; female: 90.6% (2010 est.)
Health: life expectancy at birth: total population: 62.75 years; male: 61.75 years; female: 63.78 years (2012 est.); Infant mortality rate: total: 75.18 deaths/1,000 live births; male: 76.25 deaths/1,000 live births; female: 74.08 deaths/1,000 live births (2012 est.)
Unemployment rate: 22.3% (2009 est.)
Work force: 195,200 (2007)

Government

Type: republic
Independence: 12 October 1968
Constitution: approved by national referendum 17 November 1991; amended January 1995
Political subdivisions: 7 provinces (provincias, singular—provincia); Annobon, Bioko Norte, Bioko Sur, Centro Sur, Kie-Ntem, Litoral, Wele-Nzas
Suffrage: 18 years of age; universal

Economy

GDP (purchasing power parity): $28.03 billion (2012 est.); $26.48 billion (2011 est.); $24.73 billion (2010 est.); $24.92 billion (2009 est.)
GDP real growth rate: 5.7% (2012 est.); 7.1% (2011 est.); -0.8% (2010 est.); 5.7% (2009 est.)
GDP per capita (PPP): $20,200 (2012 est.); $19,600 (2011 est.); $18,800 (2010 est.); $19,500 (2009 est.)
Natural resources: petroleum, natural gas, timber, gold, bauxite, diamonds, tantalum, sand and gravel, clay
Agriculture products: coffee, cocoa, rice, yams, cassava (manioc), bananas, palm oil nuts; livestock; timber
Industries: petroleum, natural gas, sawmilling
Exports: $18.31 billion (2012 est.); $15.64 billion (2011 est.); $10 billion (2010 est.)
Exports—commodities: petroleum products, timber
Exports—partners: Spain 14.6%, China 13%, Italy 10.8%, Japan 10.5%, US 9.5%, Netherlands 7.5%, Canada 5.5%, Brazil 5%, France 4.7%, South Korea 4.1% (2011)
Imports: $7.59 billion (2012 est.); $7.322 billion (2011 est.); $5.7 billion (2010 est.)
Imports—commodities: petroleum sector equipment, other equipment, construction materials, vehicles
Imports—partners: Spain 16.7%, US 12.8%, France 12.1%, China 12%, Italy 6.6%, Cote dIvoire 5.8%, Morocco 4.7% (2011)
Debt—external: $1.232 billion (31 December 2012 est.); $1.051 billion (31 December 2011 est.); $829.1 million (31 December 2010 est.)
Exchange rates: Cooperation Financiere en Afrique Centrale francs per US dollar; 511.4 (2012 est.); 471.87 (2011 est.); 495.28 (2010 est.); 472.19 (2009)

GEOGRAPHY

The Republic of Equatorial Guinea is located in west central Africa. Bioko Island lies about 40 kilometers (25 mi.) from Cameroon. Annobon Island lies about 595 kilometers (370 mi.) southwest of Bioko Island. The larger continental region of Rio Muni lies between Cameroon and Gabon on the mainland; Equatorial Guinea includes the islands of Corisco, Elobey Grande, Elobey Chico, and adjacent islets.

Bioko Island, called Fernando Po until the 1970s, is the largest island in the Gulf of Guinea—2,017 square kilometers (780 sq. mi.). Two large volcanic formations are separated by a valley that bisects the island at its narrowest point. The 195-kilometer (120-mi.) coastline is steep and rugged in the south but lower and more accessible in the north, with excellent harbors at Malabo and Luba, and several scenic beaches between those towns.

On the continent, Rio Muni covers 26,003 square kilometers (10,040 sq. mi.). The coastal plain gives way to a succession of valleys separated by low hills and spurs of the Crystal Mountains. The Rio Benito (Mbini), which divides Rio Muni in half, is not navigable except for a 20-kilometer stretch at its estuary. Temperatures and humidity in Rio Muni are slightly lower than on Bioko Island.

Annobon Island, named for its discovery on New Year's Day 1472, is a small volcanic island covering 18 square kilometers (7 sq. mi.). The coastline is abrupt except in the north; the principal volcanic cone contains a small lake.

Most of the estimated 1,900 inhabitants are fisherman specializing in traditional, small-scale tuna fishing and whaling. The climate is tropical—heavy rainfall, high humidity, and frequent seasonal changes with violent windstorms.

PEOPLE

The majority of the Equatoguinean people are of Bantu origin. The largest tribe, the Fang, is indigenous to the mainland, but substantial migration to Bioko Island has resulted in Fang dominance over the earlier Bubi inhabitants.

The Fang constitute 80% of the population and are themselves divided into 67 clans. Those in the northern part of Rio Muni speak Fang-Ntumu, while those in the south speak Fang-Okah; the two dialects are mutually unintelligible. The Bubi, who constitute 15% of the population, are indigenous to Bioko Island.

In addition, there are coastal tribes, sometimes referred to as "Playeros," consisting of Ndowes, Bujebas, Balengues, and Bengas on the mainland and small islands, and "Fernandinos," a Creole community, on Bioko. Together, these groups comprise 5% of the population. There are also a growing number of foreigners from neighboring Cameroon, Nigeria, and Gabon.

National/Racial/Ethnic Minorities

Undocumented residents from Nigeria, Ghana, Cameroon, Mali, Togo, Gabon, and other African countries represented a significant portion of the labor force and continued to grow, despite police attempts to enforce immigration laws. Foreigners routinely were stopped at checkpoints and asked to provide documentation.

Language

Spanish, French, and Portuguese are the official languages, though use of Spanish predominates.

Religion

An estimated 93 percent of the population is Christian, of which 87 percent is Roman Catholic and 6 percent Protestant and members of independent denominations. Many Catholics reportedly follow traditional beliefs as well. Five percent of the population practices indigenous religious beliefs exclusively. Muslims, Baha'is, and practitioners of other religious beliefs each constitute less than 1 percent of the population. The number of Muslims is increasing due to the growing number of West African and Middle Eastern immigrants.

HISTORY

The first inhabitants of the region that is now Equatorial Guinea are believed to have been Pygmies, of whom only isolated pockets remain in northern Rio Muni. Bantu migrations between the 17th and 19th centuries brought the coastal tribes and later the Fang. Elements of the latter may have generated the Bubi, who immigrated to Bioko from Cameroon and Rio Muni in several waves and succeeded former Neolithic populations. The Annobon population, native to Angola, was introduced by the Portuguese via Sao Tome.

The Portuguese explorer, Fernando Po (Fernao do Poo) discovered the island of Bioko in 1471. He called it Formosa ("pretty flower"), but it quickly took on the name of its European discoverer. The Portuguese retained control until 1778, when the island, adjacent islets, and commercial rights to the mainland between the Niger and Ogoue Rivers were ceded to Spain in exchange for territory in South America (Treaty of El Pardo). From 1827 to 1843, Britain established a base on the island to combat the slave trade. The Treaty of Paris settled conflicting claims to the mainland in 1900, and the mainland territories were united administratively under Spanish rule.

Spain did not develop an extensive economic infrastructure but did develop large cacao plantations for internal consumption for which thousands of Nigerian workers were imported as laborers. At independence in 1968 Equatorial Guinea had one of the highest per capita incomes in Africa. The Spanish also helped Equatorial Guinea achieve one of the continent's highest literacy rates and developed a good network of health

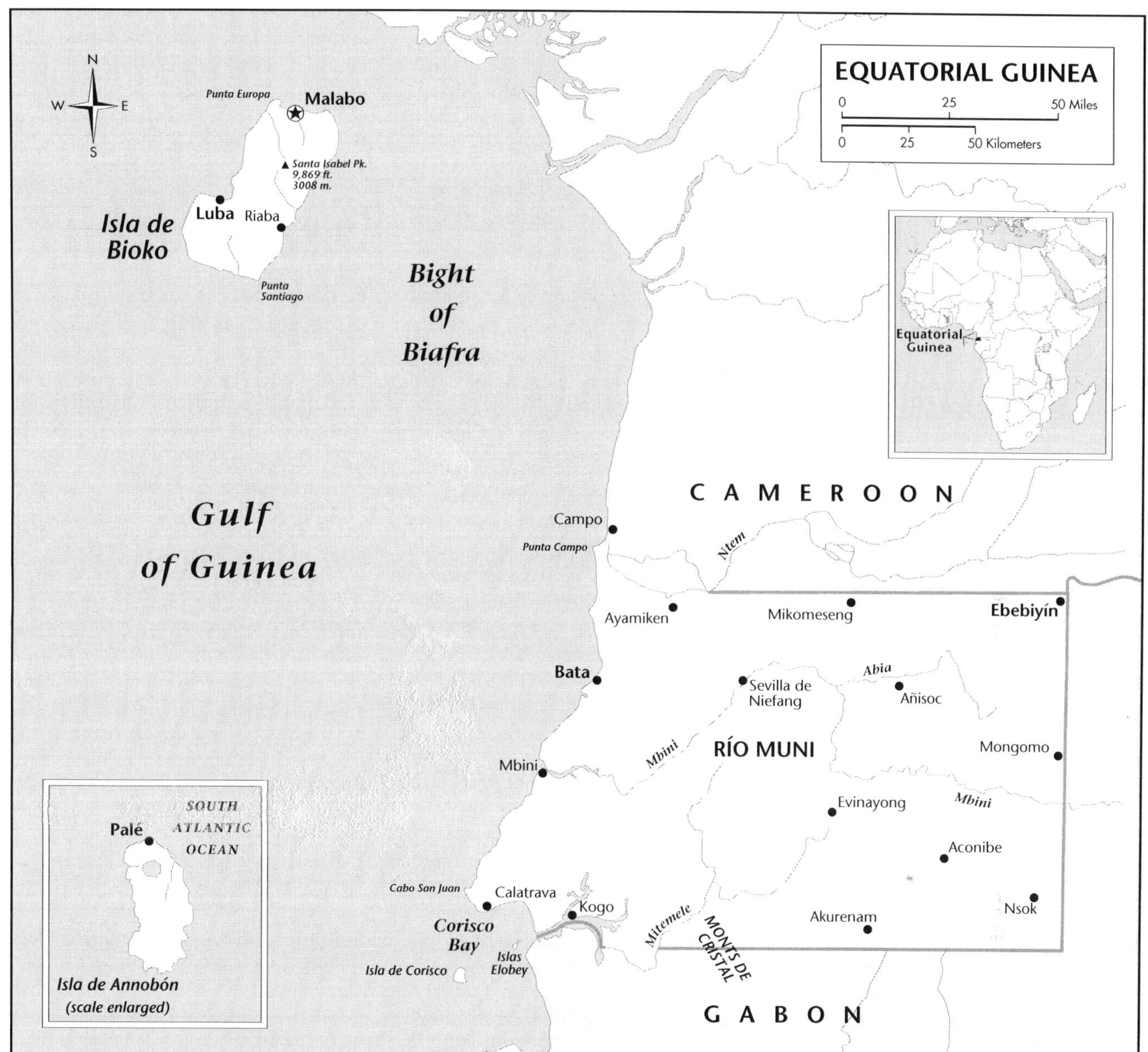

care facilities. In 1959, the Spanish territory of the Gulf of Guinea was established with status similar to the provinces of metropolitan Spain. As the Spanish Equatorial Region, a governor general ruled it exercising military and civilian powers.

The first local elections were held in 1959, and the first Equatoguinean representatives were seated in the Spanish parliament. Under the Basic Law of December 1963, limited autonomy was authorized under a joint legislative body for the territory's two provinces. The name of the country was changed to Equatorial Guinea. Although Spain's commissioner general had extensive powers, the Equatorial Guinean General Assembly had considerable initiative in formulating laws and regulations.

In March 1968, under pressure from Equatoguinean nationalists and the United Nations, Spain announced that it would grant independence to Equatorial Guinea. A constitutional convention produced an electoral law and draft constitution. A referendum was held on August 11, 1968, and 63% of the electorate voted in favor of the constitution, which provided for a government with a General Assembly and a Supreme Court with judges appointed by the president. In September 1968, Francisco Macias Nguema was elected first president of Equatorial Guinea, and independence was granted in October. In July 1970, Macias created a single-party state and by May 1971, key portions of the constitution were abrogated. In 1972 Macias took complete control of the government and assumed the title of President-for-Life.

The Macias regime was characterized by abandonment of all government functions except internal security, which was accomplished by terror;

this led to the death or exile of up to one-third of the country's population. Due to pilferage, ignorance, and neglect, the country's infrastructure—electrical, water, road, transportation, and health—fell into ruin. Religion was repressed, and education ceased. The private and public sectors of the economy were devastated. Nigerian contract laborers on Bioko, estimated to have been 60,000, left en masse in early 1976. The economy collapsed, and skilled citizens and foreigners left.

On August 3, 1979 Teodoro Obiang Nguema Mbasogo led a successful coup d'etat; Macias was arrested, tried, and executed. Obiang assumed the presidency in October 1979. Obiang initially ruled Equatorial Guinea with the assistance of a Supreme Military Council. A new constitution, drafted in 1982 with the help of the United Nations Commission on Human Rights, came into effect after a popular vote on August 15, 1982; the Council was abolished, and Obiang remained in the presidency for a 7-year term. He was reelected in 1989.

A new constitution was approved in 1991 and amended in 1995. One-party rule formally ended in 1991 and political activities in Equatorial Guinea were legalized, but the opposition had few electoral successes in the 1990s. In September 1995, the country had its first freely contested municipal elections. Most observers agree that the elections themselves were relatively free and transparent and that the opposition parties garnered between two-thirds and three-quarters of the total vote. The government, however, delayed announcement of the results and then claimed a highly dubious 52% victory overall and the capture of 19 of 27 municipal councils.

In early January 1996 Obiang called for presidential elections. International observers agreed that the campaign was marred by fraud, and most of the opposition candidates withdrew in the final week. Obiang claimed re-election with 98% of the vote. In an attempt to mollify his critics, Obiang gave minor portfolios in his cabinet to people identified as opposition figures. In the legislative election in March 1999, the party increased its majority in the 80-seat parliament from 68 to 75. The main opposition parties refused the seats they had allegedly won. By early 2000, the President's Democratic Party of Equatorial Guinea (PDGE) party fully dominated government at all levels. In May 2000, the ruling PDGE overwhelmed its rivals in local elections.

Opposition parties rejected as invalid the December 2002 presidential election, which they boycotted. President Obiang was re-elected with 97% of the vote. Reportedly, 95% of eligible voters voted in this election, although many observers noted numerous irregularities. Following his re-election Obiang formed a government based on national unity encompassing all opposition parties, except for the Convergence for Social Democracy (CPDS), which declined to join after Obiang refused to release one of their jailed leaders.

In the April 2004 parliamentary and municipal elections President Obiang's Democratic Party of Equatorial Guinea and allied parties won 98 of 100 seats in parliament and all but seven of 244 municipal posts. International observers criticized both the election and its results.

The May 4, 2008 legislative elections resulted in an overwhelming victory for the PDGE. Ninety-nine of the 100 seats in the assembly went to the PDGE while the Convergence for Social Democracy only received one. Results were similar in the municipal elections held the same day, granting PDGE 319 councilor seats while CPDS only gained 13. Some international election observers reported that the elections were generally conducted in a free and fair manner.

Nevertheless, irregularities were reported, which included the barring of certain members of the international press. In November 2009, President Obiang won a new 7-year mandate with 95.4% of the vote in an election that was not boycotted by the opposition. The main opposition leader won 3.6% of the vote. He stated that he viewed the elections as neither fair nor free, but with the approval of the executive committee of his party, did not formally object to the election results.

GOVERNMENT AND POLITICAL CONDITIONS

Equatorial Guinea is nominally a multiparty constitutional republic. Since a military coup in 1979, President Obiang Nguema Mbasogo dominated all branches of government in collaboration with his clan and his political party, the Democratic Party of Equatorial Guinea (PDGE). In 2009 voters reelected President Obiang with a claimed 95.37 percent of votes cast. The lopsided results and weak independent monitoring of the electoral process raised suspicions of systematic vote fraud. Foreign diplomatic observers noted numerous irregularities and the presence of military personnel at all voting stations.

Recent Elections

In 2009 President Obiang was reelected, winning a claimed 95.37 percent of votes cast; opposition candidate Placido Mico of the CPDS won 3.55 percent of the vote. The lopsided results and weak independent monitoring of the electoral process raised the suspicion of systematic voting fraud.

The government's insistence on coordinating the movement of election observers, prohibition on criticism of the elections, and control of media access to cover the elections limited the participation of international election observers at the 1,289 polling stations.

Procedural irregularities at some polling stations included multiple voting, failure to respect secrecy of the vote, and the absence of a posted list of registered candidates. At some stations family voting was allowed, unregistered voters were allowed to vote, and ballot boxes were unsealed.

Soldiers were deployed to all polling stations. In October 2009 President Obiang announced the election would be on November 29, with campaigning to begin officially on November 5. According to Human Rights Watch, the tight election timetable and the government's refusal to make the voter rolls public severely limited the opposition's ability to campaign and win support.

The voter registration process was seriously flawed. The registration committee was composed primarily of PDGE members and routinely decided issues in favor of the PDGE. When registering a PDGE member, the committee registered all members of the family as PDGE voters, including children. Persons who were dead or underage were included as PDGE registrants.

No independent and impartial body existed to oversee the electoral process or consider election-related complaints. The National Electoral Commission, which was separate from the voter registration committee and charged with ensuring the fairness of the elections and handling formal post-election complaints, was controlled by the ruling party and headed by the interior minister, a prominent member of the party. While its membership included a representative of each political party that fielded candidates, it also included representatives from the government and lacked civil society representation.

In addition, a majority of its members were ruling party officials. The opposition CPDS party claimed that one of its electoral officials was forced with a pistol held to his head to approve a vote count.

Opposition party members and candidates operated at a significant disadvantage when attempting to gain voter support. On the whole, opposition parties and their candidates were poorly organized, inadequately financed, and unsupported by the public. Several peaceful political parties banned in recent years were not allowed to participate in the elections. The government denied the opposition equal access to the media. Opposition members and leaders also claimed the government monitored their activities.

Unlike in previous elections, no opposition members were arbitrarily arrested, detained, or tortured, but opposition candidates were harassed and intimidated during the presidential campaign.

Political Parties: The ruling PDGE party ruled through a complex arrangement built around family, clan, and ethnic loyalties. Indirect pressure for public employees to join the PDGE continued. Opposition party members continued to report they had been discriminated against in hiring, job retention, scholarships, and obtaining business licenses. Opposition members contended government pressure precluded them from obtaining jobs with foreign companies. Opposition party members claimed businesses found to have hired employees with direct links to families, individuals, parties, or groups out of favor with the government often were forced to dismiss those employees or face reprisals.

On January 27, 2011, the government appointed four deputy prime ministers from opposition parties. At least two serving ministers were also from the opposition.

The legal opposition parties faced restrictions on freedoms of speech, association, and assembly. Some political parties that existed before the 1992 law establishing procedures to legalize political parties remained banned, generally for "supporting terrorism."

The president exercised strong powers as head of state, commander of the armed forces, head of the judiciary, and founder and head of the ruling party. In general, leadership positions within government were restricted to the president's party or the coalition of "loyal opposition" parties. On November 13, the government held a popular vote on a constitutional referendum to limit the president to two seven-year terms and create a vice president, a second chamber of the legislature, an anti-corruption body, and a "Defender of the People" to serve as a human rights ombudsman.

The referendum passed with 97.7 percent support. The margin of the positive vote and the lack of any credible oversight of the voting process raised doubts about the legitimacy of the referendum. International NGOs and local opposition parties claimed that the process was marred by reports of voting fraud, harassment of opposition supporters, and intimidation of voters. There were scattered confrontations between regime authorities and opposition activists in the continental city of Bata.

Because the ruling party overwhelmingly dominated the commissions established to review electoral practices and recommend reforms, few changes were made.

Participation of Women and Minorities: The government did not overtly limit participation of minorities in politics; however, the predominant Fang ethnic group, estimated to constitute more than 85 percent of the population, continued to exercise strong political and economic power. Women constituted more than 10 percent of the 100-member parliament, including its vice president. There were two women in the 22 member cabinet, and four of the 24 vice ministers were women.

Principal Government Officials

Last Updated: 1/31/2013

Pres.: **Teodoro OBIANG Nguema Mbasogo, Brig. Gen. (Ret.)**

Prime Min.: **Ignacio MILAM Tang**

First Vice Prime Min. in Charge of Economic & Financial Affairs: **Aniceto EBIAKA Moete**

Second Vice Prime Min. in Charge of Political & Democracy Affairs: **Demetrio ELO Ndong Nsefumu**

Third Vice Prime Min. in Charge of Social & Human Rights Affairs: **Salomon Nguema OWONO**

Sec. Gen. of the Govt. in Charge of Admin. Coordination: **Vicente Ehate TOMI**

Min. of Agriculture & Forests: **Teodoro Nguema OBIANG Mangu**

Min. of Economy, Commerce, & Business Development: **Francisca TATCHOUP Belope**

Min. of Education, Science, & Sports: **Joaquin NBANA Nchama**

Min. of Finance & Budget: **Melchor Esono EDJO**

Min. of Fishing & the Environment: **Anastasio ASUMU Mum Munoz**

Min. of Foreign Affairs, Intl. Cooperation, & Francophone Affairs: **Pastor Micha ONDO BILE**

Min. of Health & Social Welfare: **Salomon Nguema OWONO**

Min. of Information, Culture, Tourism, & Govt. Spokesman: **Jeronimo Osa Osa ECORO**

Min. of Justice, Religious Affairs, & Penitentiary Institutions: **Francisco Javier Ngomo MBENONO**

Min. of Labor & Social Security: **Estanislao Don MALAVO**

Min. of Mines, Industry, & Energy: **Marcelino Owono EDU**

Min. of National Defense: **Antonio MBA Nguema, Gen.**

Min. of National Security: **Nicolas OBAMA Nchama**

Min. of Planning, Economic Development, & Public Investment: **Jose ELA Oyana**

Min. of Public Admin. & Admin. Planning: **Tomas ESONO Ava**

Min. of Public Works & Infrastructures: **Marcelino OYONO Ntutumu**

Min. of Social Affairs & the Promotion of Women: **Eulalia ENVO Bela**

Min. of Transportation, Technology, & Posts & Telecommunications: **Mauricio BOKUNG Asumu**

Min. at the Presidency in Charge of Civil Cabinet: **Braulio Ncogo ABEGUE**

Min. at the Presidency in Charge of Missions: **Alejandro EVUNA Owono Asangono**

Min. at the Presidency in Charge of Regional Integration: **Baltasar Engonga EDJO**

Min. in Charge of Relations With Parliament: **Angel MASIE Mibuy**

Ambassador to the US: **Purificacion ANGUE ONDO**

Permanent Representative to the UN, New York: **Anatolio NDONG MBA**

ECONOMY

The discovery and exploitation of large oil and gas reserves have contributed to dramatic economic growth, but fluctuating oil prices have produced huge swings in GDP growth in recent years. Forestry and farming are also minor components of GDP. Subsistence farming is the dominate form of livelihood.

Although pre-independence Equatorial Guinea counted on cocoa production for hard currency earnings, the neglect of the rural economy under successive regimes has diminished potential for agriculture-led growth (the government has stated its intention to reinvest some oil revenue into agriculture). A number of aid programs sponsored by the World Bank and the IMF have been cut off since 1993 because of corruption and mismanagement.

The government has been widely criticized for its lack of transparency and misuse of oil revenues; however, in 2010, under Equatorial Guinea's candidacy in the Extractive Industries Transparency Initiative, the government published oil revenue figures for the first time. Undeveloped natural resources include gold, zinc, diamonds, columbite-tantalite, and other base metals. The economy recovered from the global recession in 2011–12 stimulated by higher oil prices and large investments in public infrastructure and hotels.

Labor Conditions

The law prohibits children under the age of 14 from working and provides that persons found guilty of illegally forcing a minor to work may be punished with a fine of approximately 50,000 to 250,000 CFA francs ($98 to $490). Children younger than age 16 are prohibited from participating in work that may endanger their health, security, or morals. A limited number of children were recruited and transported from nearby countries, primarily Nigeria, Benin, Cameroon, and Gabon, and forced to work as domestic servants, market laborers, and ambulant vendors. Children involved in street work sold food, water, and clothes; transported water; and washed cars. Young women ages 15 to 18 reportedly were involved also in transactional sex, particularly girls studying in urban centers such as Malabo and Bata. There was no reliable data available on the extent of child labor, although observers believed it was not a major problem.

In September the government increased the monthly minimum wage from 95,400 CFA francs ($188) to 129,035 CFA francs ($255) for all workers in the country. Many formal-sector companies paid more than this, but workers in the informal sector and domestic workers were not covered under the minimum wage law.

The law exempts domestic workers, except those working for business executives, and those working within the family or the informal sector from the minimum wage law. By law hydrocarbon industry workers received salaries many times higher than those in other sectors, worsening disparities within society and fueling inflation for some goods and services. The Ministry of Labor is responsible for enforcing minimum wage rules.

The law prescribes a standard 35-hour workweek and a 48-hour weekly rest period; these requirements were generally observed in the formal economy. Exceptions were made for some jobs, such as those in offshore oil industry work. Premium pay for overtime was required, but the requirement was not always effectively enforced.

U.S.-EQUATORIAL GUINEA RELATIONS

The United States established diplomatic relations with Equatorial Guinea in 1968, following the country's independence from Spain. Equatorial Guinea's President has held office for more than three decades, and his party dominates the legislature. Three major U.S. foreign policy issues form the cornerstone of the bilateral relationship with Equatorial Guinea — good governance and democracy; the protection of human rights; and U.S. national security, especially access to energy resources.

The United States seeks to encourage improved human rights, the development of a working civil society, greater fiscal transparency, and increased government investment in Equatorial Guinea's people in areas such as health and education.

U.S. Assistance to Equatorial Guinea

U.S. assistance to Equatorial Guinea has focused on introducing the country's military and police forces to the principles of human rights, good governance, and democracy, and on improving regional maritime security. The U.S. Agency for International Development has several small regional projects, but does not have a presence within the country.

The Ambassador's Self-Help Fund annually finances a number of small grassroots projects. Equatoguineans visit the U.S. under programs sponsored by the U.S. Government, U.S. oil companies, and educational institutions.

Bilateral Economic Relations

Equatorial Guinea's hydrocarbon riches dwarf all other economic activity; the country's oil reserves are located mainly in the Gulf of Guinea. U.S. oil companies are one of Equatorial Guinea's largest investors, and they have a lead role in oil and gas exploration and extraction. Equatorial Guinea's exports to the U.S. are dominated by petroleum products. In an effort to attract increased U.S. investment, U.S. passport-holders are entitled to visa-free entry for short visits. Imports from the United States include machinery, iron and steel products, optic and medical instruments, and inorganic chemical and rare earth minerals.

Equatorial Guinea's Membership in International Organizations

Equatorial Guinea has used its oil wealth to expand its foreign presence, establishing diplomatic missions in other countries. Equatorial Guinea and the United States belong to a number of the same international organizations, including the United Nations, International Monetary Fund, and World Bank. The country also is an observer to the Organization of American States and World Trade Organization.

Bilateral Representation

Equatorial Guinea maintains an embassy at 2020 16th Street NW, Washington, DC 20009 (Tel. (202) 518-5700.

Principal U.S. Embassy Officials

Last Updated: 1/14/2013

MALABO (E) Carretera de Aeropuerto KM-3 (El Paraiso), Apartado 95, Malabo Equatorial Guinea, (240) 333 098895, Fax (240) 333 098894, INMARSAT Tel 8707-722-38353, Workweek: 8:00-5:30 M-R; 8:00-12:00 F, Website: http://malabo.usembassy.gov/

AMB OMS:	Christine McNab Visick
MGT:	Baylor M. Duncan
AMB:	Mark Asquino
CON:	Ashley White
DCM:	Rafael Foley
GSO:	Richard Woodhouse
ECON:	Denise M. Taylor
ISSO:	John Visick

TRAVEL

Consular Information Sheet

September 24, 2012

Country Description: Equatorial Guinea is an oil-rich, developing country on the western coast of central Africa. Its capital and main port, Malabo, is located on the island of Bioko, off the coast of Cameroon. A secondary port, Luba, is also on Bioko. The mainland territory of Equatorial Guinea is bordered by Cameroon and Gabon. The principal city on the mainland is Bata. Official languages are Spanish, which is widely spoken, and French, which is not widely understood, but sometimes used in business dealings.

Equatorial Guinea is nominally a multiparty constitutional republic. All branches of government are dominated by President Teodoro Obiang Nguema Mbasogo, who has ruled since 1979. In November 2009, he was declared the winner of the presidential election with over 95 percent of the vote.

Facilities for tourism are limited but growing. Cash machines are rare and often broken. The cash machine located at Malabo's airport and one at the SGBGE Bank in downtown Malabo are open to the public; other cash machines that do exist require membership in the local bank. There are no ATMs outside of Malabo and Bata. Equatorial Guinea is a beautiful country with many interesting sites and beautiful beaches, but there is little tourism information to assist in planning a vacation.

There is no public transportation and renting a vehicle is difficult. Rental vehicle choices are limited and can be expensive. Taxis are readily available in the larger cities and are generally inexpensive. Unless you pay a significantly higher price, drivers will pick up additional people until the vehicle is full. Passengers are delivered to their destinations at the convenience of the driver, not the passenger.

Smart Traveler Enrollment Program (STEP)/Embassy Locations: If you are going to live in or visit Equatorial Guinea, please take the time to tell us about your trip by enrolling in the Smart Traveler Enrollment Program (STEP). If you enroll, we can keep you up to date with important, local and world-wide safety and security announcements. It will also help your friends and family get in touch with you in an emergency. You should remember to keep all of your information in STEP up to date. It is important during enrollment or updating of information to include your current phone number and current email address where you can be reached in case of an emergency.

U.S. citizens without Internet access may register directly with the nearest U.S. embassy or consulate. By registering, you make it easier for the Embassy in Malabo to contact you in case of emergency.

U.S. Embassy Malabo
Carretera de Aeropuerto KM-3 (El Paraiso)
Apartado 95
Malabo
Telephone: 240-333-098-895

Immigrant Visa services are provided through the U.S. Embassy in Yaoundé, Cameroon, Avenue Rosa Parks in the Mbankolo Quartier, adjacent to the Mount Febe Golf Club.

Mailing Address: P.O. Box 817, Yaounde, Cameroon
Telephone: 237-2220–1500
Emergency after-hours telephone: 237-2220–1500
Facsimile: 237-2220–1572

Entry/Exit Requirements for U.S. Citizens: According the Government of Equatorial Guinea's website, visas are not required for U.S. citizens but they must fill out a visa application and present two passport photos and a letter of invitation from the employer at the point of entry. In addition, a certification of vaccination for small pox, yellow fever, and cholera are required to enter Equatorial Guinea.

Of the three vaccines listed, the CDC recommends only the Yellow Fever vaccination. Small pox and cholera vaccinations are generally not available in the United States. Immigration officials may bar entry into the country for those that cannot comply with the vaccination requirements. All other nationals must acquire a visa prior to arriving in country. It is extremely difficult to obtain a visa upon entry into Equatorial Guinea. U.S. citizens staying longer than 90 days should register with the local police station.

Private ships landing at an Equato-Guinean port must get clearance prior to approaching the shore.

You can obtain the latest information and details from the Embassy of the Republic of Equatorial Guinea, 2020 16th Street NW, Washington, DC 20009, telephone (202) 518-5700, fax (202) 518-5252.

The U.S. Department of State is unaware of any HIV/AIDS entry restrictions for visitors to or foreign residents of Equatorial Guinea.

Threats to Safety and Security: Although large public demonstrations are uncommon, you should avoid large crowds, political rallies, and street demonstrations.

In February 2009, approximately 50 gunmen arriving by speedboats attacked government buildings in Malabo but were repelled by Equato-Guinean military and police.

Stay up to date by:

- Bookmarking our Bureau of Consular Affairs website, which contains the current Travel Warnings and Travel Alerts as well as the Worldwide Caution.
- Following us on Twitter and the Bureau of Consular Affairs page on Facebook as well.
- Downloading our freeSmart Traveler App, available through iTunes and the Android marketplace, to have travel information at your fingertips.
- Calling 1-888-407-4747 toll-free within the United States and Canada, or a regular toll line, 1-202-501-4444, from other countries.
- Taking some time before travel to consider your personal security.

The Department of State urges you to take responsibility for your personal security while traveling overseas. For general information about appropriate measures travelers can take to protect themselves in an overseas environment, see the Department of State's extensive tips and advice on traveling safely abroad.

Crime: Violent crime is rare and the overall level of criminal activity is low in comparison to other countries in the region. However, there has been a rise in non-violent street crime and residential burglaries. You should exercise prudence and normal caution, including avoiding dark alleys, remote locations, and traveling alone. Sexual assault is rare and there is no specific group of people (the elderly, women, or gays) suffering from victimization. There is little evidence of racially motivated hate crimes and U.S. citizens are not specifically targeted. There is also limited evidence of scams or confidence schemes.

In many countries around the world, counterfeit and pirated goods are widely available. You will find such products widely available on the streets, local shops, and in market places. Transactions involving such products may be illegal under local law. In addition, carrying them back to the United States may result in forfeitures and/or fines.

Victims of Crime: If you or someone you know becomes the victim of a crime abroad, you should contact the local police and the nearest U.S. embassy or consulate. We can:

- Replace a stolen passport.
- Help you find appropriate medical care if you are the victim of violent crimes such as assault or rape.
- Put you in contact with the appropriate police authorities, and if you want us to, we can contact family members or friends.
- Help you understand the local criminal justice process and direct you to local attorneys, although it is important to

remember that local authorities are responsible for investigating and prosecuting the crime.

There is no local equivalent to the "911" emergency line in Equatorial Guinea.

Criminal Penalties: While you are traveling in Equatorial Guinea, you are subject to its laws even if you are a U.S. citizen. Foreign laws and legal systems can be vastly different than our own. In some places you may be taken in for questioning if you don't have your passport with you. In some places, it is illegal to take pictures of certain buildings. In some places driving under the influence could land you immediately in jail. These criminal penalties will vary from country to country.

Persons violating Equato-Guinean laws, even unknowingly, may be expelled, arrested or imprisoned. Penalties for possession, use, or trafficking in illegal drugs in Equatorial Guinea are severe, and convicted offenders can expect long jail sentences and heavy fines. There are also some things that might be legal in the country you visit, but still illegal in the United States, and you can be prosecuted under U.S. law. Engaging in sexual conduct with children or using or disseminating child pornography in a foreign country is a crime prosecutable in the United States.

If you break local laws in Equatorial Guinea, your U.S. passport won't help you avoid arrest or prosecution. It's very important to know what's legal and what's not where you are going.

Official Corruption: It is not uncommon for a uniformed member of the security forces to stop motorists on the pretext of minor or nonexistent violations of the local motor vehicle regulations in order to extort small bribes. Visitors are advised not to pay bribes, and to request that the officer provide a citation to be paid at the local court or a receipt stating the violation, amount due, and the officer's name. If visitors encounter any of these problems, they should contact the Embassy Duty Officer at 516-008 to report the situation.

Currency: Equatorial Guinea is a strictly cash economy. The country has very few hotels that accept credit cards. Generally, credit cards and checks are not accepted, and credit card cash advances are not available. Most local businesses do not accept travelers' checks, dollars, or Euros. However, dollars can be exchanged at local banks for Central African Francs (CFA). Cash in CFA is usually the only form of payment accepted throughout the country.

Photography: In the recent past a special permit from the Ministry of Information and Tourism (or from the local delegation if outside Malabo) was required for virtually all types of photography. This law changed, but many police or security officials may still attempt to impose a fine on people taking photographs.

It is still forbidden to take photos of the Presidential Palace and its surroundings, military installations, airports, harbors, government buildings and any other area deemed sensitive by the local government. Police and security officials may attempt to take a violator into custody, or seize the camera of persons photographing in the country.

Unusual Customs: Possession of camouflage-patterned clothing, large knives, binoculars, firearms, and a variety of other items may be deemed suspicious by the security forces, and grounds for confiscation of the item(s) and detention of the carrier.

Medical Facilities and Health Information: Medical facilities are extremely limited. Pharmacies in Malabo and Bata stock basic medicines including antibiotics, but cannot becounted on to supply advanced medications. Outside of these cities, many medicines are unavailable. You are advised to carry a supply of properly-labeled prescription drugs and other medications that you require for your entire stay; an adequate supply of prescription or over-the-counter drugs in local stores or pharmacies is generally not available.

The sanitation levels in even the best hospitals are very low, except for the new La Paz Hospitals in Bata and Malabo, which meet the medical standards of a modern hospital in a developed country. Doctors and hospitals often require immediate payment for health services, and patients are sometimes expected to supply their own bandages, linen, and toiletries.

Malaria is a serious and sometimes fatal disease. The national government, along with U.S. oil companies in the country, has taken aggressive steps to control the mosquito population and limit the impact of malaria on the population centers in Malabo and Bata. Plasmodium falciparum malaria, the type that predominates in Equatorial Guinea, is resistant to the anti-malarial drug chloroquine. Travelers to the country are at high risk for contracting malaria; the Centers for Disease Control and Prevention (CDC) advise that you take one of the following anti-malarial drugs: mefloquinedoxycycline, or atovaquone/proguanil (Malarone).

If you become ill with a fever or flu-like illness while traveling in a malaria-risk area, and up to one year after returning home, you should seek prompt medical attention and tell your physician your travel history and what anti-malarials you have been taking. Visit the CDC's Travelers' Health page for additional information on malaria, including protective measures.

There are periodic outbreaks of cholera in Equatorial Guinea. Yellow fever can cause serious medical problems, but the vaccine, required for entry, is very effective in preventing the disease. Tuberculosis is an increasingly serious health concern in Equatorial Guinea. For further information, please consult the CDC's information on TB.

Many insect-borne illnesses are present. Insect precautions are encouraged at all times. Avoid non-chlorinated freshwater contact on the mainland to lessen the risk of Schistosomiasis.

Information on vaccinations and other health precautions, such as safe food and water precautions and insect bite protection, may be obtained from the Centers for Disease Control and Prevention's (CDC) hotline for international travelers at 1-877-FYI-TRIP (1-877-394-8747) or via the CDC.

For information about outbreaks of infectious diseases abroad, consult the infectious diseases section of the World Health Organization (WHO). The WHO also contains additional health information for travelers, including detailed country-specific health information.

Medical Insurance: You can't assume your insurance will go with you when you travel. It's very important to find out BEFORE you leave whether or not your medical insurance will cover you overseas. You need to ask your insurance company two questions:

- Does my policy apply when I'm out of the United States?
- Will it cover emergencies like a trip to a foreign hospital or a medical evacuation?

In many places, doctors and hospitals still expect payment in cash at the time of service. Your regular U.S. health insurance may not cover doctor and hospital visits in other countries. If your policy doesn't go with you when you travel, it's a very good idea to take out another one for your trip.

Traffic Safety and Road Conditions: While in a foreign country, you may encounter road conditions that differ significantly from those in the United States. The information below concerning Equatorial Guinea is provided for general reference only, and may not be totally accurate in a particular location or circumstance.

Generally, Equatorial Guinea's road networks are increasingly well developed. Nevertheless, livestock and pedestrians still create road hazards. New road construction and repair is taking place all over the country, and road conditions have improved markedly over the course of the past year. If you plan on staying in Equatorial Guinea and driving around the country for any length of time, you should attempt to purchase a cell phone for assistance in case of an emergency.

Travelers outside the limits of Malabo and Bata will encounter military roadblocks. You should be prepared to show proper identification (for example, a U.S. passport) and to explain your reason for being at that particular location.

The personnel staffing these checkpoints normally do not speak or understand English or French; travelers who do not speak Spanish should have their reason for being in the country and their itinerary written down in Spanish before venturing into the countryside.

There are currently no distracted driving laws in effect in the Equatorial Guinea, but police may pull over drivers who talk or text while driving for not following unspecific safe driving procedures.

Aviation Safety Oversight: As there is no direct commercial air service to the United States by carriers registered in Equatorial Guinea, the U.S. Federal Aviation Administration (FAA) has not assessed Equatorial Guinea's Civil Aviation Authority (CAA) for compliance with International Civil Aviation Organization (ICAO) aviation safety standards. Further information may be found on the FAA's safety assessment page.

Commercial air travel options to and from Equatorial Guinea continue to improve. Malabo is now served by Air France, Lufthansa, and Iberia Airlines which allow service to Europe seven days a week. Additionally, Ethiopian Airlines has begun regular service to Addis Ababa.

The island of Bioko and the African mainland are connected by several small local airlines offering daily service. Schedules are subject to change or cancellation without notice; flights are often overbooked andreservations may not guarantee seats. Malabo Airport has navigational aids and can accommodate night landings. There are no navigational aids at Bata Airport. Special clearances are required to land in or overfly Equatorial Guinea territory.

Children's Issues: Please see the U.S. Dept. of State Office of Children's Issues web pages on intercountry adoption and international parental child abduction.

Intercountry Adoption

May 2012

The information in this section has been edited from the latest report available as of February 2013 from the State Department Bureau of Consular Affairs, Office of Overseas Citizens Services. For more information, please read the *Intercountry Adoption* section of this book and review current reports online at http://adoption.state.gov.

Equatorial Guinea is not party to the Hague Convention on Protection of Children and Co-operation in Respect of Intercountry Adoption (the Hague Adoption Convention). Intercountry adoptions of children from non-Hague countries are processed in accordance with 8 Code of Federal Regulations, Section 204.3 as it relates to orphans as defined under the Immigration and Nationality Act, Section 101(b)(1)(F).

Below is the limited adoption information that the Department has obtained from the adoption authority of Equatorial Guinea. U.S. citizens adopting children from Equatorial Guinea, as well as U.S. citizen prospective adoptive parents living in Equatorial Guinea who would like to adopt from the United States or from a third country, should contact the adoption authority of Equatorial Guinea to inquire about applicable laws and procedures.

There is no adoption law governing intercountry adoption in Equatorial Guinea. Additionally, there is no designated adoption authority. U.S. Citizens considering adoption from Equatorial Guinea should contact the

Embassy of Equatorial Guinea in the United States for information on how to contact the appropriate government entity in Equatorial Guinea.

Prospective adoptive parents should be aware that not all children in orphanages or children's homes are adoptable. In many countries, birth parents place their child(ren) temporarily in an orphanage or children's home due to financial or other hardship, with the intention of returning for the child when they are able to do so. In such cases, the birth parent(s) rarely would have relinquished their parental rights or consented to their child(ren)'s adoption.

Equatorial Guinea's Adoption Authority: There is no adoption authority. We encourage you to inquire as to the appropriate government entity with the Embassy of Equatorial Guinea to the United States.

Embassy of Equatorial Guinea
2020 16th Street, NW, Washington DC 20009
Tel: (202) 518-5700
Fax: (202) 518-5252

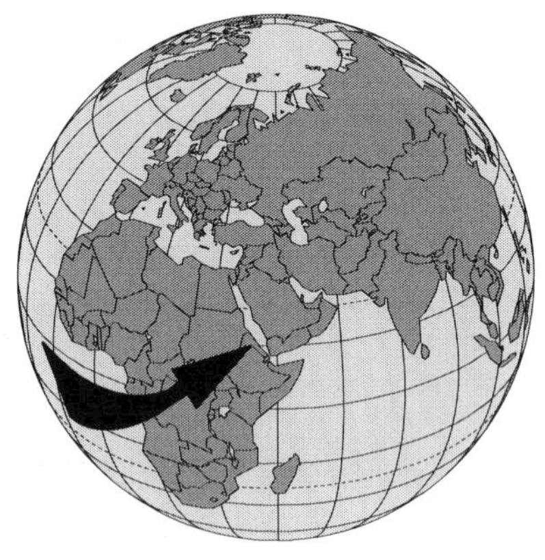

ERITREA

Compiled from publications that were available as of February 2013 from the U.S. Department of State, the U.S. Department of Commerce, and the Central Intelligence Agency (CIA). See the introduction to this set for explanatory notes.

Official Name:
State of Eritrea

PROFILE

Geography

Area: total: 117,600 sq km; country comparison to the world: 101; land: 101,000 sq km; water: 16,600 sq km
Major cities: Asmara (capital) 649,000 (2009)
Climate: hot, dry desert strip along Red Sea coast; cooler and wetter in the central highlands (up to 61 cm of rainfall annually, heaviest June to September); semiarid in western hills and lowlands
Terrain: dominated by extension of Ethiopian north-south trending highlands, descending on the east to a coastal desert plain, on the northwest to hilly terrain and on the southwest to flat-to-rolling plains

People

Nationality: noun: Eritrean(s); adjective: Eritrean
Population: 6,086,495 (July 2012 est.)
Population growth rate: 2.418% (2012 est.)
Ethnic groups: nine recognized ethnic groups: Tigrinya 55%, Tigre 30%, Saho 4%, Kunama 2%, Rashaida 2%, Bilen 2%, other (Afar, Beni Amir, Nera) 5% (2010 est.)
Religions: Muslim, Coptic Christian, Roman Catholic, Protestant
Languages: Tigrinya (official), Arabic (official), English (official), Tigre, Kunama, Afar, other Cushitic languages
Literacy: definition: age 15 and over can read and write; total population: 67.8%; male: 78.7%; female: 57.5% (2010 est.)
Health: life expectancy at birth: total population: 62.86 years; male: 60.73 years; female: 65.06 years (2012 est.); Infant mortality rate: total: 40.34 deaths/1,000 live births; male: 45.69 deaths/1,000 live births; female: 34.82 deaths/1,000 live births (2012 est.)
Unemployment rate: NA%
Work force: 1.935 million (2007)

Government

Type: transitional government
Independence: 24 May 1993
Constitution: adopted 23 May 1997, but has not yet been fully implemented
Political subdivisions: 6 regions (zobatat, singular—zoba); Anseba, Debub (South), Debubawi K'eyih Bahri (Southern Red Sea), Gash Barka, Ma'akel (Central), Semenawi Keyih Bahri (Northern Red Sea)
Suffrage: 18 years of age; universal

Economy

GDP (purchasing power parity): $4.412 billion (2012 est.); $4.089 billion (2011 est.); $3.761 billion (2010 est.); $3.68 billion (2009 est.)
GDP real growth rate: 7.5% (2012 est.); 8.7% (2011 est.); 2.2% (2010 est.); 3.9% (2009 est.)
GDP per capita (PPP): $800 (2012 est.); $700 (2011 est.); $700 (2010 est.); $700 (2009 est.)
Natural resources: gold, potash, zinc, copper, salt, possibly oil and natural gas, fish
Agriculture products: sorghum, lentils, vegetables, corn, cotton, tobacco, sisal; livestock, goats; fish
Industries: food processing, beverages, clothing and textiles, light manufacturing, salt, cement
Exports: $304.5 million (2012 est.); $415.4 million (2011 est.); $29 million (2010 est.)
Exports—commodities: livestock, sorghum, textiles, food, small manufactures
Exports—partners: Italy 30.5%, Sudan 24%, Saudi Arabia 8.8%, China 8.5%, UK 5.7%, Egypt 4.8% (2008)
Imports: $939.7 million (2012 est.); $900 million (2011 est.); $689.5 million (2010 est.)
Imports—commodities: machinery, petroleum products, food, manufactured goods
Imports—partners: Saudi Arabia 15.7%, Egypt 11.9%, China 11.1%, India 8.9%, Germany 7.2%, Italy 7.2%, South Africa 6.5%, Brazil 5.9%, South Korea 4.3% (2008)

Debt—external: $1.026 billion (31 December 2012 est.); $1.077 billion (31 December 2011 est.); $1.032 billion (31 December 2010 est.)
Exchange rates: nakfa (ERN) per US dollar; 15.38 (2012 est.); 15.375 (2011 est.); 15.375 (2010 est.); 15.375 (2009); 15.38 (2008); 15.5 (2007)

GEOGRAPHY

Eritrea is located in the Horn of Africa and is bordered on the northeast and east by the Red Sea, on the west and northwest by Sudan, on the south by Ethiopia, and on the southeast by Djibouti. The country has a high central plateau that varies from 1,800 to 3,000 meters (6,000-10,000 ft.) above sea level. A coastal plain, western lowlands, and some 300 islands comprise the remainder of Eritrea's landmass. Eritrea has no year-round rivers.

The climate is temperate in the mountains and hot in the lowlands. Asmara, the capital, is about 2,300 meters (7,500 ft.) above sea level. Maximum temperature is 26o C (80o F). The weather is usually sunny and dry, with the short or belg rains occurring February-April and the big or meher rains beginning in late June and ending in mid-September.

PEOPLE

Eritrea's population comprises nine ethnic groups, most of whom speak Semitic or Cushitic languages. The Tigrinya and Tigre make up four-fifths of the population and speak different, but somewhat mutually intelligible, Semitic languages. Tigrinya and Arabic are the most frequently used languages for commercial and official transactions. In urban areas, English is widely spoken and is the language used for secondary and university education.

Religion

Although reliable statistics are not available, the government claims that 50 percent of the population is Christian and 50 percent Sunni Muslim. Reliable international sources estimate that the population is approximately 40 percent Christian and 60 percent Muslim. The Christian population is roughly 24 percent Orthodox Christian, 10 percent Roman Catholic, and 4 percent other groups (Protestants, Seventh-day Adventists, and Jehovah's Witnesses). There is a small Baha'i community, and 2 percent of the population is animist. NGOs often estimate that there is a significant Muslim majority and larger populations of unregistered and unrecognized religious groups such as Pentecostals. The population is predominantly Muslim in the eastern and western lowlands and mainly Christian in the highlands. There are high levels of religious participation among all ethnic groups.

HISTORY

Prior to Italian colonization in 1885, what is now Eritrea had been ruled by the various local or international powers that successively dominated the Red Sea region. In 1896, the Italians used Eritrea as a springboard for their disastrous attempt to conquer Ethiopia. Eritrea was placed under British military administration after the Italian surrender in World War II. In 1952, a UN resolution federating Eritrea with Ethiopia went into effect. The resolution ignored Eritrean pleas for independence but guaranteed Eritreans some democratic rights and a measure of autonomy. Almost immediately after the federation went into effect, however, these rights began to be abridged or violated.

In 1962, Emperor Haile Sellassie unilaterally dissolved the Eritrean parliament and annexed the country, sparking the Eritrean fight for independence from Ethiopia that continued after Haile Sellassie was ousted in a coup in 1974. The new Ethiopian Government, known as the Derg, was a Marxist military junta led by Ethiopian strongman Mengistu Haile Miriam.

During the 1960s, the Eritrean Liberation Front (ELF) led the Eritrean independence struggle. In 1970, some members of the group broke away to form the Eritrean People's Liberation Front (EPLF). By the late 1970s, the EPLF had become the dominant armed Eritrean group fighting against the Ethiopian Government, with Isaias Afwerki as its leader. The EPLF used material captured from the Ethiopian Army to fight against the government.

By 1977, the EPLF was poised to drive the Ethiopians out of Eritrea. That same year, however, a massive airlift of Soviet arms to Ethiopia enabled the Ethiopian Army to regain the initiative and forced the EPLF to retreat to the bush. Between 1978 and 1986, the Derg launched eight major offensives against the independence movement—all of which failed.

In 1988, the EPLF captured Afabet, headquarters of the Ethiopian Army in northeastern Eritrea, prompting the Ethiopian Army to withdraw from its garrisons in Eritrea's western lowlands. EPLF fighters then moved into position around Keren, Eritrea's second-largest city. Meanwhile, other dissident movements were making headway throughout Ethiopia. At the end of the 1980s, the Soviet Union informed Mengistu that it would not be renewing the existing bilateral defense and cooperation agreement. With the withdrawal of Soviet support and supplies, the Ethiopian Army's morale plummeted, and the EPLF—along with other Ethiopian rebel forces—advanced on Ethiopian positions.

The United States played a facilitative role in the peace talks in Washington during the months leading up to the May 1991 fall of the Mengistu regime. In mid-May, Mengistu resigned as head of the Ethiopian Government and went into exile in Zimbabwe, leaving a caretaker government in Addis Ababa. Later that month, the United States chaired talks in London to formalize the end of the war. The four major combatant groups, including the EPLF, attended these talks.

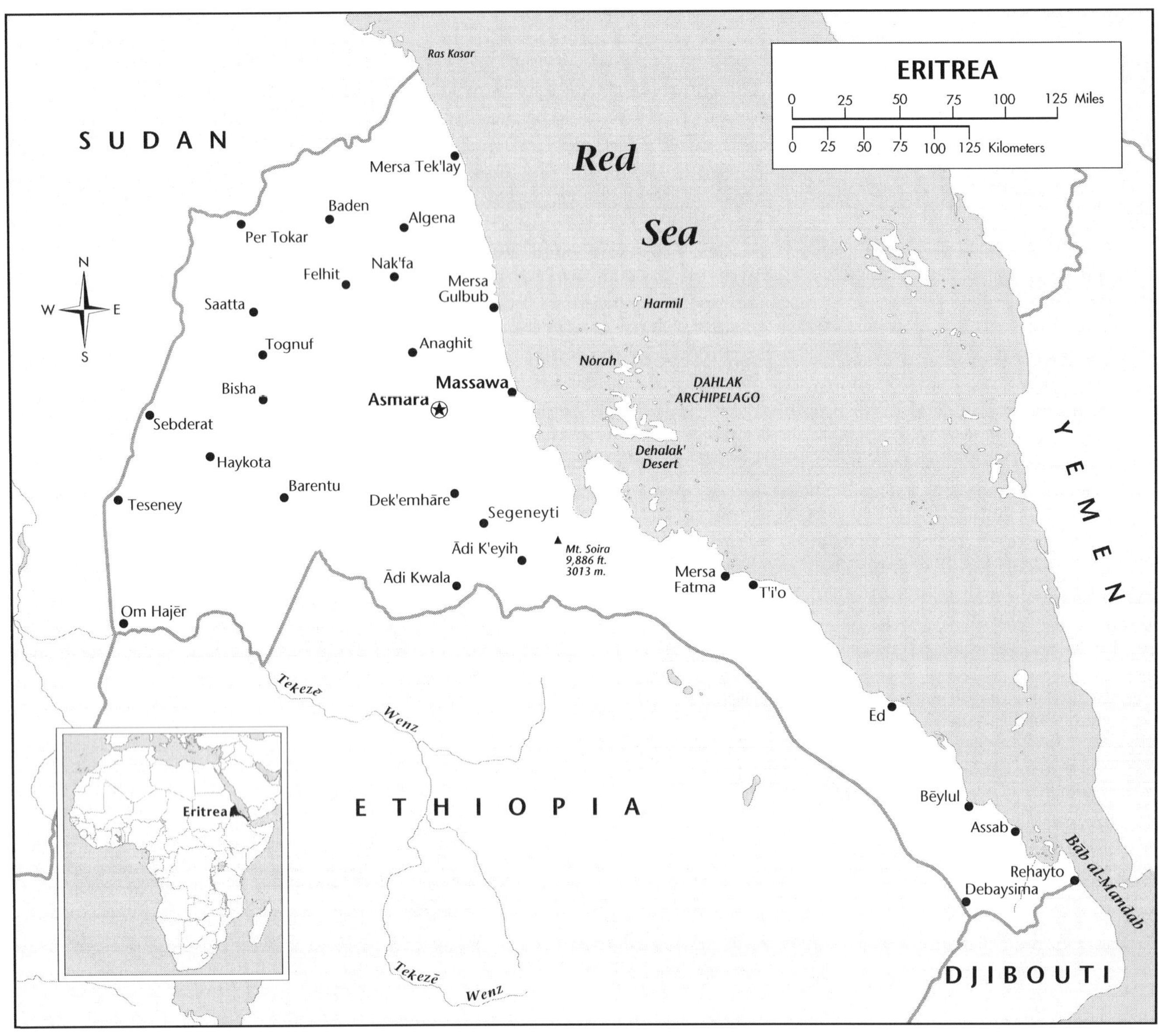

Having defeated the Ethiopian forces in Eritrea, EPLF troops took control of their homeland. In May 1991, the EPLF established the Provisional Government of Eritrea (PGE) to administer Eritrean affairs until a referendum could be held on independence and a permanent government established. EPLF leader Isaias became the head of the PGE, and the EPLF Central Committee served as its legislative body.

A high-level U.S. delegation was present in Addis Ababa for the July 1-5, 1991 conference that established a transitional government in Ethiopia. The EPLF attended the July conference as an observer and held talks with the new transitional government regarding Eritrea's relationship to Ethiopia. The outcome of those talks was an agreement in which the Ethiopians recognized the right of the Eritreans to hold a referendum on independence.

Although some EPLF cadres had espoused a Marxist ideology, Soviet assistance for Mengistu limited the level of Eritrean interest in seeking Soviet support. The fall of communist regimes in the former Soviet Union and the Eastern Bloc convinced the Eritreans it was a failed system. The EPLF (and later its successor, the PFDJ) expressed commitment to establishing a democratic form of government and a free-market economy in Eritrea. The United States agreed to provide assistance to both Ethiopia and Eritrea, conditional on continued progress toward democracy and human rights.

On April 23-25, 1993, Eritreans voted overwhelmingly for independence from Ethiopia in a UN-monitored free and fair referendum. The Eritrean authorities declared Eritrea an independent state on April 27, and Eritrea officially celebrated its independence on May 24, 1993.

GOVERNMENT AND POLITICAL CONDITIONS

The Government of Eritrea is an authoritarian regime under the control of President Isaias Afwerki. The People's Front for Democracy and Justice (PFDJ), headed by President Afwerki, is the sole political party. The PFDJ has controlled the country since 1991. Elections have not taken place since the country's independence from Ethiopia in 1993.

Recent Elections

The government came to power in a 1993 popular referendum in which voters chose to have an independent country managed by a transitional government; however, the transitional government did not permit the formation of a democratic system. The government twice scheduled elections in accordance with the constitution but cancelled them without explanation.

An official declaration in 2003 claimed that, "in accordance with the prevailing wish of the people, it is not the time to establish political parties, and discussion of the establishment has been postponed." Government officials also stated that implementation of the constitution was not possible until the border demarcation with Ethiopia was finalized. In 2008 the president claimed in an Al-Jazeera interview that elections might not take place for another 30 or 40 years.

Political Parties: The country is a one-party state. Power rested with the PFDJ and its institutions. At times the government coerced persons to join the PFDJ. Although no other political parties operated in the country, citizens living abroad established several political parties and a shadow government in Ethiopia. During 2011 the government continued to label individuals as gay, traitors, rapists, pedophiles, and traffickers if they were deemed not loyal to the government.

Participation of Women and Minorities: Almost all high-level government officials were former liberation fighters who had been in power since 1993. Women held four nominal ministerial positions in the government: justice, labor and human welfare, tourism, and health. Women also served in other government positions, such as mayors and regional administrators.

A few members of ethnic minorities were on the PFDJ's Executive Council or served on the Central Council. Some senior government and party officials were members of minority groups such as the Tigre. The head of the navy was an ethnic Afar.

Principal Government Officials

Last Updated: 1/31/2013

Pres.: **ISAIAS Afworki**
Vice Pres.:
Min. of Agriculture: **AREFAINE Berhe**
Min. of Defense: **SEBHAT Ephrem**
Min. of Education: **SEMERE Russom**
Min. of Energy & Mines: **AHMED Hajj Ali**
Min. of Finance: **BERHANE Abrehe**
Min. of Foreign Affairs: **OSMAN Saleh Mohammed**
Min. of Health: **AMINA Nurhussein**
Min. of Information: **ALI Abdu**
Min. of Justice: **FOZIA Hashim**
Min. of Labor & Human Welfare: **SALMA Hassen**
Min. of Land, Water, & Environment: **TESFAI Ghebreselassie**
Min. of Maritime Resources: **SALEH Meki**
Min. of National Development: **GHIORGHISH Teklemichael, Dr.**
Min. of Public Works: **ABRAHA Asfaha**
Min. of Tourism: **ASKALU Menkerios**
Min. of Trade & Industry
Min. of Transport & Communications: **WOLDENKIEL Abraha**
Governor, Bank of Eritrea (Acting): **KIBREAB Woldemariam**
Charge d'Affaires, Embassy, Washington: **BERHANE Gebrehiwet Solomon**
Permanent Representative to the UN, New York: **ARAYA Desta**

ECONOMY

Since independence from Ethiopia in 1993, Eritrea has faced the economic problems of a small, desperately poor country, accentuated by the recent implementation of restrictive economic policies. Eritrea has a command economy under the control of the sole political party, the People's Front for Democracy and Justice (PFDJ). Like the economies of many African nations, a large share of the population—nearly 80%—is engaged in subsistence agriculture, but they produce only a small share of total output.

Since the conclusion of the Ethiopian-Eritrea war in 2000, the government has maintained a firm grip on the economy, expanding the use of the military and party-owned businesses to complete Eritrea's development agenda. The government strictly controls the use of foreign currency by limiting access and availability. Few private enterprises remain in Eritrea. Eritrea's economy depends heavily on taxes paid by members of the diaspora.

Erratic rainfall and the delayed demobilization of agriculturalists from the military continue to interfere with agricultural production, and Eritrea's recent harvests have been unable to meet the food needs of the country. The Government continues to place its hope for additional revenue on the development of several international mining projects. Despite difficulties for international companies in working with the Eritrean Government, a Canadian mining company signed a contract with the government in 2007 and began mineral extraction in 2010.

Eritrea's economic future depends upon its ability to master social problems such as illiteracy, unemployment, and low skills, and more importantly, on the government's willingness to support a true market economy.

Labor Conditions

The legal minimum age for employment is 14, although this does not apply to self-employed workers. The minimum age for hazardous work is 18. The law prohibits minors from working in transport industries or working underground, such as in mines and sewers. However, children in apprenticeships may engage in these hazardous work assignments, provided they are supervised by a competent authority. It was unclear at what age a child may become an apprentice.

Labor inspectors from the Ministry of Labor and Human Welfare are responsible for enforcing child labor laws; however, laws were not enforced. Children were engaged in child labor, including the worst forms of child labor, many of them in agriculture, domestic service, and automotive repair; however, data on the extent of child labor was not available. Children in rural areas assisted with farming, fetched firewood and water, and herded livestock. In urban areas children worked in small-scale manufacturing, car and bicycle repair shops, tea and coffee shops, or the transportation of grain and other goods via donkey carts. Some children worked in the streets cleaning cars or selling cigarettes, newspapers, or chewing gum.

The government sets wages for union workers, employees of PFDJ-owned enterprises, and government employees. There is no national minimum wage for the private sector. The standard workweek was 44.5 hours, but forced overtime without fair compensation was often required by employers. There are no prohibitions against excessive overtime. Workers were legally entitled to overtime pay, except for those employed under national service, but this was not enforced. Workers were entitled to one rest day per week; most received one to one-and-one-half days off. There were no known occupational health and safety standards or enforcement mechanisms.

Civil service employees and national service recruits were paid according to a fixed scale, the most common salary being 500 nakfa ($33) per month. For most professions wages had not increased for more than a decade despite high inflation. Inspection and enforcement were nonexistent or varied widely among work places. In practice some workers removed themselves from dangerous work sites without retaliation.

Abuses pertaining to wage, overtime, or safety and health standards were common in all sectors. During 2011 there was discrimination against foreign or migrant workers, especially Ethiopians, who could not receive food coupons and were periodically arrested without cause and not released until they paid a fine.

U.S.-ERITREAN RELATIONS

The United States established diplomatic relations with Eritrea in 1993, following its independence and separation from Ethiopia. The United States supported Eritrea's independence, but U.S.-Eritrea relations became strained as a result of the 2001 government crackdown against political dissidents and others, the closure of the independent press, and limits on civil liberties, which has persisted to this day.

Eritrea's authoritarian regime is controlled entirely by the president, who heads the sole political party; that party has ruled the country since 1991. Elections have not taken place since then. Regionally, Eritrea has had military confrontations with Ethiopia and Djibouti over border disputes It has also been cited by the UN for destabilizing activities in the broader Horn of Africa.

U.S. interests in Eritrea include encouraging Eritrea to contribute to regional stability, reconciling ongoing disputes with Ethiopia and Djibouti, urging progress toward a democratic political culture, citing and addresses human rights issues, and promoting economic reform.

U.S. Assistance to Eritrea

At the Eritrean Government's request, the United States no longer provides bilateral assistance to Eritrea. The U.S. has no military-to-military cooperation with Eritrea.

Bilateral Economic Relations

Eritrea's Government and ruling party control the economy. The United States and Eritrea have very little bilateral trade. Eritrea is a member of the Common Market for Eastern and Southern Africa, which has a Trade and Investment Framework Agreement with the United States.

Eritrea's Membership in International Organizations

Eritrea and the United States belong to a number of the same international organizations, including the United Nations, International Monetary Fund, and World Bank.

Bilateral Representation

Eritrea maintains an embassy in the United States at 1708 New Hampshire Ave., NW, Washington, DC 20009 (tel. 202-319-1991).

Principal U.S. Embassy Officials

Last Updated: 1/14/2013

ASMARA (E) 179 Alaa Street. P.O.Box 211, Asmara, 291-1-120004, Fax 291-1-127584, INMARSAT Tel 00-871-683-142-188, Workweek: Mon-Thu 0800-1800; Fri 0800-1200, http://asmara.usembassy.gov/

DCM OMS:	Vacant
AMB OMS:	Maria Fotheringham
MGT:	Acting DCM Peter Wessel
POL/ECON:	Debra Johnson
POSHO:	Michael Fotheringham
SPSH:	Vacant
AMB:	Vacant
CON:	John Paul Schutz
DCM:	Charge Sue Bremner
PAO:	Debra Johnson
GSO:	Michael Fotheringham

RSO: Lisa Baisden
AFSA: Vacant
CLO: Vacant
EEO: Vacant
ICASS Chair: Vacant
IMO: Michael Fotheringham
ISSO: Ken Wolf
State ICASS: Vacant

TRAVEL

Consular Information Sheet

December 10, 2012

Country Description: Eritrea is a poor East African country, the capital of which is Asmara. Formerly a province of Ethiopia, Eritrea became an independent country on May 24, 1993, following a 30-year struggle that culminated in an overwhelming referendum vote for independence. Tourism facilities are very limited.

Smart Traveler Enrollment Program (STEP)/Embassy Locations: If you are going to live in or visit Eritrea, please take the time to tell our Embassy about your trip. If you enroll, we can keep you up to date with important safety and security announcements. It will also help your friends and family get in touch with you in an emergency.

U.S. Embassy Eritrea
179 Alaa Street, PO Box 211, Asmara
Telephone: (291-1) 12-00-04
Facsimile: (291-1) 124-255
and (291-1) 127-584

Entry/Exit Requirements for U.S. Citizens: You should have a passport and valid visa prior to arrival; visas are not generally available at the airport. Travelers visiting Eritrea using a foreign passport do not need an exit visa, provided they leave before the expiration of their entrance visa. Persons staying beyond the visa expiration date may be subject to fines or imprisonment, or be required to remain in Eritrea for an extended period while their case is reviewed in court. All long-term residents regardless of citizenship must obtain an exit visa prior to departure, unless they hold a difficult-to-obtain multiple entry visas. Upon entry and exit, visitors must declare all foreign currency, and may be asked to declare electronic equipment such as cameras, computers, and video equipment. Visitors must save all receipts for foreign exchange and present these upon departure to account for all foreign currency spent in Eritrea. Failure to report foreign currency or meet customs requirements usually results in both a fine and imprisonment. There is a $20 airport departure tax.

With a valid local residence ID it is possible to pay in local currency; otherwise payment must be made in U.S. dollars. Information about the airport tax and entry/exit requirements is available from the Embassy of Eritrea, 1708 New Hampshire Avenue NW, Washington, DC 20009; telephone (202) 319-1991; fax (202) 319-1304. Overseas, inquiries may be made at the nearest Eritrean embassy or consulate.

U.S. citizens born in Eritrea, to Eritrean parents, or who in any other way appear to have Eritrean origins, are required by the Government of Eritrea to register with the Immigration and Nationality office in Asmara within seven business days of their entry into the country. The Eritrean government sometimes subjects U.S. citizens of Eritrean heritage to the same entry/exit requirements as Eritrean citizens.

HIV/AIDS Restrictions: The U.S. Department of State is unaware of any HIV/AIDS entry restrictions for visitors to or foreign residents of Eritrea.

Threats to Safety and Security: Eritrea and Ethiopia fought a border war from 1998–2000. United Nations peacekeepers patrolled the border until March 2008, when Government of Eritrea diesel fuel restrictions resulted in the peacekeepers' withdrawal. Both Eritrea and Ethiopia maintain large military presences along the border and all border crossings into Ethiopia from Eritrea remain closed. U.S. citizens are strongly advised to avoid travel near the Eritrean-Ethiopian border and to the Southern Red Sea region, including the port of Assab, as there have been military tensions in these areas.

Landmines and unexploded ordnance remain a serious problem throughout the country. There are reports of accidents and incidents where vehicles and people occasionally detonate mines. Many detonations occurred on relatively well-traveled roads in and near the Gash Barka region of western Eritrea; subsequent investigations indicated that several mines were recently laid. In September 2011, press reported that a vehicle in Senafe, 60 miles south of Asmara, ran over a landmine, killing five persons and injuring the 34 others. Vast areas of the country still have not been certified free of mines and unexploded ordnance left over from both the 30-year war for independence and the subsequent 1998–2000 conflict with Ethiopia. U.S. citizens should avoid walking alone and hiking in riverbeds or areas that local government officials have not certified as safe.

Although Eritrea and Sudan have diplomatic relations, the procedures for crossing their common border are variable and subject to change. Overland travel between the two countries is dangerous and ill-advised. Travelers crossing from Eritrea to Sudan north and west of the Keren-Barentu road risk becoming victims of banditry, kidnapping or insurgent activity. Numerous incidents have been reported since 2008, apparently involving insurgents or criminals in this area. The U.S. Embassy also received reports of sporadic bombings of vehicles and government facilities in the Gash Barka region near Sudan in 2007 and 2008. If travel near the Eritrean-Sudanese border is essential, travelers should consult both the Eritrean authorities and the U.S. Embassy in advance. Foreign travelers who wish to visit any area outside of Asmara must apply at least ten days in advance for a travel permit from the Eritrean government.

U.S. citizens are urged to avoid sailing off the coast of Eritrea. In August 2011, three separate incidents of piracy were reported off the Eritrean coast near the port of Assab. Multiple high-speed skiffs with armed persons onboard continue to attack merchant vessels. If transit around the Horn of Africa is necessary, it is strongly recommended that vessels travel in convoys, maintain good communications contact at all times, and follow the guidance provided by the Maritime Security Center—Horn of Africa (MSC-HOA). U.S. citizens should consult the Maritime Administration's Horn of Africa Piracy page for information on maritime advisories, self-protection measures, and naval forces in the region.

U.S. citizens are also urged to avoid remote Eritrean islands, some which have Eritrean military facilities.

Stay up to date by:

- Bookmarking our Bureau of Consular Affairs website, which contains the current Travel Warnings and Travel Alerts as well as the Worldwide Caution.
- Following us on Twitter and the Bureau of Consular Affairs page on Facebook as well.
- You can also download our free Smart Traveler App, available through iTunes and the Android market, to have travel information at your fingertips. Calling 1-888-407-4747 toll-free within the U.S. and Canada, or a regular toll line, 1-202-501-4444, from other countries.
- Taking some time before travel to consider your personal security.

Crime: Crime in Asmara has increased due to deteriorating economic conditions along with persistent food, water, and fuel shortages, and rapid price inflation. Travelers should exercise vigilance in their personal security and take safety precautions regarding the valuables they carry and areas they visit. Eritrean authorities have limited capacity to deter or investigate crime or prosecute perpetrators.

Don't buy counterfeit and pirated goods, even if they are widely available. Not only are the bootlegs illegal in the United States, if you purchase them you may also be breaking local law. Do not attempt to take advantage of street or black market exchange in foreign currency. It is illegal and there are extremely stiff penalties. Utilize government exchange at the airport, hotel or bank.

Victims of Crime: If you or someone you know becomes the victim of a crime abroad, you should contact the local police and the nearest U.S. embassy or consulate. We can:

- Replace a stolen passport.
- Help you find appropriate medical care if you are the victim of violent crimes such as assault or rape.
- Put you in contact with the appropriate police authorities, and if you want us to, we cancontact family members or friend.
- Help you understand the local criminal justice process and direct you to local attorneys, although it is important to remember that local authorities are responsible for investigating and prosecuting the crime.

Criminal Penalties: While you are in Eritrea, you are subject to its laws even if you are a U.S. citizen. Foreign laws and legal systems are vastly different than our own. You may be taken in for questioning if you don't have your passport or identification with you. It is illegal to take pictures of government buildings.

Driving under the influence could land you immediately in jail, as could a traffic accident, whether or not you are at fault. There are also some things that might be legal in the country you visit, but still illegal in the United States; for example you can be prosecuted under U.S. law if you buy pirated goods in Eritrea, even if you are not prosecuted in Eritrea.

Engaging in sexual conduct with children or using or disseminating child pornography in a foreign country is a crime prosecutable in the United States. If you break local laws in Eritrea, your U.S. passport won't help you avoid arrest or prosecution. It's very important to know what's legal and what's not where you are going.

Persons violating Eritrea's laws, even unknowingly, may be expelled, arrested, or imprisoned. Penalties for possessing, using, or trafficking in illegal drugs in Eritrea are severe, and convicted offenders can expect long jail sentences and heavy fines.

Arrest notifications in Eritrea: Based on the Vienna Convention on Consular Relations, bilateral agreements with certain countries, and customary international law, if you are arrested in Eritrea, you have the option to request that the police, prison officials, or other authorities alert the nearest U.S. embassy or consulate of your arrest, and to have communications from you forwarded to the nearest U.S. embassy or consulate. However, in Eritrea, contrary to the Vienna Convention, such requests are not generally granted.

Special Circumstances: The Government of Eritrea requires all foreign residents including diplomats to apply 10 days in advance for travel outside of Asmara city limits. This restriction can delay or prevent the Embassy from providing emergency assistance to U.S. citizens outside of Asmara since U.S. diplomatic personnel are not excluded from this restriction.

The consular section of the U.S. Embassy in Asmara has been closed for most visa services since February 2007. It is fully open for American Citizen Services in Eritrea, including reports of birth, passports, and notarial services. Currency exchange on the street is illegal.

Eritrea has complicated citizenship laws and does not recognize renunciation of Eritrean citizenship. Dual nationals who enter the country on Eritrean travel documents are treated as Eritrean citizens, regardless of their other citizenship. U.S. citizens born in Eritrea, or who otherwise are considered to have acquired Eritrean citizenship, may be subject to certain obligations, including being drafted into national service, regardless of the documents they present at entry. (National service is approximately nine months of military training, followed by an often unspecified and open-ended number of years in military or other government service.) In some cases, U.S. citizens of dual nationality and Eritrean Lawful Permanent Residents of the United States have not been allowed to leave Eritrea as they have been drafted into national service.

U.S.-Eritrean dual nationals who enter the country on an Eritrean passport or national ID card must obtain an exit visa prior to departure. The exit visa application process can significantly delay travel plans. Exit visas may be denied, even for persons who entered Eritrea legally. Eritrean dual nationals are required to pay a 2% income tax on overseas earnings to the Eritrean Government prior to being granted an exit visa. Additionally, Eritrean authorities sometimes do not allow Eritreans who left the country after 1993 to depart Eritrea after visiting the country, even if they have a U.S. passport and a valid Eritrean visa.

Dual nationals cannot obtain civil documents such as birth and death certificates, marriage and divorce certificates, educational transcripts, property ownership records, or court records without proof of payment of the 2% income tax. The only exception is for hardship purposes (students and those unable to work) and this must be stated in writing by an Eritrean Embassy abroad only after registering there.

Persons of dual nationality are at risk of being arrested or held without charge for questioning. The Eritrean government does not recognize the U.S. citizenship of dual nationals. It will not inform the U.S. Embassy of the arrest of U.S. citizens, and has not responded favorably to requests by Embassy officials to visit incarcerated U.S. citizens. When arrested, a person may be held for many days without being told the purpose of his or her incarceration. Conditions are harsh—those incarcerated may be held in very small quarters without access to restrooms, bedding, food or clean water. Visitors are advised to exercise caution when taking photographs in Eritrea. Foreigners in Asmara have been harassed and detained by local police and plainclothes security officials for taking photographs of street scenes in the city. No law has been cited, but the justifications given have been that unmarked government buildings are in the background and/or that the pictures are being taken illegally for commercial reasons.

All foreign nationals in Eritrea are required to apply for permits to travel outside of Asmara. Travel permits must be presented upon request. Although formal police checkpoints no longer exist, persons have been asked to present travel permits at beaches, restaurants, and social events, so lack of formal police checkpoints should not discourage travelers from legally obtaining a travel permit. Persons have been jailed for not being able to show a valid travel permit. Applications for travel permits are available at the two Ministry of Tourism offices located on Harnet Avenue and Airport Road.

Accessibility: While in Eritrea, individuals with disabilities may find accessibility and accommodation limited, although the government is committed to equal access for the handicapped. Eritrea is not able to comply with ADA standards but there are more accommodations for handicapped persons in Eritrea than in most developing countries. The majority of persons using wheelchairs do so in the streets rather than on the sidewalks, due to lack of sidewalks. Pedestrians must also often walk on the street for the same reason.

Medical Facilities and Health Information: Medical facilities and physicians in Eritrea are limited. In 2010, the Eritrean government closed all private medical clinics and laboratories. Travelers should carry their own supplies of prescription drugs and preventative medicines because pharmaceuticals may be in short supply. Food and water-borne illnesses are very common among travelers, so drink only bottled or purified water and eat foods that are cooked or peeled. Malaria and dengue fever are serious risks to travelers in the lowlands of Eritrea, particularly during the rainy season (November to February). One of the worst dengue fever outbreaks in recent Eritrean history occurred during the winter of 2009–10 in Massawa. Asmara, because of its altitude, is generally considered free of these mosquito-borne illnesses. Travelers to the lowlands are urged to carry mosquito repellent and mosquito nets, especially during the rainy season.

You can find detailed information on vaccinations and other health precautions on the CDC website. For information about outbreaks of infectious diseases abroad, consult the World Health Organization (WHO) website. The WHO website also contains additional health information for travelers, including detailed country-specific health information.

Medical Insurance: You can't assume your insurance will go with you when you travel. It's very important to find out BEFORE you leave whether or not your medical insurance will cover you overseas. You need to ask your insurance company two questions:

- Does my policy apply when I'm out of the United States?
- Will it cover emergencies like a trip to a foreign hospital or a medical evacuation?

In many places, doctors and hospitals still expect payment in cash at the time of service. Your regular U.S. health insurance may not cover doctor and hospital visits in other countries. If your policy doesn't go with you when you travel, it's a very good idea to take out another one for your trip.

Traffic Safety and Road Conditions: While in Eritrea, you may encounter road conditions that differ significantly from those in the United States. According to the World Health Organization's first report on global road safety in September 2009, Eritrea's roads are deadly. The roads between major cities (Asmara, Massawa, Mendefera, Dekemhare, Barentu, and Keren) are paved and in relatively good condition, though winding mountain roads do not generally have guardrails.

Secondary roads and roads in remote areas are usually unpaved and in poor condition. U.S. citizens should avoid traveling on these roads, especially at night. Bad weather can also make the condition of poor roads worse. If you must take unpaved roads, check first with local government and village officials as new minefields continue to be discovered. Even in Asmara city, some road surfaces have deteriorated to dangerous conditions. Eritreans are found travelling on foot nearly everywhere due to lack of transportation, often dressed in dark clothing and in unlit areas at night, which creates unpredictable and dangerous situations on roads. Street lighting may not exist in some locations, and power outages continue to leave some neighborhoods in the dark. Speed limits may not be obeyed. Travelers should check with the Embassy of Eritrea regarding drivers' license requirements prior to your traveling to Eritrea.

Landmines and unexploded ordnance litter the countryside in many areas, occasionally causing injuries and deaths. Although the UN conducted de-mining efforts until late 2007, evidence of new mines has been reported, particularly in areas near the Ethiopian border. All areas that are not well traveled are potentially dangerous due to live mines, especially north and west of Keren. There are also minefields near Massawa, Ghinda, Agordat, Barentu, south of Tessenae, Nakfa, Adi Keih, Arezza, Dekemhare, and in a roughly 40-kilometer (24.8 mile) wide region just west of the Eritrean-Ethiopian border between the Setit and Mereb Rivers.

Many Eritreans use inexpensive public transportation, especially bus service. Travelers should avoid taking buses due to extreme over-crowding. Taxis are plentiful and inexpensive in Asmara, but usually carry multiple passengers along pre-defined routes. If an empty taxi is available, a customer may request a "contract" taxi, which accepts no additional passengers, for a higher fixed price. Drivers should be aware of heavy and erratic pedestrian, livestock, and bicycle traffic obstructing vehicle flow. Children and the elderly sometimes wander into the path of moving traffic, as do slow, motorized carts. Elderly or disabled people may not always yield to faster moving traffic.

Aviation Safety Oversight: As there is no direct commercial air service to the United States by carriers registered in Eritrea, the U.S. Federal Aviation Administration (FAA) has not assessed the government of Eritrea's Civil Aviation Authority for compliance with International Civil Aviation Organization (ICAO) aviation safety standards. Further information may be found on the FAA's safety assessment page.

Children's Issues: Please see the U.S. Dept. of State Office of Children's Issues web pages on intercountry adoption and international parental child abduction.

Travel Warning

November 29, 2012

The U.S. Department of State continues to warn U.S. citizens of the risks of travel to Eritrea and strongly recommends U.S. citizens defer all travel to the country. This replaces the Travel Warning for Eritrea of April 18, 2012, to update information on security incidents, including attacks near the border with Ethiopia, and to remind U.S. citizens of ongoing security concerns in Eritrea.

The Eritrean government continues to restrict the travel of all foreign nationals. These restrictions require all visitors and residents, including U.S. diplomats, to apply 10 days in advance for permission to travel outside Asmara's city limits. Permission is rarely granted. As a result, the U.S. Embassy is extremely limited in its ability to provide emergency consular assistance outside of Asmara.

A number of Eritrean-U.S. dual citizens have been arrested and some are currently being held without apparent cause. Once arrested, detainees may be held for extended periods without being told the reason for their incarceration. Conditions are harsh—those incarcerated may be held in very small quarters without access to restrooms, bedding, food, or clean water. The Eritrean government does not inform the U.S. Embassy when U.S. citizens, including those who are not dual nationals, have been arrested or detained. Should the U.S. Embassy learn of the arrest of a U.S. citizen, the Eritrean government rarely allows consular access, regardless of the reason the U.S. citizen is being held.

U.S. citizens are cautioned to carry appropriate documentation with them at all times. Those not carrying documentation of their identity and military status may be subject to round-ups, sometimes by armed persons. U.S. citizens are advised to exercise caution around armed persons.

The Eritrean government-controlled media frequently broadcasts anti-U.S. rhetoric, and has done so repeatedly since December 2009, when the United Nations Security Council (UNSC) first imposed sanctions on Eritrea. Anti-U.S. messages scripted by the current regime, which often appear as cover stories in the sole English-language state-run newspaper in Eritrea, have grown even stronger since UNSC sanctions were strengthened in December 2011.

Although there have been no specific incidents of violence targeting U.S. citizens, U.S. citizens are urged to exercise caution, stay current with media coverage of local events, and be aware of their surroundings at all times.

U.S. citizens are strongly advised to avoid travel near the Eritrean-Ethiopian border and the Southern Red Sea region. U.S. citizens should be aware of the presence of large numbers of Eritrean and Ethiopian troops along the Eritrean-Ethiopian border and of political and military tensions between the two countries. On March 15, 2012, Ethiopian troops attacked three locations approximately 10 miles inside Eritrean territory. On January 16, 2012, a group of tourists was attacked in Ethiopia not far from the Eritrean-Ethiopian border. Five tourists were killed and four others kidnapped. In May 2010, 13 people were injured when a bomb exploded on a bus just over the border in Ethiopia. In April 2010, a bomb near the border in Ethiopia killed five people and injured 20. In January and February 2010, skirmishes between Eritrean and Ethiopian troops resulted in military fatalities.

Although Eritrean forces have withdrawn from disputed territory at the border with Djibouti, tensions in this area remain high.

U.S. citizens on ships and sailing vessels are strongly advised not to sail off the Eritrean coast nor to attempt to dock in Eritrean ports or travel through Eritrean waters. U.S. citizens are also urged to avoid remote Eritrean islands, some of which may be used for Eritrean military training and could therefore be unsafe. The Eritrean government does not issue visas to persons arriving by marine vessel. Additionally, fuel and provisions are often unavailable in Massawa and other parts of Eritrea, and are often scarce in the capital city of Asmara.

In April 2012, the Yemeni government reported that three Yemeni sailors continue to be held in Eritrean prisons three years after their boat inadvertently sailed into Eritrean waters. Yemen also reported at the end of March 2012 that Eritrean boats had attacked four Yemeni fishing boats in international waters. In February 2012, a U.S. company reported that two of its vessels were seized by Eritrean authorities in the Port of Massawa, where they had sought assistance after one vessel was distressed while off the Eritrean coast. To date, neither vessels nor crew have been released. In December 2010, a British ship attempting to refuel in Massawa was detained by Eritrean authorities, and its crew of four was held without consular access for six months before being released. There are reports of additional vessels carrying nationals from other countries being detained for several months. In nearly all cases, the Eritrean government has neither given a reason for detention nor granted consular access. The port of Assab is closed to private marine vessels.

In August 2011, three separate incidents of piracy were reported off the Eritrean coast near the port of Assab. High-speed skiffs with armed persons on board continue to attack merchant vessels. If transit around the Horn of Africa is necessary, vessels should travel in convoys, maintain good communications contact at all times, and follow the guidance provided by the Maritime Security Center—Horn of Africa (MSC-HOA). U.S. citizens should consult the Maritime Administration's Horn of Africa Piracy page for information on maritime advisories, self-protection measures, and naval forces in the region.

Landmines and unexploded ordnance remain a serious problem throughout the country. There are reports of accidents and incidents in which vehicles or people occasionally detonate mines. Many detonations occurred on relatively well-traveled roads in and near the Gash Barka region of western Eritrea; subsequent investigations indicated that several mines were recently laid. In September 2011, press reported that a vehicle in Senafe, 60 miles south of Asmara, ran over a landmine; five people were killed and another 34 injured in the incident. Vast areas of the country still have not been certified free of mines and unexploded ordnance following the 30-year war for independence and the subsequent 1998–2000 conflict with Ethiopia. You should avoid walking alone and hiking in riverbeds or areas that local government officials have not certified as safe.

U.S. citizens choosing to travel to Eritrea despite this Travel Warning must obtain an Eritrean visa before their arrival. Persons arriving in Eritrea without a visa are generally refused admission and returned on the next flight back to their point of origin. However, the Embassy is aware of persons being jailed for several months after arriving without a visa. The Embassy urges Eritrean-U.S. dual citizens to obtain an Eritrean visa in their U.S. passport before travelling to Eritrea and to enter the country as U.S. citizens. Eritrean-U.S. dual citizens who enter Eritrea with an Eritrean ID card may find it difficult to obtain the required visa to legally exit the country. The Embassy is aware of numerous cases where dual Eritrean-U.S. citizens have not been permitted to leave the country. The Embassy cautions travelers not to stay beyond the period of time granted at the time of admission by Eritrean Immigration.

Crime in Asmara has increased as a result of deteriorating economic conditions accompanied by persistent food, water, and fuel shortages, and rapid price inflation. The combination of forced, open-ended, low-paying, national service for many Eritreans and severe unemployment leads some Eritreans to commit crime to support their families. Eritrean authorities have limited capacity to deter or investigate crime or prosecute perpetrators.

Modern telecommunications options are limited in Eritrea and cannot be counted upon in an emergency. International cell phone service plans do not work on Eritrean networks. Local cellular phone service is tightly controlled by the Eritrean government and difficult to obtain. When available, international cell phone calls are extremely expensive and only available using pre-paid minutes. Internet cafés are rare and hours are limited. Internet service is limited and slow, and generally does not support Voice over Internet Protocol (VoIP) services such as Skype.

The U.S. Embassy in Asmara strongly encourages U.S. citizens who travel to or remain in Eritrea despite this Travel Warning to enroll in the Smart Traveler Enrollment Program (STEP) so you can receive the most up-to-date security information.

Please keep all of your information in STEP current. It is important when enrolling or updating information to include multiple phone numbers and email addresses to facilitate communication in the event of an emergency.

The consular section of the U.S. Embassy in Asmara, though closed for most visa services, is open for all U.S. citizen services between the hours of 2:00 pm and 4:00 pm Monday through Thursday, or by appointment. The U.S. Embassy in Asmara is located at 179 Alaa Street, P.O. Box 211, Asmara; telephone +291-1-12-00-04, available 24 hours in case of emergency; fax +291-1-124-255 and +291-1-127-584.

Current information on safety and security can also be obtained by calling 1-888-407-4747 toll-free in the United States and Canada or, a regular toll line at-1-202-501-4444 for callers from other countries. These numbers are available from 8:00 a.m. to 8:00 p.m. Eastern Time, Monday through Friday (except U.S. federal holidays). You can also stay up to date by bookmarking our Bureau of Consular Affairs website, which contains the current Worldwide Caution. Follow us on Twitter and the Bureau of Consular Affairs page on Facebook as well. You can also download our free Smart Traveler App, available through iTunes and the Android market, to have travel information at your fingertips.

Intercountry Adoption

May 2012

The information in this section has been edited from the latest report available as of February 2013 from the State Department Bureau of Consular Affairs, Office of Overseas Citizens Services. For more information, please read the *Intercountry Adoption* section of this book and review current reports online at http://adoption.state.gov.

Eritrea is not party to the Hague Convention on Protection of Children and Co-operation in Respect of Intercountry Adoption (Hague Adoption Convention). Intercountry adoptions of children from non-Hague countries are processed in accordance with 8 Code of Federal Regulations, Section 204.3 as it relates to orphans as defined under the Immigration and Nationality Act, Section 101(b)(1)(F).

The body of law that applies to adoptions in the State of Eritrea is not codified as a single adoption law. Regulations change often and without notice to the U.S. Embassy in Asmara, Eritrea or other foreign entities. Enforcement of laws and regulations is irregular at times. The Department of State recommends prospective adoptive parents verify requirements with legal counsel experienced in adoption law in Eritrea or directly with the Eritrean authorities. In the U.S. Embassy's experience, all adoptions by U.S. citizens are by Eritrean-American dual nationals, because Eritrean law requires at least one parent to be of Eritrean heritage. Most adoption cases involve older teen-aged children where one parent has died and one parent has abandoned the child. It is usually difficult to prove that the child meets the U.S. immigration requirements for "orphan."

Who Can Adopt? To bring an adopted child to the United States from Eritrea you must meet eligibility and suitability requirements. The U.S. Department of Homeland Security, U.S. Citizenship and Immigration Services (USCIS) determines who can adopt under U.S. immigration law. Additionally, a child must meet the definition of orphan under U.S. immigration law in order to be eligible to immigrate to the United States on an IR-3 or IR-4 immigrant visa. In addition to U.S. immigration requirements, you must also meet the following requirements in order to adopt a child from Eritrea.

Residency: A 2011 Eritrean proclamation stipulates that at least one adoptive parent must be of Eritrean heritage and have completed national service in order to adopt an Eritrean child.

Age of Adopting Parents: Not specified.

Marriage: Prospective adoptive parents may be single or married.

Income: Not specified.

Other Requirements: Eritrea is an extremely conservative country, and same-sex couples would likely not be allowed to adopt in Eritrea.

Who Can Be Adopted? In addition to U.S. immigration requirements, Eritrea has specific requirements that a child must meet in order to be eligible for adoption:

Relinquishment: Not specified.

Abandonment: Not specified.

Age of Adoptive Child: Not specified. The U.S. Embassy is aware of final, local adoptions of infants younger than one year and teenagers older than 18 years.

Sibling Adoptions: Not specified.

Special Needs or Medical Conditions: Not specified.

Waiting Period or Foster Care: Not specified.

Eritrea's Adoption Authority: Ministry of Labor and Human Welfare

The Process: The recommended first step in adopting a child from Eritrea is to decide whether or not to use a licensed adoption service provider in the United States that can help you with your adoption. Adoption service providers must be licensed by the U.S. state in which they operate.

There are no official adoption agencies in Eritrea. However, the Ministry of Labor and Human Welfare facilitates and oversees both domestic and intercountry adoptions.

If there is a request regarding an intercountry adoption, the Ministry of Labor and Human Welfare assists with the processing and obtaining documentation regarding the adoption. In the event prospective adoptive parents wish to consult an attorney, a list of attorneys can be obtained from the U.S. Embassy in Asmara website. Neither the U.S. Embassy nor the Department of State can vouch for the efficacy or professionalism of attorneys on this list.

In order to adopt a child from Eritrea, you will need to meet the requirements of the Government of Eritrea and U.S. immigration law. You must submit an application to be found eligible to adopt with the Ministry of Labor and Human Welfare of Eritrea.

You may also file an I-600A, Application for Advance Processing of an Orphan Petition with U.S. Department of Homeland Security's U.S. Citizenship and Immigration Services to be found eligible and suitable to adopt.

If you are eligible to adopt, and a child is available for intercountry adoption, the central adoption authority or other authorized entity in Eritrea will provide you with a referral. Each family must decide for itself whether or not it will be able to meet the needs of and provide a permanent home for a particular child.

Role of the Adoption Authority: The Ministry of Labor and Human Welfare facilitates and oversees both domestic and intercountry adoptions.

Role of the Court: All adoptions must be finalized through the office of the Ministry of Labor and Human Welfare and/or by the High Court. Prospective adoptive parents must first work with local clerks of the municipal government of the area where the child resides to obtain a statement that transfers authority from the biological parent(s) or relative (if available) or the Ministry of Labor and Human Welfare to the prospective adoptive parents. Prospective adoptive parents submit the request for transfer of authority and the application to adopt to the High Court. The High Court issues a decision based on their statement and the court's satisfaction of the decision done in the best interests of the child. The adoption goes into effect as of the date the High Court's judge signs the petition.

Role of Adoption Agencies: There are no official adoption agencies in Eritrea.

Adoption Application: Most children in orphanages are abandoned children, i.e., they have no living parents or relatives to care for them. The Ministry of Labor and Human Welfare has custody of abandoned children and the authority to place these children with prospective adoptive parents.

However, some children residing in orphanages also have surviving parent(s) and/or distant relatives. Before adopting a child, prospective adoptive parents should consider speaking with legal counsel to ensure the child meets the definition of orphan under U.S. immigration law.

For the child to exit Eritrea, an exit visa is required. Eritrean Immigration will place an exit visa in the child's Eritrean passport. The fee for this service is about $7.

If the child will transit through Frankfurt, Germany, or Amsterdam, Netherlands, en route to the United States, a Schengen States transit visa is required. Adoptive parents can apply for a Schengen States transit visa at the Dutch Embassy in Asmara (about $45). However, if the child remains in the Frankfurt airport, the child doesn't need a transit visa. An adopted Eritrean child transiting the Amsterdam airport will still need a transit visa.

Time Frame: The adoption process takes approximately six months, but can take longer.

Adoption Fees: Prospective adoptive parents are required under Eritrean law to retain an attorney for adoption proceedings. Adoption fees paid to the attorney vary.

Documents Required:

- A written statement from the prospective adoptive parents explaining why an Eritrean child is preferred;
- Original birth certificate(s) of the prospective adoptive parent(s);
- Original marriage license/certificate, if applicable. Note - If originals are not available, certified copies must be authenticated by the Department of State or U.S. Embassy Asmara;
- An original Eritrean police clearance for each of the prospective adoptive parent(s) including those residing in Eritrea;
- A medical certificate/clearance for each of the prospective adoptive parent(s);
- The original home study prepared by a qualified social worker and the agency's recommendation regarding your suitability as an adoptive parent with an original translation into Tigrigna.);
- Evidence of economic status, which must include a letter from prospective adoptive parents' employer showing salary, date of employment, position in the organization and a bank statement;
- Proof of life insurance and health insurance, other proof of income or assets may also be submitted;
- Three letters of reference from friends, relatives, church or other sources qualified to assess prospective adoptive parents' character, the stability of marriage, and ability to parent;
- Two passport-size photographs of the prospective adopting parent(s);
- If the prospective adoptive parent(s) do not come to Eritrea together to oversee this entire process, then they must execute a power of attorney for their adoption agency, or if only one parent will travel to Eritrea, the other parent must execute a power of attorney for him/her;
- "Obligation of Adoption or Social Welfare Agency" signed by the adoption agency handling the

adoption, or for private adopters, from the organization that provided the home study, or by the parents' employer;

- Verification by the adoption agency or home study organization on the child's qualification for naturalization under the laws of the parents' country of residence with an original translation into Tigrigna.

Additional documents may be requested. You may be asked to provide proof that a document from the United States is authentic.

Bringing Your Child Home: Once your adoption is complete (or you have obtained legal custody of the child), there are a few more steps to take before you can head home. Specifically, you need to apply for several documents for your child before he or she can travel to the United States, such as a birth certificate, a passport or travel document for your child from the country in which he or she was born, and a U.S. Immigration Visa. For detailed and updated information on how to obtain these documents, review the *Intercountry Adoption* section in this publication and visit the U.S. Department of State Intercountry Adoption website at http://adoption.state.gov.

Child Citizenship Act: For adoptions finalized abroad, the Child Citizenship Act of 2000 allows your new child to acquire American citizenship automatically when he or she enters the United States as lawful permanent residents. For adoptions finalized in the United States, the Child Citizenship Act of 2000 allows your new child to acquire American citizenship automatically when the court in the United States issues the final adoption decree. To learn more, review the *Intercountry Adoption* section in this publication and visit the U.S. Department of State Intercountry Adoption website at http://adoption.state.gov.

After Adoption: There are no post-adoption reporting requirements.

U.S. Embassy in Eritrea
Address: 179 Alaa Street
P.O. Box 211
Asmara, Eritrea
Tel: (291)(1) 12-00-04
Fax: (291)(1) 12-75-84
Email: ConsularAsmara@state.gov
Internet: eritrea.usembassy.gov/

Eritrea's Adoption Authority
Address: Ministry of Labor and Human Welfare
P. O. Box 5252
Asmara, Eritrea
Tel: (291) 1-151846

Embassy of Eritrea
Address: 1708 New Hampshire Ave, NW
Washington, DC 20009
Tel: (202) 319-1991
Fax: (202) 319-1304
Email: girma@embassyeritrea.org
Internet: embassyeritrea.org/

Office of Children's Issues
U.S. Department of State
2201 C Street, NW
SA-29
Washington, DC 20520
Tel: 1-888-407-4747
E-mail: AskCI@state.gov
http://adoption.state.gov

For questions about immigration procedures, call the National Customer Service Center (NCSC) at 1-800-375-5283 (TTY 1-800-767-1833).

ESTONIA

Compiled from publications that were available as of February 2013 from the U.S. Department of State, the U.S. Department of Commerce, and the Central Intelligence Agency (CIA). See the introduction to this set for explanatory notes.

Official Name:
Republic of Estonia

PROFILE

Geography

Area: total: 45,228 sq km; country comparison to the world: 133; land: 42,388 sq km; water: 2,840 sq km

Major cities: Tallinn (capital) 399,000 (2009)

Climate: maritime; wet, moderate winters, cool summers

Terrain: marshy, lowlands; flat in the north, hilly in the south

People

Nationality: noun: Estonian(s); adjective: Estonian

Population: 1,274,709 (July 2012 est.)

Population growth rate: -0.65% (2012 est.)

Ethnic groups: Estonian 68.7%, Russian 25.6%, Ukrainian 2.1%, Belarusian 1.2%, Finn 0.8%, other 1.6% (2008 census)

Religions: Evangelical Lutheran 13.6%, Orthodox 12.8%, other Christian (including Methodist, Seventh-Day Adventist, Roman Catholic, Pentecostal) 1.4%, unaffiliated 34.1%, other and unspecified 32%, none 6.1% (2000 census)

Languages: Estonian (official) 67.3%, Russian 29.7%, other 2.3%, unknown 0.7% (2000 census)

Literacy: definition: age 15 and over can read and write; total population: 99.8%; male: 99.8%; female: 99.8% (2010 census)

Health: life expectancy at birth: total population: 73.58 years; male: 68.3 years; female: 79.19 years (2012 est.); Infant mortality rate: total: 6.94 deaths/1,000 live births; male: 8.07 deaths/1,000 live births; female: 5.74 deaths/1,000 live births (2012 est.)

Unemployment rate: 11.5% (2012 est.)

Work force: 675,900 (2012 est.)

Government

Type: parliamentary republic

Independence: 20 August 1991

Constitution: adopted 28 June 1992

Political subdivisions: 15 counties (maakonnad, singular—maakond); Harjumaa (Tallinn), Hiiumaa (Kardla), Ida-Virumaa (Johvi), Jarvamaa (Paide), Jogevamaa (Jogeva), Laanemaa (Haapsalu), Laane-Virumaa (Rakvere), Parnumaa (Parnu), Polvamaa (Polva), Raplamaa (Rapla), Saaremaa (Kuressaare), Tartumaa (Tartu), Valgamaa (Valga), Viljandimaa (Viljandi), Vorumaa (Voru)

Suffrage: 18 years of age; universal for all Estonian citizens

Economy

GDP (purchasing power parity): $28.44 billion (2012 est.); $27.66 billion (2011 est.); $25.7 billion (2010 est.); $25.13 billion (2009 est.)

GDP real growth rate: 2.4% (2012 est.); 7.6% (2011 est.); 2.3% (2010 est.); -14.3% (2009 est.)

GDP per capita (PPP): $21,200 (2012 est.); $20,600 (2011 est.); $19,200 (2010 est.); $18,700 (2009 est.)

Natural resources: oil shale, peat, rare earth elements, phosphorite, clay, limestone, sand, dolomite, arable land, sea mud

Agriculture products: grain, potatoes, vegetables; livestock and dairy products; fish

Industries: engineering, electronics, wood and wood products, textiles; information technology, telecommunications

Exports: $17.38 billion (2012 est.); $16.84 billion (2011 est.); $11.66 billion (2010 est.)

Exports—commodities: machinery and electrical equipment 21%, wood and wood products 9%, metals 9%, furniture 7%, vehicles and parts 5%, food products and beverages 4%, textiles 4%, plastics 3%

Exports—partners: Sweden 17%, Finland 16.3%, Russia 11.9%, Latvia 8.6%, Germany 4.9%, Lithuania 4.9% (2011)

Imports: $17.87 billion (2012 est.); $17.09 billion (2011 est.); $11.94 billion (2010 est.)
Imports—commodities: machinery and electrical equipment 22%, mineral fuels 18%, chemical products 3%, foodstuffs 6%, plastics 6%, textiles 5%
Imports—partners: Finland 13.4%, Latvia 11.6%, Sweden 11.3%, Germany 10.9%, Lithuania 8.7%, Poland 7.2%, China 4.7% (2011)
Debt—external: $25.92 billion (31 December 2012 est.); $25.22 billion (31 December 2011 est.); $22.03 billion (31 December 2010 est.)
Exchange rates: kroon (EEK) per US dollar; 0.782 (2012 est.); 0.71 (2011 est.); 11.81 (2010 est.); 11.23 (2009); 10.7 (2008); 11.535 (2007)

GEOGRAPHY

Between 57.3 and 59.5 degrees latitude and 21.5 and 28.1 degrees longitude, Estonia lies on the eastern shores of the Baltic Sea on the level, northwestern part of the rising East European platform. Average elevation reaches only 50 meters (160 ft.).

The climate resembles New England's. Oil shale and limestone deposits, along with forests that cover 47% of the land, play key economic roles in this generally resource-poor country. Estonia has more than 1,500 lakes, numerous bogs, and 3,794 kilometers of coastline marked by numerous bays, straits, and inlets. Tallinn's Muuga port offers one of Europe's finest warm water harbor facilities.

Estonia's strategic location has precipitated many wars fought on its territory between other powers at its expense. In 1944, the Union of Soviet Socialist Republics (U.S.S.R.) granted Russia the trans-Narva and Petseri regions on Estonia's eastern frontier. Russia and Estonia signed a border treaty in 2005 recognizing the current border. Estonia ratified the treaty in June 2005, but Russia subsequently revoked its signature to the treaty, due to a reference the Estonian parliament inserted regarding the Peace Treaty of Tartu.

PEOPLE

Estonians belong to the Finno-Ugric peoples, as do the Finns and the Hungarians. Archaeological research confirms the existence of human activity in the region as early as 8000 BC; by 3500 BC the principal ancestors of the Estonians had arrived from the east.

Estonians have strong ties to the Nordic countries today stemming from deep cultural and religious influences gained over centuries during Scandinavian colonization and settlement. This highly literate society places great emphasis upon education, which is free and compulsory until age 17.

As of January 1, 2011, 84.2% of Estonia's population held Estonian citizenship, 8.7% were citizens of other countries (primarily Russia), and 7.1% were of undetermined citizenship.

National/Racial/Ethnic Minorities

Knowledge of Estonian is required to obtain citizenship, and all public servants and public sector employees, service personnel, medical professionals, and other workers who have contact with the public must possess a minimum competence in the language.

Roma, who numbered fewer than 1,000, reportedly faced discrimination in employment and other areas. The government took steps to emphasize the importance of education for Romani children, but their dropout rate remained high.

Language

Written with the Latin alphabet, Estonian is the language of the Estonian people and the official language of the country. Estonian is one of the world's most difficult languages to learn for English-speakers: it has 14 cases, which can be a challenge even for skilled linguists. During the Soviet era, the Russian language was imposed for official use.

Religion

Approximately 14 percent of the population is Evangelical Lutheran, and approximately 15 percent of the population belongs to one of the two Orthodox Churches in the country: the Estonian Orthodox Church, subordinate to the Moscow Patriarchate (EOCMP), and the Estonian Apostolic Orthodox Church (EAOC). Other Christian groups, including Methodists, Seventh-day Adventists, Roman Catholics, and Pentecostals, together constitute 1.4 percent of the population. The Russian Old Believers, who live primarily along the west bank of Lake Peipsi in the east, constitute another distinctive community. There are also small Jewish and Muslim communities. Thirty-two percent of the population is unspecified or other, approximately 34 percent is unaffiliated, and 6 percent does not identify with a religion. According to the government, as of September 2010, there were more than 500 religious associations registered in the country.

Most religious adherents among the Russian-speaking population, who mainly reside in the capital or the northeastern part of the country, are Orthodox.

HISTORY

Estonians are one of the longest-settled European peoples and have lived along the Baltic Sea for over 5,000 years. The Estonians were an independent nation until the 13th century A.D. The country was subsequently conquered by Denmark, Germany, Poland, Sweden, and finally Russia, whose defeat of Sweden in 1721 resulted in the Uusikaupunki Peace Treaty, granting Russia rule over what became modern Estonia.

Independence remained out of reach for Estonia until the collapse of the Russian empire during World War I. Estonia declared itself an independent democratic republic on February 24, 1918. In 1920, by the Peace Treaty of Tartu, Soviet Russia recognized Estonia's independence and renounced in perpetuity all rights to its territory.

The first constitution of the Republic of Estonia was adopted in 1920 and established a parliamentary form of government. Estonia's independence lasted for 22 years, during which time Estonia guaranteed cultural autonomy to all minorities, including its small Jewish population, an act that was unique in Western Europe at the time.

Leading up to World War II (WWII), Estonia pursued a policy of neutrality. However, the Soviet Union forcibly incorporated Estonia as a result of the Molotov-Ribbentrop Pact of 1939, in which Nazi Germany gave control of Estonia, Latvia, and Lithuania to the Soviet Union in return for control of much of Poland. In August 1940, the U.S.S.R. proclaimed Estonia a part of the Soviet Union as the Estonian Soviet Socialist Republic (E.S.S.R.). The United States never recognized Soviet sovereignty over Estonia, Latvia, or Lithuania.

During World War II, between 1939 and 1945, through both the Nazi and Soviet occupations, Estonia's direct human losses reached 180,000 residents, which amounted to 17% of its total population. During the Nazi occupation from 1941 to 1944, 7,800 citizens of the Republic of Estonia (70% ethnic Estonians, 15% ethnic Russians, 12.8% Estonian Jews, and 2.2% representing other nationalities) were executed in Nazi prison camps. Of the total number executed during the period of Nazi occupation, an estimated 1,000 were Estonian Jews—or roughly 25% of the pre-war Jewish population of Estonia. Additionally, an estimated 10,000 Jews were transported to Estonia from elsewhere in Eastern Europe and killed there. Soviet authorities conducted mass deportations in 1940–41, 1944, and 1949, with smaller deportations running through 1956. In total, an estimated 60,000 Estonians were murdered or deported by the Soviet Union. Another 70,000 fled to the West in 1944.

In the late 1980s, looser controls on freedom of expression under Soviet leader Mikhail Gorbachev reignited the Estonians' call for self-determination. By 1988, hundreds of thousands of people were gathering across Estonia to sing previously banned national songs in what became known as the "Singing Revolution."

In November 1988, Estonia's Supreme Soviet passed a declaration of sovereignty; in 1990, the name of the Republic of Estonia was restored, and during the August 1991 coup in the U.S.S.R., Estonia declared full independence. The U.S.S.R. Supreme Soviet recognized independent Estonia on September 6, 1991. Unlike the experiences of Latvia and Lithuania, Estonia's revolution ended without blood spilled. After more than 3 years of negotiations, on August 31, 1994, the armed forces of the Russian Federation withdrew from Estonia.

In 1992, a constitutional assembly introduced amendments to the 1938 constitution. After the draft constitution was approved by popular referendum, it came into effect July 3, 1992. Presidential elections were held on September 20, 1992, with Lennart Meri as victor. Lennart Meri served two terms as president, implementing many reforms during his tenure. Meri was constitutionally barred from a third term. Arnold Ruutel became president in 2001, and Toomas Hendrik Ilves in 2006 and again in 2011.

Since fully regaining independence, Estonia has had 10 governments with 7 different prime ministers elected: Mart Laar, Andres Tarand, Tiit Vahi, Mart Siimann, Siim Kallas, Juhan Parts, and Andrus Ansip. In March 2011 Ansip was reelected as Prime Minister.

GOVERNMENT AND POLITICAL CONDITIONS

Estonia is a multiparty, constitutional democracy with a unicameral parliament, a prime minister as head of government, and a president as head of state. The prime minister and cabinet generally represent the party or coalition of parties that have a majority of seats in parliament. Parliamentary elections held on March 6, 2011 were generally free and fair.

Recent Elections

On March 6, 2011, the country held parliamentary elections that were considered free and fair and led to the formation of a two-party coalition government, which took office on April 6.

Political Parties: Political parties could operate without restriction or outside interference. Only citizens may be members of political parties.

Participation of Women and Minorities: There were 20 women in the 101-seat parliament. The speaker and deputy speaker of the parliament were women. There was one female minister in the 13-member cabinet. The 24 percent of the country's non-Estonian population that were stateless could not participate in the election process at the national level. Noncitizens who are long-term residents may vote in local elections, but cannot vote in national elections or hold office. Citizens of the European Union who have established permanent residency may also vote in local elections, and those who are entered into the country's population register may vote in elections for Estonian representatives to the European Parliament. Ten members of ethnic minorities served in the 101-seat parliament.

Principal Government Officials

Last Updated: 1/31/2013

Pres.: **Toomas Hendrik ILVES**
Prime Min.: **Andrus ANSIP**
Min. of Agriculture: **Helir-Valdor SEEDER**
Min. of Culture: **Rein LANG**
Min. of Defense: **Urmas REINSALU**
Min. of Economic Affairs & Communications: **Juhan PARTS**
Min. of Education & Research: **Jaak AAVIKSOO**
Min. of Environment: **Keit PENTUS**
Min. of Finance: **Jurgen LIGI**
Min. of Foreign Affairs: **Urmas PAET**
Min. of the Interior: **Ken MARTI-VAHER**
Min. of Justice: **Hanno PEVKUR**
Min. of Regional Affairs: **Siim-Valmar KIISLER**
Min. of Social Affairs: **Taavi ROIVAS**
Governor, Bank of Estonia: **Ardo HANSSON**
Ambassador to the US: **Marina KALJURAND**
Permanent Representative to the UN, New York: **Margus KOLGA**

ECONOMY

Estonia, a member of the European Union and the eurozone since 2004, has a modern market-based economy and one of the higher per capita income levels in Central Europe and the Baltic region. Estonia's successive governments have pursued a free market, pro-business economic agenda and have wavered little in their commitment to pro-market reforms. The current government has followed sound fiscal policies that have resulted in balanced budgets and low public debt.

The economy benefits from strong electronics and telecommunications sectors and strong trade ties with Finland, Sweden, Russia, and Germany. Tallinn's priority has been to sustain high growth rates - on average 8% per year from 2003 to 2007. Estonia's economy fell into recession in mid-2008 with GDP contracting 14.3% in 2009, as a result of an investment and consumption slump following the bursting of the real estate market bubble and a decrease in export demand as result of economic slowdown in the rest of Europe.

Estonia rebounded nearly 8% in 2011 and the Estonian economy now has one of the higher GDP growth rates in Europe. Estonia adopted the euro on 1 January 2011.

Labor Conditions

The law sets the minimum age for employment at 18, with some exceptions. Children 15 to 17 years old may work with the consent of a parent or guardian and minors seven to 12 may do light work in the areas of culture, art, sports, or advertising with the consent of the Labor Inspectorate. Children under the age of 18 may not perform hazardous work. The law limits the hours that children may work and prohibits overtime or night work. The Labor Inspectorate was responsible for enforcing these laws. The government effectively enforced laws and policies to protect children from exploitation in the workplace.

In 2010 there was a national monthly minimum wage of 4,350 kroon ($372). It has remained the same for several years despite the rising cost of utilities, food, and other basic items.

The standard workweek is 40 hours. The law requires a rest period of at least 11 hours in sequence for every 24-hour period. Reduced working time is required for minors and for employees who perform work that is underground, poses a health hazard, or is of an otherwise special nature. The law requires overtime pay of not less than 150 percent of the employee's hourly wage. These requirements were effectively enforced. There is no prohibition of excessive compulsory overtime.

U.S.-ESTONIA RELATIONS

The United States and Estonia are strong allies and partners. The United States established diplomatic relations with Estonia in 1922 following its declaration of independence during World War I. Estonia was annexed by the Soviet Union in 1940 during World War II. In 1991, Estonia declared full independence, and international recognition followed. The United States had never recognized the forcible incorporation of Estonia into the Soviet Union, and it views the present Government of Estonia as the legal continuation of the interwar republic.

Since 1991, Estonia has undergone a tremendous transformation. Through hard work, innovation, and a pursuit of strong democratic ideals, enhanced security, and greater cooperation, Estonia has emerged as an example to the region and the world. The country's integration of technology into public and private partnerships demonstrates the endless possibilities that technology can have when harnessed to benefit societies. Estonia is an effective and reliable trans-Atlantic partner in advancing peace, stability, and democracy in Europe and beyond. Its cooperation with the region has made it an invaluable ally in the North Atlantic Treaty Organization (NATO), and the United States appreciates Estonia's commitment to the shared mission in Afghanistan.

U.S. Assistance to Estonia

U.S. security assistance to Estonia provides the opportunity to sustain and expand the partnership the United States has formed with Estonia, contribute to improved NATO interoperability, and support Estonia's military commitments abroad.

Bilateral Economic Relations

The United States and Estonia have signed a bilateral investment treaty. Principal imports from the United States include computer and electronic products; chemicals; machinery; transportation equipment; and wood products. U.S. imports from Estonia include computer and electronic products; petroleum products; chemicals; electrical equipment; and optical, medical, or precision instruments. Estonia participates in the Visa Waiver Program, which allows nationals of participating countries to travel to the United States for certain business or tourism purposes for stays of 90 days or less without obtaining a visa.

Estonia is a member of the European Union (EU). The U.S. economic relationship with the EU is the largest and most complex in the world, and the United States and the EU continue to pursue initiatives to create new opportunities for transatlantic commerce.

Estonia's Membership in International Organizations

Estonia and the United States belong to a number of the same international organizations, including the United Nations, North Atlantic Treaty Organization, Euro-Atlantic Partnership Council, Organization for Security and Cooperation in Europe, Organization for Economic Cooperation and Development, International Monetary Fund, World Bank, and World Trade Organization. Estonia also is an observer to the Organization of American States.

Bilateral Representation

Estonia maintains an embassy in the United States at 2131 Massachusetts Avenue, NW, Washington DC 20008; tel: (202) 588-0101.

Principal U.S. Embassy Officials

Last Updated: 1/14/2013

TALLINN (E) Kentmanni 20, Tallinn 15099, Estonia, (372) 668-8100, Fax (372) 668-8266, Workweek: 8:30–17:30, Website: http://estonia.usembassy.gov/

DCM OMS:	Marsha Philipak Chambers
AMB OMS:	Rebecca Eggert
HRO:	Michael Bradecamp
MGT:	Michael Bradecamp
POL/ECON:	Mary Glantz
POSHO:	Wayne Crawford
SDO/DATT:	LTC Darren Smith
AMB:	Jeffrey Levine
CON:	Rachel Crawford
DCM:	Bob Gilchrist
PAO:	Michelle Schohn
GSO:	Wayne Crawford
RSO:	Josh Weisman
CLO:	Natalia Smith
EEO:	Crawford, Rachel
FMO:	Michael Bradecamp
ICASS Chair:	Tony Lippold
IMO:	Garland Saunders
ISSO:	Garland Saunders
LEGATT:	Scott Janezic
State ICASS:	Nathan Doyel

TRAVEL

Consular Information Sheet

April 17, 2012

Country Description: Estonia is a stable democracy with an economy that is rebounding after facing sharp decline in 2008 and 2009. Tourist facilities in the capital, Tallinn, are comparable to those found in western European cities, but some amenities may be lacking in rural areas. In Tallinn, as well as in other locations frequented by tourists, many people can communicate in English.

Smart Traveler Enrollment Program (STEP)/Embassy Locations: If you are going to live in or travel to Estonia, please take the time to tell our Embassy about your trip. If you enroll in the Smart Traveler Enrollment Program, we can keep you up to date with important safety and security announcements. It will also help your friends and family get in touch with you in an emergency.

The U.S. Embassy in Tallinn is available 24 hours a day for emergency assistance for U.S. citizens visiting or residing in Estonia. Our embassy is located just a short walk from Tallinn's "Old Town" at Kentmanni 20 (postal code 15099). The embassy's main switchboard number is 372-668-8100 (please see our dialing instructions, below). You can call the Consular Section directly during business hours (08:30-17:30) at 372-668-8128, 8129, 8111, or 8197; send a fax to 372-668-8267; or e-mail us at ACSTallinn@state.gov. For after-hours emergencies, you may call our Embassy's duty officer at 372-509-2129, or if there is no answer, our Embassy's 24-hour guard booth at 372-668-8169. Most information that U.S. citizens may need, including full information on our hours (including holidays) and how to contact us, is on our website.

Dialing instructions: Where you see the " " sign, you must begin by dialing the prefix required for international calls. If you are in the United States, you should start by dialing "011." If you are calling from most other countries, you begin by dialing "00." Thus, if you are in the United States, you can reach the embassy's switchboard by dialing 011-372-668-8100. If you are calling from within Estonia, you can omit the country code (372).

Entry/Exit Requirements for U.S. Citizens: Estonia is a party to the Schengen Agreement. This means that U.S. citizens may enter Estonia for up to 90 days within a six month period for tourist or business purposes without a visa. Your passport should be valid for at least three months beyond the period of stay. You need to prove you have sufficient funds and a return airline ticket. Your passport will be stamped (and the 90 days will begin) at your first stop in the Schengen Zone. The period of stay does not end until you completely depart the Schengen Zone, at which point your passport will again be stamped. Most countries in Western and Central Europe, including most of Estonia's neighboring countries (e.g., Lithuania, Latvia, Finland, Sweden, etc.) are members of the Schengen Zone as well. Accordingly, there is no mandatory immigration control when you travel between Estonia and these countries (and the 90-day period you are allowed to stay continues to run, even if you leave Estonia). You should always have your passport with you, however, as each country has the right to conduct passport checks. Other countries in the region, such as Russia and Ukraine, are not parties to the Schengen Agreement, so there is mandatory immigration control for persons entering or exiting Estonia by land or air to/from those countries.

If you would like to stay in Estonia (and the other countries in the Schengen Zone) longer than 90 days, you can apply for a longer-term visa from the Consulate General of Estonia in New York (telephone 212-883-0636) before you begin your trip. You can find more information about visiting Estonia, including a list of all Estonian embassies and consulates worldwide, on the website of the Estonian Ministry of Foreign Affairs. Residency permits, visa extensions, and other rules applicable to foreigners visiting Estonia (such as students, temporary workers, etc.) are processed by the Estonian Citizenship and Migration Bureau, part of the Estonian Police & Border Guard Board. You can find comprehensive information on residency permits by visiting the Police & Border Guard's website and clicking on "Services." You can also obtain additional information about Estonia from the Embassy of Estonia in Washington, DC (telephone 202-588-0101).

There are no restrictions in Estonia to visitors or residents with HIV/AIDS. You can find general information about dual nationality on the Department of State's website, as well as specific information about dual nationality in Estonia, below. You can also find information about the prevention of international child abduction, as well information about customs regulations, in our Customs Information sheet.

Threats to Safety and Security: Estonian authorities are vigilant in combating terrorism and other threats to security. There have been no incidents of terrorism directed toward U.S. citizens in Estonia. Furthermore, civil unrest is rarely a problem in Estonia. Nevertheless, large public gatherings and demonstrations may occur on occasion in response to political issues, but these (with few exceptions) have proceeded without incident in the past. If you hear of or encounter a demonstration, you should avoid the area and check local media for updates on the situation. You can also contact the U.S. Embassy in Tallinn for current information.

Estonia is quite dark during the winter months (roughly October through April), and Estonian law requires pedestrians to wear small reflectors, which people generally pin to their coats or handbags. Although this law is rarely enforced in cities, reflectors are very important in rural areas where it may be difficult for motorists to see pedestrians. Violators of this law may be subject to a fine of around US$50, or a higher fine up to around US$500 if the pedestrian is under the influence of alcohol. Reflectors are inexpensive and you should be able to find them at many supermarkets, kiosks, and other shops.

Stay up to date by:

- Bookmarking our Bureau of Consular Affairs website, which contains the current Travel Warnings and Travel Alerts as well as the Worldwide Caution;
- Following us on Twitter and the Bureau of Consular Affairs page on Facebook;
- Downloading our free Smart Traveler iPhone App to have travel information at your fingertips;
- Calling 1-888-407-4747 toll-free within the U.S. and Canada, or a regular toll line, 1-202-501-4444, from other countries; and
- Taking some time before travel to consider your personal security.

Crime: Estonia is a relatively safe country, although sporadic crime in Tallinn's Old Town is an ongoing concern, particularly during the summer tourist season. You should exercise the same precautions with regard to your personal safety and belongings that you would take in major U.S. cities. The most common crime encountered by foreign tourists in Estonia is pick-pocketing. Tourists are often targeted by individuals and small groups of thieves working together. In public places such as Tallinn's Old Town, in particular the Town Hall Square ("Raekoja Plats"), the airport, train stations, bus stations, and the Central Market, you should exercise special care in safeguarding valuables against pick-pockets. Guard your valuables (especially purses and bags) while visiting busy cafés and restaurants. Do not leave valuables unattended in vehicles, and make sure car doors are locked at all times.

From time to time, especially late at night near bars and night clubs, foreigners have been subject to scams, or have become involved in altercations (some violent) with inebriated individuals. One late night scam has involved attractive women enticing tourists in a reputable bar to visit a nearby bar where they are grossly overcharged. Although Estonian police have shut down several suspect bars over the past year, this remains a concern.

On occasion, U.S. citizens have reported that they were harassed for racial reasons or because they appeared or sounded "foreign." These incidents have generally occurred outside of major tourist areas. Credit-card fraud is also an ongoing concern, as is Internet-based financial fraud and "Internet dating" fraud. You should take precautions to safeguard your credit cards and report any suspected unauthorized transaction to the credit card company immediately. If an incident occurs, you should report it promptly to the local police. The Estonian police agencies are modern, well-equipped law enforcement entities on a standard comparable to most Western European police, with only isolated instances of corruption

Don't buy counterfeit and pirated goods, even if they are widely available. Not only are the bootlegs illegal to bring back into the United States, by purchasing them you may also be breaking local law.

Victims of Crime: If you or someone you know becomes the victim of a crime abroad, you should contact the local police and the nearest the U.S. Embassy or consulate. We can:

- Replace a stolen passport;
- Help you find appropriate medical care if you are the victim of a violent crime such as assault or rape;
- Put you in contact with the appropriate police authorities, and contact family members or friends; and
- Help you understand the local criminal justice process and can direct you to local attorneys, although the local authorities are responsible for investigating and prosecuting the crime.

Even if you decide not to report a crime while in Estonia, but still believe that some action should be taken, you can still file a police report after returning home to the United States by sending a letter or e-mail to the Estonian police. Please contact the Embassy so we can facilitate your communication with the police.

The local equivalent to the "911" emergency line for ambulance or fire in Estonia is 112. The emergency line for the police is 110. The non-emergency local number for the Estonian police is (372) 612-3000. Although many operators speak English, at times those answering this line may have minimal English speaking skills.

Criminal Penalties: While traveling in Estonia, you are subject to its laws and regulations. Foreign laws and legal systems can be vastly different than our own. If you break local laws in Estonia, your U.S. passport won't help you avoid arrest or prosecution. It's very important to know what's legal and what's not where you are going.

There are also some things that might be legal in the country you visit, but still illegal in the United States. For example, you can be prosecuted under U.S. law if you buy pirated goods abroad. Engaging in sexual conduct with children or using or disseminating child pornography in a foreign country is a crime prosecutable in the United States.

Based on the Vienna Convention on Consular Relations, bilateral agreements with certain countries, and customary international law, if you are arrested in Estonia, you have the option to request that the police, prison officials, or other authorities alert the U.S. embassy of your arrest, and to have communications from you forwarded to the embassy.

Special Circumstances: As of 2011, Estonia replaced its currency, the kroon, with the euro. Only euros are now accepted, although persons holding cash kroons can continue exchanging them for euros at the official rate for an indefinite period at the Bank of Estonia (Eesti Pank) in Tallinn and at selected bank branches elsewhere in Estonia. You can also get local currency from ATMs using your U.S. debit card. Please note that some ATMs will function only if your ATM card has a computer chip. You can use a regular U.S. credit card for payment in most shops and restaurants in Estonia. If you plan to exchange U.S. cash for euros while visiting Estonia, you should be aware that many banks and currency exchanges do not accept old U.S. bills. Accordingly, please try to bring newer bills (preferably those issued after 2000).

Dual Nationality: Although Estonian law generally does not permit dual nationality, Estonian law does provide that a person who has the right to Estonian citizenship from birth cannot have his/her citizenship taken away. Accordingly, a number of individuals who have claims to Estonian citizenship from birth (generally ethnic Estonians) carry both Estonian and U.S. passports (such as Estonians who move to the United States and naturalize as U.S. citizens, and their children). If you are not ethnic Estonian, but wish to naturalize as an Estonian citizen, you could risk losing your U.S. citizenship. You are strongly advised to contact us and discuss your case with a consul if you are considering becoming an Estonian citizen (or renouncing your U.S. citizenship for any other purpose). You should note that getting an Estonian residency permit (an "elamisluba") would have no effect on your U.S. citizenship. If you are an Estonian-American who carries both U.S. and Estonian passports, you should be aware that you must show your U.S. passport when entering the United States. U.S. citizens cannot enter the United States under the Visa Waiver Program using an Estonian passport.

Accessibility: While in Estonia, individuals with disabilities may find accessibility and accommodation very different from what you find in the

United States. Estonian law requires that most new public buildings and others with community space (e.g., shopping centers) be accessible for persons with disabilities. However, many older buildings are not required to meet these requirements.

Getting around in Estonian cities and towns may be difficult at times since many sidewalks are narrow and uneven, and cobblestone streets—particularly in Tallinn's popular old town—make access difficult. In general, mobility is easier in cities such as Tallinn, Tartu, and Pärnu, compared to smaller towns and rural areas. Roads and sidewalks in the winter can get quite icy, which makes getting around more difficult. In general, public transport is not accommodating to people with mobility disabilities, although selected Tallinn public buses are specially equipped to assist persons in wheelchairs, and many Tallinn buses, trolleys and trams have travel escorts (reisisaatjad) who will assist riders with disabilities. Many of these escorts will not speak English, however.

The English-language website of the Estonian visitors bureau contains general information for disabled visitors, specific information for visually-impaired travelers and those using wheelchairs, and general accessibility information for hotels and other accommodations in Estonia. An Estonian advocacy group for the disabled, Freedom of Movement (Liikumisvabadus) has a site that provides specific accessibility ratings for hundreds of businesses and public buildings in Estonia, as well as other useful information. You may also e-mail the U.S. Embassy in Tallinn for further information on this topic.

Medical Facilities and Health Information: Although medical care in Estonia still falls short of Western standards, Estonia's medical care is generally good, especially in Tallinn, and in some other cities such as Tartu and Pärnu. Estonia has many highly-trained medical professionals, but some hospitals and clinics still suffer from a lack of equipment and resources. You may find that some hospital staff and nurses, including those who work in emergency rooms, speak only limited English. You can find good information on vaccinations and other health precautions, such as safe food and water precautions and insect bite protection, on the Centers for Disease Control and Prevention's (CDC) website, or by calling their hotline for international travelers at 1-877-FYI-TRIP (1-877-394-8747). You can also consult the World Health Organization's (WHO) website, which contains additional health information for travelers, including detailed country-specific health information.

If you plan to visit forested areas of Estonia in the summertime, you should take steps to avoid ticks because of occasional cases of tick-borne encephalitis. Although there is no vaccine against this disease currently licensed for use in the United States, a vaccine (requiring a series of injections) is available under two different brand names in Estonia, both of which can be obtained from many local physicians. Serious cases of seasonal influenza, including H1N1, have been reported in recent years and you should consider getting a flu shot before traveling to Estonia during flu season.

Medical Insurance: You can't assume your insurance will go with you when you travel. It's very important to find out BEFORE you leave. You need to ask your insurance company two questions:

- Does my policy apply when I'm out of the U.S.?
- Will it cover emergencies like a trip to a foreign hospital or an evacuation?

Your regular U.S. health insurance may not cover doctor and hospital visits in other countries. If your policy doesn't go with you when you travel, it's a very good idea to take out another one for your trip.

Even if you have insurance covering you while traveling overseas, Estonian hospitals and clinics generally will require you to pay for the medical services immediately.

Traffic Safety and Road Conditions: While in Estonia, you may encounter road conditions that differ significantly from those in the United States. In order to drive in Estonia, you must have the correct license. Estonian authorities strictly enforce their rules on driving with a proper license, and many U.S. citizens have been subjected to hefty fines in recent years due to confusion about Estonian rules, so please read the following information carefully. If you are a visitor to Estonia, you may drive only if you carry both your valid U.S. driver's license and a valid International Driving Permit (IDP). You should obtain your IDP from either the American Automobile Association (AAA) or the American Automobile Touring Alliance (part of the National Auto Club) before you leave the United States. These are the only two entities in the United States that are authorized by international agreements to provide IDPs. Other entities purport to offer "international driver's licenses," but such documents are not recognized by Estonian authorities. If you are a resident of Estonia, you can initially drive in Estonia with your valid U.S. driver's license and valid IDP, but upon receipt of an Estonian residence permit or after living in Estonia for more than one year (whichever is shorter), American citizens must obtain an Estonian driving license. However, licenses cannot be issued until you have been in Estonia for 185 days within the past year. All individuals required to obtain an Estonian license must pass both a theoretical (written) and a practical driver's exam. An English-language version of the written exam is available and the Road Administration will ensure that an English-speaking examiner is available for the practical driving portion. Although testing may take place at several locations around the country, it is recommended that you contact the Road Administration headquarters at Mäepealse 19 in Tallinn, tel: 620-1200. Your U.S. license and International Drivering Permit must have been issued before your "residency" began, so it is imperative that you obtain these documents before you move to Estonia. If you are caught driving without a proper license, you likely will be subject to a fine and your driving privileges may be revoked. Any U.S. citizen who wishes to obtain an Estonian driver's license should contact the Estonian Road Administration authority (known by the Estonian acronym "ARK").

Although road conditions in Estonia are generally good, especially roads between Estonian cities, some roads—especially in rural areas—are poorly lighted and are not up to Western standards. You may find that, compared to U.S. drivers, some drivers in Estonia can be aggressive, recklessly overtaking vehicles and traveling at high speed, even in crowded urban areas. Despite strict Estonian laws against driving under the influence of alcohol, accidents involving intoxicated drivers are frequent. It is not uncommon for the police to set up checkpoints on major streets and highways; you should pull over when asked by a police officer. You should always remain alert to the possibility of drunk drivers and pedestrians.

If driving, you must always stop for all pedestrians in marked crosswalks. Some Estonian motorists do not comply with this rule, so if you are walking, you should always be careful when crossing the streets. In rural areas, wild animals, such as deer and moose, and icy road conditions can create unexpected hazards. You should also watch out for dark-clothed or drunk pedestrians walking along unlighted roads or darting across dimly-lighted streets or highways. Winter roads are usually treated and cleared of snow, but you still should remain vigilant for icy patches and large potholes.

Estonian police very strictly enforce laws against driving under the influence. The basic rule is zero tolerance. Thus, you can be subject to severe penalties if stopped by the police and even a trace of alcohol is detected, so please do not drive in Estonia if you have consumed any alcohol whatsoever. You should also comply with other important traffic rules, including the following: You should always keep your headlights illuminated while driving; the driver and all passengers should use seatbelts (and children too small to be secure in seatbelts must use child car seats); you should carefully comply with posted speed limits; you should not be using a cell phone without a hands-free device while driving; and right turns on a red light are prohibited unless otherwise indicated by a green arrow. According to Estonian law, if you are involved in an accident, you should not attempt to move the vehicle to the side of the road until the police reach the scene. The Eesti Autoklubi (Estonian Auto Club), which is affiliated with AAA, provides emergency roadside assistance. You do not need to be a member to receive assistance, although fees are lower for members. To request roadside assistance or towing service, dial 1888. For ambulance or fire assistance the number is 112. For emergency police assistance, call 110. Please note that for both numbers, the level of English spoken by the operator answering may be minimal.

The Estonian National Tourist Office website also has useful information about traveling around Estonia by car.

Aviation Safety Oversight: As there is no direct commercial air service to the United States by carriers registered in Estonia, the U.S. Federal Aviation Administration (FAA) has not assessed the Estonian Civil Aviation Authority for compliance with International Civil Aviation Organization (ICAO) aviation safety standards. For more information, travelers may visit the FAA's website.

Children's Issues: Estonia is a party to the Hague Convention on the Civil Aspects of International Child Abduction. The Estonian central authority for implementation and enforcement of this convention is the International Judicial Cooperation Division (Rahvusvahelise Õigusabi Talitus) of the Estonian Ministry of Justice. For more information, please see the U.S. Department of State's Office of Children's Issues web pages on intercountry adoption and international parental child abduction.

Intercountry Adoption

January 2012

The information in this section has been edited from the latest report available as of February 2013 from the State Department Bureau of Consular Affairs, Office of Overseas Citizens Services. For more information, please read the *Intercountry Adoption* section of this book and review current reports online at http://adoption.state.gov.

Estonia is party to the Hague Convention on Protection of Children and Co-operation in Respect of Intercountry Adoption (Hague Adoption Convention). Therefore, all adoptions between Estonia and the United States must meet the requirements of the Convention; the U.S. implementing legislation, the Intercountry Act of 2000 (IAA); and the IAA implementing regulations.

Who Can Adopt? Adoption between the United States and Estonia is governed by the Hague Adoption Convention. Therefore to adopt from Estonia, you must first be found eligible to adopt by the U.S. Government. The U.S. Government agency responsible for making this determination is the Department of Homeland Security, U.S. Citizenship and Immigration Services (USCIS). According to the Estonian Family Law only those children whose parents are deceased or whose parents have had their parental rights taken away may be adopted. There are few such children and long waiting lists of Estonian families who by law take precedence. Consequently, identifying a child for adoption can be lengthy (several years or more) as the number of children that can be adopted by foreigners is quite limited (only about 20 children a year). Since foreign parents with Estonian background are given preference over foreigners with no Estonian heritage, prospective adoptive parents should explain their ties to Estonia.

Residency Requirements: There are no residency requirements for prospective adoptive parents in Estonia.

Age Requirements: A prospective adoptive parent must be at least 25 years old. In exceptional cases, the Court may give permission to a younger person.

Marriage Requirements: Both single individuals and legally married couples can adopt. Married couples must have the written consent of the spouse. Per the Estonian Family Law Act, an adoption can occur without the consent of the spouse if the conjugal relations of the spouses have terminated and they live apart.

Income Requirements: Estonia does not have any income requirements for intercountry adoptions.

Other Requirements: Same-sex couples cannot adopt in Estonia.

Who Can Be Adopted? Because Estonia is party to The Hague Adoption Convention, children from Estonia must meet the requirements of the Convention in order to be eligible for adoption. For example, the Convention requires that Estonia attempt to place a child with a family in Estonia before determining that a child is eligible for intercountry adoption. In addition to Estonia's requirements, a child must meet the definition of a Convention adoptee for you to bring him or her back to the United States.

Relinquishment Requirements: No known relinquishment requirements

Abandonment Requirements: According to the Estonian Family Law only those children whose parents are deceased or whose parents have had their parental rights taken away may be adopted.

Age Requirements: No known age requirements

Sibling Requirements: No known sibling requirements

Requirements for Special Needs or Medical Conditions: Unknown

Waiting Period: Unknown

Estonia's Adoption Authority: Ministry of Social Affairs (Sotsiaal Ministeerium)

The Process: Because Estonia is party to the Hague Adoption Convention, adopting from Estonia must follow a specific process designed to meet the Convention's requirements. For detailed and updated information on these requirements, please review the *Intercountry Adoption* section of this publication and visit the U.S. Department of State Intercountry Adoption website at http://adoption.state.gov.

The first step in adopting a child from Estonia is to select an adoption service provider in the United States that has been accredited. Only these agencies and attorneys can provide adoption services between the United States and Estonia. Adoption Hope International is currently the only registered U.S. adoption agency working in Estonia. The address and website for Adoption Hope International is:

Adoption Hope International, Inc.
284 Shoreward Drive
Myrtle Beach, SC 29579
http://www.adopts.com/estonia.html

After you choose an accredited adoption service provider, you apply to be found eligible to adopt (Form I-800A) by the U.S. Government, Department of Homeland Security, U.S. Citizenship and Immigration Services (USCIS). Once the U.S. Government determines that you are "eligible" and "suitable" to adopt, you or your agency will forward your information to the adoption authority in Estonia. Estonia's adoption authority will review your application to determine whether you are also eligible to adopt under Estonia's law. Once prospective adoptive parents have been approved to adopt, the Ministry places them on a list and begins the process of locating a suitable match Once a match is found, the Ministry notifies the prospective adoptive parents (through the adoption agency). According to the Estonian Family Law only those children whose parents are deceased or whose parents have had their parental rights taken away may be adopted. There are few such children and long waiting lists of Estonian families who by law take precedence. Consequently, identifying a child for adoption can be lengthy (several years or more) as the number of children that can be adopted by foreigners is quite limited (only about 20 children a year). Since foreign parents with Estonian background are given preference over foreigners with no Estonian heritage, prospective adoptive parents should explain their ties to Estonia. The Ministry of Social Affairs cautions that prospective adoptive parents should not visit orphanages to locate a child since it is unlikely that the child they choose will be permitted to be adopted by foreigners. According to the new adoption law, international adoptions may be processed through an adoption agency in the parents' home country which has signed an agreement with the Ministry. After you accept a match with a child, you will apply to the Department of Homeland Security, U.S. Citizenship and Immigration Services (USCIS) for provisional approval to adopt that particular child (Form I-800). USCIS will determine whether the child is eligible under U.S. law to be adopted and enter the United States. The consular officer will review the child's information and evaluate the child for possible visa ineligibilities. If the consular officer determines that the child appears eligible to immigrate to the United States, he or she will send a letter (an "Article 5 Letter") to the Estonian Central Authority. Do not adopt or obtain custody of a child in Estonia before a U.S. consular officer issues the Article 5 Letter.

Role of the Adoption Authority: The Ministry of Social Affairs prepares the entire package of adoption documents for approval first by the Minister of Social Affairs and then for the county or city court to make the adoption decision. Once prospective adoptive parents have been approved to adopt, the Ministry places them on a list and begins the process of locating a suitable match Once a match is found, the Ministry notifies the prospective adoptive parents (through the adoption agency).

Role of the Court: Estonian adoption law requires court approval of international adoptions and the adoptive parents' presence at the court hearing when the adoption is finalized. The Domiciliary County Government's Children Protection Officer represents the child's rights and will release the child into the adoptive parents' custody.

Role of Adoption Agencies: The adoption agency sends a letter of interest, on behalf of the prospective adoptive parents, to the Ministry of Social Affairs indicating the sex and age of the child(ren) they would be interested in adopting as well as information regarding the prospective adoptive parents' age and profession. Once a child is identified, the adoption agency notifies the prospective adoptive parents. The adoption agency then notifies the Ministry of Social Affairs of the prospective adoptive parents' decision to accept or decline a proposed child. (It should be noted that no more than three successive children will be offered to the prospective adoptive parents.)

Time Frame: Once a child has been identified, the adoption process takes approximately one year. This estimate includes matching the child and prospective parents, documentation, and the court hearing.

Adoption Application: The adoption agency forwards the letter of interest and the adoption application to the Ministry of Social Affairs.

Adpotion Fees: While there is no official adoption fee in Estonia, some fees prospective adoptive parents should anticipate include court fees ($10 USD) and new Estonian passports ($25 USD). In the adoption services contract that you sign at the beginning of the adoption process, your agency will itemize the fees and estimated expenses related to your adoption process.

Documents Required: The following is a list of documents needed for adoptions in Estonia:

- Home study
- Medical examination indicating the prospective adoptive parents' state of health;
- Documents pertaining to the financial condition of the prospective adoptive parents;
- Copy of marriage certificate;
- Copies of the prospective adoptive parents' passports;
- Any other information the parents feel would be useful for the MSW to know, including family heritage, ties to Estonia, letters of reference, etc.; and
- Documents determining that there is no open criminal record of the prospective adoption parents.

Bringing Your Child Home: Once your adoption is complete (or you have obtained legal custody of the child), there are a few more steps to take before you can head home. Specifically, you need to apply for several documents for your child before he or she can travel to the United States, such as a birth certificate, a passport or travel document for your child from the country in which he or she was born, and a U.S. Immigration Visa. For detailed and updated information on how to obtain these documents, review the *Intercountry Adoption* section in this publication and visit the U.S. Department of State Intercountry Adoption website at http://adoption.state.gov.

Child Citizenship Act: For adoptions finalized abroad, the Child Citizenship Act of 2000 allows your new child to acquire American citizenship automatically when he or she enters the United States as lawful permanent residents. For adoptions finalized in the United States, the Child Citizenship Act of 2000 allows your new child to acquire American citizenship automatically when the court in the United States issues the final adoption decree. To learn more, review the *Intercountry Adoption* section in this publication and visit the U.S. Department of State Intercountry Adoption website at http://adoption.state.gov.

After Adoption: Estonia does not have any post-adoption requirements.

U.S. Embassy in Estonia
Kentmanni 20
Tallinn, Estonia
Tel: 011–372–668–8100
Fax: 011–372–668–8267
Email: ACSTallinn@state.gov

Estonia's Adoption Authority
Ministry of Social Affairs
(Sotsiaal Ministeerium)
Gonsiori 29, 15027 Tallinn, Estonia
Internet: http://www.sm.ee/eng/pages/index.html

Embassy of Estonia
2131 Massachusetts Ave, N.W.
Washington D.C. 20008
Tel: (202) 588–0101
Fax: (202) 588–0108

Consulate General of Estonia
600 Third Avenue, 26th Floor
New York, N.Y. 10016–2001
Tel: (212) 883–0636
Fax:(212) 883–0648
Email: nyconsulate@nyc.estemb.org
Internet: http://www.nyc.estemb.org

Office of Children's Issues
U.S. Department of State
2201 C Street, NW
SA-29
Washington, DC 20520
Tel: 1–888–407–4747
E-mail: AskCI@state.gov
http://adoption.state.gov

For questions about intercountry adoption and related immigration procedures, call the USCIS National Benefits Center (NBC) 1-877-3424-8374.

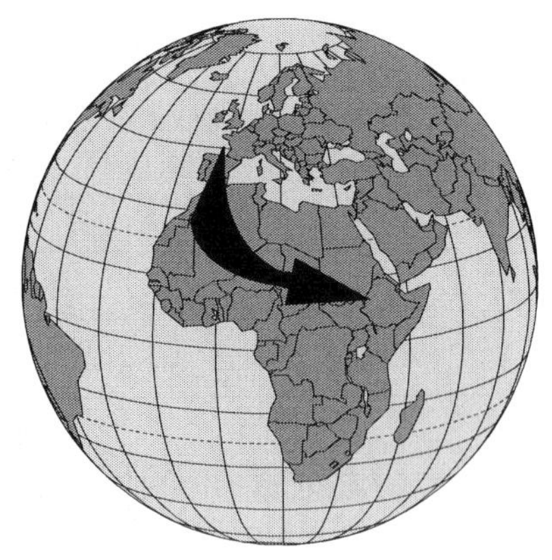

ETHIOPIA

Compiled from publications that were available as of February 2013 from the U.S. Department of State, the U.S. Department of Commerce, and the Central Intelligence Agency (CIA). See the introduction to this set for explanatory notes.

Official Name:
Federal Democratic Republic of Ethiopia

PROFILE

Geography

Area: total: 1,104,300 sq km; country comparison to the world: 27; land: 1 million sq km; water: 104,300 sq km
Major cities: Addis Ababa (capital) 2.863 million (2009)
Climate: tropical monsoon with wide topographic-induced variation
Terrain: high plateau with central mountain range divided by Great Rift Valley

People

Nationality: noun: Ethiopian(s); adjective: Ethiopian
Population: 91,195,675 (July 2012 est.)
Population growth rate: 3.179% (2012 est.)
Ethnic groups: Oromo 34.5%, Amara 26.9%, Somalie 6.2%, Tigraway 6.1%, Sidama 4%, Guragie 2.5%, Welaita 2.3%, Hadiya 1.7%, Affar 1.7%, Gamo 1.5%, Gedeo 1.3%, other 11.3% (2007 Census)
Religions: Orthodox 43.5%, Muslim 33.9%, Protestant 18.6%, traditional 2.6%, Catholic 0.7%, other 0.7% (2007 Census)
Languages: Oromigna (official regional) 33.8%, Amarigna (Amharic) (official) 29.3%, Somaligna 6.2%, Tigrigna (official regional) 5.9%, Sidamigna 4%, Wolayitigna 2.2%, Guaragigna 2%, Affarigna 1.7%, Hadiyigna 1.7%, Gamogna 1.5%, other 11.7%, English (official) (major foreign language taught in schools), Arabic (official) (1994 census)
Literacy: definition: age 15 and over can read and write; total population: 42.7%; male: 50.3%; female: 35.1% (2003 est.)
Health: life expectancy at birth: total population: 56.56 years; male: 53.99 years; female: 59.21 years (2012 est.); Infant mortality rate: total: 75.29 deaths/1,000 live births; male: 86.03 deaths/1,000 live births; female: 64.23 deaths/1,000 live births (2012 est.)
Unemployment rate: NA%
Work force: 37.9 million (2007)

Government

Type: federal republic
Independence: oldest independent country in Africa and one of the oldest in the world—at least 2,000 years
Constitution: ratified 8 December 1994, effective 22 August 1995
Political subdivisions: 9 ethnically based states (kililoch, singular—kilil) and 2 self-governing administrations (astedaderoch, singular—astedader); Adis Abeba (Addis Ababa), Afar, Amara (Amhara), Binshangul Gumuz, Dire Dawa, Gambela Hizboch (Gambela Peoples), Hareri Hizb (Harari People), Oromiya (Oromia), Sumale (Somali), Tigray, Ye Debub Biheroch Bihereseboch na Hizboch (Southern Nations, Nationalities and Peoples)
Suffrage: 18 years of age; universal

Economy

GDP (purchasing power parity): $103.1 billion (2012 est.); $96.09 billion (2011 est.); $89.36 billion (2010 est.); $82.74 billion (2009 est.)
GDP real growth rate: 7% (2012 est.); 7.5% (2011 est.); 8% (2010 est.); 10% (2009 est.)
GDP per capita (PPP): $1,200 (2012 est.); $1,100 (2011 est.); $1,100 (2010 est.); $1,000 (2009 est.)
Natural resources: small reserves of gold, platinum, copper, potash, natural gas, hydropower
Agriculture products: cereals, pulses, coffee, oilseed, cotton, sugarcane, potatoes, khat, cut flowers; hides, cattle, sheep, goats; fish
Industries: food processing, beverages, textiles, leather, chemicals, metals processing, cement
Exports: $3.163 billion (2012 est.); $2.75 billion (2011 est.); $2.4 billion (2010 est.)
Exports—commodities: coffee, khat, gold, leather products, live animals, oilseeds
Exports—partners: Germany 13.7%, China 11.8%, Belgium 7.5%, Saudi Arabia 6.5%, US 6%, Italy 4.9%, Sudan 4.1% (2011)
Imports: $10.6 billion (2012 est.); $8.25 billion (2011 est.); $7.365 billion (2010 est.)

Imports—commodities: food and live animals, petroleum and petroleum products, chemicals, machinery, motor vehicles, cereals, textiles

Imports—partners: Saudi Arabia 10.2%, China 10.2%, US 7.8% (2011)

Debt—external: $9.956 billion (31 December 2012 est.); $7.989 billion (31 December 2011 est.); $7.147 billion (31 December 2010 est.)

Exchange rates: birr (ETB) per US dollar; 17.8 (2012 est.); 16.899 (2011 est.); 14.41 (2010 est.); 11.78 (2009); 9.57 (2008); 8.96 (2007)

GEOGRAPHY

Ethiopia is located in the Horn of Africa and is bordered by Eritrea, Djibouti, Somalia, Kenya, South Sudan, and Sudan. The country has a high central plateau that varies from 1,800 to 3,000 meters (6,000 ft.-10,000 ft.) above sea level, with some mountains reaching 4,620 meters (15,158 ft.).

Elevation is generally highest just before the point of descent to the Great Rift Valley, which splits the plateau diagonally. A number of rivers cross the plateau—notably the Blue Nile flowing from Lake Tana. The plateau gradually slopes to the lowlands of Ethiopia's neighbors to the west and the Somali-inhabited plains to the southeast.

The climate is temperate on the plateau and hot in the lowlands. At Addis Ababa, which ranges from 2,200 to 2,600 meters (7,000 ft.-8,500 ft.), maximum temperature is 26o C (80o F) and minimum 4o C (40o F). The weather is usually sunny and dry with the short (belg) rains occurring February-April and the big (meher) rains beginning in mid-June and ending in mid-September.

PEOPLE

Ethiopia's population is highly diverse. The Oromo, Amhara, and Tigreans make up more than two-thirds of the population.

Language

There are more than 80 major language groups in Ethiopia, although the national language, Amharic, is spoken throughout the country. Oromiffa and Tigrinya are other widely-used Ethiopian languages. English is the second official language and is understood in most towns among the more educated segments of the population.

Religion

According to the most recent census (2007), 44 percent of the population belongs to the Ethiopian Orthodox Church (EOC), which is predominant in the northern regions of Tigray and Amhara. Thirty-four percent of the population is Sunni Muslim, of which the majority is Sufi. Islam is most prevalent in the Somali and Afar regions, and in Oromia. Christian evangelical and Pentecostal groups constitute 19 percent of the population. Established Protestant churches are strongest in the Southern Nations, Nationalities, and Peoples' Region (SNNPR), Gambella, and parts of Oromia.

There are small numbers of Eastern Rite and Roman Catholics, Jehovah's Witnesses, Jews, members of The Church of Jesus Christ of Latter-day Saints (Mormons), animists, and practitioners of indigenous religions.

HISTORY

Hominid bones discovered in eastern Ethiopia dating back 4.4 million years make Ethiopia one of the earliest known locations of human ancestors. Ethiopia is the oldest independent country in Africa and one of the oldest in the world. Herodotus, the Greek historian of the fifth century B.C., describes ancient Ethiopia in his writings.

The Old Testament of the Bible records the Queen of Sheba's visit to Jerusalem. According to legend, Menelik I, the son of King Solomon and the Queen of Sheba, founded the Ethiopian Empire. Missionaries from Egypt and Syria introduced Christianity in the fourth century A.D. Following the rise of Islam in the seventh century, Ethiopia was gradually cut off from European Christendom. The Portuguese established contact with Ethiopia in 1493, primarily to strengthen their influence over the Indian Ocean and to convert Ethiopia to Roman Catholicism. There followed a century of conflict between pro- and anti-Catholic factions, resulting in the expulsion of all foreign missionaries in the 1630s. This period of bitter religious conflict contributed to hostility toward foreign Christians and Europeans, which persisted into the 20th century and was a factor in Ethiopia's isolation until the mid-19th century.

Under the Emperors Tewodros II (1855–68), Johannes IV (1872–89), and Menelik II (1889–1913), the kingdom was consolidated and began to emerge from its medieval isolation. When Menelik II died, his grandson, Lij Iyassu, succeeded to the throne but soon lost support because of his Muslim ties. The Christian nobility deposed him in 1916, and Menelik's daughter, Zewditu, was made empress. Her cousin, Ras Tafari Makonnen (1892–1975), was made regent and successor to the throne. In 1930, after the empress died, the regent, adopting the throne name Haile Selassie, was crowned emperor.

His reign was interrupted in 1936 when Italian Fascist forces invaded and occupied Ethiopia. The emperor was forced into exile in England. Five years later, British and Ethiopian forces defeated the Italians, and the emperor returned to the throne.

Following civil unrest, which began in February 1974, the aging Haile Selassie I was deposed on September 12, 1974, by a provisional administrative council of soldiers, known as the Derg ("committee"). The Derg seized power, installing a government that was socialist in name and military in style. It then summarily executed 59 members of the royal family and ministers and generals of the emperor's government; Emperor Haile Selassie I was strangled in the basement of his palace on August 22, 1975.

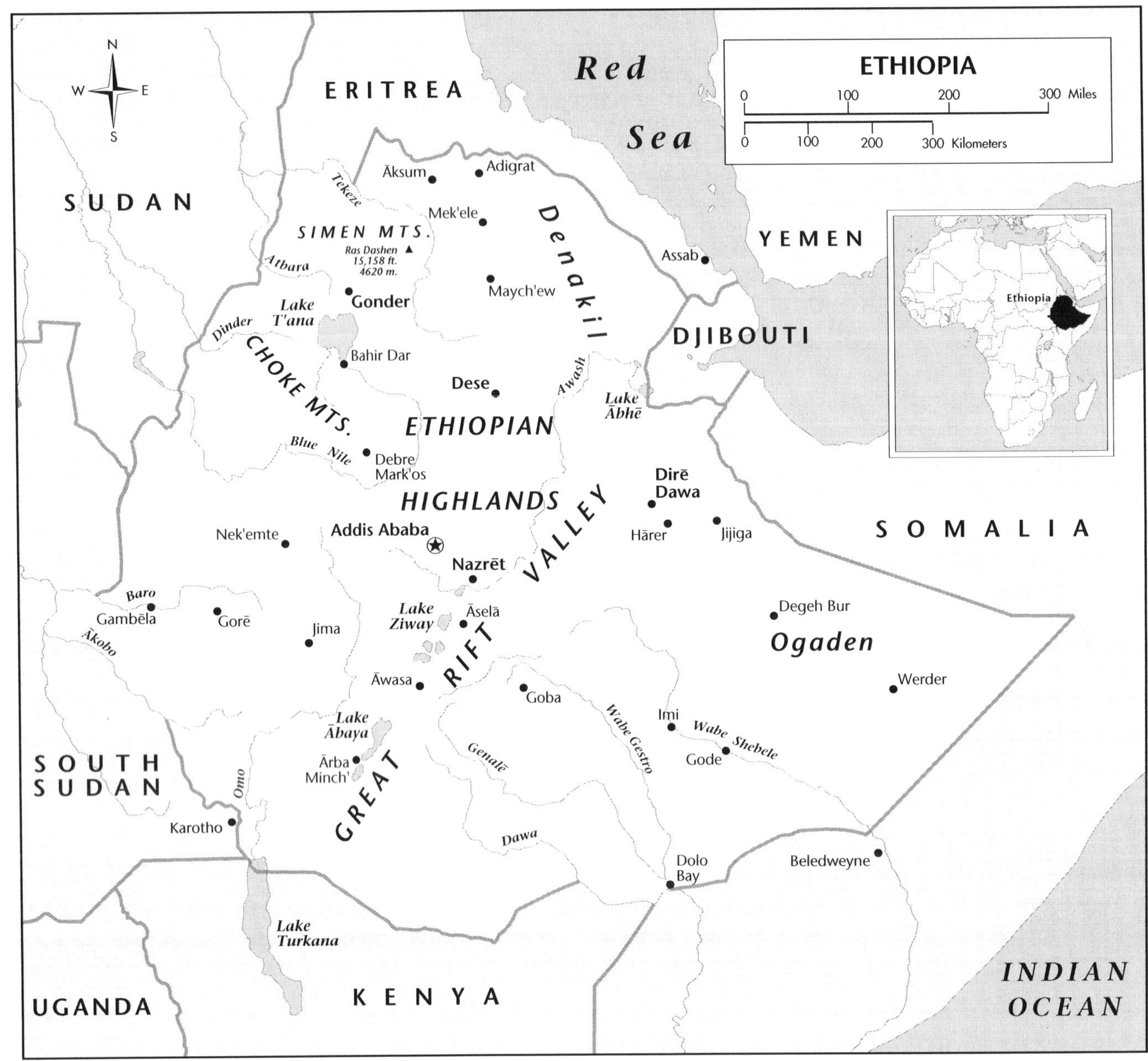

The Derg's collapse was hastened by droughts, famine, and insurrections, particularly in the northern regions of Tigray and Eritrea. In 1989, the Tigrayan People's Liberation Front (TPLF) merged with other ethnically based opposition movements to form the Ethiopian Peoples' Revolutionary Democratic Front (EPRDF). In May 1991, EPRDF forces advanced on Addis Ababa. Mengistu fled the country for asylum in Zimbabwe, where he still resides.

In July 1991, the EPRDF, the Oromo Liberation Front (OLF), and others established the Transitional Government of Ethiopia (TGE), composed of an 87-member Council of Representatives and guided by a national charter that functioned as a transitional constitution. In June 1992, the OLF withdrew from the government; in March 1993, members of the Southern Ethiopia Peoples' Democratic Coalition left the government.

In May 1991, the Eritrean People's Liberation Front (EPLF), led by Isaias Afwerki, assumed control of Eritrea and established a provisional government. This provisional government independently administered Eritrea until April 23-25, 1993, when Eritreans voted overwhelmingly for independence in a UN-monitored free and fair referendum. Eritrea, with Ethiopia's consent, was declared independent on April 27. The United States recognized its independence the next day.

In Ethiopia, President Meles Zenawi and members of the TGE pledged to oversee the formation of a multiparty democracy. The election for a 547-member constituent assembly was held in June 1994. The assembly adopted the constitution of the Federal Democratic Republic of Ethiopia in December 1994. The elections for

Ethiopia's first popularly chosen national parliament and regional legislatures were held in May and June 1995. Most opposition parties chose to boycott these elections, ensuring a landslide victory for the EPRDF. International and non-governmental observers concluded that opposition parties would have been able to participate had they chosen to do so. The Government of the Federal Democratic Republic of Ethiopia was installed in August 1995.

In May 1998, Eritrean forces attacked part of the Ethiopia-Eritrea border region, seizing some Ethiopian-controlled territory. The strike spurred a 2-year war between the neighboring states that cost more than 70,000 lives. On June 18, 2000, Ethiopian and Eritrean leaders signed an Agreement on Cessation of Hostilities and on December 12, 2000, a peace agreement known as the Algiers Agreement.

Opposition candidates won 12 seats in national parliamentary elections in 2000. In controversial national elections in May 2005, the opposition was awarded 170 of 547 seats but claimed fraud; violence ensued. Ethiopian security forces responded and in the process killed more than 200 people, arrested scores of opposition leaders, as well as journalists and human rights advocates, and detained tens of thousands of civilians for up to 3 months in rural detention camps.

In December 2005, the government charged 131 opposition, media, and civil society leaders—including the prominent opposition leader Birtukan Mideksa, a former judge and the vice-chairperson of the opposition Coalition for Unity and Democracy (CUD) party—with capital offenses including "outrages against the constitution." Birtukan was sentenced to life imprisonment, though she and other key opposition leaders and the majority of the 131 arrested were pardoned and released from prison 18 months later. The opposition largely boycotted local elections in 2008 with the result that EPRDF won more than 99% of all local seats.

In June 2008, Birtukan was elected the party chairman of the new Unity for Democracy and Justice (UDJ) party at its inaugural session in Addis Ababa. In October 2008, the Ethiopian Government arrested more than 100 Oromo leaders, accusing some of being members of the outlawed Oromo Liberation Front (OLF).

At the end of December 2008, after briefly detaining Birtukan several times during the month, the government re-arrested her, saying she had violated the conditions of her summer 2007 pardon. Her original sentence of life imprisonment was reinstated and she remained in prison until she was pardoned again and released on October 6, 2010.

In April 2009, the Ethiopian Government arrested 41 individuals, mostly Amhara military or ex-military members allegedly affiliated with external opposition party Ginbot 7, for suspected involvement in a terrorist assassination plot of government leaders.

The Ginbot 7 party was founded in May 2008 in the United States by Berhanu Nega, one of the opposition leaders in the 2005 elections, and advocates for change in the government "by any means." In August 2009, the Federal High Court found 13 of the defendants guilty in absentia and one not guilty in absentia. In November 2009, the court found another 27 guilty.

In simultaneous national and regional parliamentary elections in May 2010, the ruling EPRDF won more than 99% of all legislative seats in the country. In a tally of the popular vote, 91.95% voted for EPRDF and affiliate parties, while only 8.05% voted for the opposition countrywide. Election day was peaceful as 89% of registered voters cast ballots, but independent observation of the vote was severely limited.

Only European Union and African Union observers were permitted, and they were restricted to the capital and barred from proximity to polling places. Although those few independent observers allowed access to the process did not question the EPRDF victory, there was ample evidence that unsavory government tactics—including intimidation of opposition candidates and supporters—influenced the extent of the victory.

Observers declared the 2010 elections not up to international standards because an environment conducive to free and fair elections was not in place. According to observers, the EPRDF used the advantage of incumbency to restrict political space for opposition candidates and activists.

At the local level, thousands of opposition activists complained of EPRDF-sponsored mistreatment, ranging from harassment in submitting candidacy forms to beatings by local militia members, and complained further that there was no forum free of EPRDF control to which to present those complaints.

In June 2011, the Ethiopian parliament officially designated five groups as terrorist organizations under Ethiopian law, including the OLF, the Ogaden National Liberation Front (ONLF), Ginbot 7, al-Qaida, and al-Shabaab.

Later in 2011, the Ethiopian Government arrested large numbers of activists, journalists, and political leaders for alleged involvement in terrorist activities and charged many of them under Ethiopia's controversial 2009 anti-terrorism proclamation. In December 2011, two Swedish journalists were sentenced to 11 years in prison on charges of entering Ethiopia illegally and allegedly supporting the ONLF.

On January 26, 2012, the Federal High Court sentenced Elias Kifle, a blogger, to life imprisonment in absentia; Zerihun Gebre Egziabhier, Chairman of Ethiopian National Unity Party, to 17 years in prison; Wubishet Taye, deputy editor-in-chief of a local newspaper, to 14 years; Reeyot Alemu, a columnist, to 14 years; and Hirut Kifle, a political activist, to 19 years, for conspiring and attempting to commit terrorist acts and participation in a terrorist organization.

GOVERNMENT AND POLITICAL CONDITIONS

Ethiopia is a federal republic led by Prime Minister Meles Zenawi and the Ethiopian People's Revolutionary Democratic Front (EPRDF). In national parliamentary elections in May 2010, the EPRDF and affiliated parties won 545 of 547 seats to remain in power for a fourth consecutive five-year term.

The EPRDF is made up of four ethnically based political organizations: the Tigrayan People's Liberation Front, Amhara National Democratic Movement, Oromo People's Democratic Organization, and Southern Ethiopian People's Democratic Movement. Although the relatively few international officials allowed to observe the elections concluded that technical aspects of the vote were handled competently, some also noted that an environment conducive to free and fair elections was not in place prior to election day.

Several laws, regulations, and procedures implemented since the 2005 national elections created a clear advantage for the EPRDF throughout the electoral process.

Recent Elections

In the May 2010 national parliamentary elections, the EPRDF and affiliated parties won 545 of 547 seats to remain in power for a fourth consecutive five-year term. In simultaneous elections for regional parliaments, the EPRDF and its affiliates won 1,903 of 1,904 seats. The EPRDF and its affiliates received approximately 79 percent of total votes cast but won more than 99 percent of all seats at all levels. Independent observation of the vote was severely limited due to government restrictions.

Although the relatively few international officials allowed to observe the elections concluded that technical aspects of the vote were handled competently, some also noted that an environment conducive to free and fair elections was not in place prior to election day. Several laws, regulations, and procedures implemented since the 2005 national elections created a clear advantage for the EPRDF throughout the electoral process.

There was ample evidence that unfair government tactics—including intimidation of opposition candidates and supporters—influenced the extent of the EPRDF victory. In addition voter education was limited in scope to information about technical voting procedures and done only by the National Electoral Board, and then only days before voting began.

The African Union, whose observers arrived one week before the vote, pronounced the elections as free and fair. The European Union, some of whose observers arrived a few months before the vote, concluded that the elections fell short of international standards for transparency and failed to provide a level playing field for opposition parties.

Overall the EU observed a "climate of apprehension and insecurity," noting that the volume and consistency of complaints of harassment and intimidation by opposition parties was "a matter of concern" and had to be taken into consideration "in the overall assessment of the electoral process."

Political Parties: Political parties were predominantly ethnically based. Membership in the EPRDF conferred advantages upon its members; the party directly owned many businesses and was broadly perceived to award jobs and business contracts to loyal supporters.

The opposition reported that in many instances local authorities told its members to renounce their party membership and join the EPRDF if they wanted access to subsidized seeds and fertilizer; food relief; civil service job assignment, promotion, or retention; student university assignment and postgraduate employment; and other benefits controlled by the government.

During 2011 there were credible reports that teachers and other government workers had their employment terminated if they belonged to opposition political parties.

According to opposition groups such as the OFDM and the OPC, the Oromia regional government continued to threaten to dismiss opposition party members—particularly teachers—from their jobs. At the university level, however, members of Medrek and its constituent parties were able to teach.

Registered political parties must receive permission from regional governments to open and occupy local offices.

In early 2010 a system of public campaign finance was announced. Under this system parties are to receive public funds based in part on the number of parliamentary seats they hold.

Participation of Women and Minorities: No laws or cultural or traditional practices prevented women or minorities from voting or participating in political life on the same basis as men or nonminority citizens.

The government policy of ethnic federalism led to the creation of individual constituencies to provide for representation of all major ethnic groups in the House of People's Representatives. There were more than 80 ethnic groups, and small groups lacked representation in the legislature.

There were 24 nationality groups in six regional states (Tigray, Amhara, Beneshangul-Gumuz, SNNPR, Gambella, and Harar) that did not have a sufficient population to qualify for constituency seats based on the 2007 census result; however, in the May 2010 elections, individuals from these nationality groups competed for 24 special seats in the House of People's Representatives. Additionally these 24 nationality groups have one seat each in the unelected, largely ceremonial House of Federation.

Principal Government Officials

Last Updated: 1/31/2013

Pres.: **GIRMA Woldegiorgis**
Prime Min.: **HAILEMARIAM Desalegn**
Dep. Prime Min.: **DEBRETSION Gebre-Michael**
Dep. Prime Min.: **DEMEKE Mekonnen Hassen**
Dep. Prime Min.: **MUKTAR Kedir**
Min. of Agriculture: **TEFERA Deribew**
Min. of Cabinet Affairs: **DEMISSE Shito**
Min. of Civil Service: **MUKTAR Kedir**
Min. of Communication & Information Technology: **DEBRETSION Gebre-Michael**
Min. of Culture & Tourism: **AMIN Abdulkadir**
Min. of Defense: **SIRAJ Fegessa Shereffa**
Min. of Education: **DEMEKE Mekonnen**
Min. of Federal Affairs: **SHIFERAW Tekle-Mariam**
Min. of Finance & Economic Development: **SUFIAN Ahmed**
Min. of Foreign Affairs: **TEWODROS Adhanom**
Min. of Govt. Communications Affairs Office: **BEREKET Simon**
Min. of Health: **KESETE-BERHAN Admasu**
Min. of Industry: **MEKONNEN Manyazewal**
Min. of Justice: **BIRHAN Hailu**
Min. of Labor & Social Affairs: **ABDULFETAH Abdulahi Hassen**
Min. of Mines: **SINKINESH Ejigu**
Min. of Science & Technology: **DESSIE Dalke**
Min. of Trade: **KEBEDE Chane**
Min. of Transport: **DIRIBA Kuma**
Min. of Urban Development & Construction: **MEKURIA Haile**
Min. of Water & Energy: **ALEMAYEHU Tegenu**
Min. of Women, Children, & Youth Affairs: **ZENEBU Tadesse**
Governor, National Bank of Ethiopia: **TEKLEWOLD Atnafu**
Ambassador to the US: **GIRMA Birru Geda**
Permanent Representative to the UN, New York: **TEKEDA Alemu Wolde Mariam**

ECONOMY

Ethiopia's economy is based on agriculture, which accounts for 46% of GDP and 85% of total employment. Coffee has been a major export crop. The agricultural sector suffers from poor cultivation practices and frequent drought, but recent joint efforts by the Government of Ethiopia and donors have strengthened Ethiopia's agricultural resilience, contributing to a reduction in the number of Ethiopians threatened with starvation.

The banking, insurance, and micro-credit industries are restricted to domestic investors, but Ethiopia has attracted significant foreign investment in textiles, leather, commercial agriculture and manufacturing. Under Ethiopia's constitution, the state owns all land and provides long-term leases to the tenants; land use certificates are now being issued in some areas so that tenants have more recognizable rights to continued occupancy and hence make more concerted efforts to improve their leaseholds.

While GDP growth has remained high, per capita income is among the lowest in the world. Ethiopia's economy continues on its state-led Growth and Transformation Plan under its new leadership after Prime Minister Meles's death. The five-year economic plan has achieved high single-digit growth rates through government-led infrastructure expansion and commercial agriculture development. Ethiopia in 2013 plans to continue construction of its Grand Renassiance Dam on the Nile-the controversial multi-billion dollar effort to develop electricity for domestic consumption and export.

Labor Conditions

By law the minimum age for wage or salary employment is 14 years. The minimum age provisions, however, do not apply to self-employed children. Special provisions cover children between the ages of 14 and 18, including the prohibition of hazardous or night work. By law children between the ages of 14 and 18 are not permitted to work more than seven hours per day or between 10 p.m. and 6 a.m., on public holidays or rest days, or overtime.

The law defines hazardous work as work in factories or involving machinery with moving parts or any work that could jeopardize a child's health. Prohibited work sectors include passenger transport, electric generation plants, underground work, street cleaning, and many other sectors.

The government did not effectively enforce these laws in practice. Child labor was particularly pervasive in subsistence agricultural production, traditional weaving, and small-scale gold mining. Children in rural areas, especially boys, also engaged in activities such as cattle herding, petty trading, plowing, harvesting, and weeding, while other children, mostly girls, collected firewood and fetched water.

Children in urban areas, including orphans, also worked in domestic service, often working long hours, which prevented many from attending school regularly. Children in urban areas also worked in construction, manufacturing, shining shoes, making clothes, portering, directing customers to taxis, parking, public transport, petty trading, and occasionally herding animals. Child laborers often faced physical, sexual, and emotional abuse at the hands of their employers.

There is no national minimum wage. Some government institutions and public enterprises, however, set their own minimum wages. Public sector employees, the largest group of wage earners, earned a monthly minimum wage of approximately 420 birr ($24); employees in the banking and insurance sector had a minimum monthly wage of 336 birr ($20).

Wages in the informal sector were generally below subsistence levels. Consequently, most families in the wage sector required at least two wage earners to survive, which forced many children to leave school early. Only a small percentage of the population was involved in wage-labor employment, which was concentrated in urban areas. The law provides for a 48-hour maximum legal workweek with a 24-hour rest period, premium pay for overtime, and prohibition of excessive compulsory overtime. The country has 13 paid public holidays per year. The law entitles employees in public enterprise and government financial institutions to overtime pay; civil servants receive compensatory time for overtime work.

Compensation, benefits, and working conditions of seasonal agricultural workers were far below those of unionized permanent agricultural employees. Although the government did little to enforce the law, in practice most employees in the formal sector worked a 39-hour workweek. However, many foreign, migrant, and informal sector workers worked more than 48 hours per week.

U.S.-ETHIOPIA RELATIONS

The United States established diplomatic relations with Ethiopia in 1903. Italy, which had neighboring possessions in Africa, invaded and occupied Ethiopia from 1935 until its expulsion in 1941 during World War II. The United States never publicly recognized Italian authority in Ethiopia. After Ethiopia's 1974 revolution, U.S.-Ethiopian relations began to cool due to the government's linkage with international communism and U.S. revulsion at its human rights abuses. Bilateral relations improved with the 1991 downfall of Ethiopia's regime.

The United States and the people of Ethiopia share a strong history as friends and partners. Today, the three pillars of the bilateral relationship are economic growth and development; democracy, governance, and human rights; and regional peace and security. The United States and Ethiopia work together to enhance food security, improve health services, strengthen education, promote trade, and expand development. The United States has welcomed Ethiopia's dedication to maintaining security in the region, including through peacekeeping missions in Sudan and South Sudan.

U.S. Assistance to Ethiopia

Ethiopia is prone to drought, and the United States has provided emergency resources to it in the form of food aid and humanitarian assistance. U.S. development assistance to Ethiopia is focused on reducing famine vulnerability, hunger, and poverty and emphasizes economic, governance, and social sector policy reforms.

Some military training funds, including training in such issues as the laws of war and observance of human rights, also are provided but are explicitly limited to nonlethal assistance, training, and peacekeeping support at present.

Bilateral Economic Relations

Ethiopia is eligible for preferential trade benefits under the African Growth and Opportunity Act. U.S. exports to Ethiopia include aircraft, wheat, machinery, low-value shipments and repaired products, and vegetables. U.S. imports from Ethiopia include coffee, niger seeds, returns, and apparel. The United States has signed a trade and investment framework agreement with the Common Market for Eastern and Southern Africa, of which Ethiopia is a member.

Ethiopia's Membership in International Organizations

Ethiopia and the United States belong to a number of the same international organizations, including the United Nations, International Monetary Fund, and World Bank. Ethiopia is an observer to the World Trade Organization.

Bilateral Representation

Ethiopia maintains an embassy in the United States at 3506 International Drive, NW, Washington, DC 20008 (tel. 202-364-1200)

Principal U.S. Embassy Officials

Last Updated: 1/14/2013

ADDIS ABABA (E) 1014 Entoto Rd, Addis Ababa, +251 011-130-6000, Fax +251 011-130-6100, INMARSAT Tel 00871761258488, Workweek: Mon-Th 0730-1700, Fri 0730-1230.

DCM OMS: Chris Call
AMB OMS: Diane Corbin
CA: Louise Guallpa-Lliquichuxhca
CDC: Tom Kenyon
Co-CLO: Renate Cunningham
ECON/COM: Daniel Rosenthal
FM: Ron Saunders
HRO: Thomas Zeitler
MGT: Joyce Currie
PAO/ADV: Diane Brandt
POL: /ADV Jeffrey Graham
POL/ECON: Shannon Cazeau
SDO/DATT: COL Thomas B Sweeney
SPSH: Patrick Wozny
AMB: Donald Booth
CON: Scott Riedmann
DCM: Molly Phee
PAO: Robert Post
GSO: Dwight Samuels
RSO: Donald Jurczyk
AFSA: Daniel Rosenthal
AGR: Merritt Chesley
AID: Dennis Weller
ATO: Merritt Chesley
CLO: Mark Lovejoy
EEO: Diane Corbin
EST: Stephen Cunningham
FAA/CASLO: Daniel Rosenthal
FMO: Richard Nicholson
ICASS Chair: Thomas Kenyon
IMO: Matthew Michaud
IPO: Daniel Siebert
LEGATT: David Snyder
State ICASS: Robert Post

US MISSION TO AFRICAN UNION (M) 1014 Entoto Rd, Addis Ababa, (251-11) 130-7001, Fax +251-11-124-2459, Workweek: Mo-Th 0730–1700, Fr 0730-1230.

AMB OMS: Ginger Richeter
POL/ECON: John Yang
SDO/DATT: COL Tony Curtis
AMB: Michael A. Battle
DCM: Wallace Bain
PAO: Jasmine White
AID: Glenn Rogers
ECON: Darrow Godeski Merton
POL: Jasmine White

TRAVEL

Consular Information Sheet

May 1, 2012

Country Description: The Federal Democratic Republic of Ethiopia is a developing country in East Africa. It is comprised of nine states and two city administrations (Addis Ababa and Dire Dawa). The capital is Addis Ababa. Tourism facilities can be found in the most populous regions of Ethiopia, but infrastructure is basic. The government is led by the Ethiopian People's Revolutionary Democratic Front (EPRDF) and Prime Minister Meles Zenawi. Despite several years of high economic growth, the country remains vulnerable to external economic shocks.

Registration/Embassy Location: If you are going to live in or visit Ethiopia, please take the time to tell our Embassy about your trip. If you sign up, we can keep you up to date with important safety and security announcements. We can also help your friends and family get in touch with you in an emergency.

U.S. Embassy
Addis Ababa, Ethiopia Telephone: +251- 11 130-6000
Emergency after-hours telephone: 011 130-6000
Facsimile:+251- 11 124-2435 and+251- 11 124-2419

Entry/Exit Requirements for U.S. Citizens: To avoid possible confusion or delays, travelers are strongly advised to obtain a valid Ethiopian visa at the nearest Ethiopian Embassy prior to arrival. This is a necessary step if you plan to enter Ethiopia by any land port-of-entry. For example: travelers wishing to enter Ethiopia from Kenya at the land border at Moyale must obtain an Ethiopian visa first. Ethiopian visas ARE NOT available at the border crossing point at Moyale or at any other land border in Ethiopia.

Ethiopian tourist visas (one month or three month, single entry) may be available to U.S. citizens upon arrival at Bole International Airport in Addis Ababa in some cases. A Government of Ethiopia policy prevents travelers born in Eritrea, regardless of their current nationality, from receiving tourist visas at the airport. The on-arrival visa process is available only at Bole International Airport and is not available at any of the other airports in Ethiopia. The visa fee at Bole International Airport is payable in U.S. dollars.

Business visas of up to three months validity can also be obtained at Bole International Airport upon arrival, but only if the traveler has a sponsoring organization in Ethiopia that has made prior arrangements for issuance through the Main Immigration Office in Addis Ababa. In some cases, U.S. tourist and business travelers have not been permitted to receive visas at Bole International Airport or have been significantly delayed.

Travelers whose entry visa expires before they depart Ethiopia must obtain a visa extension through the Main Immigration Office in Addis Ababa and pay a monthly penalty fee of $20 USD per month. Such travelers may also be required to pay a court fine of up to 4000 ETB (USD $300) before being permitted to depart Ethiopia. Court fees must be paid in Ethiopian Birr. Travelers may be detained by immigration officials and/or required to appear in immigration court, and are required to pay the penalty fee before they will be able to obtain an exit visa (USD $20, payable in dollars) permitting them to leave Ethiopia.

Business travelers or employees of non-governental organizations (NGOs) who intend to stay for 90 days or more must apply for a residence card/work permit in order to continue working and living in Ethiopia. Travelers must apply for this permit within the first 30 days of their stay in Ethiopia and must not work until this permit is approved.

Travelers should check with their sponsoring organization to ensure they have the correct documentation in place, or risk penalties, including detention, fines, and deportation. The Govement of Ethiopia's regulations also allow for similar penalties for those who assist others to reside illegally in Ethiopia.

If you plan to stay in Ethiopia for a prolonged period of time, you are advised to contact the Ethiopian Embassy in Washington prior to traveling. Some long-term visitors may be eligible to apply for a residence permit before they depart for Ethiopia. The Ethiopian Embassy is located at 3506 International Drive NW, Washington, DC 20008; telephone (202) 364-1200; fax (202) 587-0195.

Customs Requirements: Non-residents traveling to Ethiopia must declare any/all foreign currency in excess of 3000 USD (or its equivalent). Non-residents departing Ethiopia may carry a maximum of 3000 USD (or its equivalent), unless they can produce a customs declaration, bank slip showing the purchase of foreign currency, or letter confirming that they were paid by an embassy or foreign organization in Ethiopia. Residents of Ethiopia must produce a bank slip showing the purchase of foreign currency, or customs declaration that is not more than 45 days old, in order to carry any foreign currency out of Ethiopia.

Any traveler entering or exiting Ethiopia may carry a maximum of 200 Ethiopian Birr on their person or in their luggage.

Ethiopian customs rules limit the amount of precious metals or minerals imported or exported for personal use to a) 100 grams for gold and other precious metals; b) 30 grams for precious stones; c) 100 grams for semi-precious stones.

Permits are required before exporting either antiques or animal skins from Ethiopia. Antique religious artifacts, including "Ethiopian" crosses, require a permit for export. These permits can be processed by the Export Section of the Airport customs office. Even tourist souveniers, especially crosses, may require such documentation if customs authorities deem it necessary, and/or may be confiscated by customs authorites if in excess of the allowable limit of precious metals as noted above.

Animal skins must have an export permit, which can be obtained from the Ethiopian Wildlife Conservation Authority. Please also note that large Ethiopian crosses may not be taken on aircraft as hand luggage, as some airlines consider them to be potential weapons.

The ivory trade is banned in Ethiopia. Recently, travelers wearing ivory jewelry have been detained, even if the jewelry pre-dates the ivory ban. Jewelry has been confiscated and fines imposed for violating this ban.

Travelers found violating any of the above customs rules have been detained at the airport and in some cases have been sentenced to prison terms of three months or more. For the most current visa and travel information, visit the Ethiopian Embassy website or the Ethiopian Revenue and Customs Authority website. U.S. citizens located overseas may also inquire at the nearest Ethiopian embassy or consulate.

The U.S. Department of State is unaware of any HIV/AIDS entry restrictions for visitors to or foreign residents of Ethiopia.

Threats to Safety and Security: Throughout Ethiopia: U.S. citizens are strongly advised to review their personal safety and security posture, to remain vigilant, and to be cautious when frequenting prominent public places and landmarks. While Ethiopia is generally stable, domestic insurgent groups, extremists from Somalia, and the heavy military presence along the border with Eritrea pose risks to safety and security.

A number of al-Qaida operatives and other extremists are believed to be operating in and around Africa. Since the July 11, 2010, terrorist bombings in Kampala, Uganda, for which the Somalia-based, U.S. government-designated Foreign Terrorist Organization al-Shabaab has claimed responsibility, there have been increased threats against public areas across East Africa.

Current information suggests that al-Qaida and affiliated organizations continue to plan terrorist attacks against US interests in multiple regions, including Africa. In February 2012, leaders of al-Shabaab and al-Qaida announced a merger of the two groups.

U.S. citizens should strongly consider the risk of attending or being near large public gatherings, or venues where westerners gather on a routine or predictable basis, and which have no visible security presence. Such gatherings or venues can provide vulnerable targets for extremist or terrorist groups. U.S. citizens should avoid, if possible, using public transportation, including mini-buses. You are advised to avoid unattended baggage or packages left in any location, including in taxis.

There are periodic attacks on civilians as well as security forces in the Somali region of Ethiopia. In 2011, Kenyan and Ethiopian forces initiated an offensive against al-Shabab in Somalia, together with the African Union Mission in Somalia (AMISOM) which has been in Mogadishu since 2007, resulting in an increase in the threat level in Ethiopia and neighboring countries.

In southern Ethiopia, along the Kenyan border, banditry and incidents involving ethnic conflicts are also common. You should exercise caution when traveling to any remote area of the country, including the borders with Eritrea, Somalia, Kenya, Sudan, and South Sudan, and avoid travel outside of the major towns in these border areas.

Ethiopia/Eritrea Border (Northern Ethiopia): Ethiopia and Eritrea signed a peace agreement in December 2000 that ended their border war. However, the border remains an issue of contention between the governments of Ethiopia and Eritrea. The border area is a militarized zone where the possibility of armed conflict between Ethiopian and Eritrean forces continues. U.S. government personnel are restricted from travel north of the Shire (Inda Silassie)-Axum-Adigrat road in the Tigray region of Ethiopia. Personnel are further restricted from travel north of the road from Dessie through Semera to the Galafi border crossing with Djibouti, including the Danakil Depression and the Erta Ale volcano.

In January 2012, a group of foreign tourists were attacked near the Erta Ale volcano in the Afar region near the Eritrean border, approximately 100 miles southeast of Adigrat in the Danakil Depression. The attack resulted in five deaths, three wounded, and four people kidnapped. The victims were European and Ethiopian citizens. The two Europeans who were kidnapped were subsequently released.

On February 15, 2012, Ethiopia, which blamed Eritrea for the attack, retaliated by striking military camps in Eritrea where the attackers were allegedly trained. This episode illustrates the continuing volatility of the border area. Please see this restricted area indicated in red on the map below.

Somali Region (Eastern Ethiopia): Travel to Ethiopia's Somali region is restricted for U.S. government employees, although essential travel to Jijiga town and zone, as well as the Shimeli zone is permitted. Since the mid-1990's, members of the Ogaden National Liberation Front (ONLF) have conducted attacks on civilian targets near the city of Harar and in the Somali regional state, particularly in the Ogaden zones.

Expatriates have been killed in these attacks. In 2010, the Government of Ethiopia initiated peace talks with the ONLF, which are ongoing. Despite these talks, there have been isolated incidents of violence. In May 2011, gunmen affiliated with the ONLF attacked a vehicle belonging to the United Nations World Food Program (WFP), killing the vehicle's driver, wounding one other, and kidnapping two other WFP employees. The kidnapped employees were later released.

Gambella Region (Western Ethiopia): Sporadic inter-ethnic clashes are a concern throughout the Gambella region of western Ethiopia. While the security situation in the town of Gambella is generally calm, it remains unpredictable throughout the rest of the region. Intensified conflict between Sudan and the Republic of South Sudan has increased refugee flows into Western Ethiopia. Travel to the border areas in the Beneshangul (Asosa) region is restricted to major towns. U.S. government personnel are restricted from travel in the areas of Ethiopia indicated on the map above. Blue indicates the Somali region; Red indicates the Ethiopian/Eritrean border area; and Green indicates the Gambella region.

Important Note: The Government of Ethiopia rarely informs the Embassy of arrested or detained U.S. citizens, even those detained at the airport by immigration or customs authorities. In some instances, U.S. citizens have been detained for weeks or even months without Embassy notification.

If you are arrested or detained in Ethiopia, you have the right to request that Ethiopian authorities alert the U.S. Embassy of your detention or arrest in accordance with the 1951 Treaty of Amity and Economic Relations between the United States and Ethiopia. If you are detained or arrested in Ethiopia you should use whatever means of communication available to alert the U.S. Embassy of your situation.

Stay up to date by:

- Bookmarking our Bureau of Consular Affairs website, which contains the current Travel Warnings and Travel Alerts as well as the Worldwide Caution.
- Following us on Twitter and the Bureau of Consular Affairs page on Facebook as well.
- Downloading our free Smart Traveler IPhone App to have travel information at your fingertips.
- Calling 1-888-407-4747 toll-free within the United States and Canada, or a regular toll line, 1-202-501-4444, from other countries.
- Taking some time before travel to consider your personal security.

Crime: U.S. citizens are strongly advised to review their personal safety and security posture, to remain vigilant and to be cautious when frequenting prominent public places and landmarks. Pick-pocketing, "snatch and run" thefts, including from occupied vehicles and other petty crimes are common in Addis Ababa.

These are generally crimes of opportunity rather than planned attacks. Beginning in 2011, purse snatchings and harassment by gangs of youths in the Bole area of Addis Ababa have increased. These incidents have occurred in both the daytime and nighttime. There were also beatings and stabbings of expats in the area. The number of residential burglaries has also increased.

Travelers should exercise caution in crowded areas, and especially the Mercato in Addis Ababa, a large open-air market. You should limit the amount of cash you carry and leave valuables, such as passports, jewelry, and airline tickets in a hotel safe or other secure place. You should keep wallets and other valuables where they will be less susceptible to pickpockets. If you have a cellular phone, carry it with you.

You should be cautious at all times when traveling on roads in Ethiopia. Highway robbery by armed bandits in some border areas have been reported. Some of these incidents have been accompanied by violence. You are cautioned to limit road travel outside major towns or cities to daylight hours and travel in convoys, if possible, in case of breakdowns.

When driving, be wary of other motorists warning you of a mechanical problem or loose tire. This may be a ruse used by thieves to get you to stop the vehicle. Most of all be alert and aware of your surroundings at all times to ensure that you aren't being followed.

Don't buy counterfeit and pirated goods, even if they are widely available. Not only are the bootlegs illegal in the United States, if you purchase them you may also be breaking local law.

Victims of Crime: If you or someone you know becomes the victim of a crime abroad, you should contact the local police and the nearest U.S. embassy or consulate. We can:

- Replace a stolen passport.
- Help you find appropriate medical care if you are the victim of violent crimes such as assault or rape.
- Put you in contact with the appropriate police authorities, and if you want us to, we can contact family members or friend.
- Help you understand the local criminal justice process and direct you to local attorneys, although it is important to remember that local authorities are responsible for investigating and prosecuting the crime.

The local equivalent to the "911" emergency line in Ethiopia is 991.

Criminal Penalties: While you are traveling in another country, you are subject to its laws even if you are a U.S. citizen. Foreign laws and legal systems can be vastly different than our own. Criminal penalties vary from country to country. There are also some things that might be legal in the country you visit, but still illegal in the United States, and you can be prosecuted under U.S. law if you buy pirated goods.

Engaging in sexual conduct with children or using or disseminating child pornography in a foreign country is a crime prosecutable in the United States. If you break local laws in your host country, your U.S. passport won't help you avoid arrest or prosecution. It's very important to know what's legal and what's not where you are going. Ethiopian law strictly prohibits the photographing of military installations, police/military personnel, industrial facilities, government buildings, and infrastructure (roads, bridges, dams, airfields, etc.). Such sites are rarely marked clearly. Travel guides, police, and Ethiopian officials can advise if a particular site may be photographed. Photographing prohibited sites may result in the confiscation of film and camera and arrest.

Persons violating Ethiopian laws, even unknowingly, may be expelled, arrested, or imprisoned. Penalties for possessing, using, or trafficking in illegal drugs in Ethiopia are severe, and convicted offenders can expect long jail sentences and heavy fines.

If you are arrested in Ethiopia, you have the right to request that authorities alert the U.S. Embassy of your detention or arrest in accordance with the 1951 Treaty of Amity and Economic Relations between the United States and Ethiopia.

If you are detained or arrested in Ethiopia you should use whatever means of communication available to alert the U.S. Embassy of your situation. Please be aware that the Government of Ethiopia does not recognize dual nationality, so U.S. citizens born in Ethiopia are accorded the same rights as any other U.S. citizens in the case of arrest or detention.

Dual nationality: Ethiopia does not recognize dual nationality. The government of Ethiopia considers Ethiopians who have naturalized as U.S. citizens to be U.S. citizens only. Such individuals are not subject to Ethiopian military service. The Ethiopian government has stated that Ethiopian-Americans in almost all cases are given the same opportunity to invest in Ethiopia as Ethiopians. Ethiopian officials have stated that Eritrean-Americans are treated as U.S. citizens and are not subject to arrest simply because of their ties to Eritrea although, as noted above, they are not permitted to receive tourist visas at the airport.

Currency: Ethiopia is still primarily a cash economy. Dollars and some of the more popular travelers checks can be changed at the airport, and at some banks. There are some ATM machines at the major hotels and commercial centers that accept the major international credit and debit cards, although connectivity problems sometimes limit their availability. While credit cards are gaining acceptance with some hotels, travel agencies, and merchants, it is best to check ahead and ensure you have sufficient cash reserves.

Foreign currency should be exchanged in authorized banks, hotels, and other legally authorized outlets and proper receipts should be obtained for the transactions. Exchange receipts are required to convert unused Ethiopian currency back to the original foreign currency. Penalties for exchanging money on the black market range from fines to imprisonment. Credit cards are not accepted at most hotels, restaurants, shops, or other local facilities, although they are accepted at the Hilton, Sheraton, and Raddison Hotels in Addis Ababa. Some hotels and car rental companies, particularly in Addis Ababa, may require foreigners to pay in foreign currency or show a receipt for the source of foreign exchange if paying in local currency. Many hotels and establishments, however, are not permitted to accept foreign currency or may be reluctant to do so.

All travelers are permitted to carry $3,000 in foreign currency in and out of Ethiopia with proper evidence of its source. Employees of embassies and foreign organizations or individuals entering into the country through embassies or foreign organizations on temporary employment (e.g., to attend seminars, to give training) may leave the country carrying more than $3,000 in cash only when they can produce evidence that they were paid directly from a bank.

Residents may carry foreign currency upon departure, but only by producing evidence that the currency was purchased from a bank, or by producing a customs declaration not more than 45 days after it was issued. Travelers can only carry up to 200 Ethiopian Birr out of the country.

Ethiopian institutions have on occasion refused to accept 1996 series U.S. currency, although official policy is that such currency should be treated as legal tender.

Residence Permit: Business travelers or employees of non-goverentel organizations (NGOs) who intend to stay for 90 days or more must apply for a residence card/work permit in order to continue working and living in Ethiopia. Travelers must apply for this permit within the first 30 days of their stay in Ethiopia and may not work until this permit is approved.

Travelers should check with their sponsoring organziation to ensure they have the correct documentation in place, or risk penalties, including detention, fines, and deportation. The Govement of Ethiopia's regulations also allow for similar penalties for those who assist others to reside illegally in Ethiopia.

If you are arrested or detained in Ethiopia, it is unlikely that government authorities will notify the U.S. Embassy. Therefore, you should use should use whatever means of communication available to alert the U.S. Embassy of your situation.

Earthquakes: There is a risk of earthquakes in Ethiopia. Buildings may collapse due to strong tremors. General information about natural disaster preparedness is available via the Internet from the U.S. Federal Emergency Management Agency (FEMA).

Accessibility: While in Ethiopia, individuals with disabilities may find accessibility and accommodation very different from what you find in the United States. The Ethiopian Building Proclamation (no. 624), gazetted in May 2010, contains an article that mandates building accessibility and accessible toilet facilities for persons with physical disabilities.

In addition, landlords are required to give persons with disabilities preference for ground floor apartments, and this is respected in practice. In general, public buildings are not accessible to individuals with disabilities.

Medical Facilities and Health Information: Health facilities in Ethiopia are very limited and are generally inadequate outside the capital. Even the best hospitals in Addis Ababa suffer from inadequate facilities, antiquated equipment, and shortages of supplies (particularly medicines). There is a shortage of physicians. Emergency assistance is limited.

Psychiatric services and medications are practically nonexistent. Serious illnesses and injuries often require travelers to be medically evacuated from Ethiopia to a location where adequate medical attention is available. Such "medevac" services are very expensive and are generally available only to travelers who either have travel insurance that covers medevac services or who are able to pay for the service in advance (often in excess of USD 40,000). (See Medical Insurance below.)

Travelers must carry their own supplies of prescription drugs and preventive medicines, as well as a doctor's note describing the medication. If the quantity of drugs exceeds that which would be expected for personal use, a permit from the Ministry of Health is required.

Malaria is prevalent in Ethiopia outside of the highland areas. Travelers who become ill with a fever or flu-like illness while traveling in a malaria-risk area and up to one year after returning home should seek prompt medical attention and explain to the health care provider their travel history and which anti-malarials they have been taking.

For additional information on malaria, protection from insect bites, and anti-malarial drugs, please visit the Centers for Disease Control and Prevention malaria website.

Ethiopia is a mountainous country and the high altitude may cause health problems, even for healthy travelers. Addis Ababa is the third highest capital city in the world, at an altitude of 8,300 feet. Travelers may experience shortness of breath, fatigue, nausea, headaches and an inability to sleep. Individuals with respiratory (including asthma) or heart conditions should consult with a health care professional before traveling to Ethiopia. Travelers to Ethiopia should also avoid swimming in any lakes, rivers, or still bodies of water (other than Lake Langano). Most bodies of water have been found to contain parasites. Travelers should be aware that Ethiopia has a high prevalence of HIV/AIDS.

Ethiopia has had outbreaks of acute watery diarrhea, possible cholera, typhoid, and other bacterial diarrhea in the recent past, and the conditions for reoccurrences continue to exist in both urban and rural settings. Further information on prevention and treatment of cholera and other diarrheal diseases can be found at the Centers for Disease Control and Prevention Foodborne, Bacterial and Mycotic Diseases webpage. To avoid such diseases, health professionals strongly recommend:

- Strict adherence to personal hygiene, hand washing with soap and water before handling or eating food.
- Eating food that is cooked and served hot.
- Avoiding fruits and vegetables unless they have been personally peeled and soaked in a bleach-treated solution before eating.
- Drinking only distilled or bottled water/beverages and using ice made from distilled, boiled or chlorinated water. This includes avoidance of rinsing toothbrushes with tap water.

Travelers developing voluminous watery diarrhea should start oral rehydration quickly and seek medical care immediately for possible IV rehydration.

Ethiopian authorities are monitoring the possibility of avian influenza following the deaths of poultry and birds; preliminary results have been negative. For additional information on avian flu please visit the Centers for Disease Control and Prevention Avian Influenza website.

The U.S. Department of State is unaware of any HIV/AIDS entry restrictions for visitors to or foreign residents of Ethiopia. Please verify this with the Embassy of Ethiopia before you travel. Please refer to the "Entry Restrictions" section of this notice, or the Ethiopian Embassy website.

You can find good information on vaccinations and other health precautions, on the CDC website. For information about outbreaks of infectious diseases abroad, consult the the World Health Organization (WHO) website. The WHO website also contains additional health information for travelers, including detailed country-specific health information.

Tuberculosis is an increasingly serious health concern in Ethiopia. For further information, please consult the CDC's information on TB.

Medical Insurance: You can't assume your insurance will go with you when you travel. It's very important to find out BEFORE you leave whether or not your medical insurance will cover you overseas. You need to ask your insurance company two questions:

- Does my policy apply when I'm out of the United States?
- Will it cover emergencies like a trip to a foreign hospital or a medical evacuation?

In many places, doctors and hospitals still expect payment in cash at the time of service. Your regular U.S. health insurance may not cover doctors' and hospital visits in other countries. If your policy doesn't go with you when you travel, it's a very good idea to take out another one for your trip.

Traffic Safety and Road Conditions: While in a foreign country, you may encounter road conditions that differ significantly from those in the United States.

According to the World Health Organization (WHO), Ethiopia has the highest rate of traffic fatalities per vehicle in the world. Roads in Ethiopia are poorly maintained, inadequately marked, and poorly lighted. Road travel after dark outside Addis Ababa and other cities is dangerous and discouraged due to hazards posed by broken-down vehicles left in the road, pedestrians walking in the road, stray animals, and the possibility of armed robbery.

Road lighting in cities is inadequate at best and nonexistent outside of cities. Excessive speed, unpredictable local driving habits, pedestrians and livestock in the roadway, and the lack of adherence to basic safety standards for vehicles are daily hazards on Ethiopian roads. Many vehicles are unlicensed and many drivers lack basic driver training or insurance. Emergency services are limited or nonexistent in many parts of the country.

Drivers should always carry spare tires, fuel, and tools on long trips as there is no roadside assistance. USG personnel must limit road travel outside towns or cities to daylight hours and travel in convoys, if possible, in case of breakdowns. Public transport is unregulated and unsafe; if travelers do use public transport, they should use taxis, not minibuses or large buses and should ensure they are the only passengers in the vehicle.

While travel during daylight hours on both paved and unpaved roads is generally considered safe, land mines and other anti-personnel devices can be encountered on isolated dirt roads that were targeted during various conflicts, especially along the Eritrean border. Before undertaking any off-road travel, it is advisable to inquire of local authorities to ensure that the area has been cleared of mines.

It is unlawful to use a cell phone or other electronic communications device while driving in Ethiopia (even if it has a hands-free feature), and use of seat belts is required. Be sure to carry your valid Ethiopian driver's license with you, as well as proof of comprehensive local insurance coverage, and your Ethiopian Identification card. While in a vehicle, keep your doors locked and the windows rolled up at all times. Keep bags, purses, and valuables out of sight—in the trunk, on the floor, or in the glove compartment. Do not carry unnecessary items in your bag; leave your credit cards, social security card, etc, at home. Do not open your doors or windows to give to beggars. Police can fine people for giving money to beggars.

If you are in a traffic accident, do not leave the scene unless you fear for your personal safety. Special units of the traffic police investigate traffic accidents. Normal investigative procedures require the police to conduct on on-scene investigation, after which all involved parties go to the Traffic Department for a vehicle inspection and to provide details about the accident for a final report. If possible, obtain the names and contact information of all persons involved in the accident and make a note of the extent of any injuries; make a note of any registration information (tag number) of other vehicle(s) involved; and obtain the other driver's permit data, and give similar information or registration/permit data to the other driver and to the police upon request.

Aviation Safety Oversight: The U.S. Federal Aviation Administration (FAA) has assessed the government of Ethiopia's Civil Aviation Authority as being in compliance with International Civil Aviation Organization (ICAO) aviation safety standards for oversight of Ethiopia's air carrier operations. Further information may be found on the FAA's safety assessment page.

The Ethiopian government has closed air routes near the border with Eritrea and has referred to the airspace as a "no-fly zone." The FAA currently prohibits U.S. aircraft and U.S. pilots from flying in Ethiopian airspace north of 12 degrees north latitude, the area along the country's northern border with Eritrea. For complete information on this flight prohibition, travelers may visit the FAA NOTAM website.

Children's Issues: Please see the U.S. Dept. of State Office of Children's Issues web pages on intercountry adoption and international parental child abduction.

Intercountry Adoption

July 2011

The information in this section has been edited from the latest report available as of February 2013 from the State Department Bureau of Consular Affairs, Office of Overseas Citizens Services. For more information, please read the *Intercountry Adoption* section of this book and review current reports online at http://adoption.state.gov.

Ethiopia is not party to the Hague Convention on Protection of Children and Co-operation in Respect of Intercountry Adoption (Hague Adoption Convention). Therefore, when the Hague Adoption Convention entered into force for the United States on April 1, 2008, intercountry adoption processing for Ethiopia did not change. The Department of State shares families' concerns about recent media reports alleging direct recruitment of children from birth parents by adoption service providers or their employees. In response to these reports, the U.S. Embassy in Addis Ababa has increased scrutiny of its adoption visa processing. Adoptive parents should be aware that in all adoption visa cases worldwide, an I-604 (Determination on Child for Adoption, sometimes referred to as " orphan investigation") must be completed in connection with every I-600 application.

Depending on the circumstances of the case, this investigation may take up to several weeks or even months to complete. Therefore, adoptive parents should not plan to travel to Ethiopia until they have confirmed with their adoption agency that their visa interview appointment has been confirmed. Adoption agencies submit case paperwork to the U.S. Embassy for review before the Embassy schedules the immigrant visa appointment. At that point, consular officers may begin the I-604 determination, which could take several weeks or more to complete. We understand that this may result in a longer period before parents are able to bring their adopted children to the U.S.

However, this additional scrutiny is required to ensure that the adoption is legal under both U.S. and Ethiopian law. The U.S. Embassy will work with adoptive parents and their adoption agency to ensure that each case is processed in the most expeditious manner possible in accordance laws and regulations. Families should continue to work through their agency to schedule immigrant visa appointments and answer questions regarding pending cases.

If families have concerns about their adoption, we ask that they share this information with the Embassy, particularly if it involves possible fraud or misconduct specific to your child's case. The Embassy takes all allegations of fraud or misconduct seriously.

The best way to contact the Embassy is by email at ConsAdoptionAddis@state.gov. Please include your name, your child's name, your adoption agency, the date of the adoption (month and year), and, if possible, the immigrant visa case number for your child's case (this number begins with the letters ADD followed several numbers and can be found on any document sent to you by the National Visa Center). Please let us know if we have your permission to share concerns about your specific case with Ethiopian government officials.

Who Can Adopt? To bring an adopted child to United States from Ethiopia, you must be found eligible to adopt by the U.S. Government. The U.S. Government agency responsible for making this determination is the Department of Homeland Security, U.S. Citizenship and Immigration Services (USCIS).

Residency Requirements: There are no residency requirements for prospective adoptive parents.

Age Requirements: If single, the prospective adoptive parent must be at least 25 years of age. If married, there is no minimum age. There also is no maximum age limit for adoptive parents. However, Ethiopian Government practice is to limit the age difference between the prospective adoptive parent and the adopted child to no more than 40 years.

Marriage Requirements: The Ethiopian Government has shown a preference for placing children with married couples who have been married for at least five years. Ethiopian government policy regarding adoptions by unmarried women is one of the issues being studied as part of the government's overall review of adoption regulations and practices. It is unclear whether Ethiopian government's policy about single adoptive mothers will change, and if so, when it might change.

Thus, adoption service providers in Ethiopia may have different policies regarding whether or not they make referrals of adoptable children to unmarried women and under what circumstances. The U.S. Embassy in Addis Ababa urges adoptive parents to contact their agency to clarify what their current policies are.

Income Requirements: Prospective parent(s) must prove financial ability as determined by the Ethiopian courts, although there is no set minimum income requirement.

Other Requirements: Ethiopian law prohibits adoption by gay and/or lesbian parents.

Who Can Be Adopted? Ethiopia has specific requirements that a child must meet in order to be eligible for adoption. You cannot adopt a child in Ethiopia unless he or she meets the requirements outlined below. Additional adoption information is available on the Ethiopian Embassy in Washington, D.C. website.

In addition to these requirements, a child must meet the definition of an orphan under U.S. law for the adoptive parent(s) to bring him or her immediately back to the United States.

The Ethiopian Ministry of Women's Affairs (MOWA) identifies orphans in need of permanent family placement through intercountry adoption. Generally, orphans identified for intercountry adoption have been abandoned by their parents or have lost their parents to disease or other misfortune.

Relinquishment Requirements: The Contract of Adoption is signed between the child's legal guardian and the adoptive parents or their agency representative. This contract is the basis for the issuance of the adoption decree, which shows that the guardian or the orphanage has relinquished their legal rights to the adopted child. The contract must be taken to the Inland Revenue Administration office to be stamped. There is a nominal fee.

Abandonment Requirements: When a child is abandoned, by law s/he comes into the custody of the Government of Ethiopia. When a child is found to have two HIV/AIDS-infected parents, or one living HIV/AIDS-infected parent, the Government routinely declares that the child is an orphan and assumes legal guardianship of the child.

Waiting Period: Typically, the Government of Ethiopia requires that a child be resident in an orphanage for three months before being adopted.

Ethiopian Adoption Authority: The Adoption Team in the Children and Youth Affairs Office (CYAO) operating under the Ministry of Women's Affairs (MOWA) is the primary adoption authority in Ethiopia.

The Process: The first step in adopting a child from Ethiopia is usually to select a licensed agency in the United States that can help with your adoption. Adoption service providers must be licensed by the U.S. state in which they operate. There are more than twenty U.S.-based adoption agencies authorized by the government of Ethiopia to provide adoption services that are actively referring children to American families.

Americans contemplating adopting in Ethiopia should take great care in selecting an agency. They should research different agencies, seeking the input of families who have used these agencies in the past and looking at independent NGO evaluations of agencies' performance and ethics.

Intercountry adoptions from Ethiopia are handled by the Adoption Team in the Children and Youth Affairs Office (CYAO), a part of the Ministry of Women's Affairs (MOWA). There are currently more than 20 U.S.-based adoption agencies authorized by the Ethiopian Government to provide adoption services for American adoptive parents. For a current list, contact MOWA (see Contacts section below) or the Ethiopian Embassy in Washington, D.C. website.

To bring an adopted child from Ethiopia to the United States, you must apply to be found eligible to adopt (Form I-600A) by the U.S. Government, Department of Homeland Security, U.S. Citizenship and Immigration Services (USCIS). Before they can be matched with a child, prospective adoptive parents must first take or send all of the required documents (see below), certified and authenticated, to the Ethiopian Embassy in Washington, D.C. for additional authentication.

Once it has completed its authentication, the Ethiopian Embassy returns the documents to the parents and the parents forward them to MOWA, Children and Youth Affairs Office, Adoption Team (CYAO). Parents who have received MOWA permission to adopt privately must come to Ethiopia to complete adoption requirements. Only one parent has to appear, but, if married, must bring a power of attorney from the other parent. If these parents plan to file the I-600 at the U.S. Embassy in Addis Ababa, they need to make sure that the parent who comes to finalize the adoption is an American citizen and that the I-600 has been signed by the non-traveling parent prior to the Embassy interview.

Ethiopian-Americans who are adopting orphaned relatives do not have to come to Ethiopia to process their adoptions. They can have a representative with a power of attorney represent them in court. Married adoptive parents need to make sure that both parents have given the representative a power of attorney so that both parents' names appear on the adoption decree.

Upon approval of the Adoption Request by the Adoption Committee, a child is selected and referred to the prospective parents to adopt, according to the parents' preferences for age and sex. The child must be eligible to be adopted according to Ethiopia's requirements. The child must also meet the definition of an orphan under U.S. law.

At this time Ethiopian authorities publish in the local press a notice seeking any other claimants to the child, stating the child's name and the name of the prospective adoptive parents. The notice advises that any parties opposed to the adoption must appear at MOWA by a certain date and time. Upon acceptance of the referral, a Contract of Adoption is signed by the child's legal guardian and the adoptive parents or the agency representative. The contract is taken to the Inland Revenue Administration office to be stamped. A nominal fee is charged. CYAO opens a file at the Federal First Instance Court to apply for an appointment date for an adoption hearing. The court date set for the hearing is often one to two months from the date of filing, and may be rescheduled more than once based on the Court and CYAO's schedules.

All Ethiopian adoptions are full and final and irrevocable under Ethiopian law. Adoption hearings take place before the Federal First Instance Court. The court date scheduled for an intercountry adoption could be one to two months from the date the CYAO files the adoption petition. The prospective parents or their representative (usually their agency's local representative) appear at the court hearing. The Court sometimes makes a final decision quickly. However, decisions are sometimes delayed for weeks. The Court's decision is made via a Court Decree. Adoptive parents must obtain at least two originals of the Court Decree. One will be retained by MOWA and one must be submitted to the U.S. Embassy at the time of the visa application. The Embassy will return the Court Decree to the parents at the conclusion of the visa application process.

The Private Adoption Process: Private adoption is an alternate process available ONLY to adoptive parents of Ethiopian descent or to Americans who are resident in Ethiopia. Private adoptions are permitted in Ethiopia, but the Embassy encourages all parents using the private adoption process to ensure that their cases are approved by the Federal First Instance Court and MOWA. These steps will ensure that private adoptions do not bypass the process and protections put in place by the government of Ethiopia relating to international adoption.

Adoptive parents considering a private adoption are also urged to consult with USCIS or an immigration attorney regarding the child's orphan status as it pertains to U.S. immigration law before the adoption is finalized. All Ethiopian adoptions are full, final, and irrevocable, so it is important to know whether or not a child qualifies as an orphan before completing the adoption.

Bringing Your Child Home: Once your adoption is complete (or you have obtained legal custody of the child), there are a few more steps to take before you can head home. Specifically, you need to apply for several documents for your child before he or she can travel to the United States, such as a birth certificate, a passport or travel document for your child from the country in which he or she was born, and a U.S. Immigration Visa. For detailed and updated information on how to obtain these documents, review the *Intercountry Adoption* section in this publication and visit the U.S. Department of State Intercountry Adoption website at http://adoption.state.gov.

Child Citizenship Act: For adoptions finalized abroad, the Child Citizenship Act of 2000 allows your new child to acquire American citizenship automatically when he or she enters the United States as lawful permanent residents. For adoptions finalized in the United States, the Child Citizenship Act of 2000 allows your new child to acquire American citizenship automatically when the court in the United States issues the final adoption decree. To learn more, review the *Intercountry Adoption* section in this publication and visit the U.S. Department of State Intercountry Adoption website at http://adoption.state.gov.

After Adoption: Pursuant to Ethiopian law, adoptive parents must submit post adoption reports at three months, six months, and one year. After the first year, the reports must be filed yearly until the child turns 18. This is a commitment that the adopting parents, home study agency, and adoption agency must sign when submitting documents for the adoption.

Adoptive parents are strongly urged to comply with these requirements and to complete all post-adoption reports in a timely manner. Your adoption agency may be able to help you with this process. Your cooperation will contribute to that country's history of positive experiences with American adoptive parents and helps keep the intercountry adoptions viable in Ethiopia.

U.S. Embassy in Ethiopia
Entoto Road
Addis Ababa
Tel: (251–11) 130–6000
Fax: (251–11) 124–24–35
Email: consaddis@state.gov
http://ethiopia.usembassy.gov/service.html.

Ethopian Adoption Authority
Ministry Of Women's Affairs (MOWA)
Children and Youth Affairs Office, Adoption Team (CYAO)
P.O. Box 1293
Addis Ababa
Ethiopia
The head of the Adoption Team can be reached at:
Tel: (251)- 251–11–554–5676
Fax: (251)-11–416–6362

Embassy of Ethiopia
3506 International Drive, N.W.
Washington, D.C. 20008
Phone: 202–364–1200
Fax: 202–587–0195
info@ethiopianembassy.org
http://www.ethiopianembassy.org/contact.shtml

Office of Children's Issues
U.S. Department of State
2201 C Street, NW
SA-29
Washington, DC 20520
Tel: 1–888–407–4747
E-mail: AskCI@state.gov
http://adoption.state.gov

For questions about immigration procedures, call the National Customer Service Center (NCSC) 1-800-375-5283 (TTY 1-800-767-1833).

FIJI

Compiled from publications that were available as of February 2013 from the U.S. Department of State, the U.S. Department of Commerce, and the Central Intelligence Agency (CIA). See the introduction to this set for explanatory notes.

Official Name:
Republic of the Fiji Islands

PROFILE

Geography

Area: total: 18,274 sq km; country comparison to the world: 157; land: 18,274 sq km; water: 0 sq km

Major cities: Suva (capital) 174,000 (2009)

Climate: tropical marine; only slight seasonal temperature variation

Terrain: mostly mountains of volcanic origin

People

Nationality: noun: Fijian(s); adjective: Fijian

Population: 890,057 (July 2012 est.)

Population growth rate: 0.766% (2012 est.)

Ethnic groups: Fijian 57.3% (predominantly Melanesian with a Polynesian admixture), Indian 37.6%, Rotuman 1.2%, other 3.9% (European, other Pacific Islanders, Chinese) (2007 census)

Religions: Protestant 55.4% (Methodist 34.6%, Assembly of God 5.7%, Seventh-Day Adventist 3.9%, Anglican 0.8%, other 10.4%), Hindu 27.9%, Roman Catholic 9.1%, Muslim 6.3%, Sikh 0.3%, other or unspecified 0.3%, none 0.7% (2007 census)

Languages: English (official), Fijian (official), Hindustani

Literacy: definition: age 15 and over can read and write; total population: 93.7%; male: 95.5%; female: 91.9% (2003 est.)

Health: life expectancy at birth: total population: 71.59 years; male: 69 years; female: 74.32 years (2012 est.); Infant mortality rate: total: 10.73 deaths/1,000 live births; male: 11.82 deaths/1,000 live births; female: 9.58 deaths/1,000 live births (2012 est.)

Unemployment rate: 7.6% (1999)

Work force: 335,000 (2007 est.)

Government

Type: republic

Independence: 10 October 1970

Constitution: enacted 25 July 1997; effective 28 July 1998; note—constitution encourages multiculturalism and makes multiparty government mandatory

Political subdivisions: 4 divisions and 1 dependency; Central, Eastern, Northern, Rotuma, Western

Suffrage: 21 years of age; universal

Economy

GDP (purchasing power parity): $4.307 billion (2012 est.); $4.186 billion (2011 est.); $4.106 billion (2010 est.)

GDP real growth rate: 2% (2012 est.); 2% (2011 est.); -0.2% (2010 est.); -1.3% (2009 est.)

GDP per capita (PPP): $4,800 (2012 est.); $4,700 (2011 est.); $4,600 (2010 est.); $4,700 (2009 est.)

Natural resources: timber, fish, gold, copper, offshore oil potential, hydropower

Agriculture products: sugarcane, coconuts, cassava (manioc), rice, sweet potatoes, bananas; cattle, pigs, horses, goats; fish

Industries: tourism, sugar, clothing, copra, gold, silver, lumber, small cottage industries

Exports: $991.6 million (2012 est.); $901.5 million (2011 est.)

Exports—commodities: sugar, garments, gold, timber, fish, molasses, coconut oil

Exports—partners: Australia 14.3%, US 11%, Japan 6.3%, UK 5.9%, Samoa 5.8%, Tonga 5.1% (2011)

Imports: $1.938 billion (2012 est.); $1.762 billion (2011 est.)

Imports—commodities: manufactured goods, machinery and transport equipment, petroleum products, food, chemicals

Imports—partners: Singapore 34.1%, Australia 16.3%, NZ 14.1%, China 8.9% (2011)

Debt—external: $268 million (31 December 2012 est.); $258.7 million (31 December 2011 est.)

Exchange rates: Fijian dollars (FJD) per US dollar; 1.792 (2012 est.); 1.7932 (2011 est.); 1.9183 (2010 est.)

GEOGRAPHY

Fiji is comprised of a group of volcanic islands in the South Pacific lying about 4,450 km. (2,775 mi.) southwest of Honolulu and 1,770 km. (1,100 mi.) north of New Zealand. Its 322 islands vary dramatically in size. The largest islands are Viti Levu, about the size of the "Big Island" of Hawaii, and where the capital and 70% of the population are located, and Vanua Levu. Just over 100 of the smaller islands are inhabited.

The larger islands contain mountains as high as 1,200 meters (4,000 ft.) rising abruptly from the shore. Heavy rains—up to 304 cm. (120 in.) annually—fall on the windward (southeastern) sides of the islands, covering these sections with dense tropical forest. Lowlands on the western portions of each of the main islands are sheltered by the mountains and have a well-marked dry season favorable to crops such as sugarcane.

PEOPLE

Most of Fiji's population lives on Viti Levu's coasts, either in Suva or in smaller urban centers. The interior of Viti Levu is sparsely populated due to its rough terrain.

Indigenous Fijians are a mixture of Polynesian and Melanesian, resulting from the original migrations to the South Pacific many centuries ago. The Indo-Fijian population grew rapidly from the 60,000 indentured laborers brought from India between 1879 and 1916 to work in the sugarcane fields. Thousands more Indians migrated voluntarily in the 1920s and 1930s and formed the core of Fiji's business class. Native Fijians live throughout the country, while Indo-Fijians reside primarily near the urban centers and in the cane-producing areas of the two main islands.

Some Indo-Fijians have been displaced by the expiration of land leases in cane-producing areas and have moved into urban centers in pursuit of jobs. Similarly, a number of indigenous Fijians have moved into urban areas, especially Suva, in search of a better life. Meanwhile, the Indo-Fijian population has declined due to emigration and a declining birth rate. Indo-Fijians currently constitute 37% of the total population, although they were the largest ethnic group from the 1940s until the late 1980s. Indo-Fijians continue to dominate the professions and commerce, while ethnic Fijians dominate government and the military.

National/Racial/Ethnic Minorities

Tension between ethnic Fijians and Indian-Fijians has been a longstanding problem. Indigenous Fijians make up 57 percent of the population, Indian-Fijians comprise 37 percent, and the remaining 6 percent is composed of Europeans, Chinese, and Rotuman and other Pacific Islander communities.

In an effort to address the sensitive question of ethnic and national identity, in 2010 the government decreed that the country's citizens would henceforth be known as "Fijians," a term that previously was understood to refer only to the ethnic indigenous population. Indigenous Fiji Islanders would become known as "iTaukei" (literally, "owners" in the Fijian language). The decree requires that anywhere the word "indigenous" or "native" appears in the law and in government publications and communications, it is to be replaced by the term "iTaukei."

Some commentators, writing in blogs or overseas publications, observed that the lack of prior consultations with the indigenous community about the change and its promulgation by decree could complicate its implementation, given the historical opposition by indigenous Fijians to making "Fijian" the common name for all citizens. (The 1997 constitution used the term "Fiji Islander" to refer to all citizens.)

Language

Fiji is an English-speaking country, although Fijian and Hindustani are also widely spoken.

Religion

Estimates of the country's religious affiliation are: 52 percent of the population is Christian, 30 percent Hindu, and 7 percent Muslim. The largest Christian denomination is the Methodist Church, which claims approximately 218,000 members, nearly one-quarter of the population. Other Protestant denominations and the Roman Catholic Church also have significant followings. The Methodist Church is supported by the majority of the country's chiefs and remains influential in the ethnic Fijian community, particularly in rural areas. There is also a small number of active nondenominational Christian groups.

Religious affiliation runs largely along ethnic lines. Most indigenous Fijians, who constitute 57 percent of the population, are Christian. Most Indo-Fijians, who account for 37 percent, are Hindu, while 20 percent of the Indo-Fijians are Muslim and 6 percent of Indo-Fijians are Christian. Approximately 60 percent of the small Chinese community is Christian. The very small European community is predominantly Christian.

Hindu and Muslim communities maintained a number of active religious and cultural organizations.

Numerous Christian missionary organizations are nationally and regionally active in social welfare, health, and education. Many major Christian denominations have missionaries in the country. The Adventist, Anglican, Catholic, Hindu, Methodist, Mormon, Muslim, and other communities operate numerous schools, including colleges, which are not subsidized by the government.

HISTORY

Melanesian and Polynesian peoples settled the Fijian islands some 3,500 years ago. European traders and mis-

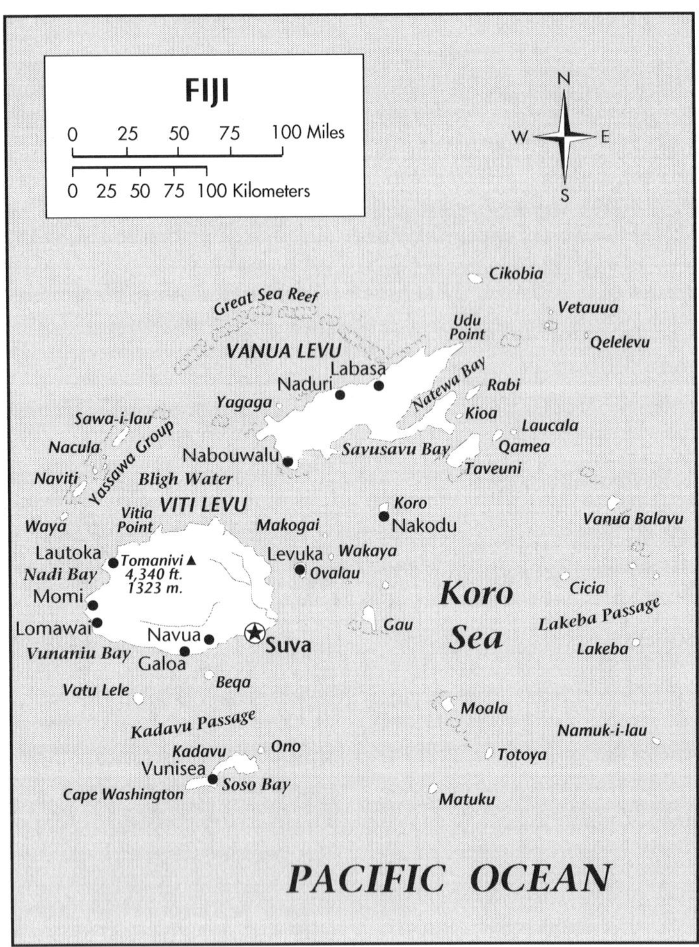

sionaries arrived in the first half of the 19th century, and the resulting disruption led to increasingly serious wars among the native Fijian confederacies. One Ratu (chief), Cakobau, gained limited control over the western islands by the 1850s, but the continuing unrest led him and a convention of chiefs to cede Fiji unconditionally to the British in 1874.

The pattern of colonialism in Fiji during the following century was similar to that in many other British possessions: the pacification of the countryside, the spread of plantation agriculture, and the introduction of Indian indentured labor. Many traditional institutions, including the system of communal land ownership, were maintained.

Fiji soldiers fought alongside the Allies in the Second World War, gaining a fine reputation in the tough Solomon Islands campaign. The United States and other Allied countries maintained military installations in Fiji during the war, but Fiji itself never came under attack.

In April 1970, a constitutional conference in London agreed that Fiji should become a fully sovereign and independent nation within the Commonwealth. Fiji became independent on October 10, 1970. Post-independence politics came to be dominated by the Alliance Party of Ratu Sir Kamisese Mara. The Indian-led opposition won a majority of House seats in 1977, but failed to form a government out of concern that indigenous Fijians would not accept Indo-Fijian leadership. In April 1987, a coalition led by Dr. Timoci Bavadra, an ethnic Fijian supported by the Indo-Fijian community, won the general election and formed Fiji's first majority Indian government, with Dr. Bavadra serving as Prime Minister. Less than a month later, Dr. Bavadra was forcibly removed from power during a military coup led by Lt. Col. Sitiveni Rabuka on May 14, 1987.

After a period of deadlocked negotiations involving the Governor-General, who had denounced the coup, Rabuka staged a second coup on September 25, 1987. The military government revoked the 1970 constitution and declared Fiji a republic on October 10. This action, coupled with protests by the Government of India, led to Fiji's expulsion from the Commonwealth of Nations and official non-recognition of the Rabuka regime from foreign governments, including Australia and New Zealand. On December 6, 1987, Rabuka resigned as head of state and Governor-General Ratu Sir Penaia Ganilau was appointed the first President of the Fijian Republic. The interim government that governed Fiji from December 1987–1992 was led by former Prime Minister Mara who was reappointed interim Prime Minister, and Rabuka became Minister of Home Affairs.

The new government drafted a new constitution, effective July 1990. Under its terms, majorities were reserved for ethnic Fijians in both houses of the legislature. Previously, in 1989, the government had released statistical information showing that for the first time since 1946, ethnic Fijians were a majority of the population. More than 12,000 Indo-Fijians and other minorities had left the country in the 2 years following the 1987 coups. After resigning from the military, Rabuka became prime minister in 1993 after elections under the new constitution.

Tensions simmered in 1995–96 over the renewal of land leases and political maneuvering surrounding the mandated 5-year review of the 1990 constitution. A Constitutional Review Commission recommended a new constitution that expanded the size of the legislature, lowered the proportion of seats reserved by ethnic group, gave to the unelected Council of Chiefs authority to appoint the president and vice president, and opened the position of prime minister to all races. Ethnic Fijians and Indo-Fijians were allocated communal seats proportional to their numbers in the population at the time. Twenty-five seats were "open" to all. Prime Minister Rabuka and President Mara supported the proposal, while the nationalist indigenous Fijian parties opposed it. The constitution amendment act was unanimously approved by parliamentarians in July 1997. The new constitution mandated the formation of a multi-party cabinet (each party with 10% of members of Parliament was entitled to nominate a cabinet minister). Fiji was readmitted to the Commonwealth.

The first legislative elections held under the new constitution took place in May 1999. Rabuka's coalition was defeated by the Fiji Labor Party (FLP), which formed a coalition, led by Mahendra Chaudhry, with two small Fijian parties. Chaudhry became Fiji's first Indo-Fijian prime minister. One year later, in May 2000, Chaudhry and most other members of Parliament were taken hostage in the House of Representatives by gunmen led by ethnic Fijian nationalist George Speight. The standoff dragged on for 8 weeks—during which time Chaudhry was removed from office by then-president Mara due to his inability to govern while a hostage. The Republic of Fiji military forces abrogated the constitution, convinced President Mara to resign, and brokered a negotiated end to the situation. Speight was later arrested when he violated the settlement's terms. In February 2002, Speight was convicted of treason and is currently serving a life sentence.

In July 2000, the military commander Voreqe "Frank" Bainimarama and the Great Council of Chiefs appointed former banker Laisenia Qarase interim Prime Minister and head of the interim civilian administration. The Vice President, Ratu Josefa Iloilo, was named President. The Court of Appeal in March 2001 reaffirmed the validity of the constitution and ordered the President to recall the elected Parliament. However, the President dissolved the Parliament elected in 2000 and appointed Qarase head of a caretaker government to take Fiji to general elections that were held in August. Qarase's newly formed Soqosoqo Duavata ni Lewenivanua (SDL) party won the elections but did not invite into the cabinet representatives of the FLP as required by the constitution. In May 2006, the SDL was re-elected to a majority in the Parliament. Qarase continued as Prime Minister and formed a multiparty cabinet, which included nine members of the FLP.

In the lead-up to the May 2006 election and beginning again in September, tensions grew between Commander of the Fiji Military Forces Commodore Frank Bainimarama and the Qarase government. Bainimarama demanded the Qarase government not pursue certain legislation and policies favorable to the former mutineers and indigenous interests. On December 5, 2006 Bainimarama assumed executive authority, removed elected Prime Minister Qarase from his position, and dissolved Parliament in a military coup d'etat. Qarase was exiled to an outer island. On January 4, 2007, Bainimarama reinstated President Iloilo, who stated the military was justified in its behavior and promised them amnesty. The following day Iloilo appointed Bainimarama interim Prime Minister. Over the following weeks Bainimarama formed an "interim government" that included, among others, former Prime Minister Chaudhry and former Republic of Fiji Military Forces heads Epeli Ganilau and Epeli Nailatikau. On January 15, 2007, President Iloilo decreed amnesty to Bainimarama, the Republic of Fiji Military Forces (RFMF), and all those involved in the coup from December 5, 2006 to January 5, 2007, and he claimed to ratify all the actions of Bainimarama and the RFMF.

The coup was widely condemned by regional partners, including Australia, New Zealand, the United States, and the European Union. In April 2007, the interim government suspended the Great Council of Chiefs after the council declined to appoint the interim government's choice as vice president. In October 2007, the interim government launched a "People's Charter" initiative, ostensibly to remove communal or ethnic voting and improve governance arrangements. There was little progress made toward elections. In October 2008, the High Court ruled that President Iloilo's January 2007 appointment of Bainimarama as Prime Minister, the granting of amnesty to coup perpetrators, and rule by decree, was not unconstitutional. However, on April 9, 2009, the Court of Appeal ruled that that the 2006 coup had been illegal. The following day President Iloilo abrogated the constitution, and removed all officials appointed under the constitution including all judges and the Governor of the Central Bank. He then reappointed Bainimarama as Prime Minister and imposed a "Public Emergency Regulation" (PER) that allowed press censorship.

GOVERNMENT AND POLITICAL CONDITIONS

Fiji is a republic under a military-led government since armed forces commander Commodore Josaia Voreqe (Frank) Bainimarama overthrew the elected government in a bloodless coup in 2006. In 2009 the interim government headed by Prime Minister Bainimarama abrogated the constitution, imposed a state of emergency, and continued its rule by decree, a situation that remained at year's end. During 2011 the country had no constitution or parliament. Security forces did not report to civilian authorities.

Recent Elections

The most recent elections, held in 2006, were judged generally free and fair. Party politics was largely race based, although this did not limit participation in the political process. The governing Soqosoqo Duavata ni Lewenivanua (SDL) party was primarily ethnic Fijian, and the Fiji Labour Party (FLP), the second-largest party, was primarily Indian-Fijian, although both had membership across racial lines. After the elections the SDL established a multiparty cabinet with the FLP as required by the constitution. This government was removed by the RFMF under Bainimarama's leadership during the 2006 coup.

At the end of 2011, the PER continued in force, and the government continued to rule by decree. Bainimarama has declared that political reforms are necessary before elections can resume and repeatedly postponed national elections. In September the government announced it would start electronic voter registration in 2012 as part of preparations for promised 2014 parliamentary elections and invited tenders from interested companies. A government official also announced in September that political party "manifestos" or published platforms would not be allowed in future elections, and that all competing parties would have to uphold the government's Charter for Peace, Change, and Progress.

Participation of Women and Minorities: There was one woman in the 11-member cabinet. Indigenous women played important roles in the traditional system of chiefs, and some became chiefs in their own right.

There were two Indian-Fijian ministers in the cabinet and no other minority ministers. Indian-Fijians, who accounted for 37 percent of the population, continued to be underrepresented at senior levels of the civil service and greatly so in the military. Indian-Fijians comprised approximately 35 percent of the civil service overall. The "disciplined services"—the military, police, and prison services—were predominantly ethnic Fijian; however, Indian-Fijians comprised approximately one-third of the police force.

Principal Government Officials

Last Updated: 1/31/2013

The US has not recognized the interim government formed after the illegal coup of 5 December 2006.

Pres.: **Epeli NAILATIKAU**
Prime Min.: **Josaia Voreqe BAINIMARAMA, Commodore**
Min. for Anticorruption: **Aiyaz SAYED-KHAIYUM**
Min. for Defense, National Security, & Immigration (Acting): **Joketani COKANASIGA**
Min. for Education, National Heritage, & Culture & Arts: **Filipe BOLE**
Min. for Finance: **Josaia Voreqe BAINIMARAMA, Commodore**
Min. for Foreign Affairs & Intl. Cooperation: **Inoke KUBUABOLA**
Min. for Health: **Neil SHARMA, Dr.**
Min. for Industry & Trade: **Aiyaz SAYED-KHAIYUM**
Min. for Information, National Archives, & Library Services of Fiji: **Josaia Voreqe BAINIMARAMA, Commodore**
Min. for Intl. Trade: **Aiyaz SAYED-KHAIYUM**
Min. for Justice, Electoral Reform, & Anticorruption: **Aiyaz SAYED-KHAIYUM**
Min. for Labor, Industrial Relations, & Employment: **Jone USAMATE**
Min. for Lands & Mineral Resources (Acting): **Josaia Voreqe BAINIMARAMA, Commodore**
Min. for Local Govt., Urban Development, Housing, & Environment: **Samuela SAUMATUA, Col.**
Min. for People's Charter for Change & Progress: **Josaia Voreqe BAINIMARAMA, Commodore**
Min. for Primary Industries: **Joketani COKANASIGA**
Min. for Provincial Development: **Josaia Voreqe BAINIMARAMA, Commodore**
Min. for Public Enterprises, Communications, Civil Aviation, & Tourism: **Aiyaz SAYED-KHAIYUM**
Min. for Public Service: **Josaia Voreqe BAINIMARAMA, Commodore**
Min. for Public Utilities, Works, & Transport: **Timoci Lesi NATUVA, Cdr.**
Min. for Strategic Planning, National Development, & Statistics: **Josaia Voreqe BAINIMARAMA, Commodore**
Min. for Sugar Industry: **Josaia Voreqe BAINIMARAMA, Commodore**
Min. for Taukei & Multiethnic Affairs: **Josaia Voreqe BAINIMARAMA, Commodore**
Min. for Women, Social Welfare, & Poverty Alleviation: **Jiko LUVENI**
Min. for Youth & Sports: **Viliame NAUPOTO, Cdr.**
Attorney Gen.: **Aiyaz SAYED-KHAIYUM**
Governor, Reserve Bank: **Barry WHITESIDE**
Ambassador to the US: **Winston THOMPSON**
Permanent Representative to the UN, New York: **Peter THOMSON**

POLITICAL CONDITIONS

For 17 years after independence, Fiji was a parliamentary democracy. During that time, political life was dominated by Ratu Sir Kamisese Mara and the Alliance Party, which combined the traditional Fijian chiefly system with leading elements of the European, part-European, and Indian communities. The main parliamentary opposition, the National Federation Party, represented mainly rural Indo-Fijians. Intercommunal relations were managed without serious confrontation. However, when a cabinet with substantial ethnic Indian representation was installed after the April 1987 election, extremist elements played on ethnic Fijian fears of domination by the Indo-Fijian community, resulting in an indigenous-led military coup d'etat.

The 1987 coups began what many now refer to as the "coup cycle." The most recent coup took place in December 2006, and was the first coup ostensibly to restrain, rather than promote, indigenous grievances. Military commander Commodore Bainimarama had resolved the 2000 crisis by imposing martial law and bringing about new elections. Bainimarama appointed an interim government led by interim Prime Minister Laisenia Qarase. Subsequently, Qarase was elected in 2001 and 2006, but increasingly pursued policies favoring the indigenous Fijian community that alarmed the country's commercial sector and ethnic minorities.

In 2005 and 2006, tensions rose between Bainimarama and Qarase over legislation proposed by the Qarase government concerning land ownership, traditional non-public ownership of the foreshore ("Qoliqoli rights"), and a reconciliation bill that opened granting immunity to some coup participants and attempted assassins from 2000. Bainimarama began to make demands and threats, and engaged in shows of military force to intimidate the Qarase government into backing away from the controversial policies.

When the Qarase government did not accede to all military demands, on December 5, 2006, Bainimarama assumed the powers of the presidency, dismissed Parliament, and declared a temporary military government.

Commodore Bainimarama was appointed interim Prime Minister in 2007; his interim government has pursued what he terms a "clean-up campaign" to root out what he considers to be large-scale corruption in Fiji. A number of civil servants, including the former Chief Justice, were summarily suspended or dismissed due to unspecified corruption concerns. Many individuals who have spoken out against the coup government have been taken to military camps where they have been questioned and sometimes abused.

After his assumption of power, Bainimarama quickly promised national parliamentary elections, to take place in 2009. Given his record in restoring order and new elections during 2000–2001, many in the international community took him at his word, and while the United States, Australia, the European Union, New Zealand, and the United Kingdom imposed varying degrees of aid limits and travel restrictions, international observers and regional organizations expected a restoration of elected government in 2009. The coup government organized a "People's Charter" dialogue and report, which included many academics and non-governmental organization (NGO) figures and attempted to define and outline solutions for the internecine disruptions of Fiji's politics over the last 20 years. But Bainimarama surprised the international community by postponing elections to 2014, and with the constitution abrogated indefinitely, organizations such as the Commonwealth of Nations and Pacific Islands Forum suspended Fiji's membership.

After several years without concrete progress toward democratization, constitutional dialogue, or election preparation, the government in late 2011 and early 2012 combined steps moving forward toward elections with the announcement of policies that further strengthened the regime's hold on society and security. The September 2011 Essential National Industries Decree limited union participation in designated sectors (airlines, utilities, banks, and public broadcasting). Prime Minister Bainimarama announced on January 1, 2012, the lifting of the PER effective January 7, and the PER including press censorship in media offices ended on that date. On January 5, 2012, however, Bainimarama announced that a new Public Order Amendment Decree (POAD) had come into effect, which repeated many of the PER's restrictions, defined conditions for public political meetings, and gave military and police forces authority to use armed force against the public while rendering all provisions of the POAD unchallengeable in court. Although media have begun covering more sensitive political topics since the end of the PER, criticism in print is rare as media may be subject to lawsuits under the 2010 Media Decree. In February, a decree amending the State Proceedings Act (the State Proceedings Amendment Decree or SPAD) gave government ministers and the press immunity from suits for publication of any libelous statements against others made by ministers, under the guise of granting the government "parliamentary privilege." With no parliament or due process guarantee, the decree appears to strengthen the government's position in the media while upholding its immunity from criticism.

Electoral preparations and constitutional dialogue showed progress in early 2012, with the award of an electronic voter registration contract to be implemented in early 2012, and the beginning of government briefings on "constitutional awareness" to select communities. NGOs and academic presentations began to discuss a new constitutional dialogue process.

ECONOMY

Fiji, endowed with forest, mineral, and fish resources, is one of the most developed of the Pacific island economies though still with a large subsistence sector. Sugar exports, remittances from Fijians working abroad, and a growing tourist industry - with 400,000 to 500,000 tourists annually - are the major sources of foreign exchange.

Fiji's sugar has special access to European Union markets but will be harmed by the EU's decision to cut sugar subsidies. Sugar processing makes up one-third of industrial activity but is not efficient. Fiji's tourism industry was damaged by the December 2006 coup and is facing an uncertain recovery time. In 2007 tourist arrivals were down almost 6%, with substantial job losses in the service sector, and GDP dipped. The coup has created a difficult business climate.

The EU has suspended all aid until the interim government takes steps toward new elections. Long-term problems include low investment, uncertain land ownership rights, and the government's inability to manage its budget. Overseas remittances from Fijians working in Kuwait and Iraq have decreased significantly. Fiji's current account deficit peaked at 23% of GDP in 2006, and declined to 12.5% of GDP in 2012.

Labor Conditions

Under the law children under age 12 may not be employed except in a family-owned business or agricultural enterprise. Any such employment must not interfere with school attendance and is to be of limited duration. Although the law provides that education is compulsory up to age 15, children between 12 and 15 may be employed on a daily wage basis in nonindustrial "light" work not involving machinery, provided they return to their parents or guardian every night. Children between ages 15 and 17 may be employed in certain occupations not involving heavy machinery, hazardous materials, mines, or heavy physical labor; however, they must be given specified hours and rest breaks.

The Ministry of Labor deployed inspectors nationwide to enforce compliance with labor laws, including those covering child labor. However, enforcement of existing child labor regulations was inadequate. Increasing poverty led to more children working as casual laborers, often with no safeguards against abuse or injury. Children as young as age 11 worked as full-time laborers in the sugar cane industry. Children also worked in the production of other agricultural products, including coconuts and root vegetables.

There was no single, national minimum wage, although the Wages Councils, comprising representatives of both workers and employers, set minimum wages for certain sectors. The 11 corporations designated by the ENID are excluded from the ambit of the Wages Councils. There was no current official poverty-level income figure, but minimum wage levels in regulated industries and entry-level wages in unregulated and informal sectors did not provide a decent standard of living for a worker and family.

There is no single national limitation on maximum working hours for adults, but there are restrictions and overtime provisions in certain sectors. The ENID bans overtime payments for work in the 11 designated corporations unless agreed upon by the employer.

U.S.-FIJI RELATIONS

The United States established diplomatic relations with Fiji in 1971 following its independence from the United Kingdom. Relations between Fiji and the United States have traditionally been excellent. The two countries share a multi-ethnic heritage and an outlook on Pacific Islands regional issues, and often align on major UN voting questions.

Post-independence, Fiji saw a mix of parliamentary democracy, ethnic tensions, and four coups, the most recent occurring in 2006. The United States continues to encourage the government of Fiji to return to democracy and hold elections. The United States is also concerned by the government's targeting of opponents and human rights and labor activists for harassment, arbitrary arrest, and abuse. The three pillars of U.S. policy toward Fiji under the coup government are upholding U.S. law-based sanctions, protecting and promoting U.S. interests in the region, and doing no harm to the people of Fiji. The United States, in concert with allies, is supporting Fiji's process to form a new constitution and hold credible elections in 2014.

U.S. Assistance to Fiji

Although the United States provides relatively little direct bilateral development assistance to Fiji, it contributes through its membership in multilateral agencies and USAID funding of regional environmental projects. Small U.S. grants contribute to civil society, journalism, environmental protection, and anti-human-trafficking efforts. Non-military law enforcement cooperation assists port security, rule of law professionalism, intellectual property rights, and disaster preparedness and response. Assistance in 2012 included an $800,000 grant through a U.S.-based consortium to support the drafting of a new constitution. There is a Peace Corps program in Fiji.

Bilateral Economic Relations

Fiji's economy is shifting from a reliance on sugar and textiles to a focus on tourism and related industries. The United States has been among Fiji's principal trading partners. The main products imported to the U.S. from Fiji include bottled water, tuna, and sugar. U.S. exports to Fiji are mainly machinery, transport equipment, and food. Fiji and the United States do not have a bilateral investment agreement. Tourism including from the United States contributes significantly to the Fijian economy.

Fiji's Membership in International Organizations

Fiji and the United States belong to a number of the same international organizations, including the United Nations, International Monetary Fund, World Bank, Asian Development Bank, and World Trade Organization.

Bilateral Representation

Fiji maintains an embassy at 2000 M Street NW, Suite 710, Washington, DC 20036 (tel: 202-337-8320).

Principal U.S. Embassy Officials

Last Updated: 1/14/2013

SUVA (E) 158 Princes Road, Tamavua, 679-331-4466, Fax 679-330-5106, Workweek: 0800–1730 (Mon-Thu), 0800–1500 (Fri), Website: http://suva.usembassy.gov/

DCM OMS:	Gigi M. Dever
AMB OMS:	Roniece Briscoe
COM/CON:	Cyndee Crook
FM:	Robert Russell
HRO:	Paul S. Dever
MGT:	Paul S. Dever
POL/ECON:	Michael Via
SDO/DATT:	CDR Scott Sherard
AMB:	Frankie A. Reed
CON:	Wayne Schmidt
DCM:	Jeffrey J. Robertson
PAO:	Joseph Crook
GSO:	Matthew Boullioun
RSO:	Bleu Lawless
AFSA:	John C. Carleton
CLO:	Liza Valverde
EEO:	Brooke Petitti
EST:	Norman Barth
FMO:	John C. Carleton
IMO:	Barry Hall
IPO:	Richard Alex
ISO:	Barry Hall
ISSO:	Rich Alex
LAB:	Noah Geesaman

TRAVEL

Consular Information Sheet

January 13, 2012

Country Description: Fiji is a South Pacific island nation with over 350 islands and islets, approximately 100 of which are inhabited. The capital of Fiji is Suva. Once a leader of Pacific democracies, Fiji has been under military rule since 2006. Since the government's abrogation of Fiji's Constitution in April 2009, the government has ruled by decree and enforced Public Emergency Regulations that limit basic freedoms. Tourism is a major industry in Fiji, and a full range of services are available. The Fiji Visitors Bureau has a wide range of information for travelers and that can be accessed by visiting the Fiji Visitors Bureau's website.

Smart Traveler Enrollment Program/Embassy Location: If you are going to live in or visit Fiji, please take the time to tell our Embassy about your trip. If you enroll, we can keep you up to date with important safety and security announcements. It will also help your friends and family get in touch with you in an emergency.

U.S. Embassy
158 Princes Road, Suva, Fiji
Telephone: (679) 331-4466
Emergency after-hours telephone: (679) 772-8049
Facsimile: (679) 330-2267

Entry/Exit Requirements for U.S. Citizens: To enter Fiji, you will need a passport valid for at least three months after your scheduled departure date from Fiji. You will also need proof that you have enough money to travel and that you have an onward or return ticket. You do not need a visa if you are a tourist staying less than four months. If you are traveling to the Lau group of islands by yacht, you need special permission from your first port of entry into Fiji. For more information on entry/exit requirements, you can contact the Embassy of the Republic of Fiji at 2000 M Street NW, Suite 710, Washington DC 20036, by phone at (202) 466-8320 and fax at (202) 466-8325. You can also contact the Fiji Mission to the United Nations in New York. If you are entering Fiji by boat, please pay special attention to the important requirements for access into Fiji. Visit the Embassy of Fiji website for the most current visa information.

HIV/AIDS Restrictions: Some HIV/AIDS entry restrictions exist for visitors to and foreign residents of Fiji. There may be travel restrictions for people applying for visa work permits if they have HIV/AIDS. Once medical clearance is obtained, the work permit committee will decide on a case-by-case basis whether or not to approve the permit.

H1N1 Influenza Screening: Although international passengers are not currently being screened for influenza, Fiji has a standby process to screen for possible cases of the H1N1 influenza known as 'swine Flu.' The Ministry of Health monitors H1N1 cases in Fiji. If the Ministry detects an H1N1 problem, international passengers arriving by air who show flu-like symptoms may be separated from the public and evaluated. Those infected with the H1N1 influenza receive treatment as required. Please verify this information with the Embassy of Fiji before you travel.

Threats to Safety and Security: The Department of State advises U.S. Citizens to exercise caution when traveling to or within Fiji. The political situation is unpredictable, and the rule of law has deteriorated since the December 2006 military coup. The independence of the judicial system is compromised and basic freedoms are limited. The Government of Fiji rules by decree, maintaining Public Emergency Regulations that limit freedom of speech, freedom of the media, and freedom of assembly. Additionally, the U.S. Embassy has noted growing anti-U.S rhetoric in the government-controlled media.

U.S. Citizens in Fiji should remain cautious and alert in public places and near military activities in the greater Suva area. You should avoid demonstrations and large crowds, remembering that even peaceful demonstrations can turn violent unexpectedly.

Stay up to date by:

- Bookmarking our Bureau of Consular Affairs website, which contains the current Travel Warnings and Travel Alerts as well as the Worldwide Caution.
- Following us on Twitter and the Bureau of Consular Affairs page on Facebook as well.
- Downloading our free Smart Traveler iPhone App to have travel information at your fingertips.
- Calling 1-888-407-4747 toll-free within the U.S. and Canada, or a regular toll line, 1-202-501-4444, from other countries.
- Taking some time before travel to consider your personal security.

Crime: Urban areas experience a higher incidence of crime when compared with rural areas. You should always protect your valuables and be aware that theft from hotel rooms and purse snatching or pick pocketing is the most common crimes against tourists. Be attentive of your personal safety and be cautious about sharing too much personal information about where you are from and where you are staying while traveling. If you are not familiar with the area, ask hotel staff about areas to avoid. You should not walk alone after dark and always be sure to avoid isolated and deserted areas. Since there is crime directed at taxi drivers, do not allow taxis to pick up other passengers while you are en route. Similarly, you should not enter a taxi already carrying other passengers.

Don't buy counterfeit and pirated goods, even if they are widely available. Not only are the bootlegs illegal in the United States, if you purchase them you may also be breaking local law.

Victims of Crime: If you or someone you know becomes the victim of a crime abroad, you should contact the local police and the nearest U.S. embassy or consulate. We can:

- Replace a stolen passport.
- Help you find appropriate medical care if you are the victim of violent crimes such as assault or rape.
- Put you in contact with the appropriate police authorities, and if you want us to, we can contact family members or friend.
- Help you understand the local criminal justice process and direct you to local attorneys, although it is important to remember that local authorities are responsible for investigating and prosecuting the crime.

The local equivalent to the "911" emergency line in Fiji is also "911."

Criminal Penalties: While you are traveling in Fiji, you are subject to its laws even if you are a U.S. citizen. Foreign laws and legal systems can be vastly different than our own. You should carry photo identification with you at all times. If you are suspected of being involved in criminal activities, you will be taken in for questioning and will be asked for identification. Respect any sites that for cultural or security reasons have warnings posted against photography. Fiji enforces driving under the influence of alcohol laws, and offenders may be taken to jail. If you are stopped and found of driving under the influence of alcohol, you will be taken in for further tests at the police station. If the second test is affirmative, you will be locked up in a prison cell to sober up, typically overnight, and then you will be charged the following morning. If you do not have a permanent address in Fiji, the local police will keep you in custody and will arrange for a special court hearing with a Magistrate. These hearings take place generally during weekends and holidays. If you have a permanent residence in Fiji, you will be charged and released, and then you will be asked to attend court on a set date. Criminal penalties vary from country to country. There are also some things that might be legal in the country you visit, but still illegal in the United States, and you can be prosecuted under U.S. law if you buy pirated goods. Engaging in sexual conduct with children or using or disseminating child pornography in a foreign country is a crime prosecutable in the United States. If you break local laws in Fiji, your U.S. passport won't help you avoid arrest or prosecution. It's very important to know what's legal and what's not where you are going.

While some countries will automatically notify the nearest U.S. embassy or consulate if a U.S. citizen is detained or arrested in a foreign country, that might not always be the case. To ensure that the United States is aware of your circumstances, request that the police and prison officials notify the nearest U.S. embassy or consulate as soon as you are arrested or detained overseas.

Accessibility: While in Fiji, individuals with disabilities may find accessibility and accommodation very different from what you find in the United States. Under the constitution abrogated in April 2009, all persons are considered equal under the law, and discrimination against persons with disabilities in employment, education, provision of housing and land, or provision of other state services is illegal. Since the constitution's abrogation, no new decree has addressed specifically the rights of persons with disabilities; however, existing statutes provide for the right of access to places and all modes of transport generally open to the public. Public health regulations provide penalties for noncompliance; however, there is very little enabling legislation on accessibility for persons with disabilities, and there is little or no enforcement of laws protecting them.

Building regulations require new public buildings to be accessible to persons with disabilities, but only a few existing buildings meet this requirement. Under the Health and Safety at Work Act, all new office spaces must be accessible to persons with disabilities. The number of disabled-accessible vehicles in the country is small.

There some special schools for persons with physical, cognitive, and sensory disabilities, but cost and location limit access. Opportunities for a secondary school education for those with disabilities are very limited.

Water Sports: Many visitors to Fiji participate in water sports, including surfing, scuba diving, snorkeling, and operating jet-skis. Surfing on Fiji's numerous reef breaks can be highly dangerous. If you scuba dive or snorkel while in Fiji, please be sure to check the references, licenses, and equipment of tour operators before agreeing to or paying for a tour. Only rent equipment from trustworthy operators and ensure you receive training before using the equipment. Some rental diving equipment may not be properly maintained or inspected. Local dive masters may not consider your skill level when they organize the trip. Deaths and serious accidents have occurred in the past since basic safety measures were not taken during diving and snorkeling trips. Remember that safety precautions and emergency responses may not be similar to U.S. standards. Fiji has only one decompression chamber to provide medical assistance for dive related injuries. The chamber is located in Suva, which is far from most resorts. Please note that the chamber is not always fully functioning.

Trekking: Terrain in the Fiji islands can be hazardous. You should speak with local guides and/or hotel staff before starting a trek. It is best to hike with a companion and stay on trails that are clearly marked.

Customs: There may be strict regulations and customs enforcement for importing and exporting items such as alcohol and tobacco products in Fiji. You should contact the Embassy of Fiji in Washington, DC, at (202) 466-8320 for specific information regarding customs requirements. Bringing animals into Fiji is strictly controlled. Pets may be imported only from certain designated, rabies-free areas. If you want to bring a pet into Fiji, contact the Ministry of Agriculture in Suva about six months in advance to find out the details. Also, please see the Customs Information sheet for additional information.

Purchase of Real Estate: Purchasing real estate in Fiji can be risky. Be cautious before you enter into commitments to invest in property. You should gather reliable information and hire experienced Fijian legal counsel regarding any real estate investment. Fijian law and practices about real estate differ substantially from those in the United States.

Notification of Arrest: You should carry a copy of your U.S. passport at all times. If questioned by local authorities, you will need to show proof of identity and U.S. citizenship. According to Fijian law, a person detained for criminal actions may be held for a maximum of 48 hours before being charged. Police authorities should contact the U.S. Embassy if there is a detention or arrest of a U.S. citizen within 24 hours of the incident. Nevertheless, if you are detained you should request that a consular officer at the U.S. Embassy in Suva be notified.

Natural Disasters: Fiji is located in an area of high seismic activity. Although the probability of a major earthquake occurring during your trip is rare, please remember that earthquakes can and do occur. Undersea earthquakes in the South Pacific can generate destructive tsunamis. Fiji does not have a siren warning system in place; instead, tsunami warnings are transmitted through local radio and television stations. Most coastal resorts and hotels have tsunami evacuation plans in place, and guests should carefully follow staff instructions in the event of a tsunami warning.

Cyclones: The cyclone season is November through April. The Fiji Meteorological Service maintains a Tropical Cyclone Warning Center in Nadi serving the Southwest Pacific Region. General information regarding disaster preparedness is available by visiting the Bureau of Consular Affairs web site and the U.S. Federal Emergency Management Agency (FEMA) home page.

Medical Facilities and Health Information: Health-care facilities in Fiji's urban areas are adequate for routine medical problems. In the rural areas, staff training is limited and there are often shortages of supplies and medications. Emergency response is extremely limited. Ambulance availability is minimal, and ambulances are often poorly equipped and staffed.

Two major hospitals, the Lautoka Hospital in the western city of Lautoka and the Colonial War Memorial Hospital in Suva, provide limited emergency and outpatient services. A recompression chamber at the Colonial War Memorial Hospital in Suva can treat decompression sickness (See also Special Circumstances, Water Sports).

A private hospital in Suva provides Western-style medical care, and other hospitals and clinics provide only a limited range of health services. Medical emergencies may be evacuated to Australia, New Zealand, or the United States. Serious medical problems requiring hospitalization and/or medical evacuation to the United States or elsewhere can cost tens of thousands of dollars. Doctors and hospitals expect immediate cash payment for health services.

Dengue fever, carried by infected mosquitoes, occurs throughout the country of Fiji, especially during the rainy season. You can find good information on vaccinations and other health precautions, on the CDC website. For information about outbreaks of infectious diseases abroad, consult the World Health Organization (WHO) website. The WHO website also contains additional health information for travelers, including detailed country-specific health information.

Medical Insurance: You can't assume your insurance will go with you when you travel. It's very important to find out BEFORE you leave whether or not your medical insurance will cover you overseas. You need to ask your insurance company two questions:

- Does my policy apply when I'm out of the United States?
- Will it cover emergencies like a trip to a foreign hospital or a medical evacuation?

In many places, doctors and hospitals still expect payment in cash at the time of service. Your regular U.S. health insurance may not cover doctors' and hospital visits in other countries. If your policy doesn't go with you when you travel, it's a very good idea to take out another one for your trip.

Traffic Safety and Road Conditions: While in Fiji, you may encounter road conditions that differ significantly from those in the United States. Traffic moves on the left in Fiji. While most roads in urban areas are paved, they are poorly maintained. Roads outside the city are usually not paved. In the city, driving after dark requires heightened attentiveness. Outside of the city, it is discouraged to drive after dark except in emergency or exceptional circumstances. Stray animals, unwary pedestrians, and potholes make driving dangerous and particularly hazardous at night.

Aviation Safety Oversight: The U.S. Federal Aviation Administration (FAA) assessed the government of Fiji's Civil Aviation Authority as being in compliance with International Civil Aviation Organization (ICAO) aviation safety standards for oversight of Fiji's air carrier operations. Further information may be found on the FAA safety assessment page.

Children's Issues: Please see the Office of Children's Issues web pages on intercountry adoption and international parental child abduction.

Intercountry Adoption

The Hague Adoption Convention Enters Into Force for Fiji September 4, 2012

On August 1, 2012, the Hague Convention on Protection of Children and Co-Operation in Respect of Intercountry Adoption entered into force for Fiji. The Department of State has not received information from the Government of Fiji on its plans for implementing the Convention. The United States cannot process Convention intercountry adoptions until the Government of Fiji implements an effective Convention intercountry adoption process.

We caution adoption service providers and prospective adoptive parents that, to ensure that adoptions from Fiji will comply with the Convention, important steps must take place before intercountry adoptions between the United States and Fiji resume. Adoption service providers should neither initiate nor claim to initiate adoption programs in Fiji until the Department of State notifies them that it has resumed adoptions in Fiji. The Department of State will provide updated information on adoption.state.gov as it becomes available. If you have any questions about this notice, please contact the Office of Children's Issues at 1-888-407-4747 within the United States, or 202-501-4444 from outside the United States. E-mail inquiries may be directed to AdoptionUSCA@state.gov.

Adoption Overview February 2009

The information in this section has been edited from the latest report available as of February 2013 from the State Department Bureau of Consular Affairs, Office of Overseas Citizens Services. For more information, please read the *Intercountry Adoption* section of this book and review current reports online at http://adoption.state.gov.

According to Fiji law American citizens wishing to adopt orphans from that country MUST be residents in the Republic of Fiji. The Social Welfare Department, under the Ministry of Women, Social Welfare and Poverty, is in charge of overseeing intercountry adoptions. Fiji has specific intercountry adoption administrative arrangements established with Australia, New Zealand and Pacific Island countries for the purpose of adoption of infants from Fiji to those countries. There are no intercountry arrangements between Fiji and the United States because the Government of Fiji has determined that it is not feasible. This generally means that persons currently residing in the United States cannot adopt from the Fiji Islands, but in practice the courts have occasionally waived the residency requirement if the prospective adoptive parents/children are blood relations and/or the prospective adoptive parents were previously citizens of Fiji.

Who Can Adopt? To bring an adopted child to United States from Fiji, you must be found eligible to adopt by the U.S. Government. The U.S. Government agency responsible for making this determination is the Department of Homeland Security, U.S. Citizenship and Immigration Services (USCIS).

Residency Requirements: According to Fiji law American citizens wishing to adopt orphans from that country MUST be residents in the Republic of Fiji. This means applicants are living and/or working in Fiji, or have property or other demonstrated connections to Fiji. Prospective adoptive parents must be long-term residents of Fiji (at least 3 months) in order for them to apply for and be granted a full and final adoption order. Prospective adoptive parents must be physically present in court to file an application for adoption and must remain in Fiji until the final adoption order is granted. In addition, applicants must reside with a child or contribute to a child's welfare for a minimum of three months prior to application.

Age Requirements: At least one prospective adoptive parent must have attained the age of 25. Applicants must be at least 21 years older than the child.

Marriage Requirements: A single male applicant cannot adopt a female child. Fiji law permits both single and married foreigners to adopt Fijian children.

Income Requirements: Income should be above average and prospective adoptive parents should live in a conducive environment. Proof of income will have to be submitted to the Department of Social Welfare.

Other requirements: The applicants must have no adverse police record relating to any offense involving violence towards a child or abuse of child. The applicant must be able to provide a secure and stable home environment for the child. The court and the Department of Social Welfare are inclined to look more favorable on cases where the child and the adoptive parents are related by blood. Most orphan visa cases involve prospective adoptive parents who are former residents of Fiji and who have family ties in Fiji. The Fijian court takes these issues into account when deciding whether the prospective adoptive parents have fulfilled Fiji's residency requirements.

Who Can Be Adopted? Fiji has specific requirements that a child must meet in order to be eligible for adoption. In addition to these requirements, a child must meet the definition of an orphan under U.S. law for you to bring him or her back to the United States.

Eligibility Requirements: An adoption order shall not be made in the case of any child unless the child has been continuously in the care and possession of the prospective adoptive parents for at least three consecutive months immediately preceding the date of the order. An adoption order shall not be made except with the consent of every person or body who is a parent or guardian of the infant, or who is liable by virtue of any order or agreement to contribute to the maintenance of the infant. Provided that the court may dispense with any consent required by this subsection if it is satisfied:

- In the case of a parent or guardian of the infant, that he has abandoned, neglected or persistently ill-treated the infant, or has made no contribution to its maintenance for a period in excess of five years;

- In the case of a person liable as aforesaid to contribute to the maintenance of the infant, that he has persistently neglected or refused so to contribute;

- In any case, that the person whose consent is required cannot be found, or is incapable of giving his consent or that his consent is unreasonably withheld.

Abandoned children are usually wards of the state and the local Government appoints the Social Welfare Department to be their legal guardians.

Age Requirements: The child should be under the age of 21 years old.

Sibling Requirements: The Social Welfare Department prefers that a sibling of the prospective adoptive child be adopted by the same family, if the sibling is also available for adoption.

Requirements for Special Needs or Medical Conditions: Living conditions of prospective adoptive parents must be conducive to the child's needs.

Waiting Period: Prospective adoptive parents must have had the child in their care and possession for a period of three continuous months before an adoption order will be issued by the court. The total waiting period could be less than four months.

Fijian Adoption Authority: The Social Welfare Department, under the Ministry of Women, Social Welfare and Poverty, is in charge of overseeing intercountry adoptions.

For people residing in Fiji, the adoption authority in Fiji is the Magistrate's court having jurisdiction over the adopted child's place of residence. Almost every town and city in Fiji has a court.

The Process: The first step in adopting a child from Fiji is usually to select a licensed agency in the United States that can help with your adoption. Adoption service providers must be licensed by the U.S. state in which they operate. If you are eligible to adopt, you will have to make your own arrangements to identify a child available for adoption.

Fiji has specific intercountry-adoption administrative arrangements established with Australia, New Zealand and Pacific Island Countires. Unfortunately, there are no intercountry arrangements between Fiji and the USA.

Role of the Adoption Authority: The Social Welfare Department, under the Ministry of Women Social Welfare and Poverty Alleviation, oversees all adoptions. The Social Welfare Department is appointed by the court to conduct home studies. The magistrate considers the Social Welfare Department's report as highly persuasive when deciding cases. There are no lists of local attorneys in Fiji who specialize in adoptions but almost all legal firms in Fiji can assist in facilitating adoption cases in Fiji.

Role of the Court: The prospective adoptive parents file an Application for Adoption with the Magistrate's Court. The Court appoints the Fiji Social Welfare Department as Guardian Ad Litem. The Social Welfare Department conducts a home-study investigation that assesses the prospective adoptive parents' character, financial competence and suitability. The Magistrate's Court considers whether to grant an Adoption Order based on the Social Welfare Department's report. If the Social Welfare report is favorable, the court tends to grant the Adoption Order.

Adoption Application: Tips for working the adoption through the local system:

- Seek legal advice from a local lawyer.

- Have the Department of Social Welfare involved from the beginning. It is best to contact it in writing.

- Being related to the infant is not necessary but often speeds up the process.

Time Frame: The time frame from the filing of the motion/application until the adoption order is issued is approximately four to five months. If the prospective adoptive parents are biologically related to the child, the process may be quicker.

Adoption Fees: A court fee of $45 is required to file the motion and receive the Adoption Order. Additional attorney fees will apply if the family uses a lawyer. There is no charge for the Social Welfare Department (home study) report.

Documents Required: To file the application at the court prospective adoptive parents generally need to include:

- Motion/Application for Adoption (drafted by an attorney).

- Affidavits (including original marriage certificates for the perspective adopting parents and consent of release from the biological parent(s) or legal guardian for adoption and immigration)

- Notice for an Application for an Adoption Order (Social Welfare report attached).

The Social Welfare Department will require the prospective adoptive parents to submit:

- Child's original birth certificate.

- Written consent of release for adoption of the child from a parent or guardian.

- Financial documents, such as bank statements.

- Reference from employer and/or evidence of property.
- Character reference from the prospective adoptive parents' community.

After you finalize the adoption (or gain legal custody) in Fiji, the U.S Government, Department of Homeland Security, U.S. Citizenship and Immigration Services (USCIS) MUST determine whether the child is eligible under U.S. law to be adopted (Form I-600).

Bringing Your Child Home: Once your adoption is complete (or you have obtained legal custody of the child), there are a few more steps to take before you can head home. Specifically, you need to apply for several documents for your child before he or she can travel to the United States, such as a birth certificate, a passport or travel document for your child from the country in which he or she was born, and a U.S. Immigration Visa. For detailed and updated information on how to obtain these documents, review the *Intercountry Adoption* section on this publication and visit the USCIS Intercountry Adoption website at http://adoption.state.gov.

Child Citizenship Act: For adoptions finalized abroad, the Child Citizenship Act of 2000 allows your new child to acquire American citizenship automatically when he or she enters the United States as lawful permanent residents. For adoptions finalized in the United States, the Child Citizenship Act of 2000 allows your new child to acquire American citizenship automatically when the court in the United States issues the final adoption decree. To learn more, visit the USCIS Intercountry Adoption website at http://adoption.state.gov.

U.S. Embassy in Fiji
31 Loftus Street
P.O. Box 218
Suva, Fiji
Tel: (679) 331-4466
Fax: (679) 330-2267
Recorded Information: (679) 330-3888
Email: consularsuva@state.gov
http://suva.usembassy.gov/index.html

Fijian Adoption Authority
Social Welfare Department
P.O. Box 2127
Government Buildings
72 Suva Street, Toorak
Suva, Fiji
Tel: (679) 331-5585

Embassy of Fiji
2233 Wisconsin Avenue, N.W.
Suite 240
Washington, D.C. 20007
Tel: 202-337-8320
Fax: 202-337-1996
Email: info@fijiembassydc.com
Internet: www.fijiembassydc.com

Office of Children's Issues
U.S. Department of State
2201 C Street, NW
SA-29
Washington, DC 20520
Tel: 1-888-407-4747
E-mail: AskCI@state.gov
http://adoption.state.gov

For questions about immigration procedures, call the National Customer Service Center (NCSC) 1-800-375-5283 (TTY 1-800-767-1833).

FINLAND

Compiled from publications that were available as of February 2013 from the U.S. Department of State, the U.S. Department of Commerce, and the Central Intelligence Agency (CIA). See the introduction to this set for explanatory notes.

Official Name:
Republic of Finland

PROFILE

Geography

Area: total: 338,145 sq km; country comparison to the world: 65; land: 303,815 sq km; water: 34,330 sq km

Major cities: Helsinki (capital) 1.107 million (2009)

Climate: cold temperate; potentially subarctic but comparatively mild because of moderating influence of the North Atlantic Current, Baltic Sea, and more than 60,000 lakes

Terrain: mostly low, flat to rolling plains interspersed with lakes and low hills

People

Nationality: noun: Finn(s); adjective: Finnish

Population: 5,262,930 (July 2012 est.)

Population growth rate: 0.065% (2012 est.)

Ethnic groups: Finn 93.4%, Swede 5.6%, Russian 0.5%, Estonian 0.3%, Roma (Gypsy) 0.1%, Sami 0.1% (2006)

Religions: Lutheran Church of Finland 82.5%, Orthodox Church 1.1%, other Christian 1.1%, other 0.1%, none 15.1% (2006)

Languages: Finnish (official) 91.2%, Swedish (official) 5.5%, other (small Sami- and Russian-speaking minorities) 3.3% (2007)

Literacy: definition: age 15 and over can read and write; total population: 100%; male: 100%; female: 100% (2000 est.)

Health: life expectancy at birth: total population: 79.41 years; male: 75.94 years; female: 83.02 years (2012 est.); Infant mortality rate: total: 3.4 deaths/1,000 live births; male: 3.7 deaths/1,000 live births; female: 3.09 deaths/1,000 live births (2012 est.)

Unemployment rate: 7.3% (2012 est.)

Work force: 2.679 million (2012 est.)

Government

Type: republic

Independence: 6 December 1917

Constitution: 1 March 2000

Political subdivisions: 19 regions (maakunnat, singular—maakunta (Finnish); landskapen, singular—landskapet (Swedish)

Suffrage: 18 years of age; universal

Economy

GDP (purchasing power parity): $198.1 billion (2012 est.); $198.2 billion (2011 est.); $192.7 billion (2010 est.); $185.8 billion (2009 est.)

GDP real growth rate: 0.3% (2012 est.); 2.9% (2011 est.); 3.7% (2010 est.); -8.4% (2009 est.)

GDP per capita (PPP): $36,500 (2012 est.); $36,700 (2011 est.); $35,900 (2010 est.); $34,700 (2009 est.)

Natural resources: timber, iron ore, copper, lead, zinc, chromite, nickel, gold, silver, limestone

Agriculture products: barley, wheat, sugar beets, potatoes; dairy cattle; fish

Industries: metals and metal products, electronics, machinery and scientific instruments, shipbuilding, pulp and paper, foodstuffs, chemicals, textiles, clothing

Exports: $72.7 billion (2012 est.); $78.8 billion (2011 est.); $69.63 billion (2010 est.)

Exports—commodities: electrical and optical equipment, machinery, transport equipment, paper and pulp, chemicals, basic metals; timber

Exports—partners: Sweden 12.1%, Germany 10.2%, Russia 9.5%, Netherlands 6.9%, UK 5.3%, US 5.1%, China 4.8% (2011)

Imports: $72.23 billion (2012 est.); $80.4 billion (2011 est.); $66.23 billion (2010 est.)

Imports—commodities: foodstuffs, petroleum and petroleum products, chemicals, transport equipment, iron and steel, machinery, computers, electronic industry products, textile yarn and fabrics, grains

Imports—partners: Russia 18%, Sweden 14.1%, Germany 13.9%, Netherlands 7.8%, China 4.3% (2011)
Debt—external: $577 billion (31 December 2011); $370.8 billion (30 June 2010)
Exchange rates: euros (EUR) per US dollar; 0.7838 (2012 est.); 0.7194 (2011 est.); 0.755 (2010 est.); 0.7198 (2009 est.); 0.6827 (2008 est.)

PEOPLE

National/Racial/Ethnic Minorities

There was some societal tension between ethnic Finns and minority groups, and there were reports of racist or xenophobic incidents.

Groups of Roma have lived in the country for centuries. According to the minority ombudsman, discrimination against the country's approximately 10,000 to 12,000 Roma extended to all areas of life, resulting in their effective exclusion from society. Roma are classified as a "traditional ethnic minority" in the ombudsman's report. The Romani minority was the most frequent target of racially motivated discrimination, followed by Russian speakers, Somalis, Turks, Iraqis, Sami, and Thais. Ethnic Finns were also occasionally victims of racially motivated crimes for associating with members of minority communities.

A new, significant influx of adult Romani beggars from Romania started in 2007 after Romania joined the EU, with an increase in Roma in Helsinki and other large cities. The number of beggars varied significantly over the year, ranging from approximately 200-300 during the summer months and only a few dozen during the winter.

At the end of 2010 there were 54,500 Russian-speaking persons living in the country, principally in Helsinki and areas along the Russian border. They were by far the largest minority not speaking Finnish or Swedish, the country's two official languages. In April 2009, the latest date for which data was available, unemployment among immigrants from the former Soviet Union (excluding Estonia) was 31 percent, compared to 17.6 percent for all immigrants and 8.8 percent in the country overall.

The government strongly encouraged tolerance and respect for minority groups and sought to address racial discrimination.

The constitution provides for the protection of the Sami language and culture, and the government financially supported these protections. The Sami, who constitute less than 0.1 percent of the population, have full political and civil rights as citizens as well as a measure of autonomy in their civil and administrative affairs.

A 21-member Sami parliament (Samediggi), popularly elected by the Sami, is responsible for the group's language, culture, and matters concerning their status as an indigenous people. The Sami parliament is an independent body but operates under the purview of the Interior Ministry. It can adopt legally binding resolutions, propose initiatives, and provide policy guidance. Despite constitutional protections, members of the Sami community continued to protest the lack of explicit legislation to safeguard Sami land, resources, and economic livelihood.

The government owns 90 percent of the land in the Sami home region, much of it in the form of national parks. Sami have alleged for decades that the government used their land for logging and other purposes without consulting them.

Language

The two official languages in Finland are Finnish and Swedish. Both languages are compulsory at school. English is widely spoken in Finland, especially among younger people and in major cities.

Religion

Approximately 78 percent of the population belongs to the Evangelical Lutheran Church (ELC) and 1 percent to the Orthodox Church. Other religious groups, each accounting for less than 1 percent of the population, include Jehovah's Witnesses, the Free Church of Finland, Roman Catholics, Muslims, Pentecostals, Seventh-Day Adventists, The Church of Jesus Christ of Latter-day Saints, and Jews.

There are approximately 40,000 Muslims, a 100 percent increase since 1999, primarily due to immigration and high birth rates. An estimated 30,000 Muslims are Sunni and 10,000 are Shiite. The largest Muslim group is ethnic Somali; there are also communities of North Africans, Bosnians, peninsular Arabs, Tartars, Turks, and Iraqis.

The government statistics agency reported on September 30 that the number of persons with no religious affiliation is over one million. An estimated 19 percent of the population either does not belong to any religious group or practices religion "in private," including non-registered Pentecostal worshippers and Muslims.

HISTORICAL HIGHLIGHTS

The origins of the Finnish people are still a matter of conjecture, although many scholars argue that their original home was in what is now west-central Siberia. The Finns arrived in their present territory thousands of years ago, pushing the indigenous Lapps into the more remote northern regions. Finnish and Lappish—the language of Finland's small Lapp minority—both are Finno-Ugric languages and are in the Uralic rather than the Indo-European family.

Finland's nearly 700-year association with the Kingdom of Sweden began in 1154 with the introduction of Christianity by Sweden's King Eric. During the ensuing centuries, Finland played an important role in the political life of the Swedish-Finnish realm, and Finnish soldiers often predominated in Swedish armies. Finns also formed a significant proportion of the first "Swedish" settlers in 17th-century America.

Following Finland's incorporation into Sweden in the 12th century, Swedish became the dominant language, although Finnish recovered its predominance after a 19th-century resurgence of Finnish nationalism. Publication in 1835 of the Finnish national epic, The Kalevala—a collection of traditional myths and legends—first stirred the nationalism that later led to Finland's independence from Russia.

In 1809, Finland was conquered by the armies of Czar Alexander I and thereafter remained an autonomous grand duchy connected with the Russian Empire until the end of 1917. On December 6, 1917, shortly after the Bolshevik Revolution in Russia, Finland declared its independence.

In 1918, the country experienced a brief but bitter civil war that colored domestic politics for many years. During World War II, Finland fought the Soviet Union twice—in the Winter War of 1939–40 and again in the Continuation War of 1941–44. This was followed by the Lapland War of 1944–45, when Finland fought against the Germans as they withdrew their forces from northern Finland.

During the Continuation War (1941–1944) Finland was a co-belligerent with Germany. However, Finnish Jews were not persecuted. Of the approximately 500 Jewish refugees who arrived in Finland, eight were handed over to the Germans, for which Finland submitted an official apology in 2000. Also during the war, approximately 2,600 Soviet prisoners of war were exchanged for 2,100 Finnish prisoners of war from Germany. In 2003, the Simon Wiesenthal Center submitted an official request for a full-scale investigation by the Finnish authorities of the prisoner exchange. It was established there were about 70 Jews among the extradited prisoners.

However, none was extradited as a result of ethnic background or religious belief. Treaties signed in 1947 and 1948 with the Soviet Union included obligations and restraints on Finland vis-a-vis the U.S.S.R. as well as territorial concessions by Finland; both have been abrogated by Finland since the 1991 dissolution of the Soviet Union (see Foreign Relations).

GOVERNMENT AND POLITICAL CONDITIONS

The Republic of Finland is a constitutional republic with a directly elected president and a unicameral parliament (Eduskunta). The prime minister heads a six-party coalition government.

Recent Elections

Parliamentary elections held on April 17, 2011, were considered free and fair.

Participation of Women and Minorities: As a result of the April elections, 86 women entered the 200-seat parliament and nine women took portfolios in the 19-member Council of State (cabinet). The president of the republic and the president of the Supreme Court were women. Four of the eight parties in parliament went into the election campaign under female leaders. Women were in the majority in two parliamentary groups: the Social Democratic Party (27 women and 15 men) and the Swedish People's Party (five women and four men).

There were 10 members of minority groups in parliament and two in the cabinet. Jani Toivola, a Kenyan-Finn from the Greens Party, became the first member of a racial minority to win a parliamentary seat as well as one of the few openly gay members of parliament. The autonomous region of the Aland Islands elects one representative to the national parliament and has its own parliament. The indigenous Sami minority enjoys semiautonomous status and has its own parliament as well as full representation as citizens in the national parliament; however, no Sami were members of the national parliament.

Principal Government Officials

Last Updated: 1/31/2013

Pres.: **Sauli NIINISTO**
Prime Min.: **Jyrki Tapani KATAINEN**
Dep. Prime Min.: **Jutta URPILAINEN**
Min. of Agriculture & Forestry: **Jari KOSKINEN**
Min. of Culture & Sport: **Paavo ARHINMAKI**
Min. of Defense: **Carl HAGLUND**
Min. of Development Cooperation: **Heidi HAUTALA**
Min. of Economic Affairs: **Jan VAPAAVUORI**
Min. of Education: **Jukka GUSTAFSSON**
Min. of the Environment: **Ville NIINISTO**
Min. of Finance: **Jutta URPILAINEN**
Min. of Foreign Affairs: **Erkki Sakari TUOMIOJA**
Min. of Foreign Trade & European Affairs: **Cai-Goran Alexander STUBB**
Min. of Health & Social Affairs: **Paula RISIKKO**
Min. of Housing & Communications: **Krista KIURU**
Min. of Interior: **Paivi RASANEN**
Min. of Justice: **Anna-Maija HENRIKSSON**
Min. of Labor: **Lauri IHALAINEN**
Min. of Public Admin. & Local Govt.: **Henna VIRKKUNEN**
Min. of Social Services: **Maria GUZENINA-RICHARDSON**
Min. of Transport: **Merja KYLLONEN**
Governor, Bank of Finland: **Erkki LIIKANEN**
Ambassador to the US: **Ritva Inkeri KOUKKU-RONDE**
Permanent Representative to the UN, New York: **Jarmo VIINANEN**

ECONOMY

Finland has a highly industrialized, largely free-market economy with per capita output roughly that of Austria, Belgium, the Netherlands, and Sweden. Trade is important with exports accounting for over one third of GDP in recent years.

Finland is strongly competitive in manufacturing - principally the wood, metals, engineering, telecommunications, and electronics industries. Finland excels in high-tech exports such as mobile phones. Except for timber and several minerals, Finland depends on imports of raw materials, energy, and some components for manufactured goods. Because of the climate, agricultural development is limited to maintaining self-sufficiency in basic products. Forestry, an important export earner, provides a secondary occupation for the rural population. Finland had been one of the best performing economies within the EU in recent years and its banks and financial markets avoided the worst of global financial crisis. However, the world slowdown hit exports and domestic demand hard in 2009, with Finland experiencing one of the deepest contractions in the euro zone. A recovery of exports, domestic trade, and household consumption stimulated economic growth in 2010–11. The recession affected general government finances and the debt ratio, turning previously strong budget surpluses into deficits, but Finland has taken action to ensure it will meet EU deficit targets by 2013 and retains its triple-A credit rating. Finland's main challenge in 2013 will be to stimulate growth in the face of weak demand in EU export markets and government austerity measures meant to reduce its budget deficit. Longer-term, Finland must address a rapidly aging population and decreasing productivity that threaten competitiveness, fiscal sustainability, and economic growth.

Labor Conditions

The law allows children over the age of 15 to enter a valid employment contract as long as work does not interrupt compulsory education. Such employment is restricted to no more than nine hours per day and 48 hours per week with mandatory minimum daily rest of 12 hours. Young workers may not work at night after 10:00 p.m. or under conditions that risk health and safety.

Children under the age of 15 may be employed for summer work, school-related events, modeling, and other similar purposes, but the approval of both their guardians and OSHA is required, and their working hours are limited in all cases. Employers are required to provide work insurance, social payments, and a letter of reference for all young workers. The law applies to work done by all persons under 18 years of age, whether in the private or public sector. In addition to employment relationships, the provisions of the act on occupational safety and health apply to the practical training of under-18-year-old pupils or practical work done at school. The Ministry of Employment and the Economy enforces child labor regulations.

There is no national minimum wage law; however, the law requires all employers, including nonunionized employers, to pay minimum wages stipulated in collective bargaining agreements. The Ministry of Employment and the Economy is responsible for labor policy strategy and implementation, improving the viability of working life and its quality, and promoting employment.

The standard workweek established by law is eight hours per day with no more than 40 hours of work per week. According to Statistics Finland, the full-time workweek averaged 37.8 hours for all workers in 2010, the most recent year for which data was available. Certain occupations, such as seamen, household workers, road-transport workers, and workers in bakeries, are subject to separate workweek regulations. Employees working shifts or during the weekend are entitled to one 24-hour rest period per week. Workers are entitled to time-and-a-half pay for the first hour of overtime work and double-time pay for time beyond the first hour. The law limits a worker to 250 hours of overtime per year and 138 overtime hours in any four-month period.

U.S.-FINLAND RELATIONS

The United States established diplomatic relations with Finland in 1919, following its 1917 declaration of independence from the Russian Empire. The United States severed diplomatic relations with Finland in 1944 during World War II, due to Finland's alliance with Nazi Germany. U.S.-Finland diplomatic relations were reestablished in 1945. Finland is bordered on the east by Russia and, as one of the former Soviet Union's neighbors, was of particular interest and importance to the United States both during the Cold War and in its aftermath. Before the Soviet Union dissolved in 1991, longstanding U.S. policy was to support Finnish neutrality while maintaining and reinforcing Finland's historic, cultural, and economic ties with the West.

The United States and Finland have enjoyed an enduring partnership and friendship. Finland has contributed to the advancement of technology and research, promotion of international economic development, and the defense of human rights and peace.

The United States has welcomed Finland's integration into Western economic and political structures. In 1994, Finland joined the North Atlantic Treaty Organization's (NATO) Partnership for Peace program. It became a full member of the European Union (EU) in 1995 and joined the EU's Economic and Monetary Union in 1999.

U.S. Assistance to Finland

The United States provides no development assistance to Finland.

Bilateral Economic Relations

Finland welcomes foreign investment. Areas of particular interest for U.S. investors are specialized high-tech companies and investments that take advantage of Finland's position as a gateway to Russia and the Baltic countries. Exports from the United States to Finland include machinery, telecommunications equipment and parts, metalliferous ores, road vehicles and transport equipment, computers, peripherals and software, electronic components, chemicals, medical equipment, and some agricultural products. Imports from Finland to the United States include electronics, machinery, ships and boats, paper and paperboard, refined petroleum products, and telecommunications equipment and parts. Finland participates in the Visa Waiver Program, which allows nationals of participating countries to travel to the United States for certain business or tourism purposes for stays of 90 days or less without obtaining a visa.

Finland is a member of the European Union. The U.S. economic relationship with the EU is the largest and most complex in the world, and the United States and the EU continue to pursue initiatives to create new opportunities for transatlantic commerce.

Finland's Membership in International Organizations

Finland and the United States belong to a number of the same international organizations, including the United Nations, Euro-Atlantic Partnership Council, Organization for Security and Cooperation in Europe, Organization for Economic Cooperation and Development, International Monetary Fund, World Bank, and World Trade Organization. Finland also is an observer to the Organization of American States and a participant in the North Atlantic Treaty Organization's (NATO) Partnership for Peace program.

Bilateral Representation

Finland maintains an embassy in the United States at 3301 Massachusetts Avenue, NW, Washington, DC 20008; tel: 202-298-5800.

Principal U.S. Embassy Officials

Last Updated: 1/14/2013

HELSINKI (E) Itainen Puistotie 14, 00140 Helsinki, 358-9-6162-50, Fax +358-9-6162-5135, Workweek: Monday-Friday 0830-1700, Website: http://helsinki.usembassy.gov/

DCM OMS:	Patty Hennessy
AMB OMS:	Anni Pirinen Valme
Co-CLO:	Chris Hernandez
DHS/TSA:	Jesus (Jess) Presas
FCS:	Nicholas Kuchova
FM:	Kato Smith
IBB:	Arto Mujunen
MGT:	Steve Rider
MLO/ODC:	COL Scott Davis
POL/ECON:	Juha Salin
SDO/DATT:	COL Scott Davis, Datt
AMB:	Bruce Oreck
CON:	Susan Carl
DCM:	Danny Hall
PAO:	Marjut Robinson
GSO:	Wayne Hemmings
RSO:	Joseph Castro
AGR:	Steve Huete–The Hague
CLO:	Rebekah Newquist
ECON:	Dan Daley

EEO: Patricia Hennessy
FMO: Steve Rider
ICASS Chair: Nicholas Kuchova
IMO: Craig Bowman
IRS: Kelli D. Winegardner–London
ISSO: Devin Hendriksen
LEGATT: Gregory D. Cox (Copenhagen)
State ICASS: Marjut Robinson

TRAVEL

Consular Information Sheet

June 25, 2012

Country Description: Finland is a highly developed democracy with a modern economy. It is a member of the European Union. Tourist facilities are widely available.

Smart Traveler Enrollment Program (STEP)/Embassy Locations: If you are going to live in or visit Finland, please take the time to tell our Embassy about your trip. If you enroll in the Smart Traveler Enrollment Program, we can keep you up to date with important safety and security announcements. It will also help your friends and family get in touch with you in an emergency.

U.S. Embassy Helsinki
Itäinen Puistotie 14B
Hours: Mon—Fri, 0830—1700
Tel: 358-9-616-250 (24 hour switchboard number)
Fax: 358-9-612-3003
e-mail: HelsinkiACS@state.gov

Entry/Exit Requirements: Visit the Embassy of Finland website for the most current visa information. The U.S. Embassy in Helsinki is not able to assist private U.S. citizens in obtaining necessary visas for neighboring countries, including Russia and other countries of the former Soviet Union.

Finland is a party to the Schengen agreement. As such, U.S. citizens may enter Finland for up to 90 days for tourist or business purposes without a visa. Your passport should be valid for at least three months beyond the period of stay. You need sufficient funds and a return airline ticket.

The U.S. Department of State is unaware of any HIV/AIDS entry restrictions for visitors to or foreign residents of Finland.

Threats to Safety and Security: Finland remains largely free of terrorist incidents. However, like other countries in the Schengen area, Finland's open borders with its Western European neighbors allow the possibility of terrorist groups anonymously entering and exiting the country. Elements of organized crime groups operating in the former Soviet Union and Eastern Europe are present in Finland, but do not represent a specific danger to U.S. citizen residents or tourists. U.S. citizens are reminded to remain vigilant with regard to their personal security and to exercise caution.

Stay up to date by:

- Bookmarking our Bureau of Consular Affairs website, which contains the current Travel Warnings and Travel Alerts as well as the Worldwide Caution;
- Following us on Twitter and the Bureau of Consular Affairs page on Facebook as well;
- Downloading our free Smart Traveler iPhone App to have travel information at your fingertips;
- Calling 1-888-407-4747 toll-free within the U.S. and Canada, or a regular toll line, 1-202-501-4444, from other countries.
- Taking some time before travel to consider your personal security.

Crime: Although the crime rate in Finland is low compared to the United States and most European countries, it has increased in recent years. However, Finland remains relatively safe. U.S. citizens visiting Finland are seldom victims of crime, but visitors should not be complacent regarding personal safety or the protection of valuables. The same precautions employed in the United States should be followed in Finland. Finnish police services are excellent. Travelers should be aware that some police officers speak little English. Due to the low crime rate, Finland has fewer police officers than most European nations. Outside of key sites in major urban centers, police rarely project a visible presence; consequently, response times to crisis situations may be unpredictable. All forms of public transportation are considered safe. Street crimes, such as mugging and pick-pocketing, remain uncommon, but do occur.

Don't buy counterfeit and pirated goods, even if they are widely available. Not only are the bootlegs illegal in the United States, if you purchase them you may also be breaking local law.

Victims of Crime: If you or someone you know becomes the victim of a crime abroad, you should contact the local police and the nearest U.S. embassy or consulate. We can:

- Replace a stolen passport;
- Help you find appropriate medical care if you are the victim of a violent crime such as assault or rape;
- Put you in contact with the appropriate police authorities and, if you want us to, contact family members or friends.
- Help you understand the local criminal justice process and direct you to local attorneys, although it is important to remember that local authorities are responsible for investigating and prosecuting the crime.

Finland has a program to provide financial compensation to victims who suffer serious criminal injuries. According to existing regulations, the victim must report the incident to the police and file an application for compensation within 10 years of the date of the crime. Finnish police routinely inform victims of serious crime of their right to seek compensation. The relevant forms and further information can be obtained from the State Treasury of Finland website.

The local equivalent to the "911" emergency line in Finland is 112.

Criminal Penalties: While you are traveling in Finland, you are subject to its laws even if you are a U.S. citizen. Foreign laws and legal systems can be vastly different than our own.

There are also some things that might be legal in the country you visit, but still illegal in the United States; for instance, you can be prosecuted under U.S. law if you buy pirated goods. Engaging in sexual conduct with children or using or disseminating child pornography in a foreign country is a crime prosecutable in the United States. If you break local laws in Finland, your U.S. passport won't help you avoid arrest or prosecution. It's very important to know what's legal and what's not wherever you go.

Arrest notifications in host country: While some countries will automatically notify the nearest U.S. embassy or consulate if a U.S. citizen is detained or arrested in a foreign country, that might not always be the case. To ensure that the United States is aware of your circumstances, request that the police and prison officials notify the nearest U.S. embassy or consulate as soon as you are arrested or detained overseas.

Special Circumstances: Commercial and financial transactions in Finland are increasingly automated and on-line. Cash is almost always acceptable (the currency is the euro), but most major credit cards are widely accepted. Automatic Teller Machines (ATMs) are very common and many U.S.-issued bankcards are compatible with them. We are not aware of any special currency or customs circumstances for this country.

Accessibility: While in Finland, individuals with disabilities may find accessibility and accommodation very different from what is found in the United States. Many existing buildings as well as public transportation systems are less adapted to individuals with disabilities. You should check ahead with your hotel/destination to learn more about options to accommodate disabled traveler needs before visiting Finland.

Laws mandating access to buildings for persons with disabilities are generally enforced, but many older buildings remain inaccessible. Most forms of public transportation are accessible, but geographically isolated areas can be especially problematic for travelers with disabilities. Call ahead to restaurants, museums, and other facilities to find out if they are wheelchair-accessible. Assistance for train travelers is available at most stations, but must be requested in advance. For more information, visit the Finnish National Tourist Board's website.

Medical Facilities and Health Information: In Finland, medical facilities and staff are generally excellent and widely available for emergency services. English is commonly spoken by Finnish medical personnel. Helsinki is a frequent medical evacuation point for emergency cases from the countries of the former Soviet Union. The public hospital system and many private hospitals honor foreign credit cards. Most pharmacies (apteekki in Finnish) are open during normal shopping hours and major cities have at least one 24-hour service pharmacy.

If you are a tourist or temporary visitor to Finland and you require immediate emergency medical assistance, you may visit a local medical center, clinic, or first-aid station (ensiapuasema in Finnish). Usually these stations are located at hospitals and will provide a full range of services. The emergency telephone number, 112, can be used throughout Finland to contact emergency medical services.

Travelers with special medical needs should consult with their personal physicians and take appropriate precautions, including bringing adequate supplies of necessary medication. Medicines may be brought into the country as long as they are intended for the traveler's personal use; however, there are special requirements concerning the quantity. Finland allows travelers from the European Economic Area to bring personal prescription medicines (up to a one year supply) without a customs declaration. All others may bring a 90-day supply of personal prescription drugs to Finland. A formal doctor's note may be requested by Finnish customs officials. Prescribed narcotics are more highly restricted, however, and may only be brought into the country for the traveler's personal use for a maximum of 14 days and must be accompanied by a medical certificate stating why the traveler needs them.

In addition, stringent Finnish customs regulations prohibit travelers from receiving drugs from abroad after having arrived in the country. Travelers may also find local physicians reluctant to prescribe equivalent quantities of dosages. For more detailed information, please visit the Finnish National Tourist Board website or contact the Embassy of Finland.

You can find detailed information on vaccinations and other health precautions on the Centers for Disease Control and Prevention (CDC) website. For information about outbreaks of infectious diseases abroad, consult the World Health Organization (WHO) website, which also contains additional health information for travelers, including detailed country-specific health information.

Medical Insurance: You can't assume your insurance will go with you when you travel. It's very important to find out BEFORE you leave whether or not your medical insurance will cover you overseas. You need to ask your insurance company two questions:

- Does my policy apply when I'm out of the United States?
- Will it cover emergencies like a trip to a foreign hospital or a medical evacuation?

In many places, doctors and hospitals still expect payment in cash at the time of service. Your regular U.S. health insurance may not cover doctors' and hospital visits in other countries. If your policy doesn't go with you when you travel, it's a very good idea to take out another one for your trip.

Traffic Safety and Road Conditions: While in Finland, you may encounter road conditions that differ significantly from those in the United States. Finnish roads are comparable to those in the United States, but the traffic rules are not.

Finland has an extensive network of highways, as well as excellent public transportation services throughout the country. A valid U.S. driver's license may be used while visiting Finland, but drivers must be at least 18 years of age. Driving in Finland is on the right. Traffic approaching from the right has priority, even if entering a primary roadway from a secondary one; as such, stop signs are rarely used in Finland, which can cause confusion if cars converge at the same time at an intersection. In addition, it is common practice in Finland, including in large cities, to turn off traffic lights at major intersections early in the evening. Some roads in Helsinki designated as two-way are narrow, making passing difficult. Road signs use standard international symbols and Finnish text. Many urban streets have traffic lanes reserved for public transportation only. Unless otherwise noted on traffic signs, the speed limit varies from 30km/h to 40 km/h in urban areas, to 80 km/h on open roads, and 120 km/h on expressways during summer (reduced to 100 km/h during winter). Vehicles must use headlights at all times. Use of seatbelts is mandatory for drivers and all passengers. Children under 135cm (approx. 53 inches) in height must be seated in approved child or booster seats or use appropriate safety equipment as stated on the Finnish police website and the Finnish Department of Transportation fact sheets.

Public transport in Finland is good quality and is the recommended method of travel. Passenger trains, intercity buses, and air flights provide regular service over longer distances. Public transportation in urban centers includes buses, subways, trams, suburban trains, and taxis. Taxis are more expensive than in major U.S. cities. Most local residents use public transport in Helsinki as parking can be hard to find and expensive. The bus, train, and subway systems are relatively safe.

You should be aware that drunk-driving laws are strict and acceptable blood-alcohol levels are much lower in Finland than in the United States. Police strictly enforce all traffic laws and institute random roadside breath-analyzer tests. Drivers who register a 0.05 or higher blood-alcohol content are subject to immediate arrest. For more information, please review the Finnish Police website.

Driving in Finland during the winter months can be hazardous. Daylight hours are very short and drivers should be comfortable with driving in darkness. Icy road conditions are common. Your vehicle must be winterized with snow tires from December to February. Engine heaters are strongly recommended. When driving at night, drivers must be alert to moose wandering onto major roadways. Striking a moose can severely damage a vehicle and even fatally injure its occupants. If you are in a car accident, it is important to have your insurance paperwork with you. In the event of an emergency, call 112 for emergency services.

Aviation Safety Oversight: The U.S. Federal Aviation Administration (FAA) has assessed the Government of Finland's Civil Aviation Authority as being in compliance with International Civil Aviation Organization (ICAO) aviation safety standards for oversight of Finland's air carrier operations. Further information may be found on FAA's safety assessment page.

Children's Issues: Please see the U.S. Dept. of State Office of Children's Issues web pages on intercountry adoption and international parental child abduction.

Intercountry Adoption

July 2009

Finland is party to the Hague Convention on Protection of Children and Co-operation in Respect of Intercountry Adoption (Hague Adoption Convention). Therefore, adoptions between Finland and the United States are governed by the requirements of the Convention and the laws and regulations implementing the Convention in both the United States and Finland.

The Department of State does not maintain files on the adoption process in Finland because adoptions from Finland are rare. Fewer than five adoptions by American citizen parents have taken place since 2000.

The Finnish Board of Intercountry Adoption Affairs, of the Ministry of Social Affairs and Health is the Central Authority for the purposes of the Hague Adoption Convention in Finland. American Citizens living in Finland who wish to adopt from the U.S. or a third country should contact the the Finish Central Authority to learn about Finish requirements that may apply to their adoption. Contact information for the Finish Central Authority is available on their website http://www.stm.fi.

FRANCE

Compiled from publications that were available as of February 2013 from the U.S. Department of State, the U.S. Department of Commerce, and the Central Intelligence Agency (CIA). See the introduction to this set for explanatory notes.

Official Name:
French Republic

PROFILE

Geography

Area: total: 643,801 sq km; 551,500 sq km (metropolitan France); country comparison to the world: 43; land: 640,427 sq km; 549,970 sq km (metropolitan France); water: 3,374 sq km; 1,530 sq km (metropolitan France)

Major cities: Paris (capital) 10.41 million; Marseille-Aix-en-Provence 1.457 million; Lyon 1.456 million; Lille 1.028 million; Nice-Cannes 977,000 (2009)

Climate: metropolitan France: generally cool winters and mild summers, but mild winters and hot summers along the Mediterranean; occasional strong, cold, dry, north-to-northwesterly wind known as mistral

Terrain: metropolitan France: mostly flat plains or gently rolling hills in north and west; remainder is mountainous, especially Pyrenees in south, Alps in east

People

Nationality: noun: Frenchman(men), Frenchwoman(women); adjective: French

Population: 65,630,692 (July 2012 est.)

Population growth rate: 0.497% (2012 est.)

Ethnic groups: Celtic and Latin with Teutonic, Slavic, North African, Indochinese, Basque minorities

Religions: Roman Catholic 83%-88%, Protestant 2%, Jewish 1%, Muslim 5%-10%, unaffiliated 4%

Languages: French (official) 100%, rapidly declining regional dialects and languages (Provencal, Breton, Alsatian, Corsican, Catalan, Basque, Flemish)

Literacy: definition: age 15 and over can read and write; total population: 99%; male: 99%; female: 99% (2003 est.)

Health: life expectancy at birth: total population: 81.46 years; male: 78.35 years; female: 84.73 years (2012 est.); Infant mortality rate: total: 3.37 deaths/1,000 live births; male: 3.7 deaths/1,000 live births; female: 3.01 deaths/1,000 live births (2012 est.)

Unemployment rate: 9.8% (2012 est.)

Work force: 29.62 million (2012 est.)

Government

Type: republic

Independence: no official date of independence: 486

Constitution: adopted by referendum 28 September 1958; effective 4 October 1958; amended many times

Political subdivisions: 27 regions (regions, singular—region)

Suffrage: 18 years of age; universal

Economy

GDP (purchasing power parity): $2.253 trillion (2012 est.); $2.246 trillion (2011 est.); $2.208 trillion (2010 est.); $2.178 trillion (2009 est.)

GDP real growth rate: 0.1% (2012 est.); 1.7% (2011 est.); 1.4% (2010 est.); -2.6% (2009 est.)

GDP per capita (PPP): $35,500 (2012 est.); $35,600 (2011 est.); $35,200 (2010 est.); $34,800 (2009 est.)

Natural resources: metropolitan France: coal, iron ore, bauxite, zinc, uranium, antimony, arsenic, potash, feldspar, fluorspar, gypsum, timber, fish

Agriculture products: wheat, cereals, sugar beets, potatoes, wine grapes; beef, dairy products; fish

Industries: machinery, chemicals, automobiles, metallurgy, aircraft, electronics; textiles, food processing; tourism

Exports: $567.5 billion (2012 est.); $587.1 billion (2011 est.); $517.2 billion (2010 est.)

Exports—commodities: machinery and transportation equipment, aircraft, plastics, chemicals, pharmaceutical products, iron and steel, beverages

Exports—partners: Germany 16.7%, Italy 8.3%, Spain 7.4%, Belgium 7.4%, UK 6.7%, US 5%, Netherlands 4.3% (2011)

Imports: $658.9 billion (2012 est.); $688.5 billion (2011 est.); $588.4 billion (2010 est.)

Imports—commodities: machinery and equipment, vehicles, crude oil, aircraft, plastics, chemicals
Imports—partners: Germany 19.1%, Belgium 11.3%, Italy 7.7%, Netherlands 7.5%, Spain 6.6%, UK 5.1%, China 4.8% (2011)
Debt—external: $5.633 trillion (30 June 2011); $4.698 trillion (30 June 2010)
Exchange rates: euros (EUR) per US dollar; 0.7838 (2012 est.); 0.7194 (2011 est.); 0.755 (2010 est.); 0.7198 (2009 est.); 0.6827 (2008 est.); 0.7345 (2007 est.)

PEOPLE

Since prehistoric times, France has been a crossroads of trade, travel, and invasion. Three basic European ethnic stocks—Celtic, Latin, and Teutonic (Frankish)—have blended over the centuries to make up its present population. France's birth rate was among the highest in Europe from 1945 until the late 1960s. Since then, its birth rate has fallen but remains higher than that of most other west European countries. Traditionally, France has had a high level of immigration.

Education

Education is free, beginning at age 2 and mandatory between ages 6 and 16. The public education system is highly centralized. Private education is primarily Roman Catholic. Higher education in France began with the founding of the University of Paris in 1150. It now consists of 91 public universities and 175 professional schools, including the post-graduate Grandes Ecoles. Private, college-level institutions focusing on business and management with curriculums structured on the American system of credits and semesters have been growing in recent years.

National/Racial/Ethnic Minorities

Societal violence and discrimination against immigrants of North African origin, Roma, and other ethnic minorities remained a problem. During 2011 several French NGOs reported deteriorating living conditions for Roma. A study by Doctors without Borders highlighted declining health within the Romani community, due in part to poor access to medical care. The study claimed that 2.5 percent of Roma living in itinerant camps had tuberculosis and only 8 percent were fully vaccinated. The newborn death rate among Roma was reportedly nine times higher than the national average.

Language

The French language derives from the vernacular Latin spoken by the Romans in Gaul, although it includes many Celtic and Germanic words. Historically, French has been used as the international language of diplomacy and commerce. Today it remains one of six official languages at the United Nations and has been a unifying factor in Africa, Asia, the Pacific, and the Caribbean.

Religion

In accordance with its definition of separation of state and religion, the government does not keep statistics on religious affiliation. According to a poll published in Le Parisien in February, 36 percent believe in God, 34 percent do not, and 30 percent are uncertain.

A December 2009 poll in the Catholic daily La Croix found that 64 percent of the population, about 41 million people, identify themselves as Roman Catholic, 4.5 percent of whom are observant. The Interior Ministry estimates that 8 to 10 percent of the population, or five to six million people, are Muslim, 25 percent of whom attend Friday prayers. The Muslim population primarily consists of immigrants from former French North African and sub-Saharan colonies and their descendents.

All other religious groups combined constitute less than 7 percent of the population. Le Figaro estimates that there are 1.5 million Protestants, 400,000-600,000 of whom are evangelical. Many evangelical churches are African-style "prosperity" churches composed primarily of African and Antillean immigrants. Le Parisien estimates there are 800,000 Buddhist sympathizers and practitioners. The Buddhist population mainly consists of Chinese and Vietnamese immigrants and their descendants. The Jewish community numbers approximately 600,000, of whom 40 percent are highly observant, according to press reports. The Jewish community is comprised of approximately 70 percent Sephardic and 30 percent Ashkenazi Jews. Jehovah's Witnesses claim that there are approximately 120,000 observant members. Orthodox Christians number between 80,000 and 100,000; most are associated with the Greek or Russian Orthodox churches. The Church of Scientology estimates 50,000 members. The Church of Jesus Christ of Latter-day Saints (Mormons) estimates its numbers at 35,000-36,000, 30 percent of whom are observant. According to the press, there are between 7,000 and 15,000 Sikhs.

HISTORY

France was one of the earliest countries to progress from feudalism to the nation-state. Its monarchs surrounded themselves with capable ministers, and French armies were among the most innovative, disciplined, and professional of their day. During the reign of Louis XIV (1643–1715), France was the dominant power in Europe. But overly ambitious projects and military campaigns of Louis and his successors led to chronic financial problems in the 18th century. Deteriorating economic conditions and popular resentment against the complicated system of privileges granted the nobility and clerics were among the principal causes of the French Revolution (1789–94). Although the revolutionaries advocated republican and egalitarian principles of government, France reverted to forms of absolute rule or constitutional monarchy four times—the Empire of Napoleon, the Restoration of Louis XVIII, the reign of Louis-Philippe, and the Second Empire of Napoleon III. After the

Franco-Prussian War (1870), the Third Republic was established and lasted until the military defeat of 1940.

World War I (1914–18) brought great losses of troops and material. In the 1920s, France established an elaborate system of border defenses (the Maginot Line) and alliances to offset resurgent German strength. France was defeated early in World War II, however, and was occupied in June 1940. That July, the country was divided into two: one section being ruled directly by the Germans, and a second controlled by the French ("Vichy" France) and which the Germans did not occupy. German and Italian forces occupied all of France, including the "Vichy" zone, following the Allied invasion of North Africa in November 1942. The "Vichy" government largely acquiesced to German plans, namely in the plunder of French resources and the forceful deportations of tens of thousands of French Jews living in France to concentration camps across Europe, and was even more completely under German control following the German military occupation of November 1942. Economically, a full one-half of France's public sector revenue was appropriated by Germany. After 4 years of occupation and strife in France, Allied forces liberated the country in 1944.

France emerged from World War II to face a series of new problems. After a short period of provisional government initially led by Gen. Charles de Gaulle, the Fourth Republic was set up by a new constitution and established as a parliamentary form of government controlled by a series of coalitions. French military involvement in both Indochina and Algeria combined with the mixed nature of the coalitions and a consequent lack of agreement caused successive cabinet crises and changes of government.

Finally, on May 13, 1958, the government structure collapsed as a result of the tremendous opposing pressures generated by 4 years of war with Algeria. A threatened coup led the Parliament to call on General de Gaulle to head the government and prevent civil war. Marking the beginning of the Fifth Republic, he became prime minister in June 1958 and was elected president in December of that year. The Algerian conflict also spurred decades of increased immigration from the Maghreb states, changing the composition of French society.

Seven years later, for the first time in the 20th century, the people of France went to the polls to elect a president by direct ballot. De Gaulle won reelection with a 55% share of the vote, defeating Francois Mitterrand. In April 1969, President de Gaulle's government conducted a national referendum on the creation of 21 regions with limited political powers. The government's proposals were defeated, and de Gaulle subsequently resigned. Succeeding him as president of France have been Gaullist Georges Pompidou (1969–74), Independent Republican Valery Giscard d'Estaing (1974–81), Socialist Francois Mitterrand (1981–95), neo-Gaullist Jacques Chirac (1995–2007), center-right Nicolas Sarkozy (2007–12), and Socialist Francois Hollande (2012). While France continues to revere its rich history and independence, French leaders have increasingly tied the future of France to the European Union (EU). France was integral in establishing the European Coal and Steel Community in 1951 and was among the EU's six founding states. During his tenure, President Mitterrand stressed the importance of European integration and advocated the ratification of the Maastricht Treaty on European economic and political union, which France's electorate narrowly approved in 1992.

Since the September 11, 2001 terrorist attacks in the U.S., France has played a central role in counterterrorism efforts. French forces have participated in Operation Enduring Freedom and in the International Security Assistance Force (ISAF) for Afghanistan. France did not, however, join the coalition that liberated Iraq in 2003.

In October and November 2005, 3 weeks of violent unrest in France's largely immigrant suburbs focused the country's attention on its minority communities. In the spring of 2006, students protested widely over restrictive employment legislation. In May 2007, Nicolas Sarkozy was elected as France's sixth president under the Fifth Republic, signaling French approval of widespread economic and social reforms, as well as closer cooperation with the United States. By midway through his 5-year term, Sarkozy faced mounting pressure to revive the economy, lower unemployment, and reduce the government's sizable budget deficit. The most notable reform in 2010 was raising the minimum retirement age from 60 to 62 and from 65 to 67 for full benefits. A poll in November 2011 showed a 40% approval rating for Sarkozy, a 12-month high and up from 29% in April. On the international front, President Sarkozy has reintegrated France into the North Atlantic Treaty Organization (NATO), confirmed France's commitments to Afghanistan, and worked closely with the United States on the Iran nuclear issue. Although a 2005 French referendum was responsible for the defeat of a treaty to establish a constitution for Europe, France later backed the Lisbon Treaty—a main priority of Sarkozy during France's EU presidency in the latter half of 2008. The Lisbon Treaty took effect in December 2009. France continues to play a leading role in the EU, particularly in the development of a Common Security and Defense Policy (CSDP).

In July 2008, France was instrumental in launching the Union for the Mediterranean (UM), a continuation of the EU Barcelona Process. France and Egypt held the first rotating copresidency, which serves as a forum for political and economic cooperation between the EU and its Mediterranean neighbors. The second biennial conference scheduled for 2010 was indefinitely postponed due to heightened tensions in the Middle East. France has held the rotating presidencies of the G-8 and G-20 and was instrumental in spring 2011 in assembling the international coalition that engaged in military operations in Libya.

GOVERNMENT AND POLITICAL CONDITIONS

France is a multiparty constitutional democracy. The president of the republic is elected by popular vote for a five-year term. Francois Hollande is the incumbent. The upper house (Senate) of the bicameral parliament is elected indirectly through an electoral college, while the lower house (National Assembly) is elected directly. Elections for seats in the National Assembly and for the presidency in 2007 and 2013 and for seats in the Senate in 2011 were considered free and fair. The Union for a Popular Movement (UMP) is the majority party in parliament.

Recent Elections

The 2007 national parliamentary and presidential elections were deemed free and fair. In March 2010 the country held regional elections that independent observers considered free and fair. Cantonal elections took place in March 2011 and were free and fair.

Participation of Women and Minorities: As a result of the September 25 senatorial elections, there were 185 women in the two chambers of the 925-seat parliament, 108 in the National Assembly and 77 in the Senate. There were nine female ministers in the 34-member ministerial cabinet. Women made up 48 percent of regional council members, 13.8 percent of departmental council members, and 34.8 percent of municipal council members. They held two presidencies of the 22 regional councils, four presidencies of the 101 departmental councils, and 14 percent of mayoral positions. The law requires political parties to present candidate lists containing equal numbers of male and female candidates or face fines.

Because the law prohibits the government from collecting information on the racial or ethnic background of residents of the country, no statistics on minority participation in government were available. With the exception of parliamentary representatives from some of the overseas territories where the populations were predominantly of non-European origin, minorities appeared to be significantly underrepresented in the government. At the end of 2011, there was only one black member of the National Assembly. As of year's end, President Sarkozy had appointed six female minority officials to his cabinet.

Principal Government Officials

Last Updated: 1/31/2013

Pres.: **Francois HOLLANDE**
Prime Min.: **Jean-Marc AYRAULT**
Min. of Agriculture, Agribusiness, & Forestry: **Stephane LE FOLL**
Min. of Culture & Communication: **Aurelie FILIPPETTI**
Min. of Defense: **Jean-Yves LE DRIAN**
Min. of Ecology, Sustainable Development, & Energy: **Delphine BATHO**
Min. of the Equality of the Territories & Housing: **Cecile DUFLOT**
Min. of Finance, Economy, & Trade: **Pierre MOSCOVICI**
Min. of Foreign Affairs: **Laurent FABIUS**
Min. of Foreign Trade: **Nicole BRICQ**
Min. of Higher Education & Research: **Genevieve FIORASO**
Min. of Industrial Renewal: **Arnaud MONTEBOURG**
Min. of the Interior: **Manuel VALLS**
Min. of Justice & Keeper of the Seals: **Christiane TAUBIRA**
Min. of Labor, Employment, Professional Development, & Social Dialogue: **Michel SAPIN**
Min. of National Education: **Vincent PEILLON**
Min. of Overseas France: **Victorin LUREL**
Min. of Social Affairs & Health: **Marisol TOURAINE**
Min. of Sports, Youth, Further Education, & Community Outreach: **Valerie FOURNEYRON**
Min. of State Reform, Decentralization, & Civil Service: **Marylise LEBRANCHU**
Min. of Women's Rights & Govt. Spokesperson: **Najat VALLAUD-BELKACEM**
Governor, Bank of France: **Christian NOYER**
Ambassador to the US: **Francois DELATTRE**
Permanent Representative to the UN, New York: **Gerard ARAUD**

ECONOMY

The French economy is diversified across all sectors. The government has partially or fully privatized many large companies, including Air France, France Telecom, Renault, and Thales. However, the government maintains a strong presence in some sectors, particularly power, public transport, and defense industries. With at least 79 million foreign tourists per year,

France is the most visited country in the world and maintains the third largest income in the world from tourism. France's leaders remain committed to a capitalism in which they maintain social equity by means of laws, tax policies, and social spending that reduce income disparity and the impact of free markets on public health and welfare. France's real GDP contracted 2.6% in 2009, but recovered somewhat in 2010 and 2011, before stagnating in 2012. The unemployment rate increased from 7.4% in 2008 and has remained above 9% per year since then. Lower-than-expected growth and increased unemployment have strained France's public finances.

The budget deficit rose sharply from 3.4% of GDP in 2008 to 7.5% of GDP in 2009 before improving to 4.5% of GDP in 2012, while France's public debt rose from 68% of GDP to 89% over the same period. Under President Sarkozy, Paris implemented some austerity measures to bring the budget deficit under the 3% euro-zone ceiling by 2013 and to highlight France's commitment to fiscal discipline at a time of intense financial market scrutiny of euro-zone debt.

Socialist Party candidate Francois Hollande won the May 2012 presidential election, after advocating pro-growth economic policies, the separation of banks' traditional deposit taking and lending activities from more speculative businesses, increasing the top corporate and personal tax rates, and hiring an additional 60,000 teachers during his five-year term. France ratified the EU fiscal stability treaty in October 2012 and Hollande's government has maintained France's commitment to meeting the budget deficit target of 3% of GDP during 2013 even amid signs that economic growth will be lower than the government's forecast of 0.8%. Despite stagnant growth and fiscal challenges, France's borrowing costs declined during the second half of 2012 to euro-era lows.

Labor Conditions

The minimum age for employment is 16. There are exceptions for those enrolled in certain apprenticeship programs or working in the entertainment industry; however, these industries are subject to further regulation of conditions and work hours for minors. Persons under the age of 18 generally are prohibited from performing work considered arduous or working between 10 p.m. and 6 a.m. Inspectors from the Ministry of Labor, Employment, and Health investigated workplaces and generally enforced compliance with child labor laws.

On November 30, the Council of Ministers raised the national minimum wage to 9.19 euros ($11.95) per hour. The Ministry of the Economy, Industry, and Employment enforced the minimum wage. The poverty-level income rate was 954 euros ($1,240) a month for an individual, 1,431 euros ($1,860) for a couple, and 2,000 euros ($2,600) for a couple with two children under the age of 14. Salaries below the minimum wage were permitted for certain categories of employment, such as persons in subsidized jobs and internships, which must conform to separate, clearly defined standards. Employers, except those in the informal economy, generally adhered to the minimum wage requirement.

The official workweek is 35 hours. Companies may negotiate opt-outs with employees. The maximum number of working days for white-collar workers is 235 days per year. Maximum hours of work are fixed at 10 hours per day, 48 hours per week, and an average of 44 hours per week over a 12-week work period. Employees are entitled to a daily rest of at least 11 hours and a weekly break of at least 24 hours total, not including the daily rest period. Employers are required to give workers a 20-minute break during a six-hour workday. Premium pay of 25 percent is mandatory for overtime and on weekends and holidays. These standards were effectively enforced.

U.S.-FRENCH RELATIONS

The United States and France established diplomatic relations in 1778 following the United States' declaration of independence from Great Britain, and France provided key assistance to the United States as an ally during its war of independence. The Vichy Government of France severed diplomatic relations with the United States in 1942 during World War II; relations were normalized in 1944. The United States and France are among the five permanent members of the UN Security Council (P5).

Relations between the United States and France are active and friendly. The two countries share common values and have parallel policies on most political, economic, and security issues. Differences are discussed frankly and have not generally been allowed to impair the pattern of close cooperation that characterizes relations between the two countries.

The U.S. and France work closely on many issues, most notably in combating terrorism, efforts to stem the proliferation of weapons of mass destruction, and on regional problems, including in Africa, the Middle East, the Balkans, and Central Asia. As one of the P5+1 powers and as a leader of the European Union, France is working to prevent Iran from developing nuclear weapons. In the Israeli-Palestinian conflict, France fully supports U.S. engagement in the peace process. France is one of the North Atlantic Treaty Organization's (NATO) top five troop contributors. The French support NATO modernization efforts and are leading contributors to the NATO Response Force.

U.S. Assistance to France

The United States provides no development assistance to France.

Bilateral Economic Relations

France is a member of the European Union and is the United States' third-largest trading partner in Europe (after Germany and the U.K.). Trade and investment between the United States and France are strong. On average, over $1 billion in commercial transactions, including sales of U.S. and French foreign affiliates, take place every day. U.S. exports to France include industrial chemicals, aircraft and engines, electronic components, telecommunications, computer software, computers and peripherals, analytical and scientific instrumentation, medical instruments and supplies, and broadcasting equipment. The United States is the top destination for French investment and the United States is the largest foreign investor in France. The United States and France have a bilateral convention on investment and a bilateral tax treaty addressing, among other things, double taxation and tax evasion.

France's Membership in International Organizations

France and the United States belong to a number of the same international organizations, including the United Nations, North Atlantic Treaty Organization, Euro-Atlantic Partnership Council, Organization for Security and Cooperation in Europe, G-20, G-8, Organization for Economic Cooperation and Development, International Monetary Fund, World Bank, and World Trade Organization. France also is an observer to the Organization of American States.

Bilateral Representation

France maintains its embassy in the U.S. at 4101 Reservoir Rd. NW, Washington, DC 20007 (tel. 202-944-6000).

Principal U.S. Embassy Officials

Last Updated: 1/14/2013

PARIS (E) 2, avenue Gabriel, 75382 Paris Cedex 08, (33) (1) 4312-2222, Fax 33-1-4266-9783, INMARSAT Tel 011-8816-4142-8701, 011–8816-4142-8702, 011-8816-4142-8703, Workweek: Mon–Fri 9 a.m–6 p.m., Website: http://paris.usembassy.gov/

DCM OMS:	James Bryant
AMB OMS:	Abigail Erickson
CDC:	Mary-Kathleen Glynn
CG OMS:	Debbie Rodriguez
DHS/ICE:	Steve Andres

DHS/TSA: Annemarie Pellerin
FCS: Reginald Miller
FM: Ken Hunter
GFS: Philip Anstead
HRO: Gilda Weech-House
MGT: J. Patrick Truhn
POSHO: Ken Hunter
SDO/DATT: COL Brendan McAloon
AMB: Charles H. Rivkin
CG: Lisa Piascik
CON: Lisa Piascik
DCM: Mark Taplin
PAO: Philip Breeden
GSO: Christa Dupuis
RSO: Greg Hays
AFSA: Brian Ferinden
AGR: Daryl A. Brehm
AID: Pending
APHIS: Alejandro Thiermann
CLO: Regina Prince
DEA: Thomas Varvitsiotis
ECON: Wendela Moore
EEO: Mark Atkisson And Kristen Grauer
EST: Candy Green
FAA: David Knorr
FMO: N. Scott Einhorn
IMO: Karen Finer
IPO: Steve Lewis
IRS: Aziz Benbrahim
ISO: Steve McCain
ISSO: Kevin Desrosiers
LEGATT: Katherine L. Andrews
POL: Jonathan Cohen
State ICASS: Candy Green

MARSEILLE (CG) Place Varian Fry, 13286 Marseille France, 33 (0) 4-91-54-92-00, Fax 33 (0) 4-91-55-09-47, Workweek: Monday–Friday, 8:30–5:00, Website: http://france.usembassy.gov/marseille.

PO: Diane Kelly
CON: Philip Richards

BORDEAUX (C) 89, quai des Chartrons, 33300 bordeaux, 33–(0)5-56-48-63-80, Fax 33–(0)5-56-51-61-97, Workweek: M-F 9-6, Website: http://www.amb-usa.fr/bordeaux/default.htm

PO: Joel F. Maybury

RENNES (C) 30 quai Duguay-Trouin, 35000 Rennes, France, 33 (0) 2-23-44-09-60, Fax +33.2.99.35.00.92, Workweek: Mon-Fri, 9 am-6pm, Website: http://paris.usembassy.gov/rennes.

PO: Robert Tate

STRASBOURG (C) 14, avenue d'Alsace, 67082 Strasbourg, France, 33–(0)3-88-35-31-04, Fax 33 (0)3-88-24-06-95, Workweek: M-F 9:00 to 13:00, 14:00 to 17:00, Website: http://france.usembassy.gov/strasbourg.

CG: Evan Reade

TOULOUSE (C) 25 allee Jean Jaures, 3100 Toulouse, 33–(0)5-34-41-36-50, Fax 33–(0)5-34-41-16-19, Workweek: Mon–Fri 9a.m–5 p.m, Website: http://france.usembassy.gov/toulouse.

PO: Rachel Schneller

US UNESCO (PARIS) (M) 12 Avenue Raphael, Paris 75116, 9-011-33-1-45 24 74 56, Fax 9-011-33-1-45 24 74 58, Workweek: 0900-1800, Website: http://unesco.usmission.gov/

DCM OMS: Robin Taylor
AMB OMS: Robin Taylor
Co-CLO: Christine Murphy
AMB: David T. Killion
DCM: Kathleen Kavalec
PAO: Shaila Manyam
GSO: Howard Zappia
RSO: John Hicks
AFSA: Frederic W. Maerkle
CLO: Francois Gentil
IMO: Kevin Desrosiers
LEGATT: Carolyn Willson
POL: David Ostroff

USOECD (M) 12, ave Raphael Paris 75016 France, 33 1-45-24-74-77, Fax 33 (0)1-45-24-74-80, Workweek: M-F; 9-6, Website: http://usoecd.usmission.gov/

DCM OMS: Mishele Ainsley
AMB OMS: Mishele Ainsley
Co-CLO: Regina Prince
DEP US REP:Giulia Bisconti
MGT: Robert F. Ensslin
US EXEC DIR:D.A. Brown
US REP: Michael Koplovsky
US REP OMS:Abby Bylotas
AMB: Charge Jeri Guthrie-Corn
DCM: Acting DCM Michael Koplovsky
PAO: Zoe L. Mezin
RSO: Jonathan Emory
AFSA: Brian Ferinden
AGR: Derek Christensen, Trade And Agr. Advisor
AID: Vacant
APHIS: Alejandro Thiermann
EST: Edu. & Envir. Advisor
FIN Nicholle Manz, ECON:Advisor
IPO: Kevin Desrosiers
ISSO: Kevin Desrosiers
LAB: Jennifer Harwood, Labor & Governance Advisor

LYON 1, quai Jules Courmont, 69289 Lyon cedex 02, 33–(0)4-78-38-36-88, Fax 33–(0)4-72-41-71-81, Workweek: M-F 09h00–12h00 and 14h00–18h00, Website: http://paris.usembassy.gov/lyon.

PO: Mark A. Schapiro

TRAVEL

Consular Information Sheet—France and Monaco

July 27, 2012

Country Description: France is a developed and stable democracy with a modern economy. Tourist facilities are widely available.

Smart Traveler Enrollment Program (STEP)/Embassy Locations: If you are going to live in or visit France, please take the time to tell us about your trip. By enrolling in the Smart Traveler Enrollment Program, you can keep up to date with important safety and security announcements. It will also help your friends and family get in touch with you in an emergency.

Please check the individual webpage for the embassy or consulate you will be visiting to verify public hours and security regulations. Generally, you won't be allowed to bring electronic devices such as cell phones and laptops with you inside our facilities.

There are two Consulates General, four American Presence Posts and one Consular Agency in France, in addition to the Embassy in Paris. Only the consular sections in Paris and Marseille are authorized to issue passports. The other offices provide limited services to American citizens. Appointments are required for most services. Appointments can be scheduled online for Embassy Paris and Consulate General Marseille. Call or email posts in other locations to schedule an appointment. Please note that the emergency after-hours telephone number for all U.S. posts in France is: (33) 1 43 12 22 22. Ask to speak to the duty officer if you need emergency assistance after business hours. All of our telephone numbers below are written the way you would dial them from the United States. When calling from within France, drop the country code and add a zero. For example: (33) 1 43 12 22 becomes 01 43 12 22 22.

Entry/Exit Requirements for U.S. Citizens: U.S. citizens may enter France for up to 90 days for tourist or business purposes without a visa. France is a party to the Schengen Agreement, which allows for visa-free travel between member countries. U.S. citizens traveling with either an official or diplomatic passport do require a valid Schengen visa. If you are traveling for reasons other than business or tourism—such as employment, study, or internship—you must obtain a French visa for that purpose before you leave the United States. You should be aware that it is nearly impossible to obtain or change visa status while in France.

If you are transiting France en route to other countries, make sure you know all of the entry and exit requirements for your trip and final destination. If you don't have the right documentation, you might be denied boarding to your connecting flight. Some countries require a certain number of blank visa pages or more than six months remaining validity on your passport.

The Department of State is unaware of any HIV/AIDS entry restrictions for visitors to, or foreign residents of, France.

Contact the French Embassy in Washington at 4101 Reservoir Road NW, Washington, DC 20007, tel. (202) 944 6000, or one of the French Consulates General in Atlanta, Boston, Chicago, Houston, Los Angeles, Miami, New Orleans, New York, or San Francisco for the most current visa information.

Threats to Safety and Security: Political violence in Paris and throughout France is still relatively uncommon, although there are occasional instances of extremely large demonstrations occurring in many French cities simultaneously. Large demonstrations in Paris are generally managed by a strong police presence, but even demonstrations intended to be peaceful can turn confrontational and possibly escalate into violence. U.S. citizens are therefore urged to avoid the areas of demonstrations if possible, and to exercise caution if within the vicinity of any demonstrations. In addition, the congestion caused by large demonstrations can cause serious inconveniences for a visitor on a tight schedule. Likewise, some sporting events, such as soccer matches, have occasionally degenerated into violence that continued into the streets.

Political unrest has developed in some Francophone countries with historic ties to France (e.g., Algeria, Cote d'Ivoire, and Tunisia). Some French citizens and residents with ties to such countries have protested in front of those countries' embassies or consulates located in France in response to the unrest. Although these protests are infrequent and do not target Americans, visitors should avoid such demonstrations.

The Government of France maintains a threat rating system, known locally as "Vigipirate," similar to the U.S. Department of Homeland Security Advisory System. Under this plan, the government routinely augments police with armed forces and increases visibility at airports, train and metro stations, and other high-profile locations such as schools, major tourist attractions, and government installations. Over the last few years, there have been arrests of suspected Islamic militants involved in terrorist plots. French authorities have periodically spoken publicly about the heightened threat conditions for terrorist attacks in Europe. Information is routinely shared between the United States and France in order to disrupt terrorist plotting, identify and take action against potential operatives, and strengthen defenses against potential threats. Although U.S. citizens have not been specifically targeted in terrorist attacks in France within the past few years, travelers should remain vigilant. Immediately report unattended packages observed in public places or any other suspicious activities to French law enforcement authorities. French law enforcement authorities are proactive and will respond immediately. If there is a security incident or suspicious package, do not linger in the area to observe.

Public safety and security in France are maintained by three different forces: Municipal Police, National Police, and the military Gendarmerie. These services are professional, competent, and pro-active in fighting crime and violence and maintaining overall state security.

In an emergency, dialing 17 will connect the caller to the Police. You can also dial the Europe-wide emergency response number 112 to reach an operator for all kinds of emergency services (similar to the U.S. 911 system). Non-French speakers may experience a delay while an English speaker is located.

For non-emergency assistance, visitors should go to the nearest police station (commissariat) in order to file an official report.

Stay up to date:

- Bookmark our Bureau of Consular Affairs website, which contains the current Travel Warnings and Travel Alerts as well as the Worldwide Caution;
- Follow us on Twitter and the Bureau of Consular Affairs page on Facebook as well;
- Download our free Smart Traveler iPhone App to have travel information at your fingertips;
- Call 1-888-407-4747 toll-free within the U.S. and Canada, or a regular toll line, 1-202-501-4444, from other countries; and

- Taking some time before travel to consider your personal security.

Crime: Prior to travel to France, the United States State Department recommends that all visitors check the Department's website for updated security advisories.

France is a relatively safe country. Most crimes are non-violent, but pick-pocketing is a significant problem. See section below entitled Tips on How to Avoid Becoming a Victim.

The majority of crimes directed against foreign visitors, including U.S. citizens, involve pick-pocketing, residential break-ins, bicycle theft, and other forms of theft with minimal violence. However, as in any big city, robberies involving physical assault do occur in Paris and other major urban areas. Visitors to congested areas and known tourist sites (e.g., museums, monuments, train stations, airports, and subways) should be particularly attentive to their surroundings. Crimes against visitors are generally crimes of opportunity, though these crimes are more likely to involve violence on the street late at night or when the victim detects the theft and resists the criminal. As in any major city, women should exercise extra caution when out alone at night and/or consider traveling out at night with companions. In general, Paris taxis are safe and professionally operated, but we have noted an increase in reported harassment and assaults on women by taxi drivers.

Caution is required throughout France when driving through economically depressed areas, where there is a high incidence of "smash and grab" robberies. Thieves will approach a vehicle that is stopped in traffic, smash a window, reach into the vehicle to grab a purse or other valuable item, and then flee. Keep doors locked and valuables out of sight.

Throughout August, the month when most French residents take summer vacations, and in December, there is generally an increase in the number of residential break-ins. The majority are attributed to residents not using security measures already in place, including double locking doors and locking windows. Home invasions are often preceded by phone calls to see if the resident is at home. Often thieves who manage to gain access to the apartment building will knock on apartment doors to see if anyone answers, offering the excuse they are taking a survey or representing a utility company.

Paris: Crime in Paris is similar to that in most large cities. Violent crime is relatively uncommon in the city center, but women should exercise extra caution when out alone at night and/or consider traveling out at night with companions. There has been an increase recently in reported sexual harassment, and sometimes assault, by taxi drivers. Pickpockets are by far the most significant problem. In addition to purses and wallets, smart phones and small electronic devices are particular targets. In Paris, pickpockets can be any gender, race, or age and are commonly children under the age of 16 because they are difficult to prosecute. Pickpockets are very active on the rail link (RER B) from Charles de Gaulle Airport to the city center. Travelers may want to consider using a shuttle service or one of the express buses to central Paris rather than the RER. In addition, passengers on the Metro line 1, which traverses the city center from east to west and services many major tourist sites, are often targeted. A common method is for one thief to distract the tourist with questions or disturbances, while an accomplice picks pockets, a backpack, or a purse. Schemes in Paris include asking if you would sign a petition or take a survey and presenting a ring and asking if you dropped it. Thieves often time their pickpocket attempts to coincide with the closing of the automatic doors on the Metro, leaving the victim secured on the departing train. Many thefts also occur at the major department stores (e.g., Galeries Lafayette, Printemps, and Le Bon Marché), where tourists may leave wallets, passports, and credit cards on cashier counters during transactions. Popular tourist sites are also popular with thieves, who favor congested areas to mask their activities. The crowded elevators at the Eiffel Tower, escalators at museums, and the area surrounding Sacré Coeur Basilica in Montmartre are all favored by pickpockets and snatch-and-grab thieves. There have been some instances of tourists being robbed and assaulted near less utilized Metro stations. The area around the Moulin Rouge, known as Pigalle, requires extra security precautions to avoid becoming a victim. Pigalle is an adult entertainment area known for prostitution, sex shows, and illegal drugs. Unsuspecting tourists have run up exorbitant bar bills and been forced to pay before being permitted to leave. Other areas in Paris where extra security precautions are warranted after dark are Les Halles and the Bois de Boulogne.

Provence Alpes Maritimes (PACA)/Languedoc-Roussillon (Marseille, Montpellier, Perpignan, Carcassonne Avignon, Aix en Provence, Arles, Cannes, Nice): The PACA/Languedoc-Roussillon region enjoys a fairly low rate of violent crime directed at tourists. The most common problems in the region are thefts from cars (both stopped in traffic and parked) and from luggage trolleys at the major transportation hubs (e.g., Nice Airport, and the railway stations at Marseille, Avignon, and Aix en Provence). U.S. citizen victims reported to the U.S. Consulate General in Marseille fifty cases of theft from cars and twenty purse snatchings in transportation hubs during the May-June 2011 period. The U.S. Consulate General in Marseille has also noted an increase in holiday rental-home burglaries and in necklace snatching. Keep your car doors locked and windows rolled up at all times. Valuables should be hidden out of site to prevent snatch-and-grab attempts. Maintain visual contact with your car when visiting tourist sites, when using rest facilities at gas stations, or stopping to enjoy panoramic views, even for a short period, as thieves will break windows to access items left in cars. Victims are reporting car break-ins within minutes of leaving a car unattended. Passports should be kept separate from other valuables.

Strasbourg: Strasbourg's historic center enjoys a fairly low rate of violent crime. Pickpockets and snatch-and-grab thieves tend to concentrate their efforts in the Petite France historic district popular with visitors.

Bordeaux: This large city is considered fairly safe; general crimes and offenses have been on the decline since 2005. As with any big city, you should be watchful of pickpockets and other tourist-aimed crimes, especially around public transportation. However, local police are considered professional and responsive to persons who are victims of crime. Stolen purses, ID cards, and passports left in cars—particularly around renowned landmarks– routinely lead to requests for emergency issuance of passports.

Lyon: Although levels of violent crime are low, Lyon has a fair amount of petty crime and vandalism. Late-night weekend rowdiness is common in the center of town and in areas with night clubs. But the public transportation system is safe at night (generally a concern for U.S. citizens), and there is extensive police video surveillance utilized on the streets. To combat reckless and drunk drivers and prevent them from fleeing accident scenes, Lyon initiated 30 KPH zones in commercial districts, and the local police have increased controls for drunken driving. They have also installed speed and red-light radar systems. Despite these efforts, in 2010 six pedestrians were killed by moving vehicles. The number of stolen passports and personal items in the district remains relatively low, and attacks are rare. Home break-ins have increased recently; according to the local news, there are 30 per day, which represents a 16% increase over 2010. A recent wave of armed robberies in luxury goods stores and cash exchange businesses ended with the arrest of an organized gang of delinquents. Bicycle thefts are also a risk, as Lyon becomes increasingly bicycle-friendly and more people cycle around town.

Normandy: Break-ins and thefts from cars in the parking lots at the Normandy beaches and American cemeteries are common. Do not leave valuables unattended in a car. Locking valuables in the trunk is not an adequate safeguard as thieves often pry open car trunks to steal bags.

Rennes: In general, the city of Rennes is a relatively safe and secure environment, and crime rates throughout the consular district tend to be lower than in larger cities elsewhere. There are occasional crimes in the center of Rennes related to drunkenness and rowdy behavior, with the largest and most boisterous crowds tending to gather on Thursday nights in the area around Rue Saint Michel (a.k.a. "Rue de la Soif" or "Thirst Street") and the adjacent Place Sainte Anne. The local authorities, both police and political, make security a priority. The Rennes police are well informed about potential threats and respond quickly to any criminal issues occurring in the city. Tourists do occasionally encounter theft of valuables and/or passports. Valuables left unattended in rental cars overnight, or for extended amounts of time, are particularly susceptible to theft. In particular, tourist sites around Brittany warn travelers against leaving expensive items in plain view in parked cars, due to frequent vehicle break-ins. Do not leave luggage unattended on trains.

Toulouse and the Midi-Pyrenees: Toulouse and the Midi-Pyrenees region are considered generally safe. Car theft, vehicle break-ins, petty theft and burglary are the most common crimes, and they are relatively more frequent in areas near the railway station. Car-jackings and home invasions may occur, particularly in wealthier areas surrounding Toulouse. Home invasions, although usually targeting valuables and cars, may include violence. Police are usually very helpful to travelers who are victims of crime. Itinerant street people, often in groups accompanied by dogs, are increasingly prevalent in downtown Toulouse, particularly in warmer weather. While alcohol and drug abuse can make them unpredictable, incidents of crime are relatively rare.

Tips on How to Avoid Becoming a Victim: Common-sense security precautions will help you enjoy a trouble-free stay. Most problems can be avoided by being aware of one's surroundings and avoiding high-risk areas.

When going out, carry only essential items: ONE credit/ATM card, ONE piece of identification, and no more than 40-50 euros. Avoid carrying high-value jewelry and large amounts of cash. Valuables should be kept out of sight and in places difficult for thieves to reach, such as internal coat pockets or in pouches hung around the neck or inside clothes. Shoulder bags and wallets in back pockets are an invitation to a thief.

Keep photocopies of travel documents and credit cards separate from the originals, along with key telephone numbers to contact banks for credit card replacement.

Crowded elevators and escalators at tourist sites and crowded metro cars should raise awareness levels. When possible, take a seat or stand against a wall to deter pickpockets and try to maintain a 360-degree awareness of the surrounding area.

Carry only a purse that zips closed and ensure that it is carried under the arm and slightly in front of the body. For a backpack-type purse, swing it around so that it is slightly in front of the body. Wallets that are carried on the body should be in a front pocket. While on foot, remain aware of your surroundings at all times and keep bags slung across the body, with the bag hanging away from the street.

Many U.S. citizens have had purses or bags stolen from the back of a chair or from under the table while in cafes, restaurants and nightclubs/bars, including higher end establishments. Again, keep your valuables with you and never leave them unattended or out of your sight.

Do not leave valuables in hotel rooms. If you must leave valuables in the hotel, consider using the hotel safe.

Be aware that thieves often operate in groups and will come to each other's aid if confronted. If a thief is caught in the act, a simple pick-pocketing could turn into an assault (or worse) if an attempt is made to capture the thief. You can shout out for police assistance to attract attention, but do not pursue whomever you think stole your wallet or bag.

Do not use ATMs in isolated, poorly lighted areas or where loiterers are present. Be especially aware of persons standing close enough to see the Personal Identification Number (PIN) being entered into the machine. Thieves often conduct successful scams by simply watching the PIN as it is entered and then stealing the card from the user in some other location. If the card gets stuck in the machine, you should immediately report it to the bank where the machine is located as well as to your bank back home.

Many theft and assault victims are targeted when making their way home from a late night out after drinking alcohol. If you go out late at night, do so with a group of friends. There is safety in numbers.

Use only authorized taxis. Authorized taxis in Paris have the following equipment:

- An illuminated "Taxi Parisien" sign on the roof,
- A display meter showing the cost of the trip,
- A display at the rear of the vehicle and visible from the exterior which enables the monitoring of the daily duration of use of the vehicle,
- A plate fixed to the front fender bearing the license number.

Over the past year, there has been an increase in reports by women of sexual harassment and assault by the driver. Women may want to consider having another individual walk them to a taxi and, in plain view of the driver, note the license number of the vehicle, or call a friend while in the taxi and communicate the license number. Letting the driver know that others are aware of your trip and the license number of the taxi may reduce the chances of becoming a victim.

Public parks should be avoided after dark as they are often frequented by drug dealers and prostitutes.

The Paris Police Prefecture publishes a pamphlet entitled "Paris in Complete Safety " that provides practical advice and useful telephone numbers for visitors.

Victims of Crime: If you or someone you know becomes the victim of a crime abroad, you should contact the local police and the nearest U.S. embassy or consulate. We can:

- Replace a lost or stolen passport.
- Provide information on the most rapid means for money transfer.
- Assist with contacting family members or friends.
- Help you find appropriate medical care following violent crimes such as assault or rape.
- Put you in contact with the appropriate police authorities.
- Although the local authorities are responsible for investigating and prosecuting the crime, consular officers can help you understand the local criminal justice process and can direct you to local attorneys.

For more serious crimes, compensation is available under French law to victims of crime committed on French soil under certain circumstances. We recommend that you read our information on victims of crime, including possible victim-compensation programs in the United States. The European equivalent to the U.S. 911 emergency line is 112. Non-French speakers may experience a delay while an English speaker is located. Alternatively, one can call French emergency numbers specific to the type of incident: 17 (police emergency); 18 (fire department/paramedics); and 15 (medical emergency/paramedic team/ambulance).

For private legal matters, commercial disputes, tourist, trade, or property complaints, you may refer to the website of the Department of State concerning retaining a foreign attorney. Consular staff is prohibited from providing legal representation or guidance, but we can refer inquiries to French law directories, bar associations or other organizations in order to assist you. You may also refer to our list of attorneys for legal assistance in France.

Criminal Penalties: While you are traveling in France, you are subject to its laws even if you are a U.S. citizen. Criminal penalties vary from country to country and there are some things that might be legal in the country you visit, but are still illegal in the United States. For example, you can be prosecuted under U.S. law if you buy pirated goods in another country. Engaging in sexual conduct with children or using or disseminating child pornography in a foreign country is also a crime prosecutable in the United States. If you do something illegal in another country, your U.S. passport won't help you avoid arrest or prosecution. It's very important to know what's legal and what's not where you are going.

Persons violating French laws, even unknowingly, may be expelled, arrested, or imprisoned. Penalties for possession, use, or trafficking in illegal drugs in France are severe, and convicted offenders can expect long jail sentences and heavy fines. For legal assistance in France, you may refer to this list of attorneys.

If you use any of France's excellent public transportation services, take particular care to retain your used or "validated" ticket. Inspectors conduct periodic, random checks, and passengers who fail to present the correct validated ticket for their journey are subject to stiff and immediate fines. Inspectors may show no interest in explanations and no sympathy for an honest mistake. Failure to cooperate with these inspectors can result in a visit to the police station. While some countries will automatically notify the nearest U.S. embassy or consulate if a U.S. citizen is detained or arrested in a foreign country, that might not always be the case. To ensure that the United States is aware of your circumstances, request that the police and prison officials notify the nearest U.S. embassy or consulate as soon as you are arrested or detained.

There are strict regulations concerning temporary importation into or export from France of items such as firearms, antiquities, medications, business equipment, sales samples, and other items. You should contact the Embassy of France in Washington, D.C. or one of France's consulates in the United States for specific information regarding customs requirements.

Accessibility: In France, accessibility and accommodation for individuals with disabilities are very different from what you find in the United States. French law requires that any new building with public or community space and any existing public building be accessible for persons with disabilities. However, many existing buildings, as well as transportation systems, do not yet meet these requirements.

Getting around in French cities may be difficult at times since many sidewalks are narrow and uneven, and cobblestone streets make access difficult, but the major tourist areas have better facilities. Although the Paris métro is a very efficient method for traveling throughout central Paris, most métro stations are not readily accessible for people with disabilities. Very few stations have elevators, and most have stairways and long corridors for changing trains or exiting to the street. However many Parisian buses and tramways are equipped with lowering platforms for travelers with limited-mobility, or who are sight- or hearing-disabled. Taxis are also a good means of transportation.

The English language website of the Paris Visitors Bureau and the French language, government sponsored internet site contain additional information and include links to a downloadable local transportation map specifically designed for travelers with special mobility needs. There are many other resources available on the internet for disabled persons traveling to, or living in, France. You may also contact any of our consular offices by e-mail for further information on this topic.

Medical Facilities and Health Information: Medical care is comparable to that found in the United States. In an emergency, dialing 15 will connect the caller to emergency medical services. You can also dial the Europe-wide emergency response number 112 to reach an operator for all kinds of emergency services (similar to the U.S. 911 system). Non-French speakers may experience a delay while an English speaker is located. For non-emergency medical assistance in France, you may refer to this list of medical professionals. You can find good information on vaccinations and other health precautions on the Centers for Disease Control (CDC) website. For information about outbreaks of infectious diseases abroad, consult the World Health Organization (WHO) website, which also contains additional health information for travelers, including detailed country-specific health information.

Medical Insurance: You cannot assume that your insurance will go with you when you travel. It's very important to find out BEFORE you leave. You need to ask your insurance company two questions:

- Does my policy apply when I'm out of the United States?
- Will it cover emergencies like a trip to a foreign hospital or an evacuation?

In many places, doctors and hospitals still expect payment in cash at the time of service. Your regular U.S. health insurance may not cover doctor and hospital visits in other countries. If your policy doesn't cover you when you travel, it's a very good idea to take out another one for your trip.

NOTE: The U.S. Social Security Medicare Program does not provide coverage for hospital or medical costs outside the United States.

Traffic Safety and Road Conditions: While in France, you may encounter road conditions that are very different from those in the United States.

Roads in France are generally comparable to those in the United States, but traffic engineering and driving habits pose special dangers. Lane markings and sign placements may not be clear. Drivers should be prepared to make last-minute maneuvers, as most French drivers do. The French typically drive more aggressively and faster than Americans, and tend to exceed posted speed limits. Right-of-way rules in France may differ from those in the United States. Drivers entering intersections from the right have priority over those on the left (unless specifically indicated otherwise), even when entering relatively large boulevards from small side streets. Many intersections in France are traffic circles, where the right-of-way belongs to drivers in the circle.

On major highways, there are service stations at least every 25 miles. Service stations are not as common on secondary roads in France as they are in the United States. Paris, the capital and largest city in France, has an extensive and efficient public transportation system. The interconnecting system of buses, subways, and commuter rails serves more than four million people a day with a safety record comparable to, or better than, the systems of major American cities. Similar transportation systems are found in all major French cities. Between cities, France is served by an equally extensive rail service, which is safe and reliable. High-speed rail links connect the major cities in France. Many cities are also served by frequent air service. Traveling by train is safer than driving.

Pedestrians make up 13 percent of the deaths in motor vehicle accidents in France (roughly the same as in the United States), but this percentage is increasing. Most of these accidents occur when a pedestrian steps out onto the street, often when a car or motorcycle is making a turn onto a pedestrian crosswalk. Pedestrians should be cautious even when they have a green walking signal since this is no guarantee against aggressive drivers.

While Paris, Marseille, Lyon, and other French cities actively encourage the renting of bicycles through widely available city-sponsored systems, you should be cautious about this means of transportation, especially in a busy and unfamiliar urban environment. Helmets are neither required nor readily available near these rental stations. If you choose to ride a bicycle in France, you should bring your own helmet.

Visit the website of the French National Tourist Office, which contains specific information concerning French driver's permits, vehicle inspection, road tax, and mandatory insurance. The Embassy page on Driving in France provides information on the use of U.S. licenses in France. Note that as of July 1 2012, road safety equipment in all private vehicles in France must include a breathalyzer kit.

Aviation Safety Oversight: The U.S. Federal Aviation Administration (FAA) has assessed the government of France's Civil Aviation Authority as being in compliance with International Civil Aviation Organization (ICAO) aviation safety standards for oversight of France's air carrier operations. Further information may be found on the FAA's safety assessment page.

Children's Issues: For information see the U.S. Dept. of State Office of Children's Issues web pages on intercountry adoption and international parental child abduction.

Intercountry Adoption

January 2012

The information in this section has been edited from the latest report available as of February 2013 from the State Department Bureau of Consular Affairs, Office of Overseas Citizens Services. For more information, please read the *Intercountry Adoption* section of this book and review current reports online at http://adoption.state.gov.

France is party to the Hague Convention on Protection of Children and Co-operation in Respect of Intercountry Adoption (Hague Adoption Convention). Therefore all adoptions between France and the United States must meet the requirements of the Convention and U.S. law implementing the Convention. France is not considered a country of origin in intercountry adoption. There are few children eligible for adoption in France, with a long waiting list of French prospective adoptive parents. Most intercountry adoptions in France are by legal residents of France who adopt in third countries. While legally possible, intercountry adoption of a French orphan by foreigners is unlikely. No French orphans have received U.S. immigrant visas in the past five fiscal years. The information provided is intended primarily to assist in rare adoption cases from France, including adoptions of French children by relatives in the United States, as well as adoptions from third countries by Americans living in France.

Who Can Adopt? Adoption between the United States and France is governed by the Hague Adoption Convention. Therefore to adopt from France, you must first be found eligible to adopt by the U.S. Government. The U.S. Government agency responsible for making this determination is the Department of Homeland Security, U.S. Citizenship and Immigration Services (USCIS).

Residency Requirements: A foreigner who resides outside of France, and wishes to complete an intercountry adoption of a child residing in France, does not need to establish residency in France. A foreigner who wishes to adopt a child, whether in France or elsewhere, for the purpose of residing in France with the child, must be a permanent resident of France.

Age And Marriage Requirements: For domestic and intercountry adoptions, a couple must be married for a minimum of two years or, if married less than two years, both spouses must be at least 28 years old. A single person can adopt provided he/she is at least 28 years old; however, in practice, it is very difficult to get approval. There is no age limit if one of the spouses wishes to adopt the other spouse's child. Adopting parents must be at least 15 years older than the child they want to adopt (10 years in the case of the other spouse's child).

Income Requirements: Prospective parents must prove that they can provide for the child but there is no minimum income requirement.

Who Can Be Adopted? Because France is party to the Hague Adoption Convention, children from France must meet the requirements of the Convention in order to be eligible for adoption. For example, the Convention requires that France attempt to place a child with a family in France before determining that a child is eligible for intercountry adoption. In addition to France's requirements, a child must meet the definition of a Convention adoptee for you to bring him or her back to the United States.

France's Central Authority: Since January 2009, the Central Authority for adoptions in France is the Ministry of Foreign and European Affairs.

The Process: Because France is party to the Hague Adoption Convention, adopting from France must follow a specific process designed to meet the Convention's requirements. For detailed and updated information on these requirements, please review the *Intercountry Adoption* section of this publication and visit the U.S. Department of State Intercountry Adoption website at http://adoption.state.gov.

The first step in adopting a child from France is to select an adoption service provider in the United States that has been accredited. Only these agencies and attorneys can provide adoption services between the United States and France. After you choose an accredited adoption service provider, you apply to be found eligible to adopt (Form I-800A) by the U.S. Government, Department of Homeland Security, U.S. Citizenship and Immigration Services (USCIS).

Eligibility Requirements.: Once the U.S. government determines that you are "eligible" and "suitable" to adopt, you or your agency will forward your information to the adoption authority in France. France's adoption authority will review your application to determine whether you are also eligible to adopt under France's law. If both the United States and France determine that you are eligible to adopt, and a child is available for intercountry adoption, the central adoption authority in France may provide you with a referral for a child.

After you accept a match with a child, you will apply to the U.S. Government, Department of Homeland Security, U.S. Citizenship and Immigration Services (USCIS) for provisional approval to adopt that particular child (Form I-800). USCIS will determine whether the child is eligible under U.S. law to be adopted and enter the United States.

After this, your adoption service provider or you will submit a visa application to a Consular Officer at the U.S. Embassy in Paris. The Consular Officer will review the child's information and evaluate the child for possible visa ineligibilities. If the consular officer determines that the child appears eligible to immigrate to the United States, he or she will send a letter (an "Article 5 Letter") to the French Central Authority. Do not adopt or obtain custody of a child in France before a U.S. consular officer issues the Article 5 Letter.

Role of the Adoption Authority: American citizens interested in or considering adopting a child in France should consult the website of the Agence Française de l'Adoption, provided in the section under "Contact Information."

Role of the Court: Prospective parents must file for adoption at the Tribunal de Grande Instance having jurisdiction over their place of residence. Although it is not mandatory, it is advisable to retain a lawyer. The court has six months to determine if the conditions for adoption have been respected and if the adoption is in the best interest of the child. Once adoption is granted, the prosecutor asks the city hall of the adoptee's place of birth to record the adoption. There is no indication of the biological parents.

Role of the Adoption Agencies: In cases of domestic adoption, prospective parents deal directly with social services. Other adoption agencies specialize in international adoption.

Time Frame: Intercountry adoption in France is a lengthy process, sometimes taking several years. The domestic adoption process takes about a year on average.

Adoption Application: Necessary documents are generally prepared by an attorney.

Adoption Fees: There are no "adoption fees" in France but adopting parents often hire an attorney to assist them with the administrative and legal proceedings.

Documents Required: American citizens interested in or considering adopting a child in France or bringing a child to be adopted elsewhere to reside with them in France should consult the French government internet site provide above under Adoption Authority in France for information concerning documentary requirements.

Americans who are legally resident in France but are considering adopting a child from a different country should first consult the country-specific information on adoption for that country. It is critical to remember, however, that in addition to meeting U.S. legal requirements, such children adopted from a third country must also have a French visa to enter and reside in France. Adopted children of a number of Americans have been denied entry into France because they did not have the appropriate French visas. Once in France, they will need to obtain a U.S. visa, if they choose to bring their child to the United States at a later time.

Bringing Your Child Home: Once your adoption is complete (or you have obtained legal custody of the child), there are a few more steps to take before you can head home. Specifically, you need to apply for several documents for your child before he or she can travel to the United States, such as a birth certificate, a passport or travel document for your child from the country in which he or she was born, and a U.S. Immigration Visa.

For detailed and updated information on how to obtain these documents, review the *Intercountry Adoption* section in this publication and visit the U.S. Department of State Intercountry Adoption website at http://adoption.state.gov.

Child Citizenship Act: For adoptions finalized abroad, the Child Citizenship Act of 2000 allows your new child to acquire American citizenship automatically when he or she enters the United States as lawful permanent residents. For adoptions finalized in the United States, the Child Citizenship Act of 2000 allows your new child to acquire American citizenship automatically when the court in the United States issues the final adoption decree. To learn more, review the *Intercountry Adoption* section in this publication and visit the U.S. Department of State Intercountry Adoption website at http://adoption.state.gov.

After Adoption: France has no requirements of the adoptive parents after the adoption.

U.S. Embassy in France
2, avenue Gabriel
75382 Paris Cedex 08
Switchboard: +33 1 43 12 22 22
Fax: +33 1 42 66 97 83
http://france.usembassy.gov

The French Central Authority
Service de l'Adoption Internationale

(SAI), Autorité Centrale
(International Adoption Service, Central Authority)
Ministère des Affaires Etrangères et Européennes (Ministry of Foreign and European Affairs)
244 boulevard Saint-Germain
75303 PARIS 07 SP
France
Telephone number: +33 (1) 4317 9118
Fax number: +33 (1) 4317 9344
E-mail:
courrier.fae-sai@diplomatie.gouv.fr
Websites: diplomatie.gouv.fr/
www.adoption.gouv.fr

Embassy of France
4101 Reservoir Road, NW
Washington, DC 20007
Telephone: (202) 944–6000
Fax: (202) 944–6166
http://www.info-france-usa.org

France has Consulates General in Atlanta, Boston, Chicago, Houston, Los Angeles, Miami, New Orleans, New York and San Francisco.

Office of Children's Issues
U.S. Department of State
2201 C Street, NW
SA-29
Washington, DC 20520
Tel: 1–888–407–4747
E-mail: AskCI@state.gov
http://adoption.state.gov

For questions about intercountry adoption and related immigration procedures, call the USCIS National Benefits Center (NBC) 1–877–3424–8374.

International Parental Child Abduction
October 2012

The information in this section has been edited from a report of the Bureau of Consular Affairs, Office of Overseas Citizens Services of the U.S. Department of State. For more information, please read the *International Parental Child Abduction* section of this book and review current reports online at www.travel.state.gov/abduction.

Disclaimer: The information on this page relating to the legal requirements of specific foreign countries is provided for general information only. Questions involving interpretation of specific foreign laws should be addressed to foreign legal counsel.

General Information: France is a signatory to the Hague Abduction Convention. The U.S. Embassy in Paris has not observed any gender/nationalistic bias in court decisions related to custody, or enforcement of the Hague Convention.

Parents need to gather different documents to obtain a passport for children under age18 depending on their status as married or unmarried at the time the child was born. France does not have exit controls.

Hague Abduction Convention: The U.S. Department of State serves as the U.S. Central Authority (USCA) for the Hague Abduction Convention. In this capacity, the Department's Bureau of Consular Affairs, Directorate for Overseas Citizens Services, Office of Children's Issues facilitates the submission of applications under the Hague Abduction Convention for the return of, or access to, children located in countries that are U.S. treaty partners, including France. Parents are strongly encouraged to contact the Department of State for assistance prior to initiating the Hague process directly with the foreign Central Authority.

United States Department of State
Office of Children's Issues
2201 C Street, N.W.
Washington, DC 20520
Telephone: 1-888-407-4747
Outside the United States or Canada: 1-202-501-4444
Fax: 202-736-9132

The French Central Authority for the Hague Abduction Convention is the Ministère de la Justice et des Libertés. The Ministère de la Justice et des Libertés forwards completed Hague applications to the appropriate Public Prosecutor attached to the civil court of general jurisdiction in the jurisdiction where the defendant resides. The Prosecutor brings the case on behalf of France. Parents or legal guardians and other parties (e.g., the child) have the right to their own counsel. The French Central Authority can be reached at:

Ministère de la Justice et des Libertés
Direction des Affaires Civiles et du Sceau
13, Place Vendôme
75042 PARIS Cedex 01
France
Telephone: +33 (1) 4477 6105/6380
Fax: +33 (1) 4477 6122
E-mail:
entraide-civile-internationale@justice.gouv.fr
Website: www.justice.gouv.fr

To initiate a Hague case for return of, or access to, a child in France, a parent or legal guardian is encouraged to review the eligibility criteria and instructions for completing the Hague application form located at the Department of State website and contact the Department of State for assistance prior to initiating the Hague process directly with the foreign Central Authority. It is extremely important that each document written in English be translated into French. Please note, however, that certified translations are not necessary. Any competent person or organization may translate the documents. The USCA is available to answer questions about the Hague application process, to forward a completed application to the Ministère de la Justice et des Libertés, and to subsequently monitor its progress through the foreign administrative and legal processes.

Legal System: France has a civil law legal system, in which codified legislation is interpreted and applied by the courts. France has two court systems, judicial and administrative. The judicial courts hear civil and criminal cases, including those arising under the Hague Convention.

French law uses the term autorité parentale (parental responsibility) to encompass the right and the duties of the parents to live with their child. If a parent does not have parental responsibilities, or if the child does not live with the parent, the parent has a right and duty of contact (droit de visite, d'hébergement et de correspondence). The Procureur de la République (public prosecutor) will work with the local police to locate a missing child.

Absent a court order, married parents have equal rights of parental authority over their minor children. Unmarried parents (whose parentage is established) have equal rights of parental authority to children born out-of-wedlock; however, if only one parent recognizes his/her parentage within a year of the child's birth, he or she has sole parental responsibility. Likewise, if one parent's parentage is established by court order, the parent who acknowledged his/her own parentage holds sole parental responsibility.

Judicial courts handle civil cases. Specifically, judges in the Tribunal de Grande Instance (superior court) in charge of family cases hear divorce and custody cases. The French Department of Justice created a website in French dedicated to child abduction matters; please see http://www.justice.gouv.fr/justice-civile-11861/enlevement-parental-12063/.

Retaining an Attorney: In a Hague Abduction Convention case, the French Central Authority will assign a Public Prosecutor to present the case to the court, and it is not mandatory for a petitioner to retain a private attorney. The Public Prosecutor, however, does not represent the left-behind parent who submitted the Hague Abduction Convention application; the Prosecutor represents the French Republic and submits the request for return on behalf of the French Central Authority. The parent or legal guardian who has submitted the application may hire a private attorney in France to join the Prosecutor in presenting the Hague Abduction Convention case, however, legal aid is only available to French citizens. A privately hired attorney should contact the French Central Authority as soon as possible after the Hague Abduction Convention application has been filed with the French Central Authority.

The U.S. Embassy in Paris, France, posts a list of attorneys including those who specialize in family law at: http://photos.state.gov/libraries/france/5/acs/paris-attorneys.pdf. This list is provided as a courtesy service only and does not constitute an endorsement of any individual attorney. The Department of State assumes no responsibility or liability for the professional ability or reputation of, or the quality of services provided by, the persons or firms included in this list. Professional credentials and areas of expertise are provided directly by the lawyers.

Citizenship & Passport Matters: If one parent is a citizen of France, the child of that parent automatically acquires French citizenship regardless of where the birth takes place. However, not all children born in France acquire citizenship automatically. France does recognize dual citizenship. For additional information, please see the French Embassy website page.

An application for a French passport for a child can be processed with the authorization of a parent exercising custody over the child. For more information on passports, please see the French Embassy website.

A passport application for a child does not typically require both parents' signatures unless there is a court order (usually a divorce judgment) that states that both parents must consent. Such judgments can be entered in the passport software of the Préfecture (as a "lookout"), and, if only one parent shows up, the other parent's consent will be demanded. (French minors can no longer be put on their parents' passports.)

A child can travel through the region on a national ID card without processing through customs (i.e., travel through the European Union).

Exit Permits: France does not require an exit stamp or exit visa. The consent of the non-traveling parent is required only if a court order states that both parents must consent.

Civil Remedies: The Family Law Division of the Tribunal de Grande Instance hears custody cases.

Left-behind parents may wish to file for custody in the French courts or may wish to file for recognition and enforcement of a U.S. court order in the French courts. It is important to note that either of these options may be construed as acquiescence to the jurisdiction of the foreign court. An attorney can provide advice on the option that would be most effective in a particular case.

A U.S. court order cannot be enforced automatically in France. An exequatur (a French court order enforcing the U.S. decision) must be obtained from a French court. A left-behind parent seeking an exequatur must hire an attorney in France to seek such an order.

French local court orders are directly enforceable in France, and they can also be appealed, although the appeal does not necessarily suspend the execution of the first judgment or part of it. It is possible to petition the court for a stay of execution. In most cases, the judgment mentions specifically that the appeal suspends the execution or that the judgment in question is immediately enforceable.

In the event that parents no longer live together (under legal separation, divorce, or other circumstances), both parents still share joint custody, and French law allows each parent to maintain personal relationships with the child. However, the judge may decide, based on the child's best interests, that only one parent should have the exercise of the parental responsibilities and that the other parent should have a contact right. The judge has full discretion to determine the child's best interests. Still, sole custody is very seldom granted in France.

A final appeal can be lodged with the Cour de Cassation, the French Supreme Court, but this court examines only if the law was applied properly. It does not review the facts of the case. If the Cour de Cassation determines that the court of appeal did not apply the law properly, it sends the case back before a different court of appeal.

Married parents in France have equal and joint custody over their children. An unwed father has custody rights equal to those of the mother, provided the father has officially recognized the child (by filing a statement with the city hall of the town where the child was born). After parents separate or divorce, they usually retain joint custody, though the mother typically has "residential custody," especially in cases where the child is very young. The parent without residential custody generally has access rights, which are enforceable in court. The Tribunal de Grande Instance is the court of first instance for hearing child custody disputes and family law matters.

Custody decisions are made "in the best interest of the child." The U.S. Embassy in Paris has not observed any gender/nationalistic bias in court decisions related to custody. Divorce/custody disputes are common in France. Such disputes can take months to resolve depending on the specifics of the case and the backlogs at the court in question, but courts issue temporary orders that can be enforced immediately pending a final decision.

Criminal Remedies: International parental child kidnapping is a crime in France. The criminal law related to child abduction and withholding of access rights is set out in the French Criminal Code, under the heading "Encroachment on the Exercise of Parental Authority." Please take note that pursuing criminal charges against the abducting parent may adversely affect a Hague Abduction Convention case.

The United States has an extradition treaty with France and international parental child abduction is an extraditable offense. However, France does not extradite its own citizens. French authorities will not arrest on an Interpol notice (unless a Council of Europe country requested the flag) but will notify law enforcement authorities if a subject of a red notice is encountered.

A left-behind parent may also wish to file a missing persons report with his/her local law enforcement agency, and have them follow up with an NCIC (National Crime Information Center) entry, as well as a yellow Interpol notice. These actions do not necessarily have any criminal implications, but will serve to document the case and may assist in locating the child should s/he cross U.S. or international borders. In the event that a TP refuses to return the child or the prosecutor is not active in pursuing a return, the LBP can file a criminal complaint in France for non-presentation of the child/children.

Visitation/Access: A person may file an application under the Hague Abduction Convention for access to a child living in France. The criteria for acceptance of a Hague access application vary from country to country. The U.S. Department of State can assist parents living in the United States to understand country-specific criteria and provide information on the process for submitting a Hague application.

Mediation: The International Mediation Mission for Families, created at the Ministry of Justice in France in April 2001, provides mediation services to facilitate Hague procedures when the French Central Authority finds it appropriate or upon a prosecutor's request. The French Central Authority promotes mediation in abduction cases and will attempt to initiate mediation in most Hague Abduction Convention cases.

U.S. Embassy France
Mailing Address
2 avenue Gabriel
75382 Paris Cedex 08
France
Physical Address (GPS & Google maps)
2 avenue Gabriel
75008 Paris
France
Telephone: [33] (1)43122222
Fax: 33 (1)42669783
Website: http://france.usembassy.gov/

Embassy of France
4101 Reservoir Road, NW
Washington, DC 20007
Telephone: 202-944-6000
Email: info@ambafrance-us.org
Website:
http://ambafrance-us.org/spip.php?rubrique2

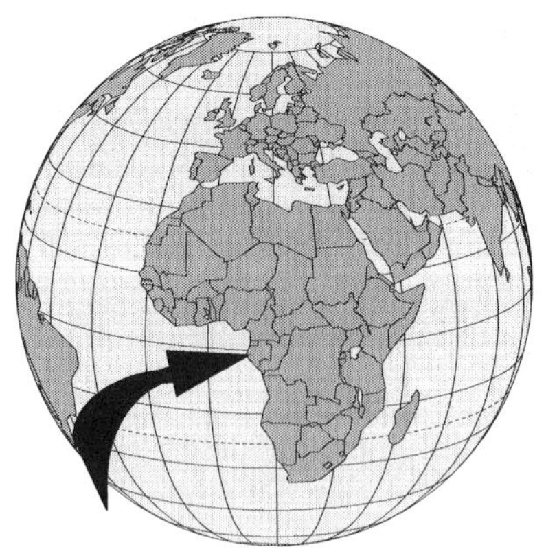

GABON

Compiled from publications that were available as of February 2013 from the U.S. Department of State, the U.S. Department of Commerce, and the Central Intelligence Agency (CIA). See the introduction to this set for explanatory notes.

Official Name:
Gabonese Republic

PROFILE

Geography

Area: total: 267,667 sq km; country comparison to the world: 77; land: 257,667 sq km; water: 10,000 sq km
Major cities: Libreville (capital) 619,000 (2009)
Climate: tropical; always hot, humid
Terrain: narrow coastal plain; hilly interior; savanna in east and south

People

Nationality: noun: Gabonese (singular and plural); adjective: Gabonese
Population: 1,608,321 (July 2012 est.)
Population growth rate: 1.977% (2012 est.)
Ethnic groups: Bantu tribes, including four major tribal groupings (Fang, Bapounou, Nzebi, Obamba); other Africans and Europeans, 154,000, including 10,700 French and 11,000 persons of dual nationality
Religions: Christian 55%-75%, animist, Muslim less than 1%
Languages: French (official), Fang, Myene, Nzebi, Bapounou/Eschira, Bandjabi
Literacy: definition: age 15 and over can read and write; total population: 88.4%; male: 91.9%; female: 84.9% (2010 est.)
Health: life expectancy at birth: total population: 52.29 years; male: 51.65 years; female: 52.93 years (2012 est.); Infant mortality rate: total: 49 deaths/1,000 live births; male: 56.68 deaths/1,000 live births; female: 41.09 deaths/1,000 live births (2012 est.)
Unemployment rate: 21% (2006 est.)
Work force: 756,200 (2012 est.)

Government

Type: republic; multiparty presidential regime
Independence: 17 August 1960
Constitution: adopted 14 March 1991
Political subdivisions: 9 provinces; Estuaire, Haut-Ogooue, Moyen-Ogooue, Ngounie, Nyanga, Ogooue-Ivindo, Ogooue-Lolo, Ogooue-Maritime, Woleu-Ntem
Suffrage: 18 years of age; universal

Economy

GDP (purchasing power parity): $26.71 billion (2012 est.); $24.89 billion (2011 est.); $23.53 billion (2010 est.); $22.07 billion (2009 est.)
GDP real growth rate: 6.1% (2012 est.); 5.8% (2011 est.); 6.6% (2010 est.); -1.4% (2009 est.)
GDP per capita (PPP): $17,300 (2012 est.); $16,400 (2011 est.); $15,700 (2010 est.); $15,000 (2009 est.)
Natural resources: petroleum, natural gas, diamond, niobium, manganese, uranium, gold, timber, iron ore, hydropower
Agriculture products: cocoa, coffee, sugar, palm oil, rubber; cattle; okoume (a tropical softwood); fish
Industries: petroleum extraction and refining; manganese, gold; chemicals, ship repair, food and beverages, textiles, lumbering and plywood, cement
Exports: $10.82 billion (2012 est.); $10.86 billion (2011 est.); $9.371 billion (2010 est.)
Exports—commodities: crude oil, timber, manganese, uranium
Exports—partners: US 40.9%, Australia 9.1%, Malaysia 8.6%, Japan 5.9%, China 5%, Spain 4.8% (2011)
Imports: $3.496 billion (2012 est.); $3.194 billion (2011 est.); $2.5 billion (2010 est.)
Imports—commodities: machinery and equipment, foodstuffs, chemicals, construction materials
Imports—partners: France 32.9%, China 8.4%, US 6.3%, Belgium 5.8%, Cameroon 4.3% (2011)
Debt—external: $2.758 billion (31 December 2012 est.); $2.726 billion (31 December 2011 est.)
Exchange rates: Cooperation Financiere en Afrique Centrale francs per US dollar; 515.1 (2012 est.) ; 471.87 (2011 est.); 495.28 (2010 est.); 472.19 (2009); 447.81 (2008)

PEOPLE

Gabon is one of the least densely inhabited countries in Africa. Almost all Gabonese are of Bantu origin. Gabon has at least 40 ethnic groups, with separate languages and cultures. The largest ethnicity is the Fang (about 30%). Other ethnic groups include the Nzebi, Myene, Bandjabi, Eshira, Bapounou, Bateke/ Obamba, and Bakota.

Ethnic group boundaries are less sharply drawn in Gabon than elsewhere in Africa. Most ethnicities are spread throughout Gabon, leading to constant contact and interaction among the groups. Intermarriage between the ethnicities is quite common, helping reduce ethnic tensions. French, the official language, is a unifying force. The Democratic Party of Gabon's historical dominance also has served to unite various ethnicities and local interests into a larger whole.

More than 10,000 native French live in Gabon, including an estimated 2,000 dual nationals. France dominates foreign cultural and commercial influences.

National/Racial/Ethnic Minorities

Pygmies are the earliest known inhabitants of the country. Small numbers of Pygmies continued to live in large tracts of rainforest in the northeast. Most Pygmies, however, were relocated to communities along the major roads during the late colonial and early post-independence period. The law grants them the same civil rights as other citizens, but Pygmies remained largely outside of formal authority, keeping their own traditions, independent communities, and local decision-making structures.

Pygmies suffered societal discrimination, often lived in extreme poverty, and did not have easy access to public services. Their Bantu neighbors often exploited their labor by paying them much less than the minimum wage. Despite their equal status under the law, Pygmies had little recourse if mistreated by Bantu. There were no specific government programs or policies to assist Pygmies.

Religion

Approximately 70 percent of the population, including noncitizens, is Christian; 10 to 15 percent is Muslim (of whom 80 to 90 percent are foreigners); 10 percent practices animism exclusively; and 5 percent of the population is not religious. Many persons practice a syncretistic religious belief that combines elements of Christianity, traditional mystical religious beliefs, Voodoo, or animism.

HISTORY

Over the last 7 centuries, Bantu ethnic groups arrived in the area from several directions to escape enemies or find new land. In the process they displaced other groups in the region, among them the pygmies who now inhabit the jungle in the country's far east. Gabon's first European visitors were Portuguese traders who arrived in the 15th century. They named the area after the Portuguese word "gabao," a coat with sleeves and hood resembling the shape of the Komo River estuary. Dutch, British, and French traders followed the Portuguese in the 16th century, and the coast became a center of the slave trade. In a bid to beat the other European powers, France began to formalize its status in Gabon by signing treaties with Gabonese coastal chiefs in 1839 and 1841.

Libreville, the capital, grew out of a series of small settlements along the Komo River estuary. The first settlement was started in 1842 by American missionaries from New England who established a Presbyterian mission on a hilltop overlooking the estuary. The mission, called Baraka, is now located in the section of Libreville called Glass. In 1849, the population along the Komo River estuary swelled when the French captured an illegal slave ship and released the passengers at the mouth of the Komo River. The slaves named their settlement Libreville—"free town."

The interior remained relatively unexplored by outsiders until the mid-19th century. An American, Paul du Chaillu, was among the first foreigners to explore the interior of the region in the 1850s. Between 1862 and 1887, French explorers penetrated the dense jungles of what would become Gabon. The most famous, Savorgnan de Brazza, used local Bantu bearers and guides in his search for the headwaters of the Congo River.

Capitalizing on treaties signed with indigenous chiefs earlier in the century, France occupied Gabon in 1885 during the European scramble for Africa. However, it did not begin to administer it until 1903. In 1910, Gabon became one of the four territories of French Equatorial Africa, a federation that survived until 1959. The territories became independent in 1960—forming the independent nations of the Central African Republic, Chad, Congo (Brazzaville), and Gabon.

At the time of Gabon's independence in 1960, two principal political parties existed: the Bloc Democratique Gabonais (BDG), led by Leon M'Ba, and the Union Democratique et Sociale Gabonaise (UDSG), led by J.H. Aubame. In the first post-independence election, held under a parliamentary system, neither party was able to win a majority. The BDG obtained support from three of the four independent legislative deputies, and M'Ba was named Prime Minister. Soon after this the two parties agreed that Gabon did not have enough people to support a two-party system, and the two party leaders agreed on a single list of candidates, starting with the 1961 presidential election. In that election, held under the new presidential system, M'Ba became President and Aubame became Foreign Minister.

This one-party system appeared to work until February 1963. Then, the larger BDG element forced the UDSG members to choose between a merger of the parties or resignation. The UDSG cabinet ministers resigned, and M'Ba called an election for February 1964 and at the same time

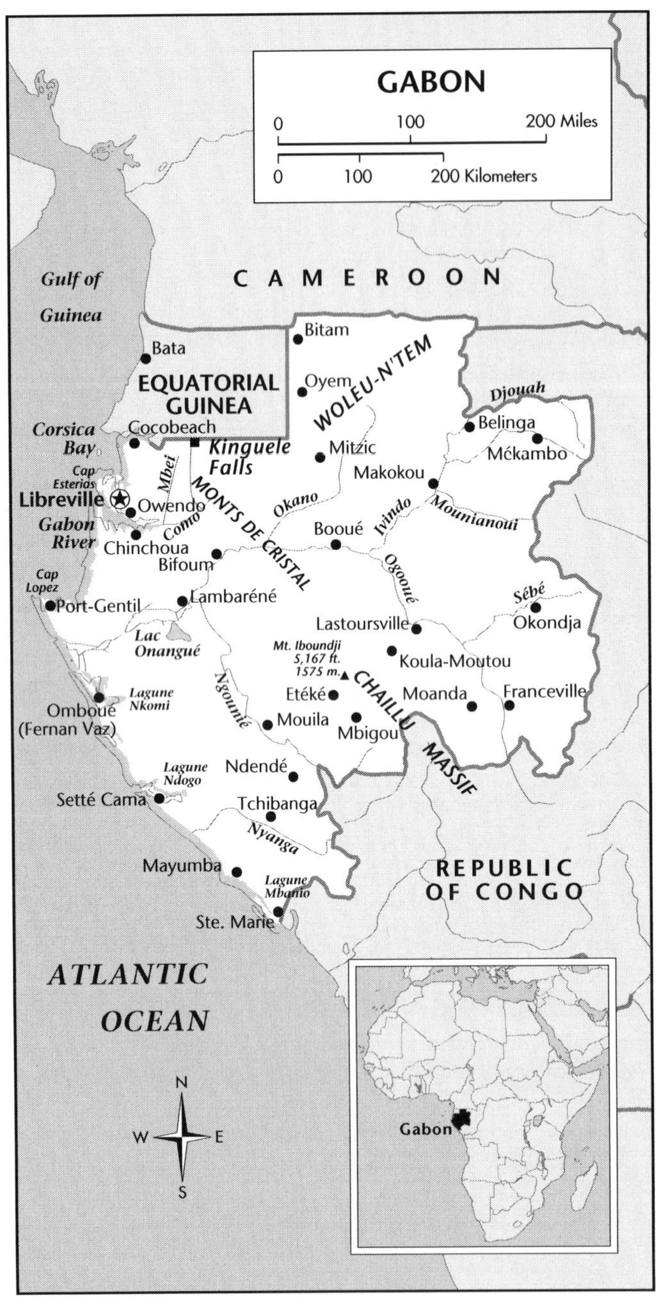

reduced the number of National Assembly deputies from 67 to 47. The UDSG failed to muster a list of candidates able to meet the requirements of the electoral decrees. When the BDG appeared likely to win the election by default, the Gabonese military toppled M'Ba in a bloodless coup on February 18, 1964. French troops re-established his government the next day. Elections were held in April 1964 with many opposition participants. BDG-supported candidates won 31 seats and the opposition 16. Late in 1966, the constitution was revised to provide for automatic succession of the vice president should the president die in office. In March 1967, Leon M'Ba and Omar Bongo (then Albert Bongo) were elected President and Vice President. M'Ba died later that year, and Omar Bongo became President.

In March 1968, Bongo declared Gabon a one-party state by dissolving the BDG and establishing a new party—the Parti Democratique Gabonais (PDG). He invited all Gabonese, regardless of previous political affiliation, to participate. Bongo sought to forge a single national movement in support of the government's development policies, using the PDG as a tool to submerge the regional and tribal rivalries that had divided Gabonese politics in the past. Bongo was elected President in February 1975; in April 1975, the position of vice president was abolished and replaced by the position of prime minister, who had no right to automatic succession. Bongo was re-elected President in both December 1979 and November 1986 to 7-year terms.

Economic discontent and a desire for political liberalization provoked violent demonstrations and strikes by students and workers in early 1990. In response to grievances by workers, Bongo negotiated with them on a sector-by-sector basis, making significant wage concessions. In addition, he promised to open up the PDG and to organize a national political conference in March-April 1990 to discuss Gabon's future political system. The PDG and 74 political organizations attended the conference. Participants essentially divided into two loose coalitions, the ruling PDG and its allies, and the United Front of Opposition Associations and Parties, consisting of the breakaway Morena Fundamental and the Gabonese Progress Party.

The April 1990 conference approved sweeping political reforms and major changes to Gabon's political system, including creation of a national Senate, decentralization of the budgetary process, freedom of assembly and press, and cancellation of an exit visa requirement. In an attempt to guide the political system's transformation to multiparty democracy, Bongo resigned as PDG chairman and created a transitional government headed by a new Prime Minister, Casimir Oye-Mba. The Gabonese Social Democratic Grouping (RSDG), as the resulting government was called, was smaller than the previous government and included representatives from several opposition parties in its cabinet. The RSDG drafted a provisional constitution in May 1990 that provided a basic Western-style bill of rights, a National Council of Democracy to oversee the guarantee of those rights, a governmental advisory board on economic and social issues, and an independent judiciary; the constitution retained strong executive powers for the president.

Opposition to the PDG continued after the April 1990 conference, and in September 1990, two coup d'etat attempts were uncovered and aborted. The untimely death of an opposition leader was followed by anti-government demonstrations. In September-October 1990 the first multiparty National Assembly elections in almost 30 years took place, although opposition parties had not formally been declared legal. Despite the PDG garnering a large majority, the elections produced a representative, multiparty National Assembly.

In January 1991, the National Assembly unanimously passed a law governing the legalization of opposition parties. After review by a constitutional committee, the National Assembly, the PDG Central Committee, and the President, the Assembly in March 1991 unanimously adopted the May 1990–drafted constitution. Although the Senate was created in the 1990–91 constitutional rewrite, it was not brought into being until after 1997 local elections.

Following President Omar Bongo's re-election in December 1993 with 51% of the vote, opposition candidates refused to validate the election results. Serious civil disturbances led to an agreement between the government and opposition factions to work toward a political settlement. These talks led to the Paris Accords in November 1994, under which several opposition figures were included in a government of national unity. The Accords also provided a framework for the next elections. Legislative and local elections were delayed until 1996–97. This unity arrangement soon broke down, however, and the 1996 and 1997 legislative and municipal elections provided the background for renewed partisan politics. The PDG won a landslide victory in the legislative election, but several major cities, including Libreville, elected opposition mayors during the 1997 local election. In 1997, constitutional amendments put forward years earlier were adopted to create the Senate, re-establish the position of vice president, and set the president's term at 7 years.

President Omar Bongo coasted to easy re-election in December 1998, with large majorities of the vote due to a divided opposition. While Bongo's major opponents rejected the outcome as fraudulent, some international observers characterized the results as representative despite many perceived irregularities, and there were none of the civil disturbances that followed the 1993 election. Peaceful though flawed legislative elections held in 2001–2002, which were boycotted by a number of smaller opposition parties and were widely criticized for their administrative weaknesses, produced a National Assembly almost completely dominated by the PDG and allied independents. In November 2005, President Omar Bongo was elected for his sixth term. He won re-election easily, but opponents claim that the balloting process was marred by irregularities. There were some instances of violence following the announcement of Omar Bongo's win, but Gabon generally remained peaceful.

National Assembly elections were held again in December 2006. Several seats contested because of voting irregularities were overturned by the Constitutional Court, but the subsequent run-off elections in early 2007 again yielded a PDG-controlled National Assembly.

On June 8, 2009, President Omar Bongo died of cardiac arrest at a Spanish hospital in Barcelona, ushering in a new era in Gabonese politics. In accordance with the amended constitution, Rose Francine Rogombe, the President of the Senate, became Interim President on June 10, 2009. The first contested elections in Gabon's history that did not include Omar Bongo as a candidate were held on August 30, 2009 with 18 candidates for president. The lead-up to the elections saw some isolated protests, but no significant disturbances. Omar Bongo's son, ruling party leader Ali Bongo Ondimba, was formally declared the winner after a 3-week review by the Constitutional Court; his inauguration took place on October 16, 2009. The same month, President Bongo Ondimba began efforts to streamline the government, eliminating 17 minister-level positions. He also abolished the vice president position and reorganized the portfolios of numerous ministries, bureaus, and directorates with the intention of reducing corruption and government bloat.

The court's review of the 2009 elections had been prompted by claims of fraud by the many opposition candidates, with the initial announcement of election results sparking unprecedented violent protests in Port-Gentil, the country's second-largest city and a long-time bastion of opposition to PDG rule. The citizens of Port-Gentil took to the streets, and numerous shops and residences were burned, including the French Consulate and a local prison. Officially, only four deaths occurred during the riots, but opposition and local leaders claim many more. Gendarmes and the military were deployed to Port-Gentil to support the beleaguered police, and a curfew was in effect for more than 3 months.

A partial legislative by-election was held in June 2010. A newly created coalition of parties, the Union Nationale (UN), participated for the first time. The UN was composed largely of PDG defectors who left the party after Omar Bongo's death. Of the five hotly contested seats, the PDG won three and the UN won two; both sides claimed victory.

In January 2011, Andre Mba Obame, the Secretary General of the UN coalition, swore himself in as President, established a parallel government, and occupied the United Nations Development Program headquarters in Libreville for a month. Mba Obame believed himself the rightful winner of the 2009 presidential election despite coming in third according to the official count. In response to Mba Obame's self-proclamation, the government dissolved the UN for violating the country's unity (per Article 94 of the constitution). Further, on May 5, 2011, Gabon's National Assembly voted to dissolve Mba Obame's immunity as a member of parliament. Mba Obame departed the country for medical treatment.

On June 17, 2011, the Gabonese parliament adopted a law on the protection of personal data to allow for the introduction of biometrics in Gabon's future elections. In the lead-up to legislative elections held December 17, 2011, opposition groups threatened a boycott based on the failure to implement a biometrics system. Voter turnout remained historically low. The ruling PDG won by a landslide, gaining 114 of the 120 seats in the National Assembly. The elections were deemed free and fair by external observers. In February 2012, Raymond Ndong Sima was selected as Prime Minister. Several new ministers also were named.

GOVERNMENT AND POLITICAL CONDITIONS

Gabon is a republic dominated by a strong presidency and the Democratic Party of Gabon (PDG), which has held power since 1968. In 2009 President Ali Bongo Ondimba was elected in a poll characterized by international observers as generally free and fair, although irregularities and post-election violence occurred.

In January 2011, Andre Mba Obame, the secretary general of the former National Union (UN) political party, swore himself in as president, established a parallel government, and occupied the UN Development Program headquarters in Libreville for a month. Mba Obame considered himself the rightful winner of the 2009 presidential election despite coming in third, according to the official count. On January 27, security forces briefly detained seven members of the UN party and charged them with disturbing the peace for refusing to move out of the street during morning traffic. An eighth UN member, Paulin Obiang Ndong, also was briefly detained for distributing videos of Mba Obame's "investiture." In response to Mba Obame's self-proclamation, the government dissolved the UN party for violating the country's unity. On May 5, the National Assembly voted to remove Mba Obame's immunity as a member of parliament. Mba Obame subsequently departed the country for medical treatment.

Recent Elections

President Ali Bongo Ondimba was elected in August 2009 with 41 percent of the vote. The president succeeded his father, former president Omar Bongo, who died in 2009 after a 41-year rule. The two leading opposition candidates each received approximately 25 percent of the vote. International observers characterized the election as largely free and fair, although the election was marred by post-election violence, significant restrictions on human rights, and accusations of political tampering with the electoral process. Irregularities included problems with voter lists and registration, polls that opened late, improperly secured ballot boxes, and armed security personnel in or near voting sites. Authorities censored news coverage and harassed the press. Numerous candidates contested the election results, which were subsequently validated by the Constitutional Court.

In legislative elections held on December 17, 2011, the ruling PDG won 144 of 120 seats in the National Assembly. Regional and local observers deemed the election generally free and fair despite minor irregularities. Voter abstention was estimated at 65 percent. Opposition and civil society leaders who had called for a boycott claimed victory for the low voter turnout. Other observers noted that abstention rates during legislative elections were generally high, primarily due to lack of interest.

On June 17, 2011, parliament passed the Personal Data Protection Law, which provides for the introduction of biometrics by 2013 to increase transparency in future elections. Critics viewed the law, which includes criminal penalties for the unlawful handling of personal information, as a significant step toward reducing electoral irregularities. No identity document using the proposed new technology had been produced by year's end.

Political Parties: The PDG has dominated the government since its creation by former president Omar Bongo in 1968. PDG membership conferred advantage in obtaining government positions.

Participation of Women and Minorities: Women held governmental positions, including at the ministerial level, in all branches of government. In the 31-member cabinet, five were women. The president of the Senate and the head of the Constitutional Court also were women.

Members of the president's Bateke ethnic group and other southerners held a disproportionately large number of key positions in the security forces, although members of all major ethnic groups continued to occupy prominent government positions. Indigenous Pygmies rarely participated in the political process.

Principal Government Officials

Last Updated: 1/31/2013

Pres.: **Ali Ben BONGO Ondimba**
Prime Min.: **Raymond NDONG SIMA**
Min. of Agriculture, Livestock Farming, Fisheries, & Rural Development: **Julien Nkoghe BEKALE**
Min. of Budget & Accounting: **Christian Rose OSSOUCAH RAPONDA**
Min. of Defense: **Pacome Rufin ONDZOUNGA**
Min. of Digital Economy, Communication, & Postal Services: **Blaise LOUEMBE**
Min. of Economy, Employment, & Sustainable Development: **Luc OYOUBI**
Min. of Education, Culture, Youth, & Sports: **Seraphin MOUNDOUNGA**
Min. of Family & Social Affairs: **Honorine Nzet BITEGHE**
Min. of Foreign Affairs: **Emmanuel ISSOZE-NGONDET**
Min. of Health: **Leon NZOUBA**

Min. of Industry & Mines: **Regis Immongault TATAGANI**
Min. of Interior, Decentralization, Security, & Immigration: **Jean Francois NDONGOU**
Min. of Investment Promotion, Public Works, Transport, Habitat, &Tourism: **Magloire NGAMBIA**
Min. of Justice, Human Rights, & Constitutional Institutions: **Ida Reteno ASSOUNOUET**
Min. of Oil, Energy, & Hydraulic Resources: **Etienne NGOUBOU**
Min. of Small & Medium-Size Enterprises, Artisans, & Commerce: **Fidele Mengue M'ENGOUANG**
Min. of Water & Forests: **Gabriel NTCHANGO**
Ambassador to the US: **Carlos Victor BOUNGOU**
Permanent Representative to the UN, New York: **Noel Nelson MESSONE**

ECONOMY

Gabon enjoys a per capita income four times that of most sub-Saharan African nations, but because of high income inequality, a large proportion of the population remains poor. Gabon depended on timber and manganese until oil was discovered offshore in the early 1970s.

The economy was reliant on oil for about 50% of its GDP, about 70% of revenues, and 87% of goods exports for 2010, although some fields have passed their peak production. A rebound of oil prices from 1999 to 2008 helped growth, but declining production has hampered Gabon from fully realizing potential gains. Gabon signed a 14-month Stand-By Arrangement with the IMF in May 2007, and later that year issued a $1 billion sovereign bond to buy back a sizable portion of its Paris Club debt. Gabon continues to face fluctuating prices for its oil, timber, and manganese exports.

Despite the abundance of natural wealth, poor fiscal management has stifled the economy. However, President BONGO has made efforts to increase transparency and is taking steps to make Gabon a more attractive investment destination to diversify the economy. BONGO has attempted to boost growth by increasing government investment in human resources and infrastructure. GDP grew more than 6% per year over the 2010–12 period.

Labor Conditions

The law prohibits employment of children below the age of 16 without the expressed consent of the ministries of labor, education, and public health. The law provides for fines of between 290,000 and 480,000 CFA francs ($602 to $996) and prison sentences of up to two years for violations of the minimum age for work. The ministries rigorously enforced this law in urban areas with respect to citizen children, and few citizens under the age of 18 worked in the formal wage sector. The law was not enforced in rural areas and within the informal sectors, however, primarily because the inspection force was inadequate.

Child labor was a problem, particularly in rural areas, where the law was seldom enforced. Noncitizen children were more likely to work in informal or illegal sectors of the economy, where laws against child labor were less rigorously enforced. An unknown number of children, primarily noncitizens, worked in marketplaces or performed domestic work. Many of these children were reportedly the victims of child trafficking.

During 2011 the national monthly minimum wage was increased from 80,000 CFA francs ($166) to 150,000 CFA francs ($311). Government workers received an additional monthly allowance of 20,000 CFA francs ($41) per child and transportation, housing, and family benefits. There was no minimum wage in the informal sector.

The labor code stipulates a 40-hour workweek with a minimum rest period of 48 consecutive hours. Employers must compensate workers for overtime work, which is determined by collective agreements or government regulations. According to the law, the daily limit for compulsory overtime can be extended from 30 minutes to two hours to perform specified preparatory or complementary work, such as starting machines in a factory or supervising a workplace. It also can be extended for urgent work to prevent or repair accidents. The daily limit does not apply to establishments in which work is performed on a continuous basis and those providing services that cannot be subject to a daily limit, including retail, transport, dock work, hotels and catering, housekeeping, guarding, security, medical establishments, domestic work, and the press.

U.S.-GABONESE RELATIONS

The United States established diplomatic relations with Gabon in 1960, following its independence from France. Although structurally multiparty, in practice, Gabon had a one-party system until 1963. This was followed over the next few years by a military coup, French military intervention, elections, and the establishment of a one-party state. The 1990s saw protests and some moves toward political reform and multiparty democracy. After Gabon's 42-year president died in 2009, elections were held, and his son, Ali Bongo Ondimba became president.

Relations between the United States and Gabon are excellent. The United States has welcomed the reforms that Gabon has taken to bring more transparency and accountability to government, at the same time urging Gabon to take bold steps to root out corruption and to reform the judiciary and other key institutions to ensure the protection of human rights. The United States applauds Gabon's efforts toward greater regional cooperation on environmental issues. The two countries work together to help diversify Gabon's economic potential, ensure security in the Gulf of Guinea, and expand their bilateral trade.

Gabon is a key player in conflict resolution efforts in the Central African region. It provides peacekeepers to the Economic Community of Central African States (ECCAS) peacekeeping mission to stabilize the Central African Republic. Gabon also hosts and acts as a driving force behind ECCAS, which is establishing a regional standby peacekeeping brigade under the auspices of the African Union's African Standby Force.

U.S. Assistance to Gabon

U.S. assistance to Gabon seeks to improve the professionalism of the country's military officers and senior enlisted personnel by providing training that will help prepare the military to operate effectively in regional peacekeeping and security efforts. Gabon, a leader in maritime security efforts, is a participant in the Africa Partnership Station program supported through the Africa Maritime Security Initiative.

Bilateral Economic Relations

Gabon's economy is dominated by oil, although the government is diversifying it, most notably in agribusiness. Most foreign investment, including U.S. investment, is concentrated in the oil and mineral sectors. Gabon is eligible for preferential trade benefits under the African Growth and Opportunity Act. U.S. exports to Gabon include machinery, agricultural products, vehicles, and optic and medical instruments. U.S. imports from Gabon include crude oil, manganese ores, agricultural products, returns, and wood.

Gabon's Membership in International Organizations

Gabon is a member of the African Union and Gabon and the United States belong to a number of the same international organizations, including the United Nations, International Monetary Fund, World Bank, and World Trade Organization.

Bilateral Representation

Gabon maintains an embassy in the United States at 1630 Connecticut Ave. NW, Suite 700, Washington, DC, 20009 (tel. 202-797-1000).

Principal U.S. Embassy Officials

Last Updated: 1/14/2013

LIBREVILLE (E) Sabliere, BP 4000, Libreville, Gabon, [241] 01-45-71-00, Fax [241] 01-45-11-78, Workweek: MON-THU 08:00-17:15 and FRI 08:00-14:00.

AMB OMS:	Erne Guzman
FM:	Chris Grawburg
HRO:	Michael Moody
IBB:	Kenneth Tripp
MGT:	Gaspar Guzman
MLO/ODC:	Jason Neal
POSHO:	Chris Grawburg
SDO/DATT:	LTC Scott Roxburgh
AMB:	Eric Benjaminson
CON:	Jessica Munson
DCM:	Dante Paradiso
PAO:	Kevin Krapf
GSO:	Michael Agner
RSO:	Matt Becht
CLO:	Jerry Wright
ECON:	Hilleary Smith
FMO:	Michael Moody
ICASS Chair:	Jessica Munson
IMO:	Joshua Kim
IPO:	Joshua Kim
POL:	Jenny Bah
State ICASS:	Jessica Munson

TRAVEL

Consular Information Sheet

April 5, 2012

Country Description: The Gabonese Republic is a developing nation on the western coast of central Africa with a multiparty presidential government. French is the official language; few Gabonese speak English. Facilities for tourism outside the capital city of Libreville are available, but they are often limited and can be expensive.

Smart Traveler Enrollment Program (STEP)/Embassy Locations: If you are going to live in or travel to Gabon, please take the time to tell our Embassy about your trip by enrolling in the Smart Traveler Enrollment Program (STEP). If you enroll, we can keep you up to date with important safety and security announcements. It will also help your friends and family get in touch with you in an emergency. You should remember to keep all of your information in STEP up to date. It is important during enrollment or when you update your information to include your current phone number and email address where you can be reached in case of an emergency.

U.S. Embassy Libreville
Bord du Mer, B.P. 4000
Libreville, Gabon
Telephone: 241 76-20-03
or 241 76-20-04
Facsimile: 241 74-55-07

Entry/Exit Requirements for U.S. Citizens: A passport, visa, and proof of vaccination against yellow fever are required. You will need to get your visa in advance, as airport visas are not available. U.S. citizen travelers without the required visa have been refused entry into Gabon. Tourist and business visas to Gabon are issued at the Embassy of Gabon, 2034 20th Street NW, Washington, DC 20009, and the Consulate of Gabon at 18 East 41st Street, Ninth Floor, New York, NY 10017 (email ConsulatGabon@aol.com). To obtain a visa for Gabon, you will need the application form, your passport, your itinerary and reservations, the visa fee, a photo, your International Certificate of Vaccination (Yellow Card) proving that you have been vaccinated against yellow fever at least 10 days before entering the country, and a prepaid return envelope. You may call the Gabonese Embassy at (202) 797-1000 or the Consulate at (212) 683-7371 to obtain the latest visa information. You should bring the supporting documentation that you provided with your visa application to prevent delays upon arrival in Gabon. Overseas, the nearest Gabonese Embassy or Consulate can assist you. All non-Gabonese citizens, with the exception of those bearing diplomatic or official passports, must obtain exit visas from the Direction Générale à la Documentation et l'Immigration (DGDI, formerly known as CEDOC) before departing Gabon.

The U.S. Department of State is unaware of any HIV/AIDS entry restrictions for visitors to or foreign residents of Gabon.

Threats to Safety and Security: You should be aware of your surroundings and personal security at all times. There have been incidents of civil unrest and, in 2009, there was some post-election violence in Libreville and Port Gentil. You should avoid large gatherings, protests, demonstrations, and any other event where crowds congregate.

In the event of a fire, dial the following phone numbers for fire departments in Gabon's major cities: Libreville (74-09-55 or 76-15-20), Port Gentil (56-27-75 or 56-27-76), and Franceville (67-75-67, 67-75-68, or 67-75-69).

Stay up to date by:

- Bookmarking our Bureau of Consular Affairs website, which contains the current Travel Warnings and Travel Alerts as well as the Worldwide Caution.
- Following uson Twitter and the Bureau of Consular Affairs page on Facebook as well.
- Downloading our free Smart Traveler IPhone App to have travel information at your fingertips.
- Calling 1-888-407-4747 toll-free within the United States and Canada, or a regular toll line, 1-202-501-4444, from other countries.
- Taking some time before travel to consider your personal security.

Crime: Petty theft is common in Gabon. Violent crime is more common in urban areas, and there have been armed robberies in homes, restaurants, and at beaches frequented by foreigners. On some occasions, Americans and Europeans have been the victims of crime.

The U.S. Embassy in Gabon encourages you to take extra precautions when traveling in Libreville. To prevent carjacking and petty theft, you should travel with your car windows up, doors locked, and items of value hidden from view. You should avoid marginal neighborhoods, poorly lit streets, and unfamiliar areas of the city, especially at night. You should not walk, run, or stay on the beach alone or in groups after dusk. When dining in restaurants or visiting markets, you should carry a minimal amount of cash and avoid wearing flashy or expensive jewelry. If you are the victim of an attempted robbery or carjacking, you are encouraged to comply with the attacker to avoid injury and to report all incidents to the police and the U.S. Embassy. Police response time to reports of crime is often slow.

Scams or confidence schemes do occur in Gabon. For general information on scams, see the Department of State's Financial Scams web page.

Credit cards are not widely accepted except at hotels, and because of the high rate of credit card fraud, you should exercise caution when using them. Some hotels only accept credit cards with a European-style microchip. While withdrawing funds from ATMs, you should exercise the same safety precautions as in the U.S. as they are targeted by thieves.

In many countries around the world, counterfeit and pirated goods are widely available. You will find these products being sold on the streets, local shops, and in market places. Transactions involving such products may be illegal under local law. In addition, carrying them back to the United States may result in forfeitures and/or fines.

Victims of Crime: If you or someone you know becomes the victim of a crime abroad, you should contact the local police and the nearest U.S. embassy or consulate. We can:

- Replace a stolen passport.
- Help you find appropriate medical care if you are the victim of violent crimes such as assault or rape.
- Put you in contact with the appropriate police authorities, and if you want us to, we can contact family members or friend.
- Help you understand the local criminal justice process and direct you to local attorneys, although it is important to remember that local authorities are responsible for investigating and prosecuting the crime.

The local equivalent to the "911" emergency line to reach the police in Gabon's major cities are the following phone numbers: Libreville (72-00-37,) Port Gentil (55-22-36) and Franceville (67-72-76 or 67-72-94).

Criminal Penalties: While you are traveling in Gabon, you are subject to its laws. Foreign laws and legal systems can be vastly different than our own and criminal penalties will vary from country to country. There are also some things that might be legal in the country you visit, but still illegal in the United States. You can be prosecuted under U.S. law if you buy pirated goods. Engaging in sexual conduct with children or using or disseminating child pornography in a foreign country is a crime prosecutable in the United States. If you break local laws in Gabon, your U.S. passport won't help you avoid arrest or prosecution. It's very important to know what's legal and what's not wherever you are.

Based on the Vienna Convention on Consular Relations, bilateral agreements with certain countries, and customary international law, if you are arrested in Gabon, you have the option to request that the police, prison officials, or other authorities alert the nearest U.S. embassy or consulate of your arrest, and to have communications from you forwarded to the nearest U.S. embassy or consulate.

Language: The official language of Gabon is French; if you do not speak French, you will face difficulties in communication associated with the language barrier.

Identification: You should always carry identification with you in case you are stopped at a police checkpoint. You should carry photocopies of your U.S. passport biographic information page and your Gabonese visa.

Photography: Taking photographs of the Presidential Palace, airport, military or other government buildings is strictly forbidden.

Official Corruption: Official corruption is common, but paying bribes is not recommended.

Currency: Gabon is largely a cash economy. Credit cards are accepted at only a few major hotels. Travelers' checks can be cashed or dollars exchanged for Central African Francs (CFA) at hotels and banks. ATMs are available in major urban centers, and dispense CFA. You should exercise the same safety precautions as in the U.S. while withdrawing funds from ATMs as they are commonly targeted by thieves.

Accessibility: While in Gabon, individuals with disabilities may find accessibility and accommodation very different from what you find in the United States. There are no laws prohibiting discrimination against persons with disabilities or providing for access to transportation, communication, buildings or services. There is some societal discrimination against persons with disabilities, and employment opportunities and treatment facilities are limited.

Medical Facilities and Health Information: Medical facilities in Gabon's major cities are limited, but they are generally adequate for routine or basic needs. Medical services in rural areas are either unavailable or of very poor quality. Additionally, some medicines are not available; you should carry your own supply of properly-labeled medications to cover your entire stay. For medical emergencies in Libreville, the emergency room at El Rapha Polyclinic, a private clinic can be reached at 44-70-00, 20-01-03 or 07 98 66 60and an ambulance can be requested through them or by calling 13-00 from a Gabon telecom landline.

Due to the presence of schistosomiasis, you should avoid exposure to non-chlorinated fresh water. Tuberculosis (TB) is an increasingly serious health concern in Gabon. For further information, please consult the CDC's information on TB.

You can find more information on vaccinations and other health precautions on the CDC website. For information about outbreaks of infectious diseases abroad, consult the World Health Organization (WHO) website. The WHO website also contains additional health information for travelers, including detailed country-specific health information.

Medical Insurance: You can't assume your insurance will go with you when you travel. It's very important to find out BEFORE you leave whether or not your medical insurance will cover you overseas. You need to ask your insurance company two questions:

- Does my policy apply when I'm out of the United States?
- Will it cover emergencies like a trip to a foreign hospital or a medical evacuation?

In many places, doctors and hospitals expect payment in cash at the time of service. Your regular U.S. health insurance may not cover doctors' and hospital visits in other countries. Medicare does not pay for any medical care received outside of the United States or its territories. If your policy doesn't cover you when you travel, it is a good idea to take out another policy for your trip.

Traffic Safety and Road Conditions: While in a foreign country, U.S. citizens may encounter road conditions that differ significantly from those in the United States.

Travel by road in Gabon can be hazardous. You should drive with your car windows up and the doors locked. Travelers are routinely stopped at police checkpoints within cities and on roads to the interior. You should comply politely if stopped, but avoid encouraging requests for bribery if possible. You should use extreme caution when driving after dark. Two-lane roads are the norm throughout Gabon. Roads to outlying cities have many visible and hidden dangers including large potholes, absence of road signs, poor to non-existent streetlights, timber-laden trucks, and the presence of pedestrians and animals. Construction work is generally poorly indicated. Drivers may change lanes or stop unexpectedly. Lane markings are frequently ignored. Four-wheel drive vehicles are recommended for travel beyond the paved road to Lambarene, especially during the rainy season.

Roadside assistance and emergency medical services are available in Libreville, but they may not be dependable. These services are non-existent outside of the city. Service stations are available along main roads, but vehicle repair facilities are not always available. Drivers must have a valid international driver's license (available from AAA and the American Automobile Routing Alliance) when driving in Gabon.

Bus service exists in Libreville, but buses are infrequent and routes are not generally convenient, so most people use taxis to get around the city. Use of taxis is generally safe, but does pose added risks. You should use a hotel taxi when possible. Before entering a taxi, check that the taxi has seatbelts and negotiate the rate for your trip. Riding in a taxi alone or during late hours of the evening is not recommended and increases your risk of becoming the victim of crime. Rail services remain available, but infrequent, and travelers should expect lengthy delays.

Talking or texting on a cell phone while driving in Gabon is against the law.

Aviation Safety Oversight: As there is no direct commercial air service to the United States by carriers registered in Gabon, the U.S. Federal Aviation Administration (FAA) has not assessed the Government of Gabon's Civil Aviation Authority for compliance with International Civil Aviation Organization (ICAO) aviation safety standards. Further information may be found on the FAA's safety assessment page.

Children's Issues: Please see the U.S. Dept. of State Office of Children's Issues web pages on intercountry adoption and international parental child abduction.

Intercountry Adoption

July 2012

Gabon is not party to the Hague Convention on Protection of Children and Co-operation in Respect of Intercountry Adoption (Hague Adoption Convention). Intercountry adoptions of children from non-Hague countries are processed in accordance with 8 Code of Federal Regulations, Section 204.3 as it relates to orphans as defined under the Immigration and Nationality Act, Section 101(b)(1)(F).

Below is the limited adoption information that the Department has obtained from the adoption authority of Gabon. U.S. citizens adopting children in rare adoption cases from Gabon, as well as U.S. citizen prospective adoptive parents living in Gabon who would like to adopt from the United States or from a third country, should contact the adoption authority of Gabon to inquire about applicable laws and procedures. See contact information below.

Potential adoptive parents begin the process by sending a letter to the Ministry of Social Affairs explaining why they would like to adopt and providing a description of a child they are seeking to adopt. Preferably, the potential adoptive parents reside in Gabon. If not, they will need to travel to Gabon to meet the child. The potential adoptive parents can spend time with the child on weekends and school holidays. After the police have approved the parents and the social worker has determined that the potential adoptive parents and the child have developed a strong relationship, the court can finalize the adoption.

Prospective adoptive parents should be aware that not all children in orphanages or children's homes are adoptable. In many countries, birth parents place their child(ren) temporarily in an orphanage or children's home due to financial or other hardship, intending that the child return home when this becomes possible. In such cases, the birth parent(s) have rarely relinquished their parental rights or consented to their child(ren)'s adoption.

The Gabonese Republic's Adoption Authority
Ministère de la Famille et des Affaires Sociales
B.P. 50, Libreville
Phone +241 76 35 90

THE GAMBIA

Compiled from publications that were available as of February 2013 from the U.S. Department of State, the U.S. Department of Commerce, and the Central Intelligence Agency (CIA). See the introduction to this set for explanatory notes.

Official Name:
Republic of The Gambia

PROFILE

Geography

Area: total: 11,295 sq km; country comparison to the world: 167; land: 10,000 sq km; water: 1,295 sq km

Major cities: Banjul (capital) 436,000 (2009)

Climate: tropical; hot, rainy season (June to November); cooler, dry season (November to May)

Terrain: flood plain of the Gambia River flanked by some low hills

People

Nationality: noun: Gambian(s); adjective: Gambian

Population: 1,840,454 (July 2012 est.)

Population growth rate: 2.344% (2012 est.)

Ethnic groups: African 99% (Mandinka 42%, Fula 18%, Wolof 16%, Jola 10%, Serahuli 9%, other 4%), non-African 1% (2003 census)

Religions: Muslim 90%, Christian 8%, indigenous beliefs 2%

Languages: English (official), Mandinka, Wolof, Fula, other indigenous vernaculars

Literacy: definition: age 15 and over can read and write; total population: 50%; male: 60%; female: 40.4% (2010 est.)

Health: life expectancy at birth: total population: 63.82 years; male: 61.52 years; female: 66.18 years (2012 est.); Infant mortality rate: total: 69.58 deaths/1,000 live births; male: 75.15 deaths/1,000 live births; female: 63.84 deaths/1,000 live births (2012 est.)

Unemployment rate: NA%

Work force: 777,100 (2007)

Government

Type: republic

Independence: 18 February 1965

Constitution: approved by national referendum 8 August 1996; effective 16 January 1997

Political subdivisions: 5 divisions and 1 city; Banjul, Central River, Lower River, North Bank, Upper River, Western

Suffrage: 18 years of age; universal

Economy

GDP (purchasing power parity): $3.495 billion (2012 est.); $3.541 billion (2011 est.); $3.429 billion (2010 est.); $3.25 billion (2009 est.)

GDP real growth rate: -1.6% (2012 est.); 3.3% (2011 est.); 5.5% (2010 est.); 6.7% (2009 est.)

GDP per capita (PPP): $1,900 (2012 est.); $2,000 (2011 est.); $2,000 (2010 est.); $1,900 (2009 est.)

Natural resources: fish, clay, silica sand, titanium (rutile and ilmenite), tin, zircon

Agriculture products: rice, millet, sorghum, peanuts, corn, sesame, cassava (manioc), palm kernels; cattle, sheep, goats

Industries: processing peanuts, fish, and hides; tourism, beverages, agricultural machinery assembly, woodworking, metalworking, clothing

Exports: $103.3 million (2012 est.); $103.9 million (2011 est.); $98.2 million (2010 est.)

Exports—commodities: peanut products, fish, cotton lint, palm kernels

Exports—partners: China 41.8%, India 20.8%, France 10.4%, UK 6.3% (2011)

Imports: $354.1 million (2012 est.); $327 million (2011 est.); $313.1 million (2010 est.)

Imports—commodities: foodstuffs, manufactures, fuel, machinery and transport equipment

Imports—partners: China 29.2%, Brazil 10.1%, Senegal 8.7%, India 5.5%, Netherlands 4.1%, Turkey 4% (2011)

Debt—external: $545.8 million (31 December 2012 est.); $642.3 million (31 December 2011 est.); $573.8 million (31 December 2010 est.)

Exchange rates: dalasis (GMD) per US dollar; 31.5 (2012 est.); 29.462 (2011 est.); 28.012 (2010 est.); 26.6444 (2009); 22.75 (2008); 27.79 (2007)

PEOPLE

A wide variety of ethnic groups live in The Gambia with a minimum of intertribal friction, each preserving its own language and traditions. The Mandinka tribe is the largest, followed by the Fula, Wolof, Jola, and Sarahule. Approximately 3,500 non-Africans live in The Gambia, including Europeans and families of Lebanese origin.

According to the 1993 census, more than 63% of Gambians lived in rural villages, although more and more young people were coming to the capital in search of work and education. Provisional figures from the 2003 census showed that the gap between the urban and rural populations was narrowing as more areas were declared urban. While urban migration, development projects, and modernization are bringing more Gambians into contact with Western habits and values, the traditional emphasis on the extended family, as well as indigenous forms of dress and celebration, remain integral parts of everyday life.

Religion

Sunni Muslims constitute more than 90 percent of the population. The great majority is Malikite Sufi; the main orders represented are Tijaniyah, Qadiriyah, and Muridiyah. Sufi orders pray together at common mosques. There also are a small number of non-Sufi Muslims, including members of the Ahmadiyya order and some immigrants from South Asia.

An estimated 9 percent of the population is Christian, and less than 1 percent practices indigenous animist religious beliefs. The Christian community, situated mostly in the west and south, is predominantly Roman Catholic; there are also Anglicans, Methodists, Baptists, Seventh-day Adventists, Jehovah's Witnesses, and members of various evangelical denominations. There is a small group of Baha'is and a small community of Hindus among South Asian immigrants and business persons.

HISTORY

The Gambia was once part of the Mali and Kaabu Empires. The first written accounts of the region come from records of Arab traders in the 9th and 10th centuries A.D. Arab traders established the trans-Saharan trade route for slaves, gold, and ivory. In the 15th century, the Portuguese took over this trade using maritime routes. At that time, The Gambia was part of the Kingdom of Mali.

In 1588, the claimant to the Portuguese throne, Antonio, Prior of Crato, sold exclusive trade rights on The Gambia River to English merchants; this grant was confirmed by letters patent from Queen Elizabeth I. In 1618, King James I granted a charter to a British company for trade with The Gambia and the Gold Coast (now Ghana). During the late 17th century and throughout the 18th, England and France struggled continuously for political and commercial supremacy in the regions of the Senegal and Gambia Rivers. The 1783 Treaty of Versailles gave Great Britain possession of The Gambia, but the French retained a tiny enclave at Albreda on the north bank of the river, which was ceded to the United Kingdom in 1857.

As many as 3 million slaves may have been taken from the region during the 3 centuries that the transatlantic slave trade operated. It is not known how many slaves were taken by Arab traders prior to and simultaneous with the transatlantic slave trade. Most of those taken were sold to Europeans by other Africans; some were prisoners of intertribal wars; some were sold because of unpaid debts, while others were kidnapped. Slaves were initially sent to Europe to work as servants until the market for labor expanded in the West Indies and North America in the 18th century. In 1807, slave trading was abolished throughout the British Empire, and the British tried unsuccessfully to end the slave traffic in The Gambia. They established the military post of Bathurst (now Banjul) in 1816. In the ensuing years, Banjul was at times under the jurisdiction of the British governor general in Sierra Leone. In 1888, The Gambia became a separate colonial entity. An 1889 agreement with France established the present boundaries, and The Gambia became a British Crown Colony, divided for administrative purposes into the colony (city of Banjul and the surrounding area) and the protectorate (remainder of the territory). The Gambia received its own executive and legislative councils in 1901 and gradually progressed toward self-government. A 1906 ordinance abolished slavery.

During World War II, Gambian troops fought with the Allies in Burma. Banjul served as an air stop for the U.S. Army Air Corps and a port of call for Allied naval convoys. U.S. President Franklin D. Roosevelt stopped overnight in Banjul en route to and from the Casablanca Conference in 1943, marking the first visit to the African Continent by an American president while in office.

After World War II, the pace of constitutional reform quickened. Following general elections in 1962, full internal self-government was granted in 1963. The Gambia achieved independence on February 18, 1965, as a constitutional monarchy within the British Commonwealth. Shortly thereafter, the government proposed conversion from a monarchy to a republic with an elected president replacing the British monarch as chief of state. The proposal failed to receive the two-thirds majority required to amend the constitution, but the results won widespread attention abroad as testimony to The Gambia's observance of secret balloting, honest elections, and civil rights and liberties. On April 24, 1970, The Gambia became a republic following a referendum.

Until a military coup in July 1994, The Gambia was led by President Sir Dawda Kairaba Jawara, who was re-elected five times. The relative stability of the Jawara era was first broken by a violent, unsuccessful coup attempt in 1981. The coup was led by Kukoi Samba Sanyang, who, on two occasions, had unsuccessfully sought election to parliament. After a week of violence which left several hundred

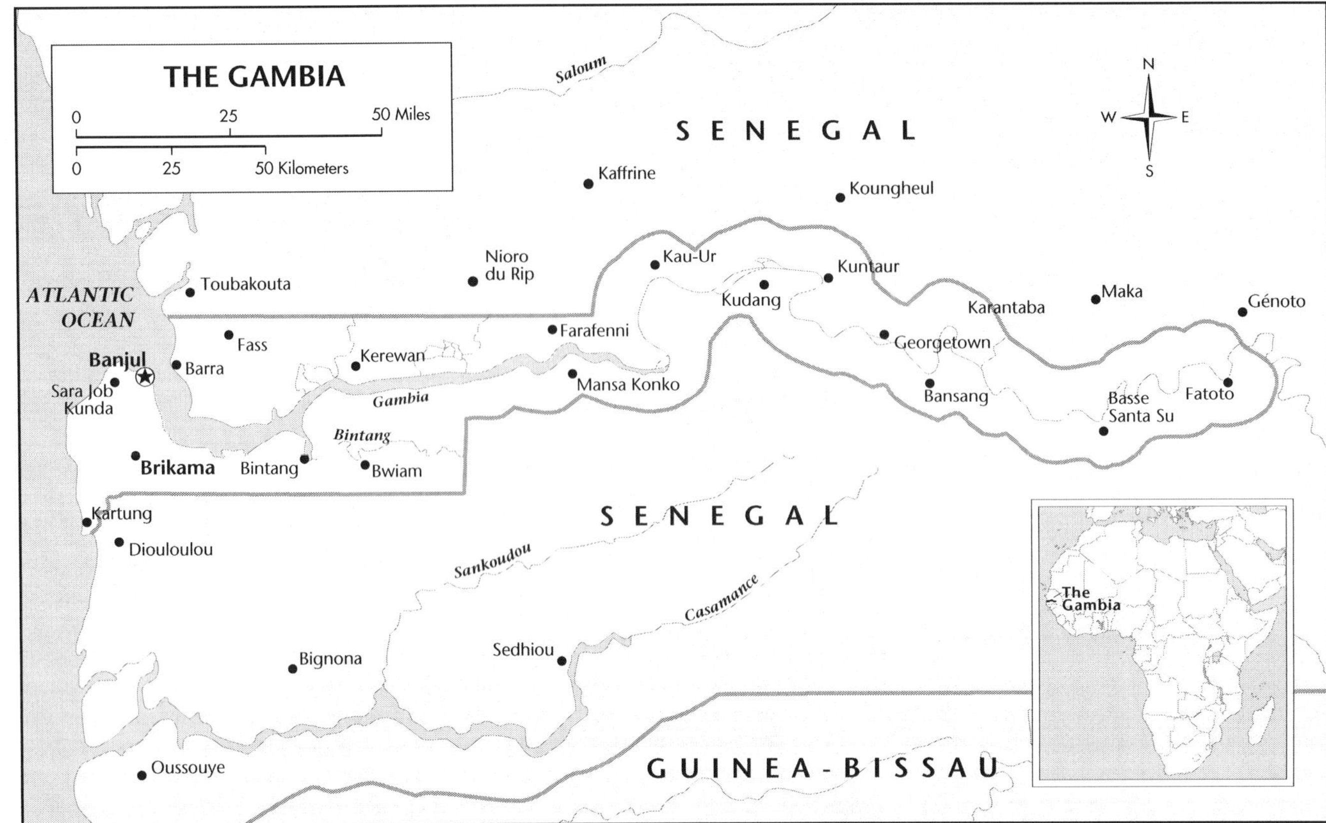

dead, President Jawara, in London when the attack began, appealed to Senegal for help. Senegalese troops defeated the rebel force.

In the aftermath of the attempted coup, Senegal and The Gambia signed the 1982 Treaty of Confederation. The result, the Senegambia Confederation, aimed eventually to combine the armed forces of the two nations and to unify economies and currencies. The Gambia withdrew from the confederation in 1989.

In July 1994, the Armed Forces Provisional Ruling Council (AFPRC) seized power in a military coup d'etat, deposing the government of Sir Dawda Jawara. Lieutenant Yahya A.J.J. Jammeh, chairman of the AFPRC, became head of state. The AFPRC announced a transition plan for return to democratic civilian government. The Provisional Independent Electoral Commission (PIEC) was established in 1996 to conduct national elections. The transition process included the compilation of a new electoral register, adoption of a new constitution by referendum in August 1996, and presidential and legislative elections in September 1996 and January 1997, respectively. Foreign observers did not deem these elections free and fair. Retired Col. Yahya A.J.J. Jammeh was sworn into office as President of the Republic of The Gambia in November 1996. The PIEC was transformed to the Independent Electoral Commission (IEC) in 1997 and became responsible for registration of voters and conduct of elections and referenda.

In late 2001 and early 2002, The Gambia completed a full cycle of presidential, legislative, and local elections, which foreign observers deemed free, fair, and transparent, albeit with some shortcomings. President Yahya Jammeh, who was re-elected, took the oath of office again on December 21, 2001. The APRC maintained its strong majority in the National Assembly, particularly after the main opposition United Democratic Party (UDP) boycotted the legislative elections. President Jammeh was re-elected for a third 5-year term on September 22, 2006 with 67% of the vote. The UDP received 27% of the vote, and instead of boycotting future elections, vowed to take part in the 2007 National Assembly elections. In the January 2007 parliamentary elections the ruling Alliance for Patriotic Reorientation and Construction (APRC) won 42 of the available 48 elected seats.

GOVERNMENT AND POLITICAL CONDITIONS

The Gambia is a multiparty democratic republic. On November 25, voters reelected President Alhaji Yahya Jammeh to a fourth term in a peaceful, orderly election that was neither free nor fair. President Jammeh's party, the Alliance for Patriotic Reorientation and Construction (APRC), continued to dominate the political landscape. There were instances in which elements of the security forces acted independently of civilian control.

Recent Elections

On November 24, 2011, voters reelected President Jammeh to a fourth term with 72 percent of the vote. The election was peaceful and orderly, and more than 83 percent of voters participated. UDP leader Ousainu Darboe came in second with 17 percent, and independent candidate Hamat Bah received 11 percent.

Prior to the election, ECOWAS said its investigations found "an opposition and electorate cowed by repression and intimidation." Explaining its decision not to send election observers, ECOWAS added that the preparations and political environment were not conducive to the conduct of free, fair, and transparent polls. Mustapha Carayol, the chairman of the Independent Electoral Commission, characterized the ECOWAS criticism as lies.

Other government sources claimed the ECOWAS boycott was the result of a personal dispute rather than based on fact. The opposition criticized government control of the state-owned media, a shortened official campaign period, use of state resources by the ruling party, and the overt participation in political activity by government officials and members of the security forces. However, the UDP and its alliance partners did not challenge election results in court, claiming that they were not given sufficient time to do so.

Political Parties: President Jammeh's party, the APRC, held 42 of 48 seats in the National Assembly and continued to dominate the political landscape. APRC membership conferred advantages, such as expediting government transactions, facilitating access to certain documents, and securing employment contracts.

Participation of Women and Minorities: There were four women in the 53-seat National Assembly; two were elected and two were nominated by the president. At the end of 2011, there were five women in the 16-member cabinet, including the vice president. No statistics were available on the percentage of minorities included in the legislature or the cabinet. However, President Jammeh and many members of his administration were from the minority Jola ethnic group.

Principal Government Officials

Last Updated: 1/31/2013

Pres.: **Yahya JAMMEH**

Vice Pres.: **Isatou NJIE-SAIDY**

Min. of Agriculture: **Khalifa KAMBI**

Min. of Basic & Secondary Education: **Fatou Lamin FAYE**

Min. of Communications, Information, & Technology: **Alhaji Abdoulie CHAM**

Min. of Defense: **Yahya JAMMEH**

Min. of Finance & Economic Affairs: **Abdou KOLLEY**

Min. of Fisheries, Water Resources, & National Assembly Matters: **Mamadou TANGARA**

Min. of Foreign Affairs, Intl. Cooperation, & Gambians Abroad: **Mambury NJIE**

Min. of Forestry & Environment: **Jato SILLAH**

Min. of Health & Social Welfare: **Fatim BADJIE**

Min. of Higher Education & Research, Science, & Technology: **Mariama SARR-CEESAY**

Min. of Interior: **Ousman SONKO**

Min. of Justice & Attorney Gen.: **Edward GOMEZ**

Min. of Local Govt. & Lands: **Pierre Biram TAMBA**

Min. of Petroleum & Mineral Resources: **Teneng M. JAITEH**

Min. of Tourism & Culture: **Fatou Mas JOBE-NJIE**

Min. of Trade, Regional Integration, & Employment: **Abdou KOLLEY**

Min. of Women's Affairs: **Isatou NJIE-SAIDY**

Min. of Works, Construction, & Infrastructure: **Njogou L. BAH**

Min. of Youth & Sports: **Sheriff M. L. GOMEZ**

Ambassador to the US: **Alieu Momodou NGUM**

Permanent Representative to the UN, New York: **Susan WAFFA-OGOO**

ECONOMY

The Gambia has sparse natural resource deposits and a limited agricultural base, and relies in part on remittances from workers overseas and tourist receipts. About three-quarters of the population depends on the agricultural sector for its livelihood and the sector provides for about one-quarter of GDP. The agricultural sector has untapped potential - less than half of arable land is cultivated. Small-scale manufacturing activity features the processing of peanuts, fish, and hides.

The Gambia's natural beauty and proximity to Europe has made it one of the larger markets for tourism in West Africa, boosted by government and private sector investments in eco-tourism and upscale facilities. In 2012, however, sluggish tourism led to a decline in GDP. Tourism brings in about one-fifth of GDP. Agriculture also took a hit in 2012 due to unfavorable weather patterns.

The Gambia's re-export trade accounts for almost 80% of goods exports. Unemployment and underemployment rates remain high. Economic progress depends on sustained bilateral and multilateral aid, on responsible government economic management, and on continued technical assistance from multilateral and bilateral donors. International donors and lenders continue to be concerned about the quality of fiscal management and The Gambia's debt burden.

Labor Conditions

The constitution prohibits economic exploitation of children under 16 years of age, and the law prohibits exploitive labor or hazardous employment of children under the age of 18; however, the government did not effectively enforce the law. The Children's Act sets the minimum age for light work at 16 years and for apprenticeship in the informal sector at 12 years. Most children completed their formal education by the age of 14 and then began work. The law implicitly applies only to the formal sector.

Child labor in the informal sector was difficult to regulate. Rising costs of school fees combined with stagnating incomes prohibited some families from sending their children to school, contributing to child labor. In urban areas some children worked as street vendors, domestics, or taxi and bus assistants. Other sectors where children between the ages of 14 and 17 were known to work include carpentry, masonry, plumbing, tailoring, and auto repair. Children in rural areas worked on family farms.

The minimum wage was 50 dalasi ($1.75) per day, although this only covered the 20 percent of the workforce employed in the formal sector. The government considered the national poverty baseline to be 38 dalasi ($1.33) per person per day. Most workers were paid above the minimum wage. The Department of Labor is responsible for enforcing the minimum wage. A majority of workers were employed privately or were self-employed, often in agriculture. Most citizens did not live on a single worker's earnings and shared resources within extended families.

The basic legal workweek is 48 hours within a period not to exceed six consecutive days. Nationwide the workweek included four eight-hour workdays and two four-hour workdays (Friday and Saturday). There are no limits on hours worked per week and no prohibition of excessive compulsory overtime.

A 30-minute lunch break is mandated. Government employees are entitled to one month of paid annual leave after one year of service. Most government employees were not paid overtime. However, government workers holding temporary positions and private sector workers received overtime pay calculated per hour. Private sector employees received between 14 and 30 days of paid annual leave, depending on length of service. There was no exception for foreign or migrant workers.

The Department of Labor effectively enforced the wage law and workweek standards when cases were brought to its attention.

U.S.-GAMBIAN RELATIONS

During World War II, Gambian troops fought with the Allies in Burma. The Gambia's capital city served as an air stop for the U.S. Army Air Corps and a port of call for Allied naval convoys. The Gambia became independent from the United Kingdom in 1965. The country has been headed by the same president since he took power in a 1994 military coup d'etat. Presidential elections have been held every 5 years since 1996. U.S. policy seeks to build improved relations with The Gambia on the basis of historical ties; mutual respect; democratic rule; human rights; and adherence to United Nations resolutions on counterterrorism, conflict diamonds, and other forms of trafficking.

U.S. Assistance to The Gambia

U.S. assistance supports democracy, human rights, girls' education, and the fight against HIV/AIDS. In addition, the Peace Corps maintains a large program with about 100 volunteers engaged in the environment, public health, and education sectors, mainly at the village level. The United States also provides military assistance to The Gambia.

Bilateral Economic Relations

The Gambia is eligible for preferential trade benefits under the African Growth and Opportunity Act. A number of U.S. citizens have set up small businesses in The Gambia and several U.S. brand companies such as Western Union, MoneyGram, UPS, Sheraton, Motorola, and Coca Cola are represented there.

The Gambia's Membership in International Organizations

The Gambia plays an active role in international affairs, especially West African and Islamic affairs. The Gambia and the United States belong to a number of the same international organizations, including the United Nations, International Monetary Fund, World Bank, and World Trade Organization.

Bilateral Representation

The Gambia maintains an embassy at 2233 Wisconsin Avenue, NW, Suite 240, Washington, DC 20007. Tel. (202) 785-1399.

Principal U.S. Embassy Officials

Last Updated: 1/14/2013

BANJUL (E) Kairaba Avenue, Fajara PMB 19, [220] 439-2856, Fax [220] 439-2475, Workweek: Monday-Thursday 0800-1730, Friday 0800-1200, http://banjul.usembassy.gov/

AMB OMS:	Michelle Donnelly
HRO:	Karolyn Pifer
MGT:	Jason Brenden
POL/ECON:	Stubbs John
POSHO:	Kerrie Nanni
AMB:	Edward Alford
CON:	Andrew Utschig
DCM:	Richard Yoneoka
PAO:	Joshua Shrager
GSO:	Nanni, Kerrie
RSO:	Tommy Jones
CLO:	Lovette Singleton
EEO:	Andrew Utschig
FMO:	Daniel Driggers
ICASS Chair:	Wilson Keverenge
IMO:	Dwayne Singleton
ISSO:	Wilson Keverenge

TRAVEL

Consular Information Sheet

June 1, 2011

Country Description: The Gambia is a developing country in western Africa. Its capital is Banjul. The official language is English, but many inhabitants speak indigeneous languages such as Wolof or Mandinka. Facilities for tourism in the Banjul area are good; however, outside the capital region tourist facilities are limited in availability and quality.

Smart Traveler Enrollment Program (STEP)/Embassy Locations: If you are going to live in, or visit, The Gambia, please take the time to tell our Embassy about your trip. If you register online, we can keep you up to date with important safety and security announcements. It will also help your friends and family get in touch with you in an emergency.

U.S. Embassy Banjul
Address:
The U.S. Embassy is located 92 Kairaba Avenue in Fajara, a suburb of the capital city of Banjul.
The mailing address is P.M.B.19, Banjul, The Gambia.
Telephone: 220-439-2856,
220-439-2858 and 220-439-1971
(Available 24 hours a day.)
Facsimile: 220-439-2475.

Entry/Exit Requirements for U.S. Citizens: A passport, visa, and evidence of yellow fever vaccination are required. The current fee for a five-year visa for U.S. citizens is $100. The Gambian government requires a visa if a traveler resides in a country which has a Gambian Embassy, the only exception being for those travelling on chartered tourist flights. If you enter The Gambia without a visa, you will most likely be allowed to enter, but given only two working days in which to obtain a visa from the Department of Immigration in downtown Banjul. To avoid this hassle, the Embassy strongly recommends that travelers obtain visas before leaving the U.S.

New Fee: The Gambia has begun charging an "airport development" fee of 20 Euros (or its equivalent in Dollars or Dalasi) in cash from all departing travelers. Travelers are urged to obtain the latest information on customs and entry requirements from the Embassy of The Gambia,, 2233 Wisconsin Avenue, NW, Suite 240, Georgetown Plaza Washington, DC 20007; telephone (202) 785-1399, -1379, -1425 fax (202) 785-1430; or from the Permanent Mission of The Gambia to the U.N. at 800 Second Avenue, Suite 400-F, New York, NY, 10017; Telephone (212) 949-6640 or Fax: (212) 856-9820. Overseas, inquiries should be made at the nearest Gambian embassy or consulate. Visit the Embassy of The Gambia website for the most current visa information.

The U.S. Department of State is unaware of any HIV/AIDS entry restrictions for visitors to or foreign residents of The Gambia.

Threats to Safety and Security: The Gambia has not experienced any acts of terrorism or large scale violence; however, much of its southern region borders the Casamance region of Senegal, which is home to a long-running low-intensity conflict. Like most countries in the region, conditions are always subject to change and travelers should check with the U.S. Embassy if they have specific concerns. Demonstrations are rare in The Gambia. Travelers driving a vehicle in The Gambia are obligated to stop at all roadblocks or road checkpoints in the country. Drivers should not reverse direction to avoid a road checkpoint or make any movements that security personnel may view as suspicious or provocative.

For travel to the nearby Casamance region of Senegal, please see the Country Specific Information for Senegal.

Stay up to date by bookmarking our Bureau of Consular Affairs website, which contains the current Travel Warnings and Travel Alerts as well as the Worldwide Caution. Follow us on Twitter and the Bureau of Consular Affairs page on Facebook as well. You can also call 1-888-407-4747 toll-free within the United States and Canada, or 1-202-501-4444 by regular toll line from other countries. These numbers are available from 8 a.m. to 8 p.m. Eastern Time, Monday through Friday (except U.S. federal holidays). Take some time before travel to improve your personal security—things are not the same everywhere as they are in the United States.

Crime: Petty street crime is a problem in The Gambia. Travelers should be careful of pickpockets in crowded markets areas and on ferries. Packages or luggage should never be left unattended, especially in taxis. U.S. citizens in The Gambia should be careful not to leave valuables or identity documents unsecured in hotel rooms or cars. Travelers should also be cautious of individuals who persistently offer unsolicited help.

Visitors and resident U.S. citizens should leave their windows up and doors locked while driving due to several reported automobile burglaries, including theft from occupied cars stopped in traffic with the windows open or doors unlocked. Long-term residents should consider hiring a security guard for their home to prevent burglary and theft. Women should avoid walking alone especially after dark, including in beach and tourist areas. In addition, female visitors to The Gambia should be particularly cautious of men locally known as "bumsters," who approach females wishing "just to get to know you" or offering to be tour guides. Bumsters often use romance in hopes of gaining money and other assistance, or in the hope of departing The Gambia through marriage to a Westerner. Travelers are advised to be polite but decisive in turning down unwanted help or attempts at conversation.

Business fraud, long associated with other parts of West Africa, has also been reported in The Gambia. The U.S. embassy has received reports of several scams in which U.S. businesses sent, but did not receive, payment for shipments. U.S. citizens should be very suspicious of any unsolicited offers to participate in lucrative business opportunities, especially if they require financial disclosures, money transfers, large up-front investments or promises of confidentiality. The best way to avoid becoming a victim of fraud is common sense—if it looks too good to be true, it probably is. You should be suspicious of any unsolicited business proposal originating in The Gambia. Carefully scrutinize all proposals before you commit any funds, provide any goods or services, or undertake any travel. For additional information, please see the Department of State's information on International Financial Scams.

The U.S. Embassy has also been contacted by several victims of romantic Internet scams perpetrated in The Gambia. Generally, a U.S. citizen befriends someone or gets engaged to someone over the Internet. This person, who can claims to be a U.S. citizen or a Gambian citizen, eventually requests financial assistance from the U.S. citizen to help pay for urgent medical treatment, to tide him or her over after a recent robbery, or to pay some form of alleged exit tax or government fine. In the vast majority of cases, the person with whom the U.S. citizen has been corresponding is using a fake identity and is in no need of assistance. In general, U.S. citizens are advised not to send money to anyone they have not met in person.

Don't buy counterfeit and pirated goods, even if they are widely available. Not only are the bootlegs illegal in the United States, you may be breaking local law too.

Victims of Crime: If you or someone you know becomes the victim of a crime abroad, you should contact the local police and the nearest U.S. embassy (see the Department of State list of embassies and consulates). If your passport is stolen we can help you replace it. For violent crimes such as assault and rape, we can help you find appropriate medical care, contact family members or friends, and help them send you money if needed. Although the investigation and prosecution of the crime are solely the responsibility of local authorities, consular officers can help you understand the local criminal justice process and find an attorney, if needed. Please contact the U.S. Embassy in Banjul for a list of lawyers practicing in The Gambia, or visit the Embassy's website.

The local equivalent to the "911" emergency line in The Gambia is 116 for Ambulatory services, 117 for police assistance, and 118 for fire. The Gambian Police Force operates another 24 hour emergency line at (220) 422-4914. Please be advised that the emergency numbers listed may or may not have an English-speaking operator available.

Criminal Penalties: While you are traveling in The Gambia, you are subject to its laws even if you are a U.S. citizen. Foreign laws and legal systems can be vastly different than our own. In some places you may be taken in for questioning if you don't have your passport with you. In some places, it is illegal to take pictures of certain buildings. In some places, driving under the influence could land you immediately in jail. These criminal penalties will vary from country to country. There are also some things that might be legal in the country you visit, but still illegal in the United States; for instance, you can be prosecuted under U.S. law if you buy pirated goods. Engaging in sexual conduct with children, or using or disseminating child pornography in a foreign country, is a crime and is prosecutable in the United States. If you break local laws in The Gambia, your U.S. passport won't help you avoid arrest or prosecution. It is very important to know what is legal and what is not wherever you are traveling.

The Gambia is a party to a bilateral agreement that requires mandatory notification.

If you are arrested in The Gambia, The Gambian authorities are required to notify the U.S. embassy of your arrest. If you are concerned that the Department of State may not be aware of your situation, you should request the police or prison officials to notify the U.S. embassy of your arrest.

Special Circumstances: In addition to being subject to all of The Gambia's laws affecting foreigners, U.S. citizens who are also Gambian citizens may be subject to additional provisions of Gambian law while in The Gambia. Dual nationals should inquire at a Gambian embassy or consulate regarding their status.

In May 2008, Gambian government leaders, including the country's president, strongly condemned homosexuality and advocated for greatly increased penalties for anyone harboring homosexuals. However, no legislative action has resulted. The Gambia's existing laws already criminalize homosexual sex acts, but current laws do not include the death penalty. Violations of the laws against homosexual sex acts are occasionally pursued and Gambian citizens have been prosecuted under these laws. In June 2008, two Western tourists were detained but not charged under this section of the criminal code.

The Gambia has strict laws on the import and export of skin-bleaching creams and some medications. Visitors who arrive with substances containing 1% or more of: hydroquinone (in any form), hydrocortisone (unless in trace amounts and for specific purposes such anti-itch products), betamethasone, flucinonide, clobestatol, or clobestatone are subject to fines up to $2,000 and/or three years imprisonment. Airport police and customs officials routinely inspect incoming and outgoing luggage. Airline passengers are required to put their luggage through an x-ray machine before departing the airport. Travelers in possession of prescription drugs should carry proof of their prescriptions, such as labeled containers. Police have, on occasion, arrested foreigners carrying unlabeled pills. For a list of prohibited items, travelers should contact the nearest Gambian embassy or consulate.

It is against the law for tourists to photograph or film government buildings, including airports, military installations or embassies due to security concerns.

The Gambia's currency, the dalasi, is freely convertible but is not widely available outside the country. The Gambia has a cash economy and travelers should carry sufficient currency to cover all expenses for their visit. Visitors can exchange currency at banks or exchange bureaus. Changing money unofficially is prohibited and individuals who do so may face prosecution. Travelers should be aware that The Gambia has many last-minute holidays requiring banks and other businesses to close. Travelers should always have enough cash to carry them through unexpected bank closures. Credit cards are accepted only at major hotels, some grocery stores, and a few restaurants. Local personal checks from U.S. citizens are accepted only at exchange bureaus and only from U.S. citizens who are resident in The Gambia. There are a few ATMs in the Banjul area, but they often malfunction or fail to issue receipts. ATMs only accept VISA cards for international transactions and only dispense a maximum of about $140.00 (in local currency) per transaction, with three transactions allowed per day. Money transfers are widely available at Western Union branch offices in The Gambia.

Accessibility: While in The Gambia, individuals with disabilities may find accessibility and accommodation to be different from the United States. As per Department of State's Human Rights Report, the Gambian constitution protects persons with disabilities in terms of access to health services, education, and employment. However, there are no laws to ensure access to buildings for persons with disabilities, and very few buildings in the country are accessible to them.

Medical Facilities and Health Information: Medical facilities in The Gambia are very limited, some treatments are unavailable, and emergency services can be unpredictable and unreliable. Travelers should carry their own supplies of prescription, as well as over-the-counter medicines or treatments.

You can find good information on vaccinations and other health precautions on the CDC website. For information about outbreaks of infectious diseases abroad, consult the World Health Organization (WHO) website. The WHO website also contains additional health information for travelers, including detailed country-specific health information.

Malaria is a serious risk to travelers in The Gambia. Travelers who become ill with a fever or flu-like illness while traveling in a malaria-risk area (and for up to one year after returning home) should seek prompt medical attention and tell the physician their travel history, as well as what anti-malarial medications they have been taking. For additional information on malaria, protection from insect bites, and anti-malarial drugs, visit the CDC website.

Medical Insurance: You can't assume your insurance will go with you when you travel. It's very important to find out BEFORE you leave whether or not your medical insurance will cover you overseas. You need to ask your insurance company two questions:

- Does my policy apply when I'm out of the United States?
- Will it cover emergencies like a trip to a foreign hospital or a medical evacuation?

In many places, doctors and hospitals still expect payment in cash (local currency) at the time of service. Your regular U.S. health insurance may not cover doctors' and hospital visits in other countries. If your policy doesn't go with you when you travel, it's a very good idea to take out another one for your trip.

Traffic Safety and Road Conditions: While in The Gambia, you may encounter road conditions that differ significantly from those in the United States. The information below concerning The Gambia is provided for general reference only, and may not be totally accurate in a particular location or circumstance.

Travel in The Gambia is difficult due to poor road conditions, particularly during the rainy season, which generally lasts from June through October. Although there are paved main roads in the greater Banjul area, many are poorly maintained and poorly lit. With the installation of street lights on roads in the Banjul area, some drivers no longer use their vehicle lights at night. Most roads outside the Banjul area are still unlit and unpaved. Caution should be exercised when using taxis, particularly at night. Most taxis lack safety belts and some are not road-worthy. Livestock and pedestrians pose road hazards throughout the country, including in the greater Banjul area. Drivers and pedestrians should exercise extreme caution to prevent accidents.

Numerous accidents are caused by intoxicated drivers. Tests are rarely done to determine levels of intoxication. If you are suspected of causing an accident while intoxicated, and the case is taken to trial, you may be subject to a substantial fine or imprisonment.

The police do not consistently apply traffic laws and regulations, and sometimes compel drivers to pay fines on the spot for violations, real or contrived. Written citations/tickets are rarely given. Police periodically set up impromptu traffic stops on major streets to check for drivers' licenses and proper insurance. Drivers should not attempt to drive around these traffic stops. Government convoys frequently travel at high speeds and often in either or both lanes of traffic, including in the oncoming traffic lane, requiring cars to move off the road. Whenever there are police lights or sirens, drivers should move off the road immediately and completely to avoid collisions. There are no trauma centers in The Gambia and severe accidents often require evacuation to Senegal or Europe.

Water transportation in the region can be unpredictable and risky. Ferries rarely keep to their posted schedules. The ferries, which are often overcrowded, usually lack sufficient numbers of life preservers for all passengers. In particular, the wooden dugout "pirogues" that cross the Gambia River often leave shore overloaded and occasionally sink in the middle of the river. U.S. citizens are advised to exit their cars during the crossing. U.S. citizens who must cross the Gambia River are advised to use the Gambia Port Authority's Banjul-Barra or Yelitenda-Farafenni ferries, which are slower but safer than the privately operated pirogues.

Aviation Safety Oversight: The U.S. Federal Aviation Administration (FAA) has assessed the government of The Gambia's Civil Aviation

Authority as not being in compliance with International Civil Aviation Organization (ICAO) aviation safety standards for oversight of The Gambia's air carrier operations. Further information may be found on the FAA safety assessment page.

Gambian airlines do not offer service to the United States. Services provided by the West African regional air carriers that service Banjul are sometimes unreliable. The airlines are known to alter scheduled stops, cancel or postpone flights on short notice, and regularly overbook flights. Travelers may experience unexpected delays even after check-in, and should be prepared to handle alternate ticketing and/or increased food and lodging expenses.

Children's Issues: Please see the U.S. Dept. of State Office of Children's Issues web pages on intercountry adoption and international parental child abduction.

Intercountry Adoption

July 2012

The Gambia is not party to the Hague Convention on Protection of Children and Co-operation in Respect of Intercountry Adoption (Hague Adoption Convention). Intercountry adoptions of children from non-Hague countries are processed in accordance with 8 Code of Federal Regulations, Section 204.3 as it relates to orphans as defined under the Immigration and Nationality Act, Section 101(b)(1)(F).

Below is the limited adoption information that the Department has obtained from the adoption authority of the Gambia. U.S. citizens adopting children in rare adoption cases from the Gambia, as well as U.S. citizen prospective adoptive parents living in The Gambia who would like to adopt from the United States or from a third country, should contact the adoption authority of the Gambia to inquire about applicable laws and procedures. See contact information below.

Foreigners are allowed to adopt Gambian children only in exceptional circumstances. Prospective adoptive parents usually must be resident in The Gambia at least six months prior to applying to adopt. The U.S. Embassy in Dakar, Senegal issues immigrant visas for Gambian citizens, including adopted orphans.

Prospective adoptive parents should be aware that not all children in orphanages or children's homes are adoptable. In many countries, birth parents place their child(ren) temporarily in an orphanage or children's home due to financial or other hardship, intending that the child return home when this becomes possible. In such cases, the birth parent(s) have rarely relinquished their parental rights or consented to their child(ren)'s adoption.

The Gambian Adoption Authority
The Kanifing Children's Court
Address: Mamadi Maniyang Highway, Kanifing, KMC, The Gambia
Tel: +(220) 437-4525 or 439-2202

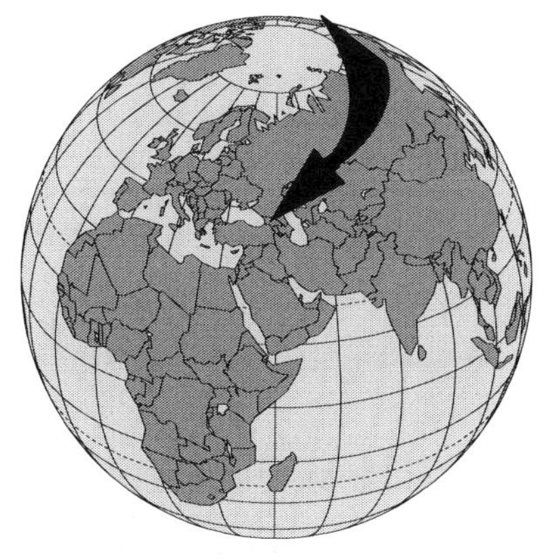

GEORGIA

Compiled from publications that were available as of February 2013 from the U.S. Department of State, the U.S. Department of Commerce, and the Central Intelligence Agency (CIA). See the introduction to this set for explanatory notes.

Official Name:
Republic of Georgia

PROFILE

Geography

Area: total: 69,700 sq km; country comparison to the world: 121; land: 69,700 sq km; water: 0 sq km
Major cities: Tbilisi (capital) 1.115 million (2009)
Climate: warm and pleasant; Mediterranean-like on Black Sea coast
Terrain: largely mountainous with Great Caucasus Mountains in the north and Lesser Caucasus Mountains in the south; Kolkhet'is Dablobi (Kolkhida Lowland) opens to the Black Sea in the west; Mtkvari River Basin in the east; good soils in river valley flood plains, foothills of Kolkhida Lowland

People

Nationality: noun: Georgian(s); adjective: Georgian
Population: 4,570,934 (July 2012 est.)
Population growth rate: -0.327% (2012 est.)
Ethnic groups: Georgian 83.8%, Azeri 6.5%, Armenian 5.7%, Russian 1.5%, other 2.5% (2002 census)
Religions: Orthodox Christian (official) 83.9%, Muslim 9.9%, Armenian-Gregorian 3.9%, Catholic 0.8%, other 0.8%, none 0.7% (2002 census)
Languages: Georgian (official) 71%, Russian 9%, Armenian 7%, Azeri 6%, other 7%
Literacy: definition: age 15 and over can read and write; total population: 99.7%; male: 99.8%; female: 99.7% (2010 est.)
Health: life expectancy at birth: total population: 77.32 years; male: 73.99 years; female: 81 years (2012 est.); Infant mortality rate: total: 14.68 deaths/1,000 live births; male: 16.58 deaths/1,000 live births; female: 12.59 deaths/1,000 live births (2012 est.)
Unemployment rate: 16.3% (2010 est.)
Work force: 1.945 million (2010 est.)

Government

Type: republic
Independence: 9 April 1991
Constitution: adopted 24 August 1995
Political subdivisions: 9 regions (mkharebi, singular—mkhare), 1 city (k'alak'i), and 2 autonomous republics (avtomnoy respubliki, singular—avtom respublika)
Suffrage: 18 years of age; universal

Economy

GDP (purchasing power parity): $26.4 billion (2012 est.); $24.86 billion (2011 est.); $23.24 billion (2010 est.); $21.87 billion (2009 est.)
GDP real growth rate: 6% (2012 est.); 7% (2011 est.); 6.3% (2010 est.); -3.8% (2009 est.)
GDP per capita (PPP): $5,900 (2012 est.); $5,600 (2011 est.); $5,200 (2010 est.); $5,000 (2009 est.)
Natural resources: timber, hydropower, manganese deposits, iron ore, copper, minor coal and oil deposits; coastal climate and soils allow for important tea and citrus growth
Agriculture products: citrus, grapes, tea, hazelnuts, vegetables; livestock
Industries: steel, machine tools, electrical appliances, mining (manganese, copper, and gold), chemicals, wood products, wine
Exports: $3.324 billion (2012 est.); $2.189 billion (2011 est.); $2.462 billion (2010 est.)
Exports—commodities: vehicles, ferro-alloys, fertilizers, nuts, scrap metal, gold, copper ores
Exports—partners: Azerbaijan 17.5%, Turkey 10.5%, Armenia 10%, Kazakhstan 7.3%, Ukraine 6.2%, US 5.5%, Canada 5.2%, Bulgaria 4.7% (2011)
Imports: $6.623 billion (2012 est.); $7.058 billion (2011 est.); $5.049 billion (2010 est.)
Imports—commodities: fuels, vehicles, machinery and parts, grain and other foods, pharmaceuticals

Imports—partners: Turkey 17.8%, Ukraine 10%, Azerbaijan 8.3%, China 7.6%, Germany 6.9%, Russia 5.7% (2011)
Debt—external: $8.2 billion (31 December 2012); $11.08 billion (31 December 2011); $10.77 billion (31 December 2010)
Exchange rates: laris (GEL) per US dollar; 1.66 (2012 est.); 1.6865 (2011 est.); 1.7823 (2010 est.); 1.6705 (2009); 1.47 (2008); 1.7 (2007)

PEOPLE

Language

Georgian, a South Caucasian (or "Kartvelian") language, unrelated to any outside the immediate region, is one of the oldest living languages in the world and has its own distinct alphabet. The official language is Georgian, but almost all business executives speak Russian. English is the most widely used language after Russian, and is gaining in popularity.

Ethnic Armenians, Azeris, Abkhaz, South Ossetians, and Russians usually communicated in their native languages or in Russian in the areas where they were the dominant ethnic groups. The law requires that ethnic minority students learn Georgian as a second language. The government continued to provide education in the state language and minority languages in minority regions.

Religion

In the early 4th century, Georgia became the second nation in the world to officially adopt Christianity. Most ethnic Georgians (84 percent of the population, according to the 2002 census) associate with the Georgian Orthodox Church. There are also a small number of mostly ethnic Russian adherents of several dissident Orthodox schools not affiliated with the GOC, including the Molokani, Staroveriy (Old Believers), and Dukhoboriy (Spirit Wrestlers).

The Armenian Apostolic Church (AAC), the Roman Catholic Church (RCC), Judaism, and Islam have coexisted with Georgian Orthodoxy for centuries. There are strong correlations between ethnicity, religious affiliation, and region of residence. Overall, 10 percent of the population is Muslim. Azeris, who are predominantly Muslim, constitute the second largest ethnic group (7 percent of the population) and form the majority of the population in the southeastern region of Kvemo-Kartli. Other Muslim groups include the ethnic Georgian Muslims of Ajara and Chechen Kists in the northeastern region. Armenians are the third largest ethnic group (6 percent of the population) and primarily belong to the AAC; they constitute the majority of the population in the southern Samtskhe-Javakheti region.

Roman Catholics, Kurdish Yezidis, Greek Orthodox, and Jews together make up less than 5 percent of the population. Protestant and other "nontraditional" denominations such as Baptists, Jehovah's Witnesses, Pentecostals, and Hare Krishnas, who are growing in number, constitute less than 1 percent of the population.

HISTORY

Georgia has historically been situated on the margins of great empires, and Georgians have lived together in a unified state for only a fraction of their existence as a people. Since at least the 1st century B.C. through the 18th century, much of Georgia's territory was fought over by Persian, Roman, Byzantine, Arab, Mongol, and Turkish armies. The zenith of Georgia's power as an independent kingdom came in the 11th and 12th centuries, during the reigns of King David the Builder and Queen Tamar, who rank among the most celebrated of all Georgian rulers.

In 1783, the king of Kartli (in eastern Georgia) signed the Treaty of Georgievsk with the Russians, by which Russia agreed to take the kingdom as its protectorate. In 1801, the Russian empire began the piecemeal process of unifying and annexing Georgian territory, and for most of the next 2 centuries (1801–1991) Georgia was ruled from St. Petersburg or Moscow. Exposed to modern European ideas of nationalism under Russian tutelage, Georgians, like the influential writer Ilya Chavchavadze, began calling for greater Georgian independence.

The independent Republic of Georgia was established on May 26, 1918, in the wake of the Russian Revolution. Pro-Menshevik president Noe Zhordania and a social-democratic government led the country until March 1921, when it was occupied by the Bolshevik Red Army. Georgia became a Soviet Socialist Republic the following year. Several of the Soviet Union's most well-known leaders in the 1920s and 1930s were Georgian, such as Joseph Stalin, Sergo Orjonikidze, and Lavrenti Beria, the head of Stalin's secret police. During the Soviet period, Georgia was one of the wealthiest and most privileged republics, and its Black Sea coastline was a popular holiday destination for the Soviet elite. On April 9, 1991, shortly before the collapse of the Soviet Union, the Supreme Council of the Republic of Georgia declared independence from the U.S.S.R.

Like other former Soviet Republics, Georgia's newly declared independence was followed by ethnic and civil strife. Secessionists took control of parts of South Ossetia and most of Abkhazia prior to cease-fire agreements brokered in 1992 and 1994, respectively. Georgia began to stabilize in 1995. However, the separatist conflicts in Georgia's regions of Abkhazia and South Ossetia remain unresolved. Periodic flare-ups in tension and violence culminated in a 5-day war in August 2008 between Georgia and Russia. French President Nicolas Sarkozy negotiated a cease-fire between Presidents Mikheil Saakashvili and Dmitriy Medvedev on August 12, 2008, which remains in effect, although Russia has not fulfilled some of its cease-fire commitments, including withdrawal of its forces to pre-war positions. As part of the Saakashvili-Medvedev cease-fire agreement, the European Union established the EU Monitoring Mission (EUMM), which patrols the undisputed Georgian side of the

administrative boundary lines with Abkhazia and South Ossetia but does not have access into those regions of Georgia. The cease-fire also called for international peace talks on the situation, which have taken place regularly in Geneva since October 2008 among the EU, United Nations (UN), Organization for Security and Cooperation in Europe (OSCE), Georgia, Russia, and the United States, with the participation of de facto representatives from Abkhazia and South Ossetia.

In August 2008, Russia recognized the independence of both Abkhazia and South Ossetia. With a handful of exceptions, all other countries, including the United States, have confirmed their continuing support for Georgia's political sovereignty and territorial integrity within its internationally recognized borders.

GOVERNMENT AND POLITICAL CONDITIONS

The constitution of Georgia provides for an executive branch that reports to the president, a unicameral parliament, and an independent judiciary. President Mikheil Saakashvili was reelected in January 2008 in an election that international observers found consistent with most Organization of Security and Cooperation in Europe (OSCE) democratic election commitments. However, the OSCE also highlighted significant problems, including widespread allegations of intimidation and pressure, flawed vote-counting and tabulation processes, and shortcomings in the complaints and appeals process. These and other problems were also seen in parliamentary elections in May 2008, which OSCE observers concluded were uneven and incomplete in their adherence to international standards. Despite a large number of opposition parties, the executive and parliament were dominated by a single party.

De facto authorities in the separatist regions of Abkhazia and South Ossetia remained outside the control of the central government. These authorities continued to be supported by several thousand Russian troops and border guards occupying the areas since the 2008 armed conflict between Russia and Georgia. A cease-fire remained in effect in both Abkhazia and South Ossetia, although incidents of violence occurred in both areas. Russian border guards restricted the movement of the local populations. De facto authorities continued to restrict the rights, primarily of ethnic Georgians, to vote, otherwise participate in the political process, own property, register businesses, and travel. The de facto South Ossetian authorities refused to permit most ethnic Georgians driven out during and after the 2008 conflict to return to South Ossetia. With the exception of the International Committee of the Red Cross (ICRC), international organizations were not allowed regular access to South Ossetia to provide humanitarian assistance.

Recent Elections

International observers found presidential elections in January 2008 consistent with most Organization of Security and Cooperation in Europe (OSCE) democratic election commitments. However, there were significant problems, including widespread allegations of intimidation and pressure, flawed vote-counting and tabulation processes, and shortcomings in the complaints and appeals process. These and other problems also marred parliamentary elections in May 2008, which OSCE observers concluded were uneven and incomplete in their adherence to international standards.

According to the OSCE election observation mission, while the May 2010 municipal elections marked progress towards meeting OSCE and Council of Europe commitments, there were still significant shortcomings, including deficiencies in the legal framework and its implementation, an uneven playing field for candidates, and isolated cases of election-day fraud. Observers reported a variety of violations including instances of likely ballot box stuffing, cases of multiple voting, proxy voting, and series of seemingly identical signatures of voters on voters' lists. The observers also noted procedural violations in one-fifth of the vote counts and one-fourth of the vote tabulations they monitored. The OSCE mission received allegations of violations from opposition parties and NGOs, including reports of pressure on opposition candidates to withdraw. NGOs and opposition parties reported that supervisors pressured government employees to vote for and donate to the ruling party with the implication that failure to do so might result in a loss of employment. The OSCE also reported allegations that businesses were reluctant to donate to some opposition parties due to fear of reprisals. The OSCE mission noted that election materials were available in minority languages but not in all areas inhabited by minorities.

The Ministry of Justice reported five election commission members were charged and convicted of election fraud or election interference in various regions of the country for acts committed during the 2010 municipal elections. In most cases election results for the districts were annulled. The investigation of several cases in Mestia continued.

In preparation for 2012 parliamentary elections, parliament adopted a new electoral code on December 27 which incorporated many recommendations from NGOs and the Venice Commission. The new code provides that any party that receives 5 percent of the total vote would win at least six seats in parliament and be accorded a parliamentary faction and corresponding privileges, prohibits the use of administrative resources for political purposes, improves postelection complaint procedures, reduces residency requirements for candidates for parliament, requires media to treat candidates equitably, and provides financial incentives for parties to increase the number of women on their parliamentary lists. The code also provides for the establishment of a commission to address pre-election complaints beginning in July 2012. However, the new code fails to address the Venice Commission's primary recommendation to strengthen the equality of the vote by reconstituting single mandate election districts to be comparable in size.

Political Parties: There are no legal restrictions on political party formation beyond registration requirements, and the electoral code adopted in December allows an individual to run for office without party affiliation. However, members of some organizations linked to the political opposition asserted that they were unduly singled out for harassment and prosecution. Members of some opposition parties reported threatening calls warning them to refrain from party participation and surveillance by local police from unmarked cars. An NGO reported being filmed while entering a hotel conference room to meet with an opposition party. Opposition party members also alleged teacher dismissals due to party affiliation.

After billionaire Bidzina Ivanishvili announced in October that he intended to establish an opposition political party to compete in the 2012 parliamentary elections, there were reports that government officials targeted individuals and businesses associated with him for politically motivated harassment. In one illustrative example, materials imported by Ivanishvili for business and political purposes were repeatedly and inexplicably found to be damaged following their release from customs. Moreover, representatives from Ivanishvili's Cartu Group reported the percentage of their imports delayed by additional inspection increased from 10 percent to 100 percent since Ivanishvili entered politics. An independent monitoring company contracted by Cartu Group confirmed that Cartu imports were undamaged prior to customs entry and damaged after customs released the cargo.

Pursuant to Article 32 of the Law on Citizenship, the government canceled the Georgian citizenship of Ivanishvili and his wife, Ekaterine Khvedelidze, on October 11, several days after Ivanishvili publicly acknowledged possessing French citizenship while declaring his intention to renounce it. Article 32 provides that a person loses his or her Georgian citizenship if he or she acquires another citizenship. Both Ivanishvili and Khvedelidze challenged their loss of citizenship in court. In a December 27 decision, the Tbilisi City Court found that the government had overreached in the case of Khvedelidze, since she had acquired her Georgian citizenship after her French citizenship, and annulled the government's order revoking her Georgian citizenship. The court upheld the government's decision in the case of Ivanishvili, who had acquired his Georgian citizenship before his French citizenship. Ivanishvili's appeal of the court's decision was pending at year's end.

Opposition-linked individuals and organizations continued to report pressure on potential donors. On December 28, parliament amended the Law on Political Unions to regulate campaign and political party financing. The amended law prohibited corporate donations to political parties and provision of money, goods, or services to voters by parties; required all financial contributions to parties be made by wire transfer to ensure transparency; limited the overall amount a party can receive from public and private sources in a year to 0.2 percent of the country's GDP; and delegated financial oversight of party financing to the government's auditing agency, the Chamber of Control. However, local and international observers raised concerns about several amendments, including the vagueness of the criteria for determining political bribery and which individuals and organizations would be subject to the law.

Participation of Women and Minorities: There were nine women in the 150-seat parliament. One of the seven vice speakers was a woman, as was the chair of parliament's procedural committee. There were three women in the 19-member cabinet and six women on the 19-judge Supreme Court.

According to the final OSCE report on the May 2010 municipal elections, women were underrepresented in leadership positions in the election administration as well as among the candidates for and members of city councils. However, they were well represented in lower-level election commissions. The OSCE mission found that many parties put forward candidates belonging to national minorities and that election materials were made available in minority languages, but not in all areas inhabited by minorities. The new electoral code provided financial incentives for parties to increase the number of women on their parliamentary lists, as recommended by the Venice Commission.

There were three ethnic Armenians and three ethnic Azeris in parliament, as well as one member of a minority in the cabinet. There were no members of minorities in the Supreme Court or Constitutional Court. Higher-level city managers included ethnic minority leaders.

The de facto authorities in Abkhazia continued to restrict the rights of citizens to vote and to participate in the political process through a "citizenship" law that forced ethnic Georgians to give up their Georgian citizenship to vote or participate in regional elections. Even those ethnic Georgians willing to apply for Abkhaz "passports" generally did not receive them because of extensive delays and were, therefore, unable to participate. Ethnic Georgians in South Ossetia were also required to accept a South Ossetian "passport" and "citizenship" to participate in political life.

Abkhazia held de facto "presidential elections" in August, and South Ossetia did likewise in November. Neither contest was considered free and fair due to the large number of internally displaced persons who were prohibited from voting. In South Ossetia public concerns about the integrity of the election results, including a seemingly biased decision by the de facto "supreme court," led to public demonstrations and a political crisis that was settled through Russian mediation.

Principal Government Officials

Last Updated: 1/31/2013

Pres.: **Mikheil SAAKASHVILI**
Speaker of Parliament: **Davit USUPASHVILI**
Prime Min.: **Bidzina IVANISHVILI**
First Dep. Prime Min.: **Irakli ALASANIA**
Dep. Prime Min.: **Kakha KALADZE**
Min. of Agriculture: **Davit KIRVALIDZE**
Min. of Corrections & Legal Assistance: **Sozar SUBARI**
Min. of Culture & Monument Protection: **Guram ODISHARIA**
Min. of Defense: **Irakli ALASANIA**
Min. of Economy & Sustainable Development: **Giorgi KVIRIKASHVILI**
Min. of Education & Science: **Giorgi MARGELASHVILI**
Min. of Energy: **Kakha KALADZE**
Min. of Environmental Protection & Natural Resources: **Khatuna GOGOLADZE**
Min. of Finance: **Nodar KHADURI**
Min. of Foreign Affairs: **Maia PANJIKIDZE**
Min. of Internal Affairs: **Irakli GHARIBASHVILI**
Min. of Justice: **Tea TSULUKIANI**
Min. of Labor, Health & Social Affairs: **Davit SERGIENKO**
Min. of Regional Development & Infrastructure: **David NARMANIA**
Min. of Sports & Youth Affairs: **Levan KIPIANI**
State Min. for Diaspora Issues: **Kote SURGULADZE**
State Min. for European & Euro-Atlantic Integration: **Alexi PETRIASHVILI**
State Min. for Internally Displaced Persons From the Occupied Territories, Accommodation, & Refugees of Georgia: **Davit DARAKHVELIDZE**
State Min. for Reintegration: **Paata ZAKAREISHVILI**
Sec., National Security Council: **Giorgi "Giga" BOKERIA**
Chmn., National Bank: **Giorgi KADAGIDZE**
Ambassador to the US:
Permanent Representative to the UN, New York:

ECONOMY

Georgia's main economic activities include the cultivation of agricultural products such as grapes, citrus fruits, and hazelnuts; mining of manganese, copper, and gold; and output of a small industrial sector producing alcoholic and nonalcoholic beverages, metals, machinery, and chemicals. The country imports nearly all its needed supplies of natural gas and oil products. It has sizeable hydropower capacity that now provides most of its energy needs.

Georgia has overcome the chronic energy shortages and gas supply interruptions of the past by renovating hydropower plants and by increasingly relying on natural gas imports from Azerbaijan instead of from Russia. Construction of the Baku-T'bilisi-Ceyhan oil pipeline, the Baku-T'bilisi-Erzerum gas pipeline, and the Kars-Akhalkalaki Railroad are part of a strategy to capitalize on Georgia's strategic location between Europe and Asia and develop its role as a transit point for gas, oil, and other goods. Georgia's economy sustained GDP growth of more than 10% in 2006–07, based on strong inflows of foreign investment and robust government spending.

However, GDP growth slowed following the August 2008 conflict with Russia, and sunk to negative 4 percent in 2009 as foreign direct investment and workers' remittances declined in the wake of the global financial crisis. The economy rebounded in 2010–12, with growth rates above 6% per year, but FDI inflows, the engine of Georgian economic growth prior to the 2008 conflict, have not recovered fully. Unemployment has also remained high at above 16%. Georgia has historically suffered from a chronic failure to collect tax revenues; however, the government, since coming to power in 2004, has simplified the tax code, improved tax administration, increased tax enforcement, and cracked down on petty corruption, leading to higher revenues.

The country is pinning its hopes for renewed growth on a determined effort to continue to liberalize the economy by reducing regulation, taxes, and corruption in order to attract foreign investment, with a focus on hydropower, agriculture, tourism, and textiles production. Since 2004, the government has taken a series of actions against endemic corruption, including reform of the traffic police and implementation of a fair examination system for entering the university system. The government has received high marks from the World Bank for its anti-corruption efforts.

Labor Conditions

In most situations the minimum legal age for employment is 16. In exceptional cases, children may work with parental consent at the ages of 14 and 15. Children under the age of 18 may not engage in unhealthy or underground work, and children between the ages of 16 and 18 are subject to reduced working hours and prohibited from working at night. The labor code permits employment agreements with persons under the age of 14 in sports, arts, cultural activities, and for performing advertising services.

Although official data was not available, a 2007 survey estimated that 77.4 percent of working children were employed intermittently on family farms, while 18.4 percent worked in family enterprises. Many minors under the age of 16 worked and performed chores on small family-owned farms in rural areas. In most cases this work was not abusive and not categorized as child labor. However, in some ethnic minority areas, family farm obligations were reported to disrupt the ability to attend school.

The monthly minimum wage for public sector employees is 115 lari ($68) and has remained the same since 2005. Minimum wage for private sector employees is 90 lari ($54) per month. The official subsistence level income is 138 lari ($82) for the average consumer and 276 lari ($164) for a family of four. The labor code provides for a 41-hour work week and for a weekly 24-hour rest period unless otherwise determined by a labor contract. According to the code, shifts must be at least 12 hours apart.

Pregnant women or women who have recently given birth may not be forced to work overtime without their consent. Overtime is defined as work that exceeds the work hours addressed in the employment agreement. If the employment agreement does not specify business hours, then overtime is considered to be performance exceeding 41 work hours per week. Terms of overtime labor are defined by agreement between the parties. The labor code also permits an employer to change the hours of work by 90 minutes without renegotiating the terms of any labor contact. NGOs contended that this provision would effectively require employees to work overtime without compensation, a violation of the constitutional prohibition against compulsory labor. The law does not explicitly prohibit excessive overtime.

U.S.-GEORGIA RELATIONS

The United States established diplomatic relations with Georgia in 1992 following Georgia's 1991 independence from the Soviet Union. Since 1991, Georgia has made impressive progress fighting corruption, developing modern state institutions, and enhancing global security. The United States is committed to helping Georgia deepen Euro-Atlantic ties and strengthen its democratic institutions. The United States supports Georgia's sovereignty and territorial integrity within its internationally recognized borders, and does not recognize the independence of Abkhazia and South Ossetia, two regions of Georgia currently occupied by Russia. As a participant of the Geneva International Discussions on the conflict in Georgia, the United States continues to play an active role in support of these principles.

The strength of U.S.-Georgia relations is codified in the 2009 U.S.-Georgia Charter on Strategic Partnership. The U.S.-Georgia Strategic Partnership Commission comprises four bilateral working groups on priority areas identified in the Charter: democracy; defense and security; economic, trade, and energy issues; and people-to-people and cultural exchanges. In addition to holding a high-level plenary session of the Commission each year, senior-level U.S. and Georgian policymakers lead yearly meetings of each working group to review commitments, update activities, and establish future objectives.

Since the signing of the Charter, the United States and Georgia have strengthened their mutual cooperation based on U.S. support for Georgia's sovereignty and territorial integrity, and its commitment to further democratic and economic reforms.

U.S. Assistance to Georgia

U.S. Government assistance to Georgia supports the consolidation of Georgia's democracy; its eventual integration into Euro-Atlantic institutions; progress toward a peacefully unified nation, secure in its borders; and further development of its free-market economy. A fact sheet on U.S. assistance to Georgia can be found here.

Bilateral Economic Relations

The United States and Georgia seek to identify opportunities for U.S. businesses to invest in Georgia, and for both countries to sell goods and services to each other. They have signed a bilateral investment treaty and a bilateral trade and investment framework agreement. Georgia can export many products duty-free to the United States under the Generalized System of Preferences program. Through a high-level trade and investment dialogue, the two countries have discussed a range of options to improve economic cooperation and bilateral trade, including the possibility of a free trade agreement. They have also discussed ways to improve Georgia's business climate to attract more investment, underscoring the importance of continued improvements in rule of law, respect for labor rights, and protecting intellectual property rights. From 2006 to 2011, a Millennium Challenge Corporation Compact helped promote Georgian enterprise and economic growth. Georgia is currently working with the MCC to finalize the design of a second compact, focused instead on education.

Georgia's Membership in International Organizations

Georgia and the United States belong to a number of the same international organizations, including the United Nations, Euro-Atlantic Partnership Council, Organization for Security and Cooperation in Europe, International Monetary Fund, World Bank, and World Trade Organization. Georgia also is an observer to the Organization of American States and a participant in the North Atlantic Treaty Organization's (NATO) Partnership for Peace program.

Bilateral Representation

Georgia maintains an embassy in the United States at 2209 Massachusetts Avenue, NW, Washington, DC 20008, telephone (202) 387-2390.

Principal U.S. Embassy Officials

Last Updated: 1/14/2013

TBILISI (E) 11 George Balanchini Street, Tbilisi, Georgia, 0131, 995-32-227-7000, Fax 995-32-227-7701, Workweek: M-F; 0900-1800, Website: http://georgia.usembassy.gov/

DCM OMS:	Tonya Reardon
AMB OMS:	Patricia Lara
CDC:	Ed Maes
DHS/CIS:	Ronald Grimes
FM:	Bruce R. Moore
HRO:	Conard C. Hamilton
MGT:	Robert C. Ruehle
NAS/INL:	Aaron Fishman
POL/ECON:	Alan Meltzer
POL/MIL:	Kurt Lichtfuss
POSHO:	Bruce Moore
SDO/DATT:	COL Jeffrey Hartman
TREAS:	Ann Green
AMB:	Richard B. Norland
CON:	Shannon Behaj
DCM:	Bridget Brink
PAO:	Michael R.Turner
GSO:	Kevin Allen
RSO:	Mathieu Souliere
AGR:	Lawrence F. Barbieri
AID:	Stephen Haykin
CLO:	Riley Ganz
EEO:	Harvey K. Heard
FMO:	James Barber
ICASS Chair:	Jared Kimball
IMO:	Harvey K. Heard
IPO:	Henly Cheng
ISO:	Greg Morris
ISSO:	Henly Cheng
LEGATT:	Mark Nowak
State ICASS:	Joshua S. Fischel

TRAVEL

Consular Information Sheet

September 10, 2012

Country Description: Georgia is a constitutional republic with a developing democracy and economy. Tourist facilities outside of Tbilisi and Batumi are not highly developed, and many of the goods and services taken for granted in other countries are not yet available.

Smart Traveler Enrollment Program (STEP)/Embassy Locations: If you are going to live in or visit Georgia, please take the time to tell our Embassy about your trip. If you enroll, we can keep you up to date with important safety and security announcements. It will also help your friends and family get in touch with you in an emergency.

U.S. Embassy Tbilisi
11 George Balanchine Street
Tbilisi 0131
Tel: (995 32) 227-70-00 or Consular Section: (995 32) 227-77-24
Duty officer for emergencies after hours: (995 32) 227-71-33
Email: AskConsulTbilisi@state.gov

Entry/Exit Requirements for U.S. Citizens: You will need a valid passport to enter Georgia. U.S. citizens visiting for 360 days or less do not need a visa. For further information concerning entry requirements for Georgia, travelers should contact the Embassy of Georgia at 2209 Massachusetts Avenue NW, Washington DC, 20008 tel. (202) 387-2390, fax: (202) 387-0864.

HIV/AIDS Restrictions: There are no restrictions on travel for HIV/AIDS positive tourist visitors to Georgia who plan to stay for 360 days or less.

Threats to Safety and Security: The Department of State warns U.S. citizens against travel to the occupied regions of South Ossetia, in north-central Georgia, and Abkhazia, in northwest Georgia. These regions are not under the control of the central government following civil wars in the early 1990s, and the conflict with Russia in August 2008. Tensions remain high between the de facto authorities in Abkhazia and South Ossetia and the central government. Russian troops and border guards continue to occupy both regions. Due to the volatility of the political situation, reported high levels of crime, and inability of embassy personnel to travel freely to Abkhazia or South Ossetia, the U.S. Embassy strongly discourages travel to these areas. The restricted access of U.S. officials to Abkhazia and South Ossetia significantly limits the ability of the U.S. government to assist U.S. citizens in these regions, even in emergencies. All travelers to these regions should enroll in the Smart Traveler Enrollment Program (STEP). The U.S. Embassy recommends that any travel to Abkhazia or South Ossetia be conducted in accordance with applicable Georgian laws (specifically that U.S. citizens enter the two regions from undisputed Georgia) and that U.S. citizens regularly monitor Emergency Messages on the Embassy website for the latest information on the security situation throughout Georgia.

The situation near both Abkhazia and South Ossetia remains unpredictable, and a number of attacks, criminal incidents, and kidnappings have occurred in and around these regions over the past several years. U. S. citizens are advised to exercise caution when traveling near the administrative boundary lines of Abkhazia and South Ossetia, as there is a possibility of encountering unexploded ordnance near the administrative boundary lines of both regions, particularly on the North side of the South Ossetia administrative boundary line. Abkhaz de facto "border officials" and their Russian counterparts may demand that travelers entering the region purchase "visas" from the so-called "Ministry of Foreign Affairs of Abkhazia," but the U.S. Government and the majority of the international community do not recognize any jurisdiction of de facto authorities in either Abkhazia or South Ossetia. Entering the Abkhazia or South Ossetia area without the proper documentation can lead to arrest, imprisonment by border officials, and/or fines.

Political demonstrations take place from time to time in Tbilisi, sometimes in front of the Parliament building on Rustaveli Avenue. While these demonstrations are generally peaceful, some confrontations between the government and protesters have occurred, as recently as May 2011. All U. S. citizens should be aware that even peaceful demonstrations can escalate into violence with little or no notice. Demonstration Notices are posted on the U.S. Embassy Tbilisi website.

Review your security practices and be aware of your surroundings at all times. Vary your times and routes, especially from places of residence to work locations. Maintain a low profile—do not carry large amounts of cash or otherwise draw unnecessary attention to yourself. Report any security-related incidents such as suspicious vehicles, individuals, or activities, to the Georgian authorities, and also inform the U.S. Embassy as soon as possible.

Travel in pairs or groups, and stay on main streets and routes. The U.S. Embassy recommends that if you are traveling throughout the country you do so during daylight hours only and provide a travel itinerary and contact telephone numbers to someone. See below for more details on road safety in Georgia.

In the past, some members of religious minorities in Georgia have been targets of attacks. U.S. citizens should remain cautious when engaging in missionary activity in Georgia.

Stay up-to-date by:

- Bookmarking our Bureau of Consular Affairs website, which contains the current Travel Warnings and Travel Alerts as well as the Worldwide Caution;
- Following us on Twitter and the Bureau of Consular Affairs Facebook page;
- Downloading our free Smart Traveler iPhone App to have travel information at your fingertips;
- Calling 1-888-407-4747 toll-free within the U.S. and Canada, or a regular toll line, 1-202-501-4444, from other countries;
- Taking some time before travel to consider your personal security.

Terrorism: Georgia has experienced several improvised explosive device (IED) attacks and attempted attacks, both in Tbilisi and elsewhere in the country, since September 2010. Most of these attacks are believed to have originated in the occupied territories of South Ossetia and Abkhazia, though at least one attack had its origins outside of Georgia. Targets have included government facilities, public places, and diplomatic missions.

Crime: There is a great disparity in affluence between foreigners and most Georgians. U.S. citizens in particular are perceived as being wealthy, and therefore may be targeted for economic and property-based crimes. Petty street crime, such as theft by pickpocket, has been reported throughout the country, particularly in crowded places such as tourist sites or on public transportation. Firearms are readily available in Georgia and assailants may be armed with firearms or other weapons. There are also disputes, sometimes in areas where Americans frequent, which include firearms and may endanger American citizens.

Personal vehicles and established (clearly marked) taxis and public transportation are generally safe for overland travel in Georgia. As stated above, however, crowded and "off the beaten path" conditions of some public transportation increase passengers' vulnerability to robbery.

Reports of sexual assaults of U.S. citizens, including date or acquaintance rape, have increased in Georgia. Women should avoid being alone in isolated areas with people whom they do not know well. In many of the reported cases, alcohol was involved. Avoid traveling alone in a private taxi or a "marshrutka" mini-bus, especially after dark. Victims of sexual assault should first get to a safe location and then call the U.S. Embassy and the local police. Women victimized overseas may be entitled to receive compensation for counseling and/or other services, including relocation back to the United States. For further information, visit the U.S. Department of Justice's Office on Violence Against Women.

Crime levels in Abkhazia and South Ossetia are known to be high, including targeted violence such as murder, and could easily endanger U.S. citizen travelers. For this reason, and others noted above, the Department of State warns Americans against travel to Abkhazia and South Ossetia.

Victims of Crime: If you or someone you know becomes the victim of a crime abroad, you should contact the local police and the nearest U.S. Embassy or Consulate. We can:

- Replace a stolen passport;
- Help you find appropriate medical care if you are the victim of a violent crime such as assault or rape;
- Put you in contact with the appropriate police authorities, and if you want us to, we can contact family members or friends; and,
- Help you understand the local criminal justice process and direct you to local attorneys, although it is important to remember that local authorities are responsible for investigating and prosecuting the crime.

Recently the Georgian Ministry of Internal Affairs (MOIA) has established a 24-hour emergency response center equivalent to "911." The new emergency-response center services all of Georgia via united emergency number "112," and transmits received emergency calls to the fire and rescue service, p atrol police, and the nearest medical-emergency center.

Please note that the dispatcher speaks Georgian and Russian, but will transfer a call to an English-speaking operator.

Criminal Penalties: While you are traveling in Georgia, you are subject to its laws even if you are a U.S. citizen. Foreign laws and legal systems can be vastly different than our own, and criminal penalties vary from country to country. Penalties for possessing, using, or trafficking in illegal drugs in Georgia are severe, and convicted offenders can expect long jail sentences and heavy fines.

There are also some things that might be legal in the country you visit, but still illegal in the United States. For example, you can be prosecuted under U.S. law if you buy pirated goods. Engaging in sexual conduct with children or using or disseminating child pornography in a foreign country is a crime prosecutable in the United States. If you break local laws in Georgia, your U.S. passport won't help you avoid arrest or prosecution. It's very important to know what's legal and what's not wherever you go.

Arrest notifications in host country: While some countries will automatically notify the nearest U.S. embassy or consulate if a U.S. citizen is detained or arrested in a foreign country, that might not always be the case. To ensure that the United States is aware of your circumstances, request that the police and prison officials notify the nearest U.S. embassy or consulate as soon as you are arrested or detained overseas.

If you are arrested in Georgia, the local authorities are required to notify the U.S. Embassy of your arrest. If you are concerned that the Department of State may not be aware of your situation, you should request the police or prison officials to notify the U.S. Embassy of your arrest. A consular officer from the Embassy will visit you but will not be able to get you out of jail. You will need to consult an attorney. A list of English-speaking attorneys can be found on the embassy's website. The Georgian authorities will provide you with an attorney and translator if you cannot afford one.

Special Circumstances: The lack of lighting in some public places, particularly outside of Tbilisi and Batumi, heightens your vulnerability to crime.

Georgia's customs authorities enforce regulations concerning the temporary import into or export from Georgia of items such as alcohol, tobacco, jewelry, religious materials, art or artifacts, antiquities, and business equipment. Only personal medicines with a doctor's statement can be imported without the permission of the Georgian Drug Agency section of the Ministry of Health.

You may not import firearms into Georgia; however, you may bring hunting weapons into the country for a two-week period, based on a valid Georgian hunting license. While there is no limit to the amount of currency that you can import, if you try to take out more money than you declared at the time of entry, you are obligated to prove it was legally obtained. There are limits on the amount of Georgian currency that may be exported. For additional customs information, U. S. citizens should contact the Embassy of Georgia in Washington DC.

The U.S. Embassy strongly discourages the purchase of property in the Abkhazia or South Ossetia regions of Georgia. Land for sale in those regions may rightfully belong to internally displaced persons forced to leave the breakaway regions in the early 1990s and may have been placed improperly on the market. In such cases, the Government of Georgia considers the sale of property in Abkhazia and South Ossetia illegal and the property could be reclaimed by original owners at a future date.

The Ministry of Culture's Department of Expertise and Evaluation must license any valuables such as artwork, antiques, jewelry, or paintings. This license describes the object, assesses its value, and provides permission to export it from Georgia. Please contact the Embassy of Georgia in Washington, D.C. for specific information regarding customs requirements.

While the Georgian lari is the only legal tender, dollars can be exchanged freely for lari at market rates. ATMs are widespread within Tbilisi. Credit cards are accepted in upscale hotels and restaurants, but travelers' checks are difficult to cash. U. S. citizens in Georgia have reported incidents of credit card fraud and identity theft. You should closely monitor your credit card statements.

Military Draft: U.S.-Georgian dual-national males between the ages of 18 and 27 may be subject to military conscription under Georgian law.

Accessibility: Individuals with disabilities may find accessibility and accommodation very different in Georgia from what you find in the United States. While the Georgian administrative code mandates access to buildings for persons with disabilities and stipulates fines for noncompliance, very few public or private facilities or buildings are accessible. Public and private transportation offer no accommodation for persons with disabilities. There are few sidewalks outside of Tbilisi or Batumi.

Medical Facilities and Health Information: Western-standard medical care in Georgia is limited, but Georgian healthcare continues to improve. There is a shortage of medical supplies and capabilities outside of Tbilisi, Kutaisi, and Batumi. Elderly travelers and those with pre-existing health problems may be at risk due to inadequate medical facilities. We strongly recommend that travelers who intend to visit Georgia for at least two weeks get the Hepatitis A vaccine and a pre-exposure rabies vaccine. Travelers are also encouraged to bring medicine to treat diarrhea, which regularly afflicts newcomers. Georgian doctors and hospitals often expect immediate cash payment before rendering medical services.

You can find detailed information on vaccinations and other health precautions on the Centers for Disease Control and Prevention (CDC) website. For information about outbreaks of infectious diseases abroad, consult the World Health Organization (WHO) website,which also contains additional health information for travelers, including detailed country-specific health information.

Tuberculosis is an increasingly serious health concern in Georgia. For further information, please refer to CDC guidance.

Medical Insurance: You can't assume your insurance will cover you when you travel. It's very important to find out BEFORE you leave whether or not your medical insurance will cover you overseas. You need to ask your insurance company two questions:

- Does my policy apply when I'm out of the United States?
- Will it cover emergencies like a trip to a foreign hospital or a medical evacuation?

In many places, doctors and hospitals still expect payment in cash at the time of service. Your regular U.S. health insurance may not cover doctor and hospital visits in other countries. If your policy doesn't cover you when you travel, it's a very good idea to take out another one for your trip.

Traffic Safety and Road Conditions: While in Georgia, you will encounter road conditions that differ significantly from those in the United States. As in the United States, vehicular traffic in Georgia moves along the right side of roadways. Speed limits range from 80 to 100 km/hr on highways, and from 30 to 60 km/hr on urban thoroughfares. Motorists are not permitted to make right turns at red traffic lights. Front-seat passengers are required by law to fasten their seat belts in moving vehicles. Georgian law requires that children under four (4) years of age be restrained in child-safety seats, however these are not widely available or used. Children under twelve (12) years of age may not legally ride in the front seat, but this law is also not widely observed. A driver with any blood-alcohol concentration exceeding 0.00% is considered to be driving under the influence of alcohol.

You should exercise extreme caution when driving in Georgia, as many local drivers do not operate their vehicles in accordance with established traffic laws. Traffic signals and rules of the road are often completely ignored. Motorists drive erratically, often recklessly, at excessive speeds, and many times under the influence of alcohol or drugs. Motorists frequently encounter oncoming high-speed traffic attempting to pass other vehicles at blind turns or over hilltops. Pedestrians enjoy no right-of-way and need to be extremely careful when crossing streets. The Georgian Patrol Police, who come under the authority of the Ministry of Internal Affairs, are responsible for maintaining traffic safety in Georgia, but enforcement of traffic regulations is haphazard. There is no requirement that vehicles are certified safe to drive, and some vehicles may not have working headlights or tail lights.

Undivided two-lane roads connect most major cities in Georgia. Outside of major highways, roads are generally in poor condition, unpaved, and often lack shoulder markings, center lines, and lighting. In addition, traffic signals may not work due to poor maintenance. Driving at night can be especially dangerous. Travel on mountain roads is treacherous in both rain and snow, and during winter, heavy snowfalls may make some roads impassable.

Aviation Safety Oversight: As there is no direct commercial air service to the United States by carriers registered in Georgia, the U.S. Federal Aviation Administration (FAA) has not assessed the government of Georgia's Civil Aviation Authority for compliance with International Civil

Aviation Organization (ICAO) aviation safety standards. Further information may be found on the FAA's safety assessment page. Regional airlines among the countries of the Caucasus may experience prolonged delays and sudden cancellations of flights. In addition to frequent delays, flights are sometimes overbooked. Basic safety features such as seat belts are sometimes missing. Air travel to Georgia on international carriers via Europe is typically more reliable. Ticketed passengers on flights departing from Georgia should reconfirm reservations with the airline 24 hours prior to departure.

Children's Issues: Please see the U.S. Dept. of State Office of Children's Issues web pages on intercountry adoption and international parental child abduction.

Intercountry Adoption

August 2011

The information in this section has been edited from the latest report available as of February 2013 from the State Department Bureau of Consular Affairs, Office of Overseas Citizens Services. For more information, please read the *Intercountry Adoption* section of this book and review current reports online at http://adoption.state.gov. Georgia is party to the Hague Convention on Protection of Children and Co-operation in Respect of Intercountry Adoption (Hague Adoption Convention). Therefore, all adoptions between Georgia and the United States must meet the requirements of the Convention, the U.S. implementing legislation, the Intercountry Act of 2000 (IAA), and the IAA implementing regulations.

Who Can Adopt? Adoption between the United States and Georgia is governed by the Hague Adoption Convention. Therefore, to adopt from Georgia, you must first be found eligible to adopt by the U.S. Government. The U.S. Government agency responsible for making this determination is the Department of Homeland Security, U.S. Citizenship and Immigration Services (USCIS).

Residency Requirements: There are no residency requirements for prospective adoptive parents in Georgia.

Age Requirements: An adoptive parent may be any person who is of legal age and who is has legal capacity. Persons who have previously adopted or have been deprived of parental rights, or were the guardians/caregivers of an underage child or had a person in foster care, and have had these relationships terminated due to not properly carrying out their duties, may not adopt.

The age difference between the adoptive parent and the child to be adopted must not be less than sixteen years. However, a court may waive this age difference requirement if a valid reason exists.

Marriage Requirements: Both single individuals and legally married couples can adopt.

Income Requirements: Prospective parents must prove that they can provide for the child but there is no minimum income requirement.

Who Can Be Adopted? Because Georgia is party to the Hague Adoption Convention, children from Georgia must meet the requirements of the Convention in order to be eligible for adoption. For example, the Convention requires that Georgia attempt to place a child with a family in-country before determining that a child is eligible for intercountry adoption. In addition to Georgia's requirements, a child must meet the definition of a Convention adoptee in order to be brought back to the United States.

Eligibility Requirements: Foreign citizens can adopt Georgian children who have been registered in the Registry of Adoptable Children and have not been adopted by a Georgian citizen within eight months of registry, and who have been given the status of a child to be adopted.

Relinquishment Requirements: Children whose every legal representative has given consent to his/her being adopted; Whose parent(s) has (have) been deprived of the parental right.

Abandonment Requirements: Persons whose parent(s) has (have) been deemed legally incapable, recognized as missing or been declared deceased by a court of law.

Age Requirements: Any child under the age of eighteen who has been registered in the Registry of Adoptable Children and who has not been adopted in Georgia within eight months of being registered, may be selected for adoption abroad.

Sibling Requirements: Sibling relationships are given consideration in adoption proceedings, but are considered on a case-by-case basis, with particular emphasis given to the possibility of adopting them together.

Requirements for Special Needs or Medical Conditions: On a case-by-case basis, evidence may be required that an adopting family is aware of and able to cope with a child's special needs and may require families to submit to follow up assessments.

Waiting Period: The child will be placed in the permanent, full-time care of the prospective adoptive parents (PAPs) only after, and not before, the court has made a final decision on the adoption proceedings.

Georgia's Adoption Authority: Social Service Agency

The Process: Because Georgia is party to the Hague Adoption Convention, adopting from Georgia must follow a specific process designed to meet the Convention's requirements. For detailed and updated information on these requirements, please review the *Intercountry Adoption* section of this publication and visit the U.S. Department of State Intercountry Adoption website at http://adoption.state.gov.

The first step in adopting a child from Georgia is to select an adoption service provider in the United States that has been accredited. Only these agencies and attorneys can provide adoption services between the United States and Georgia. In accordance with Georgian law, it is prohibited for any persons or legal entities other than the Social Service Agency to carry out any actions in the adoption process. After you choose an accredited adoption service provider, you must apply to be found eligible to adopt (Form I-800A) by the U.S. Government, Department of Homeland Security, U.S. Citizenship and Immigration Services (USCIS). Once the U.S. government determines that you are "eligible" and "suitable" to adopt, you or your agency will forward your information to the adoption authority in Georgia. Georgia's adoption authority will review your application to determine whether you are also eligible to adopt under Georgia's law. If both the United States and Georgia determine that you are eligible to adopt, and a child is available for intercountry adoption, the central adoption authority in Georgia may provide you with a referral for a child.

After you accept a match with a child, you must apply to the U.S Government, Department of Homeland Security, U.S. Citizenship and Immigration Services (USCIS) for provisional approval to adopt that particular child (Form I-800). USCIS will determine whether the child is eligible under U.S. law to be adopted and enter the United States.

After this, you or your adoption service provider will submit a visa application to a consular officer at the U.S. Embassy. The consular officer will review the child's information and evaluate the child for possible visa ineligibilities. If the consular officer determines that the child appears eligible to immigrate to the United States, he or she will send a letter (an "Article 5 Letter") to the Georgian Central Authority. Do not adopt or obtain custody of a child in Georgia before a U.S. consular officer issues the Article 5 Letter.

Role of the Adoption Authority:

- Issues the adoption decree and the Certificate under Article 23;
- Prepares the adoption case for Court hearing;
- Is involved in the court proceedings of intercountry adoption cases;
- Counsels the adoptive parents on the requirements of the child;
- Ensures the psychological preparation of the child for entrustment to the PAPs and assists them in travel arrangements.

Role of the Court: Processes all adoption cases and takes appropriate decisions. In accordance with Georgian law, the court makes the final decision in all adoption cases.

Role of the Adoption Agencies: Foreign accredited bodies are permitted to work as intermediaries between the Central Authorities of Receiving States and Social Service Agency. They ensure the preparation of documents related to adoption (translation, notarization, transmission etc.) and provide PAPs with attorney services.

Time Frame:

- Select the PAPs, notify the Central Authority of the Receiving State about the match—one week.
- Acceptance of the match by the PAPs (to receive the document, under the Article 17). Largely depends on the Receiving State—two weeks.
- Notify the Ministry of Internal affairs of Georgia about the acceptance of the match by PAPs—one week.
- Final examination of the case and preparation of the decree on adoption for the Court Hearing by the Central Authority—one week.
- Court Hearing, including the final decision—two—five months.
- Issuance of the Certificate under Article 23—one week.

Adoption Application: The PAPs' adoption application must be submitted to the Central Authority of Georgia

Adoption Fees: In the adoption services contract that you sign at the beginning of the adoption process, your agency will itemize fees and estimate related expenses.

Some of the fees specifically associated with adopting from Georgia include:

- Fees at Court—50 GEL.
- Notarial service (translation, notarization) 50–150 GEL (depending on the number of pages).
- Preparation of the passport for the child—100–205 GEL (depending on the amount of time necessary).
- Legal fees—(varies).

Documents Required:

- Application form.
- Spouse's consent, if the child is being adopted by one of the spouses.
- Copy of the ID document (personal ID, passport, residence ID).
- Copy of the marriage certificate (if applicable).
- Reference sheet on health condition.
- Reference sheet of the medical-narcological inspection.
- Reference sheet on the criminal record.
- Research concerning the family, conducted by the authorized body on adoption of the Receiving State.

All documents must be legalized or certified with Apostille, translated into Georgian and notarized.

Bringing Your Child Home: Once your adoption is complete (or you have obtained legal custody of the child), there are a few more steps to take before you can head home. Specifically, you need to apply for several documents for your child before he or she can travel to the United States, such as a birth certificate, a passport or travel document for your child from the country in which he or she was born, and a U.S. Immigration Visa. For detailed and updated information on how to obtain these documents, review the *Intercountry Adoption* section in this publication and visit the U.S. Department of State Intercountry Adoption website at http://adoption.state.gov.

Child Citizenship Act: For adoptions finalized abroad, the Child Citizenship Act of 2000 allows your new child to acquire American citizenship automatically when he or she enters the United States as lawful permanent residents. For adoptions finalized in the United States, the Child Citizenship Act of 2000 allows your new child to acquire American citizenship automatically when the court in the United States issues the final adoption decree. To learn more, review the *Intercountry Adoption* section in this publication and visit the U.S. Department of State Intercountry Adoption website at http://adoption.state.gov.

After Adoption: Based on a special agreement, the Georgian adoption authority is obliged to request the adopting parents, via the adoptive country's relevant government agency (or, in the case of non-existence of such agency, with the licensed and/or accredited relevant authorized organization) to annually submit information about the health and social condition of the child, until the adopted child becomes of eighteen years of age.

U.S. Embassy in Georgia
11 Balanchine street, Tbilisi, Georgia
Tel: (995 32) 27–77–24
Email: askconsultbilisi@state.gov
Internet:
http://georgia.usembassy.gov

Georgia's Adoption Authority
LEPL Social Service Agency of the Ministry of Labour, Health and Social Affairs of Georgia
144 Akaki tsereteli Ave., 0119 Tbilisi, Georgia
Tel: (995 32) 251–00–47
(995 32) 251–00–48
(995 32) 251–00–49
Email: esaneblidze@ssa.gov.ge
Internet: www.ssa.gov.ge

Embassy of Georgia
2209 Massachusetts Avenue NW
Washington DC, 20008
Tel: (202) 387–2390
Fax: (202) 387–0864
Email: embgeorgia.usa@mfa.gov.ge; washington.emb@mfa.gov.ge
Internet: www.usa.mfa.gov.ge

Georgian Consulate
144, East 44th ST., 5th Floor
New York, NY 10017
Tel: (212) 867–3617; (212) 867–3272
Fax: (212) 867–3654
Email: georgianconsulate1@verizon.net; newyork.con@mfa.gov.ge

Office of Children's Issues
U.S. Department of State
2201 C Street, NW
SA-29
Washington, DC 20520
Tel: 1–888–407–4747
E-mail: AskCI@state.gov
http://adoption.state.gov

For questions about immigration procedures, call the National Customer Service Center (NCSC) at 1-800-375-5283 (TTY 1-800-767-1833).

GERMANY

Compiled from publications that were available as of February 2013 from the U.S. Department of State, the U.S. Department of Commerce, and the Central Intelligence Agency (CIA). See the introduction to this set for explanatory notes.

Official Name:
Federal Republic of Germany

PROFILE

Geography

Area: total: 357,022 sq km; country comparison to the world: 63; land: 348,672 sq km; water: 8,350 sq km

Major cities: Berlin (capital) 3.438 million; Hamburg 1.786 million; Munich 1.349 million; Cologne 1.001 million (2009)

Climate: temperate and marine; cool, cloudy, wet winters and summers; occasional warm mountain (foehn) wind

Terrain: lowlands in north, uplands in center, Bavarian Alps in south

People

Nationality: noun: German(s); adjective: German

Population: 81,305,856 (July 2012 est.)

Population growth rate: -0.2% (2012 est.)

Ethnic groups: German 91.5%, Turkish 2.4%, other 6.1% (made up largely of Greek, Italian, Polish, Russian, Serbo-Croatian, Spanish)

Religions: Protestant 34%, Roman Catholic 34%, Muslim 3.7%, unaffiliated or other 28.3%

Languages: German

Literacy: definition: age 15 and over can read and write; total population: 99%; male: 99%; female: 99% (2003 est.)

Health: life expectancy at birth: total population: 80.19 years; male: 77.93 years; female: 82.58 years (2012 est.); Infant mortality rate: total: 3.51 deaths/1,000 live births; male: 3.81 deaths/1,000 live births; female: 3.19 deaths/1,000 live births (2012 est.)

Unemployment rate: 6.5% (2012 est.)

Work force: 44.01 million (2012 est.)

Government

Type: federal republic

Independence: 18 January 1871

Constitution: 23 May 1949, known as Basic Law; became constitution of the united Germany 3 October 1990

Political subdivisions: 16 states (Laender, singular—Land); Baden-Wurttemberg, Bayern (Bavaria), Berlin, Brandenburg, Bremen, Hamburg, Hessen (Hesse), Mecklenburg-Vorpommern (Mecklenburg-Western Pomerania), Niedersachsen (Lower Saxony), Nordrhein-Westfalen (North Rhine-Westphalia), Rheinland-Pfalz (Rhineland-Palatinate), Saarland, Sachsen (Saxony), Sachsen-Anhalt (Saxony-Anhalt), Schleswig-Holstein, Thuringen (Thuringia); note—Bayern, Sachsen, and Thuringen refer to themselves as free states (Freistaaten, singular—Freistaat)

Suffrage: 18 years of age; universal

Economy

GDP (purchasing power parity): $3.194 trillion (2012 est.); $3.139 trillion (2011 est.); $3.046 trillion (2010 est.); $2.941 trillion (2009 est.)

GDP real growth rate: 0.9% (2012 est.); 3.1% (2011 est.); 3.6% (2010 est.); -5.1% (2009 est.)

GDP per capita (PPP): $39,100 (2012 est.); $38,400 (2011 est.); $37,300 (2010 est.); $35,900 (2009 est.)

Natural resources: coal, lignite, natural gas, iron ore, copper, nickel, uranium, potash, salt, construction materials, timber, arable land

Agriculture products: potatoes, wheat, barley, sugar beets, fruit, cabbages; cattle, pigs, poultry

Industries: among the world's largest and most technologically advanced producers of iron, steel, coal, cement, chemicals, machinery, vehicles, machine tools, electronics, food and beverages, shipbuilding, textiles

Exports: $1.492 trillion (2012 est.); $1.408 trillion (2011 est.); $1.303 trillion (2010 est.)

Exports—commodities: motor vehicles, machinery, chemicals, computer and electronic products, electri-

cal equipment, pharmaceuticals, metals, transport equipment, foodstuffs, textiles, rubber and plastic products
Exports—partners: France 9.4%, US 6.8%, Netherlands 6.6%, UK 6.2%, Italy 6.2%, China 5.7%, Austria 5.5%, Belgium 4.7%, Switzerland 4.4% (2009 est.)
Imports: $1.276 trillion (2012 est.); $1.198 trillion (2011 est.); $1.099 trillion (2010 est.)
Imports—commodities: machinery, data processing equipment, vehicles, chemicals, oil and gas, metals, electric equipment, pharmaceuticals, foodstuffs, agricultural products
Imports—partners: China 9.7%, Netherlands 8.4%, France 7.6%, US 5.7%, Italy 5.2%, UK 4.7%, Belgium 4.2%, Austria 4.1%, Switzerland 4.1% (2009 est.)
Debt—external: $5.624 trillion (30 June 2011); $4.713 trillion (30 June 2010)
Exchange rates: euros (EUR) per US dollar; 0.7838 (2012 est.); 0.7194 (2011 est.); 0.755 (2010 est.); 0.7198 (2009 est.); 0.6827 (2008 est.); 0.7345 (2007 est.)

PEOPLE

Most inhabitants of Germany are ethnic German. There are, however, more than 7 million foreign residents, many of whom are the families and descendents of so-called "guest workers" (foreign workers, mostly from Turkey, invited to Germany in the 1950s and 1960s to fill labor shortages) who remained in Germany.

Germany has a sizable ethnic Turkish. Germany is also a prime destination for political and economic refugees from many developing countries. An ethnic Danish minority lives in the north, and a small Slavic minority known as the Sorbs lives in eastern Germany. Due to restrictive German citizenship laws, most "foreigners" do not hold German citizenship even when born and raised in Germany. However, since the German Government undertook citizenship and immigration law reforms in 2002, more foreign residents have had the ability to naturalize.

Germany has one of the world's highest levels of education, technological development, and economic productivity. Since the end of World War II, the number of youths entering universities has more than tripled, and the trade and technical schools of the Federal Republic of Germany (F.R.G.) are among the world's best. Germany is a broadly middle class society. A generous social welfare system provides for universal medical care, unemployment compensation, and other social needs. Millions of Germans travel abroad each year. It is estimated that the population of Germany will decline from the current 81 million people to around 77 million people by 2050.

Due to this demographic change, the available workforce aged 20-64 will shrink by more than six million by 2030, resulting in a marked shortage of skilled workers. In the absence of appropriate and timely policy action, demographic change threatens to become a constraining factor for prosperity and growth.

With unification on October 3, 1990, Germany began the major task of bringing the standard of living of Germans in the former German Democratic Republic (G.D.R.) up to that of western Germany. This has been a lengthy and difficult process due to the relative inefficiency of industrial enterprises in the former G.D.R., difficulties in resolving property ownership in eastern Germany, and the inadequate infrastructure and environmental damage that resulted from years of mismanagement under communist rule.

Economic uncertainty in eastern Germany is often cited as one factor contributing to extremist violence, primarily from the political right. Confusion about the causes of the current hardships and a need to place blame has found expression in harassment and violence by some Germans directed toward foreigners, particularly non-Europeans. The vast majority of Germans condemn such violence.

Language

German is the official language. In larger towns, many people can communicate in English.

Religion

There are no official statistics on religious groups. Unofficial estimates and figures provided by religious organizations indicate the Roman Catholic Church has a membership of approximately 25 million, and the Protestant Church (which is a confederation of the Lutheran, Uniate, and Reformed Protestant denominations) has approximately 24 million members.

Together, these two churches account for more than three-fifths of the population. Other Protestant denominations include the New Apostolic Church with approximately 360,000 members, Baptist communities (Evangelical Christian Baptists, International Baptist Convention, Reformed Baptists, Bible Baptists, and others) with approximately 75,000 to 100,000 members, and evangelical nondenominational Baptists with approximately 85,000 members.

Muslims number approximately 4 million, including 2.9 million Sunnis, 500,000 Alevis, and 280,000 Shia. Orthodox Christians number approximately 1.4 million. Buddhists number 245,000 and Hindus 97,500. Other religious groups in the country include Jehovah's Witnesses, the Church of Scientology (COS), and a Jewish community of approximately 200,000 members. Approximately 28 million persons (one-third of the population) either have no religious affiliation or are members of unrecorded religious organizations.

HISTORY

Two of Germany's most famous writers, Goethe and Schiller, identified the central aspect of most of Germany's history with their poetic lament, "Germany? But where is it? I cannot find that country." Until 1871, there was no "Germany." Instead,

Europe's German-speaking territories were divided into several hundred kingdoms, principalities, duchies, bishoprics, fiefdoms and independent cities and towns.

Finding the answer to "the German question"—what form of statehood for the German speaking lands would arise, and which form could provide central Europe with peace and stability—has defined most of German history.

This history of many independent polities has found continuity in the F.R.G.'s federal structure. It is also the basis for the decentralized nature of German political, economic, and cultural life that lasts to this day.

The Holy Roman Empire

Between 962 and the beginning of the 19th century, the German territories were loosely organized into the Holy Roman Empire of the German Nation. The initially non-hereditary Emperor, elected by the many princes, dukes, and bishops of the constituent lands and confirmed by the Pope, nominally governed over a vast territory, but had very limited ability to intervene in the affairs of the hundreds of entities that made up the Empire, many of which would often wage war against each other. The Empire was never able to develop into a centralized state.

Beginning in 1517 with Martin Luther's posting of his 95 Theses on the door of the Wittenberg Castle church, the German-speaking territories bore the brunt of the pan-European struggles unleashed by the Reformation. The leaders of the German kingdoms and principalities chose sides, leading to a split of the Empire into Protestant and Catholic regions, with the Protestant strongholds mostly in the North and East, the Catholic in the South and West. The split along confessional lines also laid the groundwork for the later development of the most powerful German states—Prussia and Austria—as the Prussian Hohenzollern line adopted Protestantism and the Hapsburgs remained Catholic.

The tension culminated in the 30 Years War (1618–1648), a combination of wars within the Empire and between outside European states that were fought on German land.

These wars, which ended in a rough stalemate, devastated the German people and economy, definitively strengthened the rule of the various German rulers at the cost of the (Habsburg) Emperor (though Habsburg Austria remained the dominant single German entity within the Empire), and established the continued presence of both Catholics and Protestants in German territories.

The Rise of Prussia

The 18th and 19th centuries were marked by the rise of Prussia as the second powerful, dominant state in the German-speaking territories alongside Austria, and Austrian-Prussian rivalry became the dominant political factor in German affairs. Successive Prussian kings succeeded in modernizing, centralizing, and expanding the Prussian state, creating a modern bureaucracy and the Continent's strongest military. Despite Prussia's emphasis on militarism and authority, Prussia also became a center of the German Enlightenment and was known for its religious tolerance, with its western regions being predominantly Catholic and Jews being granted complete legal equality by 1812. After humiliating losses to Napoleon's armies, Prussia embarked on a series of administrative, military, economic, and education reforms that eventually succeeded in turning Prussia into the Continent's strongest state.

Following Napoleon's defeat, the 1814–1815 Congress of Vienna replaced the Holy Roman Empire with the German Confederation, made up of 38 independent states. A loose confederation, this construct had no common citizenship, legal system, or administrative or executive organs.

It did, however, provide for a Federal Diet that met in Frankfurt—a Congress of deputies of the constituent states who would meet to discuss issues affecting the Confederation as a whole.

The Path to Unification: The Customs Union and the 1848 Revolutions

Prussia led a group of 18 German states that formed the German Customs Union in 1834, and the Prussian Thaler eventually became the common currency used in this region. The Customs Union greatly enhanced economic efficiency, and paved the way for Germany to become a single economic unit during the 19th century's period of rapid industrialization. Austria chose to remain outside the German Customs Union, preferring instead to form its own customs union with the Hapsburg territories—a further step down the path of a unified Germany that did not include Austria.

France's 1848 February Revolution that overthrew King Louis Phillipe of France also sparked a series of popular uprisings throughout the German states. Panicking local leaders provided several political, social, and economic concessions to the demonstrators, including agreeing to a national assembly that would discuss the constitutional form of a united Germany, individual rights, and economic order.

The assembly rapidly devolved into competing factions; meanwhile, the conservative leaders of the German states reconstituted their power. When the assembly finally determined that there should be a united, federal Germany (excluding Austria) with universal male suffrage, organized as a constitutional monarchy under an Emperor—and offered that emperor title to the King of Prussia—there was no longer any interest or political reason (least of all in absolutist, powerful Prussia) for the leaders to assent. The Prussian monarch rejected the assembly's offer, and the assembly was forcefully disbanded without achieving any of the stated goals of the 1848 revolutionaries.

Nevertheless, the 1848 Revolutions did leave a lasting legacy. The factions of the ill-fated national assembly went on to develop into political parties. Certain economic and social reforms, such as the final abolition of feudal property structures, remained. The idea of German unity was firmly established. And the revolutionaries' colors—black, red, and gold—became firmly ensconced as the colors of German democratic and liberal aspirations.

Unification and Imperial Germany

German nationalism developed into an important unifying and sometimes liberalizing force during this time, though it became increasingly marked by an exclusionary, racially-based definition of nationhood that included anti-Semitic tendencies. However, eventual unification of Germany was essentially the result of Prussian expansionism rather than the victory of nationalist sentiment. Prussia's economic growth outstripped Austria's during the latter half of the 19th century and Prussia-controlled Germany became one of Europe's industrial powerhouses. Under Chancellor Otto von Bismarck, Prussia defeated Austria

(1866) and France (1870) in wars that paved the way for the formation of the German Empire under Emperor Wilhelm I in 1871. Germany became a federal state, with foreign and military policy determined at the national level, but many other policies remained the purview of the states.

Internally, Bismarck waged a struggle against Catholicism, which he viewed as an agent of Austria (ironically, these anti-Catholic efforts—which eventually failed—actually ended up consolidating a lasting political role for Germany's Catholics), and tried to both co-opt and repress the emerging socialist movement by passing the age's most progressive social insurance and worker protection legislation while clamping down on Socialist activities. Externally, Bismarck then moved to consolidate the stability of the new Empire, launching a string of diplomatic initiatives to form a complex web of alliances with other European powers to ensure that Germany did not become surrounded by hostile powers and avoid Germany's involvement in further wars.

However, Emperor William II disagreed vehemently with Bismarck, firing him in 1890. Wilhelm II had global aspirations for Germany, including acquisition of overseas colonies. His dynamic expansion of military power and confrontational foreign policies contributed to tensions on the continent. The fragile European balance of power, which Bismarck had helped to create, broke down in 1914. World War I and its aftermath, including the Treaty of Versailles, ended the German Empire.

The Weimar Republic and Fascism's Rise and Defeat

The postwar Weimar Republic (1919–33) was established as a broadly democratic state, but the government was severely handicapped and eventually doomed by economic problems and the rise of the political extremes. The dozens of political parties represented in the federal parliament never allowed stable government formation, creating political chaos. (This lesson led to the decision by the creators of the F.R.G. to limit parliamentary representation to parties that garner at least 5% of the vote, and to install other safeguards designed to enhance the stability of German governments.) The hyperinflation of 1923, the world depression that began in 1929, and the social unrest stemming from resentment toward the conditions of the Versailles Treaty worked to destroy the Weimar government.

The National Socialist (Nazi) Party, led by Adolf Hitler, stressed nationalist and racist themes while promising to put the unemployed back to work. The party blamed many of Germany's ills on the alleged influence of Jewish and non-German ethnic groups. The party also gained support in response to fears of growing communist strength.

In the 1932 elections, the Nazis won a third of the vote. In a fragmented party structure, this gave the Nazis a powerful parliamentary caucus, which they used to undermine the Republic. Continued instability resulted in President Paul von Hindenburg offering the chancellorship to Hitler in January 1933. After President von Hindenburg died in 1934, Hitler assumed that office as well.

Once in power, Hitler and his party first undermined and then abolished democratic institutions and opposition parties. The Nazi leadership immediately jailed many Jewish citizens and opposition figures and withdrew their political rights. Hitler's Nuremburg Laws subsequently deprived all of Germany's Jews of their political rights and also of their economic assets and professional licenses, foreshadowing the systematic plundering of Jewish assets throughout Nazi-occupied territory.

The Nazis implemented a program of genocide, at first through incarceration and forced labor and then by establishing death camps. In a catastrophe generally known as the Holocaust or Shoah, roughly six million European Jews from Germany and Nazi-occupied countries were murdered in these death camps and in the killing fields set up behind military lines on the Eastern Front. Nazi forces also carried out a campaign of ethnic extermination against Europe's Roma/Sinti and murdered thousands of Eastern Europeans, homosexuals, mentally disabled people, Freemasons, Jehovah's Witnesses, and opposition figures, among others.

Nazi revanchism and expansionism led to World War II, which resulted in the destruction of Germany's political and economic infrastructures and led to its division.

After Germany's unconditional surrender on May 8, 1945, the United States, the United Kingdom, the U.S.S.R. and, later, France occupied the country and assumed responsibility for its administration. The commanders in chief exercised supreme authority in their respective zones and acted in concert on questions affecting the whole country.

The United States, the United Kingdom, and the Soviet Union agreed at Potsdam in August 1945 to treat Germany as a single economic unit with some central administrative departments in a decentralized framework. However, Soviet policy turned increasingly toward dominating the part of Europe where Soviet armies were present, including eastern Germany.

In 1948, the Soviets, in an attempt to abrogate agreements for Four-Power control of the city, blockaded Berlin. Until May 1949, the Allied-occupied part of Berlin was kept supplied only by an Allied airlift. The "Berlin airlift" succeeded in forcing the Soviets to accept, for the time being, the Allied role and the continuation of freedom in a portion of the city, West Berlin.

Political Developments in West Germany

The United States and the United Kingdom moved to establish a nucleus for a future German government by creating a central Economic

Council for their two zones. The program later provided for a constituent assembly, an occupation statute governing relations between the Allies and the German authorities, and the political and economic merger of the French with the British and American zones. The western portion of the country became the Federal Republic of Germany.

On May 23, 1949, the Basic Law, which came to be known as the constitution of the Federal Republic of Germany, was promulgated. Konrad Adenauer became the first federal Chancellor on September 20, 1949. The next day, the occupation statute came into force, granting powers of self-government with certain exceptions.

As part of an ongoing commitment to deal with its historic responsibility, the Federal Republic of Germany took upon itself a leading role in the field of Holocaust education and support for research into this dark period of history. It has also paid out nearly 63 billion Euros as a measure of compensation to Jewish survivors and heirs of the Holocaust and other victims of Nazism, such as forced laborers from many European countries.

The F.R.G. quickly progressed toward fuller sovereignty and association with its European neighbors and the Atlantic community. The London and Paris agreements of 1954 restored full sovereignty (with some exceptions) to the F.R.G. in May 1955 and opened the way for German membership in the North Atlantic Treaty Organization (NATO) and the Western European Union (WEU).

The three Western Allies retained occupation powers in Berlin and certain responsibilities for Germany as a whole, including responsibility for the determination of Germany's eastern borders. Under the new arrangements, the Allies stationed troops within the F.R.G. for NATO defense, pursuant to stationing and status-of-forces agreements. With the exception of 45,000 French troops, Allied forces were under NATO's joint defense command. (France withdrew from NATO's military command structure in 1966.) Political life in the F.R.G. was remarkably stable and orderly. After Adenauer's chancellorship (1949–63), Ludwig Erhard (1963–66) and Kurt Georg Kiesinger (1966–69) served as Chancellor. Between 1949 and 1966 the united caucus of the Christian Democratic Union (CDU) and Christian Social Union (CSU), either alone or with the smaller Free Democratic Party (FDP), formed the government. Kiesinger's 1966–69 "Grand Coalition" included the F.R.G.'s two largest parties, CDU/CSU and the Social Democratic Party (SPD). After the 1969 election, the SPD, headed by Willy Brandt, formed a coalition government with the FDP. Brandt resigned in May 1974, after a senior member of his staff was uncovered as an East German spy.

Helmut Schmidt (SPD) succeeded Brandt, serving as Chancellor from 1974 to 1982. Hans-Dietrich Genscher, a leading FDP official, became Vice Chancellor and Foreign Minister, a position he would hold until 1992.

In October 1982, the FDP joined forces with the CDU/CSU to make CDU Chairman Helmut Kohl the Chancellor. Following national elections in March 1983, Kohl emerged in firm control of both the government and the CDU. He served until the CDU's election defeat in 1998. In 1983, a new political party, the Greens, entered the Bundestag for the first time.

Political Developments in East Germany

In the Soviet zone, the Communist Party forced the Social Democratic Party to merge in 1946 to form the Socialist Unity Party (SED). Under Soviet direction, a constitution was drafted on May 30, 1949, and adopted on October 7 when the German Democratic Republic was proclaimed. On October 11, 1949, a SED government under Wilhelm Pieck was established. The Soviet Union and its East European allies immediately recognized the G.D.R. The United States and most other countries did not recognize the G.D.R. until a series of agreements in 1972–73. The G.D.R. established the structures of a single-party, centralized, communist state. On July 23, 1952, the G.D.R. abolished the traditional Laender and established 14 Bezirke (districts). Formally, there existed a "National Front"—an umbrella organization nominally consisting of the SED, four other political parties controlled and directed by the SED, and the four principal mass organizations (youth, trade unions, women, and culture). However, control was clearly and solely in the hands of the SED. Balloting in G.D.R. elections was not secret. On July 17, 1953, East Germans revolted against totalitarian rule. The F.R.G. marked the bloody revolt by making the date the West German National Day, which remained until reunification.

Inter-German Relations

During the 1950s, East Germans fled to the West by the millions. The Soviets made the inner German border increasingly tight, but Berlin's Four-Power status countered such restrictions. Berlin thus became an escape point for even greater numbers of East Germans. On August 13, 1961, the G.D.R. began building a wall through the center of Berlin, slowing down the flood of refugees and dividing the city. The Berlin Wall became the symbol of the East's political debility and the division of Europe.

In 1969, Chancellor Brandt announced that the F.R.G. would remain firmly rooted in the Atlantic Alliance but would intensify efforts to improve relations with Eastern Europe and the G.D.R. The F.R.G. commenced this "Ostpolitik" by negotiating nonaggression treaties with the Soviet Union, Poland, Czechoslovakia, Bulgaria, and Hungary. Based upon Brandt's policies, in 1971 the Four Powers concluded a Quadripartite Agreement on Berlin to address practical questions the division posed, without prejudice to each party's view of the city's Four Power status.

The F.R.G.'s relations with the G.D.R. posed particularly difficult questions. Though anxious to relieve serious hardships for divided families and to reduce friction, the F.R.G. under Brandt was intent on holding to its concept of "two German states in one German nation." Relations improved, however, and in September 1973, the F.R.G. and the G.D.R. were admitted to the United Nations. The two Germanys exchanged permanent representatives in 1974, and, in 1987, G.D.R. head of state Erich Honecker paid an official visit to the F.R.G.

Berlin

Shortly after World War II, Berlin became the seat of the Allied Control Council, which was to have governed Germany as a whole until the conclusion of a peace settlement. In 1948, however, the Soviets refused to participate any longer in the quadripartite administration of Germany. They also refused to continue the joint administration of Berlin and drove the government elected by the people of Berlin out of its seat in the Soviet sector and installed a communist regime in its place. From then until unification, the Western Allies continued to exercise supreme authority—effective only in their sectors—through the Allied Kommandatura. To the degree compatible with the city's special status, however, they turned over control and management of city affairs to the Berlin Senat (executive) and House of Representatives, governing bodies established by constitutional process and chosen by free elections. The Allies and German authorities in the F.R.G. and West Berlin never recognized the communist city regime in East Berlin or G.D.R. authority there.

During the years of Berlin's isolation—176 kilometers (110 mi.) inside the former G.D.R.—the Western Allies encouraged a close relationship between the Government of West Berlin and that of the F.R.G. Representatives of the city participated as non-voting members in the F.R.G. parliament; appropriate West German agencies, such as the supreme administrative court, had their permanent seats in the city; and the governing mayor of Berlin took his turn as President of the Bundesrat. In addition, the Allies carefully consulted with the F.R.G. and Berlin Governments on foreign policy questions involving unification and the status of Berlin.

Between 1948 and 1990, major events such as fairs and festivals took place in West Berlin, and the F.R.G. encouraged investment in commerce by special concessionary tax legislation. The results of such efforts, combined with effective city administration and the Berliners' energy and spirit, were encouraging. Berlin's morale remained high, and its industrial production considerably surpassed its prewar level.

German Unification

During the summer of 1989, rapid changes took place in the G.D.R. Pressures for political opening throughout Eastern Europe had not seemed to affect the G.D.R. regime. However, Hungary ended its border restrictions with Austria, and a growing flood of East Germans began to take advantage of this route to West Germany. Thousands of East Germans also tried to reach the West by staging sit-ins at F.R.G. diplomatic facilities in other East European capitals. The exodus generated demands within the G.D.R. for political change, and mass demonstrations in several cities—particularly in Leipzig—continued to grow. On October 7, Soviet leader Mikhail Gorbachev visited Berlin to celebrate the 40th anniversary of the establishment of the G.D.R. and urged the East German leadership to pursue reform.

On October 18, Erich Honecker resigned and was replaced by Egon Krenz. The exodus continued unabated, and pressure for political reform mounted. Finally, on November 9, the G.D.R. allowed East Germans to travel freely. Thousands poured through the Berlin Wall into the western sectors of Berlin. The Wall was opened.

On November 28, F.R.G. Chancellor Kohl outlined a 10-point plan for the peaceful unification of the two Germanys. In December, the G.D.R. Volkskammer eliminated the SED's monopoly on power. The SED changed its name to the Party of Democratic Socialism (PDS), and numerous political groups and parties formed. The communist system had been eliminated. A new Prime Minister, Hans Modrow, headed a caretaker government that shared power with the new, democratically oriented parties.

In early February 1990, Chancellor Kohl rejected the Modrow government's proposal for a unified, neutral Germany. Kohl affirmed that a unified Germany must be a member of NATO. Finally, on March 18, the first free elections were held in the G.D.R., and Lothar de Maiziere (CDU) formed a government under a policy of expeditious unification with the F.R.G. The freely elected representatives of the Volkskammer held their first session on April 5, and the G.D.R. peacefully evolved from a communist to a democratically elected government.

Four Power Control Ends

In 1990, as a necessary step for German unification and in parallel with internal German developments, the two German states and the Four Powers—the United States, U.K., France, and the Soviet Union—negotiated to end Four Power reserved rights for Berlin and Germany as a whole. These "Two-plus-Four" negotiations were mandated at the Ottawa Open Skies conference on February 13, 1990. The six foreign ministers met four times in the ensuing months in Bonn (May 5), Berlin (June 22), Paris (July 17), and Moscow (September 12). The Polish Foreign Minister participated in the part of the Paris meeting that dealt with the Polish-German borders.

Of key importance was overcoming Soviet objections to a united Germany's membership in NATO. The Alliance was already responding to the changing circumstances, and, in NATO, issued the London Declaration on a transformed NATO. On July 16, after a bilateral meeting, Gorbachev and Kohl announced an agreement in principle to permit a united Germany in NATO. This cleared the way for the signing of the "Treaty on the Final Settlement With Respect to Germany" in Moscow on September 12. In addition to terminating Four Power rights, the treaty mandated the withdrawal of all Soviet forces from Germany by the end of 1994. This made it clear that the current borders were final and definitive, and specified the right of a united Germany to belong to NATO. It also provided for the continued presence of British, French, and American troops in Berlin during the interim period of the Soviet withdrawal. In the treaty, the Germans renounced nuclear, biological, and chemical weapons and stated their intention to reduce German armed forces to 370,000 within 3 to 4 years after the Conventional Armed Forces in Europe (CFE) Treaty, signed in Paris on November 19, 1990, entered into force.

German unification could then proceed. In accordance with Article 23 of the F.R.G.'s Basic Law, the five Laender (which had been reestablished in the G.D.R.) acceded to the F.R.G. on October 3, 1990. The F.R.G. proclaimed October 3 as its new national day. On December 2, 1990, all-German elections were held for the first time since 1933.

The Final Settlement Treaty ended Berlin's special status as a separate area under Four Power control. Under the terms of the treaty between the F.R.G. and the G.D.R., Berlin became the capital of a unified Germany. The Bundestag voted in June 1991 to make Berlin the seat of government.

The Government of Germany asked the Allies to maintain a military presence in Berlin until the complete withdrawal of the Western Group of Forces (ex-Soviet) from the territory of the former G.D.R. The Russian withdrawal was completed August 31, 1994. On September 8, 1994, ceremonies marked the final departure of Western Allied troops from Berlin.

In 1999, the formal seat of the federal government moved from Bonn to Berlin. Berlin also is one of the Federal Republic's 16 Laender.

GOVERNMENT AND POLITICAL CONDITIONS

Germany is a constitutional, parliamentary democracy. Citizens choose their representatives periodically in free and fair multiparty elections. The head of the federal government, the chancellor, is elected by the Federal Parliament (Bundestag). The second legislative chamber, the Federal Council (Bundesrat), represents the 16 states at the federal level and is composed of members of the state governments. The most recent national elections for the Bundestag took place in 2009.

Recent Elections

In 2009 the country held parliamentary elections that were considered free and fair.

Political Parties: Political parties generally operated without restriction or outside interference unless they were deemed a threat to the federal constitution. Even when the federal authorities perceive such a threat, they have no authority to ban a party; they can only petition to the Federal Constitutional Court to do so.

A total of 31 splinter parties were denied approval to participate in the 2009 federal parliamentary elections. A report on the parliamentary elections released in 2009 by the Office for Democratic Institutions and Human Rights of the Organization for Security and Cooperation in Europe (OSCE) criticized certain provisions of the law for the admission of new parties for conflicts of interest in the federal election committee, which decides on such admissions, and a lack of judicial review of election administration decisions.

Participation of Women and Minorities: The federal chancellor and five of the 16 cabinet members were women. There were 204 women in the 620-seat Federal Parliament. Five judges on the 16-member Federal Constitutional Court were women. There were 16 members of ethnic minorities or members with an immigrant background in the parliament, one on the Federal Constitutional Court, and one in the cabinet. There were three female state-level ministers for integration with a Turkish background and three female minister presidents.

Principal Government Officials

Last Updated: 1/31/2013

Fed. Pres.: **Joachim GAUCK**
Chancellor: **Angela MERKEL**
Vice Chancellor: **Philipp ROESLER**
Min. for Consumer Protection & Agriculture: **Ilse AIGNER**
Min. of Defense: **Thomas DE MAIZIERE**
Min. for Economic Cooperation & Development: **Dirk NIEBEL**
Min. for Economics & Technology: **Philipp ROESLER**
Min. for Education & Research: **Annette SCHAVAN**
Min. for Environment & Nuclear Safety: **Peter ALTMAIER**
Min. for Family, Seniors, Women, & Youth: **Kristina SCHROEDER**
Min. of Finance: **Wolfgang SCHAEUBLE**
Min. of Foreign Affairs: **Guido WESTERWELLE**
Min. for Health: **Daniel BAHR**
Min. of Interior: **Hans-Peter FRIEDRICH**
Min. of Justice: **Sabine LEUTHEUSSER-SCHNARRENBERGER**
Min. for Labor & Social Affairs: **Ursula VON DER LEYEN**
Min. for Transportation, Construction, & Urban Development: **Peter RAMSAUER**
Min. Without Portfolio & Chancellery Chief: **Ronald POFALLA**
Pres., Bundesbank: **Jens WEIDMANN**
Ambassador to the US: **Peter AMMON**
Permanent Representative to the UN, New York: **Peter WITTIG**

ECONOMY

The German economy - the fifth largest economy in the world in PPP terms and Europe's largest - is a leading exporter of machinery, vehicles, chemicals, and household equipment and benefits from a highly skilled labor force. Like its Western European neighbors, Germany faces significant demographic challenges to sustained long-term growth. Low fertility rates and declining net immigration are increasing pressure on the country's social welfare system and necessitate structural reforms. Reforms launched by the government of Chancellor Gerhard Schroeder (1998–2005), deemed necessary to address chronically high unemployment and low average growth, contributed to strong growth in 2006 and 2007 and falling unemployment.

These advances, as well as a government subsidized, reduced working hour scheme, help explain the relatively modest increase in unemployment during the 2008–09 recession - the deepest since World War II—and its decrease to 6.5% in 2012.

GDP contracted 5.1% in 2009 but grew by 3.7% in 2010, and 3.0% in 2011, before dipping to 0.9% in 2012—a reflection of the worsening euro-zone financial crisis and the financial burden it places on Germany as well as falling demand for German exports. Stimulus and stabilization efforts initiated in 2008 and 2009 and tax cuts introduced in Chancellor Angela Merkel's second term increased Germany's budget deficit to 3.3% in 2010, but slower spending and higher tax revenues reduce the deficit to 1.7% in 2011, and the government estimates it had a balanced budget in 2012.

A constitutional amendment approved in 2009 limits the federal government to structural deficits of no more than 0.35% of GDP per annum as of 2016. Following the March 2011 Fukushima nuclear disaster, Chancellor Angela Merkel announced in May 2011 that eight of the country's 17 nuclear reactors would be shut down immediately and the remaining plants would close by 2022. Germany hopes to replace nuclear power with renewable energy. Before the shutdown of the eight reactors, Germany relied on nuclear power for 23% of its electricity generating capacity and 46% of its base-load electricity production.

Labor Conditions

Comprehensive legislation protects children from exploitation in the workplace, and the government enforced these laws.

The law prohibits the employment of children younger than 15 with a few exceptions: children 13 or 14 years of age may do farm work for up to three hours per day or deliver newspapers for up to two hours per day, and children three to 14 years of age may take part in cultural performances under strict limits on the kinds of activity, number of hours, and times of the day. Exploitative child labor was not a serious problem, although violations did occur mainly in small, often family-owned businesses such as bars, restaurants, and grocery stores. The Federal Ministry of Labor and Social Affairs enforced the law effectively through its Factory Inspection Bureau.

The country does not have a statutory minimum wage. As of December 31, binding minimum wages were in place for approximately four groups of construction occupations, electrical trades, painting, postal service, waste management, large-scale laundries, nursing care, security services, special mining services, and temporary employment agencies, covering approximately 8 percent of the workforce.

Minimum wages vary between eastern and western Germany. In eastern Germany wages ranged from 6.53 euros ($8.49) per hour in security activities up to 10.80 euros ($14.04) per hour for erection of roof coverings and frames; minimum wages in the west ranged from 7.65 euros ($9.95) per hour in commercial cleaning up to 13.00 euros ($16.90) per hour for skilled construction work. Official social indicators on poverty and social exclusion ("federal indicators") revealed that persons who had a disposable income of less than 11,151 euros ($14,496) per year), after inclusion of government transfer payments, were at risk of poverty. While in the eastern German states (including Berlin), 19.5 percent of the population was at risk of poverty, the rate in the former West Germany (excluding Berlin) was significantly lower (12.9 percent). The reference period for collecting the income data was 2008.

The minimum wage rates set by collective bargaining agreements are enforceable by law. Sector-wide collective bargaining agreements determined wages and working conditions in most industries, but company-level agreements frequently deviated from them. Multicompany, industry-wide contracts covered directly approximately 32 percent of all firms; company-level agreements covered 4 percent, 40 percent were guided by a respective industry agreement, and 24 percent were not covered at all. Collective bargaining agreements covered approximately 65 percent of the labor force in the western part of the country and approximately 51 percent in the eastern part.

The law provides for equal treatment of foreign workers, who generally worked in conditions equal to those of citizens, although such workers faced some wage discrimination. For example, some schools paid foreign teachers less than their citizen counterparts. Employers also often paid lower wages to seasonal workers from Eastern Europe who came to the country on temporary work permits. At times employers paid workers from other EU countries the same wages they would receive in their home country, even if the corresponding citizen worker would receive a higher wage.

Federal regulations limit the workweek to 48 hours, but collective bargaining agreements may stipulate lower maximums. Contracts directly or indirectly affecting 80 percent of the working population regulated the number of hours of work per week. According to the European Labor Force Survey, in 2010 the average full-time employee's workweek was 39.8 hours for women and 41 hours for men; rest periods for lunch were accepted practices.

Provisions for overtime, holiday, and weekend pay varied depending upon the applicable collective bargaining agreement. Excessive compulsory overtime is prohibited, and workers are covered and protected against arbitrary employer requests either by collective bargaining agreements or individual contracts. Employees who refuse to work overtime cannot lose their jobs or face other reprisals such as demotion or assignment to unattractive work or to less desirable shift times such as nights or weekends.

U.S.-GERMAN RELATIONS

Following U.S. independence from Great Britain, the United States established diplomatic relations with first the Kingdom of Prussia in 1797, then the German Empire in 1871. U.S.-German relations were terminated in 1917 during World War I, and the United States declared war on Germany. Relations were reestablished in 1921, but were severed again in 1941 during World War II when Nazi Germany declared war on the United States. After the war, Germany was divided into four zones occupied by Allied powers; Berlin also was divided. In 1955, the United States established diplomatic relations with West Germany, which had been created out of the U.S., British, and French zones. The United States established diplomatic relations in 1974 with East Germany, which had been created from the Soviet Union's zone. West Germany and East Germany were unified in 1990.

The United States is committed to preserving peace and security in Europe, and U.S.-German relations have been a focal point of U.S. involvement in Europe since the end of World War II. Germany stands at the center of European affairs and is a key partner in U.S. relations with Europeans in the North Atlantic Treaty Organization (NATO) and the European Union. U.S. policy toward Germany is to preserve and consolidate a close and vital relationship with Germany, not only as friends and trading partners, but also as allies sharing common institutions. The United States recognizes that the security and prosperity of the United States and Germany significantly depend on each other. The bilateral political, economic, and security relationships are based on close consultation and coordination at the most senior levels, and the United States and Germany cooperate actively in international forums.

As allies in NATO, the United States and Germany work side by side to maintain peace and freedom. U.S. and German troops work together effectively in NATO and UN operations worldwide due in part to the joint training and capacity-building performed at U.S. military installations in Germany. The two countries have extended their diplomatic cooperation into military cooperation by maintaining peacekeeping efforts in the Balkans and working together to encourage the evolution of open and democratic states throughout central and eastern Europe. Germany has been an integral part of the UN-mandated International Security Assistance Force in Afghanistan. German and U.S. maritime forces also are deployed to combat piracy off the Horn of Africa. Following the September 11, 2001, terrorist attacks in the United States, Germany has been a reliable U.S. ally in efforts against terrorism.

U.S. Assistance to Germany

The United States provides no development assistance to Germany.

Bilateral Economic Relations

As two of the world's leading trading nations, the United States and Germany share a commitment to an open and expanding world economy. Germany is a member of the European Union, and in 2007 was the main driver behind the creation of the Transatlantic Economic Council (TEC), a political body that seeks to deepen cooperation between the United States and the European Union by promoting economic growth through increased trade and job creation. Germany and the United States hold regular Informal Commercial Exchange (ICE) Talks to informally address economic issues on a bilateral basis. The United States is Germany's leading export market outside the EU (in 2011). Counting EU-countries, the United States still ranks second, topped only by France. In 2011, Germany exported goods worth $97 billion to the United States. Germany is the 5th largest U.S. trading partner globally and the top importer of U.S. goods in the EU (in 2011). In 2011, U.S. exports totaled slightly over $49 billion to Germany.

The U.S. and German trade relationship is driven by massive mutual investment. In 2010, German direct investment in the United States was worth $213 billion, while U.S. direct investment in Germany was worth $106 billion. German investments include key industries such as chemicals and transportation equipment, as well as services sectors such as financial industries. Altogether, German firms employ approximately half-a-million American workers.

The U.S.-German Treaty of Friendship, Commerce and Navigation affords U.S. investors national treatment and provides for the free movement of capital between the United States and Germany. Taxation of U.S. firms within Germany is governed by a protocol on the avoidance of double taxation.

Germany's Membership in International Organizations

Germany and the United States belong to a number of the same international organizations, including the United Nations, North Atlantic Treaty Organization, Euro-Atlantic Partnership Council, Organization for Security and Cooperation in Europe, G-20, G-8, Organization for Economic Cooperation and Development, International Monetary Fund, World Bank, and World Trade Organization. Germany also is an observer to the Organization of American States.

Bilateral Representation

Germany maintains an embassy in the United States at 2300 M Street NW, Washington, DC 20037 (tel. 202-298-4000).

Principal U.S. Embassy Officials

Last Updated: 1/14/2013

BERLIN (E) Pariser Platz 2, 10117 Berlin, Germany, [49] (30) 8305-0, Fax [49] (30) 238-6290, Workweek: Monday-Friday, 0830-1730, Website: http://germany.usembassy.gov/

DCM OMS:	Sarah G. Gowen
AMB OMS:	Theresa R. Dowling
FM:	Michael R. Wilson
HRO:	Helen G. Recinos
MGT:	Frank Ledahawsky
POSHO:	Tommy D. Heard
SDO/DATT:	COL Gregory J. Broecker
AMB:	Philip D. Murphy
CON:	Karen L. Christensen
DCM:	James D. Melville
PAO:	Thomas Miller
COM:	Dale Tasharski
GSO:	Melissa A. Coskuner
RSO:	Robert D. Barton
AGR:	Paul Spencer-Macgregor
CLO:	Hema Crockett
ECON:	Seth D. Winnick
EEO:	Gail Sims
FMO:	Joseph C. Johnson
IMO:	Jeffrey S. Myers
IPO:	Jonathan W. Kirkpatrick
IRS:	Thomas E. Stevens
ISO:	Daniel D. Fern
ISSO:	Richard A. Marafino
LEGATT:	Stuart Wirtz
POL:	Robin Quinville
State ICASS:	Karen L. Christensen

DUSSELDORF (CG) Willi-Becker-Alle 10 40227 Dusseldorf, +49-211-4706-125, Fax +49-211-788-8936, Workweek: Monday–Friday 08:00–17:00, Website: http://duesseldorf.usconsulate.gov/

CG OMS:	Nicole Leick
FCS:	Lora Baker
MGT:	Whitney S Wiedeman
POL/ECON:	Richard Volk
CG:	Steve Hubler
RSO:	Jeff Horkey (Frankfurt), Whitney S. Wiedeman–Pso
IMO:	Ken Curry
ISSO:	Rick Marafino

FRANKFURT (CG) Giessener Strasse 30, 60435 Frankfurt, 49-69-7535-0, Fax 49-69-7535-5410 (Mgmt), Workweek: 8:00 a.m.–4:30 p.m. M-F, http://frankfurt.usconsulate.gov/

CG OMS:	Mary Thomas
DHS/CIS:	Kristina Carty-Pratt
DPO:	Charisse Phillips
FM:	Thomas Murphy
HRO:	Sandra Acevedokoosha And Lisa Davis
MGT:	Michael McCarthy
POL/ECON:	Barry Belknap
CG:	Kevin Milas
CON:	Charles Wintheiser
PAO:	Jeff Hill
GSO:	Marcia Cole
RSO:	Charles Horkey
CLO:	Janet Hartnett
DEA:	Michael Barbuti
EEO:	Ruben Solis
FAA:	John Benning
FAA/CASLO:	Anthony Monreal Dhs/Tsa
FMO:	Marcia Cole
IMO:	William Curry
IPO:	Randy Kreft
IRS:	Thomas Stevens
ISO:	Holly McRea
LEGATT:	Lesley Buckler

HAMBURG (CG) Alsterufer 27/28, 20354 Hamburg, Germany, +49-40-41171-300, Fax +49-40-41171-222; +49-40-41171-777, Workweek: M–F; 0830–1730 local, http://hamburg.usconsulate.gov/

CG OMS:	Goschka M Witoslawski
MGT:	Wilbur A. Velarde
POL/ECON:	Robert Stevens
CG:	Inmi Patterson
RSO:	Evan M Matthiesen
ICASS Chair:	Am Emb Berlin
ISSO:	Scott Alper

LEIPZIG (CG) Wilhelm-Seyfferth-Str. 4, (49) (341) 213-840, Fax (49) (341) 213-8475, Workweek: 8:00 am to 5:00 pm, Mo thru Fri, Website: http://leipzig.usconsulate.gov/

POL/ECON:	Helena P. Schrader
CG:	Mark Powell
PAO:	Teta Moehs

MUNICH (CG) Koeniginstrasse 5, +49-89-2888-0, Fax +49-89-283-047, INMARSAT Tel Iridium: 8816-7631-0884, Workweek: Monday–Friday, 0830-1730, Website: http://munich.usconsulate.gov/

CG OMS:	Maria D. Schamber
FCS:	Christina Sharkey
HRO:	Andrea Proctor
MGT:	John K. Moyer
POL/ECON:	John A. Crosby
POSHO:	John K. Moyer
CG:	William E. Moeller
CON:	Randall T. Merideth
PAO:	Leyla L. Ones
GSO:	Dieter Hackl
RSO:	John K. Keith
CLO:	Sharon M. Keith
EEO:	John Nixon
IPO:	Glen R. Jardine
ISSO:	Glen R. Jardine

TRAVEL

Consular Information Sheet

June 7, 2012

Country Description: Germany is a modern and stable democracy located in Western Europe. Tourist facilities are highly developed. In larger towns, many people can communicate in English.

Smart Traveler Enrollment Program (STEP)/Embassy Locations: If you are going to live in or travel to Germany, please take the time to tell us about your trip. If you enroll, we can keep you up to date with important safety and security announcements. It will also help your friends and family get in touch with you in an emergency.

U.S. Embassy Berlin
Clayallee 170, 14191 Berlin
Tel. (49) (30) 8305–0
(emergency services only)
Tel. (49) (30) 8305–1200
(routine calls, 2-4 p.m.
Monday-Thursday)
Fax (49) (30) 8305–1215
American Citizen Services e-mail: ACSBerlin@state.gov

U.S. Consulate General Frankfurt
Giessener Str. 30, 60435
Frankfurt am Main
Tel. (49) (69) 7535–0 (emergency services only)
Tel. (49) (69) 7535–2102
(routine calls, 2-4 p.m.
Monday-Friday)

Fax (49) (69) 7535–2252
American Citizen Services e-mail: GermanyACS@state.gov
Passport Inquiries e-mail: FrankfurtPassports@state.gov

U.S. Consulate General Munich
Koeniginstrasse 5, 80539 Munich
Tel. (49) (89) 2888–0
Fax (49) (89) 280-9998
American Citizen Services e-mail: ConsMunich@state.gov

U.S. Consulate Leipzig (emergency services only)
Wilhelm-Seyfferth-Strasse 4
04107 Leipzig
Tel. (49) (341) 21-8418
Fax: (49) (341) 213-8417

There is also a U.S. consular agency in Bremen at:

Flughafenallee 18, 28199 Bremen
Tel. (49) (421) 301-5860
Fax: (49) (421) 301-5861

Consular services are only provided at the Consulates General in Hamburg and Dusseldorf through periodic visits by consular staff from Berlin and Frankfurt, respectively.

Entry/Exit Requirements for U.S. Citizens: Germany is a party to the Schengen Agreement. As a U.S. citizen, you may enter Germany for up to 90 days for tourist or business purposes without a visa. Your entry into Germany begins the 90-day limit for the entire Schengen area. You may also contact the German Embassy in Washington, for the location of German consulates in Atlanta, Boston, Chicago, Houston, Los Angeles, Miami, New York, or San Francisco to obtain the most current visa information.

If you are transiting Germany en route to other countries, make sure you know all of the entry and exit requirements for your final destination. If you don't have the right documentation, you might be denied boarding to your connecting flight. For example, some countries (e.g., South Africa) require a certain number of blank visa pages, or more than six month's remaining validity on your passport.

We are unaware of any HIV/AIDS entry restrictions for visitors to, or foreign residents of, Germany.

Threats to Safety and Security: German authorities are vigilant in combating terrorism and other threats to security. They have uncovered specific threats and prosecuted suspects, though Germany itself has been largely free of terror incidents.

However, like other countries in the Schengen area, Germany's open borders with its European neighbors limits its ability to track suspect individuals entering and exiting the country with anonymity. Germany's robust democracy is often expressed in large, public demonstrations on a variety of political and economic issues. Such demonstrations are common on politically significant holidays, such as German Labor Day on May 1, and during international summits hosted in Germany.

In order to stage a demonstration, groups must obtain prior police approval, and police routinely oversee participants and passersby. Nonetheless, these demonstrations can attract counter-demonstrations and have the potential to turn violent. Avoid areas around protests and demonstrations and check local media for updates on the situation and traffic advisories.

In addition, hooligans, most often drunken "skinheads," have been known to harass or even attack people whom they believe to be foreigners or members of rival groups. On occasion, U.S. citizens have reported that they were assaulted for racial reasons or because they appeared "foreign." In addition, U.S. citizens should also exercise caution when congregating in areas known as expatriate hangouts such as restaurants, bars, and discos frequented by high numbers of resident U.S. citizens and/or U.S. citizen tourists, as this could attract unwanted attention from disorganized groups of rowdy patrons seeking to start a fight.

Stay up to date by:

- Bookmarking our Bureau of Consular Affairs website, which contains the current Travel Warnings and Travel Alerts as well as the Worldwide Caution;
- Following us on Twitter and the Bureau of Consular Affairs page on Facebook as well;
- Downloading our free Smart Traveler iPhone App to have travel information at your fingertips;
- Calling 1-888-407-4747 toll-free within the U.S. and Canada, or a regular toll line, 1-202-501-4444, from other countries; and
- Taking some time before travel to consider your personal security.

Crime: Violent crime is rare in Germany, but can occur, especially in larger cities or high-risk areas such as train stations. There have been several reports of aggravated assault against U.S. citizens in higher-risk urban areas. However, most incidents of street crime involve the theft of unattended items and pick pocketing. Take the same precautions that you would in any large city.

Don't buy counterfeit and pirated goods, even if they are widely available. Not only are the bootlegs illegal in the United States, if you purchase them, you could also be breaking local law.

Victims of Crime: If you or someone you know becomes the victim of a crime abroad, you should contact the local police and the nearest U.S. embassy or consulate. We can:

- Replace a stolen passport;
- Help you find appropriate medical care if you are the victim of violent crimes such as assault or rape;
- Put you in contact with the appropriate police authorities, and if you want us to, we can contact family members or friends; and

- Help you understand the local criminal justice process and direct you to local attorneys, although it is important to remember that local authorities are responsible for investigating and prosecuting the crime.

In Germany, there are two separate phone numbers that correspond to 911 in the United States: In an emergency, dial 112 for an ambulance and 110 for the police.

Criminal Penalties: While traveling in Germany, you are subject to its laws, even if you are a U.S. citizen. Foreign laws and legal systems can be vastly different from our own.While you are overseas, U.S. laws do not apply, and if you do something illegal in your host country, your U.S. passport won't help you. It is very important to know what is legal and what is not, and criminal penalties vary from country to country. There are also some things that may be legal where you are traveling, but illegal in the United States. If you engage in sexual conduct with children or use or disseminate child pornography in a foreign country, you can be prosecuted in the United States.

The Embassy has learned of some incidents of German lawyers, working on behalf of media companies, aggressively identifying individuals who are illegally downloading copyrighted content and then billing those people 1000 euros or more per incident. If these cases are brought to court, German courts will likely rule in favor of the companies. You are strongly advised not to download media content except from reputable legal sites.

Arrest Notifications in Germany: While some countries will automatically notify the nearest U.S. embassy or consulate if a U.S. citizen is detained or arrested in a foreign country, that might not always be the case. To ensure that the United States is aware of your circumstances, request that the police and prison officials notify the nearest U.S. embassy or consulate as soon as you are arrested or detained overseas.

Special Circumstances: Germany has strict customs regulations concerning temporary importation into or export from Germany of items such as firearms, military artifacts (particularly those pertaining to the Second World War), antiques, medications/pharmaceuticals, and business equipment. Under German law it is also illegal to bring into, or take out of, Germany literature, music CDs, or paraphernalia that glorifies fascism, the Nazi past, or the "Third Reich." Contact the German Embassy in Washington or one of the German consulates in the United States for specific information regarding customs requirements.

Surprisingly, credit cards are not accepted as widely as they are in the United States. However, automatic teller machines (ATMs) are widely available throughout Germany. They utilize many of the same account networks that are found in the United States, so it is possible in most cases to get Euros directly from your U.S. bank while you are in Germany, without paying inordinate currency exchange fees.

Accessibility: While in Germany, individuals with disabilities may find accessibility and accommodation different from what is found in the United States. Many existing buildings, as well as public transportation systems, are less adapted to individuals with disabilities.

You should check with your hotel or destination to learn more about options to accommodate disabled traveler needs before visiting Germany. At German airports, Lufthansa and Air Berlin offer services for disabled travelers, and the German National Railway, Deutsche Bahn, maintains a mobility resource webpage. The German Hotel and Restaurant Association (DEHOGA) and the German Hotel Association (IHA) maintain directories of accessible accommodations. You can find more information on accessibility by visiting the German National Tourist Board website.

Medical Facilities and Health Information: Germany has good medical care and facilities. If you are not a resident of Germany, doctors and hospitals may expect immediate payment, in cash. Most doctors, hospitals and pharmacies do not accept credit cards.

Due to Germany's strict customs regulations, generally you are not allowed to receive prescription medication by mail without special permission. During your trip, you should only carry the amount you plan to use. For more information, please visit the German Customs website regarding medicine.

You can find detailed information on vaccinations and other health precautions on the CDC website. For information about outbreaks of infectious diseases abroad, consult the World Health Organization (WHO) website. The WHO website also contains additional health information for travelers, including detailed country-specific health information.

Medical Insurance: You cannot assume your insurance coverage will go with you when you travel. It's very important to find out BEFORE you leave whether or not your medical insurance will cover you overseas. You need to ask your insurance company two questions:

- Does my policy apply when I am outside of the U.S.?
- Will it cover emergency expenses like a trip to a foreign hospital or an evacuation?

In many places, doctors and hospitals still expect payment in cash at the time of service. Your regular U.S. health insurance may not cover doctor and hospital visits in other countries. If your policy doesn't go with you when you travel, it's a very good idea to take out another one for your trip.

Traffic Safety and Road Conditions: In Germany, road conditions can be significantly different from those in the United States. If you hold a valid U.S. driver's license, you can drive in Germany for up to six months without acquiring a German driver's license. German road conditions in general are excellent, although you should exercise caution while traveling on older roads in eastern Germany. Contrary to popular belief, there are posted speed limits on large stretches of the highway, or Autobahn, mostly when traveling through urban areas or when the road has many curves. The high speed permitted on the Autobahn, adverse weather conditions, and unfamiliar road markings can pose significant hazards. Driver error is a leading cause of accidents involving U.S. citizen motorists in Germany. Bicycles are another cause of mishaps. Many German streets and sidewalks have dedicated bike lanes. Whether you are driving or walking, be aware that bicycles have priority use of these lanes. If you are walking, watch for bicyclists before crossing or stepping into bike lanes. Bicyclists also have priority over cars when turning onto side streets.

If you are driving, check whether a bicyclist is approaching from either direction before attempting to enter side streets, even when the light is in your favor. If you are turning into a side street and hit a bicyclist using a marked bike lane, you will be held responsible for any injury or damage caused. Driver right-of-way rules are different from the United States. Unless you are traveling on a priority road, vehicles coming from the right have the right-of-way. It is generally illegal in Germany to pass vehicles on the right. The threshold for determining whether a person has been driving under the influence of alcohol is lower than in the United States. Under German law it is illegal to operate a vehicle if the blood level is 0.5 per mill or higher. The law imposes a penalty and the withdrawal of the driver's license for specified periods of time depending upon the gravity of each violation. For more information, please visit the U.S. Embassy's webpage on" Driving in Germany." It is illegal to use your cell phone while driving in Germany. If you would like more specific information on travel within Germany, please visit the website of the German National Tourist Board

Aviation Safety Oversight: The U.S. Federal Aviation Administration (FAA) has assessed the government of Germany's Civil Aviation Authority as being in compliance with International Civil Aviation Organization (ICAO) aviation safety standards for oversight of Germany's air carrier operations. Further information may be found on the FAA's safety assessment page.

Children's Issues: Please see the U.S. Dept. of State Office of Children's Issues web pages on intercountry adoption and international parental child abduction.

Intercountry Adoption

January 2013

The information in this section has been edited from a report available through the U.S. Department of State Office of Children's Issues. For more detailed information, please read the *Intercountry Adoption* section of this book and review current reports online at http://www.adoption.state.gov.

Germany is party to the Hague Convention on Protection of Children and Co-operation in Respect of Intercountry Adoption(Hague Adoption Convention). Intercountry adoption processing in Hague countries is done in accordance with the requirements of the Convention; the U.S. implementing legislation, the Intercountry Adoption Act of 2000 (IAA); and the IAA;s implementing regulations, as well as the implementing legislation and regulations of Germany. Germany is not generally considered a country of origin in intercountry adoption. Only five German orphans have received U.S. immigrant visas since 2007.

The information provided is intended primarily to assist in rare adoption cases from Germany, including adoptions of German children by relatives in the United States, as well as adoptions from third countries by U.S. citizens living in Germany.

Who Can Adopt? To bring an adopted child to the United States from Germany, you must meet eligibility and suitability requirements. The U.S. Department of Homeland Security, U.S. Citizenship and Immigration Services (USCIS) determines who can adopt under U.S. immigration law. Additionally, a child must meet the definition of Convention adoptee under U.S. law in order to immigrate to the United States on an IH-3 or IH-4 immigrant visa.

Residency: There are no residency requirements to adopt a child from Germany. There is no restriction on the nationality or citizenship of the adopting parent. Germany allows non-Germans to adopt a German child. U.S. citizens who are resident in Germany may apply to adopt from other countries through the German intercountry adoption process. These prospective adoptive parents may contact the relevant central authority for the area of their residence in order to initiate the process.

Age of Adopting Parents: The minimum age for an adopting parent is 25 years old. However, in the case of an adoption of a stepchild, the lower age limit of the adopting parent is 21 years. There is no legal upper age limit of an adopting parent. If a child is being adopted in Germany by foreign parents, the court has the right to take age restrictions in the laws of the parents' home country into consideration. Although there is no statutory limit, pursuant to a recommendation by the Federal Working Group of the State Youth Welfare Offices, the age gap between the adopting parents and the child being adopted should not be greater than 40 years.

Marriage: Unmarried, single people, as well as one member of an unmarried heterosexual couple, can adopt a child in Germany. Married couples can only adopt together as husband and wife, with the minimum age for one parent being 25 years old and the minimum age of the second parent being at least 21 years old. Same-sex couples may register as a partnership, but partners cannot adopt jointly, as a married couple can. However, one member of a registered partnership may adopt the biological child of his or her registered partner. Also, one member of a registered partnership may adopt alone.

Income: No specific requirements.

Who Can Be Adopted? Because Germany is party to the Hague Adoption Convention, children from Germany must meet the requirements of the Convention in order to be eligible for adoption. For example, the Convention requires that Germany attempt to place a child with a family in-country before determining that a child is eligible for intercountry adoption. In addition to Germany's requirements, a child must meet the definition of a Convention adoptee for you to bring him or her back to the United States.

Relinquishment/Consent: The parents of the child must provide consent to the adoption; this consent cannot be accepted by the court if the child is less than eight weeks of age. If the child is over eight weeks old and under the age of 14, the child's legal guardian (sometimes, but not always, the parents) must also consent to the adoption on the child's behalf. If the child is over the age of 14, s/he must personally consent to the adoption, with the concurrence of his/her legal guardian. In the case of children born out of wedlock, the biological father can surrender parental rights and consent to the adoption any time after conception and prior to the child's birth. In this case, the mother must still wait until the child is eight weeks old to consent to adoption. As an additional requirement in cases where the citizenship of the adopting parent and the child being adopted are different, this consent has to be approved by the family court. However, it does not apply in the case of a domestic adoption subject to German law.

Abandonment: Consent is not required from a parent whose whereabouts are unknown (the court will determine the whereabouts unknown after six months of searching unsuccessfully). In addition, the court may waive the need for parental consent in several circumstances, including those related to the parent's treatment of the child and the parent's mental capacity. Ultimately, the courts will look at each case individually to determine if consent of a biological parent is needed.

Age of Adoptive Child: A person can be adopted at any age. Parents must wait until the child is eight weeks of age before consenting to adoption. Adoption of a person who has reached age 18, the age of majority in Germany, must be justifiable. Sibling Adoptions: Sibling relationships are given consideration in adoption proceedings, but are considered on a case-by-case basis, with particular emphasis given to the positive or negative nature of the relationship between the siblings.

Special Needs or Medical Conditions: On a case-by-case basis, the court may require evidence that an adopting family is aware of and able to cope with a child's special needs and may require families to submit to follow up assessment.

Waiting Period or Foster Care: Typically, the child must live with the prospective adoptive parents for a probationary period prior to the court issuing the adoption order.

Germany's Adoption Authority: There is no centralized court system governing adoption cases in Germany. Each of Germany's 16 Federal States is locally responsible for the effectiveness and legality of an adoption. The main point of contact is:

Bundesamt für Justiz
(Federal Office of Justice)
Zentrale Behörde
Adenauerallee 99-103
53113 Bonn
Tel: +49 22899 410-5414 or -5415
Fax: +49 22899 410-5402
E-mail:auslandsadoption@bfj.bund.de
www.bundesjustizamt.de/auslandsadoption

Persons wishing to adopt a child in Germany should contact either one of the following institutions:

- Youth Welfare Office (Jugendamt) of each district/major city
- Youth Welfare Office (Landesjugendamt) of each German state (Bundesland).

These organizations will be able to assist in arranging an adoption and in facilitating legal proceedings.

The Process: Because Germany is party to the Hague Adoption Convention, adopting from Germany must follow a specific process designed to meet the Convention's requirements. For detailed and updated information on these requirements, please review the *Intercountry Adoption* section of this publication and visit the USCIS Intercountry Adoption website at http://adoption.state.gov.

Role of the Adoption Authority: Each of Germany's 16 Federal States has a central adoption agency that oversees international adoptions.

Role of the Court: The guardianship court (Vormundschaftsgericht) hears an application for an order to change the legal status to that of parent and child and, if appropriate, issues such an order. The court must investigate and review all relevant facts, including information from the adoption agency or public authority involved and the child (as permitted by age).

Role of Adoption Agencies: Adoption services are provided by public youth welfare agencies as well as private, nonprofit agencies that have been qualified to provide adoption services in international adoptions under Germany's Adoption Placement Act. The adoption agency is responsible for key aspects of the adoption process, including providing information to the guardianship court on the prospective adoptive parents.

Adoption Application: For both domestic and intercountry adoption, the prospective adoptive parent(s) must first approach one of four sources for an initial consultation: 1) either one of the youth offices listed above, 2) the German Central Authority for intercountry adoption, 3) the Central Authority in the country of the child's habitual abode, or 4) an international adoption agency. After a favorable evaluation, the parents will be subject to a home study by their local youth welfare office. Their translated home study will be sent to the adoption authority office. When a child has been identified, the adopting parent(s) and the child's legal guardian sign an agreement before a German court or notary public. Before the family court decides if the adoption may take place and issues the final decree, the adopting parent(s) have to prove that the child will be lawfully admitted into their home country.

Time Frame: After an investigation and interview, the Jugendamt issues an initial approval valid for two years. There is no specific time frame for the adoption process. It varies from case to case and primarily depends upon the duration of the qualifying process and/or the difficulty of identifying a child for adoption. The paperwork and investigation process generally takes between four and nine months. A foster period is required to adopt a German child. By law the foster period should be "adequate in length." The court will decide in each case individually whether a parent-child-relationship between the adopting parent and the child to be adopted has been developed.

Adoption Fees: In the adoption services contract that you sign at the beginning of the adoption process, your agency will itemize the fees and estimated expenses related to your adoption process.

Documents Required: Both the German Youth Welfare Department ("Jugendamt") and the adoption agencies require the following documents at the start of the adoption process:

- An application for adoption;
- Birth certificates;
- Proof of citizenship;
- Resume/curriculum vitae for both parents;
- Police certificate for both parents;
- Identification (passport, photo identification, etc.);
- Marriage certificate (if applicable);
- Termination of previous marriage(s) (death certificate, divorce decree, etc.);
- Medical attestation;
- Proof of parents' income (including bank statements);
- Parents' police certificates; and
- Character references.

Bringing Your Child Home: Once your adoption is complete (or you have obtained legal custody of the child), there are a few more steps to take before you can head home. Specifically, you need to apply for several documents for your child before he or she can travel to the United States, such as a birth certificate, a passport or travel document for your child from the country in which he or she was born, and a U.S. Immigration Visa. For detailed and updated information on how to obtain these documents, visit the USCIS Intercountry Adoption website at http://adoption.state.gov.

Child Citizenship Act: For adoptions finalized abroad, the Child Citizenship Act of 2000 allows your new child to acquire American citizenship automatically when he or she enters the United States as lawful permanent residents. For adoptions finalized in the United States, the Child Citizenship Act of 2000 allows your new child to acquire American citizenship automatically when the court in the United States issues the final adoption decree. To learn more, visit the USCIS Intercountry Adoption website at http://adoption.state.gov.

After Adoption: While there are no post-adoption/post-placement reporting requirements in Germany, the placing agency must offer consultation and support after the adoption is finalized upon the request of the adopting parents. This may include, but is not limited to, the provision of contact information for and liaison with local and national adoption networks and support groups. In general, the German authorities also encourage agencies to facilitate contact between adopting families and birth parents and assist with the provision of updates on the child's development, pictures, etc.

U.S. Consulate General
Immigrant Visa Unit
Giessener Strasse 30
60435 Frankfurt Am Main
Tel: (069) 7535-0
http://frankfurt.usconsulate.gov/index.html

Germany's Adoption Authority
Bundesamt für Justiz
(Federal Office of Justice)
Address: Zentrale Behörde, Adenauerallee 99-103, 53113 Bonn
Tel: + 49-228-99-410-0
Fax: +49-228-99-410-5050
www.bundeszentralregister.de

Embassy of Germany
4645 Reservoir Road NW
Washington, DC, 20007-1998
(202) 298-4000
http://www.germany.info/relaunch/index.html

Germany also has consulates in: Atlanta, Boston, Chicago, Houston, Los Angeles, Miami, New York, and San Francisco.

Office of Children's Issues
U.S. Department of State
2201 C Street, NW
SA-29
Washington, DC 20520
Tel: 1-888-407-4747
E-mail: AskCI@state.gov
http://adoption.state.gov

International Parental Child Abduction

October 2012

The information in this section has been edited from a report of the State Department Bureau of Consular Affairs, Office of Overseas Citizens Services. For more information, please read the *International*

Parental Child Abduction section of this book and review current reports online at www.travel.state.gov/abduction.

Disclaimer: The information on this page relating to the legal requirements of specific foreign countries is provided for general information only. Questions involving interpretation of specific foreign laws should be addressed to foreign legal counsel.

General Information: Germany and the United States have been treaty partners under the 1980 Hague Convention on the Civil Aspects of International Child Abduction (Hague Abduction Convention) since December 1, 1990.

Legal System: The Basic Law (constitution) provides the basis for Germany's legal system, which is based on Roman law and uses a comprehensive system of legal codes, as opposed to the Common Law system used in the United States where precedents from prior cases guide court decisions. Courts may also consider the laws of the European Union and the international community. The German Police conduct searches for missing children. Absent a court order, married parents have equal rights of custody to their minor children under German law. Absent a court order, the mother has custody of a child born out-of-wedlock, and the child's father has visitation rights. Family law courts handle divorce, custody, and Hague cases.

Hague Abduction Convention: The U.S. Department of State serves as the U.S. Central Authority (USCA) for the Hague Abduction Convention. In this capacity, the Department's Bureau of Consular Affairs, Directorate for Overseas Citizens Services, Office of Children's Issues facilitates the submission of applications under the Hague Abduction Convention for the return of, or access to, children located in countries that are U.S. treaty partners, including Germany. Parents are strongly encouraged to contact the Department of State for assistance prior to initiating the Hague process directly with the foreign Central Authority.

United States Department of State
Office of Children's Issues
2201 C Street, N.W.
Washington, DC 20520
Telephone: 1-888-407-4747
Outside the United States or Canada: 1-202-501-4444
Fax: 202-736-9132

The German Central Authority (GCA) for the Hague Abduction Convention is the Bundesamt für Justiz, located in the Ministry of Justice. The GCA has an administrative role in processing Hague applications. The Ministry of Justice forwards completed Hague petitions to the appropriate German family court. Among the more than 600 German family courts, only 22 have jurisdiction in proceedings concerning return, access, and recognition and enforcement under the Hague Child Abduction Convention. You can find the list of competent German courts here. Parents or legal guardians and other parties (e.g., the child) have the right to their own counsel. The German Central Authority can be reached at:

German Central Authority
Zentrale Behörde, Adenauerallee 99-103
53113 Bonn.
Tel: +49-228-99-410-5212
Fax:+49-228-99-410-5401
Email: int.sorgerecht@bfj.bund.de

To initiate a Hague case for return of, or access to, a a child in Germany, the USCA encourages a parent or legal guardian to review the eligibility criteria and instructions for completing the Hague application form located at the Department of State website and contact the Department of State for assistance prior to initiating the Hague process directly with the GCA. It is extremely important that each document written in English be translated into German in order to be accepted by a German court. Official documents (court orders, etc.) must be translated by a sworn translator (vereidigter Übersetzer). Letters, statements, and other documentation may be translated unofficially. The USCA is available to answer questions about the Hague application process, to forward a completed application to the GCA, and to subsequently monitor its progress through the foreign administrative and legal processes.

There are no fees for filing Hague applications with either the U.S. or the German central authorities. Attorney fees are the responsibility of the applicant parent. Additional costs may include airplane tickets for court appearances and for the return of the child, if so ordered.

Return: A parent or legal guardian may file an application under the Hague Abduction Convention for return to the United States of a child abducted to, or wrongfully retained in, Germany. The U.S. Department of State can assist parents living in the United States to understand whether the Convention is an available civil remedy and can provide information on the process for submitting a Hague application.

Visitation/Access: A person may file an application under the Hague Abduction Convention for access to a child living in Germany. The criteria for acceptance of a Hague access application vary from country to country. The U.S. Department of State can assist parents living in the United States to understand country-specific criteria and provide information on the process for submitting a Hague application

Retaining an Attorney: The GCA can appoint an English-speaking attorney with Hague experience to represent left-behind parents in Hague cases. The fee for these legal services is 1500 Euros and must be paid at the time the applicant submits the Hague application. A parent who is unable to pay the fee may apply for German legal aid. Under certain circumstances, legal aid may also be available in cases of international child abduction from some non-governmental organizations, including Weisser Ring. For more information, contact: info@weisser-ring.de.

Parents may also choose to retain private legal counsel in Germany to handle their Hague case. A parent who hires private counsel should notify both the German and the U.S. central authorities. The U.S. Embassy in Berlin, Germany, posts lists of attorneys including those who specialize in family law at: http://germany.usembassy.gov/acs/lists/. This list is provided as a courtesy service only and does not constitute an endorsement of any individual attorney. The Department of State assumes no responsibility or liability for the professional ability or reputation of, or the quality of services provided by, the persons or firms included in this list. Professional credentials and areas of expertise are provided directly by the lawyers.

Citizenship & Passport Matters: Children born in Germany and/or to parents of German citizenship acquire German citizenship according to specific laws. While Germany recognizes the concept of dual nationality, Germany generally considers a dual national in Germany to be a German citizen only. German law generally does not recognize more than one citizenship unless an individual acquires two citizenships by birth. Germany does not allow a child to be included on a parent's passport. Children under the age of 12 are routinely issued a Kinderreisepass (or children's passport) valid for six years or until the child turns 13.

The United States does not accept these documents for travel to the United States without a visa, but European nations and other countries around the world do accept them for visa-free travel. Germany requires both parents' signatures or proof of sole custody to obtain a Kinderreisepass, but the child does not have to appear when the parents submit an application. If both parents share custody, either parent's refusal to sign the application will prevent issuance of the passport. Germany also issues 6-year maximum validity passports to children under the age of 18. Germany requires the consent of both parents (or proof of sole custody) before issuing a 6-year passport to a child. Like the United States, it also requires a child to appear in person at the time of application. Children under age 16 must have a passport (Kinderreisepass or regular passport) to fly between Schengen countries. When traveling by car/train from one Schengen country to another, however, there are no border controls.

Exit Permits: Germany requires both an entry and exit stamp in the passport, but border police do not keep immigration records. On the basis of a German court order, German immigration can place a departure hold on a child to prohibit the child's removal from Germany. Removal of the hold can only be executed at the request of the court. Any minor traveling alone or with a noncustodial parent should carry an authorization from the custodial parent; however, neither border officials nor airlines routinely request proof of this consent.

Mediation: The German federal government is extremely supportive of mediation programs to resolve international parental abduction cases. While courts cannot order cases into mediation, judges can and do strongly encourage mediated resolutions and can stay hearings to permit parties the time to mediate. In general, social workers, family lawyers, and judges not hearing the case can serve as mediators in their particular geographic region. Fees are normally based on hourly rates, but a sliding scale or negotiated rate is sometimes available. The Bundes-Arbeitgemeinschaft für Familien-Mediation (BAFM), or the Federal Consortium for Family Mediation, is a privately-funded, countrywide mediation organization with a network of multi-lingual mediators in all 16 German states. The German Central Authority and the judge hearing the Hague case work together to identify cases that are potentially suitable for mediated resolutions and make recommendations accordingly. Participation in mediation is voluntary.

The non-governmental organization MiKK (Mediation in international Conflicts involving Parents and Children) deals with mediation in cross-border child abduction, custody, and visitation cases. This is a joint project of the two largest mediation associations in Germany, and their network includes 60 specialized and experienced family mediators who are fluent in 17 languages.

Embassy of the United States Berlin
Clayallee 170
14191 Berlin
Federal Republic of Germany
Tel.: +49-30-8305–0

Embassy of the Federal Republic of Germany
2300 M Street NW
Washington, DC 20037
Phone (202) 298-4000

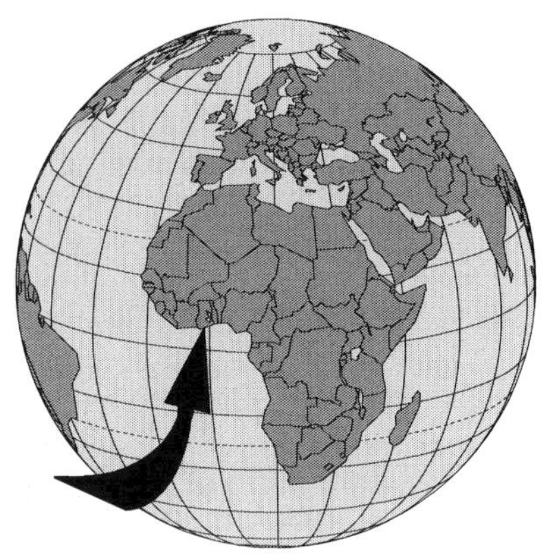

GHANA

Compiled from publications that were available as of February 2013 from the U.S. Department of State, the U.S. Department of Commerce, and the Central Intelligence Agency (CIA). See the introduction to this set for explanatory notes.

Official Name:
Republic of Ghana

PROFILE

Geography

Area: total: 238,533 sq km; country comparison to the world: 82; land: 227,533 sq km; water: 11,000 sq km

Major cities: Accra (capital) 2.269 million; Kumasi 1.773 million (2009)

Climate: tropical; warm and comparatively dry along southeast coast; hot and humid in southwest; hot and dry in north

Terrain: mostly low plains with dissected plateau in south-central area

People

Nationality: noun: Ghanaian(s); adjective: Ghanaian

Population: 24,652,402 (July 2012 est.)

Population growth rate: 1.787% (2012 est.)

Ethnic groups: Akan 45.3%, Mole-Dagbon 15.2%, Ewe 11.7%, Ga-Dangme 7.3%, Guan 4%, Gurma 3.6%, Grusi 2.6%, Mande-Busanga 1%, other tribes 1.4%, other 7.8% (2000 census)

Religions: Christian 68.8% (Pentecostal/Charismatic 24.1%, Protestant 18.6%, Catholic 15.1%, other 11%), Muslim 15.9%, traditional 8.5%, other 0.7%, none 6.1% (2000 census)

Languages: Asante 14.8%, Ewe 12.7%, Fante 9.9%, Boron (Brong) 4.6%, Dagomba 4.3%, Dangme 4.3%, Dagarte (Dagaba) 3.7%, Akyem 3.4%, Ga 3.4%, Akuapem 2.9%, other (includes English (official) 36.1% (2000 census)

Literacy: definition: age 15 and over can read and write; total population: 67.3%; male: 73.2%; female: 61.2% (2010 census)

Health: life expectancy at birth: total population: 61.45 years; male: 60.22 years; female: 62.73 years (2012 est.); Infant mortality rate: total: 47.26 deaths/1,000 live births; male: 50.64 deaths/1,000 live births; female: 43.79 deaths/1,000 live births (2012 est.)

Unemployment rate: 11% (2000 est.)

Work force: 11.67 million (2012 est.)

Government

Type: constitutional democracy

Independence: 6 March 1957

Constitution: approved 28 April 1992

Political subdivisions: 10 regions; Ashanti, Brong-Ahafo, Central, Eastern, Greater Accra, Northern, Upper East, Upper West, Volta, Western

Suffrage: 18 years of age; universal

Economy

GDP (purchasing power parity): $83.18 billion (2012 est.); $75.9 billion (2011 est.); $66.81 billion (2010 est.); $62.02 billion (2009 est.)

GDP real growth rate: 8.2% (2012 est.); 13.6% (2011 est.); 7.7% (2010 est.); 4% (2009 est.)

GDP per capita (PPP): $3,300 (2012 est.); $3,100 (2011 est.); $2,800 (2010 est.); $2,700 (2009 est.)

Natural resources: gold, timber, industrial diamonds, bauxite, manganese, fish, rubber, hydropower, petroleum, silver, salt, limestone

Agriculture products: cocoa, rice, cassava (manioc), peanuts, corn, shea nuts, bananas; timber

Industries: mining, lumbering, light manufacturing, aluminum smelting, food processing, cement, small commercial ship building

Exports: $13.58 billion (2012 est.); $12.75 billion (2011 est.); $7.96 billion (2010 est.)

Exports—commodities: gold, cocoa, timber, tuna, bauxite, aluminum, manganese ore, diamonds, horticultural products

Exports—partners: France 19.5%, Netherlands 10.4%, US 8.8%, Italy 8.3%, UK 4.8% (2011)

Imports: $17.52 billion (2012 est.); $15.32 billion (2011 est.); $10.92 billion (2010 est.)

Imports—commodities: capital equipment, petroleum, foodstuffs

Imports—partners: China 20.5%, Nigeria 12.4%, US 7.8%, India 5.1%, Netherlands 5.1%, UK 4.2% (2011)

Debt—external: $11.23 billion (31 December 2012 est.); $7.511 billion (31 December 2011 est.); $6.541 billion (31 December 2010 est.)

Exchange rates: cedis (GHC) per US dollar; 1.512 (2011 est.); 1.815 (2012 est.); 1.431 (2010 est.); 1.409 (2009); 1.1 (2008); 0.95 (2007)

GEOGRAPHY

Ghana is located on West Africa's Gulf of Guinea only a few degrees north of the Equator. Half of the country lies less than 152 meters (500 ft.) above sea level, and the highest point is 883 meters (2,900 ft.). The 537-kilometer (334-mi.) coastline is mostly a low, sandy shore backed by plains and scrub and intersected by several rivers and streams, most of which are navigable only by canoe. A tropical rain forest belt, broken by heavily forested hills and many streams and rivers, extends northward from the shore, near the Cote d'Ivoire frontier. This area produces most of the country's cocoa, minerals, and timber. North of this belt, the country varies from 91 to 396 meters (300 ft.-1,300 ft.) above sea level and is covered by low bush, park-like savanna, and grassy plains.

The climate is tropical. The eastern coastal belt is warm and comparatively dry; the southwest corner, hot and humid; and the north, hot and dry. There are two distinct rainy seasons in the south—May-June and August-September; in the north, the rainy seasons tend to merge. A dry, northeasterly wind, the Harmattan, blows in January and February. Annual rainfall in the coastal zone averages 83 centimeters (33 in.).

Volta Lake, the largest manmade lake by surface area in the world, extends from the Akosombo Dam in southeastern Ghana to the town of Yapei, 520 kilometers (325 mi.) to the north. The lake generates electricity, provides inland transportation, and is a potentially valuable resource for irrigation and fish farming.

PEOPLE

Ghana's population is concentrated along the coast and in the principal cities of Accra and Kumasi. Most Ghanaians descended from migrating tribes that probably came down the Volta River valley at the beginning of the 13th century. Ethnically, Ghana is divided into small groups speaking more than 50 languages and dialects. Among the more important linguistic groups are the Akans, which include the Fantis along the coast and the Ashantis in the forest region north of the coast; the Guans, on the plains of the Volta River; the Ga- and Ewe-speaking peoples of the south and southeast; and the Moshi-Dagomba-speaking tribes of the northern and upper regions. English, the official and commercial language, is taught in all the schools.

Education

Primary and junior secondary school education is tuition-free and mandatory. The Government of Ghana's support for basic education is unequivocal. Article 39 of the constitution mandates the major tenets of the free, compulsory, universal basic education (FCUBE) initiative. Launched in 1996, it is one of the most ambitious pre-tertiary education programs in West Africa.

Since the early 1980s, Government of Ghana expenditures on education have risen from 1.5% to nearly 3.5% of GDP. Since 1987, the share of basic education in total education spending has averaged around 67%. The units of the Ministry of Education, Science and Sports (MOESS) responsible for education are: the Ghana Education Service (GES), which administers pre-university education; the National Council on Tertiary Education; the National Accreditation Board; and the National Board for Professional and Technician Examinations (NABPTEX).

The West African Examinations Council (WAEC), a consortium of five Anglophone West African Countries (Ghana, Nigeria, Sierra Leone, Gambia, and Liberia) is responsible for developing, administering, and grading school-leaving examinations at the secondary level.

Since 1986, pre-tertiary education in Ghana includes 6 years of primary education, 3 years at the junior secondary school level, and 3 years at the senior secondary school level. A new educational reform, beginning September 1, 2007, introduced 2 years of kindergarten education beginning at age 4 and increased the 3 years senior secondary to 4 years. In early 2009, the government reverted senior secondary school back to 3 years. Successful completion of senior secondary school leads to admission eligibility at training colleges, polytechnics, and universities.

In 2006 there were approximately 5.1 million students attending schools at these three levels: 68% at the primary level, 23% at the junior secondary level, and 10% at the senior secondary level. There were over 600 public senior secondary schools in Ghana that graduated a total of 90,000 students in 2004, representing a huge expansion over the old system (which was transformed in 1987), which consisted of 300 institutions graduating 27,000 students a year. However, access to each successive level of education remains severely limited by lack of facilities.

About 99.1% of junior secondary school graduates are able to gain admission to senior secondary schools, and only about 34.4% of senior secondary school graduates are able to gain admission to universities and polytechnics, plus another 10%-20% to diploma-level postsecondary education. Private secondary schools play a very small role in Ghana, with only a handful of institutions offering international curricula such as the British-based A-levels, International Baccalaureate, and U.S. high school. Combined, they graduate fewer than 200 students a year.

Entrance to one of the five Ghanaian public universities is by examination following completion of senior secondary school. There are now five public and 12 private degree-granting universities in Ghana, along with 10 public polytechnics offering the British Higher National Diploma (HND), a 3-year tertiary system in applied fields of study. Ghana's first private Catholic university opened in 2003 in Sunyani. The polytechnics also offer vocational, non-tertiary diploma programs. In addition, there are approximately 40 teacher-training colleges and 15 nurses' training colleges.

Private tertiary education is a recent but rapid development in Ghana, meticulously regulated by the National Accreditation Board. Over 84,078 undergraduates are now enrolled in secular degree-granting programs in 17 public and private universities, 29,047 students enrolled in polytechnics, and 26,025 trainees enrolled in teacher training colleges.

Religion

Approximately 69 percent of the population is Christian, 16 percent is Muslim, 8 percent adheres to indigenous religious beliefs, and 7 percent identifies as belonging to other religious groups, including those who profess no religious beliefs. Other religious groups include those adhering to the Baha'i Faith, Buddhism, Judaism, Hinduism, Shintoism, Eckankar, and Rastafarianism.

Christian groups include Roman Catholic, Methodist, Anglican, Mennonite, Evangelical Presbyterian, African Methodist Episcopal Zionist, Christian Methodist, Evangelical Lutheran, F'eden, The Church of Jesus Christ of Latter-day Saints (Mormon), Seventh-day Adventist, Pentecostal, Baptist, African independent churches, the Society of Friends (Quaker), and numerous charismatic religious groups.

Several Islamic traditions are present in the country: orthodox Sunni, Ahmadi, the Tijani and Qadiriyya orders of Sufism, and a small number of Shia.

Many individuals who are nominally Christian or Muslim also practice some aspects of traditional beliefs. There are also some syncretistic groups that combine elements of Christianity and Islam with traditional beliefs. Zetahil, a practice unique to the country, combines elements of Christianity and Islam.

There is not a significant link between ethnicity and religion; however, geography is often associated with religious identity. The majority of the Muslim population resides in northern areas as well as in the urban centers of Accra, Kumasi, Sekondi-Takoradi, Tamale, and Wa, while the majority of the followers of traditional religious beliefs resides in rural areas. Christians live throughout the country.

HISTORY

The history of the Gold Coast before the last quarter of the 15th century is derived primarily from oral tradition that refers to migrations from the ancient kingdoms of the western Soudan (the area of Mauritania and Mali). The Gold Coast was renamed Ghana upon independence in 1957 because of indications that present-day inhabitants descended from migrants who moved south from the ancient kingdom of Ghana. The first contact between Europe and the Gold Coast dates from 1470, when a party of Portuguese landed. In 1482, the Portuguese built Elmina Castle as a permanent trading base. Thomas Windham made the first recorded English trading voyage to the coast in 1553. During the next 3 centuries, the English, Danes, Dutch, Germans, and Portuguese controlled various parts of the coastal areas.

In 1821, the British Government took control of the British trading forts on the Gold Coast. In 1844, Fanti chiefs in the area signed an agreement with the British that became the legal steppingstone to colonial status for the coastal area.

From 1826 to 1900, the British fought a series of campaigns against the Ashantis, whose kingdom was located inland. In 1902, they succeeded in establishing firm control over the Ashanti region and making the northern territories a protectorate. British Togoland, the fourth territorial element eventually to form the nation, was part of a former German colony administered by the United Kingdom from Accra as a League of Nations mandate after 1922. In December 1946, British Togoland became a UN Trust Territory, and in 1957, following a 1956 plebiscite, the United Nations agreed that the territory would become part of Ghana when the Gold Coast achieved independence.

The four territorial divisions were administered separately until 1946, when the British Government ruled them as a single unit. In 1951, a constitution was promulgated that called for a greatly enlarged legislature composed principally of members elected by popular vote directly or indirectly. An executive council was responsible for formulating policy, with most African members drawn from the legislature and including three ex officio members appointed by the governor.

A new constitution, approved on April 29, 1954, established a cabinet comprised of African ministers drawn from an all-African legislature chosen by direct election. In the elections that followed, the Convention People's Party (CPP), led by Kwame Nkrumah, won the majority of seats in the new Legislative Assembly. In May 1956, Prime Minister Nkrumah's Gold Coast government issued a white paper containing proposals for Gold Coast independence.

The British Government stated it would agree to a firm date for independence if a reasonable majority for such a step were obtained in the Gold Coast Legislative Assembly after a general election. This election, held in 1956, returned the CPP to power with 71 of the 104 seats in the Legislative Assembly. Ghana became an independent state on March 6, 1957, when the United Kingdom relinquished its control over the Colony of the Gold Coast and Ashanti, the Northern Territories Protectorate, and British Togoland.

In subsequent reorganizations, the country was divided into 10 regions,

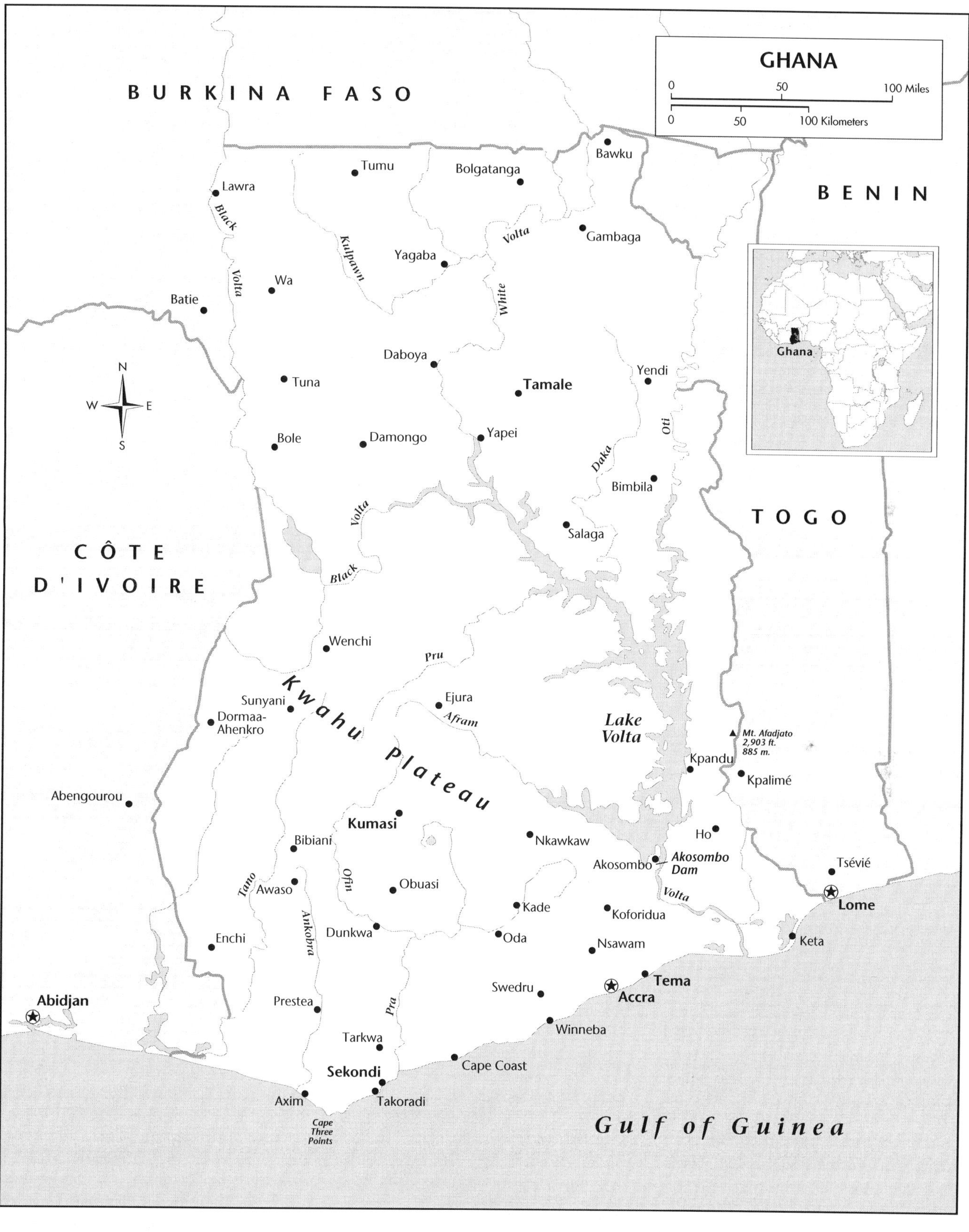
GHANA
0 50 100 Miles
0 50 100 Kilometers
BURKINA FASO
BENIN
TOGO
CÔTE D'IVOIRE
Ghana
Gulf of Guinea
Lake Volta
Kwahu Plateau
Bawku
Tumu
Bolgatanga
Lawra
Gambaga
Yagaba
Wa
Batie
Daboya
Tamale
Yendi
Tuna
Bole
Damongo
Yapei
Bimbila
Salaga
Wenchi
Sunyani
Dormaa-Ahenkro
Ejura
Mt. Afadjato 2,903 ft. 885 m.
Kpandu
Kpalimé
Abengourou
Kumasi
Bibiani
Nkawkaw
Ho
Akosombo
Akosombo Dam
Tsévié
Awaso
Obuasi
Kade
Koforidua
Lome
Enchi
Dunkwa
Oda
Nsawam
Keta
Tema
Accra
Swedru
Abidjan
Prestea
Winneba
Tarkwa
Cape Coast
Sekondi
Axim
Takoradi
Cape Three Points
Black Volta
White Volta
Volta
Kulpawn
Oti
Daka
Pru
Afram
Tano
Ankobra
Ofin
Pra
N
S
E
W

which currently are subdivided into 138 districts. The original Gold Coast Colony now comprises the Western, Central, Eastern, and Greater Accra Regions, with a small portion at the mouth of the Volta River assigned to the Volta Region; the Ashanti area was divided into the Ashanti and Brong-Ahafo Regions; the Northern Territories into the Northern, Upper East, and Upper West Regions; and British Togoland essentially is the same area as the Volta Region.

Post-Independence Politics

After independence, the CPP government under Nkrumah sought to develop Ghana as a modern, semi-industrialized, unitary socialist state. The government emphasized political and economic organization, endeavoring to increase stability and productivity through labor, youth, farmers, cooperatives, and other organizations integrated with the CPP.

The government, according to Nkrumah, acted only as "the agent of the CPP" in seeking to accomplish these goals. The CPP's control was challenged and criticized, and Prime Minister Nkrumah used the Preventive Detention Act (1958), which provided for detention without trial for up to 5 years (later extended to 10 years). On July 1, 1960, a new constitution was adopted, changing Ghana from a parliamentary system with a prime minister to a republican form of government headed by a powerful president. In August 1960, Nkrumah was given authority to scrutinize newspapers and other publications before publication. This political evolution continued into early 1964, when a constitutional referendum changed the country to a one-party state.

On February 24, 1966, the Ghanaian Army and police overthrew Nkrumah's regime. Nkrumah and all his ministers were dismissed, the CPP and National Assembly were dissolved, and the constitution was suspended. The new regime cited Nkrumah's flagrant abuse of individual rights and liberties, his regime's corrupt, oppressive, and dictatorial practices, and the rapidly deteriorating economy as the principal reasons for its action.

Post-Nkrumah Politics

The leaders of the February 24, 1966 coup established the new government around the National Liberation Council (NLC) and pledged an early return to a duly constituted civilian government. Members of the judiciary and civil service remained at their posts and committees of civil servants were established to handle the administration of the country.

Ghana's government returned to civilian authority under the Second Republic in October 1969 after a parliamentary election in which the Progress Party, led by Kofi A. Busia, won 105 of the 140 seats. Until mid-1970, a presidential commission led by Brigadier A.A. Afrifa held the powers of the chief of state. In a special election on August 31, 1970, former Chief Justice Edward Akufo-Addo was chosen President, and Dr. Busia became Prime Minister.

Faced with mounting economic problems, Prime Minister Busia's government undertook a drastic devaluation of the currency in December 1971. The government's inability to control the subsequent inflationary pressures stimulated further discontent, and military officers seized power in a bloodless coup on January 13, 1972.

The coup leaders, led by Col. I.K. Acheampong, formed the National Redemption Council (NRC) to which they admitted other officers, the head of the police, and one civilian. The NRC promised improvements in the quality of life for all Ghanaians and based its programs on nationalism, economic development, and self-reliance. In 1975, government reorganization resulted in the NRC's replacement by the Supreme Military Council (SMC), also headed by now-General Acheampong.

Unable to deliver on its promises, the NRC/SMC became increasingly marked by mismanagement and rampant corruption. In 1977, General Acheampong brought forward the concept of union government (UNIGOV), which would make Ghana a non-party state. Perceiving this as a ploy by Acheampong to retain power, professional groups and students launched strikes and demonstrations against the government in 1977 and 1978. The steady erosion in Acheampong's power led to his arrest in July 1978 by his chief of staff, Lt. Gen. Frederick Akuffo, who replaced him as head of state and leader of what became known as the SMC-2.

Akuffo abandoned UNIGOV and established a plan to return to constitutional and democratic government. A Constitutional Assembly was established, and political party activity was revived. Akuffo was unable to solve Ghana's economic problems, however, or to reduce the rampant corruption in which senior military officers played a major role. On June 4, 1979, his government was deposed in a violent coup by a group of junior and noncommissioned officers—Armed Forces Revolutionary Council (AFRC)—with Flt. Lt. Jerry John Rawlings as its chairman.

The AFRC executed eight senior military officers, including former chiefs of state Acheampong and Akuffo; established Special Tribunals that, secretly and without due process, tried dozens of military officers, other government officials, and private individuals for corruption, sentencing them to long prison terms and confiscating their property; and, through a combination of force and exhortation, attempted to rid Ghanaian society of corruption and profiteering.

At the same time, the AFRC accepted, with a few amendments, the draft constitution that had been submitted; permitted the scheduled presidential and parliamentary elections to take place in June and July; promulgated the constitution; and handed over power to the newly elected President and Parliament of the Third Republic on September 24, 1979.

The 1979 constitution was modeled on those of Western democracies. It provided for the separation of powers between an elected president and a unicameral Parliament, an independent judiciary headed by a Supreme Court, which protected individual rights, and other autonomous institutions, such as the Electoral Commissioner and the Ombudsman.

The new President, Dr. Hilla Limann, was a career diplomat from the north and the candidate of the People's National Party (PNP), the political heir of Nkrumah's CPP. Of the 140 members of Parliament, 71 were PNP. The PNP government established the constitutional institutions and generally respected democracy and individual human rights. It failed, however, to halt the continuing decline in the economy; corruption flourished, and the gap between rich and poor widened. On December 31, 1981, Flight Lt. Rawlings and a small group of enlisted and former soldiers launched a coup that succeeded against little opposition in toppling President Limann.

The PNDC Era

Rawlings and his colleagues suspended the 1979 constitution, dismissed the President and his cabinet, dissolved the Parliament, and proscribed existing political parties. They established the Provisional National Defense Council (PNDC), initially composed of seven members with Rawlings as chairman, to exercise executive and legislative powers. The existing judicial system was preserved, but alongside it the PNDC created the National Investigation Committee to root out corruption and other economic offenses; the anonymous Citizens' Vetting Committee to punish tax evasion; and the Public Tribunals to try various crimes.

The PNDC proclaimed its intent to allow the people to exercise political power through defense committees to be established in communities, workplaces, and in units of the armed forces and police. Under the PNDC, Ghana remained a unitary government.

In December 1982, the PNDC announced a plan to decentralize government from Accra to the regions, the districts, and local communities, but it maintained overall control by appointing regional and district secretaries who exercised executive powers and also chaired regional and district councils. Local councils, however, were expected progressively to take over the payment of salaries, with regions and districts assuming more powers from the national government. In 1984, the PNDC created a National Appeals Tribunal to hear appeals from the public tribunals; changed the Citizens' Vetting Committee into the Office of Revenue Collection; and replaced the system of defense committees with Committees for the Defense of the Revolution.

In 1984, the PNDC also created a National Commission on Democracy to study ways to establish participatory democracy in Ghana. The commission issued a "Blue Book" in July 1987 outlining modalities for district-level elections, which were held in late 1988 and early 1989, for newly created district assemblies. The government appointed one-third of the assembly members.

The Fourth Republic

Under international and domestic pressure for a return to democracy, the PNDC allowed the establishment of a 258-member Consultative Assembly made up of members representing geographic districts as well as established civic or business organizations. The assembly was charged to draw up a draft constitution to establish a Fourth Republic, using PNDC proposals. The PNDC accepted the final product without revision, and it was put to a national referendum on April 28, 1992, in which it received 92% approval. On May 18, 1992, the ban on party politics was lifted in preparation for multi-party elections.

The PNDC and its supporters formed a new party, the National Democratic Congress (NDC), to contest the elections. Presidential elections were held on November 3 and parliamentary elections on December 29, 1992. Members of the opposition boycotted the parliamentary elections, however, which resulted in a 200-seat Parliament with only 17 opposition party members and two independents.

The constitution entered into force on January 7, 1993, to found the Fourth Republic. On that day, Flt. Lt. Jerry John Rawlings was inaugurated as President and members of Parliament swore their oaths of office. In 1996, the opposition fully contested the presidential and parliamentary elections, which were described as peaceful, free, and transparent by domestic and international observers.

In that election, President Rawlings was re-elected with 57% of the popular vote. In addition, Rawlings' NDC party won 133 of the Parliament's 200 seats, just one seat short of the two-thirds majority needed to amend the constitution, although the election returns of two parliamentary seats faced legal challenges.

The December 2000 elections ushered in the first democratic presidential change of power in Ghana's history when John Agyekum Kufuor of the New Patriotic Party (NPP) defeated the NDC's John Atta Mills, Rawlings' Vice President and hand-picked successor. Kufuor defeated Mills by winning 56.73% of the vote, while the NPP picked up 100 of 200 seats in Parliament.

The elections were declared free and fair by a large contingent of domestic and international monitors. After several by-elections were held to fill vacated seats, the NPP majorityhad 103 of the 200 seats in Parliament, the NDC held 89, and independent and small party members held eight.

In December 2004, eight political parties contested parliamentary elections and four parties, including the NPP and NDC, contested presidential elections. This election was reported to have a remarkable turnout of 85.12% according to the Election Commission. Despite a few incidents of intimidation and minor irregularities, domestic and international observers judged the elections generally free and fair.

There were several isolated incidents of election-related violence, but the election was generally peaceful in most of Ghana. John A. Kufuor was re-elected president with 52.45% of the vote against three other presidential candidates, including former Vice-President John Atta Mills of the NDC. Thirty constituencies were created in the period between the 2000 and 2004 elections, resulting in a 230-member Parliament. On March 6, 2007, Ghana celebrated its 50th anniversary since becoming independent. As the first African nation to win its struggle for independence, Ghana hosted delegations from around the world during its year-long Jubilee event.

Ghana held presidential and legislative elections on December 7, 2008. Eight candidates contested the election but none of the candidates achieved over 50% of the vote. A runoff was held between NPP candidate Nana Akufo-Addo and NDC candidate John Atta Mills on December 28, 2008. After voting was conducted in the last voting district on January 2, John Atta Mills emerged as the winner with a margin of just over 40,000 votes.

The new administration was sworn into office on January 7, 2009. The next election is scheduled to take place in 2012, with John Atta Mills running for his second term and Nana Akufo-Addo running as the primary opposition for the NPP.

GOVERNMENT AND POLITICAL CONDITIONS

Ghana is a constitutional democracy with a strong presidency and a unicameral, 230-seat parliament. In late 2008 the opposition National Democratic Congress (NDC) won both the presidency and a small majority in parliament in an election deemed generally free and fair by domestic and international observers. NDC candidate Professor John Evans Atta Mills was inaugurated president in early 2009 for a four-year term.

Recent Elections

Following a narrow victory in 2008 over New Patriotic Party (NPP) candidate Nana Akufo-Addo, opposition NDC candidate John Evans Atta Mills was inaugurated president in 2009. There were reports of voter intimidation and election irregularities; however, observers and the Independent Electoral Commission deemed these irregularities too insufficient to have altered the outcome of the election. Incidents of preelection violence occurred.

In 2008 NPP and NDC supporters clashed in Gushiegu District, Northern Region, resulting in six deaths and the burning of houses and vehicles. During the same period, an NPP rally in Tamale was disrupted by gunfire, forcing the party's vice presidential candidate to flee. The incident led to attacks on NDC supporters returning from their own rally and the destruction of houses and vehicles. The 2010 by-elections were held with few incidents reported.

Political Parties: Political parties operated without restriction or outside interference. The NDC held 116 seats in the parliament, the NPP 107, minor parties three, and independents four.

Participation of Women and Minorities: There are no laws preventing women from voting or participating in political life on the same basis as men, but women traditionally had less access to leadership positions than men. There were 19 women in the 230-seat parliament, four women in the cabinet, and five women on the Supreme Court. Seven of 38 ministers were women.

Nana Konadu Agyeman Rawlings, wife of former president John Jerry Rawlings, sought to become the NDC's presidential candidate for the 2012 general election but lost to incumbent Mills at the party's 2011 convention.

There are no laws or practices that keep members of minorities from equal participation in political life. According to the 2000 census, the country had more than 80 ethnic groups, none of which constituted a majority. The Ashanti, the largest ethnic group, made up 14.8 percent of the population.

Principal Government Officials

Last Updated: 1/31/2013

Pres.: **John Dramani MAHAMA**
Vice Pres.
Min. of Chieftancy & Culture: **Alexander ASUM-AHENSAH**
Min. of Communications: **Haruna IDDRISSU**
Min. of Defense: **Joseph Henry SMITH, Lt. Gen. (Ret.)**
Min. of Education: **Lee OCRAN**
Min. of Employment & Social Welfare: **Moses ASAGA**
Min. of Energy: **Joe Oteng ADJEI**
Min. of Environment, Science, & Technology: **Sherry AYITTEY**
Min. of Finance & Economic Planning: **Kwabena DUFFUOR**
Min. of Food & Agriculture: **Kwesi AHWOI**
Min. of Foreign Affairs & Regional Integration: **Muhammed MUMUNI**
Min. of Health: **Alban Sumana BAGBIN**
Min. of Information & National Orientation: **Fritz BAFFOUR**
Min. of Interior: **William Kwesi ABOAH**
Min. of Justice & Attorney Gen.: **Benjamin KUMBUOR**
Min. of Lands & Natural Resources: **Mike HAMMAH**
Min. of Local Govt. & Rural Development: **Samuel Ofosu AMPOFO**
Min. of Roads & Highways: **Joseph GIDISU**
Min. of Tourism: **Akua Sena DANSUA**
Min. of Trade, Industry, & Private-Sector Development: **Hanna TETTEH**
Min. of Transportation: **Collins DAUDU**
Min. of Water Resources, Works, & Housing: **E. T. MENSAH**
Min. of Women's & Children's Affairs: **Julinana AZUMAH-MENSAH**
Min. of Youth & Sports: **Kofi HUMADO**
Min. of State, Office of the Pres.: **Stephen Kwao AMOANOR**
Min. of State, Office of the Pres.: **John GYETUAH**
Governor, Bank of Ghana: **K. B. AMMISSAH-ARTHUR**
Ambassador to the US: **Kwame BAWUAH-EDUSEI**
Permanent Representative to the UN, New York: **Kenneth Kweku KANDA**

ECONOMY

Ghana's economy has been strengthened by a quarter century of relatively sound management, a competitive business environment, and sustained reductions in poverty levels. Ghana is well endowed with natural resources and agriculture accounts for roughly one-quarter of GDP and employs more than half of the workforce, mainly small landholders.

The services sector accounts for 50% of GDP. Gold and cocoa production and individual remittances are major sources of foreign exchange. Oil production at Ghana's offshore Jubilee field began in mid-December, 2010, and is expected to boost economic growth. President MILLS faces challenges in managing new oil revenue while maintaining fiscal discipline and resisting debt accumulation. Estimated oil reserves have jumped to almost 700 million barrels.

Ghana signed a Millennium Challenge Corporation (MCC) Compact in 2006, which aims to assist in transforming Ghana's agricultural sector. Ghana opted for debt relief under the Heavily Indebted Poor Country (HIPC) program in 2002, and is also benefiting from the Multilateral Debt Relief Initiative that took effect in 2006. In 2009 Ghana signed a three-year Poverty Reduction and Growth Facility with the IMF to improve macroeconomic stability, private sector competitiveness, human resource development, and good governance and civic responsibility. Sound macroeconomic management along with higher prices for oil, gold and, cocoa helped sustain high GDP growth in 2008–12.

Labor Conditions

The law sets the minimum employment age at 15 years, or 13 years for light work that was not likely to be harmful to the child and does not affect the child's attendance at or capacity to benefit from school.

The law prohibits night work and certain types of hazardous labor for those under 18 and provides for fines and imprisonment for violators. The law allows for children age 15 and above to have an apprenticeship under which craftsmen and employers have the obligation to provide a safe and healthy work environment along with training and tools. Child labor laws were not enforced effectively or consistently, and law enforcement officials, including judges, police, and labor officials, were sometimes unfamiliar with the provisions of the law that protected children.

According to government labor officials, ILO, and the Ghana Employers Association, child labor problems were infrequent in the formal labor sector. However, local custom and poverty encouraged children to work to help support their families and eroded societal observance of child labor laws, particularly in the informal sector.

Children as young as seven worked in agriculture and as domestic laborers, porters, hawkers, miners, quarry workers, and fare collectors. Children also engaged in herding livestock, fetching firewood, and bricklaying. In the fishing industry in the Lake Volta region child laborers engaged in potentially hazardous work, such as diving into deep waters to untangle fishing nets caught on submerged tree roots.

Girls in the region also engaged in work as domestic servants, cooks, servers, and porters. Children were also forced to work, and in some cases parents reportedly sold, leased, or gave away their children to work in fishing villages, shops, or homes. It was difficult to determine the extent to which forced and bonded labor by children was practiced.

A National Tripartite Committee composed of representatives of the government, labor, and employers set a daily minimum wage, which was 3.73 cedis ($2.49) during 2011. There was no official minimum wage for the growing informal labor force. The law sets the maximum workweek at 40 hours, with a break of at least 48 consecutive hours every seven days. Workers were entitled to at least 15 working days of leave with full pay in a calendar year of continuous service or after having worked at least 200 days in a particular year. However, such provisions do not apply to task workers or domestic workers in private homes, nor elsewhere in the informal sector. The law does not prescribe overtime rates and does not prohibit excessive compulsory overtime.

Occupational safety and health (OSH) regulations are set by the government. The Factories Department within the MESW was responsible for imposing sanctions on violators of the OSH standards. Employers who failed to comply were liable to a fine not exceeding 1,000 penalty units, imprisonment for a term not exceeding three years, or both. The law requires that employers report occupational accidents and diseases no later than seven days from the date of occurrence. Only workers in the formal sector, which employed less than 20 percent of the labor force, are covered by this legislation.

The MESW was unable to effectively enforce the wage law. There was widespread violation of the minimum wage law in the formal economy across all sectors. The minimum wage law was not enforced in the informal sector. Legislation governing working hours was largely followed in the formal sector but widely flouted and not enforced in the informal sector.

U.S.-GHANAIAN RELATIONS

The United States established diplomatic relations with Ghana in 1957 following its independence from the United Kingdom. The United States and Ghana share a long history promoting democracy, human rights, and the rule of law. Ghana has set an example for countries throughout Africa in promoting governance and regional stability.

The U.S. and Ghanaian militaries have cooperated in numerous joint training exercises through U.S. Africa Command, and there is a bilateral International Military Education and Training (IMET) program, a Foreign Military Financing program, as well as numerous Humanitarian Affairs projects. Ghana continues to participate in the African Contingency Operations Training and Assistance (ACOTA) program, in which the U.S. facilitates the development of an interoperable peacekeeping capacity among African nations. Ghana also enjoys a relationship with the North Dakota National Guard, under the auspices of the State Partnership Program.

Through the U.S. International Visitor Program, Ghanaian parliamentarians and other government officials have become acquainted with U.S. congressional and state legislative practices and have participated in programs designed to address other issues of interest. Youth exchanges and study abroad programs are also robust and growing between U.S. and Ghanaian universities and NGO's. At the U.S. state level, the State Partnership Program aims to promote greater economic ties between Ghana and U.S. institutions, including the National Guard.

The United States has enjoyed good relations with Ghana at a nonofficial, people-to-people level since Ghana's independence. Thousands of Ghanaians have been educated in the United States. Close relations are maintained between educational and scientific institutions, and cultural links are strong, particularly between Ghanaians and African-Americans.

U.S. Assistance to Ghana

U.S. development assistance to Ghana is implemented by the U.S. Agency for International Development (USAID), the Millennium Challenge Corporation (MCC), the African Development Foundation, and others. USAID-managed development assistance to Ghana has supported the country in increasing food security, improving basic health care, enhancing access to quality basic education, and strengthening local governance to benefit all Ghanaians. The West Africa Trade Hub, located in Accra, provides technical assistance to help small businesspersons to grow their businesses and access new customers in the United States and the West African region. The Peace Corps has a large program in Ghana, with volunteers working in education, agriculture, and health (including HIV/AIDS, malaria, sanitation, and nutrition).

Bilateral Economic Relations

The United States is among Ghana's principal trading partners, with two-way trade between the two countries rapidly increasing and reaching nearly $2 billion in 2011. A number of major U.S. companies operate in the country. Political stability, overall sound economic management, a low crime rate, competitive wages, and an educated, English-speaking workforce enhance Ghana's potential as a West African hub for American businesses.

The discovery of major oil reserves in deep water in the Gulf of Guinea has led numerous international petroleum exploration firms to enter the Ghanaian market, and many other firms involved in oil and gas auxiliary services have expressed interest in starting operations in the country.

Ghana's Membership in International Organizations

In foreign affairs, Ghana generally follows the consensus of the Nonaligned Movement and the African Union on economic and political issues that do not directly affect its own interests. Ghana and the United States belong to a number of the same international organizations, including the United Nations, International Monetary Fund, World Bank, and World Trade Organization. Ghana also is an observer to the Organization of American States.

Bilateral Representation

Ghana maintains an embassy in the United States at 3512 International Drive, NW, Washington, DC 20008 (tel. 202-686-4500).

Principal U.S. Embassy Officials

Last Updated: 1/14/2013

ACCRA (E) No. 24 4th Circular Rd Cantonments Accra, Ghana, (233) (30) 2741-000, Fax (233) (30) 2741-389, INMARSAT Tel BGAN 870-77-223-8330; IRIDIUM 881-6-414-5573/881-6-934-55773, Workweek: M-Th 0730-1700 Fri 0730-1230 Lunch 1230-1:15, Website: http://ghana.usembassy.gov/

DCM OMS:	Kathryn Chelsen
AMB OMS:	Carol Johnson
CDC:	Fazel Khan
Co-CLO:	Marie Murphy
DHS/CIS:	Vacant
FCS:	Vacant
FM:	Richard McManaway
HRO:	Teena Ege
IBB:	Joyce Ngoh
MGT:	Vacant
POSHO:	Richard McManaway
SDO/DATT:	Keith Blakley
TREAS:	Ted Webber
AMB:	Gene Cretz
CON:	Mark Strege
DCM:	C. Pat Alsup
PAO:	Sara Stryker
GSO:	Dennie Ege
RSO:	James Suor
AGR:	Rusell Nicely
AID:	Cheryl Anderson
DEA:	Hayward Lampley
ECON:	Vancant
EEO:	Jennifer Nikolaef
EST:	Kent Healey
FMO:	Sherrie Szymeczek
ICASS Chair:	Travis Turner
IMO:	Stacey Hopkins
IPO:	William White
IRS:	Ted Webber
ISO:	Rodrigo Sandoval
ISSO:	Rodrigo Sandavol
LEGATT:	Vacant
POL:	Vernelle Trim
State ICASS:	Vacant

TRAVEL

Consular Information Sheet

April 30, 2012

Country Description: Ghana is a developing country on the west coast of Africa. The capital is Accra. Tourist facilities are available in the population centers of the greater Accra region, Kumasi in the Ashanti region, and in the Cape Coast area of the Central region. They are limited in the more remote areas of the country. English is the official language.

Smart Traveler Enrollment Program (STEP)/Embassy Locations: If you are going to live in or visit Ghana, please take the time to tell our Embassy or Consulate about your trip. If you enroll, we can keep you up to date with important safety and security announcements. It will also help your friends and family get in touch with you in an emergency.

Embassy Accra
Address: The U.S. Embassy is located at No. 24 Fourth Circular Road, Cantonments, Accra
Telephone: (233)-(030) 274-1000
Emergency after-hours telephone: (233)-(030) 274-1775
Facsimile: (233)-(030) 274-1362 or 274-1426

Entry/Exit Requirements for U.S. Citizens: A passport and a visa are required, as is evidence of a yellow fever vaccination. Travelers should obtain the latest information and details from the Embassy of Ghana, 3512 International Drive NW, Washington, DC 20008; telephone (202) 686-4520. Consular services are also available at the Ghana Permanent Mission to the United Nations at 19 East 47th Street, New York, NY 10017, telephone (212) 832-1300; and the Honorary Consulate of Ghana, 3434 Locke Lane, Houston, TX, telephone (713) 960-8833. Overseas, inquiries should be made at the nearest Ghanaian embassy or consulate. Visit the Embassy of Ghana website for the most current visa information.

The U.S. Department of State is unaware of any HIV/AIDS entry restrictions for visitors to or foreign residents of Ghana.

Threats to Safety and Security: Due to the potential for violence, U.S. citizens should avoid political rallies and street demonstrations and stay aware of their safety at all times.

There are a number of ongoing chieftaincy disputes in Ghana that generally involve competition over limited resources. Several of these disputes have erupted into violence and unrest during recent years, most notably in Yendi in the Northern Region and Bawku in the Upper East Region. Visitors should exercise caution when traveling in these areas and remain alert to outbreaks of unrest.

Stay up to date by:

- Bookmarking our Bureau of Consular Affairs website, which contains the current Travel Warnings and Travel Alerts as well as the Worldwide Caution.
- Following us on Twitter and the Bureau of Consular Affairs page on Facebook as well.
- Downloading our free Smart Traveler IPhone App to have travel information at your fingertips.
- Calling 1-888-407-4747 toll-free within the United States and Canada, or a regular toll line, 1-202-501-4444, from other countries.
- Taking some time before travel to consider your personal security.

Crime: Pick-pocketing, purse-snatching, and various types of scams are the most common forms of crime confronting visitors. Travelers have reported these types of theft at crowded markets, beaches, parks, and tourist attractions. Incidences of violent crime, such as armed robbery, are on the rise, including reports of armed robberies in expatriate residential areas. Victims who resist attackers run a high risk of serious physical injury. Take security measures, such as traveling in groups and avoiding travel at night. Avoid travel in communal taxis. Travelers who limit their display of jewelry and handle their cash discreetly reduce their vulnerability to crime. Travelers are advised to carry limited amounts of cash and only photocopies of key documents.

Thefts of both luggage and travel documents occur at Kotoka International Airport in Accra and in hotels across Ghana. All U.S. citizens should ensure that documents are kept secure at all times (including when leaving the airport) and that baggage is never left unattended.

Travelers should be wary of all offers of unsolicited assistance at the airport unless from uniformed porters or officials. All permanent staff at the airport are issued current ID cards bearing their name and photograph. ID cards without a photograph are not valid. Travelers who are met at the airport should confirm the identity of their driver, either by requesting proper identification or otherwise verifying that the driver is an official from an organization or a hotel.

There have been increasing incidences of impostors who approach travelers before the main arrivals area claiming to be the traveler's driver or contact. The impostor will have obtained the traveler's name from the board displayed by the official driver in the arrivals area outside the airport. The impostor then attempts to extort money from the traveler once the traveler is in the impostor's vehicle.

Use of credit cards in Ghana should be avoided if possible, as a growing number of travelers have been victims of credit card fraud.

In recent years, U.S. citizens have reported substantial financial losses from questionable transactions involving gold and other precious metals. The Government of Ghana maintains strict regulations on these natural resources. All agents must be licensed and all transactions must be certified.

Perpetrators of business fraud often target foreigners, including U.S. citizens. Such fraud schemes are now prevalent throughout West Africa, including Ghana. Please refer to the Country Commercial Guide for Ghana for further information.

U.S. citizens frequently consult the Embassy regarding questionable business offers sent from Ghana. These are scams and typically begin with an unsolicited communication (usually by e-mail) from an unknown individual who describes a situation that promises quick financial gain, often by assisting in the transfer of a large sum of money or valuables out of the country.

A series of "advance fees" must be paid in order to conclude the transaction, such as fees to open a bank account or to pay certain taxes. In fact, the final payoff does not exist; the purpose of the scam is simply to collect money from the victim. The Embassy has also received reports of fraudulent charities soliciting contributions through the Internet or direct mail. If you receive such business offers or charity requests, carefully check them out before you commit any funds, provide any goods or services, or undertake any travel

Another type of fraud is committed by persons claiming to live in Ghana or traveling to Ghana on business, and who profess friendship or romantic interest over the Internet. Once a relationship has been established, the correspondent typically asks the U.S. citizen to send money for living expenses, travel expenses, or visa costs. Sometimes a "hospital" or "doctor" telephones to say that the friend has suffered an "accident" and needs immediate financial assistance to cover medical bills.

There are other variations of this scam, but the common goal is to fraudulently obtain as much money as possible from the victim. U.S. citizens have reported losing thousands of dollars through such scams. The anonymity of the Internet means that the victim cannot be sure of the real name, age, marital status, nationality, or even gender of the correspondent. In most cases reported to the Embassy, the correspondent turned out to be a fictitious persona created to lure U.S. citizens into sending money.

Visitors to Ghana should also be wary of overly-friendly locals offering tours, discounted lodging, or other services that seem too good to be true. Tourists are often targeted by touts and scam artists. Some U.S. citizens have been victims of false criminal accusations and have lost time and money as they seek to resolve these difficult situations.

Don't buy counterfeit and pirated goods, even if they are widely available. Not only are the goods illegal in the United States, you may be breaking the local law too.

Victims of Crime: If you or someone you know becomes the victim of a crime abroad, you should contact the local police and the nearest U.S. embassy or consulate (see the Department of State's list of embassies and consulates). We can:

- Replace a stolen passport.
- Help you find appropriate medical care if you are the victim of violent crimes such as assault or rape.
- Put you in contact with the appropriate police authorities, and if you want us to, we can contact family members or friend.
- Help you understand the local criminal justice process and direct you to local attorneys, although it is important to remember that local authorities are responsible for investigating and prosecuting the crime.

Ghana maintains a specialized Domestic Violence Victim Support Unit (DOVVSU) within the Ghana Police Service to assist victims of domestic violence, especially women and children. In addition to its law enforcement responsibilities, the Unit can refer victims to medical providers and counselors, as well as to community support services.

The local equivalent to the "911" emergency line in Ghana is 191.

Criminal Penalties: While you are traveling in Ghana, you are subject to its laws. Foreign laws and legal systems can be significantly different than our own and may not afford the protections available to the individual under U.S. law.

Penalties for breaking the law can be more severe than in the United States for similar offenses. In some places you may be taken in for questioning if you don't have your passport with you. In some places, it is illegal to take pictures of certain buildings.

In some places, driving under the influence could land you immediately in jail. These criminal penalties will vary from country to country. There are also some things that might be legal in the country you visit, but still illegal in the United States, and you can be prosecuted under U.S. law if you buy pirated goods.

Engaging in sexual conduct with children or using or disseminating child pornography in a foreign country is a crime prosecutable in the United States. If you break local laws in Ghana, your U.S. passport won't help you avoid arrest or prosecution. It's very important to know what's legal and what's not wherever you go.

Persons violating Ghanaian laws, even unknowingly, may be expelled, arrested, or imprisoned. Penalties for possessing, using, or trafficking in illegal drugs in Ghana are severe, and convicted offenders can expect long jail sentences and heavy fines.

The use of illegal drugs procured in Ghana may have life-threatening consequences. There have been several deaths of U.S. citizens resulting from the use of narcotics procured locally.

While some countries will automatically notify the nearest U.S. embassy or consulate if a U.S. citizen is detained or arrested in a foreign country, that might not always be the case. To ensure that the United

States is aware of your circumstances, request that the police and prison officials notify the nearest U.S. embassy or consulate as soon as you are arrested or detained overseas.

Special Circumstances: Effective July 1, 2007, the Government of Ghana redenominated the local currency, the cedi, introducing new banknotes (Ghana Cedi) and coins (Ghana Pesewa). 10,000 cedis = 1 Ghana Cedi = 100 Ghana Pesewas. The old cedi was taken out of circulation on December 31, 2007, and as of January 1, 2008, can be converted only at commercial banks or the Bank of Ghana. Travelers should be alert to persons who may try to defraud them with the old and new bills. The Government of Ghana established a website in 2007 to inform the public about the redenomination exercise. The website includes a useful currency converter.

Visitors arriving or departing Ghana with more than $$10,000 in cash are required to declare the amount at the border. Currency exchange is available at most banks and at licensed foreign exchange bureaus, but currency transactions with private citizens are illegal. The Government of Ghana also prohibits departing travelers from carrying more than 5,000 Ghana Cedi out of the country. Ghanaian currency must either be spent or exchanged before departure, or it will be confiscated.

Strict customs regulations govern temporary importation into or export from Ghana of items such as gold, diamonds and precious natural resources. Only agents licensed by the Precious Metals and Mining Commission, telephone (233)(030) 266-4635 or 266-4579, may handle import-export transactions of these natural resources. Any transaction without the commission's endorsement is illegal and/or fraudulent.

All transactions must be completed through the commission at the price set daily by the London exchange. Any transaction that discounts this price, or includes a previously negotiated price, is either illegal or fraudulent. Export of gold dust is rare as it encourages dangerous and environmentally destructive practices, and transactions involving the export of gold dust are probably fraudulent. Attempts to evade regulations are punishable by imprisonment. It is advisable to contact the Embassy of Ghana in Washington, D.C., or one of the Ghanaian consulates in the United States, for specific information regarding customs requirements.

In rare instances, visitors arriving in Ghana with sophisticated electronic equipment (e.g., video cameras and laptop computers) may have to deposit 17.5 percent of the item's value with the Customs and Excise office at the airport. To get the deposit refunded, visitors must apply to the Customs and Excise Office in central Accra 48 hours before departure.

Taking pictures near sensitive installations, including military sites and some government buildings, is prohibited. These sites are not always clearly marked and application of these restrictions is subject to interpretation. Permission may be obtained from Ghanaian security personnel. Permission should also be obtained before photographing anyone in uniform (e.g., police and military officers). In some cases, film and cameras have been confiscated. For security reasons, taking photographs of the U.S. Embassy is also prohibited.

It is strictly prohibited to wear any military apparel such as camouflage jackets or trousers, or any clothing or items that may appear military in nature.

Medical Facilities and Health Information: Medical facilities in Ghana are limited, particularly outside Accra, the capital. Travelers should carry adequate supplies of any needed prescription medicines, along with copies of their prescriptions, the generic name of the drugs, and a supply of preferred over-the-counter medications. For information on avian influenza (bird flu), please refer to the Department of State's Pandemic Influenza Fact Sheet.

Documentation of yellow fever vaccination is required upon arrival from all countries. Motor vehicle accidents, drownings, and water-related accidents due to Ghana's rough surf have been reporter by U.S. citizens. Muggings, and other violent attacks, as well as the risk of contracting sexually transmitted diseases—including HIV—are health and safety concerns that have been reported by U.S. citizens and can be at least partially mitigated by using common-sense safety precautions.

Information on vaccinations and other health precautions, such as safe food and water precautions and insect bite protection, may be obtained from the Centers for Disease Control and Prevention's (CDC) hotline for international travelers at 1-877-FYI-TRIP (1-877-394-8747) or via the CDC website. For information about outbreaks of infectious diseases abroad, consult the infectious diseases section of the World Health Organization (WHO) website. The WHO website also contains additional health information for travelers, including detailed country-specific health information.

Medical Insurance: You should not assume your health insurance will be valid when you travel overseas. It's very important to find out BEFORE you leave. You need to ask your insurance company two questions:

- Does my policy apply when I'm out of the United States?
- Will it cover emergencies like a trip to a foreign hospital or an evacuation?

In many places, doctors and hospitals still expect payment in cash at the time of service. Your regular U.S. health insurance may not cover doctors' and hospital visits in other countries. If your policy isn't valid overseas, it's a very good idea to take out another one, created especially for your trip.

Traffic Safety and Road Conditions: While in a foreign country, U.S. citizens may encounter road conditions that differ significantly from those in the United States. The information below concerning Ghana is provided for general reference only, and may not be totally accurate in a particular location or circumstance.

Primary roads are generally paved and well maintained. However, some side roads within major cities and many roads outside of major cities are in poor condition. The road from Accra to the central region tourist area of Cape Coast continues to be the site of many accidents. Travel in darkness, particularly outside the major cities, is extremely hazardous, due to poor street lighting and the unpredictable behavior of pedestrians, bicyclists and farm animals, particularly goats and sheep. Aggressive drivers, poorly maintained vehicles, and overloaded vehicles pose serious threats to road safety.

Another hazard are pedestrians who intentionally bump vehicles and pretend to be hit. They then attempt to extort money from the vehicle occupants. Scams of this nature most commonly occur in congested urban areas. The safety standards of the small private buses that transit roads and highways are uncertain. Travelers are encouraged to consider this when making travel arrangements.

Armed robbers have targeted travellers following their arrival at Kotoka airport. An increasingly used tactic is to deliberately cause a minor road traffic accident to make a car stop, and to then rob the occupants. If your car is hit by another car it is best to drive to the nearest police station to sort out the incident. Otherwise, all drivers, particularly at night, should remain vigilant, and drive with doors locked.

There has been an increase in incidents of highway robbery on the road from Kintampo to Tamale in the Brong Ahafo and Northern regions. Travelers along this route should exercise due caution.

Travelers are routinely stopped at police checkpoints throughout Ghana, and vehicles and passengers may be searched. Foreign nationals should carry documentation of their status, such as a passport and a visa. You can drive up to one year on your U.S. driver's license, after which you must obtain an international driver's license (available from AAA and the American Automobile Touring Alliance). It is illegal in Ghana to maneuver a vehicle while talking on a mobile phone.

Aviation Safety Oversight: The U.S. Federal Aviation Administration (FAA) has assessed the government of Ghana's Civil Aviation Authority as not being in compliance with International Civil Aviation Organization (ICAO) aviation safety standards for oversight of Ghana's air carrier operations. Further information may be found on the FAA's safety assessment page. Service provided by a number of regional air carriers is reported to be unreliable. The airlines may alter scheduled stops, cancel or postpone flights on short notice, and regularly overbook flights. Travelers may experience unexpected delays even after checking in. Passengers should get the required seat reconfirmation stamped on the ticket, have enough emergency funds for food and lodging in case of unexpected delays, and arrive at the airport at least two hours before the scheduled departure time.

Children's Issues: Please see the U.S. Dept. of State Office of Children's Issues web pages on intercountry adoption and international parental child abduction.

Intercountry Adoption
October 2010

The information in this section has been edited from the latest report available as of February 2013 from the State Department Bureau of Consular Affairs, Office of Overseas Citizens Services. For more information, please read the *Intercountry Adoption* section of this book and review current reports online at http://adoption.state.gov.

Ghana is not party to the Hague Convention on Protection of Children and Co-operation in Respect of Intercountry Adoption (Hague Adoption Convention). Therefore, when the Hague Adoption Convention entered into force for the United States on April 1, 2008, intercountry adoption processing for Ghana did not change. The Department of Social Welfare may consider an application for intercountry adoption as an alternative means of child care, if a child cannot be placed in a foster or adoptive family in Ghana or cannot in any suitable matter be cared for in Ghana. A court may grant an intercountry adoption order if it is in the best interests of the child.

Who Can Adopt? To bring an adopted child to United States from Ghana, you must be found eligible to adopt by the U.S. government. The U.S. government agency responsible for making this determination is the Department of Homeland Security, U.S. Citizenship and Immigration Services (USCIS).

Residency Requirements: Prospective adoptive parents must be resident in Ghana a minimum of three months prior to adopting a child. The prospective adoptive parents may request a waiver of the residency requirement through the court. The courts will approve a waiver of the residency requirement with the recommendation of the Ministry of Social Welfare if it is in the best interest of the child.

Age Requirements: Applicants must be at least 25 years of age and at least 21 years older than the child.

Marriage Requirements: An application for adoption may be made jointly by a husband and wife. Application for adoption may be made by a single person, but only if that person is a citizen of Ghana. Same-sex couples are not allowed to adopt children in Ghana, nor are single males unless the child to be adopted is their biological child.

Income Requirements: Applicants must be gainfully employed.

Other Requirements: Applicants must be of sound mind and must undergo a medical exam as part of the pre-approval process.

Who Can Be Adopted? Ghana has specific requirements that a child must meet in order to be eligible for adoption. In addition to these requirements, a child must meet the definition of an orphan under U.S. law for you to bring him or her immediately to the United States.

Ghanian Adoption Authority: The Department of Social Welfare, Client Services Unit

The Process: Prospective adoptive parents will work with a Ghanaian Social Welfare Officer in the region from which they will adopt to be pre-approved for adoption.

Prospective adoptive parents must work with an attorney to complete the legal requirements for adoption in Ghana. The GOG does not accredit foreign adoption service providers. The Ministry of Social Welfare is the only agency to provide adoption services.

To bring an adopted child from Ghana to the United States, you must apply to be found eligible to adopt by the U.S. Government, Department of Homeland Security, U.S. Citizenship and Immigration Services (USCIS). In addition to meeting the U.S. requirements for adoptive parents, you need to meet the requirements of Ghana.

Applicants purchase the adoption form from the Director of Social Welfare ad any regional Social Welfare office for 10 Cedis (subject to change but current as of February 2009) and submit the completed form along with the attachments specified in the form to the Director of Social Welfare or his/her representative at the Regional Office for processing.

The processing of the application begins with visits to the applicant's home by a Social Welfare Officer who interviews the applicants and submits the report to the Placement Committee, the head officer for adoptions in the Department of Social Welfare. The Placement Committee will review the application and determine eligibility. This process can take approximately three months. If you are eligible to adopt, and a child is available for intercountry adoption, the central adoption authority in Ghana will provide you with a referral to a child. Depending on the availability of children, a suitable child is placed with would-be parents for a trial period of three months, during which time the Social Welfare Officer undertakes monthly visits. The Director of Social Welfare submits the comprehensive report, which covers the social investigation of the applicants, background checks, mental stability, financial stability, etc. to the High Court. An adoption order may then be granted by the High Court upon recommendations from the Director of Social Welfare. The adoption is incomplete without the granting of an Adoption Order by the High Court.

Time Frame: It takes one year to complete an adoption in Ghana. An additional one to six months may be required for the U.S. immigration petition and visa process. USCIS and the Department of Homeland Security in Accra, conducts investigations of all adoption cases in Ghana, which can prolong the process.

Documents Required: In general, the documents required are the same as for an adoption in the United States, including birth, marriage and divorce records, medical examination and clearance, and evidence of financial stability and gainful employment.

Bringing Your Child Home: Once your adoption is complete (or you have obtained legal custody of the child), there are a few more steps to take before you can head home.

Specifically, you need to apply for several documents for your child before he or she can travel to the United States, such as a birth certificate, a passport or travel document for your child from the country in which he or she was born, and a U.S. Immigration Visa.

For detailed and updated information on how to obtain these documents, review the *Intercountry Adoption* section in this publication and visit the U.S. Department of State Intercountry Adoption website at http://adoption.state.gov.

Child Citizenship Act: For adoptions finalized abroad, the Child Citizenship Act of 2000 allows your new child to acquire American citizenship automatically when he or she enters the United States as lawful permanent residents.

For adoptions finalized in the United States, the Child Citizenship Act of 2000 allows your new child to acquire American citizenship automatically when the court in the United States issues the final adoption decree. To learn more, review the *Intercountry Adoption* section in this publication and visit the U.S. Department of State Intercountry Adoption website at http://adoption.state.gov.

After Adoption: Ghana has no post-adoption requirements.

U.S. Embassy in Ghana
The Consular Section is located in the Embassy at:
24 Fourth Circular Road.
Cantonments, Accra
Telephone (233) (21) 741–000
Fax (233) (21) 741–389http://ghana.usembassy.gov
E-mail: consulateaccra@state.gov or AccraAdoption@state.gov

Ghanaian Adoption Authority
The Department of Social Welfare
Client Services Unit
P.O. Box M230
Accra, Ghana
Tel: 233–21–662–857

Embassy of Ghana
3512 International Drive, N.W.
Washington, D.C. 20008
Telephone (202) 686–4520.

Ghana also has consulates in Houston, TX, and Consular Services are available at the Ghana Permanent Mission to the United Nations in New York, NY.

Office of Children's Issues
U.S. Department of State
2201 C Street, NW
SA-29
Washington, DC 20520

Tel: 1–888–407–4747
E-mail: AskCI@state.gov
http://adoption.state.gov

U.S. Citizenship and Immigration Services (USCIS) Accra Field Office
Department of Homeland Security
P.O. Box 194
24 Fourth Circular Rd
Accra, Ghana
Tel: (233–21)-741646 or 741561
Fax: (233–21)-741 455
Email: USCIS.Accra@dhs.gov

For questions about immigration procedures, call the National Customer Service Center (NCSC) 1-800-375-5283 (TTY 1-800-767-1833).

International Parental Child Abduction

February 2013

The information in this section has been edited from a report from the State Department Bureau of Consular Affairs, Office of Overseas Citizens Services. For more information, please read the *International Parental Child Abduction* section of this book and check for updated reports online at www.travel.state.gov/abduction.

Disclaimer: The information in this flyer is provided for general information only, is not intended to be legal advice, and may change without notice. Questions involving interpretation of law should be addressed to an attorney licensed to practice in the relevant jurisdiction.

Hague Abduction Convention: Ghana is not a signatory to the 1980 Hague Convention on the Civil Aspects of International Child Abduction (Hague Abduction Convention), nor are there any bilateral agreements in force between Ghana and the United States concerning international parental child abduction.

Return: Legal systems and laws pertaining to custody, divorce, and parental abduction vary widely from country to country. Parents are encouraged to consult with an attorney who specializes in family law in Ghana and who can provide accurate legal guidance that is specific to their circumstances. The Department of State's Bureau of Consular Affairs, Directorate for Overseas Citizens Services, Office of Children's Issues provides assistance in cases of international parental child abduction. Parents are strongly encouraged to contact the Department of State for assistance.

United States Department of State
Office of Children's Issues
2201 C Street, N.W.
Washington, DC 20520
Telephone: 1-888-407-4747
Outside the United States or Canada: 1-202-501-4444
Fax: 202-736-9132
Email: AskCI@state.gov

Parental child abduction is a criminal offense in Ghana. The Children's Act of 1998 makes removal of a child from a person who has legal custody an offense with possible fines or imprisonment. Links to Ghanaian law regarding children are available at the Ghanaian Ministry of Women and Children's website. The Children's Act 1998 is available here.

Parents may wish to consult with an attorney in the United States and in the country to which the child has been removed or retained to learn more about how filing criminal charges may impact a custody case in the foreign court.

Visitation/Access: Legal systems and laws pertaining to custody, divorce, and parental abduction vary widely from country to country. Parents are encouraged to consult with an attorney who specializes in family law in Ghana and who can provide accurate legal guidance that is specific to their circumstances. The Office of Children's Issues may be able to assist parents seeking access to children who have been wrongfully removed from or retained outside the United States. Parents who are seeking access to children who were not wrongfully removed from or retained outside the United States should contact the appropriate U.S. Embassy in Ghana for information and possible assistance.

Retaining an Attorney: Neither the Office of Children's Issues nor consular officials at the U.S. Embassy in Ghana are authorized to provide legal advice. The U.S. Embassy in Accra, Ghana, posts a list of attorneys, including those who specialize in family law. This list is provided as a courtesy service only and does not constitute an endorsement of any individual attorney. The Department of State assumes no responsibility or liability for the professional ability or reputation of, or the quality of services provided by, the following persons or firms. Professional credentials and areas of expertise are provided directly by the lawyers..

Mediation: While mediation is not a process used in custody disputes in Ghana, occasionally the court will refer a case to the Department of Social Welfare to work with the families.

U.S. Embassy—Accra
No. 24 Fourth Circular Road
Cantonments, Accra
Phone: (233)-(030) 274-1000
Fax: (233)-(030) 274-1362
or 274-1426
E-Mail: ACSaccra@state.gov
http://ghana.usembassy.gov/

Embassy of the Republic of Ghana
3512 International Drive NW
Washington, DC 20008
Telephone: (202) 686-4520
Website:
http://www.ghanaembassy.org/

GREECE

Compiled from publications that were available as of February 2013 from the U.S. Department of State, the U.S. Department of Commerce, and the Central Intelligence Agency (CIA). See the introduction to this set for explanatory notes.

Official Name:
Hellenic Republic

PROFILE

Geography

Area: total: 131,957 sq km; country comparison to the world: 97; land: 130,647 sq km; water: 1,310 sq km

Major cities: Athens (capital) 3.252 million; Thessaloniki 834,000 (2009)

Climate: temperate; mild, wet winters; hot, dry summers

Terrain: mostly mountains with ranges extending into the sea as peninsulas or chains of islands

People

Nationality: noun: Greek(s); adjective: Greek

Population: 10,767,827 (July 2012 est.)

Population growth rate: 0.06% (2012 est.)

Ethnic groups: population: Greek 93%, other (foreign citizens) 7% (2001 census)

Religions: Greek Orthodox (official) 98%, Muslim 1.3%, other 0.7%

Languages: Greek (official) 99%, other (includes English and French) 1%

Literacy: definition: age 15 and over can read and write; total population: 96%; male: 97.8%; female: 94.2% (2001 census)

Health: life expectancy at birth: total population: 80.05 years; male: 77.48 years; female: 82.79 years (2012 est.); Infant mortality rate: total: 4.92 deaths/1,000 live births; male: 5.41 deaths/1,000 live births; female: 4.41 deaths/1,000 live births (2012 est.)

Unemployment rate: 24.4% (2012 est.)

Work force: 4.951 million (2012 est.)

Government

Type: parliamentary republic

Independence: 1830

Constitution: 11 June 1975; amended March 1986, April 2001, and May 2008

Political subdivisions: 13 regions (perifereies, singular—perifereia) and 1 autonomous monastic state (aftonomi monastiki politeia); Agion Oros (Mount Athos), Anatoliki Makedonia kai Thraki (East Macedonia and Thrace), Attiki (Attica), Dytiki Ellada (West Greece), Dytiki Makedonia (West Macedonia), Ionia Nisia (Ionian Islands), Ipeiros (Epirus), Kentriki Makedonia (Central Macedonia), Kriti (Crete), Notio Aigaio (South Aegean), Peloponnisos (Peloponnese), Sterea Ellada (Central Greece), Thessalia (Thessaly), Voreio Aigaio (North Aegean)

Suffrage: 18 years of age; universal and compulsory

Economy

GDP (purchasing power parity): $280.8 billion (2012 est.); $298.1 billion (2011 est.); $320.1 billion (2010 est.); $331.7 billion (2009 est.)

GDP real growth rate: -6% (2012 est.); -6.9% (2011 est.); -3.5% (2010 est.); -3.3% (2009 est.)

GDP per capita (PPP): $25,100 (2012 est.); $26,600 (2011 est.); $28,600 (2010 est.); $29,700 (2009 est.)

Natural resources: lignite, petroleum, iron ore, bauxite, lead, zinc, nickel, magnesite, marble, salt, hydropower potential

Agriculture products: wheat, corn, barley, sugar beets, olives, tomatoes, wine, tobacco, potatoes; beef, dairy products

Industries: tourism, food and tobacco processing, textiles, chemicals, metal products; mining, petroleum

Exports: $26.67 billion (2012 est.); $28.16 billion (2011 est.); $22.66 billion (2010 est.)

Exports—commodities: food and beverages, manufactured goods, petroleum products, chemicals, textiles

Exports—partners: Italy 9.6%, Germany 8%, UK 6.5%, Italy 6.2%, Bulgaria 5.6%, US 5.1%, China 5.1%, Switzerland 4.7%, Belgium 4.7%, Poland 4.4% (2011)

Imports: $57.92 billion (2012 est.); $66.04 billion (2011 est.); $60.19 billion (2010 est.)
Imports—commodities: machinery, transport equipment, fuels, chemicals
Imports—partners: Germany 10.7%, Italy 9.3%, China 7.1%, China 5.7%, Netherlands 5.5%, France 5.1%, Austria 4.5%, Russia 4.2%, Czech Republic 4.1% (2011)
Debt—external: $583.3 billion (30 June 2011); $532.9 billion (30 June 2010)
Exchange rates: euros (EUR) per US dollar; 0.7838 (2012 est.); 0.7194 (2011 est.); 0.755 (2010 est.); 0.7198 (2009 est.); 0.6827 (2008 est.); 0.7345 (2007 est.)

PEOPLE

Greece was inhabited as early as the Paleolithic period and by 3000 BC had become home, in the Cycladic Islands, to a culture whose art remains among the most evocative in world history. In the second millennium BC, the island of Crete nurtured the maritime empire of the Minoans, whose trade reached from Egypt to Sicily. The Minoans were supplanted by the Mycenaeans of the Greek mainland, who spoke a dialect of ancient Greek. During the Roman, Byzantine, and Ottoman Empires (1st-19th centuries), Greece's ethnic composition became more diverse.

National/Racial/Ethnic Minorities

According to NGOs, Roma continued to face widespread governmental and societal discrimination, including alleged police abuse or mistreatment while in police custody; regular raids and searches of their neighborhoods for criminal suspects, drugs, and weapons; limited access to education; and segregated schooling. Their dwellings lacked running water, electricity, or waste removal and were at times demolished by municipal authorities. NGOs and representatives of the Romani community reported that government efforts to address these problems were inconsistent, especially at the municipal level. The government did not recognize the existence of a Slavic dialect, called "Macedonian" by its speakers, in the northwestern area of the country. Nevertheless, a small number of its speakers insisted on identifying themselves as "Macedonian," a designation that generated strong opposition from other citizens.

These individuals claimed that the government pursued a policy designed to discourage the use of their language. Government officials and the courts denied requests by Slavic groups to identify themselves using the term "Macedonian," stating that approximately 2.2 million ethnically (and linguistically) Greek citizens also use the term "Macedonian" to identify themselves.

The UN independent expert on minority issues, in a 2009 report, urged the government to withdraw from the dispute over whether there was a "Macedonian" or a "Turkish" ethnic minority in the country. She advised focusing instead on protecting the rights to self-identification, freedom of expression, and freedom of association of those communities and on complying fully with the rulings of the ECHR that associations should be allowed to use the words "Macedonian" and "Turkish" in their names and to express their ethnic identities freely.

The independent expert found that those identifying themselves as ethnic Macedonians continued to report discrimination and harassment. Representatives of the minority claimed they were denied the right to freedom of association, citing unsuccessful efforts since 1990 to register the organization "Home of Macedonian Culture" in Florina.

Education

Greek education is free and compulsory for children between the ages of 6 and 15. Overall responsibility for education rests with the Ministry of National Education and Religious Affairs. Private colleges and universities (mostly foreign) have campuses in Greece despite the fact that their degrees are not recognized by the Greek state. Entrance to public universities is determined by state-administered exams.

Language

Greek is the official language of Greece. The roots of Greek language and culture date back at least 3,500 years, and modern Greek preserves many elements of its classical predecessor. A high percentage of Greek business people and government officials speak English. Also, many speak German and/or French.

Religion

The government does not keep statistics on religious groups. An estimated 98 percent of the population, however, identifies itself as Greek Orthodox. The 1923 Treaty of Lausanne created an officially recognized "Muslim minority," which consists of an estimated 140,000 to 150,000 individuals (approximately 1.3 percent of the Greek population) residing in Thrace. The remaining population is composed of Roman Catholics, Protestants, Jews, Old Calendarist Orthodox, Jehovah's Witnesses, members of The Church of Jesus Christ of Latter-day Saints (Mormons), Scientologists, Baha'is, Hare Krishna devotees, and followers of polytheistic Hellenic religions. Church leaders estimated that 30 percent of self-identified Orthodox regularly participates in religious services.

NGOs estimate that between 500,000 and 700,000 Muslims reside in Attica as a result of longstanding migration from Albania and a recent influx of illegal immigrants and refugees from Afghanistan, Pakistan, North Africa, and South Asia.

HISTORY

The Greek War of Independence began in 1821 and concluded in 1830 when England, France, and Russia forced the Ottoman Empire to grant Greece its independence under a European monarch.

At independence, Greece had an area of 47,515 square kilometers (18,346 square mi.), and its northern boundary extended from the Gulf of Volos to the Gulf of Arta. Under the influence of the "Megali Idea," which in its most broad interpretation meant the expansion of the Greek state to include all areas where significant Greek communities existed, Greece acquired the Ionian islands in 1864; Thessaly and part of Epirus in 1881; part of Macedonia, Crete, Epirus, and the Aegean islands in 1913; western Thrace in 1918; and the Dodecanese islands in 1947.

Greece entered World War I in 1917 on the side of the Allies. After the war, Greece took part in the Allied occupation of Turkey, where many Greeks still lived. In 1921, the Greek army marched toward Ankara, but was defeated by Turkish forces led by Kemal Mustapha Ataturk and was forced to withdraw. In an exchange of populations under the Treaty of Lausanne, more than 1.3 million refugees from Turkey poured into Greece, and nearly 800,000 Greek Turks were sent to Turkey. This large influx of people created enormous challenges for the Greek economy and society.

Greek politics, particularly between the two world wars, involved a struggle for power between monarchists and republicans. Greece was proclaimed a republic in 1924, but George II returned to the throne in 1935. A plebiscite in 1946 upheld the monarchy, which was finally abolished by referendum on December 8, 1974.

Greece's entry into World War II was precipitated by the Italian invasion on October 28, 1940. Despite Italian superiority in numbers and equipment, determined Greek defenders drove the invaders back into Albania. Hitler was forced to divert German troops to protect his southern flank and overran Greece in 1941. Following a very severe German occupation in which many Greeks died (including over 90% of Greece's Jewish community) German forces withdrew in October 1944, and the government-in-exile returned to Athens.

After the German withdrawal, the principal Greek resistance movement, which was controlled by the communists, refused to disarm. A banned demonstration by resistance forces in Athens in December 1944 ended in battles with Greek Government and British forces. Continuing tensions led to the outbreak of full-fledged civil war in 1946. First the United Kingdom and later the U.S. gave extensive military and economic aid to the Greek Government. In 1947, Secretary of State George C. Marshall implemented the Marshall Plan under President Truman, which focused on the economic recovery and the rebuilding of Europe. The U.S. contributed hundreds of millions of dollars to rebuild Greece's buildings, agriculture, and industry.

In August 1949, the Greek national army forced the remaining insurgents to surrender or flee to Greece's communist neighbors. The insurgency resulted in 100,000 killed, 700,000 displaced persons inside the country, and catastrophic economic disruption. This civil war left Greek society deeply divided between leftists and rightists.

Greece became a member of NATO in 1952. From 1952 to late 1963, Greece was governed by conservative parties—the Greek Rally of Marshal Alexandros Papagos and its successor, the National Radical Union (ERE) of Konstantinos Karamanlis. In 1963, the Center Union Party of George Papandreou was elected and governed until July 1965. It was followed by a succession of unstable coalition governments.

On April 21, 1967, just before scheduled elections, a group of colonels led by Col. George Papadopoulos seized power in a coup d'état. The junta suppressed civil liberties, established special military courts, and dissolved political parties. Several thousand political opponents were imprisoned or exiled to remote Greek islands. In November 1973, following an uprising of students at the Athens Polytechnic University, General Dimitrios Ioannides replaced Papadopoulos and tried to continue the dictatorship.

In July 1974, the Greek junta sponsored a coup in Cyprus led by extremist Greek Cypriots against the government of President Makarios, citing his alleged pro-communist leanings and his perceived abandonment of enosis, or political union with Greece. Turkey, citing the 1960 Treaty of Guarantee, intervened militarily to protect Turkish Cypriots. In a two-stage offensive, Turkish troops took control of 38% of the island. Almost all Greek Cypriots subsequently fled south while almost all Turkish Cypriots moved to the north.

Senior Greek military officers withdrew their support from the junta, which toppled. Leading citizens persuaded Karamanlis to return from exile in France to establish a government of national unity until elections could be held. Karamanlis' newly organized party, New Democracy (ND), won elections held in November 1974, and he became Prime Minister.

Following the 1974 referendum, the parliament approved a new constitution and elected Constantine Tsatsos as president of the republic. On January 1, 1981, Greece became the 10th member of the European Community (now the European Union—EU). Parliamentary elections were held March 8, 2004, and ND won 165 seats to the Panhellenic Socialist Movement's (PASOK) 117; Konstantinos Karamanlis, ND leader and the nephew of the former prime minister of the same name, became Prime Minister. Karolos Papoulias was elected President by parliament in February 2005. On October 4, 2009, PASOK won an early parliamentary election with 160 seats to ND's 91. PASOK leader George Papandreou succeeded Karamanlis as Prime Minister.

On February 3, 2010, Papoulias was re-elected President by parliament with a majority of 266 votes out of 300. On November 11, 2011, Papandreou stepped down as prime minister to make way for a coalition government led by Lucas Papademos (PASOK).

GOVERNMENT AND POLITICAL CONDITIONS

Greece is a constitutional republic and multiparty parliamentary democracy. On November 11, 2011, a new "unity" government composed of the Pan-Hellenic Socialist Movement (PASOK), the New Democracy (ND) party, and the Popular Orthodox Rally (LAOS) party was sworn in, with Lucas Papademos as prime minister.

Recent Elections

The country's parliamentary elections in 2009 were considered free and fair.

Participation of Women and Minorities: There were 51 women in the 300-seat parliament and two women in the 18-member cabinet. A quota system requires that 30 percent of all parties' candidates for local government be women. At the three highest courts, 14 of 61 Council of State justices, 28 of 59 Supreme Administrative Court justices, and three of 62 Supreme Court justices were women. There were two members of the Muslim minority of Thrace in the parliament; there were no minority members in the cabinet.

Approximately one-third of the Romani population was not registered to vote.

Principal Government Officials

Last Updated: 1/31/2013

Pres.: **Karolos PAPOULIAS**

Prime Min.: **Antonios SAMARAS**

Min. of Admin. Reform & Electronic Governance: **Antonios MANITAKIS**

Min. of Development & Infrastructure: **Konstantinos HATZIDAKIS**

Min. of Education & Culture: **Konstantinos ARVANITOPOULOS**

Min. of Environment, Energy, & Climate Change: **Evangelos LIVIERATOS**

Min. of Finance: **Ioannis STOURNARAS**

Min. of Foreign Affairs: **Dimitrios AVRAMOPOULOS**

Min. of Health: **Andreas LYKOURENTZOS**

Min. of Interior: **Euripides STYLIANIDIS**

Min. of Justice: **Antonios ROUPAKIOTIS**

Min. of Labor & Social Security: **Ioannis VROUTSIS**

Min. of Macedonia-Thrace: **Theodoros KARAOGLOU**

Min. of National Defense: **Panagiotis PANAGIOTOPOULOS**

Min. of Public Order & Citizen Protection: **Nikolaos DENDIAS**

Min. of Rural Development & Food: **Athanasios TSAFTARIS**

Min. of Shipping & Aegean: **Konstantinos MOUSOUROULIS**

Min. of State: **Dimitrios STAMATIS**

Min. of Tourism: **Olga KEFALOGIANNI**

Govt. Spokesman: **Simeon KEDIKOGLOU**

Governor, Bank of Greece: **Georgios PROVOPOULOS**

Ambassador to the US: **Vasileios KASKARELIS**

Permanent Representative to the UN, New York: **Anastasios MITSIALIS**

ECONOMY

Greece has a capitalist economy with a public sector accounting for about 40% of GDP and with per capita GDP about two-thirds that of the leading euro-zone economies. Tourism provides 15% of GDP. Immigrants make up nearly one-fifth of the work force, mainly in agricultural and unskilled jobs. Greece is a major beneficiary of EU aid, equal to about 3.3% of annual GDP.

The Greek economy grew by nearly 4% per year between 2003 and 2007, due partly to infrastructural spending related to the 2004 Athens Olympic Games, and in part to an increased availability of credit, which has sustained record levels of consumer spending. But the economy went into recession in 2009 as a result of the world financial crisis, tightening credit conditions, and Athens' failure to address a growing budget deficit. The economy contracted by 2.3% in 2009, 3.5% in 2010, 6.9% in 2011, and 6.0% in 2012. Greece violated the EU's Growth and Stability Pact budget deficit criterion of no more than 3% of GDP from 2001 to 2006, but finally met that criterion in 2007–08, before exceeding it again in 2009, with the deficit reaching 15% of GDP. Austerity measures reduced the deficit to about 8% in 2012.

Deteriorating public finances, inaccurate and misreported statistics, and consistent underperformance on reforms prompted major credit rating agencies to downgrade Greece's international debt rating in late 2009, and has led the country into a financial crisis. Under intense pressure from the EU and international market participants, the government adopted a medium-term austerity program that includes cutting government spending, decreasing tax evasion, overhauling the health-care and pension systems, and reforming the labor and product markets.

Athens, however, faces long-term challenges to push through unpopular reforms in the face of widespread unrest from the country's powerful labor unions and the general public. In April 2010 a leading credit agency assigned Greek debt its lowest possible credit rating; in May 2010, the International Monetary Fund and Euro-Zone governments provided Greece emergency short- and medium-term loans worth $147 billion so that the country could make debt repayments to creditors. In exchange for the largest bailout ever assembled, the government announced combined spending cuts and tax increases totaling $40 billion over three years, on top of the tough austerity measures already taken.

Greece, however, struggled to meet 2010 targets set by the EU and the IMF, especially after Eurostat—the EU's statistical office—revised upward Greece's deficit and debt numbers for 2009 and 2010. European leaders and the IMF agreed in October 2011 to provide Athens a second bailout package of $169 billion. The second deal however, calls for Greece's creditors to write down a significant portion of their Greek government bond holdings.

In exchange for the second loan Greece has promised to introduce an additional $7.8 billion in austerity measures during 2013–15. However, these massive austerity cuts are lengthening Greece's economic recession and depressing tax revenues. Greece's lenders are calling on Athens to step up efforts to increase tax collection, privatize public enterprises, and rein in health spending, and are planning to give Greece more time to shore up its economy and finances. Many investors doubt that Greece can sustain fiscal efforts in the face of a bleak economic outlook, public discontent, and political instability.

Labor Conditions

Although the law protects children from exploitation in the workplace and prohibits forced or compulsory labor, the government did not adequately protect children, primarily Roma, who were trafficked for begging, pickpocketing, or selling merchandise on the street.

The minimum age for employment in the industrial sector is 15, with higher limits for some activities. The minimum age is 12 in family businesses, theaters, and the cinema. The Labor Inspectorate enforced these limits by occasional spot checks, and they were generally observed. Younger family members often assisted families in agriculture, food service, and merchandising on at least a part-time basis.

Child labor was a problem. The Labor Inspectorate is responsible for enforcing child labor legislation; however, trade unions alleged that enforcement was inadequate due to inspectorate understaffing.

The gross national minimum wage in the private sector was 34 euros ($44) per day and 751 euros ($976) per month. Public sector salaries, including the minimum wage, were determined by the government without negotiations with civil servant unions. The minimum gross salary for the public sector was 780 euros ($1,014) per month. The National Statistical Authority estimated in 2008 (the latest statistics available) that the poverty income level for an individual was 6,480 euros ($8,424) per year. Wages were officially the same for local and foreign workers, but there were numerous reports of exploitation of documented, and even more reports of exploitation of undocumented, foreign workers by employers who paid low wages and made no social security contributions. Workers in the shadow economy, estimated to comprise approximately 25-35 percent of gross domestic product, usually received less than the minimum wage and had no social security coverage. The Labor Inspectorate estimated in September that more than 35 percent of migrants received salaries below the minimum and did not have social security coverage. The law allows employers to pay workers under the age of 25 wages amounting to 84 percent of the national minimum wage.

The maximum legal workweek is 40 hours. The law provides for at least one 24-hour rest period per week, mandates paid vacation of one month per year, and sets limits on the amount of overtime. Premium pay and authorization by the Ministry of Employment and Social Security are required by law for overtime work.

U.S.-GREECE RELATIONS

The United States appointed its first Consul to Greece in 1837, following Greece's independence from the Ottoman Empire, and established diplomatic relations with Greece in 1868. After World War II, the United States contributed hundreds of millions of dollars to rebuild Greece's buildings, agriculture, and industry as part of the Marshall Plan. Today, an estimated three million Americans resident in the United States claim Greek descent. This large, well-organized community cultivates close political and cultural ties with Greece.

Greece is an important partner of the United States on many policy priorities. As a leader in the region, Greece has been an ally to the U.S. in promoting Balkan stability and economic development, supporting Turkey's bid for accession to the European Union, and supporting the diversification of Europe's energy supplies. Greece's geostrategic position also makes it an important ally in engagement and dialogue with the Muslim world. Greece is the primary entry point into the Schengen visa area for migrants from the Middle East, North and Sub-Saharan Africa, and Southwest Asia.

Greece occupies a strategic location in the Eastern Mediterranean on the southern flank of the North Atlantic Treaty Organization (NATO). The U.S.-Greece mutual defense cooperation agreement provides for the operation by the United States of a naval support facility at the deep-water port and airfield at Souda Bay in Crete. Greece contributes to NATO operations in Afghanistan and Kosovo, as well as to counterterrorism and counter-piracy maritime efforts.

U.S. Assistance to Greece

U.S. assistance fosters strong bilateral military-to-military relations and contributes toward the interoperability of Greek forces within NATO.

Bilateral Economic Relations

Greece is a member of the European Union and the Eurozone. The United States has expressed consistent strong support for Greece's ongoing effort to restore fiscal stability, implement structural reforms, recover competitiveness and restart growth. There are no significant non-tariff barriers to U.S. exports. The top U.S. exports to Greece are defense articles, although. U.S. business activity is expected to grow in the tourism development, medical, construction, food processing, specialty agriculture and packaging and franchising sectors. U.S. companies are interested and involved in Greece's ambitious but slow-moving privatization efforts. Further deregulation of Greece's energy sector and the country's central location as a transportation hub for Europe may offer additional opportunities in electricity, gas, refinery, and related sectors. Greece participates in the Visa Waiver Program, which allows nationals of participating countries to travel to the United States for certain business or tourism purposes for stays of 90 days or less without obtaining a visa.

Greece's Membership in International Organizations

Greece and the United States belong to a number of the same international organizations, including the United Nations, North Atlantic Treaty Organization, Euro-Atlantic Partnership Council, Organization for Security and Cooperation in Europe, Organization for Economic Cooperation and Development, International Monetary Fund, World Bank, and World Trade Organization. Greece also is a permanent observer to the Organization of American States.

Bilateral Representation

Greece maintains an embassy in the United States at 2217 Massachusetts Ave., NW, Washington, DC 20008; tel: (202) 939-1300.

Principal U.S. Embassy Officials

Last Updated: 1/14/2013

ATHENS (E) 91 Vasillissis Sophias Ave, 30 210 721-2951, Fax 30 210 645 6282, INMARSAT Tel (EATL) 871 683 131 245, Workweek: M-F, 8:30-5:00.

DCM OMS:	Angela Fresne
AMB OMS:	Betsy Zouroudis
Co-CLO:	Letise Lafeir
DHS/CIS:	Adonis Rubinstein
DHS/ICE:	Andrew Diamond
FCS:	David McNeill
FM:	Eric Lee
HRO:	Suzanne Inzerillo
MGT:	Mary J. Teirlynck
PO/CON:	Marsha Lance
POL/MIL:	Amy Scanlon
POSHO:	Eric Lee
SDO/DATT:	COL David Chapman
AMB:	Daniel B. Smith
CON:	Mark Marrano
DCM:	Virginia Bennett
PAO:	Laurie Weitzenkorn
GSO:	Doug Ellrich
RSO:	Thomas Barnard
CLO:	Tchrieyah Napier
DEA:	Nikos Eliopoulos
ECON:	David Lippeatt
EEO:	Laurie Weitzenkorn
FMO:	Tahwanda Lambert
IMO:	Michael Chiaventone
ISSO:	Steve Labocki
LEGATT:	William Peterson
POL:	Daniel J. Lawton

THESSALONIKI (CG) 43, Tsimiski Street, Thessaloniki 546 23, 0030-2310-242-905, Fax 0030-2310-242 924, Workweek: Mon–Fri 08:30–17:00, Website: http://thessaloniki.usconsulate.gov/

DPO:	Marsha A. Lance
FM:	Eric Lee (Athens)
MGT:	Marsha A. Lance
POL/ECON:	Robert P. Sanders
POSHO:	Marsha A. Lance
PO:	Robert P. Sanders
CON:	Marsha A. Lance
RSO:	Pso-Marsha A. Lance
EEO:	Robert P. Sanders
FMO:	Tahwanda Lambert (Athens)
IMO:	Michael Chiaventone (Athens)
IPO:	Susan Lee (Athens)
ISSO:	Raul Claud (Athens)

TRAVEL

Consular Information Sheet

August 23, 2012

Country Description: Greece is a developed and stable democracy with a modern economy. Tourist facilities are widely available.

Smart Traveler Enrollment Program (STEP)/Embassy Locations: If you are going to live in or visit Greece, please take the time to tell our Embassy or Consulate about your trip. If you enroll, we can keep you up to date with important safety and security announcements. Enrolling also will help your friends and family get in touch with you in an emergency.

U. S. Embassy Athens
91 Vasilissis Sophias Boulevard
Telephone: (30) (210) 721-2951
Emergency after-hours telephone: (30) (210) 729-4444
or (30) (210) 729-4301
Fax: (30) (210) 724-5313

U.S. Consulate General Thessaloniki
Plateia Commercial Center
43 Tsimiski Street, 7th floor
Telephone: (30) (2310) 242-905
Fax: (30) (2310) 242-927

Entry/Exit Requirements for U.S. Citizens: Greece is a party to the Schengen Agreement. As such, U.S. Citizens may enter Greece for up to 90 days for tourist or business purposes without a visa. Stiff fines may be imposed for overstaying the 90-day period. Your passport should be valid for at least three months beyond the period of your stay. You may also need to demonstrate at the port of entry (or during the visa interview if you are applying for a visa) that you have sufficient funds for your trip and that you have a return airline ticket.

For other entry requirements, travelers should contact the Embassy of Greece at 2221 Massachusetts Avenue NW, Washington, DC 20008, telephone (202) 939-1300, or the Greek Consulate in Atlanta, Boston, Chicago, Houston, Los Angeles, Tampa, New York, or San Francisco. Visit the Embassy of Greece for the most current visa information. If you are a U.S. citizen born in the Republic of Macedonia, please note Greek Immigration Officers at all ports of entry (land, air and sea) will not place entry stamps in passports listing the traveler's place of birth as Macedonia or the Republic of Macedonia. These travelers are required to complete a short form on which the entry stamp will be placed and which the traveler should keep with their passport for the duration of their stay in Greece and present upon departure.

Please note: If you are traveling with a U.S. official or diplomatic passport, you MUST obtain a visa prior to arrival. Travelers arriving with official or diplomatic passports without visas will not be allowed to enter the country.

The U.S. Department of State is unaware of any HIV/AIDS entry restrictions for visitors to or foreign residents of Greece.

Threats to Safety and Security: The U.S. Government remains deeply concerned about the heightened threat of terrorist attacks against U.S. citizens and interests abroad. Like other countries that are members of the Schengen Agreement for free cross-border movement, Greece's open borders with other members of the EU's Schengen zone allow for the possibility of terrorist groups entering/exiting the country with anonymity. As the first entry point into Schengen from points south and east, Greece's long coastline and many islands increase the possibility that foreign-based terrorists might try to enter Europe through its borders.

Domestic terrorist organizations such as Revolutionary Struggle (RS), Sect of Revolutionaries, and the Conspiracy of Fire Nuclei (CFN) have been the most active anarchist terrorist groups in recent years striking both domestic and foreign targets in Greece. For example, in December 2010, a powerful bomb exploded outside of the Court of the First Instance in Athens, approximately a mile from the U.S. Embassy.

In November 2010, a number of package bombs were sent to courier services for delivery to several foreign embassies in Athens; some exploded, resulting in minor injuries to a courier office employee, and others were detonated by police. In June 2010, an assistant to the Minister of Citizen Protection was killed when he opened a package bomb delivered to police headquarters. In March 2010, a fifteen-year-old Afghan immigrant was killed when he apparently disturbed a bomb placed outside an Athens business.

In January 2010, a bomb exploded near the Tomb of the Unknown Soldier on Syntagma square, a site popular with tourists. Other attacks and attempted attacks have included the use of Molotov cocktails (gasoline bombs), small arms and rifle fire, targeted assassinations, and improvised explosive devices, the largest being a 100-kilo ammonium nitrate car bomb detonated at the Athens Stock Exchange in September 2009.

Greek police forces, other Greek government agencies, banks, and private U.S. and Greek businesses have been attacked in the last four years; the U.S. Embassy was attacked in 2007. A positive development, however, is that Greek police made a large number of arrests in 2010 and 2011 of suspected members of both RS and CFN, and trials involving these suspects are currently underway in Athens. 2011 saw a noticeable drop in the number of major terrorist incidents. Only three planned bomb attacks in 2011 appear to have had the potential to cause major damage, and all were discovered or defused with no injuries; the last such attempt was in March 2011.

Nonetheless, it is assumed that some members of RS and CFN are still at large, and no suspected members of Sect of Revolutionaries have yet been apprehended. Despite the downturn in serious terrorist incidents in 2011, the risk of "being in the wrong place at the wrong time" in the event of a terrorist action remains a concern for residents and visitors.

Strikes and demonstrations are a regular occurrence. Greece is a stable democracy and these activities for the most part are orderly and lawful, although early 2012 protests signaled an uptick in the level of violence with extensive fire-bombings and vandalism in Central Athens. A wave of incidents that started in December 2008 when a teenager was shot and killed in an encounter with police was marked by violent confrontations with the police and destructive vandalism and rioting,, including areas frequented by tourists, injuring numerous police officers. The subsequent anniversaries of the event have been marked by demonstrations. In May 2010, three bank employees were killed when anarchists participating in a general strike-related demonstration fire-bombed their bank. Demonstrations also occur annually on November 17, the anniversary of the 1973 student uprising against the military regime in power at the time.

As a result of recent austerity measures imposed by the government, labor unions, certain professions, and other groups affected by the current financial crisis hold frequent demonstrations, work-stoppages, and marches throughout the center of Athens. Strikes in the transportation sector often affect traffic and public transportation, to include taxis, ports, and airports; most are of short duration, but you should always reconfirm domestic and international flights before heading to the airport. If you plan to rent a car, ask your rental agent about possible interruptions to fuel supplies. Riot control procedures often include the use of tear gas. Visitors should stay informed about demonstrations from local news sources and hotel security. Information regarding demonstrations that have been brought to the attention of the U.S. Embassy can be found on the Embassy website and on our Consular Section Facebook page. U.S. citizens are urged to carry a copy of their passport or some form of photo identification with them at all times when traveling in Greece. You should be aware of and avoid places where demonstrators frequently congregate such as the Polytechnic University area; Exarchia, Omonia, and Syntagma Squares in Athens; and Aristotle Square in Thessaloniki. University campuses are exploited as refuges by anarchists and criminals. The Omonia and Exarchia areas of Athens are at particular risk for crime and politically-motivated violence. U.S. Embassy personnel and their families are strongly urged to avoid these areas between 9 p.m. and dawn. There have been recent reports of violent attacks by extremists in Athens and other major urban areas against persons who are perceived to be foreign migrants.

Stay up to date by:

- Bookmarking our Bureau of Consular Affairs website, which contains the current Travel Warnings and Travel Alerts as well as the Worldwide Caution;
- Following us on Twitter and the Bureau of Consular Affairs page on Facebook as well;;
- Downloading our free Smart Traveler iPhone App to have travel information at your fingertips;;
- Calling 1-888-407-4747 toll-free within the U.S. and Canada, or a regular toll line, 1-202-501-4444, from other countries; and
- Taking some time before travel to consider your personal security.

Crime: You should take the usual safety precautions you would in any urban or tourist area during a visit to Greece. Crimes against tourists (such as pick-pocketing and purse-snatching) occur at popular tourist sites and on public transportation—especially the Metro—and in some shopping areas in and around Thessaloniki. If you travel by Metro, keep track of your purse/backpack/wallet at all times. Thieves will often try to create a diversion to draw your attention away from your immediate surroundings. These diversions can include "accidentally" sneezing or spilling something on you and loudly accusing you of having bumped into them. Thieves ride the trains in from the Athens Airport, so be especially careful when you first arrive. You may be tired and a bit disoriented and you may have just visited the ATM or exchanged money. Always keep a close eye on your suitcase. Try to avoid standing near the doors, as thieves will often wait to strike just as the train/bus doors open and then dash onto the platform and disappear into the crowd. Omonia, Vathi, and Kolokotroni Squares in Athens, while very close to the tourist sites, are areas with high crime rates; Glyfada Square has a significant organized crime network associated with clubs, which should be avoided if you get a "hard-sell" pitch for business. Never agree to go to a bar or club with someone you have just met on the street. Sexual assaults of U.S. citizens, including date or acquaintance rape, are not uncommon. Drink alcohol in moderation and stay in control. Never leave your drink unattended in a bar or club. Some bars and clubs serve counterfeit or homemade spirits of unknown potency. Don't buy counterfeit and pirated goods, even those widely available, along the sidewalks in Central Athens or Thessaloniki. Not only are these goods illegal to bring back into the United States, the purchase of bootlegs and "knock-offs" in Greece violates Greek law.

Victims of Crime: If you or someone you know becomes the victim of a crime abroad, you should contact the local police and the nearest U.S. embassy or consulate. We can:

- Replace a stolen passport;;
- Help you find appropriate medical care if you are a victim of a violent crime such as assault or rape;
- Put you in contact with the appropriate police authorities and, if you want us to, we can contact family members or friends; and
- Although the local authorities are responsible for investigating and prosecuting the crime, consular officers can help you understand the local criminal justice process and can direct you to local attorneys.

The local equivalents to the "911" emergency line in Greece are 112 for life-threatening emergencies (this is a Europe-wide emergency number and has English-speaking operators), 100 for the Police, 166 for an Ambulance, and 199 for the Fire Brigade.

Criminal Penalties: While you are traveling in Greece, you are subject to its laws, even if you are a U.S. citizen. Foreign laws and legal systems can be vastly different than our own. Penalties for breaking the law can be more severe than in the United States for similar offenses. Persons violating Greek laws, even unknowingly, may be expelled, arrested, or imprisoned.

Penalties for possessing, using, or trafficking in illegal drugs in Greece are severe, and convicted offenders can expect long jail sentences and heavy fines. Engaging in sexual conduct with children or using or disseminating child pornography in a foreign country is a crime prosecutable in the United States. Mace or pepper spray canisters, though legal in the U.S., are illegal in Greece. Such items will be confiscated and may result in detention and arrest.

If you are arrested in Greece, the authorities are required to notify the nearest U.S. embassy or consulate of your arrest. If you are concerned the Department of State may not be aware of your situation, you should request the police or prison officials to notify the nearest U.S. embassy or consulate on your behalf.

Special Circumstances: Greek customs authorities have strict regulations concerning the export from Greece of antiquities, including rocks from archaeological sites. Penalties range from large fines to prison terms. You should ensure that you get a receipt for any item that you buy. In addition to being subject to all Greek laws affecting U.S. citizens, dual nationals may also be subject to other laws that impose special obligations on Greek citizens. Greek males between the ages of 20 and 45 are required by Greek law to perform military service. This applies to any individual whom the Greek authorities consider to be Greek citizen, regardless of whether or not the individual considers himself Greek, has a foreign citizenship and passport, or was born or lives outside of Greece.

If remaining in Greece for more than the 90-day period permitted for tourism or business, men of Greek descent may be prevented from leaving Greece until they complete their military obligations. Generally, obligatory, non-voluntary military service in Greece will not affect U.S. citizenship. Specific questions on this subject should be addressed to the citizenship section of the U.S. Embassy in Athens.

If you plan to use public transportation, be sure to buy the appropriate ticket and to validate it correctly, mindful that service to the airport is more expensive than other bus and Metro services, and that ticket inspectors circulate among passengers on trains and buses, and in stations, assuring compliance with ticketing regulations. Currently, the fine for passengers without tickets or with the wrong ticket is 60 times the basic fare, or 84 Euros. The Government of Greece does not permit the photographing of military installations; violators are subject to arrest.

Disaster Preparedness: Greece often experiences forest fires during the dry summer months. Travelers should be particularly mindful of the risk of fires, taking care not to spark one inadvertently through carelessness. The Government of Greece has also produced an earthquake-safety pamphlet for tourists and visitors. Greece experiences frequent seismic activity; tremors are common and serious earthquakes have occurred. Detailed information on Greece's earthquake fault lines is available from the U.S. Geological Survey (USGS.)

Disaster preparedness information and specific suggestions to help mitigate the impact of wildfires and earthquakes is available from the U.S. Federal Emergency Management Agency (FEMA.) In any natural disaster, follow the instructions of local authorities. The General Secretariat for Civil Protection, which responds to emergencies, may be reached at 210-3359932/33.

Accessibility: While in Greece, individuals with disabilities will find accessibility and accommodation very different from what you find in the United States. While Greek law prohibits discrimination against persons with physical and intellectual disabilities in employment, education, access to health care, or the provision of other government services, in practice, enforcement of these provisions is uneven.

The law mandates access to buildings for persons with disabilities and special ramps for the sidewalks and means of public transportation; however, enforcement is inconsistent and is a work in progress. While handicapped parking spaces and sidewalk ramps exist or are being constructed throughout the country, they are often occupied or blocked by parked vehicles, thus hindering accessibility for disabled persons.

The general condition of the sidewalks can be problematic. They are very narrow in places and there are often broken paving stones, large holes, and poorly-positioned signs. A small but growing percentage of public buildings are fully accessible to persons with physical disabilities, with the majority in Athens. Many buildings with special ramps might not have accessible elevators or lavatories. You should ask your hotel before booking. The Athens Metro and Athens International Airport are fully accessible and have ramps and elevators installed. The Deputy Ombudsman for Social Welfare handles complaints related to persons with disabilities, especially those related to employment, social security, and transportation.

Many sidewalks in Athens have detectable warning and way finding systems of bumps and lines for visually impaired travelers and a few traffic lights are equipped with audible crosswalk signals.

Scams: In the last few months, we have seen a number of instances of "Grandparent Scams." This scam targets elderly citizens in the United States and convinces them to wire money to assist a relative (often a grandchild) in distress overseas. Review our Financial Scams page for the full picture on this and many other scams.

Medical Facilities and Health Information: Medical facilities are adequate, and some, particularly the private clinics and hospitals in Athens and Thessaloniki, are quite good. Some private hospitals have affiliations with U.S. facilities, and generally their staff doctors have been trained in the United States or Europe.

Public medical clinics, especially on the islands, may lack resources; care can be inadequate by U.S. standards, and often, little English is spoken. Many patients— Greeks and visitors alike— are transferred from the provinces and islands to Athens hospitals for more sophisticated care. Others may choose to transfer from a public to a private hospital within Athens or Thessaloniki. U.S. citizens choosing to do so would arrange for an ambulance belonging to the private hospital to transport them from the public hospital to the private one. The cost of the ambulance for this transfer, as well as all expenses in a private hospital, must be borne by the patient. Private hospitals will usually demand proof of adequate insurance or cash before admitting a patient.

Nursing care, particularly in public hospitals, may be less than adequate. For special or through-the-night nursing care, it is suggested that a private nurse be hired or a family member or friend be available to assist. One parent or a private nurse should always plan to stay with a hospitalized child on a 24-hour basis, as even the best hospitals generally maintain only a minimal nursing staff from midnight to dawn on non-emergency floors or wards. You can find good information on vaccinations and other health precautions on the U.S. Centers for Disease Control and Prevention (CDC) website. For information about outbreaks of infectious diseases abroad, consult the infectious diseases section of the World Health Organization (WHO) website, which also contains additional health information for travelers, including detailed, country-specific health information.

Medical Insurance: It's very important to find out BEFORE you leave whether or not your medical insurance will cover you overseas. You need to ask your insurance company two questions:

- Does my policy cover me when I am outside of the United States?
- Will it cover emergencies like a trip to a foreign hospital or a medical evacuation?

In many places, doctors and hospitals still expect payment in cash at the time of service. If your policy doesn't go with you when you travel, it is a really good idea to take out travelers' insurance specifically for your trip. If you plan to participate in even slightly "extreme" sports that are popular in Greece, such as SCUBA, white-water rafting, or water-skiing, you might consider adventure travel insurance options.

Traffic Safety and Road Conditions: While in Greece, you will encounter road conditions that differ significantly from those in the United States. Drivers and pedestrians alike should exercise extreme caution when operating motor vehicles or when walking along roadways or crossing streets, mindful that Greece's traffic fatality rates are the fourth-highest in the 27 nations that make up the European Union. Visitors to Greece must be prepared to drive defensively. Heavy traffic, poor roads, and high speeds pose hazards, especially at night or in inclement weather. Be especially careful if you are riding a motorbike. The law in

Greece requires motorcyclists to wear a helmet. You may see many "wearing" theirs on the arm, but do not be tempted to follow their example. When driving, be sure to double-check rear and side mirrors, as motorbikes will often ride between lanes and pass on both the left and right. On many two-lane highways, slower traffic will drive on the shoulder and cars will pass straddling the center, double yellow line. Talking on a cell phone while driving is illegal in Greece and the police check cell phone call records when investigating accidents. Driving while under the influence of alcoholic substance is illegal,.05 is the legal limit in Greece, as compared to.08 in the US. Exceeding that limit may result in arrest, heavy fines and/or license confiscation. There are a number of nationwide auto-service clubs and plans, similar to those in the United States, which provide towing and roadside service, which a tourist can call and pay for per service; the largest, quite similar to AAA, is ELPA, whose nationwide phone number is 10400.

Tourists and temporary residents who will stay in Greece for fewer than 185 days, and plan to drive, must carry a valid U.S. license as well as an international driver's permit (IDP). Failure to have both documents may result in police detention or other problems. The U.S. Department of State has designated two organizations to issue IDPs to those who hold valid U.S. driver's licenses: AAA and the American Automobile Touring Alliance. Issuance of an IDP is quick and inexpensive, but must generally be done before a traveler leaves the United States.

Vehicles may not properly be rented without the IDP, although sometimes they are. A driver without one, however, will be cited for failure to have one in the event of an accident, and may be open to civil suit as well. Fines are high. Small motorbike rental firms frequently do not insure their vehicles; customers are responsible for damages and should review their coverage before renting. Individuals who expect to spend more than 185 days in Greece should either obtain a Greek license or convert their valid U.S. license for use in Greece through their local Nomarchy's Office of Transportation and Communications.

Aviation Safety Oversight: The U.S. Federal Aviation Administration (FAA) has assessed the government of Greece's Civil Aviation Authority as being in compliance with International Civil Aviation Organization (ICAO) aviation safety standards for oversight of Greece's air carrier operations. Further information may be found on the FAA's safety assessment page.

Children's Issues: Please see the U.S. Dept. of State Office of Children's Issues web pages on intercountry adoption and international parental child abduction.

Intercountry Adoption

September 2009

The information in this section has been edited from the latest report available as of February 2013 from the State Department Bureau of Consular Affairs, Office of Overseas Citizens Services. For more information, please read the *Intercountry Adoption* section of this book and review current reports online at http://adoption.state.gov.

Greece is not a major Country of Origin for children adopted through intercountry adoption. There are many more prospective adoptive parents in Greece than there are children eligible for adoption. Over the recent 5 years, only 3 Greek children have received orphan immigrant visas to the U.S. following their adoptions by U.S. citizen parents. Although there are no private adoption agencies in Greece, children may be adopted with the involvement of an attorney or gynecologist who will act as a facilitator. Whether a child is adopted through one of the government-run institutions and orphanages, or privately, a lawyer is required.

Who Can Adopt? Adoption between the United States and Greece is governed by the Hague Adoption Convention. Therefore to adopt from Greece, you must first be found eligible to adopt by the U.S. Government. The U.S. Government agency responsible for making this determination is the Department of Homeland Security, U.S. Citizenship and Immigration Services (USCIS). In addition to these U.S. requirements for adoptive parents, Greece also has the following requirements for adoptive parents.

Residency Requirements: You must be a resident of Greece to adopt a child from any of the governmental institutions and orphanages in Greece which care for orphaned or abandoned infants. Exceptions for prospective adoptive parents who do not reside in Greece will be made only for children with health problems who live in Greek institutions. In the case of a private adoption, no restriction applies as to the place of residence of the prospective parents.

Age Requirements: You must be between the ages of 30 and 60 in order to adopt a child. At least one of the adoptive parents must be at least 18 years older but not more than 50 years older than the adopted child. Only minors can be adopted, except in the case of step-parent adoption. Although the legal process of adoption cannot be started before the child reaches 3 months of age, in almost all cases of private adoption biological parents give the child to prospective adoptive parents immediately after birth.

Marriage Requirements: Prospective adoptive parents may be married or single.

Income Requirements: You must provide evidence of financial status.

Other Requirements: There is no religious requirement in order to adopt a child in Greece.

Who Can Be Adopted? Because Greece is party to the Hague Adoption Convention, children from Greece must meet the requirements of the Convention in order to be eligible for adoption. For example, the Convention requires that Greece attempt to place a child with a family in-country before determining that a child is eligible for intercountry adoption. In addition to Greece's requirements, a child must meet the definition of a Convention adoptee for you to bring him or her back to the United States.

Age Requirements: Only minors can be adopted, except in the case of step-parent adoption.

Sibling Requirements: The court takes into consideration the perspectives of the children of the adopting family.

Requirements for Special Needs or Medical Conditions: Medical Reports are needed in addition to all other documents.

Waiting Period: Due to a limited number of children available for adoption and a large number of prospective adoptive parents, the waiting period to finalize an adoption is approximately five years for a child living in an institution. For children with health problems, the waiting period usually takes up to three years. An attorney is necessary in order to present the case in court and finalize the adoption. Court decisions concerning adoption cases usually take from 1-6 months before a final decision is made.

Greece's Adoption Authority
Ministry of Health and Social Solidarity
Aristotelous 17
104 33 Athens, Greece
Tel. 210-5232821-9
Fax: 210-5234768
E-mail: www.mohaw.gr

The Process: Because Greece is party to the Hague Adoption Convention, adopting from Greece must follow a specific process designed to meet the Convention's requirements. For detailed and updated information on these requirements, please review the *Intercountry Adoption* section of this publication and visit the USCIS Intercountry Adoption website at http://adoption.state.gov. The process for finalizing the adoption (or gaining legal custody) in Greece generally includes the following.

Role of the Adoption Authority: According to Greek Law, 2447/1996, all petitions submitted to local orphanages by the prospective adoptive parents are followed by an extensive and thorough field investigation performed by the social services of the institution, which is supervised by the Greek Ministry of Health and Social Solidarity. When the investigation is over, the case file is forwarded to the local institution's committee. The local institution's committee approves or disapproves the petition of the prospective parents. This committee then matches prospective adoptive parents with children, taking into account the specific needs of specific children and the corresponding ability of prospective parents to meet those needs. If the child is 12 years of age and over and of sound psychological condition, the court takes the child's wishes into consideration.

In addition, the court takes into consideration the perspectives of the children of the adopting family. Because of the relatively small number of adoptions in Greece, this matching process can be detailed and precise. Adoptive parents' applications are processed by the local institutions strictly in chronological order; with the exception that priority is given to persons willing to adopt a child with special physical or psychological needs. If the petition is approved, the case file is forwarded to the appropriate court for endorsement. In order for prospective parents who live abroad to initiate an adoption, they must communicate with the respective office of the International Social Services in their country of residence, www.iss-ssi.org (for the Greek branch, issgr@otenet.gr). For private adoptions within Greece, the social service arm of the respective Prefecture (Nomarchy) of the area where the parents reside will conduct the field investigation. The law requires that a home study be conducted by local social services, prior to the court hearing, so that the family and the social status of the adoptive parents can be determined. There is a 15-20 day fostering period for children living in institutions.

Role of the Court: Adoptions done privately are also legal in Greece. In case of a private adoption, no restriction applies as to the place of residence of the prospective parents. There are no private adoption agencies in Greece; however, children may be adopted with the involvement of an attorney or gynecologist who will act as a facilitator. A court decision must be issued following the field investigation by the relevant social service. The majority of private adoption mediators ensure that biological parents do not know the details of the adoptive parents, to exclude the possibility of blackmail attempt or other unlawful action. The documents that comprise the legal file submitted to the court in order to issue a final decision for the adoption are:

- Field investigation report by the Institution's social service department;
- Marriage certificate;
- Penal record;
- Family status certificate;
- Written consent of biological parent(s);
- Proof of good financial status of prospective adoptive parents;
- Medical examination of the adoptive parents (excluding those with chronic diseases).

In the abandonment context, a court process replaces the consent of biological parents as necessary and facilitates procedures between the adoptive parents and the interested party. Specifically, the consent of parents for adoption of their child is replaced with a specially reasoned decision of the court if:

- Parents are unknown or the child is abandoned;
- Both parents have been denied parental responsibility or are in a situation where they have been

forbidden to exercise parental control regarding their ability to consent to adoption of the child;

- Parents have an unknown residence;
- The child is protected by a recognized social organization, if he/she has been removed from the parent's custody and the parents refuse to give consent; or
- The child is delivered with the consent of parents to a (foster) family for care and upbringing, with the intent to adopt, and the child has been integrated into that family for at least a year, and the parents later refuse to give consent.

Role of Adoption Agencies: There are no private adoption agencies in Greece. Children may be adopted with the involvement of an attorney or gynecologist who will act as a facilitator. Whether an individual adopts a child from one of the government-run institutions and orphanages, or privately, a lawyer is required.

Adoption Application: An application signed by the adoptive parents is submitted to the institution.

Time Frame: Due to the limited number of children available for adoption, and the large number of prospective adoptive parents, the waiting period to finalize an adoption is approximately five years for a child living in an institution. An attorney is required in order to present the case to court and finalize the adoption.

Court decisions concerning adoption cases usually take from 1-6 months before a final decision is issued. For children with health problems it usually takes up to three years. The timeframe for private adoptions varies.

Adoption Fees: In the adoption services contract that you sign at the beginning of the adoption process, your accredited U.S. agency will itemize the fees and estimated expenses related to your adoption process.

There are also some fees specifically associated with adopting from Greece. The U.S. Embassy in Athens is aware that prospective adoptive parents will have to obtain a "revenue stamp" (Greek Government fee) before a child is released to him or her by a local institution. Court and attorney fees generally may be approximately 1,000 Euros for adoption of children living in local institutions. Fees may change. Fees and expenses may exist for private adoptions and they can be substantial.

Documents Required: In the case of an intercountry adoption, the International Social Service in Athens requires the following documents from prospective adoptive parents in order to proceed with a field investigation:

- An application to show their interest to adopt a child, notarized by the Greek police if they happen to be here in Greece, or sent through their International Social Services office from the United States;
- Certified copies of birth certificates, and baptismal certificates if applicable, of the adoptive parents;
- Certified copy of their marriage certificate;
- Medical certificates concerning the general health condition, and separate certificates concerning the mental health of the adoptive parents;
- Evidence of the financial status of the adoptive parents; and
- Penal records of both adoptive parents. A "penal record" is a document that Greek citizens can obtain from the appropriate area judicial authority regard to their "conviction free" background.

Bringing Your Child Home: Once your adoption is complete (or you have obtained legal custody of the child), there are a few more steps to take before you can head home. Specifically, you need to apply for several documents for your child before he or she can travel to the United States, such as a birth certificate, a passport or travel document for your child from the country in which he or she was born, and a U.S. Immigration Visa. For detailed and updated information on how to obtain these documents, visit the USCIS Intercountry Adoption website at http://adoption.state.gov.

Child Citizenship Act: For adoptions finalized abroad, the Child Citizenship Act of 2000 allows your new child to acquire American citizenship automatically when he or she enters the United States as lawful permanent residents. For adoptions finalized in the United States, the Child Citizenship Act of 2000 allows your new child to acquire American citizenship automatically when the court in the United States issues the final adoption decree.

After Adoption: There are no post-adoption reporting requirements. However, within Greece, there is mutual cooperation between adopted parents and the social workers from Governmental institutions. Psychologists assist adopted parents with any problems that may arise. The welfare Department of the Ministry of Health follows up on the wellbeing of adopted children in their new homes for as long as needed.

U.S. Embassy in Greece
Vasilissis Sophias 91
101 60 Athens, Greece
210-7202404

Greece's Adoption Authority
Ministry of Health and Social Solidarity
Aristotelous 17
104 33 Athens, Greece
Tel: 210-5232820-9
Fax: 210-5234768

Embassy of Greece
2217 Massachusetts Ave., N.W.
Washington, D.C. 20008
Tel: 202-939-1300
Fax: 202-234-2803
http://www/greekembassy.org

Office of Children's Issues
U.S. Department of State

2201 C Street, NW
SA-29
Washington, DC 20520
Tel: 1-888-407-4747
E-mail: AskCI@state.gov
http://adoption.state.gov

For questions about immigration procedures, call the National Customer Service Center (NCSC) 1-800-375-5283 (TTY 1-800-767-1833).

International Parental Child Abduction

November 2012

The information in this section has been edited from a report from the State Department Bureau of Consular Affairs, Office of Overseas Citizens Services. For more information, please read the *International Parental Child Abduction* section of this book and check for updated reports online at www.travel.state.gov/abduction.

Disclaimer: The information in this flyer is provided for general information only, is not intended to be legal advice, and may change without notice. Questions involving interpretation of law should be addressed to an attorney licensed to practice in the relevant jurisdiction.

General Information: Greece and the United States have been treaty partners under the 1980 Hague Convention on the Civil Aspects of International Child Abduction (Hague Abduction Convention) since June 1, 1993.

Hague Abduction Convention: The U.S. Department of State serves as the U.S. Central Authority (USCA) for the Hague Abduction Convention. Parents are strongly encouraged to contact the Department of State for assistance prior to initiating the Hague process directly with the foreign Central Authority.

United States Department of State
Bureau of Consular Affairs
Office of Children's Issues
2201 C Street, N.W.
Washington, DC 20520
Telephone: 1-888-407-4747
Outside the United States or Canada: 1-202-501-4444
Fax: 202-736-9132

The Greek Central Authority (GCA) for the Hague Abduction Convention is the Ministry of Justice. The Ministry of Justice has an administrative role in processing Hague Abduction Convention applications. The Ministry of Justice forwards completed Hague applications to the Legal Council of the State, which in turn will assign the case to a legal representative. Parents or legal guardians and other parties (e.g., the child) have the right to their own legal counsel.

The Greek Central Authority
Ministry of Justice, Transparency and Human Rights
96 Mesogeion Avenue
11527 Athens
Greece
Telephone: 011 [30] (210) 776-7312
Fax: 011 [30] (210) 776-7499

To initiate a Hague case for return of, or access to, a child in Greece, the USCA encourages a parent or legal guardian to review the eligibility criteria and instructions for completing the Hague application. For more information on the Hague Convention and the application process, please read the *International Parental Child Abduction* section of this book and review current reports online at www.travel.state.gov/abduction.

Return: A parent or legal guardian may file an application under the Hague Abduction Convention for return to the United States of a child abducted to, or wrongfully retained in, Greece. The U.S. Department of State can assist parents living in the United States to understand whether the Convention is an available civil remedy and can provide information on the process for submitting a Hague application.

Visitation/Access: A person may file an application under the Hague Abduction Convention for access to a child living in Greece. The criteria for acceptance of a Hague access application vary from country to country. The U.S. Department of State can assist parents living in the United States to understand country-specific criteria and provide information on the process for submitting a Hague application

Retaining an Attorney: In a Hague Abduction Convention case, it is not mandatory for a petitioner to retain a private attorney because the GCA will assign a legal representative to present the case to the court. However, the legal representative does not represent the left-behind parent or legal guardian who submitted the Hague Abduction Convention application; instead, the legal representative represents Greece and submits the request for return on behalf of the Greek Minister of Justice. Applicant parents or legal guardians have the option to hire a private attorney at their own expense. The U.S. Embassy in Athens, Greece, posts a list of attorneys including those who specialize in family law at: http://photos.state.gov/libraries/greece/38517/uscitizens/attorneys_jan11.pdf. This list is provided as a courtesy service only and does not constitute an endorsement of any individual attorney.

Mediation: Mediation may be available for both abduction and access cases. Although the GCA does not provide mediation services directly, there are registered attorneys who act as mediators and offer mediation services in every Greek Bar Association.

U.S. Embassy Athens
91 Vasilisis Avenue
10160 Athens, Greece
Telephone: 30-210-721-2951
Email:
AthensAmericanCitizenServices@state.gov
Website:
http://athens.usembassy.gov/

Embassy of Greece
2217 Massachusetts Avenue
Washington, D.C. 20008
Telephone: (202) 939-1300
Fax: (202) 939-1324
Email: gremb.was@mfa.gr

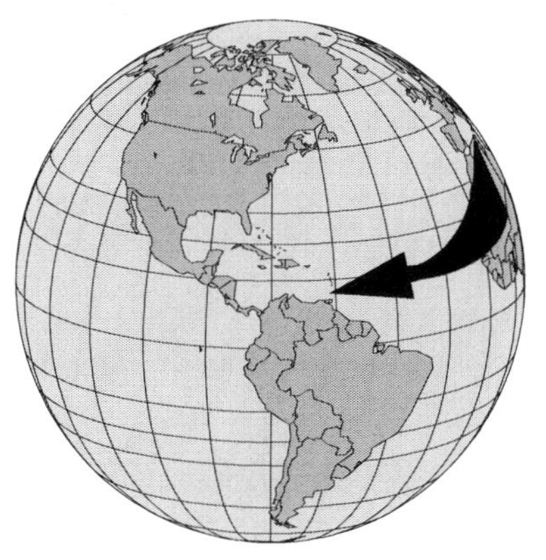

GRENADA

Compiled from publications that were available as of February 2013 from the U.S. Department of State, the U.S. Department of Commerce, and the Central Intelligence Agency (CIA). See the introduction to this set for explanatory notes.

Official Name:
Grenada

PROFILE

Geography

Area: total: 344 sq km; country comparison to the world: 207; land: 344 sq km; water: 0 sq km
Major cities: Saint George's (capital) 40,000 (2009)
Climate: tropical; tempered by northeast trade winds
Terrain: volcanic in origin with central mountains

People

Nationality: noun: Grenadian(s); adjective: Grenadian
Population: 109,011 (July 2012 est.)
Population growth rate: 0.538% (2012 est.)
Ethnic groups: black 82%, mixed black and European 13%, European and East Indian 5%, and trace of Arawak/Carib Amerindian
Religions: Roman Catholic 53%, Anglican 13.8%, other Protestant 33.2%
Languages: English (official), French patois
Literacy: definition: age 15 and over can read and write; total population: 96%; male: NA; female: NA (2003 est.)
Health: life expectancy at birth: total population: 73.3 years; male: 70.76 years; female: 76.09 years (2012 est.); Infant mortality rate: total: 11.12 deaths/1,000 live births; male: 10.3 deaths/1,000 live births; female: 12.02 deaths/1,000 live births (2012 est.)
Unemployment rate: 25% (2008)
Work force: 47,580 (2008)

Government

Type: parliamentary democracy and a Commonwealth realm
Independence: 7 February 1974
Constitution: 19 December 1973
Political subdivisions: 6 parishes and 1 dependency; Carriacou and Petite Martinique, Saint Andrew, Saint David, Saint George, Saint John, Saint Mark, Saint Patrick
Suffrage: 18 years of age; universal

Economy

GDP (purchasing power parity): $1.471 billion (2012 est.); $1.468 billion (2011 est.); $1.452 billion (2010 est.); $1.471 billion (2009 est.)
GDP real growth rate: 0.5% (2012 est.); 1.1% (2011 est.); -1.3% (2010 est.); -5.7% (2009 est.)
GDP per capita (PPP): $14,100 (2012 est.); $14,100 (2011 est.); $14,000 (2010 est.); $14,100 (2009 est.)
Natural resources: timber, tropical fruit, deepwater harbors
Agriculture products: bananas, cocoa, nutmeg, mace, citrus, avocados, root crops, sugarcane, corn, vegetables
Industries: food and beverages, textiles, light assembly operations, tourism, construction
Exports: $38.69 million (2009 est.); $30.26 million (2010 est.)
Exports—commodities: nutmeg, bananas, cocoa, fruit and vegetables, clothing, mace
Exports—partners: St. Lucia 19.9%, Antigua and Barbuda 13.5%, St. Kitts and Nevis 12.2%, Dominica 12.1%, US 10.2% (2011)
Imports: $284.4 million (2010 est.); $252.8 million
Imports—commodities: food, manufactured goods, machinery, chemicals, fuel
Imports—partners: Trinidad and Tobago 43.4%, US 19.1% (2011)
Debt—external: $531 million (2009); $347 million (2004)
Exchange rates: East Caribbean dollars (XCD) per US dollar; 2.7 (2012 est.); 2.7 (2011 est.); 2.7 (2010 est.); 2.7 (2009)

PEOPLE

Nearly 90% of Grenada's population is of African descent. An additional 8% are of mixed East Indian, African, and/or Caucasian ancestry, reflecting Grenada's history of African slaves, East Indian indentured servants, and European settlers. An additional 2% of the population considers itself East Indian, which includes some descendents of the indentured servants brought to Grenada from 1857 to the 1890s, as well as immigrants arriving from Trinidad and Tobago, Guyana, and Indians since the 1970s. A small community (less than 1% of the population) of the descendants of early European settlers resides in Grenada. About 60% of Grenada's population is under the age of 25.

Language

English is the official language; few people still speak French patois, though there has been a recent resurgence of interest in re-learning the language.

Religion

According to the 2001 census, 44 percent of the population is Roman Catholic, 12 percent Anglican, 11 percent Pentecostal, and 11 percent Seventh-day Adventist. Religious groups whose adherents number at least 2 percent of the population include Methodist, Presbyterian, Church of God, Baptist, and evangelical.

Smaller groups include Jehovah's Witnesses, Brethren, the Baha'is, Hindus, Moravians, Muslims, Rastafarians, the Salvation Army, The Church of Jesus Christ of Latter-day Saints (Mormons), and Mennonites. Approximately 4 percent of the population view themselves as nonbelievers. There are two mosques. There is no organized Jewish community. Saint George's University hosts Christian, Jewish, and Muslim student organizations; the government does not count its 3,700 foreign students in the census data.

HISTORY

Before the arrival of Europeans, Carib Indians had driven the more peaceful Arawaks from the island. Columbus landed on Grenada in 1498 during his third voyage to the new world. He named the island "Concepcion." The origin of the name "Grenada" is obscure, but it is likely that Spanish sailors renamed the island for the city of Granada. By the beginning of the 18th century, the name "Grenada," or "la Grenade" in French, was in common use.

Partly because of the Caribs, Grenada remained un-colonized for more than 100 years after its discovery; early English efforts to settle the island were unsuccessful. In 1650, a French company founded by Cardinal Richelieu purchased Grenada from the English and established a small settlement. After several skirmishes with the Caribs, the French brought in reinforcements from Martinique and defeated the Caribs.

The island remained under French control until its capture by the British in 1762, during the Seven Years' War. The Treaty of Paris formally ceded Grenada to Great Britain in 1763. Although the French regained control in 1779, the Treaty of Versailles restored the island to Britain in 1783. Britain overcame a pro-French revolt in 1795, and Grenada remained British for the remainder of the colonial period.

During the 18th century, Grenada's economy underwent an important transition. Like much of the rest of the West Indies it was originally settled to cultivate sugar, which was grown on estates using slave labor. But natural disasters paved the way for the introduction of other crops. In 1782, Sir Joseph Banks, the botanical adviser to King George III, introduced nutmeg to Grenada. The island's soil was ideal for growing the spice, and because Grenada was a closer source of spices for Europe than the Dutch East Indies the island assumed a new importance to European traders. The collapse of the sugar estates and the introduction of nutmeg and cocoa encouraged the development of smaller landholdings, and the island developed a land-owning yeoman farmer class. Slavery was outlawed in 1834.

In 1833, Grenada became part of the British Windward Islands Administration. The governor of the Windward Islands administered the island for the rest of the colonial period. In 1958, the Windward Islands Administration was dissolved, and Grenada joined the Federation of the West Indies. After that federation collapsed in 1962, the British Government tried to form a small federation out of its remaining dependencies in the Eastern Caribbean.

Following the failure of this second effort, the British and the islands developed the concept of associated statehood. Under the Associated Statehood Act of 1967, Grenada was granted full autonomy over its internal affairs in March 1967. Full independence was granted on February 7, 1974.

After obtaining independence, Grenada adopted a modified Westminster parliamentary system based on the British model, with a governor general appointed by and representing the British monarch (head of state) and a prime minister who is both leader of the majority party and the head of government. Sir Eric Gairy was Grenada's first Prime Minister.

On March 13, 1979, the New Joint Endeavor for Welfare, Education, and Liberation Movement (New Jewel Movement—NJM), ousted Gairy in a coup and established a People's Revolutionary Government (PRG) headed by Maurice Bishop, who became Prime Minister. His Marxist-Leninist government established close ties with Cuba, the Soviet Union, and other communist bloc countries.

In October 1983, a power struggle within the government resulted in the arrest and execution of Bishop and several members of his cabinet and the killing of dozens of his supporters by elements of the People's Revolutionary Army (PRA).

A U.S.-Caribbean force landed on Grenada on October 25, 1983, in response to an appeal from the Governor General and to a request for assistance from Barbados and other Eastern Caribbean states. U.S. citizens were evacuated, and order was restored.

An advisory council named by the Governor General administered the country until general elections were held in December 1984. The New National Party (NNP) led by Herbert Blaize won 14 out of 15 seats in free and fair elections and formed a democratic government. Grenada's constitution had been suspended in 1979 by the PRG, but it was restored after the 1984 elections.

The NNP continued in power until 1989 but with a reduced majority. Five NNP parliamentary members, including two cabinet ministers, left the party in 1986–87 and formed the National Democratic Congress (NDC), which became the official opposition.

In August 1989, Prime Minister Blaize broke with the NNP to form another new party, The National Party (TNP), from the ranks of the NNP. This split in the NNP resulted in the formation of a minority government until constitutionally scheduled elections in March 1990. Prime Minister Blaize died in December 1989 and was succeeded as Prime Minister by Ben Jones until the elections.

The NDC emerged from the 1990 elections as the strongest party, winning seven of the 15 available seats. Nicholas Brathwaite added two TNP members and one member of the Grenada United Labor Party (GULP) to create a 10-seat majority coalition. The Governor General appointed him to be Prime Minister.

In parliamentary elections on June 20, 1995, the NNP won eight seats and formed a government headed by Keith Mitchell. The NNP continued to hold power for the next 13 years, with varying levels of representation in parliament, taking all 15 parliamentary seats in the January 1999 elections and 8 of 15 seats in the November 2003 elections. The National Democratic Congress (NDC) led by Tillman Thomas established itself as the official opposition.

Keith Mitchell lost his bid to win an unprecedented fourth term in the July 2008 election. While he won his own seat by a huge margin, only three other NNP candidates were voted in a very close election. Tillman Thomas led his NDC cohort to an 11 to 4 victory over their long-time rivals. Mitchell became the leader of the official opposition.

GOVERNMENT AND POLITICAL CONDITIONS

Grenada is a parliamentary democracy with a bicameral legislature. In generally free and fair elections in February 2013, the New National Party won 15 of 15 seats in Parliament, and Keith Mitchell was sworn in as prime minister.

Recent Elections

The most recent general elections were held in February 2013, when the New National Party won all 15 seats in the House of Representatives, defeating the National Democratic Congress, which had temporarily displaced the NNP in 2008. The elections were deemed free and fair.

Principal Government Officials

Last Updated: 1/31/2013

Governor Gen.: **Carlyle Arnold GLEAN**
Prime Min.: **Keith MITCHELL**
Dep. Prime Min.: **Elvin NIMROD**
Min. of Agriculture, Land, Forestry, Fisheries, & the Environment: **Roland BHOLA**
Min. of Carriacou & Petite Martinique Affairs: **Elvin NIMROD**
Min. of Communications & Works, Physical Development, Public Utilities, & Information Communications Technology: **Gregory BOWEN**
Min. of Economic Development, Trade, Planning, & Cooperatives: **Oliver JOSEPH**
Min. of Education & Human Resources Development: **Anthony BOATSWAIN**
Min. of Energy: **Keith MITCHELL**
Min. of Finance: **Keith MITCHELL**
Min. of Foreign Affairs & Intl. Business: **Nikolas STEELE**
Min. of Health & Social Security: **Clarice MODESTE-CURWEN**
Min. of Labor & Local Govt.: **Elvin NIMROD**
Min. of Legal Affairs: **Elvin NIMROD**
Min. of National Security, Disaster Preparedness, & Home Affairs: **Keith MITCHELL**
Min. of Public Affairs, Public Admin., Implementation, & Information: **Keith MITCHELL**
Min. of Social Development, Housing, & Community Development: **Delma THOMAS**
Min. of Tourism, Civil Aviation, & Culture: **Alexandra OTWAY-NOEL**
Min. of Youth, Sports, & Ecclesiastical Relations: **Emmalin PIERRE**
Min. in the Min. of Communications & Works, Physical Development, Public Utilities, & Information Communications Technology (ICT) With Responsibility for ICT: **Alvin DABREO**
Attorney Gen.: **Elvin NIMROD**
Ambassador to the US: **Gillian BRISTOL**
Permanent Representative to the UN, New York: **Dessima WILLIAMS**

ECONOMY

Grenada relies on tourism as its main source of foreign exchange especially since the construction of an international airport in 1985. Hurricanes Ivan (2004) and Emily (2005) severely damaged the agricultural sector - particularly nutmeg and cocoa cultivation - which had been a key driver of economic growth. Grenada has rebounded from the devastating effects of the hurricanes but is now saddled with the debt burden from the rebuilding process.

Public debt-to-GDP is nearly 110%, leaving the Thomas administration limited room to engage in public investments and social spending. Strong performances in construction and manufacturing, together with the development of tourism and an offshore financial industry, have also contributed to growth in national output; however, economic growth remained stagnant in 2010–12 after a sizeable contraction in 2009, because of the global economic slowdown's effects on tourism and remittances.

Labor Conditions

The statutory minimum age for employment of children is 16 years.

Background Notes

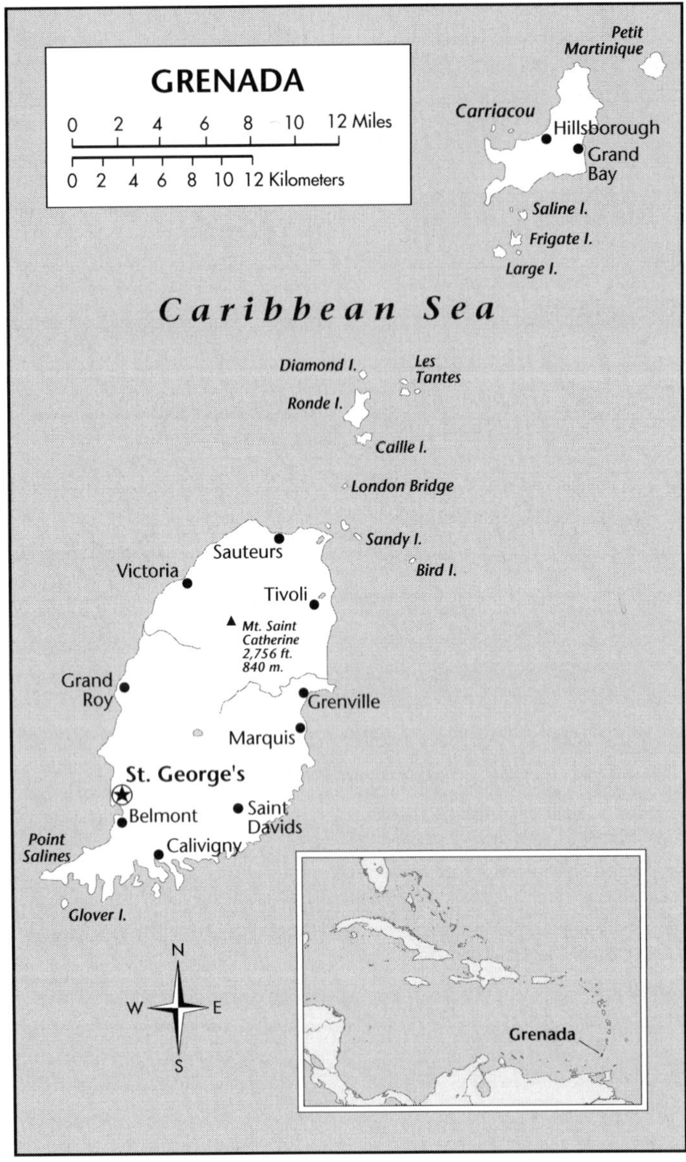

Employment for minors under 18 is permitted so long as certain conditions related to hours, insurance and working conditions set forth in the Labor Code are met. It was common practice for children to undertake summer jobs or for school-leavers to take on part-time employment following secondary school graduation at age 16.

Inspectors from the Labor Ministry enforced the minimum age provision in the formal sector through periodic checks. Enforcement in the informal sector was insufficient, particularly for family farms. The Labor Ministry inspected family farms for child workers upon receipt of child labor allegations. The labor code does not specifically prohibit the sale or trafficking of children for exploitive labor.

The minimum wage schedules set pay by occupation and, in the case of agricultural workers, by sex. The minimum wage for domestic workers, for example, was EC$400 ($148) monthly, while that for a security guard was EC $4.00 ($1.48) per hour.

The law provides for a 40-hour maximum workweek. The law does not stipulate rest periods, although no one can be asked to work for longer than five hours consecutively without a one-hour meal break. In addition, domestic employees may not, by law, be asked to work longer than a 10-hour period without at least two hours of breaks for meals and rest periods. The law requires a premium for work above the standard workweek and prohibits excessive or compulsory overtime. The law mandates paid annual vacation—two weeks in the first year and three weeks thereafter.

U.S.-GRENADIAN RELATIONS

The United States established diplomatic relations with Grenada in 1974 following its independence from the United Kingdom. After obtaining independence, Grenada adopted a modified Westminster parliamentary system based on the British model, which includes a governor general appointed by and representing the British monarch (head of state). In 1979, the opposition staged a coup and established the People's Revolutionary Government. In 1983, a power struggle within the ruling party resulted in the arrest and execution of the prime minister and several members of his cabinet and the killing of dozens of his supporters by elements of the People's Revolutionary Army. A U.S.-Caribbean force landed on Grenada in response to an appeal from Grenada's governor general and a request for assistance from other Eastern Caribbean states. U.S. citizens were evacuated, and order was restored.

Grenada has shown a commitment to protecting its democratic traditions and delivering educational and economic opportunities to its citizens, and the United States seeks to strengthen the ties of friendship between the two countries. The United States and Grenada cooperate through partnerships including the Partnership Framework for HIV and AIDS, the Energy and Climate Partnership of the Americas, and the Caribbean Youth Empowerment Program. The two also cooperate closely in fighting narcotics smuggling and other forms of transnational crime. They have signed a maritime law enforcement treaty, including an overflight/order-to-land amendment; a mutual legal assistance treaty; and an extradition treaty.

U.S. Assistance to Grenada

The U.S. Agency for International Development plays a role in Grenada's development through its office in Bridgetown, Barbados. Peace Corps volunteers in Grenada teach special education, remedial reading, and vocational training and assist with HIV/AIDS work. Grenada receives counter-narcotics assistance from the United States and is eligible to be considered for U.S. military exercise-related construction and humanitarian civic action projects. The United States provides training, equipment, and material to Grenadian security and defense forces, including through the Caribbean Basin Security Initiative. Some U.S. military training is provided as well.

Bilateral Economic Relations

Grenada is a beneficiary of the U.S. Caribbean Basin Initiative (CBI), which grants duty-free entry into the United States for many goods. The CBI aims to facilitate the economic development and export diversification of the Caribbean Basin economies. Grenada is a member of the Caribbean Community and Common Market (CARICOM). At the 2012 meeting of the U.S.-CARICOM Trade and Investment Council, the parties approved an action agenda outlining priorities for strengthening and deepening the trading relationship.

Grenada's Membership in International Organizations

Grenada and the United States belong to a number of the same international organizations, including the United Nations, Organization of American States, International Monetary Fund, World Bank, and World Trade Organization.

Bilateral Representation

Grenada maintains an embassy in the United States at 1701 New Hampshire Avenue, NW, Washington, DC 20009 (tel: 202-265-2561).

Principal U.S. Embassy Officials

Last Updated: 1/14/2013

ST. GEORGE'S (E) Lance Aux Epines, 1-473-444-1173/7, Fax 1-473–444-4820, Workweek: Mon. thru Fri., 8AM-4:30 PM, http://bridgetown.usembassy.gov/

AMB OMS:	Ellen Benjamin-Leon
CDC:	Dr. Rachel Albalak (Bridgetown)
DCM/CHG:	Charge Louis J. Crishock
FM:	Bruce Youmans (Bridgtown)
HRO:	Willette Gooding (Resident Frc)
MGT:	Jeremey Neitzke (Bridgetown)
MLO/ODC:	Cdr Michael Long (Bridgetown)
NAS/INL:	Kurt Van Der Walde (Bridgetown)
PAO/ADV:	Rachel Zaspel (Bridgetown)
POSHO:	Bruce Youmans
AMB:	Larry Palmer
PAO:	Rebecca Ross (Bridgetown)
GSO:	M.Holly Peirce (Bridgetown)
RSO:	Thomas Baker (Bridgetown)
AID:	Daniel Smolka (Bridgetown)
DEA:	Charles Graham (Bridgetown)
EEO:	Gregory Floyd (Bridgetown)
FMO:	W. Lee Thompson (Bridgetown)
IMO:	Michael Cassilly (Bridgetown)
IRS:	Andrew Thornton (Bridgetown)
ISO:	Michael Cassilly (Bridgetown)
ISSO:	Frederick Melton
LAB:	Gregory Floyd (Bridgetown)
LEGATT:	David Brooks (Bridgetown)
POL:	Brian Greaney (Bridgetown)

TRAVEL

Consular Information Sheet

October 16, 2009

Country Description: Grenada is a developing Caribbean island nation. The capital is St. George's. Tourism facilities vary, according to price and area.

Smart Traveler Enrollment Program (STEP)/Embassy Location: If you are going to work, live, or travel abroad, please take the time to tell the local U.S. Embassy about your trip. If you enroll, the Embassy can keep you up to date with important safety and security announcements. It will also help your friends and family get in touch with you in an emergency.

The U.S. Embassy is located on the main road to L'Anse aux Epines after the Christian Scientist Church, and is approximately 15 minutes from the Point Salines International Airport. Telephone: 1-(473) 444-1173/4/5; fax: 1-(473) 444-4820. Embassy Grenada's consulate's hours are 8:00 am to 12:30 pm by appointment, Monday to Friday except local and American holidays.

Entry/Exit Requirements: All Americans traveling by air outside of the United States are required to present a passport or other valid travel document to enter the United States. This requirement will be extended to sea travel (except closed-loop cruises), including ferry service, on June 1, 2009. Until then, U.S. citizens traveling by sea may present government-issued photo identification and a document showing their U.S. citizenship (for example, a birth certificate or certificate of naturalization). Starting June 1, 2009, all travelers must present a Western Hemisphere Travel Initiative (WHTI) compliant document such as a passport or a passport card for entry to the United States. While passport cards and enhanced driver's licenses are sufficient for entry into the

United States, they may not be accepted by the particular country you plan to visit; please be sure to check with your cruise line and countries of destination for any foreign entry requirements. For additional information concerning entry/exit requirements, travelers may contact the Embassy of Grenada, 1701 New Hampshire Avenue, NW, Washington, DC 20009, telephone: (202) 265-2561, fax: (202) 265-2468, or the Consulate of Grenada in New York. Sea travelers must have a valid U.S. passport (or other original proof of U.S. citizenship, such as a certified U.S. birth certificate with a government-issued photo ID).

There is no visa requirement for stays up to three months. However, now that the United States requires a passport to re-enter, Grenadian immigration authorities have been more closely scrutinizing the documentation of arriving American citizens and may deny entry for insufficient documentation of citizenship. There is an airport departure fee of US$20 for adults and US$10 for children between the ages of five and twelve.

The U.S. Department of State is unaware of any HIV/AIDS entry restrictions for visitors to or foreign residents of Grenada.

Threats to Safety and Security: Many parts of Grenada have no sidewalks and few streetlights, forcing pedestrians to walk in the road. Visitors should take care if walking along the road after dark and wear light, reflective clothing. For the latest security information, Americans traveling abroad should regularly monitor the Department's Internet web site, where the current Worldwide Caution Travel Alert, Travel Warnings and Travel Alerts can be found. Up-to-date information on safety and security can also be obtained by calling 1-888-407-4747 toll free in the U.S. and Canada, or for callers outside the U.S. and Canada, a regular toll-line at 1-202-501-4444. These numbers are available from 8:00 a.m. to 8:00 p.m. Eastern Time, Monday through Friday (except U.S. federal holidays).

Crime: Crime in Grenada is mostly opportunistic. Tourists have been the victims of robbery, especially in isolated areas, and thieves frequently steal credit cards, jewelry, cameras, U.S. passports and money. Muggings, purse snatchings and other robberies may occur in areas near hotels, beaches and restaurants, particularly after dark. Recently, the St. George's main market square and the Grand Anse area known as Wall Street have experienced decreases in crime since the vendors have been working as a team and now have employed security in the area.

Visitors should exercise appropriate caution when walking after dark or when using the local bus system or taxis hired on the road. It is advisable to hire taxis to and from restaurants and to ask whether the driver is a member of the Grenada Taxi Association (GTA). Members of the GTA are required to pass additional driving tests and receive training from the Grenada Tourism Board. They are generally reliable and knowledgeable about the country and its attractions.

In many countries around the world, counterfeit and pirated goods are widely available. Transactions involving such products may be illegal under local law. In addition, bringing them back to the United States may result in forfeitures and/ or fines.

Victims of Crime: If you are the victim of a crime abroad, you should contact the local police and the nearest U.S. embassy or consulate (see end of this sheet or see the Department of State's list of embassies and consulates). This includes the loss or theft of a U.S. passport. The embassy/consulate staff can, for example, help you find appropriate medical care, contact family members or friends and explain how funds may be transferred. Although the investigation and prosecution of the crime are solely the responsibility of local authorities, consular officers can help you to understand the local criminal justice process and to find an attorney if needed. The local equivalent to the "911" emergency line in Grenada is "911."

Criminal Penalties: While in a foreign country, a U.S. citizen is subject to that country's laws and regulations, which sometimes differ significantly from those in the United States and may not afford the protections available to the individual under U.S. law. Engaging in sexual conduct with children or using or disseminating child pornography in a foreign country is a crime, prosecutable in the United States. Penalties for possessing, using, or trafficking in illegal drugs in Grenada are severe, and convicted offenders can expect long jail sentences and heavy fines. A person can be prosecuted for using foul language in the presence of an officer of the law. The police began cracking down in 2008 on inappropriate dress (indecent exposure), including baggy pants with the belt below the waist and beach attire on the street.

Special Circumstances: Since 2007, the local air carrier, LIAT, has significantly reduced flights into and out of Grenada. Travelers coming into the region from the U.S. and elsewhere should verify in advance directly with LIAT that they have a valid reservation. The sharp increase in oil prices in 2008 resulted in steeply higher airline ticket prices, impacting especially inter-island travel dominated by LIAT. Ticket prices have not fallen as quickly as fuel prices have. From October a company 'Bedy Oceanlines', will ply daily routes to Barbados, Trinidad and Tobago, St. Lucia, St. Vincent and the Grenadines and Grenada making travel between the islands more affordable. Hotels may now legally include a surcharge for fuel costs on their bills, and at least one hotel is adding the surcharge.

Grenada experiences tropical storms and hurricanes during the hurricane season, from June through November. Sea surges occasionally flood low lying areas, including parts of downtown St. George's and Hillsborough on the island of Carriacou. Heavy winds periodically close local beaches to swimming. General information about natural disaster preparedness is available from the U.S. Federal Emergency Management Agency

(FEMA). Travel from Grenada to Carriacou is possible by sea and by air. Petite Martinique can only be reached by sea. The Osprey ferry service, with two boats, travels every day between the three islands and is reliable with a good safety record. The trip takes about 1 ½ hours in the large boat and 2 hours in the smaller one. SVG Airline flies a small propeller plane (4-6 passengers) to Carriacou and back daily. Small boat owners may offer to take tourists to the other islands. Before accepting, travelers should check to be sure that the boat carries life preservers and a radio. Though now required, many small boats do not carry this equipment.

Grenada has several qualified dive operations. Travelers should check with the Grenada Tourism Board at 473-444-4140 or their hotels for further information. There is no hyperbaric chamber in Grenada.

It is difficult to cash personal U.S. checks in Grenada. If accepted, they will take approximately six weeks to clear by a local bank. Major credit cards are widely accepted, and ATM facilities are available at most banks. Most hotels and restaurants take U.S. currency; however, change will be in local currency.

Medical Facilities and Health Information: Medical care is limited. U.S. citizens requiring medical treatment may contact the U.S Embassy in St. George's for a list of local doctors, dentists, pharmacies and hospitals. Serious medical problems requiring hospitalization and/or medical evacuation to the U.S. can cost thousands of dollars. Doctors and hospitals often expect immediate cash payment for health services.

Pharmacies are usually well stocked and prescription medicine is available. They periodically suffer shortages when deliveries from abroad are delayed though most pharmacies will check with others in the area to see if they can get what is needed. Travelers are advised to bring with them sufficient prescription medicine for the length of their stay. Grenada chlorinates its water, making it generally safe to drink. However, during especially heavy rains, quality control can slip, particularly in the city of St. George's. It is recommended that visitors to Grenada request bottled water, which is widely available and relatively inexpensive. Ambulance service is available but response times vary greatly. Malaria is not found in Grenada, but there are low levels of dengue fever. The government periodically fogs public areas to reduce the mosquito population.

Information on vaccinations and other health precautions, such as safe food and water precautions and insect bite protection, may be obtained from the Centers for Disease Control and Prevention's hotline for international travelers at 1-877-FYI-TRIP (1-877-394-8747) or via the CDC's Internet site at http://www.cdc.gov/travel. For information about outbreaks of infectious diseases abroad consult the World Health Organization's (WHO) website at http://www.who.int/en. Further health information for travelers is available at http://www.who. int/ith.

Medical Insurance: The Department of State strongly urges Americans to consult with their medical insurance company prior to traveling abroad to confirm whether their policy applies overseas and whether it will cover emergency expenses such as a medical evacuation.

Traffic Safety and Road Conditions: While in a foreign country,U.S. citizens may encounter road conditions that differ significantly from those in the United States. The information below concerning Grenada is provided for general reference only, and may not be totally accurate in a particular location or circumstance.

Traffic moves on the left in Grenada; the majority of vehicles are right-hand drive. Grenada's roads, paved and unpaved, are mostly narrow and winding, with many blind corners, narrow or no shoulders, and steep drops into the many ravines found on Grenada's three islands. There are few sidewalks, and cars vie with pedestrians for road space. Road lighting varies on all three islands, which compounds the dangers at night. Road surfaces often deteriorate, especially during the rainy season (June–November) before maintenance work begins. Driving conditions in Grenada, including road conditions, increasing numbers of vehicles, and sometimes undisciplined minibus drivers all require caution and reduced speed for safety. The Government of Grenada has a seat belt law; drivers and passengers found not wearing seat belts are subject to a fine of EC$1,000 (US$400). Getting a local temporary driver's license, based on a valid U.S. driver's license plus EC$30 (US$12), is highly recommended. In the event of an accident, not having a valid local driver's license may result in a fine, regardless of who is at fault. Rental vehicle companies are available; most of them will assist in applying for temporary driver's licenses. The adequacy of road signage varies, but is generally poor to nonexistent.

Aviation Safety Oversight: The U.S. Federal Aviation Administration (FAA) has assessed the Government of Grenada's Civil Aviation Authority as being in compliance with International Civil Aviation Organization (ICAO) aviation safety standards for the oversight of Grenada's air carrier operations. For more information, travelers may visit the FAA's internet website at http://www.faa.gov.

Children's Issues: For information on intercountry adoption of children and international parental child abduction, see the Office of Children's Issues website at http://travel.state.gov.

Intercountry Adoption

July 2005

The information in this section has been edited from the latest report available as of February 2013 from the State Department Bureau of Consular Affairs, Office of Overseas Citizens Services. For more information, please read the *Intercountry Adoption* section of this book and review current reports online at http://adoption.state.gov.

Disclaimer: The information in this flyer relating to the legal requirements of specific foreign countries is based on public sources and current understanding. Questions involving foreign and U.S. immigration laws and legal interpretation should be addressed respectively to qualified foreign or U.S. legal counsel.

Please Note: If you are not resident or domiciled in Grenada, you may not adopt. Furthermore, no adoption is possible for children who are not resident in Grenada.

Patterns of Immigration: Please review current reports online at http://adoption.state.gov.

Adoption Authority: The government office responsible for adoptions in Grenada is the Grenada adoption board:

Ministry of Social Services
Tanteen, St. George's
Grenada.
Tel: (473) 440-6575, (473) 440-8717
Fax: (473) 440-4780

Eligibility Requirements for Adoptive Parents: The government of Grenada requires that the adoptive parent(s) must be age twenty-five or at least twenty-one years older than the child.

Residential Requirements: Grenada requires that applicants for adoption be resident and domiciled in Grenada. The child must also be in the continuous physical care of the applicant for at least three consecutive months immediately preceding the adoption order.

Time Frame: This can vary greatly, depending on the number of cases before the courts. Adoptions can take from three months to a year.

Adoption Agencies and Attorneys: Prospective adopting parents are advised to fully research any adoption agency or facilitator they plan to use for adoption services. For U.S.- based agencies, it is suggested that prospective adopting parents contact the Better Business Bureau and licensing office of the Department of Health and Family Services in the state where the agency is located.

Adoption Fees: The cost for adoptions is approximately US $2,000.00, though this can vary depending on the fees charged by the local attorney.

Adoption Procedures: An initial adoption request is done through a local attorney in Grenada. Subject to the provisions of the Grenada Adoption Act, the court may make an order authorizing the applicant to adopt a child upon an application made in the prescribed manner by a person domiciled in Grenada if the applicant:

- Has attained the age of twenty five and is at least twenty one years older than the infant; or
- Has attained the age of twenty one and is a relative of the infant; or
- Is the biological mother or biological father of the infant.

Required Documents: The prospective parents are required to have valid passports, naturalization certificate, marriage certificate, divorce certificate, birth certificate, bank statements, and medical history. The child will need a valid passport, original birth certificate and naturalization certificate.

Please see the *Intercountry Adoption* section of this book for more details and review current reports online at http://travel. state.gov.

Embassy of Grenada
1701 New Hampshire Avenue, N.W.
Washington, DC 20009
Tel: (202) 265-2561
Email: grenada@oas.org

Grenada Consulate
820 2ND Avenue, Suite 900 D,
New York, N.Y. 10017.
Tel: 212-599-0301

U.S. Immigration Requirements: Prospective adopting parents are strongly encouraged to consult USCIS publication M-249, *The Immigration of Adopted and Prospective Adoptive Children,* as well as the Department of State publication, *Intercountry Adoptions.*

Please see the *Intercountry Adoption* section of this book for more details and review current reports online at http://adoption.state.gov.

U.S. Embassy
Lance Aux Epines Main Road,
St. George's, Grenada
Mailing address:
P.O. Box 54
St. George's, Grenada
Tel: (473) 444-1173
Fax: (473) 444-4820
E-mail: usemb_gd@caribsurf.com

Additional Information: Specific questions about adoption in Grenada may be addressed to the U.S. Embassy in Grenada. General questions regarding intercountry adoption may be addressed to the Office of Children's Issues, U.S. Department of State, CA/OCS/CI, SA-29, 4 th Floor, 2201 C Street, NW, Washington, D.C. 20520-4818, toll-free Tel: 1-888-407-4747.

International Parental Child Abduction

January 2012

The information in this section has been edited from the latest report available as of February 2013 from the State Department Bureau of Consular Affairs, Office of Overseas Citizens Services. For more information, please read the *International Parental Child Abduction* section of this book and check for updated reports online at www.travel.state.gov/abduction.

Disclaimer: The information in this flyer relating to the legal requirements of specific foreign countries is provided for general information only. Questions involving interpretation of specific foreign laws should be addressed to foreign legal counsel.

General Information: Grenada is not a party to the Hague Convention on the Civil Aspects of International Child Abduction, nor are there any international or bilateral treaties in force between Grenada and the United States dealing with international parental child abduction. American citizens who travel to Grenada place themselves under the jurisdiction of local courts. American citizens planning a trip to Grenada with dual national children should bear this in mind.

Custody Disputes: In Grenada, if parents are legally married they share the custody of their children. If they are not married, custody is granted to the mother by law unless there are known facts of inappropriate behavior, mental or social problems. Foreign court orders are not automatically recognized.

Enforcement of Foreign Judgments: Custody orders and judgments of foreign courts are not enforceable in Grenada.

Visitation Rights: In cases where one parent has been granted custody of a child, the other parent is usually granted visitation rights. If a custodial parent fails to allow visitation, the non-custodial parent may appeal to the court.

Dual Nationality: Dual nationality is not recognized under Grenadine law.

Passports for Minors and the Children's Passport Issuance Alert Program: For more information on these topics, see the International Parental Child Abduction section of this publication and review current reports from the U.S. Department of State at www.travel.state.gov/abduction.

Travel Restrictions: No exit visas are required to leave Grenada.

Criminal Remedies: For information on possible criminal remedies, please contact your local law enforcement authorities or the nearest office of the Federal Bureau of Investigation (FBI).

Information is also available on the Internet at the web site of the U.S. Department of Justice, Office of Juvenile Justice and Delinquency Prevention (OJJDP) at http://www.ojjdp.ncjrs.org. Persons who wish to pursue a child custody claim in a Grenadian court should retain an attorney in Grenada. The U.S. Embassy in Grenada maintains a list of attorneys willing to represent American clients. A copy of this list may be obtained by requesting one from the Embassy at:

U.S. Embassy St. George's
Consular Section
P O Box 54
St. George's
Grenada
Tel: 473-444-1173
e-mail: usemb_gd@caribsurf.com

Questions involving Grenadian law should be addressed to a Grenadian attorney or to the Embassy of Grenada in the United States at:

Embassy of Grenada
1701 New Hampshire Avenue, NW
Washington, DC 20009
Telephone: (202) 265-2561

For further information on international parental child abduction, contact the Office of Children's Issues, U.S. Department of State at 1-888-407-4747 or visit its web site on the Internet at http://travel.state.gov/abduction.

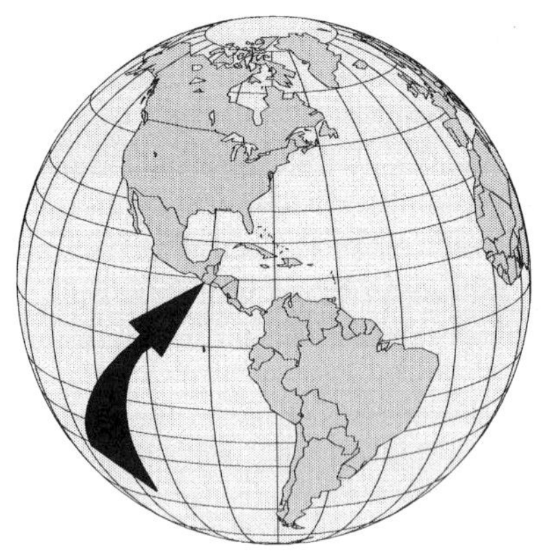

GUATEMALA

Compiled from publications that were available as of February 2013 from the U.S. Department of State, the U.S. Department of Commerce, and the Central Intelligence Agency (CIA). See the introduction to this set for explanatory notes.

Official Name:
Republic of Guatemala

PROFILE

Geography

Area: total: 108,889 sq km; country comparison to the world: 107; land: 107,159 sq km; water: 1,730 sq km
Major cities: Guatemala City (capital) 1.075 million (2009)
Climate: tropical; hot, humid in lowlands; cooler in highlands
Terrain: mostly mountains with narrow coastal plains and rolling limestone plateau

People

Nationality: noun: Guatemalan(s); adjective: Guatemalan
Population: 14,099,032 (July 2012 est.)
Population growth rate: 1.948% (2012 est.)
Ethnic groups: Mestizo (mixed Amerindian-Spanish—in local Spanish called Ladino) and European 59.4%, K'iche 9.1%, Kaqchikel 8.4%, Mam 7.9%, Q'eqchi 6.3%, other Mayan 8.6%, indigenous non-Mayan 0.2%, other 0.1% (2001 census)
Religions: Roman Catholic, Protestant, indigenous Mayan beliefs
Languages: Spanish (official) 60%, Amerindian languages 40%
Literacy: definition: age 15 and over can read and write; total population: 69.1%; male: 75.4%; female: 63.3% (2002 census)
Health: life expectancy at birth: total population: 71.17 years; male: 69.29 years; female: 73.14 years (2012 est.); Infant mortality rate: total: 25.16 deaths/1,000 live births; male: 27.34 deaths/1,000 live births; female: 22.87 deaths/1,000 live births (2012 est.)
Unemployment rate: 4.1% (2011 est.)
Work force: 5.571 million (2011 est.)

Government

Type: constitutional democratic republic
Independence: 15 September 1821
Constitution: 31 May 1985, effective 14 January 1986; suspended 25 May 1993; reinstated 5 June 1993; amended November 1993
Political subdivisions: 22 departments (departamentos, singular—departamento)
Suffrage: 18 years of age; universal; note—active duty members of the armed forces and police may not vote by law and are restricted to their barracks on election day

Economy

GDP (purchasing power parity): $78.42 billion (2012 est.); $75.67 billion (2011 est.); $72.91 billion (2010 est.); $70.93 billion (2009 est.)
GDP real growth rate: 3.1% (2012 est.); 3.8% (2011 est.); 2.8% (2010 est.); 0.5% (2009 est.)
GDP per capita (PPP): $5,200 (2012 est.); $5,100 (2011 est.); $5,100 (2010 est.); $5,100 (2009 est.)
Natural resources: petroleum, nickel, rare woods, fish, chicle, hydropower
Agriculture products: sugarcane, corn, bananas, coffee, beans, cardamom; cattle, sheep, pigs, chickens
Industries: sugar, textiles and clothing, furniture, chemicals, petroleum, metals, rubber, tourism
Exports: $9.864 billion (2012 est.); $10.46 billion (2011 est.); $8.566 billion (2010 est.)
Exports—commodities: coffee, sugar, petroleum, apparel, bananas, fruits and vegetables, cardamom
Exports—partners: US 38%, El Salvador 10.6%, Honduras 6.9%, Mexico 4.8% (2011)
Imports: $15.57 billion (2012 est.); $16.6 billion (2011 est.); $12.86 billion (2010 est.)
Imports—commodities: fuels, machinery and transport equipment, construction materials, grain, fertilizers, electricity, mineral products, chemical products, plastic materials and products
Imports—partners: US 41.5%, Mexico 10.5%, China 8.4%, El Salvador 4.6% (2011)
Debt—external: $16.17 billion (31 December 2012 est.); $15.67 billion (31 December 2011 est.)
Exchange rates: quetzales (GTQ) per US dollar; 7.88 (2012 est.); 7.7854 (2011 est.); 8.0578 (2010 est.)

PEOPLE

More than half of Guatemalans are descendants of indigenous Mayan peoples. Westernized Mayans and mestizos (mixed European and indigenous ancestry) are known as Ladinos. Most of Guatemala's population is rural, though urbanization is accelerating.

National/Racial/Ethnic Minorities

Indigenous persons from 22 ethnic groups constituted an estimated 43 percent of the population. Many indigenous persons were illiterate, and approximately 29 percent did not speak Spanish, according to the 2006 National Statistics Institute National Survey of Life Conditions report, the latest data available.

While the average nonindigenous child from seven to 17 years of age had received 4.4 years of schooling, indigenous children of the same age range had received an average of 3.7 years, according to the same report. More than 50 percent of indigenous women over the age of 15 were illiterate, and a disproportionate number of indigenous girls did not attend school. According to the Ministry of Education, approximately 82,970 preschool- and kindergarten-age indigenous children were enrolled in Spanish-indigenous language bilingual education programs.

Language

Though the official language is Spanish, it is not universally understood among the indigenous population. The peace accords signed in December 1996 provide for the translation of some official documents and voting materials into several indigenous languages. Many international businesses are accustomed to working in English.

Religion

There is no official census of religious affiliation. The Roman Catholic Episcopal Conference of Guatemala has estimated that 65 to 70 percent of the population is Catholic. Alianza Evangelica, the official umbrella organization for Protestants, has estimated that 35 to 40 percent of the population is Protestant. The largest Protestant group is the Full Gospel Church, followed by the Assemblies of God, the Central American Church, and the Prince of Peace Church, as well as many independent evangelical groups. Other religious groups include Baptists, Presbyterians, Lutherans, Episcopalians, Seventh-day Adventists, The Church of Jesus Christ of Latter-day Saints (Mormons), Russian Orthodox, and Jehovah's Witnesses. Approximately 2,000 Jews and a small Muslim population reside primarily in Guatemala City.

Catholics and Protestants are present throughout the country, and their adherents are found among all major ethnic groups and political parties. According to leaders of Mayan spiritual organizations and Catholic and Protestant missionaries, many indigenous Catholics and some Protestants also practice some form of indigenous spiritual ritual.

HISTORY

The Mayan civilization flourished throughout much of Guatemala and the surrounding region long before the Spanish arrived, but it was already in decline when the Mayans were defeated by Pedro de Alvarado in 1523–24. The first colonial capital, Ciudad Vieja, was ruined by floods and an earthquake in 1542. Survivors founded Antigua, the second capital, in 1543. Antigua was destroyed by two earthquakes in 1773. The remnants of its Spanish colonial architecture have been preserved as a national monument. The third capital, Guatemala City, was founded in 1776.

Guatemala gained independence from Spain on September 15, 1821; it briefly became part of the Mexican Empire, and then for a period belonged to a federation called the United Provinces of Central America. From the mid-19th century until the mid-1980s, the country passed through a series of dictatorships, insurgencies (particularly beginning in the 1960s), coups, and stretches of military rule with only occasional periods of representative government.

1944 to 1986

In 1944, Gen. Jorge Ubico's dictatorship was overthrown by the "October Revolutionaries," a group of dissident military officers, students, and liberal professionals. A civilian President, Juan Jose Arevalo, was elected in 1945 and held the presidency until 1951. Social reforms initiated by Arevalo were continued by his successor, Col. Jacobo Arbenz. Arbenz permitted the communist Guatemalan Labor Party to gain legal status in 1952. The army refused to defend the Arbenz government when a U.S.-backed group led by Col. Carlos Castillo Armas invaded the country from Honduras in 1954 and quickly took over the government. Gen. Miguel Ydigoras Fuentes took power in 1958 following the murder of Colonel Castillo Armas.

In response to the increasingly autocratic rule of Ydigoras Fuentes, a group of junior military officers revolted in 1960. When they failed, several went into hiding and established close ties with Cuba. This group became the nucleus of the forces that were in armed insurrection against the government for the next 36 years. Four principal left-wing guerrilla groups—the Guerrilla Army of the Poor (EGP), the Revolutionary Organization of Armed People (ORPA), the Rebel Armed Forces (FAR), and the Guatemalan Labor Party (PGT)—conducted economic sabotage and targeted government installations and members of government security forces in armed attacks. These organizations combined to form the Guatemalan National Revolutionary Unity (URNG) in 1982.

Shortly after President Julio Cesar Mendez Montenegro took office in 1966, the army launched a major counterinsurgency campaign that largely broke up the guerrilla move-

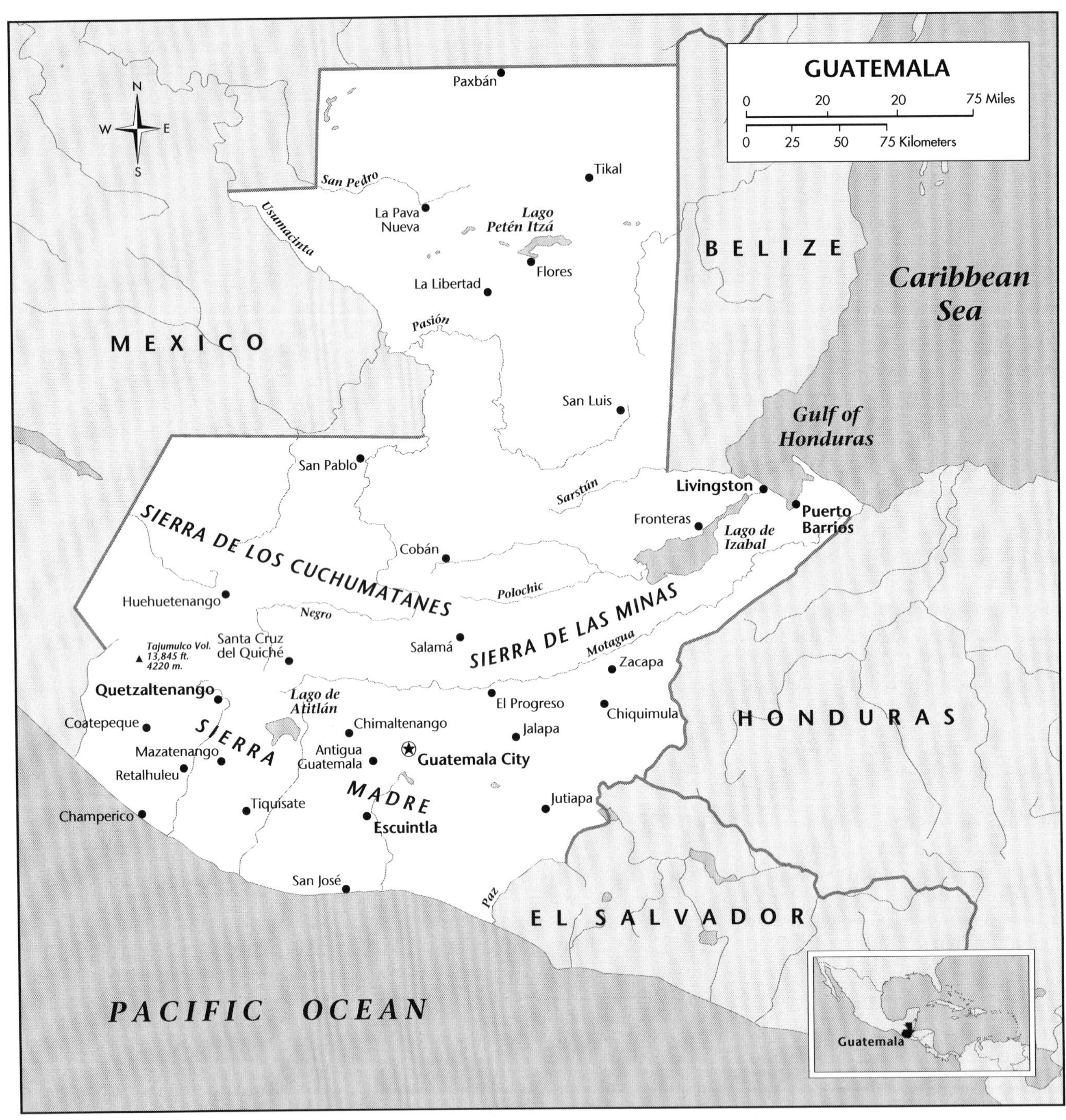

ment in the countryside. The guerrillas then concentrated their attacks in Guatemala City, where they assassinated many leading figures, including U.S. Ambassador John Gordon Mein in 1968. Between 1966 and 1982, there was a series of military or military-dominated governments.

On March 23, 1982, army troops commanded by junior officers staged a coup to prevent the assumption of power by Gen. Angel Anibal Guevara, the hand-picked candidate of outgoing President and Gen. Romeo Lucas Garcia. They denounced Guevara's electoral victory as fraudulent. The coup leaders asked retired Gen. Efrain Rios Montt to negotiate the departure of Lucas and Guevara.

Rios Montt was at this time a lay pastor in the evangelical protestant "Church of the Word." He formed a three-member military junta that annulled the 1965 constitution, dissolved Congress, suspended political parties, and canceled the electoral law. After a few months, Rios Montt dismissed his junta colleagues and assumed the de facto title of "President of the Republic."

Guerrilla forces and their leftist allies denounced Rios Montt. Rios Montt sought to defeat the guerrillas with military actions and economic reforms; in his words, "rifles and beans." The government began to form local civilian defense patrols (PACs). Participation was in theory voluntary, but in reality, many Guatemalans, especially in the heavily indigenous northwest, had no choice but to join either the PACs or the guerrillas. Rios Montt's conscript army and PACs recaptured essentially all guerrilla territory—guerrilla activity lessened and was largely limited to hit-and-run operations. However, Rios Montt won this partial victory at an enormous cost in civilian deaths, in what was probably the most violent period of the 36-year internal conflict, resulting in about 200,000 deaths of mostly unarmed indigenous civilians.

On August 8, 1983, Rios Montt was deposed by his own Minister of Defense, Gen. Oscar Humberto Mejia Victores, who succeeded him as de facto President of Guatemala. Rios Montt survived to found a political party (the Guatemalan Republican Front) and to be elected President of Congress in 1995 and 2000. Awareness in the United States of the conflict in Guatemala, and its ethnic dimension, increased with the 1983 publication of the book I, Rigoberta Menchu, An Indian Woman in Guatemala.

General Mejia allowed a managed return to democracy in Guatemala, starting with a July 1, 1984 election for a Constituent Assembly to draft a democratic constitution. On May 30, 1985, after 9 months of debate, the Constituent Assembly finished drafting a new constitution, which took effect immediately. Vinicio Cerezo, a civilian politician and the presidential candidate of the Christian Democracy Party, won the first election held under the new constitution with almost 70% of the vote, and took office on January 14, 1986.

1986 to 2011

Upon its inauguration in January 1986, President Cerezo's civilian government announced that its top priorities would be to end the political violence and establish the rule of law. Reforms included new laws of habeas corpus and amparo (injunction), the creation of a legislative human rights committee, and the establishment in 1987 of the Office of the Human Rights Ombudsman. Cerezo survived coup attempts in 1988 and 1989, and the final 2 years of Cerezo's government were also marked by a failing economy, strikes, protest marches, and allegations of widespread corruption.

Presidential and congressional elections were held on November 11, 1990. After a runoff ballot, Jorge Serrano was inaugurated on January 14, 1991, thus completing the first transition from one democratically-elected civilian government to another.

The Serrano administration's record was mixed. It had some success in consolidating civilian control over the army, replacing a number of senior officers and persuading the military to participate in peace talks with the URNG. Serrano took the politically unpopular step of recognizing the sovereignty of Belize. The Serrano government reversed the economic slide it inherited, reducing inflation and boosting real growth.

On May 25, 1993, Serrano illegally dissolved Congress and the Supreme Court and tried to restrict civil freedoms, allegedly to fight corruption. The "autogolpe" (or self-initiated coup) failed due to unified, strong protests by most elements of Guatemalan society, international pressure, and the army's enforcement of the decisions of the Court of Constitutionality, which ruled against the attempted takeover. Serrano fled the country.

On June 5, 1993, the Congress, pursuant to the 1985 constitution, elected the Human Rights Ombudsman, Ramiro De Leon Carpio, to complete Serrano's presidential term. De Leon, not a member of any political party and lacking a political base but with strong popular support, launched an ambitious anticorruption campaign to "purify" Congress and the Supreme Court, demanding the resignations of all members of the two bodies. Despite considerable congressional resistance, presidential and popular pressure led to a November 1993 agreement brokered by the Catholic Church between the administration and Congress. This package of constitutional reforms was approved by popular referendum on January 30, 1994. In August 1994, a new Congress was elected to complete the unexpired term.

Under De Leon, the peace process, now brokered by the United Nations, took on new life. The government and the URNG signed agreements on human rights (March 1994), resettlement of displaced persons (June 1994), historical clarification (June 1994), and indigenous rights (March 1995). They also made significant progress on a socioeconomic and agrarian agreement. National elections for president, the Congress, and municipal offices were held in November 1995. With almost 20 parties competing in the first round, the presidential election came down to a January 7, 1996 runoff in which National Advancement Party (PAN) candidate Alvaro Arzu defeated Alfonso Portillo of the Guatemalan Republican Front (FRG) by just over 2% of the vote. Under the Arzu administration, peace negotiations were concluded, and the government signed peace accords ending the 36-year internal conflict in December 1996. The human rights situation also improved during Arzu's tenure, and steps were taken to reduce the influence of the military in national affairs.

In a December 1999 presidential runoff, the FRG's Portillo won 68% of the vote to 32% for Oscar Berger (PAN). Portillo's impressive electoral triumph, with two-thirds of the vote in the second round, gave him a claim to a mandate from the people to carry out his reform program. Berger, representing the Grand National Alliance (GANA) party, won the November 9, 2003 presidential election, receiving 54.1% of the vote. His opponent, Alvaro Colom Caballeros of the National Unity of Hope (UNE) party, received 45.9% of the vote.

In February 2004, after his 2000–2004 term ended, Portillo fled to Mexico to escape corruption charges. In October 2008, Mexican authorities extradited him to Guatemala to face the charges. In March 2010, a Guatemalan court ruled to approve Portillo's extradition to the United States to face money-laundering charges after resolution of domestic charges. Portillo appealed that decision, but in August 2011, the Guatemalan Constitutional Court issued a ruling disposing of his appeal. On November 15, outgoing President Colom publicly announced that he authorized Portillo's extradition to the United States. His extradition to the United States has been deferred, however, pending the outcome of an appeal by Guatemalan authorities on domestic embezzlement charges; he remains in prison.

Colom won the November 2007 presidential election against retired General Otto Perez Molina, with 52.8% of the vote versus 47.2%. Perez Molina won the November 6, 2011 election, defeating Manuel Baldizon of the Renewed Democratic Liberty Party with 54% of votes.

GOVERNMENT AND POLITICAL CONDITIONS

Guatemala is a multiparty constitutional republic. On November 6, 2011, Otto Perez Molina of the Patriot Party (PP) won the presidential election for a four-year term beginning January 2012. International observers considered the election generally free and fair.

Recent Elections

On November 6, 2011 Otto Perez Molina of the PP won a four-year term as president. The OAS international observation mission characterized the elections as generally free and fair. The Office of the Human Rights Ombudsman reported 36 killings of political activists or candidates, mostly at the municipal level, during the election cycle. There were few arrests or convictions for such killings, and the actors behind them were generally unknown.

Participation of Women and Minorities: There were 20 women in the 158-seat Congress. A total of 343 women served as judges nationwide, including one on the Supreme Court and one on the Constitutional Court. In October a woman was elected to serve a one-year term as president of the Supreme Court. There were no women in the 13-member cabinet. Six of the country's 333 mayors were women.

Despite a sizable indigenous population, there were no indigenous cabinet members or Supreme Court justices. There were 113 indigenous mayors and approximately 20 indigenous members of Congress.

Principal Government Officials

Last Updated: 1/31/2013

Pres.: **Otto Fernando PEREZ MOLINA**
Vice Pres.: **Ingrid Roxana BALDETTI Elias**
Min. of Agriculture, Livestock, & Food: **Efrain MEDINA**
Min. of Communications, Infrastructure, & Housing: **Alejandro SINIBALDI**
Min. of Culture & Sports: **Carlos BATZIN**
Min. of Defense: **Ulises Noe ANZUETO Giron, Maj. Gen.**
Min. of Economy: **Sergio DE LA TORRE**
Min. of Education: **Cynthia DEL AGUILA**
Min. of Energy & Mines: **Erick ARCHILA**
Min. of Environment & Natural Resources: **Roxana SOBENES**
Min. of Foreign Relations: **Harold Osberto CABALLEROS Lopez**
Min. of Finance: **Pavel CENTENO**
Min. of Govt.: **Hector Mauricio LOPEZ BONILLA**
Min. of Labor: **Carlos CONTRERAS**
Min. of Public Health & Social Assistance: **Jorge VILLAVICENCIO Alvarez**
Attorney Gen.: **Claudia PAZ Y PAZ Bailey**
Solicitor Gen.: **Larry Mark ROBLES Guibert**
Sec. Gen. of the Presidency: **Gustavo MARTINEZ**
Pres., Bank of Guatemala: **Edgar BARQUIN**
Ambassador to the US:
Permanent Representative to the UN, New York: **Gert ROSENTHAL Koenigsberger**

ECONOMY

Guatemala is the most populous country in Central America with a GDP per capita roughly one-half that of the average for Latin America and the Caribbean. The agricultural sector accounts for 13% of GDP and 38% of the labor force; key agricultural exports include coffee, sugar, bananas, and vegetables. The 1996 peace accords, which ended 36 years of civil war, removed a major obstacle to foreign investment, and since then Guatemala has pursued important reforms and macroeconomic stabilization.

The Dominican Republic-Central American Free Trade Agreement (CAFTA-DR) entered into force in July 2006 spurring increased investment and diversification of exports, with the largest increases in ethanol and non-traditional agricultural exports. While CAFTA-DR has helped improve the investment climate, concerns over security, the lack of skilled workers and poor infrastructure continue to hamper foreign direct investment.

The distribution of income remains highly unequal with the richest 20% of the population accountingfor more than 51% of Guatemala's overall consumption. More than half of the population is below the national poverty line and 13% of the population lives in extreme poverty. Poverty among indigenous groups, which make up 38% of the population, averages 73% and extreme poverty rises to 28%.

Nearly one-half of Guatemala's children under age five are chronically malnourished, one of the highest malnutrition rates in the world. Given Guatemala's large expatriate community in the United States, it is the top remittance recipient in Central America, with inflows serving as a primary source of foreign income equivalent to nearly two-fifths of exports or one-tenth of GDP. Economic growth fell in 2009 as export demand from US and other Central American markets dropped and foreign investment slowed amid the global recession. The economy gradually recovered in 2010–12.

Labor Conditions

The law bars employment of minors under the age of 14 without written permission from parents and the Ministry of Labor. The law prohibits persons under the age of 18 from work where alcoholic beverages are served, in unhealthy or dangerous conditions, and at night or overtime. The legal workday for persons younger than 14 is six hours, and for persons 14 to 17 years of age, seven hours.

The Ministry of Labor's Child Worker Protection Unit is charged with enforcing restrictions on child labor and educating minors, their parents, and employers on the rights of minors in the labor market. While penalties in theory are adequate to deter child labor, the government did not effectively enforce these laws, a situation exacerbated by the weakness of the labor-inspection and labor-court systems.

Child labor was a widespread problem. The NGO Conrad Project Association of the Cross estimated that the workforce included approximately one million children between the ages of five and 17. Most child labor occurred in rural indigenous areas. The informal and agricultural sectors regularly employed children below 14 years of age, usually in small family enterprises, and there were reports during the year that child labor existed in the production of broccoli, coffee, corn, fireworks, gravel, and sugar. Indigenous children also worked frequently in street sales and rubber and timber production and as shoe shiners and bricklayer assistants. Some child laborers worked an average of 45 hours per week.

An estimated 39,000 children, primarily indigenous girls, worked as domestic servants and were often vulnerable to physical and sexual abuse. In the Mexican border area, there were reports of forced child labor in municipal dumps and in street begging.

The law sets national minimum wages for agricultural and nonagricultural work and work in garment factories. The minimum wage was 63.70 quetzales ($8.16) per day for agricultural and nonagricultural work and 59.45 quetzales ($7.61) per day for work in garment factories. In December the National Statistics Institute estimated that the minimum food budget for a family of five was 2,440 quetzales ($312) per month. The basic basket for vital needs, including food and housing, was 4,452 quetzales ($570). Labor representatives noted that even where both parents worked, the minimum wage did not enable a family to meet the basic basket of vital needs.

The legal workweek is 48 hours with at least one paid 24-hour rest period. Daily and weekly maximum hour limits do not apply to domestic workers. Workers in the formal sector receive the standard pay for a day's work for official annual holidays. Time-and-a-half pay is required for overtime work, and the law prohibits excessive compulsory overtime.

U.S.-GUATEMALAN RELATIONS

The United States established diplomatic relations with Guatemala in 1849 following its independence from Spain and the later dissolution of a federation of Central American states. In 1954, the United States assisted in the overthrow of the Guatemalan government due to concerns about the threat of communism. A new government took power in Guatemala the same year, and the United States established diplomatic relations with it. Beginning in 1960, forces carried out armed insurrection against the Guatemalan government. Peace accords ending the 36-year internal conflict were signed in 1996. Guatemala continues to face major challenges to successful development, including poverty, malnutrition, and vulnerability to economic fluctuations and natural disasters. The Guatemalan government also faces the challenges of corruption and the presence of transnational organized crime.

U.S. policy objectives in Guatemala include:

- Supporting the institutionalization of democracy and implementation of the peace accords;
- Encouraging respect for human rights and the rule of law, and the efficient functioning of the International Commission Against Impunity in Guatemala, which was inaugurated in 2008;
- Supporting broad-based economic growth and sustainable development and maintaining mutually beneficial trade and commercial relations, including ensuring that benefits of the U.S.-Central America-Dominican Republic Free Trade Agreement (CAFTA-DR) reach all sectors of the Guatemalan populace;
- Cooperating to combat money laundering, corruption, narcotics trafficking, alien-smuggling, and other transnational crime, including through programs funded under the Central American Regional Security Initiative; and
- Supporting Central American integration through support for resolution of border/territorial disputes.

U.S. Assistance to Guatemala

U.S. assistance focuses on improving citizen security and justice, increasing levels of economic growth and social development in the Western Highlands, fostering sustainable management of natural resources, and mitigating the effects of global climate change.

Bilateral Economic Relations

The United States is one of Guatemala's largest trading partners. The two countries are parties to the U.S.-Central America-Dominican Republic Free Trade Agreement, which aims to facilitate trade and investment and further regional integration by eliminating tariffs, opening markets, reducing barriers to services, and promoting transparency. CAFTA-DR contains a chapter on investment similar to a bilateral investment treaty with the United States. U.S. exports to Guatemala include oil, agricultural products, articles donated for relief and low-value shipments, and machinery. U.S. imports from Guatemala include agricultural products, apparel, gold, and silver.

Guatemala's Membership in International Organizations

Guatemala and the United States belong to a number of the same international organizations, including the United Nations, Organization of American States, International Monetary Fund, World Bank, and World Trade Organization.

Bilateral Representation

The Guatemalan embassy is located at 2220 R Street, NW, Washington, DC 20008 (tel. 202-745-4952).

Principal U.S. Embassy Officials

Last Updated: 1/14/2013

GUATEMALA (E) Ave. Reforma 7-01, Zona 10, (502) 2326-4000, Fax (502) 2326-4658, INMARSAT Tel 683133345, Workweek: Mon-Thu: 7:30 to 5:00 p.m.; Fri: 7:30 to 12:30, http://guatemala.usembassy.gov/

DCM OMS:	Beatriz Beroud
AMB OMS:	Judy Reed
CDC:	Dr. Nelson Arboleda
DHS/CIS:	Miriam Moreno
DHS/ICE:	Angel Ortiz
FM:	Bill Sherrill
GFS:	Patricia Baid
HRO:	Paula Bravo
MGT:	Paula M. Bravo
MLO/ODC:	COL Michael Knutson
NAS/INL:	Alberto Rodriguez
POL/ECON:	Jean Ellen Preston
SDO/DATT:	COL Michael Knutson
TREAS:	Arturo Girona
AMB:	Arnold Chacon
CG:	Dennis Offutt
DCM:	Bruce Williamson
PAO:	Lilian Devalcourt-Ayala
GSO:	Richard Behnke
RSO:	Christopher Rooks
AGR:	Henry Schmick
AID:	Kevin Kelly
APHIS:	Gary Greene
CLO:	Adriana Gonzalez-Girona/ Jennifer Benecke
DEA:	Dial Johnson
ECON:	Susanne Kuester
EEO:	Kathleen Guerra;Barnett Sporkin-Morrison
FMO:	Joseph Strzalka
ICASS Chair:	Bernard Benecke
IMO:	Marc Beroud
IPO:	Raymond Harger
ISO:	Jerry A. Lopez
ISSO:	Jerry A. Lopez
LAB:	William Ayala
State ICASS:	Denisson Offutt

Other Contact Information

U.S. Department of Commerce International Trade Administration Trade Information Center
14th and Constitution, NW
Washington, DC 20230
Tel: 800-USA-TRADE
Internet: http://trade.gov

American Chamber of Commerce in Guatemala
5a avenida 5-55 zona 14 Europlaza, Torre I Nivel 5
01014 Guatemala City, Guatemala
Tel: (502) 2333–3899
Fax: (502) 2368–3536
E-Mail: trade@amchamguate.com

Caribbean/Latin American Action (C/LAA)
1818 N Street, NW, Suite 310
Washington, DC 20036
Tel.: 202-466-7464

TRAVEL

Consular Information Sheet

November 13, 2012

Country Description: Guatemala is a developing country characterized by wide income disparities. Violent crime is a serious concern due to endemic poverty, an abundance of weapons, a legacy of societal violence, and weak law enforcement and judicial systems. Spanish is the official and most commonly spoken language. Please read the Department of State Fact Sheet on Guatemala for additional information.

Smart Traveler Enrollment Program (STEP)/Embassy Location: If you are going to live in or visit Guatemala, please take the time to tell our embassy about your trip. Enrolling in the Smart Traveler Enrollment Program will keep you up to date with important safety and security announcements, and help your friends and family get in touch with you in an emergency.

Embassy of the United States in Guatemala
Avenida Reforma 7-01, Zona 10
Guatemala Ciudad, Guatemala
Telephone: (502) 2326–4000 during embassy business hours (8:00 a.m. to 5:00 p.m. Mo-Thu and 8:00 a.m. to 12:00 p.m. Fridays).
Emergency after-hours telephone: (502)2331–2354
Facsimile: (502)2331–3804
Internet website: http://guatemala.usembassy.gov
Other emergency numbers:
Police (911 equivalent): 110 or 120
Tourist emergency assistance: 502 2421–2810
Tourist Police (POLITUR): 1 500
Fire Department: 122 or 123

Entry/Exit Requirements for U.S. Citizens: A valid U.S. passport is required for all U.S. citizens to enter Guatemala and to depart Guatemala for return to the United States, regardless of age. Even if dual nationals are permitted to enter Guatemala on a second nationality passport, U.S. citizens returning to the United States from Guatemala are not allowed to board their flights without a valid U.S. passport. Certificates of Naturalization, birth certificates, driver's licenses, and photocopies are not accepted by Guatemalan authorities as alternative travel documents. While in Guatemala, U.S. citizens should carry a photocopy of their passports with them at all times due to the high rate of passport theft and leave the original passport in a safe place. Visit the Ministry of Foreign Affairs website (Spanish only) for the most current visa information.

An exit tax must be paid when departing Guatemala by air. The exit tax (currently $30) is generally included in an airline ticket price, but may be charged separately. There is an additional airport security fee (currently 20 quetzals, or approximately $2.60) that all travelers must pay at the airport.

Minors under 18 years old traveling with a valid U.S. passport do not need special permission from their parents to enter or leave Guatemala. U.S. citizens do not need a visa for a stay of 90 days or less. That period can be extended for an additional 90 days upon application to Guatemalan immigration. (If the initial period of stay granted upon entry is less than 90 days, any extension would be granted only for the same number of days as the initial authorization.) There is a daily fine of 10 quetzals for each day that a traveler overstays his/her permission to be in Guatemala, which must be paid directly to the Guatemalan Immigration Agency. (U.S. citizens born in Guatemala are currently exempted from this fine.)

In June 2006, Guatemala entered a "Central America-4 (CA-4) Border Control Agreement" with El Salvador, Honduras, and Nicaragua. Under the terms of the agreement, citizens of the four countries may travel freely across land borders from one of the countries to any of the others without completing entry and exit formalities at immigration checkpoints. U.S. citizens and other eligible foreign nationals who legally enter any of the four countries may similarly travel among the four without obtaining additional visas or tourist entry permits for the other three countries. Immigration officials at the first port of entry determine the length of stay, up to a maximum period of 90 days. Foreign tourists who wish to remain in the region beyond the period initially granted for their visit are required either to request a one-time extension of stay from local immigration authorities in the country where the traveler is physically present, or to travel outside the CA-4 countries and reapply for admission to the region.

Foreigners "expelled" from any of the four countries are excluded from the entire CA-4 region. In isolated cases, the lack of clarity in the implementation of the CA-4 Border Control Agreement has caused temporary inconvenience to travelers. U.S. citizens who are also citizens of another country and who choose to travel within the CA-4 region using their non-U.S. passport should consult in advance with the appropriate regional authorities regarding visa requirements within the CA-4 zone.

A U.S. citizen whose passport is lost or stolen in Guatemala must obtain a new passport at the U.S. Embassy as soon as possible and present it, together with a police report on the loss or theft, to the Guatemalan Immigration Agency (Dirección de Migración), Sub-Director for Migratory Control (Sub-director de Control Migratorio) in order to obtain permission to depart Guatemala. The agency is located in Guatemala City at 6a Avenida 3-11, Zone 4. Office hours are weekdays from 8:00 a.m. to 4:30 p.m.; the telephone number is 2411–2411. No fee is charged by Guatemalan immigration for this service.

For further information regarding entry, exit and customs requirements, travelers should contact the Guatemalan Embassy at 2220 R Street NW, Washington, DC 20008; telephone (202) 745-4953, extension 102; fax (202) 745-1908; Visit their website; or contact the nearest Guatemalan consulate (Atlanta, Chicago, Denver, Houston, Los Angeles, Miami, New York, Providence, Phoenix or San Francisco).

Threats to Safety and Security: Large demonstrations occur throughout Guatemala, often with little or no notice, and can cause serious traffic disruptions. Although most demonstrations are peaceful, they can turn violent, and travelers should avoid areas where demonstrations are taking place. The use of roadblocks and/or blocking of public facilities, including the international airport, has increased and demonstrators may prevent tourists caught behind the blockades from leaving. When acts of violence are particularly severe, such as those caused by drug traffickers in the Petén region, a state of siege can be declared by the authorities. That means a curfew will be set and increased police patrols in the areas affected. Americans traveling through these places should be very cautious, cooperate with the authorities and stay indoors after the curfew.

Due to uncontrolled drug and alien smuggling, the Guatemalan border with Mexico (and in particular the northwestern corner of Petén) is a high-risk area. The border areas including the Sierra de Lacandon and Laguna del Tigre National Parks are among the most dangerous areas in Guatemala due to drug trafficking activity. The U.S. Embassy takes extra precautions when U.S. government personnel travel to the region.

Guatemala is a country with many different and firmly held local beliefs and customs. Particularly in small villages, residents are often wary and suspicious of outsiders. In the past, Guatemalan citizens have been lynched for suspicion of child abduction, so we recommend that U.S. citizens keep a distance from local children, and refrain from actions that could fuel such suspicions. In addition, U.S. citizens are advised to be aware of and avoid activities that might unintentionally violate a cultural or religious belief. The following recommendations will help residents and visitors alike to increase their safety:

- Avoid gatherings of agitated people. Attempting to intervene may put you at risk of attacks from mobs.

- Avoid close contact with local children, including taking photographs, especially in rural areas. Such contact can be viewed with deep suspicion and may provoke panic and violence.

- Keep informed of possible demonstrations by following the local news and consulting hotel personnel and tour guides. Avoid areas where demonstrations are occurring.

Stay up to date by:

- Bookmarking our Bureau of Consular Affairs website, which contains the current Travel Warnings and Travel Alerts as well as the Worldwide Caution.

- Following us on Twitter and the Bureau of Consular Affairs page on Facebook as well.

- Downloading our free Smart Traveler App, available through iTunes or the Android market, to have travel information at your fingertips.

- Calling 1-888-407-4747 toll-free within the U.S. and Canada, or a regular toll line, 1-202-501-4444, from other countries.

- Taking some time before travel to consider your personal security.

The Department of State urges U.S. citizens to take responsibility for their own personal security while traveling overseas. For general information about appropriate measures travelers can take to protect themselves in an overseas environment, see the Department of State's extensive tips and advice on traveling safely abroad.

Crime and Safety Tips: Guatemala has one of the highest violent crime rates in Central America. Between January and September 2012, an average of 95 murders per week were reported countrywide in Guatemala. The vast majority of murders do not involve foreigners; however, the sheer volume of activity means that local officials, who are often inexperienced and underpaid, are unable to cope with the problem. Rule of law is lacking as the judicial system is weak, overworked, and inefficient. Criminals know there is little chance they will be caught or punished as the rate of convictions/resolution are very low.

The number of violent crimes reported by U.S. citizens and other foreigners has remained high and incidents have included, but are not limited to, assault, theft, armed robbery, carjacking, rape, kidnapping, and murder, even in areas of Guatemala City once considered safe, such as Zones 10, 14, and 15. Since December 2008, 31 murders of U.S. citizens have been reported in Guatemala, including six in 2011 and three in 2012. To decrease the likelihood of becoming a victim, do not display items of value such as laptops, iPods, cameras, and jewelry and refrain from using a cell phone on the street. Carry a photocopy of your passport when out and about to avoid losing it to a robbery.

The Embassy discourages carrying large sums of money. Do not resist if you are being robbed. Victims have been killed when they resisted attack or refused to give up their money or other valuables. Assailants are often armed with guns and do not hesitate to use them if you resist.

Emboldened armed robbers have attacked vehicles on main roads in broad daylight. Travel on rural roads increases the risk of being stopped by a criminal roadblock or ambush. Widespread narcotics and alien-smuggling activities make remote areas especially dangerous. There is no evidence that U.S. citizens are specifically targeted, although an appearance of wealth could increase the chances of your becoming a focus of attention for criminal gangs. Criminals look for any opportunity to strike, so all travelers should remain constantly vigilant.

U.S. Embassy personnel observe heightened security precautions in Guatemala City and throughout the country:

- Rather than traveling alone, use a reputable tour organization.

- Stay in groups, travel in a caravan consisting of two or more vehicles, and stay on the main roads.

- Ensure that someone not traveling with you is aware of your itinerary.

- Avoid hotels that do not have adequate security.

- Intercity travel after dark anywhere in Guatemala is extremely dangerous and should be avoided altogether.

- It is preferable to stay in the main tourist destinations.

- Pay close attention to your surroundings, especially when walking or driving in Guatemala City.

A number of travelers have experienced carjackings and armed robberies after just having arrived on international flights, most frequently in the evening. In the most common scenario, tourists or business travelers who land at the airport after dark are held up by armed men as their vehicle departs the airport, but similar incidents have occurred at other times of the day.

Private vehicles, taxis and shuttle buses have all been targeted. Typically, the assailants steal money, passports, and luggage, and in some but not all cases, the assailants steal the vehicle as well. In some cases, assailants have been wearing full or partial police uniforms and have used vehicles that resemble police vehicles, indicating that some elements of the police might be involved. Armed robberies have occurred within minutes of a tourist's vehicle having been stopped by the police. Recently, many of these attacks have taken place far from the airport, just as travelers were arriving at their homes, or in less busy areas of the city. Victims who did not resist the attackers were not physically injured.

Security Escorts: for tourist groups and security information are available from the Tourist Assistance Office (PROATUR) of INGUAT (the Guatemalan Tourism Institute) at 7a Avenida 1-17, Zona 4, Centro Cívico, Guatemala City. INGUAT's PROATUR division has 24-hour/seven days per week direct telephone numbers for tourist assistance and emergencies. You may call them at (502) 2421–2810, fax them at (502) 2421–2891, or simply dial 1500 in Guatemala to reach INGUAT Tourist Assistance. You can also contact INGUAT by email. PROATUR also maintains regional offices in all major tourist destinations in Guatemala, and the regional delegates provide rapid and appropriate assistance to crime and accident victims. Travelers may also wish to visit INGUAT's web site (Spanish only). Tourist groups are advised to request security escorts from INGUAT. There have been no incidents of armed robbery of groups escorted through the Tourist Protection Program. The request should be submitted by mail, fax, or e-mail and should arrive at INGUAT at least three business days in advance of the proposed travel. Requests should be directed to the attention of the Coordinator of the National Tourist Assistance Program, and should provide the itinerary, names of travelers, and model and color of the vehicle in which they will be traveling. Travelers should be aware that INGUAT might not be able to accommodate all requests.

Taxis: If you need a taxi upon arrival (particularly in the evening) call the Guatemalan tourist assistance agency, PROATUR, by dialing 1500and they will call a radiotaxi to pick you up at the airport. Alternatively, you can contact the Taxi Seguro booth at the airport and they will send you off on a police-vetted taxi. Taxi Seguro may not always be available, especially late at night. Additional hints for travel safety include:

- Coordinating arrival times with those picking up passengers, minimize time spent standing outside in the airport passenger pick-up area, and do not walk out of the airport with valuables in plain sight.
- Laptops are frequently targeted, so carry them inconspicuously in a backpack or other carry-on luggage.
- Avoid using electronic devices in traffic or leaving purses on seats in plain sight.

Buses: Avoid low-priced intra- and inter-city public buses (recycled U.S. school buses). They are often attacked by armed robbers and are poorly maintained and dangerously driven. In the first three months of 2012, nine bus drivers were killed and in 2011, 91 bus drivers were murdered in robberies staged by holdup gangs targeting public transportation, both urban and inter-city. Outside the capital, shuttles and buses carrying tourists have been stopped and robbed, including incidents on the road to Tikal. Do not hail taxis on the street in Guatemala City. For shorter trips, the safest option is to take radio-dispatched (Taxi Amarillo) or hotel taxis.

The use of modern inter-city buses somewhat improves security and safety; however, several travelers have been attacked on first-class buses on highway CA-2 near the border areas with both Mexico and El Salvador, and on highways CA-1 and CA-9 near the border with El Salvador, and in the highlands between Quetzaltenango and Sololá. Be cautious with personal items such as backpacks, fanny packs, and passports while riding buses, as tourists' possessions are a favorite target of thieves.

Highway Safety: There have been numerous reports of violent criminal activity along Guatemala's main highways, including the Carretera a El Salvador (Inter-American Highway CA-2). There has also been an increase in alcohol-related traffic accidents on this same road at night. Embassy employees are discouraged from driving at night. There has also been a series of violent highway robberies along National Route #14 (RN-14) between Antigua and Escuintla, along National Route #4 (RN-4) on the south side and west shores of Lake Atitlán between San Lucas Tolimán and Chacala, and along National Route #11 (RN-11) on the east shore between San Lucas Tolimán and CA-1. Several tourists of various nationalities have been targeted along these routes in brazen daylight robberies. One of these incidents occurred on CA-2 in Santa Rosa while the van was traveling from the El Salvador border to Antigua. Another incident occurred on CA-1 in Totonicapan as a private bus traveled from the Mexican border to Panajachel. At least two others occurred in 2009 on Route #11 near Patulul.

The main road to Lake Atitlán via the Inter-American Highway (CA-1) and Sololá is safer than the alternative secondary roads near the lake. Specifically, the main road is preferable to the alternative road through Las Trampas and Godinez to Panajachel (RN-11) where robbery, rape, and assault are known to have occurred in the past. Armed attacks have occurred on roads between Guatemala City and the Petén as well as between Tikal and the Belize border. Visitors to the Mayan ruins at Tikal are urged to fly to nearby Flores and then travel by bus or tour van to the site. Violent attacks have occurred in the Mayan ruins in the Petén, including in the Cerro Cahui Conservation Park, Yaxha, the road to and inside Tikal Park, and in the Tikal ruins, particularly during early morning sunrise tours of the ruins. However, tourist police (POLITUR) patrols have significantly reduced the incidence of violent crime inside the park and there have been no reports of armed assaults on tourists there in the past year. Travelers should remain in groups, stay on the principal trails leading to the Central Plaza and the Temple IV complex, and avoid remote areas of the park.

Theft of items from occupied vehicles is becoming more common. Often the assailants are on motorcycles and pull up alongside a car stopped at a traffic light. The passenger on the motorcycle is armed and the assailants are able to flee the scene quickly. In some cases, the vehicle occupants were visibly using their cell phones or other handheld devices. Leaving cars unattended in parking lots of fast food franchises can also invite break-ins in spite of the presence of armed guards. Make sure you leave the car just long enough to complete the meal—the armed guards are for decoration only.

Flat-tire Scam: In one popular scam, robbers place a nail in a parked vehicle's tire. The vehicle is then followed by the robbers who pose as "good Samaritans" when the tire becomes flat and the victims pull to the side of the road. While "help" is being rendered, the contents of the car are stolen, often without the knowledge of the victims. However, in some cases, the robbers have threatened the tourists with weapons. Parking areas in and around the Guatemala City International Airport are particularly prone to this crime.

Parking Lot Scam: Victims are approached in a hotel, restaurant or other public place by an individual claiming that there is some sort of problem with his or the would-be victim's automobile in the parking lot. On the way to investigate the "problem," usually in a remote or concealed area near the parking lot, the robber pulls a gun on the victim and demands cash, credit cards and other valuables.

Rape: Women should be especially careful when traveling alone and avoid staying out late without an escort. Support for victims of sexual assault is lacking outside of major cities, and there are not enough trained personnel who can help victims either in the capital or outlying areas. A U.S. citizen teenager attending a party was raped by four teens in June 2010 in Jutiapa. In August 2010, a U.S. citizen woman was raped on the beach in Monterrico by a person claiming to be hotel security who offered to escort her to her hotel. In March 2011, a U.S. citizen student was accosted by two men on a street in Panajachel and raped by one when she left a bar late in the evening. In August 2011, two U.S. citizen tourists traveling from El Salvador were raped by five armed men when their vehicle was hijacked on the Carretera a El Salvador (CA-2), 16 miles away from Guatemala City.. Arrest and prosecution of assailants in sexual assault cases is uncommon at best and can be more difficult without private legal assistance.

Swimming and Boating Safety and Indigenous Areas: Travelers should be aware that basic safety precautions commonly required in the United States for swimming, boating and other outdoor activities may not be observed in Guatemala. Multiple boaters in the Rio Dulce area of the Department of Izabal have been victimized in violent armed attacks while on their boats. Indigenous activists have taken foreign tourists hostage in the Rio Dulce and Livingston area. Although all hostages have been released unharmed, tensions between indigenous activists and authorities remain. In January 2012, a group of National Geographic explorers, including U.S. citizens, were detained in Quiche by local residents when they jumped into a pond considered sacred in the Mayan tradition. They were released unharmed but the incident serves as a warning to be mindful of local traditional practices when visiting indigenous Mayan communities.

Kidnapping Gangs: who are often connected to narcotraffickers, are a concern in both Guatemala City and rural Guatemala. Gang members are often well armed with sophisticated weaponry and they sometimes use massive amounts of force to extort, kidnap and kill. There have been "express" kidnappings in recent years, primarily in Guatemala City, in which kidnappers demand a relatively small ransom that they believe can be quickly gathered. U.S. citizens, although not specifically targeted, have been kidnap victims. Some kidnapping gangs are known to kill their victims whether or not the ransom is paid. In January 2012, a U.S. citizen was kidnapped in Santa Rosa and was reportedly killed when kidnappers did not get the demanded ransom. In August 2012, kidnappers seized a 17 year old in Chiquimula; the child was returned after the family paid a ransom.

Armed robberies: including those committed during daylight hours, are becoming more common in all areas of the country. Persons carrying laptop computers and expensive cell phones are often targets. Areas that offer wi-fi computer services have been targeted. Several individuals have been killed and their laptops taken upon departure from these establishments after they were seen using their computers in public. Avoid carrying laptop cases or anything that resembles one, even if they do not contain laptops.

Pickpockets: and purse-snatchers are active in all major cities and tourist sites, especially the central market and other parts of Zone 1 in Guatemala City. For security reasons, the Embassy does not allow U.S. government employees to stay in hotels in Zone 1 and urges private travelers to avoid staying in this area. In a common scenario, an accomplice distracts the victim while an assailant slashes or simply steals a bag or backpack. In recent months, U.S. citizens have increasingly reported to the Embassy about armed robberies in Antigua, mostly at night but with some occurring in plain daylight, targeting pedestrians on less frequented roads. The Embassy advises tourists and residents to be very vigilant of their surroundings and report any crime incidents promptly to the police.

Extortion: Simple extortion involves an anonymous phone call threatening harm if money is not sent to the caller. A sophisticated scam involves extortionists calling elderly relatives of a U.S. youth worker in Guatemala and warning them that their relative has been arrested or kidnapped and asking for money to be wired to Guatemala to get him/her released. The elderly relative then becomes alarmed and sends money before the facts are checked.

Report extortions promptly to the police. Do not engage in negotiations with extortionists over the phone. If they persist, consider changing your phone number or temporarily leaving the area.

Use of ATMs: Another popular scam involves various attempts to acquire a victim's ATM card and personal identification number (PIN). Some sophisticated criminals have even placed electronic boxes outside ATM kiosks to record the PIN of unsuspecting victims who believe they must enter their PIN to gain entry to the ATM foyer. After recording the PIN, robbers then steal the owner's ATM card to complete their crimes. There have been a number of incidents in which foreigners have been robbed immediately after making a large withdrawal from local banks. While complicity by bank employees is strongly suspected in these crimes, the police have only arrested credit card forgers.

There are dozens of techniques scammers can use to rob victims of money and possessions. While most people mean no harm, always be cautious when strangers approach you for any reason or make unusual requests. Dozens of victims (mostly foreign tourists) have had their bank accounts emptied remotely from places such as Bogota, Lima, Caracas and the Dominican Republic shortly after using their ATM cards at a slew of banks in Antigua and other places. We strongly encourage persons not to use ATMs and if at all possible to withdraw money from a teller inside a bank with your credit card.

Victims of Crime: If you are the victim of a crime abroad, you should contact the local police and the nearest U.S. embassy or consulate (see the Department of State's list of embassies and consulates). We can:

- Replace a stolen passport.
- For violent crimes such as assault or rape, help you find appropriate medical care.
- Put you in contact with the appropriate police authorities and, if you want us to, we can contact family members or friends.
- Although the local authorities are responsible for investigating and prosecuting the crime, consular officers can help you understand the local criminal justice process and can direct you to local attorneys.
- Victims of crime in Guatemala should contact the following phone numbers for assistance: POLICE: The local equivalent to the "911" emergency line in Guatemala is 110/120
- FIRE DEPARTMENT: 122/123
- TOURIST POLICE: 1500 POLITUR is a joint national police/INGUAT initiative and is present in all major tourist destinations.

Criminal Penalties: While in a foreign country, you are subject to that country's laws and regulations, which sometimes differ significantly from those in the United States and may not afford the protections available to the individual under U.S. law. Penalties for breaking the law can be more severe than in the United States for similar offenses. Engaging in sexual conduct with children or using or disseminating child pornography in a foreign country is a crime, prosecutable in the United States.

Persons violating Guatemalan laws, even unknowingly, may be expelled, arrested, or imprisoned. Penalties for possession, use, or trafficking in illegal drugs in Guatemala are severe, and convicted offenders can expect long jail sentences and heavy fines. Pseudoephedrine is banned in Guatemala since it can be used in the manufacture of methamphetamines. Possession or distribution of drugs containing pseudoephedrine is illegal and can result in arrest of violators.

Arrest notifications in Guatemala: Based on the Vienna Convention on Consular Relations, bilateral agreements with certain countries, and customary international law, if you are arrested in Guatemala, you have the option to request that the police, prison officials, or other authorities alert the U.S. embassy or consulate of your arrest, and to have communications from you forwarded to the nearest U.S. embassy or consulate.

Customs: Guatemalan customs authorities may enforce strict regulations concerning temporary importation into or export from Guatemala of items such as antiquities and other cultural property. You should declare any amount of cash exceeding $10,000 that you bring into the country or the money may be confiscated by the authorities. It is advisable to contact the Embassy of Guatemala in Washington, D.C. or one of Guatemala's consulates in the United States for specific information regarding customs requirements. Enforcement of laws to protect intellectual property rights in Guatemala has been inconsistent. In Guatemala, counterfeit CDs and DVDs are openly sold on the streets of major cities in violation of copyright laws. A number of raids, cases, and prosecutions have been pursued; however, resource constraints and lack of coordinated government action impede efficient enforcement efforts. Piracy of works protected by copyright and infringement of other forms of intellectual property, such as trademarks, remain problematic. Transactions involving such products are illegal and bringing them back to the United States may result in forfeitures and/or fines.

Access for the disabled: Travelers who are disabled and need to use a wheelchair will find access for the disabled limited in Guatemala. Except for major hotels, some government buildings and major museums that have special access ramps for the disabled, most buildings remain wheelchair-inaccessible. Visitors in wheelchairs to Mayan ruins such as Tikal are advised that these sites do not provide special access for the disabled.

Marriage: Non-Guatemalan citizens who wish to marry in Guatemala are required to provide proof of identity and civil status (indicating whether they are single or divorced). Prior notice of the marriage must be given in the Diario de Centro América (Guatemala's Official Record) and any large-circulation daily newspaper for fifteen days. The marriage must take place within six months of the publication of the notice or the publication loses validity and a new one is required with additional expense.

Volcano Hiking: Tourists planning to climb Pacaya and Agua volcanoes during Guatemala's rainy season (May through October) should plan their climb for the morning hours when thunderstorms are less likely to occur. Climbers should monitor the weather situation and return to the base of the volcano as quickly and safely as possible if thunderstorms gather. INGUAT has organized an active community-based tourism program in San Vicente Pacaya to minimize the risk of armed robbery on Pacaya. Climbing volcanoes in groups is still highly advisable to reduce the risk of assault. (Inguat website)

Pacific Beaches: Beware of strong currents, riptides, and undertow along Guatemala's Pacific coast beaches. They pose a serious threat to even the strongest swimmers. In July 2011, a U.S. citizen drowned as a result of the undertow in this area and two U.S. citizens drowned in the same area in February 2012. Signs warning of treacherous surf are rare and confined mostly to private beaches owned by hotels. Lifeguards are rarely present on beaches.

Earthquakes: Guatemala is a geologically active country. Visitors should be aware of the possibility of earthquakes at any time and the need for contingency plans. There are also four active volcanoes. Volcanic activity has on occasion forced evacuations of nearby villages. In September 2012, increased activity of Volcan Fuego caused the evacuation of several villages. The May 2010 eruption of Pacaya Volcano near Guatemala City briefly closed Guatemala City's international airport. Both the Caribbean and Pacific coasts of Guatemala are vulnerable to hurricanes and tropical storms from mid-May through November. Mudslides and flooding during the May to November rainy season often kill dozens of people and close roads. General information about natural disaster preparedness is available locally from the National Disaster Reduction Coordination Office (CONRED) and from the U.S. Federal Emergency Management Agency (FEMA). Please consult CONRED for updates on natural disasters or tropical storms and hurricanes.

Grandparent Scams: Scams targeting grandparents which involve claims that their grandchildren have been arrested are an increasingly common occurrence in Guatemala. Typically the caller will claim that the grandchild has been arrested in Guatemala and urgently needs bail money (about $2,000). Before you send any money, please contact your grandchild (who most likely is not in Guatemala and never has been) or the child's parents to make sure you are not being scammed. If in doubt, call the U.S. Embassy at 011-(502) 2326–4501. Do not call the number the callers give you, as it will only help them reinforce the scam by having fictitious embassy officials answer the phone.

Medical Facilities and Health Information: The full range of medical care is available in Guatemala City, but medical care outside the city is limited. Guatemala's public hospitals frequently experience serious shortages of basic medicines and equipment. Care in private hospitals is generally adequate for most common illnesses and injuries, and many of the medical specialists working in them are U.S.-trained and -certified.

The U.S. Department of State is unaware of any HIV/AIDS entry restrictions for visitors to or foreign residents of Guatemala.

Information on vaccinations and other health precautions, such as safe food and water precautions and insect bite protection, may be obtained from the Centers for Disease Control and Prevention's (CDC) hotline for international travelers at 1-877-FYI-TRIP (1-877-394-8747) or via the CDC website. For information about outbreaks of infectious diseases abroad, consult the infectious diseases section of the World Health Organization (WHO) website. The WHO website also contains additional health information for travelers, including detailed country-specific health information.

Medical Insurance: You can't assume your insurance will go with you when you travel. It's very important to find out BEFORE you leave whether or not your medical insurance will cover you overseas. You need to ask your insurance company two questions:

- Does my policy apply when I am out of the United States?
- Will it cover emergencies like a trip to a foreign hospital or a medical evacuation?

The Department of State strongly urges U.S. citizens to consult their medical insurance company prior to traveling abroad to determine whether the policy applies overseas and whether it covers emergency expenses such as a medical evacuation. Many hospitals in Guatemala require payment prior to treating patients, even if personal insurance will cover the treatment. They do not typically enter into payment plan agreements. Travelers should be aware that they may have to pay in advance and seek reimbursement.

Traffic Safety Road Conditions: While in a foreign country, U.S. citizens may encounter road conditions that differ significantly from those in the United States. The information below concerning Guatemala is provided for general reference only, and may not apply to all locations or circumstances.

Driving in Guatemala requires one's full attention, and safe drivers must take extraordinary efforts to drive defensively to avoid dangerous situations. Traffic rules are only casually observed. Many drivers do not use their turn signals to alert other drivers. Instead, a common custom is for a driver or passenger to stick a hand out the window and wave it to indicate that they will be taking an unspecified action. Speed limits, lane markings, and stop signs are frequently ignored. Passing blindly on winding and/or steep mountain roads, poorly designed surfaces, and unmarked hazards, including frequent landslides and precarious temporary highway repairs, present additional risks to motorists. Lethal head-on collisions are common.

All drivers involved in accidents resulting in injury may be detained and held in protective custody pending investigation. In several instances, police officers have been posted outside hospital rooms of drivers who were injured and they were not allowed to depart the country without judicial intervention. Such cases require the assistance of private local attorneys.

Common public transportation is by local brightly-painted recycled school buses, which serve almost every town in the country. Criminal activity and frequent fatal accidents, however, make the low-priced inter-city buses particularly dangerous. Modern inter-city buses offer some security from highway violence, but armed attacks are increasing, indicating that all buses are vulnerable. (See additional information in the CRIME section.)

Although city streets are lit, secondary and rural roads have little to no illumination. Driving outside of urban areas at night is dangerous and not recommended. The Inter-American Highway (CA-1) and the road from Guatemala City to the Caribbean coast (CA-9) are especially dangerous due to heavy traffic, including large trucks and trailers. There are no roadside assistance clubs; however, a roadside assistance force (PROVIAL) patrols most of the major highways in the country. PROVIAL can be contacted by calling 2419–2121. Their vehicles are equipped with basic tools and first aid supplies, and their services are free. Police patrol the major roadways and may assist travelers, but the patrols are sporadic and may be suspended due to budget constraints. For roadside assistance, travelers may call the police by dialing 110 or 120 or the fire department by dialing 122 or 123. Cellular telephone service covers most areas frequented by tourists. Cars and trucks are often stalled or parked in the middle of the road. Tree branches are sometimes placed in the road a hundred meters or so before the stalled vehicle to warn approaching traffic of the hazard. While driving in or near large cities, be vigilant of pedestrians who unexpectedly dart across roads, even in heavy traffic due to the lack of cross walks.

Valid U.S. driver's licenses are accepted for the first 30 days of a visit, and international driving permits are accepted in Guatemala for extended stays. Guatemala's road safety authorities are the Department of Transit and the Joint Operations Center of the National Police. Drivers use the right-hand side of the road in Guatemala, and speed limits are posted (in kilometers) depending on the condition of the road. Speed limits are rarely enforced, and drivers often drive at the absolute maximum speed their vehicle can handle at that particular time. These drivers share the road with slow vehicles, some barely able to manage 20 miles per hour, creating a hazardous mix of velocities. Turning right on red is not permitted unless otherwise posted, and drivers must yield when entering a traffic circle. Seat belts must be worn in Guatemala, but there are no laws regarding the use of child safety seats. It is against the law for drivers to operate cellular phones while driving but cell phone usage while driving remains commonplace. People found driving under the influence of alcohol or other drugs are arrested and may serve jail time. For accidents resulting in death, every driver involved is taken into custody and the vehicle(s) impounded until a judge determines responsibility following a re-enactment of the accident. For accidents resulting in injury, the non-injured party may be taken into custody until a judge determines fault and financial responsibility.

In April 2009, Guatemala passed a new transportation law primarily aimed to limit the number of individuals on motorcycles and mopeds. Under this new law, motorcycles and mopeds may carry only one person, the driver. In addition, motorcycle and moped drivers must wear a helmet and a vest. The helmet and vest must each have a reflective band that displays the motorcycle or moped's license plate number to be visible from five meters away. The law is applicable in Guatemala City and the seven municipalities of the Department of Guatemala: Villa Nueva, Villa Canales, Mixco, Chinautla, Santa Catarina Pinula, San José Pinula, and San Miguel Petapa. It does not provide exceptions to tourists and non-residents. All individuals are subject to the law and non-compliance could result in fines ranging from approximately $65 to $3,125. The law also has provisions limiting the number of passengers in any vehicle to the number stated in the vehicle's registration papers. Bicycles may only carry one passenger unless designed for more. Also, we suggest that you visit the website of the Guatemala's national tourist office and national authority responsible for road safety or contact them via e-mail.

Aviation Safety Oversight: The U.S. Federal Aviation Administration (FAA) has assessed the Government of Guatemala's Civil Aviation Authority as being in compliance with International Civil Aviation Organization (ICAO) aviation safety standards for oversight of Guatemala's air carrier operations. Further information may be found on the FAA's safety assessment page. In August 2008, seven U.S. citizen tourists died in a charter aircraft accident due to engine failure, caused by improper maintenance procedures which led to excessive high combustion temperatures and turbine blade fracture. In May 2010, a private aircraft crashed in adverse weather conditions in Zone 3 of Guatemala City, killing a U.S. citizen pilot and three passengers. The cause of the crash was attributed to failure of the altimeter due to poor maintenance. In January 2011, a private aircraft carrying two U.S. citizens crashed while attempting to land at an airstrip in Panajachel, killing the pilot.

Children's Issues: Guatemala is a signatory of the Hague Convention on Child Abduction. For information see the U.S. Dept. of State Office of Children's Issues web pages on intercountry adoption and international parental child abduction.

Intercountry Adoption

January 2013

The information in this section has been edited from the latest report of the State Department Bureau of Consular Affairs, Office of Overseas Citizens Services. For more information, please read the *Intercountry Adoption* section of this book and review current reports online at http://adoption.state.gov.

Guatemala is party to the Hague Convention on Protection of Children and Co-operation in Respect of Intercountry Adoption(Hague Adoption Convention). Intercountry adoption processing in Hague countries is done in accordance with the requirements of the Convention; the U.S. implementing legislation, the Intercountry Adoption Act of 2000 (IAA); and the IAA's implementing regulations, as well as the implementing legislation and regulations of the child's country of origin.

The Department of State has determined that Guatemala has not yet fully implemented legislation that would create a Convention-compliant adoption process. U.S. Citizenship and Immigration Services (USCIS) is therefore unable to approve any Form I-800 petition filed on behalf of a Guatemalan child because the Department of State is unable to verify that the requirements of the Hague Adoption Convention have been met in cases from Guatemala, per Section 301(a) of the Intercountry Adoption Act (IAA). The only intercountry adoption cases that USCIS and the U.S. Embassy in Guatemala are currently processing are cases that were filed before December 31, 2007, and were not completed when Guatemala joined the Convention and implemented its new adoption code.

The Guatemalan National Adoption Council (CNA) announced in September 2008 that it would not accept any new adoption cases at that time in order for the CNA to work on establishing guidelines to use in accrediting adoption agencies and to focus on completing transition cases. More information about the CNA's September 2008 decision may be found on its website, cna.gob.gt.

In August 2011, the CNA announced a plan, referred to as the "Acuerdo," which provides a general processing framework for a limited group of pending adoption cases already under CNA processing authority. This process applies only to cases pending with the CNA and not to cases pending with the Procuraduría General de la Nación (PGN) as "notario" cases. In December 2011, the CNA confirmed the details of the processing plan for a limited group of pending adoption cases already under CNA processing authority filed before December 31, 2007. Since January 2012, the CNA has referred17 cases to the U.S. Embassy for final adoption processing as acuerdo cases, and has identified others that it considered eligible to move through the acuerdo process.

U.S. Embassy in Guatemala
Avenida Reforma 7-01, Zona 10
Guatemala City, Guatemala
Fax: 011-502-2326-4674
Email: adoptguatemala@state.gov
http://guatemala.usembassy.gov

Guatemalan Central Authority
National Council on Adoption (CNA)
Tel: 011-502-23390825/26
Fax: 011-502-23390835
Email: cna@cna.gob.gt
Website: http://www.cna.gob.gt

Embassy of Guatemala
2220 R Street, N.W.
Washington, DC. 20008
Tel: (202) 745-4952
Fax: (202) 745-1908
consul@guatemala-embassy.org

Office of Children's Issues
U.S. Department of State
2201 C Street, NW
SA-29
Washington, DC 20520
Tel: 1-888-407-4747
E-mail: AskCI@state.gov
http://adoption.state.gov

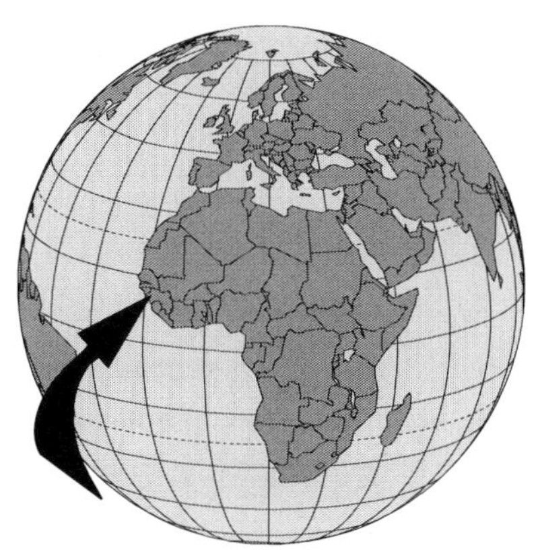

GUINEA

Compiled from publications that were available as of February 2013 from the U.S. Department of State, the U.S. Department of Commerce, and the Central Intelligence Agency (CIA). See the introduction to this set for explanatory notes.

Official Name:
Republic of Guinea (République de Guinée)

PROFILE

Geography

Area: total: 245,857 sq km; country comparison to the world: 79; land: 245,717 sq km; water: 140 sq km

Major cities: Conakry (capital) 1.597 million (2009)

Climate: generally hot and humid; monsoonal-type rainy season (June to November) with southwesterly winds; dry season (December to May) with northeasterly harmattan winds

Terrain: generally flat coastal plain, hilly to mountainous interior

People

Nationality: noun: Guinean(s); adjective: Guinean

Population: 10,884,958 (July 2012 est.)

Population growth rate: 2.641% (2012 est.)

Ethnic groups: Peuhl 40%, Malinke 30%, Soussou 20%, smaller ethnic groups 10%

Religions: Muslim 85%, Christian 8%, indigenous beliefs 7%

Languages: French (official)

Literacy: definition: age 15 and over can read and write; total population: 41%; male: 52%; female: 30% (2010 est.)

Health: life expectancy at birth: total population: 58.61 years; male: 57.12 years; female: 60.15 years (2012 est.); Infant mortality rate: total: 59.04 deaths/1,000 live births; male: 62.18 deaths/1,000 live births; female: 55.81 deaths/1,000 live births (2012 est.)

Unemployment rate: NA%

Work force: 4.778 million (2012 est.)

Government

Type: republic

Independence: 2 October 1958

Constitution: 7 May 2010 (Loi Fundamentale)

Political subdivisions: 33 prefectures and 1 special zone (zone special)

Suffrage: 18 years of age; universal

Economy

GDP (purchasing power parity): $12.25 billion (2012 est.); $11.61 billion (2011 est.); $11.21 billion (2010 est.); $11 billion (2009 est.)

GDP real growth rate: 4.8% (2012 est.); 3.6% (2011 est.); 1.9% (2010 est.); -0.3% (2009 est.)

GDP per capita (PPP): $1,100 (2012 est.); $1,100 (2011 est.); $1,100 (2010 est.); $1,100 (2009 est.)

Natural resources: bauxite, iron ore, diamonds, gold, uranium, hydropower, fish, salt

Agriculture products: rice, coffee, pineapples, palm kernels, cassava (manioc), bananas, sweet potatoes; cattle, sheep, goats; timber

Industries: bauxite, gold, diamonds, iron; alumina refining; light manufacturing, and agricultural processing

Exports: $1.785 billion (2012 est.); $1.615 billion (2011 est.); $1.471 billion (2010 est.)

Exports—commodities: bauxite, alumina, gold, diamonds, coffee, fish, agricultural products

Exports—partners: Chile 24.4%, Spain 9.1%, India 7.9%, Russia 7.4%, Germany 5.1%, Ireland 5%, US 4.9%, Ukraine 4.4% (2011)

Imports: $2.708 billion (2012 est.); $1.761 billion (2011 est.); $1.405 billion (2010 est.)

Imports—commodities: petroleum products, metals, machinery, transport equipment, textiles, grain and other foodstuffs

Imports—partners: China 13.4%, Netherlands 8.2%, US 5.4%, France 4% (2011)

Debt—external: $2.652 billion (31 December 2012 est.); $3.034 billion (31 December 2011 est.); $2.923 billion (31 December 2010 est.)

Exchange rates: Guinean francs (GNF) per US dollar; 7,100 (2012 est.); 6,658 (2011 est.); 5,726.1 (2010 est.); 5,500 (2009); 5,500 (2008); 4,122.8 (2007)

GEOGRAPHY

Guinea is located on the Atlantic Coast of West Africa and is bordered by Guinea-Bissau, Senegal, Mali, Cote d'Ivoire, Liberia, and Sierra Leone. The country is divided into four geographic regions: a narrow coastal belt (Lower Guinea); the pastoral Fouta Djallon highlands (Middle Guinea); the northern savannah (Upper Guinea); and a southeastern rainforest region (Forest Guinea). The Niger, Gambia, and Senegal Rivers are among the 22 West African rivers that have their origins in Guinea.

The coastal region of Guinea and most of the inland have a tropical climate, with a rainy season lasting from April to November, relatively high and uniform temperatures, and high humidity. Conakry's year-round average high is 29oC (85oF), and the low is 23oC (74oF); its average annual rainfall is 430 centimeters (169 inches). Sahelian Upper Guinea has a shorter rainy season and greater daily temperature variations.

PEOPLE

Guinea has four main ethnic groups: Peuhl (Foula or Foulani), who inhabit the mountainous Fouta Djallon; Malinke (or Mandingo), in the savannah and forest regions; Soussous in the coastal areas; and several other ethnic groups (Gerze, Toma, etc.) in the forest region.

Other West Africans make up the largest non-Guinean population. Non-Africans total about 10,000 (mostly Lebanese, French, and other Europeans).

Language

French is the official language of government, education, and business. Local languages (Soussou, Peular, Malinké, etc) are also widely spoken, particularly outside of Conakry. Major written languages are French and Arabic.

Religion

Approximately 85 percent of the population is Muslim, 10 percent is Christian, and 5 percent holds indigenous religious beliefs, although much of the population incorporates some indigenous beliefs and rituals into their religious practices. Muslims are generally Sunni, although the few Shia are increasing in number. Christian groups include Roman Catholics, Anglicans, Baptists, Jehovah's Witnesses, Seventh-day Adventists, and several evangelical groups. There is a small Baha'i community. There are also small numbers of Hindus, Buddhists, and practitioners of traditional Chinese religious beliefs among foreign residents.

Muslims constitute a majority in all four major regions. Christians are most numerous in Conakry, large cities, the south, and the eastern Forest Region. Indigenous religious beliefs are most prevalent in the Forest Region.

Participation in formal religious services and rituals is high as a result of the close ties between cultural rituals and religious practices.

HISTORY

The area occupied by Guinea today was included in several large West African political groupings, including the Ghana, Mali, and Songhai empires, at various times from the 10th to the 15th century, when the region came into contact with European commerce. Guinea's colonial period began with French military penetration into the area in the mid-19th century. French domination was assured by the defeat in 1898 of the armies of Almamy Samory Toure, warlord and leader of Malinke descent, which gave France control of what today is Guinea and adjacent areas.

France negotiated Guinea's present boundaries in the late 19th and early 20th centuries with the British for Sierra Leone, the Portuguese for their Guinea colony (now Guinea-Bissau), and Liberia. Under the French, the country formed the Territory of Guinea within French West Africa, administered by a governor general resident in Dakar. Lieutenant governors administered the individual colonies, including Guinea.

Led by Ahmed Sekou Toure, head of the Democratic Party of Guinea (PDG), which won 56 of 60 seats in 1957 territorial elections, the people of Guinea in a September 1958 plebiscite overwhelmingly rejected membership in the proposed French Community. The French withdrew quickly, and on October 2, 1958, Guinea proclaimed itself a sovereign and independent republic, with Sekou Toure as President. Under Toure, Guinea became a one-party dictatorship, with a closed, socialized economy and no tolerance for human rights, free expression, or political opposition, which was ruthlessly suppressed. Originally credited for his advocacy of cross-ethnic nationalism, Toure gradually came to rely on his own Malinke ethnic group to fill positions in the party and government. Alleging plots and conspiracies against him at home and abroad, Toure's regime targeted real and imagined opponents, imprisoning many thousands in Soviet-style prison gulags, where many perished. The regime's repression drove more than a million Guineans into exile, and Toure's paranoia ruined relations with foreign nations, including neighboring African states, increasing Guinea's isolation and further devastating its economy.

Sekou Toure and the PDG remained in power until his death on April 3, 1984. A military junta—the Military Committee of National Recovery (CMRN)—headed by then-Lt. Col. Lansana Conte, seized power just 1 week after the death of Sekou Toure. The CMRN immediately abolished the constitution, the sole political party (PDG) and its mass youth and women's organizations, and announced the establishment of the Second Republic. In lieu of a constitution, the government was initially based on ordinances, decrees, and decisions issued by the president and various ministers.

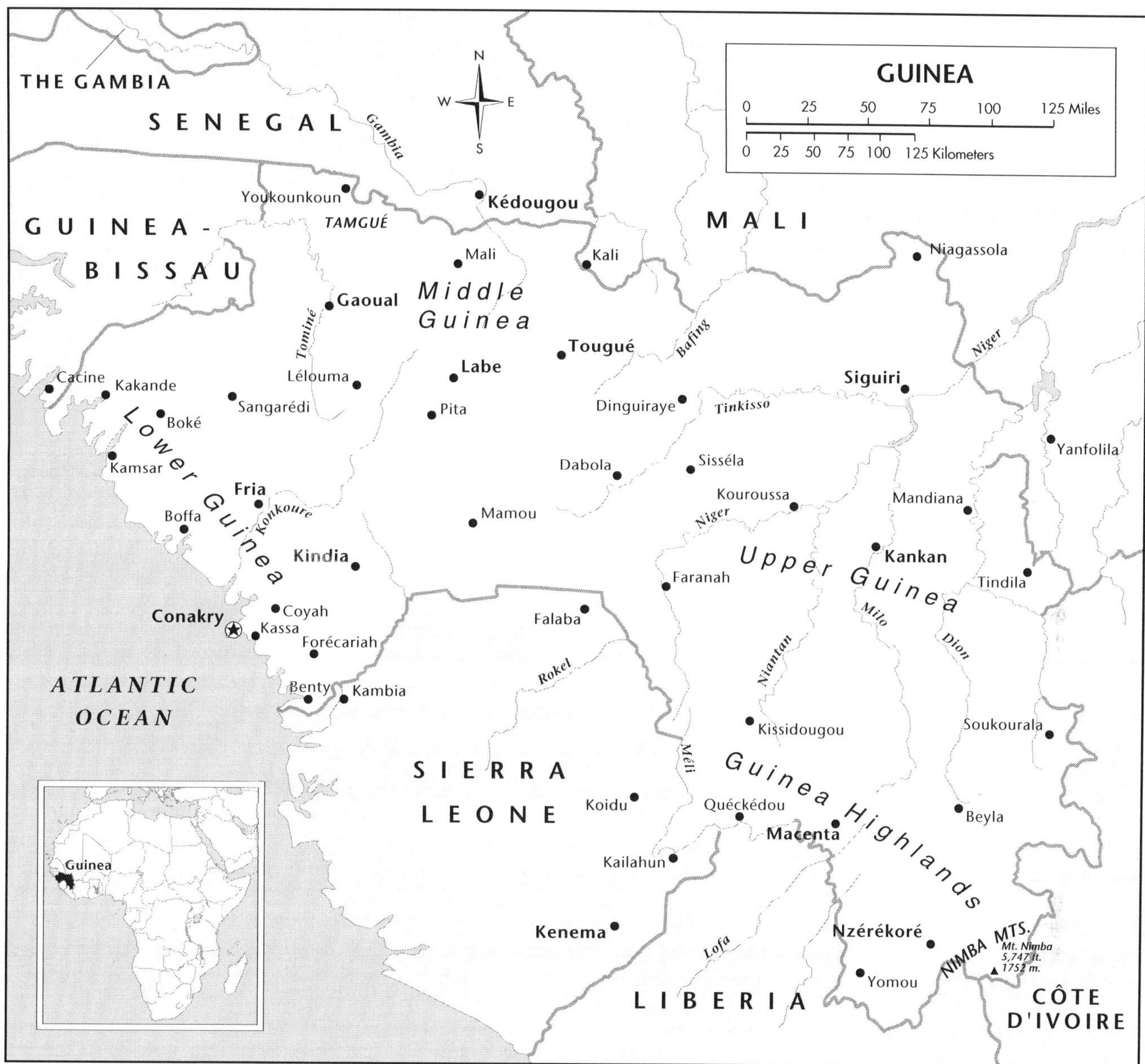

Political parties were proscribed. The new government also released all prisoners and declared the protection of human rights as one of its primary objectives. It reorganized the judicial system and decentralized the administration. The CMRN also announced its intention to liberalize the economy, promote private enterprise, and encourage foreign investment in order to develop the country's rich natural resources.

The CMRN formed a transitional parliament, the "Transitional Council for National Recovery" (CTRN), which created a new constitution (La Loi Fundamental) and Supreme Court in 1990. The country's first multi-party presidential election took place in 1993. These elections were marred by irregularities and lack of transparency on the part of the government. Legislative and municipal elections were held in 1995. Conte's ruling Party for Unity and Progress (PUP) won 76 of 114 seats in the National Assembly, amid opposition claims of irregularities and government tampering. The new National Assembly held its first session in October 1995.

Several thousand malcontent troops mutinied in Conakry in February 1996, destroying the presidential offices and killing several dozen civilians. Mid-level officers attempted, unsuccessfully, to turn the rebellion into a coup d'etat. The Government of Guinea made hundreds of arrests in connection to the mutiny, and put 98 soldiers and civilians on trial in 1998. A number of them were executed.

In December 1998, Conte was reelected to another 5-year term in a flawed election that was, nevertheless, an improvement over 1993. Following his reelection and the improvement of economic conditions through 1999, Conte reversed direction, making wholesale and regressive changes to his cabinet. He replaced many technocrats and members of the Guinean diaspora that had previously held important positions with "homegrown" ministers, particularly from his own Soussou ethnic group. These changes led to increased cronyism, corruption, and a retrenchment on economic and political reforms.

Despite his failing health, in December 2003, President Conte easily won a third presidential term against a single, relatively unknown candidate after the opposition parties boycotted the elections. Conte insisted in a late 2006 interview that regardless of his health he would remain in office until his term ended in 2010. In 2006 and 2007, Guinea's labor union alliance launched a series of historic, increasingly violent labor strikes. Whereas the unions' demands during the March and June 2006 strikes were primarily economic, the January 2007 strike was more political. Security forces were responsible for the deaths of several protesters in June 2006. The 2007 strike also turned violent after President Conte ignored the unions' demand that he resign from office. Nationwide, protesters began barricading roads, throwing rocks, burning tires, and skirmishing with police. Violence peaked on January 22 when several thousand ordinary Guineans poured into the streets, primarily in the capital, calling for change. Guinean security forces and the military's "red beret" presidential guard reacted by opening fire on the peaceful crowds.

On January 27, 2007, unions, employers associations, and the government entered a tripartite agreement to suspend the strike. President Conte agreed to name a new "consensus" prime minister, with delegated executive powers. For the first time, the new prime minister of Guinea would carry the title of "head of government" and exercise certain powers previously held by the president of the republic. However, President Conte's February 9 appointment of a longtime associate, Eugene Camara, as Guinea's new prime minister sparked another wave of violence and protests. In an attempt to quell the violence, on February 12 President Conte declared a "state of siege," which conferred broad powers on the military, and implemented a strict curfew. According to media reports, the following days saw military and police forces scour Conakry and towns in the hinterlands where they committed serious human rights abuses.

When Guinea's National Assembly rejected Conte's effort to extend the "state of siege," it became clear that the popular protests had widespread support, even among leaders of Conte's own ruling party. Soon after, an Economic Community of West African States (ECOWAS) delegation led by former Nigerian President Babangida announced that President Conte had agreed to name a new "consensus" prime minister in consultations with the unions and civil society. Lansana Kouyate arrived in Conakry on February 27, 2007, just hours after being announced as the new Prime Minister and head of the government. Security forces are believed responsible for having killed at least 137 people and injuring more than 1,700 others during the strike-related violence in January and February 2007.

During his premiership, Kouyate faced constant speculation that the president and his associates opposed his reform efforts. His failure to alleviate social and economic conditions contributed to the steady decline of his popularity. In May 2008, President Conte replaced Kouyate with Ahmed Tidiane Souare, a former minister of mines from a previous cabinet. The Souare administration quickly began to reinstate presidential loyalists. President Conte's death on December 22, 2008 sparked an immediate coup d'etat by elements of the military.

Captain Moussa Dadis Camara seized power on December 23, 2008, declaring himself President of the Republic and suspending the constitution, but promising elections and an eventual restoration of civilian authority. By August 2009, it was increasingly clear that Camara intended to run for president. In response, Guinea's opposition coalition, Les Forces Vives, organized a protest on September 28, 2009, which attracted tens of thousands of protesters to the national stadium in Conakry. The Guinean military responded by opening fire on the crowd, killing at least 157 protesters, wounding more than a 1,000 others, and sexually assaulting more than 100 women, triggering widespread condemnation from the international community and increasing isolation for the junta. On December 3, 2009, Camara was wounded by his aide-de-camp in a failed assassination attempt and evacuated to Morocco for medical treatment. National Council for Democracy and Development (CNDD) Minister of Defense Brigadier General Sekouba Konate stepped in as interim President of the Republic. Camara's wounds were not fatal, but necessitated a prolonged period of rehabilitation.

Camara was flown to Ouagadougou in January 2010, at the invitation of Burkinabe President Blaise Compaore, the ECOWAS-appointed mediator to the Guinean political crisis. Compaore helped broker a deal between Camara and Konate, known as the January 15 Ouagadougou Accords, in which Camara agreed to remain outside of Guinea for an extended recuperation and to officially appoint General Konate as the interim President of the Republic. Konate appointed former speaker for Les Forces Vives, Jean Marie Dore, as Prime Minister. In February, Dore formed a government that included 11 ministers from political parties, 11 from civil society, and 11 from the junta government. In addition, a National Transition Council (CNT) consisting of 150 members from civil society, labor unions, political parties, the private sector, security forces, and other important organizations, was formed to act as the legislative body until legislative elections could be held. The CNT rewrote and enacted the constitution in March. It also enacted new electoral and media codes.

On June 27, Guinea had its first round of presidential elections, with 24 candidates running for the office of President. As per the Ouagadougou

Accords, no member of the military or the transition government ran in the elections. International and national observer groups declared the elections credible and fair, though they cited major technical problems that needed to be addressed before the second round could credibly take place. Cellou Dalein Diallo of the Union of Democratic Forces of Guinea (UFDG) party received 43% of the vote; Alpha Conde of the Rally for the Guinean People (RPG) party received 18%; and Sidya Toure of the Union of Republican Forces (UFR) party received 13%. Diallo and Conde went on to compete in the second round of elections that, after several delays, took place on November 7. In the weeks leading up to and immediately after the elections, ethnic violence broke out between the Peuhl and Malinke support bases of the two candidates, resulting in several hundred internally displaced people and at least a dozen deaths. The transition government imposed a state of emergency and imposed a curfew, which successfully stopped the violence.

On December 2, the Guinean Supreme Court determined Alpha Conde the winner of the elections with 53% of the vote, which was declared free and credible by international observer missions. On December 3, Cellou Diallo publicly accepted the results of the election and called for his supporters to support the newly elected president. President Conde was peacefully inaugurated on December 21, 2010. On December 24, Mohamed Said Fofana, an economist, was appointed as Guinea's Prime Minister.

After inauguration, the government lifted security checkpoints throughout the country. Following a July 19, 2011 attack on the president's personal residence, the government temporarily reinstated the checkpoints, citing security concerns. By the end of July the checkpoints were reduced to operating during the hours of 11:00 p.m. to 6:00 a.m.

Although legislative elections were mandated to take place 6 months after the completion of presidential elections, as of November 2011 legislative elections had not yet been held. The Independent National Commission for Elections announced that elections would take place on December 29, 2011, but election experts and outside observers stated that the commission's timeline was unrealistic and elections would not take place in 2011.

GOVERNMENT AND POLITICAL CONDITIONS

Guinea is a republic. In December 2010 Alpha Conde, the candidate of the Rally of the Guinean People (RPG) Party and longtime opposition leader, was inaugurated as the country's first democratically elected president since independence from France in 1958. Conde defeated Cellou Dalein Diallo of the Union of Democratic Forces of Guinea (UFDG). While the elections generally were regarded as free and fair, the second round was accompanied by widespread violence. Prior to Conde's inauguration, Guinea was headed by a transition government led by former interim president General Sekouba Konate, the defense minister in the military junta that seized control of the country in 2008.

Recent Elections

In June 2010 UFDG candidate Cellou Diallo and RPG candidate Alpha Conde emerged as the front-runners in the first round of presidential elections, which international observers characterized as credible and free. The second round of presidential elections, originally scheduled for September 2010, was repeatedly postponed until November 2010 due to a dispute over alleged bias in the Independent National Electoral Commission (CENI) leadership and inadequate preparation for the elections. Widespread violence occurred in the months leading up to the November 2010 election and for several weeks afterward.

The violence was largely drawn along ethnic lines between Diallo's Peuhl supporters and Conde's supporters—mostly Malinke, Soussou, and Forestier residents of the Forest Region. Numerous deaths, injuries, and the displacement of thousands of ethnic Peuhl resulted from beatings, shootings, and the vandalizing of homes by mobs. While security forces sought to quell the violence, there were some reports that FOSSEPEL officers—who generally supported the RPG—targeted individuals on the basis of their ethnicity.

Before election results were announced, Diallo declared that he would not accept the outcome of the vote due to interethnic clashes that left some of his supporters unable to vote. CENI subsequently announced the provisional results of the election, which gave Alpha Conde the victory with 52.52 percent of the vote. Despite the violence, international observers characterized the election as generally free and fair. Diallo challenged the results in the Supreme Court, and two days of violence between UFDG and RPG supporters ensued. In early December 2010 the Supreme Court validated the election results.

Despite the constitutional provision that legislative elections be held no longer than 14 days after presidential elections, they still had not been held by year's end. Legislative elections scheduled for December 29 were postponed until 2013.

Political Parties: There were no government restrictions on political party formation beyond registration requirements. According to the Ministry of Territorial Affairs and Decentralization, there were 140 registered political parties.

On February 12, the minister of youth threatened members of the civil service with lay-offs if they supported opposition candidates during the legislative elections. Two days later he retracted his remarks.

Opposition parties questioned the legitimacy of the planned legislative elections, noting that the government was proceeding with unilateral preparations that lacked transparency.

Opposition access to state media was limited or nonexistent throughout the year, although private media criticized the government's election preparations without restriction. These concerns led to the opposition call for nationwide street protests on September 27 and 28 (see section 1.a.).

Participation of Women and Minorities: There were 36 women in the 155-seat CNT, including the CNT president. Six of 38 cabinet ministers were women, and there were two female justices out of 14 on the Supreme Court. Minority ethnic groups were represented in CENI, the CNT, and the cabinet.

Although the law states that all persons are equal before the law regardless of gender, race, ethnicity, language, beliefs, political opinions, philosophy, or creed, the government did not enforce these provisions uniformly.

Principal Government Officials

Last Updated: 1/31/2013

Pres.: **Alpha CONDE**
Prime Min.: **Mohamed Said FOFANA**
Min. of Agriculture: **Emile YOMBOUNO**
Min. of Audit, Economic, & Financial Controls: **Aboubacar Sidiki KOULIBALY**
Min. of Commerce: **Mohamed Dorval DOUMBOUYA**
Min. of Communication: **Togba Cesaire KPOGHOMOU**
Min. of Culture & Heritage: **Ahmed Tidiane CISSE**
Min. of Defense: **Alpha CONDE**
Min. of Economy & Finance: **Kerfalla YANSANE**
Min. of Employment, Technical Education, & Vocational Training Damantan: **Albert CAMARA**
Min. of Energy: **Papa Koly KOUROUMA**
Min. of Environment, Waters, & Forests: **Saramady TOURE**
Min. of Fisheries & Aquaculture: **Moussa CONDE**
Min. of Foreign Affairs & Guineans Abroad: **Francois Lonseny FALL**
Min. of Health & Public Hygiene: **Edouard Gnankoye LAMA, Dr.**
Min. of Higher Education & Scientific Research: **Teliwel Bailo DIALLO**
Min. of Hotel Management, Tourism, & the Arts: **Mariame BALDE**
Min. of Human Rights & Public Liberties: **Kalifa Gassama DIABY**
Min. of Industry & Small & Medium Enterprises: **Ramatoulaye BAH**
Min. of Information: **Dirus Diale DORE**
Min. of Intl. Cooperation: **Koutoubou Moustapha SANO**
Min. of Justice & Keeper of the Seals: **Me Christian SOW**
Min. of Labor & Public Service: **Fatoumata TOUNKARA**
Min. of Literacy & the Promotion of National Languages: **Bamba CAMARA**
Min. of Livestock
Min. of Mines & Geology: **Mohamed Lamine FOFANA**
Min. of Planning: **Sekou TRAORE**
Min. of Pre-University Education: **Ibrahima KOUROUMA**
Min. of Public Works & Transportation: **Ousmane BAH**
Min. of Security, Civil Protection, & Reform of Security Services: **Mouramani CISSE**
Min. of Social Affairs & Female Promotion: **Diaka DIAKITE**
Min. of Sports: **Aboubacar Sidiki CAMARA**
Min. of Territorial Admin. & Decentralization: **Alhassane CONDE**
Min. of Urbanism, Habitat, & Construction: **Ibrahima BANGOURA**
Min. of Youth & Youth Employment: **Sanoussy Gbatama SOW**
Governor, Central Bank: **Louceny NABE**
Ambassador to the US: **Blaise CHERIF**
Permanent Representative to the UN, New York: **Mamadi TOURE**

ECONOMY

Guinea is a poor country that possesses major mineral, hydropower, and agricultural resources. The country has almost half of the world's bauxite reserves and significant iron ore, gold, and diamond reserves. However, Guinea has been unable to profit from this potential, as rampant corruption, dilapidated infrastructure, and political uncertainty have drained investor confidence.

In the time since a 2008 coup following the death of long-term President Lansana Conte, international donors, including the G-8, the IMF, and the World Bank, have significantly curtailed their development programs.

Throughout 2009, policies of the ruling military junta severely weakened the economy. The junta leaders spent and printed money at an accelerating rate, driving inflation and debt to perilously high levels. In early 2010, the junta collapsed and was replaced by a Transition Government, which ceded power in December 2010 to the country's first-ever democratically elected president, Alpha Conde. International assistance and investment are expected to return to Guinea, but the levels will depend upon the ability of the new government to combat corruption, reform its banking system, improve its business environment, and build infrastructure. IMF and World Bank programs will be especially critical as Guinea attempts to gain debt relief.

International investors have expressed keen interest in Guinea's vast iron ore reserves, which could further propel the country's growth. The government put forward a new mining code in September 2011 that includes provisions to combat corruption, protect the environment, and review all existing mining contracts. Longer range plans to deploy broadband Internet throughout the country could spur economic growth as well.

Labor Conditions

The law prohibits all forms of child labor and sets forth penalties of three to 10 years' imprisonment, and disgorgement of resulting profits, for violations.

The minimum age for employment is 16 years, although children may begin to work at 12 years of age as apprentices for light work in such sectors as domestic service and agriculture, and at 14 years of age for other work. Workers and apprentices under the age of 18 are not permitted to work at night, more than 10 consecutive hours, more than 12 consecutive days, or on Sundays. The Ministry of Labor maintained a list of occupations in which women and youth under the age of 18 cannot be employed, but enforcement was limited to large firms in the modern sector of the economy.

Child labor by boys occurred most frequently in the informal sectors of subsistence farming, small-scale commerce, and mining. Child labor by girls most often involved commercial sexual exploitation and put them at risk for face beatings, sexual harassment, and rape. Family members or employers forced some children to prostitute themselves to earn enough money to survive. The government did not take action when prostitution of minors was brought to its attention, and it did not monitor child or adult prostitution.

Many children between the ages of five and 16 worked 10 to 15 hours a day in the diamond and gold mines for minimal compensation and little food. Child laborers extracted, transported, and cleaned the minerals. They operated in extreme conditions, lacked protective gear, did not have access to water or electricity, and faced a constant threat of disease and sickness. A 2006 study by the NGO AGRAAD reported that 45 percent of workers at the Dandano gold mine were children, approximately 30 percent of whom were working with an adult relative in the mine. Children also worked in granite and gravel pits.

Although the labor code allows the government to set a minimum hourly wage enforced by the Ministry of Labor, the government has neither exercised this provision nor promoted a standard wage. Prevailing wages routinely did not provide a decent standard of living for a worker and family.

The law mandates that regular work should not exceed 10-hour days or 48-hour weeks, and it mandates a period of at least 24 consecutive hours of rest each week, usually on Sunday. Every salaried worker has the legal right to an annual paid vacation, accumulated at the rate of at least two workdays per month of work. There also are provisions in the law for overtime and night wages, which are fixed percentages of the regular wage. In practice, authorities rarely monitored work practices or enforced these rules. The law provides for a maximum of 100 hours of compulsory overtime a year.

In practice, teachers' wages were extremely low, and teachers sometimes went six months or more without pay. Salary arrears were not paid, and some teachers lived in abject poverty.

U.S.-GUINEAN RELATIONS

The United States maintained close relations with Guinea prior to the country's 2008 military coup d'etat, which the U.S. condemned. Following Guinea's presidential elections in 2010, the United States reestablished strong diplomatic relations with the government. U.S. policy seeks to encourage Guinea's democratic reforms, its positive contribution to regional stability, and sustainable economic and social development.

The United States has called on the Government of Guinea to establish an electoral timeline for free, fair, and timely legislative elections, which have been repeatedly delayed. Dialogue between Guinea's Government and political party leadership is essential, and the U.S. has strongly encouraged all political players to reconcile their differences.

U.S. Assistance to Guinea

The U.S. Agency for International Development (USAID) mission in Guinea has a core program that supports democratic transition and election processes, good governance at the local level, and improved service delivery by government institutions through key interventions at the national level. USAID also has significant programming intended to improve health outcomes through improved standards of care and community engagement. Regional programming supports preservation of World Heritage forest sites and critical biodiversity hotspots in Guinea. Peace Corps volunteers work in four project areas: secondary education, environment/agro-forestry, public health and HIV/AIDS prevention, and small enterprise development.

Bilateral Economic Relations

In late 2011, the U.S. Government reinstated Guinea's African Growth and Opportunity Act (AGOA) benefits, which had been lost in early 2010. The reinstatement followed a review by the U.S. Government to examine whether the country had made "continual progress" in meeting AGOA's eligibility criteria. Those criteria include establishment of a market-based economy, rule of law, economic policies to reduce poverty, protection of internationally recognized worker rights, and efforts to combat corruption; political progress was a key factor. Restoring AGOA eligibility provided opportunities to increase mutually beneficial trade and investment between Guinea and the United States.

The United States and Guinea have signed an investment guarantee agreement offering political risk insurance to U.S. investors through the Overseas Private Investment Corporation.

Guinea's Membership in International Organizations

Guinea has been active in efforts toward regional integration and cooperation. Guinea and the United States belong to a number of the same international organizations, including the United Nations, International Monetary Fund, World Bank, and World Trade Organization.

Bilateral Representation

Guinea maintains an embassy in the United States at 2112 Leroy Place, NW, Washington, DC 20008 (tel. 202-483-9420).

Principal U.S. Embassy Officials

Last Updated: 1/14/2013

CONAKRY (E) Transversale No. 2, Ratoma, +224-65-10-40-00, Fax +224-65-10-42-74, Workweek: M-Th, 7:30-16:30; F, 7:30-13:30, Website: http://usembassy.state.gov/conakry

DCM OMS:	Andrea Rogers
AMB OMS:	Pauline Maurantonio
Co-CLO:	Dave Landes
FM:	Mike Dzingleski
HRO:	Jim Nunno
MGT:	Jim Nunno
POL/ECON:	{Vacant}
POSHO:	Mike Dzingleski
SDO/DATT:	MAJ Lance Sells
AMB:	Alexander Laskaris
CON:	John Marietti
DCM:	Stephen Fakan
PAO:	Leigh Rieder
GSO:	Paula Cassell
RSO:	Keith Harris
AFSA:	Leigh Rieder
AID:	Nancy Estes
CLO:	Carrie Smith
ECON:	Brad Coley
EEO:	Lisa Landes
FMO:	Jim Nunno
ICASS Chair:	MAJ Lance Sells
IMO:	Calvin Mcqueen
ISSO:	Donal Godfrey
POL:	Caleb Goddard
State ICASS:	Stephen Fakan

TRAVEL

Consular Information Sheet

August 9, 2012

Country Description: Guinea is a developing country in western Africa with minimal facilities for tourism. Travelers who plan to stay in Conakry, the capital, should make reservations well in advance. French is the official language; Pular, Malinké, and Soussou are also widely spoken.

Smart Traveler Enrollment Program (STEP)/Embassy Locations: If you are going to live in or visit Guinea, please take the time to tell our Embassy about your trip. If you enroll, we can keep you up-to-date with important safety and security announcements. It will also help your friends and family get in touch with you in an emergency.

Embassy Conakry
The U.S. Embassy is located on the Transversale No. 2, Centre Administratif de Koloma opposite the New Radio Station in Ratoma, Conakry, Guinea.
Telephone: 224-65-10-4000
Emergency after-hours telephone: 224-67-10-4311
Facsimile: 224-65-10-4297

Entry/Exit Requirements for U.S. Citizens: A passport, visa, international vaccination record (WHO card), and current yellow fever vaccination are all required to enter Guinea. Please contact the Embassy of the Republic of Guinea for the most current visa information. The Embassy of the Republic of Guinea in Washington is located at 2112 Leroy Street, NW, Washington, DC 20008, tel. (202) 986-4300, fax (202) 478-3010. When overseas, inquiries should be made at the nearest Guinean embassy or consulate.

The U.S. Department of State is unaware of any HIV/AIDS entry restrictions for visitors to or foreign residents of Guinea.

Threats to Safety and Security: Guinea's first democratically-elected President, Alpha Condé, was inaugurated in December 2010. The presidential election was supposed to be followed by elections for the national legislature, but these have been repeatedly delayed. Although the situation has remained calm despite these delays, there is a residual potential for violence in Guinea.

Since 2010, discipline among security forces, including elements of the army, gendarmerie, and police, has been good. Before 2011, the United States Government would not permit minor children of U.S. citizen employees of the U.S. Embassy to be stationed with their parent(s) in Guinea. These restrictions for U.S. citizen minors have since been lifted. There are currently no restrictions on the travel of U.S. citizen employees of the Embassy within Guinea.

While not specifically targeted, U.S. citizens have been victims of crime. Motorists traveling outside of Conakry have encountered improvised checkpoint-barricades manned by persons in military uniforms who demand money and search through personal belongings, confiscating items of value. On rare occasions, persons, including U.S. citizens, have reported abusive treatment by security forces and being taken into custody for purposes of extortion.

Civilian groups occasionally stage impromptu strikes or demonstrations, a practice which seems more likely when legislative elections occur. In some instances and in some locales, these demonstrations can involve violence. While U.S. citizens have not been targeted in past outbreaks of violence, being in the wrong place at the wrong time can be very dangerous. During periods of civil unrest, public services such as transportation and medical care, as well as the availability of goods and services, can be affected.

During many demonstrations, crowds of people gather and burn tires, create roadblocks, and damage vehicles by throwing rocks and bricks. The military has also been known to demonstrate and incite unrest due to their grievances with the government. Because of the potential for violence, U.S. citizens should avoid large crowds, political rallies, and street demonstrations. They should also avoid sensitive government installations, including the Presidential Palace, official government buildings, and military bases. U.S. citizens should maintain security awareness at all times.

Most border crossings are controlled jointly by Guinean armed forces, gendarmes, police, and immigration officials. A relatively long land border and the military's lack of physical and monetary resources mean, however, that borders are lightly patrolled. U.S. citizens considering travel to the border regions with Liberia, Mali, Sierra Leone, or Côte d'Ivoire should consult the latest Travel Warnings and Country Specific Information for these countries.

Crossing land borders requires visas and complete paperwork, and can be difficult.

Stay up to date by:

- Bookmarking our Bureau of Consular Affairs website, which contains the current Travel Warnings and Travel Alerts as well as the Worldwide Caution.
- Following us on Twitter and the Bureau of Consular Affairs page on Facebook as well.
- Downloading our free Smart Traveler I Phone App to have travel information at your fingertips.
- Calling 1-888-407-4747 toll-free within the United States and Canada, or a regular toll line, 1-202-501-4444, from other countries.
- Taking some time before travel to consider your personal security.

Crime: In Conakry, as in many large cities, crime is a fact of daily life. Residential and street crimes are very common. Some crime is perpetrated by individuals in military uniforms. Sentiments toward U.S. citizens in Guinea are generally positive, but criminals regularly target foreigners, including U.S. citizens, because they are perceived as lucrative targets. Nonviolent and violent crime are both problems. Most nonviolent crime involves acts of pick-pocketing and purse-snatching, while armed robbery, muggings, and assaults are the most common violent crimes. Despite the police's good intentions, they have been unable to prevent the rapid escalation of crime. Police and military officials have also been known to make direct and indirect requests for bribes. Criminals particularly target visitors at the airport, in the traditional markets, and near hotels and restaurants frequented by foreigners. Visitors should avoid unsolicited offers of assistance at the airport and hotels because such offers often mask an intention to steal luggage, purses, or wallets. Travelers should arrange for hotel personnel, family members, or business contacts to meet them at the airport to reduce their vulnerability to these crimes of opportunity.

Commercial scams and disputes with local business partners can create legal difficulties for U.S. citizens because corruption is widespread in Guinea. Business is routinely based on bribes rather than the law, and enforcement of the law is irregular and inefficient. The U.S. Embassy has extremely limited recourse in assisting U.S. citizens who are victims of illegal business deals.

Business fraud is rampant and the targets are usually foreigners, including U.S. citizens. Schemes previously associated exclusively with Nigeria are now prevalent throughout West Africa, including Guinea, and pose a danger of severe financial loss. Typically these scams begin with the receipt of an unsolicited communication (usually by e-mail) from a stranger who promises quick financial gain, often by transferring large sums of money or valuables out of the country, but then requires a series of "advance fees" to be paid—such as fees for legal documents or taxes—to finalize the release of funds. The final payoff does not exist; the purpose of the scam is simply to collect the advance fees. A common variation is the scammer's claim to be a refugee or émigré from a prominent West African family, or a relative of a present or former political leader who needs assistance in transferring large sums of cash. Still other variations appear to be legitimate business deals that require advance payments on contracts. Sometimes victims are convinced to provide bank account and credit card information and financial authorization that drain their accounts, incur large debts against their credit, and take their life savings.

The best way to avoid becoming a victim of advance-fee fraud is common sense—if a proposition looks too good to be true, it probably is. You should carefully check into and research any unsolicited business proposal before committing funds, providing goods or services, or undertaking any travel. A good clue to a scam is the phone number given to the victim; legitimate businesses and offices provide fixed-line numbers, while scams typically involve the use of only cell phones. It is virtually impossible to recover money lost through these scams.

Don't buy counterfeit and pirated goods, even if they are widely available. Not only are the bootlegs illegal in the United States, you may be breaking local law too.

Victims of Crime: If you or someone you know becomes the victim of a crime abroad, you should contact the local police and the nearest U.S. embassy or consulate. We can:

- Replace a stolen passport.
- Help you find appropriate medical care if you are the victim of violent crimes such as assault or rape.
- Put you in contact with the appropriate police authorities, and if you want us to, we can contact family members or friend.
- Help you understand the local criminal justice process and direct you to local attorneys, although it is important to remember that local authorities are responsible for investigating and prosecuting the crime.

There is no emergency assistance in Guinea that is similar to the "911" system in the United States.

Criminal Penalties: While you are traveling in Guinea, you are subject to its laws even if you are a U.S. citizen. Foreign laws and legal systems can be vastly different than our own. In some places, you may be taken in for questioning if you don't have your passport with you. In some places, it is illegal to take pictures of certain buildings. In some places, driving under the influence could land you immediately in jail. These criminal penalties will vary from country to country. There are also some things that might be legal in the country you visit, but still illegal in the United States. For example, you can be prosecuted under U.S. law if you buy pirated goods. Engaging in sexual conduct with children or using or disseminating child pornography in a foreign country is a crime prosecutable in the United States. If your break the local laws in Guinea, your U.S. passport won't help you avoid arrest or prosecution. It is very important to know what is legal and what is not legal where you are going. Persons violating Guinean laws, even unknowingly, may be expelled, arrested, or imprisoned. Penalties for possessing, using, or trafficking in illegal drugs in Guinea are severe, and convicted offenders can expect long jail sentences and heavy fines. It is common for criminal cases to take months, if not years, to reach a verdict.

Arrest notifications in host country: While some countries will automatically notify the nearest U.S. embassy or consulate if a U.S. citizen is detained or arrested, that might not always be the case. To ensure that the United States is aware of your circumstances, request that the police and prison officials notify the nearest U.S. embassy or consular if you are arrested or detained overseas.

Special Circumstances: Guinean customs authorities may enforce strict regulations concerning the temporary import or export of items such as firearms, antiquities, medications, business equipment, and ivory. You should contact the Embassy of Guinea in Washington (see contact information above in the Entry Requirements section) for specific information regarding customs requirements.

The local currency is the Guinean franc (FG). Travelers may not depart Guinea carrying more than 100,000 FG (currently about $15.00) or more than $5,000 U.S. dollars. Guinea has a cash economy. ATMs are mostly unavailable, and traveler's checks are accepted only at some banks and hotels. Credit cards are accepted at some larger hotels in Conakry, but should be used only at reputable hotels and banks. Cash advances on Visa credit cards are available at various branches of BICIGUI, a local bank. Inter-bank fund transfers are possible at BICIGUI branches but can be difficult and expensive. Money transfers from the United States have worked successfully in the past. Western Union has several offices in Conakry, and MoneyGram has an office in downtown Conakry as well.

Visitors should restrict photography to private gatherings and should obtain explicit permission from the Guinean government before photographing military and transportation facilities, government buildings, or public works. Photographing without permission in any public area may provoke a response from security personnel or a dangerous confrontation with people who find being photographed offensive.

Accessibility: While in Guinea, individuals with disabilities may find accessibility and accommodation very different from what you find in the United States. Guinea does not have legislation that mandates access to transportation, communication and public buildings for persons with disabilities.

Medical Facilities and Health Information: Medical facilities are poorly equipped and extremely limited, both in the capital city and throughout Guinea. Medicines are in short supply and of questionable quality, sterility of equipment should not be assumed, and treatment is frequently unreliable. Some private medical facilities provide a better range of treatment options than public facilities, but are still well below western standards. There is one ambulance in Conakry but there are no ambulance or emergency rescue services in Guinea. Trauma care is extremely limited. Water in Guinea is presumed to be contaminated, so travelers should use only bottled or distilled water for drinking. Malaria is a serious risk to travelers in Guinea. For additional information on malaria, including protective measures, visit CDC's malaria web page.

You can find good information on vaccinations and other health precautions, on the CDC website. For information about outbreaks of infectious diseases abroad, consult the World Health Organization (WHO) website. The WHO website also contains additional health information for travelers, including detailed country-specific health information.

Medical Insurance: You cannot assume that your insurance will go with you when you travel or that it will cover all of your needs while traveling in Guinea. It is very important to find out BEFORE you leave. You need to ask your insurance company two questions:

- Does my policy apply when I am out of the United States?
- Will it cover emergencies like a trip to a foreign hospital or a full emergency medical evacuation?

In many places, doctors and hospitals still expect payment in cash at the time of service. Your regular U.S. health insurance may not cover doctors' and hospital visits in other countries. If your policy does not go with you when you travel, it is a very good idea to take out another one for your trip.

Traffic Safety and Road Conditions: While in Guinea, you may encounter road conditions that differ significantly from those in the United States. The information below concerning Guinea is provided for general reference only, and may not be totally accurate in a particular location or circumstance.

Drivers in Guinea tend to be poorly trained and routinely ignore road safety rules. Guinea's road network, which is only partly paved, is underdeveloped and unsafe. Roads and vehicles are poorly maintained, road signs are insufficient, and roads and vehicles are frequently unlit. Livestock and pedestrians create constant road hazards and make nighttime travel inadvisable. The police and the military often set up roadblocks, making inter- and intra-city travel difficult from 10:00 p.m. to 6:00 a.m. During the rainy season (July through September), flash floods make some roads temporarily impassable. There is also a significant increase in banditry along the roadways between towns and upcountry during evening hours. U.S. citizens and other foreigners are strongly discouraged from traveling after dark outside of populated areas. Roadside assistance is not available in Guinea.

Guinea has no reliable public transportation. Taxis, including small cars and larger vans, are often poorly maintained and overcrowded. Taxis frequently stop and start without regard to other vehicles, making driving hazardous. Hired vehicles and drivers are available from agencies at major hotels in Conakry.

Aviation Safety Oversight: As there is no direct commercial air service to the United States by carriers registered in Guinea, the U.S. Federal Aviation Administration (FAA) has not assessed the government of Guinea's Civil Aviation Authority for compliance with International Civil Aviation Organization (ICAO) safety standards. Further information may be found on the FAA's safety assessment page.

Children's Issues: Please see the U.S. Dept. of State Office of Children's Issues web pages on intercountry adoption and international parental child abduction.

Travel Warning

September 7, 2012

The Department of State warns U.S. citizens of the risks of travel to Guinea because the political situation there remains unpredictable. This replaces the Travel Warning of November 4, 2011, to update information on the political situation and accompanying security issues.

Although Guinea has been relatively calm since the democratically elected President took office in December 2010, legislative elections, which should have taken place shortly after the presidential elections, have been repeatedly delayed, causing increasing frustration and anger. On several occasions, large crowds of demonstrators representing partisans of various opposition parties have gathered at thoroughfares to express their dissatisfaction. If the legislative election cycle is further delayed or postponed, which seems likely, political rhetoric could turn peaceful demonstrations into violent ones.

U.S. citizens are urged to exercise caution, to be particularly alert to their surroundings, and to avoid crowds, demonstrations, or any other form of public gathering. Visitors to Guinea should be familiar with their hotel evacuation plans, policies, or procedures.

U.S. citizens in Guinea should carry their travel documents (i.e., passport, birth certificate, picture ID, etc.) with them at all times. Additionally, U.S. citizens in Guinea are reminded to stay in contact with friends and family in the United States to keep them apprised of their current welfare and whereabouts.

U.S. citizens traveling to or remaining in Guinea despite this Travel Warning are strongly urged to enroll in the State Department's Smart Traveler Enrollment Program (STEP) to receive the most up-to-date security information. By enrolling, you make it easier for the U.S. Embassy to contact you in case of emergency.

U.S. citizens should consult the Country Specific Information for Guinea and the Worldwide Caution, both located on the Department of State's Bureau of Consular Affairs website. Current information on safety and security can also be obtained by calling 1-888-407-4747 toll-free in the United States and Canada, or a regular toll line at 1-202-501-4444 from other countries. These numbers are available from 8:00 a.m. to 8:00 p.m. Eastern Time, Monday through Friday (except U.S. federal holidays).

The U.S. Embassy is located on the Transversale No. 2, Centre Administratif de Koloma, opposite the New Radio Station in Ratoma, Conakry, Guinea. You can call the Embassy switchboard at 224-65-10-4000, or reach the consular section directly by calling 224-67-10-4444. For after-hours emergencies, please call 224-67-10-4311. 2000 at Rue 243, Porte 297. The Embassy's mailing address is B.P. 34, Bamako, Mali. The telephone number, including for after-hour emergencies, is 223 2070–2300. The consular fax number is 223 2070–2340.

Intercountry Adoption

October 2012

The information in this section has been edited from a report available through the U.S. Department of State Office of Children's Issues. For more detailed information, please read the *Intercountry Adoption* section of this book and review current reports online at http://www.adoption.state.gov.

Guinea is party to the Hague Convention on Protection of Children and Co-operation in Respect of Intercountry Adoption (Hague Adoption Convention). Intercountry adoption processing in Hague countries is done in accordance with the requirements of the Convention; the U.S. implementing legislation, the Intercountry Adoption Act of 2000 (IAA); and the IAA's implementing regulations, as well as the implementing legislation and regulations of Guinea. Guinea does not allow adoption service providers or orphanages to assist with intercountry adoptions. Prospective adoptive parents must work with an accredited or approved adoption service provider for U.S. processing elements, but should expect to work directly with Guinean authorities or a licensed Guinean attorney for services in Guinea.

Who Can Adopt? To bring an adopted child to the United States from Guinea, you must meet eligibility and suitability requirements. The U.S. Department of Homeland Security, U.S. Citizenship and Immigration Services (USCIS) determines who can adopt under U.S. immigration law. Additionally, a child must meet the definition of Convention adoptee under U.S. law in order to immigrate to the United States on an IH-3 or IH-4 immigrant visa. Guinea also has the following requirements for prospective adoptive parents.

Background Notes

Residency: The Government of Guinea requires prospective adoptive parent(s) to be present for the final step in the adoption process in order to witness the child's acceptance of the prospective adoptive parent(s). Prospective adoptive parent(s) should plan to be in Guinea for one to three weeks.

Age of Adopting Parents: Prospective adoptive parent(s) must be at least 15 years older than the child they propose to adopt.

Marriage: A married couple must have been together at least five (5) years.

Income: None specified.

Other: There is no statutory bar to adoption by a single parent or same-sex parents apart from the age requirement above.

Who Can Be Adopted? Because Guinea is party to the Hague Adoption Convention, children from Guinea must meet the requirements of the Convention in order to be eligible for adoption. For example, the Convention requires that Guinea attempt to place a child with a family in Guinea before determining that a child is eligible for intercountry adoption. In addition to Guinea's requirements, a child must meet the definition of a Convention adoptee for you to bring him or her back to the United States.

Relinquishment: An Affidavit of Consent must be obtained from the parent in the case of a single parent relinquishing a child for intercountry adoption, or from a representative of the child's family if the parents are deceased or abandoned the child.

Abandonment: Local police authorities will obtain an Order of Abandonment from the court for any child found to be without parents or known family.

Age of Adoptive Child: To be adopted, a child must be under the age of 15; a child age 13 or 14 must consent to a prospective adoption.

Sibling Adoptions: Nothing specified.

Special Needs or Medical Conditions: Nothing specified.

Waiting Period or Foster Care: Nothing specified.

Guinea's Adoption Authority: Ministry of Social Affairs, Women and Children

The Process: Because Guinea is party to the Hague Adoption Convention, adopting from Guinea must follow a specific process designed to meet the Convention's requirements. For detailed and updated information on these requirements, please review the *Intercountry Adoption* section of this publication and visit the USCIS Intercountry Adoption website at http://adoption.state.gov.

The recommended first step in adopting a child from Guinea is to select an adoption service provider in the United States that has been accredited or approved to provide services to U.S. citizens in Convention cases. Only accredited or approved adoption services providers may provide adoption services between the United States and Guinea. The U.S. accredited or approved adoption service provider will act as the primary provider in your case. The primary adoption service provider is responsible for ensuring that all adoption services in the case are done in accordance with The Hague Adoption Convention and U.S. laws and regulations. Learn more about Agency Accreditation. Note: No adoption agency or orphanage, foreign or domestic, is approved or accredited to assist prospective adoptive parents with the in-country process. The process for finalizing the adoption (or gaining legal custody) in Guinea generally includes the following.

Role of Adoption Authority: Adoptions from Guinea begin with a letter addressed to the Minister of Social Affairs. After conducting an investigation into the background of the child to be adopted and determining that the child is eligible for adoption, the Ministry will send an Article 16 report on the child for inclusion with the Form I-800 filed with USCIS. After an adoption is finalized, the Ministry will certify that everything was done according to the provisions of the Hague Convention (Article 23 Certificate). You will need to take this certificate with you when you appear for the visa interview at the U.S. Embassy in Dakar, Senegal.

Role of the Court: A court in Conakry, called the Tribunal of First Instance, will issue the Decree of Adoption. The Tribunal can also issue a Jugement Suppletif in place of a birth certificate, if needed.

Role of Adoption Agencies: An adoption agency or orphanage in Guinea may offer or attempt to assist in processing your application for adoption in Guinea. Note that no adoption agency or orphanage in Guinea is approved or accredited to assist you, and no payment should be made to anyone other than a Guinean attorney hired by you to undertake specific tasks, or to the Government of Guinea for specific assessed fees.

Time Frame: There is no set time frame for an adoption from Guinea.

Adoption Application: Adoptions from Guinea begin with a letter addressed to the Minister of Social Affairs, accompanied by your dossier and the Form I-800A approval notice. If you have already identified a child that you would like to adopt, you should be prepared to supply the Guinean Central Authority with all known information about the child and the child's family.

Adoption Fees: The Government of Guinea is working to publish a schedule of fees. In the meantime, fees are assessed on a case-by-case basis according to an estimation of actual costs. For example, an investigation that requires travel to a distant location would incur a higher fee that an investigation undertaken in the capital. In the adoption services contract that you sign at the beginning of the adoption process, your agency will itemize the fees and estimated expenses related to your adoption process.

Some of the fees specifically associated with adopting from Guinea include those charged by the Government of Guinea for investigations.

Documents Required: Prospective adoptive parent(s) should provide a letter addressed to the Minister of Social Affairs stating the desire to adopt a child in Guinea. The letter must be signed by both prospective adoptive parents (if a married couple), and by every child in the household age 13 or older. The letter should accompany your dossier and the Form I-800A approval notice. Additional documents may be requested.

Bringing Your Child Home: Once your adoption is complete (or you have obtained legal custody of the child), there are a few more steps to take before you can head home. Specifically, you need to apply for several documents for your child before he or she can travel to the United States, such as a birth certificate, a passport or travel document for your child from the country in which he or she was born, and a U.S. Immigration Visa. For detailed and updated information on how to obtain these documents, visit the USCIS Intercountry Adoption website at http://adoption.state.gov.

Child Citizenship Act: For adoptions finalized abroad, the Child Citizenship Act of 2000 allows your new child to acquire American citizenship automatically when he or she enters the United States as lawful permanent residents. For adoptions finalized in the United States, the Child Citizenship Act of 2000 allows your new child to acquire American citizenship automatically when the court in the United States issues the final adoption decree. To learn more, review the *Intercountry Adoption* section on this publication and visit the USCIS Intercountry Adoption website at http://adoption.state.gov.

U.S. Embassy
BP 603
Conakry, Guinea
Tel: + (224) 65-10-4000
Fax: + (224) 65-19-4297
Email: conconakry@state.gov
Internet: conakry.state.gov

U.S. Embassy in Dakar, Senegal
Consular Section
Avenue Jean XXIII
Dakar, Senegal
Tel: + (221) 33-829-2100
Fax: + (221) 33-822-5903
Email: consulardakar@state.gov
Internet: dakar.usembassy.gov

Guinea's Adoption Authority
Address: Ministry of Social Affairs, Women and Children
B. P. 527
Conakry, Republic of Guinea
Tel: + (224) 64-36-4299
Email: bafodekeith2000@yahoo.fr

Embassy of Republic of Guinea
2112 Leroy Place, N.W.
Washington, D.C. 20008
Tel: (202) 986-4300
Internet: guineaembassyusa.com

Office of Children's Issues
U.S. Department of State
2201 C Street, NW
SA-29
Washington, DC 20520
Tel: 1-888-407-4747
E-mail: AskCI@state.gov
http://adoption.state.gov

GUINEA-BISSAU

Compiled from publications that were available as of February 2013 from the U.S. Department of State, the U.S. Department of Commerce, and the Central Intelligence Agency (CIA). See the introduction to this set for explanatory notes.

Official Name:
Republic of Guinea-Bissau

PROFILE

Geography

Area: total: 36,125 sq km; country comparison to the world: 138; land: 28,120 sq km; water: 8,005 sq km

Major cities: Bissau (capital) 302,000 (2009)

Climate: tropical; generally hot and humid; monsoonal-type rainy season (June to November) with southwesterly winds; dry season (December to May) with northeasterly harmattan winds

Terrain: mostly low coastal plain rising to savanna in east

People

Nationality: noun: Guinean(s); adjective: Guinean

Population: 1,628,603 (July 2012 est.)

Population growth rate: 1.971% (2012 est.)

Ethnic groups: African 99% (includes Balanta 30%, Fula 20%, Manjaca 14%, Mandinga 13%, Papel 7%), European and mulatto less than 1%

Religions: Muslim 50%, indigenous beliefs 40%, Christian 10%

Languages: Portuguese (official), Crioulo, African languages

Literacy: definition: age 15 and over can read and write; total population: 54.2%; male: 68.2%; female: 40.6% (2010 est.)

Health: life expectancy at birth: total population: 49.11 years; male: 47.16 years; female: 51.11 years (2012 est.); Infant mortality rate: total: 94.4 deaths/1,000 live births; male: 104.25 deaths/1,000 live births; female: 84.26 deaths/1,000 live births (2012 est.)

Unemployment rate: NA%

Work force: 632,700 (2007)

Government

Type: republic

Independence: 24 September 1973

Constitution: 16 May 1984; amended several times

Political subdivisions: 9 regions (regioes, singular—regiao); Bafata, Biombo, Bissau, Bolama, Cacheu, Gabu, Oio, Quinara, Tombali; note—Bolama may have been renamed Bolama/Bijagos

Suffrage: 18 years of age; universal

Economy

GDP (purchasing power parity): $1.902 billion (2012 est.); $1.95 billion (2011 est.); $1.852 billion (2010 est.); $1.789 billion (2009 est.)

GDP real growth rate: -2.8% (2012 est.); 5.3% (2011 est.); 3.5% (2010 est.); 3% (2009 est.)

GDP per capita (PPP): $1,100 (2012 est.); $1,200 (2011 est.); $1,100 (2010 est.); $1,100 (2009 est.)

Natural resources: fish, timber, phosphates, bauxite, clay, granite, limestone, unexploited deposits of petroleum

Agriculture products: rice, corn, beans, cassava (manioc), cashew nuts, peanuts, palm kernels, cotton; timber; fish

Industries: agricultural products processing, beer, soft drinks

Exports: $125 million (2012 est.); $244.6 million (2011 est.); $126 million (2010 est.)

Exports—commodities: fish, shrimp; cashew nuts, peanuts, palm kernels, sawn lumber

Exports—partners: India 41.5%, Nigeria 33.9%, Brazil 8.7%, Togo 7.9% (2011)

Imports: $254.1 million (2012 est.); $327.6 million (2011 est.); $206.1 million (2010 est.)

Imports—commodities: foodstuffs, machinery and transport equipment, petroleum products

Imports—partners: Portugal 28.3%, Senegal 15.6%, China 4.7% (2011)

Debt—external: $1.095 billion (31 December 2010 est.); $941.5 million (31 December 2000 est.)

Exchange rates: Communaute Financiere Africaine francs (XOF) per US dollar; 514.1 (2012 est.); 471.87 (2011 est.); 495.28 (2010 est.); 472.19 (2009); 447.81 (2008); 493.51 (2007)

PEOPLE

The population of Guinea-Bissau is ethnically diverse with distinct languages, customs, and social structures. According to the 2009 census, 42.5% of the population is under 15 years of age; 3.2% is 65 and older, and 49.6% are women aged between 15 and 49. The country has 1,361 schools and 537 health centers.

Religion

Approximately 50 percent of the population follows indigenous religious practices. Forty percent is Muslim, and 10 percent is Christian.

The Fula (Peuhl or Fulani) and Mandinka ethnic groups are the most numerous followers of Islam. Muslims generally live in the north and northeast, and most Muslims are Sunni. Practitioners of indigenous religious beliefs generally live in all but the northern parts of the country. Christians belong to a number of groups, including the Roman Catholic Church and various Protestant denominations. Christians are concentrated in Bissau and other large towns.

HISTORY

The rivers of Guinea and the islands of Cape Verde were among the first areas in Africa explored by the Portuguese in the 15th century. Portugal claimed Portuguese Guinea in 1446, but few trading posts were established before 1600. In 1630, a "captaincy-general" of Portuguese Guinea was established to administer the territory. With the cooperation of some local tribes, the Portuguese entered the slave trade and exported large numbers of Africans to the Western Hemisphere via the Cape Verde Islands. Cacheu became one of the major slave centers, and a small fort still stands in the town. The slave trade declined in the 19th century, and Bissau, originally founded as a military and slave-trading center in 1765, grew to become the major commercial center.

Portuguese conquest and consolidation of the interior did not begin until the latter half of the 19th century. Portugal lost part of Guinea to French West Africa, including the center of earlier Portuguese commercial interest, the Casamance River region. A dispute with Great Britain over the island of Bolama was settled in Portugal's favor with the involvement of U.S. President Ulysses S. Grant.

Before World War I, Portuguese forces, with some assistance from the Muslim population, subdued animist tribes and eventually established the territory's borders. The interior of Portuguese Guinea was brought under control after more than 30 years of fighting; final subjugation of the Bijagos Islands did not occur until 1936. The administrative capital was moved from Bolama to Bissau in 1941, and in 1952, by constitutional amendment, the colony of Portuguese Guinea became an overseas province of Portugal.

In 1956, Amilcar Cabral and Raphael Barbosa organized the African Party for the Independence of Guinea and Cape Verde (PAIGC) clandestinely. The PAIGC moved its headquarters to Conakry, Guinea, in 1960 and started an armed rebellion against the Portuguese in 1961. Despite the presence of Portuguese troops, which grew to more than 35,000, the PAIGC steadily expanded its influence until, by 1968, it controlled most of the country.

It established civilian rule in the territory under its control and held elections for a National Assembly. Portuguese forces and civilians increasingly were confined to their garrisons and larger towns. The Portuguese Governor and Commander in Chief from 1968 to 1973, Gen. Antonio de Spinola, returned to Portugal and led the movement that brought democracy to Portugal and independence for its colonies.

Amilcar Cabral was assassinated in Conakry in 1973, and party leadership fell to Aristides Pereira, who later became the first president of the Republic of Cape Verde. The PAIGC National Assembly met at Boe in the southeastern region and declared the independence of Guinea-Bissau on September 24, 1973. Following Portugal's April 1974 revolution, it granted independence to Guinea-Bissau on September 10, 1974. The United States recognized the new nation that day. Luis Cabral, Amilcar Cabral's half-brother, became president of Guinea-Bissau. In late 1980, the government was overthrown in a relatively bloodless coup led by Prime Minister and former armed forces commander Joao Bernardo "Nino" Vieira.

From November 1980 to May 1984, power was held by a provisional government responsible to a Revolutionary Council headed by President Joao Bernardo Vieira. In 1984, the council was dissolved, and the National Popular Assembly (ANP) was reconstituted. The single-party assembly approved a new constitution, elected President Vieira to a new 5-year term, and elected a Council of State, which was the executive agent of the ANP. Under this system, the president presided over the Council of State and served as head of state and government. The president also was head of the PAIGC and commander in chief of the armed forces.

There were alleged coup plots against the Vieira government in 1983, 1985, and 1993. In 1986, first Vice President Paulo Correia and five others were executed for treason following a lengthy trial. In 1994, the country's first multi-party legislative and presidential elections were held. An army uprising against the Vieira government in June 1998 triggered a bloody civil war that created hundreds of thousands of displaced persons and resulted in President Vieira having to request assistance from the governments of Senegal and Guinea, who provided troops to quell the uprising. The President was ousted by a military junta in May 1999. An interim government turned over power in February 2000 when opposition leader Kumba Yala, founder of the Social Renovation Party (PRS), took office following two rounds of transparent presidential elections.

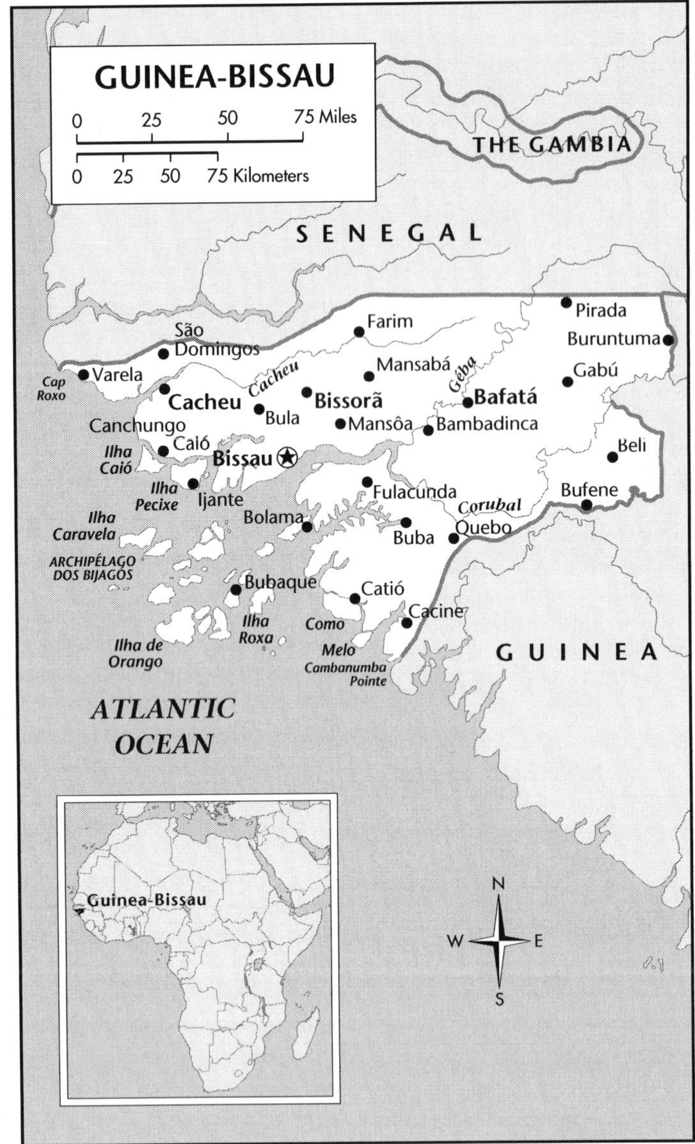

Despite the elections, democracy did not take root in the succeeding 3 years. President Yala neither vetoed nor promulgated the new constitution that was approved by the National Assembly in April 2001. The resulting ambiguity undermined the rule of law. Impulsive presidential interventions in ministerial operations hampered effective governance. On November 14, 2002, the President dismissed the government of Prime Minister Alamara Nhasse, dissolved the National Assembly, and called for legislative elections. Two days later, he appointed Prime Minister Mario Pires to lead a caretaker government controlled by presidential decree. Elections for the National Assembly were scheduled for April 2003, but later postponed until June and then October. On September 12, 2003, the President of the National Elections Commission announced that it would be impossible to hold the elections on October 12, 2003, as scheduled. The army, led by Chief of Defense General Verrisimo Correia Seabra, intervened on September 14, 2003. President Yala announced his "voluntary" resignation and was placed under house arrest. The government was dissolved and a 25-member Committee for Restoration of Democracy and Constitutional Order was established. On September 28, 2003, businessman Henrique Rosa was sworn in as President. He had the support of most political parties and of civil society. Artur Sanha, PRS President, was sworn in as Prime Minister. On March 28 and 30, 2004, Guinea-Bissau held legislative elections which international observers deemed acceptably free and fair. On May 9, 2004, Carlos Gomes Junior became Prime Minister.

GOVERNMENT AND POLITICAL CONDITIONS

Guinea-Bissau is a multiparty republic. In July 2009 Malam Bacai Sanha of the African Party for the Independence of Guinea and Cape Verde (PAIGC) was elected president in elections following the assassination of Joao Bernardo Vieira by the military. International observers declared the election to be generally free and fair despite election-related violence preceding the polls. As in the previous year, there were multiple instances in which elements of the security forces acted independently of civilian control.

Recent Elections

Following the March 2009 military assassination of President Vieira, interim President Raimundo Pereira postponed the first round of the presidential election until June 2009 although the constitution provides that an election be held within 60 days of a president's death. The PAIGC candidate, Malam Bacai Sanha, won the June 2009 first round with 39 percent of the vote, and the July 2009 second round with 63 percent.

International observers characterized the polling process as generally free and fair.

Political Parties: Formal membership in the dominant party conferred some informal advantages. The Balanta ethnic group, mainly through its predominance in the armed forces, controlled the political system.

Unlike previous years, the political opposition was not subjected to restrictions on political activity or overt violence such as torture or killings.

Participation of Women and Minorities: The 98-member National Assembly had 10 female members. The Supreme Court president, two of the 19 government ministers, and one of nine state secretaries also were women.

All ethnic groups were represented in the government.

Principal Government Officials

Last Updated: 1/31/2013

Guinea-Bissau since the coup d'etat on 12 April 2012 has been ruled by a junta-selected Transitional National Council. All leaders are serving in an acting capacity.

Pres.: **Manuel Serifo NHAMADJO**
Prime Min.: **Rui Duarte de BARROS**
Min. for the Presidency of the Council of Ministers: **Fernando VAZ**
Min. of Agriculture & Fisheries: **Malam MANE**
Min. of Civil Service & State Modernization: **Carlos Joaquim VAMAIN**
Min. of Defense & War Veterans: **Celestino de CARVALHO**
Min. of Economy, Planning, & Regional Integration: **Degol MENDES**
Min. of Energy, Industry, & Natural Resources: **Daniel GOMES**
Min. of Finance: **Abubacar Demba DAHABA**
Min. of Foreign Affairs, Intl. Cooperation, & Diaspora: **Faustino Fudut IMBALI**
Min. of Infrastructures: **Fernando GOMES**
Min. of Interior: **Antonio Suka NTCHAMA**
Min. of Justice: **Mamadu Saido BALDE**
Min. of National Education, Culture, Science, Youth, & Sports: **Vincente PUNGURA**
Min. of Public Health & Social Solidarity: **Agostinho CA**
Min. of Social Communication & Parliamentary Affairs: **Fernando VAZ**
Min. of Territorial Admin. & Local Govt.: **Baptista TE**
Min. of Trade: **Abubacar BALDE**
Permanent Representative to the UN, New York:

ECONOMY

One of the poorest countries in the world, Guinea-Bissau's legal economy depends mainly on farming and fishing, but trafficking in narcotics is probably the most lucrative trade. The combination of limited economic prospects, a weak and faction-ridden government, and favorable geography have made this West African country a way station for drugs bound for Europe. Cashew crops have increased remarkably in recent years; low rainfall hindered cereals and other crops in 2011.

Guinea-Bissau exports fish and seafood along with small amounts of peanuts, palm kernels, and timber. Rice is the major crop and staple food. However, intermittent fighting between Senegalese-backed government troops and a military junta destroyed much of the country's infrastructure and caused widespread damage to the economy in 1998; the civil war led to a 28% drop in GDP that year, with partial recovery in 1999–2002.

In December 2003, the World Bank, IMF, and UNDP were forced to step in to provide emergency budgetary support in the amount of $107 million for 2004, representing over 80% of the total national budget. The government is successfully implementing a three-year $33 million extended credit arrangement with the IMF that runs through 2012.

In December 2010 the World Bank and IMF announced support for $1.2 billion worth of debt relief. Guinea-Bissau made progress with debt relief in 2011 when members of the Paris Club opted to write-off much of the country's obligations.

Labor Conditions

There are no specific laws that protect children from exploitation in the workplace. The legal minimum age is 14 for general factory labor and 18 for heavy or dangerous labor, including labor in mines. Minors are prohibited from working overtime.

The small formal sector generally adhered to these minimum age requirements. The Ministries of Justice and of Civil Service and Labor did not effectively enforce these requirements, particularly in informal work settings, where most child labor occurred. According to the 2010 Multiple Indicator Cluster Survey, almost 60 percent of children ages five to 14 work—65 percent in rural areas and 45 percent in urban areas. Children in rural communities performed domestic and fieldwork without pay to help support their families. They also lacked educational opportunities. Some children were partially or completely withdrawn from school to work in the fields during the annual cashew harvest.

The Council of Ministers annually establishes minimum wage rates for all categories of work, but it did not enforce them. The lowest monthly wage was approximately 19,030 CFA francs ($34) per month plus a bag of rice.

The law provides for a maximum 45-hour workweek; however, many employees were forced to work longer hours. The law also provides for overtime pay, as long as overtime does not exceed 200 hours per year, and a mandatory 12-hour rest period between workdays; however, these provisions were not enforced.

U.S.-GUINEA-BISSAU RELATIONS

The United States established diplomatic relations with Guinea-Bissau in 1975, following its independence from Portugal. Post-independence, the country has seen a mix of coups, attempted coups, civil war, assassinations, and democratic elections. The United States strongly condemned the April 2012 attempt by elements of the military to forcibly seize power, called for maximum restraint on all sides and the restoration of legitimate civilian leadership, and continues to work with its partners in the region and beyond as it monitors developments on the ground. Now that the Economic Community of West African States (ECOWAS) has returned Bissau-Guinean military factions to their barracks and a civilian government is in power, the United States is working with its partners and the Transitional Government of Guinea-Bissau to facilitate free and fair elections by Spring 2013, and to promote basic reforms on governance, justice, and economic development.

There is no U.S. Embassy in Guinea-Bissau. All official U.S. contact with Guinea-Bissau is handled by the U.S. Embassy in Senegal. Local employees staff the U.S. Office in Bissau, and U.S. diplomats from the Embassy in Dakar travel frequently to Bissau.

U.S. Assistance to Guinea-Bissau

Given the April 12, 2012 coup, the United States was obliged to terminate foreign assistance to the Government of Guinea-Bissau consistent with the requirements of section 7008 of the Department of State, Foreign Operations and Related Programs Appropriations Act for 2012. Previous limited non-humanitarian assistance focused primarily on the justice sector as well as demining and proper weapons storage programs.

Bilateral Economic Relations

At least until a democratically elected government resumes office, Guinea-Bissau is ineligible for preferential trade benefits under the African Growth and Opportunity Act. U.S. exports to Guinea-Bissau include agricultural products and machinery. The top import to the U.S. from Guinea-Bissau is diamonds. The United States has a trade and investment framework agreement with the West African Economic and Monetary Union, of which Guinea-Bissau is a member.

Guinea-Bissau's Membership in International Organizations

Guinea-Bissau and the United States belong to a number of the same international organizations, including the United Nations, International Monetary Fund, World Bank, and World Trade Organization.

Bilateral Representation

Although Guinea-Bissau has a mission to the United Nations in New York, it currently does not have an embassy in, or diplomatic accreditation to, Washington DC .

Principal U.S. Embassy Officials

Last Updated: 1/14/2013
(Operations suspended in 1998. Covered by Embassy Dakar)

BISSAU (BO) P.O. Box 297 Bissau Codex, Bairro de Penha, Rua Ulysses Grant, 00-245-252-282, Fax 00-245-222-273, Workweek: M-F, 0800-1700, Website: http://dakar.usembassy.gov/

HRO:	Thomas Zeitler
MGT:	Stephen Dodson
SDO/DATT:	LTC Matthew Sousa
GSO:	Carla Mudgett
RSO:	Thad Osterhout
POL:	David Whiting

TRAVEL

Consular Information Sheet

March 7, 2012

Country Description: The Republic of Guinea-Bissau, a small country in western Africa, is one of the world's poorest nations. The capital is Bissau and the official language is Portuguese, though many people outside of Bissau only speak an indigenous language or creole. The country's 1998–99 civil war devastated the economy. Tourist facilities and infrastructure in general are very limited and not up to U.S. standards.

Smart Traveler Enrollment Program/Embassy Location: If you are going to live in or visit Guinea-Bissau, please take the time to tell our Embassy in Dakar, Senegal about your trip by enrolling in the Smart Traveler Enrollment Program. If you enroll, we can keep you up to date with important safety and security announcements. It will also help your friends and family get in touch with you in an emergency. If you don't have Internet access you may enroll directly with the nearest U.S. embassy.

The nearest U.S. embassies are located in Banjul, The Gambia; Conakry, Guinea; and Dakar, Senegal (which also maintains a U.S. Liaison Office in Bissau). The U.S. Embassy in Dakar has jurisdiction over Guinea-Bissau and U.S. citizens travelling or residing in Guinea-Bissau are encouraged to enroll with the U.S. Embassy in Dakar.

U.S. Embassy Dakar
Avenue Jean XXIII—B.P. 49
Dakar, Senegal
Telephone: (221) 33-829-2100
Emergency after-hours telephone: (221) 33-829-2209
Regional Security Office:
(221) 33-829-2142
Facsimile: (221) 33-822-5903

U.S. Bissau Liaison Office
Edifício SITEC
Rua José Carlos Schwarz 245
Bairro d'Ajuda
Bissau, Guinea-Bissau
Telephone/Facsimile: (245) 325-6382

Entry/Exit Requirements: A valid passport, visa, and proof of onward/return ticket are required. The Bissau-Guinean Embassy in Washington, DC, suspended operations in January 2007. The Embassy of Guinea-Bissau does not have a website. Due to Guinea-Bissau's lack of consular representation in the United States, it can be difficult for you to obtain the required visa for entry into Guinea-Bissau. Since most flights destined for Guinea-Bissau must pass through Dakar, Senegal, or Lisbon, Portugal, most travelers are able to apply for visas at the Bissau-Guinean embassies in those countries. Although it is possible to obtain a visa upon arrival in Bissau if arrangements are made in advance, there are no clear instructions for how to make those arrangements.

Guinea-Bissau remains an unstable threat environment for which additional security precautions are required. The U.S. State Department rates Guinea-Bissau as a high threat country for political violence and crime. All official U.S. government travelers (including personnel assigned to the U.S. Embassy in Dakar), must have Regional Security Office (RSO) approval and are required to receive an RSO country-specific security briefing prior to travel.

The U.S. Department of State is unaware of any HIV/AIDS entry restrictions for visitors to or foreign residents of Guinea-Bissau.

Threats to Safety and Security: Guinea-Bissau is one of the poorest countries in West Africa and lacks sufficient resources and infrastructure to insure a stable security environment. Since Guinea-Bissau gained independence from Portugal in 1974, the country has been plagued by coups, political assassinations, and a civil war. The country's fragile political system and weak governance allows for widespread corruption directly influenced by illicit activity. Criminals, corrupt officials, and drug cartels continue to undermine the rule of law and utilize the country for criminal activity, including using Guinea-Bissau as a major transit-point for cocaine and light arms trafficking, and for illegal immigration. Guinea-Bissau's unprotected coastline and archipelago, with over 90 islands, many un-policed, and remote airstrips,is a haven for narcotics trafficking and other criminal activity. Due to the current political, economic and security instability in Guinea-Bissau, all U.S. citizens and organizations should exercise heightened personal security awareness.

Guinea-Bissau continues to experience periodic political violence and instability and all travelers to the country should closely monitor the political situation. On December 26, 2011, forces allegedly under the command of Navy Chief of Staff Admiral Jose Americo Bubo Na Tchuto attacked the headquarters of the Army Chief of Staff, General Antonio Indjai. At least one person was killed and Na Tchuto, who is listed on the U.S. Treasury Department's Drug Kingpin List, was arrested along with many of his alleged supporters. In January 2012, Bissau-Guinean President Malam Bacai Sanhá died from natural causes.The government plans to hold Presidential Elections on March 18.

Avoid political gatherings and street demonstrations. Demonstrations typically begin or end in front of the former Presidential Palace in "Praca dos Herois Nacionaisalso. While most demonstrations in Bissau are non-violent, the imbalance of power in the country can lead to violent demonstrations. For guidelines on dealing safely with public demonstrations, please see the American Citizen Services page of the U.S. Embassy Dakar web site.

Unexploded military ordnance and landmines remain scattered throughout the country. Although the capital city of Bissau was declared "mine-free" in June 2006 by the national demining center (CAAMI), there have been occasional findings or unintentional mine explosions. Two non-governmental organizations (NGOs) have been active in successfully removing mines. Avoid driving in rural areas at night and remain on well-traveled roads at all times to minimize the risks posed by landmines

The U.S. Embassy in Bissau suspended operations on June 14, 1998, at the outbreak of a violent civil war. There is currently no permanent U.S. diplomatic or consular presence in Guinea-Bissau. The U.S. Embassy in Dakar, Senegal is accredited for all diplomatic and security concerns. In 2007, the U.S. government opened a U.S. Liaison Office in Bissau (BLO), which is staffed by locally employed personnel. The BLO provides limited services to U.S. citizens in the event of an emergency. However, all security and consular services should be coordinated through the American Citizens Services Section and the Regional Security Office at the U.S. Embassy in Dakar, Senegal. The U.S. Liaison Office is located at: Edifício SITEC, Rua José Carlos Schwarz 245, Bairro d'Ajuda (Telephone: 245-325-6382).

Stay up to date by:

- Bookmarking our Bureau of Consular Affairs website, which contains the current Travel Warnings and Travel Alerts as well as the Worldwide Caution.
- Following us on Twitter and the Bureau of Consular Affairs page on Facebook as well.
- Downloading our free Smart Traveler IPhone App to have travel information at your fingertips.
- Calling 1-888-407-4747 toll-free within the United States and Canada, or a regular toll line, 1-202-501-4444, from other countries.
- Taking some time before travel to consider your personal security.

Crime: Guinea-Bissau is rated high for crime due to the frequency of crimes committed and lack of law enforcement resources and capabilities. Foreigners are primarily the targets of crimes of opportunity to include, petty-theft, pick-pocketing, theft of valuables from vehicles, and minor assaults. In particular, low-level criminal activity occurs in crowded areas such as the Bandim Market and port in central Bissau. Criminals take advantage of foreigners attempting to navigate through the crowded markets. Exercise good personal security practices to reduce the risks of becoming victimized. Keep a low profile, remain vigilant, and avoid potential conflict situations. Do not wear flashy clothing or jewelry, and be cautious about displaying any amount of currency in public.

To avoid theft do not walking alone in isolated areas, particularly at night and lock all doors and close all windows when driving. Do not walk on dark streets at night, even in groups. To minimize inconvenience in the event of theft, carry copies, rather than originals, of your passport and other identification documents. Avoid carrying credit cards if not being used.

In conjunction with the high crime rate, the poor infrastructure and lack of lighting at night also present a more opportune environment for criminals to exploit. It is recommended to arrange for transportation and limit walking around Bissau at night to reduce the risk of being a victim of a crime. In addition, banditry also occurs with some regularity on the main highways throughout the country after dark. The U.S. Embassy recommends that travel be completed during daylight hours only and, if possible, in convoy.

The unstable security environment and high rates of unemployment strongly influence criminals to go to extreme measures to achieve their goals. While most criminals in Guinea-Bissau seek crimes of opportunity with low risks of confrontation, they are not afraid to exert violence. In many cases, criminal elements in Bissau operate in small, loosely affiliated groups to perpetrate a crime. Criminals use one or two individuals to cause a distraction or remain on lookout, while the others conduct the crime.

While violent crime towards foreigners are not common in Guinea-Bissau, the increase in both drug use and narcotics trafficking has contributed to an increase in criminal activity and aggressive assaults among the local population in more rural areas of Guinea-Bissau. There is a direct correlation between increased crimes rates and the increased drug use that is fueled by the international narcotics trafficking in Bissau.

The Bandim market and other vendors in Bissau offer a wide variety of illicit and counterfeit goods. While the items are widely available, all travelers are urged to not purchase any illicit items to prevent breaking local laws and U.S. laws if brought back in the country.

Victims of Crime: Police and emergency personnel in Guinea-Bissau lack the basic resources necessary to effectively respond to crime and emergency situations. Due to the deficiency in resources, response time to emergency situations may not be timely or may be non-existent.

- Replace a stolen passport.
- Help you find appropriate medical care if you are the victim of violent crimes such as assault or rape.
- Put you in contact with the appropriate police authorities, and if you want us to, we can contact family members or friend.
- Help you understand the local criminal justice process and direct you to local attorneys, although it is important to remember that local authorities are responsible for investigating and prosecuting the crime.

There is no local equivalent to the "911" emergency line in Guinea-Bissau.

Criminal Penalties: While you are traveling in Guinea-Bissau, you are subject to its laws even if you are a U.S. citizen. Foreign laws and legal systems can be vastly different than our own. In some places, you may be taken in for questioning if you don't have your passport with you. In some places, it is illegal to take pictures of certain buildings. In some places, driving under the influence could land you immediately in jail. These criminal penalties will vary from country to country. There are also some things that might be legal in the country you visit, but still illegal in the United States, and you can be prosecuted under U.S. law if you buy pirated goods.Engaging in sexual conduct with children or using or disseminating child pornography in a foreign country is a crime prosecutable in the United States. If you break local laws in Guinea-Bissau, your U.S. passport won't help you avoid arrest or prosecution. It's very important to know what's legal and what's not wherever you go.

Persons violating Bissau-Guinean laws, even unknowingly, may be expelled, arrested, or imprisoned. Penalties for possessing, using, or trafficking in illegal drugs in Guinea-Bissau are severe, and convicted offenders can expect long jail sentences and heavy fines. Drug trafficking is endemic in Guinea-Bissau.

The United States does not have an agreement with Guinea-Bissau requiring notification of the U.S. Embassy of your arrest. If you are arrested in Guinea-Bissau, you should use whatever means of communication available to alert the closest U.S. Embassy or consulate of your situation.

Special Circumstances: Guinea-Bissau's customs authorities may enforce strict regulations concerning the temporary import or export of items such as firearms, antiquities, medications, and business equipment.

International banking and finance is problematic due to a limited formal banking sector. ATMs are not available, credit cards are not accepted, currency exchange only exists at banks and hotels, wire transfer possibilities are extremely limited, and repatriation of funds is problematic. Purchases of goods and services are possible only in cash and in the local currency, the Franc CFA of the West African Economic and Monetary Zone. It is recommended that travelers secure more than adequate sums of CFA before arriving in Guinea-Bissau. There is no money available for travelers at the U.S. Liaison Office in Bissau.

As there is currently no functioning U.S. Embassy in Guinea-Bissau, and no consular notification agreement between Guinea-Bissau and the United States, U.S. consular officials may not be properly notified when a U.S. citizen is arrested or detained in Guinea-Bissau. U.S. citizens are encouraged to carry a notarized copy of their U.S. passports with them at all times so that, if questioned by local officials, proof of identity and U.S. citizenship is readily available.

Accessibility: While in Guinea-Bissau, individuals with disabilities may find accessibility and accommodation very different from what you find in the United States.

Medical Facilities and Health Information: Modern medical facilities are virtually nonexistent in Guinea-Bissau, and travelers should not rely on them. More acceptable levels of medical care are available in Dakar, Senegal; however, as of this writing, there are extremely limited air travel options available between Dakar and Bissau. In addition, malaria, a serious and sometimes fatal disease, is a risk for travelers to Guinea-Bissau. Guinea-Bissau has a high HIV/AIDS infection rate.

You can find good information on vaccinations and other health precautions on the CDC website. For information about outbreaks of infectious diseases abroad, consult the infectious diseases section of the World Health Organization (WHO) website. The WHO website also contains additional health information for travelers, including detailed country-specific health information.

Medical Insurance: You can't assume your insurance will go with you when you travel. It's very important to find out BEFORE you leave whether or not your medical insurance will cover treatment overseas. You will need to ask your insurance company two questions:

- Does my policy apply when I'm out of the United States?
- Will it cover emergencies like a trip to a foreign hospital or a medical evacuation?

In many places, doctors and hospitals still expect payment in cash at the time of service. Your regular U.S. health insurance may not cover doctors' and hospital visits in other countries. If your policy doesn't go with you when you travel, it's a very good idea to purchase travelers' medical insurance.

Traffic Safety and Road Conditions: While in Guinea-Bissau, you may encounter road conditions that differ significantly from those in the United States. The information below concerning Guinea-Bissau is provided for general reference only, and may not be totally accurate in a particular location or circumstance.

The public transportation system, urban and rural road conditions, and availability of roadside assistance are all poor. There is no consistent public electricity in the capital, and the lack of lighting at night makes careful driving essential. Since there are mines left in place from the civil war and the war of independence, travelers should not leave designated roads and pathways. The landmines are scattered in several areas throughout Guinea-Bissau, including the Bafata, Oio, Biombo, Quinara, and Tombali regions. While there has been significant progress in locating and removing landmines, a substantial number remains. Speak with local authorities first and use caution if leaving a main road or highway to enter a trail network or to make other types of cross-country movement.

Passengers should also exercise caution if choosing to use a taxi for transportation because many are in substandard condition. If a taxi is used, it is important for passengers to inform taxi drivers that they do not want additional patrons to be picked up along the route. Taxis in Bissau serve as a bus service, in which each passenger pays for their seat. Furthermore, the Embassy does not recommend that visitors use the unconventional bus system in Bissau, the "Bus Rapides" or "Toca-Tocas."

Aviation Safety Oversight: As there is no direct commercial air service to the United States by carriers registered in Guinea-Bissau, the U.S. Federal Aviation Administration (FAA) has not assessed the government of Guinea-Bissau's Civil Aviation Authority for compliance with International Civil Aviation Organization (ICAO) aviation safety standards. Further information may be found on the FAA's safety assessment page.

Children's Issues: Please see the U.S. Dept. of State Office of Children's Issues web pages on intercountry adoption and international parental child abduction.

Intercountry Adoption

July 2012

Guinea-Bissau is not party to the Hague Convention on Protection of Children and Co-operation in Respect of Intercountry Adoption (Hague Adoption Convention). Intercountry adoptions of children from non-Hague countries are processed in accordance with 8 Code of Federal Regulations, Section 204.3 as it relates to orphans as defined under the Immigration and Nationality Act, Section 101(b)(1)(F).

Below is the limited adoption information that the Department has obtained from the adoption authority of Guinea-Bissau. U.S. citizens adopting children in rare adoption cases from Guinea-Bissau, as well as U.S. citizen prospective adoptive parents living in Guinea-Bissau who would like to adopt from the United States or from a third country, should contact the adoption authority of Guinea-Bissau to inquire about applicable laws and procedures.

The U.S. Embassy in Dakar, Senegal issues immigrant visas for Bissau-Guinean citizens, including adopted orphans.

Prospective adoptive parents should be aware that not all children in orphanages or children's homes are adoptable. In many countries, birth parents place their child(ren) temporarily in an orphanage or children's home due to financial or other hardship, intending that the child return home when this becomes possible. In such cases, the birth parent(s) have rarely relinquished their parental rights or consented to their child(ren)'s adoption.

There are two types of adoptions in Guinea Bissau: 1) simple adoption (adopcao restrita) and 2) full adoption (adopcao plena). Simple adoption is a form of legal custody that may specifically permit immigration of the child and adoption abroad. In a simple adoption, the birth family is usually still living and the child may continue to have contact with his or her birth family. The birth family must have consented to the simple adoption, and the adopting family must have met the prerequisite care requirements before obtaining guardianship of the child. Simple adoptions are revocable, but can be converted to full adoptions if the requirements for full adoption are met. Prospective adoptive parents should be aware a child must meet the definition of orphan under U.S. immigration law in order to be eligible to immigrate to the United States on an IR-3 or IR-4 immigrant visa.

In contrast, full adoptions are irrevocable and are granted when one or both birth parents have died and/or any living biological parent has severed ties with the child, or when simple adoptions are converted to full adoptions after the biological parents consent and the child has been in the care of the adopting family for at least 12 months. In these cases, the child will take the last name of the adopting parents and be considered their legitimate child. Adoption lawyers and authorities in Guinea-Bissau should be aware that only full adoption is legally equivalent to an adoption in the United States. In order to adopt, the prospective adoptive parents must have a local lawyer and meet the eligibility requirements.

Guinea-Bissau Adoption Authority: The Ministry of Child Protection is responsible for intercountry adoptions in Guinea-Bissau.

Ministry of Social Solidarity and Fight Against Poverty
Address: Rua Unidade Africana
P.O. P: 716
Tel: (245) 3204605
Fax: (245) 3204785
Email:
Helenasaid2005@yahoo.com.br

GUYANA

Compiled from publications that were available as of February 2013 from the U.S. Department of State, the U.S. Department of Commerce, and the Central Intelligence Agency (CIA). See the introduction to this set for explanatory notes.

Official Name:
Co-operative Republic of Guyana

PROFILE

Geography

Area: total: 214,969 sq km; country comparison to the world: 85; land: 196,849 sq km; water: 18,120 sq km

Major cities: Georgetown (capital) 132,000 (2009)

Climate: tropical; hot, humid, moderated by northeast trade winds; two rainy seasons (May to August, November to January)

Terrain: mostly rolling highlands; low coastal plain; savanna in south

People

Nationality: noun: Guyanese (singular and plural); adjective: Guyanese

Population: 741,908 (July 2012 est.)

Population growth rate: -0.327% (2012 est.)

Ethnic groups: East Indian 43.5%, black (African) 30.2%, mixed 16.7%, Amerindian 9.1%, other 0.5% (2002 census)

Religions: Protestant 30.5% (Pentecostal 16.9%, Anglican 6.9%, Seventh-Day Adventist 5%, Methodist 1.7%), Hindu 28.4%, Roman Catholic 8.1%, Jehovah's Witnesses 1.1%, Muslim 7.2%, other Christian 17.7%, other 4.3%, none 4.3% (2002 census)

Languages: English, Amerindian dialects, Creole, Caribbean Hindustani (a dialect of Hindi), Urdu

Literacy: definition: age 15 and over has ever attended school; total population: 91.8%; male: 92%; female: 91.6% (2002 Census)

Health: life expectancy at birth: total population: 67.39 years; male: 63.57 years; female: 71.4 years (2012 est.); Infant mortality rate: total: 35.59 deaths/1,000 live births; male: 39.74 deaths/1,000 live births; female: 31.25 deaths/1,000 live births (2012 est.)

Unemployment rate: 11% (2007)

Work force: 313,100 (2009 est.)

Government

Type: republic

Independence: 26 May 1966

Constitution: 6 October 1980

Political subdivisions: 10 regions; Barima-Waini, Cuyuni-Mazaruni, Demerara-Mahaica, East Berbice-Corentyne, Essequibo Islands-West Demerara, Mahaica-Berbice, Pomeroon-Supenaam, Potaro-Siparuni, Upper Demerara-Berbice, Upper Takutu-Upper Essequibo

Suffrage: 18 years of age; universal

Economy

GDP (purchasing power parity): $6.164 billion (2012 est.); $5.857 billion (2011 est.); $5.62 billion (2010 est.); $5.386 billion (2009 est.)

GDP real growth rate: 3.7% (2012 est.); 4.2% (2011 est.); 4.4% (2010 est.); 3.3% (2009 est.)

GDP per capita (PPP): $8,000 (2012 est.); $7,600 (2011 est.); $7,300 (2010 est.); $7,000 (2009 est.)

Natural resources: bauxite, gold, diamonds, hardwood timber, shrimp, fish

Agriculture products: sugarcane, rice, edible oils; beef, pork, poultry; shrimp, fish

Industries: bauxite, sugar, rice milling, timber, textiles, gold mining

Exports: $1.229 billion (2012 est.); $1.178 billion (2011 est.); $884.5 million (2010 est.)

Exports—commodities: sugar, gold, bauxite, alumina, rice, shrimp, molasses, rum, timber

Exports—partners: Canada 29%, US 28.6%, UK 4.9%, Trinidad and Tobago 4.3%, Jamaica 4.3% (2011)

Imports: $1.85 billion (2012 est.); $1.456 billion (2011 est.); $1.299 billion (2010 est.)

Imports—commodities: manufactures, machinery, petroleum, food

Imports—partners: US 23.1%, Trinidad and Tobago 21.7%, China 9%, Cuba 6% (2011)

Debt—external: $1.234 billion (31 December 2010); $804.3 million (30 September 2008)

Exchange rates: Guyanese dollars (GYD) per US dollar; 204.4 (2012 est.); 204.02 (2011 est.); 203.64 (2010 est.); 203.95 (2009); 203.86 (2008); 201.89 (2007)

PEOPLE

Guyana's population is made up of five main ethnic groups—East Indian, African, Amerindian, Chinese, and Portuguese. Ninety percent of the inhabitants live on the narrow coastal plain, where population density is more than 115 persons per square kilometer (380 per sq. mi.). The population density for Guyana as a whole is low—less than four persons per square kilometer. The government has provided free primary and secondary education since 1975.

National/Racial/Ethnic Minorities

According to the 2002 census, the indigenous population constituted 9 percent of the population. There were nine recognized tribal groups, and 90 percent of indigenous communities were located in the remote interior. Indigenous communities' standard of living was lower than that of most citizens, and they had limited access to education and health care.

Religion

A 2002 census on religious affiliation indicated that approximately 57 percent of the population is Christian with 17 percent Pentecostal, 8 percent Roman Catholic, 7 percent Anglican, 5 percent Seventh-day Adventist, and 20 percent other Christian groups. Approximately 28 percent of the population is Hindu, 7 percent Muslim (mostly Sunni), and 2 percent practice other beliefs, including the Rastafari Movement and the Baha'i Faith. An estimated 4 percent of the population does not profess any religion. Some religious groups claim greater numbers of members than reported in the 2002 census.

The country is ethnically diverse, reflecting East Indian, African, Chinese, and European ancestry, as well as a significant indigenous population. Most religious groups can claim membership from a cross section of ethnic groups, with two exceptions: most Hindus are Indo-Guyanese, and nearly all Rastafarians are Afro-Guyanese.

HISTORY

Before the arrival of Europeans, the region was inhabited by both Carib and Arawak tribes, who named it Guiana, which means "land of many waters." The Dutch settled in Guyana in the late 16th century, but their control ended when the British became the de facto rulers in 1796. In 1815, the colonies of Essequibo, Demerara, and Berbice were officially ceded to Great Britain at the Congress of Vienna and, in 1831, were consolidated as British Guiana. Following the abolition of slavery in 1834, thousands of indentured laborers were brought to Guyana to replace the slaves on the sugarcane plantations, primarily from India but also from Portugal and China. The British stopped the practice in 1917. Many of the Afro-Guyanese former slaves moved to the towns and became the majority urban population, whereas the Indo-Guyanese remained predominantly rural. A scheme in 1862 to bring black workers from the United States was unsuccessful. The small Amerindian population lives in the country's interior.

The people drawn from these diverse origins have coexisted peacefully for the most part. Slave revolts, such as the one in 1763 led by Guyana's national hero, Cuffy, demonstrated the desire for basic rights but also a willingness to compromise. Politically inspired racial disturbances between Indo-Guyanese and Afro-Guyanese erupted in 1962–64, and again following elections in 1997 and 2001. The conservative and cooperative nature of Guyanese society has contributed to a cooling of racial tensions; however, such tensions do constitute Guyana's most sensitive social stress point.

Guyanese political history has been turbulent. The first modern political party in Guyana was the People's Progressive Party (PPP), established on January 1, 1950, with Forbes Burnham, a British-educated Afro-Guyanese, as chairman; Dr. Cheddi Jagan, a U.S.-educated Indo-Guyanese, as second vice chairman; and Dr. Jagan's American-born wife, Janet Jagan, as secretary general. The PPP won 18 out of 24 seats in the first popular elections permitted by the colonial government in 1953, and Dr. Jagan became leader of the house and minister of agriculture in the colonial government. Five months later, on October 9, 1953, the British suspended the constitution and landed troops because, they said, the Jagans and the PPP were planning to make Guyana a communist state. These events led to a split in the PPP, in which Burnham broke away and founded what eventually became the People's National Congress (PNC).

Elections were permitted again in 1957 and 1961, and Cheddi Jagan's PPP ticket won on both occasions, with 48% of the vote in 1957 and 43% in 1961. Cheddi Jagan became the first premier of British Guiana, a position he held for 7 years. At a constitutional conference in London in 1963, the U.K. Government agreed to grant independence to the colony but only after another election in which proportional representation would be introduced for the first time. It was widely believed that this system would reduce the number of seats won by the PPP and prevent it from obtaining a clear majority in Parliament. The December 1964 elections gave the PPP 46%, the PNC 41%, and the United Force (TUF), a conservative party, 12%. TUF threw its votes in the legislature to Forbes Burnham, who became prime minister.

Guyana achieved independence in May 1966, and became a republic on February 23, 1970—the anniversary of the Cuffy slave rebellion. From December 1964 until his death in August 1985, Forbes Burnham ruled Guyana in an increasingly autocratic manner, first as prime minister and later, after the adoption of a new constitution in 1980, as executive president. During that timeframe, elections were viewed in Guyana and abroad as fraudulent. Human rights and civil liberties were suppressed, and two major political assassinations occurred: the Jesuit Priest and journalist Bernard Darke in July 1979, and the distinguished historian and WPA Party leader Walter Rodney in June 1980. Agents of President Burnham are widely believed to have been responsible for both deaths.

Following Burnham's own death in 1985, Prime Minister Hugh Desmond Hoyte acceded to the presidency and was formally elected in the December 1985 national elections. Hoyte gradually reversed Burnham's policies, moving from state socialism and one-party control to a market economy and unrestricted freedom of the press and assembly. On October 5, 1992, a new National Assembly and regional councils were elected in the first Guyanese election since 1964 to be internationally recognized as free and fair. Cheddi Jagan was elected and sworn in as president on October 9, 1992.

When President Jagan died in March 1997, Prime Minister Samuel Hinds replaced him in accordance with constitutional provisions. President Jagan's widow, Janet Jagan, was elected president in December 1997. She resigned in August 1999 due to ill health and was succeeded by Finance Minister Bharrat Jagdeo, who had been named prime minister a day earlier. National elections were held on March 19, 2001. Incumbent President Jagdeo won re-election with a voter turnout of over 90%. President Jagdeo won re-election again in national elections held on August 28, 2006, the first non-violent elections held in more than 20 years.

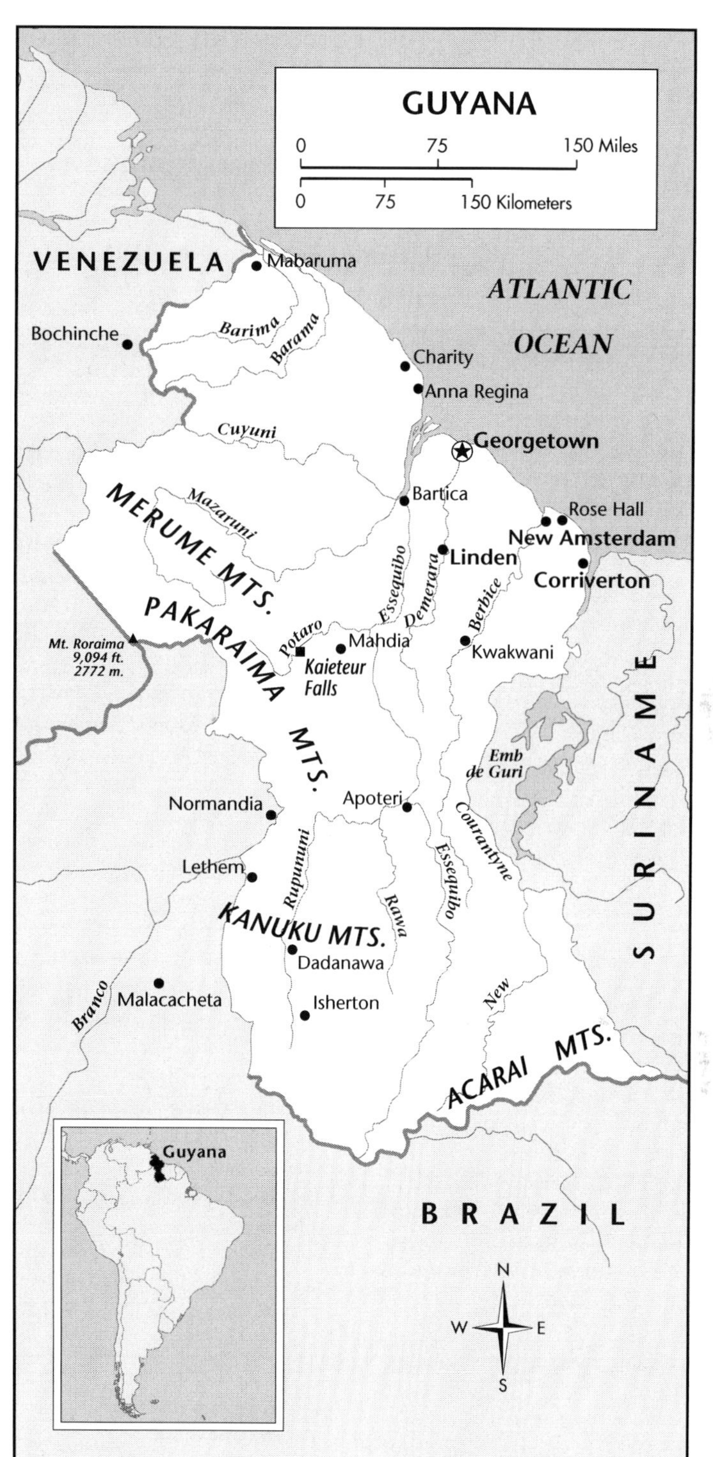

GOVERNMENT AND POLITICAL CONDITIONS

The Cooperative Republic of Guyana is a multiparty democracy. On November 28, 2011, voters elected Donald Ramotar of the People's Progressive Party Civic (PPP/C) to be president, replacing Bharrat Jagdeo of the same party. However, the PPP/C won only 48.6 percent of the vote, and President Ramotar presides over the first minority government in parliament since independence in 1966. International and local observers considered the elections to be generally free, transparent, and peaceful.

Recent Elections

On November 28, 2011, voters elected PPP/C candidate Donald Ramotar to a five-year term as president, replacing outgoing PPP/C president Jagdeo. However, the PPP/C gained only 48.6 percent of the vote, and President Ramotar therefore presides over the first minority government in parliament since independence in 1966. International observers, including teams from the Organization of American States, Caribbean Community, Commonwealth, and Union of South American Nations, generally concluded that the elections were substantially free, transparent, and peaceful and that they were well administered. Electoral observer criticisms centered on the need for greater timeliness in transmission of preliminary and final results and for increased women's participation in the electoral process. Observers also noted that Guyana Elections Commission (GECOM) members are political appointees, saying this "compromises the effectiveness and integrity of the commission, which needs to be independent and above politics at all levels."

Although all five parties competing in the elections signed a code of conduct prepared by the GECOM, hours after the ceremony the opposition coalition, A Partnership for National Unity (APNU), accused the ruling PPP/C of violating the code by distributing leases for land to residents of the Essequibo Coast. During the campaign GECOM's Media Monitoring Unit highlighted three problem areas in media portrayal of political parties, including inequitable reporting by certain outlets, publication of two racially divisive articles, and use of unscientific polling data. Nonetheless, the unit concluded that there were few major infringements of a separate media code of conduct.

Participation of Women and Minorities: The constitution requires that one-third of each party list of candidates be women but does not require the parties to select women for seats. Parties selected 21 female representatives for the 65-seat National Assembly, and President Ramotar named five women to his 21-member cabinet.

While supporters of the two major parties (the PPP/C and APNU) were drawn largely from the Indo-Guyanese and Afro-Guyanese communities, respectively, political party leadership was more diverse. The cabinet was also ethnically diverse, mirroring the ethnic makeup of the general population. Seven cabinet members were Afro-Guyanese, including the prime minister and the head of the presidential secretariat. The ethnically diverse National Assembly included seven indigenous members; there were also two Amerindian cabinet ministers.

Principal Government Officials

Last Updated: 1/31/2013

Pres.: **Donald RAMOTAR**
First Vice Pres.
Second Vice Pres.
Prime Min.: **Samuel HINDS**
Min. of Agriculture: **Leslie RAMSAMMY, Dr.**
Min. of Amerindian Affairs: **Pauline CAMPBELL-SUKHAI**
Min. of Education: **Priya MANICKCHAND**
Min. of Finance: **Ashni SINGH, Dr.**
Min. of Foreign Affairs: **Carolyn RODRIGUES-BIRKETT**
Min. of Health: **Bheri RAMSARRAN, Dr.**
Min. of Home Affairs: **Clement ROHEE**
Min. of Housing & Water: **Irfaan ALI**
Min. of Human Services & Social Security: **Jennifer WEBSTER**
Min. of Labor: **Nanda GOPAUL**
Min. of Legal Affairs: **Anil NANDLALL**
Min. of Local Govt. & Regional Development: **Ganga PERSAUD**
Min. of Natural Resources & the Environment: **Robert PERSAUD**
Min. of Parliamentary Affairs: **Samuel HINDS**
Min. of Public Service Management: **Jennifer WESTFORD, Dr.**
Min. of Public Works: **Robeson BENN**
Min. of Tourism, Industry, & Commerce
Min. of Culture, Youth, & Sports: **Frank ANTHONY, Dr.**
Head, Presidential Secretariat: **Roger LUNCHEON**
Attorney Gen.: **Anil NANDLALL**
Governor, Bank of Guyana: **Dolly S. SINGH**
Ambassador to the US: **Bayney KARRAN**
Permanent Representative to the UN, New York: **George Wilfred TALBOT**

ECONOMY

The Guyanese economy exhibited moderate economic growth in recent years and is based largely on agriculture and extractive industries. The economy is heavily dependent upon the export of six commodities—sugar, gold, bauxite, shrimp, timber, and rice—which represent nearly 60% of the country's GDP and are highly susceptible to adverse weather conditions and fluctuations in commodity prices.

Guyana's entrance into the Caricom Single Market and Economy (CSME) in January 2006 has broadened the country's export market, primarily in the raw materials sector. Guyana has experienced positive growth almost every year over the past decade. Inflation has been kept under control. Recent years have seen the govern

ment's stock of debt reduced significantly - with external debt now less than half of what it was in the early 1990s. Chronic problems include a shortage of skilled labor and a deficient infrastructure. Despite recent improvements, the government is still juggling a sizable external debt against the urgent need for expanded public investment. In March 2007, the Inter-American Development Bank, Guyana's principal donor, canceled Guyana's nearly $470 million debt, equivalent to 21% of GDP, which along with other Highly Indebted Poor Country (HIPC) debt forgiveness brought the debt-to-GDP ratio down from 183% in 2006 to 120% in 2007.

Guyana became heavily indebted as a result of the inward-looking, state-led development model pursued in the 1970s and 1980s. Growth slowed in 2009 as a result of the world recession, but picked up in 2010–11, before slowing again in 2012, as a result of a second recession, this focused mainly in Europe. The slowdown in the domestic economy and lower import costs has helped to narrow the country's current account deficit, despite generally lower earnings from exports.

Labor Conditions

The law prohibits the employment of children younger than 15 with some exceptions. Technical schools may employ children as young as age 14 provided a competent authority approves and supervises such work.

No person under 18 may be employed in industrial work at night, with exceptions for those aged 16 and 17 whose work requires continuity through day and night, including certain gold mining processes and the production of iron, steel, glass, paper, and raw sugar. The law permits children under 15 to be employed only in enterprises in which members of the same family are also employed. The law prohibits children under 15 from working in factories and stipulates that those under 18 may be removed from factory work if authorities determine they are engaged in activities that are hazardous to their health or safety.

Child labor was most prevalent in family-based businesses, farming, bars and restaurants, domestic work, and street vending. Small numbers of children also performed hazardous work in the construction, logging, farming, fishing, manufacturing, and mining industries.

The minimum wage is 35,863 Guyanese dollars ($178) per month. Public sector employees also receive unilateral wage increases. The law sets hours of employment, which vary by industry and sector. In general, work in excess of a 44-hour workweek requires an overtime payment rate. The law prohibits compulsory overtime and provides for paid annual holidays. The law establishes workplace safety and health standards. The Occupational Health and Safety Division of the Ministry of Labor is charged with conducting factory inspections and investigating complaints of substandard workplace conditions. The Ministry of Labor is also responsible for enforcing legislation regarding the minimum wage and working hours. According to local trade unions and NGOs, enforcement of minimum wage legislation was not effective, and unorganized workers, particularly women in the informal sector, often were paid less than the minimum wage. The ministry reported that standards regarding working hours were effectively enforced.

U.S.-GUYANA RELATIONS

U.S. policy toward Guyana seeks to develop robust, sustainable democratic institutions, laws, and political practices; support economic growth and development; promote an active, organized, and empowered civil society; and promote stability and security. Beginning in the late 1980s, Guyana sought to improve relations with the United States as part of a decision to shift toward political nonalignment, moving from state socialism and one-party control to a market economy and greater freedom of the press and assembly. This shift, recent free and fair democratic elections, closer security cooperation, and expanding trade and investment have helped place U.S.-Guyanese relations on an excellent footing.

The United States values Guyana's partnership and cooperation on issues of mutual interest. Together, the two countries promote democracy and respect for human rights; empower youth, women, the private sector, and civic/opinion leaders to formulate grassroots responses to social and economic challenges; support new initiatives to improve the health of the Guyanese people; and, through the Caribbean Basin Security Initiative, enhance the security and prosperity of the region.

U.S. Assistance to Guyana

Working together through the Caribbean Basin Security Initiative (CBSI), the United States and Guyana, along with other nations of the Caribbean, are combating drug trafficking and other transnational crimes that threaten regional security. The United States also works closely with Guyana in the fight against HIV/AIDS through the President's Emergency Plan for AIDS Relief (PEPFAR) program. U.S. agencies, including the U.S. Centers for Disease Control and Prevention (CDC), and the U.S. Agency for International Development (USAID), are administering a multi-million dollar program of education, prevention, and treatment for those infected and affected by HIV/AIDS, and contributing to the country's health care capacity. USAID also supports an activity designed to strengthen political processes and institutions. The Public Affairs Section is developing people-to-people ties through exchange programs and by supporting meaningful discourse and programs with civil society, the private sector, and government on issues of bilateral importance. U.S. military medical and engineering teams continue to conduct training exercises in Guyana, digging wells, building schools and clinics, and providing medical treatment.

Bilateral Economic Relations

Guyana's 2011 nominal Gross Domestic Product (GDP) was USD 1.9 billion, and with an estimated population of 751,000 people, its per capita GDP was USD 2,500. In 2011, the service sector, led by construction services, contributed to 65 percent of the GDP, followed by the agricultural and mining sectors which contributed 23 percent and 10 percent respectively. The manufacturing sector accounted for 4 percent of the GDP.

Guyana's leading export goods in 2011 were gold, rice, and bauxite which accounted for 45 percent, 15 percent and 11 percent of export earnings respectively. Sugar accounted for 11 percent of total export earnings. In 2011, Guyana's exports to all countries were $1.128 billion and its imports were $1.747 billion. Guyana traded more with the United States in 2011 than with any other country, exporting $424.5 million of goods to the U.S. while importing $363.6 million of U.S. goods. Guyanese products such as apparel knit with U.S.-made material, sugar, seafood, fruit, and other agricultural products enjoy duty-free access to the U.S. market under the Caribbean Basin Trade Partnership Act, which has been extended to 2020.

The United States Geological Survey (USGS) has identified the Guyana Suriname basin as having the second highest resource potential among unexplored oil basins in the world and estimates mean recoverable oil reserves of 15 billion barrels of oil and gas reserves of 42 trillion cubic feet. Under the Energy Governance and Capacity Initiative (EGCI), the United Stated Government provides a range of technical and capacity building assistance as Guyana seeks to develop financial and regulatory regimes and address capacity issues that would maximize the development potential from prospective offshore oil and gas resources.

Guyana's Membership in International Organizations

Following its independence from the United Kingdom in 1966, Guyana sought an influential role in international affairs, particularly among developing countries and nonaligned nations. Guyana and the United States belong to a number of the same international organizations, including the United Nations, Organization of American States, and International Monetary Fund. The Caribbean Community (CARICOM) Secretariat is headquartered in Guyana.

Bilateral Representation

Guyana maintains an embassy in the United States at 2490 Tracy Place NW, Washington, DC 20008 (tel. 202-265-6900), and a Consulate at 370 7th Avenue, Room 402, New York, NY 10001.

Principal U.S. Embassy Officials

Last Updated: 1/14/2013

GEORGETOWN (E) 100 Young & Duke Sts, (592) 225-4900/9, Fax (592) 225-8497/ 747-0303, Workweek: M-F 07:30-16:00, Website: http://georgetown.usembassy.gov/

DCM OMS:	Claire S. Rotering
AMB OMS:	Karen S Ramroop
CDC:	Barbara Allen
FM:	Terry L. Vice
GFS:	Post Accountant Brandi Thacker
HRO:	Anita A Brown (Frc)
MGT:	Hormazd J. Kanga
MLO/ODC:	Ryan Brooks; Lt, Usn
POL/ECON:	Eric C Moore
AMB:	D. Brent Hardt
CON:	Mark O'Connor
DCM:	Thomas C. Pierce
PAO:	Tabatha L Fairclough
GSO:	Ms. Jessi M. Copeland
RSO:	Brett R. Ramsey
AFSA:	Vacant
AID:	Dan Smolka
CLO:	Sandra M Parra
DEA:	Henry Cuervo
FMO:	Michael R Wagoner
ICASS Chair:	Lt.Ryan Brooks
IMO:	Frank Sauer
ISSO:	Imo Frank Sauer
LEGATT:	Maximo Delancer
POL:	P/E Chief: Michael Fraser
State ICASS:	Mark O'Connor

Other Contact Information

U.S. Department of Commerce
International Trade Administration
Trade Information Center
14th and Constitution, NW
Washington, DC 20230
Tel: 800-USA-TRADE

Caribbean/Latin American Action
1818 N Street, NW, Suite 310
Washington, DC 20036
Tel: (202) 466-7464
Fax: (202) 822-0075

TRAVEL

Consular Information Sheet

July 27, 2012

Country Description: Guyana is a developing nation on the north coast of South America. Tourist facilities are generally not developed, except for a few hotels in the capital city of Georgetown and a limited number of eco-resorts. The vast majority of Guyanese nationals live along the coast, leaving the interior largely unpopulated and undeveloped. Travel in the interior of Guyana can be difficult; many interior regions can only be reached by plane or boat, and the limited roads are often impassable in the rainy seasons.

Smart Traveler Enrollment Program (STEP)/Embassy Locations: If you are going to live or visit Guyana, please take the time to tell our Embassy about your trip. If you enroll, we can keep you up to date with important safety and security announcements. It will also help your friends and family get in touch with you in an emergency.

100 Young & Duke Streets
Georgetown, Guyana
Telephone: 011-592-225-4900
Emergency after-hours telephone: 011-592-623-1992
Facsimile: 011-592- 227-0221
http://georgetown.usembassy.gov/

Entry/Exit Requirements for U.S. Citizens: You will need a valid U.S. passport to enter and depart Guyana. On arrival, Guyanese Immigration normally grants U.S. visitors a stay of thirty days. When traveling to Guyana you should ensure that your passport has at least six months of remaining validity. You may request an extension from the Ministry of Home Affairs at 60 Brickdam Street, Georgetown. The Central Office of Immigration, located on Camp Street, Georgetown, must also note the extension in your passport. If your purposes are other than tourism, you should check with the Ministry of Home Affairs for information about requirements for work permits and extended stays. If you are a U.S.-Guyanese dual national departing Guyana for the United States using a Guyanese passport, you must present to Guyanese authorities a U.S. passport, Certificate of Naturalization, or other document establishing that you may legally enter the United States. U.S. citizens with dual nationality are not eligible for U.S. visas and must use their U.S. passports to enter and depart the United States. For further information about entry, exit and customs requirements, you may consult the Embassy of Guyana at 2490 Tracy Place NW, Washington, DC 20008, telephone (202) 265-6900, the Consulate General in New York, or honorary consuls in California, Florida, Ohio, and Texas.

The U.S. Department of State is unaware of any HIV/AIDS entry restrictions for visitors to or foreign residents of Guyana.

Threats to Safety and Security: Demonstrations and protests are rare in Georgetown. Past demonstrations have not been directed at U.S. citizens, and violence against U.S. citizens in general is not common. You should nevertheless remain alert and take prudent personal security measures to deal with the unexpected while in Guyana. It is advisable to avoid areas where crowds have congregated and to maintain a low profile when moving about Georgetown and other Guyanese locales. As with any elections, demonstrations and protests can occur. The Embassy reminds U.S. citizens to be cautious and vigilant, particularly near any sites associated with political activity.

Most major eco-tourist resorts and hotels in Guyana do not have written emergency plans in place, and many of them have safety deficiencies, including a lack of easily identifiable lifeguards, or none at all. Many of these resorts also do not have adequately stocked first aid supplies.

Stay up to date by:

- Bookmarking our Bureau of Consular Affairs website, which contains the current Travel Warnings and Travel Alerts as well as the Worldwide Caution.
- Follow us on Twitter and the Bureau of Consular Affairs page on Facebook as well.
- Calling 1-888-407-4747 toll-free within the U.S. and Canada, or a regular toll line, 1-202-501-4444, from other countries.
- Taking some time before travel to consider your personal security.

Crime: Serious crime, including murder and armed robbery, continues to be a major problem. The murder rate in Guyana is three times higher than the murder rate in the United States.

Armed robberies continue to occur intermittently, especially in major business and shopping districts. Hotel room strong-arm break-ins also occur; you should use caution when opening your hotel room doors and should safeguard any valuables left in hotel rooms. Criminals may act brazenly, and police officers themselves have been the victims of assaults and shootings. When traveling in a vehicle you should keep the doors locked and be aware of your surroundings at all times.

Pick pocketing, purse snatching, assault, and robbery can occur in all areas of Georgetown. The sea wall, from east of the Pegasus Hotel extending to Sheriff Street and adjacent areas, has been the site of several crimes; you should avoid these areas after dark. As cars parked in Georgetown have been subject to theft, you are urged to avoid leaving any valuables in vehicles left unattended and are encouraged to lock your vehicles at all times (when in or out of the vehicle). The National Park in Georgetown and the seawall from Sheriff Road to UG Road are frequented by joggers, dog walkers, and families and are generally considered safe during daylight hours but are not recommended at all after dusk.

Petty crimes also occur in the general area of Stabroek Market and to a lesser extent in the area behind Bourda Market. Care should be taken to safeguard personal property when shopping in these markets. The area around St. George's cathedral is known for having pickpockets and should be avoided after dark. Guyana's commercial downtown between Main Street and Water Street from Lamaha Road to Stabroek Market, including "Tiger Bay," is largely deserted outside of business hours and should be avoided after dark. U.S. passports and permanent residency cards are prized by thieves, as they may be used for smuggling and identity theft.

You should avoid walking around Georgetown alone, even in the main areas and especially after dark. Although bandits have been known to attack taxis, they are generally safe and remain the safest means of getting around town and to and from the airport. Only use taxis that are connected to major hotels or are painted yellow. All yellow taxies are registered with the Government of Guyana's licensing office. Exercise constant vigilance, and prior to entering any taxi, make note of the vehicle's license plate. This can be used to track down the driver in the event of being overcharged or if luggage is lost. Do not dress ostentatiously, as there have also been reports of gold chains or other jewelry being snatched off of pedestrians.

Local law-enforcement authorities are generally cooperative but lack the resources to respond effectively to serious criminal incidents. Nevertheless, if you are a victim of crime you are encouraged to contact the police as well as the American Citizens Services Unit of the U.S. Embassy's Consular Section.

Don't buy counterfeit and pirated goods, even if they are widely available. Not only are the bootlegs illegal in the United States, if you purchase them you may also be breaking local law.

Victims of Crime: If you or someone you know becomes the victim of a crime abroad, you should contact the local police and the nearest U.S. embassy or consulate (see the Department of State's list of embassies and consulates). If your passport is stolen we can help you replace it; you will need to present a police report when you come to the Embassy for a new passport. For violent crimes, such as assault and rape, we can help you find appropriate medical care, contact family members or friends and help them send you money if you need it. Although the investigation and prosecution of the crime are solely the responsibility of local authorities, consular officers can help you to understand the local criminal justice process and to find an attorney if needed.

The local equivalent to the "911" emergency line in Guyana is 911.

Criminal Penalties: While you are traveling in Guyana, you are subject to its laws even if you are a U.S. citizen. Foreign laws and legal systems can be vastly different than our own. In Guyana you may be taken in for questioning if you don't have your passport with you. It is illegal to take pictures of certain buildings, especially government buildings. Repercussions for driving under the influence result in a fine for the initial offense, a suspension of your license for the second offence and a jail term for succeeding offenses. It's very important to know what's legal and what's not where you are going.

Criminal penalties will vary from country to country. There are also some things that might be legal in the country you visit, but still illegal in the United States. You can be prosecuted under U.S. law if you buy pirated goods. Engaging in sexual conduct with children or disseminating child pornography in a foreign country is a crime prosecutable in the United States.

If you break local laws in Guyana, your U.S. passport won't help you avoid arrest or prosecution. Persons violating Guyanese laws, even unknowingly, may be expelled, arrested, or imprisoned. Penalties for possessing, using, or trafficking in illegal drugs in Guyana are severe, and convicted offenders can expect long jail sentences and heavy fines. Incarceration time prior to conviction and sentencing does not count toward time served.

If you are arrested in Guyana, Guyanese authorities are required by the Vienna Convention on Consular Notification to notify the U.S. Embassy of your arrest. If you are concerned the Department of State may not be aware of your situation, you should request that police or prison officials notify the nearest U.S. embassy or consulate of your arrest.

Special Circumstances: Flights on all airlines can be delayed, rerouted, or canceled without notice. Air travel within Guyana generally depends on demand. On small domestic airlines, flights that are not full may be canceled or passengers may be expected to pay for the empty seats. Travelers to the United States from Guyana have found narcotics planted in their luggage, both in bags registered under their names and in items they were carrying for others. You should not carry any items you did not personally purchase and pack and should take care that no additional bags are registered in your name. Every year several U.S. citizens are arrested at the airport attempting to carry drugs to the United States. Persons arrested usually end up serving lengthy prison sentences in Guyana, as drug laws are strict and pre-trial detention can last for years. In addition, due to the risks of checked baggage being lost, delayed, or rifled through, you should hand carry medications, valuables, and perishable items and make sure to carry a prescription for any medications that you are required to take.

Travel in the interior: The interior of the country is largely not policed and emergency services are generally not available. There is no cellular phone reception in much of the interior.

Flooding: There are two main rainy seasons in Guyana (December—January and May—July). However, even at other times of the year, heavy rains are possible and flash flooding can occur. The coastal plain floods occasionally, and there was significant flooding in Greater Georgetown and along the East Coast in January 2005 and in the Mahaica-Mahaicony Abrary area, Canals 1 and 2, on the West Coast Demerara and the Pomeroon River catchment area in January 2006. There was also isolated flooding on the East Coast in early 2009. The incidence of waterborne diseases increases during periods of flooding. Rains are expected to be heavier than normal during the 2011–2012 rainy seasons.

Drinking Water: The water supply system throughout the country should be considered contaminated, and travelers should treat or boil water before consumption, or purchase bottled water.

Changing Currency and Credit Card Use: You should have enough cash or travelers checks to meet your expenses. Although credit cards are accepted at certain institutions in Georgetown, travelers should consider the risk of using credit cards and ATM cards to withdraw cash from an overseas account, due to a high risk of stolen PIN data. You are advised to exchange currency only with banks, hotels, and licensed money exchange houses ("cambios"). Many foreigners who opt to exchange money on the streets, lured by promises of higher exchange rates, become victims of fraud or receive counterfeit currency. Foreigners have been mugged after completing bank transactions. There is no legal recourse unless the police are successful in apprehending the perpetrator; even then there is no guarantee that the money will be recovered.

Firearms: Guyanese customs authorities may enforce strict regulations concerning temporary importation into or export from Guyana of items such as firearms. If you plan to take your firearms or ammunition to or through Guyana, you should contact officials at the Embassy of Guyana to learn about local regulations and fully comply with those regulations before traveling. Even innocuous items like jewelry that looks like ammunition could result in arrest. You may consult the U.S. Customs and Border Protection web site for information on importing firearms into the United States.

Wildlife: Many plants and animals common in Guyana are globally threatened or endangered species protected by the Convention on International Trade in Endangered Species of Wild Fauna and Flora (CITES). More information may be found at the CITES web site. The Guyanese Ministry of Agriculture will grant an export permit for taking an exotic bird out of the country only to those persons who have been legally residing in Guyana for more than one year.

There have been several U.S. citizens arrested for attempting to leave Guyana carrying birds without having obtained an export permit. If you have legally resided in Guyana for more than a year and would like to take back to the United States any birds or animals, including pets that are listed in CITES Appendices I, II, and III, you must also have an appropriate U.S. import permit from the

U.S. Fish and Wildlife Service (USFWS). This is a U.S. regulation that applies regardless of distinctions among the three CITES Appendices. You can obtain fact sheets and permit applications from the USFWS Office of Management Authority, Branch of Permits, 4401 N. Fairfax Drive, Arlington, VA 22203, telephone (703) 358-2104, fax (703) 358-2281.

Accessibility: While in Guyana, individuals with disabilities may find accessibility and accommodation very different from what you find in the United States. The constitution mandates the state to take measures to protect persons with disabilities but there is no law that mandates provision of access for such persons. There is also a lack of appropriate infrastructure that provides access to both public and private facilities.

Medical Facilities and Health Information: Medical care in Guyana does not meet U.S. standards. Care is available for minor medical conditions, although quality is very inconsistent. Emergency care and hospitalization for major medical illnesses or surgery are very limited, due to a lack of appropriately trained specialists, below standard in-hospital care, and poor sanitation.

There are very few ambulances in Guyana. Ambulance service is limited to transportation without any medical care and is frequently not available for emergencies. An MRI (linked to the United States for interpretation) has been installed and is operational, but results may take up to 4 days. It is located on the compound of St. Joseph Mercy Hospital, immediately behind the Embassy on Parade Street.

In the event of an emergency, the number for an ambulance is 913, but this number is not always operational and an ambulance may not be available. You are advised to bring prescription medicine sufficient for your length of stay and should be aware that Guyana's humid climate may affect some medicines. Some prescription medicines (mainly generic rather than name-brand) are available.

Special attention should be paid to HIV/AIDS in Guyana. In addition to elevated infection rates among high-risk populations, such as commercial sex workers, and mobile populations such as miners or loggers, data from the World Health Organization estimate that Guyana has among the highest prevalence rates in Latin America and the Caribbean.

Insect borne illnesses are common and include malaria, dengue, Leishmaniasis, and Chagas disease. Insect precautions and anti-malarial chemoprophylaxis are encouraged. You can find good information on vaccinations and other health precautions, on the CDC website. For information about outbreaks of infectious diseases abroad, consult the World Health Organization (WHO) website. The WHO website also contains additional health information for travelers, including detailed country-specific health information.

Tuberculosis is an increasingly serious health concern in Guyana. For further information, please consult the CDC's information on TB.

Medical Insurance: You can't assume your insurance will go with you when you travel. It's very important to find out before you leave whether your medical insurance will cover you overseas. You need to ask your insurance company two questions:

- Does my policy apply when I'm out of the U.S.?
- Will it cover emergencies like a trip to a foreign hospital or an evacuation?

In many places, doctors and hospitals still expect payment in cash at the time of service. Your regular U.S. health insurance may not cover doctors' and hospital visits in other countries. If your policy doesn't go with you when you travel, it's a very good idea to take out another one for your trip.

Traffic Safety and Road Conditions: While in a Guyana, you may encounter road conditions that differ significantly from those in the United States. The information below concerning Guyana is provided for general reference only, and may not be totally accurate in a particular location or circumstance.

Driving in Guyana can be potentially very hazardous. The rate of traffic accident fatalities in Guyana is higher than in the United States. Cars, large commercial vehicles, horse drawn carts, bicyclists, motorcycles, free range livestock, stray dogs, pedestrians, aggressive "minibuses" and sleeping animals all share narrow, poorly maintained roads.

Aggressive, speeding vehicles on the same roads with slow-moving vehicles makes driving in Guyana especially dangerous. Driving at unsafe speeds, reckless driving, tail-gating, quick stops without signaling, passing at intersections, and passing on crowded streets is commonplace. Driving at night poses additional concerns as many roads are not lit, some drivers do not lower high beam lights, livestock sleep on the road and many pedestrians congregate by the roadside. You should exercise caution at all times while driving and avoid driving outside of Georgetown at night when possible.

The Traffic Division of Guyana's National Police Force is responsible for road safety but is ill-trained and ill-equipped. The Department of State recommends that Embassy staff travel in groups of two or more vehicles when traveling outside Georgetown.

You are advised to use caution traveling to and from Cheddi Jagan International Airport, especially at night. The Embassy requires its staff to use official vehicles when traveling this route between dusk and dawn due to a combination of most of the aforementioned characteristics of driving in Guyana.

Penalties for drivers involved in an accident resulting in injury or death are severe, including life imprisonment. If involved in an accident, call 911 for police and 913 for an ambulance. Please note that these numbers are not always operational, police may be slow to respond and an ambulance may not be available.

Drivers use the left side of the road in Guyana. Seatbelt use is required by law and is enforced; failure to use a seatbelt when riding in the front seat of any vehicle can result in a fine. There presently are no laws in Guyana concerning use of child car seats, but the use of age-appropriate seats is strongly recommended for child passengers. Both drivers of and passengers on motorcycles must wear protective helmets that meet certain specifications. Talking on cellular telephones while driving is illegal; however, it is legal if a driver uses a hands free set. Mini-buses (small 12- to 15-passenger vans) ply various routes both within and between cities. Mini-bus drivers have come under severe criticism from the government, press, and private citizens for speeding, aggressive and reckless driving, overloading of vehicles, poor vehicle maintenance and repair, and offensive remarks directed at passengers, but little change in their driving behavior has been noted. Mini-buses have been involved in the majority of fatal vehicular accidents in recent years, and official Americans are barred from using them. You should use taxis for transportation.

Aviation Safety Oversight: The U.S. Federal Aviation Administration (FAA) has assessed the Government of Guyana's Civil Aviation Authority as not being in compliance with International Civil Aviation Organization (ICAO) aviation safety standards for oversight of Guyana's air carrier operations. Further information may be found on the FAA's safety assessment page.

The U.S. Embassy in Guyana wishes to draw attention to information released by the U.S. Embassy in Suriname in regard to Suriname-based airline, Blue Wing. While not based in Guyana, Blue Wing does have flights between Guyana and Suriname. The U.S. Embassy in Suriname has prohibited its employees from using Blue Wing Airlines for official travel on domestic flights within Suriname due to safety concerns arising from the airline's three crashes since 2008, the latest on May 15, 2010.

All three accidents involved Antonov 28 planes. Consequently, the Government of Suriname's Civil Aviation and Safety Authority (CASAS) has grounded all Antonov planes pending further investigation. Blue Wing uses the Antonovs only for domestic flights. Following up on the action taken by CASAS, the U.S. Embassy in Suriname has prohibited the use of Blue Wing Airlines for official domestic travel and advised against its use for personal travel until safety issues are resolved. You should use discretion regarding plans to travel on Blue Wing international flights.

Children's Issues: Please see the U.S. Dept. of State Office of Children's Issues web pages on intercountry adoption and international parental child abduction

Intercountry Adoption

September 2010

The information in this section has been edited from the latest report available as of February 2013 from the State Department Bureau of Consular Affairs, Office of Overseas Citizens Services. For more information, please read the *Intercountry Adoption* section of this book and review current reports online at http://adoption.state.gov.

Guyana is not party to the Hague Convention on Protection of Children and Co-operation in Respect of Intercountry Adoption (Hague Adoption Convention). Therefore, when the Hague Adoption Convention entered into force for the United States on April 1, 2008, intercountry adoption processing for Guyana did not change. Under Guyanese law only Guyanese nationals, former Guyanese nationals or non-Guyanese domiciled in Guyana may adopt Guyanese children. Prospective adoptive parents should note that their presence is required at most stages during the adoption process.

Who Can Adopt? To bring an adopted child to United States from Guyana, you must be found eligible to adopt by the U.S. government. The U.S. government agency responsible for making this determination is the Department of Homeland Security, U.S. Citizenship and Immigration Services (USCIS). In addition to these U.S. requirements for adoptive parents, Guyana also has the following requirements for adoptive parents.

Residency Requirements: Guyanese law dictates that Guyanese children can only be adopted by a person domiciled in Guyana; a Guyanese national who is resident outside Guyana; or a former Guyanese national who has acquired, by registration or other voluntary and formal act (including marriage), the citizenship of another country. Non-Guyanese nationals who are not domiciled in Guyana cannot adopt Guyanese children.

Age Requirements: The prospective adoptive parent (if married, at least one member of the couple) must be 25 years of age and at least 21 years older than the adoptive child (18 years older if the child is a relative).

Marriage Requirements: Both married and single individuals can adopt in Guyana.

Income Requirements: Prospective adoptive parents must prove financial stability.

Who Can Be Adopted? Guyana has specific requirements that a child must meet in order to be eligible for adoption. You cannot adopt a child in Guyana unless he or she meets the requirements outlined below. In addition to these requirements, a child must meet the definition of an orphan under U.S. law for you to bring him or her back to the United States.

Eligibility Requirements: Consent of each birth parent or guardian of the child is required unless the birth parent or guardian has abandoned, neglected, or mistreated the child, cannot be found, or is incapable of giving consent. In cases where the biological parent cannot be found, an advertisement of the pending adoption must be placed for three consecutive Saturdays in a daily newspaper. In the event that the child's biological parents are deceased, death certificates must be shown.

Guyana's Adoption Authority: Adoption Board, Ministry of Labor, Human Services and Social Security

The Process: The first step in adopting a child is usually to select a licensed agency in the United States that can help with your adoption. Adoption service providers must be licensed by the U.S. state in which they operate.

There are no private adoption agencies in Guyana. A list of attorneys who can provide legal services related to adoption can be obtained from the U.S. Embassy in Georgetown or via the Embassy's website at http://georgetown.usembassy.gov.

To bring an adopted child from Guyana to the United States, you must apply to be found eligible to adopt (Form I-600A) by the U.S. Government, Department of Homeland Security, U.S. Citizenship and Immigration Services (USCIS).

Prospective adoptive parents must apply in person to the Adoption Board ("the Board"). The application form, First Schedule, consist of two parts, Form A and Form B. Form A is completed and signed by the prospective adoptive parents and consists of biographical data for the applicants and prospective child. It also includes references for the prospective adoptive parents. Form B is a medical certificate for the child or children to be adopted, which must be completed by a duly qualified medical practitioner. Prospective adoptive parents must obtain these forms in person from the Board.

When the prospective adoptive parents file the First Schedule, they will received an acknowledgement slip with an appointment date for the initial adoption interview. The prospective adoptive parents, child, and biological parents must appear before the Board at the interview. The appointments are usually scheduled within 4-6 weeks after the application is filed. The Board will undertake a request for an expedited appointment but it is not guaranteed.

A social worker interviews the birth parents, prospective adoptive parents, and children separately at the initial adoption interview. At the conclusion of the interview, assuming a signed and witnessed consent is obtained from the biological parents, or, if absent, the Board is satisfied that the birth parent(s) cannot be located, the prospective adoptive parents are given an informational letter from the Board. This letter provides instructions for the prospective adoptive parents' attorney to begin preparing the court papers for the adoption process. Two copies of this letter must also be filed in the High Court by the attorney for the applicants, along with an application to appoint the Board guardian ad litem of the child. Obtaining the order may take up to six months depending on the attorney's skill and the court calendar. If you are eligible to adopt, and a child is available for intercountry adoption, the central adoption authority in Guyana will provide you with a referral to a child.

The Adoption Board will grant guardian ad litem (also called first order) to the prospective adoptive parents, then, the Board conducts a more thorough investigation of the case. The investigation includes a visit by an officer of the Board to the home of the prospective adoptive parents to ensure that the welfare of the child is being met. If the child does not live with the prospective adoptive parents, a probationary period is allowed for bonding between the prospective adoptive parents and the child. The bonding period must take place in Guyana. The Board receives a report of the investigation. In addition to the investigation, a home study must be conducted by a certified social worker.

After the investigation is complete and the home study received by the Board, the case is placed on the Adoption Board's calendar. Cases are usually scheduled 2-3 months in advance. The prospective adoptive parents, children, and birth parents are required to be present for the meeting. The prospective adoptive parents must also be physically present in Guyana at least one month prior to the Board meeting. The Adoption Board meets on the last Wednesday of every month, except December, at 1:30 pm. The social worker's report based on the investigation and home study is discussed and the Board seeks a consensus. A decision in favor of the prospective adoptive parents would be followed within a week by a recommendation (Form C) of the case to the High Court for the making of a Final Order. The Board can defer a case until it is fully convinced about the competence of the applicant, or can reject it because there are no justifiable grounds for the adoption. At a later date the parties involved will be given notice to attend court before a judge in chambers for the issuance of the Final Order. Once the Final Order is issued, a copy of the child's Adoption Certificate can be obtained from the office of the Registrar General.

Role of the Adoption Authority: The Adoption Board provides the adoption application. After the prospective adoptive parents file the First Schedule, the Adoption Board provides the acknowledgement slip with the initial adoption interview appointment date.

Role of the Court: The High Court reviews the Board's informational letter and if approved, appoints the Board guardian ad litem for the child. After the Adoption Board's has made their decision, the parties involved will be given notice to attend court before a judge in chambers for the issuance of the Final Order. Once the Final Order is issued, a copy of the child's Adoption Certificate can be obtained from the office of the Registrar General.

Role of Adoption Agencies: While there are no adoption agencies in Guyana, an attorney assists the prospective adoptive parents with the adoption.

Adoption Application: Prospective adoptive parents must obtain the adoption application in person from the Adoption Board. Office hours are Monday—Friday from 8:00 a.m.—Noon and 1:00 p.m.—4:30 p.m. The office closes at 3:30 p.m. on Fridays. The Application is called the First Schedule and consists of two parts, Form A and Form B.

Time Frame: Adoptions in Guyana typically take one year to complete.

Adoption Fees: There are no government fees. Prospective adoptive parents should be aware that attorneys determine the fees for adoption services rendered and may vary significantly among different attorneys.

Documents Required: The following certified documents are required for adoptions in Guyana:

- Birth and marriage certificates
- Bank statements
- Employment verification
- Police clearance
- Home study
- National identity cards or passports (if non-Guyanese)

In addition to the above documents for prospective adoptive parents', the following documents pertaining to the child are needed for the initial adoption interview:

- Death Certificate, if biological parents are deceased
- Child's birth certificate
- Most recent school records

Bringing Your Child Home: Once your adoption is complete (or you have obtained legal custody of the child), there are a few more steps to take before you can head home. Specifically, you need to apply for several documents for your child before he or she can travel to the United States, such as a birth certificate, a passport or travel document for your child from the country in which he or she was born, and a U.S. Immigration Visa.

For detailed and updated information on how to obtain these documents, review the *Intercountry Adoption* section on this publication and visit the USCIS Intercountry Adoption website at http://adoption. state.gov.

Child Citizenship Act: For adoptions finalized abroad, the Child Citizenship Act of 2000 allows your new child to acquire American citizenship automatically when he or she enters the United States as lawful permanent residents.

For adoptions finalized in the United States, the Child Citizenship Act of 2000 allows your new child to acquire American citizenship automatically when the court in the United States issues the final adoption decree. To learn more, review the *Intercountry Adoption* section on this publication and visit the USCIS Intercountry Adoption website at http://adoption. state.gov.

After Adoption: There are no post-adoption requirements for Guyana.

U.S. Embassy in Guyana
99/100 Young & Duke Streets
Kingston, Georgetown
Tel: 592-225-7965; 592-225-7966
Fax: 592-227-0221
Email: visageorge@state.gov
http://georgetown.usembassy.gov

Guyanese Adoption Authority
Adoption Board, Ministry of Labor, Human Services and Social Security
1 Water and Cornhill Streets
Georgetown, Guyana
Tel: 592-225-7450
Fax: 592-227-1308

Embassy of Guyana
2490 Tracy Place, N.W.
Washington, D.C. 20008
Tel: (202) 265-3834; (202) 265-6900
Fax: (202) 232-1297

Consulate General of Guyana
370 7th Avenue, Room 402
New York, N.Y. 10001
Tel: (212) 947-5115; (212) 947-5116
Fax: (212) 947-5163

Guyana also has honorary consulates in Los Angeles, Miami, East Chicago, and Waco (TX).

Office of Children's Issues
U.S. Department of State
2201 C Street, NW
SA-29
Washington, DC 20520
Tel: 1-888-407-4747
E-mail: AskCI@state.gov
http://adoption.state.gov

For questions about immigration procedures, call the National Customer Service Center (NCSC) 1-800-375-5283 (TTY 1-800-767-1833).

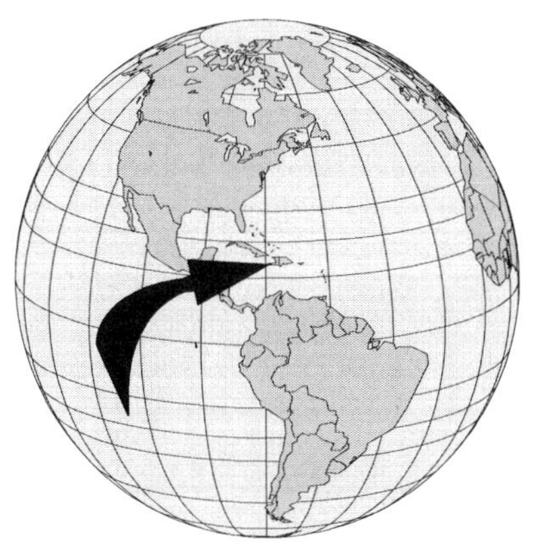

HAITI

Compiled from publications that were available as of February 2013 from the U.S. Department of State, the U.S. Department of Commerce, and the Central Intelligence Agency (CIA). See the introduction to this set for explanatory notes.

Official Name:
Republic of Haiti

PROFILE

Geography

Area: total: 27,750 sq km; country comparison to the world: 148; land: 27,560 sq km; water: 190 sq km
Major cities: Port-Au-Prince (capital) 2.143 million (2010)
Climate: tropical; semiarid where mountains in east cut off trade winds
Terrain: mostly rough and mountainous

People

Nationality: noun: Haitian(s); adjective: Haitian
Population: 9,801,664 (July 2012 est.)
Population growth rate: 0.888%
Ethnic groups: black 95%, mulatto and white 5%
Religions: Roman Catholic 80%, Protestant 16% (Baptist 10%, Pentecostal 4%, Adventist 1%, other 1%), none 1%, other 3%
Languages: French (official), Creole (official)
Literacy: definition: age 15 and over can read and write; total population: 52.9%; male: 54.8%; female: 51.2% (2003 est.)
Health: life expectancy at birth: total population: 62.51 years; male: 61.15 years; female: 63.89 years; Infant mortality rate: total: 52.44 deaths/1,000 live births; male: 56.47 deaths/1,000 live births; female: 48.37 deaths/1,000 live births
Unemployment rate: 40.6% (2010 est.)
Work force: 4.81 million

Government

Type: republic
Independence: 1 January 1804
Constitution: approved March 1987; this is Haiti's 23rd constitution
Political subdivisions: 10 departments (departements, singular—departement); Artibonite, Centre, Grand'Anse, Nippes, Nord, Nord-Est, Nord-Ouest, Ouest, Sud, Sud-Est
Suffrage: 18 years of age; universal

Economy

GDP (purchasing power parity): $13.13 billion (2012 est.); $12.52 billion (2011 est.); $11.86 billion (2010 est.); $12.54 billion (2009 est.)
GDP real growth rate: 4.5% (2012 est.); 5.6% (2011 est.); -5.4% (2010 est.); 2.9% (2009 est.)
GDP per capita (PPP): $1,300 (2012 est.); $1,300 (2011 est.); $1,200 (2010 est.); $1,300 (2009 est.)
Natural resources: bauxite, copper, calcium carbonate, gold, marble, hydropower
Agriculture products: coffee, mangoes, sugarcane, rice, corn, sorghum; wood
Industries: textiles, sugar refining, flour milling, cement, light assembly based on imported parts
Exports: $801.7 million (2012 est.); $721.3 million (2011 est.); $561.5 million (2010 est.)
Exports—commodities: apparel, manufactures, oils, cocoa, mangoes, coffee
Exports—partners: US 83.3% (2011)
Imports: $2.928 billion (2012 est.); $3.352 billion (2011 est.); $2.809 billion (2010 est.)
Imports—commodities: food, manufactured goods, machinery and transport equipment, fuels, raw materials
Imports—partners: Dominican Republic 31.9%, US 25.3%, Netherlands Antilles 8.7%, China 7.2% (2011)
Debt—external: $854.7 million (31 December 2012 est.); $665.1 million (31 December 2011 est.); $482.1 million (31 December 2010 est.)
Exchange rates: gourdes (HTG) per US dollar; 40.52 (2012 est.); 40.523 (2011 est.); 39.8 (2010 est.); 42.02 (2009); 39.216 (2008); 37.138 (2007)

PEOPLE

Although Haiti averages about 350 people per square kilometer, its population is concentrated most heavily in urban areas, coastal plains, and valleys. About 95% of Haitians are of African descent. The rest of the population is mostly of mixed Caucasian-African ancestry. A few are of European or Levantine heritage. Sixty percent of the population lives in rural areas.

Large-scale emigration, principally to the U.S.—but also to Canada, the Dominican Republic, The Bahamas and other Caribbean neighbors, and France—has created what Haitians refer to as the Eleventh Department or the Diaspora. About one of every eight Haitians lives abroad, with more than 80% of Haitians with college degrees emigrating mostly to Canada.

Although the expatriate Haitian community has a strong interest in Haiti's future and a positive financial impact on the Haitian economy, the Haitian Diaspora is constrained by Article 15 of Haiti's 1987 constitution, which prohibits dual citizenship. Consequently, Haitian Americans lack political rights in their homeland, including voting rights; property rights are restricted for foreign nationals.

Language

French is one of two official languages, but it is spoken fluently by only about 10% of the people. All Haitians speak Creole, the country's other official language. English and Spanish are increasingly used as second languages among the young and in the business sector.

Religion

A UN Population Fund census released in 2006 (based on 2003 data) lists the following religious demographics: 55 percent of the population is Roman Catholic, 15 percent Baptist, 8 percent Pentecostal, and 3 percent Seventh-day Adventist. Other religious groups include Episcopalians, Jehovah's Witnesses, Methodists, members of The Church of Jesus Christ of Latter-day Saints (Mormons), Muslims, Scientologists, and practitioners of Vodou (voodoo). Recent estimates indicate that half of the population practices Vodou. Vodou is often practiced along with other religions, most often Catholicism.

Education

Although public education is free, the cost is still quite high for Haitian families who must pay for uniforms, textbooks, supplies, and other inputs. Due to weak state provision of education services, private and parochial schools account for approximately 90% of primary schools, and only 65% of primary school-aged children are actually enrolled.

At the secondary level, the figure drops to around 20%. Less than 35% of those who enter will complete primary school. Though Haitians place a high value on education, few can afford to send their children to secondary school and primary school enrollment is dropping due to economic factors.

Remittances sent by Haitians living abroad are important in paying educational costs. After the January 12, 2010 earthquake most schools in the greater Port-au-Prince area were not operating, though some schools reopened on April 5. As of July 1, 2010, 75% of students in earthquake-affected areas had returned to school.

HISTORY

The Spaniards used the island of Hispaniola (of which Haiti is the western part and the Dominican Republic the eastern) as a launching point from which to explore the rest of the Western Hemisphere. French buccaneers later used the western third of the island as a point from which to harass English and Spanish ships. In 1697, Spain ceded the western third of Hispaniola to France. As piracy was gradually suppressed, some French adventurers became planters, making Saint Domingue, as the French portion of the island was known, the "pearl of the Antilles"—one of the richest colonies in the 18th-century French empire.

During this period, African slaves were brought to work on sugarcane and coffee plantations. In 1791, the slave population revolted—led by Toussaint L'Ouverture, Jean Jacques Dessalines, and Henri Christophe—and gained control of the northern part of the French colony, waging a war of attrition against the French.

By January 1804, local forces defeated an army sent by Napoleon Bonaparte, established independence from France, and renamed the area Haiti. The impending defeat of the French in Haiti is widely credited with contributing to Napoleon's decision to sell the Louisiana territory to the United States in 1803.

Haiti is the world's oldest black republic and the second-oldest republic in the Western Hemisphere, after the United States. Although Haiti actively assisted the independence movements of many Latin American countries, the independent nation of former slaves was excluded from the hemisphere's first regional meeting of independent nations, in Panama in 1826, and did not receive U.S. diplomatic recognition until 1862.

Two separate regimes—north and south—emerged after independence but were unified in 1820. Two years later, Haiti occupied Santo Domingo, the eastern, Spanish-speaking part of Hispaniola. In 1844, however, Santo Domingo broke away from Haiti and became the Dominican Republic. With 22 changes of government from 1843 to 1915, Haiti experienced numerous periods of intense political and economic disorder, prompting the United States military intervention of 1915. Following a 19-year occupation, U.S. military forces were withdrawn in 1934, and Haiti regained sovereign rule.

The late 1950s saw the start of the violent and repressive dictatorship of Francois "Papa Doc" Duvalier. Elected president in 1957, he

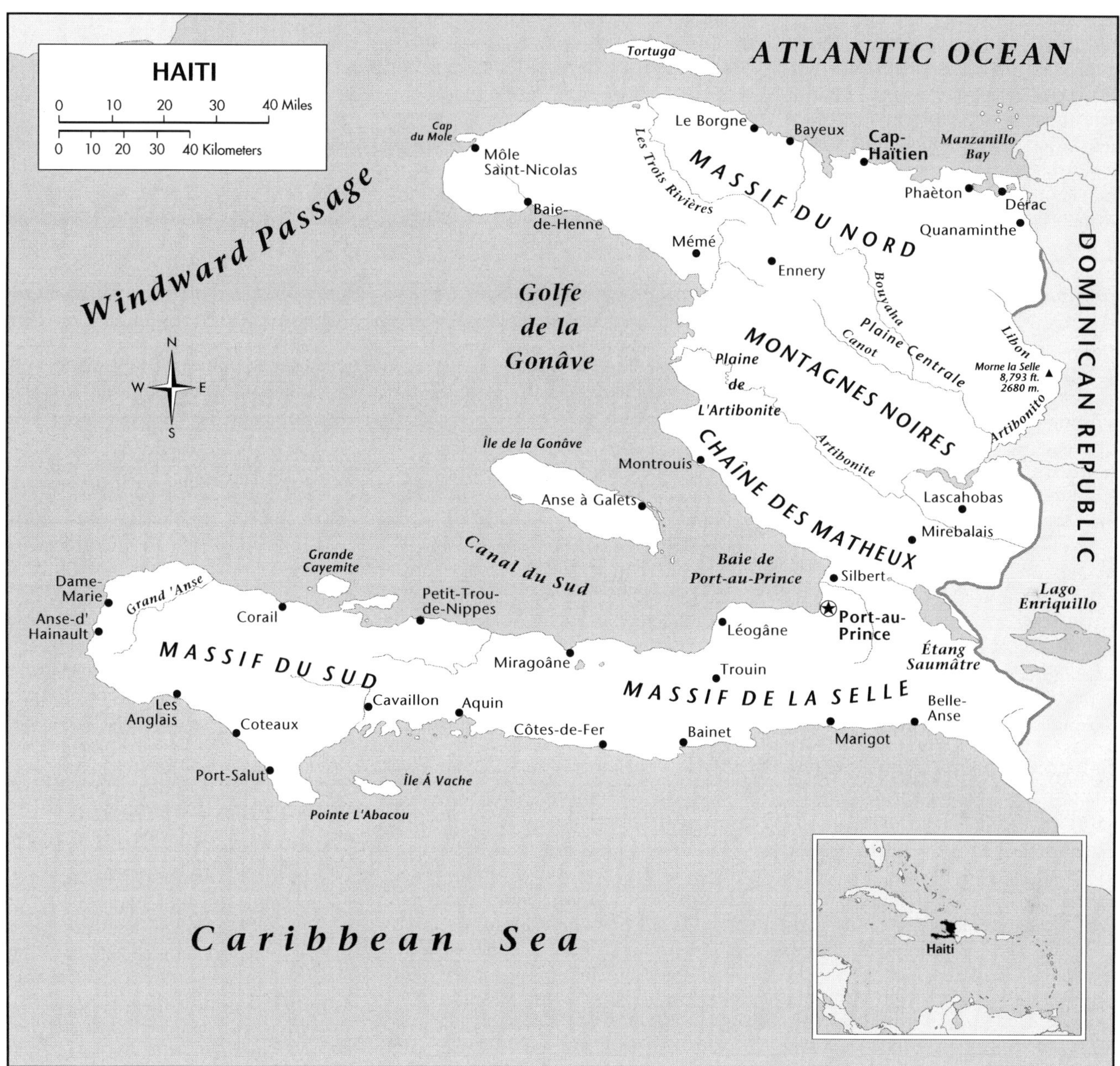

declared himself president-for-life in 1964 and ruled until his death in 1971 with the help of his paramilitary force, the Tontons Macoutes. Francois Duvalier was succeeded by his son, Jean-Claude "Baby Doc" Duvalier, who also declared himself president-for-life. The Duvaliers' rule was characterized by repressive state controls, including the lack of basic democratic rights.

Faced with economic collapse and a popular uprising, Jean-Claude Duvalier fled to France on February 7, 1986. The period immediately after his departure was marked by mob vengeance against members of the Tontons Macoutes. From 1986 to 1990, Haiti was ruled by a series of provisional governments.

In March 1987, a constitution was ratified that provided for an elected, bicameral parliament; an elected president as head of state; and a prime minister, cabinet, ministers, and Supreme Court appointed by the president with the parliament's consent.

The constitution also provided for political decentralization through the election of mayors and administrative bodies responsible for local government.

In December 1990, Jean-Bertrand Aristide won 67% of the vote in a presidential election that international observers deemed largely free and fair. Aristide took office on February 7, 1991, but was overthrown that September in a violent coup led by army elements and supported by many of the country's economic elite.

The coup contributed to a large-scale exodus of Haitians by boat. From October 1991 to September 1994 a de facto military regime governed Haiti. Several thousand Haitians may have been killed during the de facto military rule. Various Organization of American States (OAS) and United Nations initiatives to end the political crisis through the peaceful restoration of the constitutionally elected government failed.

On July 31, 1994, the UN Security Council (UNSC) authorized member states to use all necessary means to facilitate the departure of Haiti's military leadership and to restore Haiti's constitutionally elected government to power. In mid-September, with troops prepared to enter Haiti by force, Gen. Raoul Cedras and other top leaders agreed to accept the intervention of the U.S.-led multinational force. President Aristide and other elected officials in exile returned on October 15.

Nationwide local and parliamentary elections in June 1995 returned a pro-Aristide, multi-party coalition called the Lavalas Political Organization (OPL) to power at all levels. In accordance with the constitutional bar on succeeding himself, President Aristide agreed to step aside and support a presidential election in December 1995. Rene Preval, a prominent Aristide political ally, took 88% of the vote, and was sworn in to a 5-year term on February 7, 1996, during what was Haiti's first-ever transition between two democratically elected presidents.

In late 1996, former President Aristide broke from the OPL and created a new political party, the Lavalas Family (FL). The OPL, holding the majority of the Parliament, renamed itself the Struggling People's Organization. Initial results of elections in April 1997 for the renewal of one-third of the Senate and creation of commune-level assemblies and town delegations showed victories for FL candidates in most races.

However, the elections, which drew only about 5% of registered voters, were plagued with allegations of fraud and not certified by most international observers as free and fair. Preval's first term was marked by political wrangling. The opposition blocked his initiatives, and he failed to organize timely legislative elections. Following parliamentary elections that the opposition deemed deeply flawed on August 28, 2000, Haiti's main bilateral donors re-channeled their assistance away from the government and announced they would not support or send observers to the November elections. Most opposition parties regrouped in an alliance that became the Democratic Convergence.

Elections for President and nine Senators took place on November 26, 2000. All major opposition parties boycotted these elections, in which voter participation was estimated at 5%. Jean-Bertrand Aristide emerged as the easy victor of these controversial elections, and the candidates of his FL party swept all contested Senate seats. On February 7, 2001, Jean-Bertrand Aristide was inaugurated as President.

The political stalemate continued, and violence ensued. On July 28, 2001, unknown gunmen attacked police facilities in Port-au-Prince and the provinces. A subsequent government crackdown on opposition party members and former soldiers further increased tensions between Lavalas and Convergence. On December 17, 2001, unidentified gunmen attacked the National Palace in Port-au-Prince. Following the assault, pro-government groups attacked the offices and homes of several opposition leaders. One opposition member was killed. Negotiations between FL and Democratic Convergence were suspended indefinitely.

Despite the creation of an OAS Special Mission designed to strengthen Haiti's democratic institutions in security, justice, human rights, and governance, security continued to deteriorate.

Events spiraled downward throughout 2003, as President Aristide and the opposition failed to agree on a political resolution. Following a meeting with Aristide at the Summit of the Americas in January 2004, Caribbean Community leaders proposed a plan to resolve the political crisis, which President Aristide said he accepted. A high-level international delegation went to Haiti February 21 to obtain agreement on a specific implementation timetable. President Aristide agreed, but the opposition "Democratic Platform" group of political parties and civil society expressed reservations.

Meanwhile, violence in Gonaives culminated February 5 in the "Artibonite Resistance Front" seizing control of the city. Other armed groups opposed to the Aristide government quickly emerged and succeeded in seizing control of many towns, mostly with little resistance from government authorities. By February 28, 2004, a rebel group led by a former police chief, Guy Philippe, advanced to within 25 miles of the capital. On February 29, 2004 Aristide submitted his resignation as President of Haiti and flew on a chartered plane to Africa.

2004–2009 —Interim Government Gives Way to a New Democracy

Following the constitutional line of succession, Supreme Court Chief Justice Boniface Alexandre assumed the presidency and Gerard Latortue was appointed prime minister of the Interim Government of Haiti (IGOH) with the mandate of organizing elections to choose a new government.

The interim government managed to organize three rounds of elections with the help of the OAS and UN. The first round of elections for President and Parliament took place peacefully on February 7, 2006, with a turnout estimated at over 60% of registered voters. The elections were considered generally free, fair, transparent, and democratic by national and international observers.

Rene Preval, former President (1996–2001) and former ally to Aristide, won the presidential election with 51.15%. Partial results first showed he fell short of an absolute majority, which triggered demonstrations against alleged fraud. The later decision of the Electoral Council not to count blank ballots gave the victory to Preval. The Parliament, composed of a 30-seat Senate and a 99-member Chamber of Deputies, was elected in two rounds held on February 7 and April 21, 2006. Lespwa was the main political force in both chambers but fell short of the majority.

Fusion, UNION, Alyans, OPL, and Fanmi Lavalas had many representatives in both chambers. Preval chose his long-time political associate and former Prime Minister Jacques-Edouard Alexis to serve again as his Prime Minister. Municipal elections were held December 3, 2006 and April 29, 2007. Some of these local government positions had not been filled in over a decade.

A series of crises in 2008 threatened Haiti's democratic consolidation. Nationwide civil disturbances broke out in April 2008, sparked by sharp increases in food and fuel prices. The April riots caused widespread disruption and suffering, toppled the government of Prime Minister Alexis, and forced postponement of a donor conference.

In August and September, four tropical storms and hurricanes killed 800, affected nearly one million, exacerbated food shortages and pushed yet more Haitians into poverty. In early September 2008, Prime Minister Michele Pierre-Louis's government took office and acted decisively within its means to provide relief and reconstruction. Pierre-Louis initially received cooperation from Parliament in crafting a relief package, but soon after Parliament summoned both her and her ministers to explain perceived delays in delivering relief assistance and to criticize her 2008–2009 budget.

Despite the devastating hurricanes and food riots in 2008, the Preval administration made substantial gains in the overall physical security throughout Haiti. The international community took notice of Haiti's relative stability, and in January 2009, UN Secretary General Ban Ki-moon commissioned British economist Paul Collier to draft an economic development strategy for Haiti. In February, shortly after taking office, Secretary of State Hillary Clinton identified Haiti as a policy priority.

By March, Collier's report, "Haiti: From Natural Catastrophe to Economic Security" was adapted by the Government of Haiti as a template for its own economic growth strategy, presented at the Haiti Donor's Conference hosted by the Inter-American Development Bank in April. The strategy called on donors to assist the Haitian Government by investing in the country's roads, export zones, agriculture, electricity, schools, hospitals, and ports. In May 2009, the Secretary General named former U.S. President William J. Clinton as UN Special Envoy for Haiti and charged him with coordinating donors and attracting private investment to Haiti.

On October 20, 2009, Prime Minister Pierre-Louis was dismissed by the Senate, 1 year after taking office. Prime Minister Jean-Max Bellerive, former Minister of Planning and External Cooperation, took office in November 2009. By most accounts, Haiti prior to the January 2010 earthquake enjoyed relative internal stability.

The country had a fully functioning legislature, and although it had risked instability by ousting Prime Minister Pierre-Louis, it demonstrated a marked readiness to act by promptly approving new Prime Minister Bellerive.

January 12, 2010 Earthquake

On January 12, 2010, a 7.0-magnitude earthquake struck Haiti, with its epicenter near Port-au-Prince. The quake caused severe damage in Port-au-Prince, Leogane, Jacmel, and surrounding communities. Search and rescue teams were on the ground in Port-au-Prince immediately following the earthquake and worked 24 hours a day using listening devices, cameras, and trained dogs to detect any sign of human life.

Rescue efforts eventually transitioned into recovery efforts on January 27, 15 days after the earthquake. The government estimated 230,000 deaths, about one million displaced people within the Port-au-Prince metropolitan area, and 598,000 people who migrated from the affected areas to other locations in Haiti. Most of those people are thought to have returned to Port-au-Prince, as the communities of origin lacked the capacity to sustain the increase in population.

Following the earthquake, the U.S. military and representatives from the U.S. Department of Health and Human Services' Disaster Mortuary Operational Response Team (DMORT) worked side by side to recover, identify, and repatriate any American citizen that was recovered. All U.S. citizens believed to be in the Hotel Montana, which had collapsed in the earthquake, were repatriated back to the United States, and families of victims recovered from other locations were given the choice of repatriation or local disposition.

The U.S. Embassy and the Bureau of Consular Affairs' Office of American Citizens Services and Crisis Management were in regular and direct contact with the families of all of the missing.

U.S. Southern Command established Joint Task Force Haiti to support the relief effort following the earthquake. At the height of the task force's initial response, the U.S. contributed more than 20,000 U.S. troops, 20 ships, and 130 aircraft. U.S. military forces were focused on mitigating the negative weather effects on displacement camps in Port-au-Prince, supporting efforts to relocate displacement camps to transitional resettlement sites, and positioning the task force for a seamless transition.

By March 15, all Canadian troops had left Haiti. Joint Task Force Haiti completed its mission on June 1, 2010. A small military liaison office of eight people remained in Port-au-Prince to coordinate further humanitarian missions with the lead U.S. federal agency, the U.S. Agency for

International Development (USAID), and the Government of Haiti during the already-scheduled theater security cooperation exercise called New Horizons.

The exercise brought in about 500 soldiers—mainly from the Louisiana National Guard along with soldiers from the Arizona, Montana, Nevada, Puerto Rican, and Virgin Island National Guards—to conduct engineering activities and medical readiness training exercises in the vicinity of Gonaives, north of Port-au-Prince.

The earthquake's enormous devastation threatened political and socioeconomic stability and posed huge recovery and reconstruction challenges. The earthquake was the worst in Haiti in the previous 200 years, and generated an estimated $11.5 billion (173% of GDP) in damages and reconstruction costs. Assisting Haiti in recovery and rebuilding is a massive undertaking and requires a well-coordinated, well-funded, Government of Haiti-led effort by the Haitian people, the United States, the United Nations, other nations, international organizations, the Haitian Diaspora, and non-governmental organizations (NGOs).

The outpouring of international support has been tremendous, as has the resolve of the Haitian people. The U.S. Government continues to work with the Haitian Government, NGOs, the UN, and partner nations to provide humanitarian assistance in Haiti. U.S. Government humanitarian relief efforts in Haiti total over $1 billion. The United States and other donor countries, international organizations, and other partners have pledged resources, coordinated support of Haiti's long-term recovery, and committed to a sustained, long-term effort to support Haiti.

At the "International Donors' Conference Toward a New Future for Haiti," co-hosted by the United States and the United Nations on March 31, 2010 in New York, UN member states and international organizations pledged $9.9 billion toward reconstruction. The United States pledged $1.15 billion toward reconstruction efforts in the areas of energy, health, agriculture, governance, and security. The Government of Haiti presented its action plan outlining its vision for the future, which donors unanimously endorsed.

On April 15, 2010, the Haitian Parliament ratified a law extending by 18 months the state of emergency that President Preval had declared after the earthquake. The law also created the Interim Commission for the Reconstruction of Haiti (IHRC), allowing for Haitian-led planning with a role for international partners to provide input.

The earthquake prompted postponement of legislative elections and cast uncertainty over whether presidential elections could be held at the end of 2010 as planned. On May 10, the mandates of one-third of the Senators and all of the 99 Deputies in the Haitian Parliament expired, leaving 19 Senators in office. In the interim, President Preval had the authority to rule by decree. Just before the mandates expired, Parliament passed a bill allowing President Preval to remain in office until May 2011, 3 months beyond the February date when he originally intended to step down.

Presidential and parliamentary elections were held in November 2010 (first round) and March 2011 (second round).

GOVERNMENT AND POLITICAL CONDITIONS

Haiti is a constitutional republic with a multiparty political system. There were some allegations of fraud and irregularities in the second round of presidential and legislative elections on March 20, 2011, but international observers considered the elections generally free and fair. Voters elected President Michel Martelly, who took office on May 14 but was unable to secure the required parliamentary approval of a prime minister until October 4. Thus day-to-day government operations and budgetary discretion remained in the hands of the outgoing Preval government for six months, during which time there were multiple allegations of human rights abuses, corruption, and embezzlement of public funds.

Since 2004 the UN Peacekeeping Force in Haiti (MINUSTAH), made up of approximately 13,000 military and police officers and civilians, has operated in the country with a mandate to assist and advise government and security authorities.

Following the January 2010 earthquake, foreign governments, the international community, and many nongovernmental organizations provided assistance in rebuilding the country, while MINUSTAH continued to help maintain security. The earthquake effectively destroyed much of the government's infrastructure, and approximately 550,000 persons remained homeless and lived in camps for the internally displaced.

Recent Elections

There were isolated incidents of fraud, flawed voter registration lists, ballot stuffing, intimidation, and some violence at the polls during the March 20, 2011, second round of elections for deputies, senators, and president. Despite incidents of civil unrest, the police remained largely neutral during the political process.

The first round of elections in November 2010 was also marred by fraud, flawed voter registration lists, ballot stuffing, intimidation, and some violence at the polls. Despite a relatively low (22 percent) participation rate, international observers and civil society generally considered the second round to be free and fair. Voters elected Michel Martelly by a wide margin, and he was peacefully inaugurated as president on May 14, all the more remarkable since the outgoing and incoming presidents were from opposing political parties.

Political Parties: There were some restrictions on certain political parties. In 2009 the Provisional Electoral Council (CEP) considered 69 political parties for the 2010 parliamentary elections and approved 53. The CEP rejected 16 parties, including former president Jean-Bertrand Aristide's party, Fanmi Lavalas, for documentation that was inconsistent, lacked notarization, or did not conform to legal requirements.

Other rejected major parties included Union, Popular Solidarity Alliance, Struggling People's Organization, and Fusion. The latter two groups allied under a new party banner, Alternative, which officially boycotted the elections, although many of the party's legislative candidates participated in the elections.

The constitution requires that, following local and municipal elections, local officials must hold a series of indirect elections to staff departmental organs of self-government and an interdepartmental council to advise the national government and nominate candidates for the CEP.

The law requires that the three branches of the national government select from among these nominees the council's nine members. Since these indirect elections have not taken place since the constitution was written, the country continued to operate with the presidentially appointed CEP.

Participation of Women and Minorities: Electoral legislation mandates that political parties nominating at least 30 percent female candidates and electing 20 percent of those nominated receive twice as much public financing for those same positions in the next election. None of the political parties met these criteria in the November or March elections.

The monetary deposit required of female candidates for political office (if sponsored by a recognized party) was one-half that required of male candidates. In the 2010 elections, two women ran as candidates for president, eight for the Senate, and 45 for deputy seats. Of the deputy candidates, two won their seats outright in the first round, and seven qualified to run in the second round. Mirlande Manigat, one of the female presidential candidates, won approximately 30 percent of the vote, qualifying her to run in the second round.

Voters elected five women to the 99-member Chamber of Deputies. The sole female member of 30 senators was elected in 2006, and her term expired during 2011. President Martelly appointed three women into ministerial positions (women's affairs, tourism, and health), of which there were 16, and four female secretaries of state out of 19. Martelly also appointed women to be director general and vice director general of the Haitian Popular Bank, one of two state-owned banks.

Principal Government Officials

Last Updated: 1/31/2013

Pres.: **Michel MARTELLY**
Prime Min.: **Laurent LAMOTHE**
Min. of Agriculture, Natural Resources, & Rural Development: **Thomas JACQUES**
Min. of Commerce & Industry: **Wilson LALEAU**
Min. of Communication: **Ady Jean GARDY**
Min. of Culture: **Jean Mario DUPUY**
Min. of the Economy & Finance: **Marie Carmelle JEAN-MARIE**
Min. of Environment: **Jean Vilamond HILAIRE**
Min. of Foreign Affairs & Worship: **Pierre-Richard CASIMIR**
Min. of Haitians Living Abroad: **Daniel SUPPLICE**
Min. of Interior & Territorial Collectivities: **Ronsard ST.-CYR**
Min. of Justice & Public Security: **Jean Renel SANON**
Min. of National Defense: **Jean Rodolphe JOAZILE**
Min. of National Education & Professional Training: **Vanneur PIERRE**
Min. of Planning & External Cooperation: **Laurent LAMOTHE**
Min. of Public Health & Population: **Florence Duperval GUILLAUME**
Min. of Public Works, Transport, & Energy: **Jacques ROUSSEAU**
Min. of Social Affairs & Labor: **Josepha Raymond GAUTHIER**
Min. of Tourism: **Stephanie Balmir VILLEDROUIN**
Min. of Women's Affairs & Rights: **Yanick MEZIL**
Min. of Youth, Sports, & Civic Action: **Rene Jean ROOSEVELT**
Min.-Del. to the Prime Min. in Charge of Promoting the Peasantry: **Marie Mimose FELIX**
Min.-Del. to the Prime Min. in Charge of Relations With Parliament: **Ralph Ricardo THEANO**
Min.-Del. to the Prime Min. for Human Rights & the Fight Against Extreme Poverty: **Marie Carmelle Rose Anne AUGUSTE**
Governor, Bank of the Republic of Haiti: **Charles CASTEL**
Ambassador to the US: **Paul ALTIDOR**
Permanent Representative to the UN, New York: **Jean Wesley CAZEAU**

ECONOMY

Haiti is a free market economy that enjoys the advantages of low labor costs and tariff-free access to the US for many of its exports. Poverty, corruption, and poor access to education for much of the population are among Haiti's most serious disadvantages. Haiti's economy suffered a severe setback in January 2010 when a 7.0 magnitude earthquake destroyed much of its capital city, Port-au-Prince, and neighboring areas.

Already the poorest country in the Western Hemisphere with 80% of the population living under the poverty line and 54% in abject poverty, the earthquake inflicted $7.8 billion in damage and caused the country's GDP to contract 5.4% in 2010. Following the earthquake, Haiti received $4.59 billion in internatioonal pledges for reconstruction, which has proceeded slowly.

Two-fifths of all Haitians depend on the agricultural sector, mainly small-scale subsistence farming, and remain vulnerable to damage from frequent natural disasters, exacerbated by the country's widespread deforestation. US economic engagement under the Haitian Hemispheric Opportunity through Partnership Encouragement (HOPE) Act, passed in December 2006, has boosted apparel exports and investment by providing duty-free access to the US. Congress voted in 2010 to extend the legislation until 2020 under the Haiti Economic Lift Program Act (HELP); the apparel sector accounts for about 90% of Haitian exports and nearly one-tenth of GDP.

Remittances are the primary source of foreign exchange, equaling nearly 20% of GDP and more than twice the earnings from exports. Haiti suffers from a lack of investment, partly because of limited infrastructure and a lack of security. I

n 2005, Haiti paid its arrears to the World Bank, paving the way for reengagement with the Bank. Haiti received debt forgiveness for over $1 billion through the Highly-Indebted Poor Country initiative in mid-2009. The remainder of its outstanding external debt was cancelled by donor countries following the 2010 earthquake but has since risen to over $600 million.

The government relies on formal international economic assistance for fiscal sustainability, with over half of its annual budget coming from outside sources. The Martelly administration in 2011 launched a campaign aimed at drawing foreign investment into Haiti as a means for sustainable development.

Labor Conditions

The minimum age for employment in industrial, agricultural, or commercial companies is 15. The minimum age for apprenticeships is 14. The law prohibits young persons and children from performing any work that is likely to be hazardous, interferes with their education, or is harmful to their physical, mental, spiritual, moral, or social health and development, including the use of children in criminal activities.

The law also prohibits minors from working under dangerous or hazardous conditions, such as mining, construction, or sanitation services, and prohibits night work in industrial enterprises for minors under 18. There is no minimum age restriction for work in domestic service, and there are no legal penalties for employing children in domestic labor unless the nature or condition of domestic service harms their health, safety, or morals.

The law requires employers to pay domestic workers over the age of 15, thereby allowing employers of domestic workers to use "food and shelter" as a means of unregulated compensation for those under 15. Although the law guarantees free and compulsory primary education for all children, children are only required to attend school for six years, making children ages 12 to 14 (who are not required to attend school but are also not legally allowed to work) particularly vulnerable to child labor, including the worst forms of child labor.

Young people ages 15 to 18 seeking employment must obtain a work authorization from the Ministry of Social Affairs and Labor, unless they are employed in domestic service. Companies that employ minors without work authorization risk punishment with fines of between 3,000 and 5,000 gourdes ($78 and $125). The government does not report statistics on investigations into child labor law violations or the penalties imposed.

The daily minimum wage was 150 gourdes (approximately $3.75) in the textile sector and 200 gourdes (approximately $5.00) in the commercial and industrial sectors. Workers paid at a piecework rate received a minimum of 200 gourdes per day. For all other industrial and commercial work, the daily minimum wage was fixed at 200 gourdes for eight hours of work.

The law sets the standard workday for industrial, commercial, and agricultural establishments at eight hours and the workweek at 48 hours, with 24 hours of rest and paid annual holidays. It also provides for the payment of overtime and prohibits excessive compulsory overtime. However, the law grants exemptions to healthcare, lodging, food and beverage, and entertainment establishments; managerial positions; and family establishments that employ only family members. The Labor Directorate may grant exemptions for other employers not specifically exempted by the law. The law is also silent with respect to prohibiting overtime for public sector employees.

Labor law is very vague regarding domestic workers' rights including working hours, salary, vacation, and severance. The law establishes minimum health and safety regulations.

Most citizens worked in the informal sector and subsistence agriculture, for which minimum wage legislation does not apply, and where daily wages of 20-30 gourdes ($0.50-0.75) were common. Many women worked in domestic service, which was also exempted from minimum wage legislation. Due to staff shortages and special events, salaried HNP officers sometimes worked 12-hour shifts six days per week and received no overtime, although they received standardized bonuses at year's end.

U.S.-HAITI RELATIONS

U.S. policy toward Haiti is designed to foster economic growth, enhance government capacity, and strengthen democracy; help alleviate poverty, illiteracy, and malnutrition; promote respect for human rights; counter illegal migration and drug trafficking; and assist in the reconstruction of the country after the January 2010 earthquake.

The U.S. also supports and facilitates bilateral trade and investment along with legal migration and travel. U.S. policy goals are met through direct bilateral action and by working with the international community. The Haitian diaspora is a potentially powerful ally in the effort to strengthen U.S. policy initiatives in Haiti.

Maintaining good relations with and fostering democracy in Haiti are important for many reasons, not least of which is the country's geographical proximity to the continental United

States. In addition to the many Haitians who receive visas to immigrate into the U.S. (averaging over 15,000 annually in FY 2007–2011), there is a flow of illegal migrants. Over 100,000 undocumented Haitian migrants were intercepted at sea by the U.S. Coast Guard in the past two decades, particularly during the 1991–94 period of illegal military rule when more than 67,000 migrants were interdicted.

Since the return of the legitimate government in 1994, the interdiction of illegal migrants by U.S. Coast Guard vessels has decreased dramatically, averaging fewer than 1,500 annually. The prospect remains, however, for the renewal of higher flows of illegal migrants, particularly under conditions of political unrest or further economic downturn.

In January 2010, the U.S. granted temporary protected status (TPS) for 18 months to Haitians living illegally in the U.S. During that period, they were allowed to live and work in the U.S. upon submission and approval of a TPS application. On May 17, 2011, the Department of Homeland Security (DHS) announced an extension and re-designation of TPS for Haiti. The extension will allow Haitians who have already been granted TPS following the earthquake to re-register and remain in the United States through January 22, 2013. In addition, DHS re-designated Haiti for TPS—meaning that Haitian nationals who have continuously resided in the United States since January 12, 2011, may now also be eligible to apply for TPS and will be allowed to stay in the United States through January 22, 2013. The extension and re-designation of TPS became effective July 23, 2011.

U.S. Assistance to Haiti

Political insecurity, embargo and debt policies, and the failure of Haiti's government to invest in developing the country's natural and human resources have contributed significantly to the country's current state of underdevelopment. U.S. efforts to strengthen democracy and help build the foundation for economic growth aim to rectify this condition. The U.S. has been Haiti's largest donor since 1973. Following the January 2010 earthquake, the U.S. Government, working with the Government of Haiti and the United Nations system, executed what became the largest international humanitarian response to a natural disaster in U.S. history.

Haiti's recovery is a strategic imperative for the United States. The U.S. Government's development strategy focuses on stimulating economic activity and enhancing the delivery of basic services in designated development corridors, or areas of the country, while engaging the private sector in the reconstruction process. Consistent with the Haitian Government's action plan, the U.S. Government's reconstruction and long-term development plan seeks to support new and diverse economic opportunities outside of Port-au-Prince using focused and catalytic investments in housing, energy, agriculture, health, security, and national and local governance.

The U.S. Government strategy consists of investments in four focus areas or "pillars" critical to achieving economic growth and stability: infrastructure and energy; food and economic security; health and other basic services; and governance and rule of law. For more information on the strategy, see http://www.state.gov/s/hsc/rpt/index.htm.

Bilateral Economic Relations

The U.S. remains Haiti's largest trading partner. Many Haitian entrepreneurs conduct business in English, and U.S. currency circulates freely in Haiti. A number of U.S. firms, including commercial banks, telecommunications, airlines, oil and agribusiness companies, and U.S.-owned assembly plants are present in Haiti.

Opportunities for U.S. businesses include the development and trade of raw and processed agricultural products; medical supplies and equipment; rebuilding and modernizing Haiti's infrastructure (particularly relevant in the wake of the January 2010 earthquake); developing tourism and allied sectors—including arts and crafts; and improving capacity in waste disposal, transportation, energy, telecommunications, and export assembly operations.

Benefits for both Haitian and American importers and exporters are available under the Caribbean Basin Trade Partnership Act—which provides for duty-free export of many Haitian products assembled from U.S. components or materials—the successor program to the Caribbean Basin Initiative. The Haitian Hemispheric Opportunity through Partnership Encouragement Act provides additional duty-free preferences for qualifying apparel/textiles products and automotive wire harnesses.

The U.S. and Haiti have a bilateral agreement on investment guarantees that permits the U.S. Overseas Private Investment Corporation to offer programs in Haiti. The Haitian Government encourages the inflow of new capital and technological innovations and has made a commitment to improving the business environment and attracting foreign investors. Its Center of Investment Facilitation (CFI) aims to facilitate and promote local investment by reducing administrative delays, streamlining the creation of enterprises, and facilitating the provision of inducements. For more information on the CFI, see http://www.cfihaiti.net/j10/index.php/en/.

Additional information on business opportunities in Haiti can be found at www.export.gov under opportunities, market research, Country Commercial Guides.

Haiti's Membership in International Organizations

Haiti and the United States belong to a number of the same international organizations, including the United Nations, Organization of American States (OAS), International Monetary Fund, World Bank, and World Trade Organization. The United States has taken a leading role in organizing international involvement with Haiti. The United States works closely with the OAS, particularly through the Secretary General's "Friends of Haiti" group, the Caribbean Community (CARICOM), and individual countries to achieve policy goals.

Bilateral Representation

Haiti maintains an embassy in the United States at 2311 Massachusetts Ave., NW, Washington, DC 20008 (tel. 202-332-4090).

Principal U.S. Embassy Officials

Last Updated: 1/14/2013

PORT AU PRINCE (E) Tabarre 41, Blvd du 15 Octobre–Tabarre, Haiti, (509) 2-229-8000, Fax (509) 2-229-8028, Workweek: 0700–1530, Website: http://portauprince.usembassy.gov/

DCM OMS:	Carol Hazzard
AMB OMS:	Robin Goertz
CDC:	John F. Vertefeuille, D/Dir
DHS/CIS:	Hichem Kefi
FM:	Lawrence Ragan
HRO:	Robert Young
MGT:	George W. Indyke
MLO/ODC:	CDR Richter Tipton
NAS/INL:	Carl R. Siebentritt
POSHO:	Lawrence Ragan
SDO/DATT:	JCS Richter Tipton
TREAS:	Elizabeth Morris
AMB:	Pamela White
CG:	Jay T. Smith
DCM:	Marc L. Desjardins
PAO:	Arnaldo Arbesu, A.I.
GSO:	Monique C. Austin
RSO:	Jeffrey Roberts
AFSA:	Pamela Hack
AID:	Herbert Smith, Acting
APHIS:	(Vacant)
CLO:	Meredith Whitney
DEA:	Shawn Alexander
ECON:	John G. Robinson
EEO:	Stephanie Schmid
FMO:	Stephen Hartwell
ICASS Chair:	Hichem Kefi
IMO:	Raemona Willis-Middlebrooks
IPO:	Bryan Martin
ISO:	Bill Geschwind
ISSO:	Bill Geschwind
POL:	Henry M. Rector

Additional Contact Information

Office of the Haiti Special Coordinator
U.S. Department of State
http://www.state.gov/s/hsc/

The U.S. Commercial Service does not have a separate office in Haiti. Interested parties may contact the U.S. Commercial Service in Santo Domingo:

U.S. Commercial Service
American Embassy
Ave. Pedro Henriquez Urena No. 133
Santo Domingo, Dominican Republic
Tel: (809) 227-2121
Fax: (809) 920-0267
http://export.gov/caribbean/

Alternatively, they may contact the Port-au-Prince Embassy economic section at papecon@state.gov. For more Embassy contacts, visit the Embassy's website. (Note: As of mid-2010, Haiti's land line telephone system was not operating because of damage caused by the earthquake. Therefore, e-mail communication with the Embassy and other organizations located in Haiti is recommended.)

Overseas Private Investment Corporation (OPIC)
1615 M Street, NW
Washington, DC 20527
Tel: (202) 457-7200
Fax: (202) 331-4234

U.S. Department of Commerce
14th and Constitution Ave., NW
Washington, DC 20230
Haiti Desk: Tel: (202) 482-1810

Caribbean/Latin American Action
1818 N Street, NW, Suite 310
Washington, DC 20036
Tel: (202) 466-7464
Fax: (202) 822-0075

Association des Industries d'Haiti (ADIH)
Bldg. Le Triangle Delmas 31, #139
Port-au-Prince
Tel: (509) 2246–4509/4510 or 2211
www.adih.ht
e-mail: info@adih.ht

Centre Pour la Libre Entreprise et la Democratie (CLED)
37, Avenue Marie-Jeanne
No. 8 B.P. 1316
Port-au-Prince
Tel: (509) 2244–0901
or (509) 2245–6039
Fax: (509) 2222–8252

Chambre de Commerce et d'Industrie d'Haiti
P.O. Box 982
Port-au-Prince
Tel: (509) 2222–0281 or (509) 2222–2475

Haitian-American Chamber of Commerce and Industry (AMCHAM)
Rue Oge, A-5
Petionville
Republic of Haiti
Tel: (509) 2511–3024
fax not available

TRAVEL

Consular Information Sheet

August 29, 2011

Country Description: Haiti covers the western third of the Caribbean island of Hispaniola. The capital city is Port-au-Prince. The January 12, 2010 earthquake significantly damaged key infrastructure and greatly reduced the capacity of Haiti's medical facilities.

Despite the passage of time, Haiti's infrastructure remains in very poor condition, unable to support normal activity, much less crisis situations. Last year's cholera outbreak—exacerbated by inadequate public sanitation—killed thousands of Haitians, further straining the capacity of medical facilities and personnel and undermining their ability to attend to emergencies.

While the Embassy's ability to provide emergency consular services has improved since the earthquake, it is still limited. The Haitian National Police (HNP), with assistance from

UN Police (UN Pol), are responsible for keeping peace in Haiti and rendering assistance during times of civil unrest. The level of violent crime in Port-au-Prince, including murder and kidnapping, remains a concern and Haiti is considered a 'critical threat' post for crime.

Smart Traveler Enrollment Program (STEP)/Embassy Locations: If you are going to live in or visit Haiti, please take the time to tell our Embassy (and/or Consulate) about your trip. If you enroll, we can keep you up to date with important safety and security announcements. This will also help your friends and family get in touch with you in an emergency.

Embassy of the United States
Port-au-Prince Haiti
Boulevard du 15 October, Tabarre 41, Tabarre, Haiti
Telephone: (509) (2) 229-8000
Facsimile: (509) (2) 229-8027
Email: acspap@state.gov
After hours, weekend & holidays: Please call (509) (2) 229-8000.

American Citizens Services Unit office hours are 7:00 a.m. to 3:30 p.m., Monday through Friday. The Consular Section is closed on U.S. and local holidays.

Entry/Exit Requirements: All U.S. Citizens traveling by air from outside of the United States are required to present a passport to enter or re-enter the United States. Haitian law requires U.S. citizens to have a passport to enter and exit Haiti. An undocumented U.S. citizen can experience delays of several weeks for the issuance of a U.S. passport in Haiti, as it is often more difficult to establish identity and citizenship overseas than in the United States.

U.S. citizens are encouraged to contact the Embassy of the Republic of Haiti for more details regarding current entry, departure and customs requirements for Haiti. The Embassy of the Republic of Haiti is located at 2311 Massachusetts Avenue NW, Washington, DC 20008; the telephone number is (202) 332-4090. There are Haitian consulates in Miami and Orlando, Florida; Atlanta, GA; Boston, Massachusetts; New York, New York; Chicago, Illinois; and San Juan, Puerto Rico. Visit the Embassy of the Republic of Haiti web site for the most current visa information.

The U.S. Department of State is unaware of any HIV/AIDS entry restrictions for visitors to or foreign residents of Haiti.

Threats to Safety and Security: The Department of State strongly urges U.S. citizens to consider carefully all travel to Haiti. Travel fully supported by organizations with solid infrastructure, evacuation options, and medical support systems in place is recommended and preferable to travel in country without such support structures in place.

Those wishing to assist in Haiti relief efforts should be aware that despite their good intentions, travel to Haiti will increase the burden on a system already struggling to support those in need on the ground. If you intend to work for an organization involved in relief efforts in Haiti, be aware that living conditions are difficult and the availability of food supplies, clean drinking water and adequate shelter is limited.

If you are seeking work with a relief organization you should confirm before traveling to Haiti that the organization has the capability to provide food, water, transportation, and shelter for its paid and volunteer workers. All relief organizations should have a security plan in place for their personnel. Please note that space in hotels is extremely limited.

If you travel to or reside in Haiti despite this warning we remind you that there remains a persistent danger of violent crime, including armed robbery, homicide, rape, and kidnapping. While the capacity and capabilities of the Haitian National Police have improved since 2006, the presence of UN stabilization force (MINUSTAH) peacekeeping troops and UN-formed police units remain critical to maintaining an adequate level of security throughout the country.

The limited capability of local law enforcement to resolve crime further compounds the security threat to U.S. citizens. In particular, there have been cases in which travelers arriving in Port-au-Prince on flights from the United States were attacked and robbed while traveling in cars away from the airport. Several U.S. citizens were shot and killed in such incidents in 2010 and 2011.

Police authorities believe criminals may be targeting travelers arriving on flights from the United States, following them, and attacking once they are out of the area. Use extra caution in arranging transportation from the airport. Most kidnappings are criminal in nature, and kidnappers make no distinctions of nationality, race, gender, or age. Some kidnap victims have been killed, shot, sexually assaulted, or physically abused.

While MINUSTAH remains fully deployed and is assisting the Government of Haiti in providing security, travel within Port-au-Prince can be hazardous. U.S. embassy personnel are under an embassy-imposed curfew and must remain in their homes or in U.S. government facilities during the curfew. Some areas are off-limits to Embassy staff after dark, including downtown Port-au-Prince, Cite Soleil, Martissant, Carrefour, Croix Des Bouquets, and other areas.

The embassy restricts travel by its staff to some areas outside of Port-au-Prince because of the prevailing road, weather, or security conditions. Embassy personnel are not authorized to travel outside Port-au-Prince after dark. This may constrain the embassy's ability to provide emergency services to U.S. citizens outside Port-au-Prince.

Demonstrations and violence, which are common occurrences in Haiti,may occasionally limit embassy operations to emergency services, even within Port-au-Prince. We recommend that you avoid all large gatherings, as crowd behavior can be unpredictable.

Visitors encountering roadblocks, demonstrations, or large crowds should remain calm and depart the area quickly and avoid confrontation. Assistance from Haitian authorities is often unavailable.

Be particularly cautious on days when there are political activities planned in Haiti. Take common-sense precautions and avoid any event where crowds may congregate.

Stay up-to-date by:

- Bookmarking our Bureau of Consular Affairs website, which contains the current Travel Warnings and Travel Alerts as well as the Worldwide Caution.
- Following us on Twitter and the Bureau of Consular Affairs page on Facebook as well.
- Downloading our free Smart Traveler iPhone App to have travel information at your fingertips.
- Calling 1-888-407-4747 toll-free within the U.S. and Canada, or a regular toll line, 1-202-501-4444, from other countries.
- Taking some time before travel to consider your personal security.

Crime: Haiti is a key transit point for drugs coming to the United States. Law and order in Haiti is negatively impacted as a result. Kidnapping, death threats, murders, drug-related shootouts, armed robberies, home break-ins and car-jacking are common in Haiti. Generally, these crimes are committed by Haitians against other Haitians, but foreigners and U.S. citizens have been victimized.

The incidence of kidnapping in Haiti has diminished from its peak in 2006 when 60 U.S. citizens were reported kidnapped. In 2010, there were twelve reported kidnappings of U.S. citizens, twelve homicides, six aggravated assaults, two sexual assaults, and 82 reported robberies. Many U.S. citizens who were kidnapped reported being beaten and/or raped by their hostage takers.

Kidnapping remains the most critical security concern, and kidnappers frequently target children. It is important to exercise a high degree of caution throughout the country. Keep valuables well hidden, ensure possessions are not left in parked vehicles, use private transportation, alternate your travel routes, and keep doors and windows in homes and vehicles closed and locked. You should avoid all night-time travel due to poor road conditions and increased criminal activity after dark. Remain alert for suspicious onlookers when entering and exiting banks, as criminals often watch and subsequently attack bank customers. Withdrawals of large amounts of cash should be avoided.

Criminal perpetrators often operate in groups of two to four individuals, and may occasionally be confrontational and gratuitously violent. Criminals sometimes will seriously injure or kill those who resist their attempts to commit crime. In robberies or home invasions, it is not uncommon for the assailants to beat or shoot the victim in order to limit the victim's ability to resist. If an armed individual demands the surrender of a vehicle or other valuables, we recommend that you comply. This recommendation also applies in the event of a kidnapping.

Exercise caution at all times and review basic personal security procedures frequently. While in Haiti, you must be particularly alert when arriving from overseas at the Port-au-Prince airport, as criminals have often targeted arriving passengers for later assaults and robberies. Avoid using public transportation, including "tap-taps" (private transportation used for commercial purposes).

All public transportation is prohibited for Embassy personnel due to the safety and security risks associated with its use. Instead, arrange for someone you know to meet you at the airport. You should decline all requests to carry items for others to or from Haiti. Traffickers of illegal drugs have duped unsuspecting travelers into helping transport narcotics aboard commercial airlines.

Avoid certain high-crime zones in the Port-au-Prince area, including Croix-des-Bouquets, Carrefour, Martissant, the port road (Boulevard La Saline), urban route Nationale #1,route Nationale #9,the airport road (Boulevard Toussaint L'Ouverture) and its adjoining connectors to the New ("American") Road via Route Nationale #1 (which should also be avoided).

This latter area in particular has been the scene of numerous robberies, carjackings, and murders. Embassy employees are prohibited from entering Cite Soleil and La Saline and their surrounding environs due to significant criminal activity.

Neighborhoods in Port-au-Prince once considered relatively safe, such as the Delmas road area, Petionville, and Vivy Mitchel have been the scenes of an increasing number of violent crimes.

Cameras and video cameras should only be used with the permission of the subjects; violent incidents have followed unwelcome photography. Avoid photography/videography in high-crime areas.

Holiday periods, especially Christmas and Carnival, often bring a significant increase in criminal activity. Haiti's Carnival season is marked by street celebrations in the days leading up to Ash Wednesday. In recent years, Carnival has been accompanied by civil disturbances, altercations and severe traffic disruptions.

People attending Carnival events or simply caught in the resulting celebrations have been injured and killed. Random stabbings during Carnival season are frequent. Roving musical bands called "rah-rahs" operate during the period from New Year's Day through Carnival. Being caught in a rah-rah event may begin as an enjoyable experience, but the potential for injury and the destruction of property is high. A mob mentality can develop unexpectedly leaving people and cars engulfed and at risk. During Carnival, rah-rahs continuously form without warning; some rah-rahs have identified themselves with political entities, lending further potential for violence. The Haitian police are understaffed, poorly equipped and unable to respond to most calls for assistance. There are continued allegations of police complicity in criminal activity. The unsatisfactory response and enforcement capabilities of the Haitian national police and the weakness of the judiciary frustrate many victims of crime in Haiti.

In the past, U.S. citizens involved in business and property disputes in Haiti have been arrested and detained without charge, and have been released only after intervention at high levels of the Haitian government. In many countries around the world, counterfeit and pirated goods are widely available. Transactions involving such products may be illegal under local law. In addition, bringing them back to the United States may result in forfeitures and/or fines.

Victims of Crime: If you are the victim of a crime abroad, you should contact the local police and the U.S. Embassy (see above or see the Department of State's list of embassies and consulates). If your passport is stolen, we can help you replace it. For violent crimes such as assault or rape, we can, for example, help you find appropriate medical care, put you in contact with the appropriate policy authorities, and contact family members or friends.

Although the investigation and prosecution of the crime are solely the responsibility of local authorities, consular officers can help you to understand the local criminal justice process and can direct you to local attorneys.

The local equivalent to the "911" emergency line in Haiti is 114.

Criminal Penalties: While you are traveling in Haiti, you are subject to its laws even if you are a U.S. citizen. Foreign laws and legal systems can be vastly different than our own. In some places you may be taken in for questioning if you don't have your passport with you. In some places, it is illegal to take pictures of certain buildings. In some places driving under the influence could land you immediately in jail. These criminal penalties will vary from country to country. There are also some things that might be legal in the country you visit, but still illegal in the United States, and you can be prosecuted under U.S. law if you buy pirated goods.

Engaging in sexual conduct with children or using or disseminating child pornography in a foreign country is a crime prosecutable in the United States. If you break local laws in Haiti, your U.S. passport won't help you avoid arrest or prosecution. It's very important to know what's legal and what's not where you are going.

Persons violating Haiti's laws, even unknowingly, may be expelled, arrested or imprisoned. Penalties for possession, use, or trafficking in illegal drugs in Haiti are severe, and convicted offenders can expect long jail sentences and heavy fines. The judicial process in Haiti can be extremely slow; progress is often dependent on considerations not related to the specific case, including personal disputes.

Detainees have waited months or years for their cases to be heard before a judge or to have legal decisions acted upon by the authorities. Bond is not usually available to those arrested for serious crimes with the result that often suspects remain in custody for many months before formal indictment. Judges have more or less unfettered freedom to detain individuals for prolonged periods of time without the possibility of release or sanctions.

Based on the Vienna Convention on Consular Relations, bilateral agreements with certain countries, and customary international law, if you are arrested in Haiti, you have the option to request that the police, prison officials, or other authorities alert the U.S. Embassy of your arrest, and to have communications from you forwarded to the U.S. Embassy.

Special Circumstances: The official currency of Haiti is the gourde, which has a variable exchange rate (currently approximately 40 gourdes to the U.S. dollar). Visitors will notice that most establishments in Haiti price items in an unofficial currency known as the "Haitian dollar." (One Haitian dollar is equivalent to five gourdes.) Others give prices in gourdes or even in U.S. dollars.

It is always a good idea to clarify with vendors which currency — the gourde, Haitian dollar, or U.S. dollar — is being used in a given transaction, as price tags often bear a number without indicating currency. The currency itself shows a value in gourdes. U.S. dollars are the currency of choice at the Labadee Beach cruise ship port-of-call.

Travelers' checks are often difficult to change in Haiti, but credit cards are widely accepted and some establishments accept or cash personal checks. At least one local bank chain has ATMs around Port-au-Prince that are compatible with some U.S. ATM cards. These ATMs are frequently out-of-order, and there have been reports of overcharging and robberies at the ATMs.

Haiti, like most Caribbean countries, can be affected by hurricanes and other storms. Hurricane season runs from approximately June 1 - November 30 each year. During the 2008 hurricane season, the country was struck by three tropical storms and one hurricane that resulted in torrential rains, extensive flooding and mudslides, and hundreds of reported casualties.

The lack of government infrastructure and rescue services, combined with impassable roads and bridges, severely hindered rescue and relief efforts. Daily weather information in Haiti is available from national and international media. The Haitian meteorological service provides hurricane warnings via national radio. Most information local media broadcast only in Kreyol and/or French. Warnings are also available on the internet from many sources, one of which is the National Oceanic and

Atmospheric Administration (NOAA). General information about natural disaster preparedness is available from the U.S. Federal Emergency Management Agency (FEMA).

Accessibility: While in Haiti, individuals with disabilities may find accessibility and accommodation very different from what is found in the United States. Businesses and institutions in Haiti generally do not make special accommodation for persons with disabilities.

Additionally, Haitian authorities do not effectively enforce laws mandating access to transportation, communication, and public buildings by persons with disabilities. Because of widespread and chronic poverty, a shortage of public services, and limited educational opportunities, persons with disabilities are severely disadvantaged.

Pedestrian sidewalks and walkways are limited, and when present, often end abruptly, causing accidents. Accommodations and reduced fares on public transportation are not offered for elderly individuals or persons with disabilities. Pedestrian crosswalks are rarely established and not adhered to, creating risk for pedestrians traversing roads in both business and residential areas.

Medical Facilities and Health Information: Medical facilities in Haiti are scarce and for the most part sub-standard. Outside the capital standards are often even lower than in Port-au-Prince. Medical care in Port-au-Prince is limited, and the level of community sanitation is extremely low. Life-threatening emergencies often require evacuation by air ambulance at the patient's expense. Doctors and hospitals often expect immediate cash payment in advance for health services. In the event of a medical emergency requiring evacuation, a list of air ambulance or charter flight services is available at the ACS web site.

Information on vaccinations and other health precautions, such as safe food and water precautions, malaria and insect bite protection, may be obtained from the Centers for Disease Control and Prevention's hotline for international travelers at 1-877-FYI-TRIP (1-877-394-8747) or via the CDC web site. The CDC also provides specific travel and cholera information for Haiti at their Haiti Traveler's Health and Cholera in Haiti web pages.

For information about outbreaks of infectious diseases abroad, consult the World Health Organization (WHO) web site. The WHO website also contains additional health information for travelers, including detailed country-specific health information. Tuberculosis is an increasingly serious health concern in Haiti. For further information, please consult the CDC's information on Tuberculosis.

Medical Insurance: You can't assume your insurance will go with you when you travel. It's very important to find out BEFORE you leave whether or not your medical insurance will cover you overseas. You need to ask your insurance company two questions:

- Does my policy apply when I'm out of the United States? Are there banned countries?
- Will it cover emergencies like a trip to a foreign hospital or a medical evacuation?

In many places, doctors and hospitals still expect payment in cash at the time of service. Your regular U.S. health insurance may not cover doctors' and hospital visits in other countries. If your policy doesn't go with you when you travel, it's a very good idea to take out another one for your trip. The U.S. Embassy does not have funds for covering private citizens' expenses. For more information, please see our information on medical insurance overseas page.

Traffic Safety and Road Conditions: While in Haiti, you may encounter road conditions that differ significantly from those in the United States. The information below concerning Haiti is provided for general reference only, and may not be totally accurate in a particular location or circumstance.

Most of the main roads have been cleared of rubble following the earthquake, although piles of rubble remain in certain areas—increasing congestion due to traffic. A few roads remain impassable due to damage from the earthquake. People regularly walk on the side of the road and street-side vendors ply their wares on the existing sidewalks. Small animals (pigs, dogs, goats) are often encountered in the city and larger ones (cows and donkeys) will unexpectedly cross country roads.

Cars are supposed to be driven on the right side of the road in Haiti, but few roads have lane indicators and drivers use whichever side of the road is open to them. Traffic is extremely congested in urban areas, and hours-long traffic jams develop throughout the country.

Driving in Haiti must be undertaken with extreme caution. Traffic is usually chaotic; those with no knowledge of Haitian roads and traffic customs should hire a driver through a local tour operator or hotel. Roads are generally unmarked, and detailed and accurate maps are not widely available. Lanes are not marked and signs indicating the direction of traffic flow seldom exist. Huge potholes may cause drivers to execute unpredictable and dangerous maneuvers in heavy traffic.

The Haitian government lacks adequate resources to assist drivers in distress or to clear the road of accidents or broken-down vehicles blocking the flow of traffic. While drinking and driving is illegal in Haiti, people frequently drive after drinking, especially at night.

Public transportation in Haiti consists primarily of "tap-taps" that run regular routes within urban areas and between towns in the countryside. A handful of public buses exist in the capital. Neither is considered reliable nor safe. Regular marked taxis are nonexistent. We strongly discourage the use of "tap-taps," public buses, and taxis. They pose the risk of vehicular accident -"tap-taps" in particular are hazardous because they are open and passengers are often ejected during an accident—and have been the site of numerous robberies and kidnappings in the past.

Never ride in open vehicles that lack seatbelts or on motorbikes without helmets. If you are visiting Haiti, to assist in humanitarian projects, you should confirm that your sponsoring organization has arranged to provide safe, reliable transportation during your stay. U.S. citizens have suffered life-threatening injuries and some have been killed after being thrown from open vehicles or motorbikes in accidents in Haiti.

Those who drive in Haiti should do so defensively and conservatively, should avoid confrontations such as jockeying for position, and remain aware of the vehicles around them. Drivers should carry the phone numbers of people to call for assistance in an emergency, as Haitian authorities are unlikely to respond to requests for assistance. When traveling outside of Port-au-Prince, drivers should caravan with other vehicles to avoid being stranded in the event of an accident or breakdown.

Although Haitian law requires that applicants pass both a written and a driving test to qualify for a driver's license, many Haitian drivers appear unaware of traffic laws. Signaling imminent actions is not widely practiced and not all drivers use turn indicators or international hand signals properly. For instance, many drivers use their left blinker for all actions, including turning right and stopping in the road, and others flap their left arm out the window to indicate that they will be taking an unspecified action.

Drivers do not always verify that the road is clear before switching lanes, turning, or merging. When making a left-hand turn, drivers should be aware that traffic may pass on the left while they are attempting to turn. This is legal in Haiti. The driver passing on the left has the right of way even when the car being overtaken has its left-hand turn signal on and is attempting to turn left.

Speed limits are seldom posted and are generally ignored. Speeding is the cause of many fatal traffic accidents in Haiti, as are overloaded vehicles on winding, mountainous roads and vehicles without brakes. Poor maintenance and mechanical failures often cause accidents as well. Drivers should be particularly cautious at night, as unlighted vehicles can appear without warning.

Right of way is not widely observed in Haiti, and there are few operational traffic lights or traffic signs. It is advisable at most intersections to stop and verify that there is no oncoming traffic even if it appears that you have the right of way. Drivers can be quite aggressive and will seldom yield. Walls built to the edge of roads frequently make it impossible to see around corners, forcing drivers to edge their cars into the road at intersections to check for oncoming traffic.

In addition to vehicles, a variety of other objects may appear on the road in Haiti, such as wooden carts dragged by people or animals, small ice cream carts, animals, mechanics working on vehicles parked on the street, and vendors and their wares. Haiti's unwritten rule of the road is that any vehicle that breaks down, must be left exactly where it stopped until it can be repaired, even if it creates an enormous backup of traffic. Cars often remain in the roadway for hours or days while often extensive repairs are carried out in-situ. Vehicles are often abandoned in the road or by the side of the road.

These are often identified by tree branches extending from the rear of the vehicle. There are few marked crosswalks and sidewalks, and pedestrians often wend their way through traffic in urban areas. Additionally, motorcycles on Haitian roads tend to maneuver in between traffic on both the left and right sides of vehicles, as well as into on-coming traffic. Drivers should check all their rear view mirrors prior to changing lanes or making turns to avoid colliding with other traffic.

Aviation Safety Oversight: The U.S. Federal Aviation Administration (FAA) has assessed the government of Haiti's Civil Aviation Authority as not being in compliance with International Civil Aviation Organization (ICAO) aviation safety standards for oversight of Haiti's air carrier operations. Further information may be found on the FAA's safety assessment page.

Children's Issues: Please see the U.S. Dept. of State Office of Children's Issues web pages on intercountry adoption and international parental child abduction.

Travel Warning

December 28, 2012

The Department of State has issued this Travel Warning to inform U.S. citizens traveling to or living in Haiti about the current security situation. This replaces the Travel Warning dated June 18, 2012, updating information regarding the level of crime, the presence of cholera, lack of adequate infrastructure - particularly in medical facilities - seasonal severe inclement weather, and limited police protection. The United Nations' Stabilization Force for Haiti (MINUSTAH) remains in Haiti.

The Department of State urges U.S. citizens to exercise caution when visiting Haiti. Thousands of U.S. citizens safely visit Haiti each year, but the poor state of Haiti's emergency response network should be carefully considered when planning travel. Travelers to Haiti are encouraged to use organizations that have solid infrastructure, evacuation, and medical support options in place. (Please see the Country Specific Information page for Haiti.)

U.S. citizens have been victims of violent crime, including murder and kidnapping, predominantly in the Port-au-Prince area. No one is safe from kidnapping, regardless of occupation, nationality, race, gender, or age. In recent months, travelers arriving in Port-au-Prince on flights from the United States were attacked and robbed shortly after departing the airport. At least two U.S. citizens were shot and killed in robbery and kidnapping incidents in 2012. Haitian authorities have limited capacity to deter or investigate such violent acts, or prosecute perpetrators.

The ability of local authorities to respond to emergencies is limited and in some areas nonexistent. Should you find yourself in an emergency, local health, police, judicial, and physical infrastructure limitations mean there are few local resources available to help resolve the problem. For this reason, the Embassy limits its staff's travel in areas outside of Port-au-Prince. This in turn constrains our ability to provide emergency services to U.S. Citizens outside of Port-au-Prince.

U.S. Embassy personnel are under an Embassy-imposed curfew of 1:00 a.m. to 5:00 a.m. and must remain at home or at another safe facility during curfew hours. Additionally, there are restrictions on travel by Embassy staff in other areas or times. This, too, may constrain the Embassy's ability to provide emergency services to U.S. citizens outside Port-au-Prince. For additional details on restrictions on staff travel within Haiti, please see our Country Specific Information for Haiti.

The Haitian National Police (HNP), with assistance from MINUSTAH, are responsible for keeping the peace and rendering assistance. However, given the possibility and unpredictability of protests, including the potential (as with any protest) to become violent, its ability to assist U.S. citizens during disturbances is very limited. Please see our website for additional information on how the Department of State assists U.S. citizens during a crisis.

Haiti's infrastructure remains in poor condition and unable to fully support even normal activity, much less crisis situations. U.S. government-facilitated evacuations, such as the evacuation that took place after the earthquake in Haiti in 2010, occur only when no safe commercial alternatives exist. Medical facilities, including ambulance services, are particularly weak.

Some U.S. citizens injured in accidents and others with serious health concerns have been unable to find necessary medical care in Haiti and have had to arrange and pay for medical evacuation to the United States. Given these conditions and the cost of private evacuations, we strongly encourage visitors to Haiti to obtain evacuation insurance, including for medical issues that may arise.

While incidents of cholera have declined significantly, cholera persists in many areas of Haiti. Prior to travel, U.S. citizens should obtain information about cholera and other health-related issues by visiting the Centers for Disease Control and Prevention website at http://www.cdc.gov.

We urge U.S. citizens who choose to travel to Haiti to review our Country Specific Information page. U.S. private sector organizations with operations in Haiti can obtain additional information on the security situation in the country through the U.S. Department of State's Overseas Security Advisory Council (OSAC). OSAC's mission is to promote security cooperation between U.S. private sector interests worldwide and the U.S. Department of State.

OSAC also maintains an active Country Council in Haiti to promote the exchange of security-related information. The Council is comprised of security professionals and is co-chaired by the Regional Security Officer at the U.S. Embassy Port-au-Prince and a private sector representative. U.S. private sector entities can obtain additional information on OSAC by visiting the OSAC website at www.osac.gov.

U.S. citizens are also urged to enroll in the Smart Traveler Enrollment Program (STEP) in order to receive the most up-to-date security information. While the Embassy's ability to provide emergency consular services is extremely limited, by enrolling in STEP travelers can receive security messages via email. Current information on safety and security can also be obtained by calling 1-888-407-4747 toll free in the United States; callers outside the United States and Canada can receive the information by calling a regular toll-line at 1-202-501-4444.

These numbers are available from 8:00 a.m. to 8:00 p.m. Eastern Time, Monday through Friday, except U.S. federal holidays. The Embassy of the United States of America is located in Port-au-Prince at Boulevard du 15 Octobre, Tabarre 41, Tabarre, Haiti, telephone: (509) (2) 229-8000, facsimile: (509) (2) 229-8027, email: acspap@state.gov American Citizens Services (ACS) Unit office hours are 7:00 a.m. to 3:30 p.m., Monday through Friday. The Consular Section is closed on U.S. and local holidays. After hours, on weekends and on holidays, please call (509) (2) 229-8000. The Marine guard will connect you with the Embassy Duty Officer.

U.S. citizens can also stay informed about conditions in Haiti by following the Embassy and ACS on Twitter and Facebook. Travelers can have the latest travel information at their fingertips by downloading our free Smart Traveler app, available through iTunes and the Android market.

Intercountry Adoption

Notice: Haiti Announces New Adoption Procedures
September 14, 2012

Haiti's adoption authority, Institut du Bien-Être Sociale et de Recherches (IBESR), announced new administrative adoption procedures, which will take effect on October 1, 2012. Although these new procedures are part of the Government of Haiti's efforts to become a Hague Adoption Convention partner with the United States, at this time Haiti is not party to the Convention, and the U.S. government will continue to process adoptions under the non-Hague system until the Convention enters into force for Haiti.

The Department of State's understanding of the new adoption procedures is as follows: IBESR plans to regulate orphanages, crèches, and children's homes in Haiti through an authorization process. In addition, IBESR plans to implement an authorization process for certified adoption service providers (ASPs) or their agents to facilitate adoptions and to begin requiring families to use the services of an authorized ASP. Children will be eligible for adoption only if they reside in an authorized facility. We continue to seek further clarification and will update this notice as information becomes available.

IBESR informed the U.S. government that beginning September 2012, they will accept applications from ASPs wishing to facilitate adoptions in Haiti under the new procedures.

New procedures may prohibit prospective adoptive parents from establishing contact with the child they are seeking to adopt before they are officially matched to that child by IBESR in coordination with the ASP and orphanage, crèche, or children's home. Some exceptions, such as intra-family adoptions may be allowed, even with prior contact. IBESR may consider exceptions to this policy for new cases in which prospective adoptive parents have already had contact with the child on a case-by-case basis.

IBESR has informed the U.S. government that it will process adoption cases submitted prior to May 7, 2012 under pre-existing adoption procedures. IBESR has also informed the U.S. government that they will review new cases submitted up to and including September 15, 2012 to determine if they can be processed under the old procedures.

If you have questions about the status of your adoption case, please work closely with your adoption agency or facilitator. The U.S. Embassy in Port-au-Prince is continuing to seek clarification on the new procedures. Please continue to refer to our website at www.adoption.state.gov for updates on adoptions in Haiti.

Overview of Existing Adoption Process
October 2010

The information in this section has been edited from the latest report available as of February 2013 from the State Department Bureau of Consular Affairs, Office of Overseas Citizens Services. For more information, please read the *Intercountry Adoption* section of this book and review current reports online at http://adoption.state.gov.

Haiti is not party to the Hague Convention on Protection of Children and Co-operation in Respect of Intercountry Adoption (Hague Adoption Convention). Therefore, when the Hague Adoption Convention entered into force for the United States on April 1, 2008, intercountry adoption processing for Haiti did not change.

Who Can Adopt? To bring an adopted child to United States from Haiti, you must be found eligible to adopt by the U.S. Government. The U.S. Government agency responsible for making this determination is the Department of Homeland Security, U.S. Citizenship and Immigration Services (USCIS).

Residency Requirements: Haitian law does not require prospective adoptive parents to reside in Haiti, although Haitian courts and/or the Institut du Bien Etre Social et de Recherches (IBESR, the Haitian adoption authority) may require American prospective adoptive parents to travel to Haiti before the adoption is finalized. The U.S. Government does not require adoptive parents to travel to Haiti at any time during the adoption and immigrant visa process.

Age Requirements: Under Haitian law, the prospective adoptive parent must be 35 or older. For married couples, one prospective adoptive parent may be under age 35, provided the couple has been married for ten years and has no biological children.

The adoptive parent must be at least 19 years older than the child they intend to adopt. These restrictions can be waived with permission from the President of Haiti.(please see note below on "Waiver of Ineligibility.")

Marriage Requirements: Adoptions by married couples require the consent of both spouses. This restriction can be waived with permission from the President of Haiti. (please see note below on "Waiver of Ineligibility.") U.S. immigration procedures still require the signature of both spouses on the USCIS Form I-600 (Petition to Classify Orphan as Immediate Relative).

Other Requirements: Haitian law permits adoptions by single parents, provided they meet the age requirements. Adoptive parents who already have children will need to obtain a waiver from the President of Haiti. This requirement is commonly waived. Waiver of Ineligibility: While Presidential waivers of ineligibility are sometimes issued, they are difficult to obtain and require a lengthy period of time to process. Prospective adoptive parents who do not fit the guidelines should consider not adopting in Haiti.

Who Can be Adopted? Prospective adoptive parent(s) must obtain consent from the child's surviving parent(s) or legal guardian. Known as the "Extrait des Minutes du Greffe du Tribunal de Paix," this document describes the proceeding during which prospective adoptive parents and the child's biological parents or legal guardians agree to the adoption.

Such proceeding takes place at the office of the Justice of the Peace with jurisdiction over the residence of the child. In some jurisdictions, such as Port au Prince, prospective adoptive parents are required to appear personally before the Justice of the Peace to effect consent before the adoption is finalized.

In the Port-au-Prince jurisdiction, parents are also asked to appear before the Dean of the Civil Courts after appearing before the Justice of the Peace. It is feasible to accomplish both meetings in one trip. While it is our understanding that this should only take one trip to Haiti to complete the process, the number of trips will depend heavily on the local agents in scheduling and planning on behalf of their clients, the availability of the consenting parties, and of course on the availability of the magistrates.

Abandonment Requirements: If the biological parents of the child are deceased, their Extrait de l'Acte de Decès (extract of the death certificate) must be obtained from the Haitian National Archives.

The Process: The first step in adopting a child from Haiti is usually to select a licensed agency in the United States that can help with your adoption. Adoption agencies must be licensed by the U.S. state in which they operate. Under the current system, matching often occurs through the adoption service provider. Each family must decide for itself whether or not it will be able to meet the needs of a particular child and provide a permanent family placement for the child. Once the prospective adoptive parents are matched with a child, they must submit the Extrait des Minutes du Greffe du Tribunal de Paix (minutes of the legal consent proceedings) or Extrait de l'acte de Decès (extract of the death certificates of the biological parents), if applicable to IBESR, which will investigate, among other things, the medical and psychological well-being of the prospective adoptive parents and child.

Role of the Justice of the Peace: the biological parents consent to the adoption process before the Justice of the Peace. Some jurisdictions such as Port-au-Prince require American prospective adoptive parents to travel to Haiti to appear before a Justice of the Peace in consent proceedings before the adoption is finalized. . In the Port-au-Prince jurisdiction, parents are also asked to appear before the Dean of the Civil Courts after appearing before the Justice of the Peace.

While it is our understanding that this should only take one trip to Haiti to complete the process, the number of trips will depend heavily on the local agents in scheduling and planning on behalf of their clients, the availability of the consenting parties, and of course on the availability of the magistrates.

Role of the Adoption Authority: If IBESR approves the adoption, it issues an Autorisation d'Adoption, Authorization of Adoption.

Only the IBESR office in Port-au-Prince can authorize an adoption. IBESR regional offices do not have this authority. This second step is often the most time-consuming in the overall adoption process. Each case has different mitigating factors, some more complicated than others, all of which can have a direct impact on the length of time it takes IBESR to process an individual case. The Immigrant Visa Unit of the U.S. Embassy has no authority over or ability to influence how quickly IBESR processes its caseload or which cases it takes in which order.

Role of the Civil Court: Prospective adoptive parents must present the IBESR Authorization of Adoption to the Tribunal Civil (Civil Court) that has jurisdiction over the child's residence in order to obtain an Acte d'Adoption (Adoption Act), which finalizes the adoption. Adoption Application: Prospective adoptive parents should file their application with IBESR.

Time Frame: The adoption process in Haiti frequently requires as long as eighteen months, primarily because the legal process is complex. Historically, adoption applications have taken over than two years. Once an adoption case has been approved by IBESR and USCIS, the adoptive parent(s) must apply for a Haitian passport for the child; this process can take an additional two or three months after the receipt of the Acte d'Adoption. The Adoptions Unit recommends that the child obtain a valid Haitian passport once the adoption is complete.

The Adoptions Unit will conduct the visa interview in the case once the applicant files a completed DS-230, Application for Immigrant Visa and Alien Registration, and pays the required necessary fees. However, there is no guarantee that a visa will be granted after the visa interview. The granting of a visa depends on the applicant's file being documentarily complete, and the applicant overcoming any visa ineligibility. If at the time of the visa interview the adoption case is complete and the immigrant visa is issuable, the visa itself is typically available within two business days.

Adoption Fees: IBESR charges approximately $190 USD. Haiti's courts charge for judicial services, but their fees are not fixed. Prospective adoptive parents should expect to pay varying court fees and expenses. It is not possible to determine the approximate total cost to adopt a child in Haiti because there are no set adoption fees. Some adoptive parents have reported paying $3,000 USD, excluding airfare; while others reported paying much larger sums.

The Adoptions Unit recommends that prospective adoptive parents contact their local agents or adoption service providers to inquire about current fees as they are subject to change.

The adoptive parents must also pay the cost of the child's medical examination. The fee for the medical examination is $55. Children over the age of 10 are also required to obtain the necessary vaccinations—the fees for which will vary depending on which vaccinations the child is missing. These fees do change periodically.

Note that the vaccinations may be waived for completion in the United States if the child is under the age of 10. Haitian and U.S. law prohibit any payments to the child's birth parent(s) or guardian(s) by the prospective adoptive parent(s) or their agents.

Documents Required: All documents are required to be translated into French and authenticated by a Haitian consul in the United States. The following is a list of documents for the child that are required by IBESR to process an adoption application:

- Three identity photos;
- A Haitian legal document called the "Certificate of Abandonment" (this document is applicable in abandonment cases)
- Relinquishment of parental rights from each birth parent (if the birth parents are deceased, the surviving relatives or legal guardian must issue this document);
- The child's birth certificate, and the extract (official copy from the National Archives) of the birth certificate, if available;
- Death certificate of the birth parents ("l'acte de decès"), if applicable;
- The child's social history, which is a statement prepared by a social worker appointed by IBESR, stating how the child became an abandoned child;
- A psychological evaluation of the child;
- A complete medical report that includes tests for tuberculosis, HIV, and sickle cell anemia;
- A statement from the prospective adoptive parents that they plan to adopt a child in Haiti;
- Three identity photos of each of the prospective adoptive parents;
- Birth certificate of each prospective adoptive parent (or Extrait de Naissance if born in Haiti);
- Marriage certificate of the prospective adoptive parents (Extrait de Mariage if married in Haiti; not required of single adoptive parent);
- An original notarized power of attorney designating whoever may act on the parents' behalf in Haiti (if applicable; a fax copy is not sufficient);
- Financial documents, including tax returns, job letters, notarized bank account documents and copies of deeds and mortgages (prospective adoptive parents should forward the Form I-864 Affidavit of Support with the requisite attachments);
- An evaluation of the household environment in which the adoptive child will live (the home study conducted for the I-600A can be used to fulfill this requirement);
- A statement from a competent police authority in the prospective adoptive parent's town of residence indicating the absence of a criminal record (this is included in the home study and the I-171H is sufficient for this requirement);
- Medical examination reports for the prospective adoptive parent(s);
- A psychological evaluation report of the prospective adoptive parent(s); and
- Two notarized letters of reference.

Fraudulent documents are easily and cheaply available in Haiti and often can be obtained with much less effort than genuine documents. These documents may include birth certificates, death certificates, relinquishment documents purportedly issued by civil courts and even adoption authorizations.

Documents are routinely submitted to the issuing authorities for verification. Fraudulent documents submitted for an immigrant visa petition for an adoptive child will result in the I-600 petition being returned to the USCIS office that approved the petition with a memorandum requesting reconsideration and possible revocation. Submission of additional documents in an attempt to "correct" the fraudulent documents does not offer relief of the fraud after the fact. After IBESR approves the adoption, the Haitian courts require that prospective adoptive parents submit the following documents:

- The adoptive parents' birth certificates (if born in Haiti, these must be the official Extrait de l'acte de Naissance (Extract of Birth certificate) available from the Haitian National Archives);
- The child's Extrait d'acte de Naissance; this should not be confused with the Acte de Naissance, the document upon which the Extrait is based;
- The adoptive parents' marriage certificate, if applicable; and
- If the biological parents of the child are deceased, their Extrait d'acte de Decès (Extract of Death certificate) from the Haitian National Archives.

Archives Nationales d'Haiti is the National Archives in Port-au-Prince and is the only Haitian agency with the authority to issue extracts related to acts of birth, death, marriage, and divorce. Each of these documents is based on an "acte" of birth, death, marriage, and divorce; this "acte" is rarely sufficient for IBESR or U.S. immigration purposes. The Immigrant Visa Unit of the U.S. Embassy has no authority over the National Archives or ability to influence how quickly it can provide required extracts.

Bringing Your Child Home: Once your adoption is complete (or you have obtained legal custody of the child), there are a few more steps to take before you can head home. Specifically, you need to apply for several documents for your child before he or she can travel to the United States, such as a birth certificate, a passport or travel document for your child from the country in which he or she was born, and a U.S. Immigration Visa.

For detailed and updated information on how to obtain these documents, review the *Intercountry Adoption* section in this publication and visit the U.S. Department of State Intercountry Adoption website at http://adoption.state.gov.

Child Citizenship Act: For adoptions finalized abroad, the Child Citizenship Act of 2000 allows your new child to acquire American citizenship automatically when he or she enters the United States as lawful permanent residents. For adoptions finalized in the United States, the Child Citizenship Act of 2000 allows your new child to acquire American citizenship automatically when the court in the United States issues the final adoption decree.

To learn more, review the *Intercountry Adoption* section in this publication and visit the U.S. Department of State Intercountry Adoption website at http://adoption.state.gov.

After Adoption: Haiti does not have any post-adoption requirements.

U.S. Embassy in Haiti
Consular Section (Adoptions Unit)
Boulevard du 15 Octobre
Tabarre 41
Tabarre, Haiti
Tel: 509-2229-8000 (from Haiti); 1-866-829-2842 (from the United States)
Email: papadoptions@state.gov

Haitian Adoption Authority
Institut du Bien Etre Social et de Recherches" (IBESR)
13 rue des marguerites
PORT-AU-PRINCE

Embassy of Haiti
2311 Massachusetts Ave., NW
Washington, DC 20008
Tel: (202) 332-4090
Fax: (202) 745-7215
Email: embassy@haiti.org

Office of Children's Issues
U.S. Department of State
2201 C Street, NW
SA-29
Washington, DC 20520
Tel: 1-888-407-4747
E-mail: AskCI@state.gov
http://adoption.state.gov

For questions about immigration procedures, contact the National Customer Service Center (NCSC) at 1-800-375-5283 (TTY 1-800-767-1833).

Pursuing Independent Adoptions without Licensed Agencies Increases Risks of Delays and Fraud
June 27, 2011

The Department of State has seen a recent increase in U.S. citizens seeking to pursue adoptions in Haiti through independent agents instead of licensed adoption providers. While these "private" adoptions are currently permissible in Haiti, prospective adoptive parents should be aware of the risks associated with not utilizing experienced, licensed agencies. Non-licensed facilitators may lack experience in navigating the complex Haitian adoption process, and this could lead to delays and critical mistakes in processing the case. Haitian facilitators may also not be familiar with U.S. immigration law governing intercountry adoption processing.

Prospective adoptive parents pursuing an independent adoption may place their trust in private facilitators engaging in unethical or illegal practices in Haiti. The Department strongly encourages prospective adoptive parents adopting from Haiti to research U.S. immigration laws and Haitian adoption procedures through the use of a reputable, licensed agency or experienced facilitator. For more information about intercountry adoption in Haiti, please visit our website at: http://adoption.state.gov/country_information/country_specific_info.php?country-select=haiti.

International Parental Child Abduction

January 2012

The information in this section has been edited from the latest report available as of February 2013 from the State Department Bureau of Consular Affairs, Office of Overseas Citizens Services. For more information, please read the *International Parental Child Abduction* section of this book and check for updated reports online at www.travel.state.gov/abduction.

Disclaimer: The information in this flyer relating to the legal requirements of specific foreign countries is provided for general information only. Questions involving interpretation of specific foreign laws should be addressed to foreign legal counsel.

General Information: Haiti is not a party to the Hague Convention on the Civil Aspects of International Child Abduction, nor are there any international or bilateral treaties in force between Haiti and the United States dealing with international parental child abduction. American citizens who travel to Haiti place themselves under the jurisdiction of local courts. American citizens planning a trip to Haiti with dual national children should bear this in mind.

Custody Disputes: Normally, in Haiti, parents who are legally married share the custody of their children. If they are not married, custody is decided by a court.

The rights of the designated parent will be set within the scope of the court order. Culture, ethnicity, and gender do not have an impact in custody disputes. However, morality, financial resources, dependability, and availability are essential elements that are taken into account in custody disputes. Parental kidnapping is considered a crime and the length of imprisonment depends on the age of the child abducted.

Enforcement of Foreign Judgments: Custody orders and judgments of foreign courts are not enforced in Haiti.

Visitation Rights: In cases where legal custody has been granted and the judgment has been rendered, the non-custodial parent can petition the court for visitation rights within the court ordered decision or come to a verbal agreement with the custodial parent.

Dual Nationality: Dual nationality is not recognized under Haitian law.

Passports for Minors and the Children's Passport Issuance Alert Program: For more information on these topics, see the International Parental Child Abduction section of this publication and review current reports from the U.S. Department of State at www.travel.state.gov/abduction.

Travel Restrictions: No exit visas are required to leave Haiti. However, travel restrictions can be imposed on married women or children. This authorization requires certification from the Haiti immigration office before they may exit the country.

Criminal Remedies: For information on possible criminal remedies, please contact your local law enforcement authorities or the nearest office of the Federal Bureau of Investigation (FBI). Information is also available on the Internet at the web site of the U.S. Department of Justice, Office of Juvenile Justice and Delinquency Prevention (OJJDP) at http://www.ojjdp.ncjrs.org.

Persons who wish to pursue a child custody claim in a Haitian court should retain an attorney in Haiti. The U.S. Embassy in Haiti maintains a list of attorneys willing to represent American clients. A copy of this list may be obtained by requesting one from the Embassy at:

U.S. Embassy Port-Au-Prince
Consular Section
5 Harry Truman Blvd
P O Box 1761
Port-au-Prince
Haiti
Telephone: (509) 223-7011
Fax: [509] 223-9665
Web site: http://usembassy.state.gov

Questions involving Haitian law should be addressed to a Haitian attorney or to the Embassy of Haiti in the United States at:

Embassy of Haiti
2311 Massachusetts Avenue, NW
Washington, DC 20008
Telephone: (202) 332-4090
Internet: http://www.haiti.org

THE HOLY SEE

Compiled from publications that were available as of February 2013 from the U.S. Department of State, the U.S. Department of Commerce, and the Central Intelligence Agency (CIA). See the introduction to this set for explanatory notes.

Official Name:
The Holy See

PROFILE

Geography

Area: Total of 0.44 sq. km. (109 acres); land: 0.44 sq km; water: 0 sq km
Climate: temperate; mild, rainy winters (September to May) with hot, dry summers (May to September)
Terrain: urban; low hill

People

Population: 836 (July 2012 est.)
Population growth rate: 0.004% (2012 est.)
Ethnic groups: Italian, Swiss, other.
Religions: Roman Catholic.
Languages: Italian, Latin, French, various others.
Literacy: definition: age 15 and over can read and write; total population: 100%.
Work force: NA

Government

Type: Papacy; ecclesiastical, governmental, and administrative capital of the Catholic Church.
Independence: 11 February 1929 (from Italy); note—the three treaties signed with Italy on 11 February 1929 acknowledged, among other things, the full sovereignty of the Holy See and established its territorial extent; however, the origin of the Papal States, which over centuries varied considerably in extent, may be traced back to 754
Constitution: Fundamental Law promulgated by Pope John Paul II 26 November 2000, effective 22 February 2001 (replaced the first Fundamental Law of 1929)
Political subdivisions: none
Suffrage: limited to cardinals less than 80 years old

Economy

Budget: revenues: $326 million; expenditures: $313 million (2010)
Natural resources: none
Industries: printing; production of coins, medals, postage stamps; mosaics and staff uniforms; worldwide banking and financial activities
Exchange rates: euros (EUR) per US dollar—0.7838 (2012 est.); 0.7194 (2011 est.); 0.755 (2010 est.); 0.7198 (2009 est.); 0.6827 (2008 est.); 0.7345 (2007 est.)

PEOPLE AND HISTORY

The population of Vatican City includes high-ranking Catholic Church officials, priests, women religious, and Swiss Guards. The Vatican's workforce includes about 3,000 lay (non-clerical) workers who live outside Vatican City State.

The Holy See's diplomatic history began in the fourth century, but the boundaries of the papacy's temporal power have shifted over the centuries. From the 8th century through the middle of the 19th century, Popes ruled over the Papal States, which included a broad band of territory across central Italy. In 1860, after prolonged civil and regional unrest, Victor Emmanuel's army seized the Papal States, leaving only Rome and surrounding coastal regions under papal control.

In 1870, Victor Emmanuel captured Rome itself and declared it the new capital of Italy, ending papal claims to temporal power. Pope Pius IX and his successors disputed the legitimacy of these acts and proclaimed themselves to be "prisoners" in the Vatican. Finally, in 1929, the Italian Government and the Holy See signed three agreements resolving the dispute: a treaty recognizing the independence and sovereignty of the Holy See and creating Vatican City State; a Concordat defining the relations between the government and the church within Italy; and a financial convention providing the Holy See with compensation for its losses in 1870.

A revised Concordat, altering the terms of church-state relations, was signed in 1984.

GOVERNMENT AND INSTITUTIONS

The Pope exercises supreme legislative, executive, and judicial power over the Holy See and Vatican City State. Pope Francis, formerly Cardinal Jorge Bergoglio of Argentina, was elected on March 13, 2013 and formally inaugurated on March 19. The term "Holy See" refers to the composite of the authority, jurisdiction, and sovereignty vested in the Pope and his advisers to direct the worldwide Catholic Church. As the "central government" of the Catholic Church, the Holy See has a legal status that allows it to enter into treaties as the juridical equal of a state and to send and receive diplomatic representatives. The Holy See has formal diplomatic relations with 176 nations, including the United States and some predominantly Muslim countries. Created in 1929 to provide a territorial identity for the Holy See in Rome, Vatican City State is a recognized national territory under international law. The Holy See enters into international agreements and receives and sends diplomatic representatives.

Administration of Vatican City State

The Pope delegates the internal administration of Vatican City State to a Pontifical Commission. Vatican City State Gendarmerie are responsible for security. The Vatican has its own post office, commissary, bank, helicopter airfield, and electrical generating plant. The Vatican also issues its own coins and stamps and has its own Internet domain (.va).

Administration of the Holy See

The Pope exercises his authority through the Roman Curia and the Papal Civil Service. The Roman Curia consists of the Secretariat of State, nine Congregations, three Tribunals, 12 Pontifical Councils, and a complex of offices that administer Church affairs at the highest level. The Secretariat of State, under the Cardinal Secretary of State, directs and coordinates the Curia. On September 15, 2006, Pope Benedict XVI appointed Cardinal Tarcisio Bertone as Secretary of State (a role equivalent to that of prime minister) and appointed Archbishop Dominique Mamberti as Secretary for Relations with States (equivalent to foreign minister). Among the most active of the major Curial institutions are the Congregation for the Doctrine of the Faith, which oversees Church doctrine; the Congregation for Bishops, which coordinates the appointment of bishops worldwide; the Congregation for the Evangelization of Peoples, which oversees all missionary activities; and the Pontifical Council for Justice and Peace, which deals with international peace and social issues.

Three tribunals are responsible for judicial power. The Apostolic Penitentiary deals with matters of conscience; the Roman Rota is responsible for appeals, including annulments of marriage; and the Apostolic Signatura is the final court of appeal. The Prefecture for Economic Affairs coordinates the finances of the Holy See departments and supervises the administration of the Patrimony of the Holy See, an investment fund formed in 1967 from separate funds dating back to the time of the Lateran Pacts. A committee of 15 cardinals, chaired by the Secretary of State, has final oversight authority over all financial matters of the Holy See, including those of the Institute for Works of Religion, the Vatican bank. The Swiss Guard is a small military force of about 120 Swiss nationals. It shares security responsibilities with the Vatican City State Gendarmerie and falls under the authority of the Secretary of State.

Media and Communications

Vatican Radio, the official radio station, broadcasts in 40 languages to all continents. L'Osservatore Romano is the semi-official newspaper, published daily in Italian, and weekly in English, Spanish, Portuguese, German, and French (plus a monthly edition in Polish). There is also a weekly version published in Italian, as well as a weekly version in Malayalam (a language of India). Linked to the Osservatore Romano is a small publishing house, "Tipografia Vaticana." The Vatican also runs a TV production company that provides a live feed of papal events.

Principal Government Officials

Last Updated: 3/20/2013

Supreme Pontiff, Roman Catholic Church: **FRANCIS, Pope**

Sec. of State: **Tarcisio BERTONE, Cardinal**

Sec. for Relations With States: **Dominique MAMBERTI, Archbishop**

Apostolic Nuncio to the US: **Carlo Maria VIGANO, Archbishop**

Permanent Observer to the UN, New York: **Francis Assisi CHULLIKATT, Archbishop**

Papal Audiences

Requests for admission to papal audiences are handled by the U.S. Bishops Office for U.S. Visitors to the Vatican. The address is Casa Santa Maria dell'Umilta, Via dell'Umilta 30, 00187, Rome, Italy (tel. 39-06-690-0189), visitorsoffice@pnac.org.

ECONOMY

The Holy See is supported financially by a variety of sources, including investments, real estate income, and donations from Catholic individuals, dioceses, and institutions; these help fund the Roman Curia (Vatican bureaucracy), diplomatic missions, and media outlets. Moreover, an annual collection taken up in dioceses and from direct donations go to a non-budgetary fund, known as Peter's Pence, which is used directly by the Pope for charity, disaster relief, and aid to churches in developing nations. Donations increased between 2010 and 2011.

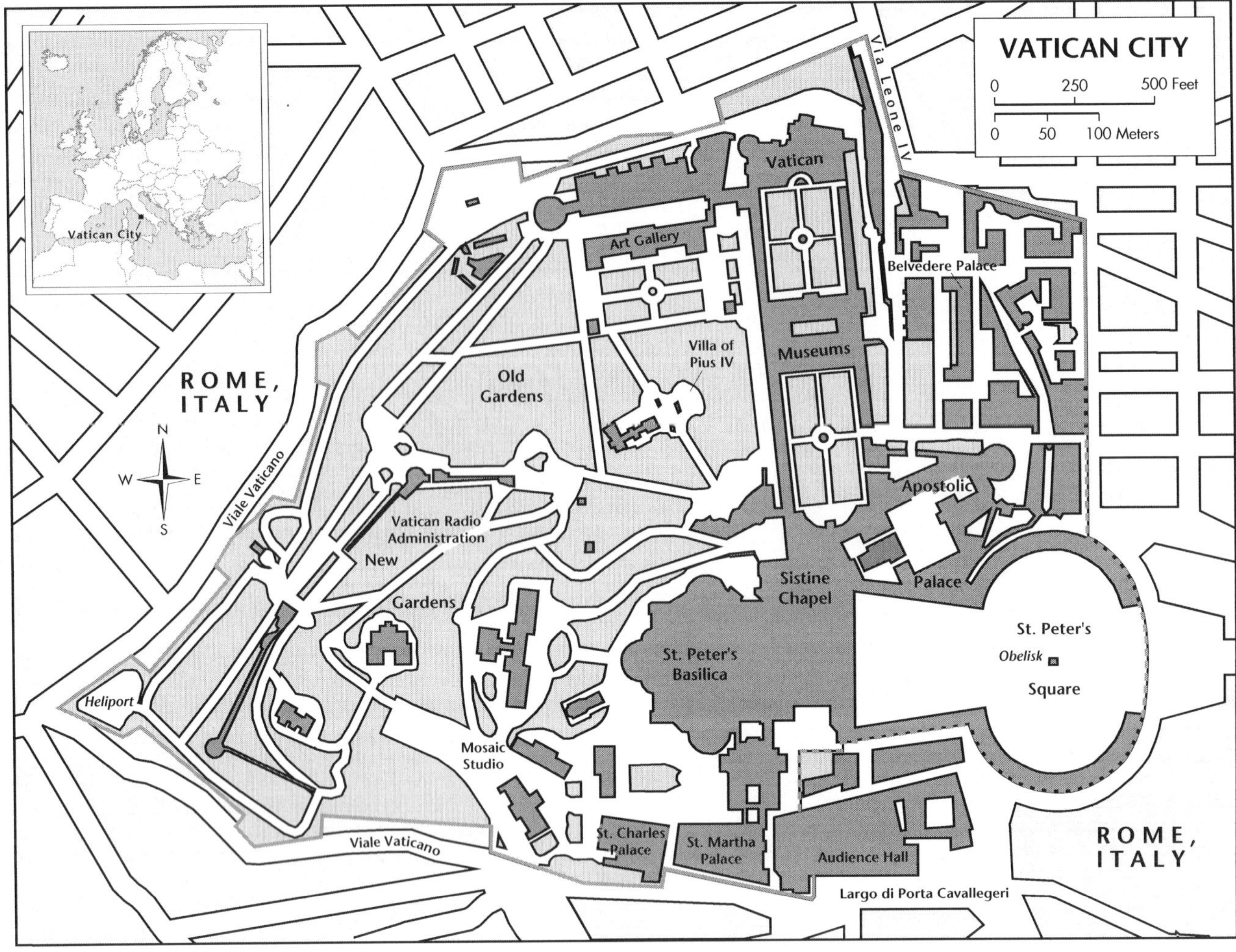

The separate Vatican City State budget includes the Vatican museums and post office and is supported financially by the sale of stamps, coins, medals, and tourist mementos; by fees for admission to museums; and by publications sales. Its revenues increased between 2010 and 2011 because of expanded opening hours and a growing number of visitors.

However, the Holy See has not escaped the financial difficulties engulfing other European countries; in 2012 it started a spending review to determine where to cut costs to reverse its 2011 budget deficit of 15 million euros. Most public expenditures go to wages and other personnel costs; the incomes and living standards of lay workers are comparable to those of counterparts who work in the city of Rome.

U.S.-HOLY SEE RELATIONS

The Holy See is the universal government of the Catholic Church and operates from Vatican City State, a sovereign, independent territory. The Pope is the ruler of both Vatican City State and the Holy See. The Holy See, as the supreme body of government of the Catholic Church, is a sovereign juridical entity under international law. The United States and the Holy See consult and cooperate on international issues of mutual interest, including human rights, inter-religious understanding, peace and conflict prevention, development, and environmental protection.

The United States maintained consular relations with the Papal States from 1797 to 1870 and diplomatic relations with the Pope, in his capacity as head of the Papal States, from 1848 to 1868, though not at the ambassadorial level.

These relations lapsed in 1870 with the loss of all papal territories during the unification of Italy. From 1870 to 1984, the United States did not have diplomatic relations with the Holy See. Several U.S. presidents, however, designated personal envoys to visit the Holy See periodically for discussions of international humanitarian and political issues.

In 1984, a revised Concordat was signed defining the relations between the government and the church within Italy. The United States and the Holy See announced the establishment of diplomatic relations in 1984.

U.S. Assistance to the Holy See

The United States provides no development assistance to the Holy See.

Bilateral Economic Relations

The United States has no significant trade or investment with the Holy See.

The Holy See's Membership in International Organizations

The Holy See and the United States both are members of the Organization for Security and Cooperation in Europe. The Holy See also is an observer to a number of international organizations of which the United States is a member, including the United Nations, Organization of American States, and World Trade Organization.

Bilateral Representation

The Holy See maintains an Apostolic Nunciature, the equivalent of an embassy, in the United States at 3339 Massachusetts Ave. NW, Washington, DC 20008, tel. (202) 333-7121.

Principal U.S. Embassy Officials

Last Updated: 1/14/2013

VATICAN CITY (E) Via delle Terme Deciane, 26, (+39) 06-4674-3425, Fax (0039) 06-575-8346, Workweek: Mon–Fri / 8:30am–5:30pm, Website: http://vatican.usembassy.gov

DCM OMS:	Jelena Lazovic
AMB OMS:	Paolina Milasi
MGT:	Daniel Mehring
POL/ECON:	Chad Miner
DCM:	Mario M. Mesquita
PAO:	Phillip Assis
IMO:	William J. Walls
POL:	Kimberly Penland

TRAVEL

Consular Information Sheet—Italy, Holy See, and San Marino

December 21, 2011

Country Description: Italy is a developed democracy with a modern economy. The Holy See is a sovereign entity that serves as the ecclesiastical, governmental, and administrative capital of the Roman Catholic Church, physically located within the State of the Vatican City inside Rome, with a unique, non-traditional economy. San Marino is a developed, constitutional democratic republic, also independent of Italy, with a modern economy. Tourist facilities are widely available.

Smart Traveler Enrollment Program (STEP)/Embassy Locations: If you are going to live or visit Italy, San Marino, or the Holy See, please take the time to tell our embassy or consulates about your trip by enrolling in the Smart Traveler Enrollment Program. If you enroll, we can keep you up to date with important safety and security announcements; it will also help your friends and family get in touch with you in an emergency.

U.S. Embassy Rome
Via V. Veneto 119/A, Rome, Italy
Telephone: 39-06-46741
Facsimile: 39-06-4674–2217
Email: uscitizensrome@state.gov

U.S. Embassy to the Holy See
Via delle Terme Deciane 26
Rome, Italy
Telephone: 39-06-4674–3428
Facsimile: 39-06-575-8346

U.S. Consulate General Florence
Lungarno Amerigo Vespucci 38
Florence, Italy
Telephone: 39-055-266-951
Facsimile: 399-055-215-550
Email: uscitizensflorence@state.gov

U.S. Consulate General Milan
Via Principe Amedeo 2/10
Milan, Italy
Telephone: 39-02-290-351
Facsimile: 39-02-290-35-273
Email: uscitizensmilan@state.gov

U.S. Consulate General Naples
Piazza della Repubblica
Naples, Italy
Telephone: 39-081-583-8111
Facsimile: 39-081-583-8275
Email: uscitizensnaples@state.gov

There are U.S. Consular Agents located in the following Italian cities:

Genoa
Via Dante 2, Genoa, Italy
Telephone: 39-010-584-492
Facsimile: 39-010-553-3033
Email: usconsge@libero.it

Palermo
Via Vaccarini 1, Palermo, Italy
Telephone: 39-091-305-857
Facsimile: 39-091-625-6026
Email: uscitizenspalermo@state.gov

Venice
Viale Galileo Galilei 30, Venice, Italy
Telephone: 39-041-541-5944
Facsimile: 39-041-541-6654
Email: uscitizensvenice@state.gov

Entry/Exit Requirements for U.S. Citizens: Italy is a party to the Schengen Agreement. As such, U.S. citizens may enter Italy for up to 90 days for tourist or business purposes without a visa. The passport should be valid for at least three months beyond the period of stay. For further details about travel into and within Schengen countries, please see our Schengen Fact sheet. For all other purposes, you need a visa, which you must get from an Italian Embassy or Consulate before entering Italy. For further information concerning visas and entry requirements for Italy, you may contact the Embassy of Italy at 3000 Whitehaven Street NW, Washington, DC 20008, or via telephone at (202) 612-4400; or Italian Consulates General in Boston, Chicago, Detroit, Houston, Los Angeles, Miami, Newark, New Orleans, New York, Philadelphia, or San Francisco, accessible through the Italian Embassy website.

Are you a non-resident? U.S. citizens staying or traveling within Italy for less than three months are considered non-residents. This includes persons on vacation, those taking professional trips, students registered at an authorized school, or persons performing research or independent study. Under Italian law, all non-residents are required to complete a dichiarazione di presenza (declaration of presence). Tourists arriving from a non-Schengen-country (e.g. the United States) should obtain a stamp in their passport at the airport on the day of arrival. This stamp is considered the equivalent of the declaration of presence. Tourists arriving from a Schengen-country (e.g. France) must request the declaration of presence form from a local police office (commissariato di zona), police headquarters (questura) or their place of stay (e.g hotel, hostel, campgrounds) and submit the form to the police or to their place of stay within eight business days of arrival. It is important that applicants keep a copy of the receipt issued by the Italian authorities. Failure to complete a declaration of presence is punishable by expulsion from Italy. Additional information may be obtained (in Italian only) from the Portale Immigrazione and the Polizia di Stato. Are you a resident? U.S. citizens staying in Italy for more than three months are considered residents and must obtain a permesso di soggiorno (permit of stay). This includes U.S. citizens who will work or transact business and persons who want simply to live in Italy. An application "kit" for the permesso di soggiorno can be requested from one of 14,000 national post offices (Poste Italiane). The kit must then be returned to one of 5,332 designated Post Office acceptance locations. It is important that applicants keep a copy of the receipt issued by the post office. Additional information may be obtained from the Italian immigration website. Within 20 days of receiving the permit to stay in Italy, U.S. citizens must go to the local Vital Statistics Bureau (Anagrafe of the Comune) to apply for residency. It generally takes one to two months to receive the certificate of residence (Certificato di Residenza).

The U.S. Department of State is unaware of any HIV/AIDS entry restrictions for visitors to or foreign residents of Italy.

Threats to Safety and Security: Several major earthquake fault lines cross Italy. Principal Italian cities, with the exception of Naples, do not lie near these faults; however, smaller tourist towns, such as Assisi, do lie near faults, and have experienced earthquakes. An earthquake severely damaged the town of L'Aquila in 2009. General information about disaster preparedness is available online from the U.S. Federal Management Agency (FEMA). Detailed information on Italy's fault lines is available from the U.S. Geological Survey (USGS).

Italy also has several active volcanoes generating geothermal events. Mt. Etna, on the eastern tip of the island of Sicily, has been erupting intermittently since 2000. Mt. Vesuvius, located near Naples, is currently capped and not active. Activity at Mt. Vesuvius is monitored by an active seismic network and sensor system, and no recent seismic activity has been recorded. Two of Italy's smaller islands, Stromboli and Vulcano, in the Aeolian Islands north of Sicily, also have active volcanoes with lava flows. Detailed information on volcano activity in Italy is available from the USGS. Politically motivated violence in Italy is most often connected to Italian internal developments or social issues. Italian authorities and foreign diplomatic facilities have found bombs outside public buildings, received bomb threats, and were subjects of letter bombs. Buildings or offices are sometimes the targets of firebombs or Molotov cocktails, although generally at night; such incidents are instigated by organized crime or anarchist movements, and have not targeted or injured U.S. citizens. Demonstrations may have an anti-American character, especially in areas hosting U.S. military bases. Even demonstrations intended to be peaceful have the potential to turn confrontational and possibly escalate into violence. You should take common sense precautions and follow news reports carefully. Stay up to date by reading the Embassy's Demonstration Notices. Italian authorities have made several high-profile arrests involving members or affiliates of transnational terror groups. Like other countries in the Schengen area, Italy's open borders with its Western European neighbors allow for the possibility of terrorist groups entering/exiting the country with anonymity.

Stay up to date by:

- Bookmarking our Bureau of Consular Affairs website, which contains the current Travel Warnings and Travel Alerts as well as the Worldwide Caution;
- Following us on Twitter and the Bureau of Consular Affairs page on Facebook;
- Downloading our free Smart Traveler IPhone App to have travel information at your fingertips; and
- Calling 1-888-407-4747 toll-free within the U.S. and Canada, or a regular toll line, 1-202-501-4444, from other countries.

Take some time before travel to consider your personal security.

Crime: Italy has a moderate rate of crime. You should exercise extra caution at night and at train stations, airports, nightclubs, bars, and outdoor cafes. If you are drinking heavily, your ability to judge situations and make decisions may be impaired and this can make you a target for crime. Young drinkers are particularly vulnerable to robbery and physical and sexual assault. Petty crimes such as pick-pocketing, theft from parked cars, and purse snatching are serious problems, especially in large cities. Pick-pockets sometimes dress like businessmen. You should not be lulled into a false sense of security by believing that well-dressed individuals are not potential pick-pockets or thieves. Most reported thefts occur at crowded tourist sites, on public buses or trains, or at the major railway stations. Rome's Termini; Milan's Centrale; Florence's Santa Maria Novella; and Naples' Centrale at Piazza Garibaldi. For more information on trains and security, please see the Italian railway police's advice for travelers at http://www.poliziadistato.it/articolo/view/22329/. You should also be alert to theft in Milan's Malpensa Airport, particularly at car rental agencies. Clients of Internet cafes in major cities are also targeted. Be careful with your bag or purse, as thieves on motor scooters are very quick and can snatch a purse off of your arm from a moving scooter. Resisting these thieves can be hazardous, as some tourists have suffered broken arms and collarbones.

Thieves in Italy often work in groups or pairs. Pairs of accomplices or groups of children are known to divert tourists' attention so that another can pick-pocket them. In one particular routine, one thief throws trash, waste, or ketchup at the victim; a second thief assists the victim in cleaning up the mess; and the third discreetly takes the victim's belongings. Criminals on crowded public transportation slit the bottoms of purses or bags with a razor blade or sharp knife removing the contents.

Some travelers in Rome, Florence, and Naples have reported incidents where criminals used drugs to assault or rob them. These incidents have been reported near Rome's Termini train station; at bars and cafes near Rome's Colosseum, Colle Oppio, Campo de Fiori, and Piazza Navona; and at bars or cafes in the center of Florence and Naples. Criminals using this tactic "befriend" you at a train station, restaurant, café, or bar, and then offer you a drink laced with a sleeping drug. When you fall asleep, criminals steal your valuables and may sexually assault you. Some victims of these assaults in Rome have required hospitalization and two cases resulted in death.

Thieves are also known to have impersonated police officers in order to steal. The thief shows you a circular plastic sign with the words "police" or "international police" and then in perfect English asks to see your identification and your money. U.S. citizens should be aware that local police will generally exit their own vehicle when speaking with members of the public. Also, plainclothes undercover units rarely attempt to pull over vehicles without a marked car accompanying them. If this happens to you, you should insist on seeing the officer's identification card (documento), before handing over your wallet as impersonators tend not to carry forged documents. You should immediately report thefts or other crimes to the actual police.

Be alert to the possibility of carjackings and thefts while you are waiting in traffic or stopped at traffic lights. This has been a particular problem in Catania, Sicily. Use particular caution driving at night on highways, when thieves are more likely to strike. Americans have reported break-ins of their rental cars during stops at highway service areas; thieves smash car windows and steal everything inside. Theft of small items such as radios, luggage, cameras, briefcases, and even cigarettes from parked cars is prevalent. Vehicles parked near beaches during the summer can be broken into and robbed of valuables. Lock car doors whenever you park, and do not leave packages in your car in plain view. The U.S. Secret Service in Rome is assisting Italian Law Enforcement authorities in investigating an increase in the appearance of ATM skimming devices. These devices are attached to legitimate bank ATMs, usually located in tourist areas, and capture the account information stored electronically on the card's magnetic strip. The devices consist of a card reader installed over the legitimate reader and a pin-hole video camera mounted above the keypad that records the customer's PIN. ATMs with skimming devices installed may also allow normal transactions to occur. The victim's information is sold, traded on-line, or encoded on another card such as a hotel key card to access the compromised account. Here are some helpful hints to protect against and identify skimming devices:

- Use ATMs located in well-lighted public areas, or secured inside a bank/business.

- Cover the keypad with one hand as you enter your PIN.

- Look for gaps, tampered appearance, or other irregularities between the metal faceplate of the ATM and the card reader.

- Avoid card readers that are not flush with the face of the ATM.

- Closely monitor your account statements for unauthorized transactions.

Organized criminal groups operate throughout Italy, but are more prevalent in the south. They occasionally resort to violence to intimidate or to settle disputes. Though the activities of such groups are not generally targeted at tourists, visitors should be aware that innocent bystanders could be injured.

Don't buy counterfeit and pirated goods, even if they are widely available. Not only are the bootlegs illegal to bring back into the United States, if you purchase them you may also be breaking local law. According to Italian Law (Law 80 of May 14, 2005), anyone caught buying counterfeit goods (for example, DVDs, CDs, watches, purses, bags, belts, sunglasses, etc.) is subject to a fine of no less than EUR 1,000. Police in major Italian cities enforce this law to varying degrees. You are advised to purchase products only from stores and other licensed retailers to avoid unknowingly buying counterfeit and illegal merchandise.

Victims of Crime: If you or someone you know becomes the victim of a crime abroad, you should contact the local police and the nearest U.S. embassy or consulate. We can:

- Replace a stolen passport.

- For violent crimes such as assault or rape, help you find appropriate medical care.

- Put you in contact with the appropriate police authorities and, if you want us to, we can contact family members or friends.

- Although the local authorities are responsible for investigating and prosecuting the crime, consular officers can help you understand the local criminal justice process and can direct you to local attorneys.

The local equivalent to the "911" emergency line in Italy is 113.

Criminal Penalties: While you are traveling in Italy, you are subject to its laws even if you are a U.S. citizen. Foreign laws and legal systems can be vastly different than our own, and criminal penalties vary from country to country. There are also some things that might be legal in the country you visit, but still illegal in the United States; for instance, you can be prosecuted under U.S. law if you buy pirated goods. Engaging in sexual conduct with children or using or disseminating child pornography in a foreign country is a crime prosecutable in the United States. If you break local laws in Italy, your U.S. passport won't help you avoid arrest or prosecution.

Arrest notifications in host country: While some countries will automatically notify the nearest U.S. embassy or consulate if a U.S. citizen is detained or arrested in a foreign country, that might not always be the case. To ensure that the United States is aware of your circumstances, request that the police and prison officials notify the nearest U.S. embassy or consulate as soon as you are arrested or detained overseas.

Special Circumstances: Strikes and other work stoppages occur frequently in the transportation sector (national airlines, airports, trains, and bus lines); most are announced in advance and are of short duration. Reconfirmation of domestic and international flight reservations is highly recommended. You must obey local transportation laws and regulations. You must purchase train tickets and validate them by punching them in validating machines usually located near the entrance of train tracks prior to boarding. Failure to follow this procedure may result in an on-the-spot fine by an inspector on the train. You must purchase bus tickets prior to boarding and validate them immediately after boarding. Tickets may be purchased at tobacco stores or kiosks. Failure to follow this procedure may result in an immediate fine imposed by an inspector on the bus. If the violator does not pay the fine on the spot, it will automatically double and will be forwarded to the violator's home address.

You must obey local driving laws and regulations. Vehicle traffic in some historic downtown areas of cities and towns throughout Italy is limited by a system of permits (called "ZTL" and functioning the same way as an electronic toll system in the United States might on the freeway). Cameras record the license plates of cars driving in parts of the city that require a permit. Although most of the automated verification stations are clearly marked, if a driver passes one it is impossible to know at the time that a violation occurred or has been recorded. Violators are not pulled over or stopped, and there is no personal contact with a police officer. Whenever possible, the fines imposed for these violations are forwarded to the driver's home in the United States to request payment. Notice from Italian authorities of a violation may take a year or longer to arrive. The fines are cumulative for each time a driver passes a control point. A similar system of automated traffic control cameras is in place in many parts of the highway system and is used to ticket speeding violations.

Accessibility: While in Italy, travelers with disabilities may find accessibility and accommodation different from what is found in the United States. Many find Italy's narrow cobbled streets and storied monuments charming; they can, however, be a challenge for physically impaired travelers. Many Italian sidewalks lack ramps, some Italian streets lack sidewalks altogether, or for instance in the case of Venice, may feature staircases and narrow pedestrian bridges. While some major sights and hotels have put time and planning into ensuring accessibility, there are others that lack ramps, elevators, or handicap-accessible bathrooms. Advance planning can go a long way in making a difference in accommodation for disabled travelers. Inform airlines and hotels of your disabilities when making reservations as some time may be needed to prepare accommodation. Call ahead to restaurants, museums, and other facilities to find out if they are wheelchair-accessible. Most, but not all train stations in Italy have accommodations for those traveling in wheelchairs. With advance notice, personal assistance can be provided to a disabled person traveling through a particular station. More information is available at Trenitalia's website addressing disabled travelers. For those who wish to rent cars, hand-controlled vehicles are available in Italy from major car-rental companies. You should contact the car rental company well in advance of your trip in order to reserve the vehicle. Remember that Italy functions on 220 volt current. To recharge an electric wheelchair motor you may require a transformer to change the 220 current to 110 volts, as well as an adaptor to adjust the plug to fit Italian electric sockets. Guide-dog owners must present the documentation required by European Union Member States in order to enter Italy with a dog.

Medical Facilities and Health Information: Medical facilities are available, but may be limited outside urban areas. Public hospitals, though generally free of charge for emergency services, sometimes do not maintain the same standards as hospitals in the United States, so you are encouraged to obtain insurance that would cover a stay in a private Italian hospital or clinic. It is almost impossible to obtain an itemized hospital bill from public hospitals, as required by many U.S. insurance companies, because the Italian National Health Service charges one inclusive rate (care services, room and board).

In parts of southern Italy, the lack of adequate trash disposal and incineration sites has led to periodic accumulations of garbage in urban and rural areas. In some cases, residents have burned garbage, resulting in toxic emissions that can aggravate respiratory problems.

The U.S. Navy initiated a public health evaluation in the Naples area in 2008. After finding levels of bacterial and chemical contamination of potential health concern, particularly in samples of area well water, the Navy recommended all personnel living off-base in the Naples area use only bottled water for drinking, cooking, ice-making, and brushing teeth. For more information on safe food and water precautions, see the Centers for Disease Control and Prevention (CDC) website. You can find good information on vaccinations and other health precautions, on the CDC website. For information about outbreaks of infectious diseases abroad, consult the World Health Organization (WHO) website, which also contains additional health information for travelers, including detailed country-specific health information.

Medical Insurance: You can't assume your insurance will go with you when you travel. It's very important to find out BEFORE you leave. You need to ask your insurance company two questions:

- Does my policy apply when I'm out of the U.S.?
- Will it cover emergencies like a trip to a foreign hospital or a medical evacuation?

In many places, doctors and hospitals still expect payment in cash at the time of service. Your regular U.S. health insurance may not cover doctors' and hospital visits in other countries. If your policy doesn't go with you when you travel, it's a very good idea to take out another one for your trip.

Traffic Safety and Road Conditions: While in Italy, you may encounter road conditions that differ significantly from those in the United States. Italy has one of the highest rates of car accident deaths in the European Union. Streets in Italian historic city centers are often narrow, winding, and congested. Motor scooters are very popular, and scooter drivers often see themselves as exempt from conventions that apply to automobiles. Pedestrians and drivers should be constantly alert to the possibility of a scooter's sudden presence. Most vehicle-related deaths and injuries involve pedestrians or cyclists who are involved in collisions with scooters or other vehicles. Be particularly cautious if you rent a scooter. You should remain vigilant and alert when walking or cycling near traffic. Pedestrians should be careful, as sidewalks can be extremely congested and uneven. Drivers of bicycles, motorcycles, and other vehicles routinely ignore traffic signals and traffic flows, and park and drive on sidewalks. For safety, pedestrians should look carefully in both directions before crossing streets, even when using a marked crosswalk with a green avanti ("walk") light illuminated. Traffic lights are limited and often disobeyed, and a different convention of right-of-way is observed. Italy has over 5,600 kilometers (3,480 mi.) of Autostrada, or superhighways. Commercial and individual vehicles travel and pass on these well-maintained roads at very high speeds. In rural areas, a wide range of speed on highways makes for hazardous driving. Roads are generally narrow and often have no guardrails. Travelers in northern Italy, especially in winter, should be aware of fog and poor visibility, responsible for multiple-car accidents each year. Most Italian automobiles are equipped with special fog lights. Roadside assistance in Italy is excellent on the well-maintained toll roads, but limited on secondary roads. Use of safety belts and child restraining devices is mandatory and headlights should be on at all times outside of urban areas.

U.S. citizens driving in Italy should also note that, according to Italian regulation, if a resident of a non-European Union country (e.g. the United States) violates a traffic law, the violator must pay the fine at the time the violation occurs to the police officer issuing the ticket. If the citizen does not or cannot pay the fine at the time, Italian regulation allows the police officer to confiscate the offender's vehicle (even if the vehicle is a rental vehicle). For specific information concerning Italian driving permits, vehicle inspection, road tax, and mandatory insurance, contact the Italian Government Tourist Board (ENIT), tel: 212-245-5618; or the A.C.I. (Automobile Club d'Italia) at Via Marsala 14A, 00185 Rome, tel: 39-06-4998–2496. For information on obtaining international drivers licenses, contact AAA or the American Automobile Touring Alliance. Visit the website of Italy's national tourist office and national authority responsible for road safety.

Aviation Safety Oversight: The U.S. Federal Aviation Administration (FAA) assessed the Government of Italy's Civil Aviation Authority as being in compliance with International Civil Aviation Organization (ICAO) aviation safety standards for oversight of Italy's air carrier operations. Further information may be found on the FAA safety assessment page.

Children's Issues: Please see the U.S. Dept. of State Office of Children's Issues web pages on intercountry adoption and international parental child abduction.

HONDURAS

Compiled from publications that were available as of February 2013 from the U.S. Department of State, the U.S. Department of Commerce, and the Central Intelligence Agency (CIA). See the introduction to this set for explanatory notes.

Official Name:
Republic of Honduras

PROFILE

Geography

Area: total: 112,090 sq km; country comparison to the world: 103; land: 111,890 sq km; water: 200 sq km
Major cities: Tegucigalpa (capital) 1 million (2009)
Climate: subtropical in lowlands, temperate in mountains
Terrain: mostly mountains in interior, narrow coastal plains

People

Nationality: noun: Honduran(s); adjective: Honduran
Population: 8,296,693 (July 2012 est.)
Population growth rate: 1.838% (2012 est.)
Ethnic groups: mestizo (mixed Amerindian and European) 90%, Amerindian 7%, black 2%, white 1%
Religions: Roman Catholic 97%, Protestant 3%
Languages: Spanish (official), Amerindian dialects
Literacy: definition: age 15 and over can read and write; total population: 80%; male: 79.8%; female: 80.2% (2001 census)
Health: life expectancy at birth: total population: 70.71 years; male: 69.03 years; female: 72.47 years (2012 est.); Infant mortality rate: total: 19.85 deaths/1,000 live births; male: 22.47 deaths/1,000 live births; female: 17.1 deaths/1,000 live births (2012 est.)
Unemployment rate: 4.5% (2012 est.)
Work force: 3.44 million (2012 est.)

Government

Type: democratic constitutional republic
Independence: 15 September 1821
Constitution: 11 January 1982, effective 20 January 1982; amended many times
Political subdivisions: 18 departments (departamentos, singular—departamento); Atlantida, Choluteca, Colon, Comayagua, Copan, Cortes, El Paraiso, Francisco Morazan, Gracias a Dios, Intibuca, Islas de la Bahia, La Paz, Lempira, Ocotepeque, Olancho, Santa Barbara, Valle, Yoro
Suffrage: 18 years of age; universal and compulsory

Economy

GDP (purchasing power parity): $37.67 billion (2012 est.); $36.15 billion (2011 est.); $34.89 billion (2010 est.); $33.95 billion (2009 est.)
GDP real growth rate: 3.8% (2012 est.); 3.6% (2011 est.); 2.8% (2010 est.); -2.1% (2009 est.)
GDP per capita (PPP): $4,600 (2012 est.); $4,400 (2011 est.); $4,300 (2010 est.); $4,300 (2009 est.)
Natural resources: timber, gold, silver, copper, lead, zinc, iron ore, antimony, coal, fish, hydropower
Agriculture products: bananas, coffee, citrus, corn, African palm; beef; timber; shrimp, tilapia, lobster
Industries: sugar, coffee, woven and knit apparel, wood products, cigars
Exports: $6.946 billion (2012 est.); $7.204 billion (2011 est.); $5.742 billion (2010 est.)
Exports—commodities: apparel, coffee, shrimp, automobile wire harnesses, cigars, bananas, gold, palm oil, fruit, lobster, lumber
Exports—partners: US 86% (2011)
Imports: $10.66 billion (2012 est.); $10.34 billion (2011 est.); $8.55 billion (2010 est.)
Imports—commodities: machinery and transport equipment, industrial raw materials, chemical products, fuels, foodstuffs
Imports—partners: US 49.8%, Guatemala 8.2%, Mexico 5%, El Salvador 4.9% (2011)
Debt—external: $4.884 billion (31 December 2012 est.); $4.564 billion (31 December 2011 est.); $4.168 billion (31 December 2010 est.)
Exchange rates: lempiras (HNL) per US dollar; 19.51 (2012 est.)18.895 (2011 est.); 18.9 (2010 est.); 18.9 (2009); 18.983 (2008); 18.9 (2007)

PEOPLE

About 90% of the population is mestizo. There also are small minorities of European, African, Asian, Arab, and indigenous Indian descent. The restored Mayan ruins near the Guatemalan border in Copan reflect the great Mayan culture that flourished there for hundreds of years until the early 9th century. Columbus landed at mainland Honduras (Trujillo) in 1502, and named the area "Honduras" (meaning "depths") for the deep water off the coast. Spaniard Hernan Cortes arrived in 1524.

National/Racial/Ethnic Minorities

Approximately 621,000 persons, constituting 8 percent of the general population, were members of indigenous and other ethnic minority groups. These groups, including the Misquitos, Tawahkas, Pech, Tolupans, Lencas, Maya-Chortis, Nahual, Bay Islanders, and Garifunas, lived in 362 communities and generally had little or no political power to make decisions affecting their lands, cultures, traditions, and the allocation of natural resources.

Language

While Spanish is the predominant language, some English is spoken along the northern coast and is prevalent on the Caribbean Bay Islands. A substantial number of Honduran professionals and business executives speak English, and many high government officials and private sector leaders were educated in the United States.Several indigenous Indian languages and Garífuna (a mixture of Afro-indigenous languages) are also spoken.

Religion

There are no reliable government statistics on religious affiliation. In a 2007 nationwide survey, CID-Gallup, a Latin American market research and public opinion company, reported 47 percent of respondents identified themselves as Roman Catholic and 36 percent as evangelical Protestant. The principal religious groups are Catholic, Episcopal, Lutheran, Jehovah's Witnesses, Mennonite, The Church of Jesus Christ of Latter-day Saints (Mormons), and approximately 300 evangelical Protestant groups.

The most prominent evangelical churches include the Abundant Life, Living Love, and Great Commission churches. A growing number of evangelical churches have no denominational affiliation. The Evangelical Confederation of Honduras represents the evangelical leadership. There are approximately 2,000 Muslims and 1,000 Jews. San Pedro Sula has a mosque and a synagogue, and Tegucigalpa has a synagogue.

HISTORY

Honduras was originally inhabited by indigenous tribes, the most powerful of which were the Mayans. The western-central part of Honduras was inhabited by the Lencas. These autonomous groups had their conflicts but maintained their commercial relationships with each other and with other populations as distant as Panama and Mexico.

On July 30, 1502, Christopher Columbus first saw Honduran soil and he claimed the territory in the name of his sovereigns, Ferdinand of Aragon and Isabella of Castile.

In 1523, the first expeditionary forces arrived under the command of Gil Gonzales de Avila, who hoped to rule the new territory. In 1524, Cristobal de Olid arrived with the same intent on behalf of Hernan Cortes. Olid founded the colony Triunfo de la Cruz and tried to establish an independent government. When Cortes learned of this, he decided to reestablish his own authority by sending a new expedition, headed by Francisco de las Casas. Olid, who managed to capture his rivals, was betrayed by his men and assassinated. Cortes then traveled to Honduras to firmly establish his government in the city of Trujillo before returning to Mexico in 1526. Honduras formed part of the colonial era Captaincy General of Guatemala. The cities of Comayagua and Tegucigalpa developed as early mining centers.

By October 1537, the Lenca chief, Lempira, a warrior of great renown, had managed to unify more than two hundred native tribes in order to offer an organized resistance against penetration by the Spanish conquerors. After a long battle, Governor Montejo gained the Valley of Comayagua, established Comayagua city in another location, and vanquished the indigenous peoples in Tenampua, Guaxeregui, and Ojuera.

Independence

Honduras gained independence from Spain in 1821. The country was then briefly annexed to the Mexican Empire. In 1823, Honduras joined the newly formed United Provinces of Central America federation, which collapsed in 1838. Gen. Francisco Morazan—a Honduran national hero—led unsuccessful efforts to maintain the federation. Honduras' agriculture-based economy was dominated in the 1900s by U.S. companies that established vast banana plantations along the north coast. Foreign capital, plantation life, and conservative politics held sway in Honduras from the late 19th century until the mid-20th century.

Military Rule

Authoritarian Gen. Tiburcio Carias Andino controlled Honduras during the Great Depression, until 1948. In 1955—after two authoritarian administrations and a strike by banana workers—young military reformists staged a coup that installed a provisional junta and paved the way for constituent assembly elections in 1957.

This assembly appointed Ramon Villeda Morales as President and transformed itself into a national legislature with a 6-year term. In 1963, conservative military officers preempted constitutional elections and deposed Villeda in a bloody coup. The armed forces, led by Gen. Lopez Arellano, governed until 1970. Popular

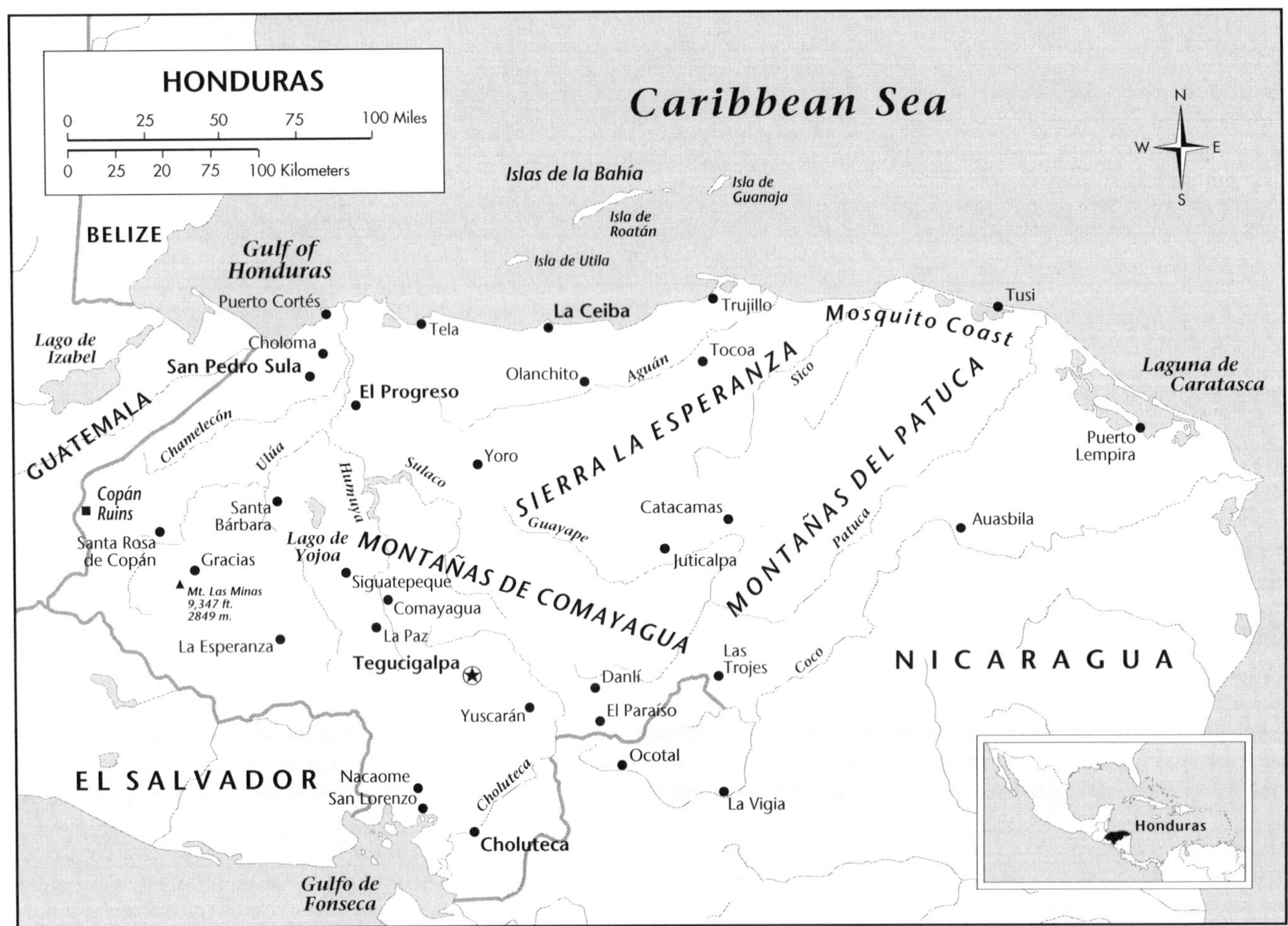

discontent continued to rise after a 1969 border war with El Salvador, known as "the Soccer War." A civilian President—Ramon Cruz of the National Party—took power briefly in 1970 but proved unable to manage the government. In 1972, Gen. Lopez staged another coup. Lopez adopted more progressive policies, including land reform, but his regime was brought down in the mid-1970s by corruption scandals.

The regimes of Gen. Melgar Castro (1975–78) and Gen. Paz Garcia (1978–82) largely built the current physical infrastructure and telecommunications system of Honduras. The country also enjoyed its most rapid economic growth during this period, due to greater international demand for its products and the availability of foreign commercial lending.

Seven Consecutive Democratic Elections

Following the overthrow of Anastasio Somoza in Nicaragua in 1979 and general instability in El Salvador at the time, Hondurans elected a constituent assembly in 1980 and voted in general elections in 1981.

A new constitution was approved in 1982, and the Liberal Party government of President Roberto Suazo Cordoba took office. Suazo relied on U.S. support during a severe economic recession, including ambitious social and economic development projects sponsored by the U.S. Agency for International Development (USAID). Honduras became host to the largest Peace Corps mission in the world, and nongovernmental and international voluntary agencies proliferated.

As the 1985 election approached, the Liberal Party interpreted election law as permitting multiple presidential candidates from one party. The Liberal Party claimed victory when its presidential candidates, who received 42% of the vote, collectively outpolled the National Party candidate, Rafael Leonardo Callejas. Jose Azcona Hoyo, the candidate receiving the most votes among the Liberals, assumed the presidency in 1986. With the endorsement of the Honduran military, the Azcona administration ushered in the first peaceful transfer of power between civilian presidents in more than 30 years.

Nationalist Rafael Callejas won the following presidential election, taking office in 1990. The nation's fiscal deficit ballooned during Callejas' last year in office. Growing public dissatisfaction with the rising cost of living and with widespread government corruption led voters in 1993 to elect Liberal Party candidate Carlos Roberto Reina with 56% of the vote. President Reina, elected on a platform calling for a "moral revolution," actively prosecuted corruption and pursued those responsible for human rights abuses in the 1980s. He created a modern attorney general's office and an investigative police force, increased civilian control over the armed forces, transferred the police from military to civilian authority, and restored national fiscal health.

Liberal Carlos Roberto Flores Facusse took office in 1998. Flores inaugurated programs of reform and modernization of the Honduran government and economy, with emphasis on helping Honduras' poorest citizens while maintaining the country's fiscal health and improving international competitiveness. In October 1998, Hurricane Mitch devastated Honduras, leaving more than 5,000 people dead and 1.5 million displaced. Damages totaled nearly $3 billion.

Ricardo Maduro Joest of the National Party won the 2001 presidential elections, and was inaugurated in 2002. Maduro's first act as President was to deploy a joint police-military force to the streets to permit wider neighborhood patrols in the ongoing fight against the country's massive crime and gang problem. Maduro was a strong supporter of U.S. counterterrorism efforts and joined the U.S.-led coalition in Iraq with an 11-month contribution of 370 troops.

Under President Maduro's guidance, Honduras also negotiated and ratified the U.S.-Central America Free Trade Agreement (CAFTA), received debt relief, became the first Latin American country to sign a Millennium Challenge Account Compact with the U.S., and actively promoted greater Central American integration. While the Maduro administration implemented a number of successful economic and security policies, reliable polling data revealed widespread popular rejection of Honduran institutions, underscoring the lack of public faith in the political class, the media, and the business community.

Jose Manuel "Mel" Zelaya Rosales of the Liberal Party won the November 27, 2005, presidential elections with less than a 4% margin of victory, the smallest margin ever in Honduran electoral history. Zelaya's campaign theme was "citizen power," and he vowed to increase transparency and combat narcotrafficking, while maintaining macroeconomic stability. The Liberal Party won 62 of the 128 congressional seats, just short of an absolute majority. Zelaya's presidency was marked by a series of controversies as his policies and rhetoric moved closer in line with that of Venezuelan President Hugo Chavez.

Zelaya signed on to Chavez' Bolivarian Alternative for the Americas (ALBA) in August 2008, and the treaty was ratified by the National Congress in October 2008. In the final year of Zelaya's term, he began advocating that a referendum be added to the November 2009 elections regarding reform of the constitution. Zelaya proposed that an informal poll be held on June 28 to gauge public support for his proposal. However, Honduran courts ruled that Zelaya's plans were unconstitutional and directed that government agencies desist from providing support to carry out the poll. Zelaya ignored the rulings.

Coup d'Etat

Army soldiers entered Zelaya's residence in the early hours of June 28, 2009, the day of the poll, forcibly seized Zelaya and transported him to Costa Rica. The National Congress met in an emergency session that same day, declared Zelaya was no longer president, and swore in President of Congress Roberto Micheletti as the new President of the Republic. Micheletti replaced all the cabinet members who did not accept Zelaya's ouster. As reflected in resolutions by the Organization of American States (OAS) and the United Nations General Assembly, and later in the findings of the Truth and Reconciliation Commission, the events of June 28 constituted a coup d'etat against a democratically elected government.

Zelaya's forced removal was universally condemned by the international community, and the OAS issued an immediate and unanimous call for Zelaya's unconditional return to office. With support from the United States, the OAS designated Nobel Peace Prize laureate and then-Costa Rican President Oscar Arias as mediator to reach a peaceful, diplomatic resolution of the crisis.

Through the Arias-led negotiations, the San Jose Accord, a 12-point plan for restoration of constitutional order, was drafted. The plan called for restoration of Zelaya as president, but with a consensus-based "unity government;" establishment of a truth commission and a verification commission under the auspices of the OAS; amnesty for political crimes committed by all sides related to the coup; and early elections to establish a successor as rapidly as possible.

In early October 2009, negotiations were moved to Tegucigalpa and renamed the Guaymuras process. On October 30, 2009, President Zelaya and Roberto Micheletti signed the Tegucigalpa-San Jose Accord. However, President Zelaya broke off his participation in the process of implementing the Tegucigalpa-San Jose Accord after Micheletti announced on November 6, 2009, that he would form a new cabinet without Zelaya.

On November 29, 2009, Hondurans elected Porfirio "Pepe" Lobo as President in a previously scheduled free and fair election that attracted broad voter participation. Lobo received the largest number of votes for a presidential candidate in Honduran history. President Lobo was sworn in on January 27, 2010. After assuming office, Lobo formed a government of national unity and convened a truth commission, as set forth in the Tegucigalpa-San Jose Accord. Zelaya returned to Honduras on May 28, 2011, paving the way for the country's return to participation in the OAS on June 1, 2011. The Truth and Reconciliation Commission released its final report on July 7, 2011.

GOVERNMENT AND POLITICAL CONDITIONS

Honduras is a constitutional, multiparty republic. Following November 2009 elections, which the international community generally recognized as free and fair, Porfirio "Pepe" Lobo assumed the presidency in January 2010 and formed a government of national unity including all five registered political parties.

Recent Elections

In January 2010 Porfirio "Pepe" Lobo assumed office for a four-year presidential term following elections in November 2009 that international observers considered to be generally free and fair.

Participation of Women and Minorities: The law states that at least 30 percent of candidates from each party for national election should be women. Women held 25 of 128 seats in the National Congress, and 30 women were alternate members. Six women sat on the 15-member executive board of congress, and 12 presided over congressional committees. One of three presidential designates in the government with equivalent status to that of a vice president was a woman. There were three female cabinet members: the secretaries of state for justice and human rights, for tourism, and for social development.

The National Congress had one Misquito community member and one Afro-Honduran member. The cabinet-level minister of the Secretariat of State for Indigenous and Afro-Honduran Affairs was an Afro-Honduran.

Principal Government Officials

Last Updated: 1/31/2013

Pres.: **Porfirio LOBO Sosa**
Vice Pres.: **Maria Antonieta GUILLEN de Bogran**
Min. of Agriculture & Livestock: **Jacobo REGALADO**
Min. of Culture, Arts, & Sports: **Tulio Mariano GONZALES**
Min. of Defense: **Marlon PASCUA Cerrato**
Min. of Education: **Marlon ESCOTO**
Min. of Finance: **Wilfredo CERRATO**
Min. of Foreign Relations: **Arturo CORRALES Alvarez**
Min. of Govt. & Justice: **Africo MADRID**
Min. of Health: **Roxana ARAUJO**
Min. of Industry & Commerce: **Jose LAVAIRE**
Min. of Justice & Human Rights: **Ana PINEDA**
Min. of Labor & Social Security: **Felicito AVILA**
Min. of Natural Resources & Environment: **Rigoberto CUELLAR**
Min. of the Presidency: **Maria Antonieta Guillen de BOGRAN**
Min. of Public Works, Transportation, & Housing: **Miguel Angel GAMEZ**
Min. of Security: **Pompeyo BONILLA Reyes**
Min. of Tourism: **Nelly JEREZ**
Attorney Gen.: **Luis RUBI**
Pres., Central Bank: **Maria Elena MONDRAGON**
Ambassador to the US: **Jorge Ramon HERNANDEZ Alcerro**
Permanent Representative to the UN, New York: **Mary Elizabeth FLORES Flake**

ECONOMY

Honduras, the second poorest country in Central America, suffers from extraordinarily unequal distribution of income, as well as high underemployment. While historically dependent on the export of bananas and coffee, Honduras has diversified its export base to include apparel and automobile wire harnessing. Nearly half of Honduras's economic activity is directly tied to the US, with exports to the US accounting for 30% of GDP and remittances for another 20%.

The US-Central America Free Trade Agreement (CAFTA) came into force in 2006 and has helped foster foreign direct investment, but physical and political insecurity, as well as crime and perceptions of corruption, may deter potential investors; about 70% of FDI is from US firms. The economy registered sluggish economic growth in 2010, insufficient to improve living standards for the nearly 65% of the population in poverty. The Lobo administration inherited a difficult fiscal position with off-budget debts accrued in previous administrations and government salaries nearly equivalent to tax collections. His government has displayed a commitment to improving tax collection and cutting expenditures, and attracting foreign investment.

This enabled Tegucigalpa to secure an IMF Precautionary Stand-By agreement in October 2010. The IMF agreement has helped renew multilateral and bilateral donor confidence in Honduras following the Zelaya administration's economic mismanagement and the 2009 coup.

Labor Conditions

The law regulates child labor, sets the minimum age for employment at 14, and regulates the hours and type of work that can be performed by minors up to age 18.

Under the law all minors between the ages of 14 and 18 must be granted special permission from the STSS to work. The STSS is expected to perform a home study to ensure that there is an economic necessity for the child to work and that the child will not work outside the country or in hazardous conditions, including offshore fishing.

If permission is granted, children between the ages of 14 and 16 are not allowed to work more than four hours per day. Children between the ages of 16 and 18 are allowed to work no more than six hours per day. The law prohibits night work and overtime for minors under the age of 18. However, the STSS can grant special permission for minors between the ages of 16 and 18 to work in the evening if it does not affect their schooling. The labor code requires that employers with more than 20 school-age children working at their business facility provide a location for a school. The law provides for between three and five years in prison for persons violating child labor laws.

In practice the vast majority of children who worked did so without STSS permits, and the government failed to enforce child labor laws effectively. Children often harvested melons, coffee, and sugarcane; rummaged at garbage dumps; worked in the forestry, hunting, and fishing sectors; and worked as deckhands and divers in the lobster industry.

Children worked as domestic servants, peddled goods such as fruit, begged, washed cars, hauled loads, and labored in limestone and lime production. Most child labor occurred in rural areas. Children often worked alongside other family members in agriculture and other sectors, such as fishing, construction, transportation, and small business.

On April 11, the STSS announced the minimum wage for the year, which was retroactive to January 1 and based on the number of employees and size of the company. Wages ranged from a low of 3,280 lempiras ($175) per month to a high of 6,592 lempiras ($350). For instance, a company with one to 10 employees working in agriculture was required to pay at least 4,368 lempiras ($230) per month, while a company with more than 151 employees in the transportation industry was required to pay at least 6,533 lempiras ($345) per month.

The law applies equally to national and foreign workers and prescribes a maximum eight-hour shift per day, a 44-hour workweek, and at least one 24-hour rest period for every six days of work. It provides for paid national holidays and annual leave. The law requires overtime payment for hours in excess of the standard, and there are prohibitions on excessive compulsory overtime. Civil society groups and unions reported that employers frequently ignored these regulations, especially in the fast food industry, because the STSS failed to enforce these requirements effectively. Worker safety standards were enforced poorly, particularly in the construction, garment assembly, and agriculture sectors.

In practice the minimum wage was rarely paid in the agricultural sector and seldom paid elsewhere. The STSS estimated that 68 percent of employers did not comply with the federal minimum wage. The law prohibits the practice of requiring workers to complete quotas before being allowed to leave.

However, civil society groups reported the government did not effectively enforce the law. There were credible allegations of compulsory overtime at apparel assembly factories (particularly for women, who made up approximately 65 percent of that sector's workforce), in the private security sector, and among household workers.

Workers were frequently denied benefits, including vacation pay and 13th- and 14th- month bonuses, and there were reports that both public and private sector employers failed to pay into the social security institute funds. In addition, unions and civil society groups reported that some employers used contract employees to avoid paying benefits due to full- and part-time employees.

The law does not protect domestic workers effectively. Human rights organizations continued to report that, in the private security and household sectors, workers were typically obliged to work more than 60 hours a week but paid for only 44 hours. Civil society organizations also reported that workers in cleaning services and the fast food industry were often obliged to work shifts of 12 or more hours. These household workers often lacked contracts and were paid salaries below the minimum wage. Since many lived in on-site housing, their work hours often varied widely based on the will of individual employers. Private security guards also often worked for salaries below the minimum wage. Many guards worked every other day on 24-hour shifts, which violated labor law restrictions regarding maximum number of hours one may work.

U.S.-HONDURAN RELATIONS

Honduras has traditionally been an ally of the United States. Following Honduras' June 2009 coup and U.S. recognition of the November 2009 presidential election, U.S. policy has sought to consolidate democracy, protect human rights, and promote the rule of law. U.S. Government programs are aimed at promoting a healthy and more open economy capable of sustainable growth, improving the climate for business and investment and protecting U.S. citizen and corporate rights, and promoting the well-being of the Honduran people.

The United States also works with Honduras to meet transnational challenges—including the fight against terrorism, narcotics trafficking, money laundering, illegal migration, and trafficking in persons—and encourages and supports Honduran efforts to protect the environment. The goals of strengthening democracy and promoting viable economic growth are especially important given the geographical proximity of Honduras to the United States. An estimated 1 million Hondurans reside in the United States, 600,000 of whom are believed to be undocumented; consequently, immigration issues are an important item on the bilateral agenda. An average of 80,000 to 110,000 U.S. citizens visit Honduras annually, and about 15,000 Americans reside there.

U.S. Assistance to Honduras

Honduras, one of Latin America's poorest nations, strives to improve its economic and democratic development with U.S. assistance. The United States has historically been the largest bilateral donor to Honduras. U.S. Agency for International Development (USAID) programs include education, health, economic policy, microenterprise, environmental conservation, food security, municipal development, and justice sector reform.

The United States maintains a small presence at a Honduran military base. U.S. forces conduct and provide logistics support for a variety of bilateral and multilateral exercises—medical, engineering, peacekeeping, counternarcotics, and disaster relief—for the benefit of the Honduran people and their Central American neighbors. Through the Central America Regional Security Initiative, the United States supports the Government of Honduras by assisting law enforcement entities in disrupting criminal networks; building investigative, prosecutorial, and judicial capacity; and implementing violence prevention programs for vulnerable communities.

In June 2005, Honduras became the first country in the hemisphere to sign a Millennium Challenge Account (MCA) Compact with the U.S. Government. Under the Compact, the U.S. Millennium Challenge Corporation invested $205 million over 5 years to help Honduras improve its road infrastructure, diversify its agriculture, and transport its products to market.

Bilateral Economic Relations

The U.S. is the chief trading partner for Honduras, supplying 46.2 percent of Honduran imports and purchasing 33.4 percent of Honduran exports in 2011 (excluding maquila trade). Bilateral trade between the two nations totaled $10.6 billion in 2011. U.S. exports to Honduras continued to perform well in 2011 reaching $6.1 billion, an increase of 33 percent over 2010. The U.S.-Central America Free Trade Agreement (CAFTA-DR) entered into force in 2006. It eliminates most tariffs and other barriers for U.S. goods destined for the Central American market, provides protection for U.S. investments and intellectual property, and creates more transparent rules and procedures for conducting business. CAFTA also aims to eliminate intra-Central American tariffs and facilitate increased regional trade, benefiting U.S. companies manufacturing in Honduras. With CAFTA implemented, about 80% of U.S. goods now enter the region duty-free, with tariffs on the remaining 20% to be phased out by 2016.

Leading U.S. exports in 2011 included petroleum products, textile and fabrics, cotton yarn, electrical equipment, chemicals, manmade staple fibers, computer and electronic products, machinery, food products and cereals (corn, wheat, rice). Nearly all textile and apparel goods that meet CAFTA-DR's rules of origin became duty-free and quota-free immediately, thus promoting new opportunities for U.S. fiber, yarn, fabric, and apparel manufacturers. Honduras is the seventh largest exporter of apparel and textile products by volume to the U.S. market behind countries such as Mexico and China, and first among Central American and Caribbean countries.

According to the U.S. Department of Commerce/Bureau of Economic Analysis, the stock of U.S. investment in Honduras was $930 million in 2011, compared to $999 million in 2010. This was concentrated largely in the transport, warehousing and communication sector; followed by the manufacturing and maquila sectors.

Honduras' Membership in International Organizations

Honduras generally supports U.S. initiatives in international fora. Honduras and the United States belong to a number of the same international organizations, including the United Nations, Organization of American States, World Trade Organization, and International Monetary Fund.

Bilateral Representation

Honduras maintains an embassy in the United States at 3007 Tilden Street NW, Washington, DC 20008 (tel. 202-966-7702).

Principal U.S. Embassy Officials

Last Updated: 1/14/2013

TEGUCIGALPA (E) Avenida La Paz, Tegucigalpa, Honduras, [504] 2236-9320 or [504] 2238-5114, Fax [504] 2236-9037, INMARSAT Tel Iridium: 8816 414-55644 or 8816-414-55648, Workweek: M-Th, 8–5:30; F 8–3 local time, http://honduras.usembassy.gov/english/index_e1.htm.

DCM OMS:	Vacant
AMB OMS:	Claudia Shaw
Co-CLO:	Chanda Zirkelbach
DHS/CIS:	Catherine Ventura
DHS/ICE:	Richard Rodriguez
FM:	Luther Sargent
HRO:	Christine Stockman (Resident Florida Regional Center)
MGT:	Mona A Kuntz
MLO/ODC:	LTC Lawrence Ott (Acting)
NAS/INL:	Andrea Lewis
POSHO:	Luther Sargent
SDO/DATT:	COL Robert W. Swisher, Usaf
AMB:	Lisa Kubiske
DCM:	Matthias Mitman
PAO:	Stephen Posivak
COM:	Ireas Cook
GSO:	Geraldine Gray Thibodeau
RSO:	Vacant
AFSA:	Kevin M. Byron
AID:	William R. Brands
CLO:	Amy Anderson
DEA:	Vacant
ECON:	Mary Grace McGeehan
FMO:	Wagih Ibrahim
ICASS Chair:	William Douglass
IMO:	Kevin M. Byron
IPO:	Kevin J. Inglis
ISO:	A Bryan Thibodeau
ISSO:	Vacant
LEGATT:	Joseph Deters
POL:	Silvia Eiriz
State ICASS:	William Douglass

Additional Contact Information

American Chamber of Commerce (AMCHAM)
Hotel Honduras Maya
Apartado Postal 1838
Tegucigalpa, Honduras
Tel: +504 2231–1379/2232–6035
Fax: +504 232-2031
Branch office in San Pedro Sula
Tel: +504 2557–6412/2557–7634
Fax: +504 2557–6402

U.S. Department of Commerce International Trade Administration
Office of Latin America and the Caribbean
14th and Constitution Avenue, NW
Washington, DC 20230

Tel: 202-482-0057
800-USA-TRADE
Fax: 202-482-0464
Internet: http://www.export.gov

U.S. Agency for International Development
1300 Pennsylvania Avenue, NW
Washington, DC 20523–0001
Tel: 202-712-4810
Fax: 202-216-3524
Internet: http://www.usaid.gov

TRAVEL

Consular Information Sheet

July 10, 2012

Country Description: Honduras has a developing economy. The national language is Spanish, although English is often spoken in the Bay Islands. The climate is generally pleasant and temperate, with dry and wet seasons. During the dry season from February into May, widespread forest fires and agricultural burning can severely degrade air quality throughout the country, possibly causing respiratory problems and airport closures. The terrain includes mountainous areas, coastal beaches, and jungle lowlands. Facilities that would normally be used by tourists, including hotels and restaurants, are generally adequate in the capital city of Tegucigalpa, in San Pedro Sula, Tela, La Ceiba, the Bay Islands, and near the Copan ruins. Large sections of the country, however, lack basic public services or even a governmental presence. Currency exchange is readily available at banks and hotels in the major cities.

Smart Traveler Enrollment Program (STEP)/Embassy Locations: If you are going to move to or visit Honduras, please take the time to tell our Embassy about your trip. If you enroll in the Smart Traveler Enrollment Program (STEP), we can keep you up to date with important safety and security announcements. It will also help your friends and family get in touch with you in an emergency.

U.S. Embassy Tegucigalpa
Avenida La Paz in Tegucigalpa, Honduras
Telephone: 011-504-2236–9320 or 011-504-2238–5114
Emergency after-hours telephone: 011-504-2236–8497
American Citizens Services Unit Fax: 011-504-2238–4357
American Citizens Services Unit Office hours: Monday through Friday from 8:00 a.m. to 11:30 a.m.

The Consulate is closed the first Tuesday of every month.

To provide better customer service and reduce waiting times, the Consular Section in Tegucigalpa uses an online appointment system for passport renewals, first-time passports and additional passport pages, reports of birth abroad, notaries, and immigrant visas. Appointments are required to submit your application for these services.

You can find more information, including how to schedule an appointment, at the U.S. Embassy's American Citizen Services website. We accept walk-ins Monday through Friday between 8:00 a.m. and 11:30 a.m. only for emergencies, reports of death, reports of birth abroad, or to pick up passports. All other services require an appointment.

Consular Agency in San Pedro Sula
Banco Atlantida Building (across from Central Park)—11th Floor
San Pedro Sula, Honduras
Telephone: 011-504-2558–1580

Office hours: Mondays, Wednesdays, and Fridays from 12:00 p.m. to 4:00 p.m.

The Consular Agent in San Pedro Sula assists the Embassy in protecting the interests of U.S. citizens in Honduras. The Agent may execute notarials, Reports of Birth Abroad, and U.S. passport applications. The Agent may also assist U.S. citizens with emergency situations such as arrests and deaths of U.S. citizens in Honduras. The Consular Agent does not provide visa information or services. For additional details about all U.S. Embassy and consular services in Honduras, please see the Embassy website or visit the Bureau of Consular Affairs website.

Entry/Exit Requirements for U.S. Citizens: If you are a U.S. traveler wishing to enter Honduras, you must present a U.S. passport with at least six months remaining validity. A visa is not required for American citizens, but tourists must provide evidence of return or onward travel. U.S. citizens are encouraged to carry a photocopy of their U.S. passports with them at all times so that if questioned by local officials proof of identity and U.S. citizenship are readily available. In June 2006, Honduras entered a "Central America-4 (CA-4) Border Control Agreement" with Guatemala, El Salvador, and Nicaragua. Under the terms of the agreement, citizens of the four countries may travel freely across land borders from one of the countries to any of the others without completing entry and exit formalities at immigration checkpoints. U.S. citizens and other eligible foreign nationals who legally enter any of the four countries may similarly travel among "CA-4" countries without obtaining additional visas or tourist entry permits for the other three countries.

Immigration officials at the first port of entry determine the length of stay, up to a maximum period of 90 days. Foreign tourists who wish to remain in the "CA-4" country region beyond the period initially granted for their visit are required to request a one-time extension of stay from local immigration authorities in the country where the traveler is physically present. Alternatively, as of December 1, 2010, travelers are allowed to leave Honduras after their initial 90 day permit has expired, enter one of the neighboring countries of the CA-4 region, and then return to Honduras, at which time a new 90 day permit will be provided.

Foreigners "expelled" from any of the four countries are excluded from the entire "CA-4" region. In isolated cases, the lack of clarity in the implementing details of the CA-4 Border Control Agreement has caused temporary inconvenience to some travelers and has resulted in others being fined more than $100 or detained for 72 hours or longer.

The Honduran immigration office nearest to the U.S. Embassy in Tegucigalpa has the following location:

Dirección General de Migración y Extranjería
Colonia Las Torres
Calle Principal
Edificio #1404
Comayagüela, DC
Tel.: (504) 2234–1996/1998

To depart Honduras, travelers must clear Honduran Immigration. Travelers by air must return the copy of their immigration document received at entry. Travelers by land or sea must also return the entrance permit they received when entering Honduras. If you are departing via air, you will be charged an airport tax of $38. The airport tax must be paid at the airport in cash in either U.S. dollars or lempiras. Checks and credit cards are not accepted. If you stay in Honduras beyond 90 days, a fine may be imposed by Honduran Immigration prior to your departure.

Special Requirements for Minors: Parents should obtain U.S. passports for infants and minors born in the United States and not rely on birth certificates for their child's travel. Honduran entry and exit control laws require that a child under age 21, traveling either unaccompanied or with one parent only, must have written and notarized permission to travel from the non-traveling parent/s (or legal guardian/s). If the non-traveling parent is the father, he must authorize travel; the law does not delegate this authority to any other male member of the family in his absence. For more information concerning entry and exit requirements, travelers may contact the Honduran consulate at 1014 M Street NW, Washington, DC 20001, telephone (202) 682-5948, or a Honduran consulate in Atlanta, Chicago, Houston, Miami, Los Angeles, New Orleans, New York, Phoenix, or San Francisco. The Honduran government also retains an Honorary Consul in San Juan, Puerto Rico.

The Honduran Embassy is located at 3007 Tilden Street NW, Washington, DC 20008. The Embassy can be contacted by phone at (202) 966-7702. Visit the Embassy of Honduras' website for the most current visa information. For tourist information or suggestions, please contact the Honduras Institute of Tourism at (800) 410-9608 (in the United States) or (800) 222-TOUR (8687) (within Honduras only), or visit the Honduras Institute of Tourism website.

HIV/AIDS Restrictions: There are no entry restrictions or requirements for persons with HIV/AIDS entering Honduras. The 2010 Report on the Global AIDS Epidemic by the UNAIDS/WHO Working Group estimates approximately 39,000 children and adults living with HIV/AIDS in Honduras. The estimated prevalence is 0.5 percent, equal to the average prevalence rate in Central and South America. There are limited health resources in Honduras, including for treatment of persons with HIV/AIDS.

For more information concerning entry and exit requirements, travelers may contact the Honduran consulate at 1014 M Street NW, Washington, DC 20001, telephone (202) 682-5948, or a Honduran consulate in Atlanta, Chicago, Houston, Miami, Los Angeles, New Orleans, New York, Phoenix, or San Francisco. The Honduran government also retains an Honorary Consul in San Juan, Puerto Rico.

Threats to Safety and Security: Political demonstrations occur frequently in the major cities of Honduras. During demonstrations, protestors frequently block public roads to press their political views or to seek concessions from the Honduran government. Police may use tear gas, water cannons, or rubber bullets to disperse demonstrators. Travelers should avoid areas where demonstrations are taking place and never try to pass roadblocks. U.S. citizens may stay informed by visiting the U.S. Embassy website, following the local news, and consulting hotel personnel and tour guides.

While the Honduran side of the Honduras-Nicaragua border has been largely cleared of land mines, travelers should exercise caution there.

Honduras is vulnerable to hurricanes, heavy rains, and flooding. The rainy season extends between June and November. Honduras' National Emergency Management Commission (COPECO)issues national alerts. COPECO announced on May 11, 2011, that meteorologists predict the possible formation of sixteen tropical storms and fourteen hurricanes in 2011.

For up-to-date information on storms, U.S. visitors are encouraged to visit the National Hurricane Center's website and read about hurricane preparedness on the State Department travel website. Stay up to date by bookmarking our Bureau of Consular Affairs website, which contains the current Travel Warnings and Travel Alerts as well as the Worldwide Caution.

Follow us on Twitter and the Bureau of Consular Affairs page on Facebook as well. You can also call (888) 407-4747 toll-free within the United States and Canada, or by calling a regular toll line, (202) 501-4444, from other countries. These numbers are available from 8:00 a.m. to 8:00 p.m. Eastern Standard Time, Monday through Friday (except U.S. federal holidays). Take some time before travel to improve your personal security.

Crime: Crime is widespread in Honduras and requires a high degree of caution by U.S. visitors and residents alike. U.S. citizens have been the victims of a wide range of crimes, including murder, kidnapping, rape, assault, and property crimes. Widespread poverty and unemployment, along with significant street gang and drug trafficking activity, have contributed to the extremely high crime rate. In January 2012, the Peace Corps suspended its program in order to review the safety and security of its volunteers.

According to the United Nations, Honduras has the highest per capita homicide rate in the world, with 86 homicides for every 100,000 inhabitants. Although crime and violent crime occurs in all parts of Honduras, the north coast and central portions of the country have historically had the country's highest crime rates. Copan, Roatan/Bay Islands, and other tourist destinations have a lower crime rate than other parts of the country.

Since 1995, 108 U.S. citizens have been reported murdered in Honduras; of these, just 29 cases have been resolved. Six U.S. citizens were reported murdered in Honduras in the first six months of 2012

Since 2010, seven U.S. citizens have been reported as victims of rape or sexual assault in Honduras, signaling an increasing trend in these types of crimes. Two U.S. citizens reported incidents of rape or sexual assault in the first six months of 2012. Perpetrators of sexual assaults are often armed, and gang rape or rapes with multiple perpetrators are not unknown.

Kidnappings have occurred in recent years, with large ransoms paid and infrequent capture of the kidnappers. Two U.S. citizens were reported kidnapped in the first six months of 2012.

U.S. citizens are primarily the victims of opportunistic crime. There is no evidence suggesting criminals specifically target U.S. citizens, but foreigners have been targeted for crime due to their perceived wealth. Weapons abound in Honduras, and armed street robberies are especially common, with criminals taking advantage of relatively isolated victims to steal their valuables. Young males working in pairs, often riding motorcycles, are perpetrating many of the armed robberies in Honduras' urban areas. Criminals and pickpockets target visitors as they enter and depart airports and hotels, so visitors should consider carrying their passports and valuables in a concealed pouch. There have also been reports of armed robbers traveling in private cars targeting pedestrians on isolated streets.

Incidents of crime along roads, including carjacking and kidnapping, are common in Honduras. There have been frequent incidents of carjacking and highway robbery on a number of roads including the main highway (CA-5) between San Pedro Sula and Siguatepeque, with the greatest risk between Potrerillos and Pito Solo in the lake area. For more information, please see the section below on Traffic Safety and Road Conditions.

Travelers should always drive with their doors locked and windows rolled up to avoid potential robberies at traffic lights and other places, such as congested downtown streets. Avoid driving at night. All bus travel should be during daylight hours and on first-class conveyances, not on economy buses. Choose taxis carefully, and note the driver's name and license number. Instruct the driver not to pick up other passengers, agree on the fare before you depart, and have small bills available for payment, as taxi drivers often do not make change. Where possible, travel in groups.

Incidents of piracy off the coast of Honduras can occur. In 2012, a U.S. citizen reported that his boat was boarded and his passengers were the victims of an armed robbery while sailing in Honduran waters near Puerto Cortez, three miles north of Punta Sal. In 2011, a Canadian citizen was killed in a similar incident. U.S. citizens should exercise caution while sailing or mooring in Honduran waters.

Travelers are encouraged to be vigilant of their surroundings at all times, especially when entering or exiting their homes, cars, garages, schools, and workplaces. It is also recommended that drivers vary their routes and schedules so as to not create a predictable routine. Individuals should also limit the sharing of personal information and closely screen personal employees. Should a U.S. citizen be kidnapped, local authorities and the Embassy should be contacted immediately.

Do not resist a robbery attempt. Most criminals have weapons, and most injuries and deaths during robberies resulted when victims resisted. Several U.S. citizens have been injured or killed while resisting armed robberies. Do not hitchhike or go home with strangers, particularly from nightspots. Whenever possible, travel in groups of two or more persons. Use the same common sense while traveling in Honduras that you would in any high crime area in the United States: do not wear excessive jewelry; do not carry large sums of money, or display cash, ATM/credit cards, or other valuables. Avoid walking at night in most areas of Honduras and exercise strong caution during the day. Do not hike alone in backcountry areas, or walk alone on beaches, historic ruins, or trails.

The Honduran government conducts occasional joint police/military patrols in major cities in an effort to reduce crime. However, the Honduran law enforcement authorities' ability to prevent, respond to, and investigate criminal incidents and prosecute criminals is limited. Honduran police generally do not speak English. The government has established a special tourist police in the resort town of Tela and other tourist destinations including Tegucigalpa, San Pedro Sula, La Ceiba, and Roatan, but the number deployed is small and coverage is limited.

The Basilica of Suyapa in Tegucigalpa, also known as Suyapa Church or Cathedral, is an important religious site and popular tourist destination. However, it is situated in a high crime area and has been the site of numerous armed robberies and thefts. Americans in Honduras on U.S. government orders are only allowed to visit the Basilica of Suyapa with an organized tour group that provides armed security for the group.

The San Pedro Sula area has seen armed robberies against tourist vans, minibuses, and cars traveling from the airport to area hotels, and there have also been armed robberies along the road to Copan. Armed men have forced vehicles transporting tourists off the road and robbed the victims, occasionally assaulting the driver or passengers. In past years, several U.S. citizens have been murdered in San Pedro Sula and La Ceiba shortly after arriving in the country. Assaults in these areas may be based on tips from sources at airport arrival areas, so visitors are strongly urged to exercise caution in discussing travel plans in public.

Although Copan, Roatan/Bay Islands, and other tourist destinations have a lower crime rate than other parts of the country, thefts, break-ins, assaults, and murders do occur. Exercise particular caution walking on isolated beaches, especially at night. Coxen Hole on the island of Roatan should be avoided after dark.

The Government of Honduras has a very limited law enforcement presence in some northern coastal areas, including parts of the departments of Olancho, Colon, and Gracias a Dios. These areas are well known for narcotics smuggling and violence. Travelers in those areas should use extra caution. See the description of highways/areas to be avoided in the Traffic Safety and Road Conditions section below for details. Do not buy counterfeit and pirated goods, even if they are widely available. Not only are the bootlegs illegal in the United States, if you purchase them you may also be breaking local law and will be subject to local penalties.

Stay up to date by:

- Bookmarking our Bureau of Consular Affairs website, which contains the currentTravel Warnings and Travel Alerts as well as the Worldwide Caution.
- Follow us on Twitter and the Bureau of Consular Affairs page on Facebook as well.
- Download our free Smart Traveler iPhone App to have travel information at your fingertips.
- Calling 1-888-407-4747 toll-free within the U.S. and Canada, or a regular toll line, 1-202-501-4444, from other countries.
- Taking some time before travel to consider your personal security.

Victims of Crime: If you or someone you know becomes the victim of a crime abroad you should contact the local police and the nearest U.S. embassy or consulate (see the Department of State's list of embassies and consulates). If your passport is stolen, we can help you replace it. For violent crimes such as assault and rape, we can help you find appropriate medical care, contact family members or friends, and help them send you money if you need it. Although the investigation and prosecution of the crime are solely the responsibility of local authorities, consular officers can help you understand the local criminal justice process and find an attorney if you need one.

The local equivalents of the "911" emergency line in Honduras is 199 for National Police; 198 for fire fighters; and 195 for the local Red Cross. The operators typically speak Spanish only.

Criminal Penalties: While you are traveling in another country, you are subject to its laws even if you are a U.S. citizen. Foreign laws and legal systems can be vastly different from our own. In some places, you may be taken in for questioning if you do not have your passport with you. Penalties for possession, use, or trafficking in illegal drugs in Honduras are severe, and convicted offenders can expect long jail sentences and heavy fines. There are also some activities that might be legal in the country you visit but illegal in the United States; for example, you can be prosecuted under U.S. law if you buy pirated goods. Engaging in sexual conduct with children or using or disseminating child pornography in a foreign country is a crime prosecutable in the United States. If you break local laws in Honduras, your U.S. passport will not help you avoid arrest or prosecution. It is very important to know what is legal and what is not where you are going.

If you are arrested in Honduras, you have the right to request the authorities to alert the U.S. Embassy.

Special Circumstances: Marine Safety and Oversight: The areas off both coasts of Honduras are the subject of maritime border disputes between Honduras and its neighbors. The Honduran Navy patrols these areas and all private vessels transiting Honduran territorial waters should be prepared to be hailed and possibly boarded by Honduran military personnel to verify documentation. While the Honduran Navy previously used private vessels as patrol vessels, this is no longer the case. In the event that any vessel is hailed in Honduran waters in the Caribbean by a non-military vessel or any suspicious vessel and directed to prepare for boarding, the vessel should immediately contact the U.S. Coast Guard Operations Center by radio or INMARSAT at (305) 415-6800. Anyone needing more information can also contact the U.S. Embassy during working hours and request to speak with the U.S. Military Group (USMILGP) office. There have been incidents of armed assaults against private sailing vessels by criminals posing as fishermen off the northeast coast of Honduras, particularly in the numerous small islands northeast of the Department of Gracias a Dios. Sailors should contact the Coast Guard and yacht facility managers in their areas of travel for current information.

Real Estate Investment: U.S. citizens should exercise extreme caution before entering into any form of commitment to invest in real estate, particularly in coastal areas and the Bay Islands. Honduran laws and practices regarding real estate differ substantially from those in the United States, and fraudulent deeds and titles are common; U.S. citizens considering investing or buying real estate in Honduras should be aware that rights to such property do not enjoy the same level of protection as in the United States. Approximately 80 percent of privately held land is either untitled or improperly titled. Inadequate land title procedures have led to numerous investment disputes involving U.S. nationals who are landowners. Historically, title insurance has not been available in Honduras. Recently, some American insurance companies have begun offering title insurance in cooperation with Honduran attorneys. In addition, there are complaints that the Honduran judicial system often prolongs disputed cases for many years before resolution. American citizens have spent thousands of dollars in legal fees and experienced years of frustration trying to resolve property disputes, even in cases where local attorneys and Honduran and U.S. real estate agents had given assurances to the investor. Violence has been used against American citizens involved in disputed property cases. Potential investors should engage competent local legal representation before making any commitments. Investors should also thoroughly check the references of attorneys and real estate agents.

Honduran law places certain restrictions on land ownership by foreigners in coastal and border areas. Squatters have claimed a number of properties owned by U.S. citizens. U.S. government officials may not act as agents, attorneys, or in a fiduciary capacity. U.S. citizens who own property abroad and who have assumed responsibilities concurrent with ownership of property in a foreign country should take steps on their own initiative to safeguard their interests and to employ private legal counsel when the need arises. For further information on investing in property in Honduras, please review the State Department's Investment Climate Statement, part of the Country Commercial Guide. For information on contracting Honduran legal representation, please check with other investors. You may also refer to the list of attorneys available on the Embassy's home page.

Financial Market Investment: Due to poor regulation and lack of guarantees, investment in the Honduran "Bolsa de Valores," or securities market, as well as banking institution bonds, "fideicomisos" (trusts), and certificates of deposit from uninsured financial institutions pose high risks to investors. Extreme caution should be exercised before and while undertaking such activities, as American citizens have lost large sums of money through investments in such markets. For further information on investing in Honduras, please review the State Department's Investment Climate Statement, part of the Country Commercial Guide.

Corruption: Many U.S. firms and citizens operating in Honduras have found corruption to be a serious problem and a constraint to successful investment. While some U.S. firms have satisfactorily resolved cases through the courts, many have difficulty navigating the legal system. There are complaints that the Honduran judicial system exhibits favoritism and vulnerability to external pressure and bribes. Corruption appears to be most pervasive in government procurement, government permits, and in the buying and selling of real estate (land titling).

Customs Regulations: U.S. citizens who intend to stay in Honduras for an extended period of time and who bring vehicles or household goods into the country should consult Honduran customs officials prior to shipment. With the exception of "antique" cars, all cars imported into Honduras by foreigners must be less than ten (10) years old. Buses, pickup trucks, and dump trucks must be less than 13 years old. For specific information regarding customs requirements, please contact the Embassy of Honduras in Washington, DC. Honduran customs authorities may enforce strict regulations concerning temporary import and export of items such as antiquities, medications, and business equipment. For example, Honduran law prohibits the export of antiques and artifacts from pre-colonial civilizations. To protect the country's biodiversity, it is illegal to export certain birds, feathers, and other flora and fauna.

Firearms: No one may bring firearms into Honduras, except for Diplomats or individuals participating in shooting or hunting sport events who have obtained a temporary firearm importation permit from the Honduran Ministry of Security prior to their travel to Honduras.

Firearms for personal safety or for purposes other than those mentioned above must be purchased locally through a store named "La Armería." These stores are regulated by the Honduran Armed Forces and are located throughout Honduras.

Diplomats or individuals participating in shooting or hunting sport events seeking a permit for the importation of firearms can contact the Ministry of Security at the following address:

Secretario de Estado en el Despacho de Seguridad Pública
Secretaría General
Cuartel General de Casamata
Tegucigalpa, M.D.C., Honduras, C.A.
Fax: (504) 2220–4352

Firearms that arrive without the requisite Honduran permit will be confiscated and the bearer will be prosecuted to the full extent of Honduran law.

Adventure Sports: Honduras' growing tourism industry attracts a number of people interested in adventure sports such as whitewater kayaking and rafting, scuba diving, and canopy tours. Travelers should be warned that in addition to the inherent risk of injury and death in these activities, there is little or no oversight of safety standards for adventure sports operators in Honduras. Five American citizens died in these sports in Honduras during the past three years. While many operators use good practices and attempt to meet internationally accepted safety standards, travelers should be diligent in researching potential adventure sports providers to make sure they are using internationally-acceptable or certified equipment, guides, safety measures, and instruction.

Medical Facilities and Health Information: Medical care in Honduras varies greatly in quality and availability. Outside of Tegucigalpa and San Pedro Sula, medical care is inadequate to address complex situations. Support staff facilities and necessary equipment and supplies are not up to U.S. standards anywhere in Honduras. Facilities for advanced surgical procedures are not available. Wide areas of the country, including the popular tourist areas of the Bay Islands, do not have a general surgery hospital. Ambulance services are limited in major cities and almost non-existent elsewhere. Emergency services may be contacted directly through their local numbers, including 199 for the national emergency line and 195 for the local Red Cross.

The U.S. Embassy encourages visitors who are considering medical care in Honduras to obtain as much information about the facility and the medical personnel as possible. Medical tourists should confirm that the facilities they are considering are accredited, purchase medical evacuation insurance before travelling, and confirm that the cost and payment for their treatment is clearly understood by both parties. In addition to other publicly available information, U.S. citizens may consult the U.S. Embassy's website for a list of hospitals and air ambulance services, or contact the U.S. Embassy prior to seeking non-emergency medical attention.

Scuba diving is popular in the Bay Islands, but the limited medical facilities there pose a special risk in the event of an emergency. There is a decompression chamber on Roatan and Utila for divers, but no advanced medical care on either island for diving related accidents.

Mosquito-borne illnesses are an ongoing problem in Honduras. All persons traveling in the northern areas of Honduras, even for a brief visit, are at risk of contracting malaria. Take a prophylactic regimen best suited to your health profile. The country regularly suffers from outbreaks of dengue fever. Unlike traditional mosquito-borne illnesses, there is no medicinal prophylactic or curative regimen for dengue fever. Travelers should take precautions against being bitten by mosquitoes to reduce the chance of contracting such illnesses, such as avoiding standing water even in the home, wearing long sleeves and pants in both day and night, and applying insect repellent regularly.

Severe air pollution, which can aggravate or lead to respiratory problems, is common throughout the country during the dry season due in large part to widespread forest fires and agricultural burning. Travelers with respiratory or cardiac conditions and those who are elderly or extremely young are at greatest risk for complications from air pollution, including coughing, difficulty breathing, wheezing, or chest pain. Acute respiratory infections are also widespread; more than 100,000 cases are reported annually.

Honduras lacks a substantial infrastructure for maintaining water purity. Travelers are strongly encouraged to avoid drinking tap water or a beverage that contains ice from an unknown source (even alcoholic drinks). Bottles and bags of purified water are widely available. It is also recommended that individuals traveling to Honduras avoid eating untreated raw vegetables, fruits that cannot be peeled on the spot, raw fish like ceviche and undercooked shellfish, and products containing mayonnaise, pastry icing, and unpasteurized dairy products. Hot cooked food, fresh bread, dry foods such as crackers, bottled carbonated beverages, coffee, tea, and beer are usually safe, provided such food items are not purchased from street vendors. All fruits and vegetables should be washed thoroughly with detergent and running water. Those that will be cooked or peeled can then be stored in a sealed container until used. Those that will be eaten raw and will not be peeled should be soaked for 15 minutes in a solution of chlorine bleach (or 5 percent household bleach) and water (one tablespoon of bleach per gallon of water), rinsed with potable water, and allowed to air dry.

Individuals traveling to Honduras should ensure that all their routine vaccinations are up to date, particularly measles and rubella vaccination. The Honduran government issued a declaration in May 2011 requiring proof of measles and rubella vaccination for all foreign travelers from North America, Europe, Africa, Argentina, Chile, and Brazil. Vaccination against Hepatitis A, Hepatitis B, and Typhoid is strongly recommended for those traveling to Honduras from the United States. Pre-exposure rabies vaccination should also be considered for travelers who may be exposed to stray animals on city streets or in rural areas. Honduras requires vaccination against yellow fever for those traveling to Honduras from countries where there is the risk of transmission. Travelers taking prescription medications should bring an adequate supply with them when coming to Honduras and ensure that their prescriptions are properly labeled.

You can find good information on vaccinations and other health precautions on the CDC website. For information about outbreaks of infectious diseases abroad, consult the World Health Organization (WHO) website. The WHO website also contains additional health information for travelers, including detailed country-specific health information.

Medical Insurance: You cannot assume your insurance will go with you when you travel. It is very important to find out BEFORE you leave whether or not your medical insurance will cover you overseas. You need to ask your insurance company two questions:

- Does my policy apply when I am out of the United States?
- Will it cover emergencies like a trip to a foreign hospital or a medical evacuation?

In many places, doctors and hospitals still expect payment in cash at the time of service. Your regular U.S. health insurance may not cover doctors' and hospital visits in other countries. If your policy does not go with you when you travel, it is a good idea to take out another one for your trip.

Traffic Safety and Road Conditions: While in a foreign country, you may encounter road conditions that differ significantly from those in the United States. The information below concerning Honduras is provided for general reference only, and may not be totally accurate in a particular location or circumstance.

Because of crime, poor road conditions, and heavy commercial truck traffic, driving can be very dangerous, and travelers should carry a cellular phone in case of an emergency. Travelers should exercise extreme caution while driving on isolated stretches of road and passing on mountainous curves. Rockslides are common, especially in the rainy season (May through December). Traffic signs, even on major highways, are often inadequate, and streets in the major cities are often unmarked. Travelers should always drive with their doors locked and windows rolled up to avoid potential robberies at traffic lights and other places such as congested downtown streets. Honduran roads are poorly lit and poorly marked. Vehicles are often driven at night without adequate illumination, and animals and people wander onto the roads at all hours. For these reasons, and because of the high incidence of crime, the U.S. Embassy discourages car and bus travel after dark.

Major cities are connected by an inconsistently maintained system of paved roads. While the main road network is being upgraded and widened in key positions, most of it consists of only two lanes.

Significant construction on the highway between Tegucigalpa and San Pedro Sula is scheduled through 2012 so drivers can expect delays. Many secondary roads in Honduras are unpaved. During the rainy season, even major highways are often closed due to rockslides and flooding from heavy rains.

In the event of an accident, contact the Honduran Transit Authority ("Transito") immediately. They may be contacted either directly through their local numbers, or through their national emergency number, 199. Honduran law requires that no vehicles involved in an accident be moved until Transit agents arrive, not even to clear a traffic obstruction, unless you are in serious physical danger. Besides informing the Transit Authority, the car insurance companies should be notified immediately or as soon as possible. Personal identification documents, including driver's licenses, copies of passports, and the vehicle registration cards should be carried while driving.

Besides the incidents of carjacking and highway robbery on the main highway, CA-5, between San Pedro Sula and Siguatepeque in the lake area, similar incidents have occurred on the highway between San Pedro Sula and Tela with the greatest risk near the palm tree plantations near El Progreso. These carjackings and robberies have targeted SUV's and usually occur at night; therefore, driving at night is highly discouraged. In Olancho, on the road from Juticalpa to Telica, and from the turn off to Gualaco on Route 39 to San Esteban and Bonito Oriental, rival criminal elements have engaged in violent acts against one another. Travelers should avoid this road. In addition, delivery trucks throughout Honduras are common targets of highway robberies.

Some of the most dangerous stretches for road travel include: Tegucigalpa to Choluteca, because of dangerous mountain curves; El Progreso to La Ceiba, because of animal crossings and the poor condition of bridges from flooding. On July 11, 2011, a bus overturned nine miles after Santa Rosa de Copan en route to San Pedro Sula killing ten people and injuring 20.

The only recommended route to the north coast from the south is CA-5 to route 21 to CA-13 via Tela to La Ceiba and Trujillo. Hijackings of private and commercial vehicles from the United States to Honduras have occurred. While Honduras and the United States have signed and ratified a Stolen Vehicle Treaty, existing Honduran laws protect good faith buyers (even of stolen vehicles), so the recovery and return of these vehicles to their original owners is not guaranteed. Vehicle insurance may mitigate loss; please check with the National Insurance Crime Bureau or with private insurance carriers about coverage details.

Aviation Safety Oversight: The U.S. Federal Aviation Administration (FAA) has assessed the Government of Honduras' Civil Aviation Authority as not being in compliance with International Civil Aviation Organization (ICAO) aviation safety standards for the oversight of Honduras' air carrier operations. Further information may be found on the FAA's safety assessment page.

Children's Issues: Please see the U.S. Dept. of State Office of Children's Issues web pages on intercountry adoption and international parental child abduction.

Travel Warning

November 21, 2012

The Department of State has issued this Travel Warning to inform U.S. citizens about the security situation in Honduras.

Tens of thousands of U.S. citizens safely visit Honduras each year for study, tourism, business, and volunteer work. However, crime and violence are serious problems throughout the country. Honduras has the highest murder rate in the world. San Pedro Sula is considered to be the world's most violent city, with 159 murders for every 100,000 residents in 2011. These threats have increased substantially over the past several years, and incidents can occur anywhere. In January 2012, the Peace Corps withdrew its volunteers from the country to conduct an administrative review of the security situation.

U.S. citizens do not appear to be targeted based on their nationality. Resort areas and tourist destinations generally have lower levels of crime and violence than other areas of the country. Moreover, tourists traveling with group tours only rarely report criminal incidents. In June 2012, the government agreed to increase police presence in areas frequented by tourists, such as the Copan Mayan ruins and Roatan. The government also established special tourist police forces in Copan and Roatan and is evaluating this option in other locations. Additionally, major hotels and other tourist installations have increased security, including with the help of police, in response to the crime epidemic.

A majority of serious crimes are never solved; of the 24 murders committed against U.S. citizens since January 2010, police have closed none. Members of the Honduran National Police have been known to engage in criminal activity, such as murder and car theft. The Government of Honduras lacks sufficient resources to properly investigate and prosecute cases, and to deter violent crime. The Honduran government is in the early stages of substantial reforms to its criminal justice institutions.

Transnational criminal organizations conduct narcotics trafficking and other unlawful activities throughout the country and use violence to control drug trafficking routes and carry out other criminal activity. Other criminals, acting both individually and in gangs in Tegucigalpa and San Pedro Sula, commit crimes such as murder, kidnapping, carjacking, armed robbery, rapes, and other aggravated assaults.

Kidnappings and disappearances are a concern throughout the country. Kidnapping affects both the local and expatriate communities, with victims sometimes paying large ransoms for the prospect of release. Kidnapping is believed to be underreported.

U.S. citizens should be vigilant of their surroundings at all times, especially when entering or exiting their homes or hotels, cars, garages, schools, and workplaces. Whenever possible, travel in groups of two or more persons. Avoid wearing jewelry and do not carry large sums of money or display cash, ATM/credit cards, or other valuables. Avoid walking at night in most areas of Honduras, and do not walk alone on beaches, historic ruins, or trails. Incidents of crime along roads, including carjacking and kidnapping, are common in Honduras. Motorists should avoid traveling at night and always drive with their doors locked to deter potential robberies at traffic lights and on congested downtown streets.

The location and timing of criminal activity is unpredictable. We recommend that all travelers exercise caution when traveling anywhere in Honduras. However, certain areas of the country demonstrate higher levels of criminal activity than others. Honduran "departments" (a geographic designation similar to U.S. states) with crime rates higher than the national average include:

- Atlantida (where La Ceiba is located)
- Colon
- Copan (where the Mayan ruins are located)
- Cortes (where San Pedro Sula is located)
- Francisco Morazan (where Tegucigalpa is located)
- Ocotepeque
- Yoro

Certain areas of Olancho, particularly the municipalities of Catacamas, Juticalpa, San Francisco de la Paz, and Santa Maria de Real, also report a significantly high crime rate.

For more detailed information regarding personal security, please see the State Department's Country Specific Information for Honduras. For the latest security information, U.S. citizens traveling abroad should regularly monitor the Bureau of Consular Affairs' Web site, where the Worldwide Caution, Travel Warnings, and Travel Alerts can be found. U.S. citizens living or traveling in Honduras are strongly encouraged to sign up for the State Department's Smart Traveler Enrollment Program to obtain updated information on travel and security within Honduras. The Embassy is located on Avenida La Paz in Tegucigalpa and can be reached by telephone at (504) 2236–9320/2238–5114 or by fax at (504) 2236–9037. For after-hours emergencies, please call (504) 2236–8497. The Embassy's American Citizen Services Unit can be reached directly by fax at (504) 2238–4357 or by e-mail at usahonduras@state.gov. The American Citizen Services Unit's Facebook page, http://www.facebook.com/acstegucigalpa, is another resource for updated security information. Travelers may register with the Consular Section of the U.S. Embassy in Tegucigalpa through the Smart Traveler Enrollment Program. Travelers may obtain up-to-date information on security conditions by calling 1-888-407-4747 toll-free in the United States or outside the U.S. and Canada on a regular toll line at 1-202-501-4444. For information on general crime and security issues, U.S. citizens should also consult the U.S. Embassy in Honduras and the U.S. Consular Agency in San Pedro Sula. Stay up to date by bookmarking our Bureau of Consular Affairs Web site, which contains Travel Warnings and Travel Alerts as well as the Worldwide Caution. Follow us on Twitter and the Bureau of Consular Affairs page on Facebook and download the Smart Traveler App for iPhone or Android.

The U.S. Consular Agency in San Pedro Sula, which accepts passport applications and performs notarial services, is located on the eleventh floor of the Banco Atlantida building (across from Central Park), telephone (504) 2558–1580. The agency is open Monday-Wednesday-Friday from 12 p.m. to 4 p.m. In case of emergency in the San Pedro Sula/north coast area, please contact the Embassy in Tegucigalpa at (504) 2236–9320/2238–5114, which will forward the call to the Consular Agent if necessary.

Intercountry Adoption

January 2010

The information in this section has been edited from the latest report available as of February 2013 from the State Department Bureau of Con-

sular Affairs, Office of Overseas Citizens Services. For more information, please read the *Intercountry Adoption* section of this book and review current reports online at http://adoption.state.gov.

Honduras is not party to the Hague Convention on Protection of Children and Co-operation in Respect of *Intercountry Adoption* (Hague Adoption Convention). Therefore, when the Hague Adoption Convention entered into force for the United States on April 1, 2008, intercountry adoption processing for Honduras did not change. The adoption process in Honduras is currently in flux. Policies regarding eligibility requirements for prospective adoptive parents, residency requirements, and time frame are under review by the Honduran Family Court (IHNFA).

Any change on the family code regarding all the above must be done by the Congress, not the family court, they can only give their opinion. This has been under review for more than 8 years, they have been studying many law projects, and however, it remains the same.

Who Can Adopt? To bring an adopted child to United States from Honduras, you must be found eligible to adopt by the U.S. Government. The U.S. Government agency responsible for making this determination is the Department of Homeland Security, U.S. Citizenship and Immigration Services (USCIS). In addition to these U.S. requirements for prospective adoptive parents, Honduras has the following eligibility requirements for prospective adoptive parents that must be met. Their eligibility requirements are currently under review by the Honduran Family Court.

Who Can Be Adopted? Honduras has specific requirements that a child must meet in order to be eligible for adoption. In addition to these requirements, a child must meet the definition of an orphan under U.S. law for you to bring him or her home back to the United States. Learn more about U.S. immigration requirements.

Honduras' Adoption Authority: Instituto Hondureño de la Niñez y la Familia (IHNFA) and Honduran Family Court

The Process: The first step in adopting a child from Honduras is usually to select a licensed agency in the United States that can help with your adoption. Adoption service providers must be licensed by the U.S. state in which they operate.

Additionally, all agencies operating in Honduras must be accredited by the government. IHNFA maintains a list of these agencies and information on registration and accreditation to operate. The U.S. Embassy in Tegucigalpa maintains a listing of attorneys in Honduras who may be able to help you on the embassy's website.

To bring an adopted child from Honduras to the United States, you must apply to be found eligible to adopt (Form I-600A) by the U.S. Government, Department of Homeland Security, U.S. Citizenship and Immigration Services (USCIS). In addition to meeting the U.S. requirements for adoptive parents, you need to meet the requirements of Honduras. If you are eligible to adopt, and a child is available for intercountry adoption, IHNFA in Honduras will provide you with a referral to a child.

Role of the Adoption Authority: The Honduran Family Court acts as the adoption authority for children 14 years of age and older. The Instituto Hondureño de la Niñez y la Familia (IHNFA) is the adoption authority representing children under 14 years of age. The Honduran Family Court and the IHNFA review the petitions submitted for adoptions.

Role of the Court: The Honduran Family Court is responsible for processing intercountry adoptions for children 14 years of age and older.

Role of Adoption Agencies: The adoption agency forwards the required petition and documentation to the appropriate adoption authority.

Adoption Application: If the child is 14 years of age and older, the adoption agency sends the adoption application (petition) to the Honduran Family Court. If the child is younger than 14 years of age, the adoption agency sends the adoption application (petition) to the IHNFA.

Time Frame: The timeframe for intercountry adoptions of Honduran children is currently under review by the Honduran Family Court.

Adoption Fees: The adoption fees are between $3,000 and $10,000 USD for attorney fees.

Documents Required: The documents necessary to adopt a Honduran child are currently under review by the Honduran Family Court (IHNFA). Please contact the IHNFA for more specific information.

After you finalize the adoption (or gain legal custody) in Honduras, the USCIS must determine whether the child is eligible under U.S. law to be adopted (Form I-600).

Bringing Your Child Home: Once your adoption is complete (or you have obtained legal custody of the child), there are a few more steps to take before you can head home. Specifically, you need to apply for several documents for your child before he or she can travel to the United States, such as a birth certificate, a passport or travel document for your child from the country in which he or she was born, and a U.S. Immigration Visa. For detailed and updated information on how to obtain these documents, review the *Intercountry Adoption* section on this publication and visit the USCIS Intercountry Adoption website at http://adoption.state.gov.

Child Citizenship Act: For adoptions finalized abroad, the Child Citizenship Act of 2000 allows your new child to acquire American citizenship automatically when he or she enters the United States as lawful permanent residents.

For adoptions finalized in the United States, the Child Citizenship Act of 2000 allows your new child to acquire American citizenship automatically when the court in the United States issues the final adoption decree.

To learn more, review the *Intercountry Adoption* section on this publication and visit the USCIS Intercountry Adoption website at http://adoption.state.gov.

After Adoption: Currently, there are no specified post-adoption requirements. This may change as the intercountry adoption process is being reviewed by the Honduran Family Court.

U.S. Embassy in Honduras
Avenida La Paz
Tegucigalpa, Honduras
Tel: (504) 238-5114 ext. 4400
Email: usahonduras@state.gov
http://honduras.usembassy.gov

Honduras' Adoption Authority
Instituto Hondureño de la Niñez y la Familia (IHNFA)
Honduras, Centro America
Tegucigalpa, Col. Humuya
Calle la salud
Apartado Postal 3234
Tel: (504) 23.57.754, (504) 23.57.755, (504) 23.57.756
Fax: (504) 23.53.598
Website: http://www.ihnfa.hn

Embassy of Honduras
3007 Tilden Street, N.W.
Washington, D.C. 20008
Tel: (202) 966-7702
Email: embassy@hondurasemb.org
http://www.hondurasemb.org

Note: Honduras also has consulates in Atlanta, Boston, Chicago, Houston, Jacksonville, Los Angeles, Miami, New Orleans, Phoenix, San Francisco, San Juan, and Tampa.

Office of Children's Issues
U.S. Department of State
2201 C Street, NW
SA-29
Washington, DC 20520
Tel: 1-888-407-4747
E-mail: AskCI@state.gov
Website: http://adoption.state.gov

For questions about immigration procedures, contact the National Customer Service Center (NCSC) at 1-800-375-5283 (TTY 1-800-767-1833).

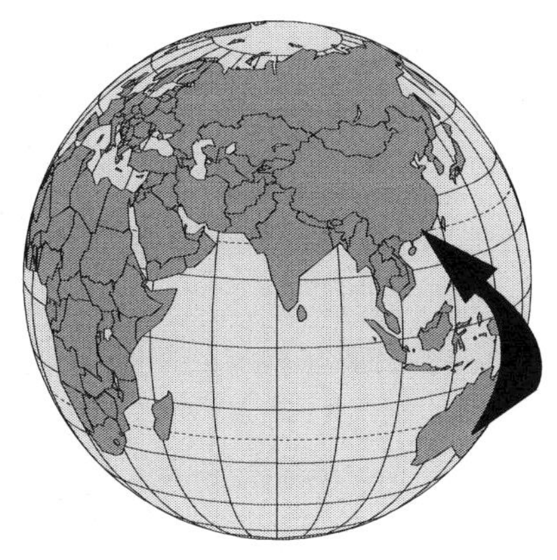

HONG KONG

Compiled from publications that were available as of February 2013 from the U.S. Department of State, the U.S. Department of Commerce, and the Central Intelligence Agency (CIA). See the introduction to this set for explanatory notes.

Official Name:
Hong Kong Special Administrative Region

PROFILE

Geography

Area: total: 1,104 sq km; country comparison to the world: 184; land: 1,054 sq km; water: 50 sq km

Climate: subtropical monsoon; cool and humid in winter, hot and rainy from spring through summer, warm and sunny in fall

Terrain: hilly to mountainous with steep slopes; lowlands in north

People

Nationality: noun: Chinese/Hong Konger; adjective: Chinese/Hong Kong

Population: 7,153,519 (July 2012 est.)

Population growth rate: 0.421% (2012 est.)

Ethnic groups: Chinese 95%, Filipino 1.6%, Indonesian 1.3%, other 2.1% (2006 census)

Religions: eclectic mixture of local religions 90%, Christian 10%

Languages: Cantonese (official) 90.8%, English (official) 2.8%, Putonghua (Mandarin) 0.9%, other Chinese dialects 4.4%, other 1.1% (2006 census)

Literacy: definition: age 15 and over has ever attended school; total population: 93.5%; male: 96.9%; female: 89.6% (2002)

Health: life expectancy at birth: total population: 82.12 years; male: 79.39 years; female: 85.05 years (2012 est.); Infant mortality rate: total: 2.9 deaths/1,000 live births; male: 3.07 deaths/1,000 live births; female: 2.71 deaths/1,000 live births (2012 est.)

Unemployment rate: 3.4% (2012 est.)

Work force: 3.705 million (2012 est.)

Government

Type: limited democracy

Independence: none

Constitution: The Basic Law, approved March 1990 by China's National People's Congress, is Hong Kong's charter

Political subdivisions: none (special administrative region of China)

Suffrage: 18 years of age in direct elections for half the legislature and a majority of seats in 18 district councils; universal for permanent residents living in the territory of Hong Kong for the past seven years; note—in indirect elections, suffrage is limited to about 220,000 members of functional constituencies for the other half of the legislature and an 1,200-member election committee for the chief executive drawn from broad sectoral groupings, central government bodies, municipal organizations, and elected Hong Kong officials

Economy

GDP (purchasing power parity): $363.7 billion (2012 est.); $355.6 billion (2011 est.); $338.8 billion (2010 est.); $316.5 billion (2009 est.)

GDP real growth rate: 1.8% (2012 est.); 5% (2011 est.); 7% (2010 est.); -2.6% (2009 est.)

GDP per capita (PPP): $50,700 (2012 est.); $49,800 (2011 est.); $47,700 (2010 est.); $44,900 (2009 est.)

Natural resources: outstanding deepwater harbor, feldspar

Agriculture products: fresh vegetables; poultry, pork; fish

Industries: textiles, clothing, tourism, banking, shipping, electronics, plastics, toys, watches, clocks

Exports: $439 billion (2012 est.); $427.9 billion (2011 est.); $394 billion (2010 est.)

Exports—commodities: electrical machinery and appliances, textiles, apparel, footwear, watches and clocks, toys, plastics, precious stones, printed material

Exports—partners: China 52.4%, US 9.9%, Japan 4% (2011 est.)

Imports: $499.4 billion (2012 est.); $482.6 billion (2011 est.); $437 billion (2010 est.)

Imports—commodities: raw materials and semi-manufactures, consumer goods, capital goods, foodstuffs, fuel (most is reexported)

Imports—partners: China 44.9%, Japan 8.9%, Taiwan 7.5%, US 4.9% (2011 est.)

Debt—external: $903.2 billion (30 June 2011 est.); $750.8 billion (31 December 2010 est.)

Exchange rates: Hong Kong dollars (HKD) per US dollar; 7.8 (2012 est.); 7.784 (2011 est.); 7.77 (2010 est.); 7.75 (2009); 7.751 (2008); 7.802 (2007)

PEOPLE

Hong Kong's population has increased steadily over the past decade, reaching 7.097 million in 2010. Hong Kong is one of the most densely populated areas in the world, with an overall density of some 6,426 people per square kilometer.

National/Racial/Ethnic Minorities

Although 95 percent ethnic Chinese, the SAR is a multiethnic society with persons from a number of ethnic groups recognized as permanent residents with full rights under the law.

Language

Cantonese, the official Chinese dialect in Hong Kong, is spoken by most of the population. English, also an official language, is widely understood and is spoken by more than one-third of the population.

Religion

According to the government's Information Services Department, approximately 43 percent of the population practice some form of religion. The two most prevalent religions are Buddhism and Taoism, which often are observed in the same temple. There are approximately 1.5 million Buddhists and Taoists; 320,000 Protestants; about 355,000 Roman Catholics; approximately 20,000 members of the Church of Jesus Christ of Latter-day Saints (Mormons); about 90,000 Muslims; over 40,000 Hindus; about 10,000 Sikhs; and approximately 5,000-6,000 Jews. Confucianism also is prevalent, although few believers practiced Confucianism as a formal religion. There are between 300 and 500 practitioners of Falun Gong, a self-described spiritual discipline. There are approximately 600 Taoist and Buddhist temples (including temples affiliated with Tibetan Buddhist schools), 800 Christian churches and chapels, five mosques, seven synagogues, one Hindu temple, and one Sikh temple.

There are 1,400 Protestant congregations, representing 50 denominations, including Baptists, Lutherans, Seventh-day Adventists, Anglicans, Christian and Missionary Alliance groups, the Church of Christ in China, Methodists, Pentecostals, and the Mormons. The Hong Kong Diocese recognizes Pope Benedict XVI as the head of the Roman Catholic Church. A bishop, as well as priests, monks, and nuns, served Catholics and maintained links to the Vatican.

Education

All children are required by law to be in full-time education between the ages of 6 and 15. Starting in 2008, the Hong Kong Government expanded the length of free education it offers from 9 to 12 years. Preschool education for most children begins at age 3. Primary school begins normally at age 6 and lasts for 6 years. At about age 12, children progress to a 3-year course of junior secondary education; at age 15, they can choose to continue with 3-year senior secondary education or to join full-time vocational training.

More than 90% of children complete upper secondary education or equivalent vocational education. In 2010, 301,200 students were enrolled in post-secondary education. Over 25.5% of the total population aged 15 and over have attended post-secondary educational institutions.

HISTORY

According to archaeological studies, human activity on Hong Kong dates back over five millennia. Excavated neolithic artifacts suggest an influence from northern Chinese stone-age cultures. The territory was settled by Han Chinese during the seventh century, A.D., evidenced by the discovery of an ancient tomb at Lei Cheung Uk in Kowloon. The first major migration from northern China to Hong Kong occurred during the Sung Dynasty (960-1279).

The British East India Company made the first successful sea venture to China in 1699, and Hong Kong's trade with British merchants developed rapidly soon after. After the Chinese defeat in the First Opium War (1839–42), Hong Kong was ceded to Britain in 1842 under the Treaty of Nanking. Britain was granted a perpetual lease on the Kowloon Peninsula under the 1860 Convention of Beijing, which formally ended hostilities in the Second Opium War (1856–58).

The United Kingdom, concerned that Hong Kong could not be defended unless surrounding areas also were under British control, executed a 99-year lease of the New Territories in 1898, significantly expanding the size of the Hong Kong colony. In the late 19th century and early 20th centuries, Hong Kong developed as a warehousing and distribution center for U.K. trade with southern China. After the end of World War II and the communist takeover of Mainland China in 1949, hundreds of thousands of people fled from China to Hong Kong. Hong Kong became an economic success and a manufacturing, commercial, finance, and tourism center. High life expectancy, literacy, per capita income, and other socioeconomic measures attest to Hong Kong's achievements over the last 5 decades.

On July 1, 1997, China resumed the exercise of sovereignty over Hong Kong, ending more than 150 years of British colonial rule. Hong Kong is a Special Administrative Region of the People's Republic of China with a high degree of autonomy in all matters except foreign and defense affairs. According to the Sino-British Joint Declaration (1984) and the Basic Law, Hong Kong will retain its political, economic, and judicial systems and unique way of life for 50 years after reversion and will continue to participate in international agreements and organizations under the name, "Hong Kong, China."

GOVERNMENT AND POLITICAL CONDITIONS

Hong Kong is a Special Administrative Region (SAR) of the People's Republic of China (PRC). The 1984 Sino-British Joint Declaration on the Question of Hong Kong and the SAR's charter, the Basic Law of the SAR (the Basic Law), specify that Hong Kong will enjoy a high degree of autonomy except in matters of defense and foreign affairs. The Fourth Term Legislative Council (Legco) was elected from a combination of geographic and functional constituencies in 2008 elections that were generally free and fair.

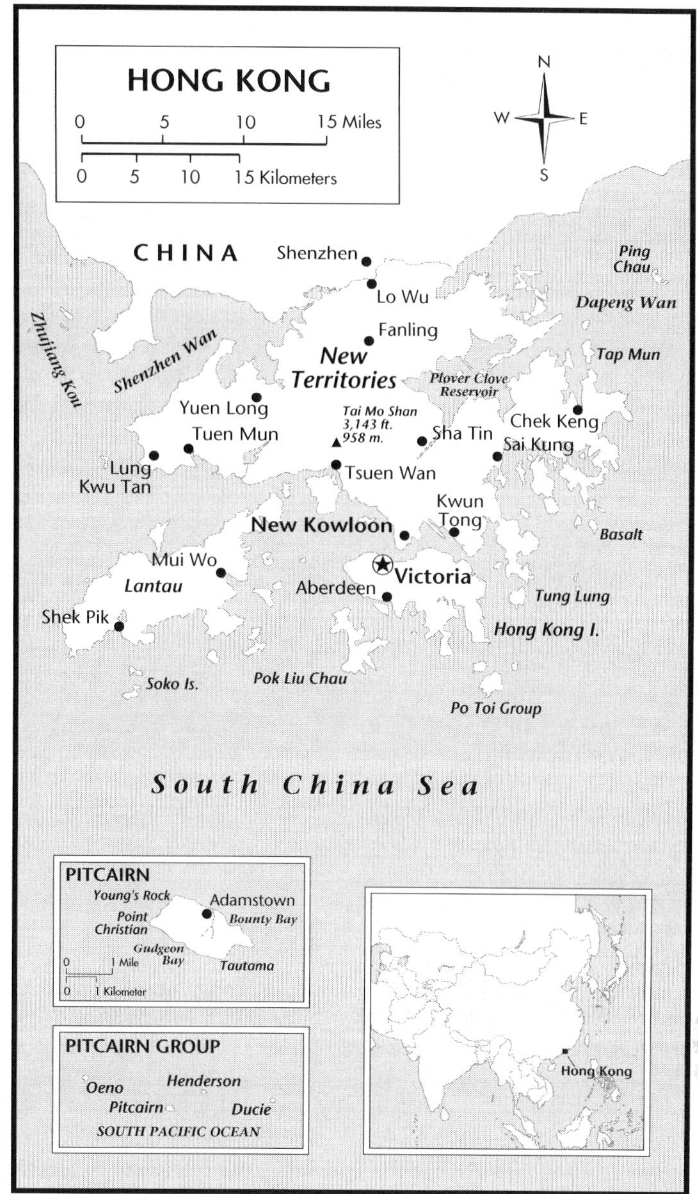

Recent Elections

In 2007, the CE Election Committee selected incumbent Donald Tsang Yam-kuen, and the PRC's State Council formally appointed him. In 2008 voters in five GCs elected 30 legislators, half of the total Legco, in elections that were generally free and fair. A record number of candidates, both party-affiliated and independent, contested the elections. Of the 30 FC seats, 14 incumbents returned uncontested.

In January 2010, five legislators resigned to force a by-election they declared to be a "referendum" on political reform, particularly on achieving universal suffrage. While the government stated that neither the Basic Law nor local law establishes a legal process by which to conduct a referendum, on May 16, the government held the by-election. Supporters of the by-election criticized the government for not making the traditional efforts to encourage citizens to vote in the by-election. They also criticized the publicly announced decision of the CE and senior officials not to cast ballots in the election. The by-election itself, which saw a turnout of approximately 17 percent, was generally free and fair, and the five "incumbents" were reelected.

Responding to this event, and arguing that the democrats used a loophole to abuse the electoral system and waste public money, the government presented draft legislation on June 8 to eliminate by-elections. Angered by the government's efforts to rush the bill through the Legco, thousands of Hong Kongers (organizers claimed 218,000 participants and the police put the number at 54,000) marched in the biggest July 1 protest since 2004. The government responded by holding a public consultation on the reforms and presenting four proposals for filling vacant seats; many commented that the government's options were undemocratic. At the end of 2011, the Constitutional and Mainland Affairs Bureau had not sent the government's draft legislation to the Legco.

Political Parties: Pan-democratic parties faced a number of institutional challenges preventing them from holding a majority of the seats in the Legco or having one of their members become chief executive. The unique nature of voting for Legco members ensures pro-business representatives and Beijing's allies control a majority. Additionally, the Central Government and its business supporters provided generous financial resources to parties that support Beijing's political agenda in Hong Kong, ensuring these organizations will control the levers of government and all senior positions.

Participation of Women and Minorities: Seven of the 30 members of the Executive Council (cabinet-level secretaries and "nonofficial" councilors who advise the CE) were women. Seven of the 30 directly elected Legco members were women, and women held four of the 30 FC seats. Two political parties represented in the Legco were headed by women. Four of the 22 most senior government officials were women.

There is no legal restriction against non-Chinese running for electoral office or participating in the civil service, although most elected or senior appointed positions require that the officeholder have a legal right of abode only in the SAR. There were no members of ethnic minorities in the Legco. The government regarded ethnic origin as irrelevant to civil service appointment and did not collect data on the number of non-ethnic Chinese serving in the civil service, a practice that some observers criticized as preventing the government from monitoring hiring and promotion rates for non-ethnic Chinese.

Principal Government Officials

Last Updated: 1/31/2013

Chief Executive: **Donald TSANG Yam-kuen**
Chief Sec. for Admin.: **Stephen LAM Sui-lung**
Sec. for Civil Service: **Denise YUE Chong-yee**
Sec. for Commerce & Economic Development: **Gregory SO Kam-leung**
Sec. for Constitutional & Mainland Affairs: **Raymond TAM Chi-yuen**
Sec. for Development: **Carrie LAM Cheng Yuet-ngor**
Sec. for Education: **Michael SUEN Ming-yueng**
Sec. for Environment: **Edward YAU Tang-wah**
Sec. for Finance: **John TSANG Chun-wah**
Sec. for Financial Services & the Treasury: **K. C. CHAN Ka-keung**
Sec. for Food & Health: **York CHOW, Dr.**
Sec. for Home Affairs: **TSANG Tak-sing**
Sec. for Justice: **WONG Yan Lung**
Sec. for Labor & Welfare: **Matthew CHEUNG Kin-chung**
Sec. for Security: **Ambrose LEE Siu-kwong**
Sec. for Transport & Housing: **Eva CHENG**
Chief Executive, Hong Kong Monetary Authority: **Norman CHAN Tak-lam**
Chief Justice: **Geoffrey MA Tao-li**
Pres., Legislative Council: **Jasper TSANG Yok-sing**
Commissioner of Police: **TSANG Wai-hung**
Commissioner, Independent Commission Against Corruption: **Timothy TONG Hin-ming**
Director of Audit: **Benjamin TANG**

ECONOMY

Hong Kong has a free market economy, highly dependent on international trade and finance - the value of goods and services trade, including the sizable share of re-exports, is about four times GDP. Hong Kong's open economy left it exposed to the global economic slowdown that began in 2008. Although increasing integration with China, through trade, tourism, and financial links, helped it to make an initial recovery more quickly than many observers anticipated, it again faces a possible slowdown as exports to the Euro zone and US slump.

The Hong Kong government is promoting the Special Administrative Region (SAR) as the site for Chinese renminbi (RMB) internationalization. Hong Kong residents are allowed to establish RMB-denominated savings accounts; RMB-denominated corporate and Chinese government bonds have been issued in Hong Kong; and RMB trade settlement is allowed. The territory far exceeded the RMB conversion quota set by Beijing for trade settlements in 2010 due to the growth of earnings from exports to the mainland. RMB deposits grew to roughly 7.8% of total system deposits in Hong Kong by the end of 2011, an increase of over 59% since the beginning of the year.

The government is pursuing efforts to introduce additional use of RMB in Hong Kong financial markets and is seeking to expand the RMB quota. The mainland has long been Hong Kong's largest trading partner, accounting for about half of Hong Kong's exports by value. Hong Kong's natural resources are limited, and food and raw materials must be imported. As a result of China's easing of travel restrictions, the number of mainland tourists to the territory has surged from 4.5 million in 2001 to 28 million in 2011, outnumbering visitors from all other countries combined.

Hong Kong has also established itself as the premier stock market for Chinese firms seeking to list abroad. In 2011 mainland Chinese companies constituted about 43% of the firms listed on the Hong Kong Stock Exchange and accounted for about 56% of the Exchange's market capitalization. During the past decade, as Hong Kong's manufacturing industry moved to the mainland, its service industry has grown rapidly. Growth slowed to 5% in 2011, and less than 2% in 2012. Credit expansion and tight housing supply conditions caused Hong Kong property prices to rise rapidly in 2010 and inflation to rise 5.3% in 2011, but the tempo slowed in 2012.

Lower and middle income segments of the population are increasingly unable to afford adequate housing. Hong Kong continues to link its currency closely to the US dollar, maintaining an arrangement established in 1983.

Labor Conditions

There were laws to protect children from exploitation in the workplace. Regulations prohibit employment of children under the age of 15 in any industrial establishment. Other regulations limit work hours in the manufacturing sector for persons 15 to 17 years of age to eight hours per day and 48 hours per week between 7 a.m. and 7 p.m., and prohibit overtime in industrial establishments with employment in dangerous trades for persons less than 18 years of age.

Children 13 and 14 years of age may work in certain nonindustrial establishments, subject to conditions aimed at ensuring a minimum of nine years of education and protection of their safety, health, and welfare.

The SAR's first statutory minimum hourly wage, HK$28 (US$3.60), came into force in May. Approximately 760,000 Hong Kong residents live under the locally defined poverty line (annual income of about HK$47,213 [US$6,053] for an individual, HK$75,598 [US$9,692] for a two-person unit, HK$100,168 [US$12,842] for a three-person family, etc.).

In practice wages were often set by employers and employer associations. Additionally, unionists alleged that workers were tricked by employers into signing contracts that changed their terms of employment to "self-employed," and thus they were not entitled to employer-provided benefits such as paid leave, sick leave, medical insurance, workers' compensation, or Mandatory Provident Fund payments.

The minimum wage for foreign domestic workers was HK$3,740 per month (US$482). The government's Standard Employment Contract requires employers to provide foreign domestic workers with housing, worker's compensation insurance, travel allowances, and food or a food allowance in addition to the minimum wage, which together provided a decent standard of living. Foreign domestic workers could be deported if dismissed.

After leaving one employer, workers have two weeks to secure new employment before they must leave the SAR. Activists contended this restriction left workers vulnerable to a range of abuses from employers. Workers who pursued complaints through legal channels may be granted leave to remain; however, they were not able to work, leaving them either to live from savings or to depend on charitable assistance.

There was no law concerning working hours, paid weekly rest, rest breaks, or compulsory overtime for most employees. For certain groups and occupations, such as security guards and certain categories of drivers, there were regulations and guidelines on working hours and rest breaks. According to the General Household Survey conducted by the Census and Statistics Department during the year, about 17.1 percent of Hong Kong employees worked 60 hours or more per week. The law stipulates that employees are entitled to 12 days of statutory holidays and employers must not make payment in lieu of granting holidays.

Domestic workers were required to live with their employers (who do not always provide separate accommodation for the worker), which made it difficult to enforce maximum working hours per day or overtime.

The government contended that the "two-week rule" was necessary to maintain effective immigration control and prevent migrant workers from overstaying and taking up unauthorized work. Regarding maximum hours and rest periods, the government stated that the rules on these issues cover local and migrant workers. However, in its explanation of why live-in domestic helpers (both local and foreign) would not be covered by the statutory minimum wage, the government explained that "the distinctive working pattern—round-the-clock presence, provision of service-on-demand, and the multifarious domestic duties expected of live-in domestic workers—makes it impossible to ascertain the actual hours worked so as to determine the wages to be paid."

There are no laws restricting work during typhoon or rainstorm warning signals except for a Labor Department recommendation that employers have only essential staff come to work during certain categories of typhoon or rainstorm warnings. Both pro-Beijing and pan-democratic unions called for a review of protections for workers during inclement weather, including legal protections.

U.S.-HONG KONG RELATIONS

In 1997, China resumed the exercise of sovereignty over Hong Kong, ending more than 150 years of British colonial rule. Hong Kong is a Special Administrative Region of the People's Republic of China. Its foreign relations and defense are the responsibility of China. However, Hong Kong is a customs territory and economic entity separate from the rest of China and is able to enter into international agreements on its own behalf in commercial and economic matters.

U.S. policy toward Hong Kong is stated in the U.S.-Hong Kong Policy Act of 1992 and grounded in the determination to promote Hong Kong's prosperity, autonomy, and way of life. The United States maintains substantial economic and political interests in Hong Kong. The U.S. supports Hong Kong's autonomy under the "One Country, Two Systems" framework by concluding and implementing bilateral agreements; promoting trade and investment; broadening law enforcement cooperation; bolstering educational, academic, and cultural links; supporting high-level visits of U.S. officials; and serving the large community of U.S. citizens and visitors.

Hong Kong is active in counterterrorism efforts. Hong Kong has joined the Container Security Initiative and remains an important partner in efforts to eliminate funding for terrorist networks and combat money laundering. Hong Kong has passed legislation designed to bring it into compliance with applicable United Nations anti-terror resolutions and with most Financial Action Task Force recommendations. In 2010, Hong Kong passed legislation allowing it to adopt the most recent globally recognized standards for exchange of tax information.

U.S. Assistance to Hong Kong

The United States provides no foreign assistance to Hong Kong.

Bilateral Economic Relations

The United States enjoys substantial economic and social ties with Hong Kong. U.S. companies have a generally favorable view of Hong Kong's business environment, including its legal system and the free flow of information, low taxation, and infrastructure. There are some 1,400 U.S. firms, including 840 regional operations (315 regional headquarters and 525 regional offices), and over 60,000 American residents in Hong Kong.

The U.S. trade surplus with Hong Kong was the largest of any U.S. surplus in 2011, owing largely to Hong Kong imports of American aircraft and spacecraft, diamonds, nonmonetary gold, telecommunications equipment, and computer processors. In 2010, the United States was one of the largest investors in Hong Kong.

Hong Kong enjoys a high degree of autonomy as a separate customs territory, with no changes to borders, staffing, or technology export controls since the 1997 handover. Intellectual property rights protection is relatively strong, and Hong Kong continues to take steps to improve both its legislation and its enforcement regime. Amendments to improve protections for copyrighted materials were passed in 2007, and additional amendments to protect on-line content have been drafted and await passage by LegCo.

Hong Kong's Membership in International Organizations

Hong Kong, independently of China, participates as a full member of several international economic organizations. The United States and Hong Kong both belong to the World Trade Organization, Asia-Pacific Economic Cooperation forum, and Financial Action Task Force. Hong Kong is an articulate and effective champion of free markets and the reduction of trade barriers.

Bilateral Representation

Hong Kong maintains three Economic and Trade Offices in the United States in Washington, D.C.; New York; and San Francisco.

China's embassy in the United States is at 3505 International Place, NW, Washington, DC 20008; Tel.: (202) 495-2266.

Principal U.S. Embassy Officials

Last Updated: 1/14/2013

HONG KONG (CG) 26 Garden Road, Central, (852) 2523-9011/Post One– (852) 2841-2230 & (852) 9091-5726 (cell), Fax (852) 2845-1598, Workweek: Monday–Friday; 0830-1730, Website: http://hongkong.usconsulate.gov/

CG OMS:	Claudia Ellingwood
Co-CLO:	Janet Malanga
DHS/ICE:	Eben Roberts
DPO:	Matthew J. Matthews
FCS:	Scott Shaw
FM:	Ronald Hernandez
HRO:	Eric Browing-Larsen
MGT:	Andrea S. Baker
POL/ECON:	Andrew Shaw
POSHO:	Ronald Hernandez
SDO/DATT:	CAPT Clayton Grindle
CG:	Stephen M. Young
CON:	George Hogeman
PAO:	Nini Forino
GSO:	Polly A. Emerick
RSO:	Mark Lewis
ATO:	Erich Kuss
CLO:	Linda Barker
DEA:	Andrew J. Malanga
FMO:	Nina Robinson
ICASS Chair:	Erich Kuss
IMO:	Mari Jain Womack
IPO:	Janet Vancoblijn
IRS:	William Cheung
ISO:	Mark C. Allen
LEGATT:	Lawrence Futa

TRAVEL

Consular Information Sheet

April 16, 2012

Description: Hong Kong, a Special Administrative Region (SAR) of the People's Republic of China (PRC) since July 1, 1997, has a high degree of autonomy, except in the areas of defense and foreign policy, and retains its own currency, laws, and border controls. It is composed of three geographic areas: the New Territories, Kowloon Peninsula, and Hong Kong Island. Hong Kong SAR is cosmopolitan and highly developed. Tourist facilities and services are widely available.

Smart Traveler Enrollment Program (STEP)/Embassy Locations: If you are going to live in or visit Hong Kong, please take the time to tell our Consulate about your trip. If you enroll in the Smart Traveler Enrollment Program, we can keep you up-to-date with important safety and security announcements. It will also help your friends and family get in touch with you in an emergency.

U.S. Consulate General Hong Kong & Macau
26 Garden Road, Central, Hong Kong
Telephone: 852-2841–2211, 852-2841–2225, 852-2841–2323 (Direct lines to American Citizen Services during regular business hours)
Emergency after-hours telephone: 852-2523–9011
Facsimile: 852-2845–4845

Entry/Exit Requirements for U.S. Citizens: To enter Hong Kong, you will need a passport that is valid for at least one month beyond the date of your intended stay, adequate funds to cover your stay without working locally, and evidence of onward/return transportation. Many neighboring areas require that your passport is valid for at least six months before they will allow you to enter, so if you plan on regional travel beyond Hong Kong, make sure that your passport is valid for at least six months beyond the date you plan to enter such areas. You do not need a visa for tourist visits of up to 90 days. You may be granted an extension of your stay if you apply to the Hong Kong SAR Immigration Department. You must have an appropriate visa to work or study in Hong Kong. Visit the Hong Kong SAR Immigration Department or the Embassy of the People's Republic of China website for the most current visa information.

You should obtain all required visas prior to departing the United States. Specifically, if you wish to travel to the PRC from Hong Kong, you will need a PRC visa and should apply at the PRC embassy or consulate where you reside.

If you are the parent of a child who holds U.S. passport, you should know that the PRC Visa Office may require a certified birth certificates or other documentation for your child. A certified U.S. birth certificated is required when applying in Hong Kong for PRC visas for U.S.-born children. Further information on travel to and around the PRC is available in our China Country Specific Sheet.

The U.S. Department of State is unaware of any HIV/AIDS entry restrictions for visitors to or foreign residents of Hong Kong SAR.

Threats to Safety and Security:

Stay up to date:

- Bookmark our Bureau of Consular Affairs website, which contains the current Travel Warnings and Travel Alerts as well as the Worldwide Caution.
- Follow us on Twitter and the Bureau of Consular Affairs page on Facebook as well.
- Download our free Smart Traveler IPhone App to have travel information at your fingertips.
- Call 1-888-407-4747 toll-free within the U.S. and Canada, or a regular toll line, 1-202-501-4444, from other countries.
- Taking some time before travel to consider your personal security.

Crime: Hong Kong has a low crime rate. Even so, you should exercise caution when in congested areas and pay particular attention to personal belongings while in crowded markets and while traveling on public transportation. Violent crime, though rare, does occur.

Don't buy counterfeit and pirated goods, even if they are widely available. Not only are the bootlegs illegal in the United States, if you purchase them you may also be breaking local law.

Victims of Crime: If you or someone you know becomes the victim of a crime abroad, you should contact the local police and the nearest U.S. embassy or consulate. We can:

- Replace a stolen passport.
- Help you find appropriate medical care if you are the victim of violent crimes such as assault or rape.
- Put you in contact with the appropriate police authorities, and if you want us to, we can contact family members or friend.
- Help you understand the local criminal justice process and direct you to local attorneys, although it is important to remember that local authorities are responsible for investigating and prosecuting the crime.

Hong Kong has a crime victim compensation program available to U.S. citizens who are legal residents or tourists in Hong Kong. For more detailed information on the program and its requirements, please see the Hong Kong Social Welfare Department webpage. More resources for victims of crime in Hong Kong are available in our Help for U.S. Victims of Crime in Hong Kong information sheet.

The local equivalent to the U.S. "911" emergency line in Hong Kong is 999.

Criminal Penalties: While you are traveling in Hong Kong, you are subject to its laws even if you are a U.S. citizen. Foreign laws and legal systems can be vastly different from our own. In Hong Kong you may be taken in for questioning if you don't have your passport with you. If you are found to be driving under the influence, you could be sent immediately to jail. There are also some things that might be legal in Hong Kong, but still illegal in the United States, and you can be prosecuted under U.S. law if you buy pirated goods. Engaging in sexual conduct with children or using or disseminating child pornography in a foreign country is a crime prosecutable in the United States. If you break local laws in Hong Kong, your U.S. passport won't help you avoid arrest or prosecution. It's very important to know what's legal and what's not where you are going.

If you violate Hong Kong laws, even unknowingly, you may be expelled, arrested, or imprisoned. Penalties for possession, use of, or trafficking in illegal drugs in Hong Kong are severe, and if you are convicted, you can expect long jail sentences and heavy fines. In Hong Kong, detained U.S. citizens have been surprised that they had been arrested for violations that would not have resulted in arrest in the United States.

Arrest notifications in Hong Kong: If you are arrested in Hong Kong, authorities of Hong Kong are required to notify the nearest U.S. embassy or consulate of your arrest. If you are concerned the Department of State may not be aware of your situation, you should request the police or prison officials to notify the U.S. Consulate General in Hong Kong of your arrest.

Special Circumstances: Hong Kong SAR customs authorities enforce strict regulations concerning controlled items you might be carrying while transiting Hong Kong (temporary importation or exportation) such as firearms and ammunition, counterfeit goods or illegally produced copies of copyright items, ivory, narcotics, medications, television decoders requiring a subscription, animals and plants, meat and poultry, textiles, and sensitive high technology or military products. If you bring such goods into Hong Kong without a license, you may be prosecuted, and the goods may be seized. The penalty for trafficking in dangerous drugs can be life imprisonment and a heavy fine. Among the other items that you must declare to customs officials are liquors, tobacco, cigarettes and cigars, methyl alcohol, and merchandise imported for commercial purposes. There are no currency restrictions for travelers.

You will be subject to prosecution and possible detention if you are caught carrying any firearm or ammunition in or out of Hong Kong. Unless otherwise exempted by laws, possession of an "imitation firearm" is also an offense. "Arms" means any firearm, air rifle/air gun/air pistol from which any shot, bullet or missile can be discharged with a muzzle energy greater than two joules, electric stunning device, gun/pistol or other propelling/releasing instrument from or by which a projectile containing any gas or chemical could be discharged, weapon for the discharge of any noxious liquid/gas/powder, and harpoon or spear gun. Paintball guns are included in this category.

You will be liable to prosecution if you carry in or out of Hong Kong any "weapon," which includes Chinese-style throwing dart, gravity knife, gravity-operated steel baton, knuckleduster, Chinese-style fighting iron, spring-loaded steel baton, any knife with a blade that can be exposed by a spring or other mechanical/electric device, and any bladed/pointed weapon. The fact that such items are openly sold in mainland China does not necessarily mean that they may be brought into Hong Kong.

Please visit the website of the Hong Kong Department of Customs and Excise for specific information regarding Hong Kong customs requirements.

U.S. Customs officials encourage the use of an ATA (Admission Temporaire/Temporary Admission) Carnet for the temporary admission of professional equipment, commercial samples, and/or goods for exhibitions and fair purposes. For additional information, please visit the U.S. Council for International Business website, and the U.S. Customs and Border Patrol web page on Traveling with Samples.

You may bring dogs and cats into Hong Kong only with a special permit that was issued in advance. Dogs and cats imported from the United States may be exempted from quarantine when they have valid health and vaccination certificates and the pets have been in the United States for at least six months immediately preceding travel.

Dual Nationality: According to PRC nationality law, if you are of Chinese descent and were born in mainland China or Hong Kong, you are a PRC citizen. However, under the U.S.—PRC Consular Convention, all U.S. citizens entering Hong Kong on their U.S. passports are considered to be U.S. citizens by the Hong Kong SAR authorities for purposes of ensuring consular access and protection for the first 90 days you are in Hong Kong.

If you are a dual national who is or previously was a Hong Kong resident, and who wishes to ensure U.S. consular access and protection after your initial 90-day period of admission into Hong Kong, you must declare your U.S. nationality by presenting your U.S. passport to the Hong Kong Immigration Department and completing an application for declaration of change of nationality. A declaration of change of nationality will ensure U.S. consular protection, but it may also result in loss of your Chinese nationality (although not necessarily you're right of abode).

If you fail to declare your U.S. nationality, you may jeopardize your U.S. consular protection, but you will not jeopardize your U.S. citizenship. If you are a dual nation resident of Hong Kong and entered on your Hong Kong identity cards but desire U.S. consular protection, you will have to declare your U.S. nationality with the Hong Kong Immigration Department. Information on how to declare your citizenship to Hong Kong authorities may be found on the Hong Kong Immigration Department's website. If you are a dual national contemplating onward travel into mainland China, you should strongly consider which passport you will use to enter and exit China. Under the U.S.-PRC Consular Convention, the U.S. Embassy and consulates general in the PRC are not able to provide you with consular protection if you do not use your U.S. passport to enter or exit China.

Typhoons: During the storm season (July through September), the Hong Kong Observatory issues typhoon warnings an average of six times a year and heavy rainstorm alerts more frequently. The Hong Kong Observatory has a good notification and monitoring system. You may find general information about natural disaster preparedness at the U.S. Federal Emergency Management Agency (FEMA). Please be advised that if the Hong Kong Government announces a Typhoon Signal 8 or above or Black Rainstorm Warning, the Consulate General will close.

Accessibility: While in Hong Kong, individuals with disabilities may find accessibility and accommodation very different from what you find in the United States. Hong Kong law prohibits discrimination against persons with physical, sensory, intellectual, and mental disabilities in employment, education, access to health care, or the provision of other state services, and the government generally enforces these provisions in practice.

The law mandates access to buildings, information, and communications for persons with disabilities The Social Welfare Department is primarily responsible for coordinating and funding public assistance programs to persons with disabilities. The Hong Kong Tourism Board publishes "Accessible Hong Kong " a guide for visitors with disabilities and the Transport Department publishes A Guide to Public Transport for People with Disabilities. In addition, the Hong Kong government has created Cyberable, a barrier free portal website, to provide one-stop information for persons with different disabilities. Despite efforts to improve accessibility, Hong Kong continues to be challenging for those with physical disabilities. It has many stairs, inclines, and steep uneven walkways and is not designed for anyone who uses a walker, cane, or wheelchair.

Medical Facilities and Health Information: Good medical facilities are available, and there are many Western-trained physicians in Hong Kong. Prescription drugs are widely available, although they may have different names than those in the United States. Hong Kong emergency service response times for police, fire, and ambulances are good.

Air pollution is increasingly serious in Hong Kong. Congested vehicle traffic and mainland factories pump out ozone, sulfur, and nitrogen oxides, leading to a visible haze in the atmosphere on most days of the year. Average roadside pollution levels exceed WHO guidelines by 200% and continue to deteriorate, creating health risks for those with allergies, asthma, or cardiac problems.

Hong Kong remains at "Alert" response status for Pandemic Influenza. Further current information about Pandemic Influenza and other health-related concerns in Hong Kong are available on the Centre for Health Protection website.

You can find good information on vaccinations and other health precautions, on the CDC website. For information about outbreaks of infectious diseases abroad, consult the World Health Organization (WHO) website. The WHO website also contains additional health information for travelers, including detailed country-specific health information.

Medical Insurance: You can't assume your insurance will go with you when you travel. It's very important to find out BEFORE you leave whether or not your medical insurance will cover you overseas. You need to ask your insurance company two questions:

- Does my policy apply when I'm out of the United States?
- Will it cover emergencies like a trip to a foreign hospital or a medical evacuation?

In many places, doctors and hospitals still expect payment in cash at the time of service. Your regular U.S. health insurance may not cover doctors' and hospital visits in other countries. If your policy doesn't go with you when you travel, it's a very good idea to take out another one for your trip.

Traffic Safety and Road Conditions: While in Hong Kong, you may encounter road conditions that differ significantly from those in the United States. About 90 percent of the population in Hong Kong depends on public transport. Taxis, buses, and the mass transit railway (MTR) are readily available, inexpensive, and generally safe. The MTR, an underground railway network, is the most popular mode of public transport, carrying an average of 3.5 million passengers a day.

In Hong Kong, traffic moves on the left. During the daytime, traffic congests Hong Kong's urban areas. Each year there are about 14,000 traffic accidents in Hong Kong involving more than 18,000 drivers, passengers, and pedestrians. Speed limits are 50 kilometers per hour (kph) (approximately 31 miles per hour (mph)) in urban areas, 80 kph (approximately 50 mph) on highways and 110 kph (approximately 68 mph) on expressways unless otherwise marked. The use of seatbelts in vehicles, if so equipped, is mandatory both in the front and back seats. The maximum penalty for dangerous driving causing death can be a fine of $50,000 HK ($6,500 US), imprisonment for five years and disqualification from driving for not less than two years on first conviction. If you are a driver involved in a traffic accident, you will be required to undergo alcohol-level testing. If you are found to exceed the prescribed limit of blood alcohol, you may face prosecution under Hong Kong law. The use of hand-held cellular phones while driving in Hong Kong is strictly prohibited. If you breach this law, you may be subject to a maximum fine of $2,000 HK ($260 US). However, you can use "hands-free devices," such as headphones and speakerphones. Hong Kong law requires that all registered vehicles carry valid third-party liability insurance.

You may be issued a Hong Kong driver's license without a test if you hold a valid U.S. driver's license, provided you have resided in the United States for not less than six months. If you do not plan to stay in Hong Kong for more than 12 months you can drive in Hong Kong on your valid U.S. driver's license.

Aviation Safety Oversight: The U.S. Federal Aviation Administration (FAA) has assessed the government of Hong Kong's Civil Aviation Authority as being in compliance with International Civil Aviation Organization (ICAO) aviation safety standards for oversight of Hong Kong's air carrier operations. Further information may be found on the FAA's safety assessment page.

Children's Issues: Please see the U.S. Dept. of State Office of Children's Issues web pages on intercountry adoption and international parental child abduction.

Intercountry Adoption

January 2010

The information in this section has been edited from the latest report available as of February 2013 from the State Department Bureau of Consular Affairs, Office of Overseas Citizens Services. For more information, please read the *Intercountry Adoption* section of this book and review current reports online at http://adoption.state.gov.

China is party to the Hague Convention on Protection of Children and Co-operation in Respect of Intercountry Adoption (Hague Adoption Convention). Since Hong Kong Special Administrative Region is a territory of China, all adoptions between Hong Kong and the United States must meet the requirements of the Convention and U.S. law implementing the Convention. The Government of Hong Kong tends to prefer that prospective adoptive parents are ethnic Chinese. However, non-ethnic Chinese may also adopt if willing to consider an older child or a child with special needs.

Who Can Adopt? Adoption between the United States and Hong Kong is governed by the Hague Adoption Convention. Therefore to adopt from Hong Kong, you must first be found eligible to adopt by the U.S. Government. The U.S. Government agency responsible for making this determination is the Department of Homeland Security, U.S. Citizenship and Immigration Services (USCIS).

Residency Requirements: Prospective adoptive parents currently living in Hong Kong must be residents of Hong Kong or should offer assurance to the Adoption Unit that they will be living in Hong Kong for a minimum of 12 months. There are no residency requirements for prospective adoptive parents residing in the United States.

Age Requirements: Prospective adoptive parents must be at least 25 years of age. Prospective adoptive parents over the age of 45 will be considered if they are willing to accept older children or children with special needs.

Marriage Requirements: Both single individuals and married couples are eligible to adopt from Hong Kong. For single prospective adoptive parents, preference is given to single parents with special parental skills, such as nursing or social work skills. Some single parents have found their chances of being approved for adoption in Hong Kong increase if they agree to adopt a child with special needs. Single parents who already have a special needs child have a better chance of being matched with a special needs adoptee.

Income Requirements: Prospective adoptive parents will have to prove their income exceeds the Medium Monthly Domestic Household Income set by the Social Welfare Department. The Medium Monthly Domestic Household Income requires that after a family has paid all the necessary monthly expenditures (e.g., mortgage, loans, insurance, helper wages, tuition, etc.), a minimum level of funds are left over for incidental expenses. For instance, a family of three must show monthly funds of HK$18,700 and a family of four must show monthly funds of HK23,500. The Medium Monthly Domestic Household Income is not available publicly. The Social Welfare Department must be contacted directly for specifics. Couples residing outside of Hong Kong must submit their tax returns and complete a questionnaire detailing their financial assets.

Other Requirements: Prospective adoptive parents should be in good physical and mental health

Who Can be Adopted? Because Hong Kong has implemented the Hague Adoption Convention, children from Hong Kong must meet the requirements of the Convention in order to be eligible for adoption. For example, the Convention requires that Hong Kong attempt to place a child with a family in-country before determining that a child is eligible for intercountry adoption.

In addition to Hong Kong's requirements, a child must meet the definition of a Convention adoptee for you to bring him or her back to the United States. Learn more about the Convention's requirements for adoptable children.

Age Requirements: Children between the ages of six months and 18 years of age can be adopted. (Statistics reflect that most children available for adoption are five years old or younger and some have health problems or are disabled.)

The Process: Because Hong Kong is party to the Hague Adoption Convention, adopting from Hong Kong must follow a specific process designed to meet the Convention's requirements. For detailed and updated information on these requirements, please review the *Intercountry Adoption* section of this publication and visit the U.S. Department of State Intercountry Adoption website at http://adoption.state.gov.

Role of the Adoption Authority: The Director of the Social Welfare Department reviews the documentation to determine if the adoption is in the best interests of the child. Upon approval, the Social Welfare Department will file a court order to pass the care and control of the child to the Director of the U.S. adoption agency. (If the prospective adoptive parents are residents of Hong Kong, the child is released into their home for at least six months.) During the six months of living with the family, an adoption social worker makes periodic visits to determine if adoption by the prospective adoptive parents is in the best interest of the child.

Role of the Court: The District Court grants the adoption order and issues the final adoption certificate. For non-residents of Hong Kong, the finalization of the adoption passes the care and control of the child from the U.S. adoption agency to the adoptive parents.

Role of Adoption Agencies: The adoption agency arranges the prospective adoptive parents' home study. The adoption agency works with one of the agencies in Hong Kong that have been accredited to facilitate *Intercountry Adoption*s. The U.S. adoption agency forwards the home study report and supporting documents to the Hong Kong accredited body. The Hong Kong agency submits the documentation to the Social Welfare Department.

Adoption Application: The adoption application is filed with the Adoption Unit of the Social Welfare Department.

Time Frame: The average amount of time required to complete an *Intercountry Adoption* ranges from 12-24 months. The timeframe may be increased if the prospective adoptive parents have specific requests regarding the child's age and/or medical conditions.

Adoption Fees: The Social Welfare Department's Adoption Unit provides an assessment of the prospective adoptive parents' suitability to adopt at no charge. Adoptive parents based in Hong Kong are required to pay $2,840 HK for acting as guardian ad litem while the adoption proceedings are finalized. Prospective adoptive parents residing outside of Hong Kong are not required to pay this fee.

In the adoption services contract that you sign at the beginning of the adoption process, your agency will itemize the fees and estimated expenses related to your adoption process.

Documents Required: The following is a list of documents required to adopt a child from Hong Kong:

- Copy of U.S. passport;
- Copy of marriage certificate (if applicable);
- Evidence of termination of previous marriage (if applicable);
- Proof of income;
- Copies of school credentials;
- Evidence of prior adoptions (if any); and
- Satisfactory home study report and medical examination reports of the adopting parents. (These documents are not required by Hong Kong to be authenticated. The agencies in the U.S. engaging in adoptions submit notarized home study and physical exam reports in adoption cases.)

Bringing Your Child Home: Once your adoption is complete (or you have obtained legal custody of the child), there are a few more steps to take before you can head home. Specifically, you need to apply for several documents for your child before he or she can travel to the United States, such as a birth certificate, a passport or travel document for your child from the country in which he or she was born, and a U.S. Immigration Visa. For detailed and updated information on how to obtain these documents, review the *Intercountry Adoption* section in this publication and visit the U.S. Department of State Intercountry Adoption website at http://adoption.state.gov.

Child Citizenship Act: For adoptions finalized abroad, the Child Citizenship Act of 2000 allows your new child to acquire American citizenship automatically when he or she enters the United States as lawful permanent residents. For adoptions finalized in the United States, the Child Citizenship Act of 2000 allows your new child to acquire American citizenship automatically when the court in the United States issues the final adoption decree.

After Adoption: Hong Kong does not have any post-adoption requirements.

U.S. Consulate General Hong Kong and Macau
26 Garden Road
Central, Hong Kong
Mailing Address:
8000 Hong Kong Place
Washington, DC 20521-8000
Tel: (852) 2841-2211
Fax: (852) 2845-4845
http://hongkong.usconsulate.gov/visa_inquiries.html

Hong Kong's Adoption Authority
Social Welfare Department
Room 201, 2/F., North Point Goverment Offices
333 Java Road, North Point, Hong Kong
Tel: (852) 3595 1935
Fax: (852) 3595 0025
grau@swd.gov.hk
http://www.info.gov.hk/swd

Diplomatic Mission for Hong Kong
The Embassy of the People's Republic of China
2300 Connecticut Ave., N.W.
Washington, D.C. 20008
Tel: (202) 328-2500
Fax: (202) 588-0032
webmaster@china-embassy.org

Office of Children's Issues
U.S. Department of State
2201 C Street, NW
SA-29
Washington, DC 20520
Tel: 1-888-407-4747
AskCI@state.gov
http://adoption.state.gov

For questions about immigration procedures, call the National Customer Service Center (NCSC) at 1-800-375-5283 (TTY 1-800-767-1833).

International Parental Child Abduction

December 2012

The information in this section has been edited from a report of the State Department Bureau of Consular Affairs, Office of Overseas Citizens Services. For more information, please review current reports online at www.travel.state.gov/abduction.

Disclaimer: The information in this flyer is provided for general information only, is not intended to be legal advice, and may change without notice. Questions involving interpretation of law should be addressed to an attorney licensed to practice in the relevant jurisdiction.

General Information: The 1980 Hague Convention on the Civil Aspects of International Child Abduction (Hague Abduction Convention) has applied between the Hong Kong Special Administrative Region (SAR) and the United States since September 1, 1997.

Hague Abduction Convention: The U.S. Department of State serves as the U.S. Central Authority (USCA) for the Hague Abduction Convention. In this capacity, the Department's Bureau of Consular Affairs, Directorate for Overseas Citizens Services, Office of Children's Issues facilitates the submission of applications under the Hague Abduction Convention for the return of, or access to, children, including applications concerning the Hong Kong SAR. Parents are strongly encouraged to contact the Department of State for assistance prior to initiating the Hague process directly with the foreign Central Authority (FCA).

United States Department of State
Office of Children's Issues
2201 C Street, N.W.
Washington, DC 20520
Telephone: 1-888-407-4747
Outside the United States or Canada: 1-202-501-4444
Fax: 202-736-9132

The Hong Kong SAR Central Authority for the Hague Abduction Convention is the Secretary for Justice, International Law Division. The Hong Kong Central Authority reviews all incoming applications, files applications with the court, monitors the case from beginning to end, updates the requesting Central Authority on the progress of the case, and provides other assistance as appropriate, including involving law enforcement or social workers. The Central Authority does not represent a parent in the court proceedings. The Hong Kong Central Authority can be reached at:

Central Authority of Hong Kong
c/o International Law Division
Mutual Legal Assistance Unit
Department of Justice
47/F, High Block
Queensway Government Offices
66 Queensway, Hong Kong
Telephone Number: (852) 2867 2062
Fax Number: (852)2523 7959
or (852) 2877 9585
Email: childabduct@doj.gov.hk

To initiate a Hague case for return of, or access to, a child in Hong Kong, the left-behind parent or the Central Authority of the left-behind parent's country must submit a Hague application to the Hong Kong Central Authority. The USCA is available to answer questions about the Hague application process, to forward a completed application to the Hong Kong Central Authority, and to subsequently monitor its progress through the foreign administrative and legal processes.

There are not fees for filing Hague applications with either the United States or Hong Kong central authorities. Attorney fees in Hong Kong can vary depending upon an attorney's experience and reputation. Additional costs may include airplane tickets for court appearances and for the return of the child, if so ordered.

Return: A parent or legal guardian may file an application under the Hague Abduction Convention for return to the United States of a child abducted to, or wrongfully retained in Hong Kong. The U.S. Department of State can assist parents living in the United States to understand whether the Convention is an available civil remedy and can provide information on the process for submitting a Hague application.

Visitation/Access: A person may file an application under the Hague Abduction Convention for access to a child living in Hong Kong. The U.S. Department of State can assist parents living in the United States to understand country-specific criteria and provide information on the process for submitting a Hague application.

Retaining an Attorney: Retaining a private attorney is not required to submit Hague Convention applications to the Hong Kong Central Authority. However, parents may wish to hire a private attorney to follow up on the case, to provide direct information to the court, and to advise as to the best course of action for their individual circumstances. A parent may be able to retain a private attorney through legal aid if the parent satisfies the merit and means tests set by the Legal Aid Department. If a parent wishes to apply for legal aid, the Hong Kong Central Authority will provide that parent direct contact information for legal aid. Parents may represent themselves if they choose not to have a private attorney. The U.S. Consulate General in Hong Kong, posts list of attorneys including those who specialize in family law. This list is provided as a courtesy service only and does not constitute an endorsement of any individual attorney. The Department of State assumes no responsibility or liability for the professional ability or reputation of, or the quality of services provided by, the persons or firms included in this list. Professional credentials and areas of expertise are provided directly by the lawyers.

Mediation: The Hong Kong Central Authority strongly recommends that parents reach an amicable settlement for the voluntary return of the child through mediation. Mediation services are available through the Social Welfare Department or via accrediting bodies such as the Hong Kong Family Welfare Society, Integrated Family Services Centre, and International Social Services (Hong Kong Branch).

U.S. Consulate General Hong Kong
26 Garden Road
Hong Kong
Telephone: 852 2841 2211
or 852 2841 2323
Fax: 852 2845 4845
Email: acshk@state.gov

Hong Kong is a Special Administrative Region of the People's Republic of China.

Embassy of the People's Republic of China
3505 International Place, N.W.
Washington, D.C. 20008 U.S.A.
Tel: +1-202-495-2266
Fax: +1-202-495-2138
Email:
chinaembpress_us@mfa.gov.cn

HUNGARY

Compiled from publications that were available as of February 2013 from the U.S. Department of State, the U.S. Department of Commerce, and the Central Intelligence Agency (CIA). See the introduction to this set for explanatory notes.

Official Name:
Republic of Hungary

PROFILE

Geography

Area: total: 93,028 sq km; country comparison to the world: 110; land: 89,608 sq km; water: 3,420 sq km

Major cities: Budapest (capital) 1.705 million (2009)

Climate: temperate; cold, cloudy, humid winters; warm summers

Terrain: mostly flat to rolling plains; hills and low mountains on the Slovakian border

People

Nationality: noun: Hungarian(s); adjective: Hungarian

Population: 9,958,453 (July 2012 est.)

Population growth rate: -0.184% (2012 est.)

Ethnic groups: Hungarian 92.3%, Roma 1.9%, other or unknown 5.8% (2001 census)

Religions: Roman Catholic 51.9%, Calvinist 15.9%, Lutheran 3%, Greek Catholic 2.6%, other Christian 1%, other or unspecified 11.1%, unaffiliated 14.5% (2001 census)

Languages: Hungarian 93.6%, other or unspecified 6.4% (2001 census)

Literacy: definition: age 15 and over can read and write; total population: 99%; male: 99.2%; female: 98.9% (2010 est.)

Health: life expectancy at birth: total population: 75.02 years; male: 71.27 years; female: 78.98 years (2012 est.); Infant mortality rate: total: 5.24 deaths/1,000 live births; male: 5.5 deaths/1,000 live births; female: 4.96 deaths/1,000 live births (2012 est.)

Unemployment rate: 11.2% (2012 est.)

Work force: 4.178 million (2012)

Government

Type: parliamentary democracy

Independence: 16 November 1918

Constitution: 25 April 2011, effective 1 January 2012

Political subdivisions: 19 counties (megyek, singular—megye), 23 urban counties (singular—megyei varos), and 1 capital city (fovaros)

Suffrage: 18 years of age; universal

Economy

GDP (purchasing power parity): $196.8 billion (2012 est.); $198.1 billion (2011 est.); $194.8 billion (2010 est.); $192.4 billion (2009 est.)

GDP real growth rate: -1% (2012 est.); 1.7% (2011 est.); 1.3% (2010 est.); -6.8% (2009 est.)

GDP per capita (PPP): $19,800 (2012 est.); $19,800 (2011 est.); $19,500 (2010 est.); $19,200 (2009 est.)

Natural resources: bauxite, coal, natural gas, fertile soils, arable land

Agriculture products: wheat, corn, sunflower seed, potatoes, sugar beets; pigs, cattle, poultry, dairy products

Industries: mining, metallurgy, construction materials, processed foods, textiles, chemicals (especially pharmaceuticals), motor vehicles

Exports: $105.1 billion (2012 est.); $103.1 billion (2011 est.); $91.45 billion (2010 est.)

Exports—commodities: machinery and equipment 55.3%, other manufactures 30.6%, food products 7.4%, raw materials 3.2%, fuels and electricity 3.3% (2009 est.)

Exports—partners: Germany 25.1%, Romania 5.7%, Austria 5.4%, Slovakia 5.4%, Italy 5%, France 4.8%, UK 4.6% (2010 est.)

Imports: $100.8 billion (2012 est.); $93.9 billion (2011 est.); $87.15 billion (2010 est.)

Imports—commodities: machinery and equipment 44.7%, other manufactures 41.3%, fuels and electricity 5.1%, food products, raw materials 6.7%

Imports—partners: Germany 24.7%, Russia 8.6%, China 8.4%, Austria 6.2%, Slovakia 4.9%, Poland 4.7%, Netherlands 4.4%, Italy 4.3% (2010 est.)

Debt—external: $170 billion (31 December 2012 est.); $184.5 billion (31 December 2011 est.); $178.9 billion (31 December 2010 est.)
Exchange rates: forints (HUF) per US dollar; 229.5 (2012 est.); 201.06 (2011 est.); 207.94 (2010 est.); 202.34 (2009); 171.8 (2008); 183.83 (2007)

PEOPLE

National/Racial/Ethnic Minorities

Ethnic groups in Hungary include Magyar (nearly 90%), Romany, German, Serb, Slovak, and others.

The Romani community remained the largest ethnic minority. According to the Central Statistics Office, in 2007 the Romani community accounted for 2 percent of the population, or approximately 200,000 persons. However, unofficial estimates varied widely and suggested the actual figure was much higher, ranging between 500,000 and 800,000 persons. Human rights NGOs reported that Roma were discriminated against in almost all fields of life, particularly in employment, education, housing, penal institutions, and access to public places, such as restaurants and bars.

Language

Hungarian is the most widely used language. English is regularly used for business in Hungary, especially among multinational firms. German is the second most common foreign language.

Religion

Data on religious affiliation is regarded as sensitive information and may not be officially recorded. However, the 2001 national census, the latest survey available, included an optional question on religious affiliation, to which 90 percent of the population responded. According to the replies, the population is 55 percent Roman Catholic, 15 percent Hungarian Reformed Church (Presbyterian), 3 percent Lutheran, and less than 1 percent Jewish. These four groups are considered the country's "historic" religions. Groups that constitute less than 5 percent of the population include Greek Catholics, the Congregation of Faith, five Orthodox Christian religious groups, a broad range of other Christian denominations, seven Buddhist groups, and three Muslim communities. Data protection regulations impeded the collection of official statistics on participation in religious life. The government held another national census during the year, but the results were not yet available.

HISTORY

Hungary has long been an integral part of Europe. It converted to Western Christianity before AD 1000. Although Hungary was a monarchy for nearly 1,000 years, its constitutional system preceded by several centuries the establishment of Western-style governments in other European countries.

Following the defeat of the Austro-Hungarian Dual Monarchy (1867–1918) at the end of World War I, Hungary lost two-thirds of its territory and one-third of its population. It experienced a brief but bloody communist dictatorship and counterrevolution in 1919, followed by a 25-year regency under Admiral Miklos Horthy. Although Hungary fought in most of World War II as a German ally, it fell under German military occupation on March 19, 1944 following an unsuccessful attempt to switch sides. Under Nazi occupation, the Hungarian Government executed or deported and seized the property of hundreds of thousands of its minority citizens, mostly members of the Jewish community. On January 20, 1945, a provisional government concluded an armistice with the Soviet Union and established the Allied Control Commission, under which Soviet, American, and British representatives held complete sovereignty over the country. The Commission's chairman was a member of Stalin's inner circle and exercised absolute control.

Communist Takeover

The provisional government, dominated by the Hungarian Communist Party (MKP), was replaced in November 1945 after elections which gave majority control of a coalition government to the Independent Smallholders' Party. The government instituted a radical land reform and gradually nationalized mines, electric plants, heavy industries, and some large banks. The communists ultimately undermined the coalition regime by discrediting leaders of rival parties and through terror, blackmail, and show trials. In elections tainted by fraud in 1947, the leftist bloc gained control of the government.

By February 1949, all opposition parties had been forced to merge with the MKP to form the Hungarian Workers' Party. In 1949, the communists held a single-list election and adopted a Soviet-style constitution, which created the Hungarian People's Republic. Between 1948 and 1953, the Hungarian economy was reorganized according to the Soviet model. In 1949, the country joined the Council for Mutual Economic Assistance (CMEA, or Comecon.) All private industrial firms with more than 10 employees were nationalized. Freedom of the press, religion, and assembly were strictly curtailed. The head of the Roman Catholic Church, Cardinal Jozsef Mindszenty, was sentenced to life imprisonment.

Forced industrialization and land collectivization soon led to serious economic difficulties, which reached crisis proportions by mid-1953. Imre Nagy replaced Rakosi as prime minister in 1953 and repudiated much of Rakosi's economic program of forced collectivization and heavy industry. He also ended political purges and freed thousands of political prisoners. However, the economic situation continued to deteriorate, and Rakosi succeeded in disrupting the reforms and in forcing Nagy from power in 1955 for "right-wing revisionism." Hungary joined the Soviet-led Warsaw Pact Treaty Organization the same year.

1956 Revolution

Pressure for change reached a climax on October 23, 1956, when security forces fired on Budapest students marching in support of Poland's confrontation with the Soviet Union. The ensuing battle quickly grew into a massive popular uprising. Fighting did not abate until the Central Committee named Imre Nagy as prime minister on October 25. Nagy dissolved the state security police, abolished the one-party system, promised free elections, and negotiated with the U.S.S.R. to withdraw its troops.

Faced with reports of new Soviet troops pouring into Hungary, despite Soviet Ambassador Andropov's assurances to the contrary, on November 1 Nagy announced Hungary's neutrality and withdrawal from the Warsaw Pact. In response, the Soviet Union launched a massive military attack on Hungary on November 3. Some 200,000 Hungarians fled to the West. Nagy and his colleagues took refuge in the Yugoslav Embassy. Party First Secretary Janos Kadar defected from the Nagy cabinet, fleeing to the Soviet Union. On November 4 he announced the formation of a new government. He returned to Budapest and, with Soviet support, carried out severe reprisals; thousands of people were executed or imprisoned. Despite a guarantee of safe conduct, Nagy was arrested and deported to Romania. In June 1958, Nagy was returned to Hungary, and, following a secret trial, was executed by the communist government.

Reform Under Kadar

In the early 1960s, Kadar announced a new policy under the motto of "He Who is Not Against Us is With Us," and introduced a relatively liberal cultural and economic course aimed at overcoming the post-1956 hostility toward him and his regime. In 1966, the Central Committee approved the "New Economic Mechanism," through which it sought to overcome the inefficiencies of central planning, increase productivity, make Hungary more competitive in world markets, and create prosperity to ensure political stability.

By the early 1980s, it had achieved some lasting economic reforms and limited political liberalization and pursued a foreign policy which encouraged more trade with the West. Nevertheless, the New Economic Mechanism led to mounting foreign debt incurred to shore up unprofitable industries.

Transition to Democracy

Hungary's transition to a Western-style parliamentary democracy was the first and the smoothest among the former Soviet bloc. By 1987, activists within the party and bureaucracy and Budapest-based intellectuals were increasingly pressing for change. Young liberals formed the Federation of Young Democrats (Fidesz); a core from the so-called Democratic Opposition formed the Association of Free Democrats (SZDSZ), and the neo-populist national opposition established the Hungarian Democratic Forum (MDF). Civic activism intensified to a level not seen since the 1956 revolution.

In 1988, Kadar was replaced as General Secretary of the MSZMP (the Communist Party), and that same year, the Parliament adopted a "democracy package," which included trade union pluralism; freedom of association, assembly, and the press; a new electoral law; and a radical revision of the constitution, among others. The Soviet Union reduced its involvement by signing an agreement in April 1989 to withdraw Soviet forces by June 1991.

National unity culminated in June 1989 as the country reburied Imre Nagy, his associates, and, symbolically, all other victims of the 1956 revolution. A national roundtable, comprising representatives of the new parties and some recreated old parties—such as the Smallholders and Social Democrats—the Communist Party, and different social groups, met in the late summer of 1989 to discuss major changes to the Hungarian constitution in preparation for free elections and the transition to a fully free and democratic political system.

Free Elections and a Democratic Hungary

The first free parliamentary election, held in March-April 1990, was a plebiscite of sorts on the communist past with the Democratic Forum (MDF) winning 43% of the vote and the Free Democrats (SZDSZ) capturing 24%. Under Prime Minister Jozsef Antall, the MDF formed a center-right coalition government with the Independent Smallholders' Party (FKGP) and the Christian Democratic People's Party (KDNP) to command a 60% majority in the Parliament. Parliamentary opposition parties included SZDSZ, the Socialists (MSZP—successors to the Communist Party), and the Alliance of Young Democrats (Fidesz). Peter Boross succeeded as Prime Minister after Antall died and the Antall/Boross coalition governments achieved a reasonably well-functioning parliamentary democracy and laid the foundation for a free market economy.

In May 1994, the Socialists came back to win a plurality of votes and 54% of the seats after an election campaign focused largely on economic issues and the substantial decline in living standards since 1990. A heavy turnout of voters swept away the right-of-center coalition but soundly rejected extremists on both right and left. The MSZP continued economic reforms and privatization, adopting a painful, but necessary, policy of fiscal austerity (the "Bokros plan") in 1995. However, dissatisfaction with the pace of economic recovery, rising crime, and cases of government corruption convinced voters to propel center-right parties into power following national elections in May 1998. Fidesz captured a plurality of parliamentary seats and forged a coalition with the Smallholders and the Democratic Forum.

The new government, headed by 35-year-old Prime Minister Viktor Orban, promised to stimulate faster growth, curb inflation, and lower taxes. Although the Orban administration also pledged continuity in foreign policy, and continued to pursue Euro-Atlantic integration as its first priority, it was a more vocal advocate of minority rights for ethnic Hungarians abroad than the previous government. During Orban's tenure, Hungary acceded to NATO on March 12, 1999.

In April 2002, the country voted to return the MSZP-Free Democrat coalition to power with Peter Medgyessy as Prime Minister. The Medgyessy government placed special emphasis on solidifying Hungary's Euro-Atlantic course, which culminated in Hungary's accession to the European Union on May 1, 2004. Prime Minister Medgyessy resigned in August 2004 after losing coalition support following an attempted cabinet reshuffle. Ferenc Gyurcsany succeeded Medgyessy as Prime Minister in September 29, 2004.

In the April 2006 election, Prime Minister Ferenc Gyurcsany and his Socialist-liberal coalition were re-elected, the first time since communism that a sitting government renewed its mandate. The SZDSZ pulled out of the coalition in April 2008, leaving the MSZP to govern alone.

The global economic crisis spilled over into Hungary in autumn 2008, and severely impacted the country. Prime Minister Gyurcsany resigned in March 2009 and was succeeded by a technocratic crisis management government led by Gordon Bajnai, the former Minister of Economy and National Development.

Parliamentary elections in April 2010 brought a Fidesz-KDNP coalition back to power with a two-thirds majority (262 seats). Viktor Orban became Prime Minister. Joining the MSZP in opposition were the newly elected far-right Jobbik party and the Green party, Politics Can Be Different (LMP). Today, Fidesz-KDNP has 263 seats. In the opposition, MSZP has 48 seats, Jobbik 46, and LMP 15; 10 Members of Parliament (MPs) have left MSZP to create a new party, the Democratic Coalition. There are four independent MPs.

The Fidesz-dominated Parliament quickly launched an ambitious legislative agenda that has promised to reduce the overall number of seats in Parliament to 199 effective for the next election in 2014, cut by half the number of local representatives, and extended citizenship and voting rights to ethnic Hungarians living beyond the country's present borders. In April 2011, Parliament adopted the country's new constitution, which entered into effect January 1, 2012. Among other changes, the document makes reference to the role of Christianity in "preserving the nation" and sets the term of local government members at 5 years. Additionally, it mandated a process requiring the passage of several dozen so-called cardinal laws on issues such as religion, the media, the restructuring of the judiciary, elections, and the central bank. The majority of these laws were passed in 2011, and their future modification would require a two-thirds majority in Parliament.

GOVERNMENT AND POLITICAL CONDITIONS

Hungary is a multiparty parliamentary democracy. Legislative authority is vested in the unicameral National Assembly (parliament). The parliament elects the president (the head of state) every five years. The president appoints a prime minister from the majority party or coalition following a two-round national election every four years. The last parliamentary elections in April 2010 were assessed as free and fair. The conservative Fidesz-Christian Democrat (KDNP) coalition won a two-thirds majority. Fidesz's prime ministerial candidate, Viktor Orban, took office in May 2010.

Recent Elections

The OSCE election observation mission reported that two-round parliamentary elections held in April 2010 were conducted in a manner consistent with international standards and commitments for democratic elections. The elections brought a Fidesz-KDNP coalition back to power with a two-thirds majority.

Participation of Women and Minorities: The 386-seat parliament elected in April 2010 included 34 women, 20 percent fewer than its predecessor. There were no women in Prime Minister Orban's eight-member cabinet until December 23, when Zsuzsanna Nemeth took the office as the new minister of national development. Women were represented at the subcabinet level. There was one woman on the Constitutional Court elected by parliament on June 6. Due to privacy laws regarding ethnic data, no statistics were available on the number of minorities in the parliament, cabinet, or Constitutional Court.

Principal Government Officials

Last Updated: 1/31/2013

Pres.: **Janos ADER**
Prime Min.: **Viktor ORBAN**
Dep. Prime Min.: **Tibor NAVRACSICS**
Dep. Prime Min.: **Zsolt SEMJEN**
Min. of Defense: **Csaba HENDE**
Min. of National Economy: **Gyorgy MATOLCSY**
Min. of Foreign Affairs: **Janos MARTONYI**
Min. of Interior: **Sandor PINTER**
Min. of National Development: **Zsuzsanna NEMETH**
Min. of National Resources: **Miklos RETHELYI**
Min. of Public Admin. & Justice: **Tibor NAVRACSICS**
Min. of Rural Development: **Sandor FAZEKAS**
Min. Without Portfolio: **Mihaly VARGA**
Governor, National Bank of Hungary: **Andras SIMOR**
Ambassador to the US: **Gyorgy SZAPARY**
Permanent Representative to the UN, New York: **Csaba KOROSI**

ECONOMY

Hungary has made the transition from a centrally planned to a market economy, with a per capita income nearly two-thirds that of the EU-27 average. The private sector accounts for more than 80% of GDP. Foreign ownership of and investment in Hungarian firms are widespread, with cumulative foreign direct investment worth more than $70 billion.

In late 2008, Hungary's impending inability to service its short-term debt - brought on by the global financial crisis—led Budapest to obtain an IMF/EU/World Bank-arranged financial assistance package worth over $25 billion. The global economic downturn, declining exports, and low domestic consumption and fixed asset accumulation, dampened by government austerity measures, resulted in an economic contraction of 6.8% in 2009.

In 2010 the new government implemented a number of changes including cutting business and personal income taxes, but imposed "crisis taxes" on financial institutions, energy and telecom companies, and retailers. The IMF/EU bail-out program lapsed at the end of the year and was replaced by Post Program Monitoring and Article IV Consultations on overall economic and fiscal processes. The economy began to recover in 2010 with a big boost from exports, especially to Germany, and achieved growth of approximately 1.7% in 2011.

At the end of 2011 the government turned to the IMF and the EU to obtain financial backstop to support its efforts to refinance foreign currency debt and bond obligations in 2012 and beyond, but Budpest's rejection of EU and IMF economic policy recommendations led to a breakdown in talks with the lenders in late 2012. Since joining the EU in 2004, Hungary has been subject to the European Commisssion's Excessive Deficit Procedure; Brussels has requested that the government outline measures to sustainably reduce the budget deficit to under 3% of GDP. Ongoing economic weakness in Western Europe caused a GDP to fall 1% in 2012. Unemployment remained high, at more than 11%.

Labor Conditions

The law prohibits children younger than 16 from working. Children between the ages of 16 and 18 may work under certain circumstances as temporary workers during school vacations. Children may not work night shifts or overtime or perform hard physical labor. The government effectively enforced child labor laws.

The national minimum monthly wage was 78,500 forints ($325). A special minimum monthly wage for jobs requiring the completion of secondary education was 94,000 forints ($389).

The law sets the official workday at eight hours, although it may vary depending on the industry. A 48-hour rest period is required during any seven-day period. The regular work-week is 40 hours with premium pay for overtime and two days of rest. The law prohibits overtime exceeding 200 hours per year and provides for paid annual national holidays. The government set occupational safety and health standards. Labor laws also apply to foreign workers with work permits.

U.S.-HUNGARIAN RELATIONS

Hungary is a member of the European Union (EU), and as a NATO Ally, it partners with the United States on our common goals in Europe, such as stability in the Balkans and promoting democracy in Europe's East, as well as on global challenges beyond Europe. The United States and Hungary have a mutual commitment to reducing the threats posed by climate change and nuclear proliferation, and supporting human rights, the rule of law, and peace and freedom for all. The two countries are bound together through myriad people-to-people contacts in business, the arts, scholarship, and a host of other exchanges.

In 1921, the United States established diplomatic relations with Hungary following its establishment of independence. During World War II, Hungary severed relations with the United States and declared war on it in 1941. Relations were reestablished in 1945. Following the war, Hungary became a satellite of the Soviet Union. As Hungary began to pull away from the Soviet orbit in the 1980s, the United States offered assistance and expertise to substantially revise its constitution, establish a democratic political system, and introduce a plan for a free market economy. Hungary acceded to the North Atlantic Treaty Organization (NATO) in 1999 and the European Union in 2004. The United States works with Hungary as a valued partner in the transatlantic relationship. Hungary has been a firm ally in coalition operations, contributing troops to NATO missions in Afghanistan and the Balkans.

U.S. Assistance to Hungary

U.S. security assistance to Hungary contributes to regional stability and helps maintain strong support in Hungary for coalition operations, including for the provision of personnel, equipment, and other resources for these operations. Funding will promote the continued development of a flexible, sustainable, and NATO-interoperable Hungarian military capable of meeting NATO commitments. Earlier assistance to promote the development of democratic institutions and a market economy was phased out as Hungary achieved its EU status.

Bilateral Economic Relations

Hungary is a member of the European Union and has transitioned from a centrally planned economy to a market-based one since the fall of communism in 1989. The United States is among the top foreign investors in the country. Hungary's strategic location in Europe, access to EU markets, highly skilled and educated workforce, and sound infrastructure have led U.S. companies to locate facilities there, both in manufacturing and services. U.S. investment has had a direct, positive impact on the Hungarian economy. The two countries have a treaty on double taxation currently pending ratification.

Hungary's Membership in International Organizations

Hungary and the United States belong to a number of the same international organizations, including the United Nations, North Atlantic Treaty Organization, Euro-Atlantic Partnership Council, Organization for Security and Cooperation in Europe, Organization for Economic Cooperation and Development, International Monetary Fund, World Bank, and World Trade Organization. Hungary also is an observer to the Organization of American States.

Bilateral Representation

The Hungarian Embassy is located at 3910 Spring of Freedom St. NW, Washington, DC 20008 (tel. 202-362-6730). Hungary has consulates in New York City and Los Angeles.

Principal U.S. Embassy Officials

Last Updated: 1/14/2013

BUDAPEST (E) 1054 Budapest Szabadsag Ter 12 Hungary, +36-1/475-4400, Fax +36-1/475-4520, Workweek: Mon–Fri; 8:00AM–5:00PM, Website: http://www.usembassy.hu/

DCM OMS:	Wojtasiewicz, Renata
AMB OMS:	Sheila Jefferson
FCS:	Robert Peaslee
FM:	Therman Campbell
HRO:	Anna Kosinska
MGT:	Eric Kettner
MLO/ODC:	COL Curtis Milam
POL/ECON:	Robert J. Riley
POSHO:	Therman Campbell
SDO/DATT:	COL Mark Karas
AMB:	Eleni Tsakopoulos Kounalakis
CON:	Meghan Moore
DCM:	Timothy Betts
PAO:	Karyn Posner-Mullen
GSO:	Anne Baker
RSO:	James Gayhart
AGR:	Paul Spencer
AID:	Monica Smith
CLO:	Heather Davenport
EEO:	Joe Klinger, Anna Kosinska
EST:	Mark Canning
FMO:	Jeffrey Perkinson
ICASS Chair:	Gregory Shaffer
IMO:	Paul Echaniz
IPO:	Ted Cross
ISO:	Brian Jetter
ISSO:	Ted Cross
LEGATT:	Gregory Shaffer
State ICASS:	Brad Hurst

TRAVEL

Consular Information Sheet

July 25, 2012

Country Description: Hungary is a stable democracy with a market economy. Tourist facilities outside Budapest are widely available, but may not be as developed as those found in Western Europe. Hungarian is the official language; English is not widely used.

Smart Traveler Enrollment Program (STEP)/Embassy Location: If you are going to live in or visit Hungary, please take the time to sign up for the Smart Traveler Enrollment Program. If you enroll, we can keep you up to date with important safety and security announcements, and help your friends and family get in touch with you in case of an emergency.

The U.S. Embassy in Budapest
Szabadság tér 12
H-1054 Budapest
Telephone: (36)(1) 475-4400
After-hours emergency calls—for U.S. citizens only: (36)(1) 475-4703/4924
The Consular Section's fax is (36)(1) 475-4188 or (36)(1) 475-4113

Entry/Exit Requirements for U.S. Citizens: Hungary is a party to the Schengen Agreement. This means that U.S. citizens may enter Hungary for up to 90 days for tourist or business purposes without a visa. Your passport should be valid for at least three months beyond your period of stay. You need sufficient funds and a return airline ticket. If you want to visit Hungary for any reason other than business or tourism, or if you want to get a residence or work permit, please contact the Embassy of the Republic of Hungary at 3910 Shoemaker Street N.W., Washington, D.C. 20008, telephone (202) 362-6730. More information can be found on the Hungarian Embassy's website, or at the Hungarian Consulates in Los Angeles and New York.

The U.S. Department of State is unaware of any HIV/AIDS entry restrictions for visitors to or foreign residents of Hungary.

Threats to Safety and Security: Although Hungary is generally a safe place to visit, you should use caution and stay alert. Be especially careful in train stations and crowded tourist areas. In addition, you should avoid demonstrations and political rallies. In recent years a few demonstrations have turned violent, and authorities have used riot police and water cannons to control crowds.

In recent years, right-wing radical groups have gained popularity in Hungary due to their nationalist messages, which include intolerance towards Jews, Roma, and homosexuals. Although these groups are not explicitly anti-U.S., you should avoid public demonstrations and confrontations with their members.

Be alert and aware of your surroundings, and pay attention to what the local news media have to say. In general, larger public demonstrations are announced on the Demonstration Notices pagewithin the U.S. Embassy Budapest website.

Stay up to date by:

- Bookmarking our Bureau of Consular Affairs website, which contains the current Travel Warnings and Travel Alerts as well as the Worldwide Caution;
- Following us on Twitter and the Bureau of Consular Affairs page on Facebook;
- Downloading our free Smart Traveler iPhone App to have travel information at your fingertips;
- Calling 1-888-407-4747 toll-free within the U.S. and Canada, or a regular toll line, 1-202-501-4444, from other countries; and
- Taking some time before travel to consider your personal security.

Crime: Crime in Budapest is a concern. Be careful during your visit, and exercise the same caution you would in any big city or tourist area at home. Do not walk alone at night; keep your belongings secure at all times. Passports, cash, and credit cards are favorite targets of thieves.

Keep items that you do not store in your hotel safe or residence in a safe place, but be aware that pockets, purses, and backpacks are especially vulnerable, even if they close with a zipper. We recommend you use a travel money belt that keeps your cash and passport under your outer clothing and well out of view. Be sure to secure these items when you get back to your hotel or residence.

If you drive, be careful at gas stations and rest areas, or while fixing flat tires or other mechanical problems, especially at night. One scam involves someone who attracts your attention by claiming there is something wrong with your car to get you to pull over and then robs you. Do not leave your luggage and valuables unattended inside any vehicle.

Another common scam involves young women asking foreign men to buy them drinks. When the bill arrives the drinks cost hundreds of dollars each. You should avoid bars and restaurants suggested by cab drivers or people on the street. Every bar and restaurant should provide a menu with prices on it. Look at the prices before you order anything, including drinks. The Embassy maintains a list of bars and restaurants that are known to engage in this scam.

Don't buy counterfeit and pirated goods, even if they are widely available. Not only are the bootlegs illegal to bring back into the United States, but you may also be breaking local law.

Victims of Crime: If you or someone you know becomes the victim of a crime abroad, you should contact the local police and the nearest U.S. embassy or consulate. We can:

- Replace a stolen passport;
- Help you find appropriate medical care if you are the victim of a violent crime such as assault or rape;
- Put you in contact with the appropriate police authorities, and if necessary, contact family members or friends; and
- Help you understand the local criminal justice process and direct you to local attorneys, although it is important to remember that local authorities are responsible for investigating and prosecuting the crime.

The local equivalent to the "911" emergency line in Hungary is 112. Operators can speak English.

Criminal Penalties: While you are traveling in Hungary, you are subject to its laws even if you are a U.S. citizen. Foreign laws and legal systems can be vastly different than our own. Criminal penalties vary from country to country. There are also some things that might be legal in the country you visit, but still illegal in the United States; for instance, you can be prosecuted under U.S. law if you buy pirated goods.

Engaging in sexual conduct with children or using or disseminating child pornography in a foreign country is a crime prosecutable in the United States. If you break local laws in Hungary, your U.S. passport won't help you avoid arrest or prosecution. It's very important to know what's legal and what's not, wherever you may be going.

You should carry your passport with you at all times when you are in Hungary. Hungarian law requires all visitors to carry their passports; a photocopy is not a valid substitute. You could be arrested or fined if you do not have your passport with you. Since expert pickpockets frequent tourist areas and train stations, it is a good idea to keep your passport in a safe place. Hungary has a "zero tolerance" policy on drinking and driving. You should not drive after drinking, regardless of the amount of alcohol you have had.

Based on the Vienna Convention on Consular Relations, bilateral agreements with certain countries, and customary international law, if you are arrested in Hungary, you have the option to request that the police, prison officials, or other authorities alert the U.S. Embassy of your arrest, and to have communications from you forwarded to the U.S. Embassy.

Special Circumstances: Traveler's checks are not universally accepted in Hungary. ATMs are prevalent in all major cities and are increasingly common in rural areas. Western Union is the most prevalent international money transfer company and has hundreds of locations throughout Hungary. Hungary's custom authorities may enforce strict regulations concerning temporary importation into or export from Hungary of firearms, antiquities, prescription medications, and other items. You should contact the Hungarian Embassy in Washington or one of Hungary's consulates in either New York of Los Angeles for specific information regarding customs.

Accessibility: Accessibility and accommodation for individuals with disabilities are quite different in Hungary than in the United States. Although Hungarian law requires all government buildings to be accessible to persons with disabilities, these regulations have only been in force during the last decade and many older buildings and areas are still not accessible. The accessibility of private buildings, restaurants, and hotels varies widely.

Getting around Hungarian cities and towns may be difficult since many sidewalks are narrow and uneven. Small towns may lack sidewalks altogether. Buses, trams, subways, and railroads provide reliable transportation in cities and throughout the country, but most stations lack the most basic facilities and equipment for disabled access. Although there are plans to upgrade municipal bus fleets, currently buses and trams are not equipped with lifts for travelers with disabilities. Taxis are a good means of transportation.

Medical Facilities and Health Information: Medical treatment in Hungary is adequate, but hospital facilities are not always comparable to what you may find in the United States. Doctors are generally well trained, but there is a lack of adequate emergency services. Some doctors speak English. The Embassy maintains a website with more details about specific medical care providers.

Good information on vaccinations and other health precautions can be found via the Centers for Disease Control and Prevention(CDC) website. For information about outbreaks of infectious diseases abroad, consult the World Health Organization (WHO) website, which also contains additional health information for travelers, including detailed country-specific health information.

Medical Insurance: You can't assume your insurance will go with you when you travel. It's very important to find out BEFORE you leave whether or not your medical insurance will cover you overseas. You need to ask your insurance company two questions:

- Does my policy apply when I'm outside of the U.S.?
- Will it cover emergencies like a trip to a foreign hospital or an evacuation?

In Hungary, doctors and hospitals expect payment in cash at the time of service and usually cannot bill your insurer directly, even if you are covered overseas. This means you may have to pay bills from your own funds and claim reimbursement from your insurer later. Your regular U.S. health insurance may not cover doctor and hospital visits abroad. If your policy isn't valid when you travel, it is a good idea to get another policy for your trip.

Traffic Safety and Road Conditions: While in Hungary, U.S. citizens may encounter road conditions that differ significantly from those in the United States. In Hungary, there are approximately 1,200 fatal traffic accidents per year, and about 7,000 traffic accidents per year resulting in serious injuries. Roadside assistance, including medical and other services, is generally available. English is usually spoken at the emergency numbers listed below. In case English is not spoken, dial 112.

Ambulance: 104 or 350-0388
Police: 107
Fire: 105
24-hour English speaker: 112

Hungarian motorways and highways are generally in good condition. Urban road maintenance is also good, although areas under construction are not always adequately marked or blockaded. In Budapest, many roads are often under construction. Outside the city, roads are often narrow, poorly lighted, and can be in a poor state of repair in some areas. Pedestrians, tractors, and farm animals often use these small rural roads, so stay alert. Additional information on road conditions is available from "Útinform" at (36)(1)336-2400.

Hungary has zero tolerance for driving under the influence of alcohol. Police often conduct routine roadside checks where breath-analysis tests are administered. If you are caught driving after drinking, you will face jail and fines. Penalties for a car accident involving injury or death are one to five years in prison. Police stop vehicles regularly to check documents. It is against the law to use a hand-held cell phone while driving anywhere in Hungary.

You can drive in Hungary with a valid U.S. driver's license for one year as long as you have a certified Hungarian translation of the license attached to it. Hungary also recognizes international driver's permits (IDP) issued by the American Automobile Association (AAA) and the American Automobile Touring Alliance, when used along with a valid state driver's license. If you have an IDP, you do not need to have the license translated, but must carry the IDP and state driver's license together. After one year in Hungary, U.S. citizens must obtain a Hungarian driver's license. For further information on this procedure visit the U.S. Embassy's website.

The speed limit for cars and motorcycles on the motorway is 130 km per hour (approximately 80 mph); on highways, it is 110 km per hour (approximately 65 mph); and in towns and villages it is 50 km per hour (approximately 30 mph). Many drivers do not observe the speed limits, and you should be extra careful on two-way roads where local drivers pass each other frequently and allow for less space than you may be used to. Car seats are required for infants. Children under age 12 may not sit in the front seat. Seats belts are mandatory for everyone in the car. You may not turn right on a red light.

The police issue tickets for traffic violations and charge fines on the spot. The police will give you a postal check (money order) on which the amount of the fine to be paid is written, and this postal check may be presented and paid at any Hungarian post office. Sometimes in disputes about fines or the offense, the police will confiscate your passport and issue a receipt for the passport with an "invitation letter" to appear at the police station the next day or day after to resolve the dispute. Your passport is returned after resolution and/or the payment of the fine.

As in most European countries, you must pay to use Hungary's motorways. Payments must be made either at a gas station or online.

For specific information about Hungarian driver's permits, vehicle inspection, road taxes, and mandatory insurance, visit the Hungarian National Tourist Organization Office in New York website.

The U.S. Federal Aviation Administration (FAA) has assessed the government of Hungary's Civil Aviation Authority as being in compliance with International Civil Aviation Organization (ICAO) aviation safety standards for oversight of Hungary's air carrier operations. Further information may be found on the FAA's safety assessment page.

Children's Issues: Please see the U.S. Dept. of State Office of Children's Issues web pages on inter country adoption and international parental child abduction.

Intercountry Adoption

April 2010

The information in this section has been edited from the latest report available as of February 2013 from the State Department Bureau of Consular Affairs, Office of Overseas Citizens Services. For more information, please read the *Intercountry Adoption* section of this book and review current reports online at http://adoption.state.gov.

Hungary is party to the Hague Convention on Protection of Children and Co-operation in Respect of Intercountry Adoption (Hague Adoption Convention). Therefore, all adoptions between Hungary and the United States must meet the requirements of the Convention; the U.S. implementing legislation, the Intercountry Act of 2000 (IAA); and the IAA implementing regulations.

Who Can Adopt? Adoption between the United States and Hungary is governed by the Hague Adoption Convention. Therefore to adopt from Hungary, you must first be found eligible to adopt by the U.S. Government. The U.S. Government agency responsible for making this determination is the Department of Homeland Security, U.S. Citizenship and Immigration Services (USCIS).

Residency Requirements: There are no residency requirements for prospective adoptive parents in Hungary.

Age Requirements: Hungarian law specifies an age limit for the adoptive parents. Adoptive parents must be at least 16 years older than their adoptive child, but no more than 45 years

Background Notes

older. The age difference is calculated based on the age of the younger adoptive parent. If the adoptive children are siblings, the age of the older sibling is taken into consideration.

Marriage Requirements: Hungarian law does allow single people to adopt. However, Hungarian authorities may not encourage these adoptions based on the strongly held opinion that a child should be raised by a married couple in a traditional family. According to information from the Hungarian Ministry of Social Affairs and Labor, adoptions are approved based on the submitted documents and a detailed study of the particular case.

Income Requirements: There is no income requirement for adoptive parents in Hungary; however, parents must submit proof of their income to the Ministry of Social Affairs and Labor.

Other Requirements: Hungarian law requires both adoptive parents to meet the child prior to the adoption.

Who Can be Adopted? Because Hungary is party to the Hague Adoption Convention, children from Hungary must meet the requirements of the Convention in order to be eligible for adoption. For example, the Convention requires that Hungary attempt to place a child with a family in-country before determining that a child is eligible for intercountry adoption.

In addition to Hungary's requirements, a child must meet the definition of a Convention adoptee for you to bring him or her back to the United States. According to the Hungarian Family Law, only orphans may be adopted by foreigners. "Private" adoption is not allowed. Hungarian citizens residing permanently in the United States are also considered as foreign adoptive parents.

The Process: Because Hungary is party to the Hague Adoption Convention, adopting from Hungary must follow a specific process designed to meet the Convention's requirements. For detailed and updated information on these requirements, please review the *Intercountry Adoption* section of this publication and visit the U.S. Department of State Intercountry Adoption website at http://adoption.state.gov.

Role of the Adoption Authority: After meeting with the child, the custody of the child is granted to the adoptive parents. The Local Guardianship Authority issues an official Custody Decree regarding the placement of the child into the custody of the adoptive parents for at least one month. During that month, the child lives with you and you are regularly visited by the local child protection service.

When the one month custody is successfully completed, the adoption is finalized, and a Final Adoption Decree is issued by the local Guardianship Authority.

Time Frame: If there is a child available for intercountry adoption, and the adoptive parents accept the child for adoption, they have to meet the 30 days temporary custody requirement. The procedure after the adoption may take one or two weeks; however, there are very few children on the waiting list for intercountry adoption. The adoptive parents may wait many months or even years until the Ministry of Social Affairs and Labor offers them a child.

Adoption Fees: Although there are no fees for the adoption itself, other expenses of obtaining documents, passport and translations can be high. For a translation of one page a translator or a translation office may collect from $25 to $85. The fee for the Hungarian passport is $12. In the adoption services contract that you sign at the beginning of the adoption process, your agency will itemize the fees and estimated expenses related to your adoption process.

Documents Required: Adoptive parents need to obtain the following documents with official Hungarian translation:

- Home study
- Proof of income
- Psychological report showing suitability of the parents to adopt
- Home country's advanced permission to the adoption
- Proof of citizenship (photocopy of the passport)
- Statement of the adoptive parents regarding their motivation for adoption, and expectations about the child (child's sex, age, health)
- Accreditation of the adoption agency
- Photos of the adoptive parents, of their home, other children or other important elements of their life

Bringing Your Child Home: Once your adoption is complete (or you have obtained legal custody of the child), there are a few more steps to take before you can head home. Specifically, you need to apply for several documents for your child before he or she can travel to the United States, such as a birth certificate, a passport or travel document for your child from the country in which he or she was born, and a U.S. Immigration Visa.

Child Citizenship Act: For adoptions finalized abroad, the Child Citizenship Act of 2000 allows your new child to acquire American citizenship automatically when he or she enters the United States as lawful permanent residents.

For adoptions finalized in the United States, the Child Citizenship Act of 2000 allows your new child to acquire American citizenship automatically when the court in the United States issues the final adoption decree.

After Adoption: Hungary requires adoptive parents to submit post adoption reports about the child after two and after twelve months. Please attach photos and provide as much information about the child as you can.

We strongly urge you to comply with this requirement of the Hungarian Ministry of Social Affairs and Labor. Positive experience with American parents will contribute to the overall picture of the relations between Hungary and the United States.

U.S. Embassy in Hungary
Immigrant Visa Unit
1054 Budapest, Szabadsag ter 12.
Tel: 011-36-1-475-4394
Fax: 011-36-1-475-4188
E-mail: iv.budapest@state.gov
http://hungary.usembassy.gov

Hungarian Adoption Authority
Ministry of Social Affairs and Labor,
Department of Child and
Youth Protection
1054 Budapest, Hold u. 1.
Phone: (36-1) 428-9921
gyif@szmm.gov.hu
www.szmm.gov.hu

Embassy of Hungary
3910 Shoemaker Street, N.W.
Washington, D.C. 20008
Tel: 1-202-362-6730
E-mail: info@huembwas.org
http://www.hungaryemb.org

Office of Children's Issues
U.S. Department of State
2201 C Street, NW
SA-29
Washington, DC 20520
Tel: 1-888-407-4747
E-mail: AskCI@state.gov
http://adoption.state.gov

For questions about immigration procedures, call the National Customer Service Center (NCSC) at 1-800-375-5283 (TTY 1-800-767-1833).

ICELAND

Compiled from publications that were available as of February 2013 from the U.S. Department of State, the U.S. Department of Commerce, and the Central Intelligence Agency (CIA). See the introduction to this set for explanatory notes.

Official Name:
Republic of Iceland

PROFILE

Geography

Area: total: 103,000 sq km; country comparison to the world: 108; land: 100,250 sq km; water: 2,750 sq km

Major cities: Reykjavik (capital) 198,000 (2009)

Climate: temperate; moderated by North Atlantic Current; mild, windy winters; damp, cool summers

Terrain: mostly plateau interspersed with mountain peaks, icefields; coast deeply indented by bays and fiords

People

Nationality: noun: Icelander(s); adjective: Icelandic

Population: 313,183 (July 2012 est.)

Population growth rate: 0.674% (2012 est.)

Ethnic groups: homogeneous mixture of descendants of Norse and Celts 94%, population of foreign origin 6%

Religions: Lutheran Church of Iceland (official) 80.7%, Roman Catholic 2.5%, Reykjavik Free Church 2.4%, Hafnarfjorour Free Church 1.6%, other religions 3.6%, unaffiliated 3%, other or unspecified 6.2% (2006 est.)

Languages: Icelandic, English, Nordic languages, German widely spoken

Literacy: definition: age 15 and over can read and write; total population: 99%; male: 99%; female: 99% (2003 est.)

Health: life expectancy at birth: total population: 81 years; male: 78.81 years; female: 83.29 years (2012 est.); Infant mortality rate: total: 3.18 deaths/1,000 live births; male: 3.33 deaths/1,000 live births; female: 3.03 deaths/1,000 live births (2012 est.)

Unemployment rate: 5.6% (2012 est.)

Work force: 180,800 (2012 est.)

Government

Type: constitutional republic

Independence: 1 December 1918

Constitution: 16 June 1944, effective 17 June 1944; amended many times

Political subdivisions: 8 regions; Austurland, Hofudhborgarsvaedhi, Nordhurland Eystra, Nordhurland Vestra, Sudhurland, Sudhurnes, Vestfirdhir, Vesturland

Suffrage: 18 years of age; universal

Economy

GDP (purchasing power parity): $12.95 billion (2012 est.); $12.57 billion (2011 est.); $12.2 billion (2010 est.); $12.71 billion (2009 est.)

GDP real growth rate: 2.7% (2012 est.); 3.1% (2011 est.); -4% (2010 est.); -6.8% (2009 est.)

GDP per capita (PPP): $39,400 (2012 est.); $38,500 (2011 est.); $37,800 (2010 est.); $39,800 (2009 est.)

Natural resources: fish, hydropower, geothermal power, diatomite

Agriculture products: potatoes, green vegetables; mutton, chicken, pork, beef, dairy products; fish

Industries: fish processing; aluminum smelting, ferrosilicon production; geothermal power, hydropower, tourism

Exports: $5.1 billion (2012 est.); $5.3 billion (2011 est.); $4.603 billion (2010 est.)

Exports—commodities: fish and fish products 40%, aluminum, animal products, ferrosilicon, diatomite

Exports—partners: Netherlands 32.5%, Germany 15.1%, UK 9%, Norway 4.4% (2011)

Imports: $4.699 billion (2012 est.); $4.501 billion (2011 est.); $3.621 billion (2010 est.)

Imports—commodities: machinery and equipment, petroleum products, foodstuffs, textiles

Imports—partners: Norway 16%, US 10.9%, Germany 7.9%, Netherlands 7.4%, China 6.3%, Denmark 6.2%, Brazil 5.8%, UK 5.2% (2011)

Debt—external: $124.5 billion (30 June 2011); $3.073 billion (2002 est.)

Exchange rates: Icelandic kronur (ISK) per US dollar; 127.2 (2012 est.) ; 115.95 (2011 est.); 122.24 (2010 est.); 123.64 (2009); 85.619 (2008); 63.391 (2007)

GEOGRAPHY

Iceland is a volcanic island in the North Atlantic Ocean east of Greenland and immediately south of the Arctic Circle. It lies about 4,200 kilometers (2,600 mi.) from New York and 830 kilometers (520 mi.) from Scotland. About 79% of Iceland's land area, which is of recent volcanic origin, consists of glaciers, lakes, a mountainous lava desert (highest elevation 2,000 meters—6,590 ft.—above sea level), and other wasteland. About 28% of the land is used for grazing, and 1% is cultivated. The inhabited areas are on the coast, particularly in the southwest where about 60% of the population lives. Because of the Gulf Stream's moderating influence, the climate is characterized by damp, cool summers and relatively mild but windy winters. In Reykjavik, the average temperature is 11°C (52°F) in July and -1°C (30°F) in January.

PEOPLE

Most Icelanders are descendants of Norwegian settlers and Celts from the British Isles, and the population is remarkably homogeneous. According to Icelandic Government statistics, 94% of the nation's inhabitants live in urban areas (localities with populations greater than 200) and about 63% live in the Reykjavik metropolitan area.

Language

Of the Nordic languages, the Icelandic language is closest to the Old Norse language and has remained relatively unchanged since the 12th century. The Icelandic alphabet contains letters not found in modern English. For example, Þ is transliterated as "th," and ð is transliterated as "d."

Most Icelandic surnames are based on patronymy, or the adoption of the father's first given name. For example, Magnus and Anna, children of a man named Petur, would hold the surname Petursson and Petursdottir, respectively. Magnus' children, in turn, would inherit the surname Magnusson or Magnusdottir, while Anna's children would claim their father's first given name as their surname. Women normally maintain their original surnames after marriage. This system of surnames is required by law, except for the descendants of those who had acquired family names before 1913. Most Icelanders, while reserved by nature, rarely call each other by their surnames, and even phone directories are based on first names. Because of its small size and relative homogeneity, Iceland holds all the characteristics of a very close-knit society.

Religion

According to the National Statistical Bureau of Iceland, 245,456 persons (77 percent of the population) are members of the state ELC. In 2011, 2,735 individuals resigned from the church, while the church registered 206 new individuals other than infants. Many of those who resigned joined one of the organizationally and financially independent Lutheran Free Churches, which have a total membership of 18,187 (5.7 percent of the population). Although the majority of citizens choose traditional Lutheran rituals to mark events such as baptisms, confirmations, weddings, and funerals, most Lutherans do not regularly attend Sunday services.

A total of 21,468 persons (6.7 percent) are members of 35 small recognized and registered religious organizations ranging from the Roman Catholic Church (10,455 members) to Church of God Ministry of Jesus Christ International (three members). There are 18,662 individuals (5.8 percent) who belong to other or unspecified religious organizations and 15,802 (4.9 percent) who are not members of any religious organization. There are an estimated 1,000 to 1,500 Muslims living in the country, according to those groups. There are fewer than 100 Jews; followers of Judaism have never requested official recognition.

Foreigners constitute an estimated 80 percent of the Roman Catholic population, mostly from other European countries and the Philippines.

Cultural Achievements

The Sagas, almost all written between 1180 and 1300 A.D., remain Iceland's best-known literary accomplishment, and they have no surviving counterpart anywhere in the Nordic world. Based on Norwegian and Icelandic histories and genealogies, the Sagas present views of Nordic life and times up to 1100 A.D.

The Saga writers sought to record their heroes' great achievements and to glorify the virtues of courage, pride, and honor, focusing in the later Sagas on early Icelandic settlers. The best-known Icelandic writer of the 20th century was the 1955 Nobel Prize winner Halldor Kiljan Laxness. The literacy rate is 99.9%, and literature and poetry are legendary passions with the population. Per capita publication of books and magazines is the highest in the world.

Unlike its literature, Iceland's fine arts did not flourish until the 19th century because the population was small and scattered. Iceland's most famous painters are Asgrimur Jonsson, Jon Stefansson, and Johannes Kjarval, all of whom worked during the first half of the 20th century.

The best-known modern sculptor, Asmundur Sveinsson (1893–1982), drew his inspiration from Icelandic folklore and the Sagas for many of his works. Today, Kristjan Johannsson and Gardar Thor Cortes are Iceland's most famous opera singers, while pop singer Bjork and progressive rock band Sigur Ros are well known internationally.

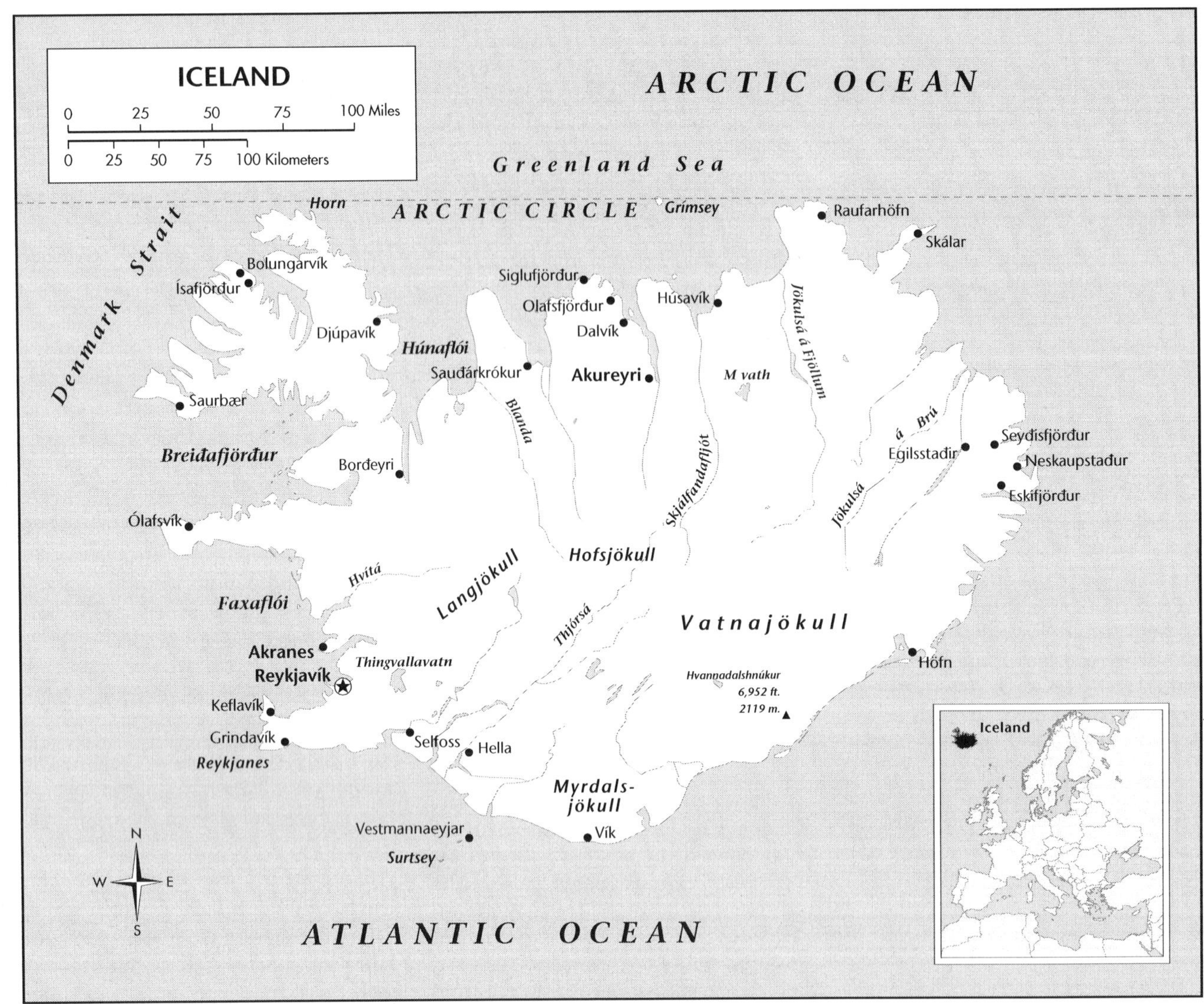

HISTORY

Iceland was settled in the late 9th and early 10th centuries, principally by people of Norse origin. In 930 A.D., the ruling chiefs established a republican constitution and an assembly called the Althingi (Alþingi) the oldest parliament in the world. Iceland remained independent until 1262, when it entered into a treaty establishing a union with the Norwegian monarchy. Iceland was then passed to Denmark in the late 14th century when Norway and Denmark were united under the Danish crown.

In the early 19th century, national consciousness was revived in Iceland. The Althingi had been abolished in 1800 but was reestablished in 1843 as a consultative assembly. In 1874, Denmark granted Iceland limited home rule, which was expanded in scope in 1904. The constitution, written in 1874, was revised in 1903. The Act of Union, a 1918 agreement with Denmark, recognized Iceland as a fully sovereign state united with Denmark under a common king. Iceland established its own flag, but Denmark continued to represent Icelandic foreign affairs and defense interests.

German occupation of Denmark in 1940 severed communications between Iceland and Denmark. Consequently, Iceland moved immediately to assume control over its own territorial waters and foreign affairs. In May 1940, British military forces occupied Iceland. Responsibility for Iceland's defense passed to the United States in July 1941. Following a plebiscite, Iceland formally became an independent republic on June 17, 1944. In October 1946, the Icelandic and U.S. Governments agreed to terminate U.S. responsibility for the defense of Iceland, but the United States retained certain rights at Keflavik. Iceland became a charter member of the North Atlantic Treaty Organization (NATO) in 1949.

After the outbreak of hostilities in Korea in 1950, and pursuant to the request of NATO military authorities, the United States and Iceland agreed that the United States should again make arrangements for Iceland's defense. A bilateral defense agreement signed on May 5, 1951 remains in force, even though the

U.S. military forces are no longer permanently stationed in Iceland. Iceland is the only NATO country with no standing military of its own.

GOVERNMENT AND POLITICAL CONDITIONS

Iceland is a constitutional parliamentary republic. The president is the head of state; a prime minister, usually the head of the majority party, is head of government. There is a unicameral parliament (Althingi). In 2008 voters reelected Olafur Ragnar Grimsson as president without opposition. After free and fair parliamentary elections in 2009, the Social Democratic Alliance (SDA) and the Left-Green Movement formed a governing coalition led by Prime Minister Johanna Sigurdardottir (SDA).

Recent Elections

In 2009 the country held parliamentary elections that were considered free and fair. In 2008 the incumbent president was reelected unopposed.

Participation of Women and Minorities: There were 25 women in the 63-seat parliament. The speaker was a woman as well as five of the six vice speakers. There were four women in the 10-member cabinet, including the prime minister. Two of the 12 Supreme Court judges, including the president of the court, and 17 of 48 district court judges were women. No members of minority groups held seats in either parliament or the cabinet.

Principal Government Officials

Last Updated: 1/31/2013

Pres.: **Olafur GRIMSSON**
Prime Min.: **Johanna SIGURDARDOTTIR**
Min. of Economic Affairs: **Steingrimur J. SIGFUSSON**
Min. of Education, Science, & Culture: **Katrin JAKOBSDOTTIR**
Min. of Environment: **Svandis SVAVARSDOTTIR**
Min. of Finance: **Oddny G. HARDARDOTTIR**
Min. of Fisheries & Agriculture: **Steingrimur J. SIGFUSSON**
Min. of Foreign Affairs & External Trade: **Ossur SKARPHEDINSSON**
Min. of Industry, Energy, & Tourism (Acting): **Oddny G. HARDARDOTTIR**
Min. of Interior: **Ogmundur JONASSON**
Min. of Welfare: **Gudbjartur HANNESSON**
Dir., Central Bank of Iceland: **Mar GUDMUNDSSON**
Ambassador to the US: **Gudmundur A. STEFANSSON**
Permanent Representative to the UN, New York: **Greta GUNNARSDOTTIR**

ECONOMY

Iceland's Scandinavian-type social-market economy combines a capitalist structure and free-market principles with an extensive welfare system. Prior to the 2008 crisis, Iceland had achieved high growth, low unemployment, and a remarkably even distribution of income. The economy depends heavily on the fishing industry, which provides 40% of export earnings, more than 12% of GDP, and employs 7% of the work force. It remains sensitive to declining fish stocks as well as to fluctuations in world prices for its main exports: fish and fish products, aluminum, and ferrosilicon.

Iceland's economy has been diversifying into manufacturing and service industries in the last decade, particularly within the fields of software production, biotechnology, and tourism. Abundant geothermal and hydropower sources have attracted substantial foreign investment in the aluminum sector, boosted economic growth, and sparked some interest from high-tech firms looking to establish data centers using cheap green energy, although the financial crisis has put several investment projects on hold.

Much of Iceland's economic growth in recent years came as the result of a boom in domestic demand following the rapid expansion of the country's financial sector. Domestic banks expanded aggressively in foreign markets, and consumers and businesses borrowed heavily in foreign currencies, following the privatization of the banking sector in the early 2000s.

Worsening global financial conditions throughout 2008 resulted in a sharp depreciation of the krona vis-a-vis other major currencies. The foreign exposure of Icelandic banks, whose loans and other assets totaled more than 10 times the country's GDP, became unsustainable. Iceland's three largest banks collapsed in late 2008. The country secured over $10 billion in loans from the IMF and other countries to stabilize its currency and financial sector, and to back government guarantees for foreign deposits in Icelandic banks. GDP fell 6.8% in 2009, and unemployment peaked at 9.4% in February 2009. GDP rose 2.7% in 2012 and unemployment declined to 5.6%.

Since the collapse of Iceland's financial sector, government economic priorities have included: stabilizing the krona, implementing capital controls, reducing Iceland's high budget deficit, containing inflation, addressing high household debt, restructuring the financial sector, and diversifying the economy. Three new banks were established to take over the domestic assets of the collapsed banks. Two of them have foreign majority ownership, while the State holds a majority of the shares of the third. Iceland began making payments to the UK, the Netherlands, and other claimants in late 2011 following Iceland's Supreme Court ruling that upheld 2008 emergency legislation that gives priority to depositors for compensation from failed Icelandic banks.

Iceland owes British and Dutch authorities approximately $5.5 billion for compensating British and Dutch citizens who lost deposits in Icesave when parent bank Landsbanki failed in 2008. Iceland began accession negotiations with the EU in July 2010; however, public support has dropped substantially because of concern about losing control over fishing resources and in reaction to worries over the ongoing Eurozone crisis.

Labor Conditions

The constitution and law prohibit the employment of persons younger than 16 in factories, on ships, or in other places that are hazardous or require hard labor; this prohibition was observed in practice. Children who are 14 or 15 years of age may work part-time or during school vacations in light, nonhazardous jobs. Their work hours must not exceed the ordinary work hours of adults in the same positions. The Administration of Occupational Safety and Health (AOSH) enforced child labor regulations effectively.

The law does not establish a minimum wage. The minimum wages negotiated in various collective bargaining agreements applied automatically to all employees in those occupations, including foreign workers, regardless of union membership. While the agreements can be either industry-wide, sector-wide, or in some cases firm-specific, the negotiated wage levels are defined by the kind of position.

The standard legal workweek is 40 hours, including nearly three hours of paid breaks a week. Paid annual holidays include 13 whole days and two half days. Work exceeding eight hours per day must be compensated as overtime. Overtime pay does not vary significantly across unions, but unions determine the terms of overtime pay when negotiating a bargaining agreement with the employer's association.

Workers are entitled to 11 hours of rest in each 24-hour period and one day off each week. Under special defined circumstances, employers may reduce the 11-hour rest period to no less than eight hours, but they must then compensate workers with one-and-a-half hours of rest for every hour of reduction. They may also postpone a worker's day off, but the worker must receive the corresponding rest time within 14 days. Foreign workers are entitled to the same protections in terms of working time and rest periods as citizens. The AOSH enforced these regulations. There were indications that undocumented foreign workers—primarily men in the construction and restaurant industries—were underpaid and required to work long hours while living in substandard housing or even sleeping at building sites. Most sources stressed that the men willingly worked illegally to earn more than they might have expected in their Eastern European or Baltic home countries.

U.S.-ICELANDIC RELATIONS

The United States was the first country to recognize Iceland's independence in 1944 following Danish rule, union with Denmark under a common king, and German and British occupation during World War II. Iceland is a member of the North Atlantic Treaty Organization (NATO) but has no standing military of its own. The United States and Iceland signed a bilateral defense agreement in 1951; it remains in force, although U.S. military forces are no longer permanently stationed in Iceland.

The U.S.-Icelandic relationship is founded on cooperation and mutual support. The two countries share a commitment to individual freedom, human rights, and democracy. U.S. policy aims to maintain close, cooperative relations with Iceland, both as a NATO ally and as a friend interested in the shared objectives of enhancing world peace; respect for human rights; economic development; arms control; and law enforcement cooperation, including the fight against terrorism, narcotics, and human trafficking. The United States and Iceland work together on a wide range of issues from enhancing peace and stability in Afghanistan, to harnessing new green energy sources, to ensuring peaceful cooperation in the Arctic.

U.S. Assistance to Iceland

The 1951 bilateral defense agreement stipulated that the U.S. would make arrangements for Iceland's defense on behalf of NATO and provided for basing rights for U.S. forces in Iceland. In 2006 the U.S. announced it would continue to provide for Iceland's defense but without permanently basing forces in the country.

That year, Naval Air Station Keflavik closed and thc two countrics signed a technical agreement on base closure issues (e.g., facilities return, environmental cleanup, residual value) and a "joint understanding" on future bilateral security cooperation (focusing on defending Iceland and the North Atlantic region against emerging threats such as terrorism and trafficking).

The United States also worked with local officials to mitigate the impact of job losses at the Air Station, notably by encouraging U.S. investment in industry and tourism development in the Keflavik area. Cooperative activities in the context of the new agreements have included joint search and rescue, disaster surveillance, and maritime interdiction training with U.S. Navy and U.S. Coast Guard units; and U.S. deployments to support the NATO air surveillance mission in Iceland.

Bilateral Economic Relations

The United States seeks to strengthen bilateral economic and trade relations. Most of Iceland's exports go to the European Union (EU) and the European Free Trade Association (EFTA) countries, followed by the United States and Japan. The U.S. is one of the largest foreign investors in Iceland, primarily in the aluminum sector. The United States and Iceland signed a Trade and Investment Framework Agreement in 2009.

Iceland's Membership in International Organizations

Iceland's ties with other Nordic states, the United States, and other NATO member states are particularly close. Iceland and the United States belong to a number of the same international organizations, including the United Nations, NATO, the Organization for Security and Cooperation in Europe, Arctic Council, Organization for Economic Cooperation and Development, International Monetary Fund, World Bank, and World Trade Organization.

Bilateral Representation

Iceland maintains an embassy in the United States at the House of Sweden, 2900 K Street, NW, #509, Washington, DC 20007-1704 [tel. (202) 265-6653].

Principal U.S. Embassy Officials

Last Updated: 1/14/2013

REYKJAVIK (E) Laufasvegur 21, IS-101 Reykjavik, Iceland, (354) 562-9100, Fax (354) 562-9118, Workweek: Monday to Friday/0800-1700, Website: http://iceland.usembassy.gov/

DCM OMS:	Adrienne Gersnoviez-Frybarger
AMB OMS:	Elizabeth Skopowski
ECON/COM:	Bradley K. Stilwell
MGT:	Andrew B. Graves
SDO/DATT:	Vacant
AMB:	Luis Arreaga
CON:	Marcy S. Brown
DCM:	Eric F. Green
PAO:	Paul M. Cunningham
RSO:	Jason Crosby
IMO:	Stevephen Skopowski
IPO:	David S Yeager
ISSO:	Steve Skowpowski
POL:	Daniel S. Katz
State ICASS:	Vacant

TRAVEL

Consular Information Sheet

June 6, 2012

Country Description: Iceland is an island located in the North Atlantic Ocean east of Greenland and immediately south of the Arctic Circle. Iceland is a highly developed country with a stable democracy. The country has a population of approximately 320,000 people and is about the size of Virginia.

Iceland is home to active volcanoes and was a focal point in international news following the April 2010 eruption of the Eyjafjallajokull volcano and the May 2011 eruption of the Grimsvotn volcano Both volcanoes have since ceased all eruption activity. The national language is Icelandic, but English is widely spoken, especially in the capital city of Reykjavik. Tourist facilities in Iceland are well developed and widely available.

Smart Traveler Enrollment Program (STEP)/Embassy Locations: If you are going to live in or visit Iceland, please take the time to tell our embassy about your trip. If you enroll in the Smart Traveler Enrollment Program, we can keep you up to date with important safety and security announcements. It will also help your friends and family get in touch with you in an emergency. The Embassy in Iceland is located at the following address:

U.S. Embassy Reykjavik
Laufásvegur 21
101 Reykjavik
Telephone: 354-562-9100
Emergency After Hours Telephone: 354-693-9207
Fax: 354-562-9110

You can also follow the U.S. Embassy Iceland on Twitter (@usembreykjavik) and Facebook.

Entry/Exit Requirements for U.S. Citizens: Iceland is a party to the Schengen Agreement. This means that U.S. citizens may enter Iceland for up to 90 days for tourist or business purposes without a visa. Your passport should be valid for at least three months beyond the period of stay. You also need to show that you have sufficient funds and a return airline ticket. For the most current visa information, contact the Embassy of Iceland at 2900 K Street, N.W., Washington, D.C. 20007–1704, tel: 1-202-265-6653. Information can also be obtained from the Icelandic Directorate of Immigration website (available in English).

The U.S. Department of State is unaware of any HIV/AIDS entry restrictions for visitors to, or foreign residents of, Iceland.

Threats to Safety and Security: There have been no terrorist attacks and very few criminal attacks affecting U.S. citizens in Iceland. However, like other countries in the Schengen area, Iceland's open borders with its Western European neighbors allow the possibility of members of terrorist organizations entering/exiting the country with anonymity. You should remain vigilant about your personal security and exercise caution while traveling abroad.

Stay up to date by:

- Bookmarking our Bureau of Consular Affairs website, which contains the current Travel Warnings and Travel Alerts as well as the Worldwide Caution;
- Following us on Twitter and the Bureau of Consular Affairs page on Facebook as well;
- Downloading our free Smart Traveler iPhone App to have travel information at your fingertips;
- Calling 1-888-407-4747 toll-free within the U.S. and Canada, or a regular toll line, 1-202-501-4444, from other countries; and,
- Taking some time before travel to consider your personal security.

Crime: Iceland has a low crime rate with rare instances of violent crime. Most crimes involve the theft of personal property from cars in public areas or residences. Pick-pocketing has increased in the last few years, usually attributed to an organized group looking for easy targets.

Many U.S. citizens fall victim to these highly skilled thieves, especially at the major tourist attractions in Reykjavik. Do not put any bags containing valuables, such as your passport, down on the ground. Do not leave your valuables in parked vehicles, even if the vehicle is locked. In addition, be aware that downtown Reykjavik can become disorderly in the early morning hours on weekends.

Outside of the Reykjavik metropolitan area, police services and emergency services are short-staffed, but are augmented by a corps of civilian volunteer civil defense and rescue units. These civil defense and rescue units are composed of volunteers from several sectors of Icelandic society and are generally well-trained to handle most emergencies.

Don't buy counterfeit and pirated goods, even if they are widely available. Not only are the bootlegs illegal to bring back into the United States, if you purchase them you may also be breaking local law.

Victims of Crime: If you or someone you know becomes the victim of a crime abroad, you should contact the local police and the nearest U.S. embassy or consulate. We can:

- Replace a stolen passport.
- Help you find appropriate medical care if you are the victim of violent crimes such as assault or rape.
- Put you in contact with the appropriate police authorities, and if you want us to, we can contact family members or friends.
- Help you understand the local criminal justice process and direct you to local attorneys, although it is important to remember that local authorities are responsible for investigating and prosecuting the crime.

The Icelandic Red Cross has a helpline that is open 24 hours a day, every day, for anyone needing assistance with grief, anxiety, fear, depression or suicidal thoughts. Dial 1717 to reach Red Cross volunteers in Iceland.

The local equivalent to the "911" emergency line in Iceland is 112.

Criminal Penalties: While you are traveling in Iceland you are subject to its laws even if you are a U.S. citizen. Foreign laws and legal systems can be vastly different than our own. Iceland's drunk driving laws are very strict. Penalties for possessing, using or trafficking in illegal drugs in Iceland are severe, and convicted offenders can expect long jail sentences and heavy fines.

Engaging in sexual conduct with children or using or disseminating child pornography in a foreign country is a crime prosecutable in the United States. If you break local laws in Iceland, your U.S. passport won't help you avoid arrest or prosecution. It's very important to know what's legal and what's not at your destination. Some activities that might be legal in the country you visit are still illegal in the United States.

While some countries will automatically notify the nearest U.S. embassy or consulate if a U.S. citizen is detained or arrested in a foreign country, that might not always be the case. To ensure that the United States is aware of your circumstances, request that the police and prison officials notify the nearest U.S. embassy or consulate as soon as you are arrested or detained overseas.

Importation Of Whale Meat To The U.S.: All persons are barred from importing whale meat to the United States. Even though whale meat is sold throughout Iceland, the Marine Mammal Protection Act makes it illegal to bring back whale meat into the U.S. Any importation of whale meat to the U.S. will result in the seizure of the goods and possible criminal prosecution. Penalties include jail time and fines of up to $10,000.

Special Circumstances: Be extremely careful if you are going to Iceland's numerous natural attractions, which include glaciers, volcanic craters, lava fields, ice caves, hot springs, boiling mud pots, geysers, waterfalls, and glacial rivers. There are few warning signs or barriers to alert you to potential hazards. Several tourists are scalded each year because they get too close to an erupting geyser or because they fall or step into a hot spring or boiling mud pot. High winds and icy conditions can make it more dangerous when visiting these nature areas. Hikers and backpackers should stay on marked trails, travel with another person, notify a third party about their travel plans, and check weather reports before visiting such areas. This is especially important as weather conditions in Iceland are subject to frequent and unexpected changes. Be sure to leave a travel itinerary with family, friends, or local guides/officials if you are planning to trek through remote parts of the country.

Iceland is home to active volcanoes. If a volcanic eruption occurs while you are in Iceland you should closely follow any instructions from the Icelandic authorities. Although there has been no indication of an imminent eruption at Katla, a large volcano located over 90 miles southeast of Reykjavik, it could erupt at any time. A Katla eruption could range from small and insignificant to large in scale. Be aware that airports in Iceland, including Keflavik International Airport, may need to close in the event of future eruptions. You can find updates on volcanic activity in Iceland though the Icelandic Office of Civil Defense.

Accessibility: While in Iceland, individuals with disabilities may find accessibility and accommodation very different from what you find in the United States. Icelandic law prohibits discrimination against persons with disabilities and requires that public accommodations and government buildings, including elevators, be accessible to individuals with disabilities.

All government buildings in Iceland are wheelchair accessible, as are most museums, malls, and large shopping centers in the capital area. The public bus system and taxis both provide transportation services for individuals with disabilities. However, many stores in the old downtown area in Reykjavik, such as around the popular shopping street of Laugavegur, are not wheelchair accessible. Many sidewalks in downtown Reykjavik lack curb ramps, and the streets in the area are steep. Smaller hotels and hotels outside the major cities are not all accessible to individuals with disabilities. There are very few paths or marked trails at natural attractions found outside of urban areas.

Medical Facilities and Health Information: Medical care in Iceland is of high quality, but limited services are available outside of large urban areas. For emergency medical assistance anywhere in the country, dial 112. For non-emergency medical assistance in the Reykjavik metropolitan area dial 544-4114 during business hours. Outside of normal business hours, dial 1770. The nurse who answers will do one of three things: offer advice on how to handle the problem on your own, suggest that you come to an after-hours clinic, or send a physician to you for a house call. The Icelandic medical system does not offer coverage to people who do not live in Iceland. Nonresidents are expected to pay their own medical costs and you should be prepared to pay your bill in full before leaving the hospital or clinic.

You can find good information on vaccines and other health precautions on theCenters for Disease Control and Prevention (CDC) website. For information about outbreaks of infectious diseases abroad, consult the infectious diseases section of the World Health Organization (WHO) website, whichalso contains additional health informationfor travelers, including detailed country-specific health information.

Medical Insurance: You can't assume your insurance will go with you when you travel. It's very important to find out BEFORE you leave whether or not your medical insurance will cover you overseas.

You need to ask your insurance company two questions:

- Does my policy apply when I'm out of the United States?
- Will it cover emergencies like a trip to a foreign hospital or a medical evacuation?

In many places, doctors and hospitals still expect payment in cash at the time of service. Your regular U.S. health insurance may not cover doctors' and hospital visits in other countries. If your policy doesn't go with you when you travel, it's a very good idea to take out another one for your trip.

Traffic Safety and Road Conditions: While in Iceland, you may encounter road conditions that differ significantly from those in the United States. You must be at least 17 years old to drive in Iceland. You can use your U.S. driver's license for stays of 90 days or less in Iceland.

Less than one-third of Iceland's total road network is paved (2,262 miles of paved road vs. 5,774 miles of gravel or dirt road). Most of the 900-mile ring road (Highway 1) that encircles the country is paved, but that highway sometimes closes in certain places for road repair. Many other roads outside the capital, especially those that run through the center of the country, are dirt or gravel tracks. Even paved roads tend to be narrow and lack a shoulder or margin. Most bridges are only one lane wide, requiring drivers to be alert to oncoming traffic.

Extreme care should be taken when driving in rural areas during the winter (October through April), when daylight hours are limited and the weather and road conditions can change rapidly. Drivers should pay special attention to signs marking roads as impassable. If you drive on a road that the Icelandic authorities have marked as closed or impassable, and then become stuck, you may incur fines of up to $1500 for emergency assistance. Off-road driving is strictly prohibited in Iceland and can incur fines of up to $2000.

Many routes in the interior of the country are impassable until July due to muddy conditions caused by snowmelt. If you are driving in the interior of Iceland, you should consider traveling with a second vehicle. Always inform someone of your travel plans. For information on current road conditions throughout the country, please consult the Public Roads Administration (Vegagerðin) website or call 1777. For recorded weather information in English, call the Icelandic Weather Office (Veðurstofa Islands): 522-6000 (during regular office hours) or 902-0600; press 1 for English (pay-per-minute service available 24 hours a day).

Icelandic law requires drivers to keep headlights on at all times. Talking on cell phones while driving is prohibited, except when using a hands-free system, and is subject to a fine of 5000 Icelandic Kronur (approximately 45 US Dollars). Unless otherwise posted, the speed limit is 50 km/h in urban areas and 30 km/h in residential areas. In rural areas, the speed limit depends on the type of road: on dirt and gravel roads, the speed limit is 80 km/h; on paved highways, the speed limit is 90 km/h. It is illegal to turn right on a red light. At four-way intersections, the right of way goes to the driver on the right; in traffic circles, drivers in the inside lane have the right of way. Many intersections in the capital have cameras to catch traffic violators.

The use of seatbelts is mandatory in both the front and rear seats, and children under the age of six must be secured in a special car seat designed for their size and weight. Drivers are held responsible for any passenger under the age of 15 not wearing a seatbelt. No one shorter than 140 centimeters, lighter than 40 kilograms, or younger than 12 years of age is allowed to ride in a front seat equipped with an airbag.

Driving under the influence of alcohol is considered a serious offense in Iceland. The threshold blood alcohol test (BAT) level is very low. Drivers can be charged with DUI (Driving Under the Influence) with a BAT as low as.05%. Drivers stopped under suspicion of DUI are usually given a "balloon" or Breathalyzer test. If the test is positive, a blood test is routinely administered. Under Icelandic law, a blood test cannot be refused and will be administered by force if necessary. The minimum punishment for a first offense is a fine of 70,000 Icelandic Kronur (approximately 625 US Dollars) and the loss of driving privileges for two months.

Aviation Safety Oversight: The U.S. Federal Aviation Administration (FAA) has assessed the government of Iceland's Civil Aviation Authority as being in compliance with International Civil Aviation Organization (ICAO) aviation safety standards for oversight of Iceland's air carrier operations. Further information may be found on the FAA's safety assessment page.

Children's Issues: Please see the U.S. Dept. of State Office of Children's Issues web pages on intercountry adoption and international parental child abduction.

Intercountry Adoption

March 2009

The information in this section has been edited from the latest report available as of February 2013 from the State Department Bureau of Consular Affairs, Office of Overseas Citizens Services. For more information, please read the *Intercountry Adoption* section of this book and review current reports online at http://adoption.state.gov.

While legally possible, intercountry adoption of an Icelandic orphan by foreigners is unlikely. No Icelandic orphans have received U.S. immigrant visas in the past five fiscal years.

Who Can Adopt? Adoption between the United States and Iceland is governed by the Hague Adoption Convention. Therefore to adopt from Iceland, you must first be found eligible to adopt by the U.S. Government. The U.S. Government agency responsible for making this determination is the Department of Homeland Security, U.S. Citizenship and Immigration Services (USCIS). In addition to these U.S. requirements for prospective adoptive parents, Iceland also has the following requirements for prospective adoptive parents.

Residency Requirements: Prospective adoptive parents must be residents of Iceland or "have a special connection to the country" to be allowed to adopt children in Iceland

Age and Marriage Requirements:

- Applicants must be at least 25 years old, but not more than 45 years old;
- Married couples or a male and a female that have lived together in a proxy marriage (cohabitation registered with the National Registry) for at least 5 years can adopt together;
- One of the married individuals or a male/female in a proxy marriage can adopt the partner's child or foster child with the partner's permission;
- One of the married individuals or a male/female in a proxy marriage can adopt a child without the partner's permission if the partner has vanished or his/her mental state would impede the adoption process;
- Individuals can adopt children in special circumstances and if the adoption benefits the welfare of the child;
- Same-sex couples can adopt (since 2006) as long as they fulfill all other requirements, such as length of marriage/ proxy marriage, age, health and no criminal record.

Other Requirements:

- Applicants must be in good mental and physical state;
- Must not have a criminal record;
- Must be able to financially support a family.

Who Can Be Adopted? Because Iceland is party to The Hague Adoption Convention, children from Iceland must meet the requirements of the Convention in order to be eligible for adoption. For example, the Convention requires that Iceland attempt to place a child with a family in-country before determining that a child is eligible for intercountry adoption. In addition to Iceland's requirements, a child must meet the definition of a Convention adoptee for you to bring him or her back to the United States.

Iceland's Adoption Authority: The Ministry of Judicial and Ecclesiastical Affairs—The National Commissioner on Adoptions

The Process: Because Iceland is party to The Hague Adoption Convention, adopting from Iceland must follow a specific process designed to meet the Convention's requirements. For more detailed information, please read the *International Adoption* section of this book and review current reports online at http://www.adoption.state.gov.

Adoption Application and Role of Adoption Authority: The first step to adopt a child is to apply for a pre-approval from The National Commissioner on Adoptions. Applicants can get the application forms on the Ministry of Judicial and Ecclesiastical Affairs website. Then they return the forms to Íslensk Ættleiðing (Icelandic Adoption Society -IAS) and the agency will send the forms to The National commissioner on adoptions and attach necessary documents.

The application with attached documents is sent to The National Commissioner on Adoptions which then asks the social services and the child protection agency in the applicants' home town to give a report about the applicant's home and family environment. An employee from social services will contact the applicant and do a home study. This report is sent to the ministry which will take the decision based on this report. If the pre-approval is granted, then it is sent in English to IAS and the applicant gets a copy. The approval notice, which is valid for two years, will state that the applicant is permitted to adopt a child from a specific third country.

Role of Adoption Agencies: Íslensk Ættleiðing (Icelandic Adoption Society) is the only adoption agency in Iceland. Please see their website (only in Icelandic): http://www.isadopt.is

Time Frame: The pre-approval process, described below, will take three to six months. The length of time to adopt in a third country will depend on the child's country of origin.

Documents Required:

- Application for pre-approval, Ministry of Judicial and Ecclesiastical Affairs—The National Commissioner on Adoptions. Skuggasundi, 150 Reykjavík. Telephone: 354-545-9000;
- Birth certificate from applicant;
- Information about applicant on this form. (1. Re Application For Permission to Adopt. 2. Re Application for Pre-Approval);
- Marriage certificate or certificate that proves proxy marriage of applicant;
- Certificate from the National Registry to show how long applicants have been living together. Marriage must have lasted at least three years and Proxy Marriage at least five years. The certificate can be sought at the National Registry in Iceland, Borgartúni 21a, 104 Reykjavík. Telephone: 354-569-2900. Business hours: Mon-Fri. 8:30-16:00;
- Police certificates from countries prospective adoptive parents resided for 3 months after the age of 16;
- Information about the applicant's health on the Information on Health Re application for Pre-Approval to Adopt a Child form;
- Doctors certificate for the adopting parent. Here you can get the Medical Certificate for Prospective Adoption Parent form, needs to be filled out by a doctor and the applicant;
- Certified copy of tax returns for the last two years.

Bringing Your Child Home: Once your adoption is complete (or you have obtained legal custody of the child), there are a few more steps to take before you can head home.

Specifically, you need to apply for several documents for your child before he or she can travel to the United States, such as a birth certificate, a passport or travel document for your child from the country in which he or she was born, and a U.S. Immigration Visa. For detailed and updated information on how to obtain these documents, review the *Intercountry Adoption* section on this publication.

Child Citizenship Act: For adoptions finalized abroad, the Child Citizenship Act of 2000 allows your new child to acquire American citizenship automatically when he or she enters the United States as lawful permanent residents.

For adoptions finalized in the United States, the Child Citizenship Act of 2000 allows your new child to acquire American citizenship automatically when the court in the United States issues the final adoption decree. To learn more, visit the USCIS Intercountry Adoption website at http://adoption.state.gov.

After Adoption: Iceland does not have any post-adoption or post-placement reporting requirements at this time.

U.S. Embassy in Iceland
Laufasvegur 21
101 Reykjavik, Iceland
Tel: (354) 562-9100
E-mail: reykjavikconsular@state.gov

Iceland's Adoption Authority
The Ministry of Judicial and Ecclesiastical Affairs
Arnarhvall on Lindargata
150 Reykjavik, Iceland
Tel: 011-354-560-9010
Fax: 011-354-552-7340
E-mail: postur@dkm.stjr.is
Internet: www.stjr.is

Embassy of Iceland
1156 15th Street N.W., Suite 1200
Washington, D.C. 20005-1704
Tel.: (202) 265 6653
E-mail: icemb.wash@mfa.is
http://www.iceland.org/us

Office of Children's Issues
U.S. Department of State
2201 C Street, NW
SA-29
Washington, DC 20520
Tel: 1-888-407-4747
E-mail: AskCI@state.gov
Internet: http://adoption.state.gov

For questions about immigration procedures, call the National Customer Service Center (NCSC) 1-800-375-5283 (TTY 1-800-767-1833).

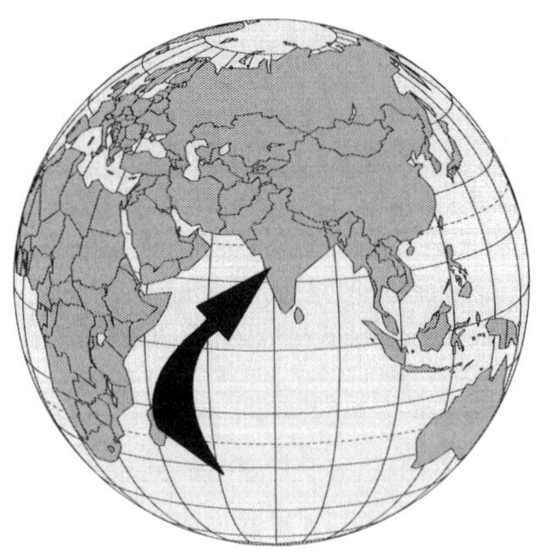

INDIA

Compiled from publications that were available as of February 2013 from the U.S. Department of State, the U.S. Department of Commerce, and the Central Intelligence Agency (CIA). See the introduction to this set for explanatory notes.

Official Name:
Republic of India

PROFILE

Geography

Area: total: 3,287,263 sq km; country comparison to the world: 7; land: 2,973,193 sq km; water: 314,070 sq km

Major cities: New Delhi (capital) 21.72 million; Mumbai 19.695 million; Kolkata 15.294 million; Chennai 7.416 million; Bangalore 7.079 million (2009)

Climate: varies from tropical monsoon in south to temperate in north

Terrain: upland plain (Deccan Plateau) in south, flat to rolling plain along the Ganges, deserts in west, Himalayas in north

People

Nationality: noun: Indian(s); adjective: Indian

Population: 1,205,073,612 (July 2012 est.)

Population growth rate: 1.312% (2012 est.)

Ethnic groups: Indo-Aryan 72%, Dravidian 25%, Mongoloid and other 3% (2000)

Religions: Hindu 80.5%, Muslim 13.4%, Christian 2.3%, Sikh 1.9%, other 1.8%, unspecified 0.1% (2001 census)

Languages: Hindi 41%, Bengali 8.1%, Telugu 7.2%, Marathi 7%, Tamil 5.9%, Urdu 5%, Gujarati 4.5%, Kannada 3.7%, Malayalam 3.2%, Oriya 3.2%, Punjabi 2.8%, Assamese 1.3%, Maithili 1.2%, other 5.9%

Literacy: definition: age 15 and over can read and write; total population: 61%; male: 73.4%; female: 47.8% (2001 census)

Health: life expectancy at birth: total population: 67.14 years; male: 66.08 years; female: 68.33 years (2012 est.); Infant mortality rate: total: 46.07 deaths/1,000 live births; male: 44.71 deaths/1,000 live births; female: 47.59 deaths/1,000 live births (2012 est.)

Unemployment rate: 9.9% (2012 est.)

Work force: 498.4 million (2012 est.)

Government

Type: federal republic

Independence: 15 August 1947

Constitution: 26 January 1950; amended many times

Political subdivisions: 28 states and 7 union territories; Andaman and Nicobar Islands, Andhra Pradesh, Arunachal Pradesh, Assam, Bihar, Chandigarh, Chhattisgarh, Dadra and Nagar Haveli, Daman and Diu, Delhi, Goa, Gujarat, Haryana, Himachal Pradesh, Jammu and Kashmir, Jharkhand, Karnataka, Kerala, Lakshadweep, Madhya Pradesh, Maharashtra, Manipur, Meghalaya, Mizoram, Nagaland, Odisha, Puducherry, Punjab, Rajasthan, Sikkim, Tamil Nadu, Tripura, Uttar Pradesh, Uttarakhand, West Bengal

Suffrage: 18 years of age; universal

Economy

GDP (purchasing power parity): $4.735 trillion (2012 est.); $4.515 trillion (2011 est.)

GDP real growth rate: 5.4% (2012 est.); 7.2% (2011 est.); 10.6% (2010 est.); 6.6% (2009 est.)

GDP per capita (PPP): $3,900 (2012 est.); $3,700 (2011 est.); $3,500 (2010 est.); $3,200 (2009 est.)

Natural resources: coal (fourth-largest reserves in the world), iron ore, manganese, mica, bauxite, rare earth elements, titanium ore, chromite, natural gas, diamonds, petroleum, limestone, arable land

Agriculture products: rice, wheat, oilseed, cotton, jute, tea, sugarcane, lentils, onions, potatoes; dairy products, sheep, goats, poultry; fish

Industries: textiles, chemicals, food processing, steel, transportation equipment, cement, mining, petroleum, machinery, software, pharmaceuticals

Exports: $309.1 billion (2012 est.); $299.4 billion (2011 est.); $225.3 billion (2010 est.)

Exports—commodities: petroleum products, precious stones, machinery, iron and steel, chemicals, vehicles, apparel

Exports—partners: UAE 13%, US 11.4%, China 6.3%, Singapore 5.3% (2011)

Imports: $500.3 billion (2012 est.); $461.4 billion (2011 est.); $357.5 billion (2010 est.)

Imports—commodities: crude oil, precious stones, machinery, fertilizer, iron and steel, chemicals

Imports—partners: China 12.1%, UAE 8.3%, Saudi Arabia 5.8%, US 5.1%, Switzerland 4.7% (2011)

Debt—external: $299.2 billion (31 December 2012 est.); $289.7 billion (31 December 2011 est.); $290.3 billion (31 December 2010 est.)

Exchange rates: Indian rupees (INR) per US dollar; 53.17 (2012 est.); 46.67 (2011 est.); 45.726 (2010 est.); 48.405 (2009); 43.319 (2008); 41.487 (2007)

PEOPLE

Although India occupies only 2.4% of the world's land area, it supports over 15% of the world's population. Only China has a larger population. India's median age is 25, one of the youngest among large economies. About 70% live in more than 550,000 villages, and the remainder in more than 200 towns and cities. Over the thousands of years of its history, India has been invaded from the Iranian plateau, Central Asia, Arabia, Afghanistan, and the West; Indian people and culture have absorbed and modified these influences to produce a remarkable racial and cultural synthesis.

Language

Religion, caste, and language are major determinants of social and political organization in India today. However, with more job opportunities in the private sector and better chances of upward social mobility, India has begun a quiet social transformation in this area. The government has recognized 18 official languages; Hindi, the national language, is the most widely spoken, although English is a national lingua franca.

Religion

According to the 2001 census, Hindus constitute 80.5 percent of the population, Muslims 13.4 percent, Christians 2.3 percent, and Sikhs 1.9 percent. Groups that together constitute less than 1.1 percent of the population include Buddhists, Jains, Parsis (Zoroastrians), Jews, and Baha'is. Tribal groups, indigenous groups historically outside the caste system and generally included among Hindus in government statistics, often practice traditional indigenous religious beliefs (animism).

There are large Muslim populations in the states of Uttar Pradesh, Bihar, Maharashtra, West Bengal, Andhra Pradesh, Karnataka, and Kerala; Muslims are the majority in Jammu and Kashmir. Although Muslims are a minority nationally, the country has the world's third-largest Muslim population. Slightly more than 85 percent of Muslims are Sunni; the rest are Shia. Christian populations are found across the country but in greater concentrations in the northeast, as well as in the southern states of Kerala, Tamil Nadu, and Goa. Three small northeastern states (Nagaland, Mizoram, and Meghalaya) have large Christian majorities. Sikhs are the majority in the state of Punjab.

Caste

The Hindu caste system reflects Indian occupational and socially defined hierarchies. Ancient Sanskrit sources divide society into four major categories, priests (Brahmin), warriors (Kshatriya), traders/artisans (Vaishya) and farmers/laborers (Shudra). Although these categories are understood throughout India, they describe reality only in the most general terms. They omit, for example, the tribal people and those outside the caste system formerly known as "untouchables," or dalits. In reality, Indian society is divided into thousands of jatis—local, endogamous groups based on occupation—and organized hierarchically according to complex ideas of purity and pollution. Discrimination based on caste is officially illegal, but remains prevalent, especially in rural areas. Nevertheless, the government has made strong efforts to minimize the importance of caste through active affirmative action and social policies. Moreover, caste is often diluted if not subsumed in the economically prosperous and heterogeneous cities, where an increasing percentage of India's population lives. In the countryside, expanding education, land reform and economic opportunity through access to information, communication, transport, and credit are helping to lessen the harshest elements of the caste system.

HISTORY

The people of India have had a continuous civilization since 2500 B.C.E., when the inhabitants of the Indus River valley developed an urban culture based on commerce and sustained by agricultural trade. The Harappan Civilization, as it came to be known, declined around 1500 B.C.E., most likely due to ecological changes.

During the second millennium B.C.E., pastoral, Aryan-speaking tribes migrated from the northwest into the subcontinent, settled in the middle Ganges River valley, and adapted to antecedent cultures. Alexander the Great expanded across Central Asia during the 4th century B.C.E., exposing India to Grecian influences. The Maurya Empire came to dominate the Indian subcontinent during the 3rd century B.C.E., reaching its greatest height under Emperor Ashoka. The political map of ancient and medieval India was made up of myriad kingdoms with fluctuating boundaries. At the height of the Roman Empire under Emperor Hadrian during the 2nd century C.E., the Kushan Empire, originating in ancient Bactria, conquered north India and the trans-Indus region ushering in a period of trade and prosperity. In the 4th and 5th centuries C.E., northern India was unified under the Gupta Dynasty. During this period, known as India's Golden Age, Hindu culture and political administration reached new heights.

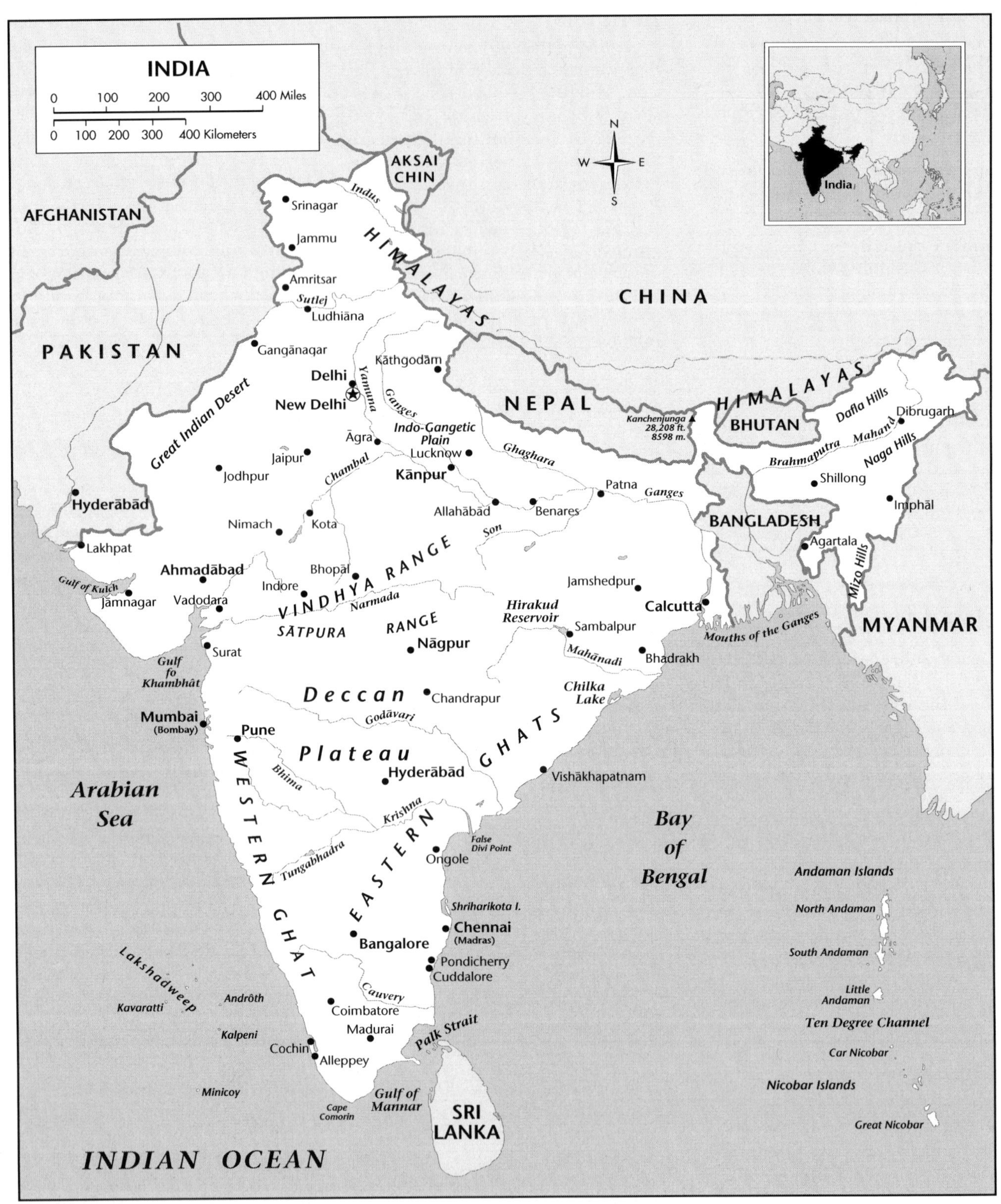

Islam spread across the subcontinent over a period of 700 years. In the 10th and 11th centuries, Turks and Afghans invaded India and established the Delhi Sultanate. In the early 16th century, Babur, a Turkish-Mongol adventurer and distant relative of Timurlane and Genghis Khan, established the Mughal Dynasty, which lasted for 200 years. South India followed an independent path, but by the 17th century large areas of South India came under the direct rule or influence of the expanding Mughal Empire. While most of Indian society in its thousands of villages remained untouched by the political struggles going on around them, Indian courtly culture evolved into a unique blend of Hindu and Muslim traditions.

The first British outpost in South Asia was established by the English East India Company in 1619 at Surat on the northwestern coast. Later in the century, the Company opened permanent trading stations at Madras (now Chennai), Bombay (now Mumbai), and Calcutta (now Kolkata), each under the protection of native rulers.

The British expanded their influence from these footholds until, by the 1850s, they controlled most of present-day India, Pakistan, Sri Lanka, and Bangladesh. In 1857, an unsuccessful rebellion in north India led by Indian soldiers seeking the restoration of the Mughal Emperor led the British Parliament to transfer political power from the East India Company to the Crown. Great Britain began administering most of India directly and maintained both political and economic control, while controlling the rest through treaties with local rulers. Imperial India became the "crown jewel" of the rapidly expanding British Empire.

In the late 1800s, the first steps were taken toward self-government in British India with the appointment of Indian councilors to advise the British Viceroy and the establishment of Provincial Councils with Indian members; the British subsequently widened participation in Legislative Councils. Beginning in 1920, Indian leader Mohandas K. Gandhi transformed the Indian National Congress political party into a mass movement to campaign against British colonial rule. The party used both parliamentary and nonviolent resistance and non-cooperation to agitate for independence. During this period, however, millions of Indians served with honor and distinction in the British Indian Army, including service in both World Wars and countless other overseas actions in service of the Empire.

With Indians increasingly united in their quest for independence, a war-weary Britain led by Labor Prime Minister Clement Attlee began in earnest to plan for the end of its suzerainty in India. On August 15, 1947, India became a dominion within the Commonwealth, with Jawaharlal Nehru as Prime Minister. Strategic colonial considerations, as well as political tensions between Hindus and Muslims, led the British to partition British India into two separate states: India, with a Hindu majority; and Pakistan, which consisted of two "wings," East and West Pakistan—now Bangladesh and Pakistan—with Muslim majorities. India became a republic, but chose to continue as a member of the British Commonwealth, after promulgating its constitution on January 26, 1950.

After independence, the Indian National Congress, the party of Gandhi and Nehru, ruled India under the leadership first of Nehru and then his daughter (Indira Gandhi) and grandson (Rajiv Gandhi), with the exception of brief periods in the 1970s and 1980s and during a short period in 1996. From 1998–2004, a coalition led by the Bharatiya Janata Party governed.

Prime Minister Nehru governed the nation until his death in May 1964. Nehru was succeeded by Lal Bahadur Shastri, who also died in office in January 1966. In 1 month, power passed to Nehru's daughter, Indira Gandhi, Prime Minister from 1966 to 1977. In June 1975, beset with deepening political and economic problems, Mrs. Gandhi declared a state of emergency and suspended many civil liberties. Seeking a mandate at the polls for her policies, she called for elections in March 1977, only to be defeated by Morarji Desai, who headed the Janata Party, an amalgam of five opposition parties.

In 1979, Desai's government crumbled. Charan Singh formed an interim government, which was followed by Mrs. Gandhi's return to power in January 1980. On October 31, 1984, Mrs. Gandhi was assassinated by her Sikh bodyguards, which led to the killings of thousands of Sikhs in New Delhi. Her son, Rajiv, was chosen by the Congress (I)—for "Indira"—Party to take her place. His Congress government was plagued with allegations of corruption resulting in an early call for national elections in November 1989.

Although Rajiv Gandhi's Congress Party won more seats than any other single party in the 1989 elections, he was unable to form a government with a clear majority. The Janata Dal, a union of opposition parties, then joined with the Hindu-nationalist Bharatiya Janata Party (BJP) on the right and the Communists on the left to form the government. This loose coalition collapsed in November 1990, and the Janata Dal, supported by the Congress (I), came to power for a short period, with Chandra Shekhar as Prime Minister. That alliance also collapsed, resulting in national elections in June 1991.

While campaigning in Tamil Nadu on behalf of his Congress (I) party, Rajiv Gandhi was assassinated on May 21, 1991 by Tamil extremists from Sri Lanka unhappy with India's military intervention in that country's civil war. In the elections, Congress (I) won 213 parliamentary seats and returned to power at the head of a coalition, under the leadership of P.V. Narasimha Rao. This Congress-led government, which served a full 5-year term, initiated a gradual process of economic liberalization under then-Finance Minister Manmohan Singh. These reforms opened the Indian economy to global trade and investment. India's domestic politics also took new shape, as the nationalist appeal of the Congress Party gave way to traditional caste, creed, regional, and ethnic alignments, leading to the founding of a plethora of small, regionally based political parties.

The final months of the Rao-led government in the spring of 1996 were marred by several major corruption scandals, which contributed to the worst electoral performance by the Congress Party in its history. The Hindu-nationalist BJP emerged from the May 1996 national elections as the single-largest party in the Lok Sabha but without a parliamentary majority. Under Prime Minister Atal Bihari Vajpayee, the subsequent BJP coalition lasted only 13 days. With all political parties wishing to avoid another round of elections, a 14-party coalition led by the Janata Dal formed a government known as the

United Front, under the former Chief Minister of Karnataka, H.D. Deve Gowda. His government collapsed after less than a year, when the Congress Party withdrew its support in March 1997. Inder Kumar Gujral replaced Deve Gowda as the consensus choice for Prime Minister at the head of a 16-party United Front coalition.

In November 1997, the Congress Party again withdrew support from the United Front. In new elections in February 1998, the BJP won the largest number of seats in parliament—182—but fell far short of a majority. On March 20, 1998, the President approved a BJP-led coalition government with Vajpayee again serving as Prime Minister. On May 11 and 13, 1998, this government conducted a series of underground nuclear tests, spurring U.S. President Bill Clinton to impose economic sanctions on India pursuant to the 1994 Nuclear Proliferation Prevention Act.

In April 1999, the BJP-led coalition government fell apart, leading to fresh elections in September-October. The National Democratic Alliance—a new coalition led by the BJP—won a majority to form the government with Vajpayee as Prime Minister in October 1999. The NDA government was the first coalition in many years to serve a full 5-year term, providing much-needed political stability.

The Kargil conflict in May-July 1999 and an attack by terrorists on the Indian parliament in December 2001 led to increased tensions with Pakistan.

Hindu nationalists supportive of the BJP agitated to build a temple on a disputed site in Ayodhya, destroying a 17th-century mosque there in December 1992, and sparking widespread religious riots in which thousands, mostly Muslims, were killed. In February 2002, 57 Hindu volunteers returning from Ayodhya were burnt alive when their train caught fire. Alleging that the fire was caused by Muslim attackers, anti-Muslim rioters throughout the state of Gujarat killed over 2,000 people and left 100,000 homeless. The Gujarat state government and the police were criticized for failing to stop the violence and in some cases for participating in or encouraging it.

The ruling BJP-led coalition was defeated in a five-stage election held in April and May of 2004. The Congress Party, under the leadership Sonia Gandhi, the widow of Rajiv Gandhi, formed a coalition government, known as the United Progressive Alliance (UPA). It took power on May 22 with Manmohan Singh as Prime Minister. The UPA's victory was attributed to dissatisfaction among poorer rural voters that the prosperity of the cities had not filtered down to them, and rejection of the BJP's Hindu nationalist agenda.

The Congress-led UPA government continued many of the BJP's foreign policies, particularly improving relations with the U.S. Prime Minister Singh and President George W. Bush concluded a landmark U.S.-India strategic partnership framework agreement on July 18, 2005. In March 2006, President Bush visited India to further the many initiatives underlying the agreement. The strategic partnership is anchored by a historic civil nuclear cooperation initiative and includes cooperation in the fields of space, high-technology commerce, health issues, democracy promotion, agriculture, and trade and investment.

In July 2008, the UPA won a confidence motion with 275 votes in its favor and 256 against. In late November 2008, terrorists killed at least 164 people in a series of coordinated attacks around Mumbai. Prime Minister Singh promised a thorough investigation and Home Minister Chidambaram pledged significant reforms to improve India's counterterrorism agencies.

The Congress-led UPA coalition gained a more stable majority following May 2009 elections, riding mainly on the support of rural voters. Singh became the first prime minister since Nehru to return to power after completing a full 5-year term.

GOVERNMENT AND POLITICAL CONDITIONS

India is a multiparty, federal, parliamentary democracy with a bicameral parliament. The president, elected by an electoral college, is the chief of state, and the prime minister is the head of the government. Under the constitution the 28 states and seven union territories have a high degree of autonomy and have primary responsibility for issues of law and order. President Pratibha Patil was elected in 2007 to a five-year term, and Manmohan Singh became prime minister for a second term following the Congress Party-led coalition's victory in the 2009 general elections, which were considered free and fair, despite scattered instances of violence.

Recent Elections

The country held a five-phase national election in April and May 2009 that included 714 million eligible voters. National and local security forces helped to ensure a relatively smooth election, although 65 persons were killed in voting-related violence. The Congress-led United Progress Alliance government (a coalition of parties), headed by Prime Minister Manmohan Singh, continued in power for a second term.

The country held state assembly elections in four states (Bihar, Kerala, Jharkhand, and Tamil Nadu) and one Union Territory (Puducherry) from April to May in which 140 million eligible voters participated. The elections were largely peaceful and free of major violence.

Participation of Women and Minorities: The law requires one-third of the seats in local bodies (panchayats and municipal councils) to be reserved for women. In addition, the country has no cultural or traditional practices that prevented women from participating in political life on the same basis as men, and women held many high-level political offices. Women participated in politics throughout the country at all levels. The constitution stipulates that to protect historically marginalized groups and to ensure representation in the lower house of parliament, each state must reserve seats for scheduled castes and scheduled tribes in proportion to their population in the state. Only candidates belonging to these groups can contest elections in reserved constituencies. In the 2009 elections, 84 seats for candidates from scheduled castes and 47 seats from scheduled tribes were reserved, representing 24 percent of the total seats in the lower house.

Principal Government Officials

Last Updated: 1/31/2013

Pres.: **Pranab MUKHERJEE**
Vice Pres.: **Mohammad Hamid ANSARI**
Prime Min.: **Manmohan SINGH**
National Security Adviser: **Shivshankar MENON**
Dep. Chmn., Planning Commission: **Montek Singh AHLUWALIA**
Min. of Agriculture: **Sharad PAWAR**
Min. of Chemicals & Fertilizers: **M. K. ALAGIRI**
Min. of Civil Aviation: **Ajit SINGH**
Min. of Coal: **Shriprakash JAISWAL**
Min. of Commerce & Industry: **Anand SHARMA**
Min. of Communications & Information Technology: **Kapil SIBAL**
Min. of Culture: **Chandresh Kumari KATOCH**
Min. of Defense: **A. K. ANTONY**
Min. of Earth Sciences: **Jaipal Sudini REDDY**
Min. of External Affairs: **Salman KHURSHID**
Min. of Finance: **Palaniappan CHIDAMBARAM**
Min. of Food Processing Industries: **Sharad PAWAR**
Min. of Health & Family Welfare: **Ghulam Nabi AZAD**
Min. of Heavy Industries & Public Enterprises: **Praful PATEL**
Min. of Home Affairs: **Sushil Kumar SHINDE**
Min. of Housing & Urban Poverty Alleviation: **Ajay MAKEN**
Min. of Human Resource Development: **Mallipudi Mangapati Pallam RAJU**
Min. of Labor & Employment: **Mallikarjun KHARGE**
Min. of Law & Justice: **Ashwani KUMAR**
Min. of Mines: **Dinsha J. PATEL**
Min. of Minority Affairs: **K. Rahman KHAN**
Min. of New & Renewable Energy: **Farooq ABDULLAH**
Min. of Overseas Indian Affairs: **Vayalar RAVI**
Min. of Panchayati Raj: **V. Kishore Chandra DEO**
Min. of Parliamentary Affairs: **Kamal NATH**
Min. of Personnel, Public Grievances, & Pensions: **Manmohan SINGH**
Min. of Petroleum & Natural Gas: **M. Veerappa MOILY**
Min. of Planning: **Manmohan SINGH**
Min. of Railways: **Pawan Kumar BANSAL**
Min. of Road Transport & Highways: **C. P. JOSHI**
Min. of Rural Development: **Jairam RAMESH**
Min. of Science & Technology: **Jaipal Sudini REDDY**
Min. of Shipping: **Govind Karuppiah VASAN**
Min. of Social Justice & Empowerment: **Kumari SELJA**
Min. of Steel: **Beni Prasad VERMA**
Min. of Textiles: **Anand SHARMA**
Min. of Tribal Affairs: **V. Kishore Chandra DEO**
Min. of Urban Development: **Kamal NATH**
Min. of Water Resources: **Harish RAWAT**
Min. of State (Independent Charge) for Consumer Affairs, Food, & Public Distribution: **K. V. THOMAS**
Min. of State (Independent Charge) for Corporate Affairs: **Sachin PILOT**
Min. of State (Independent Charge) for Development of North-Eastern Region: **Paban Singh GHATOWAR**
Min. of State (Independent Charge) for Drinking Water & Sanitation: **Bharatsinh Madhavsinh SOLANKI**
Min. of State (Independent Charge) for Environment & Forests: **Jayanthi NATARAJAN**
Min. of State (Independent Charge) for Information & Broadcasting: **Manish TEWARI**
Min. of State (Independent Charge) for Micro-, Small, & Medium Enterprises: **K. H. MUNIYAPPA**
Min. of State (Independent Charge) for Power: **Jyotiraditya Madhavrao SCINDIA**
Min. of State (Independent Charge) for Statistics & Program Implementation: **Srikant JENA**
Min. of State (Independent Charge) for Tourism: **K. CHIRANJEEVI**
Min. of State (Independent Charge) for Women & Child Development: **Krishna TIRATH**
Min. of State (Independent Charge) for Youth Affairs & Sports: **Jitendra SINGH**
Head, Dept. of Atomic Energy: **Manmohan SINGH**
Head, Dept. of Space: **Manmohan SINGH**
Governor, Reserve Bank of India: **Duvvuri SUBBARAO**
Ambassador to the US: **Nirupama RAO**
Permanent Representative to the UN, New York: **Hardeep Singh PURI**

ECONOMY

India is developing into an open-market economy, yet traces of its past autarkic policies remain. Economic liberalization, including industrial deregulation, privatization of state-owned enterprises, and reduced controls on foreign trade and investment, began in the early 1990s and has served to accelerate the country's growth, which has averaged more than 7% per year since 1997.

India's diverse economy encompasses traditional village farming, modern agriculture, handicrafts, a wide range of modern industries, and a multitude of services. Slightly more than half of the work force is in agriculture, but services are the major source of economic growth, accounting for nearly two-thirds of India's output, with less than one-third of its labor force. India has capitalized on its large educated English-speaking population to become a major exporter of information technology services and software workers. In 2010, the Indian economy rebounded robustly from the global financial crisis—in large part because of strong domestic demand—and growth exceeded 8% year-on-year in real terms.

However, India's economic growth began slowing in 2011 because of a tight monetary policy, intended to address persistent inflation, and a decline in investment, caused by investor pessimism about domestic economic reforms and about the global situation. High international crude prices have exacerbated the government's fuel subsidy expenditures, contributing to a higher fiscal deficit and a worsening current account deficit.

In late 2012, the Indian Government announced reforms and deficit reduction measures to reverse India's slowdown. The outlook India's medium-term growth is positive due to a young population and corresponding low dependency ratio, healthy savings and investment rates, and increasing integration into the global economy. India has many long-term challenges that it has not yet fully addressed, including poverty, inadequate physical and social infrastructure, limited non-agricultural employment opportunities, inadequate availability of quality basic and higher education, and accommodating rural-to-urban migration.

Labor Conditions

There is no overall minimum age for child labor. The law permits child labor with some restrictions. Children may work only for six hours a day, between 8 a.m. and 7 p.m., with one day's rest weekly. The government defines hazardous occupations and processes and prohibits work by children under age 14 in factories, mines, domestic service, carpet weaving, roadside eateries, and other areas. On April 18, 2011, the Supreme Court banned the employment of children in the circus industry and directed state governments to devise comprehensive plans to remove and rehabilitate children working in the circus industry.

The incidence of child labor remained widespread. The government estimated the number of child laborers at 1.2 million; UNICEF recently estimated the number of child workers at 29 million. Some NGOs estimated that there were between 50 and 115 million child workers. Among factors contributing to the prevalence of child labor were social tolerance of the practice, weak state and federal government enforcement of existing laws, and poverty. The absence of a minimum age for employment increased the risk of children falling victim to the worst forms of child labor. The majority of child labor occurred in agriculture and the informal economy.

State government laws set minimum wages, hours of work, and safety and health standards. Federal law is applicable to all industries and sets safety and health standards, but enforcement is by state governments. In 2010 the federal government set the floor minimum wage at 100 rupees per day (approximately $2) for its flagship Mahatma Gandhi National Rural Employment Guarantee program. Minimum wages varied according to the state and to the sector of industry. State governments set a separate minimum wage for agricultural workers. The law mandates a maximum eight-hour workday and 48-hour workweek, as well as safe working conditions, which include adequate provisions for restrooms, canteens, medical facilities, and ventilation. The law mandates a minimum rest period of 30 minutes after every four hours of work and premium pay for overtime. It does not mandate paid holidays and prohibits compulsory overtime. The law does not give workers the right to leave workplaces that endanger health and safety without jeopardizing their continued employment.

Enforcement of all labor laws is done by respective state governments. State labor inspectors typically are required to enforce a minimum of at least 10 labor-related laws. Penalties are not sufficient to deter violations, and the number of inspectors was insufficient to enforce the diverse array of labor laws.

Laws on wages, hours, and occupational health and safety do not apply to the informal sector, which employed nearly 93 percent of the workforce. Violations of wage, overtime, and occupational safety and health standards were common in the informal sector. State governments did not effectively enforce minimum wage laws for agricultural workers. Enforcement of safety and health standards was poor, especially in the informal sector but also in some formal sector industries. Workers in small, low technology factories were often exposed to hazardous working conditions. The country's undocumented foreign workers did not receive basic occupational health and safety protections.

Members of Scheduled Castes and Tribes, including children, often worked as rag pickers, recycling trash under hazardous and generally substandard conditions. Workers from these groups also cleaned sewers and drains of human excrement without proper equipment and under extremely unsanitary conditions.

U.S.-INDIA RELATIONS

President Obama has called India one of the defining partnerships of the 21st century, one which will be vital to U.S. strategic interests in Asia-Pacific and across the globe. Presidents Clinton, Bush and Obama all visited India, underscoring the increasing importance of the bilateral relationship. Our relationship is rooted in common values, including the rule of law, respect for diversity, and democratic government. We have a shared interest in promoting global security, stability, and economic prosperity through trade, investment, and connectivity. The United States and India have a common interest in the free flow of global trade and commerce, including through the vital sea lanes of the Indian Ocean.

The U.S. supports India's critical role as a leader in maintaining regional stability. Security ties are robust and growing with bilateral defense and counterterrorism cooperation reaching unprecedented levels. The United States and India also look continue to develop their defense partnership through military sales and joint research, co-production and co-development efforts.

The U.S.-India Strategic Dialogue, launched in 2009, provides opportunities to strengthen collaboration in areas including energy, climate change, trade, education, and counterterrorism. The third annual meeting was held in June 2012. In 2012 alone, seven Cabinet-level officials made visits to India to deepen bilateral ties.

The strength of people to people linkages between the United States and India has come to define the indispensable relationship between our two countries. The increased cooperation of state and local officials to create ties has enhanced engagement in education. Additionally, state to state and city to city engagements have created new partnerships in business and the private sector and enhance our robust government to government engagement.

Bilateral Economic Relations

The United States is one of India's largest trade and investment partners. U.S.- India bilateral trade in goods and services has increased four and a half times over the last decade, to more than $86 billion in 2011. Bilateral trade between our two countries is up 40 percent since we began our Strategic Dialogue three years ago. The stock of Indian FDI in the United States has increased from $227 million in 2002 to almost $4.9 billion in 2011, supporting thousands of U.S. jobs.

The United States and India are negotiating a bilateral investment treaty as a key part of the effort to deepen the economic relationship, improve investor confidence, and support economic growth in both countries. India continues to move forward, albeit haltingly, with market-oriented economic reforms that began in 1991. Recent reforms have included an increasingly liberal foreign investment regime in many sectors.

On energy cooperation, the United States and India also share a strong commitment to work collaboratively in bilateral and multilateral fora to help ensure mutual energy security, combat global climate change, and support the development of low-carbon economies that will create opportunities and fuel job growth in both countries. The two countries consult regularly on the future of global oil and gas markets, expanding sustainable energy access to support jobs and economic growth in both countries, collaborating in research and technology, and increasing U.S. exports of clean energy technology. U.S. exports to India include diamonds and gold, machinery, oil, and fertilizers. U.S. imports from India include diamonds, pharmaceutical products, oil, agricultural products, organic chemicals, and apparel. U.S. direct investment in India is led by the information, professional, scientific, and technical services, and manufacturing sectors. India direct investment in the U.S. is primarily concentrated in the professional, scientific, and technical services sector.

India's Membership in International Organizations

India and the United States share membership in a variety of international organizations, including the United Nations, G-20, Association of Southeast Asian Nations (ASEAN) Regional Forum, International Monetary Fund, World Bank, and World Trade Organization. The United States supports a reformed UN Security Council that includes India as a permanent member. India is an ASEAN dialogue partner, an Organization for Economic Cooperation and Development partner under its Enhanced Engagement program, and an observer to the Organization of American States. India is also a member and the current chair of the Indian Ocean Rim-Association for Regional Cooperation (IOR-ARC). In November 2012, the United States was admitted as a dialogue partner in the IOR-ARC with India's support.

Bilateral Representation

India maintains an embassy in the United States at 2107 Massachusetts Avenue NW, Washington, DC 20008 (tel. 202-939-7000).

Principal U.S. Embassy Officials

Last Updated: 1/14/2013

NEW DELHI (E) Shanti Path, Chanakya Puri New Delhi–110021, India, 91-11-24198000, Fax 91-11-24190017, Workweek: Monday thru Friday; 0830 hrs to 1700 hrs, Website: http://newdelhi.usembassy.gov/

DCM OMS:	Lisa Cantonwine
AMB OMS:	Suzonne M. Woytovech
CDC:	Kenneth Earhart
Co-CLO:	Cassandra Davis
DHS/CBP:	Steven King
DHS/CIS:	Bobbie Johnson
DHS/ICE:	Vacant
FCS:	Judy Reinke
FDA:	Bruce Ross
FM:	James Horner
HHS:	Steven T. Smith
HRO:	Thomas Steyer
MGT:	Michael Mullins
MLO/ODC:	CAPT Kenneth Spurlock
POSHO:	James Horner
SDO/DATT:	CAPT Timothy J. Maricle
AMB:	Nancy J. Powell
CON:	Julia R. Stanley
DCM:	Donald Lu
PAO:	Walter T. Douglas
GSO:	William McClure
RSO:	Tim Haley
AFSA:	Isabelle Chan
AGR:	Allan Mustard
AID:	William Hammink
CLO:	Alicia May
DEA:	Michael Brown
ECON:	Blair P. Hall
EEO:	Lisa Cantonwine
EST:	Blair P. Hall
FAA:	Aaron Wilkins
FMO:	Mary Jo Rasing
ICASS Chair:	Judy Reinke
IMO:	Aziz Ahmed
IPO:	Wesley M. Tompkins
IRS:	Elizabeth Kinney
ISO:	Joseph Conners
ISSO:	Michael Meaux
LEGATT:	Daniel Clegg
POL:	Herro Mustafa
State ICASS:	Julia R. Stanley

CHENNAI (CG) 220 Anna Salai Rd, Chennai 600 006, India, 91-44-2857-4000, Fax 91-44-2811-2020, Workweek: Mon–Fri 0815–1700, Website: http://chennai.usconsulate.gov/

CDC:	Sharel Patel
CG OMS:	Roland Elliot
FCS:	James Golsen
HRO:	Kristin Grajales)
MGT:	Joy K. Bhattacharyya (A/Mo)

POL/ECON:	Monica A. Sledjeski
CG:	Jennifer A McIntyre
PO:	Jennifer A McIntyre
CON:	Nicholas J Manring
PAO:	David J. Gainer
GSO:	Kris Arvind
RSO:	Marlon Grullon
CLO:	Darin P. Volyes
IPO:	Joy K. Bhattacharyya
ISSO:	Ligang Chen
POL:	Matthew Beh

HYDERABAD (CG) 1-8-323, Chiran Fort Lane, Begumpet, Secunderabad-500 003, 91-40-4033-8300, Fax 91-40-40338301, Workweek: Mon–Fri 0830-1730, Website: Hyderabad.state.gov/

CG OMS:	Elizabeth Tillman
FM:	Noemi Davila
MGT:	Daniel F. McCullough
POL/ECON:	Travis Coberly
POSHO:	Noemi Davila
CG:	Katherine S. Dhanani
CON:	Martha Haas
PAO:	Carla Benini
GSO:	Noemi Davila
RSO:	Jason Kephart
ECON:	Paul C. Mueller
IMO:	Aziz Ahmed
IPO:	Mahmood Khattak
ISSO:	Mahmood Khattak

KOLKATA (CG) 5/1 Ho Chi Minh Sarani, Kolkata 700071, 91-33-3984-2400, Fax 91-33-2282-2335, Workweek: Mon-Fri, 0800 hours-1700 hours, http://kolkata.usconsulate.gov/

CG OMS:	Christine Marks
FCS:	Richard Craig
MGT:	Daley C. O'Neil
PAO/ADV:	Rachel Sunden
POL/ECON:	Clinton S. Brown
POSHO:	Matthew Hetrick
CG:	Dean R. Thompson
CON:	Wendy Kennedy
PAO:	Jeffrey K. Reneau
GSO:	Matthew Hetrick
RSO:	John P. Walsh
CLO:	Vandana Kaiser
IPO:	Mahmud H. Khan
ISSO:	Mahmud H. Khan

MUMBAI (CG) C-49, G-Block Bandra Kurla Complex, Bandra East, Mumbai, India 40051, 91-22-2672-4000, Fax 91-22-2672-4755, Workweek: Mon-Fri 0800-1630 hrs, Website: http://mumbai.usconsulate.gov/

CG OMS:	Jennifer A. Koon
Co-CLO:	Valerie Aguirre
FCS:	Richard Rothman
FDA:	Muralidhara B. Gavini
FM:	David Bodycoat
HRO:	Ana Bien Walker
MGT:	Paul C. Cox
POL/ECON:	Robert W. Carlson
CG:	Peter D. Haas
CON:	Aaron Hellman
PAO:	Anne E. Grimes
GSO:	Ana Maria L. Chiaventone
RSO:	Chris Gillis
AFSA:	Daniel Gedacht
AGR:	David J. Williams
CLO:	Noemi Hellman
ECON:	Eva D'Ambrosio
FMO:	Ana Bien Walker
IPO:	James E. Davis
ISO:	Enrico Walker
ISSO:	Noah Dietrich
POL:	Braphus E. Kaalund

TRAVEL

Consular Information Sheet

April 3, 2012

Country Description: India, the world's largest democracy, has a very diverse population, geography, and climate. India is the world's second most populous country, and the world's seventh largest country in area. Tourist facilities offer varying degrees of comfort. Amenities are widely available in large cities and tourist areas.

Smart Traveler Enrollment Program (STEP)/Embassy Locations: If you are traveling to India, please take the time to tell our Embassy and/or Consulate about your trip so we can keep you up to date with important safety and security announcements. We can also help your friends and family get in touch with you in an emergency.

The U.S. Embassy in New Delhi is located at Shanti Path, Chanakya Puri 110021; telephone 91-11-2419–8000; fax 91-11-2419–8407. In case of emergency involving an American citizen, please call the 24-hour operator at (91-11) 2419–8000 and ask for American Citizen Services.

The U.S. Consulate General in Mumbai (Bombay) is located C-49, G-Block, Bandra Kurla Complex, Bandra East, Mumbai 400051, telephone 91-22-2672–4000. In case of an emergency involving an American citizen, please call the 24-hour operator at (91-22) 2672–4000 and ask for American Citizens Services. If you are calling from within India, but outside Mumbai, first dial 022.

The U.S. Consulate General in Kolkata (Calcutta) is at 5/1 Ho Chi Minh Sarani, 700071; telephone 91-33-3984–2400; fax 91-33-2282 2335. If you are an American citizen with an after hours emergency (arrest, death or loss of passport), please call our primary hotline cell phone (91) 99030 42956. If unable to reach the cell phone, please call (91) (33) 3984–2400 and dial "0" and ask for Duty Officer.

The U.S. Consulate General in Chennai (Madras) is at 220 Anna Salai, Gemini Circle, 600006; telephone 91-44-2857–4000; fax 91-44-2857–4443. In case of emergency involving an American citizen, please call the 24-hour operator at (91-44) 2857–4000 and ask for American Citizen Services.

The U.S. Consulate General in Hyderabad is at Paigah Palace, 1-8-323 Chiran Fort Lane, Begumpet, Secunderabad, Andhra Pradesh, 500003; telephone 91-40-4033–8300; fax 91-40-4033–8301. In case of emergency involving an American citizen, please call the 24-hour operator at (91-40) 4033–8300 and ask for American Citizen Services.

Entry/Exit Requirements for U.S. Citizens: All U.S. citizens need a valid passport and valid Indian visa to enter and exit India for any purpose (also see Special Circumstances below). Visitors, including those on official U.S. government business, must apply for visas at an Indian Embassy or Consulate abroad before entering the country. Visas are not available upon arrival for U.S. citizens. If you don't have a valid passport and visa you may be immediately deported. The U.S. Embassy and Consulates in India cannot assist you if you arrive without proper documentation. Please carry photocopies of the bio-data page of your U.S. passport and the pages containing the Indian visa and Indian immigration stamps. If your passport is lost or stolen, copies will help you apply for a replacement passport and an exit visa from the Indian government. Replacing a lost visa, which is required in order to exit the country, may take three to four business days.

U.S. citizens wishing to visit India are responsible for requesting the correct type of visa from the Indian Embassy or Consulate. There are generally no provisions for changing your immigration category (e.g., from tourist to work visa) once you have been admitted into the country. Indian visa regulations change frequently, often with little advance notice, and changes may be poorly advertised and inconsistently enforced. Travelers are urged to check the Indian Government's Ministry of Home Affairs website before any travel to India to review the most current information. If you travel on a tourist visa, you are generally given six months of legal stay upon entering India; extensions are rarely granted. Indian visas may be obtained in the U.S. through Travisa Visa Outsourcing (www.travisa.com), the Government of India's visa contractor. Diplomatic and Official visa applications, however, are accepted directly at the Indian Embassy and Consulates. Please review the information on the Travisa website to determine your purpose for travel and the most appropriate visa category. All U.S. government employees, including military personnel, must obtain country clearance for travel to India.

U.S. citizens of Pakistani origin should expect additional delays when applying for Indian visas due to administrative processing.

Foreign citizens who visit India to study, do research, work, or act as missionaries, as well as all travelers planning to stay more than 180 days, are required to register their visit to India within 14 days of arrival with the Foreigners Regional Registration Office (FRRO) closest to where they will be staying. The FRRO maintains offices in New Delhi, Mumbai, Chennai (known as the "Bureau of Immigration"), Hyderabad, Kolkata, Bengaluru, and Amritsar. District Superintendents of Police serve as Foreigners Registration Officers (FROs) in all states. If you are traveling to India on a tourist visa you may not be allowed re-entry to India within two months of departure without specific permission from an Indian embassy or consulate abroad. For more information on this requirement, please review the Frequently Asked Question (FAQ) section on the Indian Bureau of Immigration website. Travelers have reported that enforcement of this rule at ports of entry may be inconsistent.

If you overstay your Indian visa, or otherwise violate Indian visa regulations, you may require a clearance from the Ministry of Home Affairs in order to leave the country. Generally you will be fined, and in some cases may be jailed, until deportation can be arranged. Visa violators seeking an exit clearance are requested to schedule an online appointment at the Ministry of Home Affairs website before visiting the Visa Facilitation Center at The Ministry of Home Affairs, Foreigners Division, Jaisalmer House, 26 Man Singh Road, New Delhi 110 011(tel. 91-11-2338–5748). Processing of an exit visa under these circumstances may take up to 60 days.

For the most current information on entry and exit requirements, please contact the Embassy of India at 2536 Massachusetts Avenue NW, Washington, DC 20008, telephone (202) 939-9806 or the Indian Consulates in Chicago, New York, San Francisco, or Houston. Outside the United States, inquiries should be made at the nearest Indian Embassy or consulate.

There are no disclosure requirements or restrictions for HIV/AIDS patients who enter India on a tourist visa. Disclosure regarding HIV/AIDS is required of anyone seeking a resident permit in India. Foreign residents found to be suffering from HIV/AIDS will be deported. Please verify this information with the Embassy of India before you travel. General information regarding Indian visa and immigration rules, including the addresses and telephone numbers for the FRRO offices, can be found at the Indian Ministry of Home Affairs Bureau of Immigration website.

Threats to Safety and Security: India continues to experience terrorist and insurgent activities which may affect U.S. citizens directly or indirectly. Anti-Western terrorist groups, some on the U.S. government's list of foreign terrorist organizations, are active in India, including Islamist extremist groups such as Harkat-ul-Jihad-i-Islami, Harakat ul-Mujahidin, Indian Mujahideen, Jaish-e-Mohammed, and Lashkar-e Tayyiba. The U.S. government continues to receive information that terrorist groups are planning attacks that could take place in locations throughout India.

Past attacks have targeted public places, including some frequented by Westerners, such as luxury and other hotels, trains, train stations, markets, cinemas, mosques, and restaurants in large urban areas. Attacks have taken place during the busy evening hours in markets and other crowded places, but could occur at any time. Recent incidents include the February 13, 2012 bombing of an Israeli diplomatic vehicle near the diplomatic enclave in New Delhi that injured four persons; the September 7, 2011 bomb blast at New Delhi's High Court that killed 12 people; and the July 13, 2011 bombings in crowded areas in Mumbai, where three separate explosions killed 21 people and injured more than 100. In December 2010 an explosive device that detonated at Shitla Ghat in Varanasi during evening "aarti," or prayers, killed two persons and injured 30, including several foreigners. In February 2010, an explosive device detonated at a café in Pune, Maharashtra and killed 10 people, including two foreign nationals, and injured 50. Beginning in May 2008, several coordinated terrorist attacks occurred in major cities throughout India, to include New Delhi, culminating in the November attacks in

Mumbai where over 170 people were killed, including six U.S. citizens. The most prominent insurgent groups in India are the Maoists (also known as "Naxalites"). The Naxalites typically attack Indian government officials, but have also derailed rail lines and targeted other government buildings such as police stations. They operate mostly in the more remote areas of the country.

U.S. citizens should always practice good security. Be aware of your surroundings and keep a low profile. Monitor local news reports, vary your routes and times in carrying out daily activities, and consider the level of security present when you visit public places, including religious sites, or choosing hotels, restaurants, and entertainment and recreation venues.

Beyond the threat from terrorism and insurgencies, demonstrations and general strikes, or "bandh," often cause inconvenience. Large religious ceremonies that attract hundreds of thousands of people can result in dangerous and often life-threatening stampedes. Local demonstrations can begin spontaneously and escalate with little warning, disrupting transportation systems and city services and posing risks to travelers. In response to such events, Indian authorities occasionally impose curfews and/or restrict travel. You are urged to avoid demonstrations and rallies as they have the potential for violence, especially immediately preceding and following elections and religious festivals (particularly when Hindu and Muslim festivals coincide). Tensions between castes and religious groups can also result in disruptions and violence. In some cases, demonstrators specifically block roads near popular tourist sites and disrupt train operations in order to gain the attention of Indian authorities; occasionally vehicles transporting tourists are attacked in these incidents. India generally goes on "High Alert" status prior to major holidays or events. You should monitor local television, print media, Mission India's Facebook page, and enroll with the program forfurther information about the current situation in areas where you will travel. Religious violence occasionally occurs in India, especially when tensions between different religious communities are purposefully exacerbated by groups pushing religiously chauvinistic agendas. Violence against Indian Christians in a remote part of Odisha (formerly known as Orissa) in 2008 resulted in the displacement of thousands of villagers and the deaths of 40 people. There are active "anti-conversion" laws in some Indian states, and acts of conversion sometimes elicit violent reactions from Hindu extremists. Foreigners suspected of proselytizing Hindus have been attacked and killed in conservative, rural areas in India in the past.

Swimming in India: You should exercise caution if you intend to swim in open waters along the Indian coastline, particularly during the monsoon season. Every year, several people in Goa, Mumbai, Puri (Odisha), off the Eastern Coast in the Bay of Bengal, and other areas drown due to strong undertows. It is important to heed warnings posted or advised at beaches and to avoid swimming in the ocean during the monsoon season. Trained lifeguards are very rare along beaches.

If you visit the Andaman Islands, be aware that there have been 24 reports of salt-water crocodile attacks in the past 25 years in the Islands. Four have resulted in fatalities, including a U.S. citizen tourist in April 2010. Ask local residents about dangerous sea life before swimming and keep a safe distance from animals at all times.

Wildlife safaris: India offers opportunities for observation of wildlife in its natural habitat and many tour operators and lodges advertise structured, safe excursions into parks and other wildlife viewing areas for close observation of flora and fauna. However, safety standards and training vary, and it is a good idea to ascertain whether operators are trained and licensed. Even animals marketed as "tame" should be respected as wild and extremely dangerous. Keep a safe distance from animals at all times, remaining in vehicles or other protected enclosures when venturing into game parks.

Trekking in India: Trekking expeditions should be limited to routes identified for this purpose by local authorities. Use only registered trekking agencies, porters, and guides, suspend trekking after dark, camp at designated camping places, and travel in groups rather than individually or with one or two companions. Altitudes in popular trekking spots can be as high as 25,170 feet (7,672 m); please make sure that you have had a recent medical checkup to ensure that you are fit to trek at these altitudes and carry sufficient medical insurance that includes medical evacuation coverage.

Jammu & Kashmir: The Department of State strongly recommends that you avoid travel to the state of Jammu & Kashmir (with the exception of visits to the eastern Ladakh region and its capital, Leh) because of the potential for terrorist incidents, as well as violent public unrest. U.S. government employees are prohibited from traveling to Jammu & Kashmir (except for Ladakh) without permission, which is only granted by the U.S. Embassy in New Delhi in exceptional circumstances. A number of terrorist groups operate in the state, targeting security forces in the region, particularly along the Line of Control (LOC) separating Indian and Pakistani-controlled Kashmir, and those stationed in primary tourist destinations in the Kashmir Valley: Srinagar, Gulmarg, and Pahalgam. Since 1989, as many as 60,000 people (terrorists, security forces, and civilians) have been killed in the Kashmir conflict. Foreigners are particularly visible, vulnerable, and at risk. In the past, serious communal violence left the state mostly paralyzed due to massive strikes and business shut downs, and U.S. citizens have had to be evacuated by local police. The Indian government prohibits foreign tourists from visiting certain areas along the LOC (see the section on Restricted Areas, below).

India-Pakistan Border: The State Department recommends that you avoid travel to areas within ten kilometers of the border between India and Pakistan. Both India and Pakistan maintain a strong military presence on both sides of the border. The only official India-Pakistan border crossing point for persons who are not citizens of India or Pakistan is in the state of Punjab between Atari, India, and Wagah, Pakistan. The border crossing is usually open, but you are advised to confirm the current status of the border crossing prior to commencing travel. A Pakistani visa is required to enter Pakistan. Only U.S. citizens residing in India may apply for a Pakistani visa in India. Otherwise you should apply for a Pakistani visa in your country of residence before traveling to India. The Pakistani government requires that U.S. citizen residents of India must first come to the U.S. Embassy in New Delhi to sign an affidavit of intent to apply for the Pakistani visa before submitting their application.

Both India and Pakistan claim an area of the Karakoram mountain range that includes the Siachen glacier. Travel or mountain climbing in this area is highly dangerous. The disputed area includes the following peaks: Rimo Peak; Apsarasas I, II, and III; Tegam Kangri I, II and III; Suingri Kangri; Ghiant I and II; Indira Col; and Sia Kangri. Check with the U.S. Embassy in New Delhi for information on current conditions. (Please see the section on "Smart Traveler Enrollment Program (STEP)/Embassy Location" above.)

Northeastern states: Incidents of violence by ethnic insurgent groups, including bombings of buses, trains, rail lines, and markets, occur with some frequency in the northeast. While U.S. citizens have not been specifically targeted, it is possible that you could be affected as a bystander. If you travel to the northeast, you should avoid travel by train at night, travel outside major cities at night, and crowds. Security laws are in force in the region, in recognition that these areas have a higher level of instability, and the central government has deployed security personnel. U.S. government employees are prohibited from traveling to the states of Assam, Arunachal Pradesh, Mizoram, Nagaland, Meghalaya, Tripura, and Manipur without permission from the U.S. Consulate in Kolkata. Restricted Area Permits are required for foreigners to visit certain Northeastern states (see the section on Restricted Areas, below.) Contact the U.S. Consulate in Kolkata for information on current conditions. (Please see the section on Smart Traveler Enrollment Program (STEP)/Embassy Location, above.)

East Central and Southern India: Maoist extremist groups, or "Naxalites," are active in East Central India primarily in rural areas. The Naxalites have a long history of conflict with state and national authorities, including frequent attacks on local police, paramilitary forces, and government officials, and are responsible for more terrorist attacks in the country than any other organization through an ongoing campaign of violence and intimidation. In February 2012, four officers of the Border Security Force (BSF) were killed in an ambush by Communist Party of India-Maoist rebels in the Malkangiri district of Odisha. In March 2012 Naxalite guerrillas abducted four persons including two Italian nationals from a remote area of southern Odisha. Naxalites have not specifically targeted U.S. citizens but have attacked symbolic targets that have included Western companies and rail lines. While Naxalite violence does not normally occur in places frequented by foreigners, there is a risk that visitors could become victims of violence.

Naxalites are active in a large swath of India from eastern Maharashtra and northern Andhra Pradesh through western West Bengal, particularly in rural parts of Chhattisgarh and Jharkhand and on the borders of Andhra Pradesh, Maharashtra, Madhya Pradesh, Uttar Pradesh, Bihar, West Bengal, and Odisha. Due to the fluid nature of the threat, all U.S. government travelers to states with Naxalite activity must receive prior authorization from the Regional Security Officer responsible for the area to be visited. U.S. officials traveling only to the capital cities in these states do not need prior authorization from the Regional Security Officer.

Civil unrest continues in the south-central Indian state of Andhra Pradesh over the contentious issue of creating a separate state called Telangana within Andhra Pradesh. Until the issue is resolved definitively, there may continue to be tension, especially in the Telangana Region of Andhra Pradesh, which includes the districts of Rangareddi, Warangal, Medak, Nizamabad, Karimnagar, Adilabad, Khammam, Nalgonda, and Mahbubnagar. You should avoid political rallies, demonstrations, and large crowds of any kind. The campus of Osmania University in Hyderabad has been the site of recurring civil disturbances regarding the Telangana statehood issue. Also, organized demonstrations are often held at Indira Park, located on Lower Tank Bund Road. Other locations where protests have occurred are at the State Legislative Assembly, Gun Park, and Nizam College in Bashir Bagh. Use caution when visiting these sites, and avoid them altogether during periods of unrest. If you are residing or traveling in Andhra Pradesh you should monitor the situation via media sources, including TV, radio and via the internet, and enroll in the STEP program to receive updated security information from the U.S. Embassy or Consulate.

Restricted/Protected areas: Certain parts of India are designated as "restricted areas" by the Indian government and require special advance permission to visit. These areas include:

- The state of Arunachal Pradesh
- Portions of the state of Sikkim
- Portions of the state of Himachal Pradesh near the Chinese border
- Portions of the state of Uttarakhand (Uttaranchal) near the Chinese border

- Portions of the state of Rajasthan near the Pakistani border
- Portions of the state of Jammu & Kashmir near the Line of Control with Pakistan and certain portions of Ladakh
- The Andaman & Nicobar Islands
- The Union Territory of the Laccadives Islands (Lakshadweep)
- The Tibetan colony in Mundgod, Karnataka

More information on travel to/in restricted/protected areas can be found at India's Bureau of Immigration. "Restricted Area Permits" are available outside India at Indian embassies and consulates abroad, or in India from the Ministry of Home Affairs (Foreigners Division) at Jaisalmer House, 26 Man Singh Road, New Delhi. The states of Arunachal Pradesh and Sikkim maintain official guesthouses in New Delhi, which can also issue Restricted Area Permits for their respective states for certain travelers. You should exercise caution while visiting Mamallapuram (Mahabalipuram) in Tamil Nadu as the Indira Gandhi Atomic Research Center, Kalpakkam, is located just south of the site and is not clearly marked as a restricted and dangerous area. For the latest security information, travelers should enroll in the STEP program to receive updated security information and regularly monitor travel information available from the U.S. Embassy in New Delhi as well as the U.S. Consulates General in Mumbai (Bombay), Chennai (Madras), Hyderabad, and Kolkata (Calcutta).

Stay up to date by:

- Bookmarking our Bureau of Consular Affairs website, which contains the current Travel Warnings and Travel Alerts as well as the Worldwide Caution.
- Follow us on Twitter and the Bureau of Consular Affairs page on Facebook as well.
- Download our free Smart Traveler iPhone App to have travel information at your fingertips.
- Calling 1-888-407-4747 toll-free within the United States and Canada, or a regular toll line, 1-202-501-4444, from other countries.
- Taking some time before travel to consider your personal security.

Crime: Petty crime, especially theft of personal property, is common, particularly on trains or buses. Pickpockets can be very adept and women have reported having their bags snatched, purse-straps cut, or the bottom of their purses slit without their knowledge. Theft of U.S. passports is common, particularly in major tourist areas, on overnight trains, and at airports and train stations. If you are traveling by train, lock your sleeping compartments and take your valuables with you when leaving your berth. If you travel by air, be careful with your bags in the arrival and departure areas outside airports. Violent crime, especially directed against foreigners, has traditionally been uncommon, although in recent years there has been a modest increase. Be cautious about displaying cash or expensive items to reduce the chance of being a target for robbery or other crime, and be aware of your surroundings when you use ATMs. Gangs and criminal elements operate in major cities and have sometimes targeted unsuspecting business travelers and their family members for kidnapping or extortion.

U.S. citizens, particularly women, are cautioned not to travel alone in India. Western women, especially those of African descent, continue to report incidents of verbal and physical harassment by groups of men. Known locally as "Eve-teasing," these incidents can be quite frightening. Eve-teasing can occur anytime or anywhere, but most frequently has happened in crowded areas such as in market places, train stations, buses, and public streets. The harassment can range from sexually suggestive or lewd comments, to catcalls, to outright groping. Southern India is very distinct from the other major cities and has a strong reputation for being very traditional. If you are a woman traveling in India, you are advised to respect local dress and customs. While India is generally safe for foreign visitors, according to the latest figures by Indian authorities, rape is the fastest growing crime in India. Among large cities, Delhi experienced the highest number of crimes against women. Although most victims have been local residents, recent sexual attacks against female visitors in tourist areas underline the fact that foreign women are at risk and should exercise vigilance.

Women should observe stringent security precautions, including avoiding use of public transport after dark without the company of known and trustworthy companions, restricting evening entertainment to well-known venues, and avoiding isolated areas when alone at any time of day. If you are a woman traveling in India, you are advised to respect conservative local dress and customs. Keep your hotel room number confidential and make sure hotel room doors have chains, deadlocks, and spy-holes. In addition, only hire reliable cars and drivers and avoid traveling alone in hired taxis, especially at night. Use taxis from hotels and pre-paid taxis at airports rather than hailing them on the street. If you encounter threatening situations, call "100" for police assistance.

Scams: Major airports, train stations, popular restaurants, and tourist sites are often used by scam artists looking to prey on visitors, often by creating a distraction. Beware of taxi drivers and others, including train porters, who solicit travelers with "come-on" offers of cheap transportation and/or hotels. Travelers accepting such offers have frequently found themselves the victims of scams, including offers to assist with "necessary" transfers to the domestic airport, disproportionately expensive hotel rooms, unwanted "tours," unwelcome "purchases," extended cab rides, substandard hotel rooms at overly expensive rates and even threats when the tourists decline to pay. There have been reports of tourists being lured, held hostage and forced to pay thousands of dollars in the face of threats of violence against the traveler and his/her family members.

You should exercise care when hiring transportation and/or guides and use only well-known travel agents to book trips. Some scam artists have lured travelers by displaying their name on a sign when they leave the airport. Another popular scam is to drop money or to squirt something on the clothing of an unsuspecting traveler and during the distraction to rob them of their valuables. Tourists have also been given drugged drinks or tainted food to make them more vulnerable to theft, particularly at train stations. Even food or drink purchased in front of the traveler from a canteen or vendor could be tainted.

Some vendors sell carpets, jewelry, gemstones, or other expensive items that may not be of the quality promised. Deal only with reputable businesses and do not hand over your credit cards or money unless you are certain that goods being shipped are the goods you purchased. If a deal sounds too good to be true, it is best avoided. Most Indian states have official tourism bureaus set up to handle complaints.

There have been a number of other scams perpetrated against foreign travelers, particularly in Goa, Jaipur, and Agra that target younger travelers and involve suggestions that money can be made by privately transporting gems or gold (both of which can result in arrest) or by taking delivery abroad of expensive carpets, supposedly while avoiding customs duties. The scam artists describe profits that can be made upon delivery of the goods, and require the traveler to pay a "deposit" as part of the transaction.

U.S. citizens have had problems with business partners, usually involving property investments. You may wish to seek professional legal advice in reviewing any contracts for business or services offered in India. A list of attorneys is available on the Embassy and Consulate websites.

In another common scam, family members in the U.S., particularly older people, are approached for funds to help grandchildren or relatives who claim to be in jail or without money to return home. Do not send money without contacting the U.S. Embassy or Consulate to confirm the caller's situation. You can also call our office of Overseas Citizens Services at 888-407-4747 (from overseas: 202-501-4444). Review our information on Emergency Assistance to Americans Abroad.

Don't buy counterfeit and pirated goods, even if they are widely available. Not only are the bootlegs illegal in the United States, if you purchase them you may also be breaking local law.

Victims of Crime: If you or someone you know becomes the victim of a crime abroad, you should contact the local police and the nearest U.S. embassy or consulate. We can:

- Replace a stolen passport.
- Help you find appropriate medical care if you are the victim of violent crimes such as assault or rape.
- Put you in contact with the appropriate police authorities, and if you want us to, we can contact family members or friend.
- Help you understand the local criminal justice process and direct you to local attorneys, although it is important to remember that local authorities are responsible for investigating and prosecuting the crime. You will need to obtain a copy of the police report (FIR) from local police when you report the incident. Local authorities generally are unable to take any meaningful action without the filing of a police report.

If your passport is stolen you should immediately report the theft or loss to the police in the location where your passport was stolen. A police report, called an FIR (First Information Report) is required by the Indian government in order to obtain an exit visa to leave India if the lost passport contained your Indian visa. Although the Embassy or Consulate is able to replace a stolen or lost passport, the Ministry of Home Affairs and the Foreigners Regional Registration Office (FRRO) are responsible for approving an exit permit. This process can take three to four working days. You will need to obtain a copy of the police report (FIR) from local police when you report the incident. Local authorities generally are unable to take any meaningful action without the filing of a police report.

The local equivalent to the "911" emergency line in India is "100." An additional emergency number, "112," can be accessed from mobile phones.

Criminal Penalties: While you are traveling in another country, you are subject to its laws even if you are a U.S. citizen. Foreign laws and legal systems can be vastly different from our own. In some places, you may be taken in for questioning if you don't have your passport with you. In some places, it is illegal to take pictures of certain buildings. In some places, driving under the influence could land you immediately in jail. These criminal penalties will vary from country to country. While you are physically overseas, U.S. laws don't apply. If you do something illegal in your host country, your U.S. passport won't help. It's very important to know what's legal and what's not where you are going. It is also important to note that there are also some things that might be legal in the country you visit, but still illegal in the United States. For example, you can be prosecuted in the United States if you buy pirated goods, engage in sexual conduct with children, or use or disseminate child pornography in a foreign country even if those activities do not happen to be illegal in that country.

While some countries will automatically notify the nearest U.S. embassy or consulate if a U.S. citizen is detained or arrested in a foreign country, that might not always be the case. To ensure that the United States is aware of your circumstances, request that the police and prison officials notify the nearest U.S. embassy or consulate as soon as you are arrested or detained overseas.

Special Circumstances: Dual nationality: India does not permit its citizens to hold dual nationality. In 2006, India launched the "Overseas Citizens of India" (OCI) program, which has often been mischaracterized as a dual nationality program. It does not grant Indian citizenship. If you are a U.S. citizen and obtain an OCI card you will not become a citizen of India; you will remain a citizen of the United States. An OCI card is similar to a U.S. "green card" in that a holder can travel to and from India indefinitely, work in India, study in India, and own property in India (except for certain agricultural and plantation properties). An OCI card holder, however, does not receive an Indian passport, cannot vote in Indian elections, and is not eligible for Indian government employment. The OCI program is similar to the Persons of Indian Origin (PIO) card introduced by the Indian government several years ago, except that PIO holders must still register with Indian immigration authorities, and PIO cards are not issued for an indefinite period. U.S. citizens of Indian descent can apply for PIO or OCI cards at the Indian Embassy in Washington, or at the Indian Consulates in Chicago, New York, San Francisco, and Houston. Inside India, U.S. citizens can apply at the nearest FRRO office (please see "Entry/Exit Requirements" section above for more information on the FRRO).

Religious activities: If you plan to engage in religious proselytizing, you are required by Indian law to have a "missionary" visa. Immigration authorities have determined that certain activities, including speaking at religious meetings to which the general public is invited, may violate immigration law if the traveler does not hold a missionary visa. Foreigners with tourist visas who engage in missionary activity are subject to deportation and possible criminal prosecution. The states of Odisha, Chhattisgarh, Gujarat, Himachal Pradesh, and Madhya Pradesh have active "anti-conversion" legislation regulating conversion from one religious faith to another. Arunachal Pradesh currently has an inactive "anti-conversion" law awaiting accompanying regulations needed for enforcement. If you intend to engage in missionary activity, you may wish to seek legal advice to determine whether the activities you intend to pursue are permitted under Indian law.

Tourists should also be mindful of restrictions and observances when planning to visit any religious establishment, whether Hindu temples, mosques, churches, or other locations considered sacred by the local population. Many individual temples and mosques do not permit non-members to enter all or parts of the facilities, and may require the removal of shoes, headwear or have other specific requirements for appropriate attire.

Customs restrictions: Before traveling to or from India, you are urged to thoroughly inspect all bags and clothing that might inadvertently contain prohibited items. Since January 2010, at least seven U.S. citizens have been arrested or detained when airport security officials discovered loose ammunition in their luggage. If you are found to have loose ammunition or bullets on your person, you could be charged with violation of the Indian Arms Act, incarcerated, and/or deported from India. In addition to firearms and ammunition, Indian customs authorities enforce strict regulations concerning temporary importation into or export from India of such items as, antiquities, electronic equipment, currency, ivory, gold objects, and other prohibited materials. Permission from the Government of India is required to bring in restricted items, even if you are transiting through India. If you do not comply with these regulations, you risk arrest or fine or both and confiscation of these items. If you are charged with any alleged legal violations by Indian law enforcement, have an attorney review any document before you sign it. The Government of India requires the registration of antique items with the local police along with a photograph of the item. It is advisable to contact the Embassy of India in Washington or one of India's consulates in the United States for specific information regarding customs requirements. More information is available from the Indian Central Board of Excise and Customs.

Indian customs authorities encourage the use of an ATA (Admission Temporaire/Temporary Admission) Carnet for the temporary admission of professional equipment, commercial samples, and/or goods for exhibitions and fair purposes. ATA Carnet Headquarters, located at the U.S. Council for International Business, 1212 Avenue of the Americas, New York, NY 10036, issues and guarantees the ATA Carnet in the United States. For additional information call (212) 354-4480, or email USCIB for details.

Natural disaster threats: Parts of northern India are highly susceptible to earthquakes. Regions of highest risk, ranked 5 on a scale of 1 to 5, include areas around Srinagar, Himachal Pradesh, Rishikesh and Dehra Dun, the northern parts of Punjab, northwest Gujarat, northern Bihar, and the entire northeast. Ranked 4 (high damage risk) is an area that sweeps along the north through Jammu and Kashmir, Eastern Punjab, Haryana, Northern Uttar Pradesh, central Bihar and the northern parts of West Bengal. New Delhi is located in zone 4. Severe flooding is common in Bihar, Assam, and Odisha. In August 2010 flash flooding and mudslides in Leh killed 300 people and stranded hundreds more for several days.

Accessibility: While in India, individuals with disabilities may find accessibility and accommodation very different from what you find in the United States. Despite legislation that all public buildings and transport be accessible to the disabled, accessibility remains limited. One notable exception is the recently constructed Delhi metro system, designed to be accessible to those with physical disabilities.

Medical Facilities and Health Information: The quality of medical care in India varies considerably. Medical care in the major population centers approaches and occasionally meets Western standards, but adequate medical care is usually very limited or unavailable in rural areas.

If you are arriving in India from Sub-Saharan Africa or other yellow-fever areas, Indian health regulations require that you present evidence of vaccination against yellow fever. If you do not have such proof, you could be subjected to immediate deportation or a six-day detention in the yellow-fever quarantine center. If you transit through any part of sub-Saharan Africa, even for one day, you are advised to carry proof of yellow fever immunization.

Good information on vaccinations and other health precautions is available from the Centers for Disease Control and Prevention (CDC) or by calling the hotline for international travelers at 1-877-FYI-TRIP (1-877-394-8747). Some vaccines such as Typhoid, Influenza, and Hepatitis A are recommended for all travelers and other vaccines such as Hepatitis B, Japanese Encephalitis, and Rabies are recommended for high-risk travelers. For information about outbreaks of infectious diseases abroad, consult the World Health Organization (WHO). The WHO website also contains additional health information for travelers, including detailed country-specific health information. These websites provide useful information, such as suggested vaccinations for visitors to India, safe food and water precautions, appropriate measures to avoid contraction of mosquito-borne diseases (such as malaria and Japanese B encephalitis), suggestions to avoid altitude sickness, etc. Further, these sites provide information on disease outbreaks that may arise from time to time. Outbreaks of mosquito-borne viral diseases such as dengue fever and chikungunya occur in various parts of India each year. You should check these sites shortly before traveling to India. Further health information for travelers is available from the WHO.

Outbreaks of Avian Influenza (H5N1 virus) occur intermittently in eastern India, including West Bengal, Manipur, Sikkim, and Assam. For further information on avian influenza (bird flu), please refer to the Department of State's Avian Influenza Fact Sheet.

Malaria prophylaxis depends on time of year and area the traveler is going to. Please consult the CDC website for more information.

H1N1, also known as the swine flu, has been reported in India in travelers coming from or transiting through the United States, and has spread locally throughout India. Individuals traveling with flu-like symptoms should strongly consider delaying their travel until their symptoms have resolved for the protection of other passengers and the risk of being quarantined in a communicable public hospital on arrival in India. H1N1 vaccine and seasonal influenza vaccine are available in India.

Tuberculosis is an increasingly serious health concern in India. For further information, please consult the CDC's Travel Notice on TB.

Medical tourism is a rapidly growing industry. Companies offering vacation packages bundled with medical consultations and financing options provide direct-to-consumer advertising over the internet. Such medical packages often claim to provide high quality care, but the quality of health care in India is highly variable. People seeking health care in India should understand that medical systems operate differently from those in the United States and are not subject to the same rules and regulations. Anyone interested in traveling for medical purposes should consult with their local physician before traveling and refer to the information from CDC. Persons traveling to India for medical purposes require the proper "medical" visa. Please check with the nearest Indian Embassy or consulate for more information.

Despite reports of antibiotic-resistant bacteria in hospitals, in general travelers should not delay or avoid treatment for urgent or emergent medical situations. However, health tourists and other travelers who may be contemplating elective procedures in this country should carefully research individual hospital infection control practices. Rh-negative blood may be difficult to obtain as it is not common in Asia.

Monkeys can transmit rabies and herpes B, among other diseases, to human victims. Avoid feeding monkeys. If bitten, you should immediately soak and scrub the bite for at least 15 minutes and seek urgent medical attention.

Commercial surrogacy, a growing industry in India, remains unregulated, operating solely under non-binding government guidelines. There are concerns that the interests and rights of commissioning parents, surrogates, egg donors, and the resulting children may not always be adequately protected.

In order for a child born of surrogacy to acquire U.S. citizenship and obtain a U.S. passport, sufficient proof must be submitted showing a genetic relationship between the newborn child and an American parent. This is best accomplished through DNA testing. Newborns found not to have acquired U.S. citizenship at birth risk becoming stateless persons unable to obtain travel documents as Indian law prohibits the issuance of Indian passports to children born of surrogacy. With no right to other citizenship, infants may find themselves stranded in India.

If you are considering traveling to India for assisted reproductive technology (ART) procedures, please contact the Embassy or one of the Consulates well in advance and review the available information to learn if your child born from ART may be documented as a U.S. citizen.

After the birth of your child, you should count on staying in India at least two weeks to complete the Consular Report of Birth Abroad of a U.S. Citizen (CRBA) and passport application and to obtain an Indian exit visa.

The U.S. Embassy and Consulates in India maintain lists of local doctors and hospitals, all of which are published on their respective websites under "U.S. Citizen Services." We cannot endorse or recommend any specific medical provider or clinic.

Medical Insurance: You can't assume your insurance will go with you when you travel. It's very important to find out BEFORE you leave. You need to ask your insurance company two questions:

- Does my policy apply when I'm out of the United States?
- Will it cover emergencies like a trip to a foreign hospital or an evacuation?

In many places, doctors and hospitals still expect payment in cash at the time of service. Your regular U.S. health insurance may not cover doctors' and hospital visits in other countries. If your policy doesn't go with you when you travel, it's a very good idea to take out another one for your trip. Medical evacuation coverage is strongly advised.

Traffic Safety and Road Conditions: Travel by road in India is dangerous. India leads the world in traffic-related deaths and a number of U.S. citizens have suffered fatal traffic accidents in recent years. You should exercise extreme caution when crossing streets, even in marked pedestrian areas, and try to use only cars that have seatbelts. Seat belts are not common in taxis. Helmets should always be worn on motorcycles and bicycles.

Travel at night is particularly hazardous. Buses, patronized by hundreds of millions of Indians, are convenient in that they serve almost every city of any size. However, they are usually driven fast, recklessly, and without consideration for the rules of the road. Accidents are quite common. Trains are safer than buses, but train accidents still occur more frequently than in other countries.

In order to drive in India, you must have either a valid Indian driver's license or a valid international driver's license. Because of difficult road and traffic conditions, you may wish to consider hiring a local driver.

On Indian roads, the safest driving policy is to always assume that other drivers will not respond to a traffic situation in the same way you would in the United States. On Indian roads, might makes right, and buses and trucks epitomize this fact. Buses and trucks often run red lights and merge directly into traffic at yield points and traffic circles. Cars, auto-rickshaws, bicycles, and pedestrians behave only slightly more cautiously. Use your horn or flash your headlights frequently to announce your presence. It is both customary and wise.

Outside major cities, main roads and other roads are often poorly maintained and congested. Even main roads frequently have only two lanes, with poor visibility and inadequate warning markers. On the few divided highways one can expect to meet local transportation traveling in the wrong direction, often without lights. Heavy traffic is the norm and includes (but is not limited to) overloaded trucks and buses, scooters, pedestrians, bullock and camel carts, horse or elephant riders en route to weddings, bicycles, and free-roaming livestock. Traffic in India moves on the left. It is important to be alert while crossing streets and intersections, especially after dark as traffic is coming in the "wrong" direction. Travelers should remember to use seatbelts in both rear and front seats where available, and to ask their drivers to maintain a safe speed.

If a driver hits a pedestrian or a cow, the vehicle and its occupants are at risk of being attacked by passersby. Such attacks pose significant risk of injury or death to the vehicle's occupants or at least of incineration of the vehicle. It is unsafe to remain at the scene of an accident of this nature, and drivers may instead wish to seek out the nearest police station.

Protestors often use road blockage as a means of publicizing their grievances, causing severe inconvenience to travelers. Visitors should monitor local news reports for any reports of road disturbances.

Emergency Numbers: The following emergency numbers work in New Delhi, Mumbai, Chennai, Hyderabad, and Kolkata:

- Police 100
- Fire Brigade 101
- Ambulance 102

Aviation Safety Oversight: The U.S. Federal Aviation Administration (FAA) has assessed the Government of India's Civil Aviation Authority as being in compliance with International Civil Aviation Organization (ICAO) aviation safety standards for oversight of India's air carrier operations. For more information, travelers may visit the FAA's website. In the wake of a series of crashes in the northeast, travelers are urged to use caution while booking private helicopters for travel, especially in the northeast.

Children's Issues: Please see the U.S. Dept. of State Office of Children's Issues web pages on intercountry adoption and international parental child abduction.

Intercountry Adoption

Freeze on New Intercountry Adoption Applications November 30, 2012

Effective December 1, 2012, India will not accept new applications for intercountry adoptions from the United States. or other foreign adoption service providers until further notice, in order to clear a backlog of existing cases.

Central Adoption Resource Authority (CARA) will continue to process applications registered prior to December 1, 2012. We will provide an update when CARA begins accepting new applications. If you have any questions, please contact us by phone at 1-888-407-4747 or e-mail us at adoptionUSCA@state.gov.

Overview
November 2010

The information in this section has been edited from the latest report available as of February 2013 from the State Department Bureau of Consular Affairs, Office of Overseas Citizens Services. For more information, please read the *Intercountry Adoption* section of this book and review current reports online at http://adoption.state.gov. India is a party to the Hague Convention on Protection of Children and Co-operation in Respect of Intercountry Adoption (Hague Adoption Convention). Therefore, all adoptions between India and the United States must meet the requirements of the Convention and the U.S. law implementing the Convention.

Who Can Adopt? Adoptions between the United States and India are governed by the Hague Adoption Convention. Therefore to adopt from India, you must first be found eligible to be an adoptive parent by the U.S. Government by filing Form I-800A. The U.S. Government agency responsible for making this determination is the Department of Homeland Security, U.S. Citizenship and Immigration Services (USCIS).

Residency Requirements: The Central Adoption Resource Authority (CARA) does not have any residency requirement. However, some Recognized Indian Placement Agencies (RIPAs) may ask prospective adoptive parents (PAPs) to reside with the child for seven days in India cumulative from the time of identifying the child to the time of departure from India.

Age Requirements: PAPs should be at least 30 and no more than 55 years of age. Married couples may not have a combined age of more than 90 years. These provisions may be relaxed in exceptional cases, such as the adoption of older children, sibling groups, and children with special needs. However, in no case should the age of any one of the PAPs exceed 55 years. Single parents up to age 45 can adopt. PAPs should be at least 21 years older than the child.

Marriage Requirements: A married couple that has been in a stable relationship for at least 5 years. Single persons (never married, widowed, divorced) up to 45 years can also adopt.

Income Requirements: There are no income requirements.

Other Requirements: The financial status and health of PAPs should be covered in the Home Study Report. A second adoption from India will be considered only after the legal adoption of the first child is completed, except in the case of siblings adopted at the same time. Same sex couples are not eligible to adopt.

Who Can be Adopted? Because India is a member of the Hague Adoption Convention, children from India must meet the requirements of the Convention in order to be eligible for adoption. For example, the Convention requires that the sending country attempt to place a child with a family in India before determining that a child is eligible for intercountry adoption. In addition to India's requirements, a child must meet the definition of a Convention adoptee before you can bring him or her immediately back to the United States.

The Process: Because India is party to the Hague Adoption Convention, adopting from India must follow a specific process designed to meet the Convention's requirements. For detailed and updated information on these requirements, please review the *Intercountry Adoption* section of this publication and visit the U.S. Department of State Intercountry Adoption website at http://adoption.state.gov.

Intra-Family Adoption: While the adoption of a relative is possible under the Hague Adoption Convention, the prospective adoptive child must meet the definition of Convention Adoptee. Furthermore, in the case of a child having two living birth parents, it must be demonstrated that they are incapable of providing proper care for the child in accordance with local standards (for information on the definition of Convention Adoptee, please see: http://adoption.state.gov/hague/laws.html *Intercountry Adoption* Act of 2000, Sec. 302. Immigration and Nationality Act Amendments Relating to Children Adopted from Convention Countries.)

Adoption of Tibetan Children: Tibetan refugees living in India are considered stateless persons. Tibetan children come under the jurisdiction of the Child Protection Standard of India. CARA has forwarded draft guidelines relating to the adoption of Tibetan children pursuant to the Hague Adoption Convention to the Ministry of Law for its consideration. These guidelines are still pending the Ministry's approval. Until these guidelines are approved and implemented, the adoption of Tibetan children is on hold.

Role of the Adoption Authority: The Central Adoption Resource Agency (CARA) regulates and monitors intercountry adoptions. CARA implements the Hague Adoption Convention, acts as a clearing house for information regarding abandoned/relinquished/orphaned children available for intercountry adoption, issues No-Objection Certificates in intercountry adoption cases. Frames and implements guidelines for intercountry adoption, issues guidelines on policies, procedures and practices relating to Intercountry Adoption, renews recognition of recognized Indian Placement Agencies (RIPAs) and Enlisted Foreign Adoption Agencies (EFAAs), and issues confirmatory certificates (Article 23) for cases were adoption is completed in India.

Role of Adoption Agencies: All Indian orphanages (referred to in India as placement agencies) must be registered with their Indian state Voluntary Coordinating Agency (VCA). Placement agencies do not provide national coverage, so prospective adoptive parents must determine the Indian state from which they propose to adopt. The Central Adoption Resource Agency (CARA), established in 1990, licenses all the VCAs and all Indian placement agencies. The Indian placement agency usually files the paperwork with the court, minimizing the need for a private attorney.

Time Frame: The time frame can vary from two to six months for the Indian courts to provide the court order for adoption or legal guardianship. Be mindful that this time frame is after the Embassy has sent the Article 5 letter to CARA and CARA has issued its NOC.

Adoption Application: Your ASP may indicate their preference of a particular Indian placement agency, if any. On receiving the adoption dossier, a case file will be opened by CARA and CARA will advise the ASP if any additional documents are required. Any application from foreigners (including Non-Resident Indians (NRIs), Persons of Indian Origin (PIOs). and those with Overseas Citizens of India (OCI) status) for adoption of an Indian child received by a RIPA shall not be entertained without prior consent of CARA. For more information, see the intercountry adoption website at http://adoption.state.gov.

Adoption Fees: The U.S. Embassy in India discourages the payment of any fees that are not properly receipted, "donations," or "expediting" fees, that may be requested from prospective adoptive parents. Such fees have the appearance of "buying" a baby and put all future adoptions in India at risk. In the adoption services contract that you sign at the beginning of the adoption process, your ASP will itemize the fees and estimated expenses related to your adoption process.

Documents Required: Your ASP will submit one attested/notarized copy of the adoption application (not original) along with the below mentioned documents to CARA for approval:

- Home Study Report (see information below for Home Study Reports for Americans Residing in India);
- Recent photographs of the adoptive parents/family;
- Marriage certificate (if applicable);
- Certificate of medical fitness of PAP(s) certified by a medical doctor;
- Declaration regarding the financial status of PAPs along with supporting documents, such as job letters, income tax returns, and bank statements;
- Three reference letters from relatives/friends regarding the suitability of PAPs to adopt;
- Adoption decrees of previously adopted child/children, if any;
- Police clearance report(s);
- Birth certificate/passport of PAPs, as proof of age;
- Approval of the U.S. Central Authority (the Article 5 letter, discussed under Apply for the Child to be Found Eligible for Adoption above);
- Documentary proof of citizenship/ nationality of PAPs (copy of U.S. passport);
- Statement from ASP that the child will be legally adopted by the PAP(s) pursuant to the laws of the receiving country within a period not to exceed two years from the time of arrival of the child in the receiving country and that as soon as a full and final adoption has been completed the ASP will send certified copies of the adoption order to all concerned agencies/entities;
- Statement from the ASP that follow up reports relating to the progress of the child along with his/her recent photograph will be sent semi-annually for a period of 2 years or until such time as the legal adoption is completed and citizenship is acquired in the receiving country;
- Power of Attorney from PAPs in favor of office/official of the recognized Indian placement agency required to process the case. Such Power of Attorney should authorize the office/official of the Indian placement agency to handle the case on behalf of the foreigner should the foreigner not be in a position to come to India;
- Statement from the ASP that it will care for the child and find a suitable alternative placement in case of disruption of the adoption before a legal adoption has been completed but only with the approval of CARA. After seeking the necessary approval from CARA, it will report the alternative placement to the concerned Indian court handling guardianship/adoption proceedings with the help of the concerned Indian placement agency and such information shall be passed to all concerned departments;
- Statement from the ASP that it will pay any required adoption fees to the concerned Indian placement agency.
- In cases where PAP(s) have a biological and/or adopted child(ren), and if they are old enough, they will be required to express their views.
- A copy of the adoption decree, if the PAP(s) have adopted a child or children earlier.
- Divorce decree in case the PAP(s) have ever been divorced.
- In case where a couples' composite age is over 90 years, a document from a younger family member expressing their willingness to look after the child in case of any short-or long-term eventuality.

Bringing Your Child Home: Once your adoption is complete (or you have obtained legal custody of the child), there are a few more steps to take before you can head home. Specifically, you need to apply for several documents for your child before he or she can travel to the United States, such as a birth certificate, a passport or travel document for your child from the country in which he or she was born, and a U.S. Immigration Visa. For detailed and updated information on how to obtain these documents, review the *Intercountry Adoption* section in this publication and visit the U.S. Department of State Intercountry Adoption website at http://adoption.state.gov.

Child Citizenship Act: For adoptions finalized abroad, the Child Citizenship Act of 2000 allows your new child to acquire American citizenship automatically when he or she enters the United States as lawful permanent residents. For adoptions finalized in the United States, the Child Citizenship Act of 2000 allows your new child to acquire American citizenship automatically when the court in the United States issues the final adoption decree. To learn more, review the *Intercountry Adoption* section in this publication and visit the U.S. Department of State Intercountry Adoption website at http://adoption.state.gov.

After Adoption: Some Indian courts require regular follow-up visits and post-adoption counseling by a licensed social worker until the child has adjusted to his/her new environment. The follow-ups are generally for a period of one year or as directed by the Court. Copies of the follow-up reports should be sent to the District Social Welfare Officer or other concerned State Government Department, concerned Voluntary Scrutinizing Agency and the Court from where the adoption or guardianship order was obtained. In addition, CARA normally requires post-placement reports to be completed by PAPs until the adopted child reaches 18 years of age. In case of a disruption (i.e., the PAP(s) decides after brining the child home that they are do not wish to complete a full and final adoption in the U.S., if required, or are no able to parent the adopted child), the ASP is expected to report such information to CARA immediately. The ASP would attempt to identify other PAP(s) who would be interested in adopting the child. Failing that, the ASP, CARA and the U.S. central authority would determine whether it is in the best interest of the child to repatriate him/her. In such cases the child would return to the Indian orphanage where they had originally been residing.

U.S. Embassy in India
Shantipath, Chanakyapuri
New Delhi—110021
Tel: 091-011-24198000
091-011-24198062 (10:00 a.m. and 12:00 p.m.)
Fax: 091-011-24198407
Email: ACSnd@state.gov

India's Adoption Authority
Central Adoption Resource Agency (CARA)
Ministry of Social Justice
and Empowerment
West Block VIII, Wing II
2nd Floor, R.K. Puram
New Delhi—110 066
Tel: 91-011 618-0194
Fax: 91-011 618-0198
Email: CARA@bol.net.in
www.adoptionindia.nic.in

Embassy of India
2107 Massachusetts Ave, N.W.
Washington, D.C. 20008
Tel: (202) 939-7000
Fax: (202) 939-7027
http://www.indianembassy.org/newsite/embassy.asp

Office of Children's Issues
U.S. Department of State
2201 C Street, NW
SA-29
Washington, DC 20520
Tel: 1-888-407-4747
E-mail: AskCI@state.gov
http://adoption.state.gov

International Parental Child Abduction

December 2012

The information in this section has been edited from a report of the State Department Bureau of Consular Affairs, Office of Overseas Citizens Services. For more information, please read the *International Parental Child Abduction* section of this book and review current reports online at www.travel.state.gov/abduction.

Disclaimer: The information in this flyer is provided for general information only, is not intended to be legal advice, and may change without notice. Questions involving interpretation of law should be addressed to an attorney licensed to practice in the relevant jurisdiction.

Hague Abduction Convention: India is not a signatory to the 1980 Hague Convention on the Civil Aspects of International Child Abduction (Hague Abduction Convention), nor are there any bilateral agreements in force between India and the United States concerning international parental child abduction.

Return: Legal systems and laws pertaining to custody, divorce, and parental abduction vary widely from country to country. The government of India maintains information about custody, visitation, and family law on the Internet at the India Code Legislation Web site Parents are encouraged to consult with a local attorney who specializes in family law in India and who can provide accurate legal guidance that is specific to their circumstances.

The Department of State's Bureau of Consular Affairs, Directorate for Overseas Citizens Services, Office of Children's Issues provides assistance in cases of international parental child abduction. For U.S. citizen parents whose children have been wrongfully removed to or retained in countries that are not U.S. partners under the Hague Abduction Convention, the Office of Children's Issues can provide information and resources about country-specific options for pursuing the return of or access to an abducted child. The Office of Children's Issues may also coordinate with appropriate foreign and U.S. government authorities about the welfare of abducted U.S. citizen children. Parents are strongly encouraged to contact the Department of State for assistance.

United States Department of State
Office of Children's Issues
2201 C Street, N.W.

Washington, DC 20520
Telephone: 1-888-407-4747
Outside the United States or Canada: 1-202-501-4444
Fax: 202-736-9132
Email: AskCI@state.gov

Parental child abduction is not a crime in India. Parents may wish to consult with an attorney in the United States and in the country to which the child has been removed or retained to learn more about how filing criminal charges may impact a custody case in the foreign court.

Visitation/Access: Legal systems and laws pertaining to custody, divorce, and parental abduction vary widely from country to country. Parents are encouraged to consult with an attorney who specializes in family law in India and who can provide accurate legal guidance that is specific to their circumstances.

The Office of Children's Issues may be able to assist parents seeking access to children who have been wrongfully removed from or retained outside the United States. Parents who are seeking access to children who were not wrongfully removed from or retained outside the United States should contact the appropriate U.S. Embassy or Consulate in India for information and possible assistance.

Retaining an Attorney: Neither the Office of Children's Issues nor consular officials at the U.S. Embassy or Consulates in India are authorized to provide legal advice.

The U.S. Embassy and Consulates in India posts a list of attorneys, including those who specialize in family law. This list is provided as a courtesy service only and does not constitute an endorsement of any individual attorney. The Department of State assumes no responsibility or liability for the professional ability or reputation of, or the quality of services provided by, the persons or firms included in this list. Professional credentials and areas of expertise are provided directly by the lawyers.

Mediation: Mediation may be available in different states in India as an alternative to litigation for couples interested in attempting to reach a voluntary agreement.

U.S. Embassy New Delhi
American Citizen Services Unit
U.S. Embassy
Shantipath
Chanakyapuri
New Delhi, India 110021
Telephone: 91-11-2419–8000
Fax: 91-11-2419–8407
Email: acsnd@state.gov

U.S. Consulate General Mumbai
American Citizen Services Unit
C-49, G-Block
Bandra Kulra, Bandra East
Mumbai 400051
Telephone: 91-22-2672–4000
Fax: 91-(0)22-2672–4786
Email: mumbaiacs@state.gov

U.S Consulate General Kolkata
5/1 Ho Chi Minh Sarani 700071
Telephone: 91-33-3984–2400
Fax: 91-33-2282–2335
Email: kolkataACS@state.gov

U.S. Consulate General Chennai
220 Anna Salai
Gemini Circle, 600006
Telephone: 91-44-2857–4000
Fax: 91-44-2857–4443
Email: chennaics@state.gov

U.S. Consulate General Hyderabad
Paigah Palace
1-8-323 Chiran Fort Lane Begumpet
Secunderabad
Andhra Pradesh, 500003
Telephone: 91-40-4033–8300
Fax: 91-40-4033–8301
Email: hydacs@state.gov

Embassy of India
2107 Massachusetts Avenue, NW
Washington, DC 20008
Telephone: (202) 939-7000
Fax: (202) 265-4351

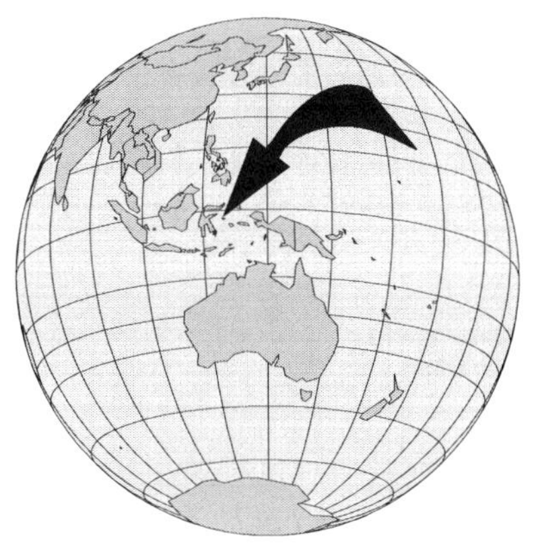

INDONESIA

Compiled from publications that were available as of February 2013 from the U.S. Department of State, the U.S. Department of Commerce, and the Central Intelligence Agency (CIA). See the introduction to this set for explanatory notes.

Official Name:
Republic of Indonesia

PROFILE

Geography

Area: total: 1,904,569 sq km; country comparison to the world: 15; land: 1,811,569 sq km; water: 93,000 sq km

Major cities: Jakarta (capital) 9.121 million; Surabaya 2.509 million; Bandung 2.412 million; Medan 2.131 million; Semarang 1.296 million (2009)

Climate: tropical; hot, humid; more moderate in highlands

Terrain: mostly coastal lowlands; larger islands have interior mountains

People

Nationality: noun: Indonesian(s); adjective: Indonesian

Population: 248,645,008 (July 2012 est.)

Population growth rate: 1.04% (2012 est.)

Ethnic groups: Javanese 40.6%, Sundanese 15%, Madurese 3.3%, Minangkabau 2.7%, Betawi 2.4%, Bugis 2.4%, Banten 2%, Banjar 1.7%, other or unspecified 29.9% (2000 census)

Religions: Muslim 86.1%, Protestant 5.7%, Roman Catholic 3%, Hindu 1.8%, other or unspecified 3.4% (2000 census)

Languages: Bahasa Indonesia (official, modified form of Malay), English, Dutch, local dialects (of which the most widely spoken is Javanese)

Literacy: definition: age 15 and over can read and write; total population: 90.4%; male: 94%; female: 86.8% (2004 est.)

Health: life expectancy at birth: total population: 71.62 years; male: 69.07 years; female: 74.29 years (2012 est.); Infant mortality rate: total: 26.99 deaths/1,000 live births; male: 31.54 deaths/1,000 live births; female: 22.21 deaths/1,000 live births (2012 est.)

Unemployment rate: 6.7% (2012 est.)

Work force: 119.5 million (2012 est.)

Government

Type: republic

Independence: 17 August 1945

Constitution: August 1945; abrogated by Federal Constitution of 1949 and Provisional Constitution of 1950, restored 5 July 1959; series of amendments concluded in 2002

Political subdivisions: 30 provinces (provinsi-provinsi, singular—provinsi), 2 special regions (daerah-daerah istimewa, singular—daerah istimewa), and 1 special capital city district (daerah khusus ibukota)

Suffrage: 17 years of age; universal and married persons regardless of age

Economy

GDP (purchasing power parity): $1.212 trillion (2012 est.); $1.139 trillion (2011 est.); $1.07 trillion (2010 est.); $1.008 trillion (2009 est.)

GDP real growth rate: 6% (2012 est.); 6.5% (2011 est.); 6.2% (2010 est.); 4.6% (2009 est.)

GDP per capita (PPP): $5,000 (2012 est.); $4,700 (2011 est.); $4,500 (2010 est.); $4,300 (2009 est.)

Natural resources: petroleum, tin, natural gas, nickel, timber, bauxite, copper, fertile soils, coal, gold, silver

Agriculture products: rice, cassava (manioc), peanuts, rubber, cocoa, coffee, palm oil, copra; poultry, beef, pork, eggs

Industries: petroleum and natural gas, textiles, apparel, footwear, mining, cement, chemical fertilizers, plywood, rubber, food, tourism

Exports: $199.1 billion (2012 est.); $201.5 billion (2011 est.); $158.1 billion (2010 est.)

Exports—commodities: oil and gas, electrical appliances, plywood, textiles, rubber

Exports—partners: Japan 16.6%, China 11.3%, Singapore 9.1%, US 8.1%, South Korea 8.1%, India 6.6%, Malaysia 5.4% (2011)

Imports: $185 billion (2012 est.); $166.1 billion (2011 est.); $127.4 billion (2010 est.)

Imports—commodities: machinery and equipment, chemicals, fuels, foodstuffs

Imports—partners: China 14.8%, Singapore 14.6%, Japan 11%, South Korea 7.3%, US 6.1%, Thailand 5.9%, Malaysia 5.9% (2011)

Debt—external: $187.1 billion (31 December 2012 est.); $186.9 billion (31 December 2011 est.); $179.1 billion (31 December 2010 est.)

Exchange rates: Indonesian rupiah (IDR) per US dollar; 9,348.3 (2012 est.); 8,770.4 (2011 est.); 9,090.4 (2010 est.); 10,389.9 (2009); 9,698.9 (2008); 9,143 (2007)

PEOPLE

Indonesia's approximately 237.6 million people make it the world's fourth-most populous nation. The island of Java, roughly the size of New York State, is the most populous island in the world (136.6 million, 2010 est.) and one of the most densely populated areas in the world. Indonesia includes numerous related but distinct cultural and linguistic groups, many of which are ethnically Malay.

National/Racial/Ethnic Minorities

Ethnic Chinese, which accounted for approximately 3 percent of the population, played a major role in the economy, and increasingly participated in politics. However, some ethnic Chinese noted that, despite recent reforms, public servants still discriminated against them when issuing marriage licenses and in other services.

Language

Since independence, Bahasa Indonesia (the national language, a form of Malay) has spread throughout the archipelago and has become the language of most written communication, education, government, business, and media. Local languages are still important in many areas, however. English is the most widely spoken foreign language.

Religion

According to the 2010 census, the most recent available, approximately 87 percent of the population is Muslim, 7 percent Protestant, 3 percent Roman Catholic, and 1.5 percent Hindu. Other religions (Buddhism, followers of traditional indigenous religions, Confucianism, other Christian denominations, and those that did not respond to the census question) comprise approximately 1.25 percent of the population.

Muslims in the country are overwhelmingly Sunni. Of the more than 207 million Muslims in the country, there is an estimated one to three million Shia Muslims. Many smaller Muslim organizations exist, including approximately 200,000-400,000 persons who subscribe to the Ahmadiyya Qadiyani interpretation of Islam. A smaller group, known as Ahmadiyya Lahore, is also present. Other small Islamic minorities include al-Qiyadah al-Islamiya, Darul Arqam, Jamaah Salamulla (Salamulla Congregation), and members of the Indonesian Islamic Propagation Institute.

Some indigenous religious groups, including the "Naurus" on Seram Island in Maluku Province, incorporate Hindu and animist beliefs, and many have also adopted some Protestant teachings.

The country has a small Sikh population, estimated at between 10,000 and 15,000, residing primarily in Medan and Jakarta.

An estimated 20 million persons, primarily in Java, Kalimantan, and Papua, practice various traditional belief systems, often referred to collectively as "Aliran Kepercayaan." Many combine their beliefs with one of the government-recognized religions and register under that recognized religion.

There are small Jewish communities in Jakarta and Surabaya. The Baha'i community reported thousands of members, but no reliable figures are available. Falun Dafa (or Falun Gong), which considers itself a spiritual organization rather than a religion, claims several thousand followers, nearly half of whom live in Yogyakarta, Bali, and Medan. However, specific numbers of followers were unavailable.

HISTORY

By the time of the Renaissance, the islands of Java and Sumatra had already enjoyed a 1,000-year heritage of advanced civilization spanning two major empires. During the 7th-14th centuries, the Buddhist kingdom of Srivijaya flourished on Sumatra. At its peak, the Srivijaya Empire reached as far as West Java and the Malay Peninsula. Also by the 14th century, the Hindu Kingdom of Majapahit had risen in eastern Java. Gadjah Mada, the empire's chief minister from 1331 to 1364, succeeded in gaining allegiance from most of what is now modern Indonesia and much of the Malay archipelago as well.

Legacies from Gadjah Mada's time include a codification of law and an epic poem. Islam arrived in Indonesia sometime during the 12th century and supplanted Hinduism by the end of the 16th century in Java and Sumatra. Bali, however, remains overwhelmingly Hindu. In the eastern archipelago, both Christian and Islamic proselytizing took place in the 16th and 17th centuries, and, currently, there are large communities of both religions on these islands.

Beginning in 1602, the Dutch slowly established themselves as rulers of Indonesia, exploiting the weakness of the small kingdoms that had replaced that of Majapahit. The only exception was East Timor, which remained under Portugal's control until 1975. During 300 years of rule, the Dutch developed the Netherlands East Indies into one of the world's richest colonial possessions, extracting natural resources through co-opted local elites but doing little to modernize Indonesia.

During the first decade of the 20th century, an Indonesian independence movement began and expanded rapidly, particularly between the two

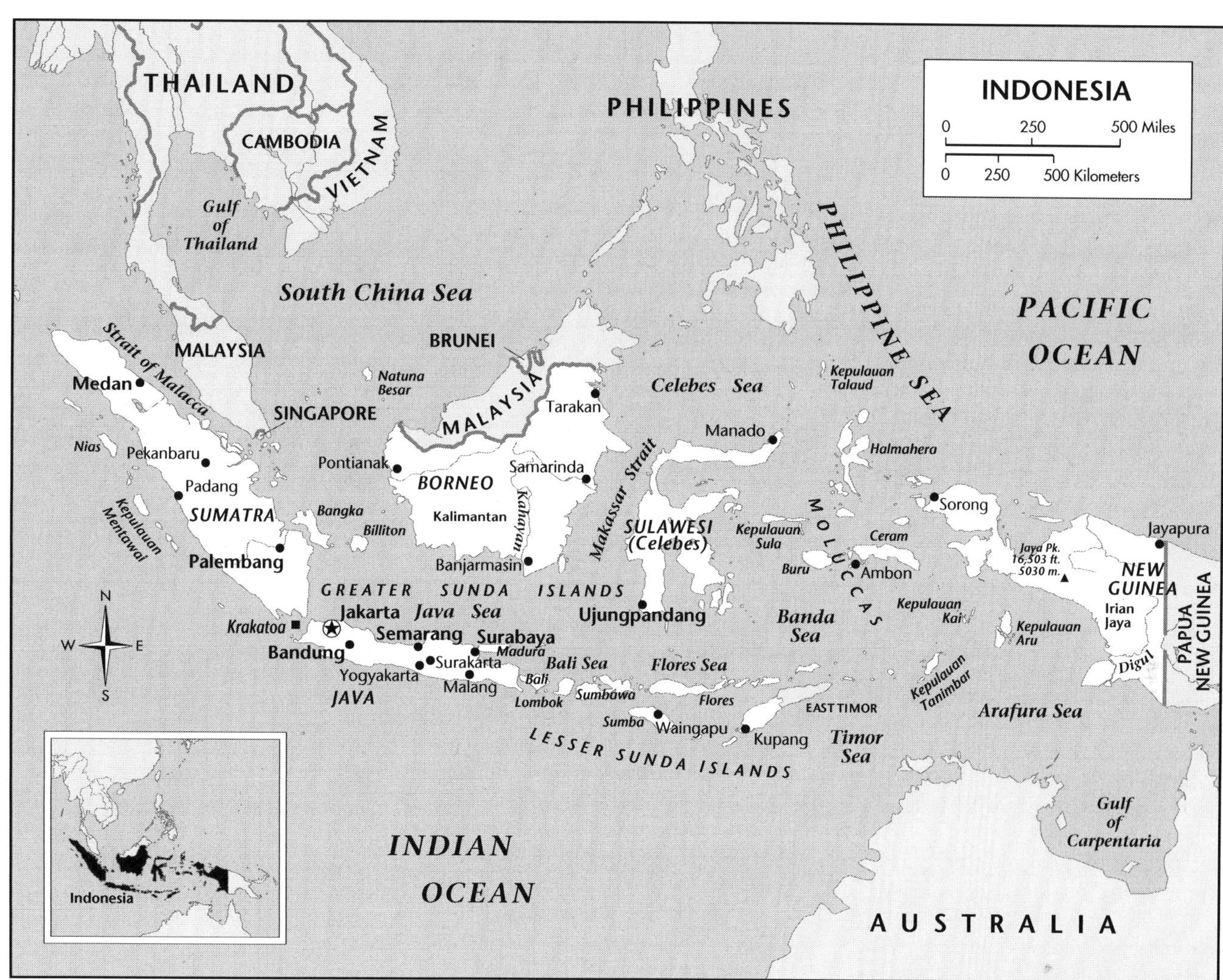

World Wars. Its leaders came from a small group of young professionals and students, some of whom had been educated in the Netherlands. Many, including Indonesia's first president, Soekarno (1945–67), were imprisoned for political activities.

During World War II, Japan invaded Indonesia (in early 1942), outclassing a combined American, British, Dutch, and Australian military command. Sizeable U.S. naval forces and smaller air and ground forces sent to defend Indonesia were defeated, with heavy losses in ships and large numbers of Americans killed or captured. The Japanese treated captured Allied troops and interned Western civilians with extreme cruelty. Because of local animosity toward Dutch colonial rule, there was no anti-Japanese guerilla movement as in the Philippines and Malaysia, and most Indonesians initially welcomed the Japanese as liberators. But increasingly harsh Japanese rule strengthened the prewar independence movement, and on August 17, 1945, 3 days after Japan's surrender to the Allies, a small group of Indonesians, led by Soekarno and Mohammad Hatta, proclaimed independence and established the Republic of Indonesia. They set up a provisional government and adopted a constitution to govern the republic until elections could be held and a new constitution written. Fighting soon broke out between Indonesian independence groups and Allied forces—mainly British, Indian, and Australian forces—sent to accept the Japanese surrender. Dutch efforts later to reestablish complete control met resistance. Following the Philippines' independence in 1946, the U.S. was unwilling to see the Netherlands use post-war Marshall Plan support to indirectly fund the suppression of Indonesia's independence. Negotiations and on-and-off fighting in Indonesia continued until 1949. The stalemate, combined with reduced international support and a devastated economy in the Netherlands, led to the Dutch decision to withdraw from Indonesia. Colonial rule and its violent end left a legacy in Indonesia of mistrusting foreign motives, especially those of large powers. In 1950, Indonesia became the 60th member of the United Nations.

Shortly after hostilities with the Dutch ended in 1949, Indonesia adopted a new constitution, providing for a parliamentary system of government in which the executive was chosen by and accountable to parliament. Parliament was divided among many political parties before and after the country's first nationwide election in 1955, and stable governmental coalitions were difficult to achieve. The role of Islam in Indonesia was debated. Soekarno defended a secular state based on Pancasila, five principles of the state philosophy—monotheism, humanitarianism, national unity, representative democracy by consensus, and social justice—codified in the 1945 constitution, while some Muslim groups preferred either an Islamic state or a constitution that included a preambular provision requiring adherents of Islam to be subject to Islamic law.

At the time of independence, the Dutch retained control over the western half of New Guinea (known as Irian Jaya in the Soekarno and Suharto eras and as Papua since 2000) and permitted steps toward self-government and independence. Negotiations with the Dutch on the incorporation of Irian Jaya into Indonesia failed, and armed clashes broke out between Indonesian and Dutch troops in 1961. In August 1962, the two sides reached an agreement, and Indonesia assumed administrative responsibility for Irian Jaya on May 1, 1963. The Indonesian Government conducted an "Act of Free Choice" in Irian Jaya under UN supervision in 1969 in which 1,025 Papuan representatives of local councils agreed by consensus to remain a part of Indonesia.

A subsequent UN General Assembly resolution confirmed the transfer of sovereignty to Indonesia. Opposition to Indonesian administration of Papua gave rise to small-scale guerrilla activity in the years following Jakarta's assumption of control. In the more open atmosphere since 1998, there have been more explicit expressions within Papua calling for independence from Indonesia. Unsuccessful rebellions on Sumatra, Sulawesi, West Java, and other islands beginning in 1958, plus a failure by the constituent assembly to develop a new constitution, weakened the parliamentary system. Consequently, in 1959, when President Soekarno unilaterally revived the provisional 1945 constitution that provided for broad presidential powers, he met little resistance. From 1959 to 1965, President Soekarno imposed an authoritarian regime under the label of "Guided Democracy."

Soekarno favored a foreign policy of nonalignment, a stance supported by other prominent leaders of former colonies who rejected formal alliances with either the West or Soviet bloc. Under Soekarno's auspices, these leaders gathered in Bandung, West Java, in 1955 to lay the groundwork for what became known as the Non-Aligned Movement. In the late 1950s and early 1960s, President Soekarno moved closer to Asian communist states and toward the Indonesian Communist Party (PKI) in domestic affairs. The PKI represented the largest communist party outside the Soviet Union and China.

By 1965, the PKI controlled many of the mass civic and cultural organizations that Soekarno had established to mobilize support for his regime and, with Soekarno's acquiescence, embarked on a campaign to establish a "Fifth Column" by arming its supporters. Army leaders resisted this campaign. Under circumstances that have never been fully explained, on October 1, 1965, PKI sympathizers within the military, including elements from Soekarno's palace guard, occupied key locations in Jakarta and kidnapped and murdered six senior generals. Major General Suharto, the commander of the Army Strategic Reserve, rallied army troops opposed to the PKI to reestablish control over the city. Violence swept throughout Indonesia in the aftermath of the October 1 events, and unsettled conditions persisted through 1966. Right-wing groups killed tens of thousands of alleged communists in rural areas. Estimates of the number of deaths range between 160,000 and 500,000. The violence was especially brutal in Java and Bali. During this period, PKI members by the tens of thousands turned in their membership cards. The emotions and fears of instability created by this crisis persisted for many years as the communist party remains banned from Indonesia.

Throughout the 1965–66 period, President Soekarno vainly attempted to restore his political stature and shift the country back to its pre-October 1965 position. Although he remained President, in March 1966, Soekarno transferred key political and military powers to General Suharto, who by that time had become head of the armed forces. In March 1967, the Provisional People's Consultative Assembly (MPRS) named General Suharto acting President. Soekarno ceased to be a political force and lived under virtual house arrest until his death in 1970.

President Suharto proclaimed a "New Order" in Indonesian politics and dramatically shifted foreign and domestic policies away from the course set in Soekarno's final years. The New Order established economic rehabilitation and development as its primary goals and pursued its policies through an administrative structure dominated by the military but with advice from Western-educated economic experts. In 1968, the People's Consultative Assembly (MPR) formally selected Suharto to a full 5-year term as President, and he was reelected to successive 5-year terms in 1973, 1978, 1983, 1988, 1993, and 1998. In mid-1997, Indonesia suffered from the Asian financial and economic crisis, accompanied by the worst drought in 50 years and falling prices for commodity exports. As the exchange rate changed from a fixed to a managed float to fully floating, the rupiah (IDR or Rp) depreciated in value, inflation increased significantly, and capital flight accelerated. Demonstrators, initially led by students, called for Suharto's resignation. Amid widespread civil unrest, Suharto resigned on May 21, 1998, 3 months after the MPR had selected him for a seventh term. Suharto's hand-picked Vice President, B.J. Habibie, became Indonesia's third President. President Habibie reestablished International Monetary Fund (IMF) and donor community support for an economic stabilization program. He released several prominent political and labor prisoners, initiated investigations into the unrest, and lifted controls on the press, political parties, and labor unions.

In January 1999, Habibie and the Indonesian Government agreed to a process, with UN involvement, under which the people of East Timor would be allowed to choose between autonomy and independence through a direct ballot held on August 30, 1999. Some 98% of registered voters cast their ballots, and 78.5% of the voters chose independence over continued integration with Indonesia. Many people were killed by Indonesian military forces and military-backed militias in a wave of violence and destruction after the announcement of the pro-independence vote.

Indonesia's first elections in the post-Suharto period were held for the national, provincial, and sub-provincial parliaments on June 7, 1999. Forty-eight political parties participated in the elections. For the national parliament, Partai Demokrasi Indonesia Perjuangan (PDI-P, Indonesian Democratic Party of Struggle, led by Megawati Sukarnoputri) won 34% of the vote; Golkar ("Functional Groups" party) 22%; Partai Kebangkitan Bangsa (PKB, National Awakening Party, linked to the moderate Islamic organization Nadhlatul Ulama headed by former President Abdurrahman Wahid) 13%; and the conservative Islamic Partai Persatuan Pembangunan (PPP, United Development Party, led by Hamzah Haz) 11%. The MPR selected Abdurrahman Wahid as Indonesia's fourth President in November 1999 and replaced him with Megawati Sukarnoputri in July 2001.

The constitution, as amended in the post-Suharto era, now provides for the direct election by popular vote of the president and vice president. Under the 2004 amendment, only parties or coalitions of parties that gained at least 3% of the House of Representatives (DPR) seats or 5% of the vote in national legislative elections were eligible to nominate a presidential and vice presidential ticket.

The 2004 legislative elections took place on April 5 and were considered to be generally free and fair. Twenty-four parties took part in the elections. Big parties lost ground, while small parties gained larger shares of the vote. However, the two Suharto-era nationalist parties, PDI-P and Golkar, remained in the lead. PDI-P (opposition party during the Suharto era) lost its plurality in the House of Representatives, dropping from 33% to 18.5% of the total vote (and from 33% to 20% of the seats). The Golkar Party (Suharto's political party) declined slightly from 1999 levels, going from 22% to 21% of the national vote (from 26% to 23% of DPR seats). The third- and fourth-largest parties (by vote share) were two Islamic-oriented parties, the United Development Party (PPP) (8% of the votes, 10.5% of the seats) and National Awakening Party (PKB) (10.5% of the vote, 9.45% of the seats). Susilo Bambang Yudhoyono's nationalist Democratic Party (PD) won 7.45% of the national vote and 10% of the DPR seats, making it the fourth-largest party in the DPR. Seven of the 24 parties won no DPR seats; six won 1-2 seats, and the other six won between 2%-6% of the national vote (between 5-52 DPR seats).

The first direct presidential election was held on July 5, 2004, contested by five tickets. As no candidate won at least 50% of the vote, a runoff election was held on September 20, 2004, between the top two candidates, President Megawati Sukarnoputri and retired General Susilo Bambang Yudhoyono. In this final round, Yudhoyono won 60.6% of the vote. Approximately 76.6% of the eligible voters participated, a total of roughly 117 million people, making Indonesia's presidential election the largest single-day election in the world. The Carter Center, which sent a delegation of election observers, issued a statement congratulating "the people and leaders of Indonesia for the successful conduct of the presidential election and the peaceful atmosphere that has prevailed throughout the ongoing democratic transition."

In 2009, national legislative elections were held on April 9 and presidential elections were held in July. They were peaceful and considered free and fair. New electoral rules required that a party win 2.5% of the national vote in order to enter parliament. A total of thirty-eight national and six local (Aceh only) parties contested the 2009 legislative elections. At least 171 million voters registered to vote in these elections. Voter turnout was estimated to be 71% of the electorate. Nine parties won parliamentary seats in the House of Representatives (DPR). The top three winners were secular nationalist parties: President Yudhoyono's Partai Demokrat, with 20.85% of the vote; Vice President Jusuf Kalla's Golkar Party, 14.45%; and former president Megawati's opposition PDI-P party, with 14.03%. The next four largest parties were all Islamic-oriented parties: PKS, PAN (6%), PPP (5.3%), and PKB (4.9%). Only PKS maintained its 2004 vote share (7.88%); the other three declined in popularity. The smallest two parties in Parliament, Gerindra and Hanura, with 4.46 and 3.77% of the vote respectively, were headed by retired Suharto-era army generals Prabowo Subianto and Wiranto (one name only). The 2009 DPR members took their seats October 1.

Also in 2009, the threshold was revised so that only parties or coalitions of parties that gained at least 20% of the House of Representatives (DPR) seats or 25% of the vote in the 2009 national legislative elections would be eligible to nominate a presidential and vice presidential ticket. Partai Demokrat, Golkar, and PDI-P parties, the top winners in the legislative elections, nominated presidential candidates. To win in one round, a presidential candidate was required to receive more than 50% of the vote and more than 20% of the vote in 17 of Indonesia's 33 provinces. If no candidate did so, the top two candidates would have competed in a second round in September 2009.

Three tickets competed in the presidential elections. Incumbent President Yudhoyono and his running mate, non-partisan former Central Bank Chair and Economics Minister Boediono, won the election with such a significant plurality—60.6%—that it obviated the need for a second round of elections. Main challenger and former president and opposition leader Megawati Sukarnoputri and running mate Prabowo Subianto trailed with 28%. Meanwhile, Vice President Jusuf Kalla and running mate Wiranto came in last at 12.7%. Indonesia's Consultative Assembly (MPR) inaugurated President Susilo Bambang Yudhoyono for his second term as president on October 20, 2009.

Natural disasters have devastated many parts of Indonesia over the past few years. On December 26, 2004, a 9.1 to 9.3 magnitude earthquake took place in the Indian Ocean, and the resulting tsunami killed over 130,000 people in Aceh and left more than 500,000 homeless.

On March 26, 2005, an 8.7 magnitude earthquake struck between Aceh and northern Sumatra, killing 905 people and displacing tens of thousands. After much media attention on the seismic activity on Mt. Merapi in April and May 2006, a 6.2 magnitude earthquake occurred 30 miles to the southwest. It killed more than 5,000 people and left an estimated 200,000 people homeless in the Yogyakarta region. An earthquake of 7.4 struck Tasikmalaya, West Java, on September 2, 2009, killing approximately 100 people. On September 30, 2009, a 7.6 magnitude earthquake struck Western Sumatra. No official statistics were released on deaths and injuries; however, press reports indicated more than 1,100 fatalities.

GOVERNMENT AND POLITICAL CONDITIONS

Indonesia is a multiparty democracy. In 2009 Susilo Bambang Yudhoyono was reelected president in free and fair elections. Domestic and international observers judged the 2009 legislative elections free and fair as well.

Recent Elections

In 2009 President Yudhoyono was reelected overwhelmingly. Also in 2009 the country conducted its third democratic legislative elections. In general, domestic and foreign observers found the elections free and fair. The elections were a complex affair with voters receiving ballots for the DPR, the DPD, provincial parliaments, and regency and city councils. Thirty-eight national parties competed in the elections, with an additional six parties in Aceh Province only. Irregularities occurred, requiring 245 reruns in 10 provinces. Observers concluded the vast majority of irregularities involved logistical difficulties (primarily due to faulty voter list data) rather than malfeasance. Some violence and intimidation also marred the legislative election campaign in Aceh, Papua, and West Papua.

Political parties were required to win a minimum of 2.5 percent of the national vote to qualify for a seat in the DPR. In 2009 nine parties met this threshold and won seats in parliament. The top three vote getters were secular, nationalist parties, followed by the four largest Islamic-oriented parties. President Yudhoyono's Democrat Party won a plurality of seats, while then-vice president Kalla's Golkar Party finished in second place. The major opposition party, the Indonesia Democratic Party-Struggle, led by Megawati Sukarnoputri, finished in third place.

All adult citizens, age 17 or older, are eligible to vote except active members of the military and the police, convicts serving a sentence of five years or more, persons suffering from mental disorders, and persons deprived of voting rights by an irrevocable verdict of a court of justice. Married juveniles are legally adults and allowed to vote.

According to the Elections Commission (KPU) 63 regional elections were held in 2011. This number includes 49 new elections in 2011, eight elections originally scheduled for 2010, four elections carried over from 2010, and two repeat elections from 2010; there were also elections scheduled for four governors and 59 mayors/regents.

During 2011 the Constitutional Court received 132 requests to adjudicate election disputes, and carried over six pending cases from 2010. Of these, 131 were decided, with 15 rulings in favor of complainants. As a result of the decisions, there were election reruns in several cases, including the West Papua gubernatorial election. At the end of 2011, seven cases were pending.

The General Elections Monitoring Body, which handles reports of electoral violations, received 1,718 reports of violations in 92 local elections in 2011. Of these, 565 were considered administrative and handed over to the KPU for follow-up. There were 372 considered to be poll violations that involved criminal acts and which the police were investigating.

In a few isolated cases, local elections led to civil disturbances. For example, in Puncak, Papua, various reports indicated that on July 30-31, 19 people were killed in conflict stemming from clashes between rival politicians. In another case, individuals blockaded roads, damaged public facilities, and burned down the recently re-elected West Papua Governor Abraham Ataruri's residence on December 19. At the end of 2011,, police had arrested 13 people and named 11 other suspects.

Participation of Women and Minorities: There are no legal restrictions on the role of women in politics. A law on political parties mandated that women make up 30 percent of the founding members of a new political party. An election law, which included a nonbinding clause for parties to select women for at least 30 percent of the candidate slots on their party lists, encouraged parties to include more women candidates.

The Constitutional Court invalidated this clause when it struck down the law and ruled voters could directly elect their representatives, regardless of their position on party lists. The number of women in parliament increased significantly, from 11 percent to 18 percent of the DPR seats in the 2009 elections. During 2011 women held four of 37 cabinet-level positions.

At the provincial level, there was one female governor and one vice governor. Women held disproportionately few leadership positions in local government in some provinces; for example, in Aceh the highest position held by a woman was that of deputy mayor, in the city of Banda Aceh.

With the exception of Aceh Province, where non-Muslims effectively were blocked from political office by a requirement that all candidates must demonstrate their ability to read the Qur'an in Arabic, there were no legal restrictions on the role of minorities in politics. There were no official statistics on the ethnic backgrounds of legislators in the DPR. President Yudhoyono's cabinet consisted of a plurality of Javanese, with others being of Sundanese, Bugis, Batak, Acehnese, Papuan, Balinese, and Chinese heritage.

Principal Government Officials

Last Updated: 1/31/2013

Pres.: **Susilo Bambang YUDHOYONO**
Vice Pres.: **BOEDIONO**
Coordinating Min. for Economic Affairs: **Hatta RAJASA**
Coordinating Min. for the People's Welfare: **Agung LAKSONO**
Coordinating Min. for Political, Legal, & Security Affairs: **Djoko SUYANTO**
State Sec.: **Sudi SILALAHI**
Min. of Agriculture: **SUSWONO**
Min. of Communication & Information: **Tifatul SEMBIRING**
Min. of Defense: **Purnomo YUSGIANTORO**
Min. of Education & Culture: **Muhammad NUH**
Min. of Energy & Mineral Resources: **Jero WACIK**
Min. of Finance: **Agus Dermawan Wintarto MARTOWARDOJO**
Min. of Foreign Affairs: **Raden Mohammad Marty Muliana NATALEGAWA**
Min. of Forestry: **Zulkifli HASAN**
Min. of Health: **NAFSIAH Mboi**
Min. of Home Affairs: **Gamawan FAUZI**
Min. of Industry: **Mohamad Suleman HIDAYAT**
Min. of Justice & Human Rights: **Amir SYAMSUDDIN**
Min. of Manpower & Transmigration: **Muhaimin ISKANDAR**
Min. of Maritime Affairs & Fisheries: **Cicip SUTARJO**
Min. of Public Works: **Djoko KIRMANTO**
Min. of Religious Affairs: **SURYADHARMA Ali**
Min. of Social Affairs: **Salim Segaf AL-JUFRIE**
Min. of Tourism & Creative Economy: **Mari Elka PANGESTU**
Min. of Trade: **Gita Irawan WIRJAWAN**
Min. of Transportation: **Evert Erenst MANGINDAAN**
State Min. for Cooperatives & Small & Medium Enterprises: **Syarifuddin HASAN**
State Min. for the Development of Disadvantaged Regions: **Helmy Faishal ZAINI**
State Min. for the Environment: **Balthazar "Berth" KAMBUAYA**
State Min. for National Development Planning: **Armida ALISJAHBANA**
State Min. for Public Housing: **Djan FARIDZ**
State Min. of Research & Technology: **Gusti Muhammad HATTA**
State Min. for State Apparatus Reform: **Azwar ABUBAKAR**
State Min. for State-Owned Enterprises: **Dahlan ISKAN**
State Min. for Women's Empowerment & Child Protection: **Linda Amalia Sari GUMELAR**
State Min. for Youth & Sports (Acting): **Agung LAKSONO**
Attorney Gen.: **Basrief ARIEF**
Cabinet Sec.: **Dipo ALAM**
Dir., State Intelligence Agency (BIN): **Marciano NORMAN**
Governor, Bank Indonesia: **Darmin NASUTION**
Ambassador to the US: **Dino Patti DJALAL**
Permanent Representative to the UN, New York: **Desra PERCAYA**

ECONOMY

Indonesia, a vast polyglot nation, grew an estimated 6.1% and 6.4% in 2010 and 2011, respectively. The government made economic advances under the first administration of President YUDHOYONO (2004–09), introducing significant reforms in the financial sector, including tax and customs reforms, the use of Treasury bills, and capital market development and supervision.

During the global financial crisis, Indonesia outperformed its regional neighbors and joined China and India as the only G20 members posting growth in 2009. The government has promoted fiscally conservative policies, resulting in a debt-to-GDP ratio of less than 25%, a fiscal deficit below 3%, and historically low rates of inflation. Fitch and Moody's upgraded Indonesia's credit rating to investment grade in December 2011. Indonesia still struggles with poverty and unemployment, inadequate infrastructure, corruption, a complex regulatory environment, and unequal resource distribution among regions. The government in 2013 faces the ongoing challenge of improving Indonesia's insufficient infrastructure to remove impediments to economic growth, labor unrest over wages, and reducing its fuel subsidy program in the face of high oil prices.

Labor Conditions

The Manpower Act establishes 15 as the minimum age for work and prohibits children under the age of 18 from working in hazardous sectors. Children 13 to 15 years of age may work in light work for no more than three hours per day and only under a number of other conditions, such as parental consent, no work during school hours, and payment of legal wages. Entrepreneurs hiring children must also meet their occupational safety and health requirements.

A strong legal framework and National Action Plans address economic and sexual exploitation, including child prostitution, child trafficking, and the involvement of children in the narcotics trade, and provide severe criminal penalties and jail terms for persons who violate children's rights. The law and regulations explicitly prohibit forced labor by children.

The government did not enforce minimum age laws effectively, and furthermore did not act effectively to eliminate forced child labor. An estimated six to eight million children exceeded the legal three-hour-daily work limit, working in agriculture, street vending, mining, clothing manufacture, and other areas. A 2009 survey from by the International Labor Organization and the National Statistics Agency reported that about four million working children age 10 to 17 are considered employed in wage work by the standard definition.

Children worked in agriculture primarily on palm oil, tobacco, rubber, and tea plantations. Children also worked in fisheries, manufacturing (such as cottage factory footwear production, textiles, and cigarette production), logging, toy making, food processing (e.g., bird-nest gathering), and in the small-scale mining sector. Other children work in the informal sector selling newspapers, shining shoes, street vending, scavenging, and working with their parents in family businesses or cottage industries.

A domestic worker advocacy group estimated that there were four million domestic workers in the country, of whom at least 1.3 million were under age 18.

The minimum wage levels set by most local governments did not provide a worker and family with a decent standard of living. Most province-level minimum wage rates fell below the government's own calculation of basic minimum needs. During 2011 West Papua Province offered the highest minimum wage at 1.41 million rupiah (approximately $160) per month, while the Manpower Ministry reported official minimum wages as low as 705,000 rupiah ($80) per month in East Java. Jakarta's minimum wage was 1.29 million rupiah ($145) per month. As of March, the official poverty line was 233,740 rupiah (approximately $26) per capita per month.

The law establishes a 40-hour workweek, with one 30-minute rest period for every four hours of work. Companies often required a five-and-a-half- or six-day workweek. The law also requires at least one day of rest weekly. The daily overtime rate was 1.5 times the normal hourly rate for the first hour and twice the hourly rate for additional overtime, with a maximum of three hours of overtime per day and no more than 14 hours per week. The law also requires employers to register workers with and pay contributions to the state-owned insurance agency.

The practical observance of laws regulating benefits and labor standards, including wage and hours, varied by sector and region. Unions complained that companies relied upon excessive overtime in some garment and electronics assembly plants, to the detriment of workers' health and safety. Employer violations of legal requirements were fairly common, sometimes resulting in strikes and protests. The American Center for International Labor Solidarity reported workers in the garment industry worked extremely long hours, but because their pay slips did not specify the amount of overtime paid, they could not be certain they were fully compensated for overtime.

Although labor law and ministerial regulations provide workers with a variety of benefits, it was estimated that, aside from government officials, only 10 percent of workers received social security benefits. Persons who worked at formal sector companies often received health benefits, meal privileges, and transportation, which was rarely provided for workers in the informal sector. The Manpower Act also requires employers to provide a safe and healthy workplace and to treat workers with dignity. Enforcement of health and safety standards in smaller companies and in the informal sector tended to be weaker or nonexistent.

U.S.-INDONESIAN RELATIONS

The United States established diplomatic relations with Indonesia in 1949, following its independence from the Netherlands. The United States has important economic, commercial, and security interests in Indonesia, and relations are positive and cooperative. Indonesia is a stable, democratic nation committed to a comprehensive partnership with the United States. The country is a linchpin of regional security due to its strategic location astride a number of key international maritime straits, particularly the Malacca Strait. Friction points in the bilateral political relationship have included human rights and differences in foreign policy, such as on Palestine statehood.

U.S. Assistance to Indonesia

Indonesia faces domestic development challenges; uneven benefits from democratic and economic progress; fragile institutions that are ill-equipped to address social service needs; and risks from climate change and environmental degradation. The U.S.-Indonesia Comprehensive Partnership focuses on a forward-looking agenda that promotes cooperation across a wide range of key development areas: strengthening education and professional ties, improving governance, building public support for shared values, improving trade and investment, advancing security, partnering on international issues, cooperating on health, and supporting environmental sustainability.

U.S. development assistance is delivered through U.S. Agency for International Development programs, Millennium Challenge Corporation funding, and Peace Corps projects.

Bilateral Economic Relations

Indonesia has a market-based economy in which the government plays a significant role. U.S. exports to Indonesia include agricultural products, aircraft, machinery, and cotton yarn and fabric. U.S. imports from Indonesia include agricultural products, apparel, electrical machinery, and oil. U.S. companies have invested heavily in the petroleum sector. Two U.S. firms operate two copper/gold mines in Indonesia. The United States and Indonesia have an agreement on the avoidance of double taxation.

Indonesia's Membership in International Organizations

Indonesia and the United States belong to a number of the same international organizations, including the United Nations, ASEAN Regional Forum, Asia-Pacific Economic Cooperation forum, G-20, International Monetary Fund, World Bank, and World Trade Organization. Indonesia also participates as a key partner in the Organization for Economic Cooperation and Development's Enhanced Engagement program.

Bilateral Representation

Indonesia maintains an embassy in the United States at 2020 Massachusetts Avenue NW, Washington, DC 20036 (tel. 202-775-5200).

Principal U.S. Embassy Officials

Last Updated: 1/14/2013

JAKARTA (E) Medan Merdeka Selatan 5, (62-21) 3435-9000, Fax (62) (21) 386-2259, INMARSAT Tel 683-142-927, Workweek: M-F 7:30 a.m.-4:00 p.m., Website: http://jakarta.usembassy.gov/

DCM OMS: Jan Cordell
ALT US REP AMB:(Asean) David Carden
AMB OMS: Johanna Villemarette
Co-CLO: Linda Schnaible
DHS/ICE: Timothy Dwyer
FCS: David Gossack
FM: John Rexford
HRO: Darion Akins
ICITAP: Gerald Heuett
MGT: Jacqueline Holland-Craig
MLO/ODC: Col Michael Janser
NAS/INL: Terry Mobley
OPDAT: Terry Kinney
POSHO: John Rexford
SDO/DATT: COL Col. Russell Bailey
AMB: Scot Marciel
CG: Thurmond Borden
DCM: Kristen Bauer
PAO: Don Q. Washington
GSO: Margaret C. Sula
RSO: Jim Schnaible
AFSA: John Rexford
AGR: Ali Abdi
AID: Andrew Sisson
CLO: Jeannine Toder
DEA: Eric Williams
ECON: Jim Carouso
EEO: Martha Crunkleton
EST: Benjamin V. Wohlauer
FMO: Robert R. Haynie
ICASS Chair: COL Russell Bailey
IMO: Elizabeth Slater
IPO: Steve Mort
ISO: Kenneth Hill
ISSO: Rodney Cordell
LEGATT: Robert Coble
POL: Ted Lyng
State ICASS: Jim Carouso

US MISSION TO ASEAN (E) Medan Merdeka Selatan 5, (62) (21) 3435-9000, Fax (62) (21)3435-9971, INMARSAT Tel 683-142-927, Workweek: M-F 7:30 a.m.–4:00 p.m.

AMB OMS: Renae Stein
AMB: David Carden

SURABAYA (CG) Jl. Citra Raya Niaga no. 2 Surabaya 60213, 62-31-297-5300, Fax (62-31) 297-5301, INMARSAT Tel 383-134-370, Workweek: M-F 7:30 a.m to 4:00 p.m., Website: http://jakarta.usembassy.gov/sby/

CG OMS: Patti Limeri
MGT: Erika Zielke
POL/ECON: Heather Coble
POSHO: Erika Zielke
CG: Joaquin Monserrate
CON: R. Chris Santoro
PAO: Andrew Veveiros
RSO: Jonathan Loden
CLO: Julie Veveiors
IPO: Maurizio Visani

MEDAN Jl. Let.Jend.MT Haryono, No.A-1

DPO: Trevor Olson
MGT: Fsn Henni Zulfah
PO: Kathryn Crockart
POL: Fsn Rachma Jaurinata

TRAVEL

Consular Information Sheet

November 2, 2011

Country Description: Indonesia is an independent republic consisting of more than 17,500 islands spread over 3,400 miles along the Equator. The main islands are Java, Sumatra, Bali, Kalimantan (Borneo), Sulawesi (Celebes), Papua, Halmahera, and Seram. The capital city of Jakarta lies in the lowlands of West Java, the most populated island. The country has approximately 246,000,000 people and more than 300 ethnic groups. Indonesia's geographic location and topography make the country prone to natural disasters, especially seismic upheaval due to its location on the "Ring of Fire," an arc of volcanoes and fault lines encircling the Pacific Basin. Indonesia is a developing country with a growing economy and many infrastructure shortcomings, especially in rural areas.

Smart Traveler Enrollment Program (STEP)/Embassy Locations: If you are going to live or visit Indonesia, please take the time to tell our Embassy in Jakarta or Consulate in Surabaya about your trip. If you enroll in the Smart Traveler Enrollment Program, we can keep you up to date with important safety and security announcements. It will also help your friends and family get in touch with you in an emergency.

U.S. Embassy Jakarta is located at Medan Merdeka Selatan 5, Jakarta 10110; telephone: (62)(21) 3435–9000; fax (62)(21) 385-7189. The most secure international mail address is: U.S. Embassy Jakarta, DPO, AP 96520 USA.

U.S. Consulate General in Surabaya is at Jalan Raya Dr. Sutomo 33; telephone: (62) (31) 295-6400; fax (62) (31) 567-4492, after-hours duty officer (62) (811) 334-183. The consulate can also be reached by e-mail. The consulate should be the first point of contact for assistance to U.S. citizens who are present or residing in the Indonesian provinces of East Java, Nusa Tenggara Timor, Nusa Tenggara Barat, all of Sulawesi and North and South Maluku.

There is a Consular Agency in Bali at Jalan Hayam Wuruk 310, Denpasar, Bali; telephone: (62) (361) 233-605; fax (62) (361) 222-426; or BaliConsularAgency@state.gov. The U.S. Consulate in Surabaya is an alternate contact for U.S. citizens in Bali.

The American Presence Post in Medan, North Sumatra, provides only emergency assistance to U.S. citizens and does not offer routine consular services. U.S. citizens needing emergency consular assistance in Sumatra should call (62) (61) 451-9000.

Entry/Exit Requirements for U.S. Citizens: You will need a passport valid for at least six months following the date of your arrival to Indonesia. The U.S. Embassy cannot obtain entry permission for U.S. citizens with expiring passports. If you arrive and your passport has less than six month's validity, Indonesian authorities will require you to depart Indonesia immediately to obtain a new U.S. passport elsewhere; you will not be allowed to renew your passport here and follow-up later with Indonesian authorities. Also, if your passport does not have the required six month's validity remaining on your passport, you may be denied boarding at your point of origin or at a transit point en route. Generally, you should expect to wait two weeks for a U.S. passport to be issued outside of the United States.

You are required to have a visa to enter Indonesia, obtained either beforehand or, in limited circumstances, on arrival. Tourist passport holders traveling for private purposes may apply for a 30-day visitor visa on arrival at the airports in Jakarta, Bali, Surabaya, Banda Aceh, Medan, Padang, Pekanbaru, Manado, Biak, Ambon, Balikpapan, Pontianak, Kupang, Batam, and South Sumatra. Visas-on-Arrival are also available at a limited number of seaports, including the Batam and Bintan ferry terminals opposite Singapore, but they are unavailable at any land border crossing. Visas-on-Arrival are only for private, temporary business or pleasure visits. Travel for other purposes requires the appropriate Indonesian visa before arrival. Visas-on-Arrival are valid for 30 days and cost U.S. $25. A Visa-on-Arrival may be extended one time only. An onward/return ticket is required to apply for a Visa-on-Arrival at these ports of entry. The Indonesian Embassy website indicates that Visas-on-Arrival are unavailable to government travelers who want to enter Indonesia on a diplomatic or official passport for an official purpose or mission. For details on Visas-on-Arrival and other visa information please visit the Embassy of the Republic of Indonesia website.

If you are entering Indonesia through Bali, you must have two fully blank passport pages in your passport. If you are entering through other ports of entry, you must have at least one blank page. Indonesian immigration inspectors do not consider amendment pages in your passport as blank pages. If your passport is nearly full, be sure to obtain extra blank passport pages before you travel. If you don't meet Indonesian entry criteria properly, you may be denied entry on the spot with no recourse and put on the next available flight departing Indonesia.

Please be advised that Indonesian entry and visa procedures may be inconsistently applied at different ports of entry, and when faced with making a decision, Indonesian authorities usually make the more conservative, restrictive decision. Entry requirements are subject to change at the sole discretion of the Indonesian authorities, a process over which the U.S. government has no control.

You may apply for a visa at the Indonesian Embassy in Washington, D.C., or at an Indonesian consulate elsewhere in the United States. In some cases, you may also apply at Indonesian embassies and consulates in other countries. If you are traveling overseas and wish to apply for an Indonesian visa, you should inquire with the local Indonesian embassy in the country where you are currently traveling. For up-to-date information, travelers may contact the Embassy of the Republic of Indonesia: 2020 Massachusetts Avenue NW, Washington D.C. 20036, phone: (202) 775-5200, or at Indonesian Consulates in Los Angeles (213) 383-5126; San Francisco (415) 474-9571; Chicago (312) 920-1880; New York (212) 879-0600; and Houston (713) 785-1691. Visit the Embassy of Indonesia website for the most current visa information.

Indonesia strictly enforces its immigration/visa requirements. Travelers who overstay the date stamped in their Visa-on-Arrival are subject to a fine of 200,000 Rupiah, approximately U.S. $22, per day, and other sanctions. Westerners, including U.S. citizens, have been jailed for visa violations and/or overstays. Violators may also be subject to substantial fines and/or deportation from Indonesia for immigration and visa violations. Immigration officials have also detained foreigners for conducting work, academic, or other non-tourist activities while on visitor status. Even gratis volunteer work with local or international NGOs is not permitted on visitor status. Penalties for such immigration/visa violations have included a prison sentence of up to five years and a fine of Rupiah 25 million. Travelers should contact an Indonesian consular office to determine the appropriate visa category before traveling to Indonesia.

All airline passengers, including children, diplomats, and officials, are subject to a departure tax, which must be paid in Rupiah, cash only. The international departure tax as of February 2010 is 150,000 Rupiah in Jakarta and varies at other international airports. The domestic departure tax in Jakarta is 30,000 Rupiah and also varies elsewhere.

The U.S. Department of State is unaware of any HIV/AIDS entry restrictions for visitors to or foreign residents of Indonesia. The Indonesian Government screens incoming passengers in response to reported outbreaks of pandemic illnesses.

Threats to Safety and Security: Since 2005, the Indonesian police and security forces have disrupted a number of terrorist cells, including Jemaah Islamiyah (JI), a U.S. government-designated terrorist organization that carried out several bombings at various times from 2000 to 2009. Indonesia suffered its worst terrorist attack in 2002, when more than 200 foreign tourists and Indonesian citizens were killed in Bali. Deadly car bombs have exploded outside hotels and resorts frequented by Westerners in Jakarta and Bali in

2003 and 2005 and outside of the Australian Embassy in Jakarta in 2004. In July 2009, JI-affiliated elements bombed two Western hotels in Jakarta, killing nine Indonesians and foreigners and injuring over 50, including six U.S. citizens. Since these attacks, Indonesia has effectively pursued counterterrorism efforts through legislation and law enforcement. In 2010, security forces arrested more than 100 individuals on terrorism-related charges. However, violent elements in Indonesia continue to demonstrate a willingness and ability to carry out violent attacks with little or no warning.

Extremists may target both official and private interests, including hotels, nightclubs, shopping areas, and restaurants. Whether at work, pursuing daily activities, and/or while traveling, you should be vigilant and prudent at all times. Monitor local news reports, vary your routes and times, and maintain a low profile. Be sure to consider the security and safety preparedness of hotels, residences, restaurants, and entertainment or recreational venues that you frequent.

In November 2009, unknown assailants shot at foreigners in Banda Aceh, North Sumatra, an area that was devastated by the 2004 tsunami and the scene of a long-running separatist conflict that ended in 2005. The gunfire wounded a European development worker. In the same area, a house occupied by U.S. citizen teachers was targeted and hit by gunfire, but there were no U.S. citizen casualties.

Indonesian security forces are engaged in combat and policing operations to suppress the Free Papua Movement (OPM), a low-intensity separatist insurgency. However, separatists in Papua continue to conduct occasional, violent attacks against police and civilians in the province that resulted in the deaths of and injuries to local residents and expatriate workers.

Be aware that a real or even perceived offense may generate a violent response from local people. For example, in June 2008, two U.S. citizens in western Sumatra were beaten after they reportedly accused a local man of theft. In the same month, another U.S. citizen in Sumatra was threatened by members of a local mosque when he complained about being awakened from his sleep by the morning call to prayer.

Indonesia's location on the "Ring of Fire" results in often severe seismic events that pose grave threats, and disrupt daily life and regional air travel. There is little warning and Indonesian emergency response capabilities are limited in the best of circumstances. U.S. citizens must prepare for unforeseen emergencies when living or traveling in Indonesia.

Please update your passports and important personal papers in case you must depart Indonesia quickly in an emergency. Travel distances, poor communications, and an inadequate infrastructure make it extremely difficult for the Embassy to respond to U.S. citizen emergencies. Many parts of Indonesia (including many tourist destinations) are isolated and difficult to reach or contact.

Stay up to date by:

- Bookmarking our Bureau of Consular Affairs website, which contains current Travel Warnings and Travel Alerts as well as the Worldwide Caution.
- Following us on Twitter and the Bureau of Consular Affairs page on Facebook as well.
- Downloading our free Smart Traveler iPhone App to have travel information at your fingertips.
- Calling 1-888-407-4747 toll-free within the U.S. and Canada, or a regular toll line, 1-202-501-4444, from other countries.
- Taking some time before travel to consider your personal security.

Crime: Crime can be a problem in some major metropolitan areas in Indonesia. Crimes of opportunity such as pick-pocketing and theft occur throughout the country. If you are in Jakarta and Surabaya, hire a taxi either at a major hotel or shopping center queue, or by calling or hailing a reputable taxi company, such as Silver Bird, Blue Bird or White Express. If you are arriving at Soekarno-Hatta International Airport in Jakarta, use only these taxis obtained at a designated taxi queue or clearly marked taxi stand. Politely decline all offers of help from touts or anyone who approaches you. Major hotels have staff on duty to offer safe meet-and-greet service at airports and can also direct their hotel guests to a reliable taxi. It is best to request meet and greet services from your hotel in advance. Add about 25,000 Rupiah to the metered fare for required airport taxes and toll road fees. Depending on traffic, a minimum metered fare is 150,000-200,000 Rupiah from Soekarno-Hatta airport to central Jakarta. Criminals in Jakarta regularly rob customers in taxis painted to look like taxis from reputable companies; booking taxis by telephone directly from the company or through hotels is the best way to avoid falling victim to this scam.

Indonesian police have noted an upward trend in burglaries and armed robberies in Jakarta, an increase of 25 percent in 2010, particularly in wealthier areas where expatriates tend to live. The best defense is to proactively take personal responsibility for your own security: know the layout of your dwelling, have someone at home at all times, discuss security procedures with your family and household staff, and know your neighborhood.

Claiming to act in the name of religious or moral standards, certain extremist groups have, on occasion, attacked nightspots and places of entertainment. Most of these attacks have sought to destroy property rather than to injure individuals. International news events can sometimes trigger anti-American or anti-Western demonstrations.

Credit card fraud and theft is a serious and growing problem in Indonesia, particularly for Westerners. Travelers should minimize use of credit cards and instead use cash. If used, credit card numbers should be closely safeguarded at all times. There have been many reports of shop, restaurant, and hotel staff writing down the credit card numbers of customers and then making purchases using the credit card number after the card owner has departed the retail location. Travelers should also avoid using credit cards for online transactions at Internet cafes and similar venues. Travelers who decide to use credit cards should monitor their credit card activity carefully and immediately report any unauthorized use to their financial institution. ATM cards have been skimmed and cloned, resulting in bank accounts being drained. If you choose to use an ATM, exercise the same level of caution you would in the United States when using unfamiliar ATM machines and monitor your statements closely. Selecting tour guides, hotels, and business partners based on their reputation, competence, and ability to help can be very useful when considering a stay in Indonesia.

You are encouraged to carry a copy of your U.S. passport with you at all times so that if questioned by local officials, proof of identity and proof of U.S. citizenship are readily available. If you are arrested or detained, formal notification of the arrest is normally provided in writing to the U.S. Embassy in Jakarta, a process that can take several weeks. If detained, telephone the U.S. Embassy in Jakarta, or the nearest U.S. consular office immediately.

"Drink-spiking" incidents have been of increasing concern as there have been many reports of males being targeted for this ruse in clubs and nightspots. One drug used in these incidents is believed to be an animal tranquilizer, and its effects are extremely powerful. Besides putting the victim in an unconscious state for a long time, the side effects include memory loss, nausea, headaches, and vomiting. Although most of these incidents involve male victims, it is important to remember that females have been victimized in the past with "Date-Rape" drugs. Local, "home brew" alcoholic drinks may also be spiked. The best advice is: do not go out alone; do not leave drinks unattended; drink brand name beverages; and drink responsibly, in moderation. Even though alcohol is widely available, public inebriation is highly frowned upon.

Maritime piracy in Indonesian waters continues, although incidents have decreased steadily in recent years. The most recent reports are of thefts of valuables or cargo from boats that are in port and not at sea. Regardless, before traveling by sea, especially in the Straits of Malacca between the Riau Province and Singapore and in the waters north of Sulawesi and Kalimantan, review the current security situation with local authorities.

Don't buy counterfeit and pirated goods, even if they are widely available. Not only are the bootleg items illegal in the United States, if you purchase them you may also be breaking local law.

Victims of Crime: If you or someone you know becomes the victim of a crime abroad, you should contact the local police and the nearest U.S. embassy or consulate. We can:

- Replace a stolen passport.
- Help you find appropriate medical care for violent crimes such as assault or rape.
- Put you in contact with the appropriate police authorities, and contact family members or friends.
- Although the local authorities are responsible for investigating and prosecuting the crime, consular officers can help you understand the local criminal justice process and can direct you to local attorneys.

The local equivalents to the "911" emergency telephone line in Indonesia are 110 for police, 113 for fire, and 118 for ambulance. While these numbers exist, they are not always answered. It is often more effective to physically go to Indonesian authorities to ask for their help rather than to wait for emergency services to respond to your phone call. There are sets of local direct emergency numbers in each district and you should learn and keep these emergency numbers at hand. However all Indonesian emergency services, police, fire and ambulance, if available at all, are often rudimentary at best.

Criminal Penalties: While you are traveling in Indonesia, you are subject to its laws even if you are a U.S. citizen. Foreign laws and legal systems can be vastly different than our own. There are also some things that might be legal in the country you visit, but still illegal in the United States; for example, you can be prosecuted under U.S. law if you buy pirated goods. In Indonesia, you may be taken in for questioning if you don't have your passport with you. It is also illegal to take pictures of certain buildings, and driving under the influence could land you immediately in jail. If you break local laws in Indonesia, your U.S. passport won't help you avoid arrest or prosecution. It's very important to know what's legal and what's not where you are going.

In March 2008, the Indonesian parliament passed a bill criminalizing the access of internet sites containing violent or pornographic material. Anyone found guilty of the new offense could be jailed for up to three years or have to pay a heavy fine.

Engaging in sexual conduct with children, using, and/or disseminating child pornography is a crime prosecutable in the United States regardless of the country where the activity occurs. The Indonesian child protection law imposes up to 15 years in prison for those convicted of engaging in sexual contact with a child, and the anti-trafficking in persons law imposes 15 years in prison for anyone engaging in sex with a victim of trafficking.

Penalties for possession, use, or trafficking in illegal drugs in Indonesia are severe, and convicted offenders can expect long jail sentences and heavy fines. A life sentence or the death penalty can be given in cases of drug trafficking; several foreigners have been sentenced to death in recent years. One U.S. citizen was given a life sentence for drug trafficking. Indonesian prisons are harsh and do not meet Western standards. Many prisoners are required to supplement their prison diets and clothing with funds from relatives. Medical and dental care in Indonesian prisons, while available, is below Western standards, and access to medical testing to diagnose illness as well as medications to treat conditions are often difficult to obtain.

Arrest notifications in Indonesia: While some countries will automatically notify the nearest U.S. embassy or consulate if a U.S. citizen is detained or arrested in a foreign country, that might not always be the case. To ensure that the United States Government is aware of your circumstances, request that the police and prison officials notify the nearest U.S. embassy or consulate as soon as you are arrested or detained overseas.

Special Circumstances: The Regional Security Officer of the U.S. Embassy must receive prior notice from U.S. government employees of their travel to Papua, Aceh, Central Sulawesi, and Maluku. Separate pre-travel procedures apply to U.S. Armed Forces personnel who intend to travel to Indonesia for any reason.

Accessibility: Indonesia enacted laws in 1997, 1998, 2004, 2007, and 2008 regarding accessibility for the disabled. However, except for buildings constructed under international standards, most public places and transportation facilities are not accessible, and applicable laws are not enforced. Persons with disabilities will face severe difficulties in Indonesia as walkways, road crossings, rest rooms, and tourist and other areas are not equipped with accommodating features.

Sharia law: Sharia law is enforced in Aceh, northern Sumatra, by a separate police force. In a few other areas, it exists unofficially or through local legislation. In these areas, implementation is uneven, processes are opaque, and enforcement can be arbitrary. Sharia authorities rarely confront non-Muslims about violations of Sharia law, but this has occurred. Visitors to all areas are encouraged to respect local tradition, dress modestly, and seek guidance from local police if confronted by Sharia authorities. Many women, both Muslim and non-Muslim, carry a scarf to drape around their head while traveling in Aceh, although wearing a headscarf is not compulsory, and non-Muslim women are not necessarily expected to wear one. The Sharia concept of "khalwat" forbids an unmarried man and unmarried woman (who are not close relatives) to be alone together in closed rooms or secluded areas.

Natural Disasters: Many areas of Indonesia are at high risk for natural disasters due to the country's geographic location and topography. If you are planning hikes or other outdoor activities in Indonesia, obtain up-to-date information on local conditions, travel with a reputable local guide, have overseas medical insurance, and carry a local mobile phone. Obey instructions from security and emergency personnel, and do not enter restricted areas. Organized and trained rescue services are rudimentary in populated areas and do not exist in remote areas. If you get into trouble, you may find yourself at great risk even if you can communicate your plight.

Earthquakes and Tsunamis: The Indian Ocean earthquake and tsunami in December 2004 killed more than 130,000 people and left over 37,000 missing in Aceh and North Sumatra. In January 2009, a magnitude 7.7 quake struck the north coast of Papua between the cities of Sorong and Manokwari causing deaths and heavy damage. In September 2009, magnitude 7.6 and 7.9 earthquakes struck the towns of Jambi and Padang in Sumatra, causing widespread damage and 700 deaths and many more injuries. Another earthquake in the Mentawai islands in October 2010 caused a tsunami which killed over 450 locals and displaced up to tens of thousands for several weeks. Because of the islands' remoteness, emergency response personnel needed several days to evacuate tourists and bring in emergency relief supplies. In places where tsunamis are a potential threat, you should head inland for high ground immediately when large tremors are felt as tsunami warning systems may not be operable or reports delayed; be sure to establish an escape route beforehand. The city of Jakarta lacks an earthquake plan, according to its own 2010 report, which is a common problem replicated throughout the country.

Volcanoes: Mt. Merapi, a volcano near Yogyakarta, erupted with massive pyroclastic flows from April to early July 2006 and again in late 2010, disrupting air travel as far away as Jakarta and causing hundreds of casualties in the volcano's vicinity. Mount Sinabung in the Tanah Karo Highlands of North Sumatra erupted in August 2010. The eruption caused the evacuation of 30,000 people.

Flooding and Landslides: These frequently follow heavy rains, and travelers should exercise caution both in and outside of cities. On the roads, be aware of the possibility of land slippage, road washouts, and potholes.

Fires: Fire departments lack modern equipment and training. Seventy percent of Jakarta's fire hydrants are inoperative, and the city fire department is only manned at fifty percent of its recommended level. Outside of Jakarta, fire prevention is no better. Occupants of high floors and crowded markets are at great risk, since fire departments are unable to reach those places.

Environmental Quality: Air quality outside of Jakarta and other major cities is acceptable most of the time. However, within Indonesia's major cities, air quality can range from "unhealthy for sensitive groups" to "unhealthy." Some expatriate residents of Jakarta have tested positive for highly elevated levels of carbon monoxide in their blood. The air and water quality in Jakarta is particularly polluted. Individuals susceptible to chronic respiratory illnesses should consult with their doctor before spending significant amounts of time in Jakarta. Open burning of rain forests continues, although to a lesser degree than in the early 2000s. Water is not potable. A 2008 study showed that 100 percent of Jakarta's water is contaminated by fecal coliform bacteria (see below). Only bottled water should be consumed. Sewage and drainage systems are incomplete.

Scuba Diving, Snorkeling, and Surfing: Exercise prudence when scuba diving, snorkeling, or surfing and when visiting remote tourist locations. Strong seasonal undercurrents in coastal waters pose a fatal threat to surfers and swimmers; every year, several U.S. citizens drown in unstable water. Surfers and divers should also be aware that local fishermen in coastal waters may use explosives and poisons to catch fish, although this practice is illegal in Indonesia.

Rescue services are mostly ad hoc and cannot be relied upon. Dangerous marine life such as cnidaria (jellyfish) and physalia (Portugese Man-O-War) are common, and divers and swimmers should be prepared to provide first aid if encountered. Divers should contact the Divers Alert Network (DAN) and obtain diving medical insurance in the event decompression is required as air evacuation is usually the only way to get to the nearest decompression chamber. DAN has a large network of dive physicians that are available for consultation and emergency response to its members.

Papua: All travelers to Papua and West Papua provinces, whether traveling as a private citizen or in an official capacity, must obtain prior approval to travel from the Indonesian government. Low-intensity communal conflict exists in Papua and has caused numerous deaths and injuries. Travelers should strictly avoid situations involving armed tribal members. Anti-government protests have caused numerous deaths and injuries and led to temporary closures of the airport in Timika. In 2009 and January 2010, sniper fire from unknown attackers on the private road from Kuala Kencana to Tembagapura caused several casualties, including deaths, of government forces, local workers, and expatriates.

Mountain Hiking: Hikers on Puncak Jaya or other mountains in Papua and elsewhere in Indonesia should organize their trip through a reputable tour operator and ensure that they have firm, realistic, primary and backup plans for climbing down the mountain. In the past, some local tour operators have abandoned climbers after they reached the summit.

Climbers should be aware that transiting private or commercial properties on the way down the mountain is considered trespassing and not a safe or legal alternative to a proper plan. Hikers should assume that they will be completely on their own in case of any emergency. Hikers should be aware that severe seismic events occur frequently and without notice.

Teaching English in Indonesia: If you would like to teach English in Indonesia, carefully review employment contracts before traveling to Indonesia. Most contracts include a monetary penalty for early termination. English schools may hold passports to insure that the employee complies with the terms of the contract or pays the appropriate penalty. There have been many U.S. citizens who were unable to depart Indonesia after having terminated their employment contracts early because their employer would not release their passports.

Commercial Disputes: If you are involved in commercial or property matters, be aware that the business environment is complex, and formal, regulated, transparent dispute settlement mechanisms are not fully developed. Local and foreign businesses often cite corruption and ineffective courts as serious problems. Business and regulatory disputes, which would be generally considered administrative or civil matters in the United States, may in some cases be treated as criminal cases in Indonesia. It can be challenging to resolve trade disputes.

Internet Purchases: U.S. citizens frequently may be defrauded when purchasing goods by Internet from Indonesian suppliers whom the buyer has not met personally.

Currency: The widespread use of counterfeit currency causes banks, exchange facilities, and most commercial establishments to not accept U.S. currency that is worn, defaced, torn, or issued before 1996.

Dual Nationality: Indonesian law does not recognize dual nationality for adults over 18 years of age. Because of this law, U.S. citizens who are also documented as Indonesian nationals may experience difficulties with immigration formalities in Indonesia. Holding dual citizenship may also hamper the U.S. Embassy's ability to provide consular protection to dual national U.S. citizens. In addition to being subject to all Indonesian laws affecting U.S. citizens, dual nationals may also be subject to other laws that impose special obligations on Indonesian citizens. In July 2006, the Indonesian Parliament passed new legislation allowing children under age 18 to hold foreign as well as Indonesian citizenship. Parents whose children hold both Indonesian and U.S. citizenship continue to experience difficulties with entry and exit immigration procedures.

Transportation: There has been a rapid rise in all manners of public and private transportation within Indonesia. New private airlines have begun operations over the past several years, as have new bus and ferry lines. Air, ferry, and road accidents resulting in fatalities, injuries, and significant damage are common.

While all forms of transportation are ostensibly regulated in Indonesia, oversight is spotty, equipment tends to be less well maintained than that operated in the United States, amenities do not typically meet Western standards, and rescue/emergency response is notably lacking. Travelers by boat or ferry should not board before confirming that adequate personal floatation devices are provided. Ferries are frequently overcrowded and lack basic safety equipment, and there have been a number of ferry sinkings resulting in significant loss of life.

Customs Regulations: Indonesian customs authorities strictly regulate the import and export of items such as prescription medicines and foreign language materials or videotapes/discs. You should contact the Embassy of Indonesia in Washington or Indonesian consulates elsewhere in the United States for specific information about customs requirements. Transactions involving such products may be illegal, and bringing them back to the United States may result in forfeiture and/or fines.

Medical Facilities and Health Information: The general level of sanitation and health care in Indonesia is far below U.S. standards. Some routine medical care is available in all major cities, although most expatriates leave the country for all but the simplest medical procedures. Psychological and psychiatric services are limited throughout Indonesia. Medical procedures requiring hospitalization and/or medical evacuation to locations with acceptable medical care, such as Singapore, Australia, or the United States can cost thousands of dollars. Physicians and hospitals often expect immediate cash payment or sizable deposits before offering medical care. A non-exhaustive list of English-speaking doctors and hospitals is accessible via the U.S. Embassy Jakarta's website. Many places in Indonesia are inaccessible to the physically handicapped. What sidewalks that exist are uneven and difficult to navigate, and many buildings do not have elevators.

Ambulance services are individually run by hospitals and clinics. Indonesian ambulance attendants lack paramedical training equivalent to U.S. standards, and there is no reliable emergency ambulance service in Indonesia. If you are staying in Indonesia for an extended period, especially if you have known health problems, you are advised to investigate private ambulance services in your area, and to provide family and close contacts with the direct telephone number(s) of their preferred service. Traffic congestion is a significant problem in urban Indonesia and roads are generally in poor condition in rural Indonesia, so ambulance transport, if it exists at all, even over short distances can take hours.

Community sanitation and public health programs are inadequate throughout Indonesia and subject to frequent breakdowns. Water and air pollution and traffic congestion have rapidly increased with the unstructured growth of major cities. Almost all maladies of the developing world are endemic to Indonesia, and immediate treatment is problematic. Residents are subject to water- and food-borne illnesses such as typhoid, hepatitis, cholera, worms, amebiasis, giardia, cyclospora, and bacterial dysentery. Mosquito-borne dengue fever and tuberculosis exist throughout Indonesia and have been serious in Jakarta. Indonesia has the highest incidence of dengue fever in Asia. Multiple drug-resistant strains of malaria are endemic in some parts of Indonesia but not in metropolitan Jakarta, Medan, Surabaya, and Bali; even short stays can be disastrous without malaria prophylaxis. Malaria prophylaxis is highly recommended for travel to malaria-endemic areas outside major cities. Travelers to Sulawesi should be tested for schistosomiasis. Asthma and other respiratory difficulties are common and generally worse in Jakarta than in other areas, exacerbated by the high pollution levels. Skin allergies are also common. Avian (H5N1) and swine (H1N1) influenza are endemic in Indonesia. Rabies is endemic in Indonesia and a particular problem in Bali, where it has caused over 100 deaths from 2008 to 2010. Polio reemerged in Western Java in 2005. Travelers are urged to consult with their personal physicians and to get updated information on prevalent diseases before traveling to Indonesia. Travelers should be current on all recommended immunizations; those planning on traveling extensively should consider the series of three pre-exposure inoculations against rabies. Local pharmacies carry a range of products of variable quality, availability, and cost. Counterfeit pharmaceuticals are a significant risk and U.S. citizens should patronize only reputable pharmacies. Tap water is not potable. In 2008, Indonesian authorities found that 100 percent of tap water samples from the Jakarta area tested positive for coliform bacteria, as well as high concentrations of toxic chemicals, including lead and mercury. Bottled water should be used for consumption, including for cooking. Factory bottled soft drinks, and juices and milk sold in sealed containers are generally safe. Take extra care preparing fresh fruits, vegetables, and meats. If you cannot see refrigerators, expect that any food, especially street food, is preserved with high concentrations of formaldehyde derivatives. Consider that unprocessed or raw food may be unsafe even in higher end establishments. Washing, soaking, peeling, and/or thoroughly cooking food are mandatory procedures to minimize insecticide, bacterial, and parasitic contamination. Gastrointestinal disorders are common. A wide variety of foods are available in local markets and supermarkets, and with some care and effort, it is possible to eat a well-balanced diet.

Car and motorcycle accidents are the primary causes of severe injury to foreigners living and traveling in Indonesia. Defensive driving and use of seatbelts are encouraged. Use of motorcycles and bicycling in traffic are both discouraged. Rh negative blood may be difficult to obtain in an area with very few Westerners. Therefore, it is important to know your blood type and recognize that scarcity may be a problem.

Updated information and links to the World Health Organization (WHO) and Centers for Disease Control and Prevention (CDC) are posted on the U.S. Embassy Jakarta's website.

Information on vaccinations and other health precautions, such as safe food and water precautions and insect bite protection, may be obtained from the Centers for Disease Control and Prevention's (CDC) hotline for international travelers at 1-877-FYI-TRIP (1-877-394-8747) or via the CDC website. For information about outbreaks of infectious diseases abroad, consult the infectious diseases section of the World Health Organization (WHO) website. The WHO website also contains additional health information for travelers, including detailed country-specific health information. Tuberculosis is an increasingly serious health concern in Indonesia.

Medical Insurance: You can't assume your insurance will go with you when you travel. It's very important to find out BEFORE you leave whether or not your medical insurance will cover you overseas. You need to ask your insurance company two questions:

- Does my policy cover me when I'm out of the United States?
- Will it cover emergencies such as treatment in a foreign hospital, medical evacuation or an air ambulance?

In many places, doctors and hospitals still expect payment in cash at the time of service. Your regular U.S. health insurance may not cover doctor and hospital visits in other countries. If your policy doesn't provide overseas coverage when you travel, it's a very good idea to take out another one for your trip.

Traffic Safety and Road Conditions: While in Indonesia, U.S. citizens may encounter road conditions that differ significantly from those in the United States. Traffic in Indonesia is highly dangerous, congested, and undisciplined. Traffic signals are frequently ignored and often in disrepair. The number and variety of vehicles on the road far exceed the capacity of existing roadways. Road conditions vary from good (in the case of toll roads and major city roads) to dangerously poor. Generally, road safety awareness is very low in Indonesia. Buses and trucks are often dangerously overloaded and travel at high speeds. Most roads outside major urban areas have a single lane of traffic in each direction, making passing dangerous. Most Indonesian drivers do not maintain a safe-following distance in a manner familiar to U.S. drivers and tend to pass or maneuver with considerably less margin for error than in the United States. Although traffic in Indonesia moves on the left side of the road, drivers tend to pass on both sides and may use the shoulder for this purpose. It is common for drivers to create extra lanes regardless of the lane markings on the roads. Nails are frequently sprinkled on roads to cause punctures and create business for tire-repair services.

Throughout Indonesia, there is an overabundance of motorcycles claiming the right of way. Many motorcycle drivers weave recklessly in and out of traffic with complete disregard for traffic regulations and simple safety precautions. Throughout the country, motor vehicles share the roads with other forms of transportation such as pedicabs, horse and ox carts, push-carts, and domestic animals such as cows, sheep, and goats.

Indonesia requires the use of seat belts in front seats; most Indonesian automobiles do not have seat belts in the rear passenger seats. The use of infant and child car seats is uncommon, and it can be very difficult to rent a car seat. Helmets are required for all motorcycle passengers, the laws for which are inconsistently enforced. Passengers often do not wear helmets. Accidents on rented motorcycles constitute the largest cause of death and serious injury among foreign visitors to Indonesia. Given the poor quality of emergency services, an injury considered to be minor in the United States might result in greater bodily harm in Indonesia.

Accidents between a car and a motorcycle are invariably viewed as the fault of the driver of the car. Groups of motorcycle riders will sometimes threaten the driver of a car who is involved in an accident regardless of who is at fault. Expatriates and affluent Indonesians often use professional drivers. All car rental firms provide drivers for a nominal additional fee. Travelers unfamiliar with Indonesian driving conditions are strongly encouraged to hire drivers. Driving at night can be extremely dangerous outside of major urban areas. Drivers often refuse to use their lights until it is completely dark, and most rural roads are unlit. Sometimes residents in rural areas use road surfaces as public gathering areas, congregating on them after dark.

When an accident involving personal injury occurs, Indonesian law requires both drivers to await the arrival of a police officer to report the accident. Although Indonesian law requires third party insurance, most Indonesian drivers are uninsured, and even when a vehicle is insured, it is common for insurance companies to refuse to pay damages. Nevertheless, foreigners who plan to drive while in Indonesia should ensure they have appropriate insurance coverage and a driver's license.

Ambulance service in Indonesia is unreliable, and taxis or private cars are often used to transport the injured to a medical facility. In cases of serious injury to a pedestrian, the driver of the vehicle could be required to help transport the injured person to the hospital. When an accident occurs outside a major city, it may be advisable, before stopping, to drive to the nearest police station to seek assistance.

Aviation Safety Oversight: The U.S. Federal Aviation Administration (FAA) has assessed the Indonesian Directorate General of Civil Aviation as not being in compliance with International Civil Aviation Organization (ICAO) aviation safety standards for oversight of Indonesian's air carrier operations. Further information may be found on the FAA's safety assessment page.

Indonesian air carriers continue to experience air incidents and accidents. U.S. citizens traveling to and from Indonesia are encouraged to fly directly to their destinations on international carriers from countries whose civil aviation authorities meet international aviation safety standards for the oversight of their air carrier operations under the FAA's International Aviation Safety Assessment (IASA) program.

Children's Issues: Please see the U.S. Dept. of State Office of Children's Issues web pages on intercountry adoption and international parental child abduction.

Intercountry Adoption

August 2009

The information in this section has been edited from the latest report available as of February 2013 from the State Department Bureau of Consular Affairs, Office of Overseas Citizens Services. For more information, please read the *Intercountry Adoption* section of this book and review current reports online at http://adoption.state.gov.

Indonesia is not party to the Hague Convention on Protection of Children and Co-operation in Respect of Intercountry Adoption (Hague Adoption Convention).

Who Can Adopt? To bring an adopted child to United States from Indonesia, you must be found eligible to adopt by the U.S. Government. The U.S. Government agency responsible for making this determination is the Department of Homeland Security, U.S. Citizenship and Immigration Services (USCIS). In addition to these U.S. requirements for adoptive parents, Indonesia also has the following requirements for adoptive parents.

Residency Requirements: Couples must be a resident of Indonesia for at least 2 years with a permit issued by the local authorities (Rukun Tetangga, Rukun Warga, Kelurahan, Kecamatan), and a letter from the Embassy in Jakarta (a statement of Domicile). Foreign national prospective adoptive parents must be resident in Indonesia and must have been working and living in Indonesia for at least two years prior to the application to adopt. Past experience has shown that if one foreign national parent is resident in Indonesia before the other, he or she may initiate the process as long as s/he has already been resident in Indonesia for at least two years. In cases where one prospective adoptive parent is a foreign national and the other is an Indonesian citizen, the residency requirement has not applied as long as the Indonesian national has resided in Indonesia to see the adoption process through completion. Such cases, however, are necessarily more complicated, and different courts may interpret the law differently.

As was noted above, the U.S. Embassy strongly recommends that prospective adoptive parents contact the Immigrant Visa Unit at U.S. Embassy Jakarta or Yayasan Sayap Ibu for further details. Please note that regardless of residency, both adopting parents must appear at the court hearing. Also, the adoptive parents need to obtain separate domicile statements issued by the local authorities (Rukun Tetangga, Rukun Warga, Kelurahan, Kecamatan), and by the U.S. Embassy in Jakarta. The domicile statement issued by the U.S. Embassy in Jakarta will indicate the prospective adoptive parents' local address and their dates of residency in Indonesia. The U.S. Embassy determines the dates of residency according to the parents' KIMS/KITAS (Temporary Residence Card).

Age Requirements: Couples must be between 30 and 45 years of age.

Marriage Requirements: Individuals wanting to adopt must be married for a minimum of five years. Couples can be either childless, have one of their own children or have previously adopted an Indonesian child. If the prospective adoptive mother has had birth children in the past, she must no longer be capable of bearing children.

Other Requirements: Indonesian Government stipulates that an adoptive child must be of the same religion as the adoptive parents. Where the religion of the child's birth parents is not known, the child will be deemed to be Muslim. The prospective adoptive parents must believe in God and both must appear at the court hearing.

Who Can Be Adopted? Indonesia has specific requirements that a child must meet in order to be eligible for adoption. You cannot adopt a child in Indonesia unless he or she meets the requirements outlined below. In addition to these requirements, a child must meet the definition of an orphan under U.S. law for you to bring him or her back to the United States.

Eligibility Requirements: The adoptive child must be in the care of a registered and authorized social welfare organization.

Age Requirements: The adoptive child must be less than five years old.

Indonesia's Adoption Authority: The Ministry of Social Affairs of the Republic of Indonesia, Directorate of Child Social Service Development

The Process: The first step in adopting a child usually to select a licensed agency in the United States that can help with your adoption. Adoption service providers must be licensed by the U.S. state in which they operate. The U.S. Embassy in Jakarta is not aware of any legally recognized Indonesian agencies who can assist adoptive parents. Foreigners may seek private legal assistance to facilitate the process of adoption and seek advice and information from certain orphanages. To bring an adopted child from Indonesia to the United States, you must apply to be found eligible to adopt (Form I-600A) by the U.S. Government, Department of Homeland Security, U.S. Citizenship and Immigration Services (USCIS).

There are several documents that must be completed by the adoptive parents. When all required paperwork is completed, application for adoption are directed through Yayasan Sayap Ibu or another designed social organization to the Department of Social Affairs, which usually grants permission for the child to be released into the prospective adoptive parents' foster care.

If you are eligible to adopt, and a child is available for intercountry adoption, the central adoption authority in Indonesia will provide you with a referral to a child. The child will be released into prospective adoptive parents' foster care. The adoptive parent must complete a minimum period of six months of foster parenting the child before commencing the court process to finalize the adoption. Monitoring by an Indonesian social worker appointed by the Department of Social Affairs (DSP-SOS) is a part of this fostering process. After the parents have completed the requisite six months of foster parenting, fulfilled the two year residency requirement, and have delivered all the necessary paperwork to the Sayap Ibu Orphanage, a court date will be set. The court hearing will officially establish the foster parents as the child's adoptive parents. Approximately two weeks after the court hearing approving the adoption, the adoptive parents will receive the official court adoption document. The process for finalizing the adoption (or gaining legal custody) in Indonesia generally includes the following.

Role of the Adoption Authority: The Ministry of Social Affairs of the Republic of Indonesia, Directorate of Child Social Service Development is the agency designated by the Indonesian government to manage the administration of Indonesian adoption law and regulations. This office may be reached in writing or by phone at:

Jalan Salemba Raya No. 28
Jakarta Pusat, Indonesia
Telephone: 62-21-310-0375

Role of Adoption Agencies: Yayasan Sayap Ibu (the Sayap Ibu Foundation has been designated by the Ministry of Social Affairs to handle adoptions by foreigners. In areas of Indonesia where Yayasan Sayap Ibu is not represented, the first point of contact should be the Ministry itself. The Yayasan Sayap Ibu office in Jakarta is located at:

Yayasan Sayap Ibu
Jalan Barito II # 55
Telephone: 62-21-722-1763

Adoption Application: There are several required documents that must be completed by the adoptive parents. When all the required paperwork is completed, applications for adoption are directed through Yayasan Sayap Ibu or another designated social organization to the Department of Social Affairs, which usually grants permission for the child to be released into the prospective adoptive parents' foster care. Americans intending to adopt a child in Indonesia should not attempt to circumvent the proper processes. In order to obtain a valid court order, all adoptions must be vetted by an Inter-Departmental Committee (Tim Pertimbangan Perizinan Pangangkatan Anak Antara Warganegara Indonesia dan Warganegara Asing) that authorizes foreign adoptions. The final court decision must refer to the approval decision made by this committee.

Time Frame: Adoption procedures can take from 12 to 18 months.

Adoption Fees: The legal fees paid to the Indonesian authorities for adoption are approximately US$ 400. However, some adoptive parents have indicated that the cost can run up to $600 or more total.

Documents Required:

- Letter of no objection to the adoption from the American Embassy (issued by the Consular Section);
- Marriage Certificate (authenticated by the Indonesian Embassy/Consulate in the country of issuance);
- Birth Certificates of both parents (authenticated by the Indonesian Embassy/Consulate in the country of issuance);
- Birth Certificates of previous children (authenticated by the Indonesian Embassy/Consulate in the country of issuance);
- Reference letters from the parents or close relatives of both prospective adoptive parents stating that they approve of the prospective parents' desire to adopt an Indonesian child;
- Health statement for the husband and wife by a medical practitioner at an Indonesian government hospital. Statement from an Indonesian government hospital gynecologist regarding involuntary childlessness (i.e. the mother is infertile or can no longer have any more children even if she has had children previously);
- Income statement;
- Good conduct certificates from the Indonesian police for both husband and wife;
- Family photos and photos of the home and surroundings;
- Three photos each (3cm x 4cm) of husband and wife;
- Statement from the adoptive parents that they will report the condition of the adopted child to the Indonesian Embassy or Consulate in future areas of residence;
- Statement of motivation for adopting an Indonesian child (with U.S. Embassy seal);
- Separate statements of domicile issued by the U.S. Embassy in Jakarta and from the local authorities (Rukun Tangga/ Rukun Warga/Kelurahan/Kecamatan);
- Photocopy of Work or Residence Permits;
- Photocopy of passports; and
- A letter from the U.S. Embassy in Jakarta stating that the child will be allowed to enter the United States after the adoption is granted, and that under U.S. adoption legislation an adopted child becomes a child of the adopters as if he/she had been born to them in marriage.

All documents must be translated into Indonesian (Bahasa Indonesia) by a translator that has registered their signature with the Embassy so that translations may be certified with greater ease.

Prospective adoptive parents may obtain the list of sworn translators from the U.S. Embassy in Jakarta. The Sayap Ibu Foundation can assist if required. The Foundation can also provide assistance in court to couples planning to adopt children who are not under the care of the Foundation.

Bringing Your Child Home: Once your adoption is complete (or you have obtained legal custody of the child), there are a few more steps to take before you can head home. Specifically, you need to apply for several documents for your child before he or she can travel to the United States, such as a birth certificate, a passport or travel document for your child from the country in which he or she was born, and a U.S. Immigration Visa. For detailed and updated information on how to obtain these documents, review the *Intercountry Adoption* section on this publication and visit the USCIS Intercountry Adoption website at http://adoption.state.gov.

Child Citizenship Act: For adoptions finalized abroad, the Child Citizenship Act of 2000 allows your new child to acquire American citizenship automatically when he or she enters the United States as lawful permanent residents. For adoptions finalized in the United States, the Child Citizenship Act of 2000 allows your new child to acquire American citizenship automatically when the court in the United States issues the final adoption decree. To learn more, review the *Intercountry Adoption* section on this publication and visit the USCIS Intercountry Adoption website at http://adoption.state.gov.

After Adoption: There are no post-adoption requirements in Indonesia.

U.S. Embassy in Jakarta, Indonesia
Jalan Medan Merdeka Selatan #4-5
Jakarta—10110
Tel: 62-21-3435-9000
Fax: 62-21-385-7189

Indonesian Adoption Authority
The Ministry of Social Affairs of the Republic of Indonesia, Directorate of Child Social Service Development
Jalan Salemba Raya No. 28
Jakarta Pusat, Indonesia
Telephone: 62-21-310-0375

Embassy of Indonesia
2020 Massachusetts Ave. N.W.
Washington, D.C. 20036
Tel: 202-775-5200
Fax: 202-775–5365

Office of Children's Issues
U.S. Department of State
2201 C Street, NW
SA-29
Washington, DC 20520
Tel: 1-888-407-4747
E-mail: AskCI@state.gov
http://adoption.state.gov

For questions about immigration procedures, call the National Customer Service Center (NCSC) 1-800-375-5283 (TTY 1-800-767-1833).

International Parental Child Abduction
January 2012

The information in this section has been edited from the latest report available as of February 2013 from the State Department Bureau of Consular Affairs, Office of Overseas Citizens Services. For more information, please read the *International Parental Child Abduction* section of this book and check for updated reports online at www.travel.state.gov/abduction.

Disclaimer: The information in this flyer relating to the legal requirements of specific foreign countries is provided for general information only. Questions involving interpretation of specific foreign laws should be addressed to foreign legal counsel.

General Information: Indonesia is not a party to the Hague Convention on the Civil Aspects of International Child Abduction, nor are there any international or bilateral treaties in force between Indonesia and the United States dealing with international parental child abduction. Therefore, there is no treaty remedy by which the left-behind parent would be able to pursue recovery of the child or children should they be abducted or wrongfully retained in Indonesia. Once in Indonesia, the child or children would be completely subject to Indonesian law for all matters including custody. The United States is not a party to any treaty or convention on the enforcement of court orders. A custody decree issued by a court in the U.S. has no binding legal force abroad, although it may have a persuasive force in some countries. Furthermore, a U.S. custody decree may be considered by foreign courts and authorities as evidence and, in some cases, foreign courts may voluntarily recognize and enforce it on the basis of comity (the voluntary recognition by courts of one jurisdiction of the laws and judicial decisions of another).

Custody Disputes: Parental child abduction is not a crime under Indonesian law. Custody disputes are considered civil legal matters that must be resolved between the concerned parties or through the courts in Indonesia. The district/religious courts will hear and process child custody cases only as part of a divorce petition. Family issues and custody disputes are adjudicated based on Indonesian's Civil Code.

In order to bring a case/petition before the local court, the left-behind parent will require the assistance of an attorney licensed to practice in Indonesia. Ideally, these orders and proceedings ensure due process under the local laws as well as providing protection for the child/ren. The court will also consider a child's relationship with each of the disputing parties and will evaluate each parent's ability to provide education and general living conditions and welfare for the child/ren. Although there is no treaty in force between the United States and Indonesia on enforcement of judgments, the Indonesia courts will also take into consideration child custody decrees issued by foreign courts in deciding disputes regarding children residing in Indonesia. Domestic law does not provide visitation rights to the non-custodian parent unless the parent(s) ask the court to incorporate visitation orders before the final divorce decree is issued. Indonesian authorities advise the U.S. Embassy in Jakarta that non-compliance or violation of a local court order can result in a prison sentence. It should also be noted that Indonesian police or local law enforcement are reluctant to get involved in custody disputes and could not be counted on to enforce custody decrees issued by the Indonesian courts.

The district and religious courts have jurisdiction on civil law cases, including child custody disputes. Indonesia does not have an official religion. However, the constitution enshrines belief in one God and officially "embraces" five specific religions (Islam, Catholicism, Protestantism, Buddhism, and Hinduism), though other religions are permitted. For Muslims, Islamic (Sharia) law can apply in family and religious matters. Questions on specific Islamic laws as they pertain to custody rights should be addressed to a lawyer licensed to practice in Indonesia. U.S. consular officers are prohibited by U.S. federal regulations from providing legal advice, from taking custody of a child, from forcing a child to be returned to the United States, from providing assistance or refuge to parents attempting to violate local law, or from initiating or attempting to influence child custody proceedings in foreign courts. The American Citizen Services division of the Consular Section at the U.S. Embassy can assist in locating children believed to be in Indonesia and in verifying the child's welfare. If a child is in danger or if there is evidence of abuse, consular officers will request assistance from the local authorities in safeguarding the child's welfare. Consular officers maintain lists of attorneys practicing in the particular areas of Indonesia, as well as general information regarding child custody practices. For further information on international parental child abduction, contact the Office of Children's Issues, U.S. Department of State at 1-888-407-4747 or visit its web site on the Internet at http://www.travel.state.gov/abduction.

Deportation: There is no extradition treaty between the United States and Indonesia. However, if the taking parent is a U.S. citizen whose U.S. passport has been revoked due to an outstanding federal Unlawful Flight to avoid Prosecution (UFAP) warrant or indictment on charges of International Parental Kidnapping (IPKCA) in violation of 18 USC Section 1204, Indonesian authorities may consider deportation based on lack of a valid travel document.

Exit permits are required for foreigners who stay in Indonesia for more than six months. Exit/re-entry permits are given to foreigners who are holding "KITAS" (temporary stay permit).

Dual Nationality: A child with a parent who was born outside of the U.S. or who has acquired a second nationality through naturalization in another country may have a claim to citizenship in that country.

There is no requirement that a U.S. citizen parent consent to the acquisition by his/her child of another nationality and in many cases a parent is unaware that his/her child may have dual citizenship. The Embassy of Indonesia in Washington D.C. will be able to provide more detailed information on whether your child has a claim.

Passports for Minors and the Children's Passport Issuance Alert Program: For more information on these topics, see the *International Parental Child Abduction* section of this publication and review current reports from the U.S. Department of State at www.travel.state.gov/abduction.

Initiating Foreign Enforcement Proceedings Under Local Law: If a country is not a signatory to the Hague Convention on the Civil Aspects of International Child Abduction, it may be necessary for you to initiate a child custody action in the courts in the foreign country. This usually will require retaining the services of an attorney abroad. The Department of State, Office of Children's Issues is not a repository for foreign laws. However, selected information may be available concerning general procedures on child custody in particular countries. Contact the Office of Children's Issues to see if such information is available.

Retaining A Foreign Attorney: A list of English-speaking attorneys is available from the U.S. State Department, Office of American Citizens Services. See also the Martindale-Hubbell Law Directory available in law libraries.

It may be helpful to provide your foreign attorney with copies of any state laws concerning child custody orders and their enforcement in the U.S.

Criminal Remedies: The Department of State is not a law enforcement agency. The Department of Justice, Office of International Affairs works with U.S. prosecuting attorneys, the Federal Bureau of Investigation and with Interpol (an international police agency) in a joint cooperative effort to return persons charged with U.S. crimes from foreign countries. Extradition of the abducting adult may not result in the return of the child. Foreign countries may refuse to extradite a person to the United States if that person is also a citizen of the foreign country. Foreign countries may not recognize parental abduction as a crime. Please note that the extradition process applies only to the abducting adult/fugitive and not the child. The proper channel for the return of the child is through civil mechanisms or voluntary return arrangements.

Additional information is also available on the Internet at the web site of the U.S. Department of Justice, Office of Juvenile Justice and Delinquency Prevention (OJJDP) at http://www.ojjdp.ncjrs.org.

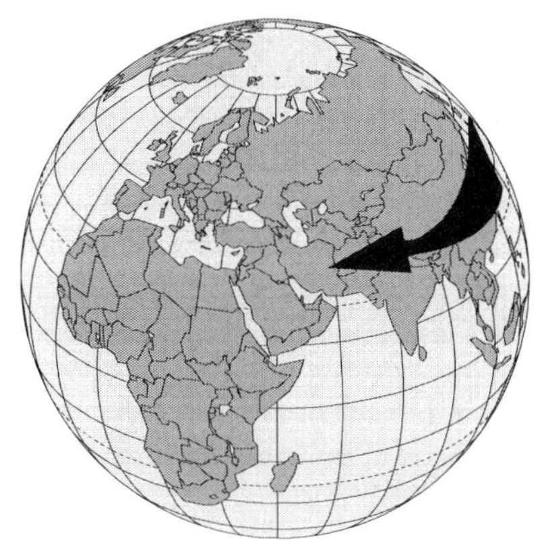

IRAN

Compiled from publications that were available as of February 2013 from the U.S. Department of State, the U.S. Department of Commerce, and the Central Intelligence Agency (CIA). See the introduction to this set for explanatory notes.

Official Name:
Islamic Republic of Iran

PROFILE

Geography

Area: total: 1,648,195 sq km; country comparison to the world: 18; land: 1,531,595 sq km; water: 116,600 sq km
Major cities: Tehran (capital) 7.19 million; Mashhad 2.592 million; Esfahan 1.704 million; Karaj 1.531 million; Tabriz 1.459 million (2009)
Climate: mostly arid or semiarid, subtropical along Caspian coast
Terrain: rugged, mountainous rim; high, central basin with deserts, mountains; small, discontinuous plains along both coasts

People

Nationality: noun: Iranian(s); adjective: Iranian
Population: 78,868,711 (July 2012 est.)
Population growth rate: 1.247% (2012 est.)
Ethnic groups: Persian 61%, Azeri 16%, Kurd 10%, Lur 6%, Baloch 2%, Arab 2%, Turkmen and Turkic tribes 2%, other 1%
Religions: Muslim (official) 98% (Shia 89%, Sunni 9%), other (includes Zoroastrian, Jewish, Christian, and Baha'i) 2%
Languages: Persian (official) 53%, Azeri Turkic and Turkic dialects 18%, Kurdish 10%, Gilaki and Mazandarani 7%, Luri 6%, Balochi 2%, Arabic 2%, other 2%
Literacy: definition: age 15 and over can read and write; total population: 77%; male: 83.5%; female: 70.4% (2002 est.)
Health: life expectancy at birth: total population: 70.35 years; male: 68.84 years; female: 71.93 years (2012 est.); Infant mortality rate: total: 41.11 deaths/1,000 live births; male: 41.61 deaths/1,000 live births; female: 40.58 deaths/1,000 live births (2012 est.)
Unemployment rate: 15.5% (2012 est.)
Work force: 27.05 million (2012 est.)

Government

Type: theocratic republic
Independence: 1 April 1979
Constitution: 2-3 December 1979; revised 1989
Political subdivisions: 31 provinces (ostanha, singular—ostan)
Suffrage: 18 years of age; universal

Economy

GDP (purchasing power parity): $997.4 billion (2012 est.); $1.003 trillion (2011 est.); $983.5 billion (2010 est.); $928.7 billion (2009 est.)
GDP real growth rate: -0.9% (2012 est.); 2% (2011 est.); 5.9% (2010 est.); 4% (2009 est.)
GDP per capita (PPP): $13,100 (2012 est.); $13,200 (2011 est.); $13,200 (2010 est.); $12,600 (2009 est.)
Natural resources: petroleum, natural gas, coal, chromium, copper, iron ore, lead, manganese, zinc, sulfur
Agriculture products: wheat, rice, other grains, sugar beets, sugarcane, fruits, nuts, cotton; dairy products, wool; caviar
Industries: petroleum, petrochemicals, fertilizers, caustic soda, textiles, cement and other construction materials, food processing (particularly sugar refining and vegetable oil production), ferrous and non-ferrous metal fabrication, armaments
Exports: $66.37 billion (2012 est.); $131.8 billion (2011 est.); $108.6 billion (2010 est.)
Exports—commodities: petroleum 80%, chemical and petrochemical products, fruits and nuts, carpets
Exports—partners: China 21%, India 9.3%, Japan 8.9%, Turkey 8.7%, South Korea 7.9%, Italy 5.2% (2011)
Imports: $66.97 billion (2012 est.); $76.1 billion (2011 est.); $68.45 billion (2010 est.)
Imports—commodities: industrial supplies, capital goods, foodstuffs and other consumer goods, technical services
Imports—partners: UAE 30.6%, China 17.2%, South Korea 8.4%, Germany 4.8%, Turkey 4.2% (2011)

Debt—external: $9.452 billion (31 December 2012 est.); $17.9 billion (31 December 2011 est.); $22.1 billion (31 December 2010 est.)

Exchange rates: Iranian rials (IRR) per US dollar; 12,260 (2012 est.); 10,616.3 (2011 est.); 10,254.18 (2010 est.); 9,864.3 (2009); 9,142.8 (2008); 9,407.5 (2007)

PEOPLE

Iran is a pluralistic society. Persians are the largest ethnic group in Iran, though many are actually of mixed ancestry. The population of the country has important Turkic elements (e.g., Azeris) and Arabs predominate in the southwest. In addition, Iran's population includes Kurds, Balochi, Bakhtyari, Lurs, and other smaller minorities, such as Armenians, Assyrians, Jews, and Brahuis (or Brohi).

The 1979 Islamic Revolution and the 1980–88 Iran-Iraq war transformed Iran's class structure politically, socially, and economically. During this period, Shi'a clerics took a more dominant position in politics and nearly all aspects of Iranian life, both urban and rural. After the fall of the Pahlavi dynasty in 1979, much of the urban upper class of prominent merchants, industrialists, and professionals, favored by the former monarch, Shah Mohammad Reza Pahlavi, lost standing and influence to the senior clergy and their supporters. However, Bazaar merchants, who were allied with the clergy against the Shah, gained significant political and economic power after the revolution. The urban working class has enjoyed a somewhat enhanced status and economic mobility, spurred in part by opportunities provided by revolutionary organizations and the government bureaucracy. Though the number of clergy holding senior positions in the Majles and elsewhere in government has declined since the 1979 revolution, Iran has nevertheless witnessed the rise of a post-revolutionary elite among clerics who are strongly committed to the preservation of the Islamic Republic. In addition, service in the Islamic Revolutionary Guard Corps (IRGC) provides veterans with employment opportunities as the IRGC controls larger parts of the economy and government bureaucracy.

National/Racial/Ethnic Minorities

There are between five and 11 million ethnic Kurds in the country, who have frequently campaigned for greater regional autonomy. There were two terrorist organizations inside the Kurdish province; however, they did not represent the majority of the Kurdish population. Nevertheless, the government persecuted the entire minority for criminal acts sponsored by the two organizations.

According to a 2009 HRW report, the government used security laws, media laws, and other legislation to arrest and persecute Kurds solely for exercising their right to freedom of expression and association. The government reportedly banned Kurdish-language newspapers, journals, and books and punished publishers, journalists, and writers for opposing and criticizing government policies. Although the Kurdish language is not banned, schools did not teach it.

Authorities suppressed legitimate activities of Kurdish NGOs by denying them registration permits or bringing spurious charges of security offenses against individuals working with such organizations. Kurds were not allowed to register certain names for their children in official registries.

Religion

The population is 98 percent Muslim--89 percent Shia and 9 percent Sunni (mostly Turkmen and Arabs, Baluchs, and Kurds living in the southwest, southeast, and northwest, respectively). There were no official statistics available on the size of the Sufi Muslim population; however, some reports estimated that between two and five million persons practice Sufism.

Unofficial estimates from religious organizations claimed that Baha'is, Jews, Christians, Sabean-Mandaeans, and Zoroastrians constitute 2 percent of the population. The largest non-Muslim minority is the Baha'is, who number 300,000 to 350,000. Unofficial estimates of the Jewish community's size varied from 20,000 to 30,000.

According to UN figures, 300,000 Christians live in the country, and the majority of them are ethnic Armenians. Unofficial estimates for the Assyrian Christian population ranged between 10,000 and 20,000. There are also Protestant denominations, including evangelical groups. Christian groups outside the country estimate the size of the Protestant Christian community to be less than 10,000, although many Protestant Christians reportedly practice in secret. Sabean-Mandaeans number 5,000 to 10,000 persons. The government estimated there are 30,000 to 35,000 Zoroastrians, who are primarily ethnic Persians; however, Zoroastrian groups claim to have 60,000 adherents.

HISTORY

The ancient nation of Iran, historically known as Persia, has traditionally been a major power in the region. Despite invasions by Arabs, Seljuk Turks, and Mongols, Iran has always reasserted its national identity and taken pride in its unique cultural and political heritage.

Archeological findings indicate that human activity in Iran dates back to the middle Paleolithic era, about 100,000 years ago. The sixth millennium B.C. saw the emergence of a fairly sophisticated agricultural society and the rise of proto-urban population centers. Many dynasties have ruled Iran, beginning with the Achaemenid (559-330 B.C.), which was founded by Cyrus the Great. After the conquest of Persia by Alexander the Great ushered in the Hellenistic period (300-250 B.C.), ancient Iran was ruled by the Parthian (250 B.C.-226 A.D.) and the Sassanian (226-651) dynasties.

The seventh-century Arab conquest of Iran, which introduced Islam to the population, was followed by invasions by the Seljuk Turks and the Mongols. Iran experienced a political and cultural revival under the Safavid dynasty (1502–1736), during which Shah Abbas expelled the Uzbeks and Ottomans from Persia. The conqueror Nadir Shah and his Afsharid dynasty (1736–1749) were succeeded by the Zand dynasty (1750–1794), which was founded by Karim Khan, and later the Qajar (1795–1925) and the Pahlavi (1925–1979) dynasties.

Many date the beginning of modern Iranian history to the nationalist uprisings against the Shah in 1905 and the establishment of a limited constitutional monarchy in 1906. The discovery of oil in 1908 would later become a key factor in Iranian history and development.

In 1921, Reza Khan, an Iranian officer of the Persian Cossack Brigade, seized control of the government. In 1925, after finally ousting the Qajar dynasty, he declared himself Shah and established the Pahlavi dynasty.

Reza Shah forcibly enacted policies of modernization and secularization in Iran and reasserted government authority over the country's tribes and provinces. In 1935, Reza Shah Pahlavi changed the country's name to Iran to accentuate Persia's Aryan roots. During World War Two, the Allies feared that the Shah's close relations with Nazi Germany would jeopardize Iran as a source of oil and a vital supply link to the Soviet Union. In September 1941, following the occupation of western Iran by the Soviet Union and the United Kingdom, Reza Shah was forced to abdicate. His son, Mohammad Reza Pahlavi, ascended to the throne.

After the war, Soviet troops stationed in northwestern Iran refused to withdraw across the border and, instead, supported short-lived, pro-Soviet separatist regimes in the northern provinces of Azerbaijan and Kurdistan. In 1946, under U.S. and United Nations pressure, the Soviets were forced to withdraw their troops. The Shah's forces then moved in to suppress the Azerbaijani and Kurdish revolts. In 1951, the government of nationalist Prime Minister Mohammed Mossadegh (alternatively spelled Mossadeq) nationalized the British-owned Anglo-Iranian Oil Company. In the face of strong public support for Mossadegh, the Shah fled to Rome. Although Mossadegh was not a communist, the U.S. and U.K. feared that his links to the communist Tudeh party would cause Iran to align with the Eastern Bloc. Consequently, in August 1953, the U.S. and U.K. supported a coup against the democratically elected Mossadegh, during which pro-Shah army forces arrested the Prime Minister. The Shah returned to Iran soon thereafter and, fearing further opposition, began to govern Iran in an increasingly authoritarian manner.

In 1961, Iran administered a series of economic, social, and administrative reforms—pushed by the Kennedy administration—that became known as the White Revolution. As a result of this program, which was driven by reform, modernization and economic growth proceeded at an unprecedented rate. This tremendous growth was fueled by Iran's vast petroleum reserves, which were then the third-largest in the world. However, while Iran's economy prospered, democratic reform and civil liberties deteriorated. The Shah's autocratic method of rule and the abusive practices of SAVAK (his internal security and intelligence service) alienated large sectors of the population, including the Shi'a clergy. The clergy also objected to land reforms that led to the breaking up of their large land holdings. In 1978, domestic turmoil turned to revolution driven by several disparate groups—nationalists, Islamists, Marxists, and students—who joined together in opposition to the Shah. In January 1979, the Shah fled Iran for Egypt, later traveling to the U.S. to seek medical treatment for cancer; he died in exile in Egypt 1 year later.

On February 1, 1979, exiled religious leader Ayatollah Ruhollah Khomeini returned from France to assume control of the revolution and establish himself as Supreme Leader of a new, theocratic republic guided by Islamic principles. As Supreme Leader, Khomeini steered Iran's foreign policy sharply away from its close alignment with the West. In September 1980, during the U.S. hostage crisis, Iraq invaded Iran to prevent the spread of the Islamic Revolution to Iraq's Shi'a, seize the heavily Arab province of Khuzestan. After 8 punishing years of war, in July 1988 the Islamic Republic of Iran at last agreed to the cease-fire implemented in UN Security Council Resolution 598. Neither nation made any significant territorial gains in the war, although both suffered massive casualties.

Iran's relations with many of its Arab neighbors were strained during the early years of the Islamic Republic because of fears that the Islamic Revolution would spread abroad.

Following Khomeini's death on June 3, 1989, the Assembly of Experts chose the outgoing president of the republic, Ali Khamenei, to succeed him as Supreme Leader, despite Khamenei's relative lack of religious credentials.

In August 1989, Akbar Hashemi-Rafsanjani, Speaker of the Majles, was elected President by an overwhelming majority. He was re-elected June 1993, albeit with a more modest majority. Some Western observers attributed the reduced support for Rafsanjani in 1993 to popular disenchantment with Iran's deteriorating economy. In August 1997, an overwhelming majority of Iranians elected reformist cleric Mohammad Khatami as President, hoping he would usher in a new era of freedom and reform. Khatami had modest successes in broadening the participation of Iranians in government by holding popular elections for local government councils and encouraging the development of civil society. Although many liberal-minded Iranians were disappointed that Khatami did not support student protesters in 1999, he retained enough popular support to secure re-election in June 2001.

In February 2004, elections were held for the Seventh Majles, in which many reformists were prohibited from running, resulting in a more conservative group of parliamentarians in control of the Majles. In March 2008, the Iranian Government again interfered in parliamentary elections. Although reformist candidates managed to hold onto their positions, the Eighth Majles remained under the control of conservative blocs.None of the seven presidential candidates on the ballot for the June 17, 2005 elections received a majority, resulting in a two-candidate runoff on June 24 between Tehran mayor (and IRGC veteran) Mahmoud Ahmadi-Nejad and former president Akbar Hashemi Rafsanjani. Some Iranian politicians alleged voter fraud and electoral interference by the IRGC-controlled Basij militia forces during the first round of voting. Ahmadi-Nejad, who won in the second round with nearly 62% of the vote according to Iranian Government figures, assumed office in August 2005. Ahmadi-Nejad was re-elected as Iran's president in June 2009, in a multiparty election that many Iranians considered neither free nor fair. Due to a lack of independent international election monitors, international organizations could not verify the results. Although the final vote tallies remain disputed, the Iranian Government's official results allocated 62.6% of the vote to Ahmadi-Nejad, with his closest challenger, Mir Hossein Mousavi, receiving 33.8%.

GOVERNMENT AND POLITICAL CONDITIONS

The Islamic Republic of Iran is a constitutional, theocratic republic in which Shia Muslim clergy and political leaders vetted by the clergy dominate the key power structures. Government legitimacy is based on the twin pillars of popular sovereignty—albeit restricted—and the rule of the supreme leader of the Islamic Revolution. The current supreme leader, Ayatollah Ali Khamenei, was chosen by a directly elected body of religious leaders, the Assembly of Experts, in 1989. Khamenei's writ dominates the legislative, executive, and judicial branches of government. He directly controls the armed forces and indirectly controls internal security forces, the judiciary, and other key institutions. The legislative branch is the popularly elected 290-seat Islamic Consultative Assembly, or Majlis. The unelected 12-member Guardian Council reviews all legislation the Majlis passes to ensure adherence to Islamic and constitutional principles; it also screens presidential and Majlis candidates for eligibility. Mahmoud Ahmadinejad was reelected president in June 2009 in a multiparty election that was generally considered neither free nor fair. There were numerous instances in which elements of the security forces acted independently of civilian control.

Demonstrations by opposition groups, university students, and others increased during the first few months of 2011, inspired in part by events of the Arab Spring. In February hundreds of protesters throughout the country staged rallies to show solidarity with protesters in Tunisia and Egypt. The government responded harshly to protesters and critics, arresting, torturing, and prosecuting them for their dissent. As part of its crackdown, the government increased its oppression of media and the arts, arresting and imprisoning dozens of journalists, bloggers, poets, actors, filmmakers, and artists throughout the year. The government's suppression and intimidation of voices of opposition continued at a rapid pace at year's end.

Recent Elections

In 2009 the country held a presidential election, which outside observers regarded as neither free nor fair. International observers were not allowed entry to monitor the election results. The Guardian Council approved only four of more than 450 prospective candidates, including 42 women and former officials. No women were approved to run as candidates. Authorities increased censorship and surveillance during the campaign, blocking cellular telephone signals and access to social networking and opposition Web sites. The government also harassed and arbitrarily arrested political activists, members of the country's religious and ethnic minority communities, students, trade unionists, and women's rights activists during the preelection period (see section 1.e., Political Prisoners and Detainees). Anecdotal evidence suggested that authorities forced some election observers representing opposition candidates to leave polling stations and that millions of unused paper ballots disappeared.

Before all polls closed and ballot counting had commenced, government-controlled media announced that President Ahmadinejad had been reelected in the first round of elections, obtaining a majority of the votes. Contrary to the election law, Khamenei approved the election results before the Guardian Council certified the election and before the Interior Ministry announced the final results. Independent analysts studied election data and concluded there were a number of irregularities, including at least two provinces showing a turnout of more than 100 percent in some districts and the absence of longstanding regional variations in turnout, which appeared abnormal despite regulations that allow voters to use any polling station. On November 20, 2011, Ali Saeedi, the supreme leader's representative to the IRGC, reportedly stated that those who challenged the 2009 election results were "worthy of death" and that the IRGC and the Basij should not have "any hesitations" about crushing them.

Majlis elections were scheduled for March 2012. In preparation for the elections, the government increased actions and rhetoric against the opposition. In a January 5 press statement, the chief of the Guardian Council, Ayatollah Ahmad Jannati, stated that it was better for the opposition to "stay out of the political arena." He further stated on February 11 in a public address on the anniversary of the 1979 Islamic Revolution that the council "will not allow any unsavory individuals to obtain the smallest position in the country, regardless of their popularity."

Political Parties: The constitution allows for the formation of political parties; however, the Interior Ministry granted licenses only to parties with ideological and practical adherence to the system of government embodied in the constitution. There were more than 230 registered political organizations that generally operated without restriction or outside interference, but most were small entities, often focused around an individual, and did not have nationwide membership. Members of political parties and individuals with any political affiliation that the government deemed unacceptable faced harassment, violence, and sometimes imprisonment. Reformist university students and professors faced dismissal (see section 2.a., Academic Freedom and Cultural Events).

The government banned several opposition organizations and political parties during 2011. For example, in March authorities banned the Assembly of Lecturers and Scholars of Qom Seminary, a clerical organization formed by supporters of former reformist president Mohammad Khatami. Also, on November 4, the election office banned three reformist political parties from participating in the March 2012 legislative elections. The Islamic Participation Front, Islamic Revolution Mujaheddin Organization, and Freedom Movement of Iran allegedly did not have the licenses required to run for the Majlis. The Islamic Participation Front and the Islamic Revolution Mujaheddin Organization were banned in September 2010 after they protested the controversial results from the 2009 presidential elections.

Security officials continued a campaign of harassment, intimidation, and arrests against members of the political opposition (see also section 1.e., Political Prisoners and Detainees). Many analysts indicated such tactics were carried out in an effort to further stifle dissent in advance of the anticipated March 2012 Majlis elections.

Former presidential candidates Mehdi Karroubi and Mir Hossein Mousavi were being held under de facto house arrest since 2009.

Participation of Women and Minorities: According to the Guardian Council's interpretation, the constitution barred women and persons of non-Iranian origin or religions other than Shia Islam from becoming president or from running in parliament. Women were also barred from serving as supreme leader; as members of the Assembly of Experts, Guardian Council, or Expediency Council (a body responsible for mediating between the Majlis and the Guardian Council and serving as a consultative council for the supreme leader); and as certain types of judges (see section 6, Women). On November 20, ISNA reported that Minou Kianirad was appointed the first female deputy governor of the central bank since the 1979 revolution. Four women served in the cabinet: the vice presidents for legal affairs and science and technology, the minister of health, and the head of the National Youth Organization. Eight women, in a total of 290 seats, served in the Majlis during 2011. Five Majlis seats were reserved for recognized religious minorities. Other ethnic minorities in the Majlis included Arabs and Kurds. There were no non-Muslims in the cabinet or on the Supreme Court.

Principal Government Officials

Last Updated: 1/31/2013

Supreme Leader: **Ali Hoseini-KHAMENEI, Ayatollah**
Pres.: **Mahmud AHMADI-NEJAD**
Speaker of the Islamic Consultative Assembly (Majles): **Ali Ardeshir-LARIJANI**
Sec. of the Cabinet: **Ali SADUQI**
Chief of Staff, Presidential Office, & Adviser to the Pres.: **Esfandiar Rahim MASHAIE**
First Vice Pres.: **Mohammad Reza RAHIMI**
Vice Pres. for Atomic Energy: **Fereidun ABBASI-Davani**
Vice Pres. for Cultural Heritage & Tourism: **Hasan MUSAVI**
Vice Pres. for Environmental Protection: **Mohammad Javad MOHAMMADIZADEH**
Vice Pres. for Executive Affairs: **Hamid BAQAI**
Vice Pres. for Implementation of the Constitution: **Mohammad Reza MIR-TAJODINI**
Vice Pres. for Intl. Affairs: **Ali SAIDLU**
Vice Pres. for Legal & Parliamentary Affairs: **Lotfollah FARUZANDEH-Dehkardi**
Vice Pres. for Management, Development, & Human Resources: **Ebrahim AZIZI**
Vice Pres. for Martyrs & War Veterans Affairs: **Masud ZARIBAFAN**
Vice Pres. for Planning & Strategic Supervision: **Behruz MORADI**
Vice Pres. for Scientific & Technological Affairs: **Nasrin SOLTANKHAH**
Min. of Agricultural Jihad: **Sadeq KHALILIAN**
Min. of Communication & Information Technology: **Reza TAQI-PUR**
Min. of Defense & Armed Forces Logistics: **Ahmad VAHIDI**
Min. of Economic Affairs & Finance: **Shams-ed-Din HOSEINI**
Min. of Education: **Hamed Reza HAJI-BABAI**
Min. of Energy: **Majid NAMJU**
Min. of Foreign Affairs: **Ali Akbar SALEHI**
Min. of Health, Treatment, & Medical Education: **Marzieh VAHID-DASTJERDI**
Min. of Industry, Mining, & Trade: **Mehdi QAZANFARI**
Min. of Intelligence & Security: **Heidar MOSLEHI**
Min. of Interior: **Mostafa Mohammad NAJAR, Brig. Gen. (Ret.)**
Min. of Islamic Culture & Guidance: **Mohammad HOSEINI**
Min. of Justice: **Morteza BAKHTIARI**
Min. of Labor, Cooperatives, & Social Welfare: **Abdol Reza SHEIKH-OL-ESLAMI**
Min. of Petroleum: **Rostam QASEMI, Brig. Gen.**
Min. of Roads & Urban Development: **Ali NIKZAD**
Min. of Science, Research, & Technology: **Kamran DANESHJU**
Min. of Sports & Youth: **Mohammad ABBASI**
Govt. Spokesman
Governor, Central Bank of Iran: **Mahmud BAHMANI**
Head of Interest Section in the US: **Mostafa RAHMANI**
Permanent Representative to the UN, New York: **Mohammad KHAZAI-Torshizi**

ECONOMY

Iran's economy is marked by statist policies and an inefficient state sector, which create major distortions throughout the system, and reliance on oil, which provides the majority of government revenues. Price controls, subsidies, and other rigidities weigh down the economy, undermining the potential for private-sector-led growth. Private sector activity is typically limited to small-scale workshops, farming, and services. Significant informal market activity flourishes and corruption is widespread.

Tehran since the early 1990s has recognized the need to reduce these inefficiencies, and in December 2010 the legislature passed President Mahmud Ahmadi_Nejad's Targeted Subsidies Law (TSL) to reduce state subsidies on food and energy. This was the most extensive economic reform since the government implemented gasoline rationing in 2007. Over a five-year period the bill will phase out subsidies that previously cost Tehran $60-$100 billion annually and mostly benefited Iran's upper and middle classes. Cash payouts of $45 per person to more than 90% of Iranian households mitigated initial widespread resistance to the TSL program, though popular acceptance remains vulnerable to rising inflation.

A rise in world oil prices in 2011 increased Iran's oil export revenue by roughly $28 billion over 2010, easing some of the financial impact of international sanctions. However, expansionary fiscal and monetary policies, government mismanagement, the sanctions, and a depreciating currency are fueling inflation, and GDP growth remains stagnant. Iran also continues to suffer from double-digit unemployment and underemployment. Underemployment among Iran's educated youth has convinced many to seek jobs overseas, resulting in a significant "brain drain."

Labor Conditions

The law prohibits employment of minors younger than 15 and places restrictions on employment of minors younger than 18, such as prohibitions on hard labor or night work; however, the law permits children to work in agriculture, domestic service, and some small businesses from the age of 12. The government did not adequately monitor or enforce laws pertaining to child labor, and child labor was a serious problem.

In March the government increased the minimum wage to 303,048 toman (approximately $303) per month. According to a May report, the nationwide average income level below which a family with 3.7 members was considered to be living in poverty was 653,000 toman ($653) a month. In Tehran the poverty income level was 813,000 toman ($813) a month.

The law establishes a maximum six-day, 48-hour workweek with a weekly rest day (normally Friday), at least 12 days of paid annual leave, and several paid public holidays. Any hours worked above this entitles a worker to overtime. The law mandates a payment of 40 percent above the hourly wage to employees for any accrued overtime. Employees must consent to work the overtime; it is not compulsory under the law. However, the law does not fully cover workers in workplaces with fewer than 10 workers, nor does it apply at all to those in workplaces with fewer than five workers, to noncitizens, or to any workers in export processing zones. Afghan workers, especially those working illegally, were subject to abusive working conditions, including below minimum wage remuneration, nonpayment of wages, and compulsory overtime. Such informal employment was common in construction, agriculture, transportation, retail, and the textile industry.

According to the International Alliance in Support of Workers in Iran, approximately 80 percent of workers employed by public and private companies were on temporary contracts, including teachers. Workers on temporary contracts can be dismissed at any time without reason. Low wages and the lack of job security due to contracting practices continued to be major drivers of worker strikes and protests, notably in the oil and petrochemical industry.

U.S.-IRANIAN RELATIONS

The United States and Iran (then called Persia) established diplomatic relations in 1883. In the following years, Iran saw the 1906 establishment of a limited constitutional monarchy, a 1953 coup against its democratically elected prime minister that was supported by the United States and the United Kingdom, and a 1978 revolution against the country's hereditary ruler, the shah. The United States broke diplomatic relations with Iran in 1980 after the seizure of the U.S. Embassy and 52 Americans by Iranian students. The U.S. Government does not have diplomatic or consular relations with Iran.

The United States has long-standing concerns over Iran's nuclear program, sponsorship of terrorism, and human rights record. Numerous sanctions have been imposed on Iran by the United States and the international community to compel Iran to engage seriously in discussions with the international community and address concerns over its nuclear program. Iran still has not recognized Israel's right to exist and has hindered the Middle East peace process by arming militants, including Hamas, Hizballah, and Palestinian Islamic Jihad. Despite these obstacles, U.S. and Iranian representatives have discussed a number of issues of concern over the years, including Iran's nuclear program, Afghanistan, and Iraq.

U.S. Assistance to Iran

The United States provides no development assistance to Iran.

Bilateral Economic Relations

The U.S. Government, through executive orders issued by the President as well as congressional legislation, prohibits nearly all trade and investment with Iran. Sanctions have been imposed on Iran because of its sponsorship of terrorism, its refusal to comply with international obligations on its nuclear program, and its human rights violations.

Iran's Membership in International Organizations

Iran and the United States belong to a number of the same international organizations, including the United Nations, International Monetary Fund, and World Bank. Iran also is an observer to the World Trade Organization.

Bilateral Representation

The Embassy of Switzerland in Iran represents U.S. interests, and the Embassy of Pakistan in the United States represents Iranian interests.

TRAVEL

Consular Information Sheet

July 16, 2012

Country Description: Iran is a constitutional Islamic republic with a theocratic system of government where ultimate political authority is vested in the highest religious authority, the Supreme Leader, Ayatollah Ali Khamenei. He has final say on all domestic, foreign, and security policies for Iran, though he establishes and supervises those policies in consultation with other political bodies. Shia Islam is the official religion of Iran, and Islamic law is the basis of the authority of the state. The Iranian constitution guarantees freedom of worship to Jews, Christians, and Zoroastrians, though they and followers of other faiths are often the subject of discrimination and repression. The work week in Iran is Saturday through Thursday; however, many government offices and private companies are closed on Thursdays. Friday is the day of rest when all establishments are closed. Offices in Iran are generally open to the public during the morning hours only.

Smart Traveler Enrollment Program (STEP)/Embassy Locations: The U.S. government does not have diplomatic or consular relations with the Islamic Republic of Iran and therefore cannot provide protection or routine consular services to U.S. citizens in Iran. The Swiss government, acting through its Embassy in Tehran, serves as protecting power for U.S. interests in Iran. If you are going to live in or visit Iran, please take the time to tell the Swiss Embassy about your trip. If you enroll, we can keep you up to date with important safety and security announcements. It will also help your friends and family get in touch with you in an emergency.

Embassy of Switzerland—
U.S. Interests Section
No. 39, Shahid Mousavi (
Golestan 5th)
Pasdaran Avenue
Tehran, Iran
Telephone: (98) (21) 2254–2178 and (98) (21) 2256–5273
Facsimile: (98) (21) 2258–0432
Contact via e-mail:
tie.vertretung@eda.admin.ch

The workweek is Sunday through Thursday. Public service hours are 8:00 am—12:00 noon. The Interests Section does not issue U.S. visas or accept visa applications. The limited consular services provided to U.S. citizens in Tehran include: (a) Registering U.S. citizens; (b) Responding to inquiries concerning the welfare and whereabouts of U.S. citizens in Iran; (c) Rendering assistance in times of distress or physical danger; (d) Providing U.S. citizens with passport and Social Security card applications and other citizenship forms for processing at the U.S. Embassy in Bern, Switzerland; (e) Performing notarial services; and (f) Taking provisional custody of the personal effects of deceased U.S. citizens.

Entry/Exit Requirements for U.S. Citizens: Should you decide to travel to Iran despite the current Travel Warning, a passport, valid for six months beyond duration of stay, and visa are required, except for travel to Kish Island where a visa is not required. Travelers should not attempt to enter mainland Iran from Kish without a visa. To obtain a visa, contact the Iranian Interests Section of the Embassy of Pakistan located at 2209 Wisconsin Ave. NW, Washington, DC. 20007; tel. 202-965-4990, 91, 92, 93, 94, 99; fax 202-965-1073, 202-965-4990 (Automated Fax-On-Demand after office hours); email: requests@daftar.org.

U.S. citizens traveling to Iran are fingerprinted upon entry. The Iranian press has reported that foreign tourists may obtain seven-day tourist visas at the airport in Tehran. However, U.S. citizens are not eligible to receive these visas and must obtain valid visas from the Iranian Interests Section in Washington. Note: possession of a valid Iranian visa will not guarantee entry into the country. Some U.S. citizen travelers with valid visas have been refused entry at the border without explanation. U.S. citizens do not have to obtain a visa for travel from Dubai, United Arab Emirates, to Kish Island.

U.S. passports are valid for travel to Iran. However, the Iranian government does not recognize dual nationality and will treat U.S.—Iranian dual nationals solely as Iranian citizens subject to Iranian laws. Thus, U.S. citizens who were born in Iran, who became naturalized citizens of Iran (e.g., through marriage to an Iranian citizen), and children of such persons—even those without Iranian passports who do not consider themselves Iranian—are considered Iranian nationals by Iranian authorities. Therefore, despite the fact that these individuals hold U.S. citizenship, under Iranian law, they must enter and exit Iran on an Iranian passport, unless the Iranian government has recognized a formal renunciation or loss of Iranian citizenship. Dual nationals may be subject to harsher legal treatment than visitors with only U.S. citizenship. (See section on Special Circumstances below.)

Iranian authorities have prevented a number of U.S. citizen academics, scientists, journalists, and others who traveled to Iran for personal/cultural/business reasons from leaving the country and in some cases have detained, interrogated, and imprisoned them on unknown or various charges, including espionage and being a threat to the regime. U.S. citizens of Iranian origin should consider the risk of being targeted by authorities before planning travel to Iran. Iranian authorities may deny dual nationals access to the U.S. Interests Section of the Embassy of Switzerland in Tehran, because they are considered to be solely Iranian citizens.

As a precaution, it is advisable for U.S.—Iranian dual nationals to obtain, in their Iranian passports, the necessary visas for the countries they will transit upon their return to the United States so that if their U.S. passports are confiscated in Iran, they may depart Iran with their Iranian passport. These individuals can then apply for a new U.S. passport in the country they are transiting.

No visa is required for Iranian nationals traveling to Turkey, Malaysia, Sri Lanka, Maldives, Indonesia and Armenia.

Dual nationals whose U.S. passports are confiscated may also obtain a "Confirmation of Nationality" from the U.S. Interests Section of the Embassy of Switzerland, the U.S. protecting power. This statement, addressed to the relevant foreign embassies in Tehran, enables the travelers to apply for third-country visas in Tehran, provided they meet Schengen States' criteria for a visa. Dual nationals finding themselves in this situation should note in advance that the Swiss Embassy would issue this statement only after the traveler's U.S. nationality is confirmed and after some processing delay. A "Confirmation of Nationality" would be considered in lieu of the standard invitation letter that all Schengen visa applicants are required to present; however, it does not guarantee issuance of an entry visa. Dual nationals must enter and depart the United States on U.S. passports.

Visa extensions are time-consuming and must be filed at least one week in advance of the expiration date. A foreign national and anyone accompanying him/her will pay a fine of 300,000 rials or 30,000 tomans per day for each day of unauthorized stay in Iran.

U.S. citizens, whose stay surpasses six months and whose domicile is outside Iran, need to obtain an exit permit to leave the country. U.S. citizens residing in Iran on permanent resident visas must obtain an exit permit each and every time they depart Iran, regardless of the period of stay. Although an exit stamp is no longer inserted into the passport, the exit tax must still be paid. U.S.—Iranian dual nationals are no longer required to pay an exit tax regardless of the duration of their stay in Iran. More specific information on Iranian passport and exit visa requirements may be obtained from the Iranian Interests Section of the Embassy of Pakistan in Washington, D.C.

Non-Iranian-national women who marry Iranian citizens gain Iranian nationality upon marriage. If the marriage takes place in Iran, the woman's U.S. passport will be confiscated by Iranian authorities. A woman must have the consent of her husband to leave Iran or, in his absence, must gain the permission of the local prosecutor. Iranian law, combined with the lack of diplomatic relations between the United States and Iran, means that the U.S. Interests Section in Tehran can provide only very limited assistance if a U.S. citizen woman married to an Iranian man has marital difficulties and/or encounters difficulty in leaving Iran.

After divorce or death of the husband, a foreign-born woman has the choice to renounce her Iranian citizenship, but any of the couple's children will automatically be Iranian citizens and their citizenship is irrevocable. They will be required to enter and depart Iran on Iranian passports. For a divorce to be recognized it should be carried out in Iran or, if outside Iran, in accordance with Sharia law. Upon divorce, custody of the children normally goes to the mother until children reach age 7, at which point custody automatically transfers to the father. However, if the courts determine that the father is unsuitable to raise the children, they may grant custody to the paternal grandfather or to the mother, if the mother has not renounced her Iranian citizenship and is normally resident in Iran. If the courts grant custody to the mother, she will need permission from the paternal grandfather or the courts to obtain exit visas for children under age 18 to leave the country. The term "custody" in the United States does not have the same legal meaning in Iran. In Iran a woman is granted "guardianship," and only in very rare cases is actually granted "custody." Even if the woman has "custody/guardianship," all legal decisions, e.g., application for a passport, permission to exit Iran, etc., would still require the consent of the father. Iran is not a signatory to the Hague Convention on the Civil Aspects of International Child Abduction. The U.S. Department of State is unaware of any HIV/AIDS entry restrictions for visitors to or foreign residents of Iran.

Threats to Safety and Security: U.S. citizens who travel to Iran despite the Travel Warning should exercise caution throughout the country, but especially in the southeastern region where Westerners have been victims of criminal gangs often involved in the smuggling of drugs and other contraband. U.S. citizens should avoid travel to areas within 100 kilometers of the border with Afghanistan, within 10 kilometers of the border with Iraq, and generally anywhere east of the line from Bam and Bandar Abbas toward the Pakistan border.

Terrorist explosions have killed a number of people since 2005. Be aware that the Iranian government has blamed the U.S. and/or UK governments for involvement in the February 2007 bombing that killed Iranian military forces in Zahedan in the southeast, the 2005/2006 bombings in Ahvaz/Khuzestan in the southwest, and the May 2009 bombing of a mosque in the south-east Iranian city of Zahedan.

U.S. citizens are advised to avoid demonstrations and large public gatherings. Increased tension between Iran and the West over the past several years is a cause of concern for U.S. citizen travelers. Large-scale demonstrations in response to politically motivated events, such as the 2009 presidential election, have taken place sporadically throughout the country, resulting in a significant security presence, arrests, and occasional clashes between demonstrators and security officials. U.S. citizens should stay current with media coverage of local events and be aware of their surroundings at all times. U.S. passport holders who are arrested or detained by Iranian authorities should request assistance from the U.S. Interests Section at the Swiss Embassy in Tehran.

Iranian security personnel may at times place foreign visitors under surveillance. Hotel rooms, telephones, and fax machines may be monitored, and personal possessions in hotel rooms may be searched. Photography near military and other government installations is strictly prohibited and could result in serious criminal charges, including espionage, which carries the death penalty.

The United States Maritime Administration (MARAD) has advised that elevated regional tensions have increased the risk of maritime attacks being conducted by extremist to vessels operating in the Gulf of

Oman, North Arabian Sea, Gulf of Aden, and the Bab el Mandeb regions.

MARAD recommends vessels at anchor, operating in restricted maneuvering environments, or at slow speeds should be especially vigilant, and report suspicious activity. U.S. flag vessels that observe suspicious activity in the area are advised to report such suspicious activity or any hostile or potentially hostile action to COMUSNAVCENT battlewatch captain at phone number 011-973-1785–3879. All suspicious activities and events are also to be reported to the U.S. Coast Guard National Response Center at the following toll free telephone: 1-800-424-8802, direct telephone 202-267-2675, or TDD 202-267-4477. The complete advisory is available on the MARAD website at www.MARAD.DOT.gov.

Stay up to date by:

- Bookmarking our Bureau of Consular Affairs website, which contains the current Travel Warnings and Travel Alerts as well as the Worldwide Caution.
- Following us on Twitter and the Bureau of Consular Affairs page on Facebook as well.
- Downloading our free Smart Traveler iPhone App to have travel information at your fingertips.
- Calling 1-888-407-4747 toll-free within the U.S. and Canada, or a regular toll line, 1-202-501-4444, from other countries.
- Taking some time before travel to consider your personal security.

Crime: Major crime is generally not a problem for travelers in Iran, although foreigners occasionally become victims of petty street crime. Young men in unmarked cars have robbed foreigners and young men on motor bikes have snatched bags. There have been reports of robberies by police impersonators, usually in civilian clothing. Insist on seeing the officer's identity card and request the presence of a uniformed officer/marked patrol car. Travelers should not surrender any documents or cash. You are advised to make a copy of your U.S. passport (biographical data page and the page with your Iranian visa) and to keep it separate from your original passport.

Travelers should not carry large amounts of hard currency while on the streets. In view of the possibility of theft, passports, disembarkation cards, other important documents and valuables should be kept in hotel safes or other secure locations. Pre-booked taxis are safer than those hailed from the street. U.S. citizens should check with their hotel or tour guide for information on local scams.

Don't buy counterfeit and pirated goods, even if they are widely available. Not only are the bootlegs illegal in the United States, if you purchase them you may also be breaking local law.

Victims of Crime: If you or someone you know becomes the victim of a crime abroad, you should contact the local police and the nearest U.S. embassy or consulate (see the Department of State's list of embassies and consulates). We can:

- Provide an application to replace a stolen passport, for processing at the U.S. Embassy in Bern, Switzerland.
- Help you find appropriate medical care if you are the victim of violent crimes such as assault or rape.
- Put you in contact with the appropriate police authorities, and if you want us to, we can contact family members or friend.
- Help you understand the local criminal justice process and direct you to local attorneys, although it is important to remember that local authorities are responsible for investigating and prosecuting the crime.

The local equivalent to the "911" emergency line in Iran is: 115 for ambulance service, 125 for fire and 110 for police. English speakers, however, are generally unavailable.

Criminal Penalties: While you are traveling in Iran, you are subject to its laws even if you are a U.S. citizen. Foreign laws and legal systems can be vastly different from our own. In some places you may be taken in for questioning if you don't have your passport with you. In some places, it is illegal to take pictures of certain buildings. In some places driving under the influence could land you immediately in jail. These criminal penalties will vary from country to country. There are also some things that might be legal in the country you visit, but still illegal in the United States, and you can be prosecuted under U.S. law if you buy pirated goods. Engaging in sexual conduct with children or using or disseminating child pornography in a foreign country is a crime prosecutable in the United States. If you break local laws in Iran your U.S. passport won't help you avoid arrest or prosecution. It's very important to know what's legal and what's not where you are going.

Persons violating Iranian laws, even unknowingly, may be expelled, arrested, or imprisoned. Fines, public floggings, and long prison terms are common. Former Muslims who have converted to other religions, as well as persons who encourage Muslims to convert, are subject to arrest and possible execution. Drinking, possession of alcoholic beverages and drugs, un-Islamic dress, as well as public displays of affection with a member of the opposite sex are considered to be crimes. Relations between non-Muslim men and Muslim women are illegal. Adultery, sex outside marriage, and homosexual sex are all illegal under Iranian law and carry the death penalty. DVDs depicting sexual relations and magazines showing unveiled women are forbidden. Penalties for possession, use, or trafficking in illegal drugs in Iran are severe and convicted offenders can expect long jail sentences and heavy fines. Iran executes many people each year on drug-related charges.

Engaging in sexual conduct with children or using or disseminating child pornography in a foreign country is a crime, prosecutable in the United States. U.S. citizens in Iran who violate Iranian laws, including laws unfamiliar to Westerners (such as those regarding the proper wearing of apparel), may face severe penalties.

The Iranian government reportedly has the names of all individuals who filed claims against Iran at the Iran-U.S. Claims Tribunal at The Hague pursuant to the 1981 Algerian Accords. In addition, the Iranian government reportedly has compiled a list of the claimants who were awarded compensation in the Iran Claims Program administered by the Foreign Claims Settlement Commission. The Iranian government has allegedly been targeting award-holders who travel to Iran. It has been reported that upon some claimants' entry into Iran, Iranian authorities have questioned them as to the status of payment of their respective awards with a view to recouping the award money. The Iranian government has also reportedly threatened to prevent U.S. claimants who visit Iran from departing the country until they make arrangements to repay part of or their entire award.

Based on the Vienna Convention on Consular Relations, bilateral agreements with certain countries, and customary international law, if you are arrested in Iran, you have the option to request that the police, prison officials, or other authorities alert the U.S. Interests Section at the Swiss Embassy in Tehran of your arrest, and to have communications from you forwarded to the nearest U.S. embassy or consulate.

Special Circumstances: The Iranian government has seized the passports and blocked the departure of foreigners who work in Iran on tax/commercial disputes. In addition to being subject to all Iranian laws, U.S. citizens who also possess Iranian citizenship are also subject to other laws that impose special obligations on citizens of Iran, such as military service or taxes. Iranian-citizen males aged 18-34 are required to perform military service, unless exempt. This requirement includes Iranian-Americans, even those born in the United States. Young men who have turned 17 years of age will no longer be allowed to leave Iran without first having completed their military service.

Dual nationals sometimes have their U.S. passports confiscated and may be denied permission to leave Iran, or encounter other problems with Iranian authorities. Likewise, Iranian authorities may deny dual nationals' access to the U.S. Interests Section in Tehran, because they are considered to be solely Iranian citizens. Refer to the above section entitled "Entry/Exit Requirements" for additional information concerning dual nationality. U.S. citizens who are not dual U.S.-Iranian nationals are encouraged to carry a copy of their U.S. passport (biodata page and page with Iranian visa) with them at all times so that, if questioned by local officials, proof of U.S. citizenship is readily available. Carry some other form of identification with you at all times as well, such as a driver's license or other photo identification.

Credit cards and bank cards cannot be used in Iran. It is easy to exchange U.S. dollars for rials, either at banks or with certified money changers; however, you will not be able to access U.S. bank accounts using ATMs in Iran. While in Iran, avoid accessing a U.S. bank account via Internet, since the account will immediately be frozen or blocked by the bank due to U.S. government economic sanctions. Traveler's checks can be difficult to exchange. Bring enough hard currency to cover your stay, but make sure you declare this currency upon entry. There is no Western Union or similar institution and bank transfers may not be possible. Exchange money only at banks or an authorized currency exchange facility, not on the street, and keep your exchange receipts.

Pre-paid overseas calling cards are available at most newsagents. The Internet is widely used in Iran. There are Internet cafes in most hotels; usage may be monitored. The Iranian government blocks access to social media such as Facebook, Twitter and YouTube.

Do not work illegally. You will be deported, fined, and/or imprisoned. You may also be prevented from reentering the country.

Islamic law is strictly enforced in Iran. Alcohol is forbidden. Importation of pork products is banned. Consult a guide book on Iran to determine how to dress and behave properly and respectfully. Women should expect to wear a headscarf and a long jacket that covers the arms and upper legs while in public. There may be additional dress requirements at certain religious sites; e.g., women might need to put on a chador (which covers the whole body except the face) at some shrines. During the holy month of Ramadan, you should generally observe the Muslim tradition of not eating, drinking, or smoking in public from sunrise to sunset each day, though there are exemptions for foreign travelers who eat in hotel restaurants.

In general, it is best to ask before taking photographs of people. Hobbies like photography and those involving the use of binoculars (e.g., bird-watching) can be misunderstood and get you in trouble with security officials. (See Threats to Safety and Security section above for warnings on photography.)

For specific information regarding Iranian customs regulations, contact the Iranian Interests Section of the Embassy of Pakistan in Washington, D.C.

OFAC provides guidance to the public on the interpretation of the current economic sanctions on Iran. For further information, consult OFAC's Iran sanctions resource page or contact OFAC's Compliance Programs Division at 202-622-2490, visit OFAC's web site, or obtain information via fax at 202-622-0077.

Licensing Division
Office of Foreign Assets Control
U.S. Department of the Treasury
1500 Pennsylvania Avenue NW

Treasury Annex
Washington, DC 20220
Telephone (202) 622-2480
Fax (202) 622-1657

Iran is prone to earthquakes, many of them severe. An earthquake in the city of Bam in 2003, for example, claimed 30,000 lives. To learn more about the seismic regions of Iran including the most recent earthquakes please visit the U.S. Geological Survey website.

Accessibility: While in Iran, individuals with disabilities may find accessibility and accommodations very different from what you find in the United States. On October 23, 2009, the Islamic Republic of Iran declared its accession to the respective UN Convention on the Rights of Persons with Disabilities, however with regard to Article 46, the Islamic Republic of Iran declared it does not consider itself bound by any provisions of the Convention that may be incompatible with its applicable rules. There are no laws in Iran to mandate access to transportation, communication, and public buildings for persons with disabilities. In general, it is not recommended for individuals with disabilities to travel to Iran.

Medical Facilities and Health Information: Basic medical care and medicines are available in the principal cities, but may not be available in rural areas. Medical facilities do not meet U.S. standards and sometimes lack medicines and supplies. Iranian authorities confirmed outbreaks of avian influenza (bird flu) in January 2008 in northern Iran, as well as earlier reports of outbreaks among wild swans in the Anzali Wetlands and in domestic poultry in the northern provinces of Azerbaijan and Gilan. There were a number of confirmed cases of H1N1 influenza in 2009.

You can find good information on vaccinations and other health precautions on the Centers for Disease Control and Prevention (CDC) website. For information about outbreaks of infectious diseases abroad, consult the World Health Organization (WHO) website. The WHO website also contains additional health information for travelers, including detailed country-specific health information.

Medical Insurance: You can't assume your insurance will go with you when you travel. It's very important to find out BEFORE you leave. You need to ask your insurance company two questions:

- Does my policy apply when I'm out of the United States?
- Will it cover emergencies like a trip to a foreign hospital or an evacuation?

In many places, doctors and hospitals still expect payment in cash at the time of service. Your regular U.S. health insurance may not cover doctor and hospital visits in other countries. If your policy doesn't go with you when you travel, it's a very good idea to take out another one for your trip.

Traffic Safety and Road Conditions: While in Iran, you may encounter road conditions that differ significantly from those in the United States. Travelers in possession of International Driver's Permits may drive in Iran, though the U.S. Interests Section in Iran does not recommend that tourists drive in Iran. Iran has a very high rate of traffic accidents, the second highest cause of mortality in the country. Drivers throughout Iran tend to ignore traffic lights, traffic signs, and lane markers. Urban streets are not well lit. It is therefore particularly dangerous to drive at night. Sidewalks in urban areas only exist on main roads and are usually obstructed by parked cars. In residential areas, few sidewalks exist. Drivers almost never yield to pedestrians at crosswalks. If you are involved in an accident, no matter how minor, do not leave the scene: wait until the police arrive to file a report.

Iranian authorities sometimes set up informal roadblocks, both in cities and on highways, often manned by young, inexperienced officers who are often suspicious of foreigners. Ensure you carry a form of identification with you and avoid getting into disputes.

Very high pollution levels from cars, particularly in Tehran, can trigger respiratory problems.

Aviation Safety Oversight: As there is no direct commercial air service to the United States by carriers registered in Iran, the U.S. Federal Aviation Administration (FAA) has not assessed the government of Iran's Civil Aviation Authority for compliance with International Civil Aviation Organization (ICAO) aviation safety standards. Further information may be found on the FAA's safety assessment page.

Children's Issues: Please see the U.S. Dept. of State Office of Children's Issues web pages on intercountry adoption and international parental child abduction.

Travel Warning

December 7, 2012

The Department of State warns U.S. citizens to carefully consider the risks of travel to Iran. Dual national Iranian-American citizens may encounter difficulty in departing Iran. U.S. citizens should stay current with media coverage of local events and carefully consider nonessential travel. This replaces the Travel Warning for Iran issued April 27, 2012 to add additional contact information for the U.S. Interests Section in Tehran.

Some elements in Iran remain hostile to the United States. As a result, U.S. citizens may be subject to harassment or arrest while traveling or residing in Iran. Since 2009, Iranian authorities have prevented the departure, in some cases for several months, of a number of Iranian-American citizens, including journalists and academics, who traveled to Iran for personal or professional reasons. Iranian authorities also have unjustly detained or imprisoned U.S. citizens on various charges, including espionage and posing a threat to national security. U.S. citizens of Iranian origin should consider the risk of being targeted by authorities before planning travel to Iran. Iranian authorities deny the U.S. Interests Section in Tehran access to imprisoned dual national Iranian-American citizens because Iranian authorities consider them to be solely Iranian citizens; access to U.S. citizens is often denied as well.

The Iranian government continues to repress some minority religious and ethnic groups, including Baha'i, Arabs, Kurds, Azeris, and others. Consequently, some areas within the country where these minorities reside, including the Baluchistan border area near Pakistan and Afghanistan, the Kurdish northwest of the country, and areas near the Iraqi border, remain unsafe. Iranian authorities have detained and harassed U.S. citizens of Iranian origin. Former Muslims who have converted to other religions, as well as persons who encourage Muslims to convert, are subject to arrest and prosecution.

The U.S. government does not have diplomatic or consular relations with the Islamic Republic of Iran and therefore cannot provide protection or routine consular services to U.S. citizens in Iran. The Swiss government, acting through its Embassy in Tehran, serves as protecting power for U.S. interests in Iran. The range of consular services provided by the U.S. Interests Section at the Swiss Embassy is limited and may require significantly more processing time than at U.S. Embassies or Consulates. The Iranian government does not recognize dual citizenship and will not allow the Swiss to provide protective services for U.S. citizens who are also Iranian nationals.

Our ability to assist U.S. citizens in Iran in the event of an emergency is extremely limited. U.S. citizens in Iran should ensure that they have updated documentation at all times and make their own plans in the event of an emergency. For more information, see "What the Department of State Can and Can't Do in a Crisis" at the Department's website. U.S. citizens who travel or reside in Iran are strongly encouraged to enroll in the State Department's Smart Traveler Enrollment Program. U.S. citizens may also enroll in person at the U.S. Interests Section at the Swiss Embassy, located at No. 39, Shahid Mousavi (Golestan 5th), Pasdaran, Tehran. The telephone numbers for the U.S. Interests Section are (98)(21)2279–3912, (98)(21)2279–3697,(98)(21) 2254–2178, and (98)(21) 2256–5273, fax (98)(21) 2258–0432, email: tie.vertretung@eda.admin.ch, website: http://www.eda.admin.ch/tehran.

U.S. citizens should also review the Department of State's Country Specific Information for Iran and stay up to date by bookmarking the Bureau of Consular Affairs website, which contains the current Travel Warnings and Travel Alerts as well as the Worldwide Caution. You may follow us on Twitter and the Bureau of Consular Affairs page on Facebook as well; however, both Twitter and Facebook are filtered in Iran and will not be accessible without a virtual private network (VPN).

If you don't have internet access, current information on safety and security can also be obtained by calling 1-888-407-4747 toll-free in the United States and Canada or, for callers from other countries, a regular toll line at 1-202-501-4444. These numbers are available from 8:00 a.m. to 8:00 p.m. Eastern Time, Monday through Friday (except U.S. federal holidays).

Intercountry Adoption

January 2012

The information in this section has been edited from the latest report available as of February 2013 from the State Department Bureau of Consular Affairs, Office of Overseas Citizens Services. For more information, please read the *Intercountry Adoption* section of this book and review current reports online at http://adoption.state.gov.

Iran is not party to the Hague Convention on Protection of Children and Co-operation in Respect of Intercountry Adoption (Hague Adoption Convention). Therefore, when the Hague Adoption Convention entered into force for the United States on April 1, 2008, intercountry adoption processing for Iran did not change. In accordance with current Iranian practice, adoptions by parents residing outside of Iran are possible provided the adoptive parents are Iranian citizens and fulfill all other required conditions for adoption. Applications from close family members have the greatest chance of being approved.

Only the Iranian Welfare Organization and an appropriate court can decide each case on its own merits in the best interest of the child. Muslim children will be given exclusively to Muslim parents. Children of Christian faiths may be adopted by Christian parents.

Before an adoption can take place, strict rules are applied in order to protect the children and to establish the suitability of prospective adoptive parents. The process is complicated and time-consuming. After a child has been placed with a family, surveillance by Iranian authorities continues and periodic checks are made to ensure the child's physical and mental well-being.

Iranians living abroad can file adoption applications through relatives living in Iran. Applications must be submitted to the Iranian Welfare Organization.

Who Can Adopt? To bring an adopted child to United States from Iran, you must be found eligible to adopt by the U.S. Government. The U.S. Government agency responsible for making this determination is the Department of Homeland Security, U.S. Citizenship and Immigration Services (USCIS).

Residency Requirements: Parents who intend to adopt children in Iran must be physically present in the country for fingerprinting and medical examinations. One of the parents may leave the country if desired. After completing all requirements, the power of attorney may rest with the parent staying in the country to assume custody.

Age Requirements: One of the adoptive parents must be at least 29 years old

Marriage Requirements: The adoptive couple must be married for at least five years with no children

Income Requirements: The adoptive couple is expected to have sufficient financial capacity to support the child.

Other Requirements: The adoptive couple must be Muslims, with no criminal records, no addiction to drugs or alcohol and no contagious and/or terminal disease(s). Couple should be able to submit a medical report to prove that at least one of the spouses is incapable of conceiving.

Who Can Be Adopted? Iran has specific requirements that a child must meet in order to be eligible for adoption. You cannot adopt a child in Iran unless he or she meets the requirements outlined below.

Eligibility Requirements: Relinquishment Requirements: The child's father, paternal grandfather and mother must all be either unknown or dead.

Abandonment Requirements: The child must be one who has been placed under the care of a public institution with none of the above-mentioned relatives having shown up for 3 full years.

Age Requirements: The child must be under 12 full years of age.

Sibling Requirements: None

Requirements for Special Needs or Medical Conditions: None

Waiting Period: After consulting the institution or person in charge of the child's temporary care, and prior to issuance of guardianship approval, the court will place the child in the care of the applying couple for a six-month probation period. Disagreement of the said institution or person will not be binding to the court should it find such disagreement contrary to the child's interests. During the probation period the court may terminate the guardianship in consideration of the request of the Public Prosecutor, the National Society for the Protection of Children or the institution where the child was previously under care, or on the basis of its own conclusion reached through appropriate methods of investigation. Likewise the applying couple may declare their change of mind during the probation period, in which case the court will terminate the guardianship.

In addition to these requirements, a child must meet the definition of an orphan under U.S. law for you to bring him or her back to the United States. Learn more about these U.S. requirements.

Iran Adoption Authority: Iranian Welfare Organization (Edareh Beh Zistiti, Bakhshe Farzand Khandegi); Address: 188 Karimkhan St., Tehran.

The Process: The first step in adopting a child from Iran is to decide whether or not to use a licensed agency in the United States that can help with your adoption. Adoption service providers must be licensed by the U.S. state in which they operate. Learn more about choosing the right adoption service provider here.

There are no formal adoption agencies in Iran assisting individuals in the Iranian adoption process. Iranian NGOs such as "The Society for Protecting the Rights of the Child" may be helpful resources.

To bring an adopted child from Iran to the United States, you must apply to be found eligible to adopt (Form I-600A) by the U.S. Government, Department of Homeland Security, U.S. Citizenship and Immigration Services (USCIS).

At this stage the Iranian authorities assess the adoptive family's eligibility to adopt in Iran. This includes financial, medical and moral eligibility of the prospective adoptive family.

If you are eligible to adopt, and a child is available for intercountry adoption, the central adoption authority in Iran will provide you with a referral to a child. Each family must decide for itself whether or not it will be able to meet the needs of a particular child and provide a permanent family placement for the referred child.

The child must be eligible to be adopted according to the requirements, as described in the Who can be Adopted section. The child must also meet the definition of an orphan under U.S. law. Learn more about this critical decision.

Role of the Adoption Authority: The Iranian Welfare Organization is the decision making authority in the adoption cases. Parents intending to adopt a child should contact the Iranian Welfare Organization and inform them of their intent. The organization may be able to open a file for the family and assign a case number.

Role of the Court: A file at Judicial Center(s) should be created as a part of the adoption process by submitting the required formal documents with necessary translations.

Role of Adoption Agencies: Adoption agencies do not operate in Iran.

Adoption Application: After a formal application is filed, participation in court sessions is required. Prospective parents also will go through tests on their physical and mental conditions and will submit documents to the court regarding their criminal background. The court issues an introduction letter to the Iranian Welfare Organization. A series of interviews take place at the Iranian Welfare Organization. A file in the orphanage is established. The head nurse at the orphanage will refer the file to the Adoption Affairs office. Interviews and visits by a social worker and referral to relevant offices(s) will follow.

The parents meet with an adoption council who refers them to the orphanage's social office. The family is put in a waiting list and the child selection process begins. After the selection, the child goes through a medical examination by a physician selected by the parents. Mental and physical health certificates of the child are issued by a specialist. At the end of this process, the Iranian Welfare Organization refers the case to the court. The court issues a temporary custody document and puts the family in a six month probationary period.

Time Frame: The complete process may take up to 3 years. After temporary custody is granted to the parents, they are put on a six month probationary period. The final judgment is made at the end of this period if the parents are found to be qualified.

Adoption Fees: Not known

Documents Required:

- Translation of English documents into Farsi in two copies certified by Iranian authorities.
- Request form
- Originals and notarized copies of birth certificates (Shenasnameh)
- Original and notarized copy of the marriage certificate
- Infertility certificate (original/translation/notarized copy)
- Test results on physical and mental health of the parents (including addiction tests)
- Police records
- Proof of financial status
- Last education document (diploma)

Additional documents may be requested.

Bringing Your Child Home: Once your adoption is complete (or you have obtained legal custody of the child), there are a few more steps to take before you can head home. Specifically, you need to apply for several documents for your child before he or she can travel to the United States, such as a birth certificate, a passport or travel document for your child from the country in which he or she was born, and a U.S. Immigration Visa. For detailed and updated information on how to obtain these documents, review the *Intercountry Adoption* section in this publication and visit the U.S. Department of State Intercountry Adoption website at http://adoption.state.gov.

Child Citizenship Act: For adoptions finalized abroad, the Child Citizenship Act of 2000 allows your new child to acquire American citizenship automatically when he or she enters the United States as lawful permanent residents. For adoptions finalized in the United States, the Child Citizenship Act of 2000 allows your new child to acquire American citizenship automatically when the court in the United States issues the final adoption decree. To learn more, review the *Intercountry Adoption* section in this publication and visit the U.S. Department of State Intercountry Adoption website at http://adoption.state.gov.

After Adoption: We strongly urge you to comply with and complete all Iranian post-adoption requirements in a timely manner. Your adoption agency may be able to help you with this process. Your cooperation will contribute to that country's history of positive experiences with American parents.

U.S. Embassy in Ankara, Turkey
110 Ataturk Blvd.
Kavaklidere
06100 Ankara, Turkey
Phone: 90-312-455 5555
Fax: 90-312-468 6103
Internet:
http://turkey.usembassy.gov/

Iran Adoption Authority
Iranian Welfare Organization
(Edareh Beh Zistiti, Bakhshe Farzand Khandegi)
Address: 188 Karimkhan St., Tehran

Embassy of Iran
Address: 2209 Wisconsin Avenue, N.W.
Washington, D.C. 20007
Tel: (202) 965-4990
Fax: (202) 965-1073
Email: requests@daftar.org
Internet: http://www.daftar.org/ENG/default.asp?lang=eng

Office of Children's Issues
U.S. Department of State
2201 C Street, NW
SA-29
Washington, DC 20520
Tel: 1-888-407-4747
E-mail: AskCI@state.gov
http://adoption.state.gov

For questions about immigration procedures, call the National Customer Service Center (NCSC) at 1-800-375-5283 (TTY 1-800-767-1833).

International Parental Child Abduction

January 2012

The information in this section has been edited from the latest report available as of February 2013 from the State Department Bureau of Consular Affairs, Office of Overseas Citizens Services. For more information, please read the *International Parental Child Abduction* section of this book and check for updated reports online at www.travel.state.gov/abduction.

Disclaimer: The information in this flyer relating to the legal requirements of specific foreign countries is provided for general information only. Questions involving interpretation of specific foreign laws should be addressed to foreign legal counsel.

The Office of Overseas Citizens Services has taken an active role in almost 80 cases of children taken to or wrongfully retained in Iran. To our knowledge, the majority of these cases have not been resolved. However, in a number of cases, the left-behind parent has kept open the lines of communication, negotiated with the abducting parent, and eventually persuaded the other parent to travel out of Iran with the children.

The United States severed diplomatic and consular relations with the Government of Iran on April 7, 1980 as a result of the events surrounding the seizure of our Embassy in Tehran,

Iran on November 4, 1979. In April of 1980, the United States Government formally asked the Swiss Government if it would assume diplomatic and consular representation of the United States in Iran. The Swiss agreed to perform specific consular and administrative functions on behalf of the U.S. Government.

One of their responsibilities is to provide consular services to children who have been taken by one parent to Iran without the other parent's knowledge or consent. In this regard, Swiss officials are permitted to ascertain the child's welfare, process applications for U.S. passports and to inform appropriate officials if there are allegations of child abuse. However, the Iranian government has placed strict limits on the ability of Swiss diplomats to intervene in such cases because they do not recognize the concept of dual nationality and therefore, when one parent is an Iranian citizen, consider the children involved to be Iranian citizens only.

Swiss diplomats in Iran do not have the authority to take custody of and return a child to the United States, just as foreign diplomats in the U.S. cannot remove children from this country. Such an action would be considered kidnapping under local law.

If you are concerned about a potential abduction, one of the first steps you should take is to notify the Department's Office of Passport Services by entering your child into the Children's Passport Issuance Alert Program. If the child's father is an Iranian citizen, the child is considered an Iranian citizen under Iranian law and could travel abroad on an Iranian passport. There is nothing the Department of State can do to prevent the issuance of an Iranian passport by the Iranian Interests Section of the Embassy of Algeria.

You may wish to notify the Iranian Interests Section that you would object to your child receiving a passport without your consent. At that time, you could ask whether they have already issued a passport for the child. The address and the telephone number of the Iranian Interests Section of the Embassy of Algeria are: 2209 Wisconsin Avenue, N.W., Washington D.C. 20007; (202) 965-4999. Unfortunately, it has been our experience that a parent encounters little or no difficulty obtaining travel documentation from the Interests Section for a dual U.S.-Iranian citizen child, despite the existence of a U.S. court order barring departure without the court's consent.

As you may already know, a custody decree issued by a court in the United States has no force or effect in a foreign country. When a child is abducted by a parent, the deprived parent must usually initiate legal proceedings in the foreign country to regain custody of the child or to enforce visitation rights. However, the difficulties in recovering a child from an Islamic country without the full support and consent of the father can be insurmountable.

It is the Department's understanding that in Iran, all matters concerning family law are governed by the religious courts. While you would be free to seek legal custody through the Iranian religious courts, you should be aware that Islamic courts rarely, if ever, grant custody of children to a parent who will not raise them as Muslims, does not plan to remain in Iran or has remarried. Islamic courts attach great importance to having children reside near their father so that he can visit frequently and oversee their upbringing. Even if the mother is granted custody, (The children would still need his permission to leave the country).

Currently, the only treaties which have any application to abductions of children from the United States are the Hague Convention on the Civil Aspects of International Child Abduction and the extradition treaties which the United States has with individual countries. Iran is not a party to the Hague Convention, and since the U.S. and Iran do not maintain diplomatic relations, there is no bilateral treaty in effect which would cover parental child abduction.

The U.S. Immigration and Naturalization Act was recently reformed by adding a Section which addressed the issue of child abduction. Under its provisions, which became effective June 1, 1991, a left-behind parent can, upon presentation of a custody decree, ask the Department of State to exclude an international child abductor from the United States. If you have further questions about this procedure or other aspects of child abduction, please contact the Office of Children's Issues at 1-888-407-4747.

IRAQ

Compiled from publications that were available as of February 2013 from the U.S. Department of State, the U.S. Department of Commerce, and the Central Intelligence Agency (CIA). See the introduction to this set for explanatory notes.

Official Name:
Republic of Iraq

PROFILE

Geography

Area: total: 438,317 sq km; country comparison to the world: 59; land: 437,367 sq km; water: 950 sq km

Major cities: Baghdad (capital) 5.751 million; Mosul 1.447 million; Erbil 1.009 million; Basra 923,000; As Sulaymaniyah 836,000 (2009)

Climate: mostly desert; mild to cool winters with dry, hot, cloudless summers; northern mountainous regions along Iranian and Turkish borders experience cold winters with occasionally heavy snows that melt in early spring, sometimes causing extensive flooding in central and southern Iraq

Terrain: mostly broad plains; reedy marshes along Iranian border in south with large flooded areas; mountains along borders with Iran and Turkey

People

Nationality: noun: Iraqi(s); adjective: Iraqi

Population: 31,129,225 (July 2012 est.)

Population growth rate: 2.345% (2012 est.)

Ethnic groups: Arab 75%-80%, Kurdish 15%-20%, Turkoman, Assyrian, or other 5%

Religions: Muslim (official) 97% (Shia 60%-65%, Sunni 32%-37%), Christian or other 3%

Languages: Arabic (official), Kurdish (official), Turkmen (a Turkish dialect) and Assyrian (Neo-Aramaic) are official in areas where they constitute a majority of the population), Armenian

Literacy: definition: age 15 and over can read and write; total population: 78.2%; male: 86%; female: 70.6% (2010 est.)

Health: life expectancy at birth: total population: 70.85 years; male: 69.41 years; female: 72.35 years (2012 est.); Infant mortality rate: total: 40.25 deaths/1,000 live births; male: 44.43 deaths/1,000 live births; female: 35.86 deaths/1,000 live births (2012 est.)

Unemployment rate: 15% (2010 est.)

Work force: 8.9 million (2010 est.)

Government

Type: parliamentary democracy

Independence: 3 October 1932

Constitution: ratified 15 October 2005 (subject to review by the Constitutional Review Committee and a possible public referendum)

Political subdivisions: 18 governorates (muhafazat, singular—muhafazah) and 1 region; Al Anbar, Al Basrah, Al Muthanna, Al Qadisiyah (Ad Diwaniyah), An Najaf, Arbil (Erbil), As Sulaymaniyah, Babil, Baghdad, Dahuk, Dhi Qar, Diyala, Karbala', Kirkuk, Kurdistan Regional Government, Maysan, Ninawa, Salah ad Din, Wasit

Suffrage: 18 years of age; universal

Economy

GDP (purchasing power parity): $155.4 billion (2012 est.); $129.3 billion (2011 est.); $117.6 billion (2010 est.); $116.6 billion (2009 est.)

GDP real growth rate: 10.2% (2012 est.); 9.9% (2011 est.); 0.8% (2010 est.); 4.2% (2009 est.)

GDP per capita (PPP): $4,600 (2012 est.); $3,900 (2011 est.); $3,700 (2010 est.); $3,700 (2009 est.)

Natural resources: petroleum, natural gas, phosphates, sulfur

Agriculture products: wheat, barley, rice, vegetables, dates, cotton; cattle, sheep, poultry

Industries: petroleum, chemicals, textiles, leather, construction materials, food processing, fertilizer, metal fabrication/processing

Exports: $88.27 billion (2012 est.); $82.77 billion (2011 est.); $51.76 billion (2010 est.)

Exports—commodities: crude oil 84%, crude materials excluding fuels, food and live animals

Exports—partners: US 23.3%, India 19.2%, China 14%, South Korea 12.2%, Japan 5%, Netherlands 4.5% (2011)

Imports: $56.89 billion (2012 est.); $53.93 billion (2011 est.); $43.92 billion (2010 est.)
Imports—commodities: food, medicine, manufactures
Imports—partners: Turkey 25%, Syria 18.1%, China 11.5%, US 7.3%, South Korea 4.6% (2011)
Debt—external: $50.79 billion (31 December 2011 est.); $52.58 billion (31 December 2010 est.)
Exchange rates: Iraqi dinars (IQD) per US dollar; 1,170 (2011 est.); 1,170 (2010 est.); 1,170 (2009); 1,176 (2008); 1,255 (2007)

GEOGRAPHY

Iraq is bordered by Kuwait, Iran, Turkey, Syria, Jordan, and Saudi Arabia. The country slopes from mountains over 3,000 meters (10,000 ft.) above sea level along the border with Iran and Turkey to the remnants of sea-level marshes in the southeast. Much of the land is desert or non-arable. The mountains in the northeast are an extension of the alpine system that runs eastward from the Balkans into southern Turkey, northern Iraq, Iran, and Afghanistan, terminating in the Himalayas.

Average temperatures range from higher than 48°C (120°F) in July and August to below freezing in January. Most of the rainfall occurs from December through April and averages between 10 and 18 centimeters (4-7 in.) annually. The mountainous region of northern Iraq receives appreciably more precipitation than the central or southern desert region.

PEOPLE

Almost 75% of Iraq's population lives in the flat, alluvial plain stretching southeast from Baghdad and Basrah to the Persian Gulf. The Tigris and Euphrates Rivers carry about 70 million cubic meters of silt annually to the delta. Known in ancient times as Mesopotamia, the region is the legendary locale of the Garden of Eden. The ruins of Ur, Babylon, and other ancient cities are located in Iraq.

In recent years, a large number of Iraqis have been displaced, and there are currently a reported 177,376 Iraqi refugees registered with the UN High Commissioner for Refugees (UNHCR) in Jordan, Syria, Lebanon, and other neighboring countries. UNHCR estimates that approximately 1.2 million Iraqis were displaced by sectarian violence following the Samarra Mosque bombing of February 2006 and remain internally displaced inside Iraq. For more information on Iraqi refugees, internally displaced persons, and conflict victims, please visit: http://www.state.gov/j/prm/ra/index.htm.

National/Racial/Ethnic Minorities

The country's population includes Arabs, Kurds, Turkmen, as well as religious minorities including Chaldeans, Assyrians, Armenians, Yezidis, Sabean-Mandaeans, Baha'i, Shabak, Kakai, and a small number of Jews. Many consider the Assyrians and Chaldeans to be a distinct ethnic group. These communities speak a different language, preserve Christian traditions, and do not define themselves as Arabs. The country also has citizens of African descent, "Black Iraqis," a population that community representatives estimated to number more than one million.

The constitution identifies Arabic and Kurdish as the two official languages of the state. It also provides the right of citizens to educate their children in their mother tongue, such as Turkmen, Syriac, or Armenian, in government educational institutions in accordance with educational guidelines or in any other language in private educational institutions.

During 2011 discrimination against ethnic minorities was a problem. There were numerous reports of Kurdish authorities discriminating against minorities, including Turkmen, Arabs, Yezidis, and Assyrians, in the disputed territories under the de facto control of the KRG.

According to press reports, Palestinians continued to experience arrest, detention, harassment, and abuse by authorities. A 2006 citizenship law prevents Palestinians from obtaining citizenship and Jews who emigrated to other countries from reclaiming citizenship.

Black Iraqis reported widespread economic and social discrimination. Black Iraqi leaders estimate that more than 20 percent of the Black Iraqi population was unemployed, compared to an overall unemployment rate of 15 percent. Minority Rights Group International reported that many were laborers or worked as domestic workers.

Language

In Iraq, there are two official languages: Arabic and Kurdish. More than three-fourths of the Iraqi population speak Arabic, which has several major dialects; these are generally mutually intelligible, but significant variations do exist within the country. Modern Standard Arabic-the benchmark of literacy-is taught in schools, and most Arabs and many non-Arabs, even those who lack schooling, are able to understand it. Roughly one-fifth of the population speaks Kurdish, in one of its two main dialects. Kurdish is the official language in the Kurdish Autonomous Region in the north. A number of other languages are spoken by smaller ethnic groups, including Turkish, Turkmen, and Assyrian. Bilingualism is fairly common, particularly among minorities who are conversant in Arabic. English is widely used in commerce.

Religion

Due to violence, internal migration, and lack of governmental capacity, religious demography statistics varied. Numbers were often estimates from nongovernmental organizations (NGOs) rather than census data or other official sources. The government passed a census law in 2008; however, no census has yet been conducted.

According to statistics provided in 2010 by the government, 97 percent of the population is Muslim. Shia Muslims--predominantly Arabs but

also Turkmen, Faili (Shia) Kurds, and other groups--constitute a 60 to 65 percent majority. Arab and Kurdish Sunni Muslims make up 32 to 37 percent of the population--18 to 20 percent are Sunni Kurds, 12 to 16 percent are Sunni Arabs, and the remaining 1 to 2 percent are Sunni Turkmen. Approximately 3 percent of the population is composed of Christians, Yezidis, Sabean-Mandaeans, Baha'is, Shabaks, Kaka'is (sometimes referred to as Ahl-e Haqq), and a very small number of Jews. Shia, although predominantly located in the south and east, are also a majority in Baghdad and have communities in most parts of the country. Sunnis form the majority in the west, center, and the north of the country.

Current Christian population estimates by Christian leaders range from 400,000 to 600,000. Approximately two-thirds of Christians are Chaldeans (an eastern rite of the Catholic Church), nearly one-fifth are Assyrians (Church of the East), and the remainder are Syriacs (Eastern Orthodox), Armenians (Roman Catholic and Eastern Orthodox), Anglicans, and other Protestants. The archbishop of the Armenian Orthodox Diocese reported that approximately 15, 000 Armenian Christians remained in the country, primarily in the cities of Baghdad, Basrah, Kirkuk, and Mosul. Evangelical Christians reportedly number approximately 5,000.

Yezidi leaders reported that most of the country's 500,000 to 600,000 Yezidis reside in the north, with 15 percent in Dohuk Province and the rest in Ninewa Province. Shabak leaders stated there are 400,000 to 500,000 Shabaks, who reside mainly in the north, near Mosul. Estimates of the size of the Sabean-Mandaean community vary widely; according to Sabean-Mandaean leaders, about 4,000 remained in the country. The Baha'i leadership reported their members number fewer than 2,000 and are spread throughout the country in small groups. The Kakai'i community around Kirkuk is estimated at 24,500 people. Eight Jews reside in Baghdad, and none are known to live in other parts of the country.

UNHCR reported that 67,080 Iraqi refugees and 193,610 internally displaced persons (IDPs) registered returns in 2011. A majority of these refugees originally fled Iraq and sought ayslum in Syria and Iran due to sectarian violence. According to UNHCR's 2011 mid-year monitoring report, the majority of the Iraqi refugees who had sought asylum in Iran were Shia families who had fled Iraq prior to 2003; those who returned in 2011 mostly settled in Najaf and Kerbala.

In addition to Iraqi refugees, an estimated 1.3 million people of all religious backgrounds remained internally displaced due to the sectarian violence between 2006 and 2008. The number of religious minorities internally displaced by violence remains uncertain because many stay with relatives and friends. At year's end, the International Organization for Migration (IOM) reported that 489 Christian families remained internally displaced in Iraq, down from 1,354 families at the beginning of the year. IOM attributed the decrease to families choosing to leave Iraq or deciding to return to their home areas due to growing security fears, lack of work opportunities, and difficulty with education transfers for their children in the area of displacement. Christian IDP families frequently found temporary residence in rental houses or with relatives. Humanitarian organizations working with this vulnerable population noted that Christian families were often unable to sell their homes at a reasonable price. They also faced increasing rental costs in their area of displacement. Approximately 150 of the families that did not integrate into their area of displacement returned to Baghdad.

HISTORY

Once known as Mesopotamia, Iraq was the site of flourishing ancient civilizations, including the Sumerian, Babylonian, and Parthian cultures. Muslims conquered Iraq in the seventh century A.D. In the eighth century, the Abassid caliphate established its capital at Baghdad. The territory of modern Iraq came under the rule of the Ottoman Turks early in the 1500s.

At the end of World War I, Ottoman control ended and Iraq came under the authority of a British mandate. When it was declared independent in 1932, the Hashemite family, a branch of which also ruled Jordan, ruled as a constitutional monarchy. In 1945, Iraq joined the United Nations and became a founding member of the Arab League. In 1956, the Baghdad Pact allied Iraq, Turkey, Iran, Pakistan, and the United Kingdom, and established its headquarters in Baghdad.

Gen. Abdul Karim Qasim took power in a July 1958 coup, during which King Faysal II and Prime Minister Nuri as-Said were killed. Qasim ended Iraq's membership in the Baghdad Pact in 1959. Qasim was assassinated in February 1963, when the Arab Socialist Renaissance Party (Ba'ath Party) took power under the leadership of Gen. Ahmad Hasan al-Bakr as prime minister and Col. Abdul Salam Arif as president. Nine months later, Arif led a coup ousting the Ba'ath government. In April 1966, Arif was killed in a plane crash and was succeeded by his brother, Gen. Abdul Rahman Mohammad Arif. On July 17, 1968, a group of Ba'athists and military elements overthrew the Arif regime. Ahmad Hasan al-Bakr reemerged as the President of Iraq and Chairman of the Revolutionary Command Council (RCC).

In July 1979, Bakr resigned, and his cousin Saddam Hussein, already a key figure in the Ba'ath party and the RCC, assumed the two offices of President and RCC Chairman. The Iran-Iraq war (1980–88) devastated the economy of Iraq. Iraq declared victory over Iran in 1988 but actually achieved only a weary return to the pre-war status quo. The war left Iraq with the largest military establishment in the Gulf region and with huge debts.

Iraq invaded Kuwait in August 1990, but a U.S.-led coalition acting under United Nations (UN) resolutions expelled Iraq in February 1991. After the war, Kurds in the north and Shi'a Muslims in the south rebelled against the government of Saddam Hussein. The government responded quickly and with crushing force, killing thousands, and pursued damaging environmental and agricultural policies meant to drain the marshes of the south. Coalition forces enforced no-fly zones in southern and northern Iraq to protect Iraqi citizens from attack by the regime and a no-drive zone in southern Iraq to prevent the regime from massing forces to threaten or again invade Kuwait. In addition, the UN Security Council required the regime to surrender its weapons of mass destruction (WMD) and submit to UN inspections. When the regime refused to fully cooperate with the UN inspections, the Security Council passed a series of Chapter VII sanctions to prevent further WMD development and compel Iraqi adherence to international obligations.

Citing Iraq's failure to comply with UN inspections, a U.S.-led coalition invaded Iraq in March 2003 and removed the Ba'ath regime, leading to the overthrow of the dictator Saddam Hussein. Following his capture in December 2003 and subsequent trial, Saddam Hussein was executed on December 30, 2006, by the Government of Iraq. The Coalition Provisional Authority (CPA) assumed security and administrative responsibility for Iraq while Iraqi political leaders and the Iraqi people established a transitional administration. The CPA's mission was to restore conditions of security and stability and to create conditions in which the Iraqi people could freely determine their own political future. The UN Security Council acknowledged the authority of the Coalition Provisional Authority and provided a role for the UN and other parties to assist in fulfilling these objectives.

The CPA disbanded on June 28, 2004, transferring sovereign authority for governing Iraq to the Iraqi Interim Government (IIG). Based on the timetable laid out in the Transitional Administrative Law (TAL), the IIG governed Iraq until elections were held on January 30, 2005; thereafter, the Iraqi Transitional Government assumed authority.

In May 2005, the Iraqi Transitional Government appointed a multi-ethnic committee to draft a new Iraqi constitution. The new constitution was finalized in September 2005, and was ratified in a nationwide referendum on October 15, 2005. On December 15, 2005, Iraqis again went to the polls to participate in the first national legislative elections as established by the new constitution. The new 4-year, constitutionally-based government took office in March 2006, and the new cabinet was approved and installed in May 2006. By that time, following the February 2006 bombing of the Golden Mosque in Samarra, violence in the country was widespread. The ongoing violence and instability prompted the United States to increase troop numbers in Iraq (the "surge" in U.S. forces) in an attempt to improve the security situation and give Iraqi political leaders an opportunity to address the many problems that plagued the Iraqi people. Following the troop increase and adjustments to military strategy, violence declined, thereby providing political space and an improved environment for leaders to make progress on difficult national issues.

In January 2009, two bilateral agreements between the United States and the Government of Iraq took effect: 1) the "Agreement between the United States of America and the Republic of Iraq On the Withdrawal of United States Forces from Iraq and the Organization of Their Activities During Their Temporary Presence in Iraq" (referred to as the "Security Agreement"), which governed the presence and status of U.S. forces in Iraq and addressed the withdrawal of these forces; and, 2) the "Strategic Framework Agreement for a Relationship of Friendship and Cooperation between the United States of America and the Republic of Iraq" (referred to as the "Strategic Framework Agreement" or "SFA"), which set out a variety of areas and aims for bilateral cooperation and formed the basis for a long-term partnership with the people and Government of Iraq and which remains in effect.

On January 31, 2009, Iraq held elections for provincial councils in all provinces except the three provinces comprising the Iraqi Kurdistan Region, and Kirkuk province. On March 7, 2010, Iraq held national elections in which parties competed for positions in the Council of Representatives and the executive branch.

In June 2009, in accordance with the bilateral Security Agreement, U.S. forces withdrew from cities, villages, and localities in Iraq. On August 31, 2010, President Barack Obama announced the end of major combat operations, the completion of the withdrawal of all U.S. combat brigades, and the transition of the role of the remaining U.S. military force of 50,000 troops to advising and assisting Iraqi security forces. On October 21, 2011, President Obama announced the full withdrawal of U.S. forces from Iraq by year's end pursuant to the Security Agreement. U.S. Forces-Iraq completed the withdrawal by December 18, 2011. A traditional security cooperation relationship is maintained through the presence of the Office of Security Cooperation-Iraq, which is comprised of a small group of U.S. military and civilian advisors and contractors who work with the Iraqi security forces, helping them to receive, maintain, and operate defense-related articles.

GOVERNMENT AND POLITICAL CONDITIONS

Iraq is a constitutional parliamentary republic. Prime Minister Nouri Kamal al-Maliki was sworn in following free and fair elections in March 2010, once the major political parties reached a power-sharing agreement that allowed the government to be seated in December 2010. While the government is inclusive of all major political parties, significant unresolved issues continued to hamper its operation as permanent ministers of defense and interior had yet to be appointed at year's end. However, during the year, the role of the Council of Representatives (COR) and provincial governments increased. Iraqi Security Forces (ISF) reported to civilian authorities, but continuing violence, corruption, and organizational dysfunction undermined the government's protection of human rights.

Recent Elections

In the March 2010 parliamentary elections, nearly 12 million persons voted, from a pool of more than 18.9 million registered voters. International observer missions and indigenous observers declared the elections free from widespread or systemic fraud.

The Independent High Electoral Commission announced preliminary election results based on the tabulation of 100 percent of the vote and resolution of approximately 200 complaints. Despite the controversy surrounding the electoral commission decision to ban approximately 500 candidates for alleged ties to the banned Ba'ath Party and violence before and on election day, the elections were considered free and fair.

Provincial elections in the IKR scheduled during the year were postponed pending passage in the Iraqi Kurdistan Parliament (IKP) of a package of laws related to provincial council elections, provincial powers, and the establishment of a Kurdish electoral commission. However, the IKP passed the Provincial Council Elections Law in November and signed it into law in December. On December 28, the KRG set September 27, 2012, as the date for Provincial Council elections.

Political Parties: While political parties did not formally restrict membership to certain societal groups, they tended to be organized along either religious or ethnic lines. Shia Islamist parties, such as the Islamic Supreme Council of Iraq, al-Dawa al-Islamiyya Party, and Sadrist Trend, as well as Kurdish nationalist parties such as the KDP and PUK, were the predominant political forces. Other political players included the secular Iraqiyya, Sunni Iraqi Islamic Party, the Goran (Change) Party in the IKR, and ethnic minority parties, such as the Assyrian Democratic Movement, the Kurdish Islamic Union, and the Kurdish Islamic Group. Membership in some political parties conferred special privileges and advantages in employment and education. The KDP and PUK gave preference in KRG government employment to their respective members. In total, 160 regular parties, 36 independents, and 10 minority parties and candidates participated in the elections.

Participation of Women and Minorities: The constitution mandates that female members of parliament constitute 25 percent of the COR. There were 81 women elected to the COR, including candidates elected through the open list system. However, female parliamentarians were often marginalized. There was one female minister out of 29 in the cabinet (minister of state for women's affairs), and four cabinet members from religious and ethnic minority groups: the ministers of agriculture, environment, youth and sports, and provincial affairs. In the COR there were five women chairing standing committees: services and construction; woman, family, and childhood; members affairs and parliamentary development; health and environment; and deportees, immigrants, and expatriates.

Of the 325 seats in the parliament, the law reserves eight compensatory seats for minorities: five for Christian candidates from Baghdad, Ninewa, Kirkuk, Erbil, and Dohuk; one Yezidi representing Ninewa; one Sabean-Mandaean representing Baghdad; and, one Shabak representing Ninewa. The law also opened the process to out-of-country voting for refugees and citizens abroad.

Principal Government Officials

Last Updated: 1/31/2013

Pres.: **Jalal TALABANI**
Vice Pres.: **Tariq al-HASHIMI**
Vice Pres.: **Khudayr Musa Jafar Abbas al-KHUZAI**
Prime Min.: **Nuri al-MALIKI**
Dep. Prime Min. for Economic Affairs: **Rowsch Nuri SHAWAYS**
Dep. Prime Min. for Energy Affairs: **Husayn Ibrahim Salih al-SHAHRISTANI**
Dep. Prime Min. for Services: **Salih al-MUTLAQ**
Min. of Agriculture: **Izz al-Din al-DAWLAH**
Min. of Communications: **Muhammad Tawfiq ALLAWI**
Min. of Culture: **Sadun Farhan al-DULAYMI**
Min. of Defense (Acting): **Sadun Farhan al-DULAYMI**
Min. of Displacement & Migration: **Dindar Najam Shafiq DOSKI**
Min. of Education: **Muhammad Khalaf Tamim al-JUBURI**
Min. of Electricity: **Abd al-Karim AFTAN Ahmad al-Jumayli**
Min. of Environment: **Sargon Lazar SULAYWAH**
Min. of Finance: **Rafi Hiyad al-ISSAWI, Dr.**
Min. of Foreign Affairs: **Hoshyar Mahmud ZEBARI**
Min. of Health: **Majid Hamad Amin JAMIL**
Min. of Higher Education & Scientific Research: **Ali Muhammad al-ADIB**
Min. of Housing & Construction: **Muhammad Sahib al-DARAJI**
Min. of Human Rights: **Muhammad Shia al-SUDANI**
Min. of Industry & Minerals: **Ahmad Nasir Dilli al-KARBULI**
Min. of Interior (Acting): **Nuri al-MALIKI**
Min. of Justice: **Hasan al-SHAMMARI**
Min. of Labor & Social Affairs: **Nasar al-RUBAI**
Min. of Municipalities & Public Works: **Adil Muhudir Radi al-MALIKI**
Min. of Oil: **Abd al-Karim LUAYBI**
Min. of Planning: **Ali al-SHUKRI**
Min. of Science & Technology: **Abd al-Karim al-SAMARRAI**
Min. of Trade: **Khayrallah Hasan BABAKIR**
Min. of Transportation: **Hadi Farhan al-AMIRI**
Min. of Water Resources: **Muhannad al-SA'DI**
Min. of Youth & Sports: **Jasim Muhammad JAFAR**
Min. of State for Council of Representatives Affairs: **Safa al-Din al-SAFI**
Min. of State for Foreign Affairs: **Ali al-SAJRI**
Min. of State for Provincial Affairs: **Turhan Mudhir al-MUFTI**
Min. of State for Women's Affairs: **Ibtihal Qasid al-ZAYDI**
Governor, Central Bank of Iraq: **Sinan Muhammad Ridha al-SHABIBI**
Ambassador to the US: **Jabir Habib JABIR**
Permanent Representative to the UN, New York: **Hamid al-BAYATI**

ECONOMY

An improving security environment and foreign investment are helping to spur economic activity, particularly in the energy, construction, and retail sectors. Broader economic development, long-term fiscal health, and sustained improvements in the overall standard of living still depend on the central government passing major policy reforms. Iraq's largely state-run economy is dominated by the oil sector, which provides more than 90% of government revenue and 80% of foreign exchange earnings. Iraq in 2012 boosted oil exports to a 30-year high of 2.6 million barrels per day, a significant increase from Iraq's average of 2.2 million in 2011.

Government revenues increased as global oil prices remained persistently high for much of 2012. Iraq's contracts with major oil companies have the potential to further expand oil exports and revenues, but Iraq will need to make significant upgrades to its oil processing, pipeline, and export infrastructure to enable these deals to reach their economic potential. Iraq is making slow progress enacting laws and developing the institutions needed to implement economic policy, and political reforms are still needed to assuage investors' concerns regarding the uncertain business climate, which may have been harmed by the November 2012 standoff between Baghdad and Erbil.

The government of Iraq is eager to attract additional foreign direct investment, but it faces a number of obstacles including a tenuous political system and concerns about security and societal stability. Rampant corruption, outdated infrastructure, insufficient essential services, skilled labor shortages, and antiquated commercial laws stifle investment and continue to constrain growth of private, nonoil sectors. In 2010, Baghdad signed agreements with both the IMF and World Bank for conditional aid programs designed to help strengthen Iraq's economic institutions. Iraq is considering a package of laws to establish a modern legal framework for the oil sector and a mechanism to equitably divide oil revenues within the nation, although these reforms are still under contentious and sporadic negotiation.

Political and economic tensions between Baghdad and local governments have led some provincial councils to use their budgets to independently promote and facilitate investment at the local level. The Central Bank has successfully held the exchange rate at about 1,170 Iraqi dinar/US dollar since January 2009. Inflation has remained under control since 2006 as security improved. However, Iraqi leaders remain hard pressed to translate macroeconomic gains into an improved standard of living for the Iraqi populace. Unemployment remains a problem throughout the country despite a bloated public sector.

Encouraging private enterprise through deregulation would make it easier for Iraqi citizens and foreign investors to start new businesses. Rooting out corruption and implementing reforms - such as restructuring banks and developing the private sector - would be important steps in this direction.

Labor Conditions

The law limits working hours for persons younger than 18 and prohibits their employment in dangerous occupations.

The minimum age for employment is 15. The law prohibits employment of anyone younger than 16 in work that is detrimental to health, safety, or morals. Article 34 of the constitution guarantees the right of free education and citizen children are required to attend school until age 11. This left children ages 12 to 15 vulnerable to child labor, as they were not required to be in school but were not permitted to work. Children employed in family enterprises were exempt from some protections with regard to employment conditions (see section 6).

Data on child labor was limited. Poor families routinely used child labor to augment their incomes. This work often took the form of seasonal labor in rural areas, or begging or peddling in urban settings. There were anecdotal reports of children performing hazardous work in family-owned automobile shops or on construction sites. Unconfirmed reports alleged the sale of children for indentured servitude. Sunni and Shia militias, as well as al-Qaida in Iraq, recruited and used children for spying, working as couriers, scouting, and planting improvised explosive devices.

The national minimum wage for a skilled worker was less than 12,000 dinars (approximately $10) per day and for an unskilled worker less than 5,250 dinars ($4.50) per day. Wages were set by contract in the private sector and by the government in the public sector. The Central Organization of Statistics and Information Technology reported that the average salary in 2009—the latest year for which information was available—was approximately 2.4 million dinars ($2,060) per year, an increase over the previous year's figure of 1.78 million dinars ($1,528). These earnings remained two to three times poverty level, defined in the 2009 Central Organization of Statistics and Information Technology report as 923,000 dinars ($792) per person per year.

The standard workday is eight hours with one or more rest periods. Up to four hours of overtime work per day is permitted, and premium pay for overtime is required. Regulations on working conditions existed but were almost entirely unenforced.

There was little information available on the number of foreign workers in the country. Migrant workers have no legal protections. Some foreign workers in the country were subjected to abusive treatment and conditions associated with forced labor, including confiscation of travel and identity documents, restrictions on movement and communication, physical abuse, sexual harassment and rape, withholding of wages, forced overtime, and hazardous working conditions.

U.S.-IRAQ RELATIONS

The U.S. Mission in Iraq remains dedicated to building a strategic partnership with Iraq and the Iraqi people. The December 2011 departure of U.S. troops from Iraq marked a milestone in our relationship as Iraq continues to develop as a sovereign, stable, and self-reliant country. Iraq is now a key partner for the U.S. in the region as well as a voice of moderation and democracy in the Middle East. Iraq has functioning government institutions including an active legislature, is playing an increasingly constructive role in the region, and has a bright economic future as oil revenues surpass pre-Saddam production levels with continued rapid growth to come. The U.S. maintains vigorous and broad engagement with Iraq on diplomatic, political, economic, and security issues in accordance with the U.S.-Iraq Strategic Framework Agreement.

The Strategic Framework Agreement (SFA) between Iraq and the U.S. provides the basis for the U.S.-Iraq bilateral relationship. It covers the range of bilateral issues including political relations and diplomacy, defense and security, trade and finance, energy, judicial and law enforcement issues, services, science, culture, education, and environment. Efforts to implement the SFA are overseen by the Higher Coordinating Committee and several Joint Coordination Committees, which meet periodically.

U.S. Assistance to Iraq

U.S. assistance to Iraq has changed over the last several years, shifting from large scale infrastructure projects to focus on capacity-building, long-term development, assistance to vulnerable groups, and democracy and governance. U.S. assistance also continues to help build the capacity of Iraq's civil society organizations and elected representatives, including assistance in the modernization of Iraqi law and seeks to increase participation in the democratic process. U.S. bilateral assistance aims to preserve the strategic, political, and economic importance of the U.S.-Iraq partnership in a changing Middle East region.

U.S. security assistance supports the development of a modern, accountable, and professional Iraqi military capable of defending Iraq and its borders. U.S. security assistance programs also promote civilian oversight of the military, adherence to the rule of law, and the respect for human rights, while simultaneously increasing the Iraqi military's capability to respond to threats and conduct counter-terrorism operations. Embassy Baghdad maintains the Office of Security Cooperation—Iraq to further these goals and to facilitate Iraq's role as a responsible security partner, contributing to the peace and security of the region.

The U.S. Government strives to work in partnership with Iraqis on initiatives that they support with their own funds. The U.S. Government seeks to utilize assistance to help Iraq marshal its own financial resources for the self-sustaining benefit of its people.

Bilateral Economic Relations

The Iraqi Government has stated its desire to transition from a centrally run economy to one that is more market-oriented, though progress has been slow and uneven. Iraq is gradually deepening its trade with the international community, with both exports and imports showing rapid growth in recent years. Turkey is currently Iraq's largest trading partner The United States has designated Iraq as a beneficiary developing country under the Generalized System of Preferences program and a number of U.S. companies are active in Iraq, including in the energy, defense, Information technology, automotive, transportation sectors.

Two-way trade in 2011 was $19.3 billion, with U.S. exports to Iraq at $2.4 billion (a 46.8% increase over 2010), and Iraqi exports to the United States at $16.9 billion, almost entirely consisting of crude oil. In the first half of 2012, U.S. exports totaled $951.7 million, down from $1.365 billion in the first half of 2011.

Iraq's Membership in International Organizations

Iraq's re-integration into the international community has been underscored by their cooperation with international organizations, including the United Nations, International Monetary Fund,World Bank and Arab League,. Iraq is also a candidate for accession to the World Trade Organization (WTO).

Bilateral Representation

Iraq maintains an embassy in the United States at 3421 Massachusetts Ave., NW, Washington, DC 20007; tel. 202-742-1600.

Principal U.S. Embassy Officials

Last Updated: 1/14/2013

BAGHDAD (E) Unit 6060 Box ####, 240-553-0581; IDDD 964-760-030-3000, 4 or 7 digit extension, Fax 703-343-8485, Workweek: Sunday–Thursday 0800-1700, Website: http://iraq.usembassy.gov/

DCM OMS:	Goodall, Laney L
AMB OMS:	Parish, Frances C
Co-CLO:	Roberts, Nicole
DHS/CBP:	Leonard, Raleigh
FCS:	Reed, Christian
HRO:	Lemelin, Steven
MGT:	Aycock, Barbara
PAO/ADV:	Finver, Frank
POL/MIL:	Jones, Deby
POSHO:	Hutchinson, Vicki
SDO/DATT:	Ruffing, John D (Boone)
TREAS:	Cohen, Carol
AMB:	Charge Beecroft, Robert
CON:	Garrote, Michael
DCM:	Silliman, Douglas
PAO:	Ziff, Benjamin
RSO:	Hunter, Mark
AFSA:	Nelson, Lynn
AGR:	Salmon, David G
CLO:	Parmentier, Marina
ECON:	Zate, Steven
EEO:	Nelson, Lynn
FMO:	Osborne, Kathi
IMO:	Keegan, Howard
IPO:	Clayton, Donald
ISO:	Kane, Mike
ISSO:	Owens, Kenya
LEGATT:	Anderson, Scott R
POL:	Godfrey, Anthony

BASRAH (CG) U.S. Consulate General, Basrah, Iraq, 1-240-553-0650, Workweek: Mon-Thur, Sat 8:00-5:00, Sun 12:00-5:00 Closed Friday, Website: http://iraq.usembassy.gov/

CG OMS:	Mary Ann Durham
CON/POL/ECON:	Ryan Alexander
FM:	David Stewart
MGT:	David Chinn
OMS:	Susan Bidou (Rso)

POSHO:	David Stewart
CG:	William Grant
PAO:	Brent Maier
GSO:	Dennis McCann
RSO:	Steven Jones
AID:	Garret Harries
ECON:	Anton Smith
IPO:	Kim Long
LEGATT:	Vacant
POL:	Mark Rincon

ERBIL (CG), (240) 553-0590, Workweek: Sun-Thurs/8-1700, Website: http://erbil.usconsulate.gov/

CA:	William Quick
CG OMS:	Georgette Corral
MGT:	Marco Sims
NAS/INL:	Kim Krhounek
POL/ECON:	Steve Gee
SDO/DATT:	LTC Tim Maynard
CG:	Paul Sutphin
PAO:	Jinnie Lee
GSO:	Roinel Arriola
RSO:	Tom Colin
AID:	Ken Maclean
IPO:	Tim Demerse
LEGATT:	Damian Bricko

KIRKUK (C) U.S. Embassy Office, Kirkuk, Iraq, 240 553 0590 VoIP (No operator, see Opennet GAL for extensions), INMARSAT Tel 873 763 603 853, Workweek: Saturday–Thursday 8 am–8 pm, Website: http://iraq.usembassy.gov/

MGT:	John Marten
RSO:	Mike Rohlfs
IPO:	Naseem Ioane
ISSO:	Naseem Ioane

TRAVEL

Consular Information Sheet

December 17, 2012

Country Description: Iraq is a parliamentary democracy located in the Middle East with a population of over 31 million people. Iraq held parliamentary elections in March 2010 and has a coalition government. Iraq is a country with a developing infrastructure and extremely limited tourist facilities. Iraqi forces have full responsibility for providing security in Iraq. The Government of Iraq (GOI) has made significant political, economic, and security progress in recent years, but the country still faces many challenges. Those challenges include overcoming three decades of war and government mismanagement that stunted Iraq's economy; sectarian and ethnic tensions that have slowed progress toward national reconciliation; and ongoing criminal and terrorist violence. The slight decline and leveling off in the number of insurgent attacks and overall improvements in security have spurred economic growth in Iraq; however, conditions in the country remain dangerous.

Smart Traveler Enrollment Program (STEP)/Embassy Locations: If you are going to live in or visit Iraq, we strongly encourage you to register with the Smart Traveler Enrollment Program (STEP). If you enroll, we can keep you up to date with important safety and security announcements. It will also help your friends and family get in touch with you in an emergency.

U.S. citizens who choose to visit or reside in Iraq despite the Department of State's Travel Warning are urged to take responsibility for their own personal security and belongings (including their U.S. passports); avoid crowds, especially rallies or demonstrations; and to inform the U.S. Embassy of their presence in Iraq. A list of private security companies is available on the U.S. Embassy website. The Embassy takes substantial security precautions when moving personnel. State Department guidance to U.S. businesses in Iraq advises the use of Protective Security Details (PSDs).

In addition to the Embassy in Baghdad, the U.S. Mission in Iraq includes Consulates General in Basrah and Erbil, and a Consulate inKirkuk. These constituent posts do not offer routine consular services for U.S.citizens. The full range of consular services typically provided at U.S. embassies and consulates (passports, notarials, and Consular Reports of Birth Abroad, among others) are currently available only at Embassy Baghdad.

U.S. Embassy Baghdad
Located in the International Zone
Telephone: 240-553-0581, ext. 4293 or 2413 (U.S. dial numbers that ring in Baghdad).

U.S. Citizen Emergency After-hours Telephone: 011-964-770-443-1286 from the U.S. or 0770–443-1286 from within Iraq (for emergency matters involving U.S. citizens that cannot wait until normal business hours only).Visa questions will not be answered on this phone.

Constituent Posts
U.S. Consulate General Basrah
Basrah, Iraq (near Basrah International Airport)
U.S. citizens in Basrah requiring emergency assistance, should call the U.S. Embassy in Baghdad at 0770–443-1286 or from the U.S. 011-964-770-443-1286.

U.S. Consulate General Erbil
413 Ishtar, Ankawa
Erbil, Iraq
Telephone: 0770–443-4396
Email: ErbilACS@state.gov

U.S. Consulate for Kirkuk
KirkukPublicAffairs@state.gov
Website:
http://kirkuk.usconsulate.gov/

U.S. citizens who have questions are encouraged to contact the American Citizens Services (ACS) Unit via e-mail whenever possible. ACS strives to answer all inquiries within one business day.

The International Zone (IZ) is a restricted-access area. Iraqi authorities control access to the IZ. U.S. citizens seeking to enter the IZ to obtain consular services at the U.S. Embassy should email the American Citizens Services unit for IZ entry information.

Entry/Exit Requirements for U.S. Citizens: Entry and exit requirements for foreign citizens in Iraq, as stipulated by the Iraqi Ministry of Interior (MOI) require all U.S. citizens tohold passports valid for at least six months after dates of travel. Visas are required for all U.S. citizens. An Iraqi visa may be obtained through the Iraqi Embassy in Washington, D.C. Visas are available upon arrival at the port of entry only if the traveler receives prior visa approval in the form of an Entry Visa Approval Memorandum from the Ministry of Interior Residency Office. Travelers who obtain this approval must enter Iraq within 90 days of the issuance of the memorandum for a single entry visa or within 6 months of the issuance of the memorandum for a multi entry visa. Once admitted into the country, visitors must obtain an arrival sticker and submit a blood sample taken by the Iraq Ministry of Health within 10 days of entry. Arriving passengers are reminded of this requirement upon admission.

The Government of Iraq's requirements for entry and residency for U.S. government contractors differ. Persons traveling to Iraq to work on U.S. government contracts should check with their contracting company and contracting officer's representative to determine entry and residency procedures and requirements.

Visitors who plan to stay for more than 10 days must also obtain a residency stamp. Visitors who exceed the 10-day period will be fined USD $125. Diplomatic and official passport holders have up to 30 days to obtain a residency stamp. In Baghdad, the arrival stickers and residency stamps are available for all visitors at the main Residency Office near the National Theater.

There is a USD $40 penalty (subject to change) for visitors who do not obtain the required residency stamp. A U.S. citizen who plans to stay longer than two months must apply at the Residency Office for an extension. U.S. citizens traveling to Iraq for the purpose of employment should check with their employers and with the Iraqi Embassy in Washington, D.C. for any special entry or exit requirements related to employment. Contractors receive an Iraqi visa tied specifically to the contract and will be in violation of Iraqi immigration law if found to be violating the terms of the visa, including by overstaying.

U.S. citizens must also obtain an exit stamp at a Residency Office before departing the country. In Baghdad, they are available for all visitors at the main Residency Office near the National Theater. Contractors in the IZ may also obtain exit stamps at the Karadah Mariam Police Station (available Sunday and Wednesday, 10:00-14:00). In Basrah, the Residency Office is located on Kuwait Street in Ashar. Exit stamp fees vary from USD $20 to USD $200, depending on length of stay, type of entry visa, and other factors. Travelers who hold a tourist passport with no visa or an expired visa are required to purchase an exit visa for USD $80 and pay a fine of USD $45 for a total of USD $125. Visitors who arrive via official aircraft but depart on commercial airlines must pay USD $82 single entry visa departure fee at the airport. Visitors who intend to return to Iraq will require a re-entry visa, also available through a local residency office.

As of the date of this report, immigration officials in the Iraqi Kurdistan Region (IKR) were routinely allowing U.S. citizens to enter Iraq without a valid Iraqi visa; however, the airport-issued IKR visa is not valid outside the IKR, and U.S. citizens are not permitted to travel within the rest of Iraq with only the IKR-issued visa. This visa is valid only in the IKR for a period of 10 days. U.S. citizens who plan to stay for longer than 10 days require an extension to their visa; this can be obtained by visiting the local residency office. In addition, it is difficult for U.S. citizens to obtain residency authorization outside the IKR without first obtaining a valid Iraqi visa.

Iraq recognizes dual nationality. Travellers to Iraq should check the MFA's website and the Ministry of Interior's website for the most current information about rights and responsibilities regarding dual citizens and their stay in Iraq.

Iraq has imposed HIV/AIDS travel restrictions on all visitors. At this time, there is no waiver available for this ineligibility. Please verify this information with the Embassy of Iraq before you travel. There are legal restrictions on the transfer of currency outside Iraq. Transporting large amounts of currency is not advisable. Iraqi law prohibits adult Iraqis and foreigners from holding and transporting more than USD $10,000 in cash out of Iraq. In addition, adult Iraqi and resident foreigners may hold and transport out of the country no more than 200,000 Iraqi dinars to cover travel expenses. Iraqi law also prohibits taking more than 100 grams of gold out of the country. Iraqi customs personnel are taking action to enforce these laws and may pose related questions to travelers during immigration and customs exit procedures. (Civil customs personnel also will verify passport annotations related to any items such as foreign currency, gold jewelry, or merchandise that were declared by passengers upon entry into Iraq on Form-8.)

For additional details, please consult the website for the General Commission for Customs (available in English).If you are detained at the airport or at any other point of exit regarding your attempt to transfer currency out of Iraq, you should contact, or ask that Iraqi authorities immediately contact, the U.S. Embassy.

Visit the Embassy of Iraq for the most current visa information. The Embassy of Iraq is located at 3421 Massachusetts Ave, NW, Washington, DC 20007; phone number is 202-742-1600; fax number is 202-333-1129.

Threats to Safety and Security: Some regions within Iraq have experienced fewer violent incidents than others in recent years, in particular the Iraqi Kurdistan Region (IKR). However, violence and threats against U.S. citizens persist. While violence and threats against U.S. citizens have lessened in the past six months, threats of attack against U.S. citizens in Iraq continue. U.S. citizens in Iraq remain at risk for kidnapping. Methods of attack in the past have included roadside improvised explosive devices (IEDs), including Explosively Formed Penetrators (EFPs); magnetic IEDs placed on vehicles; human and vehicle-borne IEDs, mines placed on or concealed near roads; mortars and rockets, and shootings using various direct fire weapons. Numerous insurgent groups, including Al Qaida in Iraq, remain active throughout Iraq. Although Iraqi Security Forces (ISF) operations against these groups continue, terrorist activity persists in many areas of the country. While sectarian and terrorist violence occurs at levels lower than in previous years, it occurs often, particularly in the provinces of Baghdad, Ninewa, Salahad Din, Anbar, and Diyala.

The security situation in the Iraqi Kurdistan Region (IKR), which includes the provinces of Sulymaniya, Erbil, and Dohuk, has been more stable relative to the rest of Iraq in recent years, but threats remain. U.S. government personnel in northern Iraq are required to be accompanied by a protective security detail when traveling outside secure facilities. Although there have been significantly fewer terrorist attacks and lower levels of insurgent violence in the IKR than in other parts of Iraq, the security situation throughout the country remains dangerous. Increasingly, many U.S. and third-country business people travel throughout much of Iraq; however, they do so under restricted movement conditions and almost always with security advisors and teams.

The Turkish military continues to carry out operations against elements of the Kongra-Gel terrorist group (formerly Kurdistan Workers' Party or PKK) located along Iraq's northern border. Additionally, extensive unmarked minefields remain along the same border. The Governments of Turkey and Iran continue to carry out military operations against insurgent groups in the mountain regions bordering Iraq. These operations have included troop movements and both aerial and artillery bombardments. U.S. citizens should avoid areas near the Turkish or Iranian borders because of these ongoing military operations. Borders in these areas are not always clearly defined. In 2009, three U.S. citizens were detained by Iranian authorities while hiking in the vicinity of the Iranian border in the Kurdistan region. The resources available to the U.S. Embassy to assist U.S. citizens who venture close to or cross the border with Iran are extremely limited. The Department of State discourages travel in close proximity to the Iranian border.

The U.S. government considers the potential threat to U.S. government personnel in Iraq to be serious enough to require them to live and work under strict security guidelines. All U.S. government employees under the authority of the U.S. Chief of Mission must follow strict safety and security procedures when traveling outside the Embassy. State Department guidance to U.S. businesses in Iraq advises the use of protective security details. Detailed security information is available at the U.S. Embassy website.

Stay up to date by:

- Bookmarking our Bureau of Consular Affairs website, which contains the current Travel Warnings and Travel Alerts as well as the Worldwide Caution.
- Following us on Twitter and the Bureau of Consular Affairs page on Facebook as well.
- Downloading our freeSmart Traveler Appavailable through iTunes and the Android market to have travel information at your fingertips.
- Taking some time before travel to consider your personal security.
- Travelers are also referred to the U.S. Embassy Baghdad's Messages for U.S. Citizens, which are available on the U.S. Embassy Baghdad's website. Detailed security information is available on the U.S. Embassy Baghdad's website.

Crime: Petty theft is common in Iraq; this includes pick-pocketing in busy areas (e.g. markets), as well as the theft of money, jewelry, or other valuables from hotel rooms. Historically, carjacking by armed thieves has been very common, even during daylight hours, and particularly on the highways from Jordan and Kuwait to Baghdad. Both foreigners - especially dual American-Iraqi citizens - and Iraqi citizens are targets of kidnapping. Kidnappers often demand money but have also carried out kidnappings for political/religious reasons. Many hostages have been killed.

Do not buy counterfeit and pirated goods, even if they are widely available. Not only are the bootlegs illegal in the United States, if you purchase them you may also be breaking local law.

Victims of Crime: If you or someone you know becomes the victim of a crime abroad, you should contact the local police and the nearest U.S. embassy or consulate. We can:

- Replace a stolen passport.
- Help you find appropriate medical care if you are the victim of violent crimes such as assault or rape.
- Put you in contact with the appropriate police authorities, and if you want us to, we can contact family members or friend.
- Help you understand the local criminal justice process and direct you to local attorneys, although it is important to remember that local authorities are responsible for investigating and prosecuting the crime.

The local equivalent to the "911" emergency line in Iraq is "130" from both mobile and fixed line telephones. Please note that responders do not speak English.

Criminal Penalties: While you are traveling in Iraq, you are subject to its laws even if you are a U.S. citizen. Foreign laws and legal systems can be vastly different than our own. In some places you may be taken in for questioning if you do not have your passport with you. In some places, driving under the influence could land you immediately in jail. Criminal penalties will vary. There are also some things that might be legal in the country you visit, but still illegal in the United States, for example, you can be prosecuted under U.S. law if you buy pirated goods. Engaging in sexual conduct with children or using or disseminating child pornography in a foreign country is a crime prosecutable in the United States.If you break local laws in Iraq, your U.S. passport will not help you avoid arrest or prosecution. It is very important to know what is legal and what is not wherever you go. Persons violating Iraq's laws, even unknowingly, may be expelled, arrested, or imprisoned.

Penalties for the possession, use, or trafficking of illegal drugs in Iraq are severe, and convicted offenders may anticipate long jail sentences and heavy fines, and in some cases may be subject to the death penalty.

U.S. citizens should avoid unauthorized photography, especially of Iraqi security forces, which is strictly prohibited. Iraqi military personnel may confiscate equipment and temporarily detain individuals taking unauthorized photographs. Pictures inside the International Zone are forbidden. In some places, it is illegal to take pictures of certain buildings.

While some countries will automatically notify the nearest U.S. embassy or consulate if a U.S. citizen is detained or arrested, that might not always be the case. To ensure that the United States is aware of your circumstances, request that the police and prison officials notify the nearest U.S. embassy or consulate as soon as you are arrested or detained overseas.

Special Circumstances: The ability of the U.S. Embassy to provide consular services to U.S. citizens outside Baghdad is particularly limited given the security environment. Host government emergency services and support are limited.

Iraq continues to suffer from serious problems in all public services. Many areas have only a few hours of electricity per day; many families supplement their state-provided electricity through local cooperatives that share generators.

Travelers should be aware that Iraqi fire and rescue services are still developing, and hotels may not be fully equipped with fire safety equipment. When staying in a hotel, you should request a room on a lower floor and make sure you have identified the exits nearest your room.

Telephone (landline) service is very limited; however, calls may be made from hotels, restaurants, and shops. While cellular service (mobile wireless) has expanded rapidly into urban areas, reliability can vary by region. Even in urban areas, users may frequently experience dropped calls. Internet service is available through Internet cafes, but broadband Internet service to homes is currently limited. Please be aware that large wire transfers may require Central Bank of Iraq approval due to measures in place to combat money laundering. Such approvals can be obtained by the sending bank if a customer provides information on the origin of the funds and the reason for their transfer. Additional information on banking in Iraq is available on the Central Bank of Iraq's website.

Customs officers have the broad authority to search persons or vehicles at Iraqi ports of entry. Officers may confiscate any goods they deem may pose a threat to the peace, security, health, environment, or social order of Iraq. Antiquities or cultural items suspected of being illegally exported may also be confiscated, as with goods that are not declared. Visitors may also be ordered to return such goods, at their expense, to the jurisdiction from which they came. The banking and financial infrastructure is in the process of rebuilding. Hotels usually require payment in foreign currency. Automatic Teller Machines (ATMs) are extremely rare in most of Iraq, but the Trade Bank of Iraq (TBI) provides ATM services in dinars and USD at its main branch in central Baghdad. The work week in Iraq is Sunday through Thursday.

Accessibility: While in Iraq, individuals with disabilities may find accessibility and accommodation very different from what you find in the United States. The law prohibits discrimination against persons with disabilities in employment, education, access to health care, and other state services. The government enforces the law in the public sector, but not in the private sector. Access for persons with disabilities to buildings and in educational and work settings remains inconsistent. Public and government buildings, as well as public bathrooms, may not be accessible.

Medical Facilities and Health Information: Basic modern medical care and medicines are not widely available in Iraq. Conflict has left some medical facilities non-operational and medical stocks and supplies severely depleted. The facilities in operation do not meet U.S. standards, and the majority lack medicines, equipment, and supplies. Some private companies facilitate medical evacuations.

Blood banks exist in Iraq, though blood supply may not be sufficient in the event of an emergency. In addition, many areas suffer rolling power outages and generators are not always available for back-up. You can find detailed information on vaccinations and other health precautions on the CDC website. For information about outbreaks of infectious diseases abroad, consult the World Health Organization (WHO) website. The WHO website also contains additional health information for travelers, including detailed country-specific health information.

Tuberculosis is an increasingly serious health concern in Iraq. For further information, please consult the CDC's information on TB.

Medical Insurance: You cannot assume that your insurance will cover you when you travel. It is very important to find out BEFORE you leave whether or not your medical insurance will cover you overseas. You need to ask your insurance company two questions:

- Does my policy apply when I am out of the United States?
- Will it cover emergencies like a trip to a foreign hospital or a medical evacuation?

In many places, doctors and hospitals will expect payment in cash at the time of service. Your regular U.S. health insurance may not cover doctors' and hospital visits in other countries. If your policy does not cover you when you travel, it is a very good idea to take out another one for your trip.

Traffic Safety and Road Conditions: While in Iraq, U.S. citizens may encounter road conditions that differ significantly from those in the United States. Vehicular travel in Iraq can be extremely dangerous. There have been attacks on civilian vehicles as well as Iraqi military and security convoys on roads and highways throughout Iraq, both in and outside metropolitan areas. Attacks occur throughout the day, but travel at night is more dangerous and should be avoided. Such attacks have been random and unpredictable, and have involved small arms fire and Improvised Explosive Devices (IEDs) capable of destroying the average vehicle. Travel throughout the country by road involves the significant potential for attacks. While Baghdad has seen the majority of insurgent activity over the past year, significant incidents have also occurred in outlying cities, indicating a high risk to travelers on roadways. Anyone traveling by vehicle through Iraq should consider the risk of IED attacks carefully and plan accordingly. Buses run irregularly and frequently change routes. Poorly-maintained city transit vehicles are often involved in accidents. Long-distance buses are available, but are often in poor condition and drive at unsafe speeds. Jaywalking is common. Drivers usually do not yield to pedestrians at crosswalks and ignore traffic lights (if available), traffic rules, andregulations. Roads are congested. Some cars do not use lights at night and urban street lights may not be functioning. Some motorists drive at excessive speeds, tailgate, and force other drivers to yield the right of way.

Aviation Safety Oversight: There is no direct commercial air service to the United States by carriers registered in Iraq, the U.S. Federal Aviation Administration (FAA) has not assessed the Government of Iraq's Civil Aviation Authority for compliance with International Civil Aviation Organization (ICAO) aviation safety standards. The FAA maintains prohibitions on certain flight operations within Iraq by U.S. commercial operaters and airmen under a Special Federal Aviation Regulation, however beginning January 7, 2013 these prohibitions do not apply to the airports at Erbil (ORER) or Sulaymaniyah (ORSU).

Children's Issues: The U.S. Embassy has encountered multiple cases of female U.S. citizens whose Iraqi-born husbands will not allow them or their children to depart Iraq; in certain cases, their husbands have withheld U.S. travel documents to prevent them and their children from leaving the country. The U.S. Embassy will seek to assist U.S. citizens in these situations, but Iraqi family law differs substantially from U.S. law, and individuals in these situations may find it difficult to obtain legal relief. Please see the U.S. Dept. of State Office of Children's Issues web pages on intercountry adoption and international parental child abduction.

Travel Warning

August 9, 2012

The Department of State warns U.S. citizens against all but essential travel to Iraq given the security situation. Travel within Iraq remains dangerous. This Travel Warning replaces the Travel Warning dated January 19, 2012, to update information on security incidents and to remind U.S. citizens of ongoing security concerns for U.S. citizens in Iraq, including kidnapping and terrorist violence. The United States completed its withdrawal of military forces from Iraq as of December 31, 2011. The ability of the Embassy to respond to situations where U.S. citizens face difficulty, including arrests, is extremely limited.

Some regions within Iraq have experienced fewer violent incidents than others in recent years, in particular the Iraqi Kurdistan Region (IKR). Although violence and threats against U.S. citizens persist, reported instances have lessened in the past six months. U.S. citizens in Iraq also remain at risk for kidnapping. Methods of attack have, in the past, included roadside improvised explosive devices (IEDs), including explosively formed penetrators (EFPs); magnetic IEDs placed on vehicles; human and vehicle-borne IEDs, mines placed on or concealed near roads; mortars and rockets, and shootings using various direct fire weapons.

Numerous insurgent groups, including Al Qaida in Iraq, remain active throughout Iraq. Although Iraqi Security Forces (ISF) operations against these groups continue, terrorist activity persists in many areas of the country. While terrorist violence occurs at levels lower than in previous years, it occurs frequently, particularly in the provinces of Baghdad, Ninewa, Salah ad Din, Anbar, and Diyala.

The security situation in the Iraqi Kurdistan Region (IKR), which includes the governorates of Sulymaniya, Erbil, and Dohuk, has been more stable relative to the rest of Iraq in recent years, but threats remain. U.S. government personnel in northern Iraq are required to be accompanied by a protective security escort when traveling outsidesecure facilities.

Although there have been significantly fewer terrorist attacks and lower levels of insurgent violence in the IKR than in other parts of Iraq, the security situation throughout the IKR remains dangerous. Increasingly, many U.S. and third-country business people travel throughout much of Iraq; however, they do so under restricted movement conditions and almost always with security advisors and teams. U.S. citizens should avoid areas near the Turkish or Iranian borders. The Turkish military continues to carry out operations against elements of the Kongra-Gel terrorist group (KGK, formerly Kurdistan Workers' Party or PKK) located along Iraq's northern border. Additionally, extensive unmarked minefields remain along the same border. The Governments of Turkey and Iran continue to carry out military operations against insurgent groups in the mountain regions.

These operations have included troop movements and both aerial and artillery bombardments. Borders in these areas are not always clearly defined. Iranian authorities previously detained, for an extended period, U.S. citizens who were hiking in the vicinity of the Iranian border in the IKR. The resources available to the U.S. Embassy to assist U.S. citizens who venture close to or cross the border with Iran are extremely limited. The U.S. Embassy is located in the International Zone (IZ) in Baghdad. The IZ is a restricted access area. Iraqi authorities are responsible for control of the IZ. Travelers to the IZ should be aware that Iraqi authorities may require special identification to enter the IZ or may issue IZ-specific access badges. Individuals residing and traveling within the IZ should continue to exercise good personal safety precautions.

The U.S. government considers the potential threat to U.S. government personnel in Iraq to be serious enough to require them to live and work under strict security guidelines. All U.S. government employees under the authority of the U.S. Chief of Mission must follow strict safety and security procedures when traveling outside the Embassy. State Department guidance to U.S. businesses in Iraq advises the use of protective security details. Detailed security information is available at the U.S. Embassy website. The ability of the U.S. Embassy to provide consular services to U.S. citizens throughout Iraq, including Baghdad, is particularly limited given the security environment. The U.S. Consulates in Basrah Erbil, and Kirkuk cannot provide routine services such as passport applications, extra visa pages, and Consular Reports of Birth Abroad. U.S. citizens in need of these services while in Iraq must travel to the U.S. Embassy in Baghdad. The Embassy's website (http://iraq.usembassy.gov) includes consular information and the most recent messages to U.S. citizens in Iraq. U.S. citizens in Iraq who are in need of emergency assistance should call 0770–443-1286.

For information on "What the Department of State Can and Can't Do in a Crisis," please visit the Bureau of Consular Affairs' Emergencies and Crisis link at www.travel.state.gov. Up-to-date information on security can also be obtained by calling 1-888-407-4747 toll-free in the United States and Canada or, for callers outside the United States and Canada, on a regular toll line at 1-202-501-4444. These numbers are available from 8:00 a.m. to 8:00 p.m. Eastern Daylight Time, Monday through Friday (except U.S. federal holidays). U.S. citizens who choose to visit or reside in Iraq despite this Travel Warning are urged to take responsibility for their own personal security and belongings (including their U.S. passports) and to avoid crowds, especially rallies or demonstrations. U.S. citizens who choose to travel in Iraq should be aware that Iraqi authorities have arrested or detained U.S. citizens whose purpose of travel is not readily apparent. Persons also have been detained for taking photographs of buildings, monuments, or other sites, especially in the IZ in Baghdad.

The Government of Iraq is strictly enforcing requirements regarding visas and stamps for entry and exit; vehicle registration; authorizations for weapons and movements through check points, as well as other matters. This list is subject to revision.

The Embassy highly recommends that all U.S. citizens in Iraq carefully review the status of their government documents and any necessary licenses and government authorizations to ensure that they are current and valid. U.S. citizens are urged to immediately correct any deficiencies in their government documents. U.S. citizens are strongly advised against traveling throughout the country with deficient or invalid documents.

All U.S. citizens in Iraq, including those working on contract for the U.S. government, are urged to inform the U.S. Embassy of their presence in Iraq by enrolling in the Smart Traveler Enrollment Program (STEP) at www.travel.state.govin order to obtain updated travel information. By enrolling, U.S. citizens make it easier for the Embassy to provide updated security information or to contact them in emergencies. U.S. citizens may obtain the latest security information or other information about Iraq by contacting the U.S. Embassy, located in the International Zone, via email, or by accessing U.S. Embassy Baghdad's website. The after-hours emergency numbers are 011-964-770-443-1286 (from the United States) or 0770–443-1286 (within Iraq). As cell phone service is unreliable in Iraq, emergency calls may also be placed through the Department of State at 1-888-407-4747.

Intercountry Adoption

May 2011

Iraq is not party to the Hague Convention on Protection of Children and Co-operation in Respect of Intercountry Adoption (Hague Adoption Convention). Therefore, when the Hague Adoption Convention entered into force for the United States on April 1, 2008, intercountry adoption processing for Iraq did not change. The Department of State does not maintain files on the adoption process in Iraq because adoptions from Iraq are rare; fewer than five adoptions by American citizen parents have taken place since 2000. Islamic Law does not allow for adoption as it is recognized in the United States; rather, they allow for "guardianship." American Citizens interested in adopting from Iraq are encouraged to read more about Islamic Law.

IRELAND

Compiled from publications that were available as of February 2013 from the U.S. Department of State, the U.S. Department of Commerce, and the Central Intelligence Agency (CIA). See the introduction to this set for explanatory notes.

Official Name:
Republic of Ireland

PROFILE

Geography

Area: total: 70,273 sq km; country comparison to the world: 120; land: 68,883 sq km; water: 1,390 sq km
Major cities: Dublin (capital) 1.084 million (2009)
Climate: temperate maritime; modified by North Atlantic Current; mild winters, cool summers; consistently humid; overcast about half the time
Terrain: mostly level to rolling interior plain surrounded by rugged hills and low mountains; sea cliffs on west coast

People

Nationality: noun: Irishman(men), Irishwoman(women), Irish (collective plural); adjective: Irish
Population: 4,722,028 (July 2012 est.)
Population growth rate: 1.112% (2012 est.)
Ethnic groups: Irish 87.4%, other white 7.5%, Asian 1.3%, black 1.1%, mixed 1.1%, unspecified 1.6% (2006 census)
Religions: Roman Catholic 87.4%, Church of Ireland 2.9%, other Christian 1.9%, other 2.1%, unspecified 1.5%, none 4.2% (2006 census)
Languages: English (official, the language generally used), Irish (Gaelic or Gaeilge) (official, spoken mainly in areas along the western coast)
Literacy: definition: age 15 and over can read and write; total population: 99%; male: 99%; female: 99% (2003 est.)
Health: life expectancy at birth: total population: 80.32 years; male: 78.07 years; female: 82.69 years (2012 est.); Infant mortality rate: total: 3.81 deaths/1,000 live births; male: 4.2 deaths/1,000 live births; female: 3.41 deaths/1,000 live births (2012 est.)
Unemployment rate: 14.6% (2012 est.)
Work force: 2.104 million (2012 est.)

Government

Type: republic, parliamentary democracy
Independence: 6 December 1921
Constitution: adopted 1 July 1937 by plebiscite; effective 29 December 1937
Political subdivisions: 29 counties and 5 cities
Suffrage: 18 years of age; universal

Economy

GDP (purchasing power parity): $191.5 billion (2012 est.); $183.9 billion (2011 est.); $182.6 billion (2010 est.); $183.4 billion (2009 est.)
GDP real growth rate: 0.7% (2012 est.); 0.7% (2011 est.); -0.4% (2010 est.); -7% (2009 est.)
GDP per capita (PPP): $41,700 (2012 est.); $40,100 (2011 est.); $40,900 (2010 est.); $41,100 (2009 est.)
Natural resources: natural gas, peat, copper, lead, zinc, silver, barite, gypsum, limestone, dolomite
Agriculture products: barley, potatoes, wheat; beef, dairy products
Industries: pharmaceuticals, chemicals, computer hardware and software, food products, beverages and brewing; medical devices
Exports: $113.6 billion (2012 est.); $118.7 billion (2011 est.); $110.1 billion (2010 est.)
Exports—commodities: machinery and equipment, computers, chemicals, medical devices, pharmaceuticals; food products, animal products
Exports—partners: US 22.3%, UK 16.2%, Belgium 15.3%, Germany 7.1%, France 5.7%, Switzerland 4.2% (2011)
Imports: $63.1 billion (2012 est.); $68 billion (2011 est.); $61.63 billion (2010 est.)
Imports—commodities: data processing equipment, other machinery and equipment, chemicals, petroleum and petroleum products, textiles, clothing

Imports—partners: UK 39.8%, US 13%, Germany 7.8%, Netherlands 5.8% (2011)

Debt—external: $2.352 trillion (30 September 2011); $2.283 trillion (31 December 2010)

Exchange rates: euros (EUR) per US dollar; 0.7838 (2012 est.) ; 0.7194 (2011 est.); 0.755 (2010 est.); 0.7198 (2009 est.); 0.6827 (2008 est.); 0.7345 (2007 est.)

PEOPLE

The Irish people are mainly of Celtic origin, with the country's only significant sized minority having descended from the Anglo-Normans.

National/Racial/Ethnic Minorities

The Irish people are mainly of Celtic origin, with the country's only significant sized minority having descended from the Anglo-Normans.

According to the 2006 census, 22,369 persons identified themselves as members of an indigenous nomadic group called Travellers, with a distinct history and culture. Despite applicable antidiscrimination laws and longstanding government policies to redress imbalances, Travellers faced societal discrimination and occasionally were denied access to education, employment, premises, facilities, and basic services. However, Travellers also received substantial funding from the government, particularly for education and housing.

Language

There are two official languages in Ireland-Irish and English. While English is used predominantly, the Irish language, Gaelic, can be heard in the western part of the country and found on signage around the country. English is used for business contracts and correspondence; however, some expressions and terms may have different meanings from those in the United States.

Anglo-Irish writers such as Swift, Sheridan, Goldsmith, Burke, Wilde, Joyce, Yeats, Shaw, and Beckett have made a major contribution to world literature over the past 300 years, with four Irish writers having won the Nobel Prize for Literature.

Religion

According to the 2011 census, the religious affiliation of the population is 84.1 percent Catholic, 2.8 percent Church of Ireland, 1.07 percent Muslim, 0.99 percent Orthodox Christian, 0.90 percent unspecified Christian, 0.53 percent Presbyterian, less than 0.1 percent Jewish, and 5.88 percent unaffiliated.

Christian and Muslim Africans, Muslims from North Africa and the Middle East, Muslims and Hindus from South Asia, and Orthodox Christian communities in particular continued to grow, especially in larger urban areas.

HISTORY

The earliest inhabitants—people of a mid-Stone Age culture—arrived about 6000 BC. About 4,000 years later, tribes from southern Europe arrived and established a high Neolithic culture, leaving behind gold ornaments and huge stone monuments. The Bronze Age people, who arrived during the next 1,000 years, produced elaborate gold and bronze ornaments and weapons.

The Iron Age arrived abruptly in the fourth century BC with the invasion of the Celts, a tall, energetic people who had spread across Europe and Great Britain in the preceding centuries. The Celts, or Gaels, and their more numerous predecessors divided into five kingdoms in which, despite constant strife, a rich culture flourished.

The coming of Christianity from across the Irish Sea brought major changes and civilizing influences. Tradition maintains that St. Patrick arrived on the island in AD 432 and, in the years that followed, worked to convert the Irish to Christianity. The pagan druid tradition collapsed before the spread of the new faith, and Irish scholars excelled in the study of Latin learning and Christian theology in the monasteries that flourished. Missionaries went forth from Ireland to England and the continent, spreading news of the flowering of learning, and scholars from other nations came to Irish monasteries. The excellence and isolation of these monasteries helped preserve Latin and Greek learning during the Dark Ages. The arts of manuscript illumination, metalworking, and sculpture flourished and produced such treasures as the Book of Kells, ornate jewelry, and the many carved stone crosses that dot the island.

Two hundred years of Viking invasion and settlement was later followed by a Norman conquest in the 12th century. The Norman conquest resulted in the assimilation of the Norman settlers into Irish society. The early 17th century saw the arrival of Scottish and English Protestants, sent as colonists to the north of Ireland and the Pale around Dublin.

In 1800 the Irish parliament passed the Act of Union with Great Britain, and Ireland was an official part of the United Kingdom until 1921. Religious freedom, outlawed in the 18th century, was restored in 1829, but this victory for the Irish Catholic majority was overshadowed by a severe economic depression and the great famine of 1846–48 when the potato crop failed. Millions died, and millions more emigrated, spawning the first mass wave of Irish emigration to the United States. A decade later, in 1858, the Irish Republican Brotherhood (IRB—also known as the Fenians) was founded as a secret society dedicated to armed rebellion against the British. An above-ground political counterpart, the Home Rule Movement, was created in 1874, advocating constitutional change for independence. Galvanized by the leadership of Charles Stewart Parnell, the party was able to force British governments after 1885 to introduce several home rule bills. The turn of the century witnessed a surge of interest in Irish nationalism, including the founding of Sinn Fein ("Ourselves Alone") as an open political movement.

Nationalism was and is a potent populist force in Irish politics. A home rule bill was passed in 1914, but its implementation was suspended until war in Europe ended. Believing the mantra: "England's problem is Ireland's opportunity," and tapping into a mood of Gaelic revivalism, Padraic Pearse and James Connolly led the unsuccessful Easter Rising of 1916. Pearse and the other 1916 leaders declared an independent Irish republic, but a lack of popular support doomed the rebellion, which lasted a week and destroyed large portions of Dublin. The decision by the British military government to execute the leaders of the rebellion, coupled with the British Government's threat of conscripting the Irish to fight in the Great War, alienated public opinion and produced massive support for Sinn Fein in the 1918 general election. Under the leadership of Eamon de Valera, the elected Sinn Fein deputies constituted themselves as the first Dail. Tensions only increased: British attempts to smash Sinn Fein ignited the Anglo-Irish War of 1919–1921.

The end of the war brought the Anglo-Irish treaty of 1921, which established the Irish Free State of 26 counties within the British Commonwealth and recognized the partition of the island into Ireland and Northern Ireland, although this was supposedly a temporary measure. The six predominantly Protestant counties of northeast Ulster—Northern Ireland—remained a part of the United Kingdom with limited self-government. A significant Irish minority repudiated the treaty settlement because of the continuance of subordinate ties to the British monarch and the partition of the island. This opposition led to further hostilities—a civil war (1922–23), which was won by the pro-treaty forces.

In 1932, New York-born Eamon de Valera, the political leader of the forces initially opposed to the treaty, became Prime Minister, and a new Irish constitution was enacted in 1937. The last British military bases were soon withdrawn, and the ports were returned to Irish control. Ireland was neutral in World War II. The government formally declared Ireland a republic in 1948; however, it does not normally use the term "Republic of Ireland," which tacitly acknowledges the partition, but refers to the country simply as "Ireland."

GOVERNMENT AND POLITICAL CONDITIONS

Ireland is a multiparty parliamentary democracy with an executive branch headed by a prime minister, a bicameral parliament (Oireachtas), and a directly elected president. The country held free and fair parliamentary and presidential elections in February 2011.

Recent Elections

Observers reported that the parliamentary and presidential elections were free and fair. Political parties could operate without restriction or outside interference.

Participation of Women and Minorities: There were 25 women in the 166-seat parliament (Dail Eireann) and 18 in the 60-seat senate (Seanad Eireann). The outgoing president of the republic was a woman, as were two of the 15 government ministers. There were two female candidates for the presidency. The chief justice of the Supreme Court, the director of public prosecutions, and the attorney general were women. There were no minorities in the lower house, the senate, or the cabinet.

Principal Government Officials

Last Updated: 1/31/2013

Pres.: **Michael D. HIGGINS**
Taoiseach (Prime Min.): **Enda KENNY**
Dep. Prime Min.: **Eamon GILMORE**
Min. for Agriculture, Food, & the Marine: **Simon COVENEY**
Min. for Arts, Heritage, & Gaeltacht Affairs: **Jimmy DEENIHAN**
Min. for Children: **Frances FITZGERALD**
Min. for Communications, Energy, & Natural Resources: **Pat RABBITTE**
Min. for Defense: **Alan Joseph SHATTER**
Min. for Education & Skills: **Ruairi QUINN**
Min. for Enterprise, Jobs, & Innovation: **Richard BRUTON**
Min. for Environment, Community, & Local Govt.: **Phil HOGAN**
Min. for Finance: **Michael NOONAN**
Min. for Foreign Affairs & Trade: **Eamon GILMORE**
Min. for Health: **James REILLY**
Min. for Justice & Equality: **Alan Joseph SHATTER**
Min. for Public Expenditure & Reform: **Brendan HOWLIN**
Min. for Social Protection: **Joan BURTON**
Min. for Transport, Tourism, & Sport: **Leo VARADKAR**
Attorney Gen.: **Maire WHELAN**
Governor, Central Bank of Ireland: **Patrick HONOHAN**
Ambassador to the US: **Michael COLLINS**
Permanent Representative to the UN, New York: **Anne ANDERSON**

ECONOMY

Ireland is a small, modern, trade-dependent economy. Ireland was among the initial group of 12 EU nations that began circulating the euro on 1 January 2002. GDP growth averaged 6% in 1995–2007, but economic activity has dropped sharply since the onset of the world financial crisis, with GDP falling by over 3% in 2008, nearly 7% in 2009, and less than 1% in 2010.

Ireland entered into a recession in 2008 for the first time in more than a decade, with the subsequent collapse of its domestic property and construction markets. Property prices rose more rapidly in Ireland in the decade up to 2007 than in any other developed economy. Since their 2007 peak, average house prices have fallen 47%. In the wake of the collapse of the construction sector and the downturn in

consumer spending and business investment, the export sector, dominated by foreign multinationals, has become a key component of Ireland's economy. Agriculture, once the most important sector, is now dwarfed by industry and services. In 2008 the COWEN government moved to guarantee all bank deposits, recapitalize the banking system, and establish partly-public venture capital funds in response to the country's economic downturn. In 2009, in continued efforts to stabilize the banking sector, the Irish Government established the National Asset Management Agency (NAMA) to acquire problem commercial property and development loans from Irish banks. Faced with sharply reduced revenues and a burgeoning budget deficit, the Irish Government introduced the first in a series of draconian budgets in 2009. In addition to across-the-board cuts in spending, the 2009 budget included wage reductions for all public servants.

These measures were not sufficient. In 2010, the budget deficit reached 32.4% of GDP - the world's largest deficit, as a percentage of GDP - because of additional government support for the banking sector. In late 2010, the former Cowen Government agreed to a $112 billion loan package from the EU and IMF to help Dublin further increase the capitalization of its banking sector and avoid defaulting on its sovereign debt.

Since entering office in March 2011, the Kenny government has intensified austerity measures to try to meet the deficit targets under Ireland's EU-IMF program. Ireland achieved moderate growth of 1.4% in 2011 and cut the budget deficit to 9.1% of GDP. Although the recovery slowed in 2012 because of weaker EU demand for Irish exports, Dublin managed to trim the deficit to about 8.5% of GDP.

Labor Conditions

The law prohibits employment of children under age 16 in full-time jobs. However, employers may hire children ages 14 or 15 for light work on school holidays as part of an approved work experience or educational program. Employers may hire children over age 15 on a part-time basis during the school year. The law establishes rest intervals and maximum working hours, prohibits the employment of 18-year-olds for late night work, and requires employers to keep detailed records of workers under age 18. The Office of the Labor Inspectorate at the Department of Enterprise, Trade, and Employment is responsible for enforcement and was generally effective. The government implemented laws and policies to protect children from exploitation in the workplace, and these laws were effectively enforced.

The national minimum hourly wage was 8.65 euros ($11.20). Approximately 6 percent of the population is below the poverty level for a family in Ireland; the official poverty rate was 10,831 euros ($14,080) a year. During 2011 reports persisted that the pay of foreign migrant workers was at times below the minimum wage, particularly in the rural agricultural and construction sectors.

Laws establishing and regulating wage levels do not explicitly cover foreign migrant workers. The standard workweek is 39 hours. The law limits industrial sector to nine hours per day and 48 hours per week. The law limits overtime work to two hours per day, 12 hours per week, and 240 hours per year. The government effectively enforced these standards. Although there is no statutory entitlement, premium pay for overtime could be arranged between employer and employee.

The gray or informal market for labor is small. While largely undocumented and not reported, the agriculture and services sectors have historically had the most informal labor representation. However, recent reports indicated that the underground economy, which encompassed everything from narcotics to cash-only employment, may be growing as the country deals with a prolonged economic slump.

U.S.-IRISH RELATIONS

U.S. relations with Ireland have long been based on common ancestral ties and shared values, and emigration has been a foundation of the U.S.-Irish relationship. Besides regular dialogue on political and economic issues, the U.S. and Irish Governments have official exchanges in areas such as medical research and education.

With Ireland's membership in the European Union (EU), discussions of EU trade and economic policies as well as other aspects of EU policy have also become key elements in the U.S.-Irish relationship. Irish citizens have continued a common practice of taking temporary residence overseas for work or study, mainly in Australia, the U.S., Canada, the United Kingdom (U.K.), and elsewhere in Europe. Along with an increased interest in long-term emigration, there has been a surge of interest in "mid-term" emigration for 3-5 years, which has been mirrored in Irish Government interest in a specialized extended-stay visa for mid-career professionals to live/work in the U.S.

The U.S. J-1 visa program is popular means for Irish youths to work temporarily in the United States; a bilateral program expansion in 2008 that provides further opportunities for recent graduates to spend up to 1 year in the United States has been undersubscribed. A high priority of the Irish Government is the need to find a legal remedy for those Irish living out of status in the United States. Regarding Northern Ireland, which is part of the United Kingdom, "Nationalist" and "Republican" groups seek a united Ireland that includes Northern Ireland, while "Unionists" and "Loyalists" want Northern Ireland to remain part of the United Kingdom. U.S. priorities continue to be supporting the peace process and devolved political institutions in Northern Ireland and encouraging the implementation of the U.S.-brokered 1998 Belfast Agreement, also known as the Good Friday Agreement, and the 2006 St. Andrews Agreement.

U.S. Assistance to Ireland

The International Fund for Ireland (IFI), created in 1986, provides funding for projects to generate cross-community engagement and economic opportunity in Northern Ireland (the United Kingdom) and the border counties of Ireland. Since the IFI's establishment, the U.S. Government has contributed over $500 million, roughly half of total IFI funding. The other major donor to IFI is the European Union.

Bilateral Economic Relations

Economic and trade ties are an important facet of overall U.S.-Irish relations. U.S. exports to Ireland include electrical components and equipment, computers and peripherals, drugs and pharmaceuticals, and livestock feed.

Irish exports to the United States include alcoholic beverages, chemicals and related products, electronic data processing equipment, electrical machinery, textiles and clothing, and glassware. U.S. firms year after year account for over half of Ireland's total exports. U.S. investment has been particularly important to the growth and modernization of Irish industry over the past 25 years, providing new technology, export capabilities, and employment opportunities.

There are approximately 600 U.S. subsidiaries in Ireland that employ roughly 100,000 people and span activities from manufacturing of high-tech electronics, computer products, medical supplies, and pharmaceuticals to retailing, banking, finance, and other services. In more recent years, Ireland has also become an important research and development center for U.S. firms in Europe.

Ireland's Membership in International Organizations

Ireland and the United States belong to a number of the same international organizations, including the United Nations, Organization for Security and Cooperation in Europe, Organization for Economic Cooperation and Development, International Monetary Fund, World Bank, and World Trade Organization. Ireland is also a member of the North Atlantic Treaty Organization's (NATO) Partnership for Peace program.

Bilateral Representation

Ireland maintains an embassy in the United States at 2234 Massachusetts Ave. NW, Washington, DC 20008 (tel. 202-462-3939). Ireland also maintains consulates general in Atlanta, Boston, Chicago, New York, and San Francisco.

Principal U.S. Embassy Officials

Last Updated: 1/14/2013

DUBLIN (E) 42 Elgin Road, Ballsbridge, Dublin 4, +353-1-668-8777, Fax +353-1-668-2896, Workweek: 8:30 am–5:00 pm, Website: http://dublin.usembassy.gov/

DCM OMS:	Stacy Elliott
AMB OMS:	Vacant
DHS/CBP:	Matt Davies
DHS/ICE:	Joe Trias/London
DHS/TSA:	Craig Lynes/London
FCS:	Vacant
FM:	Ed Eng
HRO:	Stephanie Arnold
MGT:	Greg Morrison
POL/ECON:	Mark Erickson
SDO/DATT:	LTC Sean Cosden
AMB:	Daniel M. Rooney
CON:	Kees Davison
DCM:	John Hennessey-Niland
PAO:	Susan Cleary
GSO:	Ann Granatino
RSO:	Stephen Marquette
AGR:	Daryl Brehm/Paris
CLO:	Heather Sanchez
DEA:	William Fallen/London
EEO:	Kerry Hyre
FAA:	Roberto Gonzalez/London
FMO:	Stephanie Arnold
IMO:	William Mincks
IPO:	Leo Ruiz
IRS:	Kelli Winegardner/London
ISSO:	Leo Ruiz
LEGATT:	Deron Roberts/London
POL:	Lynne Gadkowski
State ICASS:	Bradley Wilde

TRAVEL

Consular Information Sheet

June 11, 2012

Country Description: Ireland is a highly developed democracy with a modern economy. Tourist facilities are widely available. The global economic downturn affected the Irish economy severely and resulted in the end of a prolonged property market boom and problems within the domestic banking system.

Smart Traveler Enrollment Program (STEP)/Embassy Locations: If you are going to live in or visit Ireland, please take the time to tell our embassy about your trip. If you enroll in the Smart Traveler Enrollment Program, we can keep you up to date with important safety and security announcements. It will also help your friends and family get in touch with you in an emergency.

U.S. Embassy Dublin
42 Elgin Road
Ballsbridge
Dublin 4
Telephone: 353-1-668-8777
Emergency after-hours telephone: 353-1-630-6200
Facsimile: 353-1-668-8056

Entry/Exit Requirements for U.S. Citizens: You will need your valid passport to enter Ireland, but you will not need a visa for tourist or business stays of up to three months. Visit the Embassy of Ireland website for the most current visa information. You may also contact the Irish Embassy at 2234 Massachusetts Avenue, NW, Washington, DC 20008, Tel: 1-202-462-3939, or the Irish consulate nearest you; these are located in Boston, Chicago, New York, San Francisco and Atlanta.

Irish Immigration strictly enforces national immigration laws and regulations. You will be expected to present all documentation relating to the purpose of your trip to Ireland to the Irish Immigration officer upon your entry into Ireland. Irish Immigration may grant a stay of up to three months; however, they may grant a lesser period than three months depending on the documentation provided. I n the past two years, an increased number of U.S. citizens have been refused entry or have been granted limited stays because they failed to comply with and/or satisfy Irish immigration laws. S ome cases have also involved other EU states' immigration authorities when U.S. citizens traveling from Ireland to another EU state have been deported back to Ireland due to visa-related matters.

The U.S. Department of State is unaware of any HIV/AIDS entry restrictions for visitors to or foreign residents of Ireland.

Threats to Safety and Security: Travelers should exercise sound personal safety practices to minimize their chance of becoming a victim. Travelers should be aware of their surroundings and avoid unlit, non-tourist areas, public demonstrations and showing signs of affluence.

Northern Ireland is part of the United Kingdom. The political situation in Northern Ireland has improved substantially since the days of the "Troubles." Nevertheless, the Police Service of Northern Ireland assesses the dissident republican threat in Northern Ireland to be severe. Attacks by violent dissident groups primarily have focused on police and military targets.

Recent attacks have targeted the private vehicles and homes of security personnel, police stations, and other justice sector buildings, increasing the potential for travelers to be caught in the wrong place at the wrong time. U.S. citizens traveling to Northern Ireland should remain alert to their surroundings and should be aware that if they choose to visit potential flashpoints or attend parades, sporadic violence remains a possibility.

Tensions may be heightened during the summer marching season (April to August), particularly during the month of July (around the July 12th public holiday). Travelers to Northern Ireland should consult the Country Specific Information for the United Kingdom and Gibraltar

Stay up to date by:

- Bookmarking our Bureau of Consular Affairs website, which contains the current Travel Warnings and Travel Alerts as well as the Worldwide Caution;
- Following us on Twitter and the Bureau of Consular Affairs page on Facebook;
- Downloading our free Smart Traveler iPhone App to have travel information at your fingertips;

- Calling 1-888-407-4747 toll-free within the U.S. and Canada, or a regular toll line, 1-202-501-4444, from other countries; and,
- Taking some time before travel to consider your personal security.

Crime: Ireland's national police, An Garda Síochána, is responsible for law and immigration enforcement in Ireland. Although Ireland has a low rate of violent crime, there is a high incidence of petty crime in major tourist areas—namely theft, burglary, and purse-snatching. And these types of crime have been on the rise over the past several years. Thieves often target rental cars and tourists, particularly in the vicinity of tourist attractions. In rare cases, purse- and bag-snatching have involved physical assault or violence, especially in Dublin. Take extra caution to guard your passport and wallet. We recommend you leave your passport in a secure location separate from your purse or luggage. Do not leave your drinks unattended at bars or restaurants, as there have been some instances of drinks being spiked with illegal substances, leading to incidents of robbery and sexual assaults. Please practice personal vigilance during your stay in Ireland.

ATM Fraud: Crimes involving automated teller machines (ATMs) are also a concern. Protect your PIN at all times and look closely at ATMs for evidence of tampering before use. Ireland has seen an increase in the use of "skimmers" on ATMs, especially in tourist areas. Skimmers are usually small electronic devices that are attached to the outside of an ATM in order to steal the ATM or credit card data. Most ATMs in Ireland now have signs or electronic warnings that advise customers to look closely at the ATM for evidence of tampering before using. Be aware that in busy areas, thieves use distraction techniques such as waiting until the PIN has been entered and then pointing to money on the ground or asking for loose change.

While the ATM user is distracted, another person will quickly withdraw the cash and leave. If you are distracted in any way, cancel the transaction immediately. If the machine does not return your card, report the incident to the issuing bank right away.

Internet scams: Online fraud scams have increased in recent years and travelers should verify through local authorities, family or friends, the authenticity of any solicited or unsolicited requests for assistance. If you receive an email from family or friends requesting assistance, we advise you to try first to contact the loved one at the last known phone number and/or to verify the story/circumstances with a neutral third party you know and trust before sending any funds. You should view with skepticism any unsolicited invitations to travel to Ireland to collect winnings or an inheritance.

There are no licenses or fees required when transiting Irish airports, emergency medical treatment is never withheld pending payment of fees, and hotels in Ireland will not detain guests for lack of funds without involving the police. A claim that a hospital or hotel will not let someone depart until the bill is settled is usually a sign of a scam. Do not buy counterfeit and pirated goods, even if they are widely available. Not only are the bootlegs illegal to bring back into the United States, you may be breaking local law, too.

Victims of Crime: If you or someone you know becomes the victim of a crime abroad, you should contact the local police and the nearest U.S. embassy or consulate. We can:

- Replace a stolen passport;
- Help you find appropriate medical care if you are the victim of a violent crime such as assault or rape;
- Put you in contact with the appropriate police authorities, and if you want us to, we can contact family members or friend; and,
- Help you understand the local criminal justice process and direct you to local attorneys, although it is important to remember that local authorities are responsible for investigating and prosecuting the crime.

The Irish Tourist Assistance Service (ITAS) is a free nationwide service offering support and assistance to tourists who are victimized while visiting Ireland. If you are a tourist victim of crime, report the incident to the nearest Garda Station (police station), which will contact ITAS. All tourist victims are referred to ITAS by the police.

The local equivalent to the "911" emergency line in Ireland is 999 and/or 112. The number 112 is used throughout the EU and is accessible from any phone, free of charge.

Criminal Penalties: While you are traveling in Ireland, you are subject to local laws even if you are a U.S. citizen. Foreign laws and legal systems can be vastly different from our own. If you break local laws in Ireland, your U.S. passport won't help you avoid arrest or prosecution. It is very important to know what's legal and what's not where you are going. In some circumstances, driving under the influence could land you immediately in jail. These criminal penalties will vary from country to country. There are also some things that might be legal in the country you visit, but still illegal in the United States. Engaging in sexual conduct with children or using or disseminating child pornography in a foreign country is a crime prosecutable in the United States.

Persons violating Ireland's laws, including its tough drunk-driving rules, even unknowingly, may be arrested, imprisoned and/or deported. Penalties for possessing, using, or trafficking illegal drugs in Ireland are severe, and convicted offenders can expect long jail sentences and heavy fines.

Arrest notifications in host country: Based on the Vienna Convention on Consular Relations, bilateral agreements with certain countries, and customary international law, if you are arrested in Ireland you have the option to request that the police, prison officials, or other authorities alert the U.S. Embassy of your arrest, and to have communications from you forwarded to the Embassy.

Special Circumstances: Most Irish banks will not accept U.S. $100 bills. Many Irish financial institutions have recently stopped accepting or cashing traveler's checks. Credit cards are widely accepted throughout Ireland. ATMs are widely available, but some, particularly in rural areas, may not accept debit cards from U.S. banks.

Some airlines have advised their passengers that their passport must remain valid for six months after their entry into Ireland; however, the Government of Ireland states that this is a recommendation of the airline industry and is not an Irish legal requirement. Travelers must be in possession of a valid passport to enter Ireland.

Accessibility: While in Ireland, individuals with disabilities may find accessibility and accommodation very different from what you find in the United States. Irish law requires access to public buildings for persons with disabilities, and this requirement is enforced. Under Irish law, public service providers should ensure the service is accessible to those with mobility, sensory, and/or cognitive impairments. Significant changes have been made in recent years to having an accessible public transportation system. People who live in Ireland and meet the medical conditions of a disability allowance may apply for free travel passes; there is also a blind/invalidity pension from the Irish Department of Social Protection for those who qualify. The majority of buses and trains in the main city areas of Ireland are now equipped for those with limited-mobility, sight, or hearing disabilities, although some train stations and pathways may not be as easily accessible. Local authorities and commercial premises such as shopping outlets have no legal obligation to provide external disabled parking facilities for their customers; however, on-street parking, public building parking lots, and internal parking lots always have a certain number of disabled spaces available. Mainline and suburban trains require special portable ramps to permit boarding from the platforms to the carriages. These are available at all terminal points and major junctions and stations that have staff on duty. They are also available on some trains. Travelers are advised to contact the local railway station in advance to ensure such facilities are available. The website for Dublin Bus provides information on its travel assistance scheme. Regional and intercity bus services are provided by Bus Eireann.

All service providers at state airports are required to have specific facilities for air travelers with disabilities. Air travelers are advised to notify the airline/airport authority in advance if they require any specific facilities. There are many resources available online for those with mobility, sensory and cognitive impairments traveling to, or living in Ireland. You may contact our consular office at acsdublin@state.gov for further information on this topic.

Medical Facilities and Health Information: Modern medical facilities and highly skilled medical practitioners are available in Ireland, but due to high demand, access to medical specialists and admissions to hospitals for certain non-life-threatening medical conditions may result in extensive waiting lists. It is not unusual for emergency room (ER) services to be very busy or for post-treatment admissions to include a long wait (sometimes overnight) on a gurney in a hallway rather than in a shared or private room.

Over-the-counter medications of most types are available, but many U.S. brands are not. (Ask the pharmacist about substitutes.) Some medications available over the counter in the United States may require a prescription in Ireland. Irish pharmacists may not be able to dispense medication prescribed by U.S. physicians and may direct you to obtain a prescription from an Irish doctor before providing your required medication.

If you are traveling to Ireland and may require medical treatment while in the country, consult your personal physician prior to traveling. A list of Irish general practitioners in each area of Ireland may be obtained from the website of the Irish College of General Practitioners. Emergency services usually respond quickly. Good information on vaccinations and other health precautions can be found via the Centers for Disease Control and Prevention (CDC) website. For information about outbreaks of infectious diseases abroad, consult the World Health Organization (WHO) website, which also contains additional health information for travelers, including detailed country-specific health information.

Medical Insurance: You can't assume your insurance will go with you when you travel. It's very important to find out BEFORE you leave whether or not your medical insurance will cover you overseas. You need to ask your insurance company two questions:

- Does my policy apply when I'm out of the United States?
- Will it cover emergencies like a trip to a foreign hospital or a medical evacuation?

In many places, doctors and hospitals still expect payment in cash at the time of service. Your regular U.S. health insurance may not cover doctor and hospital visits in other countries. If your policy doesn't go with you when you travel, it's a very good idea to take out another one for your trip.

Traffic Safety and Road Conditions: Motorists drive on the left side of the road in Ireland, and road conditions can differ significantly from those in the United States. If you do not have experience driving on the left, you should be especially cautious as tourists driving on the incorrect side of the road are the cause of several serious accidents each year. Most intersections in Ireland use circular "roundabouts" instead of signals, and it is important that motorists pay close attention to signs and yield the right of way to those already in the roundabout. At signals, turning on red is illegal; you must wait for either a full green (any direction turn permitted) or directional green light (which could be straight, left, or right). Most rental cars in Ireland have manual transmission; it can be difficult to find automatic transmission rental cars.

Road conditions are generally good, but once you exit the main highways, country roads are likely to be narrow, uneven, and winding. Roads are more dangerous during the summer and on holiday weekends due to increased traffic. Police periodically set up road blocks to check for drunk drivers. Penalties for driving under the influence can be severe.

You may use your existing U.S. driving license in Ireland for a temporary stay; this can be for any period of time up to a maximum of one year. Some insurance and car rental companies may request an International Driving Permit in addition to your existing driving license. Should you wish to apply for an International Driving Permit, please contact the American Automobile Association. You are required to apply for an Irish driving license if you become a resident of Ireland.

More information on driving in Ireland can be found on the U.S. Embassy Dublin's website. For specific information concerning Irish driving permits, vehicle inspection, road tax and mandatory insurance, please visit the official tourism guide for Ireland.

Taxi rates vary with time of day and location. Ask your hotel or innkeeper for the number of a call-dispatched taxi service if you plan to be out during less busy times. Bus service in the cities is generally adequate, although many buses are crowded and they frequently run late. Pay close attention to where bus stops are in both directions, as the drop-off and pick-up locations could be several blocks away from each other. Intercity bus and train services are good.

Aviation Safety Oversight: The U.S. Federal Aviation Administration (FAA) has assessed the government of Ireland's Civil Aviation Authority as being in compliance with International Civil Aviation Organization (ICAO) aviation safety standards for oversight of Ireland's air carrier operations. Further information may be found on the FAA's safety assessment page.

Children's Issues: Please see the U.S. Dept. of State Office of Children's Issues web pages on intercountry adoption and international parental child abduction.

Intercountry Adoption

November 2010

The information in this section has been edited from the latest report available as of February 2013 from the State Department Bureau of Consular Affairs, Office of Overseas Citizens Services. For more information, please read the *Intercountry Adoption* section of this book and review current reports online at http://adoption.state.gov.

Ireland ratified the Hague Convention on Protection of Children and Cooperation in Respect of Intercountry Adoption (Hague Adoption Convention) and established the new Adoption Authority of Ireland with the enactment of the Adoption Act 2010. The Hague Adoption Convention entered into force for Ireland on November 1, 2010. Prospective adoptive parents residing in Ireland who wish to adopt from another Hague Convention country, including the United States, after November 1, 2010 should contact the Adoption Authority of Ireland to learn about the Hague Convention requirements.

Adoption Authority of Ireland
Telephone from Ireland: 01-2309300
Telephone from U.S.: 011-353-1-2309300
Email: info@aai.gov.ie
Website: www.aai.gov.ie

Ireland is considered to be a receiving country, rather than a country of origin of children adopted through intercountry adoption. Only one Irish orphan has been adopted by a U.S. citizen during the past five years.

International Parental Child Abduction

January 2012

The information in this section has been edited from the latest report available as of February 2013 from the State Department Bureau of Consular Affairs, Office of Overseas Citizens Services. For more information, please read the *International Parental Child Abduction* section of this book and check for updated reports online at www.travel.state.gov/abduction.

Disclaimer: The information in this flyer relating to the legal requirements of specific foreign countries is provided for general information only. Questions involving interpretation of specific foreign laws should be addressed to foreign legal counsel.

General Information: Absent a court order, married parents in Ireland are assumed to share joint custody of any minor children. In divorce and custodial proceedings, it is rare, but not unheard of, for the father to be awarded custody. The mother of a child born out-of-wedlock in Ireland is assumed to have sole and full custody of the child. If the father's name does not appear on the birth certificate, he may have a difficult time even obtaining access to the child even though he can still be brought to court and ordered to pay child support. A U.S. court order regarding custody is not enforceable in Ireland, but will be taken into account as a courtesy, if presented to the Irish court during a custody hearing in Ireland. The child of an Irish citizen automatically acquires Irish citizenship regardless of where the birth occurred (with a few exceptions). The signatures of both parents are required on an application for an Irish passport for a minor child. If your child has a claim to Irish citizenship, you may be able to prevent the issuance of an Irish passport to your child upon presentation of a court order certified by the clerk of the court. For more information, please read the *International Parental Child Abduction* section of this book and review current reports online at www.travel.state.gov/abduction.

Passports for Minors and the Children's Passport Issuance Alert Program: For more information on these topics, see the International Parental Child Abduction section of this publication and review current reports from the U.S. Department of State at www.travel.state.gov/abduction.

The Hague Convention: The Hague Convention on the Civil Aspects of International Child Abduction (Hague Convention) came into force between the United States and the Republic of Ireland on October 1, 1991. Therefore, Hague Convention provisions for return would apply to children abducted or retained after October 1, 1991. Parents and legal guardians of children taken to the Republic of Ireland prior to October 1, 1991 may still submit applications for access/visitation to the child under the Hague Convention. All countries party to the Hague Convention have a Central Authority that is responsible for processing Hague applications. For more information, please read the *International Parental Child Abduction* section of this book and review current reports online at www.travel.state.gov/abduction. The designated Central Authority for the Republic of Ireland is the Department of Justice, Equality and Law Reform. They are located at 43/49 Mespil Road, Dublin 4, Ireland. The international telephone number is 011-353-1-667-0344 and the international telefax number is 011-353-1-667-0367. The Central Authority e-mail address is child_abduction@justice.ie.

Criminal Remedies: For information on possible criminal remedies, please contact your local law enforcement authorities, or the nearest office of the Federal Bureau of Investigation. Information is also available on the Internet at the web site of the U.S. Department of Justice, Office of Juvenile Justice and Delinquency Prevention at http://www.ojjdp.ncjrs.org. You should be aware that filing criminal child abduction charges in the United States against a taking parent could jeopardize an Irish Hague Convention case.

For further information on international parental child abduction, contact the Office of Children's Issues, U.S. Department of State at 1-888-407-4747 or visit its web site on the Internet at http://travel.state.gov/abduction.

ISRAEL

Compiled from publications that were available as of February 2013 from the U.S. Department of State, the U.S. Department of Commerce, and the Central Intelligence Agency (CIA). See the introduction to this set for explanatory notes.

Official Name:
State of Israel

PROFILE

Geography

Area: total: 20,770 sq km; country comparison to the world: 154; land: 20,330 sq km; water: 440 sq km

Major cities: Tel Aviv-Yafo 3.219 million; Haifa 1.027 million; Jerusalem (capital) 768,000 (2009)

Climate: temperate; hot and dry in southern and eastern desert areas

Terrain: Negev desert in the south; low coastal plain; central mountains; Jordan Rift Valley

People

Nationality: noun: Israeli(s); adjective: Israeli

Population: 7,590,758 (July 2012 est.)

Population growth rate: 1.541% (2012 est.)

Ethnic groups: Jewish 76.4% (of which Israel-born 67.1%, Europe/America-born 22.6%, Africa-born 5.9%, Asia-born 4.2%), non-Jewish 23.6% (mostly Arab) (2004)

Religions: Jewish 75.6%, Muslim 16.9%, Christian 2%, Druze 1.7%, other 3.8% (2008)

Languages: Hebrew (official), Arabic (used officially for Arab minority), English (most commonly used foreign language)

Literacy: definition: age 15 and over can read and write; total population: 97.1%; male: 98.5%; female: 95.9% (2004 est.)

Health: life expectancy at birth: total population: 81.07 years; male: 78.88 years; female: 83.36 years (2012 est.); Infant mortality rate: total: 4.07 deaths/1,000 live births; male: 4.25 deaths/1,000 live births; female: 3.89 deaths/1,000 live births (2012 est.)

Unemployment rate: 6.3% (2012 est.)

Work force: 3.269 million (2012 est.)

Government

Type: parliamentary democracy

Independence: 14 May 1948

Constitution: no formal constitution; some of the functions of a constitution are filled by the Declaration of Establishment (1948), the Basic Laws of the parliament (Knesset), and the Israeli citizenship law; note—since May 2003 the Constitution, Law, and Justice Committee of the Knesset has been working on a draft constitution

Political subdivisions: 6 districts (mehozot, singular—mehoz); Central, Haifa, Jerusalem, Northern, Southern, Tel Aviv

Suffrage: 18 years of age; universal

Economy

GDP (purchasing power parity): $247.9 billion (2012 est.); $238.2 billion (2011 est.); $227.5 billion (2010 est.); $217 billion (2009 est.)

GDP real growth rate: 2.9% (2012 est.); 4.7% (2011 est.); 4.8% (2010 est.); 0.8% (2009 est.)

GDP per capita (PPP): $32,200 (2012 est.); $31,400 (2011 est.); $30,600 (2010 est.); $29,800 (2009 est.)

Natural resources: timber, potash, copper ore, natural gas, phosphate rock, magnesium bromide, clays, sand

Agriculture products: citrus, vegetables, cotton; beef, poultry, dairy products

Industries: high-technology products (including aviation, communications, computer-aided design and manufactures, medical electronics, fiber optics), wood and paper products, potash and phosphates, food, beverages, and tobacco, caustic soda, cement, construction, metals products, chemical products, plastics, diamond cutting, textiles, footwear

Exports: $64.74 billion (2012 est.); $62.85 billion (2011 est.); $56.09 billion (2010 est.)

Exports—commodities: machinery and equipment, software, cut diamonds, agricultural products, chemicals, textiles and apparel

Exports—partners: US 28.8%, Hong Kong 7.9%, Belgium 5.6%, UK 5%, India 4.5%, China 4% (2011)

Imports: $77.59 billion (2012 est.); $71.93 billion (2011 est.); $58.04 billion (2010 est.)

Imports—commodities: raw materials, military equipment, investment goods, rough diamonds, fuels, grain, consumer goods

Imports—partners: US 11.8%, China 7.4%, Germany 6.2%, Belgium 6.1%, Switzerland 5.4%, Italy 4.2% (2011)

Debt—external: $104.2 billion (31 December 2012 est.); $102.3 billion (31 December 2011 est.); $106.4 billion (31 December 2010 est.)

Exchange rates: new Israeli shekels (ILS) per US dollar; 3.903 (2012 est.) ; 3.5781 (2011 est.); 3.739 (2010 est.); 3.93 (2009); 3.588 (2008); 4.14 (2007)

PEOPLE

Population and Religion

The country has a population of 7.8 million (including settlers living in the Occupied Territories), of which 5.8 million are Jews; 1.6 million are Muslims and Christians; and 322,000 are classified as "other" —mostly persons from the former Soviet Union who immigrated under the Law of Return but did not qualify as Jews according to the Orthodox Jewish definition used by the government for civil procedures, although many identify themselves as Jewish.

According to the 2009 report of the Central Bureau of Statistics (CBS), 8 percent of the Jewish population is Haredi (also known as "ultra-Orthodox"); 12 percent identify themselves as Orthodox; 13 percent describe themselves as "traditional, religious;" 25 percent say they are "traditional, not so religious;" and 42 percent describe themselves as "nonreligious/ secular" Jews, most of whom observed some Jewish traditions. About 30 percent of the country's Jewish population was born outside the country. Over 15,000 traditional and secular Jews associated themselves with the Conservative (Masorti) or Reform streams of Judaism, while a few held Reconstructionist beliefs. There is a small but growing community of approximately 20,000 Messianic Jews. Slightly more than 20 percent of the population are non-Jews, primarily ethnic Arabs. Of the country's total population, Muslims (nearly all Sunnis) constitute 16.6 percent; Christians 1.6 percent; Druze 1.6 percent; and other religious groups collectively constitute approximately 0.5 percent, including relatively small communities of Samaritans, Karaites, Jehovah's Witnesses, and Baha'is. Religious communities often are concentrated in geographical areas according to religious beliefs. The country continues to undergo demographic change owing to the higher birth rates of the Haredi community.

During the year, there were nearly 90,000 foreigners permitted to work in the country and an estimated 118,000 illegal foreign workers residing in the country. Foreign workers were members of many different religious groups, including Protestants, Roman Catholics, Orthodox Christians, Buddhists, Hindus, and Muslims.Approximately 98 percent of Palestinian residents of the Occupied Territories are Sunni Muslims. Although there is no official count, there are 51,710 Christians in the West Bank, Gaza, and East Jerusalem, according to the Diyar Consortium, a Lutheran ecumenical institution.

A majority of Christians are Greek Orthodox; the remainder consists of Armenian Orthodox, Copts, Episcopalians, Ethiopian Orthodox, Greek Catholics, Lutherans, Maronites, Roman Catholics, Syrian Orthodox, and several other Protestant denominations. Christians are concentrated primarily in Jerusalem, Ramallah, Nablus, and Bethlehem, but smaller communities exist elsewhere. A very small number of adherents of several denominations of evangelical Christians, as well as Jehovah's Witnesses, reside in the West Bank. There is also a community of approximately 400 Samaritans in the West Bank. According to local Christian leaders, Palestinian Christian emigration has accelerated since 2001, reducing the number of Christians in Jerusalem and the Occupied Territories. Lower birth rates among Palestinian Christians also contribute to their shrinking numbers.

National/Racial/Ethnic Minorities

Arab citizens of the country faced institutional and societal discrimination. Tensions between Arabs and Jews were sometimes high in areas where the two communities overlap, such as Jerusalem, the Galilee, and Negev, and in some cities with historically separate Jewish and Arab neighborhoods. The law exempts Arab citizens, except for Druze, from mandatory military service, but some serve voluntarily. Citizens who do not perform military service enjoy fewer societal and economic benefits and are sometimes discriminated against in hiring practices. Citizens generally were ineligible to work in companies with defense contracts or in security-related fields if they had not served in the military. The government managed a National Civil Service program for citizens not drafted for military service, giving Arabs, haredi Jews, Orthodox Jewish women, and others the opportunity to provide public service in their own communities and thus be eligible for the same financial benefits accorded military veterans.

Language

Hebrew and Arabic are the two official languages of Israel. English is the third and principal international language, and Russian is also prevalent. Many signs in public places are in all three languages. Most Israelis are multilingual.

Education

Education is compulsory from age 6 to 16 and is free up to age 18. The school system is organized into kindergartens, 6-year primary schools, 3-year junior secondary schools, and 3-year senior secondary schools, after which a comprehensive examination is offered for university admissions. There are seven university-level institutions in Israel, a number of regional colleges, and an Open University program.

Culture

With a population drawn from more than 100 countries on 5 continents, Israeli society is rich in cultural diversity and artistic creativity. The arts are actively encouraged and supported by the government. The Israeli Philharmonic Orchestra performs throughout the country and frequently tours abroad. The Jerusalem Symphony and the New Israel Opera also tour frequently, as do other musical ensembles.

Almost every municipality has a chamber orchestra or ensemble, many boasting the talents of gifted performers from the countries of the former Soviet Union. Israel has several professional ballet and modern dance companies, and folk dancing, which draws upon the cultural heritage of many immigrant groups, continues to be very popular.

There is great public interest in the theater; the repertoire covers the entire range of classical and contemporary drama in translation as well as plays by Israeli authors. Of the three major repertory companies, the most famous, Habimah, was founded in 1917.

Active artist colonies thrive in Safed, Jaffa, and Ein Hod, and Israeli painters and sculptors exhibit works worldwide. Israel boasts more than 120 museums, including the Israel Museum in Jerusalem, which houses the Dead Sea Scrolls along with an extensive collection of regional archaeological artifacts, art, and Jewish religious and folk exhibits. Israelis are avid newspaper readers, with more than 90% of Israeli adults reading a newspaper at least once a week. Major daily papers are in Hebrew; others are in Arabic, English, French, Polish, Yiddish, Russian, Hungarian, and German.

HISTORY

The creation of the State of Israel in 1948 was preceded by more than 50 years of efforts to establish a sovereign state as a homeland for Jews. These efforts were initiated by Theodore Herzl, founder of the Zionist movement, and were given added impetus by the Balfour Declaration of 1917, which asserted the British Government's support for the creation of a Jewish homeland in Palestine.

In the years following World War I, Palestine became a British Mandate and Jewish immigration steadily increased, as did violence between Palestine's Jewish and Arab communities. Mounting British efforts to restrict this immigration were countered by international support for Jewish national aspirations following the near-extermination of European Jewry by the Nazis during World War II. This support led to the 1947 UN partition plan, which would have divided Palestine into separate Jewish and Arab states, with Jerusalem under UN administration.

On May 14, 1948, soon after the British quit Palestine, the State of Israel was proclaimed and was immediately invaded by armies from neighboring Arab states, which rejected the UN partition plan. This conflict, Israel's War of Independence, was concluded by armistice agreements between Israel, Egypt, Jordan, Lebanon, and Syria in 1949 and resulted in a 50% increase in Israeli territory.

In 1956, French, British, and Israeli forces engaged Egypt in response to its nationalization of the Suez Canal and blockade of the Straits of Tiran. Israeli forces withdrew in March 1957, after the United Nations established the UN Emergency Force (UNEF) in the Gaza Strip and Sinai. This war resulted in no territorial shifts and was followed by several years of terrorist incidents and retaliatory acts across Israel's borders.

In June 1967, Israeli forces struck targets in Egypt, Jordan, and Syria in response to Egyptian President Nasser's ordered withdrawal of UN peacekeepers from the Sinai Peninsula and the buildup of Arab armies along Israel's borders. After 6 days, all parties agreed to a cease-fire, under which Israel retained control of the Sinai Peninsula, the Golan Heights, the Gaza Strip, the formerly Jordanian-controlled West Bank of the Jordan River, and East Jerusalem. On November 22, 1967, the Security Council adopted Resolution 242, the "land for peace" formula, which called for the establishment of a just and lasting peace based on Israeli withdrawal from territories occupied in 1967 in return for the end of all states of belligerency, respect for the sovereignty of all states in the area, and the right to live in peace within secure, recognized boundaries.

The following years were marked by continuing violence across the Suez Canal, punctuated by the 1969–70 war of attrition. On October 6, 1973—Yom Kippur (the Jewish Day of Atonement), the armies of Syria and Egypt launched an attack against Israel. Although the Egyptians and Syrians initially made significant advances, Israel was able to push the invading armies back beyond the 1967 cease-fire lines by the time the United States and the Soviet Union helped bring an end to the fighting. In the UN Security Council, the United States supported Resolution 338, which reaffirmed Resolution 242 as the framework for peace and called for peace negotiations between the parties.

In the years that followed, sporadic clashes continued along the cease-fire lines, but guided by the U.S., Egypt and Israel continued negotiations. In November 1977, Egyptian President Anwar Sadat made a historic visit to Jerusalem, which opened the door for the 1978 Israeli-Egyptian peace summit convened at Camp David by President Jimmy Carter. These negotiations led to a 1979 peace treaty between Israel and Egypt, signed by President Sadat of Egypt and Prime Minister Menachem Begin of Israel, after which Israel withdrew from the Sinai in 1982.

In the years following the 1948 war, Israel's border with Lebanon was

quiet relative to its borders with other neighbors. After the expulsion of Palestinian fighters from Jordan in 1970 and their influx into southern Lebanon, however, hostilities along Israel's northern border increased and Israeli forces crossed into Lebanon in 1978. After passage of Security Council Resolution 425, calling for Israeli withdrawal and the creation of the UN Interim Force in Lebanon peacekeeping force (UNIFIL), Israel withdrew its troops.

In June 1982, following a series of cross-border terrorist attacks and the attempted assassination of the Israeli Ambassador to the U.K., Israel invaded Lebanon to fight the forces of Yasser Arafat's Palestine Liberation Organization (PLO). The PLO withdrew its forces from Lebanon in August 1982. Israel, having failed to finalize an agreement with Lebanon, withdrew most of its troops in June 1985 save for a residual force which remained in southern Lebanon to act as a buffer against attacks on northern Israel. These remaining forces were completely withdrawn in May 2000 behind a UN-brokered delineation of the Israel-Lebanon border (the Blue Line). Hezbollah forces in Southern Lebanon continued to attack Israeli positions south of the Blue Line in the Shaaba Farms/Har Dov area of the Golan Heights.

The victory of the U.S.-led coalition in the Persian Gulf War of 1991 opened new possibilities for regional peace. In October 1991, the United States and the Soviet Union convened the Madrid Conference, in which Israeli, Lebanese, Jordanian, Syrian, and Palestinian leaders laid the foundations for ongoing negotiations designed to bring peace and economic development to the region.

Within this framework, Israel and the PLO signed a Declaration of Principles on September 13, 1993, which established an ambitious set of objectives relating to a transfer of authority from Israel to an interim Palestinian authority. Israel and the PLO subsequently signed the Gaza-Jericho Agreement on May 4, 1994, and the Agreement on Preparatory Transfer of Powers and Responsibilities on August 29, 1994, which began the process of transferring authority from Israel to the Palestinians.

On October 26, 1994, Israel and Jordan signed a historic peace treaty, witnessed by President Bill Clinton. This was followed by Israeli Prime Minister Rabin and PLO Chairman Arafat's signing of the historic Israeli-Palestinian Interim Agreement on September 28, 1995. This accord, which incorporated and superseded previous agreements, broadened Palestinian self-government and provided for cooperation between Israel and the Palestinians in several areas.

Israeli Prime Minister Yitzhak Rabin was assassinated on November 4, 1995, by a right-wing Jewish radical, bringing the increasingly bitter national debate over the peace process to a climax. Subsequent Israeli governments continued to negotiate with the PLO resulting in additional agreements, including the Wye River and the Sharm el-Sheikh memoranda. However, a summit hosted by President Clinton at Camp David in July 2000 to address permanent status issues—including the status of Jerusalem, Palestinian refugees, Israeli settlements in the West Bank and Gaza, final security arrangements, borders, and relations and cooperation with neighboring states—failed to produce an agreement.

Following the failed talks, widespread violence broke out in Israel, the West Bank, and Gaza in September 2000. In April 2001 the Sharm el-Sheikh Fact Finding Committee, commissioned by the October 2000 Middle East Peace Summit and chaired by former U.S. Senator George Mitchell, submitted its report, which recommended an immediate end to the violence followed by confidence-building measures and a resumption of security cooperation and peace negotiations. Building on the Mitchell report, in April 2003, the Quartet (the U.S., UN, European Union (EU), and the Russian Federation) announced the "roadmap," a performance-based plan to bring about two states, Israel and a democratic, viable Palestine, living side by side in peace and security. Despite the promising developments of spring 2003, violence continued and in September 2003 the first Palestinian Prime Minister, Mahmoud Abbas (Abu Mazen), resigned after failing to win true authority to restore law and order, fight terror, and reform Palestinian institutions. In response to the deadlock, in the winter of 2003–2004 Prime Minister Sharon put forward his Gaza disengagement initiative, proposing the withdrawal of Israeli settlements from Gaza as well as parts of the northern West Bank.

President George W. Bush endorsed this initiative in an exchange of letters with Prime Minister Sharon on April 14, 2004, viewing Gaza disengagement as an opportunity to move towards implementation of the two-state vision and begin the development of Palestinian institutions. In a meeting in May 2004 the Quartet endorsed the initiative, which was approved by the Knesset in October 2004.

The run-up to disengagement saw a flurry of diplomatic activity, including the February 2005 announcement of Lieutenant General William Ward and subsequently Lieutenant General Keith Dayton as U.S. Security Coordinator; the March 2005 Sharon-Abbas summit in Sharm el-Sheikh; the return of Egyptian and Jordanian ambassadors to Israel; and the May 2005 appointment of former World Bank president James D. Wolfensohn as Special Envoy for Gaza Disengagement to work for a revitalization of the Palestinian economy after disengagement.

On August 15, 2005, Israel began implementing its disengagement from the Gaza Strip, and the Israeli Defense Forces completed their withdrawal, including the dismantling of 17 settlements, on September 12. After broad recognition for Prime Minister Sharon's accomplishment at that fall's UN General Assembly, international attention quickly turned to efforts to strengthen Palestinian governance and the economy in Gaza. The United States brokered a landmark Agreement on Movement and Access between the parties in November 2005 to facilitate further progress on Palestinian economic issues. However, the terrorist organization Hamas—building on popular support for its "resistance" to Israeli occupation and a commitment to clean up the notorious corruption of the Palestinian Authority (PA)—took a majority in the January 2006 Palestinian Legislative Council (PLC) elections, with Hamas leader Ismail Haniya as Prime Minister. The Israeli leadership pledged not to work with a Palestinian government in which Hamas had a role.

Shortly following Hamas' PLC victory, the Quartet—comprised of the United States, European Union, United Nations, and Russia—outlined three basic principles the Hamas-led PA must meet in order for the U.S. and the international community to reengage with the PA: renounce violence and terror, recognize Israel, and respect previous agreements, including the roadmap. The Hamas-led PA government rejected these principles, resulting in a Quartet statement of "grave concern" on March 30, 2006 and the suspension of U.S. assistance to the PA, complete prohibition on U.S. Government contacts with the PA, and prohibition of unlicensed transactions with the PA government. The Palestine Liberation Organization (PLO) under the leadership of PLO Chairman and PA President Mahmud Abbas (Abu Mazen), by contrast, remained consistently committed to the Quartet principles.

Despite several negotiated cease-fires between Hamas and Fatah, violent clashes in the Gaza Strip—and to a lesser extent in the West Bank—were commonplace between December 2006 and February 2007 and resulted in dozens of deaths and injuries. In an attempt to end the intra-Palestinian violence, the King of Saudi Arabia invited Palestinian rivals to Mecca, and on February 9, 2007, Abbas and Hamas leader Haniya agreed to the formation of a Palestinian national unity government and a cessation of violence. Hamas' rejectionist policies and violent behavior continued despite the formation of the national unity government. In June 2007, Hamas effectively orchestrated a violent coup in Gaza. Hamas also launched scores of Qassam rockets into southern Israel in an attempt to involve Israel in the Hamas-Fatah conflict. On June 14, Palestinian Authority President Mahmoud Abbas exercised his lawful authority by declaring a state of emergency, dissolving the national unity government, and replacing it with a new government with Salam Fayyad as Prime Minister.

The Palestinian Authority (PA) government under President Abbas and Prime Minister Fayyad has no elements controlled by Hamas. The government is dedicated to pursuing a negotiated solution to the Arab-Israeli conflict, and the Quartet principles. As a result, the PA has been supported politically and financially by the international community, and engaged by Israel. The U.S. reinstated its assistance to the PA in 2007 and provides budget and development assistance as well as support for the PA's efforts to reform and improve security and rule of law in the West Bank.

In November 2007, Israeli and Palestinian leaders participated in an international conference in Annapolis, at which they committed to launch bilateral negotiations towards the establishment of a Palestinian state in the West Bank and Gaza, and the realization of Israeli-Palestinian peace. During the year that followed, Israeli Prime Minister Olmert and Palestinian Authority President Abbas and other members of their governments engaged in regular bilateral negotiations on final status issues. Although the two sides reportedly narrowed their differences on some issues, the negotiations were suspended in December 2008 when conflict broke out between Israel and Hamas in Gaza.

On December 27, 2008, in response to a sharp increase in the number and frequency of rocket attacks into Israel shortly prior to and following the formal expiration of a 6-month "calm" between Israel and Hamas, the Israel Defense Forces launched Operation Cast Lead, targeting Hamas security installations, personnel, and other facilities in the Gaza Strip. The Israeli military operation continued until January 18, 2009, when Israel and Hamas each declared a unilateral cease-fire.

On January 22, 2009, President Barack Obama named Senator Mitchell his and Secretary of State Hillary Clinton's special envoy for Middle East peace. Special Envoy Mitchell immediately traveled to the region and subsequently returned on a nearly monthly basis in an effort to help create the conditions that would support a two-state solution and to re-launch credible and productive negotiations. The President has visited Turkey, Egypt, and Saudi Arabia and hosted Prime Minister Netanyahu and numerous Arab heads of state in Washington, DC. On September 22, 2009 he hosted a trilateral meeting with Prime Minister Netanyahu and President Abbas, and he has written to over a dozen Arab heads of state asking for their assistance in ending the Arab-Israeli conflict. Senator Mitchell began indirect talks between the two parties in March 2010, and direct talks were launched on September 2, 2010 in Washington, DC. Secretary Clinton has met many leaders from the region and has traveled to the Middle East multiple times since her appointment to promote a Middle East peace settlement.

GOVERNMENT AND POLITICAL CONDITIONS

Israel is a multiparty parliamentary democracy. Although it has no constitution, Israel's parliament, the unicameral 120-member Knesset, has enacted a series of "Basic Laws" that enumerate fundamental rights. Certain fundamental laws, orders, and regulations legally depend on the existence of a "State of Emergency," which has been in effect since 1948. The Knesset has the power to dissolve the government and mandate elections. The 2009 nationwide Knesset elections, considered free and fair, resulted in a coalition government led by Prime Minister Benjamin Netanyahu. Israeli

Recent Elections

Parliamentary elections held in 2009 were considered free and fair.

Political Parties: The Basic Law prohibits the candidacy of any party or individual that denies the existence of the State of Israel as the state of the Jewish people or the democratic character of the state, or that incites racism. Otherwise, political parties operated without restriction or interference.

Participation of Women and Minorities: Women and minorities were participants in political life on the same legal basis as men or nonminority citizens. Although the senior leaders have traditionally come from the predominantly male IDF, women generally do not face cultural barriers in politics, including in leadership positions up to prime minister. Women face significant cultural barriers in political parties representing conservative religious movements and the Arab minority. At the end of 2011, the 120-member Knesset had 24 female and 14 Arab members. The 30-member cabinet included three women but no Arabs; two women and one Arab were deputy ministers. Five members of the 15-member Supreme Court, including its president, were women. One Arab was a justice of the Supreme Court.

Principal Government Officials

Last Updated: 1/31/2013

Pres.: **Shimon PERES**
Prime Min.: **Binyamin "Bibi" NETANYAHU**
Vice Prime Min.: **Silvan SHALOM**
Vice Prime Min.: **Moshe "Boogie" YAALON**
Min. of Agriculture & Rural Development: **Orit NOKED**
Min. of Communications: **Moshe KAHLON**
Min. of Culture & Sport: **Limor LIVNAT**
Min. of Defense: **Ehud BARAK**

Min. for Development of the Negev & Galilee: **Silvan SHALOM**
Min. of Economic Strategy: **Binyamin "Bibi" NETANYAHU**
Min. of Education: **Gideon SA'AR**
Min. of Environmental Protection: **Gilad ERDAN**
Min. of Finance: **Yuval STEINITZ**
Min. of Foreign Affairs: **Binyamin "Bibi" NETANYAHU**
Min. of Health: **Binyamin "Bibi" NETANYAHU**
Min. of Home Front Defense: **Avraham "Avi" DICHTER**
Min. of Housing & Construction: **Ariel ATIAS**
Min. of Immigrant Absorption: **Sofa LANDVER**
Min. of Improvement to Govt. Services: **Michael EITAN**
Min. of Industry, Trade, & Labor: **Shalom SIMHON**
Min. of Information & Diaspora Affairs: **Yuli EDELSTEIN**
Min. of Intelligence & Atomic Energy: **Dan MERIDOR**
Min. of Interior: **Eliyahu "Eli" YISHAI**
Min. of Internal (Public) Security: **Yitzhak AHARONOVITCH**
Min. of Justice: **Yaakov NEEMAN**
Min. of Minority Affairs: **Shalom SIMHON**
Min. of National Infrastructures: **Uzi LANDAU**
Min. of Pensioner Affairs: **Binyamin "Bibi" NETANYAHU**
Min. of Regional Development: **Silvan SHALOM**
Min. of Religious Services: **Yaakov MARGI**
Min. of Science & Technology: **Daniel HERSHKOWITZ**
Min. of Strategic Affairs: **Moshe "Boogie" YAALON**
Min. of Tourism: **Stas MISEZHNIKOV**
Min. of Transportation & Road Safety: **Yisrael KATZ**
Min. of Welfare & Social Services: **Moshe KAHLON**
Min. Without Portfolio: **Ze'ev Binyamin "Benny" BEGIN**
Min. Without Portfolio: **Meshulam NAHARI**
Min. Without Portfolio: **Yosef "Yossi" PELED**
Attorney Gen.: **Yehuda WEINSTEIN**
Governor, Bank of Israel: **Stanley FISCHER**
Ambassador to the US: **Michael OREN**
Permanent Representative to the UN, New York: **Ron PROSOR**

ECONOMY

Israel has a technologically advanced market economy. Its major imports include crude oil, grains, raw materials, and military equipment. Cut diamonds, high-technology equipment, and pharmaceuticals are among the leading exports. Israel usually posts sizable trade deficits, which are covered by tourism and other service exports, as well as significant foreign investment inflows. The global financial crisis of 2008–09 spurred a brief recession in Israel, but the country entered the crisis with solid fundamentals - following years of prudent fiscal policy and a resilient banking sector. The economy has recovered better than most advanced, comparably sized economies.

In 2010, Israel formally acceded to the OECD. Israel's economy also has weathered the Arab Spring because strong trade ties outside the Middle East have insulated the economy from spillover effects. Natural gas-fields discovered off Israel's coast during the past two years have brightened Israel's energy security outlook. The Leviathan field was one of the world's largest offshore natural gas finds this past decade, and production from the Tama field is expected to meet all of Israel's natural gas demand beginning mid-2013. In mid-2011, public protests arose around income inequality and rising housing and commodity prices. The government formed committees to address some of the grievances but has maintained that it will not engage in deficit spending to satisfy populist demands.

Labor Conditions

Laws provide for protection of children from exploitation in the workplace and prohibit forced or compulsory labor; the government generally enforced these laws. Children at least 14 years old may be employed during official school holidays in light work that will not harm their health. Children at least 15 years old who have completed education through grade nine may be employed as apprentices. Working hours for those children between16 and 18 years old are restricted in all sectors.

The national minimum wage was 21 NIS ($5.50) per hour; many foreign workers received less. The official poverty line was 2,413 NIS ($632) for one person per month and 5,116 NIS ($1,340) for a family of three. Persons with disabilities whose working capacity was reduced due to their disability earned between 19 and 50 percent of minimum wage. Youth below the age of 18 earned between 60 and 83 percent of the minimum wage. The law allows a maximum 43-hour workweek at regular pay and paid annual holidays. Premium pay for overtime was 125 percent for the first two hours and 150 percent for any additional hours, with a limit of 15 hours of overtime per week. Some workers, such as migrant workers in the homecare sector, were not covered by the law.

U.S.-ISRAELI RELATIONS

The United States played a key supporting role in Israel's 1948 founding, Israel and the United States are bound closely by historic and cultural ties as well as by mutual interests. Commitment to Israel's security has been a cornerstone of U.S. policy in the Middle East since Israel's creation. Israel's founding was preceded by more than 50 years of efforts to establish a sovereign state as a homeland for Jews. The1917 Balfour Declaration asserted the British Government's support for the creation of a Jewish homeland in Palestine. Palestine became a British mandate following the end of World War I (1914–1918). Immediately after the end of British mandate on May 14, 1948, the State of Israel was proclaimed, and the U.S. recognized Israel that same day. Palestinians in Palestine and neighboring Arab states rejected a 1947 UN partition plan that would have divided Palestine into separate Jewish and Arab states, and the area has seen periods of invasions and armed conflict since

1948. The broad issues of Arab-Israeli and Palestinian-Israeli peace continue to be a major focus of the U.S.-Israel relationship. The basis of U.S. efforts to reach a Middle East peace settlement includes UN Security Council Resolutions 242 and 338 and have been based on the premise that as Israel takes calculated risks for peace,, the United States will help minimize those risks.

Bilateral relations between the United States and Israel cover many areas. The two countries have a thriving two-way trade relationship and deep social and cultural connections, They participate in security dialogues, joint military planning, and combined exercises, and have collaborated on military research and weapons development. There also are bilateral science and technology efforts (including the Binational Science Foundation and the Binational Agricultural Research and Development Foundation); the U.S.-Israeli Education Foundation, which sponsors educational and cultural programs; the Joint Economic Development Group, which maintains a high-level dialogue on economic issues; the Joint Counterterrorism Group, designed to enhance cooperation in fighting terrorism; and a high-level, semi-annualStrategic Dialogue.

U.S. Assistance to Israel

U.S. security assistance to Israel acknowledges strong bilateral ties and reflects the unshakable commitment of the United States to Israel's security. Annually, the U.S. provides Israel $3.1 billion in security assistance.

Bilateral Economic Relations

The United States is Israel's largest single trading partner. The top five U.S. exports to Israel are: diamonds, machinery, agricultural products, aircraft, and optic and medical instruments. The top five U.S. imports from Israel are: include diamonds, pharmaceutical products, machinery, optic and medical instruments, and agricultural products. U.S. direct investment in Israel is primarily in the manufacturing sector, as is Israeli investment in the United States. The United States and Israel have had a free trade agreement since 1985, serving as the foundation for expanding trade and investment between the two countries by reducing barriers and promoting regulatory transparency.

Israel's Membership in International Organizations

Israel and the United States belong to a number of the same international organizations, including the United Nations, Organization for Economic Cooperation and Development, International Monetary Fund, World Bank, and World Trade Organization. Israel also is a Partner for Cooperation with the Organization for Security and Cooperation in Europe and an observer to the Organization of American States.

Bilateral Representation

Israel maintains an embassy in the United States at 3514 International Drive NW, Washington DC, 20008 (tel. 202-364-5500).

Principal U.S. Embassy Officials

Last Updated: 1/14/2013

TEL AVIV (E) 71 Hayarkon, Tel Aviv, Israel 6343229, 972-3-519-7575, Fax 972-3-517-3227, INMARSAT Tel 873-783-133-445, Workweek: M-F / 0800–1630, Website: http://telaviv.usembassy.gov/

DCM OMS: Judith Brooks
AMB OMS: Joyce E. Harley
CG OMS: Maytal Raymond-Bossem
DHS/ICE: Richard A. Jolles
FCS: Maria Andrews
FM: Sergio Tristan
HRO: Ronald Coles
MGT: Michelle M. Esperdy
POSHO: Sergio Tristan
SDO/DATT: COL Jeffrey L. Hood
AMB: Daniel B. Shapiro
CG: Lawrence J. Mire
DCM: Thomas H. Goldberger
PAO: Hilary Olsin-Windecker
GSO: Charles W. Davis
RSO: Christian J. Schurman
AFSA: David J. Cummings
AID: Michael Harvey
CLO: Michelle Tamburello
ECON: Robert W. Forden
EEO: David Cummings
EST: Ingrid Kollist
FAA: Roy Barnett (Dubai)
FMO: Dianne M. Hand
ICASS Chair: Brian Carney
IMO: Jan Cote-Cartwright
IPO: Kelley Razer
IRS: Aziz Benbrahim
ISO: Walter Yates, III
ISSO: Amanda Gilke
LEGATT: Omer Meisel
POL: Acting: Eva Anne Weigold Shultz
State ICASS: Robert W. Forden

JERUSALEM (CG) 18-20 Agronmon Rd., Jerusalem 91002; 14 David Flusser Rd. Arnona, Jerusalem 93392; 27 Nablus Rd., Jerusalem 97200, +972-2-622-7230, Fax +972-2-622-3551, Workweek: Mon-Fri 0800-1630, Website: http://jerusalem.usconsulate.gov

CG OMS: Michael Jahncke
DHS/ICE: Lance Lueck
DPO: Yael Lempert
HRO: Edwin Eustaquio
MGT: Martin Kelly
NAS/INL: Alyce Tidball
POSHO: Alfredo Biteng
CG: Michael Ratney
CON: Jeremy Cornforth
PAO: Michael Richards
GSO: Michael Longhauser
RSO: Robert Grech
AID: Karen Exel
CLO: Juliet C. Craven
ECON: Mark Johnson
FMO: Jeanne Miller
ICASS Chair: Mark Herzberg
IMO: Edward D. Jefferson
IPO: A/Ipo Stephen Craven
ISO: Ricardo Perez
POL: Jennifer Gavito
State ICASS: Douglas Haidle

TRAVEL

Consular Information Sheet

August 9, 2012

Country Description: The State of Israel is a parliamentary democracy with a modern economy. Israel occupied the West Bank, Gaza Strip, Golan Heights, and East Jerusalem as a result of the 1967 War. Pursuant to negotiations between Israel and the Palestinians, the Palestinian Authority (PA) was established in the Gaza Strip and West Bank in 1994. HAMAS, a U.S.-designated terrorist organization, took control of the Gaza Strip in June 2007 and exercises control there. The division of responsibilities and jurisdiction in the West Bank between Israel and the PA is complex and subject to change. PA security forces are responsible for keeping order in certain areas, and the PA exercises a range of civil functions in those areas of the West Bank. Official guidance on entry, customs requirements, arrests, and other matters in the West Bank and Gaza is subject to change without prior notice or may not be available. Tourist facilities are widely available with certain exceptions, including Gaza. Travelers may visit the websites of the Israeli Ministry of Tourism and the Palestinian Ministry of Tourism for tourist information.

Smart Traveler Enrollment Program (STEP)/Embassy Locations: If you are going to live or visit Israel, the West Bank, or Gaza, please take the time to tell our Embassy and/or Consulate about your trip. If you enroll, we can keep you up to date with important safety and security announcements. It will also help your friends and family get in touch with you in an emergency.

The U.S. Embassy is located at 71 Hayarkon Street in Tel Aviv. The U.S. mailing address is 9700 Tel Aviv Place, Washington, DC 20521–9700. The telephone number is (972) (3) 519-7575 Monday through Friday. The after hours emergency number on weekends and after 4:30 p.m. and before 8:00 a.m. local time on weekdays is (972) (3) 519-7551. The fax number is (972) (3) 516-4390, or 516-0315. The Embassy can be contacted by e-mail.

The Consular Section of the U.S. Embassy should be contacted for information and assistance in the following areas: Israel, the Golan Heights, and ports of entry at Ben Gurion Airport, Haifa Port, the northern (Jordan River) and southern (Arava) border crossings connecting Israel and Jordan, and the border crossings between Israel and Egypt.

A U.S. Consular Agent who reports to the Embassy in Tel Aviv maintains an office in Haifa at 26 Ben Gurion Boulevard, telephone (972) (4) 853-1470. The Consular Agent can provide both routine and emergency services in the northern part of Israel. The Consular Section of the U.S. Consulate General in Jerusalem is located at14 David Flusser, Jerusalem 93392 (Near the former Diplomat Hotel, now the Caprice Diamond Center). The U.S. mailing address is 6350 Jerusalem Place, Dulles, VA 20189–6350. The telephone number is (972) (2) 622-7230. The Consular Section's public telephone number for information and assistance is (972) (2)630-4000, Monday through Friday. For after-hours emergencies directly involving an American citizen on weekends and after 4:30 p.m. and before 8:00 a.m. local time on weekdays, calls should be directed to (972) (2) 622-7250. The Consular Section's fax number is (972) (2) 630-4070.You may contact the Consulate by e-mail.

The Consular Section of the U.S. Consulate General in Jerusalem should be contacted for information and assistance in the following areas: Jerusalem, the West Bank, the Gaza Strip, and the Allenby Bridge crossing connecting the West Bank and Jordan.

Entry/Exit Requirements for U.S. Citizens: The general entry and exit requirements for U.S. citizens traveling to Israel, the West Bank, and Gaza are listed below. U.S. citizens are advised to read all sections of this sheet very carefully for special regulations that may affect their travel.

The U.S. government seeks equal treatment and freedom to travel for all U.S. citizens regardless of national origin or ethnicity. U.S. citizens who encounter difficulties are encouraged to contact the U.S. Embassy in Tel Aviv or the U.S. Consulate General in Jerusalem by e-mail or at the numbers above.

Security Screening: U.S. citizens are advised that all persons applying for entry to Israel, the West Bank, or Gaza are subject to security and police record checks by the Government of Israel, and may be denied entry or exit without explanation.

U.S. citizen visitors have been subjected to prolonged questioning and thorough searches by Israeli authorities upon entry or departure. U.S. citizens whom Israeli authorities suspect of being of Arab, Middle Eastern, or Muslim origin; those who have been involved in missionary or activist activity; and those who ask that Israeli stamps not be entered into their passport may face additional, often time-consuming, and probing questioning by immigration and border authorities, or may even be denied entry into Israel, the West Bank, or Gaza. U.S. citizens of similar background who are suspected of wishing to enter those areas deemed prohibited to them by the Ministry of Interior (MOI) are requested by the MOI to sign a standard agreement. This agreement stipulates that they will refrain from entering those prohibited areas. U.S. citizens have been detained and/or arrested at the airport and at other border crossings on suspicion of security-related offenses. Members of religious groups have been monitored, arrested, and deported for suspicion of intent to proselytize in Israel. In some cases, Israeli authorities have denied U.S. citizens access to U.S. consular officers, lawyers, and family members during temporary detention.

Additional security-related delays are not unusual for travelers carrying audio-visual or data storage/processing equipment, and some have had their laptop computers and other electronic equipment confiscated at Ben Gurion Airport. While most items are returned prior to the traveler's departure, some equipment has been retained by the authorities for lengthy periods and has reportedly been damaged, destroyed, lost or never returned. U.S. citizens who have had personal property damaged due to security procedures at Ben Gurion may contact the Commissioner for Public Complaints at the airport for redress by fax to 972-3-9752387. Israeli security officials have also requested access to travelers' personal e-mail accounts or other social media accounts as a condition of entry. In such circumstances, travelers should have no expectation of privacy for any data stored on such devices or accounts.

U.S. citizens who feel they have been wrongly denied entry to Israel or the West Bank or unnecessarily subjected to additional security screening may contact the American Citizen Services (ACS) unit of the U.S. Consulate General in Jerusalem or the ACS unit of the U.S. Embassy in Tel Aviv.

Israeli-Americans: The Government of Israel considers U.S. citizens who also hold Israeli citizenship or have a claim to dual nationality to be Israeli citizens for immigration and other legal purposes. For example, an American citizen child of an Israeli parent will be considered an Israeli citizen by Israeli immigration officials, even if the child was born outside of Israel, and Israeli law will apply to the child's travel to and departure from Israel. U.S. citizens who are also citizens of Israel must enter and depart Israel using their current Israeli passport. Israeli citizens are currently not permitted to enter Gaza and are generally restricted from traveling to parts of the West Bank under PA control ("Area A"). Contact the Israeli Ministry of Interior or your nearest Israeli embassy or consulate for more information on citizenship and travel restrictions for Israeli citizens.

Palestinian-Americans: U.S. citizens who have a PA identification number or whom the Government of Israel considers to have residency status in the West Bank or Gaza are advised to read this section very carefully.

Israeli authorities might consider as Palestinian anyone who has a Palestinian identification number, was born in the West Bank or Gaza, or was born in the United States but has parents or grandparents who were born or lived in the West Bank or Gaza. Any such U.S. citizen might be required by the Government of Israel to travel to Israel using a PA passport. Without the PA passport, such U.S. citizens might be barred from entering or exiting Israel, the West Bank, or Gaza, or may face serious delays at the ports of entry. At the Allenby crossing between Jordan and the West Bank, however, Palestinian-Americans may depart using PA identity cards and PA exit permits, provided they have Jordanian visas in their U.S. passports.

Individuals who hold a PA ID, as well as persons judged by Israeli authorities to have claim to a PA ID by virtue of ancestry, will be considered subject to Israeli law and to regulations that Israel applies to residents of the West Bank and Gaza, regardless of whether they also hold U.S. citizenship. In most cases, such individuals will be required by Israeli authorities to enter the West Bank via the Allenby Bridge (also known as King Hussein Bridge) crossing with Jordan, rather than via Ben Gurion International Airport, unless they obtain advance permission from an Israeli embassy or consulate for that purpose. Even if they have entered Israel via Ben Gurion Airport, these individuals may be required to depart via the Allenby Bridge. Upon arrival at any of the ports of entry, such persons may wish to consider asking Israeli immigration authorities from where they will be required to depart.

Entering Israel: An onward or return ticket and proof of sufficient funds are required for entry. Although a passport valid for six months from the date of entering Israel is not required by the Government of Israel, airlines routinely require this and may prevent boarding if a traveler does not have at least six months validity on his or her passport. A no-charge, three-month tourist visa may be issued upon arrival and may be renewed. Travelers carrying official or diplomatic U.S. passports must obtain visas from an Israeli embassy or consulate prior to arrival. Anyone who has been refused entry, experienced difficulties with his/her status during a previous visit, overstayed the authorized duration of a previous visit, or otherwise violated the terms of his/her admission to Israel should consult the nearest Israeli embassy or consulate before attempting to return. Anyone seeking returning resident status must obtain permission from Israeli authorities before traveling. The Government of Israel at times has declined to admit U.S. citizens wishing to visit, work, or travel to the West Bank or Gaza. Persons denied entry who seek immigration court hearings to contest such denials may be detained for prolonged periods while awaiting a hearing.

Entering the Gaza Strip: The Department of State strongly urges U.S. citizens to avoid all travel to the Gaza Strip, which is under the control of HAMAS, a designated foreign terrorist organization. U.S. citizens in Gaza are advised to depart immediately. Travelers who enter the Gaza Strip through the Rafah crossing from Egypt must also exit through the Rafah crossing. The Israeli authorities do not permit such travelers to exit through the Erez crossing into Israel except in situations of extreme humanitarian need. Travelers entering the Gaza Strip may not be able to depart at a time of their choosing. Delays of days or weeks are common. Private vehicles may not cross from Israel into Gaza or from Gaza into Israel. The Rafah crossing between Gaza and Egypt allows for some passenger travel, though coordination with local authorities—which could take days or weeks to process—is reportedly required. U.S. citizens should be aware that as a consequence of a longstanding prohibition on travel by U.S. citizen employees of the U.S. government into the Gaza Strip, the ability of consular staff to offer timely assistance to U.S. citizens there is extremely limited, including the provision of routine consular services. Please contact the U.S. Consulate General in Jerusalem for updated guidance. See the latest Travel Warning for Israel, the West Bank, and Gaza for the latest information concerning travel to the Gaza Strip.

Entering the West Bank: The Department of State urges U.S. citizens to exercise caution when traveling to the West Bank. Please contact the U.S. Consulate General in Jerusalem for updated guidance. See the Travel Warning for Israel, the West Bank, and Gaza for the latest information concerning travel to the West Bank.

Israel-Jordan Crossings: The international crossing points between Israel and Jordan are the Arava crossing (Wadi al-'Arabah) in the south, near Eilat; and the Jordan River crossing (Sheikh Hussein Bridge) in the north, near Beit Shean. U.S. citizens using these two crossing points to enter either Israel or Jordan need not obtain prior visas, but they will be required to pay fees, which are subject to change.

Allenby Bridge (King Hussein Bridge): For detailed information, please refer to the Consulate General's web site. Visas should be obtained in advance for those wanting to cross the Allenby Bridge between Jordan and the West Bank. (Note: The Government of Israel requires that Palestinian-Americans with residency status in the West Bank enter Jordan via the Allenby Bridge.) Persons with residency status in Gaza seeking to cross the Allenby Bridge from Jordan should contact the Jordanian authorities for information concerning special clearance procedures for PA ID holders before traveling to the bridge.

Procedures for all three crossings into Jordan are subject to frequent changes. Visit the Embassy of Israel web site for the most current visa information.

The Israeli Ministry of Health imposes some HIV/AIDS entry restrictions for visitors to and foreign residents of Israel, and the Ministry of Health reserves the right to deny entry to visitors who declare their status. Please verify this information with the Embassy of Israel before you travel.

Threats to Safety and Security: Several groups operating in Israel, the West Bank, and Gaza have been designated as Foreign Terrorist Organizations (FTO) by the U.S. Department of State. FTOs include, but are not limited to, the Al-Aqsa Martyrs Brigade, Kahane Chai (Kach), and HAMAS (the Islamic Resistance Movement). It is unlawful for a U.S. citizen or a person who is located in the United States or is subject to the jurisdiction of the United States to knowingly provide material support or resources to a designated FTO.

U.S. citizens, including tourists, students, residents, and U.S. government personnel, have been injured or killed by terrorists while in Israel, the West Bank, and Gaza. Attacks have occurred in highly frequented shopping and pedestrian areas and on public buses. U.S. citizen employees of the U.S. Embassy and Consulate General and their families are prohibited from using public buses and their associated terminals. U.S. citizens should use good judgment and exercise caution when visiting public areas and using transportation facilities in order to minimize exposure to possible terrorist attacks. Strategies to minimize risk include avoiding demonstrations and large crowds; being aware of one's immediate surroundings, especially while visiting contentious religious sites, military areas, and bus stops where large groups of soldiers congregate; and by avoiding suspicious objects.

Small clashes continue to occur along the boundary of the Gaza Strip. Rockets and mortars are still fired into Israel from Gaza, and Israel continues to conduct military operations inside Gaza, including airstrikes. Israel has also declared an exclusion zone inside Gaza along its boundary with Israel and has taken lethal measures against individuals who enter the exclusion zone.In the past, some rockets have traveled more than 40 km (24 miles) from Gaza and landed as far north as Yavne and Gadera and as far east as Beersheva. As a result of possible military operations by the Government of Israel in Gaza and the ever-present risk of rocket and mortar attacks into Israel from Gaza, U.S. government personnel traveling in the vicinity of the Gaza Strip boundary, to include the city of Sderot, must make prior notification to the Embassy's Regional Security Office. U.S. citizens in the area should be aware of the risks and should take note of announcements by the Government of Israel's office of Homefront Command.

Kidnapping: In the past, armed gunmen have kidnapped foreigners, including several Americans, in Gaza and the West Bank. Gunmen have sometimes used such foreign hostages as bartering tools. The threat of hostage-taking remains a concern for U.S. citizens and foreigners within the Gaza Strip. Any U.S. citizens traveling to Gaza despite the Department of State's Travel Warning should enroll with the U.S. Consulate General in Jerusalem prior to entry and maintain a very low profile while moving within Gaza. They should also carry the telephone numbers of the U.S. Consulate General and utilize them in the event of an emergency. The ability of the U.S. Government to assist U.S. citizens in Gaza is extremely limited.

There have been multiple kidnappings of U.S. citizens in the Sinai over the past four years and kidnappings of foreign tourists in the Sinai have increased since January 2012. In May 2012, two U.S. citizens were kidnapped and released a day later; in July 2012, two U.S. citizens were kidnapped and released a few days later. While thus far all known foreign kidnapping victims have been released unharmed in 2012, the danger of overland travel in the Sinai is significant. Overland travel from Israel to the Sinai is strongly discouraged. U.S. government personnel are currently prohibited from traveling to the Sinai, except by air to Sharm El Sheikh. Overland travel by U.S. government (USG) employees anywhere in the Sinai outside of Sharm El Sheikh is prohibited.

Demonstrations and Civil Unrest: U.S. citizens are advised to avoid demonstrations. Demonstrations or altercations can occur spontaneously, and all demonstrations have the potential to become violent without warning. If such disturbances occur, U.S. citizen visitors should leave the area immediately.

U.S. citizens have been seriously injured in demonstrations that have turned violent. In Jerusalem's Old City, where exit routes are limited, U.S. citizen visitors should seek safe haven inside a shop or restaurant until the incident is over. Demonstrations can be particularly dangerous in areas such as checkpoints, settlements, military areas, and major thoroughfares where protesters are likely to encounter Israeli security forces. Within Israel, U.S. citizens should be aware that demonstrations in predominantly Arab areas and confrontations between Arab and Jewish residents in ethnically mixed towns can occur with little or no advance warning.

U.S. government personnel at the Embassy in Tel Aviv or the Consulate General in Jerusalem, whether stationed there or on temporary duty may be prohibited on occasion from traveling to sections of Jerusalem and parts of Israel and the West Bank, depending on prevailing security conditions.

Jerusalem: In Jerusalem, travelers should exercise caution at religious sites on holy days, Fridays, Saturdays, and Sundays, and dress appropriately when visiting the Old City and ultra-orthodox Jewish neighborhoods. Most roads into ultra-orthodox Jewish neighborhoods are blocked off on Friday nights, Saturdays, and Jewish holidays. Assaults on secular visitors, either for being in cars or for being "immodestly dressed," continue to occur in these neighborhoods. Isolated street protests and demonstrations can occur in the predominantly Arab commercial districts of East Jerusalem (Salah Ed-Din Street and Damascus Gate areas) during periods of unrest. U.S. government employees are prohibited from entering the Old City on Fridays during the month of Ramadan due to overall congestion and security-related access restrictions. Visitors are urged to exercise caution and be aware of their surroundings at all times. This is especially true when entering or exiting the Old City at times of high pedestrian traffic. Some tourists have reported harassment by vendors in tourist areas of Jerusalem.

West Bank: Personal travel in the West Bank for U.S. government personnel and their families is allowed in the areas described below. They may travel to Bethlehem and Jericho. They may also transit the West Bank using only Routes 1 and 90. Personal travel is also permitted to Qumran off Route 90 by the Dead Sea and all areas south of Highway 1 and east of route 90 in the Dead Sea area.

U.S. government personnel and family members are permitted both official and personal travel on Route 443 between Modi'in and Jerusalem. All other personal travel in the West Bank, unless specifically authorized for mission-approved purposes, is prohibited.

PA security forces are currently deployed in all major cities of the West Bank, and violence in these areas has decreased markedly since a series of PA security campaigns that started in 2007.Among major West Bank cities, the level of violence is lowest in Jericho, Bethlehem, and Ramallah. Bethlehem, one of the most important religious sites to members of the Christian faith, is a significant stop for many pilgrims. U.S. government employees frequently travel in the West Bank with appropriate security measures.

Gaza: Travel to the Gaza Strip by U.S. government personnel is currently prohibited. Private U.S. citizens are strongly encouraged to avoid travel to the area.

During periods of unrest, the Israeli government sometimes closes off access to the West Bank and Gaza and those areas may be placed under curfew. All persons in areas under curfew should remain indoors to avoid risking arrest or injury. U.S. citizens have been killed, seriously injured, or detained and deported as a result of encounters with Israel Defense Forces (IDF) operations in Gaza and the West Bank. Travel restrictions may be imposed with little or no warning. Strict measures have frequently been imposed following terrorist actions, and the movement of Palestinian-Americans, both those with residency status in the West Bank or Gaza as well as foreign passport holders, has been severely impeded. Due to current limitations on travel by U.S. government employees to the West Bank and Gaza made necessary by security conditions, the ability of consular staff to offer timely assistance to U.S. citizens in need in these areas is considerably reduced at present.

Golan Heights: There are live land mines in many areas of the Golan Heights, so visitors should walk only on established roads or trails. Near the northern border of Israel, rocket attacks from Lebanese territory can and have occurred without warning.

Stay up to date by:

- Bookmarking our Bureau of Consular Affairs website, which contains the current Travel Warnings and Travel Alerts as well as the Worldwide Caution.
- Following us on Twitter and the Bureau of Consular Affairs page on Facebook as well.
- Downloading our free Smart Traveler iPhone App to have travel information at your fingertips.
- Calling 1-888-407-4747 toll-free within the U.S. and Canada, or a regular toll line, 1-202-501-4444, from other countries. These numbers are available from 8:00 a.m. to 8:00 p.m. Eastern Time, Monday through Friday (except U.S. federal holidays).
- Taking some time before travel to consider your personal security.

Crime: The crime rate is moderate in Israel, the West Bank, and Gaza. Break-ins of parked vehicles are common at beach areas, the Dead Sea, cemeteries, and national parks (especially Caesarea National Park). Car break-ins and purse snatchings in cities and cemeteries occur regularly throughout Israel. U.S. citizens should not leave their valuables (including passports) unattended, in parked vehicles or unsecured in hotels.

Don't buy counterfeit and pirated goods, even if they are widely available. Not only are the bootlegs illegal in the United States, if you purchase them you may also be breaking local law.

Victims of Crime: If you or someone you know becomes the victim of a crime abroad, you should contact the local police and the nearest U.S. embassy or consulate (see the Department of State's list of embassies and consulates). We can:

- Replace a stolen passport.
- Help you find appropriate medical care if you are the victim of violent crimes such as assault or rape.
- Put you in contact with the appropriate police authorities, and if you want us to, we can contact family members or friends.

Help you understand the local criminal justice process and direct you to local attorneys, although it is important to remember that local authorities are responsible for investigating and prosecuting the crime.

The local equivalent to the "911" emergency line in Israel is 100.

The local equivalent to the "911" emergency line in the West Bank and Gaza is 101.

The Government of Israel provides assistance to victims of terrorist acts. Please contact the National Insurance Institute for more information.

Criminal Penalties: While you are traveling in Israel, the West Bank, or Gaza, you are subject to its laws even if you are a U.S. citizen. Foreign laws and legal systems can be vastly different from our own. In some places you may be taken in for questioning if you don't have your passport with you. In some places, it is illegal to take pictures of certain buildings. In some places, driving under the influence of drugs or alcohol could land you immediately in jail. Penalties for breaking the law can be more serious than those in the United States for similar offenses. Persons violating Israeli or PA laws, even unknowingly, may be arrested or imprisoned. Penalties for possession, use, or trafficking illegal drugs in Israel and PA-administered areas are severe, and convicted offenders can expect long jail sentences and heavy fines. Engaging in sexual conduct with children or using or disseminating child pornography in a foreign country is a crime prosecutable in the United States. If you break local laws in Israel, the West Bank, or Gaza, your U.S. passport won't help you avoid arrest or prosecution.

While some countries will automatically notify the nearest U.S. embassy or consulate if a U.S. citizen is detained or arrested in a foreign country, that might not always be the case. To ensure that the United States is aware of your circumstances, request that the police and prison officials notify the U.S. Embassy as soon as you are arrested or detained in Israel. If you are arrested in the West Bank or Gaza, you should use whatever means of communication available to alert the U.S. Consulate in Jerusalem of your situation.

Special Circumstances: Video cameras and other electronic items must be declared upon entry to Israel. In the past, Israeli customs and security officials have seized electronic equipment at ports of entry and prior to boarding aircraft; the equipment is usually returned, but not always expeditiously, and equipment has sometimes been returned damaged. It is advisable to contact the Embassy of Israel in Washington, DC, or one of Israel's consulates in the United States for specific information regarding customs requirements. Definitive information on customs requirements for the PA is not available.

Arrests and Detentions: U.S. citizens arrested by the Israel National Police (INP) and charged with crimes are entitled to legal representation provided by the Israeli government and to consular notification and visitation, per Vienna Convention agreement. In some cases, there are significant delays between the time of arrest and the time when the INP notifies the Embassy or Consulate General and grants consular access. This is particularly true in the arrest of dual American-Israeli and American-Palestinian citizens. The notification procedure may be expedited if the arrested U.S. citizen shows a U.S. passport to the police and asks the police or prison authority to contact the U.S. Embassy or Consulate General. When access to a detained U.S. citizen is delayed or denied, the U.S. government can protest the lack of consular access to the Israeli government.

U.S. citizens arrested by Israeli security forces for security offenses and U.S. citizens arrested by Israeli authorities in the West Bank or Gaza for criminal or security offenses may be prevented from communicating with lawyers, family members, or consular officers for lengthy periods. The U.S. Consulate General and the U.S. Embassy sometimes are not notified of such arrests or are not notified in a timely manner. Consular access to the arrested individual is frequently delayed. On occasion, arrestees have been subject to mistreatment during interrogation and pressured to sign statements. Under local law, arrestees may be detained for up to six months without charges. Youths over the age of 14 have been detained and tried as adults. The U.S. government may formally protest any report of mistreatment to the relevant authorities.

U.S. citizens arrested by PA security forces in the West Bank for crimes are entitled to legal representation and consular notification and access. PA security forces normally notify the Consulate General of non-security-related arrests for criminal offenses, but not always in a timely manner. Consular access is normally granted within four days. This procedure may be expedited if the arrested U.S. citizen shows a U.S. passport to the police or asks the police to contact the U.S. Consulate General.

Palestinian-Americans living in the West Bank may be detained or arrested by the IDF. In such instances, the Government of Israel may not recognize the detainee's U.S. citizenship and will instead consider the arrested person a Palestinian. In such cases the U.S. Consulate General may not be notified.

Dual Palestinian-American citizens arrested by PA security forces in the West Bank for security offenses may be prevented from communicating with lawyers, family members, or consular officers for lengthy periods. In addition, they may be held in custody for protracted periods without formal charges or before being brought before a judge for an arrest extension. The PA often does not notify the U.S. Consulate General of such arrests in a timely manner, and consular access to arrestees is occasionally delayed. Since HAMAS seized control of the Gaza Strip in June 2007, its Executive Forces (EF) have dominated security matters there. The U.S. government has no contact with the EF.

Dual Nationality: Israeli citizens naturalized in the United States retain their Israeli citizenship, and children born in the United States to Israeli parents usually acquire both U.S. and Israeli nationality at birth. Israeli citizens, including dual nationals, are subject to Israeli laws requiring service in Israel's armed forces, as well as other laws pertaining to passports and nationality. American-Israeli dual nationals of military age, including females, who do not wish to serve in the Israeli armed forces should contact the Israeli Embassy in Washington, D.C., to learn more about an exemption or deferment from Israeli military service and should obtain written confirmation of military service exemption or deferment before traveling to Israel. Without this exemption or deferment document, such dual nationals may not be able to depart Israel without completing military service or may be subject to criminal penalties for failure to serve. Israeli citizens, including dual nationals, must enter and depart Israel on their Israeli passports, and Israeli authorities may require persons whom they consider to have acquired Israeli nationality at birth to obtain an Israeli passport prior to departing Israel. Bearers of PA passports or identity numbers who have become naturalized U. S. citizens are considered by the Israeli government to retain their Palestinian nationality, and Israeli authorities will view them as Palestinians. Palestinian-Americans whom the Government of Israel considers residents of the West Bank or Gaza may face certain travel restrictions (see "Entry/Exit Requirements for U.S. Citizens," above). These individuals are subject to restrictions on movements between Israel, the West Bank, and Gaza and within the West Bank and Gaza that are imposed by the Israeli government on all Palestinians. Some Jerusalem ID holders who hold residency or citizenship elsewhere may encounter problems retaining their Jerusalem residence status.

During periods of heightened security concern, these travel restrictions can be onerous. Palestinian-American residents of Jerusalem are normally required to use laissez-passers (travel documents issued by the Israeli government) that contain reentry permits approved by the Israeli Ministry of Interior for any out-of-country travel. U.S. citizens who are residents of East Jerusalem and hold blue Israeli ID cards may also enter and exit Israel using their U.S. passports, provided they have a prior reentry stamp in their passports from the Israeli Interior Ministry. All U.S. citizens must enter and exit the United States on their U.S. passports.

Court Jurisdiction: Civil courts in Israel actively exercise their authority to bar certain individuals, including nonresidents, from leaving the country until monetary and other legal claims against them are resolved. Israel's religious courts exercise jurisdiction over all citizens and residents of Israel in cases of marriage, divorce, child custody and child support. In some cases, U.S. citizens who entered Israel as tourists have become defendants in divorce or custody cases filed by their spouses in Israeli religious courts. These U.S. citizens have been detained in Israel for prolonged periods while the Israeli courts consider whether the individuals have sufficient ties to Israel to establish jurisdiction. Such visitors should be aware that they might be subject to involuntary and prolonged stays in Israel if a case is filed against them in a religious court, even if their marriage took place in the United States and regardless of whether their spouse is present in Israel.

Purchases of Property: U.S. citizens who buy or lease property in the occupied territories of East Jerusalem, the West Bank, and Gaza may find their ownership challenged by people earlier displaced from those lands. Prospective property buyers should always seek legal advice before buying in these areas. The possible establishment of a Palestinian state may have legal consequences for property owners in Israeli settlements in the West Bank and in East Jerusalem.

Accessibility: While in Israel, the West Bank and Gaza, individuals with disabilities may find accessibility and accommodation very different from that in the United States. Israeli law prohibits discrimination against persons with disabilities in employment, education, and access to health care or in the provision of other state services. Legislation mandates access to buildings and transportation, as well as accommodations for persons with disabilities in services and the work place. The government enforces the laws with limited success. Societal discrimination and lack of accessibility persist in employment and housing. Television stations include subtitles or sign language, and the courts accommodate testimony from persons with intellectual disabilities or mental illness. The law mandates accessibility to urban public transportation but not interurban buses. Most train stations maintain access for persons with disabilities; however, many buses still do not have such access.

Tourists will find restaurants, foot paths, and public transportation less accessible than in the United States.

Medical Facilities and Health Information: Modern medical care and medicines are available in Israel. A few hospitals in Israel and most hospitals in the West Bank and Gaza, however, fall below Western standards. It is recommended that visitors have health insurance. Travelers can find information in English about emergency medical facilities and after-hours pharmacies in the Jerusalem Post and the English-language edition of the Ha'aretz newspaper, or refer to the Embassy's or Consulate General's medical lists.

You can find detailed information on vaccinations and other health precautions on the Centers for Disease Control's (CDC) website. For information about outbreaks of infectious diseases abroad, consult the World Health Organization (WHO) website. The WHO website also contains additional health information for travelers, including detailed country-specific health information.

Medical Insurance: You can't assume your insurance will go with you when you travel. It's very important to find out BEFORE you leave whether or not your medical insurance will cover you overseas. You need to ask your insurance company two questions:

- Does my policy apply when I'm out of the United States?
- Will it cover emergencies like a trip to a foreign hospital or a medical evacuation?
- Will it cover hospitalization in a mental health facility?

In many places, doctors and hospitals still expect payment in cash at the time of service. Your regular U.S. health insurance may not cover doctors' and hospital visits in other countries. If your policy doesn't go with you when you travel, it's a very good idea to take out another one for your trip.

Traffic Safety and Road Conditions: While in Israel, the West Bank, and Gaza, U.S. citizens may encounter road conditions that differ significantly from those in the United States. The information below concerning Israel, the West Bank, and Gaza is provided for general reference only and may not be totally accurate in a particular location or circumstance.

Israeli roads and highways tend to be crowded, especially in urban areas. Aggressive driving is commonplace, and many drivers fail to maintain safe following distances or signal before changing lanes or making turns. Overtaking on high-speed undivided two-lane roads is common and results in frequent accidents. Drivers are also prone to stop suddenly on roads without warning, especially in the right lane. Drivers should use caution, as Israel has a high rate of fatalities from automobile accidents.

U.S. citizen employees of the U.S. Embassy in Tel Aviv and the U.S. Consulate General Jerusalem and their families have been prohibited from using public buses and light rail networks. (Please review the earlier section entitled Terrorism under the section Threats to Safety and Security.)

The Government of Israel requires that all passenger car occupants use their seat belts at all times and that headlights be used during all intercity travel, both day and night, during winter. As of January 1, 2006, all drivers are required to carry fluorescent vests in the car with them at all times, and they are required to wear these vests whenever they get out of their cars to make repairs, change tires, etc. If a vehicle is stopped for a traffic violation and it does not contain a fluorescent vest, the driver will be fined. These vests can be purchased for a nominal price in all local gas stations. While cellular handset phone use is prohibited while driving, hands-free units are authorized.

West Bank and Gaza: Crowded roads are common in the West Bank and Gaza. During periods of heightened tension, cars with Israeli license plates have been stoned and fired upon. Emergency services may be delayed by the need for Palestinian authorities to coordinate with Israeli officials. Seat belt use is required and drivers may not drink alcohol. Individuals involved in accidents resulting in death or injury may be detained by police pending an investigation.

We also suggest that you visit the website of the national tourist office and the Israeli Bureau of Motor Vehicles.

Aviation Safety Oversight: The U.S. Federal Aviation Administration (FAA) has assessed the government of Israel's Civil Aviation Authority as not being in compliance with International Civil Aviation Organization (ICAO) aviation safety standards for oversight of Israel's air carrier operations. Further information may be found on the FAA's safety assessment page.

Children's Issues: Please see the U.S. Dept. of State Office of Children's Issues web pages on intercountry adoption and international parental child abduction.

Travel Warning

December 20, 2012

The security environment remains complex in Israel and the West Bank, and U.S. citizens need to be aware of the continuing risks of travel to these areas, particularly to areas described in this travel warning, where there are heightened tensions and security risks. The Department of State strongly warns U.S. citizens against travel to the Gaza Strip. Furthermore, it cautions them that, with the exception of Jericho and Bethlehem, personal travel to the West Bank by U.S. Government employees is prohibited. This replaces the Travel Warning issued August 10, 2012, to update information on the general security environment.

Over three million foreign citizens, including hundreds of thousands of U.S. citizens, safely visit Israel and the West Bank each year for study, tourism, and business. The Government of Israel and the Palestinian Authority make considerable efforts to protect U.S. citizens and other visitors to major tourist destinations.

Nonetheless, U.S. citizens should also take into consideration that U.S. government personnel are not permitted to use public buses due to past attacks on public transportation and that U.S. government personnel must notify the Embassy's Regional Security Officer before traveling in the areas surrounding Gaza and south of Beersheva. Furthermore, U.S. government personnel are restricted from conducting personal travel to most parts of the West Bank.

Major Metropolitan Areas in Israel: Personal safety conditions in major metropolitan areas, including Tel Aviv and Haifa and their surrounding regions, are comparable to or better than those in other major global cities. Tourists, students, and businesspeople from around the world are welcome. Visitors should observe appropriate personal security practices to reduce their vulnerability to crime, particularly late at night or in isolated or economically depressed areas, including in the countryside. Visitors are advised to avoid large gatherings or demonstrations and keep current with local news, which is available through numerous English language sources.

U.S. citizen employees of the U.S. Embassy and Consulate General and their families are prohibited from using public buses and their associated terminals and bus stops throughout the country. On November 21, 2012, a bomb exploded on a public bus in downtown Tel Aviv, causing several injuries. Additionally, between November 15 and 20, 2012, long-range rockets launched from Gaza reached as far north as Tel Aviv. In light of the threat of rocket or missile attacks, visitors and U.S. citizens living in Israel should also familiarize themselves with the location of the nearest bomb shelter (often referred to as a secure or protected room). Since the early 1990s, the Government of Israel has required that all new homes and buildings include a designated shelter. Visitors should seek information on shelters from hotel staff or building managers. For further emergency preparedness guidance, please visit the website of the Government of Israel's Home Front Command, which provides information on how to choose a secure space in a home or apartment.

Gaza Vicinity: Travelers to areas of Israel in the vicinity of the Gaza Strip should be aware of the risks presented by small arms fire, anti-tank weapons, rockets, and mortars launched from inside Gaza toward Israeli cities and towns. These attacks can come with little warning. Some rockets have traveled more than 40 km (24 miles) from Gaza and landed as far north as Yavne and Gadera and as far east as Beersheva. Gunfire, rocket, and mortar attacks in the regions bordering Gaza have been a regular occurrence.

Visitors to these areas should remain aware of their surroundings and of the location of bomb shelters and should take note of announcements and guidance provided by the Home Front Command.

Travelers should also be aware of the heightened state of alert maintained by Israeli authorities along Israel's border with Egypt since an August 18, 2011, terrorist attack that killed eight and injured nearly 40 people along Route 12, north of Eilat. There have been subsequent cross-border incidents from Egypt including rocket attacks and ground incursions, such as an attack that took place on August 5, 2012.

Due to the threats in these areas, U.S. Government personnel must notify the Embassy's Regional Security Office in advance if they plan to visit the vicinity of the Gaza Strip or south of Beersheva. Added security measures, such as the use of armored vehicles, are commonly used for such travel. U.S. citizens considering travel overland into Egypt from Israel should review the Department of State's Country Specific Information for Egypt.

Northern Israel: Rocket attacks into Israel from Lebanon have occurred without warning along the Israeli-Lebanese border, such as three rockets that were fired from Lebanon on November 29, 2011. There are active land mines in areas of the Golan Heights, so visitors should walk only on established roads or trails.

Jerusalem: U.S. citizens should be aware of the possibility of isolated street protests, particularly within the Old City and areas around Salah Ed-Din Street, Damascus Gate, Silwan, and the Sheikh Jarrah neighborhood. Travelers should exercise caution at religious sites on holy days, Fridays, Saturdays, and Sundays. U.S. Government employees are prohibited from entering the Old City on Fridays during the month of Ramadan due to congestion and security-related access restrictions.

U.S. government employees are also prohibited from transiting Independence Park in central Jerusalem during the hours of darkness due to reports of criminal activity.

In October 2012, a tour bus operating on an established route within East Jerusalem was the target of a stone-throwing attack that resulted in injury to a U.S. citizen tourist. Such attacks, however, are not common in the city of Jerusalem.

In mid-November 2012, long-range rockets launched from Gaza in the direction of Jerusalem reached as far as the outskirts of Bethlehem.

The West Bank: The Department of State urges U.S. citizens to exercise caution when traveling to the West Bank. Demonstrations and violent incidents can occur without warning, and vehicles are regularly targeted by rocks, Molotov cocktails, and gunfire on West Bank roads. U.S. citizens can be caught in the middle of potentially dangerous situations, and some U.S. citizens involved in political demonstrations in the West Bank have sustained serious injuries.

The Department of State recommends that U.S. citizens, for their own safety, avoid demonstrations. During periods of unrest, the Israeli Government may restrict access to the West Bank, and some areas may be placed under curfew. All persons in areas under curfew should remain indoors to avoid arrest or injury.

Security conditions in the West Bank may hinder the ability of consular staff to offer timely assistance to U.S. citizens. Personal travel in the West Bank by U.S. Government personnel and their families is permitted to the towns of Bethlehem and Jericho and to transit the West Bank using Routes 1, 443, and 90. Personal travel is also permitted to Qumran off Route 90 by the Dead Sea, as are stops at roadside facilities along routes 1 and 90. All other personal travel in the West Bank, unless specifically authorized for official purposes, is prohibited.

The Gaza Strip: The Department of State strongly urges U.S. citizens to avoid travel to the Gaza Strip, which is under the control of Hamas, a foreign terrorist organization, by any means, including by sea. U.S. citizens in Gaza are advised to depart immediately. The security environment within Gaza, including its border with Egypt and its seacoast, is dangerous and volatile. Exchanges of fire between the Israel Defense Forces and militant groups in Gaza take place regularly, and civilians have been caught in the crossfire in the past. Although the Rafah crossing between Gaza and Egypt allows for some passenger travel, prior coordination with local authorities — which could take days or weeks to process — is generally required, and crossing points may be closed for days or weeks. Travelers who enter the Gaza Strip through the Rafah crossing must also exit through the Rafah crossing, and those entering the Gaza Strip may not be able to depart at a time of their choosing. Because U.S. citizen employees of the U.S. Government are not allowed to enter the Gaza Strip or have contact with Hamas, the ability of consular staff to offer timely assistance to U.S. citizens is extremely limited.

Entry/Exit Difficulties: Some U.S. citizens holding Israeli nationality, possessing a Palestinian identity card, or of Arab or Muslim origin have experienced significant difficulties in entering or exiting Israel or the West Bank. Such U.S. citizens planning to travel to Israel, the West Bank, or Gaza should consult the detailed information concerning entry and exit difficulties in the Country Specific Information. Contact the Consular Section of the U.S. Embassy for information and assistance in Israel, the Golan Heights, and ports of entry at Ben Gurion Airport, Haifa Port, the northern (Jordan River/Sheikh Hussein) and southern (Arava) border crossings connecting Israel and Jordan, and the border crossings between Israel and Egypt. An embassy officer can be contacted at (972) (3) 519-7575 from Monday through Friday during working hours. The after-hours emergency number is (972) (3) 519-7551. Contact the Consular Section of the U.S. Consulate General in Jerusalem for information and assistance in Jerusalem, the West Bank, the Gaza Strip, and the Allenby/King Hussein Bridge crossing connecting the West Bank and Jordan, at (972) (2) 630-4000 from Monday through Friday during working hours. The after-hours emergency number is (972) (2) 622-7250.

For More Information: Occasional public messages issued by the Embassy and the Consulate General are e-mailed to registered U.S. citizens and are posted on State Department websites to highlight time-sensitive security concerns. To receive such messages, travelers should register with the Embassy or the Consulate General via the Smart Traveler Enrollment Program and visit the consular affairs website. Current information on travel and security in Israel, the West Bank, and the Gaza Strip may be obtained from the Department of State by calling 1-888-407-4747 within the United States and Canada, or, from overseas, 1-202-501-4444. For additional and more in-depth information about specific aspects of travel to these areas, travelers should consult the Country Specific Information for Israel, the West Bank and Gaza and the Worldwide Caution. Travelers transiting or visiting Jordan and Egypt during their trip to Israel should also consult their respective Travel Warnings, Travel Alerts and Country Specific Information, all of which are available on the Department of State's Consular Affairs website.

Intercountry Adoption

April 2008

The information in this section has been edited from the latest report available as of February 2013 from the State Department Bureau of Consular Affairs, Office of Overseas Citizens Services. For more information, please read the *Intercountry Adoption* section of this book and review current reports online at http://adoption.state.gov.

Who Can Adopt? Adoption between the United States and Israel is governed by the Hague Adoption Convention. Therefore to adopt from Israel, you must first be found eligible to adopt by the U.S. Government. The U.S. Government agency responsible for making this determination is the Department of Homeland Security, U.S. Citizenship and Immigration Services (USCIS).

Residency Requirements: Adoptive parents must stay in Israel for the duration of the adoption process. In order to adopt a baby up to age 2, the parents must be Israeli citizens. Non-Israeli citizens can only adopt a baby or a child with special needs for whom no adoptive parents could be found in Israel. Preference will be given to adoptive parents of the same religion or ethnic origin as the child.

Age Requirements: The age difference between either of the parents and the child may not be greater than 43 years.

Marriage Requirements: Partners whose cohabitation is not recognized by the government as a legal marriage or single parents can only adopt children with special needs.

Income Requirements: The adopting parents' financial situation must be strong enough to allow adequate support of the child. Prospective adoptive parents must also submit salary slips to prove financial stability. The adoption officer will verify the information by interviewing the adoptive parents and conducting a home visit.

Other Requirements: All prospective adoptive parents must undergo a psychological test conducted by a psychologist as well as a social worker. The prospective adopting parents must also be judged in good physical health.

Who Can Be Adopted? Because Israel is party to the Hague Adoption Convention, children from Israel must meet the requirements of the Convention in order to be eligible for adoption.

For example, the Convention requires that Israel attempt to place a child with a family in Israel before determining that a child is eligible for intercountry adoption. In addition to Israeli requirements, a child must meet the definition of a Convention adoptee for you to bring him or her back to the United States.

Eligibility Requirements: Either the birth parents must provide a signed statement that they are willing to abandon the child or a court must declare the birth parents as unknown or unable to raise the child.

Adoption Authority: The Central Agency for International Adoption, managed by Ms. Orna Hirshfeld, is the national adoption authority. Ms. Nehama Tal has been assigned to be the inspector on international adoption.

The Process: Because Israel is party to the Hague Adoption Convention, adopting from Israel must follow a specific process designed to meet the Convention's requirements.

For detailed and updated information on these requirements, please review the *Intercountry Adoption* section of this publication and visit the USCIS Intercountry Adoption website at http://adoption.state.gov.

Time Frame: To adopt a baby in Israel, there is approximately a 5-year waiting list. When adopting a child with special needs, there is at least a six-month wait (depending on the age of the child and the parents' abilities).

Adoption Application/Procedure: All prospective adopting parents must go through the following process when adopting an Israeli child:

- Preliminary medical examination of the parents;
- The child must first be declared adoptable. Either the birth parents must provide a signed statement that they are willing to abandon the child or a court must declare the birth parents as unknown or unable to raise the child;
- Written evaluation of the child's medical condition;
- The adoptive parents must physically arrive in Israel, meet the child and appear in court. At that point the court will grant them full guardianship;
- The Ministry of Labor will conduct a follow-up investigation as to the child's successful integration into the family;
- If the results of the Ministry's investigation are satisfactory after a period of six months residency with the adoptive parents, an adoption decree will be granted by the applicable Israeli court;
- Additionally, an adoption decree must be received from the country of the adoptive parents. The adoptive parents will then proceed with obtaining an immigrant visa for the child;
- The child is then registered in the Israeli adoption registry.

Palestinian Adoption Procedures: These are the Palestinian adoption procedures in the West bank and Gaza according to the consulate in Jerusalem.

- **Christian Adoption:** Prospective adoptive parents can obtain an adoption decree from the ecclesiastical court of their community (e.g. Latin, Greek, Armenian, etc).

  On the basis of the adoption decree issued by the court of the respective church, a Palestinian Birth Certificate can be issued and subsequently a Palestinian Passport (please note that there are sometimes difficulties in receiving civil documents from the Palestinian Authority).

- **Muslim Adoption:** The Palestinian Authority opposes adoption by foreign parents, because, according to an unnamed source, Palestinian children must remain in Palestine. Additionally, Islamic Shari'a Law does not allow for adoption as it is recognized in the United States ; rather, they allow for "guardianship". Please view our flyer on "Adoption of Children from Countries in which Islamic Shari'a Law is observed."

If a couple is able to locate a child, the couple must pursue custody with the Palestinian Authority District Court. Only after this is granted, can U.S. Embassy Tel Aviv pursue an IR-4 immigrant visa for the child under the category "to be adopted in the U.S." All adoption cases that were handled in the Jerusalem Consulate were from the West Bank, and they have not yet encountered one from Gaza. According to the Israeli adoption agency representative, adoption in Gaza is not possible since Islam does not enable adoption. According to the agency representative, about three years ago Chairman Arafat ordered that only Muslim couples could adopt children from Gaza.

Adoption Fees: In the adoption services contract that you sign at the beginning of the adoption process, your agency will itemize the fees and estimated expenses related to your adoption process. There are no government processing fees associated with adoption in Israel. The U.S. Embassy in Israel discourages the payment of any fees that are not properly receipted, "donations," or "expediting" fees, that may be requested from prospective adoptive parents. Such fees have the appearance of "buying" a baby and put all future adoptions in Israel at risk.

Documents Required: The following items are required prior to adoption in Israel:

- Home study of the adoptive parents,
- Salary slips attesting to their income,
- Proof of adequate housing,
- Police certificate showing no previous criminal record,
- Medical report proving the good health of the adoptive parents.
- Guarantee that the child will obtain their citizenship once the adoption has been finalized.
- Report completed by an Israeli social worker concerning the prospective adopting parents' financial situation and ability to support the child as well as stating that there is no history of family violence or harassment of minors.

Bringing Your Child Home: Once your adoption is complete (or you have obtained legal custody of the child), there are a few more steps to take before you can head home. Specifically, you need to apply for several documents for your child before he or she can travel to the United States, such as a birth certificate, a passport or travel document for your child from the country in which he or she was born, and a U.S. Immigration Visa. For detailed and updated information on how to obtain these documents, review the *Intercountry Adoption* section on this publication and visit the USCIS Intercountry Adoption website at http://adoption.state.gov.

Child Citizenship Act: For adoptions finalized abroad, the Child Citizenship Act of 2000 allows your new child to acquire American citizenship automatically when he or she enters the United States as lawful permanent residents.

For adoptions finalized in the United States, the Child Citizenship Act of 2000 allows your new child to acquire American citizenship automatically when the court in the United States issues the final adoption decree. To learn more, visit the USCIS Intercountry Adoption website at http://adoption.state.gov.

U.S. Embassy in Israel
Immigration Visa Unit
71 Hayarkon Street
Tel Aviv , Israel 63903
Tel: (972) (03) 519-7601
Fax: (972) (03) 519-7619
Email: IVtelaviv@state.gov
Internet: http://telaviv.usembassy.gov

Israel's Adoption Authority
Central Agency for International Adoption
Ministry of Labor
10 Yad Harutzim Street
Jerusalem 91012
Tel: 972-2-6708177/8
Fax: 972-2-6708451

Embassy of Israel
3514 International Dr. N.W.
Washington DC 20008
Tel: 202-364-5500
Fax: 202-364-5527
E-mail: info@israelemb.org
http://www.israelemb.org/index.htm

Office of Children's Issues
U.S. Department of State
2201 C Street, NW
SA-29
Washington, DC 20520
Tel: 1-888-407-4747
E-mail: AskCI@state.gov
http://adoption.state.gov

ITALY

Compiled from publications that were available as of February 2013 from the U.S. Department of State, the U.S. Department of Commerce, and the Central Intelligence Agency (CIA). See the introduction to this set for explanatory notes.

Official Name:
Italian Republic

PROFILE

Geography

Area: total: 301,340 sq km; country comparison to the world: 72; land: 294,140 sq km; water: 7,200 sq km

Major cities: Rome (capital) 3.357 million; Milan 2.962 million; Naples 2.27 million; Turin 1.662 million; Palermo 872,000 (2009)

Climate: predominantly Mediterranean; Alpine in far north; hot, dry in south

Terrain: mostly rugged and mountainous; some plains, coastal lowlands

People

Nationality: noun: Italian(s); adjective: Italian

Population: 61,261,254 (July 2012 est.)

Population growth rate: 0.38% (2012 est.)

Ethnic groups: Italian (includes small clusters of German-, French-, and Slovene-Italians in the north and Albanian-Italians and Greek-Italians in the south)

Religions: Christian 80% (overwhelming Roman Catholic with very small groups of Jehova Witnesses and Protestants), Muslims NEGL (about 700,000 but growing), Atheists and Agnostics 20%

Languages: Italian (official), German (parts of Trentino-Alto Adige region are predominantly German speaking), French (small French-speaking minority in Valle d'Aosta region), Slovene (Slovene-speaking minority in the Trieste-Gorizia area)

Literacy: definition: age 15 and over can read and write; total population: 98.4%; male: 98.8%; female: 98% (2001 census)

Health: life expectancy at birth: total population: 81.86 years; male: 79.24 years; female: 84.63 years (2012 est.); Infant mortality rate: total: 3.36 deaths/1,000 live births; male: 3.56 deaths/1,000 live births; female: 3.14 deaths/1,000 live births (2012 est.)

Unemployment rate: 10.9% (2012 est.)

Work force: 25.28 million (2012 est.)

Government

Type: republic

Independence: 17 March 1861

Constitution: passed 11 December 1947, effective 1 January 1948; amended many times

Political subdivisions: 15 regions (regioni, singular—regione) and 5 autonomous regions (regioni autonome, singular—regione autonoma)

Suffrage: 18 years of age; universal (except in senatorial elections, where minimum age is 25)

Economy

GDP (purchasing power parity): $1.834 trillion (2012 est.); $1.871 trillion (2011 est.); $1.863 trillion (2010 est.); $1.83 trillion (2009 est.)

GDP real growth rate: -2.3% (2012 est.); 0.4% (2011 est.); 1.8% (2010 est.); -5.5% (2009 est.)

GDP per capita (PPP): $30,100 (2012 est.); $30,900 (2011 est.); $30,900 (2010 est.); $30,500 (2009 est.)

Natural resources: coal, mercury, zinc, potash, marble, barite, asbestos, pumice, fluorspar, feldspar, pyrite (sulfur), natural gas and crude oil reserves, fish, arable land

Agriculture products: fruits, vegetables, grapes, potatoes, sugar beets, soybeans, grain, olives; beef, dairy products; fish

Industries: tourism, machinery, iron and steel, chemicals, food processing, textiles, motor vehicles, clothing, footwear, ceramics

Exports: $483.3 billion (2012 est.); $523.9 billion (2011 est.); $448.4 billion (2010 est.)

Exports—commodities: engineering products, textiles and clothing, production machinery, motor vehicles, transport equipment, chemicals; food, beverages and tobacco; minerals, and nonferrous metals

Exports—partners: Germany 13.3%, France 11.8%, US 5.9%, Spain 5.4%, Switzerland 5.4%, UK 4.7% (2011)

Imports: $469.7 billion (2012 est.); $556.4 billion (2011 est.); $475.7 billion (2010 est.)

Imports—commodities: engineering products, chemicals, transport equipment, energy products, minerals and nonferrous metals, textiles and clothing; food, beverages, and tobacco

Imports—partners: Germany 16.5%, France 8.9%, China 7.7%, Netherlands 5.5%, Spain 4.7% (2011)

Debt—external: $2.46 trillion (30 June 2012 est.); $2.684 trillion (30 June 2011 est.); $2.223 trillion (30 June 2010 est.)

Exchange rates: euros (EUR) per US dollar; 0.7838 (2012 est.); 0.7194 (2011 est.); 0.755 (2010 est.); 0.7198 (2009 est.); 0.6827 (2008 est.); 0.7345 (2007 est.)

PEOPLE

Italy is largely homogeneous linguistically and religiously but is diverse culturally, economically, and politically. Italy has the fifth-highest population density in Europe—about 200 persons per square kilometer (about 500 per sq. mi.). Minority groups are small, the largest being the German-speaking people of Bolzano Province and the Slovenes around Trieste. There are also small communities of Albanian, Greek, Ladino, and French origin. Immigration has increased in recent years; however, the Italian population is declining overall due to low birth rates. National/Racial/Ethnic Minorities

There were no accurate statistics on the number of Roma in the country. NGOs estimated that between 120,000 and 170,000 Roma, including 75,000 citizens, were concentrated on the fringes of urban areas in the central and southern parts of the country.

Language

Italian is the official language and is spoken in all parts of Italy, although some minority groups in the Alto Adige and Aosta regions speak German and French, respectively.

Religion

An estimated 87 percent of native-born citizens were Roman Catholic in 2009; however, according to an independent research institute, in 2010 only 24 percent regularly participated in Catholic worship services. Less than 5 percent of the population consists of members of non-Catholic Christian groups, Muslims, Jews, Hindus, the Baha'i faith, and Buddhists. Significant Christian communities include Christian Orthodox, Jehovah's Witnesses, Assemblies of God, the Confederation of Methodist and Waldensian Churches, The Church of Jesus Christ of Latter-day Saints (Mormons), and other small Protestant groups.

Immigration continued to add large groups of non-Christian residents, mainly Muslims, from North Africa, South Asia, Albania, and the Middle East.

In 2011 there were reportedly 764 places of worship for Muslims (often officially labeled "cultural centers" and unofficially called "garage" mosques), concentrated in the regions of Lombardy, Veneto, Lazio, Emilia Romagna, and Tuscany. Roughly 90 percent of Italy's mosques are located in regions in the North, with the remaining 10 percent concentrated in the southern regions of Calabria, Campania, and Puglia. The Jewish community is estimated at 30,000 and maintains synagogues in 21 cities.

HISTORY

Greeks settled in the southern tip of the Italian Peninsula in the eighth and seventh centuries B.C.; Etruscans, Romans, and others inhabited the central and northern mainland. The peninsula was subsequently unified under the Roman Republic. The neighboring islands came under Roman control by the third century B.C.; by the first century A.D., the Roman Empire effectively dominated the Mediterranean world. After the collapse of the Roman Empire in the West in the fifth century A.D., the peninsula and islands were subjected to a series of invasions and lost political unity. Italy became an oft-changing succession of small states, principalities, and kingdoms, which fought among themselves and were subject to ambitions of foreign powers. Popes of Rome ruled central Italy; rivalries between the popes and the Holy Roman Emperors, who claimed Italy as their domain, often made the peninsula a battleground. Beginning in the 11th century, the commercial prosperity of northern and central Italian cities, combined with the influence of the Renaissance, somewhat mitigated the effects of these medieval political rivalries.

Although Italy declined after the 16th century, the Renaissance had strengthened the idea of a single Italian nationality. By the early 19th century, a nationalist movement developed and led to the reunification of Italy—except for Rome—in the 1860s. In 1861, Victor Emmanuel II of the House of Savoy was proclaimed King of Italy. Rome was incorporated in 1870. From 1870 until 1922, Italy was a constitutional monarchy with a parliament elected under limited suffrage.

20th-Century History

During World War I, Italy renounced its standing alliance with Germany and Austria-Hungary and, in 1915, entered the war on the side of the Allies. Under the postwar settlement, Italy received some former Austrian territory along the northeast frontier. In 1922, Benito Mussolini came to power and, over the next few years, eliminated political parties, curtailed personal liberties, and installed a fascist dictatorship termed the Corporate State. The king, with little or no effective power, remained titular head of state.

Italy allied with Germany and declared war on the United Kingdom and France in 1940. In 1941, Italy—with the other Axis powers, Germany and Japan—declared war on the United States and the Soviet Union.

Following the Allied invasion of Sicily in 1943, the King dismissed Musso-

lini and appointed Marshal Pietro Badoglio as Premier. The Badoglio government declared war on Germany, which quickly occupied most of the country and freed Mussolini, who led a brief-lived regime in the north. An anti-fascist popular resistance movement grew during the last 2 years of the war, harassing German forces before they were driven out by Allied forces in April 1945. A 1946 plebiscite ended the monarchy, and a constituent assembly was elected to draw up plans for the republic. Under the 1947 peace treaty, minor adjustments were made in Italy's frontier with France, the eastern border area was transferred to Yugoslavia, and the area around the city of Trieste was designated a free territory.

In 1954, the free territory, which had remained under the administration of U.S.-U.K. forces (Zone A, including the city of Trieste) and Yugoslav forces (Zone B), was divided between Italy and Yugoslavia, principally along the zonal boundary. This arrangement was made permanent by the Italian-Yugoslav Treaty of Osimo, ratified in 1977 (currently being discussed by Italy, Slovenia, and Croatia). Under the 1947 peace treaty, Italy also relinquished its overseas territories and certain Mediterranean islands.

The Roman Catholic Church's status in Italy has been determined, since its temporal powers ended in 1870, by a series of accords with the Italian Government. Under the Lateran Pacts of 1929, which were confirmed by the present constitution, Vatican City is recognized by Italy as an independent, sovereign entity. While preserving that recognition, in 1984, Italy and the Vatican updated several provisions of the 1929 accords. Included was the end of Roman Catholicism as Italy's formal state religion.

Italy's Cultural Contributions

Europe's Renaissance period began in Italy during the 14th and 15th centuries. Literary achievements—such as the poetry of Petrarch, Tasso, and Ariosto and the prose of Boccaccio, Machiavelli, and Castiglione—exerted a tremendous and lasting influence on the subsequent development of Western civilization, as did the painting, sculpture, and architecture contributed by giants such as da Vinci, Raphael, Botticelli, Fra Angelico, and Michelangelo.

The musical influence of Italian composers Monteverdi, Palestrina, and Vivaldi proved epochal; in the 19th century, Italian romantic opera flourished under composers Gioacchino Rossini, Giuseppe Verdi, and Giacomo Puccini. Contemporary Italian artists, writers, filmmakers, architects, composers, and designers contribute significantly to Western culture.

GOVERNMENT AND POLITICAL CONDITIONS

Italy is a multiparty parliamentary democracy with a bicameral parliament consisting of the Chamber of Deputies and the Senate. The constitution vests executive authority in the Council of Ministers, headed by the prime minister, who is the president of the council. The president, who is the head of state, nominates the prime minister after consulting with the leaders of all political forces in the parliament. International observers considered the 2008 national parliamentary elections free and fair.

Recent Elections

National and international observers, including the Organization for Security and Cooperation in Europe, considered the 2008 parliamentary elections free and fair.

Participation of Women and Minorities: There were 60 women in the 321-seat Senate and 135 women in the 630-seat Chamber of Deputies. Women held five of 23 positions in the Council of Ministers. The proportion of female judges is 7 percent.

Two legally defined minority groups had representatives in parliament; the French-speaking Valdostani and the German-speaking Altoatesini/Suedtiroler had a total of four senators and three deputies. In a predominantly ethnically homogenous society, immigrants represented approximately 6.5 percent of the population, and fewer than half of these qualified as ethnic/racial minorities. Two representatives of ethnically diverse groups (of Moroccan and Congolese origin) were members of the Chamber of Deputies.

Principal Government Officials

Last Updated: 1/31/2013

Pres.: **Giorgio NAPOLITANO**
Prime Min.: **Mario MONTI**
Under Sec. for the Presidency of the Council of Ministers: **Antonio CATRICALA**
Min. of Agriculture: **Mario CATANIA**
Min. of Community Policy: **Enzo Moavero MILANESI**
Min. of Cultural Assets: **Lorenzo ORNAGHI**
Min. of Defense: **Giampaolo DI PAOLA**
Min. of Economic Development: **Corrado PASSERA**
Min. of Economy & Finance: **Vittorio GRILLI**
Min. of Education: **Franceso PROFUMO**
Min. of Environment: **Corrado CLINI**
Min. of Foreign Affairs: **Giulio TERZI di Sant' Agata**
Min. of Health: **Renato BALDUZZI**
Min. of Infrastructure & Transport: **Corrado PASSERA**
Min. of Interior: **Anna Maria CANCELLIERI**
Min. of Intl. Cooperation: **Andrea RICCARDI**
Min. of Justice: **Paola SEVERINO**
Min. of Labor, Welfare, & Equal Opportunity: **Elsa FORNERO**
Min. of Relations With Parliament: **Piero GIARDA**
Min. of Territorial Cohesion: **Fabrizio BARCA**
Min. of Tourism & Sport: **Piero GNUDI**
Governor, Bank of Italy: **Ignazio VISCO**
Ambassador to the US: **Claudio BISOGNIERO**
Permanent Representative to the UN, New York: **Cesare Maria RAGAGLINI**

ECONOMY

Italy has a diversified industrial economy, which is divided into a developed industrial north, dominated by private companies, and a less-developed, highly subsidized, agricultural south, with high unemployment. The Italian economy is driven in large part by the manufacture of high-quality consumer goods produced by small and medium-sized enterprises, many of them family owned. Italy also has a sizable underground economy, which by some estimates accounts for as much as 17% of GDP.

These activities are most common within the agriculture, construction, and service sectors. Italy is the third-largest economy in the euro-zone, but its exceptionally high public debt and structural impediments to growth have rendered it vulnerable to scrutiny by financial markets. Public debt has increased steadily since 2007, topping 126% of GDP in 2012, and investor concerns about the broader euro-zone crisis at times have caused borrowing costs on sovereign government debt to rise to euro-era records.

During the second half of 2011 the government passed a series of three austerity packages to balance its budget and decrease its public debt. These measures included a hike in the value-added tax, pension reforms, and cuts to public administration.

The government also faces pressure from investors and European partners to sustain its recent efforts to address Italy's long-standing structural impediments to growth, such as an inflexible labor market and widespread tax evasion. In 2012 economic growth and labor market conditions deteriorated, with growth at -2.3% and unemployment rising to nearly 11%. Although the government has undertaken several economic reform iniatiatives, in the longer-term Italy's low fertility rate, productivity, and foreign investment will increasingly strain its economy. Italy's GDP is now 7% below its 2007 pre-crisis level.

Labor Conditions

The government sought to enforce laws and policies designed to protect children from exploitation in the workplace; however, there were a number of reports of child labor.

The law prohibits employment of children under age 15 with some limited exceptions, and there are specific restrictions on employment in hazardous or unhealthy occupations for boys under the age of 18 and girls under the age of 21. Enforcement was generally effective in the formal economy; however, enforcement was difficult in the relatively extensive informal economy.

The law does not provide for a minimum wage. Instead, collective bargaining labor contracts negotiated by unions set minimum wage levels for different sectors of employment. The official poverty line was set at 992 euros ($1,290) per month for a family of two. Workers in the informal sector often worked for less than the comparable minimum wage in the formal sector. The estimated three million workers in the informal sector accounted for 11.3 percent of the total workforce and worked primarily in the south in the agricultural and service sectors during the year, according to ISTAT.

The legal workweek is 40 hours. Overtime work may not exceed two hours per day or an average of 12 hours per week. Unless limited by a collective bargaining agreement, the law sets maximum overtime hours in industrial sector firms at no more than 80 per quarter and 250 annually. The law requires rest periods of one day per week and 11 hours per day. Premium pay is required for overtime. The government, with regular union input, effectively enforced these standards.

U.S.-ITALY RELATIONS

The United States established diplomatic relations with Italy in 1861 following the unification of most of the peninsula into one state. In 1941, Italy - with the other World War II Axis powers Germany and Japan - declared war on the United States. U.S. relations with Italy were reestablished in 1944.

Today, the United States and Italy enjoy warm and friendly relations. Italy is a strong and active transatlantic partner. The two countries have sought to foster democratic ideals and international cooperation, especially in areas of strife and civil conflict.

The United States and Italy are North Atlantic Treaty Organization (NATO) allies and cooperate in the United Nations, in various regional organizations, and bilaterally for peace, prosperity, and security. Italy has worked closely with the United States and others on such issues as NATO and UN operations; assistance to Russia and the New Independent States; Lebanon; Libya; Syria; Afghanistan; the Middle East peace process; Somalia and Mozambique peacekeeping; and combating drug trafficking, trafficking in women and children, and counterterrorism.

Under bilateral agreements flowing from NATO membership, Italy hosts U.S. military forces at Vicenza and Livorno (army); Aviano (air force); and Sigonella, Gaeta, and Naples - home port for the U.S. Navy Sixth Fleet. Italy hosts the NATO Defense College in Rome.

U.S. Assistance to Italy

The United States provides no development assistance to Italy.

Bilateral Economic Relations

The United States and Italy cooperate closely on major economic issues, including within the G-8. The United States is one of Italy's most important trade partners. As a member of the European Union (EU), Italy is bound by EU treaties and laws, including those directly governing or indirectly impacting business investments. Under both the EU treaty's Right of Establishment, and the Friendship, Commerce and Navigation Treaty with the United States, Italy is generally obliged to provide national treatment to U.S. investors established in Italy or in another EU member state. The two countries have enacted an income tax agreement to prevent double taxation.

Italy's Membership in International Organizations

Italy and the United States belong to a number of the same international organizations, including the United Nations, North Atlantic Treaty Organization, Euro-Atlantic Partnership Council, Organization for Security and Cooperation in Europe, Organization for Economic Cooperation and Development, G-20, G-8, International Monetary Fund, World Bank, and World Trade Organization. Italy also is an observer to the Organization of American States.

Bilateral Representation

Italy maintains an embassy in the United States at 3000 Whitehaven Street, NW, Washington, DC 20008 (tel. 202-612-4400).

Principal U.S. Embassy Officials

Last Updated: 1/14/2013

ROME (E) 119/a Via Vittorio Veneto, (+39) 06-4674-1, Fax (+39) 06-488-2672, Workweek: Mon-Fri from 08:30 to 17:30, http://rome.usembassy.gov/

DCM OMS:	Mary Jo Fuhrer
AMB OMS:	Theresa G. Chupp
CG OMS:	Claudia Ghirardi
Co-CLO:	Anne Kemp
DHS/CBP:	Richard F. Quinn
DHS/CIS:	John L. Lafferty
DHS/ICE:	Miguel Unzueta
DHS/TSA:	Raymond E. Montgomery
FCS:	Carmine G. D'Aloisio
FM:	Chad M. Shelley
HRO:	Ellen M. Flanagan
MGT:	Theresa M. Leech
MLO/ODC:	Salvatore A. Arria
PO/CON:	Donald F. Mulligan
POL/MIL:	Eric Carlson
POSHO:	Chad M. Shelley
SDO/DATT:	CAPT Anthony J. Parisi
AMB:	David H. Thorne
CG:	Richard C. Beer
DCM:	Douglas C. Hengel
PAO:	Maria E. McKay
GSO:	Kirby D. Nelson
RSO:	Peter S. Hargraves
AGR:	Christine Sloop
CLO:	Linda Sieben
DEA:	Russell F. Benson
ECON:	John L. Carwile
EST:	Elizabeth Fritschie
FMO:	Matthew T. Simiskey
ICASS Chair:	John L. Lafferty
IMO:	William J. Walls
IPO:	Cory D. Wilcox
IRS:	Mr. Benbrahim
ISO:	Perry M. Romeo
ISSO:	Melinda Isachsen
LEGATT:	Stewart B. Roberts
POL:	Daniel J. O'Grady
State ICASS:	Maria E. McKay

FLORENCE (CG) Lungarno A. Vespucci, 38, +39-055-266-951, Fax 39-055-284088, Workweek: 8:30–5:30 Mon to Fri, Website: http://florence.usconsulate.gov/

CG OMS:	Kathryn Rakich
DPO:	Stephen Barneby
MGT:	Stephen Barneby
POSHO:	Stephen Barneby
CG:	Sarah Morrison
CON:	Stephen Barneby

MILAN (CG) Via Principe Amedeo 2/10, 20121 Milano, +39-02-29035-1, Fax +39-02-29035-440, Workweek: 8:30-12:30 13:30-17:30, Website: http://milan.usconsulate.gov/

CG OMS:	Judy C. Schwartz
MGT:	David S. Elmo
POSHO:	Tyler J. Johnston
CG:	Kyle R. Scott
CON:	Joan E. Kane
PAO:	Robert J Palladino
COM:	Michael Richardson
GSO:	Tyler J. Johnston
RSO:	Donovan F. Williams
CLO:	Zinna Saud
ECON:	Matthew J Zamary
IPO:	Gerard R Breton
ISO:	Gerard R Breton
ISSO:	Kevin J. Sloan
LEGATT:	Richard A Mains
POL:	Richard W. Snelsire

NAPLES (CG) Piazza della Repubblica, ++39-081-583-8111, Fax ++39-081-761-1869, Workweek: Mon-Fri 08:00–17:00, Website: http://naples.usconsulate.gov/

MGT:	Michelle Galstaun
OMS:	Kevin M. Wood
POL/ECON:	Lori E Balbi
POSHO:	Michelle Galstaun
CG:	Donald Moore
PO:	Donald Moore
CON:	William D. Howard
PAO:	James Rodriguez
RSO:	Shannon Conrad
CLO:	Vacant
EEO:	James Rodriguez
IPO:	Louis Fleitz
ISSO:	Louis Fleitz

USUN ROME (M) Via Boncompagni 2, 00187 Rome, Italy, 39-06-4674-3501, Fax 39-06-4674-3535, INMARSAT Tel 88-163-145-8979, Workweek: 8:30M to 5:30 PM, Website: usunrome.usmission.gov/

DCM OMS:	Terentia (Terry) Stefani
AMB OMS:	Jeffrey Bing
CDC:	Dr. James Zingeser
MGT:	Sarah Hall
POL/ECON:	Stetson A. Sanders
AMB:	David Lane
DCM:	Karen E. Johnson
PAO:	Sharon Ketchum
AGR:	Michael Michener
AID:	Christopher Shepherd-Pratt
APHIS:	Dr. Edgardo Arza
POL:	Gregory S. Groth

TRAVEL

Consular Information Sheet—Italy, Holy See, and San Marino

December 21, 2011

Country Description: Italy is a developed democracy with a modern economy. The Holy See is a sovereign entity that serves as the ecclesiastical, governmental, and administrative capital of the Roman Catholic Church, physically located within the State of the Vatican City inside Rome, with a unique, non-traditional economy. San Marino is a developed, constitutional democratio republic, also independent of Italy, with a modern economy. Tourist facilities are widely available.

Smart Traveler Enrollment Program (STEP)/Embassy Locations: If you are going to live or visit Italy, San Marino, or the Holy See, please take the time to tell our embassy or consulates about your trip by enrolling in the Smart Traveler Enrollment Program.

If you enroll, we can keep you up to date with important safety and security announcements; it will also help your friends and family get in touch with you in an emergency.

U.S. Embassy Rome
Via V. Veneto 119/A, Rome, Italy
Telephone: 39-06-46741
Facsimile: 39-06-4674–2217
Email: uscitizensrome@state.gov

U.S. Embassy to the Holy See
Via delle Terme Deciane 26
Rome, Italy
Telephone: 39-06-4674–3428
Facsimile: 39-06-575-8346

U.S. Consulate General Florence
Lungarno Amerigo Vespucci 38
Florence, Italy
Telephone: 39-055-266-951
Facsimile: 399-055-215-550
Email: uscitizensflorence@state.gov

U.S. Consulate General Milan
Via Principe Amedeo 2/10
Milan, Italy
Telephone: 39-02-290-351
Facsimile: 39-02-290-35-273
Email: uscitizensmilan@state.gov

U.S. Consulate General Naples
Piazza della Repubblica
Naples, Italy
Telephone: 39-081-583-8111
Facsimile: 39-081-583-8275
Email: uscitizensnaples@state.gov

There are U.S. Consular Agents located in the following Italian cities:

Genoa
Via Dante 2, Genoa, Italy
Telephone: 39-010-584-492
Facsimile: 39-010-553-3033
Email: usconsge@libero.it

Palermo
Via Vaccarini 1, Palermo, Italy
Telephone: 39-091-305-857
Facsimile: 39-091-625-6026
Email: uscitizenspalermo@state.gov

Venice
Viale Galileo Galilei 30, Venice, Italy
Telephone: 39-041-541-5944
Facsimile: 39-041-541-6654
Email: uscitizensvenice@state.gov

Entry/Exit Requirements for U.S. Citizens: Italy is a party to the Schengen Agreement. As such, U.S. citizens may enter Italy for up to 90 days for tourist or business purposes without a visa. The passport should be valid for at least three months beyond the period of stay. For further details about travel into and within Schengen countries, please see our Schengen Fact sheet.

For all other purposes, you need a visa, which you must get from an Italian Embassy or Consulate before entering Italy. For further information concerning visas and entry requirements for Italy, you may contact the Embassy of Italy at 3000 Whitehaven Street NW, Washington, DC 20008, or via telephone at (202) 612-4400; or Italian Consulates General in Boston, Chicago, Detroit, Houston, Los Angeles, Miami, Newark, New Orleans, New York, Philadelphia, or San Francisco, accessible through the Italian Embassy website. Are you a non-resident? U.S. citizens staying or traveling within Italy for less than three months are considered non-residents. This includes persons on vacation, those taking professional trips, students registered at an authorized school, or persons performing research or independent study.

Under Italian law, all non-residents are required to complete a dichiarazione di presenza (declaration of presence). Tourists arriving from a non-Schengen-country (e.g. the United States) should obtain a stamp in their passport at the airport on the day of arrival. This stamp is considered the equivalent of the declaration of presence. Tourists arriving from a Schengen-country (e.g. France) must request the declaration of presence form from a local police office (commissariato di zona), police headquarters (questura) or their place of stay (e.g hotel, hostel, campgrounds) and submit the form to the police or to their place of stay within eight business days of arrival. It is important that applicants keep a copy of the receipt issued by the Italian authorities. Failure to complete a declaration of presence is punishable by expulsion from Italy. Additional information may be obtained (in Italian only) from the Portale Immigrazione and the Polizia di Stato.

Are you a resident? U.S. citizens staying in Italy for more than three months are considered residents and must obtain a permesso di soggiorno (permit of stay). This includes U.S. citizens who will work or transact business and persons who want simply to live in Italy. An application "kit" for the permesso di soggiorno can be requested from one of 14,000 national post offices (Poste Italiane). The kit must then be returned to one of 5,332 designated Post Office acceptance locations.

It is important that applicants keep a copy of the receipt issued by the post office. Additional information may be obtained from the Italian immigration website. Within 20 days of receiving the permit to stay in Italy, U.S. citizens must go to the local Vital Statistics Bureau (Anagrafe of the Comune) to apply for residency. It generally takes one to two months to receive the certificate of residence (Certificato di Residenza). The U.S. Department of State is unaware of any HIV/AIDS entry restrictions for visitors to or foreign residents of Italy.

Threats to Safety and Security: Several major earthquake fault lines cross Italy. Principal Italian cities, with the exception of Naples, do not lie near these faults; however, smaller tourist towns, such as Assisi, do lie near faults, and have experienced earthquakes. An earthquake severely damaged the town of L'Aquila in 2009. General information about disaster preparedness is available online from the U.S. Federal Management Agency (FEMA). Detailed information on Italy's fault lines is available from the U.S. Geological Survey (USGS).

Italy also has several active volcanoes generating geothermal events. Mt. Etna, on the eastern tip of the island of Sicily, has been erupting intermittently since 2000. Mt. Vesuvius, located near Naples, is currently capped and not active. Activity at Mt. Vesuvius is monitored by an active seismic network and sensor system, and no recent seismic activity has been recorded. Two of Italy's smaller islands, Stromboli and Vulcano, in the Aeolian Islands north of Sicily, also have active volcanoes with lava flows. Detailed information on volcano activity in Italy is available from the USGS.

Politically motivated violence in Italy is most often connected to Italian internal developments or social issues. Italian authorities and foreign diplomatic facilities have found bombs outside public buildings, received bomb threats, and were subjects of letter bombs. Buildings or offices are sometimes the targets of firebombs or Molotov cocktails, although generally at night; such incidents are instigated by organized crime or anarchist movements, and have not targeted or injured U.S. citizens.

Demonstrations may have an anti-American character, especially in areas hosting U.S. military bases. Even demonstrations intended to be peaceful have the potential to turn confrontational and possibly escalate into violence. You should take common sense precautions and follow news reports carefully.

Italian authorities have made several high-profile arrests involving members or affiliates of transnational terror groups. Like other countries in the Schengen area, Italy's open borders with its Western European neighbors allow for the possibility of terrorist groups entering/exiting the country with anonymity.

Stay up to date by:

- Bookmarking our Bureau of Consular Affairs website, which contains the current Travel Warnings and Travel Alerts as well as the Worldwide Caution;
- Following us on Twitter and the Bureau of Consular Affairs page on Facebook;
- Downloading our free Smart Traveler IPhone App to have travel information at your fingertips; and
- Calling 1-888-407-4747 toll-free within the U.S. and Canada, or a regular toll line, 1-202-501-4444, from other countries.
- Taking some time before travel to consider your personal security.

Crime: Italy has a moderate rate of crime. You should exercise extra caution at night and at train stations, airports, nightclubs, bars, and outdoor cafes. If you are drinking heavily, your ability to judge situations and make decisions may be impaired and this can make you a target for crime. Young drinkers are particularly vulnerable to robbery and physical and sexual assault.

Petty crimes such as pick-pocketing, theft from parked cars, and purse snatching are serious problems, especially in large cities. Pick-pockets sometimes dress like businessmen. You should not be lulled into a false sense of security by believing that well-dressed individuals are not potential pick-pockets or thieves. Most reported thefts occur at crowded tourist sites, on public buses or trains, or at the major railway stations. Rome's Termini; Milan's Centrale; Florence's Santa Maria Novella; and Naples' Centrale at Piazza Garibaldi.

For more information on trains and security, please see the Italian railway police's advice for travelers at http://www.poliziadistato.it/articolo/view/22329/. You should also be alert to theft in Milan's Malpensa Airport, particularly at car rental agencies. Clients of Internet cafes in major cities are also targeted. Be careful with your bag or purse, as thieves on motor scooters are very quick and can snatch a purse off of your arm from a moving scooter. Resisting these thieves can be hazardous, as some tourists have suffered broken arms and collarbones.

Thieves in Italy often work in groups or pairs. Pairs of accomplices or groups of children are known to divert tourists' attention so that another can pick-pocket them. In one particular routine, one thief throws trash, waste, or ketchup at the victim; a second thief assists the victim in cleaning up the mess; and the third discreetly takes the victim's belongings. Criminals on crowded public transportation slit the bottoms of purses or bags with a razor blade or sharp knife removing the contents.

Some travelers in Rome, Florence, and Naples have reported incidents where criminals used drugs to assault or rob them. These incidents have been reported near Rome's Termini train station; at bars and cafes near Rome's Colosseum, Colle Oppio, Campo de Fiori, and Piazza Navona; and at bars or cafes in the center of Florence and Naples. Criminals using this tactic "befriend" you at a train station, restaurant, café, or bar, and then offer you a drink laced with a sleeping drug. When you fall asleep, criminals steal your valuables and may sexually assault you. Some victims of these assaults in Rome have required hospitalization and two cases resulted in death.

Thieves are also known to have impersonated police officers in order to steal. The thief shows you a circular plastic sign with the words "police" or "international police" and then in perfect English asks to see your identification and your money. U.S. citizens should be aware that local police will generally exit their own vehicle when speaking with members of the public. Also, plainclothes undercover units rarely attempt to pull over vehicles without a marked car accompanying them.

If this happens to you, you should insist on seeing the officer's identification card (documento), before handing over your wallet as impersonators tend not to carry forged documents. You should immediately report thefts or other crimes to the actual police.

Be alert to the possibility of carjackings and thefts while you are waiting in traffic or stopped at traffic lights. This has been a particular problem in Catania, Sicily. Use particular caution driving at night on highways, when thieves are more likely to strike. Americans have reported break-ins of their rental cars during stops at highway service areas; thieves smash car windows and steal everything inside.

Theft of small items such as radios, luggage, cameras, briefcases, and even cigarettes from parked cars is prevalent. Vehicles parked near beaches during the summer can be broken into and robbed of valuables. Lock car doors whenever you park, and do not leave packages in your car in plain view.

The U.S. Secret Service in Rome is assisting Italian Law Enforcement authorities in investigating an increase in the appearance of ATM skimming devices. These devices are attached to legitimate bank ATMs, usually located in tourist areas, and capture the account information stored electronically on the card's magnetic strip. The devices consist of a card reader installed over the legitimate reader and a pin-hole video camera mounted above the keypad that records the customer's PIN. ATMs with skimming devices installed may also allow normal transactions to occur.

The victim's information is sold, traded on-line, or encoded on another card such as a hotel key card to access the compromised account. Here are some helpful hints to protect against and identify skimming devices:

- Use ATMs located in well-lighted public areas, or secured inside a bank/business
- Cover the keypad with one hand as you enter your PIN
- Look for gaps, tampered appearance, or other irregularities between the metal faceplate of the ATM and the card reader
- Avoid card readers that are not flush with the face of the ATM
- Closely monitor your account statements for unauthorized transactions

Organized criminal groups operate throughout Italy, but are more prevalent in the south. They occasionally resort to violence to intimidate or to settle disputes. Though the activities of such groups are not generally targeted at tourists, visitors should be aware that innocent bystanders could be injured. Don't buy counterfeit and pirated goods, even if they are widely available. Not only are the bootlegs illegal to bring back into the United States, if you purchase them you may also be breaking local law. According to Italian Law (Law 80 of May 14, 2005), anyone caught buying counterfeit goods (for example, DVDs, CDs, watches, purses, bags, belts, sunglasses, etc.) is subject to a fine of no less than EUR 1,000. Police in major Italian cities enforce this law to varying degrees.

You are advised to purchase products only from stores and other licensed retailers to avoid unknowingly buying counterfeit and illegal merchandise.

Victims of Crime: If you or someone you know becomes the victim of a crime abroad, you should contact the local police and the nearest U.S. embassy or consulate. We can:

- Replace a stolen passport.
- For violent crimes such as assault or rape, help you find appropriate medical care.
- Put you in contact with the appropriate police authorities and, if you want us to, we can contact family members or friends.
- Although the local authorities are responsible for investigating and prosecuting the crime, consular officers can help you understand the local criminal justice process and can direct you to local attorneys.

The local equivalent to the "911" emergency line in Italy is 113.

Criminal Penalties: While you are traveling in Italy, you are subject to its laws even if you are a U.S. citizen. Foreign laws and legal systems can be vastly different than our own, and criminal penalties vary from country to country. There are also some things that might be legal in the country you visit, but still illegal in the United States; for instance, you can be prosecuted under U.S. law if you buy pirated goods.

Engaging in sexual conduct with children or using or disseminating child pornography in a foreign country is a crime prosecutable in the United States. If you break local laws in Italy, your U.S. passport won't help you avoid arrest or prosecution. It's very important to know what's legal and what's not where you are going.

Arrest notifications in host country: While some countries will automatically notify the nearest U.S. embassy or consulate if a U.S. citizen is detained or arrested in a foreign country, that might not always be the case.

To ensure that the United States is aware of your circumstances, request that the police and prison officials notify the nearest U.S. embassy or consulate as soon as you are arrested or detained overseas.

Special Circumstances: Strikes and other work stoppages occur frequently in the transportation sector (national airlines, airports, trains, and bus lines); most are announced in advance and are of short duration. Reconfirmation of domestic and international flight reservations is highly recommended. You must obey local transportation laws and regulations. You must purchase train tickets and validate them by punching them in validating machines usually located near the entrance of train tracks prior to boarding. Failure to follow this procedure may result in an on-the-spot fine by an inspector on the train. You must purchase bus tickets prior to boarding and validate them immediately after boarding.

Tickets may be purchased at tobacco stores or kiosks. Failure to follow this procedure may result in an immediate fine imposed by an inspector on the bus. If the violator does not pay the fine on the spot, it will automatically double and will be forwarded to the violator's home address. You must obey local driving laws and regulations. Vehicle traffic in some historic downtown areas of cities and towns throughout Italy is limited by a system of permits (called "ZTL" and functioning the same way as an electronic toll system in the United States might on the freeway). Cameras record the license plates of cars driving in parts of the city that require a permit. Although most of the automated verification stations are clearly marked, if a driver passes one it is impossible to know at the time that a violation occurred or has been recorded. Violators are not pulled over or stopped, and there is no personal contact with a police officer. Whenever possible, the fines imposed for these violations are forwarded to the driver's home in the United States to request payment. Notice from Italian authorities of a violation may take a year or longer to arrive. The fines are cumulative for each time a driver passes a control point. A similar system of automated traffic control cameras is in place in many parts of the highway system and is used to ticket speeding violations.

Accessibility: While in Italy, travelers with disabilities may find accessibility and accommodation different from what is found in the United States. Many find Italy's narrow cobbled streets and storied monuments charming; they can, however, be a challenge for physically impaired travelers. Many Italian sidewalks lack ramps, some Italian streets lack sidewalks altogether, or for instance in the case of Venice, may feature staircases and narrow pedestrian bridges. While some major sights and hotels have put time and planning into ensuring accessibility, there are others that lack ramps, elevators, or handicap-accessible bathrooms. Advance planning can go a long way in making a difference in accommodation for disabled travelers. Inform airlines and hotels of your disabilities when making reservations as some time may be needed to prepare accommodation. Call ahead to restaurants, museums, and other facilities to find out if they are wheelchair-accessible. Most, but not all train stations in Italy have accommodations for those traveling in wheelchairs. With advance notice, personal assistance can be provided to a disabled person traveling through a particular station.

More information is available at Trenitalia's website addressing disabled travelers. For those who wish to rent cars, hand-controlled vehicles are available in Italy from major car-rental companies. You should contact the car rental company well in advance of your trip in order to reserve the vehicle. Remember that Italy functions on 220 volt current. To recharge an electric wheelchair motor you may require a transformer to change the 220 current to 110 volts, as well as an adaptor to adjust the plug to fit Italian electric sockets.

Guide-dog owners must present the documentation required by European Union Member States in order to enter Italy with a dog.

Medical Facilities and Health Information: Medical facilities are available, but may be limited outside urban areas. Public hospitals, though generally free of charge for emergency services, sometimes do not maintain the same standards as hospitals in the United States, so you are encouraged to obtain insurance that would cover a stay in a private Italian hospital or clinic. It is almost impossible to obtain an itemized hospital bill from public hospitals, as required by many U.S. insurance companies, because the Italian National Health Service charges one inclusive rate (care services, room and board). In parts of southern Italy, the lack of adequate trash disposal and incineration sites has led to periodic accumulations of garbage in urban and rural areas. In some cases, residents have burned garbage, resulting in toxic emissions that can aggravate respiratory problems.

The U.S. Navy initiated a public health evaluation in the Naples area in 2008. After finding levels of bacterial and chemical contamination of potential health concern, particularly in samples of area well water, the Navy recommended all personnel living off-base in the Naples area use only bottled water for drinking, cooking, ice-making, and brushing teeth. For more information on safe food and water precautions, see the Centers for Disease Control and Prevention (CDC) website.

You can find good information on vaccinations and other health precautions, on the CDC website. For information about outbreaks of infectious diseases abroad, consult the World Health Organization (WHO) website, which also contains additional health information for travelers, including detailed country-specific health information.

Medical Insurance: You can't assume your insurance will go with you when you travel. It's very important to find out BEFORE you leave. You need to ask your insurance company two questions:

- Does my policy apply when I'm out of the U.S.?
- Will it cover emergencies like a trip to a foreign hospital or a medical evacuation?

In many places, doctors and hospitals still expect payment in cash at the time of service. Your regular U.S. health insurance may not cover doctors' and hospital visits in other countries. If your policy doesn't go with you when you travel, it's a very good idea to take out another one for your trip.

Traffic Safety and Road Conditions: While in Italy, you may encounter road conditions that differ significantly from those in the United States. Italy has one of the highest rates of car accident deaths in the European Union. Streets in Italian historic city centers are often narrow, winding, and congested. Motor scooters are very popular, and scooter drivers often see themselves as exempt from conventions that apply to automobiles. Pedestrians and drivers should be constantly alert to the possibility of a scooter's sudden presence. Most vehicle-related deaths and injuries involve pedestrians or cyclists who are involved in collisions with scooters or other vehicles. Be particularly cautious if you rent a scooter. You should remain vigilant and alert when walking or cycling near traffic. Pedestrians should be careful, as sidewalks can be extremely congested and uneven. Drivers of bicycles, motorcycles, and other vehicles routinely ignore traffic signals and traffic flows, and park and drive on sidewalks. For safety, pedestrians should look carefully in both directions before crossing streets, even when using a marked crosswalk with a green avanti ("walk") light illuminated.

Traffic lights are limited and often disobeyed, and a different convention of right-of-way is observed. Italy has over 5,600 kilometers (3,480 mi.) of Autostrada, or superhighways. Commercial and individual vehicles travel and pass on these well-maintained roads at very high speeds. In rural areas, a wide range of speed on highways makes for hazardous driving. Roads are generally narrow and often have no guardrails.

Travelers in northern Italy, especially in winter, should be aware of fog and poor visibility, responsible for multiple-car accidents each year. Most Italian automobiles are equipped with special fog lights. Use of safety belts and child restraining devices is mandatory and headlights should be on at all times outside of urban areas. U.S. citizens driving in Italy should also note that, according to Italian regulation, if a resident of a non-European Union country (e.g. the United States) violates a traffic law, the violator must pay the fine at the time the violation occurs to the police officer issuing the ticket. If the citizen does not or cannot pay the fine at the time, Italian regulation allows the police officer to confiscate the offender's vehicle (even if the vehicle is a rental vehicle). For specific information concerning Italian driving permits, vehicle inspection, road tax, and mandatory insurance, contact the Italian Government Tourist Board (ENIT), tel: 212-245-5618; or the A.C.I. (Automobile Club d'Italia) at Via Marsala 14A, 00185 Rome, tel: 39-06-4998–2496. For information on obtaining international drivers licenses, contact AAA or the American Automobile Touring Alliance.

Aviation Safety Oversight: The U.S. Federal Aviation Administration (FAA) assessed the Government of Italy's Civil Aviation Authority as being in compliance with International Civil Aviation Organization (ICAO) aviation safety standards for oversight of Italy's air carrier operations. Further information may be found on the FAA safety assessment page.

Children's Issues: Please see the U.S. Dept. of State Office of Children's Issues web pages on intercountry adoption and international parental child abduction.

Intercountry Adoption

September 2009

The information in this section has been edited from the latest report available as of February 2013 from the State Department Bureau of Consular Affairs, Office of Overseas Citizens Services. For more information, please read the *Intercountry Adoption* section of this book and review current reports online at http://adoption.state.gov.

Who Can Adopt? Adoption between the United States and Italy is governed by the Hague Adoption Convention. Therefore to adopt from Italy, you must first be found eligible to adopt by the U.S. Government. The U.S. Government agency responsible for making this determination is the Department of Homeland Security, U.S. Citizenship and Immigration Services (USCIS).

Residency Requirements: Prospective adoptive parents must legally reside in Italy.

Age Requirements: Adoptive parents must be at least eighteen years old and no more than forty-five years over the age of the adoptee.

Marriage Requirements: Only married couples may adopt. The couple must have been married for at least three years (without separation during the three-year period prior to the adoption) and must reside in Italy. Single persons can only adopt in very limited circumstances.

Other Requirements: Same-sex couples cannot adopt in Italy.

Who Can Be Adopted? Because Italy is party to the Hague Adoption Convention, children from Italy must meet the requirements of the Convention in order to be eligible for adoption. For example, the Convention requires that Italy attempt to place a child with a family in-country before determining that a child is eligible for intercountry adoption. In addition to Italy's requirements, a child must meet the definition of a Convention adoptee for you to bring him or her back to the United States.

Eligibility Requirements: The judge can terminate the parental custody when the parent violates or neglects his/her parental duties or abuses of his/her powers, with serious prejudice to the child. Therefore, due to serious reasons, the judge can order the removal of either the child or the parent, who mistreats or abuses the minor, from the family's residence. In order to be declared "adoptable," the child must be in a state of abandonment, meaning that the child cannot live in his or her own family. The minor who is deprived of moral and material assistance by the parents or relatives, who are considered responsible for his/her support, is considered abandoned.

Age Requirements: Children age 14 and older can only be adopted if they personally consent to the adoption.

Sibling Requirements: Prospective adoptive parents are allowed to apply for more adoptions. If prospective adoptive parents have already adopted a sibling or if they apply for the adoption of siblings at the same time, this is considered preferential criteria for the adoption.

Waiting Period: Up to three years.

Adoption Authority: Commissione per le Adozioni Internazionali (Commission for Intercountry Adoption). NOTE: City Juvenile Courts oversee the handling of adoption cases. For a complete listing of these courts, prospective adoptive parents should visit the following website: http://www.commissioneadozioni.it.

The Process: Because Italy is party to the Hague Adoption Convention, adopting from Italy must follow a specific process designed to meet the Convention's requirements.

For detailed and updated information on these requirements, please review the *Intercountry Adoption* section of this publication and visit the USCIS Intercountry Adoption website at http://adoption.state.gov.

Role of the Adoption Authority: The Adoption authority in Italy has the following roles:

- collect, preserve and exchange information about the situation of the child and the prospective adoptive parents, so far as is necessary to complete the adoption;

- facilitate, follow and expedite proceedings with a view to obtaining the adoption;
- promote the development of adoption counseling and post-adoption services in their States;
- provide each other with general evaluation reports about experience with intercountry adoption;
- reply, in so far as is permitted by the law of their State, to justified requests from other Central Authorities or public authorities for information about a particular adoption situation.

Role of the Court: City Juvenile Courts oversee the handling of adoption cases. For a complete listing of these courts, prospective adoptive parents should visit http://www.commissioneadozioni.it. Prospective adoptive parents start the adoption procedure by submitting a request called "Dicharazione alla Disponabilità per l'Adozione" (Declaration of Willingness to Adopt) to the Juvenile Court in the city of their choice. Prospective adoption parents can submit more than one request to Juvenile Courts in various cities as long as all of the Juvenile Courts are aware of all of the requests made. Based on the information provided by the prospective adoptive parents, the Juvenile Court selects the child that better matches the prospective adoptive parents. There are no further details on how the child is selected by the Juvenile Court. There is a fostering period of one year which can be extended to two years. During that period, the local Juvenile Court monitors and provides support to the prospective adoptive parents. At the end of the fostering period, the Juvenile Court either confirms or revokes the adoption. The Court will request the intervention of the local social services agency to assist and evaluate the couple, prepare a home study, and report the findings to the Court. The Juvenile Court can also appoint a judge and/or a team of specialists, who will hold meetings with the prospective adoptive parents in order to evaluate them and/or to provide additional information.

Role of Adoption Agencies: The appointed local social services agency will then conduct a study on the prospective adoptive parents in order to evaluate their capacity to bring up the minor, their personal economic situation, their personal health conditions, the family environment and the motivation of their request.

Time Frame: An adoption in Italy can take up to three years from the time the application is filed with the juvenile court until the child is in the new family's home and the adoption is finalized.

Adoption Fees: In the adoption services contract that you sign at the beginning of the adoption process, your agency will itemize the fees and estimated expenses related to your adoption process. In Italy, national adoption services are free of charge.

Documents Required: The Declaration of Willingness to Adopt should be accompanied by the following documents:

- Birth Certificates of the prospective adoptive parents;
- Registry Office certificate ("Stato di Famiglia");
- Declaration of consent to adopt by the prospective adoptive parents' parents, given in the form of an affidavit or, should they be deceased, death certificate(s) of adoptive parents' parents;
- Medical certificate issued by family doctor;
- Evidence of economic means (i.e. tax returns; pay stubs);
- Criminal record of adoptive parents;
- Notarial act, or equivalent declaration, attesting that there is neither legal nor de facto separation between the adoptive couple.

Bringing Your Child Home: Once your adoption is complete (or you have obtained legal custody of the child), there are a few more steps to take before you can head home. Specifically, you need to apply for several documents for your child before he or she can travel to the United States, such as a birth certificate, a passport or travel document for your child from the country in which he or she was born, and a U.S. Immigration Visa.

Child Citizenship Act: For adoptions finalized abroad, the Child Citizenship Act of 2000 allows your new child to acquire American citizenship automatically when he or she enters the United States as lawful permanent residents. For adoptions finalized in the United States, the Child Citizenship Act of 2000 allows your new child to acquire American citizenship automatically when the court in the United States issues the final adoption decree. To learn more, review the *Intercountry Adoption* section on this publication and visit the USCIS Intercountry Adoption website at http://adoption.state.gov.

After Adoption: Italy has no requirements for the adoptive parents after the adoption requirements

U.S. Embassy in Italy
Via Vittorio Veneto 121—00187
ROMA
Tel: (switchboard): (+39) 06.46741
Fax: (+39) 06.4674.2244
Email: uscitizensrome@state.gov
Internet:
http://italy.usembassy.gov/english

Italy's Adoption Authority
Commissione per le Adozioni
Internazionali
Largo Chigi, 19
00187 ROMA
Telephone numbers: +39 (06) 6779 2060/66/68
Fax: number: +39 (06) 6779 2165
cai.segreteria-enti@palazzochigi.it
http://www.commissioneadozioni.it

Embassy of Italy
Address: 3000 Whitehaven Street, NW, Washington, DC 20008
Tel.: (202) 612-4400
Fax: (202) 518-2151
http://www.ambwashingtondc.esteri.it/ambasciata_washington

Office of Children's Issues
U.S. Department of State
2201 C Street, NW
SA-29
Washington, DC 20520
Tel: 1-888-407-4747
E-mail: AskCI@state.gov
http://adoption.state.gov

For questions about immigration procedures, call the National Customer Service Center (NCSC) 1-800-375-5283 (TTY 1-800-767-1833).

International Parental Child Abduction

November 2012

Disclaimer: The information in this flyer is provided for general information only, is not intended to be legal advice, and may change without notice. Questions involving interpretation of law should be addressed to an attorney licensed to practice in the relevant jurisdiction.

General Information: Italy and the United States have been treaty partners under the 1980 Hague Convention on the Civil Aspects of International Child Abduction (Hague Abduction Convention) since May 1, 1995.

Hague Abduction Convention: The U.S. Department of State serves as the U.S. Central Authority (USCA) for the Hague Abduction Convention. Parents are strongly encouraged to contact the Department of State for assistance prior to initiating the Hague process directly with the foreign Central Authority

United States Department of State
Office of Children's Issues
2201 C Street, N.W.
Washington, DC 20520
Telephone: 1-888-407-4747
Outside the United States or Canada: 1-202-501-4444
Fax: 202-736-9132

The Italian Central Authority (ICA) for the Hague Abduction Convention is the Ministero della Giustizia. The ICA has an administrative role in processing Hague Abduction Convention applications. The ICA forwards completed Hague applications to the appropriate Public Prosecutor attached to the civil court of general jurisdiction in the jurisdiction where the defendant resides. The Prosecutor brings the case on behalf of Italy. The ICA can be reached at:

Ministero della Giustizia
Dipartimento per la Giustizia Minorile
Via Damiano Chiesa No 24
00136 Rome
Italia
Email:
autoritacentrali.dgm@giustizia.it
Website: www.giustiziaminorle.it

To initiate a Hague case for return of, or access to, a child in Italy, the USCA encourages a parent or legal guardian to review the eligibility criteria and instructions for completing the Hague application. For more information on the Hague Convention and the application process, please read the *International Parental Child Abduction* section of this book and review current reports online at www.travel.state.gov/abduction.

Return: A parent or legal guardian may file an application under the Hague Abduction Convention for return to the United States of a child abducted to, or wrongfully retained in, Italy. The U.S. Department of State can assist parents living in the United States to understand whether the Convention is an available civil remedy and can provide information on the process for submitting a Hague application.

Visitation/Access: A person may file an application under the Hague Abduction Convention for access to a child living in Italy. The criteria for acceptance of a Hague access application vary from country to country. The U.S. Department of State can assist parents living in the United States to understand country-specific criteria and provide information on the process for submitting a Hague application.

Retaining an Attorney: Parents or legal guardians are not required to retain a private attorney in order to file a Hague Abduction Convention application with a court in Italy. The ICA assigns a legal representative to present the case to the court. However, the legal representative does not represent the left-behind parent or the legal guardian who submitted the Hague Abduction Convention application; instead, the legal representative represents Italy and submits the request for return on behalf of the Italian Minister of Justice. Parents or legal guardians have the option to hire a private attorney at their own expense. The U.S. Embassy in Rome, Italy, posts a list of attorneys including those who specialize in family law at: http://italy.usembassy.gov/acs/professionals/lawyers/lawyers-main.html. This list is provided as a courtesy service only and does not constitute an endorsement of any individual attorney.

Mediation: The USCA is not aware of any government or private organizations in Italy that offer mediation services in either abduction or access cases.

U.S. Embassy Rome
via Vittorio Veneto 121
00187 Rome
Italy
Telephone: (39) 06 4674 2406
Email: uscitizensrome@state.gov
Website: italy.usembassy.gov

The Embassy of Italy is located in Washington, D.C., at:

Embassy of Italy
3000 Whitehaven Street, NW
Washington, DC 20008
Telephone: (202) 612-4400
Fax: (202) 518-2154
Website:
http://www.ambwashingondc.esteri.it

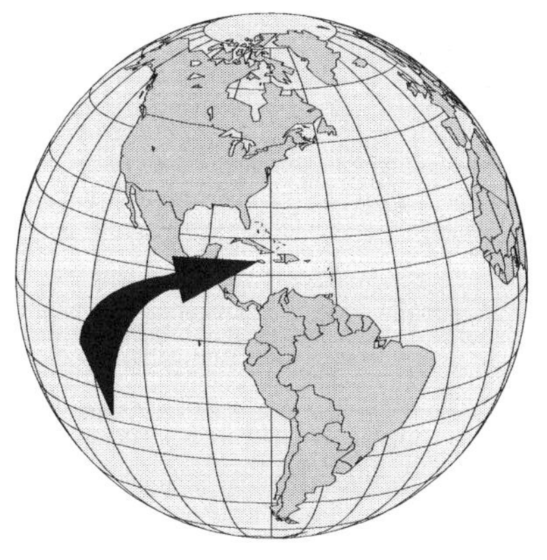

JAMAICA

Compiled from publications that were available as of February 2013 from the U.S. Department of State, the U.S. Department of Commerce, and the Central Intelligence Agency (CIA). See the introduction to this set for explanatory notes.

Official Name:
Jamaica

PROFILE

Geography

Area: total: 10,991 sq km; country comparison to the world: 168; land: 10,831 sq km; water: 160 sq km

Major cities: kingston (capital) 580,000 (2009)

Climate: tropical; hot, humid; temperate interior

Terrain: mostly mountains, with narrow, discontinuous coastal plain

People

Nationality: noun: Jamaican(s); adjective: Jamaican

Population: 2,889,187 (July 2012 est.)

Population growth rate: 0.714% (2012 est.)

Ethnic groups: black 91.2%, mixed 6.2%, other or unknown 2.6% (2001 census)

Religions: Protestant 62.5% (Seventh-Day Adventist 10.8%, Pentecostal 9.5%, Other Church of God 8.3%, Baptist 7.2%, New Testament Church of God 6.3%, Church of God in Jamaica 4.8%, Church of God of Prophecy 4.3%, Anglican 3.6%, other Christian 7.7%), Roman Catholic 2.6%, other or unspecified 14.2%, none 20.9%, (2001 census)

Languages: English, English patois

Literacy: definition: age 15 and over has ever attended school; total population: 87.9%; male: 84.1%; female: 91.6% (2003 est.)

Health: life expectancy at birth: total population: 73.43 years; male: 71.78 years; female: 75.15 years (2012 est.); Infant mortality rate: total: 14.3 deaths/1,000 live births; male: 14.87 deaths/1,000 live births; female: 13.69 deaths/1,000 live births (2012 est.)

Unemployment rate: 14.2% (2012 est.)

Work force: 1.325 million (2012 est.)

Government

Type: constitutional parliamentary democracy and a Commonwealth realm

Independence: 6 August 1962

Constitution: 6 August 1962

Political subdivisions: 14 parishes; Clarendon, Hanover, Kingston, Manchester, Portland, Saint Andrew, Saint Ann, Saint Catherine, Saint Elizabeth, Saint James, Saint Mary, Saint Thomas, Trelawny, Westmoreland

Suffrage: 18 years of age; universal

Economy

GDP (purchasing power parity): $25.18 billion (2012 est.); $25.07 billion (2011 est.); $24.69 billion (2010 est.); $25.05 billion (2009 est.)

GDP real growth rate: 0.9% (2012 est.); 1.5% (2011 est.); -1.4% (2010 est.); -3.1% (2009 est.)

GDP per capita (PPP): $9,100 (2012 est.); $9,100 (2011 est.); $9,000 (2010 est.); $9,200 (2009 est.)

Natural resources: bauxite, gypsum, limestone

Agriculture products: sugarcane, bananas, coffee, citrus, yams, ackees, vegetables; poultry, goats, milk; shellfish

Industries: tourism, bauxite/alumina, agro processing, light manufactures, rum, cement, metal, paper, chemical products, telecommunications

Exports: $1.718 billion (2012 est.); $1.613 billion (2011 est.); $1.37 billion (2010 est.)

Exports—commodities: alumina, bauxite, sugar, rum, coffee, yams, beverages, chemicals, wearing apparel, mineral fuels

Exports—partners: US 37%, Canada 18.1%, Netherlands 7.3%, UK 5.4%, Norway 4.3% (2011)

Imports: $6.019 billion (2012 est.); $6.292 billion (2011 est.); $4.629 billion (2010 est.)

Imports—commodities: food and other consumer goods, industrial supplies, fuel, parts and accessories of capital goods, machinery and transport equipment, construction materials

Imports—partners: US 33.9%, Venezuela 15.5%, Trinidad and Tobago 14.6%, China 6.6% (2011)

Debt—external: $14.7 billion (31 December 2011 est.); $13.87 billion (31 December 2010 est.)

Exchange rates: Jamaican dollars (JMD) per US dollar; 88.59 (2012 est.); 85.892 (2011 est.); 87.196 (2010 est.); 87.89 (2009); 72.236 (2008); 69.034 (2007)

PEOPLE AND HISTORY

Arawaks from South America had settled in Jamaica prior to Christopher Columbus' first arrival at the island in 1494. During Spain's occupation of the island, starting in 1510, the Arawaks were exterminated by disease, slavery, and war. Spain brought the first African slaves to Jamaica in 1517. In 1655, British forces seized the island, and in 1670, Great Britain gained formal possession.

Sugar made Jamaica one of the most valuable possessions in the world for more than 150 years. The British Parliament abolished slavery as of August 1, 1834. After a long period of direct British colonial rule, Jamaica gained a degree of local political control in the late 1930s, and held its first election under full universal adult suffrage in 1944. Jamaica joined nine other U.K. territories in the West Indies Federation in 1958 but withdrew after Jamaican voters rejected membership in 1961. Jamaica gained independence in 1962, remaining a member of the Commonwealth.

Historically, Jamaican emigration has been heavy. Since the United Kingdom restricted emigration in 1967, the major flow has been to the United States and Canada. About 20,000 Jamaicans emigrate to the United States each year; another 200,000 visit annually. New York, Miami, Chicago, and Hartford are among the U.S. cities with a significant Jamaican population.

Religion

According to the most recent census (2001), religious affiliation as a proportion of the population is: Church of God, 24 percent; Seventh-day Adventist, 11 percent; Pentecostal, 10 percent; Baptist, 7 percent; Anglican, 4 percent; Roman Catholic, 2 percent; United Church, 2 percent; Methodist, 2 percent; Jehovah's Witnesses, 2 percent; Moravian, 1 percent; Brethren, 1 percent; unstated, 3 percent; and "other," 10 percent. The category "other" included 24,020 Rastafarians, an estimated 5,000 Muslims, 1,453 Hindus, approximately 350 Jews, and 279 Baha'is. The census reported 21 percent claimed no religious affiliation.

GOVERNMENT AND POLITICAL CONDITIONS

Jamaica is a constitutional parliamentary democracy. On December 29, 2011, the opposition Peoples National Party (PNP) won 42 of the 63 seats in the House of Representatives, and PNP leader Portia Simpson Miller was sworn in as prime minister on January 5, 2012. International election observers deemed the elections transparent, free and fair, and without violence.

Recent Elections

In general elections held on December 29, 2011, the opposition PNP won 42 of the 63 seats in the House of Representatives, and PNP leader Portia Simpson Miller was to be sworn in as prime minister on January 5, 2012. Simpson Miller, who also served as prime minister in 2006–07, defeated the JLP led by Prime Minister Andrew Holness. International election observers from the Caribbean Community and the OAS deemed the elections transparent, free and fair, and without violence. A local organization, Citizen Action for Free and Fair Elections, also provided volunteer election observers, as it did in every election since 1998. In a preliminary assessment, the OAS cited adherence to agreements negotiated by the country's Electoral Office between the parties on media, advertising protocols, and campaigning rules as important elements that helped strengthen the democratic process. The OAS recommendations included ensuring adequate space to guarantee voter privacy, clarifying the duties of political liaison officers, providing copies of the voters' lists at polling stations, and improving signage at the entrance to polling stations.

All citizens age 18 and over have the right to vote by secret ballot. The relative lack of violence and intimidation in the December elections was notable, especially because in past elections voters living in "garrison communities," inner-city areas dominated by one of the two major political parties, often faced substantial influence and pressure from politically connected gangs and young men helping one political party by intimidating supporters of the opposing political party. Unlike in the past, however, civil society activism and pressure from the private sector, churches, and civic watchdogs made it difficult for either party to continue past practices of intimidation, lack of transparency, and back-room deals.

Participation of Women and Minorities: On December 29, 2011, voters elected eight women to the new Parliament, including three of the JLP's 13 female candidates and five of the six PNP nominees, including the party leader and candidate for prime minister. During 2011 there were eight female members in the 60-seat House of Representatives and three women appointed to the 21-seat Senate. One of the 16 cabinet ministers was a woman. A woman was elected speaker of the house on July 12, the second woman in the country's history to hold the position.

Principal Government Officials

Last Updated: 1/31/2013

Governor Gen.: **Patrick Linton ALLEN**
Prime Min.: **Portia SIMPSON-MILLER**

Min. of Agriculture & Fisheries: **Roger CLARKE**
Min. of Education: **Ronald THWAITES**
Min. of Finance, Planning, & the Public Service: **Peter PHILLIPS**
Min. of Foreign Affairs & Foreign Trade: **Arnold J. NICHOLSON**
Min. of Health: **Fenton FERGUSON**
Min. of Industry, Investment, & Commerce: **Anthony HYLTON**
Min. of Justice: **Mark GOLDING**
Min. of Labor & Social Security: **Derrick KELLIER**
Min. of Local Govt. & Community Development: **Noel ARSCOTT**
Min. of National Security: **Peter BUNTING**
Min. of Science, Technology, Energy, & Mining: **Phillip PAULWELL**
Min. of Tourism & Entertainment: **Wykeham MCNEILL**
Min. of Transport, Works, & Housing: **Omar DAVIES**
Min. of Water, Land, Environment, & Climate Change: **Robert PICKERSGILL**
Min. of Youth & Culture: **Lisa HANNA**
Min. Without Portfolio With Responsibility for Housing: **Morais GUY**
Min. Without Portfolio With Responsibility for Information: **Sandrea FALCONER**
Min. Without Portfolio With Responsibility for Public Service: **Horace DALLEY**
Min. Without Portfolio With Responsibility for Sports: **Natalie NEITA-HEADLEY**
Attorney Gen.: **Patrick ATKINSON**
Governor, Central Bank: **Bryan WYNTER**
Ambassador to the US: **Stephen VASCIANNIE**
Permanent Representative to the UN, New York: **Raymond Osbourne WOLFE**

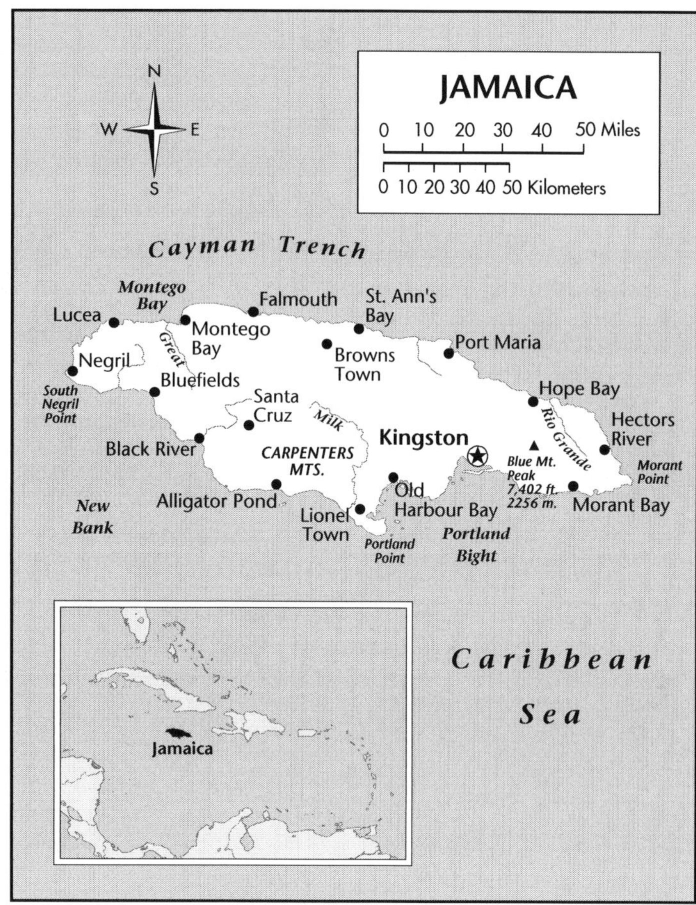

ECONOMY

The Jamaican economy is heavily dependent on services, which now account for nearly 65% of GDP. The country continues to derive most of its foreign exchange from tourism, remittances, and bauxite/alumina. Remittances account for nearly 15% of GDP and exports of bauxite and alumina make up about 10%. The bauxite/alumina sector was most affected by the global downturn while the tourism industry was resilient, experiencing an increase of 4% in tourist arrivals. Tourism revenues account for roughly 10% of GDP, and both arrivals and revenues grew in 2010, up 4% and 6% respectively. Jamaica's economy faces many challenges to growth: high crime and corruption, large-scale unemployment and underemployment, and a debt-to-GDP ratio of more than 120%.

Jamaica's onerous public debt burden is the result of government bailouts to ailing sectors of the economy, most notably to the financial sector in the mid-to-late 1990s. In early 2010, the Jamaican government created the Jamaica Debt Exchange in order to retire high-priced domestic bonds and significantly reduce annual debt servicing.

The Government of Jamaica signed a $1.27 billion, 27-month Standby Agreement with the International Monetary Fund for balance of payment support in February 2010. Other multilaterals have also provided millions of dollars in loans and grants. Despite the improvement, debt servicing costs still hinder the government's ability to spend on infrastructure and social programs, particularly as job losses rise in a shrinking economy.

The Simpson-Miller administration faces the difficult prospect of having to achieve fiscal discipline in order to maintain debt payments, while simultaneously attacking a serious crime problem that is hampering economic growth. High unemployment exacerbates the crime problem, including gang violence that is fueled by the drug trade. As of late 2012, the Simpson-Miller government was working to negotiate a new IMF Stand-by agreement to gain access to additional funds.

Labor Conditions

The law protects children from exploitation in the workplace and stipulates that every citizen has a duty to report child abuse. The minimum age for employment is 15 years, and the law prohibits the employment of children under age 13 in any type of work. Children between ages 13 and 15 are permitted to engage in "light work," as defined by the Ministry of Labor, which will not disrupt their education or be harmful to their health. Children are not to work more than four hours in a day. The law prohibits hazardous work for all children under 18.

The minimum wage was J$4,500 ($55.15) per week for all workers. In practice some minimum-wage earners worked two or more jobs, but most workers were paid more than the legal minimum. There were, however, some reports of domestic workers receiving less than the minimum wage.

The law provides for a standard 40-hour workweek and mandates at least one day of rest per week. Work in excess of 40 hours per week or eight hours per day must be compensated at overtime rates, a provision that was generally respected. The law also provides for paid annual holidays. The law does not prohibit excessive compulsory overtime. Some employees, notably security guards, were regularly required to work 12-hour shifts without overtime compensation. The Ministry of Labor's Industrial Safety Division sets industrial health and safety standards.

U.S.-JAMAICAN RELATIONS

The United States established diplomatic relations with Jamaica in 1962 following its independence from the United Kingdom. The United States and Jamaica maintain close and productive relations. The two countries enjoy a close friendship based on trust and mutual interest, strengthened by people-to-people ties and a vibrant Jamaican-American community. The United States and Jamaica collaborate within the Caribbean Basin Security Initiative to foster a safer and more secure environment and increased prosperity and stability for both countries. They work together to promote sustainable economic development, including through the Caribbean IdEA Marketplace. This is a business competition that connects local entrepreneurs with members of the Caribbean diaspora, with the goal of forming new partnerships that will create jobs and economic opportunities in the region.

U.S. Assistance to Jamaica

The United States seeks to strengthen its partnership with Jamaica by providing assistance to address key social issues that contribute to high levels of violent crime and transnational criminal activity. Priority goals include reducing corruption; promoting greater transparency and good governance; fostering Jamaican participation in regional security efforts; strengthening basic education; and increasing adaptation to climate change. Regional HIV/AIDS and security programs complement U.S. assistance.

Bilateral Economic Relations

The United States is Jamaica's most important trading partner. Jamaica seeks to attract U.S. investment and generally supports efforts to liberalize trade. The country is a beneficiary of the Caribbean Basin Trade Partner Act, and it has an investment treaty and a double taxation agreement with the United States. More than 80 U.S. firms have operations in the country. Jamaica is a popular destination for American tourists.

Jamaica's Membership in International Organizations

Jamaica and the United States belong to a number of the same international organizations, including the United Nations, Organization of American States, International Monetary Fund, World Bank, and World Trade Organization.

Bilateral Representation

Italy maintains an embassy in the United States at 3000 Whitehaven Street, NW, Washington, DC 20008 (tel. 202-612-4400).

Principal U.S. Embassy Officials

Last Updated: 1/14/2013

KINGSTON (E) 142 Old Hope Road, Kingston 6, 876-702-6000, Fax 876-702-6001, Workweek: M-F; 07:15 to 16:00; most offices allow flex time; all offices staffed core hours, some staff take Friday afternoons off, working longer on other days, Website: http://kingston.usembassy.gov/

DCM OMS:	Janelle Walker
AMB OMS:	Jacqueline Lawrence
CDC:	Rachel Albalak
CG OMS:	Cheri Champ
DHS/CIS:	Adijatu Abiose
DHS/ICE:	James Stitzel
FM:	Wall, David
HRO:	Judith Glen
MGT:	Leslie Degraffenried
NAS/INL:	Gary Rex
POL/ECON:	Alexander Martschenko
POSHO:	Wall, David
SDO/DATT:	LTC Thomas Newman
AMB:	Pamela Bridgewater
CG:	David Stone
DCM:	Brown, Raymond
PAO:	Yolonda Kerney
GSO:	Lloyd Champ
RSO:	Vincent Cooper
AGR:	Margaret Bauer
AID:	Denise Herbol
APHIS:	Steve Crook
CLO:	Newman, Jade
DEA:	Gavin Kersellius
EEO:	Alexander Martschenko
FAA:	Allan B. Hurr
FMO:	Melissa Huth
ICASS Chair:	Gavin Kersellius
IMO:	Anbess Keffelew
ISO:	Cynthia Atnip
ISSO:	Anbess Keffelew
LEGATT:	Donitta Clark
State ICASS:	David Stone

Other Contact Information

U.S. Department of Commerce International Trade Administration Trade Information Center
14th and Constitution Avenue, NW
Washington, DC 20230
Tel: 800-USA-TRADE
or 800-872-8723
Web site: http://trade.gov/

American Chamber of Commerce of Jamaica
The Jamaica Pegasus
81 Knutsford Blvd
Kingston 5, Jamaica
Tel: (876) 929-7866/67
Fax: (876) 929-8597
Web site:
http://www.amchamjamaica.org/
E-mail: amcham@cwjamaica.com

Caribbean-Central American Action
1710 Rhode Island Ave, NW
Suite 300, Washington, DC 20036
Tel: (202) 331-9467
Fax: (202) 785-0376
Web site: http://www.c-caa.org/

TRAVEL

Consular Information Sheet

January 8, 2013

Country Description: Jamaica is a developing nation of over 2.6 million people. Facilities for tourists are widely available. International airports are located in Kingston and Montego Bay

Smart Traveler Enrollment Program (STEP)/Embassy Locations: If you are going to live in or visit Jamaica, please take the time to tell our Embassy or Consulate about your trip. If you check in, we can keep you up to date with important safety and security announcements. It will also help your friends and family get in touch with you in an emergency.

U.S. Embassy Kingston
142 Old Hope Road
Kingston, Jamaica
Telephone: (876) 702-6000
Facsimile: (876) 702-6018
Email: KingstonACS@state.gov

U.S. Consular Agency
in Montego Bay
Whitter Village, Unit EU-1
Ironshore (across from Burger King)
Montego Bay
Tel: (876) 953-0620
Fax: (876) 953-3898
Public Hours are M-F,
from 9:00 a.m.-12:30 p.m.
Email: MobayACS@state.gov

The U.S. Embassy in Kingston also has consular responsibility for the Cayman Islands, a British dependent territory.

U.S. Consular Agency
Cayman Islands
Cayman Center Unit B-1
118 Dorcy Drive
Georgetown, Grand Cayman Island
Public Hours are M-F,
from 8:00 a.m.-1:00 p.m.
Telephone: (345) 945-8173
Email: CaymanACS@state.gov

Entry/Exit Requirements for U.S. Citizens: All U.S. citizens traveling by air outside of the United States are required to present a passport or other valid travel document to exit or enter the United States. U.S. citizens traveling by sea must present a Western Hemisphere Travel Initiative (WHTI) compliant document such as a passport or a passport card for entry to the United States. While passport cards are sufficient for entry into the United States, they may not be accepted by the particular country you plan to visit; please be sure to check with your cruise line and countries of destination for any foreign entry requirements. Passport cards are an acceptable travel document for entry into Jamaica for sea travelers only.

Visitors to Jamaica must have a return ticket and be able to show sufficient funds for their visit. U.S. citizens traveling to Jamaica for work or extended stays are required to have a current U.S. passport and a visa issued by the Jamaican Embassy or a Jamaican Consulate. There is a departure tax for travelers, which is regularly included in airfare. For further information, travelers may contact the Embassy of Jamaica at 1520 New Hampshire Avenue NW, Washington, DC 20036, telephone (202) 452-0660; the Jamaican Consulate General in Miami (25 SE 2nd Ave # 850 Miami, FL 33131–1699, tel:(305) 374-8431) or the Jamaican Consulate General in New York (767 3rd Ave # 2 New York, NY 10017–9032, tel: (212) 935-9000); or honorary consuls in Atlanta, Boston, Chicago, Houston, Seattle or Los Angeles.

The U.S. Department of State is unaware of any HIV/AIDS entry restrictions for visitors to or foreign residents of Jamaica.

Threats to Safety and Security: Violence and shootings occur regularly in certain areas of Kingston and Montego Bay. Embassy employees as well as private U.S. citizens are advised to avoid traveling into high-threat areas including, but not limited to, Mountain View, Trench Town, Tivoli Gardens, Cassava Piece, and Arnett Gardens in Kingston, and Flankers, Canterbury, Norwood, Rose Heights, Clavers Street and Hart Street in Montego Bay. Sudden demonstrations can occur, during which demonstrators often construct roadblocks or otherwise block streets.

Jamaican media reports on fire safety indicate that compliance with fire safety regulations among nightclubs and other places of entertainment is low. Overcrowding is common and travelers should remain aware of their surroundings at all times. Jamaica currently lacks the infrastructure to provide shelter and protection for travelers who temporarily become destitute during their stay on the island. U.S. citizens should be aware that under such circumstances they may be stranded without recourse unless and until the Embassy can provide appropriate assistance.

Stay up to date by bookmarking our Bureau of Consular Affairs website, which contains the current Travel Warnings and Travel Alerts as well as the Worldwide Caution. Follow us on Twitter and the Bureau of Consular Affairs page on facebook as well. You can also call 1-888-407-4747 toll-free within the United States and Canada, or by calling a regular toll line, 1-202-501-4444, from other countries. These numbers are available from 8:00 a.m. to 8:00 p.m. Eastern Time, Monday through Friday (except U.S. federal holidays). Take some time before travel to improve your personal security—things are not the same everywhere as they are in the United States.

Crime: Crime, including violent crime, is a serious problem in Jamaica, particularly in Kingston and Montego Bay. While the vast majority of crimes occur in impoverished areas, random acts of violence, such as gunfire, may occur anywhere. The primary criminal concern for tourists is becoming a victim of theft. In several cases, armed robberies of U.S. citizens have turned violent when the victims resisted handing over valuables. Crime is exacerbated by the fact that police are understaffed and often ineffective. Additionally, there have been frequent allegations of police corruption. Tourists should take all necessary precautions, always pay extra attention to their surroundings when traveling, and keep windows up and doors locked while in a vehicle. Travelers should avoid walking alone, exercise special care after dark, and always avoid areas known for high crime rates. Under no circumstances should travelers accept rides from unknown individuals, as this is often a pretext for attempted robbery and/or sexual assault.

Each year the Embassy receives a number of reports of sexual assaults against U.S. citizens, including cases of alleged sexual assaults at tourist resorts, some of which involve resort staff. It is important to realize that sexual assault allegations generally do not receive the same type of law enforcement attention in Jamaica that they would in the United States. Local law also requires the presence of the victim at each stage of the judicial process in order for a case to move forward, and as a result most sexual assault cases languish in the Jamaican courts until they are eventually dismissed. In addition, victims in Jamaica cannot expect the totatility of victim's assistance that is routinely offered in the United States. This includes hesitation to and/or lack of knowledge of how to perform rape kits, a prosecutorial/interrogation approach to victims on the part of the police and hotels, as well as a lack of counseling for victims.

U.S. citizens traveling in Jamaica should maintain careful watchfulness, avoid secluded places or situations (even within resort properties), go out in groups, and watch out for each other. Don't be afraid to ask or call out for help if you feel threatened or encounter individuals who make you feel uncomfortable. Report any suspicious activity to the U.S. Embassy, local police and, if appropriate, to the hotel's management. As a general rule, do not leave valuables unattended or in plain view, including in hotel rooms and on the beach. Take care when carrying high value items such as cameras and expensive cell phones or when wearing expensive jewelry on the street. Women's handbags should be zipped and held close to the body. Men should carry wallets in their front pants pocket. Large amounts of cash should always be handled discreetly.

In the last several years, a number of U.S. visitors have reported being robbed inside their resort hotel rooms while they slept. Particular care is called for when staying at isolated villas and smaller establishments that may have fewer security arrangements. You may wish to ask your villa or small establishment if they have met Jamaica Tourist Board certification standards for safety and security.

The U.S. Embassy advises its staff to avoid inner-city areas of Kingston and other urban centers, such as those listed in the section on Safety and Security, whenever possible. Particular caution is advised after dark and in downtown Kingston and New Kingston. The U.S. Embassy also cautions U.S. citizens not to use public buses, which are often overcrowded and are a frequent venue for crime.

To enhance security in the principal resort areas, the Government of Jamaica has taken a number of steps, including assignment of special police foot and bicycle patrols. Some street vendors, beggars, and taxi drivers in tourist areas aggressively confront and harass tourists to buy their wares or employ their services. If a firm "No, thank you," does not solve the problem, visitors may wish to seek the assistance of a tourist police officer, identified by their white hats, white shirts, and black trousers. These officers are only located at or near tourist areas.

Drugs: Illegal drug use is prevalent in some tourist areas, leading to numerous U.S. citizen arrests and incarcerations in Jamaica every year. Possession or use of marijuana or other illicit drugs is illegal in Jamaica. U.S. citizens should avoid buying, selling, holding, or taking illegal drugs under any circumstances. There is anecdotal evidence that the use of so-called date rape drugs, such as Rohypnol, has become more common at clubs and private parties. Marijuana, cocaine, heroin, and other illegal narcotics are especially potent in Jamaica, and their use may lead to severe or even disastrous health consequences.

Scams: U.S. Citizens are often the target of international financial scams originating in Jamaica. In addition to numerouslottery and investment scams, relatives of U.S. citizens visiting Jamaica and U.S. citizens who are prisoners in Jamaica have received telephone calls from people claiming to be Jamaican police officers, other public officials, or medical professionals. The callers usually state that the visitor or prisoner has had trouble and needs financial help. In almost every case these claims are untrue. The caller insists that money should be sent by wire transfer to either themselves or a third party who will assist the visitor or prisoner, but when money is sent, it fails to reach the U.S. citizens in alleged need. U.S. citizens who receive calls such as these should never send money before consulting the embassy for additional information.

The U.S. Embassy has also received reports of extortion attempts originating in Jamaica where the caller threatens the victim if they do not send a sum of money. Another financial scam reported is the ' Damsel in Distress ' where a partner met over the Internet falls into a series of alleged mishaps and requests money with the promise of rewards at a later date, such as an in-person meeting. Contact the American Citizen Services Unit of the Embassy's Consular Section at KingstonACS@state.gov and provide as much detail as possible regarding the nature of the communication. Additional guidance on such crimes is available at the Department of State's web page on International Financial Scams.

Don't buy counterfeit and pirated goods, even if they are widely available. Not only are the bootlegs illegal in the United States, if you purchase them you may also be breaking local law.

Victims of Crime: If you or someone you know becomes the victim of a crime abroad, you should contact the local police and the nearest U.S. embassy or consulate (see the Department of State's list of embassies and consulates). If your passport is stolen we can help you replace it. For violent crimes such as assault and rape, we can help you find appropriate medical care, contact family members or friends, and help them send you money if you need it. Although the investigation and prosecution of the crime are solely the responsibility of local authorities, consular officers can help you to understand the local criminal justice process and to find a local attorney if you need one.

The local equivalent to the "911" emergency line in Jamaica is "119."

Criminal Penalties: While you are traveling in Jamaica, you are subject to its laws even if you are a U.S. citizen. Foreign laws and legal systems can be vastly different than our own. In some places you may be taken in for questioning if you don't have some form of identification with you. In some places driving under the influence could land you immediately in jail. These criminal penalties will vary from country to country. There are also some things that might be legal in the country you visit, but still illegal in the United States, and you can be prosecuted under U.S. law if you buy pirated goods. Engaging in sexual conduct with children or using or disseminating child pornography in a foreign country is a crime prosecutable in the United States. If you break local laws in Jamaica, your U.S. passport won't help you avoid arrest or prosecution. It's very important to know what's legal and what's not where you are going. Persons violating Jamaica's laws, even unknowingly, may be expelled, arrested or imprisoned. Penalties for possession, use, or trafficking in illegal drugs in Jamaica are severe, and convicted offenders can expect long jail sentences and heavy fines. Airport searches are thorough and people attempting to smuggle narcotics are often apprehended. Several U.S. citizens currently serving time in Jamaica for drug smuggling say they were arrested for carrying bags that friends or acquaintances asked them to deliver to someone in the United States. In one case, the U.S. arrestee claimed that she express mailed a package for a local taxi driver who claimed not to have his identification with him. U.S. citizens should never accept packages/baggage in such circumstances. Prison conditions in Jamaica differ greatly from prison conditions in the United States. Prisoners are provided only the most basic meals and must rely upon personal funds, family and friends to supplement their diets, provide clothing, and supply personal care items such as toothpaste and shampoo. Packages shipped from the United States to prisoners are subject to Jamaican import taxes and are undeliverable when the recipient lacks the funds to pay the duties. Jamaican law contains specific prohibitions on certain sexual activities. These prohibitions have been used to target homosexuals and trans-gendered individuals. Violations can result in lengthy imprisonment.

If you are arrested in Jamaica, authorities of Jamaica are required to notify the nearest U.S. embassy or consulate of your arrest. If you are concerned the Department of State may not be aware of your situation, perhaps because you are also a Jamaican citizen, you should request the police or prison officials to notify the nearest U.S. embassy or consulate of your arrest.

Special Circumstances: *Attitudes towards homosexuals*—Harassment, threats, and acts of violence have been targeted at homosexuals in Jamaica. Government officials have been known to make derogatory comments toward homosexuals, and discrimination on the basis of sexual orientation is widespread. It has been reported that police do not always investigate reports of harassment, threats, or violence targeted on the basis of sexual orientation of the victim.

Firearms and ammunition: The Department of State warns U.S. citizens against taking any type of firearm or ammunition into Jamaica without authorization from the Jamaican Ministry of National Security. Entering Jamaica with a firearm or even a single round of ammunition is a serious crime that can result in a long prison sentence. Mace, pepper spray and knives also are prohibited and may not be brought into Jamaica without specific authorization from the Jamaican Ministry of National Security.

Import/export of foodstuffs: Fresh fruits, vegetables and uncooked meats are not permitted to be brought in or out of the country and may be confiscated by customs officials. Pets may not be brought into Jamaica, except for dogs from the United Kingdom that have been vaccinated for rabies and then only after six months quarantine. It is advisable to contact the Embassy of Jamaica in Washington or one of the Jamaican consulates in the United States for specific information regarding customs requirements.

Hurricanes: Jamaica, like all Caribbean countries, can be affected by hurricanes. Hurricane season runs from June 1 to November 30 each year. The Jamaican Office of Disaster Preparedness and Emergency Management (ODPEM) has responsibility for emergency management on the island. General information on hurricane preparedness is also available via the Internet from the U.S. Federal Emergency Management Agency (FEMA).

Accessibility: While in Jamaica, individuals with disabilities may find accessibility and accommodation very different from what you find in the United States. Jamaican law does not mandate access to transportation, communication and public buildings for persons with disabilities. In general, popular tourist venues in Jamaica are not equipped to accommodate physically challenged visitors. While some of the country's all-inclusive resorts are accessible, most transportation, entertainment and even medical facility options are not. You may wish to consult websites and blogs that focus on accessible travel for practical information and first-hand accounts of traveling in Jamaica.

Medical Facilities and Health Information: Medical care is more limited than in the United States. Comprehensive emergency medical services are located only in Kingston and Montego Bay, and smaller public hospitals are located in each parish. Emergency medical and ambulance services, and the availability of prescription drugs, are limited in outlying parishes. Ambulance service is limited both in the quality of emergency care and in the availability of vehicles in remote parts of the country. Serious medical problems requiring hospitalization and/or medical evacuation to the United States can cost thousands of dollars or more. Doctors and hospitals in Jamaica often require cash payment prior to providing services. If a medical evacuation is required, the Embassy recommends you contact the American Citizen Services Unit at (876) 702-6000 for assistance. You can find good information on vaccinations and other health precautions, on the CDC website. For information about outbreaks of infectious diseases abroad, consult the World Health Organization (WHO) website. The WHO website also contains additional health information for travelers, including detailed country-specific health information.

Medical Insurance: You can't assume your insurance will go with you when you travel. It's very important to find out BEFORE you leave whether or not your medical insurance will cover you overseas. You need to ask your insurance company two questions:

- Does my policy apply when I'm out of the United States?
- Will it cover emergencies like a trip to a foreign hospital or a medical evacuation?

In many places, doctors and hospitals still expect payment in cash at the time or before the service is performed. This is particularly true with private hospitals. Depending on the extent of your injury, it may be advisable to go to a regional public hospital to be stabilized for evacuation rather than spend time waiting for a getting funds to pay for the same a private hospital. Your regular U.S. health insurance may not cover doctors' and hospital visits in other countries. If your policy doesn't go with you when you travel, it's a very good idea to take out another one for your trip.

Traffic Safety and Road Conditions: While in Jamaica, you may encounter road conditions that differ significantly from those in the United States. Drivers and pedestrians should remember that, unlike the United States, driving in Jamaica is on the left-hand side of the road. Breakdown assistance is limited in urban areas and virtually unavailable in rural areas. Nighttime driving is especially dangerous and should be avoided whenever possible. U.S. Embassy personnel are prohibited from driving at night outside of the cities of Kingston, Ocho Rios, Montego Bay, and Negril. Heavy rains, which can occur at any time of the year, frequently leave roads impassable and result in life-threatening flash floods. Drivers should monitor media reports for information on road conditions and closures. Gullies in particular should be avoided as they are prone to flash floods capable of sweeping away vehicles. As noted above in the section on Crime, public buses are often overcrowded and are frequently a venue of crime. Travelers who use taxicabs should take only licensed taxicabs having red-and-white PP license plates or taxis recommended by their hotels.

Most roads are paved, but suffer from ill repair, inadequate signage, large pot holes, and poor traffic control markings. Roads are often subject to poorly marked construction zones, pedestrians, bicyclists, and, occasionally, livestock. The lack of pedestrian crosswalks requires special vigilance for all pedestrians. Driving habits range from aggressive speeding and disregard for others to inexperience and over-polite behaviors creating uncertainty and hazards to pedestrians. In February 2009, an American tourist in Jamaica was killed while attempting to cross a busy stretch of road to his hotel. The American was hit by an overtaking car after another vehicle had stopped and waved him across. Roads in rural areas (including near major tourist resorts in Montego Bay and Negril) are often traveled at very high speeds and pedestrians should take special care when attempting to cross.

Drivers should maintain special care when entering traffic circles ("roundabouts"), which are often poorly marked and require traffic to move in a clockwise direction. Motorists entering a roundabout must yield to those already in it. Labeling of roundabout exit points is exceptionally confusing, often making it difficult to determine which exit to take to continue toward the desired destination. Failure to turn into the correct flow of traffic can result in a head-on collision. The A1, A2 and A3 highways are the primary links between the most important cities and tourist destinations on the island. These roads are not comparable to American highways, and road conditions are hazardous due to poor repair, inadequate signage and poor traffic control markings. The B highways and rural roads are often very narrow and frequented by large trucks, buses, pedestrians, bicyclists and open range livestock. Highways are traveled at high speeds, but are not limited-access. Drivers and passengers in the front seat are required to wear seat belts, and motorcycle riders are required to wear helmets. Extreme caution should be used in operating motor driven cycles. Several serious and even fatal accidents take place each year involving U.S. tourists riding in taxis without seat belts. All passengers are strongly encouraged to use vehicles equipped with seat belts. Official emergency response to a road accident can be slow, given traffic, road conditions, distance from metropolitan areas and a limited number of responders. In practice, many victims of vehicular accidents are assisted by fellow motorists.

Aviation Safety Oversight: The U.S. Federal Aviation Administration (FAA) has assessed the government of Jamaica's Civil Aviation Authority as being in compliance with International Civil Aviation Organization (ICAO) aviation safety standards for oversight of Jamaica's air carrier operations. Further information may be found on the FAA's safety assessment page.

Children's Issues: Please see the U.S. Dept. of State Office of Children's Issues web pages on intercountry adoption and international parental child abduction.

Intercountry Adoption

February 2013

The information in this section has been edited from a report available through the U.S. Department of State Office of Children's Issues. For more information detailed, please read the *Intercountry Adoption* section of this book and review current reports online at http://adoption.state.gov.

Jamaica is not party to the Hague Convention on Protection of Children and Co-operation in Respect of Intercountry Adoption (Hague Adoption Convention). Intercountry adoptions of children from non-Hague countries are processed in accordance with 8 Code of Federal Regulations, Section 204.3 as it relates to orphans as defined under the Immigration and Nationality Act, Section 101(b)(1)(F). There are two types of adoption in Jamaica–Adoption Licenses and Adoption Orders. An Adoption License allows a Jamaican citizen child to be taken to a "scheduled country" (in these cases, the United States) and adopted there. An Adoption Order provides for an orphan to be adopted in Jamaica. An Order legally supersedes a birth certificate, as it shows date of birth, (new) parentage, and (new) name. The child's Jamaican passport information may also be superseded by the new parentage and name.

Who Can Adopt? To bring an adopted child to the United States from Jamaica, you must meet eligibility and suitability requirements. The U.S. Department of Homeland Security, U.S. Citizenship and Immigration Services (USCIS) determines who can adopt under U.S. immigration law. Additionally, a child must meet the definition of orphanunder U.S. immigration law in order to be eligible to immigrate to the United States on an IR-3 or IR-4 immigrant visa.

Residency: Prospective adoptive parents seeking an Adoption License can generally expect to travel to Jamaica at least twice, once to meet with the Child Development Agency (CDA) and again to apply for a visa. However, they are not required to reside in Jamaica, nor are they required to attend the court hearing, though the judge can request their presence. Prospective adoptive parents seeking an Adoption Order are required by Jamaican law to reside with the child under the supervision of a local social worker for at least three months before the court will approve the full adoption. The court may waive the pre-adoption placement requirement if the prospective adoptive parents are Jamaican nationals adopting a relative.

Age of Adopting Parents: Prospective adoptive parents who are not related to the potential adopted child must be 25 years of age or older. If the child is a brother, sister, niece, or nephew of the prospective adoptive parent(s), at least one parent must be 18 years of age or older. There are no laws establishing a required age difference between the adoptee and the prospective adoptive parent when they are related.

Marriage: Both single individuals and married couples can adopt, though Jamaica does not recognize same-sex marriage. As such, a Jamaican court may not issue an Adoption Order or License to a same-sex couple.

Income: While there are no specific income requirements, prospective adoptive parents will have to provide documents relaying their financial status.

Other: Each potential adoption is evaluated on a case-by-case basis by the CDA and the Jamaican Adoption Board. Under Jamaican law, the CDA and the Jamaican Adoption Board have the authority to take prospective adoptive parents' medical conditions into consideration when evaluating their eligibility to adopt. In practice, however, it is extremely rare for a prospective parent to be denied eligibility due to an existing medical condition.

Who Can Be Adopted? In addition to U.S. immigration requirements, Jamaica has specific requirements that a child must meet in order to be eligible for adoption. In all cases, the CDA will assess the child's suitability for adoption by conducting visits to the child's place of residence, as well as interviews and counseling with the child, the birth parents, if applicable, and the prospective adoptive parents.

Relinquishment: If the birth parents have not already relinquished their parental rights or had their rights separated by the state, Jamaica requires the child's birth parents to provide consent before the adoption can be finalized.

Age of Adoptive Child: Only children between the ages of six weeks and 18 years old are eligible for adoption.

Sibling Adoptions: The Jamaican Adoption of Children Act does not include any provision prioritizing sibling placement in order to preserve sibling unity. However, the CDA and the Adoption Board are concerned about child welfare and are willing to work with prospective adoptive parents to ensure that siblings are placed together.

Special Needs or Medical Conditions: Each child must undergo a medical examination in Jamaica by a registered Jamaican medical practitioner before the Adoption Order or License can be approved. This is separate from the medical examination the child must undergo prior to obtaining an immigrant visa.

Jamaica's Adoption Authority: Child Development Agency (CDA).

The Process: The first step in adopting a child from Jamaica is usually to select a licensed agency in the United States that can help with your adoption. Adoption service providers must be licensed by the United States state in which they operate. The CDA is the only agency legally authorized to provide adoption services in Jamaica. There are one or two private agencies operating in Jamaica, but they do so without government sanction. The CDA verifies the contents of the home study by writing to the home study agency. This verifies the home study authorship and obtains the home study agency's agreement to supervise the placement in the future. If you are eligible to adopt, and a child is available for intercountry adoption, the CDA in Jamaica will provide you with a referral to a child. The process for finalizing the adoption (or gaining legal custody) in Jamaica generally includes the following.

Role of Adoption Authority: Once the CDA conducts their assessment of the child's suitability for adoption, the CDA report is forwarded to the independent Jamaican Adoption Board which decides whether the adoption should be approved. The Adoption Board reviews the CDA's report on the child as well as information on the prospective adoptive parent.

Role of the Court: If the Jamaican Adoption Board approves the adoption, the case is sent to a family court which will review the relevant case facts and determine if the Adoption License or Adoption Order should be issued. In the Kingston, St. Andrew, Westmoreland, and St. James parishes, special Family Courts exercise jurisdiction over adoptions. In the remaining parishes, the local Resident Magistrate's Court supervises adoptions.

Time Frame: Prospective adoptive parents seeking an Adoption License can usually complete an adoption in Jamaica in four months. Those seeking an Adoption Order may need more time, as Jamaican adoption regulations require a locally placed child to be supervised by local social workers for at least three months. However, the court may waive the pre-adoption placement requirement if the prospective adoptive parents are Jamaican nationals adopting a relative.

Adoption Fees: Jamaica does not charge any fees for adoptions. However, each child is required to have an extensive physical before the child is found eligible for adoption by the Adoption Board. Costs for the pre-adoption medical vary by physician, but can be up to $100 USD.

Documents Required: The following documents are required to obtain an Adoption License:

- Application form (available from the CDA);
- Home Study—Certified original home study plus two additional copies to be sent directly to the Board by the Department of Health (in most cases, this can be the same home study conducted in the United States for the I-600A or I-600);
- Medical Examination (examination of both the prospective adoptive parents and the child);
- Letter of Undertaking–The agency that conducted the home study submits the letter agreeing to supervise the placement until the adoption is complete, and beyond, as determined on a case-by-case basis by the CDA;
- Bank Statement; and
- Letter(s) from Employer(s)–The letter(s) should indicate the annual income and the nature of employment.

The following documents are required to obtain an Adoption Order:

- Application form (available from the CDA);
- Home Study—certified original home study plus two additional copies to be sent directly to the Board by the Department of Health (can be the same home study conducted in the United States for the I-600A or I-600);
- Medical Examination (examination of both the prospective adoptive parents and the child);
- Income Statement;
- Personal References (two); and
- Letter of Undertaking–provided by the Jamaican agency that conducted the home study to supervise placement.

Bringing Your Child Home: Once your adoption is complete (or you have obtained legal custody of the child), there are a few more steps to take before you can head home. Specifically, you need to apply for several documents for your child before he or she can travel to the United States, such as a birth certificate, a passport or travel document for your child from the country in which he or she was born, and a U.S. Immigration Visa. For detailed and updated information on how to obtain these documents, review the *Intercountry Adoption* section on this publication and visit the USCIS Intercountry Adoption website at http://adoption.state.gov.

Child Citizenship Act: For adoptions finalized abroad, the Child Citizenship Act of 2000 allows your new child to acquire American citizenship automatically when he or she enters the United States as lawful permanent residents. For adoptions finalized in the United States, the Child Citizenship Act of 2000 allows your new child to acquire American citizenship automatically when the court in the United States issues the final adoption decree. To learn more, review the *Intercountry Adoption* section on this publication and visit the USCIS Intercountry Adoption website at http://adoption.state.gov.

After Adoption: The CDA may, on a case-by-case basis, require the agency that conducted the home study to submit reports to the CDA on a regular basis for up to two years after an Adoption License is issued. Post-adoption reporting is not mandated in cases that receive Adoption Orders.

United States Embassy in Jamaica
16 Oxford Road
Kingston 5
Jamaica, West Indies
Tel: 876-935-6000
Fax: 876-935-6019
Mailing Address:
P.O. Box 541
Kingston
Jamaica

Jamaica's Adoption Authority
Child Development Agency (CDA)
2-4 King Street
Kingston 5, Jamaica
Tel: 876-948-6678
Fax: 876-924-9401
Website: http://www.cda.gov.jm

Embassy of Jamaica
1520 New Hampshire Ave. NW
Washington, DC 20036
Tel: 202-452-0660

Office of Children's Issues
United States Department of State
2201 C Street, NW; SA-29
Washington, DC 20520
Tel: 1-888-407-4747
Website: http://adoption.state.gov

International Parental Child Abduction

January 2012

The information in this section has been edited from the latest report available as of February 2013 from the State Department Bureau of Consular Affairs, Office of Overseas Citizens Services. For more information, please read the *International Parental Child Abduction* section of this book and check for updated reports online at www.travel.state.gov/abduction.

Disclaimer: The information in this flyer relating to the legal requirements of specific foreign countries is provided for general information only. Questions involving interpretation of specific foreign laws should be addressed to foreign legal counsel.

General Information: Jamaica is not party to the Hague Convention on the Civil Aspects of International Child Abduction, nor are there any other international or bilateral treaties in force between Jamaica and the United States dealing with international parental child abduction. American citizens who travel to Jamaica place themselves under the jurisdiction of local courts. American citizens planning a trip to Jamaica with dual national children should bear this in mind.

Custody Disputes: In Jamaica, if parents are legally married they share the custody of their children. If they are not married, custody is granted by law to the mother unless there are known facts of inappropriate behavior mental or social problems. Foreign court orders are not automatically recognized.

Enforcement of Foreign Judgments: Custody orders and judgments of foreign courts are not automatically enforced in Jamaica, but may be formally recognized by a Jamaican court.

Visitation Rights: In cases where one parent has been granted custody of a child, the other parent is usually granted visitation rights. The American Embassy in Kingston has reported few problems for non-custodial parents exercising their visitation rights. If a custodial parent fails to allow visitation, the non-custodial parent may appeal to the court.

Dual Nationality: Dual nationality is recognized under Jamaican law.

Passports for Minors and the Children's Passport Issuance Alert Program: For more information on these topics, see the International Parental Child Abduction section of this publication and review current reports from the U.S. Department of State at www.travel.state.gov/abduction.

Travel Restrictions: No exit visas are required to leave Jamaica. However, a child leaving the country with a person other than a parent needs written authorization from one parent. This authorization requires certification from the Jamaican immigration office before minors may exit the country.

Criminal Remedies: For information on possible criminal remedies, please contact your local law enforcement authorities or the nearest office of the Federal Bureau of Investigation (FBI). Information is also available on the Internet at the web site of the U.S. Department of Justice, Office of Juvenile Justice and Delinquency Prevention (OJJDP) at http://www.ojjdp.ncjrs.org.

U.S. Embassy Kingston
Consular Section
Jamaica Mutual Life Center
2 Oxford Road, 3rd Floor
Kingston, Jamaica
Telephone: (876) 929-4850
Fax: [876] 935-6001
Web site: www.state.gov/kingston

Questions involving Jamaican law should be addressed to a Jamaican attorney or to the Embassy of Jamaica in the United States at:

Embassy of Jamaica
1520 New Hampshire Avenue N.W.
Washington, DC 20036
Telephone: (202) 452-0660

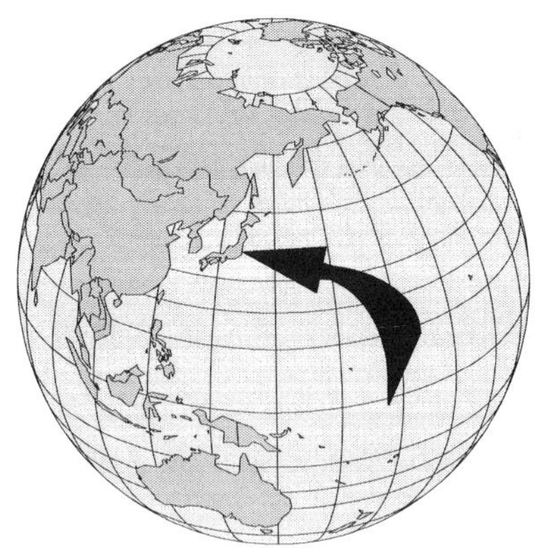

JAPAN

Compiled from publications that were available as of February 2013 from the U.S. Department of State, the U.S. Department of Commerce, and the Central Intelligence Agency (CIA). See the introduction to this set for explanatory notes.

Official Name:
Japan

PROFILE

Geography

Area: total: 377,915 sq km; country comparison to the world: 62; land: 364,485 sq km; water: 13,430 sq km
Major cities: Tokyo (capital) 36.507 million; Osaka-Kobe 11.325 million; Nagoya 3.257 million; Fukuoka-Kitakyushu 2.809 million; Sapporo 2.673 million (2009)
Climate: varies from tropical in south to cool temperate in north
Terrain: mostly rugged and mountainous

People

Nationality: noun: Japanese (singular and plural); adjective: Japanese
Population: 127,368,088 (July 2012 est.)
Population growth rate: -0.077% (2012 est.)
Ethnic groups: Japanese 98.5%, Koreans 0.5%, Chinese 0.4%, other 0.6%
Religions: Shintoism 83.9%, Buddhism 71.4%, Christianity 2%, other 7.8%
Languages: Japanese
Literacy: definition: age 15 and over can read and write; total population: 99%; male: 99%; female: 99% (2002)
Health: life expectancy at birth: total population: 83.91 years; male: 80.57 years; female: 87.43 years (2012 est.); Infant mortality rate: total: 2.21 deaths/1,000 live births; male: 2.44 deaths/1,000 live births; female: 1.97 deaths/1,000 live births (2012 est.)
Unemployment rate: 4.4% (2012 est.)
Work force: 65.27 million (2012 est.)

Government

Type: a parliamentary government with a constitutional monarchy
Independence: 3 May 1947
Constitution: 3 May 1947
Political subdivisions: 47 prefectures
Suffrage: 20 years of age; universal

Economy

GDP (purchasing power parity): $4.617 trillion (2012 est.); $4.497 trillion (2011 est.); $4.531 trillion (2010 est.); $4.339 trillion (2009 est.)
GDP real growth rate: 2.2% (2012 est.); -0.7% (2011 est.); 4.4% (2010 est.); -5.5% (2009 est.)
GDP per capita (PPP): $36,200 (2012 est.); $35,200 (2011 est.); $35,500 (2010 est.); $34,000 (2009 est.)
Natural resources: negligible mineral resources, fish
Agriculture products: rice, sugar beets, vegetables, fruit; pork, poultry, dairy products, eggs; fish
Industries: among world's largest and technologically advanced producers of motor vehicles, electronic equipment, machine tools, steel and nonferrous metals, ships, chemicals, textiles, processed foods

Exports: $792.9 billion (2012 est.); $788 billion (2011 est.); $730.1 billion (2010 est.)

Exports—commodities: motor vehicles 13.6%; semiconductors 6.2%; iron and steel products 5.5%; auto parts 4.6%; plastic materials 3.5%; power generating machinery 3.5%

Exports—partners: China 19.7%, US 15.5%, South Korea 8%, Hong Kong 5.2%, Thailand 4.6% (2011)

Imports: $856.9 billion (2012 est.); $808.4 billion (2011 est.); $639.1 billion (2010 est.)

Imports—commodities: petroleum 15.5%; liquid natural gas 5.7%; clothing 3.9%; semiconductors 3.5%; coal 3.5%; audio and visual apparatus 2.7%

Imports—partners: China 21.5%, US 8.9%, Australia 6.6%, Saudi Arabia 5.9%, UAE 5%, South Korea 4.7% (2011)

Debt—external: $2.719 trillion (30 June 2011); $2.441 trillion (30 September 2010)

Exchange rates: yen (JPY) per US dollar; 79.42 (2012 est.); 79.81 (2011 est.); 87.78 (2010 est.); 93.57 (2009); 103.58 (2008); 117.99 (2007)

GEOGRAPHY

Japan, a country of islands, extends along the eastern or Pacific coast of Asia. The four main islands, running from north to south, are Hokkaido, Honshu (or the mainland), Shikoku, and Kyushu. Okinawa Island is about 380 miles southwest of Kyushu. About 3,000 smaller islands are included in the archipelago. In total land area, Japan is slightly smaller than California. About 73% of the country is mountainous, with a chain running through each of the main islands. Japan's highest mountain is the world-famous Mt. Fuji (12,388 feet).

Since so little flat area exists, many hills and mountainsides are cultivated all the way to the summits. As Japan is situated in a volcanic zone along the Pacific depth, frequent low-intensity earth tremors and occasional volcanic activity are felt throughout the islands. Destructive earthquakes occur several times a century. A massive earthquake (magnitude 9.0) and tsunami struck northeastern Japan on March 11, 2011. Hot springs are numerous and have been developed as resorts.

Temperature extremes are less pronounced than in the United States, but the climate varies considerably. Sapporo, on the northernmost main island, has warm summers and long, cold winters with heavy snowfall. Tokyo, Nagoya, Kyoto, Osaka, and Kobe, in central and western parts of the largest island of Honshu, experience relatively mild winters with little or no snowfall and hot, humid summers. Fukuoka, on the island of Kyushu, has a climate similar to that of Charleston, South Carolina, with mild winters and wet summers. Okinawa is subtropical.

PEOPLE

Japan's population experienced a phenomenal growth rate for much of the 20th century as a result of scientific, industrial, and sociological changes, but birth rates have fallen steadily since the 1970s. In 2005, Japan's population declined for the first time, 2 years earlier than predicted. However, high sanitary and health standards produce a life expectancy exceeding that of the United States.

Japan is an urban society with only about 1% of the labor force engaged in agriculture. Many farmers supplement their income with part-time jobs in nearby towns and cities. About 80 million of the urban population is heavily concentrated on the Pacific shore of Honshu and in northern Kyushu. Japan faces the same problems that confront urban industrialized societies throughout the world: overcrowded cities, congested roads, air pollution, and juvenile delinquency.

Language

The national language of Japan is Japanese (nihongo) and is spoken and understood all over the country. English is a required subject in Japanese high schools, and it is by far the most widely known foreign language in Japan. International business correspondence and negotiations in Japan are almost always conducted in English.

Religion

Shintoism and Buddhism are Japan's two principal religions. Shintoism is founded on myths and legends emanating from the early animistic worship of natural phenomena. Since it was unconcerned with problems of afterlife which dominate Buddhist thought, and since Buddhism easily accommodated itself to local faiths, the two religions comfortably coexisted, and Shinto shrines and Buddhist temples often became administratively linked. Today many Japanese are adherents of both faiths.

From the 16th to the 19th century Shintoism flourished. Adopted by the leaders of the Meiji restoration, Shintoism received state support and was cultivated as a spur to patriotic and nationalistic feelings. Following World War II, state support was discontinued, and the emperor disavowed divinity. Today Shintoism plays a more peripheral role in the life of the Japanese people. The numerous shrines are visited regularly by a few believers and, if they are historically famous or known for natural beauty, by many sightseers. Many marriages are held in the shrines, and children are taken there after birth and on certain anniversary dates; special shrine days are celebrated for certain occasions, and numerous festivals are held throughout the year. Many homes have "god shelves" where offerings can be made to Shinto deities.

Buddhism first came to Japan in the 6th century and for the next 10 centuries exerted profound influence on its intellectual, artistic, social, and political life. Most funerals are conducted by Buddhist priests, and many Japanese visit family graves and Buddhist temples to pay respects to ancestors.

Confucianism arrived with the first great wave of Chinese influence into Japan between the 6th and 9th centuries. Overshadowed by Buddhism, it survived as an organized philosophy into the late 19th century and remains today as an important influence on Japanese thought and values.

Christianity, first introduced into Japan in 1549, was virtually stamped out by the government a century later; it was reintroduced in the late 1800s and has spread slowly.

Beyond the three traditional religions, many Japanese today are turning to a great variety of popular religious movements normally lumped together under the name "new religions." These religions draw on the concept of Shinto, Buddhism, and folk superstition and have developed in part to meet the social needs of elements of the population. The officially recognized new religions number in the hundreds, and total membership is reportedly in the tens of millions.

Since the government does not require religious groups to report their membership, it is difficult to determine accurately the number of adherents of different religious

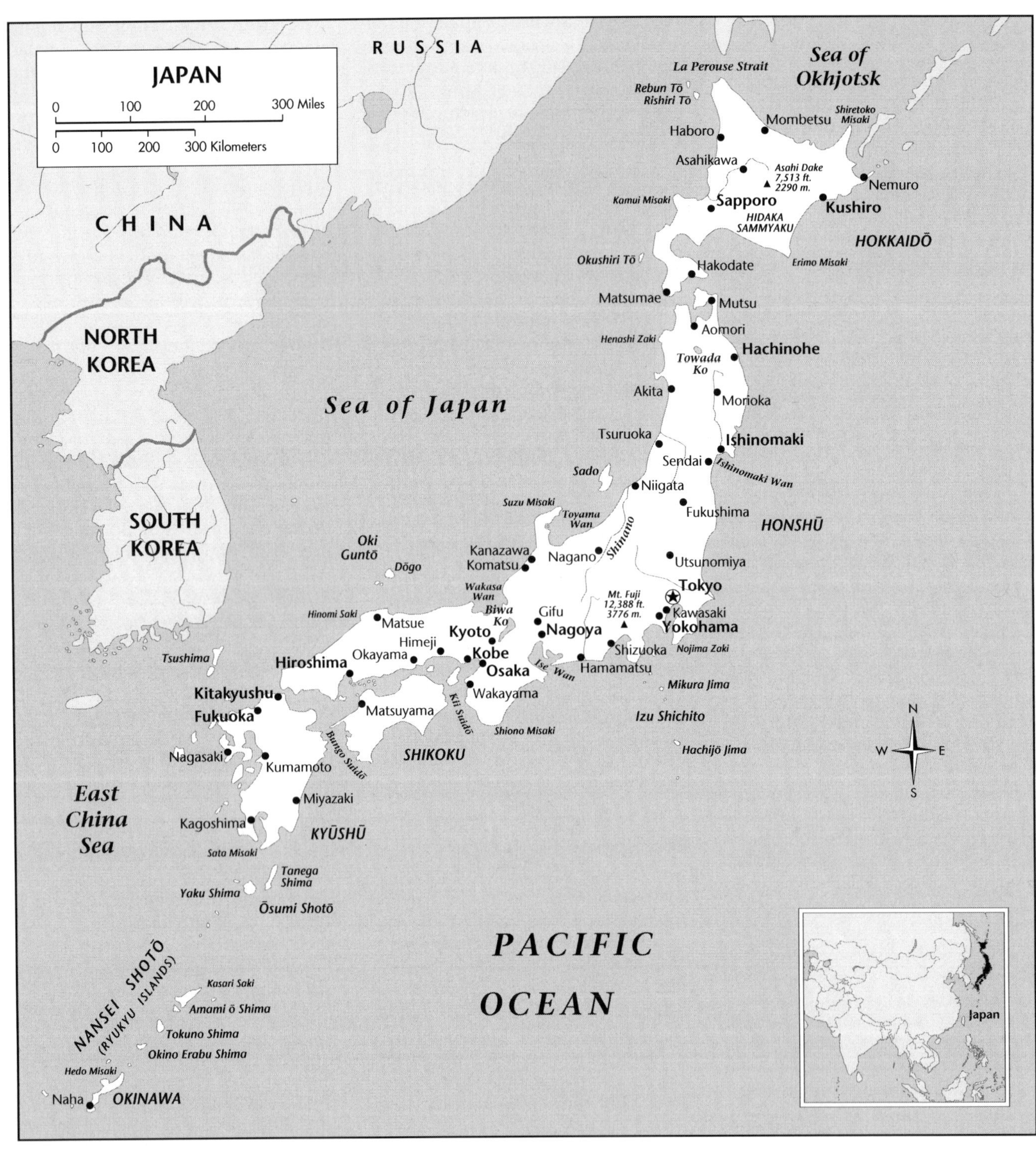

groups. The Agency for Cultural Affairs reported that membership claims by religious groups totaled 207 million as of December 2008.

This number, substantially more than the country's population of 127.4 million, reflects many citizens' affiliation with multiple religions. For example, it is common to practice both Buddhist and Shinto rites. According to the agency's current yearbook which shows statistics for 2008, 108 million people identified themselves as Shinto, 88 million as Buddhist, and 2.3 million as Christian, while 8.9 million followed "other" religions. There are no governmental statistics on the number of Muslims in the country.

HISTORY

Japanese legend maintains that Japan was founded in 600 BC by the Emperor Jimmu, a direct descendant of the sun goddess and ancestor of the present ruling imperial family. In about AD 405, the Japanese court officially adopted the Chinese writing system. Together with the introduction of Buddhism in the 6th century, these two events revolutionized Japanese culture and marked the beginning of a long period of Chinese cultural influence. From the establishment of the first fixed capital at Nara in 710 until 1867, the emperors of the Yamato dynasty were the nominal rulers, but actual power was usually held by influential court nobles, regents, or "shoguns" (military governors).

Contact With the West

The first recorded contact with the West occurred in about 1542, when a Portuguese ship, blown off its course to China, landed in Japan. During the next century, traders from Portugal, the Netherlands, England, and Spain arrived, as did Jesuit, Dominican, and Franciscan missionaries. During the early part of the 17th century, Japan's shogunate suspected that the traders and missionaries were actually forerunners of a military conquest by European powers. This caused the shogunate to place foreigners under progressively tighter restrictions. Ultimately, Japan forced all foreigners to leave and barred all relations with the outside world except for severely restricted commercial contacts with Dutch and Chinese merchants at Nagasaki. This isolation lasted for 200 years, until Commodore Matthew Perry of the U.S. Navy negotiated the opening of Japan to the West with the Convention of Kanagawa in 1854.

Within several years, renewed contact with the West profoundly altered Japanese society. The shogunate resigned, and the emperor was restored to power. The "Meiji restoration" of 1868 initiated many reforms. The feudal system was abolished, and numerous Western institutions were adopted, including a Western legal and educational system and constitutional government along parliamentary lines.

In 1898, the last of the "unequal treaties" with Western powers was removed, signaling Japan's new status among the nations of the world. In a few decades, by creating modern social, educational, economic, military, and industrial systems, the Emperor Meiji's "controlled revolution" had transformed a feudal and isolated state into a world power.

Wars With China and Russia

Japanese leaders of the late 19th century regarded the Korean Peninsula as a potential threat to Japan. It was over Korea that Japan became involved in war with the Chinese Empire in 1894–95 and with Russia in 1904–05. The war with China established Japan's domination of Korea, while also giving it the Pescadores Islands and Formosa (now Taiwan). After Japan defeated Russia in 1905, the resulting Treaty of Portsmouth awarded Japan certain rights in Manchuria and in southern Sakhalin, which Russia had received in 1875 in exchange for the Kurile Islands. Both wars gave Japan a free hand in Korea, which it formally annexed in 1910.

World War I to 1952

World War I permitted Japan, which fought on the side of the victorious Allies, to expand its influence in Asia and its territorial holdings in the Pacific. The postwar era brought Japan unprecedented prosperity. Japan went to the peace conference at Versailles in 1919 as one of the great military and industrial powers of the world and received official recognition as one of the "Big Five" of the new international order. It joined the League of Nations and received a mandate over Pacific islands north of the Equator formerly held by Germany.

During the 1920s, Japan progressed toward a democratic system of government. However, parliamentary government was not rooted deeply enough to withstand the economic and political pressures of the 1930s, during which military leaders became increasingly influential.

Japan invaded Manchuria in 1931 and set up the puppet state of Manchukuo. In 1933, Japan resigned from the League of Nations. The Japanese invasion of China in 1937 followed Japan's signing of the Anti-Comintern Pact with Nazi Germany the previous year and was part of a chain of developments culminating in the Japanese attack on the United States at Pearl Harbor, Hawaii, on December 7, 1941.

After years of war, resulting in the loss of 3 million Japanese lives and the atomic bombings of Hiroshima and Nagasaki, Japan signed an instrument of surrender on the U.S.S. Missouri in Tokyo Harbor on September 2, 1945. As a result of World War II, Japan lost all of its overseas possessions and retained only the home islands. Manchukuo was dissolved, and Manchuria was returned to China; Japan renounced all claims to Formosa; Korea was occupied and divided by the U.S. and the U.S.S.R.; southern Sakhalin and the Kuriles were occupied by the U.S.S.R.; and the U.S. became the sole administering authority of the Ryukyu, Bonin, and Volcano Islands. The 1972 reversion of Okinawa completed the U.S. return of control of these islands to Japan.

After the war, Japan was placed under international control of the Allies through the Supreme Commander, Gen. Douglas MacArthur. U.S. objectives were to ensure that Japan would become a peaceful nation and to establish democratic self-government supported by the freely expressed will of the people. Political, economic, and social reforms were introduced, such as a freely elected Japanese Diet (legislature) and universal adult suffrage.

The country's constitution took effect on May 3, 1947. The United States and 45 other Allied nations signed the Treaty of Peace with Japan in September 1951. The U.S. Senate ratified the treaty in March 1952, and under the terms of the treaty, Japan regained full sovereignty on April 28, 1952.

GOVERNMENT AND POLITICAL CONDITIONS

Japan is a constitutional monarchy with a parliamentary government. Prime Minister Yoshihiko Noda, leader of the Democratic Party of Japan, derives his authority to govern from the constitution. July 2010 upper-house elections were considered free and fair.

Recent Elections

In July 2010 the country held national elections for the House of Councillors, the upper house of the Diet, which were considered free and fair.

Participation of Women and Minorities: Women held 52 of 480 seats in the House of Representatives, the lower house of the Diet, and 44 of 242 seats in the upper house. At the end of 2011, there were three female governors and one woman in the 18-member cabinet.

Because some ethnic minorities are of mixed heritage and do not self-identify, it was difficult to determine the number of minorities that served in the Diet. Three Diet members acknowledged being naturalized Japanese citizens.

Principal Government Officials

Last Updated: 1/31/2013

Emperor: **AKIHITO**
Prime Min.: **Shinzo ABE**
Dep. Prime Min.: **Taro ASO**
Chief Cabinet Sec.: **Yoshihide SUGA**
Min. for the Abduction Issue: **Keiji FURUYA**
Min. for Admin. Reform: **Tomomi INADA**
Min. of Agriculture, Forestry, & Fisheries: **Yoshimasa HAYASHI**
Min. for Civil Service Reform: **Tomomi INADA**
Min. of Defense: **Itsunori ONODERA**
Min. of Economy, Trade, & Industry: **Toshimitsu MOTEGI**
Min. of Education, Culture, Sports, Science, & Technology: **Hakubun SHIMOMURA**
Min. of the Environment: **Nobutera ISHIHARA**
Min. of Finance: **Taro ASO**
Min. of Foreign Affairs: **Fumio KISHIDA**
Min. of Health, Labor, & Welfare: **Norihisa TAMURA**
Min. of Justice: **Sadakazu TANIGAKI**
Min. of Land, Infrastructure, Transport, & Tourism: **Akihiro OTA**
Min. in Charge of "Challenge Again" Initiative: **Tomomi INADA**
Min. in Charge of Comprehensive Policy Coordination for Revival From the Nuclear Accident at Fukushima: **Takumi NEMOTO**
Min. in Charge of "Cool Japan" Strategy: **Tomomi INADA**
Min. in Charge of Economic Revitalization: **Akira AMARI**
Min. in Charge of Industrial Competitiveness: **Toshimitsu MOTEGI**
Min. in Charge of Information Technology Policy: **Ichita YAMAMOTO**
Min. in Charge of Internal Affairs & Communications: **Yoshitaka SHINDO**
Min. in Charge of National Infrastructure Resilience: **Keiji FURUYA**
Min. in Charge of Nuclear Incident Economic Countermeasures: **Toshimitsu MOTEGI**
Min. in Charge of Overcoming Deflation & Yen Appreciation: **Taro ASO**
Min. in Charge of Rebuilding Education: **Hakubun SHIMOMURA**
Min. in Charge of Reconstruction: **Takumi NEMOTO**
Min. in Charge of Regional Govt.: **Yoshitaka SHINDO**
Min. in Charge of Regional Revitalization: **Yoshitaka SHINDO**
Min. in Charge of Support for Women's Empowerment & Child-Rearing: **Masako MORI**
Min. in Charge of Total Reform of Social Security & Tax: **Akira AMARI**
Min. of State for Consumer Affairs & Food Safety: **Masako MORI**
Min. of State for the Corporation in Support of Compensation for Nuclear Damage: **Toshimitsu MOTEGI**
Min. of State for Decentralization Reform: **Yoshitaka SHINDO**
Min. of State for Disaster Management: **Keiji FURUYA**
Min. of State for Economic & Fiscal Policy: **Akira AMARI**
Min. of State for Financial Services: **Taro ASO**
Min. of State for Gender Equality: **Masako MORI**
Min. of State for Measures for Declining Birthrate: **Masako MORI**
Min. of State for Nuclear Emergency Preparedness: **Nobuteru ISHIHARA**
Min. of State for Okinawa & Northern Territories Affairs: **Ichita YAMAMOTO**
Min. of State for Regulatory Reform: **Tomomi INADA**
Min. of State for Science & Technology Policy: **Ichita YAMAMOTO**
Min. of State for Space Policy: **Ichita YAMAMOTO**
Chmn., National Public Safety Commission: **Keiji FURUYA**
Governor, Bank of Japan: **Masaaki SHIRAKAWA**
Ambassador to the US:
Permanent Representative to the UN, New York: **Tsuneo NISHIDA**

ECONOMY

In the years following World War II, government-industry cooperation, a strong work ethic, mastery of high technology, and a comparatively small defense allocation (1% of GDP) helped Japan develop a technologically advanced economy. Two notable characteristics of the post-war economy were the close interlocking structures of manufacturers, suppliers, and distributors, known as keiretsu, and the guarantee of lifetime employment for a substantial portion of the urban labor force.

Both features are now eroding under the dual pressures of global competition and domestic demographic change. Japan's industrial sector is heavily dependent on imported raw materials and fuels. A tiny agricultural sector is highly subsidized and protected, with crop yields among the highest in the world. Usually self-sufficient in rice, Japan imports about 60% of its food on a caloric basis. Japan maintains one of the world's largest fishing fleets and accounts for nearly 15% of the global catch.

For three decades, overall real economic growth had been spectacular—

a 10% average in the 1960s, a 5% average in the 1970s, and a 4% average in the 1980s. Growth slowed markedly in the 1990s, averaging just 1.7%, largely because of the after effects of inefficient investment and an asset price bubble in the late 1980s that required a protracted period of time for firms to reduce excess debt, capital, and labor.

Modest economic growth continued after 2000, but the economy has fallen into recession three times since 2008. A sharp downturn in business investment and global demand for Japan's exports in late 2008 pushed Japan into recession. Government stimulus spending helped the economy recover in late 2009 and 2010, but the economy contracted again in 2011 as the massive 9.0 magnitude earthquake in March disrupted manufacturing.

Recovery spending helped boost GDP in early 2012, but slower global economic growth began weakening Japan's export-oriented economy by mid-year. Electricity supplies remain tight because Japan tentatively shut down almost all of its nuclear power plants after the Fukushima Daiichi nuclear reactors were crippled by the earthquake and resulting tsunami. Newly-elected Prime Minister Shinzo ABE has declared the economy his government's top priority; he has pledged to reconsider his predecessor's plan to permanently close nuclear power plants and has said he will increase stimulus spending and press the Bank of Japan to loosen monetary policy. Measured on a purchasing power parity (PPP) basis that adjusts for price differences, Japan in 2012 stood as the fourth-largest economy in the world after second-place China, which surpassed Japan in 2001, and third-place India, which edged out Japan in 2012.

The new government will continue a longstanding debate on restructuring the economy and reining in Japan's huge government debt, which exceeds 200% of GDP. Persistent deflation, reliance on exports to drive growth, and an aging and shrinking population are other major long-term challenges for the economy.

Labor Conditions

By law children between the ages of 15 and 18 may perform any job that is not designated as dangerous or harmful. Children between the ages of 13 and 15 may perform "light labor" only, and children under 13 may work only in the entertainment industry. These laws were effectively enforced in practice.

Minimum wages ranged from 645 yen (approximately $8.40) to 837 yen ($10.85) per hour, depending on the industry and prefecture. The law imposes a fine of up to 500,000 yen ($6,500) for employers who fail to pay a minimum wage. In 2009, 16 percent of the population earned an annual income below the poverty line of 1.12 million yen (approximately $14,500).

The law provides for a 40-hour workweek for most industries, mandates premium pay for hours worked above 40 in a week or eight in a day, sets limits on the number of overtime hours permitted in a fixed period, and prohibits excessive compulsory overtime. The law mandates paid leave on national holidays as well as at least 10 days of paid leave accrued per year following six months of full-time employment. The government sets occupational safety and health (OSH) standards.

U.S.-JAPAN RELATIONS

The United States established diplomatic relations with Japan in 1858. During World War II, diplomatic relations between the United States and Japan were severed when both nations declared war on each other in the wake of Japan's 1941 attack on Pearl Harbor, Hawaii. After years of fighting in the Pacific region, which included the U.S. atomic bombings of Hiroshima and Nagasaki, Japan signed an instrument of surrender in 1945. Normal diplomatic relations were reestablished in 1952, when the Supreme Commander for the Allied Powers, which had overseen the postwar Allied occupation of Japan since 1945, disbanded.

Japan has become one of Asia's most successful democracies and largest economies. The U.S.-Japan alliance is the cornerstone of U.S. security interests in Asia and is fundamental to regional stability and prosperity. It is based on shared vital interests and values. These include stability in the Asia-Pacific region, the preservation and promotion of political and economic freedoms, support for human rights and democratic institutions, and securing of prosperity for the people of both countries and the international community as a whole.

Japan provides bases as well as financial and material support to U.S. forward-deployed forces, which are essential for maintaining stability in the region. Over the past decade the alliance has been strengthened through revised defense guidelines, which expand Japan's noncombatant role in a regional contingency, the renewal of the agreement on host nation support of U.S. forces stationed in Japan, and an ongoing process called the Defense Policy Review Initiative (DPRI). The DPRI redefines roles, missions, and capabilities of alliance forces and outlines key realignment and transformation initiatives, including reducing the number of U.S. troops stationed in Okinawa, enhancing interoperability and communication between the two countries' respective commands, and broadening cooperation in the area of ballistic missile defense.

Because of the two countries' combined economic and technological impact on the world, the U.S.-Japan relationship has become global in scope. The United States and Japan cooperate on a broad range of global issues, including development assistance, combating communicable disease such as the spread of HIV/AIDS and avian influenza, and protecting the environment and natural resources. The countries also collaborate in science and technology in such areas as mapping the human genome, research on aging, and international space exploration.

Japan contributes irreplaceable political, financial, and moral support to U.S.-Japan diplomatic efforts. The

United States consults closely with Japan and the Republic of Korea on policy regarding North Korea. The United States works closely with Japan and Australia under the auspices of the Trilateral Strategic Dialogue and the Security and Defense Cooperation Forum to exchange views and increase coordination on global and regional initiatives.

In Southeast Asia, U.S.-Japan cooperation is vital for stability and for political and economic reform. Outside Asia, Japanese political and financial support has substantially strengthened the U.S. position on a variety of global geopolitical problems, including the Persian Gulf, Middle East peace efforts, and the Balkans. Japan is an indispensable partner in the United Nations and the second-largest contributor to the UN budget. Japan broadly supports the United States on nonproliferation and nuclear issues.

U.S. Assistance to Japan

The United States provides no development assistance to Japan.

Bilateral Economic Relations

U.S. economic policy toward Japan is aimed at increasing access to Japan's markets and two-way investment, stimulating domestic demand-led economic growth, promoting economic restructuring, improving the climate for U.S. investors, and raising the standard of living in both the United States and Japan.

The U.S.-Japan bilateral economic relationship—based on enormous flows of trade, investment, and finance—is strong, mature, and increasingly interdependent. It also is firmly rooted in the shared interest and responsibility of the United States and Japan to promote global growth, open markets, and a vital world trading system.

Japan is a major market for many U.S. products, including agricultural products, chemicals, pharmaceuticals, films and music, commercial aircraft, nonferrous metals, plastics, medical and scientific supplies, and machinery. U.S. imports from Japan include vehicles, machinery, optic and medical instruments, and organic chemicals. U.S. direct investment in Japan is mostly in the finance/insurance, manufacturing, nonbank holding companies, and wholesale sectors. Japanese direct investment in the U.S. is mostly in the wholesale trade and manufacturing sectors.

The United States and Japan cooperate in a number of international economic forums. In 2011, Japan announced its intention to begin consultations with Trans-Pacific Partnership countries, including the United States, about joining negotiations that seek to develop a regional trade agreement.

Japan's Membership in International Organizations

Japan and the United States belong to a number of the same international organizations, including the United Nations, G-8, G-20, Organization for Economic Cooperation and Development, Asia-Pacific Economic Cooperation forum, ASEAN Regional Forum, International Monetary Fund, World Bank, and World Trade Organization. Japan also is a Partner for Cooperation with the Organization for Security and Cooperation in Europe and an observer to the Organization of American States.

Bilateral Representation

Japan maintains an embassy in the United States at 2520 Massachusetts Avenue NW, Washington, DC 20008 (tel: 202-238-6700).

Principal U.S. Embassy Officials

Last Updated: 1/14/2013

TOKYO (E) 10-5 Akasaka 1-chome, Minato-ku, Tokyo 107-8420, 81-3-3224-5000, Fax 81-3-3505-1862, Workweek: 0830–1730, Website: http://tokyo.usembassy.gov/

DCM OMS: Joyce Ogier
AMB OMS: Bonnie Angelov
DHS/CBP: Robert Thommen; Edward V. Bayron
DHS/ICE: William Wallrapp
DHS/TSA: Christopher Baden
FCS: Andrew Wylegala
FM: Thomas Martyn
HRO: David Osgood
MGT: Gregory Stanford
MLO/ODC: Shanan Farmer
POL/MIL: David Schlaefer
SDO/DATT: CAPT Justin Cooper
TREAS: Christopher Winship
AMB: John V. Roos
CG: Paul Fitzgerald
CON: Hugues Ogier
DCM: Kurt Tong
PAO: Mark Davidson
GSO: Timothy Bullington
RSO: Alan Chipman
AFSA: Cynthia Hoof, Vi Nhan
AGR: David Miller
AID: Jaidev Singh
APHIS: Dr. Kelly Preston
ATO: Steven Shnitzler
CLO: Aye Aye Maw, Scott Clever & Melody Walker
DEA: Louis D'Ambrosio
ECON: Jessica Webster
EEO: Mark Copeland
FAA: James Spillane
FIN: Christopher Winship
FMO: Robert Wert
ICASS Chair: Christopher Quade
IMO: Barry Peterson
IPO: James Jessee
ISO: Mark Copeland
ISSO: Mark Copeland/Paul Lewis
LEGATT: Edward Shaw
POL: Robert Luke

NAHA (CG) 2-1-1 Toyama Urasoe City, Okinawa Japan 901-2104, (81) (98) 876-4211, Fax (81) (98) 876-4243, INMARSAT Tel 872-76-344-9547, Workweek: 08:30–17:30, Website: http://naha.usconsulate.gov/

CG OMS: John E. Buhler
DPO: Matt O'Connor
MGT: Timothy W. Martin
POL/ECON: Matt O'Connor
POL/MIL: Matt O'Connor
CG: Alfred R. Magleby
CON: Clark Ledger
PAO: Heather Eaton
RSO: Timothy W. Martin
ECON: Heather L. Dresser
IPO: John E. Buhler
ISO: Timothy W. Martin
ISSO: John E. Buhler

OSAKA KOBE (CG) American Consulate General, 11-5, Nishitenma 2-Chome, Kita-ku, Osaka 530-8543, Japan, 81-6-6315-5900, Fax 81-66315 5915, INMARSAT Tel 76 344 9547, Workweek: Mon-Fri/0800-1700, Website: http://osaka.usconsulate.gov/

DHS/CIS:	Chi Siu
FCS:	John Fleming
MGT:	Brian Himmelsteib
POL/ECON:	Christopher Bishop
CG:	Patrick Linehan
CON:	Benjamin Brown
PAO:	Gregory Kay
COM:	John Fleming
RSO:	Darby Knox
AFSA:	Vi Nhan
AGR:	Resident In Tokyo
CLO:	Mieko Brown
IPO:	Ricardo Pereira
ISSO:	Ricardo Pereira

SAPPORO (CG) Kita 1-Jo Nishi 28-Chome, Chuo-Ku, Sapporo 064-0821, 81-11-641-1115, Fax 81-11-643-1283, Workweek: 8:30 a.m.–5:30 p.m. except designated holidays, Website: http://sapporo.usconsulate.gov/

MGT:	Carlton L. Benson
CG:	John N. Ries
CON:	Carlton L. Benson
PAO:	Jeffry W. Duffy
ECON:	Carlton L. Benson
IMO:	Barry R. Peterson
ISO:	Mark S. Copeland
POL:	Jeffry W. Duffy

FUKUOKA (C) 5-26 Ohori 2-chome, Chuo-ku, Fukuoka 810-0052, 81-92-751-9331, Fax 81-92-713-9222, Workweek: 8:45 a.m.–5:30 p.m., Mon–Friday, Website: http://fukuoka.usconsulate.gov/

MGT:	Timothy P. Dougherty
POL/ECON:	Daniel C. Callahan
PO:	Jason R. Cubas
CON:	Timothy P. Dougherty
PAO:	Mike Chadwick
RSO:	Darby Knox (In Osaka)
ISSO:	Timothy P. Dougherty

NAGOYA (C) Nagoya Kokusai Center Bldg., 6th Fl., 1-47-1, Nagono, Nakamura-ku, Nagoya, Japan 450-0001, 81-52-581-4501, Fax 81-52-581-3190, INMARSAT Tel 00763449534, Workweek: 8:30–17:30 MF, Website: http://nagoya.usconsulate.gov/

DHS/CBP:	Ryan Santino
PO:	Harry R. Sullivan
CON:	Stephen S. Wheeler
PAO:	Stephen S. Wheeler

YOKOHAMA 152-3 Yamate-cho, Naka-ku, Yokohama, Japan 231-0862, (81) (45) 622-6514, Fax (81) (45) 622-6516, INMARSAT Tel 8816 2145-4473 (iridium), Workweek: 08:30-17:30, Website: http://intranet.tokyo.state.gov/usmissionjpn/Docs/FSI/index.htm/

PO:	John Maher

TRAVEL

Consular Information Sheet

December 6, 2012

Country Description: Japan is a stable, highly developed parliamentary democracy with a modern economy. Tourist facilities are widely available, except in coastal areas of Northeast Japan still recovering from the aftermath of the March 11, 2011, earthquake and tsunami.

Smart Traveler Enrollment Program (STEP)/Embassy Locations: If you are going to live in or visit Japan, please take the time to tell our Embassy or one of our Consulates in Japan about your trip. If you enroll in the Smart Traveler Enrollment Program, we can keep you up-to-date with important safety and security announcements. It will also help your friends and family get in touch with you in an emergency. In accordance with the Privacy Act, information on your welfare or whereabouts may not be released to inquirers without your expressed written authorization.

U.S. Embassy in Tokyo
1-10-5 Akasaka, Minato-ku,
Tokyo 107-8420 Japan
Telephone: 81-3-3224–5000
Emergency after-hours telephone:
81-3-3224–5000
Facsimile: 81-3-3224–5856

U.S. Consulate General in
Osaka-Kobe
2-11-5 Nishitenma, Kita-ku,
Osaka 530-8543
Telephone: 81-6-6315–5900
Emergency after-hours telephone:
81-6-6315–5900
Facsimile: 81-6-6315–5914

U.S. Consulate General in Naha
2-1-1 Toyama, Urasoe,
Okinawa 901-2104
Telephone: 81-98-876-4211
Emergency after-hours telephone:
81-3-3224–5000 (Emergency calls are routed through the Embassy switchboard after hours)
Facsimile: 81-98-876-4243

U.S. Consulate General in Sapporo
Kita 1-Jo Nishi 28-chome, Chuo-ku,
Sapporo 064-0821
Telephone: 81-11-641-1115
Emergency after-hours telephone:
81-11-641-1115
Facsimile: 81-11-643-1283.

U.S. Consulate in Fukuoka
2-5-26 Ohori, Chuo-ku,
Fukuoka 810-0052
Telephone: 81-92-751-9331
Emergency after-hours telephone:
81-3-3224–5000 (Emergency calls are routed through the Embassy switchboard after hours)
Facsimile: 81-92-713-9222

U.S. Consulate in Nagoya
Nagoya International Center Bldg.
6th floor, 1-47-1 Nagono,
Nakamura-ku, Nagoya 450-0001
Telephone: 81-52-581-4501
Emergency after-hours telephone:
81-52-581-4501
Facsimile: 81-52-581-3190.

Entry/Exit Requirements for U.S. Citizens: You must have a valid passport and an onward/return ticket for tourist/business "visa free" stays of up to 90 days. Your passports must be valid for the entire time you are staying in Japan. U.S. citizens cannot work on a 90-day "visa free" entry. As a general rule, "visa free" entry status may not be changed to another visa status without departing and then re-entering Japan with the appropriate visa, such as a spouse, work, or study visa.

For more information about the Japanese visa waiver program for tourists, Japan's rules on work visas, special visas for taking depositions, and other visa issues, you should consult the Consular Section of the Embassy of Japan at 2520 Massachusetts Avenue NW, Washington, DC 20008, tel. (202) 238-6800, or the nearest Japanese consulate. Please visit the Japanese Embassy's website for location details. The U.S. Embassy and U.S. consulates in Japan cannot assist in obtaining visas for Japan.

All foreign nationals entering Japan, with the exception of certain categories listed below, are required to provide fingerprint scans and to be photographed at the port of entry. This requirement is in addition to any existing visa or passport requirements. Foreign nationals exempt from this requirement include special permanent residents, persons under 16 years of age, holders of diplomatic or official visas, and persons invited by the head of a national administrative organization.

U.S. travelers on official business must have a diplomatic or official visa specifying the nature of travel as "As Diplomat," "As Official," or "In Transit" to be exempt from biometric collection. All other visa holders, including those with diplomatic and official visas stating "As Temporary Visitor," are subject to this requirement. Status of Forces Agreement (SOFA) personnel, are exempt from biometrics entry requirements under SOFA Article IX.2.

If you are a U.S. citizen entering or transiting Japan, you should ensure that your passport and visa are valid and up to date before you leave the United States. Occasionally, airlines mistakenly board U.S. citizens coming to Japan even though their passports have already expired.

The U.S. Embassy and U.S. consulates cannot "vouch for" you without a valid passport, and passport services are not available at the airport. In some prior instances, travelers have been returned immediately to the United States, while in other cases, they have been issued 24-hour "shore passes" and required to return the next day to Japanese Immigration for lengthy processing.

Many Asian countries require you to hold a passport valid for at least six months after you enter the country. Airlines in Japan will deny you boarding for transit if you don't have the required travel documents for an onward destination in Asia. For the entry requirements of the country you're traveling to, visit the State Department's Country Specific Information website

Airlines in Japan will deny you boarding for onward flights to China if your passport does not have a valid Chinese visa. U.S. citizen travelers who are not legally resident in Japan have reported difficulties in obtaining a Chinese visa during a short stay in Japan. The U.S. embassy and U.S. consulates in Japan cannot assist in obtaining Chinese visas.

Military/SOFA Travelers: While active-duty U.S. military personnel may enter Japan under the Status of Forces Agreement (SOFA) with proper Department of Defense (DOD) identification and travel orders, all SOFA family members, civilian employees, and contractors must have valid passports and, in some cases, SOFA visas to enter Japan. Military members with non-U.S. citizen family members seeking to have them accompany them to Japan should consult with their command and Japan Immigration for requirements, as entry to Japan may differ depending on nationality. Active-duty military personnel should obtain a tourist passport before leaving the United States to accommodate off-duty travel elsewhere in Asia, as obtaining one in Japan can take several weeks. Personnel whose duties will include official travel should also obtain an Official Passport before coming to Japan to avoid delays of up to two months, as overseas applications for these passports must be referred to a special office in Washington, which increases the processing times. DOD travelers should consult the DOD Foreign Clearance Guide, DOD 4500.54, before leaving the United States.

Long-Term Residency Requirements: Japan amended its Immigration Control and Refugee Recognition Act in 2009, and the changes took effect on July 9, 2012. In addition, under the 2006 revision of the same law, if you are a long-term resident who obtained residence through your Japanese ancestry, you may have to provide evidence that you do not have a criminal record in your home country before you can renew residency status in Japan. As Japanese Immigration regulations are complex and changing, the Embassy recommends that you consult directly with your local immigration office for specific guidance. You can obtain a Proof of no U.S. criminal record through the FBI Identification Record Request..

The current residency system, instituted by the Japanese government on July 9, 2012, impacts the following groups:

- Foreign nationals with Permanent Resident status;
- Foreign nationals who have long-term residence in Japan based on familial relationships with Japanese citizens;
- Foreign nationals with "College Student" status; and
- Foreign nationals issued a working visa in various professional classifications such as Engineer, Specialist in Humanities/International Services, Research, Business Management, Designated Activities, etc.

PLEASE NOTE: "Long-Term Resident" (teijusha) and "Permanent Resident" (eijusha) are different and therefore are subject to different requirements. The current residency system includes updated residency cards with a maximum stay of five years, a revised re-entry permit system, updated requirements for reporting to the Japanese Immigration Bureau, as well as a regulation requiring legal resident aliens in Japan to report to their local city offices. As part of the current policy, a Residence Card (zairyu kaado) has replaced the previous Alien Registration Certificate (ARC). Resident aliens are also required to register their households in the same manner as Japanese citizens.

The current procedures also updated and changed penalties for those who fail to maintain legal status in Japan or do not comply with current reporting requirements. Both prospective and current resident aliens in Japan should be familiar with updated procedures to ensure compliance with current policies.

As the changes in Japanese immigration and resident registration procedures and the affected groups described above are not a comprehensive listing, please check directly with the Japan Immigration Bureau or the Ministry of Internal Affairs and Communications (MIC). The Japanese government websites below have more information on these changes:

http://www.soumu.go.jp/main_sosiki/jichi_gyousei/c-gyousei/qa_en.html

http://www.soumu.go.jp/main_sosiki/jichi_gyousei/c-gyousei/zairyu_english.html

http://www.immi-moj.go.jp/newimmiact_1/en/index.html

http://www.immi-moj.go.jp/english/newimmiact/newimmiact_english.html

For a renewal of visa status or a change in visa status, you should bring your Japanese health insurance card (social insurance or national health insurance) to immigration offices in addition to your passport. Immigration officials will urge those applicants without a health insurance card to join the Japanese public health insurance system.

HIV/AIDS Restrictions: The U.S. Department of State is unaware of any HIV/AIDS entry restrictions for visitors or foreign residents of Japan.

Threats to Safety and Security: There have been no major terrorist incidents in Japan since 1995. However, you should be aware of the potential risks and take these into consideration when making travel plans.

The Government of Japan maintains heightened security measures at key facilities and ports of entry as anti-terrorism precautions. At times, these security measures may increase because of regional tensions with North Korea. The Government of Japan is vigilant in tracking terrorist threat indicators and remains at a high state of alert. You can contact local police substations (koban) and police emergency dispatchers (tel. 110) to report any suspicious activity.

Our offices in Japan communicate threat information through the Smart Traveler Enrollment Program (STEP) and post current threat information on the U.S. Embassy's American Citizens Services (ACS) web page. If you reside in or visit Japan, we encourage you to enroll in STEP, so that the Embassy can keep you up-to-date with important safety and security announcements.

Stay up to date by:

- Bookmarking our Bureau of Consular Affairs website, which contains the current Travel Warnings and Travel Alerts as well as the Worldwide Caution.
- Following us on Twitter and the Bureau of Consular Affairs page on Facebook as well.
- Downloading our free Smart Traveler app, available through iTunes or the Android market, to have travel information at your fingertips.
- Calling 1-888-407-4747 toll-free within the United States and Canada, or a regular toll line, 1-202-501-4444, from other countries.
- Taking some time before travel to consider your personal security.

Crime: The general crime rate in Japan is well below the U.S. national average. Crimes against U.S. citizens in Japan usually involve personal disputes, theft, or vandalism. Violent crime is rare but does exist. Sexual assaults do not happen often but do occur, and females may be randomly targeted. Hate-related violent crimes rarely occur, though some U.S. citizens have reported being the target of comments or actions because of their nationality or their race. There have been some incidents of pick pocketing of foreigners in crowded shopping areas, on trains, and at airports. Every year, a number of U.S. citizens report their passports lost or stolen at international airports, especially passports that were carried in their pockets.

Some U.S. citizens report that Japanese police procedures appear to be less sensitive and responsive to a victim's concerns compared to the procedures in the United States, particularly in cases of domestic violence or sexual assault, or when both the victim and the perpetrator are foreigners. Few victim's assistance resources or battered women's shelters exist in major urban areas, and they are generally unavailable in rural areas. Investigations of sexual assault crimes are often conducted without female police officers present and police typically ask about the victim's sexual history and previous relationships. The quality of Japanese-English interpretation services can vary, and for some U.S. citizen victims, this has caused a problem.

Don't buy counterfeit and pirated goods, even if they are widely available. Not only are such goods illegal in the United States, if you purchase them you may also be breaking local law.

Concerns Regarding Roppongi and other Entertainment and Nightlife Districts: Roppongi is an entertainment district in Tokyo that caters to foreign clientele and is considered a high-risk area for crime, particularly misappropriation of credit card information in bars to make fraudulent credit card charges. Other high-risk areas for crime in the Tokyo area include Shinjuku (especially the area of Kabuki-cho), Shibuya, and Ikebukuro. However, you should use caution in all entertainment and nightlife districts throughout Japan. Incidents involving U.S. citizens since the spring of 2008 in these areas include physical and sexual assaults, drug overdoses, theft of purses, wallets, cash and credit cards at bars or clubs, and drugs allegedly slipped into drinks.

Drink-spiking at bars and entertainment venues, especially in areas such as Roppongi and Kabuki-cho, near Shinjuku, has routinely led to robbery and has also resulted in physical and sexual assaults. In most drink-spiking reports, the victim unknowingly drinks a beverage that has been mixed with a drug that makes the victim unconscious or dazed for several hours, during which time the victim's credit card is used for large purchases or the card is stolen. Some victims regain consciousness in the bar or club; other victims may awaken on the street or in other unknown locations. Several U.S. citizens have also reported being charged exorbitant bar tabs in some bars and clubs in Roppongi and other entertainment and nightlife districts. Although firearms and brandishing knives in public are illegal in Japan, there have been reports by U.S. citizens of being threatened with gun or knife violence in such venues in order to force them to pay bar tabs or withdraw money. There have also been reports of beatings of U.S. citizens who have refused to pay or hand over money.

There have been recent reports of U.S. citizens being forcibly taken to ATM machines and robbed, or to withdraw funds after being unable to pay exhorbitant bar tabs. Please be aware that Roppongi and other entertainment and nightlife districts have also been the scenes of violence between criminal syndicates in the past. In 2012, a member of a Japanese criminal organization was beaten to death in a bar in Roppongi by several masked men.

We urge you to keep these incidents in mind and use caution in all entertainment areas and nightlife districts.

Victims of Crime: If you or someone you know becomes the victim of a crime abroad, you should contact the local police and the nearest U.S. embassy or consulate. We can:

- Replace a stolen passport.
- Help you find appropriate medical care if you are the victim of violent crimes such as assault or rape.
- Put you in contact with the appropriate police authorities, and if you want us to, we cancontact family members or a friend.
- Help you understand the local criminal justice process and direct you to local attorneys, although it is important to remember that local authorities are responsible for investigating and prosecuting the crime.

The local equivalents to the "911" emergency line in Japan are 110 (police) or 119 (ambulance/fire).

Contacting Police, Fire and Ambulance Services: You can reach the police throughout Japan by dialing 110. Fire and ambulance services can be contacted by dialing 119. Note that these numbers may not work from cell phones and English-speaking dispatchers may not be available. Please review advice on how to call for help. If you need assistance, you should be able to describe your address/location in Japanese or find someone who can do so, since few police officers speak English.

Criminal Penalties: While you are traveling in another country, you are subject to its laws even if you are a U.S. citizen. Foreign laws and legal systems can be vastly different than our own. In Japan, you may be taken in for questioning if you don't have your passport or Japanese residence card to show your identity and visa status. Driving under the influence could also land you immediately in jail. If you violate Japanese law, even unknowingly, you may be arrested, imprisoned, or deported. If you are arrested in Japan, even for a minor offense, you may be held in detention without bail for several months or more during the investigation and legal proceedings. A list of English-speaking lawyers located throughout Japan is available on our website. There are also some things that might be legal in the country you visit, but still illegal in the United States, and you can be prosecuted under U.S. law if you buy pirated goods or purchase child pornography. While you are overseas, U.S. laws don't apply. If you do something illegal in your host country, you are subject to the laws of the country even though you arc a U.S. citizen. It's very important to know what's legal and what's not wherever you go.

Illegal Drugs: Penalties for possessing, using, or trafficking in illegal drugs, including marijuana, are severe, and convicted offenders can expect long jail sentences and fines. In most drug cases, suspects are detained and barred from receiving visitors or corresponding with anyone other than a lawyer or a U.S. consular officer until after the first hearing. Solitary confinement is common.

You could be convicted of drug use based on positive blood or urine tests alone, and several U.S. citizens are now serving time in Japanese prisons as the result of sting operations that used informants. The Japanese police routinely share information on drug arrests with Interpol, assuring that notification of the arrest will reach U.S. law enforcement agencies.

A large proportion of all U.S. citizens now in prison in Japan are incarcerated for drug-related crimes. In recent months, there have been arrests of individuals selling and possessing synthetic drug—like substances, such as the synthetic marijuana called "spice."

Japanese authorities aggressively pursue drug smugglers with sophisticated detection equipment, "sniffing" dogs, and other methods. When entering Japan, you and your luggage will be screened at ports of entry. Incoming and outgoing mail, as well as international packages sent via DHL or FedEx, is also checked carefully. The Japanese police make arrests for even the smallest amounts of illegal drugs. Several U.S. citizens have been arrested, tried, and convicted after having mailed illegal drugs to themselves from other countries, or for having tried to bring drugs into Japan as paid couriers working out of Southeast Asia or Europe.

Knives: Possession of a knife with a locking blade, or a folding blade that is longer than 5.5 cm (a little more than two inches), is illegal in Japan. U.S. citizens have been arrested and detained for more than 10 days for carrying pocket knives that are legal in the United States but illegal in Japan.

Immigration Penalties: Japanese work visas are not transferable and are issued outside of Japan for a specific job with a specific employer at a specific place of employment. It is illegal for you to work in Japan while in tourist or visa-waiver status. Japanese authorities do not allow foreigners to change their immigration status from visa-waiver status to work status while in Japan. Japanese immigration officers may deny you entry if you appear to have no visible means of support. Please contact the Japanese Embassy or nearest Japanese consulate in the United States for information on what is considered enough financial support. If you work in Japan without a work visa, you may be subject to arrest, which can involve several weeks or months of incarceration, followed by conviction and imprisonment or deportation. If you are deported, you will have to pay the cost of deportation, including legal expenses and airfare.

Overstaying your visa or working illegally may lead to fines of several thousands of dollars, and in some cases, re-entry bans can be as long as ten years or indefinitely for drug offenders.

Arrest notifications in Japan: Generally, when you are arrested in Japan, the police will ask if you would like the U.S. embassy or consulate to be notified of your arrest. To ensure that the United States is aware of your circumstances, request that the police and prison officials notify the nearest U.S. embassy or consulate as soon as you are arrested or detained overseas.

Customs Regulations: Japan has very strict laws regarding the importation and possession of firearms and other weapons. Persons bringing a firearm or sword into Japan (including target and trophy pistols, air guns, some pocket knives, and even Japanese-origin swords) may have these items confiscated by Japanese customs authorities and may be arrested, prosecuted, and deported or jailed. Some prescription medications, as well as some over-the-counter medications, cannot be imported into Japan. (Please see the "Confiscation of Prescription Drugs and other Medication" section below.) Please contact the Japanese Embassy or nearest Japanese consulate in the United States, or visit the Japanese Customs website for specific information regarding import restrictions and customs requirements.

Japanese customs authorities encourage the use of an Admission Temporaire/Temporary Admission (ATA) Carnet in order to temporarily import professional equipment, commercial samples and/or goods for exhibitions and trade fairs into Japan. The ATA Carnet Headquarters is located at the U.S. Council for International Business (U.S. CIB), 1212 Avenue of the Americas, New York, NY 10036 issues and guarantees the ATA Carnet in the United States. For additional information, please call (212) 354-4480, or email the U.S. CIB for details.

Confiscation of Prescription Drugs and Other Medication: The Japanese government decides which medications may be imported legally into Japan. The Embassy and Consulates of Japan in the United States have limited information available and do not have comprehensive lists of specific medications or ingredients.

You can bring up to a two-month supply of allowable over-the-counter medication and up to a two-month supply of allowable vitamins into Japan duty-free. However, it is illegal to bring some over-the-counter medicines commonly used in the United States, including inhalers and some allergy and sinus medications into Japan. Specifically, products that contain stimulants (medicines that contain pseudoephedrine, such as Actifed, Sudafed, and Vicks inhalers) or codeine are prohibited. You can generally bring up to one month's supply of allowable prescription medicine into Japan. You must bring a copy of your doctor's prescription as well as a letter stating the purpose of the drug.

However, some U.S. prescription medications cannot be imported into Japan, even when accompanied by a customs declaration and a copy of the prescription. You should not mail prescription medicines, including insulin and injectors, without obtaining an import certification called "Yakkan-Syoumei" from the Ministry of Health, Labor, and Welfare. Please see more information on importing medicines into Japan.

Japanese physicians can often prescribe similar but not identical substitutes for medicines available in the United States. You can consult a Japanese doctor by phone before you travel to Japan, to find out what medications are available and/or permitted in Japan. See the list of English-speaking medical facilities throughout Japan on our website. Some popular medications that are legal in the United States, such as Prozac and Viagra, are sold illegally in Japan on the black market. You risk arrest and imprisonment if you purchase such drugs illegally while in Japan.

If you travel to Japan carrying prescription and non-prescription medications, you should consult the Japanese Embassy or a Japanese consulate in the United States before leaving the United States to confirm whether or not you will be allowed to bring the particular medication into Japan.

Pets: The Japanese Animal Quarantine Service (AQS) sets procedures for importing pets. At a minimum, the process will take 7-8 months, though the process can take up to a year before a pet may enter Japan. Advance planning is critical. You can find more information about importing a pet into Japan or information about exporting a pet from Japan on our embassy website.

Consular Access: You must carry your U.S. passport or Japanese Residence Card with you at all times so that if questioned by local officials, you can prove your identity, citizenship, and immigration status. Under Japanese law, the police may stop any person on the street at any time and demand to see identification. If you do not have with you either a passport or valid Japanese Residence Card, you are subject to arrest. In accordance with the U.S.-Japan Consular Convention, U.S. consular officers are generally notified within 24 hours of the arrest of a U.S. citizen, if the U.S. citizen requests consular notification.

Conditions at Prisons and Detention Facilities: Japanese prisons and detention facilities maintain internal order through a regime of very strict discipline. U.S. citizen prisoners often complain of stark, austere living conditions and psychological isolation. No one arrested in Japan is allowed access to personal medication of any type, often causing problems and health risks to those arrested with medical conditions, as substitute medication provided by prison medical officials is seldom the same in effect or strength. As a prisoner, you can become eligible for parole only after serving about 60-70% of your sentence. Early parole is not allowed for any reason — humanitarian, medical, or otherwise. Access to interpreters is not always required under Japanese criminal law. Additional information on arrests in Japan is available on our embassy website. Japan acceded to the Council of Europe Convention on the Transfer of Sentenced Persons on June 1, 2003. Please see our information on Prisoner Transfer Treaties.

Employment Issues: U.S. citizens should not come to Japan to work without having the proper employment visa arranged ahead of time, or in the hopes of earning a large salary. Teaching English, even privately, and serving as hosts/hostesses are both considered "work" in Japan and are illegal without the proper visa.

Some U.S.-based employment agencies and Japanese employers do not fully discuss or correctly represent the true nature of employment terms and conditions. U.S. consular officers in Japan receive numerous complaints from U.S. citizens who come to Japan to work as English teachers, carpenters, models, actors, entertainers, exotic dancers, and bar hosts/hostesses. The complaints include contract violations, non-payment of salary for months at a time, sexual harassment, intimidation, and threats of arrest, deportation, and physical assault.

A minimum requirement for effectively seeking the protection of Japanese labor law is a written and signed work contract. Without a signed contract, Japanese authorities do not get involved on behalf of foreign workers. If you're coming to Japan to work, carefully review your contracts and the history and reputation of your Japanese employer before traveling to Japan. We cannot confirm information about prospective Japanese employers although we may be familiar with organizations or have received complaints in the past.

If you are asked to do something you find troubling, you should reconsider being in Japan and think about terminating your employment and returning to the United States. Complaints against U.S.-based employment agencies or recruiters may be directed to the Better Business Bureau or the Office of the Attorney General in that particular state.

Living and Travel Expenses: Japan's cost of living is one of the highest in the world. The use of credit/debit cards is not widespread, particularly outside major cities. While there are ATMs in Japan, most are not open 24 hours a day, and only a very limited number accept U.S.-issued cards. ATMs at major airports, foreign bank branches, Japanese post offices, 7-11 stores and some convenience stores are more likely to accept foreign cards than are those at other locations. You should make sure that you have access to sufficient funds through credit cards, debit cards, or cash to carry out your travel, and know how to contact your banking or credit card establishments in an emergency.

In summer 2010, Western Union resumed service in Japan, offering cash-to-cash transfers across 200 countries and territories to and from some areas in Japan. Western Union money transfer service is available at Travelex offices. More information can be found in English at http://www.westernunion.com/ and in Japanese at http://www.travelex.co.jp.

Taxi fares from airports to downtown Osaka and Tokyo can cost hundreds of dollars; bus fare can run US$40 or more. The airport departure fee is generally included in the ticket prices for flights departing from international airports in Japan. Bus fare between Narita (Tokyo) International Airport and Haneda Airport in Tokyo is approximately $40 and takes from 90 to 120 minutes.

English Help and Information Lines: As a tourist or foreign resident in Japan, you can have access to valuable information, including professional counseling, through help and information telephone hotlines. The Tokyo English Lifeline ("TELL") provides English-speaking counseling and referrals at 03-5774–0992. The Japan Help Line provides similar assistance nationwide at 0570–000-911 (domestic), 813-3435–8017 (international).

Disaster Preparedness: Japan is faced with the ever-present danger of deadly earthquakes, tsunamis, and typhoons. Japan is one of the most seismically active locations in the world; minor tremors are felt regularly throughout the islands. On March 11, 2011, an earthquake registering 9.0 on the Richter scale struck the northeastern coast of Japan and triggered tsunami waves that caused extensive damage to life and property and severely damaged the Fukushima Daiichi Nuclear Power Plant. Additional information on the aftermath of the March 11 earthquake is available on the U.S. Embassy's American Citizens Services (ACS) web page. While responsibility for caring for disaster victims, including foreigners, rests with the Japanese authorities, one of the first things you should do upon arriving in Japan is to learn about earthquake and disaster preparedness from hotel or local government officials. Self-preparedness information is available on the on the U.S. Embassy's American Citizens Services (ACS) web page and on the U.S. Federal Emergency Management Agency (FEMA) home page.

Radiation: Fukushima Daiichi Nuclear Power Plant: The Government of Japan and agencies of the U.S. government continue to work together to monitor the conditions at and around the Fukushima Daiichi Nuclear Power Plant. In addition, on September 19, 2012, Japan established an independent organization to oversee the safety of its atomic reactors, the Nuclear Regulation Authority.

Areas We Recommend U.S. Citizens Avoid: Based on current data from Japan, we recommend that U.S. citizens avoid all unnecessary travel to areas described by the Japanese government on the following map (Japanese version map). In addition, U.S. citizens should avoid all unnecessary travel to the area northwest of the Plant that the Government of Japan has designated the "Deliberate Evacuation Area" that includes Iitate-mura, the Yamagiya district of Kawamata-machi, Katsurao-mura, Namie-machi and parts of Minamisoma. For a more detailed description of the differences in travel restrictions between the variouszones click here. Out of an abundance of caution, we recommend that those considering travel to affected areas in Fukushima Prefecture consult with local authorities to receive current guidance on expected levels of radiation and recommendations for reducing exposure to radiation in these areas.

Areas We Recommend Caution for Long Term Residence by U.S. Citizens: Out of an abundance of caution, we recommend that U.S. citizens who choose to reside for more than one year within 80 kilometers of the Fukushima Daiichi Nuclear Power Plant, and especially within the current Deliberate Evacuation Area, consult with local authorities to receive current guidance on expected levels of radiation and recommendations for reducing exposure to radiation.

Additional information about radiation and its effects on human health may be found at the following websites:

http://japan2.usembassy.gov/e/acs/tacs-health.html

http://emergency.cdc.gov/radiation/japan2011.asp

http://epa.gov/radiation/understanding-radiation-overview.html

http://www.kantei.go.jp/foreign/incident/health_and_safety.html

http://registry.csd.disa.mil/otr.

Please note that many of the coastal areas in the Fukushima, Iwate, and Miyaga Prefectures affected by the earthquake/tsunami/nuclear disaster in 2011 are still undergoing significant reconstruction. If you wish to travel to these areas, you should exercise caution as you may experience disruption in travel or infrastructure. We recommend that you contact local authorities, or travel/accommodation service providers in advance.

Accessibility: While in Japan, individuals with disabilities may find accessibility and accommodation very different from what they are in the United States. Although Japan's accessibility laws mandate that new construction projects for public use include provisions for persons with disabilities, older buildings are not likely to have been retrofitted for accessibility. At major train stations, airports, and hotels, travelers with disabilities should encounter few accessibility problems. Accessibility at other public facilities continues to improve through the installation of elevators and wheelchair ramps. However, travelers should note that many smaller stations are inaccessible to those who cannot climb stairs. Most major urban hotels have wheelchair accessible rooms, while smaller "business hotels" and traditional Japanese-style inns may not accommodate wheelchair users.

Information on travel in Japan for travelers with disabilities is available at Tesco Premium Search Co., Ltd. website "the Travel Guide for Wheelchair Users." American travelers in wheelchairs should be aware that wheelchairs must be no more than 120 centimeters in length/height and no more than 70 centimeters in width in order to be allowed in trains. Accessibility information regarding the East Japan Railway Company is also available at the company's website. Reduced train fares for individuals with disabilities are not available for temporary visitors to Japan. If you do not speak Japanese, you may wish to ask your travel agent to make advance arrangements for your travel in Japan.

Medical Facilities and Health Information: While medical care in Japan is good, English-speaking physicians and medical facilities that cater to U.S. citizens' expectations are expensive and not widespread. Japan has a national health insurance system which is available only to those foreigners with long-term visas for Japan. National health insurance does not pay for medical evacuation. Medical caregivers in Japan require payment in full at the time of treatment or concrete proof of ability to pay before they will treat a foreigner who is not a member of the national health insurance plan.

U.S.-style and standard psychiatric care can be difficult to locate in major urban centers in Japan and generally is not available outside of Japan's major cities. Extended psychiatric care for foreigners in Japan is difficult to obtain at any price.

U.S. prescriptions are not honored in Japan, so if you need ongoing prescription medicine you should arrive with a sufficient supply for your stay in Japan or enough until you are able to see a local care provider. Certain medications, including some commonly prescribed for depression and Attention Deficient Hyperactivity Disorder (ADHD), are not widely available. Please see the section above entitled, "Confiscation of Prescription Drugs and Other Medication," regarding the importation of medicine into Japan. Also see information on importing medicines into Japan and a list of medical facilities in Japan with English-speaking staff.

You can find detailed information on vaccinations and other health precautions, on the Centers for Diseases Control (CDC) website. For information about outbreaks of infectious diseases abroad, consult the World Health Organization (WHO) website. The WHO website also contains additional health information for travelers, including detailed country-specific health information.

Medical Insurance: Serious medical problems requiring hospitalization and/or medical evacuation can cost anywhere from \$30,000 to \$120,000 or more, depending on your location and medical condition. U.S. military hospitals in Japan do not treat or provide military medical evacuation to private U.S. citizens. The military strictly controls access to U.S. military facilities; veterans with service-connected disabilities should contact the appropriate U.S. military hospital before traveling to Japan. The embassy is unable to arrange for treatment of veterans at any U.S. military hospitals in Japan. Most small clinics and some large hospitals do not accept credit/debit cards. No facility accepts checks drawn on U.S. bank accounts.

You can't assume your insurance will go with you when you travel. It's very important to find out BEFORE you leave whether or not your medical insurance will cover you overseas. You need to ask your insurance company two questions:

- Does my policy apply when I'm out of the U.S.?
- Will it cover emergencies like a trip to a foreign hospital or an evacuation?

In many places, doctors and hospitals still expect payment in cash at the time of service. Your regular U.S. health insurance may not cover doctors' and hospital visits in other countries. If your policy doesn't go with you when you travel, it's a very good idea to take out another one for your trip.

Traffic Safety and Road Conditions: While in a foreign country, you may encounter road conditions that differ significantly from those in the United States. The information below concerning Japan is provided for general reference only, and it may not be totally accurate in a particular location or circumstance.

Driving in Japan is quite complicated and expensive. Traffic moves on the left side of the road. Those who cannot read the language will have trouble understanding road signs. Highway tolls can be as high as \$1 (U.S.) or more per mile. City traffic is often very congested. A 20-mile trip in the Tokyo area may take two hours. There is virtually no legal roadside parking, however, traffic is commonly blocked or partially-blocked by those illegally parked curbside. In mountainous areas, roads are often closed during the winter, and cars should be equipped with tire chains.

Roads in Japan are much narrower than those in the United States. Japanese compulsory insurance (JCI) is mandatory for all automobile owners and drivers in Japan. Most short-term visitors choose not to drive in Japan. Other than a few exceptions, turning on red lights is generally not permitted.

Japanese law provides that all drivers in Japan are held liable in the event of an accident, and assesses fault in an accident on all parties. Japan has a national zero percent blood-alcohol level standard for driving, and drivers stopped for driving under the influence of intoxicants will have their licenses confiscated. If you're found guilty of "drunken, speeding, or blatantly careless driving resulting in injury" you are subject to up to 15 years in prison.

All passengers are required to fasten their seat belts.

The National Police Agency (NPA) oversees the administration and enforcement of traffic laws in Japan. You can find further information in English on the NPA's website.

Emergency Assistance: Within Japan, please dial 110 for police, and 119 for ambulance. For roadside assistance, please contact the Japan Automobile Federation (JAF) at 03-5730–0111 in Tokyo, 072-645-0111 in Osaka, 011-857-8139 in Sapporo, 092-841-5000 in Fukuoka, or 098-877-9163 in Okinawa.

For specific information concerning Japanese driving permits, vehicle inspection, road tax and mandatory insurance, please refer to the Japan National Tourist Organization website for locations in Chicago, Los Angeles, New York, or San Francisco. In addition, information about roadside assistance, rules of the road, and obtaining a Japanese driver's license is available in English from the Japan Automobile Federation (JAF) web site.

International Driving Permits (IDPs): An international driving permit (IDP) issued in the United States by the American Automobile Association (AAA) or the American Automobile Touring Alliance (AATA) is required of short-term visitors who drive in Japan. You must obtain an IDP issued in your country of residence prior to arriving in Japan. The U.S. Embassy or its consulates do not issue IDPs. IDPs issued via the Internet and/or by other organizations are not valid in Japan.

"Residents"—the exact definition is unclear - must convert to or obtain a Japanese driver's license. Residents in Japan who use an international driver's license may be fined or arrested. In practice, the term "resident" involves more than simply visa status or length of stay in Japan and is determined by the police. In short, an international license is not a substitute for a valid Japanese license. See our website for more information on driving in Japan.

Aviation Safety Oversight: The U.S. Federal Aviation Administration (FAA) has assessed the government of Japan's Civil Aviation Authority as being in compliance with International Civil Aviation Organization (ICAO) aviation safety standards for oversight of Japan's air carrier operations. Further information may be found on the FAA's safety assessment page.

Children's Issues: Please see the U.S. Dept. of State Office of Children's Issues web pages on intercountry adoption and international parental child abduction. Japan-specific information on international parental child abduction may be found here.

Intercountry Adoption

June 2010

The information in this section has been edited from the latest report available as of February 2013 from the State Department Bureau of Consular Affairs, Office of Overseas Citizens Services. For more information, please read the *Intercountry Adoption* section of this book and review current reports online at http://adoption.state.gov.

Japan is not party to the Hague Convention on Protection of Children and Co-operation in Respect of Intercountry Adoption (Hague Adoption Convention). Japan has two distinct procedures for intercountry adoption: full and final adoption or legal custody. Both alternatives require that the child meet the definition of "orphan" in the Immigration and Nationality Act (INA) Section 101(b)(1)(F) in order to qualify for issuance of an immediate immigrant visa to enter the United States in either category IR-3 (option 1) or IR-4 (option 2).

"Special" and "Regular" Adoptions: For adoptions that are finalized in Japan, there are two types of adoptions under Japanese law—regular and special. "Regular" adoptions are not considered an option for American citizens wishing to adopt in Japan as they are based on Japanese cultural and family traditions and do not legally sever the ties between the child and his or her birth family.

To date there have been no known cases of Americans applying for immigrant visas for children adopted under the Japanese "regular" adoption process. To be a valid adoption for U.S. immigration purposes there must be an irrevocable termination of the biological parent(s)—child relationship. "Special" adoptions in the Japanese context are an option for Americans who are resident in Japan.

The law on special adoptions went into effect on January 1, 1988, having been created to protect children. Special adoptions more closely resemble Western-style adoptions. As in U.S. adoptions, a special adoption legally severs the child's ties, rights and privileges with regard to the birth parent(s) and any prior adoptive parents.

Who Can Adopt? To bring an adopted child to United States from Japan, you must be found eligible to adopt by the U.S. Government. The U.S. Government agency responsible for making this determination is the Department of Homeland Security, U.S. Citizenship and Immigration Services (USCIS).

Residency Requirements: There are no laws concerning the visa status of prospective adoptive parents. However, parents almost always must reside in Japan during the entire court process, which takes a minimum of six months and possibly as long as 18 months. When the adoption is finalized at least one parent must be present at court. Proxy adoptions are not permitted.

Age Requirements: In special adoptions, prospective adoptive parents must be over 25 years of age. However, if one parent is over 25, the other parent can be younger than 25 so long as he or she is at least 20 years old. In regular adoptions, prospective adoptive parents must be at least 20 years of age.

Marriage Requirements: In special adoptions, prospective adoptive parents must be a married couple. In regular adoptions, there may be circumstances in which single people can adopt.

Income Requirements: While there are no specific income requirements required by Japanese law, the prospective adoptive parents likely will have to provide documentation on their income and finances.

Other Requirements: There are no laws regulating or addressing same-sex couples adopting in Japan, but there have been no known cases of this happening. However, it may be permitted if the prospective adoptive parents' state recognizes the marriage as legal.

Who Can Be Adopted? Japan has specific requirements that a child must meet in order to be eligible for adoption. You cannot adopt a child in Japan unless he or she meets the requirements outlined below. In addition to these requirements, a child must meet the definition of an orphan under U.S. law for you to bring him or her back to the United States.

Age Requirements: For a child to be adopted under the special adoption law, the child must be under the age of 6 at the time the petition to adopt is filed. However, the adoption can still proceed if the child is under the age of 8 and the prospective adoptive parents have had custody of the child and continually cared for the child since before the child was 6 years of age. Abandonment/ Japanese law does not specify that the child must be an "orphan" (i.e., as defined in U.S. immigration law) in order for the adoption to proceed.

A special adoption can be granted when:

- It is extremely difficult for the biological parents to take care of the child;

- It is considered inappropriate for the biological parents to raise the child; and/or
- It is in the interests of the child.

Adoption Authority: Japan's principal adoption authorities are the Family Courts and the Child Guidance Centers (CGC), both of which are administered at the prefectural level.

The Process: The first step in adopting a child from Japan is usually to select a licensed agency in the United States that can help with your adoption, including those requirements related to the child's immigration to the United States. Adoption service providers in the United States must be licensed by the U.S. state in which they operate.

To bring an adopted child to the U.S. or to obtain custody of a child for the purpose of adoption in the U.S., you must apply to be found eligible to adopt (Form I-600A) by the U.S. Government, Department of Homeland Security, U.S. Citizenship and Immigration Services (USCIS). If you are eligible to adopt, and a child is available for intercountry adoption, the Japanese adoption service provider or the Child Guidance Center that has custody of the child arranges for child/prospective adoptive parent matches. In some cases the biological parent is asked to provide input concerning who will adopt the child.

Final Adoption (Special Adoption): For those who are finalizing the adoption in Japan, the Family Court reviews the adoption application. Please note that you may never actually appear in court in front of a judge; the paperwork may be done at the clerk's office. In reviewing the application, the Court examines the law governing intercountry adoptions in the prospective adoptive parents' U.S. state of legal domicile.

The Court informs the prospective adoptive parents of their court hearing date. This first hearing date generally occurs at the end of the trial six-month period, during which time a court representative conducts an interview with the prospective adoptive parents and conducts at least one home visit.

Approximately two to three weeks after the final hearing, the judge will decide whether or not to approve the adoption. If the judge approves the petition, the Court issues a certificate allowing "Permission to adopt" (yoshi no kyoka). If the biological parents or any interested parties do not object within two weeks of the parents' registering the adoption at the ward office or two weeks after the date provided on the final decree, it is considered final.

Legal Custody for Purpose of Adoption in the United States: For those who are obtaining legal custody of a child to complete the adoption in their U.S. state of residence, the Japanese court is not involved and the Japanese adoption agency is responsible for transferring custody. In such circumstances, the biological parent signs a form in English and her native language stating that she is the sole remaining parent of the child, that she is incapable of providing care for the child, and that she consents irrevocably to the adoption of the child by the prospective adoptive parents as well as the emigration of the child to the United States.

Role of Adoption Agencies: When finalizing the adoption in Japan, the adoption agency can match the prospective adoptive parents with a child, provide all of the necessary forms and instructions on how to complete the adoption process in Japan, and help collect the documents necessary for the U.S. immigrant visa, including the birth certificate and adoption decree. When obtaining legal custody of a child for a full and final adoption in the U.S., the adoption agency can match the prospective adoptive parents with a child and assist with the forms and documents necessary to secure a U.S. immigrant visa.

Adoption Application: When finalizing an adoption in Japan, the prospective adoptive parents submit their adoption application to the Family Court with jurisdiction over the child's residence. When obtaining custody of a child for a full and final adoption in the United States, the application to adopt is submitted to the proper authorities in the U.S. state of residence after the child enters the United States on an immigrant visa. Please note that in this case, the adopted child will acquire U.S. citizenship only after a full and final adoption in the United States.

Time Frame: Intercountry adoptions through the Family Court require at least six months and sometimes longer, possibly up to 18 months. The Japanese court system will take into account the laws of your state of residence and will try to comply with those laws. In practice, this may mean that finalization of the adoption takes several months longer than it otherwise would. The Family Court does not mandate a time limit on when an adoption must be completed. Prospective adoptive parents who are gaining custody to complete a full and final adoption in the United States report that the process takes between nine and eighteen months to take custody of the child, plus additional time in the United States to finalize the adoption in their state of residence.

Adoption Fees: For those who are resident in Japan and adopting a child through the Japanese court system, the costs vary widely; however, the average total cost is approximately US$20,000. This includes fees for the Family Court, adoption agency, immigration processing, and document translations and authentications. It should be noted that Japanese adoption service provider fees can range from US$5,000 to US$50,000 or higher, so the overall cost of adoption depends on the agency the prospective adoptive parents select.

Japanese law prohibits adoption service providers operating in Japan from profiting from adoptions, and the provider is required to give you an itemized invoice. That list may include fees to cover the birth of the child, as such costs are not covered by Japanese health insurance. Prospective adoptive parents may incur additional fees when adopting a child with medical conditions. Adoption service providers in Japan are prohibited from receiving donations before the completion of the adoption process, and a donation may not be a condition for providing services. Providers that violate these regulations should be reported to the prefectural government and may be suspended or closed by that government.

Documents Required:

- When completing a full and final adoption under Japanese law, the Japanese adoption agency should provide you with a complete list of required documents. These may include: Birth certificate and/or family register of all parties
- Passport, Japanese visas and Alien Registration cards for all parties
- Copy of U.S. military ID (where applicable)
- Marriage, divorce, and death certificates (where applicable)
- Copy of any property ownership deeds and/or bank statements
- Certificate of foster parent registration (where applicable)
- Certificate of good conduct/no criminal record for each adoptive parent (issued by their home city or state police department)
- Certificate of legal address, employment, and income
- Biographic history of all parties
- Statement of consent to adopt by the child's biological parent(s) or guardian
- Statement of prospective parent(s)' intent to adopt the identified child
- Home Study (approved by an authorized and licensed adoption agency)
- Two character references

When taking custody of a child for a full and final adoption in the United States, again the adoption service provider will assist you with documentation.

For example, you will need a family registry (koseki) for the child, a passport for the child, signed release statements from the biological mother, and descriptions of the situation of the biological mother. After you finalize the adoption (or gain legal custody) in Japan, the U.S Government, Department of Homeland Security, U.S. Citizenship and Immigration Services (USCIS) MUST determine whether the child is eligible under U.S. law to be adopted (Form I-600).

Because Japan does not have a USCIS office, the U.S. Embassy in Tokyo and the U.S. Consulate General in Naha, Okinawa are authorized to accept the Form I-600 when the parent(s) already have an approved and valid I-600A.

Bringing Your Child Home: Once your adoption is complete (or you have obtained legal custody of the child), there are a few more steps to take before you can head home. Specifically, you need to apply for several documents for your child before he or she can travel to the United States, such as a birth certificate, a passport or travel document for your child from the country in which he or she was born, and a U.S. Immigration Visa. For detailed and updated information on how to obtain these documents, review the *Intercountry Adoption* section on this publication and visit the USCIS Intercountry Adoption website at http://adoption.state.gov.

Child Citizenship Act: For adoptions finalized abroad, the Child Citizenship Act of 2000 allows your new child to acquire American citizenship automatically when he or she enters the United States as lawful permanent residents. For adoptions finalized in the United States, the Child Citizenship Act of 2000 allows your new child to acquire American citizenship automatically when the court in the United States issues the final adoption decree. To learn more, review the *Intercountry Adoption* section on this publication and visit the USCIS Intercountry Adoption website at http://adoption.state.gov.

After Adoption: Once a special adoption is completed in Japan or the child is adopted in the United States, the adoptive parents need to work with the Japanese adoption service provider to have the child's name removed from the birth mother's family registry (koseki).

This is important to the birth mother because she may have chosen intercountry adoption so that the child would be removed from her family registry. Japanese children who are adopted by foreign parents and acquire a second nationality retain Japanese citizenship because they are not viewed as having acquired a second nationality by their own choice.

According to Japanese law they should select their citizenship before reaching the age of 22. For more information, click here.

U.S. Embassy in Japan
Box 114
1-10-5 Akasaka Minato-ku
Tokyo 107-8420, Japan
Tel: (81)(3) 3224-5000
Fax: (81)(3) 3224-5929
http://tokyo.usembassy.gov

Embassy of Japan
2520 Massachusetts Ave., NW
Washington, D.C. 20008-2869
Tel: (202) 939-6700

Office of Children's Issues
U.S. Department of State
2201 C Street, NW
SA-29
Washington, DC 20520
Tel: 1-888-407-4747
E-mail: AskCI@state.gov
http://adoption.state.gov

For questions about immigration procedures, call the National Customer Service Center (NCSC) 1-800-375-5283 (TTY 1-800-767-1833).

International Parental Child Abduction

April 2012

The information in this section has been edited from the latest report available as of February 2013 from the State Department Bureau of Consular Affairs, Office of Overseas Citizens Services. For more information, please read the *International Parental Child Abduction* section of this book and check for updated reports online at www.travel.state.gov/abduction.

General Information: Abductions to Japan represent one of the largest portfolios in the State Department, Bureau of Consular Affairs, Office of Children's Issues and are among the most difficult to resolve. Japan has not ratified the 1980 Hague Convention on the Civil Aspects of International Child Abduction (Convention) and does not consider international parental child abduction to be a crime. Japan signaled its intent to ratify the Convention during 2012.

Japanese law and custom favor one parent having sole custody, making it extremely difficult for foreign left-behind parents to obtain the return of or access to abducted children. Returns from Japan have occurred primarily through voluntary measures or agreements between the parents. Success for left-behind parents in the Japanese courts is rare and difficult to enforce.

Legal System: A general description of Japan's legal system is available at the Japanese Federation of Bar Associations website. According to the Japan Federation of Bar Associations (JFBA) website, joint custody is not customary under Japanese law. The JFBA website provides a description of how the Japanese Family Court system conducts closed proceedings.

Children typically reside with their mother after a divorce. U.S. citizens involved in international custody disputes in Japan report to the U.S. Embassy in Tokyo that Japanese mothers are more likely to win sole custody. They also state that closed Family Court proceedings impede due process because of the inability for both parties to access information about the proceedings. They additionally report that Japan lacks a mechanism to uniformly enforce court orders, whether issued by a Japanese or foreign court.

Today, there is a movement in Japan advocating that it is in the best interest of the child to maintain contact with both parents after a divorce.

For left-behind parents trying to locate a child in Japan, a child's Appendix to the Family Register includes the current address of everyone listed. A parent or a designated proxy may request an appendix of the child's Japanese Family Register (koseki no fuhyou kakunin) from the local municipal office where the child is domiciled if the parent's name was ever listed on the Family Register (koseki tohon).

The Ministry of Foreign Affairs in Japan informed Embassy Tokyo, however, that a Family Register will not be released if a claim of domestic violence was made by the taking parent to police or the municipal office. Administrative steps to acquire an appendix may be numerous. Left-behind parents should consider retaining an attorney in the prefecture where the taking parent resides or resided and possibly in the prefecture where the children's Japanese grandparents reside.

Retaining an Attorney: In order to bring a custody issue before the Family Court, a left-behind parent may want to consult with a Japanese attorney, especially if the parent is not fluent in written and spoken Japanese and is unfamiliar with the Japanese legal system. The U.S. Embassy in Tokyo maintains a list of attorneys, including those who specialize in family law.

This list is provided as a courtesy service only and does not constitute an endorsement of any individual attorney. The State Department assumes no responsibility or liability for the professional ability or reputation of, or the quality of services provided by, any persons or firms. Professional credentials and areas of expertise are provided directly by the lawyers and should be vetted prior to retaining the attorney. Japan offers free or reduced fee legal aid services for divorce and custody matters to persons in legal visa/immigration status in Japan whose income is below specified levels. Interested parties should contact Houterasu (The Japan Legal Support Center) which is a nationwide legal support center which helps callers locate professional support in civil and criminal matters. Call Center: 0570–078374.

Citizenship & Passport Matters: According to Article 3 of the Nationality Act, a child acquires Japanese citizenship if either parent is a Japanese national at the time of birth. A child of an unmarried Japanese father or mother and non-Japanese father or mother may acquire Japanese citizenship if the child's legal representative notifies the Ministry of Justice and the Japanese parent recognizes the child. Under Article 14 of the Nationality Act, Japan permits dual nationality for children up to the age of 22; however, after the age of 22, the individual must choose one and renounce the other.

Japanese law requires the consent of both parents before issuing a child a passport; however, the consent of the non-applying parent is presumed when only one parent applies. The consular officer in a Japanese Embassy or consulate should ask the applying parent to affirm that the non-applying parent consents to Japanese passport issuance.

If a parent objects to the issuance of a Japanese passport to a minor, he/she should notify a passport office in Japan, or a Japanese Embassy or consulate in writing and include documentation that shows that the objecting parent has legal custody of the child. Japanese Ministry of Foreign Affairs policy states that Japanese authorities should contact the objecting parent and request a letter of consent from the objecting parent prior to issuing the child a passport. Instructions are on the Japanese

Ministry of Foreign Affairs website. The State Department cannot confirm the reliability of Japan's reported procedures for preventing the unlawful removal of a child to Japan given reports of inconsistent application of MOFA's policy.

Japan does not allow a child to be included on a parent's passport.

Exit Permits: Upon departure from Japan, immigration officers will examine passports and provide an exit stamp. A traveler may be denied departure if he/she overstayed or has an outstanding warrant issued by Japanese police or an Interpol notice.

There is no "exit hold" by which a non-traveling parent can request that Japanese Immigration prevent a child (and accompanying adult) from departing Japan. If the left-behind parent contacts Japanese police, however, it is possible that the police may contact Japanese immigration, which would then handle the matter on a case-by-case basis. Similarly, there is no "entry hold" by which a parent can request that Japanese Immigration prevent a child from entering Japan.

The consent of the non-traveling parent is not required for a child to depart Japan. However, if required by the destination country, airlines in Japan may require a letter of consent from the non-traveling parent, or proof that the traveling adult has legal custody or guardianship.

Mediation: Family Court mediation is required in many custody disputes; however, the U.S. State Department observes that few outcomes are favorable to left-behind parents. Mediated agreements are difficult to enforce. For more information, please contact an attorney in Japan.

Hague Abduction Convention: Japan is not a party to the Hague Abduction Convention. The Government of Japan announced on May 20, 2011, that it will ratify the Hague Abduction Convention, and Ministry of Foreign Affairs (MOFA) officials told officers in the U.S. Embassy Tokyo that the Convention and the domestic implementing legislation will be concurrently presented in the 2012 Diet session. MOFA and the Ministry of Justice (MOJ) drafted the domestic law changes.

During MOFA's public comment period on the draft implementing legislation, the U.S. and a multilateral group of Convention parties commented that implementing legislation should closely reflect the language provided in the Convention. Once passed, the State Department will determine if the legislation is consistent with the Convention.

Civil Remedies: U.S. parents' and local attorneys report that Japanese courts generally do not recognize U.S. court orders. A parent holding a custody decree issued in U.S. courts should retain local Japanese counsel for advice to determine whether to apply to the Japanese district courts (not family courts) for recognition of the U.S. court order. Even if the U.S. court order is recognized by the district court and a judge agrees that the child should be returned to the United States, attorneys have informed the embassy that there are no clear, reliable enforcement mechanisms to ensure compliance with the order.

Japan's Ministry of Foreign Affairs informed U.S. government representatives about some of the many obstacles involved in gaining recognition of a U.S. custody order in Japanese courts. In order to recognize a foreign court order, the Japanese court must find that it is a final and binding judgment under conditions in which both sides had procedural protections of their legal rights.

The Japanese family law system draws an important distinction between custody orders that merely determine or transfer custody (keisei hanketsu or a 'formative judgment') and a decision that explicitly orders one party to surrender a child to another (kyufu hanketsu or 'judgment ordering performance').

It is only this second type of order (kyufu hanketsu) that the Japanese courts will recognize as a full and binding judgment. At this time, the State Department knows of very few instances in which a U.S. custody order significantly influenced the outcome of custody proceedings in Japan.

The Japanese Family Court hears custody disputes and normally resolves the issue based on the best interests of the child. However, there are no statutory factors to guide courts charged with determining the child's best interests. Also, there are limited mechanisms to enforce Family Court orders. While a parent can request the court to recommend fining the non-compliant parent, there is no evidence that these fines are effective. Compliance is essentially voluntary and dependent upon the agreement of both parents. Embassy experience is that Japanese police are reluctant to get involved in custody disputes or to enforce custody decrees issued by Japanese courts.

Family Court orders can be appealed to a high court. High court orders may be appealed to the Supreme Court in limited circumstances.

Criminal Remedies: International parental child abduction is not a crime in Japan. Because the extradition treaty between Japan and the United States requires "dual criminality;" that the crime for which a Japanese national is charged in the United States is also a crime in Japan, a Japanese taking-parent has never been extradited from Japan to face criminal charges for international parental child abduction in the United States.

Interpol notices that inform immigration authorities about an international parental child abduction case from the United States may be useful to help locate a child when a Japanese taking-parent transits a third country with whom the U.S. has an extradition treaty relationship. Please read Japan's Ministry of Foreign Affairs notice to Japanese parents considering international travel for more information.

Although international parental child abduction is not a crime in Japan, using force to take children is, and both Japanese citizens and foreigners have been arrested for using force when allegedly kidnapping their children. Also, foreigners have been arrested for attempting to flee Japan with their children. The embassy is not aware of any Japanese parent being charged with child abduction for bringing his/her child to Japan from another country, notwithstanding charges of child abduction filed in the other country.

The embassy's experience has shown that the police will not assist with the search for a child abducted by a parent (domestically or internationally) because of the widely-accepted cultural view that custody should be handled within families and there is no cause for concern if the child is with one of the parents. Japan's strict privacy laws prevent police and other officials from releasing information about the location of an abducted child.

Visitation/Access: As of April 1, 2012, changes to Japanese Civil Code Article 766 came into force. Previously, Civil Code Article 766 did not address visitation and only required a divorcing couple with a child to specify the custody arrangement in the divorce documentation. Now, Civil Code Article 766 requires a divorcing couple with a child to specify, in addition to custody, visitation arrangements between the child and the father and mother as well as the arrangements for childcare expenses. It remains unknown how such agreements regarding visitation will work in practice.

U.S. Embassy in Tokyo, Japan: http://japan.usembassy.gov/

Embassy of Japan in the United States: http://www.us.emb-japan.go.jp/english/html/index.html

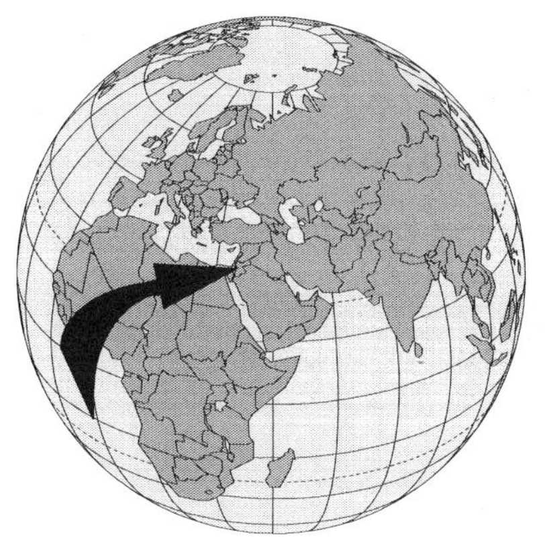

JORDAN

Compiled from publications that were available as of February 2013 from the U.S. Department of State, the U.S. Department of Commerce, and the Central Intelligence Agency (CIA). See the introduction to this set for explanatory notes.

Official Name:
Hashemite Kingdom of Jordan

PROFILE

Geography

Area: total: 89,342 sq km; country comparison to the world: 112; land: 88,802 sq km; water: 540 sq km

Major cities: Amman (capital) 1.088 million (2009)

Climate: mostly arid desert; rainy season in west (November to April)

Terrain: mostly desert plateau in east, highland area in west; Great Rift Valley separates East and West Banks of the Jordan River

People

Nationality: noun: Jordanian(s); adjective: Jordanian

Population: 6,508,887 (July 2012 est.)

Population growth rate: -0.965% (2012 est.)

Ethnic groups: Arab 98%, Circassian 1%, Armenian 1%

Religions: Sunni Muslim 92% (official), Christian 6% (majority Greek Orthodox, but some Greek and Roman Catholics, Syrian Orthodox, Coptic Orthodox, Armenian Orthodox, and Protestant denominations), other 2% (several small Shia Muslim and Druze populations) (2001 est.)

Languages: Arabic (official), English (widely understood among upper and middle classes)

Literacy: definition: age 15 and over can read and write; total population: 92.6%; male: 95.8%; female: 89.2% (2010 est.)

Health: life expectancy at birth: total population: 80.18 years; male: 78.82 years; female: 81.61 years (2012 est.); Infant mortality rate: total: 15.83 deaths/1,000 live births; male: 16.42 deaths/1,000 live births; female: 15.2 deaths/1,000 live births (2012 est.)

Unemployment rate: 12.3% (2012 est.)

Work force: 1.824 million (2012 est.)

Government

Type: constitutional monarchy

Independence: 25 May 1946

Constitution: 1 January 1952; amended many times

Political subdivisions: 12 governorates (muhafazat, singular—muhafazah); Ajlun, Al 'Aqabah, Al Balqa', Al Karak, Al Mafraq, 'Amman, At Tafilah, Az Zarqa', Irbid, Jarash, Ma'an, Madaba

Suffrage: 18 years of age; universal

Economy

GDP (purchasing power parity): $38.67 billion (2012 est.); $37.37 billion (2011 est.); $36.47 billion (2010 est.); $35.64 billion (2009 est.)

GDP real growth rate: 3% (2012 est.); 2.5% (2011 est.); 2.3% (2010 est.); 5.5% (2009 est.)

GDP per capita (PPP): $6,000 (2012 est.); $6,000 (2011 est.); $6,000 (2010 est.); $6,000 (2009 est.)

Natural resources: phosphates, potash, shale oil

Agriculture products: citrus, tomatoes, cucumbers, olives, strawberries, stone fruits; sheep, poultry, dairy

Industries: clothing, fertilizers, potash, phosphate mining, pharmaceuticals, petroleum refining, cement, inorganic chemicals, light manufacturing, tourism

Exports: $8.218 billion (2012 est.); $7.986 billion (2011 est.); $7.028 billion (2010 est.)

Exports—commodities: clothing, fertilizers, potash, phosphates, vegetables, pharmaceuticals

Exports—partners: Iraq 15.3%, US 14.7%, India 12.5%, Saudi Arabia 9.6%, Lebanon 4.4% (2011)

Imports: $17.73 billion (2012 est.); $16.21 billion (2011 est.); $13.68 billion (2010 est.)

Imports—commodities: crude oil, machinery, transport equipment, iron, cereals

Imports—partners: Saudi Arabia 22.4%, China 10.6%, US 6.2%, Italy 5.1%, Germany 4.2%, Egypt 4.1% (2011)

Debt—external: $8.345 billion (31 December 2012 est.); $7.644 billion (31 December 2011 est.); $7.645 billion (31 December 2010 est.)

Exchange rates: Jordanian dinars (JOD) per US dollar; 0.709 (2012 est.); 0.71 (2011 est.); 0.71 (2010 est.); 0.709 (2009); 0.709 (2008); 0.709 (2007)

PEOPLE

Jordanians are Arabs, except for a few small communities of Circassians, Armenians, and Chechens who have adapted to Arab culture. The official language is Arabic, but English is used widely in commerce and government. About 70% of Jordan's population is urban; less than 6% of the rural population is nomadic or semi-nomadic. Approximately 1.7 million registered Palestinian refugees and other displaced persons, including Iraqis, reside in Jordan.

National/Racial/Ethnic Minorities

There were three groups of Palestinians residing in the country, many of whom faced some discrimination. Palestinians were underrepresented in parliament and senior positions in the government and the military, as well as in admissions to public universities. They had limited access to university scholarships.

Religion

Approximately 95 percent of the population is Sunni Muslim. Estimates of the number of Christian citizens vary from 1.5 to 3 percent of the population. Shia Muslims, Baha'i, and Druze constitute an estimated 2 percent of the population.

Officially recognized Christian denominations include the Greek Orthodox, Roman Catholic, Greek Catholic (Melkite), Armenian Orthodox, Maronite Catholic, Assyrian, Coptic, Anglican, Lutheran, Seventh-day Adventist, and Presbyterian churches. Christian churches not officially recognized but registered as "societies" include the Free Evangelical Church, Nazarene Church, Assemblies of God, Christian and Missionary Alliance, and The Church of Jesus Christ of Latter-day Saints (Mormons). Unrecognized Christian denominations not registered as "societies" include United Pentecostal and Jehovah's Witnesses. There are Chaldean and Syriac Christians among the Iraqi refugee population, referred to as "guests" by the government. The Baptist Church is registered as a "denomination," but does not enjoy the full privileges of other registered denominations in the country. The government does not recognize the Baha'i Faith as a religion.

HISTORY

The land that became Jordan is part of the richly historical Fertile Crescent region. Around 2000 B.C., Semitic Amorites settled around the Jordan River in the area called Canaan. Subsequent invaders and settlers included Hittites, Egyptians, Israelites, Assyrians, Babylonians, Persians, Greeks, Romans, Arab Muslims, Christian Crusaders, Mameluks, Ottoman Turks, and, finally, the British. At the end of World War I, the League of Nations awarded the territory now comprising Israel, Jordan, the West Bank, Gaza, and Jerusalem to the United Kingdom as the mandate for Palestine and Transjordan.

In 1922, the British divided the mandate by establishing the semiautonomous Emirate of Transjordan, ruled by the Hashemite Prince Abdullah, while continuing the administration of Palestine under a British High Commissioner. The mandate over Transjordan ended on May 22, 1946; on May 25, the country became the independent Hashemite Kingdom of Transjordan. It ended its special defense treaty relationship with the United Kingdom in 1957.

Transjordan was one of the Arab states which moved to assist Palestinian nationalists opposed to the creation of Israel in May 1948, and took part in the warfare between the Arab states and the newly founded State of Israel. The armistice agreements of April 3, 1949 left Jordan in control of the West Bank and provided that the armistice demarcation lines were without prejudice to future territorial settlements or boundary lines. In 1950, the country was renamed the Hashemite Kingdom of Jordan to include those portions of Palestine annexed by King Abdullah I. While recognizing Jordanian administration over the West Bank, the United States maintained the position that ultimate sovereignty was subject to future agreement.

Jordan signed a mutual defense pact in May 1967 with Egypt, and it participated in the June 1967 war between Israel and the Arab states of Syria, Egypt, and Iraq. During the war, Israel gained control of the West Bank and all of Jerusalem. In 1988, Jordan renounced all claims to the West Bank but retained an administrative role pending a final settlement, and its 1994 treaty with Israel allowed for a continuing Jordanian role in Muslim holy places in Jerusalem.

The U.S. Government considers the West Bank to be territory occupied by Israel and believes that its final status should be determined through direct negotiations among the parties concerned on the basis of UN Security Council Resolutions 242 and 338. The 1967 war led to a dramatic increase in the number of Palestinians living in Jordan. Its Palestinian refugee population—700,000 in 1966—grew by another 300,000 from the West Bank.

The period following the 1967 war saw an upsurge in the power and importance of Palestinian resistance elements (fedayeen) in Jordan. The heavily armed fedayeen constituted a growing threat to the sovereignty and security of the Hashemite state, and open fighting erupted in September 1970.

No fighting occurred along the 1967 Jordan River cease-fire line during the October 1973 Arab-Israeli war, but Jordan sent a brigade to Syria to fight Israeli units on Syrian territory.

Jordan did not participate in the Gulf war of 1990–91. In 1991, Jordan agreed, along with Syria, Lebanon, and Palestinian representatives, to participate in direct peace negotiations with Israel sponsored by the U.S. and Russia. It negotiated an end to hostilities with Israel and signed a peace treaty in 1994. Jordan has since sought to remain at peace with all of its neighbors.

GOVERNMENT AND POLITICAL CONDITIONS

The Hashemite Kingdom of Jordan is a constitutional monarchy ruled by King Abdullah II bin Hussein. The constitution concentrates executive and legislative authority in the king. The multiparty parliament consists of the 60-member House of Notables (Majlis al-Ayan) appointed by the king and a 120-member elected lower house, the Chamber of Deputies (Majlis al-Nuwwab). Parliamentary elections, which international observers deemed credible, took place in November 2010.

Throughout 2011 citizens staged weekly demonstrations calling for various political and economic reforms. The demonstrations were mostly peaceful; however, there were incidents of violence by counterprotesters and security forces against protesters. The government did not investigate or prosecute individuals and security officials accused of inciting violence during the demonstrations.

Recent Elections

In November 2010 the country held parliamentary elections, which international observers considered "a clear improvement over the nation's 2007 polls." However, observers recommended future reforms such as establishing an independent electoral management body, preprinting ballots to mitigate concerns over voting procedures for the illiterate, strengthening representation for all citizens, and introducing regulations to allow for systematic appeals of the election results. Gerrymandering districts to minimize the impact of votes by citizens of Palestinian origin in favor of tribal interests was a significant problem. The law allows voters to choose one candidate in their district, which in the largely tribal society meant citizens tended to cast their vote for members of their own tribe.

On September 30, 2011, the government amended the constitution to establish an independent electoral commission.

Political Parties: The government licensed political parties and other associations but prohibited membership in unlicensed political parties. The High Court of Justice may dissolve a party if it concludes that the party violated the constitution or the law. Political parties, NGOs, and independent candidates found the registration process both onerous and costly and criticized the GID's annual screening process of founding party members.

Participation of Women and Minorities: Many human rights activists cited cultural bias against women as an impediment to women participating in political life on the same scale as men. On September 14, the government increased the quota for women in municipal council seats to 25 percent. The law provides a 10 percent quota for women in the lower house of parliament. In the November 2010 elections, voters elected 13 women to parliament, exceeding the quota by one. Unlike in the previous year, there were no female governors; however, two women served in the appointed 27-member cabinet.

Citizens of Palestinian origin were underrepresented at all levels of government and the military. The law reserves nine seats in the lower house of parliament for Christians and three seats for the Circassian and Chechen ethnic minorities combined, constituting an overrepresentation for these minorities. No seats were reserved for the relatively small Druze population, but they were permitted to hold office under their government classification as Muslims. The law also stipulates that Muslims must hold all seats not reserved for specified minority religions. Christians served as cabinet ministers and ambassadors.

The government traditionally reserves some positions in the upper levels of the military for Christians (4 percent); however, Muslims held all senior command positions.

Principal Government Officials

Last Updated: 1/31/2013

King: **ABDALLAH II**
Prime Min.: **Abdullah NSOUR**
Dep. Prime Min.: **Awad KHULAYFAT**
Min. of Agriculture: **Ahmad al-KHATTAB**
Min. of Awqaf & Islamic Affairs: **Abdul Salam ABBADI**
Min. of Defense: **Abdullah NSOUR**
Min. of Education: **Wajih OWAIS**
Min. of Energy & Mineral Resources: **Alaa BATAYNEH**
Min. of the Environment: **Nayef Hmeidi al-FAYEZ**
Min. of Finance: **Sulayman al-HAFIZ**
Min. of Foreign Affairs: **Nasser JUDEH**
Min. of Health: **Abdul Latif WREIKAT**
Min. of Higher Education & Scientific Research: **Wajih OWAIS**
Min. of Information & Communication Technology: **Hatem Hafez Al HALAWANI**
Min. of Industry & Trade: **Hatem Hafez Al HALAWANI**
Min. of Interior: **Awad KHULAYFAT**
Min. of Justice: **Ghaleb ZUBI**
Min. of Labor: **Nidal Mardi Al QATAMIN**
Min. of Municipal Affairs: **Mahir ABUL SAMIN**
Min. of Parliamentary Affairs: **Bassam Salamah HADDADIN**
Min. of Planning & Intl. Cooperation: **Jafar HASSAN**
Min. of Political Development: **Bassam Salamah HADDADIN**
Min. of Public Sector Development: **Khleif al-KHAWALDEH**
Min. of Public Works & Housing: **Yahya al-KISBI**
Min. of Social Development: **Wajeeh AZAYZEH**
Min. of Tourism & Antiquities: **Nayef Hmeidi al-FAYEZ**

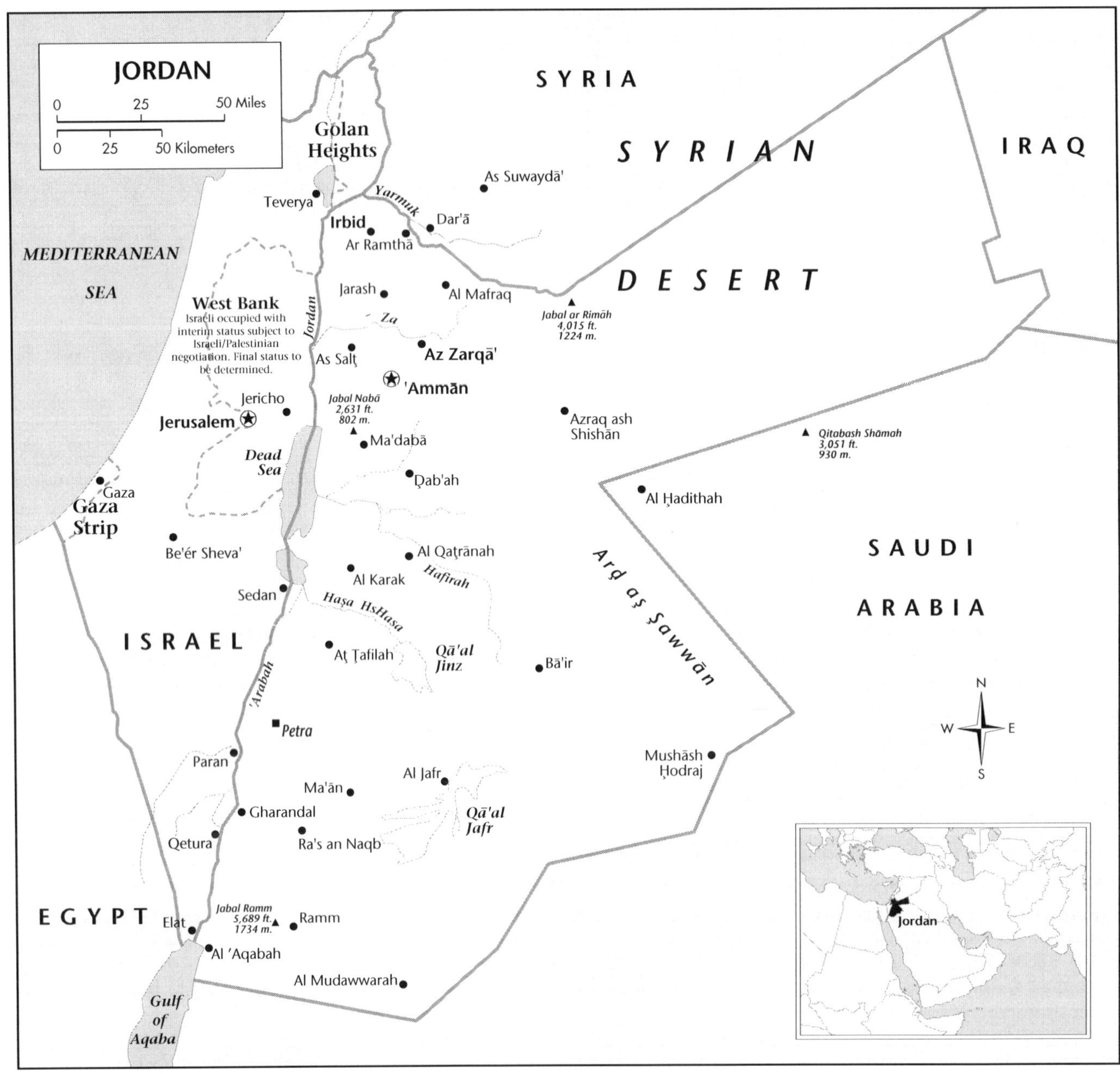

Min. of Transportation: **Alaa BATAYNEH**

Min. of Water & Irrigation: **Mahir ABUL SAMIN**

Min. of State for Media Affairs & Communication & Govt. Spokesman: **Sami MA'AYTAH**

Min. of State for Prime-Ministerial Affairs & Legislation: **Nofan Al AJARMEH**

Governor, Central Bank of Jordan: **Mohammad Said SHAHEEN**

Ambassador to the US: **Alia Hatough-BOURAN**

Permanent Representative to the UN, New York: **ZEID Ra'ad Zeid al-Hussein**

ECONOMY

Jordan's economy is among the smallest in the Middle East, with insufficient supplies of water, oil, and other natural resources, underlying the government's heavy reliance on foreign assistance. Other economic challenges for the government include chronic high rates of poverty, unemployment, inflation, and a large budget deficit. Since assuming the throne in 1999, King Abdallah has implemented significant economic reforms, such as opening the trade regime, privatizing state-owned companies, and eliminating some fuel subsidies, which in the last decade spurred economic growth by attracting foreign investment and creating some jobs.

The global economic slowdown and regional turmoil, however, have depressed Jordan's GDP growth, impacting export-oriented sectors, construction, and tourism. In 2011 the government approved two economic relief packages and a budgetary supplement, largely to improve the living conditions for the middle and poor classes. Jordan's finances have also been strained by a series of natural gas pipeline attacks in Egypt, causing Jordan to substitute more expensive heavy fuel oils to generate electricity. An influx of foreign aid, especially from Gulf countries, has helped to somewhat offset these extrabudgetary expenditures, but the budget deficit is likely to remain high, at more than 11% of GDP in 2012 excluding grants. Amman likely will continue to depend heavily on foreign assistance to finance the deficit in 2012. Jordan's financial sector has been relatively isolated from the international financial crisis because of its limited exposure to overseas capital markets. Jordan is currently exploring nuclear power generation to forestall energy shortfalls.

Labor Conditions

The law forbids employment of children younger than 16 years of age, except as apprentices in nonhazardous positions. The law provides that employers who hire a child younger than 16 must pay a fine of as much as 500 dinars ($710), which is doubled for repeat offenses. The law bans those between the ages of 16 and 18 from working in potentially hazardous jobs, limits working hours for such children to six hours per day, mandates one-hour breaks for every four consecutive working hours, and prohibits these children from working after 8 p.m. on national or religious holidays and on weekends.

In practice children worked in mechanical repair, agriculture, construction, and the hotel and restaurant industry; in the informal sector as street vendors, carpenters, blacksmiths, domestic workers, and painters; and in small family businesses. Child labor appeared concentrated in larger cities, such as Amman, Zarqa, and Irbid. A 2008 Department of Statistics study estimated that more than 32,000 children between the ages of five and 17 were working in the country. Activists estimated the number to be significantly higher, as many businesses and families tended to hide the practice. The government lacked recent statistics on the problem.

During 2011 the national minimum wage was 150 dinars ($212) per month, and the poverty level was set at 323 dinars ($455) per month for a family of six. Ministry of Labor inspectors enforced the minimum wage but were unable to ensure full compliance due to limited resources. The garment sector and workers in domestic jobs did not receive the 2008 minimum wage increase; these workers had a minimum wage of 110 dinars ($155) per month. This exemption was granted in part because of an understanding that employers often provide room and board for workers in these sectors. However, some garment factories continued to deduct room and board from workers' already below-minimum-wage salaries. Many domestic workers reported to local NGOs and their embassies that they received insufficient food, no private accommodations, and long delays in payment.

The law requires overtime pay for hours worked in excess of the 48-hour standard workweek. The law permits compulsory overtime under certain circumstances such as conducting an annual inventory, closing accounts, preparing to sell goods at discounted prices, avoiding loss to goods that would otherwise be exposed to damage, and receiving special deliveries. In such cases actual working hours may not exceed 10 hours per day, the employee must be paid overtime, and the period may not last more than 30 days. There is no cap on the amount of consensual overtime. Thus the Ministry of Labor permitted employees in some industries, such as the garment sector, to work excessive workweeks, reportedly as much as 80-100 hours per week. Employees can lodge a complaint directly with the Ministry of Labor or through organizations such as their union or the NCHR. Employees are entitled to one day off per week. Provisions for domestic workers were similar.

The law specifies a number of health and safety requirements that the Ministry of Labor is authorized to enforce; however, workers do not have a statutory right to remove themselves from hazardous conditions without risking the loss of their jobs and may be fired if they attempt to do so. Foreign workers, who make up the vast majority of workers in the QIZ garment factories and Export Processing Zones, were more susceptible to dangerous or unfair conditions, including mandatory overtime, delayed payment of wages, deductions for room and board, and unacceptable dormitory conditions.

Some workers in the agricultural sector, the vast majority of whom were Egyptian, were subject to exploitative conditions. According to a domestic NGO, it was common for agricultural workers to be paid less than the minimum wage, work excessive hours without adequate compensation, and live in substandard housing. Some employers in the agricultural sector also reportedly confiscated passports.

During 2011 hundreds of domestic workers from the Philippines, Indonesia, and Sri Lanka were sheltered at their respective embassies in Amman. Most had reportedly fled some form of forced labor or abuse, including unpaid wages and, to a lesser extent, sexual or physical abuse. By law employers are responsible for renewing residency permits but often failed to do this for domestic employees. As a result most of the embassy-sheltered domestic workers were considered illegal residents, and many were stranded because they were unable to pay the daily overstay fees of 1.5 dinars ($2) to depart the country. The Philippines, Indonesia, and for part of the year Sri Lanka prohibited the emigration of migrant workers for domestic work because of these problems. However, the prohibition did not reduce the flow of migrant workers. Some human rights organizations argued the bans heightened the vulnerability of foreign domestic workers by shutting scrupulous recruitment agencies out of the market.

U.S.-JORDANIAN RELATIONS

The United States deeply values its long history of cooperation and friendship with Jordan, with which it established diplomatic relations in 1949. The United States appreciates the special leadership role that Jordan plays in advancing peace and moderation in the region. The United States and Jordan share the mutual goals of a comprehensive, just, and lasting peace in the Middle East and an end to violent extremism that threatens the security of Jordan, the region, and the entire globe.

The peace process and Jordan's opposition to terrorism parallel and indirectly assist wider U.S. interests. U.S. policy seeks to reinforce Jordan's commitment to peace, stability, and moderation. Through economic and military assistance and through close political cooperation, the United States has helped Jordan maintain its stability and prosperity. The United States encourages Jordanian efforts to implement reforms that will secure a better future for the Jordanian people.

From 1949 to 1967, Jordan administered the West Bank. Since the 1967 war between Israel and several Arab states, when Israel took control of this territory, the United States has considered the West Bank to be territory occupied by Israel. The United States believes that the final status of the West Bank can be determined only through negotiations among the concerned parties based on UN Security Council Resolutions 242 and 338.

U.S. Assistance to Jordan

The United States has worked with Jordan to improve the lives of Jordanian citizens. Assistance programs contribute to a strong bilateral relationship centered on a stable, reform-oriented Jordan. Development assistance has resulted in improved health indicators, road and water networks, hundreds of schools built, thousands of Jordanians in various fields educated and trained in the U.S., and grants and loans for U.S. agricultural commodities.

Current focus areas include education, access to water, resource management and conservation, energy, youth and poverty alleviation programs, maternal/child health, energy, governance, macroeconomic policy, workforce development, and competitiveness. A strong U.S. military assistance program is designed to meet Jordan's legitimate defense needs, including preservation of border integrity and regional stability through the provision of materiel and training.

In 2008, the U.S. and Jordan signed a non-binding memorandum of understanding (MOU) to provide assistance to Jordan over a 5-year period, subject to the appropriation and availability of funds for this purpose.

The MOU also reinforces the commitment to broaden cooperation and dialogue in a variety of areas. In 2011, a Millennium Challenge Corporation compact for Jordan entered into force that aims to increase income and reduce poverty in Zarqa Governorate. The compact seeks to increase water supplies available to households and businesses and improve the efficiency of water delivery, extend wastewater collection, and expand wastewater treatment.

Bilateral Economic Relations

Qualifying Industrial Zones established by the U.S. Congress allow products to enter the United States duty-free if manufactured in Israel, Jordan, Egypt, or the West Bank and Gaza. The U.S.-Jordan free trade agreement has expanded the trade relationship by reducing barriers for services, providing cutting-edge protection for intellectual property, ensuring regulatory transparency, and requiring effective labor and environmental enforcement.

The United States and Jordan have an "open skies" civil aviation agreement; a bilateral investment treaty; a science and technology cooperation agreement; and a memorandum of understanding on nuclear energy cooperation. Such agreements bolster efforts to help diversify Jordan's economy and promote growth.

Jordan's Membership in International Organizations

Jordan and the United States belong to a number of the same international organizations, including the United Nations, International Monetary Fund, World Bank, and World Trade Organization. Jordan also is a Partner for Cooperation with the Organization for Security and Cooperation in Europe.

Bilateral Representation

Jordan maintains an embassy in the United States at 3504 International Drive NW, Washington, DC 20008 (tel. 202-966-2664).

Principal U.S. Embassy Officials

Last Updated: 1/14/2013

AMMAN (E) Al-Umawyeen Street, Abdoun, Amman, Jordan 11118, +(962) 6 590-6000, Fax +962-6-592-0163 (Admin), Workweek: Sun-Thurs 0800-1630, Website: http://amman.usembassy.gov/

DCM OMS:	Angelica Mendez
AMB OMS:	Cecilia Wylie
Co-CLO:	Suzi Russell
DHS/CIS:	Suzanne Sinclair-Smith
DHS/TSA:	Nouri Larbi
DIR:	Vacant
FM:	Derrick Bullock
HRO:	Anthony Blenke
MGT:	Eric W. Stromayer
POSHO:	Derrick Bullock
SDO/DATT:	COL Joseph Rank
AMB:	Stuart Jones
CON:	Ian Hopper
DCM:	Madelyn Spirnak
PAO:	Vacant
GSO:	John Marten
RSO:	Bartle Gorman
AGR:	Mohammad Khraishy
AID:	Beth S. Paige
APHIS:	Mohammad Khraishy
CLO:	Paula Vernon
ECON:	Joyce Wong
EEO:	Lisa Kenna
EST:	Caron De Mars
FMO:	Don Simmons
IMO:	Frank Landymore
IPO:	Joshua Rush
ISO:	Sean Kelley

ISSO: Sean Kelley
LEGATT: Rajiv Maan
POL: Lisa Kenna
State ICASS: Joyce Wong

TRAVEL

Consular Information Sheet

August 24, 2012

Country Description: The Hashemite Kingdom of Jordan is a constitutional monarchy with a developing economy and a modern infrastructure. Western culture features prominently in the lives of many Jordanians. At the same time, traditional Islamic ideals and beliefs provide a conservative foundation for the country's customs, laws, and practices. Businesses and facilities catering to tourists are widely available, although quality may vary depending on price and location.

Smart Traveler Enrollment Program (STEP)/Embassy Locations: If you are going to live in or visit Jordan, please take the time to tell our Embassy about your trip. If you enroll, we can keep you up to date with important safety and security announcements. It will also help your friends and family get in touch with you in an emergency.

U.S. Embassy in Amman
Al-Umayyaween Street, Abdoun neighborhood, PO Box 354,
Amman 11118
Telephone: [962] (6) 590-6000
Emergency after-hours telephone: [962] (6) 590-6500
Facsimile: [962] (6) 592-4102
Email: Amman-ACS@state.gov

The U.S. Embassy is open Sunday through Thursday, and is closed all U.S. and Jordanian holidays as well as the last business day of every month.

Entry/Exit Requirements for U.S. Citizens: A passport with a validity of at least three months and a visa are required. Jordan issues visas to U.S. citizens for a fee at most international ports of entry and at most international land border crossings upon arrival. The visa currently costs 20 JD ($28 USD) for a single entry, 40 JD ($56 USD) for two entries, and 60 JD ($84 USD) for a multiple entry. Please note that visas are not issued upon arrival at the King Hussein/Allenby Bridge land border crossing. U.S. citizens must already have a valid visa to Jordan or have a special entry permit from the Jordanian Ministry of Interior to enter Jordan at this crossing. U.S. Citizens who depart Jordan by the King Hussein/Allenby Bridge may return to Jordan through the same bridge without a new visa as long as the current visa is still valid. An exit fee of 8 JD ($11) is assessed to all visitors departing through the Allenby Bridge. For more information regarding travel to the West Bank and Jerusalem, please contact the U.S. Consulate General in Jerusalem.

U.S. citizens are typically given visas that are valid for 30 days. Foreigners who wish to stay longer than the time limit given to them by Jordanian immigration upon entry into Jordan must register at a Jordanian police station before expiration of that time limit. Travelers who fail to register properly subject themselves to a fine of 1.5 JD (approximately $2.10 USD) per day of overstay. This fine is usually assessed at departure.

Some HIV/AIDS entry restrictions exist for visitors to and foreign residents of Jordan. Jordan does not permit entry or residency for foreign nationals with HIV/AIDS. Travelers known to have HIV are denied entry at ports of entry, including land border crossings. Travelers seeking to extend their stay beyond the initial timeframe are legally required to have an AIDS test performed at a government medical facility. Those who fail to submit to the test or who test positive for HIV are deported. For further information, please see the Embassy of Hashemite Kingdom of Jordan website before you travel.

Travelers should check the Country Specific Information and any existing Travel Warnings and Travel Alerts for all countries they plan to visit during their travel to the region. Border crossing requirements may change and borders may be closed during periods of heightened security. For further information travelers may contact the Embassy of the Hashemite Kingdom of Jordan at 3504 International Drive NW, Washington, DC 20008, or by telephone at (202) 966-. 2861 or (202) 966-2887Jordan also maintains Honorary Consulates in Detroit, MI, Chicago, IL, and San Francisco, CA.

Threats to Safety and Security: The threat of terrorism remains high in Jordan. Transnational and indigenous terrorist groups have demonstrated the capability to plan and implement attacks in Jordan. In August 2010, a roadside improvised explosive device (IED) detonated next to a vehicle carrying three USG contractors as it was traveling through an Amman suburb; the contractors did not suffer any serious injuries. In January 2010, an official Israeli motorcade was struck by an IED as it was traveling from Amman to the King Hussein/Allenby Bridge border crossing; passengers in the vehicles were unharmed and the vehicles sustained minor damage. Several rockets believed to have been launched from the Sinai Peninsula struck the port city of Aqaba in April and August 2010. In the latter attack, one rocket destroyed a taxi cab outside of a hotel, killing the driver.

Following the death of Usama bin Laden in May 2011, the Department issued a worldwide Travel Alert to all U.S. citizens traveling or residing overseas regarding the possibility of enhanced anti-American violence. Travelers to Jordan should be cognizant of the fact that Al-Qaida in Iraq affiliates have carried out terrorist activities against U.S. and Government of Jordan (GOJ) targets in Jordan.

Terrorists often do not distinguish between U.S. government personnel and private U.S. citizens. Terrorists may target areas frequented by Westerners, such as tourist sites, hotels, restaurants, bars, nightclubs, liquor stores, shopping malls, transportation hubs, places of worship, expatriate residential areas, and schools. In light of these security concerns, U.S. citizens should maintain a high level of vigilance, be aware of their surroundings, and take appropriate steps to increase their security awareness. It is especially important for travelers to be unpredictable in their movements by varying their times and routes and maintaining a low profile. Moreover, U.S. citizens should avoid contact with any suspicious or unfamiliar objects and immediately report the presence of such objects to local authorities. U.S. government personnel overseas have been advised to take the same precautions.

Demonstrations are common. Some, especially smaller ones, have turned violent leading security officials to intercede. Because demonstrations intended to be peaceful can turn confrontational and possibly escalate into violence, travelers should avoid all protests and large gatherings of people. Many demonstrations occur on Fridays near mosques following noon prayers. Consequently, you should exercise special sensitivity and caution when visiting or traveling near mosques and religious sites during holy days and Fridays. Demonstrations and other forms of unrest have occurred on public university campuses in Jordan. Some acts of violence on university campuses have involved the use of firearms. Anti-American demonstrations have also taken place in front of the U.S. Embassy. Travelers should avoid any demonstrations or large gatherings of people.

Tribal violence in Jordan remains a concern. Clashes between feuding clans or families periodically erupt without notice and sometimes involve an escalation in violence, including the use of firearms. In some cases, Jordanian security services are slow to respond or may opt to let the violence peter out before intervening. When necessary, authorities have closed major roads, including a key road near Amman's international airport, or parts of cities to contain the violence.

U.S. citizens should avoid the border area with Syria. Police and security officials have arrested weapons and drug smugglers, as well as foreign fighters attempting to enter Syria to fight in the country's ongoing civil war. Some riots have occurred at the Ramtha/Jaber border crossing, resulting in the burning of key municipal facilities. The Department of State also advises against travel into Iraq.

Stay up to date by:

- Bookmarking our Bureau of Consular Affairs website, which contains the current Travel Warnings and Travel Alerts as well as the Worldwide Caution.
- Follow us on Twitter and the Bureau of Consular Affairs page on Facebook as well.
- Download our free Smart Traveler App through iTunes and the Android market to have travel information at your fingertips.
- Calling 1-888-407-4747 toll-free within the U.S. and Canada, or a regular toll line, 1-202-501-4444, from other countries.
- Takes ome time before travel to consider your personal security.

Crime: Statistically, petty crime is the most common form that U.S. citizens and other Western nationals, experience in Jordan especially at tourist sites and in crowded areas. Pickpockets, purse snatchers and opportunistic thieves are known to target foreigners in the narrow and crowded streets of the older parts of Amman's city center. Travelers should be more guarded in these areas and in all tourist locations in Jordan to lessen the likelihood of becoming a victim of petty thefts. Jordanian police have warned the public to exercise vigilance when leaving banks or ATMs, as thieves have reportedly preyed upon persons soon after using these services.

Women from Western countries visiting and residing in Jordan have periodically reported incidents of sexual harassment, stalking, and indecent exposure. The Embassy continues to receive a limited number of reports regarding incidents of sexual assaults involving taxis and taxi drivers. Many of the incidents have involved verbal sexual harassment, staring, or following the victim. To decrease the likelihood of being victimized while using a taxi, foreign women should take reasonable precautions such as avoiding travel to unfamiliar areas at night, not traveling alone, not riding in the front seat of a taxi and dressing modestly when in public. We also recommend c a cellular telephone at all times.

Violent crime is infrequent and rarely targets U.S. citizens or other Westerners. In the past year, the Embassy has received reports of firearms being discharged at vehicles being driven by Westerners. A dispute between two rival protection rackets led to shots being fired at multiple nightclubs, bars, liquor stores and similar establishments in March 2011. While not common, thefts of vehicles, assaults, robbery and attempted residential break-ins have also been reported. Don't buy counterfeit and pirated goods, even if they are widely available. Not only are the bootlegs illegal in the United States, if you purchase them you may also be breaking local law.

Victims of Crime: If you or someone you know becomes the victim of a crime abroad, you should contact the local police and the nearest U.S. embassy or consulate. We can:

- Replace a stolen passport.
- For violent crimes such as assault or rape, help you find appropriate medical care.
- Put you in contact with the appropriate police authorities and, contact family members or friends.
- Although the local authorities are responsible for investigating and prosecuting the crime, consular officers can help you understand the local criminal justice process and can direct you to local attorneys.

The local equivalent to the "911" emergency line in Jordan is 191. In some areas of Amman, however, you may dial 911 for emergencies.

Criminal Penalties: While you are traveling in Jordan, you are subject to its laws even if you are a U.S. citizen. Foreign laws and legal systems can be vastly different from our own. In some places driving under the influence could land you immediately in jail. Criminal penalties will vary from country to country. There are also some things that might be legal in the country you visit, but still illegal in the United States, and you can be prosecuted under U.S. law. Engaging in sexual conduct with children or using or disseminating child pornography in a foreign country is a crime prosecutable in the United States. If you break local laws in Jordan, your U.S. passport won't help you avoid arrest or prosecution. It's very important to know what's legal and what's not wherever you are go.

The Jordanian constitution provides for freedom of speech and of the press; however, in practice the government has imposed some restrictions on these rights. In particular, insulting the King or members of the Royal Family may lead to detainment or imprisonment. Additionally, activities that the Jordanian government considers proselytizing to Muslims are forbidden under the law. Please see the information below on Islam as the state religion of Jordan.

While some countries will automatically notify the nearest U.S. embassy or consulate if a U.S. citizen is detained or arrested in a foreign country, that might not always be the case. To ensure that the United States is aware of your circumstances, request that the police and prison officials notify the nearest U.S. embassy or consulate as soon as you are arrested or detained overseas.

Special Circumstances: Under Jordanian law any adult male may prevent a female or child relative from leaving Jordan by registering a hold on their travel with the Jordanian authorities. This is possible even if the child or woman only holds U.S. nationality. Jordanian authorities consider disputes surrounding travel holds as private family matters and the Embassy is limited in its ability to intervene. Travel holds may only be removed by the person who placed them or by a court. Please see the section below on Children's Issues. U.S. citizens are subject to Jordanian laws while in Jordan. U.S. citizens who possess Jordanian nationality may also be subject to laws that impose special obligations on Jordanians.

For example, all Jordanian men under the age of 37 are required to register for service in the Jordanian military. Those subject to registration may be prevented from leaving Jordan until exit permission is obtained from appropriate Jordanian authorities. This permission is often granted to U.S. citizens, but may take some time to obtain and may be limited to a single exit.

The Government of Jordan considers U.S.-Jordanian dual nationals to be Jordanian citizens. Local authorities typically do not notify the U.S. Embassy of arrests, detentions, or accidents involving dual nationals. For this reason, dual nationals in particular should carry a copy of their U.S. passport with them at all times so that evidence of their identity and U.S. citizenship is readily available for local authorities.

Islam is the state religion of Jordan. The Jordanian government generally does not interfere in religious practices. However, some religious groups cannot obtain legal recognition of their denominations. On official documents such as birth and wedding certificates, the Government of Jordan only allows affiliation with legally recognized faiths, including Islam, Christianity, and Judaism. Not listing an affiliated faith, or listing a faith outside those recognized by the government, is not permitted. Activities such as proselytizing or encouraging conversion to any faith other than Islam are prohibited. U.S. citizens have been deported, detained, and arrested for discussing or trying to engage Jordanians in debate about religion.

Jordanian customs authorities may enforce strict regulations concerning temporary importation into or export from Jordan of items such as drugs, firearms, poisons, chemicals, explosives, and pornographic materials, among other items. You should contact the Embassy of the Hashemite Kingdom of Jordan in Washington, D.C., or one of the Jordanian consulates in the United States, if you seek specific information regarding customs requirements.

The local work week for Jordanian government offices and most businesses is Sunday through Thursday.

Accessibility: While in Jordan, individuals with disabilities may find accessibility and accommodation very different from what you find in the United States. Outside of a few of the more expensive hotels in the capital, individuals with disabilities will find almost no accessible accommodations. Similarly there are very few accessible restaurants, shops, or historical sites. Transportation is not accessible, and sidewalks and crosswalks, even in the main cities, are not accessible. Handicap-accessible toilets and bathrooms, even in major hospitals, are generally not available.

Medical Facilities and Health Information: Modern medical care and medicines are generally available in the principal cities of Jordan, but not necessarily in outlying areas. Most acute and chronic medical conditions can be appropriately managed. When called, ambulance vehicles are often slow to arrive and personnel generally have only a basic level of training. Seasonal dust storms that envelop the country for days or weeks each spring may significantly aggravate respiratory conditions such as asthma or sinus problems. Most hospitals in Jordan, especially in Amman, are privately owned. Doctors and hospitals often expect immediate cash payment for services. Because serious medical problems requiring hospitalization and/or medical evacuation to the United States could cost over US $150,000, we strongly advise travelers to carry medical evacuation insurance.

You can find good information on vaccinations and other health precautions on the CDC website. For information about outbreaks of infectious diseases abroad, consult the World Health Organization (WHO) website. The WHO website also contains additional health information for travelers, including detailed country-specific health information.

Travelers should take normal precautions against contracting the flu, including frequent handwashing and covering sneezes. It is a good idea to postpone traveling while ill.

Medical Insurance: You can't assume your insurance will go with you when you travel. It's very important to find out BEFORE you leave whether or not your medical insurance will cover you overseas. You need to ask your insurance company two questions:

- Does my policy apply when I'm out of the U.S.?
- Will it cover emergencies like a trip to a foreign hospital or an evacuation?

In many places, doctors and hospitals still expect payment in cash at the time of service. Your regular U.S. health insurance may not cover doctors' and hospital visits in other countries. If your policy doesn't go with you when you travel, it's a very good idea to take out another one for your trip.

Traffic Safety and Road Conditions: While in Jordan, U.S. citizens may encounter road conditions that differ significantly from those in the United States. The information below concerning Jordan is provided for general reference only and may not be completely accurate in a particular location or circumstance.

It is typical for drivers in Jordan to not signal turns or lane changes. Drivers can also be aggressive and cars operate very closely together on the highways. Jordanian roads are particularly treacherous during the rainy season, which runs from December to March. City driving in Amman is also more hazardous in the summer months of June to September when Jordan experiences an influx of visitors from other countries in the region. Highways are more crowded around the Muslim holidays when many Jordanian expatriates return to Jordan for family visits. Poor lighting and road conditions prevail, so extra caution must be exercised at all times, especially when driving at night.

The Desert Highway outside Aqaba, a popular tourist destination, is particularly dangerous because it is narrow, winding, steep, and crowded with trucks. If possible,you should try to avoid this area at night. When driving in both urban and rural areas, motorists should beware of both unmarked speed bumps and livestock, including camels, sheep, and goats. Collisions between livestock and automobiles are common.

As a result of all these factors, traffic accidents are very frequent and continue to be the largest cause of injury and death in Jordan. Drivers and passengers are required to wear seatbelts and all cars must have a fire extinguisher and warning triangle in the vehicle. Child car seats are not required by law. Violators of speed limits may be assessed fines up to US$140. Police routinely pull over reckless drivers as well as those believed to be driving under the influence of drugs or alcohol. Driving and talking on a cell phone is prohibited. If stopped by police, drivers may face a fine. Licensed drivers must carry local third-party insurance with sufficient coverage for accidents resulting in injury or death. Landmines are often located within two miles of military installations and borders, including the popular Dead Sea area. Minefields are usually fenced off and marked with skull-and-crossbones notices, but the fences and signs may be in poor repair or hard to see. Avoiding these areas reduces the risk of accidentally setting off a mine.

Jordan has abundant bus and taxi services. Please see the Crime section for more information about incidents of sexual harassment and assault involving taxi drivers and important safety tips when using public or private transportation in Jordan. Visitors should arrange for their transportation needs via their hotel and should request that drivers not pick up additional passengers en route to their destinations. We do not recommend other forms of public transportation. Jordanian security authorities often establish checkpoints, especially on roads leading to popular tourist destinations, where drivers are expected to stop and present their identity documents. All drivers should stop when directed to do so and comply with the instructions provided to them by the authorities. Emergencies should be referred to the Civil Defense Department at telephone number 199. Visit the website of Jordan's Ministry of Tourism and Antiquities. For information on driving regulations please contact the Embassy of the Hashemite Kingdom of Jordan at 3504 International Drive NW, Washington, DC 20008, by telephone at (202) 966-2664.

Aviation Safety Oversight: The U.S. Federal Aviation Administration (FAA) has assessed the Government of Jordan's Civil Aviation Authority as being in compliance with International Civil Aviation Organization (ICAO) aviation safety standards for oversight of Jordan's air carrier operations. Further information may be found on the FAA's safety assessment page.

Children's Issues: Please see the U.S. Dept. of State Office of Children's Issues web pages on intercountry adoption and international parental child abduction.

Intercountry Adoption

February 2010

The information in this section has been edited from the latest report available as of February 2013 from the State Department Bureau of Consular Affairs, Office of Overseas Citizens Services. For more information, please read the *Intercountry Adoption* section of this book and review current reports online at http://adoption.state.gov.

Jordan is not party to the Hague Convention on Protection of Children and Co-operation in Respect of Intercountry Adoption (Hague Adoption Convention). Adoption is not legal in Jordan. However, the Ministry of Social Development (MSD) may grant guardianship of children to people who are not the child's parents and who intend to adopt the child in a different country.

In addition, Jordanian law does not allow for full adoptions of Jordanian children. Americans considering adoption of Jordanian children must obtain guardianship from a Jordanian court and subsequently adopt the child in the United States. Prospective American guardians may also want to review our Sharia Adoption Flyer on Guardianship in Islamic Countries.

Who Can Adopt? To bring an adopted child to United States from Jordan, you must be found eligible to adopt by the U.S. Government. The U.S. Government agency responsible for making this determination is the Department of Homeland Security, U.S. Citizenship and Immigration Services (USCIS). By law, all adoptive parents must be Muslim.

Residency Requirements: There are no Jordanian residency requirements for prospective adoptive parents.

Age Requirements: The husband must be between 35 and 55 years of age and the wife must be between 30 and 50 years of age.

Marriage Requirements: Prospective adoptive parents must be married for five or more years. Single people cannot "adopt" children in Jordan.

Other Requirements: Parents must be medically certified as infertile. They may have up to two children total, including adopted children.

If the parents have one child already, then the adopted Jordanian child must be of the same sex. Parents who have previously adopted in Jordan must wait a minimum of two years before adopting another child of the same sex from Jordan.

Who Can be Adopted? Jordanian children who are under the care of the Ministry of Social Development (MSD).

The Process: To bring a foster child from Jordan to the United States, you must apply to be found eligible to adopt (Form I-600A) by the U.S. Department of Homeland Security, U.S. Citizenship and Immigration Services (USCIS).

If you are eligible to adopt, and a child is available for guardianship with the goal of completing an intercountry adoption, the central adoption authority in Jordan will provide you with a referral to a child. Each family must decide for itself whether or not it will be able to meet the needs of a particular child and provide a permanent family placement for the referred child.

Adoption Agencies/Attorneys: There are no adoption agencies in Jordan as Jordan, under Islamic Sharia law, does not permit adoptions. In certain cases, the MSD will award guardianship of a child to people who are not the child's parents. The Embassy maintains a list of attorneys practicing in Jordan.

Time Frame: The MSD reports that adoptive parents can expect to wait an average of three months from the time they initiate contact with the MSD to when they are given custody of a child.

Adoption Fees: The MSD does not charge any fees. However, adoptive parents can expect to pay fees for the baby's birth certificate, passport, and family book issuance. The "family book," issued by the Jordanian government, contains biographical information about each member of the family. The fee for obtaining a Jordanian passport for a child (under 16) is 10 JD; for the birth certificate is 1 JD; and for the Jordanian family book is 2 JD.

Assume Legal Guardianship of the child in Jordan: Regardless of nationality, all couples are required to apply to the MSD to qualify to become foster parents. The pre-qualification process is similar to those in most U.S. states. To begin this process, prospective adoptive parents are asked to submit a fostering request to the MSD. Requests should be sent by fax or letter to:

Ministry of Social Development
Family and Childhood Section/Fostering Program
P.O. Box 925379
Jabal Al Hussein
Amman, Jordan
Fax: 962-6-569-4953
or 962-6-569-4346

This request should include the following information: name, age, profession, and religion of both parents. Contact information, including full mailing address, must be provided.

Once the MSD has received and processed the request, it will direct the Jordanian Embassy in Washington (through the Foreign Ministry) to request additional documentation from the prospective foster parents.

Documents Required for Jordanian Guardianship: The following documents are required:

- Copies of the marriage certificate;
- Copies of each parent's valid passport;
- Social (home) study (forms will be provided through the Jordanian Embassy);
- Employment letters;
- Original health reports of both parents, including medical proof of the parents' infertility, and;
- If applicable, copy of the conversion certificate to Islam.

All of these documents must be translated into Arabic and certified by the Jordanian Embassy in Washington, which will forward them to the MSD (through the Foreign Ministry). If an

American Citizen is resident in Jordan, then these documents should be translated into Arabic and certified directly with the Jordanian Ministry of Foreign Affairs' (MFA) Authentication Department located in Jabal Amman, 3rd Circle, Amman. The current fee for certifying documents is between 1-5 JD.

The parents' employer(s) must provide detailed information about their income, employment status, etc. Original doctor's reports about the health of the parents must also be provided, including medical proof of the parents' infertility. If either or both of the parents are converts to Islam, a copy of the conversion certificate must be provided. All of these documents must be translated into Arabic and certified by the Jordanian Embassy in Washington, which will forward them to the MSD (through the Foreign Ministry). Once received, an MSD committee reviews the request to foster a child. If all conditions are met, the Minister of Social Development issues his/her approval or denial. Foster parents are notified by mail that they are approved and invited to travel to Jordan to locate a child. Couples who are approved will then be escorted to a government-run orphanage to choose from children whose parents are unknown.

There are no court proceedings involved with guardianship in Jordan. MSD is the only entity authorized to grant guardianship. According to the precepts of Islam and the laws of Jordan governing the guardianship of infants of unknown parentage, the guardian parents are permitted to choose the first name of the child. The Ministry of Interior, Department of Civil Status chooses fictitious names for the unknown mother and father, which along with the child's first name are placed on the Jordanian birth certificate.

These fictitious parents' names, which are chosen at random and do not identify with any common Jordanian family or tribal names, are required for issuance of a Jordanian birth certificate. The child, per Jordanian law, will carry the names of the fictitious father. Once a birth certificate has been issued, the child is also issued a Jordanian Family Book and a Jordanian passport. At this point, the guardian parents may petition for an immigrant visa for their child at the U.S. Embassy in Amman, Jordan (see below).

Bringing Your Child Home: Once your adoption is complete (or you have obtained legal custody of the child), there are a few more steps to take before you can head home. Specifically, you need to apply for several documents for your child before he or she can travel to the United States, such as a birth certificate, a passport or travel document for your child from the country in which he or she was born, and a U.S. Immigration Visa. For detailed and updated information on how to obtain these documents, review the *Intercountry Adoption* section in this publication and visit the U.S. Department of State Intercountry Adoption website at http://adoption.state.gov.

Child Citizenship Act: For adoptions finalized abroad, the Child Citizenship Act of 2000 allows your new child to acquire American citizenship automatically when he or she enters the United States as lawful permanent residents. For adoptions finalized in the United States, the Child Citizenship Act of 2000 allows your new child to acquire American citizenship automatically when the court in the United States issues the final adoption decree. To learn more, review the *Intercountry Adoption* section in this publication and visit the U.S. Department of State Intercountry Adoption website at http://adoption.state.gov.

After Adoption: After the child has immigrated to the United States, adoptive parents are required to inform the nearest Jordanian embassy or consulate of any change in address. This facilitates the follow up that the MSD performs for all adopted Jordanian children abroad.

U.S. Embassy in Jordan
Address al Umawayeen Street
Abdoun
Tel: 962-6-590-6000
Fax: 962-6-592-4102
Email: Amman-IV@state.gov
or ACSAmman@state.gov
Internet: http://jordan.usembassy.gov

Jordanian Adoption Authority
Ministry of Social Development (MSD)
Family and Childhood
Section/Fostering Program
P.O. Box 925379
Jabal Al Hussein
Amman, Jordan
Fax 962-6-569-4953or 962-6-569-4346
www.cspd.gov.jo

Embassy of Jordan
3504 International Drive, N.W.
Washington, D.C. 20008
Phone: (202) 966-2664
Fax: (202) 966-3110
http://www.jordanembassyus.org
E-mail: HKJEmbassyDC@jordanembassyus.org

Office of Children's Issues
U.S. Department of State
2201 C Street, NW
SA-29
Washington, DC 20520
Tel: 1-888-407-4747
E-mail: AskCI@state.gov
http://adoption.state.gov

For questions about immigration procedures, call the National Customer Service Center (NCSC) at 1-800-375-5283 (TTY 1-800-767-1833).

International Parental Child Abduction

January 2013

The information in this section has been edited from reports from the State Department Bureau of Consular Affairs, Office of Overseas Citizens Services. For more information, please review current reports online at www.travel.state.gov/ abduction.

Disclaimer: The information in this flyer is provided for general information only, is not intended to be legal advice, and may change without notice. Questions involving interpretation of law should be addressed to an attorney licensed to practice in the relevant jurisdiction.

Hague Abduction Convention: Jordan is not a signatory to the 1980 Hague Convention on the Civil Aspects of International Child Abduction (Hague Abduction Convention), nor are there any bilateral agreements in force between Jordan and the United States concerning international parental child abduction.

The Department of State's Bureau of Consular Affairs, Directorate for Overseas Citizens Services, Office of Children's Issues provides assistance in cases of international parental child abduction. Parents are strongly encouraged to contact the Department of State for assistance.

United States Department of State
Office of Children's Issues
2201 C Street, N.W.
Washington, DC 20520
Telephone: 1-888-407-4747
Outside the United States or Canada: 1-202-501-4444
Fax: 202-736-9132
Email: AskCI@state.gov

Parental child abduction may be considered a crime in Jordan depending on the circumstances surrounding the child's removal. Parents are encouraged to consult with a Jordanian attorney to determine if their particular case qualifies as a crime under Jordanian law.

Parents may wish to consult with an attorney in the United States and in the country to which the child has been removed or retained to learn more about how filing criminal charges may impact a custody case in the foreign court.

General Information: Jordanian laws regarding divorce and custody of minor children are adjudicated in religious courts. If the marriage partners are Muslim, disputes will be resolved before a Sharia court judge who will apply principles of Islamic law. In the case of Christians, the court will be an Ecclesiastical Court composed of clergymen from the appropriate religious community. For Christians, the law will be derived from principles governing family status in the Greek Orthodox Church, Roman Catholic Church or other Christian denominations. Effective January 2010, Jordan re-established a general rule requiring the father to sign a child's Jordanian passport application. A mother's signature is not required for a father to renew the child's Jordanian passport. The Jordanian Embassy provides procedures for applying for a child's Jordanian passport at http://www. jordanembassyus.org/new/consular/passport. shtml (English text follows Arabic text throughout the form).

Jordanian citizens may depart Jordan on a valid Jordanian passport. Foreigners, however, must depart on a valid passport, including evidence of entry into Jordan, accompanied by their valid residency permit, if applicable. A foreigner cannot depart Jordan without evidence of entry into Jordan. If a Jordanian-American citizen enters Jordan on a U.S. passport, s/he can depart on a Jordanian passport without incurring overstay fines, or without showing evidence of entry into Jordan.

Legal System: Jordan has three main types of courts: Civil courts, military courts and religious courts. Religious courts have jurisdiction over all matters of "personal status." This includes most family law matters such as marriage, divorce, child custody, and adoption or guardianship. Consequently, there is no civil marriage or divorce in Jordan. Under Sharia law, a mother retains physical custody of her children until puberty, which, in Jordan, may be interpreted as 15 years of age. In Jordan, it is illegal to have a child out of wedlock. A woman must present a marriage certificate to the hospital at the time of admission. Under Jordanian law, it is impossible to document a child born out of wedlock. The Department of State's Office of Children's Issues seeks assistance from Jordanian authorities on reports of missing children.

Retaining an Attorney: Neither the Office of Children's Issues nor consular officials at the U.S. Embassy or Consulates in Jordan are authorized to provide legal advice. The U.S. Embassy in Amman, Jordan, posts list of attorneys, including those who specialize in family law. This list is provided as a courtesy service only and does not constitute an endorsement of any individual attorney. The Department of State assumes no responsibility or liability for the professional ability or reputation of, or the quality of services provided by, the persons or firms included in this list. Professional credentials and areas of expertise are provided directly by the lawyers.

Citizenship & Passport Matters: A child acquires Jordanian citizenship by: 1) being born to a Jordanian father, regardless of the location of the child's birth, 2) by maintaining residence in Jordan for at least 15 years. Jordan does recognize dual citizenship. Although the Government of Jordan does not require an exit visa to depart the country, there is a system by which the departure from Jordan can be prevented for any individual who has been granted entry. The "travel hold" is a method by which Jordanian citizens and legal residents can prevent the travel of any individual from Jordan. The ability to place a travel hold against another depends on the circumstances of the request. In the case of the parent-child relationship, a Jordanian father may place a travel hold against his child at any time. Custody is not a consideration in a father's ability to place a travel hold against his child. A father has the ability to place a travel hold against his son until the age of 18, and against his daughter, forever. He retains this right throughout her marriage, as well. Only a custodial mother has the ability to place a travel hold against her child. Once she loses physical custody, she loses her right to place a travel hold. A father who resides outside of Jordan retains the right to grant any adult, male family member the authority to place a travel hold against his child. If the child's parents are still considered married under Jordanian law, a travel hold can also be placed against the man's wife. The initiation of a travel hold against anyone will prevent the issuance of a Jordanian passport or travel document. In the case of children, a travel hold can prevent the issuance of a passport, even upon the request of the custodial parent. Jordan does allow a child to be entered on a parent's passport until the age of 16. However, a child may be issued a passport in his/her own name, as well. The father makes the determination. A child, traveling through the region, cannot process through customs on a national ID card. Travelers must possess a Jordanian passport or Jordanian travel document, a document issued by the Jordanian Government to Palestinians resident in Jordan. The Jordanian travel document does not confer citizenship.

Effective January 2010, Jordan reestablished a general rule requiring a father's permission for a child to depart the country under certain circumstances, e.g., if the child has his own Jordanian passport, and the mother is a foreign national, written approval from the father, notarized by the police, is required to depart the country. If the child is included in either the mother's or the father's Jordanian passport and the father is not present, written authorization from the father, notarized by the police, is required. Exceptions to this general rule are as follows, a Jordanian mother and Jordanian child departing on their individual Jordanian passports do not require a father's permission to the depart the country. A foreign national child departing Jordan on the same nationality passport used at the time of entry does not require a father's permission to depart the country.

Exit Permits: A travel hold can be initiated through a request at any local police station, as well as through a court order. It can also be withdrawn through the police by the person who initiated it or by any adult, male family member with the authority to do so, as well as by court order.

Civil Remedies: Custody orders and judgments of foreign courts are not enforceable in Jordan if they potentially contradict or violate local laws and practices. For example, an order from a U.S. court granting custody to an American mother will not be honored in Jordan if the mother intends to take the child to the United States and live outside of Jordan. Nor will Jordanian courts enforce a U.S. court decree ordering a parent in Jordan to pay for child support, since Jordanian law states that the parent with custody is responsible for providing financial support for the child.

Married or divorced, under Sharia law, parents do not enjoy equal rights of custody to their children. According to Article 162 of the Personal Status Law, a mother retains custody of her children until puberty. In Jordan, puberty may be interpreted as 15 years of age. At the age of puberty, a son may choose to stay with his mother, but a daughter must transfer into the custody of her father. However, the court will hear the wishes of a child at the age of puberty in considering custodial matters. Again, there is no steadfast ruling in such matters. If a custodial mother remarries, she automatically loses custody of her children to their father. If it is determined that a custodial mother is in a relationship with another man, she may lose custody of her children to their father. A custodial father does not lose custody of his children upon entering into a relationship or marriage.

Religion is a consideration in custody matters. A non-Muslim, divorced, foreign mother may not be awarded custody of her child in Sharia court. Both maternal and paternal grandparents have the right to visitation through a request of the Sharia court. Parents who come to an agreement themselves on the custody of their children are more likely to have equal access to their children than through a court-ordered, custodial agreement.

Criminal Remedies: Parental child abduction is a serious criminal offense in Jordan. Any person who abducts a child in order to deprive the legal guardian of custody faces a prison sentence of three months to three years and a fine. This applies equally to a parent committing such an offense in order to unlawfully obtain custody of a child. A mother may also face serious legal difficulties if she attempts to take her children out of Jordan without the permission of the father. In certain circumstances, border officials will ask to see permission in writing before allowing children to exit. The United States has an extradition treaty with Jordan; however, it does not include international parental child abduction as an extraditable offense. Jordan is a member country of Interpol.

Visitation/Access: Legal systems and laws pertaining to custody, divorce, and parental abduction vary widely from country to country. Parents are encouraged to consult with an attorney who specializes in family law in Jordan and who can provide accurate legal guidance that is specific to their circumstances. The Office of Children's Issues may be able to assist parents seeking access to children who have been wrongfully removed from or retained outside the United States. Parents who are seeking access to children who were not wrongfully removed from or retained outside the United States should contact the appropriate U.S. Embassy or Consulate in Jordan for information and possible assistance.

Mediation: Mediation in Jordan is voluntary. There are no government agencies or non-governmental organizations that offer mediation services for custody disputes.

U.S. Embassy Jordan
Abdoun, Al-Umawyeen St.
Amman—Jordan
Mailing Address: American Embassy
P.O. Box 354, Amman
11118 Jordan
Telephone: 962-6-590-6000
Email: Amman-ACS@state.gov

Embassy of Jordan
3504 International Drive, N.W.
Washington, D.C. 20008
Telephone: (202) 966-2664
Email:
hkjembassydc@jordanembassyus.org

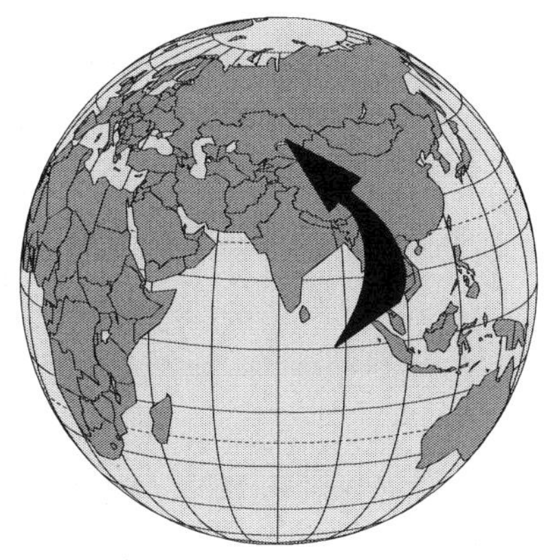

KAZAKHSTAN

Compiled from publications that were available as of February 2013 from the U.S. Department of State, the U.S. Department of Commerce, and the Central Intelligence Agency (CIA). See the introduction to this set for explanatory notes.

Official Name:
Republic of Kazakhstan

PROFILE

Geography

Area: total: 2,724,900 sq km; country comparison to the world: 9; land: 2,699,700 sq km; water: 25,200 sq km
Major cities: Almaty 1.383 million; Astana (capital) 650,000 (2009)
Climate: continental, cold winters and hot summers, arid and semiarid
Terrain: vast flat steppe extending from the Volga in the west to the Altai Mountains in the east and from the plains of western Siberia in the north to oases and deserts of Central Asia in the south

People

Nationality: noun: Kazakhstani(s); adjective: Kazakhstani
Population: 17,522,010 (July 2012 est.)
Population growth rate: 1.235% (2012 est.)
Ethnic groups: Kazakh (Qazaq) 63.1%, Russian 23.7%, Uzbek 2.8%, Ukrainian 2.1%, Uighur 1.4%, Tatar 1.3%, German 1.1%, other 4.5% (1999 census)
Religions: Muslim 47%, Russian Orthodox 44%, Protestant 2%, other 7%
Languages: Kazakh (Qazaq, state language) 64.4%, Russian (official, used in everyday business, designated the "language of interethnic communication") 95% (2001 est.)
Literacy: definition: age 15 and over can read and write; total population: 99.5%; male: 99.8%; female: 99.3% (1999 est.)
Health: life expectancy at birth: total population: 69.63 years; male: 64.34 years; female: 74.59 years (2012 est.); Infant mortality rate: total: 23.06 deaths/1,000 live births; male: 25.83 deaths/1,000 live births; female: 20.46 deaths/1,000 live births (2012 est.)
Unemployment rate: 5.3% (2012 est.)
Work force: 8.973 million (2012 est.)

Government

Type: republic; authoritarian presidential rule, with little power outside the executive branch
Independence: 16 December 1991
Constitution: first post-independence constitution adopted 28 January 1993; new constitution adopted by national referendum 30 August 1995, amended May 2007
Political subdivisions: 14 provinces (oblystar, singular—oblys) and 3 cities (qalalar, singular—qala); Almaty Oblysy, Almaty Qalasy, Aqmola Oblysy (Astana), Aqtobe Oblysy, Astana Qalasy, Atyrau Oblysy, Batys Qazaqstan Oblysy [West Kazakhstan] (Oral), Bayqongyr Qalasy [Baykonur], Mangghystau Oblysy (Aqtau), Ongtustik Qazaqstan Oblysy [South Kazakhstan] (Shymkent), Pavlodar Oblysy, Qaraghandy Oblysy, Qostanay Oblysy, Qyzylorda Oblysy, Shyghys Qazaqstan Oblysy [East Kazakhstan] (Oskemen), Soltustik Qazaqstan Oblysy (Petropavlovsk), Zhambyl Oblysy (Taraz)
Suffrage: 18 years of age; universal

Economy

GDP (purchasing power parity): $232.3 billion (2012 est.); $219.6 billion (2011 est.); $204.2 billion (2010 est.); $190.4 billion (2009 est.)
GDP real growth rate: $200.6 billion (2012 est.); 7.5% (2011 est.); 7.3% (2010 est.); 1.2% (2009 est.)
GDP per capita (PPP): $13,900 (2012 est.); $13,200 (2011 est.); $12,400 (2010 est.); $11,800 (2009 est.)
Natural resources: major deposits of petroleum, natural gas, coal, iron ore, manganese, chrome ore, nickel, cobalt, copper, molybdenum, lead, zinc, bauxite, gold, uranium
Agriculture products: grain (mostly spring wheat), cotton; livestock
Industries: oil, coal, iron ore, manganese, chromite, lead, zinc, copper, titanium, bauxite, gold, silver, phosphates, sulfur, uranium, iron and

steel; tractors and other agricultural machinery, electric motors, construction materials
Exports: $88.61 billion (2012 est.); $88.89 billion (2011 est.); $60.84 billion (2010 est.)
Exports—commodities: oil and oil products 59%, ferrous metals 19%, chemicals 5%, machinery 3%, grain, wool, meat, coal
Exports—partners: China 21.7%, France 9.4%, Germany 8.3%, Russia 5.3%, Italy 5.2%, Canada 4.5%, Romania 4.5% (2011)
Imports: $42.82 billion (2012 est.); $42.13 billion (2011 est.); $31.96 billion (2010 est.)
Imports—commodities: machinery and equipment, metal products, foodstuffs
Imports—partners: China 30.2%, Russia 20%, Germany 7.4%, Ukraine 5% (2011)
Debt—external: $122.9 billion (31 December 2011 est.); $108.8 billion (31 December 2010 est.)
Exchange rates: tenge (KZT) per US dollar; 148.6 (2012 est.); 146.62 (2011 est.); 147.36 (2010 est.); 147.5 (2009); 120.25 (2008); 122.55 (2007)

PEOPLE

Kazakhstan is very ethnically diverse, with only a slight majority of Kazakhstanis being ethnic Kazakh. Other ethnic groups include Russian, Ukrainian, Uzbek, German, and Uyghur. Religions are Sunni Muslim, Russian Orthodox, Protestant, and other.

National/Racial/Ethnic Minorities

The government continued to discriminate in favor of ethnic Kazakhs in senior government employment. Minorities experienced ethnic prejudice and hostility; encountered incidents of insult, humiliation, or other offenses; and were discriminated against in employment or job retention.

Ethnic Kazakh migrants (oralmans) who returned to the country from abroad experienced domestic discrimination including problems with housing, employment, and access to social services. Kazakh is the official state language, although organizations and bodies of local self-administration officially may use Russian on an equal basis with Kazakh. The language law was intended to strengthen the use of Kazakh without infringing on the rights of citizens to use other languages. By law the ability to speak Kazakh is not required for entry into the civil service, but most government agencies officially have switched to conducting business in Kazakh. Non-Kazakh speakers have protested that this is language discrimination. The Election Law requires presidential candidates to be fluent in Kazakh.

Among other forms of discrimination, critics have noted a scarcity of representatives of non-Kazakh ethnicities in the government and a reduction in the number of Russian-language schools.

Language

Despite a national movement to encourage the use of the Kazakh language, Russian is still widely used in business as well as on the street. Both Kazakh and Russian languages appear on road signs, at stores and on product packaging. English is one of Kazakhstan's three official languages and occasionally appears on some signs. English skills are quite strong in the service industries.

Religion

Due in part to the country's nomadic and Soviet past, many residents describe themselves as nonbelievers. The government maintains statistics on the number of registered congregations and organizations but not on the size of each group. The most recent reliable statistics on religious affiliation are based on the 1999 census.

Approximately 65 percent of the population professes to be Muslim. Ethnic Kazakhs, who constitute an estimated 60 percent of the population, and ethnic Uzbeks, Uighurs, and Tatars, who collectively make up less than 10 percent, are historically mostly Sunni Muslims of the Hanafi school. Other Islamic groups that account for less than 1 percent of the population include Shafi'i Sunni (traditionally associated with Chechens), Shia, Sufi, and Ahmadi. The highest concentration of self-identified practicing Muslims is in the southern region bordering Uzbekistan.

Approximately one-third of the population, consisting of sizeable numbers of ethnic Russians and smaller populations of ethnic Ukrainians and ethnic Belarusians, are mostly Russian Orthodox by tradition. Non-Muslim groups that constitute less than 5 percent of the population include Roman Catholics, Greek Catholics, Jehovah's Witnesses, Lutherans, Presbyterians, Seventh-day Adventists, Methodists, Mennonites, The Church of Jesus Christ of Latter-day Saints (Mormons), Jews, Buddhists, Hare Krishnas, Baha'is, Christian Scientists, Scientologists, Grace Church, New Life Church, and the Unification Church.

HISTORY

Nomadic tribes have been living in the region that is now Kazakhstan since the first century BC, although the land has been inhabited at least as far back as the Stone Age. From the fourth century AD through the beginning of the 13th century, the territory of Kazakhstan was ruled by a series of nomadic nations.

Following the Mongolian invasion in the early 13th century, administrative districts were established under the Mongol Empire, which eventually became the territories of the Kazakh Khanate. The major medieval cities of Taraz and Turkestan were founded along the northern route of the Great Silk Road during this period.

Traditional nomadic life on the vast steppe and semi-desert lands was characterized by a constant search for new pasture to support the livestock-based economy. The Kazakhs emerged from a mixture of tribes living in the region in about the 15th century and by the middle of the 16th

century had developed a common language, culture, and economy. In the early 1600s, the Kazakh Khanate separated into the Great, Middle and Little (or Small) Hordes—confederations based on extended family networks. Political disunion, competition among the hordes, and a lack of an internal market weakened the Kazakh Khanate. The beginning of the 18th century marked the zenith of the Kazakh Khanate. The following 150 years saw the gradual colonization of the Kazakh-controlled territories by tsarist Russia.

The process of colonization was a combination of voluntary integration into the Russian Empire and outright seizure. The Little Horde and part of the Middle Horde signed treaties of protection with Russia in the 1730s and 1740s. Major parts of the northeast and central Kazakh territories were incorporated into the Russian Empire by 1840. With the Russian seizure of territories belonging to the Senior Horde in the 1860s, the tsars effectively ruled over most of the territory belonging to what is now the Republic of Kazakhstan.

The Russian Empire introduced a system of administration and built military garrisons in its effort to establish a presence in Central Asia in the so-called "Great Game" between it and Great Britain. Russian efforts to impose its system aroused the resentment of the Kazakh people, and by the 1860s, most Kazakhs resisted Russia's annexation largely because of the disruption it wrought upon the traditional nomadic lifestyle and livestock-based economy.

The Kazakh national movement, which began in the late 1800s, sought to preserve the Kazakh language and identity. There were uprisings against colonial rule during the final years of tsarist Russia, with the most serious occurring in 1916. The destruction of the nomadic life, prior to and during the Communist period, created a Kazakh diaspora in neighboring countries, especially western China. Since independence in 1991, the government has encouraged the return of ethnic Kazakhs by offering subsidies for returnees. Although there was a brief period of autonomy during the tumultuous period following the collapse of the Russian Empire, the Kazakhs eventually succumbed to Soviet rule. In 1920, the area of present-day Kazakhstan became an autonomous republic within Russia and, in 1936, a Soviet republic.

Soviet repression of the traditional elites, along with forced collectivization in late 1920s-1930s, brought about mass hunger and led to unrest. Soviet rule, however, took hold, and a communist apparatus steadily worked to fully integrate Kazakhstan into the Soviet system. Kazakhstan experienced population inflows of thousands exiled from other parts of the Soviet Union during the 1930s and later became home for hundreds of thousands evacuated from the Second World War battlefields. The Kazakh Soviet Socialist Republic (SSR) contributed five national divisions to the Soviet Union's World War II effort.

The period of the Second World War marked an increase in industrialization and increased mineral extraction in support of the war effort. At the time of Soviet leader Josif Stalin's death, however, Kazakhstan still had an overwhelmingly agricultural-based economy. In 1953, Soviet leader Nikita Khrushchev initiated the ambitious "Virgin Lands" program to turn the traditional pasturelands of Kazakhstan into a major grain-producing region for the Soviet Union. The Virgin Lands policy, along with later modernizations under Soviet leader Leonid Brezhnev, sped up the development of the agricultural sector, which to this day remains the source of livelihood for a large percentage of Kazakhstan's population.

Growing tensions within Soviet society led to a demand for political and economic reforms, which came to a head in the 1980s. In December 1986, mass demonstrations by young ethnic Kazakhs took place in Almaty to protest Moscow's installment of a non-Kazakhstani First Secretary as leader. Soviet troops suppressed the unrest, and dozens of demonstrators were jailed. In the waning days of Soviet rule, discontent continued to grow and find expression under Soviet leader Mikhail Gorbachev's policy of glasnost.

Caught up in the groundswell of Soviet republics seeking greater autonomy, Kazakhstan declared its sovereignty as a republic within the Union of Soviet Socialist Republics (U.S.S.R.) in October 1990. Following the August 1991 abortive coup attempt in Moscow and the subsequent dissolution of the Soviet Union, Kazakhstan declared independence on December 16, 1991.

The years following independence have been marked by significant reforms to the Soviet command-economy and political monopoly on power. Under Nursultan Nazarbayev, who initially came to power in 1989 as the head of the Kazakh Communist Party and was eventually elected President in 1991, Kazakhstan has made significant progress toward developing a market economy, for which it was recognized by the United States in 2002. The country has enjoyed significant economic growth since 2000, partly due to its large oil, gas, and mineral reserves.

GOVERNMENT AND POLITICAL CONDITIONS

The Republic of Kazakhstan has a parliamentary system dominated by President Nursultan Nazarbayev and the ruling Nur Otan Party. The constitution concentrates power in the presidency. The president controls the legislature and the judiciary as well as the regional and local government. Changes or amendments to the constitution require presidential consent. The April 3 presidential election, in which President Nazarbayev received 95 percent of the vote, fell short of international standards.

The 2007 national elections for the Mazhilis (lower house of parliament), in which Nur Otan won every seat in the chamber with 88 percent of the vote, also were flawed. Although the 2007 constitutional amendments increased legislative authority in some spheres, the constitution continues to concentrate power in the presidency.

The president appoints and dismisses most high-level government officials, including the prime minister, the cabinet, the prosecutor general, the KNB chief, supreme court and lower-level judges, regional governors, and the chairman and two members of the Central Election Commission (CEC), which oversees presidential and parliamentary elections. The Mazhilis must confirm the president's choice of prime minister, and the senate must confirm the president's choice of prosecutor general, chief of the KNB, supreme court judges, and the head of the national bank. The parliament has never failed to confirm a presidential nomination. Modifying or amending the constitution effectively requires the president's consent. The 2007 constitutional amendments exempt President Nazarbayev from the two-term presidential term limit, and an amendment passed during the year gives him protection from prosecution.

Two June 2010 leader-of-the-nation laws establish President Nazarbayev as chair of the Kazakhstan People's Assembly, grant him lifetime membership on the Constitutional and Security Councils, allow him "to address the people of Kazakhstan at any time," and stipulate that all "initiatives on the country's development" must be coordinated through him.

Recent Elections

In December 2010, in accordance with the law, a group of government supporters initiated a petition process to replace two scheduled presidential elections with a 2011 referendum to extend President Nazarbayev's term until 2020. The referendum movement collected over 5 million signatures—well above the required 200,000—although there were credible reports that many were obtained by coercion.

The referendum bid ultimately failed and was replaced by an early presidential election. In the April 3 election, President Nazarbayev won 95 percent of the vote with a turnout of almost 90 percent. Following the 2011 cancellation of a referendum to extend Nazarbayev's term until 2020, parliament hastily amended the constitution and election legislation to allow for the early presidential election, which had been scheduled previously for December 2012.

Despite efforts by the authorities to improve the election-related legislation, the legal framework remained inconsistent with the government's commitments to the Organization for Security and Cooperation in Europe (OSCE), as well as other international standards, including excessive restrictions on candidates' eligibility—particularly the Kazakh-language fluency requirement—as well as freedoms of assembly and expression. The lack of vibrant political discourse or opposition candidates resulted in a non-competitive environment and reflected systemic restrictions on political freedom.

The OSCE election assessment cited efforts to improve the quality of the voter lists and a high degree of professionalism demonstrated by members of the CEC. International observers rated the voting process positively in 90 percent of polling stations but negatively in 10 percent. OSCE observers cited irregularities in the counting procedure in 20 percent of precincts. According to the election law, the CEC is not required to publish detailed election results, which further diminished transparency.

The OSCE and some international observation missions noted systemic problems and serious irregularities, including numerous instances of seemingly identical signatures on voter lists; cases of ballot box stuffing; and proxy, multiple, and family voting, primarily caused by continued deficiencies in poll worker and voter education. Domestic observers reported significantly inflated turnout numbers, exceeding observed turnout by as much as 21 percent.

In indirect elections on August 19, local representative bodies (Maslikhats) elected 16 Nur Otan party members to the senate. The CEC reported no complaints or irregularities. Maslikhats elect 32 of 47 senate deputies, and the president appoints 15 members, with the requirement that the appointments facilitate representation of different ethnic and cultural groups.

The 2007 elections for the Mazhilis were flawed, and President Nazarbayev's Nur Otan party, which dominates local and national government bodies, received 88 percent of the vote, winning every seat in the chamber. No other party received the 7 percent of the vote then required to obtain Mazhilis seats. The 2009 amendments to the law on elections require that the party with the second-highest vote count automatically receive seats in the Mazhilis, even if it fails to reach the 7 percent threshold.

Political Parties: Political parties must register members' personal information, including date and place of birth, address, and place of employment. This requirement discouraged many citizens from joining political parties. There were credible allegations that authorities pressured persons entering government service to join the Nur Otan party.

At the end of 2011,, there were nine registered political parties, including the opposition parties Ak Zhol, Rukhaniyat, Auyl, and the National Social Democratic Party. On October 4, a Kazakhstani court issued a six-month ban on the Communist Party of Kazakhstan because it formed an illegal alliance with the unregistered Alga opposition party.

In order to register, a political party must hold a founding congress with minimum attendance of 1,000 delegates from two-thirds of the oblasts and the cities of Astana and Almaty. Parties must obtain at least 700 signatures from each oblast and the cities of Astana and Almaty, registration from the CEC, and registration from each oblast-level election commission.

Participation of Women and Minorities: Traditional attitudes sometimes hindered women from holding high office or playing active roles in political life, although there were no legal restrictions on the participation of women and minorities in politics.

Principal Government Officials

Last Updated: 1/31/2013

Pres.: **Nursultan NAZARBAYEV**
Prime Min.: **Serik AKHMETOV**
Dep. Prime Min.: **Aset ISEKESHEV**
Dep. Prime Min.: **Kairat KELIMBETOV**
Dep. Prime Min.: **Krymbek KUSHERBAYEV**
Dep. Prime Min.: **Yerbol ORYNBAYEV**
Min. of Agriculture: **Asylzhan MAMYTBEKOV**
Min. of Culture & Information: **Darkan MYNBAI**
Min. of Defense: **Adilbek DZHAKSYBEKOV**
Min. of Economic Development & Trade: **Yerbolat DOSAYEV**
Min. of Economic Integration: **Zhanar AYTZHANOVA**
Min. of Education & Science: **Bakytzhan ZHUMAGULOV**
Min. of Emergency Situations: **Vladimir BOZHKO**
Min. of Environmental Protection: **Nurlan KAPPAROV**
Min. of Finance: **Bolat ZHAMISHEV**
Min. of Foreign Affairs: **Yerlan IDRISOV**
Min. of Health: **Salidat KAIRBEKOVA**
Min. of Industry & New Technologies: **Aset ISEKESHEV**
Min. of Internal Affairs: **Kalmukhanbet KASYMOV**
Min. of Justice: **Berik IMASHEV**
Min. of Labor & Social Protection: **Serik ABDENOV**
Min. of Oil & Gas: **Sauat MYNBAYEV**
Min. of Transport & Communications: **Askar ZHUMAGALIYEV**
Sec., Security Council: **Marat TAZHIN**
Chmn., Ctte. for National Security (KNB): **Nurtay ABYKAYEV**
Chmn., National Bank: **Grigoriy MARCHENKO**
Ambassador to the US
Permanent Representative to the UN, New York: **Byrganym AITIMOVA**

ECONOMY

Kazakhstan, geographically the largest of the former Soviet republics, excluding Russia, possesses enormous fossil fuel reserves and plentiful supplies of other minerals and metals, such as uranium, copper, and zinc. It also has a large agricultural sector featuring livestock and grain. In 2002 Kazakhstan became the first country in the former Soviet Union to receive an investment-grade credit rating.

Extractive industries have been and will continue to be the engine of Kazakhstan's growth, although the country is aggressively pursuing diversification strategies. Landlocked, with restricted access to the high seas, Kazakhstan relies on its neighbors to export its products, especially oil and grain. Although its Caspian Sea ports, pipelines, and rail lines carrying oil have been upgraded, civil aviation and roadways continue to need attention. Telecoms are improving, but require considerable investment, as does the information technology base. Supply and distribution of electricity can be erratic because of regional dependencies, but the country is moving forward with plans to improve reliability of electricity and gas supply to its population.

At the end of 2007, global financial markets froze up and the loss of capital inflows to Kazakhstani banks caused a credit crunch. The subsequent and sharp fall of oil and commodity prices in 2008 aggravated the economic situation, and Kazakhstan plunged into recession. While the global financial crisis took a significant toll on Kazakhstan's economy, it has rebounded well, helped by prudent government measures. GDP increased 7.5% year-on-year in 2011, and 5.5% in 2012. Rising commodity prices have helped the recovery.

Despite solid macroeconomic indicators, the government realizes that its economy suffers from an overreliance on oil and extractive industries, the so-called "Dutch disease." In response, Kazakhstan has embarked on an ambitious diversification program, aimed at developing targeted sectors like transport, pharmaceuticals, telecommunications, petrochemicals and food processing. In 2010 Kazakhstan joined the Belarus-Kazakhstan-Russia Customs Union in an effort to boost foreign investment and improve trade relationships and is planning to accede to the World Trade Organization in 2013.

Labor Conditions

The law protects children from exploitation in the workplace. The minimum age for employment is 16. With parental permission, children who are between 14 and 16 years of age can perform light work that does not interfere with their health or education. The law also restricts the length of the workday for employees younger than 18. The government conducted labor inspections to enforce the minimum age for employment, but enforcement was uneven.

The government did not maintain statistics on child labor. NGOs and activists reported that child labor occurred in agriculture, especially during harvest season. Children were involved in growing cotton and tobacco. Past NGO studies have found that more than 70 percent of the children employed in this work were from migrant families, primarily Uzbek and Kyrgyz.

The national monthly minimum wage was 15,999 tenge (approximately $109). It was common for working-class families to have more than one wage earner. Most workers earned above the minimum wage in urban areas. As of 2009, 8.2 percent of the population lived below the poverty line. According to the government, the poverty line is 40 percent of the subsistence level income and is currently 6,259.6 tenge ($42.30).

The law stipulates that the normal workweek should not exceed 40 hours and limits heavy manual labor or hazardous work to no more than 36 hours a week. The law limits overtime to two hours a day or one hour a day for heavy manual labor, and requires overtime to be paid at least a 50-percent premium. Overtime is prohibited for work in hazardous conditions. The law provides that labor agreements may stipulate the length of working time, holidays, and paid annual leave for each worker.

The Ministry of Labor and Social Protection enforced minimum wages, work hours restrictions, and overtime. Ministry inspectors conducted random inspections of employers. Labor advocates reported that some employers regularly violated these laws. The law provides for the right to safe and hygienic working conditions, but working and safety conditions in the industrial, agricultural, and construction sectors were often substandard. Workers in factories usually lacked protective clothing and worked in conditions of poor visibility and ventilation.

U.S.-KAZAKHSTAN RELATIONS

Following the dissolution of the Soviet Union, the United States, on December 25, 1991, was the first country to recognize Kazakhstan's independence. The United States opened its Embassy in Almaty in January 1992 and then relocated to Astana in 2006. The United States opened a Consulate General in Almaty in 2009. In the years since Kazakhstan's independence, the two countries have developed a strong and wide-ranging bilateral relationship.

U.S.-Kazakhstani cooperation in security and nuclear non-proliferation is a cornerstone of the relationship, as evidenced by Kazakhstan's participation in the Nuclear Security Summit in Washington, D.C, in 2010 and again in Seoul, South Korea in 2012. Kazakhstan showed leadership when it renounced its nuclear weapons in 1993 and closed the Semipalatinsk Test Site (STS). The United States assisted Kazakhstan in the removal of nuclear warheads, weapons-grade materials, and their supporting infrastructure. In 1994, Kazakhstan transferred more than a half-ton of weapons-grade uranium to the United States. In 1995 Kazakhstan removed its last nuclear warheads and, with U.S. assistance, completed the sealing of 181 nuclear test tunnels at the STS in May 2000. In the following decade, the United States and Kazakhstan worked together to seal 40 more nuclear test tunnels at the STS. Kazakhstan signed the Conventional Armed Forces in Europe Treaty (1992), the START Treaty (1992), the nuclear Non-Proliferation Treaty (1993), the Chemical Weapons Convention, and the Comprehensive Test Ban Treaty (2001). Under the Cooperative Threat Reduction program, the United States spent $240 million to assist Kazakhstan in eliminating weapons of mass destruction and weapons of mass destruction-related infrastructure. Kazakhstan's military participates in the U.S.'s International Military Education and Training program and Foreign Military Financing.

Bilateral Economic Relations

Kazakhstan is currently the United States' 78th largest goods trading partner, with $2.5 billion in total two-way trade in 2011. The stock of U.S. foreign direct investment in Kazakhstan was $9.6 billion in 2010 (latest data available), up 23.9% from 2009. These companies are concentrated in the oil and gas, business services, telecommunications, and electrical energy sectors. Kazakhstan has made progress in creating a favorable investment climate, although serious problems, including arbitrary enforcement of laws, remain. A U.S.-Kazakhstan Bilateral Investment Treaty and a Treaty on the Avoidance of Dual Taxation have been in place since 1994 and 1996, respectively. In 2001, Kazakhstan and the United States established the U.S.-Kazakhstan Energy Partnership. Accession to the World Trade Organization remains a top priority for the government of Kazakhstan. Sections 402 and 409 of the United States 1974 Trade Act require that the President submit semi-annually a report to Congress on continued compliance with the Act's freedom of emigration provisions by those countries, including Kazakhstan, that fall under the Trade Act's Jackson-Vanik Amendment. The U.S. Commercial Service provides U.S. business internships for Kazakhstanis, supports Kazakhstani businesses through a matchmaker program and disseminates information on U.S. goods and services.

U.S. Assistance to Kazakhstan

U.S. Government assistance to Kazakhstan focuses on combating transnational threats (trafficking in persons, narcotics, terrorists, and weapons of mass destruction materiel), improving the functioning of the judiciary, promoting an increased public role for civil society and mass media, maintaining Kazakhstan's open investment and trade environment, and helping the government provide effective social services. For more detailed information on U.S. Government assistance to Kazakhstan, please see the annual reports to Congress on U.S. Government Assistance to and Cooperative Activities with Eurasia, which are available in the Bureau of European and Eurasian Affairs section on the State Department's website. A fact sheet on U.S. assistance to Kazakhstan can be found here.

Kazakhstan's Membership in International Organizations

Kazakhstan and the United States belong to a number of the same international organizations. Kazakhstan is a member of the United Nations, Organization for Security and Cooperation in Europe (OSCE), and North Atlantic Cooperation Council. Kazakhstan held the chairmanship of the OSCE in 2010 and held an OSCE summit in Astana in December 2010. It is an active participant in the North Atlantic Treaty Organization's (NATO) Partnership for Peace program. Kazakhstan also engages in regional security dialogue with the Association of Southeast Asian Nations (ASEAN). Kazakhstan, in June, 2011 became the chairman of the Foreign Ministers' Council of the Organization of Islamic Cooperation, and in 2012 hosted a ministerial meeting for the Conference on Interaction and Confidence Building Measures in Asia. Kazakhstan is also a member of the Collective Security Treaty Organization and the Shanghai Cooperation Organization.

The United States and the European Union worked together with the Ministry of Environmental Protection to establish an independent, nonprofit, and nonpolitical Regional Environmental Center in Kazakhstan to strengthen civil society and support sustainable development by promoting public awareness and participation in environmental decision-making among the countries of Central Asia. Kazakhstan is a signatory to the Convention on International Trade in Endangered Species (CITES).

Bilateral Representation

The Kazakhstan maintains an embassy at 1401 16th Street, NW, Washington, DC 20036 (tel. 202-232-5488).

Principal U.S. Embassy Officials

Last Updated: 1/14/2013

ASTANA (E) Rakhymzhan Koshkarbayev Avenue, No. 3, Astana, 010010, +8 (7172) 70-21-00, Fax +8 (7172) 54-09-14, Workweek: 9:00–18:00, Website: http://www.usembassy.kz/

DCM OMS:	Susan Rogers
AMB OMS:	Jane Kane
FM:	Carroll Webb
HRO:	Seth Magarian
MGT:	Patricia Miller
MLO/ODC:	MAJ Justin Colbert
NAS/INL:	Marko Velikonja
POL/ECON:	Michael Dixon
POL/MIL:	Jennifer Bixler
SDO/DATT:	COL Rob Timm
AMB:	Kenneth Fairfax
CON:	Martin Ryan
DCM:	Elisabeth Millard
PAO:	Catherine J. Jarvis
GSO:	Wanda Washington
RSO:	David Hodson
AGR:	Zhamal Zharmagambetova

AID:	Nils Bergeson
CLO:	Lesley Bell
EEO:	Matt Golden
EST:	David Paradise
FMO:	Paul Kenul
ICASS Chair:	Rob Timm
IMO:	Mark Hodgson
IPO:	Steve McFall
ISO:	Robert Weed
ISSO:	Robert Weed
LEGATT:	Kenneth Jones
State ICASS:	Catherine J. Jarvis

ALMATY (CG) 97 Zholdasbekov St., Almaty, 7-727-250-4802, Fax 7-727-250-4867, Workweek: 9:00 am to 6:00 pm, Website: http://www.usembassy.kz/

CDC:	George Schmid
CG OMS:	James Clarkson
FCS:	Justin Kimmons-Gilbert (State)
HRO:	Seth Magarian (Astana)
MGT:	Markus Dausses
POSHO:	Sam Matthews (Usaid/Exo)
CG:	Michael Snowden
CON:	Ian Turner
PAO:	Tristram Perry
RSO:	Jason Repchak
AID:	Clay Epperson (Acting)
CLO:	Frank Southfield
DEA:	Donald Barnes
EEO:	Justin Kimmons-Gilbert
ICASS Chair:	Robert Timm (Astana)

TRAVEL

Consular Information Sheet

April 26, 2012

Country Description: Kazakhstan is a constitutional republic with a strong presidency and a market economy. Kazakhstan's tourist facilities are not highly developed; the availability of goods and services is better than in most neighboring countries, but not up to the standards found in North America and Western Europe. Internal travel and travel to neighboring countries, by air and land, can be subject to delays due to infrastructure shortcomings and winter weather.

Smart Traveler Enrollment Program (STEP)/Embassy Locations: If you are going to live in or visit Kazakhstan, please take the time to tell our Embassy or Consulate about your trip. If you enroll, we can keep you up to date with important safety and security announcements. It will also help your friends and family get in touch with you in an emergency.

United States Embassy Astana
Akbulak-4
Street 22-23, Building 3
Astana, Kazakhstan 010010
Telephone: 7-7172–70-21-00
Facsimile: 7-7172–70-22-80
Emergency after-hours telephone: 8-7172–70-22-00
Email: USAKZ@state.gov

U.S. Consulate General Almaty
97 Zholdasbekov Street
Samal-2
Almaty, Kazakhstan 050059
Telephone: 7-727-250-49-00
Facsimile: 7-727-250-48-84
Email: USAKZ@state.gov

Entry/Exit Requirements for U.S. Citizens: A valid passport and visa are required. The Embassy of Kazakhstan in Washington, D.C., and the Consulate of Kazakhstan in New York issue visas. The Embassy of Kazakhstan is located at 1401 16th Street NW, Washington, DC 20036, telephone (202) 232-5488 or 550-9617, fax (202) 232-5845, and the Consulate at 866 United Nations Plaza, Suite 586 A, New York, NY 10017, telephone (212) 230-1900 or 230-1192, fax (212) 230-1172. An invitation is not required for single-entry business and tourist visas, but multiple-entry visas require an invitation from an individual or organizational sponsor in Kazakhstan.

The U.S. Embassy in Astana and the U.S. Consulate General in Almaty do not issue letters of invitation to citizens interested in private travel to Kazakhstan. All travelers, even those simply transiting Kazakhstan, must obtain a Kazakhstani visa before entering the country. Travelers should be aware that overstaying the validity period of a visa will result in fines and delays upon exit. Travelers may be asked to provide proof at the border of their subsequent travel arrangements. Travelers transiting through Kazakhstan are reminded to check that their visas allow for a sufficient number of entries to cover each transit trip and to check the length of validity of the visa.

Most visa categories cannot be extended in Kazakhstan. Exceptions to this rule are student visas, visas for medical treatment, visas for permanent residents of Kazakhstan, and work visas, which can be extended in Kazakhstan up to the expiration date of the holder's work permit, a separate document issued only in Kazakhstan.

Business visas can be extended domestically if the traveler is in Kazakhstan at the invitation of the Government of Kazakhstan, a diplomatic mission, or an international organization in Kazakhstan. Please note that the application process for work permits—including extensions—requires a U.S. police clearance. It is highly recommended that you obtain the clearance before your travel to Kazakhstan, as it may be difficult to have fingerprints taken in Kazakhstan. For more information about U.S. background checks, please see www.FBI.gov.

Travel to certain areas bordering China and cities in close proximity to military installations require prior permission from the Kazakhstani government. In 2008, the government declared the following areas closed to foreigners: the town of Baikonur and surrounding areas in Kyzylorda Oblast, and the town of Gvardeysk near Almaty.

U.S. citizens traveling within Kazakhstan have on occasion reported local officials demanding documentation authorizing travel within their area of jurisdiction, even though they received permission from the Department of Migration Police. U.S. citizens should report any trouble with local authorities to the U.S. Embassy in Astana or the U.S. Consulate General in Almaty. Registration of U.S. passports is conducted at the same time as the issuance of the visa in one of Kazakhstan's embassies and consulates abroad or at the time of a border crossing. At airports and border posts, Kazakhstani immigration officers present travelers with a white registration card. Travelers must retain this card throughout their stay in Kazakhstan. Two stamps on the card indicate that the traveler is registered. If the card contains only one stamp, the traveler must register with the Migration Police within five days.

All registrations are valid for three months, regardless of where they are issued. To extend your registration beyond three months, or if you are not sure if you have been properly registered at the time of visa issuance or border crossing, please contact your local office of the Department of Migration Police. Foreigners must inform the Migration Police of changes of address. Penalties for violating registration rules include imprisonment for up to 15 days, and deportation.

New visa rules that went into effect on March 1, 2010, create a new visa category for missionaries. Visitors to Kazakhstan engaging in missionary work or other religious activities must register with the Department of Justice office in the region (Akimat) where the activities will take place. This applies even if the religious activities are not the primary purpose of the visit. Attendance at a religious service does not itself require registration, but participation in the delivery of the service may. U.S. citizens have been fined and deported from Kazakhstan for addressing a congregation, leading prayers, and performing religious music without proper religious worker registration.

In addition, representatives of faith-based non-governmental organizations are often considered subject to the registration requirement even if their activities are not religious in nature. If in doubt whether registration is required, visitors should contact the Department of Justice office responsible for the area of Kazakhstan where they intend to engage in religious activities and request a written decision. Religious worker registration is only valid for the locality where it is granted and visitors must register in each jurisdiction where they wish to engage in religious activities.

In an effort to prevent international child abduction, many governments have initiated procedures at entry/exit points. These often include requiring documentary evidence of relationship and permission for a child's travel from the parent(s) or legal guardian if not present. Having such documentation on hand, even if not required, may facilitate entry/departure. All children adopted in Kazakhstan after May 2003 must obtain exit stamps from both the Ministry of the Interior and the Ministry of Foreign Affairs before departing the country.

Some HIV/AIDS restrictions exist for visitors to and foreign residents of Kazakhstan. Visitors applying for a work or residency permit, required for U.S. citizens who wish to spend more than 6 months in Kazakhstan, must submit negative HIV test results with their application to the Migration Police in the city where they intend to work or reside.

The results must be less than three months old. The city HIV clinic in the place of registration can conduct the test or may certify test results performed abroad. If the original test results are in a language other than Russian or Kazakh, they must be accompanied by an official translation. If a foreigner tests positive for HIV in Kazakhstan, he or she must depart the country. Please verify this information with the Embassy of Kazakhstan before you travel.

Threats to Safety and Security: Supporters of extremist groups such as the Islamic Jihad Union, the Islamic Movement of Uzbekistan, al-Qaida, and the Eastern Turkistan Islamic Movement remain active across Central Asia. These groups have expressed anti-U.S. sentiments and may attempt to target U.S. Government or private interests in the region, including in Kazakhstan. Attacks against foreign interests in Central Asia have occurred and new tactics, including the use of suicide bombers, have been employed by extremists in Kazakhstan and in neighboring Uzbekistan. Terrorists do not distinguish between official and civilian targets. Because of increased security at official U.S. facilities, terrorists are also targeting "soft" civilian targets such as residential areas, clubs and restaurants, places of worship, hotels, schools, outdoor recreation events, resorts, beaches, maritime facilities, and aircraft.

Kazakhstani security personnel may at times place foreign visitors under surveillance. Hotel rooms, telephones and fax machines may be monitored, and personal possessions in hotel rooms may be searched. Taking photographs of anything that could be perceived as being of military or security interest may result in problems with authorities.

Stay up to date by:

- Bookmarking our Bureau of Consular Affairs website, which contains the current Travel Warnings and Travel Alerts as well as the Worldwide Caution.
- Following us on Twitter and the Bureau of Consular Affairs page on Facebook as well.
- Downloading our free Smart Traveler iPhone App to have travel information at your fingertips.
- Calling 1-888-407-4747 toll-free within the U.S. and Canada, or a regular toll line, 1-202-501-4444, from other countries.
- Taking some time before travel to consider your personal security.

Crime: Travelers in Kazakhstan should exercise the same precautions concerning personal safety and protection of valuables as they would in any major U.S. city. Using good judgment and avoiding high-risk areas can reduce the crime threat.

The most common crimes foreign tourists encounter are purse snatching, pick pocketing, assaults, and robberies. Pick pocketing or robberies occur most frequently in the vicinity of Western hotels, transportation sites, and at open-air markets, including the central open-air market in Almaty (known locally as the "green market"). U.S. citizens are advised to exercise caution in the vicinity of hotels, bus or train stations, and when shopping. The U.S. Embassy strongly recommends that U.S. citizens do not carry large sums of money on the street.

Identification checks by the police are common practice. U.S. visitors must produce either a passport or an Embassy-certified copy thereof upon request. Police are not required to demonstrate probable cause or reasonable suspicion to initiate ID checks. Given concerns with crime, the U.S. Embassy has an agreement with the Kazakhstani government to allow U.S. citizens to carry a certified copy of their passport and visa rather than the original.

These copies can be obtained from either the U.S. Embassy's Consular Section in Astana or the U.S. Consulate General in Almaty during American Citizens Services hours. Please check the Embassy website for the American Citizens Services hours in Almaty and Astana.

Be wary of persons representing themselves as police or other local officials. It is not uncommon for U.S. citizens to become victims of harassment and extortion by imposters, genuine law enforcement, and other officials. A genuine police official should always present his own credentials when approaching someone on the street. If the officer cannot produce identification, he is most likely an imposter.

Never voluntarily hand over your wallet to a police officer. If pressured, tell the officer that you will report his behavior to the U.S. Embassy and his supervisors. Authorities are concerned about these incidents and have cooperated in investigating such cases. Try to obtain the officer's name, badge number, and license plate number, and note where the incident happened because this information assists local officials in identifying the perpetrators. Report crimes committed against you by persons presenting themselves as police or other governmental authorities to a police station and the U.S. Embassy.

The "lost wallet" scam continues to be common in Kazakhstan. One version of this swindle involves the discovery of a lost wallet in your presence. A first person will discover the wallet and offer to divide its contents with you. Then, a second person will appear, claim to be the owner of the wallet, and demand compensation for the missing money.

A second version involves a person looking for a lost wallet, asking you if have seen it. The person asks you to reveal the contents of your pockets or bag to prove that you do not have the missing wallet. The wallet seeker will then surreptitiously steal your exposed valuables. When initially approached by the "finder" or "seeker" of the lost wallet, simply walk away.

The Embassy highly discourages taking unlicensed cabs in lieu of licensed taxicabs while in Kazakhstan. This applies especially to travel from the airport to the city upon arrival, where men posing as "meet and greet" airport facilitators have lured foreigners into cars purportedly to take them to their hotels. However, the driver then takes the passengers to a secluded destination and demands approximately $100 for gas to take the foreigner back to the city. At the airport, U.S. citizens should not leave with anyone who does not show prearranged identification, even if the person is holding a sign with the traveler's name.

The Embassy has received reports from U.S. citizen residents and visitors of being victims of violent, late-night muggings. U.S. citizens are advised to travel in groups or pairs. Lone individuals often make easy targets for muggers. At night, try to remain in well-lit, populated areas. Visitors are encouraged to leave restaurants or bars if fights break out. Corruption by public officials, including law enforcement, has been reported frequently, especially at the airport in Almaty. Some foreigners have been told by customs or border guard officials that they must pay a $50-$500 fine for violating an undisclosed local regulation, despite the fact that the foreign citizen has fully complied with local laws. Some U.S. citizens have reportedly been asked to pay a large fine upon exiting Kazakhstan. When encountering such irregularities, U.S. citizens are advised to seek clarification from supervisory airport officials or contact the U.S. Embassy before paying.

Don't buy counterfeit and pirated goods, even if they are widely available. Not only are the bootlegs illegal in the United States, you may also be breaking local law.

Victims of Crime: If you or someone you know becomes the victim of a crime abroad, you should contact the local police and the nearest U.S. embassy or consulate. We can:

- Replace a stolen passport.
- Help you find appropriate medical care if you are the victim of violent crimes such as assault or rape.
- Put you in contact with the appropriate police authorities, and if you want us to, we can contact family members or friend.
- Help you understand the local criminal justice process and direct you to local attorneys, although it is important to remember that local authorities are responsible for investigating and prosecuting the crime.

The local equivalent to the "911" emergency line in Kazakhstan is 103.

Criminal Penalties: While you are traveling in another country, you are subject to its laws even if you are a U.S. citizen. Foreign laws and legal systems can be vastly different from our own. In some places you may be taken in for questioning if you don't have your passport with you. In some places it is illegal to take pictures of certain buildings. In some places driving under the influence could land you immediately in jail. These criminal penalties will vary from country to country. There are also some things that might be legal in the country you visit, but still illegal in the United States, and you can be prosecuted under U.S. law if you buy pirated goods. Engaging in sexual conduct with children or using or disseminating child pornography in a foreign country is a crime prosecutable in the United States. If you break local laws in your host country, your U.S. passport won't help you avoid arrest or prosecution. It's very important to know what's legal and what's not where you are going. Penalties for possessing, using, or trafficking in illegal drugs in Kazakhstan are severe, and convicted offenders can expect long jail sentences and heavy fines.

While some countries will automatically notify the nearest U.S. embassy or consulate if a U.S. citizen is detained or arrested in a foreign country, that might not always be the case. To ensure that the United States is aware of your circumstances, request that the police and prison officials notify the nearest U.S. embassy or consulate as soon as you are arrested or detained overseas.

Special Circumstances: Kazakhstan remains largely a cash economy. Travelers' checks and credit cards are not widely accepted, except at large hotels and restaurants catering to international visitors. U.S. dollars can easily be exchanged for the local currency (Tenge) at local and authorized currency exchanges, but all denominations of U.S. currency except $1 bills must be new series (large portraits) and all must have been issued after 2000 and be in good condition (not worn or torn and without any writing or marks).

Kazakhstan, especially in the mountainous southeast region, is an earthquake-prone country. The U.S. Department of State has ranked the earthquake threat level within Almaty as a Level 4 (the highest level assigned). Building practices within Kazakhstan do not generally meet U.S. seismic standards. In addition, local authorities do not have sufficient resources to respond to a large-scale disaster. U.S. citizens traveling to Kazakhstan are encouraged to register with either the Consular Section of the U.S. Embassy in Astana or the U.S. Consulate General in Almaty to facilitate contact in the event of an emergency. General information about natural disaster preparedness is available from the U.S. Federal Emergency Management Agency (FEMA).

Kazakhstani customs authorities may enforce strict regulations concerning export from Kazakhstan of items such as antiques. Foreigners must complete a customs declaration upon entering Kazakhstan and may face fines upon departure if unable to produce certificates verifying legal conversion of foreign currency.

Travelers are strongly encouraged to declare all valuables, including computers, video cameras, and mobile telephones, upon entry in order to avoid paying duty on those items upon departure. Tenge, Kazakhstan's currency can be exported by residents of Kazakhstan (including foreigners) in amounts up to $3,000 without declaration and without written certification of the origin of funds. Residents exporting between $3,000 and $10,000 must complete a customs declaration and prove the origin of the funds (e.g. proof of locally paid salary). Travelers visiting Kazakhstan for short periods of time may not leave the country with more currency than they declared when entering Kazakhstan. For legal requirements on the export of Tenge, travelers should consult with local Customs officials. In practice, however, travelers should be wary of such officials at the airport, as visitors have been erroneously charged duty on Tenge exports or asked to surrender Tenge in the past. It is advisable to contact the Embassy of the Republic of Kazakhstan in Washington, DC, for specific information at 1401 16th Street NW, Washington, DC 20036, telephone (202) 232-5488.

Foreigners are required to carry a valid passport while in Kazakhstan. U.S. citizens are strongly urged to have a certified copy of their U.S. passport made at either of the U.S. Embassy's Consular Sections at the Embassy in Astana or the Consulate General in Almaty. Having a certified copy in possession satisfies the local requirement to carry a passport and reduces the chances of a passport being lost or stolen.

Accessibility: While in Kazakhstan, individuals with disabilities may find accessibility and accommodation very different from what you find in the United States. Although Kazakhstani law mandates access to buildings and transportation for persons with disabilities, implementation and enforcement of this law has not yet resulted in widespread accommodations for persons with disabilities. As such many buildings, public walkways and public transportation remain inaccessible to persons with disabilities.

Medical Facilities and Health Information: Medical care in Kazakhstan is limited and well below North American and West European standards. The U.S. Embassy maintains a list of English-speaking physicians. Elderly travelers and those with pre-existing health problems may be at risk due to inadequate medical facilities. Most resident U.S. citizens travel to Western Europe for serious medical treatment. Such travel can be extremely expensive if undertaken under emergency conditions. Travelers requiring prescription medications or specific brand-name medicines should bring sufficient supplies of medications and not rely on local availability.

You can find good information on vaccinations and other health precautions on the CDC website. For information about outbreaks of infectious diseases abroad, consult the World Health Organization (WHO) website. The WHO website also contains additional health information for travelers, including detailed country-specific health information.

Tuberculosis is an increasingly serious health concern in Kazakhstan. For further information, please consult the CDC's information on TB.

Medical Insurance: You can't assume your insurance will go with you when you travel. It's very important to find out BEFORE you leave whether or not your medical insurance will cover you overseas. You need to ask your insurance company two questions:

- Does my policy apply when I'm out of the United States?
- Will it cover emergencies like a trip to a foreign hospital or a medical evacuation?

In many places, doctors and hospitals still expect payment in cash at the time of service. Your regular U.S. health insurance may not cover doctors' and hospital visits in other countries. If your policy doesn't go with you when you travel, it's a very good idea to take out another one for your trip.

Traffic Safety and Road Conditions: While in a foreign country, you may encounter road conditions that differ significantly from those in the United States. The information below concerning Kazakhstan is provided for general reference only, and may not be totally accurate in a particular location or circumstance.

Roads in Kazakhstan are in poor repair, especially in rural areas. Poor signage is common. Street lighting, especially on side streets, may be turned off at night. Drivers often ignore lane markings. Potholes are common, and are often dangerously deep. Pedestrians frequently dart out in front of cars. Visitors should drive defensively at all times as many local drivers do not follow traffic laws. Special caution should be taken if driving at night. Road rage can be a problem, especially in and around Almaty, and a non-confrontational response to such behavior is strongly recommended. Accidents involving severe injury and/or death are common. Traffic police have reportedly stopped cars to extort bribes on main city streets and at periodic checkpoints on major highways. The road between Almaty and Bishkek, Kyrgyzstan, is especially treacherous at night or during poor weather. U.S. citizens and other travelers have been killed in traffic accidents on that road, and travel at night should be avoided. Travelers should be particularly careful when using public transportation and taxis. Buses tend to be very crowded and can be unsafe and unreliable. Due to the danger of theft or assault, travelers should be selective regarding which taxi they contract and always avoid entering a cab that already contains persons other than the driver.

Kazakhstan has a zero-tolerance policy for driving under the influence of alcohol. A driver may be detained by police and convicted of drunk driving for driving a vehicle after consuming one drink of alcohol, regardless of whether the driver is actually intoxicated. U.S. citizens wishing to drive in Kazakhstan should possess a valid international driver's license. For specific information, travelers may contact the Embassy of the Republic of Kazakhstan at 1401 16th Street NW, Washington, DC 20036, telephone (202) 232-5488.

Aviation Safety Oversight: As there is no direct commercial air service to the United States by carriers registered in Kazakhstan, the U.S. Federal Aviation Administration (FAA) has not assessed the government of Kazakhstan's Civil Aviation Authority for compliance with International Civil Aviation Organization (ICAO) aviation safety standards. Further information may be found on the FAA's safety assessment page.

Children's Issues: Please see the U.S. Dept. of State Office of Children's Issues web pages on intercountry adoption and international parental child abduction.

Intercountry Adoption

Kazakhstan Suspends Intercountry Adoptions August 2012

The Ministry of Foreign Affairs of Kazakhstan informed the U.S. Embassy in Astana on August 9 that Kazakhstan is suspending intercountry adoptions to the United States, effective immediately. Ambassador Susan Jacobs, Special Advisor for Children's Issues, met with government officials in Kazakhstan on August 16 to address the Ministry's concerns. The Ministry clarified that the suspension involves a pause in adoption referrals, but does not affect Kazakhstan's ongoing process to authorize U.S. adoption service providers. The Department of State is continuing discussions with Kazakhstan as a Hague Adoption Convention partner, and will provide updated information on adoption.state.gov as it becomes available.

U.S. Consulate General Almaty
97 Zholdasbekov St.
Samal-2
Almaty, Kazakhstan 480099
Tel: +7 (7272) 50-76-12
Fax: +7 (7272) 50-48-67
Email: USAKZ@state.gov
Internet: kazakhstan.usembassy.gov

Kazakhstan's Adoption Authority
Children Rights Protection Committee
Ministry of Education and Science
010000, Republic of Kazakhstan
Astana City
Government House
11th Entrance
939, 941 Rooms
Tel: + 10 (7172) 742343/742154/742341/742033
Internet: bala-kkk.kz

Embassy of the Republic of Kazakhstan
1401 16th Street, NW
Washington, D.C. 20036
Tel: (202) 232-5488
Fax: (202) 232-5845
Email:
washington@kazakhembus.com
Internet: kazakhembus.com

Kazakhstan also has a consulate in New York City.

Office of Children's Issues
U.S. Department of State
2201 C Street, NW
SA-29
Washington, DC 20520
Tel: 1-888-407-4747
E-mail: AskCI@state.gov
http://adoption.state.gov

For questions about immigration procedures, call the National Customer Service Center (NCSC) at 1-800-375-5283 (TTY 1-800-767-1833).

Overview of Existing Adoption Process July 2012

The information in this section has been edited from a report of the Bureau of Consular Affairs, Office of Overseas Citizens Services of the U.S. Department of State. For more information, please read the Intercountry Adoption section of this book and review current reports online at http://adoption.state.gov.

Hague Convention Information: Kazakhstan is party to the Hague Convention on Protection of Children and Co-operation in Respect of Intercountry Adoption (Hague Adoption Convention). Intercountry adoption processing in Hague countries is done in accordance with the requirements of the Convention; the U.S. implementing legislation, the Intercountry Adoption Act of 2000 (IAA); and the IAA's implementing regulations, as well as the implementing legislation and regulations of Kazakhstan.

In May 2012, the Central Authority of Kazakhstan approved the first U.S. accredited adoption service providers (ASPs) to process intercountry adoptions from Kazakhstan to the United States under the Hague Adoption Convention. Approval of ASPs was the final step needed for Kazakhstan to complete its implementation of the Convention and to become a full Convention partner to the United States. Each U.S. ASP approved by Kazakhstan may begin accepting applications for adoptions under the new procedures as of the date of its authorization.

Who Can Adopt? To bring an adopted child to the United States from Kazakhstan you must meet eligibility and suitability requirements. The U.S. Department of Homeland Security, U.S. Citizenship and Immigration Services (USCIS) determines who can adopt under U.S. immigration law. Additionally, a child must meet the definition of Convention adoptee under U.S. law in order to immigrate to the United States on an IH-3 or IH-4 immigrant visa. In addition to the U.S. requirements, Kazakhstan obliges prospective adoptive parents (PAPs) to meet the following requirements in order to adopt a child from Kazakhstan.

Residency: The PAPs must have a permanent residence/abode.

Age of Adopting Parents: The age difference between the parents and the child must be at least 16 years and not more than 45 years.

Marital Status: A couple must be legally married.

Income: No specifications in the laws or regulations.

Legally Qualified to Adopt: The PAPs must not have committed any actions that would legally prohibit them from adopting. Completed Psychological and Medical Condition Exams, including alcohol and drug tests. Police Clearance including referral from authorized agencies on moral character. Four-week bonding period: You must spend four weeks in the child's place of residence in order to establish a bond with the child.

Other: Gay and lesbian couples cannot adopt in Kazakhstan.Single prospective fathers are not allowed to adopt.

Who Can Be Adopted? Because Kazakhstan is party to the Hague Adoption Convention, children from Kazakhstan must meet the requirements of the Convention in order to be eligible for adoption. For example, the adoption may take place only if the competent authorities of Kazakhstan have determined that placement of the child within Kazakhstan has been given due consideration and that an intercountry adoption is in the child's best interests. In addition to Kazakhstan's requirements, a child must meet the definition of Convention adoptee to be eligible for an immigrant visa that will allow you to bring him or her to the United States.

Relinquishment: The child can be adopted if his or her biological parents are unknown, have died, relinquished their parental rights, agreed to adoption, had their parental rights taken away, or have been recognized by the court as legally incapable of caring for the child.

Age of Adoptive Child: The child must consent to adoption if he or she is 10 years old or older.

Sibling Adoptions: Prospective adoptive parents are permitted to adopt more than one child; either siblings or unrelated children.

Special Needs or Medical Conditions: Many of the orphans eligible for intercountry adoption in Kazakhstan will have special needs.

Kazakhstan's Adoption Authority: Children Rights Protection Committee, Ministry of Education and Science

The Process: Because Kazakhstan is party to the Hague Adoption Convention, adopting from Kazakhstan must follow a specific process designed to meet the Convention's requirements. The first step in adopting a child from Kazakhstan is to select an adoption service provider in the United States that has been accredited or approved to provide services to U.S. citizens in Convention cases. Only accredited or approved adoption service providers that also have received Kazakhstan's approval may provide adoption services between the United States and Kazakhstan. The U.S. accredited or approved adoption service provider will act as the primary provider in your case. The primary adoption service provider is responsible for ensuring that all adoption services in the case are done in accordance with the Hague Adoption Convention and U.S. laws and regulations.

The Ministry of Education and Science has authorized the following U.S. accredited agencies to work in Kazakhstan:

- Little Miracles

- Across the World
- Child Adoption Associates
- Love Basket
- American World Adoption Associates

After you choose an accredited or approved adoption service provider, you must apply to be found eligible to adopt by the responsible U.S. government agency, the Department of Homeland Security, U.S. Citizenship and Immigration Services (USCIS), by submitting Form I-800A. Once USCIS determines that you are "eligible" and "suited" to adopt by approving the Form I-800A, your adoption service provider will provide your approval notice, home study, and any other required information to the adoption authority in Kazakhstan as part of your adoption dossier. Kazakhstan's adoption authority will review your application to determine whether you are also eligible to adopt under Kazakhstan's law.

If both the United States and Kazakhstan determine that you are eligible to adopt, and the central authority for Convention adoptions has determined that a child is available for adoption and that intercountry adoption is in that child's best interests, the central authority for Convention adoptions in Kazakhstan may provide you with a referral for a child. The referral is a proposed match between you and a specific child based on a review of your dossier and the needs of a specific child in Kazakhstan.

The adoption authority in Kazakhstan will provide a background study and other information, if available, about the child to help you decide whether to accept the referral or not. Each family must decide for itself whether or not it will be able to meet the needs and provide a permanent home for a particular child. If you accept the referral, the adoption service provider communicates that to the adoption authority in Kazakhstan. Learn more about this critical decision. After you accept a match with a child, you will apply to the U.S. Department of Homeland Security, U.S. Citizenship and Immigration Services (USCIS) for provisional approval for the child to immigrate to the United States (Form I-800). USCIS will make a provisional determination as to whether the child meets the definition of a Convention Adoptee and will be eligible to enter the United States and reside permanently as an immigrant.

After provisional approval of Form I-800, your adoption service provider or you will submit a visa application to the Consular Section of the U.S. Consulate General in Almaty, Kazakhstan, which is responsible for issuing immigrant visas to children from Kazakhstan. A consular officer will review the Form I-800 and the visa application for possible visa ineligibilities and advise you of options for the waiver of any noted ineligibilities.

The consular officer will send a letter (referred to as an "Article 5 Letter") to the Kazakhstan's Central Authority in any intercountry adoption involving U.S. citizen parents and a child from Kazakhstan where all Convention requirements are met and the consular officer determines that the child appears eligible to immigrate to the United States. This letter will inform the Kazakhstan's Central Authority that the parents are eligible and suited to adopt, that all indications are that the child may enter and reside permanently in the United States, and that the U.S. Central Authority agrees that the adoption may proceed.

Do not attempt to adopt or obtain custody of a child in Kazakhstan before a U.S. consular officer issues the Article 5 Letter in any adoption case.

The adoption in Kazakhstan is concluded by the court based on the prospective parents' application. The process requires the physical presence of the prospective adoptive parents, guardianship or custodian representatives, and representatives of the General Prosecutor.

The individuals or state agencies who have custody of the child must agree to the adoption. After the court decision (15-day appeal period) the court must forward the adoption decree to the local registration office for civil documents.

In the adoption services contract that you sign at the beginning of the adoption process, your agency will itemize the fees and estimated expenses related to your adoption process.

Bringing Your Child Home: Once your adoption is complete (or you have obtained legal custody of the child), there are a few more steps to take before you can head home. Specifically, you need to apply for several documents for your child before he or she can travel to the United States, such as a birth certificate, a passport or travel document for your child from the country in which he or she was born, and a U.S. Immigration Visa. For detailed and updated information on how to obtain these documents, review the *Intercountry Adoption* section in this publication and visit the U.S. Department of State Intercountry Adoption website at http://adoption.state.gov.

Child Citizenship Act: For adoptions finalized abroad, the Child Citizenship Act of 2000 allows your new child to acquire American citizenship automatically when he or she enters the United States as lawful permanent residents. For adoptions finalized in the United States, the Child Citizenship Act of 2000 allows your new child to acquire American citizenship automatically when the court in the United States issues the final adoption decree. To learn more, review the *Intercountry Adoption* section in this publication and visit the U.S. Department of State Intercountry Adoption website at http://adoption.state.gov.

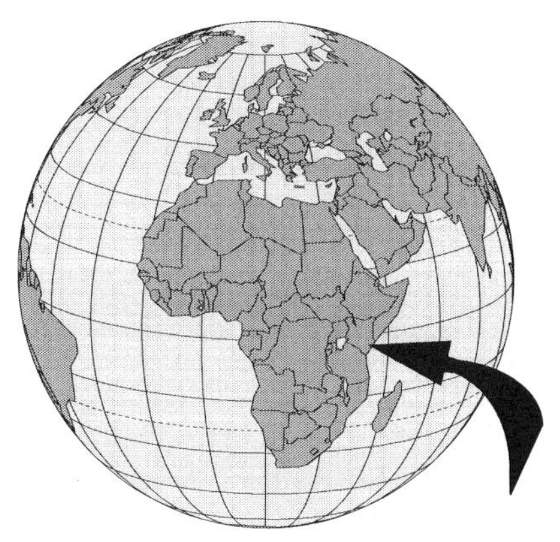

KENYA

Compiled from publications that were available as of February 2013 from the U.S. Department of State, the U.S. Department of Commerce, and the Central Intelligence Agency (CIA). See the introduction to this set for explanatory notes.

Official Name:
Republic of Kenya

PROFILE

Geography

Area: total: 580,367 sq km; country comparison to the world: 49; land: 569,140 sq km; water: 11,227 sq km
Major cities: Nairobi (capital) 3.375 million; Mombassa 966,000 (2009)
Climate: varies from tropical along coast to arid in interior
Terrain: low plains rise to central highlands bisected by Great Rift Valley; fertile plateau in west

People

Nationality: noun: Kenyan(s); adjective: Kenyan
Population: 43,013,341 (July 2012 est.)
Population growth rate: 2.444% (2012 est.)
Ethnic groups: Kikuyu 22%, Luhya 14%, Luo 13%, Kalenjin 12%, Kamba 11%, Kisii 6%, Meru 6%, other African 15%, non-African (Asian, European, and Arab) 1%
Religions: Protestant 45%, Roman Catholic 33%, Muslim 10%, indigenous beliefs 10%, other 2%
Languages: English (official), Kiswahili (officia12291), numerous indigenous languages
Literacy: definition: age 15 and over can read and write; total population: 87.4%; male: 90.6%; female: 84.2% (2010 est.)
Health: life expectancy at birth: total population: 63.07 years; male: 61.62 years; female: 64.55 years (2012 est.); Infant mortality rate: total: 43.61 deaths/1,000 live births; male: 48.41 deaths/1,000 live births; female: 38.71 deaths/1,000 live births (2012 est.)
Unemployment rate: 40% (2008 est.)
Work force: 18.89 million (2012 est.)

Government

Type: republic
Independence: 12 December 1963
Constitution: 27 August 2010; the new constitution abolishes the position of prime minister and establishes a bicameral legislature; many details have yet to be finalized and will require significant legislative action
Political subdivisions: 7 provinces and 1 area; Central, Coast, Eastern, Nairobi Area, North Eastern, Nyanza, Rift Valley, Western; note—the constitution promulgated in August 2010 designates 47 yet-to-be-defined counties as first-order administrative units
Suffrage: 18 years of age; universal

Economy

GDP (purchasing power parity): $76.07 billion (2012 est.); $72.34 billion (2011 est.); $68.9 billion (2010 est.); $65.27 billion (2009 est.)
GDP real growth rate: $41.84 billion (2012 est.); 5.1% (2012 est.)5% (2011 est.); 5.6% (2010 est.); 2.6% (2009 est.)
GDP per capita (PPP): $1,800 (2012 est.); $1,800 (2011 est.); $1,700 (2010 est.); $1,700 (2009 est.)
Natural resources: limestone, soda ash, salt, gemstones, fluorspar, zinc, diatomite, gypsum, wildlife, hydropower
Agriculture products: tea, coffee, corn, wheat, sugarcane, fruit, vegetables; dairy products, beef, pork, poultry, eggs
Industries: small-scale consumer goods (plastic, furniture, batteries, textiles, clothing, soap, cigarettes, flour), agricultural products, horticulture, oil refining; aluminum, steel, lead; cement, commercial ship repair, tourism
Exports: $5.942 billion (2012 est.); $5.768 billion (2011 est.); $5.225 billion (2010 est.)
Exports—commodities: tea, horticultural products, coffee, petroleum products, fish, cement
Exports—partners: Uganda 10%, Tanzania 9.7%, Netherlands 8.5%, UK 8.2%, US 6.2%, Democratic Republic of the Congo 4.2% (2011)
Imports: $14.39 billion (2012 est.); $13.49 billion (2011 est.); $11.53 billion (2010 est.)
Imports—commodities: machinery and transportation equipment, petroleum products, motor vehicles, iron and steel, resins and plastics

Imports—partners: China 14.8%, India 14%, UAE 10.1%, South Africa 7.8%, Saudi Arabia 7.1% (2011)

Debt—external: $8.947 billion (31 December 2011 est.); $8.4 billion (31 December 2010 est.)

Exchange rates: Kenyan shillings (KES) per US dollar; 85.82 (2012 est.) ; 88.811 (2011 est.); 79.233 (2010 est.); 77.352 (2009); 68.358 (2008); 68.309 (2007)

PEOPLE

Kenya has a very diverse population that includes three of Africa's major sociolinguistic groups: Bantu, Nilotic, and Cushitic. Most city residents retain links with their rural, extended families and leave the city periodically to help work on the family farm. About 75% of the work force is engaged in agriculture, mainly as subsistence farmers. The national motto of Kenya is Harambee, meaning "pull together." In that spirit, volunteers in hundreds of communities build schools, clinics, and other facilities each year and collect funds to send students abroad.

National/Racial/Ethnic Minorities

The population is divided into approximately 42 ethnic groups, among which discrimination and occasional violence were frequent. The 2009 census released in August 2010 revealed that the major ethnic communities were: Kikuyu, 6.6 million; Luhya, 5.3 million; Kalenjin, 5 million; Luo, 4 million; Kamba, 3.9 million; Kenyan Somali, 2.3 million; Kisii, 2.2 million; and Mijikenda, 1.9 million. The Kikuyu and related groups dominated much of private commerce and industry and often purchased land outside their traditional home areas, which sometimes resulted in fierce resentment from other ethnic groups. The numerically small and shrinking South Asian community controlled a disproportionate share of commerce.

Education

Kenya has six full-pledged public universities: University of Nairobi, Jomo Kenyatta University of Agriculture and Technology, Egerton University, Moi University, Maseno University, Masinde Muliro University (most of these universities also have constituent colleges); and approximately 13 private universities, including United States International University. Public and private universities have a total enrollment of approximately 50,000 students with about 80% of these being enrolled in public universities (representing 25% of students who qualify for university admission). In addition, more than 60,000 students enroll in middle-level colleges where they study career courses leading to certificate, diploma, and higher diploma awards. International universities and colleges have also established campuses in Kenya where students enroll for distance learning and other flexible programs. Other Kenyan students pursue their university education abroad. More than 5,000 Kenyans are studying in the United States.

Language

The official languages of Kenya are English and Kiswahili. However, many different languages and dialects are spoken throughout the country. The commercial language is English.

Religion

Approximately 80 percent of the population is Christian and approximately 10 percent is Muslim. Groups that constitute less than 1 percent of the population include Hindus, Sikhs, and Baha'is. Most of the remaining population follows various traditional religions. Among Christians, 58 percent are Protestant and 42 percent are Roman Catholic.

HISTORY

Fossils found in East Africa suggest that protohumans roamed the area more than 20 million years ago. Recent finds near Kenya's Lake Turkana indicate that hominids lived in the area 2.6 million years ago. Cushitic-speaking people from what became Sudan, South Sudan, and Ethiopia moved into the area that is now Kenya beginning around 2000 BC. Arab traders began frequenting the Kenya coast around the first century AD. Kenya's proximity to the Arabian Peninsula invited colonization, and Arab and Persian settlements sprouted along the coast by the eighth century. During the first millennium AD, Nilotic and Bantu peoples moved into the region, and the latter now comprise two thirds of Kenya's population. Swahili, a Bantu language with significant Arabic vocabulary, developed as a trade language for the region.

Arab dominance on the coast was interrupted for about 150 years following the arrival of the Portuguese in 1498. British exploration of East Africa in the mid-1800s eventually led to the establishment of Britain's East African Protectorate in 1895. The Protectorate promoted settlement of the fertile central highlands by Europeans, dispossessing the Kikuyu and others of their land. Some fertile and well watered parts of the Rift Valley inhabited by the Maasai and the western highlands inhabited by the Kalenjin were also handed over to European settlers. For other Kenyan communities, the British presence was slight, especially in the arid northern half of the country. The settlers were allowed a voice in government even before Kenya was officially made a British colony in 1920, but Africans were prohibited from direct political participation until 1944 when a few appointed (but not elected) African representatives were permitted to sit in the legislature.

From 1952 to 1959, Kenya was under a state of emergency arising from the "Mau Mau" insurgency against British colonial rule in general and its land policies in particular. This rebellion took place almost exclusively in the highlands of central Kenya among the Kikuyu people. Tens of thousands of Kikuyu died in the fighting or in the detention camps and restricted villages. British losses

were about 650. During this period, African participation in the political process increased rapidly.

The first direct elections for Africans to the Legislative Council took place in 1957. Kenya became independent on December 12, 1963, and the next year joined the Commonwealth. Jomo Kenyatta, an ethnic Kikuyu and head of the Kenya African National Union (KANU), became Kenya's first President. The minority party, Kenya African Democratic Union (KADU), representing a coalition of small ethnic groups that had feared dominance by larger ones, dissolved itself in 1964 and joined KANU. A small but significant leftist opposition party, the Kenya People's Union (KPU), was formed in 1966, led by Jaramogi Oginga Odinga, a former Vice President and Luo elder. The KPU was banned shortly thereafter, however, and its leader detained. KANU became Kenya's sole political party. At Kenyatta's death in August 1978, Vice President Daniel arap Moi, a Kalenjin from Rift Valley province, became interim President. By October of that year, Moi became President formally after he was elected head of KANU and designated its sole nominee for the presidential election.

In June 1982, the National Assembly amended the constitution, making Kenya officially a one-party state. Two months later, young military officers in league with some opposition elements attempted to overthrow the government in a violent but ultimately unsuccessful coup. In response to street protests and donor pressure, parliament repealed the one-party section of the constitution in December 1991. In 1992, independent Kenya's first multiparty elections were held. Divisions in the opposition contributed to Moi's retention of the presidency in 1992 and again in the 1997 election. Following the 1997 election Kenya experienced its first coalition government as KANU was forced to cobble together a majority by bringing into government a few minor parties.

In October 2002, a coalition of opposition parties formed the National Rainbow Coalition (NARC). In December 2002, the NARC candidate, Mwai Kibaki, was elected the country's third President. President Kibaki received 62% of the vote, and NARC also won 59% of the parliamentary seats. Kibaki, a Kikuyu from Central province, had served as a member of parliament since Kenya's independence in 1963. He served in senior posts in both the Kenyatta and Moi governments, including Vice President and Finance Minister. In 2003, internal conflicts disrupted the NARC government. In 2005 these conflicts came into the open when the government put its draft constitution to a public referendum—key government ministers organized the opposition to the draft constitution, which was defeated soundly. In 2007, two principal leaders of the movement to defeat the draft constitution, Raila Odinga and Kalonzo Musyoka—both former Kibaki allies—were presidential candidates for the Orange Democratic Movement (ODM) party and the Orange Democratic Movement-Kenya (ODM-K) party, respectively. In September 2007, President Kibaki and his allies formed the coalition Party of National Unity (PNU). KANU joined the PNU coalition, although it was serving in parliament as the official opposition party.

On December 27, 2007, Kenya held presidential, parliamentary, and local government elections. While the parliamentary and local government elections were largely credible, the presidential election was seriously flawed, with irregularities in the vote tabulation process as well as turnout in excess of 100% in some constituencies. On December 30, the chairman of the Electoral Commission of Kenya declared incumbent Mwai Kibaki the winner of the presidential election. Violence erupted in different parts of Kenya as supporters of opposition candidate Raila Odinga and supporters of Kibaki clashed with police and each other. The post-election crisis left about 1,300 Kenyans dead and about 500,000 people displaced. In order to resolve the crisis, negotiation teams representing PNU and ODM began talks under the auspices of former UN Secretary General Kofi Annan and the Panel of Eminent African Persons (Benjamin Mkapa of Tanzania and Graca Machel of Mozambique).

On February 28, 2008, President Kibaki and Raila Odinga signed a power-sharing agreement, which provided for the establishment of a prime minister position (to be filled by Odinga) and two deputy prime minister positions, as well as the division of an expanded list of cabinet posts according to the parties' proportional representation in parliament. On March 18, 2008, the Kenyan parliament amended the constitution and adopted legislation to give legal force to the agreement. On April 17, 2008 the new coalition cabinet and Prime Minister Odinga were sworn in. The Kofi Annan-led political settlement also set out a reform agenda to address underlying causes of the post-election violence. The focus is on constitutional, electoral, land, and institutional reform as well as increased accountability for corruption and political violence. The new constitution was approved in a referendum on August 4, 2010.

GOVERNMENT AND POLITICAL CONDITIONS

Kenya is a republic with an institutionally strong president and a prime minister with unclearly defined executive powers. There is a unicameral national assembly.

In 2007 the government held local, parliamentary, and presidential elections. Observers judged the parliamentary and local elections to be generally free and fair. In the presidential election, incumbent Mwai Kibaki was proclaimed the winner by a narrow margin under controversial circumstances. Serious irregularities undermined the integrity of the presidential election results. Raila Odinga, the main opposition candidate, disputed the results, and violence erupted in sections of Nairobi and opposition strongholds in Nyanza, Rift Valley, Western, and Coast provinces. Approximately 1,150 persons were killed and more than 350,000 displaced between December 2007 and February 2008, when the two sides agreed to form a coalition government as a result of international mediation. Under the terms of the agreement, President Kibaki retained his office, and Odinga was appointed to a newly created position of prime minister. The parties also agreed to undertake a series of constitutional, electoral, institutional, and land reforms to address underlying causes of the crisis.

In a peaceful August 2010 referendum, 67 percent of voters approved a new constitution, which provides for a bill of rights and reforms the electoral system, administration of land, and judiciary. The new constitution provides parliamentary representation for women, youth, persons with disabilities, ethnic minorities, and marginalized communities. Implementation of constitutional reforms continued during the year, although full implementation was expected to take years.

Recent Elections

In 2007 the country held local, parliamentary, and presidential elections. Observers judged the parliamentary and local elections to be generally free and fair. In the presidential election, incumbent Mwai Kibaki was proclaimed the winner by a narrow margin under controversial circumstances. Serious irregularities undermined the integrity of the presidential election results. Raila Odinga, the main opposition candidate, disputed the results, and violence erupted in sections of Nairobi and opposition strongholds in Nyanza, Rift Valley, Western, and Coast provinces. Approximately 1,150 persons were killed and more than 350,000 displaced between December 2007 and February 2008.

A mixed Kenyan-international commission appointed in 2008 to evaluate the elections found that the results were "irretrievably polluted." The commission also reported that the election results, and especially the presidential election results, lacked integrity. While nearly 14.3 million citizens registered to vote, an independent review commission concluded that voter rolls contained the names of approximately 1.3 million deceased persons. Voting and counting at polling stations for the 2007 elections generally were conducted in accordance with democratic standards, although there were irregularities in both opposition and progovernment strongholds. International observers concluded that tallying irregularities by the Election Commission of Kenya (ECK) in Nairobi undermined the credibility of the ECK.

During the campaign there were instances of violence between supporters of rival parties, especially among progovernment parties. Although the government required parties to register prior to political rallies, the government generally did not interfere with party campaign activities. Text messages, pamphlets, and Web logs sometimes were used to disseminate hate speech that was banned under the election code of conduct. The KNCHR and other civil society organizations accused the government of misusing state resources by providing transport and funding rallies and election materials for some candidates in the election campaign. In accordance with the National Accord, the ECK was abolished in 2008 and replaced in 2009 by the Interim Independent Electoral Commission (IIEC). In 2009 the IIEC conducted two parliamentary by-elections, which international observers deemed free and fair, although there were problems with the voter registry and bribery of voters. During 2011 several by-elections were held, all of which were peaceful and undisputed.

Political Parties: There were numerous political parties. In the 2007 elections, 117 parties with 15,332 candidates competed in local elections; 138 parties with 2,548 candidates competed in parliamentary elections; and nine parties nominated presidential candidates. The Political Parties Act, which came into effect in November 2010, sets stringent conditions for political parties but does not discriminate against any particular party.

Participation of Women and Minorities: Women's participation in electoral politics remained low; however, a record number of female candidates ran for parliament and local office in 2007, despite harassment and attacks. Women constituted 10 percent of all parliamentary candidates. The new constitution provides for the representation in parliament of ethnic minorities; however, implementation posed hazards. The political system was characterized by alliances and hardened divisions among ethnic groups and subgroups. A political gain by one group was often perceived as a loss by other ethnic groups and, as evidenced by the postelection violence in 2007 and 2008, could trigger violence.

Principal Government Officials

Last Updated: 1/31/2013

Pres.: **Mwai KIBAKI**
Vice Pres.: **Stephene Kalonzo MUSYOKA**
Prime Min.: **Raila Amolo ODINGA**
Dep. Prime Min.: **Uhuru KENYATTA**
Dep. Prime Min.: **Wycliffe Musalia MUDAVADI**
Min. for Agriculture: **Sally Jepngetich KOSGEY**
Min. for Cooperative Development: **Joseph NYAGAH**
Min. for the East African Community: **Amason Kingi JEFFAH**
Min. for Education: **Mutula KILONZO**
Min. for Energy: **Kiraitu MURUNGI**
Min. for Environment & Mineral Resources: **Chirau Ali MWAKWERE**
Min. for Finance: **Njeru GITHAE**
Min. for Fisheries Development: **Paul Nyongesa OTUOMA**
Min. for Foreign Affairs: **Samson ONGERI**
Min. for Forestry & Wildlife: **Noah WEKESA**
Min. for Gender & Children Affairs: **Esther Murugi MATHENGE**
Min. for Higher Education, Science, & Technology: **Margaret KAMAR**
Min. for Home Affairs: **Stephene Kalonzo MUSYOKA**
Min. for Housing: **Peter Soita SHITANDA**
Min. for Industrialization: **Henry Kiprono KOSGEY**
Min. for Information & Communications: **Samuel Lesuron POGHISIO**
Min. for Justice, National Cohesion, & Constitutional Affairs: **Eugene WAMALWA**
Min. for Labor: **John Kiyonga MUNYES**
Min. for Lands: **Aggrey James ORENGO**
Min. for Livestock Development: **Mohamed Abdi KUTI**
Min. for Local Govt.
Min. for Medical Services: **Peter Anyang' NYONG'O**
Min. for Nairobi Metropolitan Development: **Jamleck KAMAU**
Min. for Public Health & Sanitation: **Beth Wambui MUGO**
Min. for Public Works: **Chris OBURE**
Min. for Regional Development Authorities: **Fredrick Omulo GUMO**
Min. for Roads: **Kipkalya KONES**
Min. for Tourism: **Danson MWAZO**
Min. for Trade: **Moses WETANGULA**
Min. for Transport: **Amos KIMUNYA**
Min. for Water & Irrigation: **Charity Kaluki NGILU**
Min. for Youth & Sports: **Helen Jepkemoi SAMBILI**
Min. of State for Defense: **Yussuf Mohamed HAJI**

Min. of State for Immigration & Registration of Persons: **Gerald Otieno KAJWANG**
Min. of State for National Heritage & Culture: **William Ole NTIMAMA**
Min. of State for Planning, National Development, & Vision 2030: **Wycliffe Ambetsa OPARANYA**
Min. of State for Provincial Admin. & National Security (Acting): **Yusuf HAJI**
Min. of State for Public Service: **Dalmas Anyango OTIENO**
Min. of State for Special Programs: **Naomi Namsi SHABAN**
Attorney Gen.: **Githu MUIGAI**
Governor, Central Bank of Kenya: **Njuguna S. NDUNGU**
Ambassador to the US: **Elkanah ODEMBO**
Permanent Representative to the UN, New York: **Macharia KAMAU**

ECONOMY

Kenya has been hampered by corruption and by reliance upon several primary goods whose prices have remained low. Low infrastructure investment threatens Kenya's long-term position as the largest East African economy. In the key December 2002 elections, Daniel Arap MOI's 24-year-old reign ended, and a new opposition government took on the formidable economic problems facing the nation.

After some early progress in rooting out corruption and encouraging donor support, the Kibaki government was rocked by high-level graft scandals in 2005 and 2006. In 2006, the World Bank and IMF delayed loans pending action by the government on corruption. The international financial institutions and donors have since resumed lending, despite little action on the government's part to deal with corruption. Unemployment is very high. The country has experienced cronic budget deficits, inflationary pressures, and sharp currency depreciation—as a result of high food and fuel import prices.

The discovery of oil in March 2012 provides an opportunity for Kenya to balance its growing trade deficit if the deposits are found to be commercially viable and Kenya is able to develop a port and pipeline to export its oil.

Labor Conditions

The law prohibits the employment of a child (defined as a person under age 18) in any activity that constitutes a worst form of child labor or that would prevent children under age 16 from attending school. Children under age 13 are prohibited from working, and the government's policy of free and compulsory education through age 13 continued to be one of the most successful means to combat child labor. Children between ages 13 and 16 may perform only "light work" that is not harmful to their health or development and does not interfere with their schooling. However, the law does not apply minimum age restrictions to children serving as apprentices under the terms of the Industrial Training Act.

Persons under age 18 may not be employed in any industrial undertaking at night, employment should not cause children to reside away from home without parental approval, and permission to work in a bar, hotel, or restaurant requires renewed consent annually from the labor commissioner. The law provides fines of up to 200,000 shillings ($2,350) and/or imprisonment for up to 12 months for employing children in such activities.

Despite legal restrictions, child labor was widespread, particularly in the informal sector, where children often worked in hazardous conditions, including in subsistence agriculture, fishing, and on small-holder and family farms. Child labor was no longer widespread on commercial farms. Children also worked as domestic servants. An estimated one million children between five and 17 years of age—most between ages 13 and 17—worked.

The 2005 Kenya Integrated Household Budget survey indicated that 951,273 children under age 18 were employed: 79.9 percent worked in agriculture (coffee, tea, rice, sisal, sugar, tobacco, and miraa—a stimulant plant) and 11.6 percent worked in domestic services. Many children worked on family plots or in family units on tea, coffee, sugar, sisal, tobacco, and rice plantations. Children also were used in the production of flowers and miraa. Children also worked in mining, including abandoned gold mines and small quarries, breaking rocks and sifting through tailings. Children often worked long hours as domestic servants in private homes for little or no pay, and there were reports of physical and sexual abuse of child domestics. Parents sometimes initiated forced or compulsory labor by children, such as agricultural labor, prostitution, and domestic servitude.

Regulation of wages is part of the Labor Institutions Act, and the government established basic minimum wages by occupation and location, setting minimum standards for monthly, daily, and hourly work in each category.

During 2011 the Productivity Center of Kenya, a tripartite institution including the Ministry of Labor, the Federation of Kenyan Employers, and the COTU, continued to set wage guidelines for various sectors based on productivity, inflation, and cost of living indices. While the center continued to set guidelines, it did not have personnel with sufficient expertise to gain the respect of industry. On May 1, the government raised the minimum wage by 12.5 percent. In many industries workers were paid the legal minimum wage; however, in most cases these wages were far outpaced by the cost of living. The lowest legal urban minimum wage was increased to 7,586 shillings ($85) per month, and the lowest agricultural minimum wage for unskilled employees was increased to 3,765 shillings ($44) per month, excluding housing allowances. Many employers did not follow the authority's recommendations. Most workers relied on second jobs, subsistence farming, other informal work, or the extended family for additional support. A large percentage of the labor force worked in the informal sector and was not covered by these provisions.

The law limits the normal workweek to 52 hours (60 hours for night workers); some categories of workers had lower limits. The law specifically excludes agricultural workers from such limitations. An employee in the nonagricultural sector is entitled to one rest day per week and 21 days of combined annual and sick leave.

The law also requires that total hours worked (regular time plus overtime) in any two-week period not exceed 120 hours (144 hours for night workers). Labor laws require two weeks' paternity leave, three months' maternity leave with full pay, and compensation for both public and private employees for work-related injuries and diseases.

While employees in the public sector enjoyed the benefits of paternity/maternity leave and workplace compensation, those in the private sector did not fully enjoy such benefits. Many employers did not allow paternity leave, but most respected the maternity leave provisions of the law. However, in 2008 private employers challenged the workers' compensation provisions in court. At the end of 2011, the case continued.

Workweek and overtime violations also were reported during 2011. Workers in some enterprises, particularly in the EPZs and road construction, claimed that employers forced them to work extra hours without overtime pay to meet production targets. In addition employers often did not provide nighttime transport, leaving workers vulnerable to assault, robbery, and sexual harassment. During 2011 trade unionists complained that employers bribed some government labor inspectors to avoid penalties for labor violations. The extremely low salaries and the lack of vehicles, fuel, and other resources made it very difficult for labor inspectors to do their work and left them vulnerable to bribes and other forms of corruption. Employers in all sectors routinely bribed labor inspectors to prevent them from reporting infractions, especially in the area of child labor.

The law details environmental, health, and safety standards. Fines generally were too low to deter unsafe practices.

U.S.-KENYAN RELATIONS

The United States established diplomatic relations with Kenya in 1964, following its December 1963 independence from the United Kingdom. The United States and Kenya have enjoyed cordial relations and an enduring strategic partnership since Kenya's independence. Relations became closer after Kenya's democratic transition of 2002 and subsequent improvements in civil liberties. In the wake of widespread violence following the disputed 2007 presidential election, the United States has supported the sweeping political and institutional reform agenda adopted by the coalition government, the centerpiece of which was constitutional reform. Kenyans adopted a new constitution in a national referendum in August 2010.

With frequent drought conditions due to climate changes, Kenya is facing economic, health, and environmental challenges that threaten progress made in these sectors. Corruption and insecurity are the two greatest impediments to Kenya achieving sustained, rapid economic growth, and the United States has urged the government to take effective action against them. Conflict and instability in neighboring Somalia pose serious security and humanitarian challenges for Kenya and the region. The United States provides equipment and training to Kenyan security forces, both civilian and military.

Bilateral Economic Relations

Kenya is eligible for preferential trade benefits under the African Growth and Opportunity Act. U.S. exports to Kenya include agricultural products, aircraft, and machinery. U.S. imports from Kenya include apparel, coffee, and tea. U.S. business investment is primarily in commerce, light manufacturing, and the tourism industry. The United States has signed trade and investment framework agreements with the East African Community and with the Common Market for Eastern and Southern Africa. Kenya is a member of both regional organizations.

Kenya's Membership in International Organizations

Kenya and the United States belong to a number of the same international organizations, including the United Nations, International Monetary Fund, World Bank, and World Trade Organization.

Bilateral Representation

Kenya maintains an embassy in the United States at 2249 R Street NW, Washington, DC 20008 (tel. 202-387-6101).

Principal U.S. Embassy Officials

Last Updated: 1/14/2013

NAIROBI (E) United Nations Avenue, Gigiri , Nairobi, 254-20-363-6000, Fax 254-20-363-6157, INMARSAT Tel 683-142-148, Workweek: Monday-Thursday, 0715-1630; Friday, 0715-1215, Website: http://nairobi.usembassy.gov/

DCM OMS:	Lindy Ransom
AMB OMS:	Joan Bower
CDC:	Robert F. Breiman
CG OMS:	Carla Cabrejo Walde
DHS/CBP:	Charles Stemple
DHS/CIS:	Sonia Gulati
DHS/TSA:	Bradely Geno
FCS:	Camille Richardson
FM:	William Connerley
HRO:	Beryl Bentley-Anderson
MGT:	Russell Le Clair
POSHO:	David Simpkins
SDO/DATT:	COL Leslie Brehm
TREAS:	Francis Obubekun
US PERM REP:	Lynette Poulton
AMB:	Charge Robert Godec
CG:	Elizabeth Jordan
CON:	Kirsten Thompson
DCM:	Isiah Parnell
PAO:	Michael Greenwald
GSO:	Chris Matthews-Tiffany
RSO:	Marian Cotter

AFSA:	Newman Waters
AGR:	Kathryn Snipes
AID:	Karen Freeman
CLO:	Nury Stemple
DEA:	Scott Linn
ECON:	David Renz
EEO:	Helaena White
FMO:	Kevin Doyle
IMO:	Ryan Korpi
IPO:	John Combs
ISO:	Paul Phipps
ISSO:	Miller Vinson
LEGATT:	Thomas Relford
POL:	John Haynes
State ICASS:	Elizabeth Jordan

US UNEP (NAIROBI) (M) U.N. Avenue, Gigiri, 254-20-363-6304, Fax 254-20-363-6427, INMARSAT Tel 881-631-437-281, Workweek: M-Th: 7.15-16.30; F 7.15-12.15.

US PERM REP:Joseph P. Murphy

TRAVEL

Consular Information Sheet

September 20, 2012

Country Description: Kenya is a developing East African country known for its wildlife and national parks. The capital city is Nairobi. The second largest city is Mombasa, located on the southeast coast. Tourist facilities are widely available in Nairobi, the game parks, the reserves, and on the coast.

Smart Traveler Enrollment Program (STEP)/Embassy Locations: If you are going to live in or visit Kenya, please take the time to tell our Embassy about your trip. If you enroll, we can keep you up to date with important safety and security announcements. It will also help your friends and family get in touch with you in an emergency.

U.S. Embassy Kenya
United Nations Avenue
Gigiri, Nairobi, Kenya
Telephone: (254) (20) 363-6451
Emergency after-hours telephone: (254) (20) 363-6000

Entry/Exit Requirements for U.S. Citizens: A passport and visa are required for entry into Kenya. Visas may be obtained in advance, although airport visas are available for U.S. citizens. Travelers who opt to obtain an airport visa should expect delays upon arrival.

Effective July 1, 2011, the fee is $50 for single-entry visas, and $100 for multiple entry visas for each applicant regardless of age, and whether obtained in advance or at the airport. Evidence of yellow fever immunization may be requested, and some travelers have been turned around at immigration for not having sufficient proof of immunization. Travelers to Kenya and neighboring African countries should ensure that the validity of their passports is at least six months beyond the end of their intended stay. Kenyan immigration authorities require a minimum oftwo blank (unstamped) visa pages in the passport to enter the country; some travelers have experienced difficulties when they arrive without the requisite blank pages. Travelers should make sure there are sufficient pages for visas and immigration stamps to enter into Kenya and other countries to be visited en route to Kenya or elsewhere in the region.

Travelers may obtain the latest information on visas as well as any additional details regarding entry requirements from the Embassy of Kenya, 2249 R Street NW, Washington, DC 20008, telephone (202) 387-6101, or the Kenyan Consulates General in Los Angeles and New York City. Persons outside the United States should contact the nearest Kenyan embassy or consulate.

HIV/AIDS Restrictions: The U.S. Department of State is unaware of any HIV/AIDS entry restrictions for visitors to or foreign residents of Kenya.

Threats to Safety and Security: The U.S. government continues to receive information regarding potential terrorist threats aimed at U.S., Western, and Kenyan interests in Kenya, particularly after the death of Osama Bin Laden. Terrorist acts could include suicide operations, bomb and grenade attacks, kidnappings, attacks on civil aviation, and attacks on maritime vessels in or near Kenyan ports. Although there have been recent gains in the pursuit of those responsible for previous terrorist activities, many of those involved remain at large and continue to operate in the region. Travelers should consult the Worldwide Caution for further information and details.

On October 14, 2011, two Spanish nationals working for an NGO were kidnapped in Dadaab refugee camp, in northeastern Kenya. On October 1, 2011, a French national was kidnapped from a private residence on Lamu Island, a popular tourist destination on Kenya's north coast. She died while in captivity in Somalia. On September 11, 2011, a British national wife and husband were kidnapped—and the husband murdered—at a coastal resort near the Kenya–Somali border. Four expatriate staff of Norwegian Refugee Council were kidnapped from Dadaab on June 29, 2012. They were rescued by Kenyan and Somali forces inside Somalia 3 days later.The motivation for these kidnappings is unclear, but the perpetrators took all of the hostages into areas of Somalia controlled by al-Shabaab, a designated terrorist organization with links to Al Qaeda. On October 16, 2011, Kenya initiated military action against al-Shabaab, declaring self-defense. Kenyan troops crossed into Somalia with the stated aim of pursuing al-Shabaab in southeastern Somalia. Al-Shabaab has responded to the Kenyan incursion into Somalia by threatening retaliation against civilian targets in Kenya.

In the past year, there have been at least 19 attacks involving grenades or explosive devices in Kenya, but not all of them have been fatal. At least 48 people died in these attacks, and around 200 people were injured. There were no U.S. citizens among the casualties. Eleven of these attacks occurred in North Eastern Province, including locations in Dadaab, Wajir, and Garissa. Several other attacks have occurred in both Nairobi, and Mombasa. Targets included police stations and police vehicles, nightclubs and bars, churches, a religious gathering, a downtown building of small shops, and a bus station.

Responsibility for these incidents has not been determined, though an individual was sentenced on October 28 for his role in the grenade attack on the nightclub. U.S. citizens traveling to Kenya for business or pleasure should take these events into account when planning their travel.

As a result of recent events and threats, the areas to which travel by U.S. government employees, contractors, grantees, and their dependents is restricted have been expanded, now encompassing Lamu District and the Northeastern Province, including El Wak, Wajir, Garissa, Dadaab, Mandera and Liboi. Although this restriction does not apply to travelers not associated with the U.S. government, it should be taken into account when planning travel. The security of these areas will be regularly reviewed for possible modification.

Presidential and parliamentary elections were held on December 27, 2007. In the wake of the announcement by the Electoral Commission of Kenya on December 30 declaring the incumbent candidate Mwai Kibaki as the presidential winner, violence erupted in strongholds of the opposition party. The violence, which appeared to be ethnically and politically based, was concentrated in Nyanza, Rift Valley, and Western provinces, as well as Nairobi and parts of Coast province.

At least 1,100 people died as a result of the post-electoral civil unrest and more than 300,000 were internally displaced. Additionally, disruptions in public transportation services occurred as a result of political violence, strikes, or work stoppages. There continues to be the potential for spontaneous violence due to simmering political grievances. The next Kenyan presidential election is set to take place in March 2013.

Political demonstrations can occur sporadically throughout Kenya. On August 27, sporadic rioting and violence erupted in Majengo, Saba Saba, Kisauni, and other areas of Mombasa in response to the killing of a Muslim cleric. Protestors burned four churches, three policemen were killed, and several protestors were injured the following day. Additionally, four policemen were injured by grenade attacks on August 29. Some roads have been intermittently barricaded.

The Kenyan government deployed additional police in Mombasa to calm the situation. Travelers should maintain security awareness at all times and avoid public gatherings and street demonstrations. Violence, including gunfire exchange, has occurred at demonstrations in the past. Demonstrations tend to occur near government buildings, university campuses, or gathering places such as public parks. Police are generally unable to properly manage large demonstrations and they often resort to excessive force to break up large crowds. Most major tourist attractions, particularly outside Nairobi, are not generally affected by protests. However, tribal conflict in rural areas has been known to erupt into violence.

Some sparsely populated rural areas of Kenya, principally in the north, experience recurrent, localized incidents of violent cattle rustling, counter-raids, ethnic conflict, tribal or clan rivalry, and armed banditry. During the past several years, incidents have occurred in the Keiro Valley, Northern Rift Valley sections of Laikipia and Nakuru Districts, and other areas north of Mount Kenya. A number of incidents have also occurred near the game parks or lodges north of Mwingi, Meru, and Isiolo, which are frequented by tourists.

Locations tend to shift over time. Recent cattle rustling incidents have involved firefights between hundreds of members of rival tribal groups and the theft of thousands of head of cattle at a time. For these reasons, U.S. citizens who plan to visit Kenya are urged to take basic security precautions to maximize their safety. Travel to northern Kenya should be undertaken with at least two vehicles to ensure a backup in the case of a breakdown or other emergency.

Similarly, in August 2012, sporadic violence erupted in remote villages in the Tana River delta area of Coast Province. What started with armed cattle rustling has escalated to household raids and deadly firefights between rival tribes. As many as one hundred Kenyans have been killed. These clashes have occurred in remote, isolated villages and have not involved tourists. However, U.S. citizens who plan to visit the Tana River delta area are urged to monitor local media and be prepared to alter their travel plans if necessary.

Villagers in rural areas are sometimes suspicious of strangers. There have been several incidents of violence against Kenyan and foreign adults in rural areas who are suspected of stealing children.

U.S. visitors to rural areas should be aware that close contact with children, including taking their pictures or giving them candy, can be viewed with deep alarm and may provoke panic and violence. Adoptive parents traveling with their adopted child should exercise particular caution and are urged to carry complete copies of their adoption paperwork with them at all times.

Travelers should keep informed of local developments by following local press, radio, and television reports prior to their visits. Visitors should also consult their hosts, including U.S. and Kenyan business contacts, hotels, tour guides, and travel organizers.

Stay up to date by:

- Bookmarking our Bureau of Consular Affairs website, which contains the current Travel Warnings and Travel Alerts as well as the Worldwide Caution.
- Following us on Twitter and the Bureau of Consular Affairs page on Facebook as well.

- Downloading our free Smart Traveler IPhone App to have travel information at your fingertips.
- Calling 1-888-407-4747 toll-free within the U.S. and Canada, or a regular toll line, 1-202-501-4444, from other countries.
- Taking some time before travel to consider your personal security.

Crime: Crime is high in all regions of Kenya, particularly Nairobi, Mombasa, Kisumu, and at coastal beach resorts. There are regular reports of attacks against tourists by groups of armed assailants. Pickpockets and thieves carry out "snatch and run" crimes on city streets and near crowds. Visitors have found it safer not to carry valuables, but rather to store them in hotel safety deposit boxes or safe rooms. However, there have been reports of safes being stolen from hotel rooms and hotel desk staff being forced to open safes. Walking alone or at night, especially in downtown areas, public parks, along footpaths, on beaches, and in poorly lit areas, is dangerous and discouraged.

Violent and sometimes fatal criminal attacks, including armed carjackings, home invasions/burglaries, and kidnappings can occur at any time and in any location, most particularly in Nairobi. Nairobi averages about ten vehicle hijackings per day and Kenyan authorities have limited capacity to deter and investigate such acts. Matatus (public transportation) tend to be targeted since they carry up to 14 passengers. Although these attacks are often violent, victims are generally not injured if they do not resist. There is also a high incidence of residential break-ins and occupants should take additional security measures to protect their property. Thieves and con artists have been known to impersonate police officers, thus U.S. citizens are strongly encouraged to ask for identification if approached by individuals identifying themselves as police officials, uniformed or not. U.S. citizens have fallen victim to such crimes within the past year. U.S. citizens in Kenya should be extremely vigilant with regard to their personal security, particularly in public places frequented by foreigners such as clubs, hotels, resorts, upscale shopping centers, restaurants, and places of worship. U.S. citizens should also remain alert in residential areas, at schools, and at outdoor recreational events.

Thieves routinely snatch jewelry and other objects from open vehicle windows while motorists are either stopped at traffic lights or in heavy traffic. Vehicle windows should be up and doors locked regardless of the time of day or weather. Thieves on matatus, buses and trains may steal valuables from inattentive passengers. U.S. citizens should guard their backpacks or hand luggage and ensure these items are not left unattended. Purchasing items from street vendors is strongly discouraged—visitors should only use reputable stores or businesses. Many scams, perpetrated against unsuspecting tourists, are prevalent in and around the city of Nairobi. Many of these involve people impersonating police officers and using fake police ID badges and other credentials. Nevertheless, police checkpoints are common in Kenya and all vehicles are required to stop if directed to do so.

Highway banditry is common in much of North Eastern Province, Eastern Province, the northern part of Coast Province, and the northern part of the Rift Valley Province. These areas are remote and sparsely populated. Incidents also occur occasionally on Kenya's main highways, particularly after dark. Due to increased bandit activity, air travel is the recommended means of transportation when visiting any of the coastal resorts north of Malindi. Travelers to North Eastern Kenya and the North Rift Valley Region should travel with police escorts or convoys organized by the government of Kenya.

There have been reports of armed banditry in or near many of Kenya's national parks and game reserves, particularly the Samburu, Leshaba, and Masai Mara game reserves. In response, the Kenya Wildlife Service and police have taken steps to strengthen security in the affected areas, but the problem has not been eliminated. Travelers who do not use the services of reputable travel firms or knowledgeable guides or drivers are especially at risk. Safaris are best undertaken with a minimum of two vehicles so that there is a backup in case of mechanical failure or other emergency. Camping alone is always risky.

The Kenyan mail system can be unreliable and monetary instruments (credit cards, checks, etc.) are frequently stolen. International couriers provide the safest means of shipping envelopes and packages, although anything of value should be insured.

Don't buy counterfeit and pirated goods, even if they are widely available. Not only are the bootlegs illegal in the United States, if you purchase them you may also be breaking local law.

Victims of Crime: If you or someone you know becomes the victim of a crime abroad, you should contact the local police and the nearest U.S. embassy or consulate. We can:

- Replace a stolen passport.
- Help you find appropriate medical care if you are the victim of violent crimes such as assault or rape.
- Put you in contact with the appropriate police authorities, and if you want us to, we can contact family members or friend.
- Help you understand the local criminal justice process and direct you to local attorneys, although it is important to remember that local authorities are responsible for investigating and prosecuting the crime.

Criminal Penalties: While you are traveling in Kenya, you are subject to its laws even if you are a U.S. citizen. Foreign laws and legal systems can be vastly different than our own. In some places, you may be taken in for questioning if you don't have your passport with you. In some places, it is illegal to take pictures of certain buildings. In some places, driving under the influence could land you immediately in jail. There are also some things that might be legal in Kenya, but still illegal in the United States, and you can be prosecuted under U.S. law. Engaging in sexual conduct with children or using or disseminating child pornography in a foreign country is a crime prosecutable in the United States. If you break local laws in Kenya, your U.S. passport won't help you avoid arrest or prosecution. It's very important to know what's legal and what's not where you are going.

Persons violating Kenya's laws, even unknowingly, may be expelled, arrested, or imprisoned. Penalties for possessing, using, or trafficking in illegal drugs in Kenya are severe, and convicted offenders can expect long jail sentences and heavy fines. Kenya has recently enacted strict legislation regulating the sale and consumption of alcohol and cigarettes.

Arrest notifications in host country: Kenya is a signatory to the Vienna Convention on Consular Relations (VCCR), and is required by the VCCR to ask any detained U.S. citizen if he/she would like the U.S. Embassy to be notified and to notify the U.S. Embassy if the detained U.S. citizen requests it. Kenya does not routinely comply with its VCCR obligation. Any U.S. citizen who is detained should request U.S. Embassy notification if he/she would like consular assistance. U.S. citizens are encouraged to carry a copy of their U.S. passport with them at all times, so that proof of identity and U.S. citizenship is readily available if questioned by local officials.

Special Circumstances: Kenyan customs authorities may enforce strict regulations concerning temporary importation into or export from Kenya of items such as firearms, religious materials, antiquities, medications, business equipment, currency, ivory, etc. In 2009 and 2010, a number of U.S. citizens were detained or arrested for attempting to bring contraband into Kenya. It is advisable to contact the Embassy of Kenya or one of Kenya's consulates in the United States for specific information regarding customs requirements.

Kenya is a relatively conservative society. Overt public displays of affection between persons of the opposite gender will likely garner serious disapproval, particularly in rural areas. Public displays of affection between persons of the same gender risk serious disapproval, and possibly violence. Same sex sexual activity is a criminal act. Although authorities have rarely prosecuted persons under this provision, travelers should be aware of cultural norms as well as the risk of possible arrest and imprisonment for such activities.

Visitors should be aware of Kenya's Alcoholic Drinks Control Act of 2010, which regulates when and where alcoholic drinks may be consumed in public. The regulations are strict and difficult to follow. For example, certain restaurants are authorized to sell alcoholic drinks on any day of the week to persons having meals in the restaurant, for consumption with such meals, from Monday to Friday during the hours of 5.00 p.m. to 11.00 p.m., and during weekends and public holidays during the hours of 2.00 p.m. to 11.00 p.m. Nightclubs have different licenses, most of which allow alcohol to be consumed until 3:00 a.m., while hotels do not have any restrictions on alcohol consumption. More information on this law may be found on Kenya's substance abuse website, NACADA. The police sporadically enforce these laws and have arrested some tourists if found in violation. The Tobacco Control Act 2007 regulates public smoking and the marketing and sale of tobacco products in Kenya. In public places, smoking is allowed only in designated smoking areas. If an individual is discovered smoking outside these designated areas, a substantial fine may be imposed.

Up to 100,000 Kenyan shillings may be taken out of the country. Destruction of Kenyan currency, even in small amounts, is illegal, and almost always results in arrest and a fine. Visitors to Kenya carrying U.S. Dollars should ensure that the bills are relatively new, as banks in Kenya have been known not to accept older U.S. currency.

Wild animals may pose danger to travelers in some regions of Kenya. Serious injuries and deaths have occurred in Kenya's national reserves, forests, andwilderness areas. Travelers are advised that, even in the most serene settings, animals are wild and can present a threat to life and safety. In addition, potentially dangerous areas may lack fences and warning signs. Travelers are cautioned to observe all local or park regulations and exercise appropriate caution in unfamiliar surroundings. Travelers are advised to thoroughly check the qualifications and safety record of all tourist lodges and guides before engaging their services and venturing into the wild in their care. The governing body of Kenya's national parks, Kenya Wildlife Service (KWS), announced in March 2010 that all tour operators and safari lodges must purchase a nationally-mandated insurance policy. Visitors should inquire whether prospective safari camps or tour operators are in compliance with this requirement.

Use of firearms is strictly forbidden in wildlife reserves and national parks. Permission to carry firearms must be obtained from local authorities prior to entry.

Local tap water is not potable. Sealed bottled water is safe to drink and can be purchased in hotels, restaurants, and grocery stores.

Kenya Telephone and Telegraph has discontinued its "collect call" facility and 1-800 numbers cannot be accessed from Kenyan landlines, though they can be called through a mobile phone by using the prefix. Use of international long-distance calling cards is very limited in Kenya. International long-distance costs from Kenya on a landline are significantly higher than corresponding long-distance rates in the United States, but calling to the United States on a mobile phone is very inexpensive. Several local companies offer computer Internet access, including on an hourly rate basis. Many hotels have fax machines but often limit access to guests; some fax services are also available at office supply shops. Travelers are urged to consider their method of maintaining contact with family and friends when making their travel preparations.

While the new constitution recognizes dual nationality, this portion of the law is not yet officially enacted. In addition to being subject to all Kenyan laws affecting U.S. citizens, dual nationals may also be subject to other laws that impose special obligations on Kenyan citizens. For additional information, see the Bureau of Consular Affairs Dual Nationality flyer.

Accessibility: While in Kenya, individuals with disabilities may find accessibility and accommodation very different from what you find in the United States. Although Kenyan law prohibits discrimination against persons with disabilities, the government has not effectively enforced these provisions and implementation has been slow. The government has equipped some public buildings with wheelchair ramps, and wheelchair-accessible elevators and sanitary facilities, and assigned each region a sign-language interpreter for court proceedings. Travelers to Kenya will find very little accessibility to public transportation or taxis. There is no functioning bus system in Nairobi, but rather an extensive use of vans ("matatus") that travel along designated routes, or taxis. Neither of these options can easily accommodate a wheelchair and most often are hailed from the side of a busy road. Footpaths at the side of the roads are generally unpaved, bumpy, dirt paths with unmarked road crossings. Very few government buildings, medical facilities, restaurants or accommodations have disabled access.

Medical Facilities and Health Information: Adequate medical services are available in Nairobi. Frequent outbreaks of cholera and malaria are endemic in Kenya outside Nairobi. In addition, diseases such as Ebola, Rift Valley Fever, and anthrax from handling sheep skins occur periodically. Travelers who become ill with a fever or flu-like illness while traveling in a malaria-risk area, and up to one year after returning home, should seek prompt medical attention and tell the physician their travel history and what anti-malarial drugs they have been taking. For additional information on malaria, protection from insect bites, and anti-malarial drugs, please visit the CDC Travelers' Health web site.

Tuberculosis is an increasingly serious health concern in Kenya. For further information, please consult the CDC's Information on TB.

You can find good information on vaccinations and other health precautions, on the CDC website. For information about outbreaks of infectious diseases abroad, consult the World Health Organization (WHO) website. The WHO website also contains additional health information for travelers, including detailed country-specific health information.

Medical Insurance: You can't assume your insurance will go with you when you travel. It's very important to find out BEFORE you leave whether or not your medical insurance will cover you overseas. You need to ask your insurance company two questions:

- Does my policy apply when I'm out of the United States?
- Will it cover emergencies like a trip to a foreign hospital or a medical evacuation?

In many places, doctors and hospitals still expect payment in cash at the time of service. Your regular U.S. health insurance may not cover doctor and hospital visits in other countries. If your policy doesn't go with you when you travel, it's a very good idea to take out another one for your trip.

Traffic Safety and Road Conditions: While in Kenya, you may encounter road conditions that differ significantly from those in the United States. One of the greatest threats to travelers in Kenya is road safety. The information below concerning Kenya is provided for general reference only and may not be totally accurate in a particular location or circumstance.

In Kenya, traffic circulates on the left side of the road, which can be very disorienting to those not accustomed to it. Excessive speed, unpredictable local driving habits and manners, poor vehicle maintenance, bumpy, potholed and unpaved roads, and the lack of basic safety equipment on many vehicles are daily hazards on Kenyan roads. When there is a heavy traffic jam, either due to rush hour or because of an accident, drivers will drive across the median strip and drive directly toward oncoming traffic.

There are often fatal accidents involving long-distance, inter-city buses, or local buses called "matatus." Matatus are known to be the greatest danger to other vehicles or pedestrians on the road. Many U.S. citizens have been killed or seriously injured in motor vehicle-related accidents. Inter-city night-time road travel should be avoided due to the poor road and street light conditions, and the threat of banditry throughout the country.

During the rainy season, some unpaved roads are impassable even with four-wheel drive vehicles with high clearance. Travelers are urged to consult with local officials regarding road conditions.

Travel via passenger train in Kenya is considered unsafe, particularly during rainy seasons, because of the lack of routine maintenance and safety checks. The Kenya Railway service operates only two days a week. The service from Nairobi to Malaba is now only a cargo service and is no longer transports passengers.

For specific information concerning Kenyan driving permits, vehicle inspection, road tax and mandatory insurance, contact the Kenyan National Tourist Organization offices in New York at telephone 212-486-1300 or in California at telephone 310-274-6635. Visitors contemplating adventure tours should contact the Kenya Tourist Board Offices in Minneapolis, Minnesota via the Internet or via telephone at 1-866-44-KENYA.

Aviation Safety Oversight: As there is no direct commercial air service to the United States by carriers registered in Kenya, the U.S. Federal Aviation Administration (FAA) has not assessed the government of Kenya's Civil Aviation Authority for compliance with International Civil Aviation Organization (ICAO) aviation safety standards. Further information may be found on the FAA's Safety Assessment page.

Children's Issues: Please see the U.S. Dept. of State Office of Children's Issues web pages on Intercountry Adoption and International Parental Child Abduction.

Travel Warning

January 14, 2013

The U.S. Department of State warns U.S. citizens of the risks of travel to Kenya. U.S. citizens in Kenya, and those considering travel to Kenya, should evaluate their personal security situation in light of continuing and recently heightened threats from terrorism and the high rate of violent crime in some areas. The levels of risk vary throughout the country. The Embassy will continue to monitor the security situation and provide updates. This replaces the Travel Warning of July 3, 2012, to update information about the current security situation.

The U.S. government continues to receive information about potential terrorist threats aimed at U.S., Western, and Kenyan interests in Kenya. Terrorist acts can include suicide operations, bombings, kidnappings, attacks on civil aviation, and attacks on maritime vessels in or near Kenyan ports. Although the pursuit of those responsible for previous terrorist activities continues, many of those involved remain at large and still operate in the region. Travelers should consult the Worldwide Caution for further information and details.

Kenya initiated military action against al-Shabaab by crossing into Somalia on October 16, 2011, and, on June 2, 2012, signed a Memorandum of Understanding (MOU) whereby it formally joined the African Union Mission in Somalia (AMISOM). Kenyan troops within AMISOM are now actively pursuing al-Shabaab in southeastern Somalia. In response to the Kenyan intervention, al-Shabaab and its sympathizers have conducted retaliatory attacks against civilian and government targets in Kenya.

In the past year, there have been over 30 attacks involving grenades or explosive devices in Kenya. At least 76 people died in these attacks, and around 220 people were injured. There were no U.S. citizens among the casualties. Ten of these attacks occurred in North Eastern Province, mainly in Dadaab, Wajir, and Garissa. Four attacks occurred in Mombasa. Six grenade and improvised explosive device (IED) attacks have occurred in Nairobi, illustrating an increase in the number of attacks and an advance in the sophistication of attacks. Targets included police stations and police vehicles, nightclubs and bars, churches, a mosque, a religious gathering, a downtown building of small shops, and a bus station. One of the deadliest attacks occurred in Nairobi on November 18, 2012, when an IED detonated on a passenger bus in Eastleigh, killing ten. The most fatal attack in Kenya this past year occurred on July 1, 2012, with two simultaneous assaults on churches in Garissa. In this attack, 17 people were killed and about 50 people were injured. Additionally, Kenyan law enforcement has disrupted several terrorist plots, which resulted in the discoveries of weapons caches and other dangerous materials, and the arrests of several individuals.

Multiple kidnappings of Westerners have occurred in Kenya. In September 2011, a British woman was kidnapped and her husband murdered at a coastal resort near the Kenya-Somali border. The British hostage was released in March 2012 after payment of ransom. In October 2011, a French national was kidnapped from a private residence on the popular tourist destination of Lamu Island on Kenya's north coast. She died while in captivity in Somalia. Also in October 2011, two Spanish nationals working for a NGO were kidnapped in a Dadaab refugee camp, in northeastern Kenya. They are still being held. On June 29, 2012, four international aid workers (from Canada, Pakistan, Norway, and the Philippines) were kidnapped in Dadaab. All were rescued on July 1, 2012.

In response to the security threats within Kenya posed by violent extremists, including al-Shabaab, the Government of Kenya announced on December 13, 2012 that all urban refugees (primarily Somalis) should relocate to refugee camps. The Kenyan government is currently conducting sweeps at checkpoints and in predominantly Somali-inhabited areas of Kenya searching for proof of status in Kenya and sending those who are refugees to camps. U.S. citizens of Somali descent should be aware that they may encounter interruptions in their travel due to these directives. It is very important to carry proof of identity and legal status in Kenya (i.e., valid visa). If you are detained by police or immigration officials, you should request to speak to someone from the Consular Section of the U.S. Embassy in Nairobi. As a result of these recent events and threats, U.S. government employees, contractors, grantees, and their dependents are prohibited from traveling to the North Eastern Province, including the cities of El Wak, Wajir, Garissa, Dadaab, Mandera, and Liboi. Although the U.S. government travel restriction for Lamu has been lifted, U.S. citizens should consider ongoing security concerns following recent events involving U.S. citizens in Lamu, including a sexual assault and threatened kidnapping. U.S. government personnel are restricted from traveling to the coastal area north of Pate Island, including Kiwayu and north to Kiunga on the Kenya/Somalia border. Although these restrictions do not apply to travelers not associated with the U.S. government, U.S. citizens already in Kenya should take these restrictions into account when planning travel.

The Embassy regularly reviews the security of these areas for possible modification.

Clashes occasionally occur in and around Isiolo and Moyale, both in Eastern province, and in 2012 there were numerous instances of sporadic violence and protests elsewhere in the country. Rioting occurred in Mombasa shortly after a local Muslim cleric with alleged ties to al-Shabaab was killed in a drive-by shooting, resulting in the deaths of three policemen and four church burnings. Demonstrations in Kisumu (Western Kenya) following the murder of two prominent Kenyan citizens in October 2012 turned violent, leaving at least four protestors dead.

More than 160 people have been killed in recent clashes between two communities in Tana River County, in Kenya's Coast Province. While this violence is not directed at foreigners, protests and ethnic clashes are unpredictable. U.S. citizens are advised to check conditions and monitor local media reports before traveling to these areas.

Violent and sometimes fatal criminal attacks, including armed carjackings, grenade attacks, home invasions and burglaries, and kidnappings can occur at any time and in any location, particularly in Nairobi. U.S. citizens, including U.S. Embassy employees, have been victims of such crimes within the past year.

U.S. citizens in Kenya should be extremely vigilant with regard to their personal security, particularly in crowded public places such as clubs, hotels, resorts, shopping centers, restaurants, bus stations, and places of worship. U.S. citizens should also remain alert in residential areas, at schools, and at outdoor recreational events. U.S. citizens should use commonsense precautions at all times, to include the following practices: avoid crowded transportation venues; visit only legitimate businesses and tourist areas only during daylight hours; use well-marked taxis and be sure to lock vehicle doors and keep windows up; lock all lodging doors and windows; carry minimal amounts of cash and credit cards; do not wear jewelry which attracts undue attention; know emergency phone numbers; do not resist or antagonize armed criminals; and always be aware of your surroundings. These measures can help ensure your travel to Kenya is safe and enjoyable. U.S. citizens should avoid demonstrations, political rallies of all kinds, and voter polling places, particularly in the lead up to Kenya's political primaries on January 17 and 18, 2013, general elections on March 4, and during a possible presidential run-off election to occur no later than April 18.

Kenya's last national election, in December 2007, resulted in widespread unrest and violence. Isolated instances of suspected political violence have already occurred in some regions of the country. U.S. citizens considering travel to Kenya during the election period should consider the possibility of civil disturbances, and disruptions of transportation and/or communication systems.

U.S. citizens who travel to or reside in Kenya are urged to enroll in the Smart Traveler Enrollment Program (STEP)in order to receive the most up-to-date security information. By enrolling, U.S. citizens make it easier for the Embassy to contact them in case of emergency. U.S. citizens without internet access may enroll directly with the U.S. Embassy in Nairobi. The U.S. Embassy in Nairobi is located on United Nations Avenue, Gigiri, Nairobi, Kenya; telephone (254) (20) 363-6000; fax (254) (20) 363-6410. In the event of an after-hours emergency, the Embassy duty officer may be contacted at (254) (20) 363-6000. Travelers may also consult the U.S. Embassy Nairobi website for more information.

U.S. citizens should also consult the Department of State's Country Specific Information for Kenya, the Worldwide Caution, Travel Warnings, and Travel Alerts, which are all available on the U.S. Department of State's, Bureau of Consular Affairs website. Travelers may obtain up-to-date information on security conditions by calling 1-888-407-4747 toll-free in the United States and Canada, or on a regular toll line at 1-202-501-4444 from other countries. Stay up to date by bookmarking our Bureau of Consular Affairs website, which contains current Travel Warnings and Travel Alerts. Follow us on Twitter and the Bureau of Consular Affairs page on Facebook, and download our Smart Traveler app, available through iTunes and the Android market, to have travel information at your fingertips.

Intercountry Adoption

August 2012

The information in this section has been edited from a report of the Bureau of Consular Affairs, Office of Overseas Citizens Services of the U.S. Department of State. For more information, please read the *Intercountry Adoption* section of this book and review current reports online at http://adoption.state.gov.

Kenya is party to the Hague Convention on Protection of Children and Co-operation in Respect of Intercountry Adoption (Hague Adoption Convention). Intercountry adoption processing in Hague countries is done in accordance with the requirements of the Convention; the U.S. implementing legislation, the Intercountry Adoption Act of 2000 (IAA); and the IAA's implementing regulations, as well as the implementing legislation and regulations of Kenya.

Alert: Expect Adoption Delays: Kenya and the United States are party to the Hague Convention on Protection of Children and Co-operation in Respect of Intercountry Adoption ("Hague"). As such, all adoptions between Kenya and the United States initiated after April 1, 2008, must meet the requirements of the Hague Convention and its U.S. and Kenya law counterparts. The Government of Kenya is still in the process of amending its laws to mirror the procedural requirements of the Convention.

In late 2010, Kenya adopted a new constitution and the government is currently drafting hundreds of pieces of new legislation required to implement the provisions of the new constitution. Due to this legislative backlog, legislation that will bring Kenya into full compliance with the Hague Convention may not be enacted for quite some time. Until it is, Kenya's Department of Children's Services is willing to make administrative adjustments that will allow it to follow the procedural framework required by the Hague Convention.

International adoptions that meet Hague Convention requirements can now be processed in Kenya. However, until Kenya's Intercountry Adoption laws are finalized, serious delays, expense, uncertainly, and difficulties could still arise with the Hague adoption process. The Department of State therefore advises American citizens to proceed with caution when deciding whether or not to adopt from Kenya.

The U.S. Embassy in Nairobi continues to be in contact with the High Court of Kenya and their Department of Children's Services concerning the processing requirements of Hague adoption cases.

Who Can Adopt? To bring an adopted child to the United States from Kenya, you must meet eligibility and suitability requirements. The U.S. Department of Homeland Security, U.S. Citizenship and Immigration Services (USCIS) determines who can adopt under U.S. immigration law. Additionally, a child must meet the definition of Convention adoptee under U.S. law in order to immigrate to the United States on an IH-3 immigrant visa. In addition to U.S. requirements, Kenya obliges prospective adoptive parents to meet the following requirements in order to adopt a child from Kenya.

Residency: After parent-child placement, prospective adoptive parents must reside in Kenya with the child for at least three months before legal procedures begin. This requirement may be waived for prospective adoptive parents who are adopting direct blood relatives with whom they already have a familial relationship. Prospective adoptive parents may need to remain in Kenya for up to six to nine additional months in order to meet all the legal requirements to finalize their adoption. The adoption hearing cannot occur until the three-month "homestay" (bonding period) is complete. The hearing process may take an additional six to nine months to complete.

Age of Adopting Parents: One of the prospective adoptive parents must be at least twenty-five years old, but neither parent can be older than sixty-five. Prospective adoptive parents must also be at least twenty-one years older than the child they adopt.

Marriage: Under Kenyan law, adoption orders will not be granted to joint prospective adoptive parents not married to each other. Prospective adoptive parents must be married for at least three years prior to being placed with a child. Single foreign male prospective adoptive parents are not permitted to adopt from Kenya. Single female prospective adoptive parents can adopt from Kenya if the court is satisfied of the existence of special circumstances. One or more of the following circumstances may be considered:

- The child is a relative;
- The child has special needs and the applicant is willing and has the capacity to care for the child;
- The applicant has adopted or has another biological child or children over whom she exercises parental responsibility;
- The child has a sibling who is also being adopted by the applicant;
- The proposed applicant is the only person available to adopt the child; or
- Where the applicant is the legal guardian of the child or children appointed by will or in adoption proceedings and the parents die or become permanently incapacitated.

Income: While no minimum income is required to adopt from Kenya, the prospective adoptive parents' homestudy report must show that they can adequately support the child they seek to adopt.

Prior Contact Prohibition: Kenyan law strictly prohibits any contact between prospective adoptive parents and prospective adoptees prior to parent-child placement by a Kenyan adoption society. Child pre-selection is not permitted. The Adoption Committee will likely reject placements of prospective adoptive parents and children to be adopted who have had prior contact. Exceptions are made where prospective adoptive parents are adopting a direct blood relative.

Adopting Relatives: Prospective adoptive parents may adopt relative children. However, the child must still be declared eligible for adoption and be entered on the register of children to be adopted.

Adopting Special Needs Children: The prospective adoptive parents' homestudy report must reflect that they can care for a child with special needs or with medical conditions if the prospective adoptive parents are to be placed with such a child and the prospective adoptive parents intend to proceed with the adoption.

Gay and Lesbian Adoptions: Under Kenyan law, adoption orders will not be granted to gay and lesbian individuals or couples.

Prospective Adoptive Parents' Mental Health: Prospective adoptive parents must be of sound mind, as defined by the Kenyan Mental Health Act.

Prior Convictions for offences Against Children: Under Kenyan law, adoption orders will not be granted to prospective adoptive parents who have been charged and convicted by a court of competent jurisdiction for any offence against children under Kenyan laws.

Note: USCIS also requires a criminal background check to be done on all petitioners and may find families ineligible based on prior criminal convictions as well.

Who Can Be Adopted? Because Kenya is party to The Hague Adoption Convention, children from Kenya must meet the requirements of the Convention in order to be eligible for adoption.

For example, the adoption may take place only if the competent authorities of Kenya have determined that placement of the child within Kenya has been given due consideration and that an intercountry adoption is in the child's best interests. In addition to Kenyan requirements, a child must meet the definition of Convention adoptee to be eligible for an immigrant visa that will allow you to bring him or her to the United States.

Eligibility Requirements: Any child who is resident in Kenya can be legally adopted, whether or not the child is a Kenyan citizen or was born in Kenya. However, only children who have been declared eligible for adoption may be matched with prospective adoptive parents for adoption.

The child to be adopted must not be previously adopted or subject to a grant of custody (and has not had prior contact with the prospective adoptive parents) before processing begins.

Relinquishment: When prospective adoptive parents seek to adopt a child who has existing parents or legal guardians, consents must be obtained from:

- Existing parents, guardians, or anyone else contributing to the maintenance of the child under any agreement or order;
- If applicable, parents or guardian(s) of the mother of the child in a case where the mother is a minor;
- If applicable, the step-father who has acquired parental responsibility; and
- The spouse of the prospective adoptive parent, if the spouse is not available in person.

A children's court must commit a relinquished child to a children's home before he/she becomes eligible to be adopted.

Abandonment: A children's court must commit an abandoned child to a children's home before he/she becomes eligible to be adopted.

Age of Adoptive Child: Only children who are at least two years old are eligible for intercountry adoption. If the child being adopted is age 14 or older, he/she must consent to the proposed intercountry adoption.

Sibling Adoptions: Prospective adoptive parents may adopt siblings in Kenya.

Special Needs or Medical Conditions: Unknown.

Waiting Period or Foster Care: A children's court commits an abandoned or relinquished child to a children's home. After six months, if no relatives can be located and no one has come forward to claim the child, a licensed Kenyan adoption society will have the child entered into the registry of children to be adopted. Children available for fostering in Kenya are generally in temporary need of care, and are usually not declared eligible for adoption.

Foreigners are only allowed to foster in Kenya if they have been residents for at least one year and are generally not permitted to travel outside of the country with the fostered child. In the past, U.S. citizens have grown attached to children they foster in Kenya and have been unable to take them to the United States. The U.S. Embassy in Nairobi strongly advises U.S. citizens living in Kenya against fostering children if their underlying intention is to adopt them.

Kenya is party to the Hague Adoption Convention. Do not adopt or obtain legal custody of a child in Kenya before a U.S. consular officer issues an "Article 5 Letter" in the case.

Kenya's Adoption Authority
The Adoption Committee
P.O. Box 46205–00100
Nairobi, Kenya
Tel: 254-020-2228–411 ext 30040

The Process: Because Kenya is party to The Hague Adoption Convention, adopting from Kenya must follow a specific process designed to meet the Convention's requirements. The recommended first step in adopting a child from Kenya is to select an adoption service provider in the United States that has been accredited or approved to provide services to U.S. citizens in Convention cases. Only accredited or approved adoption services providers may provide adoption services between the United States and Kenya.

The U.S. accredited or approved adoption service provider will act as the primary provider in your case. The primary adoption service provider is responsible for ensuring that all adoption services in the case are done in accordance with The Hague Adoption Convention and U.S. laws and regulations. Additionally, Kenyan law requires that U.S. adoption service providers be licensed by Kenya's Adoption Committee and partnered with a licensed Kenyan adoption society. Prospective adoptive parents can obtain a current list of licensed U.S. adoption service providers and Kenyan adoption societies from the Adoption Committee by calling +254 (0)20 2228–411.

After you choose an accredited or approved adoption service provider, you must apply to be found eligible to adopt by the responsible U.S. government agency, the Department of Homeland Security, U.S. Citizenship and Immigration Services (USCIS), by submitting Form I-800A. Once USCIS determines that you are "eligible" and "suited" to adopt by approving the Form I-800A, your adoption service provider will provide your approval notice, home study, and any other required information to the Kenyan adoption authority as part of your adoption dossier.

The Kenyan adoption authority will review your application to determine whether you are also eligible to adopt under Kenyan law. If both the United States and Kenya determine that you are eligible to adopt, and the central authority for Convention adoptions has determined that a child is available for adoption and that intercountry adoption is in that child's best interests, the Kenyan adoption society may provide you with a referral for a child. The referral is a proposed match between you and a specific child based on a review of your dossier and the needs of a specific child in Kenya.

The Kenyan adoption society will provide a background study and other information, if available, about the child to help you decide whether to accept the referral or not. Each family must decide for itself whether or not it will be able to meet the needs and provide a permanent home for a particular child. If you accept the referral, the adoption service provider communicates that to the Kenyan adoption society.

After you accept a match with a child, you will apply to the U.S. Department of Homeland Security, U.S. Citizenship and Immigration Services (USCIS) for provisional approval for the child to immigrate to the United States (Form I-800). USCIS will make a provisional determination as to whether the child meets the definition of a Convention Adoptee and will be eligible to enter the United States and reside permanently as an immigrant.

After provisional approval of Form I-800, your adoption service provider or you will submit a visa application to the Consular Section of the U.S. Embassy in Nairobi, Kenya, that is responsible for issuing immigrant visas to children from Kenya. A consular officer will review the Form I-800 and the visa application for possible visa ineligibilities and advise you of options for the waiver of any noted ineligibilities. The consular officer will send a letter (referred to as an "Article 5 Letter") to the Kenyan Central Authority in any intercountry adoption involving U.S. citizen parents and a child from Kenya where all Convention requirements are met and the consular officer determines that the child appears eligible to immigrate to the United States. This letter will inform the Kenyan Central Authority that the parents are eligible and suited to adopt, that all indications are that the child may enter and reside permanently in the United States, and that the U.S. Central Authority agrees that the adoption may proceed. Do not attempt to adopt or obtain custody of a child in Kenya before a U.S. consular officer issues the Article 5 Letter in any adoption case. The consular officer will make a final decision about a child's eligibility for an immigrant visa later in the adoption process.

Role of Adoption Authority: Kenya's central authority is the Adoption Committee. The Adoption Committee:

- Approves prospective adoptive parents to adopt under Kenyan law after USCIS has approved them to adopt under U.S. law;
- Reviews the prospective adoptive parent-child placement recommendations of licensed Kenyan adoption societies;
- Reviews Article 16 reports on the child to be adopted; and
- Issues the Article 23 Certificates of Conformity once the child has been adopted and entered into the register of adopted children.

The Adoption Committee authorizes licensed Kenyan adoption societies to:

- Approve of children to be adopted;
- Make prospective adoptive parent-child placement recommendations to the Adoption Committee; and
- Issue Article 16 reports on the child to be adopted. The reports should include information on the child's social, medical, and psychological history.

Role of the Court: Kenyan courts participate in the intercountry adoption process at three stages of the process: A children's court commits an abandoned or relinquished child to a children's home. After six months, if no relatives can be located and no one has come forward to claim the child, a licensed Kenyan adoption society will have the child entered into the registry of children to be adopted.

After the Form I-800 is provisionally approved by USCIS and the U.S. Embassy in Nairobi issues an Article 5 Letter, the High Court will grant temporary custody of the child to the prospective adoptive parents for a three-month bonding period. The High Court also appoints a guardian ad litem. At the final hearing, the Director of Children's Services will submit a comprehensive report on the prospective adoptive parents and the child to be adopted. If the High Court is satisfied that all the conditions are met for Intercountry Adoption in the Kenya Children's Act and the Convention, a final adoption order will be made, terminating any existing custody rights and granting full legal custody rights to the adoptive parents. The High Court will also issue an order to have the child placed in the register of adopted children. The adoptive parents can take that order to the Registrar General to get an adoption certificate. They can also take their final adoption order to the Adoption Committee to get an Article 23 Certificate of Conformity.

Role of Adoption Agencies: The U.S. accredited adoption service provider works with a Kenyan adoption society to facilitate adoptions by U.S. prospective adoptive parents in Kenya. The U.S. adoption service provider either conducts or oversees the prospective adoptive parents' home-study to ensure that it complies with U.S. and state law where the prospective adoptive parents' reside. Once the adoption is complete, the visa is issued, and the adoptive parents and child move back to the United States, the U.S. adoption service provider can help the adoptive parents report on the development of the child to the Kenyan adoption society involved in the adoption. Such reports are required under the Kenya Children Act.

Time Frame: Once prospective adoptive parents have a provisionally approved Form I-800, they should expect to spend up to one year in Kenya completing the adoption and securing the necessary documentation. This includes a three month mandatory bonding period with the child, followed by an additional six to nine months for adoption proceedings and administrative matters.

Adoption Application: Please consult with your accredited adoption service provider for more information.

Adoption Fees: Kenyan law prohibits financial transactions between individuals involved in an adoption proceeding. Some payments are permitted, for example, to an adoption society for maintenance of the child, or to an attorney who acts for any of the parties or in connection with an application for an adoption order. Any payment or reward made by prospective adoptive parents or a third party facilitating the adoption for the purpose of making an adoption order is considered illegal. The U.S. Embassy in Kenya discourages the payment of any fees that are not properly receipted, donations, or expediting fees that may be requested of prospective adoptive parents. Such fees have the appearance of "buying" a baby and put the present adoption and all future adoptions in Kenya at risk. In the adoption services contract that you sign at the beginning of the adoption process, your agency will itemize the fees and estimated expenses related to your adoption process.

Documents Required: When applicable, prospective adoptive parents are required to submit the following documents:

- Home study report that was prepared or overseen by an accredited U.S. adoption service provider;
- Recent photographs of the prospective adoptive family;
- Marriage certificate, if married;
- Prospective adoptive parents' Health Assessment or Declaration and a certificate of medical fitness of the prospective adoptive parents, duly certified by a medical doctor;
- Declaration regarding the prospective adoptive parents' financial status, along with supporting documents;
- Employment certificate(s);
- Income tax records;
- Bank references;
- Property ownership records;
- Declaration of prospective adoptive parents' willingness to adopt the child;
- Letter from the U.S. adoption service provider stating that child would be legally recognized as a citizen of the United States without any form of discrimination and that the child would be entitled to the same rights as other U.S. citizens;
- Affidavit from the prospective adoptive parents stating that they will raise and educate the adopted child in accordance with the standards of their community;
- Letter from the prospective adoptive parents and their U.S. adoption service provider showing a commitment to sending reports related to the progress of the child, along with his/her recent photograph to the Kenyan adoption society that matched the prospective adoptive parents and child. Reports must be sent every three months during first two years, and every six months for the next three years, for a total of five years; and
- Certificate from a Kenyan adoption society and a U.S. adoption service provider sponsoring the prospective adoptive parents' application and stating that they are permitted to adopt a child according to the laws of their country.

Additional documents may be requested. All documents submitted to the Adoption Committee must be authenticated.

Bringing Your Child Home: Once your adoption is complete (or you have obtained legal custody of the child), there are a few more steps to take before you can head home. Specifically, you need to apply for several documents for your child before he or she can travel to the United States, such as a birth certificate, a passport or travel document for your child from the country in which he or she was born, and a U.S. Immigration Visa. Review the *Intercountry Adoption* section in this publication and visit the U.S. Department of State Intercountry Adoption website at http://adoption.state.gov.

Child Citizenship Act: For adoptions finalized abroad, the Child Citizenship Act of 2000 allows your new child to acquire American citizenship automatically when he or she enters the United States as lawful permanent residents. For adoptions finalized in the United States, the Child Citizenship Act of 2000 allows your new child to acquire American citizenship automatically when the court in the United States issues the final adoption decree. To learn more, review the *Intercountry Adoption* section in this publication and visit the U.S. Department of State Intercountry Adoption website at http://adoption.state.gov.

After Adoption: Adoptive parents must submit post adoption reports on the child's welfare (with pictures) for five years, every three months for the first two years immediately following the adoption and then every six months for the last three years. Post-adoption reports can be submitted through your U.S. adoption service provider to the Kenya adoption society that made the adoptive parent and child placement. We strongly urge you to comply with Kenya's post-adoption requirements in a timely manner. Your adoption service provider may be able to help you with this process.

U.S. Embassy in Kenya
P.O. Box 606
Village Market
00621 Nairobi, Kenya
Tel: +254 (0)20 363-6622
Fax: +254 (0)20 363-6410
Email: NairobiAdoptions@State.gov
Internet: Nairobi.USEmbassy.gov

Kenya's Adoption Authority
he Adoption Committee
P.O. Box 46205–00100
Nairobi, Kenya
Tel: +254 (0)20 222-8411 ext 30040

Embassy of Kenya
2249 R Street, N.W.
Washington, D.C. 20008
Tel: (202) 387-6101
Fax: (202) 462-3829
Internet: kenyaembassy.com

Office of Children's Issues
U.S. Department of State
2201 C Street, NW
SA-29
Washington, DC 20520
Tel: 1-888-407-4747
E-mail: AskCI@state.gov
http://adoption.state.gov

For questions about immigration procedures, call the National Customer Service Center (NCSC) at 1-800-375-5283 (TTY 1-800-767-1833).

International Parental Child Abduction

December 2012

The information in this section has been edited from a report of the State Department Bureau of Consular Affairs, Office of Overseas Citizens Services. For more information, please review current reports online at www.travel.state.gov/abduction.

Disclaimer: The information in this flyer is provided for general information only, is not intended to be legal advice, and may change without notice. Questions involving interpretation of law should be addressed to an attorney licensed to practice in the relevant jurisdiction.

Hague Abduction Convention: Kenya is not a signatory to the 1980 Hague Convention on the Civil Aspects of International Child Abduction (Hague Abduction Convention), nor are there any bilateral agreements in force between Kenya and the United States concerning international parental child abduction.

Return: Legal systems and laws pertaining to custody, divorce, and parental abduction vary widely from country to country. The government of Kenya maintains information about custody, visitation, and family law on the Internet at Kenya Law Reports on Gender and Family. Parents are encouraged to consult with an attorney who specializes in family law in Kenya and who can provide accurate legal guidance that is specific to their circumstances. The Department of State's Bureau of Consular Affairs, Directorate for Overseas Citizens Services, Office of Children's Issues provides assistance in cases of international parental child abduction. Parents are strongly encouraged to contact the Department of State for assistance.

United States Department of State
Office of Children's Issues
2201 C Street, N.W.
Washington, DC 20520
Telephone: 1-888-407-4747
Outside the United States or Canada: 1-202-501-4444
Fax: 202-736-9132
Email: AskCI@state.gov

Parental child abduction is a crime in Kenya. Parents may wish to consult with an attorney in the United States and in the country to which the child has been removed or retained to learn more about how filing criminal charges may impact a custody case in the foreign court.

Visitation/Access: Legal systems and laws pertaining to custody, divorce, and parental abduction vary widely from country to country. Parents are encouraged to consult with an attorney who specializes in family law in Kenya and who can provide accurate legal guidance that is specific to their circumstances. The Office of Children's Issues may be able to assist parents seeking access to children who have been wrongfully removed from or retained outside the United States. Parents who are seeking access to children who were not wrongfully removed from or retained outside the United States should contact the appropriate U.S. Embassy or Consulate in Kenya for information and possible assistance.

Retaining an Attorney: Neither the Office of Children's Issues nor consular officials at the U.S. Embassy or Consulates in Kenya are authorized to provide legal advice. The U.S. Embassy in Nairobi, Kenya, posts a list of attorneys. This list is provided as a courtesy service only and does not constitute an endorsement of any individual attorney.

Mediation: Mediation may be available for both abduction and access cases. The Chartered Institute of Arbitrators (CIArb), Kenya branch, is a professional body for Mediators and Arbitrators in Kenya and can assist in locating a mediator. The CIArb, Kenya branch, does not provide mediation services directly; it provides referrals to private and non-governmental organizations that offer mediation services specific to a client's needs. Mediation is voluntary.

U.S. Embassy-Kenya
U.N. Avenue, Gigiri
Nairobi, Kenya
Telephone: 254-20-363-6000
Website:
http://nairobi.usembassy.gov/
Email: kenya_Acs@state.gov

Embassy of Kenya
2249 R Street NW
Washington, DC 20008
Telephone: 202-387-6101
Website:
http://www.kenyaembassy.com/
Email:
information@kenyaembassy.com

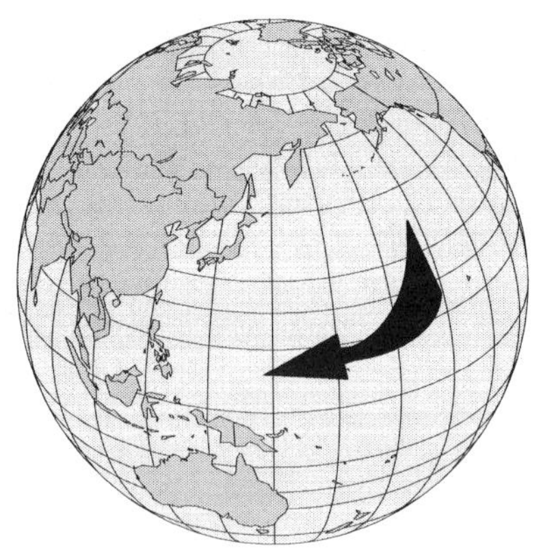

KIRIBATI

Compiled from publications that were available as of February 2013 from the U.S. Department of State, the U.S. Department of Commerce, and the Central Intelligence Agency (CIA). See the introduction to this set for explanatory notes.

Official Name:
Republic of Kiribati

PROFILE

Geography

Area: total: 811 sq km; country comparison to the world: 187; land: 811 sq km; water: 0 sq km
Major cities: Tarawa (capital) 43,000 (2009)
Climate: tropical; marine, hot and humid, moderated by trade winds
Terrain: mostly low-lying coral atolls surrounded by extensive reefs

People

Nationality: noun: I-Kiribati (singular and plural); adjective: I-Kiribati
Population: 101,998 (July 2012 est.)
Population growth rate: 1.228% (2012 est.)
Ethnic groups: Micronesian 98.8%, other 1.2% (2000 census)
Religions: Roman Catholic 55%, Protestant 36%, Mormon 3.1%, Baha'i 2.2%, Seventh-Day Adventist 1.9%, other 1.8% (2005 census)
Languages: I-Kiribati, English (official)
Literacy: NA
Health: life expectancy at birth: total population: 64.76 years; male: 62.37 years; female: 67.26 years (2012 est.); Infant mortality rate: total: 37.68 deaths/1,000 live births; male: 38.91 deaths/1,000 live births; female: 36.38 deaths/1,000 live births (2012 est.)
Unemployment rate: 2% (1992 est.)
Work force: 7,870

Government

Type: republic
Independence: 12 July 1979
Constitution: 12 July 1979
Political subdivisions: 3 units; Gilbert Islands, Line Islands, Phoenix Islands; note—in addition, there are 6 districts (Banaba, Central Gilberts, Line Islands, Northern Gilberts, Southern Gilberts, Tarawa) and 21 island councils—one for each of the inhabited islands
Suffrage: 18 years of age; universal

Economy

GDP (purchasing power parity): $624 million (2012 est.); $606.7 million (2011 est.); $595.8 million (2010 est.); $588 million (2009 est.)
GDP real growth rate: 2.5% (2012 est.); 1.8% (2011 est.); 1.4% (2010 est.); -2.4% (2009 est.)
GDP per capita (PPP): $5,900 (2012 est.); $5,800 (2011 est.); $5,800 (2010 est.); $5,800 (2009 est.)
Natural resources: phosphate (production discontinued in 1979)
Agriculture products: copra, taro, breadfruit, sweet potatoes, vegetables; fish
Industries: fishing, handicrafts
Exports: $7.066 million (2010 est.); $17 million (2004 est.);
Exports—commodities: copra 62%, coconuts, seaweed, fish
Imports: $80.09 million (2010 est.); $62 million (2004 est.);
Imports—commodities: foodstuffs, machinery and equipment, miscellaneous manufactured goods, fuel
Debt—external: $10 million (1999 est.)
Exchange rates: Australian dollars (AUD) per US dollar; 0.963 (2011); 1.0902 (2010); 1.2822 (2009); 1.2059 (2008); 1.2137 (2007)

GEOGRAPHY

Kiribati (pronounced "keer-ah-bhass") consists of 32 low-lying atolls and one raised island scattered over an expanse of ocean equivalent in size to the continental United States. The islands straddle the Equator and lie roughly halfway between Hawaii and Australia.

The three main groupings are the Gilbert Islands, Phoenix Islands, and Line Islands. In 1995 Kiribati unilaterally moved its date line to include its easternmost islands, putting the country in the same date and time zone. Kiribati includes Kiritimati (Christmas Island), the largest coral atoll in the world, and Banaba (Ocean Island), one of the three great phosphate islands in the Pacific. Except on Banaba, very little land is more than three meters above sea level.

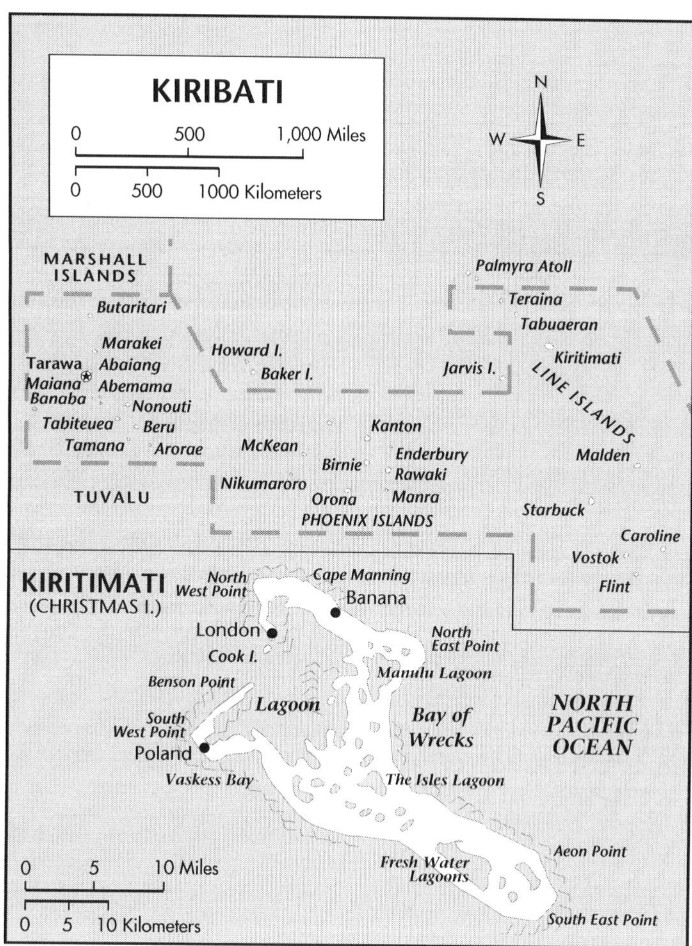

PEOPLE

The original inhabitants of Kiribati are Gilbertese, a Micronesian people. Approximately 90% of the population of Kiribati lives on the atolls of the Gilbert Islands. Although the Line Islands are about 2,000 miles east of the Gilbert Islands, most inhabitants of the Line Islands are also Gilbertese. Owing to severe overcrowding in the capital on South Tarawa, in the 1990s a program of directed migration moved nearly 5,000 inhabitants to outlying atolls, mainly in the Line Islands.

The Phoenix Islands have never had any significant permanent population. A British effort to settle Gilbertese there in the 1930s lasted until the 1960s when it was determined the inhabitants could not be self-sustaining.

Religion

The 2005 census showed that the major religious groups include the Roman Catholic Church, 55 percent; Kiribati Protestant Church, 36 percent; The Church of Jesus Christ of Latter-day Saints (Mormons), 3 percent; the Baha'i Faith, 2 percent; and the Seventh-day Adventist Church, 2 percent. The growing Mormon group claims to have higher numbers of adherents, totaling 15,364 members or 15 percent of the estimated population. Persons with no religious affiliation account for less than 1 percent of the population. Members of the Catholic Church are concentrated in the northern islands, while Protestants are the majority in the southern islands.

HISTORY

The I-Kiribati people settled what would become known as the Gilbert Islands between 1000 and 1300 AD. Subsequent invasions by Fijians and Tongans introduced Melanesian and Polynesian elements to the Micronesian culture, but extensive intermarriage has produced a population reasonably homogeneous in appearance and traditions.

European contact began in the 16th century. Whalers, slave traders, and merchant vessels arrived in great numbers in the 1800s, fomenting local tribal conflicts and introducing often-fatal European diseases. In an effort to restore a measure of order, the Gilbert and Ellice Islands (the Ellice Islands are now the independent country of Tuvalu) consented to becoming British protectorates in 1892. Banaba (Ocean Island) was annexed in 1900 after the discovery of phosphate-rich guano deposits, and the entire group was made a British colony in 1916. The Line and Phoenix Islands were incorporated piecemeal over the next 20 years.

Japan seized some of the islands during World War II. In November 1943, U.S. forces assaulted heavily fortified Japanese positions on Tarawa Atoll in the Gilberts, resulting in some of the bloodiest fighting of the Pacific campaign. The battle was a turning point for the war in the Central Pacific. Britain began expanding self-government in the islands during the 1960s. In 1975 the Ellice Islands separated from the colony and in 1978 declared their independence. The Gilberts obtained internal self-government in 1977, and became an independent nation on July 12, 1979, under the name of Kiribati. Post-independence politics were initially dominated by Ieremia Tabai, Kiribati's first President, who served from 1979 to 1991, stepping down due to Kiribati's three-term limit for presidents. The tenure of Teburoro Tito, Kiribati's second-longest serving President, was from 1994 to 2003. His third term lasted only a matter of months before he lost a no confidence motion in Parliament. (See the next section for an explanation of Kiribati's unique presidential system.) In July 2003, Anote Tong defeated his elder brother, Harry Tong, who was backed by former President Tito and his allies. Tong was re-elected for a second term as president in October 2007, and most recently defeated candidates Tetaua Taitai and Rimeta Beniamina to win a third term as president in January 2012.

GOVERNMENT AND POLITICAL CONDITIONS

Kiribati is a constitutional multiparty republic. The president exercises executive authority and is popularly elected for a four-year term. The legislative assembly nominates at least three, and no more than four, presidential candidates from among its members. Parliamentary elections held in October 2011 were considered generally free and fair.

Recent Elections

The legislature has 45 members: 43 are elected by universal adult suffrage; the Rabi Island Council of I-Kiribati (persons of Kiribati ancestry) in Fiji selects one; and the attorney general is an ex officio member. Parliamentary elections held in October were considered generally free and fair.

Participation of Women and Minorities: There were four women in the legislature, two of whom were also cabinet ministers. Several permanent secretaries and deputy secretaries were women. The president and several members of the legislature were of mixed descent.

Principal Government Officials

Last Updated: 1/31/2013

Pres.: **Anote TONG**
Vice Pres.: **Teima ONORIO**
Min. for Commerce, Industry, & Cooperatives: **Pinto KATIA**
Min. for Communications, Transport, & Tourism Development Taberannang "Peter" TIMEON
Min. for Education, Youth, & Sports Development: **Maere TEKANENE**
Min. for Environment, Lands, & Agricultural Development: **Tiarite KWONG**
Min. for Finance & Economic Development: **Tom MURDOCH**
Min. for Fisheries & Marine Resources Development: **Tinian REIHER**
Min. for Foreign Affairs & Immigration: **Anote TONG**
Min. for Health & Medical Services: **Kautu TENAUA, Dr.**
Min. for Internal Affairs & Social Development: **Teima ONORIO**
Min. for Labor & Human Resource Development: **Boutu BATERIKI**
Min. for the Line and Phoenix Islands Development: **Tawita TEMOKU**
Min. for Public Works & Utilities: **Kirabuke TEIAUA**
Attorney Gen.: **Titabu TABANE**

ECONOMY

A remote country of 33 scattered coral atolls, Kiribati has few natural resources and is one of the least developed Pacific Islands. Commercially viable phosphate deposits were exhausted at the time of independence from the UK in 1979. Copra and fish now represent the bulk of production and exports. The economy has fluctuated widely in recent years. Economic development is constrained by a shortage of skilled workers, weak infrastructure, and remoteness from international markets.

Tourism provides more than one-fifth of GDP. Private sector initiatives and a financial sector are in the early stages of development. Foreign financial aid from the EU, UK, US, Japan, Australia, New Zealand, Canada, UN agencies, and Taiwan accounts for 20-25% of GDP. Remittances from seamen on merchant ships abroad account for more than $5 million each year. Kiribati receives around $15 million annually for the government budget from an Australian trust fund.

Labor Conditions

The law prohibits the employment of children under age 14. Children through age 15 are prohibited from industrial employment and employment aboard ships. Officers from the Ministry of Labor and Human Resources Development generally enforced these laws effectively. Children rarely were employed outside the traditional economy. Some girls worked as prostitutes in bars frequented by crews of foreign fishing vessels.

There is no official minimum wage, but the Labor Ministry estimated the "non-legislated" minimum to be between A$1.60 and A$1.70 (approximately $1.63 and $1.73) per hour. There is provision for a minimum wage at the discretion of the Labor Ministry, but it has never been implemented. The standard wage income provided a marginally decent standard of living for a worker and family, but most of the working population worked within a subsistence economy.

There is no legislatively prescribed workweek. Workers in the public sector worked 36.25 hours per week, with overtime pay for additional hours. There is no law or regulation governing the amount of overtime an employee may work, but there were no known reports of excessive compulsory overtime. Employment laws provide rudimentary health and safety standards for the workplace, which the Labor Ministry is responsible for enforcing.

U.S.-KIRIBATI RELATIONS

The United States and Kiribati signed a treaty of friendship in 1979 following Kiribati's independence from the United Kingdom, and they established diplomatic relations in 1980. The United States and Kiribati have enjoyed a close relationship based on mutual respect and shared interests. The two countries work closely together on a broad range of issues, from strengthening regional security, to promoting sustainable development and addressing climate change, to protecting fisheries and the environment. The United States and Kiribati have signed a cooperative maritime enforcement agreement, or "ship rider agreement," allowing I-Kiribati law enforcement officers to embark on select U.S. Coast Guard vessels and aircraft to patrol their waters. The United States has no consular or diplomatic facilities in the country. Officers of the U.S. Embassy in Fiji are concurrently accredited to Kiribati and make periodic visits.

U.S. Assistance to Kiribati

U.S. development assistance is provided primarily through multilateral institutions.

Bilateral Economic Relations

The United States has no significant trade or investment with Kiribati. Fishing fleets from the United States pay licensing fees to operate in Kiribati's territorial waters. The majority of U.S. tourists visit Christmas Island (Kiritimati) in the Line Islands on fishing and diving vacations.

Kiribati's Membership in International Organizations

Kiribati and the United States belong to a number of the same international organizations, including the United Nations, International Monetary Fund, World Bank, and Asian Development Bank.

Bilateral Representation

Kiribati does not maintain an embassy in the United States.

Principal U.S. Embassy Officials

Last Updated: 1/14/2013

SUVA (E) 158 Princes Road, Tamavua, 679-331-4466, Fax 679-330-5106, Workweek: 0800–1730 (Mon-Thu), 0800–1500 (Fri), Website: http://suva.usembassy.gov/

DCM OMS:	Gigi M. Dever
AMB OMS:	Roniece Briscoe
COM/CON:	Cyndee Crook
FM:	Robert Russell
HRO:	Paul S. Dever
MGT:	Paul S. Dever
POL/ECON:	Michael Via
SDO/DATT:	CDR Scott Sherard
AMB:	Frankie A. Reed
CON:	Wayne Schmidt
DCM:	Jeffrey J. Robertson
PAO:	Joseph Crook
GSO:	Matthew Boullioun
RSO:	Bleu Lawless
AFSA:	John C. Carleton
CLO:	Liza Valverde
EEO:	Brooke Petitti
EST:	Norman Barth
FMO:	John C. Carleton
IMO:	Barry Hall
IPO:	Richard Alex
ISO:	Barry Hall
ISSO:	Rich Alex
LAB:	Noah Geesaman

TRAVEL

Consular Information Sheet

November 3, 2011

Country Description: The Republic of Kiribati (pronounced kir-ree-bas) is an island group in the Western Pacific Ocean. It consists of an archipelago of 33 low-lying coral atolls surrounded by extensive reefs, with a total land area of 800 square kilometers. Kiribati gained independence from the United Kingdom in 1979. Kiribati has an elected president and a legislative assembly.

The capital city is Tarawa. Kiribati has few natural resources, and its economy is very small. Tourist facilities are not widely available.

Smart Traveler Enrollment Program (STEP)/Embassy Locations: If you are going to live in or visit Kiribati, please take the time to tell our Embassy in Fiji about your trip. If you enroll, we can keep you up to date with important safety and security announcements. It will also help your friends and family get in touch with you in an emergency. There is no U.S. Embassy or diplomatic post in Kiribati. The U.S. Embassy in Fiji provides assistance for U.S. citizens in Kiribati.

U.S. Embassy Suva
158 Princes Road,Suva, Fiji
(679) 331-4466
Emergency after-hours telephone: (679) 772-8049
Facsimile: (679) 330-2267

Entry/Exit Requirements for U.S. Citizens: You will need a valid passport with a minimum of six months validity until the expiration date is required for entry. U.S. citizens are not required to obtain visas prior to travel to Kiribati. To see this and other general immigration and visa information, please go to the Kiribati National Tourism Office web site. For information on long-term visit or residency requirements, please contact the Consulate of the Republic of Kiribati, 95 Nakolo Place, Rm. 265, Honolulu, Hawaii 96819, tel. (808) 834-6775, fax (808) 834-7604, or via email.

There is an Airport Embarkation Tax of 20 AUD (Australian Dollars) levied on all passengers leaving Kiribati. Children under two years of age and transit passengers who do not leave the airport and continue their journey by the same aircraft are exempt from this tax. The U.S. Department of State is unaware of any HIV/AIDS entry restrictions for visitors to or foreign residents of Kiribati.

Threats to Safety and Security:

Stay up to date by:

- Bookmarking our Bureau of Consular Affairs website, which contains the current Travel Warnings and Travel Alerts as well as the Worldwide Caution.

- Following us on Twitter and the Bureau of Consular Affairs page on Facebook as well.
- Downloading our free Smart Traveler iPhone App to have travel information at your fingertips.
- Calling 1-888-407-4747 toll-free within the U.S. and Canada, or a regular toll line, 1-202-501-4444, from other countries.
- Taking some time before travel to consider your personal security.

Crime: Although the crime rate in Kiribati is low, visitors should not be complacent regarding their personal safety or protecting valuables. Don't buy counterfeit and pirated goods, even if they are widely available. Not only are the bootlegs illegal in the United States, if you purchase them you may also be breaking local law.

Victims of Crime: If you or someone you know becomes the victim of a crime abroad, you should contact the local police and the nearest U.S. embassy or consulate. We can:

- Replace a stolen passport.
- Help you find appropriate medical care if you are the victim of violent crimes such as assault or rape.
- Put you in contact with the appropriate police authorities, and if you want us to, we cancontact family members or friend.
- Help you understand the local criminal justice process and direct you to local attorneys, although it is important to remember that local authorities are responsible for investigating and prosecuting the crime.

Emergency numbers in Kiribati: The general emergency equivalent to "911" is 999. You can also reach individual emergency services by directly dialing 992 for police, 993 for fire, and 994 for ambulance.

Criminal Penalties: While you are traveling in Kiribati, you are subject to its laws even if you are a U.S. citizen. Foreign laws and legal systems can be vastly different than our own. In Kiribati, you may be taken in for questioning if you don't have your passport with you. It is illegal to take pictures of certain buildings. Driving under the influence could land you immediately in jail. These criminal penalties will vary from country to country. There are also some things that might be legal in the country you visit, but still illegal in the United States, and you can be prosecuted under U.S. law if you buy pirated goods. Engaging in sexual conduct with children or using or disseminating child pornography in a foreign country is a crime prosecutable in the United States. If you break local laws in Kiribati, your U.S. passport won't help you avoid arrest or prosecution. It's very important to know what's legal and what's not where you are going. While some countries will automatically notify the nearest U.S. embassy or consulate if a U.S. citizen is detained or arrested in a foreign country, that might not always be the case. To ensure that the United States is aware of your circumstances, request that the police and prison officials notify the nearest U.S. embassy or consulate as soon as you are arrested or detained overseas.

Special Circumstances: Accessibility: While in Kiribati, individuals with disabilities may find accessibility and accommodation very different from what you find in the United States. Accessibility of buildings, communications, and information for persons with disabilities is not mandated, and there are no special accommodations for persons with disabilities.

Customs: Kiribati's customs authorities strictly prohibit the importation of firearms, ammunition, explosives and indecent publications or pornography. Strict quarantine laws govern the import of any part of plants, fruits, or vegetables, as well as soil, animals, and animal products. Visitors are not allowed to export human remains, artifacts that are 30 or more years old, traditional fighting swords, traditional tools, dancing ornaments, or suits of armor. For more information, please contact the Consulate of the Republic of Kiribati in Honolulu at (808) 834-6775 or via e-mail.

Currency: The Australian dollar is the legal currency in Kiribati. Traveler's checks and all major currencies are accepted by banks and may also be exchanged for local currency at some local hotels. Visa and MasterCard are accepted at most hotels.

Natural Disasters: Kiribati is located in an area of high seismic activity. Undersea earthquakes in the South Pacific region can also generate destructive tsunamis. The government of Kiribati has only limited capability for notifying residents and visitors in the event of a tsunami warning. Visitors should take immediate precautions, such as seeking higher ground or refuge on an upper floor in a sturdy building, if you notice seismic activity and/or unusual tidal activity. Strong winds are common, especially during the cyclone season from November to April. General information about natural disaster preparedness is available from the U.S. Federal Emergency Management Agency (FEMA).

Medical Facilities and Health Information: Health care throughout Kiribati, including Tarawa, is substandard. Medication and supplies are limited and hospital accommodations are inadequate throughout the country. Serious medical conditions requiring hospitalization or evacuation to the United States or elsewhere may cost thousands of dollars. There are currently no direct flights from Kiribati to the United States, and there are only very limited flights from any of the islands of Kiribati to Fiji. A serious medical condition could require an expensive medical evacuation. All water should be regarded as a potential health risk. Visitors should refrain from drinking any water that is not bottled, boiled, or otherwise sterilized. Vegetables should be cooked and fruit should be peeled before being eaten. You can find good information on vaccinations and other health precautions, on the CDC website. For information about outbreaks of infectious diseases abroad, consult the World Health Organization (WHO) website. The WHO website also contains additional health information for travelers, including detailed country-specific health information.

Medical Insurance: You can't assume your insurance will go with you when you travel. It's very important to find out BEFORE you leave whether or not your medical insurance will cover you overseas. You need to ask your insurance company two questions:

- Does my policy apply when I'm out of the United States?
- Will it cover emergencies like a trip to a foreign hospital or a medical evacuation?

In many places, doctors and hospitals still expect payment in cash at the time of service. Your regular U.S. health insurance may not cover doctors' and hospital visits in other countries. If your policy doesn't go with you when you travel, it's a very good idea to take out another one for your trip.

Traffic Safety and Road Conditions: While in Kiribati, U.S. citizens may encounter road conditions that differ significantly from those in the United States. Traffic moves on the left side of the road in Kiribati. Roads in urban Tarawa and Christmas Island, while satisfactory in some areas, are generally in need of repair. After heavy rains, some road sections experience temporary flooding. Vehicle traffic proceeds at a relatively slow rate. Drinking and driving is a common practice, especially on the weekends. Since visibility is poor with no streetlights, drivers should be especially careful when driving at night. For specific information concerning Kiribati drivers' permits, vehicle inspection, road tax and mandatory insurance, please contact the Consulate of the Republic of Kiribati in Honolulu, Hawaii at (808) 834-6775.

Aviation Safety Oversight: The U.S. Federal Aviation Administration (FAA) has assessed the government of Kiribati's Civil Aviation Authority as not being in compliance with International Civil Aviation Organization (ICAO) aviation safety standards for oversight of Kiribati's air carrier operations. Further information may be found on the FAA safety assessment page.

Children's Issues: Please see the U.S. Dept. of State Office of Children's Issues web pages on intercountry adoption and international parental child abduction.

Intercountry Adoption

February 2009

The information in this section has been edited from the latest report available as of February 2013 from the State Department Bureau of Consular Affairs, Office of Overseas Citizens Services. For more information, please read the *Intercountry Adoption* section of this book and review current reports online at http://adoption.state.gov. Kiribati is not party to the Hague Convention on Protection of Children and Co-operation in Respect of Intercountry Adoption (Hague Adoption Convention).

Who Can Adopt? To bring an adopted child to United States from Kiribati, you must be found eligible to adopt by the U.S. Government. The U.S. Government agency responsible for making this determination is the Department of Homeland Security, U.S. Citizenship and Immigration Services (USCIS). In addition to these U.S. requirements for prospective adoptive parents, Kiribati also has the following requirements for prospective adoptive parents.

Residency Requirements: The law governing adoptions requires that applicants for an adoption order be domiciled in Kiribati.

Age Requirements: One prospective adoptive parent must be at least 25 years old, and the other at least 21 years old.

Marriage Requirements: Kiribati law permits both single and married foreigners to adopt a child from Kiribati.

Income Requirements: Income should be above average and prospective adoptive parents should live in a suitable environment. Proof of income will have to be submitted to the central adoption authority.

Other Requirements: An adoption agency shall in placing a child for adoption have regard (so far as is practicable) to any wishes of the child's adopted parents and guardians as to the religious upbringing of the child.

Who Can Be Adopted? Kiribati has specific requirements that a child must meet in order to be eligible for adoption. You cannot adopt a child in Kiribai unless he or she meets the requirements outlined below. In addition to these requirements, a child must meet the definition of an orphan under U.S. law for you to bring him or her back to the United States.

Eligibility Requirements: The prospective adoptive parents, who are domiciled in Kiribati, must obtain written consent from the child's parents or guardians. The prospective adoptive parents, who are domiciled in Kiribati, must obtain written consent from the child's parents or guardians.

Age Requirements: The child must be at least 19 weeks old before an adoption order is made. If a child is above 15 years of age, the prospective adoptive parents will need three months advance notice to the local authorities of the intention to apply for an adoption order.

Requirements for Special Needs or Medical Conditions: In reaching any decision relating to the adoption of a child, a court or adoption agency shall have regard to all the circumstances, being given to the need to safeguard and promote the welfare of the child throughout his childhood.

Waiting Period: Prospective adoptive parents must have had the child in their care and possession for a period of six continuous months before an adoption order will be issued by the court.

Adoption Authority: The Kiribati High Court handles international adoptions.

The Process: The first step in adopting a child from Kiribati is usually to select a licensed agency in the United States that can help with your adoption. Adoption service providers must be licensed by the U.S. state in which they operate. There are no adoption agencies or any non-government lawyers in Kiribati. Attorneys resident in Suva, Fiji, occasionally handle cases in Kiribati. There are two government lawyers in Kiribati, known as "People's Lawyers," who are on volunteer contracts with the Kiribati Government. The People's Lawyer may be contacted at:

Office of the People's Lawyer
Post Office Box 501
Betio, Tarawa
Telephone: (+686) 26312

Prospective adoptive parents may have to seek the assistance of the People's Lawyer. Alternatively, prospective adoptive parents may seek assistance from the Attorney General's office.

Office of the Attorney General
Post Office Box 62
Bairiki, Tarawa
Republic of Kiribati, Central Pacific
Telephone: (+686) 21242

If you are eligible to adopt, prospective adoptive parents have the responsibility of identifying the child themselves and then lodge an application for adoption with the central authority. The central authority does not assist in identifying a child for adoption.

Adoption Application: There is no support system or government body in Kiribati that oversees international adoptions, nor a central point of contact for persons wishing to inquire about adoption in Kiribati. Very generally, and in summary, the process is as follows:

- The prospective adoptive parents, who are domiciled in Kiribati, must obtain written consent from the child's parents or guardians.
- The prospective adoptive parents may then file an Application for Adoption with the Kiribati High Court.
- The High Court will not issue an adoption order unless the child has been continuously in the care and possession of the prospective adoptive parents for at least three months, not counting time before the child turned six weeks of age.
- The prospective adoptive parents must obtain and submit the consent of the child's guardians. The High Court will dispense with this requirement if the relevant persons cannot be located or have abandoned the child.
- The High Court appoints the Solicitor General's Office to conduct an investigation. The Solicitor General's representative conducts a home-study that assesses the prospective adoptive parents' character, financial competence and suitability, and reports back to the High Court.
- The High Court considers whether to grant an Adoption Order based on the report. If favorable, the court grants the Adoption Order.
- The parents take the Adoption Order to the Kiribati Registrar General in order to amend the original birth record to reflect the completion of the adoption.

Time Frame: It generally requires about two months to complete an adoption in Kiribati, from filing the application until issuance of the adoption order.

Adoption Fees: Australian currency is used in Kiribati. A court fee of Australian $13.00 is required to file the motion and receive the Adoption Order.

Documents Required: Kiribati's legislation does not specify any documents that must be presented other than consent of the child's guardians. However, the Solicitor General's representative and the High Court will generally request prospective adoptive parents to submit the following documents:

- Written consent of the child and the child's parents or guardians.
- The child's original birth certificate.
- Adoptive parents' criminal background, financial documents, employment references, evidence of property, etc.
- Prospective adoptive parents' birth certificates, marriage license, and any divorce decrees from previous marriages.
- Any written character references for the adoptive parents, preferably from people of high standing, such as church ministers, school principals, or government officials.
- Any other information tending to show that the adoption is in the best interest of the child. (e.g., a statement as to motives for adoption).

After you finalize the adoption (or gain legal custody) in Kiribati, the U.S Government, Department of Homeland Security, U.S. Citizenship and Immigration Services (USCIS) MUST determine whether the child is eligible under U.S. law to be adopted (Form I-600).

Bringing Your Child Home: Once your adoption is complete (or you have obtained legal custody of the child), there are a few more steps to take before you can head home. Specifically, you need to apply for several documents for your child before he or she can travel to the United States, such as a birth certificate, a passport or travel document for your child from the country in which he or she was born, and a U.S. Immigration Visa. For detailed and updated information on how to obtain these documents, visit the USCIS Intercountry Adoption website at http://adoption.state.gov.

Child Citizenship Act: For adoptions finalized abroad, the Child Citizenship Act of 2000 allows your new child to acquire American citizenship automatically when he or she enters the United States as lawful permanent residents.

For adoptions finalized in the United States, the Child Citizenship Act of 2000 allows your new child to acquire American citizenship automatically when the court in the United States issues the final adoption decree.

The Embassy of the United States, Suva, Fiji

31 Loftus Street
P.O. Box 218
Suva, Fiji
Tel: (679) 331-4466
Fax: (679) 330-2267
E-mail: consularsuva@state.gov
Website: http://suva.usembassy.gov

Kiribati Adoption Authority

High Court of Kiribati
Post Office Box 501
Betio, Tarawa
Tel: (+686) 26451

Office of Children's Issues

U.S. Department of State
2201 C Street, NW
SA-29
Washington, DC 20520
Tel: 1-888-407-4747
E-mail: AskCI@state.gov
http://adoption.state.gov

KOSOVO

Compiled from publications that were available as of February 2013 from the U.S. Department of State, the U.S. Department of Commerce, and the Central Intelligence Agency (CIA). See the introduction to this set for explanatory notes.

Official Name:
Republic of Kosovo

PROFILE

Geography

Area: total: 10,887 sq km; country comparison to the world: 169; land: 10,887 sq km; water: 0 sq km
Major cities: Pristina (capital)
Climate: influenced by continental air masses resulting in relatively cold winters with heavy snowfall and hot, dry summers and autumns; Mediterranean and alpine influences create regional variation; maximum rainfall between October and December
Terrain: flat fluvial basin with an elevation of 400-700 m above sea level surrounded by several high mountain ranges with elevations of 2,000 to 2,500 m

People

Nationality: noun: Kosovar (Albanian), Kosovac (Serbian); adjective: Kosovar (Albanian), Kosovski (Serbian)
Population: 1,836,529 (July 2012 est.)
Population growth rate:
Ethnic groups: Albanians 92%, other (Serb, Bosniak, Gorani, Roma, Turk, Ashkali, Egyptian) 8% (2008)
Religions: Muslim, Serbian Orthodox, Roman Catholic
Languages: Albanian (official), Serbian (official), Bosnian, Turkish, Roma
Unemployment rate: 45.3% (2011 est.)
Work force: 800,000 (2011 est.

Government

Type: republic
Independence: 17 February 2008
Constitution: adopted by the Kosovo Assembly 9 April 2008; effective 15 June 2008
Political subdivisions: 37 municipalities (Albanian: komunat, singular—komuna; Serbian: opstine, singular—opstina)
Suffrage: 18 years of age; universal

Economy

GDP (purchasing power parity): $13.56 billion (2012 est.); $13.02 billion (2011 est.); $12.41 billion (2010 est.); $11.94 billion (2009 est.)
GDP real growth rate: 3.8% (2012 est.); 5% (2011 est.); 3.9% (2010 est.); 2.9% (2009 est.)
GDP per capita (PPP): $7,400 (2011 est.); $6,500 (2011 est.); $6,400 (2010 est.); $5,300 (2009 est.)
Natural resources: nickel, lead, zinc, magnesium, lignite, kaolin, chrome, bauxite
Agriculture products: wheat, corn, berries, potatoes, peppers, fruit; dairy, livestock; fish
Industries: mineral mining, construction materials, base metals, leather, machinery, appliances, foodstuffs and beverages, textiles
Exports: $419 million (2011 est.); $400 million (2007 est.)
Exports—commodities: mining and processed metal products, scrap metals, leather products, machinery, appliances, prepared foodstuffs, beverages and tobacco, vegetable products, textile and textile articles
Imports: $3.3 billion (2011 est.); $2.7 billion (2010 est.) (2007 est.)
Imports—commodities: foodstuffs, livestock, wood, petroleum, chemicals, machinery, minerals, textiles, stone, ceramic and glass products and electrical equipment
Debt—external: $326 million; $900 million
Exchange rates: euros (EUR) per US dollar; 0.7838 (2012 est.) ; 0.7194 (2011 est.); 0.755 (2010 est.); 0.7198 (2009 est.); 0.6827 (2008 est.); 0.7345 (2007 est.)

PEOPLE

National/Racial/Ethnic Minorities

Ethnic minorities, which included Serb, Romani, Ashkali, Egyptian, Turkish, Bosniak, Gorani, Croat, and

Montenegrin communities, faced varied levels of institutional and societal discrimination, in areas such as employment, education, social services, language use, freedom of movement, IDPs' right to return, and other basic rights.

Religion

Islam is the predominant faith of the majority ethnic Albanian population; the Bosniak, Gorani, and Turkish communities; and some members of the Romani/Ashkali/Egyptian communities. The ethnic Serb population, estimated at 100,000 to 120,000, is largely Serbian Orthodox. Groups that constitute less than 5 percent of the population include Roman Catholics, Protestants, and Jews. Catholic communities are concentrated around Catholic churches in Gjakove/Djakovica, Kline/Klina, Prizren, Janjevo, and Pristina. Protestants have small populations in most cities, with the largest concentration in Pristina. The Jewish community's largest population is in Prizren.

HISTORY

Kosovo has been inhabited since the Neolithic Era. During the medieval period, Kosovo was the center of the Serbian empire and saw the construction of many important Serb religious sites, including many architecturally significant Serbian Orthodox monasteries. It was the site of a 14th-century battle in which invading Ottoman Turks defeated an army led by Serbian Prince Lazar.

The Ottomans ruled Kosovo for more than 4 centuries, until Serbia reacquired the territory during the First Balkan War in 1912–13. First partitioned in 1913 between Serbia and Montenegro, Kosovo was then incorporated into the Kingdom of the Serbs, Croats, and Slovenes (later named Yugoslavia) after World War I. During World War II, parts of Kosovo were absorbed into Italian-occupied Albania. After the Italian capitulation, Nazi Germany assumed control over Kosovo until Tito's Yugoslav Partisans entered at the end of the war. After World War II, Kosovo became an autonomous province of Serbia in the Socialist Federal Republic of Yugoslavia (S.F.R.Y.). The 1974 Yugoslav Constitution gave Kosovo (along with Vojvodina) the status of a Socialist Autonomous Province within Serbia. As such, it possessed rights nearly equal to the six constituent Socialist Republics of the S.F.R.Y. In 1981, riots broke out and were violently suppressed after Kosovo Albanians demonstrated to demand that Kosovo be granted full Republic status.

The Kosovo Conflict and NATO Intervention

In the late 1980s, Slobodan Milosevic propelled himself to power in Belgrade by exploiting Serbian nationalism and the question of Kosovo. In 1989, he eliminated Kosovo's autonomy and imposed direct rule from Belgrade. Belgrade ordered the firing of most ethnic Albanian state employees, whose jobs were then assumed by Serbs.

In response, Kosovo Albanian leaders began a peaceful resistance movement in the early 1990s, led by Ibrahim Rugova. They established a parallel government funded mainly by the Albanian diaspora. When this movement failed to yield results, an armed resistance emerged in 1997 in the form of the Kosovo Liberation Army (KLA). The KLA's main goal was to secure the independence of Kosovo.

In late 1998, Milosevic unleashed a brutal police and military campaign against the KLA, which included widespread atrocities against civilians. As Milosevic's ethnic cleansing campaign progressed, over 800,000 ethnic Albanians were forced from their homes in Kosovo. Intense international mediation efforts led to the Rambouillet Accords, which called for Kosovo autonomy and the involvement of NATO troops to preserve the peace. Milosevic's failure to agree to the Rambouillet Accords triggered a NATO military campaign to halt the violence in Kosovo. This campaign consisted primarily of aerial bombing of the Federal Republic of Yugoslavia (F.R.Y.), including Belgrade, and continued from March through June 1999. After 78 days, Milosevic capitulated. Shortly thereafter, the UN Security Council adopted Resolution 1244 (1999), which suspended Belgrade's governance over Kosovo, established the United Nations Interim Administration Mission in Kosovo (UNMIK), and authorized a NATO peacekeeping force. Resolution 1244 also envisioned a political process designed to determine Kosovo's future status.

As ethnic Albanians returned to their homes, elements of the KLA conducted reprisal killings and abductions of ethnic Serbs, Roma, and, to a limited extent, other minorities in Kosovo. Thousands of ethnic Serbs, Roma, and other minorities fled from their homes during the latter half of 1999, and many remain displaced.

Kosovo Under UN Administration

The UN established the UN Interim Administration Mission in Kosovo (UNMIK), under the control of a Special Representative of the Secretary General (SRSG). In 2001, UNMIK promulgated a constitutional framework that provided for the establishment of Provisional Institutions of Self-Government (PISG).

Under UNMIK's guidance, Kosovo established new institutions (both at the municipal and central levels), held free elections, and established a multi-ethnic Kosovo Police Service (KPS). The KLA was demobilized, with many of its members incorporated into the Kosovo Protection Corps (KPC), a civilian emergency services organization. UNMIK gradually turned over more governing competencies to local authorities.

In March 2004, Kosovo experienced its worst inter-ethnic violence since the Kosovo war. The unrest in 2004 was sparked by a series of minor events that soon cascaded into large-scale riots. Kosovo Serb communities and Serbian Orthodox churches were targeted in the violence. In October 2004, Kosovo held elections for the second 3-year term of the Kosovo

Assembly. For the first time, Kosovo's own Central Election Commission administered these elections, under Organization for Security and Cooperation in Europe (OSCE) guidance.

The main ethnic Albanian political parties were the same as in the 2001 elections, but with the addition of the new party ORA, led by Veton Surroi, and two new Kosovo Serb parties: the Serbian List for Kosovo and Metohija (SLKM) led by Oliver Ivanovic, and the Citizens Initiative of Serbia led by Slavisa Petkovic. In contrast to the previous Kosovo Government, this election produced a "narrow" coalition of two parties, the LDK and AAK. The December 3, 2004 inaugural session of the Kosovo Assembly re-elected Ibrahim Rugova as President and Ramush Haradinaj as Prime Minister.

In March 2005, Haradinaj resigned as Prime Minister after being indicted for war crimes by the International Criminal Tribunal for the former Yugoslavia (ICTY); Haradinaj voluntarily surrendered to authorities and traveled to The Hague to face charges. (Haradinaj was acquitted of all charges on April 3, 2008, but ICTY's Office of the Prosecutor successfully appealed the acquittal and the ICTY ordered a partial re-trial that started August 18, 2011 and continues. Haradinaj is in custody in The Hague.) The Kosovo Assembly subsequently elected Bajram Kosumi (AAK) as Prime Minister; Kosumi's resignation in March 2006 led to his replacement by Agim Ceku. After President Rugova's death in January 2006, he was succeeded by Fatmir Sejdiu.

Kosovo's Status Process

After 6 years of international administration, Kosovo Albanian authorities continued to press the international community to begin a process to define Kosovo's future status.

In 2005, a UN envoy, Norwegian diplomat Kai Eide, was appointed to review progress in Kosovo. Eide reported that there was no advantage to be gained by further delaying a future status process. In November 2005, the Contact Group (France, Germany, Italy, Russia, the United Kingdom, and the United States) produced a set of "Guiding Principles" for the resolution of Kosovo's future status. Key principles agreed by the Contact Group included: no return to the situation prior to 1999, no changes in Kosovo's borders, and no partition or union of Kosovo with a neighboring state. The Contact Group later said that Kosovo's future status had to be acceptable to the people of Kosovo.

The Ahtisaari Process

In November 2005, United Nations Secretary General Kofi Annan appointed Martti Ahtisaari, former president of Finland, to lead a future status process. Special Envoy Ahtisaari's diplomatic efforts addressed a broad range of issues important to Kosovo's future, including decentralizing local government, protecting cultural and religious heritage in Kosovo, economic issues, and safeguarding the rights of minorities. Over the course of 2006 and early 2007, Ahtisaari brought together officials from Belgrade and Pristina to discuss these practical issues and the question of status itself.

Ahtisaari subsequently developed a comprehensive proposal for Kosovo's future status, which set forth a series of recommendations on Kosovo's democratic governance and substantial protections for minorities. Ahtisaari also recommended that Kosovo become independent, subject to a period of international supervision.

He proposed that a new International Civilian Office (ICO) be established to supervise Kosovo's implementation of its obligations under the Ahtisaari Plan. A European Union (EU)-led rule of law mission (subsequently named EULEX) would also be deployed to focus on the police and justice sector, while a NATO-led stabilization force would continue to provide for a safe and secure environment. Pristina accepted the Ahtisaari recommendations, but Belgrade rejected them.

On April 3, 2007, Ahtisaari presented his plan to the UN Security Council. Due to Russian opposition, the Security Council could not reach agreement on a new Security Council resolution that would pave the way for the implementation of the Ahtisaari recommendations.

After several months of inconclusive discussions in the Security Council, the Contact Group agreed to support a new period of intensive engagement to try to find an agreement between Belgrade and Pristina on Kosovo's status. A "Troika" of representatives from the European Union, the Russian Federation, and the United States began this effort in August 2007.

UN Secretary General Ban Ki-moon asked them to report on their efforts no later than December 10, 2007. The German ambassador to the United Kingdom, Wolfgang Ischinger, represented the EU; Alexander Botsan-Kharchenko represented the Russian Federation; and Ambassador Frank Wisner represented the United States.

After an intense series of Troika-led negotiations, including a high-level conference in Baden, Austria, the Troika's mandate ended in December 2007 without an agreement between the parties. In its final report, the Troika stated that it had explored with the parties every realistic option for an agreement, but that it was not possible to find a mutually acceptable outcome.

Independence

Kosovo declared its independence from Serbia on February 17, 2008. In its declaration of independence, Kosovo committed to fulfilling its obligations under the Ahtisaari Plan and embraced multi-ethnicity as a fundamental principle of good governance, welcoming a period of international supervision.

The United States formally recognized Kosovo as a sovereign and independent state on February 18, 2008. As of October 2011, over 80 countries had recognized Kosovo's independence, including 22 of 27 EU member states, all of its neighbors (except Serbia), and other states from the Americas, Africa, and Asia.

Shortly after independence, a number of states established an International Steering Group (ISG) for Kosovo that appointed Dutch diplomat Pieter Feith as International Civilian Representative (ICR) and head of the International Civilian Office (ICO), charged with ensuring Kosovo's implementation of the Ahtisaari Plan and supporting Kosovo's European integration. As part of its commitment to the Ahtisaari Plan, the Kosovo Government rapidly enacted after independence laws on minority protection, decentralization, special protection zones for Serb cultural and religious sites, local self-government, and municipal boundaries.

The Kosovo Assembly approved a constitution in April 2008, which entered into force on June 15, 2008. ICR Feith certified that the constitution was in accordance with the Ahtisaari Plan. At the time of certification, ICR Feith also congratulated Kosovo on a modern constitution that "provides comprehensive rights for members of communities as well as effective guarantees for the protection of the national, linguistic and religious identity of all communities." More information on the role of the ICO in Kosovo can be found at: http://www.ico-kos.org/.

Post-Independence

In 2008, the North Atlantic Council authorized NATO's Kosovo Force (KFOR) to initiate Ahtisaari-recommended tasks to supervise the dissolution of the Kosovo Protection Corps (KPC) and to supervise and support the stand-up of a multi-ethnic, civilian-controlled Kosovo Security Force (KSF). KFOR coordinates with EULEX and the Kosovo Police as third responder to security events as well as with other international institutions to support the development of a stable, democratic, multi-ethnic, and secure Kosovo. U.S. KFOR's area of responsibility encompasses a number of significant Kosovo Serb enclaves in Kosovo. It has made a concerted effort to build confidence in local communities, supporting local infrastructure improvements such as building a new community center and reaching out to local leaders in person and on Serb radio and TV.

The KPC was deactivated on January 20, 2009, and officially dissolved on June 14, 2009. The KSF was activated on January 21, 2009, with Lt. General Sylejman Selimi as the commander and the selection of 1,400 KPC members to join the KSF. KFOR began the process of organizing, training, and equipping the new force, as well as recruiting multi-ethnic personnel to join the KSF. The KSF and its ministry reached initial operating capability in September 2009.

On December 9, 2008, the EU rule of law mission, EULEX, reached initial operating capability by deploying more than 1,000 police, judges, prosecutors, and customs officers throughout Kosovo. As EULEX ramped up, UNMIK ended its police role in Kosovo and scaled back its presence drastically, as directed by UN Secretary General Ban Ki-Moon. EULEX reached full operational capability in April 2009.

In 2009, NATO decided to begin downsizing KFOR, through a conditions-based assessments of an improved security and political situation in Kosovo. KFOR completed the first phase of downsizing in early 2010, bringing troop levels to approximately 10,000. Based on the improving security situation in Kosovo, in March 2011 KFOR completed the second phase of downsizing, bringing troop levels to approximately 6,200, plus a temporarily-deployed operational reserve force

In October 2008, Serbia requested an International Court of Justice (ICJ) advisory opinion on the legality of Kosovo's declaration of independence. Written briefs were presented by 36 countries in April 2009 and by 14 countries in July 2009, with oral statements offered in December 2009. The ICJ released the advisory opinion on July 22, 2010, affirming that Kosovo's declaration of independence did not violate general principles of international law, UN Security Council Resolution 1244, or the Constitutive Framework. The opinion was closely tailored to Kosovo's unique history and circumstances.

In March 2011, the EU launched a facilitated dialogue between Kosovo and Serbia with the declared goals of promoting cooperation and good neighborly relations, achieving progress on the path to Europe, and improving the lives of the people. As of December 2011, agreements had been reached on issues including customs stamps, university diplomas, civil registries, land records, and cross-border freedom of movement. The parties also reached an agreement on integrated border management, whose implementation awaits conclusion of a technical protocol.

GOVERNMENT AND POLITICAL CONDITIONS

Kosovo is a parliamentary democracy. The constitution and laws provide for the authorities and responsibilities of the freely elected unicameral national Assembly, the Assembly-approved government, and the Assembly-elected president. The country declared its independence in 2008 after it accepted the Ahtisaari plan, which provided for internationally sponsored mechanisms, including an International Civilian Office and the EU Rule of Law Mission (EULEX), to support the new government. Multiparty elections for the Assembly, conducted beginning in December 2010, met many international standards, but serious irregularities and electoral manipulations in some areas raised concerns and resulted in a limited re-vote in some municipalities.

The Serbian government continued to operate illegal parallel government structures in Kosovo-Serb enclaves.

Recent Elections

In December 2010 the country held snap Assembly elections, following a November 2010 Assembly vote of no confidence in the government. The elections carried into 2011. On January 9, the government held a re-vote in the municipalities of Skenderaj/Srbica, Gllogovac/Drenas, and Decan/Decani as well as in three polling stations in Malisheve/Malisevo and Lipjan/Lipljan, where the Central Election Commission annulled results due to irregularities and electoral manipulations. On January 23, the government organized a re-vote in the municipality of Mitrovice/Mitrovica as a result of a Supreme Court decision on a political party's appeal regarding failures of the ultraviolet ink and lamps used in the December 2010 round of elections.

Domestic and international observers stated the elections met many international standards but noted serious irregularities and electoral manipulations in some areas, including breeches of election procedures, falsification of signatures on the voters' list, and irregularities in counting. They reported incidences of family voting (male heads of household voting on behalf of female family members) throughout the country. Observers also cited instances of pressure and intimidation of domestic observers.

Following its constitutive session the Assembly approved the new coalition government, led by Prime Minister Hashim Thaci's Democratic Party of Kosovo, and elected Behgjet Pacolli as president on February 22.

On March 30, following a request by opposition parties, the Constitutional Court ruled that the Assembly's election of President Pacolli violated the constitution because there was not a valid quorum to conduct the vote and due to the failure of more than one candidate to contest the election. In its decision the court declared that the Assembly's vote was no longer in force and immediately ended Pacolli's mandate. Political leaders subsequently agreed on a consensus candidate, and on April 7, the Assembly elected Atifete Jahjaga as president. The political agreement was based on significant electoral reform, which continued at year's end.

Political Parties: Political parties could operate without restriction or outside interference, but party affiliation played an important role in access to government services and social and employment opportunities. Clan loyalties also played an important, although unofficial, role in political organizations.

Participation of Women and Minorities: There were 40 women in the 120-seat Assembly. The electoral law requires a 30 percent quota for female parliamentarians. There were no women on the six-member Assembly presidency. In the government there were two female deputy prime ministers and two female ministers (one served concurrently as a deputy prime minister). There were no female deputy ministers. While no women were elected in the 2010 mayoral elections, women represented 31 percent of elected municipal representatives.

There were 25 ethnic minority members in the Assembly, including 13 Kosovo-Serbs and 12 members of other groups, including ethnic Turks, Bosniaks, Gorani, Roma, Ashkali, and Egyptians.

The constitution requires that the Assembly reserve 10 seats for Kosovo-Serbs and 10 for members of other ethnic groups.

Principal Government Officials

Last Updated: 1/31/2013

Pres.: **Atifete JAHJAGA**
Prime Min.: **Hashim THACI**
First Dep. Prime Min.: **Behgjet PACOLLI**
Dep. Prime Min.: **Bujar BUKOSHI**
Dep. Prime Min.: **Hajredin KUCI**
Dep. Prime Min.: **Mimoza KUSARI**
Dep. Prime Min.: **Slobodan PETROVIC**
Dep. Prime Min.: **Edita TAHIRI**
Min. of Agriculture: **Blerand STAVILECI**
Min. of Culture, Youth, & Sport: **Memli KRASNIQI**
Min. of Economic Development: **Besim BEQAJ**
Min. of Education, Science, & Technology: **Rame BUJA**
Min. of Environment & Spatial Planning: **Dardan GASHI**
Min. for European Integration: **Vlora CITAKU**
Min. of Finance: **Bedri HAMZA**
Min. of Foreign Affairs: **Enver HOXHAJ**
Min. of Health: **Ferid AGANI**
Min. of Infrastructure: **Fehmi MUJOTA**
Min. of Internal Affairs: **Bajram REXHEPI**
Min. of Justice: **Hajredin KUCI**
Min. of the Kosovo Security Force: **Agim CEKU**
Min. of Labor & Social Welfare: **Nenad RASIC**
Min. of Local Govt. Admin.: **Slobodan PETROVIC**
Min. of Public Admin.: **Mahir JAGCILAR**
Min. of Returns & Communities: **Radojica TOMIC**
Min. of Trade & Industry: **Mimoza KUSARI-Lila**
Managing Dir., Central Banking Authority of Kosovo: **Michel SVETCHINE**
Ambassador to the US: **Akan ISMAILI**

ECONOMY

Over the past few years Kosovo's economy has shown significant progress in transitioning to a market-based system and maintaining macroeconomic stability, but it is still highly dependent on the international community and the diaspora for financial and technical assistance. Remittances from the diaspora—located mainly in Germany, Switzerland, and the Nordic countries—are estimated to account for about 18% of GDP, and donor-financed activities and aid for approximately 10%. Kosovo's citizens are the poorest in Europe with an average annual per capita income (PPP) of $7,400. Unemployment, around 45%, is a significant problem that encourages outward migration and a significant informal, unreported economy. Most of Kosovo's population lives in rural towns outside of the capital, Pristina. Inefficient, near-subsistence farming is common - the result of small plots, limited mechanization, and lack of technical expertise.

With international assistance, Kosovo has been able to privatize a majority of its state-owned-enterprises. Minerals and metals - including lignite, lead, zinc, nickel, chrome, aluminum, magnesium, and a wide variety of construction materials - once formed the backbone of industry, but output has declined because of ageing equipment and insufficient investment. A limited and unreliable electricity supply due to technical and financial problems is a major impediment to economic development, but Kosovo has received technical assistance to help improve accounting and controls and, in 2012, privatized its distribution network.

The US Government is cooperating with the Ministry for Energy and Mines and the World Bank to prepare commercial tenders for the construction of a new power plant, rehabilitation of an old plant, and the development of a coal mine that could supply both. In July 2008, Kosovo received pledges of $1.9 billion from 37 countries in support of its reform priorities, but the global financial crisis has limited this assistance and also negatively affected remittance inflows.

In June 2009, Kosovo joined the World Bank and International Monetary Fund, and Kosovo began servicing its share of the former Yugoslavia's debt. In order to help integrate Kosovo into regional economic structures, UNMIK signed (on behalf of Kosovo) its accession to the Central Europe Free Trade Area (CEFTA) in 2006. Serbia and Bosnia previously had refused to recognize Kosovo's customs stamp or extend reduced tariff privileges for Kosovo products under CEFTA, but both countries resumed trade with Kosovo in 2011.

The official currency of Kosovo is the euro, but the Serbian dinar is also used illegally in Serb enclaves. Kosovo's tie to the euro has helped keep core inflation low. Kosovo maintained a budget surplus until 2011, when government expenditures climbed sharply.

Labor Conditions

Regulations prohibit exploitation of children in the workplace, including a prohibition of forced or compulsory labor; however, with the exception of trafficking, the government rarely challenged these practices.

Regulations permit children to work at the age of 15, provided the employment is not harmful or prejudicial to school attendance. Regulations set 18 as the minimum age for any work likely to jeopardize the health, safety, or morals of a young person.

Child labor remained a problem. According to UNICEF, in recent years the number of children begging on the streets of towns and cities rose, although the overall number of child beggars remained unknown. While most children were not their families' main wage earners, child labor served as a major contribution to many families' income. In rural areas young children typically assisted their families in agricultural labor. Urban children often worked in a variety of unofficial retail jobs, such as selling newspapers, cigarettes, and phone cards on the street. Some children were also engaged in physical labor, such as transportation of goods.

There is no law establishing a minimum wage. The Social Economic Council, comprised of the government, chamber of commerce, and an association of trade unions agreed in 2010 to set the national minimum wage at 170 euros ($221) per month, which was generally respected albeit not enforceable as law.

The World Bank's Consumption Poverty Report 2009 indicated that slightly more than one-third of the population lived below the poverty line of 1.55 euros ($2.02) per adult equivalent per day, and 12 percent lived below the extreme poverty line of 1.02 euros ($1.33) per day. The average monthly salary in the country was 345 euros ($449).

Regulations provide for a standard 40-hour workweek, require rest periods, limit the number of regular hours worked to 12 hours per day, limit overtime to 20 hours per week and 40 hours per month, require payment of a premium for overtime work, and prohibit excessive compulsory overtime. The law provides for 20 days of paid leave per year for employees and up to12 months of maternity leave.

During 2011 employers often failed to abide by official labor standards due to a lack of government enforcement, particularly with regard to the standard workweek and compulsory and unpaid overtime. Employees often did not report such violations due to fear of reprisals. According to the BSPK, many individuals worked long hours in the private sector as at-will employees without employment contracts, regular pay, or pension contributions paid on their behalf. Employees reported being fired without cause in violation of existing laws and being denied holidays. Women's rights organizations indicated that sexual abuse occurred on the job but went unreported due to fear of expulsion or physical retaliation.

According to union officials, workers in the public sector commonly faced similar mistreatment, including sexual harassment and the loss of employment due to political party affiliation.

U.S.-KOSOVO RELATIONS

The United States established diplomatic relations with Kosovo in 2008, following its declaration of independence from Serbia. The United States has been joined by more than 85 countries in its recognition of Kosovo as an independent, sovereign state.

The United States remains committed to working with the Government of Kosovo and international partners to strengthen Kosovo's institutions, rule of law, and economy and build a democratic, law-abiding, multi-ethnic, tolerant, and prosperous country. U.S. policy priorities are: encouraging private sector-led economic growth so that Kosovo's citizens can prosper; ensuring that Kosovo's society and government are firmly grounded in the rule of law; ensuring Kosovo remains a home for all its diverse peoples; strengthening the institutions of Kosovo's government and civil society required for a strong democratic society; and working with European partners to realize Kosovo's European and Euro-Atlantic integration aspirations.

The United States contributes troops to the NATO-led Kosovo Force to maintain a safe and secure environment and freedom of movement for all of Kosovo's citizens. Since 2008, the United States has been a member of the International Steering Group (ISG) and contributed staff to the International Civilian Office (ICO), which supervised the Government of Kosovo's implementation of the Comprehensive Settlement Proposal, commonly known as the Ahtisaari Plan.

In July 2012, the United States joined our colleagues in the International Steering Group in recognizing the enormous progress Kosovo has achieved, including upholding its commitments to implement the provisions embodied in Special Envoy Ahtisaari's plan and enshrining these into Kosovo law, allowing the end of supervised independence.

Since its deployment in 2008, the United States has contributed staff to the EU Rule of Law Mission (EULEX), marking the first time the United States participated in an EU Common Security and Defense Policy mission. EULEX works with the Government of Kosovo to strengthen rule of law throughout the country and to monitor, mentor, and advise Kosovo police, justice, and customs officials.

In 2011, a European Union (EU)-facilitated dialogue on practical issues, such as the mutual acceptance of university diplomas, began between Serbia and Kosovo, a process that the United States supports.

U.S. Assistance to Kosovo

U.S. Government assistance aims to help Kosovo become a stable, democratic, and economically viable country within Europe, offering equal opportunity and protections to all its citizens. A fact sheet on U.S. assistance to Kosovo can be found here.

Bilateral Economic Relations

U.S. investors in Kosovo are involved with projects in the construction, energy, and real estate development sectors. Kosovo has been designated as a beneficiary country under the Generalized System of Preferences (GSP) program, under which a wide range of products that Kosovo might seek to export are eligible for duty-free entry to the United States. While there are few companies that have taken advantage of this designation, the GSP program provides an incentive for investors to produce in Kosovo and export selected products duty-free to the U.S. market.

Kosovo's Membership in International Organizations

Kosovo joined the International Monetary Fund and the World Bank in 2009. It is is not a member of the United Nations. It has a number of diplomatic missions and consular posts worldwide.

Bilateral Representation

Kosovo maintains an embassy in the United States at 1101 30th Street, NW, Suite 330/340, Washington, DC, 20007 (tel. 202-380-3581).

Principal U.S. Embassy Officials

Last Updated: 1/14/2013

PRISTINA (E) Nazim Hikmet St. No. 30, 381-38-59593000, Fax 381-38-549890, INMARSAT Tel 873-762-029-495, Workweek: M-F, 8:00-17:00, Website: http://pristina.state.gov/

DCM OMS:	Veronica D. Boring
AMB OMS:	Mary Anne Green
DHS/ICE:	James Plitt (Vienna)
ECON/COM:	Andrea J. Tomaszewicz
HRO:	Connie Oestreich
ICITAP:	Darrel Hart
MGT:	Terry A. Alston
POL/ECON:	Dana M. Brown
SDO/DATT:	COL James Kott
AMB:	Tracey Jacobson
CON:	Carolyn M. Gorman
DCM:	Kelly Degnan
PAO:	Paul Engelstad
RSO:	Stephen W. Dewitt
AID:	Maureen Shauket
FMO:	Connie Oestreich
ICASS Chair:	Darrel Hart
IMO:	Ricardo Cabrera
ISO:	Sean Crago
ISSO:	Sean Crago
State ICASS:	Brett Oestreich

TRAVEL

Consular Information Sheet

March 12, 2012

Country Description: Kosovo declared independence in February 2008. While Kosovo's government and institutions have sole responsibility for administration of the state, the international presence remains active, including police and NATO military forces. The UN Interim Administration Mission in Kosovo (UNMIK) transferred rule of law functions to the European Union Rule of Law Mission (EULEX) on December 9, 2008. Civilian institutions, including the criminal justice system, are not yet fully functioning at a level consistent with Western standards. Kosovo is a cash economy. The currency used throughout Kosovo is the Euro. Tourist facilities are very limited.

Traveler Enrollment Program (STEP)/Embassy Location: If you are going to live in or visit Kosovo, please take the time to tell our Embassy in Skopje, Macedonia about your trip. If you enroll, we can keep you up to date with important safety and security announcements. It will also help your friends and family get in touch with you in an emergency.

U.S. Embassy Pristina
30 Nazim Hikmet Street (Dragodan area)
Pristina, Kosovo
Telephone: (381) 38-5959–3000
Facsimile: (381) 38-548-614 or (381) 38-549-890
Email address:
consularpristina@state.gov

At this time U.S. Embassy Pristina provides only emergency services to U.S. citizens. U.S. Embassy Skopje, Macedonia, provides all routine consular services such as passport and visa processing.

U.S. Embassy Skopje
Samoilova 21, 1000 Skopje, Macedonia
Telephone: (389) (2) 310-2000
Emergency after-hours telephone: (389) (2) 310-2000
Facsimile: (389) (2) 310-2299
Email address:
SkopjeACSMailbox@state.gov

Entry/Exit Requirements for U.S. Citizens: Contact the Embassy of Kosovo for additional information about visa types. Visit the Kosovo Ministry of Foreign Affairs website for updates on general visa information. U.S. citizens need a passport to enter Kosovo. No visa is required, but visitors might need documentation stating the purpose of their visit. Generally, visitors entering Kosovo are permitted to stay for up to 90 days. Persons who wish to stay beyond 90 days will need to register with the Directorate for Migration and Foreigners located in the Main Police Headquarters in Pristina. If you intend to work, study, or remain longer than 90 days in Kosovo, you should contact the Directorate for Migration and Foreigners prior to your arrival in Kosovo to obtain information about requirements for visitors in these categories.

The telephone numbers are (381) 38-5080–1224; (381) 38-5080–1422; (381) 38-5080–1296; Fax is (381) 38-5080–1419 and by email. The Kosovo Ministry of Foreign Affairs website includes contact information for the Embassy of Kosovo in the United States, which can help you with additional information on how to apply for a residency permit.

Kosovo is an independent, sovereign country, but Serbia still considers Kosovo to be part of Serbia. As a consequence, Serbian border officials will prevent U.S. citizens from entering Serbia from Kosovo without first having entered Serbia and obtained a Serbian entry stamp from a border crossing point that is not a border crossing point between Kosovo and Serbia.

For example, if travelers enter Serbia from Belgrade airport or neighboring Macedonia or Montenegro, and receive a Serbian entry stamp upon entry, they may travel through Serbia to Kosovo, and then back into Serbia from Kosovo without a problem. If they first enter Kosovo from a country other than Serbia, and then try to cross into Serbia from Kosovo, the Serbian authorities will not allow the traveler to enter Serbia. Serbia does not recognize entry stamps by Kosovo border authorities at Kosovo ports of entry, including Pristina Airport.

The U.S. Department of State is unaware of any HIV/AIDS entry restrictions for visitors to or foreign residents of Kosovo.

Threats to Safety and Security: The NATO-led Kosovo Force (KFOR), along with local police and assisted by EULEX police, are responsible for security and stability in Kosovo. Although the overall security situation has improved, inter-ethnic tensions and sporadic incidents of violence continue to occur.

Per standing security instructions, U.S. Government officials assigned to Kosovo may only travel to Leposavic, Zubin Potok, and Zvecanfor official business; these restrictions will remain in place for the foreseeable future. U.S. citizens should be especially cognizant of security conditions at borders between northern Kosovo and Serbia—specifically Gates 1 and 31 at Jarinje

and Brnjak—where political violence has occurred on many occasions U.S. citizens should avoid demonstrations and other sites, such as roadblocks, where large crowds are gathered. U.S. citizens should particularly try to avoid events involving political/ethnic causes, and should be cognizant of important political/ethnic holidays and observances, when the likelihood of political/ethnic violence increases. Even demonstrations that are meant to be peaceful can become violent and unpredictable.

While de-mining programs have proven effective, unexploded ordnance and mines remain in some areas. Telecommunications, electricity, and water systems remain unpredictable.

Stay up to date:

- Bookmark our Bureau of Consular Affairs website, which contains the current Travel Warnings and Travel Alerts as well as the Worldwide Caution.
- Follow us on Twitter and the Bureau of Consular Affairs page on Facebook as well.
- Download our free Smart Traveler iPhone App to have travel information at your fingertips.
- Call 1-888-407-4747 toll-free within the U.S. and Canada, or a regular toll line, 1-202-501-4444, from other countries.
- Taking some time before travel to consider your personal security.

.**Crime:** High unemployment and other economic factors encourage criminal activity. Street crimes, in particular thefts and purse snatchings, are serious problems in Kosovo, especially in Pristina. Criminals often commit crimes while armed, often with handguns. Foreigners can be targets of crime, as criminals assume that they carry cash. Likewise, foreigners' homes and vehicles, and international non-governmental organization (NGO) offices can be targeted for burglaries.

The Kosovo Police (KP)_ carry out normal police functions. EULEX personnel mentor, advise and monitor both the police and other local authorities and institutions; EULEX police also have a limited policing role on certain issues. The judicial system is still developing with international oversight.

Do not buy counterfeit and pirated goods. Not only are the bootlegs illegal to bring back into the United States, by purchasing them you may also be breaking local law.

Victims of Crime: If you or someone you know becomes the victim of a crime abroad, you should contact the local police and the nearest U.S. embassy or consulate. We can:

- Replace a stolen passport.
- Help you find appropriate medical care if you are the victim of violent crimes such as assault or rape.
- Put you in contact with the appropriate police authorities, and if you want us to, we can contact family members or friend.
- Help you understand the local criminal justice process and direct you to local attorneys, although it is important to remember that local authorities are responsible for investigating and prosecuting the crime.

The local equivalents to the "911" emergency line in Kosovo are: Police: 92 from a landline; 192 from VALA (044) cellular carrier, 922 from IPKO (049) cellular carrier; Fire Department: 93 from a landline, 193 from VALA, 933 from IPKO; and Ambulance: 94 from a landline, 194 from VALA, and 944 from IPKO.

Criminal Penalties: While you are traveling in Kosovo, you are subject to its laws even if you are a U.S. citizen. Foreign laws and legal systems can be vastly different from our own. In Kosovo you may be taken in for questioning if you do not have your passport with you. In some places, it is illegal to take pictures of certain buildings. Driving under the influence of alchol is illegal and you may be immediately taken to jail.

There are also some things that might be legal in the country you visit, but are still illegal in the United States; for instance, you can be prosecuted under U.S. law if you buy pirated goods while abroad. Engaging in sexual conduct with children or using or disseminating child pornography in a foreign country is a crime prosecutable in the United States.

If you break local laws in Kosovo, your U.S. passport will not help you avoid arrest or prosecution. It's very important to know what's legal and what's not wherever you go.

Persons violating Kosovo's laws, even unknowingly, may be expelled, arrested, or imprisoned. Penalties for possessing, using, or trafficking in illegal drugs in Kosovo are severe, and convicted offenders can expect long jail sentences and heavy fines.

While some countries will automatically notify the nearest U.S. embassy or consulate if a U.S. citizen is detained or arrested in a foreign country, that might not always be the case. To ensure that the United States is aware of your circumstances, request that the police and prison officials notify the nearest U.S. embassy or consulate as soon as you are arrested or detained overseas.

Special Circumstances: Banking services are available in Pristina and other major towns, although they are not fully developed. There are now a number of banks with international ties that offer limited banking services, including Automated Teller Machines (ATMs), in Pristina and other major towns. If you need emergency funds from abroad, Western Union and MoneyGram have offices throughout Kosovo. While credit cards are accepted in larger stores and in some restaurants, we recommend having cash in local currency for purchases in small establishments.

Travelers entering Kosovo by air or land with more than 10,000 Euros in cash must declare all currency upon entry. Travelers must also obtain and complete a declaration form from the customs officials at the port of entry. This declaration form must be presented upon departure from Kosovo. Failure to comply may result in the confiscation of all funds.

Accessibility: While in Kosovo, individuals with disabilities may find accessibility and accommodation very different from what you find in the United States. The Kosovar Constitution and legislation prohibit discrimination against persons with disabilities in employment, education, access to health care, and in the provision of other state services; however, the situation for persons with disabilities remains difficult. Although the relevant law mandates access to official buildings, it is not enforced and such access is rarely available in practice.

Medical Facilities and Health Information: Health facilities in Kosovo are limited, and medications are in short supply. KFOR cannot provide basic health care to non-military personnel, nor can they provide medical evacuation out of Kosovo.

You can find information on vaccinations and other health precautions on the CDC website. For information about outbreaks of infectious diseases abroad, consult the World Health Organization (WHO) website. The WHO website also contains additional health information for travelers, including detailed country-specific health information.

Medical Insurance: You can't assume your insurance will go with you when you travel. It's very important to find out BEFORE you leave whether or not your medical insurance will cover you overseas. You need to ask your insurance company two questions:

- Does my policy apply when I'm out of the United States?
- Will it cover emergencies like a trip to a foreign hospital or a medical evacuation?

In many places, doctors and hospitals still expect payment in cash at the time of service. Your regular U.S. health insurance may not cover doctor and hospital visits in other countries. If your policy doesn't go with you when you travel, it's a very good idea to take out another one for your trip.

Traffic Safety and Road Conditions: While in Kosovo, you may encounter road conditions that differ significantly from those in the United States. In Kosovo, road conditions can be extremely hazardous because roads are narrow, crowded, and used by a variety of vehicles, from KFOR armored personnel carriers to horse-drawn carts. Many vehicles are old and lack standard front or rear lights. Mountain roads can be narrow and poorly marked, and lack guardrails, quickly becoming dangerous in inclement weather. During winter months, fog can obscure visibility while driving.

Driving safely in Kosovo requires excellent defensive driving skills. Many drivers routinely ignore speed limits and other traffic regulations, such as stopping for red lights and stop signs. Drivers also routinely make illegal left turns from the far right lane, or drive into oncoming lanes of traffic.

The combination of speeding, unsafe driving practices, poor vehicle maintenance, the mixture of new and old vehicles on the roads, and poor lighting contributes to unsafe driving conditions. Pedestrians should exercise extreme caution when crossing the street, even when using crosswalks, as local drivers sometimes do not slow down or stop for pedestrians. A valid U.S. driver's license is required for U.S. citizens driving in Kosovo. The use of seat belts and headlights is mandatory, at all times.

A driver with a blood alcohol level higher than 0.05 is considered intoxicated. Travelers entering Kosovo by road must purchase local third-party insurance. In Kosovo, it is illegal to use a cell phone while driving unless you are using a hands-free device. The penalty for illegal cell phone usage is 35 Euros. Drivers travelling between Serbia and Kosovo are subject to insurance, license plate and other regulations.

Aviation Safety Oversight: As there is no direct commercial air service to the United States by carriers registered in Kosovo, the U.S. Federal Aviation Administration (FAA) has not assessed the government of Kosovo's Civil Aviation Authority for compliance with International Civil Aviation Organization (ICAO) aviation safety standards. Further information may be found on the FAA's safety assessment page.

Children's Issues: Please see the U.S. Dept. of State Office of Children's Issues web pages on intercountry adoption and international parental child abduction.

Intercountry Adoption

July 2010

The information in this section has been edited from the latest report available as of February 2013 from the State Department Bureau of Consular Affairs, Office of Overseas Citizens Services. For more information, please read the *Intercountry Adoption* section of this book and review current reports online at http://adoption.state.gov.

Kosovo is not party to the Hague Convention on Protection of Children and Co-operation in Respect of Intercountry Adoption (Hague Adoption Convention). Therefore, when the Hague Adoption Convention entered into force for the United States on April 1, 2008, intercountry adoption processing for Kosovo did not change.

Who Can Adopt? To bring an adopted child to United States from Kosovo, you must be found eligible to adopt by the U.S. Government. The U.S. Government agency responsible for making this determination is the Department of Homeland Security, U.S. Citizenship and Immigration Services (USCIS).

Residency Requirements: According to the law, there are no residency requirements to complete an intercountry adoption in Kosovo.

However, there is a fostering period of 2 to 3 months prior to the final adoption of the child, where the prospective adoptive parents are required to live with the child in Kosovo, before the final approval for adoption is given to the parents.

Age Requirements: According to the applicable law in Kosovo, the minimum age for prospective parents is 21. If spouses intend to adopt a child, one of the spouses must have reached 25 years of age and the other spouse must have reached 21 years of age. The law has not established an age limit or civil status requirement(single, married or divorced) and how old the prospective parents must be in order to adopt, although it is preferred that at least one of the prospective parents be not older than 55 years.

Marriage Requirements: Marriage certificate (not older than six months)

Income Requirements: Letter of employment with salary or income information (for both spouses, if applicable)

Other Requirements:

- Written request for adoption—signed by both spouses;
- Birth certificate—for each spouse;
- Identification document (true copy of photo ID and passport, issued by State or Federal government agency) for both spouses;
- Proof of Nationality;
- Medical certificate regarding health condition and adoption capability—for both spouses, i.e., general health, illnesses that might impact on one's ability to care for a child, etc.;
- Evidence of economic condition (i.e., property ownership, bank statements);
- Statement from local police authorities that applicants have no criminal record;
- Certificate from a competent authority certifying that parental rights have never been taken away from either spouse;
- Home Study by competent adoption authority in the parents' place of residence.

All documents must be translated into Albanian or Serbian depending on the child's nationality. If a child's nationality is unknown, then documents only need to be translated into Albanian. (Include information about gay and lesbian adoption, and/or adoption by same-sex couples, if available.)

Who Can be Adopted? Prospective parents should contact the adoption authority to learn the requirements concerning children who can be adopted.

The Process: The first step in adopting a child from Kosovo is usually to select a licensed agency in the United States that can help with your adoption. Adoption service providers must be licensed by the U.S. state in which they operate.

If you are eligible to adopt, and a child is available for intercountry adoption, the central adoption authority in Kosovo will provide you with a referral to a child. Each family must decide for itself whether or not it will be able to meet the needs of a particular child and provide a permanent family placement for the referred child.

Bringing Your Child Home: Once your adoption is complete (or you have obtained legal custody of the child), there are a few more steps to take before you can head home. Specifically, you need to apply for several documents for your child before he or she can travel to the United States, such as a birth certificate, a passport or travel document for your child from the country in which he or she was born, and a U.S. Immigration Visa.

For detailed and updated information on how to obtain these documents, review the *Intercountry Adoption* section in this publication and visit the U.S. Department of State Intercountry Adoption website at http://adoption.state.gov.

Child Citizenship Act: For adoptions finalized abroad, the Child Citizenship Act of 2000 allows your new child to acquire American citizenship automatically when he or she enters the United States as lawful permanent residents. For adoptions finalized in the United States, the Child Citizenship Act of 2000 allows your new child to acquire American citizenship automatically when the court in the United States issues the final adoption decree. To learn more, review the *Intercountry Adoption* section in this publication and visit the U.S. Department of State Intercountry Adoption website at http://adoption.state.gov.

U.S. Embassy in Macedonia
Samoilova Street, No.21, 1000 Skopje, Macedonia
Tel: (02) 310 2000
Fax: (02) 310 2299
Email: SkopjeACSmailbox@state.gov
http://macedonia.usembassy.gov

Kosovo's Adoption Authority
Tel: +381-38-200-26-052 or +381-38-212-503
Fax: +381-38-211-940
Email: Fitore.s.rexhaj@ks-gov.net

Embassy of Kosovo
Presidential Plaza
900 19th Street, NW, Suite 400
Washington DC, 20006
Tel: +1 202 380 3581
Fax: +1 202 380 36 28
E-mail: embassy.usa@ks-gov.net

Office of Children's Issues
U.S. Department of State
2201 C Street, NW
SA-29
Washington, DC 20520
Tel: 1-888-407-4747
E-mail: AskCI@state.gov
http://adoption.state.gov

For questions about immigration procedures, call the National Customer Service Center (NCSC) at 1-800-375-5283 (TTY 1-800-767-1833).

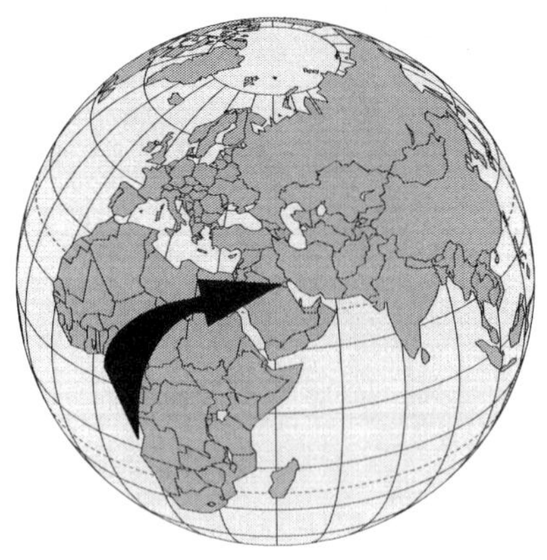

KUWAIT

Compiled from publications that were available as of February 2013 from the U.S. Department of State, the U.S. Department of Commerce, and the Central Intelligence Agency (CIA). See the introduction to this set for explanatory notes.

Official Name:
State of Kuwait

PROFILE

Geography

Area: total: 17,818 sq km; country comparison to the world: 158; land: 17,818 sq km; water: 0 sq km
Major cities: Kuwait (capital) 2.23 million (2009)
Climate: dry desert; intensely hot summers; short, cool winters
Terrain: flat to slightly undulating desert plain

People

Nationality: noun: Kuwaiti(s); adjective: Kuwaiti
Population: 2,646,314 (July 2012 est.)
Population growth rate: 1.883%
Ethnic groups: Kuwaiti 45%, other Arab 35%, South Asian 9%, Iranian 4%, other 7%
Religions: Muslim (official) 85% (Sunni 70%, Shia 30%), other (includes Christian, Hindu, Parsi) 15%
Languages: Arabic (official), English widely spoken
Literacy: definition: age 15 and over can read and write; total population: 93.3%; male: 94.4%; female: 91% (2005 census)
Health: life expectancy at birth: total population: 77.28 years; male: 76.09 years; female: 78.51 years (2012 est.); Infant mortality rate: total: 7.87 deaths/1,000 live births; male: 7.56 deaths/1,000 live births; female: 8.19 deaths/1,000 live births (2012 est.)
Unemployment rate: 2.2% (2004 est.)
Work force: 2.304 million (2012 est.)

Government

Type: constitutional emirate
Independence: 19 June 1961
Constitution: approved and promulgated 11 November 1962
Political subdivisions: 6 governorates (muhafazat, singular—muhafazah); Al Ahmadi, Al 'Asimah, Al Farwaniyah, Al Jahra', Hawalli, Mubarak al Kabir
Suffrage: 21 years of age; universal; note—males in the military or police are by law not allowed to vote; all voters must have been citizens for 20 years

Economy

GDP (purchasing power parity): $165.9 billion (2012 est.); $155.5 billion (2011 est.); $143.7 billion (2010 est.); $138.9 billion (2009 est.)
GDP real growth rate: 6.3% (2012 est.); 8.2% (2011 est.); 3.4% (2010 est.); -5.2% (2009 est.)
GDP per capita (PPP): $43,800 (2012 est.); $42,200 (2011 est.); $40,100 (2010 est.); $39,900 (2009 est.)
Natural resources: petroleum, fish, shrimp, natural gas
Agriculture products: fish
Industries: petroleum, petrochemicals, cement, shipbuilding and repair, water desalination, food processing, construction materials
Exports: $109.4 billion (2012 est.); $104.3 billion (2011 est.); $67.62 billion (2010 est.)
Exports—commodities: oil and refined products, fertilizers
Exports—partners: South Korea 18.3%, Japan 14.2%, India 13.4%, China 9.9%, US 8.7% (2011)
Imports: $24.1 billion (2012 est.); $21.96 billion (2011 est.); $20.07 billion (2010 est.)
Imports—commodities: food, construction materials, vehicles and parts, clothing
Imports—partners: US 11.9%, India 10%, China 9.3%, Saudi Arabia 8%, South Korea 6.3%, Japan 5.9%, Germany 4.8%, UAE 4.1% (2011)
Debt—external: $28.21 billion (31 December 2012 est.); $41.73 billion (31 December 2011 est.); $44.88 billion (31 December 2010 est.)
Exchange rates: Kuwaiti dinars (KD) per US dollar; 0.2801 (2012 est.); 0.276 (2011 est.); 0.2866 (2010 est.); 0.2877 (2009); 0.2679 (2008); 0.2844 (2007)

PEOPLE

Over 90% of the population lives within a 500-square kilometer area surrounding Kuwait City and its harbor. Although the majority of people residing in the State of Kuwait are of Arab origin, fewer than half are originally from the Arabian Peninsula. The discovery of oil in 1938 drew many Arabs from nearby states. Following the liberation of Kuwait from Iraqi occupation in 1991, the Kuwaiti Government undertook a serious effort to reduce the expatriate population by specifically limiting the entry of workers from nations whose leaders had supported Iraq during the Gulf War. Kuwait later abandoned this policy, and it has a sizable foreign labor force (approximately 68% of the total population is non-Kuwaiti).

National/Racial/Ethnic Minorities

Approximately 68 percent of the country's residents were noncitizens, many originating from the Indian subcontinent and Southeast Asia. Societal discrimination against noncitizens was prevalent and occurred in most areas of daily life, including employment, education, housing, social interaction, and health care.

Education

Public school education, including Kuwait University, is free, but access is restricted for foreign residents. The government sponsors the foreign study of qualified students abroad for degrees not offered at Kuwait University. In 2009, approximately 3,318 Kuwaitis were enrolled in U.S. universities.

Language

The official language of the State of Kuwait is Arabic. English is widely spoken in the business community.

Religion

Estimates derived from voting records and personal status documents indicate that 70 percent of citizens, including the ruling family, belong to the Sunni branch of Islam. The national census does not distinguish between Shia and Sunni Muslims. Most of the remaining 30 percent of citizens are Shia Muslims. There are approximately 150-200 Christian citizens and a small number of Baha'i citizens. An estimated 150,000 noncitizen residents are Shia. While some areas have relatively high concentrations of either Sunnis or Shia, most areas are religiously well integrated.

The largely non-citizen Christian population is estimated to be more than 450,000. The government-recognized Christian communities include the Roman Catholic Church, the Coptic Orthodox Church, and the National Evangelical (Protestant) Church. Other recognized denominations include the Armenian Orthodox Church, the Greek Orthodox Church (referred to in Arabic as the Roman Orthodox Church), the Greek Catholic (Melkite) Church, and the Anglican Church. There are also many unrecognized Christian religious groups with smaller populations. There are also an estimated 300,000 Hindus, 100,000 Buddhists, 10,000 Sikhs, and 400 Baha'is.

HISTORY

Archaeological finds on Failaka, the largest of Kuwait's nine islands, suggest that Failaka was a trading post at the time of the ancient Sumerians. Failaka appears to have continued to serve as a market for approximately 2,000 years, and was known to the ancient Greeks. Despite its long history as a market and sanctuary for traders, Failaka appears to have been abandoned as a permanent settlement in the 1st century A.D. Kuwait's modern history began in the 18th century with the founding of the city of Kuwait by the Uteiba, a subsection of the Anaiza tribe, who are believed to have traveled north from Qatar.

Threatened in the 19th century by the Ottoman Turks and various powerful Arabian Peninsula groups, Kuwait sought the same treaty relationship Britain had already signed with the Trucial States (U.A.E.) and Bahrain. In January 1899, the ruler Sheikh Mubarak Al Sabah—"the Great"—signed an agreement with the British Government that pledged himself and his successors neither to cede any territory, nor to receive agents or representatives of any foreign power without the British Government's consent, in exchange for protection and an annual subsidy. When Mubarak died in 1915, the population of Kuwait of about 35,000 was heavily dependent on shipbuilding (using wood imported from India) and pearl diving.

Mubarak was succeeded as ruler by his sons Jabir (1915–17) and Salim (1917–21). Kuwait's subsequent rulers have descended from these two brothers. Sheikh Ahmed al-Jabir Al Sabah ruled Kuwait from 1921 until his death in 1950, a period in which oil was discovered and in which the government attempted to establish the first internationally recognized boundaries; the 1922 Treaty of Uqair set Kuwait's border with Saudi Arabia and also established the Kuwait-Saudi Arabia Neutral Zone, an area of about 5,180 sq. km. (2,000 sq. mi.) adjoining Kuwait's southern border.

Kuwait achieved independence from the British under Sheikh Ahmed's successor, Sheikh Abdullah al-Salim Al Sabah. By early 1961, the British had already withdrawn their special court system, which handled the cases of foreigners resident in Kuwait, and the Kuwaiti Government began to exercise legal jurisdiction under new laws drawn up by an Egyptian jurist. On June 19, 1961, Kuwait became fully independent following an exchange of notes with the United Kingdom.

Kuwait enjoyed an unprecedented period of prosperity under Amir Sabah al-Salim Al Sabah, who died in 1977 after ruling for 12 years. Under his rule, Kuwait and Saudi Arabia signed an agreement dividing the Neutral Zone (now called the Divided Zone) and demarcating a new international boundary. Both countries share equally the Divided Zone's petroleum, onshore and offshore. The

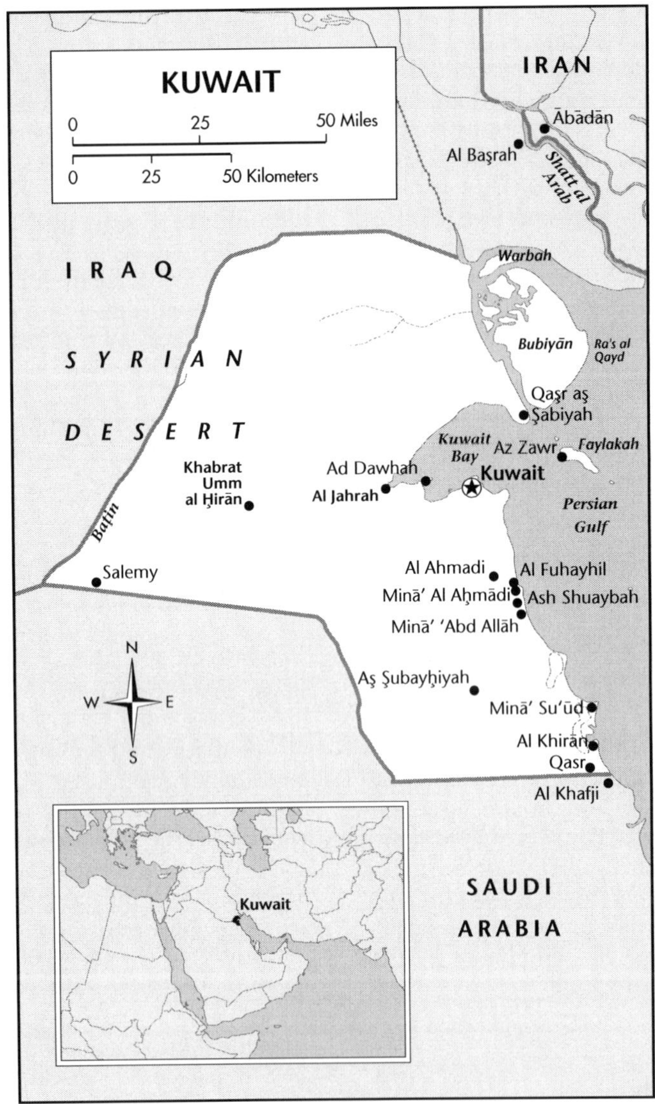

country was transformed into a highly developed welfare state with a free market economy. In August 1990, Iraq attacked and invaded Kuwait. Kuwait's northern border with Iraq dates from an agreement reached with Turkey in 1913. Iraq accepted this claim in 1932 upon its independence from Turkey. However, following Kuwait's independence in 1961, Iraq claimed Kuwait, arguing that Kuwait had been part of the Ottoman Empire subject to Iraqi suzerainty. In 1963, Iraq reaffirmed its acceptance of Kuwaiti sovereignty and the boundary it agreed to in 1913 and 1932, in the "Agreed Minutes between the State of Kuwait and the Republic of Iraq Regarding the Restoration of Friendly Relations, Recognition, and Related Matters."

Following several weeks of aerial bombardment, a UN-mandated coalition led by the United States began a ground assault in February 1991 that liberated Kuwait. During the 7-month occupation by Iraq, the Amir, the Government of Kuwait, and many Kuwaitis took refuge in Saudi Arabia and other nations. The Amir and the government successfully managed Kuwaiti affairs from Saudi Arabia, London, and elsewhere during the period, relying on substantial Kuwaiti investments available outside Kuwait for funding and war-related expenses.

Following liberation, the UN, under Security Council Resolution 687, demarcated the Iraq-Kuwait boundary on the basis of the 1932 and 1963 agreements between the two states. In November 1994, Iraq formally accepted the UN-demarcated border with Kuwait, which had been further spelled out in UN Security Council Resolutions 773 and 883. Despite these steps, bilateral relations between Kuwait and Iraq continued to be troubled into 2010 by unresolved problems related to border demarcation, debt, reparations, and the return of missing persons and archives seized during the 1990 invasion.

GOVERNMENT AND POLITICAL CONDITIONS

Kuwait is a constitutional, hereditary emirate ruled by the Al Sabah family. The country has a population of 3.44 million, of whom 1.1 million are citizens. The May 2009 parliamentary elections were considered generally free and fair.

Recent Elections

The 2009 parliamentary election, held two months after the emir dissolved the National Assembly, was generally considered free and fair. It was the third election in three years, due to the emir's previous constitutional dissolutions of parliament in 2006 and 2008.

Political Parties: The government did not recognize any political parties or allow their formation, although no formal law bans political parties. Well-organized, unofficial blocs operated as political groupings, and members of parliament formed loose alliances. Some tribes held illegal primaries to maximize their members' chances for election to the National Assembly. Assembly candidates must nominate themselves as individuals.

Participation of Women and Minorities: Tribal leaders excluded women from the tribal primaries. Four women served as elected parliamentarians in the 50-member National Assembly.

There are no laws or cultural practices preventing minorities from participating in political life. Members of the minority Shia community held nine of 50 seats in the National Assembly.

Principal Government Officials

Last Updated: 1/31/2013

Amir: **SABAH al-Ahmad al-Jabir al-Sabah**
Prime Min.: **JABIR AL-MUBARAK al-Hamad al-Sabah**
First Dep. Prime Min.: **AHMAD al-Hamud al-Jabir al-Sabah**
Dep. Prime Min.: **AHMAD AL-KHALID al-Hamad al-Sabah**
Dep. Prime Min.: **SABAH AL-KHALID al-Hamad al-Sabah**
Dep. Prime Min.: **Mustafa al-Jassim al-SHAMALI**
Dep. Prime Min. for Economic Affairs
Dep. Prime Min. for Legal Affairs: **Rashid abd al-Muhsin al-HAMMAD**
Min. of Commerce & Industry: **Anas al-Khalid al-SALIH**
Min. of Communications: **Salim al-UTHAYNA**
Min. of Defense: **AHMAD AL-KHALID al-Hamad al-Sabah**
Min. of Education & Higher Education: **Nayif Falah al-HAJ**
Min. of Electricity & Water: **Abdulaziz Abdulatif al-IBRAHIM**
Min. of Finance: **Mustafa al-Jassim al-SHAMALI**
Min. of Foreign Affairs: **SABAH AL-KHALID al-Hamad al-Sabah**
Min. of Health: **Muhammad Barak al-HAIFI**
Min. of Information: **SALMAN al-Sabah al-Sabah**
Min. of Interior: **AHMAD al-Hamud al-Jabir al-Sabah**
Min. of Justice: **Sharida al-MAUSHARJI**
Min. of Oil: **Hani Abd al-Aziz HUSAYN**
Min. of Public Works: **Abdulaziz Abdulatif al-IBRAHIM**
Min. of Religious Endowment & Islamic Affairs: **Sharida al-MAUSHARJI**
Min. of Social Affairs & Labor: **Thikra al-RASHIDI**
Min. of State for Cabinet Affairs: **MUHAMMAD Abdallah al-Mubarak al-Sabah**
Min. of State for Development Affairs: **Rawla DASHTI**
Min. of State for Housing Affairs: **Salim al-UTHAYNA**
Min. of State for Municipal Affairs: **MUHAMMAD Abdallah al-Mubarak al-Sabah**
Min. of State for National Assembly Affairs: **Rawla DASHTI**
Governor, Central Bank of Kuwait: **Muhammad al-HASHIL**
Ambassador to the US: **SALIM al-Abdallah al-Jabir al-Sabah**
Permanent Representative to the UN, New York: **Mansur Ayad al-UTAYBI**

ECONOMY

Kuwait has a geographically small, but wealthy, relatively open economy with crude oil reserves of about 104 billion barrels—about 7% of world reserves. Petroleum accounts for nearly half of GDP, 95% of export revenues, and 95% of government income. Kuwaiti officials have committed to increasing oil production to 4 million barrels per day by 2020.

The rise in global oil prices throughout 2011 is reviving government consumption and economic growth. Kuwait has experienced a 20% increase in government budget revenue, which has led to higher budget expenditures, particularly wage hikes for many public sector employees. Kuwait has done little to diversify its economy, in part, because of this positive fiscal situation, and, in part, due to the poor business climate and the acrimonious relationship between the National Assembly and the executive branch, which has stymied most movement on economic reforms.

In 2010, Kuwait passed an economic development plan that pledges to spend up to $130 billion over five years to diversify the economy away from oil, attract more investment, and boost private sector participation in the economy.

Labor Conditions

The law prohibits child labor. The legal minimum age for employment is 18; however, employers may obtain permits from the ministry to employ juveniles between the ages of 15 and 18 in some nonhazardous trades. Juveniles may work a maximum of six hours a day with no more than four consecutive hours followed by a one-hour rest period. The government made efforts to enforce the law effectively.

The law set the national minimum private sector wage at 60 dinars ($215) per month, which does not provide a decent standard of living for a worker and a family. The government will not issue visas for dependents to accompany workers earning less than 250 dinars per month ($900).

The law limits the standard workweek to 48 hours (40 hours for the petroleum industry), and gives private sector workers 30 days of annual leave. The law also forbids requiring employees to work more than 60 hours per week or 10 hours per day. The law allows for 13 designated national holiday days off annually. Workers are entitled to 125 percent of base pay for working overtime and 150 percent of base pay for working on their designated weekly day off.

Minimum wage guarantees and overtime protections do not apply to domestic workers.

Workers submitted complaints to the Ministry of Labor's Labor Disputes Department; however, the government did not enforce the standards well, and domestic servants and other unskilled foreign workers in the private sector frequently worked in excess of 48 hours a week, often with no day of rest. There were also reports that employers forced domestic workers to work overtime without additional compensation.

The government issued occupational health and safety standards; however, compliance and enforcement by the Labor Ministry appeared poor, especially with respect to unskilled foreign laborers.

The law provides that all outdoor work stop between 11 a.m. and 4 p.m. during the months of June, July, and August, or when the temperature rises to 50 degrees Celsius (122 Fahrenheit) in the shade. The Ministry of Labor monitored work sites to ensure compliance with these rules and recorded 142 violations during 2011.

U.S.-KUWAITI RELATIONS

The United States established diplomatic relations with Kuwait in 1961 following its full independence from the United Kingdom. The United States shares a long history of friendship and cooperation with Kuwait, rooted in shared values, democratic traditions, and institutions. In 1990, Iraq invaded Kuwait. Military forces of the United States and a multinational coalition expelled Iraq in 1991. The United States supports Kuwait's sovereignty, security, and independence, as well as its multilateral diplomatic efforts to build greater cooperation among the Gulf Cooperation Council countries. From 2003, Kuwait provided the main platform for U.S. and coalition operations in Iraq. Kuwait played a key role in facilitating the withdrawal of U.S. combat troops and associated equipment from Iraq, which concluded in 2011. Kuwait is an important partner in U.S. counterterrorism efforts, providing assistance in the military, diplomatic, and intelligence arenas and also supporting efforts to block financing of terrorist groups.

U.S. Assistance to Kuwait

The United States provides no development assistance to Kuwait. The United States provides military and defense technical assistance to Kuwait from both foreign military sales and commercial sources. U.S. personnel assist the Kuwait military with training, education, readiness, and war fighting.

Bilateral Economic Relations

The U.S. and Kuwaiti governments have signed a trade and investment framework agreement, providing a forum to address mutual trade concerns and needed economic reforms. The United States is Kuwait's largest supplier of goods and services, and Kuwait is one of the largest markets in the Middle East. Provided their prices are reasonable, U.S. firms have a competitive advantage in many areas requiring advanced technology, such as oil field equipment and services, electric power generation and distribution equipment, telecommunications gear, consumer goods, and military equipment.

Kuwait's Membership in International Organizations

Kuwait and the United States belong to a number of the same international organizations, including the United Nations, International Monetary Fund, World Bank, and World Trade Organization.

Bilateral Representation

Kuwait maintains an embassy in the United States at 2940 Tilden Street NW, Washington, DC 20008; tel. (202) 966-0702.

Principal U.S. Embassy Officials

Last Updated: 1/14/2013

KUWAIT (E) Al-Masjed Al-Aqsa Street, Bayan, Plot 14, (965) 2259-1001, Fax 965-2538-0282, Workweek: Sun-Thur/0800-1600, Website: http://Kuwait.usembassy.gov/

DCM OMS:	Carol A. Bourne
AMB OMS:	Margaret R. Gray
DHS/ICE:	Edward Richardson (Acting)
FCS:	Dao Le
FM:	Mark D. Mishler
HRO:	Mika I. Mcbride
IBB:	Gaines Johnson
MGT:	Matthew S. Cook
MLO/ODC:	BG Rick B. Mattson
POL/MIL:	Charles R. Broome
POSHO:	Mark D. Mishler
SDO/DATT:	LTC Mark Lewis
AMB:	Matthew H. Tueller (Eta 09/11)
CON:	Wendy C. Ryde
DCM:	Michael J. Adler
PAO:	Tracy Roberts-Pounds
GSO:	Omar Ali (Acting)
RSO:	Assiya Ashraf-Miller
AFSA:	Scott Bolz
CLO:	Cheryl Ray
DEA:	Amembassy Cairo
ECON:	Natalie A. Baker
EEO:	Kimberly A. Morales
FAA/CASLO:	Faa-Amemb Manama
FMO:	Calvin D. Levo
ICASS Chair:	COL Tracy Szczepaniak
IMO:	Stephen Ryde (Acting)
IPO:	Faye P. McClendon
ISO:	Stephen P. Ryde
ISSO:	Stephen P. Ryde
POL:	Catherine E. Sweet
State ICASS:	Emily Katkar

TRAVEL

Consular Information Sheet

August 28, 2012

Country Description: Kuwait is a small, oil-rich constitutional emirate. Foreign workers constitute approximately 90 percent of the labor force. Kuwaiti citizens number 1.1 million of the country's population of 3.4 million, and enjoy the benefits of a generous social welfare system that guarantees employment, housing, education, and medical care. Facilities for travelers are widely available.

Smart Traveler Enrollment Program (STEP)/Embassy Locations: If you are going to live in or visit Kuwait, please take the time to tell our Embassy about your trip. If you enroll, we can keep you up to date with important safety and security announcements. It will also help your friends and family get in touch with you in an emergency.

U.S. Embassy Kuwait
Al-Masjid Al-Aqsa Street, Block 6, Plot 14,
Bayan, Kuwait
Telephone: [965] 2259–1001
or 2259–1002
Emergency after-hours telephone: [965] 2259–1001
Facsimile: [965] 2259–1438
or 2538–0282
Email: KuwaitACS@state.gov

The U.S. Embassy is open Sunday through Thursday.

Entry/Exit Requirements for U.S. Citizens: Passports and visas are required for U.S. citizens traveling to Kuwait. U.S. citizens can obtain visitor visas for a fee at the port of entry in Kuwait. Travelers who overstay their visas may be required to pay large fines before leaving Kuwait. Travelers who leave Kuwait without completing Kuwaiti exit procedures may also be required to pay large fines and/or be imprisoned if they return and attempt to depart from Kuwait. This includes official and unofficial travelers proceeding via Kuwait to and from Iraq and Afghanistan.

Visas can be obtained upon arrival in Kuwait and at this time, U.S. citizens are not charged a fee. Please note that employment in Kuwait requires the issuance of a work visa prior to arriving in country. Working without the proper authorization may result in immigration penalties including deportation or denial of admission to Kuwait. For further information on entry and exit requirements, travelers should contact the Embassy of Kuwait at 2940 Tilden Street NW, Washington, DC 20008, telephone (202) 966-0702, or the Kuwaiti Consulate in New York City, telephone (212) 973-4318. U.S. citizens are urged to remain aware of their visa status while in Kuwait and to strictly follow Kuwaiti immigration laws and regulations.

Kuwaiti officials are extremely sensitive about travel to Iraq. There have been instances in which U.S. citizens, especially dual nationals, have been detained for questioning at ports of entry/exit. U.S. citizens seeking to travel to Iraq through Kuwait have also on occasion been turned around and/or detained. Kuwaitis and non-Kuwaitis, including U.S. citizens, who have been charged with criminal offenses, placed under investigation, involved in unresolved financial disputes, or have unpaid debts, are subject to Kuwaiti government travel bans. The U.S. Embassy can provide U.S. citizens with a list of attorneys. However, the embassy has no authority to remove travel bans. These bans, which are rigidly enforced, prevent the individual from leaving Kuwait for any reason until the matter is resolved. Travel bans can also be initiated by private citizens for almost any reason and may remain in place for a substantial period of time while the case is being investigated.

The Government of Kuwait has strict regulations regarding certain diseases such as HIV/AIDS and Hepatitis. Medical examinations are required for all residency applications and any applicants who are found positive for these restricted diseases will be asked to leave the country immediately and will be permanently barred from re-entry. Please inquire directly with the Embassy of Kuwait before travelling.

Threats to Safety and Security: U.S. citizens in Kuwait should exercise a high level of security awareness and are advised to monitor local news broadcasts and consular messages. The Department of State remains concerned about the possibility of further terrorist actions against U.S. citizens and interests abroad, specifically in the Middle East, including the Persian Gulf and Arabian Peninsula. U.S. citizens considering travel to Kuwait should review the Worldwide Caution.

The threat of terrorism remains high in Kuwait. Terrorists do not distinguish between official and civilian targets. Terrorist actions may include bombings, hijackings, hostage taking, kidnappings, and assassinations. Increased security at official U.S. facilities may lead terrorists and their sympathizers to seek softer targets such as public transportation, residential areas and apartment complexes, schools and places of worship, oil-related facilities and personnel, and public areas where people congregate including restaurants, hotels, clubs, and shopping areas. U.S. citizens are advised to immediately report any unusual or suspicious activity in Kuwait to the Kuwaiti police or to the U.S. Embassy.

Kuwaiti law permits freedom of assembly, although groups larger than 20 individuals must obtain prior approval from the Ministry of the Interior. Still, spontaneous demonstrations take place in Kuwait in response to world events or local developments. At times, even demonstrations intended to be peaceful can turn confrontational and possibly escalate into violence. The Embassy advises U.S. citizens to avoid areas of large gatherings and demonstrations. Exercise caution if within the vicinity of any large gatherings and demonstrations and monitor media coverage of local and regional events.

U.S. citizens in Kuwait should also maintain a low profile, and avoid areas where Westerners are known to congregate. Heightened security awareness should be exercised at hotels and residential complexes, as terrorists have specifically targeted hotel chains perceived as Western along with a variety of Western housing facilities. Military members, as well as civilians and contractors related to military interests, are also potential targets. U.S. citizens should also exercise particular caution with respect to travel to the city of al-Jahra, the Kuwait/Iraq border, and the tank graveyard near Ali Al Salem.

U.S. citizens are also reminded that desert areas and certain beaches contain unexploded ordnance and war materials left over from the 1990–1991 war. Unexploded ordnance results in deaths each year throughout the country. The Embassy urges U.S. citizens to avoid areas "off the beaten path" and not to touch or move objects that are potentially unexploded ordnance.

Stay up to date by:

- Bookmarking our Bureau of Consular Affairs website, which contains current Travel Warnings and Travel Alerts as well as the Worldwide Caution.
- Following us on Twitter and the Bureau of Consular Affairs page on Facebook as well.
- Downloading our free Smart Traveler App, available through iTunes and the Android market,to have travel information at your fingertips.

- Calling 1-888-407-4747 toll-free within the U.S. and Canada, or a regular toll line, 1-202-501-4444, from other countries.

- Taking some time before travel to consider your personal security.

Crime: The crime threat in Kuwait is assessed as low. Violent crimes against Western expatriates are rare, but do occur. The U.S. Embassy advises all U.S. citizens to take the same personal security precautions in Kuwait that one would practice in the United States or any other large city abroad. Reports from Westerners of petty theft and vehicle break-ins are crimes of opportunity and usually a result of practicing poor personal security, i.e. not locking vehicle or hotel room doors, exposing money and jewelry, or leaving valuables in plain sight and unattended. Physical and verbal harassment of women have been reported in Kuwait. Female travelers should keep in mind the cultural differences among the many people who coexist in Kuwait and should be cognizant that unwitting actions may invite unwanted attention. Modest dress, not engaging in "small talk," not making constant eye contact, and maintaining a low profile may deter harassment.

The Kuwaiti police accept crime reports at the police station with jurisdiction over the area where the crime occurred. If filing a crime report, it is advisable that the U.S. citizen be accompanied by a person who speaks Arabic or by a local attorney. The Embassy's List of Attorneys is available on the Embassy website. Filing a crime report can take several hours as a police investigator will take the victim's statement orally while composing his investigative report. In all cases of abuse, the victim must obtain a medical report from a Kuwaiti hospital in order to file a police report.

Don't buy counterfeit and pirated goods, even if they are widely available. Not only are the bootlegs illegal in the United States, if you purchase them you may also be breaking local law.

Victims of Crime: If you or someone you know becomes the victim of a crime abroad, you should contact the local police and the nearest U.S. embassy or consulate. We can:

- Replace a stolen passport.

- Help you find appropriate medical care if you are the victim of violent crimes such as assault or rape.

- Put you in contact with the appropriate police authorities, and if you want us to, we can contact family members or friend.

- Help you understand the local criminal justice process and direct you to local attorneys, although it is important to remember that local authorities are responsible for investigating and prosecuting the crime.

The local equivalent of the "911" emergency line in Kuwait is "112" and can be reached 24 hours a day, seven days a week. The quality and range of services provided by the emergency line are not equivalent to those provided in the United States. All U.S. citizens are advised to carry a mobile phone at all times in Kuwait.

Criminal Penalties: While you are traveling in Kuwait, you are subject to its laws even if you are a U.S. citizen. Foreign laws and legal systems can be vastly different than our own. In some places you may be taken in for questioning if you don't have your passport with you. In some places, it is illegal to take pictures of certain buildings. In some places driving under the influence could land you immediately in jail. These criminal penalties will vary from country to country. There are also some things that might be legal in the country you visit, but still illegal in the United States, and you can be prosecuted under U.S. law if you buy pirated goods. Engaging in sexual conduct with children or using or disseminating child pornography in a foreign country is a crime prosecutable in the United States. If you break local laws in Kuwait, your U.S. passport won't help you avoid arrest or prosecution. It's very important to know what's legal and what's not where you are going. If arrested abroad, a citizen must go through the foreign legal process for being charged or indicted, prosecuted, possibly convicted and sentenced, and for any appeals process. Within this framework, U.S. consular officers provide a wide variety of services to U.S. citizens arrested abroad and their families. Persons violating Kuwaiti laws, even unknowingly, may be expelled, arrested, or imprisoned. Alcohol is illegal; possession of it or driving under the influence could result in your immediate imprisonment. Penalties for possession, use, or trafficking in illegal drugs in Kuwait are severe, and convicted offenders can expect long jail sentences and heavy fines.

While some countries will automatically notify the nearest U.S. Embassy or Consulate if a U.S. citizen is detained or arrested in a foreign country, that might not always be the case. To ensure that the United States is aware of your circumstances, request that the police and prison officials notify the nearest U.S. embassy or consulate as soon as you are arrested or detained overseas.

Special Circumstances: The workweek in Kuwait is Sunday through Thursday for most businesses, government offices, and commercial banks.

The Government of Kuwait does not recognize dual nationality. Kuwaiti authorities have confiscated the U.S. passports of U.S. citizens and U.S.-Kuwaiti dual nationals when they have applied for Kuwaiti citizenship documents such as passports. This does not constitute loss of U.S. citizenship but should be reported to the U.S. Embassy in Kuwait.

Kuwaiti customs authorities enforce strict regulations concerning temporary importation into or export from Kuwait of such items as firearms, religious materials, pornography, and alcohol. Alcohol, pork products, and pornography are illegal in Kuwait. Travelers with prescription medications should carry them in their original packaging or bottle, as dispensed, and carry a copy of their prescription in case customs authorities question their importation into Kuwait. Kuwaiti customs authorities screen the baggage of all travelers entering Kuwait. It is advisable to contact the Embassy of Kuwait in Washington, D.C. or Kuwait's Consulates in Los Angeles or New York for specific information regarding customs requirements.

Photographing government and public buildings, military installations, and economic infrastructure, particularly that related to the oil industry, is against the law and can result in arrest, investigation, and prosecution. Also, some traditionally dressed women find being photographed to be offensive and may complain to the local police. If photographing public scenes or persons, visitors should take care to ask permission beforehand so as to not cause offense that could lead to an official complaint to the authorities.

Humiliating or insulting a person, including a police officer or a public official, is a crime in Kuwait similar to disorderly conduct or harassment in the United States. A person charged with humiliating or insulting another is subject to police investigation and possible prosecution and imprisonment. Persons under investigation can be prevented from departing Kuwait. Proselytizing is prohibited for all religions except Islam.

Accessibility: While in Kuwait, individuals with disabilities may find accessibility and accommodation very different from what you find in the United States. Kuwaiti law mandates access to buildings for persons with disabilities. The government generally enforces these provisions. The Kuwaiti government also supervises and contributes to schools and job and training programs that cater to persons with special needs.

Medical Facilities and Health Information: The health care system continues to develop, with many government and private medical facilities available in Kuwait. Medical care at government-run clinics and hospitals is provided at low cost to legal residents of Kuwait. Private physicians and hospitals charge fees for services, and some do not accept local health insurance. Many hospital and clinic services do not compare to U.S. standards.

You can find detailed information on vaccinations and other health precautions on the CDC website. For information about outbreaks of infectious diseases abroad, consult the World Health Organization (WHO) website. The WHO website also contains additional health information for travelers, including detailed country-specific health information.

Medical Insurance: You can't assume your insurance will go with you when you travel. It's very important to find out BEFORE you leave whether or not your medical insurance will cover you overseas. You need to ask your insurance company two questions:

- Does my policy apply when I'm out of the United States?
- Will it cover emergencies like a trip to a foreign hospital or a medical evacuation?

In many places, doctors and hospitals still expect payment in cash at the time of service. Your regular U.S. health insurance may not cover doctors' and hospital visits in other countries. If your policy doesn't go with you when you travel, it's a very good idea to take out another one for your trip.

Traffic Safety and Road Conditions: While in Kuwait, you may encounter road conditions that differ significantly from those in the United States. The information below concerning Kuwait is provided for general reference only, and may not be totally accurate in a particular location or circumstance.

Driving in Kuwait is extremely hazardous. Although Kuwait has an extensive and modern system of well-lit roads, excessive speed on both primary and secondary roads, coupled with lax enforcement of traffic regulations and a high density of vehicles (one vehicle for every 2.8 residents), leads to frequent and often fatal accidents. Incidents of road rage, distraction on the part of drivers, poor driving skills, and highway brinksmanship are common in Kuwait, and can be unsettling to Western drivers in Kuwait who are accustomed to more rigid adherence to traffic laws.

The government-owned Kuwait Public Transportation Company operates bus services throughout the Kuwait City metropolitan area on 50 different routes, which are widely used by the low-income expatriate labor force. Taxis are available at major hotels and may be telephoned to pick up passengers at other locations. It is sometimes possible to hail taxis on streets; taxis have meters, but fares are more commonly negotiated. U.S. citizens are advised to use only marked taxis with meters. U.S. citizens, especially those traveling alone and/or in darkness hours, should avoid sitting in the front seat of a taxi, do not travel to unfamiliar areas, do not enter taxis with unknown passengers, and not engage in "small talk" that can be misinterpreted as interest in the taxi driver. Visitors can use international driving permits issued by their respective countries within the time limit of their visas; however, the visitor must also have liability insurance. It is illegal to drive in Kuwait without a license and car registration documents. If an individual is stopped and cannot produce these documents, the individual may be taken to a police station and held until the documents are presented on his/her behalf.

The Government of Kuwait may provide U.S. citizens with a Kuwaiti driver's license. Visitors and residents should consult the Ministry of Interior website for the most up-to-date information on obtaining a driver's license.

If an individual is involved in an accident, Kuwaiti law mandates that he/she must immediately notify the police and remain at the scene until the police arrive. Involvement in an accident, even if not at fault, can lead to arrest and temporary incarceration. At-fault accidents can result in arrests, demands for financial restitution, and/or travel bans preventing individuals from departing Kuwait.

The use of front seat belts is mandatory in Kuwait. Driving is on the right side of the road. Speed limits are posted. Making a right turn on a red light is not permitted unless there is a special lane to do so with a yield sign. When a driver flashes his/her high beams in Kuwait, it is meant as a request to move the car into a slower lane to allow the driver with the flashing beams to proceed ahead. Parking is not allowed where the curb is painted black and yellow. Digital cameras for registering traffic violations, including speeding, are in use on Kuwaiti roads. Non-payment of traffic and parking fines may result in travel bans which remain in place until the fines are paid, often with penalties.

Possession or consumption of alcohol is illegal in Kuwait. Driving while under the influence of alcohol is a serious offense, which may result in fines, imprisonment, and/or deportation. Repeat traffic violations or violations of a serious nature may also result in the deportation of an expatriate offender.

Kuwait has one of the highest per capita rates of cellular telephone ownership in the world; using a cellular telephone for phone calls or text messaging while driving remains illegal, although it is widely practiced. Local emergency service organizations may be contacted by dialing 112. Ambulance crews do not respond as quickly as in the United States and do not often include trained paramedics. Visit the website of the Kuwaiti Ministry of Interior for information and statistics in Arabic about traffic safety and road conditions in Kuwait.

Aviation Safety Oversight: The U.S. Federal Aviation Administration (FAA) has assessed the government of Kuwait's Civil Aviation Authority as being in compliance with International Civil Aviation Organization (ICAO) aviation safety standards for oversight of Kuwait's air carrier operations. Further information may be found on the FAA's safety assessment page.

Children's Issues: Please see the U.S. Dept. of State Office of Children's Issues web pages on intercountry adoption and international parental child abduction.

Intercountry Adoption
May 2011

Kuwait is not party to the Hague Convention on Protection of Children and Co-operation in Respect of Intercountry Adoption (Hague Adoption Convention). Therefore, when the Hague Adoption Convention entered into force for the United States on April 1, 2008, intercountry adoption processing for Kuwait did not change. The Department of State does not maintain files on the adoption process in Kuwait because adoptions from Kuwait are rare. Fewer than five adoptions by American citizen parents have taken place in over a decade.

International Parental Child Abduction
January 2012

The information in this section has been edited from the latest report available as of February 2013 from the State Department Bureau of Consular Affairs, Office of Overseas Citizens Services. For more information, please read the *International Parental Child Abduction* section of this book and check for updated reports online at www.travel.state.gov/abduction.

Disclaimer: The information in this flyer relating to the legal requirements of specific foreign countries is provided for general information only. Questions involving interpretation of specific foreign laws should be addressed to foreign legal counsel.

General Information: Kuwait is not a party to the Hague Convention on the Civil Aspects of International Child Abduction, nor are there any international or bilateral treaties in force between Kuwait and the United States dealing with international parental child abduction. American citizens who travel to Kuwait are subject to the jurisdiction of Kuwait courts, as well as to the country's laws and regulations. American citizens planning a trip to Kuwait with dual national children should bear this in mind.

Custody Disputes: Cases involving divorce and the custody of minor children are adjudicated in religious courts. If the marriage partners are Muslim, disputes will be resolved before an Islamic Sharia court which will apply principles of the Islamic sect (Shia or Sunni or mixed) of the parties involved. A Sharia court would also hear a dispute between a Muslim husband and non-Muslim wife. Marriage between a Muslim woman and non-Muslim man is prohibited in Kuwait. In the case of Christians, the court will be an Ecclesiastical Court composed of clergymen from the appropriate religious community, who will refer to the principles governing family status in the Greek Orthodox Church, Roman Catholic Church or other Christian denomination.

In both theory and practice, Muslim and Christian courts in Kuwait differ very little in how they resolve disputes over the custody of children of divorced or separated parents. The relevant laws all give priority for custodianship to the mother as long as certain restrictive conditions are met. However, once the children reach adolescence, the father can appeal for custody, except in the Sunni sect where the daughter stays with her mother until marriage. If a court finds the mother not fit to have custody, a maternal grandmother living in Kuwait or a paternal grandmother (if the maternal grandmother is not living in Kuwait) will be given custody until the children reach the age at which the father may appeal for custody.

In actual practice, the conditions placed on the mother's primary right to custody often enable the father to maintain a great deal of influence over the rearing of the children, even though he may not have legal custody. For example, the mother must seek his approval to depart Kuwait with the children. Frequently, the father is actually able to assume legal custody against the wishes of the mother when she is unable or unwilling to meet the conditions set by law for her to maintain her custodial rights. A mother can lose her primary right to custody of a child in a number of ways. The court can determine that she is incapable of safeguarding the child or of bringing the child up in accordance with the appropriate religious standards. The mother can void her right to custody by re-marrying a party considered "unmarriageable," or by residing in a home with people who might be "strangers" to the child.

The mother may not deny visitation rights to the father or the paternal grandfather and may not travel outside Kuwait with the child without the father's approval and the approval of the court. In general, a Kuwaiti man divorcing his non-Kuwaiti wife may be awarded legal custody of their children if the court determines that any of the above conditions have not been met. Under Sharia law, if a mother removes a child from the father thus denying him access, the mother's custody rights can be severed. An attempt to remove children from Kuwait without permission from the father is considered a criminal act in Kuwait. The U.S. Embassy cannot prevent the Kuwaiti government from arresting and either deporting or prosecuting an American citizen who violates Kuwaiti law. A Kuwaiti father can remove his children from Kuwait without approval from the mother. A mother can seek a travel ban to prevent the father from taking the children out of Kuwait. Persons who wish to pursue a child custody claim in a Kuwaiti court should retain an attorney in Kuwait. The U.S. State Department and the U.S. Embassy in Kuwait maintain a list of attorneys willing to represent American clients. A copy of this list may be obtained by contacting either office.

U.S. Embassy Kuwait
P.O. Box 77 Safat
13001 Safat
Kuwait
Phone: [965] 539-5307/5308
After hours emergency phone number: [965] 538-2097/2098
Fax: [965] 539-2484
Workweek: Saturday through Wednesday

Enforcement of Foreign Judgments: Custody orders and judgments of foreign courts are not enforceable in Kuwait if they potentially contradict or violate local laws and practices. For example, an order from a U.S. court granting custody to a parent will not be honored in Kuwait if the parent intends to take the child to live outside Kuwait. Nor will Kuwaiti courts enforce U.S. court decrees ordering a parent in Kuwait to pay child support. However, a court hearing a custody case in Kuwait may take into consideration the law of the country of the father's nationality. An American father with a U.S. court order granting him custody might find that order helpful (though not binding) in a custody proceeding in Kuwait.

Visitation Rights: In cases where the father has custody of a child, the mother is guaranteed visitation rights. It has been the experience of the U.S. Embassy in Kuwait that the father and the paternal grandparents of the child are generally very open and accommodating in facilitating the right of the mother to visit and maintain contact with the child.

Dual Nationality: Dual nationality is not recognized under Kuwaiti law. Children of Kuwaiti fathers automatically acquire Kuwaiti citizenship at birth, regardless of where the child was born. Women cannot transmit citizenship. Kuwaiti citizens must enter and exit the country on Kuwaiti passports.

Travel Restrictions: Exit visas are not required to leave Kuwait. However, a mother may face serious legal difficulties if she attempts to take her children out of Kuwait without the permission of the father. Immigration officials at the airport or border often ask to see permission from the father in writing before allowing children to exit, and have even been known to confirm a written request by contacting the father. If a woman has not placed a travel ban preventing a father from removing children from Kuwait, a father will usually be permitted to exit Kuwait with his children without difficulty.

Criminal Remedies: For information on possible criminal remedies, please contact your local law enforcement authorities or the nearest office of the Federal Bureau of Investigation (FBI). Information is also available on the Internet at the web site of the U.S. Department of Justice, Office of Juvenile Justice and Delinquency Prevention (OJJDP) at http://www.ojjdp.ncjrs.org.

Specific questions regarding child custody in Kuwait should be addressed to an attorney practicing in Kuwait or to the Embassy of Kuwait at:

Embassy of the State of Kuwait
2940 Tilden Street, NW
Washington, DC 20008
Phone: (202) 966-0702
Fax: (202) 966-0517

Passports for Minors and the Children's Passport Issuance Alert Program: For more information on these topics, see the *International Parental Child Abduction* section of this publication and review current reports from the U.S. Department of State at www.travel.state.gov/abduction.

For further information on international parental child abduction, contact the Office of Children's Issues, U.S. Department of State at 1-888-407-4747 or visit its web site on the Internet at http://travel.state.gov/abduction.

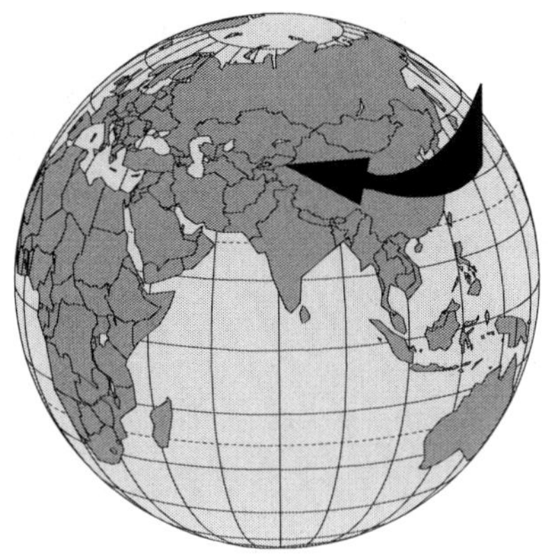

KYRGYZSTAN

Compiled from publications that were available as of February 2013 from the U.S. Department of State, the U.S. Department of Commerce, and the Central Intelligence Agency (CIA). See the introduction to this set for explanatory notes.

Official Name:
Kyrgyz Republic

PROFILE

Geography

Area: total: 199,951 sq km; country comparison to the world: 87; land: 191,801 sq km; water: 8,150 sq km

Major cities: Bishkek (capital) 854,000 (2009)

Climate: dry continental to polar in high Tien Shan Mountains; subtropical in southwest (Fergana Valley); temperate in northern foothill zone

Terrain: peaks of Tien Shan and associated valleys and basins encompass entire nation

People

Nationality: noun: Kyrgyzstani(s); adjective: Kyrgyzstani

Population: 5,496,737 (July 2012 est.)

Population growth rate: 0.887% (2012 est.)

Ethnic groups: Kyrgyz 64.9%, Uzbek 13.8%, Russian 12.5%, Dungan 1.1%, Ukrainian 1%, Uighur 1%, other 5.7% (1999 census)

Religions: Muslim 75%, Russian Orthodox 20%, other 5%

Languages: Kyrgyz (official) 64.7%, Uzbek 13.6%, Russian (official) 12.5%, Dungun 1%, other 8.2% (1999 census)

Literacy: definition: age 15 and over can read and write; total population: 98.7%; male: 99.3%; female: 98.1% (1999 census)

Health: life expectancy at birth: total population: 69.45 years; male: 65.27 years; female: 73.91 years (2012 est.); Infant mortality rate: total: 30.78 deaths/1,000 live births; male: 35.15 deaths/1,000 live births; female: 26.11 deaths/1,000 live births (2012 est.)

Unemployment rate: 8.6% (2011 est.)

Work force: 2.344 million (2007)

Government

Type: republic

Independence: 31 August 1991

Constitution: 27 June 2010

Political subdivisions: 7 provinces (oblastlar, singular—oblasty) and 1 city (shaar); Batken Oblasty, Bishkek Shaary, Chuy Oblasty (Bishkek), Jalal-Abad Oblasty, Naryn Oblasty, Osh Oblasty, Talas Oblasty, Ysyk-Kol Oblasty (Karakol)

Suffrage: 18 years of age; universal

Economy

GDP (purchasing power parity): $13.47 billion (2012 est.); $13.29 billion (2011 est.); $12.58 billion (2010 est.); $12.64 billion (2009 est.)

GDP real growth rate: 1% (2012 est.); 5.7% (2011 est.); -0.5% (2010 est.); 2.9% (2009 est.)

GDP per capita (PPP): $2,400 (2012 est.); $2,400 (2011 est.); $2,300 (2010 est.); $2,300 (2009 est.)

Natural resources: abundant hydropower; significant deposits of gold and rare earth metals; locally exploitable coal, oil, and natural gas; other deposits of nepheline, mercury, bismuth, lead, and zinc

Agriculture products: tobacco, cotton, potatoes, vegetables, grapes, fruits and berries; sheep, goats, cattle, wool

Industries: small machinery, textiles, food processing, cement, shoes, sawn logs, refrigerators, furniture, electric motors, gold, rare earth metals

Exports: $2.294 billion (2012 est.); $2.278 billion (2011 est.); $1.779 billion (2010 est.)

Exports—commodities: gold, cotton, wool, garments, meat, tobacco; mercury, uranium, hydropower; machinery; shoes

Exports—partners: Uzbekistan 25.4%, Russia 22.2%, Kazakhstan 20.1%, China 7.8%, UAE 5.5%, Afghanistan 5%, Turkey 4.2% (2011)

Imports: $4.272 billion (2012 est.); $3.947 billion (2011 est.); $2.981 billion (2010 est.)

Imports—commodities: oil and gas, machinery and equipment, chemicals, foodstuffs

Imports—partners: China 59.8%, Russia 13.9%, Kazakhstan 5.2% (2011)

Debt—external: $3.666 billion (31 December 2012 est.); $3.601 billion (31 December 2011 est.); $3.984 billion (31 December 2010 est.)

Exchange rates: soms (KGS) per US dollar; 47.33 (2012 est.); 46.144 (2011 est.); 45.964 (2010 est.); 42.905 (2009); 36.108 (2008); 37.746 (2007)

PEOPLE

According to recent findings of Kyrgyz and Chinese historians, Kyrgyz history dates back to 201 B.C. The earliest descendents of the Kyrgyz people, who are believed to be of Turkic descent, lived in the northeastern part of what is currently Mongolia. Later, some of their tribes migrated to the region that is currently southern Siberia and settled along the Yenisey River, where they lived from the 6th until the 8th centuries. They spread across what is now the Tuva region of the Russian Federation, remaining in that area until the rise of the Mongol Empire in the 13th century, when the Kyrgyz began migrating south. In the 12th century, Islam became the predominant religion in the region. Most Kyrgyz are Sunni Muslims of the Hanafi school.

During the 15th-16th centuries, the Kyrgyz people settled in the territory currently known as the Kyrgyz Republic. In the early 19th century, the southern territory of the Kyrgyz Republic came under the control of the Khanate of Kokand, and the territory was formally incorporated into the Russian Empire in 1876. The Russian takeover instigated numerous revolts against tsarist authority, and many Kyrgyz opted to move into the Pamir mountains or to Afghanistan. The suppression of the 1916 rebellion in Central Asia caused many Kyrgyz to migrate to China.

National/Racial/Ethnic Minorities

The interethnic situation between ethnic Kyrgyz and ethnic Uzbeks in the south remained tense, characterized by arbitrary arrests, detention, torture, and extortion of ethnic Uzbeks by members of security services. Ethnic Uzbek citizens in Osh and Jalalabad reported discrimination in finding jobs, particularly with the government. There were multiple reports of seizure of ethnic Uzbek businesses and property.

Minorities alleged discrimination in hiring, promotion, and housing, but no official reports were registered with local authorities.

Language

The law designates Kyrgyz as the state language and Russian as an official language, and it provides for the preservation and equal and free development of minority languages. Non-Kyrgyz-speaking citizens alleged that a ceiling precluded promotion beyond a certain level in government service. They also alleged that unfair language examinations disqualified some candidates for office. A government initiative to increase official use of Kyrgyz further raised concerns among non-Kyrgyz ethnic groups about possible discrimination.

Religion

Islam is the predominant religion, accounting for approximately 75 percent of the population. Except for approximately 1,000 Shia, all are Sunni. As of 2009 there were 1,706 mosques and seven institutes for higher Islamic teaching. Approximately 7 percent of the population is Russian Orthodox, and there were 44 Russian Orthodox churches, one convent, and one parochial school.

Of the remaining population, Protestant Christians are the largest group with approximately 11,000 members, of whom 40 percent are ethnic Kyrgyz. Protestant denominations include 48 registered Baptist, 21 Lutheran, 49 Pentecostal, 35 Presbyterian, 43 "Charismatic," and 30 Seventh-day Adventist communities. Jehovah's Witnesses number around 4,800. There are three Roman Catholic churches. The Jewish community with approximately 1,500 adherents has one synagogue. The Buddhist community includes approximately1, 000 members and is served by one temple. There are 12 registered Baha'i houses of worship that serve approximately 300 members.

Islam is practiced throughout the country in both urban and rural areas. Russian Orthodox communities and other religious groups are concentrated in cities. Ethnic Kyrgyz and Uzbeks are primarily Muslims, while ethnic Russians most often belong to the Russian Orthodox Church or one of the several Protestant denominations.

HISTORY

Soviet power was initially established in the region in 1918, and in 1924, the Kara-Kyrgyz Autonomous Oblast was created within the Russian Federal Socialist Republic. (The term Kara-Kyrgyz was used until the mid-1920s by the Russians to distinguish them from the Kazakhs, who were also referred to as Kyrgyz.) In 1926, it became the Kyrgyz Autonomous Soviet Socialist Republic. On December 5, 1936, the Kyrgyz Soviet Socialist Republic (SSR) was established as a full Union Republic of the U.S.S.R.

During the 1920s, the Kyrgyz Republic saw considerable cultural, educational, and social change. Economic and social development also was notable. Literacy increased, and a standard literary language was introduced. The Kyrgyz language belongs to the Southern Turkic group of languages. In 1924, an Arabic-based Kyrgyz alphabet was introduced, which was replaced by Latin script in 1928. In 1941 Cyrillic script was adopted. Many aspects of the Kyrgyz national culture were retained despite suppression of nationalist activity under Joseph Stalin, who controlled the Soviet Union from the late 1920s until 1953.

The early years of glasnost in the late 1980s had little effect on the political climate in the Kyrgyz Republic. However, the republic's press was permitted to adopt a more liberal stance and to establish a new publication, Literaturny Kirghizstan, by the Union of Writers. Unofficial political groups were forbidden, but several groups that emerged in 1989 to deal with an acute housing crisis were permitted to function.

In June 1990, ethnic tensions between Uzbeks and Kyrgyz surfaced in an area of the Osh Oblast, where Uzbeks form a majority of the population. Violent confrontations ensued, and a state of emergency and curfew were introduced. Order was not restored until August 1990.

The early 1990s brought measurable change to the Kyrgyz Republic. The Kyrgyzstan Democratic Movement (KDM) had developed into a significant political force with support in parliament. In an upset victory, Askar Akayev, the president of the Kyrgyz Academy of Sciences, was elected to the presidency in October 1990. The following January, Akayev introduced new government structures and appointed a new government comprised mainly of younger, reform-oriented politicians. In December 1990, the Supreme Soviet voted to change the republic's name to the Republic of Kyrgyzstan. (In 1993, it became the Kyrgyz Republic.) In February 1991, the name of the capital, Frunze, was changed back to its pre-revolutionary name—Bishkek.

Despite these moves toward independence, economic realities seemed to work against secession from the U.S.S.R. In a referendum on the preservation of the U.S.S.R. in March 1991, 88.7% of the voters approved a proposal to retain the U.S.S.R. as a "renewed federation."

On August 19, 1991, when the State Committee for the State of Emergency (SCSE) assumed power in Moscow, there was an attempt to depose Akayev in Kyrgyzstan. After the coup collapsed the following week, Akayev and Vice President German Kuznetsov announced their resignations from the Communist Party of the Soviet Union (CPSU), and the entire politburo and secretariat resigned. This was followed by the Supreme Soviet vote declaring independence from the U.S.S.R. on August 31, 1991. Kyrgyz was announced as the state language in September 1991. (In December 2001, through a constitutional amendment, the Russian language was given official status.)

In October 1991, Akayev ran unopposed and was elected President of the new independent republic by direct ballot, receiving 95% of the votes cast. Together with the representatives of seven other republics, he signed the Treaty of the New Economic Community that same month. On December 21, 1991, the Kyrgyz Republic formally entered the new Commonwealth of Independent States (CIS).

In 1993, allegations of corruption against Akayev's closest political associates blossomed into a major scandal. One of those accused of improprieties was Prime Minister Chyngyshev, who was dismissed for ethical reasons in December. Following Chyngyshev's dismissal, Akayev dismissed the government and called upon the last communist premier, Apas Djumagulov, to form a new one. In January 1994, Akayev initiated a referendum asking for a renewed mandate to complete his term of office. He received 96.2% of the vote.

A new constitution was passed by the parliament in May 1993. In 1994, however, the parliament failed to produce a quorum for its last scheduled session prior to the expiration of its term in February 1995. President Akayev was widely accused of having manipulated a boycott by a majority of the parliamentarians. Akayev, in turn, asserted that the communists had caused a political crisis by preventing the legislature from fulfilling its role. Akayev scheduled an October 1994 referendum, overwhelmingly approved by voters, which proposed two amendments to the constitution—one that would allow the constitution to be amended by means of a referendum, and the other creating a new bicameral parliament called the Jogorku Kenesh.

Elections for the two legislative chambers—a 35-seat full-time assembly and a 70-seat part-time assembly—were held in February 1995 after campaigns considered remarkably free and open by most international observers, although the election-day proceedings were marred by widespread irregularities. Independent candidates won most of the seats, suggesting that personalities prevailed over ideologies. The new parliament convened its initial session in March 1995. One of its first orders of business was the approval of the precise constitutional language on the role of the legislature.

On December 24, 1995, President Akayev was reelected for another 5-year term with wide support (75% of vote) over two opposing candidates. President Akayev used government resources and state-owned media to carry out his campaign. Three (out of six) candidates were deregistered shortly before the election. A February 1996 referendum—in violation of the constitution and the law on referendums—amended the constitution to give President Akayev more power. Although the changes gave the president the power to dissolve parliament, it also more clearly defined the parliament's powers. Since that time, the parliament has demonstrated real independence from the executive branch.

An October 1998 referendum approved constitutional changes, including increasing the number of deputies in the lower house, reducing the number of deputies in the upper house, providing for 25% of lower house deputies to be elected by party lists, rolling back parliamentary immunity, introducing private property, prohibiting adoption of laws restricting freedom of speech and mass media, and reforming the state budget.

Two rounds of parliamentary elections were held on February 20, 2000 and March 12, 2000. With the full backing of the United States, the Organization for Security and Cooperation in Europe (OSCE) reported that the elections failed to comply with commitments to free and fair elections and hence were invalid. Questionable judicial proceedings against opposition candidates and parties limited the choice of candidates available to Kyrgyz voters, while state-controlled media only reported favorably on official candidates. Government officials put pressure on independent media outlets that favored the opposition. The presidential election that followed later in 2000 also was marred by irregularities and was not declared free and fair by international observers.

March 2002 events in the southern district of Aksy, where six people protesting the arbitrary arrest of an opposition politician were shot dead by police, engendered nationwide protests. President Akayev initiated a constitutional reform process, which initially included the participation of a broad range of government, civil, and social representatives in an open dialogue. The reform process resulted in a February 2003 referendum, which was marred by voting irregularities. The amendments to the constitution approved by the referendum resulted in further control by the president and weakened the parliament and the Constitutional Court. Under the new constitution, the previously bicameral parliament became a 75-seat unicameral legislature following the 2005 parliamentary elections.

Parliamentary elections were held February 27 and March 13, 2005. The United States agreed with the findings of the OSCE that while the elections failed to comply with commitments to free and fair elections, there were improvements over the 2000 elections, notably the use of indelible ink, transparent ballot boxes, and generally good access by election observers.

Sporadic protests against widespread fraud during the parliamentary runoff elections in March 2005 erupted into calls for the government to resign. By March 24, 15,000 pro-opposition demonstrators called for the resignation of the president and his regime in Bishkek. Some injuries were reported when opposition demonstrators were attacked by police and pro-government thugs. Protestors seized the presidential administration building, after which President Akayev left the country for Kazakhstan, and then Russia. Looting broke out in parts of Bishkek on the evening of March 24, causing an estimated $100 million in damage.

Opposition leaders, caught by surprise by developments, moved to form a broadly inclusive "Committee of National Unity." Opposition leader Kurmanbek Bakiyev was named acting President and Prime Minister. Bakiyev formed an alliance with primary rival Feliks Kulov whereby Kulov agreed to drop out of the presidential race if Bakiyev appointed him Prime Minister upon winning the elections.

Bakiyev easily won the July 10, 2005 presidential elections with over 88% of the vote. An unprecedented number of domestic and international observers monitored the elections and noted significant improvements in the electoral process over the parliamentary elections, although there were some reports of irregularities.

Opposition groups held a series of demonstrations in 2006, including the entire first week of November, to protest the lack of progress on reform, in particular of the constitution, promised by President Bakiyev in 2005. The Kyrgyz parliament adopted amendments to the constitution and President Bakiyev signed the amended constitution on November 9, 2006, which limited the powers of the president and increased the role of parliament. After the government resigned on December 19, the Kyrgyz parliament voted on December 30 to adopt new amendments restoring some of the presidential powers lost in November. President Bakiyev signed the changes into law January 15, 2007.

In March 2007, President Bakiyev appointed opposition leader Almaz Atambayev as Prime Minister. A week-long opposition protest in April 2007 ended when police cleared the main Ala-Too Square in Bishkek.

In September 2007, the Constitutional Court invalidated the November 2006 and December 2006 versions of the constitution. President Bakiyev then called a snap national referendum on a new version of the constitution, which strengthened the powers of the president and provided for a parliament elected by party lists. The new constitution was approved in an October 2007 referendum that was marked by serious irregularities, including massive inflation of turnout figures. President Bakiyev then dissolved the parliament, calling for new elections. The December 2007 elections were deeply flawed, with the new pro-presidential Ak Jol party gaining 71 out of 90 seats. The largest opposition party, Ata Meken, did not gain any seats, despite probably receiving enough votes to meet the regional thresholds required to enter parliament. Following the elections, a government was formed headed by the former energy minister, Igor Chudinov, as Prime Minister. On July 23, 2009 President Bakiyev was overwhelmingly reelected with 76% of the vote, although the OSCE noted numerous voting irregularities. In October 2009, Daniyar Usenov was nominated as Prime Minister. Protests in April 2010 in the town of Talas and in Bishkek ousted Bakiyev and his government from office. A provisional government headed by President Roza Otunbayeva took office in April and navigated through brief but intense interethnic clashes in June 2010 to organize a referendum on June 27, 2010, by which voters approved a new constitution. The referendum also confirmed Otunbayeva as President until December 31, 2011.

The 2010 constitution is intended to limit presidential power and enhance the role of parliament and the prime minister. Parliamentary elections were held in October 2010. The elections were highly competitive and peaceful, Five parties entered parliament, led by the Ata Jurt party (28 seats), and followed by the Social Democratic Party of Kyrgyzstan (26 seats), Ar-Namys (25 seats), Respublika (23 seats) and Ata-Meken (18 seats). Three parties (Ata Jurt, SDPK, and Respublika) formed a governing coalition with Almazbek Atambayev as prime minister.

Because the 2010 constitutional referendum limited Roza Otunbayeva's term in office until the end of 2011, Kyrgyzstan held a presidential election on October 30, 2011. Almazbek Atambayev of the Social Democratic Party of Kyrgyzstan won the first round with 63 percent of the vote, thus avoiding the possibility of a second-round runoff. The 2011 election was democratic and peaceful, but some observers noted areas for improvement. Atambayev's inauguration on December 1, 2011 marked the first peaceful and democratic transfer of presidential power in Central Asia. With Atambayev vacating the office of prime minister, party factions consulted to organize a new government. A new governing coalition was formed consisting of SDPK, Respublika, Ata-Meken and Ar-Namys. Parliament approved the new government on December 23, 2011, with Omurbek Babanov (leader of the Respublika faction) as the new prime minister.

GOVERNMENT AND POLITICAL CONDITIONS

The Kyrgyz Republic has a parliamentary form of government that limits presidential power and enhances the role of parliament and the prime minister. The October 2010 parliamentary elections, considered relatively free and fair, led to a three-party coalition that took power in December 2010. In the 2011 presidential election held on October 30, Almazbek Atambayev, the then prime minister, received more than 60 percent of the vote. Independent observers considered the election generally transparent and competitive, despite some irregularities. This was the country's first peaceful transfer of power in its 20-year history. Following Atambayev's inauguration on December 1, parliament formed a new governing coalition that included four of the five parties that held seats.

While security forces officially reported to civilian authorities, in some regions, particularly in the south, there were instances in which elements of the security forces acted independently of civilian control.

Under the new constitution, the powers of the president, parliament, and government (headed by a prime minister) are divided. The president, who serves a six-year term, can veto legislation and appoints the heads of national security bodies. Members of parliament are elected to five-year terms on party lists and vote to approve a proposed government. Parliament can also vote to express no confidence in the government, after which the president may dissolve it. The constitution does not provide any officeholder with immunity from prosecution after the individual leaves office.

Recent Elections

On October 30, 2011, the country held a presidential election that was judged to be open and transparent, but not without problems and accusations of fraud by both local and international observers. Prime Minister Almazbek Atambayev defeated 15 other candidates with 62.52 percent of the vote. By attaining more than 50 percent of the vote, Atambayev prevented a runoff election. He assumed office December 1. The election was widely observed with nearly 800 international observers and thousands of local observers, representing domestic NGOs, political parties, and the candidates themselves. Although not widespread, instances of fraud, including ballot stuffing and manipulation of polling station and precinct results, were observed and reported, as were problems with voter lists.

For the first time, the country required citizens to register in advance and appear on voter lists in order to cast ballots. Although more than 300,000 people reportedly changed the location of their voter registration, thousands who went to the polls did not find themselves on the final voter list and were not allowed to vote. International and local observation missions noted the problems, but the general consensus was that they did not change the outcome of the election. Atambayev's two closest competitors, who each received approximately 15 percent of the vote, alleged widespread fraud and challenged the results. Nonetheless, the Central Election Commission certified the results on November 12.

Participation of Women and Minorities: There were no legal restrictions on the participation of women in politics; however, with the notable exception of President Roza Otunbayeva, traditional attitudes at times hindered women from holding high office or playing active roles in political life. There were no female candidates on the 2011 presidential ballot. Twenty-five women representing five political parties occupied seats in parliament due to parliamentary election code mandates aimed at ensuring gender diversity. The code requires that male and female candidates be no more than three spaces apart on party lists and that no more than 70 percent of candidates on a party list be of the same gender.

National minorities, which made up 35 percent of the population, were underrepresented in government positions, particularly Russians and Uzbeks, the two largest ethnic minority groups. Fourteen of the 120 parliament members belonged to a national minority. The law requires that at least 15 percent of candidates on party lists be ethnic minorities.

The Minister of Social Protection was the only ministerial position held by a woman during 2011. From April through the end of the year, the position of prosecutor general was also held by a woman. No one known to be of an ethnic minority held a cabinet-level government position. As of October women occupied 19 percent of the 675 government positions.

Principal Government Officials

Last Updated: 1/31/2013

Pres.: **Almazbek ATAMBAEV**
Prime Min.: **Jantoro SATYBALDIEV**
First Dep. Prime Min.: **Joomart OTORBAEV**
Dep. Prime Min.: **Tayyrbek SARPASHEV**
Dep. Prime Min.: **Kamila TALIEVA**
Min. & Chief of the Govt. Apparatus: **Nurkhanbek MOMUNALIEV**
Min. of Agriculture & Water Management: **Chynggysbek UZAKBAEV**
Min. of Culture & Tourism: **Ibragim JUNUSOV**
Min. of Defense: **Taalaybek OMURALIEV, Maj. Gen.**
Min. of Economy & Antimonopoly Policies: **Temir SARIEV**
Min. of Education & Science: **Kanat SADYKOV**
Min. of Emergency Situations: **Kubatbek BORONOV**
Min. of Energy & Industry: **Avtandil KALMAMBETOV**
Min. of Finance: **Olga LAVROVA**
Min. of Foreign Affairs: **Erlan ABDYLDAEV**
Min. of Health Care: **Dinara SAGIMBAEVA**
Min. of Internal Affairs: **Shamil ATAKHANOV**
Min. of Justice: **Almambet SHYKMAMATOV**
Min. of Social Development: **Kylychbek SULTANOV**
Min. of Transportation & Communication: **Kalykbek SULTANOV**
Min. of Youth & Labor: **Alisbek ALYMKULOV**
Chmn., State Ctte. for National Security (GKNB): **Beyshenbay JUNUSOV**
Prosecutor Gen.: **Aida SALYANOVA**
Chmn., National Bank of Kyrgyzstan: **Zina ASANKOJOEVA**
Ambassador to the US: **Mukhtar JUMALIEV**
Permanent Representative to the UN, New York: **Taalaybek KYDYROV**

ECONOMY

Kyrgyzstan is a poor, mountainous country with a dominant agricultural sector. Cotton, tobacco, wool, and meat are the main agricultural products, although only tobacco and cotton are exported in any quantity. Industrial exports include gold, mercury, uranium, natural gas, and electricity. The economy depends heavily on gold exports - mainly from output at the Kumtor gold mine - and on remittances from Kyrgyzstani migrant workers priimarily in Russia.

Following independence, Kyrgyzstan was progressive in carrying out market reforms, such as an improved regulatory system and land reform. Kyrgyzstan was the first Commonwealth of Independent States (CIS) country to be accepted into the World Trade Organization. Much of the government's stock in enterprises has been sold. Drops in production had been severe after the breakup of the Soviet Union in December 1991, but by mid-1995, production began to recover and exports began to increase.

In 2005, the Bakiev government and international financial institutions initiated a comprehensive medium-term poverty reduction and economic growth strategy. The government made steady strides in controlling its substantial fiscal deficit, nearly closing the gap between revenues and expenditures in 2006, before boosting expenditures more than 20% in 2007–08. GDP grew about 8% annually in 2007–08, partly due to higher gold prices internationally, but slowed to 2.9% in 2009.

The overthrow of President Bakiev in April 2010 and subsequent ethnic clashes left hundreds dead and damaged infrastructure. Shrinking trade and agricultural production, as well as political instability, caused GDP to contract 0.5% in 2010. The fiscal deficit widened to 11% of GDP, reflecting significant increases in crisis-related spending, including both rehabilitation of damaged infrastructure and bank recapitalization. The economy grew 5.7% in 2011, but slowed to around 1% in 2012, primarily because of decreased production from Kumtor; the budget deficit has been reduced to under 8% of GDP. Progress in reconstruction, fighting corruption, restructuring domestic industry, and attracting foreign aid and investment are key to future growth.

Labor Conditions

The law provides for the protection of children from economic exploitation and from work that poses a danger to their health or development; however, child labor remained a widespread problem. The minimum legal age for basic employment is 16, except for work considered by the government to be "light," such as selling newspapers. In addition, children as young as 14 may work with the permission of a parent or guardian.

The law prohibits the employment of persons under 18 at night, underground, or in difficult or dangerous conditions, including the metal, oil, and gas industries; mining and prospecting; the food industry; entertainment; and machine building. Children who are 14 or 15 may work up to five hours a day; children who are 16 to 18 may work up to seven hours a day. These laws also apply to children with disabilities.

A UNICEF report covering the period of 2003 through 2009 cited NGO reports of child labor in coal mining in the village of Sulukta and in sifting uranium tailings in the village of Orlovka.

According to a 2010 speech by the deputy minister of labor, employment, and migration, 670,000 children between the ages of five and 17 were working, primarily in agriculture on tobacco, rice, and cotton plantations, but also in car washes, trading, and other activities.

The 2011 official national minimum monthly wage was KGS 600 ($13). Minimum wage serves as an indicator for different types of official government fines, rather than an actual minimum wage requirement for employers. Employers generally paid somewhat higher wages. The law on minimum wage states that it should be raised gradually to meet the cost of living.

The government does not set an official poverty level, but it estimated the monthly minimum cost of living for a family of four to be KGS 17,690 ($383), which is above the country's reported average monthly wage. In August the National Statistics Committee reported that the average monthly salary was KGS 8,185 ($177).

The standard workweek is 40 hours, usually within a five-day week. For state-owned industries, there is a mandated 24-hour rest period in the workweek. According to the labor code, overtime work cannot exceed four hours per day or 20 hours per week and must be compensated with compensatory leave or with premium pay of between 150 and 200 percent of the hourly wage. These provisions were mainly enforced at large companies and organizations with strong trade unions. Small and informal firms had no union representation.

Safety and health conditions in factories were poor. The law establishes occupational health and safety standards, but the government generally did not enforce them. Unregistered foreign workers in the country could not exercise the same rights as registered workers because they cannot register complaints with the authorities and do not pay into and receive benefits from the social fund.

Government licensing rules place strict requirements on companies recruiting Kyrgyz citizens to work abroad, and companies must be licensed by the Ministry of Labor, Employment, and Migration before they can recruit. The government regularly published a list of licensed and vetted firms.

Recruiters are required to monitor employer compliance with employment terms and the working conditions of labor migrants while a work contract is in effect. Recruiters are also required to provide workers with their employment contract prior to their departure. The government also took steps to streamline labor migration by adopting a program on the regulation of migration processes and collaborating with the governments of Russia, South Korea, and Kazakhstan to improve the protection of rights of Kyrgyz labor migrants working abroad. The Ministry of Labor had representatives in several Russian cities to assist Kyrgyz labor migrants, who sometimes encountered discrimination, poor working conditions, or violence.

U.S.-KYRGYZ RELATIONS

The United States established diplomatic relations with Kyrgyzstan in 1991 following Kyrgyzstan's independence from the Soviet Union. The two countries have a strong partnership. The United States supports Kyrgyzstan in its development of an inclusive democracy based upon the rule of law and respect for human rights. Kyrgyzstan's 2011 presidential election marked the first peaceful transfer of presidential power in post-Soviet Central Asia.

Kyrgyzstan hosts the Transit Center at Manas International Airport, an important logistical hub for the coalition effort in Afghanistan. Significant impediments to Kyrgyzstan's development include corruption, aging infrastructure, high unemployment, and endemic poverty. Kyrgyzstan, however, benefits from a robust civil society and a relatively free media sector.

U.S. Assistance to Kyrgyzstan

U.S. Government assistance goals in Kyrgyzstan are to strengthen democratic institutions, promote greater respect for human rights and the rule of law, enhance regional security, support broad-based economic opportunity, basic humanitarian needs and development challenges in the health and education areas. A fact sheet on U.S. assistance to Kyrgyzstan can be found here.

Bilateral Economic Relations

Kyrgyzstan exports antimony, mercury, rare-earth metals, and chemical products to the United States. It imports grain, medicine and medical equipment, vegetable oil, paper products, rice, machinery, agricultural equipment, and meat from the United States. U.S. direct investment in Kyrgyzstan is concentrated in the hotel and telecommunications sectors, with increasing interest in construction and mining. Kyrgyzstan has signed a bilateral investment treaty with the United States. The treaty on double taxation that was signed by the United States and the Soviet Union remains in effect between the United States and Kyrgyzstan. Kyrgyzstan also has signed a trade and investment framework agreement with the United States and other Central Asian countries establishing a regional forum to discuss ways to improve investment climates and expand trade within Central Asia.

Kyrgyzstan's Membership in International Organizations

Kyrgyzstan and the United States belong to a number of the same international organizations, including the United Nations, Euro-Atlantic Partnership Council, Organization for Security and Cooperation in Europe, International Monetary Fund, World Bank, and World Trade Organization. Kyrgyzstan also is a participant in the North Atlantic Treaty Organization's (NATO) Partnership for Peace program.

Bilateral Representation

Kyrgyzstan maintains an embassy in the United States at 2360 Massachusetts Ave, NW, Washington, DC 20008; tel. (202) 449-9822.

Principal U.S. Embassy Officials

Last Updated: 1/14/2013

BISHKEK (E) 171 Prospekt Mira, Bishkek Kyrgyz Republic 720016, [996] {312} 551-241, Fax [996] {312} 551-264, Workweek: 8:00–1730, Website: http://kyrgyz.usembassy.gov.

DCM OMS:	Cheryl Michaels
AMB OMS:	Jenny Jeras
CDC:	George Schmid
DHS/ICE:	Matthew Siuda
FM:	Dennis Garde
HRO:	Evengeline Gohoure
MGT:	Jack Anderson
NAS/INL:	Robert Coburn
POL/ECON:	David McCormick
POSHO:	Dennis Garde
SDO/DATT:	LTC Daniel Manning
AMB:	Pamela Spratlen
CON:	Alden Greene
DCM:	Laura Griesmer
PAO:	Christian Wright
GSO:	Daniel White
RSO:	Vacant
AFSA:	Vacant
AID:	Carey Gordon
CLO:	Andrea Pullella
DEA:	Patrick Apel
EEO:	Doug Culver, Jennifer Nashashibi
EST:	Kathryn Porch
FMO:	Jennifer Nashashibi
ICASS Chair:	Anne Turner
IMO:	Douglas Culver
ISSO:	Stephen Kraemer
State ICASS:	David McCormick

TRAVEL

Consular Information Sheet

January 18, 2013

Country Description: The Kyrgyz Republic is a mountainous country of 5.5 million people. In April 2010, violence led to the collapse of the previous government leading to the formation of a provisional government. In June 2010, inter-ethnic violence killed hundreds of people and wounded thousands in the south of the country. The provisional government successfully held a constitutional referendum in June and parliamentary elections took place without violence in October 2010. A new government was formed on December 17, 2010. The country held competitive presidential elections in October 2011, and President Atambayev took office on December 1, 2011. Though the referendum and both elections took place without incident, unrest and ethnic tensions could flare up unexpectedly.

Despite recent economic growth and modest natural resources, the country grapples with substantial poverty, and the tourist industry is not highly developed. Air and land travel internally and to neighboring countries is limited and can be subject to delays due to infrastructure shortcomings and winter weather. Rural and urban areas have been subject to power, natural gas, and water outages, leaving many homes without running water, heat, or electricity at times.

Smart Traveler Enrollment Program (STEP)/Embassy Locations: If you are going to live in or visit the Kyrgyz Republic, please take the time to tell our Embassy about your plans. If you enroll, we can keep you up to date with important safety and security announcements. It will also help your friends and family get in touch with you in an emergency.

Embassy of the United States of America in the Kyrgyz Republic
171 Prospect Mira, Bishkek 720016

Kyrgyz Republic
Telephone: (996-312) 551-241
Facsimile: (996-312) 551-264
consularbishkek@state.gov

Entry/Exit Requirements for U.S. Citizens: You must have a valid U.S. passport to visit Kyrgyzstan. Your passport must be valid for a minimum period of three months from the date of entry into Kyrgyzstan and must have at least one full blank page if you are applying for a visa.

A visa-free regime for citizens of some states, including the United States of America, was introduced in July 2012. U.S. citizens are permitted to enter the country for tourism for up to 60 days without a Kyrgyz visa.

US citizens present in the Kyrgyz Republic for more than 60 days mustobtain a Kyrgyz visa at the Department of Consular Services of the Ministry of Foreign Affairs of the Kyrgyz Republic located at 10A Togolok Moldo Street, Bishkek, telephone: 0(312) 663270, or at the Department of Visa and Passport Control under the Ministry of Internal Affairs located in the main building of GUVD (Bishkek City Police Department), intersection of Pravda & Toktogul Street, telephone 0(312) 431179.Individuals traveling to the Kyrgyz Republic to perform religious work or work in affiliation with any religious organization in any capacity are required by Kyrgyz law to declare so on their visa applications. Individuals engaging in any type of missionary activity must obtain a work visa and register with the Office of Religious Affairs after arrival. It is illegal to engage in religious activity on a tourist visa. Travelers should apply for the correct category of visa for their purpose of travel. The Embassy recommends that U.S. citizens traveling in the Kyrgyz Republic also obtain Kazakh visas, as commercial air travel out of the Kyrgyz Republic is limited and U.S. citizens may need to travel through Kazakhstan to return to the United States. Travelers intending to transit through Russia en route to a third country must have a Russian transit visa. Even travelers who are simply changing planes in Moscow or another international airport in Russia for an onward destination will be asked to present a transit visa issued by a Russian Embassy or Consulate. Russian authorities may refuse entry to travelers who do not have visas. For further information regarding entry/exit requirements, contact the Embassy of the Kyrgyz Republic at 2630 Massachusetts Avenue, NW, Washington, DC 20008, telephone:(202) 338-5141, fax:(202) 742 6501.

Some HIV/AIDS entry restrictions exist for visitors and foreign residents in the Kyrgyz Republic. The law states that visitors staying more than one month must present evidence that they are HIV negative. This restriction has not been actively enforced, but enforcement could begin without notice. Please verify the status of this requirement with the Embassy of the Kyrgyz Republic before you travel.

Threats to Safety and Security: Bishkek is a large city of 1.1 million people. The greatest threats to tourists and travelers are traffic accidents and street crime. That said, the country continues to stabilize itself after the violence of 2010. Terrorism is an enduring threat, especially in the southern part of the country.

The Department of State suggests that U.S. citizens limit travel to the Batken Oblast where violence broke out several times in recent years. Ethnic, political, and socio-economic tensions continue to exist in southern Kyrgyzstan, including the cities of Osh and Jalalabad, the second and third largest cities in Kyrgyzstan, although there have been no widespread incidents of violence since 2010. As of December 2012, however, the immediate threat of violence appears to have subsided in the south, although ethnic, political, and socio-economic tensions continue to exist.

Travel of U.S. government employees to Batken is currently restricted. Land mines in Batken Oblast and near the Kyrgyz-Tajik border continue to be a concern. Areas along the Kyrgyz-Uzbek and Kyrgyz-Tajik borders continue to have small, but sometimes violent and deadly, skirmishes between border guards on both sides, and often include civilians. Organized crime and narcotics trafficking are widespread in southern Kyrgyzstan.

In late 2010, Kyrgyz security forces carried out a series of operations against groups the government claims are Islamic extremists seeking to destabilize the country. These security operations resulted in the death or arrest of several suspects, and several members of the Kyrgyz security forces. These militants are blamed for carrying out a home invasion, planting a car bomb near a Bishkek police station, and detonating an improvised explosive device outside the venue of a large trial in downtown Bishkek resulting in some property damage and minor injuries.

In late November 2010, Kyrgyz Special Forces mounted an operation against suspected terrorists in Osh, resulting in the deaths of all four suspects and the wounding of two special-forces officers. In October 2012, the Kyrgyz government also arrested five individuals with alleged ties to terrorists and extremist groups. Additionally, Kyrgyz security officials found and confiscated large caches of weapons, including machine guns and explosive materials.

Though the situation is now relatively stable, demonstrations can break out without advance notice. During times of political unrest, demonstrators often gather in front of the Presidential Administration building (White House), the Parliament, and on Alatoo Square in Bishkek's city center.

The Embassy does not always have advance information regarding demonstrations. All U.S. citizens are reminded to avoid the vicinity of any protests, because even protests that are intended to be peaceful can turn confrontational and possibly escalate into violence.

Stay up to date by:

- Bookmarking our Bureau of Consular Affairs website, which contains the current Travel Warnings and Travel Alerts as well as the Worldwide Caution.

- Following us on Twitter and the Bureau of Consular Affairs page on Facebook as well.

- Downloading our free Smart Traveler app, available through iTunes and the Androidmarket, for travel information at your fingertips.

- Calling 1-888-407-4747 toll-free within the U.S. and Canada, or a regular toll line, 1-202-501-4444, from other countries.

- Taking some time before travel to consider your personal security.

Crime: The U.S. Embassy advises U.S. citizens to exercise caution in urban areas of the Kyrgyz Republic due to the high rate of violent crime against foreigners. There have been reports of violent muggings of foreigners in downtown Bishkek at night. Other common crimes include auto theft and pick pocketing in crowded places such as markets, internet cafes, and on public transportation.

After dark, travelers should not take public transportation or walk outside and should be extremely cautious in or near hotels, bars, parks, and all places that attract an expatriate clientele. The U.S. Embassy advises its employees to avoid the use of unlicensed cabs and recommends using only radio dispatched taxis. Travelers arriving at Manas International Airport should arrange their transportation from the airport in advance. There have been reports of U.S. citizens who were robbed by groups of young men who had followed them back to their residences from hotels and bars. In addition, U.S. citizens have been victims of rape, assault, and kidnapping in the past in the Kyrgyz Republic. Police officers rarely speak English and there are no victims' assistance programs available. Medical care and counseling services for victims are limited.

Harassment and extortion by people who purport to be Kyrgyz police officers take place occasionally. According to Kyrgyz law, any person claiming to be a police officer must show identifying documents on demand. U.S. citizens should not act upon requests by people, whether in civilian dress or in police uniform, if they have no official identification.

U.S. citizens also should not get into cars with anyone they do not know, even if the person claims to be a police officer.

Don't buy counterfeit and pirated goods, even if they are widely available. Not only are the bootlegs illegal in the United States, if you purchase them you may be breaking local law. You could be prosecuted under U.S. law for pirated goods you purchased in the Kyrgyz Republic.

Victims of Crime: If you or someone you know becomes the victim of a crime abroad, you should contact the local police and the nearest U.S. embassy or consulate. We can:

- Replace a stolen passport.

- Help you find appropriate medical care if you are the victim of violent crimes such as assault or rape.

- Put you in contact with the appropriate police authorities, and if you want us to, we cancontact family members or friend.

- Help direct you to local attorneys. Please note that local authorities are responsible for investigating and prosecuting the crime.

The local equivalent to the "911" emergency line in the Kyrgyz Republic is 101 in case of fire, 102 for police, and 103 for emergency ambulance service.

Criminal Penalties: While you are traveling in the Kyrgyz Republic, you are subject to its laws even if you are a U.S. citizen. Foreign laws and legal systems can be vastly different than our own. In some places you may be taken in for questioning if you don't have your passport with you. In some places, it is illegal to take pictures of certain buildings. In some places, driving under the influence could land you immediately in jail. These criminal penalties will vary from country to country. There are also some things that might be legal in the country you visit, but still illegal in the United States, and you can be prosecuted under U.S. law if you buy pirated goods.

Engaging in sexual conduct with children or using or disseminating child pornography in a foreign country is a crime prosecutable in the United States. If you break local laws in the Kyrgyz Republic, your U.S. passport won't help you avoid arrest or prosecution. It's very important to know what's legal and what's not wherever you go.

In the Kyrgyz Republic, you may be taken in by police for questioning if you do not have your passport with you. Driving under the influence of alcohol, no matter how little you have consumed, is considered a serious offense.

Persons violating Kyrgyz Republic laws, even unknowingly, may be expelled, arrested, or imprisoned. Penalties for possessing, using, or trafficking in illegal drugs in the Kyrgyz Republic are severe, and convicted offenders can expect long jail sentences and heavy fines.

While some countries will automatically notify the nearest U.S. embassy or consulate if a U.S. citizen is detained or arrested in a foreign country, that might not always be the case. To ensure that the United States is aware of your circumstances, request that the police and prison officials notify the nearest U.S. embassy or consulate as soon as you are arrested or detained overseas.

Special Circumstances: The borders between the Kyrgyz Republic and its neighbors are poorly delineated and often unmarked, and several areas are in dispute. Border guards on both sides have been known to apprehend travelers in disputed territories to check travel documents. There have been a number of cases along the Tajikistan and Uzbekistan borders where foreign travelers were detained by immigration officials of those countries because the visitor entered the country without a proper visa, even though the traveler had no intention of leaving the Kyrgyz Republic and entering another country. Anyone traveling in those border areas should be especially careful and it is advised that travelers there have multiple entry visas for the Kyrgyz Republic and a visa for the neighboring country, as well.

Kyrgyz customs authorities may enforce strict regulations concerning temporary importation into or export from the Kyrgyz Republic of items such as antiquities or hunting trophies. It is advisable to contact the Embassy of the Kyrgyz Republic at 2630 Massachusetts Avenue, NW, Washington, D.C., 20008, telephone:(202) 338-5141, fax:(202) 742-6501, for specific information regarding customs requirements.

The Kyrgyz Republic is a mostly cash-based economy, although credit cards can be used at major Western-style stores and some restaurants. ATMs are available, although you should use only those installed at bank branches or large, reputable hotels. A hotel or bank may, on occasion, accept traveler's checks, but the fees can be as high as 20 percent.

U.S. citizens are encouraged to carry a copy of their U.S. passport and Kyrgyz visa with them at all times, so that, if questioned by local officials, proof of identity and citizenship are readily available.

The Kyrgyz Republic is an earthquake-prone country. Flooding is also common at some times of the year and in some locations. General information about natural disaster preparedness is available from the U.S. Federal Emergency Management Agency (FEMA).

Hunting and trekking are popular sports for locals and tourists in the Kyrgyz Republic; however, U.S. citizens traveling to the Kyrgyz Republic should be aware that hunting in the Kyrgyz Republic without proper licenses is illegal. It is also illegal to import or own firearms in the Kyrgyz Republic without a permit issued by the Kyrgyz government.

Foreign hunters who do not have official permission to hunt or take trophies out of the country may face criminal and/or civil charges. Both hunting and trekking infrastructures are underdeveloped with limited services, especially in the high mountainous regions. Avalanches and landslides are common in these mountainous regions, often cutting off villages for weeks at a time. These villages and hunting areas are in isolated, rugged, mountainous areas inaccessible by the limited rescue services available in the Kyrgyz Republic. U.S. citizens traveling to the Kyrgyz Republic to hunt or trek need to be aware of the risks involved.

Accessibility: While in the Kyrgyz Republic, individuals with disabilities may find accessibility and accommodation very different from what you find in the United States. The law in the Kyrgyz Republic mandates access to buildings for persons with disabilities and requires access to public transportation and parking. It also authorizes subsidies to make mass media available to persons with hearing or visual disabilities. However, the government generally does not ensure that these provisions of the law are implemented.

Public transportation, sidewalks and road crossings, hotels, and restaurants are in practice rarely made accessible. As a result, it is very unusual to see people in wheelchairs independently traveling around Bishkek.

Medical Facilities and Health Information: Medical services in the Kyrgyz Republic are extremely limited. Elderly travelers and those with existing health problems may be at risk due to inadequate medical facilities. Medications such as insulin and pain medications that are commonly available elsewhere may not be available in the Kyrgyz Republic or may be restricted. The U.S. Embassy strongly recommends that travelers to the Kyrgyz Republic carry medical evacuation insurance in case of emergency. The Consular Section of the U.S. Embassy in Bishkek maintains a list of local clinics that have agreed to provide medical care to U.S. citizens.

You can find detailed information on vaccinations and other health precautions on the CDC website. For information about outbreaks of infectious diseases abroad, consult the World Health Organization (WHO) website. The WHO website also contains additional health information for travelers, including detailed country-specific health information. Tuberculosis is an increasingly serious health concern in the Kyrgyz Republic. For further information, please consult the CDC's information on TB.

Medical Insurance: You can't assume your insurance will go with you when you travel. It's very important to find out BEFORE you leave whether or not your medical insurance will cover you overseas. You need to ask your insurance company two questions:

- Does my policy apply when I'm out of the United States?
- Will it cover emergencies like a trip to a foreign hospital or a medical evacuation?

In many places, doctors and hospitals still expect payment in cash at the time of service. Your regular U.S. health insurance may not cover doctor and hospital visits in other countries. If your policy doesn't go with you when you travel, it's a very good idea to take out another one for your trip.

Traffic Safety and Road Conditions: While in the Kyrgyz Republic, you may encounter road conditions that differ significantly from those in the United States. Accidents involving severe injury and/or death are not uncommon.

Drunk driving and hit-and-run accidents are significant problems, and drivers should exercise particular caution and use defensive driving techniques, especially at night and on holidays. In the event of an accident where there is injury, emergency medical assistance may be very slow to respond. Even if medical assistance does arrive in a timely manner, treatment and facilities available at local clinics may not meet U.S. standards.

Most of the Kyrgyz Republic's road infrastructure consists of two-lane roads, many of which have fallen into disrepair and are poorly marked and lit. Many local drivers disobey fundamental traffic laws by not stopping at red lights, driving while intoxicated, passing vehicles when it is dangerous or prohibited to do so, or not stopping for pedestrians at crosswalks and intersections.

Drivers must exercise particular caution to avoid uneven pavement, potholes, open drains, and uncovered manholes. Night driving should be avoided, as roads are inadequately lit. In winter, roads are seldom plowed and ice and snow make the poor driving conditions even more hazardous. Pedestrians routinely walk in the road, often wearing dark clothes at night. Mountain roads in the Kyrgyz Republic are often narrow and treacherous, and may close without notice due to snow, ice, or rockslides. Guardrails and barriers preventing falling rocks are often missing.

The Kyrgyz Republic does not have a roadside assistance infrastructure. Towing companies do not exist. Although mechanics are available in cities there is little organized oversight or certification of their practices or abilities. Rest areas are infrequent and basic. Service stations are generally available in and near cities, but the fuel they provide may be adulterated or of poor quality.

The road between Almaty, Kazakhstan, and Bishkek, Kyrgyz Republic, is especially unsafe at night or during poor weather. Travel on this route after dark by U.S. Embassy personnel is restricted.

The legal blood alcohol level for driving in the Kyrgyz Republic is zero. Generally, speed limits are 60 km per hour in the cities and 90 km per hour in rural areas. Kyrgyz law mandates that all automobile passengers wear seat belts and that motorcycle riders wear helmets. International driving permits are recognized in the Kyrgyz Republic.

Drivers may face harassment by traffic police, who have been known to demand payment of arbitrary "fines" for purported infractions. According to Kyrgyz law, payment of traffic fines must be made at local banks rather than directly to the traffic police. Public transportation in the Kyrgyz Republic is limited to buses, taxis, and very few intercity trains.

Travelers should be particularly careful when using public transportation. Buses tend to be very crowded and can be unsafe and unreliable. Taxis too can be dangerous. Due to the danger of theft or assault, travelers should avoid entering a cab that already contains passengers. Taxis are seldom metered, and travelers should negotiate a fare prior to entering a cab and be aware that cab drivers often try to charge foreigners a high fare. Drivers of vehicles that are not taxis are often willing to drive people for fares. However, U.S. citizens should avoid using these "private taxis" and unmarked taxis.

Aviation Safety Oversight: As there is no direct commercial air service to the United States by carriers registered in the Kyrgyz Republic, the U.S. Federal Aviation Administration (FAA) has not assessed the government of the Kyrgyz Republic's Civil Aviation Authority for compliance with International Civil Aviation Organization (ICAO) aviation safety standards. Further information may be found on the FAA's safety assessment page.

Children's Issues: Please see the U.S. Dept. of State Office of Children's Issues web pages on intercountry adoption and international parental child abduction.

Intercountry Adoption

June 2, 2011

In October 2008, the previous government of Kyrgyzstan halted all intercountry adoptions in response to allegations of corruption and illegal processing. The new government has not yet implemented a new processing system, and at this time it is not possible for new intercountry adoption cases to move forward.

The Department of State continues to reach out to the Kyrgyzstan government in an effort to seek a resolution for US citizen prospective adoptive families who were in various stages of the process prior to adoptions being suspended.

A draft Law amending the Family Code to enable the government of Kyrgyzstan to establish new adoption regulations has passed its 2nd and 3rd readings in the Kyrgyz Parliament. President Otunbaeva signed the Law on May 6, 2011 and tasked the Government to bring legislation into conformity with this new Law within 3 months.

At this time, we are unable to estimate when new adoptions from Kyrgyzstan may resume. Updated information will be provided on www.adoption.state.gov as it becomes available..

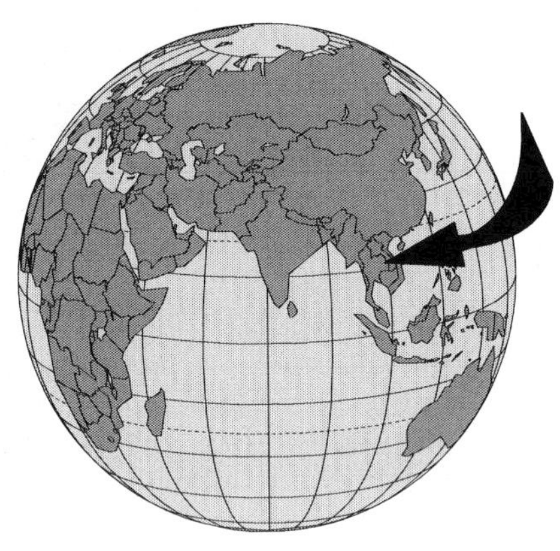

LAOS

Compiled from publications that were available as of February 2013 from the U.S. Department of State, the U.S. Department of Commerce, and the Central Intelligence Agency (CIA). See the introduction to this set for explanatory notes.

Official Name:
Lao People's Democratic Republic

PROFILE

Geography

Area: total: 236,800 sq km; country comparison to the world: 84; land: 230,800 sq km; water: 6,000 sq km

Major cities: Vientiane (capital) 799,000 (2009)

Climate: tropical monsoon; rainy season (May to November); dry season (December to April)

Terrain: mostly rugged mountains; some plains and plateaus

People

Nationality: noun: Lao(s) or Laotian(s); adjective: Lao or Laotian

Population: 6,586,266 (July 2012 est.)

Population growth rate: 1.655% (2012 est.)

Ethnic groups: Lao 55%, Khmou 11%, Hmong 8%, other (over 100 minor ethnic groups) 26% (2005 census)

Religions: Buddhist 67%, Christian 1.5%, other and unspecified 31.5% (2005 census)

Languages: Lao (official), French, English, various ethnic languages

Literacy: definition: age 15 and over can read and write; total population: 73%; male: 83%; female: 63% (2005 Census)

Health: life expectancy at birth: total population: 62.77 years; male: 60.85 years; female: 64.76 years (2012 est.); Infant mortality rate: total: 57.77 deaths/1,000 live births; male: 63.68 deaths/1,000 live births; female: 51.62 deaths/1,000 live births (2012 est.)

Unemployment rate: 2.5% (2009 est.)

Work force: 3.69 million (2010 est.)

Government

Type: Communist state

Independence: 19 July 1949

Constitution: promulgated 14 August 1991; amended in 2003

Political subdivisions: 16 provinces (khoueng, singular and plural) and 1 capital city (nakhon luang, singular and plural); Attapu, Bokeo, Bolikhamxai, Champasak, Houaphan, Khammouan, Louangnamtha, Louangphabang, Oudomxai, Phongsali, Salavan, Savannakhet, Viangchan (Vientiane), Viangchan, Xaignabouli, Xekong, Xiangkhouang

Suffrage: 18 years of age; universal

Economy

GDP (purchasing power parity): $19.16 billion (2012 est.); $17.66 billion (2011 est.); $16.31 billion (2010 est.); $15.11 billion (2009 est.)

GDP real growth rate: 8.3% (2012 est.); 8.3% (2011 est.); 7.9% (2010 est.); 7.6% (2009 est.)

GDP per capita (PPP): $3,000 (2012 est.); $2,700 (2011 est.); $2,500 (2010 est.); $2,400 (2009 est.)

Natural resources: timber, hydropower, gypsum, tin, gold, gemstones

Agriculture products: sweet potatoes, vegetables, corn, coffee, sugarcane, tobacco, cotton, tea, peanuts, rice; cassava (manioc), water buffalo, pigs, cattle, poultry

Industries: mining (copper, tin, gold, and gypsum); timber, electric power, agricultural processing, rubber, construction, garments, cement, tourism

Exports: $2.28 billion (2012 est.); $2.131 billion (2011 est.); $1.746 billion (2010 est.)

Exports—commodities: wood products, coffee, electricity, tin, copper, gold

Exports—partners: Thailand 34.8%, China 24.6%, Vietnam 10% (2011)

Imports: $2.645 billion (2012 est.); $2.336 billion (2011 est.); $2.06 billion (2010 est.)

Imports—commodities: machinery and equipment, vehicles, fuel, consumer goods

Imports—partners: Thailand 65.9%, China 11.3%, Vietnam 5.3% (2011)

Debt—external: $5.599 billion (31 December 2012 est.); $5.953 billion (31 December 2011 est.); $5.564 billion (31 December 2010 est.)
Exchange rates: kips (LAK) per US dollar; 8,017.7 (2012 est.); 8,043.7 (2011 est.); 8,258.8 (2010 est.); 8,516.04 (2009); 8,760.69 (2008); 9,658 (2007)

PEOPLE

Laos' population for 2012 is estimated at 6.5 million, dispersed unevenly across the country. Most people live in valleys of the Mekong River and its tributaries. Vientiane prefecture, the capital and largest city, is estimated to haveabout 853,000 residents in 2012.

The country's population density was 27/sq. km. About half the country's people are ethnic Lao, the principal lowland inhabitants as well as the politically and culturally dominant group.

The Lao are descended from the Tai people who began migrating southward from China in the first millennium A.D. Mountain tribes of Hmong-Yao, and Tibeto-Burman (Kor and Phounoy) as well as Tai ethnolinguistic heritage are found in northern Laos. Until recently, they were known as Lao Sung or highland Lao. In the central and southern mountains, Austro Asiatic (Mon-Khmer and Viet-Muong) tribes, formerly known as Lao Theung or mid-slope Lao, predominate. Some Vietnamese and Chinese minorities remain, particularly in the towns, but many left in two waves—after partial independence in the late 1940s and again after 1975.

National/Racial/Ethnic Minorities

Of the 49 official ethnic groups in the country, the Hmong are one of the largest and most prominent. There were a number of Hmong officials in the senior ranks of the government and the LPRP, including one Politburo member and five members of the LPRP Central Committee. However, some Hmong believed their ethnic group could not coexist with ethnic Lao. This belief fanned separatist or irredentist beliefs among some Hmong. The government focused limited assistance projects in Hmong areas to address regional and ethnic disparities in income, which helped ameliorate conditions in the poorest districts.

Language

The official and dominant language is Lao, a tonal language of the Tai linguistic group. Minorities speak an assortment of Mon-Khmer, Hmong-Yao, and Tibeto-Burman languages. French, once common in government and commerce, has declined in usage, while knowledge of English—the language of the Association of Southeast Asian Nations (ASEAN)—has increased in recent years. The government is encouraging officials and students to learn English. High school students are required to take either French or English; the majority today choose English. The government introduced English at the primary school level in 2010.

Religion

Theravada Buddhism is the religion of nearly all ethnic or "lowland" Lao, who constitute 40 to 50 percent of the overall population of the country. The remainder of the population belongs to at least 48 distinct ethnic minority groups. Most of these ethnic minorities are practitioners of animism and ancestor worship. Animism is predominant among most Sino-Thai groups, such as the Thai Dam and Thai Daeng, as well as among Mon-Khmer and Burmo-Tibetan groups. Even among lowland Lao, many pre-Buddhist animistic beliefs have been incorporated into Theravada Buddhist practice, particularly in the rural areas. Roman Catholics, Protestants, Muslims, Baha'is, Mahayana Buddhists, and followers of Confucianism constitute less than 3 percent of the population.

HISTORY

Laos traces its first recorded history and its origins as a unified state to the emergence of the Kingdom of Lan Xang (literally, "million elephants") in 1353. Under the rule of King Fa Ngum, this powerful and wealthy kingdom held suzerainty over much of what today is Thailand and Laos. His successors, especially King Setthathirat in the 16th century, helped establish Buddhism as the predominant religion of the country.

By the 17th century, the kingdom of Lan Xang entered a period of decline marked by dynastic struggle and conflicts with its neighbors. In the late 18th century, the Siamese (Thai) established suzerainty over much of what is now Laos. The region was divided into principalities centered on Luang Prabang in the north, Vientiane in the center, and Champassak in the south. Following their colonization of Vietnam, the French supplanted the Siamese and began to integrate all of Laos into the French empire. The Franco-Siamese treaty of 1907 defined the present Lao boundary with Thailand.

During World War II, the Japanese occupied French Indochina, including Laos. King Sisavang Vong of Luang Prabang was induced to declare independence from France in 1945, just prior to Japan's surrender. During this period, nationalist sentiment grew. In September 1945, Vientiane and Champassak united with Luang Prabang to form an independent government under the Free Laos (Lao Issara) banner. The movement, however, was short-lived. By early 1946, French troops reoccupied the country and conferred limited autonomy on Laos following elections for a constituent assembly.

During the first Indochina war between France and the communist movement in Vietnam, Prince Souphanouvong helped form the Pathet Lao (Land of Laos) resistance organization committed to the communist struggle against colonialism. Laos was not granted full sovereignty until the French defeat by the Vietnamese

and the subsequent Geneva peace conference in 1954. Elections were held in 1955, and the first coalition government, led by Prince Souvanna Phouma, was formed in 1957. The coalition government collapsed in 1958, amidst increased polarization of the political process. Rightist forces took over the government.

In 1960, Kong Le, an army captain, seized Vientiane in a coup and demanded the formation of a neutralist government to end the fighting. The neutralist government, once again led by Souvanna Phouma, was not successful in holding power. Rightist forces under Gen. Phoumi Nosavan supplanted it later that same year. Subsequently, the neutralists allied themselves with the communist insurgents and began to receive support from the Soviet Union. Phoumi Nosavan's rightist regime received support from the United States. A second Geneva conference, held in 1961–62, provided for the independence and neutrality of Laos. Soon after accord was reached, the signatories accused each other of violating the terms of the agreement, and, with superpower support on both sides, the civil war soon resumed. Although Laos was to be neutral, a growing American and North Vietnamese military presence in the country increasingly drew Laos into the second Indochina war (1954–75). For nearly a decade, Laos was subjected to extremely heavy bombing as the U.S. sought to interdict the portion of the Ho Chi Minh Trail that passed through eastern Laos. Unexploded ordnance, particularly cluster munitions, remains a major problem.

In 1972, the communist People's Party renamed itself the Lao People's Revolutionary Party (LPRP). It joined a new coalition government in Laos soon after the Vientiane cease-fire agreement in 1973. Nonetheless, the political struggle among communists, neutralists, and rightists continued. The fall of Saigon and Phnom Penh to communist forces in April 1975 hastened the decline of the coalition in Laos. Several months after these communist victories, the Pathet Lao entered Vientiane. On December 2, 1975, the king abdicated his throne and the communist Lao People's Democratic Republic (LPDR) was established.

The new communist government imposed centralized economic decision-making and broad security measures, including control of the media and the arrest and incarceration of many members of the previous government and military in "re-education camps." These draconian policies and deteriorating economic conditions, along with government efforts to enforce political control, prompted an exodus of lowland Lao and ethnic Hmong from Laos. About 10% of the Lao population sought refugee status after 1975, many of whom resettled in third countries, including the United States. From 1975 to 1996, the U.S. resettled some 250,000 Lao refugees from Thailand, including 130,000 Hmong. The last major resettlement to the United States of about 15,000 Hmong from the Wat Tham Krabok camp was in 2004. Over time, the Lao Government closed the reeducation camps and released most political prisoners. By the end of 1999, more than 28,900 Hmong and lowland Lao had voluntarily repatriated to Laos—3,500 from China and the rest from Thailand. The Office of the United Nations High Commissioner for Refugees (UNHCR) monitored returnees for a number of years and reported no evidence of systemic persecution or discrimination against returnees per se. UNHCR closed its Laos office at the end of 2001. Today, Laos is a country in transition and has set a goal of graduating from Least Developed Country status by 2020. While the Lao political system remains firmly in the control of the Lao People's Revolutionary Party (LPRP), the forces of globalization and regionalization continue to drive the Lao government to open the economy to market forces. Laos increasingly shows a willingness to engage in international fora on governance issues as well.

GOVERNMENT AND POLITICAL CONDITIONS

The Lao People's Democratic Republic is an authoritarian state ruled by the only party that the constitution legitimizes, the Lao People's Revolutionary Party (LPRP). The most recent National Assembly election was held on April 30, and almost all candidates were LPRP members vetted by the party.

The law provides for a representative national assembly, elected every five years in open, multiple-candidate, fairly tabulated elections with universal, adult-suffrage voting by secret ballot. Election committees appointed by the National Assembly must approve all candidates for local and national elections. Candidates do not need to be LPRP members, but in practice almost all were.

The National Assembly chooses members of the Standing Committee, generally based on the previous Standing Committee's recommendations. Upon such recommendations, the National Assembly elects or removes the president and vice president. The Standing Committee has the mandate to supervise all administrative and judicial organizations and the sole power to recommend presidential decrees. It also appoints the National Election Committee, which has powers over elections, including approval of candidates. Activities of the Standing Committee were not fully transparent.

The National Assembly, upon the president's recommendation, formally elects the prime minister and other government ministers.

Recent Elections

The most recent National Assembly election was on April 30, 2011. Independent observers were not allowed to monitor the election process.

Political Parties: The constitution legitimizes only the LPRP; all other political parties are outlawed.

Participation of Women and Minorities: There were 33 women in the 132-seat National Assembly, including two on the ten-member Standing Committee, and three women were members of the 13-member People's Supreme Court. The 61-seat LPRP Central Committee included five women, one of whom was also a member of the 11-member Politburo and president of the National Assembly. Of six ministers in the Prime Minister's Office, two were women. The minister of labor and social welfare also was a woman.

While 80 percent of the population lived in rural areas and the village chief and village council handled most everyday matters, fewer than 1 percent of the village chiefs were women. The LWU—the LPRP mass organization focused on women's issues with a presence in every village and at every government level—is the only organization that has representation in every village, and only one member of the LWU represented women in each village council.

There were seven members of ethnic minorities in the LPRP Central Committee, including two in the Politburo. The National Assembly included 50 members of ethnic minorities, while two of the 28 cabinet ministers were members of ethnic minority groups. The new president of the National Assembly was also a member of an ethnic minority. One of the People's Supreme Court justices was a member of an ethnic minority.

Principal Government Officials

Last Updated: 1/31/2013

Lao officials are addressed by the first element in their names.

Pres.: **CHOUMMALI Saignason, Lt. Gen.**
Vice Pres.: **BOUN-GNANG Volachit**
Prime Min.: **THONGSING Thammavong**
First Dep. Prime Min.: **ASANG Laoli, Maj. Gen.**
Dep. Prime Min.: **DOUANGCHAY Phichit, Maj. Gen.**
Dep. Prime Min.: **SOMSAVAT Lengsavat**
Dep. Prime Min.: **THONGLOUN Sisoulit**
Min. of Agriculture & Forestry: **VILAYVANH Phomkhe**
Min. of Communications, Transport, Posts, & Construction: **SOMMATH Pholsena**
Min. of Education & Sports: **PHANKHAM Viphavanh**
Min. of Energy & Mining: **SOULIVONG Daravong**
Min. of Finance: **PHOUPHET Khamphounvong**
Min. of Foreign Affairs: **THONGLOUN Sisoulit**
Min. of Industry & Commerce: **NAM Viyaketh**
Min. of Information, Culture, & Tourism: **BOSENGKHAM Vongdara**
Min. of Interior: **KHAMPANE Philavong**
Min. of Justice: **CHALEUAN Yapaoher**
Min. of Labor & Social Welfare: **ONECHANH Thammavong**
Min. of National Defense: **DOUANGCHAY Phichit, Maj. Gen.**
Min. of Natural Resources & Environment: **NOULIN Sinbandith**
Min. of Planning & Investment: **SOMDY Douangdy**
Min. of Post, Telecommunications, & Communication: **HIEM Phommachanh**
Min. of Public Health: **EKSAVANG Vongvichit, Dr.**
Min. of Public Security: **THONGBANH Sengaphone**
Min. of Public Works & Transportation: **SOMMATH Pholsena**
Min. of Science & Technology: **BOVIENGKHAM Vongdara**
Min. to the Prime Min.'s Office & Head of Public Admin. & Civil Authority: **BOUNPHENG Mounphosay**
Min. to the Prime Min.'s Office & Head of Sustainable Development: **KHAM-OUANE Bouppha**
Min. to the Prime Min.'s Office & Head of Water Resources & Environmental Authority: **KHEMPHENG Pholsena**
Min. to the Prime Min.'s Office: **BOUASY Lovansay**
Min. to the Prime Min.'s Office: **BOUNHEUANG Duangphachanh**

Min. to the Prime Min.'s Office: **BOUNTIEM Phitsamay**
Min. to the Prime Min.'s Office: **DOUANGSAVAD Souphanouvang**
Min. to the Prime Min.'s Office: **ONNEUA Phommachanh**
Min. to the Prime Min.'s Office: **SAISENGLI Tengbliachu**
Min. & Chmn. of National Mekong Ctte.: **KHAMLOUAD Sitlakone**
Min. & Chmn. of National Tourism Authority: **SOMPHONG Mongkhonvilay**
Min. & Head of Cabinet, Pres.'s Office: **SOUBANH Srithirath**
Min. & Head of Govt. Secretariats: **CHEUANG Sombounkhanh**
Chmn., National Narcotics Control Board: **SOUBANH Srithirath**
Chmn., Planning & Investment Ctte.: **SINLAVONG Khoutphaytoune**
Chmn., State Control Commission: **ASANG Laoli, Maj. Gen.**
Chmn., State Inspection Ctte., & Head, Anticorruption Agency: **BOUNTHONG Chitmani**
Governor, Bank of Laos: **SAMPAO Phaysith**
Ambassador to the US: **SENG Soukhathivong**
Permanent Representative to the UN, New York: **KANIKA Phommachanh**

ECONOMY

The government of Laos, one of the few remaining one-party communist states, began decentralizing control and encouraging private enterprise in 1986. The results, starting from an extremely low base, were striking - growth averaged 6% per year from 1988–2008 except during the short-lived drop caused by the Asian financial crisis that began in 1997. Laos' growth exceeded 7% per year during 2008–12. Despite this high growth rate, Laos remains a country with an underdeveloped infrastructure, particularly in rural areas. It has a basic, but improving, road system, and limited external and internal land-line telecommunications.

Electricity is available in urban areas and in many rural districts. Laos' economy continues to rely on subsistence agriculture, dominated by rice cultivation in lowland areas, which accounts for about 30% of GDP and 75% of total employment. Economic growth has reduced official poverty rates from 46% in 1992 to 26% in 2010. The economy also has benefited from high-profile foreign direct investment in hydropower, copper and gold mining, and construction though some projects have drawn criticism for their environmental impacts.

Laos gained Normal Trade Relations status with the US in 2004. On the fiscal side, Laos initiated a VAT tax system in 2010. Simplified investment procedures and expanded bank credits for small farmers and small entrepreneurs will improve Laos' economic prospects. The government appears committed to raising the country's profile among investors, opening the country's first stock exchange in 2011 and participating in regional economic cooperation initiatives. Laos was admitted to the WTO in 2012.

The World Bank has declared that Laos' goal of graduating from the UN Development Program's list of least-developed countries by 2020 is achievable.

Labor Conditions

The law allows for children between the ages of 14 and 18 to work up to eight hours per day, provided such work is not dangerous or difficult. There were no known reports of children working in hazardous environments. The ministries of public security and justice, and labor and social welfare, are responsible for enforcing these provisions, but enforcement was ineffective due to a lack of inspectors and other resources. Many children helped on family farms or in shops and other family businesses, but child labor was rare in industrial enterprises. Forced labor of Lao boys allegedly occurred in the agricultural sector, for example, on rubber plantations.

The government sets wages and salaries for government employees; management sets wages and salaries for private business employees. The Ministry of Labor and Social Welfare determines the minimum wage but has no regular schedule or transparent process for doing so. On November 23, the government passed a decree increasing the monthly minimum wage for private sector workers from 348,000 to 626,000 kip (approximately $42 to $75). Additionally, employers were required to pay an 8,500-kip ($1) meal allowance per day. The National Assembly, in consultation with the Ministry of Finance, last increased the minimum wage for civil servants and state enterprise employees to 405,000 kip ($49) per month in 2008. The government set the national poverty line at an average income of 192,000 kip ($23) per person per month. In addition to their minimum wage, civil servants often received housing subsidies and other government benefits. Some piecework employees, especially on construction sites, earned less than the minimum wage.

The law provides for a workweek limited to 48 hours (36 hours for employment in dangerous activities) and at least one day of rest per week. Overtime may not exceed 30 hours per month, and each period of overtime may not exceed three hours. The overtime pay rate varies from 150 to 300 percent of normal pay. The overtime law was not effectively enforced. By law the government determines public holidays. Workers employed under an employment contract for an indefinite period or for a period of more than one year and who have worked for one full year are entitled to 15 days' annual leave. Workers in sectors involving heavy work or work that is hazardous to health, as specified in the law, are entitled to 18 days' annual leave with full pay at the normal rate.

The law provides for safe working conditions and higher compensation for dangerous work.

There were a number of undocumented immigrants in Laos, particularly from Vietnam, China, and Burma, and they were vulnerable to exploitation by employers. These immigrants primarily worked in construction, plantations, casinos, and service industries. The law sets the percentage of foreign laborers allowed to be hired by a company operating in the country and requires approval of foreign workers, but it does not provide specific work-condition protections for them. The Ministry of Labor and Social Welfare estimated in October 2010 that approximately 250,000 foreigners were working in the country.

U.S.-LAO RELATIONS

The United States established diplomatic relations with Laos in 1950, following its limited independence within the French Union. Nationalists continued to push for an end to French colonialism. Laos gained full independence from France in 1954, but within a few years it entered into civil war. The United States supported a rightist regime in Laos. For nearly a decade beginning in 1964, Laos was subjected to heavy U.S. bombing as part of the wider war in Indochina. Following the change of regimes in Vietnam and Cambodia in 1975,, a communist government also came to power in Laos. The government aligned itself with Vietnam and the Soviet bloc, implementing one-party rule and a command economy. U.S.-Lao relations deteriorated after 1975, and U.S. representation was downgraded. After the collapse of the Soviet Union, Laos sought to improve relations with other countries. Full U.S.-Lao diplomatic relations were restored in 1992. In July 2012 Secretary of State Hillary Clinton visited Laos, marking the first visit by aSecretary of State since 1955.

Accounting for American personnel missing in Laos from the war was the initial focus of the post-war bilateral relationship. Since that time the relationship has broadened to include cooperation on a broad range of issues including counternarcotics, health, environment, and trade.

U.S. Assistance to Laos

Following the 1986 introduction of some economic reforms, Laos' economy is essentially a free market system with active central planning by the government. The overarching policy goals for U.S. assistance to Laos are to improve Lao governance and the rule of law, and increase the country's capacity to integrate fully within the Association for Southeast Asian Nations (ASEAN) and the global economy.

The largest part of U.S. bilateral assistance to Laos is devoted to improving health. The United States also helps improve trade policy in Laos, promotes sustainable development and biodiversity conservation, and works to strengthen the criminal justice system and law enforcement. Unexploded ordnance (UXO) from the war, particularly cluster munitions, remains a major problem. The United States has provided significant support for UXO clearance, removal and assistance for survivors.

Bilateral Economic Relations

U.S. exports to Laos include diamonds, metals, aircraft, vehicles, and agricultural products. U.S. imports from Laos include apparel, inorganic chemicals, agricultural products, and jewelry. Laos is working toward accession to the World Trade Organization (WTO) and has committed to joining the ASEAN Economic Community (AEC). Both of these processes require trade and regulatory reforms, which should make the investment climate more attractive to U.S. companies. WTO and AEC requirements also reinforce fuller implementation of the conditions of the 2005 U.S.-Laos bilateral trade agreement. The United States and Laos have a bilateral investment agreement and have signed a civil aviation agreement.

Laos's Membership in International Organizations

Laos and the United States belong to a number of the same international organizations, including the United Nations, ASEAN Regional Forum, International Monetary Fund, and World Bank. Laos also is an observer to the World Trade Organization.

Bilateral Representation

Laos maintains an embassy in the United States at 2222 S Street NW, Washington, DC 20008 (tel: 202-332-6416).

Principal U.S. Embassy Officials

Last Updated: 1/14/2013

VIENTIANE (E) Rue Bartolonie, Vientiane, (856) (21) 26-7000, Fax (856) (21) 26-7190, INMARSAT Tel 683-132825/826/827, Workweek: Monday-Friday, 8:00am-5:00pm, Website: http://vientiane.usembassy.gov/

DCM OMS:	Jackie Pryor
AMB OMS:	Nancy Walraven
CDC:	Dr. Andrew L. Corwin
MGT:	Robert L. Kingman
NAS/INL:	Lacy Wright
POL/ECON:	Tracy Taylor
POSHO:	Fritz Fuller
SDO/DATT:	LTC Matt Kent
AMB:	Karen Stewart
CON:	Long Nguyen
DCM:	Paul Mayer
PAO:	Pam Devolder
GSO:	Graham Harlow
RSO:	Jerry Tavares
AFSA:	Fritz Fuller
AID:	Tom D'Agnes
CLO:	Vacant
ECON:	Matt Younger
EEO:	Dustin Bickel
ICASS Chair:	Rod McKinley
IMO:	Tim Teas
IPO:	Patrick Kennedy
ISSO:	Patrick Kennedy
State ICASS:	Cori Bickel

TRAVEL

Consular Information Sheet

January 27, 2012

Country Description: The Lao People's Democratic Republic (Laos) is a poor, developing country ruled by an authoritarian, Communist, one-party government. Political power is centralized in the Lao People's Revolutionary Party. Services and facilities for tourists are adequate in the capital, Vientiane, and the UNESCO

World Heritage town of Luang Prabang but are extremely limited in other parts of the country.

Smart Traveler Enrollment Program (STEP)/Embassy Locations: If you are going to live in or visit Laos, please take the time to tell our Embassy in Vientiane about your trip. If you enroll, we can keep you up to date with important safety and security announcements. It will also help your friends and family get in touch with you in an emergency.

U.S. Embassy Vientiane
Rue Bartholonie (near That Dam), Vientiane—for local mail
Unit 8165, Box V, APO AP 96546—for mail from the United States
Telephone (856-21) 267-000
(856-21) 267-111 recorded emergency information for U.S. citizens
(856-20) 5550–2016 duty officer emergency cellular telephone
(856-21) 267-190. Embassy-wide fax number

Entry/Exit Requirements for U.S. Citizens: You must have both a passport and visa to enter Laos; your passport must also have at least six months validity remaining. You can get a visa on arrival in Laos if you are traveling for tourism, have two passport-size photographs and pay $35 at the following ports of entry: Wattay Airport, Vientiane; Pakse, Savannakhet, and Luang Prabang Airports; Friendship Bridge, Vientiane and Savannakhet; Nam Heuang Friendship Bridge, Sayabouly Province; and border crossings at Boten-Mohan, Dansavan-Lao Bao, Houaysay-Chiang Khong, Thakhek-Nakhon Phanom, Nong Haet-Nam Kan, Nam Phao-Kao Cheo, Veun Kham-Dong Calor and Vangtao-Chong Mek. You can also get a visa on arrival at the Tha Naleng train station in Vientiane, which connects to the train station in Nongkhai, Thailand. If you obtain a visa from a Lao embassy or consulate prior to your travel to Laos, you may also enter at the following international entry points: Napao-Chalo, Taichang-Sophoun, Pakxan-Bungkan, and Xiengkok.

You will generally be allowed to stay in Laos for 30 days after you arrive. If you were born in Laos, you may be admitted for 60 days or longer. You can extend your 30-day tourist visa up to an additional 60 days for a fee of $2 per day through the Department of Immigration in Vientiane. If you overstay your visa in Laos, you risk arrest and will be fined $10 for each day of overstay as you leave. The Lao government calculates visa fees and fines in U.S. dollars. Thai baht and Lao kip may sometimes be accepted for the fees but at unfavorable exchange rates. If you plan to visit Laos, additional information is available from the Lao National Tourism Administration.

If you wish to obtain a visa in advance, please contact a Lao embassy or consulate. In the United States, you can get visa and other information about Lao entry requirements from the Embassy of the Lao People's Democratic Republic, 2222 S St. NW, Washington DC 20008, tel: 202-332-6416, fax: 202-332-4923. If you enter Laos with a visitor visa issued at a Lao embassy abroad, you will be allowed to stay in Laos for 60 days.

Business visas can only be arranged in advance; a company or individual "sponsor" must contact the Lao Ministry of Foreign Affairs (MFA) in Vientiane and request a visa for you and offer a "guarantee." Once the Lao MFA approves the request, the approval will be sent to the Lao Embassy in Washington, DC, and business travelers may then apply for the business visa. This process usually takes one to three months. After you arrive, business visas can generally be extended for one month.

Do not attempt to enter Laos without valid travel documents or outside of official ports of entry. You should not cross the border between Laos and Thailand along the Mekong River except at official immigration check crossings. If you attempt to enter Laos outside of official ports of entry, you may be arrested, detained, fined, and deported.

Immigration offices at some of the less-used land border crossing points are not well marked. Make sure you complete all immigration and customs requirements when you enter or depart Laos. If you enter Laos without completing these formalities, you may be subject to fines, detention, imprisonment, and/or deportation.

In an effort to prevent international child abduction, many governments have initiated additional procedures at entry/exit points. These often include requiring documentary evidence of relationship, such as the child's birth certificate, and permission for the child's travel from the parent(s) or legal guardian not present. Having such documentation on hand, even if not required, may facilitate entry/departure.

At Wattay Airport (Vientiane), Pakse Airport, Savannakhet Airport, and the Luang Prabang Airport, there is an international airport departure tax of US$10. This tax may be included in the price of the airline ticket, depending on the carrier. There is also a 5,000 kip (equivalent to approximately U.S. 60 cents) departure tax for domestic flights, which may be included in the price of the airline ticket, depending on the carrier. At the Friendship Bridge (Vientiane, Laos—Nong Khai, Thailand border crossing) there is an overtime fee after 4:00 pm weekdays and during weekends. Visit the Embassy of Laos web site for the most current information.

The U.S. Department of State is unaware of any HIV/AIDS entry restrictions for visitors to or foreign residents of Laos.

Threats to Safety and Security: There have been reports in the past of violent incidents carried out by anti-government forces, including reports in 2007 of isolated clashes between Lao Government forces and unidentified opponents in the area of Vang Vieng in northern Vientiane Province and in Bokeo Province. The Department of State recommends that if you travel to or reside in Laos, exercise caution and be alert to your surroundings at all times.

The Lao Government security forces often stop and check all transport on main roads, particularly at night. You must comply with requests to stop at checkpoints and roadblocks. Especially if you are considering travel outside urban centers, please contact relevant Lao government offices, such as Lao Immigration Police Headquarters in Vientiane, the Lao Tourist Police, local police and customs offices, or the U.S. Embassy for the most current security information. To avoid trouble with the authorities, if you are traveling outside of normal tourist areas or contemplating any unusual activity (including, but not limited to, engaging in business, extensive photography, or scientific research of any kind), be sure to seek advance permission from the Village Chief, District Head, Provincial Governor, or National Tourism Authority, as appropriate.

The large amount of unexploded ordnance (UXO) left over from the Indochina War causes more than 300 casualties per year. UXO can be found in some parts of Savannakhet, Xieng Khouang, Saravane, Khammouane, Sekong, Champassak, Houaphan, Attapeu, Luang Prabang, and Vientiane Provinces. In addition, numerous mine fields are left over from the war along Route 7 (from Route 13 to the Vietnam border), Route 9 (Savannakhet to the Vietnam border), and Route 20 (Pakse to Saravane). Never pick up unknown metal objects and avoid traveling off well-used roads, tracks, and paths.

You should also exercise caution in remote areas along the Lao border with Burma. Bandits, drug traffickers and other people pursuing illegal activities operate in these border areas, as do armed insurgent groups opposed to the government of Burma.

Stay up to date:

- Bookmark our Bureau of Consular Affairs website, which contains the current Travel Warnings and Travel Alerts as well as the Worldwide Caution.
- Follow us on Twitter and the Bureau of Consular Affairs page on Facebook.
- Download our free Smart Traveler IPhone App to have travel information at your fingertips.
- Call 1-888-407-4747 toll-free within the U.S. and Canada, or a regular toll line, 1-202-501-4444, from other countries.
- Taking some time before travel to consider your personal security.

Crime: Laos generally has a low rate of violent crime, but you should remain aware of your surroundings and exercise appropriate security precautions. The number of thefts and assaults in Laos has increased, and some have turned violent. Sexual assaults also occur in Laos. You should exercise caution, particularly after dark, at roadside restaurants, bars and stalls. Foreigners are often victims of purse snatchings while eating or while riding bicycles or motorcycles. Please be careful when carrying these items on your person.

Residential burglary is commonplace. Local law enforcement responses to crimes, even violent crimes, are often limited. Foreigners attempting to report crimes have reported finding police stations closed, emergency telephone numbers unanswered, or policemen lacking transportation or authorization to investigate crimes that occur at night. If you move to Laos, please contact the U.S. Embassy Vientiane for security advice.

If you travel to Vang Vieng, be aware that some tourists have been robbed and sexually assaulted in that area. Many restaurants in the Vang Vieng area offer menu items, particularly "pizzas," "shakes," or "teas," that may contain unknown substances or opiates. These products are often advertised as "happy" or "special" items. These unknown substances or opiates can be dangerous, causing serious illness or even death. Travelers in Vang Vieng have been fined and detained for purchasing, possessing, or using illegal substances. In recent years, foreigners, including U.S. citizens, have died in Laos after using illegal drugs, such as methamphetamines, opium, or heroin. The potency of some of these drugs can be several times that of similar substances found in the United States.

Please exercise caution on overnight bus trips, particularly on buses travelling to/from Vietnam. The Embassy has received reports of scams and thefts of personal belongings.

Don't buy counterfeit and pirated goods, even if they are widely available. Not only are the bootlegs illegal in the United States, if you purchase them, you may also be breaking local law.

Victims of Crime: If you or someone you know becomes the victim of a crime abroad, you should contact the local police and the nearest U.S. embassy or consulate. We can:

- Replace a stolen passport;
- For violent crimes such as assault or rape, help you find appropriate medical care;
- Put you in contact with the appropriate police authorities and your family members or friends;
- Help you understand the local criminal justice process and direct you to local attorneys.

The local equivalent to the "911" emergency lines in Laos are 190 for fire, 191 for traffic police, and 195 for ambulance. The Tourist Police can be reached in Vientiane at 021-251-128.

Criminal Penalties: While you are traveling in Laos, you are subject to its laws even if you are a U.S. citizen. Foreign laws and legal systems can be vastly different than our own. In Cambodia, you may be taken in for questioning if you don't have your passport with you. It is also illegal to take pictures of certain buildings. Please see Special Circumstances below. Driving under the influence could land you immediately in jail. There are also some things that might be legal in Laos, but still illegal in the United States, and you can be prosecuted under U.S. law if you buy pirated goods. Engaging in sexual conduct with children or using or disseminating child pornography in a foreign country is a crime prosecutable in the United States. If you break local laws in Laos, your U.S. passport won't help you avoid arrest or prosecution. It's very important to know what's legal and what's not where you are going.

Arrest notifications in Laos: If you are arrested in Laos, you have the option to request that the police, prison officials, or other authorities alert the U.S. Embassy in Vientiane of your arrest, and to have communications from you forwarded to the embassy.

Accessibility: While in Laos, individuals with disabilities may find accessibility and accommodation very different from what you find in the United States. Lao law does not mandate accessibility to buildings or government services for persons with disabilities. Vientiane has some local regulations providing building access, but these regulations are not effectively enforced. Currently, except for buildings and hotels that have been built under international standards, most public places and public transportation are not accessible. Persons with disabilities will face difficulties in Laos as foot paths, rest rooms, road crossings and tourist areas are not equipped.

Travel of Foreigners within Laos: The Lao tourist police have informed foreign tourists that a licensed Lao tour guide must accompany any group of more than five foreign tourists; however, this regulation does not appear to be strictly enforced. The authorities may restrict travel in rural areas outside of popular tourist destinations. Restricted areas may not be marked or even widely known by local citizens. If you travel without a reputable tour guide who is aware of local conditions, please talk to local authorities before entering remote areas away from obvious tourist destinations. Lao citizens who wish to have a foreign citizen—including a family member—stay in their home must obtain prior approval from the village chief. You may be held responsible if the Lao host has not secured prior permission for your visit. U.S. citizens are strongly advised to ensure that such permission has been granted before accepting offers to stay in Lao homes.

Surveillance: Security personnel may at times place foreign visitors under surveillance. Hotel rooms, telephones, and fax machines may be monitored and personal possessions in hotel rooms may be searched. Taking photographs of anything that could be perceived as being of military or security interest may result in problems with the local authorities. Please review the section below on Photography and Other Restrictions.

Relationship with Lao Citizens: Lao law prohibits sexual contact between foreign citizens and Lao nationals except when the two parties have been married in accordance with Lao Family Law. Any foreigner who enters into a sexual relationship with a Lao national risks being interrogated, detained, arrested, or fined. Lao police have confiscated passports and imposed fines of up to $5,000 on foreigners who enter into unapproved sexual relationships. The Lao party to the relationship may be jailed without trial. Foreigners are not permitted to invite Lao nationals of the opposite sex to their hotel rooms; police may raid hotel rooms without notice or consent.

If you plan to marry a Lao national, you are required by Lao law to obtain prior permission from the Lao Government. The formal application process can take as long as a year. You can obtain information about these requirements from the U.S. Embassy in Vientiane. The Lao Government will not issue a marriage certificate unless the correct procedures are followed. Any attempt to circumvent Lao regulations may result in arrest, imprisonment, a fine of $500 to $5,000 and deportation. If you cohabit with or enter into a close relationship with a Lao national, you may be accused by Lao authorities of entering into an illegal marriage and be subject to these same penalties. If you wish to become engaged to a Lao national, you must also obtain prior permission from the chief of the village where the Lao national resides. Failure to obtain prior permission can result in a fine of $500 to $5,000. Lao police may impose a large fine on a foreign citizen a few days after he or she holds an engagement ceremony with a Lao citizen based on the suspicion that the couple subsequently had sexual relations out of wedlock.

Marriage: A Lao Prime Ministerial decree requires that marriages of Lao citizens performed abroad be registered with Lao embassies in order to be legal in Laos. If you marry a Lao citizen in the United States, when you visit or return to Laos, you may be subject to penalties under the Lao law governing sexual relationships (above) if your marriage has not been registered beforehand with a Lao embassy.

Religious Workers: Religious proselytizing or distributing religious material is strictly prohibited. If you are caught distributing religious material, you may be arrested or deported. The Government of Laos restricts the importation of religious texts and artifacts. While Lao law allows freedom of religion, the Government registers and controls all associations, including religious groups. Meetings, even in private homes, must be registered and those held outside of established locations may be broken up and the participants arrested.

Mode of Transportation: When you travel in Laos, please consider carefully and evaluate the relative risks of the three modes of transport (see sections on Aviation Safety Oversight, Traffic Safety, and River Travel) below.

River Travel: River travel is common in Laos, but safety conditions do not conform to U.S. standards. In particular, travel by speedboat (the local term is "fast boat") is dangerous and should be avoided, particularly during the dry season, which generally runs from December through April. Avoid travel on or across the Mekong River along the Thai border at night. Lao militia forces have shot at boats on the Mekong after dark.

Photography and Other Restrictions: If you photograph anything that could be perceived as being of military or security interest—including bridges, airfields, military installations, government buildings or government vehicles—you may be detained or arrested, and local authorities may confiscate your camera. Be cautious when traveling near military bases and strictly observe signs delineating military base areas. Lao military personnel have detained and questioned foreigners who have unknowingly passed by unmarked military facilities. Because of the prohibition on religious proselytizing, you should avoid taking photographs or videotaping non-Buddhist religious services. If attending public services or religious gatherings, ask permission from the local police and civil authorities to photograph or videotape. Please see the section above on Religious Workers. Local police may suspect persons using any kind of sophisticated still or video camera equipment of being professional photographers or possibly photojournalists, which may lead to questioning, detention, arrest, or deportation.

Financial Transactions: Network-connected ATMs are available in Vientiane, including those operated by the Australia and New Zealand Bank—Vientiane (ANZV) and the Foreign Commercial Bank of Laos, also known as the Banque Pour le Commerce Exterieur de Laos (BCEL). BCEL also has network-connected ATMs in Vang Vieng, and most provincial capitals, or "Muang." These machines are generally limited to withdrawals of the equivalent of about 100 U.S. dollars in Lao kip only. Credit cards are accepted at major hotels and tourist-oriented businesses. Credit card cash advances and/or Western Union money transfers are available at banks in most provincial capitals and other tourist centers. While the government requires that prices be quoted in Lao kip, prices are often given in U.S. dollars or Thai baht, especially in tourist areas or at markets. The Lao Government requires payment in U.S. dollars for some taxes and fees, including visa fees and the airport departure tax.

Customs/Currency Regulations: Lao customs authorities may enforce strict regulations concerning temporary importation into or export from Laos of items such as firearms, religious materials, antiquities, foreign currency, cameras and other items. Please contact the Embassy of the Lao People's Democratic Republic in Washington for specific information regarding customs requirements. Please also see section on "Religious Workers" above. Prohibitions exist against importing or exporting more than $2,500 (U.S. dollar equivalent) of currency without authorization. Contact the Lao Embassy or Lao customs authorities for more details.

Medical Facilities and Health Information: Medical facilities and services in Laos are limited and do not meet Western standards. In Vientiane, U.S. citizens may wish to contact the Primary Care Center, also known as the Centre medical de L'Ambassade de France (CMAF), which is supported by the French Embassy. The CMAF is located on Khou Vieng Road across the street from the Green Park Hotel, tel. 856-21-214-150, or 856-20-5558–4617, or email. The Australian government also supports a fee for service clinic located at the Australian Embassy which is located at Kilometer 4 on Thadeua Road, tel. 21-353-840. Both facilities have well trained physicians who can handle routine and urgent health problems and provide travel medicine services. In 2011 a clinic operated by the Wattana Hospital group from Thailand opened in the Honda building near the airport. It provides basic clinical services by Thai physicians.

U.S. citizens in Laos often seek medical care in Thailand. The Friendship Bridge linking Vientiane, Laos, to Nong Khai, Thailand, is open daily 6:00 a.m. to 10:00 p.m. Officials generally will allow travelers to cross after hours in cases of medical emergency. AEK International Hospital (tel: 66-42-342-555) and North Eastern Wattana General Hospital, both in Udorn, Thailand (tel: 66-1-833-4262), have English-speaking staff accustomed to dealing with foreign patients. Ambulances for both AEK International Hospital and Nong Khai Wattana Hospital have permission to cross the Friendship Bridge to collectpatients from Vientiane. In Vientiane, the Setthatirat Hospital ambulance (tel: 021-413-720) can take patients to Thailand. The Department of State assumes no responsibility for the professional ability or reputation of these hospitals.

Counterfeit pharmaceuticals are a problem throughout Southeast Asia. Please be aware of this problem and purchase pharmaceuticals only through the most reputable pharmacies and with a physician's prescription.

Avian influenza (H5N1) continues to be a concern in Laos. In Laos and other Southeast Asian countries affected by avian influenza, you should avoid poultry farms, contact with animals in live food markets, and any surfaces that appear to be contaminated with feces from poultry or other animals. For information on influenza, please refer to the Department of State's Influenza Fact Sheet.

You can find good information on vaccinations and other health precautions, on the CDC website. For information about outbreaks of infectious diseases abroad, consult the World Health Organization (WHO) website. The WHO website also contains additional health information for travelers, including detailed country-specific health information.

Medical Insurance:: You can't assume your insurance will go with you when you travel. It's very important to find out BEFORE you leave whether or not your medical insurance will cover you overseas. You need to ask your insurance company two questions:

- Does my policy apply when I'm out of the United States?
- Will it cover emergencies like a trip to a foreign hospital or a medical evacuation?

In many places, doctors and hospitals still expect payment in cash at the time of service. Your regular U.S. health insurance may not cover doctors' and hospital visits in other countries. If your policy doesn't go with you when you travel, it's a very good idea to take out another one for your trip.

Traffic Safety and Road Conditions: While in Laos, you may encounter road conditions that differ significantly from those in the United States. The information below concerning Laos is provided for general reference only and may not be totally accurate in a particular location or circumstance.

The number of road accidents and fatalities in Laos has risen sharply in the last decade as the number of motor vehicles has increased. U.S. citizens involved in traffic accidents have been barred from leaving Laos before paying compensation for property damage or injuries, regardless of who was at fault. A driver involved in a traffic accident should remain at the scene and attempt to contact the police or wait for them to arrive to prepare an accident report. If renting a car or motorcycle, contact the rental company and its insurance agent. If there is major damage, injury, or death, contact the Consular Section or the Duty Officer at the U.S. Embassy. When renting a car, motorcycle, or bicycle, do not give your original U.S. passport to the owner of the vehicle as surety against loss, theft, or damage to the vehicle.

Traffic in Laos is chaotic, and road conditions are very rough. Few roads have lane markings. Where lane markings, road signs, and stoplights do exist, they are widely ignored. Many drivers are unlicensed, inexperienced, and uninsured. Driving under the influence of alcohol or illegal drugs is not uncommon, and penalties for such offenses may not be enforced. Theoretically, traffic moves on the right, but vehicles use all parts of the road. Motorcyclists pay little or no heed to cars. Motorcycles carry as many as five people, greatly impeding the drivers' ability to react to traffic. The evening hours are particularly dangerous. Road construction sites are poorly marked, appear with no advance warning, and can be difficult to see at night. Roads are poorly lit, many vehicles have no operating lights, few bicycles have reflectors, and trucks without reflectors commonly park on unlit roads.

Exercise caution when traveling the roads of Laos, and be sure to check with local authorities, transport companies, other travelers, and/or the Embassy regarding any recent road developments prior to travel. Road obstacles, such as changes in surface conditions due to the weather, occur frequently.

Public transportation is unreliable and is limited after sunset. Automobile taxis or cars for hire are available at the airport, the Friendship Bridge, most major hotels, and near the Morning Market in Vientiane. The most common form of public transport is a three-wheeled, open-sided taxi called "tuk-tuks." Tuk-tuks and taxis are frequently in poor repair, and drivers generally speak little or no English. Inter-city transport is provided by buses, vans, pickups, and trucks, any of which may also be in poor repair.
Emergency services in Laos are either unreliable or non-existent. Lao road traffic regulations require any driver coming upon a road accident to assist in transporting injured persons to a hospital.

Aviation Safety Oversight: As there is no direct commercial air service to the United States by carriers registered in Laos, the U.S. Federal Aviation Administration (FAA) has not assessed the Lao Civil Aviation Authority for compliance with International Civil Aviation Organization (ICAO) aviation safety standards for oversight of Laos's air carrier operations. Further information may be found on the FAA safety assessment page.

Children's Issues: Please see the U.S. Dept. of State Office of Children's Issues web pages on intercountry adoption and international parental child abduction.

Intercountry Adoption

**Alert: Government of Laos Announces Suspension of Intercountry Adoption
March 2012**

The office of the Government of Laos announced on February 20, 2012, that the authorization to allow foreigners to adopt Lao children is suspended until appropriate regulations and procedures are established on intercountry adoption. Updated information will be provided as it becomes available on http://adoption.state.gov.

**Ovrview of Existing Adoption Process
June 2010**

The information in this section has been edited from the latest report available as of February 2013 from the State Department Bureau of Consular Affairs, Office of Overseas Citizens Services. For more information, please read the *Intercountry Adoption* section of this book and review current reports online at http://adoption.state.gov.

Laos is not party to the Hague Convention on Protection of Children and Co-operation in Respect of Intercountry Adoption (Hague Adoption Convention).

The Revised Family Law does not specifically state the legal procedures for foreigners to adopt Lao children. In practice, the Lao government is currently using an informal regulatory process that was in effect prior to the July 2008 revision of the Lao Family Law. Under those procedures, prospective adoptive American citizen parents obtain written authorization from the Office of the Prime Minister (OPM) to begin the intercountry adoption process. The OPM has suggested the steps listed below to obtain approval from the OPM—although these steps may not apply in all cases and Lao authorities may impose additional requirements:

- Prospective adoptive American Citizen parents send a letter of proposal of adoption to the Lao Embassy in the United States

- Ministry of Foreign Affairs (MFA) reviews and approves
- Ministry of Justice (MOJ) reviews and approves
- OPM conducts a review and final approval
- MOJ issues a Final Agreement

Because Lao Family Law is relatively new and is still being developed, regulations may not be clear and may not be fully consistent with other laws or regulations. There are no public or private institutions that operate solely as orphanages. There are no government agencies with clear authority and responsibility for orphans. Irregularities in the methods used to identify children for adoption in Laos can make it difficult to determine if some children meet the requirements established by U.S. immigration law. Such practices as payment to birth mothers to induce them to relinquish their child are clearly prohibited under U.S. immigration law. In this context, prospective adoptive parents should be prepared for a lengthy wait while a review is conducted by U.S. officials to verify a Lao child's background and eligibility for an immigrant visa.

Who Can Adopt? To bring an adopted child to United States from Laos, you must be found eligible to adopt by the U.S. Government. The U.S. Government agency responsible for making this determination is the Department of Homeland Security, U.S. Citizenship and Immigration Services (USCIS). In addition to these U.S. requirements for prospective adoptive parents, Laos also has the following requirements for prospective adoptive parents.

Residency Requirements: There are no residency requirements. Adoptive parents must provide their current residence address.

Age Requirements: Adoptive parents must be 18 years old and at least 18 years older than the adopted child.

Marriage Requirements: Both married and single individuals can adopt.

Income Requirements: While there is no specified income requirement, prospective adoptive parents must submit evidence of their ability to financially support the child. There are no specific documents required but typically this includes a job letter or copies of bank statements.

Who Can Be Adopted? Laos has specific requirements that a child must meet in order to be eligible for adoption. You cannot adopt a child in Laos unless he or she meets the requirements outlined below. In addition to these requirements, a child must meet the definition of an orphan under U.S. law for you to bring him or her back to the United States.

Eligibility Requirements: The biological parent(s) must provide a letter of agreement to release custody of the child. Normally this is accompanied by a certificate stating this from the Village Chief. If the child is 10 years of age or older, the child must also provide a letter of agreement that he/she agrees to be adopted by the adoptive parents. The Village Chief must provide a letter certifying that the biological parent(s) have abandoned the child. If this takes place at a hospital, the administration of the hospital must provide this letter.

Adoption Authority: Ministry of Justice, Office of the Prime Minister. The OPM is the sole authority which can approve adoptions of Lao children by foreign parents. The Ministry of Justice issues the final adoption agreement. It should be noted that there are no public or private institutions that function only as orphanages. There are no government agencies with clear responsibility for orphans. Currently, the Office of the Prime Minister (OPM) has sole authority to approve foreign adoptions.

The Process: The first step in adopting a child from Laos is usually to select a licensed agency in the United States that can help with your adoption. Adoption service providers must be licensed by the U.S. state in which they operate. To bring an adopted child from Laos to the United States, you must apply to be found eligible to adopt (Form I-600A) by the U.S. Government, Department of Homeland Security, U.S. Citizenship and Immigration Services (USCIS). If you are eligible to adopt, you must submit a letter of proposal for adoption to the Lao Embassy in the United States.

The Embassy will forward it to Ministry of Foreign Affairs (MFA) for review and then submit to the Ministry of Justice (MOJ). U.S. citizens resident in Laos may submit the letter directly to the Ministry of Foreign Affairs, Consular Department, in Vientiane. The MOJ will review your application and will submit it to the OPM after conducting an investigation.

The OPM is the final issuing authority. There is no formal matching process in Laos completed by government authorities. Prospective parents seeking to adopt from Laos must work with a local agency, representative or reputable foreign NGO to be matched with a prospective child.

Some hospitals in Laos maintain lists of prospective adoptive parents to contact when a newborn child is abandoned at the hospital. There are no known orphanages in Laos that arrange for the routine placement of orphaned children with adoptive parents.

Role of the Adoption Authority: After the MOJ has received the proposal from the MFA with all the documents, the MOJ may interview the prospective adoptive parents. Once the documents are reviewed and approved by the MOJ, the documents will be submitted to the Office of the Prime Minister.

Role of the Court: The OPM is the sole authority to approve adoptions of Lao children by foreign parents.

Role of Adoption Agencies: There are no approved Adoption Service Providers operating in Laos. There are also no public or private institutions that operate solely as orphanages. The Ministry of Justice (MOJ) accepts adoption applications and will provide assistance in the legal and regulatory requirements needed to process the final adoption but does not provide assistance with matching prospective adopted children with parents.

Adoption Application: The prospective adoptive parents submit a letter of their proposal of adoption to the Lao Embassy in the United States. The parents should attach to the letter a set of required documents from both Laos and the U.S.

In some cases, adopting parents have submitted the letter to the Lao Embassy in Washington and later submitted the documents to the Lao Ministry of Foreign Affairs (MFA), Consular Department, once the letter of proposal arrives at the MFA. If the prospective adoptive parents reside in Laos, the letter and supporting documents may be submitted directly to the Ministry of Foreign Affairs.

Time Frame: The time frame for adoption from Laos can vary greatly.

Adoption Fees: The application fee with the Ministry of Justice is 100,000 Lao Kip per child (approximately $12). If the application is approved by the OPM, there is an additional fee of 500,000 Lao Kip per child ($60).

Documents Required: The following documents related to the child are needed:

- Child's Lao birth certificate
- Custody certificate from the child's Laotian guardian to the adopting parents (both the husband/wife must sign)
- Residential Certificate of the Lao guardian
- Punishment record of the Lao guardian
- Certificate of economic status of the Lao guardian
- Letter of comment from the village chief and district authority to certify the reason for granting custody of the child to the adopting parent
- Medical examination of the child and the Lao guardian
- Copy of house hold registration book for the child and the Lao guardian
- Six 4X6 cm photos of the child
- Biographic data of the Lao guardian
- For children 10 year old and above, a letter of agreement from the child, agreeing to be adopted by the adoptive parents

The following documents are needed from the prospective adoptive parents:

- The birth certificate of each parent
- Residential Certificate (in Laos or abroad)
- Adoption Application
- Guarantee Statement from Adopting Parent(s)
- Punishment Record for Adopting Parent(s)
- Medical Examination
- Certificate of economic status
- Biographic data
- Copy of passport(s)
- A letter of purpose from the Adopting Parents stating the reasons why they want to adopt the child
- Six 4X6 cm photos, one set for each parent

ALERT: The U.S. Embassy must confirm the validity of Lao documents. The format of official documents varies widely from province to province. There is no centralized repository for the storage or maintenance of public records. Civil documents issued by the proper civil authority in the correct format may contain erroneous or falsified information. Although late registration is legal births are supposed to be registered with the local village authorities, either the village chief "naay baan" or district chief "jao muang". The birth certificate format is not standardized.

The death certificate format is not standardized and may be issued by a hospital, the police, or the village or district chief. Generally, pre-printed forms are acceptable, and death certificates should be on such a form. At a minimum, the death certificate should contain the name of the deceased, cause of death, date of death, and the deceased's date of birth or age at death. Late registration is legal. For more information regarding these issues please contact the U.S. Embassy in Laos.

Bringing Your Child Home: Once your adoption is complete (or you have obtained legal custody of the child), there are a few more steps to take before you can head home. Specifically, you need to apply for several documents for your child before he or she can travel to the United States, such as a birth certificate, a passport or travel document for your child from the country in which he or she was born, and a U.S. Immigration Visa. For detailed and updated information on how to obtain these documents, review the *Intercountry Adoption* section on this publication and visit the USCIS Intercountry Adoption website at http://adoption.state.gov.

Child Citizenship Act: For adoptions finalized abroad, the Child Citizenship Act of 2000 allows your new child to acquire American citizenship automatically when he or she enters the United States as lawful permanent residents.

For adoptions finalized in the United States, the Child Citizenship Act of 2000 allows your new child to acquire American citizenship automatically when the court in the United States issues the final adoption decree. To learn more, review the *Intercountry Adoption* section on this publication and visit the USCIS Intercountry Adoption website at http://adoption.state.gov.

After Adoption: Once the adoption is approved, the adopting parents should report back to the local authorities that the adoption was approved.

U.S. Embassy in Laos
Rue Bartholonie
That Dam
P.O. Box 114
Vientiane, Lao PDR
Tel: (856) 21-26 7000
Fax: (856) 21-267040
Website: http://laos.usembassy.gov

Laos' Adoption Authority
Ministry of Justice
Department of Judicial
Administration System
Nationality Division
Vientiane Capital, Lao PDR
Tel/Fax: 856-21-412-053

Embassy of the Lao People's Democratic Republic
2222 S St., NW
Washington, DC 20008
Tel: (202) 332-6416
Fax: (202) 332-4923
Email: laoemb@verizon.net

Office of Children's Issues
U.S. Department of State
2201 C Street, NW
SA-29
Washington, DC 20520
Tel: 1-888-407-4747
E-mail: AskCI@state.gov
http://adoption.state.gov

For questions about immigration procedures, call the National Customer Service Center (NCSC) 1-800-375-5283 (TTY 1-800-767-1833).

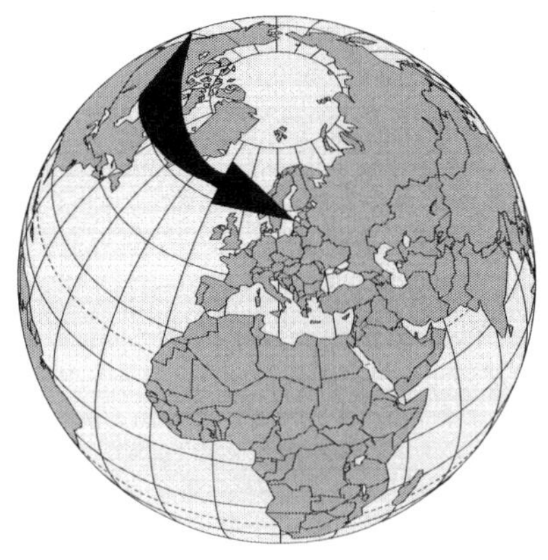

LATVIA

Compiled from publications that were available as of February 2013 from the U.S. Department of State, the U.S. Department of Commerce, and the Central Intelligence Agency (CIA). See the introduction to this set for explanatory notes.

Official Name:
Republic of Latvia

PROFILE

Geography

Area: total: 64,589 sq km; country comparison to the world: 124; land: 62,249 sq km; water: 2,340 sq km

Major cities: Riga (capital) 711,000 (2009)

Climate: maritime; wet, moderate winters

Terrain: low plain

People

Nationality: noun: Latvian(s); adjective: Latvian

Population: 2,191,580 (July 2012 est.)

Population growth rate: -0.598% (2012 est.)

Ethnic groups: Latvian 59.3%, Russian 27.8%, Belarusian 3.6%, Ukrainian 2.5%, Polish 2.4%, Lithuanian 1.3%, other 3.1% (2009)

Religions: Lutheran 19.6%, Orthodox 15.3%, other Christian 1%, other 0.4%, unspecified 63.7% (2006)

Languages: Latvian (official) 58.2%, Russian 37.5%, Lithuanian and other 4.3% (2000 census)

Literacy: definition: age 15 and over can read and write; total population: 99.8%; male: 99.8%; female: 99.8% (2010 est.)

Health: life expectancy at birth: total population: 72.93 years; male: 67.84 years; female: 78.3 years (2012 est.); Infant mortality rate: total: 8.24 deaths/1,000 live births; male: 10 deaths/1,000 live births; female: 6.39 deaths/1,000 live births (2012 est.)

Unemployment rate: 14.3% (2012 est.)

Work force: 1.139 million (2012 est.)

Government

Type: parliamentary democracy

Independence: 4 May 1990

Constitution: 15 February 1922; restored to force by the Constitutional Law of the Republic of Latvia adopted by the Supreme Council 21 August 1991; multiple amendments since

Political subdivisions: 110 municipalities (novadi, singular-novads) and 9 cities

Suffrage: 18 years of age; universal for Latvian citizens

Economy

GDP (purchasing power parity): $37.04 billion (2012 est.); $35.37 billion (2011 est.); $33.54 billion (2010 est.); $33.65 billion (2009 est.)

GDP real growth rate: 4.5% (2012 est.); 5.5% (2011 est.); -0.3% (2010 est.); -17.7% (2009 est.)

GDP per capita (PPP): $18,100 (2012 est.); $15,900 (2011 est.); $14,900 (2010 est.); $14,900 (2009 est.)

Natural resources: peat, limestone, dolomite, amber, hydropower, timber, arable land

Agriculture products: grain, rapeseed, potatoes, vegetables; pork, poultry, milk, eggs; fish

Industries: processed foods, processed wood products, textiles, processed metals, pharmaceuticals, railroad cars, synthetic fibers, electronics

Exports: $12.49 billion (2012 est.); $12.03 billion (2011 est.); $9.107 billion (2010 est.)

Exports—commodities: food products, wood and wood products, metals, machinery and equipment, textiles

Exports—partners: Russia 17.7%, Lithuania 16.5%, Estonia 12.9%, Germany 7.9%, Sweden 5.6%, Poland 5.5% (2011)

Imports: $15.92 billion (2012 est.); $14.83 billion (2011 est.); $10.8 billion (2010 est.)

Imports—commodities: machinery and equipment, consumer goods, chemicals, fuels, vehicles

Imports—partners: Lithuania 17.8%, Germany 11.8%, Russia 8.4%, Poland 7.5%, Estonia 7.1%, Finland 4.5%, Italy 4.3% (2011)

Debt—external: $38.37 billion (31 December 2011 est.); $39.56 billion (31 December 2010 est.)

Exchange rates: lati (LVL) per US dollar; 0.5519 (2012 est.); 0.5012 (2011 est.); 0.5305 (2010 est.); 0.5056 (2009); 0.4701 (2008); 0.5162 (2007)

PEOPLE

Latvia reflects the strong cultural and religious influences of centuries-long Germanic and Scandinavian colonization and settlement. Eastern Latvia (Latgale) retains strong Polish and Russian cultural influences. This highly literate society places a strong emphasis upon education, which is free and compulsory until age 16.

Traumatic wartime events, postwar emigration, deportations, and Soviet Russification policies from 1939 to 1989 reduced the percentage of ethnic Latvians in Latvia from 73% to 52%. In an attempt to preserve the Latvian language and prevent ethnic Latvians from becoming a minority in their own country, Latvia enacted language, education, and citizenship laws which require a working proficiency in the Latvian language in order to acquire citizenship as an adult. Such legislation has caused concern among many Russophone non-citizen residents, despite Latvian legal guarantees of universal human and civil rights regardless of citizenship.

National/Racial/Ethnic Minorities

The Romani community, estimated to number approximately 8,000, historically has faced widespread societal discrimination and high levels of unemployment and illiteracy.

Language

Written with the Latin alphabet, Latvian is the language of the Latvian people and the official language of the country. It is an inflective language with several analytical forms, three dialects, and German syntactical influence. The oldest known examples of written Latvian are from a 1585 catechism. Latvian and Lithuanian are the only surviving direct descendents of the Baltic languages of the Indo-European family. While Latvia was a component of the U.S.S.R., Russian was the official language, so many Latvians also speak Russian, and the resident Slavic populace generally speaks Russian as a first language.

Religion

The largest religious groups and their percentages of the population include Roman Catholic (22.7 percent), Lutheran (19.7 percent), and Orthodox Christian (16.8 percent). Sizeable religious minorities include Baptists, Pentecostals, and evangelical Protestant groups. According to the 2011 census, 6,416 persons, or 0.3 percent of the population, identified themselves as ethnically Jewish.

As of the end of the year, 1,149 congregations were registered with the government. These included Lutheran congregations (295), Catholic (250), Orthodox Christian (122), Baptist (94), Old Believer Orthodox (69), Seventh-day Adventist (51), evangelical Christian (39), Muslim (17), Jehovah's Witnesses (15), Methodist (13), Jewish (12), Hare Krishna (11), Buddhist (4), and 157 other congregations.

Interest in religion increased markedly following the restoration of independence; however, many adherents do not regularly practice their religion. Orthodox Christians, many of whom are Russian-speaking, noncitizen permanent residents, are concentrated in the major cities, while many Catholics live in the east.

HISTORY

By the 10th century, the area that is today Latvia was inhabited by several Baltic tribes who had formed their own local governments. In 1054, German sailors who shipwrecked on the Daugava River inhabited the area, which initiated a period of increasing Germanic influence. The Germans named the territory Livonia. In 1201, Riga, the current capital of Latvia, was founded by the Germanic Bishop Albert of Livonia; the city joined the Hanseatic League in 1285 and began to form important cultural and economic relationships with the rest of Europe. However, the new German nobility enserfed the indigenous people and accorded them only limited trading and property rights.

Subsequent wars and treaties led to Livonia's partition and colonization for centuries. In 1721 Russia took control over the Latvian territories as a result of its victory over Sweden in the Great Northern War. During this time there was little sense of a Latvian national identity, as both serfdom and institutional controls to migration and social mobility limited the boundaries of the indigenous people's intellectual and social geography. However, in the 1860s, the Young Latvian Movement was formed in order to promote the indigenous language against Russification policies and to publicize and counteract the socioeconomic oppression of Latvians, 60% of whom belonged to the landless, urban class. This growing proletariat base became fertile ground for the ideas of western European socialism and supported the creation in 1903 of the Latvian Social Democratic Union (LSDU), which championed national interests and Latvia's national self-determination, especially during the failed 1905 Revolution in Russia.

The onset of World War I brought German occupation of the western coastal province of Kurzeme, which Latvians heroically countered with several regiments of riflemen commanded by Czarist generals. The military campaign generally increased Latvian and LSDU support for the Bolsheviks' successful October Revolution in 1917, in the hopes of a "free Latvia within free Russia." These circumstances led to the formation of the Soviet "Iskolat Republic" in the unoccupied section of Latvia. In opposition to this government, and to the landed barons' German sympathies, stood the Latvian Provisional National Council and the Riga Democratic Bloc. These and other political

parties formed the Latvian People's Council, which on November 18, 1918 declared Latvia's independence and formed an army. The new Latvian Army won a decisive battle over the German forces and consolidated that success against Red Army forces on the eastern Latgale front. These developments led to the dissolution of the Soviet Latvian government on January 13, 1920 and to a peace treaty between Latvia and Soviet Russia on August 11 later that year. On September 22, 1921, an independent Latvia was admitted to the League of Nations.

The government, headed by Prime Minister Ulmanis, declared a democratic, parliamentary republic. It recognized Latvian as the official language, granted cultural autonomy to the country's sizeable minorities, and introduced an electoral system into the Latvian constitution, which was adopted in 1922. The ensuing decade witnessed sweeping economic reform, as the war had devastated Latvian agriculture, and most Russian factories had been evacuated to Russia. However, economic depression heightened political turmoil, and, on May 15, 1934, the Prime Minister dismissed the parliament, banned outspoken and left-wing political parties, and tightened authoritarian state control over Latvian social life and the economy.

The German-Soviet Nonaggression Pact of 1939 steadily forced Latvia under Soviet influence, culminating in Latvia's annexation by the Soviet Union on August 5, 1940. On June 14 of the following year, 15,000 Latvian citizens were forcibly deported and a large number of army officers shot. The subsequent German occupation witnessed the mobilization of many Latvians into Waffen SS legions, while some Latvians joined the Red Army and formed resistance groups, and others fled to the West and East.

An estimated 70,000, or 89.5%, of Latvian Jews were killed in Latvia under Nazi occupation. Up to one-third of Latvia's pre-war population (approximately 630,000 residents) was lost between 1940 and 1954 due to the Holocaust and the Soviet and Nazi occupations.

After World War II, the U.S.S.R. subjected the Latvian republic to a social and economic reorganization which rapidly changed the rural economy to one based on heavy industry, transformed the predominantly ethnic

Latvian population into a more multi-ethnic populace, and promoted urbanization. As part of the goal to more fully integrate Latvia into the Soviet Union, Stalin deported another 42,000 Latvians and continued to promote the policy of encouraging Soviet immigration to Latvia.

In July 1989, following the dramatic events in East Germany, the Latvian Supreme Soviet adopted a "Declaration of Sovereignty" and amended the Constitution to assert the supremacy of its laws over those of the U.S.S.R. Candidates from the pro-independence party Latvian Popular Front gained a two-thirds majority in the Supreme Council in the March 1990 democratic elections.

On May 4, the Council declared its intention to restore full Latvian independence after a "transitional" period; 3 days later, a Latvian was chosen Prime Minister. Soviet political and military forces tried unsuccessfully to overthrow the Latvian Government. On August 21, 1991, Latvia claimed de facto independence. International recognition, including that of the U.S.S.R., followed. The United States, which had never recognized Latvia's forcible annexation by the U.S.S.R. and continued to accredit a Latvian Ambassador in Washington, recognized Latvia's renewed independence on September 2.

Since regaining its independence, Latvia has rapidly moved away from the political-economic structures and socio-cultural patterns which underlay the Soviet Union. Latvia has maintained and strengthened the democratic, parliamentary republic that it revived in 1990. Through a U.S. initiative, on April 30, 1994, Latvia and Russia signed a troop withdrawal agreement; Russia withdrew the bulk of its troops by August 31 of that year. Except for some large state-owned utilities, Latvia has privatized most sectors of its economy, which enjoyed years of rapid development before slowing down in 2007.

Latvia became a member of the United Nations (UN) on September 18, 1991, and is a signatory to a number of UN organizations and other international agreements, including the International Civil Aviation Organization (ICAO), the International Monetary Fund (IMF), and the World Bank. It is also a member of the Organization on Security and Cooperation in Europe (OSCE) and officially became a member of the North Atlantic Treaty Organization (NATO) on March 29, 2004. On May 1, 2004 Latvia joined the European Union (EU).

Since 2004, Latvia has emerged as a significant player in foreign affairs, standing out as a successful post-Soviet transition society. Strong memories of occupation and oppression motivate Latvia to reach out to countries struggling to move beyond authoritarian politics and state-controlled economies. It has worked closely with the U.S. and the EU to promote democracy in Ukraine, Belarus, Moldova, and Georgia. Latvia also supports pro-market, pro-free-trade policies in European and international organizations.

Latvia has developed a policy of international security cooperation through participation in crisis management and peacekeeping operations. In 2006, Latvia deployed over 10% of its active duty military to support UN, NATO, and coalition military operations. That percentage is well above the European average in terms of per capita contributions. In 2008, Latvia increased its participation in the NATO International Security Assistance Force (ISAF) in Afghanistan to 170 soldiers and maintained the number in 2009 and 2010.

Despite major economic challenges, in 2011 Latvia again increased its NATO ISAF participation to 185. While Latvia was active in the Balkans, budget cuts forced the end of its operations there in 2009. Latvia supported the NATO mission in Kosovo with peacekeepers, and the European Union Force (EUFOR) mission in Bosnia with liaison officers. Latvia also contributed to the EU and OSCE missions to Georgia. In November 2006, Latvia hosted a NATO Summit in its capital, Riga, and in May 2010, it hosted a NATO Parliamentary Assembly.

GOVERNMENT AND POLITICAL CONDITIONS

The Republic of Latvia is a multi-party parliamentary democracy. Legislative authority is vested in the unicameral parliament (Saeima). Elections on September 17, 2011, for the 100-seat parliament were free and fair.

Recent Elections

On July 23, 2011, 95 percent of the participating electorate voted to dissolve parliament. As a result, on September 17, the country held free and fair extraordinary elections for parliament. Observers from the OSCE found that the elections were professionally run with minimal violations and offered voters a genuine choice. However, observers noted that voter education materials were only available in Latvian, potentially disadvantaging voters with low Latvian proficiency.

Political Parties: Citizens can organize political parties without restriction, but the law prohibits the country's "noncitizen residents" from organizing political parties without the participation of an equal number of citizens in the party. The election law prohibits persons who remained active in the Communist Party or various other pro-Soviet organizations after 1991 or who worked for such institutions as the former Soviet Committee for State Security (KGB) from holding elected office or certain other government positions related to security.

Participation of Women and Minorities: Following the September 17 national elections, there were 23 women in the 100-member parliament, and four women in the 14-member Cabinet of Ministers. Four of seven judges on the Constitutional Court and 23 of the 44 justices of the

Supreme Court were women. Approximately 16 percent of the country's adult population (36 percent of the non-Latvian minority population) were noncitizens. They did not participate in the elections process and were left without representation in the government. Members of minorities who were citizens, including ethnic Russians and Poles, served in various elected bodies. The mayor of Riga, the country's largest city, is a member of the ethnic Russian minority. The Harmony Center Party, which lists many ethnic Russians in its ranks, won the most seats in parliament in the September elections.

Principal Government Officials

Last Updated: 1/31/2013

Pres.: **Andris BERZINS**
Prime Min.: **Valdis DOMBROVSKIS**
Min. of Agriculture: **Laimdota STRAUJUMA**
Min. of Culture: **Zanete JAUNZEME-GRENDE**
Min. of Defense: **Artis PABRIKS**
Min. of Economics: **Daniels PAVLUTS**
Min. of Education & Science: **Roberts KILIS**
Min. of Environmental Protection & Regional Development: **Edmunds SPRUDZS**
Min. of Finance: **Andris VILKS**
Min. of Foreign Affairs: **Edgars RINKEVICS**
Min. of Health: **Ingrida CIRCENE**
Min. of Interior: **Rihards KOZLOVSKIS**
Min. of Justice: **Janis BORDANS**
Min. of Transport: **Aivis RONIS**
Min. of Welfare: **Ilze VINKELE**
Governor, Bank of Latvia: **Ilmars RIMSEVICS**
Ambassador to the US: **Andris RAZANS**
Permanent Representative to the UN, New York: **Normans PENKE**

ECONOMY

Latvia is a small, open economy with exports contributing nearly a third of GDP. Due to its geographical location, transit services are highly-developed, along with timber and wood-processing, agriculture and food products, and manufacturing of machinery and electronics industries. Corruption continues to be an impediment to attracting foreign direct investment and Latvia's low birth rate and decreasing population are major challenges to its long-term economic vitality. Latvia's economy experienced GDP growth of more than 10% per year during 2006–07, but entered a severe recession in 2008 as a result of an unsustainable current account deficit and large debt exposure amid the softening world economy. Triggered by the collapse of the second largest bank, GDP plunged 18% in 2009. The economy has not returned to pre-crisis levels despite strong growth, especially in the export sector in 2011–12.

The IMF, EU, and other international donors provided substantial financial assistance to Latvia as part of an agreement to defend the currency's peg to the euro in exchange for the government's commitment to stringent austerity measures. The IMF/EU program successfully concluded in December 2011. The government of Prime Minister Valdis DOMBROVSKIS remained committed to fiscal prudence and reducing the fiscal deficit from 7.7% of GDP in 2010, to 2.7% of GDP in 2012.

The majority of companies, banks, and real estate have been privatized, although the state still holds sizable stakes in a few large enterprises, including 99.8% ownership of the Latvian national airline. Latvia officially joined the World Trade Organization in February, 1999 and the EU in May 2004. Latvia intends to join the euro zone in 2014.

Labor Conditions

The law prohibits those under the age of 18 from nighttime or overtime work. The statutory minimum age for employment is 15, although children who are 13 years of age or older may work in certain jobs outside school hours with written permission from a parent.

Inspectors from the SLI are responsible for enforcing child labor laws and did so effectively.

The legally mandated monthly minimum wage was 200 lats ($400). By comparison, the Latvian Central Statistical Bureau's "minimum subsistence consumer basket" price index for November was 172.05 lats ($344.10).

The law provides for a mandatory 40-hour maximum workweek with at least one 42-hour rest period weekly. The maximum permitted overtime is 144 hours in a four-month period. Employees are also not allowed to work more than 24 hours consecutively, 56 hours in a week, or overtime on more than six consecutive days. The law requires a minimum of 100-percent premium pay in compensation for overtime, unless other forms of compensation are agreed to in a contract. The law establishes minimum occupational health and safety standards for the workplace. Workers have the legal right to remove themselves from situations that endanger health or safety without endangering their continued employment. The law entitles workers to 28 calendar days of paid annual holidays.

U.S.-LATVIAN RELATIONS

The U.S. and Latvia share a history as strategic allies and valued partners. The United States established diplomatic relations with Latvia in 1922 following its independence in the years after World War I. Lavia was annexed by the Soviet Union in 1940 during World War II. In 1991, Latvia claimed de facto independence, and international recognition followed. The United States had never recognized the forcible incorporation of Latvia into the Soviet Union, and it views the present Government of Latvia as the legal continuation of the interwar republic. Since regaining its independence, Latvia has embraced democracy and the principles of an open market. It embodies the success and potential of the shared vision of a Europe whole, free, and at peace. As a member of the North Atlantic Treaty Organization and the European Union, Latvia has used the knowledge it gained from political and economic reforms undertaken for accession to help others achieve security, stability, and greater prosperity.

U.S. Assistance to Latvia

The United States provides a limited amount of military assistance to Latvia. In Fiscal Year 2012, $7.5 million worth of assistance is being provided through various military programs.

Bilateral Economic Relations

U.S.-Latvian economic relations are dynamic, with room for growth. Service industries such as telecommunications, transport and logistics, and renewable energy technologies are potential areas for U.S.-Latvian investment and trade. Latvia and the United States have signed treaties on investment, trade, intellectual property protection, and avoidance of double taxation.

Latvia participates in the visa waiver program, which allows nationals of participating countries to travel to the United States for certain business or tourism purposes for stays of 90 days or less without obtaining a visa.

Latvia's Membership in International Organizations

Latvia and the United States belong to a number of the same international organizations, including the United Nations, North Atlantic Treaty Organization, Organization for Security and Cooperation in Europe, International Monetary Fund, World Bank, and World Trade Organization.

Bilateral Representation

Latvia maintains an embassy in the United States at 2306 Massachusetts Ave NW, Washington DC 20008 (tel: (202) 328-2840).

Principal U.S. Embassy Officials

Last Updated: 1/14/2013

RIGA (E) 1 Samnera Velsa iela, Riga, LV-1510, Latvia, +371 6710-7000, Fax +371 6710-7050, Workweek: Mon-Fri 08:30-17:00, Website: http://riga.usembassy.gov/

DCM OMS:	Samuel K. Tracy
AMB OMS:	Lourenda A. Block
FM:	Keith B. Ellis
HRO:	Mark D. Moody
MGT:	Mark D. Moody
MLO/ODC:	LTC Roger Bowman
POL/ECON:	Deborah A. Miller
POSHO:	Keith B. Ellis
SDO/DATT:	LTC Christopher Sill
AMB:	Mark A. Pekala
CON:	Evan McCarthy
DCM:	Caryn R. McClelland
PAO:	Amy L. Storrow
GSO:	Mark M. Bliss
RSO:	Michael J. Stutzman
CLO:	Anna Cunningham
FMO:	Mark D. Moody
IMO:	Alexander G. Miller
ISO:	Stephen L. Cunningham
LEGATT:	Kirk J. Striebich

TRAVEL

Consular Information Sheet

April 24, 2012

Country Description: Latvia is a stable democracy with a developing economy. Most tourist facilities found in a western European city are available in the capital city, Riga. However, some of the goods and services taken for granted in other countries are not yet available in other parts of the country.

Smart Traveler Enrollment Program (STEP)/Embassy Locations: If you are going to live in or visit Latvia, please take the time to tell our embassy about your trip. Registering with the Smart Traveler Enrollment Program can keep you up to date with important safety and security announcements, and help your friends and family get in touch with you in an emergency.

U.S. Embassy Riga
1 Samnera Velsa Street
Riga, LV-1510
Telephone: 371 6710–7000
Emergency After-hours telephone: 371 2920–5708
Facsimile: 371 6710–7001
e-mail: askconsular@USRiga.lv

Entry/Exit Requirements for U.S. Citizens: You needa valid passport to enter Latvia. Latvia is a party to the Schengen Agreement; as such, U.S. citizens may enter Latvia for up to 90 days for tourist or business purposes without a visa. Your passport should be valid for at least three months beyond your period of stay, and Latvian Border Guards strictly enforce this policy. Only one stay of up to 90 days is permitted in the Schengen territory within a six-month period. If you plan to visit multiple European Schengen zone countries on the same trip, you should pay attention to the total number of consecutive days spent in member countries, including Latvia. U.S. citizens are advised to carry passports when traveling to neighboring Baltic countries from Latvia—even on day trips—as random passport checks are possible.

In addition, upon entering or exiting the country, you must declare cash in excess of 10,000 Euros (or equivalent value) to Latvian customs.

If you are going to stay in Latvia for more than 90 days, you must apply for temporary residence. You must have a valid insurance policy which includes medical expenses while in Latvia. Repatriation costs, including funeral and disposition of remains costs, also have to be covered by the policy. One of the requirements for the temporary residence application is a criminal record check from the United States, which can be requested through the FBI. You must submit proof of identity, which consists of name, date and place of birth, and a set of ink-rolled fingerprint impressions.

We cannot take your fingerprints at the Embassy, but the Latvian State Criminal Police Department is able to provide such service at Bruninieku iela 72, Riga, tel: 371 6720–8662. For more information, contact the Latvian Embassy at 2306 Massachusetts Avenue NW, Washington, DC 20008, tel. (202)328-2840, fax (202)328-2860. Within Latvia, contact the Ministry of Interior's Office of Citizenship and Migration Affairs at Ciekurkalna 1st line, building 3, Riga, LV-1026. Tel. (371) 67588675, email: pmlp@pmlp.gov.lv

If you are planning to travel to the Russian Federation from Latvia, even just in transit, we recommend you obtain a visa prior to entry into Latvia. The process to apply for a visa at the Russian Embassy in Riga can be lengthy, and may involve submission of your passport for an undetermined period of time.

The U.S. Department of State is unaware of any HIV/AIDS-related entry restrictions for visitors to or foreign residents in Latvia.

Threats to Safety and Security: Civil unrest is generally not a problem in Riga, and there have been no incidents of terrorism directed toward American interests. Incidents of anti-Americanism are rare.

Nonetheless, in the past, Riga has experienced large, peaceful demonstrations related to internal political issues. While such events have generally been peaceful, we remind you that gatherings intended to be peaceful can become confrontational. Therefore, you should avoid the areas of demonstrations, if possible, and exercise caution if within the vicinity of any event. Each winter, several people in Latvia sustain serious injuries from falling icicles. Pay careful attention to sidewalks that are blocked by rope or tape and be cautious of work crews clearing ice and snow from building rooftops. Sidewalks and roads can also be extremely slippery in the winter months; exercise caution while crossing streets, even if you have the right of way.

Stay up to date by:

- Bookmarking our Bureau of Consular Affairs website, which contains the current Travel Warnings and Travel Alerts, as well as the Worldwide Caution;
- Following us on Twitter and Facebook as well;
- Downloading our free Smart Traveler iPhone App to have travel information at your fingertips;
- Calling 1-888-407-4747 toll-free within the U.S. and Canada, or a regular toll line, 1-202-501-4444, from other countries; and
- Taking some time before travel to consider your personal security.

Crime: Latvia is a relatively safe country, and crime is generally nonviolent in nature; however, serious violent assaults and robberies have occurred. Harassment of foreigners, ethnic minorities, and homosexuals has also occurred in Latvia

The most common crimes encountered by foreign tourists are purse snatching, pick-pocketing, and mugging, especially during the summer tourism season. Tourists—particularly those carrying backpacks—are targeted by individuals or small groups of thieves working together. Riga's Old Town (Vecriga), Central train station (Dzelzcela stacija), Central bus station (Autoosta) and Central market (Centraltirgus) are crowded public places that are targeted by thieves.

Please be aware that there are numerous scam artists targeting foreigners in the tourist pubs and restaurants. There have been a number of reports of foreign tourists being charged exorbitant prices for drinks in bars; some have then been assaulted or forced to withdraw money from an ATM to pay the bill. You can avoid situations like this by ensuring that you check the price of drinks before ordering, pay for one round at a time, and seek recommendations for bars from trustworthy sources. If possible, you should avoid walking alone at night and avoid using ATMs after dark.

The Riga Tourist Police Unit has a 24/7 English-speaking operator at 371 67181818 and English-speaking officers who frequently patrol the Old City.

In addition, Internet crime is a growing concern in Latvia. Common fraudulent schemes involve both Internet auction sites and Internet job-search sites. In the first scam, criminals offer you valuable items for sale at low prices on Internet auctions and request that your payments be sent by wire transfer to a bank in Latvia or through a fraudulent escrow site that they have created themselves. In this scheme, your money passes through a bank in Latvia and is quickly withdrawn at an ATM or transferred to a bank in another country. It is very difficult in these cases to discover the identities of the account holders or recover the funds.

The second common scam involves identity theft through false job offers. In this scheme, a company claiming to be located in Latvia, but which has a non-existent address, offers you employment as a U.S.-based agent or freight forwarder. When you respond to the job offer, commonly posted on one of several popular Internet job sites, you are asked for a Social Security Number and other identifying information under the guise of conducting a background check.

Victims of Crime: If you or someone you know becomes the victim of a crime abroad, you should contact the local police and the U.S. Embassy. We can:

- Replace a stolen passport;
- Help you find appropriate medical care if you are a victim of a violent crime such as assault and rape;
- Put you in contact with the appropriate police authorities, and contact family members or friends; and
- Help you understand the local criminal justice process and can direct you to local attorneys,

although local authorities are responsible for investigating and prosecuting the crime.

The local equivalent to the "911" emergency line in Latvia is 112, which can be called for fire and police assistance. The primary number for ambulance service is 113, but the 112 operator can also help dispatch an ambulance.

Criminal Penalties: Don't buy counterfeit and pirated goods, even if they are widely available. Not only are the bootlegs illegal to bring back into the United States, by buying them you may also be breaking local law. While you are traveling in another country, you are subject to its laws even if you are a U.S. citizen.

Foreign laws and legal systems can be vastly different than our own, and criminal penalties vary from country to country. There are also some things that might be legal in the country you visit, but still illegal in the United States; for instance, you can be prosecuted under U.S. law if you buy pirated goods or engage in child pornography.

If you do something illegal in Latvia, your U.S. passport won't help you avoid arrest or prosecution. Persons violating Latvian laws, even unknowingly, may be expelled, arrested, or imprisoned. Penalties for possessing, using, or trafficking in illegal drugs in Latvia are severe, and convicted offenders can expect long jail sentences and heavy fines.

Based on the Vienna Convention on Consular Relations, bilateral agreements with certain countries, and customary international law, if you are arrested in Latvia, you have the option to request that the police, prison officials, or other authorities alert the U.S. Embassy of your arrest, and to have communications from you forwarded to the U.S. Embassy.

Special Circumstances: Bank and currency exchange counters may refuse to accept U.S. currency that is crumpled, torn, discolored, or defaced (even small pen strokes are considered defacing). If such notes are accepted for exchange, an additional processing fee, based on the size of the transaction, may be charged. ATMs are widely available in Riga and in major towns. For security purposes, it is recommended that visitors use ATMs located inside major hotels or shopping malls, versus those located on the street, in high-volume tourist areas.

Telephone connections with the United States are reliable; however, U.S. toll-free numbers cannot be accessed from Latvia. Please check with your long distance carrier before departure to see if they offer service in Latvia. Local Internet cafes offer computer access, and fax machines are widely available.

Latvian customs authorities may enforce strict regulations concerning temporary importation into or export from Latvia of items such as firearms, religious materials, antiquities, medications, business equipment, drugs, etc. It is advisable to contact the Embassy of Latvia in Washington or one of the Latvian consulates in the United States for specific information regarding customs requirements.

Accessibility: While in Latvia, individuals with disabilities may find accessibility and accommodation very different from what you find in the United States. The law prohibits discrimination against persons with disabilities in employment, education, access to health care, and other state services, and the government generally enforces these provisions. The law mandates access to buildings for persons with disabilities; however, most buildings are not yet accessible.

Although Latvia has made efforts to improve disabled access, only new and completely renovated hotels, guest houses, hostels, and public buildings provide suitable facilities for seriously disabled travelers. Easy-access public transportation and taxis are rare.

Accessibility of foot paths and road crossings is improving but, in most places, still fails to meet the legal standards. The Old City has mostly cobblestone streets which can be difficult for those with disabilities. Snow and ice are common on sidewalks during winter months and can be hazardous. Free or reduced fares in public transportation are available to Latvian residents only.

Medical Facilities and Health Information: The quality of medical care in Latvia continues to improve, but still often falls short of Western standards. Latvia has many highly trained medical professionals, but hospitals and clinics still suffer from a lack of equipment and resources. The current economic crisis has resulted in further strains in health service budgets. Many doctors speak at least some English. There are few private clinics in major cities that offer services equal to Western European or U.S. standards. Elderly travelers and those with health problems may be at increased risk.

Western-quality dental care can be obtained in Riga. Doctors and hospitals often expect immediate cash payment for health services, particularly if immigration status in Latvia is unclear.

Ambulance service for emergencies is available by dialing 113; however, response time is poor in rural areas. Air ambulance service is available for medical evacuations; however, it is very expensive and advance payment or guarantee letter from an insurance company is required before a patient is transported.

Pharmaceuticals sold in Latvia are produced by companies certified in accordance with the EU standards. Products of most major pharmaceutical manufacturers are sold in pharmacies in Latvia; however, they will not necessarily be labeled the same as in the U.S. and instructions are often not printed in English.

Tick-borne encephalitis and Lyme disease are widespread throughout the country. Those intending to visit parks or forested areas in Latvia are urged to speak with their health care practitioners. Tick-borne encephalitis vaccinations are given as a series of three doses, and are not available in the U.S. There are no vaccines against Lyme disease. Hepatitis A is also a significant problem in Latvia.

Tuberculosis is an increasingly serious health concern in Latvia. For further information, please consult the Centers for Disease Control & Prevention's(CDC) information on TB. Good Information on vaccinations and other health precautions, can also be found via the CDC website. For information about outbreaks of infectious diseases abroad, consult the World Health Organization (WHO) website, which also contains additional health information for travelers, including detailed country-specific health information.

Medical Insurance: You can't assume your insurance will go with you when you travel. It's very important to find out BEFORE you leave. You need to ask your insurance company two questions:

- Does my policy apply when I'm out of the U.S.?
- Will it cover emergencies like a trip to a foreign hospital or an evacuation?

In many places, doctors and hospitals still expect payment in cash at the time of service. Your regular U.S. health insurance may not cover doctors' and hospital visits in other countries. If your policy doesn't go with you when you travel, it's a very good idea to take out another one for your trip.

Traffic Safety and Road Conditions: While in Latvia, U.S. citizens may encounter road conditions that differ significantly from those in the United States.

Foreign visitors to Latvia planning to operate a motor vehicle are required to obtain an International Driving Permit. You may get these through the American Automobile Association (AAA) or the American Automobile Touring Alliance for a small fee. Your U.S. state driver's license is not sufficient for driving in Latvia. These requirements apply if you are using rental cars as well, whether or not the rental company chooses to enforce the requirement as a condition of rental. If you drive without an International Driving Permit, you may have your vehicle confiscated by the police. U.S. citizens resident in Latvia for more than six months are required to apply for a Latvian driver's license. Upon receipt of a Latvian driver's license, U.S. citizens are required to surrender their U.S. driver's license to the Latvian authorities. The licenses are then returned to their respective states of issuance.

Latvia's rate of automobile accidents and fatalities is one of the highest in Europe. You should be alert for pedestrians and slow-moving vehicles in traffic. Additionally, violation of traffic rules is common, and it is not unusual to be passed by other automobiles traveling at high speeds, even in crowed urban areas. Drivers do not always yield to pedestrians, even at marked intersections. During winter, most major roads are cleared of snow; however, you should be alert for fog, snow, and ice while driving. Driving while intoxicated is a very serious offense and carries heavy penalties. Local authorities use roadblocks and breathalyzer tests as enforcement tools.

Be alert to the possibility of drunk drivers and drunken pedestrians wandering on the road. You must use headlights at all times, and note that there can be as little as six hours of daylight during the winter months. Speed limits are usually 50 km/hr in the city and 90 km/hr on the highways. As of late 2011, Latvia began using an extensive photo speed enforcement program with cameras deployed throughout the country. Public transportation is generally considered safe, but travelers are encouraged to select well-marked taxis. Emergency services are fair but improving (See section on Medical Facilities above); response time may be especially slow in traffic or in rural settings. Dial 112 for police assistance, or 113 for ambulance service.

Aviation Safety Oversight: As there is no direct commercial air service to the United States by carriers registered in Latvia, the U.S. Federal Aviation Administration (FAA) has not assessed the government of Latvia's Civil Aviation Authority for compliance with International Civil Aviation Organization (ICAO) aviation safety standards. Further information may be found on the FAA's safety assessment page.

Children's Issues: Please see the U.S. Dept. of State Office of Children's Issues web pages on intercountry adoption and international parental child abduction.

Intercountry Adoption

February 2012

The information in this section has been edited from the latest report available as of February 2013 from the State Department Bureau of Consular Affairs, Office of Overseas Citizens Services. For more information, please read the *Intercountry Adoption* section of this book and review current reports online at http://adoption.state.gov.

Latvia is party to the Hague Convention on Protection of Children and Co-operation in Respect of Intercountry Adoption (Hague Adoption Convention). Therefore, all adoptions between Latvia and the United States must meet the requirements of the Convention; the U.S. implementing legislation, the Intercountry Act of 2000 (IAA); and the IAA implementing regulations. Public opposition in Latvia to the adoption of Latvian children by foreigners has contributed to reluctance to reform intercountry adoption procedures, which currently require several extended trips by adoptive parents to Latvia to complete the requirements. In addition, the Latvian government has announced that it will approve applications for intercountry adoption only if the adoptive parents file to adopt a sibling group of three or more children; a child over age 9; a child with severe health problems; or a child released for intercountry adoption because he or she has not been adopted by Latvians.

Who Can Adopt? Adoption between the United States and Latvia is governed by the Hague Adoption Convention. Therefore, to adopt from Latvia, you must first be found eligible to adopt by the U.S. government. U.S. Citizenship and Immigration Services (USCIS), a Department of Homeland Security component, makes this determination. In addition to U.S. requirements, Latvia has the following requirements for prospective adoptive parents.

Residency requirements: Parent-child relationship requirement: Latvian adoption law requires that a parent-child relationship be established before the final court decision can be made by the town or city court having jurisdiction over the child. It leaves to each orphan court to decide on a case-by-case basis the period of time required to establish the parent-child relationship. The interpretation of the child-parent relationship among courts may differ. Adoptive parents are advised that orphan courts may require them to take care of the adoptive children and share a household in Latvia for a certain amount of time, not exceeding six months.

Age requirements: Latvia requires that the adoptive parent is at least 25 years old and at least 18 years older than the adoptive child.

Marriage requirements: Both single individuals and married couples are eligible to adopt.

Income requirements: Latvia does not have any income requirements for intercountry adoptions.

Who Can Be Adopted? Because Latvia is party to the Hague Adoption Convention, children from Latvia must meet the requirements of the Convention in order to be eligible for adoption. For example, the Convention requires that Latvia attempt to place a child with a family in-country before determining that a child is eligible for intercountry adoption. In addition to Latvia's requirements, a child must meet the U.S. definition of a Convention adoptee for you to bring him or her back to the United States.

Latvia's Adoption Authority: Ministry of Welfare

The Process: Because Latvia is party to the Hague Adoption Convention, adopting from Latvia must follow a specific process designed to meet the requirements of the Convention. The first step in adopting a child from Latvia is to select an adoption service provider in the United States that has been accredited. Only these agencies and attorneys can provide adoption services between the United States and Latvia.

You must also select a U.S. adoption service provider that has been accredited by the Republic of Latvia. The following providers have received Latvian accreditation:

- About a Child
- Adoption Related Services, Inc., Shrewsbury Pennsylvania
- Angel's Haven Outreach
- Great Wall China Adoption/Children of All Nations
- Life Adoption Services, Inc.
- One World Adoption Services, Inc.
- Premier Adoption Agency, Inc.
- The Open Door Adoption Agency, Inc.
  West Sands Adoptions
- World Links Intercountry Adoption Agency

After you choose an accredited adoption service provider, file Form I-800A (Application for Determination of Suitability to Adopt a Child from a Convention Country) with USCIS. Once the U.S. government determines you are "eligible" and "suitable" to adopt, you or your agency will forward your information to the adoption authority in Latvia. Latvia's adoption authority will review your application to determine whether you are also eligible to adopt under Latvian law. The Ministry of Welfare reviews all applications and determines whether the applicant is eligible. If the judgment is favorable, the Ministry provides the prospective parents with information on children available for adoption.

If both the United States and Latvia determine you are eligible to adopt, and a child is available for intercountry adoption, the Latvian Central Authority may provide you with a referral for a child. Each family must decide for itself whether or not it will be able to meet the needs of and provide a permanent family placement for the referred child. After the prospective parents accept a match, the Ministry issues permission for them to meet the child. The Ministry is informed after the adoptive family has cared for the child for the required time period and the orphan court has established that the adoption would (or would not) be in the child's interests.

After you accept a match with a child, you will apply to USCIS for provisional approval to adopt that particular child by filing Form I-800 (Petition to Classify Convention Adoptee as an Immediate Relative). USCIS will determine whether the child is eligible under U.S. law to be adopted and enter the United States. After this, your adoption service provider or you will submit a visa application to a consular officer at U.S. Embassy Riga. The consular officer will review the child's information for possible visa ineligibilities. A visa application at this stage in the process includes: a) immigrant visa application DS-230; b) the child's pre-adoption birth certificate and English translation; c) documents showing how the child was released for intercountry adoption and English translations; d) medical examination results, if available; e) immigrant visa application fee of $404 per applicant. If the consular officer determines that the child appears eligible to immigrate to the United States, he or she will send a letter (an "Article 5 Letter") to the Latvian Central Authority. Do not adopt or obtain custody of a child in Latvia before a U.S. consular officer issues the Article 5 Letter. The consular officer will make a final decision about the immigrant visa later in the adoption process.

Role of the Adoption Authority: The Ministry of Welfare is responsible for administering intercountry adoptions. Orphan courts in Latvia carry out functions similar to those of social workers in the United States. The Ministry prepares an adoption approval (or rejection) statement for submission to the town or city court responsible for the final adoption decree. The Ministry's adoption permission is valid for three months.

Role of the Court: Orphan courts decide whether the birth parents' rights can be terminated; whether an orphan should be placed in an orphanage or whether someone else must be granted custody; and issues related to inheritance rights when a child's parents die. The main purpose of the orphan court session is to establish that the adoption will be in the child's interest and that the required parent-child relationship has been established. Town or city courts approve adoptions by granting full custody of the child to the adoptive parents. Current law provides for a 20-day period before the final court decree takes effect. Thus, the adoptive child is eligible to apply for a post-adoption birth certificate, passport, and immigrant visa only after the court decree becomes effective. After the 20-day period, the Ministry Welfare issues a statement certifying that the adoption has been completed in accordance with the Hague Adoption Convention (Article 23 Certificate).

Role of Adoption Agencies: Adoption agencies are allowed to represent parents and may do the required translations and file adoption applications at the Ministry. Under current law, however, the adoptive parents are required to personally file applications at orphan courts and participate in the orphan court and final court sessions.

Time Frame: The time needed to complete an adoption in Latvia from beginning to end varies, but can take from under a year to four years.

Adoption Fees: There are no Latvian government fees for adoption services. Prospective adoptive parents, however, should be prepared to cover fees related to the translation and certification of documents and the processing of new civil and travel documents for the adopted child.

In the adoption services contract that you sign at the beginning of the adoption process, your agency will itemize the fees and estimated expenses related to your adoption process.

Required Documents:

- Application including information about the reasons for adoption as well as information about the sex, age range, and religion of the child (children) they are interested in adopting;
- A copy of the parents' marriage certificate, if applicable, under apostille (please see information below about the authentication of documents);
- A copy of any divorce decree (if applicable), under apostille;
- A statement about the family's housing (i.e., size, location, type of residence);
- An autobiography (curriculum vitae);
- Medical statements regarding the health of the family (hereditary illnesses, if any, and any specific illnesses);
- A home study, under apostille, conducted by a U.S. state adoption agency or a private organization licensed to perform such studies. Home studies must be current in order for the adoption application to considered. Extensions of home study approval should be forwarded to the Ministry for applications to remain valid;
- A police clearance statement under apostille.

Additional documents may be requested.

Bringing Your Child Home: Once your adoption is complete (or you have obtained legal custody of the child), there are a few more steps to take before you can head home. Specifically, you need to apply for several documents for your child before he or she can travel to the United States, such as a birth certificate, a passport or travel document for your child from the country in which he or she was born, and a U.S. Immigration Visa. For detailed and updated information on how to obtain these documents, review the *Intercountry Adoption* section in this publication and visit the U.S. Department of State Intercountry Adoption website at http://adoption.state.gov.

Child Citizenship Act: For adoptions finalized abroad, the Child Citizenship Act of 2000 allows your new child to acquire American citizenship automatically when he or she enters the United States as lawful permanent residents. For adoptions finalized in the United States, the Child Citizenship Act of 2000 allows your new child to acquire American citizenship automatically when the court in the United States issues the final adoption decree. To learn more, review the *Intercountry Adoption* section in this publication and visit the U.S. Department of State Intercountry Adoption website at http://adoption.state.gov.

After Adoption: If the adoptive parents and the child continue to reside in Latvia, the orphan court having jurisdiction over the child's place of residence will monitor the adopted child's well-being for the first two years after the adoption's finalization. Latvia requires periodic post-adoption reporting on the welfare of an adopted orphan in his or her new American family. Latvian law requires that two post-adoption reports be submitted: one after the first year following adoption and one after the second year. The reports should be conducted by the adoptive family's adoption agency. The intercountry adoption process requires compliance with the laws of both the United States and the child's country of origin.

While the United States cannot enforce the laws of another country, in order for a strong country-to-country partnership on adoption matters to continue, families and agencies should respect the adoption laws of the child's country of origin. We strongly encourage agencies to comply with Latvian post-adoption reporting requirements and to submit reports on time. All agencies operating in Latvia have been notified of this requirement. Compliance will help ensure that Latvia's history of positive experiences with American adoptive families continues.

U.S. Embassy in Latvia
1 S. Velsa St. Riga, LV-1510
Latvia
Tel: 371-6710–7034; 371-6710–7000
Fax: 371-6710–7001
Email: AskConsular@USRiga.lv
Internet: http://riga.usembassy.gov/

Latvian Adoption Authority
Adoption Division, Department of Out-of-Family Care
Ministry of Welfare
28 Skolas St. Riga, LV-1010
Latvia
Tel: 371-6702–1600
Fax: 371-6727–6445
Email: lm@lm.gov.lv
Internet: http://www.lm.gov.lv

Embassy of Latvia
2306 Massachusetts Avenue NW
Washington, DC 20008
Tel: 202-328-2840
Fax: 202-328-2860
Email: embassy.usa@mfa.gov.lv
Internet: http://www.latvia-usa.org/

Latvia also has honorary consuls in several U.S. states.

Office of Children's Issues
U.S. Department of State
2201 C Street, NW
SA-29
Washington, DC 20520
Tel: 1-888-407-4747
E-mail: AskCI@state.gov
http://adoption.state.gov

LEBANON

Compiled from publications that were available as of February 2013 from the U.S. Department of State, the U.S. Department of Commerce, and the Central Intelligence Agency (CIA). See the introduction to this set for explanatory notes.

Official Name:
Lebanese Republic

PROFILE

Geography

Area: total: 10,400 sq km; country comparison to the world: 170; land: 10,230 sq km; water: 170 sq km

Major cities: Beirut (capital) 1.909 million (2009)

Climate: Mediterranean; mild to cool, wet winters with hot, dry summers; Lebanon mountains experience heavy winter snows

Terrain: narrow coastal plain; El Beqaa (Bekaa Valley) separates Lebanon and Anti-Lebanon Mountains

People

Nationality: noun: Lebanese (singular and plural); adjective: Lebanese

Population: 4,140,289 (July 2012 est.)

Population growth rate: -0.38% (2012 est.)

Ethnic groups: Arab 95%, Armenian 4%, other 1%

Religions: Muslim 59.7% (Shia, Sunni, Druze, Isma'ilite, Alawite or Nusayri), Christian 39% (Maronite Catholic, Greek Orthodox, Melkite Catholic, Armenian Orthodox, Syrian Catholic, Armenian Catholic, Syrian Orthodox, Roman Catholic, Chaldean, Assyrian, Coptic, Protestant), other 1.3%

Languages: Arabic (official), French, English, Armenian

Literacy: definition: age 15 and over can read and write; total population: 87.4%; male: 93.1%; female: 82.2% (2003 est.)

Health: life expectancy at birth: total population: 75.23 years; male: 73.67 years; female: 76.88 years (2012 est.); Infant mortality rate: total: 15.32 deaths/1,000 live births; male: 15.48 deaths/1,000 live births; female: 15.17 deaths/1,000 live births (2012 est.)

Unemployment rate: NA%

Work force: 1.481 million

Government

Type: republic

Independence: 22 November 1943

Constitution: 23 May 1926; amended a number of times, most recently in 1990 to include changes necessitated by the Charter of Lebanese National Reconciliation (Ta'if Accord) of October 1989

Political subdivisions: 6 governorates (mohafazat, singular—mohafazah); Beqaa, Beyrouth (Beirut), Liban-Nord, Liban-Sud, Mont-Liban, Nabatiye; two new governorates—Aakkar and Baalbek-Hermel—have been legislated but not yet implemented

Suffrage: 21 years of age; compulsory for all males; authorized for women at age 21 with elementary education; excludes military personnel

Economy

GDP (purchasing power parity): $63.69 billion (2012 est.); $62.23 billion (2011 est.); $61.31 billion (2010 est.); $57.3 billion (2009 est.)

GDP real growth rate: $41.77 billion (2012 est.); 1.5% (2011 est.); 7% (2010 est.); 8.5% (2009 est.)

GDP per capita (PPP): $15,900 (2012 est.); $15,700 (2011 est.); $15,700 (2010 est.); $14,900 (2009 est.)

Natural resources: limestone, iron ore, salt, water-surplus state in a water-deficit region, arable land

Agriculture products: citrus, grapes, tomatoes, apples, vegetables, potatoes, olives, tobacco; sheep, goats

Industries: banking, tourism, food processing, wine, jewelry, cement, textiles, mineral and chemical products, wood and furniture products, oil refining, metal fabricating

Exports: $5.655 billion (2012 est.); $5.482 billion (2011 est.); $5.467 billion (2010 est.)

Exports—commodities: jewelry, base metals, chemicals, miscellaneous consumer goods, fruit and vegetables, tobacco, construction minerals, electric power machinery and switchgear, textile fibers, paper

Exports—partners: UAE 11.6%, South Africa 9.3%, Iraq 7.4%, Saudi Arabia 6.8%, Turkey 6.2%, Syria 6%, Egypt 5.4%, Switzerland 4.9% (2009 est.)

Imports: $20.73 billion (2012 est.); $19.89 billion (2011 est.); $17.72 billion (2010 est.)

Imports—commodities: petroleum products, cars, medicinal products, clothing, meat and live animals, consumer goods, paper, textile fabrics, tobacco, electrical machinery and equipment, chemicals

Imports—partners: US 10.3%, Italy 9.5%, France 8.9%, China 8.3%, Germany 5.2%, Turkey 4.1% (2009 est.)

Debt—external: $32.64 billion (31 December 2012 est.); $29.46 billion (31 December 2011 est.); $28.42 billion (31 December 2010 est.)

Exchange rates: Lebanese pounds (LBP) per US dollar; 1,507.5 (2012 est.); 1,507.5 (2011 est.); 1,507.5 (2010 est.); 1,507.5 (2009); 1,507.5 (2008); 1,507.5 (2007)

PEOPLE

About 400,000 Palestinian refugees, some whose families have been in Lebanon since 1948, are registered with the United Nations Relief and Works Agency (UNRWA). They are not accorded the civil and legal rights enjoyed by the rest of the population and are not allowed access to public education or health or social services. As a result, the majority of Palestinian refugees in Lebanon rely entirely on UNRWA as the sole provider of education and health, relief, and social services. UNRWA's operations in the 12 official refugee camps in Lebanon face a number of challenges, including crumbling infrastructure, overcrowded housing, poverty, systemic unemployment, and a higher percentage of registered special hardship cases than any other field.

With no official figures available, it is estimated that 600,000-900,000 persons fled the country during the initial years of civil war (1975–76). Although some returned, continuing conflict through 1990 as well as after the 2006 war sparked further waves of emigration, casting even more doubt on population figures. As much as 7% of the population was killed during the civil war between 1975 and 1990. Approximately 17,000-20,000 people are still missing or unaccounted for from the civil war period.

Many Lebanese still derive their living from agriculture. The urban population, concentrated mainly in Beirut and Mount Lebanon, is noted for its commercial enterprise. A century and a half of migration and return have produced Lebanese commercial networks around the globe—from North and South America to Europe, the Gulf, and Africa. Lebanon has a high proportion of skilled labor compared with many other Arab countries.

Language

Arabic is the official language in Lebanon, but French and English are widely spoken.

Religion

The most recent demographic study conducted in 2011 by Statistics Lebanon, a Beirut-based research firm, indicated that 27 percent of the population are Sunni Muslim, 27 percent Shia Muslim, 21 percent Maronite Christian, 8 percent Greek Orthodox, 5 percent Druze, and 4 percent Greek Catholic, with the remaining 7 percent belonging to smaller Christian denominations. There are also very small numbers of Jews, Baha'is, Buddhists, and Hindus, and a very small number of members of The Church of Jesus Christ of Latter-day Saints (Mormons).

The 18 officially recognized religious groups include four Muslim sects, 12 Christian sects, the Druze sect, and Judaism. The main branches of Islam practiced are Shia and Sunni. The Alawites and the Ismaili ("Sevener") Shia order are the smallest Muslim communities. The Maronite community, the largest Christian group, maintains its centuries-long affiliation with the Roman Catholic Church but has its own patriarch, liturgy, and ecclesiastical customs. The second-largest Christian sect is Greek Orthodox. Other Christians are divided among Greek Catholics, Armenian Orthodox (Gregorians), Armenian Catholics, Syriac Orthodox (Jacobites), Syriac Catholics, Assyrians (Nestorians), Chaldeans, Copts, evangelicals (including Protestant groups such as Baptists and Seventh-day Adventists), and Latins (Roman Catholic). The Druze, who refer to themselves as al-Muwahhideen, or "believers in one God," are concentrated in the rural, mountainous areas east and south of Beirut.

Many persons fleeing religious mistreatment and discrimination in neighboring states have immigrated to the country, including Kurds, Shia, and Chaldeans from Iraq, as well as Coptic Christians from Egypt and Sudan. According to the secretary-general of the Syriac League, approximately 10,000 Iraqi Christians and 3,000 to 4,000 Coptic Christians reside in the country.

HISTORY

Lebanon is the historic home of the Phoenicians, Semitic traders whose maritime culture flourished there for more than 2,000 years (c.2700–450 B.C.). In later centuries, Lebanon's mountains were a refuge for Christians, and Crusaders established several strongholds there. Following the collapse of the Ottoman Empire after World War I, the League of Nations mandated the five provinces that comprise present-day Lebanon to France. Modern Lebanon's constitution, drawn up in 1926, specified a balance of political power among the various religious groups. The country gained independence in 1943, and French troops withdrew in 1946. Lebanon participated in the 1948 Arab-Israeli War and signed an armistice with Israel on March 23, 1949.

Lebanon's history since independence has been marked by periods of political turmoil interspersed with prosperity built on Beirut's position as a regional center for finance and trade. In 1958, during the last months of President Camille Chamoun's term, an insurrection broke out, and U.S. forces were briefly dispatched to Lebanon in response to an appeal by the government. During the 1960s, Lebanon enjoyed a period of relative calm

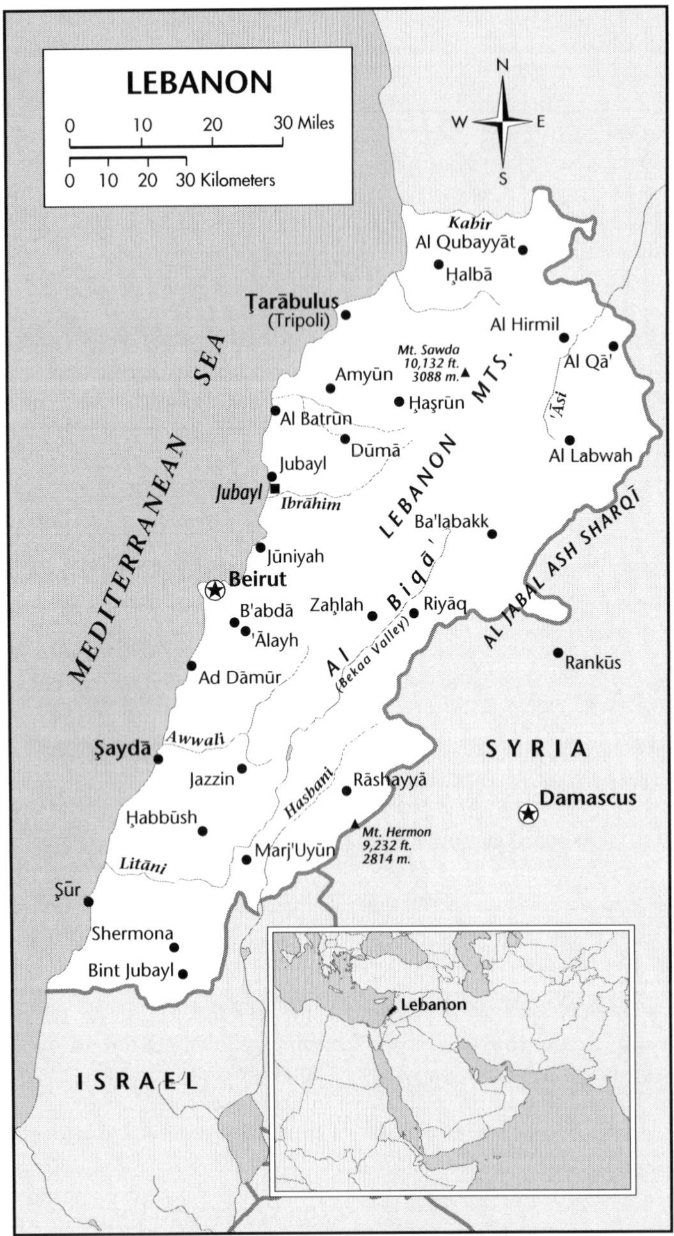

and Beirut-focused tourism and banking sector-driven prosperity. Other areas of the country, however, notably the south, north, and Bekaa Valley, remained poor in comparison.

In the early 1970s, difficulties arose over the presence of Palestinian refugees, many of whom arrived after the 1967 Arab-Israeli war, the secret 1969 Cairo Agreement permitting the establishment of Palestinian camps in Lebanon, and 1970 "Black September" hostilities in Jordan. Among the 1970 arrivals were Yasser Arafat and the Palestinian Liberation Organization (PLO). Coupled with the Palestinian problem, Muslim and Christian differences grew more intense.

Beginning of the Civil War—1975–81

Full-scale civil war broke out in April 1975. After shots were fired at a church, gunmen in Christian East Beirut ambushed a busload of Palestinians. Palestinian forces joined predominantly leftist-Muslim factions as the fighting persisted, eventually spreading to most parts of the country and precipitating the Lebanese President's call for support from Syrian troops in June 1976. In fall of 1976, Arab summits in Riyadh and Cairo set out a plan to end the war. The resulting Arab Deterrent Force, which included Syrian troops already present, moved in to help separate the combatants. As an uneasy quiet settled over Beirut, security conditions in the south began to deteriorate.

After a PLO attack on a bus in northern Israel and Israeli retaliation that caused heavy casualties, Israel invaded Lebanon in March 1978, occupying most of the area south of the Litani River. In response, the UN Security Council passed Resolution 425 calling for the immediate withdrawal of Israeli forces and creating the UN Interim Force in Lebanon (UNIFIL), charged with maintaining peace. Israeli forces withdrew later in 1978, turning over positions inside Lebanon along the border to their Lebanese ally, the South Lebanon Army (SLA) under the leadership of Maj. Saad Haddad, thus informally setting up a 12-mile wide "security zone" to protect Israeli territory from cross border attack.

U.S. Intervention—1982–84

An interim cease-fire brokered by the U.S. in 1981 among Syria, the PLO, and Israel was respected for almost a year. Several incidents, including PLO rocket attacks on northern Israel, as well as an assassination attempt on the Israeli Ambassador to the United Kingdom, led to the June 6, 1982 Israeli ground attack into Lebanon to remove PLO forces. Operation "Peace for Galilee" aimed at establishing a deeper security zone and pushing Syrian troops out of Lebanon, with a view toward paving the way for an Israeli-Lebanese peace agreement. With these aims in mind, Israeli forces drove 25 miles into Lebanon, moving into East Beirut with the support of Maronite Christian leaders and militia.

In August 1982, U.S. mediation resulted in the evacuation of Syrian troops and PLO fighters from Beirut.

The agreement also provided for the deployment of a multinational force composed of U.S. Marines along with French and Italian units. A new President, Bashir Gemayel, was elected with acknowledged Israeli backing. On September 14, however, he was assassinated. The next day, Israeli troops crossed into West Beirut to secure Muslim militia strongholds and stood aside as Lebanese Christian militias massacred almost 800 Palestinian civilians in the Sabra and Shatila refugee camps. Israel's then-Minister of Defense Ariel Sharon was held indirectly responsible for the massacre by the Kahane Commission and later resigned. With U.S. backing, Amine Gemayel, chosen by the Lebanese parliament to succeed his brother as President, focused anew on securing the withdrawal of Israeli and Syrian forces. The multinational force returned.

On May 17, 1983, Lebanon, Israel, and the United States signed an agreement on Israeli withdrawal that was conditioned on the departure of Syrian troops. Syria opposed the agreement and declined to discuss the withdrawal of its troops, effectively stalemating further progress. In August 1983, Israel withdrew from the Shuf (southeast of Beirut), thus removing the buffer between the Druze and the Christian militias and triggering another round of brutal fighting. By September, the Druze had gained control over most of the Shuf, and Israeli forces had pulled out from all but the southern security zone, where they remained until May 2000. The virtual collapse of the Lebanese Army in February 1984, following the defection of many Muslim and Druze units to militias, was a major blow to the government. With the U.S. Marines looking ready to withdraw, Syria and Muslim groups stepped up pressure on Gemayal. On March 5, 1984 the Lebanese Government canceled the May 17 agreement; the Marines departed a few weeks later.

This period of chaos witnessed the beginning of terrorist attacks launched against U.S. and Western interests. These included the April 18, 1983 suicide attack at the U.S. Embassy in West Beirut (63 dead), the bombing of the headquarters of U.S. and French forces on October 23, 1983 (298 dead), the assassination of American University of Beirut President Malcolm Kerr on January 18, 1984, and the bombing of the U.S. Embassy annex in East Beirut on September 20, 1984 (9 dead).

It also saw the rise of radicalism among a small number of Lebanese Muslim factions who believed that the successive Israeli and U.S. interventions in Lebanon were serving primarily Christian interests. It was from these factions that Hizballah emerged from a loose coalition of Shia groups. Hizballah employed terrorist tactics and was supported by Syria and Iran.

Worsening Conflict and Political Crisis—1985–89

Between 1985 and 1989, factional conflict worsened as various efforts at national reconciliation failed. Heavy fighting took place in the "War of the Camps" in 1985 and 1986 as the Shia Muslim Amal militia sought to rout the Palestinians from Lebanese strongholds. The Amal movement had been organized in mid-1975, at the beginning of the civil war, to confront what were seen as Israeli plans to displace the Lebanese population with Palestinians. (Its charismatic founder Imam Musa Sadr disappeared in Libya 3 years later. Its current leader, Nabih Berri, is the Speaker of the National Assembly.) The combat returned to Beirut in 1987, with Palestinians, leftists, and Druze fighters allied against Amal, eventually drawing further Syrian intervention. Violent confrontation flared up again in Beirut in 1988 between Amal and Hizballah.

Meanwhile, on the political front, Prime Minister Rashid Karami, head of a government of national unity set up after the failed peace efforts of 1984, was assassinated on June 1, 1987. President Gemayel's term of office expired in September 1988. Before stepping down, he appointed another Maronite Christian, Lebanese Armed Forces Commanding General Michel Aoun, as acting Prime Minister, contravening Lebanon's unwritten "National Pact," which required the prime minister to be Sunni Muslim. Muslim groups rejected the move and pledged support to Salim al-Hoss, a Sunni who had succeeded Karami. Lebanon was thus divided between a Christian government in East Beirut and a Muslim government in West Beirut, with no president.

In February 1989 Aoun attacked the rival Lebanese Forces militia. By March he turned his attention to other militias, launching what he termed a "War of Liberation" against the Syrians and their Lebanese militia allies. In the months that followed, Aoun rejected both the agreement that ultimately ended the civil war and the election of another Christian leader as president. A Lebanese-Syrian military operation in October 1990 forced him to take refuge in the French Embassy in Beirut and later to go into a 15-year exile in Paris. After Syrian troop withdrawal, Aoun returned to Lebanon on May 7, 2005 and won a seat in the 2005 parliamentary elections. His Free Patriotic Movement became a principal element of the pro-Syrian opposition bloc.

End of the Civil War—1989–91

The Taif Agreement of 1989 marked the beginning of the end of the war. In January of that year, a committee appointed by the Arab League, chaired by Kuwait and including Saudi Arabia, Algeria, and Morocco, had begun to formulate solutions to the conflict, leading to a meeting of Lebanese parliamentarians in Taif, Saudi Arabia, where they agreed to the national reconciliation accord in October. Returning to Lebanon, they ratified the agreement on November 4 and elected Rene Moawad as President the following day. Moawad was assassinated in a car bombing in Beirut on November 22 as his motorcade returned from Lebanese Independence Day ceremonies. Elias Hrawi, who remained in office until 1998, succeeded him.

In August 1990, parliament and the new President agreed on constitutional amendments embodying some of the political reforms envisioned at Taif. The National Assembly expanded to 128 seats and was divided equally between Christians and Muslims (with Druze counted as Muslims). In March 1991, parliament passed an amnesty law that pardoned all political crimes prior to its enactment. The amnesty was not extended to crimes perpetrated against foreign diplomats or certain crimes referred by the cabinet to the Higher Judicial Council. In May 1991, the militias (with the important exception of Hizballah and Palestinian militias) were dissolved, and the Lebanese Armed Forces began to slowly rebuild itself as Lebanon's only major nonsectarian institution.

In all, it is estimated that more than 100,000 were killed, and another 100,000 left handicapped, during Lebanon's 15-year civil war. Up to one-fifth of the pre-war resident population, or about 900,000 people, were displaced from their homes, of which perhaps a quarter of a million emigrated permanently. The last of the Western hostages taken during the mid-1980s were released in May 1992.

Postwar Reconstruction—1992 to 2005

Postwar social and political instability, fueled by economic uncertainty and the collapse of the Lebanese currency, led to the resignation of Prime Minister Omar Karami in May 1992, after less than 2 years in office. Former Prime Minister Rashid al Solh, who was widely viewed as a caretaker to oversee Lebanon's first parliamentary elections in 20 years, replaced him.

By early November 1992, a new parliament had been elected, and Prime Minister Rafik Hariri had formed a cabinet, retaining for himself the finance portfolio. The formation of a government headed by a successful billionaire businessman was widely seen as a sign that Lebanon would make a priority of rebuilding the country and reviving the economy. Solidere, a private real estate company set up to rebuild downtown Beirut, was a symbol of Hariri's strategy to link economic recovery to private sector investment. After the election of then-commander of the Lebanese Armed Forces Emile Lahoud in 1998, following Hrawi's extended term as President, Salim al-Hoss again served as Prime Minister. Hariri returned to office as Prime Minister in November 2000. Although problems with basic infrastructure and government services persist, and Lebanon is now highly indebted, much of the civil war damage was repaired throughout the country, and many foreign investors and tourists returned.

In early April 1996, Israel conducted a military operation dubbed "Grapes of Wrath" in response to Hizballah's continued launching of rockets at villages in northern Israel. The 16-day operation caused hundreds of thousands of civilians in south Lebanon to flee their homes. On April 18, Hizballah fired mortars at an Israeli military unit from a position near the UN compound at Qana, and the Israeli Army responded with artillery fire. Several Israeli shells struck the compound, killing 102 civilians sheltered there. In the "April Understanding" concluded on April 26, Israel and Hizballah committed themselves to avoid targeting civilians and using populated areas to launch attacks. The Israel-Lebanon Monitoring Group (ILMG), co-chaired by France and the United States, with Syria, Lebanon, and Israel all represented, was set up to implement the Understanding and assess reports of violations. ILMG ceased operations following the May 2000 Israeli withdrawal from south Lebanon.

On May 23, 2000, the Israeli military carried out a total withdrawal of Israeli troops from the south and the Bekaa Valley, effectively ending 22 years of occupation. The SLA collapsed and about 6,000 SLA members and their families fled the country, although more than 3,000 had returned by November 2003. The military court tried all of the SLA operatives who remained in the country and the average sentence handed down was 1-year imprisonment.

On June 16, 2000, the UN Security Council adopted the report of the Secretary General verifying Israeli compliance with UN Security Council Resolution 425 (1978) and the withdrawal of Israeli troops to their side of the demarcated Lebanese-Israeli line of separation (the "Blue Line") mapped out by UN cartographers. (The international border between Lebanon and Israel is still to be determined in the framework of a peace agreement.) In August 2000, the Government of Lebanon deployed over 1,000 police and soldiers to the former security zone, but Hizballah also maintained observation posts and conducted patrols along the Blue Line. While Lebanon and Syria initially agreed to respect the Blue Line, both since have registered objections and continue to argue that Israel has not fully withdrawn from Lebanese soil. As regional tension escalated with the Palestinian intifada in September 2000, Hizballah cited Blue Line discrepancies when it reengaged Israel on October 7, taking three Israeli soldiers captive in an area known as Shebaa Farms. (In 2001, the Israeli Government declared the three soldiers were believed to be dead.) Shebaa Farms, a largely unpopulated area just south of the Blue Line opposite the Lebanese town of Sheba'a, was captured by Israel when it occupied Syria's Golan Heights in 1967. The Lebanese Government has repeatedly laid claim to the area since shortly before Israel's general withdrawal. Meanwhile, the Syrian Government has verbally stated that the Shebaa Farms tract is Lebanese, but, as with the rest of the Lebanon-Syria border, has been unwilling to commit to a formal border demarcation in the area. As a result of secret mediation by the German Government, Israel released a number of Lebanese prisoners held by Israel in early 2004 in exchange for Elhanan Tannenbaum, an Israeli reservist abducted by Hizballah in late 2000.

In January 2000 the government took action against Sunni Muslim extremists in the north who had attacked its soldiers, and it continues to act against groups such as Asbat al-Ansar, which has been linked to the al-Qaida network, and other extremists. On January 24, 2002, Elie Hobeika, a former Lebanese Forces figure associated with the Sabra and Shatila massacres and who later served in three cabinets and the parliament, was assassinated in a car bombing in Beirut.

A September 2004 vote by the Chamber of Deputies to amend the constitution to extend President Lahoud's term in office by 3 years amplified the question of Lebanese sovereignty and the continuing Syrian presence. The vote was clearly taken under Syrian pressure, exercised in part through Syria's military intelligence service, whose chief in Lebanon had acted as a virtual proconsul for many years. Syria, which has historically viewed Lebanon as part of its own territory, has not signed a boundary agreement with Lebanon, although it established full diplomatic relations with Lebanon, including nominating an ambassador to Lebanon, in 2009. The UN Security Council expressed its concern over the situation by passing Resolution 1559, also in September 2004, which called for withdrawal of all remaining foreign forces from Lebanon, disbanding and disarmament of all Lebanese and non-Lebanese militias, the deployment of the Lebanese Armed Forces throughout the country, and a free and fair electoral process in the presidential election.

Syrian Withdrawal—2005

Former Prime Minister Rafik Hariri, who had resisted Syria's effort to secure Lahoud's extension, and 22 others were assassinated in Beirut by a car bomb on February 14, 2005. The assassination spurred massive protests in Beirut and international pressure that led to the withdrawal of the remaining Syrian military troops from Lebanon on April 26. In the months that followed Hariri's assassination, journalist Samir Qassir, Lebanese politician George Hawi, and journalist Gebran Tueni were murdered by car bombs, and Defense Minister Elias Murr and journalist May Chidiac narrowly avoided a similar fate when they were targeted with car bombs. The UN International Independent Investigative Commission (UNIIIC) headed by Detlev Mehlis began an investigation of Hariri's assassination and related crimes, beginning with the October 2004 attempt to assassinate Communications Minister Marwan Hamadeh. Following the investigative groundwork laid by the UNIIIC, the official opening of the Special Tribunal for Lebanon on March 1, 2009, in The Hague marked an important step toward ending impunity for political assassinations in Lebanon. The investigation into the assassination of former Prime Minister Hariri and others remains ongoing under the leadership of chief prosecutor Daniel Bellemare. On June 30, 2011, the Tribunal handed down an indictment and arrest warrants for four alleged members of Hizballah—Salim Jamil Ayyash, Mustafa Amine Badreddine, Hussein Hassan Oneissi, and Assad Hassan Sabra—for involvement in the Hariri assassination. On August 9, 2011, Lebanese Prosecutor General Said Mirza submitted a report to the Tribunal detailing the Government of Lebanon's efforts to locate and arrest the four men, and reportedly explaining that none had yet been arrested.

Parliamentary elections were held in 2005 and the anti-Syrian March 14 coalition—led by Saad Hariri, Rafik Hariri's son—won a majority of 72 seats (out of 128). Hariri ally and former Finance Minister Fouad Siniora was named Prime Minister and Nabih Berri was reelected as Speaker of Parliament. Parliament approved the first "made-in-Lebanon" cabinet in almost 30 years on July 30. The ministerial statement of the new cabinet (which included two Hizballah ministers), a summary of the new government's agenda and priorities, focused on political and economic reform, but also endorsed Hizballah's right to possess military weapons to carry out a "national resistance" against the perceived Israeli occupation of Lebanese territory.

Hizballah forces continued to launch sporadic military strikes on Israeli forces, drawing responses that produced casualties on both sides. Israel continued to violate Lebanese sovereignty by conducting overflights of Lebanese territory north of the Blue Line. UNIFIL recorded numerous violations of the Blue Line by both sides following the Israeli withdrawal. In general, however, the level of violence along the Israeli-Lebanon front decreased dramatically from May 2000 until mid-2006.

War with Israel—2006

On July 12, 2006, Hizballah guerillas crossed into Israel, killed three Israeli soldiers, and kidnapped two others, precipitating a war with Israel. Israeli air strikes hit Hizballah positions in the south and strategic targets throughout Lebanon, and Israeli ground forces moved against Hizballah in southern Lebanon. Hizballah resisted the ground attack and fired thousands of rockets at civilian targets in Israel.

By the time the war ended on August 14, an estimated 1,200 Lebanese civilians and hundreds of Hizballah fighters had died, along with 119 Israeli military and 43 Israeli civilians. UN Security Council Resolution 1701, which ended the war, provided for a ceasefire, Israeli withdrawal and lifting of blockades, disarming of Hizballah and other militias, and a ban on unauthorized weapons transfers into Lebanon. UNSCR 1701 also significantly strengthened UNIFIL's mandate and authorized its enlargement from about 2,000 up to a maximum of 15,000. Bolstered by UNIFIL, which by the beginning of 2007 had more than 11,000 personnel, the Lebanese Armed Forces (LAF) deployed to southern Lebanon and the border with Israel for the first time in almost four decades.

The war temporarily or permanently displaced roughly one-quarter of Lebanon's population and caused enormous damage to homes, businesses, and infrastructure. The country, which was already seriously indebted, suffered roughly $5 billion in damages and financial losses. The international community provided massive humanitarian relief, plus substantial aid for economic reconstruction and reform, with $940 million in aid pledged at an August 31, 2006, donors conference in Stockholm and $7.6 billion in pledges announced at a Paris conference January 25, 2007. Aid pledged in Paris was to be coordinated with the Lebanese Government's program for fiscal and economic reform.

Following its historic deployment to southern Lebanon, in May-September 2007, the LAF battled Sunni extremist group Fatah al-Islam in the Nahr al-Bared Palestinian refugee camp near Tripoli, winning a decisive victory, but destroying the camp and displacing approximately 30,000 Palestinian residents. The U.S. is the largest supporter of Nahr al-Bared relief and reconstruction, contributing a total of $91 million through FY 2010 toward UNRWA's 4-year $328 million emergency appeal.

Doha Agreement and Post-Doha Lebanon

After a cabinet walkout by Shia ministers over the issue of the Special Tribunal for Lebanon in November 2006, Lebanon's political deadlock came to a head in 2007 when Lebanese politicians were unable to agree on a successor to President Emile Lahoud. Hizballah's takeover of west Beirut in May 2008 and resulting outbreak of violence led Lebanese leaders, with Arab League mediation, to draft the Doha Agreement. The Doha Agreement paved the way for the election of a consensus candidate as President—LAF Commander Michel Sleiman—in May 2008 and the formation of a new unity government.

Parliamentary elections were held in 2009, under the new electoral law mandated by the Doha Agreement. While the new electoral law maintained the Taif Agreement's division of parliamentary seats equally between Christians and Muslims, it also divided Lebanon into 26 electoral districts and mandated that elections be held on a single day, rather than consecutive weekends. Saad Hariri's coalition secured a parliamentary majority in the 2009 elections. The new national unity cabinet headed by Prime Minister Hariri received parliament's vote of confidence on December 10, 2009, after 6 months of extensive negotiations between the majority and the opposition. As in 2005 and 2008, the new cabinet's ministerial statement focused on political and economic reform, but also endorsed Hizballah's role, along with that of the Lebanese people and army, in confronting Israeli occupation of Lebanese territory.

A number of recent security incidents in south Lebanon highlight the continuing threat to Lebanon's stability and security posed by Hizballah's arms and the need for full implementation of UN Security Council Resolutions 1559, 1680, and 1701, including the disarmament of all militias, the delineation of the Lebanon-Syria border, and enforcement of the weapons-free zone.

Unity Government Collapses

On January 12, 2011, while Prime Minister Hariri was meeting with U.S. President Barack Obama, Hizballah and its March 8 allies withdrew their ministers from Hariri's national unity cabinet over issues related to the Tribunal, thereby forcing its collapse. On January 24, President Sleiman named former Prime Minister and member of parliament Najib Mikati as Prime Minister-designate, leaving Hariri and his cabinet in caretaker status.

On June 13, following several months of negotiations, Mikati announced a government that did not include any ministers from Saad Hariri's March 14 coalition, which had refused to participate. The cabinet included a majority of ministers from the Hizballah-led March 8 alliance, with a remaining "centrist bloc" of ministers aligned with Mikati, Sleiman, and Druze leader Walid Jumblatt. The Mikati cabinet received its parliamentary vote of confidence on July 7, 2011.

GOVERNMENT AND POLITICAL CONDITIONS

Lebanon is a parliamentary republic, with a constitutionally mandated Maronite Christian president, Sunni Muslim prime minister, and Shia Muslim speaker of the chamber of deputies. Parliamentary elections in 2009 were considered free and fair. Government

Despite the presence of Lebanese and UN security forces, Hizballah retained significant influence over parts of the country, and the government made no tangible progress toward disbanding and disarming armed militia groups, including Hizballah. Palestinian refugee camps continued to act as self-governed entities and maintained security and militia forces not under the direction of government officials.

Recent Elections

Observers concluded that the 2009 parliamentary elections were generally free and fair, with minor irregularities, such as instances of vote-buying. The NGO Lebanese Transparency Association (LTA) reported that its monitors witnessed vote-buying through cash donations on election day in many electoral districts.

Political Parties: The four major political parties and numerous smaller ones were almost exclusively based on confessional affiliation, and parliamentary seats were allotted on a sectarian basis.

Participation of Women and Minorities: There were significant cultural barriers to women's participation in politics. Prior to 2004 no woman held a cabinet position. None was in the cabinet approved by parliament on July 7, and only three have been ministers since the first woman was appointed in 2004. Only four of 128 members of parliament (MPs) were women and all were close relatives of previous male MPs.

Minorities were able to participate in politics to some extent. Regardless of the number of its adherents, every government-recognized religion, except Coptic Christianity, Ismailism, and Judaism, was allocated at least one seat in parliament. Three parliamentarians representing minorities (one Syriac Orthodox and two Alawites) were elected in the 2009 elections. These groups also held high positions in government and the LAF. As Palestinian refugees are not citizens, they have no political rights. An estimated 17 Palestinian factions operated in the country, generally organized around prominent individuals. Most Palestinians lived in refugee camps that one or more factions controlled. Refugee leaders were not elected, but there were popular committees that met regularly with the UNRWA and visitors.

Principal Government Officials

Last Updated: 1/31/2013

Pres.: **Michel SULAYMAN**
Prime Min.: **Najib MIQATI**
Dep. Prime Min.: **Samir MOQBIL**
Min. of Admin. Reform: **Muhammad FNAYSH**
Min. of Agriculture: **Husayn al-Hajj HASSAN**
Min. of Culture: **Gabi LAYYOUN**
Min. of Defense: **Fayiz GHOSN**
Min. of Displaced People: **Ala al-Din TERRO**
Min. of Economy & Trade: **Nicolas NAHHAS**
Min. of Education: **Hassan DIAB**
Min. of Energy & Water: **Gibran BASSIL**
Min. of Environment: **Nazim al-KHOURY**
Min. of Finance: **Muhammad SAFADI**
Min. of Foreign Affairs & Emigrants: **Adnan MANSOUR**
Min. of Industry: **Freij SABOUNJIAN**
Min. of Information: **Walid DAOUQ**
Min. of Interior: **Marwan CHARBEL**
Min. of Justice: **Shakib QORTABAWI**
Min. of Labor: **Charbel NAHHAS**
Min. of Public Health: **Ali Hassan KHALIL**
Min. of Social Affairs: **Wael Abu FAOUR**
Min. of Telecommunications: **Nicolas SAHNAWI**
Min. of Tourism: **Fady ABBOUD**
Min. of Transport & Public Works: **Ghazi ARIDI**
Min. of Youth & Sports: **Faysal KARAMI**
Min. of State: **Salim KARAM**
Min. of State: **Ahmad KARAMI**
Min. of State: **Marwan KHAYREDDINE**
Min. of State: **Panos MANIJIAN**
Min. of State: **Ali QANSO**
Min. of State for Parliamentary Affairs: **Nicolas FATTOUSH**
Governor, Central Bank of Lebanon: **Riad Toufic SALAMEH**
Ambassador to the US: **Antoine CHEDID**
Permanent Representative to the UN, New York: **Nawaf SALAM**

ECONOMY

Lebanon has a free-market economy and a strong laissez-faire commercial tradition. The government does not restrict foreign investment; however, the investment climate suffers from red tape, corruption, arbitrary licensing decisions, complex customs procedures, high taxes, tariffs, and fees, archaic legislation, and weak intellectual property rights.

The Lebanese economy is service-oriented; main growth sectors include banking and tourism. The 1975–90 civil war seriously damaged Lebanon's economic infrastructure, cut national output by half, and derailed Lebanon's position as a Middle Eastern entrepot and banking hub.

Following the civil war Lebanon rebuilt much of its war-torn physical and financial infrastructure by borrowing heavily—mostly from domestic banks—saddling the government with a huge debt burden. Pledges of economic and financial reforms made at separate international donor conferences during the 2000s have mostly gone unfulfilled, including those made during the Paris III Donor Conference in 2007 following the July 2006 war.

The collapse of the government in early 2011 over its backing of the Special Tribunal for Lebanon and unrest in neighboring Syria slowed economic growth to 1.5% after four years of 8% average growth. In September 2011 the Cabinet endorsed a bill that would provide $1.2 billion in funding to improve Lebanon's downtrodden electricity sector, but fiscal limitations will test the government's ability to invest in other areas, such as water.

Labor Conditions

The minimum age for employment is 14 years of age, and the law lists the legal occupations for juveniles. The law requires juveniles, defined as children between 14 and 18 years of age, to undergo a medical exam by a doctor certified by the Ministry of Public Health to assure they are physically fit for the type of work they are asked to perform.

The labor code prohibits employment of juveniles younger than 18 years old for more than six hours per day and requires one hour of rest if work lasts more than four hours. Juveniles younger than 17 years old are prohibited from working in jobs that jeopardize their health, safety, or morals; they also are prohibited from working between 7 p.m. and 7 a.m. The law prohibits the employment of juveniles younger than 16 years old in industrial jobs or jobs physically demanding or harmful to their health. The penal code calls for penalties ranging from a fine of 250,000 pounds ($166), one to three months' imprisonment, or forced closing of the establishment.

The Ministry of Labor is responsible for enforcing these requirements through its Child Labor Unit. In 2010 the ministry admitted that the 130 labor inspectors and assistant inspectors employed to enforce child labor laws were not sufficient. Current figures on child labor in the country were unavailable. Anecdotal evidence suggested the number of child workers has risen and that more children were working in the informal sector, including prostitution. Child labor was predominantly concentrated in the informal sector, including in small family businesses, mechanical workshops, carpentry, construction, manufacturing, industrial sites, welding, agriculture, and fisheries. Children work under the table in some of these informal sector jobs, often in small and/or family businesses that are not part of any formal business syndicates/associations. Street children worked selling goods, polishing shoes, and washing car windows. Anecdotal evidence also suggested that child labor was prevalent within Palestinian refugee camps and among Iraqi refugees and Roma (nomadic) communities in the country.

The legal minimum wage was 500,000 pounds ($333) per month across all sectors and industries. The law prescribes a standard 48-hour workweek with a 24-hour rest period per week. The law stipulates 48 hours as the maximum duration of work per week in most corporations except agricultural entities. A 12-hour day is permitted under certain conditions, including a stipulation that the overtime provided is 50 percent higher than the pay for other hours. The law does not set limits on compulsory overtime.

The law includes specific occupational health and safety regulations and requires employers to take adequate precautions for employee safety. The Ministry of Labor is responsible for enforcing these regulations but did so unevenly. Labor organizers reported workers did not have the right to remove themselves from hazardous conditions without jeopardizing their employment. Foreign and local domestic servants are not covered under the labor law.

In practice, workers in the industrial sector worked an average of 35 hours per week, and workers in other sectors worked an average of 30 hours per week. Some private sector firms failed to provide employees with family and transport allowances as stipulated under the law and did not register them with the National Social Security Fund (NSSF). Employers sometimes registered their employees with lower salaries to decrease their contributions to the NSSF and their end-of-service pay to the employee. Some companies did not respect legal provisions governing occupational health and safety, for example, in the construction industry. Workers may report violations directly to the CGTL, Ministry of Labor, or NSSF. In most cases they preferred to remain silent for fear of arbitrary dismissal.

Some employers mistreated, abused, and raped foreign domestic workers, who were mostly of Asian and African origin. Domestic workers often worked long hours and in many cases did not receive vacations or holidays. There was no official minimum wage for domestic workers. Official contracts stipulate a wage ranging from 150,000 to 450,000 pounds ($100 to $300) per month, depending on the nationality of the worker.

Migrant domestic workers are granted increased labor protections through a unified standard contract, which is registered with the DGS in order for the worker to obtain residency. The contract covers terms and conditions of employment but the section covering wages is completed individually. Victims of abuse may file civil suits or seek legal action, often with the assistance of NGOs, but most victims, counseled by their embassies or consulates, settled for an administrative solution that usually included monetary compensation and repatriation.

Perpetrators of abuses were not further prosecuted for a number of reasons, including the victims' refusal to press charges and lack of evidence. An unknown number of other cases of nonpayment of wages were settled through negotiation. According to source country embassies and consulates, many workers did not report violations of their labor contracts until after they returned to their home countries, as they preferred not to stay in the country for a lengthy judicial process.

Foreign migrant workers arrived in the country through local recruitment agencies and source country recruitment agencies. Though all recruitment agencies must have a license from the Ministry of Labor, the government did not adequately monitor their activities.

U.S.-LEBANESE RELATIONS

Lebanon's history since its 1943 independence has been marked by periods of political turmoil interspersed with prosperity built on its position as a regional center for finance and trade. The country's 1975–90 civil war was followed by years of social and political instability. Sectarianism is a key element of Lebanese political life. Neighboring Syria has long influenced Lebanon's foreign policy and internal policies, and its military forces were in Lebanon from 1976 until 2005. The Lebanon-based Hizballah militia and Israel continued to engage in attacks and counterattacks against each other after Syria's withdrawal, and fought a brief war in 2006. Lebanon's borders with Syria and Israel are still to be resolved.

The United States seeks to maintain its traditionally close ties with Lebanon, and to help preserve its independence, sovereignty, national unity, and territorial integrity. The United States, along with the international community, supports full implementation of UN Security Council Resolutions (UNSCRs) 1559, 1680 and 1701, including the disarming of all militias, delineation of the Lebanese-Syrian border, and the deployment of the Lebanese Armed Forces (LAF) throughout Lebanon. The United States believes that a peaceful, prosperous, and stable Lebanon can make an important contribution to comprehensive peace in the Middle East.

U.S. Assistance to Lebanon

Since the 2006 war, the U.S. Government has pledged well over $1 billion in assistance for relief, recovery, rebuilding, and security. This support reflects not only humanitarian concerns and historical ties, but also the importance the United States attaches to sustainable development and the bolstering of a sovereign, stable, prosperous, and democratic Lebanon. Current funding is used to support the activities of Lebanese non-governmental organizations engaged in rural and municipal development programs nationwide, to improve the capacity of the public sector in providing transparent, quality services, to strengthen the Lebanese security services, and to reduce deep pockets of poverty, especially in areas outside metropolitan Beirut, by strengthening productive sectors and job readiness. The U.S. also supports humanitarian demining programs.

The United States also assists public school graduates to enroll at the American University of Beirut, the Lebanese American University and Haigazian University. Assistance also has been provided to the American Community School at Beirut and the International College.

In 1993, the U.S. resumed the International Military Education and Training program in Lebanon to help bolster the Lebanese Armed Forces—the country's only nonsectarian national institution—and reinforce the importance of civilian control of the military. Sales of excess defense articles resumed in 1991 and have allowed the LAF to enhance its transportation and communications capabilities, which were severely degraded during the civil war. Security assistance to both the LAF and the Internal Security Forces, representing over $600 million of the $1 billion in post-2006 assistance, increased significantly after the 2006 war in order to support the Government of Lebanon as it carries out the requirements of UNSCR 1701 and asserts its sovereignty over the whole of Lebanese territory.

Bilateral Economic Relations

Lebanon has a free-market economy and a strong laissez-faire commercial tradition. The Lebanese economy is service-oriented; main growth sectors include banking and tourism. In 2011, major U.S. exports to Lebanon were mineral fuel and oil, vehicles, machinery, pharmaceutical products, and cereals. The U.S. and Lebanon have signed a Trade and Investment Framework Agreement to help promote an attractive investment climate, expand trade relations, and remove obstacles to trade and investment between the two countries. The U.S. does not have a bilateral investment treaty with Lebanon or an agreement on the avoidance of double taxation.

Lebanon's Membership in International Organizations

Lebanon's foreign policy reflects its geographic location, the composition of its population, and its reliance on commerce and trade. Lebanon and the United States belong to a number of the same international organizations, including the United Nations, International Monetary Fund, and World Bank. Lebanon is an observer to the Organization of American States and is working toward accession to the World Trade Organization.

Bilateral Representation

Lebanon maintains an embassy in the United States at 2560 28th Street, NW, Washington, DC 20008, tel. (202) 939-6300.

Principal U.S. Embassy Officials

Last Updated: 1/14/2013

BEIRUT (E) P.O.Box70-840 Antelias-Beirut, 961-4-542600/543600, Fax 961-4-544604, INMARSAT Tel Primary:873-683-825 unsecure: 873-683-131-826 secure/alternate 761-258-233, Workweek: Monday-Friday/0800-1630, Website: http://lebanon.usembassy.gov/

DCM OMS:	Laura Birkinshaw
AMB OMS:	Katherine Ahern
DPO/PAO:	Amanda Johnson
FM:	Donald Cunningham
HRO:	Elizabeth Keene
MGT:	Robert A. Pitre
MLO/ODC:	LTC Ulises Calvo
NAS/INL:	Paul Malik
POL/ECON:	Danielle Garbe
POL/MIL:	Mohammad Shahbaz
POSHO:	Donald Cunningham
SDO/DATT:	COL David Brenner
AMB:	Maura Connelly
CON:	Sarah Kay Bellman
DCM:	Richard Mills Jr..
PAO:	Amanda Johnson
COM:	Shawn Tenbrink
GSO:	Michael J. Unglesbee
RSO:	David Brown
AFSA:	Christine Prince
AID:	Azza Al-Abd
CLO:	Norma Bryan
DEA:	James Grace
ECON:	Alexander Ted Bryan
EEO:	David Jeffrey
FMO:	Wrenn Bellamy
ICASS Chair:	Danielle Garbe
IMO:	Keith Fulton
ISO:	Ishwaran Ravindranath
ISSO:	Ishwaran Ravindranath
LEGATT:	Scott Smith
State ICASS:	Danielle Garbe

TRAVEL

Consular Information Sheet

October 11, 2012

Country Description: The Republic of Lebanon is a parliamentary republic. Political power is concentrated in the office of the President, Prime Minister, and Speaker of Parliament, each representing one of Lebanon's three largest religious sects (Maronite Christians, Sunni, and Shia Muslims). Since 1973, Lebanon has been in a state of war with Israel.

Smart Traveler Enrollment Program (STEP)/Embassy Locations: If you are going to live in or visit Lebanon, please take the time to tell our Embassy about your trip. If you enroll, we can keep you up to date with important safety and security announcements. It will also help your friends and family get in touch with you in an emergency.

U.S. Embassy, Beirut
Address: Awkar Facing the Municipality
PO Box 70-840
Telephone: (961) 4 542600 – 543600
Facsimile: (961) 4 544209
Email: BeirutACS@state.gov

U.S. citizens enrolled in STEP can receive updated information and emergency messages via e-mail by subscribing to our Message Service. U.S. citizens without Internet access may enroll directly with the U.S. Embassy in Beirut. Information on consular services and enrollment in STEP can also be found on the Embassy's website or by phone at the telephone numbers shown above between 2:00 p.m. and 4:00 p.m. Monday through Friday local time.

Public access hours for U.S. citizens are Monday through Thursday, 8:00 a.m. to 11:00 a.m. by appointment only. U.S. citizens who require emergency services outside these hours may contact the Embassy by telephone at any time.

Entry/Exit Requirements for U.S. Citizens: Passports and visas are required. U.S. citizens coming to Lebanon for tourism can purchase a short-term one-month visa at the land border with Syria, the port of Beirut, or Beirut International airport. However, official U.S. government travelers need to arrange for a visa in advance of their travel. U.S. citizens also holding Lebanese citizenship are subject to the requirements and responsibilities of that citizenship under Lebanese law. Travelers holding passports that contain visas or entry/exit stamps for Israel will likely be refused entry into Lebanon and may be subject to arrest and imprisonment. Persons seeking entry into Lebanon who have previously traveled to Israel may face arrest and/or detention even if the travel documents they are currently using do not have Israeli stamps or visas. Note that the Government of Lebanon has the authority to refuse admission to U.S. citizens and to detain U.S. citizen travelers for further inspection. Travelers who have overstayed their entry visa validity in Lebanon must adjust their status with the Central Department of Sûreté Générale (Department of Passport and Immigration) prior to their departure. Note that individuals who are detained pending deportation are expected to pay the cost of their own airline ticket and will remain under detention until they have gathered the necessary funds.

Due to security concerns, unofficial travel to Lebanon by U.S. government employees and their family members is discouraged, strictly limited, and requires prior approval by the Department of State. This is also true for U.S. government employees planning to transit through Beirut, whether for official or unofficial travel.

Further information on entry/exit requirements can be obtained from the Embassy of Lebanon, 2560 28th Street NW, Washington, DC, 20008, tel. (202) 939-6300. Travelers may also contact one of the following Consulates General:

Consulate General of Lebanon in Detroit
New Center One Building
3031 West Grand Blvd.
Suite 560
Detroit, MI 48202
(313) 758-0753 to 55

Consulate General of Lebanon in Los Angeles
660 South Figueroa St., Ste 1050
Los Angeles, CA 90017
(213) 243-0990

Consulate General of Lebanon in New York
9 E. 76th Street
New York, NY 10021
(212) 744-7905

Additional information on Lebanese Consulates General and Honorary Consulates in the United States can be found within the Consular Affairs section of the Embassy of Lebanon website.

Information about dual nationality or the prevention of international child abduction can be found on our website. For further information about customs regulations, please read our Customs Information page.

The U.S. Department of State is unaware of any HIV/AIDS entry restrictions for visitors although individuals applying for a work permit to Lebanon must submit to a laboratory exam in order to prove that s/he is free of HIV/AIDS.

Threats to Safety and Security: The current Department of State Travel Warning advises U.S. citizens against travel to Lebanon. U.S. citizens who visit or reside in Lebanon despite the Travel Warning should be aware that there are a number of serious security concerns, and should consult the Travel Warning for up-to-date information.

U.S. citizens traveling to Lebanon should also be aware that personnel from the U.S. Embassy are not able to travel in all areas of Lebanon. In the case of an emergency involving a U.S. citizen in areas where it is unsafe for Embassy personnel to travel, the Embassy may not be able to render assistance.

In the event that the security climate in the country worsens, U.S. citizens will be responsible for arranging their own travel out of Lebanon. U.S. citizens with special medical or other needs should be aware of the risks of remaining given their condition and should be prepared to seek treatment in Lebanon if they cannot arrange for travel out of the country.

Stay up to date by:

- Bookmarking our Bureau of Consular Affairs website, which contains the current Travel Warnings and Travel Alerts as well as the Worldwide Caution.
- Following us on Twitter and the Bureau of Consular Affairs page on Facebook as well.
- Downloading our free Smart Traveler App available through iTunes and the Android market to have travel information at your fingertips.
- Calling 1-888-407-4747 toll-free within the U.S. and Canada, or a regular toll line, 1-202-501-4444, from other countries.
- Taking some time before travel to consider your personal security – Here are some useful tips for traveling safely abroad.

Crime: The crime rate in Lebanon is moderate, and both car theft and burglaries occur. Violent crime and sexual assault are rare, although the

Embassy receives regular reports of domestic abuse. Petty theft—such as pick pocketing and purse snatching—is common in crowded public areas. Police are responsive but often unable to affect a positive outcome. There are no special concerns with regard to targeted victimization of U.S. citizens in scams or confidence schemes.

In the past, there have been incidents involving a theft ring that appeared to be targeting foreigners using service cars. Service cars are privately owned vehicles bearing red license plates that act as public transportation for multiple passengers at one time. Typically, a service car that already contained two people (the driver and one passenger), picked up the potential passenger. The driver then took the victim to a more isolated area or the freeway where the first "passenger" robbed the second passenger by threatening him/her with a gun. Because of the risks inherent in using any unknown transportation, U.S. citizens should be wary of these service cars and carry the number of a reputable taxi company in case of emergencies.

Do not buy counterfeit and pirated goods, even if they are widely available. Not only are the bootlegs illegal in the United States, you may also be breaking local law.

Victims of Crime: If you or someone you know becomes the victim of a crime abroad, you should contact the local police and the nearest U.S. embassy or consulate. We can:

- Replace a stolen passport.
- Help you find appropriate medical care if you are the victim of violent crimes such as assault or rape.
- Put you in contact with the appropriate police authorities, and if you want us to, we can contact family members or friend.
- Help you understand the local criminal justice process and direct you to local attorneys, although it is important to remember that local authorities are responsible for investigating and prosecuting the crime.

The local equivalent to the "911" emergency line in Lebanon is 112.

Criminal Penalties: While you are traveling in Lebanon, you are subject to its laws even if you are a U.S. citizen. Foreign laws and legal systems can be vastly different from our own. For example, you may be taken in for questioning if you do not have your passport with you. It is illegal to take pictures of certain buildings, for example, some government buildings. In some places, driving under the influence could land you immediately in jail. These criminal penalties will vary from country to country. There are also some things that might be legal in the country you visit, but still illegal in the United States; for example, you can be prosecuted under U.S. law if you buy pirated goods. Engaging in sexual conduct with children or using, or disseminating child pornography in a foreign country is a crime prosecutable in the United States. If you break local laws in Lebanon your U.S. passport will not help you avoid arrest or prosecution. It is very important to know what's legal and what's not where you are going.

While some countries will automatically notify the nearest U.S. embassy or consulate if a U.S. citizen is detained or arrested in a foreign country, that might not always be the case. To ensure that the United States is aware of your circumstances, request that the police and prison officials notify the nearest U.S. embassy or consulate as soon as you are arrested or detained overseas.

Special Circumstances: In addition to being subject to all Lebanese laws, U.S. citizens who also possess Lebanese nationality may also be subject to other laws that impose special obligations on them as Lebanese citizens. Lebanese citizens who are discovered to have associated with Israeli citizens or officials or traveled through Israel are subject to arrest and detention. Any citizen arriving at a Lebanese point of entry with an Israeli stamp in their passport may be detained, arrested, or denied entry. Penalties are especially harsh if the traveler is of Arab origin or a dual national. Travelers have also been detained if they have a family name that may be considered of Israeli or Jewish origin.

Travelers who have previously entered Lebanon illegally as refugees will be denied entry into the country even if they have since become U.S. citizens. In most cases, travelers are returned to their point of origin on the first available flight. If a U.S. citizen is detained for questioning and then subject to deportation, they are expected to pay the cost of their own airline ticket and will remain under detention until they have gathered the necessary funds.

U.S. citizens living in or traveling to Lebanon have occasionally been denied permission to leave the country because a criminal, civil, or family court has imposed a travel hold. For example, a head of household can place a travel hold against a spouse and children in family court even before the family arrives in Lebanon. Travel holds can be easily initiated and may remain in place for a substantial period of time. While the U.S. Embassy can direct U.S. citizens to options for legal representation, it cannot have travel bans removed, even in times of crisis.

U.S. citizens who come to work in Lebanon should ensure that their Lebanese employer arranges for proper documentation to remain in the country. This includes professional athletes, who should make certain that their sponsoring club/team arranges for them to receive the correct visas valid for the duration of their stay. Travelers coming to Lebanon as professional athletes should ensure that a written contract is in place before traveling as many athletes have experienced problems with scams and false offers of employment.

U.S. citizens planning to travel between Lebanon and Syria should consult the Department of State's Travel Warning for Syria. U.S. citizens planning to travel to Syria from Lebanon in spite of the Travel Warning are strongly advised to obtain a Syrian visa before leaving the United States, as they may have difficulty securing one while in Lebanon.

Mandatory military service in Lebanon was abolished on February 4, 2007. However, travelers with questions about prior military service, desertion, or failure to register in the past should contact the Military Office of the Embassy of Lebanon, 2560 28th Street, N.W., Washington, D.C. 20008, or call (202) 265-2335 or fax (202) 667-0063 for details prior to traveling to Lebanon. Information about military service can also be found at the Lebanese government website.

Lebanese Customs authorities may enforce strict regulations concerning import and export of items such as firearms or antiquities. You should contact the Embassy of Lebanon in Washington, D.C., or one or one of Lebanon's consulates in the United States, for specific information regarding customs requirements. Please see our information on customs regulations.

Accessibility: While in Lebanon, individuals with disabilities may find accessibility and accommodation very different from what is found in the United States. Lebanon has passed laws that make it illegal to discriminate against those with disabilities but the laws are not uniformly enforced. These laws include sections on building accessibility, but building codes have yet to be updated accordingly.

Most public transportation, including taxis, is not accessible. Roads are often in disrepair and there are few sidewalks or road crossings. Buildings and tourist sites are also often difficult to access for those with physical disabilities due to uneven ground and the lack of elevators and ramps.

Medical Facilities and Health Information: In Beirut and the surrounding areas, modern medical care and medicines are widely available. Modern facilities are not always available in outlying areas, although no location in the country is more than three hours from the capital. Doctors and hospitals often expect immediate cash payment for services, and without such payment, may deny service even in emergency cases. A list of doctors who speak English and a list of hospitals are available from the U.S. Embassy and at the Embassy's website.

You can find good information on vaccinations and other health precautions on the Centers for Disease Control and Prevention (CDC) website. For information about outbreaks of infectious diseases abroad, consult the World Health Organization (WHO) website. The WHO website also contains additional health information for travelers, including detailed country-specific health information.

Medical Insurance: You can't assume your insurance will go with you when you travel. It's very important to find out BEFORE you leave whether or not your medical insurance will cover you overseas. You need to ask your insurance company two questions:

- Does my policy apply when I'm out of the United States?
- Will it cover emergencies like a trip to a foreign hospital or a medical evacuation?

In many places, doctors and hospitals still expect payment in cash at the time of service. Your regular U.S. health insurance may not cover doctor and hospital visits in other countries. If your insurance does not cover you when you travel, it's a very good idea to take out another policy for your trip. Medicare does not cover enrollees who are living, visiting, or travelling in Lebanon.

Traffic Safety and Road Conditions: While in a foreign country, U.S. citizens may encounter road conditions that differ significantly from those in the United States. The information below concerning Lebanon is provided for general reference only, and may not be totally accurate in a particular location or circumstance. An international driver's license is required for visitors to Lebanon. Drivers in Lebanon often maneuver aggressively and pay little regard to traffic lights and stop signs. Lanes are generally unmarked and roads outside the capital may be poorly lighted. Pedestrians should exercise particular caution. Intercity directional signs are improving throughout the country, but side roads are often not signposted at all. Public transportation is generally safe.

While there is limited enforcement, the laws of Lebanon prohibit both drunk driving as well as cell phone usage when driving.

Emergency services in Lebanon are adequate. In case of a road accident, emergency numbers are "140" for the Red Cross and "125" for the emergency civil police.

Aviation Safety Oversight: As there is no direct commercial air service to the United States by carriers registered in Lebanon the U.S. Federal Aviation Administration (FAA) has not assessed the Government of Lebanon's Civil Aviation Authority for compliance with International Civil Aviation Organization (ICAO) aviation safety standards. Further information may be found on the FAA's safety assessment page.

Children's Issues: Please see the U.S. Dept. of State Office of Children's Issues web pages on intercountry adoption and international parental child abduction.

Travel Warning

September 17, 2012

The Department of State urges U.S. citizens to avoid all travel to Lebanon because of current safety and security concerns. U.S. citizens living and working in Lebanon should understand that they accept risks in remaining and should carefully consider those risks. This supersedes the Travel Warning issued on May 8, 2012, to emphasize information on security, kidnappings, and an upsurge in violence in Lebanon and the region.

The potential in Lebanon for a spontaneous upsurge in violence remains. Lebanese government authorities are not able to guarantee protection for citizens or visitors to the country should violence erupt suddenly. Access to borders, airports, roads, and seaports can be interrupted with little or no warning. Public demonstrations occur frequently with little warning and have the potential to become violent. Family or neighborhood disputes often escalate quickly and can lead to gunfire or other violence with little or no warning. The ability of U.S. government personnel to reach travelers or provide emergency services may be severely limited.

The Fulbright and the English Language Fellow programs that provided grants to American scholars to live and work in Lebanon during the academic year have been suspended in country because of the deteriorating security situation and the increased possibility of attacks against U.S. citizens in Lebanon.

A number of extremist groups operate in Lebanon, including some, such as Hizballah, that the U.S. government has designated as terrorist organizations. U.S. citizens have been the target of numerous terrorist attacks in Lebanon in the past, and the threat of anti-Western terrorist activity continues to exist in Lebanon. U.S. citizens traveling or residing in Lebanon despite this Travel Warning should keep a low profile, assess their personal security, and vary times and routes for all required travel. U.S. citizens also should pay close attention to their personal security at locations where Westerners generally are known to congregate, and should avoid demonstrations and large gatherings.

Hizballah maintains a strong presence in parts of the southern suburbs of Beirut, portions of the Bekaa Valley, and areas in South Lebanon. The situation remains tense, and sporadic violence involving Hizballah or other extremist or criminal organizations remains a possibility in many areas of the country. The U.S. Embassy advises U.S. citizens that clashes between Lebanese authorities and criminal elements have also recently occurred in other areas of the Bekaa and border regions.

The ongoing unrest in Syria has also resulted in numerous security incidents in the border regions between Lebanon and Syria and coincides with an increasing number of security incidents around the country. On April 9, 2012, a journalist reporting from the Lebanese border was killed by gunfire originating from Syria. Over the past several months, there have also been reports of the shelling of Lebanese border areas and villages originating from Syria, as well as armed groups originating from Syria who have kidnapped or attacked Lebanese citizens living in the border area. On August 31, 2012, a Lebanese Internal Security (ISF) officer was wounded as a result of overnight shelling. The potential for border violence remains and the U.S. Embassy advises U.S. citizens to avoid the Lebanese-Syrian border region.

U.S. citizens in Lebanon should monitor ongoing political and security developments in Syria, as this may impact the security situation in Lebanon. On August 9 the ISF arrested former Lebanese Minister Michel Samaha on charges of having plotted, at the direction of Syrian officials, to destabilize Lebanon by setting explosions and planning to assassinate certain Lebanese officials living in Tripoli or the northern region of Akkar.

Hizballah and other para-military groups have at times detained U.S. citizens or other foreigners for political motivations as well as for interrogation—sometimes for hours or longer. Kidnapping, whether for ransom or political motives, remains a problem in Lebanon. Suspects in kidnappings sometimes have been found to have ties to terrorist or criminal organizations.

On August 16, 2012, the Maqdad clan in Lebanon kidnapped numerous foreigners and claimed its actions were aimed at pressing for the release of one of their family members being held prisoner in Syria, allegedly by a group supporting the Syrian opposition. On March 23, 2011, seven Estonian bicyclists were kidnapped in Deir Zenoun, between Masnaa and Zahle in the Bekaa Valley. The kidnapping was planned and well coordinated, according to Lebanese authorities. The Estonians were ultimately released on July 14, 2011.

Although the U.S. government places the highest priority on the safe recovery of kidnapped U.S. citizens, it is U.S. policy not to pay ransom.

Demonstrators sometimes block the primary road between downtown Beirut and Rafiq Hariri International Airport for short periods of time and without warning. Access to the airport also may be cut off, sometimes for extended periods, if the security situation deteriorates.

The Special Tribunal for Lebanon (STL) is a body the United Nations and Lebanon created to investigate past political assassinations, including the 2005 assassination of former Prime Minister Rafiq Hariri. On June 30, 2011, the STL delivered to Lebanon's Prosecutor General an indictment containing arrest warrants for four Hizballah members who are still at large.

Beginning March 1, 2012 the United Nations renewed the STL's mandate for a second three-year term. U.S. citizens in Lebanon should monitor ongoing political developments, particularly in relation to the STL, as Lebanese political leaders have warned publicly that the Tribunal's findings could spark civil unrest.

Rocket attacks from southern Lebanon into Israel have occurred in the past and remain a potential threat. These attacks frequently provoke a military response from Israel. The rocket attacks and responses occur with no warning. Skirmishes and tense exchanges between the Lebanese Armed Forces and the Israeli Defense Forces, as well as protesters and civilians, along Lebanon's southern border with Israel also may occur with no warning. On May 15, 2011, several demonstrators were killed and several, including a U.S. citizen, were severely wounded near the southern Lebanese border town of Maroun ar-Ras after clashes with Israel resulted in open gunfire. Landmines and unexploded ordnance pose significant dangers throughout southern Lebanon, particularly south of the Litani River, as well as in areas of the country where fighting was intense during the civil war. More than 40 civilians have been killed and over 300 injured by unexploded ordnance remaining from the July-August 2006 Israel-Hizballah war. Travelers should watch for posted landmine warnings and strictly avoid all areas where landmines and unexploded ordnance may be present.

Palestinian groups hostile to both the Lebanese government and the United States operate largely autonomously inside refugee and military camps in different areas of the country. Intra-communal violence within the camps has resulted in violent incidents such as shootings and explosions. U.S. citizens should avoid travel to Palestinian camps. Asbat al-Ansar, a terrorist group with alleged links to Al-Qaida, has targeted Lebanese, U.S., and other foreign government interests. Although the group has been outlawed by the Lebanese government, it continues to maintain a presence in the Ain al-Hilweh refugee camp.

On December 9, 2011, an explosion in the eastern outskirts of Tyre in South Lebanon targeted a UN vehicle injuring five French peacekeepers and two civilians. This was the third attack aimed at UN Peacekeepers in 2011 with previous attacks on May 27, 2011 and July 26, 2011 when roadside bombs targeted UN convoys in which several peacekeepers were injured. These incidents took place on the coastal highway near Saida. Similar incidents could occur again without warning.

U.S. citizens traveling or resident in Lebanon despite this Travel Warning should be aware that the U.S. Embassy's ability to reach all areas of Lebanon is limited. The Embassy cannot guarantee that Embassy employees will be able to render assistance to U.S. citizens in all areas of the country.

In the event that the security climate in Lebanon and the region worsens, U.S. citizens will be responsible for arranging their own travel out of Lebanon. U.S. citizens should be aware that the embassy does not offer "protection" services to individuals who feel unsafe. U.S. citizens with special medical or other needs should be aware of the risks of remaining given their condition, and should be prepared to seek treatment in Lebanon if they cannot arrange for travel out of the country.

U.S. government-facilitated evacuations, such as the evacuation that took place from Lebanon in 2006, occur only when no safe commercial alternatives exist. Evacuation assistance is provided on a cost-recovery basis, which means the traveler must reimburse the U.S. Government for travel costs. The lack of a valid U.S. passport may hinder U.S. citizens' ability to depart the country and may slow the U.S. Embassy's ability to provide assistance. U.S. citizens in Lebanon should therefore ensure that they have proper and current documentation at all times. U.S. Legal Permanent Residents should consult with the Department of Homeland Security before they depart the United States to ensure they have proper documentation to re-enter. Further information on the Department's role during emergencies is provided within the Bureau of Consular Affairs website.

The Department of State considers the threat to U.S. Government personnel in Beirut sufficiently serious to require them to live and work under strict security restrictions. The internal security policies of the U.S. Embassy may be adjusted at any time and without advance notice. These practices limit, and may occasionally prevent, access by U.S. Embassy officials to certain areas of the country. Because of security concerns, unofficial travel to Lebanon by U.S. Government employees and their family members is discouraged and strictly limited and requires the Department of State's prior approval.

U.S. citizens living or traveling in Lebanon should enroll in the Department of State's Smart Traveler Enrollment Program (STEP) at the Bureau of Consular Affairs website to receive the latest travel updates and information and to obtain updated information on travel and security within Lebanon. U.S. citizens without Internet access may enroll directly with the U.S. Embassy in Beirut. By enrolling, U.S. citizens make it easier for the Embassy to contact them in case of emergency. The U.S. Embassy is located in Awkar, near Antelias, Beirut, Lebanon. Public access hours for U.S. citizens are Monday, Tuesday, and Thursday, 8:00 a.m. to 11:00 a.m., U.S. citizens must make appointments in advance. However, U.S. citizens who require emergency services outside these hours may contact the embassy by telephone at any time. The telephone numbers are (961-4) 542-600, 543-600, and fax 544-209.

Information on consular services and enrollment in STEP can also be found at the U.S. Embassy in Beirut's website or by phone at the above telephone numbers between 2:00 p.m. and 4:00 p.m., Monday through Friday local time. Inquiries may also be sent to BeirutACS@state.gov.

Up-to-date information on travel and security can also be obtained by calling 1-888-407-4747 toll-free in the United States and Canada or, for callers outside the United States and Canada, on a regular toll line at 1-202-501-4444. These numbers are available from 8:00 a.m. to 8:00 p.m. Eastern Daylight Time, Monday through Friday (except U.S. federal holidays).

Intercountry Adoption

November 2011

The information in this section has been edited from the latest report available as of February 2013 from the State Department Bureau of Consular Affairs, Office of Overseas Citizens Services. For more information, please read the *Intercountry Adoption* section of this book and review current reports online at http://adoption.state.gov.

Lebanon is not party to the Hague Convention on Protection of Children and Co-operation in Respect of Intercountry Adoption (Hague Adoption Convention). Therefore, when the Hague Adoption Convention entered into force for the United States on April 1, 2008, intercountry adoption processing for Lebanon did not change.

There is no civil procedure for adoption. The Government of Lebanon recognizes 19 religious confessions, each with its own court structure and laws. Because adoption is a religious procedure in Lebanon, it is supervised by authorized religious authorities and must be approved by the relevant religious court.

Islamic law does not allow for full adoptions as generally understood in the United States. However, immigrant visas can be issued in cases where the Islamic court that grants the guardianship of an orphan and where that court understands that the parents intend to obtain a full and final adoption of the child once that child is in the United States and expressly signals that agreement.

In Lebanon, only Christian institutions recognize adoptions as a legal convention and define the conditions, rights, and duties thereof. For the Catholic religious community, the relevant authorities are those of the rite of the minor child; while for the Orthodox religious communities, the forum is the court of the church of the prospective adoptive parent(s). If a child is a foundling, the child assumes the religious affiliation of the orphanage that takes accepts him/her.

Christian orphanages in Lebanon may have children available for adoption. The Lebanese Sûreté Général requires that both U.S. adoptive parents travel to Lebanon to complete the adoption procedures and accompany the child out of Lebanon. The U.S. Embassy in Beirut will be unable to obtain exceptions to this legal requirement. Parents adopting a child from Lebanon must apply for the child's U.S. immigrant visa from the U.S. Embassy in Beirut.

Who Can Adopt? To bring an adopted child to United States from Lebanon, you must be found eligible to adopt by the U.S. Government. The U.S. Government agency responsible for making this determination is the Department of Homeland Security, U.S. Citizenship and Immigration Services (USCIS). In addition to these U.S. requirements for prospective adoptive parents, Lebanon also has the following requirements for prospective adoptive parents:

Residency Requirements: There are no residency requirements for prospective adoptive parents in Lebanon.

Age Requirements: Prospective adoptive parents must be at least 40 years of age. In addition, the age difference between the prospective adoptive parents and the child must be at least 18 years. In Armenian Orthodox adoptions, the minimum age difference is 15 years.

Marriage Requirements: Both married and single individuals may adopt from Lebanon. If married, the consent of both prospective adoptive parents is needed.

Income Requirements: While there are no specific income requirements, prospective adoptive parents must provide their financial status as part of the home study.

Other Requirements: In the case of a Catholic child, at least one of the prospective adoptive parents must be Catholic. The adoptive parent(s) must not have any legal child and could not hope to have children of their own based on medical reports issued by specialists.

The adoptive parents and the child must belong to the same religious community, but not necessarily the same rite for the Catholic Church in general. Prospective adoptive parents must have a clean criminal record and general good behavior.

Who Can Be Adopted? Lebanon has specific requirements that a child must meet in order to be eligible for adoption.

Relinquishment Requirements: If the child is old enough to consent, his/her consent is required. There is no specific age of consent but practice indicates that age 10—12 or older is customary. If the child is too young to give consent, then the minor's guardian, also known as the walee, must consent. Moreover, the religious authority must consent to the adoption. Consent cannot be obtained by coercion or fraud.

Lebanon's Adoption Authority: There is no general civil adoption authority. Since adoption is overseen by religious institutions in Lebanon, they must be supervised by religious authorities and must be approved by these authorities and relevant religious courts. As a result, Lebanese governmental agencies do not get involved in registering the adoption, changing the child's name, and issuing a Lebanese passport until after the religious body has approved the adoption.

The Process: The first step in adopting a child from Lebanon is usually to select a licensed agency in the United States that can help with your adoption. Adoption service providers must be licensed by the U.S. state in which they operate. Learn more about choosing the right adoption service provider in the Working with an Agency section of our website.

There are no adoption agencies in Lebanon. The U.S. Embassy in Beirut maintains a list of lawyers here. Churches and church officials care for abandoned children but may not always have the legal expertise to process an adoption. Attorneys who specialize in family law usually handle adoption cases.

To bring an adopted child from Lebanon to the United States, you must apply to be found eligible to adopt (Form I-600A) by the U.S. Government, Department of Homeland Security, U.S. Citizenship and Immigration Services (USCIS).

In addition to meeting the U.S. requirements for adoptive parents, you need to meet the requirements of Lebanon. The adoption shall be for valid reasons and in the interest of the child. If you are eligible to adopt, and a child is available for intercountry adoption, the central adoption authority in Lebanon will provide you with a referral to a child.

The child must be eligible to be adopted according to Lebanon's requirements. The child must also meet the definition of an orphan under U.S. law.

Role of the Adoption Authority: The religious court will investigate the case, which entails proof of the good moral reputation of the prospective adoptive parent(s) and financial support for the child. If the court does not find any grounds for objection to adoption, the court will issue a decree confirming the adoption. The court's final decision on the adoption must be affirmed by the bishop of the same relevant jurisdiction.

Role of the Court: To be valid, the adoption decree must be granted exequatur, or endorsed, by the Civil Courts Enforcement Bureau. The adoption decree must then be submitted to the Lebanese Bureau of Vital Statistics so that the civil status of the adopted child can be amended in the registry book.

Role of the Adoption Agencies: There are no adoption agencies in Lebanon. Attorneys who specialize in family law usually handle adoption cases.

Adoption Application: The adoption request must be submitted to the presiding judge of the religious court of the community to which the child belongs.

Time Frame: Intercountry adoption process in Lebanon ranges from four months to one year to complete.

Adoption Fees: The following is a list of adoption fees in Lebanon:

Fees vary among confessions, and sometimes among sects within a particular confession, and are subject to change.

Documents Required: The following documents must be attached to the request for adoption filed before the religious court:

- Photocopy of the ID of the prospective parents(s) and the adopted child.
- Certificate of good behavior. This certificate must be issued by the priest (or bishop) of the church where prospective adoptive parents belong.
- A medical report stating the reasons of not having children. This is mandatory for the Orthodox Church and is based on the idea that the prospective adoptive parents are not be able to have their own biological children.
- A home study report done by the reliable authority or agency (depending on the nationality of the parents) about the prospective parent(s)' social situation and financial status. The same study submitted with the I-600A may be used.

Bringing Your Child Home: Once your adoption is complete (or you have obtained legal custody of the child), there are a few more steps to take before you can head home. Specifically, you need to apply for several documents for your child before he or she can travel to the United States, such as a birth certificate, a passport or travel document for your child from the country in which he or she was born, and a U.S. Immigration Visa. For detailed and updated information on how to obtain these documents, review the *Intercountry Adoption* section in this publication and visit the U.S. Department of State Intercountry Adoption website at http://adoption.state.gov.

Child Citizenship Act: For adoptions finalized abroad, the Child Citizenship Act of 2000 allows your new child to acquire American citizenship automatically when he or she enters the United States as lawful permanent residents. For adoptions finalized in the United States, the Child Citizenship Act of 2000 allows your new child to acquire American citizenship automatically when the court in the United States issues the final adoption decree. To learn more, review the *Intercountry Adoption* section in this publication and visit the U.S. Department of State Intercountry Adoption website at http://adoption.state.gov.

After Adoption: There are no post-adoption requirements for Lebanese adoptions.

Embassy of the United States, Beirut
Antelias, P.O. Box 70–840
Beirut, Lebanon
Tel: [961](4) 542600, 543600, 544310, 544130, and 544140
Fax: [961] (4) 543498

Embassy of Lebanon
2560 28th Street, NW
Washington, DC 20008
Tel: (202) 939–6300
Fax: (202) 939–6324
Email: info@lebanonembassyus.org
Internet:
http://www.lebanonembassyus.org

Lebanon also has consulates in Detroit, Houston, Los Angeles, Miami and New York City.

Office of Children's Issues
U.S. Department of State
2201 C Street, NW
SA-29
Washington, DC 20520
Tel: 1–888–407–4747
E-mail: AskCI@state.gov
Website:http://adoption.state.gov

For questions about immigration procedures, call the National Customer Service Center (NCSC) 1-800-375-5283 (TTY 1-800-767-1833).

International Parental Child Abduction

December 2011

The information in this section has been edited from the latest report available as of February 2013 from the State Department Bureau of Consular Affairs, Office of Overseas Citizens Services. For more information, please read the *International*

Parental Child Abduction section of this book and check for updated reports online at www.travel.state.gov/abduction.

Disclaimer: The information in this circular relating to the legal requirements of specific foreign countries is provided for general information only. Questions involving interpretation of specific foreign laws should be addressed to foreign legal counsel.

General Information: Lebanon is not a party to the Hague Abduction Convention.

Legal System: Lebanon implements a system of governance known as confessionalism and its legal system is based on Ottoman law, canon law, and French models. Jurisdiction over family matters rests in religious courts. Sharia Courts handle family matters for Sunni and Shia Muslims, as well as the Druze sect. Ecclesiastical Courts hear family matters for the different Christian denominations and the Jewish community has its own court.

Due to the absence of a civil marriage institution, Lebanese who are interested in a civil law marriage often conduct such marriages abroad. Lebanese courts uphold civil marriages provided they are duly registered at the Lebanese Personal and Family Status Department at the Ministry of Interior. Divorce and custody cases involving spouses who had a civil marriage are handled by civil courts, unless the parties submit to the jurisdiction of a religious authority. In cases where both a civil marriage and a religious marriage are conducted, the first registered marriage receives priority. Moreover, pursuant to the Civil Procedural Law, the civil courts will have exclusive jurisdiction over marriage between a Muslim and a non-Muslim and between a Lebanese national and a non-Lebanese national. However, the civil court will have to apply the law under which such marriages were conducted.

The Lebanese Internal Security Force (ISF) searches for missing children. The ISF will act according to a judicial order and/or through a request to the Ministry of Foreign Affairs. Generally speaking, the father is the legal guardian of a child absent a court order to the contrary. Under the Druze Code, a father has the right of guardianship of his children until they reach the age of majority at eighteen. In the Sunni Hanafi school of law and the Shiite Jaafari school of law, the father is the guardian of his legitimate children. Absent a court order, a mother will be granted guardianship of a child born out of wedlock; however, she cannot transmit Lebanese citizenship to her child.

Retaining an Attorney: The U.S. Embassy in Beirut, Lebanon posts a list of attorneys who specialize in personal status matters at: http://lebanon.usembassy.gov/attorneys.html. Lebanon offers free or reduced-fee legal aid services via the Justice Palace. More information in Arabic can be found at: http://www.bba.org.lb/.

Citizenship & Passport Matters: Under Lebanese law, children born to a Lebanese father, whether the birth occurs inside or outside Lebanon, are considered citizens of Lebanon. However, children born to a Lebanese mother and a non-Lebanese father may or may not be considered Lebanese citizens, depending on a variety of factors. For more specific information concerning the law governing Lebanese citizenship, contact a properly qualified attorney or the Lebanese embassy at http://www.lebanonembassyus.org/.

Lebanon does not recognize dual nationality. American/Lebanese dual nationals who carry Lebanese papers are treated as Lebanese nationals by security authorities. Lebanese civil courts will apply Lebanese law to a child who is a dual American and Lebanese citizen. Up to three children may be carried on a parent's passport. A child may be included on a parent's passport until the child is 16 years old; the child must then apply for his own passport. Under Lebanese law, no child under the age of 18 can obtain a Lebanese passport without the permission of both parents.

A Lebanese child can travel to Syria on his/her Lebanese ID card; however, a travel hold placed on a child or spouse will likely lead to discovery of the child whether traveling on a Passport or an ID.

Exit Permits: Border officials will prevent the departure from Lebanon of any individual whose passport lacks a "valid entry stamp and residency visa." Officials will issue a valid entry stamp and/or a residency visa provided that the immigration authority's records indicate the bearer's "legal" status in Lebanon.

Lebanese parents of children under 18 years of age may legally prevent their children from leaving or being taken from Lebanon through an administrative procedure that does not require court involvement, commonly referred to as a "travel hold." Likewise, a Lebanese spouse may take legal action to prevent his wife/her husband from leaving the country, regardless of nationality.

Absent a travel hold, a minor child in possession of a passport is assumed to have parental permission to travel and thus exit Lebanon.

During a custody dispute or divorce proceedings, either party can request an injunction to prevent the other's departure from the country. Once such legal orders are in place, the U.S. Embassy is unable to lift the travel restriction.

Mediation: The Juvenile Court is in charge of mediating any matters relating to the child. Currently, there are no known government agencies or non-governmental organizations that offer mediation services for custody disputes.

Hague Abduction Convention: Lebanon is not party to the Hague Abduction Convention. However, there is a Memorandum of Understanding on Consular Cooperation in Cases Concerning Parental Access to Children between the United States and Lebanon.

Civil Remedies: Lebanon has three levels of jurisdiction: courts of first instance, courts of appeal, and the court of cassation. Except in some rare cases, lower courts' orders can be appealed and are not enforceable unless they become final and unsusceptible to any recourse, such as appeal.

As a general rule, Lebanese law permits the enforcement of foreign court orders, for which the Appellate Court is responsible. To be enforceable in Lebanon, foreign court orders must not be subject to any ongoing litigation, and may not contravene any imperative rule of law or rule of public order. In practice, if a child is in the physical custody of his or her Lebanese father, it is difficult to enforce foreign custody orders that would return the child to the mother.

In Lebanon, custody disputes, like issues involving marriage and divorce, are resolved in accordance with the laws of each religious community. In general, religious courts usually award custody of boys to the mother until age seven and of girls until age nine, after which custody is transferred to the father, if he so wishes. Courts applying doctrine supported by the Christian Maronite church theoretically would award custody of a child younger than two to the mother.

If a Lebanese citizen marries outside of Lebanon, to a non-Lebanese, in a civil ceremony the civil courts in Lebanon would have jurisdiction in any custody matters.

With respect to older children, custody decisions are made in the best interests of the child. This general rule applies in each religious community provided that the custodial parent is deemed fit to raise his or her children by the court.

Lebanese courts usually address in the custody decree the conditions under which the children concerned may travel outside Lebanon. In the absence of an explicit reference to those conditions in such a decree, the authorities will require the authorization of both parents before issuing a Lebanese passport for the child. Once a child has a passport, children generally may travel with either parent unless a court orders otherwise.

Either parent can request that a custody decision be reviewed and amended by the Lebanese courts at any time based on changed circumstances.

Lebanon has codified custody laws (both civil codes and religious codes). However, there are no official versions available in English.

Criminal Remedies: Parental child abduction is a criminal offense in Lebanon. If the act occurs in Lebanon, the ISF will act according to a judicial order and/or through a request to the Ministry of Foreign Affairs based on the Memorandum of Understanding between the United States and Lebanon.

The United States does not have an extradition treaty with Lebanon, or any other bilateral treaty that that includes extradition for international parental child abduction.

Lebanon is part of the Interpol Agreement. Therefore, the General Attorney of the Supreme Court has the authority to take action for both the child and the parents based on an Interpol notice. Generally speaking, however, Lebanon does not extradite its own citizens subject to an Interpol arrest notice. Lebanese authorities may act to enforce international red notices for non-Lebanese citizens (e.g., they may confiscate a passport).

Visitation/Access: There are no generally applicable rules concerning visitation. Courts hearing custody disputes have broad discretion to issue corresponding orders depending on the facts of each case. Either the religious courts or the civil courts may determine visitation and access rights based upon the marriage of the parents. According the law, decisions about visitation and access are made with regards to the best interest of the child and are generally enforced.

U.S. Embassy Beirut:
http://lebanon.usembassy.gov/

Embassy of Lebanon, Washington D.C.:
http://www.lebanonembassyus.org/

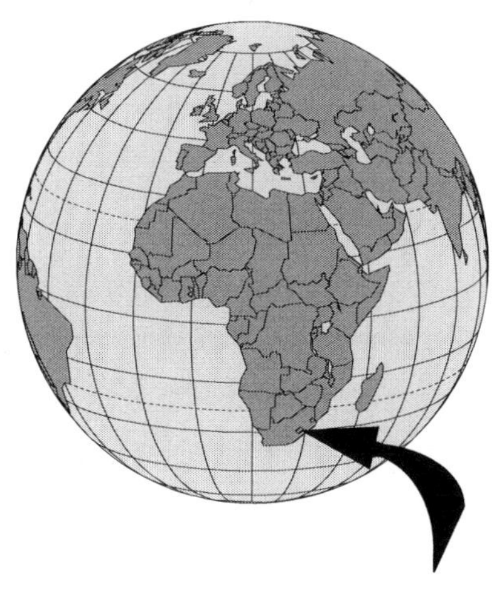

LESOTHO

Compiled from publications that were available as of February 2013 from the U.S. Department of State, the U.S. Department of Commerce, and the Central Intelligence Agency (CIA). See the introduction to this set for explanatory notes.

Official Name:
Kingdom of Lesotho

PROFILE

Geography

Area: total: 30,355 sq km; country comparison to the world: 142; land: 30,355 sq km; water: 0 sq km
Major cities: Maseru (capital) 220,000 (2009)
Climate: temperate; cool to cold, dry winters; hot, wet summers
Terrain: mostly highland with plateaus, hills, and mountains

People

Nationality: noun: Mosotho (singular), Basotho (plural); adjective: Basotho
Population: 1,930,493 (July 2012 est.)
Population growth rate: 0.332% (2012 est.)
Ethnic groups: Sotho 99.7%, Europeans, Asians, and other 0.3%,
Religions: Christian 80%, indigenous beliefs 20%
Languages: Sesotho (official) (southern Sotho), English (official), Zulu, Xhosa
Literacy: definition: age 15 and over can read and write; total population: 89.6%; male: 83.3%; female: 95.6% (2010 est.)
Health: life expectancy at birth: total population: 51.86 years; male: 51.77 years; female: 51.95 years (2012 est.); Infant mortality rate: total: 53.44 deaths/1,000 live births; male: 57.58 deaths/1,000 live births; female: 49.17 deaths/1,000 live births (2012 est.)
Unemployment rate: 45% (2002)
Work force: 854,600 (2007 est.)

Government

Type: parliamentary constitutional monarchy
Independence: 4 October 1966
Constitution: 2 April 1993
Political subdivisions: 10 districts; Berea, Butha-Buthe, Leribe, Mafeteng, Maseru, Mohale's Hoek, Mokhotlong, Qacha's Nek, Quthing, Thaba-Tseka
Suffrage: 18 years of age; universal

Economy

GDP (purchasing power parity): $3.945 billion (2012 est.); $3.853 billion (2011 est.); $3.697 billion (2010 est.); $3.497 billion (2009 est.)
GDP real growth rate: $2.62 billion (2012 est.); 4.2% (2011 est.); 5.7% (2010 est.); 3.6% (2009 est.)
GDP per capita (PPP): $2,000 (2012 est.); $2,000 (2011 est.); $1,900 (2010 est.); $1,800 (2009 est.)
Natural resources: water, agricultural and grazing land, diamonds, sand, clay, building stone
Agriculture products: corn, wheat, pulses, sorghum, barley; livestock
Industries: food, beverages, textiles, apparel assembly, handicrafts, construction, tourism
Exports: $1.039 billion (2012 est.); $1.01 billion (2011 est.); $851.8 million (2010 est.)
Exports—commodities: manufactures 75% (clothing, footwear, road vehicles), wool and mohair, food and live animals
Exports—partners: US 58.4%, Belgium 34%, Canada 3.7% (2008)
Imports: $2.469 billion (2012 est.); $2.29 billion (2011 est.); $1.998 billion (2010 est.)
Imports—commodities: food; building materials, vehicles, machinery, medicines, petroleum products
Imports—partners: South Korea 26.9%, China 23.1%, Taiwan 22.1%, Hong Kong 6.6%, US 4.4% (2008)
Debt—external: $729.9 million (31 December 2011 est.); $703.8 million (31 December 2010 est.)
Exchange rates: maloti (LSL) per US dollar; 8.095 (2012 est.); 7.2611 (2011 est.); 7.32 (2010 est.); 8.47 (2009); 7.75 (2008); 7.25 (2007)

PEOPLE

More than 99% of Lesotho's population is ethnically Basotho; other ethnic groups include Europeans,

Asians, and Xhosa. Sesotho and English are official languages, and other languages spoken include Xhosa.

Religion

Approximately 90 percent of the population is Christian. There are an estimated 4,000 Muslim families, 150 Hindu families, and 800 members of the Baha'i Faith; members of these three groups combined make up approximately 1 percent of the population. The remaining 9 percent of the population are members of indigenous religious groups, though exact figures are difficult to determine. Many Christians practice traditional cultural beliefs and rituals in conjunction with Christianity.

Muslim and Hindu numbers have declined in recent years due to emigration to South Africa. There are a small number of Jews but no practicing Jewish community. Muslims live primarily in the northern area of the country.

HISTORY

Lesotho gained independence from Britain on October 4, 1966. In January 1970 the ruling Basotho National Party (BNP) appeared set to lose the first post-independence general elections when Prime Minister Leabua Jonathan annulled the election. He refused to cede power to the Basotho Congress Party (BCP) and imprisoned its leadership.

The BNP ruled by decree until January 1986 when a military coup forced the BNP government out of office. The Military Council that came into power granted executive powers to King Moshoeshoe II, who was until then a ceremonial monarch. In 1990, however, the King was forced into exile after a falling out with the army. His son was installed as King Letsie III.

The chairman of the military junta, Major General Metsing Lekhanya, was ousted in 1991 and then replaced by Major General Phisoane Ramaema, who handed over power to a democratically elected government of the BCP in 1993. Moshoeshoe II returned from exile in 1992 as an ordinary citizen. After the return to democratic government, King Letsie III tried unsuccessfully to persuade the BCP government to reinstate his father (Moshoeshoe II) as head of state. In August 1994, Letsie III staged a coup which was backed by the military and deposed the BCP government. The new government did not receive full international recognition. Member states of the Southern African Development Community (SADC) engaged in negotiations aimed at the reinstatement of the BCP government. One of the conditions put forward by the King for the return of the BCP government was that his father should be re-installed as head of state. After protracted negotiations, the BCP government was reinstated and the King abdicated in favor of his father in 1995, but Moshoeshoe II died in a car accident in 1996 and was again succeeded by his son, Letsie III. The ruling BCP split over leadership disputes in 1997.

Prime Minister Ntsu Mokhehle formed a new party, the Lesotho Congress for Democracy (LCD), and was followed by a majority of members of parliament (MPs), which enabled him to form a new government. The LCD won the general elections in 1998 under the leadership of Pakalitha Mosisili, who had succeeded Mokhehle as party leader. Despite the elections being pronounced free and fair by local and international observers and a subsequent special commission appointed by SADC, the opposition political parties rejected the results.

Opposition protests in the country intensified, culminating in a violent demonstration outside the royal palace in August 1998. When junior members of the armed services mutinied in September, the government requested a SADC task force to intervene to prevent a coup and restore stability. A military group of South African and Botswana troops entered the country in September, put down the mutiny, and withdrew in May 1999. Looting, casualties, and widespread destruction of property followed. An Interim Political Authority (IPA), charged with reviewing the electoral structure in the country, was created in December 1998. The IPA devised a proportional electoral system to ensure that there would be opposition in the National Assembly. The new system retained the existing 80 elected Assembly seats, but added 40 seats to be filled on a proportional basis.

Elections were held under this new system in May 2002, and the LCD won again. However, for the first time, due to the inclusion of proportional seats, opposition political parties won significant numbers of seats. The February 2007 elections resulted in another LCD victory. While acknowledging the LCD victory, opposition parties continued to assert that some of the proportional seats were allocated incorrectly. Nine parties held all 40 of the proportional seats. The National Independent Party (NIP) formed an "informal alliance" with the LCD, leading to its share of 21, the largest of any minority party.

The 2007 elections remained an active point of contention for years. Opposition parties called for the reallocation of seats, revision of the electoral law, and formal designation of a leader of opposition. The Christian Council of Lesotho (CCL) began mediating the conflict in 2009. Little progress was made until early 2011. In a major breakthrough, the CCL, with the assistance of an expert facilitated by the UN Development Program (UNDP), held a meeting in which all parties agreed on the amendments to be made to the proposed electoral bill. All parties also agreed to use a single-ballot system in future elections, eliminating the possibility of the contentious informal alliances of 2007.

On April 22, 2009, a failed assassination attempt was made on Prime Minister Mosisili at his residence. Two suspects were arrested in Lesotho, and seven suspects were arrested in South Africa. Those seven were handed over to Lesotho authorities on April 19, 2011, following a prolonged extradition process. The suspected mastermind and financier of the attempted coup is in South Africa awaiting his extradition process. The eight suspects (one died of natural causes in custody) are on trial, facing charges of murder, attempted murder, robbery, kidnapping, illegal possession of firearms, contravention of the Internal Security Act of Lesotho, and conspiracy to kill the Prime Minister.

After a year of internal LCD fighting, Prime Minister Mosisili fired the Communications Minister and the Minister to the Prime Minister's Office in late January 2012. In February 2012, the Prime Minister and 44 supporters abandoned the LCD but remain in power with a new party, the Democratic Congress (DC). Of the 80 constituency-based seats, the DC now controls 45, the LCD 21, and the All Basotho Convention (ABC) 11. On February 29, parliament passed a symbolic motion of confidence in the Prime Minister as the opposition parties walked out in protest. Parliament's term ends on March 15, and national elections must follow within 90 days.

GOVERNMENT AND POLITICAL CONDITIONS

Lesotho is a constitutional monarchy. Under the constitution the king is head of state but does not actively participate in political activities. The prime minister is head of government and has executive authority. In the most recent elections in 2007, the governing Lesotho Congress for Democracy (LCD) party retained a majority of seats in parliament; domestic and international observers characterized the election as generally free and peaceful. However, some members of the leading opposition parties and nongovernmental organizations (NGOs) claimed it was not entirely fair.

Recent Elections

During the most recent 2007 national elections, the ruling LCD party maintained a legislative majority, claiming 61 of 80 constituency-based seats in the National Assembly. Domestic and international observers characterized the elections as generally free and peaceful. Other observers, including members of the leading opposition parties and some NGOs, stated they were not entirely fair. Their complaints included the method of allocating proportional parliamentary seats, the legality of appointing a leader of opposition when no opposition party controlled the stipulated 25 percent minimum of seats, and the need to review the electoral laws regarding the formation of alliances between parties. After three years of mediation by several different parties, on March 9, 2011, the government and opposition parties resolved their differences on the electoral laws and ended public arguments about the remaining issues.

Political Parties: There were no undue restrictions on political parties. The Independent Electoral Commission (IEC) had registration material on 23 political parties, but not all parties have representation in parliament, and some are completely dormant.

Participation of Women and Minorities: There are no laws preventing women or minorities from voting or otherwise participating in political life on the same basis as men or nonminority citizens. The Local

Government (Amendment) Act, 2010 provides for the allocation of one-third of the seats in the municipal, urban, and community councils to women. The National Assembly Electoral Act, 2011 also states that a political party registered with the IEC must facilitate the full participation of women, youth, and persons with disabilities. Party lists for proportional representational seats must include equal numbers of women and men.

There were 29 women in the 120-seat National Assembly and seven women in the 33-seat Senate. The speaker of the National Assembly, seven of 19 government ministers, two of three assistant ministers, and five of 10 High Court judges were women.

Approximately 98.5 percent of the population is ethnic Basotho. There were no members of minorities in the national assembly, senate, or cabinet.

Principal Government Officials

Last Updated: 1/31/2013

King: **LETSIE III**

Prime Min.: **Thomas Motsoahae THABANE**

Dep. Prime Min.: **Mothejoa METSING**

Min. of Agriculture & Food Security: **Lits'oane Simon LITS'OANE**

Min. of Communications, Science, & Technology: **Ts'eliso MOKHOSI**

Min. of Defense, Police, & National Security: **Thomas Motsoahae THABANE**

Min. of Development Planning: **Maboee MOLETSANE**

Min. of Education & Training: **'Makabelo Priscilla MOSOTHOANE**

Min. of Employment & Labor: **Lebesa MALOI**

Min. of Energy, Meteorology, & Water Affairs: **Thahane Timothy THAHANE**

Min. of Finance: **Leketekete Victor KETSO**

Min. of Foreign Affairs & Intl. Relations: **Mohlabi Kenneth TSEKOA**

Min. of Forestry & Land Reclamation: **Khotso MATLA**

Min. of Gender, Youth, Sports, & Recreation: **Thesele 'MASERIBANE**

Min. of Health: **Pinkie Rosemary MANAMOLELA, Dr.**

Min. of Home Affairs: **Joang MOLAPO**

Min. of Justice, Human Rights, Correctional Services, Law, & Constitutional Affairs: **Haae Edward PHOOFOLO**

Min. of Local Govt. & Chieftainship Affairs: **Mothejoa METSING**

Min. of Mining: **Tlali KHASU**

Min. of Public Service: **Motloheloa PHOOKO**

Min. of Public Works & Transport: **Keketso RANT'SO**

Min. of Social Development: **'Matebatso DOTI**

Min. of Tourism, Environment, & Culture: **'Mamahele RADEBE**

Min. of Trade & Industry, Cooperatives, & Marketing: **Temeki Phoenix TS'OLO**

Min. in the Prime Minister's Office: **Mophato Moshoete MONYAKE**

Min. in the Prime Minister's Office: **Molobeli SOULU**

Governor, Central Bank of Lesotho: **Rets'elisitsoe Adelaide MATLANYANE**

Ambassador to the US: **Eliachim Molapi SEBATANE**

Permanent Representative to the UN, New York: **Motlatsi RAMAFOLE**

ECONOMY

Small, landlocked, and mountainous, Lesotho relies on remittances from Basotho employed in South Africa, customs duties from the Southern Africa Customs Union (SACU), and export revenue for the majority of government revenue. However, the government has recently strengthened its tax system to reduce dependency on customs duties. Completion of a major hydropower facility in January 1998 permitted the sale of water to South Africa and generated royalties for Lesotho.

Lesotho produces about 90% of its own electrical power needs. As the number of mineworkers has declined steadily over the past several years, a small manufacturing base has developed based on farm products that support the milling, canning, leather, and jute industries, as well as an apparel-assembly sector. Despite Lesotho's market-based economy being heavily tied to its neighbor South Africa, the US is an important trade partner because of the export sector's heavy dependence on apparel exports. Exports have grown significantly because of the trade benefits contained in the Africa Growth and Opportunity Act.

Most of the labor force is engaged in subsistence agriculture, especially livestock herding, although drought has decreased agricultural activity. The extreme inequality in the distribution of income remains a major drawback. Lesotho has signed an Interim Poverty Reduction and Growth Facility with the IMF. In July 2007, Lesotho signed a Millennium Challenge Account Compact with the US worth $362.5 million. Economic growth dropped in 2009, due mainly to the effects of the global economic crisis as demand for the country's exports declined and SACU revenue fell precipitously when South Africa— the primary contributor to the SACU revenue pool—went into recession, but growth exceeded 4% per year in 2010–12. Growth is expected to increase due to major infrastructure projects, but Lesotho's weak manufacturing and agriculture sectors continue to hamper growth.

Labor Conditions

The CPWA and labor code define the legal minimum age for employment as 15 years, or 18 for hazardous employment. Hazardous work includes mining and quarrying; carrying of heavy loads; manufacturing where chemicals are produced or used; working in places where machines are used or in places such as bars, hotels, and places of entertainment where a person may be exposed to immoral behavior; herding; and producing or distributing tobacco. Any employer who breaches these provisions is liable to a fine or imprisonment or both. However, these laws were not effectively enforced outside the formal economy.

Child labor remained widespread. The high unemployment rate, high levels of poverty, and high prevalence of HIV/AIDS pressured children to work in order to support themselves and their families. The Bureau of Statistics stated that 3 percent of children ages 6-14 years participated in economic activities; this statistic did not include children aiding their families or others without compensation. UNICEF estimated 23 percent of children between 5 and 14 were working. Two-thirds of these children were engaged in subsistence farming, while the rest were engaged mainly in domestic service. Child labor was higher among male children (86.6 percent of child workers) than their female counterparts (13.4 percent).

Herd boys were sometimes attacked by armed stock thieves, caught in fights over ownership of animals, and subject to harsh weather conditions. In traditional rural society, these rigorous and occasionally dangerous working conditions were considered a prerequisite to manhood, essential to the livelihood of families, and beyond the reach of labor laws.

Children also were subject to commercial sexual exploitation. Children who had lost at least one parent to HIV/AIDS were more vulnerable to such exploitation.

There is a sector-specific national minimum wage and a general minimum wage. The general minimum monthly wage varied from 878 maloti to 958 maloti ($109 to $119). Minimum wage provisions did not cover significant portions of the workforce. Workers in agriculture or other informal sectors are not covered by labor laws.

The law stipulates standards for hours of work, including a maximum 45-hour workweek, a weekly rest period of at least 24 hours, a daily minimum rest period of one hour, at least 12 days of paid leave per year, paid sick leave, and public holidays. Required overtime is legal as long as overtime wages are paid for work in excess of the standard 45-hour workweek. The maximum overtime allowed is 11 hours per week; however, there are exemptions under special circumstances. The laws require that the premium pay for overtime be at a rate not less than one-and-one-quarter times the employee's normal wage; any employer who requires excessive compulsory overtime shall liable to a fine, imprisonment, or both.

The law empowers the Ministry of Labor and Employment to issue regulations on work safety. The Ministry of Labor and Employment is responsible for enforcing these laws and standards; however, budget resources limited the enforcement of the law. In practice businesses operating in the formal sector, including the apparel industry, were subject to more enforcement than businesses operating in the informal sector. The ministry's inspectorate reported that many locally owned businesses did not keep records of employees' salaries to facilitate labor inspections as required by law. Labor laws do not cover the agricultural and other informal sectors, where most workers are employed. The Labor Inspectorate stated that employers did not always observe these standards.

With the exception of the mining industry, employers' compliance with health and safety regulations generally was low. Trade union representatives described textile sector working conditions as poor or even harsh but not dangerous. Unions said that most textile factories were in prefabricated metal buildings with improper ventilation and air conditioning. Unions stated, however, that conditions were not detrimental to workers' health and cited few examples of serious safety violations.

Many workplace policies cover employees with HIV/AIDS. For example, the Apparel Lesotho Alliance to Fight AIDS (ALAFA) described HIV/AIDS as the primary occupational health risk in the apparel sector. ALAFA reported that 85 percent of workers were women and 43 percent of all workers were infected with HIV. Employers provided space for examinations and time off to see doctors, receive counseling, and participate in educational and antistigma programs.

Working conditions for foreign or migrant workers were similar to those of residents.

U.S.-LESOTHO RELATIONS

The United States established diplomatic relations with Lesotho in 1966, following its independence from the United Kingdom. Post-independence, the country saw a mix of rule by decree, coups, outside military intervention, and democratic government. Lesotho is a constitutional monarchy that faces challenges including poverty, income distribution inequality, and one of the highest HIV/AIDS prevalence rates in the world. Since independence, Lesotho and the United States have had productive bilateral relations. U.S. foreign policy priorities in Lesotho focus on achieving the development of a stable, prosperous, and healthy country that continues to improve its record as a voice for positive change in international fora, both regionally and globally.

U.S. Assistance to Lesotho

U.S. assistance to Lesotho focuses on reversing the devastating HIV/AIDS pandemic and promoting economic development. The Global Health Initiative, through the President's Emergency Plan for AIDS Relief program in Lesotho, complements a significant HIV/AIDS effort by the Millennium Challenge Corporation (MCC), the Government of Lesotho, and other donors, including U.S. nongovernmental organizations and universities. The Government of Lesotho has demonstrated substantial political will to fight HIV/AIDS and has undertaken many efforts to address the pandemic.

In addition to healthcare infrastructure, the $362.5 million MCC Compact includes developing Lesotho's water system infrastructure and private sector regulations. U.S. assistance also promotes disaster risk reduction through sustainable agricultural practices and promotes officer professionalism in the Lesotho Defense Force and its capacities for its roles in border security and humanitarian response.

Bilateral Economic Relations

The Government of Lesotho encourages greater U.S. participation in commercial life and welcomes interest from potential U.S. investors and suppliers. Lesotho is eligible for preferential trade benefits under the African Growth and Opportunity Act (AGOA). The top U.S. export category to Lesotho is cotton and yarn.

The primary U.S. imports from Lesotho are knit apparel and woven apparel. The country belongs to the Southern African Customs Union, which has signed a Trade, Investment, and Development Cooperative Agreement (TIDCA) with the United States. The TIDCA establishes a forum for consultative discussions, cooperative work, and possible agreements on a wide range of trade issues, with a special focus on customs and trade facilitation, technical barriers to trade, sanitary and phytosanitary measures, and trade and investment promotion.

Lesotho's Membership in International Organizations

Lesotho and the United States belong to a number of the same international organizations, including the United Nations, International Monetary Fund, World Bank, and World Trade Organization. Lesotho is a member of the Southern African Development Community (SADC), Southern African Customs Union (SACU), and the African Union (AU).

Bilateral Representation

Lesotho maintains an embassy in the United States at 2511 Massachusetts Avenue NW, Washington, DC 20008(tel: 202-797-5533).

Principal U.S. Embassy Officials

Last Updated: 1/14/2013

MASERU (E) 254 Kingsway Avenue, (266) 22-312-666, Fax (266) 22-310-116, INMARSAT Tel 881631537407 and 881631537408, Workweek: M-TH 0730-1700, F 0730-1330, Website: http://maseru.usembassy.gov/

AMB OMS:	Betty Boigenzahn
CDC:	Jim Creighton
HHS:	Dr. James Creighton
HRO:	Joy L Davies
MGT:	David McCrane
POL/ECON:	Alexander Sharp
POSHO:	Spencer Maguire
SDO/DATT:	Colonel Kelly Langdorf (Pretoria)
TREAS:	Sheryl Kelly
AMB:	Michele T. Bond
CON:	Scott Schlossberg
DCM:	Carl Fox
PAO:	Nina Lewis
GSO:	Spencer Maguire
RSO:	Gregory C Batman
AGR:	Scott Sindelar
AID:	Macarena Garcia
DEA:	Larry W. Frye (Pretoria)
FAA:	Edward Jones (Dakar)
FMO:	David McCrane
ICASS Chair:	James McCormick
IMO:	Barry W. Rice
IRS:	Kathy Beck (Paris)
LAB:	Frederick J. Kaplan (Pretoria)
LEGATT:	Donald C Przybyla (Pretoria)
State ICASS:	D. Justin Smith

TRAVEL

Consular Information Sheet

December 28, 2011

Country Description: Lesotho is a constitutional monarchy with a democratically elected lower house of parliament. The upper house, the Senate, is comprised of appointed hereditary chiefs and politicians. A Prime Minister is the head of the government. Geographically, Lesotho is an extremely mountainous developing nation located entirely within the country of South Africa. The capital, Maseru, is at 5,000 feet (1,500M) above sea level, and the mountains reach to 11,400 feet (3,500M). Facilities for tourism are limited, but are continually being developed. A limited number of restaurants are available in Maseru.

Smart Traveler Enrollment Program (STEP)/Embassy Locations: If you are going to live in or visit Lesotho, please take the time to tell our embassy about your trip. If you enroll, we can keep you up to date with important safety and security announcements. It will also help your friends and family get in touch with you in an emergency.

U.S. Embassy Maseru
254 Kingsway Avenue
Maseru 100, Lesotho
Telephone: (266) 2231–2666
Emergency after-hours telephone: (266) 5888–4035
Facsimile: (266) 2231–0116

Entry/Exit Requirements for U.S. Citizens: A passport is required, but no visa for U.S. citizens is needed for visits of 180 days or less. Vaccination for yellow fever is a common requirement and travelers should carry their international vaccination cards with them. For more information concerning entry requirements, travelers may contact the Embassy of the Kingdom of Lesotho, 2511 Massachusetts Avenue NW, Washington, DC 20008; telephone: (202) 797-5533.

Some HIV/AIDS entry restrictions exist for visitors to and foreign residents of Lesotho. Lesotho border guards have the discretion to deny entry to visitors with HIV/AIDS. Please verify this information with the Embassy of Lesotho before you travel.

While U.S. citizens normally do not need a visa for South Africa if they plan to stay less than 90 days, South African visa requirements may change for individuals who have resided in Lesotho for an extended period of time. Check with the High Commission of South Africa in Maseru if you are planning to travel in South Africa.

Threats to Safety and Security: U.S. citizens should avoid political gatherings and street demonstrations and maintain security awareness at all times. There is high potential that large gatherings could transform from non-violent to violent at anytime.

Stay up-to-date by:

- Bookmarking our Bureau of Consular Affairs website, which contains current the Travel Warnings and Travel Alerts as well as the Worldwide Caution.
- Following us on Twitter and the Bureau of Consular Affairs page on Facebook as well.
- Downloading our free Smart Traveler iPhone App to have travel information at your fingertips.
- Calling 1-888-407-4747 toll-free within the U.S. and Canada, or a regular toll line, 1-202-501-4444, from other countries.
- Taking some time before travel to consider your personal security.

Crime: Lesotho has a high rate of crime. U.S. citizens should remain vigilant about their surroundings at all times. Foreigners are frequently targeted, robbed, car-jacked and sometimes killed. While an increased number of U.S. citizens have reported incidents, including sexual assault, armed and unarmed confrontations, car-jacking, and home invasions, all occurring in broad daylight, there are no indications that U.S. citizens are targeted because of their nationality. Lesotho's high unemployment rate and the ongoing effects of social upheaval due to high HIV/AIDS rates of infection, continue to contribute to an increasing number of reported crimes.

These types of crimes occur primarily in the capital city of Maseru, but can occur elsewhere in Lesotho. Crime scenes have included popular restaurants, pedestrian overpasses, poorly lit or unlit roads, and other locations foreigners are known to frequent. Victims have included foreign diplomats, volunteer workers, employees of non-governmental organizations, and nationals of Lesotho. U.S. citizens are advised to avoid large groups and demonstrations, walking and driving at early morning hours and nighttime if possible, and casual walking in the downtown area of the capital city of Maseru even during daylight. Personal crime is more likely to occur at night and during the earlier morning hours, but, as noted above, there have been numerous recent incidents in the middle of the day. Residences with 24-hour guards are generally less likely to be targeted. Traveling alone or at night is particularly dangerous, due to limited street lighting and undeveloped road conditions.

The Lesotho Mounted Police Service (LMPS) is responsible for policing duties. Due to limited resources, the LMPS response time can vary widely. U.S. citizens should report crime to the police and to the embassy's consular section.

There is a serious baggage pilferage problem at Johannesburg International Airport, also known as Oliver Tambo International Airport, in South Africa. Persons traveling by air to Lesotho must travel via Johannesburg. The pilferage problem particularly affects travelers changing airlines and those flying on smaller airlines. Passengers flying on major international carriers may not be affected to the same degree. Travelers are encouraged to secure their luggage, use an airport plastic wrapping service, and avoid placing currency, electronics, jewelry, cameras or other valuables in checked luggage. Make an inventory of items in checked baggage to aid in claims processing if theft does occur. The claims processing procedure can be time-consuming.

Don't buy counterfeit and pirated goods, even if they are widely available. Not only ar the bootlegs illegal in the United States, if you purchase them you may also be breaking local law.

Victims of Crime: If you or someone you know becomes the victim of a crime abroad, you should contact the local police and the nearest U.S. embassy or consulate (see the Department of State's list of embassies and consulates). We can:

- Replace a stolen passport.
- Help you find appropriate medical care if you are the victim of violent crimes such as assault or rape.
- Put you in contact with the appropriate police authorities, and if you want us to, we can contact family members or friend.
- Help you understand the local criminal justice process and direct you to local attorneys, although it is important to remember that local authorities are responsible for investigating and prosecuting the crime.

Lesotho does not have a local equivalent to 911. In the event of an emergency call (266) 5888–1010 to speak to the police 24/7.

Criminal Penalties: While in Lesotho, U.S. citizens are subject to Lesotho's laws and regulations, which sometimes can differ significantly from those in the United States and may not afford the protections available to U.S. citizens under U.S. law. It is important to know what's legal and what's not in Lesotho. Penalties for breaking the law can be more severe than in the United States for similar offenses. Persons violating Lesotho laws, even unknowingly, may be expelled, arrested or imprisoned. Penalties for possession, use, or trafficking in illegal drugs in Lesotho are severe, and convicted offenders can expect long jail sentences and heavy fines. Engaging in sexual conduct with children or using or disseminating child pornography in a foreign country is a crime prosecutable in the United States.

Based on the Vienna Convention on Consular Relations, bilateral agreements with certain countries, and customary international law, if you are arrested in Lesotho, you have the option to request that the police, prison officials, or other authorities alert the nearest U.S. embassy or consulate of your arrest, and to have communications from you forwarded to the nearest U.S. embassy or consulate.

Special Circumstances: Tap water is not reliably potable. Visitors to the interior of Lesotho should bring clothing and equipment suitable for cold weather during the winter months (June - October). In the mountains, weather conditions can deteriorate rapidly. In winter, snow often closes mountain passes and temperatures often drop below freezing during the night, even in the lowlands. Lesotho has one of the highest rates of lightning strikes per square mile in the world, and lightning-related deaths are not uncommon. During a storm, find shelter in a building or car.

Accessibility: While in Lesotho, individuals with disabilities may find accessibility and accommodation very different from what you find in the United States. The only legislation that covers accessibility in Lesotho is the Buildings Control Act of 1995. The law requires all buildings be made accessible; it does not, however, mandate any penalties for non-compliance; enforcement is therefore limited. There is no mandated access to transportation, footpaths, road crossings, or parking. There are no free or reduced fares for transport, and very few accessible places of lodging, medical facilities, restaurants, cafes, and bars.

Medical Facilities and Health Information: Medical facilities in Lesotho are limited. Good medical service is available in Bloemfontein, South Africa, 90 miles west of Maseru. There is no reliable ambulance service in Lesotho. U.S. Embassy Maseru maintains a list of physicians and other health care professionals who may see U.S. citizen patients. The Embassy does not guarantee their services or provide recommendations.

Many medicines are unavailable at facilities in Lesotho; travelers should carry with them an adequate supply of needed medicines and/or prescription drugs, along with copies of prescriptions. Lesotho has a very high HIV/AIDS prevalence rate, currently estimated at 23% percent of the general population.

You can find detailed information on vaccinations and other health precautions on the CDC website. For information about outbreaks of infectious diseases abroad, consult the World Health Organization (WHO) website. The WHO website also contains additional health information for travelers, including detailed country-specific health information.

Tuberculosis is an increasingly serious health concern in Lesotho. For further information, please consult-the CDC's information on TB.

Medical Insurance: You can't assume your insurance will go with you when you travel overseas. It is very important to find out BEFORE you leave whether or not your medical insurance will cover you overseas. You need to ask your insurance provider two questions:

- Does my policy apply when I'm out of the United States?
- Will it cover emergencies like a trip to a foreign hospital or a medical evacuation?

In many places, doctors and hospitals still expect payment in cash at the time of service. Your regular U.S. health insurance may not cover doctors' and hospital visits in other countries. If your policy does not go with you when you travel overseas, it's a very good idea to take out a temporary policy for your trip.

Traffic Safety and Road Conditions: While in a foreign country, U.S. citizens may encounter road conditions that differ significantly from those in the United States. The information below concerning Lesotho is provided for general reference only, and may not be totally accurate in a particular location or circumstance.

Traffic moves on the left, with right-hand drive vehicles. Never assume right-of-way, as aggressive and undisciplined local driving habits result in frequent collisions. Lesotho has a high number of traffic-related deaths and injuries given its small size. Driving after dark is dangerous due to the absence of street lighting, livestock on the roads, and the prevalence of crime, including incidents of carjacking. Travel is best done by private car. Rental cars are available, and cars rented in neighboring South Africa may be brought into Lesotho with written permission from the rental company. Although bus and public taxi services exist, chronic overloading combined with inadequate vehicle maintenance and lack of driver training make them unsafe. Some private taxi service exists in the capital, but roving mini-bus taxis should be avoided. There is no passenger train service in the country.

Although the number of paved roads is gradually increasing, the majority of Lesotho's 5,000 miles of roads are unpaved. A few main rural highways are comparable to U.S. two-lane rural roads, but lane markings, signs, shoulders and guardrails do not meet U.S. standards, and unfenced livestock pose a particular danger. Lesotho's mountainous terrain makes driving on secondary roads hazardous. Unpaved roads in the interior, often narrow, twisty and steep, are poorly maintained. For travel in the interior, especially in wet or snowy weather, a high ground clearance or four-wheel-drive vehicle is recommended.

Four-wheel-drive is required for entering Lesotho through the Sani Pass on the eastern border. The authority for road safety issues rests with the Lesotho Mounted Police Service. There are no auto clubs or reliable ambulance services. Drivers should contact the police in emergencies.

Aviation Safety Oversight: As there is no direct commercial air service to the United States by carriers registered in Lesotho, the U.S. Federal Aviation Administration (FAA) has not assessed the government of Lesotho's Civil Aviation Authority for compliance with International Civil Aviation Organization (ICAO) aviation safety standards. Further information may be found on the FAA's safety assessment page.

Children's Issues: Please see the U.S. Dept. of State Office of Children's Issues web pages on intercountry adoption and international parental child abduction.

Intercountry Adoption

December 5, 2012
The Hague Adoption Convention Enters into Force for Lesotho

On December 1, 2012 the Hague Convention on Protection of Children and Co-Operation in Respect of Intercountry Adoption (Convention) entered into force for Lesotho. However, the Government of Lesotho notified the U.S. Embassy in Maseru that the Government of Lesotho is suspending receipt of new adoption applications from all receiving states until March 1, 2013, to give the country time to put a fully functional Convention process in place.

Adoptions initiated prior to December 1, 2012 may be considered transition cases, and therefore will be able to complete the pre-Convention adoption process. Transition cases are defined as those in which:

- Prior to December 1, 2012, a prospective adoptive parent filed a Form I-600A with U.S. Citizenship and Immigration Services identifying Lesotho as the country of origin, filed a Form I-600, or completed the adoption; and
- The child was "officially matched" with prospective adoptive parents prior to December 1, 2012. The Ministry of Social Development defines an official match as one in which the match was made during a matching meeting chaired by a Ministry official, and involving representatives of Lesotho childcare facilities and adoption service providers.

We caution adoption service providers and prospective adoptive parents that intercountry adoptions between the United States and Lesotho will not resume until steps are taken to ensure that intercountry adoptions from Lesotho comply with the Convention. Adoption service providers should neither initiate nor claim to initiate adoption programs in Lesotho until the Department of State notifies them that the Government of Lesotho has lifted its temporary suspension of intercountry adoptions and that Lesotho's procedures meet the requirements of the Convention.

The Department of State will provide updated information on adoption.state.gov as it becomes available. If you have any questions about this notice, please contact the Office of Children's Issues at 1-888-407-4747 within the United States, or 202-501-4444 from outside the United States. Email inquiries may be directed to AdoptionUSCA@state.gov.

The following information reflects the adoption requirements that applied before the Haqgue Convention went into effect and is retained here for reference only. It is likely that some of these requirements will change as the new Hague Convention process is established. For more information, please read the *Intercountry Adoption* section of this book and review current reports online at http://adoption.state.gov.

Who Can Adopt? To bring an adopted child to United States from Lesotho, you must be found eligible to adopt by the U.S. Government. The U.S. Government agency responsible for making this determination is the Department of Homeland Security, U.S. Citizenship and Immigration Services (USCIS). In addition to these U.S. requirements, you must be found eligible to adopt by the Government of Lesotho. Lesotho requires that prospective adoptive parents meet the following criteria:

Residency Requirements: The Child Welfare and Protection Act of 2011 explicitly allows for adoptions by non-residents and reduces the residency requirement for prospective adoptive parents planning to immediately return to the United States from two years to two weeks. Prospective adoptive parents who are residents of Lesotho and who do not intend to return to the United States immediately after their adoption must spend a minimum of two years in Lesotho. These residency requirements must be met before an adoption can be finalized. There is no waiver available for these requirements.

Age Requirements: The adoptive parent(s) must be at least 25-years-old and one of the prospective adoptive parents must be at least 21 years older than the child she wishes to adopt.

Marriage Requirements: There are no marriage requirements for the prospective adoptive parents. Cohabiting couples cannot adopt together; however, one of the partners may adopt as a single parent. Single men are not permitted to adopt Lesotho children, nor are same-sex couples.

Other Requirements: Prospective adoptive parent(s) are required to undergo a thorough home study by an approved social service or adoption agency and be found qualified. To locate an approved social service or adoption agency, persons interested in adopting in Lesotho should contact the Lesotho Department of Social Welfare in the Ministry of Health and Social Welfare.

Gay/lesbian prospective adoptive parents are not permitted to adopt Lesotho children.

Who Can Be Adopted? The following is a list of Lesotho's eligibility requirements, which any child must meet before he or she is qualified for adoption. In addition to these requirements, a child must meet the definition of orphan under U.S. law before he or she may be brought to the United States.

Relinquishment Requirements: To relinquish rights to a child, a parent or guardian must sign a letter stating intention to that effect. The letter must be signed in the presence of witnesses, who will preferably include members of the extended family. It will then be taken to the village chief for his concurrence and stamped by his office. The chief may choose to write a letter of endorsement at this point, but this is not required.

Abandonment Requirements: Abandoned children are placed in care facilities by police and the Department of Social Welfare. A first police report is filed upon discovery of an abandoned child, at which point an investigation is initiated. Police are required to investigate the origins of an abandoned child for a minimum of three months, at which point the child is made legally adoptable if no parent is found.

Age requirements: Prospective adoptive parents must be at least 25 years of age, and at least one of the prospective parents must be at least 21 years older than the child.

Sibling Requirements: The consent of any prospective adoptive parents' children is required if those children are over nine years of age. Matching meetings will strive to place sibling orphans into one home; however, this is a preference and not a policy.

Requirements for Children with Special Needs or Medical Issues: Children with special needs are placed with parents who specifically request them.

Waiting period: While there is no official waiting period to adopt a child from Lesotho, the entire process—from the adoption agency's initial application to the Department of Social Welfare on behalf of the prospective adoptive parents, to the parents' ultimate removal of the child to the United States—can take approximately 12 to 24 months.

Custody Law and the Rights of Birth Parents: Laws pertaining to child custody are not applied uniformly in Lesotho and may be complicated by cultural traditions. A child born out of wedlock may be recognized by the husband of his or her mother, if the husband decides to pay an agreed bride price. Such a child would otherwise be the ward of the maternal grandparent(s). According to custom, the extended family has certain custodial rights to children. Unmarried women of any age are considered legal minors and their children remain in the legal custody of the mother's parent(s). The Department of Social Welfare will ensure, prior to approving an adoption, that the concerned children are free from custody issues and all concerned family members have waived any rights to the child.

Unmarried fathers do not have legal access to or custody or guardianship of a biological child unless they have reached an understanding with the maternal grandparent(s). Customarily, the father will be involved at the invitation of the maternal grandparent(s). The Department of Social Welfare would, prior to accepting a child for adoption proceedings, ensure that any known father has waived his rights to the child.

Lesotho Adoption Authority: Department of Social Welfare, Ministry of Health and Social Welfare

The Process: The first step in adopting a child from Lesotho is to decide whether or not to use a licensed agency in the United States that can help with your adoption. Adoption service providers must be licensed by the U.S. state in which they operate.

Since early 2009, only one U.S. adoption agency—Americans for African Adoptions (AFAA)—has been authorized by the Ministry of Health and Social Welfare to coordinate intercountry adoptions in Lesotho.

To bring an adopted child from Lesotho to the United States, you must apply to be found eligible to adopt (Form I-600A) by the U.S. Government, Department of Homeland Security, U.S. Citizenship and Immigration Services (USCIS). In addition to meeting the U.S. requirements for adoptive parents, you need to meet the requirements of Lesotho. If you are found eligible to adopt by the Government of Lesotho, and if a child is available for intercountry adoption, the Ministry of Health and Social Welfare will provide you with a referral to a child. Each family must decide for itself whether or not it will be able to meet the needs of a referred child and provide a permanent family placement for that child.

Role of the Adoption Authority: Intercountry adoptions are overseen by the Department of Social Welfare in the Ministry of Health and Social Welfare. The Department of Social Welfare will consider your request to adopt and will verify the identity and status of orphaned children. A representative social worker of the Department will attend quarterly matching meetings at which prospective adoptive parents are matched with eligible orphans (parents need not appear in person at these meetings). The Minister for Health and Social Welfare then approves the match.

Role Of The Courts: Once an adoption has been approved by the Department of Social Welfare, a local representative of the relevant adoption agency contracts with a lawyer to petition the High Court for an adoption decree.

Adoption Procedure: Generally, an adoption is initiated when prospective adoptive parent(s), working with their ASP, submit a written request to adopt to the Department of Social Welfare. The Department will review the application, interview the prospective adoptive parent(s), and then complete an assessment before beginning the process. After prospective adoptive parents complete a successful home study, the Ministry of Health and Social Welfare will identify a child for referral from one of the country's orphanages or abandoned children centers.

In lieu of a Lesotho home study, the Ministry of Health and Social Welfare will accept a home study conducted in the United States and submitted as part of an approved I-600A application, which it will then forward to the High Court.

Lesotho provides children from orphanages and abandoned children centers with birth certificates confirming their orphan status. In some cases, a child may have a letter from extended family, certified by the local authorities (usually the village chief), stating that the child is eligible for adoption.

However, in order for a child to be eligible for a visa to travel to the United States, he or she must qualify for orphan status under U.S. immigration law, as evidenced by an approved Form I-600 from USCIS. Note that any documentation provided by the Government of Lesotho that confirms a child's orphan status does not automatically guarantee that the child will meet the requirements of U.S. law.

After referral to a child, the adoption agency's local representative procures the services of a lawyer, who will refer the case to the High Court for an adoption hearing. Authorization for removal of the child (which allows the child to leave Lesotho with the adoptive parents) will be noted in this same adoption decree.

An order of adoption terminates all rights and obligations existing between the child and any legally recognized parent or extended family. The adopted child is thereafter deemed by law to be the legitimate child of the adoptive parent(s). Prospective adoptive parents can then apply (through the local representative of their international adoption agency) for a revised Lesotho birth certificate and a Lesotho passport based on the official order of adoption. The revised birth certificate is available from the District Administrator and requires proof of ID, the parents' marriage certificate, a certified copy of the order of adoption, and a revenue stamp for 25c (approximately $0.05). (Stamps are available from the Lesotho Revenue Authority). The passport with revised names is available from the Ministry of Home Affairs. In order to apply, please provide a certified copy of the order of adoption, passport photos, and a fee of M/R100 (approximately $15).

Time Frame: The time frame for adoption procedures varies widely and depends in large measure on 1) residency requirements and 2) how quickly the prospective adoptive parent(s) and their agents are able to collect the necessary paperwork. Once the prospective adoptive parents arrive in Lesotho, they can expect to stay for at least four weeks. Lesotho requires a three week bonding period with the adoptive child in-country, and at least one week is required to complete a medical appointment and immigrant visa procedures in Johannesburg, South Africa. In addition, the U.S. Embassy is Maseru is required to complete a Form I-604 Determination of Child for Adoption (sometimes informally referred to as the "orphan investigation") to verify that the adopted child is an orphan as defined under U.S. immigration laws. Depending upon the circumstances of a case, the investigation could take several weeks to complete. If this is the case, the USCIS Office in Johannesburg and U.S. Embassy Maseru will work together to complete the investigation as expeditiously as possible.

Adoption Fees: The U.S. Embassy in Lesotho discourages the payment of any fees that are not properly receipted, "donations," or "expediting" fees, that may be requested from prospective adoptive parents. Such fees have the appearance of "buying" a baby and put all future adoptions in Lesotho at risk.

The Department of Social Welfare in the Ministry of Health and Social Welfare does not charge any fees for processing adoption submissions. The High Court does not charge fees for hearing adoption cases. The High Court requires revenue stamps to hear removal cases. These revenue stamps are required in the amount of M80.00 (approximately $11). The District Administrator requires revenue stamps of M1.00 (approximately $0.15) to provide your child with a new birth certificate The Ministry of Home Affairs requires a fee of M100.00 (approximately $14) to provide your child with a Lesotho Passport. One reputable law firm charges M8,400 (approx. $1,200) to process an order for adoption and an additional M8,400 for an order for removal (permission to take the child out of the country). Prospective adoptive parents do not pay this fee directly to the lawyer. Instead, it will generally appear as a distinct item on their bill from the adoption agency.

Documents Required: Prospective adoptive parent(s) must submit the following documents:

- Request for adoption to the Department of Social Welfare;
- Home Study;
- Lesotho Police record(s);
- Medical Certificate(s) from the local care facility (note that this is separate from the Panel Physician's report required as part of the immigrant visa application);
- Letter(s) of reference from the family of the prospective adoptive parent(s) (including from any children of the prospective adoptive parent(s) over the age of nine) stating that the family members acknowledge and accept the adoption. Lesotho adoption law is based on local cultural practices. By these standards, adoption is an extended family issue, not just one of the nuclear family. It is customary for the extended family to write a letter condoning the adoption. In Lesotho, these family relations would be expected to care for the child if the parents are unable to do so.
- Centers for orphaned or abandoned children will supply:
- Identification for the child
- Certification the child is eligible for adoption

You may be asked to provide proof that a document from the United States is authentic.

Bringing Your Child Home: Once your adoption is complete (or you have obtained legal custody of the child), there are a few more steps to take before you can head home. Specifically, you need to apply for several documents for your child before he or she can travel to the United States, such as a birth certificate, a passport or travel document for your child from the country in which he or she was born, and a U.S. Immigration

Visa. For detailed and updated information on how to obtain these documents, review the *Intercountry Adoption* section in this publication and visit the U.S. Department of State Intercountry Adoption website at http://adoption.state.gov.

Child Citizenship Act: For adoptions finalized abroad, the Child Citizenship Act of 2000 allows your new child to acquire American citizenship automatically when he or she enters the United States as lawful permanent residents. For adoptions finalized in the United States, the Child Citizenship Act of 2000 allows your new child to acquire American citizenship automatically when the court in the United States issues the final adoption decree. To learn more, review the *Intercountry Adoption* section in this publication and visit the U.S. Department of State Intercountry Adoption website at http://adoption.state.gov.

U.S. Embassy in Lesotho
254 Kingsway Road Maseru Lesotho
Tel: +266 22 312 666
Fax: +266 22 310 116
E-mail: usconsularmaseru@state.gov
http://maseru.usembassy.gov

Lesotho's Adoption Authority
Department of Social Welfare
Ministry of Health and Social Welfare
P/Bag A 222
Maseru, 100
Lesotho
Tel: +266 (22) 326–013
Fax: +266 (22) 317–206

Embassy of Lesotho
2511 Massachusetts Avenue, N.W.
Washington, D.C. 20008
Tel.: 1–202–797–5533
Fax: 1–202–234–6815
Email: Lesothoembassy@Verizon.Net
Internet: www.lesothoemb-usa.gov.ls

Office of Children's Issues
U.S. Department of State
2201 C Street NW
SA-29
Washington, DC 20520
Tel: 1–888–407–4747
E-mail: AskCI@state.gov
Internet:http://adoption.state.gov

For questions about immigration procedures, call the National Customer Service Center (NCSC) 1-800-375-5283 (TTY 1-800-767-1833).

LIBERIA

Compiled from publications that were available as of February 2013 from the U.S. Department of State, the U.S. Department of Commerce, and the Central Intelligence Agency (CIA). See the introduction to this set for explanatory notes.

Official Name:
Republic of Liberia

PROFILE

Geography

Area: total: 111,369 sq km; country comparison to the world: 104; land: 96,320 sq km; water: 15,049 sq km

Major cities: Monrovia (capital) 882,000 (2009)

Climate: tropical; hot, humid; dry winters with hot days and cool to cold nights; wet, cloudy summers with frequent heavy showers

Terrain: mostly flat to rolling coastal plains rising to rolling plateau and low mountains in northeast

People

Nationality: noun: Liberian(s); adjective: Liberian

Population: 3,887,886 (July 2012 est.)

Population growth rate: 2.609% (2012 est.)

Ethnic groups: Kpelle 20.3%, Bassa 13.4%, Grebo 10%, Gio 8%, Mano 7.9%, Kru 6%, Lorma 5.1%, Kissi 4.8%, Gola 4.4%, other 20.1% (2008 Census)

Religions: Christian 85.6%, Muslim 12.2%, Traditional 0.6%, other 0.2%, none 1.4% (2008 Census)

Languages: English 20% (official), some 20 ethnic group languages few of which can be written or used in correspondence

Literacy: definition: age 15 and over can read and write; total population: 60.8%; male: 64.8%; female: 56.8% (2010 est.)

Health: life expectancy at birth: total population: 57.41 years; male: 55.82 years; female: 59.04 years (2012 est.); Infant mortality rate: total: 72.71 deaths/1,000 live births; male: 77.08 deaths/1,000 live births; female: 68.2 deaths/1,000 live births (2012 est.)

Unemployment rate: 85% (2003 est.)

Work force: 1.372 million (2007)

Government

Type: republic

Independence: 26 July 1847

Constitution: 6 January 1986

Political subdivisions: 15 counties; Bomi, Bong, Gbarpolu, Grand Bassa, Grand Cape Mount, Grand Gedeh, Grand Kru, Lofa, Margibi, Maryland, Montserrado, Nimba, River Cess, River Gee, Sinoe

Suffrage: 18 years of age; universal

Economy

GDP (purchasing power parity): $2.693 billion (2012 est.); $1.792 billion (2011 est.); $1.684 billion (2010 est.); $1.604 billion (2009 est.)

GDP real growth rate: 6.4% (2011 est.); 5% (2010 est.); 2.8% (2009 est.)

GDP per capita (PPP): $700 (2012 est.); $500 (2011 est.); $400 (2010 est.); $400 (2009 est.)

Natural resources: iron ore, timber, diamonds, gold, hydropower

Agriculture products: rubber, coffee, cocoa, rice, cassava (manioc)), palm oil, sugarcane, bananas; sheep, goats; timber

Industries: rubber processing, palm oil processing, timber, diamonds

Exports: $506.5 million (2012 est.); $422.6 million (2011 est.); $241.5 million (2010 est.)

Exports—commodities: rubber, timber, iron, diamonds, cocoa, coffee

Exports—partners: South Africa 29.9%, US 15.7%, Spain 7.6%, Cote dIvoire 4.9%, Germany 4.2%, Japan 4.1%, China 4% (2011)

Imports: $785.3 million (2012 est.); $755.9 million (2011 est.); $719.9 million (2010 est.)

Imports—commodities: fuels, chemicals, machinery, transportation equipment, manufactured goods; foodstuffs

Imports—partners: South Korea 42.4%, China 28.6%, Japan 18.9% (2011)

Debt—external: $400.3 million (31 December 2012 est.); $228 million (31 December 2010 est.); $1.66 billion (31 December 2009 est.)

Exchange rates: Liberian dollars (LRD) per US dollar; 74 (2012 est.); 72.227 (2011 est.); 71.403 (2010 est.)

PEOPLE

There are 16 ethnic groups that make up Liberia's indigenous population. The Kpelle in central and western Liberia is the largest ethnic group. Americo-Liberians who are descendants of freed slaves that arrived in Liberia after 1820 make up less than 5% of the population.

There also are sizable numbers of Lebanese, Indians, and other West African nationals who comprise part of Liberia's business community. The Liberian constitution restricts citizenship to only people of Negro descent, and land ownership is restricted to citizens.

National/Racial/Ethnic Minorities

Although the law prohibits ethnic discrimination, racial discrimination is enshrined in the constitution, which provides that only "persons who are Negroes or of Negro descent" may be citizens and own land. Many persons of Lebanese and Asian descent who were born or lived most of their lives in the country were denied citizenship and property rights as a result of this discrimination.

The country has 16 indigenous ethnic groups; each speaks a distinct primary language and was concentrated regionally. Differences involving ethnic groups continued to contribute to social and political tensions.

Language

English is the official language and is generally spoken in Monrovia and its environs. There are 16 ethnic groups, each with its own language.

Religion

According to the 2008 National Population and Housing Census, Christians represent 85.5 percent of the population, Muslims 12.2 percent, adherents of indigenous religious beliefs 0.5 percent, and other religions 0.1 percent, with 1.5 percent claiming no religion. There are small numbers of Baha'is, Hindus, Sikhs, and Buddhists. Many members of religious groups practice elements of indigenous religious beliefs. Christian groups include Lutheran, Baptist, Episcopal, Presbyterian, Roman Catholic, The Church of Jesus Christ of Latter-day Saints (Mormon), Seventh-day Adventist, Jehovah's Witnesses, United Methodist, African Methodist Episcopal (AME), AME Zion, and a variety of Pentecostal churches. Many churches are affiliated with churches outside the country, while others operate independently.

Christians reside throughout the country. Muslims belong mainly to the Mandingo ethnic group, which also resides throughout the country, and the Vai ethnic group, which lives predominantly in the west. The country is also home to a Fula community that is predominantly Muslim. Ethnic groups in all regions participate in the indigenous religious practices of secret societies, such as the Poro (for men) and Sande (for women). Secret societies teach traditional customs and skills to initiate youth into adulthood.

HISTORY

Portuguese explorers established contacts with Liberia as early as 1461 and named the area Grain Coast because of the abundance of "grains of paradise" (Malegueta pepper seeds). In 1663 the British installed trading posts on the Grain Coast, but the Dutch destroyed these posts a year later. There were no further reports of European settlements along the Grain Coast until the arrival of freed slaves in the early 1800s.

Liberia, "land of the free," was founded by free African-Americans and freed slaves from the United States in 1820. An initial group of 86 immigrants, who came to be called Americo-Liberians, established a settlement in Christopolis (now Monrovia, named after U.S. President James Monroe) on February 6, 1820. Thousands of freed American slaves and free African-Americans arrived during the following years, leading to the formation of more settlements and culminating in a declaration of independence of the Republic of Liberia on July 26, 1847. The drive to resettle freed slaves in Africa was promoted by the American Colonization Society (ACS), an organization of white clergymen, abolitionists, and slave owners founded in 1816 by Robert Finley, a Presbyterian minister. Between 1821 and 1867 the ACS resettled some 10,000 African-Americans and several thousand Africans from interdicted slave ships; it governed the Commonwealth of Liberia until independence in 1847.

In Liberia's early years, the Americo-Liberian settlers periodically encountered stiff and sometimes violent opposition from indigenous Africans, who were excluded from citizenship in the new Republic until 1904. At the same time, British and French colonial expansionists encroached upon Liberia, taking over much of its territory. Politically, the country was a one-party state ruled by the True Whig Party (TWP). Joseph Jenkins Roberts, who was born and raised in America, was Liberia's first President. The style of government and constitution was fashioned on that of the United States, and the Americo-Liberian elite monopolized political power and restricted the voting rights of the indigenous population. The True Whig Party dominated all sectors of Liberia from independence in 1847 until April 12, 1980, when indigenous Liberian Master Sergeant Samuel K. Doe (from the Krahn ethnic group) seized power in a coup d'etat. Doe's forces executed President William R. Tolbert and several officials of his government, mostly of Americo-Liberian descent. One hundred and thirty-three years of Americo-Liberian political domination ended with the formation of the People's Redemption Council (PRC).

Over time, the Doe government began promoting members of Doe's Krahn ethnic group, who soon dominated political and military life in Liberia. This raised ethnic tension and caused frequent hostilities between the politically and militarily dominant Krahns and other ethnic groups in the country. After the October 1985 elections, characterized by widespread fraud, Doe solidified his control. The period after the elections saw increased human rights abuses, corruption, and ethnic tensions. The standard of living further deteriorated. On November 12, 1985, former Army Commanding Gen. Thomas Quiwonkpa almost succeeded in toppling Doe's government. The Armed Forces of Liberia repelled Quiwonkpa's attack and executed him in Monrovia. Doe's Krahn-dominated forces carried out reprisals against Mano and Gio civilians suspected of supporting Quiwonkpa. Despite Doe's poor human rights record and questionable democratic credentials, he retained close relations with Washington. A staunch U.S. ally, Doe met twice with President Ronald Reagan and enjoyed considerable U.S. financial support.

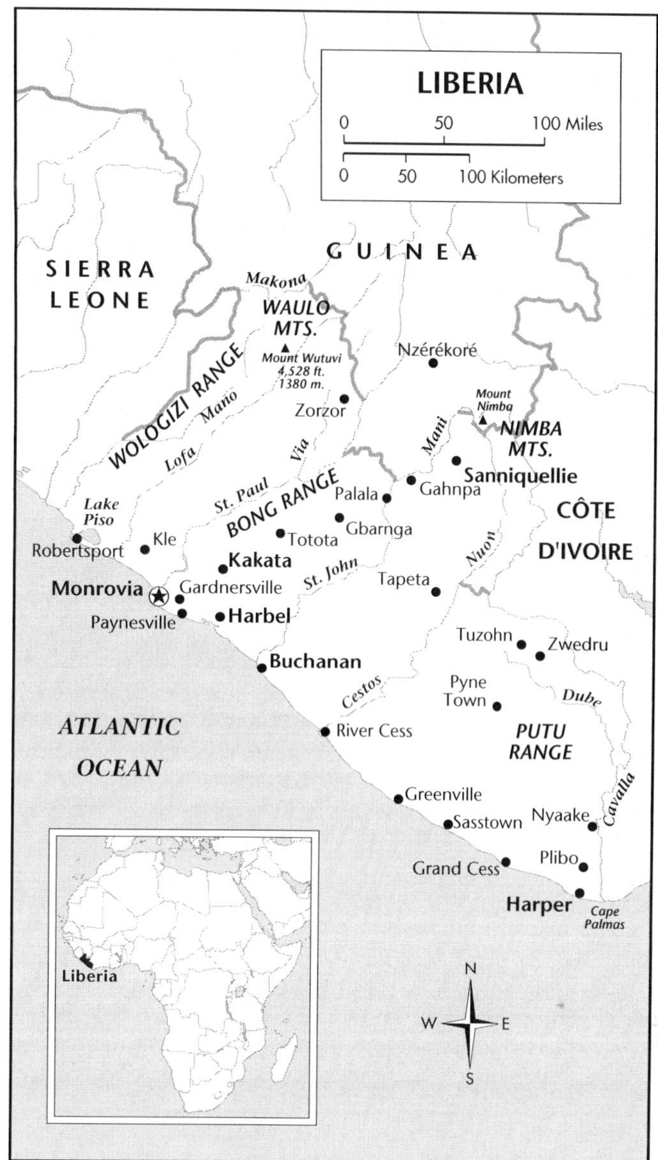

On December 24, 1989, a small band of rebels led by Doe's former procurement chief, Charles Taylor, invaded Liberia from Cote d'Ivoire. Taylor and his National Patriotic Front rebels rapidly gained the support of many Liberians and reached the outskirts of Monrovia within 6 months. From 1989 to 1996 one of Africa's bloodiest civil wars ensued, claiming the lives of more than 200,000 Liberians and displacing a million others into refugee camps in neighboring countries.

The Economic Community of West African States (ECOWAS) intervened in 1990 and succeeded in preventing Charles Taylor from capturing Monrovia. Prince Johnson—formerly a member of Taylor's National Patriotic Front of Liberia (NPFL)—formed the break-away Independent National Patriotic Front of Liberia (INPFL). Johnson's forces captured and killed Doe on September 9, 1990. Taking refuge in Sierra Leone and other neighboring countries, former AFL soldiers founded the new insurgent United Liberation Movement of Liberia for Democracy (ULIMO), fighting back Taylor's NPFL.

An Interim Government of National Unity (IGNU) was formed in Gambia under the auspices of ECOWAS in October 1990, headed by Dr. Amos C. Sawyer. Taylor (along with other Liberian factions) refused to work with the interim government and continued fighting. After more than a dozen peace accords and declining military power, Taylor finally agreed to the formation of a five-man transitional government. A hasty disarmament and demobilization of warring factions was followed by special elections on July 19, 1997. Charles Taylor and his National Patriotic Party emerged victorious. Taylor won the election by a large majority, primarily because Liberians feared a return to war had Taylor lost.

For the next 6 years, the Taylor government did not improve the lives of Liberians. Unemployment and illiteracy stood above 75%, and little investment was made in the country's infrastructure to remedy the ravages of war. Pipe-borne water and electricity were generally unavailable to most of the population, especially outside Monrovia, and schools, hospitals, roads, and infrastructure remained derelict. Rather than work to improve the lives of Liberians, Taylor supported the Revolutionary United Front in Sierra Leone (see Sierra Leone Country Background Note). Taylor's misrule led to the resumption of armed rebellion from among Taylor's former adversaries. By 2003, armed groups called "Liberians United for Reconciliation and Democracy" (LURD) and "Movement for Democracy in Liberia" (MODEL), largely representing elements of the former ULIMO-K and ULIMO-J factions that fought Taylor during Liberia's previous civil war (1989–1996), were challenging Taylor and his increasingly fragmented supporters on the outskirts of Monrovia.

On June 4, 2003 in Accra, Ghana, ECOWAS facilitated peace talks among the Government of Liberia, civil society, and the LURD and MODEL rebel groups. On the same day, the Chief Prosecutor of the Special Court for Sierra Leone issued a press statement announcing the opening of a sealed March 7, 2003 indictment of Liberian President Charles Taylor for "bearing the greatest responsibility" for atrocities in Sierra Leone since November 1996. In July 2003 the Government of Liberia, LURD, and MODEL signed a cease-fire that all sides failed to respect; bitter fighting reached downtown Monrovia in July and August 2003, creating a massive humanitarian disaster.

On August 11, 2003, under intense U.S. and international pressure, President Taylor resigned office and departed into exile in Nigeria. This move paved the way for the deployment by ECOWAS of what became a 3,600-strong peacekeeping mission in Liberia (ECOMIL). On August 18, leaders from the Liberian Government, the rebels, political parties, and civil society signed a comprehensive peace agreement that laid the framework for constructing a 2-year National Transitional Government of Liberia (NTGL), headed by businessman Charles Gyude Bryant. The UN took over security in Liberia in October 2003, subsuming ECOMIL into the United Nations Mission in Liberia (UNMIL), a force that at one point numbered more than 12,000 troops and 1,148 police officers.

The October 11, 2005 presidential and legislative elections and the subsequent November 8, 2005 presidential run-off were the most free, fair, and peaceful elections in Liberia's history. Ellen Johnson Sirleaf defeated international soccer star George Weah 59.4% to 40.6% to become Africa's first democratically elected female president. She was inaugurated in January 2006. The president's Unity Party did not win control of the legislature, in which 9 of the 20 registered political parties were represented.

The political situation remained stable after the 2005 elections. President Johnson Sirleaf has enjoyed good relations with international organizations and donor governments, with whom she has worked closely on Liberia's development. A Truth and Reconciliation Commission (TRC) was established in 2005 to investigate and report on gross human rights violations that occurred in Liberia between January 1979 and October 2003. The TRC's final, edited report was released in late 2009. The Liberian Government has yet to address many of the recommendations.

The Johnson Sirleaf government won substantial donor support for its new poverty reduction strategy at the June 2008 Liberia Poverty Reduction Forum in Berlin, Germany. In order to maintain stability through the post-conflict period, Liberia's security sector reform efforts have led to the disarmament of more than 100,000 ex-combatants, the wholesale U.S.-led reconstruction of the Armed Forces of Liberia, and a UN-led effort to overhaul the Liberian National Police. The mandate of UNMIL was extended in September 2011 to September 2012. Within UNMIL's mandate is a Peacebuilding Commission focusing on promoting rule of law, security sector reform, and national reconciliation. However, the Government of Liberia has continued to avoid taking action on freezing assets of former President Charles Taylor and his supporters, as mandated by the UN Security Council.

Liberia's executive and legislative branches brokered a compromise regarding the constitutional requirement for application of redistricting results (from the 2008 census) in preparation for 2011's presidential and legislative elections. In February, the National Elections Commission (NEC) completed voter registration (82% of the electorate) for those elections. As a necessary prelude, the NEC prepared a constitutional referendum for August 23, 2011 on individually-packaged amendments to: shorten the residency requirement from 10 to 5 years for presidential and vice-presidential candidates, increase the mandatory retirement age of Supreme Court justices from 70 to 75, move the date of national elections from the second Tuesday in October to the second Tuesday in November, and use a single-round, first-past-the-post (simple majority) method for all legislative and municipal elections while maintaining the two-round system for presidential elections. Approval by two-thirds of registered voters was required for ratification.

The October 11, 2011 presidential and legislative elections and the subsequent November 8, 2011 presidential run-off were declared free, fair, and transparent by ECOWAS, the African Union, the Carter Center, and other observers. The Congress for Democratic Change (CDC) alleged fraud in the first round and boycotted the run-off election. President Johnson Sirleaf defeated Winston Tubman of the CDC by 90.7% to 9.3% in the run-off to win re-election. She was inaugurated on January 16, 2012.\

GOVERNMENT AND POLITICAL CONDITIONS

Liberia is a constitutional republic with a bicameral National Assembly. In November Ellen Johnson Sirleaf of the Unity Party won a second term in multiparty presidential elections, which domestic and international observers considered generally free and fair.

The state is highly centralized, and the head of state appoints county superintendents. Local governments have no independent revenue base and relied entirely on the central government for funds. As a result there were very limited government services outside of Monrovia. Local officials were provided funds through the County Development Fund, but in some cases county government officials allegedly misused these funds.

Recent Elections

During 2011 Ellen Johnson Sirleaf won the national presidential election with 91 percent of the vote in a runoff election after her opponent, Winston Tubman of the Congress for Democratic Change (CDC), boycotted the second round of voting; voters also selected 15 senators and 73 representatives. The National Elections Commission (NEC) publicized its schedule for the conduct of national elections scheduled for October 2011. Sixteen candidates vied for the presidency; 865 candidates registered for the 15 contested Senate and 73 House of Representatives seats. On August 23, citizens voted on four issues during the National Referendum; the only measure that passed will allow legislative seats to be won by simple majority instead of absolute majority.

The NEC conducted the national elections on October 11; international and national observers declared them to be free, fair, transparent, and credible, although some minor irregularities were noted. Because no presidential candidate won an absolute majority of 50 percent plus one, a runoff election was held on November 8. The NEC announced that President Sirleaf and the CDC's Tubman would proceed to the second round as the top two vote-getters. On November 4, Tubman announced the CDC was boycotting the elections, citing unsubstantiated claims of widespread fraud.

International and national observers also declared the November 8 runoff free, fair, and transparent, although marred by low turnout due to the previous day's violent protest and the boycott by the CDC.

Political Parties: Registration of political parties and independent candidates took place during the year; 30 parties were registered.

Participation of Women and Minorities: There were five female ministers and nine female deputy ministers. There were four women in the 30-seat Senate and seven women in the 64-seat House of Representatives. One female associate justice sat on the five-seat Supreme Court. Women constituted 33 percent of local government officials and 31 percent of senior and junior ministers.

Muslims occupied senior government positions, including one minister, two deputy ministers, one senator, five representatives, one Supreme Court justice, and one county superintendent.

Differences stemming from the country's civil war continued to contribute to social and political tensions among ethnic groups.

Principal Government Officials

Last Updated: 1/31/2013

Pres.: **Ellen JOHNSON SIRLEAF**
Vice Pres.: **Joseph BOAKAI**
Min. of Agriculture: **Florence CHENOWETH**
Min. of Commerce & Industry: **Miatta BEYSOLOW**
Min. of Education: **Etmonia David TARPEH**
Min. of Finance: **Amara KONNEH**
Min. of Foreign Affairs: **Augustine Kpehe NGAFUAN**
Min. of Gender Development: **Julia DUNCAN-CASSELL**
Min. of Health & Social Welfare: **Walter GWENINGALE**
Min. of Information, Culture, & Tourism: **Lewis BROWN**
Min. of Internal Affairs: **Blamo NELSON**
Min. of Justice: **Christiana TAH**
Min. of Labor: **Varbah GAYFLOR**
Min. of Land, Mines, & Energy: **Patrick SENDOLO**
Min. of National Defense: **Brownie SAMUKAI**
Min. of Posts & Telecommunications: **Frederick NORKEH**
Min. of Public Works: **Samuel Koffi WOODS**
Min. of Rural Development: **E. C. B. JONES**
Min. of Transportation: **Eugene NAGBE**
Min. of Youth & Sport: **S. Tornolah VARPILAH**
Min. of State for Presidential Affairs: **Edward MCLAIN, Jr.**
Executive Governor, Central Bank of Liberia: **J. MILLS JONES**
Ambassador to the US: **Jeremiah SULUNTEH**
Permanent Representative to the UN, New York:

ECONOMY

Liberia is a low income country heavily reliant on foreign assistance for revenue. Civil war and government mismanagement destroyed much of Liberia's economy, especially the infrastructure in and around the capital, Monrovia. Many businesses fled the country, taking capital and expertise with them, but with the conclusion of fighting and the installation of a democratically-elected government in 2006, several have returned.

Liberia has the distinction of having the highest ratio of direct foreign investment to GDP in the world. Richly endowed with water, mineral resources, forests, and a climate favorable to agriculture, Liberia had been a producer and exporter of basic products, primarily raw timber and rubber and is reviving those sectors. Local manufacturing, mainly foreign owned, had been small in scope. President Johnson Sirleaf a Harvard-trained banker and administrator, has taken steps to reduce corruption, build support from international donors, and encourage private investment. Embargos on timber and diamond exports have been lifted, opening new sources of revenue for the government and Liberia shipped its first major timber exports to Europe in 2010.

The country reached its Heavily Indebted Poor Countries initiative completion point in 2010 and nearly $5 billion of international debt was permanently eliminated. This new status will enable Liberia to establish a sovereign credit rating and issue bonds. Liberia's Paris Club creditors agreed to cancel Liberia's debt as well. The IMF has completed the sixth review of Liberia's extended credit facility, bringing total disbursements to over $379 million. The African Development Bank approved a grant of $48 million in 2011 to support economic governance and competitiveness.

Rebuilding infrastructure and raising incomes will depend on generous financial and technical assistance from donor countries and foreign investment in key sectors, such as infrastructure and power generation. The country has achieved high growth during 2010–12 due to favorable world prices for its commodities.

Labor Conditions

The law prohibits the employment and apprenticeship of children under age 16 during school hours. The law does not provide for additional restrictions on working hours nor for occupational safety and health. One of the provisions of the New Education Reform Act of 2011 addresses prior inconsistencies between the minimum employment age and compulsory educational requirements. The new compulsory education requirement extends through grade nine or until age 15, also the minimum employment age. The National Children's Act has provisions intended to protect children from the worst forms of child labor and was expected to supplement other laws and efforts.

The Child Labor Commission is responsible for enforcing child labor laws and policies. However, the government did not effectively enforce child labor laws. The Child Labor Commission had inadequate staff and funding.

Child labor was widespread in almost every economic sector. In urban areas children assisted their parents as vendors in markets or hawked goods on the streets. There were also reports that children worked in conditions that were likely to harm their health and safety, such as stone cutting or work that required carrying heavy loads. Some children were engaged in hazardous labor in alluvial diamond mining and in agriculture.

The national law requires a minimum wage of 15 Liberian dollars ($0.30) per hour, not exceeding eight hours per day, excluding benefits, for unskilled laborers. The minimum wage laws apply only to the formal economic sector. The law does not fix a minimum wage for agricultural workers but requires that they be paid at the rate agreed to in the collective bargaining agreement between workers' unions and their management, excluding benefits. Skilled labor has no minimum fixed wage, and the minimum wage for civil servants was 5,600 Liberian dollars ($114) per month.

Families dependent on minimum wage incomes also engaged in subsistence farming, small-scale marketing, and begging.

The law provides for a 48-hour, six-day regular workweek with a 30-minute rest period for every five hours of work. The six-day workweek may be extended to 56 hours for service occupations and 72 hours for miners, with overtime pay beyond 48 hours. The law also provides for pay for overtime and prohibits excessive compulsory overtime.

The law provides for paid leave, severance benefits, and occupational health and safety standards. The law does not give workers the right to remove themselves from dangerous situations without risking loss of employment. Penalties were not sufficient to deter violations. The government submitted the New Labor Law and Minimum Wage Bill to the legislature for passage in an attempt to modernize current labor laws and to strengthen the government's ability to deter violations.

The Ministry of Labor's Labor Inspection Department enforced government-established health and safety standards.

Due to the continued severe economic problems, most citizens had to accept any work they could find regardless of wages or working conditions. The current minimum wage does not provide a livable income, and workers often found other activities, like street selling, to supplement their wages.

Individuals working in the formal economy, estimated at 15 percent of the workforce, were afforded labor protections, although working conditions varied from workplace to workplace. Those in the informal economy, particularly in street selling and small-scale farming, often worked more than the 48-hour workweek and faced harsher working conditions.

U.S.-LIBERIA RELATIONS

The United States established diplomatic relations with Liberia in 1864 following its independence from the American Colonization Society, an organization that resettled free African-Americans and freed slaves in Liberia. A 1980 coup ended the one-party rule that dated from independence in 1847. From 1989 to 2003, the country saw civil war, misrule, and rebellion. Elections held in 2005 and 2011 were declared free and fair.

U.S. assistance and engagement is critical to Liberia's short-term stability and long-term development. National elections in 2011 drew broad participation from the electorate, and paved the way for a peaceful transition to the incumbent president's second administration. But opposition and unrest surrounding the elections showed that security, political, and social conditions remain fragile, and that the government must continue to make progress in building and solidifying confidence in public governance, re-energizing reforms, and fostering tangible improvements in the lives of average Liberians.

U.S. Assistance to Liberia

U.S. assistance seeks to focus on professionalizing Liberia's military and civilian security forces; consolidating democratic progress; improving capacity, transparency, and accountability of governance institutions; promoting broad-based and environmentally sustainable economic growth; improving access to high-quality educational and health services; and responding to the problem of narcotics trafficking in West Africa, while helping Liberia build capacity to plan, implement, and sustain its own development efforts in each sector.

Bilateral Economic Relations

Liberia is eligible for preferential trade benefits under the African Growth and Opportunity Act. The country's revenues come primarily from rubber exports and revenues from its maritime registry program. Liberia's U.S.-owned and operated shipping and corporate registry is the world's second-largest. U.S. exports to Liberia include agricultural products (with rice as the leading category), vehicles, machinery, optic and medical instruments, and textiles. The main imports from Liberia to the United States are rubber and allied products; other imports include wood, palm oil, and diamonds. The United States and Liberia have signed a trade and investment framework agreement.

Liberia's Membership in International Organizations

Liberia and the United States belong to a number of the same international organizations, including the United Nations, International Monetary Fund, and World Bank. Liberia also is an observer to the World Trade Organization.

Bilateral Representation

Liberia maintains an embassy in the United States at 5201 16th Street, NW, Washington DC, 202-723-0437.

Principal U.S. Embassy Officials

Last Updated: 1/14/2013

MONROVIA (E) 502 Benson Street, 1000 Monrovia 10, 011-231-776-777-000, Fax 231-776-777-7370, INMARSAT Tel 00-870-772-522233, Workweek: M-Th 0800–17:30; F 0800-1300, http://monrovia.usembassy.gov/

DCM OMS: Gabrielle C. Howard
AMB OMS: Patricia Reber
CDC: Vacant
ECON/COM: Elizabeth A Wewerka
FM: Winston I Noel
HRO: Mekdim Zewde
MGT: Ronald Acuff
NAS/INL: Sally Schlegel
OMS: Gabrielle C. Howard
OPDAT: Vacant
POL/ECON: Christian Deangelis
POSHO: Winston I Noel
SDO/DATT: COL Randolph White
AMB: Deborah R. Malac
CON: Djenaba Kendrick
DCM: Karl P. Albrecht
PAO: Sara K. Hodgson
GSO: Gregory C Randolph
RSO: Adedayo Aderinto
AFSA: Vacant
AID: Patricia Rader
CLO: Sosse Nicholson
DEA: Sam Gaye (Resident In Lagos)
ECON: Sonata N Coulter
EEO: Sara K. Hodgson
FAA: Ronald L. Montgemery (Res. In Dakar)
FIN: Vacant
FMO: Janelle A. King
ICASS Chair: Patricia Rader
IMO: K Betty Barnes
IPO: Colin R Hankey
IRS: Kathy J. Beck (Resident In Paris)
ISO: Marc C Alfano
ISSO: K. Betty Barnes
LEGATT: David Brooks (Freetown)
POL: George Sarmiento
State ICASS: Vacant

TRAVEL

Consular Information Sheet

April 27, 2012

Country Description: Liberia is a country in West Africa that suffered from years of instability and conflict from 1990–2003, with attendant destruction of buildings, roads, infrastructure, and public institutions. A comprehensive peace accord ended the conflict in August 2003 and a United Nations peacekeeping force (UNMIL) was deployed to facilitate disarmament and demobilization, help arrange democratic elections, and provide for security of the country. In late 2005, Liberians went to the polls and elected Ellen Johnson-Sirleaf as president. A new government was inaugurated in January 2006, and has made progress towards restoring security and stability to the country. Presidential elections were held again in October 2011, followed by a run-off in November. President Ellen Johnson Sirleaf was re-elected in November 2011.

Despite nine years of peace and a renewal of economic growth, Liberia is still one of the poorest countries in the world and many basic services (e.g., public power, water and sewage, landline phones) are either limited or unavailable. Facilities for foreign visitors are adequate in the capital, Monrovia, but virtually non-existent in the rest of the country. The official language of Liberia is English.

Smart Traveler Enrollment Program (STEP)/Embassy Locations: If you are going to live in or travel to Liberia, please take the time to tell our Embassy about your trip by enrolling in the Smart Traveler Enrollment Program (STEP). If you enroll, we can keep you up to date with important safety and security announcements. It will also help your friends and family get in touch with you in an emergency. You should remember to keep all of your information in STEP up to date. It is important during enrollment or when you update your information to include your current phone number and email address where you can be reached in case of an emergency.

The U.S. Embassy is located at 502 Benson Street, Mamba Point, Monrovia.

U.S. citizens who wish to write to the U.S. Embassy in Monrovia may address letters to the Consular Section, 8800 Monrovia Place, U.S. Department of State, Washington, D.C. 20521–8800; Telephone: 231-77-677-7000; Emergency after-hours telephone: 231-77-677-7000; Facsimile: 231-77-677-7370.

Entry/Exit Requirements for U.S. Citizens: A passport and a visa are required for entry, as is evidence of yellow fever vaccination. Immigration officials do not issue visas at the airport. Persons arriving without a visa may be deported immediately, without being permitted to exit the airport. Persons arriving from the United States must obtain a Liberian visa before traveling. There is a U.S. $25 airport tax on departing passengers. For the latest information on entry requirements, visa fees, and the airport tax for Liberia, contact the Embassy of the Republic of Liberia at 5201 16th Street NW, Washington, DC 20011, tel. (202) 723-0437, or visit the Embassy of Liberia website. If you are overseas, inquiries should be made at the nearest Liberian embassy or consulate.

The U.S. Department of State is unaware of any HIV/AIDS entry restrictions for visitors to or foreign residents of Liberia.

Threats to Safety and Security: The Department of State urges U.S. citizens to plan proposed travel to Liberia carefully and to exercise caution when traveling in Liberia. Neither public transport nor taxis are available at the international airport, which is located 40 miles outside of Monrovia; therefore, before traveling to Liberia, U.S. citizens are urged to make arrangements for transportation from the international airport into the city center. U.S. citizens traveling to Liberia are also urged to ensure that they have confirmed reservations at a reputable hotel, as rooms can be scarce and difficult to find without advance plans.

U.S. citizens who travel to or reside in Liberia should realize that Liberia's police force has limited resources and is rebuilding. There is a UN Mission in Liberia (UNMIL), but its mandate is to ensure political stability in Liberia. U.S. citizens who travel around Liberia must realize that the role of UN Police (UNPOL) officers is to serve as advisors to the Liberia National Police. Accordingly, they do not have the authority to arrest or detain, and they are unarmed. The Liberia National Police, for its part, has a strong presence in Monrovia, but less of a presence outside of Monrovia. The police can be a source of assistance, but they can also create problems for visitors. Although corruption issues have improved, travelers may be detained by police officers who solicit bribes. U.S citizens are encouraged to carry a photocopy of their passports with them at all times so that, if questioned by local officials, proof of identity and citizenship is readily available. If detained or arrested, U.S. citizens should always ask to be allowed to contact the U.S. Embassy.

U.S. citizens in Liberia should be aware of their surroundings at all times and use caution when moving around, especially at night. Travel outside of Monrovia after dark is strongly discouraged, as roads are in poor condition and there are few public street lights, making it dangerous to navigate at night. U.S. citizens should avoid crowds, political rallies, and street demonstrations, and maintain security awareness at all times.

Stay up to date by:

- Bookmarking our Bureau of Consular Affairs website, which contains the current Travel Warnings and Travel Alerts as well as the Worldwide Caution.
- Following us on Twitter and the Bureau of Consular Affairs page on Facebook as well.
- Downloading our free Smart Traveler iPhone App to have travel information at your fingertips.
- Calling 1-888-407-4747 toll-free within the United States and Canada, or a regular toll line, 1-202-501-4444, from other countries.
- Taking some time before travel to consider your personal security.

Crime: While the Department of State has rated Liberia high for crime, most crimes that occur within the expat community are crimes of opportunity (which increase during the hours of darkness), with an occasional residential burglary and armed robbery (use of knife or machete). The Liberian National Police have limited capacity to respond to crime, thus crime is much higher in Liberian communities where police are not visible. Driving in Monrovia presents a greater danger to residents and visitors, as traffic laws are either nonexistent or unenforceable by police, thus traffic accidents are frequent and often result in injury and loss of life. The police are ill-equipped and largely incapable of providing effective protection or investigation. Criminal activity has been reported in both urban and rural areas.

Perpetrators of business fraud often target foreigners, including U.S. citizens. Formerly associated with Nigeria, these fraud schemes are now prevalent throughout western Africa, including Liberia, and pose a danger of both financial loss and physical harm. An increasing number of U.S. citizens have been the targets of such scams. The best way to avoid becoming a victim of fraud is common sense—if it looks too good to be true, it probably is. U.S. citizens should carefully check any unsolicited business proposal originating in Liberia before committing any funds, providing any goods or services, or undertaking any travel, particularly if the proposal involves the mining or sale of gold and diamonds. There has also been an increase in the number of Liberian/American Internet relationships in which there are eventual requests for financial assistance under fraudulent pretenses. For additional information, please see the Department of State's Bureau of Consular Affairs' International Financial Scams web page.

Petty corruption is rampant; poorly paid government officials are not immune from the temptation to collect fees for doing their job. The result is that travelers may be asked for bribes and inconvenienced for not paying them.

Don't buy counterfeit and pirated goods, even if they are widely available. Not only are the bootlegs illegal in the United States, you may be breaking local law too.

Victims of Crime: If you are the victim of a crime abroad, you should contact the local police and the nearest U.S. embassy or consulate (see the Department of State's list of embassies and consulates). This includes the loss or theft of a U.S. passport. We can:

- Replace a stolen passport.
- Help you find appropriate medical care if you are the victim of violent crimes such as assault or rape.
- Put you in contact with the appropriate police authorities, and if you want us to, we can contact family members or friend.
- Help you understand the local criminal justice process and direct you to local attorneys, although it is important to remember that local authorities are responsible for investigating and prosecuting the crime.

The local equivalent to the "911" emergency line in Liberia is 911.

In an emergency, dialing 911 or 355 from a cellular phone within Liberia will put you in contact with a cellular phone at the Liberian National Police (LNP) Headquarters. Please note that there is no landline telephone service in Liberia, and cellular phone communication is subject to occasional disruptions in service.

Criminal Penalties: While traveling in Liberia, you are subject to its laws even if you are a U.S. citizen. Foreign laws and legal systems can be vastly different than our own. In some places you may be taken in for questioning if you don't have your passport with you. In some places, it is illegal to take pictures of certain buildings. In some places driving under the influence could land you immediately in jail. These criminal penalties will vary from country to country. There are also some things that might be legal in the country you visit, but still illegal in the United States. You can be prosecuted under U.S. law if you buy pirated goods or engage in child pornography. If you do something illegal in your host country, your U.S. passport won't help. It's very important to know what's legal and what's not where you are going.

Persons violating Liberian laws, even unknowingly, may be expelled, arrested, or imprisoned. Penalties for possessing, using, or trafficking in illegal drugs in Liberia are severe, and convicted offenders can expect long jail sentences and heavy fines.

In 2012, the legislature of Liberia proposed legislation which will increase the penalties for same gender sexual relations and outlaw gay marriage. The legislation is currently pending.

If you are arrested in Liberia, you have the right to request that authorities alert the U.S. Embassy of your arrest.

Special Circumstances: Lodging, fuel, transportation, and telephone services are unevenly available in Liberia, and are nonexistent or severely limited in rural areas. Neither water nor electricity is commercially available in Liberia, except in some parts of Monrovia. Most hotels have utilities available, but not always on a 24-hour basis. There is no working landline telephone system in Liberia. Several cell phone companies provide service in Monrovia and some areas outside the capital. U.S. cellular phones do not always work in Liberia and it is advisable to rent or purchase a local cellular phone. The postal system is slow and unreliable. Commercial air courier service is available through UPS, Federal Express (FedEx), and other companies. The U.S. dollar is readily accepted in Liberia. Please follow the specific regulations for transferring foreign currency in and out of Liberia. Sums in excess of U.S. $10,000 must be reported at the port of entry and no more than U.S. $7,500 in foreign currency banknotes can be moved out of the country at one time. Larger sums must be transferred via bank drafts or other financial instruments; persons without a Liberian bank account are limited to two outgoing U.S. $5,000 over-the-counter cash wire transfers per month. Wire transfers are not widely used and are subject to substantial fees. ATMs are available in Monrovia, but traveler's checks and credit/debit cards are not accepted anywhere in Liberia.

Swimming Hazard: Liberia has many excellent beaches along the Atlantic coastline that tourists and those who live in the country enjoy throughout the year. However, U.S. citizens should be aware of the threat of dangerous rip currents better known as rip tides. These strong currents can occur anywhere on the coast given the right surf conditions. The Liberia Weather Service does not provide information on where and when these tides form and there are no lifeguards posted on beaches. U.S. citizens who plan to swim in the Atlantic should read from various sources about the dangers of rip currents and how to navigate them if you find yourself in such a situation; or better still, do not swim if you are unfamiliar with swimming in water where very strong rip currents occur.

Photography: Photographing military installations, air and seaports, and important government buildings is prohibited. Visitors should not take photographs of sites or activities that might be considered sensitive, or police are liable to confiscate your camera.

Accessibility: There are no accommodations for individuals with disabilities in Liberia. U.S. citizens with accessibility concerns should take this into consideration before planning travel to Liberia.

Medical Facilities and Health Information: Hospitals and medical facilities in Liberia are very poorly equipped and are incapable of providing many services. Emergency services comparable to those in the U.S. or Europe are non-existent, and the blood supply is unreliable and unsafe for transfusion. U.S. citizens with serious medical problems travel or are medically evacuated to the United States, Europe, or South Africa. Medicines are scarce, often beyond expiration dates, and generally unavailable in most areas. As there is neither an effective garbage removal service nor a functioning sewer system, the level of sanitation throughout urban areas is very poor, which increases the potential for disease. Upper respiratory infections and diarrhea are common, as well as more serious diseases such as typhoid and malaria. All travelers to Liberia must be vaccinated against yellow fever and should carry a supply of all prescription medication, including anti-malaria medication, sufficient for the duration of their entire stay. A typhoid vaccination is also recommended.

You can find information on vaccinations and other health precautions on the CDC website. For information about outbreaks of infectious diseases abroad, consult the World Health Organization (WHO) website. The WHO website also contains additional health information for travelers, including detailed country-specific health information.

Medical Insurance: You can't assume your insurance will go with you when you travel. It's very important to find out BEFORE you leave. You need to ask your insurance company two questions:

- Does my policy apply when I'm out of the United States
- Will it cover emergencies such as a trip to a foreign hospital or a medical evacuation?

In many places, doctors and hospitals still expect payment in cash at the time of service. Your regular U.S. health insurance may not cover doctors' and hospital visits in other countries. If your policy doesn't go with you when you travel, it's a very good idea to take out another one for your trip.

Traffic Safety and Road Conditions: While in a foreign country, U.S. citizens may encounter road conditions that differ significantly from those in the United States. The information below concerning Liberia is provided for general reference only, and may not be totally accurate in a particular location or circumstance.

Road travel in Liberia can be hazardous. Potholes and poor road surfaces are common, making safe driving extremely challenging. Cars, trucks, motorcycles, and taxis are often overloaded with people and goods and make frequent stops without signaling. Drivers overtake on the right as well as the left. Many vehicles operate with threadbare tires, and blowouts are frequent. Public taxis are poorly maintained and usually overloaded. Approach intersections with extreme caution. The absence of public street lights makes it difficult to see pedestrians walking in city streets or on country roads.

Drivers and pedestrians are cautioned that high-speed car convoys carrying government officials require all other vehicles to pull off the road until they have passed. Travelers should expect delays at UNMIL security checkpoints, as well as time-consuming detours around the many bridges and roads damaged by war, neglect, or the heavy annual rains, which occur from May to November. Travelers can expect strict enforcement of border controls by Liberian, Ivorian, Sierra Leonean, and Guinean authorities. At times, border crossings to neighboring countries are closed.

Aviation Safety Oversight: As there is no direct commercial air service to the United States by carriers registered in Liberia, the U.S. Federal Aviation Administration (FAA) has not assessed the government of Liberia's Civil Aviation Authority for compliance with International Civil Aviation Organization (ICAO) aviation safety standards. Further information may be found on the FAA's safety assessment page.

Children's Issues: Please see the U.S. Dept. of State Office of Children's Issues web pages on intercountry adoption and international parental child abduction.

Intercountry Adoption
September 2010

The information in this section has been edited from the latest report available as of February 2013 from the State Department Bureau of Consular Affairs, Office of Overseas Citizens Services. For more information, please read the *Intercountry Adoption* section of this book and review current reports online at http://adoption.state.gov.

Liberia is not party to the Hague Convention on Protection of Children and Co-operation in Respect of Intercountry Adoption (Hague Adoption Convention). Therefore, when the Hague Adoption Convention entered into force for the United States on April 1, 2008, intercountry adoption processing for Liberia did not change. Currently there is a moratorium on new adoptions and all approved adoptions must be approved by the ad-hoc adoption committee before the children may leave the country. Any prospective adoptive parent who is in the process of adopting from Liberia should contact the Consular Section of the U.S. Embassy in Liberia at the following e-mail address.

In July 2008, the Ministry of Justice and Ministry of Health and Social Welfare began carefully reviewing all adoption cases submitted to them for approval. This change occurred because the Government of Liberia noticed an increasing number of cases in which adoptive parents decided to terminate their parent/child relationship with Liberian adoptive children.

The Liberian Parliament is considering a revised adoption law, which was proposed in November 2007. If enacted, the new law would provide additional safeguards to protect adoptive children, birth parents, and prospective adoptive parents.

Who Can Adopt? To bring an adopted child to United States from Liberia, you must be found eligible to adopt by the U.S. Government. The U.S. Government agency responsible for making this determination is the Department of Homeland Security, U.S. Citizenship and Immigration Services (USCIS). In addition to these U.S. requirements for prospective adoptive parents, Liberia also has the following eligibility requirements for prospective adoptive parents:

Residency Requirements: There are no residency requirements for intercountry adoptions in Liberia.

Age Requirements: There are no age requirements for intercountry adoptions in Liberia.

Marriage Requirements: There are no marriage requirements for intercountry adoptions in Liberia.

Income Requirements: There are no income requirements for Liberian intercountry adoptions.

Who Can Be Adopted? Liberia has specific requirements that a child must meet in order to be eligible for adoption. You cannot adopt a child in Liberia unless he or she meets the requirements outlined below.The Consular Section of the U.S. Embassy thoroughly investigates each adoption case to verify that the child's orphan status is legitimate. Since these investigations can take a considerable amount of time, prospective adoptive parents should check with the Embassy to ensure that the investigation has been completed before making travel arrangements for the child to depart Liberia. In addition to these requirements, a child must meet the definition of an orphan under U.S. law for you to bring him or her home back to the United States.

Eligibility Requirements: In addition to a statement of relinquishment from the biological parents, the Liberian Government also requires an approved case summary from the Ministry of Health and Social Welfare (MHSW). The case summary is issued after a social worker has investigated the case thoroughly and concluded that adoption is in the best interest of the child and the Minister or one of his deputies has reviewed all the legal paperwork necessary to process an adoption in Liberia. If the child was born in wedlock, the consent of both parents is required. If the child was born out of wedlock, only the mother must consent. Parental consent is not required if the parents have abandoned the child, if the parental rights have been legally terminated, if the parents are deceased, or if a legal guardian has been appointed by the court.

Age Requirements: If the child is 16 years or older, the child must consent to the adoption. Please note that a child who is 16 years or older is not considered a "child" but the Immigration and Nationality Act and therefore may be ineligible to immigrate to the United States.

Other Requirements: In addition to obtaining a statement of relinquishment from the biological parent or legal guarding of the child being adopted, no adoption decree can be issued without an approved case summary from the Ministry of Health and Social Welfare (MHSW). A case summary from the MHSW is issued only after a social worker has investigated the case thoroughly and concluded that adoption is in the best interest of the child, and the Minister has reviewed all the legal paperwork necessary to process an adoption in Liberia. This requirement has added time to the processing of adoptions, but it is in the best interest of all parties and is strongly endorsed by the Embassy.

Adoption Authority: The Ministry of Justice

The Process: The first step in adopting a child from Liberia is usually to select a licensed agency in the United States that can help with your adoption. Adoption service providers must be licensed by the U.S. state in which they operate. To bring an adopted child from Liberia to the United States, you must apply to be found eligible to adopt (Form I-600A) by the U.S. Government, Department of Homeland Security, U.S. Citizenship and Immigration Services (USCIS). If you are eligible to adopt, and a child is available for intercountry adoption, the central adoption authority in Liberia will provide you with a referral to a child. The process for finalizing the adoption (or gaining legal custody) in Liberia generally includes the following.

Role of the Adoption Authority: No adoption decree can be issued without an approved case summary from the Ministry of Health and Social Welfare (MHSW).

Role of the Court: A petition for adoption must be filed with the Probate Court. The petition must contain the name, age, residence and marital status of the petitioners. The name, date and place of birth of the child, the date and manner in which the petitioners acquired custody of the child, facts (if any) that render consent of either parent unnecessary, the petitioners' desire to adopt the child and the child's change of name, should also be contained in the petition.

Upon receipt of a petition for adoption, the Court schedules a hearing and serves notice on all interested parties. The petitioners or their legal representative, the parent, parents, or guardian(s) of the child and the child are required to attend the hearing, though the court may waive the appearance of the child for good cause. This waiver must be stated in the order of adoption.

All hearings are public, and held in open court. The court must be satisfied that the "moral and temporal interests" of the child will be satisfied by the adoption. Upon this showing, the adoption is ordered. The court must be satisfied that the "moral and temporal interests" of the child will be satisfied by the adoption. Upon this showing, the adoption is ordered.

Role of Adoption Agencies: Most adoptive parents normally work with an adoption agency in the U.S., which in turn liases with an orphanage or organization in Liberia prior to initiating the adoption process. The organization in Liberia must be registered with the Ministry of Health and Social Welfare.

Time Frame: There are no fixed time lines or constraints on the Court's processing of adoptions. The adoption process, including formal relinquishment by the parent(s) if necessary, generally takes 3 to 4 weeks.

Since November 2007, prospective adoptive parents have experienced long delays, sometimes as long as 3 months in processing adoptions due to pending revision of the Liberian adoption law.

Adoption Fees: Official Government fees for adoptions in Liberia are minimal and consist mainly of court filing fees. These filing fees are normally less than $12,000 USD. The cost of employing local counsel varies but adoptive parents can expect to pay several hundred dollars at a minimum for an attorney. Liberia has proposed legislation that will increase fees for processing paper through the Courts and the Ministry of Justice for $5 to $1500 USD.

These funds will be used to hire additional social workers and court clerks as well as for the general operation of both Ministries.

Documents Required: The following documents are required for adoption in Liberia:

- Petition for Adoption
- Written consent of the biological parents
- Copy of adoptive parents' passports

After Adoption: Liberian law has no post-adoption requirements for adoptive parents. Parents should confirm any post-adoption requirements with their legal representatives.

U.S. Embassy in Liberia
111 U.N. Drive
Mamba Point
Monrovia, Liberia
Tel: 231-077-207-326
Fax: 231-770-010-370
Email: ConsularMonrovia@state.gov

Liberian Adoption Authority
Cllr. Philip Banks
Minister of Justice
Ministry of Justice Building
Ashmun Street (Opposite College of West Africa)
Monrovia, Liberia
Special Assistant: +231 6 520140 (Onesimus Bawon)
Secretary: +231 6 551-598 (Massa Johnson)

Embassy of Liberia
5201 16th Street, N.W.
Washington, D.C. 20011
Tel: (202) 723-0437
Fax: (202) 723-0436
Email: info@embassyofliberia.org

Office of Children's Issues
U.S. Department of State
2201 C Street, NW
SA-29
Washington, DC 20520
Tel: 1-888-407-4747
E-mail: AskCI@state.gov
http://adoption.state.gov

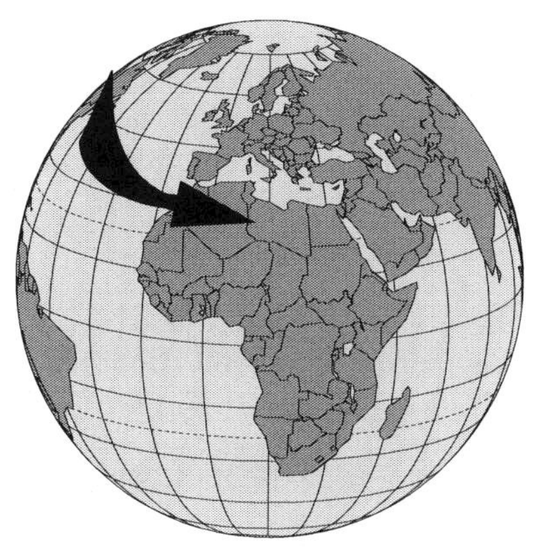

LIBYA

Compiled from publications that were available as of February 2013 from the U.S. Department of State, the U.S. Department of Commerce, and the Central Intelligence Agency (CIA). See the introduction to this set for explanatory notes.

Official Name:

Great Socialist People's Libyan Arab Jamahiriya

PROFILE

Geography

Area: total: 1,759,540 sq km; country comparison to the world: 17; land: 1,759,540 sq km; water: 0 sq km

Major cities: Tripoli (capital) 1.095 million (2009)

Climate: Mediterranean along coast; dry, extreme desert interior

Terrain: mostly barren, flat to undulating plains, plateaus, depressions

People

Nationality: noun: Libyan(s); adjective: Libyan

Population: 5,613,380 (July 2012 est.)

Population growth rate: 2.007% (2012 est.)

Ethnic groups: Berber and Arab 97%, other 3% (includes Greeks, Maltese, Italians, Egyptians, Pakistanis, Turks, Indians, and Tunisians)

Religions: Sunni Muslim (official) 97%, other 3%

Languages: Arabic (official), Italian, English (all widely understood in the major cities); Berber (Nafusi, Ghadamis, Suknah, Awjilah, Tamasheq)

Literacy: definition: age 15 and over can read and write; total population: 89.2%; male: 95.6%; female: 82.7% (2010 est.)

Health: life expectancy at birth: total population: 77.83 years; male: 75.5 years; female: 80.27 years (2012 est.); Infant mortality rate: total: 19.34 deaths/1,000 live births; male: 21.26 deaths/1,000 live births; female: 17.33 deaths/1,000 live births (2012 est.)

Unemployment rate: 30% (2004 est.)

Work force: 1.437 million (2012 est.)

Government

Type: operates under a transitional government

Independence: 24 December 1951

Constitution: 7 February 2011 draft (temporary) constitution of the Transitional National Council; note—following the September 1969 military overthrow of the Libyan government, the Revolutionary Command Council replaced the existing constitution with the Constitutional Proclamation in December 1969; in March 1977, Libya adopted the Declaration of the Establishment of the People's Authority; in September 2011 the UN recognized the Transitional National Council as the legitimate interim government

Political subdivisions: 22 districts (shabiyat, singular—shabiyat)

Suffrage: NA

Economy

GDP (purchasing power parity): $87.91 billion (2012 est.); $37.97 billion (2011 est.); $97.43 billion (2010 est.); $95.02 billion (2009 est.)

GDP real growth rate: NA% (2011 est.); 2.5% (2010 est.); -0.1% (2009 est.)

GDP per capita (PPP): $13,300 (2012 est.); $14,100 (2010 est.); $14,900 (2010 est.)

Natural resources: petroleum, natural gas, gypsum

Agriculture products: wheat, barley, olives, dates, citrus, vegetables, peanuts, soybeans; cattle

Industries: petroleum, petrochemicals, aluminum, iron and steel, food processing, textiles, handicrafts, cement

Exports: $51.48 billion (2012 est.); $16.46 billion (2011 est.); $48.94 billion (2010 est.)

Exports—commodities: crude oil, refined petroleum products, natural gas, chemicals

Exports—partners: Italy 21.5%, Germany 13.5%, France 13.4%, China 10.1%, Spain 4.9%, Tunisia 4.6%, India 4.3% (2011)

Imports: $16.31 billion (2012 est.); $10.32 billion (2011 est.); $24.56 billion (2010 est.)

Imports—commodities: machinery, semi-finished goods, food, transport equipment, consumer products

Imports—partners: Egypt 15.5%, Tunisia 11.9%, Turkey 8.1%, China 7.8%, Italy 7.5%, Syria 4.6%, France 4.4%, Germany 4.3% (2011)
Debt—external: $5.054 billion (31 December 2012 est.); $4.774 billion (31 December 2011 est.); $6.375 billion (31 December 2010 est.)
Exchange rates: Libyan dinars (LYD) per US dollar; 1.257 (2012 est.); 1.2241 (2011 est.); 1.2668 (2010 est.); 1.2535 (2009); 1.2112 (2008); 1.2604 (2007)

PEOPLE

Libya has a small population in a large land area. Population density is about 50 persons per sq. km. (80/sq. mi.) in the two northern regions of Tripolitania and Cyrenaica, but falls to less than one person per sq. km. (1.6/sq. mi.) elsewhere. Ninety percent of the people live in less than 10% of the area, primarily along the coast. More than half the population is urban, mostly concentrated in the two largest cities, Tripoli and Benghazi. Thirty-three percent of the population is estimated to be under age 15.

Native Libyans are primarily a mixture of Arabs and Berbers. Small Tebou and Tuareg tribal groups in southern Libya are nomadic or seminomadic. Among foreign residents, the largest groups are citizens of other African nations, including North Africans (primarily Egyptians and Tunisians), West Africans, and other Sub-Saharan Africans.

National/Racial/Ethnic Minorities

Arabic-speaking Muslims of mixed Arab-Amazigh (Berber) ancestry constituted 97 percent of citizenry. The principal minorities were Amazighs, Tuaregs, and Toubou. These minority groups are predominantly Sunni Muslim but identify with their respective cultural and linguistic heritage rather than with Arab traditions. Several nomadic groups live in areas along the country's desert borders, including Tuareg and Toubou. The country was home to an estimated 1.5 million to two million foreign workers and undocumented migrants, many of whom fled or were displaced during the conflict. Of those, nearly one million were thought to be of Sahelian or sub-Saharan African origin.

Under Qadhafi, Arabic was declared the only official language, and the regime denied the existence of non-Arab citizens. Amazigh people faced discrimination, including limitations on the use of their native language. Amazigh fighters participated in the revolution and were able to publicly use Amazigh symbols and the alphabet. At the end of 2011,, they pursued fledgling efforts to advocate for equal protections for Amazigh culture and language.

There was societal discrimination and violence against dark-skinned Libyans, including those of original sub-Saharan descent, in part due to allegations that Qadhafi used African mercenaries during the conflict.

Religion

The population is 97 percent Sunni Muslim. Many members of the Amazigh ethnic minority are Ibadi Muslims, and virtually all non-Sunni Muslims are resident expatriates. Small Christian communities consist almost exclusively of sub-Saharan African and Egyptian migrants and a small number of American and European workers. Bishops in Tripoli, Misurata, and Benghazi lead an estimated 50,000 Coptic Christians, most of who number among the estimated 750,000 Egyptian expatriate residents. Roman Catholic clergy are present in larger cities, working primarily in hospitals, orphanages, and with the elderly or physically impaired. A priest in Tripoli and a bishop resident in Tunis lead the Anglican community. A Greek Orthodox archbishop resident in Tripoli and priests in Tripoli and Benghazi serve 80 regular Orthodox churchgoers. The Ukrainian embassy in Tripoli also maintains a small Orthodox church for Tripoli's Russian-speaking population. There are nondenominational, evangelical Unity churches in Tripoli and Benghazi, as well as small Unity congregations located throughout the country. Nondenominational churches in Tripoli serve primarily African and Filipino migrant workers.

There are no known places of worship for members of other non-Muslim religious groups such as Hinduism, the Baha'i Faith, and Buddhism, although adherents are allowed to practice their religion in their homes. Foreign adherents of these religious groups are allowed to display and sell religious items at bazaars and other public areas.

HISTORY

For most of their history, the peoples of Libya have been subjected to varying degrees of foreign control. The Phoenicians, Carthaginians, Greeks, Romans, Vandals, and Byzantines ruled all or parts of Libya. Although the Greeks and Romans left impressive ruins at Cyrene, Leptis Magna, and Sabratha, little else remains today to testify to the presence of these ancient cultures.

The Arabs conquered Libya in the seventh century A.D. In the following centuries, most of the indigenous peoples adopted Islam and the Arabic language and culture. The Ottoman Turks conquered the country in the mid-16th century. Libya remained part of their empire, although at times virtually autonomous, until Italy invaded in 1911 and, in the face of years of resistance, made Libya a colony.

In 1934, Italy adopted the name "Libya" (used by the Greeks for all of North Africa, except Egypt) as the official name of the colony, which consisted of the Provinces of Cyrenaica, Tripolitania, and Fezzan. King Idris I, Emir of Cyrenaica, led Libyan resistance to Italian occupation between the two world wars. Allied forces removed Axis powers from Libya in February 1943. Tripolitania and Cyrenaica came under separate British administration, while the French controlled Fezzan. In 1944, Idris returned from exile in Cairo but

declined to resume permanent residence in Cyrenaica until the removal in 1947 of some aspects of foreign control. Under the terms of the 1947 peace treaty with the Allies, Italy relinquished all claims to Libya.

On November 21, 1949, the UN General Assembly passed a resolution stating that Libya should become independent before January 1, 1952. King Idris I represented Libya in the subsequent UN negotiations. When Libya declared its independence on December 24, 1951, it was the first country to achieve independence through the United Nations and one of the first former European possessions in Africa to gain independence. Libya was proclaimed a constitutional and a hereditary monarchy under King Idris. The discovery of significant oil reserves in 1959 and the subsequent income from petroleum sales enabled what had been one of the world's poorest countries to become extremely wealthy, as measured by per capita GDP. Although oil drastically improved Libya's finances, popular resentment grew as wealth was increasingly concentrated in the hands of the elite. This discontent continued to mount with the rise throughout the Arab world of Nasserism and the idea of Arab unity.

On September 1, 1969, a small group of military officers led by then 28-year-old army officer Mu'ammar Abu Minyar al-Qadhafi staged a coup d'etat against King Idris, who was subsequently exiled to Egypt. The new regime, headed by the Revolutionary Command Council (RCC), abolished the monarchy and proclaimed the new Libyan Arab Republic. Qadhafi emerged as leader of the RCC and eventually as de facto head of state, a political role he played until the February 17, 2011 uprising. The Libyan Government asserted that Qadhafi held no official position, although he was referred to in government statements and the official press as the "Brother Leader and Guide of the Revolution," among other honorifics.

An early objective of the Qadhafi regime was withdrawal of all foreign military installations from Libya. Following negotiations, British military installations at Tobruk and nearby El Adem were closed in March 1970, and U.S. facilities at Wheelus Air Force Base near Tripoli were closed in June 1970. That July, the Libyan Government ordered the expulsion of several thousand Italian residents. By 1971, libraries and cultural centers operated by foreign governments were ordered closed.

In the 1970s, Libya claimed leadership of Arab and African revolutionary forces and sought active roles in international organizations. Late in the 1970s, Libyan embassies were redesignated as "people's bureaus," as Qadhafi sought to portray Libyan foreign policy as an expression of the popular will. The people's bureaus, aided by Libyan religious, political, educational, and business institutions overseas, attempted to export Qadhafi's revolutionary philosophy abroad.

Qadhafi's confrontational foreign policies and use of terrorism, as well as Libya's growing friendship with the U.S.S.R., led to increased tensions with the West in the 1980s. Following a terrorist bombing at a discotheque in West Berlin frequented by American military personnel, in 1986 the U.S. retaliated militarily against targets in Libya, and imposed broad unilateral economic sanctions.

After Libya was implicated in the 1988 bombing of Pan Am flight 103 over Lockerbie, Scotland, UN sanctions were imposed in 1992. UN Security Council resolutions (UNSCRs) passed in 1992 and 1993 obliged Libya to fulfill requirements related to the Pan Am 103 bombing before sanctions could be lifted. Qadhafi initially refused to comply with these requirements, leading to Libya's political and economic isolation for most of the 1990s.

In 1999, Libya fulfilled one of the UNSCR requirements by surrendering two Libyans who were suspected to have been involved with the bombing for trial before a Scottish court in the Netherlands. One of these suspects, Abdel Basset Ali Mohamed al-Megrahi, was found guilty; the other was acquitted. Al-Megrahi's conviction was upheld on appeal in 2002. On August 19, 2009, al-Megrahi was released from Scottish prison on compassionate grounds due to a terminal illness and returned to Libya. In August 2003, Libya fulfilled the remaining UNSCR requirements, including acceptance of responsibility for the actions of its officials and payment of appropriate compensation to the victims' families. UN sanctions were lifted on September 12, 2003. U.S. International Emergency Economic Powers Act (IEEPA)-based sanctions were lifted September 20, 2004.

On December 19, 2003, Libya publicly announced its intention to rid itself of weapons of mass destruction (WMD) and Missile Technology Control Regime (MTCR)-class missile programs. Subsequently, Libya cooperated with the U.S., the U.K., the International Atomic Energy Agency, and the Organization for the Prohibition of Chemical Weapons toward these objectives. Libya has also signed the IAEA Additional Protocol and has become a State Party to the Chemical Weapons Convention. These were important steps toward full diplomatic relations between the U.S. and Libya.

Nationwide political violence erupted in February 2011, following the Libyan Government's brutal suppression of popular protests against Libyan leader Mu'ammar al-Qadhafi. Opposition forces quickly seized control of Benghazi, Libya's second-largest city, as well as significant portions of eastern Libya and some areas in western Libya. Drawing from the local opposition councils which formed the backbone of the "February 17" revolution, the Libyan opposition announced the formation of a Transitional National Council (TNC) on February 27, 2011. The Council stated its desire to remove Qadhafi from power and establish a unified, democratic, and free Libya that respects universal human rights principles.

On October 23, 2011, 3 days after Qadhafi's death, the TNC officially declared Libya liberated. The TNC subsequently moved from Benghazi to Tripoli and formed a transitional government (i.e., an executive branch). On February 7, 2012, it approved an election law, and the Supreme Election Commission has started preparing for June elections for the General National Conference, to consist of 200 elected representatives.

GOVERNMENT AND POLITICAL CONDITIONS

At the end of 2011,, a 38-day-old interim government began to exercise authority in Libya, formerly the Great Socialist People's Libyan Arab Jamahiriya. After eight months of civil war, ending with the ouster of the Qadhafi regime, construction of a republican form of government began. The opposition leadership in the Transitional National Council (TNC), which was formed on February 27, 2011, exercised executive authority prior to naming an interim government on November 23 and thereafter acted in a de facto legislative capacity as an arm of the government engaged in transition planning. Adopted by the TNC on August 3, Libya's Constitutional Declaration provides the basis of governance and allows for the exercise of a full range of political, civil, and judicial rights, including Article 3, which safeguards freedom of expression and assembly, and Article 8, the right to due process—rights that the Libyan people were systematically deprived of during Qadhafi's 42-year rule. While Qadhafi-era laws that did not contravene the declaration remained in force, the applicability of former laws remained unclear at year's end, due in large part to the absence of functioning courts. Although an indirect electoral system existed on paper under Qadhafi, in practice his inner circle monopolized all positions of power and

During 2011 opposition forces reportedly violated human rights and humanitarian norms. Militias and their supporters—which were not fully under the control of the TNC or transitional government authority—committed unlawful killings, other physical violence, and other abuses. Principal targets were actual or suspected detained Qadhafi soldiers or supporters, possible sub-Saharan African mercenaries or dark-skinned Libyans, and former members of the security forces. Disappearances, illegal detentions, and imprisonment of persons on political grounds occurred, as did looting and further violence. Vulnerable civilian populations, including ethnic minorities and migrants, faced discrimination and violence during and after the conflict.

Under Qadhafi the country did not have a constitution, and there were no legal means for the people to change their government. Antigovernment groups took up arms against the government in a civil war that, after eight months, resulted in Qadhafi's fall and a political transition. A temporary Constitutional Declaration and road map for political transition guided the interim government's activities. The declaration, which defines the country as a democratic state deriving authority from the people, provides for a range of political, civil, and judicial liberties.

Recent Elections

The Qadhafi-era "Jamahiriya" system of government included indirect elections for a layered pyramidal structure of committees. The most recent elections, held in 2009, were heavily influenced by Qadhafi's inner circle and the Revolutionary Committees and ultimately had no influence on the governance of the country, which was tightly controlled by Qadhafi.

Political Parties: The Qadhafi government prohibited the creation of and membership in political parties. However, the TNC and interim government promoted freedom of political parties, associations, and other civil society organizations in the Constitutional Declaration and in practice. At the end of 2011,, political groups were in the process of formation under the interim government.

Participation of Women and Minorities: The 51-member TNC had one female member, and the interim government had two women among the 24 ministers. Five Amazigh members of the TNC boycotted the government swearing-in ceremony to protest that no Amazigh were named to ministerial positions.

Principal Government Officials

Last Updated: 1/31/2013

The United States on 17 July 2011 recognized the Transitional National Council (TNC) as the legitimate governing authority for Libya until an interim government is in place. The TNC on 8 August 2011 dismissed the members of its Executive Committee, which serves as the TNC's executive branch, and only reappointed the chairman of the Executive Committee. However, many previous members of the Executive Committee have continued to be responsible for their assigned portfolios in an acting capacity.

Chmn., TNC (chief of state): **Mustafa Muhammad Abd al-JALIL**

Prime Min.: **Abd al-Rahim al-KEEB**

Dep. Prime Min.: **Amur Abdallah ABD AL-KARIM**

Dep. Prime Min.: **Haramayn Muhammad al-HARAMAYN**

Dep. Prime Min.: **Mustafa BUSHAGUR**

Min. of Agriculture, Animal, & Sea Resources: **Sulayman Abd al-Hamid BUFRUJA**

Min. of Communication & Information Technology: **Anwar al-FAYTURI**

Min. of Culture & Civil Society: **Abd al-Rahman HABIL**

Min. of Defense: **Usama JUWAYLI**

Min. of Economy: **Ahmed al-KOSHLI**

Min. of Education: **Sulayman Ali al-SAHILI**

Min. of Electricity & Renewable Energy: **Awad al-BARASI**

Min. of Endowments & Religious Affairs: **Hamzah BUFARIS**

Min. of Finance: **Hasan ZAGLAM**

Min. of Foreign Affairs & Intl. Cooperation: **Ashur BIN KHAYAL**

Min. of Health: **Fatimah al-HAMRUSH, Dr.**

Min. for Higher Education & Scientific Research: **Naim al-GHARYANI**

Min. of Housing & Utilities: **Ibrahim al-SAGUTRI**

Min. of Industry: **Muhammad al-FUTAYSI**

Min. of the Interior: **Fawzi ABD AL-AAL**

Min. of Justice: **Ali Hamidah ASHUR**

Min. of Labor & Vocational Training: **Mustafa al-RAJBANI**

Min. of Local Govt.: **Muhammad al-Hadi al-Hashimi al-HARARI**

Min. of Martyrs, Missing, & Wounded: **Ashraf BIN ISMAIL**

Min. of Oil & Gas: **Abd al-Rahman BIN YEZAH**

Min. of Planning: **Isa al-TUWAYJIR**

Min. of Social Affairs: **Mabruka Sharif JIBRIL**

Min. of Transportation: **Yusuf al-WAHISHI**

Min. of Youth & Sports: **Fathi TARBIL**

Governor, Central Bank: **Sadiq al-KABIR**

Ambassador to the US: **Ali Suleiman AUJALI**

Permanent Representative to the UN, New York: **Abd al-Rahman Muhammad SHALGHAM**

ECONOMY

Libya's economy is structured primarily around the nation's energy sector, which generates about 95% of export earnings, 80% of GDP, and 99% of government revenue. Substantial income from the energy sector coupled with a small population give Libya one of the highest per capita GDPs in Africa, but Tripoli largely has not used its significant financial resources to develop national infrastructure or the economy, leaving many citizens poor. In the final five years of Qadhafi's rule, Libya made some progress on economic reform as part of a broader campaign to reintegrate the country into the international fold.

This effort picked up steam after UN sanctions were lifted in September 2003 and after Libya announced in December 2003 that it would abandon programs to build weapons of mass destruction. The process of lifting US unilateral sanctions began in the spring of 2004; all sanctions were removed by June 2006, helping Libya attract greater foreign direct investment, especially in the energy and banking sectors.

Libyan oil and gas licensing rounds drew high international interest, but new rounds are unlikely to be successful until Libya establishes a more permanent government and is able to offer increased security and more attractive financial terms on contracts. Libya's production of crude oil, at roughly 500,000 bbl/day, is far below the 2012 target of 3 million bbl/day set by the The National Oil Corporation (NOC). Libya faces a long road ahead in liberalizing its primarily socialist economy, but the revolution probably has unleashed previously restrained entrepreneurial activity and increased the potential for the evolution of a more market-based economy.

The service and construction sectors, which account for roughly 20% of GDP, expanded over the past five years and could expand further if Tripoli prioritizes capital spending on development projects once political uncertainty subsides. Climatic conditions and poor soils severely limit agricultural output, and Libya imports about 80% of its food. Libya's primary agricultural water source remains the Great Manmade River Project.

Labor Conditions

Qadhafi-era law prohibited children younger than 18 from being employed, except when in a form of apprenticeship. No information was available concerning whether the law limited working hours or sets occupational health and safety restrictions for children. Under Qadhafi the General People's Committee for Manpower, Employment, and Training was responsible for enforcing laws on child labor. There was no information available on the prevalence of child labor or the effect that the conflict had on the practice.

The minimum wage was 250 dinars (approximately $200) per month. Although some public sector employees, such as professors, received pay increases in recent years, a freeze imposed more than a decade before continued to depress earnings. The Qadhafi government paid an additional pension of 90 dinars ($72) for a single person, 130 dinars ($104) for a married couple, and 180 dinars ($144) for a family of more than two. The interim government generally continued these payment practices, except when wages were frozen for periods during the conflict. The government heavily subsidized rent and utilities, and government workers received an additional 130 dinars ($104) per month for food staples during 2011. One-third of Libyans lived below the poverty line.

The legal workweek was 40 hours. Under Qadhafi, the law stipulated the standard working hours, night shift regulations, dismissal procedures, and training requirements. The law did not specifically prohibit excessive compulsory overtime.

While the 2006 census counted 349,040 foreigners resident in the country, observers and diplomatic missions with large migrant populations in the country estimated that the preconflict number of undocumented workers was between 1.5 and two million. Although foreign workers reportedly constituted more than 20 percent of the workforce, the labor law applies only to legal foreign workers who have work contracts, which were a fraction of the total. Contracts, generally written in Arabic, were required for the hiring business to sponsor the worker for a visa, yet such contracts were rare and generally used only if the business was closely monitored or regulated by the Qadhafi government.

Under Qadhafi, authorities permitted foreign workers to reside in the country only for the duration of their work contracts, and workers were prohibited from sending more than half of their earnings to their home countries. There was no information on whether the interim government enforced these regulations. However, there were reports that, by year's end, it had become difficult for migrants to acquire work permits.

Foreign workers were subject to arbitrary pressures, such as changes in work rules and contracts, and had little choice other than to accept such changes or depart the country. This was especially true during the conflict, when many foreign workers fled the country and others were detained in temporary camps.

U.S.-LIBYAN RELATIONS

The United States established diplomatic relations with Libya in 1951. In 1969, the army overthrew the king, and coup leader Mu'ammar al-Qadhafi became de facto head of state. Qadhafi tried to brutally suppress an uprising against his dictatorship in 2011. Under the auspices of a UN Security Council resolution, the United States, the United Kingdom, and France launched military action to protect Libyan civilians. The North Atlantic Treaty Organization continued these efforts as "Operation Unified Protector." Qadhafi was killed during the conflict. Libya faces the challenges of building democratic institutions, protecting the universal rights of all Libyans, promoting accountable and honest government, rebuilding its economy, and establishing security throughout the country. On September 11-12, 2012, armed extremists attacked the U.S. facilities in Benghazi, killing four U.S, government personnel, including Ambassador J. Christopher Stevens.

The United States continues to have a strategic interest in a stable and prosperous Libya, and following the attacks in Benghazi, U.S. officials at the highest levels reaffirmed their support for a peaceful, democratic transition in Libya,in cooperation with the UN and other international partners.

U.S. Assistance to Libya

Recognizing Libya's own substantial resources, the United States is committed to providing targeted assistance that advances primary U.S. goals: transparent, strong and accountable security sector institutions in Libya that protect the civilian population; effectively patrol the country's vast borders; contribute to regional stability; and wrest control of weapons and vast swaths of land from extragovernmental militias.

The United States also supports the creation of a democratic Libya that is secure, peaceful, prosperous, and an active member of the international community. A fact sheet on U.S. assistance to Libya can be found here.

Bilateral Economic Relations

Oil revenues constitute Libya's principal source of foreign exchange. In 2011, the U.S. imposed sanctions on the Qadhafi regime following the outbreak of violence against civilians. Most U.S. and UN sanctions against Libyan institutions were lifted at the request of the new Libyan government. Many U.S. companies, particularly in the oil sector, have resumed their operations in Libya. The United States also has signed a trade and investment framework agreement with the Common Market for Eastern and Southern Africa, of which Libya is a member.

Libya's Membership in International Organizations

Libya and the United States belong to a number of the same international organizations, including the United Nations, International Monetary Fund, and World Bank. Libya is an observer to the World Trade Organization.

Bilateral Representation

Libya maintains an embassy in the United States at 2600 Virginia Avenue NW, Suite 705, Washington DC 20037 (tel: 202-944-9601).

Principal U.S. Embassy Officials

Last Updated: 1/14/2013

TRIPOLI (E) , 218 91 220 3239, Workweek: Sun–Thurs, 08:00–16:45, Website: http://libya.usembassy.gov/

AMB OMS:	Sandra L McInturff
ECON/COM:	Hannah A Draper
FM:	Michael P Duprez
HRO:	Martin, Valerie J
MGT:	Richard L McInturff
SDO/DATT:	LTC Keith Phillips
AMB:	Charge Laurence E Pope
CON:	Jenny Cordell
DCM:	David C McFarland
PAO:	Mietek Boduszynski
GSO:	Philip J Richards
RSO:	James Bacigalupo
AID:	Maura E McCormick
FMO:	Wagih H Ibrahim
IMO:	Greg Lee
IPO:	Frank E Wierman
ISO:	Richard J. Bushby
ISSO:	Richard J. Bushby

TRAVEL

Consular Information Sheet

August 27, 2012

Country Description: Libya witnessed a popular uprising against the regime of Colonel Muammar Qadhafi that lasted from February to October 2011 and included fighting throughout the country. Libyans cast ballots July 7 in elections deemed to be free and fair according to election observers. Libya's General National Congress replaced the Transitional National Council in August 2012 and will lead the country until elections are held on the basis of a new constitution. Islamic ideals and beliefs provide the conservative foundation of the country's customs, laws, and practices.

The U.S. Embassy in Libya resumed operations on September 22, 2011. Consular services for U.S. citizens resumed August 27, 2012.

Smart Traveler Enrollment Program (STEP)/Embassy Locations: If you are going to live in or visit Libya, please take the time to tell our Embassy about your trip. If you enroll in the Smart Traveler Enrollment Program, we can keep you up to date with important safety and security announcements. It will also help your friends and family get in touch with you in an emergency.

U.S. Embassy Tripoli
Walee al-Ahad Street
Airport Road District
Telephone: 218 91 220 3239
For emergencies involving U.S. citizens only:
telephone 218 91 220 5203
Email: consulartripoli@state.gov

Entry/Exit Requirements for U.S. Citizens: Passports and visas are required for all U.S. citizens traveling to Libya. Currently, Libyan embassies abroad are operating under varying conditions; travelers are encouraged to reach out to the Libyan embassy in the country in which they reside to obtain the latest information on visa procedures. Libyan immigration officials sometimes require endorsement letters from the Transitional National Council as well.

The Government of Libya does not allow persons with passports bearing an Israeli visa or entry/exit stamps from Israel to enter Libya.

Tourist Visas: After halting the issuance of tourist visas to U.S. citizens for several years, in June 2010 the Libyan government again began issuing visas to U.S. tourists. Like European tourists, U.S. citizens must apply for tourist visas through tour operators licensed in Libya, who will file the necessary paperwork for the visa with the Libyan authorities. Through licensed tour agencies, tourist visas can be obtained for U.S. tourists within 4 to15 days. Fees for obtaining the visas vary between tour companies. Upon completion of the process, the tourist will receive a letter in Arabic listing his/her passport number and authorizing the issuance of a visa at the Libyan port of entry. This letter must be obtained prior to travel to Libya. Once the tourist is in Libya, he/she must obtain a registration stamp in his/her passport from the Libyan tourist police; this procedure can also be handled by tour agencies. Libyan authorities informed the U.S. Department of State in November 2010 that Arabic passport translations are not required for U.S. citizen tourists. Most European tourists now travel to Libya without the passport translation, and since June 2010, U.S. tourists have entered Libya without having the translation.

Note that these new procedures apply only to tourist visas and should not, under any circumstances, be used for business travel to Libya. Using a tourist visa to travel to Libya for business purposes contravenes Libyan law, and places the traveler at risk of arrest.

Business Visas: U.S. citizens traveling to Libya on business visas require an invitation from/sponsorship by a company operating in Libya. U.S. citizens who apply for Libyan business visas often experience significant delays, regularly waiting several weeks or months for their visas. All visas are vetted and approved by Libyan immigration departments in Tripoli and are only issued by the appropriate Libyan Embassy upon receipt of that approval. There may be an additional wait for actual visa issuance once approval has been received by the Embassy. The U.S. Embassy in Tripoli cannot provide assistance to U.S. citizens seeking Libyan visas.

Inquiries about obtaining a Libyan visa should be made through the Libyan Embassy in Washington, D.C. The Embassy is located at 2600 Virginia Avenue NW, Suite 705, Washington, DC 20037; 202-944-9601, fax 202-944-9606. Libya's land borders with Egypt and Tunisia are subject to periodic closures even to travelers with valid Libyan visas. Short-term closures of other land borders may occur with little notice. Within three days of arrival in Libya, visitors must register at the police station closest to where they are residing or they may encounter problems during their stay or upon departure.

The Libyan government requires all its citizens, including dual nationals, to enter and depart Libya on Libyan documents. In some cases U.S. citizens of Libyan descent have entered Libya on an old or expired Libyan identity document and then discovered that they cannot depart Libya without obtaining a valid Libyan passport, which can be a time-consuming, cumbersome process.

Some HIV/AIDS entry restrictions exist for visitors to and foreign residents of Libya. Please verify this information with the Libyan Embassy in Washington, D.C., before you travel.

Threats to Safety and Security: After the February 2011 uprising, various militias have supplanted the police in maintaining internal security. Militia members operate checkpoints within and between major cities. Libyan militia members are poorly trained and loosely affiliated with the interim government, which has not yet fully reconstituted the national army and police. The Embassy receives frequent reports of clashes between rival militias and occasional reports of vigilante revenge killings. Foreigners have been detained by militia groups, often for arbitrary or unclear reasons and without access to a lawyer. U.S. citizens are advised to carry proof of citizenship and valid immigration status on them at all times. The Embassy has extremely limited capacity to assist U.S. citizens who have been detained by militia groups. Because the Libyan government does not recognize dual citizenship, dual Libyan-U.S. citizens are not afforded access to U.S. embassy officials when they are detained.

Public demonstrations occur frequently in Libya in the central squares of cities, such as Martyrs' Square in Tripoli and Freedom Square in Benghazi. U.S. citizens are advised to avoid these demonstrations and take cover if they hear celebratory gun fire.

Recent worldwide terrorism alerts, including the Department of State's Worldwide Caution, have stated that extremist groups continue to plan terrorist attacks against U.S. interests in the Middle East region. In June 2012, an unknown group of attackers detonated an improvised explosive device outside the compound of the U.S. embassy's office in Benghazi. There have also been attacks on diplomatic vehicle convoys. Any U.S. citizen who decides to travel to Libya should maintain a strong security posture by being aware of surroundings, avoiding crowds and demonstrations, keeping a low profile, and varying times and routes for all required travel.

The Department of State advises U.S. citizens to exercise caution and comply with local regulations when traveling in desert and border regions of Libya. Terrorist attacks in Algeria, the June 2009 murder of a U.S. citizen teacher in Mauritania, kidnappings of Western tourists in desert regions of Tunisia and Egypt in 2011 and 2012, northern Niger in 2010, and Mali in January 2009, and the terrorist activity of al-Qaida in the Islamic Maghreb in North Africa are indicative of a continued threat in the region.

Filming or taking photographs of anything that could be perceived as being of military or security interest may result in problems with the Libyan authorities.

Stay up to date by:

- Bookmarking our Bureau of Consular Affairs website, which contains the current Travel Warnings and Travel Alerts as well as the Worldwide Caution.
- Following us on Twitter and the Bureau of Consular Affairs page on Facebook as well.
- Downloading our free Smart Traveler IPhone App to have travel information at your fingertips.
- Calling 1-888-407-4747 toll-free within the U.S. and Canada, or a regular toll line, 1-202-501- 4444, from other countries.
- Taking some time before travel to consider your personal security.

Crime: Crime levels in Tripoli have significantly increased since the fall of the Qadhafi regime. There have been increased reports of armed robbery, carjacking, burglary, and crimes involving weapons. The Libyan police and internal security institutions have not fully reconstituted themselves since the revolution, and the majority of the 16,000 criminals released from prisons by the former regime remain at large. Hundreds of thousands of small arms looted from government storage facilities are now in the hands of the local population, which has also contributed to the rise in violent crime.

Victims of Crime: If you or someone you know becomes the victim of a crime abroad, you should contact the local police and the nearest U.S. embassy or consulate. We can:

- Replace a stolen passport.
- Help you find appropriate medical care if you are the victim of violent crimes such as assault or rape.
- Put you in contact with the appropriate police authorities, and if you want us to, we can contact family members or friend.
- Help you understand the local criminal justice process and direct you to local attorneys, although it is important to remember that local authorities are responsible for investigating and prosecuting the crime.

The local equivalent to the "911" emergency line in Libya is 1515. This number is generally monitored only in Arabic.

Criminal Penalties: While you are traveling in Libya, you are subject to its laws even if you are a U.S. citizen. Foreign laws and legal systems can be vastly different from our own. In some places you may be taken in for questioning if you don't have your passport with you. In some places, it is illegal to take pictures of certain buildings. In some places driving under the influence could land you immediately in jail. These criminal penalties will vary from country to country. There are also some things that might be legal in the country you visit, but still illegal in the United States, and you can be prosecuted under U.S. law if you buy pirated goods. Engaging in sexual conduct with children or using or disseminating child pornography in a foreign country is a crime prosecutable in the United States. If you break local laws in Libya, your U.S. passport won't help you avoid arrest or prosecution. It's very important to know what's legal and what's not where you are going.

Persons violating Libyan laws, even unknowingly, may be expelled, arrested, or imprisoned. Penalties for possessing, using, or trafficking in illegal drugs in Libya are severe, and convicted offenders can expect long jail sentences and heavy fines. Alcohol is also prohibited in Libya, and possessing, using, or trafficking in alcohol can carry severe penalties.

While some countries will automatically notify the nearest U.S. embassy or consulate if a U.S. citizen is detained or arrested in a foreign country, that might not always be the case. To ensure that the United States is aware of your circumstances, request that the police and prison officials notify the nearest U.S. embassy or consulate as soon as you are arrested or detained overseas.

Special Circumstances: Libya's economy operates on a "cash-only" basis for most transactions, even though U.S. law now permits the use in Libya of credit cards and checks drawn on U.S. banks. A few hotels, restaurants, and major airlines are the only businesses known to accept credit cards (Visa is accepted more often than MasterCard). It is recommended that travelers consult their credit card entity prior to travel to ensure that transactions from Libya can be accepted by that entity. A number of ATMs are in service at a few large hotels, major office complexes, the airport, and one or two markets, although their availability is sporadic. Foreign visitors should be aware that the penalties for use of unauthorized currency dealers are severe. The Libyan workweek is Sunday-Thursday.

A number of Libyan entities have assets frozen by economic sanctions. For further information, please contact the Office of Foreign Assets Control at the Treasury Department.

Libyan customs authorities enforce strict regulations concerning the introduction into Libya or removal from Libya of firearms, religious materials, antiquities, medications, and currency. The importation and consumption of alcohol, pornography, and pork products are illegal in Libya.

In addition to being subject to all Libyan laws, U.S. citizens of Libyan origin may also be subject to laws that impose special obligations on Libyan citizens. The Government of Libya considers all children born to Libyan fathers to be Libyan citizens, even if they were not issued a Libyan birth certificate or a Libyan passport. Dual Libyan-American nationals may not enter or leave Libya on their U.S. passports and must obtain a Libyan travel document before traveling to Libya. Persons with dual nationality who travel to Libya on their Libyan passports are normally treated as Libyan citizens by the local government. The U.S. Embassy's ability to provide U.S. consular assistance to those traveling on Libyan passports is extremely limited.

Accessibility: While in Libya, individuals with disabilities may find accessibility and accommodation very different from what you find in the United States.

Libyan law provides for the rights of persons with physical, sensory, intellectual, and mental disabilities, and provides for monetary and other types of social care. A number of government-approved organizations care for persons with disabilities and protect access to employment, education, health care, and other state services. Few public facilities have adequate access for persons with physical disabilities.

Medical Facilities and Health Information: While some health care providers have been trained in the United States or Europe, basic modern medical care and/or medicines may not be available in Libya. Many Libyan citizens prefer to be treated outside Libya for ailments such as heart disease and diabetes.

You can find detailed information on vaccinations and other health precautions on the CDC website. For information about outbreaks of infectious diseases abroad, consult the World Health Organization (WHO) website. The WHO website also contains additional health information for travelers, including detailed country-specific health information.

Medical Insurance: You can't assume your insurance will go with you when you travel. It's very important to find out BEFORE you leave. You need to ask your insurance company two questions:

- Does my policy apply when I'm out of the United States?
- Will it cover emergencies like a trip to a foreign hospital or an evacuation?

Most health care facilities in Libya expect payment in cash at the time of service even if you are hospitalized. They will not bill your insurance. It will be up to you to file the necessary paperwork with your insurance company. Your regular U.S. health insurance may not cover doctors' and hospital visits in other countries. If your policy doesn't go with you when you travel, it's a very good idea to take out another one for your trip.

Traffic Safety and Road Conditions: While in a foreign country, U.S. citizens may encounter road conditions that differ significantly from those in the United States. The information below concerning Libya is provided for general reference only, and may not be totally accurate in a particular location or circumstance.

Driving in Libya can be hazardous, and there is a high accident rate. Enforcement of traffic laws is rare. As a result, it is often difficult to anticipate the actions of other drivers on Libyan streets and highways. Windblown sand can reduce visibility without warning. Road conditions are poor, and public transportation, which is limited to occasional bus service, is poor. Taxis are available, but many taxi drivers are reckless and untrained, and English-speaking drivers areextremely rare. The sidewalks in urban areas are often in bad condition and cluttered, but pedestrians are able to use them.

Paved roads in rural areas are satisfactory; however, many rural roads are unpaved (i.e., dirt roads). Also, major highways along the seacoast and leading south merge into single-lane highways once they are outside the cities. These roads are heavily trafficked and can be precarious to navigate, especially at night and during the winter rainy season. The presence of sand deposits, as well as domestic and wild animals that frequently cross these highways and rural roads, makes them even more hazardous.

The availability of roadside assistance is extremely limited and offered only in Arabic. In urban areas and near the outskirts of major cities there is a greater possibility of assistance by police and emergency ambulance services, although they are usually ill-equipped to deal with serious injuries or accidents. Very few streets are marked or have signage, and highway signs are normally available only in Arabic.

Aviation Safety Oversight: As there is no direct commercial air service to the United States by carriers registered in Libya, the U.S. Federal Aviation Administration (FAA) has not assessed the government of Libya's Civil Aviation Authority for compliance with International Civil Aviation Organization (ICAO) aviation safety standards. Further information may be found on the FAA's safety assessment page. In addition, the FAA maintains prohibitions on flight operations over or within Libya by U.S. air carriers, commercial operators and airmen under a Special Federal Aviation Regulation. More information is available on the FAA website.

In general, aviation safety conditions have not yet returned to pre-revolutionary levels. A number of airlines have instituted additional security checks, such as passenger screening at the gate and additional screening of all passenger luggage. To the extent possible, U.S. government direct-hire personnel are instructed to travel on commercial airlines that utilize these additional security measures. U.S. citizens departing Libya should contact their airline directly to determine what secondary screening procedures, if any, are in place.

Children's Issues: Please see the U.S. Dept. of State Office of Children's Issues web pages on intercountry adoption and international parental child abduction.

Travel Warning

January 2, 2013

The Department of State warns U.S. citizens of the risks of traveling to Libya and strongly advises against all but essential travel to Tripoli and all travel to Benghazi, Bani Walid, and southern Libya, including border areas and the regions of Sabha and Kufra. Because of ongoing instability and violence, the Department's ability to provide consular services to U.S. citizens in these regions of Libya is extremely limited. This Travel Warning supersedes the Travel Warning dated September 12, 2012.

On September 12, the Department of State ordered the departure of all non-emergency U.S. government personnel from Libya following the attack on the U.S. diplomatic mission in Benghazi. The security situation in Libya remains unpredictable. Sporadic episodes of civil unrest have occurred throughout the country. U.S. citizens should avoid areas of demonstrations and exercise caution if in the vicinity of any large gatherings, protests, or demonstrations, as even demonstrations intended to be peaceful can turn confrontational and escalate into violence. U.S. citizens traveling to, or remaining in, Libya should use caution and limit nonessential travel within the country, make their own contingency emergency plans, and maintain security awareness at all times.

We strongly recommend that U.S. citizens traveling to or residing in Libya enroll in the Department of State's Smart Traveler Enrollment Program (STEP) at https://step.state.gov/step. STEP enrollment gives you the latest security updates and makes it easier for the U.S. embassy or nearest U.S. consulate to contact you in an emergency. If you don't have internet access, enroll directly with the nearest U.S. embassy or consulate.

The Embassy's website includes consular information and the most recent messages for U.S. citizens in Libya. U.S. citizens in need of emergency assistance should call 091-379-4560 within Libya or 218-91-379-4560 if dialing from outside of Libya.

For information on "What the Department of State Can and Can't Do in a Crisis," please visit the Bureau of Consular Affairs' Emergencies and Crisis link. Up-to-date information on security can also be obtained by calling 1-888-407-4747 toll-free in the United States and Canada or, for callers outside the United States and Canada, on a regular toll line at 1-202-501-4444. These numbers are available from 8:00 a.m. to 8:00 p.m. Eastern Daylight Time, Monday through Friday (except U.S. federal holidays).

For further information, U.S. citizens should consult the Department of State's Country Specific Information for Libya. Stay up to date by bookmarking our Bureau of Consular Affairs website, which contains the current Travel Warnings and Travel Alerts as well as the Worldwide Caution. Follow us on Twitter and the Bureau of Consular Affairs page on Facebook as well. You can also download our free Smart Traveler App, available through iTunes and the Android market to have travel information at your fingertips.

Intercountry Adoption

May 2011

Libya is not party to the Hague Convention on Protection of Children and Co-operation in Respect of Intercountry Adoption (Hague Adoption Convention). Therefore, when the Hague Adoption Convention entered into force for the United States on April 1, 2008, intercountry adoption processing for Libya did not change.

The Department of State does not maintain files on the adoption process in Libya because adoptions from Libya are rare; fewer than five adoptions by American citizen parents have taken place since 2000.

LIECHTENSTEIN

Compiled from publications that were available as of February 2013 from the U.S. Department of State, the U.S. Department of Commerce, and the Central Intelligence Agency (CIA). See the introduction to this set for explanatory notes.

Official Name:
Principality of Liechtenstein

PROFILE

Geography

Area: total: 160 sq km; country comparison to the world: 219; land: 160 sq km; water: 0 sq km
Major cities: Vaduz (capital) 5,000 (2009)
Climate: continental; cold, cloudy winters with frequent snow or rain; cool to moderately warm, cloudy, humid summers
Terrain: mostly mountainous (Alps) with Rhine Valley in western third

People

Nationality: noun: Liechtensteiner(s); adjective: Liechtenstein
Population: 36,713 (July 2012 est.)
Population growth rate: 0.795% (2012 est.)
Ethnic groups: Liechtensteiner 65.6%, other 34.4% (2000 census)
Religions: Roman Catholic (official) 76.2%, Protestant 7%, unknown 10.6%, other 6.2% (June 2002)
Languages: German (official), Alemannic dialect
Literacy: definition: age 10 and over can read and write; total population: 100%; male: 100%; female: 100%
Health: life expectancy at birth: total population: 81.5 years; male: 79.37 years; female: 84.19 years (2012 est.); Infant mortality rate: total: 4.39 deaths/1,000 live births; male: 4.67 deaths/1,000 live births; female: 4.04 deaths/1,000 live births (2012 est.)
Unemployment rate: 2.8% (2009)
Work force: 34,334 (2010)

Government

Type: hereditary constitutional monarchy
Independence: 23 January 1719
Constitution: 5 October 1921; amended 15 September 2003
Political subdivisions: 11 communes (Gemeinden, singular—Gemeinde); Balzers, Eschen, Gamprin, Mauren, Planken, Ruggell, Schaan, Schellenberg, Triesen, Triesenberg, Vaduz
Suffrage: 18 years of age; universal

Economy

GDP (purchasing power parity): $5.003 billion (2009); $5.028 billion (2008); $4.16 billion (2007)
GDP real growth rate: -0.5% (2009 est.); 1.8% (2008 est.); 3.1% (2007 est.)
GDP per capita (PPP): $143,900 (2009 est.); $141,100 (2008 est.); $147,500 (2007 est.)
Natural resources: hydroelectric potential, arable land
Agriculture products: wheat, barley, corn, potatoes; livestock, dairy products
Industries: electronics, metal manufacturing, dental products, ceramics, pharmaceuticals, food products, precision instruments, tourism, optical instruments
Exports: $2.79 billion (2009); $3.92 billion (2008)
Exports—commodities: small specialty machinery, connectors for audio and video, parts for motor vehicles, dental products, hardware, prepared foodstuffs, electronic equipment, optical products
Imports: $1.73 billion (2009); $2.59 billion (2008)
Imports—commodities: agricultural products, raw materials, energy products, machinery, metal goods, textiles, foodstuffs, motor vehicles
Debt—external: $0 (2001)
Exchange rates: Swiss francs (CHF) per US dollar; 0.888 (2011); 1.0429 (2010); 1.0881 (2009); 1.0774 (2008); 1.1973 (2007)

PEOPLE

National/Racial/Ethnic Minorities

Foreign nationals, mostly Swiss, Austrian, German, and Italian, represented 33 percent of the resident population. Ethnic Turks accounted for 6.5 percent of the foreign population.

Religion

According to the 2010 census, membership in religious groups was as follows: 76 percent Roman Catholic; 7.6 percent Protestant; 5.4 percent Muslim; 2.8 percent professing no formal creed; 1.1 percent Christian Orthodox; 1.7 percent other religious groups; and 5.3 percent indicated no religious affiliation.

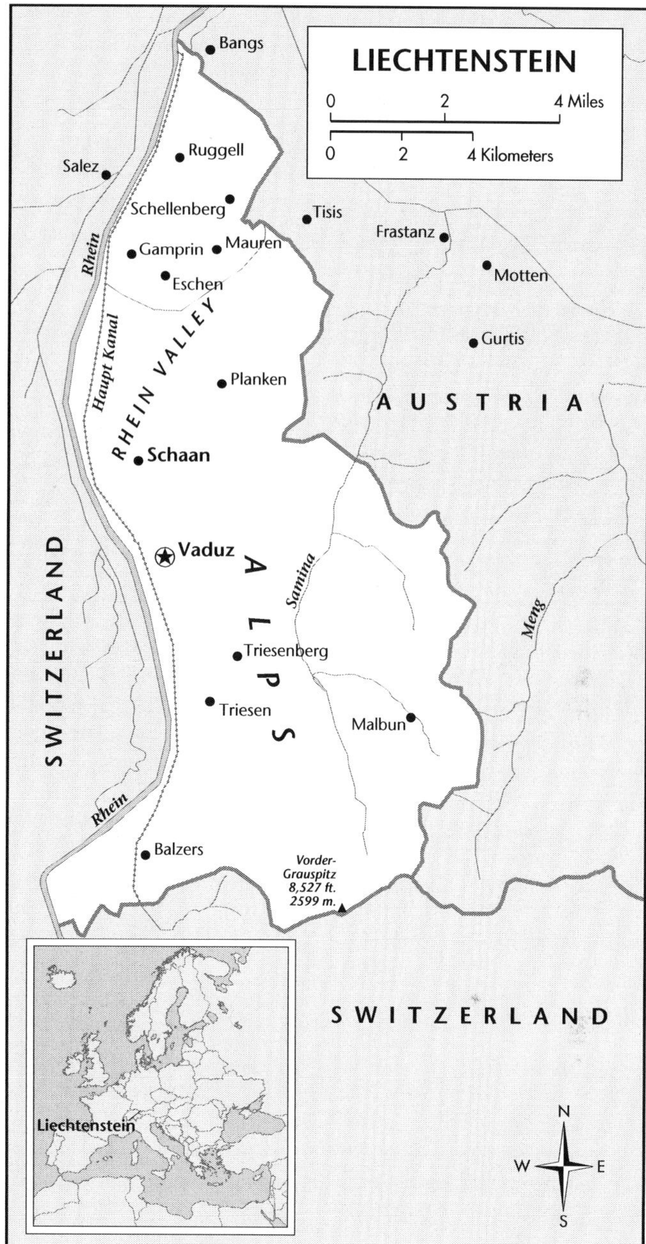

HISTORY

The Liechtenstein family, of Austrian origin, acquired the fiefs of Vaduz and Schellenberg in 1699 and 1713 respectively, and gained the status of an independent principality of the Holy Roman Empire in 1719 under the name Liechtenstein. The French, under Napoleon, occupied the country for a few years. Napoleon was the founder of the Rhine Confederation in 1806 and accepted Liechtenstein as a member.

Liechtenstein considers itself therefore to be a sovereign state since 1806. In 1815 within the new German Confederation, Liechtenstein could prove its independence once more. In 1868, after the German Confederation dissolved, Liechtenstein disbanded its army of 80 men and declared its permanent neutrality, which was declared during both world wars.

In 1919, Liechtenstein and Switzerland concluded an agreement whereby Switzerland assumed representation of Liechtenstein's diplomatic and consular interests in countries where Switzerland maintains representation and Liechtenstein does not. According to an agreement concluded with Austria in 1979, Liechtenstein citizens may seek consular assistance from Austrian representatives abroad in countries in which neither Liechtenstein nor Switzerland maintain representation.

After World War II, Liechtenstein became increasingly important as a financial center, resulting in more prosperity. In 1989, Prince Hans Adam II succeeded his father to the throne and in 1996 settled a long-running dispute with Russia over the Liechtenstein family's archives, which had been confiscated during the Soviet occupation of Vienna in 1945 and later moved to Moscow. Liechtenstein has been a participating state of the Organization for Security and Cooperation in Europe (OSCE) since the 1975 start of its predecessor, the Conference on Security and Cooperation in Europe (CSCE). Liechtenstein became a member of the Council of Europe in 1978 and joined the UN in 1990, the European Free Trade Association (EFTA) in 1991, and both the European Economic Area (EEA) and World Trade Organization (WTO) in 1995.

GOVERNMENT AND POLITICAL CONDITIONS

The Principality of Liechtenstein is a multiparty constitutional monarchy with a parliamentary government.

The unicameral Landtag (parliament) nominates, and the monarch appoints, the members of the government. A two-party coalition government was formed following free and fair parliamentary elections in 2009.

As a hereditary monarchy, the country's line of succession is restricted to male descendents of the Liechtenstein dynasty. Prince Hans Adam II is the head of state. In 2004 Hereditary Prince Alois assumed the duties of head of state, exercising the rights of office on behalf of the reigning prince. All legislation enacted by the parliament must have the concurrence of the monarch and the prime minister.

Recent Elections

In 2009 the country held free and fair parliamentary elections.

Participation of Women and Minorities: There were six women in the 25-member parliament and two women in the five-seat cabinet. There were no known members of minorities in the government.

Principal Government Officials

Last Updated: 1/31/2013

Head of State: **HANS ADAM II, Prince**
Prime Min.: **Klaus TSCHUETSCHER**
Dep. Prime Min.: **Martin MEYER**
Min. of Construction: **Martin MEYER**
Min. of Cultural Affairs: **Aurelia FRICK**
Min. of Economics: **Martin MEYER**
Min. of Education: **Hugo QUADERER**
Min. of Environmental Affairs, Land-Use Planning, Agriculture, & Forestry: **Renate MUESSNER**
Min. of Family Affairs & Equal Opportunity: **Klaus TSCHUETSCHER**
Min. of Finance: **Klaus TSCHUETSCHER**
Min. of Foreign Affairs: **Aurelia FRICK**
Min. of General Govt. Affairs: **Klaus TSCHUETSCHER**
Min. of Interior: **Hugo QUADERER**
Min. of Justice: **Aurelia FRICK**
Min. of Public Health: **Renate MUESSNER**
Min. of Social Affairs: **Renate MUESSNER**
Min. of Sports: **Hugo QUADERER**
Min. of Transportation: **Martin MEYER**
Chmn., Liechtenstein State Bank: **Josef FEHR**
Ambassador to the US: **Claudia FRITSCHE**
Permanent Representative to the UN, New York: **Christian WENAWESER**

ECONOMY

Despite its small size and limited natural resources, Liechtenstein has developed into a prosperous, highly industrialized, free-enterprise economy with a vital financial service sector and likely the second highest per capita income in the world.

The Liechtenstein economy is widely diversified with a large number of small businesses. Low business taxes—the maximum tax rate is 20%—and easy incorporation rules have induced many holding companies to establish nominal offices in Liechtenstein providing 30% of state revenues.

The country participates in a customs union with Switzerland and uses the Swiss franc as its national currency. It imports more than 90% of its energy requirements.

Liechtenstein has been a member of the European Economic Area (an organization serving as a bridge between the European Free Trade Association (EFTA) and the EU) since May 1995. The government is working to harmonize its economic policies with those of an integrated Europe.

Since 2008, Liechtenstein has faced renewed international pressure—particularly from Germany—to improve transparency in its banking and tax systems. In December 2008, Liechtenstein signed a Tax Information Exchange Agreement with the US. Upon Liechtenstein's conclusion of 12 bilateral information-sharing agreements, the OECD in October 2009 removed the principality from its "grey list" of countries that had yet to implement the organization's Model Tax Convention. By the end of 2010, Liechtenstein had signed 25 Tax Information Exchange Agreements or Double Tax Agreements. In 2011 Liechtenstein joined the Schengen area, which allows passport-free travel across 26 European countries.

Labor Conditions

There are laws and policies to protect children from exploitation in the workplace, and the government effectively enforced these laws. The law prohibits the employment of children younger than 16; exceptions may be made for the limited employment of children who are 14 and older and for those who leave school after completing nine years of compulsory education. Children who are 14 and older may be employed in light duties for not more than nine hours per week during the school year and 15 hours per week at other times.

The law prohibits labor that subjects children to physical, psychological, moral, or sexual abuse. The government devoted adequate resources and oversight to child labor policies, and the Department for Worker Safety of the Office of the National Economy effectively supervised compliance with the law.

There is no national minimum wage. The Liechtenstein Workers Association negotiates minimum wages annually with the Chamber of Commerce and the Chamber for Economic Affairs. The government estimated the poverty income level at approximately 28,000 Swiss francs ($29,300) per year, which equals 2,300 Swiss francs ($2,400) monthly, for a household (two adults and two children) and around 1,100 Swiss francs ($1,153) per month for a single person.

The law sets the maximum workweek at 45 hours for white-collar workers and employees of industrial firms and sales personnel, and 48 hours for other workers. The law provides for a daily mandatory one-hour break and an 11-hour rest period for full-time workers; with few exceptions, Sunday work is not allowed. Pay for overtime is required to be at least 25 percent higher than the standard rate, and overtime is generally restricted to two hours per day.

The average workweek, including overtime, may not exceed 48 hours over a period of four consecutive months. Thousands of workers commuted from neighboring countries daily and were covered by the same standards.

U.S.-LIECHTENSTEIN RELATIONS

The United States established diplomatic relations with Liechtenstein in 1997. The good relations between the two countries are based on close commercial interactions and common support for democracy, human rights, and free markets. The United States and Liechtenstein have signed a mutual legal assistance treaty, focused largely on jointly combating money laundering and other illegal banking activities, and a tax information exchange agreement. The United States does not have an embassy in Liechtenstein, but the U.S. Ambassador to Switzerland is also accredited to Liechtenstein.

U.S. Assistance to Liechtenstein

The United States provides no development assistance to Liechtenstein.

Bilateral Economic Relations

Liechtenstein and Switzerland represent one mutual economic area with open borders between the two countries. European Free Trade Area countries, which include Liechtenstein and Switzerland, are significant markets for U.S. exporters and investors.

Liechtenstein's Membership in International Organizations

Liechtenstein and the United States belong to a number of the same international organizations, including the United Nations, Organization for Security and Cooperation in Europe, and World Trade Organization.

Bilateral Representation

Liechtenstein maintains an embassy in the United States at 2900 K Street, NW, Suite 602B, Washington, DC 20007; tel. (202) 331-0590.

Principal U.S. Embassy Officials

Last Updated: 1/14/2013

BERN (E) Sulgeneckstrasse 19, CH-3007, Bern, 41-31-357-7011, Fax 41–31–357-7344, Workweek: Mon.–Fri., 8:30–5:30, http://bern.usembassy.gov/

DCM OMS:	Joanna Marcinkowska
AMB OMS:	Sandra Proteau
FM:	Rodney Schellack
MGT:	Matthew Shields
POL/ECON:	Marty Dale
SDO/DATT:	COL William Langan
AMB:	Donald S. Beyer
CG:	Randy Townsend
DCM:	Charge Susan Elbow
PAO:	Alex Daniels
GSO:	Gregory Robinson
RSO:	Peter Shephard
CLO:	Sylvia Shephard
DEA:	Sam Masiello
ECON:	Scott Woodard
IMO:	Demian Lamadrid
LEGATT:	Michael McGarrity

TRAVEL

Consular Information Sheet—Switzerland and Liechtenstein

November 15, 2011

Country Description: Switzerland is a highly developed democracy. The Principality of Liechtenstein is a democratically run constitutional monarchy divided into 11 municipalities.

Smart Traveler Enrollment Program (STEP)/Embassy Locations: If you are going to live in or visit Switzerland or Liechtenstein, please take the time to tell our embassy about your trip. If you sign up, we can keep you up to date with important safety and security announcements. It will also help your friends and family get in touch with you in an emergency.

United States Embassy Bern
Sulgeneckstrasse 19, 3007 Bern
Telephone: (41) (31) 357-7011
(2 p.m.—5 p.m.)
Emergency phone:
after-ours/weekends
(41) (31) 357-7777
Facsimile: (41) (31) 357-7280

United States Consular Agency Zurich, Zurich America Center
Dufourstrasse 101, 8008 Zurich
Telephone: (41) (43) 499-2960
(10 a.m.—1 p.m.)
Facsimile: (41) (43) 499-2961
Email: zurich-ca@state.gov

United States Consular Agency, Geneva
rue Versonnex 7, 1207 Geneva
Telephone: (41) (22) 840-5160
(10 a.m.—1 p.m.)
Facsimile: (41) (22) 840-5162.
Geneva-CA@state.gov

There is no U.S. embassy or consulate in Liechtenstein. For assistance and information on travel and security in Liechtenstein, U.S. citizens may contact or register with the U.S. Embassy in Bern.

Entry/Exit Requirements for U.S. Citizens: Switzerland extends visa-free entry to U.S. citizens staying in Switzerland for up to 90 days (consecutive or combined, within a six-month period) for tourist or business purposes. The passport should be valid for at least three months beyond the period of stay. Switzerland is a party to the Schengen Agreement, which allows for free travel within a multi-country zone of Europe.

Liechtenstein also has no visa requirement for U.S. citizens for stays up to 90 days. If you are planning on staying in Liechtenstein for a longer period of time, make sure to obtain a stamp in your passport from the police office in Buchs, or at the border control in Schaanwald during office hours. This will assist you in avoiding any problems when departing Liechtenstein. Liechtenstein is not a party to the Schengen Agreement. For more information on entry requirements for both countries, including for stays in excess of 90 days, travelers should contact the Embassy of Switzerland at 2900 Cathedral Avenue, N.W., Washington, D.C. 20008, telephone (202) 745-7900, or a Swiss Consulate General in Atlanta, Chicago, Los Angeles, New York, or San Francisco. The U.S. Department of State is unaware of any HIV/AIDS entry restrictions for visitors to or foreign residents of Switzerland.

Threats to Safety and Security: Switzerland remains largely free of terrorist incidents; however, like other countries in the Schengen area, Switzerland's open borders with its Western European neighbors allow for the possibility of terrorist groups entering/exiting the country anonymously. You should remain vigilant with regard to your personal security. Although there have been no recent terrorist attacks in Switzerland, violence by anti-globalization, anti-Semitic, and anti-establishment (anarchist) groups does occur from time to time. This violence is typically in the form of property damage and clashes between these groups and the police. The potential for specific threats of violence involving U.S. citizens in Switzerland is remote. Nevertheless, the Consular Agencies in Zurich and Geneva may close periodically to assess their security situation. Public demonstrations occasionally take place, mostly in Zurich, Geneva, and Bern. These events are almost always known in advance to the police, who provide appropriate personnel to observe them and maintain order. Such demonstrations rarely turn violent; nonetheless, you should avoid them if at all possible.

Stay up to date by:

- Bookmarking our Bureau of Consular Affairs website, which contains the current Travel Warnings and Travel Alerts as well as the Worldwide Caution.
- Following us on Twitter and the Bureau of Consular Affairs page on Facebook as well.
- Downloading our free Smart Traveler iPhone App to have travel information at your fingertip; and,
- Calling 1-888-407-4747 toll-free within the U.S. and Canada, or a regular toll line, 1-202-501-4444, from other countries.
- Taking some time before travel to consider your personal security.

Crime: Switzerland has a low rate of violent crime; however, crimes of all types which may include violence do occur. Pick-pocketing and purse snatching are the most common and frequently occur in the vicinity of train and bus stations, airports, and some public parks, especially during peak tourist periods (such as summer and Christmas) and when conferences, shows, or exhibits are scheduled in major cities. Be especially vigilant in the airports and railway stations in both Zurich and Geneva, as these locations experience multiple incidents of petty theft almost every day.

Liechtenstein has a low crime rate. You should be careful on trains, especially on overnight trains to neighboring countries. Thieves, who steal from passengers while they sleep, can enter even locked sleeping compartments. Thieves have been known to work in pairs to target train passengers; while one member of the pair creates a diversion at a train window or on a platform, the other steals items you have left briefly unattended. In many countries around the world, counterfeit and pirated goods are widely available. Transactions involving such products may be illegal under local law. In addition, bringing them back to the United States may result in forfeitures and/or fines.

Victims of Crime: If you or someone you know becomes the victim of a crime abroad, you should contact the local police and the nearest U.S. embassy or consulate. We can:

- Replace a stolen passport;
- Help you find appropriate medical care if you are the victim of a violent crime such as assault or rape;
- Put you in contact with the appropriate police authorities, and if you want us to, we can contact family members or friend; and,
- Help you understand the local criminal justice process and direct you to local attorneys, although it is important to remember that local authorities are responsible for investigating and prosecuting the crime.

The local equivalent to the "911" emergency line in Switzerland is 144 for medical/ambulance services; 117 for the police department; and 118 for the fire department.

Criminal Penalties: While you are traveling in Switzerland, you are subject to its laws even if you are a U.S.citizen. Foreign laws and legal systems can be vastly different than our own. In Switzerland it is expected that citizens and visitors carry an I.D. and/or a passport. Should the police stop you, and you are without an I.D., it is possible that you may be taken in for questioning. This is the decision of the individual police officer. Travelers should also be aware that photography is not allowed in certain areas (for example, at military airports). Please observe posted signs regarding photography.

Driving under the influence of alcohol can lead to heavy fines and/or a ban from driving or in severe cases, a jail sentence, depending on the percentage of alcohol in the blood;. Swiss law only allows up to 0.05% blood alcohol content (whereas the legal limit in the United States is 0.08%). Driving speeds in Switzerland are also much slower than in the rest of Europe and vary from area to area.

In residential areas the speed limit is 30 km/h (18.6 m/h), on urban roads 50 km/h (31 m/h), on rural roads 80 km/h (49.7 m/h), on minor highways 100 km/h (62 m/h) and on the Autobahn

120 km/h (74.5 m/h). Travelers are advised to carefully observe the posted speed limits.

Traffic fines are costly and vary according to where the infraction occurs and by how much one exceeds the speed limit. Fines assessed within the city limits are higher than those assessed on a highway or autobahn.

The court appearance carries a fine ranging from CHF 500-CHF 1,000 (US $683-1,270) and other penalties the court deems appropriate.

Running a red light carries a fine of CHF 250 (US $341). Drug possession carries heavy fines and prison terms in Switzerland; these can vary depending on the amount and type of narcotics carried. Any attempt to cross an international border carrying drugs (for instance transiting Switzerland via Zurich airport) automatically constitutes trafficking charges. These charges can also carry heavy penalties.

Engaging in sexual conduct with children or using or disseminating child pornography in a foreign country is a crime prosecutable in the United States. If you break local laws in Switzerland, your U.S. passport won't help you avoid arrest or prosecution. It's very important to know what's legal and what's not where you are going.

Switzerland, through its 26 cantons (states), has programs to assist victims of crime and their immediate relatives. Medical, psychological, social, financial, and legal assistance are available throughout the country. This type of assistance must be applied for, and the local police can assist if necessary. These programs also protect the rights of the victim during criminal proceedings. The victim may receive compensation for some damages, if requested during the criminal procedure. Information is available at the Swiss Department of Justice located on Bundesrain 20, 3003 Bern, telephone: 41-31-322-4750.

The United States and Switzerland do not have a bilateral agreement requiring mandatory notification of a U.S. citizen arrest to the U.S. embassy. Notification of arrests is only required if the arrested U.S. citizen so requests.

If you are arrested and concerned that the Department of State may not be aware of your situation, you should request the police or prison officials to notify the nearest U.S. embassy or consulate of your arrest. Based on the Vienna Convention on Consular Relations, bilateral agreements with certain countries, and customary international law, if you are arrested in Switzerland, you have the option to request that the police, prison officials, or other authorities alert the nearest U.S. embassy or consulate of your arrest, and to have communications from you forwarded to the nearest U.S. embassy or consulate. Switzerland is a signatory to the European Convention on Human Rights, which requires arrestees be immediately heard before an independent Magistrate to determine if they will be held for investigative detention. Individuals "highly suspected" of a crime are generally placed under police detention until such time that their case can be heard by the Magistrate.

Special Circumstances: If you are going to participate in mountain activities (summer and winter) we strongly urge you to buy mountain search and rescue insurance. Costs of search and rescue operations are your or your family's responsibility. Search and rescue insurance is available inexpensively in Switzerland and you may purchase it at many Swiss post offices. You can get more information from the Swiss National Tourist Office, at most tourist information offices or with the Swiss Air Rescue Organization. Such insurance has proved useful; an uninsured rescue can easily cost $25,000.

Switzerland's customs authorities encourage the use of an ATA (Admission Temporaire/Admission) Carnet for the temporary admission of professional equipment, commercial samples, and/or goods for exhibitions and fair purposes. ATA Carnet Headquarters, located at the U.S. Council for International Business, 1212 Avenue of the Americas, New York, N.Y. 10036, issues and guarantees the ATA Carnet in the United States. For additional information call (212) 354-4480 or email.

Accessibility: While in Switzerland, individuals with disabilities may find accessibility and accommodation different from what you find in the United States. Certain difficulties may be encountered for people with disabilities, and Switzerland is in the process of improving these facilities. Most cantons have already implemented some provisions for persons with disabilities, but there is no country-wide standard. Experts estimate that only approximately 30 percent of public buildings are wheelchair accessible.

Public transportation is good and punctual. The Swiss tourist office and train station is thebest place to obtain information about special fares for tourists.

For an excellent source of information regarding tourism in Switzerland, please refer to: www.myswitzerland.com. This site includes information on special rail passes, transport, hotel ratings, events, and weekly top news.

Medical Facilities and Health Information: Excellent medicalcare is widely available. Good information on vaccinations and other health precautions may be obtained via the CDC website. For information about outbreaks of infectious diseases abroad, consult the infectious diseases section of the World Health Organization (WHO) website.

The WHO website also contains additional health information for travelers, including detailed country-specific health information.

Medical Insurance: You can't assume your insurance will go with you when you travel. It is very important to find out BEFORE you leave. You need to ask your insurance company two questions:

- Does my policy apply when I'm outside of the U.S. and provide full coverage?
- Will it cover emergencies like a trip to a foreign hospital or an evacuation? Will my insurance policy cover treatment and/or an extended stay in a hospital or clinic, and cover a medical evacuation (medevac)?

In many places, doctors and hospitals still expect payment in cash at the time of service (this is where your insurance policy will be of assistance).

Your regular U.S. health insurance may not cover doctor and hospital visits in other countries. If your policy is not valid when you travel outside of the U.S., it's a very good idea to take out another one for your trip.

Traffic Safety and Road Conditions: While in Switzerland, you may encounter road conditions that differ significantly from those in the United States.

Although many roads are mountainous and winding, Swiss road safety standards are high. In some mountain areas, vehicle snow chains are required in winter. Road travel can be more dangerous during summer, winter holidays, the Easter break, and Whitsunday weekend (late spring) because of increased traffic. Travel on expressways (indicated by green signs with a white expressway symbol) requires purchase of a sticker ("vignette"), which must be affixed to the car's windshield.

Vignettes can be purchased at most border crossings points, gas stations and at Swiss post offices. Drivers using the highway system without a vignette are subject to hefty fines levied on the spot. Public transportation in Switzerland and Liechtenstein is excellent.

Aviation Safety Oversight: The U.S. Federal Aviation Administration (FAA) has assessed the government of Switzerland's Civil Aviation Authority as being in compliance with International Civil Aviation Organization (ICAO) aviation safety standards for oversight of Switzerland's air carrier operations. Further information may be found on the FAA's safety assessment page

Children's Issues: Please see the U.S. Dept. of State Office of Children's Issues web pages on intercountry adoption and international parental child abduction.

LITHUANIA

Compiled from publications that were available as of February 2013 from the U.S. Department of State, the U.S. Department of Commerce, and the Central Intelligence Agency (CIA). See the introduction to this set for explanatory notes.

Official Name:
Republic of Lithuania

PROFILE

Geography

Area: total: 65,300 sq km; country comparison to the world: 123; land: 62,680 sq km; water: 2,620 sq km

Major cities: Vilnius (capital) 546,000 (2009)

Climate: transitional, between maritime and continental; wet, moderate winters and summers

Terrain: lowland, many scattered small lakes, fertile soil

People

Nationality: noun: Lithuanian(s); adjective: Lithuanian

Population: 3,525,761 (July 2012 est.)

Population growth rate: -0.278% (2012 est.)

Ethnic groups: Lithuanian 84%, Polish 6.1%, Russian 4.9%, Belarusian 1.1%, other or unspecified 3.9% (2009)

Religions: Roman Catholic 79%, Russian Orthodox 4.1%, Protestant (including Lutheran and Evangelical Christian Baptist) 1.9%, other or unspecified 5.5%, none 9.5% (2001 census)

Languages: Lithuanian (official) 82%, Russian 8%, Polish 5.6%, other and unspecified 4.4% (2001 census)

Literacy: definition: age 15 and over can read and write; total population: 99.7%; male: 99.7%; female: 99.7% (2010 est.)

Health: life expectancy at birth: total population: 75.55 years; male: 70.72 years; female: 80.66 years (2012 est.); Infant mortality rate: total: 6.18 deaths/1,000 live births; male: 7.37 deaths/1,000 live births; female: 4.92 deaths/1,000 live births (2012 est.)

Unemployment rate: 15.7% (2012 est.)

Work force: 1.587 million (2012 est.)

Government

Type: parliamentary democracy

Independence: 11 March 1990

Constitution: adopted 25 October 1992; last amended 13 July 2004

Political subdivisions: 10 counties (apskritys, singular—apskritis); Alytaus, Kauno, Klaipedos, Marijampoles, Panevezio, Siauliu, Taurages, Telsiu, Utenos, Vilniaus

Suffrage: 18 years of age; universal

Economy

GDP (purchasing power parity): $64.32 billion (2012 est.); $62.39 billion (2011 est.); $58.93 billion (2010 est.); $58.1 billion (2009 est.)

GDP real growth rate: 2.7% (2012 est.); 5.9% (2011 est.); 1.4% (2010 est.); -14.8% (2009 est.)

GDP per capita (PPP): $20,100 (2012 est.); $19,100 (2011 est.); $17,900 (2010 est.); $17,400 (2009 est.)

Natural resources: peat, arable land, amber

Agriculture products: grain, potatoes, sugar beets, flax, vegetables; beef, milk, eggs; fish

Industries: metal-cutting machine tools, electric motors, television sets, refrigerators and freezers, petroleum refining, shipbuilding (small ships), furniture making, textiles, food processing, fertilizers, agricultural machinery, optical equipment, electronic components, computers, amber jewelry

Exports: $29.01 billion (2012 est.); $28.67 billion (2011 est.); $20.73 billion (2010 est.)

Exports—commodities: mineral products 22%, machinery and equipment 10%, chemicals 9%, textiles 7%, foodstuffs 7%, plastics 7%

Exports—partners: Russia 16.7%, Latvia 10.4%, Germany 9.5%, Poland 7.1%, Estonia 6.8%, Netherlands 6.2%, Belarus 5.2%, UK 4.2%, France 4.2% (2009 est.)

Imports: $31.41 billion (2012 est.); $30.83 billion (2011 est.); $22.41 billion (2010 est.)

Imports—commodities: mineral products, machinery and equipment, transport equipment, chemicals, textiles and clothing, metals

Imports—partners: Russia 33%, Germany 9.8%, Poland 9.2%, Latvia 6.7%, Netherlands 5% (2009 est.)
Debt—external: $31.37 billion (31 December 2012 est.); $31.03 billion (31 December 2011 est.); $30.15 billion (31 December 2010 est.)
Exchange rates: litai (LTL) per US dollar; 2.711 (2012 est.); 2.4811 (2011 est.); 2.6063 (2010 est.); 2.4787 (2009); 2.3251 (2008); 2.5362 (2007)

GEOGRAPHY

The largest and most populous of the Baltic states, Lithuania is situated on the eastern shore of the Baltic Sea, in northeastern Europe. It is bordered by Latvia to the north, Belarus to the southeast, Poland to the southwest, and Kaliningrad, a territory of Russia, to the west. It has 60 miles of sandy coastline, of which only 24 miles face the open Baltic Sea. Lithuania's major warm-water port of Klaipeda lies at the narrow mouth of Kursiu Gulf, a shallow lagoon extending south to Kaliningrad. The Nemunas River and some of its tributaries are used for internal shipping. Situated between the 54th and 56th latitudes and the 20th and 27th longitudes, Lithuania is glacially flat, except for the hills (of no more than 300 meters) in the western and eastern highlands. The terrain is marked by numerous small lakes and swamps, and a mixed forest zone covers 30% of the country. According to some geographers, Lithuania's capital, Vilnius, lies at the geographical center of Europe.

PEOPLE

Lithuanians are neither Slavic nor Germanic, although the union with Poland and the colonization by Germans and Russians has influenced the culture and religious beliefs of Lithuania. This highly literate society places strong emphasis upon education, which is free and compulsory until age 16.

In spite of several border changes, Soviet deportations, a massacre of its Jewish population, and German and Polish repatriations, the population of Lithuania has maintained a fairly stable percentage of ethnic Lithuanians (from 79.3% in 1959 to 83.9% in 2011). Lithuania's citizenship law and constitution meet international and Organization for Security and Cooperation in Europe (OSCE) standards, guaranteeing universal human and civil rights.

National/Racial/Ethnic Minorities

The small Romani community (approximately 3,000 persons) continued to experience problems, including discrimination in access to such services as education, housing, and health care; in employment; and in relations with police. However, there were no official charges of police abuse. Extreme poverty, illiteracy, perceived high criminality, and the negative attitudes of mainstream society kept this group locked in social exclusion, reflected in the fact that 40 percent of Roma did not know the national language. Many Roma did not have identification papers; a number of them, although born in the country, were stateless. The Romani unemployment rate continued to be more than 95 percent. Minority advocates continued to criticize the Vilnius city government for focusing on law enforcement in the Romani community but doing little to integrate Roma into the broader community.

Language

The Lithuanian language still retains the original sound system and morphological peculiarities of the prototypal Indo-European tongue and, therefore, is fascinating for linguistic study. Between 400 and 600 AD, the Lithuanian and Latvian languages split from the Eastern Baltic (Prussian) language group, which subsequently became extinct. The first known written Lithuanian text dates from a hymnal translation in 1545. Written with the Latin alphabet, Lithuanian has been the official language of Lithuania since 1989. While Lithuania was a member of the U.S.S.R., Russian was the official language; many Lithuanians speak Russian as a second language. The resident Slavic populace generally speaks Russian or Polish as a first language.

Religion

Roman Catholicism is the dominant and most influential religion. A 2007 poll commissioned by the Ministry of Justice (MOJ) indicated approximately 80 percent of respondents are Roman Catholics. According to the 2001 national census (the most recent available), the Russian Orthodox Church, the second largest religious group, has 140,000 members (approximately 4 percent of the population) living mainly along the border with Belarus. There are approximately 27,000 Old Believers, Russian Orthodox practitioners who do not accept the church's reforms in the 17th century; 20,000 Lutherans; and approximately 7,000 Reformed Evangelicals. The Jewish community numbers approximately 4,000, the Sunni Muslim community 2,700, and the Greek Catholic community 300. The Karaites, a distinct ethnic group in the country since 1397, have approximately 250 members.

Less than 0.5 percent of the population belongs to what the government refers to as "nontraditional" religious communities. The most numerous of these are Jehovah's Witnesses, Full Gospel Word of Faith Movement, Pentecostals/Charismatics, Old Baltic faith communities, Baptists, Seventh-day Adventists, New Apostolic Church, Methodists, and The Church of Jesus Christ of Latter-day Saints (Mormons).

HISTORY

Between the 7th and 2nd centuries BC, Baltic tribes established themselves on what is presently known as Lithuanian territory. These tribes were made up of a distinct Indo-European ethnic group whose descendents are the present-day Lithuanian and Latvian nations. The name of Lithuania, however, did not appear in European records until 1009 AD, when it was mentioned in the German manu-

script Annals of Quedlinburg. During the period 1236–1263, Duke Mindaugas united the various Baltic tribes and established the state of Lithuania, which was better able to resist the eastward expansion of the Teutonic Knights.

In 1253, Mindaugas embraced Christianity for political reasons and accepted the crown from the Pope of Rome, becoming the first and only king in Lithuanian history. After the assassination of Mindaugas and the ensuing civil war, Grand Duke Gediminas took control of Lithuania. He reigned from 1316 to 1341, during which the long-term expansion of Lithuania into the lands of the eastern Slavs began. He founded the modern capital city of Vilnius and started the Gediminas dynasty, which ruled Lithuania until 1572.

By the end of the 14th century, Lithuania was the largest country in Europe, stretching from the Baltic Sea to the Black Sea. In 1386, Grand Duke Jogaila of Lithuania was crowned the King of Poland, which intensified Lithuania's economic and cultural development and oriented it toward the West. It was at this time that the people of Lithuania embraced Christianity. In 1401, the formal union between Poland and Lithuania was dissolved. While Jogaila remained the King of Poland, his cousin Grand Duke Vytautas became the ruler of Lithuania. In 1410, the armies of Poland and Lithuania together defeated the Teutonic Order in the Battle of Grunewald, the biggest battle of medieval Europe.

The 16th century witnessed a number of wars against the growing Russian state over the Slavic lands ruled by Lithuania. Needing an ally in those wars, Lithuania again united with Poland through The Union of Lublin in 1569. As a member of this Commonwealth, Lithuania retained its sovereignty and its institutions, including a separate army and currency. In 1795, the joint state was dissolved by the third Partition of the Commonwealth, which forfeited its lands to Russia, Prussia, and Austria. Over 90% of Lithuania was incorporated into the Russian Empire and the remainder into Prussia. Attempts to restore independence in the uprisings of 1794, 1830–31, and 1863 were suppressed and followed by a tightened police regime and increasing Russification, including the 1864 ban on printing Lithuanian books in traditional Latin characters.

A market economy slowly developed with the abolition of serfdom in 1861. Lithuanian farmers grew stronger, and an increase in the number of intellectuals of peasant origin led to the growth of a Lithuanian national movement. In German-ruled East Prussia, also called Lithuania Minor, or Kaliningrad, Lithuanian publications were printed in large numbers and then smuggled into Russian-ruled Lithuania. The ban on the Lithuanian press was lifted in 1904.

During World War I, the German Army occupied Lithuania, and the occupation administration allowed a Lithuanian conference to convene in Vilnius in September 1917. The conference adopted a resolution demanding the restoration of an independent Lithuanian state and elected the Lithuanian Council. On February 16, 1918, the council declared Lithuania's independence. The Seimas (Parliament) of Lithuania adopted a constitution on August 1, 1922 and declared Lithuania a parliamentary republic.

The interwar period of independence gave birth to the development of Lithuanian press, literature, music, arts, and theater as well as a comprehensive system of education with Lithuanian as the language of instruction. However, territorial disputes with Poland (over the Vilnius region and the Suvalkai region) and with Germany (over the Klaipeda region) preoccupied the foreign policy of the new state. During the interwar period, the constitutional capital was Vilnius, although the city itself was annexed by Poland from 1920 to 1939. During this period the Lithuanian Government was relocated to Kaunas, which officially held the status of temporary capital.

The German-Soviet Nonaggression Pact of 1939 first pulled Lithuania into the German sphere of influence and then brought it under Soviet domination. Soviet pressure and a complicated international situation forced Lithuania to sign an agreement with the U.S.S.R. on October 10, 1939. By means of this agreement, Lithuania was given back the city of Vilnius and the part of the Vilnius region seized by the Red Army during the Soviet-Polish war; in return, some 20,000 Soviet soldiers were deployed in Lithuania. On August 3, 1940, Lithuania was proclaimed a Soviet Socialist Republic. Totalitarian rule was established, Sovietization of the economy and culture began, and Lithuanian state employees and public figures were arrested and exiled to Russia. During the mass deportation campaign of June 14-18, 1941, about 12,600 people were deported to Siberia without investigation or trial, 3,600 people were imprisoned, and more than 1,000 were killed.

Between 1940 and 1954, under the Nazi and then Soviet occupations, Lithuania lost over 780,000 residents. In World War II, German occupiers sent Lithuanians to forced labor camps in Germany. Almost 200,000, or 91%, of Lithuanian Jews were killed, one of the worst death rates of the Holocaust. After the retreat of the Wehrmacht in 1944, Lithuania was re-occupied by the Soviet Union, and an estimated 120,000 to 300,000 Lithuanians were either killed or deported to Siberia and other remote parts of the Soviet Union. Conversely, Soviet authorities encouraged the immigration to Lithuania of other Soviet workers, especially Russians, as a way of integrating Lithuania into the U.S.S.R.

With the advent of perestroika and glasnost, Gorbachev's programs of social and political reforms in the late 1980s, communist rule eroded. Lithuania, led by Sajudis, an anti-communist and anti-Soviet independence movement, proclaimed its renewed independence on March 11, 1990—the first Soviet republic to do so. The Lithuanian Supreme Soviet formed a new Cabinet of Ministers and adopted the Provisional Fundamental Law of the State with a number of by-laws. In response, on the night of January 13, 1991, the Red Army attacked the Vilnius TV Tower, killing 14 civilians and injuring 700. Soviet forces, however, were unsuccessful in suppressing Lithuania's secession.

On February 4, 1991, Iceland became the first country to recognize Lithuanian independence. Sweden was the first to open an embassy in the country. The United States never recognized the Soviet claim to Lithuania and views the present Lithuanian Government as the legal continuation of the interwar republic. In July 2007, Lithuania celebrated the 85th anniversary of continuous diplomatic relations with the United States. Lithuania joined the United Nations on September 17, 1991.

Despite Lithuania's achievement of complete independence, sizable numbers of Russian forces remained on its territory. Withdrawal of those forces was one of Lithuania's top foreign policy priorities. On August 31, 1993, Lithuania and Russia signed an agreement whereby the last Red Army troops left the country.

On May 31, 2001, Lithuania became the 141st member of the World Trade Organization. Desiring closer ties with the West, Lithuania became the first of the Baltic states to apply for membership in the North Atlantic Treaty Organization (NATO), and on March 29, 2004, it joined the Alliance. On May 1 of the same year, Lithuania also joined the European Union (EU).

Lithuania has been a staunch U.S. ally, contributing to military operations in Afghanistan and Iraq. In Afghanistan, Lithuania has led a Provincial Reconstruction Team in Ghor province since 2005, and has deployed Lithuanian Special Operation Forces to southern Afghanistan to operate under NATO's International Security Assistance Force (ISAF). In Iraq, Lithuania had an infantry platoon serving in Multinational Division Center near Al Kut until July 2008; five trainers currently serve in the NATO Training Mission-Iraq in Baghdad. Lithuania has also participated in peacekeeping operations in Bosnia and Kosovo.

Similarly, Lithuania is a strong supporter of U.S. objectives in the area of democracy promotion. In 2009 Lithuania assumed the chairmanship of the Community of Democracies. Making this a high priority for its foreign policy, Lithuania has provided development assistance and advice to Ukraine, Moldova, Georgia, and other Caucasus states. Lithuania also actively supports democratization efforts in Belarus. As a result of the broader global financial crisis, the Lithuanian economy in 2009 experienced its worst recession since gaining independence from the Soviet Union in 1991. After experiencing a boom in growth sparked by Lithuania's 2004 accession to the European Union, Lithuania's GDP contracted by 15% in 2009. To stabilize the economy, the government that took power in December 2008 approved a U.S. $2.3 billion stimulus plan as well as a fiscal austerity package that cut spending and raised taxes to shore up finances. This was followed by several more rounds of budget cuts throughout 2009, and the 2010 government budget started to cut into Lithuania's social benefit programs. Lithuania's GDP grew slightly in 2010, while economic growth in 2011 is expected to be 5%-6%.

GOVERNMENT AND POLITICAL CONDITIONS

The Republic of Lithuania is a constitutional, multiparty, parliamentary democracy. Legislative authority resides in the unicameral parliament (Seimas). Presidential elections in 2009 were considered free and fair. Parliamentary elections in 2008, also free and fair, led to the formation of a center-right coalition government.

Recent Elections

The May 2009 presidential elections and 2008 parliamentary elections were considered free and fair.

Political Parties: The government continued to ban the Communist Party; other political parties could operate without restriction or outside interference. Citizens could run for municipal councils without being on party lists.

Participation of Women and Minorities: Both the president and the speaker of the parliament were women. At the end of 2011, there were 26 women in the 141-seat parliament and two women in the 15-member cabinet of ministers. Women accounted for 5 percent of mayors, 21 percent of municipal council members, and 5 percent of local administration directors. Three members of ethnic minorities served in parliament.

Principal Government Officials

Last Updated: 1/31/2013

Pres.: **Dalia GRYBAUSKAITE**
Prime Min.: **Algirdas BUTKEVICIUS**
Min. of Agriculture: **Vigilijus JUKNA**
Min. of Culture: **Sarunas BIRUTIS**
Min. of Economy: **Birute VESAITE**
Min. of Education & Science: **Dainius PAVALKIS**
Min. of Energy: **Jaroslav NEVEROVIC**
Min. of Environment: **Valentinas MAZURONIS**
Min. of Finance: **Rimantas SADZIUS**
Min. of Foreign Affairs: **Linas LINKEVICIUS**
Min. of Health: **Vytenis Povilas ANDRIUKAITIS**
Min. of the Interior: **Dailis Alfonsas BARAKAUSKAS**
Min. of Justice: **Juozas BERNATONIS**
Min. of National Defense: **Juozas OLEKAS**
Min. of Social Security & Labor: **Algimanta PABEDINSKIENE**
Min. of Transport & Communications: **Rimantas SINKEVICIUS**
Governor, Bank of Lithuania: **Vitas VASILIAUSKAS**
Ambassador to the US: **Zygimantas PAVILIONIS**
Permanent Representative to the UN, New York: **Raimonda MURMOKAITE**

ECONOMY

Lithuania gained membership in the World Trade Organization and joined the EU in May 2004. Despite Lithuania's EU accession, Lithuania's trade with its Central and Eastern European neighbors, and Russia in particular, accounts for a significant share of total trade. Foreign investment and business support have helped in the transition from the old command economy to a market economy. Lithuania's economy grew on average 8% per year for the four years prior to 2008 driven by exports and domestic demand.

However, GDP plunged nearly 15% in 2009 - the three former Soviet Baltic republics were among the hardest hit by the 2008–09 financial crisis. The government's efforts to attract foreign investment, develop export markets, and to pursue broad economic reforms has been key to Lithuania's quick recovery from a deep recession making Lithuania one of the fastest growing economies in the EU. However, unemployment—at 15.8% in 2012—remains stubbornly high.

Labor Conditions

The law prohibits exploitation of children in the workplace, and the government generally enforced these prohibitions effectively. Statistics from 2009 indicated that 8 percent of children working did so illegally, mostly in the agricultural sector, where children sometimes received unlawfully low compensation.

The law sets the minimum employment age at 16 but allows the employment of persons as young as 14 for light labor with the written consent of the child's parents and school. The law mandates reduced work hours for children, allowing up to two hours per day or 12 hours per week during the school year and up to seven hours per day or 32 hours per week when school is not in session. Persons under the age of 18 are subject to additional restrictions, including a prohibition on night work.

The legal minimum wage was 800 litas ($300) per month. According to the National Statistics Department, the official "poverty risk level" in 2010 was 701 litas ($263) per month. The law provides that the maximum time worked in any seven-day period, including overtime, may not exceed 40 hours for white-collar work and 48 hours for blue-collar work. Overtime is allowed only in cases stipulated by law, and both overtime and night work must be compensated by at least one-and-a-half times the hourly wage. The labor laws apply to both local and foreign workers. The law gives workers the right to safe and healthy working conditions, and this provision was generally enforced.

U.S.-LITHUANIAN RELATIONS

The U.S. and Lithuania share a history as valued allies and strong partners. The United States established diplomatic relations with Lithuania in 1922, following its declaration of independence during World War I. Lithuania was annexed by the Soviet Union in 1940 during World War II. In 1990, Lithuania proclaimed its renewed independence, and international recognition followed. The United States had never recognized the forcible incorporation of Lithuania into the Soviet Union, and it views the present Government of Lithuania as the legal continuation of the interwar republic.

Since Lithuania regained its independence, the United States has worked closely with the country to help it rebuild its democratic institutions and a market economy. The U.S. welcomed Lithuania's accession to the North Atlantic Treaty Organization (NATO) and the European Union (EU) in 2004. As a NATO ally and EU member, Lithuania has become a strong, effective partner committed to democratic principles and values. The country is a strong supporter of U.S. objectives in the area of democracy promotion and has helped the people of other young European nations develop and strengthen civil institutions.

U.S. Assistance to Lithuania

The United States provides no significant foreign assistance to Lithuania.

Bilateral Economic Relations

Lithuania is a relatively small but potentially attractive market for U.S. goods and services. Steps undertaken during the country's accession to the EU and NATO helped improve its legal, tax, and customs systems, which aided economic and commercial sector development. The United States and Lithuania have signed an agreement on bilateral trade and intellectual property protection and a bilateral investment treaty. Lithuania participates in the visa waiver program, which allows nationals of participating countries to travel to the United States for certain business or tourism purposes for stays of 90 days or less without obtaining a visa.

Lithuania's Membership in International Organizations

Lithuania's foreign policy is largely informed by what it perceives as an expansionist Russia. Lithuania and the United States belong to a number of the same international organizations, including the United Nations, North Atlantic Treaty Organization, Organization for Security and Cooperation in Europe, International Monetary Fund, World Bank, and World Trade Organization.

Bilateral Representation

Lithuania maintains an embassy in the United States at 2622 16th Street NW, Washington, DC 20009, tel: (202) 234-5860.

Principal U.S. Embassy Officials

Last Updated: 1/14/2013

VILNIUS (E) Akmenu 6, LT-03106 Vilnius, 370 5 266 5500, Fax 370 5 266 5510, Workweek: M-F/8-5, Website: http://vilnius.usembassy.gov/

DCM OMS:	Sarah Bittenbender
Co-CLO:	Heather Boyers
DHS/CIS:	Gilbert L. Jacobs (Copenhagen)
DHS/ICE:	Michael Shevock (Frankfurt)
FCS:	David McNeill (Warsaw)
FM:	Colin McCarthy
MGT:	Alboino Deulus
POL/ECON:	J. Alexander Hamilton
POSHO:	Colin McCarthy
SDO/DATT:	LTC Jeffrey Jennette
AMB:	Charge Anne Hall
CON:	Anthony Beaver
DCM:	Acting DCM J. Alexander Hamilton
PAO:	Jonathan M. Berger
GSO:	John McDonald
RSO:	Michael Twining
AGR:	Eric A. Wenberg (Warsaw)
CLO:	Ana-Maria Comsa
DEA:	Timothy Moran (Copenhagen)
EEO:	Sarah Bittenbender
EST:	Erik Hall (Copenhagen)
FAA:	Paul H. Feldman (Brussels)
ICASS Chair:	Michael Twining
IMO:	Bill Potter
IPO:	James B. Cavanaugh
IRS:	Thomas E. Stevens (Frankfurt)
ISO:	Bill Potter
ISSO:	Bill Potter
LEGATT:	Kirk J. Striebich (Tallinn)
State ICASS:	Michael Twining

TRAVEL

Consular Information Sheet

January 29, 2013

Country Description: Lithuania is a stable democracy. Tourist facilities in Vilnius, the capital, and to a lesser extent in Kaunas and Klaipeda, are similar to those available in other European cities. In other parts of the country, however, some of the goods and services taken for granted in other countries may not be available.

Smart Traveler Enrollment Program (STEP)/Embassy Locations: If you are going to live or visit Lithuania, please take the time to tell us about your trip. If you enroll with the Smart Traveler Enrollment Program (STEP), we can keep you up to date with important safety and security announcements, and reach your friends and family in case of an emergency.

The U.S. Embassy Vilnius is located at Akmenu Gatve 6, Vilnius, Lithuania LT-03106. Please visit the Embassy website or call (370) (5) 266-5500, or Fax (370) (5) 266-5590 for more information.

Entry/Exit Requirements for U.S. Citizens: Lithuania is a party to the Schengen Agreement. As a U.S. citizen, you may enter Lithuania for up to 90 days for tourist or business purposes without a visa. Your passport should be valid for at least three months beyond your period of stay. For further details about travel to and within Schengen countries, please see our Schengen fact sheet. If you are staying in Lithuania for more than 90 days within any six-month period, you must apply for temporary residency. Lithuanian authorities recommend applying for a residency permit through a Lithuanian embassy or consulate before initial entry into Lithuania, as processing times can run beyond 90 days. All foreigners from non-European Union countries seeking entry into Lithuania must carry proof of a medical insurance policy contracted for payment of all costs of hospitalization and medical treatment in Lithuania. If you lack proof, you must purchase short-term insurance at the border from a Lithuanian provider for roughly $1.00 per day; the number of days will be calculated from the day of entry until the date of your return ticket. Children residing in Lithuania must have written permission from at least one parent to travel outside the country if neither parent is accompanying them on their trip. This policy is not applicable to temporary visitors. Visit the Embassy of Lithuania website for the most current visa information.

The U.S. Department of State is unaware of any HIV/AIDS entry requirements for visitors to or foreign residents of Lithuania.

Threats to Safety and Security: There have been no incidents of terrorism directed toward U.S. interests in Lithuania. Incidents of anti-Americanism are rare.

Lithuania is not experiencing any civil unrest at this time. However, marches and protests do occur, especially in larger cities. Although such events have generally been peaceful in nature, U.S. citizens are reminded that even gatherings intended to be peaceful can become confrontational. Therefore, we urge you to avoid the areas of demonstrations, if possible, and exercise caution if within the vicinity of any event. You should stay current with media coverage of local events and be aware of their surroundings at all times. From time to time, especially late at night near bars and night clubs, foreigners have been subject to violent crimes, such as muggings, or have become involved in altercations with inebriated individuals. Racially motivated verbal, and sometimes physical harassment of foreigners and ethnic minorities in major cities have occurred. In addition, LGBT individuals have experienced verbal, and sometimes physical harassment.

Stay up to date by:

- Bookmarking our Bureau of Consular Affairs website, which contains the current Travel Warnings and Travel Alerts as well as the Worldwide Caution;
- Following us on Twitter and the Bureau of Consular Affairs page on Facebook;
- Downloading our free Smart Traveler iPhone App or Smart Traveler Android App to have travel information at your fingertips; and
- Calling 1-888-407-4747 toll-free within the U.S. and Canada, or a regular toll line, 1-202-501-4444, from other countries.

Take some time before travel to improve your personal security—things are not the same everywhere as they are in the United States.

Crime: Although Lithuania is relatively safe, both violent and non-violent crimes affecting tourists have occurred throughout the country. You should maintain the same awareness and practice good personal security that you would in any U.S. metropolitan area. Large amounts of cash and expensive jewelry should be secured in a hotel safe or left at home. Common crimes against foreigners include pick-pocketing and thefts, so personal belongings should be well protected at all times. Thefts from cars and car thefts occur regularly. Valuables should not be left in plain sight in parked vehicles, as there have been increasing reports of car windows being smashed and items stolen. You should avoid walking alone at night or utilize a taxi service arranged by telephone. Isolated ATMs should be avoided after dark. Like in the United States, public inebriation should be avoided as criminals have been known to take advantage of drunken pedestrians. U.S. citizens have reported being robbed and/or scammed while intoxicated. Don't buy counterfeit and pirated goods, even if they are widely available. Not only are the bootlegs illegal to bring back into the United States, you may be breaking local law too.

Victims of Crime: If you or someone you know becomes the victim of a crime abroad, you should contact the local police and the nearest U.S. embassy or consulate (see the Department of State's list of embassies and consulates). We can:

- Replace a stolen passport;
- Help you find appropriate medical care if you are the victim of violent crimes such as assault or rape;
- Assist you in contacting the appropriate police authorities, and if you want us to, we cancontact family members or friends; and

- Help you understand the local criminal justice process and direct you to local attorneys, although it is important to remember that local authorities are responsible for investigating and prosecuting the crime.

The local equivalent to the 911 emergency number in Lithuania is 112.

Criminal Penalties: While you are traveling in Lithuania, you are subject to its laws even if you are a U.S. citizen. Foreign laws and legal systems can be vastly different than our own, and criminal penalties vary from country to country. There are also some things that might be legal in Lithuania, but still illegal in the United States; for instance, you can be prosecuted under U.S. law if you buy pirated goods. Engaging in sexual conduct with children or using or disseminating child pornography in a foreign country is a crime prosecutable in the United States. If you break local laws in Lithuania, your U.S. passport won't help you avoid arrest or prosecution. It's very important to know what's legal and what's not.

If you break Lithuanian laws, even unknowingly, you may be expelled, arrested, or imprisoned. Penalties for possession, use, or trafficking in illegal drugs in Lithuania are severe, and convicted offenders can expect long jail sentences and heavy fines. For more information about arrest procedures in Lithuania please visit the Embassy's website. While most authorities will automatically notify the U.S. embassy or consulate if a U.S. citizen is detained or arrested, this might not always be the case. To ensure that the United States is aware of your circumstances, request that the police and prison officials notify the Embassy or Consulate as soon as you are arrested or detained.

Special Circumstances: Lithuanian customs authorities may enforce strict regulations concerning the temporary importation into or export from Lithuania of items such as firearms and antiquities.

Telephone connections are generally good. U.S. 1-800 numbers can be accessed from Lithuania but not on a toll-free basis; the international long distance rate per minute will be charged. Local Internet cafes offer computer access. ATMs are widely available. Most hotels and other businesses accept major credit cards.

Accessibility: While in Lithuania, individuals with disabilities may find accessibility and accommodation very different from what is found in the United States. Lithuania'sLaw on Equal Treatment prohibits discrimination against persons with disabilities, although it does not specify what kind of disabilities. It mandates access to buildings for persons with disabilities;however, according to 2010 data from the Department of Statistics, only 40.1 percent of housing was accessible.

Medical Facilities and Health Information: Medical care in Lithuania has improved, but medical facilities do not always meet Western standards. There are a few private clinics with medical supplies and services that nearly equal Western European or U.S. standards.

Most medical supplies are now widely available, including disposable needles, anesthetics, antibiotics, and other pharmaceuticals; however, hospitals and clinics still suffer from a lack of equipment and resources. Lithuania has highly trained medical professionals, some of whom speak English, but their availability is decreasing as they leave for employment opportunities abroad.

Depending on a patient's condition, an appointment with a specialist may not be available for several weeks. Western-quality dental care can be obtained in major cities. Elderly travelers who require medical care may face difficulties. Most pharmaceuticals sold in Lithuania are from Europe; travelers will not necessarily find the same brands that they use in the United States. Serious medical problems requiring hospitalization and/or medical evacuation can cost thousands of dollars or more. Doctors and hospitals often expect immediate cash payment for health services, particularly if immigration status in Lithuania is unclear.

Tick-borne encephalitis and Lyme disease are widespread throughout the country. Those intending to visit parks or forested areas in Lithuania are urged to speak with their health care practitioners about immunization. Rabies is also increasingly prevalent in rural areas.

The Lithuanian Government does not require HIV testing for U.S. citizens; however, sexually transmitted diseases are a growing public health problem.

Good information on vaccinations and other health precautions, can be found via the Centers for Disease Control and Prevention (CDC) website. For information about outbreaks of infectious diseases abroad, consult the World Health Organization (WHO) website, whichalso contains additional health information for travelers, including detailed country-specific health information.

Medical Insurance: You can't assume your insurance will go with you when you travel. It's very important to find out BEFORE you leave. You need to ask your insurance company two questions:

- Does my policy apply when I'm out of the United States?
- Will it cover emergencies like a trip to a foreign hospital or an evacuation?

In many places, doctors and hospitals still expect payment in cash at the time of service. Your regular U.S. health insurance may not cover doctor and hospital visits in other countries. If your policy doesn't go with you when you travel, it's a very good idea to take out another one for your trip.

Traffic Safety and Road Conditions: While in Lithuania, you may encounter road conditions that differ significantly from those in the United States.

You may drive in Lithuania with a U.S. driver's license for up to 90 days. U.S. citizens who reside in Lithuania for 185 days or more in one calendar year and who wish to continue driving in Lithuania must acquire a Lithuanian driver's license. An applicant for a driver's license must take both the written and driving exams. The foreign license must be given to the Lithuanian Road Police to be processed by the Consular Department of the Lithuanian Ministry of Foreign Affairs. For more information, please visit the Embassy's website. Roads in Lithuania range from well-maintained two- to four-lane highways connecting major cities, to small dirt roads traversing the countryside. Violation of traffic rules is common. It is not unusual to be overtaken by other automobiles traveling at high speed, even in crowded urban areas.

Driving at night— especially in the countryside—can be particularly hazardous. In summer, older seasonal vehicles and inexperienced drivers can be extra hazards. Drive with caution at all times. Driving whileintoxicated is considered a very serious offense and carries heavy penalties. Be aware that such laws are significantly stricter than in many states in the United States. The speed limit is 50 km/hr in town and 90 km/hr out of town unless otherwise indicated.

The phone number for roadside assistance is 8-800-01414 from a regular phone and 1414 from a GSM mobile phone. If you are involved in a traffic accident, be aware that moving the car before the police arrive can result in your being charged with hit and run. Seatbelts are mandatory for the driver and all passengers. Children under the age of 3 must be seated in the back seat in a child seat appropriate for their age and size. Children under the age of 12 and less than 150 cm (approximately 59 inches) may not be seated in the front seat.

During the winter, most major roads are cleared of snow. Winter or all-season tires are required from November 10th through April 1st. Studded tires are not allowed from April 10th through October 31st. Drivers must have at least their low-beam lights on at all times while driving. Public transportation is generally safe, but you should maintain personal security awareness while on public transportation.

Aviation Safety Oversight: As there is no direct commercial air service to the United States by carriers registered in Lithuania, the U.S. Federal Aviation Administration (FAA) has not assessed Lithuania's Civil Aviation Authority for compliance with International Civil Aviation Organization (ICAO) aviation safety standards. Further information may be found on the FAA safety assessment page.

Children's Issues: Please see the U.S. Dept. of State Office of Children's Issues web pages on intercountry adoption and international parental child abduction

Intercountry Adoption

November 2008

The information in this section has been edited from the latest report available as of February 2013 from the State Department Bureau of Consular Affairs, Office of Overseas Citizens Services. For more information, please read the *Intercountry Adoption* section of this book and review current reports online at http://adoption.state.gov.

Lithuania is party to The Hague Convention on Protection of Children and Co-operation in Respect of Intercountry Adoption (Hague Adoption Convention). Therefore all adoptions between Lithuania and the United States must meet the requirements of the Convention and United States law implementing the Convention. For detailed information on these requirements for adoption, please review the *Intercountry Adoption* section of this publication and visit the USCIS Intercountry Adoption website at http://adoption.state.gov. According to Lithuanian law, only children whose parents are deceased or whose parents have had their parental rights taken away are eligible for adoption. There are few such children and the Lithuanian families interested in adopting are given precedence. Two United States embassies play complementary roles in the immigrant visa process for Lithuanian citizens, including adopted orphans. The United States Embassy in Warsaw, Poland ultimately issues all immigrant visas for citizens and residents of Lithuania. The United States Embassy in Vilnius, Lithuania conducts the mandatory I-604 Orphan Investigation interview for all orphan cases.

Who Can Adopt? Adoption between the United States and Lithuania is governed by The Hague Adoption Convention. Therefore to adopt from Lithuania, you must first be found eligible to adopt by the United States Government. In addition to the United States requirements for prospective adoptive parents, Lithuania also has the following requirements for prospective adoptive parents.

Residency Requirements: There are no residency requirements for prospective adoptive parents in Lithuania.

Age Requirements: Prospective adoptive parents generally cannot be over 50 years of age. There must be a minimum age difference of 18 years between the prospective adoptive parents and the child.

Marriage Requirements: Intercountry adoptions are usually limited to married couples. A single parent may be considered in exceptional cases when 1) the individual has been the foster parent of the particular child to be adopted, 2) the child has extremely serious health problems and no married couple wishes to adopt the child, or 3) the child is eight years of age or older and unable to be placed with another family.

Other Requirements: Certain medical conditions can disqualify prospective adoptive parents. The Government of Lithuania publishes a list of medical conditions. The list is maintained on the State Child Rights Protection and Adoption Service website. Some of the conditions are dipsomania (alcoholism), drug addiction "absent steady remission," mental diseases (not specified), AIDS, HIV positive status, infectious tuberculosis, chronic kidney insufficiency when dialysis is obligatory, Alzheimer's disease, Huntington's chorea, amyotrophic lateral sclerosis (ALS or Lou Gehrig's disease), epilepsy with mental and personality changes, multi-system degeneration and third or fourth stage cancers.

Who Can Be Adopted? Because Lithuania is party to The Hague Adoption Convention, children from Lithuania must meet the requirements of the Convention in order to be eligible for adoption. In addition to Lithuania's requirements, a child must meet the definition of a Convention adoptee for you to bring him or her back to the United States.

Lithuania's Adoption Authority: The State Child Rights Protection and Adoption Service

The Process: The first step in adopting a child from Lithuania is to select an adoption service provider in the United States that has been accredited. Only these agencies and attorneys can provide adoption services between the United States and Lithuania. After you choose an accredited adoption service provider, you apply to be found eligible to adopt (Form I-800A) by the USCIS. Once the United States Government determines that you are "eligible" and "suitable" to adopt, you or your agency will forward your information to the adoption authority in Lithuania. Lithuania's adoption authority will review your application to determine whether you are also eligible to adopt under Lithuania's law. If both the United States and Lithuania determine that you are eligible to adopt, and a child is available for intercountry adoption, the central adoption authority in Lithuania may provide you with a referral for a child. After you accept a match with a child, you will apply to the USCIS for provisional approval to adopt that particular child (Form I-800). After this, your adoption service provider or you will submit a visa application for to a Consular officer at the United States Embassy. If the Consular office determines that the child appears eligible to immigrate to the United States, he/she will notify the Lithuania's adoption authority (Article 5 letter). For Convention country adoptions, prospective adoptive parent(s) may not proceed with the adoption or obtain custody for the purpose of adoption until this takes place.

Role of the Adoption Authority: The State Child Rights Protection and Adoption Service places approved prospective adoptive parents on a waiting list according to the date of submission of the complete set of documents. Once a child is matched, the State Child Rights Protection and Adoption Service issues special permission for the prospective adoptive parents to meet the child.

Role of the Court: After the Chairman of the Vilnius District Court verifies that all the documents are in order, he assigns the case to one of the Vilnius District Court judges for final review. The assigned judge will set a court date. After the judge approves the adoption, there is a 40-day waiting period before the adoption is final. Adoptive parents should note that the adopted child remains in the custody of the institution where he/she resided prior to the hearing. Special permission may be granted in some cases for the child(ren) to reside with the adoptive parents in Lithuania.

Role of Adoption Agencies: The adoption agency forwards the prospective adoptive parents' letter of interest in adopting to the State Child Rights Protection and Adoption Service.

Time Frame: Once a family is approved to adopt, it can take several years for a child eligible for intercountry adoption to be matched with the prospective adoptive parents' preferences. After a referral has been made and accepted, an adoption petition can be filed with the court. There is a 40-day waiting period from the time the court issues the final approval until it comes into force.

Adoption Application: The prospective adoptive parents submit their application (letter) to the State Child Rights Protection and Adoption Service. The letter should describe the gender and age of the child(ren) they are interested in adopting, prospective adoptive parents' ages and professions, and any family ties to Lithuania.

Adoption Fees: In the adoption services contract that you sign at the beginning of the adoption process, your agency will itemize the fees and estimated expenses related to your adoption process. Some of the fees specifically associated with adopting from Lithuania include a $42 USD filing fee with the court for the adoption hearing. Prospective adoptive parents can expect to pay adoption agencies for services rendered.

Documents Required: The following is a list of documents that must accompany the letter requesting adoption:

- Information letter introducing the prospective adoptive parents (issued by the Central Governmental authority or accredited adoption association)
- Home Study copy (the socio-psychological study)
- Permit for adoption issued by a competent authority of the receiving state
- Confirmation of a competent authority of the receiving state that the adopted child will be permitted to enter the country for permanent residence
- Copies of prospective adoptive parents' passports or other personal identification documents
- Copies of birth certificates
- Copy of marriage certificate, divorce certificate (if divorced), or death certificate of the spouse (if widowed)
- Health certificates
- Certificates of the family's financial standing (income received and assets owned)

- Criminal record certificates
- Health certificates and copies of birth certificates of children residing together with prospective adoptive parents

If the family applies through an accredited adoption agency, the following documents must also be submitted:

- Power of attorney issued by the family to the agency
- Document issued by a competent authority of the receiving state certifying the authority of the agency to engage in intercountry adoption

The following is a list of documents that must accompany the letter requesting a hearing:

- Full names and addresses of the prospective adoptive parents
- Names and addresses of the Lithuanian state representative in charge of the orphanage or institution where the child resides
- Statement regarding why they want to adopt a child
- Statement as to whether the child is to be their stepchild (in cases where a foreigner wishes to adopt a child of his/her spouse in Lithuania or adoptive child)
- New name to be given to the adoptive child
- Affidavit from the birth parent(s) surrendering all rights to the child, if there are surviving biological parents or a Lithuanian court decision regarding termination of parental rights
- Statement from the institution responsible for the child agreeing to the adoption
- Financial statement of the adoptive parents indicating that they are financially able to provide for the child
- Copy of the home study (updated by the authority or accredited adoption association that prepared the original home study)
- Health certificates
- Certificates of the family's financial standing
- Criminal record certificates
- Original birth certificate of the child
- Filing fee receipt

Bringing Your Child Home: Once your adoption is complete (or you have obtained legal custody of the child), there are a few more steps to take before you can head home. Specifically, you need to apply for several documents for your child before he or she can travel to the United States, such as a birth certificate, a passport or travel document for your child from the country in which he or she was born, and a U.S. Immigration Visa.

Child Citizenship Act: For adoptions finalized abroad, the Child Citizenship Act of 2000 allows your new child to acquire American citizenship automatically when he or she enters the United States as lawful permanent residents. For adoptions finalized in the United States, the Child Citizenship Act of 2000 allows your new child to acquire American citizenship automatically when the court in the United States issues the final adoption decree. To learn more, visit the USCIS Intercountry Adoption website at http://adoption.state.gov.

After Adoption: Lithuania does not have any post-adoption requirements.

United States Embassy in Lithuania
Akmenu 6
Vilnius, Lithuania
Tel: 011-370-5-266-5500
Fax: 011-370-5-266-5590
Email: consec@state.gov
Internet: http://vilnius.usembassy.gov/service.html

Lithuania's Adoption Authority
The State Child Rights Protection and Adoption Service
Ministry of Social Security and Labour:
Sodu g. 15
LT-03211 Vilnius, Lithuania
Tel: 370-5-231-0928
Fax: 370-5-231-0927
Email: info@ivaikinimas.lt
Internet: www.ivaikinimas.lt

Embassy of the Republic of Lithuania
2300 Clarendon Boulevard, Suite 302
Arlington, VA 22201
Tel: (202) 234-5860
Fax: (202) 328-0466
Email: info@ltembassyus.org
Internet: www.ltembassyus.org

Office of Children's Issues
United States Department of State
2201 C Street, NW; SA-29
Washington, DC 20520
Tel: 1-888-407-4747
E-mail: AskCI@state.gov
http://adoption.state.gov

For questions about immigration procedures, call the National Customer Service Center (NCSC) 1-800-375-5283 (TTY 1-800-767-1833).

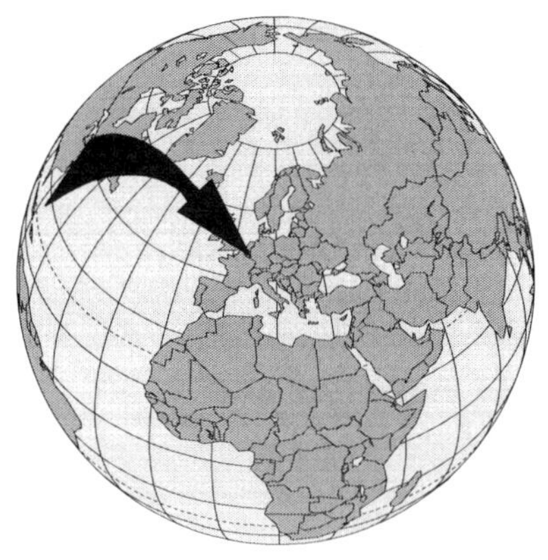

LUXEMBOURG

Compiled from publications that were available as of February 2013 from the U.S. Department of State, the U.S. Department of Commerce, and the Central Intelligence Agency (CIA). See the introduction to this set for explanatory notes.

Official Name:
Grand Duchy of Luxembourg

PROFILE

Geography

Area: total: 2,586 sq km; country comparison to the world: 179; land: 2,586 sq km; water: 0 sq km

Major cities: Luxembourg (capital) 90,000 (2009)

Climate: modified continental with mild winters, cool summers

Terrain: mostly gently rolling uplands with broad, shallow valleys; uplands to slightly mountainous in the north; steep slope down to Moselle flood plain in the southeast

People

Nationality: noun: Luxembourger(s); adjective: Luxembourg

Population: 509,074 (July 2012 est.)

Population growth rate: 1.135% (2012 est.)

Ethnic groups: Luxembourger 63.1%, Portuguese 13.3%, French 4.5%, Italian 4.3%, German 2.3%, other EU 7.3%, other 5.2% (2000 census)

Religions: Roman Catholic 87%, other (includes Protestant, Jewish, and Muslim) 13% (2000)

Languages: Luxembourgish (national language), German (administrative language), French (administrative language)

Literacy: definition: age 15 and over can read and write; total population: 100%; male: 100%; female: 100% (2000 est.)

Health: life expectancy at birth: total population: 79.75 years; male: 76.5 years; female: 83.21 years (2012 est.); Infant mortality rate: total: 4.39 deaths/1,000 live births; male: 4.41 deaths/1,000 live births; female: 4.36 deaths/1,000 live births (2012 est.)

Unemployment rate: 4.8% (2011 est.)

Work force: 208,200 (2012 est.)

Government

Type: constitutional monarchy

Independence: 1839

Constitution: 17 October 1868; occasional revisions

Political subdivisions: 3 districts; Diekirch, Grevenmacher, Luxembourg

Suffrage: 18 years of age; universal and compulsory

Economy

GDP (purchasing power parity): $42.19 billion (2012 est.); $41.75 billion (2011 est.); $41.33 billion (2010 est.); $40.26 billion (2009 est.)

GDP real growth rate: 0.2% (2012 est.); 1% (2011 est.); 2.7% (2010 est.); -5.3% (2009 est.)

GDP per capita (PPP): $80,700 (2012 est.); $81,100 (2011 est.); $81,600 (2010 est.); $80,900 (2009 est.)

Natural resources: iron ore (no longer exploited), arable land

Agriculture products: grapes, barley, oats, potatoes, wheat, fruits; dairy and livestock products

Industries: banking and financial services, iron and steel, information technology, telecommunications, cargo transportation, food processing, chemicals, metal products, engineering, tires, glass, aluminum, tourism

Exports: $15.5 billion (2012 est.); $19.9 billion (2011 est.); $16.66 billion (2010 est.)

Exports—commodities: machinery and equipment, steel products, chemicals, rubber products, glass

Exports—partners: Germany 22.2%, France 15.6%, Belgium 13.2%, UK 7.3%, Italy 5.4%, Switzerland 4.3%, Netherlands 4.1% (2011)

Imports: $25.08 billion (2012 est.); $26.27 billion (2011 est.); $22.1 billion (2010 est.)

Imports—commodities: minerals, metals, foodstuffs, quality consumer goods

Imports—partners: Belgium 30.3%, Germany 26%, France 10.8%, China 6.9%, Netherlands 5.8%, US 5.2% (2011)

Debt—external: $2.146 trillion (30 June 2011); $1.892 trillion (30 June 2010)
Exchange rates: euros (EUR) per US dollar; 0.7838 (2012 est.); 0.7194 (2011 est.); 0.755 (2010 est.); 0.7198 (2009 est.); 0.6827 (2008 est.); 0.7345 (2007 est.)

PEOPLE

Language

The national language of Luxembourg is Luxembourgish, a blend of Dutch, old German, and Frankish elements. The official language of the civil service, law, and parliament is French, although parliamentary debate and court cases are conducted mainly in Luxembourgish and police case files are recorded in German. German is the primary language of the press. French and German are taught in the schools, with German spoken mainly at the primary level and French at the secondary level. In addition, English is taught in high schools. Most Luxembourgers, as a result, speak at least some English.

Religion

The country is historically Roman Catholic, and Catholicism remains the predominant religion. While the government may not collect or maintain statistics on religious affiliation, a study by the Center for Studies of Population, Poverty and Socio-Economic Policy (CEPS/Instead) published during the year estimates more than 70 percent of the population is Catholic. Information provided by local religious communities and the aforementioned study indicates the following percentages for the country's remaining religious communities: Protestant (Lutheran, Calvinist, and Anglican), 2 percent; Muslim, 2 percent; Christian Orthodox (Greek, Serbian, Russian, and Romanian), 1 percent; and Jewish, 0.3 percent. The Baha'i Faith, the Universal Church, Jehovah's Witnesses, and The Church of Jesus Christ of Latter-day Saints (Mormons), are represented in smaller numbers.

HISTORY

After 400 years of domination by various European nations, Luxembourg was granted the status of Grand Duchy by the Congress of Vienna on June 9, 1815. Although Luxembourg considers 1835 (Treaty of London) to be its year of independence, it was not granted political autonomy until 1839 under King William I of the Netherlands, who also was the Grand Duke of Luxembourg. In 1867, Luxembourg was recognized as independent and guaranteed perpetual neutrality. After being occupied by Germany in both World Wars, Luxembourg abandoned neutrality and became a charter member of the

North Atlantic Treaty Organization (NATO) in 1949. It is also one of the six original members of the European Union (EU), formed in 1951 as the European Coal and Steel Community (ECSC).

The present sovereign, Grand Duke Henri, succeeded his father, Grand Duke Jean, on October 7, 2000. Grand Duke Jean announced his decision to abdicate in December 1999, after a 35-year reign.

GOVERNMENT AND POLITICAL CONDITIONS

The Grand Duchy of Luxembourg is a constitutional monarchy with a democratic, parliamentary form of government. Legislative authority is vested in the unicameral Chamber of Deputies (parliament). The prime minister is the leader of the dominant party in the popularly elected parliament. In 2009 the country held parliamentary elections that were considered free and fair.

Recent Elections

In 2009 the country held elections for the 60 seats in the Chamber of Deputies that were considered free and fair.

Participation of Women and Minorities: There were 15 women in the 60-member Chamber of Deputies and four women in the 15-member cabinet. There were 19 women in the 32-member Supreme Court. There was one parliamentarian of Portuguese descent and one minister of Italian descent.

Principal Government Officials

Last Updated: 1/31/2013

Grand Duke: **HENRI**
Prime Min.: **Jean-Claude JUNCKER**
Dep. Prime Min.: **Jean ASSELBORN**
Min. of Admin. Simplification: **Octavie MODERT**
Min. of Agriculture, Viticulture, & Rural Development: **Romain SCHNEIDER**
Min. of Civil Service & Admin. Reform: **Francois BILTGEN**
Min. for Communications: **Francois BILTGEN**
Min. of Culture: **Octavie MODERT**
Min. of Defense: **Jean-Marie HALSDORF**
Min. for Development Cooperation & Humanitarian Affairs: **Marie-Josee JACOBS**
Min. of Economy & Foreign Trade: **Jeannot KRECKE**
Min. of Equality of Opportunity: **Francoise HETTO-GAASCH**
Min. of Family & Integration: **Marie-Josee JACOBS**
Min. of Finance: **Luc FRIEDEN**
Min. of Foreign Affairs: **Jean ASSELBORN**
Min. of Health & of Social Security: **Mars DI BARTOLOMEO**
Min. of Higher Education & Research: **Francois BILTGEN**
Min. of Housing: **Marco SCHANK**
Min. of Interior: **Jean-Marie HALSDORF**
Min. of Justice: **Francois BILTGEN**
Min. of Labor, Employment, & Immigration: **Nicolas SCHMIT**
Min. of the Middle Class & Tourism: **Francoise HETTO-GAASCH**
Min. of National Education & Professional Training: **Mady DELVAUX-STEHRES**
Min. of Public Works: **Claude WISELER**
Min. of Relations With Parliament: **Octavie MODERT**
Min. of Religious Sects: **Francois BILTGEN**
Min. of Sports: **Romain SCHNEIDER**
Min. of State: **Jean-Claude JUNCKER**
Min. of Treasury: **Jean-Claude JUNCKER**
Chmn., Luxembourg Central Bank: **Yves MERSCH**
Ambassador to the US: **Jean-Paul SENNINGER**
Permanent Representative to the UN, New York: **Sylvie LUCAS**

ECONOMY

This small, stable, high-income economy—benefiting from its proximity to France, Belgium, and Germany—has historically featured solid growth, low inflation, and low unemployment. The industrial sector, initially dominated by steel, has become increasingly diversified to include chemicals, rubber, and other products. Growth in the financial sector, which now accounts for about 28% of GDP, has more than compensated for the decline in steel. Most banks are foreign-owned and have extensive foreign dealings, but Luxembourg has lost some of its advantages as a tax haven because of OECD and EU pressure.

The economy depends on foreign and cross-border workers for about 60% of its labor force. Luxembourg, like all EU members, suffered from the global economic crisis that began in late 2008, but unemployment has trended below the EU average. Following strong expansion from 2004 to 2007, Luxembourg's economy contracted 3.6% in 2009, but rebounded in 2010–11 before slowing again in 2012. The country continues to enjoy an extraordinarily high standard of living—GDP per capita ranks among the highest in the world, and is the highest in the euro zone.

Turmoil in the world financial markets and lower global demand during 2008–09 prompted the government to inject capital into the banking sector and implement stimulus measures to boost the economy. Government stimulus measures and support for the banking sector, however, led to a 5% government budget deficit in 2009. Nevertheless, the deficit was cut to 1.1% in 2011 and 0.9% in 2012.

Even during the financial crisis and recovery, Luxembourg retained the highest current account surplus as a share of GDP in the euro zone, owing largely to their strength in financial services. Public debt remains among the lowest of the region although it has more than doubled since 2007 as percentage of GDP.

Luxembourg's economy, while stabile, grew slowly in 2012 due to ongoing weak growth in the euro area. Authorities have strengthened supervision of domestic banks because of their exposure to the activities of foreign banks.

Labor Conditions

There are laws to protect children from exploitation in the workplace, and the government effectively enforced these laws. There were no reports of illegal child labor.

The law prohibits the employment of children under the age of 16. Apprentices who are 16 years old must attend school in addition to their job training. Workers under the age of 18 have additional legal protection, including limits on overtime and the number of hours that can be worked continuously. The Ministries of Labor and Education effectively enforced the child labor laws.

As of October 1, 2011 the national minimum wage for a worker over the age of 18 was 1,801 euros ($2,341) per month for unskilled workers and 2,161 euros ($2,809) for skilled workers. The poverty income level was 1,650 euros ($2,145) per month in 2011. The Ministry of Labor enforced the minimum wage effectively. Minimum wage provisions covered foreign and migrant workers.

The law mandates a maximum normal workweek of 40 hours. Premium pay is required for overtime or unusual hours. Sunday employment is permitted in continuous-process industries (steel, glass, and chemicals) and for certain maintenance and security personnel; other industries must request permission for Sunday work, which the government considered on a case-by-case basis and generally granted. Work on Sunday, allowed for some retail employees, must be voluntary and compensated at double the normal wage or with compensatory time off on another day, equal to the number of hours worked on Sunday. The law requires rest breaks for shift workers and limits all workers to a maximum of 10 hours per day, including overtime. The labor inspection court and the Superior Court of Justice are responsible for enforcing these laws. The government conducted investigations and transferred cases to judicial authorities regularly.

The law mandates a safe working environment. An inspection system included penalties for infractions. The labor inspectorate of the Ministry of Labor and the accident insurance agency of the Social Security Ministry carried out effective inspections. Workers have the right to ask the labor inspectorate to make a determination regarding workplace safety, and the inspectorate usually did so expeditiously. There were 50 inspectors as of 2011. In 2010 there were 19,524 work related injuries, including 17 work related deaths; figures for 2011 were not available.

U.S.-LUXEMBOURG RELATIONS

In 1867, Luxembourg gained full independence from the Netherlands, and was guaranteed perpetual neutrality by European powers. The United States established diplomatic relations with Luxembourg in 1903. Luxembourg was occupied by Germany in World War I and World War II, and was liberated by forces that included U.S. troops.

Luxembourg is a longstanding ally of the United States. The friendship between the two countries is strengthened by a shared commitment to advancing freedom and prosperity. Luxembourg has long been a prominent supporter of European political and economic integration. It is a charter member of the North Atlantic Treaty Organization (NATO) and is one of the founding members of what became the European Union (EU).

U.S. Assistance to Luxembourg

The United States provides no development assistance to Luxembourg.

Bilateral Economic Relations

Luxembourg is a member of the European Union (EU). The U.S. economic relationship with the EU is the largest and most complex in the world, and the United States and the EU continue to pursue initiatives to create new opportunities for transatlantic commerce. U.S. exports to Luxembourg include commercial aircraft and information and communications technology equipment. Luxembourg also purchases U.S. services and intellectual property, such as medical research and entertainment. U.S. firms are among the most prominent foreign investors in Luxembourg. The country is a major financial center in Europe, and U.S. banks have a significant presence. Luxembourg participates in the Visa Waiver Program, which allows nationals of participating countries to travel to the United States for certain business or tourism purposes for stays of 90 days or less without obtaining a visa.

Luxembourg's Membership in International Organizations

Luxembourg and the United States belong to a number of the same international organizations, including the United Nations, North Atlantic Treaty Organization, Euro-Atlantic Partnership Council, Organization for Security and Cooperation in Europe, Organization for Economic Cooperation and Development, International Monetary Fund, World Bank, and World Trade Organization. Luxembourg also is an observer to the Organization of American States.

Bilateral Representation

Luxembourg maintains an embassy in the United States at 2200 Massachusetts Avenue NW, Washington, DC 20008 (tel. 202-265-4171).

Principal U.S. Embassy Officials

Last Updated: 1/14/2013

LUXEMBOURG (E) 22 Blvd. Emmanuel Servais, (352) 460-123, Fax +352-461-401, INMARSAT Tel 881631437351 (Iridium), Workweek: M-F 0830–1730, Website: http://luxembourg.usembassy.gov/

DCM OMS:	Elizebeth E. Veghte
AMB OMS:	Kimberly J. Magee
DHS/CBP:	Sherri Braxton (Resident In The Hague)
DHS/ICE:	David S. Adkins (Resident In The Hague)
DHS/TSA:	Anne Marine Pellerin (Resident In Paris)
MGT:	Kevin B. Crisp
MLO/ODC:	COL Dean D. King (Resident In Brussels)
POL/ECON:	Vacant
POL/MIL:	Steve R. Nugent
SDO/DATT:	COL Jeffrey D. Saunders
AMB:	Robert A. Mandell
CON:	Carla T. Nadeau
DCM:	David R. Fetter
PAO:	Katya Thomas
GSO:	Linda Cunningham
RSO:	Mark T. Typinski
AGR:	Mary Ellen Smith (Resident In The Hague)
DEA:	Daniel D. Dodds (Resident In Brussels)
FAA:	Stephen P. Creamer
IMO:	Richard Johnson
IRS:	Aziz Benbrahim (Resident In Paris)
ISSO:	Avery Frantz
LEGATT:	Ronald P. Comers (Resident In Brussels)

TRAVEL

Consular Information Sheet

April 23, 2012

Country Description: Luxembourg is a highly developed, stable constitutional monarchy and parliamentary democracy. There are many tourist facilities in Luxembourg.

Smart Traveler Enrollment Program (STEP)/Embassy Locations: If you are going to live in or visit Luxembourg, please take the time to tell our Embassy about your trip. If you enroll, we can keep you up to date with important safety and security announcements. We can also help your friends and family get in touch with you in an emergency.

U.S. Embassy Luxembourg
22, Blvd Emmanuel Servais, L-2535
Luxembourg City
Telephone: (352) 46 01 23 (available 24/7),
Emergency after-hours telephone: (352) 621 547 133 (duty officer)
Facsimile: (352) 46 19 39

Entry/Exit Requirements for U.S. Citizens: Luxembourg is a party to the Schengen Agreement. You may enter Luxembourg for up to 90 days for tourist or business purposes without a visa. Your passport should be valid for at least three months beyond the period of stay. You are required to have sufficient funds and a return airline ticket. No immunizations are required.

If you plan to stay longer than three months, you must apply for a temporary-residence permit ("autorisation de séjour"') before entering Luxembourg. This permit, issued by the Ministry of Foreign Affairs, applies to students, employees, self-employed persons, interns, research workers, and family members. If you apply for and receive a permit, it will be mailed to you. You will then have 90 days to enter Luxembourg. You must then register your arrival ("déclaration d'arrivée") within three weekdays from your date of entry at the town office ("administration communale") of your future place of residence. You must request your official residency card ("titre de séjour") from the Immigration Directorate of the Ministry of Foreign Affairs within three months of your arrival.

For additional information about entry requirements for Luxembourg, you can contact the Embassy of Luxembourg (2200 Massachusetts Ave. NW, Washington, DC 20008; phone: (202) 265-4171 or -4172), or the Luxembourg Consulates General in New York (phone: (212) 888-6664) or San Francisco (phone: (415) 788-0816).

The U.S. Department of State is unaware of any HIV/AIDS entry restrictions for visitors to or foreign residents of Luxembourg.

Threats to Safety and Security: Terrorist incidents are rare in Luxembourg. Luxembourg's open borders, however, could possibly allow terrorist groups to enter/exit the country unnoticed.

Prior police approval is required for public demonstrations in Luxembourg. Police routinely provide supervision to ensure adequate security for participants and passers-by. Nonetheless, situations may develop which could pose threats to public safety. We advise you to avoid areas where public demonstrations are taking place.

Stay up to date by:

- Bookmarking our Bureau of Consular Affairs website, which contains the current Travel Warnings and Travel Alerts as well as the Worldwide Caution;
- Following us on Twitter and the Bureau of Consular Affairs page on Facebook as well;
- Downloading our free Smart Traveler iPhone App to have travel information at your fingertips;
- Calling 1-888-407-4747 toll-free within the U.S. and Canada, or a regular toll line, 1-202-501-4444, from other countries; and
- Taking some time before travel to consider your personal security.

Crime: The crime rate in Luxembourg is moderate as compared to other European countries. The predominant forms of crime in Luxembourg are non-violent. Such crimes include the theft of valuables through snatching of purses/bags, and breaking and entering of unoccupied homes. You should take common-sense precautions while in Luxembourg; be especially cautious while in public areas, the airport, and train terminals, where pickpockets can be a problem. Luxembourg has many public parks that are safe during the daylight hours, though the volume of low-level drug vending has increased in some of the city parks. You should avoid these parks after dark, though, because they pose a higher risk. During the summer season, you should be particularly alert to purse snatchings and confidence scams against tourists. Incidents of petty crime spike during the annual "Schueberfouer," a three-week event held every summer.

Don't buy counterfeit and pirated goods, even if they are widely available. Not only are the bootlegs illegal to bring back into the United States, if you purchase them you may also be breaking local law.

Victims of Crime: If you or someone you know becomes the victim of a crime abroad, you should contact the local police and the nearest U.S. embassy or consulate. We can:

- Replace a stolen passport;
- Help you find appropriate medical care if you are the victim of violent crimes such as assault or rape;
- Put you in contact with the appropriate police authorities, and if you want us to, we can contact family members or friend;
- Help you understand the local criminal justice process and direct you to local attorneys, although it is important to remember that local authorities are responsible for investigating and prosecuting the crime.

The Government of Luxembourg has a website that offers information about local police and justice procedures, as well as victim support services.

The local equivalent to the "911" emergency line in Luxembourg is 113 for the police.

Criminal Penalties: While you are traveling in Luxembourg, you are subject to its laws even if you are a U.S. citizen. Foreign laws and legal systems can be vastly different than our own. Criminal penalties vary from country to country. There are also some things that might be legal in the country you visit, but still illegal in the United States. You can be prosecuted under U.S. law if you buy pirated goods abroad. Engaging in sexual conduct with children or using or disseminating child pornography in a foreign country is a crime prosecutable in the United States If you break local laws in Luxembourg, your U.S. passport won't help you avoid arrest or prosecution. It's very important to know what's legal and what's not where you are going.

Persons violating Luxembourg's laws, even unknowingly, may be expelled, arrested, or imprisoned. Penalties for possessing, using, or trafficking in illegal drugs in Luxembourg are severe, and convicted offenders can expect long jail sentences and heavy fines.

Arrest notifications in host country: While some countries will automatically notify the nearest U.S. embassy or consulate if a U.S. citizen is detained or arrested in a foreign country, that might not always be the case. To ensure that the United States is aware of your circumstances, request that the police and prison officials notify the nearest U.S. embassy or consulate as soon as you are arrested or detained overseas.

Special Circumstances: Luxembourg customs authorities may enforce strict regulations on the temporary import or export of certain items into or out of Luxembourg. Such items may include live animals, plants, endangered species, medication (except for personal use), firearms and ammunition, cultural artifacts, alcoholic beverages, and tobacco products. Please contact the Embassy of Luxembourg in Washington or one of Luxembourg's consulates in the United States for specific information regarding customs requirements. You may travel with any amount of imported currency. The Euro is the official currency in Luxembourg.

Accessibility: Persons with disabilities can take advantage of a special public transportation system (Novabus) that can be requested for a small fee to transport the customer anywhere within Luxembourg. The buses operated by Luxembourg City are all accessible to persons with physical disabilities. It is also possible to book a special 'Rollibus' (minivan).

Luxembourg train station provides assistance to travelers with disabilities. This service can be requested from any platform at the station or by e-mail in advance. Luxembourg CFL (local railway system) has been improving accommodations for persons with disabilities by installing ramps, broader doors, etc.

Most public buildings, sports and cultural centers, theaters, and museums have good accessibility for disabled persons. Luxembourg has a local website that provides information for people with disabilities.

Medical Facilities and Health Information: Medical facilities are widely available. Dial 112 for a medical emergency or the fire department, and 113 for the police. Hospitals in Luxembourg operate on a 24-hour rotation system. We do not advise self-referral to any hospital, with an exception: the "Centre Hospitalier" is always on-call for emergency cases involving children under the age of 14. In Luxembourg City, three major hospitals offer comprehensive general medical and surgical treatment. Additionally, there are two pediatric clinics and two obstetric clinics in Luxembourg City. There are also hospitals in the south of the country (Esch-sur-Alzette) and in the north (Wiltz). For more specialized care, including major burns, transfer to a regional burn center in Belgium or France is necessary. Three medical services (maisons médicales) provide general medical treatment (not suitable for emergency cases) after hours, on weekends and holidays, when a treating physician is not available. Please see information on all medical facilities in Luxembourg at the following website.

Most drugstores are located in the Luxembourg City but can also be found throughout the country in all major communes. Drugstores operate on a 24-hour rotation system for after-hours services, including emergency prescriptions. The on-call pharmacy is listed daily in the local newspaper or can be ascertained by calling 112. A doctor's prescription is sometimes necessary for drugs that are sold over the counter in the United States.

You can find good information on vaccinations and other health precautions, on the Centers for Disease Control and Prevention (CDC) website. For information about outbreaks of infectious diseases abroad, consult the the World Health Organization (WHO) website, which also contains additional health information for travelers, including detailed country-specific health information.

Medical Insurance: You can't assume your insurance will go with you when you travel. It's very important to find out BEFORE you leave whether or not your medical insurance will cover you overseas. You need to ask your insurance company two questions:

- Does my policy apply when I'm out of the United States?
- Will it cover emergencies like a trip to a foreign hospital or a medical evacuation?

In many places, doctors and hospitals still expect payment in cash at the time of service. Your regular U.S. health insurance may not cover doctor and hospital visits in other countries. If your policy doesn't go with you when you travel, it's a very good idea to take out another one for your trip.

Traffic Safety and Road Conditions: If you are residing in Luxembourg, you must have your driver's license transferred within one year. To start the process, you must have been a registered resident of Luxembourg for at least 185 days and the license must have been issued in the country where you were actually residing at the time of issuance. Furthermore, you must submit a recent medical certificate, a criminal record check (affidavit from the U.S. Embassy) and a residence permit for Luxembourg. It is not possible to receive a Luxembourg driver's license and keep the foreign (U.S.) license. The foreign license must be surrendered to the driver's license office and will be returned to the issuing authority.

While in Luxembourg, you may encounter road conditions that differ significantly from those in the United States. Luxembourg has a modern, well-maintained system of highways and secondary roads. Road signs and markings are clear and primarily worded in French. Streets in the city, construction sites and crossroads are well illuminated at night. On highways, a digital alert system warns drivers of incidents or detours. Roads into and out of Luxembourg City are congested during the morning and evening rush hour. Visitors should drive defensively in high-volume commuter traffic. During the fall and winter, fog and ice can cause sudden slowdowns on highways and secondary roads.

In case of a car accident involving injury or dispute, it is a good idea to call the police at 113. The police will make an official assessment of the accident's circumstances that can subsequently be used if further legal action becomes necessary.

The daily mix of drivers from Luxembourg and its three neighboring countries results in a variety of driving practices and courtesies. While most drivers respect speed limits, traffic signals, and rules, some do not. Vehicle maintenance for cars registered in Luxembourg is controlled by the mandatory yearly car inspection; police can perform random road checks at any time. The possibility of encountering an intoxicated driver increases on weekends, especially during the late evening hours. Driving while intoxicated may result in penalties including imprisonment from eight days up to two years, plus a fine of 251 to 5,000 Euros (approximately $344 to $6,870).

Public transportation throughout the country, including bus services and taxis, is highly developed and is considered very safe.

Emergency road services in Luxembourg are excellent. For breakdown and towing service call the Automobile Club of Luxembourg (ACL) at 26000. In case of an accident, call 112 for a medical emergency and 113 for the police.

Aviation Safety Oversight: The U.S. Federal Aviation Administration (FAA) has assessed the government of Luxembourg's Civil Aviation Authority as being in compliance with International Civil Aviation Organization (ICAO) aviation safety standards for oversight of Luxembourg's air carrier operations. Further information may be found on the FAA's safety assessment page.

Children's Issues: Please see the U.S. Dept. of State Office of Children's Issues web pages on intercountry adoption and international parental child abduction.

Intercountry Adoption

July 2009

Luxembourg is party to the Hague Convention on Protection of Children and Co-operation in Respect of Intercountry Adoption (Hague Adoption Convention). Therefore, adoptions between Luxembourg and the United States are governed by the requirements of the Convention and the laws and regulations implementing the Convention in both the United States and Luxembourg.

The Department of State does not maintain files on the adoption process in Luxembourg because adoptions from Luxembourg are rare; fewer than five adoptions by American citizen parents have taken place in over a decade. The Ministry of Family and Integration (Ministère de la Famille et de l'Intégration) is the Central Authority for the purposes of the Hague Adoption Convention in Luxembourg. American Citizens living in Luxembourg who wish to adopt from the U.S. or a third country should contact the Central Authority to learn what requirements may apply to their adoption. Contact information for the Central Authority is available on their website http://www.mfi. public.lu

MACAU

Compiled from publications that were available as of February 2013 from the U.S. Department of State, the U.S. Department of Commerce, and the Central Intelligence Agency (CIA). See the introduction to this set for explanatory notes.

Official Name:
Macau Special Administrative Region

PROFILE

Geography

Area: total: 28.2 sq km; country comparison to the world: 237; land: 28.2 sq km; water: 0 sq km
Major cities:
Climate: subtropical; marine with cool winters, warm summers
Terrain: generally flat

People

Nationality: noun: Chinese; adjective: Chinese
Population: 578,025 (July 2012 est.)
Population growth rate: 0.866% (2012 est.)
Ethnic groups: Chinese 94.3%, other 5.7% (includes Macanese—mixed Portuguese and Asian ancestry) (2006 census)
Religions: Buddhist 50%, Roman Catholic 15%, none or other 35% (1997 est.)
Languages: Cantonese 85.7%, Hokkien 4%, Mandarin 3.2%, other Chinese dialects 2.7%, English 1.5%, Tagalog 1.3%, other 1.6%
Literacy: definition: age 15 and over can read and write; total population: 91.3%; male: 95.3%; female: 87.8% (2001 census)
Health: life expectancy at birth: total population: 84.43 years; male: 81.47 years; female: 87.54 years (2012 est.); Infant mortality rate: total: 3.17 deaths/1,000 live births; male: 3.32 deaths/1,000 live births; female: 3 deaths/1,000 live births (2012 est.)
Unemployment rate: 2.9% (2010)
Work force: 330,900 (2010 est.)

Government

Type: limited democracy
Independence: none
Constitution: The Basic Law, approved 31 March 1993 by China's National People's Congress, is Macau's charter
Political subdivisions: none (special administrative region of the People's Republic of China)
Suffrage: 18 years of age in direct elections for some legislative positions, universal for permanent residents living in Macau for the past seven years; note—indirect elections are limited to organizations registered as "corporate voters" (973 were registered in the 2009 legislative elections) and a 300-member Election Committee for the Chief Executive (CE) drawn from broad regional groupings, municipal organizations, central government bodies, and elected Macau officials

Economy

GDP (purchasing power parity): $18.47 billion (2009 est.); $18.14 billion (2008 est.); $14.4 billion (2006)
GDP real growth rate: 1% (2009 est.); 12.9% (2008); 26% (2007)
GDP per capita (PPP): $33,000 (2009); $31,800 (2008); $28,400 (2006)
Natural resources: NEGL
Agriculture products: only 2% of land area is cultivated, mainly by vegetable growers; fishing, mostly for crustaceans, is important; some of the catch is exported to Hong Kong
Industries: tourism, gambling, clothing, textiles, electronics, footwear, toys
Exports: $1.045 billion (2010 est.); $973 million (2009 est.)
Exports—commodities: clothing, textiles, footwear, toys, electronics, machinery and parts
Exports—partners: Hong Kong 44.1%, China 15.6%, US 8.2% (2009 est.)
Imports: $6.312 billion (2010 est.); $4.5 billion (2009 est.)
Imports—commodities: raw materials and semi-manufactured goods, consumer goods (foodstuffs, beverages, tobacco), capital goods, mineral fuels and oils
Imports—partners: China 30.8%, Hong Kong 18.8%, France 8.4%, Switzerland 6.4%, Italy 6.3%, US 5.7%, Japan 5.6% (2009 est.)
Debt—external: $0 (2010)
Exchange rates: patacas (MOP) per US dollar; 8.0182 (2011 est.); 8.0022 (2010 est.); 7.983 (2008); 8.011 (2007)

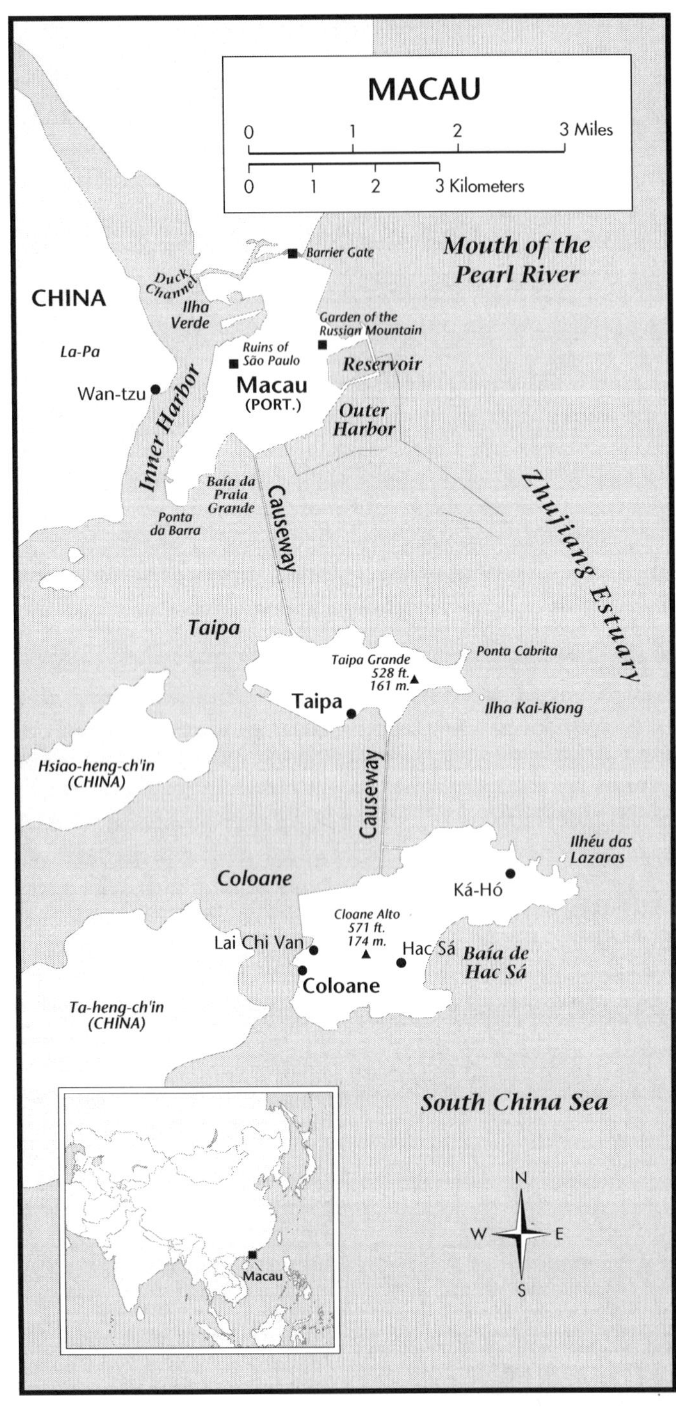

PEOPLE

Macau's resident population is mostly Chinese, primarily Cantonese and some Hakka, both from nearby Guangdong Province. The remainder is of Portuguese or mixed Chinese-Portuguese ancestry. English is spoken in tourist areas. Macau has 10 higher education institutions, including the University of Macau; about 70% of the University of Macau's students are local and 30% are from overseas.

Religion

According to the Government Information Bureau, nearly 80 percent of the population practices Buddhism. There are approximately 30,000 Roman Catholics (of whom over half are foreign domestic workers and expatriates residing in Macau) and more than 5,000 Protestants. Smaller religious groups include Baha'is (estimated at 2,500 persons); Muslims (estimated at 400 persons); and a small number of Falun Gong practitioners.

There are approximately 40 Buddhist temples, as well as dozens of village temples and houses dedicated to Buddhist deities; 30 Taoist temples; three Catholic cathedrals, 18 Catholic churches and 56 Catholic chapels within diocesan buildings; approximately 76 Protestant churches; four Baha'i centers; and one mosque.

Many Protestant denominations are represented, including Baptist, Anglican, Lutheran, Presbyterian, Methodist, and Pentecostal churches. There are also evangelical denominations and independent local churches.

An estimated 76 Protestant churches with 4,000 members conduct services in Chinese; approximately 5,000 worshippers attend every Sunday. An estimated 500 Protestants attend services conducted in foreign languages.

HISTORY

Chinese records of Macau date back to the establishment in 1152 of Xiangshan County under which Macau was administered, though it remained unpopulated through most of the next century. Portuguese traders began using Macau as a staging port as early as 1516, making it the oldest European settlement in the Far East.

In 1557, the Chinese agreed to a Portuguese settlement in Macau but did not recognize Portuguese sovereignty. Initially, the Portuguese developed Macau's port as a trading post for China-Japan trade and as a staging port on the long voyage from Lisbon to Nagasaki. When Chinese officials banned direct trade with Japan in

1547, Macau's Portuguese traders carried goods between the two countries.

The first Portuguese governor was appointed to Macau in 1680, but the Chinese continued to assert their authority, collecting land and customs taxes. Portugal continued to pay rent to China until 1849, when the Portuguese abolished the Chinese customs house and declared Macau's "independence." On March 26, 1887, the Manchu government acknowledged the Portuguese right of "perpetual occupation."

The Manchu-Portuguese agreement, known as the Protocol of Lisbon, was signed with the condition that Portugal would never surrender Macau to a third party without China's permission.

When the Chinese communists came to power in 1949, they declared the Protocol of Lisbon to be invalid as an "unequal treaty" imposed by foreigners on China. However, Beijing was not ready to settle the question, requesting maintenance of "the status quo" until a more appropriate time. Riots broke out in 1966 when pro-communist Chinese elements and the Macau police clashed. Through intervention by some of Macau's leading "patriotic" Chinese business clans, an agreement was reached which met local protestor demands and restored order under the Portuguese administration. Portugal tried in 1966 (after the riots) and again in 1974 (following the fall of the Salazar dictatorship) to return Macau to Chinese sovereignty. China, still emerging from the internal turmoil of the Cultural Revolution, declined to accept.

Portugal and China established diplomatic relations in 1979. A year later, Gen. Melo Egidio became the first Governor of Macau to visit the People's Republic of China.

The visit underscored both parties' interest in finding a mutually agreeable solution to Macau's status. In 1979, Portugal and China agreed to regard Macau as "a Chinese territory under temporary Portuguese administration." Handover negotiations began in 1985, a year after the U.K. and China reached agreement that Hong Kong would return to China in 1997. The result was a 1987 agreement returning Macau to Chinese sovereignty as a Special Administrative Region (SAR) of China on December 20, 1999.

GOVERNMENT AND POLITICAL CONDITIONS

Macau is a Special Administrative Region (SAR) of the People's Republic of China (PRC) and enjoys a high degree of autonomy, except in defense and foreign affairs, under the SAR's constitution (the Basic Law). Chief Executive Fernando Chui Sai-on, who took office in December 2009, headed the government after being elected in July 2009 by a 300-member commission.

Recent Elections

Despite calls for an increase in the number of directly elected Legislative Assembly seats, the government quickly dispelled an October 2011 news report that it was considering plans to expand the number in 2013. Of the 29 seats in the Legislative Assembly, only 12 are directly elected. The last election, held in 2009, was generally free and fair.

There are limits on the types of bills that legislators may introduce. The law stipulates that legislators may not initiate legislation related to public expenditure, the SAR's political structure, or the operation of the government. Proposed legislation related to government policies must receive the CE's written approval before it is submitted. The legislature also has no power of confirmation over executive or judicial appointments.

A 10-member Executive Council functions as an unofficial cabinet, approving draft legislation before it is presented in the Legislative Assembly. The Basic Law stipulates that the CE appoint members of the SAR Executive Council from among the principal officials of the executive authorities, members of the legislature, and public figures.

Political Parties: The SAR has no laws on political parties; politically active groups therefore registered as societies or companies. These groups were active in promoting their political agendas, and those critical of the government did not face restrictions. Such groups participated in protests over government policies or proposed legislation without restriction.

Participation of Women and Minorities: There were four women in the 29-member Legislative Assembly. Women also held a number of senior positions throughout the government, including the Secretary for Justice and Administration, the second-highest official in the SAR government. Fifteen of the SAR's 46 judges were women. Women made up more than 41 percent of the senior-level executive, 48 percent of the judiciary, and almost all of the senior legislative staff (i.e., not including legislators). There were two members of ethnic minorities in the Legislative Assembly. One Executive Council member was from an ethnic minority, as was the police commissioner general.

Principal Government Officials

Last Updated: 1/31/2013

Chief Executive: **Fernando CHUI Sai-on**
Sec. for Admin. & Justice: **Florinda Da Rosa Silva CHAN**
Sec. for Economics & Finance: **Francis TAM Pak-yuen**
Sec. for Security: **CHEONG Kuoc Va**
Sec. for Social Affairs & Culture: **CHEONG U**
Sec. for Transport & Public Works: **LAU Si Io**
Procurator Gen.: **HO Chio Meng**
Pres., Court of Final Appeal: **SAM Hou Fai**
Pres., Legislative Council: **LAU Cheok Va**
Commissioner, Audit: **HO Veng On**
Commissioner, Independent Commission Against Corruption: **FONG Man Chong**

ECONOMY

After opening up its locally-controlled casino industry to foreign competition in 2001, the territory attracted tens of billions of dollars in foreign investment, transforming Macau into one of the world's largest gaming centers. Macau's gaming and tourism businesses were fueled by China's decision to relax travel restrictions on Chinese citizens wishing to visit Macau.

By 2006, Macau's gaming revenue surpassed that of the Las Vegas strip, and gaming-related taxes accounted for more than 70% of total government revenue. In 2008, Macau introduced measures to cool the rapidly developing sector. Macau's economy slowed dramatically in 2009 as a result of the global economic slowdown, but strong growth resumed in 2010–11, largely on the back of tourism from mainland China and the gaming sectors. This city of 550,000 hosted nearly 25 million visitors in 2010. Almost 53% came from mainland China. Macau's traditional manufacturing industry slowed greatly since the termination of the Multi-Fiber Agreement in 2005.

The Closer Economic Partnership Agreement (CEPA) between Macau and mainland China that came into effect in January 2004 offers Macau-made products tariff-free access to the mainland; nevertheless, China is Macau's second largest goods export market, behind Hong Kong, and followed by the United States. However, exports in 2010 were less than US$900 million, while gaming receipts were almost US$24 billion, a 58% increase over 2009.

Macau's economy expanded at a slower pace in 2012—around 10%—reflecting continued global economic uncertainties. Macau continues to face the challenges of managing its growing casino industry, money-laundering, and the need to diversifying the economy away from heavy dependence on gaming revenues. Macau's currency, the pataca, is closely tied to the Hong Kong dollar, which is also freely accepted in the territory.

Labor Conditions

The law prohibits minors under the age of 16 from working, although minors between the ages of 14 and 16 can be authorized to work on an "exceptional basis." Some children reportedly worked in family-operated or small businesses. Local laws do not establish specific regulations governing the number of hours these children can work, but International Labor Organization conventions were applied. Additionally, the law governing the number of working hours (eight hours a day, 40 hours a week) was equally applicable to adults and minors, but minors cannot work overtime hours. Minors are forbidden from certain types of work, including but not limited to domestic work, any employment between 9 p.m. and 7 a.m., and at places where admission of minors is forbidden. The Labor Department enforced the law through periodic and targeted inspections, and violators were prosecuted.

Local labor laws establish the general principle of fair wages and mandate compliance with wage agreements. There is no mandatory minimum wage, except for government-outsourced security guards and cleaners and foreign domestic workers. The law also sets maximum hours, rest days, statutory holidays, and premium pay rules. Article 70 of the 2008 Labor Relations Law allows employers to dismiss staff "without just cause" provided that economic compensation, indexed to the employee's length of service, is paid.

Local customs normally favored employment without the benefit of written labor contracts, except in the case of migrant workers, who were issued short-term contracts. Labor groups reported that employers increasingly used temporary contracts to circumvent obligations to pay for workers' benefits, such as pensions, sick leave, and paid holidays. The short-term nature of the contracts also made it easier to dismiss workers by means of nonrenewal.

Labor legislation provides for a 48-hour workweek (many businesses operated on a 40-hour workweek), an eight-hour workday, paid overtime, annual leave, and medical and maternity care. Although the law provides for a 24-hour rest period each week, workers frequently agreed to work overtime to compensate for low wages. The Labor Department provided assistance and legal advice to workers upon request.

The Labor Department enforced occupational safety and health regulations, and failure to correct infractions could lead to prosecution. Although the law includes a requirement that employers provide a safe working environment, no explicit provisions protect employees' right to continued employment if they refused to work under dangerous conditions.

According to the government's Human Resources Office, there were approximately 90,000 imported workers at the end of September 2011, mostly from Mainland China, Hong Kong, Indonesia, the Philippines, and Vietnam. These workers, commonly engaged in the restaurant and hotel industry but also serving as foreign domestic workers, gaming and entertainment employees, and engaged in the construction and retail sectors, often complained of discrimination in the workplace. The Macau Lawyers Association claimed these foreign workers often faced unequal pay in comparison with their Macau counterparts.

U.S.-MACAU RELATIONS

In 1999, Macau returned to Chinese sovereignty from Portuguese administration. Macau is a Special Administrative Region of the People's Republic of China. Its foreign relations and defense are the responsibility of China. However, China grants Macau considerable autonomy in economic and commercial relations. Macau is a separate customs territory and economic entity from the rest of China and is able to enter into international agreements on its own behalf in commercial and economic matters. U.S. policy toward Macau is grounded in the U.S. Macau Policy Act of 1999 and reflects U.S. support for Macau's autonomy under the "One Country, Two Systems" framework established in Macau's Basic Law. The U.S. promotes trade and investment in Macau, supports broadening law enforcement cooperation, works to bolster academic, educational, and cultural links, supports official U.S. visitors to Macau, and serves the growing numbers of U.S. citizen residents and visitors in Macau. U.S. residents in Macau are estimated at over 4,000.

U.S. Assistance to Macau

The United States provides no foreign assistance to Macau.

Bilateral Economic Relations

In 2011, the United States accounted for 8.0% of Macau's exports and 6.0% of its imports. U.S. investment has played a leading role in the development of Macau's gaming and entertainment sector. According to the most recent Macau Government statistics, U.S. direct investment in Macau totaled $2.2 billion at the end of 2010, although unofficial numbers put the figure between $8 billion and $10 billion. There are over 30 U.S. firms doing business in Macau.

Macau's Membership in International Organizations

Macau and the United States belong to a number of the same international organizations, including the World Trade Organization; the Egmont Group, an informal international gathering of financial intelligence units; and the Asia/Pacific Group on Money Laundering, a Financial Action Task Force-style regional body.

Bilateral Representation

The U.S. Government has no offices in Macau. U.S. interests are represented by the U.S. Consulate General in Hong Kong.

China's embassy in the United States is at 3505 International Place, NW, Washington, DC 20008; Tel.: (202) 495-2266.

Principal U.S. Embassy Officials

Last Updated: 1/14/2013

HONG KONG (CG) 26 Garden Road, Central, (852) 2523-9011/Post One– (852) 2841-2230 & (852) 9091-5726 (cell), Fax (852) 2845-1598, Workweek: Monday–Friday; 0830-1730, Website: http://hongkong.usconsulate.gov/

CG OMS:	Claudia Ellingwood
Co-CLO:	Janet Malanga
DHS/ICE:	Eben Roberts
DPO:	Matthew J. Matthews
FCS:	Scott Shaw
FM:	Ronald Hernandez
HRO:	Eric Browing-Larsen
MGT:	Andrea S. Baker
POL/ECON:	Andrew Shaw
POSHO:	Ronald Hernandez
SDO/DATT:	CAPT Clayton Grindle
CG:	Stephen M. Young
CON:	George Hogeman
PAO:	Nini Forino
GSO:	Polly A. Emerick
RSO:	Mark Lewis
ATO:	Erich Kuss
CLO:	Linda Barker
DEA:	Andrew J. Malanga
FMO:	Nina Robinson
ICASS Chair:	Erich Kuss
IMO:	Mari Jain Womack
IPO:	Janet Vancoblijn
IRS:	William Cheung
ISO:	Mark C. Allen
LEGATT:	Lawrence Futa

TRAVEL

Consular Information Sheet

April 16, 2012

Description: Macau, a Special Administrative Region (SAR) of the People's Republic of China (PRC) since December 20, 1999, has a high degree of autonomy, except in the areas of defense and foreign policy. Macau retains its own currency, laws, and border controls. With a population of approximately 544,600, Macau covers a 29.5 square-kilometer area including the peninsula of Macau, which is connected to the PRC, and the two islands of Taipa and Coloane. Gambling and tourism are the largest sectors in Macau's economy. Facilities for tourism are well developed.

Smart Traveler Enrollment Program (STEP)/Embassy Locations: If you are going to live or visit Macau, please take the time to tell our Consulate about your trip. If you enroll, we can keep you up to date with important safety and security announcements. It will also help your friends and family get in touch with you in an emergency.

Local consulate and embassy information is available below and at the Department of State's list of embassies and consulates. There is no U.S. diplomatic or consular presence in Macau. The U.S. Consulate General in Hong Kong provides consular assistance to U.S. citizens in Macau.

U.S. Consulate General Hong Kong & Macau
26 Garden Road, Central, Hong Kong
Telephone: 852-2841–2211, 852-2841–2225, 852-2841–2323
(Direct lines to American Citizen Services during regular business hours)
Emergency after-hours telephone: 852-2841–9011
Facsimile: 852-2845–4845

Entry/Exit Requirements for U.S. Citizens: Your passport must be valid for at least 30 days beyond your intended period of stay in Macau. If you are a tourist, you may visit for up to 30 days without a visa. According to the Macau Immigration Department, if you depart and then immediately reenter Macau, when you reenter, you should expect that you will be given fewer than 30 days to remain in Macau.

Because many neighboring areas require that your passport has six months validity remaining, if you are planning to travel in these areas, be sure your passport is valid for at least six months beyond the date of your planned travel. If you hold a Hong Kong Permanent Identity Card or a Hong Kong Re-entry Permit, you may use either document to enter Macau for a maximum stay of up to one year. You must present your passport or other valid travel document upon arrival. Visit the Macau Government Tourist Office website for the most current visa information.

You should obtain all required visas prior to departing the United States. Specifically, you must have a PRC visa if you plan to travel to the PRC from Macau. You should apply for the PRC visa at the PRC embassy or consulate where you reside. In some cases you can get a PRC visa at the PRC Visa Office in Macau; however, there are limitations depending on the visa category. For example, the visa may be issued for a shorter length of validity and for fewer entries than one obtained in the United States. If you are the parent of a child who holds a U.S. passport, be aware that the PRC Visa Office may require an original birth certificate or other documentation for your child. Persons applying in Macau for PRC visas for their U.S.-born children have been unable to obtain PRC visas without the children's U.S. birth certificate. Further information on travel to and around the PRC is available in the China Country-Specific Information Sheet.

The U.S. Department of State is unaware of any HIV/AIDS entry restrictions for visitors to or foreign residents of Macau.

Threats to Safety and Security:

Stay up to date by:

- Bookmark our Bureau of Consular Affairs website, which contains the current Travel Warnings and Travel Alerts as well as the Worldwide Caution.
- Follow us on Twitter and the Bureau of Consular Affairs page on Facebook as well.
- Download our free Smart Traveler IPhone App to have travel information at your fingertips.
- Call 1-888-407-4747 toll-free within the U.S. and Canada, or a regular toll line, 1-202-501-4444, from other countries.
- Taking some time before travel to consider your personal security.

Crime: Petty street crime, including pick-pocketing, occasionally occurs in tourist areas in Macau, including in and around casinos and at the airport. You should protect your personal belongings and travel documents at all times.

Don't buy counterfeit and pirated goods, even if they are widely available. Not only are the bootlegs illegal in the United States, if you purchase them, you may also be breaking local law.

Victims of Crime: If you or someone you know becomes the victim of a crime abroad, you should contact the local police and the nearest U.S. embassy or consulate. We can:

- Replace a stolen passport.
- Help you find appropriate medical care if you are the victim of violent crimes such as assault or rape.
- Put you in contact with the appropriate police authorities, and if you want us to, we can contact family members or friend.
- Help you understand the local criminal justice process and direct you to local attorneys, although it is important to remember that local authorities are responsible for investigating and prosecuting the crime.

While the Macau government does not have an office devoted solely to crime victim assistance, the social welfare department offers support to crime victims. The support includes monetary benefits, health care, psychological services, and counseling. These are available at the local Social Service Centers. You will find more resources for victims of crime in Macau in our Help for U.S. Victims of Crime in Macau information sheet. In addition, the Macau Tourism Crisis Management Office maintains a tourism hotline (Tel: 853-2833–3000, for visitors to Macau who encounter emergency situations.

The local equivalent to the "911" emergency line in Macau is 999.

Criminal Penalties: While you are traveling in Macau, you are subject to its laws even if you are a U.S. citizen. Foreign laws and legal systems can be vastly different than our own. In some places you may be taken in for questioning if you don't have your passport with you. In some places, it is illegal to take pictures of certain buildings. In some places driving under the influence could land you immediately in jail. These criminal penalties will vary from country to country. There are also some things that might be legal in the country you visit, but still illegal in the United States, and you can be prosecuted under U.S. law if you buy pirated goods.Engaging in sexual conduct with children or using or disseminating child pornography in a foreign country is a crime prosecutable in the United States. If you break local laws in Macau, your U.S. passport won't help you avoid arrest or prosecution. It's very important to know what's legal and what's not where you are going.

If you violate Macau's laws, even unknowingly, you may be expelled, arrested, or imprisoned. Penalties for possession of, use of, or trafficking in illegal drugs in Macau are severe, and if you are convicted of these offenses, you can expect long jail sentences and heavy fines.

Arrest notifications in host country: While some countries will automatically notify the nearest U.S. embassy or consulate if a U.S. citizen is detained or arrested in a foreign country, that might not always be the case in Macau. To ensure that the United States is aware of your circumstances, request that the police and prison officials notify the nearest U.S. embassy or consulate as soon as you are arrested or detained overseas.

Currency: There are no currency restrictions for tourists in Macau. Although the pataca is the official currency in Macau, Hong Kong currency is commonly used and widely accepted in transactions, especially in tourist areas. If you are visiting Macau from Hong Kong, you may wish to bring sufficient Hong Kong dollars to cover your expenses. Credit cards and ATM network debit cards are widely accepted in Macau. Banks and major hotels accept traveler's checks.

Customs Regulations: Macau customs authorities may enforce strict regulations concerning temporary importation into or export from Macau of items such as firearms, ivory, certain categories of medications, and other goods. Please see the Macau Customs Service website for further information.

You should know that the importation into the United States of counterfeit brand-name items, such as watches, compact discs, computer software, and clothing, is prohibited by U.S. law.

Dual Nationality: According to the PRC nationality law, persons of Chinese descent who were born in the PRC, including Macau, are PRC citizens. However, under an agreement between the United States and the People's Republic of China, all U.S. citizens entering Macau on their U.S. passports, including such persons as may be considered PRC nationals by the PRC authorities, are considered to be U.S. citizens by the Macau SAR authorities for purposes of ensuring U.S. consular access and protection during their initial legal stay of up to 30 days in Macau.

If you are a dual national contemplating onward travel into mainland China, you should strongly consider which passport you will use to enter and exit China. Under the U.S.—PRC Consular Convention, the U.S. Embassy and consulates general in the PRC are not able to provide you with consular protections if you do not use your U.S. passport to enter or exit China.

In addition to being subject to all Macau SAR laws affecting U.S. citizens, dual nationals may be subject to laws of Macau that impose special obligations on Macau citizens. For further information on consular protection and dual nationality, please refer to our information on dual nationality.

Language: The official languages in the Macau SAR are Chinese (Cantonese) and Portuguese; however, English is spoken in tourist areas.

Typhoons: During the storm season (July through September), the Macau Meteorological and Geophysical Bureau issues typhoon warnings on an average of six times a year. The Bureau has a good notification and monitoring system. Please consult the Macau Meteorological and Geophysical Bureau for further information. General information about natural disaster preparedness is from the U.S. Federal Emergency Management Agency (FEMA).

Accessibility: While in Macau, individuals with disabilities may find accessibility and accommodation very different from what you find in the United States. The People's Republic of China, including the Special Administrative Region of Macau, is signatory to the Convention on the Rights of Persons with Disabilities. Macau law prohibits discrimination against persons with physical, sensory, intellectual, and mental disabilities in employment, education, access to health care, or the provision of other state services, and the government generally enforces these provisions. The law mandates access to public buildings, usually in the form of a ramp, for persons with physical disabilities. Cross-walks are also required in Macau, and they generally include audible signals for hearing-impaired and raised-treading for visually-impaired pedestrians. Handicap accessible parking is mandated in publically owned parking lots. The Social Welfare Bureau is primarily responsible for coordinating and funding public assistance programs to persons with disabilities.

In general, the historic part of Macau is hilly and the pavement uneven, but the newer parts, particularly around the CoTai strip, are flat, and the streets and sidewalks are wide. The airport is accessible, and the ferries from Hong Kong to Macau are accessible with assistance from the staff. Major hotels and casinos, taxis, and public transportation offer widely available shuttle buses, but none is equipped with special equipment to accommodate the physically disabled. For Macau residents who are mobility impaired, the Social Welfare Bureau offers free transportation to medical appointments by accessible van through their Rehabilitation Bus Service. Accessible van rental and Macau tours for the mobility impaired are available through Macau Barrier Free Tourism (tel. 853 2840 3315 or 853 6289 6796, e-mail: macaubarrierfreetourism@yahoo.com.hk Website in Chinese only).

Medical Facilities and Health Information: Several major hospitals in Macau have adequate medical facilities, and Kiang Wu and Conde de Sao Januario hospitals are able to provide emergency medical care. The U.S. Consulate General Hong Kong maintains a list of medical providers in Macau on the consulate website. Highly developed medical facilities and trained personnel are available in Hong Kong, which is about an hour by jetfoil and 10 minutes by helicopter from Macau.

You can find good information on vaccinations and other health precautions, on the CDC website. For information about outbreaks of infectious diseases abroad, consult the World Health Organization (WHO) website. The WHO website also contains additional health information for travelers, including detailed country-specific health information.

Medical Insurance: You can't assume your insurance will go with you when you travel. It's very important to find out BEFORE you leave whether your medical insurance will cover you overseas. You need to ask your insurance company two questions:

- Does my policy apply when I'm out of the United States?
- Will it cover emergencies like a trip to a foreign hospital or a medical evacuation?

In many places, doctors and hospitals still expect payment in cash at the time of service. Your regular U.S. health insurance may not cover doctors' and hospital visits in other countries. If your policy doesn't go with you when you travel, it's a very good idea to take out another one for your trip.

Traffic Safety and Road Conditions: While in Macau, you may encounter road conditions that differ significantly from those in the United States. The information below concerning Macau is provided for general reference only, and may not be totally accurate in a particular location or circumstance.

Traffic moves on the left in Macau, and roads are narrow and winding. Traffic is generally congested throughout the day. Most visitors to Macau choose not to drive. Taxis are inexpensive and plentiful at the airport, ferry terminal, and gaming venues. Public buses are also inexpensive and frequent, but you may have difficulty finding them outside major tourist areas.

For specific information concerning Macau driving permits, vehicle inspection, road tax, and mandatory insurance, email the Public Security Police Force, or contact them by telephone (853) 2837 4214 or fax (853) 2852 3407 or the Macau Transport Department, 762-804 Avenida da Praia Grande, China Plaza Bldg., 2nd floor; telephone (853) 8866–6363; fax (853) 2875 0626. (Please note: This website is available only in Chinese and Portuguese).

Aviation Safety Oversight: As there is no direct commercial air service to the United States by carriers registered in Macau, the U.S. Federal Aviation Administration (FAA) has not assessed the government of Macau's Civil Aviation Authority for compliance with International Civil Aviation Organization (ICAO) aviation safety standards. Further information may be found on the FAA's safety assessment page.

Children's Issues: Please see the U.S. Dept. of State Office of Children's Issues web pages on intercountry adoption and international parental child abduction.

Intercountry Adoption

February 2007

As of February 2013, the Department of State did not have country specific information pertaining to adoption from Macau available on its Intercountry Adoption website. The information in this section was edited from previous reports. Prospective parents should read the *Intercountry Adoption* section of this book and check for current reports online at http://adoption.state.gov for the latest information.

Please Note: U.S. citizen prospective adoptive parents who are interested in adopting from Macau are strongly encouraged to contact U.S. consular officials in Hong Kong before formalizing an adoption agreement in Macau, to ensure that appropriate procedures have been followed that will make it possible for the child to obtain an. immigrant visa.

Adoption Authority: The Social Welfare Bureau of the Macau Special Administrative Region Government is the sole Adoption Authority in Macau. Contact information is as follows:

Social Welfare Bureau
of the Macau Special Administrative Region Government
Estrada do Cemiterio, no. 6,
Macau, China;
Tel: (853) 3997716, 3997717, 3997736;
E-mail: srh@ias.gov.mo
Website: http://www.ias.gov.mo.

Adoption Agencies and Attorneys: Prospective adoptive parents are advised to fully research any adoption agency or facilitator they plan to use for adoption services. For U.S.-based agencies, it is suggested that prospective adoptive parents contact the Better Business Bureau and/or the licensing office of the appropriate state government agency in the U.S. state where the agency is located or licensed.

Adoption Procedures: Parents hoping to adopt a child in Macau should submit an application to the Social Welfare Bureau. Applications can be submitted either through the Central Authority in the country where the parent(s) habitually reside or via a licensed agency/organization engaging in intermediary adoption activities.

Prospective adoptive parents living in Macau and possessing valid Macau identity cards may submit an application directly to the Social Welfare Bureau. The Social Welfare Bureau will review the adoption application and notify the relevant agency/organization of its decision. Once an application has been accepted, the Social Welfare Bureau will start the process of matching the prospective adoptive parent(s) with a child.

Once a match has been made, the Social Welfare Bureau will compile a "feasibility study" of the adoption. If, based on the findings of the study, the application is approved, the Social Welfare Bureau will initiate judicial entrustment procedures before a civil court (Tribunal Judicial de Base). Once an authorization for judicial entrustment has been obtained, arrangements will be made for the child to live abroad with the adoptive parent(s) for a trial period. Such trial periods typically last for up to one year.

During this period, the Social Welfare Bureau will work with the relevant authorities in Singapore to determine whether the adoption by the applicant(s) would be in the best interests of the child. For the adoption to be legally finalized in Macau, a final adoption judgment must be submitted to the Social Welfare Bureau either by the relevant Central Authority of the country of the adoptive parents' habitual residence or by a certified adoption agency.

The Embassy of the People's Republic of China
2300 Connecticut Ave., NW
Washington DC 20008
Tel: (202) 328-2500
Fax: (202) 588-0032
E-mail:
webmaster@china-embassy.org
Website:
http://www.china-embassy.org

The People's Republic of China also has Consulates in Chicago, Houston, New York City, Los Angeles and San Francisco.

U.S. Immigration Requirements: Prospective adoptive parents are strongly encouraged to consult USCIS publication M-249, *The Immigration of Adopted and Prospective Adoptive Children*, as well as the Department of State publication, *Intercountry Adoptions*.

Please see the *Intercountry Adoption* section of this book for more details and review current reports online at http://adoption.state.gov.

U.S. Consulate General in Hong Kong
Street Address
26 Garden Road, Central
Hong Kong
Mailing Address from the U.S.
PSC 461, Box 5
FPO AP 96521-0006
Tel: (852) 2841-2211
Fax (852) 2845-4845
Website:
http://hongkong.usconsulate.gov/visa_inquiries.html

Additional Information: Specific questions about adoption in Macau may be addressed to the U.S. Consulate General in Hong Kong. General questions regarding intercountry adoption may be addressed to the Office of Children's Issues, U.S. Department of State, CA/OCS/CI, SA-29, 4th Floor, 2201 C Street, NW, Washington, D.C. 20520-4818, toll-free Tel: 1-888-407-4747.

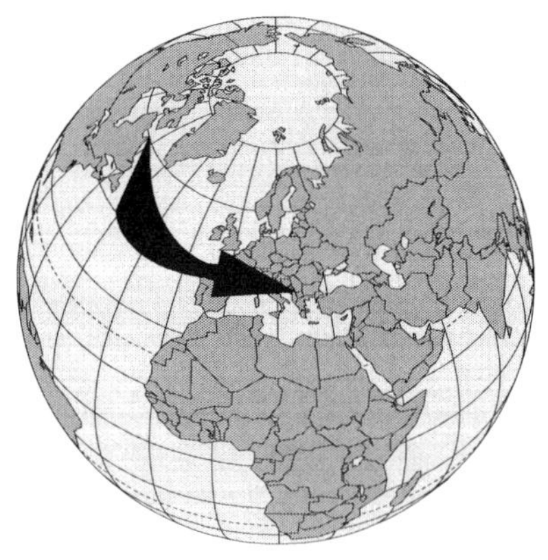

MACEDONIA

Compiled from publications that were available as of February 2013 from the U.S. Department of State, the U.S. Department of Commerce, and the Central Intelligence Agency (CIA). See the introduction to this set for explanatory notes.

Official Name:
Republic of Macedonia

PROFILE

Geography

Area: total: 25,713 sq km; country comparison to the world: 150; land: 25,433 sq km; water: 280 sq km

Major cities: Skopje (capital) 480,000 (2009)

Climate: warm, dry summers and autumns; relatively cold winters with heavy snowfall

Terrain: mountainous territory covered with deep basins and valleys; three large lakes, each divided by a frontier line; country bisected by the Vardar River

People

Nationality: noun: Macedonian(s); adjective: Macedonian

Population: 2,082,370 (July 2012 est.)

Population growth rate: 0.237% (2012 est.)

Ethnic groups: Macedonian 64.2%, Albanian 25.2%, Turkish 3.9%, Roma (Gypsy) 2.7%, Serb 1.8%, other 2.2% (2002 census)

Religions: Macedonian Orthodox 64.7%, Muslim 33.3%, other Christian 0.37%, other and unspecified 1.63% (2002 census)

Languages: Macedonian (official) 66.5%, Albanian (official) 25.1%, Turkish 3.5%, Roma 1.9%, Serbian 1.2%, other 1.8% (2002 census)

Literacy: definition: age 15 and over can read and write; total population: 97.3%; male: 98.7%; female: 95.9% (2010 est.)

Health: life expectancy at birth: total population: 75.36 years; male: 72.82 years; female: 78.1 years (2012 est.); Infant mortality rate: total: 8.32 deaths/1,000 live births; male: 8.56 deaths/1,000 live births; female: 8.07 deaths/1,000 live births (2012 est.)

Unemployment rate: 31.3% (2012 est.)

Work force: 936,000 (2012 est.)

Government

Type: parliamentary democracy

Independence: 8 September 1991

Constitution: adopted 17 November 1991, effective 20 November 1991; amended November 2001, 2005, and in 2009

Political subdivisions: 84 municipalities (opstini, singular—opstina)

Suffrage: 18 years of age; universal

Economy

GDP (purchasing power parity): $22.15 billion (2012 est.); $21.62 billion (2011 est.); $20.98 billion (2010 est.); $20.61 billion (2009 est.)

GDP real growth rate: 1% (2012 est.); 3% (2011 est.); 1.8% (2010 est.); -0.9% (2009 est.)

GDP per capita (PPP): $10,700 (2012 est.); $10,500 (2011 est.); $10,200 (2010 est.); $10,000 (2009 est.)

Natural resources: low-grade iron ore, copper, lead, zinc, chromite, manganese, nickel, tungsten, gold, silver, asbestos, gypsum, timber, arable land

Agriculture products: grapes, tobacco, vegetables, fruits; milk, eggs

Industries: food processing, beverages, textiles, chemicals, iron, steel, cement, energy, pharmaceuticals

Exports: $4.338 billion (2012 est.); $4.348 billion (2011 est.); $3.296 billion (2010 est.)

Exports—commodities: food, beverages, tobacco; textiles, miscellaneous manufactures, iron and steel

Exports—partners: Germany 28.5%, Italy 7.3%, Bulgaria 5.4%, Greece 5% (2011)

Imports: $6.188 billion (2012 est.); $7.007 billion (2011 est.); $5.241 billion (2010 est.)

Imports—commodities: machinery and equipment, automobiles, chemicals, fuels, food products

Imports—partners: Germany 13.1%, Greece 13.1%, Bulgaria 11.1%, UK 7.9%, Turkey 5.4%, Italy 5.4% (2011)

Debt—external: $6.74 billion (31 December 2012 est.); $6.609 billion (31 December 2011 est.)

Exchange rates: Macedonian denars (MKD) per US dollar; 48.1 (2012 est.); 44.231 (2011 est.); 46.485 (2010 est.); 44.1 (2009); 41.414 (2008); 44.732 (2007)

GEOGRAPHY

Macedonia is located in the heart of south central Europe. It shares a border with Greece to the south, Bulgaria to the east, Serbia and Kosovo to the north, and Albania to the west. The country is 80% mountainous, rising to its highest point at Mt. Korab (peak 2,764 meters).

PEOPLE

Since the end of the Second World War, Macedonia's population has grown steadily, with the greatest increases occurring in the ethnic Albanian community. From 1953 through the time of the official census in 2002, the percentage of ethnic Albanians living in Macedonia rose threefold. The western part of the country, where most ethnic Albanians live, is the most heavily populated, with approximately 40% of the total population. As in many countries, people have moved into the cities in search of employment. Macedonia has also experienced sustained high rates of permanent or seasonal emigration.

National/Racial/Ethnic Minorities

According to the 2002 census, the ethnic composition of the population was 64.2 percent Macedonian, 25.2 percent Albanian, 3.9 percent Turkish, 2.7 percent Romani, 1.8 percent Serbian, 0.8 percent Bosniak, and 0.5 percent Vlach.

Relations between the ethnic Macedonian and Albanian communities often are strained. Ethnic Albanians continue to complain of unequal representation in government ministries. Ethnic Macedonians have claimed that employers targeted them for reverse discrimination in downsizing, regardless of performance. Some ethnic Albanians claim that discrimination in citizenship decisions by the Ministry of Interior, which has authority to grant, revoke, interrupt, or confirm a person's citizenship, effectively disenfranchised them.

Ethnic Turks complain of discrimination. Their main concerns were slow progress in achieving equitable representation in government institutions, the absence of ethnic Turkish-majority municipalities, and the inadequacy of Turkish-language education and media.

Roma have complained of widespread societal discrimination. NGOs and international experts report that employers often deny Roma job opportunities, and some Roma complain of lack of access to public welfare funds. Roma NGOs also reported that proprietors occasionally denied Roma entrance to their establishments. Many Roma lack identity cards, which are necessary to obtain government services such as education, welfare, and health care.

Language

Although Macedonian is the official language, many of Macedonia's citizens speak foreign languages. English is the predominant foreign language, followed by German and French.

Religion

The country's two major religious groups are Orthodox Christianity and Islam. Approximately 65 percent of the population is Macedonian Orthodox, and 32 percent is Muslim. Other religious groups include Roman Catholics, various Protestant denominations, and Jews.

There is a correlation between ethnicity and religious affiliation; the majority of Orthodox believers are ethnic Macedonian, and the majority of Muslim believers are ethnic Albanian.

HISTORY

Throughout its history, the present-day territory of Macedonia has been a crossroads for both traders and conquerors moving between the European continent and Asia Minor. Each of these transiting powers left its mark upon the region, giving rise to a rich and varied cultural and historical tradition.

After the fall of the Western Roman Empire, the territory of Macedonia fell under the control of the Byzantine Empire in the 6th and 7th centuries. It was during this period that large groups of Slavic people migrated to the Balkan region. The Ottoman Turks conquered the territory in the 15th century; it remained under Ottoman Turkish rule until 1912.

After more than 4 centuries of rule, Ottoman power in the region began to wane, and by the middle of the 19th century, Greece, Bulgaria, and Serbia were competing for influence in the territory. During this time, a nationalist movement emerged and grew in Macedonia. The latter half of the 19th century, continuing into the early part of the 20th century, was marked by sporadic nationalist uprisings, culminating in the Ilinden Uprising of August 2, 1903.

Macedonian revolutionaries liberated the town of Krushevo and established the short-lived Republic of Krushevo, which was put down by Ottoman forces after 10 days. Following Ottoman Turkey's defeat by the allied Balkan countries—Bulgaria, Serbia, Montenegro, and Greece—during the First Balkan War in autumn 1912, the same allies fought the Second Balkan War over the division of Macedonia. The August 1913 Treaty of Bucharest ended this conflict by dividing the territory between Bulgaria, Greece, and Serbia. The 1919 Treaty of Versailles sanctioned partitioning the geographic region of Macedonia among the Kingdom of Serbs, Croats, and Slovenes; Bulgaria; and Greece. In the wake of the First World War, Vardar Macedonia (the present-day area of the Republic

of Macedonia) was incorporated into the newly formed Kingdom of Serbs, Croats, and Slovenes.

Throughout much of the Second World War, Bulgaria and Italy occupied Macedonia. Many citizens joined partisan movements during this time and succeeded in liberating the region in late 1944. Following the war, Macedonia became one of the constituent republics of the new Socialist Federal Republic of Yugoslavia under Marshall Tito. During this period, Macedonian culture and language flourished.

As communism fell throughout Eastern Europe in the late 20th century, Macedonia followed its other federation partners and declared its independence from Yugoslavia in late 1991. After independence, Prime Minister Nikola Kljusev remained Prime Minister, heading a government of experts, and Kiro Gligorov remained President. Macedonia was the only republic of the former Yugoslavia whose secession in 1991 was not clouded by ethnic or other armed conflict, although the ethnic Albanian population declined to participate in the referendum on independence. The new Macedonian constitution took effect November 20, 1991 and called for a system of government based on a parliamentary democracy. The first democratically elected coalition government was led by Prime Minister Branko Crvenkovski of the Social Democratic Union of Macedonia (SDSM).

President Gligorov was the first president of a former Yugoslav republic to relinquish office. In accordance with the terms of the Macedonian constitution, his presidency ended in November 1999 after 8 years in office, which included surviving a car bombing assassination attempt on October 3 in 1995. He was succeeded by former Deputy Foreign Minister Boris Trajkovski (VMRO-DPMNE), who defeated Tito Petkovski (SDSM) in a second-round run-off election for the presidency on November 14, 1999. Trajkovski's election was confirmed by a December 5, 1999 partial re-vote in 230 polling stations, which the Macedonian Supreme Court mandated due to election irregularities. In November 1998 parliamentary elections, SDSM lost its majority. A new coalition government emerged under the leadership of Prime Minister Ljubco Georgievski of the Internal Macedonian Revolutionary Organization-Democratic Party for Macedonian National Unity (VMRO-DPMNE). The initial coalition included the ethnic Albanian Democratic Party of Albanians (DPA).

During the Yugoslav period, most of Macedonia's Slavic population identified themselves as Macedonians, while several minority groups, in particular ethnic Albanians, retained their own distinct political culture and language. Although interethnic tensions simmered under Yugoslav authority and during the first decade of its independence, the country avoided ethnically motivated conflict until several years after independence. Ethnic minority grievances, which had erupted on occasion (1995 and 1997), rapidly began to gain political currency in late 2000, leading many in the ethnic Albanian community in Macedonia to question their minority protection under, and participation in, the government. Tensions erupted into open hostilities in Macedonia in February 2001, when a group of ethnic Albanians near the Kosovo border carried out armed provocations that soon escalated into an insurgency. Purporting to fight for greater civil rights for ethnic Albanians in Macedonia, the group seized territory and launched attacks against government forces. Many observers ascribed other motives to the so-called National Liberation Army (NLA), including support for criminality and the assertion of political control over affected areas. The insurgency spread through northern and western Macedonia during the first half of 2001. Under international mediation, a cease-fire was brokered in July 2001, and the government coalition was expanded in July 2001 to form a grand coalition which included the major opposition parties.

The expanded coalition of ruling ethnic Macedonian and ethnic Albanian political leaders, with facilitation by U.S. and European Union (EU) diplomats, negotiated and then signed the Ohrid Framework Agreement on August 13, 2001, which brought an end to the fighting. The agreement called for implementation of constitutional and legislative changes, which laid the foundation for improved civil rights for minority groups. The Macedonian parliament adopted the constitutional changes outlined in the accord in November 2001. The grand coalition disbanded following the signing of the Ohrid Framework Agreement and the passage of new constitutional amendments. A coalition led by Prime Minister Georgievski, including DPA and several smaller parties, completed its parliamentary term.

In September 2002 elections, an SDSM-led pre-election coalition won half of the 120 seats in parliament. Branko Crvenkovski was elected Prime Minister in coalition with the ethnic Albanian Democratic Union for Integration (DUI) party, the Liberal-Democratic Party (LDP), and a number of smaller ethnic parties.

On February 26, 2004 President Trajkovski died in a plane crash in Bosnia and Herzegovina. Presidential elections were held April 14 and 28, 2004. Then-Prime Minister Branko Crvenkovski won the second round and was inaugurated President on May 12, 2004. The parliament confirmed Hari Kostov, former Interior Minister, as Prime Minister June 2, 2004, but Kostov resigned on November 15 of the same year. On December 17, 2004, former Defense Minister Vlado Buckovski was confirmed by parliament as Prime Minister, maintaining the coalition with the ethnic Albanian Democratic Union for Integration (DUI) and the Liberal-Democratic (LDP) parties.

With international assistance, the SDSM-DUI-LDP governing coalition completed the legislative implementation of the Ohrid Framework Agreement, which is a precondition for Macedonia's integration into Euro-Atlantic institutions. A November 7, 2004 referendum opposing the law on new municipal organization failed, freeing the way for the government to complete Framework Agreement implementation.

Local elections were held in March-April 2005 under a new territorial reorganization plan that consolidated the overall number of Macedonia's municipalities and created a number of ethnically-mixed municipalities in which ethnic Albanian populations were dominant. The process of decentralization began in the new municipalities in July 2005.

The July 2006 parliamentary elections resulted in a VMRO-DPMNE-led government under Prime Minister Nikola Gruevski, in coalition with DPA, NSDP, and several smaller parties. The new government, which was confirmed in office by a parliamentary vote on August 26, 2006, stated its commitment to completing Framework Agreement implementation and reaffirmed its commitment to pursuing NATO and EU membership.

At NATO's Bucharest Summit in April 2008, all 26 NATO Allies agreed Macedonia had met the criteria for membership. Consensus on extending a NATO membership invitation could not be reached, however, due to the unresolved dispute with Greece over Macedonia's name.

Following the Bucharest Summit, the opposition DUI party, in collaboration with the governing VMRO-DPMNE and DPA parties, called for the dissolution of parliament and for early parliamentary elections, which were held in June 2008. On July 26, Prime Minister Gruevski was reconfirmed in office with a new coalition along with the DUI party and one smaller party. In 2009, Macedonia held presidential and local elections in March (first round) and April (second round). In the presidential race, VMRO-DPMNE candidate Gjorge Ivanov won with 64% of the vote. Early parliamentary elections were held in June 2011.

GOVERNMENT AND POLITICAL CONDITIONS

The Republic of Macedonia is a parliamentary democracy. A popularly elected president is head of state and commander in chief of the armed forces. A unicameral parliament (Sobranie) exercises legislative authority. On June 5, 2011, the country held national parliamentary elections that international observers assessed as meeting most international standards for democratic elections.

Recent Elections

In June 2011, the country held parliamentary elections, with high public turnout and only minor confirmed incidents. The OSCE's Office for Democratic Institutions and Human Rights reported that the elections were "transparent and well administered throughout the country"; however, insufficient separation between party and state activities and pressure on public sector employees to support the ruling coalition were problems. For the first time, citizens residing abroad could vote by absentee ballot.

Political Parties: On June 6, the day after the national election, police arrested Ljube Boskoski, leader of the United for Macedonia political party, on charges of illegal election campaign financing and misuse of official position. Boskoski was convicted on November 29 and sentenced to seven years in prison. Boskoski asserted his arrest was political retaliation for his preelection antigovernment speeches. Other sources claimed that his conviction was also retaliation for his alleged cooperation with the Office of the Prosecutor in the 2001 war crimes cases in which Boskoski received an acquittal, while the second defendant, Johan Tarculovski, was convicted and received a 12-year prison sentence.

In August 2011, the government demolished the Cosmos apartment building owned by Fiat Canovski, leader of the opposition Party for European Future, claiming that it was a few inches above code requirements. Canovski asserted that the demolition was political retaliation for his party's having joined the opposition and financing opposition-oriented A1 Television after its accounts were frozen, allowing it to remain on the air during the election campaign.

The government subsequently filed four court cases against Canovski and appointed to the case a judge who was the aunt of the minister of interior. Canovski reported difficulty in obtaining a firm to assess damages for insurance purposes (not only to his property, but to equipment belonging to the construction company as well). Canovski filed a complaint with the ECHR. On November 30, the government withdrew from parliament a draft amendment to the Construction Law, the purpose of which, according to the opposition, was to legalize the Cosmos' demolition retroactively.

Participation of Women and Minorities: There were 38 women in the 123-seat parliament and three women in the 23-member Council of Ministers. The law requires gender diversity in each political party's candidate list; at least one in every three candidates must be of the gender opposite of the majority gender on the list. Sixty percent of judges were female. None of the country's 85 mayors was a woman.

There were 24 ethnic Albanians, four ethnic Serbs, two ethnic Vlachs, two ethnic Turks, two ethnic Roma, and three ethnic Bosniaks in parliament. There were nine members of nonmajority communities in the 23-member Council of Ministers.

Principal Government Officials

Last Updated: 1/31/2013

Pres.: **Gjorge IVANOV**
Prime Min.: **Nikola GRUEVSKI**
Dep. Prime Min.: **Zoran STAVRESKI**
Dep. Prime Min. for Economic Affairs: **Vladimir PESEVSKI**
Dep. Prime Min. for European Integration: **Teuta ARIFI**
Dep. Prime Min. for Framework Agreement Implementation: **Musa XHAFERI**
Min. of Agriculture, Forestry, & Waterways: **Ljupco DIMOVSKI**
Min. of Culture: **Elizabeta KANCESKA-MILEVSKA**
Min. of Defense: **Fatmir BESIMI**
Min. of Economy: **Valon SARACINI**
Min. of Education: **Pance KRALEV**
Min. of Environment & Physical Planning: **Abdilaqim ADEMI**
Min. of Finance: **Zoran STAVRESKI**
Min. of Foreign Affairs: **Nikola POPOSKI**
Min. of Health: **Nikola TODOROV**
Min. of Information Society: **Ivo IVANOVSKI**
Min. of the Interior: **Gordana JANKULOSKA**
Min. of Justice: **Blerim BEXHETI**
Min. of Labor & Social Policy: **Spiro RISTOVSKI**
Min. of Local Self-Govt.: **Nevzat BEJTA**
Min. of Transport & Communications: **Mile JANAKIESKI**
Min. Without Portfolio: **Nezdhet MUSTAFA**
Min. Without Portfolio: **Hadi NEZIRI**
Min. Without Portfolio: **Bill PAVLESKI**
Min. Without Portfolio: **Vele SAMAK**
Governor, National Bank of the Republic of Macedonia: **Petar GOSEV**
Ambassador to the US: **Zoran JOLEVSKI**
Permanent Representative to the UN, New York: **Pajo AVIROVIK**

ECONOMY

Macedonia is vulnerable to economic developments in Europe—due to strong banking and trade ties—and dependent on regional integration and progress toward EU membership for continued economic growth.

At independence in September 1991, Macedonia was the least developed of the Yugoslav republics, producing a mere 5% of the total federal output of goods and services. The collapse of the Socialist Federal Republic of Yugoslavia ended transfer payments from the central government and eliminated advantages from inclusion in a de facto free trade area. An absence of infrastructure, UN sanctions on the downsized Yugoslavia, and a Greek economic embargo over a dispute about the country's constitutional name and flag hindered economic growth until 1996.

Since then, Macedonia has maintained macroeconomic stability with low inflation, but it has so far lagged the region in attracting foreign investment and creating jobs, despite making extensive fiscal and business sector reforms. Official unemployment remains high at 29.1%, but may be overstated based on the existence of an extensive gray market, estimated to be between 20% and 45% of GDP, that is not captured by official statistics.

In the wake of the global economic downturn, Macedonia has experienced decreased foreign direct investment, lowered credit availability, and a large trade deficit. However, as a result of conservative fiscal policies and a sound financial system, in 2010 the country credit rating improved slightly to BB+ and was kept at that level in 2011–12.

Macroeconomic stability has been maintained by a prudent monetary policy, which keeps the domestic currency pegged against the euro. As a result, GDP growth was modest, but positive, from 2010 to 2012, and inflation was under control.

Labor Conditions

The law protects children from exploitation in the workplace, including forced or compulsory labor, and the government effectively enforced the law in practice. The law mandates a prison sentence of at least eight years for anyone who buys, sells, keeps, or takes children or minors for the purpose of exploitation.

The minimum age for employment is 15. Children who are 14 years of age can work as apprentices or as part of an official education program. The law prohibits employing minors under the age of 18 in work that is detrimental to their physical or psychological health and morality. The law also prohibits minors from working nights or more than eight hours per day or 40 hours per week.

The Ministry of Labor and Social Policy is responsible for enforcing laws regulating the employment of children. Government efforts to eliminate forced begging by children were largely ineffective. Although the necessary laws were in place, officials seldom implemented them.

During 2011 a national minimum wage was established by law for the first time and was set at 8,500 denars ($177) per month. According to official statistics, the average monthly net wage in September was 20,659 denars ($430). In 2010 the government estimated that the monthly cost of basic goods, including food, gas, and transportation for a family of four, was 200 euros ($260). The government statistics office estimated that approximately 30.9 percent of the population lived in poverty in 2010.

The law establishes a 40-hour workweek with a minimum 24-hour rest period, and paid vacation and sick leave benefits. Employees may not legally work more than eight hours of overtime per week or 190 hours per year. According to the collective agreement between the government and the unions, employees in both the public and private sector have a right to overtime pay at 135 percent of their regular rate. By law collective agreements apply to all workers whether union members or not. In addition the law entitles employees who work more than 150 hours of overtime per year to a bonus of one month's salary. However, many employers hired workers without complying with the law. In particular small retail businesses often required employees to work well beyond the legal limits.

The Ministry of Labor and Social Policy did not strictly enforce laws and regulations on worker safety.

U.S.-MACEDONIAN RELATIONS

Macedonia and the United States enjoy a cooperative relationship across a broad range of political, economic, cultural, military, and social issues. The two have had good bilateral relations since Macedonia gained its independence from Yugoslavia in 1991. The United States formally recognized Macedonia in 1994, and the countries established full diplomatic relations in 1995. The United States strongly supports Macedonia's aspirations for full integration into Euro-Atlantic institutions and is committed to helping Macedonia strengthen rule of law; improve education; promote media freedom; and build greater democratic foundations in a full, inclusive multi-ethnic society.

The United States and its European allies acted swiftly to mediate an end to the 2001 civil conflict in Macedonia, which grew from ethnic tensions, and closely supported the government and major parties' successful efforts to forge a peaceful, political solution to the crisis through the Ohrid Framework Agreement. In partnership with the European Union and other international organizations active in Macedonia, the United States continues to facilitate the Macedonian Government's implementation of the Framework Agreement and fostering long-term peace and stability in the country. For the text of the 2008 bilateral Declaration of Strategic Partnership and Cooperation, please see http://2001–2009.state.gov/p/eur/rls/or/104441.htm.

U.S. Assistance to Macedonia

U.S. Government assistance to Macedonia focuses on facilitating Macedonia's continued development on the path toward full integration into the Euro-Atlantic community and assisting the Macedonian Government's efforts to sustain economic and democratic reforms to build stability and prosperity. A fact sheet on U.S. assistance to Macedonia can be found here.

Bilateral Economic Relations

The United States supports Macedonia's transition to a market-oriented economy. Macedonia is a member of the World Trade Organization seeks to join the European Union (EU); a starting date for accession negotiations has been deferred by the EU.

In 2010, total trade between Macedonia and the United States was $116.6 million, and in the first 8 months of 2011 it was $65 million. U.S. electrical machinery and equipment have been particularly attractive to Macedonian importers. Principal Macedonian exports to the United States are tobacco, apparel, iron, and steel.

Macedonia's Membership in International Organizations

Macedonia and the United States belong to a number of the same international organizations, including the United Nations, Organization for Security and Cooperation in Europe, Adriatic Charter, International Monetary Fund, World Bank, and World Trade Organization.

Macedonia seeks to join the North Atlantic Treaty Organization (NATO) and is a candidate country for the European Union. In 2008, NATO Allies determined that Macedonia met NATO membership criteria and undertook to invite Macedonia to join NATO as soon as a solution is reached in Macedonia's dispute with NATO member Greece over Macedonia's name. This decision has been reiterated at subsequent NATO Summits. Macedonia continues to make an important contribution to regional stability by supporting the logistical supply of NATO (including U.S.)

peacekeepers in Kosovo. Macedonia participated in OIF and currently participates in ISAF, the EU Althea Mission in Bosnia and Herzegovina, and the UN's observer mission in Lebanon.

Bilateral Representation

Macedonia maintains an embassy in the United States at 2129 Wyoming Ave, NW, Washington, DC 20008 (tel: (202) 667-0501).

Principal U.S. Embassy Officials

Last Updated: 1/14/2013

SKOPJE (E) ul. Samoilova 21, 1000 Skopje, Republic of Macedonia, 389-2-310-2000, Fax 389-2-310-2499, Workweek: Mon-Fri 0800-1700, Website: http://skopje.usembassy.gov/

DCM OMS:	Christney Fail
AMB OMS:	Rodica Benya
DHS/CIS:	Gary L. Cote
DHS/ICE:	James Plitt
FM:	Glen Allen
HRO:	Viviana Guerrero
ICITAP:	Timothy Faught
MGT:	Matthew Spivak
MLO/ODC:	Mark Watkins
OPDAT:	Jimmye Warren
POL/ECON:	Michele Siders
POSHO:	Glen Allen
SDO/DATT:	COL Jeffrey Predmore
AMB:	Paul Wohlers
CON:	Carolyn Gorman
DCM:	Brian Aggeler
PAO:	Angela Aggeler
GSO:	Jason Haskins
RSO:	Matthew Andrew
AGR:	Brian Goggin
AID:	Robert Wuertz
CLO:	Ann Tran
FMO:	Yuting Shao
ICASS Chair:	Timothy Faught
IMO:	James Swineford
IPO:	Thomas P. Pitts
IRS:	Linda M. Garrard
ISSO:	Thomas P. Pitts
LEGATT:	Jeffrey Harp
State ICASS:	Vacant

TRAVEL

Consular Information Sheet

April 27, 2012

Country Description: Macedonia is a parliamentary democracy that is slowly but steadily transforming its economy. Tourist facilities are available in the capital, Skopje, and other major towns. In tourist centers, such as Skopje and Ohrid, European-standard hotels and other travel amenities are available. The standard of tourist facilities throughout the rest of the country varies considerably.

Smart Traveler Enrollment Program (STEP)/Embassy Locations: If you are going to live in or visit Macedonia, please take the time to tell our embassy about your trip. If you enroll, we can keep you up to date with important safety and security announcements. It will also help your friends and family get in touch with you in an emergency.

U.S. Embassy Skopje
Samoilova 21, 1000 Skopje,
Macedonia
Telephone: (389) (2) 310-2000
Emergency after-hours
telephone: (389) (2) 310-2000
Facsimile: (389) (2) 310-2299
Email: consularskopje@state.gov

Entry/Exit Requirements for U.S. Citizens: You need a valid U.S. passport for travel to Macedonia. You don't need a visa for tourist or business trips totaling less than 90 days during a six-month period. Macedonia requires that all foreign citizens provide proof of health insurance when entering the country. Entry stamps are issued at airports or land border crossing points; these stamps let you stay for 90 days.

All foreign citizens must register with local police within 24 hours of arrival. If you are staying in private accommodations or renting an apartment, you should register in person at the police station nearest your place of residence, and you should be accompanied to the station by the owner or landlord of the apartment. Hotels are responsible for the registration of foreign guests, so you do not need to register with local police if you are staying in a hotel. If you change addresses in Macedonia, notify the police station where you initially registered and re-register with the police station closest to your new residence.

Unaccompanied U.S. citizen minors who enter Macedonia should have a notarized statement of consent from a parent or guardian to enter and stay in the country. The statement of consent must be certified by a competent authority of the country from which s/he arrives or by an embassy or consulate of the Republic of Macedonia.

A U.S. citizen who possesses more than one passport is required to leave Macedonia with the same passport they used to enter it. Also, U.S. citizens born in Macedonia are advised to read the Greece Country Specific Information if they plan to travel to Greece.

Dual citizens of U,S. and Macedonia who have stayed outside of Macedonia for more than 3 months should report to Macedonian Embassy or Consulate prior to returning to Macedonia. Another option is to report to the nearest police station after entering Macedonia. Failure to report their stay abroad may result in delays of their departure from Macedonia.

Also, if you are a U.S. citizen born in the Republic of Macedonia, please note Greek Immigration Officers at all ports of entry (land, air and sea) will not place entry stamps in passports listing the traveler's place of birth as Macedonia or the Republic of Macedonia. These travelers are required to complete a short form on which the entry stamp will be placed and which the traveler should keep with their passport for the duration of their stay in Greece and present upon departure.

If you want to work, study, or remain longer than 90 days in Macedonia you must obtain an entry visa prior to coming to Macedonia. You cannot adjust from tourist status to long-term status after arriving. Those who wish to adjust status must leave Macedonia and apply for a long-term visa at a Macedonian embassy or consulate.

Apply at the Macedonian Embassy in Washington D.C., located at 2129 Wyoming Avenue, NW, Washington, DC 20008, tel.: (202) 667-0501; fax: (202) 667-2131; email: Washington@mfa.gov.mk. You can also visit the Embassy of Macedonia website for the most current visa information.

For additional information about the conditions and procedures for visa issuance, you may visit the Macedonian Ministry of Foreign Affairs website for a list of Macedonian Embassies and Consulates. In addition to the Embassy of Macedonia in Washington, U.S. citizens may also contact the Consulates General of Macedonia in New York, Detroit, or Chicago; contact information is located on the Consular Affairs page within the Embassy of Macedonia website. You should know that all border areas apart from designated border crossings are restricted zones. Presence in these zones is forbidden without prior official permission.

The U.S. Department of State is unaware of any HIV/AIDS entry restrictions for visitors to or foreign residents of Macedonia.

Threats to Safety and Security: Macedonia has not experienced any incidents of large-scale public violence in recent years, although there have been occasions where protest activity devolved into localized violent incidents, most of which have political, ethnic, and/or religious overtones. A small number of murders and robberies involving gunfire have occurred in public areas nationwide. None of these potential risks to public safety have targeted U.S. citizens or interests, but you should be aware of current events and your surroundings.

Stay up to date by:

- Bookmarking our Bureau of Consular Affairs website, which contains the current Travel Warnings and Travel Alerts as well as the Worldwide Caution.;
- Following us on Twitter and the Bureau of Consular Affairs page on Facebook;
- Downloading our free Smart Traveler iPhone App to have travel information at your fingertips;
- Calling 1-888-407-4747 toll-free within the U.S. and Canada, or a regular toll line, 1-202-501-4444, from other countries.; and
- Taking some time before travel to consider your personal security.

Crime: You should take the same precautions against becoming crime victims as you would in any U.S. city. Violent crime against U.S. citizens is rare. Pick-pocketing, theft, and other petty street crimes do occur, particularly in areas where tourists and foreigners congregate.

Do not leave valuables, including cell phones and electronic items, in plain view in unattended vehicles. You should securely lock the windows and doors of your residence when it is not occupied. Organized crime is present in Macedonia; organized criminal activity occasionally results in violent confrontations between members of rival organizations. ATM use is generally safe; however, travelers should take standard safety precautions.

Pickpockets remain a problem in the Skopje city center, including the Main Square ("Ploshtad"), the City Center Mall ("Trgovski Center"), and the Old Town areas. Be aware of your belongings and surroundings at all times. Pickpockets use various diversionary tactics to distract victims; one method involves groups of children swarming around you and asking for money to find and take your wallet. Victims of pick-pocketing should report the crime to the police and cancel their credit cards as soon as possible.

Although taxis are a common form of transportation, you should use a licensed metered taxi to avoid getting into a dispute about the fare.

Don't buy counterfeit pirated goods, even if they are widely available. Not only are the bootlegs illegal to bring back into the United States, if you purchase them you may also be breaking local law.

Victims of Crime: If you or someone you know becomes the victim of a crime abroad, you should contact the local police and the nearest U.S. embassy or consulate. We can:

- Replace a stolen passport;
- Help you find appropriate medical care if you are the victim of a violent crime such as assault or rape;
- Put you in contact with the appropriate police authorities and, if you want us to, we can contact family members or friends; and
- Although the local authorities are responsible for investigating and prosecuting the crime, consular officers can help you understand the local criminal justice process and can direct you to local attorneys.

The local equivalent to the "911" emergency line in Macedonia is 192 for police and 194 for ambulance.

Criminal Penalties: While you are traveling in Macedonia, you are subject to its laws even if you are a U.S. citizen. Foreign laws and legal systems can be vastly different from our own. In some places you may be taken in for questioning if you do not have your passport with you. In some places, it is illegal to take pictures of certain buildings. In some places driving under the influence could land you immediately in jail. These criminal penalties will vary from country to country.

There are also some things that might be legal in the country you visit, but still illegal in the United States; for instance, you can be prosecuted under U.S. law if you buy pirated goods. Engaging in sexual conduct with children or using or disseminating child pornography in a foreign country is a crime prosecutable in theUnited States. If you break local laws in Macedonia, your U.S. passport will not help you avoid arrest or prosecution. It is very important to know what is legal and what is not where you are going. Persons violating Macedonia's laws, even unknowingly, may be expelled, arrested, or imprisoned. Penalties for possessing, using, or trafficking in illegal drugs in Macedonia are severe, and convicted offenders can expect long jail sentences and heavy fines.

While some countries will automatically notify the nearest U.S. embassy or consulate if a U.S. citizen is detained or arrested in a foreign country, that might not always be the case. To ensure that the United States is aware of your circumstances, request that the police and prison officials notify the nearest U.S. embassy or consulate as soon as you are arrested or detained overseas.

Special Circumstances: Macedonian customs authorities may enforce strict regulations on the temporary importation to or exportation from Macedonia of certain items; such items include those deemed to be of historical value or significance. Taking photographs of anything that could be perceived as being of military or security interest may result in problems with authorities.

Visitors should always observe "no photography" signs. If you are in doubt, please ask permission from authorities before taking photographs. The local currency is the denar. While credit cards are accepted in larger stores and restaurants, we recommend having cash in local currency for purchases in small establishments.

If you are entering or exiting Macedonia by air or land with more than 10,000 Euros in cash, you must declare all currency upon entry or exit at the Macedonian Customs Office and present a document from a bank or other financial institution showing the origin of the money. Customs officials will issue you a completed declaration form at the port of entry or exit. If you don't report this money, the customs service may confiscate it all. After going through the court system, you are normally required to pay a fine and the National Bank will also keep a certain percentage of the undeclared amount before it is released to you.

Accessibility: While in Macedonia, individuals with disabilities may find accessibility and accommodation very different from what you find in the United States. The law requires only that new buildings be made accessible to persons with disabilities. Most public buildings remain inaccessible and inconsistent inspection has resulted in construction of new facilities that are not accessible for persons with disabilities. Public transportation for persons with disabilities is very limited.

Medical Facilities and Health Information: You can find good information on vaccinations and other health precautions, on the Centers for Disease Control and Prevention (CDC) website. For information about outbreaks of infectious diseases abroad, consult the World Health Organization (WHO) website. The WHO website, also contains additional health information for travelers, including detailed country-specific health information.

Medical Insurance: You can't assume your insurance will go with you when you travel. It's very important to find out BEFORE you leave whether or not your medical insurance will cover you overseas. You need to ask your insurance company two questions:

- Does my policy apply when I'm out of the United States?
- Will it cover emergencies like a trip to a foreign hospital or a medical evacuation?

In many places, doctors and hospitals still expect payment in cash at the time of service. Your regular U.S. health insurance may not cover doctors' and hospital visits in other countries. If your policy doesn't go with you when you travel, it's a very good idea to take out another one for your trip.

Traffic Safety and Road Conditions: While in Macedonia, you may encounter road conditions that differ significantly from those in the United States.

Driving safely in Macedonia requires excellent defensive driving skills. Many drivers routinely ignore speed limits and other traffic regulations, such as stopping for red lights and stop signs. Drivers may make illegal left turns from the far right lane, or drive into oncoming lanes of traffic.

The combination of speeding, unsafe driving practices, poor vehicle maintenance, the mixture of new and old vehicles on the roads, and poor lighting contributes to unsafe driving conditions. Drivers and passengers should always wear seatbelts in Macedonia. Pedestrians should exercise extreme caution when crossing the street, even when using crosswalks, as local drivers often do not slow down or stop for pedestrians.

A valid U.S. driver's license in conjunction with an International Driving Permit is required for U.S. citizens driving in Macedonia. Driving is on the right side of the road. Speed limits are generally posted. Most major highways are in good repair, but many secondary urban and rural roads are poorly maintained and lighted. Horse-drawn carts, livestock, dead animals, rocks, or other objects are sometimes found in the roadway.

Some vehicles are old and lack standard front or rear lights. Secondary mountain roads can be narrow, poorly marked, and lacking guardrails, and may quickly become dangerous in inclement weather. Public transportation in Macedonia is dilapidated. Roadside emergency services are limited. In case of emergency, drivers may contact the police at telephone 192, the Ambulance Service at telephone 194, and Roadside Assistance at telephone 196.

Aviation Safety Oversight: As there is no direct commercial air service to the United States by carriers registered in Macedonia, the U.S. Federal Aviation Administration (FAA) has not assessed the Government of Macedonia's Civil Aviation Authority for compliance with International Civil Aviation Organization (ICAO) aviation safety standards. Further information may be found on the FAA's safety assessment page.

Children's Issues: Please see the U.S. Dept. of State Office of Children's Issues web pages on intercountry adoption and international parental child abduction.

Intercountry Adoption

November 2012

The Republic of Macedonia is party to the Hague Convention on Protection of Children and Co-operation in Respect of Intercountry Adoption(Hague Adoption Convention). Intercountry adoption processing in Hague countries is done in accordance with the requirements of the Convention; the U.S. implementing legislation, the Intercountry Adoption Act of 2000 (IAA); and the IAA's implementing regulations, as well as the implementing legislation and regulations of Macedonia.

Adoptions from Macedonia are rare. No adoptions by U.S. citizen parents have taken place since 2007.

Below is the limited adoption information that the Department has obtained from the adoption authority of Macedonia. U.S. citizens interested in adopting children from Macedonia should contact the Central Authority of Macedonia to inquire about applicable laws and procedures. U.S. citizen prospective adoptive parents living in Macedonia who would like to adopt a child from the United States or from a third country should also contact Macedonia's Central Authority.

Intercountry adoptions involve U.S. consular officers sending a letter (referred to as an "Article 5 Letter") to the Macedonian Central Authority in any intercountry adoption involving U.S. citizen parents and a child from Macedonia where all Convention requirements are met and the consular officer determines that the child appears eligible to immigrate to the United States. This letter will inform the Macedonian Central Authority that the parents are eligible and suited to adopt, that all indications are that the child may enter and reside permanently in the United States, and that the U.S. Central Authority agrees that the adoption may proceed.

WARNING: Do not attempt to adopt or obtain custody of a child in Macedonia before a U.S. consular officer issues the Article 5 Letter in any adoption case.

Remember: The consular officer will make a final decision about a child's eligibility for an immigrant visa later in the adoption process.

Macedonian Adoption Authority
Ministry of Labor and Social Affairs
Dame Gruev Street No. 14
1000 Skopje
Macedonia

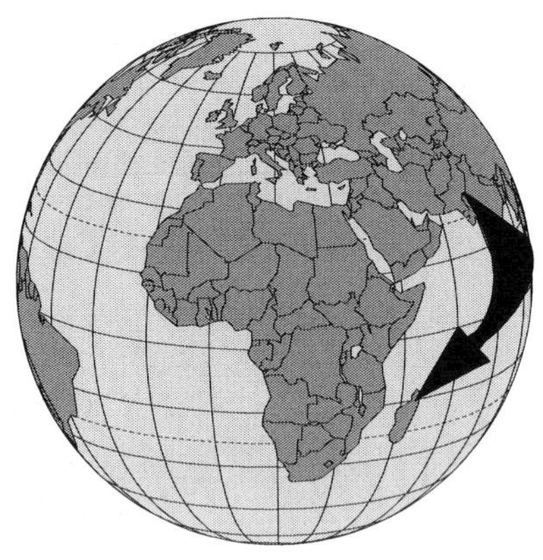

MADAGASCAR

Compiled from publications that were available as of February 2013 from the U.S. Department of State, the U.S. Department of Commerce, and the Central Intelligence Agency (CIA). See the introduction to this set for explanatory notes.

Official Name:
Republic of Madagascar

PROFILE

Geography

Area: total: 587,041 sq km; country comparison to the world: 47; land: 581,540 sq km; water: 5,501 sq km
Major cities: Antananarivo (capital) 1.816 million (2009)
Climate: tropical along coast, temperate inland, arid in south
Terrain: narrow coastal plain, high plateau and mountains in center

People

Nationality: noun: Malagasy (singular and plural); adjective: Malagasy
Population: 22,005,222 (July 2012 est.)
Population growth rate: 2.952% (2012 est.)
Ethnic groups: Malayo-Indonesian (Merina and related Betsileo), Cotiers (mixed African, Malayo-Indonesian, and Arab ancestry—Betsimisaraka, Tsimihety, Antaisaka, Sakalava), French, Indian, Creole, Comoran
Religions: indigenous beliefs 52%, Christian 41%, Muslim 7%
Languages: French (official), Malagasy (official), English
Literacy: definition: age 15 and over can read and write; total population: 64.5%; male: 67.4%; female: 61.6% (2009 est.)
Health: life expectancy at birth: total population: 64 years; male: 61.97 years; female: 66.1 years (2012 est.); Infant mortality rate: total: 50.09 deaths/1,000 live births; male: 54.8 deaths/1,000 live births; female: 45.24 deaths/1,000 live births (2012 est.)
Unemployment rate:
Work force: 9.504 million (2007)

Government

Type: republic
Independence: 26 June 1960
Constitution: passed by referendum 17 November 2010; promulgated 11 December 2010 (2010)
Political subdivisions: 6 provinces (faritany); Antananarivo, Antsiranana, Fianarantsoa, Mahajanga, Toamasina, Toliara
Suffrage: 18 years of age; universal

Economy

GDP (purchasing power parity): $21.37 billion (2012 est.); $20.66 billion (2011 est.); $20.55 billion (2010 est.); $20.44 billion (2009 est.)
GDP real growth rate: 1.9% (2012 est.); 0.5% (2011 est.); 0.5% (2010 est.); -4.1% (2009 est.)
GDP per capita (PPP): $1,000 (2012 est.); $900 (2011 est.); $1,000 (2010 est.); $1,000 (2009 est.)
Natural resources: graphite, chromite, coal, bauxite, rare earth elements, salt, quartz, tar sands, semiprecious stones, mica, fish, hydropower
Agriculture products: coffee, vanilla, sugarcane, cloves, cocoa, rice, cassava (tapioca), beans, bananas, peanuts; livestock products
Industries: meat processing, seafood, soap, breweries, tanneries, sugar, textiles, glassware, cement, automobile assembly plant, paper, petroleum, tourism
Exports: $1.533 billion (2012 est.); $1.389 billion (2011 est.); $1.173 billion (2010 est.)
Exports—commodities: coffee, vanilla, shellfish, sugar, cotton cloth, clothing, chromite, petroleum products
Exports—partners: France 23.4%, Indonesia 15.8%, Singapore 6.8%, China 5.9%, Germany 5.7%, US 5.2%, Canada 4% (2011)
Imports: $3.876 billion (2012 est.); $3.709 billion (2011 est.); $3.534 billion (2010 est.)
Imports—commodities: capital goods, petroleum, consumer goods, food
Imports—partners: China 17.4%, France 13.2%, South Africa 6.7%, Singapore 4.9%, Bahrain 4.8%, Mauritius 4.6%, Kuwait 4.5% (2011)
Debt—external: $2.631 billion (31 December 2012 est.); $2.323 billion (31 December 2011 est.); $2.228 billion (31 December 2010 est.)

Exchange rates: Malagasy ariary (MGA) per US dollar; 2,220 (2012 est.) ; 2,025.1 (2011 est.); 2,090 (2010 est.); 1,956.2 (2009); 1,654.78 (2008); 1,880 (2007)

PEOPLE

Madagascar's population is predominantly of mixed Asian and African origin. Research suggests that the island was uninhabited until Indonesian seafarers arrived in roughly the first century A.D., probably by way of southern India and East Africa, where they acquired African wives and slaves. Subsequent migrations from both the Pacific and Africa further consolidated this original mixture, and 18 separate tribal groups emerged. Asian features are most predominant in the central highlands people, the Merina and the Betsileo ; the coastal people are of more clearly African origin. The largest coastal groups are the Betsimisaraka and the Tsimihety and Sakalava.

National/Racial/Ethnic Minorities

None of the 18 tribes of the country constitute a majority. There are also minorities of Indo-Pakistani, Comoran, and Chinese heritage. Ethnicity, caste, and regional solidarity often are factors in hiring and were exploited in politics. A long history of military conquest and political dominance by highland ethnic groups of Asian origin, particularly the Merina, over coastal groups of African ancestry contributes to tension between citizens of highland and coastal descent, particularly in the political sphere.

Language

The Malagasy language is of Malayo-Polynesian origin and is generally spoken throughout the island, with significant regional variations. French is spoken among the educated population of this former French colony. English is becoming more widely spoken.

Religion

Although neither precise nor official figures were available, approximately half of the population is Christian. Four main Christian denominations compose the dominant religious association, the Council of Christian Churches in Madagascar (Fiombonan'ny Fiangonana Kristianina eto Madagasikara, or "FFKM"): Roman Catholic, Reformed Protestant Church of Jesus Christ in Madagascar (Fiangonan'i Jesoa Kristy eto Madagasikara, or "FJKM"), Lutheran, and Anglican. Smaller groups include The Church of Jesus Christ of Latter-day Saints (Mormons), Jehovah's Witnesses, and Seventh-day Adventists. A significant minority of citizens also observe indigenous religious practices.

Muslims constitute 10 to 15 percent of the population, with strong concentrations in the north, northwest, and southeast. Native-born persons and ethnic Indian and Pakistani immigrants represent the majority of Muslims; there is also a small number of Hindus.

HISTORY

The written history of Madagascar began in the seventh century A.D., when Arabs established trading posts along the northwest coast. European contact began in the 1500s, when Portuguese sea captain Diego Dias sighted the island after his ship became separated from a fleet bound for India. In the late 17th century, the French established trading posts along the east coast. From about 1774 to 1824, it was a favorite haunt for pirates, including Americans, one of whom brought Malagasy rice to South Carolina.

Beginning in the 1790s, Merina rulers succeeded in establishing hegemony over the majority of the island, including the coast. In 1817, the Merina ruler and the British governor of Mauritius concluded a treaty abolishing the slave trade, which had been important in Madagascar's economy. In return, the island received British military and financial assistance. British influence remained strong for several decades, during which the Merina court was converted to Presbyterianism, Congregationalism, and Anglicanism.

The British accepted the imposition of a French protectorate over Madagascar in 1885 in return for eventual control over Zanzibar (now part of Tanzania) and as part of an overall definition of spheres of influence in the area. Absolute French control over Madagascar was established by military force in 1895–96, and the Merina monarchy was abolished.

Malagasy troops fought in France, Morocco, and Syria during World War I. After France fell to the Germans in World War II, the Vichy government administered Madagascar. British troops occupied the strategic island in 1942 to preclude its seizure by the Japanese. The Free French received the island from the United Kingdom in 1943.

In 1947, with French prestige at a low ebb, a nationalist uprising was suppressed after several months of bitter fighting. The French subsequently established reformed institutions in 1956 under the Loi Cadre (Overseas Reform Act), and Madagascar moved peacefully toward independence. The Malagasy Republic was proclaimed on October 14, 1958, as an autonomous state within the French Community. A period of provisional government ended with the adoption of a constitution in 1959 and full independence on June 26, 1960.

GOVERNMENT AND POLITICAL CONDITIONS

Madagascar is ruled by an unelected and illegal civilian regime that assumed power in a March 2009 coup with military support. Andry Nirina Rajoelina adopted the title of president of the High Transition Authority (HAT), at the head of a loose coalition of former opposition politicians, intending to remain in this position until elections are held. Former pres-

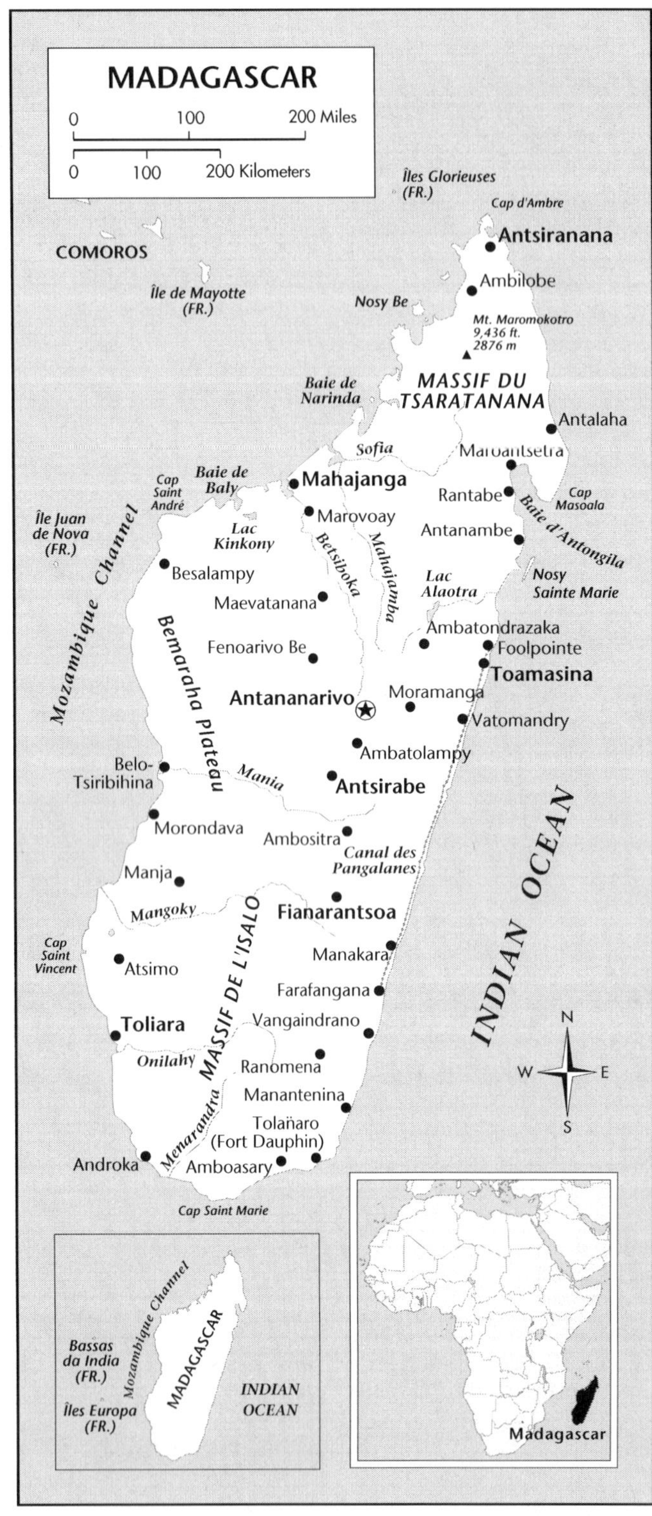

ident Marc Ravalomanana, democratically elected in 2006, is in exile. On September 17, 2011, local political leaders signed a "Roadmap For Ending the Crisis in Madagascar," brokered by mediators acting on behalf of the Southern African Development Community (SADC), which established a transitional process intended to culminate in free and open elections for the restoration of a legal government. In accordance with the letter, if not the spirit, of this roadmap, Rajoelina appointed a "Prime Minister of Consensus" on October 28, a 35-member "Government of National Unity" cabinet on November 21, and a "Transition Congress" with more than 160 members, and a "High Transitional Council" with more than 360 members on December 1. Military leaders continued to assert their autonomy from the current political leadership, despite their tacit support of Rajoelina and the SADC-endorsed roadmap. There were instances in which elements of the security forces acted independently of civilian control.

Recent Elections

Indirect elections to the 33-member senate took place in 2008. The "I Love Madagascar" Party of then president Ravalomanana won all 22 elected seats, and the president appointed the remaining 11 members. Allegations of campaign and voting irregularities surfaced during and after the election, but no conclusive legal action was taken.

Political Parties: Political parties could not operate without restriction or outside interference. Members of parties opposing the party or policies of the regime leader often had their individual rights, such as freedom of expression, violated. The regime often denied opposition parties the right to organize and publicize their opinions. Political parties also were dominated heavily by the urban elites from the more influential Malagasy tribes.

Participation of Women and Minorities: The first de facto Rajoelina government had five women in the 31-member cabinet. When reshuffled on March 26, six women were nominated to cabinet-level positions out of 31; when reshuffled again on November 21, eight women were nominated out of 35 cabinet members. At the end of 2011, 77 of the 579 members were women. Before the March 2009 coup d'etat, there were four women in the 21-member cabinet, 10 women in the 127-member national assembly, and five women in the 33-member senate.

Three of the 22 appointed regional administrators were women. Until March 2009, there were 11 Muslims and seven Chinese-Malagasy members in the national assembly and eight Muslims in the senate. Chinese-Malagasy and Muslims also held civil service positions. Residents of Indo-Pakistani origin were not well represented in regime institutions.

Principal Government Officials

Last Updated: 1/31/2013

In 2009, democratically elected President Marc Ravalomanana resigned and handed the reins of the government over to the military. The military in turn conferred the presidency on opposition leader Andry Rajoelina, who heads the High Transition Authority.

Pres.: **Andry Nirina RAJOELINA**
Prime Min.: **Jean Omer BERIZIKY**
Dep. Prime Min. in Charge of Development & Urbanization: **Hajo ANDRIANAINARIVELO**
Dep. Prime Min. in Charge of Economy & Industry: **Pierrot BOTOZAZA**
Min. of Agriculture: **Roland RAVATOMANGA**
Min. of the Armed Forces: **Andre Lucien RAKOTOARIMASY, Gen.**
Min. of Civil Service, Labor, & Social Legislation: **Tabera RANDRIAMANANTSOA**
Min. of Communication: **Harry Laurent RAHAJASON (also known as Rolly MERCIA)**
Min. of Culture & National Heritage: **Elia RAVELOMANATSOA**
Min. of Decentralization: **Ruffine TSIRANANA**
Min. of Energy: **Nestor RANDRIAKA**
Min. of Environment & Forests: **Joseph RANDRIAMIANDRISOA**
Min. of Finance & Budget: **Hery RAJAONARIMAMPIANINA**
Min. of Fisheries & Fishery Resources: **Sylvain MANDRORIKY**
Min. of Foreign Affairs: **Pierrot RAJAONARIVELO**
Min. of Higher Education & Scientific Research: **Etiene Hilaire RAZAFINDEHIBE**
Min. of Hydrocarbons: **Marcel BERNARD**
Min. of Interior: **Florent RAKOTOARISOA**
Min. of Internal Security: **Arsene RAKOTONDRAZAKA**
Min. of Justice & Keeper of the Seals: **Christine RAZANAMAHASOA**
Min. of Livestock: **Ihanta RANDRIAMANDRANTO**
Min. of Mines: **Daniella RANDRIAFENO**
Min. of National Defense: **Andre Lucien RAKOTOARIMASY, Gen.**
Min. of National Education: **Regis MANORO**
Min. of Population: **Olga VAOMALALA**
Min. of Posts, Telecommunications, & New Technology: **Ny Hasina ANDRIAMANJANTO**
Min. of Public Health: **Joanita NDAHMANJARA**
Min. of Public Service: **Tabera RANDRIAMANANTSOA**
Min. of Public Works & Meteorology: **BOTOMAMIZARA, Col.**
Min. of Sports: **Gerard BOTRALAHY**
Min. of Technical & Vocational Training: **Jean Andre NDREMANJARY**
Min. of Tourism: **Jean Max RAKOTOMAMONJY**
Min. of Trade: **Olga RAMALASON**
Min. of Transport: **Benjamina Ramarcel RAMANANTSOA**
Min. of Water Resources: **Julien REBOZA**
Min. of Youth & Leisure: **Jacques RANDRIATIANA**
Min. of Charge of the National Gendarmerie: **RANDIRANAZARY, Gen.**
Min. of Charge of Promotion of Handicrafts: **Elisa RAZAFITOMBO**
Min. of Charge of Relations With Institutions: **Victor MANANTSOA**
Governor, Central Bank: **Gaston RAVELOJAONA**
Ambassador to the US: **Jocelyn Bertin RADIFERA**
Permanent Representative to the UN, New York: **Zina ANDRIANARIVELO Razafy**

ECONOMY

After discarding socialist economic policies in the mid-1990s, Madagascar followed a World Bank- and IMF-led policy of privatization and liberalization that has been undermined since the start of the political crisis. This strategy placed the country on a slow and steady growth path from an extremely low level.

Agriculture, including fishing and forestry, is a mainstay of the economy, accounting for more than one-fourth of GDP and employing 80% of the population. Exports of apparel boomed in recent years primarily due to duty-free access to the US, however, Madagascar's failure to comply with the requirements of the African Growth and Opportunity Act (AGOA) led to the termination of the country's duty-free access in January 2010 and a sharp fall in textile production. Deforestation and erosion, aggravated by the use of firewood as the primary source of fuel, are serious concerns.

The current political crisis, which began in early 2009, has dealt additional blows to the economy. Tourism dropped more than 50% in 2009 compared with the previous year, and many investors are wary of entering the uncertain investment environment. Growth was anemic during 2010 to 2012 although expansion in mining and agricultural sectors is expected to contribute to more growth in 2013.

Labor Conditions

There were laws to protect children from exploitation in the workplace, but they were not effectively enforced. Child labor was a widespread problem.

The minimum age for employment was 15, consistent with educational requirements. However, the de facto regime did not effectively enforce the law. The law allows children to work a maximum of eight hours per day and 40 hours per week with no overtime.

The law prohibits persons under the age of 18 from working at night and at sites where there is an imminent danger to health, safety, or morals. Employers must observe a mandatory 12-hour rest period between shifts. Occupational health and safety restrictions include parental authorization and a medical visit before hiring. The International Labor Organization's 2007 National Survey on Child Labor in Madagascar indicated that approximately 28 percent of children between the ages of five and 17 (1.8 million children) were working on a full-or part-time basis, with an estimated 438,000 children involved in dangerous work. Children in rural areas worked mostly in agriculture, fishing, and livestock herding, while those in urban areas worked in occupations such as domestic labor, transport of goods by rickshaw, petty trading, stone quarrying, work in bars, and begging. Children also were engaged in salt production, deep sea diving, and the shrimp industry. The Ministry of Civil Services and Labor estimated that more than 19,000 children were working in the mining towns of Ilakaka in the south, mostly in the informal sector, helping their families mine gemstones or working as domestics. Some children were trafficked internally for the purposes of forced labor.

The Ministry of Civil Services and Labor is responsible for enforcing child labor laws and policies in the formal sector and conducted general workplace inspections during the year in response to a range of complaints. There is no enforcement in the much larger informal sector.

The monthly minimum wage was 90,235 ariary ($40) for nonagricultural workers and 91,520 ariary ($41) for agricultural workers. The official estimate for the poverty income level put the threshold at 468,800 ariary ($211) per person per year. The Ministry of Civil Services and Labor was responsible for enforcing the working conditions and minimum wages prescribed in the labor code.

The standard workweek was 40 hours in nonagricultural and service industries and 42.5 hours in the agricultural sector. Legislation limited workers to 20 hours of overtime per week and required 2.5 days of paid annual leave per month. If the hours worked exceed the legal limits for working hours (2,200 hours/year in agriculture and 173.33 hours/month in other sectors), employers are legally required to pay overtime in accordance with a Labor Council decree, which also denotes the required amount of overtime pay. The government is charged with setting occupational safety and health (OSH) standards for workers and workplaces. However, penalties for noncompliance are not defined in the labor code, which only requires an inspection before a company can open. Violations of wage, overtime, or OSH standards were common in the informal sector and in domestic work, where many are paid below minimum wage and work extensive hours.

U.S.-MALAGASY RELATIONS

During the 1800s and 1900s, Madagascar passed back and forth between British and French spheres of influence and possession. The country became independent from France in 1960. Relations between the United States and Madagascar date to the mid-1800s. The two countries concluded a commercial convention in 1867; established diplomatic relations in 1874; and concluded a treaty of peace, friendship, and commerce in 1881. Traditionally warm relations suffered considerably during the 1970s, when Madagascar expelled the U.S. Ambassador, closed a NASA tracking station, and nationalized two U.S. oil companies. In 1980, relations at the ambassadorial level were restored.

In 2009, Madagascar's democratically elected president stepped down under pressure from the military and purported to transfer his authority to a senior military figure, who in turn purported to confer the presidency on the opposition leader, who is currently heading the self-proclaimed High Transitional Authority (HAT). The United States considers the series of events in Madagascar in early 2009 to be a military coup d'état. In the aftermath of the coup d'etat, Madagascar has experienced negative economic growth and diminished government revenues, undermining the political, social, and economic stability of the country. The United States' intent is to support international efforts led by the Southern African Development Community and the African Union to ensure that a credible electoral process takes place as soon as possible, organized by an independent entity.

U.S. Assistance to Madagascar

Following the 2009 coup d'etat, the United States suspended direct assistance to or through Madagascar's governmental authorities as well as all non-humanitarian activities. The U.S. Government continues to provide assistance in health and food security through nongovernmental organizations, community associations, and other private groups. The United States is currently the largest bilateral donor to Madagascar, which is a priority country for the President's Malaria Initiative, Additionally, approximately 130 Peace Corps volunteers serve in Madagascar.

Bilateral Economic Relations

U.S. exports to Madagascar include machinery, vegetable oil, rice and wheat, aircraft, and vehicles. U.S. imports from Madagascar include apparel, vanilla beans, precious stones/metals, and perfumes/cosmetics. The United States has signed a trade and investment framework agreement with the Common Market for Eastern and Southern Africa, of which Madagascar is a member. Under the economic and political governance criteria necessary for eligibility, Madagascar is ineligible for preferential trade benefits under the African Growth and Opportunity Act.

Madagascar's Membership in International Organizations

Madagascar and the United States belong to a number of the same international organizations, including the United Nations, International Monetary Fund, World Bank, and World Trade Organization.

Bilateral Representation

Madagascar maintains an embassy in the United States at 2374 Massachusetts Avenue NW, Washington, DC 20008 (tel. 202-265-5525).

Principal U.S. Embassy Officials

Last Updated: 1/14/2013

ANTANANARIVO (E) Point Liberty, Andranoro, Antehiroka 105, Antsahavola B.P. 620 Antananarivo, Madagascar, (261) (20) 23-480 00 or 261-33-443-2000, Fax (261) (20) 23-480 35 or 261-33-443-2817, INMARSAT Tel 38-31-32673, Workweek: M-T 7:30AM–5:00PM/ F–7:30 AM–1:30 PM, http://www.antananarivo.usembassy.gov/

DCM OMS:	Tiffany Sims
AMB OMS:	Vacant
CDC:	Alyssa M. Finlay-Vickers
CG OMS:	Vacant
Co-CLO:	Bao Holy Andriamasinoro
DCM/CHG:	Charge Eric Wong
FCS:	Larry Farris
FM:	Ricardo Cruz
HRO:	Vonzett George
MGT:	Kevin Weishar
OMS:	Tiffany Sims
POL/ECON:	Jeremy Edwards
POSHO:	Ricardo Cruz
SDO/DATT:	CDR Michael Baker
AMB:	Vacant
CG:	Vacant
CON:	Jeffrey Osweiler
PAO:	Brett Bruen
GSO:	Kumi Ikeda
RSO:	Aaron Tambrini
AFSA:	Cathy Bowes
AGR:	Scott Reynolds (Pretoria)
AID:	Rudolph Thomas
CLO:	David Grist
DEA:	Jeffrey P. Breeden (Pretoria)
EEO:	Patty Baxer
FAA:	Edward Jones (Dakar)
FMO:	Tyrone Campbell
ICASS Chair:	John Reddy
IMO:	Joseph Farina
IPO:	Roger L. Smith
IRS:	Aziz Benbrahim (Paris)
ISSO:	Sonia Grigorian
LEGATT:	Wilford Rattigan
POL:	Nicolle Otallah
State ICASS:	Eric Atkins

TRAVEL

Consular Information Sheet

February 7, 2012

Country Description: Madagascar is a developing island nation off the east coast of Africa. The primary languages are French and Malagasy. French is less spoken outside of major cities. Facilities for tourism are available, but vary in quality and are in general limited. Travelers seeking high-end accommodations should make reservations in advance.

Smart Traveler Enrollment Program (STEP)/Embassy Locations: If you are going to live or visit Madagascar, please take the time to tell our Embassy about your trip. If you enroll, we can keep you up to date with important safety and security announcements. It will also help your friends and family get in touch with you in an emergency.

The U.S. Embassy is located at Lot 207 A, Point Liberty, Andranoro-Antehiroka, Antananarivo (105), Madagascar. The mailing address is B.P. 5253, Antananarivo (105) Madagascar; the telephone number is [261] (20) 23-480-00; the fax number is [261] (20) 23-480-35.

Entry/Exit Requirements for U.S. Citizens: A passport and visa are required. Tourists staying in Madagascar for less than 30 days will be able to receive a free visa upon arrival. Travelers staying for longer or who require a transformable visa are not eligible for this promotion. Visas are available at all airports servicing international flights, but travelers who opt to obtain a visa at an airport should expect delays upon arrival. Visas obtained at the airport cannot be extended. Visitors can also obtain visas from the Madagascar Embassy in Washington, DC: 2374 Massachusetts Ave. NW, Washington, DC 20008–2852; telephone (202) 265-5525/6. Visas issued by the Madagascar Embassy in Washington, DC, are extendable within Madagascar. Please be advised that in order to extend a visa within Madagascar, a current police certificate from the United States is required by the Madagascar government and cannot be provided by the U.S. Embassy in Antananarivo. All U.S. citizens must have at least one blank page and 6 months validity in their passport to gain admittance to Madagascar. Visa fees can be paid in U.S. dollars, Euros, or Madagascar Ariary. Credit cards are not accepted. Most international flights arrive in Antananarivo, but there are some limited international flights to/from the nearby islands of Comoros, Mayotte, and Reunion from airports in Mahajanga, Toamasina (Tamatave), Nosy Be, Tolagnaro (Ft. Dauphin), and Antsiranana (Diego Suarez). There are also direct flights between Italy and Nosy Be. Evidence of yellow fever immunization is required for all travelers who have been in an infected zone within six months of their arrival in Madagascar.

The U.S. Department of State is unaware of any HIV/AIDS entry restrictions for visitors to or foreign residents of Madagascar.

Travelers may obtain the latest information and details on entry requirements from the Embassy of the Republic of Madagascar, 2374 Massachusetts Avenue NW, Washington, DC 20008; telephone (202) 265-5525/6; or the Malagasy Consulate in New York City, telephone (212) 986-9491. Honorary consuls of Madagascar are located in Philadelphia and San Diego. Overseas, inquiries may be made at the nearest Malagasy embassy or consulate. Visit the Embassy of Madagascar's web site for the most current visa information.

Threats to Safety and Security: In March 2009, the democratically elected government of Madagascar resigned in actions that the U.S. government has termed a coup d'état. As of late 2011, the political situation is still unstable as the transitional government pursues legitimacy via a political road map established by international mediators. Further clashes between protesters and security forces remain possible though they have been rare since late 2009, and almost entirely restricted to Antananarivo.

Travelers should maintain security awareness at all times and should avoid political gatherings and street demonstrations. Certain large gatherings such as concerts or scenes of accidents also may pose a threat to foreigners. A downtown Antananarivo demonstration in November 2011 quickly morphed into a violent crowd of over 6,000 people that security forces were forced to disperse with tear gas.

Travel in the provincial areas is generally safe but caution should be exercised at all times. At the start of the political crisis in January 2009, a number of provincial capitals experienced political demonstrations that had, on occasion, become violent and resulted in clashes with security forces and looting. A number of route national highways connecting provincial cities and the capital experienced temporary road blocks by political demonstrators resulting in travel delays. There are random police vehicle checkpoints throughout Madagascar, so all visitors should carry photo identification (residency card, U.S. passport) in the event of police questioning. These check points are routine in nature, and should not result in vehicle and/or person searches as long as valid identification is shown.

Stay up to date by:

- Bookmarking our Bureau of Consular Affairs website, which contains the current Travel Warnings and Travel Alerts as well as the Worldwide Caution.
- Following us on Twitter and the Bureau of Consular Affairs page on Facebook as well.
- Downloading our free Smart Traveler IPhone App to have travel information at your fingertips.
- Calling 1-888-407-4747 toll-free within the U.S. and Canada, or a regular toll line, 1-202-501-4444, from other countries.
- Taking some time before travel to consider your personal security.

Crime: Madagascar is currently experiencing a dramatic spike not only in the number of crimes, but also in their severity and type. To put this into perspective, Madagascar remains, by and large, safer than many other African countries and even certain U.S. cities.

Over the last two years, there was a surge in armed attacks. The number of reported incidents has increased steadily since 2009, and, as of late 2011, the Embassy noted reports of more home invasions. The majority of those reported crimes were Malagasy on Malagasy and did not involve foreigners.

Carjackings are known to occur, though infrequent in the cities; and night time taxi brousse attacks, which used to be an occasional occurrence, are now reported weekly/monthly. There have been reports of thieves reaching into stopped vehicles, opening unlocked doors, or sometimes breaking the windows to steal cell phones, purses, and even jewelry from their victims. Keeping windows rolled up and doors locked will minimize these types of situations.

In addition, armed banditry attacks on vehicles carrying goods and people, specifically taxi be and taxi brousse, have increased drastically over the last few years and are now a regular occurrence. Groups of armed bandits often position themselves on the national routes after dark to ambush vehicles. Others have involved armed criminals who stage a "breakdown" that blocks the roadway, forcing the victimized driver to slow down, and hence become more vulnerable. Additionally, sometimes local villagers design a "trap" of sand, a tree log, or some other substance or condition that makes the only viable road impassible. Local villagers then "assist" the stranded vehicle and expect monetary compensation. Although the interim government has taken steps to increase checkpoints to deter banditry, the U.S. Embassy does not recommend night time travel outside of Antananarivo or any other city due to these attacks and the lack of security force coverage outside of city limits. All U.S. citizens are advised to avoid unknown taxis, especially if alone or at night.

Another major concerns for visitors, especially those in Antananarivo, are crimes of opportunity such as pickpocketing, purse snatching and residential and vehicular theft. Although some of these crimes are non-confrontational, incidents involving violence by assailants do occur and are on the rise, particularly when the victim resists, and especially when multiple persons confront the victim. The embassy has received reports of physical attacks against foreigners, including U.S. citizens, particularly in coastal tourist areas. A number of these attacks resulted in serious injuries and, in rare cases, fatalities. Criminal elements in Antananarivo and throughout Madagascar are becoming bolder when selecting their victims, and are also committing more crimes in areas that are considered to be "safe"—those that are generally well lit and well traveled by pedestrians and vehicles.

Criminal gangs comprised of felons, ex-military, and police are known to commit home invasions and kidnappings, sometimes targeting foreigners. Organized gangs of bandits are known to patrol areas where foreigners, who are perceived to be wealthy, tend to congregate. Crimes such as burglary and robbery do occur in areas outside the capital, and the threat of confrontational and violent crime has increased in rural and isolated areas throughout the last year.

To reduce the risk of being victimized, travel in groups and avoid wearing expensive jewelry or carrying high cost electronic items (iPods, digital cameras, or high-end cell phones) with you in public. Valuable items should never be left in an unattended vehicle or at a hotel (unless locked in the hotel safe). Walking at night, whether alone or in a group is not considered safe in urban areas, including in the vicinity of Western-standard hotels, restaurants and night clubs in Antananarivo. Visitors are strongly discouraged from traveling outside of cities after dark due to banditry, lack of lighting, poor road conditions and lack of security assets. While traveling in vehicles, remember to lock your doors and keep your windows rolled up at all times.

In major cities, the National Police is charged with maintaining peace and security. Outside of major cities, the Gendarmerie is primarily responsible for these duties. Due to the lack of resources and equipment available, police and gendarme response to victims of a crime is often limited, slow, or nonexistent.

U.S. citizens visiting Madagascar should not expect to experience any hostility or aggression solely because of their citizenship.

Don't buy counterfeit and pirated goods, even if they are widely available. Not only are the bootlegs illegal in the United States, if you purchase them you may also be breaking local law.

Victims of Crime: If you or someone you know becomes the victim of a crime abroad, you should contact the local police and the nearest U.S. embassy or consulate. We can:

- Replace a stolen passport.
- Help you find appropriate medical care if you are the victim of violent crimes such as assault or rape.
- Put you in contact with the appropriate police authorities, and if you want us to, we can contact family members or friend.
- Help you understand the local criminal justice process and direct you to local attorneys, although it is important to remember that local authorities are responsible for investigating and prosecuting the crime.

The local equivalent to the "911" emergency line in Madagascar is 117. The police can also be reached in Antananarivo at 22-227-35 and 22-281-70. We recommend you use these numbers only if you speak good Malagasy or French. Otherwise, please contact the U.S. Embassy in case of emergency.

Criminal Penalties: While you are traveling in another country, you are subject to its laws even if you are a U.S. citizen. Foreign laws and legal systems can be vastly different than our own. In some places you may be taken in for questioning if you don't have your passport with you. In some places, driving under the influence could land you immediately in jail. These criminal penalties will vary from country to country. There are also some things that might be legal in the country you visit, but still illegal in the United States, and you can be prosecuted under U.S. law if you buy pirated goods. Engaging in sexual conduct with children or using or disseminating child pornography in a foreign country is a crime prosecutable in the United States. If you break local laws in in your host country, your U.S. passport won't help you avoid arrest or prosecution. Its very important to know what's legal and what's not where you are going.

Persons violating Malagasy laws, even unknowingly, may be expelled, arrested or imprisoned. Penalties for possession, use, or trafficking in illegal drugs and child prostitution in Madagascar are severe, and convicted offenders can expect long jail sentences and heavy fines.

Arrest notifications in host country: While some countries will automatically notify the nearest U.S. embassy or consulate if a U.S. citizen is detained or arrested in a foreign country, that might not always be the case. To ensure that the United States is aware of your circumstances, request that the police and prison officials notify the nearest U.S. embassy or consulate as soon as you are arrested or detained overseas.

Special Circumstances: It is advisable to contact the Embassy of Madagascar in Washington or one of Madagascar's consulates in the United States for specific information regarding customs requirements. In many countries around the world, counterfeit and pirated goods are widely available. Transactions involving such products are illegal and bringing them back to the United States may result in forfeitures and/or fines. Taking photographs of airports or military installations is prohibited.

Madagascar is renowned for its natural resources. These include a wide variety of gemstones and other precious materials. The Government of Madagascar recently imposed restrictions on the export of precious gems; before purchasing or transporting any gemstones it is advisable to seek clarification of the applicable laws. Any precious materials should be accompanied by a certificate of authenticity and a certificate to allow for exportation from Madagascar.

Madagascar is primarily a cash-driven economy. Although some high-end establishments catering to tourists accept credit cards, normally only Visa-logo cards, most shops and restaurants are cash only. Although the government changed the local currency from the Malagasy Franc (FMG) to the Ariary several years ago, many Malagasy still think in terms of FMG. When talking about prices, it is important to quantify whether the price is in Ariary or FMG. (1 Ariary = 5 FMG). ATMs that accept Visa (generally not Mastercard) are available in large cities. Dollars are not widely accepted and $100USD bills are frequently refused at banks and local businesses.

Accessibility: While in Madagascar, individuals with disabilities may find accessibility and accommodation very different from what you find in the United States. While the constitution and law prohibit all forms of discrimination, including on the basis of race, gender, disability, language, and social status, there are no specific government institutions designated to enforce these provisions.

There is ample public transportation but entering and existing vehicles is precarious, and they are not equipped to accommodate passengers with disabilities. Vehicles are often still in motion as passengers enter and exit. There are no sidewalks in the vast majority of the country, and the roads are hazardous for foot travel with swerving vehicles and uneven surfaces. There are no pedestrian crossing signs or designated pathways, and crossing any street involves an element of risk. Pedestrian injuries are common. Public spaces are not wheelchair accessible.

Medical Facilities and Health Information: Standards of healthcare throughout Madagascar are well below U.S. standards. There are foreign physicians in Antananarivo representing a broad range of specialties, but their training is variable and often not to U.S. standards. The hospitals in Antananarivo vary greatly in standards of care. Medical care outside of Antananarivo is generally well below the care available in the capital. Caution and good judgment should be exercised when seeking hospital and medical services. The Embassy maintains a list of hospitals and specialists which can be provided on demand.

Some medications, generally of French origin, are available in Antananarivo. If you need to refill a prescription from home, it is important to carry a prescription from your doctor listing the medicine's generic name. There is limited availability of both prescription and over-the-counter medications, and outside of Antananarivo, medications may not be available. Travelers should consider consulting their health care provider about getting a supply of anti-malarial medication if traveling to high-risk areas and antibiotic prophylaxis for intestinal infections. These medications are available in Antananarivo. Travelers should have a supply of any needed medication sufficient for the entire length of a visit before arriving in Madagascar. U.S. citizens who will be carrying medications with them to Madagascar may wish to contact the Malagasy Embassy in Washington, DC, regarding any restrictions on imports.

Ambulance services are available in Antananarivo with Assistance Plus at 032 07 801 10 or 22 487 47; Polyclinique d'Ilafy at 22 425 73 or 033 11 458 48; Espace Medical at 22 625 66 or 22 481 73 or 034 05 625 66; and CDU (Centre de Diagnostic Medical d'Urgences) at 22 329 56. However, due to traffic jams, response times are often dangerously slow.

Malaria is prevalent, particularly in the coastal regions. Using preventive measures and malaria prophylaxis is strongly recommended. Rabies is endemic, and there are many street dogs. It is recommended travelers have the pre-exposure vaccination series prior to arrival in Madagascar. If bitten by an animal, wash the affected area immediately with soap and running water for ten minutes. Seek medical care immediately. Plague is also endemic to Madagascar. While the reported HIV prevalence rate is low, particularly by African standards, Madagascar suffers from a very high reported incidence of sexually transmitted infections and tuberculosis.

The East African Indian Ocean islands have seen a rise in the cases of chikungunya, a viral dengue-like ailment, and dengue itself. As with malaria, chikungunya and dengue are transmitted by mosquitoes. Every effort should be made to use bed nets, repellants, proper clothing, and barriers that discourage/prevent mosquito bites. The CDC has further information on chikungunya and dengue on their website.

Travelers should drink bottled water or carbonated beverages. Local water is not generally potable. Water purification tablets may be used as necessary. Bottled water is readily available.

You can find good information on vaccinations and other health precautions, on the CDC website. For information about outbreaks of infectious diseases abroad, consult the the World Health Organization (WHO) website. The WHO website also contains additional health information for travelers, including detailed country-specific health information

Medical Insurance: You can't assume your insurance will go with you when you travel. It's very important to find out BEFORE you leave whether or not your medical insurance will cover you overseas. You need to ask your insurance company two questions:

- Does my policy apply when I'm out of the United States?
- Will it cover emergencies like a trip to a foreign hospital or a medical evacuation?

In many places, doctors and hospitals still expect payment in cash at the time of service. Your regular U.S. health insurance may not cover doctors' and hospital visits in other countries. If your policy doesn't go with you when you travel, it's a very good idea to take out another one for your trip.

Traffic Safety and Road Conditions: While in Madagascar, you may encounter road conditions that differ significantly from those in the United States. In Madagascar, you drive on the right side of the road, generally yielding the right of way to vehicles coming in from the left. Some major intersections and traffic circles have police directing traffic. If a policeman has his back to you at an intersection, you are required to stop. Laws make seatbelt use mandatory and prohibit cell phone use while driving, even with a hands-free attachment. Child safety seats and motorcycle helmets are not required in Madagascar. If you are caught driving under the influence of alcohol, your car will be impounded for a few days and you will have to pay a fine. If you are involved in an accident involving injuries and/or deaths, there is a mandatory court case. The losing party of the court case must then pay all costs.

Except for Antananarivo's main streets and a few well-maintained routes to outlying cities, many roads are in various states of disrepair. Some may be impassable during the rainy season. Night travel by private or public transportation outside Antananarivo is strongly discouraged due to poor lighting and road conditions. Roads tend to be narrow and winding with many one-lane bridges and blind curves, and most roads outside of main routes and city centers are cobblestone, gravel, or packed dirt. Most vehicles tend to drive in the center of the road unless another vehicle is present. It is common to find livestock or human-drawn carts in the middle of the road, even at night. Local practice is to blow the horn before going around a curve, to let others know of one's presence. There are few pedestrian crosswalks and no working traffic signals.

Travel within Antananarivo can be difficult with poor road signage, streets congested with pedestrians, bicycles, animal carts, and vehicular traffic, and an abundance of one-way streets. Taxis are plentiful and are generally reasonably priced. Bargain for the fare prior to getting into a vehicle. Most accidents are pedestrian-related, due to narrow roads and lack of sidewalks on many streets. When traveling between cities, travelers must have clear directions as there are rarely signs indicating where one must turn to reach a destination. Conditions of rural roads can degrade significantly and with little notice during the rainy season. Rental cars generally come with a driver who is responsible for maintaining the vehicle and sometimes acts as a tour guide. Public transportation is unreliable and vehicles are poorly maintained. Rail services are extremely limited and unreliable.

The Ministry of Public Works, telephone (20) 22-318-02, is Madagascar's authority responsible for road safety. During an emergency, visitors to Antananarivo can contact local police by dialing 117, 22-227-35, or 22-357-09/10. U.S. citizens can also call the U.S. Embassy at (261) 20-23-480-00 if assistance is needed in communicating with law enforcement officials.

Aviation Safety Oversight: As there is no direct commercial air service to the United States by carriers registered in Madagascar, the U.S. Federal Aviation Administration (FAA) has not assessed the government of Madagascar's Civil Aviation Authority for compliance with International Civil Aviation Organization (ICAO) aviation safety standards. Further information may be found on the FAA's safety assessment page. Domestic and international air services operate regularly but are subject to delays and occasional breakdowns. Air Madagascar often changes in-country flight schedules based on demand; flights that are not full may be cancelled with little or no prior warning to passengers. Overbooking is also common. Reconfirmation of tickets prior to flight day is recommended, especially when flying from provincial airports.

Children's Issues:: Please see the U.S. Dept. of State Office of Children's Issues web pages on intercountry adoption and international parental child abduction.

Intercountry Adoption

January 2011

The information in this section has been edited from the latest report available as of February 2013 from the State Department Bureau of Consular Affairs, Office of Overseas Citizens Services. For more information, please read the *Intercountry Adoption* section of this book and review current reports online at http://adoption.state.gov.

Madagascar is party to the Hague Convention on Protection of Children and Co-operation in Respect of Intercountry Adoption (Hague Adoption Convention). Therefore all adoptions between Madagascar and the United States must meet the requirements of the Convention and U.S. law implementing the Convention. The Government of Madagascar has ratified the Hague Convention on Protection of Children and Co-Operation in Respect of Intercountry Adoption. A new adoption law in Madagascar went into effect in 2007, which closely follows Hague Convention processing requirements. Practical implementation of the new law is still being tested as cases work their way through the system. Therefore, prospective adoptive parents are advised to read the below requirements, particularly regarding timing of documents required in the initial application, and follow developments closely. Adoptive parents are advised to follow legal adoption procedures carefully. Madagascar adheres strictly to the law. Prospective adoptive parents are also advised that Madagascar has two adoption processes: simple adoption and plenary adoption. Only international plenary adoption, involving a long and sometimes difficult legal process, is recognized by both Madagascar and the United States as valid for intercountry adoption. Simple adoption, involving the mayor of the town where the child is located, is not a valid adoption for U.S. visa or Malagasy passport purposes.

Who Can Adopt? Adoption between the United States and Madagascar is governed by the Hague Adoption Convention. Therefore to adopt from Madagascar, you must first be found eligible to adopt by the U.S. Government. The U.S. Government agency responsible for making this determination is the Department of Homeland Security, U.S. Citizenship and Immigration Services (USCIS). In addition to these U.S. requirements for prospective adoptive parents, Madagascar also has the following requirements for prospective adoptive parents.

Residency Requirements: Under Malagasy law, once the case moves from the administrative to the judicial phase, at least one of the adoptive parents must come to Madagascar and live with, or otherwise become familiar with the child for a one-month probationary period. After the end of this period, the final court proceedings will take place, and one parent will need to be present for these as well. The adoption is not final until these proceedings are complete, and the child will not be able to receive a passport or a visa until after the end of the court proceedings. Although the new law imposes several specific time requirements that govern the timing of each step in the process. However, past experience under the old law suggests these time periods could be much longer. Under the old law, cases often took four to six months or longer after the probationary period.

Age Requirements: At least one spouse must be over the age of 30 to adopt in Madagascar.

Marriage Requirements: Only married heterosexual couples can adopt in Madagascar. If either spouse dies before the adoption is finalized, the process will be terminated.

Other Requirements:

- The couple can have no more than three other children, either biological or adopted.
- They must possess good moral character and demonstrate the means to care for the physical and educational needs of the child.
- They must agree to keep the Malagasy Central Authority informed, through regular written reports, of the child's well-being, and progress in integrating until the child reaches age 18.

Who Can Be Adopted? Because Madagascar is party to the Hague Adoption Convention, children from Madagascar must meet the requirements of the Convention in order to be eligible for adoption. For example, the Convention requires that Madagascar attempt to place a child with a family in Madagascar before determining that a child is eligible for intercountry adoption. In addition to Malagasy requirements, a child must meet the definition of a Convention adoptee for you to bring him or her back to the United States.

Adoption Authority: The Malagasy Central Authority is coordinated by the Director of the Protection of the Family and Children (le Directeur de la Protection de la Famille et de l'Enfance) under the Ministry of Health and Family Planning and Social Protection (Ministère en charge de la Santé, du Planning Familial et de la Protection Sociale).

The Process: Because Madagascar is party to the Hague Adoption Convention, adopting from Madagascar must follow a specific process designed to meet the Convention's requirements. For detailed and updated information on these requirements, visit the USCIS Intercountry Adoption website at http://adoption.state.gov. The process for finalizing the adoption (or gaining legal custody) in Madagascar generally includes the following.

Role of the Adoption Authority: The Malagasy Central Authority, coordinated by the Director of the Protection of the Family and Children (le Directeur de la Protection de la Famille et de l'Enfance) under the Ministry of Health and Family Planning and Social Protection (Ministère en charge de la Santé, du Planning Familial et de la Protection Sociale), oversees international plenary adoptions in Madagascar.

Time Frame: Under the prior Malagasy law, the process commonly took two to three years. The new Malagasy law promises a faster process, and Malagasy authorities informally estimate a year. Until cases are brought under the new law and processed to completion, however, it is difficult to predict how streamlined the new process actually is.

Adoption Application: The U.S. Embassy has been provided with the following as general information regarding Malagasy adoption procedures. Note that while the below time requirements are written into Malagasy law, there is no mechanism to enforce these limits. The prospective adoptive parents or the adoption agency sends the dossier of required documents to the U.S. Central Authority for forwarding to Madagascar via the Embassy of Madagascar in the U.S who in turn will transmit it to the Malagasy Ministry of Foreign Affairs. Important note: After the ratification of the Hague Convention by the American Government, the Office of Children's Issues will serve the function of the U.S. Central Authority.

- The dossier is routed to the Malagasy Central Authority (MCA);
- The MCA reviews the dossier to ensure it meets the technical standards;
- Once the dossier is deemed technically complete, it is reviewed by the MCA to determine if it will be approved.;
- Once approved by the MCA, the MCA will choose a child, under the age of 12, to be offered to the adoptive parents. Note: Under Malagasy law, the adoptive parents do not choose the child. However, with Plenary International Adoption it is possible to adopt a specific child if there is a genuine family relationship, and proof of such a relationship;
- Once the child has been identified, the MCA will prepare a dossier on the child and send it to the prospective adoptive parents;
- The prospective adoptive parents are given six months to review the dossier and accept or reject the child;
- If the parents accept the child, they send an acceptance package to the U.S. Central Authority for transmission to Madagascar;
- Within two months, the MCA reports the case to the court and gives the court a favorable recommendation of the case;
- The court case is opened;
- The court orders a one month probationary period for one or both parents to get to know the child in Madagascar;
- Before the end of the probationary period, the judge will set the hearing date, which will occur during the probationary period. The hearing requires their presence with the child;
- Once the hearing date is set, the file is sent to the prosecutor's office to complete required paperwork within three days;
- The hearing is held, at which the child, if capable of participating, participates; and a preliminary decision announced in open court;

- The written judgment is issued within 5 days, beginning a one-month objection period;
- The written decision is passed to the Civil Register of the child's place of birth to be noted on the child's birth registration;
- The child is then entitled to a copy of the birth certificate showing the adoption, a passport, and is eligible to apply for the necessary visa.

Adoption Fees: In the adoption services contract that you sign at the beginning of the adoption process, your agency will itemize the fees and estimated expenses related to your adoption process. The U.S. Embassy in Madagascar discourages the payment of any fees that are not properly receipted, "donations," or "expediting" fees, that may be requested from prospective adoptive parents. Such fees have the appearance of "buying" a baby and put all future adoptions in Madagascar at risk.

The government of Madagascar imposes a fee of 800 Euros (approximately $1,185 at current exchange rates), which goes to pay the expenses of caring for the child during the adoption proceedings as well as the costs of the Malagasy Central Authority. Attorney's fees, should the adoptive parents' choose to hire a local attorney, are additional, as are U.S. visa fees.

Documents Required: The initial dossier requires the following documents:

- A written request to adopt in Madagascar, with notarized signatures of both parents;
- Photos of the family in their everyday life;
- A signed contract with an accredited adoption agency;
- A social and psychological report prepared by an accredited agency. The home study fulfills this requirement;
- A certified copy of the marriage certificate;
- A certified birth certificate for each spouse;
- A police certificate for each spouse, from their place of residence;
- A certificate of nationality for each spouse. As this document is unusual in the U.S., certified copies of each spouse's passport, valid for at least six months form the date the dossier is submitted, can be submitted instead;
- Pay receipts for each spouse and/or the spouse's tax return;
- A certificate of morality from each employed spouse's employer. This is a recommendation letter from the employer testifying to the employee's good character;
- A certificat de bonne vie et moeurs (certificate of good citizenship) from the city or state government. As this document is not available in the U.S., Malagasy authorities have stated they will accept the approved home study;
- Medical certificates for both spouses noting they are both healthy enough to adopt; and
- A plain copy of U.S. Embassy Antananarivo Diplomatic Note 559 of September 13, 2007, available from the Consular Section of the U.S. Embassy in Antananarivo. This copy is requested by the Malagasy Central Authority so they will accept the substitutions for the livret de famille, certificate of nationality, and the certificat de bonne vie et moeurs.

All documents except the diplomatic note must be originals or certified copies. All documents not in French must be accompanied by a certified or official translation. Five copies of the dossier must also be submitted. If the parents accept the proposed child, the acceptance package must include:

- A letter of acceptance of the adoption with the notarized signatures of both parents;
- An agreement to send a report on the child's integration into the family and the U.S. every six months during the first year after adoption, and every year until the child reaches 18;
- A request for adoption addressed to the president of the Tribunal de première instance of the residence of the child, dated, signed and notarized by both parents;
- If only one parent will be present in Madagascar throughout the probationary period and adoption proceedings, a power of attorney form the absent parent;
- A passport valid for at least 6 months after the date of arrival in Madagascar. In addition, if the parent will be transiting South Africa to or from Madagascar, the passport will need to have at least two completely blank visa pages for each entry into South Africa;
- A Malagasy visa. Because of the high possibility the process could take longer than 60 days, adoptive parents should request an extendable visa from a Malagasy Embassy or Consulate in the United States prior to their trip. While available, airport visas issued upon arrival in Madagascar are not extendable and could expire before the process is complete. Without a valid visa, American Citizens are not permitted to leave Madagascar and are subject to arrest, imprisonment and deportation;
- Although not required, each traveling parent is urged to register with the U.S. Embassy in Antananarivo at https://travelregistration.state.gov prior to their trip or in person after their arrival.

Bringing Your Child Home: Once your adoption is complete (or you have obtained legal custody of the child), there are a few more steps to take before you can head home. Specifically, you need to apply for several documents for your child before he or she can travel to the United States, such as a birth certificate, a passport or travel document for your child from the country in which he or she was born, and a U.S. Immigration Visa. For detailed and updated information on how to obtain these documents, review the *Intercountry Adoption* section on this publication and visit the USCIS Intercountry Adoption website at http://adoption.state.gov.

Child Citizenship Act: For adoptions finalized abroad, the Child Citizenship Act of 2000 allows your new child to acquire American citizenship automatically when he or she enters the United States as lawful permanent residents. For adoptions finalized in the United States, the Child Citizenship Act of 2000 allows your new child to acquire American citizenship automatically when the court in the United States issues the final adoption decree. To learn more, review the *Intercountry Adoption* section on this publication and visit the USCIS Intercountry Adoption website at http://adoption.state.gov.

After Adoption: Adoptive Parents must agree to keep the Malagasy Central Authority informed, through regular written reports, of the child's well-being, and progress in integrating until the child reaches age 18. Reports should be sent to the Malagasy Central Authority every six months during the first year after adoption, and thereafter every year until the child reaches 18.

The United States Embassy in Antananarivo
14-16 Rue Rainitovo
B.P. 620, Antsahavola
Antananarivo 101
Tel: 011-261-20-22-212-57
Email: ConsAntan@state.gov

Madagascar's Adoption Authority
Coordinator of the Central Authority for Adoption
Batiment Ex Population
Ambohijatovo
101 Antananarivo
Madagascar
Tel: 261-20-22-22-018
Email: adoption_gasy@yahoo.fr

Embassy of Madagascar
2374 Massachusetts Avenue N.W.
Washington, DC 20008
Tel: 202-265-5525
Fax: 202 265 3034
Email: malagasy@embassy.org

Office of Children's Issues
U.S. Department of State
2201 C Street, NW
SA-29
Washington, DC 20520
Tel: 1-888-407-4747
E-mail: AskCI@state.gov
http://adoption.state.gov

For questions about immigration procedures, call the National Customer Service Center (NCSC) 1-800-375-5283 (TTY 1-800-767-1833).

MALAWI

Compiled from publications that were available as of February 2013 from the U.S. Department of State, the U.S. Department of Commerce, and the Central Intelligence Agency (CIA). See the introduction to this set for explanatory notes.

Official Name:
Republic of Malawi

PROFILE

Geography

Area: total: 118,484 sq km; country comparison to the world: 100; land: 94,080 sq km; water: 24,404 sq km

Major cities: Blantyre 856,000; LILONGWE (capital) 821,000 (2009)

Climate: sub-tropical; rainy season (November to May); dry season (May to November)

Terrain: narrow elongated plateau with rolling plains, rounded hills, some mountains

People

Nationality: noun: Malawian(s); adjective: Malawian

Population: 16,323,044 (July 2012 est.)

Population growth rate: 2.758% (2012 est.)

Ethnic groups: Chewa 32.6%, Lomwe 17.6%, Yao 13.5%, Ngoni 11.5%, Tumbuka 8.8%, Nyanja 5.8%, Sena 3.6%, Tonga 2.1%, Ngonde 1%, other 3.5%

Religions: Christian 82.7%, Muslim 13%, other 1.9%, none 2.5% (1998 census)

Languages: Chichewa (official) 57.2%, Chinyanja 12.8%, Chiyao 10.1%, Chitumbuka 9.5%, Chisena 2.7%, Chilomwe 2.4%, Chitonga 1.7%, other 3.6% (1998 census)

Literacy: definition: age 15 and over can read and write; total population: 74.8%; male: 81.1%; female: 68.5% (2010 est.)

Health: life expectancy at birth: total population: 52.31 years; male: 51.5 years; female: 53.13 years (2012 est.); Infant mortality rate: total: 79.02 deaths/1,000 live births; male: 83.06 deaths/1,000 live births; female: 74.92 deaths/1,000 live births (2012 est.)

Unemployment rate: NA%

Work force: 5.747 million (2007 est.)

Government

Type: multiparty democracy

Independence: 6 July 1964

Constitution: 18 May 1994

Political subdivisions: 28 districts

Suffrage: 18 years of age; universal

Economy

GDP (purchasing power parity): $14.58 billion (2012 est.); $14.08 billion (2011 est.); $13.35 billion (2010 est.); $12.53 billion (2009 est.)

GDP real growth rate: 4.3% (2012 est.); 5.5% (2011 est.); 6.5% (2010 est.); 9% (2009 est.)

GDP per capita (PPP): $900 (2012 est.); $900 (2011 est.); $800 (2010 est.); $800 (2009 est.)

Natural resources: limestone, arable land, hydropower, unexploited deposits of uranium, coal, and bauxite

Agriculture products: tobacco, sugarcane, cotton, tea, corn, potatoes, cassava (tapioca), sorghum, pulses, groundnuts, Macadamia nuts; cattle, goats

Industries: tobacco, tea, sugar, sawmill products, cement, consumer goods

Exports: $860 million (2012 est.); $911.5 million (2011 est.); $964.3 million (2010 est.)

Exports—commodities: tobacco 53%, tea, sugar, cotton, coffee, peanuts, wood products, apparel

Exports—partners: Canada 12.3%, South Africa 9%, Zimbabwe 8.9%, Germany 8.7%, US 6%, Russia 6%, UK 4.1%, China 4.1% (2011)

Imports: $1.752 billion (2012 est.); $1.687 billion (2011 est.); $1.671 billion (2010 est.)

Imports—commodities: food, petroleum products, semi-manufactures, consumer goods, transportation equipment

Imports—partners: South Africa 41.1%, India 8.4%, Zambia 8.1%, China 7.6%, Tanzania 4.9%, US 4.4% (2011)

Debt—external: $$1.214 billion (31 December 2012 est.; 1.327 billion (31 December 2011 est.); $1.24 billion (31 December 2010 est.)

Exchange rates: Malawian kwachas (MWK) per US dollar; 239 (2012 est.); 156.52 (2011 est.); 150.49 (2010 est.); 141.14 (2009); 142.41 (2008); 141.12 (2007)

GEOGRAPHY

Malawi is situated in southeastern Africa. The Great Rift Valley traverses the country from north to south. In this deep trough lies Lake Malawi, the third-largest lake in Africa, comprising about 20% of Malawi's area. The Shire River flows from the south end of the lake and joins the Zambezi River 400 kilometers (250 mi.) farther south in Mozambique. East and west of the Rift Valley, the land forms high plateaus, generally between 900 and 1,200 meters (3,000-4,000 ft.) above sea level. In the north, the Nyika Uplands rise as high as 2,600 meters (8,500 ft.); south of the lake lie the Shire Highlands, with an elevation of 600-1,600 meters (2,000-5,000 ft.), rising to Mts. Zomba and Mulanje, 2,130 and 3,048 meters (7,000 and 10,000 ft.). In the extreme south, the elevation is only 60-90 meters (200-300 ft.) above sea level.

Malawi is one of sub-Saharan Africa's most densely populated countries. All government ministries and the parliament are located in Lilongwe. Blantyre remains Malawi's major commercial center with a population of 660,000. Malawi's president resides in Lilongwe. The Supreme Court is seated in Blantyre.

Climate

Malawi's climate is generally subtropical. A rainy season runs from November through April. There is little to no rainfall throughout most of the country from May to October. It is hot and humid from October to April along the lake and in the Lower Shire Valley.

Lilongwe is also hot and humid during these months, albeit far less than in the south. The rest of the country is warm during those months. From June through August, the lake areas and far south are comfortably warm, but the rest of Malawi can be chilly at night, with temperatures ranging from 5o-14oC (41o-57oF).

PEOPLE

Malawi derives its name from the Maravi, a Bantu people who came from the southern Congo about 600 years ago. On reaching the area north of Lake Malawi, the Maravi divided. One branch, the ancestors of the present-day Chewas, moved south to the west bank of the lake. The other, the ancestors of the Nyanjas, moved down the east bank to the southern part of the country.

By AD 1500, the two divisions of the tribe had established a kingdom stretching from north of the present-day city of Nkhotakota to the Zambezi River in the south, and from Lake Malawi in the east to the Luangwa River in Zambia in the west.

Migrations and tribal conflicts precluded the formation of a cohesive Malawian society until the turn of the 20th century. Although regional distinctions and rivalries persist, ethnic and tribal distinctions have diminished as the concept of a Malawian nationality has taken hold. Despite some clear differences, no significant friction currently exists between tribal groups. Predominately a rural people, Malawians are generally conservative and traditionally nonviolent.

The Chewas constituteabout 90% of the population of the central region; the Nyanja tribe predominates in the south and the Tumbuka in the north. In addition, significant numbers of the Tongas live in the north; Ngonis—an offshoot of the Zulus who came from South Africa in the early 1800s—live in the lower northern and lower central regions; and the Yao, who are mostly Muslim, live along the southeastern border with Mozambique. Approximately 50% of the population lives in the southern region.

Language

English, the official language of Malawi, generally suffices for business communication, although few rural Malawians speak it. The most common vernacular languages include Chichewa (spoken throughout the country), Chitumbuka (spoken primarily in the North), and Chiyao (spoken primarily in the South).

Religion

The population of the country is 80 percent Christian. Among the Christian groups, the predominant denominations are the Roman Catholic Church and the Church of Central Africa Presbyterian, with smaller numbers of Anglicans, Baptists, evangelicals, and Seventh-day Adventists. Muslims constitute approximately 20 percent of the population, and the vast majority of Muslims are Sunni. There are also Hindus and Baha'is, as well as small numbers of Rastafarians and Jews.

HISTORY

Hominid remains and stone implements have been identified in Malawi dating back more than 1 million years, and early humans inhabited the vicinity of Lake Malawi 50,000 to 60,000 years ago. Human remains at a site dated about 8000 BC show physical characteristics similar to peoples living today in the Horn of Africa. At another site, dated 1500 BC, the remains possess features resembling Negro and Bushman people.

Although the Portuguese reached the area in the 16th century, the first significant Western contact was the arrival of David Livingstone along the shore of Lake Malawi in 1859. Subsequently, Scottish Presbyterian churches established missions in Malawi. One of their objectives was to end the slave trade to the Persian Gulf that continued to the end of the 19th century. In 1878, a number of traders, mostly from Glasgow, formed the African Lakes Company to supply goods and services to the missionaries. Other missionaries, traders, hunters, and planters soon followed.

In 1883, a consul of the British Government was accredited to the "Kings and Chiefs of Central Africa," and in 1891, the British established the Nyasaland Protectorate (Nyasa is the Yao word for "lake"). Although the British remained in control during the first half of the 1900s, this period was marked by a number of unsuccessful Malawian attempts to obtain independence. A growing European and U.S.-educated African elite became increasingly vocal and politically active—first through associations, and after 1944, through the Nyasaland African Congress (NAC).

During the 1950s, pressure for independence increased when Nyasaland was joined with Northern and Southern Rhodesia in 1953 to form the Federation of Rhodesia and Nyasaland. In July 1958, Dr. Hastings Kamuzu Banda returned to the country after a long absence in the United States (where he had obtained his medical degree at Meharry Medical College in Nashville, Tennessee, in 1937), the United Kingdom (where he practiced medicine), and Ghana. He assumed leadership of the NAC, which later became the Malawi Congress Party (MCP). In 1959, Banda was sent to Gwelo Prison for his political activities but was released in 1960 to participate in a constitutional conference in London.

On April 15, 1961, the MCP won an overwhelming victory in elections for a new Legislative Council. It also gained an important role in the new Executive Council and ruled Nyasaland in all but name a year later. In a second constitutional conference in London in November 1962, the British Government agreed to give Nyasaland self-governing status the following year.

Banda became Prime Minister on February 1, 1963, although the British still controlled Malawi's financial, security, and judicial systems. A new constitution took effect in May 1963, providing for virtually complete internal self-government. The Federation of Rhodesia and Nyasaland was dissolved on December 31, 1963, and Malawi became a fully independent member of the Commonwealth (formerly the British Commonwealth) on July 6, 1964. Two years later, Malawi adopted a new constitution and became a one-party state with Banda as its first president.

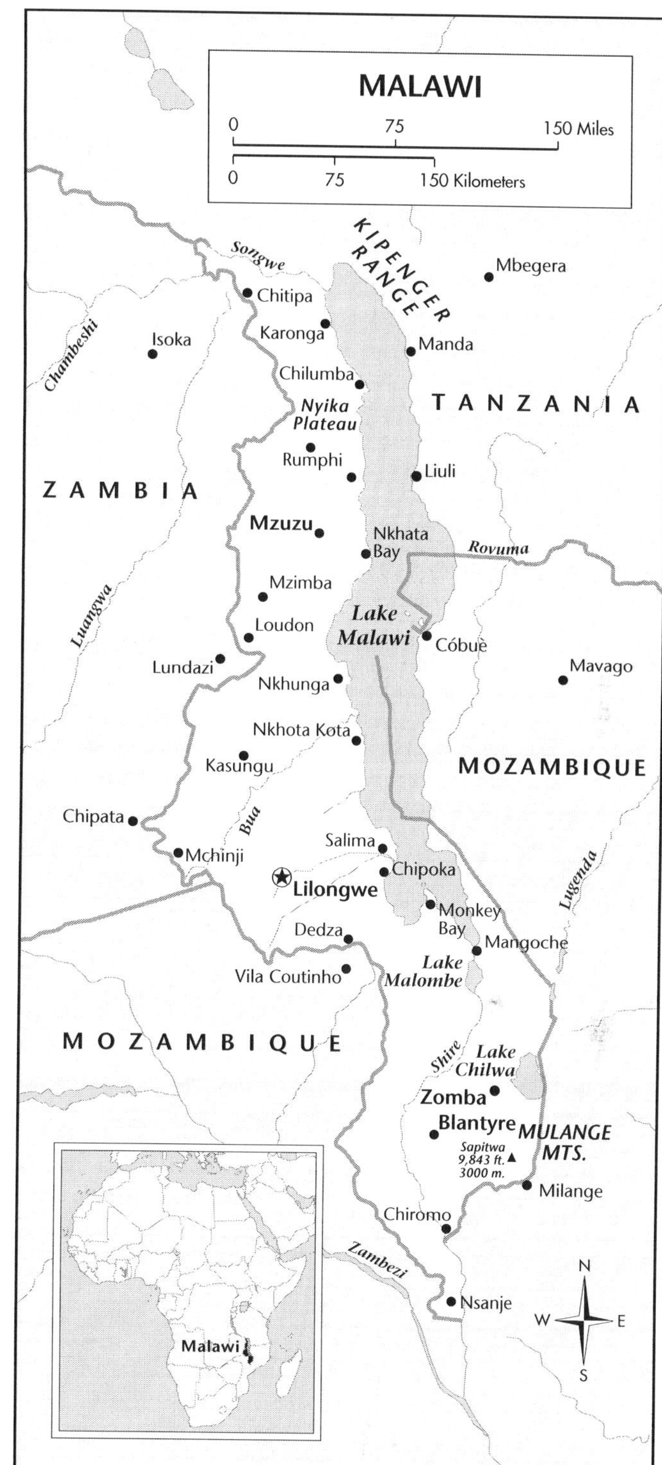

In 1970 Banda was declared President for Life of the MCP. After fully consolidating his power, Banda was named President for Life of Malawi itself in 1971. The paramilitary wing of the MCP, the Young Pioneers, helped keep Malawi under authoritarian control until the 1990s. Increasing domestic unrest and pressure from Malawian churches and from the international community led to a referendum on the continuation of the one-party state. On June 14, 1993, the people of Malawi voted overwhelmingly in favor of multi-party democracy. Free and fair national elections were held on May 17, 1994.

Bakili Muluzi, leader of the United Democratic Front (UDF), was elected President in 1994. The UDF won 82 of the 177 seats in the National Assembly and formed a coalition government with the Alliance for Democracy (AFORD). That coalition disbanded in June 1996, but some of its members remained in the government. The President was referred to as Dr. Muluzi, having received an honorary degree at Lincoln University in Missouri in 1995. Malawi's newly written constitution (1995) eliminated special powers previously reserved for the Malawi Congress Party. Accelerated economic liberalization and structural reform accompanied the political transition. When Malawi held its second democratic elections on June 15, 1999, Muluzi was reelected to serve a second 5-year term as President, despite an MCP-AFORD alliance that ran a joint slate against the UDF.

Malawi underwent its first transition between democratically elected presidents in May 2004, when the UDF's presidential candidate Bingu wa Mutharika defeated MCP candidate John Tembo and Gwanda Chakuamba, who was backed by a grouping of opposition parties. European Union and Commonwealth observers said although the election passed peacefully, they were concerned about "serious inadequacies" in the poll. The UDF did not win a majority of seats in parliament, as it had done in 1994 and 1999 elections. Through the successful maneuvering of party chairperson and former President Muluzi, the party secured a majority by forming a "government of national unity" with several opposition parties. President Mutharika left the UDF on February 5, 2005, citing differences with the party leadership, particularly over his anti-corruption campaign. He formed the Democratic Progressive Party (DPP) shortly thereafter, attracting a number of UDF and independent members of parliament (MPs) to his new party. On May 19, 2009, President Mutharika was reelected to a second 5-year term, defeating MCP candidate Tembo. Former President Muluzi attempted to run as a candidate as well, but was barred by constitutional term limits. Mutharika's DPP won a majority in parliament, and the number of women in parliament increased from 25 to 40. The May 19 elections were marked by high voter turnout, and international and domestic observers agreed that the elections were generally free and fair.

In April 2012, Vice President Joyce Banda became President following Mutharika's death.

GOVERNMENT AND POLITICAL CONDITIONS

Malawi is a multiparty democracy. In 2009 voters reelected Bingu wa Mutharika of the Democratic Progressive Party (DPP) as president in what international observers characterized as a generally free and fair election. Constitutional power is shared between the president and the 193 National Assembly members.

Recent Elections

In May 2009 the citizenry re-elected Bingu wa Mutharika of the DPP president in what international observers characterized as a generally free and fair election, although there were shortcomings. Observers criticized the inequitable access to the state-owned media faced by opposition parties and candidates. Opposition parties accused the government of using public funds for campaign purposes.

Nationwide local elections were last held in 2000 and have been repeatedly postponed since. In December 2010 the president unilaterally suspended the nine-member Malawi Electoral Commission (MEC), which was preparing for local polls scheduled for April 2011. The reason for the suspension was an investigation into missing funds. The investigation revealed the problem to be lack of documentation and not fraud, so the commissioners were reinstated on April 4. However, 10 MEC financial staff remained on suspension at year's end, which hindered MEC operations.

The executive branch exerted considerable influence over the unicameral national assembly, which followed a hybrid parliamentary system loosely based on both British and presidential-parliamentary models. All cabinet ministers were also members of the National Assembly, although they were not required to be.

Although the government did not prohibit activities of opposition political parties, the parties alleged that the government encouraged opposition party divisions. Sporadic, minor violence occurred between supporters of rival political parties.

Political Parties: While parties generally were allowed to operate without restriction or outside interference, there were instances of intimidation by members of the ruling DPP.

The government delayed the registration of new political parties, which limited their ability to operate legally. Political parties were forced to resort to the courts for judicial relief. For example, the Peoples Party applied for registration in April, but its application was rejected. The party was finally registered July 28, but only after a Supreme Court ruling compelled the government to accept the application.

Participation of Women and Minorities: There were 39 women in the 193-seat National Assembly and eight women in the 32-member cabinet, including the country's first female vice president. Women constituted approximately 25 percent of the civil service. There were three female justices among the 27 Supreme and High Court justices.

There were six members of minority groups, defined as "white," "colored" ("mixed race"), and South Asian, in the National Assembly.

Principal Government Officials

Last Updated: 1/31/2013

Pres.: **Joyce BANDA**

Vice Pres.: **Khumbo Hastings KACHALI**

Min. of Agriculture, Irrigation, & Water Development: **Peter MWANZA**

Min. of Defense: **Ken KANDODO**

Min. of Disability & Elderly Affairs: **Reene KACHERE**

Min. of Economic Planning & Development

Min. of Education, Science, & Technology: **Eunice KAEMBE**

Min. of the Environment & Climate Change Management: **Catherine Gotani HARA**

Min. of Energy: **Ibrahim MATOLA**

Min. of Finance: **Ken LIPENGA**

Min. of Foreign Affairs & Intl. Cooperation: **Ephraim Mganda CHIUME**

Min. of Gender, Children, & Community Development: **Anita KALINDE**

Min. of Health: **Khumbo Hastings KACHALI**

Min. of Home Affairs: **Uladi MUSSA**

Min. of Industry & Trade: **Sosten GWENGWE**

Min. of Information: **Moses KUNKUYU**

Min. of Justice & Constitutional Affairs: **Ralph KASAMBARA**

Min. of Labor: **Eunice MAKANGALA**

Min. of Lands & Housing: **Henry PHOYA**

Min. of Local Govt. & Rural Development: **Grace MASEKO**

Min. of Mining: **John BANDE**

Min. Responsible for Public Affairs, Statutory Corporations, Civil Service, Admin., National Relief & Disaster Management, & Nutrition, HIV, & AIDS: **Joyce BANDA**

Min. of Tourism, Wildlife, & Culture: **Daniel Symphoriana LIWIMBI**

Min. of Transport & Public Infrastructure: **Mohamed Sidik MIA**

Min. of Water Development & Irrigation: **Richie MUHEYA**

Min. of Youth, Sports, & Civic Education: **Enoch CHAKUFWA**

Attorney Gen.: **Ralph KASAMBARA**

Governor, Reserve Bank: **Charles CHUKA**

Ambassador to the US: **Hawa NDILOWE**

Permanent Representative to the UN, New York:

ECONOMY

Landlocked Malawi ranks among the world's most densely populated and least developed countries. The economy is predominately agricultural with about 80% of the population living in rural areas. Agriculture, which has benefited from fertilizer subsidies since 2006, accounts for one-third of GDP and 90% of export revenues. The performance of the tobacco sector is key to short-term growth as tobacco accounts for more than half of exports.

The economy depends on substantial inflows of economic assistance from the IMF, the World Bank, and individual donor nations. In 2006, Malawi was approved for relief under the Heavily Indebted Poor Countries (HIPC) program. In December 2007, the US granted Malawi eligibility status to receive financial support within the Millennium Challenge Corporation (MCC) initiative.

The government faces many challenges including developing a market economy, improving educational facilities, facing up to environmental problems, dealing with the rapidly growing problem of HIV/AIDS, and satisfying foreign donors that fiscal discipline is being tightened. Since 2005 President Mutharika's government has exhibited improved financial discipline under the guidance of Finance Minister Goodall Gondwe and signed a three year Poverty Reduction and Growth Facility worth $56 million with the IMF. The government has announced infrastructure projects that could yield improvements, such as a new oil pipeline for better fuel access, and the potential for a waterway link through Mozambican rivers to the ocean for better transportation options.

Since 2009, however, Malawi has experienced some setbacks, including a general shortage of foreign exchange, which has damaged its ability to pay for imports, and fuel shortages that hinder transportation and productivity. Investment fell 23% in 2009, and continued to decline in 2010. The government has failed to address barriers to investment such as unreliable power, water shortages, poor telecommunications infrastructure, and the high costs of services. Donors, who provided an average of 36% of government revenue in the past five year, suspended general budget support for Malawi in 2011 due to a negative IMF review and governance issues.

Labor Conditions

The law sets the minimum age for employment at 14, and children between the ages of 14 to 18 may not work in jobs that are considered hazardous or that interfere with their education.

The law specifies legal work hour limits, but in practice, the Ministry of Labor lacks the capacity to monitor and enforce the law. The law specifies a maximum fine of 20,000 MWK ($119) or five years' imprisonment for violations. However, the law was not effectively enforced due to lack of resources, manpower and insufficient penalties to deter offenders.

Child labor remained a serious and widespread problem. A June 2008 report from the Ministry of Labor stated that more than 1.4 million children, or one of every three children, were engaged in some form of child labor.

Child labor was common on tobacco farms, subsistence farms, and in domestic service. Many boys worked as vendors, and young girls in urban areas often worked outside of their families as domestic servants, receiving low or no wages.

The Ministry of Labor sets separate urban and rural minimum wage rates based on recommendations of the tripartite wage advisory board (TWAB), which is composed of representatives of labor, government, and the private sector. The minimum wage, revised in January, is 178.25 MWK ($1.06) per day; for both rural and urban areas. The poverty lines (at 2004 prices) were 16,165 MWK ($96) per person per year for poor households and 10,029 MWK ($60) per person per year for ultra-poor households. It is estimated that 52.4 percent of citizens live below the poverty line. There was no exception for foreign or migrant workers. The maximum legal workweek is 48 hours, with a mandatory weekly 24-hour rest period. The law requires payment for overtime work and prohibits compulsory overtime. In practice these standards were not effectively enforced, and employers frequently violated statutory time restrictions.

Official minimum wages apply only to the formal sector as the government lacks enforcement mechanisms for the informal sector. Wage earners often supplemented their incomes through farming activities. The Ministry of Labor lacked the resources to enforce the minimum wage effectively. However, the minimum wage was irrelevant for most citizens, who earned their livelihood outside the formal wage sector.

The law protects foreign workers in correct legal status. Illegal foreign workers were subject to deportation.

U.S.-MALAWIAN RELATIONS

The United States established diplomatic relations with Malawi in 1964, following its full independence from the United Kingdom. Malawi saw one-party rule from 1966 to 1994. The transition from a one-party state to a multi-party democracy in 1994 strengthened bilateral relations between the United States and Malawi.

The two countries have worked together to advance health, education, agriculture, energy, and environmental projects. In 2012, the U.S. reinstated the Millennium Challenge Corporation Compact partnership with Malawi following a number of reforms enacted by the Government of Malawi.

U.S. and Malawian views on the necessity of economic and political stability in southern Africa generally coincide. Through an assessment of its own national interests and foreign policy objectives, Malawi advocates peaceful solutions to the region's problems through negotiation. The country works to achieve these objectives in a variety of regional and international forums. The United States and Malawi engage in military-to-military programs. Malawi was the first southern African nation to receive peacekeeping training under the U.S.-sponsored African Crisis Response Force Initiative and has joined its successor, the Africa Contingency Operations Training and Assistance program.

U.S. Assistance to Malawi

U.S. assistance in Malawi seeks to promote food security and agriculture-based economic growth and poverty reduction; preserve Malawi's unique biodiversity and its ability to mitigate climate change; strengthen public and private institutions for better delivery of social services; empower the private sector and civil society; and advance democracy, human rights, and good governance. U.S. partnerships with the Government of Malawi, civil society, and other donors aim to address weaknesses and gaps that constrain the government's efforts to meet the basic needs of its citizens, support regional stability, and help the government remain a responsible actor on the international stage.

Bilateral Economic Relations

Malawi is eligible for preferential trade benefits under the African Growth and Opportunity Act. U.S. exports to Malawi include wheat, low-value shipments, pharmaceutical products, baking-related products, and machinery. U.S. imports from Malawi include tobacco, apparel, tea, macadamia nuts, and sugars.

The United States has signed a trade and investment framework agreement with the Common Market for Eastern and Southern Africa, of which Malawi is a member.

Malawi's Membership in International Organizations

Malawi and the United States belong to a number of the same international organizations, including the United Nations, International Monetary Fund, World Bank, and World Trade Organization.

Bilateral Representation

Malawi maintains an embassy in the United States at 2408 Massachusetts Avenue, NW, Washington, DC 20005 (tel. 202-721-0270).

Principal U.S. Embassy Officials

Last Updated: 1/14/2013

LILONGWE (E) Area 40, Plot No.24, Kenyatta Road, Lilongwe 3, Malawi, 265-1-773-166, Fax 265-1-772-316, Workweek: 0730-1700 Mon-Thurs.; 0730-1330 Fri/no lunch, Website: http://lilongwe.usembassy.gov/

DCM OMS:	Aisha Brown
AMB OMS:	Jennifer Little
CDC:	Sundeep Gupta
Co-CLO:	Rebekah Newquist
ECON/COM:	Chris M. Nyce
FM:	Raphael Ngotie
MGT:	Acting DCM Craig A. Anderson
POL/ECON:	Chris M Nyce
POL/MIL:	Stephanie Reed
POSHO:	Jeff Brock
SDO/DATT:	LTC Ronald J. Miller
AMB:	Jeanine Jackson
CON:	Heather Watson-Ayala
DCM:	Lisa Vickers
PAO:	David Cowhig
GSO:	Wendy Washington
RSO:	Travis Bartlett
AID:	R. Douglas Arbuckle
CLO:	Nkekeletse Anderson
EEO:	David W. Mullins
FMO:	Jeffrey Brown
ICASS Chair:	Alison McKnight
IMO:	David W. Mullins
IRS:	Kathy J. Beck (Paris)
ISSO:	David Mullins
POL:	Stephanie Reed
State ICASS:	Stephanie Reed

TRAVEL

Consular Information Sheet

December 15, 2011

Country Description: Malawi is a developing landlocked country in southern Africa. Tourist facilities in major cities and in resort areas are steadily improving, but remain limited. Aging infrastructure and lack of investment have rendered electricity, water supply, and telecommunications unreliable in rural areas.

Smart Traveler Enrollment Program (STEP)/Embassy Locations: If you are going to live or visit Malawi, please take the time to tell our Embassy about your trip. If you enroll, we can keep you up to date with important safety and security announcements.

U.S. Embassy Lilongwe
Area 40, City Center
Lilongwe, Malawi
Mailing Address:
PO Box 30016, Lilongwe 3, Malawi
Telephone: (265) 1-773-166, 1-773-342 and 1-773-367
(if dialing within Malawi add "0" before the "1"); fax (265) 1-774-976
(if dialing within Malawi add "0" before the "1").

In case of emergency, you may call the Embassy 24 hours a day and request extension 3443. In case the landlines are malfunctioning, you may also dial (265) (0)999-591024 or (265) (0) 888-734-826.

Entry/Exit Requirements for U.S. Citizens: A passport, return ticket, and adequate funds are required for entry into Malawi. U.S. citizens traveling to Malawi for tourism, transit or business for 30-days or less can receive a visitor's permit at the airports or border points of entry. The 30-day permit may be extended twice up to an additional 30 days each renewal prior to expiration. Currently, the Malawi Immigration Department is charging for all permit extensions as follows:

- A 30-day visitor's permit (or less) is granted at any port of entry and is free,
- Application for a permit extension for an additional 30-days (or less) is MK 5,000.00,
- Application for a second permit extension for an additional 30-days (or less) is MK 5,000.00.

A permit extension application must be submitted prior to the permit's expiration date. There is no guarantee the request will be granted.

U.S. citizens wishing to volunteer, study, conduct research or business for more than 90 days in Malawi are responsible for requesting the correct type of visa/permit from the Malawian Embassy or Consulate, prior to traveling to Malawi. There is no guarantee that requests for changing one's immigration category (e.g., from visitor permit or tourist visa to Temporary Employment Permit) will be granted. Foreign citizens whose primary purpose of travel is to participate in religious activities (voluntary or paid) should obtain a Temporary Employment Permit (TEP) rather than a visitor's permit through their sponsoring organization or business.

Malawian immigration authorities have fined, arrested, and deported U.S. citizens who entered Malawi with a tourist visa or on a visitor's permit and proceeded to conduct other activities inconsistent with their tourist status (e.g., business or volunteer services).

Occasionally, some airlines have required travelers to have a Malawian visa before boarding connecting flights in European airports. Malawian authorities confirmed in October 2011 that there is no requirement for obtaining a visitor's permit for short stays (30-days or less) prior to arrival in Malawi.

U.S. citizens are reminded that they are subject to Malawi's laws. Individuals that overstay on their visa, even unknowingly, have been fined, arrested and deported. For additional information on entry requirements, contact the Embassy of the Republic of Malawi in Washington, D.C. 2408 Massachusetts Ave. NW, Washington, D.C. 20008. According to Malawian Law, travelers must declare all foreign currency when entering Malawi, regardless of its purpose or amount.

Travelers should only exchange foreign currency at the bank or approved Foreign Exchange bureaus. Any currency declared at entry may be expatriated without further authorization. With bank approval, an individual may export up to $2000 per trip. Otherwise an individual is not permitted to expropriate currency and it will be confiscated at the point of departure. The U.S. Department of State is unaware of any HIV/AIDS entry restrictions for visitors to or foreign residents of Malawi.

Threats to Safety and Security: Spontaneous civil disturbances and/or demonstrations, primarily related to governance and economic issues can occur on occasion. U.S. citizens should avoid crowds, political rallies and street demonstrations and maintain security awareness at all times.

Stay up to date by:

- Bookmarking our Bureau of Consular Affairs website, which contains the current Travel Warnings and Travel Alerts as well as the Worldwide Caution.
- Following us on Twitter and the Bureau of Consular Affairs page on Facebook as well.
- Downloading our free Smart Traveler iPhone App to have travel information at your fingertips.
- Calling 1-888-407-4747 toll-free within the U.S. and Canada, or a regular toll line, 1-202-501-4444, from other countries.
- Taking some time before travel to consider your personal security.

Crime: Even though Malawi is known as "the Warm Heart of Africa," crime is common. Most crimes against Americans involve property.

Residential break-ins are prevalent throughout Malawi and perpetrators of these crimes are usually well-armed and may resort to violence with little provocation. Petty street crime (robbery and pick-pocketing) is common, and break-ins have also occurred in hotels/lodges throughout the country.

We urge you to avoid traveling on foot at night, especially in urban areas, as armed muggings and assaults have increased. Specifically, non-Malawians have been targeted in Lilongwe, and several U.S. citizens have been injured. Even when walking in a large group, city streets should be considered unsafe after dark. Pedestrians should be cautious even during daylight hours. Visitors in need of transportation should request that hotel or restaurant management call a taxi or car service.

We recommend you use caution when visiting and/or staying in isolated areas such as Mount Mulanje where the availability of public security forces is limited. You should take appropriate action to ensure your safety if traveling to remote areas, and never travel alone or at night.

Don't buy counterfeit and pirated goods, even if they are widely available. Not only are the bootlegs illegal in the United States, if you purchase them you may also be breaking local law.

Victims of Crime:: If you or someone you know becomes the victim of a crime abroad, you should contact the local police and the nearest U.S. embassy or consulate. We can:

- Replace a stolen passport.
- Help you find appropriate medical care if you are the victim of violent crimes such as assault or rape.
- Put you in contact with the appropriate police authorities, and if you want us to, we contact family members or friends.
- Help you understand the local criminal justice process and direct you to local attorneys, although it is important to remember that local authorities are responsible for investigating and prosecuting the crime.

The local equivalent to the "911" emergency line in Malawi is 199 or 997.

Criminal Penalties: While you are traveling in Malawi, you are subject to its laws even if you are a U.S. citizen. Foreign laws and legal systems can be vastly different than our own. In some places you may be taken in for questioning if you don't have your passport with you. In some places, it is illegal to take pictures of certain buildings. In some places driving under the influence could land you immediately in jail. These criminal penalties will vary from country to country. There are also some things that might be legal in the country you visit, but still illegal in the United States, and you can be prosecuted under U.S. law if you buy pirated goods. Engaging in sexual conduct with children or using or disseminating child pornography in a foreign country is a crime prosecutable in the United States. If you break local laws in Malawi, your U.S. passport won't help you avoid arrest or prosecution. It's very important to know what's legal and what's not wherever you go.

Arrest notifications in host country: While some countries will automatically notify the nearest U.S. embassy or consulate if a U.S. citizen is detained or arrested in a foreign country, that might not always be the case. To ensure that the United States is aware of your circumstances, request that the police and prison officials notify the nearest U.S. embassy or consulate as soon as you are arrested or detained overseas.

Special Circumstances: Wild animals may pose a danger, even in the most serene settings, wild animals can pose a threat to life and safety. Be sure to observe local or park regulations and heed all instructions given by tour guides.

Credit cards are not commonly accepted outside of major cities. There are a limited number of ATMs in Malawi that accept Visa, MasterCard and international ATM cards.

Dress codes against short skirts on women and long hair on men no longer exist, but travelers may wish to dress modestly, especially when visiting remote areas.

Accessibility: While in Malawi, individuals with disabilities may find accessibility and accommodation very different from what you find in the United States. There is no legislation that mandates access to transportation, public building and communication for people with disabilities. Some modern buildings may have wheelchair accessible entrances. Generally, public transportation is not accessible for travelers with disabilities.

Medical Facilities and Health Information: Medical facilities in Malawi are rudimentary and do not meet U.S. standards of medical care. While all health workers have some degree of English proficiency, communication can still be difficult. Medications are not consistently available and many U.S. medications are not available at all. Travelers should bring adequate quantities of medications to last the duration of their stay. For any major medical problems you should consider obtaining medical treatment in South Africa, where advanced medical care is available.

Diarrhea and other food borne illnesses are a common problem among travelers. We urge you to avoid tap water, ice cubes, and raw fruits and vegetables. Bottled water is recommended for drinking and food preparation. Only food that is well-cooked and served hot should be consumed.

Malaria is a potentially life-threatening disorder that is endemic to Malawi. Malaria prophylaxis is strongly advised and should be initiated prior to arriving in Malawi. Consult your doctor to learn which prophylaxis is best for you, and review possible side-effects. In addition, other measures such as the use of insect repellents and mosquito nets help to reduce the risk of malaria. If you become ill with a fever or flu-like illness while traveling in a malaria-risk area, or up to one-year after returning home should seek prompt medical attention and tell your doctor your travel history and what anti-malarial medications you have been taking.

Schistosomiasis (also known as Bilharzia) is present in most lakes and rivers in Malawi, including Lake Malawi. We recommends against swimming, wading or bathing in fresh water.

HIV infection is endemic in the Malawian population. Please take appropriate precautions to limit the risk of transmission through blood or sexual contact. You can find good information on vaccinations and other health precautions, on the CDC website. For information about outbreaks of infectious diseases abroad, consult the World Health Organization (WHO) website. The WHO website also contains additional health information for travelers, including detailed country-specific health information.

Tuberculosis is an increasingly serious health concern in Malawi. For further information, please consult the CDC's information on TB.

Medical Insurance: You can't assume your insurance will go with you when you travel. It's very important to find out BEFORE you leave whether your medical insurance will cover you overseas. You need to ask your insurance company two questions:

- Does my policy apply when I'm out of the United States?
- Will it cover emergencies like a trip to a foreign hospital or a medical evacuation?

In many places, doctors and hospitals still expect payment in cash at the time of service. Your regular U.S. health insurance may not cover doctors' and hospital visits in other countries. If your policy doesn't go with you when you travel, it's a very good idea to take out another one for your trip.

Traffic Safety and Road Conditions: While in Malawi, you may encounter road conditions that differ significantly from those in the United States. Malawi's principal highways are generally in good condition, although safety hazards include the lack of road shoulders, frequent potholes, pedestrians, bicyclists and livestock. Secondary roads are in poor repair and may be impassable to all but four-wheel drive vehicles during the rainy season (November-April). Public transportation, consisting primarily of minibuses, is unreliable and accidents are common. Modern coach buses are increasingly common on the main cross-country routes. Fuel supply, both diesel and gasoline, is often irratic and travelers should plan accordingly.

Given Malawi's high road accident rate, you should drive defensively and avoid road travel outside cities at night. Road support networks for stranded drivers do not exist. Police roadblocks are common and properly documented drivers usually pass quickly and without incident. If you intend to remain in Malawi for an extended period of time you are expected to obtain a locally-issued driver's license.

Motor vehicle accidents are the most common cause of death among travelers to Malawi due to atypical road hazards. There are no medical facilities that provide comprehensive emergency care comparable to U.S. standards. Never drive under the influence of alcohol or drugs. You should always wear your seat belt when available, try travel in well-maintained vehicles, insist that the drivers maintain a safe speed, and avoid travelling after dark.

Aviation Safety Oversight: As there is no direct commercial air service to the United States by carriers registered in Malawi, the U.S. Federal Aviation Administration (FAA) has not assessed the government of Malawi's Civil Aviation Authority for compliance with International Civil Aviation Organization (ICAO) aviation safety standards. Further information may be found on the FAA's safety assessment page.

Children's Issues: Please see the U.S. Dept. of State Office of Children's Issues web pages on intercountry adoption and international parental child abduction.

Intercountry Adoption

December 2010

The information in this section has been edited from the latest report available as of February 2013 from the State Department Bureau of Consular Affairs, Office of Overseas Citizens Services. For more information, please read the *Intercountry Adoption* section of this book and review current reports online at http://adoption.state.gov.

Malawi is not party to the Hague Convention on Protection of Children and Co-operation in Respect of Intercountry Adoption (Hague Adoption Convention). Therefore, when the Hague Adoption Convention entered into force for the United States on April 1, 2008, intercountry adoption processing for Malawi did not change.

Although the May 9, 2010 Supreme Court Decision determined that an adoption may be granted to foreign adoptive parents so long as the parent (s) were not mere sojourners in Malawi and had a serious commitment or connection to Malawi, it is must not be endorsed as set of a new law regarding intercountry adoptions for Malawi. The Courts in Malawi will asses each case on a case by case basis depending on child's conditions and orphanage status. However, the May 9, 2010 Supreme Court decision changed the residence requirement. Previous adoption practice required the adoptive parents to have lived and fostered for orphan child for a period between 18 and 24 months in order to adopt in Malawi.

Who Can Adopt? To bring an adopted child to United States from Malawi, you must be found eligible to adopt by the U.S. Government. The U.S. Government agency responsible for making this determination is the Department of Homeland Security, U.S. Citizenship and Immigration Services (USCIS). In addition to these U.S. requirements for adoptive parents, Malawi also has the following requirements for adoptive parents.

Age Requirements: Prospective adoptive parents must be at least 25 years old and at least 21 years older than the child.

Residency Requirements: Adoptive parents must be resident in Malawi to adopt. Malawi statues do not define "resident." The Ministry of Women and Child Development has not promulgated written policy regarding residency requirements for individuals seeking to adopt. Prospective adoptive parent(s) should consult with a Malawi attorney for more information.

Note: While not explicitly stated in Malawi law or required by regulation, it has been the practice of Malawian authorities to require adoptive parents to foster a prospective adoptive child for a period of not less than 18 months before an adoption may be finalized.

Time Frame: It has been the practice that before one is approved to adopt a child, s/he must first have legal custody and care for the child for a period of 18 to 24 months. This is an informal practice that has not been promulgated in writing by the Government of Malawi and is subject to change.

Marriage Requirements: Both married and single persons may adopt. However, single men may not adopt female children unless the court is satisfied that there are special circumstances, justifying an exception.

Income Requirements: None.

Other Requirements: No guidance or regulation regarding gay and lesbian adoption, and/or adoption by same-sex couples.

Who Can Be Adopted? Malawi has specific requirements that a child must meet in order to be eligible for adoption. You cannot adopt a child in Malawi unless he or she meets the requirements outlined below. In addition to these requirements, a child must meet the definition of an orphan under U.S. law for you to bring him or her back to the United States.

Eligibility Requirements: Adoption cannot take place without the consent of every person who is a parent or guardian of the child who has custody of the child or who is likely to contribute to the support to the child. If a parent is unable to care for the child, the child may be classified as an orphan by Malawi Authorities.

Age Requirements: Child must by less than 18 years old.

Sibling Requirements: Adoption of twins is permissible.

Requirements for Special Needs or Medical Conditions: No requirements promulgated.

Adoption Authority: Social Welfare Officer, Ministry of Gender, Child Welfare and Community Services

The Process: The first step in adopting a child from Malawi is usually to select a licensed agency in the United States that can help with your adoption. Adoption service providers must be licensed by the U.S. state in which they operate. There are no adoption agencies in Malawi. For information regarding home studies, interested parties should contact the Ministry of Gender, Youth and Community Services at Private Bag 330 Lilongwe 3 or Telephone 01-770-411. The U.S. Embassy in Lilongwe maintains a list of English-speaking attorneys at http://lilongwe.usembassy.gov/ainformation.html. The Embassy assumes no responsibility for the professional ability or integrity of the individuals or of the firms whose names and addresses appear on the list below.

BAZUKA AND COMPANY
Tel: 01-836-443 (Blantyre)

MVALO AND COMPANY
Tel: 01-751-186; 01-751-541;
OR CELL: 08-828-033 (Lilongwe)

BERNARD AND HARRIS
Tel: 01-823-599 (Blantyre)

KHUNZE KAPETA
Tel: 01-824-316 (Blantyre)

To bring an adopted child from Malawi to the United States, you must apply to be found eligible to adopt (Form I-600A) by the U.S. Government, Department of Homeland Security, U.S. Citizenship and Immigration Services (USCIS).

If you are eligible to adopt, and a child is available for intercountry adoption, the central adoption authority in Malawi will provide you with a referral to a child. Prospective adoptive parents often identify a child for adoption through local churches, orphanages, hospitals or missions. They then need to retain a lawyer to handle the application. The process for finalizing the adoption or gaining legal custody in Malawi generally includes the following.

Role of the Court: The lawyer files a petition with the Magistrate Court of the district in Malawi where the adoptive parents reside. Once that is done, the Court chooses a social worker to be the child's "Guardian ad Litem" who investigates the circumstances of the prospective adoptee(s) and submits a Court Social Report (a home-study) to the High Court. The Guardian ad Litem monitors the adoptive family during a required period of time. After this period of time, the Court will rule whether the adoption can be finalized.

Time Frame: Normally two to six months to complete adoption process from start to finish including investigation.

Adoption Fees: On average, depending on the complexity of the case, the fees for a lawyer range between $350 and $500. Court filing fees and Registrar fees for the new birth certificate are under five dollars. The Malawian passport fee is approximately $30. Informally, Ministry Officials indicate that an offer to pay per diem and travel expenses for the investigator can speed the process.

Documents Required: Malawi adoptions are governed by the country's Adoption of Children Act. Proof of the identity and nationality of the adoptive parents, a competed home-study and proof that the child is eligible for adoption are required. Adoption cannot take place without the consent of every person who is a parent or guardian of the child who has custody of the child or who is likely to contribute to the support to the child. After you finalize the adoption (or gain legal custody) in Liberia, the U.S Government, Department of Homeland Security, U.S. Citizenship and Immigration Services (USCIS) MUST determine whether the child is eligible under U.S. law to be adopted (Form I-600).

Bringing Your Child Home: Once your adoption is complete (or you have obtained legal custody of the child), there are a few more steps to take before you can head home. Specifically, you need to apply for several documents for your child before he or she can travel to the United States, such as a birth certificate, a passport or travel document for your child from the country in which he or she was born, and a U.S. Immigration Visa. For detailed and updated information on how to obtain these documents, visit the USCIS Intercountry Adoption website at http://adoption.state.gov.

Child Citizenship Act: For adoptions finalized abroad, the Child Citizenship Act of 2000 allows your new child to acquire American citizenship automatically when he or she enters the United States as lawful permanent residents. For adoptions finalized in the United States, the Child Citizenship Act of 2000 allows your new child to acquire American citizenship automatically when the court in the United States issues the final adoption decree. To learn more, visit the USCIS Intercountry Adoption website at http://adoption.state.gov.

U.S. Embassy in Malawi
P.O. Box 30016
16 Jomo Kenyatta Road
Lilongwe 3
Tel: 265-773-166
Fax: 265-774-976
http://lilongwe.usembassy.gov

Malawi's Adoption Authority
Mrs. H. Kulemeka/Director of Women and Child Development
Ministry of Women and Child Development
GEMINI House
Private Bag 330
Lilongwe 3
Tel: (265) 1-770-411

Embassy of Malawi
2408 Massachusetts Avenue NW
Washington, DC 20008
Tel: 202-797-1007

Office of Children's Issues
U.S. Department of State
2201 C Street, NW
SA-29
Washington, DC 20520
Tel: 1-888-407-4747
E-mail: AskCI@state.gov
http://adoption.state.gov

For questions about immigration procedures, call the National Customer Service Center (NCSC) 1-800-375-5283 (TTY 1-800-767-1833).

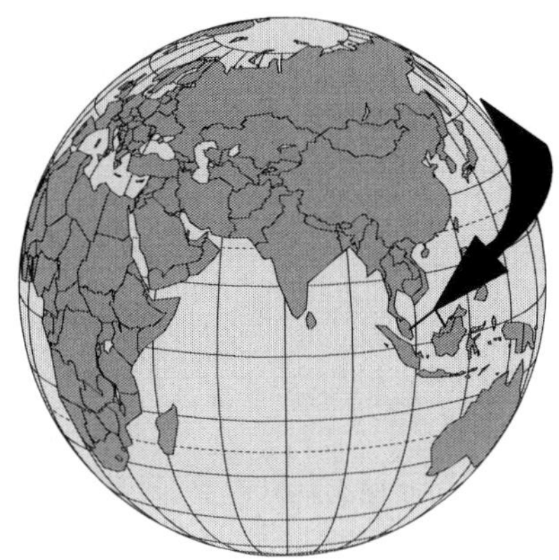

MALAYSIA

Compiled from publications that were available as of February 2013 from the U.S. Department of State, the U.S. Department of Commerce, and the Central Intelligence Agency (CIA). See the introduction to this set for explanatory notes.

Official Name:
Malaysia

PROFILE

Geography

Area: total: 329,847 sq km; country comparison to the world: 67; land: 328,657 sq km; water: 1,190 sq km

Major cities: Kuala Lumpur (capital) 1.493 million; Klang 1.071 million; Johor Bahru 958,000 (2009)

Climate: tropical; annual southwest (April to October) and northeast (October to February) monsoons

Terrain: coastal plains rising to hills and mountains

People

Nationality: noun: Malaysian(s); adjective: Malaysian

Population: 29,179,952 (July 2012 est.)

Population growth rate: 1.542% (2012 est.)

Ethnic groups: Malay 50.4%, Chinese 23.7%, indigenous 11%, Indian 7.1%, others 7.8% (2004 est.)

Religions: Muslim (or Islam—official) 60.4%, Buddhist 19.2%, Christian 9.1%, Hindu 6.3%, Confucianism, Taoism, other traditional Chinese religions 2.6%, other or unknown 1.5%, none 0.8% (2000 census)

Languages: Bahasa Malaysia (official), English, Chinese (Cantonese, Mandarin, Hokkien, Hakka, Hainan, Foochow), Tamil, Telugu, Malayalam, Panjabi, Thai

Literacy: definition: age 15 and over can read and write; total population: 88.7%; male: 92%; female: 85.4% (2000 census)

Health: life expectancy at birth: total population: 74.04 years; male: 71.28 years; female: 76.99 years (2012 est.); Infant mortality rate: total: 14.57 deaths/1,000 live births; male: 16.83 deaths/1,000 live births; female: 12.14 deaths/1,000 live births (2012 est.)

Unemployment rate: 3% (2012 est.)

Work force: 12.84 million (2012 est.)

Government

Type: constitutional monarchy

Independence: 31 August 1957

Constitution: 31 August 1957; amended many times

Political subdivisions: 13 states (negeri-negeri, singular—negeri) Johor, Kedah, Kelantan, Melaka, Negeri Sembilan, Pahang, Perak, Perlis, Pulau Pinang, Sabah, Sarawak, Selangor, Terengganu; and 1 federal territory (Wilayah Persekutuan) with three components, city of Kuala Lumpur, Labuan, and Putrajaya

Suffrage: 21 years of age; universal

Economy

GDP (purchasing power parity): $492 billion (2012 est.); $453 billion (2011 est.); $430.9 billion (2010 est.); $402 billion (2009 est.)

GDP real growth rate: 4.4% (2012 est.); 5.1% (2011 est.); 7.2% (2010 est.); -1.6% (2009 est.)

GDP per capita (PPP): $16,900 (2012 est.); $15,800 (2011 est.); $15,300 (2010 est.); $14,400 (2009 est.)

Natural resources: tin, petroleum, timber, copper, iron ore, natural gas, bauxite

Agriculture products: Peninsular Malaysia—palm oil, rubber, cocoa, rice; Sabah—palm oil, subsistence crops; rubber, timber; Sarawak—palm oil, rubber, timber; pepper

Industries: Peninsular Malaysia—rubber and oil palm processing and manufacturing, light manufacturing, pharmaceuticals, medical technology, electronics, tin mining and smelting, logging, timber processing; Sabah—logging, petroleum production; Sarawak—agriculture processing, petroleum production and refining, logging

Exports: $239.8 billion (2012 est.); $225.6 billion (2011 est.); $199 billion (2010 est.)

Exports—commodities: electronic equipment, petroleum and liquefied natural gas, wood and wood products, palm oil, rubber, textiles, chemicals

Exports—partners: China 17.9%, Singapore 12.8%, Japan 10.6%, US 8.6%, Thailand 4.4%, Hong Kong 4.1% (2010 est.)
Imports: $197.2 billion (2012 est.); $177.1 billion (2011 est.); $157.3 billion (2010 est.)
Imports—commodities: electronics, machinery, petroleum products, plastics, vehicles, iron and steel products, chemicals
Imports—partners: Singapore 20.5%, China 13.7%, Japan 10%, US 7.9%, Thailand 6%, Indonesia 5.6% (2010 est.)
Debt—external: $95.55 billion (31 December 2012 est.); $87.81 billion (31 December 2011 est.); $81.5 billion (31 December 2010 est.)
Exchange rates: ringgits (MYR) per US dollar; 3.07 (2012 est.) ; 3.06 (2011 est.); 3.22 (2010 est.); 3.52 (2009); 3.33 (2008); 3.46 (2007)

PEOPLE

Malaysia's multi-racial society contains many ethnic groups. Malays and indigenous groups comprise over 60% of the population. By constitutional definition, all Malays are Muslims. About a quarter of the population is ethnic Chinese, a group which historically has played an important role in trade and business. Malaysians of Indian descent comprise less than 10% of the population and include Hindus, Muslims, Buddhists, and Christians.

Population density is highest in peninsular Malaysia. The rest live on the Malaysian portion of the island of Borneo in the large but less densely-populated states of Sabah and Sarawak. More than half of Sarawak's residents and about two-thirds of Sabah's are from indigenous groups.

National/Racial/Ethnic Minorities

Government regulations and policy provide for extensive preferential programs designed to boost the economic position of ethnic Malays or bumiputra, who constitute a majority of the population. Such programs limit opportunities for non-bumiputra in higher education, government employment, and ownership of businesses. Many industries are subject to race-based requirements that mandated bumiputra ownership levels, limiting economic opportunities for non-bumiputra citizens. According to the government, these policies are necessary to ensure ethnic harmony and political stability.

Language

As a result of the country's ethnic diversity, most Malaysians speak at least two and even three languages-Bahasa Malaysia (the national language), English, and their own mother tongue (often Chinese Mandarin, Cantonese, Hokkien or Tamil). English is widely spoken and is commonly used in business.

Religion

According to 2010 census figures, 61.3 percent of the population practices Islam; 19.8 percent Buddhism; 9.2 percent Christianity; 6.3 percent Hinduism; and 1.3 percent Confucianism, Taoism, and other traditional Chinese religions. Other minority religious groups include animists, Sikhs, and Baha'is. Ethnic Malay Muslims account for approximately 55 percent of the population. Several of the most prominent political parties are organized along ethnic and/or religious lines. The majority of Christians reside in the eastern states of Sabah and Sarawak.

HISTORY

The early Buddhist Malay kingdom of Srivijaya, based at what is now Palembang, Sumatra, dominated much of the Malay peninsula from the 9th to the 13th centuries AD. The powerful Hindu kingdom of Majapahit, based on Java, gained control of the Malay peninsula in the 14th century. Conversion of the Malays to Islam, beginning in the early 14th century, accelerated with the rise of the state of Malacca under the rule of a Muslim prince in the 15th century. Malacca was a major regional commercial center, where Chinese, Arab, Malay, and Indian merchants traded precious goods.

Drawn by this rich trade, a Portuguese fleet conquered Malacca in 1511, marking the beginning of European expansion in Southeast Asia. The Dutch ousted the Portuguese from Malacca in 1641. The British obtained the island of Penang in 1786 and temporarily controlled Malacca with Dutch acquiescence from 1795 to 1818 to prevent it from falling to the French during the Napoleonic war. The British gained lasting possession of Malacca from the Dutch in 1824, through the Anglo-Dutch treaty, in exchange for territory on the island of Sumatra in what is today Indonesia.

In 1826, the British settlements of Malacca, Penang, and Singapore were combined to form the Colony of the Straits Settlements. From these strongholds, in the 19th and early 20th centuries the British established protectorates over the Malay sultanates on the peninsula. During their rule the British developed large-scale rubber and tin production and established a system of public administration. British control was interrupted by World War II and the Japanese occupation from 1941 to 1945.

Popular sentiment for independence swelled during and after the war. The territories of peninsular Malaysia joined together to form the Federation of Malaya in 1948 and eventually negotiated independence from the British in 1957. Tunku Abdul Rahman became the first prime minister. In 1963 the British colonies of Singapore, Sarawak, and Sabah joined the Federation, which was renamed Malaysia. Singapore's membership was short-lived, however; it left in 1965 and became an independent republic.

Neighboring Indonesia objected to the formation of Malaysia and began a program of economic, political, diplomatic, and military "confrontation" against the new country in 1963, which ended only after the fall of Indonesia's President Sukarno in

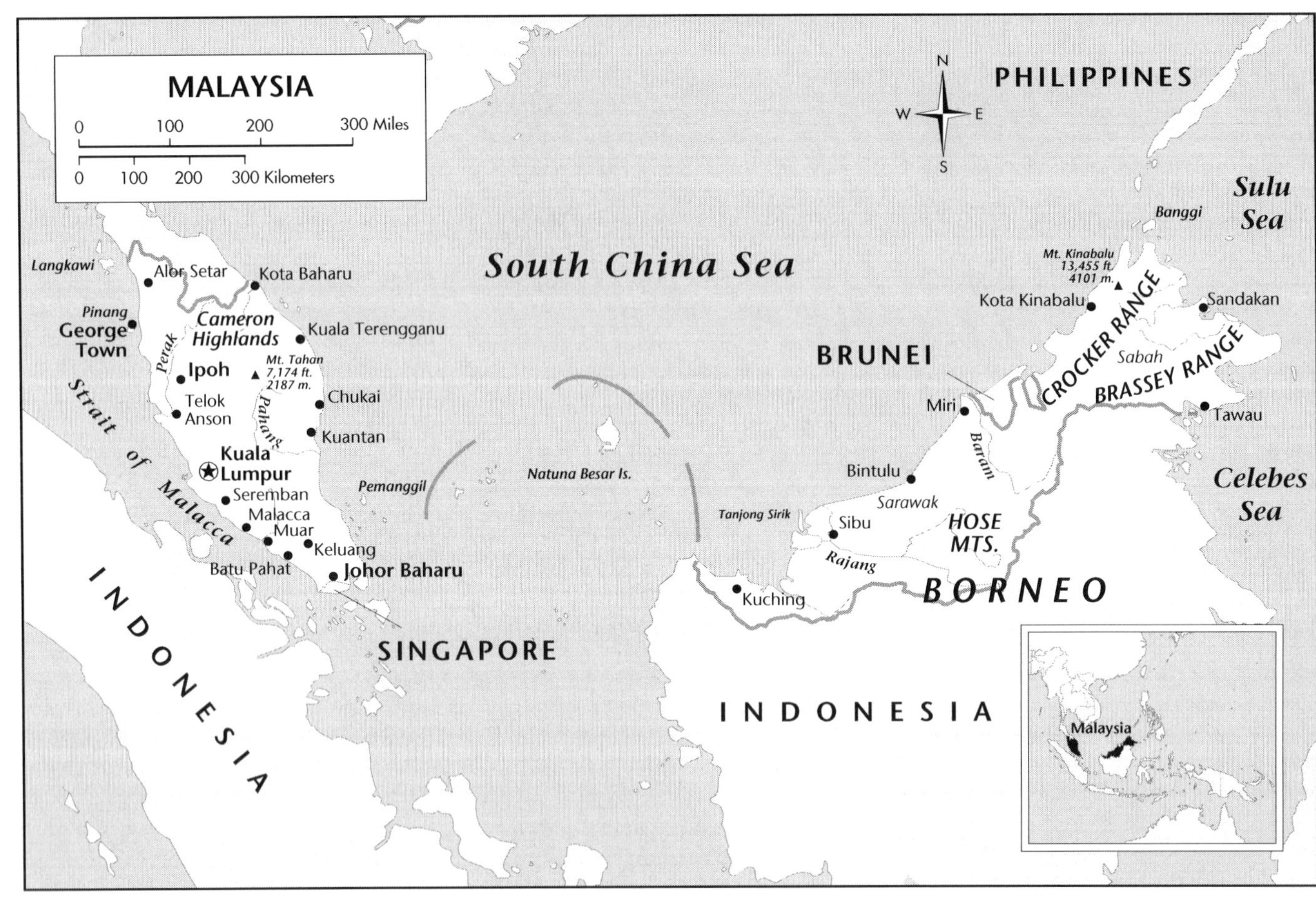

1966. Internally, local communists, nearly all Chinese, carried out a long, bitter insurgency both before and after independence, prompting the imposition of a state of emergency from 1948 to 1960. Small bands of guerrillas remained in bases along the rugged border with southern Thailand, occasionally entering northern Malaysia. These guerrillas finally signed a peace accord with the Malaysian Government in December 1989. A separate, small-scale communist insurgency that began in the mid-1960s in Sarawak also ended with the signing of a peace accord in October 1990.

GOVERNMENT AND POLITICAL CONDITIONS

Malaysia is a federal constitutional monarchy. It has a parliamentary system of government headed by a prime minister selected through periodic, multiparty elections. The United Malays National Organization (UMNO), together with a coalition of political parties known as the National Front (BN), has held power since independence in 1957. The most recent national elections, in 2008, were conducted in a generally transparent manner and witnessed significant opposition gains. In 2009 Najib Tun Razak was sworn in as prime minister.

Recent Elections

In the 2008 national elections the opposition parties won 49 percent of the popular vote, 82 of 222 parliamentary seats, 198 of 505 state assembly seats, and control of five of the 13 state governments. The opposition's electoral success for the first time since 1969 denied the ruling coalition a two-thirds majority in Parliament and thereby blocked the government's ability to amend the constitution at will. These gains came despite the fact that opposition parties were unable to compete on equal terms with the governing BN coalition, led by the UMNO party, which has held power at the national level since independence in 1957, because of restrictions on campaigning, freedom of assembly and association, and access to the media. The opposition parties won eight of 16 by-elections since the 2008 general election.

Bersih 2.0 actively campaigned for electoral reforms. Its principal demands included cleaning of the electoral roll, reform of postal voting, use of indelible ink to reduce the problem of "phantom" voters, and a longer campaign period. A parliamentary select committee on electoral reform was established effective October 3, 2011, and tabled an interim report on December 1. Among its ten recommendations were the use of indelible ink, implementation of early voting for security and armed forces personnel, extension of the postal ballot to citizens living overseas, allowing out-of-district voting, cleaning up the electoral roll, and strengthening the Election Commission (EC) to ensure its independence. On December 19, EC Chairman Abdul Aziz Mohd Yusof announced that the EC had agreed to implement seven of the commission's ten recommendations before the next general election, including the use of indelible ink. Bersih 2.0 welcomed the announcement but also criticized it as being incomplete.

Political Parties: Opposition parties were unable to compete on equal terms with the governing BN coalition, which has held power at the national level since 1957, and could not operate without restriction or outside interference. The lack of equal access to the media was one of the most serious problems for the opposition in the 2008 national elections and in the subsequent by-elections. News about the opposition was restricted and reported in a biased fashion. Opposition leaders also claimed that the Election Commission was under government control and lacked the independence needed to carry out its duties impartially. There were numerous opposition complaints of irregularities by election officials during the 2008 national election campaign; however, most observers concluded that they did not substantially alter the results. During 2011 NGOs and opposition party leaders continued to lodge allegations of illegally registered "phantom" voters, reportedly brought in from other districts to vote in tightly contested districts; inflated voter rolls; nonregistered voters using fictitious names or the names of dead voters still listed on the voter rolls; and noncitizens registered to vote.

The constitution states that parliamentary constituencies should have approximately equal numbers of eligible voters; however, in practice the numbers varied significantly, particularly between urban and rural districts. The most recently publicized data (for the 2008 general election) showed that the Putra Jaya constituency had 6,606 voters, while in urban Kuala Lumpur the Seputih constituency had 76,891 voters. In Perak, Gopeng had 74,344 voters compared with Lenggong, with 23,223 voters. Each of these constituencies had one MP.

Over the years power increasingly has been concentrated in the prime minister, and Parliament's function as a deliberative body has deteriorated. Parliament rarely amended or rejected government-proposed legislation and did not give legislation proposed by the opposition serious consideration. Parliamentary procedures allow the speaker of parliament to suspend members, establish restrictions on tabling questions, edit written copies of members' speeches before delivery, and severely restrict members' opportunities to question and debate government policies. With the increased number of opposition MPs since 2008, government officials often faced sharp questioning in Parliament, and the press reported in greater detail than in the past.

Under the Local Government Act, elections of public officials were confined to state assemblies and the federal Parliament. The central government has appointed all local and city officials since the 1969 race riots. Some politicians and NGO activists advocated reintroduction of local government elections.

In prior years opposition figures in Parliament have been suspended from Parliament from time to time for reasons such as making misleading statements to Parliament and contempt occasioned by their opposition to another's suspension.

Participation of Women and Minorities: Women faced no legal limits on participation in government and politics. As of December two of the 32 cabinet ministers were women. Women held 22 of the 222 seats in the lower house and 13 of the 65 Senate seats.

In practice the political dominance of the Malay majority meant that ethnic Malays held the most powerful senior leadership positions. Non-Malays filled 12 of the 29 ministerial posts and 21 of the 40 deputy minister positions.

Principal Government Officials

Last Updated: 1/31/2013

King: **ABDUL HALIM Mu'adzam Shah**
Prime Min.: **NAJIB Razak**
Dep. Prime Min.: **MUHYIDDIN bin Mohamed Yassin**
Min. of Agriculture: **NOH Omar**
Min. of Agricultural Development & Commodities: **Bernard Giluk DOMPOK**
Min. of Defense: **Ahmad ZAHID Hamidi**
Min. of Domestic Trade, Cooperative, & Consumerism: **ISMAIL Sabri Yaakob**
Min. of Education: **MUHYIDDIN bin Mohamed Yassin**
Min. of Energy, Green Technology, & Water: **Peter CHIN Fah Kui**
Min. of Federal Territories: **ZAINAL Abidin**
Min. of Finance: **NAJIB Razak**
Min. of Finance II: **AHMAD HUSNI Hanadzlah**
Min. of Foreign Affairs: **ANIFAH Aman**
Min. of Health: **LIOW Tiong Lai**
Min. of Higher Education: **KHALED Nordin**
Min. of Home Affairs: **HISHAMMUDDIN Tun Hussein**
Min. of Housing & Local Govt.: **CHOR Chee Heung**
Min. of Human Resources: **S. SUBRAMANIAM**
Min. of Information, Communication, Arts, & Culture: **RAIS Yatim**
Min. of Intl. Trade & Industry: **MUSTAPA Mohamed**
Min. of Natural Resources & Environment: **Douglas Unggah EMBAS**
Min. of Plantation Industries & Commodities: **Bernard DOMPOK**
Min. of Rural Development & Territories: **SHAFIE Apdal**
Min. of Science, Technology, & Innovation: **Maximus ONGKILI**
Min. of Tourism: **NG Yen Yen**
Min. of Transport: **KONG Cho Ha**
Min. of Women, Family, & Community Development: **SHARIZAT Abdul Jalil**
Min. of Works: **SHAZIMAN Abu Mansor**
Min. of Youth & Sports: **AHMAD SHABERY Cheek**
Min. in the Prime Min.'s Office: **Idris JALA**

Min. in the Prime Min.'s Office: **JAMIL KHIR bin Baharom, Maj. Gen. (Ret.)**

Min. in the Prime Min.'s Office: **KOH Tsu Koon**

Min. in the Prime Min.'s Office: **Mohamed NAZRI bin Abdul Aziz**

Min. in the Prime Min.'s Office: **NOR MOHAMED bin Yakcop**

Governor, Bank Negara Malaysia: **ZETI Akhtar Aziz**

Ambassador to the US: **OTHMAN Hashim**

Permanent Representative to the UN, New York: **Haniff HUSSEIN**

ECONOMY

Malaysia, a middle-income country, has transformed itself since the 1970s from a producer of raw materials into an emerging multi-sector economy. Under current Prime Minister Najib, Malaysia is attempting to achieve high-income status by 2020 and to move farther up the value-added production chain by attracting investments in Islamic finance, high technology industries, biotechnology, and services.

The Najib administration also is continuing efforts to boost domestic demand and reduce the economy's dependence on exports. Nevertheless, exports - particularly of electronics, oil and gas, palm oil and rubber - remain a significant driver of the economy. As an oil and gas exporter, Malaysia has profited from higher world energy prices, although the rising cost of domestic gasoline and diesel fuel, combined with strained government finances, has forced Kuala Lumpur to begin to reduce government subsidies.

The government is also trying to lessen its dependence on state oil producer Petronas. The oil and gas sector supplies more than 40% of government revenue. The central bank maintains healthy foreign exchange reserves, and a well-developed regulatory regime has limited Malaysia's exposure to riskier financial instruments and the global financial crisis. Nevertheless, Malaysia could be vulnerable to a fall in commodity prices or a general slowdown in global economic activity because exports are a major component of GDP. In order to attract increased investment, Najib has raised possible revisions to the special economic and social preferences accorded to ethnic Malays under the New Economic Policy of 1970, but he has encountered significant opposition, especially from Malay nationalists and other vested interests.

Labor Conditions

The law prohibits the employment of children younger than age 14 but permits some exceptions, such as light work in a family enterprise, work in public entertainment, work performed for the government in a school or in training institutions, or work as an approved apprentice.

In no case may a child work more than six hours per day, more than six days per week, or at night. Government officials did not deny the existence of child labor in family businesses but maintained that foreign workers had largely replaced child labor and that child labor provisions were vigorously enforced. NGOs and trade unions reported that child labor was not a significant problem.

No national minimum wage provision was in effect. Prevailing market wages generally provided a decent standard of living for citizens, although not for all migrant workers. According to the results of a 2010 survey conducted by the Federation of Malaysian Manufacturers, the mean basic monthly salary of foreign workers engaged in the manufacturing sector was RM750 ($240).

Under the Employment Act, working hours may not exceed eight hours per day or 48 hours per workweek of six days. Each workweek must include a 24-hour rest period. The act also sets overtime rates and mandates public holidays, annual leave, sick leave, and maternity allowances. Limits on overtime vary by sector. The Labor Department of the Ministry of Human Resources is responsible for enforcing the standards, but a shortage of inspectors precluded strict enforcement. The Occupational Safety and Health Act (OSHA) covers all sectors of the economy except the maritime sector and armed forces. The act establishes a national Occupational Safety and Health Council, composed of workers, employers, and government representatives, to set policy and coordinate occupational safety and health measures.

The Workmen's Compensation Act covers both local and foreign workers but provides no protection for foreign household workers. According to the government, foreign household workers are protected under the Employment Act with regard to wages and contract termination. However, these workers are excluded from provisions of the act that would otherwise ensure that they received one rest day per week, an eight-hour workday, and a 48-hour workweek. Bilateral agreements or memorandums of understanding (MOU) between Malaysia and some sending states have provisions for rest periods, compensation, and/or other conditions of employment.

Mechanisms for monitoring workplace conditions were inadequate. Private, for-profit labor agencies, themselves often guilty of abuses, were often responsible for the resolution of abuse cases. Bilateral labor agreements with Indonesia did not provide adequate protections for household workers; however, a new MOU with Indonesia signed in May calls for the creation of a joint task force to monitor the situation regarding Indonesian domestic workers. The amended MOU also provides one rest day per week (or compensation) and rules on the repayment of recruitment fees. In December 2011 the Indonesian government lifted its ban on sending domestic workers to Malaysia after a minimum monthly wage was agreed (RM700 ($221), increased from RM450 ($142).

Workers have the right to take legal action against abusive employers. The law permits migrant workers to bring employment disputes to the Industrial Court. However, the policy of the court was not to hear complaints of migrants who were undocumented. Court proceedings were time consuming, which may also prevent migrant workers from seeking redress through the court system. Once their work visas expire, migrants require "special passes" to stay in the country—they would be permitted to follow the court case but would not be allowed to work. The passes are valid for one month and cost RM100 ($32) to renew. Renewal is subject to the discretion of the director general of immigration.

Foreign migrant laborers, legal and illegal, often worked under difficult conditions, performed hazardous duties, had their pay withheld by employers, and had no meaningful access to legal counsel in cases of contract violations and abuse. Some workers alleged that their employers subjected them to inhumane living conditions, withheld their salaries, confiscated their travel documents, and physically assaulted them.

Plantation workers generally received production-related payments or daily wages. Under a "safety net" agreement, workers are bound to work for 26 days per month, unless unable due to a natural disaster such as flooding or heavy rain, and are paid a minimum of RM650 ($205). There are three main categories of plantation workers: general field, harvest (constituting the majority), and tappers. Bonus or overtime rates depend on the productivity level. For example, tappers who bring in more than the minimum eleven kilos of rubber receive extra earnings, up to RM2,000 ($631) for the most productive tappers. Such agreements are approved by Malaysian Agriculture and Plantation Association and are in line with the Employment Act.

Employers sometimes failed to honor the terms of employment and abused their household workers. For example, the contract terms for Indonesian domestic workers, who made up approximately 90 percent of all foreign household workers, were often vague and open to abuse. At the same time that arrivals from Indonesia dropped due to the 2009 ban, arrivals from Cambodia and other countries increased. An estimated 30,000 Cambodian maids arrived in the first seven months of the year, and some encountered conditions similar to those that had led to Indonesia's ban. In October 2011 the Cambodian government banned recruitment firms from sending domestic workers to Malaysia following numerous reports of abuses. The Cambodian ban remained in force at the end of 2011; the Indonesian ban was lifted in December.

On November 1, the Indian High Commission began implementing its revised guidelines for the employment of workers from India that included a minimum wage structure ranging from RM800 ($252) per month for unskilled workers (restaurant, construction) to RM1,400 ($442) per month for skilled domestic workers. According to the High Commission, Indian authorities do not grant workers clearance for travel to Malaysia unless they can produce a conforming employment contract that has been attested to by the High Commission in Kuala Lumpur as meeting the guidelines.

U.S.-MALAYSIAN RELATIONS

The United States established diplomatic relations with Malaysia in 1957, following its independence from the United Kingdom but has had a consular or commercial presence in the area since the 1800's. Today, Malaysia is a significant regional and global partner for the United States, and the two countries share a diverse and expanding partnership in trade, investment, and educational and cultural relations. Economic ties are robust, and there is a long history of people-to-people exchanges. Malaysia has a diverse democracy and is an important partner in U.S. engagement with Southeast Asia. The two countries cooperate closely on security matters, including counter-terrorism, maritime domain awareness, and regional stability and participates frequently in bilateral and multilateral training, exercises, and visits.

U.S. Assistance to Malaysia

U.S. assistance to Malaysia focuses on education, exchanges, counter-terrorism, non-proliferation, and security cooperation. The U.S. Fulbright English Teaching Assistant program in Malaysia is among the largest in the world, helping improve the English language skills of thousands of Malaysian primary and secondary school students. Exchange programs encompass secondary students, Fulbright Scholars, agricultural fellowships, and International Visitor programs. Counter-terrorism assistance builds capacity within Malaysian law enforcement and judicial entities responsible for combating terrorism, and includes improving Malaysia's ability to monitor and secure its borders. Non-proliferation assistance aims at enhancing Malaysia's ability to enforce its laws on shipments of controlled munitions, dual-use commodities, and weapons of mass destruction and related commodities through the country. Security cooperation and training builds capabilities among Malaysia's armed forces and coast guard, allowing it to take on an expanded international role, including peacekeeping operations and participation in stabilization efforts in Afghanistan.

Bilateral Economic Relations

The United States and Malaysia are both negotiating partners in the talks to form the Trans-Pacific Partnership (TPP), an ambitious next generation Asia-Pacific trade agreement. In addition to working together on TPP, the United States and Malaysia meet frequently to discuss bilateral trade and investment issues and to coordinate approaches on APEC, ASEAN, and the WTO. Malaysia was the United States' 23rd largest trading partner in 2011, and the second largest among the ten ASEAN members in Southeast Asia. The United States is Malaysia's fourth largest trading partner. U.S. exports to Malaysia include machinery,aircraft, agricultural products, optic and medical instruments, and iron and steel. U.S. imports from Malaysia include machinery, agricultural products, and optic and medical instruments. The United States remains the largest foreign investor in Malaysia both with new investments in 2011 and total stock. Reported U.S. foreign direct investment in Malaysia is led by the manufacturing, banking, and oil and gas sector. Malaysian foreign direct investment in the United States is led by the real estate and wholesale trade sectors.

Malaysia's Membership in International Organizations

Malaysia and the United States belong to a number of the same international organizations, including the United Nations, Asia-Pacific Economic Cooperation forum, ASEAN Regional Forum, International Monetary Fund, World Bank, and World Trade Organization. Malaysia and the United States participate in the East Asia Summit.

Bilateral Representation

Malaysia maintains an embassy in the United States at 3516 International Court NW, Washington, DC 20008, tel. (202) 572-9700.

Principal U.S. Embassy Officials

Last Updated: 1/14/2013

KUALA LUMPUR (E) 376 Jalan Tun Razak, [6] (03) 2168-5000, Fax [6] (03) 2142-2207, INMARSAT Tel 8816 4144 7923, Workweek: 7:45am–4:30pm, Website: http://malaysia.usembassy.gov/

DCM OMS:	Lisa Hess
AMB OMS:	Joanne Ingalls
Co-CLO:	Jessica A. Schnepple
DHS/ICE:	Steven R. Leisure
FCS:	Stephen R. Jacques
FM:	Daniel P. Hess
HRO:	Theresa E. Gillespie
MGT:	Eric Khant
MLO/ODC:	Sean D. Blundon
SDO/DATT:	CAPT John T. Segura
AMB:	Paul W. Jones
CON:	Timothy Scherer
DCM:	Lee McClenny
PAO:	Bonnie S. Gutman
GSO:	Gregory J. Campbell
RSO:	Timothy Leeds
AFSA:	Frank Tu
AGR:	Christopher P. Rittgers
CLO:	Jo Ann Sernovitz
DEA:	John Callery
ECON:	Paul A. Brown
EEO:	Anita Ghildyal
FMO:	Courtney B. Houk
ICASS Chair:	Stephen Jacques
IMO:	Keith R. Houk
ISO:	Linda L. Pohl
ISSO:	Linda L. Pohl
LEGATT:	Charles O'Neal
POL:	Jeffrey D. Rathke
State ICASS:	Vacant

TRAVEL

Consular Information Sheet

April 16, 2012

Country Description: Malaysia is a constitutional monarchy with an elected federal parliamentary government. The country comprises 13 states, 11 on the Malay Peninsula and two, Sabah and Sarawak, on the island of Borneo. There are also three federally administered territories: the capital city of Kuala Lumpur, the administrative center of Putrajaya, and the island of Labuan. Malaysia is a multi-ethnic country of 27 million people. Malays form the predominant ethnic group; the two other large ethnic groups are Chinese and Indians. Islam is the official religion and is practiced by some 60 percent of the population. Bahasa Malaysia is the official language, although English is widely spoken. Travelers to Malaysia may access information on areas of interest through the Malaysian government's website and Tourism Malaysia's website.

Smart Traveler Enrollment Program (STEP)/Embassy Location: If you are going to live or visit Malaysia, please take the time to tell our Embassy in Kuala Lumpur about your trip. If you enroll, we can keep you up to date with important safety and security announcements. It will also help your friends and family get in touch with you in an emergency.

U.S. Embassy Kuala Lumpur
376 Jalan Tun Razak 50400,
Kuala Lumpur.
P.O. Box No. 10035, 50700
Kuala Lumpur.
Emergency after-hours telephone:
(60-3) 2168–5000
(after business hours, please press 1 at the recording).
The American Citizen services unit's telephone number:
(60-3) 2168–4997/4979
Consular section's fax number:
(60-3) 2148–5801
General fax number:
(60-3) 2142 2207
E-mail—klacs@state.gov.

Entry/Exit Requirements for U.S. Citizens: To enter Malaysia, your passport must be valid for at least six months. You do not need a visa to enter Malaysia if you are coming for business or tourism for stays of 90 days or less. When you arrive, immigration officials will place an entry stamp in your passport to specify the number of days you can stay. Though immigration officials generally give 90 days, it's not a guarantee, so you should check the stamp in your passport after you enter. Generally, these entry stamps are known as social visit passes (visas) and can be extended for two months.

Travelers to Malaysia are electronically fingerprinted on arrival when arriving by air, and again on departure. While in Malaysia, you should carry your passport with you at all times. More information on the time you will be allowed to stay in Malaysia can be found on the Malaysian Ministry of Foreign Affairs' website.

If you travel into the eastern Malaysian states of Sabah and Sarawak (on the island of Borneo) from peninsular Malaysia, or between the provinces of Sabah and Sarawak, you will be required to show your passport to immigration authorities to enter these parts of Malaysia. These states have their own immigration authorities who will determine if you can enter and for how long.

You should pay attention to the amount of time you're allowed to stay and be careful not to exceed it. Entry stamps issued by Sabah and Sarawak immigration officials are also valid for other parts of Malaysia.

Visa Overstays: Malaysian immigration authorities routinely detain foreigners who overstay their social visit passes (visas). If the overstay is detected upon departure, a fine or detention and legal proceedings may be imposed. In light of the arrests of several U.S. citizens in connection with immigration sweeps conducted by Malaysian police and immigration authorities, you should carry your passport (containing the Malaysian entry stamp and associated sticker) with you at all times. Depending upon the nature of the violation, detentions may last from a few hours to several weeks, pending a formal hearing. You should check your visa status periodically while in Malaysia and strictly follow immigration laws and regulations. In December 2011 an American citizen wrongly suspected of an immigration violation was detained for twelve hours by immigration officials despite presenting a valid US passport and Malaysian social pass.

The U.S. Department of State is unaware of any HIV/AIDS entry restrictions for visitors to or foreign residents of Malaysia.

Threats to Safety and Security: The Department of State remains concerned about the possibility of terrorist attacks against U.S. citizens in Southeast Asia. Extremist groups in the region have demonstrated the capability to carry out attacks in locations where Westerners congregate, and these groups do not distinguish between civilian and official targets. The U.S. Government has designated two such groups, Jemaah Islamiyah (JI) and the Abu Sayyaf Group (ASG) as Foreign Terrorist Organizations. JI, which has a known presence in Malaysia, is linked to al-Qaeda and other regional terrorist groups and has cells operating throughout Southeast Asia.

You should be especially alert to the risks of travel to the eastern islands and coastal regions of the state of Sabah due to kidnapping that has occurred in the past perpetrated by criminal and terrorist groups. Of particular concern are resorts (and transportation to and from them) in isolated areas. If you visit these areas you should exercise caution, remain alert to your surroundings, and use good personal security measures.

In April 2000, the Abu Sayyaf Group, based in the southern Philippines, kidnapped twenty people (including 10 Westerners) in eastern Sabah and retains the capability to conduct operations in the region. Other criminal elements have committed acts of kidnapping in the region. The Government of Malaysia and other regional authorities have increased their law enforcement presence in eastern Sabah and the resort islands, enhancing their ability to deter and prevent attacks, but the size and remotenesss of the region makes it possible that there may be future security incidents affecting U.S. citizens.

Small-scale public demonstrations are occurring more frequently in Kuala Lumpur (including shopping areas frequented by U.S. citizens) and environs, sometimes arranged at short-notice via social media. There is usually a police presence. A new law makes it illegal for non-Malaysians to participate in public protests. Although such gatherings are generally peaceful, you should nevertheless avoid them.

If you travel overland from Malaysia to Thailand you should be aware of the Department of State's safety and security information for Thailand, particularly the Thai provinces of Narathiwat, Pattani and Yala bordering Malaysia. We urge you to defer non-emergency travel to those provinces. Check the U.S. Embassy of Bangkok's website for more information.

Stay up to date by:

- Bookmarking our Bureau of Consular Affairs website, which contains the current Travel Warnings and Travel Alerts as well as the Worldwide Caution.
- Following us on Twitter and the Bureau of Consular Affairs page on Facebook as well.
- Downloading our free Smart Traveler IPhone App to have travel information at your fingertips.
- Calling 1-888-407-4747 toll-free within the U.S. and Canada, or a regular toll line, 1-202-501-4444, from other countries.
- Taking some time before travel to consider your personal security.

Crime: Violent crime involving tourists and expatriates in Malaysia is relatively rare. Petty theft, particularly purse snatching and pick-pocketing, and residential burglaries are the most common crimes committed against foreigners. Other types of non-violent criminal activity include credit card fraud and automobile theft. In tourist areas such as Bukit Bintang, Petaling Street (Chinatown), Sri Hartamas and Bangsar in Kuala Lumpur, and the main square in Malacca, the police have established small "Tourist Police" stations familiar with helping visitors to Malaysia.

Scams: A large number of U.S. citizens are victims of scams originating in Malaysia. Scammers and confidence artists contact U.S. citizens through the internet, including dating websites. Scammers almost always pose as U.S. citizens who have unexpectedly experienced a medical, legal, financial or other type of "emergency" in Malaysia and who ask the U.S. citizen in the United States to send money quickly to Malaysia. Co-conspirators pose as Malaysian "lawyers" or medical professionals to verify the story and the supposed urgent need for cash. We strongly urge U.S. citizens in the United States to be very cautious about sending money to people you have not met in person and who claim to be U.S. citizens in trouble in Malaysia. If you are scammed and wish to make a formal complaint, the nearest Malaysian embassy or consulate in the U.S. will accept it (in person or via e-mail) and transmit to the police for follow-up.

For additional information on these types of scams, see the Department of State's publication, International Financial Scams.

Purse-Snatchings: In most incidents, two thieves on a motorcycle speed up from behind a victim, and the passenger on the back snatches a purse, handbag, or cellular phone. Thieves have also conducted snatch-thefts while leaning out of the passenger side of moving vehicles. Increasingly, robbers will confront a victim in larger groups. These types of thefts can occur at all hours and often in front of large groups of witnesses, even in upscale neighborhoods frequented by expatriates. Women walking by themselves or with small children are the most common targets, but men walking or jogging alone have also been targeted. Victims have been injured and even killed after falling and being dragged by thieves in cars or on motorcycles. More recently, some thieves carrying knives have slashed and cut the victim in order to shock the victim into immediately releasing valuable items.

To avoid becoming the victim of a purse snatching, be alert and aware of your surroundings. Pedestrians should walk facing traffic and keep a close eye on all vehicular traffic, particularly motorcycles. If possible, try to walk on the sidewalk away from the curb. Avoid poorly lit streets, shortcuts, and narrow alleys, but be aware that attacks may still occur anywhere. Purses or shoulder bags should be closed and tucked under the arm. Do not wrap the strap around your arm or shoulder. People have been injured or killed by being pulled to the ground by their purse straps as the thieves sped off. If your purse or bag is snatched, report the incident as soon as possible to the police.

Smash-and-Grab Robberies: The targets are motorists who are stuck in traffic or stopped at a light. The usual scenario is that a pair of thieves on a motorcycle identifies a car with a lone passenger (male or female) and with valuables (e.g., purse, bag) visible. The thieves use a hammer or crowbar to smash the window of the car, grab the bag, and speed off. If the motorist's windows are already open, the motorcyclists simply reach in and take bags off the seat of the car. You can prevent these crimes by keeping valuables like purses and laptops out of sight while driving or removing them from the car (including the trunk) when parked. GSP monitors should not be left on the windscreen or dashboard.

Credit Card Fraud: While traveling in Malaysia you should use credit cards only at reputable establishments, and you should closely safeguard your credit card numbers at all times. Credit card fraud continues to be a problem in the region, although enhanced technology has reduced reported instances of fraud. Unauthorized charges may not show on a credit card account for several months but can unexpectedly appear in amounts of $5,000 or more. One of the more common methods is for retailers to swipe the credit card under the counter where a machine containing a mobile phone SIM card receives the card's information and transmits it to a criminal organization for reproduction. You should watch retailers closely and any "under the table" transactions should be reported to the local police. In some cases, sophisticated criminal organizations have tapped into data lines emanating from retail establishments. Credit card information is then stolen while it is being transmitted to financial institutions. If you must use a credit card in Malaysia, you should check your account information frequently for fraudulent charges. ATM cards are safer as long as the machines where they are used are associated with reputable Malaysian banks. Also, keep in mind that personal identification numbers (PINs) in Malaysia are 6 digits long. Some travelers have reported having difficulty retrieving cash from ATMs using 4-digit PINs, while others have been successful.

Don't buy counterfeit or pirated goods, even if they are widely available. Not only are the bootlegs illegal in the United States, you may also be breaking local law if you buy them.

Victims of Crime: If you or someone you know becomes the victim of a crime abroad, you should contact the local police and the nearest U.S. embassy or consulate. We can:

- Replace a stolen passport.
- Help you find appropriate medical care if you are the victim of violent crimes such as assault or rape.
- Put you in contact with the appropriate police authorities, and if you want us to, we can contact family members or friend.
- Help you understand the local criminal justice process and direct you to local attorneys, although it is important to remember that local authorities are responsible for investigating and prosecuting the crime.

The local equivalent to the "911" emergency line in Malaysia is 999. An alternate number is the Royal Malaysia Police Operations Center in Kuala Lumpur, 03-2115–9999 or 03-2262–6555.

Criminal Penalties: While you are traveling in Malaysia, you are subject to its laws even if you are a U.S. citizen. Foreign laws and legal systems can be vastly different than our own. In some places you may be taken in for questioning if you don't have your passport with you. In some places, it is illegal to take pictures of certain buildings. In Malaysia, driving under the influence could land you immediately in jail. These criminal penalties will vary from country to country. There are also some things that might be legal in the country you visit, but still illegal in the United States, and you can be prosecuted under U.S. law if you buy pirated goods. Engaging in sexual conduct with children or using or disseminating child pornography in a foreign country is a crime prosecutable in the United States. If you break local laws in Malaysia, your U.S. passport won't help you avoid arrest or prosecution. It's very important to know what's legal and what's not wherever you go.

If you violate the law, even unknowingly, you may be fined, expelled, arrested, or imprisoned. Malaysia strictly enforces its drug laws. If you possess, use or traffic in illegal drugs in Malaysia, you will be sentenced to significantly longer prison sentences and much heavier fines than in the United States. Malaysian legislation provides for a mandatory death penalty for convicted drug traffickers. If you are arrested in possession of 15 grams (1/2 ounce) of heroin or 200 grams (seven ounces) of marijuana, you will be presumed by law to be trafficking in drugs. The Malaysian criminal code includes a provision for a sentence of caning for certain white-collar crimes, including criminal misappropriation, criminal breach of trust, and cheating. If you collect and/or remove local flora and fauna or protected species without authorization from the Malaysian Government, you may be prosecuted criminally and may be sentenced to heavy fines, expulsion, and/or imprisonment.

Distribution of religious leaflets or books of another faith to Malaysian Muslims is illegal; if you do so, you may be arrested and imprisoned. Occasionally, special religious authorities coordinate with local police to conduct raids on popular nightspots and hotels to deter activities among local Muslims that contravene religious customs, including drinking alcohol and having premarital sex.

Arrest notifications in Malaysia: While some countries will automatically notify the nearest U.S. embassy or consulate if a U.S. citizen is detained or arrested in a foreign country, that might not always be the case in Malaysia. To ensure that the United States is aware of your circumstances, request that the police and prison officials notify the nearest U.S. embassy or consulate as soon as you are arrested or detained overseas. You should carry your U.S. passport and current social visit pass (visa) with you at all times, so that if you are questioned by local officials, you will have proof of your identity, U.S. citizenship, and legal status in Malaysia readily available.

Currency: Currency exchange is readily available; international bank-to-bank transfers may take several days and require adequate identification. Credit cards are accepted throughout the country, but you should be aware of the risk of fraud by criminal syndicates. ATMs can be a safer means of obtaining Malaysian Ringgit. You should note that personal identification numbers (PINs) in Malaysia are 6 digits long, and that some travelers have reported having difficulty retrieving cash from ATMs using 4-digit PINs. Western Union money transfers are available through various Malaysian banks and the post office. See Western Union's website to find a Western Union location and address in Malaysia.

Customs: Malaysia's customs authorities enforce strict regulations concerning the temporary importation into or export from Malaysia of items such as firearms, narcotics, medication, business equipment, currency and books, other printed material, and video and audio recordings which might be considered obscene or in any way harmful to public interest and cultural property. You should contact the Malaysian Embassy in Washington, D.C., or one of Malaysia's consulates in the United States for specific information regarding customs requirements.

Dual Nationality: Malaysia does not recognize or permit dual nationality. If Malaysian authorities learn that you are a U.S. citizen and also a citizen of Malaysia, they may require you to immediately renounce U.S. citizenship or forfeit Malaysian citizenship. If you are a dual U.S.-Malaysian citizen you should consider this issue seriously before traveling to Malaysia.

Accessibility: While in Malaysia, individuals with disabilities may find accessibility and accommodation very different from what you find in the United States. The 2008 Persons with Disabilities Act recognizes the rights of persons with disabilities to enjoy the benefits of public transport, housing, education, employment, and health care. However, there is no penalty for those who do not comply with its provisions. For example, there are by-laws to compel new buildings to provide access for persons with disabilities but also loopholes that allow local authorities to exempt compliance. The government does not mandate accessibility to transportation for persons with disabilities, and few older public facilities are adapted for such persons. New government buildings are generally outfitted with a full range of facilities for persons with disabilities.

Medical Facilities and Health Information: Medical facilities and services are adequate in the larger cities, where you can find Western-trained doctors. The U.S. Embassy can provide a list of English-speaking doctors and hospitals upon request. Psychological and psychiatric medical and counseling services are limited. Serious medical problems requiring hospitalization and/or medical evacuation to the United States can cost thousands of dollars or more. Doctors and hospitals often expect immediate cash payment for health services although major credit cards are acceptable at some hospitals in larger cities.

Malaysian ambulance attendants do not have training equivalent to U.S. standards. Callers to Malaysia's "999" emergency number (equivalent to dialing 911 in the United States) are connected to the Red Crescent (a member of the International Federation of Red Cross and Red Crescent Societies), and patients are directed to whichever hospital the dispatcher chooses. If you are staying in Malaysia for a long time, and you have known health problems, you should investigate private ambulance services in the area and provide family and close contacts with the direct telephone number(s) of the service you prefer.

Air quality in Malaysia is acceptable most of the time. However, when Malaysia and nearby countries burn vegetation, especially from March through June and during September and October, air quality can range from "unhealthy for sensitive groups" to "unhealthy."

For information on avian influenza (bird flu), please refer to our Avian Influenza Fact Sheet. Information on H1N1 influenza (commonly referred to as swine flu) can be found at the U.S. Government pandemic influenza website.

You can find detailed information on vaccinations and other health precautions on the CDC website. For information about outbreaks of infectious diseases abroad, consult the World Health Organization (WHO) website. The WHO website also contains additional health information for travelers, including detailed country-specific health information.

Medical Insurance: You can't assume your insurance will go with you when you travel. It's very important to find out BEFORE you leave whether or not your medical insurance will cover you overseas. You need to ask your insurance company two questions:

- Does my policy apply when I'm out of the United States?
- Will it cover emergencies like a trip to a foreign hospital or a medical evacuation?

In many places, doctors and hospitals still expect payment in cash at the time of service. Your regular U.S. health insurance may not cover doctor and hospital visits in other countries. If your policy doesn't go with you when you travel, it's a very good idea to take out another one for your trip.

Traffic Safety and Road Conditions: While in Malaysia, you may encounter road conditions that differ significantly from those in the United States. The information below concerning Malaysia is for general reference only and may not be totally accurate in a particular location or circumstance.

Many car rental agencies in Malaysia are willing to rent vehicles for a short term to U.S. citizens with valid U.S. driver's licenses. Nevertheless, if you plan on driving in Malaysia, we strongly urge you to obtain an international driving permit (IDP) before leaving the United States. More information on how to obtain an IDP is available on the Road Safety Overseas section of the Department of State website. If you plan to stay in Malaysia for a longer period of time, you must obtain a local driver's permit through the Road Transport Department of Malaysia.

Traffic in Malaysia moves on the left side of the road, and most vehicles are right-hand drive. Motorcyclists attempt to circumvent traffic blockage by weaving in and out of traffic, temporarily using vacant oncoming traffic lanes, and running through red lights. This poses a hazard for both drivers and pedestrians unfamiliar with such traffic patterns. If you drive, you should use your turn signals well in advance of turning to alert motorcycles of your intent to turn. By law, you must use your front- and back—seat belts in Malaysia and must not use your cell phone while driving unless it is hands-free (e.g., Bluetooth.) Turning left at a red light is not legal unless otherwise marked.

Traffic is heavy during the morning and afternoon rush hours and slows down considerably when it rains. Monsoonal rains can quickly floods roads located in low-lying areas. Bottlenecks are common in major cities because infrastructure development has not kept pace with the proliferation of motorized vehicles. Multi-lane highways often merge into narrow two land roads in the center of town and cause added congestion. Many streets are narrow and winding.

There have been fatal and other serious accidents involving long-distance tour buses in Malaysia, particularly at night or in adverse weather conditions. If you plan to travel by bus, choose a reputable company, and avoid overnight routes.

Reports of late-night road rage incidents, especially after midnight, are rising. If you drive, avoid confrontational behavior if you are involved in an accident. If you are threatened, leave the scene and file a report with the local police within 24 hours.

Taxis are metered, but many drivers refuse to use the meter and instead charge a much higher rate, particularly during peak hours, when it is raining or when the passenger's destination is to or through a heavily congested area. Metered fares increase by regulation by 50 percent between midnight and 6 am; meters are programmed to display the higher fee automatically during these hours.

Sobriety Checkpoints: Please note that laws against drinking and driving are strictly enforced and carry serious penalties. Police operate sobriety checkpoints in many entertainment districts frequented by expatriates. At these checkpoints, all drivers must submit to alcohol breath tests. If you fail a breath test, you will be arrested.

Driver's License Requirements: International Driver's Licenses (IDL) may be used for 90 days in Malaysia. The IDL must be obtained outside of Malaysia. If you are staying longer than 90 days in Malaysia, and desire a local license, the Malaysian Road Transport Department recommends contacting a local driving school to arrange all the paperwork. In order to obtain a local license, you will also need a valid work permit. If you would like more information about Malaysian or international drivers' licenses, you can contact the Automobile Association of Malaysia, the country's national tourist office, and the national authority responsible for road safety.

Aviation Safety Oversight: The U.S. Federal Aviation Administration (FAA) has assessed the government of Malaysia's Civil Aviation Authority as being in compliance with International Civil Aviation Organization (ICAO) aviation safety standards for oversight of Malaysia's air carrier operations. Further information may be found on the FAA's safety assessment page.

Children's Issues: Please see the U.S. Dept. of State Office of Children's Issues web pages on intercountry adoption and international parental child abduction

Intercountry Adoption

April 2009

The information in this section has been edited from the latest report available as of February 2013 from the State Department Bureau of Consular Affairs, Office of Overseas Citizens Services. For more information, please read the *Intercountry Adoption* section of this book and review current reports online at http://adoption.state.gov.

Malaysia is not party to the Hague Convention on Protection of Children and Co-operation in Respect of Intercountry Adoption (Hague Adoption Convention). Adoptions are not common in Malaysia. Adoptions of non-relatives are generally difficult and time-consuming procedures. Prospective parents may be required to remain in Malaysia for two or more years during the process. Prospective adoptive parent(s) who are non-Muslims may NOT adopt Muslim children.

Who Can Adopt? To bring an adopted child to United States from Malaysia, you must be found eligible to adopt by the U.S. Government. The U.S. Government agency responsible for making this determination is the Department of Homeland Security, U.S. Citizenship and Immigration Services (USCIS). In addition to these U.S. requirements for prospective adoptive parents, Malaysia also has the following requirements for prospective adoptive parents.

Residency Requirements: The adoptive parent must be an "ordinary resident" in Malaysia, who has been working and living in Malaysia for at least two years prior to the application. Prospective parents may also be required to remain in Malaysia for two or more years during the process.

Age Requirements: One of the prospective parents in non-Muslim adoptions must be at least 25 years old and at least 21 years older than the child. If the prospective adoptive parent is a relative of the child, he/she must be at least 21 years of age. One of the prospective parents in Muslim adoptions must have attained the age of 25 and be at least 18 years older than the child. If the prospective adoptive parent is a brother, sister, uncle or aunt of the child, he/she must be at least have attained the age of 21.

Marriage Requirements: Marriage licenses from the prospective parents are required for an adoption application.

Income Requirements: There is no minimum income requirement, but all prospective parents are subject to house visits from a court-appointed guardian ad litem, usually a Social Office employee. These visits help investigate the background and circumstances of the prospective parents to verify all matters relevant to the proposed adoption.

Other Requirements: Prospective adoptive parents who are non-Muslims may NOT adopt Muslim children.

Who Can Be Adopted? Malaysia has specific requirements that a child must meet in order to be eligible for adoption. You cannot adopt a child in Malaysia unless he or she meets the requirements outlined below. In addition to these requirements, a child must meet the definition of an orphan under U.S. law for you to bring him or her back to the United States.

Eligibility Requirements: The prospective adoptive parents must obtain a statutory declaration (notarized affidavit) from the biological parent(s) relinquishing all parental rights towards the child. Both of the biological parent(s) must sign a letter of consent to relinquish their rights to the child. If they are unable to appear during court appointments, they must also sign affidavits to exempt their absences.

Age Requirements: The age limit for a child to be adopted is 18 years old. For non-Muslim adoptions, one of the prospective parents must be at least 25 years old and at least 21 years older than the child.

Waiting Period: For non-Muslim prospective parents, a notice to the Social Welfare Office and a petition must be filed to the Sessions Court through an appointed local lawyer. A court date within a few months will be assigned to appoint a guardian ad litem, after which the guardian will investigate and issue his/her findings within three months, after which the adoption order can be issued.

Adoption Authority: The government office responsible for adoptions in Malaysia is the Family and Children's Division, Social Welfare Department, Ministry of National Unity and Social Development.

The Process: The first step in adopting a child from Malaysia is usually to select a licensed agency in the United States that can help with your adoption. Adoption service providers must be licensed by the U.S. state in which they operate.

To bring an adopted child from Malaysia to the United States, you must apply to be found eligible to adopt (Form I-600A) by the U.S. Government, Department of Homeland Security, U.S. Citizenship and Immigration Services (USCIS). The process for finalizing the adoption (or gaining legal custody) in Malaysia generally includes the following.

Role of the Adoption Authority: The Social Welfare Office is responsible for providing a guardian ad litem to investigate and report on the welfare of the child and circumstances surrounding the prospective parents.

Role of the Court: The court is the primary authority on adoptions, as they issue the formal and final Adoption Order that transfers custody to the prospective parents. The Adoption Order also legally allows for the National Registration Department to change the child's birth certificate, replacing the names of the biological parents with that of the adopting parents.

Role of Adoption Agencies: There are no agencies in Malaysia. All adoption inquiries should be directed to the Social Welfare Department, Ministry of National Unity and Social Development.

Non-Muslim Adoptions: The adoption of a non-Muslim child is governed by the Adoption Act of 1952 (Act 257). The identification of a prospective child may occur privately through friends or relatives in Malaysia or through the Malaysian Social Welfare Department. Once the child has been identified, the prospective adoptive parent(s) must obtain a statutory declaration (notarized affidavit) from the biological parent(s) relinquishing all parental rights towards the child. The prospective adoptive parent notifies the Social Welfare Department of the Malaysian State in which he/she is resident of his/her intention to apply for an adoption order of the child. If the Social Welfare Department identified the child, an "offer" letter will be issued to the adoptive parents. This notification must be in writing. No matter how the child was identified, the adoptive parent(s) must reside with and care for the child not less than three (3) consecutive months before petitioning the Sessions Court or the High Court for the adoption order.

When an application for an adoption order is made, the Court appoints a guardian ad litem for the child. In most cases, the court will appoint a Social Welfare office employee. To safeguard the interests of the child before the Court, the guardian ad litem investigates the background and circumstances of the child and the adoptive parent(s), including all matters relevant to the proposed adoption. The completed guardian ad litem report is submitted to the Court on the day of the hearing. The Court may issue an adoption order or an interim order awarding custody of the child to the adoptive parent(s) for a probationary period of not less than six months and not exceeding two years, subject to provisions for the maintenance, education and supervision of the welfare of the child.

The Registrar of the Court sends a certified copy of the adoption decree to the Registrar-General at the National Registration Department and to the adoptive parent(s) within seven days. The Registrar-General enters the adoption order in the Adopted Children Register. The Register entry serves as the child's official record instead of the original birth certificate. The adoptive parent may apply for a copy through the Registrar-General.

Muslim Adoptions: Only prospective adoptive parents who are Muslims may adopt Muslim children. The Registration of Adoptions Act of 1952 and relevant Shariah laws govern the adoption of a Muslim child in Malaysia. A prospective child may be identified privately or through the Social Welfare Department. A court petition is not required.

The Muslim prospective adoptive parent applies to the National Registration Department to document the child as his/her adopted child. To qualify, the adoptive parent must have resided with and had continuous custody of the child for a period of not less than two years. The application should include evidence relating to the care, maintenance, and education of the child during the two years from the date of the biological parents statutory declaration (notarized affidavit) relinquishing all parental rights of the child.

If the National Registration Department is satisfied with the evidence submitted, an entry will be made in the Register and a certified copy of the entry delivered to the adoptive parents. If the Registration Department is not satisfied with the evidence, an officer from the Social Welfare Department will conduct an investigation on the well being of the child. Children adopted under the Registration of Adoptions Act cannot assume the name or inherit property of the adoptive parents.

Time Frame: Can take around eight months to two years or more, depending on the religion of the child.

Adoption Fees: Adoption application fees are minimal and vary by region, but a lawyer must be hired to process Adoption Orders through the Sessions Courts. Lawyers' fees range from RM2,000 (US$570) to RM10,000 (US$2850). For more information on how to obtain a list of lawyers in Malaysia, please email the U.S. Embassy Kuala Lumpur's consular section at: KLconsular@state.gov.

Documents Required: The prospective adoptive parent must present the following documents to the Malaysian Social Welfare Department under the Ministry of National Unity and Social Development:

- His/her valid passport
- The original birth certificate of the adoptive child
- Notarized letters of consent from the biological parents
- Marriage certificate from the prospective adoptive parents
- Notice letter to the Social Welfare Office stating the intentions to adopt

Bringing Your Child Home: Once your adoption is complete (or you have obtained legal custody of the child), there are a few more steps to take before you can head home. Specifically, you need to apply for several documents for your child before he or she can travel to the United States, such as a birth certificate, a passport or travel document for your child from the country in which he or she was born, and a U.S. Immigration Visa.

For detailed and updated information on how to obtain these documents, review the *Intercountry Adoption* section on this publication and visit the USCIS Intercountry Adoption website at http://adoption. state.gov.

Child Citizenship Act: For adoptions finalized abroad, the Child Citizenship Act of 2000 allows your new child to acquire American citizenship automatically when he or she enters the United States as lawful permanent residents. For adoptions finalized in the United States, the Child Citizenship Act of 2000 allows your new child to acquire American citizenship automatically when the court in the United States issues the final adoption decree. To learn more, review the *Intercountry Adoption* section on this publication and visit the USCIS Intercountry Adoption website at http://adoption.state.gov.

After Adoption: After the adoption, adoptive parents have legal custody of the child and are not subject to any other restrictions or investigations. Parents must remember to obtain the newly-worded birth certificate as stipulated in the Adoption Order from the National Registration Department for the adoption to be finalized.

U.S. Embassy in Malaysia
376 Jalan Tun Razak
50400 Kuala Lumpur
Tel: (6)(03) 2168-5000
Fax: (6)(03) 248-5801
Email: klconsular@state.gov

Malaysian Adoption Authority
Family and Children's Division
Social Welfare Department
21-23rd Floor, Menara Tun Ismail Mohd Ali
Jalan Raja Laut
50562 Kuala Lumpur, Malaysia.
Tel: (60)(3) 2616-5802—General Line
(60)(3) 2616-5865—Adoption
Email: rosmaini@kempadu.gov.my

Embassy of Malaysia
2401 Massachusetts Avenue, NW
Washington, D.C. 20008
Tel: 328-2700
Email: mwwashdc@erols.com

Office of Children's Issues
U.S. Department of State
2201 C Street, NW
SA-29
Washington, DC 20520
Tel: 1-888-407-4747
E-mail: AskCI@state.gov
http://adoption.state.gov

For questions about immigration procedures, call the National Customer Service Center (NCSC) 1-800-375-5283 (TTY 1-800-767-1833).

International Parental Child Abduction

January 2012

The information in this section has been edited from the latest report available as of February 2013 from the State Department Bureau of Consular Affairs, Office of Overseas Citizens Services. For more information, please read the *International Parental Child Abduction* section of this book and check for updated reports online at www.travel.state.gov/abduction.

Disclaimer: The information in this flyer relating to the legal requirements of specific foreign countries is provided for general information only. Questions involving interpretation of specific foreign laws should be addressed to foreign legal counsel.

General Information: Malaysia is not a party to the Hague Convention on the Civil Aspects of International Child Abduction, nor are there any international or bilateral treaties in force between Malaysia and the United States dealing with international parental child abduction. Therefore, there is no treaty remedy by which the left behind parent would be able to pursue recovery of the children should they be abducted to or wrongfully retained in Malaysia. Once in Malaysia, the child or children would be completely subject to Malaysian law for all matters including custody. The United States is not a party to any treaty or convention on the enforcement of court orders. A custody decree issued by a court in the U.S. has no binding legal force abroad, although it may have a persuasive force in some countries. Furthermore, a U.S. custody decree may be considered by foreign courts and authorities as evidence and, in some cases, foreign courts may voluntarily recognize and enforce it on the basis of comity (the voluntary recognition by courts of one jurisdiction of the laws and judicial decisions of another).

Custody Disputes: Parental child abduction is not a crime under Malaysian law. Custody disputes are considered civil legal matters that must be resolved between the concerned parties or through the courts in Malaysia. Although there is no treaty in force between the United States and Malaysia on enforcement of judgments, the Malaysian courts will also take into consideration child custody decrees issued by foreign courts in deciding disputes regarding children residing in Malaysia. The Malaysian legal system is based on English common law. The Federal courts have original jurisdiction in constitutional matters and in disputes between states and reviews decisions referred from the Court of Appeals. In addition to high courts, the Peninsular Malaysian states and the East Malaysian States of Sabah and Sarawak have magistrate courts, session courts, and juvenile courts. These courts would have jurisdiction on civil law cases, including child custody disputes among Malays or other Muslims/indigenous peoples. By Constitutional definition, all Malays are Muslim, and the "paramount ruler," customarily referred to as the "King" is also the leader of the Islamic faith in Malaysia. Malaysia's official religion is Islam and Islamic (Sharia) law applies in family and religious matter for all Muslims. Although civil law cases are adjudicated under Islamic and traditional law, certain cases involving Muslims only are heard in Sharia courts and Sharia law applies in family and religious matters. Questions on specific Islamic laws as they pertain to custody rights should be addressed to a lawyer licensed to practice in Malaysia. In order to bring a custody issue before the local court, the left-behind parent will require the assistance of an attorney licensed to practice in Malaysia. Ideally, these orders and proceedings ensure due process under the local laws as well as providing protection for the child or children. A parent holding a custody decree issued in U.S. courts must retain local Malaysian counsel to apply to the Malaysian courts for recognition and enforcement of the U.S. decree, or to petition for custody of minors. Although visitation rights for non-custodial parents are not expressly stipulated in Malaysian Civil Code, court judgments often provide visitation rights for non-custodial parents. Since compliance with the local court rulings is essentially voluntary, Malaysian police or local law enforcement are reluctant to get involved in custody disputes and could not be counted on to enforce custody decrees issued by the Malaysian courts. For more information, please read the *International Parental Child Abduction* section of this book and review current reports online at www.travel.state.gov/childabduction.

Reaching the U.S. Embassy or Consulate that serves Malaysia: The U.S. Embassy is located at 376 Jalan Tun Razak 50400, Kuala Lumpur. The mailing address is P.O. Box No. 10035, 50700 Kuala Lumpur; Telephone (60-3) 2168-5000. The fax number for the U.S. Embassy is (60-3) 242-2207; the fax number for the Consular Section is (60-3) 2148-5801. Internet: http://usembassymalaysia.org.my; e-mail address: klconsular@state.gov.

Reaching the Foreign Country's Embassy in the U.S.: For further information contact the Embassy of Malaysia, 3516 International Court, N.W., Washington, D.C. 20008; Telephone No.: (202) 572-9700 or nearest Consulate: CA (213) 892-1238 or NY (212) 490-2722. Additional information also available from malwash@kln.gov.my.

Deportation: While there is an extradition treaty between the United States and Malaysia, parental child abduction is not an extraditable offense. However, if the taking parent is a U.S. citizen whose U.S. passport has been revoked due to an outstanding federal Unlawful Flight to avoid Prosecution (UFAP) warrant or indictment on charges of International Parental Kidnapping (IPKCA) in violation of 18 USC Section 1204, Malaysian authorities may consider deportation based on lack of a valid travel document.

Dual Nationality: A child with a parent who was born outside of the U.S. or who has acquired a second nationality through naturalization in another country may have a claim to citizenship in that country. There is no requirement that a U.S. citizen parent consent to the acquisition by his/her child of another nationality and in many cases a parent is unaware that his/her child may have dual citizenship. The Embassy of Malaysia in Washington D.C. will be able to provide more detailed information on whether your child has a claim.

Passports for Minors and the Children's Passport Issuance Alert Program: For more information on these topics, see the *International Parental Child Abduction* section of this publication and review current reports from the U.S. Department of State at www.travel.state.gov/abduction.

Legal Aid: Some countries provide legal aid services in child custody cases. The legal attache or consular section of the foreign embassy in Washington, D.C. may have specific guidance. The ISS headquarters are in Geneva, Switzerland, but information or assistance may be available through its New York branch at 10 W. 40th Street, New York, N.Y. 10018, Tel. No.: 212-532-6350. The National Center for Missing and Exploited Children (NCMEC) maintains a list of attorneys interested in Hague Convention and International Child Custody cases. NCMEC handles all Hague Convention applications for return when children from other countries are abducted and believed to be in the U.S. You may obtain additional information about the attorney program at the National Center by calling 1-800-843-5678 or 703-274-3900. The Internet home page for the National Center can be reached directly at http://www.missingkids.org.

Criminal Remedies: Foreign countries may not recognize parental abduction as a crime. Please note that the extradition process applies only to the abducting adult/fugitive and not the child. The proper channel for the return of the child is through civil mechanisms or voluntary return arrangements. Additional information is also available on the Internet at the web site of the U.S. Department of Justice, Office of Juvenile Justice and Delinquency Prevention (OJJDP) at http://www.ojjdp.ncjrs.org. For further information on international parental child abduction, contact the Office of Children's Issues, U.S. Department of State at 1-888-407-4747 or visit its web site on the Internet at http://travel.state.gov/abduction.

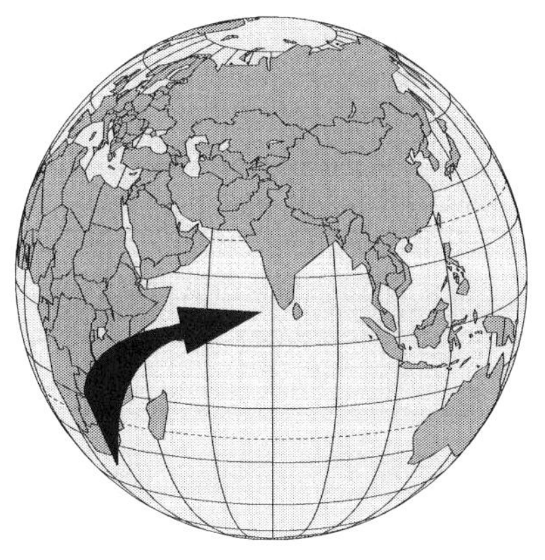

MALDIVES

Compiled from publications that were available as of February 2013 from the U.S. Department of State, the U.S. Department of Commerce, and the Central Intelligence Agency (CIA). See the introduction to this set for explanatory notes.

Official Name:
Republic of Maldives

PROFILE

Geography

Area: total: 298 sq km; country comparison to the world: 210; land: 298 sq km; water: 0 sq km

Major cities: Male (capital) 120,000 (2009)

Climate: tropical; hot, humid; dry, northeast monsoon (November to March); rainy, southwest monsoon (June to August)

Terrain: flat, with white sandy beaches

People

Nationality: noun: Maldivian(s); adjective: Maldivian

Population: 394,451 (July 2012 est.)

Population growth rate: -0.127% (2012 est.)

Ethnic groups: South Indians, Sinhalese, Arabs

Religions: Sunni Muslim (official)

Languages: Dhivehi (official, dialect of Sinhala, script derived from Arabic), English (spoken by most government officials)

Literacy: definition: age 15 and over can read and write; total population: 93.8%; male: 93%; female: 94.7% (2006 Census)

Health: life expectancy at birth: total population: 74.69 years; male: 72.44 years; female: 77.05 years (2012 est.); Infant mortality rate: total: 26.46 deaths/1,000 live births; male: 28.92 deaths/1,000 live births; female: 23.87 deaths/1,000 live births (2012 est.)

Unemployment rate: 28% (2012 est.)

Work force: 110,000 (2010)

Government

Type: republic

Independence: 26 July 1965

Constitution: new constitution ratified 7 August 2008

Political subdivisions: 7 provinces and 1 municipality; Dhekunu (South), Maale, Mathi Dhekunu (Upper South), Mathi Uthuru (Upper North), Medhu (Central), Medhu Dhekunu (South Central), Medhu Uthuru (North Central), Uthuru (North)

Suffrage: 18 years of age; universal

Economy

GDP (purchasing power parity): $2.945 billion (2012 est.); $2.877 billion (2011 est.); $2.679 billion (2010 est.); $2.534 billion (2009 est.)

GDP real growth rate: 3.5% (2012 est.); 7.4% (2011 est.); 5.7% (2010 est.); -4.7% (2009 est.)

GDP per capita (PPP): $8,700 (2012 est.); $8,800 (2011 est.); $8,400 (2010 est.); $8,100 (2009 est.)

Natural resources: fish

Agriculture products: coconuts, corn, sweet potatoes; fish

Industries: tourism, fish processing, shipping, boat building, coconut processing, garments, woven mats, rope, handicrafts, coral and sand mining

Exports: $346.4 million (2011 est.); $163 million (2009 est.); $331 million (2008 est.)

Exports—commodities: fish

Exports—partners: France 16.9%, Thailand 16.5%, India 15.2%, UK 9.1%, Sri Lanka 8.9%, Italy 7.3%, Philippines 4.4%, Germany 4.2% (2011)

Imports: $1.465 billion (2011 est.); $967 million (2009 est.); $1.388 billion (2008 est.)

Imports—commodities: petroleum products, ships, foodstuffs, clothing, intermediate and capital goods

Imports—partners: Singapore 23.1%, UAE 17.9%, India 8.9%, China 7.1%, Malaysia 6.6%, Sri Lanka 5.3%, Thailand 4.9% (2011)

Debt—external: $$1.015 billion (2011 est.); 943 million (2010 est.); $933 million (2009 est.)

Exchange rates: rufiyaa (MVR) per US dollar; 15.39 (2011); 14.602 (2010); 12.8 (2008); 12.8 (2007)

GEOGRAPHY AND ENVIRONMENT

Maldives comprises 1,191 islands in the Indian Ocean. There is growing concern about coral reef and marine life damage because of coral mining (used for building and jewelry making), sand dredging, solid waste pollution, and climate change. Mining of sand and coral have removed the natural coral reef that protected several important islands, making them highly susceptible to the erosive effects of the sea.

The practices have been banned in recent years. In April 1987, high tides swept over the Maldives, inundating much of Male and nearby islands. The December 2004 Indian Ocean tsunami inundated a number of islands, contaminating freshwater sources and damaging houses, soil, and groundwater. These events prompted high-level Maldivian interest in global climatic changes, as the country's highest point is about 8 feet (about 2.4 meters) above sea level.

PEOPLE,

The earliest settlers were probably from southern India. Indo-European speakers followed them from Sri Lanka in the fourth and fifth centuries BC. In the 12th century AD, sailors from East Africa and Arab countries came to the islands. Today, the Maldivian ethnic identity is a blend of these cultures, reinforced by religion and language. Some social stratification exists on the islands. It is not rigid, since rank is based on varied factors, including occupation, wealth, perceived Islamic virtue, and family ties. Members of the social elite are concentrated in Male.

Language

The official and common language is Dhivehi, which is related to Sinhala, a language of Sri Lanka. The writing system is from right to left. English is used widely in commerce and increasingly as the medium of instruction in government schools.

Religion

The entirety of the population belongs to a distinct ethnic group with historical roots in South Indian, Sinhalese, and Arab communities. The vast majority of the Muslim population practices Sunni Islam. Non-Muslim foreigners, including an estimated 675,000 tourists who visit annually (predominantly Chinese, Europeans, and Japanese) and 100,000 foreign workers (mainly Bangladeshis, Sri Lankans, Indians, and Pakistanis), in general were allowed to practice their religious beliefs only in private. Most Muslim tourists and Muslim foreign workers chose to practice Islam in private or at mosques located at the resorts where they worked and lived.

Education

Literacy in Maldives is high at 98%. Maldives has made great strides over the years in primary and lower secondary education, with 100% enrollment in the primary level (grades 1 to 7) since 2002. Secondary school enrollment has also improved significantly, with about 80% progressing to the secondary level. Lower secondary schools (grades 8 through 10) are located on all inhabited islands except for 5 that have less than 70 students.

Only a small proportion of children leave school with a qualification, and "Ordinary level" pass rates (at the completion of grade 10) are low for those who opt to take the examination. Access to higher secondary schools (grades 11 and 12) has improved considerably over the years. There are 38 higher secondary schools; at least one in each atoll except for two, and five in Male. Access to tertiary education is more limited. Although there is no gender bias for primary and lower secondary schools, there is a bias in favor of boys for upper secondary and tertiary education.

HISTORY

The early history of Maldives is obscure. According to Maldivian legend, a Sinhalese prince named KoiMale was stranded with his bride—daughter of the king of Sri Lanka—in a Maldivian lagoon and stayed on to rule as the first sultan.

Over the centuries, the islands have been visited and their development influenced by sailors from countries on the Arabian Sea and the Indian Ocean littorals. Mopla pirates from the Malabar Coast—present-day Kerala state in India—harassed the islands. In the 16th century, the Portuguese subjugated and ruled the islands for 15 years (1558–73) before being driven away by the warrior-patriot Muhammad Thakurufar Al-Azam.

Although governed as an independent Islamic sultanate for most of its history from 1153 to 1968, Maldives was a British protectorate from 1887 until July 26, 1965, which is now annually marked as Independence Day. In 1953, there was a brief, abortive attempt at a republican form of government, after which the sultanate was re-imposed. Following independence from Britain in 1965, the sultanate continued to operate for another 3 years. On November 11, 1968, it was abolished and replaced by a republic, and the country assumed its present name.

A 1968 referendum approved the constitution, making Maldives a republic with executive, legislative, and judicial branches of government. The constitution was amended in 1970, 1972, 1975, and again in 2008.

Ibrahim Nasir, Prime Minister under the pre-1968 sultanate, became President and held office from 1968 to 1978. He was succeeded by Maumoon Abdul Gayoom, who was elected President in 1978 and reelected in 1983, 1988, 1993, 1998, and again in October 2003. After 30 years of rule, in October 2008 Gayoom was defeated by Maldivian Democratic Party candidate Mohamed Nasheed in the first multiparty presidential elections held in 30 years.

GOVERNMENT AND POLITICAL CONDITIONS

The Republic of Maldives is a multiparty constitutional democracy. The 2008 constitution provided for the first multiparty presidential elections. In relatively free and fair elections in October 2008, Mohamed Nasheed became the country's first directly elected president.

Recent Elections

In relatively free and fair elections in October 2008, Mohamed Nasheed, a former political prisoner, became the country's first directly elected president. In May 2009 the country held its first multiparty parliamentary elections. Although there were sporadic confrontations and reports of electoral irregularities, including allegations of bribery and intimidation, election observer groups, such as Transparency Maldives and the Commonwealth, reported the elections to be generally free and fair. There were no credible reports of malfeasance in the February local elections.

Participation of Women and Minorities: There were five women in the 77-member parliament. While 213 women competed in the local council elections, only 57 of the 1,086 councilors elected were women. There were three women in the 10-person cabinet. Parliament approved a woman as commissioner of the Human Rights Commission, but the female nominee for vice commissioner was not approved by parliament because parliamentarians expressed concern about having two women leading the commission. A report published during the year by the HRCM concluded that the representation of women in public life was minimal because of lack of family support, limited experience in the political arena, inadequate access to funding, and advocacy by radicals against women's participation in political and public life. In an August 12 report, the UN Committee on the Elimination of Racial Discrimination stated that it was concerned "about the requirement that all citizens be Muslim, which restricted access to citizenship and public office...and fundamental rights and freedoms."

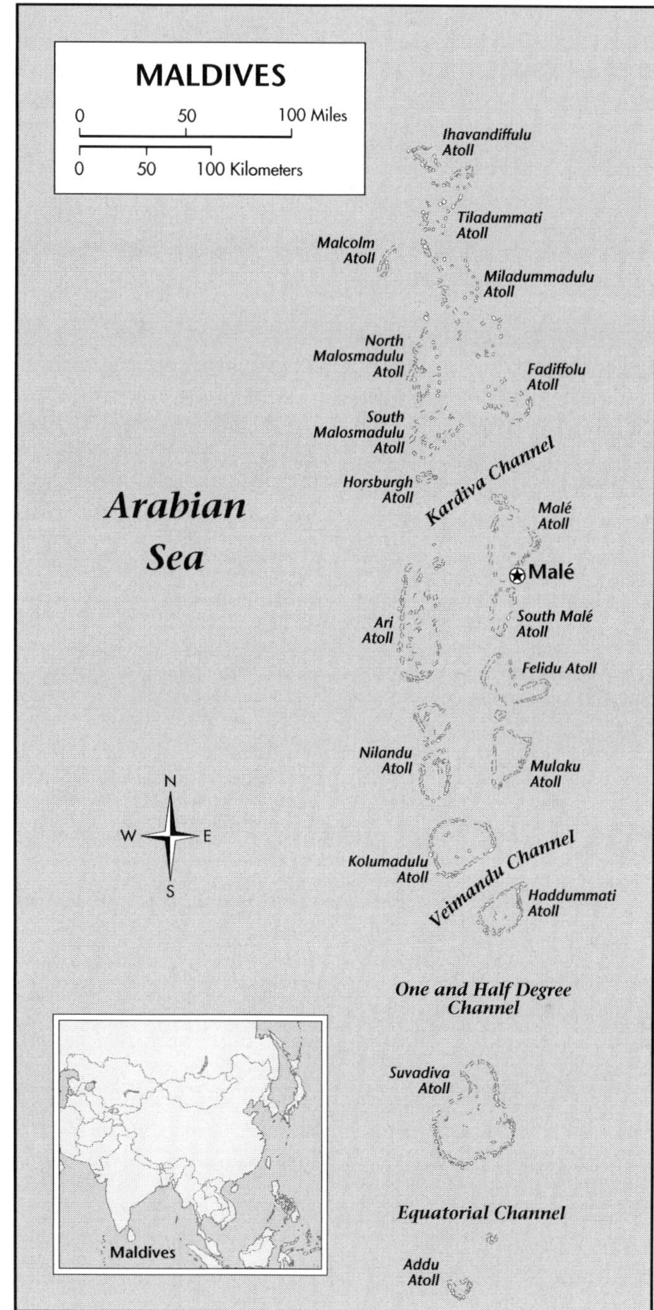

Principal Government Officials

Last Updated: 1/31/2013

Pres.: **Mohamed WAHEED Hassan Maniku**
Vice Pres.: **Mohamed Waheed DEEN**
Min. of Defense & National Security: **Mohamed NAZIM**
Min. of Economic Development: **Ahmed "Andey" MOHAMED**
Min. of Education: **Asim AHMED**
Min. of Environment & Energy: **Mariyam SHAKEELA**
Min. of Finance & Treasury: **Abdulla JIHAD**
Min. of Fisheries & Agriculture: **Ahmed SHAFEEU**
Min. of Foreign Affairs: **Abdul SAMAD Abdulla**

Min. of Gender, Family, & Human Rights (Acting): **Mariyam SHAKEELA**
Min. of Health: **Ahmed JAMSHEED Mohamed**
Min. of Home Affairs: **Mohamed Jameel AHMED**
Min. of Housing & Infrastructure: **Mohamed MUIZZU**
Min. of Human Resources, Youth, & Sports: **Mohamed "Mundhu" Hussein SHAREEF**
Min. of Islamic Affairs: **Mohamed Shaheem Ali SAEED**
Min. of Tourism, Arts, & Culture: **Ahmed Adheeb Abdul GHAFOOR**
Min. of Transport & Communication (Acting): **Mohamed NAZIM**
Attorney Gen.: **Aishath Azima SHAKOOR**
Governor, Maldives Monetary Authority: **Fazeel NAJEEB**
Ambassador to the US: **Abdul GHAFOOR Mohamed**
Permanent Representative to the UN, New York: **Ahmed SAREER**

ECONOMY

Tourism, Maldives' largest economic activity, accounts for 28% of GDP and more than 60% of foreign exchange receipts. Over 90% of government tax revenue comes from import duties and tourism-related taxes.

Fishing is the second leading sector, but the fish catch has dropped sharply in recent years. Agriculture and manufacturing continue to play a lesser role in the economy, constrained by the limited availability of cultivable land and the shortage of domestic labor.

Most staple foods must be imported. In the last decade, real GDP growth averaged around 6% per year except for 2005, when GDP declined following the Indian Ocean tsunami, and in 2009, when GDP shrank by nearly 5% as tourist arrivals declined and capital flows plunged in the wake of the global financial crisis.

Falling tourist arrivals and fish exports, combined with high government spending on social needs, subsidies, and civil servant salaries contributed to a balance of payments crisis, which was eased with a December 2009, $79.3 million IMF standby agreement. However, after the first two disbursements, the IMF withheld subsequent disbursements due to concerns over Maldives' growing budget deficit. Maldives has had chronic budget deficits in recent years and the government's plans to cut expenditures have not progressed well.

A new Goods and Services Tax (GST) on tourism was introduced in January 2011 and a new Business Profit Tax is to be introduced during 2012. These taxes are expected to increase government revenue by about 25%. The government has privatized the main airport and is partially privatizing the energy sector.

Tourism will remain the engine of the economy. The Government of the Maldives has aggressively promoted building new island resorts. Due to increasing tourist arrivals, GDP growth climbed to 8% in 2010 and around 6% in 2011. Diversifying the economy beyond tourism and fishing, reforming public finance, and increasing employment opportunities are major challenges facing the government.

Over the longer term Maldivian authorities worry about the impact of erosion and possible global warming on their low-lying country; 80% of the area is 1 meter or less above sea level.

Labor Conditions

The Employment Act sets age 16 as the minimum age for employment, with an exception for children who voluntarily participate in family businesses. The Employment Act also prohibits employment of children in "any work that may have a detrimental effect on health, education, safety, or conduct."

Child labor, however, was a problem in the fishing sector, small commercial activities, and family enterprises. There were also reports that adolescent children who were sent from islands with inadequate education facilities to Male or other areas for educational purposes sometimes worked as domestics in exchange for food and lodging. There were reports some of these children did not go to school and were sexually abused by members of the host families. According to government officials, this practice was declining as access to secondary education improved in remote parts of the country.

The 2008 Employment Act establishes maximum hours of work, overtime, annual and sick leave, maternity leave, and guidelines for work-place safety. Under the Employment Act, workers have the right to refuse work that is dangerous.

It was unclear whether workers exercised this right in practice. The Employment Act mandates the implementation of a safe work place; procurement of secure tools and machinery; ensuring the continued safety of the equipment, provision of protective equipment to eliminate health hazards, and training of employees in the use of protective gear; and the provision of appropriate medical care. All employers are obliged to provide health insurance for foreign workers. Regulatory requirements in certain industries, such as construction and transport, require employers to provide a safe working environment and ensure the observance of safety measures.

According to a 2009 HRCM report, there were no national standards for safety measures, and as a result such measures were at the discretion of employers. Some employers that produce for export adopted health and safety standards. Employers in other sectors, most notably the tourism and construction industries, reportedly had not taken similar measures. The Employment Act grants workers the right to compensation if fired without cause. The act specifically bans discrimination based on race or color, but it notes that "any preference given to Maldivians by an employer in granting employment shall not be deemed discrimination."

The Labor Relations Authority (LRA) and Employment Tribunal are charged with implementing the Employment Law. The LRA had 18 inspectors and investigators to conduct workplace inspections. It conducted investigations and provided dispute resolution mechanisms to address complaints from workers. During 2011 authorities completed an estimated 197 inspections. The most common problems were expatriates doing work other than that allowed in their work permits, illegal expatriate workers, and unpaid wages. Although the LRA can issue fines, typically it gave employers between one to three months to correct the problems. In several cases, after three months the employers continued to employ illegal expatriate workers, and the LRA had trouble enforcing its authority.

The Employment Act provides a mechanism to establish a minimum wage in the private sector. The minimum wage in the government sector was approximately Rf 3,100 ($242) per month. There is no single, nationally accepted poverty line in the Maldives, but a 2007 Asia Development Bank Study defined a "low" poverty line of Rf 300 ($23.40) per person per month and a high poverty line of Rf 450 ($35.10) per person per month. Because of the tight labor market, private sector employers generally offered competitive pay and conditions to attract skilled workers. The government approved a new pension plan covering local employees in private companies, which require contributions from both the employer and the employee. In August the Maldives Pension Administration Office reported that all tourist resorts had joined the pension fund.

The Employment Act provides for a 48-hour per week limit on work with a compulsory 24-hour break if employees work six days consecutively. Overtime is possible.

Wages in the private sector were commonly set by contract between employers and employees and were based on rates for similar work in the public sector.

Migrant workers were particularly vulnerable to exploitation and, upon arrival in the country, often found unacceptable work conditions and were forced to accept work at whatever wage was offered for debt repayment to the employment agency. The HRCM found many instances of nonpayment of wages to migrant workers and inadequate housing. Bangladesh migrant workers were exposed to dangerous working conditions, especially in the construction industry, and suffered from the effects of working in hazardous environments without proper ventilation.

The status of migrant workers employed in the categories of senior management, professionals, and skilled workers was generally better.

U.S. MALDIVIAN RELATIONS

The United States established diplomatic relations with Maldives in 1966 following its independence from the United Kingdom. Bilateral relations are friendly. The United States has sought to support Maldives' ongoing democratic initiatives and economic development agenda and seeks to ensure that Maldives addresses its social and environmental problems. Following the February 2012 transfer of power in Maldives, the United States has called on all Maldivian parties to chart a way forward that respects Maldivian democratic institutions, the rule of law, and the will of the Maldivian people.

The United States recognizes the importance of promoting security in the Indian Ocean. U.S. Naval vessels have regularly called at Maldives in recent years. Maldives has extended strong support to U.S. efforts to combat terrorism and terrorist financing. The United States has no consular or diplomatic offices in Maldives. The U.S. Ambassador and many Embassy staff in Sri Lanka are accredited to Maldives and make periodic visits.

U.S. Assistance to Maldives

U.S. foreign assistance resources aim to promote and enhance maritime security, counterterrorism, law enforcement, and counternarcotics cooperation with Maldivian forces, and to help the country's adaptive capacity and resilience to the negative effects of global climate change.

Bilateral Economic Relations

Maldives has signed a trade and investment framework agreement with the United States, providing a forum to examine ways to enhance bilateral trade and investment. Maldives has been designated as a beneficiary country under the Generalized System of Preferences (GSP) program, under which a range of products that Maldives might seek to export are eligible for duty-free entry to the United States. The GSP program provides an incentive for investors to produce in Maldives and export selected products duty-free to the U.S. market.

Maldives welcomes foreign investment, although the ambiguity of codified law acts as a damper to new investment. Areas of opportunity for U.S. businesses include tourism, construction, and simple export-oriented manufacturing, such as garments and electrical appliance assembly. There is a shortage of local skilled labor, and most industrial labor has to be imported from Sri Lanka, Bangladesh, or elsewhere.

Maldives's Membership in International Organizations

Maldives and the United States belong to a number of the same international organizations, including the United Nations, International Monetary Fund, World Bank, and World Trade Organization.

Bilateral Representation

Maldives has no embassy in Washington, DC, but its permanent representative to the United Nations in New York also is accredited as ambassador to the United States.

Principal U.S. Embassy Officials

Last Updated: 1/14/2013

COLOMBO (E) 210, Galle Road, Colombo 3, Sri Lanka, +94-11-249-8500, Fax +94-11-243-7345, INMARSAT Tel 383132989, Workweek: M-Th:0800-1730, F:0800-12:00, Website: http://colombo.usembassy.gov/

DCM OMS:	Peggy L. Matsuya
AMB OMS:	Kam T. Wong
Co-CLO:	Monica L. Rojas
DHS/CBP:	Todd Mahaun
FM:	Charles R. Baier
HRO:	Amy E. Murphy
IBB:	William S. Martin
MGT:	John W. McIntyre
MLO/ODC:	LCDR Glenda Pollard
POSHO:	Charles R. Baier
SDO/DATT:	LTC Patrick J. Schuler
AMB:	Michele J. Sison
CON:	Melissa A. Schubert
DCM:	William Weinstein
PAO:	Christopher Teal
COM:	Christopher T. Corkey
GSO:	Prasenjit R. Gupta
RSO:	Douglas C. Marvin
AFSA:	Nelson H. Wen
AID:	James F. Bednar
CLO:	Charlene J. Schuler
ECON:	Allison V. Areias
EEO:	Bryan S. Carroll
FMO:	Amy E. Murphy
ICASS Chair:	Patrick J. Schuler
IMO:	Richard L. Derousse
IPO:	Bryan S. Carroll
ISO:	Richard L. Derousse
ISSO:	Bryan S. Carroll
POL:	Michael D. Honigstein
State ICASS:	Douglas H. Ostertag

TRAVEL

Consular Information Sheet

August 23, 2012

Country Description: The Republic of Maldives consists of 1,190 islands (approximately 200 are inhabited) in the Indian Ocean, southwest of Sri Lanka. It is a presidential-parliamentary democracy and has a population of fewer than 325,000, with approximately 100,000 people residing in the capital city of Malé, and an estimated 100,000 foreign workers. Beautiful atolls, inhabited by over 1,100 species of fish and other sea life, attract hundreds of thousands of visitors each year. Tourism facilities are well developed on the resort islands.

Smart Traveler Enrollment Program (STEP)/Embassy Locations: If you are going to live in or visit Maldives, please take the time to tell our Embassy about your trip. Although there is no U.S. Embassy or Consulate in Maldives, the U.S. Embassy in Colombo, Sri Lanka, provides consular support for Maldives. If you enroll, we can keep you up to date with important safety and security announcements. It will also help your friends and family get in touch with you in an emergency.

U.S. Embassy Colombo, Sri Lanka
210 Galle Road, Colombo 3,
Sri Lanka
Telephone: (94) (11) 249-8500
Emergency after-hours telephone: (94) (11) 249-8888
Facsimile: (94) (11) 249-8590
Email: colomboacs@state.gov

Entry/Exit Requirements for U.S. Citizens: A valid passport, along with an onward/return ticket and sufficient funds, is required for entry. A no-cost visitor visa valid for 30 days is issued upon arrival.

The Department of Immigration and Emigration routinely approves requests for extension of stays up to 90 days for travelers who present evidence of sufficient funds and who stay in a resort or hotel or present a letter from a local sponsor. Anyone staying more than 60 days without proper authorization faces heavy fines and deportation.

Travelers need a yellow fever immunization if they are arriving from an infected area. Visit the Republic of the Maldives, Department of Immigration & Emigration for the most current visa information.

Arrival by private boat: Travelers arriving by private yacht or boat are granted no-cost visas, usually valid until the expected date of departure. Vessels anchoring in atolls other than Malé must have prior clearance through agents in Malé. Maldivian customs, police, and/or representatives of Maldivian immigration will meet all vessels regardless of where they anchor. Vessels arriving with a dog on board will be permitted anchorage, but the dog will not be allowed off the vessel. Any firearms or ammunition on board will be held for bond until the vessel's departure.

With the exception of the capital Malé, tourists are generally prohibited from visiting non-resort islands without the express permission of the Government of Maldives. Permission to visit non-resort islands is most commonly granted to tourists participating in trips organized by resorts or licensed tour operators.

Specific inquiries should be addressed to Maldives High Commission in Colombo, Sri Lanka, at No. 25, Melbourne Avenue, Colombo 4, telephone (94) (11) 2587824/5516302/5516303, or the Maldives Mission to the United Nations in New York, telephone (212) 599-6195.

The U.S. Department of State is unaware of any HIV/AIDS entry restrictions for visitors to or foreign residents of Maldives.

For a list of prohibited items from entry into the Republic of Maldives, visit the Maldives Customs Service website for the most current information.

Threats to Safety and Security: Maldives held its first-ever multiparty democratic election in late 2008. The capital city of Malé has had recurrent protests, sometimes violent, since the February 2012 transition of power. Political demonstrations and social unrest have resulted in the police forcibly dispersing crowds. You should exercise caution and avoid demonstrations and spontaneous gatherings. Protests are generally confined to the capital, Malé, and primarily occur during the evenings, but have been known to take place on other islands. There have not been any demonstrations on the resort islands. You should not engage in political activity in Maldives and if you encounter demonstrations or large crowds, you should remain calm and depart the area quickly and avoid confrontation. While traveling in Maldives, you should refer to news sources, check the U.S. Embassy Colombo website for possible security updates and remain aware of your surroundings at all times.

U.S. Embassy employees are not resident in Maldives. This will constrain the Embassy's ability to provide services to U.S. citizens in an emergency.

Stay up to date by:

- Bookmarking our Bureau of Consular Affairs website, which contains the current Travel Warnings and Travel Alerts as well as the Worldwide Caution.
- Following us on Twitter and the Bureau of Consular Affairs page on Facebook as well.
- Downloading our free Smart Traveler IPhone App through iTunes and the Android market to have travel information at your fingertips.
- Calling 1-888-407-4747 toll-free within the U.S. and Canada, or using a regular toll line, 1-202-501-4444, from other countries.
- Taking some time before travel to consider your personal security.

Crime: Maldives has a low crime rate, but theft of valuables left unattended on beaches or in hotels does occur. Drug use is on the rise among young Maldivians and the penalty for drug use is severe.

Don't buy counterfeit and pirated goods, even if they are widely available. Not only are bootlegs illegal in the United States, if you purchase them you may also be breaking local law.

Victims of Crime: If you or someone you know becomes the victim of a crime abroad, you should contact the local police and the nearest U.S. embassy or consulate. We can:

- Replace a stolen passport.
- Help you find appropriate medical care if you are the victim of violent crimes such as assault or rape.
- Put you in contact with the appropriate police authorities, and if you want us to, we can contact family members or friend.
- Help you understand the local criminal justice process and direct you to local attorneys, although it is important to remember that local authorities are responsible for investigating and prosecuting the crime.

The local equivalent to the "911" emergency line in Maldives is 119. Note: This number is only for the police, not emergency medical services.

Criminal Penalties: While you are traveling in Maldives, you are subject to its laws even if you are a U.S. citizen. Foreign laws and legal systems can be vastly different from our own. In some places, you may be taken in for questioning if you don't have your passport with you. In some places, it is illegal to take pictures of certain buildings. In some places, driving under the influence could land you immediately in jail. These criminal penalties will vary from country to country. There are also some things that might be legal in the country you visit, but still illegal in the United States; for example, you can be prosecuted under U.S. law if you buy pirated goods. Engaging in sexual conduct with children or using or disseminating child pornography in a foreign country is a crime prosecutable in the United States. If you break local laws in Maldives, your U.S. passport won't help you avoid arrest or prosecution. It is very important to know what is legal and what is not legal wherever you go.

While some countries will automatically notify the nearest U.S. embassy or consulate if a U.S. citizen is detained or arrested in a foreign country, that might not always be the case. To ensure that the United States is aware of your circumstances, request that the police and prison officials notify the nearest U.S. embassy or consulate as soon as you are arrested or detained overseas.

Religious Laws: Public observance of any religion other than Islam is prohibited. Religious gatherings such as Bible study groups are prohibited; however, a family unit may practice its religion, including Bible readings, within its residence. It is against the law to invite or encourage Maldivian citizens to attend these gatherings. Offenders may face jail sentences, expulsion, and/or fines.

Although Maldivian law prohibits importing "idols for religious worship," tourists traveling to the resort islands are generally allowed to bring in items and texts used for personal religious observances.

Currency: Credit cards are increasingly accepted outside large hotels and resorts; cash payment in dollars is accepted at most retail shops and restaurants and by taxi drivers.

Accessibility: While in Maldives, individuals with disabilities may find accessibility and accommodation very different from what you find in the United States. The Maldivian constitution provides for the rights and freedom from discrimination of persons with disabilities, and parliament passed a Special Needs bill last year. The new law requires public places such as supermarkets and parks to have facilities that will enable access for people with disabilities. Despite the law, most public places do not yet have access for the disabled, and implementation of the law may take some time.

Medical Facilities and Health Information: There is no 911 equivalent for medical emergencies in Maldives; 119 is for the police only, and the Coast Guard responds to 191 calls for maritime emergencies. A patient would have to call an individual hospital for ambulance services. The quality of medical care in such instances may be uncertain, as most ambulances are ill equipped.

Maldives has limited medical facilities. There are two hospitals in Malé: the government-owned Indira Gandhi Memorial Hospital (IGMH) and the privately owned Abduarahman Don Kaleyfan Hospital (ADK). ADK accepts some insurance plans, but IGMH does not. The hospitals perform limited general and orthopedic surgery, but Maldives has no trauma units and a small number of ICU beds. Persons needing treatments not offered in Maldives require evacuation to the nearest adequate medical facility, such as in Singapore.

Five recompression chambers are available in Maldives. The largest and longest operating recompression chamber is on Bandos Island (15 minutes by speedboat from Malé). The others are located on Cinnamon Alidhoo Resort, Villingili Resort in Addu, Kuramathi Resort, and Kandholhudhoo Islands.

You can find good information on vaccinations and other health precautions on the Centers for Disease Control and Prevention (CDC) website. For information about outbreaks of infectious diseases abroad, consult the World Health Organization (WHO) website. The WHO website also contains additional health information for travelers, including detailed country-specific health information.

Medical Insurance: You cannot assume your insurance will go with you when you travel. It is very important to find out BEFORE you leave whether or not your medical insurance will cover you overseas. You need to ask your insurance company two questions:

- Does my policy apply when I am out of the United States?
- Will it cover emergencies like a trip to a foreign hospital or a medical evacuation?

In many places, doctors and hospitals still expect payment in cash at the time of service. Your regular U.S. health insurance may not cover doctors' and hospital visits in other countries. If your policy does not go with you when you travel, it is a very good idea to take out another one for your trip.

Traffic Safety and Road Conditions: While in Maldives, you may encounter road conditions that differ significantly from those in the United States. The information below concerning Maldives is provided for general reference only, and may vary by location or circumstance.

Only a few of the islands are large enough to support automobiles. Most transportation in Maldives is by boat or seaplane (air taxi). Maldives has good safety standards for land, sea, and air travel. Roads in Malé and on the airport island are brick and generally well maintained. Dirt roads on resort islands are well-kept by the resorts. Transportation in Malé is either by foot, by bus, or by readily available taxis that charge a fixed fee for any single journey. Transportation between the airport and Malé, as well as to nearby resort islands, is by motorized water taxi and speedboat. Several local companies provide seaplane service to outlying islands. Air taxis stop flying one hour before sunset, and several resorts do not transport passengers by boat between the airport and the resort island later than one hour before sunset. Visitors to distant resorts arriving in the country at night can expect to stay overnight at a hotel in Malé or at the airport hotel and should confirm transfer arrangements in advance.

Aviation Safety Oversight: As there is no direct commercial air service to the United States by carriers registered in Maldives, the U.S. Federal Aviation Administration (FAA) has not assessed the government of Maldives' Civil Aviation Authority for compliance with International Civil Aviation Organization (ICAO) aviation safety standards. Further information may be found on the FAA's safety assessment page.

Children's Issues: Please see the U.S. Dept. of State Office of Children's Issues web pages on intercountry adoption and international parental child abduction.

Intercountry Adoption

May 2011

Maldives is not party to the Hague Convention on Protection of Children and Co-operation in Respect of Intercountry Adoption (Hague Adoption Convention). Therefore, when the Hague Adoption Convention entered into force for the United States on April 1, 2008, intercountry adoption processing for Maldives did not change. The Department of State does not maintain files on the adoption process in Maldives because adoptions from Maldives are rare. Fewer than five adoptions by American citizen parents have taken place in over a decade.

MALI

Compiled from publications that were available as of February 2013 from the U.S. Department of State, the U.S. Department of Commerce, and the Central Intelligence Agency (CIA). See the introduction to this set for explanatory notes.

Official Name:
Republic of Mali

PROFILE

Geography

Area: total: 1,240,192 sq km; country comparison to the world: 24; land: 1,220,190 sq km; water: 20,002 sq km

Major cities: Bamako (capital) 1.628 million (2009)

Climate: subtropical to arid; hot and dry (February to June); rainy, humid, and mild (June to November); cool and dry (November to February)

Terrain: mostly flat to rolling northern plains covered by sand; savanna in south, rugged hills in northeast

People

Nationality: noun: Malian(s); adjective: Malian

Population: 15,494,466 (July 2012 est.)

Population growth rate: 2.613% (2012 est.)

Ethnic groups: Mande 50% (Bambara, Malinke, Soninke), Peul 17%, Voltaic 12%, Songhai 6%, Tuareg and Moor 10%, other 5%

Religions: Muslim 90%, Christian 1%, indigenous beliefs 9%

Languages: French (official), Bambara 80%, numerous African languages

Literacy: definition: age 15 and over can read and write; total population: 31.1%; male: 43.4%; female: 20.3% (2010 est.)

Health: life expectancy at birth: total population: 53.06 years; male: 51.43 years; female: 54.73 years (2012 est.); Infant mortality rate: total: 109.08 deaths/1,000 live births; male: 115.85 deaths/1,000 live births; female: 102.11 deaths/1,000 live births (2012 est.)

Unemployment rate: 30% (2004 est.)

Work force: 3.241 million (2007 est.)

Government

Type: republic

Independence: 22 September 1960

Constitution: adopted 12 January 1992

Political subdivisions: 8 regions (regions, singular—region), 1 district; District de Bamako, Gao, Kayes, Kidal, Koulikoro, Mopti, Segou, Sikasso, Tombouctou (Timbuktu)

Suffrage: 18 years of age; universal

Economy

GDP (purchasing power parity): $17.35 billion (2012 est.); $18.1 billion (2011 est.); $17.63 billion (2010 est.); $16.66 billion (2009 est.)

GDP real growth rate: -4.5% (2012 est.); 2.7% (2011 est.); 5.8% (2010 est.); 4.5% (2009 est.)

GDP per capita (PPP): $1,100 (2012 est.); $1,100 (2011 est.); $1,100 (2010 est.); $1,100 (2009 est.)

Natural resources: gold, phosphates, kaolin, salt, limestone, uranium, gypsum, granite, hydropower

Agriculture products: cotton, millet, rice, corn, vegetables, peanuts; cattle, sheep, goats

Industries: food processing; construction; phosphate and gold mining

Exports: $2.557 billion (2012 est.); $2.253 billion (2011 est.); $1.873 billion (2010 est.)

Exports—commodities: cotton, gold, livestock

Exports—partners: China 32.5%, South Korea 15.2%, Indonesia 12.8%, Thailand 6.6%, Bangladesh 5.3% (2011)

Imports: $3.209 billion (2012 est.); $2.533 billion (2011 est.); $2.286 billion (2010 est.)

Imports—commodities: petroleum, machinery and equipment, construction materials, foodstuffs, textiles

Imports—partners: Senegal 15%, France 11.7%, China 8.2%, Cote dIvoire 6.3% (2011)

Debt—external: $2.725 billion (31 December 2012 est.); $3.192 billion (31 December 2011 est.)

Exchange rates: Communaute Financiere Africaine francs (XOF) per US dollar; 514.1 (2012 est.); 471.87 (2011 est.); 495.28 (2010 est.)

PEOPLE

Mali's population consists of diverse sub-Saharan ethnic groups, sharing similar historic, cultural, and religious traditions. Exceptions are the Tuaregs and Maurs, desert nomads, related to the North African Berbers.

Historically, good interethnic relations throughout much of the country were facilitated by easy mobility on the Niger River and across the country's vast savannahs. Each ethnic group was traditionally tied to a specific occupation, all working within close proximity.

The Bambara, Malinke, and Dogon are farmers; the Fulani, Maur, and Tuareg are herders; the Soninkes or Saracoles are traders; while the Bozo are fishers. In recent years, this linkage has shifted as ethnic groups seek diverse, nontraditional sources of income.

The Tuaregs have had a history of struggle since Mali's independence in 1960. A series of rebellions, which were the result of a struggle for greater autonomy, to preserve traditional Tuareg ways of life, and to share in the benefits of a modernizing Malian state, led to clashes with the military from 1963 to 1964 and 1990 to 1996. Peace accords, signed in 1992, aimed to allow greater autonomy in the north and increase government resource allocation to the impoverished region.

The peace agreement was celebrated in 1996 in Timbuktu during an official and highly publicized ceremony called Flamme de la Paix—peace flame. Since then, some Tuareg groups have criticized the government for failing to fully implement the terms of the agreement.

Language

Although each ethnic group speaks a separate language, nearly 80% of Malians communicate in Bambara, the common language of the marketplace.

Religion

Muslims constitute an estimated 90 percent of the population. Nearly all Muslims are Sunni. Most of these are Sufi, although a sizeable minority rejects Sufi traditions and refers to itself as Sunnite or Ahl-al Sunna.

The population is 4 percent Christian, of whom approximately two-thirds are Roman Catholic and one-third Protestant. The remaining 6 percent of the population practices indigenous religious beliefs or professes no religious affiliation. The majority of citizens practice their religious beliefs and traditions daily. Groups that practice indigenous religious beliefs reside throughout the country but are most active in rural areas; many Muslims and Christians also practice aspects of indigenous beliefs.

There are several mosques associated with the group Dawa al Tabligh; however, its influence appears to have declined in recent years.

HISTORY

Malians express great pride in their ancestry and pride themselves on a long history of peaceful coexistence among ethnic groups. Mali is the cultural heir to the succession of ancient African empires—Ghana, Malinke, and Songhai—that occupied the West African savannah. These empires controlled Saharan trade and were in touch with Mediterranean and Middle Eastern centers of civilization.

The Ghana Empire, dominated by the Soninke or Saracole people and centered in the area along the Malian-Mauritanian frontier, was a powerful trading state from about A.D. 700 to 1075. The Malinke Kingdom of Mali had its origins on the upper Niger River in the 11th century. Expanding rapidly in the 13th century under the leadership of Soundiata Keita, it reached its height about 1325, when it conquered Timbuktu and Gao. Thereafter, the kingdom began to decline, and by the 15th century, it controlled only a small fraction of its former domain.

The Songhai Empire expanded its power from its center in Gao during the period 1465–1530. At its peak under Askia Mohammad I, it encompassed the Hausa states as far as Kano (in present-day Nigeria) and much of the territory that had belonged to the Mali Empire in the west. It was destroyed by a Moroccan invasion in 1591. Timbuktu was a center of commerce and of the Islamic faith throughout this period, and priceless manuscripts from this epoch are still preserved in Timbuktu. The United States and other donors are making efforts to help preserve these priceless manuscripts as part of Mali's cultural heritage.

French military penetration of the Soudan (the French name for the area) began around 1880. Ten years later, the French made a concerted effort to occupy the interior. The timing and resident military governors determined methods of their advances. A French civilian governor of Soudan was appointed in 1893, but resistance to French control did not end until 1898, when the Malinke warrior Samory Toure was defeated after 7 years of war. The French attempted to rule indirectly, but in many areas they disregarded traditional authorities and governed through appointed chiefs. As the colony of French Soudan, Mali was administered with other French colonial territories as the Federation of French West Africa.

In 1956, with the passing of France's Fundamental Law (Loi Cadre), the Territorial Assembly obtained extensive powers over internal affairs and was permitted to form a cabinet with executive authority over matters within the Assembly's competence. After the 1958 French constitutional referendum, the Republique Soudanaise became a member of the French Community and enjoyed complete internal autonomy.

In January 1959, Soudan joined Senegal to form the Mali Federation, which became fully independent within the French Community on June 20, 1960. The federation collapsed on August 20, 1960, when Senegal seceded. On September 22,

Soudan proclaimed itself the Republic of Mali and withdrew from the French Community.

President Modibo Keita—whose party Union Soudanaise du Rassemblement Democratique Africain (US/RDA) had dominated preindependence politics—moved quickly to declare a single-party state and to pursue a socialist policy based on extensive nationalization. A continuously deteriorating economy led to a decision to rejoin the Franc Zone in 1967 and modify some of the economic excesses.

On November 19, 1968, a group of young officers staged a bloodless coup and set up a 14-member Military Committee for National Liberation (CMLN), with Lt. Moussa Traore as President. The military leaders attempted to pursue economic reforms but for several years faced debilitating internal political struggles and the disastrous Sahelian drought.

A new constitution, approved in 1974, created a one-party state and was designed to move Mali toward civilian rule. However, the military leaders remained in power. In September 1976, a new political party was established, the Democratic Union of the Malian People (UDPM), based on the concept of democratic centralism. Single-party presidential and legislative elections were held in June 1979, and Gen. Moussa Traore received 99% of the votes. His efforts at consolidating the single-party government were challenged in 1980 by student-led, anti-government demonstrations, which were brutally put down, and by three coup attempts.

The political situation stabilized during 1981 and 1982 and remained generally calm throughout the 1980s.

The UDPM spread its structure to cercles and arrondissements (administrative subdivisions) across the land. Shifting its attention to Mali's economic difficulties, the government approved plans for cereal marketing liberalization, reform in the state enterprise system, and new incentives to private enterprise, and worked out a new structural adjustment agreement with the International Monetary Fund (IMF). However, by 1990, there was growing dissatisfaction with the demands for austerity imposed by the IMF's economic reform programs and the perception that the President and his close associates were not themselves adhering to those demands.

As in other African countries, demands for multiparty democracy increased. The Traore government allowed some opening of the system, including the establishment of an independent press and independent political associations, but insisted that Mali was not ready for democracy. In early 1991, student-led, anti-government rioting broke out again, but this time government workers and others supported it.

On March 26, 1991, after 4 days of intense anti-government rioting, a group of 17 military officers arrested President Traore and suspended the constitution. Within days, these officers joined with the Coordinating Committee of Democratic Associations to form a predominantly civilian, 25-member ruling body, the Transitional Committee for the Salvation of the People (CTSP). The CTSP then appointed a civilian-led government. A national conference held in August 1991 produced a draft constitution (approved in a referendum January 12, 1992), a charter for political parties, and an electoral code. Political parties were allowed to form freely.

Between January and April 1992, a president, National Assembly, and municipal councils were elected. On June 8, 1992, Alpha Oumar Konare, the candidate of the Alliance for Democracy in Mali (ADEMA), was inaugurated as the President of Mali's Third Republic.

In 1997, attempts to renew national institutions through democratic elections ran into administrative difficulties, resulting in a court-ordered annulment of the legislative elections held in April 1997. The exercise, nonetheless, demonstrated the overwhelming strength of President Konare's ADEMA Party, causing some other historic parties to boycott subsequent elections. President Konare won the presidential election against scant opposition on May 11. In the two-round legislative elections conducted on July 21 and August 3, 1997, ADEMA secured more than 80% of the National Assembly seats.

General elections were organized in June and July 2002. President Konare did not seek reelection since he was serving his second and last term as required by the constitution. All political parties participated in the elections. In preparation for the elections, the government completed a new voter's list after a general census was administered a few months earlier with the support of all political parties. Retired General Amadou Toumani Toure, former head of state during Mali's transition (1991–1992) became the country's second democratically elected President as an independent candidate in 2002, and was reelected to a second 5-year term in 2007.

GOVERNMENT AND POLITICAL CONDITIONS

Mali is a constitutional democracy. International and domestic observers characterized the 2007 presidential election, which resulted in the reelection of President Amadou Toumani Toure, and the 2007 legislative elections, as generally free and fair; however, there were some administrative irregularities.

Northern Mali experienced periodic violence involving banditry, drug trafficking, clashes between rival groups, and attacks by the terrorist organization Al-Qaida in the Islamic Maghreb (AQIM).

Recent Elections

In 2007 voters elected President Amadou Toumani Toure to a second five-year term with 71 percent of the vote. Legislative elections also were held in 2007. Domestic and international observers characterized these elections as generally free, fair, and without evident fraud, but there were administrative irregularities. The next round of presidential elections was scheduled for April 2012, but was delayed indefinately as a result of a March 2012 coup.

Political Parties: Political parties generally operated without restrictions or outside interference.

Participation of Women and Minorities: There were 15 women in the 147-member National Assembly. There were five women in the 29-seat cabinet, including new Prime Minister Mariam Sidibe Kaidama Cisse. There were five women—including the chairperson—on the 33-member Supreme Court, and three women on the nine-member Constitutional Court.

The National Assembly had 15 members from historically marginalized pastoralist and nomadic ethnic minorities representing the eastern and northern regions of Gao, Timbuktu, and Kidal. The cabinet also had four members from these minorities.

Principal Government Officials

Last Updated: 1/31/2013

Mali, after the coup d'etat on 22 March 2012, returned to constitutional rule in April 2012 with an interim government.

Pres.: **Dioncounda TRAORE**
Prime Min.: **Django CISSOKO**
Min. of Agriculture: **Yaranga COULIBALY**
Min. of Communications & Spokesperson of the Govt.: **Bruno MAIGA**
Min. of Culture: **Boubacar Hamadoun KEBE**
Min. of Defense & Veterans Affairs: **Yamoussa CAMARA, Col. Maj.**

Min. of Economy & Finance: **Tiena COULIBALY**
Min. of Employment & Vocational Training: **DIALLO Dedia Mahamane Kattra, Dr.**
Min. of Energy & Water Resources: **Alfa Bocar NAFO**
Min. of Environment & Sanitation: **David SAGARA**
Min. of Equipment & Transportation: **Mamadou COULIBALY**
Min. of Foreign Affairs & Intl. Cooperation: **Tieman COULIBALY**
Min. of Health: **Soumana MAKADJI**
Min. of Housing, Land Affairs, & Town Development: **DIALLO Fadima Toure**
Min. of Industry, Investment, & Commerce: **Abdel Karim KONATE**
Min. of Internal Security & Civil Protection: **Tiefing KONATE, Gen.**
Min. of Justice & Keeper of the Seals: **Malick COULIBALY**
Min. of Livestock & Fisheries: **Makan TOUNKARA**
Min. of Malians Abroad & African Integration: **TRAORE Rokiatou Guikine**
Min. of Mines: **Amadou Baba SY**
Min. of Posts & New Technologies: **Brehima TOLO**
Min. of Primary Education, Literacy, & National Languages: **Adama OUANE**
Min. of Promotion of Women, Child, & Family Affairs: **ALWATA Ichata Sahi**
Min. of Public Functions & Admin. Reforms & Relations With Institutions: **Mamadou Namory TRAORE**
Min. of Religious Affairs: **Yacouba TRAORE**
Min. of Secondary & Higher Education & Scientific Research: **Harouna KANTE**
Min. of Social Development, Solidarity, & the Aged: **Mamadou SIDIBE**
Min. of Territorial Admin. & Local Communities: **Moussa Sinko COULIBALY, Col.**
Min. of Tourism, Arts, & Crafts: **Ousmane Ag RHISSA**
Min. of Transport & Infrastructure: **Abdoulaye KOUMARE, Lt. Col.**
Min. of Youth & Sports: **Hameye Foune MAHALMADANE**
Min.-Del. to the Prime Min. in Charge of Govt. Communication & New Technologies: **Hamadoun TOURE**
Min.-Del. to the Prime Min. in Charge of Intl. Relations: **Sadio Lamine SOW**
Min.-Del. to the Prime Min. in Charge of the Creation of Employment & Youth: **Mamadou DIAKITE**
Min.-Del. to the Min. of Economy & Finance in Charge of Budget: **Marimpa SAMOURA**
Min.-Del. to the Min. of Territorial Admin. & Local Communities in Charge of Decentralization: **Demba TRAORE**
Ambassador to the US: **Al Maamoun Baba Lamine KEITA**
Permanent Representative to the UN, New York:

ECONOMY

Among the 25 poorest countries in the world, Mali is a landlocked country highly dependent on gold mining and agricultural exports for revenue. The country's fiscal status fluctuates with gold and agricultural commodity prices and the harvest.

Mali remains dependent on foreign aid. Economic activity is largely confined to the riverine area irrigated by the Niger River and about 65% of its land area is desert or semidesert. About 10% of the population is nomadic and about 80% of the labor force is engaged in farming and fishing. Industrial activity is concentrated on processing farm commodities.

The government in 2011 completed an IMF extended credit facility program that has helped the economy grow, diversify, and attract foreign investment. Mali is developing its cotton and iron ore extraction industries to diversify foreign exchange revenue away from gold. Mali has invested in tourism but security issues are hurting the industry. Mali experienced economic growth of about 5% per year between 1996–2010, but the global recession and a military coup caused a decline in output in 2012. The interim government slashed public spending in the context of a declining state of security and declining international aid.

Labor Conditions

The labor code has provisions that pertain to child labor; however, these were often ignored in practice. Child labor was a problem. Child labor was concentrated in the agricultural sector, especially rice production, domestic services, gold mining, Koranic schools, and the informal economy.

While the labor code sets the minimum age for employment at 14, with certain exceptions, an ordinance pertaining to children sets the minimum employment age at 15. The labor code permits children between the ages of 12 and 14 to engage in domestic or light seasonal work, and limits the number of hours they may work. No child is permitted to be employed for more than eight hours per day under any circumstances. Girls who are 16 to 18 years old cannot be employed for more than six hours per day. These regulations were not enforced in practice.

Approximately half of children between the ages of seven and 14 were economically active, and more than 40 percent of children in this age group were subjected to the worst forms of child labor. Child trafficking occurred. Children, especially girls, were used for forced domestic labor. Child labor in the mining sector, including salt mining in Taoudenni and gold mining, was also a problem. Black Tamasheq children were forced to work as domestic and agricultural laborers.

The national minimum wage was 28,465 CFA francs ($58) per month, which did not provide a decent standard of living for a worker and family. The minimum wage was supplemented by a required package of benefits, including social security and health care. Persons working in the informal and subsistence sectors did not receive the minimum wage.

The labor code specifies conditions of employment, including hours, wages, and social security; however, many employers either ignored or did not comply completely with the regulations. The Ministry of Labor is also responsible for enforcing the minimum wage, but it did not do so effectively.

The legal workweek is 40 hours, except for work in the agricultural sector. The legal workweek for agricultural employees ranges from 42 to

48 hours, depending on the season. The law requires a weekly 24-hour rest period. Workers have to be paid overtime for additional hours. The law limits overtime to eight hours per week. Labor inspectors usually visited work sites only after complaints were filed by labor unions. Legal standards pertaining to hours of work were not always enforced.

The law provides a broad range of legal protections against hazards in the workplace; however, authorities did not effectively enforce these standards. Workers' groups brought pressure on employers to respect sections of the regulations. With high unemployment, workers often were reluctant to report violations of occupational safety regulations. The Labor Inspection Service oversees these standards but limited enforcement to the formal sector. It was not effective in investigating and enforcing workers' safety and was insufficiently funded for its responsibilities. Workers had the right to remove themselves from dangerous work situations and to request an investigation by the Social Security Department, which is responsible for recommending remedial action where deemed necessary; it was not known if any worker had done so.

U.S.-MALIAN RELATIONS

The United States established diplomatic relations with Mali in 1960, following its independence from France. In 1992, Mali moved from a one-party state to multiparty democracy. In March 2012, Mali's elected civilian government was removed in a military seizure of power, and an interim administration was subsequently put in place. A rebellion in northern Mali waged primarily by ethnic Tuareg groups, which began in January 2012, forced hundreds of thousands of Malians from their homes. Mali continues to face security challenges in the north from Al Qa'ida in the Islamic Maghreb (AQIM) and other armed extremist groups.

Prior to March 2012, U.S.-Malian relations were excellent and were based on shared goals of strengthening democracy and reducing poverty through economic growth. The country's stable, democratic government had been in place for almost two decades and had significantly reduced poverty and improved the quality of life for many Malians. However, Mali remained near the bottom of the Human Development Index, notably in health and education.

The United States condemned the March 2012 military seizure of power. The United States continues to call on Mali's interim government to hold presidential elections that are free of interference by the military by April 2013, the deadline set by the regional organization the Economic Community of West African States (ECOWAS), or as soon as technically feasible.

The United States also calls on the rebel groups in northern Mali to renounce any connection with terrorist groups and enter into legitimate political negotiations. A strong, stable, democratic government in Mali is essential in order for the country to deal successfully with its multiple economic, social, political, and security challenges.

U.S. Assistance to Mali

Prior to March 2012, the U.S. Agency for International Development (USAID), Peace Corps, and other U.S. Government programs aimed to foster sustainable economic and social development in Mali. USAID programs also sought to support the peace process in northern Mali and consolidate the region's socioeconomic and political integration. Defense Department security assistance programs and training support sought to build Mali's capacity to meet its various security challenges.

In 2006, the Millennium Challenge Corporation signed a 5-year compact with Mali aimed at increasing agricultural production and productivity and expanding Mali's access to markets and trade. The compact entered into force in September 2007.

As a result of the March 2012 military seizure of power, the United States terminated all assistance to the Government of Mali and suspended all assistance to Mali with the exception of humanitarian assistance, food security, health, and elections support, which are reviewed on a case-by-case basis. The ability of the United States to resume full assistance to Mali will depend on the restoration of a democratically elected government.

Bilateral Economic Relations

Mali is a small market for U.S. trade and investment, but there is potential for growth if Mali's economy expands. Exports to the United States include gold, art, and antiques, while imports from the United States include machinery, aircraft, fats and oils, pharmaceutical products, and plastics. The United States has a Trade and Investment Framework Agreement with the West African Economic and Monetary Union, of which Mali is a member.

Mali's Membership in International Organizations

Mali and the United States belong to a number of the same international organizations, including the United Nations, International Monetary Fund, World Bank, and World Trade Organization.

Bilateral Representation

Mali maintains an embassy in the United States at 2130 R Street NW, Washington, DC 20008 (tel. 202-332-2249).

Principal U.S. Embassy Officials

Last Updated: 1/14/2013

BAMAKO (E) ACI 2000, Rue 243, Porte 297, Bamako, Mali, (223) 2070-2300, Fax [223] 2070-2479, INMARSAT Tel 8816-763-11300; 8816-763-11504, Workweek: Mon.–Thur. 7:30

a.m.–5:00 p.m. , Fri. 7:30 a.m.–11:30 a.m., Website: http://mali.usembassy.gov/

DCM OMS:	Amy Griffin
AMB OMS:	Elizabeth Siletzky
CDC:	Jacques Mathiew
Co-CLO:	Kathleen Nichols
ECON/COM:	Duden Yegenoglu
HRO:	Barbara Jensen
MGT:	Robert T. Siletzky
SDO/DATT:	MAJ Michael Rue
TREAS:	Brian Morgan
AMB:	Mary Beth Leonard
CON:	Kathryn Abate
DCM:	Stephanie Syptak-Ramnath
RSO:	Corynn Stratton
AID:	Rebecca Black
EEO:	Margaret McElligott
FMO:	Robert Custodio
ICASS Chair:	Rebecca Black
IMO:	Samuel Otis Pratt

TRAVEL

Consular Information Sheet

July 27, 2011

Country Description: Mali is a developing country in western Africa with a stable and democratic government. The official language is French; however, thirteen local languages are also spoken and have status as national languages, with Bambara serving as lingua franca. The capital of Mali is Bamako (1.8 million, 2009 census estimate). Facilities for tourism are limited, though they are developing.

There is a serious threat of terrorist activities in Mali's three northern regions (Timbuktu, Gao, and Kidal, which make up nearly 60 percent of the country's area). The terrorist group Al Qaeda in the Islamic Maghreb (AQIM) continues to use northern Mali as an active area of operations as well as a safe haven, notably for detaining hostages.

Smart Traveler Enrollment/ Embassy Locations: If you are going to live in or travel to Mali, please take the time to tell us about your trip. If you enroll in our Smart Traveler Enrollment Program (STEP), we will be able to keep you up to date with the latest safety and security announcements. U.S. citizens without Internet access may enroll with STEP in person at the U.S. Embassy in Bamako.

U.S. Embassy Bamako
ACI 2000, Rue 243 Porte 297
Bamako, Mali.
Telephone: (223) 20 70 23 00
Consular Section: (223) 20 70 25 05
Emergency after-hours telephone: (223) 20 70 23 01 or 20 70 23 02
Facsimile: (223) 20 70 23 40.
Email address:
consularbamako@state.gov

Entry/Exit Requirements: If you are not able to show evidence of a current yellow fever immunization, you may be required to be re-immunized on the spot as a condition of entry into the country. The Embassy strongly discourages this option. Travelers should obtain the latest visa information and entry requirements from the Republic of Mali Embassy at 2130 R Street NW, Washington, DC 20008, telephone (202) 332-2249. Inquiries can also be made at Malian embassies or consulates worldwide.

The U.S. Department of State is unaware of any HIV/AIDS entry restrictions for visitors to Mali, or those seeking to reside in Mali.

Threats to Safety and Security: The U.S. Department of State and the U.S. Embassy in Bamako recommends against U.S. citizens traveling to the northern regions of Mali—Gao, Kidal, and Timbuktu. The terrorist group Al Qaeda in the Islamic Maghreb (AQIM) continues to use northern Mali as a safe haven and platform from which to conduct operations.

As noted in the Department of State's current Travel Warning for Mali and the Worldwide Caution, AQIM has declared its intention to attack Western targets throughout the Sahel (including Mali, Mauritania, and Niger), and has claimed responsibility for the following recent kidnappings/attempted kidnappings and other violent events:

- February 5, 2011—Italian woman kidnapped in Southern Algeria (Still being held hostage);
- February 2, 2011—Vehicle-Borne Improvised Explosive Device attack foiled by Mauritanian security forces outside of Nouakchott, Mauritania;
- January 7, 2011—Two French nationals kidnapped and executed shortly thereafter in Niamey, Niger;
- January 5, 2011—An individual claiming connections to AQIM attacked the French Embassy in Bamako, Mali with a handgun and improvised explosive device;
- September 16, 2010—Five French citizens, a Togolese citizen, and a Malagasy citizen were kidnapped in Northern Niger. The Togolese, Malagasy, and one French citizen were released, but four French citizens are still being held by AQIM.
- April 2010—French NGO worker kidnapped in Niger, executed by captors on July 24, 2010;
- December 18, 2009—Two Italian citizens kidnapped in southeastern Mauritania on the road to Mali and held in Mali (both were subsequently released);
- November 29, 2009—Three Spanish citizens kidnapped traveling between the Mauritanian capital of Nouakchott and port of Nouadhibou, and later held in Mali (all three were subsequently released);
- November 25, 2009—French citizen kidnapped near the city of Menaka (subsequently released);
- November 14, 2009—An attempted kidnapping of U.S. government employees by heavily armed individuals in Tahoua, Niger;
- August 8, 2009—Suicide-bombing against French Embassy officials in Mauritania;

- June 23, 2009—The murder of a U.S. citizen in Mauritania;
- January 22, 2009—Four European tourists kidnapped on the Mali-Niger border and held in Mali. Three were released, but a British national who was part of this group was later executed;
- December 14, 2008—Two Canadian citizen United Nations officials kidnapped north of the Nigerien capital of Niamey and held in Mali (both subsequently released).

The threat posed by AQIM, potential Tuareg unrest, sporadic banditry, run-ins with traffickers, and the porous nature of Mali's northern borders with Algeria, Niger, and Mauritania all reinforce longstanding security concerns affecting travel to northern Mali. In many, if not all, of the above listed kidnapping cases, the individuals were held in northern Mali even though most were not kidnapped there.

In addition to threats posed by AQIM and potential hostage takers, there have been confrontations between the Malian military and Tuareg rebel groups in Nampala (along Mali's frontier with Mauritania) in December 2008, and in the region of Kidal in January 2009. Additionally, the Sahel has been used by traffickers in arms, drugs, and people because of its remoteness and centralized location between Europe and Sub-Saharan Africa for hundreds of years. While these elements usually attempt to avoid contact with outsiders, even an accidental encounter could generate a violent response due to the illicit nature of their activities.

The U.S. Embassy in Bamako has designated the three northern regions of Mali as "restricted without prior authorization" for purposes of travel by U.S. government employees, contractors, grantees, and their dependents. Prior to traveling to these areas, U.S. government employees are required to have the written approval of the U.S. ambassador to Mali. Though this restriction does not apply to private U.S. citizens, it should be taken into account by all U.S. citizens contemplating travel to Mali. The restriction is in effect for the following regions:

- Kidal;
- Gao, including the road to Ansongo and the border with Niger; and
- Timbuktu (Tombouctou).

Although the we place the highest priority on the safe recovery of kidnapped U.S. citizens, it is U.S. policy not to make concessions to kidnappers. Consequently, our ability to assist kidnap victims is limited.

For the latest security information, U.S. citizens traveling abroad should regularly monitor the Bureau of Consular Affairs website, Travel Warnings and Travel Alerts, as well as the current Worldwide Caution. Up-to-date information on safety and security can also be obtained by calling 1-888-407-4747 toll-free within the United States and Canada or, for callers from other countries, at 1-202-501-4444 (international rates apply). These numbers are available from 8:00 a.m. to 8:00 p.m. Eastern Time, Monday through Friday (except U.S. federal holidays). We urge you to take responsibility for your own personal security while traveling overseas.

Crime: Violent crime in Mali is infrequent, but petty crimes, such as pick pocketing and simple theft, are common in urban areas. Passports and wallets should be closely guarded when in crowded outdoor areas and open-air markets. Individuals are advised against traveling on the Bamako-Dakar railroad and should be vigilant for pickpockets, especially at night. Criminals will not hesitate to use violence if they encounter resistance from their victims. There are sporadic reports of nighttime robberies occurring on the roads outside of the capital; tourists should not drive outside of Bamako at night. Travelers should stay alert, remain in groups, and avoid poorly lit areas after dark. Violent criminal activity does occasionally occur in Bamako. Several violent attacks were reported in January 2010, most occurring south of the Niger River in the neighborhood of Badalabougou. The reported attacks took place at night, and the majority have targeted unaccompanied individuals and ranged from muggings at gun or knife point to physical assaults. Many of the attacks occurred near the residences of the victims, both inside and outside of their vehicles.

Sporadic banditry and random carjacking have historically plagued Mali's vast northern desert region and its borders with Mauritania and Niger. While banditry has not targeted U.S. citizens specifically, such acts of violence cannot be predicted. In July 2008, six people working as USAID contractors were robbed of their vehicle and all belongings, at gunpoint, by bandits between the villages of Temera and Bourem, approximately 120 km (75 miles) northeast of Gao along the Niger River.

From May 2008 until July 2008, a series of attacks occured at various Malian government installations. While most of these have been in northeastern Mali, in May 2008, bandits attacked a military outpost in Diabali, 175 km (110 miles) north of Segou. While these actions appear directed exclusively at government security facilities, including military, gendarmerie, and national guard bases, bandits have been known to stop cars at gunpoint while making their escape. U.S. citizens traveling or living in Mali are strongly encouraged to enroll in the Smart Traveler Enrollment Program to allow e-mail notification and/or text message updates should further attacks occur.

Victims of Crime: If you or someone you know becomes the victim of a crime abroad, you should contact the local police and the nearest U.S. embassy or consulate (see the Department of State's list of embassies and consulates). If your passport is stolen we can help you replace it. For violent crimes such as assault and rape, we can help you find appropriate medical care, contact family members or friends, and help them send you money if you need it. Although the investigation and prosecution of the crime are solely the responsibility of local authorities, consular officers can help you to understand the local criminal justice process and to find an attorney if you need one.

Due to the vigilantism which often occurs when criminals are apprehended in Mali, it is best to avoid the large crowds that may gather at the scene of a crime, a vehicle accident, or any altercation.

The local equivalent to the "911" emergency line in Mali is 17 or 18.

Criminal Penalties: While in Mali, you are subject to its laws even if you are a U.S. citizen. In some places you may be taken in for questioning if you don't have your passport with you. In some places driving under the influence could land you immediately in jail. There are also some things that might be legal in the country you visit, but still illegal in the United States, and you can be prosecuted under U.S. law if you buy pirated goods.

Engaging in sexual conduct with children or using or disseminating child pornography in a foreign country is a crime prosecutable in the United States. If you break local laws in Mali, your U.S. passport won't help you avoid arrest or prosecution. It's very important to know what's legal and what's not where you are going. Persons violating Mali's laws, even unknowingly, may be expelled, arrested or imprisoned.

Penalties for possession, use, or trafficking in illegal drugs in Mali are severe, and convicted offenders can expect long jail sentences and heavy fines.

Special Circumstances: Mali is a signatory to the Treaty on Cultural Property, which restricts exportation of Malian archeological objects, in particular those from the Niger River Valley. Visitors seeking to export any such property are required by Malian law to obtain an export authorization from the National Museum in Bamako. It is advisable to contact the Embassy of Mali in Washington or the nearest Malian consulate for specific information regarding customs requirements. U.S. Customs and Border Protection may impose corresponding import restrictions in accordance with the Convention on Cultural Property Implementation Act.

Currency exchange facilities are slow and often use out-of-date exchange rates. The U.S. Embassy is unable to provide exchange facilities for private U.S. citizens. There are several ATMs in Bamako that accept U.S. citizens' credit/debit cards. Maximum withdrawals are generally limited to $400, and local banks charge up to $20 per transaction for use of their ATMs. There are no ATMs outside of Bamako. Credit cards are accepted only at the largest hotels, a few travel agencies (for an extra fee), and very few select restaurants. Cash advances from credit cards are only available via Western Union in Mali.

The U.S. Embassy does not always receive timely notification by Malian authorities of the arrest of U.S. citizens. You are encouraged to carry a copy of your passport with you at all times, so that proof of identity and citizenship are readily available in the event of questioning by local authorities. If arrested, you should always politely insist that you be allowed to contact the U.S. Embassy.

You should exercise caution when taking photographs in Mali. Photographing any official object, entity, or person is restricted. These restrictions include infrastructure, facilities, government buildings, as well as individuals. You should obtain explicit permission from the Malian government before photographing transportation facilities and government buildings. Taking a photograph without permission in any public area or around any of the above listed facilities often provokes a prompt response from security personnel or offends the people being photographed. Taking photos of the U.S. Embassy in Bamako is prohibited.

International telephone calls are expensive, and collect calls cannot be made from outside of Bamako.

Accessibility: While in Mali, individuals with disabilities may find accessibility and accommodation very different from what is available in the United States.

Medical Facilities and Health Information: Medical facilities in Mali are extremely limited, especially outside of Bamako. Psychiatric care to the same standard as that practiced in the United States does not exist. The U.S. Embassy in Bamako maintains a list of physicians and other healthcare professionals who have indicated willingness to treat U.S. citizen patients. The Embassy is unable to recommend medical professionals or facilities.

Most U.S. medicines are unavailable; European medications are more easily found, and can be obtained at pharmacies throughout Bamako, and are usually less expensive than those in the United States. Travelers should carry with them an adequate supply of needed medication and prescription drugs, along with copies of the prescriptions, including the generic names for the drugs. Be careful to avoid purchasing potentially dangerous counterfeit medications when buying on the local market in Mali.

You can find good information on vaccinations and other health precautions, on the CDC website. For information about outbreaks of infectious diseases abroad, consult the World Health Organization (WHO) website. The WHO website also contains additional health information for travelers, including detailed country-specific health information.

Medical Insurance: You can't assume your insurance will go with you when you travel. It's very important to find out BEFORE you leave. You need to ask your insurance company two questions:

- Does my policy apply when I'm out of the United States?

- Will it cover emergencies like a trip to a foreign hospital or a medical evacuation to Europe or the United States?

In many places, doctors and hospitals still expect payment in cash at the time of service. Your regular U.S. health insurance may not cover doctors' and hospital visits in other countries. If your policy doesn't cover you when you travel, it is critical that you purchase travel insurance with evacuation coverage for your trip, and carry the insurance information with you.

Traffic Safety and Road Conditions: While in a foreign country, you may encounter road conditions that differ significantly from those in the United States. The information below concerning Mali is provided for general reference only, and may not be totally accurate in a particular location or circumstance.

U.S. citizens traveling by road in Mali should exercise extreme caution. Mali has paved roads leading from Bamako to most major cities in the south. During the rainy season from mid-June to mid-September, some unpaved roads may be impassable. On many roads outside of the capital, deep sand and ditches are common. Four-wheel drive vehicles with spare tires and emergency equipment are recommended. Travelers must be prepared to repair their own vehicles should they break down or become stuck. Travelers should also carry plenty of food and water.

We strongly urge all travelers to avoid traveling after dark on roads outside of urban centers. The roads from Gao to Kidal and Menaka, and the roads around Timbuktu, are desert tracks with long isolated stretches. Travel on these roads is strongly discouraged due to the threat of kidnapping and terrorism.

Drivers travel on the right-hand side of the road in Mali. Speed limits range from 40-60 km per hour (25-40 miles per hour) within towns, to 100 km per hour (60 miles per hour) between cities. Road conditions often require much lower speeds. Due to safety concerns, we recommend against the use of motorbikes, van taxis, and public transportation. Excessive speeds, poorly maintained vehicles, lack of street lighting, and roving livestock pose serious road hazards.

Many vehicles are not well-maintained,and headlights are either extremely dim or not used at all, while rear lights or reflectors are often missing or broken. Driving conditions in the capital of Bamako can be particularly dangerous due to limited street lighting, the absence of sidewalks for pedestrians, and the number of motorcycles, mopeds, and bicycles.

Aviation Safety Oversight: Because there is no direct commercial air service to the United States by carriers registered in Mali, the U.S. Federal Aviation Administration (FAA) has not assessed the government of Mali's Civil Aviation Authority for compliance with International Civil Aviation Organization (ICAO) aviation safety standards. Further information may be found on the FAA's website.

Children's Issues: For information see the U.S. Dept. of State Office of Children's Issues web pages on intercountry adoption and international parental child abduction.

Travel Warning

January 18, 2013

The U.S. Department of State warns U.S. citizens against all travel to Mali because of ongoing fighting in northern and central Mali, fluid political conditions, the loss of government control of Mali's Northern provinces, and continuing threats of attacks and kidnappings of westerners. While the security situation in Bamako remains relatively stable, the recent escalation of hostilities around Mopti in northern Mali has heightened tensions throughout the country.

Mali continues to face challenges including food shortages, internally displaced persons, and the presence in northern Mali of factions linked to Al-Qaeda in the Islamic Maghreb (AQIM). On January 18, the Department of State ordered the departure of all dependent family members who are not employed at the U.S. Embassy in Bamako, Mali, for a period of up to 30 days. This Travel Warning replaces the Travel Warning for Mali dated January 16, 2013.

The Malian government has banned all public demonstrations and Interim President Dioncounda Traore declared a State of Emergency effective January 12. The state of emergency, which will last for 10 days with a possibility for extension, enables the government to take extraordinary measures to deal with the crisis in the north.

As a result of safety and security concerns, some organizations, including foreign companies, NGOs, and private aid organizations, have temporarily suspended operations in Mali or withdrawn some family members and/or staff. The U.S. Embassy will continue to monitor this situation closely and update U.S. citizens via Emergency Messages which it will post on the U.S. Embassy Bamako website.

Embassy Bamako instructed embassy employees to be cautious when traveling within Bamako, and encourages U.S. citizens to exercise caution, remain vigilant, maintain situational awareness at all times, and take appropriate security precautions to ensure personal safety. The Embassy strongly advises against any travel in the Segou region due to increased troop movement and the potential for checkpoints and military activity. U.S. citizens throughout Mali should develop personal contingency plans, avoid all unnecessary travel, and travel on main roads. Malian security forces are likely to increase their security safeguards, including checkpoints and other controls on movement in Bamako and around the country.

The Government of Mali may periodically impose or lift curfews as security needs may dictate. U.S. citizens should be mindful of such potential measures, stay attuned to local news announcing such curfews, and comply with such locally imposed curfews. The U.S. Embassy for internal safety and security reasons may also, without advanced notice, periodically impose temporary curfew on U.S. Embassy employees. Where possible such restrictions will be shared with the private U.S. citizen community and posted on the Embassy's website. U.S. citizens should carefully consider adopting similar safety measures by limiting any unnecessary travel or movements during such periods of heightened tension.

Northern Mali remains under the control of Ansar al-Dine, the Movement for Oneness and Jihad in West Africa (MUJAO), and other groups. The National Movement for the Liberation of Azawad (MNLA) was allied with Ansar al-Dine and shared control over Gao, Timbuktu, and Kidal. During June and July of 2012, Ansar al-Dine and MUJAO, aided by AQIM, turned on the MNLA, ejecting it from major cities and seizing control over the north.

Islamists destroyed ancient tombs in Timbuktu and implemented sharia law in the cities they hold. On November 20, 2012, a French citizen was kidnapped by MUJAO from Diema, Koulikoro region, and terrorist groups have stepped up their rhetoric calling for additional attacks or kidnapping attempts on Westerners, particularly those linked to support for international military intervention.

On January 10, Islamic extremist elements took the central town of Konna, but were driven out after French military intervention and heavy fighting. Supplies and troops are being continually transported via convoys on main roads throughout the country as the fighting continues. While the situation currently remains calm in Bamako, events in the north have heightened tensions throughout the country.

U.S. citizens should also note that the Embassy has forbidden all travel by U.S. government employees and their dependents to regions north of the city of Mopti. This designation is based on insecurity in areas adjacent to this area, including the presence of AQIM and the threat of kidnapping, as well as banditry in the region. U.S. citizens planning to travel to Mali, particularly to destinations outside of Bamako, should consult the Embassy or your host organization(s) for the most recent security assessment of the areas where you plan to travel.

Senou International Airport in Bamako is currently open for business and scheduled flights are proceeding normally. Some international flights have occasionally been canceled due to low travel volume, but travelers have been notified in advance. Persons wishing to depart the country should check with commercial airlines for the airport's operational status, and flight and seat availability, before traveling to the airport.

In this period of heightened tension, the U.S. Embassy reminds all U.S. citizens of the risk of terrorist activity in Mali, including in Bamako. U.S. citizens are urged to exercise caution, to be particularly alert to their surroundings, and to avoid crowds, demonstrations, or any other form of public gathering. U.S. citizens are further encouraged to exercise prudence if choosing to visit locations frequented by Westerners in and around Bamako.

The U.S. Embassy in Bamako may close temporarily for non-emergency business from time to time to review its security posture. U.S. citizens currently in Mali, despite this Travel Warning, should enroll in the State Department's Smart Traveler Enrollment Program (STEP). By enrolling, the U.S. embassy can contact you in case of emergency.

U.S. citizens should consult the Country Specific Information for Mali and the Worldwide Caution, both located on the Department of State's Bureau of Consular Affairs website. Current information on safety and security can also be obtained by calling 1-888-407-4747 toll-free in the United States and Canada, or a regular toll line at 1-202-501-4444 from other countries. These numbers are available from 8:00 a.m. to 8:00 p.m. Eastern Time, Monday through Friday (except U.S. federal holidays).

Stay up to date by bookmarking our Bureau of Consular Affairs website, which contains the current Travel Warnings and Travel Alerts as well as the Worldwide Caution. Follow us on Twitter and the Bureau of Consular Affairs page on Facebook as well. You can also download our free Smart Traveler App, available through iTunes and the Android market, to have travel information at your fingertips.

The U.S. Embassy in Bamako is located in ACI 2000 at Rue 243, Porte 297. The Embassy's mailing address is B.P. 34, Bamako, Mali. The telephone number, including for after-hour emergencies, is 223 2070–2300. The consular fax number is 223 2070–2340.

Intercountry Adoption

Notice: New Malian Law Potentially Restricts Intercountry Adoptions
November 26, 2012

In December 2011, the Malian National Assembly passed a new Code of Person and the Family. The Code includes a provision that could be interpreted to mean that only Malian nationals would be allowed to complete intercountry adoptions of Malian children. While the Malian Presidency did not issue a decree that the law is in effect, the U.S. Embassy in Bamako notes that some local officials and judges are applying the law. U.S. prospective adoptive parents who are adopting from Mali may encounter delays because of the confusion about the Code.

The U.S. Embassy in Bamako is seeking clarification from the Malian central authority, Direction Nationale de l'Enfant et de la Famille, on when the law will take effect and whether the relevant provision would prevent U.S. citizens who are not also Malian nationals from adopting from Mali. We encourage adoption service providers and prospective adoptive parents considering initiating new adoptions from Mali to refrain from starting the process until further information is available.

The Department of State will provide updated information on adoption.state.gov as it becomes available. If you have any questions about this notice, please contact the Office of Children's Issues at 1-888-407-4747 within the United States, or 202-501-4444 from outside the United States. Email inquiries may be directed to AdoptionUSCA@state.gov.

Overview
August 2012

The information in this section has been edited from a report of the Bureau of Consular Affairs, Office of Overseas Citizens Services of the U.S. Department of State. For more information, please read the *Intercountry Adoption* section of this book and review current reports online at http://adoption.state.gov.

Mali is a party to the Hague Convention on Protection of Children and Co-operation in Respect of Intercountry Adoption (Hague Adoption Convention). Intercountry adoption processing in Hague countries is done in accordance with the requirements of the Convention; the U.S. implementing legislation, the Intercountry Adoption Act of 2000 (IAA); and the IAA's implementing regulations, as well as the implementing legislation and regulations of Mali.

Types of adoption in Mali: Malian law distinguishes between two types of adoption. It is imperative that prospective adoptive parents understand this distinction and obtain the correct type of adoption in order for the child to be eligible to immigrate to the United States.

Adoption Protection gives the prospective adoptive parent custody over the child and obligates the custodial parent to provide for the child's food, shelter, schooling, and medical needs. In the interest of the child, Adoption Protection can be terminated at any time by the custodial party/parties, the Malian government, or the biological parent(s). Under certain circumstances, Adoption Protection can form the basis to obtain a visa to bring the child to the United States and finalize the adoption in a U.S. state court. Prospective adoptive parents must obtain an attestation from the Direction de l'Enfant et de la Famille verifying that the Adoption Protection was obtained legally in order to secure the release of the child for emigration and adoption. Please consult the U.S. Embassy in Dakar before pursuing the Adoption Protection route for intercountry adoption.

Adoption Filiation allows for parental rights to be established between the prospective adoptive parents and the adoptee. Under Malian law, an adopted child with a filiation decree becomes a full heir with the same rights as a biological child. Children under the age of five whose parents are either deceased or unknown are eligible for Adoption Filiation. The prospective adoptive parent(s) must not have any legitimate children or descendants to qualify for Adoption Filiation. Prospective adoptive parents are encouraged to use Adoption Filiation, rather than Adoption Protection, to complete an intercountry adoption in Mali.

Who Can Adopt? To bring an adopted child to the United States from Mali, you must meet eligibility and suitability requirements. The U.S. Department of Homeland Security, U.S. Citizenship and Immigration Services (USCIS) determines who can adopt under U.S. immigration law. Additionally, a child must meet the definition of Convention adoptee under U.S. law in order to immigrate to the United States on an IH-3 immigrant visa. In addition to the U.S. requirements, Mali obliges prospective adoptive parents to meet the following requirements in order to adopt a child from Mali.

Residency: There are no residency requirements for adoption. However, the Malian authorities tend to view more favorably prospective adoptive parents who are currently living in or have previously lived in Mali.

Age of Adopting Parents: For a married couple, either the husband or the wife must be at least 30 years old. An unmarried woman may adopt a Malian child if she is at least 30 years old.

Marriage: Adopted children are generally placed with married couples. An unmarried woman may adopt a Malian child if she is at least 30 years old and can demonstrate proof of sufficient economic resources to support the child. Unmarried men may not adopt Malian children.

Income: None specified.

Other: The prospective adoptive parent(s) must not have any legitimate children or descendants to qualify for Adoption Filiation.

Who Can Be Adopted? Because Mali is party to The Hague Adoption Convention, children from Mali must meet the requirements of the Convention in order to be eligible for adoption. For example, the adoption may take place only if the competent authorities of Mali have determined that placement of the child within Mali has been given due consideration and that an intercountry adoption is in the child's best interests. In addition to Mali's requirements, a child must meet the definition of Convention adoptee to be eligible for an immigrant visa that will allow you to bring him or her to the United States.

Eligibility Requirements: Relinquishment: None specified.

Abandonment: An Adoption Filiation can occur only when the child has been abandoned, with parents either unknown or deceased, and no other parent is capable of caring for the child.

Age of Adoptive Child: An Adoption Filiation can occur only when the child is under five years of age.

Sibling Adoptions: None specified.

Special Needs or Medical Conditions: None specified.

Waiting Period or Foster Care: None specified.

Mali is party to the Hague Adoption Convention. Do not adopt or obtain legal custody of a child in Mali before a U.S. consular officer issues an "Article 5 Letter" in the case. Read on for more information.

Mali's Adoption Authority: Direction Nationale de l'Enfant et de la Famille (Direction Nationale), Ministère de la Promotion de la Femme, de l'Enfant et de la Famille (MPFEF)

The Process: Because Mali is party to The Hague Adoption Convention, prospective adoptive parents must follow a specific process designed to meet the Convention's requirements. The recommended first step in adopting a child from Mali is to select an adoption service provider in the United States that has been accredited or approved to provide services to U.S. citizens in Convention cases. Only accredited or approved adoption services providers may provide adoption services between the United States and Mali.

The U.S. accredited or approved adoption service provider will act as the primary provider in your case. The primary adoption service provider is responsible for ensuring that all adoption services in the case are done in accordance with The Hague Adoption Convention and U.S. laws and regulations.

After you choose an accredited or approved adoption service provider, you must apply to be found eligible to adopt by the responsible U.S. government agency, the Department of Homeland Security, U.S. Citizenship and Immigration Services (USCIS), by submitting Form I-800A..

Once USCIS determines that you are "eligible" and "suited" to adopt by approving the Form I-800A, your adoption service provider will provide your approval notice, home study, and any other required information to the adoption authority in Mali as part of your adoption dossier. Mali's adoption authority will review your application to determine whether you are also eligible to adopt under Malian law.

If both the United States and Mali determine that you are eligible to adopt, and the central authority for Convention adoptions has determined that a child is available for adoption and that intercountry adoption is in that child's best interests, the central authority for Convention adoptions in Mali may provide you with a referral for a child.

The referral is a proposed match between you and a specific child based on a review of your dossier and the needs of a specific child in Mali. The adoption authority in Mali will provide a background study and other information, if available, about the child to help you decide whether to accept the referral or not. Each family must decide for itself whether or not it will be able to meet the needs and provide a permanent home for a particular child. If you accept the referral, the adoption service provider communicates that to the adoption authority in Mali. Learn more about this critical decision.

After you accept a match with a child, you will apply to the U.S. Department of Homeland Security, U.S. Citizenship and Immigration Services (USCIS) for provisional approval for the child to immigrate to the United States (Form I-800). USCIS will make a provisional determination as to whether the child meets the definition of a Convention Adoptee and will be eligible to enter the United States and reside permanently as an immigrant.

After provisional approval of Form I-800, your adoption service provider or you will submit a visa application to the Consular Section of the U.S. Embassy in Dakar, Senegal, that is responsible for issuing immigrant visas to children from Mali. A consular officer will review the Form I-800 and the visa application for possible visa ineligibilities and advise you of options for the waiver of any noted ineligibilities.

The consular officer will send a letter (referred to as an "Article 5 Letter") to the Malian Central Authority in any intercountry adoption involving U.S. citizen parents and a child from Mali where all Convention requirements are met and the consular officer determines that the child appears eligible to immigrate to the United States. This letter will inform the Malian Central Authority that the parents are eligible and suited to adopt, that all indications are that the child may enter and reside permanently in the United States, and that the U.S. Central Authority agrees that the adoption may proceed.

Role of Adoption Authority: Adoption Filiation must pass through the MPFEF's Direction Nationale. The MPFEF works exclusively with the only orphanage in Bamako. Malian law strictly prohibits the involvement of other agencies or associations. The Direction Nationale approves prospective adoptive parent(s) and identifies children for potential matches with prospective adoptive parent(s).

A representative from the Direction Nationale will participate in the adoption proceedings as an advocate for the prospective adoptive parent(s).

Role of the Court: The Tribunal de la Première Instance in Commune 5 in Bamako is the only court authorized to issue Adoption Filiation decrees. Prospective adoptive parent(s) may petition for the adoption of a child, along with a representative from the Direction Nationale, after the U.S. Embassy in Dakar, Senegal, issues the Article 5 Letter. There is a 15-day waiting period between the Court's decision and the adoption decree's issuance, in case someone objects to the adoption.

If the prospective adoptive parent(s) are working with a Malian lawyer, it is possible for the adoption procedures and court proceedings in Mali to be held without the presence of the prospective adopting adoptive parent(s). In this case, the adoptive parent(s) would still need to travel to Mali to accept the adopted child from the Direction Nationale once those proceedings have been completed. The MPFEF will not release newly adopted children to anyone other than the adopting parent(s).

Role of Adoption Agencies: While U.S. prospective adoptive parents must use U.S. accredited adoption service providers for the U.S. processing elements of an adoption from Mali, the MPFEF has not authorized any U.S. adoption service provider to provide services in Mali. Prospective adoptive parents are encouraged to work through a licensed Malian attorney for the in-country adoption procedures.

Time Frame: The adoption process in Mali can take from three to 18 months to complete. Once the case has been presented to the Court of Justice, final review and the issuance of the adoption decree typically take 15 days.

Adoption Application: Prospective adoptive parent(s) residing in the United States should submit all required documents, application, written statement of preferences (child's preferred age and gender), and Form I-800A approval notice to the MPFEF via the Malian Embassy in Washington, DC.

Prospective adoptive parent(s) residing in Mali should submit the application, documents, statement of preferences (child's preferred age and gender), and Form I-800A approval notice directly to the Direction Nationale de l'Enfant et de la Famille, Ministère de la Promotion de la Femme, de l'Enfant et de la Famille.

Prospective adoptive parent(s) may decline a proposed match, but if they wish to proceed with a Malian adoption of a different child, they must then submit a new application and start the process from the beginning.

Adoption Fees: Prospective adoptive parent(s) must provide their Malian attorneys with 10,000 West African Francs; this fee is then paid by the attorneys to the Court to issue the adoption decree.

In the adoption services contract that you sign at the beginning of the adoption process, your agency will itemize the fees and estimated expenses related to your adoption process.

Documents Required: Malian authorities will require:

- Certified copies of the following: Prospective adoptive parent(s) birth certificate(s), and
- Prospective adoptive parents' marriage certificate, if applicable;
- Police record or certification of the lack thereof;
- A homestudy conducted or approved by a U.S. accredited adoption service provider if the prospective adoptive parent(s) live in the United States. If the prospective adoptive parent(s) live in Mali, the home study will be conducted by the Direction Nationale du Development Social in Bamako. The homestudy must then be reviewed by an accredited U.S. adoption service provider. In both situations, the homestudy is a required component of the Form I-800A;
- Certificate attesting to the good health, both mental and physical, of the prospective adoptive parent(s);
- Residence certificate (if the prospective adoptive parent(s) reside in Mali);
- Prospective adoptive parent(s)' passport(s) or certificates attesting to their nationality, issued by the U.S. Embassy in Bamako;
- Pay statements and tax records indicating prospective adoptive parents' residency, employment and annual income;
- Notarized statement appointing a parent or friend as the child's guardian in the case of the prospective adoptive parents' death;
- Agreement to provide an annual report on the child's welfare to the MPFEF's Direction Nationale; and
- Four letters of reference.

Additional documents may be requested. You may be asked to provide proof that a document from the United States is authentic.

Bringing Your Child Home: Once your adoption is complete (or you have obtained legal custody of the child), there are a few more steps to take before you can head home.

Specifically, you need to apply for several documents for your child before he or she can travel to the United States, such as a birth certificate, a passport or travel document for your child from the country in which he or she was born, and a U.S. Immigration Visa. For detailed and updated information on how to obtain these documents, review the *Intercountry Adoption* section in this publication and visit the U.S. Department of State Intercountry Adoption website at http://adoption.state.gov.

Child Citizenship Act: For adoptions finalized abroad, the Child Citizenship Act of 2000 allows your new child to acquire American citizenship automatically when he or she enters the United States as lawful permanent residents. For adoptions finalized in the United States, the Child Citizenship Act of 2000 allows your new child to acquire American citizenship automatically when the court in the United States issues the final adoption decree.

To learn more, review the *Intercountry Adoption* section in this publication and visit the U.S. Department of State Intercountry Adoption website at http://adoption.state.gov.

After Adoption: Mali requires an agreement from the prospective adoptive parents to provide an annual report on the child's welfare to the MPFEF's Direction Nationale until an adopted child reaches the age of 16.

U.S. Embassy in Mali
Ambassade des USA
ACI 2000
Rue 243 Porte 297
B.P. 34
Bamako
Tel: +(223)-20-70-23-00

Email: consularbamako@state.gov
Internet: mali.usembassy.gov

U.S. Embassy in Senegal
Avenue Jean XXIII, angle Rue Jacques Bugnicourt - BP 49
Dakar, Senegal
Tel: +(221) 33-829-2100
Fax: +(221) 33-822-5903
Email: ConsularDakar@state.gov
Internet: dakar.usembassy.gov

Mali's Adoption Authority
Direction Nationale de l'Enfant et de la Famille
Ministère de la Promotion de la Femme, de l'Enfant et de la Famille
B.P. 2688
Bamako, Mali
Email: mpfef@cefib.com

Embassy of Mali
2130 R Street NW
Washington, D.C. 20008
Tel: (202) 332-2249
Fax: (202) 332-6603
Internet: www.maliembassy.us

Office of Children's Issues
U.S. Department of State
2201 C Street, NW
SA-29
Washington, DC 20520
Tel: 1-888-407-4747
E-mail: AskCI@state.gov
http://adoption.state.gov

For questions about immigration procedures, call the National Customer Service Center (NCSC) at 1-800-375-5283 (TTY 1-800-767-1833).

MALTA

Compiled from publications that were available as of February 2013 from the U.S. Department of State, the U.S. Department of Commerce, and the Central Intelligence Agency (CIA). See the introduction to this set for explanatory notes.

Official Name:
Malta

PROFILE

Geography

Area: total: 316 sq km; country comparison to the world: 208; land: 316 sq km; water: 0 sq km
Major cities: Valletta (capital) 199,000 (2009)
Climate: Mediterranean; mild, rainy winters; hot, dry summers
Terrain: mostly low, rocky, flat to dissected plains; many coastal cliffs

People

Nationality: noun: Maltese (singular and plural); adjective: Maltese
Population: 409,836 (July 2012 est.)
Population growth rate: 0.359% (2012 est.)
Ethnic groups: Maltese (descendants of ancient Carthaginians and Phoenicians with strong elements of Italian and other Mediterranean stock)
Religions: Roman Catholic (official) 98%
Languages: Maltese (official) 90.2%, English (official) 6%, multilingual 3%, other 0.8% (2005 census)
Literacy: definition: age 10 and over can read and write; total population: 92.8%; male: 91.7%; female: 93.9% (2005 Census)
Health: life expectancy at birth: total population: 79.85 years; male: 77.57 years; female: 82.26 years (2012 est.); Infant mortality rate: total: 3.65 deaths/1,000 live births; male: 4.08 deaths/1,000 live births; female: 3.2 deaths/1,000 live births (2012 est.)

Unemployment rate: 6.1% (2012 est.)

Work force: 170,500 (2011 est.)

Government

Type: republic

Independence: 21 September 1964

Constitution: 1964; amended many times

Political subdivisions: 68 localities (Il-lokalita)

Suffrage: 18 years of age; universal

Economy

GDP (purchasing power parity): $11.14 billion (2012 est.); $10.89 billion (2011 est.); $10.67 billion (2010 est.); $10.44 billion (2009 est.)

GDP real growth rate: 1.2% (2012 est.); 2.1% (2011 est.); 2.3% (2010 est.); -2.7% (2009 est.)

GDP per capita (PPP): $26,100 (2012 est.); $25,800 (2011 est.); $25,400 (2010 est.); $25,100 (2009 est.)

Natural resources: limestone, salt, arable land

Agriculture products: potatoes, cauliflower, grapes, wheat, barley, tomatoes, citrus, cut flowers, green peppers; pork, milk, poultry, eggs

Industries: tourism, electronics, ship building and repair, construction, food and beverages, pharmaceuticals, footwear, clothing, tobacco, aviation services, financial services, information technology services

Exports: $3.67 billion (2012 est.); $5.204 billion (2011 est.); $3.091 billion (2010 est.)

Exports—commodities: machinery and mechanical appliances; mineral fuels, oils and products; pharmaceutical products; printed books and newspapers; aircraft/spacecraft and parts thereof; toys, games, and sports requisites

Exports—partners: Germany 14.8%, France 9.3%, Italy 6.9%, UK 6.9% (2009 est.)

Imports: $4.648 billion (2012 est.); $7.336 billion (2011 est.); $6.022 billion (2010 est.)

Imports—commodities: mineral fuels, oils and products; electrical machinery; aircraft/spacecraft and parts thereof; machinery and mechanical appliances; plastic and other semi-manufactured goods; vehicles and parts thereof

Imports—partners: Italy 31.8%, France 8.6%, UK 8%, Germany 6.9% (2009 est.)

Debt—external: $48.79 billion (30 June 2011); $5.978 billion (31 December 2010)

Exchange rates: euros (EUR) per US dollar; 0.7838 (2012 est.); 0.7194 (2011 est.); 0.755 (2010 est.); 0.7198 (2009 est.); 0.6827 (2008 est.); 0.7345 (2007 est.)

PEOPLE

Malta is one of the most densely populated countries in the world, with about 3,423 inhabitants per square mile (1,322 per square kilometer). Inhabited since prehistoric times, Malta was first colonized by the Phoenicians. Subsequently, Romans, Arabs, Normans, the Knights Hospitallers of St. John of Jerusalem of Rhodes and of Malta, and the British have influenced Maltese life and culture to varying degrees. There are over 16,000 foreigners residing in Malta. The last decade saw an influx of Europe-bound migrants from sub-Saharan Africa, with some 4,000 in the country as of 2010. There was also a growing North African community of about 4,000 as of 2007.

Religion

The overwhelming majority of citizens, 95 percent (2004 estimate), are Roman Catholic, and 53 percent of Catholics (2005 estimate) attend Sunday services regularly. The country's principal political leaders are practicing Catholics.

Most congregants at the local Protestant churches are British retirees who live in the country or are vacationers from other countries. Also present are Coptic and Greek Orthodox Christians, the Bible Baptist Church, a union of 16 groups of evangelical churches consisting of Pentecostal and other nondenominational churches, Jehovah's Witnesses, The Church of Jesus Christ of Latter-day Saints (Mormons), Seventh-day Adventists, Zen Buddhists, Baha'is, and adherents of indigenous African forms of worship. Of an estimated 6,000 Muslims, approximately 5,250 are foreign citizens in either a regular or irregular immigration status, 600 are naturalized citizens, and 150 are native-born citizens. There is one mosque (and two informal mosques) and a Muslim school that teaches kindergarten through secondary school levels. There is a Jewish congregation with an estimated 100 members.

Language

Malta has two official languages—Maltese (a Semitic language with much vocabulary of Arabic origin and borrowed from Sicilian Italian) and English. The literacy rate has reached 93%, compared to 63% in 1946. Schooling is compulsory until age 16.

HISTORY

Malta was an important cultic center for earth-mother worship in the 4th millennium B.C. Archeological work shows a developed religious center there, including the world's oldest free-standing architecture, predating that of Sumer and Egypt. Malta's written history began well before the Christian era. The Phoenicians, and later the Carthaginians, established ports and trading settlements on the island. During the second Punic War (218 B.C.), Malta became part of the Roman Empire. During Roman rule, in A.D. 60, Saint Paul was shipwrecked on Malta.

In 533 A.D. Malta became part of the Byzantine Empire and in 870 came under Arab control. Arab occupation and rule left a strong imprint on Maltese life, customs, and language. The Arabs were driven out in 1090 by a band of Norman adventurers under Count Roger of Normandy, who had established a kingdom in southern Italy and Sicily. Malta thus became an appendage of Sicily for 440 years. During this period, Malta was sold and resold to various feudal lords and barons and was dominated successively by the rulers of Swabia (now part of Germany), Aquitaine (now part of France), Aragon (now part of Spain), Castile (now part of Spain), and Spain.

In 1522, Suleiman II drove the Knights of St. John out of Rhodes, where they had established themselves after being driven out of Jerusalem. They dispersed to their commanderies in Europe, and in 1530 Charles V granted them sovereignty over the Maltese islands. For the next 275 years, these famous "Knights of Malta" made the island their domain. They built towns, palaces, churches, gardens, and fortifications and embellished the island with numerous works of art. In 1565, Suleiman the Magnificent laid siege to Malta. After several months, the Knights and the Maltese population prevailed and the Turks withdrew. Over the years, the power of the Knights declined, and their rule of Malta ended with their peaceful surrender to Napoleon in 1798.

The people of Malta rose against French rule, which lasted 2 years, and with the help of the British evicted them in 1800. In 1814, Malta voluntarily became part of the British Empire. Under the United Kingdom, the island became a military and naval fortress, the headquarters of the British Mediterranean fleet. During World War II, Malta survived relentless raids from German and Italian military forces (1940–43). In recognition, King George VI in 1942 awarded the George Cross "to the island fortress of Malta—its people and defenders." A crucial moment in Maltese history was August 15, 1942, when five out of the 14 vessels that formed part of "Operation Pedestal," including the American tanker SS Ohio, broke through the Nazi blockade of Malta to deliver fuel and food to the starving population. The arrival of the vessels was the turning point in the Maltese islands' fate during World War II, and became known locally as the Santa Marija Convoy, in honor of the August 15 Feast of the Assumption, referred to locally as "Santa Marija." President Franklin Roosevelt, describing the wartime period, called Malta "one tiny bright flame in the darkness—a beacon of hope for the clearer days which have come." In September 1943, the Italian fleet's surrender was signed in Malta by U.S. General Dwight Eisenhower and Italian Marshal Pietro Badoglio.

Victory Day, celebrated on September 8, commemorates victory in the 1565 Great Siege, and the end of the World War II attacks in Malta. Malta obtained independence on September 21, 1964, became a Republic on December 13, 1974. The last British forces left in March 1979. Malta joined the European Union (EU) on May 1, 2004.

GOVERNMENT AND POLITICAL CONDITIONS

Malta is a constitutional republic and parliamentary democracy. The president is the head of state and is appointed by the unicameral parliament (House of Representatives). The president appoints as prime minister the leader of the party winning a majority of seats in parliamentary elections. General elections held in 2008 were judged free and fair.

Recent Elections

In 2008 the country held parliamentary elections that observers considered free and fair.

Participation of Women and Minorities: There were six women in the 65-seat parliament and two in the 14-member Cabinet of Ministers. Approximately 13 percent of senior government officials were women, and three women held ambassadorial rank. There were two female judges and 10 female magistrates. There were no members of minorities in the government.

Principal Government Officials

Last Updated: 1/31/2013

Pres.: **George ABELA**
Prime Min.: **Lawrence GONZI**
Dep. Prime Min.: **Tonio BORG**
Min. for Communications, Infrastructure, & Transport: **Austin GATT**
Min. for Competition, Small Business, & Consumers: **Jason AZZOPARDI**
Min. of Culture, Environment, & Tourism: **Mario DE MARCO**
Min. for Education & Employment: **Dolores CRISTINA**
Min. of Finance, Economy, & Investment: **Tonio FENECH**
Min. of Foreign Affairs: **Tonio BORG**
Min. for Gozo: **Giovanna DEBONO**
Min. of Health, the Elderly, & Community Care: **Joe CASSAR**
Min. for Home & Parliamentary Affairs
Min. for Justice, Dialogue, & the Family: **Chris SAID**
Min. of Resources & Rural Affairs: **George PULLICINO**
Governor, Central Bank: **Joseph BONNICI**
Ambassador to the US: **Joseph COLE**
Permanent Representative to the UN, New York: **Christopher GRIMA**

ECONOMY

Malta—the smallest economy in the euro zone—produces only about 20% of its food needs, has limited fresh water supplies, and has few domestic energy sources. Malta's geographic position between Europe and North Africa makes it a target for illegal immigration, which has strained Malta's political and economic resources. Malta's fertility rate is below the EU average, and population growth in recent years has largely been from immigration, putting increasing pressure on the pension system. Malta adopted the euro on 1 January 2008.

Malta's economy is dependent on foreign trade, manufacturing, and tourism, and was hurt by the global economic downturn. Malta has low unemployment relative to other European countries, and growth has recovered since the 2009 recession. Malta's financial services industry has grown in recent years and it has avoided contagion from the European financial crisis, largely because its debt is mostly held domestically and its banks have low exposure to the sovereign debt of peripheral European countries. Malta reduced its deficit below 3 percent of GDP, leading the EU to dismiss its official excessive deficit procedure against Malta in 2012.

Labor Conditions

The law prohibits the employment of children younger than 16. The director general of the directorate for educational services may grant an exemption for employment only after determining that it would not harm the health or normal development of the minor. Such exemptions were granted in practice. While no legal work was specifically restricted, children granted an exemption were not allowed to perform work that could be regarded as harmful, damaging, or dangerous to a young person.

The Employment Training Corporation (ETC), a government entity under the Ministry for Social Policy, is responsible for labor and employment issues. It generally enforced the law effectively in most formal sectors of the economy but allowed summer employment of underage youth in businesses operated by their families. No assessment was available of the effectiveness with which the ETC monitored the often-unregistered employment of children as domestic employees, restaurant workers, and street vendors.

The national weekly minimum wage was 153.45 euros ($199); in addition, there was an annual mandatory bonus of 270 euros ($351) and an annually adjusted cost-of-living increase of 242 euros ($315). The country's independent National Statistical Office estimated that approximately 15 percent of the population lives at or below the poverty income level of 5,961 euros ($7,749). Following consultations with workers and employers, the government established the minimum wage, which it revises annually based on changes in the cost of living.

Irregular migrant workers from Somalia, Eritrea, Sudan, and other sub-Saharan African countries, who comprised a small but unquantifiable percentage of the workforce, sometimes worked under conditions that did not meet the government's minimum standards for employment. In 2008 the General Workers' Union (GWU) issued a report documenting what it termed the "exploitation" of migrant workers. The general secretary of the GWU stated at a press conference that such workers often were employed in the most hazardous occupations, such as road construction and highway refuse cleanup, where traffic and environmental conditions posed a danger, and in the building construction trades, where accidents such as collapses might occur.

In many cases migrants received less than the minimum wage. In 2008 AWAS, in coordination with the ETC, established informational programs to help individuals pursue employment and obtain work permits. The GWU and AWAS believed that the programs were beneficial, but there was no data to validate this assessment. The government operated a program called Restart II, through which irregular migrants who volunteered to leave the country could receive free rail or airfare to their country of origin, plus financial assistance. The program, funded in part by the EU, was to last until June. As of September, it had provided benefits to 24 returnees.

The standard workweek was 40 hours, but in certain occupations, such as health care providers, airport workers, and civil protection services, 43 or 45 hours was the norm. Government regulations provided for a daily rest period, normally one-hour, and one day of rest per week. Premium pay is required for overtime, excessive compulsory overtime prohibited, and workers cannot be obligated to work more than 48 hours, inclusive of overtime. The Ministry of Social Policy generally enforced these requirements effectively in the formal economy. Enforcement of health and safety standards continued to be uneven; industrial accidents remained frequent, particularly in the manufacturing, and building and construction sectors.

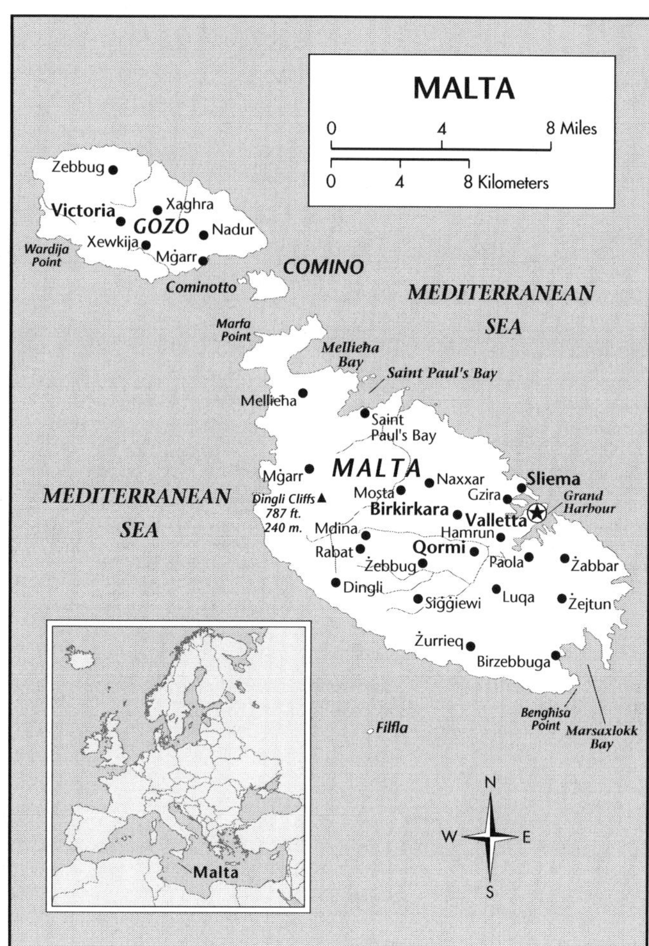

U.S.-MALTESE RELATIONS

Malta and the United States established full diplomatic relations upon Malta's independence in 1964. The government seeks close relations with the United States, with an emphasis on increased trade and private investment. U.S. Navy ships visit on a semi-regular basis. During the period of rebellion in Libya that began in February 2011, Malta played an important role in supporting evacuation of third-country nationals, including Americans; coordinating humanitarian aid to the people of Libya; and providing general assistance to forces of nations involved in enforcement of UN Security Council Resolutions 1970 and 1973.

U.S. Assistance to Malta

The U.S. foreign assistance to Malta currently provides International Military Education & Training (IMET) funding and has in the past included foreign military financing (FMF) grants and other defense assistance allowing for the acquisition of U.S. security related equipment, services and training. Under a refugee resettlement program, almost 1000 third-country migrants have been resettled in the U.S. from Malta.

Bilateral Economic Relations

The United States has been supportive of Malta's campaign to attract private investment, and a number of U.S. companies are operating in Malta. These include major hotels, light manufacturing and repair facilities, pharmaceutical and medical supply firms, and some offices servicing local and regional operations. In an effort to boost trade relations, the United States and Malta signed a double taxation agreement in 2008, which came into force in 2011. Malta joined the Visa Waiver Program in 2008. This program allows citizens of certain countries to travel to the

United States visa-free for tourist and business purposes for stays under 90 days.

Malta's Membership in International Organizations

Malta became a member of the United Nations in 1964 following independence from the United Kingdom. Malta and the United States belong to a number of the same international organizations, including the UN, International Monetary Fund, World Bank, World Trade Organization, and Organization for Security and Cooperation in Europe. Malta is a member of the North Atlantic Treaty Organization's (NATO) Partnership for Peace. Malta has been a member of the European Union since 2004, and is also a member of the Schengen Agreement on the abolition of border checks and the Euro zone.

Bilateral Representation

Malta maintains an embassy in the United States at 2017 Connecticut Avenue NW, Washington, DC 20008 (202-462-3611).

Principal U.S. Embassy Officials

Last Updated: 1/14/2013

VALLETTA (E) Ta' Qali National Park, [356] 2561-4000, Fax [356] 2561-4183, Workweek: 8:00-4:30, Website: http://malta.usembassy.gov/

DCM OMS:	Rhonda Sheppard
AMB OMS:	Maria D Valentine
COM/CON:	Michael Christie
FM:	Michael McMahon
HRO:	Laura Danylin
MGT:	Laura Danylin
POL/ECON:	Thomas Schmidt
POSHO:	Michael McMahon
SDO/DATT:	LCDR Jano Carlson
AMB:	Gina Abercrombie-Winstanley
CON:	Tracy R Brown
DCM:	Michael R. Detar
PAO:	Winifred Hofstetter
COM:	Thomas Schmidt
GSO:	Nathan Austin
RSO:	William Margulies
CLO:	Shelagh Carlson
ECON:	Joseph Sahid
FMO:	Laura Danylin
ICASS Chair:	Melissa Mills
IMO:	Robert W. Kirk
IRS:	Kathy J. Beck
ISO:	Brian V. Bielawski
ISSO:	Robert W. Kirk
LEGATT:	Martin Martinez

TRAVEL

Consular Information Sheet

April 5, 2012

Country Description: Malta is a small, developed, democratic Mediterranean island nation, positioned as a cultural stepping-stone between Europe and North Africa. Malta became a member of the European Union in 2004, and became a full member of the Schengen Area in 2008. Tourist facilities of all categories are widely available.

Smart Traveler Enrollment Program (STEP)/Embassy Locations: If you are going to live in or visit Malta, please take the time to tell our U.S. Embassy about your trip. If you enroll with the Smart Traveler Enrollment Program, we can keep you up to date with important safety and security announcements. It will also help your family and friends get in touch with you in an emergency.

U.S. Embassy—Malta
Ta'Qali National Park Street
Attard ATD 4000
MALTA
Telephone: (356) 2561–4000
Email: ConsularMalta@state.gov

The Consular Section is open for American Citizen Services Monday and Friday from 8:00-11:00 a.m. and Wednesdays from 1:00-4:00 p.m. All services are by appointment.

Entry/Exit Requirements for U.S. Citizens: Malta is a party to the Schengen Agreement. This means that U.S. citizens may enter Malta for up to 90 days for tourist or business purposes without a visa. The passport should be valid for at least three months beyond the period of stay. You need sufficient funds and a return airline ticket. For further information concerning entry requirements for Malta, travelers should contact the Embassy of Malta at 2017 Connecticut Avenue, NW, Washington DC 20008, tel.: (202) 462-3611, or the Maltese Consulate in New York City, tel.: (212) 725-2345.

The U.S. Department of State is unaware of any HIV/AIDS entry restrictions for visitors to or foreign residents of Malta.

Threats to Safety and Security: Malta remains largely free of terrorist incidents. No indigenous terrorist or extremist groups are known to be active in Malta and no foreign terrorist organization has carried out an attack against U.S. interests in Malta in recent years. U.S. Citizens are reminded to remain vigilant with regard to their personal security and to exercise caution.

Stay up to date by:

- Bookmarking our Bureau of Consular Affairs website, which contains the current Travel Warnings and Travel Alerts as well as the Worldwide Caution.
- Following us on Twitter and the Bureau of Consular Affairs page on Facebook as well.
- Downloading our free Smart Traveler IPhone App to have travel information at your fingertips.
- Calling 1-888-407-4747 toll-free within the U.S. and Canada, or a regular toll line, 1-202-501-4444, from other countries.
- Taking some time before travel to consider your personal security.

Crime: Malta has a low rate of violent crime. Practice the same good, common-sense personal security precautions that are part of everyday life in urban areas within the U.S., particularly when spending time in areas frequented by tourists. Secure your valuables and be aware of pickpockets and purse snatchers; such criminals focus on areas and establishments frequented by tourists. You should be careful in the Paceville nightclub area, where excessive drinking and poor crowd control can lead to violence, including some that appears to be racially motivated. Theft of unattended personal property and car stereos from vehicles is also a common problem. Panhandling is almost non-existent in Malta.

Don't buy counterfeit and pirated goods, even if they are widely available. Not only are the bootlegs illegal in the United States, if you purchase them you may also be breaking local law.

Victims of Crime: If you or someone you know becomes the victim of a crime abroad, you should contact the local police and the nearest U.S. embassy or consulate. We can:

- Replace a stolen passport.
- Put you in contact with the appropriate police authorities, and contact family members or friends.
- Help you locate appropriate medical care in cases of violent crimes, such as assault or rape.
- Although the local authorities are responsible for investigating and prosecuting the crime, consular officers can help you understand the local criminal justice process and can direct you to local attorneys.

Malta's crime victim assistance agency, APPOGG, can be reached by calling their support line (Tel: 179) or visiting their website.

The local equivalent to the "911" emergency line in Malta is 112.

Criminal Penalties: While you are traveling in Malta, you are subject to its laws even if you are a U.S. citizen. Foreign laws and legal systems can be vastly different than our own. These criminal penalties will vary from country to country. There are also some things that might be legal in the country you visit, but still illegal in the United States, and you can be prosecuted under U.S. law if you buy pirated goods. Engaging in sexual conduct with children or using or disseminating child pornography in a foreign country is a crime prosecutable in the United States.

If you break local laws in Malta, your U.S. passport won't help you avoid arrest or prosecution. It's very important to know what's legal and what's not where you are going. Penalties for possessing, using, or trafficking in illegal drugs in Malta are severe, and convicted offenders can expect long jail sentences and heavy fines. Judicial proceedings in Malta typically last five to seven years and are characterized by lengthy and sometimes unpredictable delays between hearings.

Foreign nationals can expect to be denied bail while a court case is ongoing, which can result in lengthy periods of pre-trial detention ranging from several months to several years. Obtaining no-fee legal aid can be a slow and difficult process, delaying already lengthy judicial proceedings.

If you are arrested in Malta, authorities of Malta are required to notify the nearest U.S. embassy or consulate of your arrest. If you are concerned the Department of State may not be aware of your situation, you should request the police or prison officials to notify the nearest U.S. embassy or consulate of your arrest.

Special Circumstances: Malta customs authorities may enforce strict regulations concerning currency restrictions and temporary importation into or export from Malta of items such as firearms, antiquities, or any item that might be deemed to have resale value. It is advisable to contact the Embassy of Malta in Washington or the Consulate of Malta in New York City for specific information regarding customs requirements. Malta's customs authorities encourage the use of an ATA (Admission Temporaire/Temporary Admission) Carnet for the temporary admission of professional equipment, commercial samples and/or goods for exhibitions and fair purposes. The U.S. Council for International Business issues and guarantees the ATA Carnet in the United States.

Accessibility: While in Malta, individuals with disabilities may find accessibility and accommodation very different from what you find in the United States. The law prohibits both the public and private sectors from discriminating against persons with disabilities in employment, education, health care, access to goods and services, housing, and insurance, and the government effectively enforced these provisions. That said, however, very few public or private spaces in Malta are wheelchair accessible. Many apartments lack elevators. Public transportation and most sidewalks or footpaths, including road crossings, are not accessible for those with mobility challenges. Taxis are readily available, but the cost is substantially higher than public buses.

Medical Facilities and Health Information: Medical care is available through public and private hospitals. The quality of medical care in Malta is excellent. Private hospitals generally offer a higher standard of service than the public hospitals.

Good information on vaccinations and other health precautions can be found via the Centers for Disease Control and Prevention (CDC) website. For information about outbreaks of infectious diseases abroad, consult the World Health Organization (WHO) website, which also contains additional health information for travelers, including detailed country-specific health information.

Medical Insurance: It's very important to find out BEFORE you leave whether or not your medical insurance will cover you overseas. You need to ask your insurance company two questions:

- Does my policy apply when I'm out of the U.S.?
- Will it cover emergencies like a trip to a foreign hospital or an evacuation?

In many places, doctors and hospitals still expect payment in cash at the time of service. Your regular U.S. health insurance may not cover doctor and hospital visits in other countries. If your policy doesn't go with you when you travel, it's a very good to take out another one for your trip.

Traffic Safety and Road Conditions: While in Malta, U.S. citizens may encounter road conditions that differ significantly from those in the United States. Traffic in Malta flows on the left, requiring attentiveness and caution from U.S. visitors accustomed to driving on the right. Additionally, Maltese drivers may drive more aggressively and with less caution than U.S. visitors are used to. Roads flood easily and are often narrow, winding and congested, with poor visibility around curves. Traffic arteries are prone to bottlenecks and accidents. Buses are the primary means of public transportation. Taxis are safe but expensive and are not metered; it is a good practice to agree with the driver in advance on the charge.

Aviation Safety Oversight: The U.S. Federal Aviation Administration (FAA) has assessed the Government of Malta's Civil Aviation Authority as being in compliance with International Civil Aviation Organization (ICAO) aviation safety standards for oversight of Malta's air carrier operations. Further information may be found on the FAA's safety assessment page.

Children's Issues: Please see the U.S. Dept. of State Office of Children's Issues web pages on intercountry adoption and international parental child abduction.

Intercountry Adoption

March 2009

The information in this section has been edited from the latest report available as of February 2013 from the State Department Bureau of Consular Affairs, Office of Overseas Citizens Services. For more information, please read the *Intercountry Adoption* section of this book and review current reports online at http://adoption.state.gov. Malta is party to the Hague Convention on Protection of Children and Co-operation in Respect of Intercountry Adoption (Hague Adoption Convention). Malta is not considered a country of origin in intercountry adoption.

While legally possible, intercountry adoption of a Maltese orphan by foreigners is unlikely. No Maltese orphans have received U.S. immigrant visas in the past five fiscal years. The information provided is intended primarily to assist in extremely rare adoption cases from Malta, including adoptions of Maltese children by relatives in the United States, as well as adoptions from third countries by Americans living in Malta.

Who Can Adopt? Adoption between the United States and Malta is governed by the Hague Adoption Convention. Therefore to adopt from Malta, you must first be found eligible to adopt by the U.S. Government. The U.S. Government agency responsible for making this determination is the Department of Homeland Security, U.S. Citizenship and Immigration Services (USCIS).

Residency Requirements: Prospective adoptive parents must be residents of Malta.

Age and Marriage Requirements: Applicants must be at least 21 years older, but not more than 45 years older, than the child to be adopted. Single persons must have reached the age of 28. A married couple must have been married and living together for at least three years, and one of the spouses must have attained the age of 28.

Other Requirements: Applicants must earn an income that meets or exceeds Malta's minimum wage. Income is evaluated during the home study phase.

Who Can Be Adopted? Because Malta is party to the Hague Adoption Convention, children from Malta must meet the requirements of the Convention in order to be eligible for adoption. For example, the Convention requires that Malta attempt to place a child with a family in-country before determining that a child is eligible for intercountry adoption. In addition to Malta's requirements, a child must meet the definition of a Convention adoptee for you to bring him or her back to the United States.

Adoption Authority: Department for Social Welfare Standards

The Process: Because Malta is party to the Hague Adoption Convention, adopting from Malta must follow a specific process designed to meet the Convention's requirements. For detailed and updated information on these requirements, please review the *Intercountry Adoption* section of this publication and visit the USCIS Intercountry Adoption website at http://adoption.state.gov.

Role of the Adoption Authority: The Department for Social Welfare Standards needs to be informed in writing of the prospective adoption and the prospective adoptive parents are required to submit a home study to the court upon notification.

Role of the Court: Adoptions in Malta are regulated by Civil Code provisions (Articles 113-130) and subsequent amendments, as well as recently enacted legislation (Adoption Administration Act of 2008) which will come into force on May 1, 2008. The laws take into account developments in child welfare, the suitability of pre-placement and placement, and are based on the principle that the adoption is done in the best interests of the child.

Adoption Application: Persons interested in adopting a child should seek the advice of the Department for Social Welfare Standards on the proper procedures to be followed. All prospective adoptive parents must complete an application form requesting a declaration of eligibility and suitability and will be required to attend preparation group sessions and a subsequent assessment. A declaration of eligibility and suitability is issued in favor of applicants who are deemed eligible as stipulated by

Act IV of the Adoption Administration Act of 2008 and by a social worker following submission of the home study report.

Role of Adoption Agencies: Persons interested in adoption in Malta should refer directly to the Ministry for Social Policy. For further information please visit their website: http://www.msp.gov.mt. For attorneys with relevant experience please consult the attorneys list on the American Embassy Website: http://malta.usembassy.gov.

Time Frame: 15 to 17 weeks.

Adoption Fees: No processing fees are incurred in making use of the service of the Department of Social Welfare Standards, Adoption Unit.

Documents Required:

- Government issued certified copy of birth certificate/s from the Government of Malta Public Registry.
- Government issued certified copy of marriage certificate from the Government of Malta Public Registry.
- Certificate/s of conduct from the police.
- Blood test for HIV and hepatitis.
- Medical report/s by a family doctor on a form obtainable from the Adoption Unit.
- Color photos of the applicants, sized 40mm x 30mm with a white background.
- Statement of family income from the Government of Malta Inland Revenue Service for the previous tax year.
- Psychological assessment.

Bringing Your Child Home: Once your adoption is complete (or you have obtained legal custody of the child), there are a few more steps to take before you can head home. Specifically, you need to apply for several documents for your child before he or she can travel to the United States, such as a birth certificate, a passport or travel document for your child from the country in which he or she was born, and a U.S. Immigration Visa. For detailed and updated information on how to obtain these documents, review the *Intercountry Adoption* section on this publication and visit the USCIS Intercountry Adoption website at http://adoption.state.gov.

Child Citizenship Act: For adoptions finalized abroad, the Child Citizenship Act of 2000 allows your new child to acquire American citizenship automatically when he or she enters the United States as lawful permanent residents. For adoptions finalized in the United States, the Child Citizenship Act of 2000 allows your new child to acquire American citizenship automatically when the court in the United States issues the final adoption decree. To learn more, review the *Intercountry Adoption* section on this publication and visit the USCIS Intercountry Adoption website at http://adoption.state.gov.

After Adoption: All adoptions are subject to Post-Adoption Reports and the adoptive parents are expected cooperate with the social worker in order for the report to be drawn up. In the case of a local adoption, the Post-Adoption Reports shall be drawn up for a period as specified by the accredited agency which in any case shall not exceed two years from the date of adoption. In the case of an inter-country adoption, the Post-Adoption Reports shall be drawn up for a specified period in accordance with the requirements of the country of origin and forwarded to the relevant authority in the country of origin, according to its requirements.

Embassy of the United States
Development House, 3rd Floor
St. Anne Street, Floriana,
Malta VLT 01
Mailing address:
P.O. Box 535, Valletta,
Malta, CMR 01
Telephone Number: (356) 2561 4000
Fax: (356) 21 243229
E-mail: usembmalta@state.gov
Internet: http://malta.usembassy.gov

U.S. Consulate General in Naples
Piazza della Republica
80122 Napoli, Italy
Tel. (+39) 081.5838.111
Fax: (+39) 081.7611.869
http://naples.usconsulate.gov

Malta's Adoption Authority
Department for Social Welfare Standards
Ministry for Social Policy
469, St. Joseph High Road
Santa Venera, Malta
Contact Person: Dr Kenneth Grech
Telephone: (356) 2144-1311
Fax: (356) 2144-7611, 2144-7621, 2149-0468

Embassy of Malta
2017 Connecticut Avenue, N.W.
Washington, D.C. 20008
Tel: (202) 387-5470
Malta_Embassy@compuserve.com

Office of Children's Issues
U.S. Department of State
2201 C Street, NW
SA-29
Washington, DC 20520
Tel: 1-888-407-4747
E-mail: AskCI@state.gov
Internet: http://adoption.state.gov

For questions about immigration procedures, call the National Customer Service Center (NCSC) 1-800-375-5283 (TTY 1-800-767-1833).

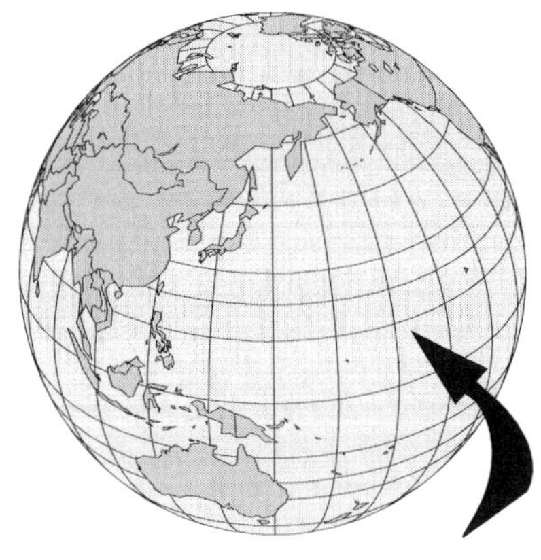

MARSHALL ISLANDS

Compiled from publications that were available as of February 2013 from the U.S. Department of State, the U.S. Department of Commerce, and the Central Intelligence Agency (CIA). See the introduction to this set for explanatory notes.

Official Name:
Republic of the Marshall Islands

PROFILE

Geography

Area: total: 181 sq km; country comparison to the world: 217; land: 181 sq km; water: 0 sq km

Major cities: Majuro (capital) 30,000 (2009)

Climate: tropical; hot and humid; wet season May to November; islands border typhoon belt

Terrain: low coral limestone and sand islands

People

Nationality: noun: Marshallese (singular and plural); adjective: Marshallese

Population: 68,480 (July 2012 est.)

Population growth rate: 1.874% (2012 est.)

Ethnic groups: Marshallese 92.1%, mixed Marshallese 5.9%, other 2% (2006)

Religions: Protestant 54.8%, Assembly of God 25.8%, Roman Catholic 8.4%, Bukot nan Jesus 2.8%, Mormon 2.1%, other Christian 3.6%, other 1%, none 1.5% (1999 census)

Languages: Marshallese (official) 98.2%, other languages 1.8% (1999 census)

Literacy: definition: age 15 and over can read and write; total population: 93.7%; male: 93.6%; female: 93.7% (1999)

Health: life expectancy at birth: total population: 72.03 years; male: 69.92 years; female: 74.25 years (2012 est.); Infant mortality rate: total: 22.93 deaths/1,000 live births; male: 25.79 deaths/1,000 live births; female: 19.92 deaths/1,000 live births (2012 est.)

Unemployment rate: 36% (2006 est.)

Work force: 14,680 (2000)

Government

Type: constitutional government in free association with the US; the Compact of Free Association entered into force on 21 October 1986 and the Amended Compact entered into force in May 2004

Independence: 21 October 1986

Constitution: 1 May 1979

Political subdivisions: 33 municipalities; Ailinginae, Ailinglaplap, Ailuk, Arno, Aur, Bikar, Bikini, Bokak, Ebon, Enewetak, Erikub, Jabat, Jaluit, Jemo, Kili, Kwajalein, Lae, Lib, Likiep, Majuro, Maloelap, Mejit, Mili, Namorik, Namu, Rongelap, Rongrik, Toke, Ujae, Ujelang, Utirik, Wotho, Wotje

Suffrage: 18 years of age; universal

Economy

GDP (purchasing power parity): $133.5 million (2008 est.); $115 million (2001 est.)

GDP real growth rate: -0.3% (2008 est.); 3.5% (2005 est.)

GDP per capita (PPP): $2,500 (2008 est.); $2,900 (2005 est.)

Natural resources: coconut products, marine products, deep seabed minerals

Agriculture products: coconuts, tomatoes, melons, taro, breadfruit, fruits; pigs, chickens

Industries: copra, tuna processing, tourism, craft items (from seashells, wood, and pearls)

Exports: $19.4 million (2008 est.); $9.1 million (2000 est.)

Exports—commodities: copra cake, coconut oil, handicrafts, fish

Imports: $79.4 million (2008 est.); $54.7 million (2000 est.)

Imports—commodities: foodstuffs, machinery and equipment, fuels, beverages and tobacco

Debt—external: $87 million (2008 est.); $86.5 million (FY99/00 est.)

Exchange rates: the US dollar is used

GEOGRAPHY

The Marshall Islands is comprised of 29 atolls and five single islands, which form two parallel groups—the

"Ratak" (sunrise) chain and the "Ralik" (sunset) chain. Over two-thirds of the nation's population lives in Majuro and Ebeye. The outer islands are sparsely populated due to lack of employment opportunities and economic development.

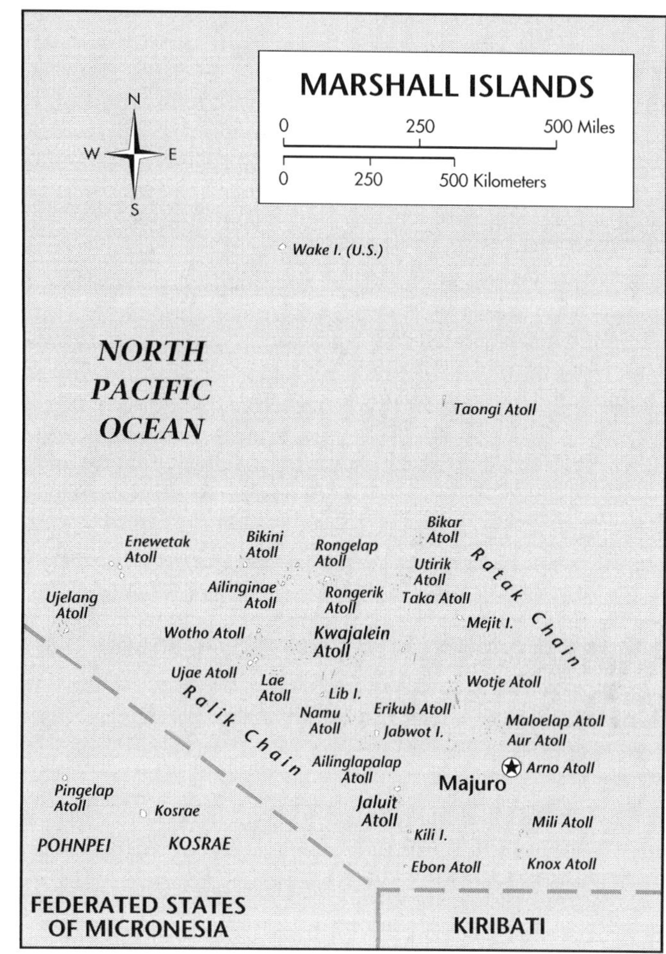

PEOPLE

The Marshallese are of Micronesian origin, which is traced to a combination of people who emigrated from Southeast Asia in the remote past. The matrilineal Marshallese culture revolves around a complex system of clans and lineages tied to land ownership.

Education

The public school system provides education through grade 12, although admission to secondary school is selective. The elementary program employs a bilingual/bicultural curriculum. English is introduced in the fourth grade. Many Marshallese and American observers have lamented the poor state of the public education system as a major stumbling block to economic development. The Marshall Islands' largest secondary institution—the 2-year College of the Marshall Islands—experienced U.S. accreditation problems between 2003 and 2008. However, thanks to an increase in funding, it has shown steady improvement and has now achieved full accreditation. The University of the South Pacific offers courses at a small campus on Majuro. Specialties taught on campus are marine resources and nursing as well as basic undergraduate education courses.

Religion

Major religious groups include the United Church of Christ (formerly Congregational), with 52 percent of the population; the Assemblies of God, 24 percent; the Roman Catholic Church, 9 percent; and The Church of Jesus Christ of Latter-day Saints (Mormons), 8 percent. Groups that constitute less than seven percent of the population include Bukot Non Jesus (also known as Assembly of God Part Two), Full Gospel, Baptists, Seventh-day Adventists, the Baha'i Faith, Jehovah's Witnesses, Jews, and Ahmadiyya Muslims.

Language

Marshallese is the official language. English is spoken to some extent by most of the adult urban population. However, both the Nitijela (parliament) and national radio use Marshallese.

HISTORY

Little is clearly understood about the prehistory of the Marshall Islands. Researchers agree on little more than that successive waves of migratory people from Southeast Asia spread across the Western Pacific about 3,000 years ago and that some of them landed on and remained on these islands. The Spanish explorer de Saavedra landed there in 1529. They were named for English explorer John Marshall, who visited them in 1799. The Marshall Islands were claimed by Spain in 1874.

Germany established a protectorate in 1885 and set up trading stations on the islands of Jaluit and Ebon to carry out the flourishing copra (dried coconut meat) trade. Marshallese iroij (high chiefs) continued to rule under indirect colonial German administration.

At the beginning of World War I, Japan assumed control of the Marshall Islands. Their headquarters remained at the German center of administration, Jaluit. U.S. Marines and Army troops took control from the Japanese in early 1944, following intense fighting on Kwajalein and Enewetak atolls. In 1947, the United States, as the occupying power, entered into an agreement with the UN Security Council to administer Micronesia, including the Marshall Islands, as the Trust Territory of the Pacific Islands.

On May 1, 1979, in recognition of the evolving political status of the Marshall Islands, the United States recognized the constitution of the Marshall Islands and the establishment of the Government of the Republic of the Marshall Islands. The constitution incorporates both American and British constitutional concepts.

GOVERNMENT AND POLITICAL CONDITIONS

The Republic of the Marshall Islands is a constitutional republic led by President Jurelang Zedkaia. On November 21, 2011, voters elected the Nitijela (parliament) in generally free and fair multiparty elections. The Nitijela, almost evenly divided between the two dominant political factions, is scheduled to elect a new president in January 2012.

Recent Elections

Executive power is centralized in the president and his cabinet. The legislature consists of the Nitijela and a council of chiefs (Iroij), the latter of which is an unelected body and serves a largely consultative function dealing with custom and traditional practices. National elections were held on November 21, 2011, and were generally free and fair.

Participation of Women and Minorities: There are no legal impediments to women's participation in government and politics; however, traditional attitudes of male dominance, women's cultural responsibilities and traditionally passive roles, and the generally early age of pregnancies made it difficult for women to obtain political qualifications or experience. There was one woman in the 33-member Nitijela who served as minister of health, and there were four women in the 12-seat House of Iroij. Since the country's founding there has always been a woman in the Nitijela, but never more than one.

In the November national election, seven women ran, and one was elected. Several women served in prominent appointed government positions, including those of minister, secretary of health, secretary of foreign affairs, director of the Social Security Administration, banking commissioner, and director of the Environmental Protection Agency.

There were no members of minorities in the legislature. There are few minorities in the country, and running for office requires land rights, which are only available to native Marshallese.

Principal Government Officials

Last Updated: 1/31/2013

Pres.: **Christopher Jorebon LOEAK**

Min. of Assistance to the Pres.: **Anton "Tony" DEBRUM**

Min. of Education: **Hilda HEINE**

Min. of Finance: **Dennis MOMOTARO**

Min. of Foreign Affairs: **Phillip H. MULLER**

Min. of Health: **David KABUA**

Min. of Internal Affairs: **Wilbur HEINE**

Min. of Justice: **Thomas HEINE**

Min. of Public Works: **Hiroshi YAMAMURA**

Min. of Resources & Development: **Michael KONELIOS**

Min. of Transportation & Communications: **Rien MORRIS**

Chief Sec.: **Casten N. NEMRA**

Commissioner, Bank of the Marshall Islands: **Ann Marie MULLER**

Ambassador to the US: **Charles Rudolph PAUL**

Permanent Representative to the UN, New York: **Amatlain Elizabeth KABUA**

ECONOMY

US Government assistance is the mainstay of this tiny island economy. The Marshall Islands received more than $1 billion in aid from the US from 1986–2002.

Agricultural production, primarily subsistence, is concentrated on small farms; the most important commercial crops are coconuts and breadfruit. Small-scale industry is limited to handicrafts, tuna processing, and copra.

The tourist industry, now a small source of foreign exchange employing less than 10% of the labor force, remains the best hope for future added income.

The islands have few natural resources, and imports far exceed exports. Under the terms of the Amended Compact of Free Association, the US will provide millions of dollars per year to the Marshall Islands (RMI) through 2023, at which time a Trust Fund made up of US and RMI contributions will begin perpetual annual payouts.

Government downsizing, drought, a drop in construction, the decline in tourism, and less income from the renewal of fishing vessel licenses have held GDP growth to an average of 1% over the past decade.

Labor Conditions

There is no law or regulation setting a minimum age for employment of children, and the government took no preventive measures during the year. Children typically were not employed in the wage economy, but it was common for children to assist their families in fishing, agriculture, retailing, and other small-scale enterprises. This was particularly true in the subsistence economies of the more remote atolls.

The law establishes a minimum wage of $2.00 per hour for both government and private-sector employees. This minimum wage has remained the same for over a decade, and there has been no legislation concerning maximum hours of work. No legislation exists that allows workers the right to remove themselves from situations that endanger their health or safety, and no legislation provides protection for workers who file official complaints about such conditions. The laws apply to foreign workers in the same workers in the same manner as indigenous citizens.

There are no official poverty levels. However, the bottom tax bracket (under which no taxes are assessed) is $1,560 annually.

Foreign employees and local trainees of private employers who had invested in or established a business in the country were exempt from minimum wage requirements. Most foreign workers—who constituted approximately 30 percent of the workforce (excluding agro-forestry) and most of the professional and technical classes in the country—earned considerably more than the minimum wage. Their earnings were estimated to average at least 50 percent higher than those of local workers.

On Sundays, most businesses are closed, and people generally refrained from working.

U.S.-MARSHALLESE RELATIONS

After gaining military control of the Marshall Islands from Japan in 1944, the United States assumed administrative control of the Marshall Islands under United Nations auspices as part of the Trust Territory of the Pacific Islands following the end of World War II. The Marshall Islands signed a Compact of Free Association with the United States in 1983 and gained independence in 1986 with the Compact's entry into force. From 1999–2003, the two countries negotiated an Amended Compact that entered into force in 2004.

The Marshall Islands is a sovereign nation. While the government is free to conduct its own foreign relations, it does so under the terms of the Compact. The United States has full authority and responsibility for security and defense of the Marshall Islands, and the Government of the Marshall Islands is obligated to refrain from taking actions that would be incompatible with these security and defense responsibilities. The United States and the Marshall Islands have full diplomatic relations.

The U.S. Department of Defense, under a subsidiary government-to-government agreement of the Compact, received permission to use parts of the lagoon and several islands on Kwajalein Atoll. The agreement allows the United States continued use of the U.S. Army Kwajalein Atoll missile test range until 2066 with an option until 2086. Another major subsidiary agreement of the original Compact provides for settlement of all claims arising from the U.S. nuclear tests conducted at Bikini and Enewetak Atolls from 1946 to 1958.

U.S. Assistance to the Marshall Islands

The Marshall Islands is an isolated, sparsely populated, low-lying Pacific island country consisting of approximately 70 sq. miles of land spread out over 750,000 sq. miles of ocean just north of the equator. These characteristics make it vulnerable to transnational threats, natural disasters, and effects of climate change. U.S. assistance focuses on supporting health, education and infrastructure in the Marshall Islands, as well as the RMI's ability to perform maritime security functions and strengthen climate resilience through disaster preparedness.

Under the Compact, as amended, the U.S. provides the Marshall Islands with approximately $70 million annually through FY 2023, including contributions to a jointly managed trust fund and financial assistance from other U.S. Federal Grants. Marshallese citizens also continue to have access to many U.S. programs and services. A Joint Economic Management and Financial Accountability Committee with members from both governments has been established to strengthen management and accountability with regard to assistance provided under the Compact, as amended, and to promote effective use of the funding provided.

A number of U.S. Government agencies operate programs or render assistance to the Marshall Islands. These include the Federal Aviation Administration, the U.S. Postal Service, the Small Business Administration, the U.S. Agency for International Development, the Department of Energy, the Department of Agriculture, the Department of Health and Human Services, the Department of Education, the Department of State, and the Department of the Interior. Compact grants are primarily funded through and implemented by the Department of the Interior.

Bilateral Economic Relations

The economy of the Marshall Islands is closely linked to that of the United States, and its GDP is derived mainly from U.S. payments under the terms of the Compact of Free Association. Through the Compact, the United States provides significant financial support to the Republic of the Marshall Islands to help achieve the Compact goals of economic self-sufficiency. The United States is one of the Marshall Islands' top trading partners, and the Marshall Islands has expressed interest in attracting U.S. investment. The Marshall Islands sells fishing rights to other nations as a source of income. Under the multilateral U.S.-Pacific Islands tuna fisheries treaty, the U.S. provides an annual grant to Pacific island parties, including the Marshall Islands, for access by licensed U.S. fishing vessels.

Marshall Islands's Membership in International Organizations

The Marshall Islands and the United States belong to a number of the same international organizations, including the United Nations, International Monetary Fund, World Bank, and Asian Development Bank. The Marshall Islands also belongs to the Pacific Islands Forum, of which the United States is a Dialogue Partner.

Bilateral Representation

The Marshall Islands maintains an embassy in the United States at 2433 Massachusetts Avenue NW, Washington, DC 20008 (tel. 202-234-5414).

Principal U.S. Embassy Officials

Last Updated: 1/14/2013

MAJURO (E) PO:BOX 1379, Majuro MH 96960, 692-247-4011, Fax 011 (692) 247-4012/5371, Workweek: 8:00 am to 5:00 pm, Website: http://majuro.usembassy.gov/

DCM OMS:	Erin Jacobs
AMB OMS:	Erin Jacobs
DCM/CHG:	Doug Carey
MGT:	Doug Carey
MLO/ODC:	Tom Maus
OMS:	Erin Jacobs
POL/ECON:	Andrew Zvirzdin
POL/MIL:	Tom Maus
POSHO:	Fred Reichard
AMB:	Tom Armbruster
CON:	Andrew Zvirzdin
DCM:	Doug Carey
PAO:	Doug Carey
GSO:	Fred Reichard
RSO:	Jeff Jacob
EEO:	Darlene Korok
IMO:	Fred Reichard
IPO:	Fred Reichard
ISO:	Fred Reichard
ISSO:	Fred Reichard
POL:	Andrew Zvirzdin
State ICASS:	Doug Carey

TRAVEL

Consular Information Sheet

April 13, 2012

Country Description: With a population of approximately 53,000, the Republic of the Marshall Islands totals 70.5 square miles. The country consists of 29 atolls and five islands. The Marshall Islands is a parliamentary democracy, and its close relationship with the United States is memorialized in the Compact of Free Association between the two nations. It has a developing agrarian and service-oriented economy. Limited tourist facilities exist, including three major hotels in Majuro, while most other areas have limited guest quarters. For general information, please visit the Marshall Islands' national tourist office website.

Smart Traveler Enrollment Program (STEP)/Embassy Locations: If you are going to live in or visit the Marshall Islands, please take the time to tell our Embassy about your trip. If you enroll, we can keep you up to date with important safety and security announcements. It will also help your friends and family get in touch with you in an emergency. If you have no access to the Internet, you may enroll directly with the U.S. Embassy in Majuro.

The U.S. Embassy in Majuro
(no street address)
Located on the ocean-side of the island's major road, approximately two miles east of the airport.
P.O. Box 1379
Majuro, MH 96960–1379
Telephone: (692) 247-4011
Facsimile: (692) 247-4012

Entry/Exit Requirements for U.S. Citizens: Under the Compact of Free Association, if you are a U.S. citizen, you do not need a visa to enter the Marshall Islands. However, there is a departure fee of $20. Diplomats are exempt from this fee. In addition, for visits over 30 days or if you arrive from an area that is having a health epidemic, a health certificate may be required. Visit the Embassy of the Republic of the Marshall Islands 'website for the most current visa information.

Some HIV/AIDS entry restrictions exist for visitors to and foreign residents of the Marshall Islands. HIV testing is required for temporary visitors staying more than 30 days and applicants for residence and work permits. Foreign test results are accepted under certain conditions. Please verify this information with the Embassy of the Republic of the Marshall Islands before you travel.

Threats to Safety and Security:

Stay up to date by:

- Bookmarking our Bureau of Consular Affairs website, which contains the current Travel Warnings and Travel Alerts as well as the Worldwide Caution.
- Following us on Twitter and the Bureau of Consular Affairs page on Facebook as well.
- Downloading our free Smart Traveler iPhone App to have travel information at your fingertips.
- Calling 1-888-407-4747 toll-free within the U.S. and Canada, or a regular toll line, 1-202-501-4444, from other countries.
- Taking some time before travel to consider your personal security.

Crime: Travel around the Marshall Islands is, by most standards, considered safe. The Marshall Islands has a relatively low crime rate. The most common crimes are break-ins and thefts from homes, hotel rooms, and vehicles, as well as occasional random acts of vandalism. There have been a few recent but isolated incidents in which non-U.S. foreigners were assaulted. It is recommended that visitors dress conservatively; skin showing above the knee, especially for females, may be considered offensive to some Marshallese citizens. Keep your hotel room or residence locked at all times. Occasionally, fights and assaults occur at nightclubs and bars. If you visit those establishments, especially late in the evening, be extra vigilant to ensure your personal security.

Don't buy counterfeit or pirated goods, even if they are widely available. Not only are the bootlegs illegal in the United States, you may be breaking local law too.

Victims of Crime: If you or someone you know becomes the victim of a crime abroad, you should contact the local police and the nearest U.S. embassy or consulate. We can:

- Replace a stolen passport.
- Help you find appropriate medical care if you are the victim of violent crimes such as assault or rape.
- Put you in contact with the appropriate police authorities, and if you want us to, we can contact family members or friend.
- Help you understand the local criminal justice process and direct you to local attorneys, although it is important to remember that local authorities are responsible for investigating and prosecuting the crime.

The local equivalent to the "911" emergency line in the Marshall Islands is "911" or "1911."

Criminal Penalties: While you are traveling in the Marshall Islands, you are subject to its laws even if you are a U.S. citizen. Foreign laws and legal systems can be vastly different than our own. There are also some things that might be legal in the country you visit, but still illegal in the United States, and you can be prosecuted under U.S. law if you buy pirated goods.

Engaging in sexual conduct with children or using or disseminating child pornography in a foreign country is a crime prosecutable in the United States. If you break local laws in the Marshall Islands, your U.S. passport won't help you avoid arrest or prosecution. It's very important to know what's legal and what's not wherever you go.

While some countries will automatically notify the nearest U.S. embassy or consulate if a U.S. citizen is detained or arrested in a foreign country, that might not always be the case. To ensure that the United States is aware of your circumstances, request that the police and prison officials notify the nearest U.S. embassy or consulate as soon as you are arrested or detained overseas.

Accessibility: While in the Marshall Islands, individuals with disabilities may find accessibility and accommodation very different from what you find in the United States. There are no mandated rules for special support for persons with disabilities. There are few ramps, almost no sidewalks, and few operational elevators in the Marshall Islands. The public transportation system is nonexistent, and the old cars used as taxis are inexpensive and widely available. The main city has one road, and there are no street addresses or house numbers. Medical facilities have generally limited and inadequate accessibility. On outer atolls, there is no transportation for evacuation to the rudimentary medical facilities on the two atolls with hospitals (Majuro and Kwajalein). Visitors to the Marshall Islands should have medical evacuation insurance and be in good health.

Currency: The Republic of the Marshall Islands uses U.S. dollars. The two ATMs on Majuro can be found at the Bank of Guam and at Robert Reimers Resort. A few hotels and restaurants accept Visa, MasterCard, and American Express credit cards. Most transactions are cash only.

Customs: Customs authorities of the Marshall Islands strictly prohibit the importation of firearms, ammunition, explosives, and indecent publications. Certification from the Quarantine Division is required to import animals, plants, and fruits. We advise you to contact the Embassy of the Republic of the Marshall Islands or one of the Marshall Islands' consulates in the United States for specific information regarding customs requirements, especially when dealing with the importation of animals into the Marshall Islands.

Communication: The Marshall Islands relies primarily on radio in the remote outer islands, which causes some communication problems. Local telephone service as well as worldwide international long distance is available on Majuro and Ebeye. The cost for international calls is quite expensive. Internet service is also available and is relatively expensive.

Flights: United Airlines flies once a day through Majuro, six days a week. Flights in and out of the Marshall Islands are three days a week to the west toward Guam, and three days a week east to Honolulu. Although Air Marshall Islands operates within the Marshall Islands; service is not reliable. Be aware that flights and boats to and from outer islands are often cancelled, sometimes leaving visitors stranded for one or more weeks.

Medical Facilities and Health Information: Health facilities in Majuro and Ebeye are adequate for routine medical problems. There are few or no health facilities available elsewhere in the Marshall Islands. Majuro has a private clinic and a public hospital. Ebeye also has a public hospital. Most outer islands have medical dispensaries. Serious medical problems requiring hospitalization and/or medical evacuation to the United States can cost tens of thousands of dollars. Prescription and over the counter medicine may not be available. We recommend that you bring a supply of your prescription medication when you visit. Doctors and hospitals often expect immediate cash payment for health services. However, the local cost for service is quite minimal.

You can find good information on vaccinations and other health precautions on the CDC website. For information about outbreaks of infectious diseases abroad, consult the World Health Organization (WHO) website. The WHO website also contains additional health information for travelers, including detailed country-specific health information.

Tuberculosis is an increasingly serious health concern in the Marshall Islands. For further information, please consult the CDC's information on TB. The incidence of tuberculosis (TB) is high, and there are a few cases of multidrug-resistant tuberculosis (MDRTB) currently under quarantine or receiving treatment.

Medical Insurance: You can't assume your insurance will go with you when you travel. It's very important to find out BEFORE you leave whether or not your medical insurance will cover you overseas. You need to ask your insurance company two questions:

- Does my policy apply when I'm out of the United States?
- Will it cover emergencies like a trip to a foreign hospital or a medical evacuation?

In many places, doctors and hospitals still expect payment in cash at the time of service. Your regular U.S. health insurance may not cover doctor and hospital visits in other countries. If your policy doesn't go with you when you travel, it's a very good idea to take out another one for your trip.

Traffic Safety and Road Conditions: While in the Marshall Islands, you may encounter road conditions that differ significantly from those in the United States. The information below concerning the Marshall Islands is provided for general reference only and may not be totally accurate in a particular location or circumstance.

Majuro atoll has only one main road. The road is paved, but there are few traffic signs and no traffic lights. While driving, you should be alert for dogs, chickens, and pigs roaming the streets and children darting into the road. Children frequently play dangerous games with vehicles, running in front of or behind vehicles. Drinking and driving is common, especially on the weekends, so use caution. Walking beside the street can be dangerous due to poor lighting, absence of sidewalks, and drivers who may have been drinking.

Vehicle traffic proceeds slowly, rarely over 25 miles per hour. Roads experience temporary flooding after heavy rains and during especially high tides. Since there are few streetlights, visibility is poor, and night driving requires special caution. For specific information concerning drivers' permits, vehicle inspection, road tax, and mandatory insurance, please contact the Embassy of the Republic of the Marshall Islands.

Aviation Safety Oversight: The U.S. Federal Aviation Administration (FAA) has assessed the government of the Marshall Islands' Civil Aviation Authority as being in compliance with International Civil Aviation Organization (ICAO) aviation safety standards for oversight of its air carrier operations. Further information may be found on the FAA's safety assessment page.

Children's Issues: Please see the U.S. Dept. of State Office of Children's Issues web pages on intercountry adoption and international parental child abduction.

Intercountry Adoption

June 2010

The information in this section has been edited from the latest report available as of February 2013 from the State Department Bureau of Consular Affairs, Office of Overseas Citizens Services. For more information, please read the *Intercountry Adoption* section of this book and review current reports online at http://adoption.state.gov.

The Republic of the Marshall Islands (Marshall Islands) is not party to the Hague Convention on Protection of Children and Co-operation in Respect of Intercountry Adoption (Hague Adoption Convention). Therefore, when the Hague Adoption Convention entered into force for the United States on April 1, 2008, intercountry adoption processing for Marshall Islands did not change.

Although the "Compact of Free Association" between Marshall Islands and the United States permits Marshallese citizens to travel to and live in the United States without a U.S. visa, this provision is NOT applicable to adopted children who will reside permanently with American families in the United States. Prospective adoptive parents of Marshallese children must go through the appropriate Marshallese adoption procedures as well as the relevant U.S. immigration procedures related to adopted foreign orphans. Adopted Marshallese children who enter the United States without a visa will later have difficulties adjusting their U.S. immigration status and, eventually, acquiring U.S. citizenship.

Who Can Adopt? To bring an adopted child to the United States from Marshall Islands, you must be found eligible to adopt by the U.S. Government. The U.S. Government agency responsible for making this determination is the Department of Homeland Security, U.S. Citizenship and Immigration Services (USCIS).

Residency Requirements: The government has no specific requirement or policy as regards the citizenship or residency of foreign prospective adoptive parents.

Age Requirements: Any person "of the age of majority" can petition to adopt a child; however the petitioner has to be at least 15 years older than the child to be adopted.

Marriage Requirements: Under Marshallese law, both married couples and single individuals may adopt Marshallese children. However, same sex couples, or an individual living as a member of a same sex couple, are not eligible to petition to adopt.

Income Requirements: There is no minimum income requirement for adoptive parents, as long as Marshallese authorities deem the prospective adoptive parents "suitable."

Other Requirements: Potential adopting family must have a home study completed by an agency that is licensed by a recognized state or government child care agency. The home study must include the following about the petitioners:

- educational background and future educational plans;
- employment history, current status and any changes in the foreseeable future;

- income history and future projections, if available;
- history of prior marriages, if any, including the basis for divorce, the age and gender of each child, the history of child support for and current relationship with those children;
- history of current marriage, age and gender of each child already in the home, and detailed report of any prior adoption experiences;
- participation in any civic or religious activity of prospective parents;
- nationwide criminal background search in the country of residence or citizenship of the prospective parent(s); and
- original child abuse records search.

The petition must also include:

- certified copy of petitioner's marriage certificate;
- certified birth certificate of each petitioner;
- photocopy of each petitioner's passport;
- doctor's statement attesting to physical; and
- mental capability of petitioner to adopt.

Who Can Be Adopted? Marshall Islands has specific requirements that a child must meet in order to be eligible for adoption. You cannot adopt a child in Marshall Islands unless he or she meets the requirements outlined below. In addition to these requirements, a child must meet the definition of an orphan under U.S. law for you to bring him or her back to the United States.

Eligibility Requirements: The Central Adoption Authority ("CAA"), the government-established office in the Ministry of Internal Affairs, oversees the adoption process. The CAA oversees the execution of an "Affidavit of Relinquishment of Parental Rights and Consent to Adoption and Emigration" by the birth parent(s).

The High Court hearing to petition the child may not occur sooner than 30 after the birth parent(s) sign the Affidavit of Relinquishment. "Abandonment" means the failure to provide financial support to the child; or knowingly failing to provide a normal parent-child relationship with the child for a period of six or more months, and deliberately failing to arrange for the provision of care and supervision of a child by another adult or adults who are willing and able to care for the child.

Age Requirements: No child 16 years of age or over may be adopted. If the child to be adopted is 12 years of age or older, the Court will examine the child to determine the child's understanding of the adoption before the child issued his/her consent to the adoption. If a child 12 years or older objects to the adoption, such objection is controlling. If a child under 12 years objects, the Court will determine whether the adoption is in the child's best interest, but the child's objection is not controlling.

Waiting Period: The High Court hearing to petition the child may not occur before 30 days have passed since the birth parent(s) sign the Affidavit of Relinquishment.

Adoption Authority: The Central Adoption Authority ("CAA") was established through the Adoptions Act of 2002. The CAA is in the Ministry of Internal Affairs and is responsible for the supervision of all adoption proceedings in the Marshall Islands. The duties of the CAA include:

- To serve as a central receiving point for all referrals of children to be adopted;
- Conduct investigations into the backgrounds and circumstances under which an adoption is being processed by the natural parents;
- Provide case management services to natural parents and children, including: birth parent counseling as to options for realistic and effective parenting, including the possibility of traditional or foreign adoption;
- Pre-natal nutrition and medical referral services to the birth mother in cooperation with other government agencies, departments, or ministries, as appropriate;
- Coordinating with licensed agencies in monitoring the quality of applications, and providing a recommendation to the Court on individual applications;
- For children whose consent to adoption is required, provide counseling to ascertain the child's wishes regarding adoption;
- Monitor post-adoption progress in coordination with the foreign agencies;
- Providing a resource to adoptive parents for post-adoption consultation on issues related to the adoption.

The Process: The first step in adopting a child from Marshall Islands is usually to select a licensed agency in the United States that can help with your adoption. Adoption service providers must be licensed by the U.S. state in which they operate. The U.S. adoption agency must contact the CAA in Marshall Islands to determine requirements. The U.S. Embassy in Majuro recommends that prospective adopting parents retain the services of a Marshallese attorney.

Role of the Court: The High Court determines the eligibility of an adopting parent(s) based on submitted evidence required by the Adoptions Act of 2002. Prospective adoptive parents must petition the High Court for adoption. There is a hearing at which the prospective adoptive parent(s) must appear.

Role of Adoption Agencies: Adoption agencies interact with the CAA to match children with prospective adoptive parent(s). These must be licensed by a state or government licensing board and need a locally licensed lawyer to appear before the High Court.

Adoption Application: Prospective adoptive parents must petition the court for adoption (see above).

Time Frame: The U.S. Embassy in Majuro has indicated that Marshallese adoptions generally take from three to seven months to complete.

Adoption Fees: Fees are determined by the Adoption Agency and can run from $17,000 to $25,000, not including travel and hotel expenses.

Documents Required: In cases where biological parents can be located, the High Court requires relinquishment and/or consent by the birth parent.

Most adoptions are orphan adoptions where the birth mother does not or cannot identify the father and no male has stepped up to claim the child or show any interest in the child.

After you finalize the adoption (or gain legal custody) in Marshall Islands, the U.S Government, Department of Homeland Security, U.S. Citizenship and Immigration Services (USCIS) MUST determine whether the child is eligible under U.S. law to be adopted (Form I-600).

Bringing Your Child Home: Once your adoption is complete (or you have obtained legal custody of the child), there are a few more steps to take before you can head home. Specifically, you need to apply for several documents for your child before he or she can travel to the United States, such as a birth certificate, a passport or travel document for your child from the country in which he or she was born, and a U.S. Immigration Visa. For detailed and updated information on how to obtain these documents, review the *Intercountry Adoption* section on this publication and visit the USCIS Intercountry Adoption website at http://adoption.state.gov.

Child Citizenship Act: For adoptions finalized abroad, the Child Citizenship Act of 2000 allows your new child to acquire American citizenship automatically when he or she enters the United States as lawful permanent residents. For adoptions finalized in the United States, the Child Citizenship Act of 2000 allows your new child to acquire American citizenship automatically when the court in the United States issues the final adoption decree.

After Adoption: The adoptive parents must arrange for a post-adoption home visit during the first six months after the adoption and must file a Post-Adoption Report with the CAA at the conclusion of the six months period. The Post-Adoption Report must contain a description of how the child and family are adjusting, whether bonding and attachment between the child and family are sufficient, whether the child's health and emotional needs are being met, what the family is doing to encourage the child's cultural heritage, and any other pertinent date sufficient to inform the natural families of the status of the child.

U.S. Embassy in Majuro
PO BOX 1379
Majuro, MH 96960
Marshall Islands
Tel: (692) 247-4011
Fax: (692) 247-4012

Embassy of The Republic of the Marshall Islands
2433 Massachusetts Ave NW
Washington, DC 20008
Tel: (202) 234-5414
www.rmiembassyus.org

Office of Children's Issues
U.S. Department of State
2201 C Street, NW
SA-29
Washington, DC 20520
Tel: 1-888-407-4747
E-mail: AskCI@state.gov
adoption.state.gov

MAURITANIA

Compiled from publications that were available as of February 2013 from the U.S. Department of State, the U.S. Department of Commerce, and the Central Intelligence Agency (CIA). See the introduction to this set for explanatory notes.

Official Name:
Islamic Republic of Mauritania

PROFILE

Geography

Area: total: 1,030,700 sq km; country comparison to the world: 29; land: 1,030,700 sq km; water: 0 sq km

Major cities: Nouakchott (capital) 709,000 (2009)

Climate: desert; constantly hot, dry, dusty

Terrain: mostly barren, flat plains of the Sahara; some central hills

People

Nationality: noun: Mauritanian(s); adjective: Mauritanian

Population: 3,359,185 (July 2012 est.)

Population growth rate: 2.323% (2012 est.)

Ethnic groups: mixed Moor/black 40%, Moor 30%, black 30%

Religions: Muslim (official) 100%

Languages: Arabic (official and national), Pulaar, Soninke, Wolof (all national languages), French, Hassaniya

Literacy: definition: age 15 and over can read and write; total population: 58%; male: 64.9%; female: 51.2% (2010 est.)

Health: life expectancy at birth: total population: 61.53 years; male: 59.3 years; female: 63.82 years (2012 est.); Infant mortality rate: total: 58.93 deaths/1,000 live births; male: 64.02 deaths/1,000 live births; female: 53.7 deaths/1,000 live births (2012 est.)

Unemployment rate: 30% (2008 est.)

Work force: 1.318 million (2007)

Government

Type: military junta

Independence: 28 November 1960

Constitution: 12 July 1991

Political subdivisions: 13 regions (wilayas, singular—wilaya); Adrar, Assaba, Brakna, Dakhlet Nouadhibou, Gorgol, Guidimaka, Hodh ech Chargui, Hodh el Gharbi, Inchiri, Nouakchott, Tagant, Tiris Zemmour, Trarza

Suffrage: 18 years of age; universal

Economy

GDP (purchasing power parity): $7.615 billion (2012 est.); $7.184 billion (2011 est.); $6.932 billion (2010 est.); $6.597 billion (2009 est.)

GDP real growth rate: 5.3% (2012 est.); 3.6% (2011 est.); 5.1% (2010 est.); -1.2% (2009 est.)

GDP per capita (PPP): $2,100 (2012 est.); $2,200 (2011 est.); $2,200 (2010 est.); $2,100 (2009 est.)

Natural resources: iron ore, gypsum, copper, phosphate, diamonds, gold, oil, fish

Agriculture products: dates, millet, sorghum, rice, corn; cattle, sheep

Industries: fish processing, oil production, mining (iron ore, gold, and copper)

Exports: $2.878 billion (2012 est.); $2.799 billion (2011 est.); $2.041 billion (2010 est.)

Exports—commodities: iron ore, fish and fish products, gold, copper, petroleum

Exports—partners: China 46.6%, Italy 8.8%, France 8.1%, Cote dIvoire 5.1%, Spain 4.6%, Japan 4.5%, Belgium 4.3%, Netherlands 4% (2011)

Imports: $3.152 billion (2012 est.); $2.854 billion (2011 est.); $2.038 billion (2010 est.)

Imports—commodities: machinery and equipment, petroleum products, capital goods, foodstuffs, consumer goods

Imports—partners: China 12.6%, Netherlands 9.1%, France 8.8%, US 7.9%, Spain 5.9%, Germany 5.5%, Brazil 5.2%, Belgium 4.4% (2011)

Debt—external: $2.942 billion (31 December 2012 est.); $2.816 billion (31 December 2011 est.); $2.351 billion (31 December 2010 est.)

Exchange rates: ouguiyas (MRO) per US dollar; 267.8 (2012 est.); 281.12 (2011 est.); 275.89 (2010 est.); 262.4 (2009); 238.2 (2008); 258.6 (2007)

PEOPLE

National/Racial/Ethnic Minorities

Ethnic minorities faced governmental discrimination. The inconsistent issuance of national identification cards, which were required for voting, effectively disenfranchised many members of southern minority groups. Racial and cultural tension and discrimination also arose from the geographic and cultural divides between Moors and Afro-Mauritanians. The Moors are divided among numerous ethnolinguistic tribal and clan groups and further distinguished as either White Moor or Black Moor, although it was often difficult to distinguish between the two by skin color. White Moor tribes and clans, many of whom are dark-skinned after centuries of intermarriage with Berbers and sub-Saharan African groups, dominated positions in government and business. The Black Moors (also called haratines or freed slaves) remained politically and economically weaker than White Moors. Afro-Mauritanian ethnic groups, which include the Halpulaar (the largest non-Moor group), Wolof, and Soninke, are concentrated in the South and urban areas. Afro-Mauritanians were underrepresented in the government and military.

Language

The constitution designates Arabic as the official language and Arabic, Pulaar, Soninke, and Wolof as the country's national languages. The government continued to encourage French and Arabic bilingualism within the school system, as opposed to earlier efforts at "arabization." Neither the Afro-Mauritanian national languages nor the local Hassaniya Arabic dialect were used as languages of instruction.

Religion

Almost the entire population practices Sunni Islam. There are very small numbers of non-Muslims, who are almost exclusively foreigners. Roman Catholic and other Christian churches are located in Nouakchott, Atar, Zouerate, Nouadhibou, and Rosso. Although there are no synagogues, a very small number of foreign residents practices Judaism.

There are several foreign faith-based nongovernmental organizations (NGOs) active in humanitarian and developmental work in the country.

HISTORY

At the crossroads of the Arab North and sub-Saharan Africa, Mauritania is a vast but sparsely populated country of some 3 million inhabitants whose capital Nouakchott (population: approximately 1 million) is on the Atlantic coast of Africa. Ancient cities in the interior were important Saharan trade centers from the Ghana Empire through the expansion of Arab civilization and into modern times. The largest of these, Chinguetti, is the seventh-holiest site in Islam.

European colonization came relatively late to Mauritania, which at its independence from France in 1960 was still administered from St. Louis, Senegal. Today's capital, Nouakchott, was a small outpost midway between that city and Port Etienne, now called Nouadhibou, Mauritania's commercial capital. At independence, much of the country's population followed a nomadic lifestyle or worked in agriculture in remote areas mostly untouched by colonial administration. Traditional slavery was formally abolished in 1980. As a result of centuries of this practice, Mauritanian society is characterized by former slave-owning groups of Arab-Berber origin, known as White Moors, and the Black Moor descendants of their liberated slaves who generally lived in the northern and eastern regions. Black African communities, also marked by slavery, traditionally resided in the southern part of the country near the Senegal River.

Ethnic tensions persist in Mauritania. In April 1989 violence broke out between communities, stemming from a schism between Arab-Berber and Black African communities. Over the next 2 years the "1989 events" resulted in Mauritania's deportation of Black African citizens to Senegal and Mali, state-sponsored killings, and the purge of tens of thousands of Black Africans from the military and government and their expulsion. In 2010, the UN High Commissioner for Refugees concluded its program of repatriating Mauritanian citizens from Senegal, a significant milestone in Mauritania's efforts to resolve this decades-long refugee problem, also known as thc passif humanitaire.

GOVERNMENT AND POLITICAL CONDITIONS

Mauritania is a highly centralized Islamic republic with a president as head of state. The legislative function is exercised by the Senate and National Assembly, the former consisting of representatives chosen indirectly by municipal councilors and the latter directly elected by the voters. The legislative bodies were weak relative to the executive. The election of Mohamed Ould Abdel Aziz as president in 2009 ended a political crisis caused by Aziz's 2008 coup d'etat against then president Sidi Ould Cheikh Abdallahi. International observers declared the 2009 presidential election to be generally free and fair. In 2009 the majority party, Union for the Republic (UPR), won most of the seats in the indirect election to refill one-third of the Senate seats. The government indefinitely postponed new Senate, National Assembly, and municipal elections scheduled to take place during the year in accordance with the opposition's initial request, although controversy over the constitutionality of the election timetable continued throughout the year.

Recent Elections

In an election held in 2009, former High State Council leader General Aziz won 53 percent of the vote. Although some opposition groups

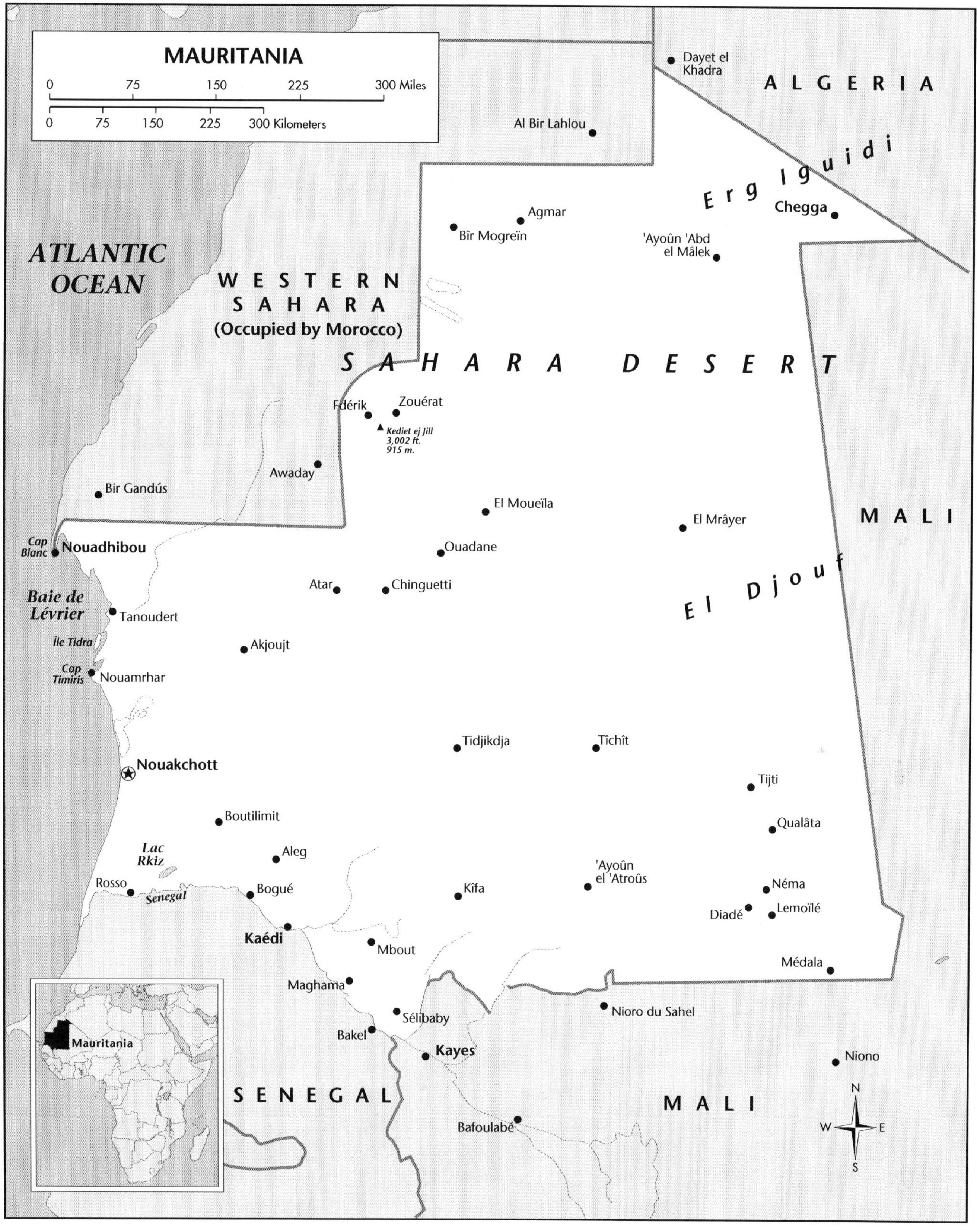
MAURITANIA
0 75 150 225 300 Miles
0 75 150 225 300 Kilometers
ATLANTIC OCEAN
WESTERN SAHARA
(Occupied by Morocco)
ALGERIA
MALI
SENEGAL
SAHARA DESERT
Erg Iguidi
El Djouf
Dayet el Khadra
Al Bir Lahlou
Agmar
Bîr Mogreïn
Chegga
'Ayoûn 'Abd el Mâlek
Fdérik
Zouérat
Kediet ej Jill 3,002 ft. 915 m.
Awaday
Bir Gandús
Cap Blanc
Nouadhibou
El Moueïla
El Mrâyer
Ouadane
Atar
Chinguetti
Baie de Lévrier
Tanoudert
Île Tidra
Akjoujt
Cap Timiris
Nouamrhar
Tidjikdja
Tîchît
Nouakchott
Tijti
Boutilimit
Qualâta
Lac Rkiz
Aleg
'Ayoûn el 'Atroûs
Rosso
Senegal
Bogué
Kîfa
Néma
Diadé
Lemoïlé
Kaédi
Mbout
Médala
Maghama
Sélibaby
Nioro du Sahel
Bakel
Kayes
Mauritania
Niono
Bafoulabé
N
W
E
S

claimed the election was fraudulent and requested an investigation, the Constitutional Council certified the election.

Elections by municipal councils to fill one-third of the seats in the Senate, also in 2009, resulted in a large win for the UPR. Opposition and independent candidates denounced what they characterized as heavy pressure on the municipal councilors to vote for majority party candidates and on independent candidates to withdraw. Authorities did not investigate these complaints.

Indirect elections for another one third of the Senate seats were originally scheduled for April 24, but they were postponed twice due to the inability of the government and a coalition of opposition parties to agree on the opposition's demand that the electoral code be rewritten, the ruling coalition dissolved, and laws regulating the media reformed. The opposition coalition indicated it would not participate in elections until its demands were met. The majority and opposition parties engaged in a national dialogue from September 17 to October 19 to resolve their political impasse, but no timetable for Senate, National Assembly, or municipal elections had been established at year's end. The Constitutional Council subsequently ruled that a delay of parliamentary elections through May 2012 would be legal.

Participation of Women and Minorities: There were 18 women in the National Assembly and six in the 56-seat Senate. The 27-member cabinet included three women, three Black Moors, and five Afro-Mauritanians. The law requires that women make up at least 20 percent of candidates on legislative candidate lists. It was observed in practice.

Principal Government Officials

Last Updated: 1/31/2013

Pres.: **Mohamed Ould Abdel AZIZ**

Prime Min.: **Moulaye Ould Mohamed LAGHDAF**

Min. of Commerce, Handicraft, & Tourism: **Bamba Ould DARAMANE**

Min. of Communications & Relations With Parliament: **Hamdi Ould MAHJOUB**

Min. of Culture, Youth, & Sports: **Cisse Mint Cheikh Ould BOIDE**

Min. of Economics & Development: **Sidi Ould TAH**

Min. of Education: **Ahmed Ould BAHYA**

Min. of Energy, Oil, & Mines: **Taleb Ould Abdi VALL**

Min. of Equipment & Transportion: **Yahya HADEMINE**

Min. of Finance: **Thiam DIOMBAR**

Min. of Fisheries & Maritime Economy: **Aghdhefna Ould EYIH**

Min. of Foreign Affairs & Cooperation: **Hamadi Ould Baba Ould HAMADI**

Min. of Habitat, Urban Affairs, & Territorial Admin.: **Ismail Bodde Cheikh SIDIYA**

Min. of Health: **Housseynou Hamady BA**

Min. of Hydrology & Sanitation: **Mohamed Lemine Ould ABOYE Ould Cheikh El Hadrami**

Min. of Interior & Decentralization: **Mohamed Ould BOILIL**

Min. of Islamic Affairs & Religious Education: **Ahmed Ould MOHAMED**

Min. of Justice: **Abidine Ould KHEIR**

Min. of National Defense: **Ahmedou Ould Idey Ould Mohamed RAHDI**

Min. of Public Services & Admin. Modernization: **Maty Mint HAMADY**

Min. of Rural Development: **Ould M'MBARECK Ould Mohamed El Moctar- Brahim**

Min. of Social, Child, & Family Affairs: **Moulaty Mint El MOCTAR**

Min. of Sec. Gen. of the Presidency: **Adama SY**

Min.-Del. to the Prime Min. for Employment & Technical Education: **Mohamed Ould KHOUNA**

Min.-Del. to the Prime Min. for Environment & Sustainable Development: **Amedi CAMARA**

Min.-Del. to the Prime Min. for Primary Education: **Hamed Ould HAMOUNY**

Min.-Del. to the Prime Min. for Secondary Education: **Oumar Ould MAATALLA**

Sec. Gen. to the Govt.: **Mohamed Ould MOHAMEDOU**

Ambassador to the US: **Mohamed Lemine El HAYCEN**

Permanent Representative to the UN, New York: **Abderrahim Ould HADRAMI**

ECONOMY

Half the population still depends on agriculture and livestock for a livelihood, even though many of the nomads and subsistence farmers were forced into the cities by recurrent droughts in the 1970s and 1980s.

Mauritania has extensive deposits of iron ore, which account for nearly 40% of total exports. The nation's coastal waters are among the richest fishing areas in the world but overexploitation by foreigners threatens this key source of revenue. The country's first deepwater port opened near Nouakchott in 1986. Before 2000, drought and economic mismanagement resulted in a buildup of foreign debt.

In February 2000, Mauritania qualified for debt relief under the Heavily Indebted Poor Countries (HIPC) initiative and nearly all of its foreign debt has since been forgiven.

A new investment code approved in December 2001 improved the opportunities for direct foreign investment. Mauritania and the IMF agreed to a three-year Poverty Reduction and Growth Facility (PRGF) arrangement in 2006. Mauritania made satisfactory progress, but the IMF, World Bank, and other international actors suspended assistance and investment in Mauritania after the August 2008 coup.

Since the presidential election in July 2009, donors have resumed assistance. Oil prospects, while initially promising, have largely failed to materialize, and the government has placed a priority on attracting private investment to spur economic growth.

The Government also emphasizes reduction of poverty, improvement of health and education, and privatization of the economy. Economic growth remained above 5% in 2010–12, mostly because of rising prices of gold, copper, iron ore, and oil.

Labor Conditions

The law prohibits employment of children under the age of 12. Those under age 13 may not be employed in the agricultural sector unless the minister of labor grants an exception due to local circumstances.

Those younger than 14 may be employed in most forms of family enterprise with authorization from the Ministry of Labor as long as the work does not affect the child's health, exceed two hours per day, or occur during school hours or holidays. The law states that employed children 14 to 16 should receive 70 percent of the minimum wage and those 17 to 18 should receive 90 percent of the minimum wage.

Children should not work more than eight hours a day with one or several one-hour breaks, and they are prohibited from engaging in night work. The law prohibits employing or inciting a child to beg with penalties ranging from one to eight months imprisonment and a fine of 180,000 to 300,000 ouguiya ($620 to $1,034). Enforcement of laws was inadequate.

Child labor in the informal sector was common and a significant problem, particularly within poorer inner city areas. Several reports suggested that young girls, as young as the age of seven, from remote regions, and possibly from western Mali, continued to be forced to work as unpaid housemaids in some wealthy urban homes. Street gang leaders forced children to steal, beg, and sell drugs in the streets of the capital. Children were reportedly forced to work in agriculture, construction, and livestock herding.

Young children in the countryside were commonly engaged in herding; cultivation of subsistence crops, such as rice, millet, and sorghum; fishing; and other significant labor in support of their families' activities. Young children in urban areas often drove donkey carts and delivered water and building materials. In keeping with longstanding tradition, many children served apprenticeships in small industries, such as metalworking, carpentry, vehicle repair, masonry, and the informal sector. Reporting by some human rights NGOs, including SOS Esclaves, strongly suggested that domestic employment of girls as young as the age of seven, often unpaid, continued to be a problem.

The nationally mandated minimum monthly wage for adults, which was not enforced, was 30,000 ouguiya ($103), increased from 21,000 ouguiya ($72) on September 24. The poverty level for 2008 was an annual income of 129,600 ouguiya ($447) and the extreme poverty level for 2008 was an annual income of 96,400 ouguiya ($332). According to the General Confederation of Workers of Mauritania, the National Agency of Social Security registered 501 workplace fatalities or injuries during the year, 189 of them at the national mining company, SNIM. It is likely that the number of accidents was greater because many accidents in the informal economy were unreported. Despite the law, labor unions pointed to conditions approaching modern slavery in several sectors, including the food processing industry. In these sectors, workers do not have contracts or receive pay stubs. Their salaries were below the official minimum wage, and they worked in very unfavorable conditions. Sometimes they were not paid for several months.

Despite the law, workers could not remove themselves from hazardous conditions without risking loss of employment.

FOREIGN RELATIONS AND U.S.–MAURITANIA RELATIONS

The United States was the first country to recognize Mauritania's independence from France in 1960. Since the late 1960s, U.S. aid and cooperation with Mauritania has varied in response to political conditions. The United States engages with Mauritania on a wide array of issues, including counterterrorism, food security, trade promotion, and efforts to strengthen human rights and the rule of law. The Departments of State and Defense, as well as the U.S. Agency for International Development (USAID), are represented at the U.S. Embassy in Nouakchott.

U.S. Assistance to Mauritania

The U.S. condemned Mauritania's 2005 and 2008 military coups. It supported Mauritania's transition to democracy following the 2005 coup, providing election-related assistance for voter education and provided elections support for the 2007 elections. Non-humanitarian U.S. aid to Mauritania was suspended after the 2008 coup. Following certification of the 2009 election by foreign observers, bilateral assistance restrictions were lifted. Mauritania is a member of the Trans-Sahara Counterterrorism Partnership (TSCTP) and receives security assistance to support its counterterrorism efforts.

Bilateral Economic Relations

The United States has limited trade and investment relations with Mauritania. The U.S.-North Africa Partnership for Economic Opportunity (NAPEO) is a regional public-private partnership that enhances the network of entrepreneurs and business leaders in the United States and each of the five Maghreb countries — Algeria, Libya, Mauritania, Morocco, and Tunisia. NAPEO is the North African regional component of Partners for a New Beginning, a collection of public-private partnerships committed to broadening and deepening engagement between the United States and local communities abroad.

Mauritania's Membership in International Organizations

Mauritania became a member of the United Nations in 1961. Mauritania and the United States belong to a number of the same international organizations, including the UN,

International Monetary Fund, World Bank, and World Trade Organization.

Bilateral Representation

Mauritania maintains an embassy in the United States at 2129 Leroy Place NW, Washington, DC 20008 (tel. 202-232-5700, fax 202-232-5701).

Principal U.S. Embassy Officials

Last Updated: 1/14/2013

NOUAKCHOTT (E) 288, Rue 42-100 Abdallaye, Nouakchott, Mauritania, 222-45-25-26-60, Fax 222-45-25-15-92, INMARSAT Tel 8816 214 57838 or 8816 214 57839, Workweek: Sunday-Thursday, 8:00–17:00, Website: http://mauritania.usembassy.gov/

DCM OMS:	Tamikka Forbes
AMB OMS:	Katrina Hourani
HRO:	Vacant
MGT:	Marika Zadva
POL/ECON:	John McKane
POSHO:	Andrew Hudson
SDO/DATT:	Scott Kastelic
AMB:	Jo Ellen Powell
CON:	Stacey Ba
DCM:	David Reimer
PAO:	Marion Wohlers
COM:	Stacey Ba
GSO:	Andrew Hudson
RSO:	Kevin Dougherty
CLO:	Vacant
ECON:	John McKane
EEO:	Vacant
FMO:	Soukeina Allaf
ICASS Chair:	Vacant
IMO:	Eleanor Wah
IRS:	Aziz Benbrahim (Resident In Paris)
ISSO:	Ibrahim Hassan
POL:	Brian Commaroto-Roverini
State ICASS:	Vacant

TRAVEL

Consular Information Sheet

October 4, 2012

Country Description: Mauritania is a developing country in northwestern Africa. Arabic is the official language, but French is widely used and several local languages are also spoken. Tourist facilities in the capital, Nouakchott, are adequate, but limited or non-existent elsewhere.

Smart Traveler Enrollment Program (STEP)/Embassy Location: If you are going to live in or visit Mauritania, please take the time to tell our Embassy about your trip.

If you enroll, we can keep you up to date with important safety and security announcements. It will also help your friends and family get in touch with you in an emergency. The U.S. Embassy is located between the Presidency building and the Spanish Embassy on Rue Abdallaye. The postal address is:

B.P. 222, Nouakchott.
Telephone: (222) 4-525-2660/2663, 4-525-1141/45, or
4-525-3038 (ext. 5441)
Emergency after-hours telephone: (222) 4-525-3288
Emergency Consular Recording (to relay messages during emergency situations): (222) 4-525-3707
Facsimile: (222) 4-525-1592

Entry/Exit Requirements: A passport and a visa are required, as is evidence of yellow fever vaccination. Mauritanian visas require an invitation or sponsor, can take up to several months to process, and must be obtained prior to travel. Visas are no longer available at border crossings or at the airport upon arrival.

For the most current visa information, contact the Embassy of the Islamic Republic of Mauritania, 2129 Leroy Place NW, Washington, DC 20008, tel. (202) 232-5700, or the Mauritanian Permanent Mission to the United Nations, 211 East 43rd Street, Suite 2000, New York, NY 10017, telephone (212) 986-7963 or 8189. Overseas, inquiries should be made at the nearest Mauritanian embassy or consulate. The U.S. Embassy in Nouakchott cannot provide assistance to private citizens seeking Mauritanian visas.

The U.S. Department of State is unaware of any HIV/AIDS entry restrictions for visitors to or foreign residents of Mauritania.

Threats to Safety and Security: The current Travel Warning for Mauritania warns U.S. citizens of the continued risks of traveling to Mauritania, and urges extreme caution when traveling there due to increased activities by the terrorist group Al Qaeda in the Islamic Maghreb (AQIM). As noted in the Department of State's Worldwide Caution dated July 18, 2012, AQIM has been designated as a terrorist organization by both the United States and the European Union.

As a result of perceived Western involvement in counterterrorism efforts, AQIM has declared its intention to attack Western targets in Mauritania and the region. It is possible that AQIM will attempt retaliatory attacks against Western targets of opportunity. AQIM has previously conducted kidnapping of Westerners for ransom and suicide bombing attempts. The Mauritanian military continues to engage in action against AQIM elements.

Because of increased AQIM activities in the following areas, travelers should avoid all non-essential travel to the Mali border regions, the Hodh El Charghi and Hodh El Gharbi regions of southeastern Mauritania, the eastern half of the Assaba region (east of Kiffa), the eastern half of the Tagant region of central Mauritania (east of Tidjika), the eastern half of the Adrar region (east of Chinguetti), and the Tiris-Zemmour region of northern Mauritania,. U.S. Embassy staff members are authorized to travel to these regions only with Mauritanian government escorts. Given AQIM threats, and because of indications of a desire to kidnap Westerners for ransom, U.S. citizens are urged to remain vigilant and be alert to surveillance or other risks to their safety. Faith-based organizations, regardless of their location, may also be particularly targeted.

Traveling Safely within Mauritania: Travelers should exercise prudence and caution when traveling in Mauritania. Be particularly vigilant when traveling by road outside of populated areas, even when traveling along main routes and highways. The U.S. Embassy discourages travel outside of urban areas unless in a convoy accompanied by an experienced guide, and even then only if equipped with sturdy vehicles and ample provisions. Driving outside of urban areas after dark is also strongly discouraged. The U.S. Embassy has received reports of banditry and smuggling in the more remote parts of Mauritania.

In Nouakchott and other major cities in Mauritania, there is an increased security presence and additional checkpoints. Police routinely conduct roadblocks at which they may ask for proof of identity and driver's licenses. These checkpoints should be respected. If you are visiting Mauritania you should be prepared for such inquiries by carrying your identification card at all times. It is best to drive cautiously and be prepared to stop at short notice. U.S. citizens driving in Mauritania are reminded to heed warnings to stop at security checkpoints, and should be particularly vigilant when traveling by road outside of populated areas, even when traveling along main routes and highways.

You should be aware of their surroundings at all times and maintain good personal security practices, including always locking your homes and cars, varying routes and time of travel, and avoiding drawing attention to themselves. When going out, avoid being part of large, highly visible groups of Westerners (but do not travel alone), and avoid sitting in areas that are easily visible from the street when in restaurants or cafes. You should be particularly alert when frequenting locales associated with Westerners, including cultural centers, social and recreation clubs, beach areas, and restaurants.

Landmines also remain a danger along the border with the Western Sahara and travelers should cross only at designated border posts. Travelers planning overland trips from Mauritania to Morocco, Algeria, Senegal, or Mali should check with the U.S. Embassy in Nouakchott before setting out.

Political Concerns: In September 2012, many countries around the world, including Mauritania, experienced political demonstrations protesting the controversial YouTube video and cartoon. Also, several political opposition parties have joined together as the Coordination of the Democratic Opposition, and organize regular demonstrations in the capital of Nouakchott seeking the departure of President Aziz. Although the political rallies are generally calm and peaceful, the possibility of political instability or of spontaneous violent protests still remains. In addition, deteriorating economic conditions could cause civil unrest. Some previous protests in Mauritania have turned violent. An anti-government group calling itself the Youth of February 25 Movement held a series of protests in the capital of Nouakchott in 2011 calling for political, economic, and social reforms.. A separate group, Do Not Touch My Nationality, organized several demonstrations in 2011 over alleged discrimination in a national registration drive in Nouakchott and in smaller towns throughout Mauritania. Most of these demonstrations turned violent and one protestor was fatally shot by security forces during a September 27, 2011 protest in Maghama. The demonstrations were generally announced in advance in the media and on the Internet. U.S. citizens are urged to avoid political rallies and street demonstrations, and to maintain security awareness at all times.

Stay up to date by:

- Bookmarking our Bureau of Consular Affairs website, which contains the current Travel Warnings and Travel Alerts as well as the Worldwide Caution.
- Follow us on Twitter and the Bureau of Consular Affairs page on Facebook as well.
- Download our free Smart Traveler iPhone App to have travel information at your fingertips.
- Calling 1-888-407-4747 toll-free within the U.S. and Canada, or a regular toll line, 1-202-501-4444, from other countries.
- Taking some time before travel to consider your personal security.

Crime: Overall, crime in Mauritania is not unlike crime in any major city in the United States. Most incidents occur in the cities and larger towns and are petty crimes, such as pickpocketing and the theft of improperly secured or openly visible valuables left in vehicles. To reduce exposure to theft and increase personal safety, lock up valuable items and keep them out of sight. Walking alone at any time is discouraged, especially for Western women. Residential burglaries and robberies, particularly at the beaches in Nouakchott, are not uncommon. In Nouakchott, travelers should avoid the beach at night.

Violent crimes and crimes involving the use of weapons are rare. Rapes and assaults have occurred and, in some instances, involved U.S. citizens. The majority of sexual assaults have occurred at night in taxi cabs. Combined with the lack of government regulation of taxi fares and poor regular maintenance, Westerners should avoid taxis and public transportation. Foreign tourists, including U.S. citizens, might be targeted for kidnapping in Mauritania.

Don't buy counterfeit and pirated goods, even if they are widely available. Not only are the bootlegs illegal in the United States, if you purchase them you may also be breaking local law.

Victims of Crime: If you are the victim of a crime abroad, you should contact the local police and the nearest U.S. embassy or consulate (see the Department of State list of embassies and consulates). We can:

- Replace stolen passports.
- Help you find appropriate medical care if you are the victim of violent crimes such as assault or rape.

- Put you in contact with the appropriate police authorities, and contact family members or friends.

- Help you to understand the local criminal justice process and direct you to attorneys, although local authorities are responsible for investigating and prosecuting the crime.

There is no local equivalent to the "911" emergency line in Mauritania.

Criminal Penalties: While you are traveling in Mauritaina, you are subject to its laws even if you are a U.S. citizen. Foreign laws and legal systems can be vastly different than our own. In some places, you may be taken in for questioning if you don't have your passport with you. In some places, it is illegal to take pictures of certain buildings. In some places, driving under the influence could land you immediately in jail. These criminal penalties will vary from country to country. There are also some things that might be legal in the country you visit, but still illegal in the United States, and you can be prosecuted under U.S. law if you buy pirated goods. Engaging in sexual conduct with children or using or disseminating child pornography in a foreign country is a crime prosecutable in the United States. If you break local laws in Mauritania, your U.S. passport won't help you avoid arrest or prosecution. It's very important to know what's legal and what's not where you are going.

Special Circumstances: Mauritanian customs authorities may enforce strict regulations concerning the temporary import or export of items such as firearms, narcotics, alcoholic drinks, and pork products. Contact the Embassy of Mauritania in Washington, DC, for specific information regarding customs regulations.

The local currency is the ouguiya, and it may not be imported or exported. Credit cards can be used only at a few hotels in the capital, Nouakchott, and in the northwestern city of Nouadhibou. However, credit card fraud is a problem, so travelers are strongly advised to pay hotel bills in cash. ATMs are available only in Nouakchott, but are not 100 percent secure. Major foreign currencies are changeable at banks and numerous currency exchanges; however, this service is not always available without advance notice or prior arrangement. There is a risk of receiving fraudulent bank notes even from banks, which often do not have the security means to detect false bank notes. Islamic ideals and beliefs in the country encourage conservative dress. Sleeved garments and below-the-knee skirts are recommended, and travelers should avoid wearing shorts.

Accessibility: While in Mauritania, individuals with disabilities may find accessibility and accommodation very different from what you find in the United States.

In December 2010, Rift Valley Fever was detected in the Adrar and Inchiri regions of Mauritania. According to the CDC, Rift Valley Fever is a viral disease that primarily affects animals, but also has the capacity to infect humans. Infection can cause severe disease and death in both animals and humans. Humans usually get Rift Valley Fever through bites from infected mosquitoes and other insects. Humans can also get the disease if they are exposed to the blood, body fluids, or tissues of infected animals. To learn more about Rift Valley Fever and preventive measures, U.S. citizens are advised to review the Centers for Disease Control and Prevention's Rift Valley Fever Fact Sheet.

You can obtain information on vaccinations and other health precautions, such as safe food and water precautions and insect bite protection, from the Centers for Disease Control and Prevention's (CDC) hotline for international travelers at 1-877-FYI-TRIP (1-877-394-8747) or via the CDC website. For information about outbreaks of infectious diseases abroad, consult the infectious diseases section of the World Health Organization (WHO) website. The WHO website also contains additional health information for travelers, including detailed country-specific health information.

Medical Insurance: You can't assume your insurance will go with you when you travel. It's very important to find out BEFORE you leave. You need to ask your insurance company two questions:

- Does my policy apply when I'm out of the United States?

- Will it cover emergencies like a trip to a foreign hospital or a medical evacuation?

In many places, doctors and hospitals still expect payment in cash at the time of service. Your regular U.S. health insurance may not cover doctors' and hospital visits in other countries. If your policy doesn't go with you when you travel, it's a very good idea to purchase travel insurance for your trip.

Traffic Safety and Road Conditions: While in a foreign country, U.S. citizens may encounter road conditions that differ significantly from those in the United States. The information below concerning Mauritania is provided for general reference only and may not be totally accurate in a particular location or circumstance.

Public transportation is not safe and road conditions in Mauritania are generally poor, particularly in the interior. Overland travel is difficult and roadside assistance is almost non-existent. The country's size (larger than Texas and New Mexico combined) and harsh climate make road maintenance and repair especially problematic. Mauritania has only about 2,070 km (1,286 miles) of surfaced roads, 710 km (441 miles) of unsurfaced roads, and 5,140 km (3,194 miles) of unimproved tracks. Drivers should not offer rides to hitchhikers, nor should visitors to Mauritania accept rides offered by strangers. Taxis and public transportation and are not considered to be secure forms of transportation for western visitors to Mauritania.

The traditional route to Nouadhibou, prior to the completion of a paved road, was along the beach during low tide. Some travelers continue to use this route, as do visitors to coastal fishing villages and other points of interest, as well as smugglers and others who try to avoid the security checkpoints that are often established along the asphalt roads. Pedestrian visitors to the beach should exercise caution because of the beach's use as a route for motorized vehicles.

U.S. citizens traveling overland for long distances in Mauritania should travel in convoys, and be sure to have suitable four-wheel drive vehicles, a local guide, an adequate supply of water and food, and a second fuel reservoir. Multiple vehicles are recommended in case of breakdown. A Global Positioning System (GPS) receiver and satellite phone are essential when traveling in remote areas. Visitors are urged not to travel alone into the desert or after dark when outside of major urban areas.

Driving in Mauritania can be treacherous, and we encourage travelers to hire a trained local driver. Traffic patterns differ considerably from U.S.-style "rules of the road," and many Mauritanians drive without regard to traffic signs or rules.

Roadway obstructions and hazards caused by drifting sand, animals, and poor roads often plague motorists. These hazards, when combined with the number of untrained drivers and poorly maintained vehicles, make heightened caution imperative at all times. Drivers should be extremely vigilant and all vehicle occupants should always wear their seat belts. Motorcycle and bicycle riders should wear helmets and protective clothing. Nighttime driving is discouraged.

The telecommunications infrastructure, including cellular telephone coverage, is limited. For those traveling outside the major urban areas, it is recommended to have a satellite telephone readily available.

Aviation Safety Oversight: As there is no direct commercial air service to the United States by carriers registered in Mauritania, the U.S. Federal Aviation Administration (FAA) has not assessed the government of Mauritania's Civil Aviation Authority for compliance with International Civil Aviation Organization (ICAO) aviation safety standards. Further information may be found on the FAA's safety assessment page.

Children's Issues: Please see the U.S. Dept. of State Office of Children's Issues web pages on intercountry adoption and international parental child abduction.

Travel Warning

November 30, 2012

The U.S. Department of State warns U.S. citizens of the risks of traveling to Mauritania, and urges extreme caution for those who choose to travel to Mauritania, because of activities by terrorist groups in the region, including al-Qaida in the Islamic Maghreb (AQIM). AQIM continues to demonstrate its intent and ability to conduct attacks against foreign nationals, including U.S. citizens. This replaces the Travel Warning for Mauritania, issued May 24, 2012, to update information on security incidents and remind travelers of security concerns.

The U.S. Embassy in Nouakchott recommends against all non-essential travel to the border regions of Guidimagha, the Hodh El Charghi and Hodh El Gharbi regions of southeastern Mauritania, the eastern half of the Assaba region (east of Kiffa), the eastern half of the Tagant region (east of Tidjika), the eastern half of the Adrar region (east of Chinguetti), and the Zemmour region of northern Mauritania because of the security risk and the threat of kidnapping to Westerners by terrorist groups.

As noted in the Department of State's Worldwide Caution, AQIM has been designated as a terrorist organization by both the United States and the European Union.

As a result of perceived Western involvement in counterterrorism efforts, AQIM has declared its intention to attack Western targets. AQIM attempts at retaliatory attacks against Western targets of opportunity cannot be discounted. While anti-terrorist military intervention has pushed terrorist operations to the Malian border regions, AQIM-affiliated support systems for logistics and information remain present in Mauritania. Additionally, the rebellion and subsequent coup in Mali has given terrorist groups the opportunity to establish territorial claims in the contested region of northern Mali. This, coupled with the influx of tens of thousands of Malian refugees into Mauritania, presents additional safety and security concerns.

AQIM and terrorists believed to be affiliated with AQIM have been operating in Mauritania since at least 2005. Actions include kidnapping and murder of Western tourists, aid workers, and Mauritanian soldiers, as well as attacks on foreign diplomatic missions in Mauritania. This culminated in the June 2009 attempted kidnapping and murder of a private U.S. citizen in the capital city of Nouakchott.

While there have been no known direct attempts against U.S. citizens since 2009, AQIM continues to threaten Westerners. A French citizen was kidnapped in southwest Mali, near the border with Mauritania, on November 20, 2012. AQIM has also focused its actions on Mauritanian military installations and personnel. The Mauritanian military continues to actively engage in action against AQIM elements, particularly along the border regions with Mali.

In August 2010, a suicide bomber attacked a Mauritanian military barracks in Nema. In February 2011, Mauritanian security forces successfully prevented a car bombing in the capital city, Nouakchott, by intercepting and destroying a vehicle containing large quantities of explosives. In July 2011, AQIM attacked a military base in Bassiknou, near Nema, in southeastern Mauritania. In December 2011, AQIM abducted a Mauritanian gendarme from his post near the eastern border with Mali.

As a result of safety and security concerns, some NGOs, private aid organizations, and Peace Corps withdrew staff and/or temporarily suspended operations in Mauritania. Peace

Corps officially closed their program in July 2011. Faith-based organizations operating in Mauritania, regardless of location, may be particularly targeted.

Travel by U.S. Embassy staff members outside of Nouakchott requires advance approval from the U.S. Embassy's security office. Travel by U.S. Embassy staff is subject to cancellation at any time. Travel to the eastern half of Mauritania occurs only with Mauritanian government escorts.

U.S. citizens should remain aware of their surroundings at all times and maintain good personal security practices, including always locking their homes and cars, varying routes and times of travel, and maintaining a low profile by not drawing attention to themselves.

When going out, they should avoid being part of large, highly visible groups of Westerners, and refrain from sitting in areas that are easily visible from the street when in restaurants or cafes. U.S. citizens should be particularly alert when frequenting locales associated with Westerners, including hotels, cultural centers, social and recreation clubs, beach areas, and restaurants. Additionally, U.S. citizens should avoid demonstrations and highly publicized events/ venues with no visible security presence.

U.S. citizens driving in Mauritania are reminded to heed warnings to stop at security checkpoints, and should be particularly vigilant when traveling by road outside of populated areas, even when traveling along main routes and highways. U.S. citizens should not venture outside urban areas unless in a convoy and accompanied by an experienced guide, and even then only if equipped with sturdy vehicles and ample provisions. Driving after dark outside of urban areas is strongly discouraged. There have been reports of banditry and smuggling in the more remote parts of Mauritania. Note also that landmines remain a danger along the border with the Western Sahara. Travelers should cross borders only at designated border posts. The U.S. Embassy in Nouakchott strongly encourages U.S. citizens who travel to or remain in Mauritania despite this Travel Warning to enroll in the Smart Traveler Enrollment Program (STEP) to receive the most up-to-date security information. Please keep all of your information in STEP current. It is important when enrolling or updating information to include multiple phone numbers and email addresses to facilitate communication in the event of an emergency.

U.S. citizens should consult the Country Specific Information sheet for the Republic of Mauritania and the Worldwide Caution, both located on the Department of State's Bureau of Consular Affairs website.

Follow us on Twitter and the Bureau of Consular Affairs page on Facebook as well. If you don't have internet access, current information on safety and security can also be obtained by calling 1-888-407-4747 toll-free in the United States, or for callers from other countries, a regular toll line at 1-202-501-4444. These numbers are available from 8:00 a.m. to 8:00 p.m. Eastern Time, Monday through Friday (except U.S. federal holidays).

The U.S. Embassy is located between the Presidency building and the Spanish Embassy on Rue Abdallaye. The postal address is B.P. 222, Nouakchott, telephone (222) 4-525-2660/2663, 4-525-1141/1145, or 4-525-3038, and fax (222) 4-525-1592. For after-hours emergencies, please call (222) 4-525-3288 or visit the U.S. Embassy Nouakchott web site. In the event of an emergency that interrupts mobile phone (SMS) or Internet communication in Mauritania, U.S. citizens may call the Embassy's dedicated Consular emergency recording at (222) 4-525-3707 to receive the most up-to-date instructions.

Intercountry Adoption

August 2012

The information in this section has been edited from a report of the Bureau of Consular Affairs, Office of Overseas Citizens Services of the U.S. Department of State. For more information, please read the *Intercountry Adoption* section of this book and review current reports online at http://adoption.state.gov.

Mauritania is not party to the Hague Convention on Protection of Children and Co-operation in Respect of Intercountry Adoption (Hague Adoption Convention). Intercountry adoptions of children from non-Hague countries are processed in accordance with 8 Code of Federal Regulations, Section 204.3 as it relates to orphans as defined under the Immigration and Nationality Act, Section 101(b)(1)(F).

Below is the limited adoption information that the Department has obtained from the adoption authority of Mauritania. U.S. citizens adopting children in rare adoption cases from Mauritania, as well as U.S. citizen prospective adoptive parents living in Mauritania who would like to adopt from the United States or from a third country, should contact the adoption authority of Mauritania to inquire about applicable laws and procedures.

Adoption is not allowed under Mauritanian law, but legal guardianship is allowed through the determination of a court. The Mauritanian judicial system is based on a strict interpretation of Islamic Sharia law.

To qualify as a guardian, one must be a blood-relative who is either Muslim or lives in a Muslim environment. In the event of the inability of a parent to care for his/her children, Mauritanian law gives a strict sequence of eligible blood relatives for guardianship. However, it is up to the discretion of a judge to determine who is most eligible for the guardianship of a child.

The 2002 Family Code, promulgated by the Mauritanian Ministry of Justice, includes sections on guardianship and custody. The Family Code does not cover scenarios in which a parent or legal guardian can pass guardianship to a foreigner.

It is possible for a lawyer to assist in obtaining approved guardianship by a Mauritanian judge. This may be sufficient to allow the child to be eligible for an immigrant visa under U.S. Immigration Laws.

However, the law prohibits non-family members from removing children from Mauritanian soil. The U.S. Embassy in Dakar, Senegal issues immigrant visas for Mauritanian citizens, including adopted orphans.

Prospective adoptive parents should be aware that not all children in orphanages or children's homes are adoptable.

In many countries, birth parents place their child(ren) temporarily in an orphanage or children's home due to financial or other hardship, intending that the child return home when this becomes possible. In such cases, the birth parent(s) have rarely relinquished their parental rights or consented to their child(ren)'s adoption.

Mauritania's Adoption Authority
Mauritanian Ministry
for the Promotion of Women,
Family, and Children
Address: Nouakchott, Mauritania
Tel: (222) 525-3860
Internet:
www.promotionfeminine.gov.mr/femme/home

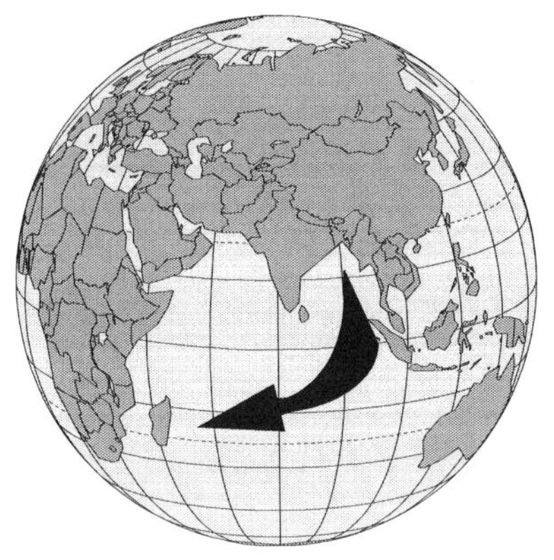

MAURITIUS

Compiled from publications that were available as of February 2013 from the U.S. Department of State, the U.S. Department of Commerce, and the Central Intelligence Agency (CIA). See the introduction to this set for explanatory notes.

Official Name:
Republic of Mauritius

PROFILE

Geography

Area: total: 2,040 sq km; country comparison to the world: 181; land: 2,030 sq km; water: 10 sq km

Major cities: Port Louis (capital) 149,000 (2009)

Climate: tropical, modified by southeast trade winds; warm, dry winter (May to November); hot, wet, humid summer (November to May)

Terrain: small coastal plain rising to discontinuous mountains encircling central plateau

People

Nationality: noun: Mauritian(s); adjective: Mauritian

Population: 1,313,095 (July 2012 est.)

Population growth rate: 0.705% (2012 est.)

Ethnic groups: Indo-Mauritian 68%, Creole 27%, Sino-Mauritian 3%, Franco-Mauritian 2%

Religions: Hindu 48%, Roman Catholic 23.6%, Muslim 16.6%, other Christian 8.6%, other 2.5%, unspecified 0.3%, none 0.4% (2000 census)

Languages: Creole 80.5%, Bhojpuri 12.1%, French 3.4%, English (official; spoken by less than 1% of the population), other 3.7%, unspecified 0.3% (2000 census)

Literacy: definition: age 15 and over can read and write; total population: 88.5%; male: 90.9%; female: 86.2% (2010 est.)

Health: life expectancy at birth: total population: 74.71 years; male: 71.25 years; female: 78.35 years (2012 est.); Infant mortality rate: total: 11.2 deaths/1,000 live births; male: 13.32 deaths/1,000 live births; female: 8.98 deaths/1,000 live births (2012 est.)

Unemployment rate: 8% (2012 est.)

Work force: 617,800 (2012 est.)

Government

Type: parliamentary democracy

Independence: 12 March 1968

Constitution: 12 March 1968; amended 12 March 1992

Political subdivisions: 9 districts and 3 dependencies; Agalega Islands, Black River, Cargados Carajos Shoals, Flacq, Grand Port, Moka, Pamplemousses, Plaines Wilhems, Port Louis, Riviere du Rempart, Rodrigues, Savanne

Suffrage: 18 years of age; universal

Economy

GDP (purchasing power parity): $20.26 billion (2012 est.); $19.52 billion (2011 est.); $18.75 billion (2010 est.); $18.01 billion (2009 est.)

GDP real growth rate: 3.4% (2012 est.); 4.1% (2011 est.); 4.1% (2010 est.); 3% (2009 est.)

GDP per capita (PPP): $15,600 (2012 est.); $15,100 (2011 est.); $14,600 (2010 est.); $14,100 (2009 est.)

Natural resources: arable land, fish

Agriculture products: sugarcane, tea, corn, potatoes, bananas, pulses; cattle, goats; fish

Industries: food processing (largely sugar milling), textiles, clothing, mining, chemicals, metal products, transport equipment, nonelectrical machinery, tourism

Exports: $2.631 billion (2012 est.); $2.645 billion (2011 est.); $2.262 billion (2010 est.)

Exports—commodities: clothing and textiles, sugar, cut flowers, molasses, fish

Exports—partners: UK 19.7%, France 17.1%, US 11.5%, Italy 8.8%, South Africa 7.3%, Spain 6.8%, Madagascar 6.5% (2011)

Imports: $5.111 billion (2012 est.); $5.159 billion (2011 est.); $4.157 billion (2010 est.)

Imports—commodities: manufactured goods, capital equipment, foodstuffs, petroleum products, chemicals

Imports—partners: India 25.6%, China 11.5%, France 9.4%, South Africa 7.3%, Singapore 5.9% (2011)

Debt—external: $5.768 billion (31 December 2012 est.); $5.205 billion (31 December 2011 est.); $4.402 billion (31 December 2010 est.)

Exchange rates: Mauritian rupees (MUR) per US dollar; 29.96 (2012 est.); 28.706 (2011 est.); 30.784 (2010 est.); 31.96 (2009); 27.973 (2008); 31.798 (2007)

PEOPLE

Language

The official language is English, but French and Creole are used in everyday life. Most business executives are bilingual in English and French. A number of Asian languages (Hindi, Urdu, and Mandarin) are also spoken.

Religion

According to the 2000 census, 48 percent of the population is Hindu, 24 percent Roman Catholic, 17 percent Muslim, and 9 percent belongs to other Christian denominations. The remaining 2 percent of the population includes Buddhists, animists, and others. Roman Catholics make up 73 percent of the Christian population, while the remaining 27 percent are members of the following groups: Seventh-day Adventist, Assemblies of God, Church of England, Pentecostal, Presbyterian, Evangelical, Jehovah's Witnesses, and The Church of Jesus Christ of Latter-day Saints (Mormons). Sunnis account for more than 90 percent of Muslims.

On the main island, the northern portion is primarily Hindu, while the central area is mainly Catholic. There are large populations of Muslims and Catholics in the cities of Port Louis, Quatre Bornes, and Curepipe. The island of Rodrigues is 92 percent Catholic. There is a strong correlation between religious affiliation and ethnicity. Citizens of Indian ethnicity are primarily Hindu or Muslim. Those of Chinese ancestry generally practice either Buddhism or Catholicism. Creoles and citizens of European descent are primarily Christian.

HISTORY

While Arab and Malay sailors knew of Mauritius as early as the 10th century AD and Portuguese sailors first visited in the 16th century, the island remained uninhabited until colonized in 1638 by the Dutch. Mauritius was populated over the next few centuries by waves of traders, planters and their slaves, indentured laborers, merchants, and artisans. The island was named in honor of Prince Maurice of Nassau by the Dutch, who abandoned the colony in 1710.

The French claimed Mauritius in 1715 and renamed it Ile de France. It became a prosperous colony under the French East India Company. The French Government took control in 1767, and the island served as a naval and privateer base during the Napoleonic wars. In 1810, Mauritius was captured by the British, whose possession of the island was confirmed 4 years later by the Treaty of Paris. French institutions, including the Napoleonic code of law, were maintained. The French language is still used more widely than English.

Mauritian Creoles trace their origins to the plantation owners and slaves who were brought to work the sugar fields. Indo-Mauritians (primarily Hindus, but also Muslims and Christians) are descended from immigrants who arrived in the 19th century from the Indian subcontinent to work as indentured laborers after slavery was abolished in 1835. Franco-Mauritians still control most of the large sugar estates and are active in business and banking. As the Indo-Mauritian population became numerically dominant and the voting franchise was extended, political power shifted from the Franco-Mauritians and their Creole allies to the Indo-Mauritian Hindus.

Elections in 1947 for the newly created Legislative Assembly marked Mauritius' first steps toward self-rule. An independence campaign gained momentum after 1961, when the British agreed to permit additional self-government and eventual independence. A coalition composed of the Mauritian Labor Party (MLP), the Muslim Committee of Action (CAM), and the Independent Forward Bloc (IFB)—a traditionalist Hindu party—won a majority in the 1967 Legislative Assembly election, despite opposition from Franco-Mauritian and Creole supporters of Gaetan Duval's Mauritian Social Democratic Party (PMSD). The contest was interpreted locally as a referendum on independence. Following a period of communal strife, brought under control with assistance from British troops, Seewoosagur Ramgoolam, MLP leader and chief minister in the colonial government, became the first prime minister at independence, on March 12, 1968.

GOVERNMENT AND POLITICAL CONDITIONS

Mauritius is a multiparty democracy governed by a prime minister, a council of ministers, and a National Assembly. The Alliance of the Future, a coalition led by Prime Minister Navinchandra Ramgoolam, won the majority of national assembly seats in the May 2010 elections, judged by international and local observers to be generally free and fair.

Recent Elections

International and local observers characterized the May 2010 National Assembly elections as free and fair. The constitution provides for 62 National Assembly seats to be filled by election. It also provides for the Electoral Supervisory Commission to allocate up to eight additional seats to unsuccessful candidates from minority communities through a system known as the "best loser system" (BLS). In the May 2010 legislative elections, the ruling coalition Alliance of the Future (AF), led by the Labor Party, won 41 parliamentary seats; the Alliance of the Heart coalition (AH), led by the Mauritian Militant Movement (MMM) won 18; the Rodrigues Movement (MR) won two; and the Mauritian Solidarity Front won one seat. Subsequently, under the

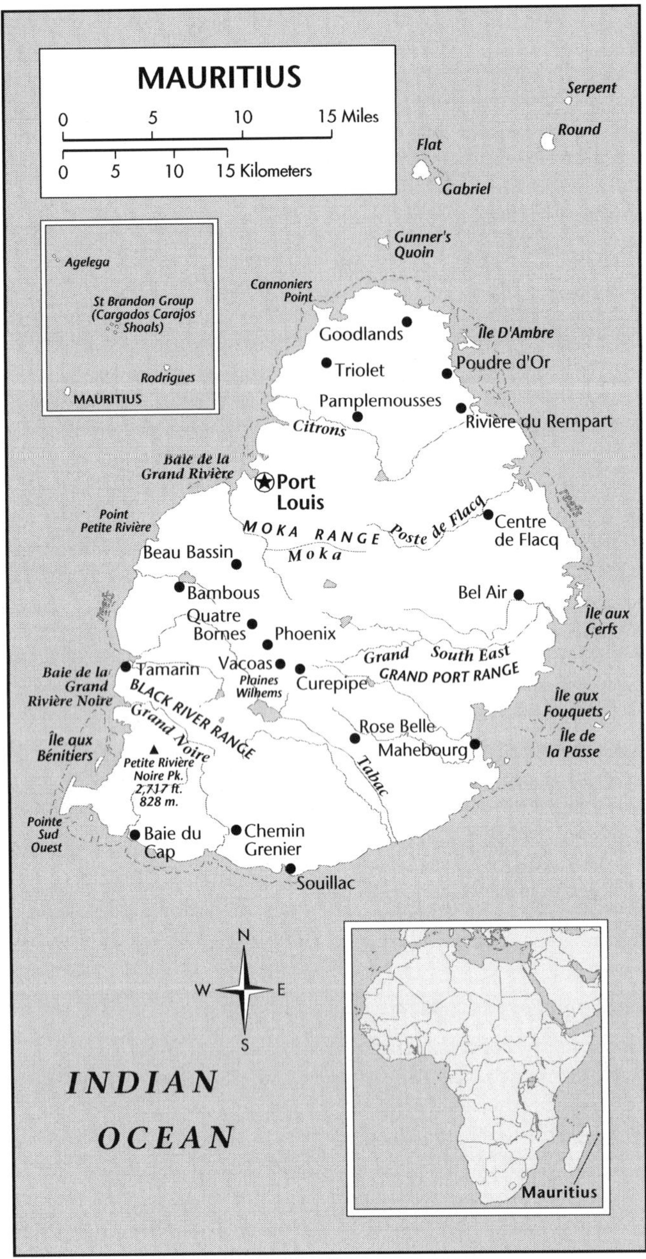

BLS, the AF obtained four additional seats, the AH two, and the Rodrigues Peoples Organization obtained one.

The constitution requires all candidates to declare themselves as belonging to one of the following four "communities": Hindu, Muslim, Sino-Mauritian, or general population (all persons who do not belong to one of the other three categories). The BLS is based on the demographic makeup of the country as found in the 1972 census. However, there were concerns the 1972 census results no longer reflected the country's demographic composition. Various political observers stated that the BLS undermined national unity and promoted discrimination. At the end of 2011,, there were active public discussions of legislative modifications to, or elimination of, the BLS.

International election observers noted some problems including unequal representation due to electoral constituencies not being redrawn, the inability of persons who turned 18 between January 2009 and May 2010 to vote due to use of the 2009 voters roll, lack of accommodations for persons with disabilities, and lack of legal provisions to provide for domestic election observers. Also various candidates stated that some politicians distributed gifts in their constituencies prior to the May 2010 election, and that some polling materials were not available in Creole, a language spoken by more than 90 percent of the population.

Political parties operated without restriction or outside interference. Opposition parties stated that the government-owned TV station, MBC TV, favored the ruling party. Opposition and MMM leader Paul Berenger stated that MBC TV provided more airtime to and better picture quality of the prime minister.

Participation of Women and Minorities: There were 13 women in the 70-seat National Assembly. Following the May 2010 National Assembly elections, there were two female ministers in the 25-member cabinet. Of the 20 Supreme Court judges, eight were women.

Although historically the Hindu majority dominated politics, no groups were excluded from the political system. In the National Assembly there were 37 Hindus, 20 members of the general population, 11 Muslims, and two Sino-Mauritian. In the cabinet there were 17 Hindus, four Muslims, four members of the general population, and one Sino-Mauritian.

Principal Government Officials

Last Updated: 1/31/2013

Pres.: **Rajkeswur Kailash PURRYAG**
Prime Min.: **Navinchandra RAMGOOLAM, Dr.**
Dep. Prime Min.: **Ahmed Rashid BEEBEEJAUN, Dr.**
Vice Prime Min.: **Anil Kumar BACHOO**
Vice Prime Min.: **Charles Gaetan Xavier-Luc DUVAL**
Min. of Agro-Industry & Food Security: **Satya Veyash FAUGOO**
Min. of Arts & Culture: **Mookeshwar CHOONEE**
Min. of Business & Enterprise: **Jangbahadoorsing Iswurdeo Mola Roopchand SEETARAM**

Min. of Civil Service & Admin. Reforms
Min. of Defense & Home Affairs: **Navinchandra RAMGOOLAM, Dr.**
Min. of Education & Human Resources: **Vasant Kumar BUNWAREE, Dr.**
Min. of Energy & Public Utilities: **Ahmed Rashid BEEBEEJAUN, Dr.**
Min. of Environment & Sustainable Development: **Devand VIRAHSAWMY**
Min. of External Communications: **Navinchandra RAMGOOLAM, Dr.**
Min. of Finance & Economic Development: **Charles Gaetan Xavier-Luc DUVAL**
Min. of Fisheries & Rodrigues Island: **Nicolas Von MALLY**
Min. of Foreign Affairs, Regional Cooperation, & Intl. Trade: **Arvin BOOLELL, Dr.**
Min. of Gender Equality, Child Development, & Family Welfare: **Sheilabhai BAPPOO**
Min. of Health & Quality of Life: **Lormus BUNDHOO**
Min. of Housing & Lands: **Abu Twalib KASENALLY, Dr.**
Min. of Industry, Commerce, & Consumer Protection: **Sayyad Abd-al-Cader SAYED-HOSSEN**
Min. of Information & Communication Technology: **Tassarajen Pillay CHEDUMBRUM**
Min. of Labor, Industrial Relations, & Employment: **Shakel MOHAMED**
Min. of Local Govt. & Outer Islands: **Louis Herve AIME**
Min. of Public Infrastructure, National Development Unit, Land Transport, & Shipping: **Anil Kumar BACHOO**
Min. of Social Integration & Economic Empowerment: **Surenda DAYAL**
Min. of Social Security, National Solidarity, & Reform Institutions .
Min. of Tertiary Education, Science, Research, & Technology: **Rajeshwar JEETAH**
Min. of Tourism & Leisure: **John Michael Tzoun Sao Yeung Sik YUEN**
Min. of Youth & Sports: **Satyaprakash RITTOO**
Attorney Gen.: **Yatrina Nath VARMA**
Governor, Central Bank: **Rundheersingh BHEENICK**
Charge d'Affaires Ad Interim, Embassy, Washington: **Joyker NAYECK**
Permanent Representative to the UN, New York: **Jaya Nyamrajsingh MEETARBHAN**

ECONOMY

Since independence in 1968, Mauritius has developed from a low-income, agriculturally based economy to a middle-income diversified economy with growing industrial, financial, and tourist sectors.

For most of the period, annual growth has been in the order of 5% to 6%. This remarkable achievement has been reflected in more equitable income distribution, increased life expectancy, lowered infant mortality, and a much-improved infrastructure. The economy rests on sugar, tourism, textiles and apparel, and financial services, and is expanding into fish processing, information and communications technology, and hospitality and property development.

Sugarcane is grown on about 90% of the cultivated land area and accounts for 15% of export earnings. The government's development strategy centers on creating vertical and horizontal clusters of development in these sectors.

Mauritius has attracted more than 32,000 offshore entities, many aimed at commerce in India, South Africa, and China. Investment in the banking sector alone has reached over $1 billion. Mauritius, with its strong textile sector, has been well poised to take advantage of the Africa Growth and Opportunity Act (AGOA).

Mauritius' sound economic policies and prudent banking practices helped to mitigate negative effects from the global financial crisis in 2008–09. GDP grew more than 4% per year in 2010–11, and the country continues to expand its trade and investment outreach around the globe.

Labor Conditions

The law prohibits the employment of children below 16 years of age and prohibits the employment of children between 16 and 18 years old in work that is dangerous, unhealthy, or otherwise unsuitable for young persons. According to the law, the penalties for employing a child are a fine of no more than 10,000 rupees ($346) and imprisonment not to exceed one year. While the government generally respected this law, it did not effectively enforce this law. Children worked in the informal sector, including as street traders, in small businesses, in restaurants, in agriculture, and in small apparel workshops.

In the private sector, the NRB sets minimum wages for nonmanagerial workers outside the EOE. The established minimum wages varied by sector. The government mandated that the minimum wage rise each year based on the inflation rate. The minimum wage for an unskilled domestic worker in the EOE was approximately 607 rupees ($21) per week, while the minimum wage for an unskilled domestic factory worker outside the EOE was approximately 794 rupees ($27) per week.

The standard legal workweek in the EOE was 45 hours. By law no worker can be forced to work more than eight hours a day, six days a week. According to the Mauritius Labor Congress, 10 hours of overtime a week is nonetheless mandatory at certain textile factories in the EOE. Those who work more than their stipulated hours must be remunerated at one and a half times the normal salary. Those who work during their stipulated hours on public holidays are remunerated at double their normal salary. For industrial positions, workers are not permitted to work more than 10 hours a day. If the worker has worked until or past 10 p.m., the employer cannot require work to resume until at least 11 hours have elapsed. The law provides that, in cases of overtime violations, the ministry is required to investigate, and employers are encouraged to take remedial actions, failing which a court action is initiated.

The government set occupational safety and health standards, and Ministry of Labor officials inspected working conditions. The ministry effectively enforced the minimum wage law. These standards were generally enforced for both foreign and domestic workers.

Although the minimum wage did not provide a decent standard of living for a worker and family, the actual market wage for most workers was much higher due to a labor shortage and collective bargaining. There were reports that full-time employees in the cleaning industry were not always paid the NRB-recommended minimum wage; they reportedly earned up to 1,500 rupees per month ($51).

Unions have reported cases of underpayment for overtime in the textile and apparel industries due to differences in existing legislation and remuneration orders for the calculation of overtime hours.

Employers did not always comply with safety regulations, resulting in occupational accidents. There were reports of foreign workers living in dormitories with unsanitary conditions. Workers had the right to remove themselves from dangerous situations without jeopardizing their continued employment, and they did so in practice.

U.S.-MAURITIAN RELATIONS

The United States established diplomatic relations with Mauritius in 1968, following its independence from the United Kingdom. In the years following independence, Mauritius became one of Africa's most stable and developed economies, as a result of its multi-party democracy and free market orientation. Relations between the United States and Mauritius are cordial, and we collaborate closely on bilateral, regional, and multilateral issues. Mauritius is a leading beneficiary of the African Growth and Opportunity Act and a U.S. partner in combating maritime piracy in the Indian Ocean.

U.S. Assistance to Mauritius

U.S. foreign assistance to Mauritius focuses on strengthening the Government of Mauritius coastal and maritime security capabilities. The United States provides training to Mauritian security officers in such fields as counterterrorism methods, forensics, seamanship, and maritime law enforcement.

Bilateral Economic Relations

Mauritius is eligible for preferential trade benefits under the African Growth and Opportunity Act. U.S. exports to Mauritius include machinery, jewelry, plastic, agricultural products, and optical/medical instruments. U.S. imports from Mauritius include apparel, diamonds, tuna, and primates. More than 200 U.S. companies are represented in Mauritius.

About 25 have offices in Mauritius, serving the domestic and/or the regional market, mainly in the information technology, textile, fast food, express courier, and financial services sectors. U.S. brands are sold widely. Several U.S. franchises have been operating for a number of years in Mauritius. The United States and Mauritius have signed a bilateral trade and investment framework agreement. The United States also has signed a trade and investment framework agreement with the Common Market for Eastern and Southern Africa, of which Mauritius is a member.

Mauritius Membership in International Organizations

Mauritius and the United States belong to a number of the same international organizations, including the United Nations, International Monetary Fund, World Bank, and World Trade Organization.

Bilateral Representation

Mauritius maintains an embassy in the United States at 1709 N Street NW, Washington, DC 20036, (tel. 202-244-1491).

Principal U.S. Embassy Officials

Last Updated: 1/14/2013

PORT LOUIS (E) 4th Floor Rogers House, John Kennedy St., Port Louis, Mauritius, (230) 202-4400, Fax (230) 208-9534, INMARSAT Tel 881631439038/881631439039, Workweek: M-Th: 0730-1645; F:0730-1230, Website: http://mauritius.usembassy.gov/

DCM OMS:	Vicki Douvres
AMB OMS:	Vacant
DHS/CIS:	Leslie A. Meeker
DHS/ICE:	Abraham Lugo
DHS/TSA:	Ronald J Malin
FCS:	Craig Allen
FM:	[Regional Support]
HRO:	[Regional Support]
MGT:	Lisa Derrickson
POL/MIL:	David Campbell
POSHO:	Kendra Kirkland
SDO/DATT:	CDR Michael Baker
AMB:	Shari Villarosa
CON:	Elizabeth Kuhse
DCM:	Charge Troy Fitrell
PAO:	Vanessa Harper
GSO:	Kendra Kirkland
RSO:	Dwight Pierce
AGR:	Scott Sindelar
APHIS:	Tom Schissel
CLO:	Jessica Pierce
DEA:	Warren Franklin
EEO:	Liz Kuhse
FAA:	Moira Keane
FMO:	[Regional Support]
IMO:	Edward Warrick
IRS:	Aziz Benbrahim
ISO:	Edward Warrick
ISSO:	Vacant
LAB:	Randy Fleitman
LEGATT:	Carol Daane
POL:	Hugo Jimenez
State ICASS:	Vanessa Harper

TRAVEL

Consular Information Sheet

December 19, 2012

Country Description: The Republic of Mauritius is a small island nation consisting of four inhabited and several other islands in the southwestern Indian Ocean. Mauritius has a stable government and a diverse economy. Its 2011 per capita GDP of

USD 8,524 is one of the highest in Africa. Facilities for tourism are well-developed. Although English is the official language, Creole and French are the languages used in daily life. English may not be understood outside of main towns and tourist areas. The capital city is Port Louis.

Smart Traveler Enrollment Program (STEP)/Embassy Locations: If you are going to live in or visit Mauritius, please take the time to tell our Embassy about your trip. If you enroll your trip with us through the Smart Traveler Enrollment Program, we can keep you up to date with important safety and security announcements. It will also help your friends and family get in touch with you in an emergency.

U.S. Embassy Mauritius
4th floor of the Rogers House on John F. Kennedy Street
Port Louis, Mauritius
Telephone: (230) 202-4400
Facsimile: (230) 208-9534

Entry/Exit Requirements for U.S. Citizens: A valid passport, onward/return ticket, and proof of sufficient funds are required. Immigration authorities require the validity of the entrant's passport to be greater than six months upon both arrival and departure. Travelers must also provide a local address where they will be staying in Mauritius. Visas are issued at the point of entry. A tourist entry fee and the airport departure tax are included in the price of a plane ticket. Travelers coming from yellow fever-infected areas may be asked to present a yellow fever vaccination certificate.

Travelers should obtain the latest information and details from the Embassy of Mauritius, 4301 Connecticut Avenue NW, Suite 441, Washington, DC 20008; telephone (202) 244-1491/2, or the Honorary Consulate in Los Angeles, telephone (310) 557-2009. Overseas, inquiries may be at the nearest Mauritian embassy or consulate. Visit the Embassy of Mauritius' web site for the most current visa information.

The U.S. Department of State is unaware of any HIV/AIDS entry restrictions for visitors to or foreign residents of Mauritius.

Threats to Safety and Security: Thefts in tourist areas are a concern, and visitors should keep track of their belongings at all times. Women are advised against walking alone, particularly on public beaches and at night. There have been reports of sexual assault and harassment of foreign travelers. U.S. citizens should avoid crowds and street demonstrations, and maintain a low profile.Stay up to date by:

- Bookmarking our Bureau of Consular Affairs website, which contains current Travel Warnings and Travel Alerts as well as the Worldwide Caution.
- Following us on Twitter and the Bureau of Consular Affairs page on Facebook as well.
- Downloading our free Smart Traveler iPhone App to have travel information at your fingertips.
- Calling 1-888-407-4747 toll-free within the U.S. and Canada, or a regular toll line, 1-202-501-4444, from other countries.
- Taking some time before travel to consider your personal security.

Crime: Although violent crime is uncommon, petty crime is a problem. There is potential for pick-pocketing and purse snatching, especially in crowded areas. Residential break-ins are reported frequently on the island. Most break-ins are surreptitious and do not involve violence, however some burglars have brandished weapons, such as knives or machetes. Although uncommon, there have been reports of armed robbery and assault. It is unwise to walk alone at night outside the immediate grounds of hotels. Foreigners should exercise caution on beaches and poorly lit or deserted areas at night.

Don't buy counterfeit and pirated goods, even if they are widely available. Not only are the bootlegs illegal in the United States, if you purchase them you may also be breaking local law.

Victims of Crime: If you or someone you know becomes the victim of a crime abroad, you should contact the local police and the nearest U.S. embassy. We can:

- Replace a stolen passport.
- Help you find appropriate medical care if you are the victim of violent crimes such as assault or rape.
- Put you in contact with the appropriate police authorities and, if you want us to, we can contact family members or friends.
- Help you understand the local criminal justice process and direct you to local attorneys, although it is important to remember that local authorities are responsible for investigating and prosecuting the crime.

The local equivalent to the "911" emergency line in Mauritius is: 999 for police, 114 for emergency medical assistance, and 115 for the fire service.

Criminal Penalties: While you are traveling in Mauritius, you are subject to its laws even if you are a U.S. citizen. Foreign laws and legal systems can be vastly different than our own. In some places you may be taken in for questioning if you don't have your passport with you. In some places, it is illegal to take pictures of certain buildings. In some places driving under the influence of alcohol could land you immediately in jail. These criminal penalties will vary from country to country. There are also some things that might be legal in the country you visit, but still illegal in the United States, and you can be prosecuted under U.S. law if you buy pirated goods. Engaging in sexual conduct with children or using or disseminating child pornography in a foreign country is a crime prosecutable in the United States. If you break local laws in Mauritius, your

U.S. passport won't help you avoid arrest or prosecution. It's very important to know what's legal and what's not where you are going.

Arrest notifications in host country: While some countries will automatically notify the nearest U.S. embassy or consulate if a U.S. citizen is detained or arrested in a foreign country, that might not always be the case. To ensure that the United States is aware of your circumstances, request that the police and prison officials notify the nearest U.S. embassy or consulate as soon as you are arrested or detained overseas.

Special Circumstances: Spear fishing equipment may not be imported into Mauritius. Animals may be required to undergo a quarantine period of up to six months,depending on the country of origin and residence history. Please contact the Mauritian Society for the Prevention of Cruelty to Animals at (230) 464-5084 for specific information related to pet importation.

Accessibility: While in Mauritius individuals with disabilities may find accessibility and accommodation very different from what is commonly provided in the United States.

The Mauritian government partially implemented a law mandating access to buildings for persons with disabilities; however, many older buildings remain difficult to access.

Medical Facilities and Health Information: Medical facilities are available, but are more limited than in the United States. Emergency assistance is limited. While public hospitals provide free care, visitors may choose to be treated by private doctors and clinics. Prescription and over-the-counter medicine is generally available, though they may not be specific U.S. brand names. Service Aide Medicale Urgence (SAMU) is a government organization that provides free ambulance and emergency assistance in response to calls to 114 (Address: Volcy Pougnet Street, Port Louis). MegaCare is a private organization that provides assistance to subscribers only (Address: 99 Draper Avenue, Quatre Bornes; phone: 116; 464-6116). Private Clinic Darne tel: 118 and Private Clinic Apollo Bramwell tel: 132 also provide for paid Ambulance Service.

You can find good information on vaccinations and other health precautions, on the CDC website. For information about outbreaks of infectious diseases abroad, consult the World Health Organization (WHO) website. The WHO website also contains additional health information for travelers, including detailed country-specific health information.

Medical Insurance: You can't assume your insurance will go with you when you travel. It's very important to find out BEFORE you leave whether or not your medical insurance will cover you overseas. You need to ask your insurance company two questions:

- Does my policy apply when I'm out of the United States?
- Will it cover emergencies like a trip to a foreign hospital or a medical evacuation?

In many places, doctors and hospitals still expect payment in cash at the time of service. Your regular U.S. health insurance may not cover doctors' and hospital visits in other countries. If your policy doesn't go with you when you travel, it's a very good idea to take out another one for your trip.

Traffic Safety and Road Conditions: While in Mauritius you may encounter road conditions that differ significantly from those in the United States.

Driving is on the left side of the road. Roads are sometimes narrow and uneven with inadequate lighting, making night driving hazardous. Speed limits are posted in kilometers per hour and all road and traffic signs are posted in English. Drivers and all passengers are required to wear seat belts.

Drivers and passengers on motorcycles are required to wear helmets. Babies and toddlers should be placed in child seats. Many accidents occur due to excessive speed and violations of road regulations.

Drivers involved in an accident are required by law to remain at the scene until the police arrive. However, if an angry crowd gathers and those involved in the accident feel threatened, police and judicial authorities have in the past not taken action against drivers who leave the scene if they have proceeded directly to a police station. In cases of minor accidents involving two parties but which involve no injuries and where drivers are not under the influence of alcohol/drugs, drivers may fill out and sign an "Agreed Statement of Facts." Police presence is not required for this. Each party should retain one copy of the statement to claim auto insurance reimbursement.

While there are organizations that provide emergency or roadside assistance, their resources and capabilities are limited and on occasion they are unable to respond in non-life threatening incidents. Public transportation by bus is available between the main towns until 11:00 p.m. and in remote areas until 6 p.m. Taxis are also available.

Aviation Safety Oversight: As there is no direct commercial air service to the United States by carriers registered in Mauritius, the U.S. Federal Aviation Administration (FAA) has not assessed the government of Mauritius' Civil Aviation Authority for compliance with International Civil Aviation Organization (ICAO) aviation safety standards. Further information may be found on the FAA's safety assessment page.

Children's Issues: Please see the U.S. Dept. of State Office of Children's Issues web pages on intercountry adoption and international parental child abduction.

Intercountry Adoption

June 2009

The information in this section has been edited from a 2009 report available through the U.S. Department of State Office of Children's Issues. As of 2013, the Department of State is in the process of revising the information to reflect current adoption laws and procedures in Mauritius. The following serves only as a reference. For more detailed information, please read the *International Adoption* section of this book and review current reports online at http://www.adoption.state.gov.

Mauritius is party to the Hague Convention on Protection of Children and Co-operation in Respect of Intercountry Adoption (Hague Adoption Convention). Therefore all adoptions between Mauritius and the United States must meet the requirements of the Convention and U.S. law implementing the Convention. Mauritius has ratified the Hague Adoption Convention; however, it is not in conformity with the Convention as the Convention requires the setting up of a Central Authority. The Government of Mauritius is in the process of establishing a central adoption authority and on amending its laws in order to be Hague-compliant.

Who Can Adopt? Adoption between the United States and Mauritius is governed by the Hague Adoption Convention. Therefore to adopt from Mauritius, you must first be found eligible to adopt by the U.S. Government. The U.S. Government agency responsible for making this determination is the Department of Homeland Security, U.S. Citizenship and Immigration Services (USCIS). In addition to these U.S. requirements for prospective adoptive parents, Mauritius also has the following requirements for prospective adoptive parents.

Residency Requirements: There are no residency requirements to complete an intercountry adoption in Mauritius.

Age Requirements: Adoptive parents must be at least 15 years older than the child.

Marriage Requirements: Adoptive parents may be single or married.

Who Can Be Adopted? Because Mauritius is party to the Hague Adoption Convention, children from Mauritius must meet the requirements of the Convention in order to be eligible for adoption. For example, the Convention requires that Mauritius attempt to place a child with a family in-country before determining that a child is eligible for intercountry adoption. In addition to Mauritius's requirements, a child must meet the definition of a Convention adoptee for you to bring him or her back to the United States.

Adoption Authority: National Adoption Council (NAC), Contact: Mrs. Baccha or Mrs. Purryag

The Process: Because Mauritius is party to the Hague Adoption Convention, adopting from Mauritius must follow a specific process designed to meet the Convention's requirements. For detailed and updated information on these requirements, please review the *Intercountry Adoption* section of this publication and visit the USCIS Intercountry Adoption website at http://adoption.state.gov.

Role of the Adoption Authority: The Mauritian National Adoption Council (NAC) does not match adoptable orphans with prospective adoptive parents. The NAC receives the adoption application, reviews it and either approves or rejects it. NAC sends approved applications on to the court.

Role of the Court: The court determines whether or not to approve the adoption.

Time Frame: The approval of the application takes approximately of 60 days, during which time the NAC verifies information regarding the biological child, including his actual home situation and information provided in the home study. There is an additional 15 days needed to complete court procedures for an adoption.

Adoptive parents will need to come to Mauritius at the time the adoption is brought before the judge for a decision. If prospective parents are residing outside Mauritius, they may request a phone interview, but the Mauritian authorities view this as the exception rather than the rule.

Adoption Application: Adoptable children are located through personal contacts with families who are unable to care for their child and are willing to give up their child for adoption. Prospective adoptive parents are advised to verify ahead of time that their Mauritian prospective adoptive child meets the definition of "legal orphan" as defined by the Immigration and Nationality Act Section 101(b)(1)(F). The application for adoption is filed with the NAC. Once it is approved, the case is brought before a judge. The judge must approve the adoption. Adoptive parents are advised to consider retaining the services of an attorney to handle the judicial proceedings. Prospective adoptive parents must attend the adoption hearing in Mauritius.

Adoption Fees: In the adoption services contract that you sign at the beginning of the adoption process, your agency will itemize the fees and estimated expenses related to your adoption process. Some of the fees specifically associated with adopting from Mauritius include a non-refundable 5,000 Mauritian Rupees (MRs) application fee together with a guarantee fee of MRs 20,000, refundable upon completion of the adoption, must be sent with the application and supporting documents to the NAC. The U.S. Embassy in Mauritius discourages the payment of any fees that are not properly receipted, "donations," or "expediting" fees, that may be requested from prospective adoptive parents. Such fees have the appearance of "buying" a baby.

Documents Required: An application form for adoption must be filed at the National Adoption Council (NAC), along with the following documents:

- 4 photos of the child duly endorsed by a lawyer (the lawyer confirms the photo is a true photo of the child being adopted);
- Birth certificate of the child;

- 2 comprehensive medical certificates for the child from two different child specialists;
- Birth and marriage certificate(s) of the biological parents (if applicable);
- Divorce decree of the biological parents, if applicable;
- Medical certificate(s) of biological parents, if applicable;
- 2 recent passport size photos of the biological parents;
- Birth certificate(s) of prospective adoptive parents;
- Marriage certificate of prospective adoptive parents, if applicable;
- A home study from an adoption services provider in the United States;
- Documentation of financial means of prospective adoptive parents;
- If applicable, documents of ownership of a house/estate;
- Report of any criminal record from the U.S. (U.S. state level will suffice);
- If either of the prospective adoptive parents is unable to have a child, medical certificate documenting this fact must be submitted;
- Guarantee that in case of an accident, a specified third party will take care of child;
- Progress report of a Mauritian child adopted by applicants, if applicable.

Bringing Your Child Home: Once your adoption is complete (or you have obtained legal custody of the child), there are a few more steps to take before you can head home. Specifically, you need to apply for several documents for your child before he or she can travel to the United States, such as a birth certificate, a passport or travel document for your child from the country in which he or she was born, and a U.S. Immigration Visa.

For detailed and updated information on how to obtain these documents, visit the USCIS Intercountry Adoption website at http://adoption.state.gov.

Child Citizenship Act: For adoptions finalized abroad, the Child Citizenship Act of 2000 allows your new child to acquire American citizenship automatically when he or she enters the United States as lawful permanent residents.

For adoptions finalized in the United States, the Child Citizenship Act of 2000 allows your new child to acquire American citizenship automatically when the court in the United States issues the final adoption decree. To learn more, review the *Intercountry Adoption* section on this publication and visit the USCIS Intercountry Adoption website at http://adoption.state.gov.

U.S. Embassy in Mauritius
4th Floor, Rogers House
John Kennedy Avenue
P.O. Box 544
Port Louis, Republic of Mauritius
Tel: (230) 202-4400
Fax: (230) 208-9534
E-mail: usembass@intnet.mu
http://mauritius.usembassy.gov

Mauritius's Adoption Authority
National Adoption Council (NAC)
Contact: Mrs. Baccha or
Mrs. Purryag
Address: 4th Floor Government
Centre, Port Louis, Mauritius
Tel: (230) 201 3549; fax: 210 8151
Internet: http://www.gov.mu

Embassy of the Republic Mauritius
4301 Connecticut Avenue, N.W.
Suite 441, Washington, DC 20008
Tel.: (202) 244-1491/1492
Fax: (202) 966-0983

Office of Children's Issues
U.S. Department of State
2201 C Street, NW
SA-29
Washington, DC 20520
Tel: 1-888-407-4747
E-mail: AskCI@state.gov
Internet: http://adoption.state.gov

For questions about immigration procedures, call the National Customer Service Center (NCSC) 1-800-375-5283 (TTY 1-800-767-1833).

MEXICO

Compiled from publications that were available as of February 2013 from the U.S. Department of State, the U.S. Department of Commerce, and the Central Intelligence Agency (CIA). See the introduction to this set for explanatory notes.

Official Name:
United Mexican States

PROFILE

Geography

Area: total: 1,964,375 sq km; country comparison to the world: 14; land: 1,943,945 sq km; water: 20,430 sq km

Major cities: Mexico City (capital) 19.319 million; Guadalajara 4.338 million; Monterrey 3.838 million; Puebla 2.278 million; Tijuana 1.629 million (2009)

Climate: varies from tropical to desert

Terrain: high, rugged mountains; low coastal plains; high plateaus; desert

People

Nationality: noun: Mexican(s); adjective: Mexican

Population: 114,975,406 (July 2012 est.)

Population growth rate: 1.086% (2012 est.)

Ethnic groups: mestizo (Amerindian-Spanish) 60%, Amerindian or predominantly Amerindian 30%, white 9%, other 1%

Religions: Roman Catholic 76.5%, Protestant 5.2% (Pentecostal 1.4%, other 3.8%), Jehovah's Witnesses 1.1%, other 0.3%, unspecified 13.8%, none 3.1% (2000 census)

Languages: Spanish only 92.7%, Spanish and indigenous languages 5.7%, indigenous only 0.8%, unspecified 0.8%

Literacy: definition: age 15 and over can read and write; total population: 86.1%; male: 86.9%; female: 85.3% (2005 Census)

Health: life expectancy at birth: total population: 76.66 years; male: 73.84 years; female: 79.63 years (2012 est.); Infant mortality rate: total: 16.77 deaths/1,000 live births; male: 18.58 deaths/1,000 live births; female: 14.86 deaths/1,000 live births (2012 est.)

Unemployment rate: 4.5% (2012 est.)

Work force: 50.01 million (2012 est.)

Government

Type: federal republic

Independence: 16 September 1810

Constitution: 5 February 1917

Political subdivisions: 31 states (estados, singular—estado) and 1 federal district (distrito federal); Aguascalientes, Baja California, Baja California Sur, Campeche, Chiapas, Chihuahua, Coahuila de Zaragoza, Colima, Distrito Federal, Durango, Guanajuato, Guerrero, Hidalgo, Jalisco, Mexico, Michoacan de Ocampo, Morelos, Nayarit, Nuevo Leon, Oaxaca, Puebla, Queretaro de Arteaga, Quintana Roo, San Luis Potosi, Sinaloa, Sonora, Tabasco, Tamaulipas, Tlaxcala, Veracruz de Ignacio de la Llave (Veracruz), Yucatan, Zacatecas

Suffrage: 18 years of age; universal and compulsory (but not enforced)

Economy

GDP (purchasing power parity): $1.758 trillion (2012 est.); $1.683 trillion (2011 est.); $1.619 trillion (2010 est.); $1.534 trillion (2009 est.)

GDP real growth rate: 3.8% (2012 est.); 4% (2011 est.); 5.5% (2010 est.); -6.3% (2009 est.)

GDP per capita (PPP): $15,300 (2012 est.); $14,800 (2011 est.); $14,400 (2010 est.); $13,900 (2009 est.)

Natural resources: petroleum, silver, copper, gold, lead, zinc, natural gas, timber

Agriculture products: corn, wheat, soybeans, rice, beans, cotton, coffee, fruit, tomatoes; beef, poultry, dairy products; wood products

Industries: food and beverages, tobacco, chemicals, iron and steel, petroleum, mining, textiles, clothing, motor vehicles, consumer durables, tourism

Exports: $377.4 billion (2012 est.); $349.7 billion (2011 est.); $298.5 billion (2010 est.)

Exports—commodities: manufactured goods, oil and oil products, silver, fruits, vegetables, coffee, cotton
Exports—partners: US 71.7%, Canada 7.4% (2009 est.)
Imports: $379.4 billion (2012 est.); $350.8 billion (2011 est.); $301.5 billion (2010 est.)
Imports—commodities: metalworking machines, steel mill products, agricultural machinery, electrical equipment, car parts for assembly, repair parts for motor vehicles, aircraft, and aircraft parts
Imports—partners: US 62.2%, China 7.5% (2009 est.)
Debt—external: $217.7 billion (31 December 2012 est.); $210.8 billion (31 December 2011 est.); $200.1 billion (31 December 2010 est.)
Exchange rates: Mexican pesos (MXN) per US dollar; 13.25 (2012 est.) ; 12.423 (2011 est.); 12.636 (2010 est.); 13.514 (2009); 11.016 (2008); 10.8 (2007)

PEOPLE

Mexico is the most populous Spanish-speaking country in the world and the second most-populous country in Latin America after Portuguese-speaking Brazil. About 76% of the people live in urban areas. Many Mexicans emigrate from rural areas that lack job opportunities—such as the underdeveloped southern states and the crowded central plateau—to the industrialized urban centers and the developing areas along the U.S.-Mexico border. According to some estimates, the population of the area around Mexico City is nearly 22 million, which would make it the largest concentration of population in the Western Hemisphere. Cities bordering on the United States—such as Tijuana and Ciudad Juarez—and cities in the interior—such as Guadalajara, Monterrey, and Puebla—have undergone sharp rises in population in recent years.

Education

Mexico has made great strides in improving access to education and literacy rates over the past few decades. According to a 2006 World Bank report, enrollment at the primary level is nearly universal, and more children are completing primary education. The average number of years of schooling for the population 15 years old and over was around 8 years during the 2004–2005 school year, a marked improvement on a decade earlier—when it was 6.8 years—but low compared with other Organization for Economic Cooperation and Development (OECD) countries.

Language

Spanish is the official language of Mexico. While many people in the large cities speak some English, it may be difficult for them to conduct detailed discussions. Many mid- and high-level government officials and business executives speak English, and many are U.S. educated.

Religion

In the 2010 census, approximately 83 percent of the population identified themselves as Roman Catholic. Approximately 8 percent stated affiliation with a Protestant or evangelical church, 2 percent identified themselves as members of other Bible-based religions, and one half of 1 percent as Jewish. More than 5 percent of the population reported not practicing any religion.

Official statistics sometimes differ from membership figures of religious groups. For example, 314,932 identified themselves as members of The Church of Jesus Christ of Latter-day Saints (Mormons) in the 2010 census; however, Mormons stated a membership of approximately 1.2 million. There are large Protestant communities in the southern states of Chiapas and Tabasco. In Chiapas, Protestant evangelicals stated that nearly half of the state's 2.4 million inhabitants are evangelicals, but less than 5 percent of the 2010 census respondents in Chiapas self-reported as evangelical.

The Jewish community numbers approximately 60,000, some 42,000 of whom live in Mexico City; there are also congregations in Guadalajara, Monterrey, Tijuana, Cancun, and San Miguel. Nearly half of the country's approximately 4,000 Muslims are concentrated in Mexico City and state. Some indigenous persons in the states of Chiapas, Oaxaca, and Yucatan practice a syncretic religion that mixes Catholic and pre-Hispanic Mayan beliefs.

In some communities, particularly in the south, there is a correlation between politics and religious affiliation. A small number of local leaders reportedly manipulated religious tensions in their communities for their own political or economic benefit, particularly in Chiapas.

HISTORY

Highly developed cultures, including those of the Olmecs, Mayas, Toltecs, and Aztecs, existed long before the Spanish conquest. Hernan Cortes conquered Mexico during the period 1519–21 and founded a Spanish colony that lasted nearly 300 years.

Independence from Spain was proclaimed by Father Miguel Hidalgo on September 16, 1810. Father Hidalgo's declaration of national independence, "Viva Mexico!," known in Mexico as the "Grito de Dolores," launched a decade-long struggle for independence from Spain. Prominent figures in Mexico's war for independence were: Father Jose Maria Morelos; Gen. Augustin de Iturbide, who defeated the Spaniards and ruled as Mexican emperor from 1822–23; and Gen. Antonio Lopez de Santa Ana, who went on to dominate Mexican politics from 1833 to 1855. An 1821 treaty recognized Mexican independence from Spain and called for a constitutional monarchy. The planned monarchy failed; a republic was proclaimed in December 1822 and established in 1824.

Throughout the rest of the 19th century, Mexico's government and economy were shaped by contentious debates among liberals and conservatives, republicans and monarchists, federalists and those who favored centralized government.

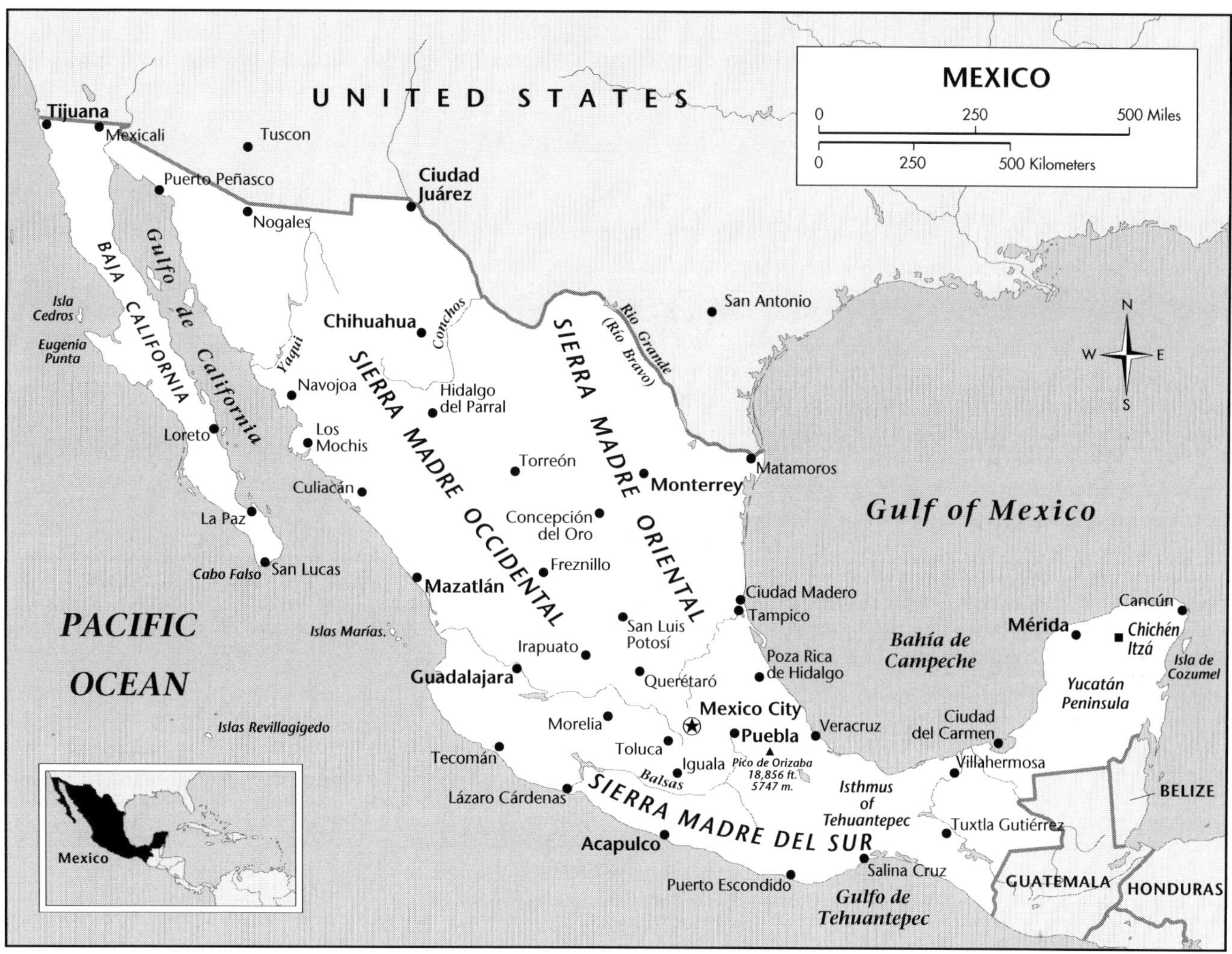

During the four presidential terms of Benito Juarez (1858–72), Mexico experimented with modern democratic and economic reforms. President Juarez' terms in office and Mexico's early experience with democracy were interrupted by the invasion of French forces in early 1862. They imposed a monarchy on the country in the form of Hapsburg archduke Ferdinand Maximilian of Austria, who ruled as emperor from 1864–67.

Liberal forces succeeded in overthrowing, and executing, the emperor in 1867 after which Juarez returned to office until his death in 1872. Following several weak governments, the authoritarian General Porfirio Diaz assumed office and was president during most of the period between 1877 and 1911. Mexico's severe social and economic problems erupted in a revolution that lasted from 1910 until 1920 and gave rise to the 1917 constitution. Prominent leaders in this period—some of whom were rivals for power—were Francisco Madero, Venustiano Carranza, Pancho Villa, Alvaro Obregon, Victoriano Huerta, and Emiliano Zapata. The Institutional Revolutionary Party (PRI), formed in 1929 under a different name, emerged from the chaos of revolution as a vehicle for keeping political competition among a coalition of interests in peaceful channels. For 71 years, Mexico's national government was controlled by the PRI, which won every presidential race and most gubernatorial races until the July 2000 presidential election of Vicente Fox Quesada of the National Action Party (PAN), in what were widely considered at the time the freest and fairest elections in Mexico's history. President Fox completed his term on December 1, 2006, when Felipe Calderon, also of the PAN, assumed the presidency. He was replaced by Enrique Pena Nieto in December 2012.

GOVERNMENT AND POLITICAL CONDITIONS

Mexico is a multiparty federal republic with an elected president and bicameral legislature. Citizens elected President Enrique Pena Nieto of the Institutional Revolutionary Party (IRP) in 2012 to a six-year term in generally free and fair multiparty elections.

Recent Elections

The December 2012 presidential election, in which Enrique Pena Nieto was elected president to a six-year term, was considered generally free and fair by most neutral observers.

Participation of Women and Minorities: As of December 2011 there were 30 women in the 128-seat Senate and 141 women in the 500-seat lower house. Two female justices sat on the 11-member Supreme Court, and there were four women in the 19-member cabinet. Many state electoral codes provide that no more than 70 to 80 percent of candidates can be of the same gender. Some political parties utilized quotas requiring that a certain percentage of candidates on a party list be female. Information on the participation of women and minorities after the 2012 elections was not available at the time of publication.

There were no established quotas for increased participation of indigenous groups in the legislative body, and no reliable statistics were available regarding minority participation in government. The law provides for the right of indigenous people to elect representatives to local office according to "usages and customs" law rather than federal and state electoral law. Usages and customs laws applied traditional practices to resolve disputes, chose local officials, and collected taxes without federal or state government interference. While such practices allowed communities to select officials according to their traditions, the usages and customs law generally excluded women from the political process and often infringed on the rights of women and religious minorities. In some villages women were not permitted to vote or hold office; in others they could vote but not hold office.

Principal Government Officials

Last Updated: 1/31/2013

Pres.: **Enrique PENA NIETO**
Sec. of Agrarian Reform: **Jorge Carlos RAMIREZ Marin**
Sec. of Agriculture, Livestock, Rural Development, Fisheries, & Nutrition: **Enrique MARTINEZ y Martinez**
Sec. of Communications & Transport: **Gerardo RUIZ Esparza**
Sec. of Economy: **Ildefonso GUAJARDO Villareal**
Sec. of Energy: **Pedro Joaquin COLDWELL**
Sec. of Environment & Natural Resources: **Juan Jose GUERRA Abud**
Sec. of Finance & Public Credit: **Luis VIDEGARAY Caso**
Sec. of Foreign Relations: **Jose Antonio MEADE Kuribrena**
Sec. of Govt.: **Miguel Angel OSORIO Chong**
Sec. of Health: **Mercedes Juan LOPEZ**
Sec. of Labor & Social Welfare: **Alfonso NAVARRETE Prida**
Sec. of National Defense: **Salvador CIENFUEGOS Zepeda, Gen.**
Sec. of the Navy: **Vidal SOBERON Sanz, Adm.**
Sec. of Public Education: **Emilio CHUAYFFET Chemor**
Sec. of Public Security
Sec. of Public Service
Sec. of Social Development: **Maria Del Rosario ROBLES Berlanga**
Sec. of Tourism: **Claudia RUIZ Massieu**
Attorney Gen.: **Jesus MURILLO Karam**
Governor, Bank of Mexico: **Agustin CARSTENS Carstens**
Ambassador to the US: **Arturo SARUKHAN Casamitjana**
Permanent Representative to the UN, New York: **Luis Alfonso DE ALBA Gongora**

ECONOMY

Mexico has a free market economy in the trillion dollar class. It contains a mixture of modern and outmoded industry and agriculture, increasingly dominated by the private sector. Recent administrations have expanded competition in seaports, railroads, telecommunications, electricity generation, natural gas distribution, and airports.

Per capita income is roughly one-third that of the US; income distribution remains highly unequal. Since the implementation of the North American Free Trade Agreement (NAFTA) in 1994, Mexico's share of US imports has increased from 7% to 12%, and its share of Canadian imports has doubled to 5%. Mexico has free trade agreements with over 50 countries including Guatemala, Honduras, El Salvador, the European Free Trade Area, and Japan - putting more than 90% of trade under free trade agreements.

In 2007, during its first year in office, the Felipe Calderon administration was able to garner support from the opposition to successfully pass pension and fiscal reforms. The administration passed an energy reform measure in 2008 and another fiscal reform in 2009. Mexico's GDP plunged 6.2% in 2009 as world demand for exports dropped, asset prices tumbled, and remittances and investment declined. GDP posted positive growth of 5.6% in 2010 with exports—particularly to the United States—leading the way. Growth slowed to 3.9% in 2011 and 3.8% in 2012, however.

The administration continues to face many economic challenges, including improving the public education system, upgrading infrastructure, modernizing labor laws, and fostering private investment in the energy sector. Calderon has stated that his top economic priorities remain reducing poverty and creating jobs.

Labor Conditions

The law prohibits children under the age of 14 from working and allows those between the ages of 14 and 17 to work limited daytime hours in non-hazardous conditions, and only with parental permission. The government did not effectively enforce such prohibitions.

According to sources including the International Labor Organization, government enforcement was reasonably effective at large and medium-sized companies, especially in factories run by U.S. companies, or the "maquila" sector, and other industries under federal jurisdiction; inadequate at many small companies and in the agriculture and construction sectors; and nearly absent in the informal sector, in which most children worked. According to the most current government child labor survey, conducted between 2007 and 2009 by the National Institute of Statistics and Geography and the Ministry of Labor, the overall child occupation rate (five to 17 years old) fell from 12.5 percent to 10.7 percent, or approximately 3 million children. Forty-two percent of child labor occurred in the livestock and the agricultural sectors. Child labor in agriculture included the production of melons, onions, sugarcane, tobacco, and tomatoes. Other sectors with significant child labor included commerce, services, manufacturing, and construction.

The minimum daily wage, determined by zone, was 59.82 pesos ($4.29) in Zone A (Baja California, Federal District, state of Mexico, and large cities); 58.13 pesos ($4.16) in Zone B (Sonora, Nuevo Leon, Tamaulipas, Veracruz, and Jalisco); and 56.70 pesos ($4.06) in Zone C (all other states). Most formal sector workers received between one and three times the minimum wage. The National Council for Evaluation of Social Development Policy estimated the poverty line at 64 pesos ($4.58) per day for 2011.

The law sets six eight-hour days and 48 hours per week as the legal workweek. Any work more than eight hours in a day is considered overtime, for which a worker receives double the hourly wage. After accumulating nine hours of overtime in a week, a worker earns triple the hourly wage; the law prohibits compulsory overtime. The law includes eight paid public holidays, and one week of paid annual leave after completing one year of work. The law requires employers to observe occupational safety and health regulations, issued jointly by the STPS and the Mexican Institute for Social Security. Legally mandated joint management and labor committees set standards and are responsible for overseeing workplace standards in plants and offices. Individual employees or unions may complain directly to inspectors or safety and health officials. By law workers may remove themselves from hazardous situations without jeopardizing their employment. In practice workers often could not remove themselves from hazardous situations without jeopardizing their employment. According to labor rights NGOs, employers in all sectors sometimes used the illegal "hours bank" approach—requiring long hours when the workload is heavy and cutting hours when it is light—to avoid compensating workers for overtime. In addition many companies evaded taxes and social security payments by employing workers informally. The Organization for Economic Cooperation and Development estimated that 43 percent of the workforce was engaged in the informal economy.

U.S.-MEXICAN RELATIONS

U.S. relations with Mexico are important and complex. The two countries share a 2,000-mile border, and relations between the two have a direct impact on the lives and livelihoods of millions of Americans—whether the issue is trade and economic reform, homeland security, drug control, migration, or the environment. The U.S. and Mexico, along with Canada, are partners in the North American Free Trade Agreement (NAFTA) and enjoy a broad and expanding trade relationship. Through the North American Leaders' Summits, the United States, Canada, and Mexico cooperate to improve North American competitiveness, ensure the safety of their citizens, and promote clean energy and a healthy environment. The three nations also cooperate on hemispheric and global challenges, such as managing transborder infectious diseases and seeking greater integration to respond to challenges of transnational organized crime.

U.S. relations with Mexico are important and complex. U.S. relations with Mexico have a direct impact on the lives and livelihoods of millions of Americans—whether the issue is trade and economic reform, homeland security drug control, migration, or the environment. The scope of U.S.-Mexican relations is broad and goes beyond diplomatic and official contacts. It entails extensive commercial, cultural, and educational ties, with over 1.25 billion dollars worth of two-way trade and roughly one million legal border crossings each day. In addition, a million American citizens live in Mexico and approximately 10 million Americans visit Mexico every year. More than 18,000 companies with U.S. investment have operations in Mexico, and U.S. companies have invested $145 billion in Mexico since 2000.

Cooperation between the United States and Mexico along the 2,000-mile common border includes state and local problem-solving mechanisms; transportation planning; and institutions to address resource, environment and health issues. Presidents Obama and Calderon created a high level Executive Steering Committee for 21st Century Border Management in 2010 to spur advancements in creating a modern, secure, and efficient border. The multi-agency U.S.-Mexico Binational Group on Bridges and Border Crossings meets twice yearly to improve the efficiency of existing crossings and coordinate planning for new ones. The ten U.S. and Mexican border states are active participants in these meetings. Chaired by U.S. and Mexican consuls, Border Liaison Mechanisms operate in "sister city" pairs and have proven to be an effective means of dealing with a variety of local issues including border infrastructure, accidental violation of sovereignty by law enforcement officials, charges of mistreatment of foreign nationals, and cooperation in public health matters.

The United States and Mexico have a long history of cooperation on environmental and natural resource issues, particularly in the border area, where there are serious environmental problems caused by rapid population growth, urbanization, and industrialization. Cooperative activities between the U.S. and Mexico take place under a number of arrangements such as the International Boundary and Water Commission; the La Paz Agreement, the U.S.-Mexico Border 2012/2020 Program; the North American Development Bank and the Border Environment Cooperation Commission; the North American Commission for Environmental Cooperation; the Border Health Commission; and a variety of other agreements that address border health, wildlife and migratory birds, national parks, forests, and marine and atmospheric resources. The International Boundary and Water Commission, United States and Mexico, is an international organization responsible for managing a wide variety of water resource and boundary preservation issues.

The two countries also have cooperated on telecommunications services in the border area for more than 50 years. There are 39 bilateral agreements that govern shared use of the radio spectrum. When the United States completed the transition to digital television in 2009, a high percentage of Mexican border cities did the same, well ahead of Mexico's deadline to complete the transition by 2021. Recent border agreements also cover mobile broadband services, including smartphones, and similar devices. The High Level Consultative Commission on Telecommunications continues to serve as the primary bilateral arena for both governments to promote growth in the sector and to ensure compatible services in the border area. The United States and Mexico have also signed an agreement to improve cross-border public security communications in the border area.

U.S. Cooperation with Mexico

The Merida Initiative is an unprecedented partnership between the United States and Mexico to fight organized crime and associated violence while furthering respect for human rights and the rule of law. Since 2010, our Merida Initiative cooperation has been organized under four strategic pillars. The first pillar aims to disrupt the capacity of organized crime to operate by capturing criminal groups and their leaders and reducing their revenues through better investigations, successful prosecutions, and shipment interdictions. The initiative's second pillar focuses on enhancing the capacity of Mexico's government and institutions to sustain the rule of law. The Merida Initiative's third pillar aims to improve border management to facilitate legitimate trade and movement of people while thwarting the flow of drugs, arms, and cash. Finally, the fourth pillar seeks to build strong and resilient communities.

U.S. cooperation with Mexico under the Merida Initiative directly supports programs to help Mexico train its police forces in modern investigative techniques, promote a culture of lawfulness, and implement key justice reforms. Merida Initiative assistance also supports Mexico's efforts to reform its judicial sector and professionalize its police forces reflect its commitment to promote the rule of law and build strong law enforcement institutions to counter the threat posed by organized crime. The U.S. Congress has appropriated $1.9 billion for the Merida Initiative since it began.

U.S. Agency for International Development (USAID) programs support Mexican efforts to address key challenges to improving citizen security and well-being, with program approaches specifically geared to the U.S.-Mexico relationship. Programs under the Merida Initiative develop and test models to mitigate the community-level impact of crime and violence, and support Mexico's implementation of criminal justice constitutional reforms that protect citizens' rights. Additional USAID programs support Mexico's commitment to reducing greenhouse gas emissions and to enhancing economic competitiveness to improve citizens' lives.

Mexico is the United States' second-largest export market (after Canada) and third-largest trading partner (after Canada and China). Mexico's exports rely heavily on supplying the U.S. market, but the country has also sought to diversify its export destinations. Nearly 80 percent of Mexico's exports in 2011 went to the United States. In 2011, Mexico was the second-largest supplier of oil to the United States. Top U.S. exports to Mexico include mechanical machinery, electronic equipment, motor vehicle parts, mineral fuels and oils, and plastics. Trade matters are generally settled through direct negotiations between the two countries or addressed via World Trade Organization or NAFTA formal dispute settlement procedures.

Mexican investment in the United States has grown by over 35 percent the past five years. It is the seventh fastest growing investor country in the United States.

Mexico is a major recipient of remittances, sent mostly from Mexicans in the United States. Remittances are a major source of foreign currency, totaling over $22.73 billion in 2011. Most remittances are used for immediate consumption — food, housing, health care, education — but some collective remittances, sent from Mexican migrants in the U.S. to their community of origin, are used for shared projects and infrastructure improvements under Mexico's 3 for 1 program that matches contributions with federal, state and local funds.

Mexico is making progress in its intellectual property rights enforcement efforts, although piracy and counterfeiting rates remain high. Mexico appeared on the Watch List in the 2012 Special 301 report. The U.S. continues to work with the Mexican Government to implement its commitment to improving intellectual property protection.

Mexico's Membership in International Organizations

Mexico is a strong supporter of the United Nations (UN) and Organization of American States (OAS) systems, and hosted the G-20 Leaders' Summit in June 2012. Mexico and the United States belong to a number of the same international organizations, including the UN, OAS, Asia-Pacific Economic Cooperation (APEC) forum, G-20, Organization for Economic Cooperation and Development (OECD), International Monetary

Fund (IMF), World Bank (WB), and World Trade Organization (WTO). In January 2012, Mexico became a member of the Wassenaar Arrangement, a multilateral export control regime for conventional arms and dual-use goods.

Bilateral Representation

Mexico maintains an embassy in the United States at 1911 Pennsylvania Ave. NW, Washington, DC 20006 (tel. 202-728-1600).

Principal U.S. Embassy Officials

Last Updated: 1/14/2013

MEXICO CITY (E) Paseo de la Reforma 305, Col. Cuauhtemoc, 06500, 011-52-55-5080-2000, Fax 011-52-55-5080-2005, INMARSAT Tel 683-142-218-172, Workweek: Monday to Friday, 8:30 a.m. to 5:30 p.m., http://mexico.usembassy.gov/

DCM OMS:	Christina Del Pozzo
AMB OMS:	Allie Almero
CG OMS:	Reyna M. Ramirez
Co-CLO:	Susan Fasciani
DHS/CBP:	Doyle Amidon
DHS/CIS:	Joseph T. Roma
DHS/ICE:	Guillermo Cano
DHS/TSA:	Alida Offenbach
FCS:	Dorothy Lutter
FDA:	Phyllis Marquitz
FM:	Lew Burkholder
HRO:	Susan Mutschler
MGT:	Marjorie R. Phillips
MLO/ODC:	COL Ronald J. Garner
NAS/INL:	Annie Pforzheimer
OPDAT:	Kevin L. Sundwall
SDO/DATT:	RADM Colin Kilrain
TREAS:	William Rondon
AMB:	Earl Anthony Wayne
CG:	Marjorie A.Ames
CON:	John B. Brennan
DCM:	Laura F. Dogu
PAO:	Mara Tekach
GSO:	Cheryl Johnson
RSO:	Paul Isaac
AGR:	Dan Berman
AID:	Tom Delaney
APHIS:	Nicholas Gutierrez
ATF:	Ari Shapira
ATO:	Garth W. Thornburn
CLO:	Sylvia Rogers
DEA:	Paul Craine
ECON:	John Sammis
EEO:	Fred Miller
EST:	Heidi Gomez
FIN:	Todd Conklin
FMO:	Philip Dubois
IMO:	Harvey Vazquez
IRS:	Alfonso Herrera
ISO:	William Jamerson
ISSO:	Jack Carollo
LAB:	Brian S. Quigley
LEGATT:	Peter Moore
POL:	Michael P. Glover
State ICASS:	Leo Brandenburg

CIUDAD JUAREZ (CG) Paseo de la Victoria 3650, 011-52-656-227-3000, Fax 011-52-656-616-9056, Workweek: MON-FRI 8A.M.-5:00P.M., Website: http://ciudadjuarez.usconsulate.gov/

CG OMS:	Cdj Staff Assistant
Co-CLO:	Ileen Park
DHS/CIS:	Yolanda Miranda
DHS/ICE:	Jaime Corona
DPO:	Douglas Koneff
FM:	Roy Wurdeman
HRO:	Marialice Burford De Castillo
MGT:	George Navadel
NAS/INL:	Leo Navarrete
POL/ECON:	Ray Hotz
POSHO:	See Fm
CG:	Ian G. Brownlee
CON:	Karen Ogle
PAO:	Olga Bashbush
GSO:	Frances Crespo
RSO:	Kieran McCambridge
AFSA:	Marlene Wurdeman
APHIS:	Alfredo Delatorre
ATF:	Richard Byrd
CLO:	Jodie Miller
EEO:	Rachel Atwood
FMO:	In Mexico City
IMO:	In Mexico City
IPO:	Thomas Murray
ISO:	See Ipo
ISSO:	Marlene Wurdeman
LEGATT:	William Hollister (Acting)

GUADALAJARA (CG) 175 Progreso Street, 52 (33) 3268-2100, Fax 52 (33) 3826-6549, INMARSAT Tel 8816-7-631-1222 & 88, Workweek: Mon-Fri 0800–1630, http://www.usembassy mexico.gov.Guadalajara.htm/

CA:	Kelly Trainor De O.
Co-CLO:	Elena Finley
DHS/ICE:	Yariel Ramos
FCS:	Vacant
MGT:	Melissa Garza
POL/ECON:	Bion N. Bliss
POSHO:	Sujoya Roy
PO:	Susan K. Abeyta
CON:	Kerry Brougham
PAO:	R. Madison Conoley
GSO:	Sujoya Roy
RSO:	Kurt Finley
APHIS:	Vacant
CLO:	Jennifer Marsh
DEA:	Kirk Seeley
IMO:	Bruce Waddell
IPO:	Bruce Waddell
ISO:	Bruce Waddell
LEGATT:	Roque Tolentino

HERMOSILLO (CG) Monterrey 141 Pte., Rosales y Galeana, CP83260 Hermosillo, Son., Mexico, (662)289-3500, Fax (662) 217-1890, INMARSAT Tel 8816 315 61540, Workweek: Mon-Fri, 0800–1630, http://hermosillo.usconsulate.gov/

CA:	Luis A. Ramirez
CG OMS:	Alejandra Escobosa
DHS/ICE:	Mario Mendez
DPO:	Alice F. Seddon
MGT:	Donald C. Emerick
POSHO:	Donald C. Emerick
CG:	John S. Tavenner
PO:	John S. Tavenner
CON:	Alice F. Seddon
RSO:	Brian Caza
DEA:	Antonio Silva
IPO:	William M. Layne
LEGATT:	Jonathan M. Tapp

MATAMOROS (CG) Calle Primera #2002, Col. Jardin, 011 (52) (868) 812-4402, Fax 011 (52) (868) 812-2517 (PO)/ 812-2171 (NIV)/ 816-2127 (Admin)/816-0883 (ACS), Workweek: Monday to Friday/8 a.m. to 5 p.m., http://matamoros.usconsulate.gov/

DHS/ICE:	Jose Ovalle/Gilberto Limon
MGT:	Jennifer Danover
PO:	Thomas Mittnacht
CON:	Joe Koen
RSO:	Robert Castro
DEA:	Stephen L. Hester
ECON:	Dorian Molina
IPO:	Francis (Mike) Ruddy
ISSO:	Francis (Mike) Ruddy
POL:	Jennifer Nilson

MERIDA (CG) Calle 60 No. 338 K x 29 y 31 Col. Alcala Martin C.P. 97050, (52) (999) 942-5700, Fax (52) (999) 942-5777, INMARSAT Tel 8816-31621411, Workweek: Monday Thru Friday 7:30 to 4:30, Website: http://merida.usconsulate.gov/

DHS/ICE:	Oscar Galarza
MGT:	Paul Nichols
PO:	Sonya Tsiros
CON:	Maureen Smith
GSO:	Paul Nichols
RSO:	Eric Jagels
ATF:	Ari C. Shapira
CLO:	Janeth K. Gehlert

DEA:	Justin Peterson
EEO:	Patricia Neira
IPO:	Andrius Ciziunas

MONTERREY (CG) Av. Constitucion #411 Pte., Monterrey, N.L., Mexico 64000, (52) (81)8047-3100, Fax (52) (81)8047-3171, Workweek: Monday–Friday/8:00 to 5:00, Website: http://monterrey.usconsulate.gov/

DHS/CIS:	Velasco, Gilda
DHS/ICE:	Lazcano, Jesus
FCS:	Howell, John
FM:	Barkenhagen, Robert
MGT:	Laycock, Chris
POL/ECON:	Michaels, Richard
POSHO:	Barkenhagen, Robert
CG:	Pomper, Joseph
CON:	Gourlay, Elizabeth
PAO:	Beale, Courtney
GSO:	Escoto, Ernesto
RSO:	Deleon, Maria
ATF:	Quinonez, Louis
ATO:	Vacant
CLO:	Baloun, Svetlana
DEA:	Silva, Leonardo
IPO:	Baloun, David
LEGATT:	Vacant

NOGALES (CG) Calle San Jose S/N Fracc. Los Alamos, Nogales Sonora 84065, 011-52-631-311-8150, Fax 011-52-631-313-4797, Workweek: M-F, 8:00 a.m.–5:00 p.m., http://nogales.usconsulate.gov/

MGT:	Ed Luchessi
POL/ECON:	Jeffery Austin
POSHO:	Ed Luchessi
PO:	Chad P. Cummins
CON:	Megan M. Phaneuf
GSO:	Ed Luchessi
RSO:	Anthony Spotti
AFSA:	Jeffery Austin
DEA:	Gregory M. Donovan
IPO:	William Layne
ISSO:	William Layne

NUEVO LAREDO (CG) Allende 3330, Col. Jardin, Nuevo Laredo, Tamps, MX 88260, (52) 867-714-0512, Fax (52) 867-714-0990, Workweek: 0800–1700, M-F, Website: http://nuevolaredo.usconsulate.gov/

MGT:	Joel Erwin
PO:	David Zimov
CON:	James Jimenez
RSO:	Lawrence Woody
CLO:	Elizabeth Herzog
IMO:	Jesus Alejandro
ISSO:	Jesus Alejandro
POL:	Kharmika Tillery

TIJUANA (CG) Paseo de las Culturas S/N, Mesa de Otay, Del. Centenario, Tijuana BC Mexico, +52-664-977-2000, Fax +52-664-977-2117, Workweek: M-F 7:30-4:15, Website: http://tijuana.usconsulate.gov/

Co-CLO:	Tomasevich, Jeffery A
DHS/ICE:	Ochoa, Salvador
FM:	Johnson, Luke
MGT:	Marquez, Panfilo
POL/ECON:	Reinert, Susan
POSHO:	Johnson, Luke
CG:	Erickson, Andrew S E
CON:	Skeirik, Lynne P.
PAO:	Grier, Amy Russell
GSO:	Bologna, Darren P.
RSO:	Kolshorn, Peter
AFSA:	Wallace, Karin S
ATF:	Hernandez, Armando
CLO:	Eggerton, Kimberly A
DEA:	Martinez, Juan A.
EEO:	Grier, Amy Russell
IMO:	Vacant
IPO:	Vacant
ISO:	Vacant
ISSO:	Vacant
LEGATT:	Embassy Mexico

Other Contact Information

American Chamber of Commerce of Mexico
Blas Pascual 205, 3rd Floor
Col. Los Morales, 11510 Mexico
D.F., Mexico
U.S. Mailing Address:
P.O. Box 60326–113
Houston, TX 77205–0326
Tel: (011)(52) 555-141-3820
Fax: (011)(52) 555-141-3836
E-Mail: amchammx@amcham.org.mx

U.S. Department of Commerce
International Trade Administration
Office of Latin America and the Caribbean
14th and Constitution, NW
Washington, DC 20230
Tel: 202-482-0305;
1-800-USA-TRADE
Internet: http://trade.gov/

TRAVEL

Consular Information Sheet

June 21, 2012

Country Description: Mexico is a Spanish-speaking country about three times the size of Texas, consisting of 31 states and one federal district. The capital is Mexico City. Mexico has a rapidly developing economy, ranked by the International Monetary Fund as the fourteenth largest in the world. The climate ranges from tropical to arid, and the terrain consists of coastal lowlands, central high plateaus, deserts and mountains of up to 18,000 feet.

Many cities throughout Mexico are popular tourist destinations for U.S. citizens. Travelers should note that location-specific information contained below is not confined solely to those cities, but can reflect conditions throughout Mexico. Although the majority of visitors to Mexico thoroughly enjoy their stay, a small number experience difficulties and serious inconveniences.

Smart Traveler Enrollment Program (STEP)/Embassy, Consulate & Consular Agency Locations: U.S. citizens living or traveling in Mexico are encouraged to sign up for the Smart Traveler Enrollment Program in order to obtain updated information on local travel and security. U.S. citizens without Internet access may sign up directly with the nearest U.S. embassy or consulate. Enrolling is important; it allows the State Department to assist U.S. citizens in an emergency and keep you up to date with important safety and security announcements.

Embassy Location: The U.S. Embassy is located in Mexico City at Paseo de la Reforma 305, Colonia Cuauhtemoc; telephone from the United States: 011-52-55-5080–2000; telephone within Mexico City: 5080–2000; telephone long distance within Mexico 01-55-5080–2000. You may contact the Embassy by e-mail or visit the Embassy website. The U.S. Embassy in Mexico City is also on Facebook & Twitter. The Embassy serves a consular district encompassing the Federal District of Mexico; the states of Guanajuato, Queretaro, Hidalgo, Veracruz, Michoacan, the State of Mexico, Tlaxcala, Morelos, Puebla, Guerrero, Oaxaca, Tabasco, and Chiapas; and the city of Tampico, Tamaulipas. In addition to the Embassy there are nine United States consulates and thirteen consular agencies located throughout Mexico. In the list below you will find the consular district covered by each consulate.

Consulates (with consular districts defined by Mexican state): Ciudad Juarez (Chihuahua): Paseo de la Victoria 3650, telephone (011) (52) (656) 227-3000. Guadalajara (Nayarit, Jalisco, Aguas Calientes, and Colima): Progreso 175, Col. Americana; telephone (011) (52) (333) 268-2100.

Hermosillo (Sinaloa and the southern part of Sonora): Calle Monterrey 141 Poniente, Col. Esqueda; telephone (011) (52) (662) 289-3500.

Matamoros (the southern part of Tamaulipas with the exception of the city of Tampico): Avenida Primera 2002 y Azaleas; telephone (011) (52) (868) 812-4402.

Merida (Campeche, Yucatan, and Quintana Roo): Calle 60 No. 338 K x 29 y 31, Col. Alcala Martin; telephone (011) (52) (999) 942-5700.

Monterrey (Nuevo Leon, Durango, Zacatecas, San Luis Potosi, and the southern part of Coahuila): Avenida Constitucion 411 Poniente; telephone (011) (52) (818) 047-3100.

Nogales (the northern part of Sonora): Calle San Jose, Fraccionamiento "Los Alamos"; telephone (011) (52) (631) 311-8150.

Nuevo Laredo (the northern part of Coahuila and the northwestern part of Tamaulipas): Calle Allende 3330, Col. Jardin; telephone (011) (52) (867) 714-0512.

Tijuana (Baja California Norte and Baja California Sur): Paseo de Las Culturas s/n Mesa de Otay, telephone (011) (52) (664) 977-2000.

Consular Agencies (mainly serving the location city only): Acapulco: Hotel Emporio, Costera Miguel Aleman 121—Suite 14; telephone (011)(52)(744) 481-0100 or (011)(52)(744) 484-0300.

Los Cabos: Tiendas de Palmilla, Carretera Transpeninsular Km 27.5

Local B221, San José del Cabo, Baja California Sur, C.P. 23406: Telephone: (624) 143-3566 Fax: (624) 143-6750

Cancun: Blvd. Kukulcan Km 13 ZH Torre La Europea, Despacho 301 Cancun, Quintana Roo, Mexico C.P. 77500; telephone (011)(52)(998) 883-0272.

Cozumel: Plaza Villa Mar en El Centro, Plaza Principal, (Parque Juárez between Melgar and 5th Ave.) 2nd floor, Locales #8 and 9; telephone (011)(52)(987) 872-4574.

Ixtapa/Zihuatanejo: Hotel Fontan, Blvd. Ixtapa; telephone (011)(52)(755) 553-2100.

Mazatlan: Hotel Playa Mazatlán, Playa Gaviotas 202, Zona Dorada; telephone (011)(52)(669) 916-5889.

Oaxaca: Macedonio Alcala No. 407, Interior 20; telephone (011)(52)(951)514-3054 or (011)(52)(951) 516-2853.

Piedras Negras: Abasolo 211, Local 3, Col. Centro; telephone (011)(52)(878) 782-5586 or (011)(52)(878) 782-8664.

Playa del Carmen: The Palapa, Calle 1 Sur, between Avenida 15 and Avenida 20; telephone (011)(52)(984) 873-0303.

Puerto Vallarta:Paseo de Los Cocoteros 85 Sur, Paradise Plaza—Local L-7, Nuevo Vallarta, Nayarit C.P.; telephone (011)(52)(322) 222-0069.

Reynosa: Calle Emilio Portes Gil #703, Col. Prado Sur; telephone: (011)(52) (899)-921-6530

San Luis Potosi: Edificio "Las Terrazas," Avenida Venustiano Carranza 2076–41, Col. Polanco; telephone (011)(52)(444) 811-7802 or (011)(52)(444) 811-7803.

San Miguel de Allende: Centro Comercial La Luciernaga, Libramiento Manuel Zavala (Pepe KBZON), telephone (011)(52)(415) 152-2357.

Entry/Exit Requirements for U.S. Citizens: For the latest entry requirements, visit the National Institute of Migration's website, the Secretary of Tourism's Manual on tourist entry, or contact the Embassy of Mexico at 1911 Pennsylvania Avenue NW, Washington, DC 20006, telephone (202) 736-1600, or any Mexican consulate in the United States.

Since March 1, 2010, all U.S. citizens—including children—have been required to present a valid passport or passport card for travel into Mexico. While documents are not routinely checked along the land border, Mexican authorities at immigration checkpoints approximately 20 to 30 kilometers from the border with the U.S. will often conduct vehicle and document inspections and will require valid travel documents and an entry permit or Forma Migratoria Multiple (FMM). All U.S. citizens entering by land and traveling farther than 20 kilometers into Mexico should stop at an immigration checkpoint to obtain an FMM, even if not explicitly directed to do so by Mexican officials. Beyond the 20-30 kilometer border zone, all non-Mexican citizens must have valid immigration documents (FMM, FM2, FM3 or FME) regardless of the original place of entry. Failure to present an FMM when checking in for an international flight departing Mexico can result in delays or missed flights as airlines may insist that a valid FMM be obtained from Mexican immigration authorities (Instituto Nacional de Migración, INM) before issuing a boarding pass.

All U.S. citizens entering Mexico by sea, including U.S. citizens engaged in recreational or commercial fishing in Mexican territorial waters, are required to have an FMM. Additionally, boats engaged in commercial activities in Mexican waters, including sports fishing vessels, must be inspected and permitted by the Secretariat of Communications and Transportations (SCT), which publishes Spanish-language information on Mexican boating permit requirements. All U.S. citizens aged 16 or older must present a valid U.S. passport book to return to the United States via an international flight.

All U.S. citizens aged 16 or older traveling outside of the United States by air, land or sea (except closed-loop cruises) are required to present a Western Hemisphere Travel Initiative (WHTI) compliant document such as a passport book or a passport card to return to the United States. Travelers with passports that are found to be washed, mutilated or damaged may be refused entry to Mexico and returned to the United States.

We strongly encourage all U.S. citizen travelers to apply for a U.S. passport well in advance of anticipated travel. U.S. citizens can visit the Bureau of Consular Affairs' website or call 1-877-4USA-PPT (1-877-487-2778) for information on how to apply for their passports.

While WHTI compliant documents other than passport books are sufficient for re-entry into the United States by land or sea, they may not be accepted as entry documents by the particular country you plan to visit; please be sure to check with your cruise line and countries of destination for any foreign entry requirements.

Although Mexican Immigration regulations allow use of the passport card for entry into Mexico by air, travelers should be aware that the card may not be used to board international flights in the U.S. or to return to the U.S. from abroad by air. The passport card is available only to U.S. citizens. Legal permanent residents in possession of their I-551 Permanent Resident card may board flights to the United States from Mexico.

HIV/AIDS Restrictions: The U.S. Department of State is unaware of any HIV/AIDS entry restrictions for visitors to or foreign residents of Mexico.

Minors: Mexican law requires that any non-Mexican citizen under the age of 18 departing Mexico must carry notarized written permission from any parent or guardian not traveling with the child to or from Mexico. This permission must include the name of the parent, the name of the child, the name of anyone traveling with the child, and the notarized signature(s) of the absent parent(s). The State Department recommends that the permission should include travel dates, destinations, airlines and a brief summary of the circumstances surrounding the travel. The child must be carrying the original letter—not a facsimile or scanned copy—as well as proof of the parent/child relationship (usually a birth certificate or court document)—and an original custody decree, if applicable. Travelers should contact the Mexican Embassy or the nearest Mexican consulate for current information.

Tourist Travel: U.S. citizens do not require a visa or a tourist card for tourist stays of 72 hours or less within the 20-30 kilometer "border zone." U.S. citizens traveling as tourists beyond the "border zone," or entering Mexico by air, must pay a fee to obtain a tourist card, also known as an FMM, available from Mexican consulates, Mexican border crossing points, Mexican tourism offices, airports within the border zone and most airlines serving Mexico. The fee for the tourist card is generally included in the price of a plane ticket for travelers arriving by air. U.S. citizens fill out the FMM form; Mexican immigration retains the large portion and the traveler is given the small right-hand portion. This FMM is normally white, blue and green in color. It is extremely important to keep this form in a safe location. Mexican immigration agents and federal police have the authority to ask for proof of legal status in Mexico, and on occasion, U.S. citizens without documents have been detained by police. Travelers should always carry a photocopy of their passport data page and FMM. Upon exiting the country at a Mexican Immigration (INM) departure check point, U.S. citizens are required to turn in this form. We are aware of cases where U.S. citizens without their FMM have been required to change their flight (at personal expense), file a police report regarding the missing document, and visit an INM office to pay a fine and obtain a valid exit visa. In other cases, travelers have been able to continue their journey after paying a fine. For more information visit the INM website.

Business Travel: Upon arrival in Mexico, business travelers must complete and submit form FMM authorizing the conduct of business, but not employment, for a 30-day period. Travelers entering Mexico for purposes other than tourism or business, or for stays of longer than 180 days, require a visa and must carry a valid U.S. passport. U.S. citizens planning to work or live in Mexico should apply for the appropriate Mexican visa at the Mexican Embassy in Washington, DC, or at the nearest Mexican consulate in the United States.

Vehicle Permits: Tourists wishing to travel beyond the border zone with their vehicle must obtain a temporary import permit or risk having their vehicle confiscated by Mexican customs officials. At present the only exceptions to the requirement are for vehicles traveling in the Baja Peninsula and those vehicles covered by the "Only Sonora" program in Western Sonora. This program generally covers the area west of Mexican Federal Highway 15 between the Arizona border and the Gulf of California, ending in Empalme. Foreign vehicles entering Mexico through land border crossings in Sonora do not need temporary import permits if they remain within the zone established by the program. All foreign tourists, however, must have their valid immigration documents (FMM, FM2, FM3 or FME) with them at all times while traveling through Mexico regardless of whether or not they must register their vehicles. For details on the program, visit the " Only Sonora " website (Spanish only).

To acquire a permit, one must submit evidence of citizenship, title for the vehicle, a vehicle registration certificate, a driver's license, and a processing fee to either a Banjercito (Mexican Army Bank) branch located at a Mexican Customs (Aduana) office at the port of entry, or at one of the Mexican consulates located in the United States. Mexican law also requires the posting of a bond at a Banjercito office to guarantee the export of the car from Mexico within a time period determined at the time of the application. For this purpose, American Express, Visa or MasterCard credit card holders will be asked to provide credit card information; others will need to make a cash deposit of between $200 and $400, depending on the make/model/year of the vehicle. In order to recover this bond or avoid credit card charges, travelers must go to any Mexican Customs office immediately prior to departing Mexico. Regardless of any official or unofficial advice to the contrary, vehicle permits cannot be obtained at checkpoints in the interior of Mexico. If the proper permit is not obtained before entering Mexico and cannot be obtained at the Banjercito branch at the port of entry, do not proceed to the interior. Travelers without the proper permit may be incarcerated, fined and/or have their vehicle seized at immigration/customs checkpoints. In addition, in November 2011, Mexico implemented a requirement for emissions certification for vehicles being permanently imported to Mexico. There are restrictions on the age of vehicles being permanently imported, but there are no such restrictions for cars under temporary permits. For further information, visit the website for Mexican Customs (Aduanas) at Acerca de Aduana Mexico ("About Mexican Customs").

Travelers should avoid individuals who wait outside vehicle permit offices and offer to obtain the permits without waiting in line, even if they appear to be government officials. There have been reports of fraudulent or counterfeit permits being issued adjacent to the vehicle import permit office in Nuevo Laredo, Ciudad Juarez and other border areas.

Dual Nationality: Mexican law recognizes dual nationality for Mexicans by birth, meaning those born in Mexico or born abroad to Mexican parents. U.S. citizens who are also Mexican nationals are considered by local authorities to be Mexican. Dual nationality status could result in the delay of notification of arrests and other emergencies or hamper U.S. Government efforts to provide consular services. Dual nationals are subject to compulsory military service in Mexico; in addition, dual national males must register for the U.S. Selective Service upon turning 18. For more information, visit the U.S. Selective Service website. Travelers possessing both U.S. and Mexican nationalities must carry with them proof of citizenship of both countries. Under Mexican law, dual nationals entering or departing Mexico must identify themselves as Mexican. Under U.S. law, dual nationals entering the United States must identify themselves as U.S. citizens.

Customs Regulations: Please refer to our information on customs regulations. U.S. citizens bringing gifts to friends and relatives in Mexico should be prepared to demonstrate to Mexican customs officials the origin and value of the gifts. U.S. citizens entering Mexico by land borders can bring in gifts with a value of up to $75.00 duty-free, except for alcohol and tobacco products. U.S. citizens entering Mexico by air or sea can bring in gifts with a value of up to $300.00 duty-free. Please refer to Mexico's customs guide for passengers for more information, including on requirements to declare cash or other financial instruments exceeding the equivalent of $3000 U.S. dollars.

Personal Effects: Tourists are allowed to bring in their personal effects duty-free. According to customs regulations, in addition to clothing, personal effects may include one camera, one video cassette player, one personal computer, one CD player, 5 DVDs, 20 music CDs or audiocassettes, 12 rolls of unused film, and one cellular phone. Any tourist carrying such items, even if duty-free, should enter the "Merchandise to Declare" lane at the first customs checkpoint. Travelers should be prepared to pay any assessed duty on items in excess of these allowances. Failure to declare personal effects may result in the seizure of the items as contraband, plus the seizure of any vehicle in which the goods were transported for attempted smuggling. Recovery of the seized vehicle may involve payment of substantial fines and attorney's fees. See also the "Firearms Penalties" section below regarding Mexico's strict laws and penalties regarding import of firearms or ammunition.

Temporary Imports/Exports: Mexican customs authorities enforce strict regulations concerning temporary importation into or exportation from Mexico of items such as trucks and autos, trailers, antiquities, medications, medical equipment, business equipment, etc. Prior to traveling, contact the Mexican Embassy or one of the Mexican consulates in the United States for specific information regarding customs requirements.

Donations of Goods: U.S. citizens traveling to Mexico with goods intended for donation within Mexico, or traveling through Mexico with goods intended for donation in another country, should be aware of Mexican Customs regulations prohibiting importation of used clothing, textiles, and other used goods into Mexico, even as charitable donations. The importation of all medicines and medical equipment for donation to charity must be approved by Mexican Customs in advance; failure to obtain the proper import permits will result in the confiscation of the medical supplies. Expired medications may not be imported for donation under any circumstances. Individuals or groups wishing to make charitable donations should check with Mexican Customs for the list of prohibited items, and should hire an experienced customs broker in the U.S. to ensure compliance with Mexican law. The charitable individual or group, not the customs broker, will be held responsible for large fines or confiscation of goods if the documentation is incorrect.

Mexican authorities require that all international transit through Mexico of persons and merchandise destined for Central or South America be handled only at the Los Indios Bridge located south of Harlingen, Texas on Route 509. The U.S. Consulate General in Matamoros is the nearest consulate to Los Indios Bridge and may be contacted for up-to-date information by calling 011-52-868-812-4402, ext. 273 or 280, or by checking their website, which lists in English the most common items prohibited from entry into Mexico. Additional customs information can be found on the U.S. Customs and Border Protection website.

Threats to Safety and Security: All travelers to Mexico should review the Department of State's Travel Warning for Mexico that provides detailed information about security issues affecting parts of the country. Millions of U.S. citizens visit Mexico safely each year. However, crime and violence, much of it fueled by transnational criminal activity, affect many parts of the country, including both urban and rural areas. Visitors should remain alert and be aware of their surroundings at all times, particularly when visiting the border region.

In its efforts to combat violence, the Government of Mexico has deployed federal police and military troops to various parts of the country. Government checkpoints, often staffed by military personnel, have been erected in many parts of the country, especially, but not exclusively, in the border area. U.S. citizens are advised to cooperate with personnel at government checkpoints when traveling on Mexican highways.

Stay up to date by:

- Bookmarking our Bureau of Consular Affairs website, which contains the current Travel Warnings and Travel Alerts as well as the Worldwide Caution.
- Following us on Twitter and the Bureau of Consular Affairs page on Facebook as well.
- Downloading our free Smart Traveler iPhone App to have travel information at your fingertips.
- Calling 1-888-407-4747 toll-free within the U.S. and Canada, or by calling a regular toll line, 1-202-501-4444, from other countries.
- Taking time before you travel to improve your personal security.

Demonstrations: The Mexican Constitution prohibits political activities by foreigners; such actions may result in detention and/or deportation. Travelers should avoid political demonstrations and other activities that might be deemed political by the Mexican authorities. Even demonstrations intended to be peaceful can turn confrontational and escalate into violence. Demonstrators in Mexico may block traffic on roads, including major arteries, or take control of toll booths on highways. U.S. citizens are urged to avoid areas of demonstrations, and to exercise caution if in the vicinity of any protests.

Crime: Crime in Mexico continues to occur at a high rate and can often be violent. Street crime, ranging from pick pocketing to armed robbery, is a serious problem in most major cities. Carjackings are also common, particularly in certain areas (see the Travel Warning for Mexico). The homicide rates in parts of Mexico have risen sharply in recent years, driven largely by violence associated with transnational criminal organizations. Ciudad Juarez and other cities along Mexico's northern border have particularly high murder rates. The Mexican government makes a considerable effort to protect U.S. citizens and other visitors traveling to major tourist destinations. Resort areas and tourist destinations in Mexico generally do not see the levels of violence and crime reported in the border region and in areas along major trafficking routes. Nevertheless, crime and violence are serious problems. While most victims of violence are Mexican citizens associated with criminal activity, the security situation poses serious risks for U.S. citizens as well. U.S. citizen victims of crime in Mexico are encouraged to report incidents to the nearest police headquarters and to the nearest U.S. consular office.

The Government of Mexico has taken significant steps to strengthen its law enforcement capabilities at the federal level, which have begun putting organized criminal networks on the defensive. However, state and local police forces continue to suffer from lack of training and funding, and are a weak deterrent to criminals acting on behalf of organized crime and armed with an impressive array of weapons. In some areas, municipal police forces are widely suspected of colluding with organized crime. In others, police officers are specifically targeted by members of transnational criminal organizations. Because of the dangerous situation in which police officers operate, all travelers are advised to take a nonthreatening posture when interacting with police and to cooperate with police instructions. We further advise travelers to avoid any areas where law enforcement operations are being carried out. Significant justice reforms are underway in certain Mexican states, as well as at the federal level; however, judicial systems are often overworked, under resourced, and inefficient.

Pirated Merchandise: Counterfeit and pirated goods are widely available in Mexico. Their sale is largely controlled by organized crime. Purchase for personal use is not criminalized in Mexico; however, bringing these goods back to the United States may result in forfeitures and/or fines.

Personal Property: Travelers should always leave valuables and irreplaceable items in a safe place, or avoid bringing them at all. All visitors are encouraged to make use of hotel safes when available, avoid wearing obviously expensive jewelry or designer clothing, and carry only the cash or credit cards that will be needed on each outing. There have been significant numbers of incidents of pick pocketing, purse snatching, and hotel-room theft. Public transportation is a particularly popular place for pickpockets. When renting a vehicle, ensure that advertisements or labels for the rental agency are not prominently displayed on the vehicle.

Avoid leaving valuables such as identification, passport, and irreplaceable property in rental vehicles, even when locked. Some travelers have had their passports stolen from their bags within the airport, particularly during peak travel seasons. Remember to secure your passport within a zipper pocket or other safe enclosure so that it cannot be easily removed. Be vigilant of your passport even after passing through security and while waiting in a departure lounge to board your flight.

Business travelers should be aware that theft can occur even in apparently secure locations. Theft of items such as briefcases and laptops occur frequently at Mexico City's Benito Juarez International Airport and at business-class hotels. Passengers arriving at Mexican airports who need to obtain pesos should use the exchange counters or ATMs in the arrival/departure gate area, where access is restricted, rather than changing money after passing through Customs, where they can be observed by criminals. A number of U.S. citizens have been arrested for passing on counterfeit currency they had earlier received in change. If you receive what you believe to be a counterfeit bank note, bring it to the attention of Mexican law enforcement.

Personal Safety: Visitors should be aware of their surroundings at all times, even when in areas generally considered safe. Women traveling alone are especially vulnerable and should exercise caution, particularly at night. Some U.S Citizens have reported being raped, robbed of personal property, or abducted and then held while their credit cards were used at various businesses or Automatic Teller Machines (ATMs). Individuals who have been targeted were often walking alone in isolated locations. Be very cautious in general when using ATMs in Mexico. If you must use an ATM, it should be accessed only during the business day at large protected facilities (preferably inside commercial establishments, rather than at glass-enclosed, highly visible ATMs on streets). Travelers to remote or isolated hunting or fishing venues should be aware that they may be some distance from ATMs, appropriate medical services, and law enforcement or consular assistance in an emergency.

Kidnapping: Kidnapping, including the kidnapping of non-Mexicans, continues to occur. So-called express kidnappings, i.e., attempts to get quick cash in exchange for the release of an individual, have occurred in almost all of Mexico's large cities and appear to target not only the wealthy but also the middle class. Review the sections above on personal property and personal safety for common sense actions you can take to reduce the risk of becoming a victim.

A common scam throughout Mexico is 'virtual' kidnapping by telephone, in which the callers typically speak in a distraught voice in a ploy to elicit information about a potential victim and then use this knowledge to demand ransom for the release of the supposed victim. Information that can be used against victims may also be obtained from social networking websites. Calls are often placed by prison inmates using smuggled cellular phones. In the event of such a call, it is important to stay calm, as the vast majority of these calls are hoaxes. Do not reveal any personal information and try to speak with the victim to corroborate his/her identity. Any kidnapping, real or virtual, should be reported to the police as well as to the Embassy or nearest consulate.

Credit/Debit Card "Skimming": Exercise caution when utilizing credit or debit cards in ATM machines or dubious locales. There have been reports of instances in which U.S. citizens in Mexico have had their card numbers "skimmed" and the money in their debit accounts stolen or their credit cards fraudulently charged. ("Skimming" is the theft of credit card information by an employee of a legitimate merchant or bank, manually copying down numbers or using a magnetic stripe reader, or using a camera and skimmer installed in an ATM machine.) In addition to skimming, the risk of physical theft of credit or debit cards also exists. To prevent such theft, the Embassy recommends that travelers keep close track of their personal belongings when out and about and that they only carry what they need. Most restaurants and other businesses will bring the credit card machine to your table so that you can keep the card in your possession at all times. If travelers choose to use credit cards, they should regularly check their account status to ensure its integrity.

Buses and Public Transportation: Whenever possible, visitors should travel by bus only during daylight hours and only by first-class conveyance. Although there have been several reports of bus hijackings and robberies on toll roads, buses on toll roads have experienced a markedly lower rate of incidents than buses (second- and third-class) that travel the less secure "free" highways. Although the police have made progress in bringing this type of crime under control, armed robberies of entire busloads of passengers still occur.

Metro (subway) robberies are frequent in Mexico City, especially during crowded rush hours. If riding the metro or the city bus system, U.S. citizens should take extreme care with valuables and belongings.

Taxis: Robberies and assaults on passengers in "libre" taxis (that is, taxis not affiliated with a taxi stand) are frequent and violent in Mexico, with passengers subjected to beating, shooting, and sexual assault. U.S. citizens visiting Mexico should avoid taking any taxi not summoned by telephone or contacted in advance. When in need of a taxi, telephone a radio taxi or "sitio" (regulated taxi stand—pronounced "C-T-O"), and ask the dispatcher for the driver's name and the taxi's license plate number. Ask the hotel concierge or other responsible individual to write down the license plate number of the cab that you entered. Avoid "libre" taxis and the Volkswagen beetle taxis altogether. Although "libre" taxis are more convenient and less expensive, these are not as well regulated, may be unregistered, and are potentially more dangerous. U.S. Embassy employees in Mexico City are prohibited from using "libre" taxis, or any taxis hailed on the street, and are authorized to use only "sitio" taxis.

Passengers arriving at any airport in Mexico should take only authorized airport taxis after pre-paying the fare at one of the special booths inside the airport.

Harassment/Extortion: In some instances, U.S. citizens have become victims of harassment, mistreatment and extortion by alleged Mexican law enforcement and other officials. Mexican authorities have cooperated in investigating such cases, but one must have the officer's name, badge number, and patrol car number to pursue a complaint effectively. Please note this information if you ever have a problem with police or other officials. In addition, tourists should be wary of persons representing themselves as police officers or other officials. When in doubt, ask for identification. Be aware that offering a bribe to a public official to avoid a ticket or other penalty is a crime in Mexico.

One of the latest extortion techniques, known as the " grandparent scam," involves calls placed by persons alleging to be attorneys or U.S. Government employees claiming that a person's relative—nearly always a purported grandchild—has been in a car accident in Mexico and has been arrested/detained. The caller asks for a large sum of money to ensure the subject's release. When the recipient of the call checks on their family member, they discover that the entire story is false. If the alleged detainee cannot be located in the U.S. and the family has reason to believe that the person did, in fact, travel to Mexico, contact the U.S. Embassy or nearest U.S. Consulate for assistance in determining if they have been detained by authorities. Further information on international financial scams is available on our website.

Beware of possible scams involving inflated prices for tourist-related goods and services and avoid patronizing restaurants and other service providers that do not have clearly listed prices. You should check with your hotel for the names of reputable establishments and service providers in the area.

Sexual Assault: Rape and sexual assault continue to be serious problems in resort areas. Many of these incidents occur at night or during the early morning hours, in hotel rooms, or on deserted beaches. Acquaintance rape is a serious problem. Hotel workers, taxi drivers, and security personnel have been implicated in many cases. Women should avoid being alone, particularly in isolated areas and at night. It is imperative that victims file a police report, which should include a rape "kit" exam, against the perpetrator(s) as soon as possible at the nearest police station. There have been several cases where the victim traveled back to the U.S. without filing a police report or submitting to a rape exam; their attempts to document their case later on did not carry weight with local Mexican authorities.

Some bars and nightclubs, especially in resort cities such as Cancun, Acapulco, Mazatlan, Cabo San Lucas, and Tijuana, can be havens for drug dealers and petty criminals. Interaction with such individuals may put a traveler at risk. There have been instances of contamination or drugging of drinks to gain control over the patron.

See the information under "Special Circumstances" below regarding Spring Break in Mexico if you are considering visiting Mexican resort areas during February through April, when thousands of U.S. college students traditionally arrive in those areas. Additional information designed specifically for traveling students is also available on our Students Abroad website.

Transnational Crime in Mexico: Since 2006, the Mexican government has engaged in an extensive effort to combat transnational criminal organizations (TCOs). Mexican TCOs, meanwhile, have been engaged in a vicious struggle to control trafficking routes and other criminal activity. According to the most recent homicide figures published by the Mexican government, 47,515 people were killed in narcotics-related violence in Mexico between December 1, 2006 and September 30, 2011, with 12,903 narcotics-related homicides in the first nine months of 2011 alone. While most of those killed in narcotics-related violence have been members of TCOs, innocent persons have also been killed. The number of U.S. citizens reported to the Department of State as murdered in Mexico increased from 35 in 2007 to 113 in 2011.

Recent violent attacks and persistent security concerns have prompted the U.S. Embassy to urge U.S. citizens to defer unnecessary travel to certain parts of Mexico, and to advise U.S. citizens residing or traveling in those areas to exercise extreme caution. For detailed information on these areas and the threats involved, please refer to the Travel Warning for Mexico.

TCOs have increasingly targeted unsuspecting individuals who cross the border on a regular and predictable basis traveling between known destinations as a way to transport drugs to the U.S. They affix drugs to the undercarriage of the car while it is parked in Mexico. Once in the U.S., members of the organization will remove the packages while the vehicle is unattended. If you are a frequent border crosser, you should vary your routes and travel times as well as closely monitor your vehicle to avoid being targeted.

Victims of Crime: If you or someone you know becomes the victim of a crime abroad, you should contact the local police and the nearest U.S. embassy or consulate (see the

Department of State's list of embassies and consulates). Do not rely on hotel/restaurant/tour company management to make the report for you. We can:

- Replace a stolen passport. The loss or theft abroad of a U.S. passport should be reported immediately to the local police and the nearest U.S. Embassy or consulate.
- Help you find appropriate medical care if you are the victim of violent crimes such as assault or rape.
- Put you in contact with the appropriate police authorities, and if you want us to, we can contact family members or friends.
- Help you understand the local criminal justice process and direct you to local attorneys, although it is important to remember that local authorities are responsible for investigating and prosecuting the crime. Under the best of circumstances, prosecution is very difficult (a fact some assailants appear to exploit knowingly), but no criminal investigation is possible without a formal complaint to Mexican authorities.

The local equivalent to the "911" emergency line in Mexico is "066." Although there may be English-speaking operators available, to avoid delay it is best to seek the assistance of a Spanish speaker to place the call.

Criminal Penalties: While in a foreign country, an individual is subject to that country's laws and regulations, which can differ significantly from those in the United States. and may not afford the protections available to the individual under U.S. law. The trial process in Mexico is different from that in the United States, and procedures may vary from state to state. Penalties for breaking the law can be more severe than in the United States for similar offenses. Persons violating Mexican laws, even unknowingly, may be expelled, arrested or imprisoned. Penalties for possession, use or trafficking in illegal drugs in Mexico are severe, and convicted offenders can expect long jail sentences and heavy fines. If you break local laws in Mexico, your U.S. passport will not help you avoid arrest or prosecution. It is very important to know what is legal and what is illegal wherever you go.

Sexual Crimes: Sexual exploitation of children or using or disseminating child pornography in a foreign country is a crime prosecutable in the United States. Soliciting sexual services of a minor is illegal in Mexico, and is punishable by imprisonment. The Mexican government has announced an aggressive program to discourage sexual tourism. Police authorities in the state of Baja California recently began enforcement of anti-pedophile legislation.

Arrests and Notifications: The Mexican government is required by international law to notify the U.S. Embassy or the nearest U.S. consulate promptly when a U.S. citizen is arrested, if the arrestee so requests. In practice, however, depending on where the arrest takes place, this notification can be months late, or may never occur at all, limiting the assistance the U.S. Government can provide. U.S. citizens should promptly identify themselves as such to the arresting officers, and should request that the Embassy or nearest consulate be notified immediately. Also see the "grandparent scam," described above in the Harrassment/Extorsion section, in which a U.S. citizen is alleged to be detained by authorities in Mexico in attempt to get relatives in the United States to wire money. Confirm an alleged detention or arrest with the Embassy or consulate before taking any other action.

Prison Facilities: Prison conditions in Mexico can be extremely poor. In many facilities food is insufficient in both quantity and quality, and prisoners must pay for adequate nutrition from their own funds. Many Mexican prisons provide poor medical care, and prisoners with urgent medical conditions may receive only a minimum of attention. U.S. citizens who are incarcerated in Mexico are sometimes forced to pay hundreds and even thousands of dollars in "protection money" to fellow prisoners. From 2008 through 2011, 30 U.S. citizen deaths in Mexican prisons have been reported, including at least 13 apparent homicides.

Prisoner Treatment/Interrogations: Mexico is party to several international anti-torture conventions, and the Mexican Constitution and Mexican law accordingly prohibit torture; however, in its annual report, Mexico's National Commission on Human Rights documents cases of Mexican security forces seeking to obtain information through torture. Convictions for torture or for any alleged abuses by security forces are rare. U.S. citizens have reported being beaten, raped, and subjected to severe interrogation techniques while in the custody of Mexican security forces.

Drug Penalties and Prescription Medications: Penalties for drug offenses are strict, and convicted offenders can expect large fines and jail sentences of up to 25 years. The purchase of controlled medications requires a prescription from a licensed Mexican physician. Some Mexican doctors have been arrested for writing prescriptions without due cause. In those instances, U.S. citizens who purchased the medications have been held in jail for months waiting for the Mexican judicial system to make a decision on their case. Marijuana prescriptions (or "medical marijuana") are not valid in Mexico. Individuals in possession of a state medical marijuana license should remember that the license is not valid outside of the borders of that state, and bringing marijuana into Mexico—even if it is accompanied by a prescription—is considered international drug trafficking, a serious federal offense.

The Mexican list of controlled medications differs from that of the United States, and Mexican public health laws concerning controlled medications are unclear and often enforced selectively. To determine whether a particular medication is controlled in

Mexico or requires a prescription from a Mexican doctor for purchase, please consult the website of the Mexican Federal Commission for Protection against Health Risks (Comisión Federal para la Protección contra Riesgos Sanitarios—COFEPRIS).

The U.S. Embassy cautions that possession of any amount of prescription medication brought from the United States, including medications to treat HIV, and psychotropic drugs such as Valium, can result in arrest if Mexican authorities suspect abuse, or if the quantity of the prescription medication exceeds the amount required for several days' use. Individuals are advised to carry a copy of the prescription. If significant quantities of the medication are required, individuals should carry a doctor's letter explaining that the quantity of medication is appropriate for their personal medical use.

Buying Prescription Drugs: Any drug classified as a controlled medicine, including antibiotics, by the government of Mexico cannot be purchased in Mexico without a Mexican prescription. This prescription must be written by a physician who is federally registered in Mexico. Purchasing a controlled medicine without a valid prescription in Mexico is a serious crime for both the purchaser and the seller. Purchasing a controlled medicine with a U.S. prescription is not sufficient and is illegal, regardless of what the Mexican pharmacy may be willing to sell to the purchaser. By law, Mexican pharmacies cannot honor foreign prescriptions. U.S. citizens have been arrested and their medicines confiscated by Mexican authorities when their prescriptions were written by a licensed U.S. physician and filled by a licensed Mexican pharmacist. There have been cases of U.S. citizens buying prescription drugs in border cities only to be arrested soon after or have money extorted by criminals impersonating police officers. Those arrested are often held for the full 48 hours allowed by Mexican law without charges being filed, then released. During this interval, the detainees are often asked for bribes or are solicited by attorneys who demand large fees to secure their release, which will normally occur without any intercession as there are insufficient grounds to bring criminal charges against the individuals. In addition, U.S. law enforcement officials believe that as many as 25 percent of the medications available in Mexico are counterfeit and substandard. Such counterfeit medications may be difficult to distinguish from the real medications and could pose serious health risks to consumers. The importation of prescription drugs into the United States can be illegal in certain circumstances. U.S. law generally permits persons to enter the United States with only an immediate supply (i.e., enough for about one month) of a prescription medication.

Criminal Penalties for Possession: Mexico has new laws that have been touted by the press as making the possession of drugs for personal use legal. Many of the allowable amounts are much less than what has been reported by the news media. Additionally, the new drug laws include stiffer penalties for many drug offenses, and the sale and distribution of drugs continues to be illegal in Mexico. U.S. citizens traveling to Mexico should review this information to avoid possible prosecution under Mexican law.

Importing Medicines into Mexico: Medications for personal use are not subject to duty when hand-carried into Mexico. Individuals are advised to carry a copy of their prescriptions in the event they are asked to prove that the medicines are for personal use. To ship (import) prescription medication into Mexico for personal use, a foreigner must obtain a permit from the Mexican Health Department prior to importing the medicine into Mexico. For a fee, a customs broker can process the permit before the Mexican authorities on behalf of an individual. If using the services of a customs broker, it is advisable to agree upon the fees before telling the broker to proceed. Current listings of local customs brokers (agencias aduanales) are available in the Mexico City yellow pages.

Firearms Penalties: Illegal firearms trafficking from the United States into Mexico is a major problem. The Department of State warns all U.S. citizens against taking any type of firearm or ammunition into Mexico. Entering Mexico with a firearm, certain types of knives, or even a single round of ammunition is illegal, even if the weapon or ammunition is taken into Mexico unintentionally. The Mexican government strictly enforces laws restricting the entry of firearms and ammunition along all land borders and at airports and seaports, and routinely x-rays all incoming luggage. U.S. citizens entering Mexico with a weapon or ammunition (including a small number of bullets), even accidentally, generally are detained for at least a few days, and violations by U.S. citizens have resulted in arrests, convictions, and long prison sentences. Travelers are strongly advised to thoroughly inspect all belongings prior to travel to Mexico to avoid the accidental import of ammunition or firearms. For more information visit the websites for the Mexican Secretary of Defense and Mexican Customs.

Vessels entering Mexican waters with firearms or ammunition on board must have a permit previously issued by the Mexican Embassy or a Mexican consulate. Mariners do not avoid prosecution by declaring their weapons at the port of entry. Before traveling, mariners who have obtained a Mexican firearm permit should contact Mexican port officials to receive guidance on the specific procedures used to report and secure weapons and ammunition.

Special Circumstances: Weather conditions in Mexico vary as they do in various parts of the United States. From June to November, the country may experience strong winds and rains as a result of hurricanes in the Gulf of Mexico or along the Pacific Coast. Some areas may experience earthquakes. It is prudent to leave a detailed itinerary, including local contact information and expected time and date of return, with a friend or family member, as well as sign up for the Smart Traveler Enrollment Program.

Water Sports: Visitors to Mexico, including to local resort areas, should carefully assess the potential risk of recreational activities. Recreational facilities such as pools may not meet U.S. safety or sanitation standards. Swimming pool drain systems may not comply with U.S. safety standards and swimmers should exercise caution. Several U.S. citizens have died in hotel pools in recent years. Do not swim in pools or at beaches without lifeguards. Parents should watch minor children closely when they are in or around water. U.S. citizens have drowned or disappeared at both remote and popular beaches along the Mexican coasts.

Warning flags on beaches should be taken seriously. If black flags are up, do not enter the water. In Cancun, there is often a very strong undertow along the beach from the Hyatt Regency all the way south to Club Med. Several drowning and near-drowning incidents have been reported on the east coast of Cozumel, particularly in the Playa San Martin-Chen Rio area. In Acapulco, avoid swimming outside the bay area. Several U.S. citizens have died while swimming in rough surf at the Revolcadero Beach near Acapulco. Despite the presence of U.S.-trained lifeguards, several U.S. citizens have drowned in the area of Zipolite Beach in Puerto Angel, Oaxaca, because of sudden waves and strong currents. Beaches on the Pacific side of the Baja California peninsula at Cabo San Lucas can be dangerous due to rip tides and rogue waves; hazardous beaches in this area are clearly marked in English and Spanish. Even people simply walking along the beaches have been washed into the ocean by rogue waves. Encounters with sharks have occurred all along Mexico's coastline, particularly in the Gulf of Mexico near Veracruz and Cancun and along the Pacific Ocean coast, including near Ixtapa. Surfers and other water sports enthusiasts should always inquire about local conditions before going into the water. Do not swim alone in isolated beach areas. Beaches may not be well-marked, and strong currents could lead to dangerous conditions for even the most experienced swimmers. Do not dive into unknown bodies of water, because hidden rocks or shallow depths can cause serious injury or death.

Rented sports and aquatic equipment may not meet U.S. safety standards or be covered by any accident insurance. Scuba diving equipment may be substandard or defective due to frequent use. Inexperienced scuba divers in particular should beware of dive shops that promise to "certify" you after only a few hours' instruction. There are several hospitals and medical centers with hyperbaric decompression chambers to treat the effects of nitrogen narcosis (commonly referred to as the "bends") in Mexico. These tend to be in large cities and near tourist destinations where scuba diving is common, such as the Yucatan Peninsula. Please note you will be expected to pay for service up front and likely in cash. Parasailing has killed U.S. citizen tourists who were dragged through palm trees or were slammed into buildings. U.S. citizen tourists have also been killed in jet-ski accidents, especially in group outings when inexperienced guides allowed clients to follow each other too closely. Accidents involving breaking zip-lines have also occurred.

Boats used for excursions may not carry adequate life jackets, radios, or tools to make repairs in the event of engine failure and may not be covered by accident insurance. Mariners preparing to depart from a Mexican harbor should visit the harbormaster and leave a detailed trip plan, including intended destination and crew and passenger information.

Resort Areas and Spring Break: Over 3 million U.S. citizens travel to Cancun and other Mexican beach resorts each year, including as many as 120,000 during "spring break" season, which normally begins in mid-February and runs for about two months. Excessive alcohol consumption, especially by U.S. citizens under the legal U.S. drinking age, is a significant problem. The legal drinking age in Mexico is 18, but it is not uniformly enforced. Alcohol is implicated in the majority of arrests, violent crimes, accidents and deaths suffered by U.S. citizen tourists. See also the section above entitled "Sexual Assault."

Mountain Climbing and Hiking: Travelers who wish to climb Pico de Orizaba in Veracruz should be aware that summer droughts in recent years have removed much of the snow coating and turned the Jamapa Glacier into a high-speed ice chute, increasing the risk of death or serious injury. At least 17 climbers have died on the mountain and 39 have been injured in recent years, including U.S. citizens. Rescue teams operate without the benefit of sophisticated equipment. Any medical treatment provided in local hospitals or clinics must be paid in cash. While regulation of the ascent is minimal and guides are not required, the U.S. Embassy recommends hiring an experienced guide.

The Popocatepetl Volcano, located 40 miles southeast of Mexico City, and the Colima Volcano, located approximately 20 miles north-northeast of Colima city in the state of Colima on the southwestern coast, are two of the most active volcanoes in Mexico. Remain within the designated tourist area and observe all safety recommendations from the Mexican Proteccion Civil that monitors the conditions of the volcano. Ash omitted from the volcano can disrupt air travel.

When departing on an outing to back-country areas to hike or climb, it is prudent to leave a detailed itinerary, including route information and expected time and date of return, with your hotel clerk or a friend or family member.

Marriage and Divorce Requirements in Mexico: In general, to marry a Mexican national in Mexico, a U.S. citizen must be physically present in Mexico and present documents required by the jurisdiction where the marriage will take place. U.S. citizens who marry U.S. citizens or other non-Mexicans are not subject to a residence requirement, but are required to present their tourist cards. For additional information on marriages in Mexico, contact the

Mexican Embassy or nearest Mexican consulate in the United States. Divorce requirements may vary according to jurisdiction. The U.S. Embassy recommends that U.S. citizens consult an attorney and/or the Mexican Embassy or nearest Mexican consulate for information on divorces in Mexico.

Real Estate and Time Shares: You should be aware of the risks inherent in purchasing real estate in Mexico, and should exercise extreme caution before entering into any form of commitment to invest in property there. Mexican law and practice regarding real estate differ substantially from the United States. Foreigners who purchase property in Mexico may find that property disputes with Mexican citizens may not be treated even-handedly by Mexican criminal justice authorities and in the courts. Consumers should consult a Mexican attorney before undertaking a real estate transaction.

U.S. citizens should exercise caution when considering time-share investments and be aware of the aggressive tactics used by some time-share sales representatives. Buyers should be fully informed and take sufficient time to consider their decisions before signing time-share contracts, ideally after consulting an independent attorney. Mexican law allows time-share purchasers five days to cancel the contract for unconditional and full reimbursement. U.S. citizens should never sign a contract that includes clauses penalizing a buyer who cancels within five days. Note that time-share companies cannot be sued in U.S. courts unless they have an office or other business presence in the U.S. The Department of State and the U.S. Embassy frequently receive complaints from U.S. citizens about extremely aggressive sales tactics, exaggerated claims of return on investment, lack of customer service, and questionable business practices by time-share companies, resulting in substantial financial losses for time-share investors.

A formal complaint against any merchant should be filed with PROFECO, Mexico's federal consumer protection agency. PROFECO has the power to mediate disputes, investigate consumer complaints, order hearings, levy fines and sanctions for not appearing at hearings, and do price-check inspections of merchants. All complaints by U.S. citizens are handled by PROFECO's English-speaking office in Mexico City at 011-52-55-5211–1723 (phone), 011-52-55-5211–2052 (fax). For more information, please see the PROFECO website.

Ownership Restrictions: The Mexican Constitution prohibits direct ownership by foreigners of real estate within 100 kilometers (about 62 miles) of any border, and within 50 kilometers (about 31 miles) of any coastline. In order to permit foreign investment in these areas, the Mexican government has created a trust mechanism in which a bank has title to the property but a trust beneficiary enjoys the benefits of ownership. However, U.S. citizens are vulnerable to title challenges that may result in years of litigation and possible eviction and even incarceration. Although title insurance is available in the Baja Peninsula and in other parts of Mexico, it is virtually unknown and remains untested in most of the country. In addition, Mexican law recognizes squatters' rights, and homeowners can spend thousands of dollars in legal fees and years of frustration in trying to remove squatters who occupy their property.

Labor Laws: U.S. citizen property owners should consult legal counsel or local authorities before hiring employees to serve in their homes or on their vessels moored in Mexico. Several U.S. citizen property owners have faced lengthy lawsuits for failure to comply with Mexican labor laws regarding severance pay and Mexican social security benefits.

Human Smuggling and Trafficking: Mexican authorities may prosecute anyone arrested for trafficking or smuggling of people into or out of Mexico in addition to any charges they may face in the other country involved, including the United States.

Medical Facilities and Health Information: Adequate medical care can be found in major cities. Excellent health facilities are available in Mexico City, but training and availability of emergency responders may be below U.S. standards. Care in more remote areas is limited. Standards of medical training, patient care and business practices vary greatly among medical facilities in beach resorts throughout Mexico. In recent years, some U.S. citizens have complained that certain health-care facilities in beach resorts have taken advantage of them by overcharging or providing unnecessary medical care. A significant number of complaints have been lodged against some of the private hospitals in the Cabo San Lucas area, including complaints about price gouging and various unlawful and/or unethical pricing schemes and collection measures. Additionally, U.S. citizens should be aware that many Mexican facilities require payment 'up front' prior to performing a procedure. Hospitals in Mexico do not accept U.S. domestic health insurance or Medicare/Medicaid and will expect payment via cash, credit, debit card or bank transfer. Elective medical procedures may be less expensive than in the United States, but providers may not adhere to U.S. standards. Additionally, visitors are cautioned that facilities may lack access to sufficient emergency support. The U.S. Embassy encourages visitors to obtain as much information about the facility and the medical personnel as possible when considering surgical or other procedures, and when possible patients should travel with a family member or another responsible party.

In addition to other publicly available information, U.S. citizens may consult the U.S. Embassy's website for a list of doctors and a list of hospitals in Mexico City or contact the U.S. Embassy, U.S. consulate, or consular agency prior to seeking non-emergency medical attention. The U.S. consulates and consular agencies also maintain lists of reputable doctors and medical facilities that are available to assist U.S. citizens in need of medical care. Before beginning international travel, U.S. citizens may wish to obtain emergency medical evacuation insurance, check with their health care providers to see of the cost for medical treatment outside the U.S. is covered, and inquire about the reimbursement process.

Procedures after the Death of a U.S. Citizen in Mexico: When a United States citizen dies in Mexico, it is critical that the next of kin act promptly to contract with a Mexican funeral home to help carry out funeral arrangements, including return of the deceased's remains to the U.S., if desired. The next of kin must also provide documents establishing the identity of both the next of kin and the decedent. Common documents used for this purpose are passports, government-issued photo identification such as a driver's license, birth certificates and marriage certificates. The next of kin is responsible for all costs associated with the funeral home, and/or shipment of remains or personal effects.

The Embassy or Consulate in the district where the U.S. citizen died can provide a list of funeral homes and location-specific requirements in the Consular District. Although Embassy staff members may not make funeral and other arrangements, staff can help locate and notify the next of kin of their loved one's passing, inform families about the Mexican legal requirements for claiming a loved one's remains, and assist in shipping personal effects to the United States. The U.S. Embassy and its Consulates also prepare a Consular Report of Death of a U.S. Citizen Abroad, based on the local Mexican death certificate. The Consular Report of Death Abroad may be used in most legal proceedings in the United States as proof of death overseas. To prepare this document, Embassy staff will need original evidence of U.S. citizenship of the decedent and the original Mexican death certificate.

Water Quality: In many areas in Mexico, tap water is unsafe and should be avoided. Bottled water and beverages are safe, although, visitors should be aware that many restaurants and hotels serve tap water unless bottled water is specifically requested. Ice may also come from tap water and should be avoided. Visitors should exercise caution when buying food or beverages from street vendors.

The quality of water along some beaches in or near Acapulco or other large coastal communities may be unsafe for swimming because of contamination. Swimming in contaminated water may cause diarrhea and/or other illnesses. Mexican government agencies monitor water quality in public beach areas but their standards and sampling techniques may differ from those in the United States.

Altitude: In high-altitude areas such as Mexico City (elevation 7,600 feet or about 1/2 mile higher than Denver, Colorado), most people need a short adjustment period. Symptoms of reaction to high altitude include a lack of energy, shortness of breath, occasional dizziness, headache, and insomnia. Those with heart problems should consult their doctor before traveling. Air pollution in Mexico City and Guadalajara is severe, especially from December to May, and combined with high altitude could affect travelers with underlying respiratory problems.

Other Health Issues: Information on vaccinations and other health precautions, such as safe food and water precautions and insect bite protection, may be obtained from the Centers for Disease Control and Prevention's hotline for international travelers at 1-877-FYI-TRIP (1-877-394-8747) or via the CDC's website. For information about outbreaks of infectious diseases abroad consult the World Health Organization's (WHO) website. Further health information for travelers is available from the WHO.

Medical Insurance: The Department of State strongly urges U.S. citizens to consult with their medical insurance company prior to traveling abroad to confirm whether their policy applies overseas and whether it will cover emergency expenses such as a medical evacuation.

Medicare coverage outside of the United States is very limited and in nearly all situations does not provide coverage for hospital or medical costs in Mexico. The Veterans Affairs health care program only reimburses registrants in the Foreign Medical Program for eligible health care costs in Mexico.

Traffic Safety and Road Conditions: Continued concerns regarding criminal activity on highways along the Mexican border (which includes placement of illegal checkpoints and the murder of persons who did not stop and/or surrender their vehicles) have prompted the U.S. Mission in Mexico to impose certain restrictions on U.S. government employees transiting the area. Effective July 15, 2010, Mission employees and their families may not travel by vehicle across the U.S.-Mexico border to or from any post in the interior of Mexico. This policy also applies to employees and their families transiting Mexico to and from Central American posts. This policy does not apply to employees and their family members assigned to border posts (Tijuana, Nogales, Ciudad Juarez, Nuevo Laredo, and Matamoros), although they may not drive to interior posts as outlined above. Travel is permitted between Hermosillo and Nogales, but not permitted from Hermosillo to any other interior posts.

While in a foreign country, U.S. citizens may encounter road conditions that differ significantly from those in the United States. The information below concerning Mexico is provided for general reference only, and may not be totally accurate in a particular location or circumstance. Public transportation vehicles, specifically taxis and city buses, often do not comply with traffic regulations, including observing speed limits and stopping at red lights.

Driving and Vehicle Regulations: U.S. driver's licenses are valid in Mexico. Mexican law requires that only owners drive their vehicles, or that the owner be inside the vehicle. If not, the vehicle may be seized by Mexican customs and will not be returned under any circumstances.

The Government of Mexico strictly regulates the entry of vehicles into Mexico. Traffic laws in Mexico are sporadically enforced and therefore often ignored by drivers, creating dangerous conditions for drivers and pedestrians. Driving under the influence of alcohol is illegal in all parts of Mexico. Using a mobile device (such as a cell phone) is also prohibited while driving in many parts of Mexico, including Mexico City, and violators may be fined.

Insurance: Mexican insurance is required for all vehicles, including rental vehicles. Mexican auto insurance is sold in most cities and towns on both sides of the border. U.S. automobile liability insurance is not valid in Mexico, nor is most collision and comprehensive coverage issued by U.S. companies. Motor vehicle insurance is considered invalid in Mexico if the driver is found to be under the influence of alcohol or drugs.

Road Emergencies and Automobile Accidents: Motor vehicle accidents are a leading cause of death of U.S. citizens in Mexico. Motorists should exercise caution and remain alert on all Mexican roads. If you have an emergency while driving, the equivalent of "911" in Mexico is "066," but this number is not always answered. If you are driving on a toll highway (or "cuota"), or any other major highway, you may contact the Green Angels (Angeles Verdes), a fleet of trucks with bilingual crews. The Green Angels may be reached directly at (01) (55) 5250–8221. If you are unable to call them, pull off to the side of the road and lift the hood of your car; chances are that they will find you.

If you are involved in an automobile accident, you may be taken into police custody until it can be determined who is liable and whether you have the ability to pay any penalty. If you do not have Mexican liability insurance, you may be prevented from departing the country even if you require life-saving medical care, and you are almost certain to spend some time in jail until all parties are satisfied that responsibility has been assigned and adequate financial satisfaction received. Drivers may face criminal charges if injuries or damages are serious.

Road Safety: Avoid driving on Mexican highways at night. Even multi-lane expressways in Mexico often have narrow lanes and steep shoulders. Single-vehicle rollover accidents involving U.S. citizens are common, often resulting in death or serious injury to vehicle occupants. Use extreme caution when approaching towns, driving on curves, and passing large trucks. All vehicle occupants should use seatbelts at all times. Criminal assaults have occurred on highways throughout Mexico; travelers should exercise extreme caution at all times and should use toll ("cuota") roads rather than the less secure "free" ("libre") roads whenever possible. Always keep car doors locked and windows up while driving, whether on the highway or in town. While in heavy traffic, or stopped in traffic, leave enough room between vehicles to maneuver and escape, if necessary. In addition, U.S. citizens should not hitchhike or accept rides from or offer rides to strangers anywhere in Mexico. Please refer to our Road Safety Overseas for more information.

Vehicular traffic in Mexico City is restricted in order to reduce air pollution. The restriction is based on the last digit of the vehicle license plate. This applies equally to permanent, temporary, and foreign (U.S.) plates. For additional information, refer to the Hoy No Circula website (Spanish only) maintained by the Mexico City government.

In recent years, moped rentals have become very widespread in Cancun and Cozumel, and the number of serious moped accidents has risen accordingly. Most operators carry no insurance and do not conduct safety checks. The U.S. Embassy recommends avoiding operators who do not provide a helmet with the rental. Some operators have been known to demand fees many times in excess of damages caused to the vehicles, even if renters have purchased insurance in advance. Vacationers at other beach resorts have encountered similar problems after accidents involving rented jet-skis. There have been cases of mobs gathering to prevent tourists from departing the scene and to intimidate them into paying exorbitant damage claims.

For additional information in English concerning Mexican driver's permits, vehicle inspection, road tax, mandatory insurance, etc., please telephone the Mexican Secretariat of Tourism (SECTUR) at 1-800-44-MEXICO (639-426). Travelers can also consult MexOnline for further information regarding vehicle inspection and importation procedures. For detailed information in Spanish only, visit Mexican Customs' website Importación Temporal de Vehículos ("Temporary Importation of Vehicles"). Travelers are advised to consult with the Mexican Embassy or the nearest Mexican consulate in the United States for additional, detailed information prior to entering Mexico. For travel information for the Baja California peninsula, you can also consult independent websites Travel to Baja or Discover Baja California.

Aviation Safety Oversight: The U.S. Federal Aviation Administration (FAA) has assessed the government of Mexico's Civil Aviation Authority as being in compliance with International Civil Aviation Organization (ICAO) aviation safety standards for oversight of Mexico's air carrier operations. Further information may be found on the FAA safety assessment page.

Maritime Safety Oversight: The Mexican maritime industry, including charter fishing and recreational vessels, is subject solely to Mexican safety regulations. Travelers should be aware that Mexican equipment and vessels may not meet U.S. safety standards or be covered by any accident insurance.

Children's Issues: Mexico is the destination country of the greatest number of children abducted from the United States by a parent. A party to the Hague Convention on the Civil Aspects of International Child Abduction since 1991, Mexico was found to be not compliant with the

Convention in the Department of State's 2009 compliance report, though compliance improved in 2010. For information, see the U.S. Dept. of State Office of Children's Issues web pages on intercountry adoption and international parental child abduction.

Travel Warning

November 20, 2012

The Department of State has issued this Travel Warning to inform U.S. citizens about the security situation in Mexico. General information on the overall security situation is provided immediately below. For information on security conditions in specific regions of Mexico, which can vary, travelers should reference the state-by-state assessments further below.

This Travel Warning supersedes the Travel Warning for Mexico dated February 8, 2012 to consolidate and update information about the security situation and to advise the public of additional restrictions on the travel of U.S. government (USG) personnel.

General Conditions: Millions of U.S. citizens safely visit Mexico each year for study, tourism, and business, including more than 150,000 who cross the border every day. The Mexican government makes a considerable effort to protect U.S. citizens and other visitors to major tourist destinations, and there is no evidence that Transnational Criminal Organizations (TCOs) have targeted U.S. visitors and residents based on their nationality. Resort areas and tourist destinations in Mexico generally do not see the levels of drug-related violence and crime reported in the border region and in areas along major trafficking routes.

Nevertheless, U.S. travelers should be aware that the Mexican government has been engaged in an extensive effort to counter TCOs which engage in narcotics trafficking and other unlawful activities throughout Mexico. The TCOs themselves are engaged in a violent struggle to control drug trafficking routes and other criminal activity. As a result, crime and violence are serious problems throughout the country and can occur anywhere. U.S. citizens have fallen victim to TCO activity, including homicide, gun battles, kidnapping, carjacking and highway robbery.

According to the statistics last published by the Mexican government in late 2011, 47,515 people were killed in narcotics-related violence in Mexico between December 1, 2006 and September 30, 2011, with 12,903 narcotics-related homicides in the first nine months of 2011 alone. While most of those killed in narcotics-related violence have been members of TCOs, innocent persons have also been killed.

The number of U.S. citizens reported to the Department of State as murdered under all circumstances in Mexico was 113 in 2011 and 32 in the first six months of 2012.

Gun battles between rival TCOs or with Mexican authorities have taken place in towns and cities in many parts of Mexico, especially in the border region. Gun battles have occurred in broad daylight on streets and in other public venues, such as restaurants and clubs. During some of these incidents, U.S. citizens have been trapped and temporarily prevented from leaving the area. TCOs use stolen cars and trucks to create roadblocks on major thoroughfares, preventing the military and police from responding to criminal activity. The location and timing of future armed engagements is unpredictable. We recommend that you defer travel to the areas indicated in this Travel Warning and to exercise extreme caution when traveling throughout the northern border region.

The number of kidnappings and disappearances throughout Mexico is of particular concern. Both local and expatriate communities have been victimized. In addition, local police have been implicated in some of these incidents. We strongly advise you to lower your profile and avoid displaying any evidence of wealth that might draw attention.

Carjacking and highway robbery are serious problems in many parts of the border region and U.S. citizens have been murdered in such incidents. Most victims who complied with carjackers at these checkpoints have reported that they were not physically harmed. Carjackers have shot at vehicles that fail to stop at checkpoints. Incidents have occurred during the day and at night, and carjackers have used a variety of techniques, including bumping/moving vehicles to force them to stop and running vehicles off the road at high speeds. There are some indications that criminals have particularly targeted newer and larger vehicles, especially dark-colored SUVs. However, victims driving a variety of vehicles, from late model SUVs to old sedans have also been targeted. While violent incidents have occurred at all hours of the day and night on both modern toll ("cuotas") highways and on secondary roads, they have occurred most frequently at night and on isolated roads. To reduce risk, if absolutely necessary to travel by road, we strongly urge you to travel between cities throughout Mexico only during daylight hours, to avoid isolated roads, and to use toll roads whenever possible. The Mexican government has deployed federal police and military personnel throughout the country as part of its efforts to combat the TCOs. U.S. citizens traveling on Mexican roads and highways may encounter government checkpoints, which are often staffed by military personnel or law enforcement personnel. TCOs have erected their own unauthorized checkpoints, and killed or abducted motorists who have failed to stop at them. You should cooperate at all checkpoints.

Effective July 15, 2010, the U.S. Mission in Mexico imposed restrictions on U.S. government employees' travel. U.S. government employees and their families are not permitted to drive for personal reasons from the U.S.-Mexico border to or from the interior of Mexico or Central America. Personal travel by vehicle is permitted between Hermosillo and Nogales but is restricted to daylight hours and the Highway 15 toll road (cuota).

U.S. government (USG) personnel (U.S. citizens working at the Embassy and nine consulates) and their families are prohibited from personal travel to all areas described as "defer non-essential travel" and when travel for official purposes is essential it is conducted with extensive security precautions. USG personnel and their families are allowed to travel for personal reasons to the areas where no advisory is in effect or where the advisory is to exercise caution. While the general public is not forbidden from visiting places described as "defer non-essential travel," USG personnel will not be able to respond quickly to an emergency situation in those areas due to security precautions that must be taken to travel to those areas.

For more information on road safety and crime along Mexico's roadways, see the Department of State's Country Specific Information.

State-by-State Assessment: Below is a state-by-state assessment of security conditions throughout Mexico divided into northern and southern regions. The accompanying map will help in identifying individual locations. Travelers should be mindful that even if no advisories are in effect for a given state, crime and violence can occur anywhere.

Baja California (north): Tijuana and Mexicali are major cities/travel destinations in the state of Baja California -see map to identify their exact locations: You should exercise caution in the northern state of Baja California, particularly at night. For the one-year period ending July 2012, the number of murders in Mexicali increased by 43%, from 127 to 181, over the preceding year. The number of murders in the city of Tijuana was 351 for the same period. In the majority of these cases, the killings appeared to be related to narcotics trafficking. Targeted TCO assassinations continue to take place in Baja California. Turf battles between criminal groups resulted in assassinations in areas of Tijuana frequented by U.S. citizens. Shooting incidents, in which innocent bystanders have been injured, have occurred during daylight hours. Twenty-five U.S. citizens were the victims of homicide in the state in the 12-month period ending July 2012.

Baja California (South): Cabo San Lucas and La Paz are major cities/travel destinations in the state of SouthernBaja California -see map to identify its exact location: No advisory is in effect.

Chihuahua: Ciudad Juarez and Chihuahua City are major cities/travel destinations in Chihuahua -see map to identify their exact locations: You should defer non-essential travel to the state of Chihuahua. The situation in the state of Chihuahua, specifically Ciudad Juarez and Chihuahua City, is of special concern. The Mexican government reports that 1,933 people were killed in Ciudad Juarez in 2011, down from 3,100 in 2010. Although there has been a further decline in homicides in 2012, Ciudad Juarez still has one of the highest homicide rates in Mexico. Chihuahua City has seen an increase in violent crime in previous years. From the United States, other areas in the state of Chihuahua are often reached through the Columbus, NM, and the Fabens and Fort Hancock, TX, ports-of-entry which also experience high levels of violence. In these areas, U.S. citizens have been victims of narcotics-related violence. There have been incidents of narcotics-related violence in the vicinity of the Copper Canyon in Chihuahua.

Coahuila: You should defer non-essential travel to the state of Coahuila. The State of Coahuila continues to experience high rates of violent crimes and narcotics-related murders. TCOs continue to compete for territory and coveted border crossings to the United States. In September 2012, more than 100 prisoners escaped from a prison in Piedras Negras. The majority of these prisoners are known or suspected to be connected with TCO activity and believed involved in a series of violent incidents since the escape. The cities of Torreón and Saltillo have seen an increase of violent crimes, including murder, kidnapping, and armed carjacking. USG personnel may not frequent casinos, sportsbooks, or other gambling establishments and adult entertainment establishments.

Durango: You should defer non-essential travel to the state of Durango. Between 2010 and 2011, the number of homicides in the State of Durango increased by 122%. Several areas in the state continue to experience high rates of violence and remained volatile and unpredictable. USG personnel may not frequent casinos, sportsbooks, or other gambling establishments and adult entertainment establishments.

Nuevo Leon: Monterrey is a major city/travel destination in Nuevo Leon -see map to identify its exact location: You should defer non-essential travel to the state of Nuevo Leon, except the metropolitan area of Monterrey where you should exercise caution. The level of violence and insecurity in Monterrey remained high. Sporadic gun battles and attacks on casinos and adult entertainment establishments continue, as do placements of "narco banners" on bridges. TCOs have kidnapped and in some cases murdered American citizens, even when ransom demands are met. TCOs continue to attack local government facilities, prisons and police stations, and engaged in public shootouts with the military and between themselves. TCOs have used vehicle-borne improvised explosive devices against military and law enforcement units as well as incendiary devices against several types of businesses. Pedestrians and innocent bystanders have been killed in these incidents. Local police and private patrols have limited capacity to deter criminal elements or respond effectively to security incidents. As a result of a Department of State assessment of the overall security situation, the Consulate General in Monterrey is a partially unaccompanied post with no minor dependents of USG personnel permitted. USG personnel serving at the U.S. Consulate General in Monterrey may not frequent casinos, sportsbooks, or other gambling establishments and may not travel outside the San Pedro Garza Garcia municipal boundaries between midnight and 6 a.m.

San Luis Potosi: You should defer non-essential travel to the state of San Luis Potosi, except the city of San Luis Potosi where you should exercise caution. The entire stretch of highway 57D in San Luis Potosi and portions of the state east of highway 57D towards Tamaulipas are particularly dangerous. A U.S. government employee was killed and another wounded when they were attacked in their U.S. government vehicle on Highway 57 near Santa Maria del Rio in 2011. Cartel violence and highway lawlessness are a continuing security concern. USG personnel may not frequent casinos, sportsbooks, or other gambling establishments and adult entertainment establishments. USG personnel may not travel outside the City of San Luis Potosi after dark and must abide by a curfew of midnight to 6 a.m.

Sinaloa: Mazatlan is a major city/travel destination in Sinaloa -see map to identify its exact location: You should defer non-essential travel to the state of Sinaloa except the city of Mazatlan where you should exercise caution particularly late at night and in the early morning. One of Mexico's most powerful TCOs is based in the state of Sinaloa. With the exception of Ciudad Juarez, since 2006 more homicides have occurred in the state's capital city of Culiacan than in any other city in Mexico. Travel off the toll roads in remote areas of Sinaloa is especially dangerous and should be avoided. We recommend that any other travel in Mazatlan be limited to Zona Dorada and the historic town center, as well as direct routes to/from these locations and the airport.

Sonora: Nogales, Puerto Peñasco, Hermosillo, and San Carlos are major cities/travel destinations in Sonora - see attached map to identify their exact locations: You should defer non-essential travel between the city of Nogales and the cities of Sonoyta and Caborca (which area also includes the smaller cities of Saric, Tubutama, and Altar), defer non-essential travel to the eastern edge of the State of Sonora which borders the State of Chihuahua (all points along that border east of the northern city of Agua Prieta and the southern town of Alamos), defer non-essential travel within the state south of the city of Ciudad Obregon with the exception of travel to Alamos (traveling only during daylight hours and using only the Highway 15 toll road, aka cuota, and Sonora State Road 162). You should exercise caution when visiting the coastal town of Puerto Peñasco. There is no recommendation against travel to San Carlos. Sonora is a key region in the international drug and human trafficking trades, and can be extremely dangerous for travelers. The region west of Nogales, east of Sonoyta, and from Caborca north, including the towns of Saric, Tubutama and Altar, and the eastern edge of Sonora bordering Chihuahua, are known centers of illegal activity. U.S. citizens in Puerto Peñasco are encouraged to maintain a high level of vigilance and to take appropriate steps to bolster their personal security following a July 2012 mid-day gun battle between TCO members and increases in reported robberies and assaults against U.S. citizens. Additionally U.S. citizens visiting Puerto Peñasco are urged to use the Lukeville, Arizona/Sonoyta, Sonora border crossing, in order to limit driving through Mexico. Travelers throughout Sonora are encouraged to limit travel to main roads during daylight hours.

Tamaulipas: Matamoros, Nuevo Laredo, Reynosa, and Tampico are major cities/travel destinations in Tamaulipas -see map to identify their exact locations: You should defer non-essential travel to the state of Tamaulipas. All USG employees are prohibited from personal travel on Tamaulipas highways outside of Matamoros, Reynosa and Nuevo Laredo due to the risks posed by armed robbery and carjacking. USG employees may not frequent casinos and adult entertainment establishments within these cities; and in Matamoros are subject to a midnight to 6 a.m. curfew. Nuevo Laredo has seen an increase in the number of grenade attacks within the past year, particularly against night clubs within city limits. In June 2012, a small car bomb exploded in front of the Nuevo Laredo city hall. Both Matamoros and Ciudad Victoria have experienced grenade attacks in the past year. All travelers should be aware of the risks posed by armed robbery and carjacking on state highways throughout Tamaulipas, particularly on highways and roads outside of urban areas along the northern border. Traveling outside of cities after dark is particularly dangerous. In August 2012 an American family was forced off the road, resulting in one death and several injuries, in an apparent robbery attempt soon after crossing the bridge from Texas into Nuevo Laredo. While no highway routes through Tamaulipas are considered safe, many of the crimes reported to the U.S. Consulate General in Matamoros have taken place along the Matamoros-Tampico highway, particularly around San Fernando and the area north of Tampico.

Zacatecas: You should defer non-essential travel to the state of Zacatecas except the city of Zacatecas where you should exercise caution. The regions of the state bordering Durango and Coahuila as well as the cities of Fresnillo and Fresnillo-Sombrete and surrounding area are particularly dangerous. The northwestern portion of the state of Zacatecas has become notably dangerous and insecure. Robberies and carjackings are occurring with increased frequency and both local authorities and residents have reported a surge in observed TCO activity. This area is remote, and local authorities are unable to regularly patrol it or quickly respond to incidents that occur there. Gun battles between criminal groups and authorities occur in the area of the state bordering the state of Jalisco. There have also been reports of roadblocks and false checkpoints on highways between the states of Zacatecas and Jalisco. The city of Fresnillo, the area extending northwest from Fresnillo along Highway 45 (Fresnillo-Sombrete) between Highways 44 and 49, and highway 49 northwards from Fresnillo through Durango and in to Chihuahua are considered dangerous. Extreme caution should be taken when traveling in the remainder of the state. USG personnel may not frequent casinos, sportsbooks, or other gambling establishments and adult entertainment establishments. USG personnel may not travel outside the City of Zacatecas after dark and must abide by a curfew of midnight to 6 a.m. within a secured venue.

Aguascalientes: You should defer non-essential travel to the areas of the state that border the state of Zacatecas. The security situation along the Zacatecas border continues to be unstable and gun battles between criminal groups and authorities occur. Concerns include roadblocks placed by individuals posing as police or military personnel and recent gun battles between rival TCOs involving automatic weapons.

Campeche: No advisory is in effect.

Chiapas: San Cristobal de las Casas is a major city/travel destination in Chiapas -see map to identify its exact location: No advisory is in effect.

Colima: Manzanillo is a major city/travel destination in Colima -see map to identify its exact location: You should defer non-essential travel to the areas of the state of Colima that border the state of Michoacán. There is no recommendation against travel to Manzanillo. You should also exercise caution when traveling at night outside of cities in the remaining portions of the state. The security situation along the Michoacán border continues to be unstable and gun battles between criminal groups and authorities occur. Concerns include roadblocks placed by individuals posing as police or military personnel and recent gun battles between rival TCOs involving automatic weapons.

Estado de Mexico: Toluca is a major city/travel destination in Estado de Mexico -see map to identify its exact location: You should exercise caution in the municipalities of Coacalco, Ecatepec, Nezahualcoyotl, La Paz, Valle del Chalco Solidaridad, Chalco, and Ixtapaluca, which are eastern portions of the greater Mexico City metropolitan area, located just to the east of the Federal District of Mexico and Benito Juarez airport. These areas have seen high rates of crime and insecurity. In September 2012, the Government of Mexico sent military and federal police forces into the Municipality of Nezahualcoyotl in an effort to combat organized crime.

Guanajuato: San Miguel de Allende and Leon are major cities/travel destinations in Guanajuato -see map to identify their exact locations: No advisory is in effect.

Guerrero: Acapulco, Ixtapa, Zihuatanejo and Taxco are major cities/travel destinations in Guerrero -see map to identify their exact locations: You should defer non-essential travel to the northwestern and southern portions of the state (the area west and south of the town of Arcelia on the border with Estado de Mexico in the north and the town of Tlapa near the border with Oaxaca), except for the cities of Acapulco, Zihuatanejo, and Ixtapa. In those cities, you should exercise caution and stay within tourist areas. You should also exercise caution and travel only during daylight hours on highway 95D (cuota/toll road) between Mexico City and Acapulco and highway 200 between Acapulco and Zihuatanejo/Ixtapa.

In Acapulco, defer non-essential travel to areas further than 2 blocks inland of the Costera Miguel Aleman Boulevard, which parallels the popular beach areas. In general, the popular tourist area of Diamante, just south of the city, has been less affected by violence. Flying into the coastal cities in southern Guerrero remains the preferred method of travel. You should also exercise caution in the northern region of Guerrero (the area north of the town of Arcelia on the border with Estado de Mexico in the north and the town of Tlapa near the border with Oaxaca).

The state of Guerrero has seen an increase in violence among rival criminal organizations. Acapulco's murder rates increased dramatically since 2009; in response, in 2011 the Government of Mexico sent additional military and federal police to the state to assist State security forces in implementing ongoing operation "Guerrero Seguro" (Secure Guerrero) that focuses on combating organized crime and returning security to the environs of popular tourist areas.

Hidalgo: No advisory is in effect.

Jalisco: Guadalajara and Puerto Vallarta are major cities/travel destinations in Jalisco -see map to identify their exact locations: You should defer non-essential travel to areas of the state that border the states of Michoacán and Zacatecas. You should also exercise caution when traveling at night outside of cities in the remaining portions of this state. There is no recommendation against travel to Guadalajara and Puerto Vallarta. There is also no recommendation against travel on principal highways in Jalisco between Guadalajara including the portions that cross in to the southern portions of the state of Nayarit.

The security situation along the Michoacán and Zacatecas borders continues to be unstable and gun battles between criminal groups and authorities occur. Concerns include roadblocks placed by individuals posing as police or military personnel and recent gun battles between rival TCOs involving automatic weapons.

Mexico City (also known as the Federal District): No advisory is in effect. See also discussion in the section on Estado de Mexico for areas within the greater Mexico City metropolitan area.

Michoacán: Morelia is a major city/travel destination in Michoacán -see attached map to identify its exact location: You should defer non-essential travel to the state of Michoacán except the cities of Morelia and Lázaro Cardenas where you should exercise caution. Flying into Morelia and Lázaro Cardenas, or driving to Lázaro Cardenas via highway 200 from Zihuatanejo/Ixtapa, are the recommended methods of travel. Attacks on Mexican government officials, law enforcement and military personnel, and other incidents of TCO-related violence, have occurred throughout Michoacán.

Morelos: Cuernavaca is a major city/travel destination in Morelos -see attached map to identify its exact location: You should exercise caution in the state of Morelos due to the unpredictable nature of TCO violence. On August 24, two USG employees were injured after being fired upon by Federal Police officers on an isolated road north of Tres Marias, Morelos. Numerous incidents of narcotics-related violence have also occurred in the city of Cuernavaca, a popular destination for U.S. students.

Nayarit: You should defer non-essential travel to all areas of the state of Nayarit north of the city of Tepic as well as to the cities of Tepic and Xalisco. The security situation north of Tepic and in these cities is unstable and travelers could encounter roadblocks or shootouts between rival criminals. There is no recommendation against travel either to Riviera Nayarit in the southern portion of the state or to principal highways in the southern portion of the state used to travel from Guadalajara to Puerto Vallarta.

Oaxaca: Oaxaca, Huatulco and Puerto Escondido are major cities/travel destinations in Oaxaca -see map to identify their exact locations: No warning is in effect.

Puebla: No advisory is in effect.

Queretaro: No advisory is in effect.

Quintana Roo: Cancun, Cozumel, Playa del Carmen, Riviera Maya and Tulum are major cities/travel destinations in Quintana Roo -see attached map to identify their exact locations: No advisory is in effect.

Tabasco: Villahermosa is a major city/travel destination in Tabasco -see attached map to identify its exact location: No advisory is in effect.

Tlaxcala: No advisory is in effect.

Veracruz: You should exercise caution when traveling in the state of Veracruz. Over the last year, the state of Veracruz has seen an increase in violence among rival criminal organizations. In response, in 2011 the Government of Mexico sent additional military and federal police to the state to assist State security forces in implementing ongoing operation "Veracruz Seguro" (Secure Veracruz) that focuses on combating organized crime.

Yucatan: Merida and Chichen Itza are major cities/travel destinations in Yucatan -see map to identify its exact location: No advisory is in effect.

We encourage you to review the U.S. Embassy's Mexico Security Update. The update contains information about recent security incidents in Mexico that could affect the safety of the traveling public. For more detailed information on staying safe in Mexico, please see the State Department's Country Specific Information for Mexico.

For the latest security information, U.S. citizens traveling abroad should regularly monitor the State Department's internet web site, where the current Worldwide Caution, Travel Warnings, and Travel Alerts can be found. Follow us on Twitter and the Bureau of Consular Affairs page on Facebook as well.

Up-to-date information on security can also be obtained by calling 1-888-407-4747 toll free in the United States and Canada or, for callers outside the United States and Canada, a regular toll line at 001-202-501-4444. These numbers are available from 8:00 a.m. to 8:00 p.m. Eastern Time, Monday through Friday (except U.S. federal holidays).

U.S. citizens traveling or residing overseas are encouraged to enroll with the State Department's Smart Traveler Enrollment Program. For any emergencies involving U.S. citizens in Mexico, please contact the U.S. Embassy or the closest U.S. Consulate (see list below). The numbers provided below for the Embassy and Consulates are available around the clock. The U.S. Embassy is located in Mexico City at Paseo de la Reforma 305, Colonia Cuauhtemoc, telephone from the United States: 011-52-55-5080–2000; telephone within Mexico City: 5080–2000; telephone long distance within Mexico 01-55-5080–2000. U.S. citizens may also contact the Embassy by e-mail.

Consulates:

Ciudad Juarez (Chihuahua): Paseo de la Victoria 3650, tel. (011)(52)(656) 227-3000.

Guadalajara (Nayarit, Jalisco, Aguas Calientes, and Colima): Progreso 175, telephone (011)(52)(333) 268-2100.

Hermosillo (Sinaloa and the southern part of the state of Sonora): Avenida Monterrey 141, telephone (011)(52)(662) 289-3500.

Matamoros (the southern part of Tamaulipas with the exception of the city of Tampico): Avenida Primera 2002, telephone (011)(52)(868) 812-4402.

Merida (Campeche, Yucatan, and Quintana Roo): Calle 60 no. 338-K x 29 y 31, Col. Alcala Martin, Merida, Yucatan, Mexico 97050, telephone (011)(52)(999) 942-5700 or 202-250-3711 (U.S. number).

Monterrey (Nuevo Leon, Durango, Zacatecas, San Luis Potosi, and the southern part of Coahuila): Avenida Constitucion 411 Poniente, telephone (011)(52)(818) 047-3100.

Nogales (the northern part of Sonora): Calle San Jose, Nogales, Sonora, telephone (011)(52)(631) 311-8150.

Nuevo Laredo (the northern part of Coahuila and the northwestern part of Tamaulipas): Calle Allende 3330, col. Jardin, telephone (011)(52)(867) 714-0512.

Nuevo Laredo (the northern part of Coahuila and the northwestern part of Tamaulipas): Paseo de Las Culturas s/n Mesa de Otay, telephone (011) (52) (664) 977-2000.

All other Mexican states, the Federal District of Mexico City, and the city of Tampico, Tamaulipas, are part of the Embassy's consular district.

Consular Agencies:

Acapulco: Hotel Emporio, Costera Miguel Aleman 121—Suite 14, telephone (011)(52)(744) 481-0100 or (011)(52)(744) 484-0300.

Cancún: Blvd. Kukulcan Km 13 ZH Torre La Europea, Despacho 301 Cancun, Quintana Roo, Mexico C.P. 77500; telephone (011)(52)(998) 883-0272.

Cozumel: Plaza Villa Mar en el Centro, Plaza Principal, (Parque Juárez between Melgar and 5th Ave.) 2nd floor, locales #8 and 9, telephone (011)(52)(987) 872-4574 or, 202-459-4661 (a U.S. number).

Ixtapa/Zihuatanejo: Hotel Fontan, Blvd. Ixtapa, telephone (011)(52)(755) 553-2100.

Los Cabos: Las Tiendas de Palmilla Local B221, Carretera Transpeninsular Km. 27.5, San José del Cabo, BCS, Mexico 23406 Telephone: (624) 143-3566 Fax: (624) 143-6750.

Mazatlán: Playa Gaviotas #202, Zona Dorada, telephone (011)(52)(669) 916-5889.

Oaxaca: Macedonio Alcalá no. 407, interior 20, telephone (011)(52)(951) 514-3054, (011) (52)(951) 516-2853.

Piedras Negras: Abasolo #211, Zona Centro, Piedras Negras, Coah., Tel. (011)(52)(878) 782-5586.

Playa del Carmen: "The Palapa," Calle 1 Sur, between Avenida 15 and Avenida 20, telephone (011)(52)(984) 873-0303 or 202-370-6708(a U.S. number).

Puerto Vallarta: Paradise Plaza, Paseo de los Cocoteros #1, Local #4, Interior #17, Nuevo Vallarta, Nayarit, telephone (011)(52)(322) 222-0069.

San Luis Potosí: Edificio "Las Terrazas," Avenida Venustiano Carranza 2076–41, Col. Polanco, telephone: (011)(52)(444) 811-7802/7803.

San Miguel de Allende: Centro Comercial La Luciernaga, Libramiento Manuel Zavala (Pepe KBZON), telephone (011)(52)(415) 152-2357.

Intercountry Adoption

October 2011

The information in this section has been edited from the latest report available as of February 2013 from the State Department Bureau of Consular Affairs, Office of Overseas Citizens Services. For more information, please read the *Intercountry Adoption* section of this book and review current reports online at http://adoption.state.gov.

Who Can Adopt? Adoption between the United States and Mexico is governed by the Hague Adoption Convention. Therefore, to adopt from Mexico, you must first be found eligible to adopt by the U.S. Government. The U.S. Government agency responsible for making this determination is the Department of Homeland Security, U.S. Citizenship and Immigration Services (USCIS).

Residency Requirements: Mexican adoption procedures include a one to three week pre-adoption trial period, during which the child lives with the prospective adoptive parent(s) in Mexico. Because of the large amount of paperwork in both the Mexican and American processes, the DIF suggests that adoptive parents be prepared to spend at least three months in Mexico including the pre-adoption trial period.

Age Requirements: Prospective adoptive parents must be over 25 years of age and at least 17 years older than the child. If married, only one parent must meet the age requirement.

Marriage Requirements: Prospective adoptive parents may be married or single, male or female.

Income Requirements: Prospective adoptive parents must demonstrate the means to support the physical and educational needs of the child. While similar, each Mexican state does have its own civil code governing adoptions. Therefore, it is important to check with each state, as the laws among states will vary.

Who Can Be Adopted? Because Mexico is party to the Hague Adoption Convention, children from Mexico must meet the requirements of the Convention in order to be eligible for adoption. For example, the Convention requires that Mexico attempt to place a child with a family in-country before determining that a child is eligible for intercountry adoption. In addition to Mexico's requirements, a child must meet the definition of a Convention adoptee in order to enter the United States to reside.

The Mexican Central Authority has informed the U.S. Department of State that Mexican children who meet any of the following conditions are eligible for placement through The Hague Convention Intercountry Adoption Process:

- Children five years and older
- Children with a physical or mental disability
- Children who suffer from a disease that is costly to treat
- Sibling groups. (Children under 5 years of age may be adopted if siblings older than five are also being adopted.)

The process for legally adopting a child in the Republic of Mexico is long, involves multiple entities, and may be characterized by uncertainty and delay. Prospective adoptive parents are cautioned that uninformed or unscrupulous agents sometimes approach couples to complete an adoption outside of the legal framework described here. However, the Hague process must be followed precisely and in the correct order for an adopted child to be issued a Hague Convention Adoption Visa. Adoptive children who enter the United States without an immigrant visa may later encounter problems with obtaining legal residence and U.S. citizenship, enrollment in school and social security, etc., and also risk being deported to Mexico after reaching their 18th birthday, even if they have legal U.S.citizen parents under Mexican law.

Mexican Central Authority: The Mexican Central Authority for Adoptions is the Secretary for Exterior Relations, or the Secretaria de Relaciones Exteriores (SRE). The SRE is responsible for policy and issues key documentation certifying Hague compliance, including the Article 23 Certificate that the adoption or grant of custody occurred in compliance with the Convention. The SRE implements the Hague Convention through the National System for the Full Development of the Family, or the Sistema Nacional de Desarollo Integral de la Familia (DIF). The DIF is a public institution in Mexico in charge of implementing national policies on all matters pertaining to the family, and the implementation of domestic and intercountry adoptions resides in their purview, along with final execution of adoptions through the legal system.

The Process: Because Mexico is party to the Hague Adoption Convention, adopting from Mexico must follow a specific process designed to meet the Convention's requirements. For detailed and updated information on these requirements, please review the *Intercountry Adoption* section of this publication and visit the U.S. Department of State Intercountry Adoption website at http://adoption.state.gov.

The first step in adopting a child from Mexico is to select an accredited or approved adoption service provider in the United States. Only these agencies and attorneys can provide adoption services between the United States and Mexico. In addition, the adoption service provider MUST ALSO is approved by the Mexican Central Authority. The Mexican Central Authority evaluates adoption service providers for approval to provide services in Mexico. In order to obtain up to date information regarding which U.S. adoption service providers are authorized by the Mexican Central Authority to provide services in Mexico, prospective adoptive parents should consult with the national DIF in Mexico City (Sistema Nacional Para El Desarrollo Integral de la Familia (DIF); website: http://dif.sip.gob.mx/dif/?contenido=15). In addition, prospective adoptive parents may also wish to consult with the DIF in the state where the adoption will take place because procedures can vary by state.

After you choose an accredited adoption service provider, the next step is to apply to be found eligible to adopt (Form I-800A) by the Department of Homeland Security, U.S. Citizenship and Immigration Services (USCIS). Once the U.S. Government determines that you are "eligible" and "suitable" to adopt, your adoption service provider will forward your information to the Central Authority in Mexico. The DIF's Technical Council on Adoptions will convene to review your application and determine whether you are also eligible to adopt under Mexican law. If approved, your name will be added to a waiting list of prospective adoptive parents maintained by DIF.

If both the United States and Mexico determine that you are eligible to adopt, and a child is available for intercountry adoption, the DIF may provide you with a referral for a child. DIF is the legal representative for abandoned children and provider of foster care for abused or orphaned minors. Though the regional or state DIF will likely play a role in the matching process, the referral must be approved by the national DIF office. Please note that the DIF matches eligible prospective adoptive parents with children who are on its list of children who are legally available for adoption, in accordance with relevant Mexican child welfare laws. Prospective adoptive parents decide at this point whether or not they will be able to meet the needs of the child referred to them by the DIF, and whether they will provide a permanent family placement for the referred child.

After you accept a match with a child, you will apply to the USCIS for provisional approval of a petition to immigrate a child through adoption (Form I-800). Form I-800, like Form I-800A, must be submitted in the United States. However, USCIS regional offices in Mexico handle cases in particular states: USCIS Tijuana handles the Mexican states of Baja California, Sinaloa and Sonora. USCIS Ciudad Juárez andes Chihuahua and Durango. USCIS Monterrey andes Coahuila, Nuevo León, Tamaulipas, San Luis Potosí, Zacatecas and Aguascalientes. The rest of Mexico is handled by USCIS Mexico City. After the I-800 is provisionally approved by USCIS, the entire case file is transferred to the U.S. Embassy via the U.S. Department of State's National Visa Center, which immediately forwards the case file to the U.S. Embassy. Upon receipt of the file the Embassy makes contact with your adoption service provider to arrange for submission of a visa application. The Embassy will ask for an immigrant visa application form known as the DS 260 Parts I and II, an original or certified birth certificate for the child, photos of the child and, if practicable, a medical exam conducted by a panel physician, Once the Consular Officer receives the visa application, the officer reviews the child's information and evaluates the case and the application for compliance with the Hague Convention and for possible visa ineligibilities. If the Consular Officer determines that the child appears eligible to immigrate to the United States, he or she will notify the SRE and DIF of this initial determination in a letter known as the Article 5 letter. When the State DIF office receives the Article 5 letter from the Embassy, it will issue a letter known as the Article 17 letter to the prospective adoptive parent(s) and the Adoption Service Provider. The Article 17 letter notifies the prospective adoptive parents that they may proceed with the adoption. For Convention country adoptions, prospective adoptive parent(s) may not proceed with the adoption or obtain custody for the purpose of adoption until both the Article 5 and Article 17 letters have been issued. Initiating the adoption process prior to issuance of the Article 5 and Article 17 letters will jeopardize the Hague adoption process.

Role of ohe Central Authority: The SRE is the competent authority that certifies that an adoption or grant of custody has occurred in accordance with the Convention by issuing an Article 23 certificate or equivalent grant of custody. The SRE implements the Hague Convention through the DIF. The DIF is a Mexican government institution with branches in each Mexican state to handle family matters. The DIF acts as the legal representative for abandoned children and provides foster care for abused or orphaned minors. Children who are abandoned or orphaned can be given up for adoption by the DIF. The DIF is assigned the responsibility to study each child's eligibility for international adoption and arrange adoptions. The DIF determines whether a family would be suitable for a particular child by ensuring that a home study has been done. Prospective adoptive parents interested in adopting in Mexico should note that the DIF makes every effort to place children with relatives or Mexican citizens living in Mexico before making intercountry placements.

Role of the Court: Judicial proceedings occur in Mexico depending on the laws of the state.

Role of the Adoption Agencies: Because Mexico is a Convention country, adoption services must be provided by a Hague-accredited agency, approved person, supervised provider, or exempted provider. Learn more Adoption service providers must also be authorized to provide adoption services by Mexican authorities.

Time Frame: The general time frame for processing a Mexico adoption after the Article 5 letter has been issued by the U.S. Embassy and issued to the Mexican Central Authority signaling that the Hague adoption may proceed ranges from three to eight months, but varies from state to state. Again, prospective adoptive parents should check with the state where the adoption will take place.

Adoption Application: The application should be filed with the SRE by the adoption service provider. Prospective adoptive parents who are dual Mexican and U.S. nationals are cautioned that only plenary or plena adoptions are considered valid for intercountry adoptions. Simple adoptions do not meet the requirements of the Hague Convention on Intercountry Adoption and it is not possible to issue a U.S. Hague adoption visa in cases for which simple adoption has been issued.

Adoption Fees: The DIF charges approximately $250 USD for adoption services but costs vary state-by-state. Generally, the fees include all applicable taxes. The DIF office also has its own lawyers and their services are also included in the fee. Using an attorney for DIF adoptions is optional for the prospective adoptive parent(s). These expenses should have been itemized in the fees and estimated expenses section of your adoption services contract.

Documents Required: Mexican authorities have informed us families must provide the following documents in order to adopt in Mexico:

- Certified copy of prospective adoptive parent's birth certificate or a U.S. passport as proof of U.S. citizenship;
- Certified copy of marriage certificate, if applicable;
- A statement from the employer of the prospective parent who is the primary supporter of the family. This statement must indicate the position, years of service with the employer, and salary;
- Copy of the most recent bank statement or other evidence of financial holdings as proof of financial solvency;
- Two letters of recommendation from people who can attest to the character of the adoptive parents. A married couple should obtain letters from persons who have known them as a married couple. Each letter should include the address and telephone number of the person writing the letter;
- Certificate from the state police from the prospective adoptive parent's state of residence in the U.S. verifying that the adoptive parents have no police record. The FBI fingerprint check for the I-800A fulfills this requirement;
- A copy of a social, economic, and psychological study of the parent's home situation conducted by an agency of the state of the child's proposed residence, or an adoption service provider authorized by that state to conduct such a study, and or by an appropriate public or private adoption service provider accredited or approved in the United States. The home study conducted for the I-800A fulfills this requirement;
- One 3x3-inch color photograph of each prospective adoptive parent; and
- Two 3x5-inch photographs of the prospective adoptive parent(s) in the home or on a family outing.

All documentation listed above must be apostilled by the Secretary of State of the U.S. state of origin of the document, translated into Spanish by an official translator of the Mexican Consulate nearest to the prospective adoptive parent's(s') place of residence in the United States. When all the documents have been assembled, they should be sent to the person or organization in Mexico acting as the adoption agent/representative for presentation to the Mexican court.

Bringing Your Child Home: Once your adoption is complete (or you have obtained legal custody of the child), there are a few more steps to take before you can head home. Specifically, you need to apply for several documents for your child before he or she can travel to the United States, such as a birth certificate, a passport or travel document for your child from the country in which he or she was born, and a U.S. Immigration Visa. For detailed and updated information on how to obtain these documents, review the *Intercountry Adoption* section in this publication and visit the U.S. Department of State Intercountry Adoption website at http://adoption.state.gov.

Child Citizenship Act: For adoptions finalized abroad, the Child Citizenship Act of 2000 allows your new child to acquire American citizenship automatically when he or she enters the United States as lawful permanent residents. For adoptions finalized in the United States, the Child Citizenship Act of 2000 allows your new child to acquire American citizenship automatically when the court in the United States issues the final adoption decree. To learn more, review the *Intercountry Adoption* section in this publication and visit the U.S. Department of State Intercountry Adoption website at http://adoption.state.gov.

U.S. Embassy in Mexico
Paseo de la Reforma 305
Colonia Cuauhtémoc
06500 Mexico, D.F.
Tel: 011–52–55–50–80–2000.

Mexican Central Authority
Secretaria de Relaciones Exteriores (SRE)
Dirección de Derecho de la Familia
Website:
http://www.sre.gob.mx/english/
Sistema Nacional Para El Desarrollo Integral de la Familia (DIF)
Website: http://dif.sip.gob.mx

Embassy of Mexico
Consular Section
2827 16th Street, NW
Washington, D.C. 20009–4260
Tel: (202) 736–1000
Website: http://www.sre.gob.mx

Mexico also has consulates General in Atlanta, Chicago, Dallas, Denver, El Paso, Houston, Los Angeles, Miami, New Orleans, New York, San Antonio, San Diego, San Francisco, and Hato Rey, Puerto Rico.

Office of Children's Issues
U.S. Department of State
2201 C Street, NW
SA-29
Washington, DC 20520
Tel: 1–888–407–4747
E-mail: AskCI@state.gov or AdoptionUSCA@state.gov
Website:http://adoption.state.gov

For questions about immigration procedures, contact the National Customer Service Center (NCSC) at 1-800-375-5283 (TTY 1-800-767-1833).

For questions on filing an I-800A and I-800 under the Hague Adoption Convention:

USCIS, National Benefits Center (Hague process):
NBC.Hague@DHS.gov
Telephone:
1–877–424–8374 (toll free)
1–816–251–2770 (local).

International Parental Child Abduction

September 2012

The information in this section has been edited from a report of the Bureau of Consular Affairs, Office of Overseas Citizens Services of the U.S. Department of State. For more information, please read the *International Child Abduction* section of this book and review current reports online at www.travel.state.gov/abduction.

General Information: Mexico is a federal republic formed by 31 states and the Federal District. A party to the Hague Convention on the Civil Aspects of International Child Abduction (Hague Abduction Convention) since 1991, Mexico is the destination country of the greatest number of children abducted from the United States by a parent. The Hague Abduction Convention provides a civil legal mechanism for parents to seek access to or the return of children wrongfully removed or retained in Mexico.

With respect to child custody, Mexican law distinguishes between parental authority (patria potestad) and custody (guarda y custodia). Patria potestad refers to parents' responsibilities and rights regarding the child, including the responsibility to care for the child, reside with the child, and provide for the child's necessities (for example, food, education and development). It also includes the right to correct the child, as well as the right to control and manage any property or rights the child may have.

Absent a court order, parents have equal patria potestad rights and responsibilities to their minor children. In reality, one parent may make all decisions for the child. If parents cannot agree over the exercise of the patria potestad, they may ask a judge to decide which parent makes the decision. If the parents are deceased or unavailable, the paternal grandparents exercise patria potestad; if they are deceased or unavailable, the maternal grandparents exercise these rights.

Most children live with their mothers after divorce. If fathers want the children to reside with them, it is typical that boys will live with the father and girls will live with their mother. At age 14, the child may decide which parent the child wishes to live with.

Mexican Immigration authorities confirm the consent of both parents before allowing any minor of any nationality to leave the country; any parent traveling alone with a minor must present a written statement from the absent parent. Mexican Foreign Ministry officials requires the signature of both parents for children younger than 18 years to obtain Mexican passports.

The Mexican agency responsible for locating missing children is the police authority. Locating missing children can be a challenge in Mexico. The Department of State's annual Compliance Report on the Hague Abduction Convention details many long unresolved child abduction cases to Mexico for which the children have not been located.

Legal System: Mexico is a civil law country, which means that court decisions in Mexico are based upon Mexican civil code. In each of the 31 states in Mexico, state law establishes the structure and function of the courts, as well as its own constitution, laws, regulations, and decrees. Generally, state courts are organized in the following way: the highest appellate court is known as the Superior Court of Justice (Tribunal Superior de Justicia); this court is followed by the Courts of First Instance (Tribunales de Primera Instancia) of ordinary jurisdiction, responsible for hearing civil, criminal and commercial causes. Immediately below, are the minor courts of special jurisdiction, such as the family courts and bankruptcy courts. Family law courts handle divorce and custody cases.

Retaining an Attorney: Mexico's National System for the Comprehensive Development of the Family, known as DIF, (Sistema Nacional para el Desarrollo Integral de la Familia) offers free legal assistance to vulnerable adults and children in Mexico. The system consists of one federal DIF institute, 32 DIF agencies (one for each state and one for the Federal District—DF in Spanish) and 2, 274 municipal DIF agencies. At the state level, the wife of the governor is often the head of the DIF.

A parent does not need to retain private counsel to file a Hague Convention petition in Mexico. The Central Authority of Mexico (Secretaria de Relaciones Exteriores) will, upon receipt of the Hague Convention application, prepare a written communiqué for the court, containing an explanation of the Hague Convention and its objectives. A parent may choose to retain an attorney, however, to follow-up on the case and to provide them with direct information on the status of the case. A retained attorney should contact the Central Authority of Mexico as soon as possible after the application is submitted.

It is important to note that while the Central Authority of Mexico does not represent Hague Convention applicants in court or assign an attorney to take the case, the Central Authority of Mexico will prepare the required documentation to submit the case in court. In Mexico, Family Court judges are authorized to intervene ex-officio in family matters and therefore have the power to enforce their decisions without the involvement of private counsel. Nevertheless, parents in the United States have said that having private legal representation resulted in fewer delays in the application process.

Citizenship/Passport Matters: Children born in Mexico or born abroad to Mexican parents are entitled to Mexican citizenship. Mexican law recognizes dual nationality for Mexicans by birth. U.S. citizens who are also Mexican nationals are considered Mexican by local authorities.

Mexican law requires that any non-Mexican citizen under the age of 18 departing Mexico must carry notarized written permission from any parent or guardian not traveling with the child to or from Mexico. This permission must include the name of the parent, the name of the child, the name of anyone traveling with the child, and the notarized signature(s) of the absent parent(s).

A parent can prevent issuance of Mexico's passport to their child, because issuance of a Mexican passport to a minor child requires the signed consent of both parents. Mexico does not allow a child to enter on a parent's passport. The child needs his/her own passport.

Exit Permits: Mexican law requires that any non-Mexican citizen under the age of 18 departing Mexico must carry notarized written permission from any parent or guardian not traveling with the child to or from Mexico. This permission must include the name of the parent, the name of the child, the name of anyone traveling with the child, and the notarized signature(s) of the absent parent(s).

Mediation: Mexico's National System for the Comprehensive Development of the Family, known as DIF, (Sistema Nacional para el Desarrollo Integral de la Familia) offers free legal assistance to vulnerable adults and children in Mexico. The system consists of one federal DIF institute, 32 DIF agencies (one for each state and one for the Federal District—DF in Spanish) and 2, 274 municipal DIF agencies. As such, this system may be a helpful tool for parents seeking mediation services. It is important to note that DIF does not represent Hague Convention applicants in court, nor do they assign attorneys to take Hague Convention cases.

Hague Abduction Convention: The Hague Convention on the Civil Aspects of International Child Abduction (the "Hague Convention") came into force between the United States and Mexico on October 1, 1991. Therefore, Hague Convention provisions for return would apply to children abducted or retained after October 1, 1991. Parents and legal guardians of children taken to Mexico prior to October 1, 1991, may still submit applications for access to the child under the Hague Convention in some cases. Mexico has been cited in the annual Compliance Report on the Hague Abduction Convention as a country demonstrating a pattern of noncompliance in the areas of law enforcement performance and judicial performance.

Mexico has no specific federal legislation for implementing the Hague Convention; rather, it is implemented under existing Mexican state law. Each state has an independent judicial organization empowered to apply and interpret the laws of that state. The judiciary in each state is headed by a Superior Court of Justice and contains civil, family, and criminal judges. Family court judges have jurisdiction for resolving disputes concerning custody, rights of access, and child abduction based on the laws of that state. They therefore receive and rule on Hague Convention cases.

Mexico has established a Central Authority charged with applying the procedures of the Hague Convention by working with state authorities. The Central Authority of Mexico is part of the Ministry of Foreign Affairs (Secretaria de Relaciones Exteriores), and is responsible for cases of children abducted from and abducted to Mexico.

The address of Mexico's Central Authority is:
ATTN: Reyna Martinez Lopez
Secretaría de Relaciones Exteriores
Dirección General de Protección y
Asuntos Consulares

Oficina de Derecho de Familia
Plaza Juárez No. 20, Piso 17
Colonia Centro, Del. Cuauhtemoc
06010 Mexico, D.F.
MEXICO

For more information on the Hague Convention and the application process, please read the *International Parental Child Abduction* section of this book and review current reports online at www.travel.state.gov/abduction.

Civil Remedies: In lieu of filing a Hague Convention application, a parent or legal guardian may seek the recognition of an U.S. custody order in the Mexican judicial system. This process takes several months and requires the services of a Mexican attorney. A parent or legal guardian may also fight for custody directly through the Mexican court system. This also requires the services of a Mexican attorney, and may preclude the option of filing a Hague Convention application, or pursuing an application already in progress. Consult with an attorney to ensure you have ample information to decide on which option to pursue. For examples of Mexico's custody laws, see the Code of Civil Procedure of the Federal District (C.P.C.D.F.) art. 94 and the Civil Code for the Federal District (C.C.D.F.) articles 283-285. The Civil Code for the Federal District is available in Spanish online.

Criminal Remedies: Parental child abduction is a crime in Mexico, and a parent may consider filing criminal charges against the taking parent. Please note, however, that this may negatively affect the outcome of a Hague Convention case and does not guarantee the child's return.

For information on possible criminal remedies, please contact local law enforcement authorities or the nearest office of the Federal Bureau of Investigation. Information is also available on the Internet at the web site of the U.S. Department of Justice, Office of Juvenile Justice and Delinquency Prevention at http://www.ojjdp.ncjrs.org. Please note that criminal charges may complicate a Hague Convention case. Contact the Mexico officer in the Office of Children's Issues for specific information.

Visitation Rights/Access Rights: A parent or legal guardian can file a Hague application for access, thereby seeking to enforce visitation rights pursuant to the Hague Abduction Convention. In the alternative, a parent or legal guardian may also retain a foreign attorney to register and then enforce a visitation agreement in family law court in Mexico. Judges generally give strong weight to the right of the children to visit their parents (derecho de convivencia con los padres), except when there is risk to the child.

The U.S. Embassy is located in Mexico City at Paseo de la Reforma 305, Colonia Cuauhtemoc; telephone from the United States: 011-52-55-5080–2000; telephone within Mexico City: 5080–2000; telephone long distance within Mexico 01-55-5080–2000. The Embassy can also be contacted by e-mail at: ccs@usembassy.net.mx. The Embassy's web page is http://mexico.usembassy.gov/eng/main.html.

In addition to the Embassy, there are several United States Consulates and Consular Agencies located throughout Mexico.

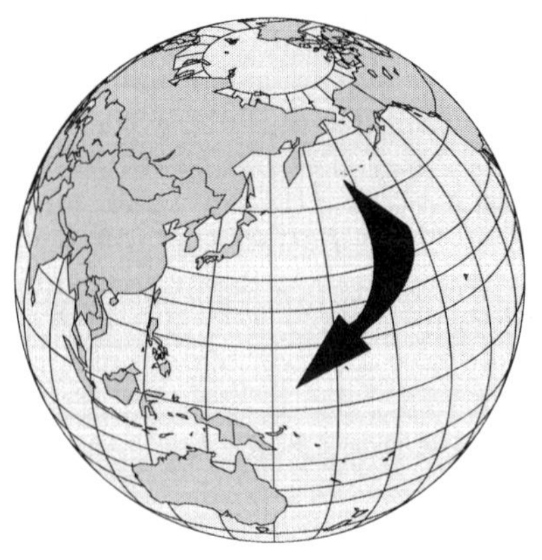

MICRONESIA

Compiled from publications that were available as of February 2013 from the U.S. Department of State, the U.S. Department of Commerce, and the Central Intelligence Agency (CIA). See the introduction to this set for explanatory notes.

Official Name:
Federated States of Micronesia (FSM)

PROFILE

Geography

Area: total: 702 sq km; country comparison to the world: 191; land: 702 sq km; water: 0 sq km (fresh water only)
Major cities: Palikir (capital) 7,000 (2009)
Climate: tropical; heavy year-round rainfall, especially in the eastern islands; located on southern edge of the typhoon belt with occasionally severe damage
Terrain: islands vary geologically from high mountainous islands to low, coral atolls; volcanic outcroppings on Pohnpei, Kosrae, and Chuuk

People

Nationality: noun: Micronesian(s); adjective: Micronesian; Chuukese, Kosraen(s), Pohnpeian(s), Yapese
Population: 106,487 (July 2012 est.)
Population growth rate: -0.343% (2012 est.)
Ethnic groups: Chuukese 48.8%, Pohnpeian 24.2%, Kosraean 6.2%, Yapese 5.2%, Yap outer islands 4.5%, Asian 1.8%, Polynesian 1.5%, other 6.4%, unknown 1.4% (2000 census)
Religions: Roman Catholic 52.7%, Protestant 41.7% (Congregational 40.1%, Baptist 0.9%, Seventh-Day Adventist 0.7%), other 3.8%, none or unspecified 0.8% (2000 Census)
Languages: English (official and common language), Chuukese, Kosrean, Pohnpeian, Yapese, Ulithian, Woleaian, Nukuoro, Kapingamarangi
Literacy: definition: age 15 and over can read and write; total population: 89%; male: 91%; female: 88% (1980 est.)
Health: life expectancy at birth: total population: 71.8 years; male: 69.84 years; female: 73.85 years (2012 est.); Infant mortality rate: total: 23.51 deaths/1,000 live births; male: 25.99 deaths/1,000 live births; female: 20.91 deaths/1,000 live births (2012 est.)
Unemployment rate: 22% (2000 est.)
Work force: 16,360 (2008)

Government

Type: constitutional government in free association with the US; the Compact of Free Association entered into force on 3 November 1986 and the Amended Compact entered into force in May 2004
Independence: 3 November 1986
Constitution: 10 May 1979
Political subdivisions: 4 states; Chuuk (Truk), Kosrae (Kosaie), Pohnpei (Ponape), Yap
Suffrage: 18 years of age; universal

Economy

GDP (purchasing power parity): $238.1 million (2008 est.); $277 million (2002 est.)

GDP real growth rate: 0.3% (2005 est.)

GDP per capita (PPP): $2,200 (2008 est.); $2,300 (2005 est.)

Natural resources: timber, marine products, deep-seabed minerals, phosphate

Agriculture products: black pepper, tropical fruits and vegetables, coconuts, bananas, cassava (tapioca), sakau (kava), Kosraen citrus, betel nuts, sweet potatoes; pigs, chickens; fish

Industries: tourism, construction; fish processing, specialized aquaculture; craft items (from shell, wood, and pearls)

Exports: $14 million (2004 est.);

Exports—commodities: fish, garments, bananas, black pepper, sakau (kava), betel nut

Imports: $132.7 million (2004);

Imports—commodities: food, manufactured goods, machinery and equipment, beverages

Debt—external: $60.8 million (FY05 est.)

Exchange rates: the US dollar is used

GEOGRAPHY

The Federated States of Micronesia (FSM) consists of 607 islands extending 1,800 miles across the archipelago of the Caroline Islands east of the Philippines. Approximately 100 islands are inhabited. The four states are the island groups of Pohnpei, Chuuk, and Yap, and the island of Kosrae. The federal capital is Palikir, on Pohnpei.

PEOPLE

The indigenous population consists of various ethno-linguistic groups. English has become the common language. The birth rate remains high at more than 3%, but the population of the four states remains almost constant due to emigration.

National/Racial/Ethnic Minorities

Each of the country's four states has a different language and culture. Traditionally the state of Yap had a caste-like social system with high-status villages, each of which had an affiliated low-status village. In the past those who came from low-status villages worked without pay for those with higher status. In exchange, those with higher status offered care and protection to those subservient to them.

The traditional hierarchical social system has been gradually breaking down, and capable people from low-status villages can rise to senior positions in society. Nonetheless, the traditional system affected contemporary life. Persons from low-status backgrounds tended to be less assertive in advocating for their communities' needs, and low-status communities sometimes continued to be underserved.

The national and state constitutions prohibit noncitizens from purchasing land, and foreign investment laws limit the types of businesses noncitizens can own and operate.

The national Congress granted citizenship to non-Micronesians only in rare cases. There is no permanent residency status. For the most part, however, noncitizens shared fully in the social and cultural life of the country.

Religion

Although there is linguistic and cultural diversity within each of the country's four states, its culture is overwhelmingly Christian. Several Protestant denominations, as well as the Roman Catholic Church, are present in every state. The United Church of Christ is the main Protestant denomination. In Kosrae, 95 percent of the population is Protestant. In Pohnpei the population is evenly divided between Protestants and Catholics. In Chuuk an estimated 60 percent is Catholic and 40 percent Protestant. In Yap an estimated 80 percent of the population is Catholic and the remainder Protestant. In addition to the United Church of Christ, Protestant denominations include Baptists, Assemblies of God, Salvation Army, and Seventh-day Adventists. Smaller groups include Jehovah's Witnesses, The Church of Jesus Christ of Latter-day Saints (Mormons), and the Baha'i Faith. The Mormon Church is growing and, in Pohnpei, with over 1,700 members, about 5 percent of the population identifies itself as Mormon. Attendance at religious services is generally high; churches are well supported by their congregations and play a significant role in civil society.

Most immigrants are Filipino Catholics who have joined local Catholic churches. The Filipino Iglesia Ni Cristo has a church in Pohnpei.

In the 1890s in Pohnpei, interdenominational rivalry and the conversion of clan leaders resulted in religious divisions along clan lines that continue today, although intermarriage has blurred the lines considerably. More Protestants live on the western side of the island, while more Catholics live on the eastern side.

HISTORY

Ancestors of the Micronesians settled the Caroline Islands over 4,000 years ago. A decentralized chieftain-based system eventually evolved into a more centralized economic and religious empire based principally in Yap and Pohnpei. European explorers—first the Portuguese in search of the Spice Islands and then the Spanish—reached the Carolines in the 16th century, with the Spanish establishing sovereignty. The current FSM passed to German control in 1899, and then through the Treaty of Versailles to the Japanese in 1919. Following World War II, these islands became part of the United Nations Trust Territory of the Pacific Islands, administered by the United States.

On May 10, 1979, four of the Trust Territory districts ratified a new constitution to become the Federated States of Micronesia. The neighboring trust districts of Palau, the Marshall Islands, and the Northern Mariana Islands chose not to participate. The FSM signed a Compact of Free Association with the United States in 1986. An Amended Compact entered into force in June 2004.

GOVERNMENT AND POLITICAL CONDITIONS

The Federated States of Micronesia is a constitutional republic composed of four states: Chuuk, Kosrae, Pohnpei, and Yap. Individual states enjoyed significant autonomy and traditional leaders retained considerable influence, especially in Pohnpei and Yap. The elected unicameral Congress selects the president from among its four members elected from at-large state districts. On May 10, 2011, Congress reelected Emanuel Mori as president. The most recent elections for Congress, held in March, were considered generally free and fair, despite technical problems and some allegations of fraud in Chuuk.

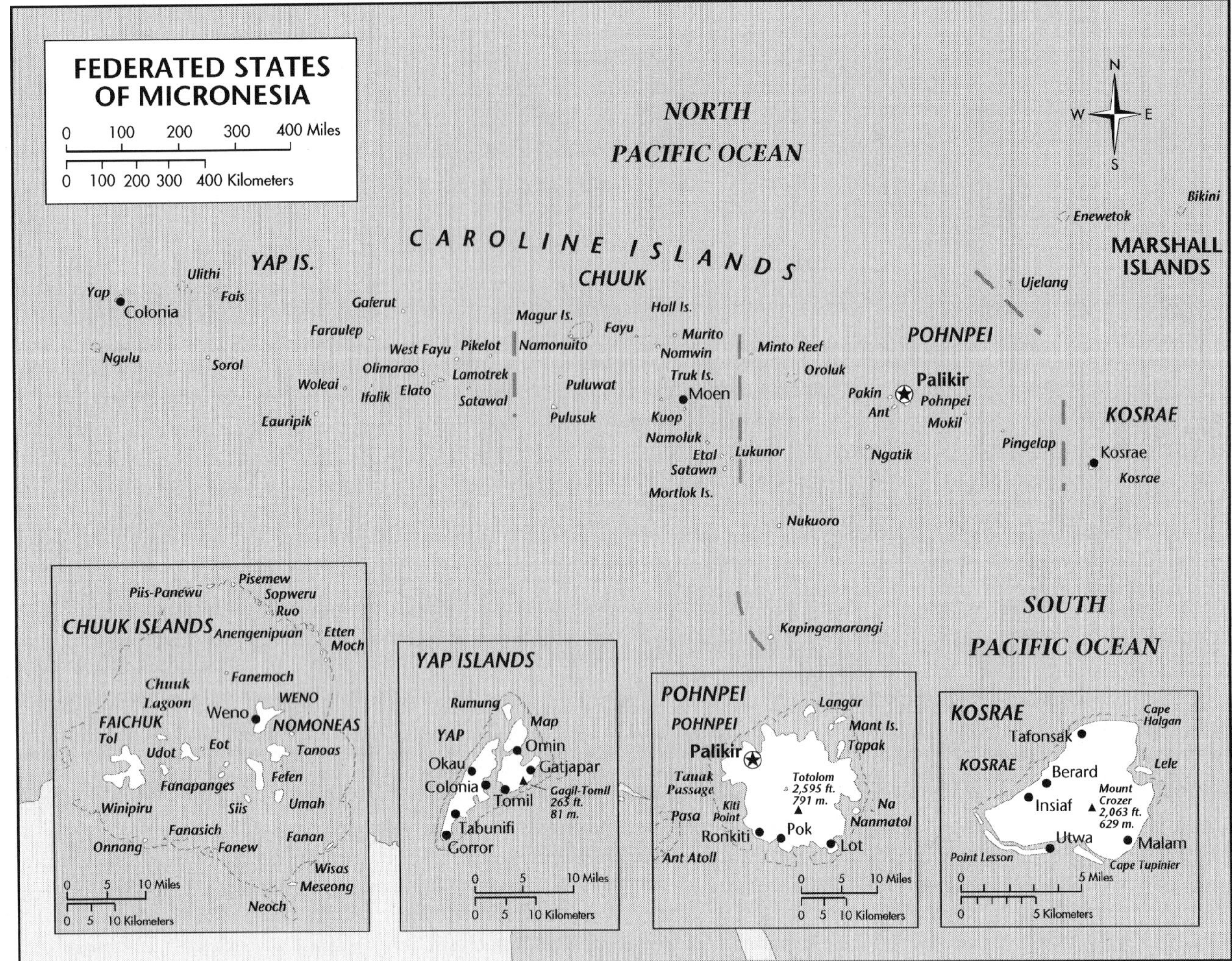

Recent Elections

National congressional elections in March 2011 generally were free and fair. There were allegations of polling fraud in a special election to replace the governor in Chuuk in August, and the losing candidate filed two complaints. The court rejected the complaints and upheld the election results.

Political Parties: There are no restrictions on the formation of political groups; however, there were no significant efforts to form organized political parties, and none existed. Candidates generally sought political support from family and allied clan groupings, religious groups, and expatriate citizen communities. Only one congressional candidate ran on a platform in March. He unseated an incumbent.

Participation of Women and Minorities: Cultural factors in the male-dominated society limited women's representation in government and politics. Women were well represented in the middle and lower ranks of government at both the federal and state level but were scarcer in the upper ranks. A woman held the cabinet-level position of secretary of health services, and there was one female associate justice on the national Supreme Court and one female associate justice on the Pohnpei State Supreme Court.

The country's first female ambassador was appointed permanent representative to the United Nations in 2010. One woman ran unsuccessfully for national office in the March elections. There were two elected women in the Pohnpei State legislature. There were no other women in the other state legislatures or in the national legislature.

To the extent that the country is a multicultural federation, both the legislature and the executive included persons from various cultural backgrounds.

Principal Government Officials

Last Updated: 1/31/2013

Pres.: **Emanuel "Manny" MORI**

Vice Pres.: **Alik L. ALIK**

Sec. of Education: **Casiano D. SHONIBER**

Sec. of Finance & Admin.: **Finley S. PERMAN**

Sec. of Foreign Affairs: **Lorin S. ROBERT**

Sec. of Health & Social Affairs: **Vita Akapito SKILLING, Dr.**
Sec. of Justice: **Maketo ROBERT**
Sec. of Resource & Development: **Marion HENRY**
Sec. of Transportation, Communication, & Infrastructure: **Francis ITIMAI**
Speaker of the Congress: **Isaac V. FIGIR**
Ambassador to the US: **Asterio R. TAKESY**
Permanent Representative to the UN, New York: **Jane J. CHIGIYAL**

ECONOMY

Economic activity consists primarily of subsistence farming and fishing. The islands have few mineral deposits worth exploiting, except for high-grade phosphate. The potential for a tourist industry exists, but the remote location, a lack of adequate facilities, and limited air connections hinder development.

Under the original terms of the Compact of Free Association, the US provided $1.3 billion in grant aid during the period 1986–2001; the level of aid has been subsequently reduced. The Amended Compact of Free Association with the US guarantees the Federated States of Micronesia (FSM) millions of dollars in annual aid through 2023, and establishes a Trust Fund into which the US and the FSM make annual contributions in order to provide annual payouts to the FSM in perpetuity after 2023.

The country's medium-term economic outlook appears fragile due not only to the reduction in US assistance but also to the current slow growth of the private sector.

Labor Conditions

National and state laws do not establish a minimum age for employment of children. In practice there was no employment of children for wages, but children often assisted their families in subsistence farming and in family-owned shops.

The minimum hourly wage for employment with the national government was $2.65. All states had a minimum hourly wage for government workers: $2.00 in Pohnpei, $1.25 in Chuuk, $1.42 in Kosrae, and $1.60 in Yap. Only Pohnpei had a minimum wage for private sector workers: $1.35 per hour. The minimum wage was enforced through the tax system, and this mechanism was believed to be effective. Statistics were not readily available, but salaried persons were relatively well-off. As of 2000, 28.4 percent of the population was in the subsistence economy.

National law sets a standard of an eight hour/five day workweek, with premium pay for overtime. A federal regulation requires that employers provide a safe workplace. No law for either the public or private sector permits workers to remove themselves from dangerous work situations without jeopardy to their continued employment.

Working conditions aboard some foreign-owned fishing vessels operating in the country's waters continued to be very poor. Crewmen reported a high incidence of injuries, beatings by officers, and nonpayment of salary.

U.S.-MICRONESIAN RELATIONS

Following World War II, the islands of what is now the Federated States of Micronesia (FSM) became part of the United Nations Trust Territory of the Pacific Islands, administered by the United States. Micronesia became independent in 1986, when it entered into a Compact of Free Association with the United States. An Amended Compact entered into force in 2004. The basic relationship of free association continues indefinitely.

The Governments of Micronesia and the United States maintain deep ties and a cooperative relationship. Reflecting a strong legacy of trusteeship cooperation, over 25 U.S. federal agencies operate programs in Micronesia. Under the Compact, the United States has full authority and responsibility for the defense and security of Micronesia. This security relationship can be changed or terminated by mutual agreement. Also under the Compact, Micronesians can live, work, and study in the United States without a visa. Micronesians volunteer to serve in the U.S. Armed Forces at approximately double the per capita rate as Americans; they are also eligible for admission to U.S. Service Academies. Americans can live and work freely in Micronesia without the need for a visa.

U.S. Assistance to Micronesia

The Compact between the two countries obligates the U.S. Government to provide grant and program assistance to Micronesia. The United States provides over $130 million in direct assistance, including additional federal grants and services, every year until 2023. This assistance also includes the systematic reallocation of a portion of the direct aid to a jointly managed Trust Fund. The Compact's overall goal is to assist Micronesia on its path to economic self sufficiency post 2023. A Joint Economic Management Committee, consisting of representatives of both nations, is responsible for ensuring that assistance funds are spent effectively, with the aim of fostering good governance and economic self-reliance. Grant assistance under the Amended Compact focuses on six sectors: education, health, infrastructure, public sector capacity building, private sector development, and the environment. The U.S. Department of the Interior is responsible for monitoring and implementing the Amended Compact.

Micronesia is highly vulnerable to natural disasters and the effects of climate change. U.S. foreign assistance focuses on strengthening Micronesia's climate resilience through disaster management.

Bilateral Economic Relations

Micronesia's national government plays a central role in the economy as recipient and domestic administrator of Compact funds. The national and state-level governments employ over half of the country's workers. The United States is Micronesia's largest trade partner.

Micronesia's Membership in International Organizations

Micronesia and the United States belong to a number of the same international organizations, including the United Nations, International Monetary Fund, and World Bank. Micronesia also belongs to the Pacific Islands Forum, of which the United States is a Dialogue Partner.

Bilateral Representation

Micronesia maintains an embassy in the United States at 1725 N Street NW, Washington, DC 20036; tel: 202-223-4383.

Principal U.S. Embassy Officials

Last Updated: 1/14/2013

KOLONIA (E) P.O. Box 1286, Pohnpei FM 96941, 691-320-2187, Fax 691-320-2186, INMARSAT Tel No INMARSAT, Workweek: Monday–Friday 8a.m. to 5 p.m., http://kolonia.usembassy.gov/

DCM OMS:	Emerlynn Shed (Les)
AMB OMS:	Emerlynn Shed (Les)
DHS/CIS:	Guam/Honolulu
DHS/ICE:	Embassy Singapore
FM:	Embassy Manila
HRO:	Randy Calvert
MGT:	Randy Calvert
POSHO:	Randy Calvert
AMB:	Doria Rosen
CON:	Charles Thomas
DCM:	Miguel Ordonez
PAO:	Patrick Maloney (Les)
GSO:	Scott Anderson (Gsa)
RSO:	Embassy Manila
APHIS:	Embassy Canberra
ECON:	Charles Thomas
EST:	Embassy Suva
FAA:	Barry Brayer
FMO:	Embassy Manila
ICASS Chair:	Paul Lake
IMO:	Robert Boylan (Ims)
IRS:	Embassy Tokyo
ISSO:	Randy Calvert
POL:	Miguel Ordonez
State ICASS:	Charles Thomas

TRAVEL

Consular Information Sheet

May 1, 2012

Country Description: The Federated States of Micronesia (FSM) is composed of over 600 islands and atolls spanning one million square miles of the western Pacific Ocean. The FSM is a voluntary federation of four semi-autonomous states (Pohnpei, Kosrae, Chuuk, and Yap), each retaining considerable autonomy to manage its domestic affairs, including civil and criminal justice systems. The federal capital is located at Palikir, on the island of Pohnpei, close to Pohnpei's largest town, Kolonia. The FSM is a constitutional democracy. The United States extends security guarantees and economic assistance to the FSM under the Compact of Free Association. Under the Compact, FSM citizens may enter the U.S. to study and work without visas.

Smart Traveler Enrollment Program (STEP)/Embassy Locations: If you are going to live in or visit the FSM, please take the time to tell our Embassy about your trip. If you enroll, we can keep you up to date with important safety and security announcements. It will also help your friends and family get in touch with you in an emergency.

U.S. Embassy in Kolonia
1286 U.S. Embassy Place, Pohnpei (near the movie theater)
P.O. Box 1286, Pohnpei, Federated States of Micronesia 96941
Telephone: (691) 320-2187
Duty Officer's telephone: (691) 920-2369.
Facsimile: (691) 320-2186

Entry/Exit Requirements for U.S. Citizens: Visit the Embassy of Micronesia website for the most current visa information. You will need a U.S. passport, a completed FSM Immigration Arrival and Departure Record (FSM Form 5004), and a completed FSM Customs Form in order to enter the FSM. Your passport must be valid for at least 120 days after you enter into the FSM. Your air carrier will distribute the FSM Immigration Arrival and Departure Record and Customs Form before you arrive into FSM. There is no limit to the length of time U.S. citizens can remain in the FSM. All states except Yap have a departure fee that you must pay when you are leaving. The fees are $10 for Pohnpei and Kosrae and $20 for Chuuk. Please make sure you have cash available as credit cards are not accepted and ATM machines are not available at any of the airports. Also note that a health certificate may be required if you are arriving from an area experiencing an epidemic. The U.S. Department of State is unaware of any HIV/AIDS entry restrictions for visitors to or foreign residents of the FSM.

For more information about FSM entry requirements, travelers may consult the Embassy of the Federated States of Micronesia at 1725 N Street NW, Washington, D.C., 20038, tel: (202) 223-4383. The FSM also has Consulates in Honolulu and Guam.

The U.S. Embassy in Kolonia accepts passport applications if you are living or traveling in the FSM; however, the passports are printed in the United States. The time between submitting an application and receiving a new passport is approximately two weeks, but can be longer. The Embassy can print limited validity passports in emergency situations only.

Threats to Safety and Security: Always maintain a high level of security, be alert to any unusual activity around your home or business, and report any suspicious incidents to local police authorities.

Unexploded ordnance remains from the heavy fighting and bombardment that took place in and around the islands of Micronesia during World War II. Exercise caution when you travel or dive in the region, especially in Yap harbor and in Chuuk Lagoon. It is illegal, as well as dangerous, to remove "souvenirs" from sunken WWII vessels and aircraft.

Stay up to date by:

- Bookmarking our Bureau of Consular Affairs website, which contains the current Travel Warnings and Travel Alerts as well as the Worldwide Caution.
- Following us on Twitter and the Bureau of Consular Affairs page on Facebook as well.
- Downloading our free Smart Traveler IPhone App to have travel information at your fingertips.
- Calling 1-888-407-4747 toll-free within the U.S. and Canada, or a regular toll line, 1-202-501-4444, from other countries.
- Taking some time before travel to consider your personal security

Crime: Throughout the country, foreigners have reported been subjected to and possibly singled out for theft and verbal and physical abuse, sometimes violent. Alcohol-related attacks as well as alcohol driving accidents are a particular concern during weekend evening hours. The Embassy encourages extra caution during the holidays, when alcohol consumption is higher. Do not attempt to intervene in disputes between local citizens. Dress conservatively, as it is considered impolite for females to wear clothing that exposes anything above the knee. Modern Western swimwear may be considered immodest by local standards, and people wearing such clothing outside of hotels that cater to tourists could be harassed. Additionally, we suggest women travel in groups and walk in well-lit areas.

Crime rates are higher in Chuuk than in the other states; you should exercise caution at all times, stay off the streets after dark on Weno (the main island), and ensure that the hotel where you are staying is prepared to assist you in an emergency. Do not buy counterfeit and pirated goods, even if they are widely available. Not only are the counterfeit items illegal in the United States, if you purchase them you may also be breaking local law.

Victims of Crime: If you or someone you know becomes the victim of a crime abroad, you should contact the local police and the nearest U.S. embassy or consulate. We can:

- Replace a stolen passport.
- Help you find appropriate medical care if you are the victim of violent crimes such as assault or rape.
- Put you in contact with the appropriate police authorities, and if you want us to, we cancontact family members or friend.
- Help you understand the local criminal justice process and direct you to local attorneys, although it is important to remember that local authorities are responsible for investigating and prosecuting the crime.

The local equivalents to the "911" emergency lines in the FSM are: In Chuuk, Kosrae, or Yap it is "911" and in Pohnpei it is "320-2221" for Police or Fire Department. Please keep in mind that the capacity of local police forces throughout the FSM is very low. There is often a significant delay for police to respond to calls or they may not respond at all. Capacity to investigate crimes is also extremely limited and victims may wait months or years for an arrest, if any. Additionally, the justice system of the FSM is slow and legal standards may not be applied evenly across all cases. Court appointed attorneys as well as judges presiding over cases, may not have the legal training or background expected in the United States.

Criminal Penalties: While you are traveling in FSM, you are subject to its laws even if you are a U.S. citizen. Foreign laws and legal systems can be vastly different from those in the United States. It is very important to know what is legal and what is not where you are going. Criminal penalties will also vary from country to country.

If you break local laws in FSM, your U.S. passport will not help you avoid arrest or prosecution. If you violate Micronesian laws, even unknowingly, you may be expelled, arrested, or imprisoned.

In Micronesia, for example, driving under the influence could land you in jail immediately. Penalties for possessing, using, or trafficking in illegal drugs in Micronesia are severe, and convicted offenders can expect long jail sentences and heavy fines.

There are also some things that might be legal in the country you visit but still illegal in the United States. You can be prosecuted under U.S. law if you buy pirated goods. Engaging in sexual conduct with children or using or disseminating child pornography in a foreign country is a crime prosecutable in the United States with very severe penalties.

While some countries will automatically notify the nearest U.S. embassy or consulate if a U.S. citizen is detained or arrested in a foreign country, that might not always be the case in FSM. To ensure that the United States is aware of your circumstances, request that the police and prison officials notify the nearest U.S. embassy or consulate as soon as you are arrested or detained overseas.

Special Circumstances: Micronesian customs authorities charge import taxes on cigarettes, tobacco, alcohol, gasoline, and other personal items that are more than the amounts allowed. All imports can be physically inspected by customs officials. Strict quarantine regulations restrict entry of plant and animal products. You should contact the Embassy of Micronesia in Washington, D.C., or one of Micronesia's consulates in Honolulu or Guam for specific information regarding customs requirements.

Accessibility: While in FSM, individuals with disabilities may find accessibility and accommodation very different from what you find in the United States. Neither laws nor regulations mandate accessibility to public facilities, services, or accomodations for persons with disabilities.

There are almost no sidewalks available in the FSM. There is no public transportation. Taxis are run by independent operators that make no provision for people with disabilities. The national Department of Health and Social Services is responsible for protecting the rights of persons with disabilities; however, action is rarely taken by the government.

Medical Facilities and Health Information: Health care facilities in the FSM consist of hospitals on each of thc four major islands and a few scattered clinics. These facilities sometimes lack basic supplies and medicines, and the quality of health care varies. Doctors and hospitals may expect immediate cash payment for health services. Medical evacuation for non-ambulatory patients may not be immediately available and can be very expensive. Scuba divers should note that although there are decompression chambers in Yap, Chuuk, and Pohnpei, their availability and staff experience in treating diving injuries vary.

You can find detailed information on vaccinations and other health precautions on the CDC website. For information about outbreaks of infectious diseases abroad, consult the World Health Organization (WHO) website. The WHO website also contains additional health information for travelers, including detailed country-specific health information.

Medical Insurance: You cannot assume your insurance will go with you when you travel. Your regular U.S. health insurance may not cover doctor and hospital visits in other countries. It is very important to find out BEFORE you leave whether or not your medical insurance will cover you overseas. You need to ask your insurance company two questions:

- Does my policy apply when I am out of the United States?
- Will it cover emergencies like a trip to a foreign hospital or a medical evacuation?

If your coverage does not go with you when you travel, it is a very good idea to take out another one for your trip.

Traffic Safety and Road Conditions: While in FSM, you may encounter road conditions that differ significantly from those in the United States. The information below concerning Micronesia is provided for general reference only, and may not be totally accurate in a particular location or circumstance.

Speed limits throughout the FSM are low: 25 miles per hour (mph) in most places; 15 mph in school zones when children are present.

Driving is on the right-hand side of the road, as in the United States. However, the majority of vehicles in FSM are right-hand drive vehicles imported from Japan; they are not designed to operate on the FSM road network. Drivers in these vehicles do not have an optimum field of vision, which can interfere with driving manoeuvres and the driver's ability to establish visual contact with the other road users.

Most roads are narrow and without sidewalks, creating hazards for both drivers and pedestrians. Many roads are in poor condition, with potholes and little or no shoulder to pull to the side. Roads outside the towns are often unpaved. All roads are used simultaneously by pedestrians, children playing, animals, and vehicles. Road conditions can worsen after heavy rains; coral surfaces are particularly likely to be slippery.

There is no formal training in road safety so many drivers are unaware of road safety rules. Drivers' skills vary and drivers often make turns or stop to pick up pedestrians without warning. Taxis are available in state capitals, but you should always be careful since some taxi drivers are reckless. Drunk drivers can create serious hazards, particularly on weekend evenings and holidays. Motorcyclists are required by law to wear helmets. If you intend to be resident to the FSM, you should acquire a local driver's license with the State Police. In most cases, the police will issue a local license to anyone who presents a U.S. driver's license. If you will be in the FSM temporarily, a U.S. driver's license itself is sufficient to rent a car and drive for the duration of your visit.

Aviation Safety Oversight: As there is no direct commercial air service to the United States by carriers registered in Micronesia, the U.S. Federal Aviation Administration (FAA) has not assessed the government of FSM's Civil Aviation Authority for compliance with International Civil Aviation Organization (ICAO) aviation safety standards. Further information may be found on the FAA's safety assessment page.

United Airlines is the only commercial carrier serving the FSM. Flight schedules and routes are limited and subject to change. There may be few alternatives if flights are canceled or missed. Flights are usually fully booked, and aircraft weight is an issue due to short runways and the type of aircraft used. Because of these limitations and the numerous transit stops made (the typical routing to get to Kolonia, for instance, would be via Honolulu with intermediate stops in Majuro, Kwajalein, and Kosrae; or via Guam with a stop in Chuuk), with debarking and embarking passengers at each location, baggage sometimes may not be loaded at the departure point or may be off-loaded by mistake and left behind at an intermediate stop. You should keep these logistical challenges in mind when traveling in the region. Missing baggage should be reported immediately to United Airlines ground personnel before onward flight departure.

Children's Issues: Please see the U.S. Dept. of State Office of Children's Issues web pages on intercountry adoption and international parental child abduction

Intercountry Adoption

May 2012

The information in this section has been edited from the latest report available as of February 2013 from the State Department Bureau of Con-

sular Affairs, Office of Overseas Citizens Services. For more information, please read the *Intercountry Adoption* section of this book and review current reports online at http://adoption.state.gov.

The Federated States of Micronesia, is not party to the Hague Convention on Protection of Children and Co-operation in Respect of Intercountry Adoption (the Hague Adoption Convention). Intercountry adoptions of children from non-Hague countries are processed in accordance with 8 Code of Federal Regulations, Section 204.3 as it relates to orphans as defined under the Immigration and Nationality Act, Section 101(b)(1)(F).

Under the Compact of Free Association between the United States and the Federated States of Micronesia (FSM), FSM citizens have the right to live, work, study and assume residence in the United States with no visa requirement. However, this does not apply to adopted children from the FSM, who must obtain a U.S. immigrant visa in order to travel to reside permanently with their adoptive families in the United States. Please see the *Intercountry Adoption* section of this book for more details. You may also review current reports online at http://adoption.state.gov.

Who Can Adopt? To bring an adopted child to the United States from the Federated States of Micronesia, you must meet eligibility and suitability requirements. The U.S. Department of Homeland Security, U.S. Citizenship and Immigration Services (USCIS) determines Who Can Adopt under U.S. immigration law. Additionally, a child must meet the definition of orphan under U.S. law in order to be eligible to immigrate to the United States on an IR-3 or IR-4 immigrant visa. In addition to U.S. immigration requirements, you must also meet the following requirements in order to adopt a child from the Federated States of Micronesia.

Residency: There is a three-year residency requirement for all U.S. citizen prospective adoptive parents in the state of Pohnpei, codified by law, meaning that the parents must have lived in the FSM for three years prior to adoption proceedings. The three other states in the FSM (Kosrae, Chuuk, and Yap) have no law specifically pertaining to adoption. Adoptions are handled in the court system and addressed entirely on a case-by-case basis.

Age of Adopting Parents: There is no codified requirement on adoptive parents related to age. This would be addressed on a case-by-case basis during the adoption proceedings. The local attorney representing the adoptive parents would be able to address and answer these issues.

Marriage: There is no codified requirement on adoptive parents related to marital status. This would be addressed on a case-by-case basis during the adoption proceedings. The local attorney representing the adoptive parents would be able to address and answer these issues.

Income: There is no codified requirement on adoptive parents related to economic eligibility. This would be addressed on a case-by-case basis during the adoption proceedings. The local attorney representing the adoptive parents would be able to address and answer these issues.

Other: None

Who Can Be Adopted? In addition to U.S. immigration requirements, FSM does not have specific requirements that a child must meet in order to be eligible for adoption.

Caution: Prospective adoptive parents should be aware that not all children in orphanages or children's homes are adoptable. In many countries, birth parents place their child(ren) temporarily in an orphanage or children's home due to financial or other hardship, with the intention of returning for the child when they are able to do so. In such cases, the birth parent(s) have rarely relinquished their parental rights or consented to their child(ren)'s adoption.

FSM Adoption Authority: There is no central (federal) FSM government office responsible for adoptions. Each state (Yap, Kosrae, Pohnpei and Chuuk) has its own court system in which adoptions take place, and prospective adoptive parents should contact the appropriate court regarding a possible adoption in that jurisdiction.

The Process: The recommended first step in adopting a child from FSM is to decide whether or not to use a licensed adoption service provider in the United States that can help you with your adoption. Adoption service providers must be licensed by the U.S. state in which they operate.

There are no adoption agencies in the FSM; however, the U.S. Embassy in Kolonia has a list of lawyers who have identified themselves as willing to assist U.S. citizen clients. Send an email request to: USEmbassy@Mail.FM.

In order to adopt a child from the FSM you will need to meet the requirements of the Government of FSM and U.S. immigration law. You must submit an application to be found eligible to adopt with the FSM. You may also file an I-600A, Application for Advance Processing of an Orphan Petition with U.S. Department of Homeland Security's U.S. Citizenship and Immigration Services to be found eligible and suitable to adopt.

If you are eligible to adopt, and a child is available for intercountry adoption, the individual state court will provide you with a referral to a child. Each family must decide for itself whether or not it will be able to meet the needs of and provide a permanent home for a particular child.

Role of Adoption Authority: There is no central adoption authority in the FSM.

Role of the Court: Each state has its own court system and these courts are responsible for making the first and final determinations related to intercountry adoption. Since each court is independent, prospective adoptive parents should contact the appropriate court regarding a possible adoption in that jurisdiction. In Pohnpei, typically both the child and the adopting parents must be present at the court. In Kosrae, Chuuk, and Yap the parents do not necessarily have to be present to complete the adoption at the discretion of the court.

Role of Adoption Agencies: There are no adoption agencies in the FSM at present.

Adoption Application: The application process may vary depending on the jurisdiction in which the adoption is taking place.

Time Frame: There are no specific time frames provided by the FSM.

Adoption Fees: Attorneys' fees vary. The adoptive parents' local attorney can advise on any FSM or local court fees.

Documents Required: There are no special documentary requirements published for any of the local courts. Certain documents are required, however, including adoptive child's birth certificate and legal status, adoptive parents' marriage certificate, proof of identity, and proof of nationality (passport). The adoptive parents' attorney would address the required documents on a case-by-case basis.

Bringing Your Child Home: Once your adoption is complete (or you have obtained legal custody of the child), there are a few more steps to take before you can head home. Specifically, you need to apply for several documents for your child before he or she can travel to the United States, such as a birth certificate, a passport or travel document for your child from the country in which he or she was born, and a U.S. Immigration Visa. For detailed and updated information on how to obtain these documents, review the *Intercountry Adoption* section in this publication and visit the U.S. Department of State Intercountry Adoption website at http://adoption.state.gov.

Child Citizenship Act: For adoptions finalized abroad, the Child Citizenship Act of 2000 allows your new child to acquire American citizenship automatically when he or she enters the United States as lawful permanent residents. For adoptions finalized in the United States, the Child Citizenship Act of 2000 allows your new child to acquire American citizenship automatically when the court in the United States issues the final adoption decree. To learn more, review the *Intercountry Adoption* section in this publication and visit the U.S. Department of State Intercountry Adoption website at http://adoption.state.gov.

After Adoption: There are no specific requirements for adoptive parents following adoption in FSM.

U.S. Embassy Kolonia
P.O. Box 1286
Pohnpei, FM 96941
Tel: (691) 320-2187
Fax: (691) 320-2186
Email: USEmbassy@mail.fm

The U.S. Embassy in Kolonia, Micronesia, does not process immigrant visa cases for adopted children. All such cases are handled at the U.S. Embassy in Manila, the Philippines.

U.S. Embassy Manila
PSC 500
APO AP 96515–1000
Telephone: +63-2-528-6300, ext 2324
Email: MNLIVCONG@state.gov

FSM Adoption Authority
The Honorable Cyprian Manmaw
Chief Justice, Yap Supreme Court
P.O. Box 435
Colonia, Yap FM 96943

The Honorable Camillo Noket
Chief Justice
Chuuk Supreme Court
P.O. Box J
Weno, Chuuk FM 96942

The Honorable Aliksa B. Aliksa
Chief Justice, Kosrae Supreme Court
P.O. Box 610 Tofol, Kosrae FM 96944

The Honorable Judah C. Johnny
Chief Justice, Pohnpei Supreme Court
P.O. Box 1449
Kolonia, Pohnpei FM 96941

Embassy of the Federated States of Micronesia
1725 N Street NW
Washington, DC 20036
Tel: 202-223-4383
Email: fsm@fsmembassy.org

Consulate of the Federated States of Micronesia
International Trade Center
590 South Marine Drive
Tamuning, Guam 96911
Telephone: 671-646-9154/55/56
Email: fsmcongm@kuentos.guam.net

Consulate of the Federated States of Micronesia
3049 Ualena St, Suite 908
Honolulu HI 96819
Telephone: 808-836-4775
Email Address: fsmcghnl@aol.com

Office of Children's Issues
U.S. Department of State
2201 C Street, NW
SA-29
Washington, DC 20520
Tel: 1-888-407-4747
E-mail: AskCI@state.gov
http://adoption.state.gov

For questions about immigration procedures, call the National Customer Service Center (NCSC) at 1-800-375-5283 (TTY 1-800-767-1833).

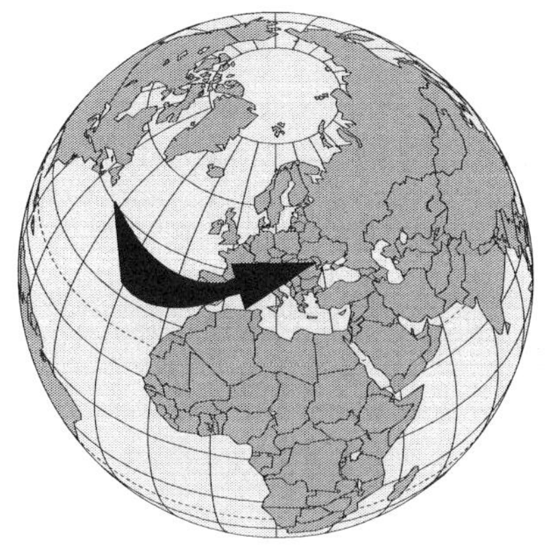

MOLDOVA

Compiled from publications that were available as of February 2013 from the U.S. Department of State, the U.S. Department of Commerce, and the Central Intelligence Agency (CIA). See the introduction to this set for explanatory notes.

Official Name:
Republic of Moldova

PROFILE

Geography

Area: total: 33,851 sq km; country comparison to the world: 140; land: 32,891 sq km; water: 960 sq km

Major cities: Chisinau (capital) 650,000 (2009)

Climate: moderate winters, warm summers

Terrain: rolling steppe, gradual slope south to Black Sea

People

Nationality: noun: Moldovan(s); adjective: Moldovan

Population: 3,656,843 (July 2012 est.)

Population growth rate: -1.014% (2012 est.)

Ethnic groups: Moldovan/Romanian 78.2%, Ukrainian 8.4%, Russian 5.8%, Gagauz 4.4%, Bulgarian 1.9%, other 1.3% (2004 census)

Religions: Eastern Orthodox 98%, Jewish 1.5%, Baptist and other 0.5% (2000)

Languages: Moldovan (official, virtually the same as the Romanian language), Russian, Gagauz (a Turkish dialect)

Literacy: definition: age 15 and over can read and write; total population: 98.5%; male: 99.1%; female: 98.1% (2010 est.)

Health: life expectancy at birth: total population: 69.51 years; male: 65.64 years; female: 73.63 years (2012 est.); Infant mortality rate: total: 13.65 deaths/1,000 live births; male: 15.59 deaths/1,000 live births; female: 11.58 deaths/1,000 live births (2012 est.)

Unemployment rate: 6.9% (2012 est.)

Work force: 1.247 million (2012 est.)

Government

Type: republic

Independence: 27 August 1991

Constitution: adopted 29 July 1994; effective 27 August 1994; note—replaced 1979 Soviet Constitution

Political subdivisions: 32 raions (raioane, singular—raion), 3 municipalities (municipii, singular—municipiul), 1 autonomous territorial unit (unitatea teritoriala autonoma), and 1 territorial unit (unitatea teritoriala)

Suffrage: 18 years of age; universal

Economy

GDP (purchasing power parity): $12.56 billion (2012 est.); $12.15 billion (2011 est.); $11.42 billion (2010 est.); $10.66 billion (2009 est.)

GDP real growth rate: 3% (2012 est.); 6.4% (2011 est.); 7.1% (2010 est.); -6% (2009 est.)

GDP per capita (PPP): $3,500 (2012 est.); $3,400 (2011 est.); $3,200 (2010 est.); $3,000 (2009 est.)

Natural resources: lignite, phosphorites, gypsum, arable land, limestone

Agriculture products: vegetables, fruits, grapes, grain, sugar beets, sunflower seed, tobacco; beef, milk; wine

Industries: sugar, vegetable oil, food processing, agricultural machinery; foundry equipment, refrigerators and freezers, washing machines; hosiery, shoes, textiles

Exports: $2.56 billion (2012 est.); $2.282 billion (2011 est.); $1.59 billion (2010 est.)

Exports—commodities: foodstuffs, textiles, machinery

Exports—partners: Italy 9.7%, Ukraine 6.9%, Germany 5%, UK 4.6% (2011)

Imports: $5.39 billion (2012 est.); $5.147 billion (2011 est.); $3.81 billion (2010 est.)

Imports—commodities: mineral products and fuel, machinery and equipment, chemicals, textiles

Imports—partners: Italy 6.7%, Ukraine 12.3%, Romania 11.1%, China 7.7%, Germany 7.7%, Turkey 7.1% (2011 est.)

Debt—external: $5.167 billion (31 December 2012 est.); $5.2 billion (31 December 2011 est.); $4.615 billion (31 December 2010 est.)

Exchange rates: 12.2 (2012 est.); Moldovan lei (MDL) per US dollar; 11.739 (2011 est.); 12.369 (2010 est.); 11.11 (2009); 10.326 (2008); 12.177 (2007)

PEOPLE

Ethnic groups represented in Moldova include Moldovan/Romanian, Ukrainian, Russian, Gagauz, and Bulgarian. Romanian (officially known as Moldovan) is the official language; Russian, Ukrainian, and Gagauz are also spoken.

Religion

The predominant religion is Orthodox Christianity. According to a 2011 Gallup poll, 97 percent of the population claims membership in one of the two Orthodox denominations: MOC with 86 percent or Bessarabian (BOC) with 11 percent.

According to the government, there are a number of other smaller denominations in the country, including the Old Rite Russian Orthodox Church (Old Believers) which has 16 parishes. Jehovah's Witnesses reported 245 congregations, including 32 in Transnistria. According to the Baptist World Alliance, the Union of Evangelical Christian Baptists of Moldova has 481 churches. The Union of Pentecostal Churches reports 223 places of worship.

Adherents of other religious groups, constituting a small portion of the population, include Roman Catholics, Seventh-day Adventists, Muslims, Baha'is, Jews, members of the Unification Church, Molokans (a Russian group), Messianic Jews, Lutherans, Presbyterians, and charismatic and evangelical Christians.

In the separatist Transnistria region, the largest religious organization is the MOC. The Tiraspol-Dubasari diocese is part of the MOC and the Russian Orthodox Church, and an estimated 80 percent of the Transnistrian population belongs to that church. Other groups include Roman Catholics, followers of Old Rite Orthodoxy, Baptists, Seventh-day Adventists, evangelical and charismatic Protestants, Jews, and Lutherans.

Language

By the country's constitution, the official language is called Moldovan, which in its standard form is identical to Romanian, with the exception of a few usage norms. The proper naming of the official language spoken in Moldova is sometimes a matter of debate, even among ethnic Moldovans, as some insist upon calling the language Moldovan, while others acknowledge that it is Romanian. During the Soviet period, the Moldovan language was written in Cyrillic and hence was clearly distinguishable from Romanian, but with the reversion to Latin script following independence, the distinction between the two disappeared. One may hear that Moldovan is roughly as similar to Romanian as American English is to British English, though the difference is that Americans acknowledge their language as being English, without insisting that it be called American.

Many Websites, including the government of Moldova's site, offer a choice among the Romanian, Russian, and English languages. Some people contend that besides the typical regional accent, the main difference between Moldovan and Romanian is that Moldovans use more Russian terms. In formal documents or settings, however, the preference is given to standard Romanian. Sometimes the debate is resolved by bypassing the name, and calling the language the state language or simply our language.

Most inhabitants of Chisinau speak both Russian and Moldovan. In Chisinau, quite often the shopkeepers and business people use the Russian language among themselves and with foreigners. At outdoor (agricultural) markets one will hear more Moldovan. In most of the villages, Moldovan is the primary language; however, there are villages where Russian is more popular. Many young people speak some English.

National/Racial/Ethnic Minorities

Roma continued to be subject to social marginalization and societal discrimination and often lacked proper access to education and other government services. According to the 2004 census, there were 12,271 Roma in Moldova. However, Romani NGOs estimate this number to be as high as 250,000, including 100,000 persons of voting age. NGOs asserted that government census forms allowed persons to identify with only one ethnic group and that many Roma declined to identify themselves as Roma. Surveys indicated that 30 percent of Roma in Moldova lived in housing in a high state of disrepair, as opposed to 7 percent for the general population.

Other concerns with respect to the Roma included denial of emergency health care services to Roma in secluded Romani settlements, unfair or arbitrary treatment by health practitioners, a gap between Roma and non-Roma in rates of coverage by health insurance, and discrimination against Roma in the job market. There were no Roma in elected office and an extremely limited number worked in any capacity in public administration. The Ministry of Labor, Social Protection, and Family opposed regarding Roma as a vulnerable group for the purpose of social inclusion policy.

In Transnistria, authorities continued to discriminate against Romanian speakers. While the use of the Latin alphabet is forbidden by the Transnistrian "constitution," and reading/writing in the Latin script is punishable by a fine of approximately 480 lei ($40.50), the extent of enforcement of this rule was unknown. However, as part of the 1992 ceasefire agreement, Transnistrian authorities allowed eight Latin-script Romanian-language schools (five high schools and three elementary schools) under the Moldovan Ministry of Education to operate in Transnistria. Approximately 7,700 children in the region attended these eight schools. According to media reports, Transnistrian authorities claimed—without presenting evidence—that the figure was much lower and that attendance levels dropped in recent years.

HISTORY

The Republic of Moldova occupies most of what has been known as Bessarabia. Moldova's location has made it a historic passageway between Asia and southern Europe, as well as the victim of frequent warfare. Greeks, Romans, Huns, and Bulgars invaded the area, which in the 13th century became part of the Mongol empire. An independent Moldovan state emerged briefly in the 14th century and grew in territory under celebrated leader Stefan the Great in the 15th century but subsequently fell under Ottoman Turkish rule in the 16th century.

After the Russo-Turkish War of 1806–12, the eastern half of Moldova (Bessarabia) between the Prut and the Dniester Rivers was ceded to Russia, while Romanian Moldavia (west of the Prut) remained with the Turks. Romania, which gained independence in 1878, took control of Russian-ruled Bessarabia in 1918. The Soviet Union never recognized the action and created an autonomous Moldavian republic on the east side of the Dniester River in 1924.

In 1940, Romania was forced to cede Bessarabia to the Union of Soviet Socialist Republics (U.S.S.R.), which established the Moldavian Soviet Socialist Republic by merging the autonomous republic east of the Dniester and the annexed Bessarabian portion. Stalin also stripped the three southern counties along the Black Sea coast from Moldova and incorporated them in the Ukrainian Soviet Socialist Republic. Romania sought to regain Bessarabia by joining with Germany in the 1941 attack on the Soviet Union. On June 22, 1941, German and Romanian troops crossed the border and deportations of the Jews from Bessarabia began immediately. By September 1941, most of the Jews of Bessarabia and Bukovina had been transported in convoys and force marched to concentration camps in Transnistria. About 185,000 Jews were in the Transnistria area in concentration camps by 1942 in abysmal conditions. Very few were left alive in these camps when the Soviets reoccupied Bessarabia in 1944.

In September 1990, the Supreme Soviet elected Mircea Snegur as President of the Soviet Socialist Republic of Moldova. A former Communist Party official, he endorsed independence from the Soviet Union and actively sought Western recognition. On May 23, 1991, the Supreme Soviet renamed itself the Parliament of the Republic of Moldova, which subsequently declared its independence from the U.S.S.R.

From August 1991, Moldova's transition to democracy confronted a series of obstacles, including an ineffective Parliament, the lack of a new constitution, a separatist movement led by the Gagauz (Christian Turkic) minority in the south, and unrest in the Transnistria region on the left bank of the Nistru/Dniester River, where a separatist movement declared a "Transdniester Moldovan Republic" in September 1990. The Russian 14th Army intervened to stem widespread violence and support the Transnistrian regime. In 1992, the government negotiated a cease-fire arrangement with Russian and Transnistrian officials, although tensions continue, and negotiations are ongoing. In February 1994, new legislative elections were held, and the ineffective Parliament that had been elected in 1990 to a 5-year term was replaced. A new constitution was adopted in July 1994. The conflict with the Gagauz minority was defused by the granting of local autonomy in 1994.

GOVERNMENT AND POLITICAL CONDITIONS

Moldova is a republic with a form of parliamentary democracy. The constitution provides for a multiparty democracy with legislative and executive branches, as well as an independent judiciary and a clear separation of powers. Legislative authority is vested in the unicameral parliament (Parliament). The Alliance for European Integration (AIE) coalition retained its parliamentary majority in November 2010 elections, which international observers stated met most Organization for Security and Cooperation in Europe (OSCE) and Council of Europe commitments.

In 1990 separatists declared a "Transdniester Moldovan Republic" (Transnistria) in the area along the eastern border with Ukraine. A 1992 ceasefire agreement established a peacekeeping force of Moldovan, Russian, and Transnistrian units. The central government did not exercise authority in the region, and Transnistrian authorities governed through parallel administrative structures. Transnistrian authorities restricted political activity and interfered with the ability of Moldovan citizens living in Transnistria to vote in Moldovan elections. In December 2011 Transnistria had an "election" that resulted in a new "president," Yevgeny Shevchuk.

Recent Elections

According to international observers, the parliamentary elections held in November 2010 met most OSCE and Council of Europe commitments. No parliamentary coalition garnered enough seats to elect a president; therefore, the election of the president remained unresolved. On September 20, the Constitutional Court affirmed that the constitutional requirement of a three-fifths majority to elect a president could not be altered, except by a constitutional amendment.

The first attempt to elect a president on November 18 was postponed due to the lack of candidates. The next attempt on December 16 failed and was later declared invalid by the Constitutional Court because the members of parliament showed their marked ballots to the press before casting their supposedly secret votes. Consequently, the election of the president remained a pending issue, and the speaker of the parliament served as acting president during 2011.

In the June local elections held throughout the country, international observers from the OSCE Office for Democratic Institutions and Human Rights and the Council of Europe's Congress of Local and Regional Authorities concluded that the elections largely met OSCE and Council of Europe commitments. Nonetheless, observers noted that legal, administrative and regulatory problems remained unresolved. The OSCE election observation mission noted that mechanisms for the oversight of political financing were insufficiently developed, lacked precision, and were inadequately enforced.

The Civic Coalition for Free and Fair elections, which also observed the elections, noted some deficiencies, including changes to the electoral code that were made after elections were announced. In addition, the coalition asserted that delays in introducing a centralized electronic voter register meant that voter lists were prepared by local authorities, raising concerns about their accuracy. Unclear residency requirements for determining the proper place of voting also complicated the election. Promo-LEX Association observers noted reports of isolated cases of violence and intimidation (22 cases), use of hate speech directed at opponents (13 cases), misuse of administrative resources (42 cases), and electoral gift-giving (99 cases).

In Transnistria authorities interfered with the right of Moldovan citizens to vote in Moldovan elections. As in previous years, the Central Electoral Commission in Chisinau failed to open a polling station in Corjova village for the June 5, 2011 local elections. Corjova was technically under the central government's authority but was effectively controlled by Transnistrian authorities. Transnistrian militia initially blocked the exit from Corjova on the morning of June 5, but later allowed voters from Corjova to travel to nearby Cocieri, where they voted. Voters from Corjova were intimidated during both the June 5 elections and runoff elections on June 19.

The Transnistria region conducted two rounds of "presidential elections" in December 2011. Consequently, after 20 years of the Smirnov regime, Transnistrian residents selected a new leader, former supreme soviet chairman Yevgeny Shevchuk, who won a landslide victory with 73.88 percent of the votes.

Participation of Women and Minorities: There were 20 women in the 101-seat parliament elected in November 2010. Members of ethnic Russian, Ukrainian, Bulgarian, Azeri, Jewish, and Gagauz communities had representation in parliament alongside members of the majority Moldovan/ethnic Romanian community.

Principal Government Officials

Last Updated: 1/31/2013

Pres.: **Nicolae TIMOFTI**
Prime Min.: **Vlad FILAT**
Dep. Prime Min.: **Eugen CARPOV**
Dep. Prime Min.: **Valeriu LAZAR**
Dep. Prime Min.: **Iurie LEANCA**
Dep. Prime Min.: **Mihai MOLDOVANU**
Min. of Agriculture & Food Industry: **Vasile BUMACOV**
Min. of Construction & Territorial Development: **Marcel RADUCAN**
Min. of Culture: **Boris FOCSA**
Min. of Defense: **Vitalie MARINUTA**
Min. of Economy: **Valeriu LAZAR**
Min. of Education: **Mihail SLEAHTITCHI**
Min. of Environment & Natural Resources: **Gheorghe SALARU**
Min. of Finance: **Veaceslav NEGRUTA**
Min. of Foreign Affairs & European Integration: **Iurie LEANCA**
Min. of Health: **Andrei USATAI**
Min. of Information Technologies & Communication: **Pavel FILIP**
Min. of Internal Affairs: **Dorin RECEAN**
Min. of Justice: **Oleg EFRIM**
Min. of Labor, Social Protection, & Family: **Valentina BULIGA**
Min. of Transport & Road Infrastructure: **Anatol SALARU**
Min. of Youth & Sport: **Ion CEBANU**
Dir., Security & Intelligence Service: **Mihai BALAN**
Sec., Supreme Security Council: **Iurie RICHICINSCHI**
Prosecutor Gen.: **Valeriu ZUBCO**
Pres., National Bank: **Dorin DRAGUTANU**
Ambassador to the US: **Igor MUNTEANU**
Permanent Representative to the UN, New York: **Vladimir LUPAN**

ECONOMY

Moldova remains one of the poorest countries in Europe despite recent progress from its small economic base. It enjoys a favorable climate and good farmland but has no major mineral deposits. As a result, the economy depends heavily on agriculture, featuring fruits, vegetables, wine, and tobacco.

Moldova must import almost all of its energy supplies. Moldova's dependence on Russian energy was underscored at the end of 2005, when a Russian-owned electrical station in Moldova's separatist Transnistria region cut off power to Moldova and Russia's Gazprom cut off natural gas in disputes over pricing. In January 2009, gas supplies were cut during a dispute between Russia and Ukraine. Previous Russian decisions to ban Moldovan wine and agricultural products, coupled with its decision to double the price Moldova paid for Russian natural gas, have hurt economic growth in the past. The onset of the global financial crisis and poor economic conditions in Moldova's main foreign markets caused GDP to fall 6% in 2009.

Unemployment almost doubled and inflation dropped to -0.1%, a record low. Moldova's IMF agreement expired in May 2009. In fall 2009, the IMF allocated $186 million to Moldova to cover its immediate budgetary needs, and the government signed a new agreement with the IMF in January 2010 for a program worth $574 million. In 2010, an upturn in the world economy boosted GDP growth to about 7% per year and inflation to more than 7%. Economic reforms have been slow because of corruption and strong political forces backing government controls. Nevertheless, the government's primary goal of EU integration has resulted in some market-oriented progress. The granting of EU trade preferences should encourage higher growth rates, but the agreements are unlikely to serve as a panacea, given the extent to which export success depends on higher quality standards and other factors.

The economy has made a modest recovery, growing by 6.4% in 2011 and 3% in 2012, but remains vulnerable to political uncertainty, weak administrative capacity, vested bureaucratic interests, higher fuel prices and the concerns of foreign investors as well as the presence of an illegal separatist regime in Moldova's Transnistria region.

Labor Conditions

The law sets standards for child labor, including the minimum age for employment, hours of work, and working conditions, and prohibits the worst forms of child labor. However, these protections were not effectively enforced, and child labor was a problem. Parents who owned or worked on farms often sent children to work in fields or to find other work.

According to a UNICEF study of working children, 18.3 percent of children fell into the category of child laborers, 63 percent of these were between five and 14 years of age, with 91 percent from rural areas.

Farms and agricultural cooperatives reportedly signed contracts with school directors to allow students to work during the harvest high season. While children were paid for the work, they were pressured to participate. According to the National Federation of Employees in Agriculture and Food Industry, school attendance in rural areas declined by 20 percent during the harvest season, with children forced to lift heavy weights and deal with hazardous chemicals.

The minimum age for unrestricted employment is 18. Juveniles between the ages of 16 and 18 are permitted to work under special conditions, including shorter workdays, but are prohibited from night, weekend, or holiday shifts and are not permitted to work overtime. Fifteen-year-old children may work only with written permission from a parent or guardian.

Children were reportedly trafficked within and outside the country for labor, and begging. Girls were mostly trafficked to Turkey, Russia, Cyprus, and the United Arab Emirates; boys were trafficked to work in the construction, agriculture, and service sectors of Russia and the region.

The minimum monthly wage for the private sector of the economy was amended in February 2010 and set at 1,100 lei ($94) per month. The amount was established after lengthy negotiations with unions and company owners. During 2011 trade unions unsuccessfully petitioned the government to increase the minimum monthly wage to 1,500 lei ($128) and adjust it to the minimum subsistence level. The minimum monthly wage for the public sector was set by the government in June at 700 lei ($60) per month. In November the National Bureau of Statistics reported that the average monthly salary was 3,231 lei ($275). The average salary in the public sector was 2,905 lei ($245), and in the production sector 3,383 lei ($285). According to official data, the minimum subsistence level was 1,471 lei ($125) in the first quarter, 1,503 lei ($126.79) in the second, and 1,386 lei ($116.92) in the third. According to the most recent data released by Prime Minister Filat, the percentage of the population below the absolute poverty line was 21.9 percent in 2010, which was 4.4 percent lower than 2009. According to official statistics, some 46 percent of the population lived on less than the minimum subsistence level. Unions maintain that 760,000 residents receive wages or pensions under the minimum subsistence level.

The law sets the maximum workweek at 40 hours with extra compensation for overtime and provides for at least one day off per week. The law prohibits excessive compulsory overtime. While the country had few foreign or migrant workers, the law gives them equal status to domestic workers.

A thriving informal economy and black market accounted for a significant portion of the country's economic activity. Union representatives believed that the shadow economy employed approximately 30 to 40 percent of the workforce. Informal economy workers did not have the same legal protections as formal employees.

Under the labor code, work contracts are required for all employment. Registration of contracts with local officials is required, and the copies are sent to the local labor inspectorate. There were no reports of such contracts offered in the agricultural sector, and the central government did not have a mechanism to monitor compliance with the requirement.

The government is required to establish and monitor safety standards in the workplace. Poor economic conditions led enterprises to economize on safety equipment and provide inadequate attention to worker safety.

U.S.-MOLDOVAN RELATIONS

Following the dissolution of the Soviet Union, the United States recognized the independence of Moldova on December 25, 1991 and opened an Embassy in its capital, Chisinau, in March 1992. The United States supports the sovereignty and territorial integrity of the Republic of Moldova and on that basis supports the 5+2 negotiations to find a comprehensive settlement that will provide a special status for the separatist region of Transnistria within Moldova. The United States co-chairs the Community of Democracies' Task Force for Moldova which provides international support to priority areas in Moldova's transition to democracy.

U.S. Assistance to Moldova

U.S. government assistance aims to help Moldova strengthen its democratic institutions, increase prosperity, secure its internationally recognized borders, and integrate with Europe and the Euro-Atlantic community. In 2010, the United States and Moldova signed a $262 million, 5-year Millennium Challenge Corporation compact for economic development and investment projects in irrigation infrastructure, high-value agricultural production, and road rehabilitation. A fact sheet on U.S. assistance to Moldova can be found here. Further details on Moldova's MCC compact are available at www.mcc.gov/pages/countries/program/moldova-compact.

Bilateral Economic Relations

As a country with a small market, Moldova benefits from liberalized trade and investment and wants to promote the export of its goods and services. A U.S.-Moldovan trade agreement providing reciprocal most-favored-nation tariff treatment took effect in 1992. The same year, an Overseas Private Investment Corporation agreement was signed, encouraging U.S. private investment in Moldova through direct loans and loan guarantees. A bilateral investment treaty was signed in 1993. The United States granted Moldova generalized system of preferences status in 1995, and some Eximbank coverage became available the same year.

Moldova's Membership in International Organizations

Moldova is a member of the United Nations, the Organization for Security and Cooperation in Europe, the North Atlantic Cooperation Council, the International Monetary Fund, the World Bank, the World Trade Organization, the GUAM Organization for Democracy and Economic Development, and the North Atlantic Treaty Organization's Partnership for Peace program. The current Government of Moldova seeks closer integration with Europe and is currently negotiating an Association Agreement, a Deep and Comprehensive Free Trade Area, and a visa liberalization plan with the European Union.

Bilateral Representation

Moldova maintains an embassy in the United States at 2101 S Street NW, Washington, DC 20008 (tel: 202-667-1130; fax 202-667-1204).

Principal U.S. Embassy Officials

Last Updated: 1/14/2013

CHISINAU (E) 103 Str. A. Mateevici, 373-22-40-8300 or 202-558-7920 (VoIP), Fax 373-22-23-3044, INMARSAT Tel 6-831-32845, Workweek: M-F 8:30 a.m.–5:30 p.m., Website: http://chisinau.usembassy.gov/

DCM OMS:	John Lackmann
AMB OMS:	Carmen Dubuque
Co-CLO:	Theresa Larson

ECON/COM:	Hayward Alto
HRO:	Donna Huss
MGT:	Jack Hardman
NAS/INL:	David Strashnoy
PAO/ADV:	Brent Israelsen
POL/ECON:	Matthew Easter
POSHO:	Gunther Fehr
SDO/DATT:	LTC Brian Stephan
AMB:	William H. Moser
CON:	Alice Easter
DCM:	Kara McDonald
PAO:	Lauren Perlaza
GSO:	Gunther Fehr
RSO:	John Childs
AFSA:	Gunther Fehr
AID:	Kent Larson
CLO:	Alejandra Porres
EEO:	Alice Easter
FMO:	Donna Huss
IMO:	Nathan Harn
IRS:	Thomas E. Stevens
ISO:	Andreas Welch
ISSO:	Nathan Harn
POL:	Gregory Winstead
State ICASS:	Hayward Alto

TRAVEL

Consular Information Sheet

August 22, 2011

Country Description: The Republic of Moldova became an independent country after the collapse of the USSR in 1991, and is now a parliamentary democracy. Moldova is a member of NATO's Partnership for Peace program as well as a member of the Council of Europe. The capital, Chisinau, offers adequate hotels and restaurants, but tourist facilities in other parts of the country are not always highly developed and some of the goods and services taken for granted in other countries are not yet available.

Smart Traveler Enrollment Program (STEP)/Embassy Locations: If you are going to visit or live in Moldova, please take the time to tell our Embassy about your trip. If you sign up, we can keep you up to date with important safety and security announcements. We can also help your friends and family get in touch with you in an emergency.

U.S. Embassy Chisinau
103, Mateevici Street
Chisinau, Moldova
Telephone: (373)(22) 40-83-00
Emergency after-hours telephone: (373)(22) 23-73-45
Fax: (373)(22) 22-63-61

Entry/Exit Requirements for U.S. Citizens: If you have a U.S. passport, you do not need a visa to enter Moldova. The Moldovan Ministry of Foreign Affairs posts a current list of countries whose citizens do not need visas to enter Moldova. For more information on entry requirements, please contact the Embassy of Moldova in Washington, D.C. or the Embassy of Moldova in a country near you. U.S. citizens can stay in Moldova for up to 90 days within a six-month period. Residence permits are required for stays over 90 days. Immigration, residence, and work permits are issued for up to five years. The Moldovan government receives applications at a "one-stop window" located at the Bureau of Migration office at 124, Stefan cel Mare Street in Chisinau. Visitors to Moldova are normally registered automatically upon arrival at Chisinau Airport or a land border with Romania or Ukraine.

U.S. citizens can enter Moldova through the separatist region of Transnistria. However, central government authorities don't register you at the border if you enter through Transnistria. If you enter through Transnistria, you must register yourself within three days of your arrival in right-bank (western) Moldova. Register at the Ministry of Information Development (MID) registration office located in central Chisinau at 49 Kogalniceanu Street. If you want to stay in Transnistria for more than three days, you should register with the "Ministry of Interior" in Tiraspol.

HIV/AIDS Restrictions: Some HIV/AIDS entry restrictions exist for visitors and foreign residents. You do not need HIV testing if you visit for less than 90 days, but if you apply for a residence permit, you need to be tested. Please check this information with the Ministry of Foreign Affairs before you travel.

Threats to Safety and Security: Although there have been no terrorist incidents or terrorist threats against U.S. citizens in Moldova, stay aware of your surroundings at all times. Because police have the legal right to ask for identification on the street, carry your passport or a photocopy with you at all times. A separatist regime controls the Transnistria region, east of the Dniester River. Be careful when visiting or crossing Transnistria, since the U.S. Embassy may not be able to help if you encounter difficulties. There are many checkpoints along roads leading into and out of Transnistria. Taking photographs of checkpoints, military facilities, and security forces is prohibited. Members of racial minority groups visiting Moldova have sometimes reported that they were stared at, verbally abused, denied entrance into some clubs and restaurants, or harassed by police. While Moldovan police can be helpful and might assist travelers in need, U. S. citizens have sometimes been harassed, mistreated, or subjected to extortion by Moldovan police. If a policeman stops you, you have a right to see his identity card ("legiti-MAT-seeya" in Romanian). Traffic police should also display a metal badge on the outside of their uniforms. If the policeman harasses you or asks for a bribe, try to remember the official's name, title, badge number, and description, and contact the U.S. Embassy. If you refuse to pay a bribe, you might be delayed, but there have been few reports of any problems beyond inconvenience.

Stay up to date by:

- Bookmarking our Bureau of Consular Affairs website, which contains the current Travel Warnings and Travel Alerts as well as the Worldwide Caution.
- Following us on Twitter and the Bureau of Consular Affairs page on Facebook as well.
- Downloading our free Smart Traveler iPhone App to have travel information at your fingertips.

- Calling 1-888-407-4747 toll-free within the U.S. and Canada, or a regular toll line, 1-202-501-4444, from other countries.

- Taking some time before travel to consider your personal security.

Crime: Most travelers to Moldova enjoy a safe and pleasant stay. Occasionally, travelers become victims of crime: usually petty theft, but sometimes more serious fraud. Foreign visitors rarely suffer physical violence or sexual assault. Some U.S. citizens have reported theft of money and small valuables from hotel rooms and local apartments, along with home and office burglaries. Be careful and protect your valuables in Chisinau, just as you would in any major U.S. city. Be cautious when using ATMs in Moldova. Some U.S. citizens have reported unauthorized access to their accounts after using ATMs (although banks sometimes post their fees later as separate transactions). They have also reported PIN theft from ATMs in Moldova, either by "skimming" devices, which record the card information, or by hidden cameras or "shoulder surfing." Train and bus services are below Western European standards, and some U.S. citizens have been robbed while traveling on international trains to and from Moldova. Be on your guard of pickpockets on public transit. U.S. citizens who use the Moldovan postal service have reported that international letters and package mail are sometimes opened or pilfered. Don't buy counterfeit and pirated goods, even if they are widely available. Not only are the bootlegs illegal to bring back into the United States, but if you purchase them you may also be breaking local law.

Victims of Crime: If you or someone you know becomes the victim of a crime abroad, you should contact the local police and the nearest U.S. embassy or consulate. We can:

- Replace a stolen passport.

- For violent crimes such as assault or rape, help you find appropriate medical care.

- Put you in contact with the appropriate police authorities, and contact family members or friends.

Although the local authorities are responsible for investigating and prosecuting the crime, consular officers can help you understand the local criminal justice process and can direct you to local attorneys. The local equivalents to the "911" emergency line in Moldova are: 901 (Fire), 902 (Police) and 903 (Ambulance). You may have difficulty finding an English-speaking operator.

Internet fraud warning: There are various Internet scams in Moldova that target foreigners. Since 2008, "phishing" schemes have hacked the bank accounts of U.S. businesses and transferred the money to Moldova. Internet auction fraud, in which buyers fail to pay for purchases or send counterfeit checks as payment, is not uncommon. Be aware of dating scams, in which someone you met over the Internet asks for money. They may say they need money to help their family, buy plane tickets, pay medical bills, provide "economic solvency funds," etc. A number of U.S. citizens have been defrauded. Fraud committed in Moldova is subject to Moldovan law and could prove difficult to prosecute. The U.S. Embassy can do little to assist U.S. citizens defrauded via the Internet. If you are arrested in Moldova, authorities of Moldova are required to notify the nearest U.S. embassy or consulate of your arrest. However, Moldovan police, particularly in Transnistria, do not always report the arrest or detention of American citizens. If you are concerned the Department of State may not be aware of your situation, you should request the police or prison officials to notify the nearest U.S. embassy or consulate of your arrest.

Criminal Penalties: While you are traveling in Moldova, you are subject to its laws even if you are a U.S. citizen. Foreign laws and legal systems can be vastly different than our own. In some places you may be taken in for questioning if you don't have your passport with you. In some places, it is illegal to take pictures of certain buildings. In some places driving under the influence could land you immediately in jail. These criminal penalties will vary from country to country. There are also some things that might be legal in the country you visit, but still illegal in the United States, and you can be prosecuted under U.S. law if you buy pirated goods. Engaging in sexual conduct with children or possessing or disseminating child pornography in a foreign country is a crime prosecutable in the United States. If you break local laws in Moldova, your U.S. passport would not help you avoid arrest or prosecution. It is very important to know what is legal and what is not where you are going.

Special Circumstances: You should register large sums of foreign currency and declare all valuable goods with Moldovan customs authorities when you arrive in Moldova. Contact the Moldovan Embassy in Washington, D.C., for more information about customs requirements.

Business in Transnistria: As noted in the "Threats to Safety and Security" section above, a separatist regime controls a narrow strip of land in eastern Moldova known as Transnistria ("Pridnestrovie" in Russian). Be very cautious doing business in Transnistria. The U.S. Embassy cannot offer consular or commercial services to U.S. citizens in Transnistria. Moldovan law requires firms (including those located in Transnistria) to register with the Moldovan Government and to use Moldovan customs seals on their exports. Under a December 2005 agreement between Moldova and Ukraine, Ukrainian customs and border officials require Moldovan customs seals on goods exported from Moldova, including Transnistria, and are enforcing this requirement with EU assistance. Transnistrian firms not legally registered with Moldovan authorities operate in contravention of Moldovan law, which complicates or even prevents the import or export of goods. The Government of Moldova has indicated that it will not recognize the validity of contracts for the privatization of firms in Transnistria that are concluded without the approval of the appropriate Moldovan authorities. A number of Internet fraud schemes also originate in Transnistria.

Telephone, internet, and postal service: Cell phone coverage in Moldova is excellent. Many restaurants, bars, and public places in Chisinau have free Wi-Fi Internet access, but availability is much less outside Chisinau. Express mail services, such as DHL, UPS, and Federal Express, are available in Chisinau.

Accessibility: While in Moldova, individuals with disabilities may find accessibility and accommodation very different from what you find in the United States. There are very few wheelchair ramps in Moldova, and most are narrow and steep. Most streets, sidewalks, and other public paths are not well maintained. You are encouraged to call ahead to inquire about accessibility with your hotel before traveling to Moldova.

Commercial transactions: Moldova is still generally a cash-only economy. Credit cards are often accepted in Chisinau, but rarely in the rest of the country. Use your credit card with caution, and protect your personal information.

Medical Facilities and Health Information: Medical care is substandard throughout Moldova, including in Chisinau. If you are sick or injured, try to go to Western Europe for treatment. In an emergency, try to contact the local ambulance service. Hospital accommodations are inadequate, technology is not advanced, and there may be shortages of routine medications and supplies. Elderly travelers and those with existing health problems may be at particular risk. The U.S. Embassy maintains a list of medical facilities and English-speaking doctors, but cannot endorse any doctors. You should bring both prescription and common over-the-counter medications. Pharmacies are not always stocked to Western standards, products are not always labeled in English, and poor quality and/or counterfeit medications have been reported. You can find good information on vaccinations and other health precautions on the Centers for Disease Control and Prevention (CDC) website. For information about outbreaks of infectious diseases abroad, consult the World Health Organization (WHO) website. The WHO website also contains additional health information for travelers, including detailed country-specific health information. Tuberculosis is an increasingly serious health concern in Moldova.

Medical Insurance: You cannot assume your insurance will go with you when you travel. It is very important to find out BEFORE you leave whether or not your medical insurance will cover you overseas. You need to ask your insurance company two questions:

- Does my policy apply when I am out of the United States?
- Will it cover emergencies like a trip to a foreign hospital or a medical evacuation?

In many places, doctors and hospitals still expect payment in cash at the time of service. Your regular U.S. health insurance may not cover doctors' and hospital visits in other countries. If your policy doesn't go with you when you travel, it's a very good idea to take out another one for your trip.

Traffic Safety and Road Conditions: While in Moldova, you may encounter very different road conditions from those in the United States. Moldova's highway infrastructure consists mainly of two-lane roads that often lack signage, are unevenly maintained, and seldom have lighting. Be careful of tractors, bicyclists, horse-drawn carts, pedestrians, and livestock on the road. Streets in Moldova are not well maintained. Try to limit driving outside cities to daylight hours. Many Moldovan drivers would be considered aggressive or erratic by U. S. standards. Many accidents involve drunk drivers. In 2009, Moldova adopted a law that established a maximum legal blood alcohol content of 0.03%, well under the levels allowed in most states in the U.S. If you drive with a blood alcohol level above 0.08%, you will be charged in criminal court. However, traffic police generally do not have testing equipment at roadside, so if they can smell alcohol on your breath, you're likely to becharged with a crime. If this happens, you have the right to request a blood test to confirm your actual blood alcohol level. To be safe, don't drink alcohol before driving. The quality and safety of public transportation vary widely. Trains, trolleybuses, and buses are often old and frequently break down. Taxis are available in most urban areas, and vary from old Soviet-era vehicles to new Western European or U.S. vehicles. Emergency services are generally responsive, although you may not find an English-speaking operator. You can call police at 902 and an ambulance at 903.

Aviation Safety Oversight: As there is no direct commercial air service to the United States by carriers registered in Moldova, the U.S. Federal Aviation Administration (FAA) has not assessed the government of Moldova's Civil Aviation Authority for compliance with International Civil Aviation Organization (ICAO) aviation safety standards. Further information may be found on the FAA's safety assessment page.

Children's Issues: Please see the U.S. Dept. of State Office of Children's Issues web pages on intercountry adoption and international parental child abduction.

Intercountry Adoption

January 2012

The information in this section has been edited from the latest report available as of February 2013 from the State Department Bureau of Consular Affairs, Office of Overseas Citizens Services. For more information, please read the *Intercountry Adoption* section of this book and review current reports online at http://adoption.state.gov.

Moldova is party to the Hague Convention on Protection of Children and Co-operation in Respect of Intercountry Adoption (Hague Adoption Convention). Therefore all adoptions between Moldova and the United States must meet the requirements of the Convention and U.S. law implementing the Convention.

Note: Special transition provisions apply to adoptions initiated before April 1, 2008.

Who Can Adopt? Adoption between the United States and Moldova is governed by the Hague Adoption Convention. Therefore to adopt from Moldova, you must first be found eligible to adopt by the U.S. Government. The U.S. Government agency responsible for making this determination is the Department of Homeland Security, U.S. Citizenship and Immigration Services (USCIS).

Adoption in Moldova can be a complicated process, sometimes involving long waits. Moldovan adoption law gives preference to Moldovan citizens and citizens of countries that have implemented the 1993 Hague Convention on Intercountry Adoption. In addition to these U.S. requirements for prospective adoptive parents, Moldova also has the following eligibility requirements for prospective adoptive parents.

Residency Requirements: There are no residency requirements for foreign adoptive parents.

Age Requirements: The minimum age requirement for adoptive parents is 25. The maximum age is 50, unless one of the couple is under the age of 50.

Marriage Requirements: Married couples and single people may adopt. Unmarried couples may not adopt from Moldova.

Income Requirements: Prospective adoptive parents must show financial stability.

Other Requirements: The presence of the following conditions disqualify prospective adoptive parents from adopting in Moldova: HIV/AIDS, psychological and behavioral disorders, drug addiction, chronic alcoholism, chronic somatic diseases (disability of the 1st and 2nd degree), various forms of cancer, Hepatitis B, C or D. The following conditions may temporarily disqualify a person from adopting: sexually transmitted diseases, tuberculosis and severe virulent diseases.

Who Can Be Adopted? Because Moldova is a member of the Hague Adoption Convention, children from Moldova must meet the requirements of the Convention in order to be eligible for adoption. For example, the Convention requires that Moldova attempt to place a child with a family in Moldova before determining that a child is eligible for intercountry adoption. Learn more about the Convention's requirements for adoptable children. In addition to Moldova's requirements, a child must meet the definition of a Convention adoptee for you to bring him or her back to the United States. Intercountry adoptions are permitted in exceptional cases, when no relatives or other Moldovan families are able to adopt orphans or become their guardians. Children who have health or developmental problems that Moldovan families cannot afford to treat are also considered exceptional cases.

Eligibility Requirements: Information about children eligible for adoption is published in the Monitorul official, the Moldovan Governments official register. For the first six months after this information is published, an adoptable child is eligible only for domestic adoption by Moldovan citizens. After six months, an adoptable child is eligible for intercountry adoption. Prospective adoptive parents may indicate the sex and age range of the child they prefer.

Moldovan Adoption Authority: The Ministry of Social Protection, Family and Child Adoption Department

The Process: Because Moldova is party to the Hague Adoption Convention, adopting from Moldova must follow a specific process designed to meet the Conventions requirements. The first step in adopting a child from Moldova is to select an adoption service provider in the United States that has been accredited. Only these agencies and attorneys can provide adoption services between the United States and Moldova.

When adopting in Moldova, prospective adoptive parents are required to use an adoption agency that is also accredited in Moldova. Please find the list of accredited adoption providers in the Contacts section. A registered adoption agency, through its Moldovan representative, forwards the foreign prospective adoptive parents file to the Adoption Department (See the list of required documents below.) The Adoption Department in turn forwards the file to the Education Directorate in the district where a prospective adoptable child resides.

After you choose an accredited adoption agency, you apply to be found eligible to adopt by the U.S. Government, Department of Homeland Security, U.S. Citizenship and Immigration Services (USCIS).

Once the U.S. Government determines you eligible and suitable to be an adoptive parent, your information will be forwarded to the adoption authority in Moldova. Moldovas adoption authority will review your application to determine whether you are also eligible to adopt under Moldovan law.

If both the United States and Moldova determine that you are eligible to adopt, and a child is available for intercountry adoption, the central adoption authority will provide you with a referral for a child. You cannot identify a specific child that you would like to adopt prior to the adoption authority providing this referral.

The local Inspector for the Protection of Children's Rights in the district, together with a physician and the director of the orphanage, examines the file and matches the family with an eligible child.

The prospective adoptive parents are then provided with complete, official information about the child, including health and family background. The Moldovan representative sends the prospective adoptive parents this information including photographs or a video of the child. The representative will also send answers from the Moldovan authorities to all additional questions the prospective adoptive parents may have about the child. The prospective adoptive parents have the option to refuse a prospective adoptive child. If they do so, they must inform the Moldovan authorities in writing of their decision.

If the prospective adoptive parents agree to accept the child, they send a letter to the Adoption Department through their agency's representative, acknowledging that they are aware of any specific health or other problems, and accept the child. The orphanage receives a copy of the letter from the Adoption Department.

After you accept a match with a child, you will apply to the U.S Government, Department of Homeland Security, U.S. Citizenship and Immigration Services (USCIS) for permission to adopt that child. USCIS will determine whether the child is eligible under U.S. law to be adopted.

In addition, a Consular officer at the U.S. Embassy must review the child's information and determine that the child appears to be eligible for a visa. As part of this process, the Consular officer may require to see the Panel Physician's medical report on the child. If the Consular office determines that the child appears eligible to immigrate to the United States, he/she will send a letter (called the Article 5 letter) to the Moldovan adoption authority.

If approved, the Directorate of Education will forward a Notice of Approval of Adoption to the Adoption Department. The Adoption Department will then decide whether to approve the adoption. Although prospective adoptive parents do not need to travel to Moldova to meet the prospective adoptive child at the time of the acceptance of the match, both parents must appear in court in Moldova to finalize the adoption.

Role of the Adoption Authority: To begin the adoption process, a registered adoption agency, through its Moldovan representative, forwards the foreign prospective adoptive parents file to the Adoption Department. The Department in turn forwards the file to the Education Directorate in the district where a prospective adoptable child resides. Once a child has been selected the prospective adoptive parents send a letter to the Adoption Department through their agency's representative, acknowledging that they are aware of any specific health or other problems, and accept the child. The orphanage receives a copy of the letter the Department.

The districts Directorate of Education must then approve the prospective adoption and provide full information on the adoptive parents and the adoptive child to the Adoption Department. If approved, the Directorate of Education will forward a Notice of Approval of Adoption to the Department. The Adoption Department will then decide whether to approve the adoption. Although prospective adoptive parents do not need to travel to Moldova to meet the prospective adoptive child at the time of the acceptance of the match, both parents must appear in court in Moldova to finalize the adoption.

Role of the Court: The approved adoption file proceeds to the court system through the districts Inspector for the Protection of Children's Rights. Once prospective adoptive parents satisfy the Moldovan adoption requirements, a judge must grant a final adoption.

Time Frame: An adoption can take six to nine months to complete from the time a child is matched with prospective adoptive parents until the completion of the adoption.

Adoption Fees: There is a Government fee of 1,500 EUR for each adopted child and cost of airfare for adoption-related travel. Separate attorneys fees can vary greatly.

The U.S. Embassy in Moldova discourages the payment of any fees that are not properly receipted. Donations or expediting fees, which may be requested from prospective adoptive parents, have the appearance of buying a baby and put all future adoptions in Moldova at risk.

In the adoption services contract that you sign at the beginning of the adoption process, your agency will itemize the fees and estimated expenses related to your adoption process.

Documents Required: The adoption application should contain:

- Name, year, month, and day of birth of prospective adoptive parent(s). Address and state of residence of the parent(s) is also required;
- Name, year, month, and day of birth of child to be adopted. Residence of the child to be adopted;
- Information regarding the biological parents and siblings of the prospective adoptive child.
- Request to change name and place of birth, and register the adoptive parents as the birth parents on the childs new birth certificate;
- Copy of prospective adoptive parent(s) birth certificate;
- Doctors Certificate of Eligibility to Adopt;
- Employment certificate, including occupation, years of service, and income;
- Authenticated copy of Deed of Sale for a home, or lease agreement for residence;
- Approval by the prospective adoptive parents Government and permission for the adopted child to reside in the United States.

Bringing Your Child Home: Once your adoption is complete (or you have obtained legal custody of the child), there are a few more steps to take before you can head home. Specifically, you need to apply for several documents for your child before he or she can travel to the United States, such as a birth certificate, a passport or travel document for your child from the country in which he or she was born, and a U.S. Immigration Visa.

For detailed and updated information on how to obtain these documents, review the *Intercountry Adoption* section in this publication and visit the U.S. Department of State Intercountry Adoption website at http://adoption.state.gov.

Child Citizenship Act: For adoptions finalized abroad, the Child Citizenship Act of 2000 allows your new child to acquire American citizenship automatically when he or she enters the United States as lawful permanent residents.

For adoptions finalized in the United States, the Child Citizenship Act of 2000 allows your new child to acquire American citizenship automatically when the court in the United States issues the final adoption decree. To learn more, review the *Intercountry Adoption* section in this publication and visit the U.S. Department of State Intercountry Adoption website at http://adoption.state.gov.

After Adoption: We strongly urge you to complete any post-adoption requirements required by Moldova in a timely manner. Your adoption agency may be able to help you with this process. Your cooperation will contribute to Moldova's history of positive experiences with American parents.

U.S. Embassy in Moldova
103, A. Mateevici Street
Chisinau, Moldova MD 2009
Tel: (373 22) 408 300
Fax: (373 22) 226 361
Email: Chisinau-ca@state.gov
Internet:
http://moldova.usembassy.gov/

Moldovan Adoption Authority
The Ministry of Labor, Social Protection and FamilyAdoption Department
Ms. Viorica Dumbraveanu
Head of Department
#1 Vasile Alecsandri Street
office
#409
Chisinau, Moldova
Tel/Fax: (373 22) 725 300

Embassy of the Republic of Moldova
2101 S Street, N.W.
Washington, D.C. 20008
Tel: (202) 667-1130
Fax: (202) 667-1204
http://www.sua.mfa.md

Office of Children's Issues
U.S. Department of State
2201 C Street, NW
SA-29
Washington, DC 20520
Tel: 1-888-407-4747
E-mail: AskCI@state.gov
http://adoption.state.gov

For questions about immigration procedures, call the National Customer Service Center (NCSC) at 1-800-375-5283 (TTY 1-800-767-1833).

MONACO

Compiled from publications that were available as of February 2013 from the U.S. Department of State, the U.S. Department of Commerce, and the Central Intelligence Agency (CIA). See the introduction to this set for explanatory notes.

Official Name:
Principality of Monaco

PROFILE

Geography

Area: total: 2 sq km; country comparison to the world: 250; land: 2 sq km; water: 0 sq km
Climate: Mediterranean with mild, wet winters and hot, dry summers
Terrain: hilly, rugged, rocky

People

Nationality: noun: Monegasque(s) or Monacan(s); adjective: Monegasque or Monacan
Population: 30,510 (July 2012 est.)
Population growth rate: -0.066% (2012 est.)
Ethnic groups: French 47%, Monegasque 16%, Italian 16%, other 21%
Religions: Roman Catholic 90% (official), other 10%
Languages: French (official), English, Italian, Monegasque
Literacy: definition: age 15 and over can read and write; total population: 99%; male: 99%; female: 99% (2003 est.)
Health: life expectancy at birth: total population: 89.68 years; male: 85.74 years; female: 93.77 years (2012 est.); Infant mortality rate: total: 1.8 deaths/1,000 live births; male: 2.04 deaths/1,000 live births; female: 1.55 deaths/1,000 live births (2012 est.)
Unemployment rate: 0% (2005)
Work force: 49,300

Government

Type: constitutional monarchy
Independence: 1419
Constitution: 17 December 1962; modified 2 April 2002
Political subdivisions: none; there are no first-order administrative divisions as defined by the US Government, but there are four quarters (quartiers, singular—quartier); Fontvieille, La Condamine, Monaco-Ville, Monte-Carlo
Suffrage: 18 years of age; universal

Economy

GDP (purchasing power parity): $5.47 billion (2010 est.); $5.337 billion (2009 est.); $6.03 billion (2008 est.)
GDP real growth rate: 2.5% (2010 est.); -11.5% (2009)
GDP per capita (PPP): $NA (2010); $63,400 (2009 est.); $71,600 (2008 est.)
Natural resources: none
Agriculture products: none
Industries: tourism, construction, small-scale industrial and consumer products
Exports: $711 million (2010); $716.3 million (2005)
Imports: $882.6 million (2010); $916.1 million (2005)
Debt—external: $NA
Exchange rates: euros (EUR) per US dollar; 0.7838 (2012 est.); 0.7194 (2011 est.); 0.755 (2010 est.); 0.7198 (2009 est.); 0.6827 (2008 est.); 0.7345 (2007 est.)

GEOGRAPHY

The Principality of Monaco is the second-smallest independent state in the world, after the Holy See (Vatican City). It is located on the Mediterranean coast, 18 kilometers (11 mi.) east of Nice, France, and is surrounded on three sides by France. Monaco is divided into four sections: Monaco-Ville, the old city on a rocky promontory extending into the Mediterranean; La Condamine, the section along the port; Monte-Carlo, the principal residential and resort area; and Fontvieille, an area constructed on land reclaimed from the sea.

The principality is noted for its beautiful natural scenery and mild, sunny climate. The average minimum temperature in January and February is 8°C (47°F); in July and August the average maximum temperature is 26°C (78°F).

PEOPLE

Language

French is the official language; English, Italian, and Monegasque (a blend of French and Italian) also are spoken. The literacy rate is 99%.

Religion

Roman Catholicism is the state religion, and an estimated 90 percent of the approximately 7,634 citizens are Catholic. There are five Catholic churches in addition to a cathedral. An archbishop presides over the Archdiocese of Monaco. Protestantism is the next most-practiced religion with two churches. There is one Greek Orthodox Church. The constitution provides the estimated 28,250 noncitizen residents the same religious freedom that citizens enjoy. A majority of noncitizens adhere to either Catholicism or Protestantism. However, there are an estimated 1,000 Jewish noncitizen residents as well as a number of noncitizens who practice Islam or other religious beliefs. There is one synagogue; there are no mosques.

HISTORY

Founded in 1215 as a colony of Genoa, Monaco has been ruled by the House of Grimaldi since 1297, except when under French control from 1789 to 1814. Designated as a protectorate of Sardinia from 1815 until 1860 by the Treaty of Vienna, Monaco's sovereignty was recognized by the Franco-Monegasque Treaty of 1861. The Prince of Monaco was an absolute ruler until a constitution was promulgated in 1911.

In July 1918, a treaty was signed providing for limited French protection over Monaco. The treaty, formally noted in the Treaty of Versailles, established that Monegasque policy would be aligned with French political, military, and economic interests.

A new constitution, proclaimed in 1962, abolished capital punishment, provided for female suffrage, and established a Supreme Court to guarantee fundamental liberties. In 1993, Monaco became an official member of the United Nations with full voting rights. It joined the Council of Europe in 2004.

Three months after the death of his father, Prince Rainier III, on April 6, Prince Albert II formally acceded to the throne on July 12, 2005.

GOVERNMENT AND POLITICAL CONDITIONS

The Principality of Monaco is a constitutional monarchy in which the sovereign prince plays the leading governmental role. The prince appoints the government consisting of a minister of state and five counselors. The prince shares the country's legislative power with the popularly elected 24-member National Council. In 2008 the country held multiparty elections for the National Council that were considered free and fair.

Recent Elections

The 2008 National Council elections were considered free and fair.

Participation of Women and Minorities: There were six women in the 24-member National Council and two women in the seven-member Crown Council. One government counselor was a woman. There were no members of minorities in the government.

Principal Government Officials

Last Updated: 1/31/2013

Chief of State: **ALBERT II, Prince**

Min. of State & Pres. of the Governing Council: **Michel ROGER**

Min. for External Relations: **Jose BADIA**

Min. for Finance & the Economy: **Marco PICCININI**

Min. for Health & Social Affairs: **Stephane VALERI**

Min. for the Interior: **Paul MASSERON**

Min. for Public Works, the Environment, & Urban Development: **Marie-Pierre GRAMAGLIA**

Ambassador to the US: **Gilles NOGHES**

Permanent Representative to the UN, New York: **Isabelle PICCO**

ECONOMY

Monaco, bordering France on the Mediterranean coast, is a popular resort, attracting tourists to its casino and pleasant climate. The principality also is a major banking center and has successfully sought to diversify into services and small, high-value-added, nonpolluting industries.

The state has no income tax and low business taxes and thrives as a tax haven both for individuals who have established residence and for foreign companies that have set up businesses and offices. Monaco, however, is not a tax-free shelter; it charges nearly 20% value-added tax, collects stamp duties, and companies face a 33% tax on profits unless they can show that three-quarters of profits are generated within the principality.

Monaco's reliance on tourism and banking for its economic growth has left it vulnerable to a downturn in France and other European economies which are the principality's main trade partners. In 2009, Monaco's GDP fell by 11.5% as the euro-zone crisis precipitated a sharp drop in tourism and retail activity and home sales. A modest recovery ensued in 2010 with GDP growth of 2.5%, but Monaco's economic prospects remain clouded in uncertainty tied to future euro-zone growth.

Weak economic growth also has deteriorated public finances as the principality recorded a budget deficit of 1.9% of GDP in 2010. Monaco was formally removed from the OECD's "grey list" of uncooperative tax jurisdictions in late 2009, but continues to face international pressure to abandon its banking secrecy laws and help combat tax evasion.

The state retains monopolies in a number of sectors, including tobacco, the telephone network, and the postal service. Living standards are high, roughly comparable to those in prosperous French metropolitan areas.

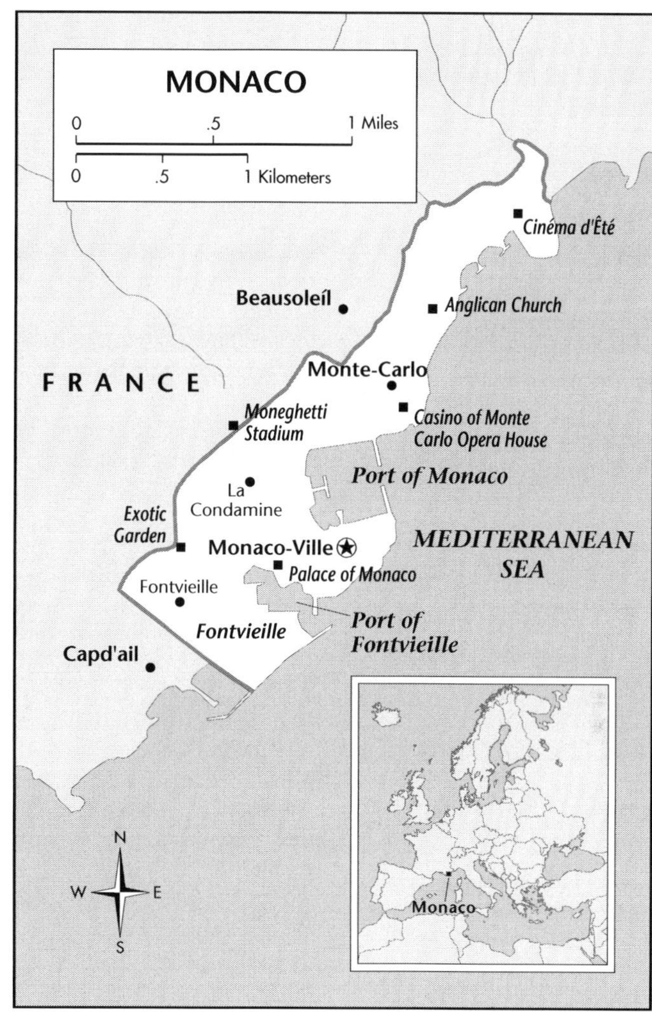

Labor Conditions

The minimum age for employment is 16 years. Those employing children under that age may be subject to a fine under criminal law. Employment between the ages of 16 and 18 is subject to severely restricted conditions. The government effectively enforced the child labor law.

The legal minimum wage for full-time work is the French minimum wage, 9.00 euros per hour ($11.64), plus a 5-percent adjustment to compensate for the travel costs of the three quarters of the workforce who commute daily. Most workers received more than the minimum wage. The legal workweek is 39 hours. The government allows companies to reduce the workweek to 35 hours if they so choose, but this option was rarely chosen. Regulations provide for a minimum number of rest periods and premium pay for overtime.

Law and government decree fix health and safety standards, which workplace health and safety committees and the government labor inspectors enforced. There were no reports of labor law violations. The Department of Employment (Ministry for Health and Social Affairs) had several labor inspectors, but the number was unknown.

The chief inspector answers directly to the director of the labor department. Labor inspectors inform employers and employees of all matters related to labor laws, and health and safety standards, reconcile—when possible—parties involved in disputes; and carry out onsite inspections to make sure all requirements of the above are respected in practice.

U.S.-MONACO RELATIONS

The United States and Monaco enjoy excellent relations, which both countries seek to maintain and strengthen. Monaco is the second-smallest independent state in the world and is linked closely to France through several treaties and agreements.

For more than 150 years, Monaco and the United States have worked together as partners and friends. The two share a strong commitment to international cooperation in addressing some of the world's greatest challenges and opportunities, seeking to promote greater freedom, transparency, and human rights. The U.S. Ambassador to France is also accredited to Monaco. The U.S. Consul General in Marseille is accredited to Monaco and handles most diplomatic and working-level contacts with Monaco.

U.S. Assistance to Monaco

The United States provides no foreign assistance to Monaco.

Bilateral Economic Relations

The United States and Monaco have a modest amount of bilateral trade in goods. Monaco has full customs integration with France, which collects and rebates Monegasque trade duties. It also participates in the European Union market system through its customs union with France. Monaco has signed a tax information exchange agreement with the United States.

Monaco's Membership in International Organizations

Monaco and the United States belong to a number of the same international organizations, including the United Nations and Organization for Security and Cooperation in Europe. Monaco also is an observer to the Organization of American States.

Bilateral Representation

Monaco maintains an embassy in the United States at 3400 International Drive, NW, Suite 2K - 100, Washington DC 20008; tel. (202) 234-1530.

Principal U.S. Embassy Officials

Last Updated: 1/14/2013

MARSEILLE (CG) Place Varian Fry, 13286 Marseille France, 33 (0) 4-91-54-92-00, Fax 33 (0) 4-91-55-09-47, Workweek: Monday–Friday, 8:30–5:00, Website: http://france.usembassy.gov/marseille/

PO:	Diane Kelly
CON:	Philip Richards

TRAVEL

Consular Information Sheet—France and Monaco

July 27, 2012

Country Description: France is a developed and stable democracy with a modern economy. Tourist facilities are widely available.

Smart Traveler Enrollment Program (STEP)/Embassy Locations: If you are going to live in or visit France, please take the time to tell us about your trip. By enrolling in the Smart Traveler Enrollment Program, you can keep up to date with important safety and security announcements. It will also help your friends and family get in touch with you in an emergency.

Please check the individual webpage for the embassy or consulate you will be visiting to verify public hours and security regulations. Generally, you won't be allowed to bring electronic devices such as cell phones and laptops with you inside our facilities.

There are two Consulates General, four American Presence Posts and one Consular Agency in France, in addition to the Embassy in Paris. Only the consular sections in Paris and Marseille are authorized to issue passports. The other offices provide limited services to American citizens. Appointments are required for most services. Appointments can be scheduled online for Embassy Paris and Consulate General Marseille. Call or email posts in other locations to schedule an appointment. Please note that the emergency after-hours telephone number for all U.S. posts in France is: (33) 1 43 12 22 22. Ask to speak to the duty officer if you need emergency assistance after business hours.

All of our telephone numbers below are written the way you would dial them from the United States. When calling from within France, drop the country code and add a zero. For example: (33) 1 43 12 22 becomes 01 43 12 22 22.

Entry/Exit Requirements for U.S. Citizens: U.S. citizens may enter France for up to 90 days for tourist or business purposes without a visa. France is a party to the Schengen Agreement, which allows for visa-free travel between member countries. U.S. citizens traveling with either an official or diplomatic passport do require a valid Schengen visa. If you are traveling for reasons other than business or tourism—such as employment, study, or internship—you must obtain a French visa for that purpose before you leave the United States. You should be aware that it is nearly impossible to obtain or change visa status while in France.

If you are transiting France en route to other countries, make sure you know all of the entry and exit requirements for your trip and final destination. If you don't have the right documentation, you might be denied boarding to your connecting flight. Some countries require a certain number of blank visa pages or more than six months remaining validity on your passport.

The Department of State is unaware of any HIV/AIDS entry restrictions for visitors to, or foreign residents of, France.

Contact the French Embassy in Washington at 4101 Reservoir Road NW, Washington, DC 20007, tel. (202) 944 6000, or one of the French Consulates General in Atlanta, Boston, Chicago, Houston, Los Angeles, Miami, New Orleans, New York, or San Francisco for the most current visa information.

Threats to Safety and Security: Political violence in Paris and throughout France is still relatively uncommon, although there are occasional instances of extremely large demonstrations occurring in many French cities simultaneously. Large demonstrations in Paris are generally managed by a strong police presence, but even demonstrations intended to be peaceful can turn confrontational and possibly escalate into violence. U.S. citizens are therefore urged to avoid the areas of demonstrations if possible, and to exercise caution if within the vicinity of any demonstrations. In addition, the congestion caused by large demonstrations can cause serious inconveniences for a visitor on a tight schedule. Likewise, some sporting events, such as soccer matches, have occasionally degenerated into violence that continued into the streets.

Political unrest has developed in some Francophone countries with historic ties to France (e.g., Algeria, Cote d'Ivoire, and Tunisia). Some French citizens and residents with ties to such countries have protested in front of those countries' embassies or consulates located in France in response to the unrest. Although these protests are infrequent and do not target Americans, visitors should avoid such demonstrations.

The Government of France maintains a threat rating system, known locally as "Vigipirate," similar to the U.S. Department of Homeland Security Advisory System. Under this plan, the government routinely augments police with armed forces and increases visibility at airports, train and metro stations, and other high-profile locations such as schools, major tourist attractions, and government installations. Over the last few years, there have been arrests of suspected Islamic militants involved in terrorist plots. French authorities have periodically spoken publicly about the heightened threat conditions for terrorist attacks in Europe. Information is routinely shared between the United States and France in order to disrupt terrorist plotting, identify and take action against potential operatives, and strengthen defenses against potential threats.

Although U.S. citizens have not been specifically targeted in terrorist attacks in France within the past few years, travelers should remain vigilant. Immediately report unattended packages observed in public places or any other suspicious activities to French law enforcement authorities. French law enforcement authorities are proactive and will respond immediately. If there is a security incident or suspicious package, do not linger in the area to observe.

Public safety and security in France are maintained by three different forces: Municipal Police, National Police, and the military Gendarmerie. These services are professional, competent, and pro-active in fighting crime and violence and maintaining overall state security.

In an emergency, dialing 17 will connect the caller to the Police. You can also dial the Europe-wide emergency response number 112 to reach an operator for all kinds of emergency services (similar to the U.S. 911 system). Non-French speakers may experience a delay while an English speaker is located. For non-emergency assistance, visitors should go to the nearest police station (commissariat) in order to file an official report.

Stay up to date:

- Bookmark our Bureau of Consular Affairs website, which contains the current Travel Warnings and Travel Alerts as well as the Worldwide Caution;
- Follow us on Twitter and the Bureau of Consular Affairs page on Facebook as well;
- Download our free Smart Traveler iPhone App to have travel information at your fingertips;
- Call 1-888-407-4747 toll-free within the U.S. and Canada, or a regular toll line, 1-202-501-4444, from other countries; and
- Taking some time before travel to consider your personal security.

Crime: Prior to travel to France, the United States State Department recommends that all visitors check the Department's website for updated security advisories.

Overall Crime Situation: France is a relatively safe country. Most crimes are non-violent, but pick-pocketing is a significant problem. See section below entitled Tips on How to Avoid Becoming a Victim.

The majority of crimes directed against foreign visitors, including U.S. citizens, involve pick-pocketing, residential break-ins, bicycle theft, and other forms of theft with minimal violence. However, as in any big city, robberies involving physical assault do occur in Paris and other major urban areas. Visitors to congested areas and known tourist sites (e.g., museums, monuments, train stations, airports, and subways) should be particularly attentive to their surroundings. Crimes against visitors are generally crimes of opportunity, though these crimes are more likely to involve violence on the street late at night or when the victim detects the theft and resists the criminal. As in any major city, women should exercise extra caution when out alone at night and/or consider traveling out at night with companions. In general, Paris taxis are safe and professionally operated, but we have noted an increase in reported harassment and assaults on women by taxi drivers.

Caution is required throughout France when driving through economically depressed areas, where there is a high incidence of "smash and grab" robberies. Thieves will approach a vehicle that is stopped in traffic, smash a window, reach into the vehicle to grab a purse or other valuable item, and then flee. Keep doors locked and valuables out of sight.

Throughout August, the month when most French residents take summer vacations, and in December, there is generally an increase in the number of residential break-ins. The majority are attributed to residents not using security measures already in place, including double locking doors and locking windows. Home invasions are often preceded by phone calls to see if the resident is at home. Often thieves who manage to gain access to the apartment building will knock on apartment doors to see if anyone answers, offering the excuse they are taking a survey or representing a utility company.

Paris: Crime in Paris is similar to that in most large cities. Violent crime is relatively uncommon in the city center, but women should exercise extra caution when out alone at night and/or consider traveling out at night with companions. There has been an increase recently in reported sexual harassment, and sometimes assault, by taxi drivers. Pickpockets are by far the most significant problem. In addition to purses and wallets, smart phones and small electronic devices are particular targets.

In Paris, pickpockets can be any gender, race, or age and are commonly children under the age of 16 because they are difficult to prosecute. Pickpockets are very active on the rail link (RER B) from Charles de Gaulle Airport to the city center. Travelers may want to consider using a shuttle service or one of the express buses to central Paris rather than the RER. In addition, passengers on the Metro line 1, which traverses the city center from east to west and services many major tourist sites, are often targeted. A common method is for one thief to distract the tourist with questions or disturbances, while an accomplice picks pockets, a backpack, or a purse. Schemes in Paris include asking if you would sign a petition or take a survey and presenting a ring and asking if you dropped it. Thieves often time their pickpocket attempts to coincide with the closing of the automatic doors on the Metro, leaving the victim secured on the departing train. Many thefts also occur at the major department stores (e.g., Galeries Lafayette, Printemps, and Le Bon Marché), where tourists may leave wallets, passports, and credit cards on cashier counters during transactions. Popular tourist sites are also popular with thieves, who favor congested areas to mask their activities. The crowded elevators at the Eiffel Tower, escalators at museums, and the area surrounding Sacré Coeur Basilica in Montmartre are all favored by pickpockets and snatch-and-grab thieves.

There have been some instances of tourists being robbed and assaulted near less utilized Metro stations. The area around the Moulin Rouge, known as Pigalle, requires extra security precautions to avoid becoming a victim. Pigalle is an adult entertainment area known for prostitution, sex shows, and illegal drugs. Unsuspecting tourists have run up exorbitant bar bills and been forced to pay before being permitted to leave. Other areas in Paris where extra security precautions are warranted after dark are Les Halles and the Bois de Boulogne.

Provence Alpes Maritimes (PACA)/Languedoc-Roussillon (Marseille, Montpellier, Perpignan, Carcassonne Avignon, Aix en Provence, Arles, Cannes, Nice): The PACA/Languedoc-Roussillon region enjoys a fairly low rate of violent crime directed at tourists. The most common problems in the region are thefts from cars (both stopped in traffic and parked) and from luggage trolleys at the major transportation hubs (e.g., Nice Airport, and the railway stations at Marseille, Avignon, and Aix en Provence). U.S. citizen victims reported to the U.S. Consulate General in Marseille fifty cases of theft from cars and twenty purse snatchings in transportation hubs during the May-June 2011 period.

The U.S. Consulate General in Marseille has also noted an increase in holiday rental-home burglaries and in necklace snatching. Keep your car doors locked and windows rolled up at all times. Valuables should be hidden out of site to prevent snatch-and-grab attempts. Maintain visual contact with your car when visiting tourist sites, when using rest facilities at gas stations, or stopping to enjoy panoramic views, even for a short period, as thieves will break windows to access items left in cars. Victims are reporting car break-ins within minutes of leaving a car unattended. Passports should be kept separate from other valuables.

Strasbourg: Strasbourg's historic center enjoys a fairly low rate of violent crime. Pickpockets and snatch-and-grab thieves tend to concentrate their efforts in the Petite France historic district popular with visitors.

Bordeaux: This large city is considered fairly safe; general crimes and offenses have been on the decline since 2005. As with any big city, you should be watchful of pickpockets and other tourist-aimed crimes, especially around public transportation. However, local police are considered professional and responsive to persons who are victims of crime. Stolen purses, ID cards, and passports left in cars—particularly around renowned landmarks– routinely lead to requests for emergency issuance of passports.

Lyon: Although levels of violent crime are low, Lyon has a fair amount of petty crime and vandalism. Late-night weekend rowdiness is common in the center of town and in areas with night clubs. But the public transportation system is safe at night (generally a concern for U.S. citizens), and there is extensive police video surveillance utilized on the streets.

To combat reckless and drunk drivers and prevent them from fleeing accident scenes, Lyon initiated 30 KPH zones in commercial districts, and the local police have increased controls for drunken driving. They have also installed speed and red-light radar systems. Despite these efforts, in 2010 six pedestrians were killed by moving vehicles. The number of stolen passports and personal items in the district remains relatively low, and attacks are rare. Home break-ins have increased recently; according to the local news, there are 30 per day, which represents a 16% increase over 2010. A recent wave of armed robberies in luxury goods stores and cash exchange businesses ended with the arrest of an organized gang of delinquents. Bicycle thefts are also a risk, as Lyon becomes increasingly bicycle-friendly and more people cycle around town.

Normandy: Break-ins and thefts from cars in the parking lots at the Normandy beaches and American cemeteries are common. Do not leave valuables unattended in a car. Locking valuables in the trunk is not an adequate safeguard as thieves often pry open car trunks to steal bags.

Rennes: In general, the city of Rennes is a relatively safe and secure environment, and crime rates throughout the consular district tend to be lower than in larger cities elsewhere. There are occasional crimes in the center of Rennes related to drunkenness and rowdy behavior, with the largest and most boisterous crowds tending to gather on Thursday nights in the area around Rue Saint Michel (a.k.a. "Rue de la Soif" or "Thirst Street") and the adjacent Place Sainte Anne. The local authorities, both police and political, make security a priority.

The Rennes police are well informed about potential threats and respond quickly to any criminal issues occurring in the city. Tourists do occasionally encounter theft of valuables and/or passports. Valuables left unattended in rental cars overnight, or for extended amounts of time, are particularly susceptible to theft. In particular, tourist sites around Brittany warn travelers against leaving expensive items in plain view in parked cars, due to frequent vehicle break-ins. Do not leave luggage unattended on trains.

Toulouse and the Midi-Pyrenees: Toulouse and the Midi-Pyrenees region are considered generally safe. Car theft, vehicle break-ins, petty theft and burglary are the most common crimes, and they are relatively more frequent in areas near the railway station. Car-jackings and home invasions may occur, particularly in wealthier areas surrounding Toulouse. Home invasions, although usually targeting valuables and cars, may include violence. Police are usually very helpful to travelers who are victims of crime. Itinerant street people, often in groups accompanied by dogs, are increasingly prevalent in downtown Toulouse, particularly in warmer weather. While alcohol and drug abuse can make them unpredictable, incidents of crime are relatively rare.

Tips on How to Avoid Becoming a Victim: Common-sense security precautions will help you enjoy a trouble-free stay. Most problems can be avoided by being aware of one's surroundings and avoiding high-risk areas.

When going out, carry only essential items: ONE credit/ATM card, ONE piece of identification, and no more than 40-50. Avoid carrying high-value jewelry and large amounts of cash. Valuables should be kept out of sight and in places difficult for thieves to reach, such as internal coat pockets or in pouches hung around the neck or inside clothes. Shoulder bags and wallets in back pockets are an invitation to a thief.

Keep photocopies of travel documents and credit cards separate from the originals, along with key telephone numbers to contact banks for credit card replacement. Crowded elevators and escalators at tourist sites and crowded metro cars should raise awareness levels. When possible, take a seat or stand against a wall to deter pickpockets and try to maintain a 360-degree awareness of the surrounding area. Carry only a purse that zips closed and ensure that it is carried under the arm and slightly in front of the body. For a backpack-type purse, swing it around so that it is slightly in front of the body. Wallets that are carried on the body should be in a front pocket. While on foot, remain aware of your surroundings at all times and keep bags slung across the body, with the bag hanging away from the street.

Many U.S. citizens have had purses or bags stolen from the back of a chair or from under the table while in cafes, restaurants and nightclubs/bars, including higher end establishments. Again, keep your valuables with you and never leave them unattended or out of your sight.

Do not leave valuables in hotel rooms. If you must leave valuables in the hotel, consider using the hotel safe.

Be aware that thieves often operate in groups and will come to each other's aid if confronted. If a thief is caught in the act, a simple pick-pocketing could turn into an assault (or worse) if an attempt is made to capture the thief. You can shout out for police assistance to attract attention, but do not pursue whomever you think stole your wallet or bag.

Do not use ATMs in isolated, poorly lighted areas or where loiterers are present. Be especially aware of persons standing close enough to see the Personal Identification Number (PIN) being entered into the machine. Thieves often conduct successful scams by simply watching the PIN as it is entered and then stealing the card from the user in some other location. If the card gets stuck in the machine, you should immediately report it to the bank where the machine is located as well as to your bank back home.

Many theft and assault victims are targeted when making their way home from a late night out after drinking alcohol. If you go out late at night, do so with a group of friends. There is safety in numbers.

Use only authorized taxis. Authorized taxis in Paris have the following equipment:

- An illuminated "Taxi Parisien" sign on the roof,
- A display meter showing the cost of the trip,
- A display at the rear of the vehicle and visible from the exterior which enables the monitoring of the daily duration of use of the vehicle,
- A plate fixed to the front fender bearing the license number.

Over the past year, there has been an increase in reports by women of sexual harassment and assault by the driver. Women may want to consider having another individual walk them to a taxi and, in plain view of the driver, note the license number of the vehicle, or call a friend while in the taxi and communicate the license number. Letting the driver know that others are aware of your trip and the license number of the taxi may reduce the chances of becoming a victim.

Public parks should be avoided after dark as they are often frequented by drug dealers and prostitutes.

The Paris Police Prefecture publishes a pamphlet entitled "Paris in Complete Safety " that provides practical advice and useful telephone numbers for visitors.

Victims of Crime: If you or someone you know becomes the victim of a crime abroad, you should contact the local police and the nearest U.S. embassy or consulate. We can:

- Replace a lost or stolen passport.
- Provide information on the most rapid means for money transfer.

- Assist with contacting family members or friends.

- Help you find appropriate medical care following violent crimes such as assault or rape.

- Put you in contact with the appropriate police authorities.

- Although the local authorities are responsible for investigating and prosecuting the crime, consular officers can help you understand the local criminal justice process and can direct you to local attorneys.

For more serious crimes, compensation is available under French law to victims of crime committed on French soil under certain circumstances. We recommend that you read our information on victims of crime, including possible victim-compensation programs in the United States. The European equivalent to the U.S. 911 emergency line is 112. Non-French speakers may experience a delay while an English speaker is located. Alternatively, one can call French emergency numbers specific to the type of incident: 17 (police emergency); 18 (fire department/paramedics); and 15 (medical emergency/paramedic team/ambulance).

For private legal matters, commercial disputes, tourist, trade, or property complaints, you may refer to the website of the Department of State concerning retaining a foreign attorney. Consular staff is prohibited from providing legal representation or guidance, but we can refer inquiries to French law directories, bar associations or other organizations in order to assist you. You may also refer to our list of attorneys for legal assistance in France.

Criminal Penalties: While you are traveling in France, you are subject to its laws even if you are a U.S. citizen. Criminal penalties vary from country to country and there are some things that might be legal in the country you visit, but are still illegal in the United States. For example, you can be prosecuted under U.S. law if you buy pirated goods in another country. Engaging in sexual conduct with children or using or disseminating child pornography in a foreign country is also a crime prosecutable in the United States. If you do something illegal in another country, your U.S. passport won't help you avoid arrest or prosecution. It's very important to know what's legal and what's not where you are going.

Persons violating French laws, even unknowingly, may be expelled, arrested, or imprisoned. Penalties for possession, use, or trafficking in illegal drugs in France are severe, and convicted offenders can expect long jail sentences and heavy fines. For legal assistance in France, you may refer to this list of attorneys.

If you use any of France's excellent public transportation services, take particular care to retain your used or "validated" ticket. Inspectors conduct periodic, random checks, and passengers who fail to present the correct validated ticket for their journey are subject to stiff and immediate fines. Inspectors may show no interest in explanations and no sympathy for an honest mistake. Failure to cooperate with these inspectors can result in a visit to the police station.

While some countries will automatically notify the nearest U.S. embassy or consulate if a U.S. citizen is detained or arrested in a foreign country, that might not always be the case. To ensure that the United States is aware of your circumstances, request that the police and prison officials notify the nearest U.S. embassy or consulate as soon as you are arrested or detained.

There are strict regulations concerning temporary importation into or export from France of items such as firearms, antiquities, medications, business equipment, sales samples, and other items. You should contact the Embassy of France in Washington, D.C. or one of France's consulates in the United States for specific information regarding customs requirements.

Accessibility: In France, accessibility and accommodation for individuals with disabilities are very different from what you find in the United States. French law requires that any new building with public or community space and any existing public building be accessible for persons with disabilities. However, many existing buildings, as well as transportation systems, do not yet meet these requirements.

Getting around in French cities may be difficult at times since many sidewalks are narrow and uneven, and cobblestone streets make access difficult, but the major tourist areas have better facilities. Although the Paris métro is a very efficient method for traveling throughout central Paris, most métro stations are not readily accessible for people with disabilities. Very few stations have elevators, and most have stairways and long corridors for changing trains or exiting to the street. However many Parisian buses and tramways are equipped with lowering platforms for travelers with limited-mobility, or who are sight- or hearing-disabled. Taxis are also a good means of transportation.

The English language website of the Paris Visitors Bureau and the French language, government-sponsored internet site contain additional information and include links to a downloadable local transportation map specifically designed for travelers with special mobility needs. There are many other resources available on the internet for disabled persons traveling to, or living in, France. You may also contact any of our consular offices by e-mail for further information on this topic.

Medical Facilities and Health Information: Medical care is comparable to that found in the United States. In an emergency, dialing 15 will connect the caller to emergency medical services. You can also dial the Europe-wide emergency response number 112 to reach an operator for all kinds of emergency services (similar to the U.S. 911 system). Non-French speakers may experience a delay while an English speaker is located. For non-emergency medical assistance in France, you may refer to this list of medical professionals.

You can find good information on vaccinations and other health precautions on the Centers for Disease Control (CDC) website. For information about outbreaks of infectious diseases abroad, consult the World Health Organization (WHO) website, which also contains additional health information for travelers, including detailed country-specific health information.

Medical Insurance: You cannot assume that your insurance will go with you when you travel. It's very important to find out BEFORE you leave. You need to ask your insurance company two questions:

- Does my policy apply when I'm out of the United States?
- Will it cover emergencies like a trip to a foreign hospital or an evacuation?

In many places, doctors and hospitals still expect payment in cash at the time of service. Your regular U.S. health insurance may not cover doctor and hospital visits in other countries. If your policy doesn't cover you when you travel, it's a very good idea to take out another one for your trip.

NOTE: The U.S. Social Security Medicare Program does not provide coverage for hospital or medical costs outside the United States.

Traffic Safety and Road Conditions: While in France, you may encounter road conditions that are very different from those in the United States.

Roads in France are generally comparable to those in the United States, but traffic engineering and driving habits pose special dangers. Lane markings and sign placements may not be clear. Drivers should be prepared to make last-minute maneuvers, as most French drivers do. The French typically drive more aggressively and faster than Americans, and tend to exceed posted speed limits.

Right-of-way rules in France may differ from those in the United States. Drivers entering intersections from the right have priority over those on the left (unless specifically indicated otherwise), even when entering relatively large boulevards from small side streets. Many intersections in France are traffic circles, where the right-of-way belongs to drivers in the circle.

On major highways, there are service stations at least every 25 miles. Service stations are not as common on secondary roads in France as they are in the United States. Paris, the capital and largest city in France, has an extensive and efficient public transportation system. The interconnecting system of buses, subways, and commuter rails serves more than four million people a day with a safety record comparable to, or better than, the systems of major American cities. Similar transportation systems are found in all major French cities. Between cities, France is served by an equally extensive rail service, which is safe and reliable. High-speed rail links connect the major cities in France. Many cities are also served by frequent air service. Traveling by train is safer than driving.

Pedestrians make up 13 percent of the deaths in motor vehicle accidents in France (roughly the same as in the United States), but this percentage is increasing. Most of these accidents occur when a pedestrian steps out onto the street, often when a car or motorcycle is making a turn onto a pedestrian crosswalk. Pedestrians should be cautious even when they have a green walking signal since this is no guarantee against aggressive drivers.

While Paris, Marseille, Lyon, and other French cities actively encourage the renting of bicycles through widely available city-sponsored systems, you should be cautious about this means of transportation, especially in a busy and unfamiliar urban environment. Helmets are neither required nor readily available near these rental stations. If you choose to ride a bicycle in France, you should bring your own helmet.

Visit the website of the French National Tourist Office, which contains specific information concerning French driver's permits, vehicle inspection, road tax, and mandatory insurance. The Embassy page on Driving in France provides information on the use of U.S. licenses in France. Note that as of July 1 2012, road safety equipment in all private vehicles in France must include a breathalyzer kit.

Aviation Safety Oversight: The U.S. Federal Aviation Administration (FAA) has assessed the government of France's Civil Aviation Authority as being in compliance with International Civil Aviation Organization (ICAO) aviation safety standards for oversight of France's air carrier operations. Further information may be found on the FAA's safety assessment page.

Children's Issues: For information see the U.S. Dept. of State Office of Children's Issues web pages on intercountry adoption and international parental child abduction.

Specific Information on Monaco: While the general information above is relevant to Monaco as well as France, this section contains information specific to Monaco.

The local point of contact for American citizens in Monaco is the U.S. Consular Agency in Nice. Additional services are available from Consulate General Marseille and the U.S. Embassy in Paris.

Consular Agency Nice
7, Avenue Gustave V
3rd floor
06000 Nice
Tel. (33) 4 93 88 89 55
Fax (33) 4 93 87 07 38
American Citizen Services Email: usanice@state.gov

Country Description: Monaco is a developed constitutional monarchy. Read the Department of State Background Notes on Monaco for additional information. A passport is required to enter Monaco but a visa is not necessary for tourist/business stays up to 90 days in Monaco.

Entry/Exit Requirements: For further information on entry requirements to Monaco, travelers may contact the Embassy of the Principality of Monaco, 3400 International Drive, NW, Suite 2K-100, Washington D.C. 20008, Tel: (202) 234-1530, Email: Embassy Monaco, or the Consulate General of Monaco, 565 Fifth Avenue–23rd floor, New York, NY 10017, Tel: (212) 286-0500, Email: Monaco Consulate. For the most current visa information, visit the Embassy of France website or the Embassy of the Principality of Monaco website. For more information please visit the official site of the Monaco Government, or the Government Tourist Office. There are strict regulations concerning temporary importation into or export of items such as firearms, antiquities, medications, business equipment, sales samples, and other items. Contact the Consulate General of Monaco in New York for specific information regarding customs requirements.

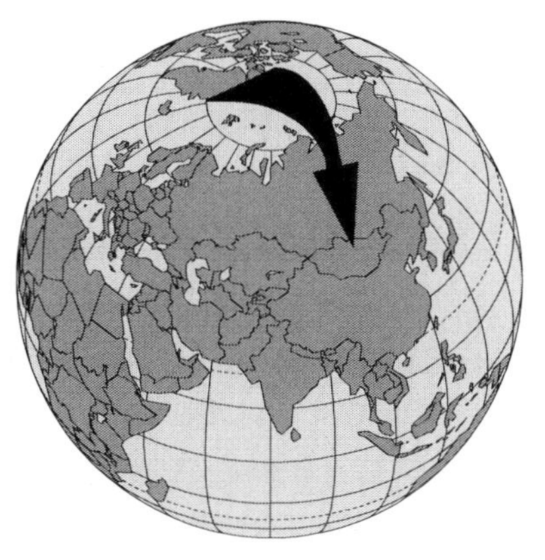

MONGOLIA

Compiled from publications that were available as of February 2013 from the U.S. Department of State, the U.S. Department of Commerce, and the Central Intelligence Agency (CIA). See the introduction to this set for explanatory notes.

Official Name:
Mongolia

PROFILE

Geography

Area: total: 1,564,116 sq km; country comparison to the world: 19; land: 1,553,556 sq km; water: 10,560 sq km

Major cities: Ulaanbaatar (capital) 949,000 (2009)

Climate: desert; continental (large daily and seasonal temperature ranges)

Terrain: vast semidesert and desert plains, grassy steppe, mountains in west and southwest; Gobi Desert in south-central

People

Nationality: noun: Mongolian(s); adjective: Mongolian

Population: 3,179,997 (July 2012 est.)

Population growth rate: 1.469% (2012 est.)

Ethnic groups: Mongol (mostly Khalkha) 94.9%, Turkic (mostly Kazakh) 5%, other (including Chinese and Russian) 0.1% (2000)

Religions: Buddhist Lamaist 50%, Shamanist and Christian 6%, Muslim 4%, none 40% (2004)

Languages: Khalkha Mongol 90% (official), Turkic, Russian (1999)

Literacy: definition: age 15 and over can read and write; total population: 97.4%; male: 96.9%; female: 97.9% (2010 est.)

Health: life expectancy at birth: total population: 68.63 years; male: 66.16 years; female: 71.23 years (2012 est.); Infant mortality rate: total: 36 deaths/1,000 live births; male: 38.94 deaths/1,000 live births; female: 32.91 deaths/1,000 live births (2012 est.)

Unemployment rate: 9.9% (2010)

Work force: 1.147 million (2010 est.)

Government

Type: parliamentary

Independence: 11 July 1921

Constitution: 13 January 1992

Political subdivisions: 21 provinces (aymguud, singular—aymag) and 1 municipality (singular—hot); Arhangay, Bayanhongor, Bayan-Olgiy, Bulgan, Darhan-Uul, Dornod, Dornogovi, Dundgovi, Dzavhan (Zavkhan), Govi-Altay, Govisumber, Hentiy, Hovd, Hovsgol, Omnogovi, Orhon, Ovorhangay, Selenge, Suhbaatar, Tov, Ulaanbaatar, Uvs

Suffrage: 18 years of age; universal

Economy

GDP (purchasing power parity): $15.22 billion (2012 est.); $13.43 billion (2011 est.); $11.46 billion (2010 est.); $10.77 billion (2009 est.)

GDP real growth rate: 12.7% (2012 est.); 17.3% (2011 est.); 6.4% (2010 est.); -1.3% (2009 est.)

GDP per capita (PPP): $5,400 (2012 est.); $4,800 (2011 est.); $4,200 (2010 est.); $4,000 (2009 est.)

Natural resources: oil, coal, copper, molybdenum, tungsten, phosphates, tin, nickel, zinc, fluorspar, gold, silver, iron

Agriculture products: wheat, barley, vegetables, forage crops; sheep, goats, cattle, camels, horses

Industries: construction and construction materials; mining (coal, copper, molybdenum, fluorspar, tin, tungsten, and gold); oil; food and beverages; processing of animal products, cashmere and natural fiber manufacturing

Exports: $4.78 billion (2011 est.); $2.909 billion (2010 est.)

Exports—commodities: copper, apparel, livestock, animal products, cashmere, wool, hides, fluorspar, other nonferrous metals, coal, crude oil

Exports—partners: China 92.1%, Russia 2%, Canada 1.9% (2011 est.)

Imports: $6.527 billion (2011 est.); $3.089 billion (2010 est.)

Imports—commodities: machinery and equipment, fuel, cars, food products, industrial consumer goods, chemicals, building materials, cigarettes and tobacco, appliances, soap and detergent

Imports—partners: China 30.7%, Russia 24.5%, US 8.1%, Japan 7.4%, South Korea 5.5% (2011 est.)

Debt—external: $1.9 billion (2011); $1.76 billion (2010)

Exchange rates: togrog/tugriks (MNT) per US dollar; 1,299.5 (2012 est.); 1,265.5 (2011 est.); 1,357.1 (2010 est.); 1,442.8 (2009); 1,170 (2007)

PEOPLE

Life in sparsely populated Mongolia has recently become more urbanized. Nearly half of the people live in urban centers, including the capital, Ulaanbaatar. Semi-nomadic life still predominates in the countryside, but settled agricultural communities are becoming more common. Mongolia's birth rate is estimated at 25.1 births per 1,000 people (2009 est.). About 58% of the total population is under age 30, 47.8% of whom are under 14.

Among ethnic Mongols, the Khalkha comprise more than 90% and the remaining groups include Dorvod, Tuvan, and Buriat Most Russians left the country following the withdrawal of economic aid and collapse of the Soviet Union in 1991.

Language

Mongol is an Altaic language—from the Altaic Mountains of Central Asia, a language family comprising the Turkic, Tungusic, and Mongolic subfamilies—and is related to Turkic (Uzbek, Turkish, and Kazakh), Korean, and, possibly, Japanese. Mongols in the north and Dariganga Mongols in the east. Turkic speakers (Kazakhs, Turvins, and Khotans) constitute about 4% of Mongolia's population, and the rest are Tungusic-speakers.

Religion

Buddhism is closely linked with the country's cultural traditions. Local scholars claim that more than 90 percent of citizens subscribe to some form of Buddhism, although practice varies widely. Lamaist Buddhism of the Tibetan variety is the traditional and dominant religion.

Ethnic Kazakhs, most of whom are Muslim, are the largest ethnic minority. They constitute approximately 5 percent of the population nationwide and 80 percent of the population of the western province of Bayan-Olgiy. The Mongolian Muslim Association estimates there are 120,000 Kazakh Muslims and 30,000 Khoton Muslims, largely in the province of Uvs. Muslims operate more than 40 mosques and ten Islamic student centers, and there are an estimated 3,000 students of Islam.

There is a small but growing number of Christians. Christian groups estimate that more than 4 percent of the population practices Christianity, of which an estimated 90 percent are Protestant and 9 percent are members of The Church of Jesus Christ of Latter-Day Saints (Mormons). Roman Catholics and members of the Russian Orthodox Church together account for the remaining 1 percent.

Some citizens practice shamanism, often in tandem with another religion, but there are no reliable statistics on their number.

At the end of the year, there were 630 registered places of worship, 272 of which were Buddhist, 293 Christian, and 65 others belonging to various religious denominations. During the year the State General Registration Office registered 50 new places of worship. According to the Evangelical Alliance nongovernmental organization (NGO), there are approximately 600 evangelical churches operating in the country. Of the 368 churches that belong to the Evangelical Alliance, over 140 are not registered. The Evangelical Alliance reported that most churches not registered are in the countryside.

HISTORY

In 1206 AD, a single Mongolian state was formed based on nomadic tribal groupings under the leadership of Chinggis ("Genghis") Khan. He and his immediate successors conquered nearly all of Asia and European Russia and sent armies as far as central Europe and Southeast Asia. Chinggis Khan's grandson Kublai Khan, who conquered China and established the Yuan dynasty (1279–1368 AD), gained fame in Europe through the writings of Marco Polo.

Although Mongol-led confederations sometimes exercised wide political power over their conquered territories, their strength declined rapidly after the Mongol dynasty in China was overthrown in 1368. The Manchus, a tribal group which conquered China in 1644 and formed the Qing dynasty, were able to bring Mongolia under Manchu control in 1691 as Outer Mongolia when the Khalkha Mongol nobles swore an oath of allegiance to the Manchu emperor. The Mongol rulers of Outer Mongolia enjoyed considerable autonomy under the Manchus, and all Chinese claims to Outer Mongolia following the establishment of the republic have rested on this oath. In 1727, Russia and Manchu China concluded the Treaty of Khiakta, delimiting the border between China and Mongolia that exists in large part today.

Outer Mongolia was a Chinese province (1691–1911), an autonomous state under Russian protection (1912–19), and again a Chinese province (1919–21). As Manchu authority in China waned, and as Russia and Japan confronted each other, Russia gave arms and diplomatic support to nationalists among the Mongol religious leaders and nobles. The Mongols accepted Russian aid and proclaimed their independence of Chinese rule in 1911, shortly after a successful Chinese revolt against the Manchus. By agreements signed in 1913 and 1915, the Russian Government forced the new Chinese Republican Government to accept Mongolian autonomy under continued Chinese control, presumably to discourage other foreign powers from approaching a newly independent Mongolian state that might seek support from as many foreign sources as possible.

The Russian revolution and civil war afforded Chinese warlords an opportunity to re-establish their rule in Outer Mongolia, and Chinese troops were dispatched there in 1919. Following Soviet military victories over White Russian forces in the early

1920s and the occupation of the Mongolian capital Urgoo in July 1921, Moscow again became the major outside influence on Mongolia. The Mongolian People's Republic was proclaimed on November 25, 1924.

Between 1925 and 1928, power under the communist regime was consolidated by the Mongolian People's Revolutionary Party (MPRP). The MPRP left gradually undermined rightist elements, seizing control of the party and the government. Several factors characterized the country during this period: The society was basically nomadic and illiterate; there was no industrial proletariat; the aristocracy and the religious establishment shared the country's wealth; there was widespread popular obedience to traditional authorities; the party lacked grassroots support; and the government had little organization or experience. In an effort at swift socioeconomic reform, the leftist government applied extreme measures that attacked the two most dominant institutions in the country—the aristocracy and the religious establishment. Between 1932 and 1945, their excess zeal, intolerance, and inexperience led to anti-communist uprisings. In the late 1930s, purges directed at the religious institution resulted in the desecration of hundreds of Buddhist institutions and imprisonment of more than 10,000 people.

During World War II, because of a growing Japanese threat over the Mongolian-Manchurian border, the Soviet Union reversed the course of Mongolian socialism in favor of a new policy of economic gradualism and buildup of the national defense. The Soviet-Mongolian army defeated Japanese forces that had invaded eastern Mongolia in the summer of 1939, and a truce was signed setting up a commission to define the Mongolian-Manchurian border in the autumn of that year. Following the war, the Soviet Union reasserted its influence in Mongolia. Secure in its relations with Moscow, the Mongolian Government shifted to postwar development, focusing on civilian enterprise. International ties were expanded, and Mongolia established relations with North Korea and the new communist governments in Eastern Europe.

It also increased its participation in communist-sponsored conferences and international organizations.

Mongolia became a member of the United Nations in 1961. In the early 1960s, Mongolia attempted to maintain a neutral position amidst increasingly contentious Sino-Soviet polemics; this orientation changed in the middle of the decade. Mongolia and the Soviet Union signed an agreement in 1966 that introduced large-scale Soviet ground forces as part of Moscow's general buildup along the Sino-Soviet frontier.

During the period of Sino-Soviet tensions, relations between Mongolia and China deteriorated. In 1983, Mongolia systematically began expelling some of the 7,000 ethnic Chinese in Mongolia to China. Many of them had lived in Mongolia since the 1950s, when they were sent there to assist in construction projects.

During the winter after the fall of the Berlin Wall in 1989, peaceful protests led to the resignation of the politburo in March 1990 and Mongolia's first multiparty elections in July 1990. In the democratic era that has followed the 1990 elections, Mongolia has sought to maintain good relationships with its two immediate neighbors as well as with democratic countries further afield (referred to as "third neighbors"), including the United States.

Mongolia has also engaged more actively in international organizations including the UN, International Atomic Energy Agency (IAEA), and Association of Southeast Asian Nations (ASEAN) Regional Forum and is seeking membership in the Organization for Security and Cooperation in Europe (OSCE). Since 2002, the Mongolian Armed Forces have trained and deployed thousands of peacekeepers to support peace operations worldwide, including missions in Iraq, Sierra Leone, Kosovo, South Sudan, Chad, and Afghanistan.

Chronology of Mongolian History 1921–Present

March 13, 1921: Provisional People's Government declared independence of Mongolia.

May 31, 1924: U.S.S.R. signed agreement with Peking government, referring to Outer Mongolia as an "integral part of the Republic of China," whose "sovereignty" therein the Soviet Union promised to respect.

May-September 16, 1939: Large scale fighting took place between Japanese and Soviet-Mongolian forces along Khalkhyn Gol on Mongolia-Manchuria border, ending in defeat of the Japanese expeditionary force. Truce negotiated between U.S.S.R. and Japan.

July 1944: Vice President Henry A. Wallace became the highest-ranking U.S. Government official to visit Mongolia.

October 6, 1949: Newly established People's Republic of China accepted recognition accorded Mongolia and agreed to establish diplomatic relations.

October 1961: Mongolia became a member of the United Nations.

January 27, 1987: Diplomatic relations established with the United States.

December 1989: First popular reform demonstrations. Mongolian Democratic Association organized.

January 1990: Large-scale demonstrations demanding democracy held in sub-zero weather.

March 2, 1990: Soviets and Mongolians announced that all Soviet troops would be withdrawn from Mongolia by 1992.

May 1990: Constitution amended to provide for multi-party system and new elections.

July 29, 1990: First democratic elections held.

September 3, 1990: First democratically elected People's Great Hural took office.

February 12, 1992: New constitution went into effect.

April 8, 1992: New election law passed.

June 28, 1992: Election for the first unicameral legislature (State Great Hural).

June 6, 1993: First direct presidential election.

June 30, 1996: Election resulted in peaceful transition of power from former communist party to coalition of democratic parties. From 1998–2000, four prime ministers and a series of cabinet changes. In early 2000, Democratic Coalition dissolved.

July 2, 2000: Election resulted in victory for the former communist Mongolian People's Revolutionary Party (MPRP); first-past-the-post electoral system enabled MPRP, with 52% of the popular vote, to win 95% of the parliamentary seats; formation of new government by Prime Minister N. Enkhbayar.

June 27, 2004: Motherland-Democracy Coalition formed in early 2004 to contest the parliamentary election. Election resulted in roughly 50/50 split of parliamentary seats between former communist party and democratic opposition and formation of new government by Prime Minister Ts. Elbegdorj (Democratic Party).

November 2005: George W. Bush became the first U.S. president to visit Mongolia.

January 2006: MPRP ministers resigned from the government, and the government dissolved. A new coalition government was formed, led by the MPRP with the participation of four smaller parties.

October 2007: MPRP ousted its leader, Prime Minister M. Enkhbold, who resigned as Prime Minister. The new leader of the MPRP, Sanjaagiin Bayar, became Prime Minister and formed a new cabinet.

December 2007: Bayar's cabinet was approved.

July 1, 2008: Two days after parliamentary elections, and 1 day after the ruling MPRP claimed a landslide victory, a sizeable protest outside the MPRP headquarters turned violent. The MPRP headquarters was burned beyond repair and clashes between civilians and security forces left at least five people dead, 13 missing, hundreds injured and hundreds in police detention. President N. Enkhbayar declared a 4-day state of emergency, imposing a curfew, a ban on public gatherings, and a broadcast-news blackout (apart from the state broadcaster).

July and August 2008: Newly elected members of parliament from the opposition Democratic Party refused to take the oath of office, demanding, among other things, that the nine-member General Election Commission resign for alleged electoral irregularities.

May 2009: Former Prime Minister and Democratic Party legislator Tsakhiagiin Elbegdorj was elected as President of Mongolia in free and fair elections.

October-November 2009: Prime Minister Sanjaagiin Bayar resigned for health reasons, and Foreign Minister Sukhbaatariin Batbold was selected as Prime Minister. Prime Minister Batbold largely retained former Prime Minister Bayar's cabinet, with only a few changes.

December 2010: The MPRP changed its name to the Mongolian People's Party (MPP).

June 2011: Former President Enkhbayar founded a new party with the name "MPRP" in response to the MPP's decision to drop the word "Revolutionary."

August 2011: Vice President Joseph R. Biden visited Ulaanbaatar to commend Mongolia on its democratic tradition and contributions to international peace and security, and to pursue more robust economic ties between the United States and Mongolia.

GOVERNMENT AND POLITICAL CONDITIONS

Mongolia is a multiparty parliamentary democracy. The most recent presidential election, held in 2009 and considered largely free and fair, was won by former prime minister Tsakhia Elbegdorj of the Democratic Party. Prime Minister Sukhbaatar Batbold and his majority Mongolian People's Party (MPP) continued to dominate the parliament but governed under a unity government with the Democratic Party. The MPP, formerly known as the Mongolian People's Revolutionary Party (MPRP), changed its name during 2011. A small remnant of the original MPRP kept the MPRP name and continued as a competing splinter party led by former president Nambar Enkhbayar.

Recent Elections

In the most recent presidential election, held in 2009, the former prime minister and candidate of the opposition Democratic Party, Tsakhia Elbegdorj, defeated MPRP incumbent Nambar Enkhbayar. Independent observers described the election as largely free and fair.

Political Parties: Political parties could operate without restrictions or outside interference, although bias within the General Election Commission was a concern, particularly for smaller political parties.

Participation of Women and Minorities: There were no legal impediments to the participation of women or minorities in government and politics, but their numbers remained small. There were three women in the 76-member parliament. One of the 15 cabinet ministers was a woman, as were seven of the 17 Supreme Court justices. Women and women's organizations were vocal in local and national politics and actively sought greater female representation in government policymaking. There were three ethnic Kazakhs serving in the parliament. There were two members of minority groups serving in the cabinet or on the Supreme Court.

Principal Government Officials

Last Updated: 1/31/2013

Pres.: **Tsakhia ELBEGDORJ**
Prime Min.: **Norov ALTANKHUYAG**
Dep. Prime Min.: **Dendev TERBISHDAGVA**
Min. of Construction & Urban Development: **Tsevelmaa BAYARSAIKHAN**
Min. of Culture, Sports, & Tourism: **Tsedevdamba OYUNGEREL**
Min. of Defense: **Dashdemberal BAT-ERDENE**
Min. of Economic Development: **Nyamjav BATBAYAR**
Min. of Education & Science: **Luvsannyam GANTMUR**
Min. of Energy: **Mishig SONOMPIL**
Min. of Environment: **Sambuu DEMBEREL**
Min. of Finance: **Mendsaikhan ENKHSAIKHAN**
Min. of Food, Agriculture, & Light Industry: **Khaltmaa BATTULGA**
Min. of Foreign Affairs & Trade: **Luvsanvandan BOLD**
Min. of Health: **Natsag UDVAL**
Min. of Justice & Home Affairs: **Khishigdemberel TEMUUJIN**
Min. of Labor: **Yadamsuren SANJMYATAV**
Min. of Mining: **Davaajav GANKHUYAG**
Min. for Population Development & Social Welfare: **Sodnomzundui ERDENE**
Min. of Road & Transportation: **Amarjargal GANSUKH**
Min. & Chief of the Govt. Secretariat: **Chimed SAIKHANBILEG**
Governor, Bank of Mongolia: **Lhanaasuren PUREVDORJ**
Ambassador to the US: **Khasbazar BEKHBAT**
Permanent Representative to the UN, New York: **Od OCH**

ECONOMY

Mongolia's extensive mineral deposits and attendant growth in mining-sector activities have transformed Mongolia's economy, which traditionally has been dependent on herding and agriculture. Mongolia's copper, gold, coal, molybdenum, fluorspar, uranium, tin, and tungsten deposits, among others, have attracted foreign direct investment. Soviet assistance, at its height one-third of GDP, disappeared almost overnight in 1990 and 1991 at the time of the dismantlement of the USSR.

The following decade saw Mongolia endure both deep recession, because of political inaction and natural disasters, as well as economic growth, because of reform-embracing, free-market economics and extensive privatization of the formerly state-run economy. The country opened a fledgling stock exchange in 1991. Mongolia joined the World Trade Organization in 1997 and seeks to expand its participation in regional economic and trade regimes. Growth averaged nearly 9% per year in 2004–08 largely because of high copper prices globally and new gold production.

By late 2008, Mongolia was hit hard by the global financial crisis. Slower global economic growth hurt the country's exports, notably copper, and slashed government revenues. As a result, Mongolia's real economy contracted 1.3% in 2009. In early 2009, the International Monetary Fund reached a $236 million Stand-by Arrangement with Mongolia and the country has largely emerged from the crisis. The banking sector is recovering and the government has started to enact greater supervision regulations.

In October 2009, Mongolia passed long-awaited legislation on an investment agreement to develop the Oyu Tolgoi mine, considered to be among the world's largest untapped copper deposits. Another similarly lengthy process is under review by the National Security Council for an investment agreement for the massive coal mine at Tavan Tolgoi. The economy grew by 6.4% in 2010, 17.5% in 2011, and by more than 12% in 2012, largely on the strength of commodity exports to nearby countries and high government spending domestically. Mongolia's economy, however, faces near-term economic risks from the government's loose fiscal policies, which are contributing to high inflation, and uncertainties in foreign demand for Mongolian exports. Trade with China represents more than half of Mongolia's total external trade—China receives more than 90% of Mongolia's exports. Mongolia purchases 95% of its petroleum products and a substantial amount of electric power from Russia, leaving it vulnerable to price increases. Due to severe winter weather in 2009–10, Mongolia lost 22% of its total livestock, and meat prices doubled. Inflation remained higher than 10% for much of 2010–12, due in part to higher food prices. Remittances from Mongolians working abroad, particularly in South Korea, are significant.

Labor Conditions

The law prohibits children under the age of 14 from working; those who are 14 or 15 years of age may work up to 30 hours per week with parental consent. The workweek for children 16 and 17 years of age is capped at 36 hours. Those under age 18 may not work at night, engage in arduous work, or work in hazardous occupations such as mining and construction.

Forced child labor occurred in the construction and mining (coal, gold, and fluorspar mineral) sectors, although largely if not exclusively in the informal, artisanal mining sector. Children worked informally in petty trade, construction, hotels, restaurants, and unauthorized small-scale mining as well as scavenging in dumpsites and herding animals. While statistics were limited, widespread alcoholism, poverty, and parental abandonment made it necessary for many children to support themselves. The National Center for Children estimated the number of children in the labor force as high as 77,000; up to 90 percent of these children were involved in traditional animal husbandry, while only 1 percent was estimated to be involved in mining.

The legal minimum wage was 140,400 tugrik ($100) per month. National poverty estimates are based on population-weighted subgroup estimates from household surveys. The surveys indicated approximately one-third of the population lived on 1,618 tugrik ($1.16) a day or less and were unable to feed themselves sufficiently. The minimum wage, which applied to both public and private sector workers and was enforced by the Ministry of Labor, did not provide a decent standard of living. The problem was exacerbated by significant inflation over the past year. Many workers received less than the minimum wage, particularly at smaller companies in rural areas.

The standard legal workweek is 40 hours, and there is a minimum rest period of 48 hours between workweeks. By law overtime work is compensated at either double the standard hourly rate or by giving time off equal to the number of hours of overtime worked. Pregnant women and nursing mothers are prohibited by law from working overtime. There is no law mandating sick leave for workers. According to the government, employers set their own rules in this regard.

These laws governing minimum wage and working hours generally were enforced, but enforcement of safety standards was inadequate.

The near-total reliance on outmoded machinery and problems with maintenance and management led to frequent industrial accidents, particularly in the construction, mining, and power sectors. While industrial accidents increased alongside industrial and mining sector growth, most accidents occurred at unofficial construction sites and private mining areas.

Foreign workers, the majority of whom were Chinese mining and construction workers, reportedly worked in conditions that did not meet government regulations. North Korean worker conditions were not fully known, and secrecy surrounded the contractual agreements, labor rights, and compensation of these workers.

However, observers stated that North Korean laborers likely failed to receive the minimum wage. In press reports, it was reported that Mongolian companies paid North Korean workers' wages directly to the government of North Korea. NGOs reported that Mongolian companies wishing to employ North Korean workers could do so through mediator companies.

There were no official reports on labor exploitation, but there were several cases in which workers, mostly Chinese, were deported without receiving their wages. In one case an employer withheld food from approximately 40 Chinese workers. Such instances were confirmed as labor exploitation only if they went to court, but few if any cases ever moved past the investigatory phase before the foreign workers raising the complaints were deported.

U.S.-MONGOLIAN RELATIONS

The United States established diplomatic relations with Mongolia in 1987. Located between Russia and China, Mongolia describes the United States as a "third neighbor." Mongolia adopted democracy in 1990 and has since conducted five presidential and six legislative elections.

The United States has sought to assist Mongolia's market-oriented reforms and to expand relations with Mongolia, primarily in the cultural and economic fields. The two countries have signed a cultural accord, Peace Corps accord, and consular convention. U.S. and Mongolian parliamentarians participate in exchange programs, and Mongolian participants have risen in prominence and spearheaded reforms. Mongolia deployed troops to Iraq from 2003 through October 2008, and now has about 345 troops in Afghanistan supporting Coalition operations.

U.S. Assistance to Mongolia

Mongolia's rate of economic growth is one of the highest in the world. Substantially increased income for both the Mongolian government and the private sector, primarily from mining, brings increased opportunities for economic diversification, improvements in education, infrastructure development, and boosted social programs and will allow Mongolia to expand its role in the international arena. Such fast income growth also brings the challenges of mismanagement and corruption.

U.S. Government assistance seeks to promote private-sector-led growth and long-term capital investment as well as other activities to aid the Mongolian government in strengthening the implementation of its laws, creating greater transparency and accountability, and addressing corruption. Training and equipment provided by the U.S. Government support the professionalization of Mongolia's defense forces and their continued support for United Nations peacekeeping operations. Because of Mongolia's long and highly porous borders, U.S. assistance also aims to support nonproliferation activities.

The U.S. Agency for International Development program and the Peace Corps both have programs in Mongolia. The United States and Mongolia have signed a Millennium Challenge Compact for September 2008 through September 2013.

Bilateral Economic Relations

U.S. exports to Mongolia, while modest, are rapidly increasing and include vehicles, machinery, optical and medical instruments, and agricultural products. U.S. imports from Mongolia include tungsten ore, art and antiques, knit apparel, jewelry, and agricultural products. The United States and Mongolia have signed an Overseas Private Investment Corporation agreement, a trade agreement, a bilateral investment treaty, and a trade and investment framework agreement.

Mongolia's Membership in International Organizations

Mongolia and the United States belong to a number of the same international organizations, including the United Nations, ASEAN Regional Forum, International Monetary Fund, World Bank, and World Trade Organization. Mongolia also is a Partner for Cooperation with the Organization for Security and Cooperation in Europe. In July 2011, Mongolia assumed the chairmanship of the Community of Democracies, a group of democratic nations focused on strengthening democratic institutions globally. In this latter role, Mongolia leads efforts to advance democracy education in emerging democracies.

Bilateral Representation

Mongolia maintains an embassy in the United States at 2833 M Street, NW, Washington, DC, 20007; tel. (202) 333-7117.

Principal U.S. Embassy Officials

Last Updated: 1/14/2013

ULAANBAATAR (E) U.S. Embassy, Big Ring Road, 11th Microdistrict, Sukhbaatar District, Ulaanbaatar-13 POB 1021, 14171, Mongolia, (976) 7007–6001, Fax (976) 7007–6016, INMARSAT Tel 38-313-0947, Workweek: M-F/0830-1230, 1300-1700, Website: http://mongolia.usembassy.gov/

AMB OMS:	Alison Millard
CDC:	(Beijing)
DHS/CBP:	(Beijing)
DHS/CIS:	(Beijing)
DHS/ICE:	(Beijing)
ECON/COM:	David Wyche
FM:	Duke Matthews
GFS:	(Bangkok)
HRO:	Joseph Zadrozny
IBB:	(Washington)
MGT:	Joseph Zadrozny
MLO/ODC:	LTC Jonathan Lau
POL/MIL:	Shawn Franz
POSHO:	Duke Matthews
SDO/DATT:	LTC Jonathan Lau
TREAS:	Patrick O'Connell
AMB:	Piper Campbell
CON:	Daniela Zadrozny

DCM:	Kathleen Morenski
PAO:	Allyson Algeo
GSO:	Larry Dagenais
RSO:	Keith Spain
AGR:	(Beijing)
AID:	Frank Donovan
APHIS:	(Beijing)
ATF:	(Beijing)
ATO:	(Bangkok)
CLO:	Joann Donovan
DEA:	(Beijing)
EEO:	Allyson Algeo
EPA:	(Beijing)
FAA:	(Beijing)
FAA/CASLO:	(Beijing)
FMO:	Joseph Zadrozny
ICASS Chair:	George Economides
IMO:	Sean Gilligan
ISO:	Ninjin Garid
ISSO:	Sean Gilligan
LAB:	(Beijing)
LEGATT:	(Beijing)
POL:	Bryan Koontz

TRAVEL

Consular Information Sheet

April 16, 2012

Country Description: Mongolia is a vast country of mountains, lakes, deserts, and grasslands. It is approximately the size of Alaska. Since 1990, Mongolia has been successfully transitioning into a parliamentary democracy. Economic reforms continue, although the country's development will depend on considerable infrastructure investment, particularly in the mining, energy, transportation, and communication sectors. You should be aware that shortcomings in these areas could affect your travel plans.

Smart Traveler Enrollment Program (STEP)/Embassy Locations: If you are going to live in or visit Mongolia, please take the time to tell our Embassy in Ulaanbaatar about your trip. If you enroll, we can keep you up to date with important safety and security announcements. It will also help your friends and family get in touch with you in an emergency.

U.S. Embassy Ulaanbaatar
Micro Region 11, Big Ring Road, Ulaanbaatar
Telephone: (976) 11-329-095
Emergency after-hours telephone: 976-9911–4168
Facsimile: (976) 11-353-788

The Consular Section can be emailed directly. The Consular Section is open for American Citizens Services by appointment Monday and Thursday from 1-3 p.m., except on U.S. and Mongolian holidays.

Entry/Exit Requirements for U.S. Citizens: You must have a valid passport to visit Mongolia. A visa is not required if you are visiting for fewer than 90 days; however, if you plan to stay in Mongolia for more than 30 days you must register with the Office of Immigration, Naturalization, and Foreign Citizens in Ulaanbaatar within seven days of arriving in Mongolia. If you do not register and you stay longer than 30 days, even for reasons beyond your control, you will be stopped at departure, not allowed to exit, and have to pay a fine.

Visitors who have been in Mongolia for more than 90 days must obtain an exit visa to leave the country. The exit visa is obtained from the Office of Immigration and usually takes 10 days to process. Visitors to Mongolia for less than 90 days do not need any kind of exit permit or visa. However, be aware that requests to exit Mongolia can be denied for reasons such as civil disputes, pending criminal investigation, or immigration violations. In such instances, you will not be allowed to leave the country until the dispute is resolved or a court has made a decision. The Mongolian government has the right to keep foreign citizens in custody for various time periods, without appeal, until a decision is made. We are aware of U.S. citizens who have been denied exit for more than two years.

If you are planning to work or study in Mongolia, you should apply for a visa at a Mongolian embassy or consulate outside of Mongolia. If you do not, the authorities may deny registration, charge you a fine, or require that you leave the country. If you arrive or depart Mongolia through China or Russia, you should be aware of Chinese and Russian visa regulations (coming and going twice will require a double- or multiple-entry visa) and note that some land-entry points have varying days and hours of operation. Many small land-border posts do not operate on a regular schedule and do not allow the entry or departure of third country nationals. Check with immigration authorities to make sure the post you intend to use will be open when you want to enter and that U.S. citizens are able to transit that post. If you plan to travel to Russia, you should get visas before you arrive in Mongolia, since it is hard to get visas at the Russian Embassy in Mongolia. For more information on these requirements, see the Country Specific Information for Russia and China.

On July 8, 2010, the Government of Mongolia passed a law requiring foreign citizens to carry their passport, and if applicable, residency permit, at all times while in Mongolia. Mongolian authorities have the legal responsibility to stop people and request their documents. Persons found not to be compliant with the law are subject to a fine.

In an effort to prevent international child abduction, many governments have initiated procedures at entry/exit points. These often include requiring documentary evidence of relationship and permission from the parent(s) or legal guardian for the child to travel. Having such documentation on hand, even if not required, may facilitate entry/departure.

Please visit the Embassy of Mongolia website for the most current visa information. You can also contact the Embassy of Mongolia at 2833 M Street NW, Washington, DC 20007, telephone (202) 333-7117 for the most current visa information.

HIV/AIDS restrictions: Some HIV/AIDS entry restrictions exist for visitors to and foreign residents of Mongolia. Please verify this information with the Embassy of Mongolia before you travel.

Threats to Safety and Security: There have been no significant acts of terrorism or extremism in Mongolia, and there are no regions of instability in the country. However, you are advised to avoid all protests, including political protests, and street demonstrations that occur occasionally in Ulaanbaatar, since demonstrations may become violent at any time.

Stay up to date by:

- Bookmarking our Bureau of Consular Affairs website, which contains the current Travel Warnings and Travel Alerts as well as the Worldwide Caution.
- Following us on Twitter and the Bureau of Consular Affairs page on Facebook as well.
- Downloading our free Smart Traveler IPhone App to have travel information at your fingertips.
- Calling 1-888-407-4747 toll-free within the U.S. and Canada or a regular toll line, 1-202-501-4444, from other countries. These numbers are available from 8:00 a.m. to 8:00 p.m. Eastern Time, Monday through Friday (except U.S. federal holidays).
- Taking some time before travel to improve your personal security.

Crime: Street crime is common in Mongolia, particularly in Ulaanbaatar, the capital. Most of the street crime is non-violent, but violent incidents do occur regularly. The most common crimes against foreigners are pickpocketing and bag snatching. There are reports of organized groups that operate in open areas, usually after dark, surrounding, grabbing, and choking an individual in order to search his or her pockets. Thieves have also cut victims' bag straps and clothing in attempts to reach wallets, cell phones, and other valuables. If you detect pickpocket attempts, you should not confront the thieves, since they may become violent. We advise you not to walk alone through Ulaanbaatar after dark.

Inter-racial couples are targeted for assault. The perpetrators usually target foreign men with local women. These assaults range from organized attacks by nationalist groups to spontaneous incidents in bars.

Since the spring of 2010, an increased number of xenophobic attacks against foreign nationals in Ulaanbaatar were reported to the U.S. Embassy. A number of these attacks occurred without provocation, and robbery was not the motive. Attackers targeted the victim(s) based solely on their ethnicity or perceived foreign nationality. Some of these attacks were directed against U.S. citizens.

Additionally, nationalist groups frequently mistake Asian-Americans for ethnic Chinese or Koreans and may attack without warning or provocation. Asian-Americans should exercise caution walking the streets of Ulaanbaatar at all times.

In general, you should be extremely cautious at these locations:

- Chinggis Khan International Airport in Ulaanbaatar: Organized groups frequently target tourists for robbery and pickpocketing at this airport.
- The State Department Store and the area around the Circus: Organized pickpocket gangs target tourists at the entries/exits/elevators of the Store and in surrounding areas, along Peace Avenue and down to the Circus.
- Naran Tuul Covered Market: Organized criminal groups target foreigners for robbery and pickpocketing.

You should also be careful in crowded public areas, such as open-air markets, the Central Post Office, and the Gandan Monastery.

In addition, you should be alert for potential criminal activity when you use public transportation or taxis. There have been several reports of foreigners being robbed and/or assaulted while riding in taxis. We recommend that your hotel, restaurant, or a store make taxi arrangements for you. Also, request that a native speaker write your destination address in Mongolian, since most cab drivers do not speak English. Private unmarked cars often act as taxis in Mongolia; their availability is high, but their consistency of performance, fare, and safety is low. We do not recommend using unmarked taxis. If you find a cab driver that you like (English speaker, trustworthy, clean car, etc.), request his mobile phone number for future use.

Crime rises sharply before, during, and after the Naadam Summer Festival in July, throughout the summer tourist season, and during and after Tsagaan Sar, the Winter Festival, in January or February.

Don't buy counterfeit and pirated goods, even if they are widely available. Not only are the bootlegged items illegal in the United States, but you may also be breaking local law.

Victims of Crime: If you or someone you know becomes the victim of a crime abroad, you should contact the local police and the nearest U.S. embassy or consulate (see the Department of State's list of embassies and consulates). We can

- Replace a stolen passport.
- Help you find appropriate medical care if you are the victim of violent crimes such as assault or rape.
- Put you in contact with the appropriate police authorities, and, if you want us to, we can contact family members or a friend.
- Help you understand the local criminal justice process and direct you to local attorneys, although it is important to remember that local authorities are responsible for investigating and prosecuting the crime.

Ulaanbaatar does not have a dedicated tourist police unit; nor do they have any centralized reporting system. You should report allegations of criminal activity to the police district responsible for the area where the crime took place. You may wish to consult with an attorney before you report a crime, since the local police can be uncooperative or aggressively question crime victims. You may be required to remain in the country for the duration of the police investigation and prosecution.

The local equivalents to the "911" emergency line in Mongolia are "102" for the police department and "103" for a medical emergency.

Criminal Penalties: While you are traveling in Mongolia, you are subject to its laws even if you are a U.S. citizen. Foreign laws and legal systems can be vastly different than our own. Criminal penalties will vary from country to country. There are also some things that might be legal in the country you visit, but still illegal in the United States, and you can be prosecuted under U.S. law if you buy pirated goods. Engaging in sexual conduct with children or using or disseminating child pornography in a foreign country is a crime prosecutable in the United States. If you break local laws in Mongolia, your U.S. passport won't help you avoid arrest or prosecution. It's very important to know what's legal and what's not where you are going.

If you are arrested in Mongolia, authorities of Mongolia are required to notify the nearest U.S. embassy or consulate of your arrest. If you are concerned the Department of State may not be aware of your situation, you should request the police or prison officials to notify the nearest U.S. embassy or consulate of your arrest. You may need to make repeated requests to authorities to speak to a consular officer. Authorities may be unaware of your rights to consular access.

Special Circumstances: In Ulaanbaatar, some hotels accept travelers' checks in U.S. dollars, and several banks convert travelers' checks to dollars or Mongolian currency, known as Tugrugs. You can use credit cards at a variety of hotels, restaurants, and shops in the city. Cash advances against credit cards are available at some commercial banks such as Trade and Development Bank, Golomt Bank, Khan Bank, and Khas Bank. International bank wire transfers are also possible. There are a handful of VISA and Maestro/Cirrus ATMs in Ulaanbaatar, but they do not always function and are not reliable. Very few ATMs exist outside the capital. Outside of Ulaanbaatar, cash is the only method of payment that is possible.

We do not always receive timely notification of the detention or arrest of a U.S. citizen, particularly outside of Ulaanbaatar. Please carry a copy of your passport with you at all times so that if questioned by local officials, evidence of your identity and citizenship are readily available.

Severe fuel shortages and problems with central heating and electrical systems may cause seriously reduced heating levels and power outages in Ulaanbaatar and other cities during the winter. Smaller towns in the countryside may have no heat or electricity at all. We recommend that you prepare to leave the country if there is a complete energy failure. General information about natural disaster preparedness is available via the internet from the U.S. Federal Emergency Management Agency (FEMA).

Mongolian customs authorities enforce strict regulations concerning import and export of items such as firearms, ammunition, and antiquities. Import of firearms or ammunition requires prior approval from the Government of Mongolia. Exporting antiquities requires a special customs clearance certificate issued by authorized antique shops at the time of purchase. For additional information contact the Embassy of Mongolia at 2833 M Street NW, Washington, DC 20007, telephone: (202) 333-7117.

Accessibility: While in Mongolia, individuals with disabilities may find accessibility and accommodation very different from what you find in the United States. The Law on Social Protection of the Disabled gives the government the responsibility to implement measures to protect the rights of persons with disabilities, including those concerning physical, sensory, and mental but not intellectual attributes. However, the government does little to execute such measures, and in practice most persons with disabilities faced significant barriers to employment, education, and participation in public life.

In February 2010, a new law took effect mandating standards of physical access for persons with disabilities to newly constructed public buildings; however, by year's end the law had not been applied. Government buildings remained largely inaccessible to persons with disabilities. Public transportation was also largely inaccessible to such persons. Despite a new law introducing standards for road construction under which some textured sidewalks meant to aid visually impaired pedestrians were installed, the persistence of open manholes, protruding obstacles, and unheeded crosswalks prevents many persons with disabilities from moving freely. There are few paved sidewalks, and those that are paved usually lack curb cuts. A few buildings have ramps, but most buildings remain inaccessible to persons with disabilities. Elevators are quite small and are unable to fit a standard-sized wheelchair. Service animals are rare here, and are often barred from public buildings due to a lack of understanding as to their purpose.

Medical Facilities and Health Information: Medical facilities in Mongolia are very limited and do not meet most Western standards, especially for emergency health care requirements. Many brand-name Western medicines are unavailable. The majority of medical facilities are located in Ulaanbaatar. Medical facilities and treatment are extremely limited or non-existent outside of Ulaanbaatar. Specialized emergency care for infants and the elderly is not available. Doctors and hospitals usually expect immediate payment in cash for health services. Infectious diseases, such as plague and meningococcal meningitis, are present at various times of the year. Tuberculosis is an increasingly serious health concern in Mongolia. For further information, please consult the CDC's information on TB. Sanitation in some restaurants is inadequate, particularly outside of Ulaanbaatar. Stomach illnesses are frequent. You should drink bottled water and use other routine safety measures to protect your health. Air pollution is a serious problem during the winter months, and travelers with breathing or other health problems should plan accordingly.

Serious medical problems requiring hospitalization and/or medical evacuation either within Mongolia or to other countries are extremely expensive and can cost more than $100,000. Evacuation companies will not take you to another location without a full fee guarantee beforehand. Please note that not all insurance companies provide medical evacuation coverage for Mongolia. Please check with your insurance provider before traveling and consider supplemental medical or travel insurance. Currently, SOS Medica Mongolia UB International Clinic is the only clinic that has medical evacuation services in Mongolia.

Local hospitals generally do not contact the Embassy about ill or injured U.S. citizens in their care. If you need assistance from the Embassy, you should ask the doctor or hospital to contact the U.S. Embassy in Ulaanbaatar.

You can find good information on vaccinations and other health precautions on the CDC website. For information about outbreaks of infectious diseases abroad, consult the World Health Organization (WHO) website. The WHO website also contains additional health information for travelers including detailed country-specific health information.

Medical Insurance: You can't assume your insurance will go with you when you travel. It's very important to find out if yours does BEFORE you leave. You need to ask your insurance company two questions:

- Does my policy apply when I'm out of the U.S.?
- Will it cover emergencies like a trip to a foreign hospital or an evacuation?

In many places, doctors and hospitals still expect payment in cash at the time of service. Your regular U.S. health insurance may not cover doctors' and hospital visits in other countries. If your policy doesn't go with you when you travel, it's a very good idea to take out another one for your trip.

Traffic Safety and Road Conditions: While in Mongolia, you may encounter road conditions that differ significantly from those in the United States. The information below concerning Mongolia is provided for general reference only and may not be totally accurate in a particular location or circumstance.

Driving in Ulaanbaatar can be extremely difficult due to poorly maintained streets, broken traffic lights, poor street lighting, a shortage of traffic signs, and undisciplined pedestrians. The knowledge and skills of the driving population have not kept pace with the dramatic growth in the number of automobiles on the streets in recent years. There are many metered taxis in Ulaanbaatar. There are a few car rental companies, but safety and maintenance standards are uncertain, so rental vehicles should be used with caution. Local tourist companies can provide cars with drivers. Public transportation within the capital is widespread, cheap, and generally reliable, but is also extremely crowded, so pickpocketing can occur. There are few paved roads outside of the capital and no street lights, and we recommend against driving outside of Ulaanbaatar after dark. For specific information concerning Mongolian drivers permits, vehicle inspection, road tax and mandatory insurance, contact the Embassy of Mongolia at 2833 M Street NW, Washington, DC 20007, telephone (202) 333-7117.

Aviation Safety Oversight: As there is no direct commercial air service to the United States by carriers registered in Mongolia, the U.S. Federal Aviation Administration (FAA) has not assessed the government of Mongolia's Civil Aviation Authority for compliance with International Civil Aviation Organization (ICAO) aviation safety standards. Further information may be found on the FAA's safety assessment page.

The U.S. Embassy prohibits U.S. government personnel from using Aero Mongolia (AM) for official travel because of uncertainties regarding service and maintenance schedules, aircraft certification, and insurance status. This prohibition does not extend to the domestic flights of other carriers.

Children's Issues: Please see the U.S. Dept. of State Office of Children's Issues web pages on intercountry adoption and international parental child abduction.

Intercountry Adoption

July 2010

The information in this section has been edited from the latest report available as of February 2013 from the State Department Bureau of Consular Affairs, Office of Overseas Citizens Services. For more information, please read the *Intercountry Adoption* section of this book and review current reports online at http://adoption.state.gov.

Who Can Adopt? Intercountry adoptions between the United States and Mongolia are governed by the Hague Adoption Convention. Therefore to adopt from Mongolia, you must first be found eligible to adopt by the U.S. Government. The U.S. Government agency responsible for making this determination is the U.S. Citizenship and Immigration Services (USCIS) an agency of the Department of Homeland Security's.

Residency Requirements: There are no residency requirements for prospective adoptive parents who apply through agencies authorized by the Mongolian Government.

Age Requirements: Prospective adoptive parents may be no more than 60 years of age.

Marriage Requirements: There are no marriage requirements for intercountry adoptions.

Income Requirements: A certification on the living and financial ability of the applicant by the relevant authority of a respective state

Other Requirements: Additional requirements include:

- A medical certification regarding whether adopter has tuberculoses, AIDS, or mental disease
- A certification regarding the place of permanent residence of the applicant by the relevant authority/ including the certification by a police authority
- Anyone who meets the criteria below is prohibited from adopting in Mongolia
- Individuals who have had their parental rights restricted, curtailed are prohibited from adopting in Mongolia
- Anyone who has returned an adopted child because his/her own fault
- Anyone who has been declared by a court decision as not having a full civil law capacity or has a restricted capacity
- Anyone who has tuberculoses or mental disease
- Anyone who habitually consumes alcoholic drinks or narcotic substances
- Anyone who has several criminal records or is currently imprisoned

Who Can be Adopted? Because Mongolia is party to the Hague Adoption Convention, children from Mongolia must meet the requirements of the Convention in order to be eligible for adoption by U.S. prospective adoptive parents. For example, the Convention requires that Mongolia attempt to place a child with a family in-country before determining that a child is eligible for inter-country adoption. In addition to Mongolia's requirements, a child must meet the definition of a Convention adoptee for you to bring him or her back to the United States.

Eligibility Requirements: The consent of parents to give their child for adoption must be in writing and certified by a notary public. A child whose parents have given up parents rights may be eligible for adoption after six months from the date when the relinquishment was recognized by the courts.

Additional Requirements: Children 7 years of age and older must consent to the adoption; Adoption must be deemed in the best interests of the child.

The Process: Because Mongolia is party to the Hague Adoption Convention, adopting from Mongolia must follow a specific process designed to meet the Convention's requirements. For detailed and updated information on these requirements, please review the *Intercountry Adoption* section of this publication and visit the U.S. Department of State Intercountry Adoption website at http://adoption.state.gov.

Role of the Adoption Authority: The MSWL reviews the home study and matches a child with the prospective adoptive parents.

Role of the Court: The Office of Immigration, naturalization and Foreign Citizens grants the final approval for the adoption.

Role of the Adoption Agencies: The adoption agency gathers documents from prospective parents and presents them to the MSWL. After a match has been made, the adoption agency then presents the documentation to the Office of Immigration, Naturalization and Foreign Citizens for final approval. This process normally takes approximately one month.

Time Frame: It is hard to predict how much time is required to complete an adoption in Mongolia. The time frames provided here are intended as guidelines only, and the specific circumstances of each case can significantly impact the length of the process.

As of March 2007, adoption procedures take approximately twelve to eighteen months from the time all of the necessary paperwork is submitted to MSWL to the time the MSWL delivers it for final approval to the Office of Immigration, Naturalization and Foreign Citizens.

Adoption Application: The adoption agency submits the adoption application to the MSWL.

Adoption Fees: In the adoption services contract that you sign at the beginning of the adoption process, your agency should itemize the fees and estimated expenses related to your adoption process. Fees will vary. There are no Mongolian government fees for adoption. Prospective adoptive parents can expect to pay notary fees and/or fees for translation of documents.

Documents Required: The following documents are required by the government of Mongolia:

- Cover letter
- Adoption application form
- Identification documents
- Passport copy-father, mother
- Drivers license copy– father, mother
- Marriage certificate copy
- Copy of highest diploma—father, mother
- Financial statement from Bank & Taxation office
- Medical documents
- Medical report—father, mother (received not later than 2 month before application)
- Medical analysis on HIV/AIDS

- Police clearance document
- I-800 approval notification
- Police clearance (received not later than 2 month before submission application)
- Court decision on permission to adopt (if any)
- Home study document
- Home study 6-8 pages (as much as possible specific)
- Home study Agency or Social worker License
- Legal and parent commitment document
- Letter from Adoption agency to the MSWL
- Copy of Accreditation from Central authority or State to work in Mongolia
- MOU with the Ministry of Social Welfare (if any)
- License of Adoption Agency (valid)
- Letter from Parents to the Agency Requesting Authorization to adopt
- Photos of family & home

Bringing Your Child Home: Once your adoption is complete (or you have obtained legal custody of the child), there are a few more steps to take before you can head home. Specifically, you need to apply for several documents for your child before he or she can travel to the United States, such as a birth certificate, a passport or travel document for your child from the country in which he or she was born, and a U.S. Immigration Visa. For detailed and updated information on how to obtain these documents, review the *Intercountry Adoption* section in this publication and visit the U.S. Department of State Intercountry Adoption website at http://adoption.state.gov.

Child Citizenship Act: For adoptions finalized abroad, the Child Citizenship Act of 2000 allows your new child to acquire American citizenship automatically when he or she enters the United States as lawful permanent residents. For adoptions finalized in the United States, the Child Citizenship Act of 2000 allows your new child to acquire American citizenship automatically when the court in the United States issues the final adoption decree. To learn more, review the Intercountry Adoption section in this publication and visit the U.S. Department of State Intercountry Adoption website at http://adoption.state.gov.

After Adoption: A report and information on the child's development (pictures, videos, etc.) made by the social worker appointed by the relevant authority shall be submitted:

- For children 1 month to 3 years old—once every half year;
- For children 4 to 8 years old—once every year;
- For children 8 to 16 years old—once every two years.

The adoption agency is responsible for translation of the reports into Mongolian and their delivery to the Immigration Agency. In necessary cases the Immigration Agency shall visit the adopted children at the expense of adopted parents and adoption agency in order to meet with the child and examine his/her conditions. According to Mongolian regulations, adoptive parents have a responsibility to introduce the child to Mongolian culture.

U.S. Embassy in Mongolia
11 Micro District
Big Ring Road, POB 1021
Ulaanbaatar-13, Mongolia
Email: cons@usembassy.mn
http://www.ulaanbaatar.usembassy.gov

Mongolia's Adoption Authority
Ministry of Social Welfare and Labor of Mongolia (MSWL)
United Nations Street 5
UB-46
Government Building No 2
Ministry of Social Welfare and Labor
Tel: 976-11-267635
Fax: 976-11-328634
sbaigalmaa@mswl.pmis.gov.mn
http://www.mswl.pmis.gov.mn

Embassy of Mongolia
2833 M Street, N.W.
Washington D.C. 20007
Email: esyam@mongolianembassy.us
http://www.mongolianembassy.us

Office of Children's Issues
U.S. Department of State
2201 C Street, NW
SA-29
Washington, DC 20520
Tel: 1-888-407-4747
E-mail: AskCI@state.gov
http://adoption.state.gov

MONTENEGRO

Compiled from publications that were available as of February 2013 from the U.S. Department of State, the U.S. Department of Commerce, and the Central Intelligence Agency (CIA). See the introduction to this set for explanatory notes.

Official Name:
Republic of Montenegro

PROFILE

Geography

Area: total: 13,812 sq km; country comparison to the world: 162; land: 13,452 sq km; water: 360 sq km

Major cities: Podgorica (capital) 144,000 (2009)

Climate: Mediterranean climate, hot dry summers and autumns and relatively cold winters with heavy snowfalls inland

Terrain: highly indented coastline with narrow coastal plain backed by rugged high limestone mountains and plateaus

People

Nationality: noun: Montenegrin(s); adjective: Montenegrin

Population: 657,394 (July 2012 est.)

Population growth rate: -0.633% (2012 est.)

Ethnic groups: Montenegrin 43%, Serbian 32%, Bosniak 8%, Albanian 5%, other (Muslims, Croats, Roma (Gypsy)) 12% (2003 census)

Religions: Orthodox 74.2%, Muslim 17.7%, Catholic 3.5%, other 0.6%, unspecified 3%, atheist 1% (2003 census)

Languages: Serbian 63.6%, Montenegrin (official) 22%, Bosnian 5.5%, Albanian 5.3%, unspecified (includes Croatian) 3.7% (2003 census)
Unemployment rate: 11.5% (2011 est.)
Work force: 251,300 (2011 est.)

Government

Type: republic
Independence: 3 June 2006
Constitution: approved 19 October 2007 (by the Assembly)
Political subdivisions: 21 municipalities (opstine, singular—opstina); Andrijevica, Bar, Berane, Bijelo Polje, Budva, Cetinje, Danilovgrad, Herceg Novi, Kolasin, Kotor, Mojkovac, Niksic, Plav, Pljevlja, Pluzine, Podgorica, Rozaje, Savnik, Tivat, Ulcinj, Zabljak
Suffrage: 18 years of age; universal

Economy

GDP (purchasing power parity): $7.288 billion (2012 est.); $7.249 billion (2011 est.); $7.075 billion (2010 est.); $6.903 billion (2009 est.)
GDP real growth rate: 0.2% (2012 est.); 2.5% (2011 est.); 2.5% (2010 est.); -5.7% (2009 est.)
GDP per capita (PPP): $11,700 (2012 est.); $11,700 (2011 est.); $11,000 (2010 est.); $10,700 (2009 est.)
Natural resources: bauxite, hydroelectricity
Agriculture products: tobacco, potatoes, citrus fruits, olives, grapes; sheep
Industries: steelmaking, aluminum, agricultural processing, consumer goods, tourism
Exports: $640 million (2011 est.); $171.3 million
Exports—commodities:
Exports—partners: Serbia 17.5%, Hungary 16.9%, Croatia 10.1% (2011 est.)
Imports: $2.5 billion (2011 est.); $601.7 million
Imports—commodities:
Imports—partners: Serbia 28.4%, Greece 7.9%, Bosnia and Herzegovina 7.6% (2011 est.)
Debt—external: $1.2 billion (2011 est.); $650 million
Exchange rates: euros (EUR) per US dollar; 0.7838 (2012 est.); 0.7194 (2011 est.); 0.755 (2010 est.); 0.7198 (2009 est.); 0.6827 (2008 est.); 0.7345 (2007 est.)

PEOPLE

National/Racial/Ethnic Minorities

The constitution and law on minority rights provide both individual and collective rights for minorities, and these provisions were generally observed for most groups, but Roma,

Ashkali, and Egyptians were disadvantaged in access to social services and continued to experience societal discrimination.

According to 2011 census, Roma, Ashkali, and Egyptians constituted approximately 1 percent of the population. According to 2009 UN data, approximately 40 percent of them lacked birth or citizenship certificates. Many, including IDPs from Kosovo, lived illegally in squatter settlements, often widely scattered, and lacked such basic services as public utilities, medical care, and sewage disposal. The 2008 Law on Citizenship and its accompanying regulations made obtaining citizenship very difficult for persons without personal identity documents (see section 2 d.). According to the UNDP, approximately 70 percent of Roma were illiterate, 50 percent were unemployed, and 36 percent lived below the poverty level.

Societal prejudice against Roma, Ashkali, and Egyptians was widespread, and local authorities often ignored or tacitly condoned it. Members of these minorities lacked political representation and generally stayed out of politics. They occasionally lacked access to advanced medical professionals, such as surgeons and other specialists, that was available to other residents. According to a study carried out by three NGOs, the Monitoring Center, Juventas, and Cazas, the greatest barriers facing Roma, Ashkali, and Egyptians in the labor sector were inability to speak the national language, lack of education, and employer discrimination.

Religion

According to the census conducted during the year by the National Statistics Office (NSO), approximately 72 percent of the population identified themselves as Orthodox (either Serbian or Montenegrin), 16 percent as Islamic, 3 percent as Muslim, and 3.4 percent as Roman Catholic. The NSO created separate categories for Muslims and followers of Islam without an official explanation. The remaining 5.4 percent is composed of members from other groups including Seventh-day Adventists, Buddhists, Protestants, Jehovah's Witnesses, Jews, and those who did not declare a religion. The Serbian Orthodox Church (SPC) had by far the largest membership, headed by Metropolitan Amfilohije in Cetinje.

HISTORY

The origins of the Montenegrin state can be traced to the emergence of Duklja, a vassal state of Byzantium, in the 9th century. In 1042, King Vojislav won a decisive battle against Byzantium, and Duklja became independent. About 120 years later, Duklja (by then known as Zeta) was conquered by Raska (Serbia). The use of the name Montenegro began in the 15th century when the Crnojevi dynasty began to rule the principality of Zeta. Over the subsequent centuries, Montenegro, while a part of the Ottoman Empire, maintained a level of autonomy. From the 16th to 19th centuries Montenegro was a theocracy ruled by a series of bishop princes, who were at first selected by popular assembly but later through heredity. In 1852, it was transformed into a secular principality when Danilo Petrovic Njegos set aside the ecclesiastical title and assumed the title of prince. Montenegro was recognized as an independent, sovereign principality by the great powers of Europe assembled at the Congress of Berlin in July 1878.

During World War I, Montenegro fought on the side of the Allies but was defeated and occupied by Austria. Upon Austrian occupation, King Nikola I and his government went into exile. In late 1918, an Assembly met in Podgorica, and under the eyes of the Serbian army, deposed King Nikola and declared unification with Serbia. The government of Montenegro in exile denounced the Assembly's action, to no avail. From 1919 to 1941, Montenegro was part of what became known as the Kingdom of Yugoslavia despite armed resistance in the early 1920s to rule from Belgrade.

When Yugoslavia was invaded and partitioned by the Axis powers in April 1941, Montenegro was occupied by Italy and ran under a nominally autonomous administration. While some Montenegrins sided with Italy, motivated by antipathy against past rule from Belgrade, the Partisan Revolt in Montenegro began early, on July 13, 1941, and initially scored impressive successes against the Italian occupiers. Throughout World War II, Montenegro served as an effective base and refuge for Josip Broz Tito's partisans. After the war, Montenegro was granted the status of a republic within the Socialist Federal Republic of Yugoslavia.

The breakup of the Yugoslav federation after 1989 left Montenegro in a precarious position. During 1991 and 1992, Slovenia, Croatia, Bosnia and Herzegovina, and Macedonia all seceded from Yugoslavia. In April 1992, Serbia and Montenegro jointly approved the Constitution of the Federal Republic of Yugoslavia (F.R.Y.), and supported Yugoslav President Slobodan Milosevic's military campaigns in the early to mid-1990s. Despite Montenegro's political attachment to Serbia, Montenegro maintained a sense of national identity. The government of Montenegro was critical of Milosevic's 1998–99 campaign in Kosovo, and the ruling coalition parties boycotted the September 2000 federal elections, which led to the eventual removal of Milosevic's regime.

In March 2002, the Belgrade Agreement was signed by the heads of the federal and republican governments, establishing the parameters for a redefinition of Montenegro's relationship with Serbia within a joint state. In February 2003, the F.R.Y. parliament ratified the Constitutional Charter, establishing a new state union and changing the name of the country from Yugoslavia to Serbia and Montenegro. On May 21, 2006, the Republic of Montenegro held a successful referendum on independence and formally declared independence on June 3, 2006.

GOVERNMENT AND POLITICAL CONDITIONS

Montenegro is a mixed parliamentary and presidential republic. Both the president and the unicameral parliament (the Assembly) are popularly elected. The president nominates, and the Assembly approves, the prime minister.

According to international observers, Assembly elections held in 2009 met international standards but underscored the need for further democratic development.

Recent Elections

According to the OSCE election observation mission, the 2009 Assembly elections met almost all OSCE and Council of Europe commitments. Nonetheless the mission's statement noted frequent allegations of electoral fraud and a blurring of state and party structures that created a negative atmosphere among many voters. As in previous elections, most opposition parties raised concerns regarding campaign and party financing and the overlap of state and political party structures. Allegations of pressure on voters and the purchase of voter identification documents were again reported by some opposition parties, the media, and certain individuals.

On September 8, 2011, legislation went into effect that brought electoral procedures into line with the 2007 constitution, one of the EU's seven key requirements for initiating negotiations for EU membership. The new law limits the suffrage to citizens, and would deprive permanent residents of this right beginning on January 31, 2012. However, amendments to legislation on citizenship, which entitled permanent residents to apply for citizenship, provided they did so by January 31, 2012, also preserved their eligibility to vote until that date. The number of persons affected was unknown, but the opposition Socialists People's Party claimed that it could be approximately 40,000.

Participation of Women and Minorities: Women remained underrepresented in higher levels of government. The president of the Supreme Court and the chief state prosecutor were women. Nine women served in the 81-seat Assembly and one in the cabinet. There were no women in four out of nine standing Assembly committees. One of the country's 21 municipalities had a female mayor. One of 10 Assembly parties had a female leader. The election law that took effect on September did not establish any quotas for women in Assembly, but instead mandated that at least 30 percent of the candidates on each party list be women.

There were 20 members of ethnic minorities in the Assembly and three in the 17-member cabinet. Almost all minority groups except Roma, Ashkali, and Egyptians were represented in the Assembly. In connection with the with the new election law, the Assembly abolished the five seats set aside for ethnic Albanians, effective with the next Assembly elections. The right of affirmative action, which sets forth the right of representation in the Assembly for ethnic minority groups that win fewer than 3 percent of the votes or constituted less than 15 percent of the population, was extended to all minority groups.

Principal Government Officials

Last Updated: 1/31/2013

Pres.: **Filip VUJANOVIC**
Prime Min.: **Milo DJUKANOVIC**
Dep. Prime Min.: **Rafet HUSOVIC**
Dep. Prime Min.: **Vujica LAZOVIC**
Dep. Prime Min.: **Igor LUKSIC**
Dep. Prime Min.: **Dusko MARKOVIC**
Min. of Agriculture: **Petar IVANOVIC**
Min. of Culture: **Branislav MICUNOVIC**
Min. of Defense: **Milica PEJANOVIC-DJURISIC**
Min. of Economy: **Vladimir KAVARIC**
Min. of Education & Sports: **Slavoljub STIJEPOVIC**
Min. of Finance: **Radoje ZUGIC**
Min. of Foreign Affairs & European Integration: **Igor LUKSIC**
Min. of Health: **Miodrag RADUNOVIC**
Min. of Human & Minority Rights: **Suad NUMANOVIC**
Min. of Information Society & Telecommunications: **Vujica LAZOVIC**
Min. of the Interior: **Rasko KONJEVIC**
Min. of Justice: **Dusko MARKOVIC**
Min. of Labor & Social Welfare: **Predrag BOSKOVIC**
Min. of Science: **Sanja VLAHOVIC**
Min. of Tourism & Sustainable Development: **Branimir GVOZDENOVIC**
Min. of Transport & Maritime Affairs: **Ivan BRAJOVIC**
Min. Without Portfolio: **Marjia VUCINOVIC**
Ambassador to the US: **Srdan DARMANOVIC**
Permanent Representative to the UN, New York: **Milorad SCEPANOVIC**

ECONOMY

Montenegro's economy is transitioning to a market system, but the state sector remains large and additional institutional changes are needed. The economy relies heavily on tourism and the export of refined metals. Unprofitable state-owned enterprises weigh on public finances. Montenegro severed its economy from federal control and from Serbia during the Milosevic era and maintained its own central bank, adopted the deutsch mark, then the euro—rather than the Yugoslav dinar—as official currency, collected customs tariffs, and managed its own budget.

The dissolution of the loose political union between Serbia and Montenegro in 2006 led to separate membership in several international financial institutions, such as the European Bank for Reconstruction and Development. In January 2007, Montenegro joined the World Bank and IMF. Montenegro became the 156th member of World Trade Organization in December 2011. The European Council (EC) granted candidate country status to Montenegro at the December 2010 session.

Montenegro began negotiations to join the EC in June, 2012, having met the conditions set down by the European Council, which called on Montenegro to take steps to fight corruption and organized crime. Unemployment and regional disparities in development are key political and economic problems. Montenegro has privatized its large aluminum complex - the dominant industry - as well as most of its financial sector, and has begun to attract foreign direct investment in the tourism sector.

The global financial crisis had a significant negative impact on the economy, due to the ongoing credit crunch, a decline in the real estate sector, and a fall in aluminum exports. In 2012, real GDP growth slipped to 0.2%, reflecting the general downturn in most of Europe.

Labor Conditions

There are laws and policies to protect children from exploitation in the workplace, and the government generally enforced these laws and regulations effectively in the formal economy. While the official minimum age for employment is 15, it was common in farming communities to find younger children assisting their families. Children under 18 may not work in jobs that involve particularly difficult physical work, overtime and night work, or underground or underwater work or in jobs that "may have a harmful effect or involve increased risk for their health and lives." The law specifies monetary penalties for violation of these provisions, with fines ranging from 10 to 300 times the minimum wage.

Romani children worked in a variety of unofficial retail jobs, typically washing car windows, collecting items such as scrap metal, or selling old newspapers.

According to the National Statistics Office, in May the average monthly wage, without taxes and contributions, was 479 euros ($ 623), a decrease of 1.6 percent from 2010. The national minimum wage in May was 143.7 euros ($187) per month. The government statistics office estimated that approximately 6.8 percent of the population lived below the absolute poverty line, set at 170 euros ($221) per person per month in 2010, compared with 4.9 percent in 2008. Significant portions of the workforce, particularly in rural areas and the informal sector, earned less than the minimum wage.

The law establishes a 40-hour workweek (except in specified unusual circumstances) and requires an unspecified premium for work in excess of 40 hours. It prescribes a 30-minute daily rest period. Overtime is limited by the Labor Law to 10 hours per week, but seasonal workers often worked much longer. Many workers, particularly in commerce, were deprived of their rights to weekly and annual leave but often did not report the violations of their rights for fear of repercussions.

The use of "temporary" workers was a major issue between trade unions and employers, since employers had considerable leverage over the terms of employment of temporary workers, particularly women, older workers, and those with disabilities. Amendments to the Labor Law adopted on November 24, restricted "temporary" employment to two years. The Ministry of Labor and Social Welfare and the Union of Free Trade Unions of Montenegro had various interpretations about the date when the amendments were to enter into force.

The government establishes health and safety regulations in the workplace. It requires employers to supply and enforce the use of safety equipment and to report any serious workplace deaths or injuries within 24 hours. Authorities did not strictly enforce the requirements, and both employers and workers violated health and safety rules, particularly in the construction industry. The machinery and tools used at construction sites were often not maintained properly, which increased the risk of injuries. The Ministry of Labor and its inspection department lacked adequate resources to enforce workplace safety.

U.S.-MONTENEGRO RELATIONS

The United States established diplomatic relations with Montenegro in 1905 following its 1878 independence from the Ottoman Empire. After World War I, Montenegro was subsumed into the Kingdom of Serbs, Croats, and Slovenes, and U.S.-Montenegro diplomatic relations ended in 1920. The United States reestablished diplomatic relations with Montenegro in 2006 following the dissolution of the state union of Serbia and Montenegro.

The relationship between the United States and Montenegro has promoted peace and prosperity in the region and around the world. U.S. policy toward Montenegro is structured to help the country transition to a prosperous, market-based democracy, fully integrated into Euro-Atlantic institutions including the North Atlantic Treaty Organization (NATO) and the European Union. The country is a participant in NATO's Partnership for Peace program. The European Union opened accession negotiations with Montenegro in June 2012. Montenegro has demonstrated its commitment to international peacekeeping efforts, including in Afghanistan where it has contributed troops to the International Security Assistance Force.

U.S. Assistance to Montenegro

U.S. Government assistance to Montenegro aims to help the country advance toward Euro-Atlantic integration, increase its ability to fight organized crime and corruption, strengthen its civil society and democratic structures, and provide stability in the Balkans. A fact sheet on U.S. assistance to Montenegro can be found here.

Bilateral Economic Relations

A number of U.S. companies are operating in Montenegro, and the Government of Montenegro has put an emphasis on attracting more U.S. investment. The Montenegrin government counts the following as incentives for U.S. investors to do business in Montenegro: a business-oriented economic system, a high level of economic freedom, a stable currency (Euro), macroeconomic predictability, and protected ownership rights. Montenegro has been designated as a beneficiary developing country under the Generalized System of Preferences program, which provides duty-free access to the U.S. market in various eligible categories.

Montenegro's Membership in International Organizations

Montenegro and the United States belong to a number of the same international organizations, including the United Nations, NATO's Euro-Atlantic Partnership Council, Organization for Security and Cooperation in Europe, International Monetary Fund, World Bank, and the World Trade Organization. Montenegro also is a participant in the North Atlantic Treaty Organization's (NATO) Partnership for Peace program.

Bilateral Representation

Montenegro maintains an embassy in the United States 1610 New Hampshire Avenue, NW, Washington, DC 20009; tel. 202-234-6108.

Principal U.S. Embassy Officials

Last Updated: 1/14/2013

PODGORICA (E) Dzona Dzeksona 2, 81000 Podgorica, Montenegro, +382-20-410-500, Fax +382-20-241-358, Workweek: Monday to Friday (0830-1700), Website: http://podgorica.usembassy.gov/

AMB OMS:	Terry Lindsey
DHS/ICE:	James Plitt
ECON/COM:	Marko Cimbaljevic
ICITAP:	Jeffrey Palmer
MGT:	Adham Loutfi
OPDAT:	J. Matthew Bressler
POL/ECON:	John Cooney
POL/MIL:	Andreja Popov

POSHO:	Maja Simovic
SDO/DATT:	LTC Bruce Murphy
AMB:	Sue K. Brown
CON:	Maria Lane Gomez
DCM:	Douglas D. Jones
PAO:	Shelly A. Seaver
GSO:	Paul G. Rey
RSO:	Timothy Kerwin
AFSA:	Shelly Seaver
CLO:	Enrique Gomez Aceff
EEO:	Maria Lane Gomez
ICASS Chair:	Shelly Seaver
IMO:	Domenic Meyer
ISO:	Domenic Meyer
ISSO:	Domenic Meyer

TRAVEL

Consular Information Sheet

August 1, 2012

Country Description: Montenegro is a small country in the Western Balkans that has experienced significant political and economic changes over the past two decades. There are many tourist facilities in Montenegro, but they vary in quality and some may not be up to Western standards.

Smart Traveler Enrollment Program (STEP)/Embassy Locations: If you are going to live in or visit Montenegro, please take the time to inform our Embassy about your trip. Registering with the Smart Traveler Enrollment Program will keep you up to date with important safety and security announcements. It will also help your friends and family get in touch with you in an emergency.

U.S. Embassy Podgorica
Dzona Dzeksona 2
81000 Podgorica
Telephone: 382 20 410 500
Email: PodgoricaACS@state.gov

Entry/Exit Requirements for U.S. Citizens: U.S. citizens with tourist, official, or diplomatic passports do not need a visa to enter and stay in Montenegro for up to 90 days. However, you must register within the first 24 hours of your stay. If you are staying in a hotel or tourist facility, the hotel will automatically register you; otherwise you are personally responsible to appear at the police station to do so. If you do not, you may be subject to a fine, incarceration, and/or expulsion. Visitors who fail to register sometimes face difficulties in departing the country.

U.S. citizens wishing to extend their stay longer than 90 days must apply for a temporary residence permit no later than one week before the 90-day period expires. Given the length of time needed for administrative procedures, we advise you to apply as soon as you learn that you will be staying in Montenegro longer than 90 days. This rule applies to bearers of all types of U.S. passports—tourist, official, or diplomatic. You can contact the Embassy of Montenegro in Washington, DC for the most current visa information.

The Embassy of Montenegro is located at 1610 New Hampshire Avenue NW, Washington, D.C. 20009; telephone (202) 234-6108; fax: (202) 234-6109; usa@mfa.gov.me. The Consulate General of Montenegro in New York is located at 801 2nd Avenue, New York, NY 10017; telephone (212) 661-5400; fax: (212) 661-5466; office@montenegroconsulatenewyork.info. Montenegro's Ministry of Foreign Affairs website contains additional contact information for its diplomatic posts in the United States.

For passenger vehicles entering Montengro, the entry tax ranges in price from 10 Euros to 50 Euros depending on the size of the vehicle. Travelers are required to declare currency exceeding 2,000 Euros upon entry. At the port of entry, travelers can ask customs officials for a currency declaration form that must be completed and presented at departure. Failure to comply with these policies may result in confiscation of funds and criminal proceedings.

The U.S. Department of State is unaware of any HIV/AIDS entry restrictions for visitors to or foreign residents of Montenegro.

Threats to Safety and Security: Demonstrations related to political activities, labor conditions, or sporting events are usually peaceful, though some have exhibited low levels of violence. Montenegrin nightclubs and tourist centers are popular with foreign tourists; patrons should be aware that these establishments can be crowded and may not comply with Western standards for occupancy control and fire safety.

Stay up to date by:

- Bookmarking our Bureau of Consular Affairs website, which contains the current Travel Warnings and Travel Alerts as well as the Worldwide Caution.
- Following us on Twitter and the Bureau of Consular Affairs page on Facebook as well.
- Downloading our free Smart Traveler iPhone App to have travel information at your fingertips.
- Calling 1-888-407-4747 toll-free within the U.S. and Canada, or a regular toll line, 1-202-501-4444, from other countries.
- Taking some time before travel to consider your personal security.

Crime: Street crime in Podgorica is at a level to be expected for a small European city of less than 200,000 people. Residential break-ins present the greatest security concern for U.S. citizens in Montenegro; however, the frequency of these crimes is still relatively low. Violent crime is infrequent. Police have a limited ability to provide services in English.

Cases of credit card fraud and theft at ATMs are minimal in the winter months, but there is a significant increase in theft at ATMs during the tourist season between May and September. Visitors should ensure that they protect their PINs at all times when using ATMs, and monitor card activity.

Don't buy counterfeit and pirated goods, even if they are widely available. Not only are the bootlegs illegal to bring into the United States, if you purchase them you may also be breaking local law.

Victims of Crime: If you or someone you know becomes the victim of a crime abroad, you should contact the local police and the nearest U.S. embassy or consulate. We can:

- Replace a stolen passport.
- Help you find appropriate medical care if you are the victim of violent crimes such as assault or rape.
- Put you in contact with the appropriate police authorities, and if you want us to, we can contact family members or friend.
- Help you understand the local criminal justice process and direct you to local attorneys, although it is important to remember that local authorities are responsible for investigating and prosecuting the crime.

The local equivalents to the "911" emergency line in Montenegro are 122 for police, 123 for the fire department, and 124 for an ambulance.

Criminal Penalties: While you are traveling in Montenegro, you are subject to its laws even if you are a U.S. citizen. Foreign laws and legal systems can be vastly different than our own. In Montenegro, you may be taken in for questioning if you don't have your passport with you. In some places, it is illegal to take pictures of certain buildings. Likewise, driving under the influence could land you immediately in jail. There are also some things that might be legal in Montenegro, but still illegal in the United States, and you can be prosecuted under U.S. law if you buy pirated goods. Engaging in sexual conduct with children or using or disseminating child pornography in a foreign country is a crime prosecutable in the United States. If you break local laws in Montenegro, your U.S. passport won't help you avoid arrest or prosecution. It's very important to know what's legal and what's not wherever you go.

Persons violating Montenegrin laws, even unknowingly, may be expelled, arrested, or imprisoned. Penalties for possessing, using, or trafficking in illegal drugs in Montenegro are severe, and convicted offenders can expect long jail sentences and heavy fines.

While some countries will automatically notify the nearest U.S. embassy or consulate if a U.S. citizen is detained or arrested in a foreign country, that might not always be the case. To ensure that the United States is aware of your circumstances, request that the police and prison officials notify the nearest U.S. embassy or consulate as soon as you are arrested or detained overseas.

Special Circumstances: Dual U.S./Montenegrin nationals may be subject to laws that impose special obligations on Montenegrin citizens. If you were considered a dual citizen of Montenegro and another country before Montenegro declared its independence on June 3, 2006, Montenegro still recognizes that dual citizenship. If you became a dual citizen after June 3, 2006, Montenegro will only recognize your dual citizenship if it is with a country with which Montenegro has signed a bilateral agreement. Currently, Montenegro has signed a bilateral citizenship agreement only with Macedonia, but it still abides by the bilateral consular agreement between Yugoslavia and the United States. As of August 30, 2006, Montenegrin men are no longer required by Montenegrin law to perform military service.

There are occasional water and electricity outages throughout the year.

Accessibility: While in Montenegro, individuals with disabilities may find accessibility and accommodation very different from what you find in the United States. While Montenegro passed a law on spatial planning and construction in August 2008 regulating the accessibility to public facilities, it only applies to future services and construction. Some structures built recently do meet those standards. The law mandates that until August 2013, all public facilities must be adjusted to allow access to persons with disabilities. The country has all normative regulations for protection of persons with disabilities, including access to transportation and communication. It also has a general anti-discrimination law. However, these regulations have not been adequately implemented in practice and everyday life. Accessibility for those with disabilities, including on public transportation, is lacking throughout the country.

Medical Facilities and Health Information: Although many physicians in Montenegro are highly trained, hospitals and clinics are generally not equipped or maintained to Western standards. Travelers may need to go to privately owned pharmacies in order to obtain medicines and basic medical supplies. Hospitals and private clinics usually require payment in cash for all services. Montenegro has only a small number of ambulances. As a consequence, emergency services are generally responsive in only the most severe cases. Otherwise, people must have their own transportation to hospitals and clinics.

You can find detailed information on vaccinations and other health precautions on the CDC website. For information about outbreaks of infectious diseases abroad, consult the World Health Organization (WHO) website. The WHO website also contains additional health information for travelers, including detailed country-specific health information.

Medical Insurance: You cannot assume your insurance will go with you when you travel. It is very important to find out BEFORE you leave whether or not your medical insurance will cover you overseas. You need to ask your insurance company two questions:

- Does my policy apply when I am out of the United States?
- Will it cover emergencies like a trip to a foreign hospital or a medical evacuation?

In many places, doctors and hospitals still expect payment in cash at the time of service. Your regular U.S. health insurance may not cover doctor and hospital visits in other countries. If your policy does not go with you when you travel, it is a very good idea to take out another one for your trip.

Traffic Safety and Road Conditions: While in Montenegro, you may encounter road conditions that differ significantly from those in the United States. Roads in Montenegro are often poorly maintained, especially in rural areas. Dangerous areas for road travel include a road through the Moraca Canyon, north of Podgorica. This twisting, two-lane road is especially overcrowded in the summer, and is the site of frequent rockslides. In the winter, the Moraca Canyon and northern parts of Montenegro are covered with snow, which may slow traffic and make the road hazardous. Roads leading to Montenegro's coastal areas are in better condition, but are overcrowded during summer season. Drivers should exercise extreme caution, as it is common for Montenegrin drivers to attempt to pass on winding roads and hills. Local drivers can be reckless and aggressive, and accidents are frequent.

The use of seat belts is mandatory and cell-phone usage while driving is prohibited. Traffic law requires that vehicle lights must be switched on at all times while driving. Police in Montenegro will test a driver's blood alcohol level on site and arrest any driver if the concentration of alcohol in the blood is more than.05%, a very strict standard. Roadside assistance is available by dialing 19807, 382 (0)20 234 467 or 382 (0)20 234 999. Other emergency numbers are police: 122; fire department: 123; and ambulance: 124.

Metered taxi service is safe and reasonably priced, although foreigners are sometimes charged higher rates. Although there are some taxi stands in each of the cities, taxis generally do not pick up passengers on the street and must be ordered by phone or SMS. We recommend negotiating a price prior to traveling by taxi between cities.

Travelers in the region may wish to consider the safety of public transportation, including trains, buses, and ferries, in view of aging and poorly maintained equipment.

Aviation Safety Oversight: When the FAA last assessed the former country of Serbia and Montenegro, the Government of Serbia and Montenegro's Civil Aviation Authority was not in compliance with International Civil Aviation Organization (ICAO) aviation safety standards for the oversight of Serbia and Montenegro's air carrier operations and the country was given a Category 2 rating. Although the independent country of Montenegro has not been assessed, Montenegro will continue to be rated Category 2, based on the earlier assessment, until the FAA verifies that the Government of Montenegro is in compliance with ICAO aviation safety oversight standards. Further information may be found on the FAA's safety assessment page.

Children's Issues: Please see the U.S. Dept. of State Office of Children's Issues web pages on intercountry adoption and international parental child abduction.

Intercountry Adoption

July 2012

On July 1, 2012, the Hague Convention on Protection of Children and Co-Operation in Respect of Intercountry Adoption entered into force for Montenegro. However, Montenegro does not yet have a fully functional Convention process in place. Therefore, the United States has determined that it will not be able to process Convention intercountry adoptions until the Government of Montenegro implements an effective Convention intercountry adoption process.

We caution adoption service providers and prospective adoptive parents that, to ensure that adoptions from Montenegro will be compliant with the Convention, important steps must take place before intercountry adoptions between the United States and Montenegro resume. Adoption service providers should neither initiate nor claim to initiate adoption programs in Montenegro until the Department of State notifies them that it has resumed adoptions in Montenegro.

The Department of State will provide updated information on adoption.state.gov as it becomes available. If you have any questions about this notice, please contact the office of Children's Issues at 1-888-407-4747 within the United States, or 202-501-4444 from outside the United States. Email inquiries may be directed to AdoptionUSCA@state.gov.

Montenegro's Adoption Authority

Ministry of Labor and Social Welfare
Department of Social Welfare and Child Protection
Mr. Remzija Ademovi
Acting Deputy Minister
Address: Rimski trg 46
81000 Podgoica
Montenegro
Tel: +382 (0)20 482 447; 234 254
Email:
remzija.ademovic@mrs.gov.me
Fax: +382 (0) 20 234 256

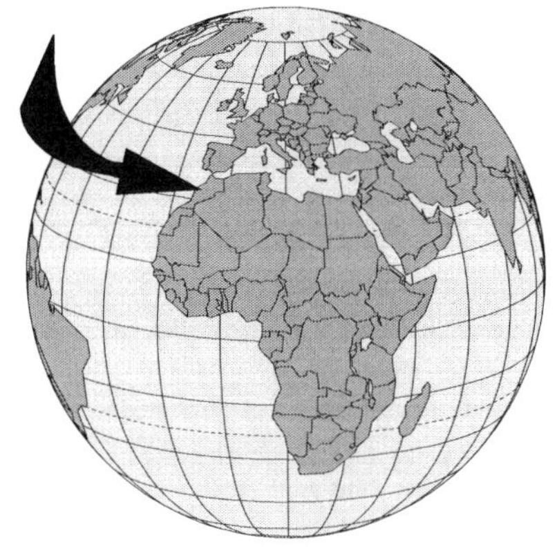

MOROCCO

Compiled from publications that were available as of February 2013 from the U.S. Department of State, the U.S. Department of Commerce, and the Central Intelligence Agency (CIA). See the introduction to this set for explanatory notes.

Official Name:
Kingdom of Morocco

PROFILE

Geography

Area: total: 446,550 sq km; country comparison to the world: 58; land: 446,300 sq km; water: 250 sq km

Major cities: Casablanca 3.245 million; Rabat (capital) 1.77 million; Fes 1.044 million; Marrakech 909,000; Tangier 768,000 (2009)

Climate: Mediterranean, becoming more extreme in the interior

Terrain: northern coast and interior are mountainous with large areas of bordering plateaus, intermontane valleys, and rich coastal plains

People

Nationality: noun: Moroccan(s); adjective: Moroccan

Population: 32,309,239 (July 2012 est.)

Population growth rate: 1.054% (2012 est.)

Ethnic groups: Arab-Berber 99%, other 1%

Religions: Muslim 99% (official), Christian 1%, Jewish about 6,000

Languages: Arabic (official), Berber languages (Tamazight (official), Tachelhit, Tarifit), French (often the language of business, government, and diplomacy)

Literacy: definition: age 15 and over can read and write; total population: 56.1%; male: 68.9%; female: 43.9% (2009 est.)

Health: life expectancy at birth: total population: 76.11 years; male: 73.04 years; female: 79.32 years (2012 est.); Infant mortality rate: total: 26.49 deaths/1,000 live births; male: 31.16 deaths/1,000 live births; female: 21.59 deaths/1,000 live births (2012 est.)

Unemployment rate: 8.8% (2012 est.)

Work force: 11.78 million (2012 est.)

Government

Type: constitutional monarchy

Independence: 2 March 1956

Constitution: 10 March 1972; revised 4 September 1992, amended September 1996; constitutional reforms weakening the King's power approved in referendum 1 July 2011

Political subdivisions: 15 regions; Grand Casablanca, Chaouia-Ouardigha, Doukkala-Abda, Fes-Boulemane, Gharb-Chrarda-Beni Hssen, Guelmim-Es Smara, Laayoune-Boujdour-Sakia El Hamra, Marrakech-Tensift-Al Haouz, Meknes-Tafilalet, Oriental, Rabat-Sale-Zemmour-Zaer, Souss-Massa-Draa, Tadla-Azilal, Tanger-Tetouan, Taza-Al Hoceima-Taounate

Suffrage: 18 years of age; universal

Economy

GDP (purchasing power parity): $171 billion (2012 est.); $164.7 billion (2011 est.); $157.9 billion (2010 est.); $152.3 billion (2009 est.)

GDP real growth rate: 2.9% (2012 est.); 4.3% (2011 est.); 3.7% (2010 est.); 4.9% (2009 est.)

GDP per capita (PPP): $5,300 (2012 est.); $5,100 (2011 est.); $5,000 (2010 est.); $4,800 (2009 est.)

Natural resources: phosphates, iron ore, manganese, lead, zinc, fish, salt

Agriculture products: barley, wheat, citrus fruits, grapes, vegetables, olives; livestock; wine

Industries: phosphate rock mining and processing, food processing, leather goods, textiles, construction, energy, tourism

Exports: $22.23 billion (2012 est.); $20.99 billion (2011 est.); $17.58 billion (2010 est.)

Exports—commodities: clothing and textiles, electric components, inorganic chemicals, transistors, crude minerals, fertilizers (including phosphates), petroleum products, citrus fruits, vegetables, fish

Exports—partners: Spain 18.6%, France 16.9%, Brazil 6%, US 4.8%, India 4.5% (2011)

Imports: $42.49 billion (2012 est.); $40.39 billion (2011 est.); $32.65 billion (2010 est.)

Imports—commodities: crude petroleum, textile fabric, telecommunications equipment, wheat, gas and electricity, transistors, plastics
Imports—partners: France 15.4%, Spain 14.4%, China 7.7%, US 7.3%, Saudi Arabia 6.1%, Italy 5.1%, Germany 4.8% (2011)
Debt—external: $29.42 billion (31 December 2012 est.); $28.08 billion (31 December 2011 est.); $26.58 billion (31 December 2010 est.)
Exchange rates: Moroccan dirhams (MAD) per US dollar; 8.689 (2012 est.); 8.0899 (2011 est.); 8.4172 (2010 est.); 8.0571 (2009); 7.526 (2008); 8.3563 (2007)

PEOPLE

Moroccans are predominantly of Arab, Berber, or mixed Arab-Berber ancestry. The Arabs brought Islam, along with Arabic language and culture, to the region from the Arabian Peninsula during the Muslim conquests of the 7th century.

Most people live west of the Atlas Mountains, a range that insulates the country from the Sahara Desert. Casablanca is the center of commerce and industry and the leading port; Rabat is the seat of government; Tangier is the gateway to Spain and also a major port; "Arab" Fes is the cultural and religious center; and "Berber" Marrakech is a major tourist center.

National/Racial/Ethnic Minorities

Approximately 60 percent of the population, including the royal family, claimed some Amazigh heritage. Amazigh cultural groups contended that their traditions and language were being lost rapidly to Arabization. The government increasingly provided television programs in the three Amazigh dialects of Tarifit, Tashelhit, and Tamazight. The government also offered Amazigh language classes in the curriculum of 3,470 schools. Expanding Amazigh language education was hindered primarily by a lack of qualified teachers, which the palace-funded Royal Institute of Amazigh Culture was addressing through the creation of university-level teacher training. Instruction in learning the Amazigh language is mandatory for students at the Ministry of Interior School for Administrators in Kenitra.

Language

Arabic is Morocco's official language, but French is widely taught and serves as the primary language of commerce and government. Moroccan colloquial Arabic, Darija, is composed of a unique combination of Arabic, Berber, and French dialects. Along with Arabic, about 10 million Moroccans, predominantly in rural areas, also speak one of the three Moroccan Berber dialects (Tarifit, Tashelhit, and Tamazight). Spanish is also used in the northern part of the country. English is increasingly becoming the foreign language of choice among educated youth and is offered in many public schools from the fourth year on.

Education

Education in Morocco is free and compulsory through primary school (age 15). Nevertheless, many children—particularly girls in rural areas—do not attend school, and most of those who do drop out after elementary school. The country's literacy rate reveals sharp gaps in education, both in terms of gender and location; while country-wide literacy rates are estimated at 39.6% among women and 65.7% among men, the female literacy rate in rural areas is estimated only at 10%.

Morocco is home to 14 public universities. Mohammed V University in Rabat is one of the country's most famous schools, with faculties of law, sciences, liberal arts, and medicine. Founded over 1,000 years ago, Karaouine University, in Fes, is the oldest center for Islamic studies in the Maghreb. Morocco's most prestigious private English-language university, Al-Akhawayn, was founded in 1993 by King Hassan II and King Fahd of Saudi Arabia in Ifrane. Its curriculum is based on an American model.

Religion

The country's population is 98.7 percent Muslim, 1.1 percent Christian, and 0.2 percent Jewish. According to Jewish community leaders, there are an estimated 3,000 to 4,000 Jews, approximately 2,500 of whom reside in Casablanca and are the remnants of a much larger community that has mostly emigrated. The most recent estimates put the size of the Rabat and Marrakesh Jewish communities at about 100 members each. The remainder of the Jewish population is dispersed throughout the country. This population is mostly elderly, with a decreasing number of young persons.

The predominantly Roman Catholic and Protestant foreign-resident Christian community consists of approximately 5,000 practicing members, although some Protestant and Catholic clergy estimate the number to be as high as 25,000. Most foreign resident Christians reside in the Casablanca, Tangier, and Rabat urban areas. Various local Christian leaders estimate that there are 4,000 citizen Christians (mostly ethnically Berber) who regularly attend "house" churches and live predominantly in the south. Some local Christian leaders estimate that there may be as many as 8,000 Christian citizens throughout the country, but many reportedly do not meet regularly due to fear of government surveillance and social persecution.

There are an estimated 3,000 to 8,000 Shia Muslims, most of them foreign residents from Lebanon or Iraq, but also a few citizen converts. Followers of several Sufi Muslim orders across the Maghreb and West Africa undertake joint annual pilgrimages to the country. The Baha'i community, located in urban areas, numbers 350 to 400 persons.

HISTORY

Morocco's strategic location has shaped its history. Beginning with the Phoenicians, many foreigners were drawn to this area. Romans, Visigoths, Vandals and Byzantine

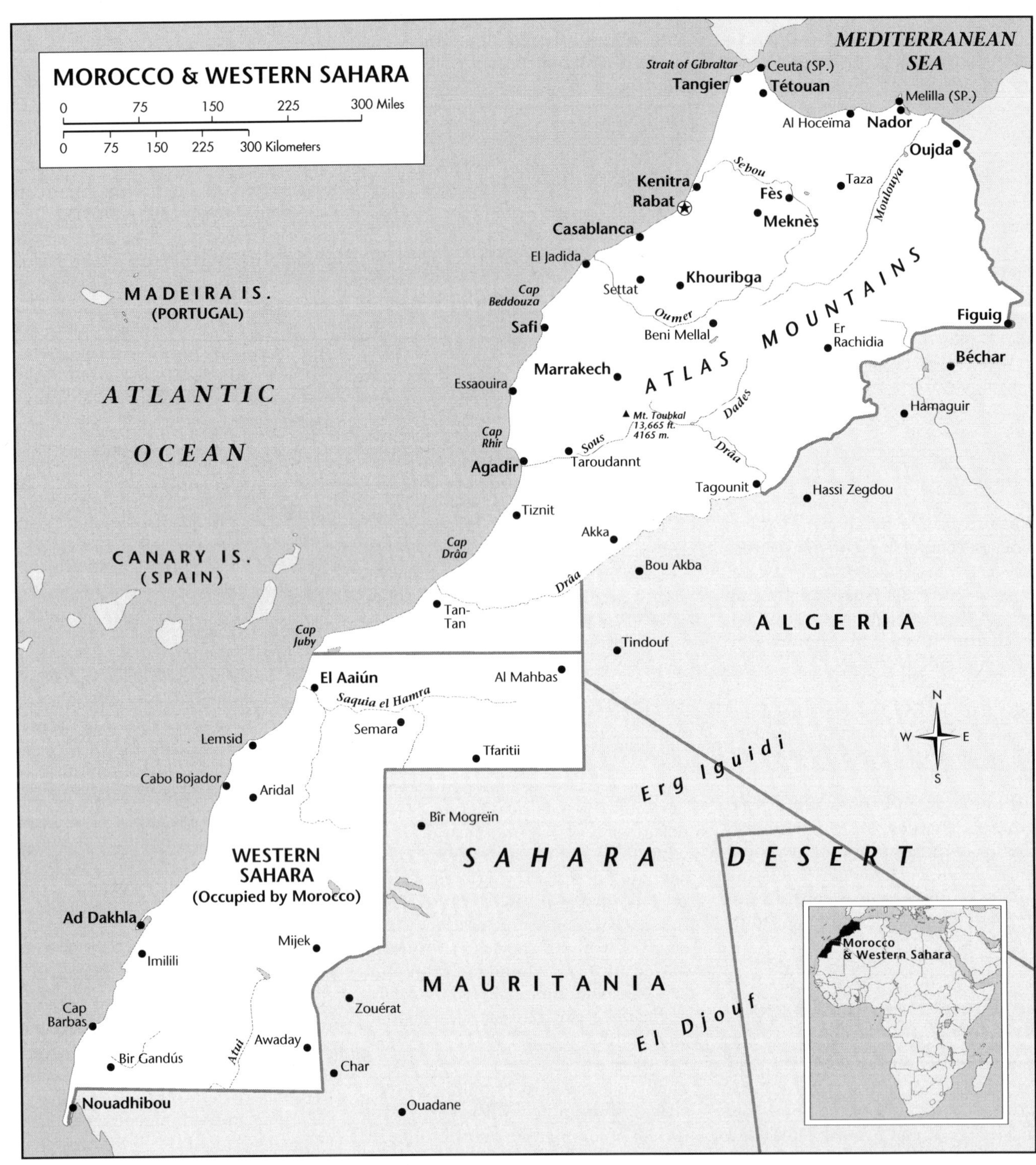

Greeks ruled successively. Arab forces began occupying Morocco in the 7th century A.D., bringing their civilization and Islam. The Alaouite dynasty, which has ruled Morocco since 1649, claims descent from the Prophet Muhammad.

Morocco's location and resources led to early competition among European powers in Africa, beginning with successful Portuguese efforts to control the Atlantic coast in the 15th century. France showed a strong interest in Morocco as early as 1830. Following recognition by the United Kingdom in 1904 of France's "sphere of influence" in Morocco, the Algeciras Conference (1906) formalized France's "special position" and entrusted policing of Morocco to France and Spain jointly. The Treaty of Fes (1912) made Morocco a protectorate of France. By the same treaty, Spain assumed the role of protecting power over the northern and southern (Saharan) zones.

Nationalist political parties, which took shape under the French protectorate, began a strong campaign for independence after World War II. Declarations such as the Atlantic Charter (a joint U.S.-British statement set forth, among other things, the right of all people to choose the form of government under which they live), served as a base for the independence movement. A manifesto of the Istiqlal (Independence) Party in 1944 was one of the earliest public demands for independence. That party subsequently provided most of the leadership for the nationalist movement and remains a strong political party.

In 1953, France exiled the highly respected Sultan Mohammed V and replaced him with the unpopular Mohammed Ben Aarafa. Ben Aarafa's reign was widely perceived as illegitimate, and sparked active opposition to French rule. France allowed Mohammed V to return in 1955, and Morocco gained independence on March 2, 1956. In 2006, Moroccans celebrated their 50th year of independence from France.

Morocco regained control over certain Spanish-ruled areas through agreements with Spain in 1956 and 1958. The internationalized city of Tangier was reintegrated into Morocco with the signing of the Tangier Protocol on October 29, 1956. The Spanish enclave of Ifni in the south became part of Morocco in 1969. Spain, however, retains control over the small coastal enclaves of Ceuta and Melilla in the north.

Hassan II became king in 1961. During the 1990s, King Hassan made great strides toward economic and political liberalization. He died on July 23, 1999, and was succeeded by his son, Mohammed VI, who pledged to continue the reforms.

GOVERNMENT AND POLITICAL CONDITIONS

Morocco is a monarchy with a constitution, under which ultimate authority rests with King Mohammed VI, who presides over the Council of Ministers. The king may dismiss ministers, dissolve parliament, and call for new elections. International and domestic observers judged that the November 25, 2011, parliamentary elections were credible and relatively free from government-sponsored irregularities.

Beginning in the spring, the country underwent a four-month constitutional reform process. In a March 9, 2011, speech, the king outlined the guidelines for the new constitution. A commission of experts whom he appointed wrote it, with input from an "accompanying mechanism" coordinating with political parties and numerous nongovernmental organizations (NGOs), associations, and individuals. The king presented the text publicly on June 17, and the populace adopted it in a referendum on July 1. This new document safeguards the essential powers of the king as the supreme arbiter among political forces, while marginally increasing the authority of parliament. The new constitution made significant steps in codifying civil liberties and advancing gender parity. Arab Spring-inspired social upheaval was relatively mild, although a new protest movement emerged, the February 20 Movement, that staged near-weekly peaceful demonstrations across the country to demand political, economic, and social reforms as well as an end to government corruption, to which the government sometimes responded with excessive force.

The law provides for, and citizens participated in, regular, free elections based on universal suffrage for the parliament's Chamber of Representatives and municipal councils. The parliament's Chamber of Counselors and the regional councils are indirectly elected through representatives. Citizens voted to accept a new constitution on July 1, 2011, and ratified it September 13.

The king may dissolve parliament in consultation with the prime minister. As head of state he appoints the head of government. According to the constitution, the king presides over the Council of Ministers—the supreme decision-making body—except in cases when he delegates that authority to the head of government. Constitutional changes outlining this division of responsibility came into effect on July 29, and it remained unclear by year's end which authorities the king might delegate and which he might maintain. Matters of religion, security, and strategic policy legally remain the purview of the king. The constitution obliges the king to choose the prime minister from the party with the most elected seats in the Chamber of Representatives. The constitution authorizes the prime minister to nominate all government ministers, although the king may dismiss them.

The constitution may not be changed without the king's approval. The king, head of government, or parliament may propose amendments to the constitution, but only the king has the power to put constitutional amendment proposals to a national referendum.

Recent Elections

In the November 25, 2011, legislative elections, which saw a turnout of approximately 45 percent of the registered electorate, the Islamist PJD won 107 of the 395 seats at stake in 92 constituencies. Of the 395 seats, 60 were reserved for women and 30 for those less than 40 years of age.

The law mandates the CNDH to supervise and facilitate the work of domestic and international observers. Accordingly, the CNDH fielded an estimated 3,500 domestic observers. The CNDH also accredited more than 300 international observers. Political parties and the vast majority of the 3,500 domestic observers considered the elections free, fair, and transparent. Most international observers considered them credible elections in which voters were able to choose freely and deemed the process relatively free of government irregularities.

Political Parties: Political parties faced fewer government-imposed restrictions as a result of the new constitution. The Ministry of Interior applied new laws that made it easier for political parties to register. By law a political party may not challenge the monarchy, Islam as the state religion, or territorial integrity.

Participation of Women and Minorities: Women's representation in political parties' decision-making structures increased during the year, and female politicians featured prominently in the press on a variety of issues. The November elections saw an increase of women in the Chamber of Representatives from 34 to 67.

Principal Government Officials

Last Updated: 1/31/2013

King: **MOHAMMED VI**
Prime Min.: **Abdelillah BENKIRANE**
Min. of Agriculture & Fisheries: **Aziz AKHANNOUCH**
Min. of Communications & Govt. Spokesperson: **Mustapha EL KHALFI**
Min. of Culture: **Mohamed Amine SBIHI**
Min. of Economy & Finance: **Nizar BARAKA**
Min. of Energy, Mines, Water, & Environment: **Fouad DOUIRI**
Min. of Equipment & Transport: **Aziz RABBAH**
Min. of Foreign Affairs & Cooperation: **Saad-Eddine AL-OTHMANI**
Min. of Habous & Islamic Affairs: **Ahmed TOUFIQ**
Min. of Handicrafts: **Abdessamad QAIOUH**
Min. of Health: **El Hossein EL OUARDI**
Min. of Higher Education, Scientific Research, & Executive Training: **Lahcen DAOUDI**
Min. of Housing, Town Planning, & Urban Policy: **Nabil BENABDELLAH**
Min. of Industry, Trade, & New Technologies: **Abdelkader AMARA**
Min. of Interior: **Mohand LAENSER**
Min. of Justice & Liberties: **Mustafa RAMID**
Min. of Labor & Vocational Training: **Abdelouahed SOUHAIL**
Min. of National Education: **Mohamed EL OUAFA**
Min. of Solidarity, Women, Family, & Social Development: **Bassima HAKKAOUI**
Min. of State: **Abdellah BAHA**
Min. of Tourism: **Lahcen HADDAD**
Min. of Youth & Sport: **Mohammed OUZZINE**
Min. in Charge of Relations With Parliament & Civil Society: **Lahbib CHOUBANI**
Sec. Gen. of the Govt.: **Driss DAHAK**
Min.-Del. to the Min. of Economy & Finance in Charge of the Budget: **Idriss Azami AL IDRISSI**
Min.-Del. to the Min. of Foreign Affairs & Cooperation: **Youssef AMRANI**
Min.-Del. to the Min. of Interior: **Draiss CHARKI**
Min.-Del. to the Prime Min. in Charge of the Admin. of National Defense: **Abdellatif LOUDIYI**
Min.-Del. to the Prime Min. in Charge of General Affairs & Governance: **Mohamed Najib BOULIF**
Min.-Del. to the Prime Min. in Charge of Moroccans Living Abroad: **Abdellatif MAAZOUZ**
Governor, Bank al-Magrib: **Abdellatif JOUAHRI**
Ambassador to the US: **Mohammed Rachad BOUHLAL**
Permanent Representative to the UN, New York: **Mohammed LOULICHKI**

ECONOMY

Morocco has capitalized on its proximity to Europe and relatively low labor costs to build a diverse, open, market-oriented economy. In the 1980s Morocco was a heavily indebted countries before pursuing austerity measures and pro-market reforms, overseen by the IMF. Since taking the throne in 1999, King Mohammed VI has presided over a stable economy marked by steady growth, low inflation, and gradually falling unemployment, although a poor harvest and economic difficulties in Europe contributed to an economic slowdown in 2012.

Industrial development strategies and infrastructure improvements—most visibly illustrated by a new port and free trade zone near Tangier —are improving Morocco's competitiveness. Key sectors of the economy include agriculture, tourism, phosphates, textiles, apparel, and subcomponents. To boost exports, Morocco entered into a bilateral Free Trade Agreement with the United States in 2006 and an Advanced Status agreement with the European Union in 2008. Despite Morocco's economic progress, the country suffers from high unemployment, poverty, and illiteracy, particularly in rural areas. In 2011 and 2012, high prices on fuel —which is subsidized and almost entirely imported—strained the government's budget and widened the country's current account deficit. Key economic challenges for Morocco include fighting corruption and reforming the the education system, the judiciary, and the government's costly subsidy program.

Labor Conditions

The minimum age for employment in all sectors is 15 years. Children younger than 16 are prohibited from working more than 10 hours per day and employers must give them a break of at least one hour. Children younger than 16 are not permitted to work between the hours of 9 p.m. and 6 a.m. in nonagricultural work, or between 8 p.m. and 5 a.m. in agriculture. The overwhelming majority of child laborers worked in rural agriculture, according to the government's statistical agency, the High Planning Commission. Seasonal agriculture work is excluded from the law. The law prohibits employment of children younger than 18 in stone quarries, mines, or any other positions the government considers hazardous. The labor code, however, does not cover domestic labor and therefore does not prohibit the employment of child maids or domestics.

The Ministry of Employment and Professional Development is responsible for implementing and enforcing child labor laws and regulations. The law provides for legal sanctions against employers who recruit children under the age of 15, with fines ranging from 27,000 to 32,000 dirhams ($3,235 to $3,835). Legal remedies to enforce child labor laws include criminal penalties, civil fines, and withdrawal or suspension of one or more civil, national, or family rights, including denial of legal residence in the country for five to 10 years. The ministry did not systematically enforce these sanctions due to a lack of resources. Child labor occurred overwhelmingly in rural areas, which accounted in 2010 for 91.2 percent of child workers, 93 percent of whom worked in agriculture, primarily on family farms. Some children were apprenticed before the age of 12, particularly in small family-run workshops in the handicraft industry. Children also worked in the informal sector in textiles, carpets, and light manufacturing. Children's safety and health conditions and wages were often substandard. In a 2011 report the High Planning Commission estimated that approximately 13,000 children between the ages of seven and 15 worked in urban areas in 2010, largely in the service sector.

The minimum wage was 80 dirhams ($9.60) per day in the industrialized sector and 52.50 dirhams ($6.30) per day for agricultural workers. The World Bank absolute poverty level threshold wage was 70 dirhams ($8.40) per day.

The law provides for a 44 to 48 hour maximum workweek with no more than 10 hours in a single day, premium pay for overtime, paid public and annual holidays, and minimum conditions for health and safety, including a prohibition on night work for women and minors. The law prohibits excessive overtime. The labor code does not cover domestic workers, who are primarily female citizens.

Occupational health and safety standards are rudimentary, except for a prohibition on the employment of women and children in certain dangerous occupations. The law outlines 33 areas of hazardous work that workers under the age of 18 are prohibited from performing, which include working in mines, handling dangerous materials, transporting explosives, and operating heavy machinery.

In practice many employers did not observe the legal provisions for condition of work, and the government did not always implement or effectively enforce basic provisions of the labor code, such as payment of the minimum wage and other basic benefits under the National Social Security Fund. The country's labor inspectors attempted to monitor working conditions and investigate accidents, but lack of resources prevented effective enforcement of labor laws, and penalties were generally not sufficient to deter violations.

Informal businesses hired approximately 60 percent of the labor force and often ignored the minimum wage requirements. In many cases several family members combined their incomes to support the family. Most workers in the industrial sector earned more than the minimum wage. Including traditional holiday-related bonuses, workers generally were paid the equivalent of 13 to 16 months' salary each year.

U.S.-MOROCCAN RELATIONS

Morocco formally recognized the United States by signing a treaty of peace and friendship in 1786. After a longstanding consular presence, permanent diplomatic relations began in 1905. Morocco entered into the status of a French protectorate from 1912 to 1956, and normal diplomatic relations were resumed after U.S. recognition of Moroccan independence in 1956. The two countries share common concerns and consult closely on regional security, political and economic transition, and sustainable development. Morocco is a strong partner in counterterrorism efforts, and it works closely with U.S. law enforcement to safeguard both countries' national security interests.

U.S. Assistance to Morocco

Since 1957, the United States and Morocco have worked together to make real and substantial improvements in the lives of Moroccan citizens. In the wake of the Arab Spring, Morocco continues to make positive strides in pursuit of political reform and remains a strong U.S. supporter. The United States Agency for International Development programs aim to increase agricultural growth and productivity; enhance teacher training; build the capacity of local governments to respond to citizen demands; and address the needs of the most at-risk youth through engagement in productive social, economic and civic activities. Funding through the Middle East Partnership Initiative (MEPI) supports the work of Moroccan civil society through programming that provides training to journalists, businesspeople, female entrepreneurs, legislators, legal professionals, and the heads of leading nongovernmental organizations. Under the Joint-Statement on Environmental Cooperation, signed in 2004, the Department of State's trade-related environmental cooperation programs focus on protecting the environment while promoting green economic development. The United States and Morocco signed a comprehensive Science and Technology Agreement in 2006. In 2008, the Millennium Challenge Corporation (MCC) commenced a five-year, $697.5 million compact with the Kingdom of Morocco to reduce poverty and stimulate economic growth. The MCC compact invests in expansion of fruit tree agriculture (including olives, nuts, and dates), support for small-scale fisheries and fish-markets, enhancement of the artisanal sector in the city of Fes, and training for small-scale businesses across all these sectors, with an emphasis on training for women and youth including literacy training.

Bilateral Economic Relations

The United States is Morocco's 6th largest trading partner, and Morocco is the 55th largest trading export market for U.S. goods. In 2006, Morocco and the United States Free Trade Agreement entered into force. Morocco has also signed a quadrilateral FTA with Tunisia, Egypt and Jordan, and a bilateral FTA with Turkey. Additionally, it is seeking trade and investment accords with other African, Asian and Latin American countries. Morocco's leading exports include phosphates and textiles. Morocco's banking system is one of the most liberalized in North

Africa; it is also highly concentrated, with the six largest banks accounting for 85 percent of banking sector assets.

Morocco's Membership in International Organizations

Morocco is a moderate Arab state that maintains close relations with Europe and the United States. It is a member of the United Nations (UN), and in January 2012 it began a 2-year term as a non-permanent member of the UN Security Council. Morocco belongs to the Arab League, Arab Maghreb Union (UMA), Organization of Islamic Cooperation (OIC), the Non-Aligned Movement, and the Community of Sahel-Saharan States (CEN-SAD). King Mohammed VI is the chairman of the OIC's Al-Quds (Jerusalem) Committee. Although not a member of the African Union (formerly the Organization of African Unity), Morocco remains involved in African diplomacy. Morocco is a party to the dispute over the Western Sahara in the UN. After Spain withdrew from its former colony there in the 1970s, Morocco claimed sovereignty over the region. A ceasefire between Morocco and the independence-seeking Polisario Front has been monitored since 1991 by a UN peacekeeping operation, the United Nations Mission for the Referendum in Western Sahara (MINURSO).

Bilateral Representation

Morocco maintains an embassy in the United States at 1601 21st Street NW, Washington, DC 20009; tel. 202-462-7979.

Principal U.S. Embassy Officials

Last Updated: 1/14/2013

RABAT (E) 2 Avenue Mohamed El Fassi, 10 000 Rabat, Morocco, 212–53-776-2265, Fax 212-53-776-5661, Workweek: Mon-Fri 0800/1700, Website: http://rabat.usembassy.gov/

DCM OMS:	Laura Craynon
AMB OMS:	Mona Skardon
CG OMS:	Karen Scott
Co-CLO:	Ashleigh Dickerson
DPO:	Jeniffer Fasiglione
FCS:	Jane Kitson
FM:	Tommy Johnson
HRO:	Carole Manley
MGT:	Howard Van Vranken
POSHO:	Tommy Johnson
SDO/DATT:	COL David Pistilli
TREAS:	Darley Steide
AMB:	Samuel Kaplan
CG:	Brian Shukan
DCM:	Judith A. Chammas
PAO:	Christopher Fitzgerald
GSO:	Fred Olivo
RSO:	Ivan Wray
AGR:	Sarah Hanson
AID:	John Groarke
CLO:	Anne Marie Ford
ECON:	Phillip Nelson
EEO:	Monica Rancher
FMO:	Karen McCarthy
ICASS Chair:	Jane Kitson
IMO:	Mark Wilson
IPO:	Richard Fasciglione
ISO:	Naseem Ioane
LEGATT:	John Morton
POL:	David Greene

CASABLANCA (CG) 8 Moulay Youssef, Casablanca, Morocco 20000, 212-52-226-4550, Fax 212-52-220-8097, INMARSAT Tel 383133250/1, Workweek: Mon-Fri/0800-1700, Website: http://casablanca.usconsulate.gov/

CG OMS:	Karen Scott
DHS/ICE:	Greg Manack
FCS:	Jane Kitson
MGT:	Linda Lee
CG:	Brian Shukan
CON:	Daniel Bazan
PAO:	Andrea Appell
RSO:	Stefan Merino
CLO:	Dez Penascino
ECON:	Erica Magallon
EEO:	Richard Page
IPO:	Richard Page
IRS:	Kathy J. Beck–Resident In Paris
ISSO:	Richard Page
POL:	Ann Meceda

TRAVEL

Consular Information Sheet

January 7, 2013

Country Description: Morocco is a constitutional monarchy with a bicameral parliament and independent judiciary; historically, the king has been the dominant authority. The population is estimated to be almost 34 million. While Morocco has a developing economy, modern tourist facilities and means of transportation are widely available, though the quality may vary depending on price and location.

Smart Traveler Enrollment Program (STEP)/Embassy Locations: If you are going to live in or visit Morocco, please take the time to tell our Embassy or Consulate about your trip. If you enroll, we can keep you up to date with important safety and security announcements. It will also help your friends and family get in touch with you in an emergency.

Embassy and Consulate information is available below and at the Department of State's list of embassies and consulates.

U.S. Embassy in Rabat
2 Avenue de Mohamed El Fassi (formerly Avenue de Marrakech), Rabat
Telephone: (212) (537) 76-22-65
Fax: (212) (537)76-56-61
For emergency services after-hours, please call the Duty Officer cell phone at (212) (661)13-19-39.

U.S. Consulate General in Casablanca
8 Boulevard Moulay Youssef, Casablanca
Telephone: (212) (522) 26-45-50
Fax number: (212) (522) 20-80-97
For emergency services after-hours, please call (212) (661) 13-19-39

Entry/Exit Requirements for U.S. Citizens: U.S. citizens traveling to Morocco must have a valid passport. Visas are not required for U.S. citizen tourists traveling to Morocco for fewer than 90 days. For visits of more than 90 days, U.S. citizens are required to apply for an extension of stay (providing a reason for the extension) and should do so as far in advance as possible. No vaccinations are required to enter Morocco. Travelers who plan to reside in Morocco must obtain a residence permit. A residence permit may be requested and obtained from immigration authorities (Service Etranger) at the central police station of the district of residence. U.S. citizens are encouraged to carry a copy of their U.S. passports with them at all times, so that, if questioned by local officials, proof of identity and U.S. citizenship is readily available.

Children born to a Moroccan father may experience difficulty leaving Morocco without the father's permission. Under Moroccan law, these children are considered Moroccan citizens. Even if the children bear U.S. passports, immigration officials may require proof that the father has approved their departure before the children will be allowed to leave Morocco. Although women, regardless of their nationality, are normally granted custody of their children in divorces, the father must approve the children's departure from Morocco. U.S. citizen women married to Moroccans do not need their spouse's permission to leave Morocco.

Visit the Embassy of the Kingdom of Morocco website for the most current visa information. The Embassy is located at 1601 21st Street NW, Washington, DC 20009, telephone (202) 462-7979 to 82, fax 202- 265-0161. There is a Moroccan Consulate General in New York at 10 E. 40th Street, New York, NY 10016, telephone (212) 758-2625, fax 212-395-8077

The U.S. Department of State is unaware of any HIV/AIDS entry restrictions for visitors to or foreign residents of Morocco.

Threats to Safety and Security: The potential for terrorist violence against U.S. interests and citizens remains high in Morocco. Moroccan authorities continue to disrupt groups seeking to attack U.S. or Western-affiliated and Moroccan government targets, arresting numerous individuals associated with international terrorist groups. With indications that such groups still seek to carry out attacks in Morocco, it is important for U.S. citizens to be keenly aware of their surroundings and adhere to prudent security practices such as avoiding predictable travel patterns and maintaining a low profile. Establishments that are readily identifiable with the United States are potential targets for attacks. These may include facilities where U.S. citizens and other foreigners congregate, including clubs, restaurants, places of worship, schools, hotels, movie theaters, U.S. brand establishments and other public areas. Such targets may also include establishments where activities occur that may offend religious sensitivities, such as casinos or places where alcoholic beverages are sold or consumed.

All U.S. citizens are urged to remain alert to local security developments and be vigilant regarding their personal security and report any suspicious incidents or problems immediately to Moroccan authorities and the U.S. Embassy or Consulate.

Demonstrations occur frequently in Morocco and are typically focused on political or social issues. During periods of heightened regional tension, large demonstrations may take place in the major cities. During most of 2011, many large cities in Morocco had weekly demonstrations ranging in size from several hundred to tens of thousands of demonstrators. In September 2012, demonstrations took place near the U.S. Consulate General in Casablanca, as well as other cities in response to a YouTube video. By law, all demonstrations require a government permit, but spontaneous unauthorized demonstrations, which have greater potential for violence, can occur. In addition, different unions or groups may organize strikes to protest an emerging issue or government policy. Travelers should be cognizant of the current levels of tension in Morocco and stay informed of regional issues that could resonate in Morocco and create an anti-American response. Avoid demonstrations if at all possible. If caught in a demonstration, remain calm and move away immediately when provided the opportunity.

The Western Sahara is an area where the legal status of the territory and the issue of its sovereignty remain unresolved. The area was long the site of armed conflict between government forces and the POLISARIO Front, which continues to seek independence for the territory. A ceasefire has been fully in effect since 1991 in the UN-administered area. There are thousands of unexploded mines in the Western Sahara and in areas of Mauritania adjacent to the Western Saharan border. Exploding mines are occasionally reported, and they have caused death and injury. There have been sporadic reports of violence in the cities of Laayoune and Dakhla stemming from sporting events and from political demonstrations.

Stay up to date by:

- Bookmarking our Bureau of Consular Affairs website, which contains the current Travel Warnings and Travel Alerts as well as the Worldwide Caution.
- Following us on Twitter and the Bureau of Consular Affairs page on Facebook as well.
- Downloading our free Smart Traveler appavailable through iTunes and the Android market to have travel information at your fingertips.
- Calling 1-888-407-4747 toll-free within the U.S. and Canada, or a regular toll line, 1-202-501-4444, from other countries.
- Taking some time before travel to consider your personal security.

Crime: Crime in Morocco is a serious concern, particularly in the major cities and tourist areas. Aggressive panhandling, pick-pocketing, purse-snatching, theft from occupied vehicles stopped in traffic, and harassment of women are the most frequently reported issues. Criminals have used weapons, primarily knives, during some street robberies and burglaries. These have occurred at any time of day or night, not only in isolated places or areas less frequented by visitors, but in crowded areas as well. It is always best to have a travel companion and utilize taxis from point to point, particularly at night and when moving about unfamiliar areas. Residential break-ins also occur and have on occasion turned violent, but most criminals look for opportunities based on stealth rather than confrontation.

Women walking alone in certain areas of cities and rural areas are particularly vulnerable to assault by men. Women are advised to travel with a companion or in a group when possible and to ignore any harassment. Responding to verbal harassment can escalate the situation. The best course of action is generally not to respond or make eye contact with the harasser. Travelers should avoid soccer stadiums and environs on days of scheduled matches as large groups of team supporters have been known to become unruly and harass and even assault bystanders.

Joggers should be mindful of traffic and remain in more heavily populated areas. It is always best to have a jogging companion and avoid isolated areas or jogging at night. The use of headphones while jogging is discouraged for personal safety reasons.

Taxis in Morocco are generally crime-free, although city buses are not considered safe. Trains are generally safe, but theft, regardless of the time of day, sometimes occurs. Avoid carrying large sums of cash and be particularly alert when using ATM machines. In the event you are victimized by crime or an attempted crime, or experience any security-related incident during your stay in Morocco, please report the incident to the local police and the U.S. Consulate General in Casablanca as soon as possible.

Fraud in Morocco may involve a wide range of situations from financial fraud to relationship fraud for the purpose of obtaining a visa. If you believe you are the victim of a fraudulent scheme, you may wish to consult with an attorney to best determine what your options are under Moroccan law. Since fraud can involve a wide range of circumstances, it is difficult to provide general guidelines on how to pursue criminal charges in these issues.

There have been instances in which a U.S. citizen has met a Moroccan online and come to live with or visit him or her in Morocco and found themselves in financial or otherwise difficult situations while in country. If you are concerned about a family member or friend who is visiting someone he or she met online, you can contact the American Citizens Services Unit of the U.S. Consulate General in Casablanca at 212-522-26-71-51.

Don't buy counterfeit and pirated goods, even if they are widely available. Not only are the bootlegs illegal in the United States, you may also be breaking local law.

Victims of Crime: If you or someone you know becomes the victim of a crime abroad, you should contact the local police and the nearest U.S. Embassy or Consulate. We can:

- Replace a stolen passport.
- Help you find appropriate medical care, if you are the victim of violent crimes such as assault or rape.
- Put you in contact with the appropriate police authorities, and if you want us to, we can contact family members or friends.
- Help you understand the local criminal justice process and can direct you to local attorneys, although it is important to remember that local authorities are responsible for investigating and prosecuting the crime.

The local equivalent to the "911" emergency line in Morocco is 190. Please note that emergency operators rarely speak English. Most police and other officials speak Arabic; some may speak French depending on their location and education.

Criminal Penalties: While you are traveling in Morocco you are subject to its laws even if you are a U.S. citizen. Foreign laws and legal systems can be vastly different from our own. In some places you may be taken in for questioning if you don't have your passport with you. There are also some things that might be legal in the country you visit, but still illegal in the United States, and you can be prosecuted under U.S. law if you buy pirated goods. Engaging in sexual conduct with children or using or disseminating child pornography in a foreign country is a crime prosecutable in the United States. If you break local laws in Morocco your U.S. passport won't help you avoid arrest or prosecution. It's very important to know what's legal and what's not wherever you go.

Arrest notifications in Morocco: While some countries will automatically notify the nearest U.S. embassy or consulate if a U.S. citizen is detained or arrested in a foreign country, that might not always be the case. To ensure that the United States is aware of your circumstances, request that the police and prison officials notify the nearest U.S. embassy or consulate as soon as you are arrested or detained overseas.

Citizenship: The Government of Morocco considers all persons born to Moroccan fathers to be Moroccan citizens. In addition to being subject to all U.S. laws, U.S. citizens who also possess the nationality of Morocco may be subject to other laws that impose special obligations on citizens of Morocco. Recently, Morocco has begun allowing Moroccan mothers of children born outside Morocco to petition for their children's citizenship. For further information on that process, please contact the Embassy of Morocco in Washington, D.C., or the Moroccan Consulate General in New York.

Foreign Currency: Current Moroccan customs procedures do not provide for accurate or reliable registration of large quantities of U.S. dollars brought into the country by tourists or other visitors. As a result, U.S. citizens may encounter difficulties when they attempt to depart with large amounts of cash. In particular, U.S. citizens with dual Moroccan nationality have been asked to provide proof of the source of the funds and have incurred heavy fines. The export of Moroccan currency (dirhams) is prohibited; however, Moroccan currency can be converted back into U.S. dollars prior to departure only if the traveler has a bank or money transfer receipt indicating he or she exchanged dollars for dirhams while in Morocco.

Import Restrictions: Moroccan customs authorities may enforce strict regulations concerning temporary importation into or export from Morocco of items such as firearms, religious materials, antiquities, business equipment, and large quantities of currency. It is advisable to contact the Embassy of Morocco in Washington, D.C., or the Moroccan Consulate General in New York for specific information concerning customs requirements.

Religion and Proselytizing: Islam is the official religion in Morocco. However, the constitution provides for the freedom to practice one's religion. The Moroccan government does not interfere with public worship by the country's Jewish minority or by expatriate Christians. Proselytizing is, however, prohibited. In the past, U.S. citizens have been arrested, detained, and/or expelled for discussing or trying to engage Moroccans in debate about Christianity. In March 2010, several U.S. citizens were expelled from Morocco for alleged proselytizing. Many of those expelled were long-time Moroccan residents. In these cases, U.S. citizens were given no more than 48 hours to gather their belongings or settle their affairs before being expelled.

Property: U.S. consular officers are prohibited by law and regulation from accepting personal property for safekeeping regardless of the circumstances involved.

If there is concern over the protection of property left behind in Morocco due to confiscation or deportation for political, legal, or other reasons, U.S. citizens should take every precaution to ensure that available legal safeguards are in place either before or immediately after purchasing property in Morocco or taking up residence there. Consultations with local attorneys concerning property rights and available protections are a prudent way of attending to these concerns. A list of attorneys who have expressed a willingness to represent U.S. citizen clients is available from the U.S. Consulate General in Casablanca; the U.S. Embassy in Rabat does not offer consular services. The U.S. Consulate cannot vouch for the reliability of attorneys on this list. They were selected for their English-speaking abilities and willingness to take on cases involving American citizens. U.S. citizens are also encouraged to consider assigning a Power of Attorney, or Procuration, to be used in Morocco if necessary. Information and sample Power of Attorney forms are available on the Consulate General of the Kingdom of Morocco in New York website.

Although rare, security personnel in Morocco may at times place foreign visitors under surveillance.

Photographing Sensitive Locations: Taking photographs of anything that could be perceived as being of military or security interest may result in problems with the authorities. As a general rule, travelers should not photograph palaces, diplomatic missions, government buildings, or other sensitive facilities and, when in doubt, they should ask for permission from the appropriate Moroccan authorities.

Internet Romance and Marriage Fraud: Many U.S. citizens befriend Moroccans through Internet dating and social networking sites and these relationships often to lead marriage or engagement. While many of the marriages between U.S. citizens and Moroccans are successful, the U.S. Consulate General in Casablanca warns against marriage fraud. It is not uncommon for foreign nationals to enter into marriages with U.S. citizens solely for immigration purposes. Relationships developed via correspondence, particularly those begun on the Internet, are especially susceptible to manipulation. Often, the marriages end in divorce in the United States when the foreign national acquires legal permanent residence ("green card") or U.S. citizenship. In some cases, the new U.S. citizen or permanent resident then remarries a wife he divorced before, around the same time as entering into a relationship with a sponsoring U.S. citizen.

Some of the signs that an Internet contact may be developing a relationship with a U.S. citizen in order to obtain an immigrant visa through marriage are:

Declarations of love within days or weeks of the initial contact;

- Proposals or discussions of marriage soon after initial contact;
- Requests to the U.S. citizen to visit the foreign national's home country soon after the declaration of love or proposal;
- Responses to messages from the U.S. citizen friend are along the lines "I love you/Sorry I missed your call," or similarly one-sided conversations;
- Once engaged, married, or an immigrant visa petition is filed, the Moroccan spouse/boy or girlfriend suddenly starts missing scheduled appointments to chat or call.

While chat rooms, dating and social networking sites are great ways to make friends across international borders, the U.S. government urges U.S. citizens who meet foreign nationals on the Internet to keep in mind the signs noted above. Entering into a marriage contract for the principal purpose of facilitating immigration to the United States for an alien is against U.S. law and can result in serious penalties, including fines and imprisonment for the U.S. citizen and the foreign national involved.

Accessibility: While in Morocco, individuals with disabilities may find accessibility and accommodation very different from what you find in the United States. Morocco does not have any significant legislation that guarantees access to public transportation, buildings, and public places.

Medical Facilities and Health Information: Adequate medical care is available in Morocco's largest cities, particularly in Rabat and Casablanca, although not all facilities meet high-quality standards. Specialized care or treatment may not be available. Medical facilities are adequate for non-emergency matters, particularly in the urban areas, but most medical staff will have limited or no English skills. Most ordinary prescription and over-the-counter medicines are widely available. However, specialized prescriptions may be difficult to fill and availability of all medicines in rural areas is unreliable.

Travelers should not ask friends or relatives to send medications through the mails or FedEx or UPS since Moroccan customs will impound the delivery and not release it to the recipient. Emergency and specialized care outside the major cities is far below U.S. standards, and in many instances may not be available at all. Travelers planning to drive in the mountains and other remote areas may wish to carry a medical kit and a Moroccan phone card for emergencies.

In the event of vehicle accidents involving injuries, immediate ambulance service usually is not available. The police emergency services telephone number is 190.

You can find detailed information on vaccinations and other health precautions on the Centers for Disease Control and Prevention (CDC) website. For information about outbreaks of infectious diseases abroad, consult the World Health Organization (WHO) website. The WHO website also contains additional health information for travelers, including detailed country-specific health information.

Medical Insurance: You can't assume your insurance will go with you when you travel. It's very important to find out BEFORE you leave whether or not your medical insurance will cover you overseas. You need to ask your insurance company two questions:

- Does my policy apply when I'm out of the U.S.?
- Will it cover emergencies like a trip to a foreign hospital or a medical evacuation?

In many places, including Morocco, doctors and hospitals still expect payment in cash at the time of service. Your regular U.S. health insurance may not cover doctors' and hospital visits in other countries. If your policy doesn't go with you when you travel, it's a very good idea to take out another one for your trip.

Traffic Safety and Road Conditions: While in Morocco, you may encounter road conditions that differ significantly from those in the United States. The information below concerning Morocco is provided for general reference only, and may not be totally accurate in a particular location or circumstance.

Traffic accidents are a significant hazard in Morocco. Driving practices are very poor and have resulted in serious injuries to and fatalities of U.S. citizens. This is particularly true at dusk during the Islamic holy month of Ramadan, when adherence to traffic regulations is lax, and from July to September when Moroccans resident abroad return from Europe by car in large numbers.

Congested streets are characteristic of urban driving. Drivers should also exercise extreme caution when driving at night due to poor lighting systems along roads. Traffic signals do not always function, and are sometimes difficult to see. Modern freeways link the cities of Tangier, Rabat, Fez, Casablanca, and Marrakesh. Two-lane highways link other major cities.

Secondary routes in rural areas are often narrow and poorly paved. Roads through the Rif and Atlas mountains are steep, narrow, windy, and dangerous. Maximum caution should be exercised when driving in the mountains. Pedestrians, scooters, and animal-drawn conveyances are common on all roadways, including the freeways, and driving at night should be avoided, if possible. During the rainy season (November - March) flash flooding is frequent and sometimes severe, washing away roads and vehicles in rural areas. Often Moroccan police officers pull over drivers for inspection within the city and on highways. Confiscation of a driver's license is possible if a violator is unable or unwilling to settle a fine at the time of a traffic stop.

In the event of a traffic accident, including accidents involving injuries, the parties are required to remain at the scene and not move their vehicles until the police have arrived and documented all necessary information. The police emergency services telephone number is 190. While public buses and taxis are inexpensive, drivers typically exhibit poor driving habits, and buses are frequently overcrowded. The train system has a good safety record. Trains, while sometimes crowded, are comfortable and generally on time.

Foreign driver's licenses are valid for use in Morocco for up to one year. After that, foreign residents must pass the Moroccan driver's test and obtain a Moroccan driver's license.

Aviation Safety Oversight: The U.S. Federal Aviation Administration (FAA) has assessed the Government ofMorocco's Civil Aviation Authority as being in compliance with International Civil Aviation Organization (ICAO) aviation safety standards for oversight of Morocco's air carrier operations. Further information may be found on the FAA's safety assessment page.

Children's Issues: Please see the U.S. Dept. of State Office of Children's Issues web pages on intercountry adoption and international parental child abduction.

Intercountry Adoption

Ministry of Justice Provides Prosecutors New Instructions on Kafala Guardianship Decrees November 6, 2012

On September 21, 2012, Justice Minister El Mostapha Ramid published a notice instructing Moroccan Prosecutors to formally oppose a petition filed with a juvenile judge seeking the granting of Kafala guardianship decrees to prospective adoptive foreign parents who are not resident in Morocco. In his notice, he asks the Prosecutors to emphasize the importance of in-country residency for the Kafala guardianship with the court judges, verify whether the prospective adoptive parents reside in Morocco, and request that judges not issue Kafala orders to foreign prospective adoptive parents (PAPs) who are not residing in Morocco. The notice states that it is difficult for the courts to ensure that conditions of the Kafala guardianship are met when the child is taken abroad by foreign parents and notes it needs to be possible for courts to cancel the guardianship in cases of failure to comply. The Minister's notice appears to indicate that Kafala guardianship should only be granted to Muslim families who are long-term residents in Morocco.

The notice states that its purpose is to ensure the implementation of the existing law. It does not contain any provisions addressing already pending Kafala guardianship petitions. At this time, it is unclear whether prosecutors will formally oppose petitions for Kafala guardianship decrees filed by U.S. citizens which were already pending with the Court at the time the notice was issued.

U.S. citizens wishing to obtain Kafala guardianship of Moroccan children should be aware that the Prosecutors are now obligated to confirm the prospective parents' Moroccan residency and the courts are requested to deny Kafala orders to foreign PAPs who do not reside in Morocco. Please continue to monitor adoption.state.gov for updated information.

Overview of Adoption Procedures September 2009

The information in this section has been edited from the latest report available as of February 2013 from the State Department Bureau of Consular Affairs, Office of Overseas Citizens Services. For more information, please read the *Intercountry Adoption* section of this book and review current reports online at http://adoption.state.gov. Morocco is not party to the Hague Convention on Protection of Children and Co-operation in Respect of Intercountry Adoption (Hague Adoption Convention).

Who Can Adopt? To bring an adopted child to the United States from Morocco, you must first be found eligible to adopt by the U.S. Government. The U.S. Government agency responsible for making this determination is the Department of Homeland Security, U.S. Citizenship and Immigration Services (USCIS). In addition to these U.S. requirements for adoptive parents, Morocco also has the following requirements for adoptive parents.

Marriage Requirements: Prospective adoptive parents must either be a single female or a married couple. Morocco does not recognize same sex marriages or domestic partnerships.

Income Requirements: The Government of Morocco requires that people seeking legal guardianship of Moroccan children be employed.

Other Requirements: Prospective adoptive parents of Moroccan children must be Muslim. Those who are not already Muslim can easily convert to Islam while in Morocco. They can obtain a conversion document from any court notary (Adul) office. Prospective adoptive parents must also have a letter from a doctor practicing in Morocco indicating that they are in good mental and physical heath and capable of caring for an adopted child.

Who Can Be Adopted? In order to qualify for immigration to the U.S., the child must meet the definition of orphan under both Moroccan and U.S. law.

Children living in Moroccan orphanages are more likely to meet the definition of orphan under U.S. law and therefore are more likely to qualify for immigration to the United States than children who do not live in orphanages.

The Process: The process for adopting a child from Morocco generally includes the following steps:

- Apply to be found eligible to adopt in the United States (I-600A petition submitted to USCIS)
- Be matched with a child that meets the U.S. definition of an orphan
- Obtain certificate of abandonment from issuing authority
- Obtain "kefala" custody of the child in a Moroccan court
- Obtain permission from Moroccan court to travel/immigrate and obtain a passport
- Apply for an Immigrant Visa for the child at the U.S. Consulate in Casablanca
- Bring the child home to the U.S. and adopt the child in your home state

Documents Required: The orphanage where the child resides should be able to provide you with an exact list of the documents required to adopt in Morocco. The documents required may vary and prospective adoptive parents should expect delays and the probability of supplementary requirements. They will most likely require that any English language documents, to include your home study, be accompanied by a sworn Arabic translation by a Moroccan translator. A list of sworn translators located throughout Morocco can be obtained by contacting the Immigrant Visa Unit at the U.S. Consulate in Casablanca, Morocco at ivcasablanca@state.gov. The following is a list of basic documents required for the kefala procedure:

- Islam Conversion Document for the prospective adoptive parents
- Birth Certificate for each prospective parent
- Marriage certificate for the prospective parents (if applicable)

- Health statement from a doctor practicing in Morocco
- Work and salary statements for each prospective adoptive parent (if applicable)
- Home study completed by a licensed U.S. home study provider
- Photographs (the exact number and size required varies)
- Copy of passports of each prospective adoptive parent

Most children residing in Moroccan orphanages will have a judgment of abandonment issued in their name. In most orphanages, this judgment of abandonment will be given to the prospective adoptive parents along with the kefala custody documentation. However, procedures may vary depending on the region. Be prepared to contact regional authorities. In order to obtain kefala custody of the child they have chosen, both prospective adoptive parents will need to appear in person in a Moroccan court. Their documents will be reviewed and the custody documents will be issued and executed. This process can take anywhere from 2 days to several weeks, depending on the local court procedures.

Attorneys/Agencies: Many orphanages in Morocco have their own legal staff that can assist you in the kefala custody process, thus alleviating the need to hire a private attorney in Morocco. Many American prospective adoptive parents who have adopted from Morocco in the last year have used orphanages that provide this service. It is always possible, however, for prospective adoptive parents to hire a private attorney to assist them in the process.

Time Frame: The time required to complete the kefala custody of a Moroccan child can vary from 3 weeks to 6 months, perhaps longer depending on the particular details of the case.

Adoption Fees: Although orphanages do not officially charge fees in Morocco, many of them may request a donation from adoptive parents. Orphanages that provide legal assistance in obtaining kefala custody usually have fees associated with this service. Anyone using an attorney can expect to pay attorneys fees for services rendered,

Documenting a Child's Eligibility for Kefala: If the child's biological parents are known, their names will usually appear on the child's birth certificate. In cases where the child was born out of wedlock to an unknown father, the father's name on the birth certificate will contain a fictitious name starting with "Abd" (Abdellah, Abdelhamid, etc) and no last name. This is a place holder name to avoid the father's portion of the birth certificate being left blank, and has no relation to the actual name of the biologic father. The prospective adoptive parents should receive a document from the Moroccan courts giving them permission to obtain a Moroccan passport and immigrate to the U.S. with the child. Prospective adoptive parents will need the child's birth certificate, kefala custody document, and permission from the court to obtain a passport. These documents are submitted to the municipality in the region where the kefala was obtained. The passport is normally ready within one week, although expedited processing can be requested. Most prospective adoptive parents who receive assistance from the orphanage in obtaining custody of the child also receive assistance in obtaining the child's Moroccan passport.

Bringing Your Child Home: Once your adoption is complete (or you have obtained legal custody of the child), there are a few more steps to take before you can head home. Specifically, you need to apply for several documents for your child before he or she can travel to the United States, such as a birth certificate, a passport or travel document for your child from the country in which he or she was born, and a U.S. Immigration Visa. For detailed and updated information on how to obtain these documents, review the *Intercountry Adoption* section on this publication and visit the USCIS Intercountry Adoption website at http://adoption.state.gov.

Child Citizenship Act: For adoptions finalized abroad, the Child Citizenship Act of 2000 allows your new child to acquire American citizenship automatically when he or she enters the United States as lawful permanent residents. For adoptions finalized in the United States, the Child Citizenship Act of 2000 allows your new child to acquire American citizenship automatically when the court in the United States issues the final adoption decree. To learn more, review the *Intercountry Adoption* section on this publication and visit the USCIS Intercountry Adoption website at http://adoption.state.gov.

After Adoption: Morocco has no post-adoption requirements.

U.S. Consulate General in Casablanca, Morocco
8 Boulevard Moulay Youssef
Tel: 212-522-26-45-50
Email: ivcasablanca@state.gov

Embassy of Morocco in the United States of America
1601 21st Street, NW Washington, DC 20009
Tel: 202-462-7979
Fax: 202-265-0161

Office of Children's Issues
U.S. Department of State
2201 C Street, NW
SA-29
Washington, DC 20520
Tel: 1-888-407-4747
E-mail: AskCI@state.gov
http://adoption.state.gov

For questions about immigration procedures, call the National Customer Service Center (NCSC) 1-800-375-5283 (TTY 1-800-767-1833).

International Parental Child Abduction

December 2012

The information in this section has been edited from a report of the Bureau of Consular Affairs, Office of Overseas Citizens Services of the U.S.

Department of State. For more information, please read the *International Parental Child Abduction* section of this book and review current reports online at www.travel.state.gov/abduction.

Disclaimer: The information in this flyer is provided for general information only, is not intended to be legal advice, and may change without notice. Questions involving interpretation of law should be addressed to an attorney licensed to practice in the relevant jurisdiction.

General Information: Morocco and the United States have been treaty partners under the 1980 Hague Convention on the Civil Aspects of International Child Abduction (Hague Abduction Convention) since December 1, 2012.

Hague Abduction Convention: The U.S. Department of State serves as the U.S. Central Authority (USCA) for the Hague Abduction Convention. Parents are strongly encouraged to contact the Department of State for assistance prior to initiating the Hague process directly with the foreign Central Authority.

United States Department of State
Office of Children's Issues
2201 C Street, N.W.
Washington, DC 20520
Telephone: 1-888-407-4747
Outside the United States or Canada: 1-202-501-4444
Fax: 202-736-9132

The Moroccan Central Authority for the Hague Abduction Convention is the Ministry of Justice and Liberty. The Ministry of Justice and Liberty has an administrative role in processing Hague Abduction Convention applications. Upon submission of a Hague application, the Moroccan Central Authority will work with the Prosecutor's Office to locate the child, attempt resolution through voluntary means if appropriate, and forward the case to the court of first instance. The Moroccan Central Authority can be reached at:

Ministère de la Justice et des Libertés
Division des Affaires Civiles
place de la Mamounia
10000 RABAT
Maroc
Tel.: +212 53 770 3348
Fax: +212 53 773 0551

To initiate a Hague case for return of, or access to, a child in Morocco, the USCA encourages parents or legal guardians to review the eligibility criteria and instructions located on the State Department website. The Moroccan Central Authority (MCA) will accept Hague applications and supporting documents in English and does not require translation into French or Arabic. The USCA is available to answer questions about the Hague application process, to forward a completed application to the Ministry of Justice and Liberty, and to subsequently monitor its progress through the foreign administrative and legal processes.

Return: A parent or legal guardian may file an application under the Hague Abduction Convention for return to the United States of a child abducted to, or wrongfully retained in, Morocco. The U.S. Department of State can assist parents living in the United States to understand whether the Convention is an available civil remedy and can provide information on the process for submitting a Hague application.

Visitation/Access: A person may file an application under the Hague Abduction Convention for access to a child living in Morocco. The criteria for acceptance of a Hague access application vary from country to country. The U.S. Department of State can assist parents living in the United States to understand country-specific criteria and provide information on the process for submitting a Hague application.

Retaining an Attorney: Retaining a private attorney is not required in order to submit a Hague Abduction Convention application to a court in Morocco. A public prosecutor presents Hague return cases to the court. Parents or legal guardians may hire a private attorney at their own expense to follow up on the case and to provide direct information to the court, and to generally advise as to the best course of action for their individual circumstances. A privately hired attorney should contact the MCA as soon as possible after the Hague Abduction Convention application has been filed with the MCA.

The U.S. Mission in Morocco posts a list of attorneys including those who specialize in family law at: http://morocco.usembassy.gov/service/professional-services/list-of-lawyers.html. This list is provided as a courtesy service only and does not constitute an endorsement of any individual attorney. The Department of State assumes no responsibility or liability for the professional ability or reputation of, or the quality of services provided by, the persons or firms included in this list. Professional credentials and areas of expertise are provided directly by the lawyers.

Mediation: The MCA encourages mediation in abduction cases; however, there are no governmental offices in place that offer these services in custody disputes.

U.S. Consulate General Casablanca
8, Bd Moulay Youssef
Casablanca
Telephone: (212) 661-79-70-00
Fax: (212) 522-20-80-97
http://morocco.usembassy.gov/hours-casa.html

Consulate General of the Kingdom of Morocco
10 East 40th Street
New York, NY 10016
Telephone: (212) 758-2625
Fax: (646) 395-8077
Email: info@moroccanconsulate.com
http://www.moroccanconsulate.com/index.cfm

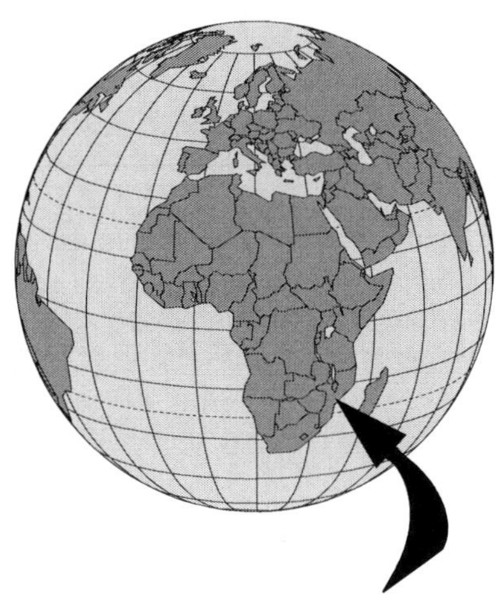

MOZAMBIQUE

Compiled from publications that were available as of February 2013 from the U.S. Department of State, the U.S. Department of Commerce, and the Central Intelligence Agency (CIA). See the introduction to this set for explanatory notes.

Official Name:
Republic of Mozambique

PROFILE

Geography

Area: total: 799,380 sq km; country comparison to the world: 35; land: 786,380 sq km; water: 13,000 sq km

Major cities: Maputo (capital) 1.589 million; Matola 761,000 (2009)

Climate: tropical to subtropical

Terrain: mostly coastal lowlands, uplands in center, high plateaus in northwest, mountains in west

People

Nationality: noun: Mozambican(s); adjective: Mozambican

Population: 23,515,934 (July 2012 est.)

Population growth rate: 2.442% (2012 est.)

Ethnic groups: African 99.66% (Makhuwa, Tsonga, Lomwe, Sena, and others), Europeans 0.06%, Euro-Africans 0.2%, Indians 0.08%

Religions: Catholic 28.4%, Protestant 27.7% (Zionist Christian 15.5%, Evangelical Pentecostal 10.9%, Anglican 1.3%), Muslim 17.9%, other 7.2%, none 18.7% (1997 census)

Languages: Emakhuwa 25.3%, Portuguese (official) 10.7%, Xichangana 10.3%, Cisena 7.5%, Elomwe 7%, Echuwabo 5.1%, other Mozambican languages 30.1%, other 4% (1997 census)

Literacy: definition: age 15 and over can read and write; total population: 56.1%; male: 70.8%; female: 42.8% (2010 est.)

Health: life expectancy at birth: total population: 52.02 years; male: 51.26 years; female: 52.8 years (2012 est.); Infant mortality rate: total: 76.85 deaths/1,000 live births; male: 79.04 deaths/1,000 live births; female: 74.62 deaths/1,000 live births (2012 est.)

Unemployment rate: 21% (1997 est.)

Work force: 10.1 million (2012 est.)

Government

Type: republic

Independence: 25 June 1975

Constitution: 30 November 1990

Political subdivisions: 10 provinces (provincias, singular—provincia), 1 city (cidade); Cabo Delgado, Gaza, Inhambane, Manica, Maputo, Cidade de Maputo, Nampula, Niassa, Sofala, Tete, Zambezia

Suffrage: 18 years of age; universal

Economy

GDP (purchasing power parity): $26.22 billion (2012 est.); $24.19 billion (2011 est.); $22.58 billion (2010 est.); $21.15 billion (2009 est.)

GDP real growth rate: 7.5% (2012 est.); 7.1% (2011 est.); 6.8% (2010 est.); 6.3% (2009 est.)

GDP per capita (PPP): $1,200 (2012 est.); $1,100 (2011 est.); $1,000 (2010 est.); $1,000 (2009 est.)

Natural resources: coal, titanium, natural gas, hydropower, tantalum, graphite

Agriculture products: cotton, cashew nuts, sugarcane, tea, cassava (tapioca), corn, coconuts, sisal, citrus and tropical fruits, potatoes, sunflowers; beef, poultry

Industries: aluminum, petroleum products, chemicals (fertilizer, soap, paints), textiles, cement, glass, asbestos, tobacco, food, beverages

Exports: $3.516 billion (2012 est.); $2.649 billion (2011 est.); $2.333 billion (2010 est.)

Exports—commodities: aluminum, prawns, cashews, cotton, sugar, citrus, timber; bulk electricity

Exports—partners: Belgium 17.8%, South Africa 17.4%, Italy 13.9%, Spain 10%, China 7.7% (2011)

Imports: $5.373 billion (2012 est.); $4.029 billion (2011 est.); $3.512 billion (2010 est.)

Imports—commodities: machinery and equipment, vehicles, fuel, chemicals, metal products, foodstuffs, textiles

Imports—partners: South Africa 22.1%, China 12.4%, India 9.1%, US 8%, Australia 7.4%, Portugal 5.4% (2011)

Debt—external: $4.88 billion (31 December 2012 est.); $4.32 billion (31 December 2011 est.); $3.804 billion (31 December 2010 est.)

Exchange rates: meticais (MZM) per US dollar; 28.13 (2012 est.); 29.068 (2011 est.); 33.96 (2010 est.); 26.28 (2009); 24.125 (2008); 26.264 (2007)

PEOPLE

Mozambique's major ethnic groups encompass numerous subgroups with diverse languages, dialects, cultures, and histories. Many are linked to similar ethnic groups living in neighboring countries. The north-central provinces of Zambezia and Nampula are the most populous, with about 45% of the population. The estimated 4 million Makhuwa are the dominant group in the northern part of the country. The Sena and Ndau are prominent in the Zambezi valley, and the Tsonga and Shangaan dominate in southern Mozambique.

Despite the influence of Islamic coastal traders and European colonizers, the people of Mozambique have largely retained an indigenous culture based on small-scale agriculture. Mozambique's most highly developed art forms are wood sculpture, for which the Makonde in northern Mozambique are particularly renowned, and dance. The middle and upper classes continue to be heavily influenced by the Portuguese colonial and linguistic heritage.

During the colonial era, Christian missionaries were active in Mozambique, and many foreign clergy remain in the country. Under the colonial regime, educational opportunities for black Mozambicans were limited, and 93% of that population was illiterate. Most of today's political leaders were educated in missionary schools. After independence, the government placed a high priority on expanding education, which reduced the illiteracy rate to about two-thirds of the population, as primary school enrollment increased. In recent years, school construction and teacher training enrollments have not kept up with population growth. With post-war enrollments reaching all-time highs, the quality of education has suffered.

Language

Portuguese is spoken in all urban areas and in much of the countryside, though in many smaller villages only the local languages are used. English is understood by some members of the business community, as well as many senior government officials.

Religion

According to the National Institute of Statistics 2007 census, 28 percent of the population is Roman Catholic; 27 percent is Protestant, Pentecostal, or evangelical; 18 percent is Muslim; 9 percent is divided among many small religious groups; and approximately 18 percent of the population does not profess a religion or belief. Religious leaders speculated that a significant portion of the population practiced some form of syncretic indigenous religion, a category not included in the 2007 census. Many Muslims believe their community accounts for closer to 25 percent of the population. There are small numbers of Jews, Hindus, and Baha'is.

The South Asian immigrant population is predominantly Muslim, and there were some differences between their practices and the traditional, Sufi-inspired Swahili Islam of Muslims of African origin. Young African Muslim clerics increasingly sought training in Egypt, Kuwait, South Africa, and Saudi Arabia, and some returned with a stricter approach to Islam.

HISTORY

Mozambique's first inhabitants were San hunter and gatherers, ancestors of the Khoisani peoples. Between the first and fourth centuries AD, waves of Bantu-speaking peoples migrated from the north through the Zambezi River valley and then gradually into the plateau and coastal areas. The Bantu were farmers and ironworkers. When Portuguese explorers reached Mozambique in 1498, Arab trading settlements had existed along the coast and outlying islands for several centuries. From about 1500, Portuguese trading posts and forts became regular ports of call on the new route to the East. Later, traders and prospectors penetrated the interior regions, seeking gold and slaves. Although Portuguese influence gradually expanded, its power was limited and exercised through individual settlers who were granted extensive autonomy. As a result, investment lagged while Lisbon devoted itself to the more lucrative trade with India and the Far East and to the colonization of Brazil.

By the early 20th century the Portuguese had shifted the administration of much of the country to large private companies, controlled and financed mostly by the British, which established railroad lines to neighboring countries and supplied cheap—often forced—African labor to the mines and plantations of the nearby British colonies and South Africa. Because policies were designed to benefit white settlers and the Portuguese homeland, little attention was paid to Mozambique's national integration, its economic infrastructure, or the skills of its population.

After World War II, while many European nations were granting independence to their colonies, Portugal clung to the concept that Mozambique and other Portuguese possessions were overseas provinces of the mother country, and emigration to the colonies soared. Mozambique's Portuguese population at the time of independence was about 250,000. The drive for Mozambican independence developed apace, and in 1962 several anti-colonial political groups formed the Front for the Liberation of Mozambique (Frelimo), which initiated an armed campaign against Portuguese colonial rule in September 1964. After 10 years of sporadic warfare and major political changes in Portugal, Mozambique became independent on June 25, 1975.

From the mid-1970s, Mozambique's history reflected political developments elsewhere in the 20th century. Following the April 1974 coup in Lisbon, Portuguese colonialism collapsed. In Mozambique, the military decision to withdraw occurred within

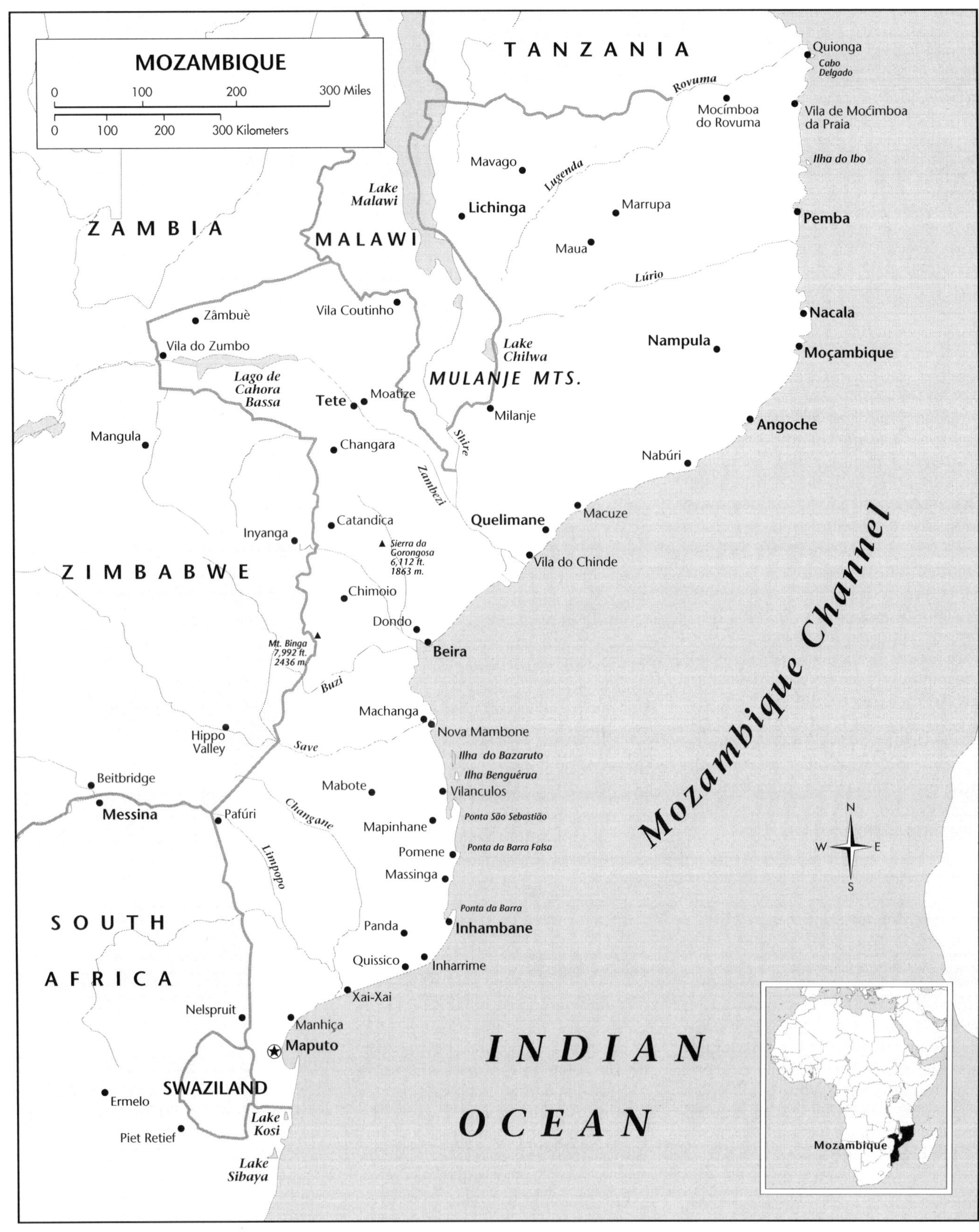
MOZAMBIQUE
0 100 200 300 Miles
0 100 200 300 Kilometers
TANZANIA
ZAMBIA
MALAWI
ZIMBABWE
SOUTH AFRICA
SWAZILAND
Quionga
Cabo Delgado
Rovuma
Mocímboa do Rovuma
Vila de Mocímboa da Praia
Ilha do Ibo
Mavago
Lugenda
Lake Malawi
Lichinga
Marrupa
Pemba
Maua
Lúrio
Vila Coutinho
Zâmbuè
Vila do Zumbo
Nacala
Lake Chilwa
Nampula
Moçambique
Lago de Cahora Bassa
MULANJE MTS.
Tete
Moatize
Milanje
Angoche
Mangula
Shire
Changara
Nabúri
Zambezi
Macuze
Catandica
Quelimane
Inyanga
Sierra da Gorongosa 6,112 ft. 1863 m.
Vila do Chinde
Chimoio
Dondo
Mt. Binga 7,992 ft. 2436 m.
Beira
Buzi
Mozambique Channel
Machanga
Nova Mambone
Hippo Valley
Save
Ilha do Bazaruto
Ilha Benguérua
Beitbridge
Mabote
Vilanculos
Messina
Pafúri
Changane
Mapinhane
Ponta São Sebastião
N
W
E
S
Limpopo
Pomene
Ponta da Barra Falsa
Massinga
Ponta da Barra
Panda
Inhambane
Quissico
Inharrime
Xai-Xai
Nelspruit
Manhiça
Maputo
INDIAN OCEAN
Ermelo
Lake Kosi
Piet Retief
Lake Sibaya
Mozambique

the context of a decade of armed anti-colonial struggle, initially led by American-educated Eduardo Mondlane, who was assassinated in 1969. When independence was achieved in 1975, the leaders of Frelimo's military campaign rapidly established a one-party state allied to the Soviet bloc and outlawed rival political activity. Frelimo eliminated political pluralism, religious educational institutions, and the role of traditional authorities.

The new government gave shelter and support to South African (ANC) and Zimbabwean (ZANU) liberation movements while the governments of first Rhodesia and later apartheid South Africa fostered and financed an armed rebel movement in central Mozambique called the Mozambican National Resistance (Renamo). Civil war, sabotage from neighboring states, and economic collapse characterized the first decade of Mozambican independence. Also marking this period were the mass exodus of Portuguese nationals, weak infrastructure, nationalization, and economic mismanagement. During most of the civil war, the government was unable to exercise effective control outside of urban areas, many of which were cut off from the capital.

An estimated 1 million Mozambicans perished during the civil war, 1.7 million took refuge in neighboring states, and several million more were internally displaced. In the third Frelimo party congress in 1983, President Samora Machel conceded the failure of socialism and the need for major political and economic reforms. He died, along with several advisers, in a 1986 plane crash which has been the subject of many conspiracy theories. A South African commission with an international membership and with access to the plane's black box found gross crew error to be the cause.

His successor, Joaquim Chissano, continued the reforms and began peace talks with Renamo. The new constitution enacted in 1990 provided for a multi-party political system, market-based economy, and free elections. The civil war ended in October 1992 with the Rome General Peace Accords. Under supervision of the ONUMOZ peacekeeping force of the United Nations, peace returned to Mozambique. By mid-1995 the more than 1.7 million Mozambican refugees who had sought asylum in neighboring Malawi, Zimbabwe, Swaziland, Zambia, Tanzania, and South Africa as a result of war and drought had returned, as part of the largest repatriation witnessed in Sub-Saharan Africa. Additionally, a further estimated 4 million internally displaced people returned to their areas of origin.

GOVERNMENT AND POLITICAL CONDITIONS

Mozambique is a constitutional democracy. In 2009 voters reelected President Armando Guebuza in a contest criticized by several national and international observers, including the EU and the Commonwealth, as lacking a "level playing field" and faulted for lacking transparency, integrity, impartiality, and independence. Domestic and foreign observers and local civil society expressed concern over the electoral procedures that preceded the balloting, particularly the exclusion of six of nine presidential candidates and the disqualification of one opposition party's parliamentary candidates from seven of 11 provinces.

There were instances in which elements of the security forces acted independently of civilian control.

Recent Elections

In the 2009 elections, Frelimo secured approximately 75 percent of the presidential vote and more than 75 percent of the seats in parliament. Frelimo mayors were elected in 42 of 43 municipalities, and it was the largest party in municipal assemblies, controlling approximately 80 percent of all seats. Frelimo gained a sufficient majority in the National Assembly to amend the constitution without the support of other parties.

The main opposition parties, Renamo and the Democratic Movement of Mozambique (MDM), complained of election fraud and noted Frelimo agitators and provocateurs routinely disrupted campaign stops, drowning out speakers and candidates by revving motors, playing instruments, shouting, and occasionally throwing stones. They alleged local authorities failed to respond to such provocative acts and that Frelimo candidates suffered no such impediments during their campaigns. Independent reporting corroborated opposition parties' accusations that Frelimo used state funds and resources for campaign purposes, in violation of electoral law.

In November 2009 the National Elections Commission (CNE) announced that Armando Guebuza of the ruling Frelimo party had been reelected president in the October general elections. While domestic and international observers noted that voting-day procedures generally followed international norms, they also documented irregularities during voter registration, the campaign, and in the vote count.

The Electoral Institute for Sustainability of Democracy in Southern Africa questioned the transparency, integrity, impartiality, and independence of the CNE, noting that improvements were required to "level the playing field, afford equal opportunity to all, and improve the transparency of the electoral process." The CNE disqualified several political parties and candidates from participating in legislative elections. The MDM, for example, was prevented from running in nine of 13 legislative districts. The CNE's action, which included backdating documents and other questionable acts, provoked protests from the diplomatic community and civil society and extensive commentary in the media. Also the Constitutional Council (CC) disqualified six of nine presidential candidates for application irregularities. In contravention of law and its own past practice, the CC did not provide the rejected candidates with notice or an opportunity to respond.

In response to these various actions by the CC and the CNE, local NGO the Center for Public Integrity (CIP) called for an independent audit of electoral processes while highlighting several significant flaws. The government granted MDM formal status in the National Assembly, which entitled its eight members of parliament to certain financial and logistical support, as well as the right to speak during parliamentary plenary sessions. The government also announced a two-year legislative process to amend the electoral code and began consultations with civil society organizations as part of this process.

Political Parties: Frelimo continued to dominate the political process, and its influence continued to grow. Opposition political parties were permitted to operate but were sometimes subject to restrictions, including unlawful arrest, and other interference by the ruling party and the government. Membership in the ruling Frelimo party was widely perceived to confer advantages.

Participation of Women and Minorities: Women and members of many ethnic groups held key positions in both the legislative and executive branches. There was no evidence that women or specific ethnic groups were excluded from participation in the political process. Eight of the 29 ministers were women. Women held 98 of the 250 seats in the National Assembly. The National Assembly also had an office dedicated to raising awareness of women's issues, including family law, domestic violence, and trafficking in persons. While there were no women on the Supreme Court, the justice minister, two of the six assistant attorneys general, and 91 of the 279 judges were women.

Principal Government Officials

Last Updated: 1/31/2013

Pres.: **Armando Emilio GUEBUZA**

Prime Min.: **Alberto Clementino VAQUINA**

Min. of Agriculture: **Jose Condugua Antonio PACHECO**

Min. for Coordination of Environmental Action: **Alcinda Antonio de ABREU**

Min. of Culture: **Armando Artur JOAO**

Min. of Defense: **Filipe Jacinto NHUSSI**

Min. of Education: **Augusto Luis JONE**

Min. of Energy: **Salvador NAMBURETE**

Min. of Finance: **Manuel CHANG**

Min. of Fisheries: **Victor Manuel BORGES**

Min. of Foreign Affairs & Cooperation: **Oldemiro Julio Marques BALOI**

Min. of Health: **Alexandre Lourenco Jaime MANGUELE**

Min. of Industry & Commerce: **Armando INROGA**

Min. of the Interior: **Alberto Ricardo MONDLANE**

Min. of Justice: **Maria Benvinda Delfina LEVI**

Min. of Labor: **Maria Helena TAIPO**

Min. of Mineral Resources: **Esperanca Laurinda Francisco Nhiuane BIAS**

Min. of Planning & Development: **Aiuba CUERENEIA**

Min. of Public Service: **Vitoria Dias DIOGO**

Min. of Public Works & Housing: **Cadmiel Feliane MUTHEMBA**

Min. of Science & Technology: **Luis Augusto PELEMBE**

Min. of State Admin.: **Carmelita Rita NAMASHALUA**

Min. of Tourism: **Carvalho MUARIA**

Min. of Transport & Communications: **Paulo Francisco ZUCULA**

Min. of Veterans Affairs: **Mateus Oscar KIDA**

Min. of Women's Affairs & Social Welfare: **Iolanda Maria Pedro Campos CINTURA**

Min. of Youth & Sport: **Fernando SUMBANA, Jr.**

Min. in the Presidency for Civil Affairs: **Antonio Correia Fernandes SUMBANA**

Min. in the Presidency for Parliamentary, Municipal, & Provincial Assembly Affairs: **Adelaide Anchia AMURANE**

Min. in the Presidency for Social Matters: **Feliciano Salomao GUNDANA**

Attorney Gen.: **Augusto PAULINO**

Governor, Bank of Mozambique: **Ernesto GOVE**

Ambassador to the US: **Amelia Matos SUMBANA**

Permanent Representative to the UN, New York: **Antonio GUMENDE**

ECONOMY

At independence in 1975, Mozambique was one of the world's poorest countries. Socialist mismanagement and a brutal civil war from 1977–92 exacerbated the situation. In 1987, the government embarked on a series of macroeconomic reforms designed to stabilize the economy. These steps, combined with donor assistance and with political stability since the multi-party elections in 1994, have led to dramatic improvements in the country's growth rate.

Fiscal reforms, including the introduction of a value-added tax and reform of the customs service, have improved the government's revenue collection abilities. Inspite of these gains, Mozambique remains dependent upon foreign assistance for more than half of its annual budget, and in 2008 54% of the population remained below the poverty line. Subsistence agriculture continues to employ the vast majority of the country's work force and smallholder agricultural productivity and productivity growth is weak. A substantial trade imbalance persists although the opening of the Mozal aluminum smelter, the country's largest foreign investment project to date, has increased export earnings.

At the end of 2007, and after years of negotiations, the government took over Portugal's majority share of the Cahora Bassa Hydroelectricity Company (HCB), a dam that was not transferred to Mozambique at independence because of the ensuing civil war and unpaid debts. More electrical power capacity is needed for additional investment projects in titanium extraction and processing and garment manufacturing that could further close the import/export gap. Mozambique's once substantial foreign debt has been reduced through forgiveness and rescheduling under the IMF's Heavily Indebted Poor Countries (HIPC) and Enhanced HIPC initiatives, and is now at a manageable level. In July 2007 the Millennium Challenge Corporation (MCC) signed a compact with Mozambique; the compact entered into force in September 2008 and will continue for five years. Compact projects will focus on improving sanitation, roads, agriculture, and the business regulation environment in an effort to spur economic growth in the four northern provinces of the country. Mozambique grew at an average annual rate of 9% in the decade up to 2007, one of Africa's strongest performances. However, heavy reliance on aluminum, which accounts for about one-third of exports, subjects the economy to volatile international prices.

The sharp decline in aluminum prices during the global economic crisis lowered GDP growth by several percentage points. Citizens rioted in September 2010, after fuel, water, electricity, and bread price increases were announced. In an attempt lessen the negative impact on people, the government implemented subsidies, decreased taxes and tariffs, and instituted other fiscal measures. Real growth of more than 7% per year was achieved in 2010–12. Investment in the country's gas sector may raise Mozambique's economic growth to 8% per year through 2017.

Labor Conditions

Child labor remained a problem. In the formal economy, the minimum working age without restrictions is 18 years of age. The law permits children between ages 15 and 18 to work, but the employer is required to provide for their education and professional training and ensure that conditions of work are not damaging to their physical and moral development.

Children between the ages of 12 and 15 are permitted to work under special conditions authorized jointly by the ministries of labor, health, and education. For children under the age of 18, the maximum workweek is 38 hours, the maximum workday is seven hours, and they are not permitted to work in occupations that are unhealthy, dangerous, or require significant physical effort. Children must undergo a medical examination before beginning work. By law children must be paid at least the minimum wage or a minimum of two-thirds of the adult salary, whichever is higher.

Although the law prohibits forced and bonded labor by children, it was a common problem, especially in rural areas. Out of economic necessity, especially in rural areas, parents often forced their children to work, particularly in commercial agriculture, as domestic employees, or in prostitution.Children, including those under age 15, commonly worked on family farms in seasonal harvests or on commercial plantations, where they picked cotton, tobacco, or tea leaves and were paid on a piecework basis for work completed rather than an hourly minimum wage. Trade unions indicated that in the northern provinces of Zambezia, Nampula, and Cabo Delgado, adults hired to work in tobacco cotton, cashew, and coconut plantations routinely had their children work also to increase their income. These children worked long hours and were prevented from attending school.

Trade unions estimated that a minimum livable monthly wage to provide for a family of five was 7,250 meticais ($268). The minimum wage varies by sector from 1,681 meticais ($62) to 5,320 meticais ($197). In April the government updated the minimum wage for various sectors, however, many employers had not implemented these minimum wages by year's end. For example, there were threats of a strike in July by employees of state-owned Radio Mocambique and a government public transport company, TPM, who complained they had not yet received the increases. The strike was called off after negotiations and an agreement for future raises, dependent on economic performance.

Although the industrial sector frequently paid above minimum wage, there were few industrial jobs outside of the Maputo area. In addition, less than 10 percent of workers held salaried positions, and the majority of the labor force worked in subsistence farming. Many workers used a variety of strategies to survive, including holding a second job, maintaining their own gardens, or depending on the income of other family members.

The Ministry of Labor is responsible for enforcing the minimum wage rates in the private sector, and the Ministry of Finance does so in the public sector. Violations of minimum wage rates usually were investigated only after workers registered a complaint. Workers generally received benefits, such as transportation and food, in addition to wages. The standard legal workweek is 40 hours but can be extended to 48 hours. After 48 hours overtime must be paid at 50 percent over the base hourly salary. Overtime is limited by law to two hours per day and 100 hours per year. The law provides for one hour of rest per day. Foreign workers are protected under the law.

Frequent worker complaints included failure by employers to deposit social security contributions that had been deducted from wages, inability to obtain social security benefits, unlawful firings, and intimidation of union members. In the small formal sector, health and environmental laws were in place to protect workers, but the Ministry of Labor did not effectively enforce these laws, and the government only occasionally closed firms for noncompliance. There continued to be significant violations of labor laws in many companies and services.

U.S.-MOZAMBICAN RELATIONS

Mozambique's independence from Portugal in 1975 was followed by years of civil conflict that ended in 1992. U.S. aid to Mozambique in the post-conflict period supported the peace and reconciliation process. The country has had one ruling political party since 1975. The United States and Mozambique share a commitment to economic development, improved living standards, and good governance for all Mozambicans.

U.S. Assistance to Mozambique

At the end of the civil war in 1992, Mozambique ranked among the least developed countries in the world and despite a strong macroeconomic performance, continues to be so today. The United States is the largest bilateral donor to the country and plays a leading role in donor efforts to assist Mozambique.

The United States seeks to strengthen democracy and inclusive governance in Mozambique as well as a continued economic growth that expands opportunity for those most at risk. Poverty reduction and job creation remain high priorities, as do improved healthcare, education, and food security. Our role as the country's largest bilateral donor continues, with such significant U.S. foreign assistance programs as the President's Emergency Plan for AIDS Relief, the Millennium Challenge Corporation, the Feed the Future Initiative, and the President's Malaria Initiative.

Bilateral Economic Relations

Bilateral trade between the United States and Mozambique rose 68% in 2011 reaching over $US 487 million according to the Office of the United States Trade Representative. A substantial amount of foreign direct investment from Mozambique comes from the United States.

The two principal U.S. investors in Mozambique are Anadarko Petroleum and Mozambique Leaf Tobacco Limitada, although interest by other U.S companies is on the rise. A Bilateral Investment Treaty (BIT) between the two nations came into effect in March, 2005.

The U.S. and Mozambique signed a Trade and Investment Framework Agreement (TIFA) in 2005, and the TIFA Council held its first meeting in October, 2006, with the most recent session in January 2012.

Mozambique's Membership in International Organizations

The twin pillars of Mozambique's foreign policy are maintenance of good relations with its neighbors and maintenance and expansion of ties to development partners. Mozambique and the United States belong to a number of the same international organizations, including the United Nations, International Monetary Fund, World Bank, and World Trade Organization.

Bilateral Representation

Mozambique maintains an embassy in the United States at 1525 New Hampshire Avenue, NW, Washington, DC 20036; tel: 202-293-7146; fax: 202-835-0245.

Principal U.S. Embassy Officials

Last Updated: 1/14/2013

MAPUTO (E) 193 Kenneth Kaunda Avenue, +258 21-492-797, Fax +258 21–490-114, Workweek: 0730-1730 Monday-Thursday–0730-1130 Friday, Website: http://Mozambique.usembassy.gov/

DCM OMS:	Catherine Lawton
AMB OMS:	Becky Cheney
CDC:	Edgar Monterroso
Co-CLO:	Rowena Zamora
ECON/COM:	Kundai Mashingaidze
FM:	Noah Swanson
HRO:	David S Reiter
MGT:	Sherry Zalika Sykes
POL/ECON:	Ruddy Wang
SDO/DATT:	Edward Dupont
AMB:	Douglas M Griffiths
CON:	Shigh Sapp
DCM:	Christine Elder
PAO:	Caroline J Savage
GSO:	John Everman
RSO:	Brian K Wood
AID:	Polly Dunford
CLO:	Christine I Twining
EEO:	Charles L Brown
FMO:	Andres Jaramillo
IMO:	M. Blaine Tyson

TRAVEL

Consular Information Sheet

April 27, 2012

Country Description: Mozambique is a developing country in southern Africa that has been steadily rebuilding its economy and civic institutions since ending a 16-year civil war in 1992. The country stabilized following Mozambique's first multi-party elections in October 1994, and the current president was reelected in October 2009. The next presidential elections will be held in 2014. Despite high economic growth rates in recent years, Mozambique remains among the world's poorest countries, with a GDP per capita of under $400. Facilities for tourism in Maputo, the capital city, are steadily improving but remain limited in other areas. Many goods and services have extremely limited availability. The official language is Portuguese, although English is spoken in many tourist areas, and in some rural areas only local languages are widely spoken.

Smart Traveler Enrollment Program (STEP)/Embassy Location: If you are going to live in or visit Mozambique, please take the time to tell our Embassy about your trip. If you enroll, we can keep you up to date with important safety and security announcements. It will also help us reach your friends and family in an emergency.

U.S. Embassy Maputo
Avenida Kenneth Kaunda, 193
Telephone: 258 21 49 2797
Emergency after-hours telephone: 258 21 49 0723
Facsimile: 258 21 49 0448

Entry/Exit Requirements for U.S. Citizens: A visa is required for entry into Mozambique. It is recommended that travelers acquire the appropriate visa prior to departing for Mozambique, although a one-entry visa can be purchased for $82 at country points of entry, including airports. Foreigners in Mozambique without a valid visa can expect to pay a substantial fine ($33) for each day they are in Mozambique illegally. The fine can be assessed upon travelers' departure or if travelers are caught by authorities while still in Mozambique. Please pay close attention to the period you are authorized to stay in Mozambique on your visa ("Autorizado a permaneçer pelo período de [number of days]"). This is the maximum number of days you may stay before you must depart Mozambique. The passports of all travelers who wish to enter Mozambique must be valid for six months upon arrival and must contain at least three clean (unstamped) visa pages each time entry is sought. The Mozambican Embassy and Consulates in South Africa charge up to five times the amount charged in the United States or at border crossing points for a tourist visa to Mozambique. In September 2007, the Mozambican Interior and Health Ministries decreed that all travelers entering Mozambique who had previously visited a country where yellow fever is present must present a valid certification of vaccination against yellow fever. We recommend all travelers be vaccinated to avoid complications at the border. Any passenger who cannot present such a certificate at the port of entry will be vaccinated at a cost of $50 US dollars or the equivalent in metical. Additionally, all travelers entering Mozambique must carry their yellow vaccination book.

The U.S. Department of State is unaware of any HIV/AIDS entry restrictions for visitors to or foreign residents of Mozambique.

We strongly urge visitors to go to the Embassy of Mozambique website before attempting to import weapons and/or artillery. Without proper documentation, permission, and a local handling agent weapons/artillery importers could face detention by local officials as was the case this past year with several U.S. citizen maritime security employees.

Threats to Safety and Security: Overland travel after dark is extremely dangerous due to the increased potential for vehicle hijacking. Visitors should be particularly vigilant when driving on the main thoroughfares connecting Mozambique and South Africa as incidents of vehicle theft, including assault and robbery, have been reported. U.S. government personnel who work at the U.S. Embassy in Mozambique are strongly discouraged from overland travel outside Maputo city limits after dark, and are encouraged to travel in convoys of two or more vehicles when outside of the city. They are prohibited from using "chapas" (local minibuses) due to frequent accidents involving these vehicles. Due to residual landmines, overland travelers are advised to remain on well-traveled roads or seek local information before going off-road outside of Maputo and other provincial capitals. Although demonstrations do occur in Mozambique, they are infrequent and there have been no recent demonstrations against U.S. interests. If any demonstrations do occur, they should be avoided. Stay up to date by bookmarking our Bureau of Consular Affairs website, which contains the current Travel Warnings and Travel Alerts as well as the Worldwide Caution. Follow us on Twitter and become a fan of the Bureau of Consular Affairs page on Facebook. Up-to-date information on safety and security can also be obtained by calling 1-888-407-4747 toll-free within the United States and Canada, or by calling a regular toll line, 1-202-501-4444, from other countries. These numbers are available from 8:00 a.m. to 8:00 p.m. Eastern Time, Monday through Friday (except U.S. federal holidays).

Stay up to date by:

- Bookmarking our Bureau of Consular Affairs website, which contains the current Travel Warnings and Travel Alerts as well as the Worldwide Caution.
- Following us on Twitter and the Bureau of Consular Affairs page on Facebook as well.
- Downloading our free Smart Traveler IPhone App to have travel information at your fingertips.
- Calling 1-888-407-4747 toll-free within the U.S. and Canada, or a regular toll line, 1-202-501-4444, from other countries.
- Taking some time before travel to consider your personal security.

Crime: Although the vast majority of visitors complete their travels in Mozambique without incident, the most serious threat facing U.S. citizens visiting Mozambique is crime. Street crimes, including mugging, purse-snatching, and pick-pocketing are common, both in Maputo and in secondary cities. Carjackings have become rare, but still do happen. Visitors must be vigilant when out in public areas and should not display jewelry or other items —even those of low value, like cell phones. Avoid isolated areas. Joggers and pedestrians have frequently been mugged, even during daylight hours. Visitors should take caution when walking at night, even in well-known tourist areas. Due to an increase in violent crime, pedestrian activity is discouraged on Maputo's Avenida Marginal between the Southern Sun hotel (formerly the Holiday Inn) and the Waterfront Restaurant.

Mozambican police are not do not operate at the standard that U.S. citizens are accustomed to in the United States. Visitors should not expect the same level of police service. Many airline trips from Mozambique to the United States, Europe, or African destinations transit Johannesburg, South Africa. Baggage pilferage is an ongoing problem at Johannesburg's Oliver Tambo International Airport. Travelers are encouraged to secure their luggage, use an airport plastic wrapping service, and avoid placing currency, electronics, jewelry, cameras, cosmetics, running shoes, or other valuables in checked luggage. Having a complete inventory of items placed in checked baggage can aid in processing a claim if theft does occur.

Don't buy counterfeit and pirated goods, even if they are widely available. Not only are the bootlegs illegal in the United States, if you purchase them you may also be breaking local law.

Victims of Crime: If you or someone you know becomes the victim of a crime abroad, you should contact the local police and the nearest U.S. embassy or consulate. We can:

- Replace a stolen passport.
- Help you find appropriate medical care if you are the victim of violent crimes such as assault or rape.
- Put you in contact with the appropriate police authorities, and if you want us to, we can contact family members or friend.
- Help you understand the local criminal justice process and direct you to local attorneys, although it is important to remember that local authorities are responsible for investigating and prosecuting the crime.

There is no local equivalent to the "911" emergency line in Mozambique.

Criminal Penalties: While you are traveling in Mozambique, you are subject to its laws even if you are a U.S. citizen. Foreign laws and legal systems can be vastly different than our own. In some places you may be taken in for questioning if you don't have your passport with you. In some places, it is illegal to take pictures of certain buildings. In some places, driving under the influence could land you immediately in jail. These criminal penalties will vary from country to country. There are also some things that might be legal in the country you visit, but still illegal in the United States, and you can be prosecuted under U.S. law if you buy pirated goods.Engaging in sexual conduct with children or using or disseminating child pornography in a foreign country is a crime prosecutable in the United States. If you break local laws in Mozambique, your U.S. passport won't help you avoid arrest or prosecution. It's very important to know what's legal and what's not wherever you go.

Persons violating Mozambican laws, even unknowingly, may be expelled, arrested or imprisoned. Penalties for possession, use, or trafficking in illegal drugs in Mozambique are severe, and convicted offenders can expect long jail sentences and heavy fines.

Arrest notifications in host country: While some countries will automatically notify the nearest U.S. embassy or consulate if a U.S. citizen is detained or arrested in a foreign country, that might not always be the case. To ensure that the United States is aware of your circumstances, request that the police and prison officials notify the nearest U.S. embassy or consulate as soon as you are arrested or detained overseas.

Special Circumstances: Mozambican law requires that all persons carry an identity document such as a passport when out in public, and that they present it to police upon request. Notarized copies of both the biographic page of a passport and a valid Mozambican visa are acceptable forms of identification, although police will occasionally demand original documents. There are certain areas in Mozambique where pedestrian traffic is prohibited and the ban is strictly enforced. These areas include the front of the presidential offices located north of the Hotel Polana on the seaside of Avenida Julius Nyerere and the Praça dos Herois on Avenida Acordos de Lusaka near the airport, both in Maputo.

It is against the law to destroy Mozambican currency; offenders can expect a jail sentence or fine. The limit for an undeclared amount of U.S. dollars one can take out of the country is $5,000. The maximum amount of local currency one can take out is 500 metical, which is less than 20 U.S. dollars. Some U.S. travelers have reported having difficulties cashing traveler's checks and have relied instead on ATMs and credit cards for money withdrawals in Mozambique. Travelers have reported that banks in Mozambique will only accept new U.S. bills. Outside of the major hotels and restaurants, credit cards are not widely accepted in Mozambique. The South African rand and U.S. dollar are sometimes accepted as legal tender, although this is more common in the southern part of the country or in tourist areas; all transactions must have a local currency (metical) payment option.

Accessibility: While in Mozambique, individuals with disabilities may find accessibility and accommodation very different from what you find in the United States. Although the government legislatively mandates access to public buildings, transportation, and government services for persons with disabilities, few buildings are accessible. In general, restaurants, hotels, and residential buildings have stairs at the entrance without wheelchair ramps, except perhaps at a few major hotels and retail areas. Pedestrian paths and transportation are extremely difficult for persons with disabilities. Sidewalks are not commonplace and, if they exist, are poorly maintained and dangerous to walk on at night. Pedestrian crossings are infrequent and drivers seldom obey traffic signals. Buses and taxis do not have special accommodations for disabled persons.

Medical Facilities and Health Information: Medical facilities are rudimentary, and most medical providers do not speak fluent English. Medicines are not always consistently available. There are both public and private medical facilities in the city of Maputo and most provincial capitals. All health care institutions and providers require payment at the time of service, and may even require payment before providing service. While some private clinics accept credit cards, many medical facilities do not. Doctors and hospitals outside Maputo generally expect immediate cash payment for health services. Outside of Maputo, available medical care ranges from very basic to nonexistent.

You can find detailed information on vaccinations and other health precautions on the CDC website. For information about outbreaks of infectious diseases abroad, consult the World Health Organization (WHO) website. The WHO website also contains additional health information for travelers, including detailed country-specific health information.

Tuberculosis is an increasingly serious health concern in Mozambique. For further information, please consult the CDC's information on TB.

Medical Insurance: You can't assume your insurance will go with you when you travel. It's very important to find out BEFORE you leave whether or not your medical insurance will cover you overseas. You need to ask your insurance company two questions:

- Does my policy apply when I'm out of the United States?
- Will it cover emergencies like a trip to a foreign hospital or a medical evacuation?

In many places, doctors and hospitals still expect payment in cash at the time of service. Your regular U.S. health insurance may not cover doctor and hospital visits in other countries. If your policy doesn't go with you when you travel, it's a very good idea to take out another one for your trip.

Traffic Safety and Road Conditions: While in Mozambique, U.S. citizens may encounter road conditions that differ significantly from those in the United States. The information below concerning Mozambique is provided for general reference only, and may not be totally accurate in a particular location or circumstance.

Serious traffic accidents, one of the greatest threats to U.S. citizens in Mozambique, occur regularly throughout the country. Several U.S. citizens have been involved in accidents this past year causing fatalities and life-threatening injuries. Accidents involving drivers and pedestrians are common, sometimes resulting in pedestrian casualty. Pedestrians often walk in the road and may not be visible to motorists, especially at night. If a serious accident occurs, or if a driver hits a pedestrian, crowds quickly gather. Some drivers involved in accidents of this nature have felt threatened by the crowds and fled the accident scene. We urge any driver involved in an accident to immediately report the accident to the nearest police station and to contact the Embassy. Drivers should obey police signals to stop at checkpoints, which are common throughout Mozambique. Foreigners visiting Mozambique for more than 90 days are required to have an International Driver's License or to obtain a Mozambican driver's license. The main north-south thoroughfare is passable north of Maputo until the city of Caia (Sofala province), where vehicle passengers must disembark and cross the Zambezi River by ferryboat. On the north side of the river, the road continues to the Northern provinces. The road network connecting provincial capitals is in fair condition, but can be riddled with potholes and other obstacles.

The EN4 toll road between Maputo and South Africa is well-maintained. U.S. government personnel are prohibited from traveling outside cities after dark because of the increased risk of banditry, poor road conditions in some areas, poor maintenance of many vehicles in the country (e.g., no headlights or rear lights), as well as the threat imposed by livestock grazing on roadsides. Travel outside Maputo often requires a four-wheel drive vehicle, which creates an additional security risk since these vehicles are high-theft items. Public transportation is limited and often has poor safety standards. The U.S. Embassy advises U.S. citizens not to use "chapas" (local minibuses) as a method of transportation due to frequent, often fatal accidents involving these vehicles.

We also suggest that travelers visit the web site of the Mozambique's national tourist office and national authority responsible for road safety.

Aviation Safety Oversight: As there is no direct commercial air service to the United States by carriers registered in Mozambique, the U.S. Federal Aviation Administration (FAA) has not assessed the government of Mozambique's Civil Aviation Authority for compliance with International Civil Aviation Organization (ICAO) aviation safety standards. Further information may be found on the FAA's safety assessment page.

Children's Issues: Please see the U.S. Dept. of State Office of Children's Issues web pages on intercountry adoption and international parental child abduction.

Intercountry Adoption

February 2013

The information in this section has been edited from a report of the State Department Bureau of Consular Affairs, Office of Overseas Citizens Services. For more information, please read the *Intercountry Adoption* section of this book and review current reports online at http://adoption.state.gov.

Mozambique is not party to the Hague Convention on Protection of Children and Co-operation in Respect of Intercountry Adoption(the Hague Adoption Convention). Intercountry adoptions of children from non-Hague countries are processed in accordance with 8 Code of Federal Regulations, Section 204.3 as it relates to orphans as defined under the Immigration and Nationality Act, Section 101(b)(1)(F).

Prospective adoptive parents must be legal residents of Mozambique and must be present in the country for the duration of the adoption process. This includes a six month integration period after a prospective adoptive child is placed in the home, and before the adoption can be finalized by the court. (Visit the Embassy of Mozambique website for current visa information.) Additionally, married prospective adoptive parents must be married for three years prior to the initiation of the adoption process. The marriage can be civil, religious, or traditional, as long as it is registered. Civil marriages are registered with the civil registrar. Religious marriages are registered with the office of the religious denomination chosen by the given couple. This is done by having the community leader, married couple, and their witnesses sign a declaration and taking it to the relevant district office.

Traditional marriages require the presence of the community leader and at least two witnesses. This is done by presenting witnesses to the appropriate district official. In cases in which the marriage took place at least three years prior to the initiation of the adoption, but was not registered, the prospective adoptive parents may invoke common law. The Government of Mozambique requires post-adoption monitoring until the child reaches 21 years of age. This requirement may be waived at the judge's discretion. However, the courts may not grant an adoption if the child will be immediately taken out of Mozambique. Changes to Mozambique's intercountry adoption laws are under consideration by Unidade Technica da Reforma Legal (UTREL), which drafts and proposes laws for the Government of Mozambique. To date, no substantial amendments have been made to the existing laws. Mozambican law does not make a distinction between intercountry and domestic adoption. This may mean that foreigners will be expected to meet the same pre- and post-adoption monitoring requirements as Mozambican families, which may become an obstacle if the court decides the child cannot be monitored outside of Mozambique.

Who Can Adopt? To bring an adopted child to United States from Mozambique, you must be found eligible to adopt by the U.S. Government. The U.S. Government agency responsible for making this determination is the Department of Homeland Security, U.S. Citizenship and Immigration Services (USCIS).

Residency: Prospective adoptive parents must be legal residents of Mozambique and must be physically present in Mozambique for the duration of the adoption process, including a six-month integration period after a prospective adoptive child is placed in the home and before the adoption can be finalized by the court.

Age of Adopting Parents: Prospective adoptive parents must be over 25 years of age and less than 50 on the date the child is entrusted to them, unless the child is the biological son or daughter of one of the prospective adoptive parents.

Marriage: Prospective adoptive parents must be married for three years prior to the initiation of the adoption process. Single people are not eligible to adopt. The Government of Mozambique does not legally permit same-sex couples to adopt.

Other: Prospective adoptive parents must undergo a home study evaluation by Mozambican social and health workers from the country's child welfare office and must be certified approved for adoption.

Who Can Be Adopted? In addition to U.S. immigration requirements, Mozambique has specific requirements that a child must meet in order to be eligible for adoption:

Relinquishment: In order to be eligible for adoption, a child must be relinquished by both parents. However, there is an exception if the prospective adoptive parent is the spouse of a biological parent or a partner with whom the biological parent has been living for at least three years. In these situations, only the biological parent who is not living with the minor child and the prospective adoptive parent must relinquish parental rights.

Abandonment: A child of unknown parents.

Age of Adoptive Child: The prospective adoptive child must be a minor under 14 years of age, or 18 years of age if s/he has been fostered by the prospective adoptive parents since 12 years of age.

Waiting Period or Foster Care: The adoption is generally preceded by a minimum adaptation period of six months, in which the prospective adopted child is integrated into the family via foster care before the legal adoption is finalized in the court. This process must take place in Mozambique.

Mozambique's Adoption Authority: Social Services National Directorate (Direcção Nacional da Acçao Social)

The Process: The recommended first step in adopting a child from Mozambique is to decide whether or not to use a licensed adoption service provider in the United States that can help you with your adoption. Adoption service providers must be licensed by the U.S. state in which they operate. In order to adopt a child from Mozambique, prospective adoptive parents will need to meet the requirements of the Government of Mozambique and U.S. immigration law. Prospective adoptive parents must submit an application to be found eligible to adopt with the municipal juvenile court (Tribunal de Menores) closest to the residence of the prospective adoptive parents.

Prospective adoptions parents must provide an application addressed to the presiding judge of the court, stating:

- Advantages of adoption for the adoptee;
- Age of adoptee;
- Age of the adoptive parents, and
- Marital status of the adoptive parents.

The prospective adoptive parents' signature on the statement must be witnessed by three people. If the judge makes a positive decision on the adoption, the case is generally transferred to the Social Services National Directorate to conduct a home study.

To meet U.S. immigration requirements, you may also file an I-600A, Application for Advance Processing of an Orphan Petition with U.S. Department of Homeland Security's U.S. Citizenship and Immigration Services to be found eligible and suitable to adopt. If you are eligible to adopt, and a child is available for intercountry adoption, Mozambique's Social Services National Directorate will provide you with a referral. Each family must decide for itself whether or not it will be able to meet the needs of and provide a permanent home for a particular child. The child must be eligible to be adopted according to Mozambique's requirements, as described in the Who Can Be Adopted section. The child must also meet the definition of an orphan under U.S. immigration law.

The process for finalizing the adoption in Mozambique generally includes the following:

Role of Adoption Authority: Municipal authorities oversee adoptions within their respective geographic areas of jurisdiction. U.S. citizens wishing to adopt in Maputo should contact Ana Maria Macuacua, the head of Maputo City's Social Service National Directorate at (258) 21 302613. Numbers for offices in other provinces can be obtained by contacting the national directorate at +258 21 302613.

Role of the Court: The Juvenile Court (Tribunal de Menores) grants official orders of adoption or guardianship.

Role of Adoption Agencies: None.

Adoption Application: The first step in the adoption process is submission of a formal adoption request to the Juvenile Court in the appropriate governing municipality. Together with the initial application, prospective parents should submit a certified copy of their marriage certificate (translated into Portuguese) and photocopies of their passports and Mozambican residency permits (known as a "DIRE"). A list of other supporting documents and required forms may be obtained from the court. If the court grants the order of adoption, the Social Services Directorate (SSD) will then begin a lengthy investigation of the prospective adoptive parents' lifestyle, economic means, mental and physical health, and other details associated with a home study evaluation. During this time, the process of identifying a child for adoption is also initiated by the SSD. As a final step, the SSD will pass the parents' petition for adoption to the Juvenile Court (Tribunal de Menores), to issue a certificate of approval officially endorsing the adoption.

Time Frame: The adoption process in Mozambique takes approximately six to nine months. U.S. immigrant visa petitions filed at the U.S. Embassy in Mozambique on behalf of adopted minors are forwarded to the U.S. Consulate General in Johannesburg for adjudication.

Adoption Fees: There is a court fee of 1,450 Meticais (approximately USD $50), in addition to minor fees for forms and documents. Adoptive parents will also be responsible for acquiring official translations of both English- and Portuguese-language documents. The U.S. Embassy in Mozambique maintains a list of Portuguese/English translators for the public use.

Documents Required: Prospective adoptive parents should be prepared to submit certified copies of their marriage certificate, Mozambican residency cards, passports (all with official translations, if required), along with bank statements and health certificates to the SSD who then submits these documents to the Juvenile court. Note: Additional documents may be requested.

Bringing Your Child Home: Once your adoption is complete (or you have obtained legal custody of the child), there are a few more steps to take before you can head home. Specifically, you need to apply for several documents for your child before he or she can travel to the United States, such as a birth certificate, a passport or travel document for your child from the country in which he or she was born, and a U.S. Immigration Visa.

Child Citizenship Act: For adoptions finalized abroad, the Child Citizenship Act of 2000 allows your new child to acquire American citizenship automatically when he or she enters the United States as lawful permanent residents. For adoptions finalized in the United States, the Child Citizenship Act of 2000 allows your new child to acquire American citizenship automatically when the court in the United States issues the final adoption decree. To learn more, review the *Intercountry Adoption* section in this publication and visit the U.S. Department of State Intercountry Adoption website at http://adoption.state.gov.

After Adoption: The government officially requires post-adoption monitoring until the child reaches 21 years. This requirement may be waived. However, if it is believed that the child will be adopted and immediately taken out of Mozambique, the courts may block an intercountry adoption.

U.S. Embassy in Mozambique
Consular Section
Avenida Kenneth Kaunda 193
Maputo, Mozambique
Tel: (258) 21 49 2797
Fax: (258) 21 49 0448
ConsularMaputo@state.gov
http://Mozambique.USEmbassy.gov

Mozambique's Adoption Authority
Direcção Nacional de Acção Social
Departamento da Crianca (Social Services National Directorate, Children's Department)
Av. Ahmed Sékou Touré 908,
Tel: +258 21 350300/301 064
Ms. Francisca Sales is the director of the Social Services National Directorate at the federal level.

Embassy of Mozambique
1990 M Street, N.W.
Suite 570
Washington, D.C. 20036
Tel: (202) 293–7146/9
Email: embamoc@aol.com

Office of Children's Issues
U.S. Department of State
2201 C Street, NW
SA-29
Washington, DC 20520
Tel: 1–888–407–4747
E-mail: AskCI@state.gov
or AdoptionUSCA@state.gov
Website:http://adoption.state.gov

For questions about immigration procedures, call the National Customer Service Center (NCSC) 1-800-375-5283 (TTY 1-800-767-1833).